TheStreet Ratings'
Guide to Stock Mutual Funds

TheStreet Ratings'
Guide to Stock Mutual Funds

A Quarterly Compilation of Investment Ratings
and Analyses Covering Equity and Balanced Mutual Funds

Spring 2015

GREY HOUSE PUBLISHING

TheStreet, Inc.
14 Wall Street, 15th Floor
New York, NY 10005
800-706-2501

TheStreet Ratings

Published by Grey House Publishing, Inc. located at 4919 Route 22, Amenia, NY, 12501; telephone 518-789-8700. Grey House Publishing neither guarantees the accuracy of the data contained herein nor assumes any responsibility for errors, omissions or discrepancies. Grey House Publishing accepts no payment for listing; inclusion in the publication of any organization agency, institution, publication, service or individual does not imply endorsement of the publisher.

Grey House
Publishing
4919 Route 22
PO Box 56
Amenia, NY 12501-0056

Edition No. 67, Spring 2015

ISBN: 978-1-61925-605-7
ISSN: 2158-6144

Contents

Terms and Conditions

This Document is prepared strictly for the confidential use of our customer(s). It has been provided to you at your specific request. It is not directed to, or intended for distribution to or use by, any person or entity who is a citizen or resident of or located in any locality, state, country or other jurisdiction where such distribution, publication, availability or use would be contrary to law or regulation or which would subject TheStreet or its affiliates to any registration or licensing requirement within such jurisdiction.

No part of the analysts' compensation was, is, or will be, directly or indirectly, related to the specific recommendations or views expressed in this research report.

This Document is not intended for the direct or indirect solicitation of business. TheStreet, Inc. and its affiliates disclaims any and all liability to any person or entity for any loss or damage caused, in whole or in part, by any error (negligent or otherwise) or other circumstances involved in, resulting from or relating to the procurement, compilation, analysis, interpretation, editing, transcribing, publishing and/or dissemination or transmittal of any information contained herein.

TheStreet has not taken any steps to ensure that the securities or investment vehicle referred to in this report are suitable for any particular investor. The investment or services contained or referred to in this report may not be suitable for you and it is recommended that you consult an independent investment advisor if you are in doubt about such investments or investment services. Nothing in this report constitutes investment, legal, accounting or tax advice or a representation that any investment or strategy is suitable or appropriate to your individual circumstances or otherwise constitutes a personal recommendation to you.

The ratings and other opinions contained in this Document must be construed solely as statements of opinion from TheStreet, Inc., and not statements of fact. Each rating or opinion must be weighed solely as a factor in your choice of an institution and should not be construed as a recommendation to buy, sell or otherwise act with respect to the particular product or company involved.

Past performance should not be taken as an indication or guarantee of future performance, and no representation or warranty, expressed or implied, is made regarding future performance. Information, opinions and estimates contained in this report reflect a judgment at its original date of publication and are subject to change without notice. TheStreet offers a notification service for rating changes on companies you specify. For more information call 1-800-706-2501 or visit www.thestreet.com/ratings. The price, value and income from any of the securities or financial instruments mentioned in this report can fall as well as rise.

This Document and the information contained herein is copyrighted by TheStreet, Inc. Any copying, displaying, selling, distributing or otherwise delivering of this information or any part of this Document to any other person, without the express written consent of TheStreet, Inc. except by a reviewer or editor who may quote brief passages in connection with a review or a news story, is prohibited.

Welcome to TheStreet Ratings
Guide to Stock Mutual Funds

With the growing popularity of mutual fund investing, consumers need a reliable source to help them track and evaluate the performance of their mutual fund holdings. Plus, they need a way of identifying and monitoring other funds as potential new investments. Unfortunately, the hundreds of performance and risk measures available – multiplied by the vast number of mutual fund investments on the market today – can make this a daunting task for even the most sophisticated investor.

TheStreet Investment Ratings simplify the evaluation process. We condense all of the available mutual fund data into a single composite opinion of each fund's risk-adjusted performance. This allows you to instantly identify those funds that have historically done well and those that have underperformed the market. While there is no guarantee of future performance, TheStreet Investment Ratings provide a solid framework for making informed investment decisions.

TheStreet Ratings' Mission Statement

TheStreet Ratings' mission is to empower consumers, professionals, and institutions with high quality advisory information for selecting or monitoring financial investments.

In doing so, TheStreet Ratings will adhere to the highest ethical standards by maintaining our independent, unbiased outlook and approach to advising our customers.

Why rely on TheStreet Ratings?

Our mission is to provide fair, objective information to help professionals and consumers alike make educated purchasing decisions.

At TheStreet Ratings, objectivity and total independence are never compromised. We never take a penny from rated companies for issuing our ratings, and we publish them without regard for the companies' preferences. TheStreet's ratings are more frequently reviewed and updated than any other ratings, so you can be sure that the information you receive is accurate and current.

Our rating scale, from A to E, is easy to understand as follows:

	Rating	Description
Top 10% of stock mutual funds	A	Excellent
Next 20% of stock mutual funds	B	Good
Middle 40% of stock mutual funds	C	Fair
Next 20% of stock mutual funds	D	Weak
Bottom 10% of stock mutual funds	E	Very Weak

In addition, a plus or minus sign designates that a fund is in the top third or bottom third of funds with the same letter grade.

Thank you for your trust and purchase of this Guide. If you have any comments, or wish to review other products from TheStreet Ratings, please call 1-800-706-2501 or visit www.thestreetratings.com. We look forward to hearing from you.

How to Use This Guide

The purpose of the *Guide to Stock Mutual Funds* is to provide investors with a reliable source of investment ratings and analyses on a timely basis. We realize that past performance is an important factor to consider when making the decision to purchase shares in a mutual fund. The ratings and analyses in this Guide can make that evaluation easier when you are considering:

- growth funds
- index funds
- balanced funds
- sector or international funds

However, this Guide does not include pure bond funds and money market funds since they are not comparable investments to funds invested exclusively or partially in equities. For information on bond and money market funds, refer to *TheStreet Ratings Guide to Bond and Money Market Mutual Funds*. The rating for a particular fund indicates our opinion regarding that fund's past risk-adjusted performance.

When evaluating a specific mutual fund, we recommend you follow these steps:

Step 1   **Confirm the fund name and ticker symbol.** To ensure you evaluate the correct mutual fund, verify the fund's exact name and ticker symbol as it was given to you in its prospectus or appears on your account statement. Many funds have similar names, so you want to make sure the fund you look up is really the one you are interested in evaluating.

Step 2   **Check the fund's Investment Rating.** Turn to Section I, the Index of Stock Mutual Funds, and locate the fund you are evaluating. This section contains all stock mutual funds analyzed by TheStreet Ratings including those that did not receive an Investment Rating. All funds are listed in alphabetical order by the name of the fund with the ticker symbol following the name for additional verification. Once you have located your specific fund, the first column after the ticker symbol shows its Investment Rating and corresponding percentile. Turn to *About TheStreet Investment Ratings* on page 7 for information about what this rating means.

Step 3   **Analyze the supporting data.** Following TheStreet Investment Rating are some of the various measures we have used in rating the fund. Refer to the Section I introduction (beginning on page 15) to see what each of these factors measures. In most cases, lower rated funds will have a low performance rating and/or a low risk rating (i.e., high volatility). Bear in mind, however, that TheStreet Investment Rating is the result of a complex computer-generated analysis which cannot be reproduced using only the data provided here.

When looking to identify a mutual fund that achieves your specific investing goals, we recommend the following:

Step 4   **Take our Investor Profile Quiz.** Turn to the Appendix and take our Investor Profile Quiz to help determine your level of risk tolerance. After you have scored yourself, the last page of the quiz will refer you to the risk category in Section VII (Top-Rated Stock Mutual Funds by Risk Category) that is best for you. There you can choose a fund that has historically provided top notch returns while keeping the risk at a level that is suited to your investment style.

Step 5   **View the 100 top performing funds.** If your priority is to achieve the highest return, regardless of the amount of risk, turn to Section V which lists the top 100 stock mutual funds with the best financial performance. Keep in mind that past performance alone is not always a true indicator of the future since these funds have already experienced a run up in price and could be due for a correction.

Step 6   **View the 100 funds with the lowest risk.** On the other hand, if capital preservation is your top priority, turn to Section VI which lists the top 100 stock mutual funds with the lowest risk. These funds will have lower performance ratings than most other funds, but can provide a safe harbor for your savings.

Step 7   **View the top-rated funds by fund type.** If you are looking to invest in a particular type of mutual fund (e.g., aggressive growth or a balanced fund), turn to Section VIII, Top-Rated Stock Mutual Funds by Fund Type. There you will find the top 100 stock mutual funds with the highest performance rating in each category. Please be careful to also consider the risk component when selecting a fund from one of these lists.

Step 8   **Refer back to Section I.** Once you have identified a particular fund that interests you, refer back to Section I, the Index of Stock Mutual Funds, for a more thorough analysis.

Always remember:

Step 9   **Read our warnings and cautions.** In order to use TheStreet Investment Ratings most effectively, we strongly recommend you consult the Important Warnings and Cautions listed on page 11. These are more than just "standard disclaimers." They are very important factors you should be aware of before using this Guide.

Step 10   **Stay up to date.** Periodically review the latest TheStreet Investment Ratings for the funds that you own to make sure they are still in line with your investment goals and level of risk tolerance. For information on how to acquire follow-up reports on a particular mutual fund, call 1-800-706-2501 or visit www.thestreetratings.com.

Data Source: Thomson Wealth Management
1455 Research Boulevard
Rockville, MD 20850

Date of data analyzed: March 31, 2015

About TheStreet Investment Ratings

TheStreet Investment Ratings represent a completely independent, unbiased opinion of a mutual fund's historical risk-adjusted performance. Each fund's rating is based on two primary components:

Primary Component #1   A fund's **Performance Rating** is based on its total return to shareholders over the last trailing three years, including share price appreciation and distributions to shareholders. This total return figure is stated net of the expenses and fees charged by the fund, and we also make additional adjustments for any front-end or deferred sales loads.

This adjusted return is then weighted to give more recent performance a slightly greater emphasis. Thus, two mutual funds may have provided identical returns to their shareholders over the last three years, but the one with the better performance in the last 12 months will receive a slightly higher performance rating.

Primary Component #2   The **Risk Rating** is based on the level of volatility in the fund's monthly returns, also over the last trailing three years. We use several statistical measures – standard deviation, semi-deviation and a drawdown factor – as our barometer of volatility. Funds with more volatility relative to other mutual funds are considered riskier, and thus receive a lower risk rating. By contrast, funds with a very stable returns are considered less risky and receive a higher risk rating.

Note that none of the mutual funds listed in this publication have received a risk rating in the A (Excellent) range. This is because all stock investments, by their very nature, involve at least some degree of risk.

The two ratings have totally independent meanings. Rarely will you ever find a mutual fund that has both a very high Performance Rating plus, at the same time, a very high Risk Rating. Therefore, the funds that receive the highest overall Investment Ratings are those that combine the ideal combination of both primary components. There is always a tradeoff between risk and reward. That is why we suggest you assess your own personal risk tolerance using the quiz in the Appendix section as a part of your decision-making process.

TheStreet Investment Ratings employ a ranking system to evaluate both safety and performance. Based on these measures, funds are divided into percentiles, and an individual performance rating and a risk rating are assigned to each fund. Then these measures are combined to derive a fund's composite percentile ranking. Finally, TheStreet Investment Ratings are assigned to their corresponding percentile rankings as shown on page 3.

How Our Ratings Differ From Those of Other Services

Balanced approach: TheStreet Investment Ratings are designed to meet the needs of aggressive *as well as* conservative investors. We realize that your investment goals can be different from those of other investors based upon your age, income, and tolerance for risk. Therefore, our ratings balance a fund's performance against the amount of risk it poses to identify those funds that have achieved the optimum mix of both factors. Some of these top funds have achieved excellent returns with only average risk. Others have achieved average returns with only moderate risk. Whatever your personal preferences, we can help you identify a top notch fund that meets your investing style.

Other Investment rating firms give a far greater weight to performance and insufficient consideration to risk. In effect, they are betting too heavily on a continuing bull market and not giving enough consideration to the risk of a decline. While performance is obviously a very important factor to consider, we believe that the riskiness of a fund is also very important. Therefore, we weigh these two components more equally when assigning TheStreet Investment Ratings.

But we don't stop there. We also assign a separate performance rating and risk rating to each fund so you can focus on the component that is most important to you. In fact, Sections V, VI, and VII are designed specifically to help you select the best stock mutual funds based on these two factors. No other source gives you the cream of the crop in this manner.

Easy to use: Unlike those of other services, TheStreet Investment Ratings are extremely intuitive and easy to use. Our rating scale (A to E) is easily understood by members of the general public based on their familiarity with school grades. So, there are no stars to count and no numbering systems to interpret.

More funds: *TheStreet Ratings Guide to Stock Mutual Funds* tracks more mutual funds than any other publication – with updates that come out more frequently than those of other rating agencies. We've included more than 15,000 funds in this edition, all of which are updated every three months. Compare that to other investment rating agencies, such as Morningstar, where coverage stops after the top 1,500 funds and it takes five months for a fund to cycle through their publication's update process.

Recency: Recognizing that every fund's performance is going to have its peaks and valleys, superior long-term performance is a major consideration in TheStreet Investment Ratings. Even so, we do not give a fund a top rating solely because it did well 10 or 15 years ago. Times change and the top performing funds in the current economic environment are often very different from those of a decade ago. Thus, our ratings are designed to keep you abreast of the best funds available *today* and in the *near future,* not the distant past.

No bias toward load funds: In keeping with our conservative, consumer-oriented nature, we adjust the performance for so-called "load" funds differently from other rating agencies. We spread the impact to you of front-end loads and back-end loads (a.k.a. deferred sales charges) over a much shorter period in our evaluation of a fund. Thus our performance rating, as well as the overall TheStreet Investment Rating, more fully reflects the actual returns the typical investor experiences when placing money in a load fund.

What Our Ratings Mean

A   **Excellent.** The mutual fund has an excellent track record for maximizing performance while minimizing risk, thus delivering the best possible combination of total return on investment and reduced volatility. It has made the most of the recent economic environment to maximize risk-adjusted returns compared to other mutual funds. While past performance is just an indication – not a guarantee – we believe this fund is among the most likely to deliver superior performance relative to risk in the future.

B   **Good.** The mutual fund has a good track record for balancing performance with risk. Compared to other mutual funds, it has achieved above-average returns given the level of risk in its underlying investments. While the risk-adjusted performance of any mutual fund is subject to change, we believe that this fund has proven to be a good investment in the recent past.

C   **Fair.** In the trade-off between performance and risk, the mutual fund has a track record which is about average. It is neither significantly better nor significantly worse than most other mutual funds. With some funds in this category, the total return may be better than average, but this can be misleading since the higher return was achieved with higher than average risk. With other funds, the risk may be lower than average, but the returns are also lower. In short, based on recent history, there is no particular advantage to investing in this fund.

D   **Weak.** The mutual fund has underperformed the universe of other funds given the level of risk in its underlying investments, resulting in a weak risk-adjusted performance. Thus, its investment strategy and/or management has not been attuned to capitalize on the recent economic environment. While the risk-adjusted performance of any mutual fund is subject to change, we believe that this fund has proven to be a bad investment over the recent past.

E   **Very Weak.** The mutual fund has significantly underperformed most other funds given the level of risk in its underlying investments, resulting in a very weak risk-adjusted performance. Thus, its investment strategy and/or management has done just the opposite of what was needed to maximize returns in the recent economic environment. While the risk-adjusted performance of any mutual fund is subject to change, we believe this fund has proven to be a very bad investment in the recent past.

+   **The plus sign** is an indication that the fund is in the top third of its letter grade.

-   **The minus sign** is an indication that the fund is in the bottom third of its letter grade.

U   **Unrated.** The mutual fund is unrated because it is too new to make a reliable assessment of its risk-adjusted performance. Typically, a fund must be established for at least three years before it is eligible to receive a TheStreet Investment Rating.

Important Warnings and Cautions

1. **A rating alone cannot tell the whole story.** Please read the explanatory information contained here, in the section introductions and in the appendix. It is provided in order to give you an understanding of our rating methodology as well as to paint a more complete picture of a mutual fund's strengths and weaknesses.

2. **Investment ratings shown in this Guide were current as of the publication date.** In the meantime, the rating may have been updated based on more recent data. TheStreet Ratings offers a notification service for ratings changes on companies that you specify. For more information call 1-800-706-2501 or visit www.thestreet.com/ratings.

3. **When deciding to buy or sell shares in a specific mutual fund, your decision must be based on a wide variety of factors in addition to TheStreet Investment Rating.** These include any charges you may incur from switching funds, to what degree it meets your long-term planning needs, and what other choices are available to you.

4. **TheStreet Investment Ratings represent our opinion of a mutual fund's past risk-adjusted performance.** As such, a high rating means we feel that the mutual fund has performed very well for its shareholders compared to other stock mutual funds. A high rating is not a guarantee that a fund will continue to perform well, nor is a low rating a prediction of continued weak performance. TheStreet Investment Ratings are not deemed to be a recommendation concerning the purchase or sale of any mutual fund.

5. **A mutual fund's individual performance is not the only factor in determining its rating.** Since TheStreet Investment Ratings are based on performance relative to other funds, it is possible for a fund's rating to be upgraded or downgraded based strictly on the improved or deteriorated performance of other funds.

6. **All funds that have the same TheStreet Investment Rating should be considered to be essentially equal from a risk/reward perspective.** This is true regardless of any differences in the underlying numbers which might appear to indicate greater strengths.

7. **Our rating standards are more consumer-oriented than those used by other rating agencies.** We make more conservative assumptions about the amortization of loads and other fees as we attempt to identify those funds that have historically provided superior returns with only little or moderate risk.

8. **We are an independent rating agency and do not depend on the cooperation of the managers operating the mutual funds we rate.** Our data are derived, for the most part, from price quotes obtained and documented on the open market. This is supplemented by information collected from the mutual fund prospectuses and regulatory filings. Although we seek to maintain an open line of communication with the mutual fund managers, we do not grant them the right to stop or influence publication of the ratings. This policy stems from the fact that this Guide is designed for the information of the consumer.

9. **This Guide does not cover bond and money market funds.** Because bond and money market funds represent a whole separate class of investments with unique risk profiles and performance expectations, they are excluded from this publication.

Section I

Index of
Stock Mutual Funds

An analysis of all rated and selected unrated

Equity Mutual Funds.

Funds are listed in alphabetical order.

Section I Contents

1.	**Fund Type**	The mutual fund's peer category based on an analysis of its investment portfolio.

AG	Aggressive Growth	HL	Health
AA	Asset Allocation	IN	Income
BA	Balanced	IX	Index
CV	Convertible	MC	Mid Cap
EM	Emerging Market	OT	Other
EN	Energy/Natural Resources	PM	Precious Metals
FS	Financial Services	RE	Real Estate
FO	Foreign	SC	Small Cap
GL	Global	TC	Technology
GR	Growth	UT	Utilities
GI	Growth and Income		

A blank fund type means that the mutual fund has not yet been categorized.

2.	**Fund Name**	The name of the mutual fund as stated in its prospectus, which can sometimes differ slightly from the name that the company uses for advertising. If you cannot find the particular mutual fund you are interested in, or if you have any doubts regarding the precise name, verify the information with your broker or on your account statement. Also, use the fund's ticker symbol for confirmation. (See column 3.)
3.	**Ticker Symbol**	The unique alphabetic symbol used for identifying and trading a specific mutual fund. No two funds can have the same ticker symbol, and the ticker symbol for mutual funds always ends with an "X".
		A handful of funds currently show no associated ticker symbol. This means that the fund is either small or new since the NASD only assigns a ticker symbol to funds with at least $25 million in assets or 1,000 shareholders.
4.	**Overall Investment Rating**	Our overall rating is measured on a scale from A to E based on each fund's risk-adjusted performance. Please see page 10 for specific descriptions of each letter grade. Also, refer to page 7 for information on how our ratings are derived. Most important, when using this rating, please be sure to consider the warnings beginning on page 11 regarding the ratings' limitations and the underlying assumptions.
5.	**Phone**	The telephone number of the company managing the fund. Call this number to receive a prospectus or other information about the fund.

6.	**Performance Rating/Points**	A letter grade rating based solely on the mutual fund's financial performance over the trailing three years, without any consideration for the amount of risk the fund poses. Like the overall Investment Rating, the Performance Rating is measured on a scale from A to E for ease of interpretation. The points score indicates where the Performance Rating falls on a scale of 0 to 10.
7.	**3-Month Total Return**	The total return the fund has provided to investors over the preceding three months. This total return figure is computed based on the fund's dividends, capital gains, and any other distributions to holders, as well as its share price appreciation/depreciation during the period, net of the expenses and fees it imposes on its shareholders. Although the total return figure does not reflect an adjustment for any loads the fund may carry, such adjustments have been made in deriving TheStreet Investment Ratings. The 3-Month Total Return shown here is not annualized.
8.	**6-Month Total Return**	The total return the fund has provided investors over the preceding six months, not annualized.
9.	**1-Year Total Return**	The total return the fund has provided investors over the preceding twelve months.
10.	**1-Year Total Return Percentile**	The fund's percentile rank based on its one-year performance compared to that of all other equity funds in existence for at least one year. A score of 99 is the best possible, indicating that the fund outperformed 99% of the other mutual funds. Zero is the worst possible percentile score.
11.	**3-Year Total Return**	The total annual return the fund has provided investors over the preceding three years.
12.	**3-Year Total Return Percentile**	The fund's percentile rank based on its three-year performance compared to that of all other equity funds in existence for at least three years. A score of 99 is the best possible, indicating that the fund outperformed 99% of the other mutual funds. Zero is the worst possible percentile score.
13.	**5-Year Total Return**	The total annual return the fund has provided investors over the preceding five years.
14.	**5-Year Total Return Percentile**	The fund's percentile rank based on its five-year performance compared to that of all other equity funds in existence for at least five years. A score of 99 is the best possible, indicating that the fund outperformed 99% of the other mutual funds. Zero is the worst possible percentile score.

15. Dividend Yield		Distributions provided to fund investors over the preceding 12 months, expressed as a percent of the fund's current share price. Dividend distributions are based on a fund's need to pass earnings from both dividends and gains on the sale of investments along to shareholders. Thus, these dividend distributions are included as a part of the fund's total return.

Keep in mind that a higher dividend yield means more current income, as opposed to capital appreciation, which in turn means a higher tax liability in the year of the distribution.

16. Expense Ratio	The expense ratio is taken directly from each fund's annual report with no further calculation. It indicates the percentage of the fund's assets that are deducted each fiscal year to cover its expenses, although for practical purposes, it is actually accrued daily. Typical fund expenses include 12b-1 fees, management fees, administrative fees, operating costs, and all other asset-based costs incurred by the fund. Brokerage costs incurred by the fund to buy or sell shares of the underlying stocks, as well as any sales loads levied on investors, are not included in the expense ratio.

If a mutual fund's net assets are small, its expense ratio can be quite high because the fund must cover its expenses from a smaller asset base. Conversely, as the net assets of the fund grow, the expense percentage should ideally diminish since the expenses are being spread across a larger asset base.

Funds with higher expense ratios are generally less attractive since the expense ratio represents a hurdle that must be met before the investment becomes profitable to its shareholders. Since a fund's expenses affect its total return though, they are already factored into its Investment Rating.

Right Pages

1. Risk Rating/Points	A letter grade rating based solely on the mutual fund's risk as determined by its monthly performance volatility over the trailing three years. The risk rating does not take into consideration the overall financial performance the fund has achieved or the total return it has provided to its shareholders. Like the overall Investment Rating, the Risk Rating is measured on a scale from A to E for ease of interpretation. The points score indicates where the Risk Rating falls on a scale of 0 to 10.
2. Standard Deviation	A statistical measure of the amount of volatility in a fund's monthly performance over the last trailing 36 months. In absolute terms, standard deviation provides a historical measure of a fund's deviation from its mean, or average, monthly total return over the period.

A high standard deviation indicates a high degree of volatility in the past, which usually means you should expect to see a high degree of volatility in the future as well. This translates into higher risk since a large negative swing could easily become a sizable loss in the event you need to liquidate your shares.

3. Beta

The level of correlation between the fund's monthly performance over the last trailing 36 months and the performance of its investment category as a whole.

A beta of 1.00 means that the fund's returns have matched those of the index one for one during the stock market's ups and downs. A beta of 1.10 means that on average the fund has outperformed the index by 10% during rising markets and underperformed it by 10% during falling markets. Conversely, a beta of 0.85 means that the fund has typically perfomed 15% worse than the overall market during up markets and 15% better during down markets.

4. Net Asset Value (NAV)

The fund's share price as of the date indicated. A fund's NAV is computed by dividing the value of the fund's asset holdings, less accrued fees and expenses, by the number of its shares outstanding.

5. Net Assets

The total value (stated in millions of dollars) of all of the fund's asset holdings including stocks, bonds, cash, and other financial instruments, less accrued expenses and fees.

Larger funds have the advantage of being able to spread their expenses over a greater asset base so that the effect per share is lessened. On the other hand, if a fund becomes too large, it can be more difficult for the fund manager to buy and sell investments for the benefit of shareholders.

6. Cash %

The percentage of the fund's assets held in cash or money market funds as of the last reporting period. Investments in this area will tend to hamper the fund's returns while adding to its stability during market swings.

7. Stocks %

The percentage of the fund's assets held in common or preferred stocks as of the last reporting period. Since stocks are inherently riskier investments than the other categories, it is common for funds invested primarily or exclusively in stocks to receive a lower risk rating.

8. Bonds %

The percentage of the fund's assets held in bonds as of the last reporting period. This category includes corporate bonds, municipal bonds, and government bonds such as T-bills and T-bonds.

9. Other %

The percentage of the fund's assets invested as of the last reporting period in other types of financial instruments such as convertible securities, options, and warrants.

10.	Portfolio Turnover Ratio	The average annual portion of the fund's holdings that have been moved from one specific investment to another over the past three years. This indicates the amount of buying and selling the fund manager engages in. A portfolio turnover ratio of 100% signifies that on average, the entire value of the fund's assets is turned over once during the course of a year.

A high portfolio turnover ratio has implications for shareholders since the fund is required to pass all realized earnings along to shareholders each year. Thus a high portfolio turnover ratio will result in higher annual distributions for shareholders, effectively increasing their annual taxable income. In contrast, a low turnover ratio means a higher level of unrealized gains that will not be taxable until you sell your shares in the fund.

11. Last Bull Market Return

The fund's performance during the most recent stock bull market. Use this field in combination with the Last Bear Market Return (next column) to assess how well the fund anticipates and reacts to changing market conditions.

Keep in mind that lower risk funds tend to under-perform higher risk funds during a bull market due to the risk/reward tradeoff.

12. Last Bear Market Return

The fund's performance during the most recent stock bear market. Use this field in combination with the Last Bull Market Return (previous column) to assess how well the fund anticipates and reacts to changing market conditions.

Keep in mind that lower risk funds tend to fare better than higher risk funds during a bear market although they may still record a net loss.

13. Manager Quality Percentile

The manager quality percentile is based on a ranking of the fund's alpha, a statistical measure representing the difference between a fund's actual returns and its expected performance given its level of risk. Fund managers who have been able to exceed the fund's statistically expected performance receive a high percentile rank with 99 representing the highest possible score. At the other end of the spectrum, fund managers who have actually detracted from the fund's expected performance receive a low percentile rank with 0 representing the lowest possible score.

14. Manager Tenure

The number of years the current manager has been managing the fund. Since fund managers who deliver substandard returns are usually replaced, a long tenure is usually a good sign that shareholders are satisfied that the fund is achieving its stated objectives.

15. Initial Purchase Minimum

The minimum investment amount, stated in dollars, that the fund management company requires in order for you to initially purchase shares in the fund. In theory, funds with high purchase minimums are able to keep expenses down because they have fewer accounts to administer. Don't be mislead, however, by the misconception that a fund with a high purchase minimum will deliver superior results simply because it is designed for "high rollers."

16. Additional Purchase Minimum

The minimum subsequent fund purchase, stated in dollars, that you can make once you have opened an existing account. This minimum may be lowered or waived if you participate in an electronic transfer plan where shares of the fund are automatically purchased at regularly scheduled intervals.

17. Front End Load

A fee charged on all new investments in the fund, stated as a percentage of the initial investment. Thus a fund with a 4% front-end load means that only 96% of your initial investment is working for you while the other 4% is immediately sacrificed to the fund company. It is generally best to avoid funds that charge a front-end load since there is usually a comparable no-load fund available to serve as an alternative.

While a fund's total return does not reflect the expense to shareholders of a front end load, we have factored this fee into our evaluation when deriving its TheStreet Investment Rating.

18. Back End Load

Also known as a deferred sales charge, this fee is levied when you sell the fund, and is stated as a percentage of your total sales price. For instance, investing in a fund with a 5% back-end load means that you will only receive 95% of your total investment when you sell the fund. The remaining 5% goes to the fund company. As with front-end loads, it is generally best to avoid funds that charge a back-end load since there is usually a comparable no-load fund available to serve as an alternative.

While a fund's total return does not reflect the expense to shareholders of a back-end load, we have factored this fee into our evaluation when deriving its TheStreet Investment Rating.

Fund Type	Fund Name	Ticker Symbol	Overall Investment Rating	Phone	Performance Rating/Pts	3 Mo	6 Mo	1Yr / Pct	3Yr / Pct	5Yr / Pct	Dividend Yield	Expense Ratio
	99 Pct = Best											
	0 Pct = Worst				PERFORMANCE							
								Total Return % through 3/31/15			Incl. in Returns	
									Annualized			
GR	13D Activist A	DDDAX	A+	(877) 413-3228	A+ / 9.7	5.33	12.73	15.64 /93	21.11 /98	--	0.00	1.75
GR	13D Activist C	DDDCX	U	(877) 413-3228	U /	5.10	12.27	14.82 /91	--	--	0.00	2.50
GR	13D Activist I	DDDIX	A+	(877) 413-3228	A+ / 9.8	5.34	12.88	15.98 /93	21.43 /98	--	0.00	1.50
SC	1492 Small Cap Core Alpha	FNTSX	D	(877) 571-1492	C- / 3.9	5.34	5.78	-7.14 / 4	11.62 /50	--	0.00	3.84
GL	1789 Growth and Income C	PSECX	C-	(888) 202-1388	C- / 3.1	0.35	2.74	5.14 /40	8.77 /31	--	0.39	2.05
FS	1919 Financial Services A	SBFAX	B-	(844) 828-1919	C+ / 6.9	-0.67	7.57	6.10 /47	16.75 /88	12.66 /65	0.35	1.45
FS	1919 Financial Services C	SFSLX	A-	(844) 828-1919	B- / 7.5	-0.82	7.23	5.41 /42	15.95 /83	11.88 /60	0.06	2.12
FS	1919 Financial Services I	LMRIX	A+	(844) 828-1919	B+ / 8.4	-0.56	7.80	6.50 /51	17.19 /91	13.03 /68	0.57	1.04
GI	1919 Socially Responsive Balanced A	SSIAX	D+	(844) 828-1919	C- / 3.2	1.58	4.41	8.28 /65	9.54 /36	8.89 /36	0.57	1.24
GI	● 1919 Socially Responsive Balanced B	SESIX	D+	(844) 828-1919	C- / 3.3	1.37	3.98	7.21 /57	8.35 /29	7.95 /30	0.00	2.38
GI	1919 Socially Responsive Balanced	SESLX	C-	(844) 828-1919	C- / 3.6	1.39	4.03	7.57 /60	8.79 /32	8.18 /31	0.00	1.96
GI	1919 Socially Responsive Balanced I	LMRNX	C-	(844) 828-1919	C / 4.3	1.60	4.50	8.57 /67	9.84 /38	9.17 /38	0.90	1.06
GL	361 Managed Futures Strategy I	AMFZX	C+	(888) 736-1227	C- / 3.2	3.49	6.94	5.42 /42	7.83 /26	--	0.00	2.15
GL	361 Managed Futures Strategy Inv	AMFQX	C+	(888) 736-1227	C- / 3.1	3.42	6.80	5.18 /40	7.57 /24	--	0.00	1.90
GL	361 Market Neutral I	ALSZX	C-	(888) 736-1227	E+ / 0.6	-0.24	-3.67	-4.31 / 6	1.88 / 6	--	0.00	10.92
GL	361 Market Neutral Inv	ALSQX	C-	(888) 736-1227	E / 0.5	-0.36	-3.82	-4.57 / 6	1.55 / 6	--	0.00	11.17
IN	AAM Bahl and Gaynor Income Gro A	AFNAX	U	(888) 966-9661	U /	0.49	3.99	9.94 /74	--	--	1.43	2.99
IN	AAM Bahl and Gaynor Income Gro I	AFNIX	U	(888) 966-9661	U /	0.47	4.20	10.29 /75	--	--	1.76	2.74
AA	AB 2000 Retirement Strat A	LTAAX	D	(800) 221-5672	E+ / 0.9	1.61	1.70	2.95 /26	4.17 /11	4.93 /12	2.00	4.50
AA	AB 2000 Retirement Strat Adv	LTAVX	D	(800) 221-5672	D- / 1.3	1.71	1.87	3.29 /28	4.50 /11	5.25 /13	2.93	4.30
AA	● AB 2000 Retirement Strat B	LTABX	D	(800) 221-5672	D- / 1.0	1.42	1.31	2.22 /23	3.40 / 9	4.19 / 9	0.00	5.04
AA	AB 2000 Retirement Strat C	LTACX	D	(800) 221-5672	D- / 1.1	1.46	1.39	2.30 /23	3.75 /10	4.37 /10	2.16	5.31
AA	AB 2000 Retirement Strat I	LTAIX	D	(800) 221-5672	D- / 1.3	1.60	1.75	3.14 /27	4.45 /11	5.21 /13	3.23	3.01
AA	AB 2000 Retirement Strat K	LTAKX	D	(800) 221-5672	D- / 1.2	1.60	1.74	3.04 /27	4.20 /11	4.99 /12	3.59	3.72
AA	AB 2000 Retirement Strat R	LTARX	D	(800) 221-5672	D- / 1.1	1.58	1.54	2.73 /25	3.93 /10	4.72 /11	3.21	4.00
AA	AB 2005 Retirement Strat A	LTBAX	D+	(800) 221-5672	D- / 1.2	1.91	2.08	3.55 /29	5.20 /14	5.68 /15	2.86	3.08
AA	AB 2005 Retirement Strat Adv	LTBVX	C-	(800) 221-5672	D / 1.7	2.01	2.31	3.87 /31	5.52 /15	5.99 /17	3.56	2.86
AA	● AB 2005 Retirement Strat B	LTCBX	D+	(800) 221-5672	D- / 1.3	1.73	1.73	2.83 /26	4.45 /11	4.91 /12	2.03	3.72
AA	AB 2005 Retirement Strat C	LTSCX	D+	(800) 221-5672	D- / 1.3	1.75	1.72	2.82 /26	4.48 /11	4.93 /12	2.55	3.84
AA	AB 2005 Retirement Strat I	LTBIX	C-	(800) 221-5672	D / 1.7	1.94	2.17	3.74 /30	5.50 /15	5.96 /17	3.80	2.43
AA	AB 2005 Retirement Strat K	LTBKX	D+	(800) 221-5672	D / 1.6	1.94	2.05	3.53 /29	5.22 /14	5.71 /15	3.41	2.85
AA	AB 2005 Retirement Strat R	LTBRX	D+	(800) 221-5672	D- / 1.5	1.81	1.94	3.29 /28	4.98 /13	5.44 /14	3.10	3.12
AA	AB 2010 Retirement Strat A	LTDAX	D+	(800) 221-5672	D- / 1.4	2.16	2.23	3.68 /30	6.12 /17	6.32 /19	3.05	1.51
AA	AB 2010 Retirement Strat Adv	LTDVX	C-	(800) 221-5672	D / 2.1	2.25	2.46	4.00 /32	6.42 /19	6.61 /21	3.57	1.20
AA	● AB 2010 Retirement Strat B	LTDBX	D+	(800) 221-5672	D / 1.6	2.07	1.91	2.99 /26	5.38 /14	5.57 /14	2.18	2.23
AA	AB 2010 Retirement Strat C	LTDCX	D+	(800) 221-5672	D / 1.6	2.00	1.93	3.02 /27	5.38 /14	5.56 /14	2.64	2.21
AA	AB 2010 Retirement Strat I	LTDIX	C-	(800) 221-5672	D / 2.1	2.26	2.47	4.01 /32	6.41 /19	6.62 /21	3.41	1.21
AA	AB 2010 Retirement Strat K	LTDKX	C-	(800) 221-5672	D / 2.0	2.16	2.30	3.75 /30	6.14 /17	6.37 /19	3.16	1.52
AA	AB 2010 Retirement Strat R	LTDRX	D+	(800) 221-5672	D / 1.8	2.15	2.17	3.53 /29	5.89 /16	6.09 /17	2.87	1.83
AA	AB 2015 Retirement Strat A	LTEAX	D+	(800) 221-5672	D / 1.8	2.38	2.47	3.88 /31	6.99 /21	6.83 /22	3.31	1.29
AA	AB 2015 Retirement Strat Adv	LTEVX	C-	(800) 221-5672	D+ / 2.6	2.46	2.57	4.15 /33	7.31 /23	7.16 /24	3.79	0.99
AA	● AB 2015 Retirement Strat B	LTGBX	D+	(800) 221-5672	D / 2.0	2.20	2.07	3.22 /28	6.25 /18	6.08 /17	2.66	2.01
AA	AB 2015 Retirement Strat C	LTECX	D+	(800) 221-5672	D / 2.0	2.13	2.02	3.17 /27	6.25 /18	6.07 /17	2.78	2.00
AA	AB 2015 Retirement Strat I	LTEIX	C-	(800) 221-5672	D+ / 2.6	2.47	2.54	4.22 /33	7.30 /23	7.16 /24	3.85	0.89
AA	AB 2015 Retirement Strat K	LTEKX	C-	(800) 221-5672	D+ / 2.4	2.45	2.48	3.97 /32	7.05 /22	6.89 /22	3.37	1.33
AA	AB 2015 Retirement Strat R	LTERX	D+	(800) 221-5672	D+ / 2.3	2.36	2.35	3.75 /30	6.78 /20	6.63 /21	3.08	1.64
AA	AB 2020 Retirement Strat A	LTHAX	D+	(800) 221-5672	D / 2.1	2.45	2.72	4.13 /33	7.66 /25	7.15 /24	3.28	1.19
AA	AB 2020 Retirement Strat Adv	LTHVX	C-	(800) 221-5672	C- / 3.0	2.62	2.88	4.55 /35	8.00 /27	7.48 /26	3.74	0.89
AA	● AB 2020 Retirement Strat B	LTHBX	D+	(800) 221-5672	D+ / 2.3	2.28	2.35	3.42 /29	6.93 /21	6.40 /19	2.41	1.91
AA	AB 2020 Retirement Strat C	LTHCX	D+	(800) 221-5672	D+ / 2.3	2.29	2.39	3.46 /29	6.91 /21	6.41 /19	2.79	1.90
AA	AB 2020 Retirement Strat I	LTHIX	C-	(800) 221-5672	C- / 3.0	2.54	2.83	4.50 /35	8.01 /27	7.50 /26	3.69	0.87
AA	AB 2020 Retirement Strat K	LTHKX	C-	(800) 221-5672	D+ / 2.8	2.52	2.78	4.18 /33	7.73 /25	7.21 /24	3.31	1.25

● Denotes fund is closed to new investors
* Denotes fund is included in Section II

www.thestreetratings.com

RISK			NET ASSETS		ASSET				Portfolio	BULL / BEAR		FUND MANAGER		MINIMUMS		LOADS	
	3 Year		NAV							Last Bull	Last Bear	Manager	Manager	Initial	Additional	Front	Back
Risk Rating/Pts	Standard Deviation	Beta	As of 3/31/15	Total $(Mil)	Cash %	Stocks %	Bonds %	Other %	Turnover Ratio	Market Return	Market Return	Quality Pct	Tenure (Years)	Purch. $	Purch. $	End Load	End Load
B- /7.0	9.9	0.86	17.78	99	6	93	0	1	85	N/A	N/A	95	4	2,500	500	5.8	2.0
U /	N/A	N/A	18.12	30	6	93	0	1	85	N/A	N/A	N/A	4	2,500	500	0.0	2.0
B- /7.0	10.0	0.86	17.95	300	6	93	0	1	85	N/A	N/A	96	4	1,000,000	0	0.0	2.0
C /4.9	16.0	1.06	14.39	6	7	92	0	1	176	N/A	N/A	10	4	5,000	250	0.0	2.0
B- /7.7	8.0	0.52	12.57	9	2	78	18	2	29	54.3	-15.7	91	4	2,000	100	0.0	1.0
B- /7.5	11.2	0.86	19.27	62	3	96	0	1	14	102.1	-18.7	82	1	1,000	50	5.8	0.0
B- /7.5	11.1	0.86	18.15	25	3	96	0	1	14	97.3	-19.0	77	1	1,000	50	0.0	0.0
B- /7.5	11.2	0.86	19.39	23	3	96	0	1	14	104.6	-18.6	84	1	1,000,000	0	0.0	0.0
C+ /6.2	6.7	0.68	18.74	114	3	68	28	1	22	55.3	-10.9	52	9	1,000	50	5.8	0.0
C+ /6.2	6.7	0.68	18.48	4	3	68	28	1	22	49.6	-11.3	34	9	1,000	50	0.0	0.0
C+ /6.3	6.7	0.68	18.94	15	3	68	28	1	22	51.7	-11.1	40	9	1,000	50	0.0	0.0
C+ /6.2	6.7	0.68	18.71	4	3	68	28	1	22	56.8	-10.7	56	9	1,000,000	0	0.0	0.0
B+ /9.3	6.5	N/A	11.57	476	0	0	0	100	0	N/A	N/A	97	4	100,000	0	0.0	0.0
B+ /9.3	6.5	-0.01	11.48	161	0	0	0	100	0	N/A	N/A	96	4	2,500	0	0.0	0.0
B+ /9.6	5.4	0.23	8.32	1	0	0	0	100	828	N/A	N/A	64	4	100,000	0	0.0	0.0
B+ /9.6	5.4	0.23	8.23	N/A	0	0	0	100	828	N/A	N/A	59	4	2,500	0	0.0	0.0
U /	N/A	N/A	13.44	25	2	97	0	1	33	N/A	N/A	N/A	3	2,500	500	5.5	2.0
U /	N/A	N/A	13.46	91	2	97	0	1	33	N/A	N/A	N/A	3	25,000	5,000	0.0	2.0
B- /7.4	4.3	0.68	10.71	1	0	28	71	1	23	21.9	-6.7	25	10	2,500	50	4.3	0.0
B- /7.2	4.3	0.68	10.70	N/A	0	28	71	1	23	23.2	-6.6	29	10	0	0	0.0	0.0
B- /7.9	4.3	0.68	10.68	N/A	0	28	71	1	23	18.9	-6.9	18	10	2,500	50	0.0	0.0
B- /7.3	4.3	0.68	10.40	N/A	0	28	71	1	23	20.0	-7.0	21	10	2,500	50	0.0	0.0
B- /7.1	4.3	0.68	10.17	N/A	0	28	71	1	23	23.0	-6.6	28	10	0	0	0.0	0.0
C+ /6.9	4.3	0.67	10.15	5	0	28	71	1	23	22.1	-6.6	27	10	0	0	0.0	0.0
B- /7.1	4.3	0.68	10.27	1	0	28	71	1	23	20.9	-6.7	23	10	0	0	0.0	0.0
B /8.4	5.4	0.86	11.19	3	0	37	62	1	15	27.8	-9.2	17	10	2,500	50	4.3	0.0
B /8.2	5.4	0.86	11.17	N/A	0	37	62	1	15	29.2	-9.0	20	10	0	0	0.0	0.0
B /8.5	5.3	0.86	11.15	N/A	0	37	62	1	15	24.8	-9.4	13	10	2,500	50	0.0	0.0
B /8.4	5.4	0.87	11.07	N/A	0	37	62	1	15	24.9	-9.4	13	10	2,500	50	0.0	0.0
B /8.2	5.3	0.86	11.02	1	0	37	62	1	15	29.2	-9.1	20	10	0	0	0.0	0.0
B /8.3	5.3	0.86	11.05	6	0	37	62	1	15	28.1	-9.2	18	10	0	0	0.0	0.0
B /8.3	5.3	0.86	11.28	N/A	0	37	62	1	15	26.9	-9.2	16	10	0	0	0.0	0.0
B- /7.9	6.4	1.04	11.35	8	0	47	52	1	16	34.2	-11.6	11	10	2,500	50	4.3	0.0
B- /7.9	6.4	1.04	11.34	16	0	47	52	1	16	35.5	-11.6	13	10	0	0	0.0	0.0
B /8.0	6.5	1.05	11.32	N/A	0	47	52	1	16	31.1	-12.0	8	10	2,500	50	0.0	0.0
B- /7.9	6.5	1.05	11.21	2	0	47	52	1	16	31.0	-11.9	8	10	2,500	50	0.0	0.0
B- /7.9	6.4	1.04	11.33	N/A	0	47	52	1	16	35.6	-11.6	13	10	0	0	0.0	0.0
B- /7.9	6.5	1.05	11.37	19	0	47	52	1	16	34.5	-11.7	11	10	0	0	0.0	0.0
B- /7.9	6.5	1.05	11.38	5	0	47	52	1	16	33.3	-11.7	10	10	0	0	0.0	0.0
B- /7.6	7.4	1.21	11.63	24	0	56	43	1	13	40.0	-13.6	7	10	2,500	50	4.3	0.0
B- /7.5	7.4	1.21	11.68	4	0	56	43	1	13	41.4	-13.4	8	10	0	0	0.0	0.0
B- /7.6	7.4	1.21	11.59	1	0	56	43	1	13	36.8	-13.8	5	10	2,500	50	0.0	0.0
B- /7.6	7.4	1.21	11.50	4	0	56	43	1	13	36.7	-13.8	5	10	2,500	50	0.0	0.0
B- /7.5	7.4	1.21	11.63	5	0	56	43	1	13	41.5	-13.4	8	10	0	0	0.0	0.0
B- /7.5	7.5	1.21	11.72	54	0	56	43	1	13	40.2	-13.5	7	10	0	0	0.0	0.0
B- /7.6	7.5	1.21	11.72	14	0	56	43	1	13	39.0	-13.6	6	10	0	0	0.0	0.0
B- /7.3	8.2	1.34	11.71	37	2	63	33	2	13	44.6	-15.3	5	10	2,500	50	4.3	0.0
B- /7.3	8.2	1.33	11.76	5	2	63	33	2	13	46.1	-15.3	6	10	0	0	0.0	0.0
B- /7.4	8.1	1.33	11.65	1	2	63	33	2	13	41.1	-15.5	4	10	2,500	50	0.0	0.0
B- /7.3	8.1	1.33	11.61	6	2	63	33	2	13	41.1	-15.6	4	10	2,500	50	0.0	0.0
B- /7.3	8.1	1.33	11.73	18	2	63	33	2	13	46.0	-15.2	6	10	0	0	0.0	0.0
B- /7.3	8.2	1.34	11.79	98	2	63	33	2	13	44.8	-15.3	6	10	0	0	0.0	0.0

99 Pct = Best
0 Pct = Worst

Fund Type	Fund Name	Ticker Symbol	Overall Investment Rating	Phone	Perfor-mance Rating/Pts	3 Mo	6 Mo	1Yr / Pct	3Yr / Pct	5Yr / Pct	Dividend Yield	Expense Ratio
AA	AB 2020 Retirement Strat R		C-	(800) 221-5672	D+ / 2.6	2.52	2.67	3.99 /32	7.46 /24	6.96 /23	2.96	1.56
AA	AB 2025 Retirement Strat A	LTIAX	D+	(800) 221-5672	D+ / 2.6	2.70	3.06	4.51 /35	8.52 /30	7.57 /27	3.16	1.20
AA	AB 2025 Retirement Strat Adv	LTIVX	C-	(800) 221-5672	C- / 3.5	2.78	3.23	4.85 /37	8.85 /32	7.89 /29	3.62	0.90
AA	● AB 2025 Retirement Strat B	LTIBX	C-	(800) 221-5672	D+ / 2.8	2.56	2.73	3.77 /30	7.76 /26	6.81 /22	2.51	1.92
AA	AB 2025 Retirement Strat C	LTICX	D+	(800) 221-5672	D+ / 2.7	2.48	2.64	3.77 /30	7.67 /25	6.77 /22	2.67	1.91
AA	AB 2025 Retirement Strat I	LTJIX	C-	(800) 221-5672	C- / 3.4	2.70	3.15	4.78 /37	8.82 /32	7.89 /29	3.47	0.92
AA	AB 2025 Retirement Strat K	LTJKX	C-	(800) 221-5672	C- / 3.3	2.70	3.05	4.50 /35	8.54 /30	7.62 /27	3.21	1.25
AA	AB 2025 Retirement Strat R	LTJRX	C-	(800) 221-5672	C- / 3.1	2.60	2.96	4.24 /33	8.26 /28	7.36 /25	2.81	1.56
AA	AB 2030 Retirement Strat A	LTJAX	C-	(800) 221-5672	C- / 3.1	2.89	3.56	5.09 /39	9.40 /36	7.99 /30	2.98	1.29
AA	AB 2030 Retirement Strat Adv	LTJVX	C	(800) 221-5672	C- / 4.0	3.06	3.79	5.49 /42	9.73 /38	8.33 /32	3.49	0.99
AA	● AB 2030 Retirement Strat B	LTJBX	C-	(800) 221-5672	C- / 3.3	2.74	3.18	4.37 /34	8.62 /31	7.23 /24	2.37	2.01
AA	AB 2030 Retirement Strat C	LTJCX	C-	(800) 221-5672	C- / 3.3	2.75	3.22	4.41 /34	8.65 /31	7.24 /25	2.48	2.00
AA	AB 2030 Retirement Strat I	LTKIX	C	(800) 221-5672	C- / 4.0	2.99	3.66	5.36 /41	9.69 /37	8.31 /32	3.36	0.98
AA	AB 2030 Retirement Strat K	LTKKX	C-	(800) 221-5672	C- / 3.8	2.98	3.56	5.17 /40	9.45 /36	8.07 /30	3.12	1.32
AA	AB 2030 Retirement Strat R	LTKRX	C-	(800) 221-5672	C- / 3.6	2.80	3.41	4.84 /37	9.16 /34	7.78 /28	2.74	1.63
AA	AB 2035 Retirement Strat A	LTKAX	C-	(800) 221-5672	C- / 3.5	3.07	3.97	5.64 /43	9.97 /39	8.28 /32	2.77	1.34
AA	AB 2035 Retirement Strat Adv	LTKVX	C	(800) 221-5672	C / 4.4	3.15	4.15	5.90 /46	10.30 /41	8.59 /34	3.21	1.04
AA	● AB 2035 Retirement Strat B	LTKBX	C-	(800) 221-5672	C- / 3.7	2.91	3.65	4.90 /38	9.21 /34	7.53 /27	1.98	2.05
AA	AB 2035 Retirement Strat C	LTKCX	C-	(800) 221-5672	C- / 3.7	2.92	3.67	4.92 /38	9.21 /34	7.52 /27	2.22	2.04
AA	AB 2035 Retirement Strat I	LTLIX	C	(800) 221-5672	C / 4.4	3.17	4.15	5.91 /46	10.30 /41	8.61 /34	3.12	1.02
AA	AB 2035 Retirement Strat K	LTLKX	C	(800) 221-5672	C- / 4.2	3.07	3.96	5.63 /43	10.04 /40	8.32 /32	2.87	1.36
AA	AB 2035 Retirement Strat R	LTLRX	C-	(800) 221-5672	C- / 4.0	2.99	3.83	5.42 /42	9.76 /38	8.07 /30	2.53	1.67
AA	AB 2040 Retirement Strat A	LTLAX	C-	(800) 221-5672	C- / 3.8	3.26	4.54	6.24 /48	10.50 /42	8.58 /34	3.09	1.39
AA	AB 2040 Retirement Strat Adv	LTLVX	C	(800) 221-5672	C / 4.7	3.34	4.69	6.55 /51	10.83 /44	8.92 /36	3.59	1.09
AA	● AB 2040 Retirement Strat B	LTLBX	C-	(800) 221-5672	C- / 4.1	3.10	4.20	5.58 /43	9.79 /38	7.83 /29	2.26	2.11
AA	AB 2040 Retirement Strat C	LTLCX	C-	(800) 221-5672	C- / 4.1	3.11	4.21	5.59 /43	9.76 /38	7.84 /29	2.55	2.10
AA	AB 2040 Retirement Strat I	LTSIX	C	(800) 221-5672	C / 4.7	3.37	4.70	6.66 /52	10.85 /45	8.92 /36	3.51	1.03
AA	AB 2040 Retirement Strat K	LTSKX	C	(800) 221-5672	C / 4.6	3.28	4.62	6.33 /49	10.60 /43	8.66 /34	3.29	1.38
AA	AB 2040 Retirement Strat R	LTSRX	C	(800) 221-5672	C / 4.4	3.18	4.45	6.07 /47	10.29 /41	8.37 /32	2.93	1.69
AA	AB 2045 Retirement Strat A	LTPAX	C-	(800) 221-5672	C- / 3.9	3.20	4.45	6.17 /48	10.62 /43	8.59 /34	2.57	1.47
AA	AB 2045 Retirement Strat Adv	LTPVX	C	(800) 221-5672	C / 4.8	3.29	4.60	6.49 /51	10.95 /45	8.95 /36	3.04	1.17
AA	● AB 2045 Retirement Strat B	LTPBX	C-	(800) 221-5672	C- / 4.1	3.06	4.09	5.49 /42	9.87 /39	7.86 /29	1.89	2.21
AA	AB 2045 Retirement Strat C	LTPCX	C-	(800) 221-5672	C- / 4.1	2.99	4.09	5.41 /42	9.84 /38	7.85 /29	2.04	2.18
AA	AB 2045 Retirement Strat I	LTPIX	C	(800) 221-5672	C / 4.8	3.25	4.61	6.44 /50	10.95 /45	8.92 /36	3.03	1.11
AA	AB 2045 Retirement Strat K	LTPKX	C	(800) 221-5672	C / 4.6	3.24	4.51	6.25 /49	10.70 /44	8.67 /34	2.80	1.45
AA	AB 2045 Retirement Strat R	LTPRX	C-	(800) 221-5672	C / 4.4	3.14	4.33	5.98 /46	10.38 /42	8.38 /32	2.41	1.76
AA	AB 2050 Retirement Strat A	LTQAX	D-	(800) 221-5672	C- / 3.9	3.19	4.41	6.03 /47	10.71 /44	8.65 /34	2.27	2.42
AA	AB 2050 Retirement Strat Adv	LTQVX	D	(800) 221-5672	C / 4.8	3.26	4.57	6.38 /50	11.06 /46	8.98 /37	2.80	2.13
AA	● AB 2050 Retirement Strat B	LTQBX	D-	(800) 221-5672	C- / 4.1	2.96	4.06	5.36 /41	9.94 /39	7.90 /29	1.76	3.21
AA	AB 2050 Retirement Strat C	LTQCX	D-	(800) 221-5672	C- / 4.1	2.97	3.90	5.30 /41	9.93 /39	7.90 /29	2.00	3.14
AA	AB 2050 Retirement Strat I	LTQIX	D	(800) 221-5672	C / 4.8	3.28	4.45	6.32 /49	11.04 /46	8.98 /37	3.06	1.75
AA	AB 2050 Retirement Strat K	LTQKX	D	(800) 221-5672	C / 4.6	3.14	4.40	6.04 /47	10.78 /44	8.70 /35	2.81	2.18
AA	AB 2050 Retirement Strat R	LTQRX	D	(800) 221-5672	C / 4.5	3.12	4.22	5.75 /44	10.49 /42	8.40 /32	2.48	2.49
AA	AB 2055 Retirement Strat A	LTWAX	D+	(800) 221-5672	C- / 3.9	3.10	4.32	6.04 /47	10.68 /43	8.64 /34	1.78	4.14
AA	AB 2055 Retirement Strat Adv	LTWVX	C-	(800) 221-5672	C / 4.8	3.24	4.58	6.46 /50	11.03 /46	8.94 /36	2.30	3.92
AA	● AB 2055 Retirement Strat B	LTWBX	D+	(800) 221-5672	C- / 4.1	2.99	4.01	5.36 /41	9.92 /39	7.88 /29	1.40	4.95
AA	AB 2055 Retirement Strat C	LTWCX	D+	(800) 221-5672	C- / 4.1	2.90	3.97	5.33 /41	9.91 /39	7.88 /29	1.55	4.92
AA	AB 2055 Retirement Strat I	LTWIX	D+	(800) 221-5672	C / 4.8	3.16	4.54	6.39 /50	11.05 /46	8.95 /36	3.24	3.12
AA	AB 2055 Retirement Strat K	LTWKX	D+	(800) 221-5672	C / 4.6	3.16	4.43	6.17 /48	10.78 /44	8.68 /34	3.04	3.61
AA	AB 2055 Retirement Strat R	LTWRX	D+	(800) 221-5672	C / 4.5	3.02	4.33	5.95 /46	10.47 /42	8.43 /33	2.67	3.87
AA	AB All Market Growth 1	ADADX	D+	(800) 221-5672	D / 1.6	2.54	2.30	2.66 /25	5.27 /14	--	2.61	4.28
AA	AB All Market Growth 2	ADAEX	C-	(800) 221-5672	D / 1.7	2.65	2.44	2.92 /26	5.53 /15	--	2.85	4.03

● Denotes fund is closed to new investors
★ Denotes fund is included in Section II

www.thestreetratings.com

Risk Rating/Pts	Standard Deviation	Beta	NAV As of 3/31/15	Total $(Mil)	Cash %	Stocks %	Bonds %	Other %	Portfolio Turnover Ratio	Last Bull Market Return	Last Bear Market Return	Manager Quality Pct	Manager Tenure (Years)	Initial Purch. $	Additional Purch. $	Front End Load	Back End Load
B- /7.3	8.2	1.34	11.78	21	2	63	33	2	13	43.5	-15.3	5	10	0	0	0.0	0.0
B- /7.1	8.9	1.46	12.15	37	5	70	24	1	16	50.4	-17.3	5	10	2,500	50	4.3	0.0
B- /7.1	8.9	1.45	12.18	5	5	70	24	1	16	52.0	-17.2	5	10	0	0	0.0	0.0
B- /7.1	8.9	1.46	12.01	1	5	70	24	1	16	46.9	-17.5	4	10	2,500	50	0.0	0.0
B- /7.1	8.8	1.45	11.97	5	5	70	24	1	16	46.7	-17.6	3	10	2,500	50	0.0	0.0
B- /7.1	8.9	1.46	12.17	5	5	70	24	1	16	52.1	-17.2	5	10	0	0	0.0	0.0
B- /7.1	8.9	1.45	12.19	117	5	70	24	1	16	50.8	-17.3	5	10	0	0	0.0	0.0
B- /7.1	8.9	1.46	12.23	22	5	70	24	1	16	49.4	-17.3	5	10	0	0	0.0	0.0
C+ /6.9	9.6	1.57	12.44	33	6	78	15	1	14	56.5	-18.9	4	10	2,500	50	4.3	0.0
C+ /6.9	9.6	1.58	12.46	5	6	78	15	1	14	58.4	-18.8	4	10	0	0	0.0	0.0
C+ /6.9	9.7	1.58	12.36	1	6	78	15	1	14	53.0	-19.2	3	10	2,500	50	0.0	0.0
C+ /6.9	9.6	1.57	12.34	5	6	78	15	1	14	53.0	-19.2	3	10	2,500	50	0.0	0.0
C+ /6.9	9.6	1.57	12.40	5	6	78	15	1	14	58.3	-18.8	4	10	0	0	0.0	0.0
C+ /6.9	9.6	1.58	12.46	88	6	78	15	1	14	56.9	-18.9	4	10	0	0	0.0	0.0
C+ /6.9	9.6	1.58	12.50	21	6	78	15	1	14	55.6	-19.0	4	10	0	0	0.0	0.0
C+ /6.7	10.1	1.65	12.76	26	5	83	11	1	17	61.2	-20.2	4	10	2,500	50	4.3	0.0
C+ /6.7	10.2	1.66	12.77	6	5	83	11	1	17	62.8	-20.1	4	10	0	0	0.0	0.0
C+ /6.7	10.2	1.66	12.74	1	5	83	11	1	17	57.4	-20.3	3	10	2,500	50	0.0	0.0
C+ /6.7	10.1	1.65	12.68	3	5	83	11	1	17	57.2	-20.3	3	10	2,500	50	0.0	0.0
C+ /6.7	10.1	1.66	12.71	5	5	83	11	1	17	62.8	-20.0	4	10	0	0	0.0	0.0
C+ /6.7	10.1	1.65	12.74	73	5	83	11	1	17	61.4	-20.1	4	10	0	0	0.0	0.0
C+ /6.7	10.1	1.65	12.75	14	5	83	11	1	17	60.0	-20.2	3	10	0	0	0.0	0.0
C+ /6.5	10.5	1.71	12.99	22	4	89	6	1	19	64.9	-20.8	3	10	2,500	50	4.3	0.0
C+ /6.4	10.5	1.72	13.01	7	4	89	6	1	19	66.7	-20.7	4	10	0	0	0.0	0.0
C+ /6.5	10.5	1.72	12.97	1	4	89	6	1	19	61.0	-21.0	3	10	2,500	50	0.0	0.0
C+ /6.5	10.5	1.72	12.93	3	4	89	6	1	19	61.1	-21.1	3	10	2,500	50	0.0	0.0
C+ /6.5	10.5	1.71	12.90	5	4	89	6	1	19	66.7	-20.7	4	10	0	0	0.0	0.0
C+ /6.4	10.5	1.72	12.92	59	4	89	6	1	19	65.3	-20.8	3	10	0	0	0.0	0.0
C+ /6.5	10.5	1.72	12.97	15	4	89	6	1	19	63.9	-20.9	3	10	0	0	0.0	0.0
C+ /6.3	10.6	1.73	12.56	16	4	89	6	1	20	66.8	-21.4	3	10	2,500	50	4.3	0.0
C+ /6.3	10.6	1.73	12.57	14	4	89	6	1	20	68.5	-21.3	4	10	0	0	0.0	0.0
C+ /6.3	10.6	1.74	12.46	N/A	4	89	6	1	20	63.0	-21.7	3	10	2,500	50	0.0	0.0
C+ /6.3	10.7	1.74	12.40	3	4	89	6	1	20	62.8	-21.7	3	10	2,500	50	0.0	0.0
C+ /6.3	10.6	1.73	12.38	3	4	89	6	1	20	68.5	-21.3	4	10	0	0	0.0	0.0
C+ /6.3	10.6	1.73	12.43	39	4	89	6	1	20	67.1	-21.4	3	10	0	0	0.0	0.0
C+ /6.3	10.6	1.73	12.47	10	4	89	6	1	20	65.6	-21.5	3	10	0	0	0.0	0.0
C- /3.7	10.7	1.75	8.41	4	3	90	6	1	31	67.6	-21.6	3	8	2,500	50	4.3	0.0
C- /3.7	10.7	1.74	8.55	N/A	3	90	6	1	31	69.4	-21.6	4	8	0	0	0.0	0.0
C- /3.8	10.7	1.74	8.35	N/A	3	90	6	1	31	63.5	-21.8	3	8	2,500	50	0.0	0.0
C- /3.7	10.7	1.75	8.32	1	3	90	6	1	31	63.8	-21.9	2	8	2,500	50	0.0	0.0
C- /3.4	10.7	1.75	8.19	3	3	90	6	1	31	69.6	-21.6	3	8	0	0	0.0	0.0
C- /3.5	10.6	1.73	8.21	12	3	90	6	1	31	68.0	-21.6	3	8	0	0	0.0	0.0
C- /3.6	10.7	1.75	8.26	3	3	90	6	1	31	66.6	-21.7	3	8	0	0	0.0	0.0
C /5.3	10.6	1.73	9.65	2	3	90	6	1	52	68.1	-22.0	3	8	2,500	50	4.3	0.0
C /5.3	10.7	1.74	9.88	N/A	3	90	6	1	52	69.8	-22.0	4	8	0	0	0.0	0.0
C /5.3	10.7	1.74	9.30	N/A	3	90	6	1	52	64.1	-22.2	3	8	2,500	50	0.0	0.0
C /5.2	10.7	1.75	9.24	N/A	3	90	6	1	52	64.1	-22.2	3	8	2,500	50	0.0	0.0
C /4.8	10.7	1.75	8.81	2	3	90	6	1	52	69.7	-21.8	3	8	0	0	0.0	0.0
C /4.8	10.7	1.74	8.82	8	3	90	6	1	52	68.2	-21.9	3	8	0	0	0.0	0.0
C /4.9	10.8	1.76	8.87	2	3	90	6	1	52	66.9	-21.9	3	8	0	0	0.0	0.0
B /8.1	7.7	1.06	9.68	N/A	20	24	55	1	132	N/A	N/A	7	4	5,000	0	0.0	0.0
B /8.2	7.7	1.06	9.69	N/A	20	24	55	1	132	N/A	N/A	8	4	0	0	0.0	0.0

Fund Type	Fund Name	Ticker Symbol	Overall Investment Rating	Phone	Perfor-mance Rating/Pts	3 Mo	6 Mo	1Yr / Pct	3Yr / Pct	5Yr / Pct	Dividend Yield	Expense Ratio
AA	AB All Market Growth A	ADAAX	D+	(800) 221-5672	D- / 1.2	2.64	2.42	2.64 /25	5.26 /14	--	1.74	5.48
AA	AB All Market Growth Adv	ADAYX	C-	(800) 221-5672	D / 1.7	2.64	2.51	2.95 /26	5.55 /15	--	2.01	5.20
AA	AB All Market Growth C	ADACX	D+	(800) 221-5672	D- / 1.3	2.33	1.95	1.89 /21	4.49 /11	--	0.92	6.21
AA	AB All Market Growth I	AMAIX	C-	(800) 221-5672	D / 1.7	2.65	2.43	2.91 /26	5.52 /15	--	2.85	4.04
AA	AB All Market Growth K	ADAKX	D+	(800) 221-5672	D / 1.6	2.54	2.39	2.63 /25	5.28 /14	--	2.58	4.31
AA	AB All Market Growth R	ADARX	D+	(800) 221-5672	D- / 1.5	2.43	2.23	2.35 /23	5.01 /13	--	2.21	4.58
AA	AB All Mkt Real Return Z	AMTZX	E+	(800) 221-5672	E- / 0.2	-3.23	-13.89	-16.91 / 2	-5.12 / 2	-0.14 / 2	2.97	0.88
BA	AB Bal Wealth Strat A	ABWAX	C-	(800) 221-5672	D+ / 2.4	2.70	3.66	5.63 /43	7.92 /26	7.24 /25	2.20	1.19
BA	AB Bal Wealth Strat Adv	ABWYX	C	(800) 221-5672	C- / 3.3	2.76	3.81	5.93 /46	8.24 /28	7.55 /27	2.51	0.94
BA	● AB Bal Wealth Strat B	ABWBX	C-	(800) 221-5672	D+ / 2.6	2.50	3.26	4.86 /38	7.16 /22	6.48 /20	1.56	1.95
BA	AB Bal Wealth Strat C	ABWCX	C-	(800) 221-5672	D+ / 2.6	2.50	3.27	4.87 /38	7.17 /22	6.48 /20	1.71	1.94
BA	AB Bal Wealth Strat I	ABWIX	C	(800) 221-5672	C- / 3.3	2.76	3.79	5.91 /46	8.22 /28	7.54 /27	2.49	0.96
BA	AB Bal Wealth Strat K	ABWKX	C-	(800) 221-5672	C- / 3.0	2.63	3.59	5.57 /43	7.87 /26	7.19 /24	2.23	1.29
BA	AB Bal Wealth Strat R	ABWRX	C-	(800) 221-5672	D+ / 2.8	2.56	3.40	5.23 /40	7.52 /24	6.84 /22	1.98	1.60
GR	AB Concentrated Growth Adv	WPSGX	B+	(800) 221-5672	B+ / 8.6	1.59	8.73	17.59 /95	15.75 /81	15.15 /88	0.00	2.06
GR	AB Concentrated Growth Z	WPSZX	B	(800) 221-5672	B+ / 8.6	1.59	8.73	17.73 /95	15.75 /81	15.15 /88	0.00	2.05
AA	AB Consv Wealth Strat A	ABPAX	C-	(800) 221-5672	D- / 1.1	1.95	2.81	4.43 /35	4.70 /12	4.92 /12	0.40	1.16
AA	AB Consv Wealth Strat Adv	ABPYX	C-	(800) 221-5672	D / 1.6	2.03	2.92	4.71 /36	5.00 /13	5.24 /13	0.61	0.91
AA	● AB Consv Wealth Strat B	ABPBX	C-	(800) 221-5672	D- / 1.2	1.73	2.40	3.60 /29	3.94 /10	4.16 / 9	0.00	1.92
AA	AB Consv Wealth Strat C	ABPCX	C-	(800) 221-5672	D- / 1.2	1.73	2.40	3.60 /29	3.95 /10	4.17 / 9	0.00	1.91
AA	AB Consv Wealth Strat I	APWIX	C-	(800) 221-5672	D / 1.6	1.95	2.90	4.61 /36	4.96 /13	5.21 /13	0.59	0.93
AA	AB Consv Wealth Strat K	APWKX	C-	(800) 221-5672	D- / 1.4	1.88	2.76	4.30 /34	4.61 /12	4.85 /11	0.36	1.26
AA	AB Consv Wealth Strat R	APPRX	C-	(800) 221-5672	D- / 1.3	1.79	2.54	3.99 /32	4.28 /11	4.52 /10	0.16	1.57
GR	AB Core Opportunities A	ADGAX	B+	(800) 221-5672	B+ / 8.3	3.09	9.20	15.57 /93	16.55 /87	15.57 /91	0.00	1.34
GR	AB Core Opportunities Adv	ADGYX	A-	(800) 221-5672	A- / 9.1	3.15	9.34	15.86 /93	16.90 /89	15.92 /93	0.00	1.04
GR	● AB Core Opportunities B	ADGBX	B+	(800) 221-5672	B+ / 8.8	3.00	9.07	15.27 /92	16.22 /85	15.19 /88	0.00	2.08
GR	AB Core Opportunities C	ADGCX	B	(800) 221-5672	B+ / 8.5	2.91	8.84	14.73 /91	15.76 /81	14.77 /85	0.00	2.05
GR	AB Core Opportunities I	ADGIX	A-	(800) 221-5672	A- / 9.2	3.17	9.37	15.90 /93	16.94 /89	15.98 /93	0.00	0.94
GR	AB Core Opportunities K	ADGKX	B+	(800) 221-5672	A- / 9.0	3.07	9.20	15.59 /93	16.62 /88	15.64 /91	0.00	1.32
GR	AB Core Opportunities R	ADGRX	B+	(800) 221-5672	B+ / 8.9	3.04	9.10	15.32 /92	16.33 /86	15.35 /89	0.00	1.59
GR	AB Core Opportunities Z	ADGZX	A	(800) 221-5672	A- / 9.1	3.17	9.37	15.90 /93	16.73 /88	15.68 /91	0.00	0.83
MC	AB Discovery Gro A	CHCLX	C	(800) 221-5672	C+ / 6.6	5.82	10.26	7.93 /62	14.51 /71	18.26 /98	0.00	1.04
MC	AB Discovery Gro Adv	CHCYX	C+	(800) 221-5672	B / 7.6	5.96	10.42	8.19 /64	14.78 /73	18.49 /98	0.00	0.81
MC	● AB Discovery Gro B	CHCBX	C	(800) 221-5672	C+ / 6.7	5.64	9.73	7.00 /55	13.53 /64	17.20 /96	0.00	1.83
MC	AB Discovery Gro C	CHCCX	C	(800) 221-5672	C+ / 6.8	5.76	10.00	7.12 /56	13.64 /64	17.35 /97	0.00	1.81
MC	AB Discovery Gro I	CHCIX	C+	(800) 221-5672	B / 7.6	5.90	10.40	8.26 /65	14.84 /74	18.60 /98	0.00	0.77
MC	AB Discovery Gro K	CHCKX	C+	(800) 221-5672	B- / 7.3	5.84	10.18	7.85 /62	14.41 /70	18.17 /98	0.00	1.13
MC	AB Discovery Gro R	CHCRX	C+	(800) 221-5672	B- / 7.1	5.81	10.18	7.65 /60	14.06 /68	17.81 /97	0.00	1.41
MC	AB Discovery Gro Z	CHCZX	C+	(800) 221-5672	B- / 7.5	5.90	10.40	8.19 /64	14.60 /72	18.32 /98	0.00	0.67
SC	AB Discovery Value A	ABASX	B-	(800) 221-5672	B / 8.0	3.11	10.70	9.13 /70	16.78 /89	13.24 /70	0.40	1.21
SC	AB Discovery Value Adv	ABYSX	B+	(800) 221-5672	B+ / 8.9	3.15	10.81	9.42 /72	17.13 /90	13.57 /74	0.72	0.91
SC	● AB Discovery Value B	ABBSX	B	(800) 221-5672	B+ / 8.6	3.02	10.60	9.01 /69	16.70 /88	13.12 /69	0.33	1.92
SC	AB Discovery Value C	ABCSX	B-	(800) 221-5672	B / 8.2	2.91	10.33	8.38 /65	15.97 /83	12.46 /64	0.00	1.91
SC	AB Discovery Value I	ABSIX	B	(800) 221-5672	B+ / 8.9	3.18	10.84	9.47 /72	17.18 /91	13.61 /74	0.75	0.89
SC	AB Discovery Value K	ABSKX	B	(800) 221-5672	B+ / 8.7	3.10	10.66	9.08 /70	16.77 /89	13.27 /71	0.42	1.23
SC	AB Discovery Value R	ABSRX	B	(800) 221-5672	B+ / 8.5	3.01	10.46	8.72 /68	16.41 /86	12.93 /67	0.11	1.54
SC	AB Discovery Value Z	ABSZX	B	(800) 221-5672	B+ / 8.9	3.18	10.90	9.58 /72	17.00 /90	13.37 /72	0.83	0.81
EM	AB Emerging Markets Multi Asset A	ABAEX	E+	(800) 221-5672	E / 0.3	1.54	-1.54	1.91 /22	-1.44 / 3	--	4.12	2.67
EM	AB Emerging Markets Multi Asset	ABYEX	E+	(800) 221-5672	E / 0.4	1.60	-1.40	2.17 /23	-1.18 / 3	--	4.67	2.40
EM	AB Emerging Markets Multi Asset C	ABCEX	E+	(800) 221-5672	E / 0.4	1.39	-1.88	1.23 /19	-2.16 / 3	--	3.49	3.34
EM	AB Emerging Markets Multi Asset I	ABIEX	E+	(800) 221-5672	E / 0.4	1.62	-1.36	2.15 /22	-1.16 / 3	--	4.78	2.33
EM	AB Emerging Markets Multi Asset K	ABKEX	E+	(800) 221-5672	E / 0.4	1.57	-1.55	1.91 /22	-1.41 / 3	--	4.42	2.68

Legend at top:
- 99 Pct = Best
- 0 Pct = Worst
- PERFORMANCE — Total Return % through 3/31/15 — Annualized — Incl. in Returns

● Denotes fund is closed to new investors
* Denotes fund is included in Section II

www.thestreetratings.com

RISK			NET ASSETS		ASSET						BULL / BEAR		FUND MANAGER		MINIMUMS		LOADS	
	3 Year		NAV							Portfolio	Last Bull	Last Bear	Manager	Manager	Initial	Additional	Front	Back
Risk	Standard		As of	Total	Cash	Stocks	Bonds	Other		Turnover	Market	Market	Quality	Tenure	Purch.	Purch.	End	End
Rating/Pts	Deviation	Beta	3/31/15	$(Mil)	%	%	%	%		Ratio	Return	Return	Pct	(Years)	$	$	Load	Load
B /8.1	7.8	1.07	10.09	1	20	24	55	1		132	N/A	N/A	7	4	2,500	50	4.3	0.0
B /8.2	7.7	1.07	10.11	2	20	24	55	1		132	N/A	N/A	8	4	0	0	0.0	0.0
B /8.0	7.8	1.07	10.09	N/A	20	24	55	1		132	N/A	N/A	5	4	2,500	50	0.0	0.0
B /8.2	7.8	1.07	9.69	9	20	24	55	1		132	N/A	N/A	7	4	0	0	0.0	0.0
B /8.1	7.7	1.06	9.69	N/A	20	24	55	1		132	N/A	N/A	7	4	0	0	0.0	0.0
B /8.1	7.7	1.07	9.70	N/A	20	24	55	1		132	N/A	N/A	6	4	0	0	0.0	0.0
C+/5.7	11.7	1.44	9.00	N/A	16	60	22	2		73	2.0	-21.3	0	5	0	0	0.0	0.0
B- /7.6	7.1	1.17	14.09	760	0	59	40	1		15	45.9	-14.7	13	12	2,500	50	4.3	0.0
B- /7.6	7.1	1.16	14.17	100	0	59	40	1		15	47.3	-14.6	15	12	0	0	0.0	0.0
B- /7.6	7.0	1.16	13.96	83	0	59	40	1		15	42.2	-14.9	10	12	2,500	50	0.0	0.0
B- /7.6	7.1	1.17	13.96	245	0	59	40	1		15	42.4	-15.0	10	12	2,500	50	0.0	0.0
B- /7.6	7.0	1.16	14.13	13	0	59	40	1		15	47.3	-14.6	15	12	0	0	0.0	0.0
B- /7.6	7.1	1.17	14.05	30	0	59	40	1		15	45.7	-14.8	13	12	0	0	0.0	0.0
B- /7.6	7.1	1.17	14.01	12	0	59	40	1		15	44.1	-14.9	11	12	0	0	0.0	0.0
C+/6.2	11.5	1.12	28.18	160	1	98	0	1		17	101.3	-11.4	36	N/A	0	0	0.0	0.0
C /5.3	11.5	1.12	28.18	32	1	98	0	1		17	101.3	-11.4	36	N/A	0	0	0.0	0.0
B+/9.0	3.9	0.63	12.52	201	0	31	68	1		11	24.2	-7.1	38	N/A	2,500	50	4.3	0.0
B+/9.1	3.9	0.63	12.57	16	0	31	68	1		11	25.3	-6.9	42	N/A	0	0	0.0	0.0
B+/9.0	3.9	0.63	12.37	28	0	31	68	1		11	21.1	-7.3	28	N/A	2,500	50	0.0	0.0
B+/9.0	3.9	0.63	12.37	90	0	31	68	1		11	21.2	-7.3	29	N/A	2,500	50	0.0	0.0
B+/9.1	3.9	0.63	12.54	N/A	0	31	68	1		11	25.2	-7.0	41	N/A	0	0	0.0	0.0
B+/9.1	3.9	0.63	12.49	9	0	31	68	1		11	23.9	-7.1	37	N/A	0	0	0.0	0.0
B+/9.1	3.9	0.63	12.51	7	0	31	68	1		11	22.6	-7.3	32	N/A	0	0	0.0	0.0
C+/5.8	9.3	0.92	18.69	111	15	84	0	1		75	102.2	-16.2	81	16	2,500	50	4.3	0.0
C+/5.9	9.2	0.92	19.01	7	15	84	0	1		75	104.3	-16.1	83	16	0	0	0.0	0.0
C+/5.6	9.3	0.92	17.16	4	15	84	0	1		75	100.2	-16.3	79	16	2,500	50	0.0	0.0
C /5.4	9.3	0.92	16.60	33	15	84	0	1		75	97.3	-16.5	76	16	2,500	50	0.0	0.0
C+/5.9	9.2	0.92	19.19	N/A	15	84	0	1		75	104.3	-16.1	83	16	0	0	0.0	0.0
C+/5.9	9.3	0.92	18.81	4	15	84	0	1		75	102.6	-16.2	81	16	0	0	0.0	0.0
C+/5.8	9.2	0.92	18.30	5	15	84	0	1		75	100.7	-16.2	80	16	0	0	0.0	0.0
C+/6.3	9.3	0.92	19.19	N/A	15	84	0	1		75	103.1	-16.2	82	16	0	0	0.0	0.0
C /4.9	12.9	1.04	9.46	893	1	98	0	1		74	96.0	-22.6	27	7	2,500	50	4.3	0.0
C /5.0	12.9	1.04	9.96	806	1	98	0	1		74	97.4	-22.5	30	7	0	0	0.0	0.0
C /4.3	12.9	1.04	6.56	3	1	98	0	1		74	90.2	-22.7	19	7	2,500	50	0.0	0.0
C /4.3	13.0	1.05	6.61	70	1	98	0	1		74	90.7	-22.8	18	7	2,500	50	0.0	0.0
C /5.0	13.0	1.04	9.87	268	1	98	0	1		74	98.1	-22.5	30	7	0	0	0.0	0.0
C /4.9	13.0	1.04	9.42	21	1	98	0	1		74	95.2	-22.5	26	7	0	0	0.0	0.0
C /4.9	13.0	1.04	9.10	30	1	98	0	1		74	93.2	-22.7	23	7	0	0	0.0	0.0
C /4.9	12.9	1.04	9.87	90	1	98	0	1		74	96.5	-22.6	28	7	0	0	0.0	0.0
C /5.2	12.8	0.88	20.90	637	0	99	0	1		50	105.2	-26.6	85	13	2,500	50	4.3	0.0
C /5.2	12.8	0.88	21.30	996	0	99	0	1		50	107.3	-26.5	87	13	0	0	0.0	0.0
C /5.1	12.8	0.88	19.79	10	0	99	0	1		50	104.7	-26.7	85	13	2,500	50	0.0	0.0
C /5.0	12.8	0.88	19.11	173	0	99	0	1		50	100.3	-26.8	81	13	2,500	50	0.0	0.0
C /5.1	12.8	0.89	20.76	312	0	99	0	1		50	107.5	-26.5	87	13	0	0	0.0	0.0
C /5.2	12.8	0.88	20.65	70	0	99	0	1		50	105.3	-26.6	85	13	0	0	0.0	0.0
C /5.2	12.8	0.88	20.53	137	0	99	0	1		50	103.1	-26.7	83	13	0	0	0.0	0.0
C /5.0	12.8	0.88	20.74	109	0	99	0	1		50	106.3	-26.6	86	13	0	0	0.0	0.0
C /5.4	11.2	0.78	8.98	1	4	64	30	2		183	12.6	N/A	37	4	2,500	50	4.3	0.0
C /5.4	11.1	0.78	8.99	16	4	64	30	2		183	13.8	N/A	41	4	0	0	0.0	0.0
C /5.4	11.1	0.78	8.96	N/A	4	64	30	2		183	10.1	N/A	28	4	2,500	50	0.0	0.0
C /5.3	11.2	0.78	8.95	16	4	64	30	2		183	13.8	N/A	41	4	0	0	0.0	0.0
C /5.3	11.1	0.78	8.94	N/A	4	64	30	2		183	12.7	N/A	38	4	0	0	0.0	0.0

99 Pct = Best
0 Pct = Worst

Fund Type	Fund Name	Ticker Symbol	Overall Investment Rating	Phone	Performance Rating/Pts	PERFORMANCE — Total Return % through 3/31/15			Annualized		Incl. in Returns	
						3 Mo	6 Mo	1Yr / Pct	3Yr / Pct	5Yr / Pct	Dividend Yield	Expense Ratio
EM	AB Emerging Markets Multi Asset R	ABREX	E+	(800) 221-5672	E / 0.4	1.63	-1.56	1.70 /21	-1.65 / 3	--	4.09	2.85
UT	AB Equity Income A	AUIAX	C+	(800) 221-5672	C / 5.3	0.89	3.97	8.83 /68	13.15 /61	14.91 /86	3.93	1.04
UT	AB Equity Income Adv	AUIYX	C+	(800) 221-5672	C+ / 6.2	0.94	4.12	9.15 /70	13.48 /63	15.25 /88	4.36	0.74
UT	● AB Equity Income B	AUIBX	C+	(800) 221-5672	C / 5.5	0.70	3.60	8.05 /63	12.33 /55	14.08 /78	3.38	1.76
UT	AB Equity Income C	AUICX	C+	(800) 221-5672	C / 5.5	0.69	3.58	8.02 /63	12.35 /55	14.10 /79	3.47	1.74
UT	AB Equity Income I	AUIIX	C+	(800) 221-5672	C+ / 6.2	0.93	4.07	9.10 /70	13.49 /63	15.27 /89	4.38	0.75
UT	AB Equity Income K	AUIKX	C+	(800) 221-5672	C+ / 6.0	0.82	3.92	8.76 /68	13.12 /60	14.91 /86	4.04	1.08
UT	AB Equity Income R	AUIRX	C+	(800) 221-5672	C+ / 5.8	0.78	3.78	8.44 /66	12.77 /58	14.57 /83	3.77	1.39
IN	AB Equity Income Z	AUIZX	C	(800) 221-5672	C+ / 6.2	0.92	4.13	9.22 /70	13.35 /62	15.03 /87	4.48	0.67
RE	AB Glbl Real Est Inv A	AREAX	C+	(800) 221-5672	C+ / 6.4	4.09	11.65	15.53 /93	12.48 /56	11.21 /54	3.52	1.32
RE	AB Glbl Real Est Inv Adv	ARSYX	B-	(800) 221-5672	B- / 7.4	4.18	11.84	15.83 /93	12.81 /58	11.54 /57	4.14	1.07
RE	● AB Glbl Real Est Inv B	AREBX	C+	(800) 221-5672	C+ / 6.6	3.92	11.32	14.73 /91	11.65 /50	10.36 /47	2.50	2.13
RE	AB Glbl Real Est Inv C	ARECX	C+	(800) 221-5672	C+ / 6.6	3.96	11.33	14.73 /91	11.69 /50	10.41 /48	2.81	2.08
RE	AB Glbl Real Est Inv I	AEEIX	B-	(800) 221-5672	B- / 7.5	4.24	11.95	16.02 /93	12.89 /59	11.65 /58	4.13	1.01
RE	AB Glbl Real Est Inv K	ARRKX	C+	(800) 221-5672	B- / 7.2	4.09	11.78	15.61 /93	12.55 /56	11.28 /55	3.74	1.34
RE	AB Glbl Real Est Inv R	ARRRX	C+	(800) 221-5672	C+ / 6.9	4.09	11.56	15.22 /92	12.18 /54	10.95 /52	3.37	1.65
BA	AB Global Risk Alloc A	CABNX	D	(800) 221-5672	D / 2.0	4.26	4.06	8.69 /67	5.83 /16	8.08 /30	6.37	1.23
BA	AB Global Risk Alloc Adv	CBSYX	D+	(800) 221-5672	D+ / 2.8	4.29	4.25	9.05 /70	6.16 /17	8.41 /32	6.87	1.00
BA	● AB Global Risk Alloc B	CABBX	D	(800) 221-5672	D / 2.1	4.07	3.69	7.88 /62	5.06 /13	7.27 /25	6.22	2.01
BA	AB Global Risk Alloc C	CBACX	D	(800) 221-5672	D / 2.1	4.05	3.70	7.92 /62	5.08 /13	7.31 /25	6.47	2.00
BA	AB Global Risk Alloc I	CABIX	D+	(800) 221-5672	D+ / 2.8	4.31	4.23	9.09 /70	6.30 /18	8.56 /33	7.09	0.83
BA	AB Global Risk Alloc K	CBSKX	D+	(800) 221-5672	D+ / 2.6	4.27	4.08	8.66 /67	5.85 /16	8.10 /30	6.68	1.27
BA	AB Global Risk Alloc R	CBSRX	D	(800) 221-5672	D+ / 2.4	4.15	3.89	8.35 /65	5.52 /15	7.77 /28	6.39	1.59
TC	AB Global Thematic Gr A	ALTFX	D	(800) 221-5672	C- / 3.6	5.32	6.23	8.17 /64	9.45 /36	6.24 /18	0.00	1.46
TC	AB Global Thematic Gr Adv	ATEYX	D+	(800) 221-5672	C / 4.5	5.37	6.37	8.47 /66	9.77 /38	6.56 /20	0.00	1.22
TC	● AB Global Thematic Gr B	ATEBX	D	(800) 221-5672	C- / 3.8	5.09	5.79	7.29 /57	8.59 /30	5.40 /14	0.00	2.28
TC	AB Global Thematic Gr C	ATECX	D	(800) 221-5672	C- / 3.8	5.11	5.83	7.37 /58	8.66 /31	5.47 /14	0.00	2.23
TC	AB Global Thematic Gr I	AGTIX	D+	(800) 221-5672	C / 4.7	5.44	6.50	8.72 /68	10.07 /40	6.86 /22	0.00	0.96
TC	AB Global Thematic Gr K	ATEKX	D+	(800) 221-5672	C / 4.5	5.34	6.32	8.36 /65	9.68 /37	6.47 /20	0.00	1.29
TC	AB Global Thematic Gr R	ATERX	D+	(800) 221-5672	C- / 4.2	5.27	6.16	8.02 /63	9.34 /35	6.15 /18	0.00	1.60
GI	AB Growth and Income A	CABDX	B-	(800) 221-5672	C+ / 6.6	0.73	5.67	8.61 /67	15.33 /77	14.55 /83	0.72	1.00
GI	AB Growth and Income Adv	CBBYX	A-	(800) 221-5672	B / 7.6	0.73	5.82	8.75 /68	15.63 /80	14.85 /86	1.08	0.68
GI	● AB Growth and Income B	CBBDX	B-	(800) 221-5672	C+ / 6.8	0.73	5.45	7.80 /61	14.54 /71	13.65 /74	0.00	1.75
GI	AB Growth and Income C	CBBCX	B-	(800) 221-5672	C+ / 6.7	0.55	5.33	7.68 /60	14.51 /71	13.71 /75	0.06	1.72
GI	AB Growth and Income I	CBBIX	A-	(800) 221-5672	B / 7.7	0.90	5.78	8.88 /69	15.78 /82	15.00 /87	1.10	0.66
GI	AB Growth and Income K	CBBKX	A-	(800) 221-5672	B- / 7.5	0.92	5.75	8.72 /68	15.47 /79	14.59 /83	0.79	1.04
GI	AB Growth and Income R	CBBRX	B+	(800) 221-5672	B- / 7.2	0.74	5.72	8.31 /65	15.11 /76	14.29 /80	0.55	1.34
GI	AB Growth and Income Z	CBBZX	B	(800) 221-5672	B- / 7.5	0.90	5.82	8.92 /69	15.55 /80	14.68 /84	1.13	0.61
GR	AB Growth Fund A	AGRFX	A-	(800) 221-5672	B+ / 8.8	5.22	11.47	19.47 /96	15.86 /82	14.83 /85	0.00	1.33
GR	AB Growth Fund Adv	AGRYX	A	(800) 221-5672	A / 9.4	5.27	11.62	19.80 /97	16.21 /85	15.17 /88	0.00	1.08
GR	● AB Growth Fund B	AGBBX	B+	(800) 221-5672	B+ / 8.9	5.00	10.93	18.48 /96	14.95 /74	13.92 /77	0.00	2.14
GR	AB Growth Fund C	AGRCX	A-	(800) 221-5672	B+ / 8.9	5.00	11.00	18.55 /96	15.02 /75	13.99 /78	0.00	2.09
GR	AB Growth Fund I	AGFIX	A	(800) 221-5672	A / 9.4	5.31	11.67	19.94 /97	16.37 /86	15.38 /89	0.00	0.95
GR	AB Growth Fund K	AGFKX	A	(800) 221-5672	A / 9.3	5.23	11.49	19.54 /96	15.99 /83	15.01 /87	0.00	1.26
GR	AB Growth Fund R	AGFRX	A	(800) 221-5672	A- / 9.2	5.14	11.30	19.15 /96	15.63 /80	14.64 /84	0.00	1.59
RE	AB Inst Global RealEst II	ARIIX	B-	(800) 221-5672	B / 7.8	4.43	12.23	16.54 /94	13.27 /61	12.12 /61	3.53	0.67
FO	AB International Port A	AIZAX	E+	(800) 221-5672	D- / 1.0	4.13	0.41	-3.54 / 8	5.40 /15	1.84 / 4	1.99	1.64
FO	● AB International Port B	AIZBX	E+	(800) 221-5672	D- / 1.1	3.95	0.09	-4.20 / 7	4.55 /12	1.03 / 3	0.92	2.49
FO	AB International Port C	AIZCX	E+	(800) 221-5672	D- / 1.1	3.98	0.11	-4.19 / 7	4.82 /13	1.22 / 4	1.26	2.41
FO	AB International Value A	ABIAX	E+	(800) 221-5672	D- / 1.5	5.44	1.48	-2.13 /10	6.82 /20	2.29 / 5	2.96	1.42
FO	AB International Value Adv	ABIYX	D-	(800) 221-5672	D / 2.1	5.49	1.61	-1.92 /10	7.13 /22	2.60 / 5	3.41	1.16
FO	● AB International Value B	ABIBX	D-	(800) 221-5672	D / 1.6	5.28	1.06	-2.84 / 9	6.03 /17	1.53 / 4	1.87	2.18

● Denotes fund is closed to new investors
* Denotes fund is included in Section II

28

RISK			NET ASSETS		ASSET					BULL / BEAR		FUND MANAGER		MINIMUMS		LOADS	
	3 Year		NAV						Portfolio	Last Bull	Last Bear	Manager	Manager	Initial	Additional	Front	Back
Risk Rating/Pts	Standard Deviation	Beta	As of 3/31/15	Total $(Mil)	Cash %	Stocks %	Bonds %	Other %	Turnover Ratio	Market Return	Market Return	Quality Pct	Tenure (Years)	Purch. $	Purch. $	End Load	End Load
C / 5.4	11.2	0.78	8.96	N/A	4	64	30	2	183	11.9	N/A	34	4	0	0	0.0	0.0
C+ / 6.6	9.7	0.20	26.73	459	0	99	0	1	101	81.4	-16.1	98	5	2,500	50	4.3	0.0
C+ / 6.6	9.8	0.20	26.95	314	0	99	0	1	101	83.3	-16.0	98	5	0	0	0.0	0.0
C+ / 6.6	9.7	0.20	26.38	7	0	99	0	1	101	77.0	-16.3	98	5	2,500	50	0.0	0.0
C+ / 6.6	9.7	0.19	26.41	150	0	99	0	1	101	77.2	-16.4	98	5	2,500	50	0.0	0.0
C+ / 6.6	9.7	0.19	26.68	3	0	99	0	1	101	83.3	-16.0	98	5	0	0	0.0	0.0
C+ / 6.6	9.7	0.20	26.72	6	0	99	0	1	101	81.3	-16.1	98	5	0	0	0.0	0.0
C+ / 6.6	9.7	0.20	26.61	18	0	99	0	1	101	79.4	-16.2	98	5	0	0	0.0	0.0
C+ / 5.6	9.7	0.99	26.67	1	0	99	0	1	101	82.4	-16.1	33	5	0	0	0.0	0.0
C / 5.5	11.9	0.86	14.73	85	10	89	0	1	90	74.3	-22.0	72	3	2,500	50	4.3	0.0
C / 5.5	11.9	0.86	14.60	34	10	89	0	1	90	76.1	-22.0	74	3	0	0	0.0	0.0
C+ / 5.6	12.0	0.86	14.58	2	10	89	0	1	90	69.8	-22.3	62	3	2,500	50	0.0	0.0
C+ / 5.6	12.0	0.86	14.59	23	10	89	0	1	90	70.2	-22.3	63	3	2,500	50	0.0	0.0
C / 5.5	11.9	0.86	14.68	3	10	89	0	1	90	76.5	-21.9	75	3	0	0	0.0	0.0
C / 5.5	12.0	0.86	14.63	12	10	89	0	1	90	74.5	-22.0	72	3	0	0	0.0	0.0
C / 5.5	11.9	0.86	14.58	11	10	89	0	1	90	72.8	-22.2	69	3	0	0	0.0	0.0
C+ / 6.6	6.8	0.84	16.17	299	30	26	42	2	96	42.0	-10.3	25	3	2,500	50	4.3	0.0
C+ / 6.6	6.7	0.84	16.27	24	30	26	42	2	96	43.4	-10.2	28	3	0	0	0.0	0.0
C+ / 6.4	6.8	0.85	14.84	10	30	26	42	2	96	38.4	-10.5	17	3	2,500	50	0.0	0.0
C+ / 6.3	6.8	0.84	14.89	56	30	26	42	2	96	38.5	-10.5	18	3	2,500	50	0.0	0.0
C+ / 6.6	6.7	0.84	16.23	N/A	30	26	42	2	96	44.1	-10.1	30	3	0	0	0.0	0.0
C+ / 6.6	6.8	0.84	16.13	2	30	26	42	2	96	42.0	-10.2	25	3	0	0	0.0	0.0
C+ / 6.6	6.8	0.84	16.06	4	30	26	42	2	96	40.5	-10.4	22	3	0	0	0.0	0.0
C / 4.9	14.2	1.18	89.13	568	0	99	0	1	44	57.5	-29.9	2	2	2,500	50	4.3	0.0
C / 4.9	14.2	1.18	93.73	38	0	99	0	1	44	59.1	-29.8	3	2	0	0	0.0	0.0
C / 4.8	14.2	1.18	74.90	16	0	99	0	1	44	53.2	-30.1	2	2	2,500	50	0.0	0.0
C / 4.9	14.2	1.18	75.46	74	0	99	0	1	44	53.6	-30.1	2	2	2,500	50	0.0	0.0
C / 4.9	14.2	1.18	90.89	10	0	99	0	1	44	58.7	-29.8	3	2	0	0	0.0	0.0
C / 4.9	14.2	1.18	88.46	4	0	99	0	1	44	57.0	-29.9	2	2	0	0	0.0	0.0
B- / 7.5	9.8	1.00	5.54	1,293	7	92	0	1	54	97.8	-16.1	58	11	2,500	50	4.3	0.0
B- / 7.5	9.8	1.00	5.55	76	7	92	0	1	54	99.2	-15.8	62	11	0	0	0.0	0.0
B- / 7.5	9.8	1.00	5.53	29	7	92	0	1	54	92.3	-16.2	47	11	2,500	50	0.0	0.0
B- / 7.5	9.9	1.00	5.52	220	7	92	0	1	54	93.1	-16.4	45	11	2,500	50	0.0	0.0
B- / 7.5	9.9	1.00	5.62	15	7	92	0	1	54	100.2	-15.9	63	11	0	0	0.0	0.0
B- / 7.5	9.8	1.00	5.50	5	7	92	0	1	54	98.0	-15.9	59	11	0	0	0.0	0.0
B- / 7.5	9.7	0.99	5.46	7	7	92	0	1	54	95.7	-16.0	57	11	0	0	0.0	0.0
C+ / 5.9	9.8	1.01	5.62	1,287	7	92	0	1	54	98.9	-16.1	59	11	0	0	0.0	0.0
C+ / 6.2	10.8	1.02	63.25	606	2	97	0	1	72	101.0	-17.1	59	7	2,500	50	4.3	0.0
C+ / 6.2	10.8	1.02	67.30	30	2	97	0	1	72	103.1	-17.0	64	7	0	0	0.0	0.0
C+ / 6.0	10.8	1.02	39.51	18	2	97	0	1	72	95.6	-17.4	47	7	2,500	50	0.0	0.0
C+ / 6.0	10.8	1.02	39.89	72	2	97	0	1	72	96.0	-17.3	48	7	2,500	50	0.0	0.0
C+ / 6.2	10.8	1.02	66.83	N/A	2	97	0	1	72	104.1	-16.9	66	7	0	0	0.0	0.0
C+ / 6.2	10.8	1.02	64.59	3	2	97	0	1	72	101.9	-17.0	61	7	0	0	0.0	0.0
C+ / 6.2	10.8	1.02	62.54	1	2	97	0	1	72	99.7	-17.1	56	7	0	0	0.0	0.0
C / 5.4	12.1	0.87	11.10	405	11	88	0	1	78	78.4	-21.4	77	3	2,000,000	0	0.0	0.0
C / 5.3	13.7	1.02	15.37	4	0	99	0	1	67	36.3	-25.8	16	N/A	2,500	50	4.3	0.0
C / 5.3	13.7	1.02	15.51	N/A	0	99	0	1	67	32.5	-26.0	11	N/A	2,500	50	0.0	0.0
C / 5.3	13.7	1.02	15.40	2	0	99	0	1	67	33.5	-26.0	12	N/A	2,500	50	0.0	0.0
C / 5.3	14.6	1.09	12.80	188	1	98	0	1	60	44.4	-27.9	22	14	2,500	50	4.3	0.0
C / 5.2	14.6	1.09	13.07	86	1	98	0	1	60	45.8	-27.9	25	14	0	0	0.0	0.0
C / 5.3	14.6	1.09	12.57	5	1	98	0	1	60	40.8	-28.2	16	14	2,500	50	0.0	0.0

					PERFORMANCE							
						Total Return % through 3/31/15					Incl. in Returns	
	99 Pct = Best		Overall		Perfor-				Annualized		Dividend	Expense
Fund	0 Pct = Worst	Ticker	Investment		mance							
Type	Fund Name	Symbol	Rating	Phone	Rating/Pts	3 Mo	6 Mo	1Yr / Pct	3Yr / Pct	5Yr / Pct	Yield	Ratio
FO	AB International Value C	ABICX	E+	(800) 221-5672	D / 1.6	5.23	1.07	-2.84 / 9	6.07 /17	1.55 / 4	2.44	2.17
FO	AB International Value I	AIVIX	D-	(800) 221-5672	D+ / 2.3	5.53	1.75	-1.64 /11	7.37 /23	2.84 / 6	3.82	0.89
FO	AB International Value K	AIVKX	D-	(800) 221-5672	D / 2.0	5.45	1.49	-2.05 /10	6.94 /21	2.41 / 5	3.27	1.32
FO	AB International Value R	AIVRX	D-	(800) 221-5672	D / 1.9	5.39	1.35	-2.35 /10	6.59 /19	2.08 / 5	2.99	1.63
FO	AB Intl Growth A	AWPAX	D-	(800) 221-5672	D- / 1.4	4.23	0.78	3.14 /27	6.14 /17	4.42 /10	0.00	1.32
FO	AB Intl Growth Adv	AWPYX	D-	(800) 221-5672	D / 2.1	4.29	0.89	3.41 /28	6.46 /19	4.73 /11	0.00	1.06
FO	● AB Intl Growth B	AWPBX	D-	(800) 221-5672	D / 1.6	3.94	0.33	2.32 /23	5.35 /14	3.62 / 7	0.00	2.11
FO	AB Intl Growth C	AWPCX	D-	(800) 221-5672	D / 1.6	4.00	0.40	2.38 /23	5.39 /14	3.66 / 7	0.00	2.07
FO	AB Intl Growth I	AWPIX	D-	(800) 221-5672	D / 2.2	4.32	1.08	3.62 /30	6.64 /20	4.91 /12	0.00	0.92
FO	AB Intl Growth K	AWPKX	D-	(800) 221-5672	D / 2.0	4.18	0.85	3.15 /27	6.22 /18	4.48 /10	0.00	1.31
FO	AB Intl Growth R	AWPRX	D-	(800) 221-5672	D / 1.8	4.14	0.67	2.85 /26	5.87 /16	4.16 / 9	0.00	1.62
GR	AB Lg Cap Growth A	APGAX	B+	(800) 221-5672	A+ / 9.6	5.84	12.19	21.43 /97	18.44 /95	15.50 /90	0.00	1.24
GR	AB Lg Cap Growth Adv	APGYX	A-	(800) 221-5672	A+ / 9.8	5.89	12.32	21.73 /97	18.72 /96	15.74 /91	0.00	0.99
GR	● AB Lg Cap Growth B	APGBX	B+	(800) 221-5672	A+ / 9.6	5.62	11.66	20.39 /97	17.45 /92	14.49 /82	0.00	2.03
GR	AB Lg Cap Growth C	APGCX	B+	(800) 221-5672	A+ / 9.6	5.63	11.76	20.50 /97	17.53 /92	14.56 /83	0.00	2.00
GR	AB Lg Cap Growth I	ALLIX	A-	(800) 221-5672	A+ / 9.8	5.90	12.31	21.80 /97	18.85 /96	15.90 /92	0.00	0.90
GR	AB Lg Cap Growth K	ALCKX	A-	(800) 221-5672	A+ / 9.8	5.82	12.12	21.37 /97	18.42 /95	15.50 /90	0.00	1.24
GR	AB Lg Cap Growth R	ABPRX	A-	(800) 221-5672	A+ / 9.7	5.76	11.99	21.04 /97	18.08 /94	15.16 /88	0.00	1.54
GR	AB Long Short Multi Manager Adv	LSYMX	U	(800) 221-5672	U /	2.43	5.50	--	--	--	0.00	N/A
GR	AB Market Neutral Str-US A	AMUAX	D	(800) 221-5672	E / 0.4	1.02	0.61	-1.10 /13	-0.41 / 4	--	0.00	26.82
GR	AB Market Neutral Str-US Adv	AMUYX	D+	(800) 221-5672	E / 0.5	1.11	0.70	-0.79 /14	-0.11 / 4	--	0.00	26.76
GR	AB Market Neutral Str-US C	AMCUX	D	(800) 221-5672	E / 0.4	0.84	0.21	-1.84 /11	-1.10 / 3	--	0.00	27.39
GR	AB Market Neutral Str-US I	AMUIX	D	(800) 221-5672	E / 0.5	1.13	0.70	-0.81 /14	-0.09 / 4	--	0.49	26.16
GR	AB Market Neutral Str-US K	AMUKX	D	(800) 221-5672	E / 0.5	1.03	0.53	-1.09 /13	-0.36 / 4	--	0.32	26.78
GR	AB Market Neutral Str-US R	AMURX	D	(800) 221-5672	E / 0.5	1.04	0.54	-1.30 /12	-0.58 / 4	--	0.22	26.72
GL	AB Multi-Manager Alt Strat Z	ALTZX	U	(800) 221-5672	U /	1.88	3.20	--	--	--	0.00	2.81
GR	AB Select US Eq A	AUUAX	A-	(800) 221-5672	B- / 7.5	1.56	6.33	13.83 /89	15.96 /83	--	0.20	1.44
GR	AB Select US Eq Adv	AUUYX	A+	(800) 221-5672	B+ / 8.6	1.56	6.50	14.15 /90	16.31 /86	--	0.37	1.19
GR	AB Select US Eq C	AUUCX	A	(800) 221-5672	B / 7.7	1.39	6.01	13.03 /87	15.14 /76	--	0.00	2.20
GR	AB Select US Eq I	AUUIX	A+	(800) 221-5672	B+ / 8.5	1.64	6.50	14.14 /90	16.26 /85	--	0.33	1.18
GR	AB Select US Eq K	AUUKX	A+	(800) 221-5672	B+ / 8.3	1.57	6.34	13.77 /89	15.93 /83	--	0.00	1.62
GR	AB Select US Eq R	AUURX	A+	(800) 221-5672	B / 8.1	1.45	6.23	13.51 /88	15.69 /81	--	0.00	1.70
GR	AB Select US LS A	ASLAX	U	(800) 221-5672	U /	0.68	1.42	4.15 /33	--	--	0.00	2.31
GR	AB Select US LS Adv	ASYLX	U	(800) 221-5672	U /	0.67	1.49	4.39 /34	--	--	0.00	2.06
GR	AB Select US LS C	ASCLX	U	(800) 221-5672	U /	0.52	1.01	3.42 /29	--	--	0.00	3.06
SC	● AB Sm Cap Growth A	QUASX	D	(800) 221-5672	C+ / 5.8	5.82	9.04	2.73 /25	14.01 /67	17.50 /97	0.00	1.25
SC	● AB Sm Cap Growth Adv	QUAYX	C-	(800) 221-5672	C+ / 6.8	5.87	9.18	2.98 /26	14.31 /69	17.81 /97	0.00	1.00
SC	● AB Sm Cap Growth B	QUABX	D	(800) 221-5672	C+ / 5.9	5.60	8.52	1.83 /21	13.08 /60	16.53 /95	0.00	2.04
SC	● AB Sm Cap Growth C	QUACX	D	(800) 221-5672	C+ / 6.0	5.61	8.60	1.92 /22	13.15 /61	16.60 /95	0.00	2.00
SC	● AB Sm Cap Growth I	QUAIX	C-	(800) 221-5672	C+ / 6.8	5.90	9.22	3.08 /27	14.43 /70	17.97 /97	0.00	0.91
SC	● AB Sm Cap Growth K	QUAKX	D+	(800) 221-5672	C+ / 6.6	5.82	9.02	2.72 /25	14.08 /68	17.60 /97	0.00	1.19
SC	● AB Sm Cap Growth R	QUARX	D+	(800) 221-5672	C+ / 6.3	5.72	8.84	2.40 /24	13.70 /65	17.21 /96	0.00	1.52
AA	AB Tax-Mgd Bal Wealth Strat A	AGIAX	C-	(800) 221-5672	D- / 1.3	1.63	2.27	4.14 /33	5.59 /15	5.31 /13	0.41	1.19
AA	AB Tax-Mgd Bal Wealth Strat Adv	AGIYX	C-	(800) 221-5672	D / 1.9	1.70	2.34	4.44 /35	5.90 /16	5.61 /15	0.57	0.94
AA	● AB Tax-Mgd Bal Wealth Strat B	AGIBX	C-	(800) 221-5672	D- / 1.4	1.48	1.82	3.38 /28	4.82 /13	4.55 /10	0.00	1.95
AA	AB Tax-Mgd Bal Wealth Strat C	AGICX	C-	(800) 221-5672	D- / 1.4	1.48	1.83	3.39 /28	4.83 /13	4.57 /10	0.09	1.94
AA	AB Tax-Mgd Csv Wealth Strat A	ACIAX	D+	(800) 221-5672	E+ / 0.8	1.32	1.48	2.88 /26	3.55 / 9	3.55 / 7	0.36	1.69
AA	AB Tax-Mgd Csv Wealth Strat Adv	ACIYX	C-	(800) 221-5672	D- / 1.1	1.32	1.63	3.20 /27	3.83 /10	3.84 / 8	0.52	1.39
AA	● AB Tax-Mgd Csv Wealth Strat B	ACIBX	D+	(800) 221-5672	E+ / 0.9	1.11	1.14	2.16 /22	2.81 / 8	2.82 / 6	0.00	2.41
AA	● AB Tax-Mgd Csv Wealth Strat C	ACICX	D+	(800) 221-5672	E+ / 0.9	1.11	1.08	2.18 /23	2.82 / 8	2.82 / 6	0.02	2.40
FO	AB Tax-Mgd Intl Port A	ABXAX	E+	(800) 221-5672	D- / 1.0	4.11	0.56	-3.50 / 8	5.57 /15	1.78 / 4	2.12	1.50
FO	● AB Tax-Mgd Intl Port B	ABXBX	E+	(800) 221-5672	D- / 1.1	3.95	0.24	-4.15 / 7	4.80 /12	1.02 / 3	1.57	2.39

● Denotes fund is closed to new investors
* Denotes fund is included in Section II

www.thestreetratings.com

RISK	3 Year		NET ASSETS		ASSET				Portfolio	BULL / BEAR		FUND MANAGER		MINIMUMS		LOADS	
Risk Rating/Pts	Standard Deviation	Beta	NAV As of 3/31/15	Total $(Mil)	Cash %	Stocks %	Bonds %	Other %	Turnover Ratio	Last Bull Market Return	Last Bear Market Return	Manager Quality Pct	Manager Tenure (Years)	Initial Purch. $	Additional Purch. $	Front End Load	Back End Load
C / 5.3	14.7	1.09	12.47	67	1	98	0	1	60	40.9	-28.2	16	14	2,500	50	0.0	0.0
C / 5.2	14.7	1.09	12.78	3	1	98	0	1	60	47.0	-27.7	27	14	0	0	0.0	0.0
C / 5.2	14.6	1.09	12.76	14	1	98	0	1	60	44.8	-27.9	23	14	0	0	0.0	0.0
C / 5.2	14.7	1.09	12.70	22	1	98	0	1	60	43.3	-27.9	20	14	0	0	0.0	0.0
C / 5.5	13.2	0.95	16.76	287	0	99	0	1	36	45.2	-27.0	29	4	2,500	50	4.3	0.0
C / 5.5	13.2	0.94	17.00	65	0	99	0	1	36	46.7	-27.0	33	4	0	0	0.0	0.0
C / 5.5	13.2	0.94	15.02	7	0	99	0	1	36	41.5	-27.2	21	4	2,500	50	0.0	0.0
C / 5.5	13.2	0.95	15.08	59	0	99	0	1	36	41.7	-27.3	21	4	2,500	50	0.0	0.0
C / 5.5	13.2	0.94	16.89	1	0	99	0	1	36	47.6	-26.9	35	4	0	0	0.0	0.0
C / 5.5	13.2	0.94	16.69	6	0	99	0	1	36	45.5	-27.0	30	4	0	0	0.0	0.0
C / 5.5	13.2	0.94	16.59	16	0	99	0	1	36	44.0	-27.1	26	4	0	0	0.0	0.0
C / 5.2	10.9	1.02	39.53	1,315	9	90	0	1	66	114.7	-18.6	82	3	2,500	50	4.3	0.0
C / 5.4	10.9	1.02	42.22	498	9	90	0	1	66	116.3	-18.5	84	3	0	0	0.0	0.0
C / 4.5	10.9	1.02	31.56	38	9	90	0	1	66	108.5	-18.9	76	3	2,500	50	0.0	0.0
C / 4.6	10.9	1.02	31.88	257	9	90	0	1	66	109.1	-18.9	77	3	2,500	50	0.0	0.0
C / 5.4	10.9	1.02	41.98	135	9	90	0	1	66	117.3	-18.5	85	3	0	0	0.0	0.0
C / 5.3	10.9	1.02	40.19	63	9	90	0	1	66	114.8	-18.6	82	3	0	0	0.0	0.0
C / 5.2	10.9	1.02	38.58	28	9	90	0	1	66	112.5	-18.7	80	3	0	0	0.0	0.0
U /	N/A	N/A	10.55	32	0	0	0	100	0	N/A	N/A	N/A	1	0	0	0.0	0.0
B / 8.6	4.2	0.06	9.87	N/A	54	0	44	2	668	-0.4	4.5	46	5	2,500	50	4.3	0.0
B / 8.7	4.2	0.07	10.00	1	54	0	44	2	668	0.7	4.7	50	5	0	0	0.0	0.0
B / 8.4	4.3	0.07	9.61	N/A	54	0	44	2	668	-2.7	4.2	34	5	2,500	50	0.0	0.0
B / 8.5	4.3	0.07	9.87	2	54	0	44	2	668	0.7	4.7	50	5	0	0	0.0	0.0
B / 8.5	4.2	0.07	9.81	N/A	54	0	44	2	668	-0.1	4.6	45	5	0	0	0.0	0.0
B / 8.4	4.2	0.07	9.72	N/A	54	0	44	2	668	-1.1	4.5	42	5	0	0	0.0	0.0
U /	N/A	N/A	10.31	393	0	0	0	100	0	N/A	N/A	N/A	N/A	0	0	0.0	0.0
B- / 7.7	8.9	0.92	15.62	30	4	95	0	1	495	N/A	N/A	78	4	2,500	50	4.3	0.0
B- / 7.7	8.9	0.92	15.65	270	4	95	0	1	495	N/A	N/A	80	4	0	0	0.0	0.0
B- / 7.7	8.9	0.92	15.28	17	4	95	0	1	495	N/A	N/A	72	4	2,500	50	0.0	0.0
B- / 7.7	8.9	0.92	15.53	39	4	95	0	1	495	N/A	N/A	80	4	0	0	0.0	0.0
B- / 7.7	8.9	0.91	15.50	4	4	95	0	1	495	N/A	N/A	78	4	0	0	0.0	0.0
B- / 7.7	8.9	0.92	15.44	N/A	4	95	0	1	495	N/A	N/A	76	4	0	0	0.0	0.0
U /	N/A	N/A	11.87	342	47	52	0	1	673	N/A	N/A	N/A	3	2,500	50	4.3	0.0
U /	N/A	N/A	11.94	1,312	47	52	0	1	673	N/A	N/A	N/A	3	0	0	0.0	0.0
U /	N/A	N/A	11.67	242	47	52	0	1	673	N/A	N/A	N/A	3	2,500	50	0.0	0.0
C- / 3.1	15.1	0.99	47.08	377	0	99	0	1	80	100.9	-24.4	39	11	2,500	50	4.3	0.0
C- / 3.2	15.1	1.00	50.10	500	0	99	0	1	80	102.7	-24.3	42	11	0	0	0.0	0.0
D+ / 2.3	15.1	1.00	34.31	3	0	99	0	1	80	95.2	-24.6	28	11	2,500	50	0.0	0.0
D+ / 2.3	15.1	1.00	34.63	60	0	99	0	1	80	95.8	-24.6	29	11	2,500	50	0.0	0.0
C- / 3.2	15.1	1.00	49.87	445	0	99	0	1	80	103.5	-24.2	44	11	0	0	0.0	0.0
C- / 3.1	15.1	1.00	48.01	84	0	99	0	1	80	101.3	-24.3	39	11	0	0	0.0	0.0
C- / 3.0	15.1	1.00	46.38	53	0	99	0	1	80	99.0	-24.4	35	11	0	0	0.0	0.0
B / 8.6	5.3	0.86	13.70	87	5	39	55	1	58	31.9	-9.1	20	23	2,500	50	4.3	0.0
B / 8.5	5.3	0.86	13.73	44	5	39	55	1	58	33.2	-8.9	23	23	0	0	0.0	0.0
B / 8.6	5.3	0.86	13.71	3	5	39	55	1	58	28.9	-9.4	15	23	2,500	50	0.0	0.0
B / 8.6	5.3	0.86	13.72	29	5	39	55	1	58	28.9	-9.4	14	23	2,500	50	0.0	0.0
B / 8.9	3.4	0.56	11.49	33	3	26	69	2	31	19.9	-5.9	33	23	2,500	50	4.3	0.0
B / 8.8	3.5	0.57	11.53	5	3	26	69	2	31	21.1	-5.7	36	23	0	0	0.0	0.0
B / 8.9	3.5	0.56	11.81	1	3	26	69	2	31	16.9	-6.1	25	23	2,500	50	0.0	0.0
B / 8.9	3.5	0.56	11.80	13	3	26	69	2	31	16.9	-6.1	24	23	2,500	50	0.0	0.0
C / 5.4	13.7	1.02	15.45	2	1	98	0	1	64	36.8	-25.8	17	3	2,500	50	4.3	0.0
C / 5.4	13.6	1.02	15.52	N/A	1	98	0	1	64	33.3	-26.1	13	3	2,500	50	0.0	0.0

					PERFORMANCE							
	99 Pct = Best			**Overall**		**Perfor-**	Total Return % through 3/31/15					Incl. in Returns
	0 Pct = Worst			**Investment**		**mance**				Annualized		Dividend Expense
Fund		Ticker		**Rating**	Phone	**Rating/Pts**	3 Mo	6 Mo	1Yr / Pct	3Yr / Pct	5Yr / Pct	Yield Ratio
Type	Fund Name	Symbol										
FO	AB Tax-Mgd Intl Port C	ABXCX	E+	(800) 221-5672	D- / 1.1	3.96	0.24	-4.17 / 7	4.83 /13	1.06 / 3	1.25	2.25
GR	AB Tax-Mgd Wlth App Strat A	ATWAX	C-	(800) 221-5672	C- / 4.2	3.04	4.29	6.90 /54	11.18 /47	8.55 /33	1.48	1.21
GR	AB Tax-Mgd Wlth App Strat Adv	ATWYX	C	(800) 221-5672	C / 5.1	3.16	4.45	7.19 /57	11.50 /49	8.86 /36	1.82	0.96
GR	● AB Tax-Mgd Wlth App Strat B	ATWBX	C-	(800) 221-5672	C / 4.4	2.94	3.93	6.09 /47	10.39 /42	7.75 /28	0.56	1.99
GR	AB Tax-Mgd Wlth App Strat C	ATWCX	C-	(800) 221-5672	C / 4.4	2.95	3.93	6.16 /48	10.42 /42	7.79 /29	0.86	1.97
IN	AB Value A	ABVAX	B-	(800) 221-5672	C+/ 6.3	-0.84	3.14	7.99 /63	15.29 /77	11.47 /57	1.42	1.04
IN	AB Value Adv	ABVYX	B+	(800) 221-5672	B- / 7.3	-0.77	3.22	8.31 /65	15.62 /80	11.79 /59	1.78	0.74
IN	● AB Value B	ABVBX	B+	(800) 221-5672	B- / 7.0	-0.83	3.06	7.98 /63	15.24 /77	11.40 /56	1.34	1.76
IN	AB Value C	ABVCX	B-	(800) 221-5672	C+/ 6.4	-1.04	2.73	7.19 /57	14.45 /70	10.67 /50	0.79	1.74
IN	AB Value I	ABVIX	B+	(800) 221-5672	B- / 7.3	-0.77	3.31	8.36 /65	15.68 /81	11.86 /60	1.85	0.68
IN	AB Value K	ABVKX	B+	(800) 221-5672	B- / 7.0	-0.85	3.08	7.93 /62	15.23 /77	11.41 /56	1.47	1.11
IN	AB Value R	ABVRX	B-	(800) 221-5672	C+/ 6.7	-0.98	2.86	7.59 /60	14.87 /74	11.07 /53	1.12	1.42
GR	AB Wealth Appreciation Strat A	AWAAX	D+	(800) 221-5672	C- / 3.6	3.07	4.14	5.88 /45	10.13 /40	8.24 /31	2.15	1.36
GR	AB Wealth Appreciation Strat Adv	AWAYX	C-	(800) 221-5672	C / 4.4	3.07	4.19	6.08 /47	10.43 /42	8.55 /33	2.55	1.11
GR	● AB Wealth Appreciation Strat B	AWABX	C-	(800) 221-5672	C- / 3.7	2.87	3.69	5.02 /39	9.30 /35	7.43 /26	1.27	2.12
GR	AB Wealth Appreciation Strat C	AWACX	C-	(800) 221-5672	C- / 3.8	2.88	3.69	5.01 /39	9.32 /35	7.47 /26	1.51	2.12
GR	AB Wealth Appreciation Strat I	AWAIX	C-	(800) 221-5672	C / 4.4	3.15	4.28	6.10 /47	10.40 /42	8.53 /33	2.50	1.15
GR	AB Wealth Appreciation Strat K	AWAKX	C-	(800) 221-5672	C- / 4.2	3.02	4.07	5.68 /44	10.04 /40	8.16 /31	2.12	1.48
GR	AB Wealth Appreciation Strat R	AWARX	C-	(800) 221-5672	C- / 4.0	2.95	3.87	5.34 /41	9.70 /37	7.84 /29	1.87	1.79
GL	Abbey Capital Futures Strategy I	ABYIX	U	(888) 261-4073	U /	8.86	19.14	--	--	--	0.00	N/A
FO	Aberdeen Asia-Pac X-Japan Eq Inst	AAPIX	D-	(866) 667-9231	D- / 1.2	3.95	-0.07	3.15 /27	4.01 /10	6.17 /18	1.32	1.27
FO	Aberdeen Asia-Pac X-Japan Eq IS	AAPEX	D-	(866) 667-9231	D- / 1.2	4.03	-0.10	3.18 /27	3.97 /10	6.13 /18	1.25	1.32
FO	Aberdeen Asia-Pacific Sm Co A	APCAX	E-	(866) 667-9231	E+/ 0.6	-2.26	-9.45	-1.46 /12	4.07 /10	--	1.25	2.69
FO	Aberdeen Asia-Pacific Sm Co C	APCCX	E-	(866) 667-9231	E+/ 0.7	-2.51	-9.82	-2.19 /10	3.23 / 8	--	0.68	3.39
FO	Aberdeen Asia-Pacific Sm Co In Sv	APCSX	E-	(866) 667-9231	E+/ 0.9	-2.23	-9.36	-1.14 /13	4.70 /12	--	1.63	2.39
FO	Aberdeen Asia-Pacific Sm Co Inst	APCIX	E-	(866) 667-9231	E+/ 0.8	-2.26	-9.38	-1.15 /13	4.33 /11	--	1.65	2.39
FO	Aberdeen Asia-Pacific Sm Co R	APCRX	E-	(866) 667-9231	E+/ 0.7	-2.26	-9.55	-1.60 /11	3.58 / 9	--	1.05	2.96
FO	Aberdeen Asia-Pacific X-Japan Eq A	APJAX	D-	(866) 667-9231	E+/ 0.8	3.88	-0.19	2.95 /26	3.75 /10	--	0.96	1.52
FO	Aberdeen Asia-Pacific X-Japan Eq C	APJCX	D	(866) 667-9231	E+/ 0.9	3.90	-0.44	2.29 /23	3.05 / 8	--	0.45	2.27
FO	Aberdeen Asia-Pacific X-Japan Eq R	APJRX	D	(866) 667-9231	D- / 1.0	3.89	-0.30	2.67 /25	3.48 / 9	--	0.83	1.77
FO	Aberdeen China Oppty A	GOPAX	E+	(866) 667-9231	E / 0.5	3.37	0.00	5.12 /39	0.62 / 5	3.69 / 7	0.76	2.30
FO	Aberdeen China Oppty C	GOPCX	E+	(866) 667-9231	E+/ 0.6	3.16	-0.31	4.38 /34	-0.10 / 4	2.96 / 6	0.20	3.03
FO	Aberdeen China Oppty Inst	GOPIX	E+	(866) 667-9231	E+/ 0.7	3.40	0.15	5.29 /41	0.87 / 5	3.97 / 8	1.05	2.03
FO	Aberdeen China Oppty Inst Svc	GOPSX	E+	(866) 667-9231	E+/ 0.8	3.40	0.14	5.37 /41	0.88 / 5	3.98 / 8	1.02	2.05
FO	Aberdeen China Oppty R	GOPRX	E+	(866) 667-9231	E+/ 0.7	3.25	-0.15	4.71 /36	0.27 / 4	3.35 / 7	0.51	2.68
AA	Aberdeen Diversified Alt A	GASAX	C-	(866) 667-9231	D / 1.6	1.37	2.44	4.74 /37	6.81 /20	6.22 /18	1.93	2.57
AA	Aberdeen Diversified Alt C	GAMCX	C-	(866) 667-9231	D / 1.9	1.18	2.01	3.87 /31	6.02 /17	5.44 /14	2.07	3.30
AA	Aberdeen Diversified Alt Inst	GASIX	C	(866) 667-9231	D+/ 2.5	1.43	2.51	4.93 /38	7.07 /22	6.49 /20	2.17	2.30
AA	Aberdeen Diversified Alt R	GASRX	C-	(866) 667-9231	D / 2.1	1.30	2.33	4.38 /34	6.44 /19	5.88 /16	2.00	2.88
AA	Aberdeen Diversified Inc A	GMAAX	D	(866) 667-9231	D- / 1.4	1.66	2.03	4.91 /38	6.13 /17	6.27 /19	2.73	1.75
AA	Aberdeen Diversified Inc C	GMACX	D	(866) 667-9231	D / 1.6	1.37	1.55	4.07 /32	5.32 /14	5.50 /14	2.37	2.49
AA	Aberdeen Diversified Inc Inst	GMAIX	D+	(866) 667-9231	D / 2.1	1.64	2.11	5.14 /40	6.39 /18	6.56 /20	3.10	1.49
AA	Aberdeen Diversified Inc R	GMRRX	D+	(866) 667-9231	D / 1.7	1.49	1.76	4.42 /34	5.62 /15	5.81 /16	2.57	2.21
AA	Aberdeen Dynamic Alloc A	GMMAX	C-	(866) 667-9231	D+/ 2.6	3.76	5.44	7.92 /62	8.13 /28	7.63 /27	2.13	1.95
AA	Aberdeen Dynamic Alloc C	GMMCX	C	(866) 667-9231	C- / 3.0	3.51	5.02	7.13 /56	7.36 /23	6.85 /22	1.73	2.68
AA	Aberdeen Dynamic Alloc Inst	GMMIX	C+	(866) 667-9231	C- / 3.7	3.77	5.55	8.20 /64	8.42 /29	7.81 /29	2.48	1.68
AA	Aberdeen Dynamic Alloc R	GAGRX	C	(866) 667-9231	C- / 3.2	3.59	5.19	7.45 /59	7.71 /25	7.30 /25	1.94	2.38
EM	● Aberdeen Emerging Markets A	GEGAX	E+	(866) 667-9231	E / 0.4	3.12	-2.71	-0.71 /14	0.36 / 5	4.46 /10	1.04	1.43
EM	● Aberdeen Emerging Markets C	GEGCX	E+	(866) 667-9231	E / 0.5	2.99	-3.03	-1.41 /12	-0.32 / 4	3.73 / 7	0.52	2.12
EM	● Aberdeen Emerging Markets Inst	ABEMX	E	(866) 667-9231	E+/ 0.6	3.19	-2.58	-0.44 /14	0.68 / 5	4.77 /11	1.38	1.12
EM	● Aberdeen Emerging Markets Inst Svc	AEMSX	E	(866) 667-9231	E / 0.5	3.19	-2.69	-0.66 /14	0.45 / 5	4.54 /10	1.15	1.36
EM	● Aberdeen Emerging Markets R	GEMRX	E+	(866) 667-9231	E / 0.5	3.13	-2.84	-1.06 /13	0.04 / 4	4.16 / 9	0.81	1.81

● Denotes fund is closed to new investors
* Denotes fund is included in Section II

www.thestreetratings.com

RISK Risk Rating/Pts	3 Year Standard Deviation	Beta	NET ASSETS NAV As of 3/31/15	Total $(Mil)	ASSET Cash %	Stocks %	Bonds %	Other %	Portfolio Turnover Ratio	BULL / BEAR Last Bull Market Return	Last Bear Market Return	FUND MANAGER Manager Quality Pct	Manager Tenure (Years)	MINIMUMS Initial Purch. $	Additional Purch. $	LOADS Front End Load	Back End Load
C / 5.4	13.7	1.02	15.50	N/A	1	98	0	1	64	33.5	-26.1	13	3	2,500	50	0.0	0.0
C+ / 6.4	10.7	1.05	16.25	37	9	87	2	2	61	70.6	-21.7	10	22	2,500	50	4.3	0.0
C+ / 6.4	10.8	1.05	16.30	695	9	87	2	2	61	72.4	-21.6	11	22	0	0	0.0	0.0
C+ / 6.4	10.7	1.05	16.08	2	9	87	2	2	61	66.3	-21.9	7	22	2,500	50	0.0	0.0
C+ / 6.4	10.7	1.05	16.03	18	9	87	2	2	61	66.6	-21.9	7	22	2,500	50	0.0	0.0
B- / 7.2	10.9	1.10	14.25	60	0	99	0	1	56	95.5	-21.4	34	6	2,500	50	4.3	0.0
B- / 7.3	10.9	1.10	14.26	325	0	99	0	1	56	97.6	-21.2	38	6	0	0	0.0	0.0
B- / 7.2	11.0	1.11	14.29	2	0	99	0	1	56	95.3	-21.4	33	6	2,500	50	0.0	0.0
B- / 7.2	11.0	1.11	14.21	18	0	99	0	1	56	91.0	-21.6	24	6	2,500	50	0.0	0.0
B- / 7.3	11.0	1.10	14.14	3	0	99	0	1	56	98.0	-21.2	38	6	0	0	0.0	0.0
B- / 7.2	11.0	1.10	14.01	13	0	99	0	1	56	95.2	-21.4	33	6	0	0	0.0	0.0
B- / 7.2	11.0	1.10	14.11	2	0	99	0	1	56	93.3	-21.5	30	6	0	0	0.0	0.0
C+ / 6.2	10.6	1.03	15.46	400	0	96	3	1	20	65.3	-22.7	7	12	2,500	50	4.3	0.0
C+ / 6.2	10.7	1.03	15.42	912	0	96	3	1	20	66.9	-22.6	8	12	0	0	0.0	0.0
C+ / 6.2	10.7	1.04	15.43	41	0	96	3	1	20	61.2	-23.0	5	12	2,500	50	0.0	0.0
C+ / 6.2	10.7	1.03	15.37	123	0	96	3	1	20	61.3	-23.0	5	12	2,500	50	0.0	0.0
C+ / 6.2	10.7	1.03	15.40	2	0	96	3	1	20	66.9	-22.7	8	12	0	0	0.0	0.0
C+ / 6.2	10.7	1.03	15.37	16	0	96	3	1	20	64.9	-22.7	7	12	0	0	0.0	0.0
C+ / 6.2	10.6	1.03	15.35	5	0	96	3	1	20	63.2	-22.8	6	12	0	0	0.0	0.0
U /	N/A	N/A	12.66	103	0	0	0	100	0	N/A	N/A	N/A	N/A	1,000,000	1,000	0.0	0.0
C+ / 6.2	12.2	0.77	11.80	1,624	2	97	0	1	36	35.6	-19.1	24	20	1,000,000	0	0.0	0.0
C+ / 6.2	12.2	0.77	11.79	4	2	97	0	1	36	35.4	-19.2	24	20	1,000,000	0	0.0	0.0
D+ / 2.6	12.2	0.66	9.07	1	7	92	0	1	52	39.9	N/A	36	4	1,000	50	5.8	0.0
D+ / 2.6	12.2	0.66	8.94	N/A	7	92	0	1	52	36.1	N/A	27	4	1,000	50	0.0	0.0
D+ / 2.8	12.0	0.65	9.22	N/A	7	92	0	1	52	42.7	N/A	46	4	1,000,000	0	0.0	0.0
D+ / 2.6	12.2	0.66	9.10	24	7	92	0	1	52	41.3	N/A	40	4	1,000,000	0	0.0	0.0
D+ / 2.7	12.2	0.66	9.08	N/A	7	92	0	1	52	37.9	N/A	31	4	0	0	0.0	0.0
B- / 7.2	12.2	0.77	11.77	1	2	97	0	1	36	N/A	N/A	22	20	1,000	50	5.8	0.0
B- / 7.2	12.2	0.77	11.73	N/A	2	97	0	1	36	N/A	N/A	16	20	1,000	50	0.0	0.0
B- / 7.2	12.1	0.77	11.75	N/A	2	97	0	1	36	N/A	N/A	19	20	0	0	0.0	0.0
C+ / 6.1	11.4	0.63	19.95	13	2	97	0	1	31	19.3	-20.1	9	8	1,000	50	5.8	0.0
C+ / 6.0	11.4	0.63	19.24	6	2	97	0	1	31	16.3	-20.3	7	8	1,000	50	0.0	0.0
C+ / 6.1	11.4	0.63	20.05	2	2	97	0	1	31	20.3	-20.0	11	8	1,000,000	0	0.0	0.0
C+ / 6.1	11.4	0.63	20.05	1	2	97	0	1	31	20.3	-20.0	11	8	1,000,000	0	0.0	0.0
C+ / 6.1	11.4	0.63	19.67	1	2	97	0	1	31	17.8	-20.2	8	8	0	0	0.0	0.0
B / 8.6	5.9	0.87	13.33	33	43	38	17	2	54	40.7	-17.9	32	N/A	1,000	50	5.8	0.0
B / 8.6	5.9	0.87	12.85	19	43	38	17	2	54	37.2	-18.2	24	N/A	1,000	50	0.0	0.0
B / 8.6	5.9	0.86	13.45	101	43	38	17	2	54	42.0	-17.9	36	N/A	1,000,000	0	0.0	0.0
B / 8.6	5.9	0.86	13.24	1	43	38	17	2	54	38.9	-18.0	28	N/A	0	0	0.0	0.0
B- / 7.5	6.1	0.91	12.28	7	9	44	46	1	29	34.2	-12.1	20	9	1,000	50	5.8	0.0
B- / 7.4	6.2	0.92	12.01	16	9	44	46	1	29	31.0	-12.5	14	9	1,000	50	0.0	0.0
B- / 7.5	6.1	0.91	12.26	2	9	44	46	1	29	35.6	-12.1	22	9	1,000,000	0	0.0	0.0
B- / 7.5	6.1	0.91	12.17	N/A	9	44	46	1	29	32.2	-12.3	17	9	0	0	0.0	0.0
B / 8.2	6.9	1.10	13.63	10	10	65	23	2	52	44.3	-15.0	20	9	1,000	50	5.8	0.0
B / 8.2	6.9	1.10	13.36	13	10	65	23	2	52	40.8	-15.2	14	9	1,000	50	0.0	0.0
B / 8.2	6.9	1.10	13.57	2	10	65	23	2	52	45.8	-14.9	22	11	1,000,000	0	0.0	0.0
B / 8.2	6.9	1.09	13.55	1	10	65	23	2	52	42.5	-15.0	17	9	0	0	0.0	0.0
C+ / 6.2	15.2	1.06	13.90	318	2	97	0	1	5	25.7	-18.2	62	8	1,000	50	5.8	0.0
C+ / 6.2	15.1	1.06	13.79	41	2	97	0	1	5	22.8	-18.4	52	8	1,000	50	0.0	0.0
C / 4.3	15.2	1.06	13.92	8,658	2	97	0	1	5	27.1	-18.1	67	8	1,000,000	0	0.0	0.0
C / 4.3	15.2	1.06	13.91	517	2	97	0	1	5	26.0	-18.3	64	8	1,000,000	0	0.0	0.0
C+ / 6.2	15.2	1.06	13.84	35	2	97	0	1	5	24.3	-18.2	58	8	0	0	0.0	0.0

					PERFORMANCE						
	99 Pct = Best 0 Pct = Worst					Total Return % through 3/31/15				Incl. in Returns	
			Overall		Perfor-				Annualized		
Fund Type	Fund Name	Ticker Symbol	Investment Rating	Phone	mance Rating/Pts	3 Mo	6 Mo	1Yr / Pct	3Yr / Pct	5Yr / Pct	Dividend Yield	Expense Ratio
GR	Aberdeen Equity Long-Short A	MLSAX	E+	(866) 667-9231	E+ / 0.6	-0.29	1.04	3.17 /27	2.90 / 8	2.68 / 5	0.00	2.85
GR	Aberdeen Equity Long-Short C	MLSCX	E-	(866) 667-9231	E+ / 0.8	-0.47	0.76	2.60 /24	2.23 / 7	1.97 / 4	0.00	3.53
GR	Aberdeen Equity Long-Short Inst	GGUIX	E+	(866) 667-9231	E+ / 0.9	-0.29	1.18	3.52 /29	3.21 / 8	2.98 / 6	0.00	2.53
GR	Aberdeen Equity Long-Short Inst Svc	AELSX	E+	(866) 667-9231	E+ / 0.9	-0.39	1.02	3.20 /27	2.95 / 8	2.75 / 5	0.00	2.78
GR	Aberdeen Equity Long-Short R	GLSRX	E+	(866) 667-9231	E+ / 0.8	-0.41	0.80	2.75 /25	2.43 / 7	2.29 / 5	0.00	3.27
GL	Aberdeen Global Equity A	GLLAX	D-	(866) 667-9231	E+ / 0.8	-0.44	-4.81	-3.79 / 7	5.34 /14	6.58 /21	1.47	1.56
GL	Aberdeen Global Equity C	GLLCX	D-	(866) 667-9231	E+ / 0.9	-0.56	-5.09	-4.35 / 6	4.70 /12	5.89 /16	1.07	2.19
GL	Aberdeen Global Equity Inst	GWLIX	D-	(866) 667-9231	D- / 1.1	-0.29	-4.60	-3.37 / 8	5.35 /14	6.71 /21	1.93	1.19
GL	Aberdeen Global Equity IS	GLLSX	D	(866) 667-9231	D- / 1.2	-0.29	-4.66	-3.44 / 8	5.73 /16	6.84 /22	1.93	1.19
GL	Aberdeen Global Equity R	GWLRX	D-	(866) 667-9231	D- / 1.0	-0.44	-4.94	-4.03 / 7	5.11 /13	6.33 /19	1.34	1.85
EN	Aberdeen Global Natural Res A	GGNAX	E-	(866) 667-9231	E- / 0.1	-6.32	-18.55	-19.15 / 1	-6.93 / 1	-3.39 / 1	1.78	1.84
EN	Aberdeen Global Natural Res C	GGNCX	E-	(866) 667-9231	E- / 0.1	-6.46	-18.78	-19.67 / 1	-7.55 / 1	-4.04 / 1	1.17	2.52
EN	Aberdeen Global Natural Res I	GGNIX	E-	(866) 667-9231	E- / 0.1	-6.24	-18.39	-18.89 / 1	-6.67 / 1	-3.10 / 1	2.29	1.52
EN	Aberdeen Global Natural Res IS	GGNSX	E-	(866) 667-9231	E- / 0.1	-6.25	-18.40	-18.90 / 1	-6.62 / 1	-3.07 / 1	2.29	1.52
EN	Aberdeen Global Natural Res R	GGNRX	E+	(866) 667-9231	E- / 0.1	-6.43	-18.69	-19.38 / 1	-7.15 / 1	-3.59 / 1	1.65	2.06
GL	Aberdeen Global Small Cap A	WVCCX	D-	(866) 667-9231	D / 2.1	1.60	1.04	1.16 /19	8.74 /31	11.84 /59	1.17	1.73
GL	Aberdeen Global Small Cap C	CPVCX	D	(866) 667-9231	D+ / 2.5	1.40	0.68	0.44 /17	7.98 /27	11.06 /53	0.71	2.43
GL	Aberdeen Global Small Cap Inst	ABNIX	D	(866) 667-9231	C- / 3.2	1.64	1.17	1.47 /20	9.08 /33	12.13 /61	1.55	1.43
GL	Aberdeen Global Small Cap Inst Svc	AGISX	D	(866) 667-9231	C- / 3.0	1.60	1.06	1.23 /19	8.82 /32	12.00 /60	1.31	1.67
GL	Aberdeen Global Small Cap R	WPVAX	D	(866) 667-9231	D+ / 2.8	1.52	0.88	0.86 /18	8.47 /30	11.57 /57	0.95	1.99
FO	Aberdeen Intl Equity A	GIGAX	E+	(866) 667-9231	E / 0.5	1.29	-5.75	-5.65 / 5	3.51 / 9	5.38 /14	2.06	1.33
FO	Aberdeen Intl Equity C	GIGCX	E+	(866) 667-9231	E+ / 0.6	1.06	-6.05	-6.28 / 4	2.81 / 8	4.65 /11	1.67	2.03
FO	Aberdeen Intl Equity Inst	GIGIX	E+	(866) 667-9231	E+ / 0.8	1.39	-5.59	-5.34 / 5	3.85 /10	5.70 /15	2.48	1.03
FO	Aberdeen Intl Equity Inst Svc	GIGSX	E+	(866) 667-9231	E+ / 0.7	1.34	-5.61	-5.42 / 5	3.71 / 9	5.57 /14	2.35	1.16
FO	Aberdeen Intl Equity R	GIRRX	E+	(866) 667-9231	E+ / 0.7	1.17	-5.87	-5.96 / 4	3.25 / 8	5.12 /12	1.98	1.62
FO	Aberdeen Select Intl Equity A	BJBIX	E	(866) 667-9231	E+ / 0.7	1.07	-6.60	-6.80 / 4	3.27 / 8	0.19 / 3	4.73	1.29
FO	Aberdeen Select Intl Equity I	JIEIX	E	(866) 667-9231	E+ / 0.7	1.09	-6.52	-6.58 / 4	3.51 / 9	0.43 / 3	4.92	1.04
FO	Aberdeen Select Intl Equity II A	JETAX	E+	(866) 667-9231	E+ / 0.8	1.36	-5.81	-6.03 / 4	3.95 /10	0.96 / 3	4.63	1.33
FO	Aberdeen Select Intl Equity II I	JETIX	E+	(866) 667-9231	E+ / 0.8	1.36	-5.77	-5.92 / 4	4.17 /11	1.20 / 4	4.93	1.11
SC	Aberdeen Small Cap A	GSXAX	B+	(866) 667-9231	B+ / 8.4	4.57	14.88	11.66 /81	16.99 /90	14.66 /84	0.00	1.59
SC	Aberdeen Small Cap C	GSXCX	A-	(866) 667-9231	B+ / 8.8	4.43	14.46	10.91 /78	16.21 /85	13.89 /77	0.00	2.27
SC	Aberdeen Small Cap Inst	GSCIX	A	(866) 667-9231	A / 9.3	4.65	15.03	11.98 /82	17.36 /92	15.01 /87	0.00	1.27
SC	Aberdeen Small Cap Inst Svc	GSXIX	A	(866) 667-9231	A / 9.3	4.68	15.06	12.01 /82	17.32 /91	15.01 /87	0.00	1.27
SC	Aberdeen Small Cap R	GNSRX	A-	(866) 667-9231	A- / 9.1	4.51	14.71	11.37 /80	16.71 /88	14.39 /81	0.00	1.82
GR	Aberdeen US Equity A	GXXAX	C	(866) 667-9231	C / 4.4	0.54	4.60	7.36 /58	12.19 /54	10.58 /49	0.90	1.25
GR	Aberdeen US Equity I C	GXXCX	C	(866) 667-9231	C / 4.8	0.27	4.23	6.56 /51	11.38 /48	9.84 /43	0.33	1.98
GR	Aberdeen US Equity Inst Svc	GXXIX	C+	(866) 667-9231	C / 5.5	0.47	4.65	7.55 /59	12.39 /55	--	1.09	1.07
GR	Aberdeen US Equity Institutional	GGLIX	C+	(866) 667-9231	C+ / 5.6	0.57	4.78	7.72 /61	12.51 /56	10.91 /52	1.18	0.98
GR	Aberdeen US Equity R	GGLRX	C+	(866) 667-9231	C / 5.2	0.44	4.45	7.10 /56	11.90 /52	10.33 /47	0.77	1.48
IX	Absolute Credit Opportunities Inst	AOFOX	D-	(800) 754-8757	E / 0.5	0.61	-0.33	4.37 /34	-0.25 / 4	0.45 / 3	0.00	2.29
GR	Absolute Strategies Inst	ASFIX	C-	(800) 754-8757	E / 0.5	-0.45	-1.87	0.27 /16	-0.09 / 4	0.92 / 3	0.00	2.47
GR	Absolute Strategies R	ASFAX	D+	(800) 754-8757	E / 0.4	-0.55	-2.07	-0.18 /15	-0.52 / 4	0.50 / 3	0.00	2.93
EM	Acadian Emerging Markets Inst	AEMGX	E+	(866) 777-7818	E+ / 0.6	0.82	-2.18	2.56 /24	1.04 / 5	2.96 / 6	1.15	1.50
FO	Acuitas International Sm Cap Inst	AISCX	U		U /	4.43	-0.23	--	--	--	0.00	N/A
SC	Acuitas US Microcap Inst	AFMCX	U		U /	5.06	15.55	--	--	--	0.00	N/A
AA	Adaptive Allocation A	AAXAX	D-	(866) 263-9260	E- / 0.2	-1.19	-3.20	-1.19 /12	-2.53 / 3	--	0.00	2.25
GI	Adaptive Allocation C	AAXCX	D-	(866) 263-9260	E / 0.3	-1.43	-3.50	-1.93 /10	-3.27 / 2	-0.35 / 2	0.00	3.00
SC	Adirondack Small Cap	ADKSX	B	(888) 686-2729	B / 7.9	4.15	11.53	2.87 /26	16.16 /85	14.58 /83	0.00	1.38
SC	Adv Inn Cir Champlain Sm Comp	CIPSX	C+	(866) 777-7818	B- / 7.2	3.10	13.65	9.25 /71	13.95 /67	14.90 /86	0.00	1.36
IN	Adv Inn Cir FMC Select Fd	FMSLX	B-	(866) 777-7818	C+ / 6.8	1.72	9.09	10.72 /77	13.72 /65	11.83 /59	0.44	0.99
SC	Adv Inn Cir ICM Sm Co I	ICSCX	D+	(866) 777-7818	C+ / 6.5	2.49	11.76	3.79 /30	13.85 /66	12.43 /64	0.17	0.96
FO	Adv Inn Cir McKee Intl Eqty I	MKIEX	D-	(866) 777-7818	D / 2.0	4.81	-0.19	-1.67 /11	7.33 /23	4.61 /11	3.80	0.97

● Denotes fund is closed to new investors
* Denotes fund is included in Section II

RISK			NET ASSETS		ASSET				Portfolio	BULL / BEAR		FUND MANAGER		MINIMUMS		LOADS	
	3 Year		NAV							Last Bull	Last Bear	Manager	Manager	Initial	Additional	Front	Back
Risk Rating/Pts	Standard Deviation	Beta	As of 3/31/15	Total $(Mil)	Cash %	Stocks %	Bonds %	Other %	Turnover Ratio	Market Return	Market Return	Quality Pct	Tenure (Years)	Purch. $	Purch. $	End Load	End Load
C / 5.2	5.2	0.51	10.16	25	57	42	0	1	31	20.3	-9.1	12	17	1,000	50	5.8	0.0
C- / 3.0	5.2	0.51	6.32	7	57	42	0	1	31	17.7	-9.4	8	17	1,000	50	0.0	0.0
C / 5.3	5.2	0.51	10.47	215	57	42	0	1	31	21.7	-9.0	13	17	1,000,000	0	0.0	0.0
C / 5.2	5.2	0.51	10.33	1	57	42	0	1	31	20.5	-9.0	12	17	1,000,000	0	0.0	0.0
C / 5.0	5.1	0.50	9.65	3	57	42	0	1	31	18.6	-9.1	10	17	0	0	0.0	0.0
C+ / 6.6	11.4	0.81	13.21	70	3	96	0	1	24	44.1	-17.6	34	6	1,000	50	5.8	0.0
C+ / 6.6	11.4	0.82	12.54	2	3	96	0	1	24	40.9	-17.8	27	6	1,000	50	0.0	0.0
C+ / 6.6	11.6	0.82	13.23	29	3	96	0	1	24	44.2	-17.5	33	6	1,000,000	0	0.0	0.0
B- / 7.2	11.4	0.81	13.23	5	3	96	0	1	24	45.8	-17.6	40	6	1,000,000	0	0.0	0.0
C+ / 6.6	11.4	0.82	12.75	2	3	96	0	1	24	42.8	-17.6	31	6	0	0	0.0	0.0
C- / 3.3	15.1	0.79	13.14	11	1	98	0	1	2	6.2	-27.3	2	5	1,000	50	5.8	0.0
C- / 3.3	15.1	0.79	12.50	2	1	98	0	1	2	3.8	-27.6	2	5	1,000	50	0.0	0.0
C- / 3.3	15.1	0.79	13.32	1	1	98	0	1	2	7.3	-27.3	2	5	1,000,000	0	0.0	0.0
C- / 3.3	15.1	0.79	13.31	1	1	98	0	1	2	7.5	-27.3	2	5	1,000,000	0	0.0	0.0
C- / 3.3	15.1	0.79	12.93	3	1	98	0	1	2	5.4	-27.4	2	5	0	0	0.0	0.0
C+ / 5.9	11.1	0.70	27.87	60	6	93	0	1	13	53.3	-16.4	84	6	1,000	50	5.8	0.0
C+ / 5.9	11.1	0.70	25.99	2	6	93	0	1	13	49.7	-16.6	80	6	1,000	50	0.0	0.0
C+ / 5.9	11.1	0.70	27.89	81	6	93	0	1	13	54.8	-16.2	86	6	1,000,000	0	0.0	0.0
C+ / 5.9	11.1	0.70	27.86	3	6	93	0	1	13	53.8	-16.2	85	6	1,000,000	0	0.0	0.0
C+ / 5.9	11.1	0.70	26.78	1	6	93	0	1	13	51.9	-16.5	83	6	0	0	0.0	0.0
C+ / 5.8	12.8	0.92	14.17	129	2	97	0	1	10	33.9	-18.3	11	6	1,000	50	5.8	0.0
C+ / 5.8	12.8	0.92	13.36	32	2	97	0	1	10	30.8	-18.6	8	6	1,000	50	0.0	0.0
C+ / 5.8	12.8	0.92	14.51	505	2	97	0	1	10	35.3	-18.2	13	6	1,000,000	0	0.0	0.0
C+ / 5.8	12.8	0.91	14.46	193	2	97	0	1	10	34.7	-18.2	12	6	1,000,000	0	0.0	0.0
C+ / 5.8	12.8	0.91	13.56	15	2	97	0	1	10	32.7	-18.4	10	6	0	0	0.0	0.0
C / 4.9	13.1	0.93	25.40	327	0	98	0	2	12	27.4	-28.4	9	2	1,000	1,000	0.0	0.0
C / 4.9	13.1	0.93	26.00	56	0	98	0	2	12	28.5	-28.3	10	2	1,000,000	0	0.0	0.0
C / 5.0	12.9	0.93	11.15	103	1	98	0	1	11	30.7	-28.0	13	2	1,000	1,000	0.0	0.0
C / 5.0	13.0	0.93	11.14	93	1	98	0	1	11	31.9	-28.0	14	2	1,000,000	0	0.0	0.0
C+ / 6.3	12.7	0.91	25.86	78	2	97	0	1	29	110.1	-27.7	84	13	1,000	50	5.8	0.0
C+ / 6.2	12.7	0.91	22.88	33	2	97	0	1	29	105.1	-27.8	80	13	1,000	50	0.0	0.0
C+ / 6.3	12.7	0.91	27.01	40	2	97	0	1	29	112.3	-27.5	86	13	1,000,000	0	0.0	0.0
C+ / 6.3	12.7	0.91	27.05	2	2	97	0	1	29	112.1	-27.5	86	13	1,000,000	0	0.0	0.0
C+ / 6.2	12.7	0.91	24.10	1	2	97	0	1	29	108.3	-27.7	83	13	0	0	0.0	0.0
C+ / 6.8	10.0	1.02	12.88	272	0	99	0	1	21	78.4	-20.2	18	15	1,000	50	5.8	0.0
C+ / 6.7	10.0	1.02	11.74	8	0	99	0	1	21	74.1	-20.3	13	15	1,000	50	0.0	0.0
C+ / 6.8	10.0	1.02	13.46	120	0	99	0	1	21	N/A	N/A	20	15	1,000,000	0	0.0	0.0
C+ / 6.8	10.0	1.02	13.48	7	0	99	0	1	21	80.2	-20.1	20	15	1,000,000	0	0.0	0.0
C+ / 6.7	10.0	1.02	12.31	N/A	0	99	0	1	21	76.9	-20.2	16	15	0	0	0.0	0.0
C+ / 6.5	2.1	N/A	9.92	48	33	17	48	2	157	0.6	-4.6	64	7	1,000,000	0	0.0	0.0
B+ / 9.4	2.7	-0.15	11.04	1,594	47	11	24	18	75	0.2	1.9	85	N/A	1,000,000	0	0.0	0.0
B+ / 9.3	2.6	-0.15	10.88	49	47	11	24	18	75	-1.4	1.8	82	N/A	250,000	100	0.0	0.0
C / 5.5	14.3	1.02	18.41	1,734	0	99	0	1	37	25.9	-26.0	71	22	2,500	1,000	0.0	2.0
U /	N/A	N/A	9.43	43	0	0	0	100	0	N/A	N/A	N/A	N/A	100,000	0	0.0	1.0
U /	N/A	N/A	11.00	35	0	0	0	100	0	N/A	N/A	N/A	N/A	100,000	0	0.0	1.0
B- / 7.7	6.4	0.79	9.98	2	6	58	35	1	79	-4.4	-10.8	2	9	5,000	100	4.8	2.0
B- / 7.6	6.4	0.44	9.64	24	6	58	35	1	79	-6.9	-11.1	2	9	5,000	100	0.0	2.0
C+ / 6.1	13.7	0.96	22.07	265	4	95	0	1	33	87.7	-21.9	73	10	3,000	50	0.0	0.0
C / 4.9	11.8	0.83	16.98	1,453	5	94	0	1	36	79.5	-19.0	73	11	10,000	0	0.0	0.0
B- / 7.7	9.0	0.90	31.36	316	3	96	0	1	11	80.6	-16.9	59	5	10,000	1,000	0.0	0.0
D+ / 2.7	13.7	0.99	29.32	1,086	3	96	0	1	24	91.9	-25.0	37	16	2,500,000	1,000	0.0	0.0
C / 5.4	13.0	0.98	12.64	183	2	97	0	1	13	46.9	-25.9	40	15	2,500	100	0.0	1.0

Fund Type	Fund Name	Ticker Symbol	Overall Investment Rating	Phone	Performance Rating/Pts	3 Mo	6 Mo	1Yr / Pct	3Yr / Pct	5Yr / Pct	Dividend Yield	Expense Ratio
GR	Adv Inn Cir Reaves Util and El A	RSRAX	C	(866) 777-7818	C / 4.6	-0.71	0.94	5.15 /40	11.68 /50	11.54 /57	0.95	1.56
GR	Adv Inn Cir Reaves Util and El I	RSRFX	C	(866) 777-7818	C / 4.8	-0.65	1.07	5.41 /42	11.93 /52	11.80 /59	1.18	1.31
GR	Adv Inn Cir TS&W Eq Port Inst	TSWEX	C	(866) 777-7818	C+ / 5.7	0.56	4.87	6.65 /52	13.03 /60	9.82 /43	0.73	1.51
GR	Adv Series Tr-Capital Adv Growth	CIAOX	B-	(866) 777-7818	B- / 7.0	1.77	6.69	12.59 /85	14.06 /68	12.54 /64	0.96	1.59
BA	Advance Capital I Balanced Inst	ADBNX	C-	(800) 345-4783	C- / 3.5	0.56	2.02	5.93 /46	9.13 /34	9.40 /40	1.63	0.85
BA	Advance Capital I Balanced Retail	ADBAX	C-	(800) 345-4783	C- / 3.3	0.50	1.89	5.70 /44	8.84 /32	9.11 /37	1.38	1.10
GR	Advance Capital I Core Eq Inst	ADCNX	D+	(800) 345-4783	C+ / 6.3	-0.17	3.09	10.56 /77	13.63 /62	11.65 /58	0.37	1.15
GR	Advance Capital I Core Eq Retail	ADCEX	D+	(800) 345-4783	C+ / 6.1	-0.27	2.83	10.18 /75	13.33 /62	11.35 /56	0.38	1.40
MC	Advance Capital I Equity Gr Inst	ADENX	E+	(800) 345-4783	C / 5.2	1.08	3.09	4.84 /37	12.37 /55	13.11 /69	0.50	0.86
MC	Advance Capital I Equity Gr Retail	ADEGX	E+	(800) 345-4783	C / 5.0	1.00	3.01	4.62 /36	12.08 /53	12.80 /66	0.50	1.11
IN	Advantus Strat Dividend Inc Instl	VSDIX	U	(800) 665-6005	U /	3.54	11.06	16.76 /94	--	--	2.26	1.23
GR	AdvisorOne CLS Domestic Equity N	CLDEX	E+	(866) 811-0225	C / 4.8	1.87	7.04	9.54 /72	10.39 /42	10.02 /45	1.15	1.65
GI	AdvisorOne CLS Enh Long/Short N	CLEIX	C-	(866) 811-0225	E+ / 0.9	0.58	-0.05	0.74 /18	3.29 / 8	3.85 / 8	0.54	1.79
GR	AdvisorOne CLS Glbl Agg Eq N	CLACX	C-	(866) 811-0225	C / 4.7	3.07	4.69	4.53 /35	11.14 /46	10.22 /46	1.57	1.92
BA	AdvisorOne CLS Glbl Dvsfd Eq C	CLCCX	C-	(866) 811-0225	C- / 3.5	1.58	1.00	3.71 /30	9.35 /35	8.07 /30	1.00	2.44
GR	AdvisorOne CLS Glbl Dvsfd Eq N	CLSAX	C	(866) 811-0225	C- / 4.0	1.78	1.40	4.65 /36	10.09 /40	8.94 /36	1.89	1.44
GI	AdvisorOne CLS Global Growth N	CLBLX	C-	(866) 811-0225	C- / 3.2	1.80	1.40	3.77 /30	8.70 /31	8.28 /32	1.13	1.54
GR	AdvisorOne CLS Growth and Income	CLERX	C-	(866) 811-0225	D / 1.7	1.12	0.78	2.46 /24	5.94 /16	6.53 /20	0.97	1.53
GI	AdvisorOne CLS International Eqty N	CLHAX	E	(866) 811-0225	D+ / 2.7	5.15	3.99	5.46 /42	6.97 /21	7.69 /28	2.18	1.66
GR	AdvisorOne CLS Shelter N	CLSHX	C+	(866) 811-0225	C / 4.3	1.87	5.12	8.49 /66	9.79 /38	5.39 /14	0.70	1.55
GL	AdvisorOne Horizon Active RA N	ARANX	U	(866) 811-0225	U /	1.03	3.90	--	--	--	0.00	N/A
GL	AdvisorOne Hrzn Active Asst Alloc N	AAANX	B-	(866) 811-0225	C / 4.9	1.24	4.09	7.48 /59	11.28 /47	--	0.13	1.84
GR	Advisory Research All Cap Value	ADVGX	C+	(888) 665-1414	C+ / 5.9	2.15	6.04	8.05 /63	13.41 /63	12.07 /61	0.45	1.14
MC	Advisory Research Emerging Mkts	ADVMX	U	(888) 665-1414	U /	-0.11	-6.84	-3.46 / 8	--	--	1.66	2.64
GL	Advisory Research Global Val	ADVWX	D	(888) 665-1414	C- / 3.4	2.71	1.95	0.43 /17	10.12 /40	--	1.12	1.86
FO	Advisory Research Intl All Cap Val	ADVEX	E+	(888) 665-1414	D / 2.2	3.60	-2.58	-4.68 / 6	8.87 /32	--	2.49	14.74
FO	Advisory Research Intl SC Val I	ADVLX	U	(888) 665-1414	U /	3.88	-2.19	-1.88 /11	--	--	1.36	1.24
FO	Advisory Research Intl SC Val Inv	ADVIX	D	(888) 665-1414	C- / 3.4	3.79	-2.16	-1.85 /11	10.83 /44	8.25 /31	1.32	1.26
EN	Advisory Research MLP & Engy Inc	MLPPX	C		C / 5.1	0.91	-5.86	9.19 /70	13.03 /60	--	5.77	1.46
EN	Advisory Research MLP & Engy Inc A	INFRX	D+		C- / 3.4	1.01	-5.65	8.80 /68	11.39 /48	--	6.12	1.51
EN	Advisory Research MLP & Engy Inc C	INFFX	U		U /	0.90	-5.99	7.98 /63	--	--	5.60	2.26
EN	Advisory Research MLP & Engy Inc I	INFIX	C		C / 5.0	1.08	-5.52	9.06 /70	12.84 /58	--	6.77	1.26
SC	Aegis Value I	AVALX	E-	(800) 528-3780	E / 0.3	-5.19	-19.64	-28.69 / 0	2.52 / 7	5.61 /15	0.00	1.38
AA	Aftershock Strategies I	SHKIX	U	(855) 745-3863	U /	-0.02	1.19	1.34 /19	--	--	1.34	1.76
GR	Akre Focus Inst	AKRIX	A+	(877) 862-9556	A / 9.3	2.50	9.71	12.29 /84	18.12 /95	18.51 /98	0.00	1.10
GR	Akre Focus Retail	AKREX	A+	(877) 862-9556	A- / 9.1	2.44	9.57	12.02 /83	17.77 /93	18.21 /98	0.00	1.35
IN	Al Frank Dividend Value Adv	VALEX	D+	(888) 263-6443	C / 5.1	0.38	1.15	2.12 /22	13.48 /63	11.93 /60	1.05	1.75
IN	Al Frank Dividend Value Inv	VALDX	D+	(888) 263-6443	C / 5.0	0.38	1.08	1.83 /21	13.21 /61	11.66 /58	0.79	2.01
GR	Al Frank Fund Adv	VALAX	C-	(888) 263-6443	C+ / 5.8	0.16	1.02	2.73 /25	14.63 /72	12.77 /66	1.39	1.29
GR	Al Frank Fund Inv	VALUX	C-	(888) 263-6443	C+ / 5.6	0.08	0.87	2.47 /24	14.35 /70	12.49 /64	1.14	1.55
GR	Alger Analyst A	SPEAX	C+	(800) 254-3796	B- / 7.2	4.80	10.85	11.94 /82	15.96 /83	12.90 /67	0.37	2.75
GR	Alger Analyst C	AACYX	B-	(800) 254-3796	B / 7.7	4.64	10.51	11.21 /79	15.24 /77	12.15 /62	0.00	3.53
GR	Alger Analyst I	AAIYX	B+	(800) 254-3796	B+ / 8.6	4.81	10.84	11.93 /82	15.97 /83	12.91 /67	0.57	2.79
BA	Alger Balanced I2	ABLOX	C	(800) 254-3796	C- / 3.5	1.52	4.58	9.71 /73	8.07 /27	7.64 /27	1.92	0.95
GR	Alger Capital Apprec I2	ALVOX	B+	(800) 254-3796	A+ / 9.6	5.26	9.66	18.65 /96	17.96 /94	15.80 /92	0.09	0.96
GR	Alger Capital Apprec S		A+	(800) 254-3796	A / 9.5	5.20	9.53	18.35 /96	17.62 /93	--	0.00	1.26
GR	Alger Capital Appreciation A	ACAAX	B	(800) 254-3796	A- / 9.1	5.41	9.67	18.27 /96	17.56 /93	15.26 /88	0.00	1.24
GR	Alger Capital Appreciation B	ACAPX	B	(800) 254-3796	A / 9.3	5.23	9.31	17.37 /95	16.64 /88	14.33 /81	0.00	2.03
GR	Alger Capital Appreciation C	ALCCX	B	(800) 254-3796	A / 9.3	5.21	9.34	17.44 /95	16.68 /88	14.37 /81	0.00	2.00
GR	Alger Capital Appreciation Focus I	ALGRX	A	(800) 254-3796	A- / 9.1	5.01	9.23	19.37 /96	15.72 /81	13.86 /76	0.00	2.36
GR	Alger Capital Appreciation Fund Z	ACAZX	B+	(800) 254-3796	A+ / 9.6	5.49	9.90	18.72 /96	17.96 /94	--	0.00	0.93
GR	Alger Capital Appreciation Inst I	ALARX	B+	(800) 254-3796	A / 9.5	5.11	9.26	18.07 /96	17.57 /93	15.33 /89	0.00	1.16

● Denotes fund is closed to new investors
* Denotes fund is included in Section II

RISK			NET ASSETS		ASSET					BULL / BEAR		FUND MANAGER		MINIMUMS		LOADS	
Risk Rating/Pts	3 Year Standard Deviation	Beta	NAV As of 3/31/15	Total $(Mil)	Cash %	Stocks %	Bonds %	Other %	Portfolio Turnover Ratio	Last Bull Market Return	Last Bear Market Return	Manager Quality Pct	Manager Tenure (Years)	Initial Purch. $	Additional Purch. $	Front End Load	Back End Load
C+ / 6.4	9.6	0.65	10.63	8	5	94	0	1	85	58.8	-10.1	80	11	1,000	0	0.0	0.0
C+ / 6.4	9.6	0.65	10.62	58	5	94	0	1	85	60.2	-10.0	81	11	1,000,000	0	0.0	0.0
C+ / 5.6	11.0	1.11	13.53	47	0	100	0	0	46	80.7	-20.9	14	15	2,500	100	0.0	1.0
C+ / 6.2	9.3	0.93	24.74	40	12	87	0	1	41	83.6	-12.8	55	14	5,000	250	0.0	0.0
B- / 7.2	6.6	1.11	19.05	1	0	60	38	2	66	51.2	-12.0	28	20	250,000	0	0.0	0.0
B- / 7.2	6.6	1.11	19.09	147	0	60	38	2	66	49.8	-12.0	25	20	10,000	0	0.0	0.0
C- / 3.1	11.0	1.12	11.48	N/A	3	96	0	1	130	83.2	-18.7	17	2	250,000	0	0.0	0.0
C- / 3.0	11.0	1.11	11.19	14	3	96	0	1	130	81.5	-18.8	15	2	10,000	0	0.0	0.0
D- / 1.3	11.7	1.02	21.58	2	1	98	0	1	118	80.3	-22.5	14	13	250,000	0	0.0	0.0
D- / 1.3	11.7	1.01	21.14	71	1	98	0	1	118	78.8	-22.6	13	13	10,000	0	0.0	0.0
U /	N/A	N/A	11.84	85	20	71	8	1	65	N/A	N/A	N/A	3	100,000	1,000	0.0	0.0
D- / 1.0	9.1	0.93	9.26	19	0	100	0	0	39	66.6	-19.4	16	2	2,500	250	0.0	0.0
B+ / 9.5	3.4	0.34	10.45	104	16	67	16	1	58	21.9	-9.7	39	6	2,500	250	0.0	0.0
C / 5.2	10.3	1.03	13.44	101	3	94	2	1	24	76.3	-23.4	11	6	2,500	250	0.0	0.0
B- / 7.1	9.8	1.65	16.69	3	3	93	3	1	27	65.0	-22.7	3	2	2,500	250	0.0	0.0
B- / 7.1	9.7	0.98	17.74	558	3	93	3	1	27	69.1	-22.4	10	2	2,500	250	0.0	0.0
B- / 7.6	7.6	0.77	11.34	296	4	74	20	2	46	55.0	-17.7	23	N/A	2,500	250	0.0	0.0
B / 8.3	5.4	0.53	10.83	419	5	53	41	1	39	38.0	-11.7	35	13	2,500	250	0.0	0.0
D- / 1.4	7.5	0.69	4.49	14	1	83	14	2	44	44.5	-13.7	19	2	2,500	250	0.0	0.0
B- / 7.6	8.5	0.83	13.10	94	1	98	0	1	158	35.6	-14.7	24	N/A	2,500	250	0.0	0.0
U /	N/A	N/A	20.52	176	0	0	0	100	0	N/A	N/A	N/A	1	2,500	250	0.0	0.0
B / 8.3	9.1	1.32	12.29	285	0	0	0	100	975	N/A	N/A	57	3	2,500	250	0.0	0.0
C+ / 5.9	10.3	1.05	15.68	36	1	98	0	1	44	77.6	-16.9	25	13	2,500	500	0.0	2.0
U /	N/A	N/A	9.39	28	6	93	0	1	67	N/A	N/A	N/A	2	2,500	500	0.0	2.0
C / 4.8	11.2	0.77	12.13	22	1	98	0	1	47	62.7	-23.2	87	6	2,500	500	0.0	2.0
C- / 3.9	12.2	0.89	8.91	1	5	94	0	1	68	46.9	N/A	72	5	2,500	500	0.0	2.0
U /	N/A	N/A	11.51	112	6	93	0	1	39	N/A	N/A	N/A	6	500,000	500	0.0	2.0
C / 5.2	12.0	0.85	11.50	37	6	93	0	1	39	53.7	-20.2	87	6	2,500	500	0.0	2.0
C+ / 6.4	10.2	0.49	13.45	206	28	51	19	2	56	70.2	-10.9	98	5	5,000,000	500	0.0	2.0
C+ / 6.4	10.3	0.51	13.48	109	31	44	24	1	38	58.6	N/A	97	5	2,500	500	5.5	2.0
U /	N/A	N/A	13.51	130	31	44	24	1	38	N/A	N/A	N/A	5	2,500	500	0.0	2.0
C+ / 6.4	10.0	0.49	13.26	692	31	44	24	1	38	66.1	-11.9	98	5	1,000,000	100,000	0.0	2.0
D- / 1.4	16.0	0.81	12.43	154	3	96	0	1	35	38.0	-23.7	2	17	1,000,000	250	0.0	0.0
U /	N/A	N/A	9.00	55	0	0	0	100	357	N/A	N/A	N/A	3	100,000	10,000	0.0	0.0
B- / 7.1	10.5	0.98	23.37	1,207	6	87	5	2	30	110.3	-5.9	84	6	250,000	25,000	0.0	1.0
B- / 7.1	10.5	0.98	23.10	2,635	6	87	5	2	30	108.3	-6.0	82	6	2,000	250	0.0	1.0
C / 4.5	11.2	1.10	13.21	N/A	2	97	0	1	25	89.9	-20.9	18	11	100,000	100	0.0	2.0
C / 4.6	11.2	1.10	13.28	16	2	97	0	1	25	88.4	-21.0	16	11	1,000	100	0.0	2.0
C / 4.6	11.8	1.17	24.75	4	3	96	0	1	19	94.2	-22.5	17	17	100,000	100	0.0	2.0
C / 4.7	11.8	1.17	24.70	85	3	96	0	1	19	92.5	-22.6	16	17	1,000	100	0.0	2.0
C / 5.5	10.7	0.93	13.76	7	4	95	0	1	170	99.3	-21.5	76	8	1,000	50	5.3	2.0
C / 5.4	10.7	0.94	13.08	N/A	4	95	0	1	170	95.1	-21.8	69	8	1,000	50	0.0	2.0
C / 5.5	10.7	0.94	13.72	2	4	95	0	1	170	99.4	-21.6	76	8	0	0	0.0	0.0
B / 8.0	6.4	1.10	14.70	96	7	61	30	2	72	45.0	-9.3	19	4	0	0	0.0	0.0
C / 4.5	10.3	1.00	75.10	550	5	94	0	1	117	110.4	-18.6	82	10	0	0	0.0	0.0
C+ / 6.9	10.3	1.00	72.67	32	5	94	0	1	117	N/A	N/A	80	10	0	0	0.0	0.0
C / 4.9	10.3	1.00	21.64	1,527	5	94	0	1	148	107.5	-18.8	79	11	1,000	50	5.3	0.0
C / 4.3	10.3	1.00	18.10	30	5	94	0	1	148	101.8	-19.1	73	11	1,000	50	0.0	0.0
C / 4.4	10.3	1.00	18.17	278	5	94	0	1	148	102.2	-19.1	73	11	1,000	50	0.0	0.0
C+ / 6.2	10.9	1.02	23.91	16	5	94	0	1	154	92.7	-16.8	58	3	0	0	0.0	0.0
C / 4.9	10.3	1.00	21.92	304	5	94	0	1	148	109.8	-18.7	81	11	500,000	0	0.0	0.0
C / 5.2	10.2	1.00	28.20	3,246	6	93	0	1	136	108.2	-19.0	79	11	0	0	0.0	0.0

99 Pct = Best
0 Pct = Worst

Fund Type	Fund Name	Ticker Symbol	Overall Investment Rating	Phone	Performance Rating/Pts	3 Mo	6 Mo	1Yr / Pct	Annualized 3Yr / Pct	Annualized 5Yr / Pct	Dividend Yield	Expense Ratio
GR	Alger Capital Appreciation Inst R	ACARX	B+	(800) 254-3796	A / 9.3	4.97	8.99	17.51 /95	16.99 /90	14.75 /85	0.00	1.64
GL	Alger Dynamic Opportunities A	SPEDX	C-	(800) 254-3796	D+ / 2.5	3.03	4.58	7.97 /63	8.61 /30	6.33 /19	0.00	2.46
GL	Alger Dynamic Opportunities C	ADOCX	C-	(800) 254-3796	D+ / 2.8	2.88	4.23	7.17 /56	7.81 /26	--	0.00	3.23
GL	Alger Dynamic Opportunities Fund Z	ADOZX	C	(800) 254-3796	C- / 3.8	3.07	4.78	8.31 /65	8.87 /32	--	0.00	2.18
EM	Alger Emerging Markets A	AAEMX	E+	(800) 254-3796	E+ / 0.6	3.01	-1.28	-0.43 /14	2.67 / 7	--	0.00	2.99
EM	Alger Emerging Markets C	ACEMX	E+	(800) 254-3796	E+ / 0.6	2.86	-1.64	-1.10 /13	1.88 / 6	--	0.00	3.79
EM	Alger Emerging Markets I	AIEMX	E+	(800) 254-3796	E+ / 0.8	3.03	-1.29	-0.43 /14	2.64 / 7	--	0.00	2.92
FO	Alger Global Growth A	CHUSX	C-	(800) 254-3796	C- / 3.6	4.47	4.32	9.63 /73	10.31 /41	7.43 /26	0.00	1.98
FO	Alger Global Growth C	CHUCX	C-	(800) 254-3796	C- / 3.9	4.26	3.89	8.78 /68	9.48 /36	6.61 /21	0.00	2.75
GR	Alger Green A	SPEGX	C+	(800) 254-3796	C / 5.1	2.53	6.73	8.66 /67	13.35 /62	10.82 /51	0.00	1.33
GR	Alger Green C	AGFCX	C+	(800) 254-3796	C / 5.4	2.43	6.47	7.98 /63	12.40 /55	9.97 /44	0.00	2.09
GR	Alger Green I	AGIFX	C+	(800) 254-3796	C+ / 6.4	2.65	6.85	8.80 /68	13.37 /62	10.84 /51	0.00	1.30
GI	Alger Growth & Income I2	AIGOX	B+	(800) 254-3796	B- / 7.4	1.22	5.45	12.51 /85	14.80 /73	13.76 /75	1.82	1.01
BA	Alger Growth and Income A	ALBAX	B-	(800) 254-3796	C+ / 6.1	1.14	5.28	12.09 /83	14.31 /69	12.68 /65	1.46	1.18
BA	Alger Growth and Income C	ALBCX	B-	(800) 254-3796	C+ / 6.4	0.98	4.91	11.28 /80	13.46 /63	11.84 /59	0.91	1.93
GI	Alger Growth and Income Z	AGIZX	A-	(800) 254-3796	B- / 7.3	1.21	5.40	12.38 /84	14.59 /72	--	1.76	1.05
GR	Alger Growth Opportunities A	AOFAX	D+	(800) 254-3796	C+ / 6.7	7.30	14.06	8.24 /64	14.40 /70	13.65 /74	0.00	2.22
GR	Alger Growth Opportunities C	AOFCX	D+	(800) 254-3796	B- / 7.1	7.25	13.72	7.66 /60	13.70 /65	12.86 /67	0.00	2.99
GR	Alger Growth Opportunities Fund Z	AGOZX	C	(800) 254-3796	B / 8.1	7.49	14.41	8.78 /68	15.00 /75	--	0.00	2.11
GR	Alger Growth Opportunities I	AOFIX	C	(800) 254-3796	B / 7.9	7.41	14.24	8.52 /66	14.72 /73	13.93 /77	0.00	2.19
HL	Alger Health Sciences Fund A	AHSAX	C+	(800) 254-3796	A+ / 9.9	11.31	17.58	30.51 /99	23.63 /99	17.14 /96	0.51	1.31
HL	Alger Health Sciences Fund B	AHSBX	C	(800) 254-3796	A+ / 9.9	11.10	17.09	29.43 /99	22.67 /98	16.22 /94	0.00	2.10
HL	Alger Health Sciences Fund C	AHSCX	C	(800) 254-3796	A+ / 9.9	11.11	17.09	29.51 /99	22.70 /98	16.25 /94	0.00	2.06
GR	Alger International Growth A	ALGAX	D	(800) 254-3796	D / 2.0	6.42	5.53	5.94 /46	6.86 /21	8.36 /32	0.89	1.32
GR	Alger International Growth B	AFGPX	D	(800) 254-3796	D+ / 2.3	6.20	5.13	5.21 /40	6.11 /17	7.60 /27	0.03	2.02
GR	Alger International Growth C	ALGCX	D	(800) 254-3796	D+ / 2.3	6.18	5.12	5.20 /40	6.02 /17	7.50 /26	0.46	2.08
GR	Alger International Growth Z	ALCZX	D+	(800) 254-3796	C- / 3.1	6.51	5.74	6.42 /50	7.31 /23	--	1.35	1.04
GR	Alger LargeCap Growth I2	AAGOX	C+	(800) 254-3796	B+ / 8.5	5.67	8.40	15.95 /93	15.09 /76	13.40 /72	0.15	0.88
GR	Alger LargeCap Growth S		B+	(800) 254-3796	B / 8.2	5.57	8.20	15.52 /92	14.64 /72	--	0.00	1.25
MC	Alger Mid Cap Growth Fund A	AMGAX	B+	(800) 254-3796	B+ / 8.3	7.26	9.92	13.16 /87	16.64 /88	13.26 /71	0.00	1.35
MC	Alger Mid Cap Growth Fund B	AMCGX	B+	(800) 254-3796	B+ / 8.6	7.06	9.43	12.31 /84	15.76 /81	12.40 /63	0.00	2.04
MC	Alger Mid Cap Growth Fund C	AMGCX	B+	(800) 254-3796	B+ / 8.5	7.00	9.39	12.29 /84	15.68 /81	12.29 /62	0.00	2.16
MC	Alger Mid Cap Growth I2	AMGOX	A-	(800) 254-3796	A- / 9.2	7.27	9.98	13.51 /88	16.93 /89	13.51 /73	0.00	1.04
MC	Alger Mid Cap Growth Inst I	ALMRX	A	(800) 254-3796	A / 9.5	7.51	10.54	15.31 /92	17.83 /94	14.03 /78	0.00	1.30
MC	Alger Mid Cap Growth Inst R	AGIRX	A	(800) 254-3796	A / 9.3	7.38	10.25	14.76 /91	17.24 /91	13.44 /72	0.00	1.80
MC	Alger Mid Cap Growth S		A-	(800) 254-3796	A- / 9.0	7.15	9.75	13.04 /87	16.48 /87	--	0.00	1.40
SC	Alger Small Cap Growth Fund A	ALSAX	D	(800) 254-3796	C / 5.5	6.86	14.95	6.67 /52	12.39 /55	12.20 /62	0.00	1.35
SC	Alger Small Cap Growth Fund B	ALSCX	D	(800) 254-3796	C+ / 5.8	6.68	14.42	5.76 /44	11.53 /49	11.52 /57	0.00	2.11
SC	Alger Small Cap Growth Fund C	AGSCX	D	(800) 254-3796	C+ / 5.7	6.68	14.42	5.75 /44	11.49 /49	11.12 /54	0.00	2.15
SC	Alger Small Cap Growth Fund Z	ASCZX	C-	(800) 254-3796	C+ / 6.6	6.92	14.93	6.96 /55	12.80 /58	--	0.00	1.03
SC	Alger Small Cap Growth Inst I	ALSRX	D-	(800) 254-3796	C+ / 6.5	7.02	15.05	6.72 /53	12.66 /57	12.44 /64	0.00	1.24
SC	Alger Small Cap Growth Inst R	ASIRX	E+	(800) 254-3796	C+ / 6.1	6.93	14.79	6.23 /48	12.12 /53	11.89 /60	0.00	1.72
SC	Alger SmallCap Growth I2	AASOX	D+	(800) 254-3796	C+ / 6.7	6.89	15.15	7.06 /55	12.95 /59	12.45 /64	0.00	0.95
MC	Alger SMid Cap Growth Fund A	ALMAX	D+	(800) 254-3796	C+ / 6.2	6.60	12.70	8.81 /68	13.60 /64	12.65 /65	0.00	1.27
MC	Alger SMid Cap Growth Fund B	ALMBX	D	(800) 254-3796	C+ / 6.4	6.32	12.21	7.93 /62	12.71 /57	11.76 /59	0.00	2.06
MC	Alger SMid Cap Growth Fund C	ALMCX	D	(800) 254-3796	C+ / 6.5	6.37	12.24	7.97 /63	12.72 /58	11.79 /59	0.00	2.03
MC	Alger SMid Cap Growth Fund I	ASIMX	C-	(800) 254-3796	B- / 7.1	6.57	12.66	8.82 /68	13.61 /64	12.72 /66	0.00	1.27
MC	Alger SMid Cap Growth Fund Z	ASMZX	C-	(800) 254-3796	B- / 7.4	6.59	12.83	9.17 /70	13.96 /67	--	0.00	0.95
MC	Alger SMidCap Growth I2	AAMOX	C-	(800) 254-3796	A+ / 9.7	6.67	12.93	9.44 /72	20.36 /98	16.79 /95	0.00	1.07
GR	Alger Spectra A	SPECX	B+	(800) 254-3796	B+ / 8.9	5.55	9.50	18.31 /96	17.75 /93	15.85 /92	0.00	1.52
GR	Alger Spectra C	ASPCX	B+	(800) 254-3796	A- / 9.1	5.41	9.11	17.44 /95	16.86 /89	14.99 /87	0.00	2.27
GR	Alger Spectra Fund Z	ASPZX	B+	(800) 254-3796	A+ / 9.6	5.67	9.64	18.64 /96	18.10 /95	--	0.00	1.23

● Denotes fund is closed to new investors
* Denotes fund is included in Section II

www.thestreetratings.com

Risk Rating/Pts	3 Year Standard Deviation	3 Year Beta	NAV As of 3/31/15	Total $(Mil)	Cash %	Stocks %	Bonds %	Other %	Portfolio Turnover Ratio	Last Bull Market Return	Last Bear Market Return	Manager Quality Pct	Manager Tenure (Years)	Initial Purch. $	Additional Purch. $	Front End Load	Back End Load
C / 5.0	10.2	1.00	26.00	625	6	93	0	1	136	104.8	-19.1	75	11	0	0	0.0	0.0
B- / 7.5	5.6	0.28	12.60	42	41	58	0	1	205	41.6	-14.8	95	6	1,000	50	5.3	2.0
B- / 7.3	5.6	0.28	12.16	7	41	58	0	1	205	38.1	-15.0	93	6	1,000	50	0.0	2.0
B- / 7.5	5.6	0.28	12.75	32	41	58	0	1	205	42.9	-14.7	95	6	500,000	0	0.0	0.0
C / 5.5	13.3	0.93	9.23	7	4	95	0	1	98	26.4	-27.7	84	5	1,000	50	5.3	2.0
C / 5.4	13.3	0.93	9.00	3	4	95	0	1	98	23.1	-27.9	79	5	1,000	50	0.0	2.0
C / 5.5	13.3	0.93	9.17	12	4	95	0	1	98	26.2	-27.7	84	5	0	0	0.0	0.0
C+ / 6.3	10.4	0.68	21.74	29	6	93	0	1	81	62.6	-29.4	91	12	1,000	50	5.3	2.0
C+ / 6.3	10.4	0.67	20.81	5	6	93	0	1	81	58.5	-29.6	88	12	1,000	50	0.0	2.0
C+ / 6.8	10.3	1.01	9.31	33	5	94	0	1	24	83.3	-17.4	29	9	1,000	50	5.3	2.0
C+ / 6.7	10.3	1.02	8.84	6	5	94	0	1	24	78.2	-17.5	20	9	1,000	50	0.0	2.0
C+ / 6.8	10.3	1.01	9.30	43	5	94	0	1	24	83.4	-17.4	30	9	0	0	0.0	0.0
B- / 7.4	9.1	0.94	16.51	35	4	95	0	1	25	90.7	-14.0	64	12	0	0	0.0	0.0
B- / 7.6	9.1	1.57	33.28	75	7	92	0	1	21	87.3	-12.9	27	4	1,000	50	5.3	0.0
B- / 7.6	9.1	1.57	32.91	21	7	92	0	1	21	82.6	-13.2	20	4	1,000	50	0.0	0.0
B- / 7.8	9.1	0.94	33.29	9	7	92	0	1	21	N/A	N/A	61	4	500,000	0	0.0	0.0
D+ / 2.9	12.5	1.03	11.47	8	3	96	0	1	92	93.1	-26.8	38	N/A	1,000	50	5.3	0.0
D+ / 2.7	12.5	1.03	10.65	5	3	96	0	1	92	88.8	-27.1	30	N/A	1,000	50	0.0	0.0
C- / 3.1	12.5	1.03	11.77	4	3	96	0	1	92	96.4	-26.7	47	N/A	500,000	0	0.0	0.0
C- / 3.0	12.5	1.02	11.74	2	3	96	0	1	92	94.8	-26.8	43	N/A	0	0	0.0	0.0
D+ / 2.5	10.1	0.67	24.40	147	2	97	0	1	168	114.9	-12.9	99	10	1,000	50	5.3	0.0
D / 1.7	10.2	0.67	20.62	9	2	97	0	1	168	109.1	-13.2	98	10	1,000	50	0.0	0.0
D / 1.7	10.1	0.66	20.70	64	2	97	0	1	168	109.2	-13.2	98	10	1,000	50	0.0	0.0
C+ / 6.3	10.5	0.95	16.08	132	2	97	0	1	98	53.3	-16.7	4	2	1,000	50	5.3	0.0
C+ / 6.3	10.5	0.95	14.22	35	2	97	0	1	98	49.5	-16.9	3	2	1,000	50	0.0	0.0
C+ / 6.3	10.5	0.94	14.08	20	2	97	0	1	98	49.0	-16.9	3	2	1,000	50	0.0	0.0
C+ / 6.3	10.5	0.95	16.20	18	2	97	0	1	98	55.3	-16.6	4	2	500,000	0	0.0	0.0
C- / 3.9	11.5	1.05	62.08	318	3	96	0	1	221	92.3	-16.7	43	14	0	0	0.0	0.0
C+ / 6.4	11.5	1.05	61.39	7	3	96	0	1	221	N/A	N/A	37	14	0	0	0.0	0.0
C+ / 6.0	11.5	0.97	11.52	150	6	93	0	1	195	98.8	-27.4	69	5	1,000	50	5.3	0.0
C+ / 6.0	11.5	0.96	9.40	31	6	93	0	1	195	93.9	-27.6	60	5	1,000	50	0.0	0.0
C+ / 6.0	11.6	0.97	9.32	27	6	93	0	1	195	92.8	-27.6	57	5	1,000	50	0.0	0.0
C+ / 5.9	11.5	0.96	21.26	157	0	99	0	1	166	99.5	-27.3	73	5	0	0	0.0	0.0
C+ / 6.0	11.4	0.96	24.33	136	4	95	0	1	192	102.5	-27.1	80	5	0	0	0.0	0.0
C+ / 6.0	11.4	0.96	22.70	21	4	95	0	1	192	99.1	-27.2	75	5	0	0	0.0	0.0
C+ / 6.2	11.5	0.96	20.37	6	0	99	0	1	166	N/A	N/A	69	5	0	0	0.0	0.0
C- / 3.3	13.7	0.97	8.72	146	3	96	0	1	89	82.9	-27.1	25	14	1,000	50	5.3	0.0
D+ / 2.5	13.7	0.97	7.19	8	3	96	0	1	89	79.5	-27.2	18	14	1,000	50	0.0	0.0
D+ / 2.4	13.7	0.98	7.03	16	3	96	0	1	89	76.5	-27.2	17	14	1,000	50	0.0	0.0
C- / 3.4	13.7	0.97	8.81	69	3	96	0	1	89	83.9	-26.9	30	14	500,000	0	0.0	0.0
E+ / 0.9	13.7	0.98	25.14	580	2	97	0	1	84	82.8	-26.6	27	14	0	0	0.0	0.0
E+ / 0.7	13.7	0.97	22.84	26	2	97	0	1	84	79.8	-26.7	22	14	0	0	0.0	0.0
D+ / 2.4	13.6	0.97	31.81	295	1	98	0	1	79	83.7	-26.7	31	14	0	0	0.0	0.0
C- / 3.1	12.3	1.05	18.09	234	1	98	0	1	92	87.5	-26.1	17	13	1,000	50	5.3	0.0
D+ / 2.4	12.3	1.05	15.64	7	1	98	0	1	92	82.4	-26.3	12	13	1,000	50	0.0	0.0
D+ / 2.4	12.3	1.05	15.70	63	1	98	0	1	92	82.7	-26.3	12	13	1,000	50	0.0	0.0
C- / 3.2	12.2	1.05	18.32	639	1	98	0	1	92	87.7	-26.0	18	13	0	0	0.0	0.0
C- / 3.3	12.3	1.06	18.44	44	1	98	0	1	92	89.8	-26.0	20	13	500,000	0	0.0	0.0
E / 0.5	15.9	1.13	8.00	43	0	99	0	1	95	123.5	-26.0	75	7	0	0	0.0	0.0
C / 5.2	10.2	0.99	18.25	2,101	4	94	0	2	149	108.1	-18.8	81	11	1,000	50	5.3	2.0
C / 5.1	10.3	0.99	17.35	781	4	94	0	2	149	102.8	-19.1	75	11	1,000	50	0.0	2.0
C / 5.2	10.2	0.99	18.46	1,029	4	94	0	2	149	110.2	-18.7	83	11	500,000	0	0.0	0.0

						PERFORMANCE							
	99 Pct = Best						Total Return % through 3/31/15					Incl. in Returns	
	0 Pct = Worst			Overall		Perfor-				Annualized		Dividend	Expense
Fund		Ticker		Investment		mance						Yield	Ratio
Type	Fund Name	Symbol		Rating	Phone	Rating/Pts	3 Mo	6 Mo	1Yr / Pct	3Yr / Pct	5Yr / Pct		
GR	Alger Spectra I	ASPIX		B+	(800) 254-3796	A+ / 9.6	5.57	9.49	18.35 /96	17.77 /93	15.90 /92	0.00	1.50
GL	AllianBerTWM GE and CovCallStr	TWMLX		D	(855) 896-3863	D+ / 2.3	1.03	0.85	2.02 /22	7.36 /23	--	1.56	1.17
GL	AllianBerTWM GE and CovCallStr Inv	TWMVX		D	(855) 896-3863	D / 2.1	0.94	-0.31	1.64 /20	7.04 /21	--	1.28	1.52
AA	AllianceBern CBF AB Agg Gr <1984			C-	(800) 221-5672	E+ / 0.9	1.49	1.95	2.62 /25	4.33 /11	4.31 / 9	0.00	0.99
AA	AllianceBern CBF AB Agg Gr <1984			C-	(800) 221-5672	D- / 1.0	1.48	1.94	2.67 /25	4.35 /11	4.32 / 9	0.00	0.99
AA	AllianceBern CBF AB Agg Gr <1984			C-	(800) 221-5672	D- / 1.0	1.29	1.59	1.95 /22	3.57 / 9	3.54 / 7	0.00	1.74
AA	AllianceBern CBF AB Agg Gr <1984			C-	(800) 221-5672	D- / 1.0	1.28	1.57	1.86 /21	3.57 / 9	3.54 / 7	0.00	1.74
AA	AllianceBern CBF AB Agg Gr <1984			C-	(800) 221-5672	D- / 1.2	1.40	1.81	2.36 /23	4.09 /10	4.06 / 9	0.00	1.24
AA	AllianceBern CBF AB Agg Gr <1984			C-	(800) 221-5672	D- / 1.3	1.49	2.07	2.90 /26	4.61 /12	4.56 /10	0.00	0.74
AA	AllianceBern CBF AB Agg Gr <1984			C-	(800) 221-5672	D- / 1.4	1.64	2.22	3.20 /27	4.91 /13	4.83 /11	0.00	0.99
AA	AllianceBern CBF AB Agg Gr <1984			C-	(800) 221-5672	D- / 1.5	1.64	2.33	3.47 /29	5.18 /14	5.11 /12	0.00	N/A
AG	AllianceBern CBF AB Agg Gr 02-04 A			D+	(800) 221-5672	D / 1.8	1.93	2.42	3.03 /27	7.16 /22	6.37 /19	0.00	1.15
AG	AllianceBern CBF AB Agg Gr 02-04			D+	(800) 221-5672	D / 1.9	1.92	2.42	3.03 /27	7.15 /22	6.36 /19	0.00	1.19
AG	AllianceBern CBF AB Agg Gr 02-04 B			D+	(800) 221-5672	D / 1.9	1.71	2.01	2.25 /23	6.34 /18	5.57 /14	0.00	1.90
AG	AllianceBern CBF AB Agg Gr 02-04			C-	(800) 221-5672	D / 2.2	1.79	2.25	2.65 /25	6.80 /20	6.00 /17	0.00	1.54
AG	AllianceBern CBF AB Agg Gr 02-04 C			D+	(800) 221-5672	D / 1.9	1.78	2.09	2.27 /23	6.38 /18	5.58 /15	0.00	1.90
AG	AllianceBern CBF AB Agg Gr 02-04			C-	(800) 221-5672	D / 2.2	1.84	2.30	2.76 /25	6.89 /21	6.12 /17	0.00	1.44
AG	AllianceBern CBF AB Agg Gr 02-04 R			C-	(800) 221-5672	D+ / 2.5	1.97	2.50	3.26 /28	7.42 /24	6.63 /21	0.00	0.94
AG	AllianceBern CBF AB Agg Gr 02-04			C-	(800) 221-5672	D+ / 2.8	2.09	2.73	3.65 /30	7.85 /26	7.00 /23	0.00	1.19
AA	AllianceBern CBF AB Agg Gr 02-04			D+	(800) 221-5672	C- / 3.0	2.17	2.89	3.95 /31	8.12 /28	--	0.00	N/A
AA	AllianceBern CBF AB Agg Gr 02-04			D+	(800) 221-5672	C- / 3.0	2.17	2.89	3.95 /31	8.12 /28	7.28 /25	0.00	N/A
AG	AllianceBern CBF AB Agg Gr 05-07 A			D+	(800) 221-5672	D / 2.2	1.76	2.16	2.36 /23	8.16 /28	7.01 /23	0.00	1.19
AG	AllianceBern CBF AB Agg Gr 05-07			D+	(800) 221-5672	D+ / 2.3	1.84	2.24	2.37 /23	8.18 /28	7.01 /23	0.00	1.19
AG	AllianceBern CBF AB Agg Gr 05-07 B			D+	(800) 221-5672	D+ / 2.3	1.62	1.83	1.62 /20	7.35 /23	6.21 /18	0.00	1.94
AG	AllianceBern CBF AB Agg Gr 05-07 C			D+	(800) 221-5672	D+ / 2.3	1.62	1.83	1.62 /20	7.37 /23	6.20 /18	0.00	1.94
AG	AllianceBern CBF AB Agg Gr 05-07			C-	(800) 221-5672	D+ / 2.7	1.75	2.09	2.16 /22	7.90 /26	6.77 /22	0.00	1.44
AG	AllianceBern CBF AB Agg Gr 05-07 R			C-	(800) 221-5672	C- / 3.0	1.85	2.30	2.63 /25	8.44 /30	7.27 /25	0.00	0.94
AG	AllianceBern CBF AB Agg Gr 05-07			C-	(800) 221-5672	C- / 3.3	1.98	2.57	3.10 /27	8.92 /32	7.69 /28	0.00	1.19
AA	AllianceBern CBF AB Agg Gr 05-07			D+	(800) 221-5672	C- / 3.4	2.04	2.61	3.25 /28	9.17 /34	--	0.00	N/A
AA	AllianceBern CBF AB Agg Gr 05-07			D+	(800) 221-5672	C- / 3.4	2.04	2.67	3.31 /28	9.16 /34	7.95 /30	0.00	N/A
AG	AllianceBern CBF AB Agg Gr 08-10 A			D+	(800) 221-5672	D+ / 2.4	1.85	2.02	2.02 /22	8.60 /30	7.24 /25	0.00	1.19
AG	AllianceBern CBF AB Agg Gr 08-10			D+	(800) 221-5672	D+ / 2.5	1.85	2.01	2.01 /22	8.54 /30	7.23 /25	0.00	N/A
AG	AllianceBern CBF AB Agg Gr 08-10 B			D+	(800) 221-5672	D+ / 2.5	1.63	1.63	1.28 /19	7.77 /26	6.45 /20	0.00	1.94
AG	AllianceBern CBF AB Agg Gr 08-10 C			D+	(800) 221-5672	D+ / 2.5	1.62	1.62	1.19 /19	7.76 /26	6.46 /20	0.00	1.94
AG	AllianceBern CBF AB Agg Gr 08-10			D+	(800) 221-5672	D+ / 2.8	1.72	1.81	1.72 /21	8.27 /29	6.98 /23	0.00	N/A
AG	AllianceBern CBF AB Agg Gr 08-10 R			C-	(800) 221-5672	C- / 3.2	1.90	2.14	2.30 /23	8.84 /32	7.53 /27	0.00	N/A
AG	AllianceBern CBF AB Agg Gr 08-10			C-	(800) 221-5672	C- / 3.5	2.03	2.35	2.75 /25	9.36 /35	7.98 /30	0.00	N/A
AA	AllianceBern CBF AB Agg Gr 08-10			D+	(800) 221-5672	C- / 3.7	2.07	2.46	3.02 /27	9.64 /37	--	0.00	N/A
AA	AllianceBern CBF AB Agg Gr 08-10			D+	(800) 221-5672	C- / 3.6	2.07	2.47	2.94 /26	9.62 /37	8.23 /31	0.00	N/A
AA	AllianceBern CBF AB Agg Gr 11-13 A			C-	(800) 221-5672	D+ / 2.6	1.90	2.22	1.98 /22	9.00 /33	--	0.00	N/A
AA	AllianceBern CBF AB Agg Gr 11-13			C-	(800) 221-5672	D+ / 2.6	1.90	2.22	1.98 /22	8.98 /33	--	0.00	N/A
AA	AllianceBern CBF AB Agg Gr 11-13 B			C-	(800) 221-5672	D+ / 2.7	1.71	1.79	1.21 /19	8.16 /28	--	0.00	N/A
AA	AllianceBern CBF AB Agg Gr 11-13 C			C-	(800) 221-5672	D+ / 2.7	1.79	1.87	1.30 /19	8.19 /28	--	0.00	N/A
AA	AllianceBern CBF AB Agg Gr 11-13			C-	(800) 221-5672	C- / 3.1	1.83	2.08	1.75 /21	8.70 /31	--	0.00	N/A
AA	AllianceBern CBF AB Agg Gr 11-13 R			C	(800) 221-5672	C- / 3.4	1.96	2.28	2.28 /23	9.27 /35	--	0.00	0.94
AA	AllianceBern CBF AB Agg Gr 11-13			C	(800) 221-5672	C- / 3.7	2.16	2.63	2.71 /25	9.78 /38	--	0.00	0.45
AA	AllianceBern CBF AB Agg Gr 11-13			C	(800) 221-5672	C- / 3.9	2.21	2.67	2.99 /26	10.14 /40	--	0.00	N/A
AA	AllianceBern CBF AB Agg Gr 11-13			C	(800) 221-5672	C- / 3.9	2.21	2.76	3.08 /27	10.10 /40	--	0.00	N/A
AA	AllianceBern CBF AB Agg Gr 84-86 A			C-	(800) 221-5672	D- / 1.1	1.49	1.95	2.68 /25	5.00 /13	4.73 /11	0.00	0.99
AA	AllianceBern CBF AB Agg Gr 84-86			C-	(800) 221-5672	D- / 1.2	1.48	1.88	2.61 /25	5.00 /13	4.74 /11	0.00	0.99
AA	AllianceBern CBF AB Agg Gr 84-86 B			C-	(800) 221-5672	D- / 1.2	1.28	1.50	1.87 /21	4.20 /11	3.95 / 8	0.00	1.74
AA	AllianceBern CBF AB Agg Gr 84-86			C-	(800) 221-5672	D- / 1.3	1.36	1.70	2.26 /23	4.59 /12	4.36 /10	0.00	1.34

● Denotes fund is closed to new investors
* Denotes fund is included in Section II

www.thestreetratings.com

RISK			NET ASSETS		ASSET						BULL / BEAR		FUND MANAGER		MINIMUMS		LOADS	
	3 Year		NAV							Portfolio	Last Bull	Last Bear	Manager	Manager	Initial	Additional	Front	Back
Risk	Standard		As of	Total	Cash	Stocks	Bonds	Other		Turnover	Market	Market	Quality	Tenure	Purch.	Purch.	End	End
Rating/Pts	Deviation	Beta	3/31/15	$(Mil)	%	%	%	%		Ratio	Return	Return	Pct	(Years)	$	$	Load	Load
C / 5.2	10.2	0.99	18.40	1,148	4	94	0	2		149	108.2	-18.8	82	11	0	0	0.0	0.0
C+ / 6.2	9.2	0.64	10.74	319	0	99	0	1		71	50.1	-14.1	79	4	25,000	250	0.0	0.0
C+ / 6.2	9.1	0.64	10.75	N/A	0	99	0	1		71	48.6	N/A	77	4	10,000	250	0.0	0.0
B+ / 9.1	4.0	0.65	15.66	2	0	31	68	1		0	22.3	-8.3	31	N/A	1,000	50	4.3	0.0
B+ / 9.1	4.0	0.65	15.75	1	0	31	68	1		0	22.2	-8.2	31	N/A	1,000	50	3.3	0.0
B+ / 9.1	4.0	0.65	14.10	N/A	0	31	68	1		0	19.0	-8.5	23	N/A	1,000	50	0.0	0.0
B+ / 9.0	4.0	0.66	14.23	1	0	31	68	1		0	19.1	-8.5	22	N/A	1,000	50	0.0	0.0
B+ / 9.1	4.0	0.65	15.18	N/A	0	31	68	1		0	21.2	-8.3	28	N/A	1,000	50	0.0	0.0
B+ / 9.1	4.0	0.65	16.30	N/A	0	31	68	1		0	23.2	-8.1	34	N/A	250	50	0.0	0.0
B+ / 9.1	4.0	0.65	16.14	N/A	0	31	68	1		0	24.5	-8.0	38	N/A	250	50	0.0	0.0
B / 8.6	4.0	0.65	16.72	N/A	0	31	68	1		0	25.5	-7.9	41	N/A	250	50	0.0	0.0
B- / 7.7	7.6	0.72	19.05	151	0	55	43	2		0	45.3	-18.0	17	N/A	1,000	50	4.3	0.0
B- / 7.7	7.6	0.72	19.07	9	0	55	43	2		0	45.3	-18.0	17	N/A	1,000	50	3.3	0.0
B- / 7.7	7.6	0.72	17.27	33	0	55	43	2		0	41.7	-18.2	12	N/A	1,000	50	0.0	0.0
B- / 7.7	7.6	0.72	18.19	N/A	0	55	43	2		0	43.7	-18.1	14	N/A	1,000	50	0.0	0.0
B- / 7.7	7.6	0.72	17.13	51	0	55	43	2		0	41.7	-18.2	12	N/A	1,000	50	0.0	0.0
B- / 7.7	7.6	0.72	18.22	4	0	55	43	2		0	44.1	-18.0	15	N/A	1,000	50	0.0	0.0
B- / 7.7	7.6	0.72	19.66	59	0	55	43	2		0	46.6	-17.9	19	N/A	250	50	0.0	0.0
B- / 7.7	7.7	0.72	19.58	5	0	55	43	2		0	48.6	-17.8	22	N/A	250	50	0.0	0.0
C+ / 6.6	7.6	1.23	20.26	11	0	55	43	2		0	49.8	-17.7	11	N/A	250	50	0.0	0.0
C+ / 6.6	7.6	1.23	20.26	1	0	55	43	2		0	49.8	-17.7	11	N/A	250	50	0.0	0.0
B- / 7.2	9.2	0.88	15.59	86	2	68	28	2		0	53.2	-20.2	9	N/A	1,000	50	4.3	0.0
B- / 7.2	9.2	0.88	15.52	6	2	68	28	2		0	53.1	-20.2	9	N/A	1,000	50	3.3	0.0
B- / 7.2	9.2	0.88	14.46	20	2	68	28	2		0	49.3	-20.4	6	N/A	1,000	50	0.0	0.0
B- / 7.2	9.2	0.88	14.47	34	2	68	28	2		0	49.4	-20.5	6	N/A	1,000	50	0.0	0.0
B- / 7.2	9.2	0.88	15.15	2	2	68	28	2		0	51.9	-20.3	8	N/A	1,000	50	0.0	0.0
B- / 7.3	9.2	0.88	15.99	47	2	68	28	2		0	54.5	-20.2	10	N/A	250	50	0.0	0.0
B- / 7.3	9.2	0.88	15.96	5	2	68	28	2		0	56.8	-20.0	13	N/A	250	50	0.0	0.0
C+ / 6.2	9.2	1.48	16.50	9	2	68	28	2		0	58.2	-19.9	5	N/A	250	50	0.0	0.0
C+ / 6.2	9.1	1.47	16.52	1	2	68	28	2		0	58.1	-19.9	5	N/A	250	50	0.0	0.0
C+ / 6.9	10.2	0.98	12.64	34	4	79	16	1		0	57.6	-22.4	6	N/A	1,000	50	4.3	0.0
C+ / 6.9	10.2	0.97	12.66	3	4	79	16	1		0	57.4	-22.4	6	N/A	1,000	50	3.3	0.0
C+ / 6.8	10.2	0.98	11.88	6	4	79	16	1		0	53.5	-22.6	4	N/A	1,000	50	0.0	0.0
C+ / 6.8	10.2	0.98	11.95	10	4	79	16	1		0	53.4	-22.5	4	N/A	1,000	50	0.0	0.0
C+ / 6.9	10.2	0.98	12.40	1	4	79	16	1		0	56.0	-22.3	5	N/A	1,000	50	0.0	0.0
C+ / 6.9	10.2	0.97	12.88	25	4	79	16	1		0	58.7	-22.2	6	N/A	250	50	0.0	0.0
C+ / 6.9	10.2	0.98	13.08	2	4	79	16	1		0	61.4	-22.1	7	N/A	250	50	0.0	0.0
C+ / 5.7	10.2	1.64	13.31	5	4	79	16	1		0	62.7	-22.0	3	N/A	250	50	0.0	0.0
C+ / 5.7	10.2	1.64	13.29	1	4	79	16	1		0	62.8	-22.0	3	N/A	250	50	0.0	0.0
B- / 7.7	10.9	1.75	12.90	14	0	0	0	100		0	60.1	-22.6	2	N/A	1,000	50	4.3	0.0
B- / 7.7	10.9	1.74	12.89	1	0	0	0	100		0	60.1	N/A	2	N/A	1,000	50	4.3	0.0
B- / 7.7	10.9	1.75	12.50	2	0	0	0	100		0	55.9	-22.8	2	N/A	1,000	50	0.0	0.0
B- / 7.7	10.9	1.74	12.51	5	0	0	0	100		0	55.9	-22.8	2	N/A	1,000	50	0.0	0.0
B- / 7.7	10.9	1.75	12.78	N/A	0	0	0	100		0	58.8	N/A	2	N/A	1,000	50	0.0	0.0
B- / 7.8	10.9	1.74	13.02	11	0	0	0	100		0	61.4	-22.5	2	N/A	250	50	0.0	0.0
B- / 7.8	10.9	1.75	13.27	1	0	0	0	100		0	64.1	-22.3	2	N/A	250	50	0.0	0.0
B- / 7.8	10.8	1.74	13.44	2	0	0	0	100		0	65.7	-22.3	3	N/A	250	50	0.0	0.0
B- / 7.8	10.9	1.74	13.40	N/A	0	0	0	100		0	65.3	-22.2	3	N/A	250	50	0.0	0.0
B+ / 9.1	4.3	0.68	15.71	1	0	31	68	1		0	24.5	-8.2	34	N/A	1,000	50	4.3	0.0
B+ / 9.1	4.2	0.67	15.73	1	0	31	68	1		0	24.6	-8.2	36	N/A	1,000	50	3.3	0.0
B+ / 9.1	4.3	0.68	14.20	N/A	0	31	68	1		0	21.4	-8.5	26	N/A	1,000	50	0.0	0.0
B+ / 9.1	4.3	0.68	14.93	N/A	0	31	68	1		0	23.0	-8.3	30	N/A	1,000	50	0.0	0.0

						PERFORMANCE							
							Total Return % through 3/31/15					Incl. in Returns	
										Annualized			
Fund Type	Fund Name	Ticker Symbol	Overall Investment Rating	Phone	Performance Rating/Pts	3 Mo	6 Mo	1Yr / Pct	3Yr / Pct	5Yr / Pct	Dividend Yield	Expense Ratio
AA	AllianceBern CBF AB Agg Gr 84-86 C		C-	(800) 221-5672	D- / 1.2	1.29	1.58	1.87 /21	4.22 /11	3.95 / 8	0.00	1.74
AA	AllianceBern CBF AB Agg Gr 84-86		C-	(800) 221-5672	D- / 1.3	1.40	1.74	2.36 /23	4.72 /12	4.47 /10	0.00	1.24
AA	AllianceBern CBF AB Agg Gr 84-86 R		C-	(800) 221-5672	D- / 1.5	1.56	2.07	2.91 /26	5.26 /14	4.99 /12	0.00	0.74
AA	AllianceBern CBF AB Agg Gr 84-86		C-	(800) 221-5672	D / 1.7	1.64	2.22	3.20 /27	5.57 /15	5.25 /13	0.00	0.99
AA	AllianceBern CBF AB Agg Gr 87-89 A		C-	(800) 221-5672	D- / 1.0	1.51	1.91	2.65 /25	4.81 /12	4.61 /11	0.00	0.99
AA	AllianceBern CBF AB Agg Gr 87-89		C-	(800) 221-5672	D- / 1.1	1.44	1.91	2.65 /25	4.81 /12	4.61 /11	0.00	0.99
AA	AllianceBern CBF AB Agg Gr 87-89 B		C-	(800) 221-5672	D- / 1.1	1.30	1.52	1.89 /21	4.01 /10	3.83 / 8	0.00	1.74
AA	AllianceBern CBF AB Agg Gr 87-89		C-	(800) 221-5672	D- / 1.2	1.37	1.72	2.29 /23	4.43 /11	4.25 / 9	0.00	1.34
AA	AllianceBern CBF AB Agg Gr 87-89 C		C-	(800) 221-5672	D- / 1.1	1.30	1.52	1.82 /21	4.01 /10	3.83 / 8	0.00	1.74
AA	AllianceBern CBF AB Agg Gr 87-89		C-	(800) 221-5672	D- / 1.3	1.42	1.83	2.39 /24	4.57 /12	4.36 /10	0.00	1.24
AA	AllianceBern CBF AB Agg Gr 87-89 R		C-	(800) 221-5672	D- / 1.5	1.51	2.02	2.87 /26	5.08 /13	4.88 /11	0.00	0.74
AA	AllianceBern CBF AB Agg Gr 87-89		C-	(800) 221-5672	D / 1.6	1.60	2.19	3.18 /27	5.37 /14	5.13 /12	0.00	0.99
AA	AllianceBern CBF AB Agg Gr 87-89		C-	(800) 221-5672	D / 1.7	1.66	2.29	3.44 /29	5.64 /15	--	0.00	N/A
AA	AllianceBern CBF AB Agg Gr 87-89		C-	(800) 221-5672	D / 1.7	1.66	2.29	3.44 /29	5.64 /15	5.39 /14	0.00	N/A
AA	AllianceBern CBF AB Agg Gr 90-92 A		C-	(800) 221-5672	D- / 1.0	1.51	1.91	2.65 /25	4.40 /11	4.35 /10	0.00	0.99
AA	AllianceBern CBF AB Agg Gr 90-92		C-	(800) 221-5672	D- / 1.0	1.44	1.91	2.65 /25	4.40 /11	4.35 /10	0.00	1.03
AA	AllianceBern CBF AB Agg Gr 90-92 B		C-	(800) 221-5672	D- / 1.0	1.30	1.60	1.89 /21	3.63 / 9	3.56 / 7	0.00	1.74
AA	AllianceBern CBF AB Agg Gr 90-92		C-	(800) 221-5672	D- / 1.2	1.38	1.73	2.29 /23	4.04 /10	3.97 / 8	0.00	1.38
AA	AllianceBern CBF AB Agg Gr 90-92 C		C-	(800) 221-5672	D- / 1.0	1.30	1.60	1.89 /21	3.63 / 9	3.57 / 7	0.00	1.74
AA	AllianceBern CBF AB Agg Gr 90-92		C-	(800) 221-5672	D- / 1.2	1.36	1.77	2.33 /23	4.12 /10	4.06 / 9	0.00	1.28
AA	AllianceBern CBF AB Agg Gr 90-92 R		C-	(800) 221-5672	D- / 1.4	1.58	2.10	2.94 /26	4.68 /12	4.60 /11	0.00	0.78
AA	AllianceBern CBF AB Agg Gr 90-92		C-	(800) 221-5672	D- / 1.5	1.60	2.19	3.18 /27	4.97 /13	4.85 /11	0.00	1.03
AA	AllianceBern CBF AB Agg Gr 90-92		C-	(800) 221-5672	D / 1.6	1.67	2.30	3.45 /29	5.22 /14	--	0.00	N/A
AA	AllianceBern CBF AB Agg Gr 90-92		C-	(800) 221-5672	D / 1.6	1.67	2.36	3.45 /29	5.22 /14	5.12 /12	0.00	N/A
AA	AllianceBern CBF AB Agg Gr 93-95 A		C-	(800) 221-5672	E+ / 0.9	1.49	1.90	2.67 /25	4.28 /11	4.29 / 9	0.00	1.03
AA	AllianceBern CBF AB Agg Gr 93-95		C-	(800) 221-5672	D- / 1.0	1.49	1.90	2.60 /25	4.25 /11	4.28 / 9	0.00	1.07
AA	AllianceBern CBF AB Agg Gr 93-95 B		C-	(800) 221-5672	D- / 1.0	1.27	1.50	1.88 /21	3.48 / 9	3.50 / 7	0.00	1.78
AA	AllianceBern CBF AB Agg Gr 93-95		C-	(800) 221-5672	D- / 1.1	1.42	1.79	2.30 /23	3.91 /10	3.93 / 8	0.00	1.42
AA	AllianceBern CBF AB Agg Gr 93-95 C		C-	(800) 221-5672	D- / 1.0	1.27	1.50	1.81 /21	3.48 / 9	3.50 / 7	0.00	1.78
AA	AllianceBern CBF AB Agg Gr 93-95		C-	(800) 221-5672	D- / 1.2	1.40	1.76	2.41 /24	4.02 /10	4.03 / 8	0.00	1.32
AA	AllianceBern CBF AB Agg Gr 93-95 R		C-	(800) 221-5672	D- / 1.3	1.51	1.97	2.85 /26	4.51 /11	4.53 /10	0.00	0.82
AA	AllianceBern CBF AB Agg Gr 93-95		C-	(800) 221-5672	D- / 1.4	1.59	2.13	3.16 /27	4.82 /13	4.79 /11	0.00	1.07
AA	AllianceBern CBF AB Agg Gr 93-95		C-	(800) 221-5672	D- / 1.5	1.66	2.32	3.45 /29	5.09 /13	--	0.00	N/A
AA	AllianceBern CBF AB Agg Gr 93-95		C-	(800) 221-5672	D- / 1.5	1.66	2.32	3.45 /29	5.11 /13	5.08 /12	0.00	N/A
AA	AllianceBern CBF AB Agg Gr 96-98 A		D+	(800) 221-5672	D- / 1.0	1.47	1.90	2.62 /25	4.52 /12	4.54 /10	0.00	1.07
AA	AllianceBern CBF AB Agg Gr 96-98		C-	(800) 221-5672	D- / 1.0	1.47	1.90	2.62 /25	4.52 /12	4.55 /10	0.00	1.11
AA	AllianceBern CBF AB Agg Gr 96-98 B		D+	(800) 221-5672	D- / 1.1	1.32	1.55	1.87 /21	3.75 /10	3.77 / 8	0.00	1.82
AA	AllianceBern CBF AB Agg Gr 96-98		C-	(800) 221-5672	D- / 1.2	1.32	1.70	2.22 /23	4.14 /11	4.19 / 9	0.00	1.46
AA	AllianceBern CBF AB Agg Gr 96-98 C		D+	(800) 221-5672	D- / 1.1	1.32	1.56	1.87 /21	3.74 /10	3.76 / 8	0.00	1.82
AA	AllianceBern CBF AB Agg Gr 96-98		C-	(800) 221-5672	D- / 1.2	1.45	1.82	2.42 /24	4.25 /11	4.30 / 9	0.00	1.36
AA	AllianceBern CBF AB Agg Gr 96-98 R		C-	(800) 221-5672	D- / 1.4	1.49	2.04	2.88 /26	4.76 /12	4.80 /11	0.00	0.86
AA	AllianceBern CBF AB Agg Gr 96-98		C-	(800) 221-5672	D- / 1.5	1.64	2.20	3.26 /28	5.12 /13	5.10 /12	0.00	1.11
AA	AllianceBern CBF AB Agg Gr 96-98		C-	(800) 221-5672	D / 1.6	1.65	2.26	3.43 /29	5.36 /14	--	0.00	N/A
AA	AllianceBern CBF AB Agg Gr 96-98		C-	(800) 221-5672	D / 1.6	1.72	2.33	3.50 /29	5.36 /14	5.35 /13	0.00	N/A
AA	AllianceBern CBF AB Agg Gr 99-01 A		D+	(800) 221-5672	D- / 1.4	1.71	2.27	2.91 /26	6.02 /17	5.54 /14	0.00	1.11
AA	AllianceBern CBF AB Agg Gr 99-01		D+	(800) 221-5672	D- / 1.5	1.71	2.27	2.98 /26	6.05 /17	5.54 /14	0.00	1.15
AA	AllianceBern CBF AB Agg Gr 99-01 B		D+	(800) 221-5672	D- / 1.5	1.51	1.82	2.13 /22	5.22 /14	4.76 /11	0.00	1.86
AA	AllianceBern CBF AB Agg Gr 99-01		C-	(800) 221-5672	D / 1.7	1.58	2.02	2.54 /24	5.67 /15	5.18 /13	0.00	1.50
AA	AllianceBern CBF AB Agg Gr 99-01 C		D+	(800) 221-5672	D- / 1.5	1.53	1.92	2.16 /22	5.26 /14	4.75 /11	0.00	1.86
AA	AllianceBern CBF AB Agg Gr 99-01		C-	(800) 221-5672	D / 1.7	1.63	2.07	2.65 /25	5.75 /16	5.28 /13	0.00	1.40
AA	AllianceBern CBF AB Agg Gr 99-01 R		C-	(800) 221-5672	D / 2.0	1.79	2.40	3.22 /28	6.31 /18	5.80 /16	0.00	0.90
AA	AllianceBern CBF AB Agg Gr 99-01		C-	(800) 221-5672	D / 2.2	1.87	2.56	3.53 /29	6.68 /20	6.12 /17	0.00	1.15

99 Pct = Best
0 Pct = Worst

● Denotes fund is closed to new investors
* Denotes fund is included in Section II

Risk Rating/Pts	Standard Deviation	Beta	NAV As of 3/31/15	Total $(Mil)	Cash %	Stocks %	Bonds %	Other %	Portfolio Turnover Ratio	Last Bull Market Return	Last Bear Market Return	Manager Quality Pct	Manager Tenure (Years)	Initial Purch. $	Additional Purch. $	Front End Load	Back End Load
B+ / 9.0	4.3	0.68	14.14	N/A	0	31	68	1	0	21.5	-8.5	26	N/A	1,000	50	0.0	0.0
B+ / 9.1	4.3	0.68	15.16	2	0	31	68	1	0	23.6	-8.3	31	N/A	1,000	50	0.0	0.0
B+ / 9.1	4.2	0.68	16.28	N/A	0	31	68	1	0	25.6	-8.1	39	N/A	250	50	0.0	0.0
B+ / 9.1	4.3	0.68	16.13	N/A	0	31	68	1	0	26.9	-8.0	42	N/A	250	50	0.0	0.0
B+ / 9.1	4.2	0.67	15.51	5	0	31	68	1	0	23.8	-8.2	34	N/A	1,000	50	4.3	0.0
B+ / 9.1	4.1	0.67	15.51	3	0	31	68	1	0	23.9	-8.3	34	N/A	1,000	50	3.3	0.0
B+ / 9.1	4.2	0.67	14.01	N/A	0	31	68	1	0	20.7	-8.5	25	N/A	1,000	50	0.0	0.0
B+ / 9.1	4.1	0.67	14.75	N/A	0	31	68	1	0	22.4	-8.3	30	N/A	1,000	50	0.0	0.0
B+ / 9.1	4.2	0.67	14.02	2	0	31	68	1	0	20.7	-8.5	25	N/A	1,000	50	0.0	0.0
B+ / 9.1	4.2	0.67	14.99	3	0	31	68	1	0	22.8	-8.3	31	N/A	1,000	50	0.0	0.0
B+ / 9.1	4.1	0.67	16.14	2	0	31	68	1	0	24.9	-8.1	37	N/A	250	50	0.0	0.0
B+ / 9.1	4.2	0.68	15.90	N/A	0	31	68	1	0	26.1	-8.0	41	N/A	250	50	0.0	0.0
B / 8.6	4.1	0.67	16.55	N/A	0	31	68	1	0	27.2	-7.9	45	N/A	250	50	0.0	0.0
B / 8.6	4.1	0.67	16.55	N/A	0	31	68	1	0	27.2	-7.9	46	N/A	250	50	0.0	0.0
B+ / 9.1	4.0	0.65	15.50	20	0	31	68	1	0	22.4	-8.2	32	N/A	1,000	50	4.3	0.0
B+ / 9.1	4.0	0.65	15.50	7	0	31	68	1	0	22.4	-8.2	32	N/A	1,000	50	3.3	0.0
B+ / 9.1	4.0	0.65	14.01	2	0	31	68	1	0	19.4	-8.5	23	N/A	1,000	50	0.0	0.0
B+ / 9.1	4.0	0.65	14.74	2	0	31	68	1	0	21.0	-8.4	28	N/A	1,000	50	0.0	0.0
B+ / 9.1	4.0	0.65	13.99	7	0	31	68	1	0	19.4	-8.6	23	N/A	1,000	50	0.0	0.0
B+ / 9.1	4.0	0.65	14.91	7	0	31	68	1	0	21.3	-8.3	28	N/A	1,000	50	0.0	0.0
B+ / 9.1	4.0	0.65	16.08	6	0	31	68	1	0	23.4	-8.1	35	N/A	250	50	0.0	0.0
B+ / 9.1	3.9	0.64	15.89	1	0	31	68	1	0	24.7	-8.0	40	N/A	250	50	0.0	0.0
B / 8.6	4.0	0.65	16.47	1	0	31	68	1	0	25.7	-7.9	42	N/A	250	50	0.0	0.0
B / 8.6	4.0	0.65	16.47	N/A	0	31	68	1	0	25.7	-7.9	42	N/A	250	50	0.0	0.0
B+ / 9.1	4.0	0.65	14.99	64	0	31	68	1	0	21.9	-8.4	30	N/A	1,000	50	4.3	0.0
B+ / 9.1	3.9	0.64	14.98	28	0	31	68	1	0	21.8	-8.3	31	N/A	1,000	50	3.3	0.0
B+ / 9.1	3.9	0.64	13.53	7	0	31	68	1	0	18.8	-8.6	23	N/A	1,000	50	0.0	0.0
B+ / 9.1	3.9	0.64	14.25	6	0	31	68	1	0	20.5	-8.5	27	N/A	1,000	50	0.0	0.0
B+ / 9.0	4.0	0.65	13.53	21	0	31	68	1	0	18.8	-8.6	22	N/A	1,000	50	0.0	0.0
B+ / 9.1	4.0	0.65	14.45	20	0	31	68	1	0	20.9	-8.5	27	N/A	1,000	50	0.0	0.0
B+ / 9.1	4.0	0.64	15.50	22	0	31	68	1	0	23.0	-8.3	33	N/A	250	50	0.0	0.0
B+ / 9.1	3.9	0.64	15.34	1	0	31	68	1	0	24.1	-8.2	38	N/A	250	50	0.0	0.0
B / 8.6	3.9	0.64	15.90	3	0	31	68	1	0	25.2	-8.1	41	N/A	250	50	0.0	0.0
B / 8.6	4.0	0.65	15.91	N/A	0	31	68	1	0	25.2	-8.0	41	N/A	250	50	0.0	0.0
B / 8.8	4.5	0.73	14.48	163	0	31	68	1	0	25.7	-11.4	24	N/A	1,000	50	4.3	0.0
B / 8.8	4.5	0.73	14.49	71	0	31	68	1	0	25.7	-11.4	24	N/A	1,000	50	3.3	0.0
B / 8.8	4.5	0.73	13.09	20	0	31	68	1	0	22.6	-11.7	17	N/A	1,000	50	0.0	0.0
B / 8.8	4.5	0.73	13.79	19	0	31	68	1	0	24.4	-11.5	20	N/A	1,000	50	0.0	0.0
B / 8.8	4.6	0.74	13.05	50	0	31	68	1	0	22.6	-11.7	16	N/A	1,000	50	0.0	0.0
B / 8.8	4.5	0.73	13.96	47	0	31	68	1	0	24.7	-11.5	21	N/A	1,000	50	0.0	0.0
B / 8.8	4.6	0.74	14.98	63	0	31	68	1	0	26.9	-11.4	25	N/A	250	50	0.0	0.0
B / 8.8	4.5	0.73	14.89	4	0	31	68	1	0	28.2	-11.2	30	N/A	250	50	0.0	0.0
B / 8.6	4.5	0.73	15.37	10	0	31	68	1	0	29.3	-11.1	33	N/A	250	50	0.0	0.0
B / 8.6	4.5	0.73	15.38	1	0	31	68	1	0	29.3	-11.1	33	N/A	250	50	0.0	0.0
B / 8.3	6.0	0.98	14.85	211	0	42	56	2	0	35.3	-15.0	14	N/A	1,000	50	4.3	0.0
B / 8.3	6.1	0.98	14.86	97	0	42	56	2	0	35.3	-15.0	14	N/A	1,000	50	3.3	0.0
B / 8.2	6.0	0.97	13.41	26	0	42	56	2	0	31.8	-15.3	10	N/A	1,000	50	0.0	0.0
B / 8.3	6.0	0.98	14.11	27	0	42	56	2	0	33.7	-15.1	12	N/A	1,000	50	0.0	0.0
B / 8.2	6.0	0.98	13.27	53	0	42	56	2	0	31.9	-15.3	10	N/A	1,000	50	0.0	0.0
B / 8.2	6.0	0.98	14.32	68	0	42	56	2	0	34.1	-15.1	13	N/A	1,000	50	0.0	0.0
B / 8.3	6.1	0.99	15.38	81	0	42	56	2	0	36.4	-14.9	16	N/A	250	50	0.0	0.0
B / 8.3	6.0	0.98	15.25	8	0	42	56	2	0	38.1	-14.8	19	N/A	250	50	0.0	0.0

Fund Type	Fund Name	Ticker Symbol	Overall Investment Rating	Phone	Perfor-mance Rating/Pts	Total Return % through 3/31/15			Annualized		Incl. in Returns	
						3 Mo	6 Mo	1Yr / Pct	3Yr / Pct	5Yr / Pct	Dividend Yield	Expense Ratio
AA	AllianceBern CBF AB Agg Gr 99-01		E-	(800) 221-5672	D+ / 2.3	1.87	2.66	3.81 /31	6.93 /21	--	0.00	N/A
AA	AllianceBern CBF AB Agg Gr 99-01		E-	(800) 221-5672	D+ / 2.3	1.87	2.66	3.81 /31	6.93 /21	6.39 /19	0.00	N/A
AA	AllianceBern CBF AB Csv Gr <1996		C-	(800) 221-5672	E+ / 0.7	1.36	2.01	2.86 /26	2.85 / 8	--	0.00	N/A
AA	AllianceBern CBF AB Csv Gr <1996		C-	(800) 221-5672	E+ / 0.8	1.21	1.68	2.07 /22	2.11 / 6	--	0.00	N/A
AA	AllianceBern CBF AB Csv Gr <1996		C-	(800) 221-5672	E+ / 0.8	1.21	1.59	2.07 /22	2.08 / 6	--	0.00	N/A
AA	AllianceBern CBF AB Csv Gr <1996		C-	(800) 221-5672	D- / 1.0	1.44	2.18	3.12 /27	3.12 / 8	--	0.00	N/A
AA	AllianceBern CBF AB Csv Gr <1996		C-	(800) 221-5672	D- / 1.1	1.51	2.33	3.63 /30	3.63 / 9	--	0.00	N/A
AA	AllianceBern CBF AB Csv Gr 02-04 A		C-	(800) 221-5672	D- / 1.0	1.42	1.93	2.70 /25	4.42 /11	--	0.00	N/A
AA	AllianceBern CBF AB Csv Gr 02-04 B		C-	(800) 221-5672	D- / 1.0	1.20	1.54	1.89 /21	3.63 / 9	--	0.00	N/A
AA	AllianceBern CBF AB Csv Gr 02-04 C		C-	(800) 221-5672	D- / 1.0	1.28	1.63	1.98 /22	3.63 / 9	--	0.00	N/A
AA	AllianceBern CBF AB Csv Gr 02-04 R		C-	(800) 221-5672	D- / 1.4	1.50	2.09	2.95 /26	4.66 /12	--	0.00	N/A
AA	AllianceBern CBF AB Csv Gr 02-04		C-	(800) 221-5672	D- / 1.5	1.64	2.31	3.34 /28	5.01 /13	--	0.00	N/A
AA	AllianceBern CBF AB Csv Gr 02-04		C-	(800) 221-5672	D- / 1.2	1.63	2.38	3.48 /29	5.26 /14	--	0.00	N/A
AA	AllianceBern CBF AB Csv Gr 05-07 A		C-	(800) 221-5672	D- / 1.4	1.79	2.51	3.40 /28	5.97 /17	--	0.00	N/A
AA	AllianceBern CBF AB Csv Gr 05-07 B		C-	(800) 221-5672	D- / 1.5	1.59	2.16	2.66 /25	5.17 /14	--	0.00	N/A
AA	AllianceBern CBF AB Csv Gr 05-07 C		C-	(800) 221-5672	D- / 1.5	1.59	2.08	2.58 /24	5.14 /14	--	0.00	N/A
AA	AllianceBern CBF AB Csv Gr 05-07 R		C	(800) 221-5672	D / 2.0	1.86	2.65	3.70 /30	6.19 /17	--	0.00	N/A
AA	AllianceBern CBF AB Csv Gr 05-07		C	(800) 221-5672	D / 2.2	1.91	2.86	3.98 /32	6.52 /19	--	0.00	N/A
AA	AllianceBern CBF AB Csv Gr 05-07		C	(800) 221-5672	D+ / 2.3	2.05	2.99	4.27 /33	6.81 /20	--	0.00	N/A
AA	AllianceBern CBF AB Csv Gr 05-07		C-	(800) 221-5672	D / 1.8	1.97	2.91	4.27 /33	6.81 /20	--	0.00	N/A
AA	AllianceBern CBF AB Csv Gr 08-10 A		D	(800) 221-5672	D / 1.7	2.03	2.65	3.43 /29	6.74 /20	--	0.00	N/A
AA	AllianceBern CBF AB Csv Gr 08-10 B		D	(800) 221-5672	D / 1.8	1.85	2.32	2.64 /25	5.97 /17	--	0.00	N/A
AA	AllianceBern CBF AB Csv Gr 08-10 C		D	(800) 221-5672	D / 1.8	1.77	2.25	2.56 /24	5.95 /17	--	0.00	N/A
AA	AllianceBern CBF AB Csv Gr 08-10 R		D+	(800) 221-5672	D+ / 2.4	2.09	2.78	3.72 /30	7.03 /21	--	0.00	N/A
AA	AllianceBern CBF AB Csv Gr 08-10		C-	(800) 221-5672	D+ / 2.6	2.14	2.98	3.98 /32	7.38 /23	--	0.00	N/A
AA	AllianceBern CBF AB Csv Gr 08-10		C-	(800) 221-5672	D+ / 2.8	2.20	3.10	4.26 /33	7.66 /25	--	0.00	N/A
AA	AllianceBern CBF AB Csv Gr 11-13 A		D+	(800) 221-5672	D / 1.9	1.97	2.54	3.13 /27	7.32 /23	--	0.00	N/A
AA	AllianceBern CBF AB Csv Gr 11-13 B		D+	(800) 221-5672	D / 2.0	1.80	2.24	2.39 /24	6.55 /19	--	0.00	N/A
AA	AllianceBern CBF AB Csv Gr 11-13 C		D+	(800) 221-5672	D / 2.0	1.80	2.17	2.32 /23	6.52 /19	--	0.00	N/A
AA	AllianceBern CBF AB Csv Gr 11-13 R		C-	(800) 221-5672	D+ / 2.6	2.09	2.74	3.39 /28	7.59 /25	--	0.00	N/A
AA	AllianceBern CBF AB Mcsv Gr 11-13		C-	(800) 221-5672	D+ / 2.9	2.13	2.84	3.78 /30	8.00 /27	--	0.00	N/A
AA	AllianceBern CBF AB Csv Gr 11-13		C-	(800) 221-5672	C- / 3.0	2.19	2.96	3.96 /31	8.24 /28	--	0.00	N/A
AA	AllianceBern CBF AB Csv Gr 11-13		C-	(800) 221-5672	D+ / 2.4	2.19	2.96	3.97 /32	8.24 /28	--	0.00	N/A
AA	AllianceBern CBF AB Csv Gr 96-98 A		C-	(800) 221-5672	E+ / 0.7	1.44	1.99	2.83 /26	2.95 / 8	--	Incl. in Returns	N/A
AA	AllianceBern CBF AB Csv Gr 96-98 B		C-	(800) 221-5672	E+ / 0.8	1.20	1.58	2.05 /22	2.16 / 6	--	0.00	N/A
AA	AllianceBern CBF AB Csv Gr 96-98 C		C-	(800) 221-5672	E+ / 0.8	1.20	1.58	2.05 /22	2.16 / 6	--	0.00	N/A
AA	AllianceBern CBF AB Csv Gr 96-98 R		C-	(800) 221-5672	D- / 1.0	1.43	2.16	3.09 /27	3.19 / 8	--	0.00	N/A
AA	AllianceBern CBF AB Csv Gr 96-98		C-	(800) 221-5672	D- / 1.1	1.51	2.23	3.34 /28	3.49 / 9	--	0.00	N/A
AA	AllianceBern CBF AB Csv Gr 96-98		C-	(800) 221-5672	D- / 1.1	1.58	2.39	3.59 /29	3.72 / 9	--	0.00	N/A
AA	AllianceBern CBF AB Csv Gr 96-98		C-	(800) 221-5672	E+ / 0.9	1.58	2.30	3.59 /29	3.73 / 9	--	0.00	N/A
AA	AllianceBern CBF AB Csv Gr 99-01 A		C-	(800) 221-5672	E+ / 0.8	1.32	1.77	2.58 /24	3.17 / 8	--	0.00	N/A
AA	AllianceBern CBF AB Csv Gr 99-01 B		C-	(800) 221-5672	E+ / 0.8	1.17	1.44	1.81 /21	2.39 / 7	--	0.00	N/A
AA	AllianceBern CBF AB Csv Gr 99-01 C		C-	(800) 221-5672	E+ / 0.8	1.08	1.45	1.81 /21	2.40 / 7	--	0.00	N/A
AA	AllianceBern CBF AB Csv Gr 99-01 R		C-	(800) 221-5672	D- / 1.0	1.40	1.93	2.83 /26	3.40 / 9	--	0.00	N/A
AA	AllianceBern CBF AB Csv Gr 99-01		C-	(800) 221-5672	D- / 1.2	1.54	2.25	3.41 /28	3.99 /10	--	0.00	N/A
AA	AllianceBern CBF AB Csv Gr 99-01		C-	(800) 221-5672	E+ / 0.9	1.54	2.25	3.41 /29	3.99 /10	--	0.00	N/A
AA	AllianceBern CBF AB Mod Gr <1984		C-	(800) 221-5672	E+ / 0.7	1.30	1.69	2.42 /24	3.15 / 8	3.31 / 7	0.00	0.97
AA	AllianceBern CBF AB Mod Gr <1984		C-	(800) 221-5672	E+ / 0.8	1.30	1.69	2.43 /24	3.16 / 8	3.30 / 7	0.00	0.97
AA	AllianceBern CBF AB Mod Gr <1984		C-	(800) 221-5672	E+ / 0.8	1.07	1.29	1.65 /21	2.37 / 7	2.55 / 5	0.00	1.72
AA	AllianceBern CBF AB Mod Gr <1984		C-	(800) 221-5672	E+ / 0.9	1.16	1.44	2.00 /22	2.78 / 7	2.94 / 6	0.00	1.32
AA	AllianceBern CBF AB Mod Gr <1984		C-	(800) 221-5672	E+ / 0.8	1.08	1.29	1.66 /21	2.38 / 7	2.54 / 5	0.00	1.72
AA	AllianceBern CBF AB Mod Gr <1984		C-	(800) 221-5672	E+ / 0.9	1.21	1.55	2.17 /23	2.88 / 8	3.05 / 6	0.00	1.22

● Denotes fund is closed to new investors
* Denotes fund is included in Section II

www.thestreetratings.com

Risk Rating/Pts	3 Year Standard Deviation	Beta	NAV As of 3/31/15	Total $(Mil)	Cash %	Stocks %	Bonds %	Other %	Portfolio Turnover Ratio	Last Bull Market Return	Last Bear Market Return	Manager Quality Pct	Manager Tenure (Years)	Initial Purch. $	Additional Purch. $	Front End Load	Back End Load
E+ / 0.9	6.0	0.98	15.81	13	0	42	56	2	0	39.2	-14.7	21	N/A	250	50	0.0	0.0
E+ / 0.9	6.0	0.98	15.81	2	0	42	56	2	0	39.3	-14.7	21	N/A	250	50	0.0	0.0
B+ / 9.5	2.7	0.44	11.14	3	4	20	74	2	0	12.1	N/A	41	N/A	1,000	50	4.3	0.0
B+ / 9.5	2.7	0.43	10.87	N/A	4	20	74	2	0	9.4	N/A	32	N/A	1,000	50	0.0	0.0
B+ / 9.5	2.7	0.42	10.87	2	4	20	74	2	0	N/A	N/A	33	N/A	1,000	50	0.0	0.0
B+ / 9.5	2.7	0.43	11.24	1	4	20	74	2	0	13.0	N/A	46	N/A	250	50	0.0	0.0
B+ / 9.5	2.7	0.43	11.43	N/A	4	20	74	2	0	N/A	N/A	54	N/A	250	50	0.0	0.0
B+ / 9.2	4.3	0.69	12.16	1	4	30	65	1	0	23.6	N/A	27	N/A	1,000	50	4.3	0.0
B+ / 9.2	4.3	0.69	11.84	N/A	4	30	65	1	0	20.4	N/A	19	N/A	1,000	50	0.0	0.0
B+ / 9.2	4.3	0.70	11.84	1	4	30	65	1	0	N/A	N/A	18	N/A	1,000	50	0.0	0.0
B+ / 9.2	4.3	0.69	12.21	1	4	30	65	1	0	N/A	N/A	29	N/A	250	50	0.0	0.0
B+ / 9.2	4.2	0.69	12.39	N/A	4	30	65	1	0	N/A	N/A	34	N/A	250	50	0.0	0.0
B+ / 9.2	4.2	0.69	12.48	N/A	4	30	65	1	0	N/A	N/A	37	N/A	250	50	4.0	0.0
B / 8.9	5.7	0.93	13.09	1	4	43	51	2	0	33.0	N/A	17	N/A	1,000	50	4.3	0.0
B / 8.9	5.7	0.93	12.75	N/A	4	43	51	2	0	29.7	N/A	12	N/A	1,000	50	0.0	0.0
B / 8.9	5.7	0.93	12.74	N/A	4	43	51	2	0	N/A	N/A	12	N/A	1,000	50	0.0	0.0
B / 8.9	5.7	0.94	13.16	N/A	4	43	51	2	0	N/A	N/A	19	N/A	250	50	0.0	0.0
B / 8.9	5.7	0.94	13.32	N/A	4	43	51	2	0	N/A	N/A	21	N/A	250	50	0.0	0.0
B / 8.9	5.8	0.94	13.44	N/A	4	43	51	2	0	N/A	N/A	24	N/A	250	50	0.0	0.0
B / 8.9	5.7	0.93	13.44	N/A	4	43	51	2	0	N/A	N/A	25	N/A	250	50	4.0	0.0
B- / 7.2	6.9	1.12	13.56	1	2	53	43	2	0	39.4	N/A	10	N/A	1,000	50	4.3	0.0
B- / 7.1	6.9	1.12	13.21	1	2	53	43	2	0	N/A	N/A	7	N/A	1,000	50	0.0	0.0
B- / 7.0	6.9	1.12	13.20	N/A	2	53	43	2	0	N/A	N/A	7	N/A	1,000	50	0.0	0.0
B- / 7.3	6.9	1.12	13.67	N/A	2	53	43	2	0	N/A	N/A	11	N/A	250	50	0.0	0.0
B- / 7.4	6.8	1.11	13.83	N/A	2	53	43	2	0	N/A	N/A	14	N/A	250	50	0.0	0.0
B- / 7.5	6.9	1.12	13.95	N/A	2	53	43	2	0	N/A	N/A	14	N/A	250	50	0.0	0.0
B- / 7.6	7.5	1.23	14.51	2	4	62	33	1	0	N/A	N/A	7	N/A	1,000	50	4.3	0.0
B- / 7.5	7.6	1.24	14.14	N/A	4	62	33	1	0	N/A	N/A	5	N/A	1,000	50	0.0	0.0
B- / 7.5	7.6	1.23	14.13	1	4	62	33	1	0	N/A	N/A	6	N/A	1,000	50	0.0	0.0
B- / 7.6	7.5	1.22	14.62	N/A	4	62	33	1	0	N/A	N/A	9	N/A	250	50	0.0	0.0
B- / 7.7	7.5	1.23	14.84	N/A	4	62	33	1	0	N/A	N/A	10	N/A	250	50	0.0	0.0
B- / 7.7	7.6	1.23	14.95	N/A	4	62	33	1	0	N/A	N/A	11	N/A	250	50	0.0	0.0
B- / 7.7	7.5	1.23	14.94	N/A	4	62	33	1	0	N/A	N/A	11	N/A	250	50	4.0	0.0
B+ / 9.5	2.7	0.43	11.26	7	4	20	74	2	0	13.1	N/A	43	N/A	1,000	50	4.3	0.0
B+ / 9.5	2.8	0.44	10.96	1	4	20	74	2	0	10.3	N/A	31	N/A	1,000	50	0.0	0.0
B+ / 9.5	2.8	0.44	10.95	4	4	20	74	2	0	Return	Return	31	N/A	1,000	50	0.0	0.0
B+ / 9.5	2.8	0.44	11.35	2	4	20	74	2	0	14.0	N/A	45	N/A	250	50	0.0	0.0
B+ / 9.5	2.8	0.44	11.45	N/A	4	20	74	2	0	N/A	N/A	50	N/A	250	50	0.0	0.0
B+ / 9.5	2.8	0.44	11.55	1	4	20	74	2	0	N/A	N/A	53	N/A	250	50	0.0	0.0
B+ / 9.5	2.8	0.44	11.54	N/A	4	20	74	2	0	N/A	N/A	53	N/A	250	50	4.0	0.0
B+ / 9.4	3.2	0.50	11.53	3	3	21	75	1	0	15.9	N/A	36	N/A	1,000	50	4.3	0.0
B+ / 9.4	3.1	0.50	11.24	N/A	3	21	75	1	0	13.1	N/A	27	N/A	1,000	50	0.0	0.0
B+ / 9.4	3.1	0.50	11.23	2	3	21	75	1	0	N/A	N/A	27	N/A	1,000	50	0.0	0.0
B+ / 9.4	3.1	0.50	11.62	1	3	21	75	1	0	N/A	N/A	40	N/A	250	50	0.0	0.0
B+ / 9.4	3.1	0.49	11.84	N/A	3	21	75	1	0	N/A	N/A	49	N/A	250	50	0.0	0.0
B+ / 9.4	3.2	0.50	11.84	N/A	3	21	75	1	0	N/A	N/A	48	N/A	250	50	4.0	0.0
B+ / 9.3	2.9	0.46	15.63	3	0	21	78	1	0	14.6	-6.3	42	N/A	1,000	50	4.3	0.0
B+ / 9.3	2.9	0.46	15.60	1	0	21	78	1	0	14.5	-6.3	41	N/A	1,000	50	3.3	0.0
B+ / 9.3	2.9	0.46	14.14	N/A	0	21	78	1	0	11.7	-6.6	32	N/A	1,000	50	0.0	0.0
B+ / 9.3	2.9	0.46	14.82	N/A	0	21	78	1	0	13.2	-6.4	36	N/A	1,000	50	0.0	0.0
B+ / 9.3	2.9	0.46	14.08	1	0	21	78	1	0	11.6	-6.5	31	N/A	1,000	50	0.0	0.0
B+ / 9.3	2.9	0.46	15.05	2	0	21	78	1	0	13.6	-6.3	37	N/A	1,000	50	0.0	0.0

99 Pct = Best
0 Pct = Worst

Fund Type	Fund Name	Ticker Symbol	Overall Investment Rating	Phone	Performance Rating/Pts	3 Mo	6 Mo	1Yr / Pct	3Yr / Pct	5Yr / Pct	Dividend Yield	Expense Ratio
AA	AllianceBern CBF AB Mod Gr <1984		C-	(800) 221-5672	D- / 1.0	1.31	1.76	2.66 /25	3.41 / 9	3.56 / 7	0.00	0.72
AA	AllianceBern CBF AB Mod Gr <1984		C-	(800) 221-5672	D- / 1.1	1.40	1.91	2.90 /26	3.67 / 9	3.82 / 8	0.00	0.97
AA	AllianceBern CBF AB Mod Gr <1984		C-	(800) 221-5672	D- / 1.2	1.47	2.09	3.24 /28	3.95 /10	--	0.00	0.20
AA	AllianceBern CBF AB Mod Gr <1984		D+	(800) 221-5672	E+ / 0.9	1.47	2.03	3.17 /27	3.93 /10	4.07 / 9	0.00	0.20
AA	AllianceBern CBF AB Mod Gr 02-04		D+	(800) 221-5672	D- / 1.4	1.87	2.55	3.29 /28	5.93 /16	5.43 /14	0.00	1.09
AA	AllianceBern CBF AB Mod Gr 02-04		D+	(800) 221-5672	D- / 1.5	1.82	2.50	3.30 /28	5.95 /17	5.43 /14	0.00	1.13
AA	AllianceBern CBF AB Mod Gr 02-04		D+	(800) 221-5672	D- / 1.5	1.70	2.14	2.51 /24	5.15 /14	4.65 /11	0.00	1.84
AA	AllianceBern CBF AB Mod Gr 02-04		C-	(800) 221-5672	D / 1.7	1.73	2.26	2.92 /26	5.56 /15	5.05 /12	0.00	1.48
AA	AllianceBern CBF AB Mod Gr 02-04		D+	(800) 221-5672	D- / 1.5	1.67	2.11	2.49 /24	5.15 /14	4.64 /11	0.00	1.84
AA	AllianceBern CBF AB Mod Gr 02-04		C-	(800) 221-5672	D / 1.7	1.74	2.34	3.00 /26	5.67 /15	5.17 /13	0.00	1.38
AA	AllianceBern CBF AB Mod Gr 02-04		C-	(800) 221-5672	D / 2.0	1.93	2.64	3.54 /29	6.22 /18	5.69 /15	0.00	0.88
AA	AllianceBern CBF AB Mod Gr 02-04		C-	(800) 221-5672	D / 2.2	1.99	2.82	3.89 /31	6.56 /19	6.01 /17	0.00	1.13
AA	AllianceBern CBF AB Mod Gr 02-04		C-	(800) 221-5672	D+ / 2.3	2.03	2.89	4.15 /33	6.84 /20	--	0.00	N/A
AA	AllianceBern CBF AB Mod Gr 02-04		D+	(800) 221-5672	D / 1.8	2.03	2.95	4.15 /33	6.83 /20	6.27 /19	0.00	N/A
AA	AllianceBern CBF AB Mod Gr 05-07		D+	(800) 221-5672	D / 1.9	2.18	2.93	3.76 /30	7.20 /22	6.32 /19	0.00	1.13
AA	AllianceBern CBF AB Mod Gr 05-07		C-	(800) 221-5672	D / 2.0	2.12	2.87	3.70 /30	7.21 /22	6.33 /19	0.00	1.17
AA	AllianceBern CBF AB Mod Gr 05-07		D+	(800) 221-5672	D / 2.0	1.99	2.50	2.95 /26	6.39 /18	5.53 /14	0.00	1.88
AA	AllianceBern CBF AB Mod Gr 05-07		C-	(800) 221-5672	D / 2.2	2.02	2.65	3.35 /28	6.81 /20	5.94 /16	0.00	1.52
AA	AllianceBern CBF AB Mod Gr 05-07		D+	(800) 221-5672	D / 2.0	1.99	2.51	2.95 /26	6.39 /18	5.53 /14	0.00	1.88
AA	AllianceBern CBF AB Mod Gr 05-07		C-	(800) 221-5672	D+ / 2.3	2.07	2.75	3.45 /29	6.94 /21	6.06 /17	0.00	1.42
AA	AllianceBern CBF AB Mod Gr 05-07		C-	(800) 221-5672	D+ / 2.7	2.26	2.99	4.00 /32	7.49 /24	6.60 /21	0.00	0.92
AA	AllianceBern CBF AB Mod Gr 05-07		C-	(800) 221-5672	D+ / 2.9	2.33	3.19	4.35 /34	7.87 /26	6.93 /23	0.00	1.17
AA	AllianceBern CBF AB Mod Gr 05-07		D+	(800) 221-5672	C- / 3.1	2.32	3.29	4.55 /35	8.13 /28	--	0.00	0.20
AA	AllianceBern CBF AB Mod Gr 05-07		D	(800) 221-5672	D+ / 2.4	2.33	3.30	4.56 /35	8.12 /28	7.20 /24	0.00	0.20
AA	AllianceBern CBF AB Mod Gr 08-10		D+	(800) 221-5672	D / 2.2	2.18	2.78	3.22 /28	7.96 /27	6.84 /22	0.00	1.17
AA	AllianceBern CBF AB Mod Gr 08-10		D+	(800) 221-5672	D+ / 2.3	2.12	2.73	3.17 /27	7.94 /27	6.80 /22	0.00	N/A
AA	AllianceBern CBF AB Mod Gr 08-10		D+	(800) 221-5672	D+ / 2.3	1.94	2.39	2.48 /24	7.17 /22	6.01 /17	0.00	1.92
AA	AllianceBern CBF AB Mod Gr 08-10		D	(800) 221-5672	D+ / 2.6	2.05	2.58	2.84 /26	7.58 /25	6.44 /20	0.00	N/A
AA	AllianceBern CBF AB Mod Gr 08-10		D+	(800) 221-5672	D+ / 2.3	2.03	2.48	2.48 /24	7.16 /22	6.03 /17	0.00	1.92
AA	AllianceBern CBF AB Mod Gr 08-10		C-	(800) 221-5672	D+ / 2.6	2.04	2.65	2.91 /26	7.66 /25	6.55 /20	0.00	N/A
AA	AllianceBern CBF AB Mod Gr 08-10		C-	(800) 221-5672	C- / 3.0	2.22	2.99	3.50 /29	8.23 /28	7.07 /23	0.00	N/A
AA	AllianceBern CBF AB Mod Gr 08-10		C-	(800) 221-5672	C- / 3.3	2.36	3.20	3.97 /32	8.70 /31	7.47 /26	0.00	N/A
AA	AllianceBern CBF AB Mod Gr 08-10		D+	(800) 221-5672	C- / 3.4	2.40	3.22	4.14 /33	8.92 /32	--	0.00	N/A
AA	AllianceBern CBF AB Mod Gr 08-10		D+	(800) 221-5672	C- / 3.4	2.40	3.23	4.16 /33	8.96 /33	7.75 /28	0.00	N/A
AA	AllianceBern CBF AB Mod Gr 11-13		C-	(800) 221-5672	D+ / 2.3	1.96	2.21	2.30 /23	8.41 /29	--	0.00	N/A
AA	AllianceBern CBF AB Mod Gr 11-13		C-	(800) 221-5672	D+ / 2.3	1.96	2.21	2.30 /23	8.41 /29	--	0.00	N/A
AA	AllianceBern CBF AB Mod Gr 11-13		C-	(800) 221-5672	D+ / 2.4	1.77	1.77	1.51 /20	7.59 /25	--	0.00	N/A
AA	AllianceBern CBF AB Mod Gr 11-13		C-	(800) 221-5672	D+ / 2.4	1.77	1.77	1.51 /20	7.59 /25	--	0.00	N/A
AA	AllianceBern CBF AB Mod Gr 11-13		C-	(800) 221-5672	D+ / 2.8	1.81	1.98	2.07 /22	8.12 /28	--	0.00	N/A
AA	AllianceBern CBF AB Mod Gr 11-13		C	(800) 221-5672	C- / 3.1	2.03	2.28	2.53 /24	8.69 /31	--	0.00	N/A
AA	AllianceBern CBF AB Mod Gr 11-13		C	(800) 221-5672	C- / 3.4	2.07	2.48	2.98 /26	9.16 /34	--	0.00	N/A
AA	AllianceBern CBF AB Mod Gr 11-13		C	(800) 221-5672	C- / 3.6	2.13	2.62	3.27 /28	9.45 /36	--	0.00	N/A
AA	AllianceBern CBF AB Mod Gr 11-13		C	(800) 221-5672	C- / 3.0	2.22	2.70	3.28 /28	9.43 /36	--	0.00	N/A
AA	AllianceBern CBF AB Mod Gr 84-86		C-	(800) 221-5672	E+ / 0.8	1.28	1.69	2.38 /23	3.50 / 9	3.53 / 7	0.00	0.97
AA	AllianceBern CBF AB Mod Gr 84-86		C-	(800) 221-5672	E+ / 0.8	1.28	1.62	2.37 /23	3.50 / 9	3.51 / 7	0.00	0.97
AA	AllianceBern CBF AB Mod Gr 84-86		C-	(800) 221-5672	E+ / 0.8	1.11	1.26	1.64 /20	2.74 / 7	2.73 / 5	0.00	1.72
AA	AllianceBern CBF AB Mod Gr 84-86		C-	(800) 221-5672	E+ / 0.9	1.20	1.49	2.06 /22	3.17 / 8	3.17 / 6	0.00	1.32
AA	AllianceBern CBF AB Mod Gr 84-86		C-	(800) 221-5672	E+ / 0.8	1.11	1.26	1.64 /20	2.73 / 7	2.75 / 5	0.00	1.72
AA	AllianceBern CBF AB Mod Gr 84-86		C-	(800) 221-5672	D- / 1.0	1.25	1.53	2.18 /23	3.24 / 8	3.26 / 6	0.00	1.22
AA	AllianceBern CBF AB Mod Gr 84-86		C-	(800) 221-5672	D- / 1.1	1.36	1.76	2.62 /25	3.76 /10	3.78 / 8	0.00	0.72
AA	AllianceBern CBF AB Mod Gr 84-86		C-	(800) 221-5672	D- / 1.2	1.38	1.91	2.93 /26	4.05 /10	4.01 / 8	0.00	0.97
AA	AllianceBern CBF AB Mod Gr 84-86		C-	(800) 221-5672	D- / 1.3	1.46	2.04	3.16 /27	4.30 /11	--	0.00	0.20

● Denotes fund is closed to new investors
* Denotes fund is included in Section II

www.thestreetratings.com

RISK	3 Year		NET ASSETS		ASSET				Portfolio	BULL / BEAR		FUND MANAGER		MINIMUMS		LOADS	
Risk Rating/Pts	Standard Deviation	Beta	NAV As of 3/31/15	Total $(Mil)	Cash %	Stocks %	Bonds %	Other %	Turnover Ratio	Last Bull Market Return	Last Bear Market Return	Manager Quality Pct	Manager Tenure (Years)	Initial Purch. $	Additional Purch. $	Front End Load	Back End Load
B+ / 9.3	2.9	0.46	16.19	N/A	0	21	78	1	0	15.5	-6.2	46	N/A	250	50	0.0	0.0
B+ / 9.3	2.9	0.46	15.99	N/A	0	21	78	1	0	16.6	-6.0	50	N/A	250	50	0.0	0.0
B / 8.9	2.9	0.46	16.59	N/A	0	21	78	1	0	17.6	-5.9	53	N/A	250	50	0.0	0.0
B / 8.9	2.9	0.46	16.58	N/A	0	21	78	1	0	17.6	-5.9	54	N/A	250	50	4.0	0.0
B / 8.3	5.9	0.97	18.51	250	1	42	55	2	0	33.0	-13.5	14	N/A	1,000	50	4.3	0.0
B / 8.3	5.9	0.97	18.48	10	1	42	55	2	0	33.1	-13.5	14	N/A	1,000	50	3.3	0.0
B / 8.3	5.9	0.96	16.72	49	1	42	55	2	0	29.8	-13.8	11	N/A	1,000	50	0.0	0.0
B / 8.3	5.9	0.97	17.62	N/A	1	42	55	2	0	31.5	-13.7	12	N/A	1,000	50	0.0	0.0
B / 8.3	5.9	0.97	16.46	89	1	42	55	2	0	29.7	-13.8	10	N/A	1,000	50	0.0	0.0
B / 8.3	5.9	0.96	17.52	5	1	42	55	2	0	31.9	-13.6	13	N/A	1,000	50	0.0	0.0
B / 8.3	5.9	0.96	19.03	55	1	42	55	2	0	34.2	-13.5	16	N/A	250	50	0.0	0.0
B / 8.3	5.9	0.96	18.96	10	1	42	55	2	0	35.8	-13.3	19	N/A	250	50	0.0	0.0
B / 8.0	5.9	0.96	19.56	12	1	42	55	2	0	36.9	-13.2	21	N/A	250	50	0.0	0.0
B / 8.0	5.9	0.96	19.57	1	1	42	55	2	0	36.9	-13.2	21	N/A	250	50	4.0	0.0
B- / 7.8	7.3	1.19	15.45	104	1	54	43	2	0	42.3	-16.0	8	N/A	1,000	50	4.3	0.0
B- / 7.8	7.4	1.20	15.43	3	1	54	43	2	0	42.4	-16.1	8	N/A	1,000	50	3.3	0.0
B- / 7.8	7.3	1.20	14.33	27	1	54	43	2	0	38.7	-16.3	6	N/A	1,000	50	0.0	0.0
B- / 7.8	7.3	1.20	15.12	N/A	1	54	43	2	0	40.6	-16.2	7	N/A	1,000	50	0.0	0.0
B- / 7.8	7.4	1.20	14.32	40	1	54	43	2	0	38.7	-16.3	6	N/A	1,000	50	0.0	0.0
B- / 7.8	7.3	1.20	15.31	1	1	54	43	2	0	41.1	-16.1	8	N/A	1,000	50	0.0	0.0
B- / 7.9	7.3	1.19	15.86	31	1	54	43	2	0	43.5	-15.9	10	N/A	250	50	0.0	0.0
B- / 7.9	7.3	1.19	15.84	6	1	54	43	2	0	45.3	-15.8	12	N/A	250	50	0.0	0.0
C+ / 6.6	7.3	1.20	16.32	7	1	54	43	2	0	46.6	-15.8	13	N/A	250	50	0.0	0.0
C+ / 6.6	7.3	1.19	16.28	1	1	54	43	2	0	46.6	-15.8	13	N/A	250	50	4.0	0.0
B- / 7.4	8.5	1.38	12.18	51	2	65	31	2	0	49.9	-18.9	5	N/A	1,000	50	4.3	0.0
B- / 7.4	8.6	1.38	12.06	2	2	65	31	2	0	49.9	-18.9	5	N/A	1,000	50	3.3	0.0
B- / 7.4	8.5	1.38	11.57	8	2	65	31	2	0	46.3	-19.3	4	N/A	1,000	50	0.0	0.0
C+ / 6.3	8.6	1.39	11.94	N/A	2	65	31	2	0	48.3	-19.1	4	N/A	1,000	50	0.0	0.0
B- / 7.4	8.6	1.39	11.58	20	2	65	31	2	0	46.1	-19.2	4	N/A	1,000	50	0.0	0.0
B- / 7.4	8.5	1.39	12.03	N/A	2	65	31	2	0	48.7	-19.1	5	N/A	1,000	50	0.0	0.0
B- / 7.4	8.6	1.39	12.41	20	2	65	31	2	0	51.2	-18.9	5	N/A	250	50	0.0	0.0
B- / 7.4	8.6	1.39	12.56	3	2	65	31	2	0	53.3	-18.7	6	N/A	250	50	0.0	0.0
C+ / 6.4	8.5	1.38	12.82	4	2	65	31	2	0	54.7	-18.6	7	N/A	250	50	0.0	0.0
C+ / 6.4	8.5	1.38	12.78	1	2	65	31	2	0	54.6	-18.6	7	N/A	250	50	0.0	0.0
B / 8.0	9.7	1.56	12.46	15	0	0	0	100	0	56.1	-21.4	3	N/A	1,000	50	4.3	0.0
B / 8.0	9.7	1.56	12.46	1	0	0	0	100	0	56.1	-21.4	3	N/A	1,000	50	4.3	0.0
B- / 7.9	9.7	1.56	12.08	2	0	0	0	100	0	52.1	-21.8	2	N/A	1,000	50	0.0	0.0
B- / 7.9	9.7	1.56	12.08	6	0	0	0	100	0	52.1	-21.7	2	N/A	1,000	50	0.0	0.0
B / 8.0	9.7	1.55	12.35	N/A	0	0	0	100	0	54.8	N/A	3	N/A	1,000	50	0.0	0.0
B / 8.0	9.7	1.56	12.57	8	0	0	0	100	0	57.4	-21.4	3	N/A	250	50	0.0	0.0
B / 8.0	9.7	1.56	12.80	1	0	0	0	100	0	59.9	-21.2	4	N/A	250	50	0.0	0.0
B / 8.1	9.6	1.55	12.94	1	0	0	0	100	0	61.2	-21.1	5	N/A	250	50	0.0	0.0
B / 8.1	9.7	1.55	12.92	N/A	0	0	0	100	0	61.1	-21.2	4	N/A	250	50	4.0	0.0
B+ / 9.3	3.1	0.48	15.08	2	0	21	78	1	0	15.7	-6.2	44	N/A	1,000	50	4.3	0.0
B+ / 9.3	3.1	0.47	15.09	2	0	21	78	1	0	15.7	-6.3	45	N/A	1,000	50	3.3	0.0
B+ / 9.3	3.0	0.47	13.63	N/A	0	21	78	1	0	12.8	-6.5	35	N/A	1,000	50	0.0	0.0
B+ / 9.3	3.0	0.47	14.34	N/A	0	21	78	1	0	14.3	-6.3	41	N/A	1,000	50	0.0	0.0
B+ / 9.3	3.1	0.48	13.65	1	0	21	78	1	0	12.8	-6.5	34	N/A	1,000	50	0.0	0.0
B+ / 9.3	3.1	0.48	14.56	3	0	21	78	1	0	14.7	-6.3	40	N/A	1,000	50	0.0	0.0
B+ / 9.3	3.1	0.47	15.64	N/A	0	21	78	1	0	16.7	-6.1	49	N/A	250	50	0.0	0.0
B+ / 9.3	3.1	0.47	15.48	N/A	0	21	78	1	0	17.8	-6.0	53	N/A	250	50	0.0	0.0
B / 8.9	3.1	0.48	16.02	N/A	0	21	78	1	0	18.7	-5.9	56	N/A	250	50	0.0	0.0

						PERFORMANCE						
			99 Pct = Best				Total Return % through 3/31/15				Incl. in Returns	
			0 Pct = Worst	Overall		Perfor-				Annualized	Dividend	Expense
Fund		Ticker	Investment		mance							
Type	Fund Name	Symbol	Rating	Phone	Rating/Pts	3 Mo	6 Mo	1Yr / Pct	3Yr / Pct	5Yr / Pct	Yield	Ratio
AA	AllianceBern CBF AB Mod Gr 87-89		C-	(800) 221-5672	E+ / 0.8	1.25	1.60	2.38 /23	3.25 / 8	3.36 / 7	0.00	0.97
AA	AllianceBern CBF AB Mod Gr 87-89		C-	(800) 221-5672	E+ / 0.8	1.25	1.60	2.38 /23	3.25 / 8	3.36 / 7	0.00	0.97
AA	AllianceBern CBF AB Mod Gr 87-89		C-	(800) 221-5672	E+ / 0.8	1.07	1.23	1.62 /20	2.50 / 7	2.58 / 5	0.00	1.72
AA	AllianceBern CBF AB Mod Gr 87-89		C-	(800) 221-5672	E+ / 0.9	1.16	1.46	1.98 /22	2.89 / 8	3.02 / 6	0.00	1.32
AA	AllianceBern CBF AB Mod Gr 87-89		C-	(800) 221-5672	E+ / 0.8	1.07	1.23	1.54 /20	2.50 / 7	2.59 / 5	0.00	1.72
AA	AllianceBern CBF AB Mod Gr 87-89		C-	(800) 221-5672	E+ / 0.9	1.22	1.51	2.10 /22	3.01 / 8	3.11 / 6	0.00	1.22
AA	AllianceBern CBF AB Mod Gr 87-89		C-	(800) 221-5672	D- / 1.0	1.34	1.74	2.64 /25	3.53 / 9	3.63 / 7	0.00	0.72
AA	AllianceBern CBF AB Mod Gr 87-89		C-	(800) 221-5672	D- / 1.1	1.42	1.90	2.88 /26	3.81 /10	3.87 / 8	0.00	0.97
AA	AllianceBern CBF AB Mod Gr 87-89		C-	(800) 221-5672	D- / 1.2	1.50	2.04	3.19 /27	4.06 /10	--	0.00	0.20
AA	AllianceBern CBF AB Mod Gr 87-89		C-	(800) 221-5672	E+ / 0.9	1.50	2.03	3.24 /28	4.12 /11	4.13 / 9	0.00	0.20
AA	AllianceBern CBF AB Mod Gr 90-92		C-	(800) 221-5672	E+ / 0.7	1.22	1.57	2.33 /23	3.06 / 8	3.24 / 6	0.00	0.97
AA	AllianceBern CBF AB Mod Gr 90-92		C-	(800) 221-5672	E+ / 0.8	1.29	1.63	2.40 /24	3.08 / 8	3.25 / 6	0.00	1.01
AA	AllianceBern CBF AB Mod Gr 90-92		C-	(800) 221-5672	E+ / 0.8	1.13	1.28	1.66 /21	2.31 / 7	2.48 / 5	0.00	1.72
AA	AllianceBern CBF AB Mod Gr 90-92		C-	(800) 221-5672	E+ / 0.9	1.21	1.50	2.01 /22	2.73 / 7	2.90 / 6	0.00	1.36
AA	AllianceBern CBF AB Mod Gr 90-92		C-	(800) 221-5672	E+ / 0.8	1.05	1.20	1.58 /20	2.30 / 7	2.48 / 5	0.00	1.72
AA	AllianceBern CBF AB Mod Gr 90-92		C-	(800) 221-5672	E+ / 0.9	1.20	1.55	2.13 /22	2.82 / 8	2.99 / 6	0.00	1.26
AA	AllianceBern CBF AB Mod Gr 90-92		C-	(800) 221-5672	D- / 1.0	1.31	1.78	2.66 /25	3.34 / 9	3.51 / 7	0.00	0.76
AA	AllianceBern CBF AB Mod Gr 90-92		C-	(800) 221-5672	D- / 1.1	1.40	1.87	2.90 /26	3.61 / 9	3.74 / 7	0.00	1.01
AA	AllianceBern CBF AB Mod Gr 90-92		C-	(800) 221-5672	D- / 1.1	1.41	2.00	3.13 /27	3.86 /10	--	0.00	0.20
AA	AllianceBern CBF AB Mod Gr 90-92		D+	(800) 221-5672	E+ / 0.9	1.41	2.00	3.13 /27	3.86 /10	3.99 / 8	0.00	0.20
AA	AllianceBern CBF AB Mod Gr 93-95		C-	(800) 221-5672	E+ / 0.7	1.27	1.63	2.36 /23	2.96 / 8	3.21 / 6	0.00	1.01
AA	AllianceBern CBF AB Mod Gr 93-95		C-	(800) 221-5672	E+ / 0.8	1.27	1.63	2.43 /24	2.98 / 8	3.22 / 6	0.00	1.03
AA	AllianceBern CBF AB Mod Gr 93-95		C-	(800) 221-5672	E+ / 0.8	1.10	1.26	1.58 /20	2.19 / 7	2.44 / 5	0.00	1.76
AA	AllianceBern CBF AB Mod Gr 93-95		C-	(800) 221-5672	E+ / 0.8	1.19	1.49	2.03 /22	2.61 / 7	2.85 / 6	0.00	1.38
AA	AllianceBern CBF AB Mod Gr 93-95		C-	(800) 221-5672	E+ / 0.8	1.10	1.25	1.57 /20	2.21 / 7	2.43 / 5	0.00	1.76
AA	AllianceBern CBF AB Mod Gr 93-95		C-	(800) 221-5672	E+ / 0.9	1.17	1.47	2.07 /22	2.70 / 7	2.94 / 6	0.00	1.28
AA	AllianceBern CBF AB Mod Gr 93-95		C-	(800) 221-5672	D- / 1.0	1.30	1.71	2.63 /25	3.23 / 8	3.46 / 7	0.00	0.78
AA	AllianceBern CBF AB Mod Gr 93-95		C-	(800) 221-5672	D- / 1.1	1.45	1.95	2.95 /26	3.51 / 9	3.71 / 7	0.00	1.03
AA	AllianceBern CBF AB Mod Gr 93-95		C-	(800) 221-5672	D- / 1.1	1.47	2.01	3.19 /27	3.75 /10	--	0.00	N/A
AA	AllianceBern CBF AB Mod Gr 93-95		C-	(800) 221-5672	D- / 1.1	1.40	2.01	3.12 /27	3.75 /10	3.96 / 8	0.00	N/A
AA	AllianceBern CBF AB Mod Gr 96-98		C-	(800) 221-5672	E+ / 0.8	1.26	1.62	2.34 /23	3.30 / 8	3.53 / 7	0.00	1.03
AA	AllianceBern CBF AB Mod Gr 96-98		C-	(800) 221-5672	E+ / 0.8	1.26	1.62	2.34 /23	3.30 / 8	3.55 / 7	0.00	1.05
AA	AllianceBern CBF AB Mod Gr 96-98		C-	(800) 221-5672	E+ / 0.8	1.09	1.25	1.64 /20	2.53 / 7	2.77 / 6	0.00	1.78
AA	AllianceBern CBF AB Mod Gr 96-98		C-	(800) 221-5672	E+ / 0.9	1.18	1.48	2.01 /22	2.96 / 8	3.18 / 6	0.00	1.40
AA	AllianceBern CBF AB Mod Gr 96-98		C-	(800) 221-5672	E+ / 0.8	1.08	1.24	1.56 /20	2.52 / 7	2.76 / 6	0.00	1.78
AA	AllianceBern CBF AB Mod Gr 96-98		C-	(800) 221-5672	E+ / 0.9	1.16	1.46	2.12 /22	3.05 / 8	3.28 / 7	0.00	1.30
AA	AllianceBern CBF AB Mod Gr 96-98		C-	(800) 221-5672	D- / 1.1	1.35	1.77	2.60 /25	3.58 / 9	3.81 / 8	0.00	0.80
AA	AllianceBern CBF AB Mod Gr 96-98		C-	(800) 221-5672	D- / 1.1	1.37	1.86	2.92 /26	3.86 /10	4.06 / 9	0.00	1.05
AA	AllianceBern CBF AB Mod Gr 96-98		C-	(800) 221-5672	D- / 1.2	1.39	1.99	3.16 /27	4.12 /11	--	0.00	N/A
AA	AllianceBern CBF AB Mod Gr 96-98		C-	(800) 221-5672	D- / 1.2	1.46	2.06	3.16 /27	4.15 /11	4.33 / 9	0.00	N/A
AA	AllianceBern CBF AB Mod Gr 99-01		D+	(800) 221-5672	D- / 1.0	1.46	1.88	2.67 /25	4.45 /11	4.35 /10	0.00	1.05
AA	AllianceBern CBF AB Mod Gr 99-01		C-	(800) 221-5672	D- / 1.0	1.46	1.96	2.67 /25	4.46 /11	4.37 /10	0.00	1.09
AA	AllianceBern CBF AB Mod Gr 99-01		D+	(800) 221-5672	D- / 1.0	1.30	1.54	1.93 /22	3.66 / 9	3.58 / 7	0.00	1.86
AA	AllianceBern CBF AB Mod Gr 99-01		C-	(800) 221-5672	D- / 1.2	1.31	1.75	2.28 /23	4.07 /10	4.00 / 8	0.00	1.44
AA	AllianceBern CBF AB Mod Gr 99-01		D+	(800) 221-5672	D- / 1.0	1.23	1.54	1.85 /21	3.66 / 9	3.58 / 7	0.00	1.80
AA	AllianceBern CBF AB Mod Gr 99-01		C-	(800) 221-5672	D- / 1.2	1.44	1.88	2.47 /24	4.20 /11	4.12 / 9	0.00	1.34
AA	AllianceBern CBF AB Mod Gr 99-01		C-	(800) 221-5672	D- / 1.4	1.54	2.08	2.99 /26	4.72 /12	4.64 /11	0.00	0.84
AA	AllianceBern CBF AB Mod Gr 99-01		C-	(800) 221-5672	D- / 1.5	1.56	2.19	3.25 /28	5.04 /13	4.90 /11	0.00	1.09
AA	AllianceBern CBF AB Mod Gr 99-01		C-	(800) 221-5672	D / 1.6	1.63	2.37	3.52 /29	5.31 /14	--	0.00	N/A
GR	AllianceBern CBF Discovery Val A		B+	(800) 221-5672	B / 8.0	3.15	10.73	9.23 /70	16.87 /89	13.31 /71	0.00	1.10
GR	AllianceBern CBF Discovery Val B		B+	(800) 221-5672	B / 8.2	2.97	10.34	8.42 /66	16.00 /83	12.47 /64	0.00	1.85
GR	AllianceBern CBF Discovery Val C		B+	(800) 221-5672	B / 8.2	2.95	10.33	8.40 /66	15.99 /83	12.46 /64	0.00	1.85

RISK			NET ASSETS		ASSET				Portfolio Turnover Ratio	BULL / BEAR		FUND MANAGER		MINIMUMS		LOADS	
Risk Rating/Pts	3 Year		NAV As of 3/31/15	Total $(Mil)	Cash %	Stocks %	Bonds %	Other %		Last Bull Market Return	Last Bear Market Return	Manager Quality Pct	Manager Tenure (Years)	Initial Purch. $	Additional Purch. $	Front End Load	Back End Load
	Standard Deviation	Beta															
B+ / 9.3	2.9	0.46	14.63	15	0	21	78	1	0	14.9	-6.3	44	N/A	1,000	50	4.3	0.0
B+ / 9.3	2.9	0.46	14.63	6	0	21	78	1	0	14.9	-6.3	44	N/A	1,000	50	3.3	0.0
B+ / 9.3	2.9	0.46	13.19	1	0	21	78	1	0	12.0	-6.6	33	N/A	1,000	50	0.0	0.0
B+ / 9.3	2.9	0.46	13.90	1	0	21	78	1	0	13.5	-6.3	38	N/A	1,000	50	0.0	0.0
B+ / 9.3	3.0	0.47	13.18	6	0	21	78	1	0	12.0	-6.5	32	N/A	1,000	50	0.0	0.0
B+ / 9.3	2.9	0.46	14.09	6	0	21	78	1	0	13.9	-6.3	39	N/A	1,000	50	0.0	0.0
B+ / 9.3	2.9	0.46	15.17	2	0	21	78	1	0	15.9	-6.1	47	N/A	250	50	0.0	0.0
B+ / 9.3	2.9	0.46	14.99	N/A	0	21	78	1	0	17.0	-6.0	51	N/A	250	50	0.0	0.0
B / 8.9	2.9	0.46	15.54	1	0	21	78	1	0	18.0	-5.9	56	N/A	250	50	0.0	0.0
B / 8.9	2.9	0.46	15.60	N/A	0	21	78	1	0	18.2	-5.9	56	N/A	250	50	4.0	0.0
B+ / 9.3	2.9	0.46	14.91	43	0	21	78	1	0	14.3	-6.2	41	N/A	1,000	50	4.3	0.0
B+ / 9.3	2.8	0.45	14.94	14	0	21	78	1	0	14.3	-6.2	42	N/A	1,000	50	3.3	0.0
B+ / 9.3	2.8	0.45	13.45	4	0	21	78	1	0	11.3	-6.5	32	N/A	1,000	50	0.0	0.0
B+ / 9.3	2.9	0.46	14.18	2	0	21	78	1	0	12.9	-6.3	36	N/A	1,000	50	0.0	0.0
B+ / 9.3	2.9	0.46	13.47	16	0	21	78	1	0	11.4	-6.6	31	N/A	1,000	50	0.0	0.0
B+ / 9.3	2.9	0.46	14.38	12	0	21	78	1	0	13.3	-6.3	38	N/A	1,000	50	0.0	0.0
B+ / 9.3	2.8	0.45	15.45	6	0	21	78	1	0	15.3	-6.2	46	N/A	250	50	0.0	0.0
B+ / 9.3	2.9	0.46	15.26	1	0	21	78	1	0	16.4	-6.0	49	N/A	250	50	0.0	0.0
B / 8.9	2.9	0.46	15.82	2	0	21	78	1	0	17.3	-5.9	52	N/A	250	50	0.0	0.0
B / 8.9	2.9	0.46	15.82	N/A	0	21	78	1	0	17.3	-5.9	53	N/A	250	50	4.0	0.0
B+ / 9.3	2.8	0.45	14.30	131	0	21	78	1	0	13.9	-6.4	41	N/A	1,000	50	4.3	0.0
B+ / 9.3	2.8	0.45	14.33	34	0	21	78	1	0	14.0	-6.4	41	N/A	1,000	50	3.3	0.0
B+ / 9.3	2.9	0.46	12.88	18	0	21	78	1	0	11.1	-6.7	30	N/A	1,000	50	0.0	0.0
B+ / 9.3	2.8	0.45	13.60	9	0	21	78	1	0	12.6	-6.5	36	N/A	1,000	50	0.0	0.0
B+ / 9.3	2.9	0.46	12.92	48	0	21	78	1	0	11.1	-6.7	30	N/A	1,000	50	0.0	0.0
B+ / 9.3	2.8	0.45	13.80	30	0	21	78	1	0	13.0	-6.5	37	N/A	1,000	50	0.0	0.0
B+ / 9.3	2.8	0.45	14.83	26	0	21	78	1	0	14.9	-6.3	45	N/A	250	50	0.0	0.0
B+ / 9.3	2.9	0.45	14.66	3	0	21	78	1	0	16.0	-6.2	48	N/A	250	50	0.0	0.0
B / 8.9	2.8	0.44	15.19	6	0	21	78	1	0	17.0	-6.1	53	N/A	250	50	0.0	0.0
B / 8.9	2.8	0.45	15.19	N/A	0	21	78	1	0	17.0	-6.1	52	N/A	250	50	0.0	0.0
B+ / 9.3	3.3	0.52	14.43	308	0	21	78	1	0	17.2	-8.5	35	N/A	1,000	50	4.3	0.0
B+ / 9.3	3.3	0.52	14.44	76	0	21	78	1	0	17.2	-8.6	35	N/A	1,000	50	3.3	0.0
B+ / 9.3	3.3	0.52	13.00	39	0	21	78	1	0	14.2	-8.8	26	N/A	1,000	50	0.0	0.0
B+ / 9.3	3.2	0.52	13.73	20	0	21	78	1	0	15.7	-8.7	31	N/A	1,000	50	0.0	0.0
B+ / 9.3	3.3	0.52	13.05	108	0	21	78	1	0	14.2	-8.9	26	N/A	1,000	50	0.0	0.0
B+ / 9.3	3.2	0.51	13.94	68	0	21	78	1	0	16.2	-8.7	33	N/A	1,000	50	0.0	0.0
B+ / 9.3	3.2	0.51	14.97	63	0	21	78	1	0	18.2	-8.5	40	N/A	250	50	0.0	0.0
B+ / 9.3	3.2	0.52	14.80	11	0	21	78	1	0	19.4	-8.4	44	N/A	250	50	0.0	0.0
B / 8.9	3.3	0.52	15.34	18	0	21	78	1	0	20.4	-8.3	47	N/A	250	50	0.0	0.0
B / 8.9	3.2	0.52	15.34	2	0	21	78	1	0	20.4	-8.3	48	N/A	0	250	0.0	0.0
B / 8.8	4.4	0.72	14.61	362	0	29	69	2	0	24.2	-11.1	24	N/A	1,000	50	4.3	0.0
B / 8.8	4.4	0.71	14.60	93	0	29	69	2	0	24.1	-11.1	25	N/A	1,000	50	3.3	0.0
B / 8.8	4.4	0.72	13.21	47	0	29	69	2	0	21.0	-11.3	17	N/A	1,000	50	0.0	0.0
B / 8.8	4.4	0.71	13.93	26	0	29	69	2	0	22.8	-11.2	21	N/A	1,000	50	0.0	0.0
B / 8.8	4.4	0.71	13.20	101	0	29	69	2	0	21.0	-11.4	18	N/A	1,000	50	0.0	0.0
B / 8.8	4.4	0.71	14.12	75	0	29	69	2	0	23.2	-11.2	22	N/A	1,000	50	0.0	0.0
B / 8.8	4.4	0.72	15.18	72	0	29	69	2	0	25.3	-11.1	27	N/A	250	50	0.0	0.0
B / 8.9	4.4	0.71	14.95	12	0	29	69	2	0	26.6	-10.9	31	N/A	250	50	0.0	0.0
B / 8.6	4.4	0.71	15.58	17	0	29	69	2	0	27.7	-10.8	35	N/A	250	50	0.0	0.0
C+ / 6.7	12.8	1.19	37.05	29	0	0	0	100	0	105.7	-26.6	35	N/A	1,000	50	4.3	0.0
C+ / 6.6	12.8	1.19	33.62	4	0	0	0	100	0	100.5	-26.8	26	N/A	1,000	50	0.0	0.0
C+ / 6.6	12.8	1.19	33.55	10	0	0	0	100	0	100.5	-26.8	26	N/A	1,000	50	0.0	0.0

	99 Pct = Best *0 Pct = Worst*				**PERFORMANCE**							
						Total Return % through 3/31/15					Incl. in Returns	
									Annualized			
Fund Type	Fund Name	Ticker Symbol	Overall Investment Rating	Phone	Perfor-mance Rating/Pts	3 Mo	6 Mo	1Yr / Pct	3Yr / Pct	5Yr / Pct	Dividend Yield	Expense Ratio
GR	AllianceBern CBF Discovery Val R		A	(800) 221-5672	B+ / 8.9	3.21	10.90	9.50 /72	17.17 /91	13.60 /74	0.00	0.85
GR	AllianceBern CBF Discovery Val RA		A	(800) 221-5672	B+ / 8.8	3.17	10.74	9.23 /70	16.87 /89	13.31 /71	0.00	1.10
SC	AllianceBern CBF Discovery Val RI		A+	(800) 221-5672	B+ / 8.9	3.24	10.90	9.50 /72	17.17 /91	--	0.00	N/A
SC	AllianceBern CBF Discovery Val RZ		A+	(800) 221-5672	B+ / 8.9	3.21	10.88	9.48 /72	17.15 /91	13.59 /74	0.00	0.93
MC	AllianceBern CBF Discvry Gr A		C+	(800) 221-5672	C+ / 6.6	5.90	10.31	7.92 /62	14.51 /71	18.20 /98	0.00	1.25
MC	AllianceBern CBF Discvry Gr B		C+	(800) 221-5672	C+ / 6.7	5.69	9.87	7.11 /56	13.64 /64	17.32 /97	0.00	2.00
MC	AllianceBern CBF Discvry Gr C		C+	(800) 221-5672	C+ / 6.7	5.69	9.86	7.10 /56	13.65 /64	17.32 /97	0.00	2.00
MC	AllianceBern CBF Discvry Gr R		B	(800) 221-5672	B / 7.6	5.94	10.42	8.19 /64	14.78 /73	18.51 /98	0.00	1.07
MC	AllianceBern CBF Discvry Gr RA		B	(800) 221-5672	B- / 7.4	5.94	10.32	7.95 /62	14.52 /71	18.21 /98	0.00	1.32
MC	AllianceBern CBF Discvry Gr RI		A-	(800) 221-5672	B / 7.6	5.98	10.46	8.23 /64	14.79 /73	--	0.00	N/A
MC	AllianceBern CBF Discvry Gr RZ		A-	(800) 221-5672	B / 7.6	5.94	10.42	8.19 /64	14.78 /73	18.49 /98	0.00	N/A
AA	AllianceBern CBF Fx Alloc Apprec A		D+	(800) 221-5672	D+ / 2.8	2.06	2.52	2.26 /23	9.32 /35	7.73 /28	0.00	1.19
AA	AllianceBern CBF Fx Alloc Apprec AX		D+	(800) 221-5672	D+ / 2.9	2.05	2.51	2.25 /23	9.32 /35	7.74 /28	0.00	1.19
AA	AllianceBern CBF Fx Alloc Apprec B		D+	(800) 221-5672	C- / 3.0	1.92	2.14	1.56 /20	8.53 /30	6.95 /23	0.00	1.94
AA	AllianceBern CBF Fx Alloc Apprec BX		D+	(800) 221-5672	C- / 3.2	1.96	2.30	1.89 /21	8.94 /32	7.37 /26	0.00	1.54
AA	AllianceBern CBF Fx Alloc Apprec C		D+	(800) 221-5672	C- / 3.0	1.92	2.21	1.56 /20	8.52 /30	6.94 /23	0.00	1.94
AA	AllianceBern CBF Fx Alloc Apprec CX		C-	(800) 221-5672	C- / 3.3	2.00	2.41	2.00 /22	9.06 /33	7.46 /26	0.00	1.44
AA	AllianceBern CBF Fx Alloc Apprec R		C-	(800) 221-5672	C- / 3.6	2.11	2.69	2.56 /24	9.61 /37	7.99 /30	0.00	0.94
AA	AllianceBern CBF Fx Alloc Apprec RA		C-	(800) 221-5672	C- / 3.4	2.06	2.52	2.26 /23	9.33 /35	7.74 /28	0.00	1.19
GL	AllianceBern CBF Fx Alloc Apprec RI		D+	(800) 221-5672	C- / 3.6	2.18	2.69	2.56 /24	9.62 /37	--	0.00	N/A
GL	AllianceBern CBF Fx Alloc Apprec RZ		D	(800) 221-5672	C- / 3.0	2.18	2.69	2.56 /24	9.63 /37	8.02 /30	0.00	N/A
BA	AllianceBern CBF Fx Alloc Bal A		C-	(800) 221-5672	D / 1.7	2.19	2.96	3.81 /31	6.71 /20	5.81 /16	0.00	1.05
BA	AllianceBern CBF Fx Alloc Bal AX		C-	(800) 221-5672	D / 1.8	2.19	2.96	3.81 /31	6.71 /20	5.81 /16	0.00	1.05
BA	AllianceBern CBF Fx Alloc Bal B		C-	(800) 221-5672	D / 1.8	2.01	2.57	3.07 /27	5.90 /16	5.03 /12	0.00	1.80
BA	AllianceBern CBF Fx Alloc Bal BX		C-	(800) 221-5672	D / 2.1	2.10	2.77	3.53 /29	6.34 /18	5.46 /14	0.00	1.40
BA	AllianceBern CBF Fx Alloc Bal C		C-	(800) 221-5672	D / 1.8	2.01	2.58	3.08 /27	5.91 /16	5.02 /12	0.00	1.80
BA	AllianceBern CBF Fx Alloc Bal CX		C-	(800) 221-5672	D / 2.1	2.08	2.81	3.55 /29	6.42 /19	5.54 /14	0.00	1.30
BA	AllianceBern CBF Fx Alloc Bal R		C-	(800) 221-5672	D+ / 2.4	2.24	3.05	4.13 /33	6.97 /21	6.09 /17	0.00	0.80
BA	AllianceBern CBF Fx Alloc Bal RA		C-	(800) 221-5672	D / 2.2	2.19	2.90	3.82 /31	6.69 /20	5.82 /16	0.00	1.05
GI	AllianceBern CBF Fx Alloc Bal RI		D	(800) 221-5672	D+ / 2.4	2.24	3.05	4.07 /32	6.95 /21	--	0.00	N/A
GI	AllianceBern CBF Fx Alloc Bal RZ		D	(800) 221-5672	D / 1.9	2.24	3.05	4.07 /32	6.98 /21	6.09 /17	0.00	N/A
BA	AllianceBern CBF Fx Alloc Cnsv A		C-	(800) 221-5672	E+ / 0.7	1.27	1.73	2.50 /24	2.92 / 8	3.16 / 6	0.00	0.97
BA	AllianceBern CBF Fx Alloc Cnsv B		C-	(800) 221-5672	E+ / 0.8	1.12	1.37	1.69 /21	2.18 / 7	2.38 / 5	0.00	1.72
BA	AllianceBern CBF Fx Alloc Cnsv C		C-	(800) 221-5672	E+ / 0.8	1.12	1.29	1.69 /21	2.15 / 6	2.38 / 5	0.00	1.72
BA	AllianceBern CBF Fx Alloc Cnsv R		C-	(800) 221-5672	D- / 1.0	1.39	1.84	2.74 /25	3.20 / 8	3.43 / 7	0.00	0.72
BA	AllianceBern CBF Fx Alloc Cnsv RA		C-	(800) 221-5672	E+ / 0.9	1.35	1.73	2.50 /24	2.95 / 8	3.16 / 6	0.00	0.97
GI	AllianceBern CBF Fx Alloc Cnsv RI		C-	(800) 221-5672	D- / 1.0	1.39	1.84	2.74 /25	3.20 / 8	--	0.00	0.72
GI	AllianceBern CBF Fx Alloc Cnsv RZ		C-	(800) 221-5672	D- / 1.0	1.39	1.84	2.74 /25	3.20 / 8	3.41 / 7	0.00	0.72
GI	AllianceBern CBF Growth & Income A		B-	(800) 221-5672	C+ / 6.6	0.69	5.68	8.51 /66	15.34 /78	14.58 /83	0.00	0.98
GI	AllianceBern CBF Growth & Income B		B-	(800) 221-5672	C+ / 6.7	0.51	5.33	7.69 /60	14.49 /71	13.71 /75	0.00	1.73
GI	AllianceBern CBF Growth & Income		B-	(800) 221-5672	C+ / 6.7	0.51	5.33	7.68 /60	14.50 /71	13.73 /75	0.00	1.73
GI	AllianceBern CBF Growth & Income		A	(800) 221-5672	B / 7.6	0.76	5.87	8.79 /68	15.64 /80	14.86 /86	0.00	0.75
GI	AllianceBern CBF Growth & Income		A-	(800) 221-5672	B- / 7.4	0.69	5.72	8.51 /66	15.36 /78	14.58 /83	0.00	1.00
GI	AllianceBern CBF Growth & Income		A+	(800) 221-5672	B / 7.6	0.76	5.83	8.80 /68	15.63 /80	--	0.00	N/A
GI	AllianceBern CBF Growth & Income		A+	(800) 221-5672	B / 7.6	0.76	5.88	8.80 /68	15.66 /80	14.86 /86	0.00	N/A
GR	AllianceBern CBF Lg Cap Growth A		A+	(800) 221-5672	A+ / 9.6	5.84	12.22	21.44 /97	18.44 /95	15.47 /90	0.00	1.43
GR	AllianceBern CBF Lg Cap Growth B		A+	(800) 221-5672	A+ / 9.7	5.68	11.83	20.58 /97	17.55 /93	14.60 /83	0.00	2.18
GR	AllianceBern CBF Lg Cap Growth C		A+	(800) 221-5672	A+ / 9.7	5.65	11.76	20.53 /97	17.57 /93	14.58 /83	0.00	2.18
GR	AllianceBern CBF Lg Cap Growth R		A+	(800) 221-5672	A+ / 9.8	5.92	12.34	21.73 /97	18.74 /96	15.74 /91	0.00	1.20
GR	AllianceBern CBF Lg Cap Growth RA		A+	(800) 221-5672	A+ / 9.8	5.84	12.21	21.48 /97	18.43 /95	15.46 /90	0.00	1.45
GR	AllianceBern CBF Lg Cap Growth RI		A+	(800) 221-5672	A+ / 9.8	5.96	12.38	21.78 /97	18.74 /96	--	0.00	N/A
GR	AllianceBern CBF Lg Cap Growth RZ		A+	(800) 221-5672	A+ / 9.8	5.91	12.33	21.77 /97	18.73 /96	15.75 /92	0.00	N/A

● Denotes fund is closed to new investors

* Denotes fund is included in Section II

RISK			NET ASSETS		ASSET					BULL / BEAR		FUND MANAGER		MINIMUMS		LOADS	
	3 Year		NAV						Portfolio	Last Bull	Last Bear	Manager	Manager	Initial	Additional	Front	Back
Risk	Standard		As of	Total	Cash	Stocks	Bonds	Other	Turnover	Market	Market	Quality	Tenure	Purch.	Purch.	End	End
Rating/Pts	Deviation	Beta	3/31/15	$(Mil)	%	%	%	%	Ratio	Return	Return	Pct	(Years)	$	$	Load	Load
C+ / 6.7	12.8	1.19	38.25	7	0	0	0	100	0	107.4	-26.5	38	N/A	250	50	0.0	0.0
C+ / 6.7	12.8	1.19	36.81	1	0	0	0	100	0	105.7	-26.6	35	N/A	250	50	0.0	0.0
B- / 7.7	12.8	0.88	38.25	3	0	0	0	100	0	107.5	-26.6	87	N/A	250	50	0.0	0.0
B- / 7.7	12.8	0.88	38.22	N/A	0	0	0	100	0	107.5	-26.5	87	N/A	250	50	0.0	0.0
C+ / 6.2	13.0	1.04	33.38	35	0	0	0	100	0	95.9	-22.6	27	N/A	1,000	50	4.3	0.0
C+ / 6.1	13.0	1.04	30.29	5	0	0	0	100	0	91.0	-22.8	19	N/A	1,000	50	0.0	0.0
C+ / 6.1	13.0	1.04	30.30	11	0	0	0	100	0	91.1	-22.9	19	N/A	1,000	50	0.0	0.0
C+ / 6.3	13.0	1.04	34.22	8	0	0	0	100	0	97.6	-22.5	29	N/A	250	50	0.0	0.0
C+ / 6.2	13.0	1.04	33.15	1	0	0	0	100	0	96.0	-22.6	27	N/A	250	50	0.0	0.0
B- / 7.6	13.0	1.04	34.21	3	0	0	0	100	0	97.6	-22.5	29	N/A	0	250	0.0	0.0
B- / 7.6	13.0	1.04	34.22	N/A	0	0	0	100	0	97.6	-22.5	30	N/A	250	50	0.0	0.0
C+ / 6.6	11.0	1.76	15.86	412	5	92	1	2	0	61.5	-22.6	2	N/A	1,000	50	4.3	0.0
C+ / 6.6	11.0	1.77	15.90	136	5	92	1	2	0	61.6	-22.6	2	N/A	1,000	50	3.3	0.0
C+ / 6.6	10.9	1.76	14.33	55	5	92	1	2	0	57.6	-22.9	2	N/A	1,000	50	0.0	0.0
C+ / 6.6	10.8	1.76	15.10	25	5	92	1	2	0	59.7	-22.7	2	N/A	1,000	50	0.0	0.0
C+ / 6.6	10.9	1.76	14.35	130	5	92	1	2	0	57.7	-22.9	2	N/A	1,000	50	0.0	0.0
C+ / 6.6	10.9	1.76	15.32	111	5	92	1	2	0	60.3	-22.7	2	N/A	1,000	50	0.0	0.0
C+ / 6.6	10.9	1.76	16.42	114	5	92	1	2	0	62.9	-22.5	2	N/A	250	50	0.0	0.0
C+ / 6.6	10.9	1.76	15.85	14	5	92	1	2	0	61.6	-22.6	2	N/A	250	50	0.0	0.0
C+ / 5.6	10.9	0.77	16.44	15	5	92	1	2	0	63.1	-22.6	85	N/A	250	50	0.0	0.0
C+ / 5.6	10.9	0.76	16.43	2	5	92	1	2	0	63.2	-22.6	85	N/A	250	50	4.0	0.0
B / 8.2	6.5	1.07	16.33	204	1	53	44	2	0	35.5	-13.4	13	N/A	1,000	50	4.3	0.0
B / 8.2	6.5	1.07	16.33	30	1	53	44	2	0	35.5	-13.4	13	N/A	1,000	50	3.3	0.0
B / 8.2	6.5	1.07	14.75	31	1	53	44	2	0	32.1	-13.7	9	N/A	1,000	50	0.0	0.0
B / 8.2	6.5	1.06	15.56	4	1	53	44	2	0	33.9	-13.6	11	N/A	1,000	50	0.0	0.0
B / 8.2	6.4	1.06	14.73	87	1	53	44	2	0	32.1	-13.6	9	N/A	1,000	50	0.0	0.0
B / 8.2	6.5	1.07	15.74	32	1	53	44	2	0	34.4	-13.5	11	N/A	1,000	50	0.0	0.0
B / 8.2	6.4	1.06	16.89	31	1	53	44	2	0	36.7	-13.3	14	N/A	250	50	0.0	0.0
B / 8.2	6.5	1.07	16.32	6	1	53	44	2	0	35.5	-13.4	13	N/A	250	50	0.0	0.0
C+ / 6.4	6.5	0.62	16.88	8	1	53	44	2	0	36.7	-13.3	30	N/A	250	50	0.0	0.0
C+ / 6.3	6.4	0.61	16.87	1	1	53	44	2	0	36.6	-13.3	31	N/A	250	50	4.0	0.0
B+ / 9.3	2.9	0.45	13.54	36	0	21	78	1	0	13.5	-6.1	40	N/A	1,000	50	4.3	0.0
B+ / 9.3	2.8	0.45	12.60	7	0	21	78	1	0	10.6	-6.4	31	N/A	1,000	50	0.0	0.0
B+ / 9.3	2.8	0.45	12.61	22	0	21	78	1	0	10.7	-6.3	30	N/A	1,000	50	0.0	0.0
B+ / 9.3	2.8	0.44	13.87	9	0	21	78	1	0	14.4	-6.0	45	N/A	250	50	0.0	0.0
B+ / 9.3	2.8	0.44	13.52	1	0	21	78	1	0	13.4	-6.1	41	N/A	250	50	0.0	0.0
B / 8.9	2.8	0.24	13.87	2	0	21	78	1	0	14.4	-6.0	60	N/A	250	50	0.0	0.0
B / 8.9	2.8	0.24	13.85	N/A	0	21	78	1	0	14.5	-6.0	60	N/A	250	50	0.0	0.0
B- / 7.8	9.8	1.00	21.94	71	0	0	0	100	0	97.5	-15.8	58	N/A	1,000	50	4.3	0.0
B- / 7.8	9.9	1.00	19.75	9	0	0	0	100	0	92.8	-16.2	46	N/A	1,000	50	0.0	0.0
B- / 7.8	9.9	1.00	19.77	28	0	0	0	100	0	92.7	-16.2	46	N/A	1,000	50	0.0	0.0
B- / 7.8	9.8	1.00	22.53	23	0	0	0	100	0	99.2	-15.7	62	N/A	250	50	0.0	0.0
B- / 7.8	9.8	1.00	21.80	4	0	0	0	100	0	97.7	-15.9	58	N/A	250	50	0.0	0.0
B / 8.5	9.8	1.00	22.51	4	0	0	0	100	0	99.2	-15.8	62	N/A	250	50	0.0	0.0
B / 8.5	9.8	1.00	22.51	1	0	0	0	100	0	99.4	-15.8	62	N/A	250	50	0.0	0.0
B- / 7.4	10.9	1.01	25.72	50	0	0	0	100	0	114.6	-18.6	83	N/A	1,000	50	4.3	0.0
B- / 7.3	10.9	1.01	23.26	7	0	0	0	100	0	109.2	-18.9	77	N/A	1,000	50	0.0	0.0
B- / 7.3	10.9	1.01	23.19	19	0	0	0	100	0	109.3	-18.9	77	N/A	1,000	50	0.0	0.0
B- / 7.4	10.9	1.02	26.50	16	0	0	0	100	0	116.4	-18.5	84	N/A	250	50	0.0	0.0
B- / 7.3	10.9	1.02	25.73	3	0	0	0	100	0	114.7	-18.6	82	N/A	250	50	0.0	0.0
B / 8.2	10.9	1.01	26.50	4	0	0	0	100	0	116.5	-18.6	84	N/A	0	250	0.0	0.0
B / 8.2	10.9	1.02	26.51	1	0	0	0	100	0	116.5	-18.5	84	N/A	250	50	0.0	0.0

Fund Type	Fund Name	Ticker Symbol	Overall Investment Rating	Phone	Performance Rating/Pts	3 Mo	6 Mo	1Yr / Pct	3Yr / Pct	5Yr / Pct	Dividend Yield	Expense Ratio
GI	AllianceBern CBF PrincPro Income RI		C-	(800) 221-5672	E+ / 0.8	0.60	1.18	2.23 /23	2.51 / 7	--	0.00	N/A
GI	AllianceBern CBF PrincPro Income		C-	(800) 221-5672	E+ / 0.8	0.57	1.17	2.26 /23	2.50 / 7	2.89 / 6	0.00	N/A
GR	AllianceBern CBF Sm Cap Growth A		C	(800) 221-5672	C+ / 5.9	5.81	9.07	2.81 /25	14.14 /68	17.69 /97	0.00	1.26
GR	AllianceBern CBF Sm Cap Growth B		C	(800) 221-5672	C+ / 6.1	5.64	8.68	2.06 /22	13.30 /62	16.81 /95	0.00	2.01
GR	AllianceBern CBF Sm Cap Growth C		C	(800) 221-5672	C+ / 6.1	5.65	8.66	2.03 /22	13.30 /62	16.81 /95	0.00	2.01
GR	AllianceBern CBF Sm Cap Growth R		C	(800) 221-5672	C+ / 6.8	5.92	9.22	3.09 /27	14.44 /70	17.98 /97	0.00	1.13
GR	AllianceBern CBF Sm Cap Growth		C	(800) 221-5672	C+ / 6.6	5.85	9.11	2.84 /26	14.14 /68	17.69 /97	0.00	1.38
SC	AllianceBern CBF Sm Cap Growth RI		B-	(800) 221-5672	C+ / 6.8	5.88	9.22	3.06 /27	14.43 /70	--	0.00	N/A
SC	AllianceBern CBF Sm Cap Growth		B-	(800) 221-5672	C+ / 6.8	5.91	9.20	3.06 /27	14.43 /70	--	0.00	N/A
GR	AllianzGI Behavioral Adv LgCap A	AZFAX	B	(800) 988-8380	B / 8.0	2.26	7.27	11.99 /82	17.29 /91	--	0.94	1.25
GR	AllianzGI Behavioral Adv LgCap C	AZFCX	A-	(800) 988-8380	B+ / 8.4	2.09	6.88	11.18 /79	16.41 /86	--	0.81	2.08
GR	AllianzGI Behavioral Adv LgCap D	AZFDX	A	(800) 988-8380	A- / 9.0	2.27	7.30	12.02 /83	17.29 /91	--	1.43	2.08
GR	AllianzGI Behavioral Adv LgCap Inst	AZFIX	A	(800) 988-8380	A- / 9.1	2.29	7.39	12.28 /84	17.64 /93	--	1.18	1.05
GR	AllianzGI Behavioral Adv LgCap P	AZFPX	A	(800) 988-8380	A- / 9.0	2.29	7.36	12.15 /83	17.50 /92	--	1.41	1.20
GL	AllianzGI Best Styles Glbl Eq R6	AGERX	U	(800) 988-8380	U /	2.76	5.39	8.17 /64	--	--	2.32	1.54
FO	AllianzGI China Equity A	ALQAX	C-	(800) 988-8380	C / 4.7	4.93	10.00	17.89 /95	8.99 /33	--	2.45	5.88
FO	AllianzGI China Equity C	ALQCX	C-	(800) 988-8380	C / 5.0	4.73	9.63	16.99 /95	8.11 /28	--	0.16	6.59
FO	AllianzGI China Equity D	ALQDX	C	(800) 988-8380	C+ / 5.6	4.86	9.99	17.82 /95	8.94 /32	--	1.71	13.23
FO	AllianzGI China Equity Inst	ALQIX	C	(800) 988-8380	C+ / 5.8	4.99	10.19	18.24 /96	9.28 /35	--	2.28	5.69
FO	AllianzGI China Equity P	ALQPX	C	(800) 988-8380	C+ / 5.8	4.96	10.16	18.10 /96	9.22 /34	--	0.14	5.73
CV	● AllianzGI Convertible A	ANZAX	C	(800) 988-8380	C / 4.5	3.53	5.26	5.94 /46	12.06 /53	11.68 /58	1.48	0.96
CV	● AllianzGI Convertible Admn	ANNAX	C+	(800) 988-8380	C / 5.5	3.54	5.28	6.05 /47	12.14 /53	11.74 /59	1.44	0.90
CV	● AllianzGI Convertible C	ANZCX	C	(800) 988-8380	C / 4.9	3.34	4.87	5.18 /40	11.24 /47	10.87 /52	0.85	1.70
CV	● AllianzGI Convertible D	ANZDX	C+	(800) 988-8380	C / 5.3	3.49	5.20	5.82 /45	11.97 /52	11.64 /58	1.40	1.02
CV	● AllianzGI Convertible Inst	ANNPX	C+	(800) 988-8380	C+ / 5.6	3.61	5.41	6.30 /49	12.42 /55	12.02 /61	1.85	0.65
CV	● AllianzGI Convertible P	ANCMX	C+	(800) 988-8380	C+ / 5.6	3.58	5.36	6.20 /48	12.30 /55	11.91 /60	1.76	0.75
CV	● AllianzGI Convertible R	ANZRX	C	(800) 988-8380	C / 5.1	3.45	5.03	5.61 /43	11.62 /50	11.31 /55	1.31	1.51
EM	AllianzGI Emerging Markets Opp A	AOTAX	E+	(800) 988-8380	E+ / 0.9	3.62	1.99	6.25 /49	3.34 / 9	3.94 / 8	1.25	1.67
EM	AllianzGI Emerging Markets Opp C	AOTCX	E+	(800) 988-8380	D- / 1.1	3.46	1.60	5.50 /42	2.58 / 7	3.17 / 6	0.44	2.42
EM	AllianzGI Emerging Markets Opp D	AOTDX	E+	(800) 988-8380	D- / 1.3	3.65	1.99	6.30 /49	3.36 / 9	3.95 / 8	1.69	1.67
EM	AllianzGI Emerging Markets Opp Inst	AOTIX	D-	(800) 988-8380	D- / 1.4	3.73	2.18	6.64 /52	3.72 / 9	4.32 / 9	1.83	1.32
EM	AllianzGI Emerging Markets Opp P	AEMPX	D-	(800) 988-8380	D- / 1.4	3.69	2.11	6.52 /51	3.61 / 9	4.20 / 9	1.95	1.42
GR	AllianzGI Focused Growth A	PGWAX	B	(800) 988-8380	B+ / 8.4	5.40	9.22	13.82 /89	17.04 /90	14.82 /85	0.35	1.11
GR	AllianzGI Focused Growth Admn	PGFAX	B+	(800) 988-8380	A- / 9.2	5.43	9.30	13.96 /89	17.17 /91	14.93 /86	0.60	1.01
GR	● AllianzGI Focused Growth B	PGFBX	B	(800) 988-8380	B+ / 8.7	5.22	8.80	12.97 /86	16.17 /85	13.96 /77	0.00	1.86
GR	AllianzGI Focused Growth C	PGWCX	B	(800) 988-8380	B+ / 8.7	5.22	8.83	12.99 /86	16.18 /85	13.96 /77	0.02	1.86
GR	AllianzGI Focused Growth D	PGRDX	B+	(800) 988-8380	A- / 9.2	5.44	9.26	13.83 /89	17.06 /90	14.82 /85	0.50	1.11
GR	AllianzGI Focused Growth Inst	PGFIX	B+	(800) 988-8380	A / 9.3	5.53	9.44	14.25 /90	17.46 /92	15.22 /88	0.79	0.76
GR	AllianzGI Focused Growth P	AOGPX	B+	(800) 988-8380	A / 9.3	5.51	9.38	14.12 /90	17.34 /92	15.11 /88	0.81	0.86
GR	AllianzGI Focused Growth R	PPGRX	B	(800) 988-8380	A- / 9.0	5.37	9.10	13.55 /88	16.75 /88	14.53 /83	0.35	1.36
AA	AllianzGI Global Allocation A	PALAX	D+	(800) 988-8380	D / 1.6	2.84	1.78	2.91 /26	6.92 /21	7.08 /24	3.81	1.64
AA	AllianzGI Global Allocation Admn	AGAMX	C-	(800) 988-8380	D / 2.2	2.77	1.70	2.91 /26	6.90 /21	7.09 /24	3.92	1.57
AA	● AllianzGI Global Allocation B	PALBX	D+	(800) 988-8380	D / 1.8	2.57	1.33	2.20 /23	6.13 /17	6.29 /19	3.13	2.40
AA	AllianzGI Global Allocation C	PALCX	D+	(800) 988-8380	D / 1.8	2.63	1.39	2.21 /23	6.13 /17	6.28 /19	3.23	2.38
AA	AllianzGI Global Allocation D	AGADX	C-	(800) 988-8380	D+ / 2.3	2.78	1.71	2.95 /26	6.91 /21	7.06 /23	4.07	1.67
AA	AllianzGI Global Allocation Inst	PALLX	C-	(800) 988-8380	D+ / 2.4	2.85	1.84	3.20 /27	7.17 /22	7.37 /26	4.33	1.41
AA	AllianzGI Global Allocation P	AGAPX	C-	(800) 988-8380	D+ / 2.4	2.82	1.81	3.16 /27	7.13 /22	7.29 /25	4.28	1.42
AA	AllianzGI Global Allocation R	AGARX	C-	(800) 988-8380	D / 2.2	2.74	1.63	2.77 /25	6.74 /20	6.86 /22	3.90	1.83
AA	AllianzGI Global Dynamic Alloc A	ASGAX	E	(800) 988-8380	D / 1.6	2.85	0.62	1.27 /19	7.33 /23	7.67 /28	3.60	4.72
AA	AllianzGI Global Dynamic Alloc Adm	AGFAX	E+	(800) 988-8380	D+ / 2.3	2.86	0.65	1.31 /19	7.36 /23	7.71 /28	3.98	4.74
AA	AllianzGI Global Dynamic Alloc C	ASACX	E+	(800) 988-8380	D / 1.8	2.67	0.23	0.52 /17	6.51 /19	6.86 /22	3.09	5.50
AA	AllianzGI Global Dynamic Alloc D	AGSDX	E+	(800) 988-8380	D+ / 2.3	2.81	0.56	1.22 /19	7.32 /23	7.66 /28	3.57	4.70

● Denotes fund is closed to new investors
* Denotes fund is included in Section II

www.thestreetratings.com

RISK Risk Rating/Pts	3 Year Standard Deviation	Beta	NET ASSETS NAV As of 3/31/15	Total $(Mil)	ASSET Cash %	Stocks %	Bonds %	Other %	Portfolio Turnover Ratio	BULL/BEAR Last Bull Market Return	Last Bear Market Return	FUND MANAGER Manager Quality Pct	Manager Tenure (Years)	MINIMUMS Initial Purch. $	Additional Purch. $	LOADS Front End Load	Back End Load
B+ / 9.9	0.1	N/A	15.70	18	0	0	0	100	0	9.3	1.5	87	N/A	250	50	0.0	0.0
B+ / 9.9	0.1	N/A	15.69	2	0	0	0	100	0	9.2	1.5	86	N/A	0	250	0.0	0.0
C / 4.9	15.1	1.13	33.32	11	0	0	0	100	0	101.7	-24.3	19	N/A	1,000	50	4.3	0.0
C / 4.8	15.1	1.13	30.18	1	0	0	0	100	0	96.7	-24.6	13	N/A	1,000	50	0.0	0.0
C / 4.9	15.1	1.13	30.12	3	0	0	0	100	0	96.7	-24.6	13	N/A	1,000	50	0.0	0.0
C / 5.0	15.1	1.13	34.35	2	0	0	0	100	0	103.5	-24.3	21	N/A	250	50	0.0	0.0
C / 4.9	15.1	1.13	33.28	1	0	0	0	100	0	101.7	-24.3	19	N/A	250	50	0.0	0.0
B- / 7.1	15.1	1.00	34.37	2	0	0	0	100	0	103.5	-24.2	44	N/A	250	50	0.0	0.0
B- / 7.1	15.1	1.00	33.70	N/A	0	0	0	100	0	103.5	-24.3	44	N/A	250	50	0.0	0.0
C+ / 5.8	9.5	0.97	24.02	11	0	99	0	1	89	110.9	N/A	81	4	1,000	50	5.5	0.0
C+ / 6.5	9.5	0.97	23.50	1	0	99	0	1	89	105.5	N/A	74	4	1,000	50	0.0	0.0
C+ / 6.4	9.5	0.97	23.87	2	0	99	0	1	89	110.9	N/A	81	4	1,000	50	0.0	0.0
C+ / 6.5	9.5	0.97	24.15	49	0	99	0	1	89	113.1	N/A	83	4	1,000,000	0	0.0	0.0
C+ / 6.5	9.5	0.97	24.09	N/A	0	99	0	1	89	112.3	N/A	82	4	1,000,000	0	0.0	0.0
U /	N/A	N/A	15.99	107	0	0	0	100	76	N/A	N/A	N/A	2	0	0	0.0	0.0
C / 5.3	14.5	0.65	17.66	N/A	4	95	0	1	123	53.8	-30.7	87	5	1,000	50	5.5	0.0
C / 5.3	14.5	0.65	17.95	N/A	4	95	0	1	123	49.7	-30.9	83	5	1,000	50	0.0	0.0
C / 5.4	14.5	0.65	17.90	N/A	4	95	0	1	123	53.7	-30.6	87	5	1,000	50	0.0	0.0
C / 5.4	14.5	0.65	17.69	5	4	95	0	1	123	55.2	-30.5	88	5	1,000,000	0	0.0	0.0
C / 5.4	14.5	0.65	18.42	N/A	4	95	0	1	123	54.9	-30.6	88	5	1,000,000	0	0.0	0.0
C+ / 6.5	8.7	1.16	34.61	480	4	10	0	86	94	67.1	-17.1	20	21	1,000	50	5.5	0.0
C+ / 6.5	8.7	1.16	34.62	2	4	10	0	86	94	67.4	-17.1	21	21	1,000,000	0	0.0	0.0
C+ / 6.5	8.7	1.16	34.68	119	4	10	0	86	94	62.9	-17.4	15	21	1,000	50	0.0	0.0
C+ / 6.5	8.7	1.16	34.60	71	4	10	0	86	94	66.7	-17.1	20	21	1,000	50	0.0	0.0
C+ / 6.5	8.7	1.16	34.49	1,586	4	10	0	86	94	68.8	-17.0	24	21	1,000,000	0	0.0	0.0
C+ / 6.5	8.7	1.16	34.54	191	4	10	0	86	94	68.3	-17.1	23	21	1,000,000	0	0.0	0.0
C+ / 6.5	8.7	1.16	34.55	2	4	10	0	86	94	65.0	-17.3	17	21	0	0	0.0	0.0
C / 5.5	13.2	0.92	26.35	26	3	96	0	1	120	31.4	-29.1	87	8	1,000	50	5.5	0.0
C+ / 5.6	13.2	0.92	25.71	15	3	96	0	1	120	28.2	-29.3	84	8	1,000	50	0.0	0.0
C / 5.5	13.2	0.92	26.70	24	3	96	0	1	120	31.5	-29.1	88	8	1,000	50	0.0	0.0
C / 5.5	13.2	0.92	26.39	54	3	96	0	1	120	33.0	-29.0	89	8	1,000,000	0	0.0	0.0
C / 5.5	13.2	0.92	25.87	6	3	96	0	1	120	32.6	-29.0	89	8	1,000,000	0	0.0	0.0
C / 5.5	11.1	1.02	41.97	292	1	98	0	1	51	105.6	-16.8	73	3	1,000	50	5.5	0.0
C / 5.2	11.1	1.02	36.86	6	1	98	0	1	51	106.3	-16.8	74	3	1,000,000	0	0.0	0.0
C / 4.8	11.1	1.02	31.03	2	1	98	0	1	51	100.4	-17.1	64	3	1,000	50	0.0	0.0
C / 4.8	11.1	1.02	31.03	227	1	98	0	1	51	100.4	-17.1	64	3	1,000	50	0.0	0.0
C / 5.1	11.1	1.02	35.66	15	1	98	0	1	51	105.6	-16.9	73	3	1,000	50	0.0	0.0
C / 5.2	11.1	1.02	38.72	116	1	98	0	1	51	108.0	-16.7	76	3	1,000,000	0	0.0	0.0
C / 4.9	11.1	1.02	33.32	19	1	98	0	1	51	107.3	-16.7	76	3	1,000,000	0	0.0	0.0
C / 5.0	11.1	1.02	33.35	16	1	98	0	1	51	103.8	-16.9	70	3	0	0	0.0	0.0
B- / 7.9	6.4	1.03	11.77	60	1	57	41	1	48	39.9	-15.4	16	13	1,000	50	5.5	0.0
B- / 7.9	6.4	1.03	12.06	N/A	1	57	41	1	48	39.9	-15.5	16	13	1,000,000	0	0.0	0.0
B- / 7.9	6.4	1.04	12.04	1	1	57	41	1	48	36.5	-15.7	11	13	1,000	50	0.0	0.0
B- / 7.9	6.4	1.03	11.93	59	1	57	41	1	48	36.5	-15.8	12	13	1,000	50	0.0	0.0
B- / 7.9	6.4	1.04	11.71	2	1	57	41	1	48	40.0	-15.5	16	13	1,000	50	0.0	0.0
B- / 7.9	6.4	1.03	11.64	80	1	57	41	1	48	41.3	-15.4	18	13	1,000,000	0	0.0	0.0
B- / 7.9	6.4	1.04	11.76	2	1	57	41	1	48	41.0	-15.4	17	13	0	0	0.0	0.0
B- / 7.9	6.4	1.04	11.71	N/A	1	57	41	1	48	39.0	-15.6	15	13	0	0	0.0	0.0
C- / 3.9	8.5	1.35	19.13	1	5	69	23	3	62	48.1	-20.7	5	6	1,000	50	5.5	0.0
C- / 3.8	8.5	1.35	19.07	N/A	5	69	23	3	62	48.3	-20.7	5	6	1,000,000	0	0.0	0.0
C- / 4.0	8.5	1.35	18.83	1	5	69	23	3	62	44.3	-21.0	3	6	1,000	50	0.0	0.0
C- / 3.9	8.5	1.35	19.03	N/A	5	69	23	3	62	48.2	-20.7	5	6	1,000	50	0.0	0.0

Fund Type	Fund Name	Ticker Symbol	Overall Investment Rating	Phone	Performance Rating/Pts	Total Return % through 3/31/15			Annualized		Incl. in Returns	
						3 Mo	6 Mo	1Yr / Pct	3Yr / Pct	5Yr / Pct	Dividend Yield	Expense Ratio
AA	AllianzGI Global Dynamic Alloc Inst	AGAIX	E+	(800) 988-8380	D+ / 2.5	2.90	0.74	1.54 /20	7.63 /25	7.97 /30	4.15	4.49
AA	AllianzGI Global Dynamic Alloc P	AGSPX	E+	(800) 988-8380	D+ / 2.4	2.86	0.68	1.39 /20	7.49 /24	7.86 /29	4.05	4.59
AA	AllianzGI Global Dynamic Alloc R	ASFRX	E+	(800) 988-8380	D / 2.2	2.76	0.51	1.03 /19	7.08 /22	7.41 /26	3.67	5.18
GL	AllianzGI Global Managed Vol A	AVYAX	C	(800) 988-8380	C- / 3.8	1.08	6.60	8.76 /68	10.52 /42	--	2.34	2.63
GL	AllianzGI Global Managed Vol C	AVYCX	C+	(800) 988-8380	C- / 4.2	0.92	6.27	8.04 /63	9.75 /38	--	1.97	3.26
GL	AllianzGI Global Managed Vol D	AVYDX	C+	(800) 988-8380	C / 4.7	1.08	6.65	8.81 /68	10.56 /43	--	2.67	2.84
GL	AllianzGI Global Managed Vol Inst	AVYIX	C+	(800) 988-8380	C / 5.0	1.19	6.80	9.14 /70	10.89 /45	--	2.51	2.32
GL	AllianzGI Global Managed Vol P	AVYPX	C+	(800) 988-8380	C / 4.9	1.13	6.78	9.05 /70	10.78 /44	--	2.43	2.38
EN	AllianzGI Global Natural Res A	ARMAX	E	(800) 988-8380	E / 0.4	4.43	-10.05	-10.38 / 3	2.12 / 6	2.03 / 4	0.00	1.41
EN	AllianzGI Global Natural Res C	ARMCX	E	(800) 988-8380	E / 0.4	4.25	-10.40	-11.09 / 2	1.35 / 6	1.26 / 4	0.00	2.16
EN	AllianzGI Global Natural Res D	ARMDX	E	(800) 988-8380	E / 0.5	4.43	-9.99	-10.37 / 3	2.13 / 6	2.03 / 4	0.00	1.41
EN	AllianzGI Global Natural Res Inst	RGLIX	E	(800) 988-8380	E / 0.5	4.59	-9.84	-10.03 / 3	2.49 / 7	2.40 / 5	0.18	1.06
EN	AllianzGI Global Natural Res P	APGPX	E	(800) 988-8380	E / 0.5	4.50	-9.89	-10.12 / 3	2.38 / 7	2.28 / 5	0.25	1.16
GL	AllianzGI Global Small Cap A	RGSAX	C+	(800) 988-8380	C+ / 6.6	7.35	9.71	4.53 /35	15.28 /77	15.75 /92	0.00	1.61
GL	● AllianzGI Global Small Cap B	RGSBX	C+	(800) 988-8380	C+ / 6.9	7.16	9.30	3.75 /30	14.41 /70	14.88 /86	0.00	2.36
GL	AllianzGI Global Small Cap C	RGSCX	C+	(800) 988-8380	C+ / 6.9	7.16	9.30	3.75 /30	14.41 /70	14.88 /86	0.00	2.36
GL	AllianzGI Global Small Cap D	DGSNX	B	(800) 988-8380	B / 7.6	7.36	9.69	4.54 /35	15.27 /77	15.74 /91	0.00	1.61
GL	AllianzGI Global Small Cap Inst	DGSCX	B+	(800) 988-8380	B / 7.9	7.46	9.90	4.91 /38	15.68 /81	16.15 /94	0.00	1.26
GL	AllianzGI Global Small Cap P	ARSPX	B	(800) 988-8380	B / 7.8	7.43	9.85	4.80 /37	15.56 /80	16.03 /93	0.00	1.36
GL	AllianzGI Global Water A	AWTAX	D	(800) 988-8380	D+ / 2.3	0.00	2.66	-2.38 /10	9.65 /37	9.70 /42	0.22	1.52
GL	AllianzGI Global Water C	AWTCX	D+	(800) 988-8380	D+ / 2.6	-0.16	2.24	-3.15 / 8	8.78 /32	8.84 /36	0.00	2.29
GL	AllianzGI Global Water D	AWTDX	D+	(800) 988-8380	C- / 3.1	0.00	2.61	-2.53 / 9	9.54 /36	9.62 /41	0.25	1.60
GL	AllianzGI Global Water Inst	AWTIX	C-	(800) 988-8380	C- / 3.4	0.08	2.80	-2.07 /10	10.00 /39	10.03 /45	0.59	1.18
GL	AllianzGI Global Water P	AWTPX	C-	(800) 988-8380	C- / 3.3	0.08	2.75	-2.19 /10	9.88 /39	9.92 /44	0.73	1.26
HL	AllianzGI Health Sciences A	RAGHX	B-	(800) 988-8380	A+ / 9.9	12.04	15.73	31.22 /99	24.94 /99	19.34 /98	0.00	1.46
HL	● AllianzGI Health Sciences B	RBGHX	C+	(800) 988-8380	A+ / 9.9	11.83	15.31	30.26 /99	24.02 /99	18.46 /98	0.00	2.21
HL	AllianzGI Health Sciences C	RCGHX	C+	(800) 988-8380	A+ / 9.9	11.82	15.29	30.22 /99	24.01 /99	18.45 /98	0.00	2.21
HL	AllianzGI Health Sciences D	DGHCX	B-	(800) 988-8380	A+ / 9.9	12.04	15.74	31.23 /99	24.95 /99	19.34 /98	0.00	1.46
GI	AllianzGI Income and Growth A	AZNAX	C-	(800) 988-8380	D+ / 2.9	1.97	3.34	4.80 /37	9.43 /36	9.51 /41	2.54	1.32
GI	AllianzGI Income and Growth C	AZNCX	C-	(800) 988-8380	C- / 3.2	1.76	2.95	4.01 /32	8.61 /30	8.68 /34	2.60	2.07
GI	AllianzGI Income and Growth D	AZNDX	C	(800) 988-8380	C- / 3.7	1.96	3.40	4.78 /37	9.44 /36	9.50 /40	2.67	1.32
GI	AllianzGI Income and Growth Inst	AZNIX	C	(800) 988-8380	C- / 4.0	2.03	3.57	5.15 /40	9.83 /38	9.89 /44	2.74	0.97
GI	AllianzGI Income and Growth P	AIGPX	C	(800) 988-8380	C- / 3.9	2.04	3.49	4.98 /38	9.70 /37	9.77 /43	2.73	1.07
GI	AllianzGI Income and Growth R	AIGRX	C-	(800) 988-8380	C- / 3.6	1.95	3.29	4.53 /35	9.18 /34	9.26 /39	2.60	1.57
FO	AllianzGI International Sm Cp A	AOPAX	D	(800) 988-8380	C / 4.6	11.04	8.92	0.31 /16	11.97 /52	10.93 /52	0.66	1.83
FO	AllianzGI International Sm Cp C	AOPCX	D	(800) 988-8380	C / 4.9	10.86	8.52	-0.41 /14	11.15 /47	10.10 /45	0.46	2.43
FO	AllianzGI International Sm Cp D	ALODX	D+	(800) 988-8380	C / 5.5	11.06	8.93	0.32 /17	11.96 /52	10.92 /52	1.50	1.73
FO	AllianzGI International Sm Cp Inst	ALOIX	D+	(800) 988-8380	C+ / 5.7	11.13	9.06	0.55 /17	12.23 /54	11.26 /55	0.30	1.44
FO	AllianzGI International Sm Cp P	ALOPX	D+	(800) 988-8380	C+ / 5.6	11.08	9.00	0.48 /17	12.14 /53	11.14 /54	0.42	1.52
FO	AllianzGI International Sm Cp R	ALORX	D	(800) 988-8380	C / 5.3	11.00	8.80	0.08 /16	11.70 /50	10.65 /50	1.33	1.96
FO	AllianzGI Internatl Mgd Vol A	PNIAX	D+	(800) 988-8380	D+ / 2.6	4.77	4.02	3.52 /29	8.82 /32	5.24 /13	3.42	1.16
FO	AllianzGI Internatl Mgd Vol C	PNICX	D+	(800) 988-8380	C- / 3.0	4.56	3.65	2.72 /25	8.01 /27	4.46 /10	2.74	1.91
FO	AllianzGI Internatl Mgd Vol D	PNIDX	C-	(800) 988-8380	C- / 3.5	4.78	3.98	3.48 /29	8.82 /32	5.18 /13	3.59	1.16
FO	AllianzGI Internatl Mgd Vol Inst	NAISX	C-	(800) 988-8380	C- / 3.7	4.87	4.20	3.91 /31	9.21 /34	5.62 /15	4.00	0.81
FO	AllianzGI Internatl Mgd Vol P	ANIPX	C-	(800) 988-8380	C- / 3.7	4.89	4.20	3.76 /30	9.09 /34	5.52 /14	3.86	0.91
FO	AllianzGI Internatl Mgd Vol R	ANIRX	C-	(800) 988-8380	C- / 3.3	4.76	3.98	3.33 /28	8.58 /30	5.01 /12	3.58	1.41
SC	AllianzGI Micro Cap A	GMCAX	C+	(800) 988-8380	B+ / 8.6	9.17	18.32	4.18 /33	17.56 /93	16.41 /94	0.00	2.07
SC	AllianzGI Micro Cap Inst	AMCIX	B-	(800) 988-8380	A / 9.3	9.17	18.42	4.28 /34	17.81 /94	16.66 /95	0.00	2.01
SC	AllianzGI Micro Cap P	AAMPX	B-	(800) 988-8380	A / 9.3	9.21	18.43	4.36 /34	17.74 /93	16.58 /95	0.00	1.90
MC	AllianzGI Mid-Cap A	RMDAX	C-	(800) 988-8380	C+ / 6.0	5.76	10.18	11.05 /78	13.40 /63	12.62 /65	0.00	1.13
MC	AllianzGI Mid-Cap Administrative	DRMAX	C	(800) 988-8380	B- / 7.0	5.80	10.36	11.20 /79	13.52 /64	12.73 /66	0.00	1.03
MC	● AllianzGI Mid-Cap B	RMDBX	C-	(800) 988-8380	C+ / 6.3	5.50	9.80	10.11 /75	12.54 /56	11.83 /59	0.00	1.88

● Denotes fund is closed to new investors
* Denotes fund is included in Section II

www.thestreetratings.com

RISK			NET ASSETS		ASSET					BULL / BEAR		FUND MANAGER		MINIMUMS		LOADS	
	3 Year		NAV						Portfolio	Last Bull	Last Bear	Manager	Manager	Initial	Additional	Front	Back
Risk	Standard		As of	Total	Cash	Stocks	Bonds	Other	Turnover	Market	Market	Quality	Tenure	Purch.	Purch.	End	End
Rating/Pts	Deviation	Beta	3/31/15	$(Mil)	%	%	%	%	Ratio	Return	Return	Pct	(Years)	$	$	Load	Load
C- / 3.8	8.5	1.36	19.14	5	5	69	23	3	62	49.6	-20.6	5	6	1,000,000	0	0.0	0.0
C- / 3.8	8.5	1.35	19.09	N/A	5	69	23	3	62	49.1	-20.7	5	6	1,000,000	0	0.0	0.0
C- / 3.8	8.5	1.35	19.00	N/A	5	69	23	3	62	47.0	-20.8	4	6	0	0	0.0	0.0
B- / 7.8	8.6	0.42	16.81	N/A	2	97	0	1	118	N/A	N/A	95	4	1,000	50	5.5	0.0
B- / 7.8	8.6	0.42	16.41	N/A	2	97	0	1	118	N/A	N/A	94	4	1,000	50	0.0	0.0
B- / 7.8	8.6	0.42	16.77	N/A	2	97	0	1	118	N/A	N/A	95	4	1,000	50	0.0	0.0
B- / 7.8	8.6	0.42	16.95	2	2	97	0	1	118	N/A	N/A	96	4	1,000,000	0	0.0	0.0
B- / 7.8	8.6	0.43	16.96	N/A	2	97	0	1	118	N/A	N/A	96	4	1,000,000	0	0.0	0.0
C- / 4.0	14.5	0.86	17.19	11	0	100	0	0	93	30.5	-31.0	50	11	1,000	50	5.5	0.0
C- / 3.9	14.6	0.86	16.20	4	0	100	0	0	93	27.2	-31.3	38	11	1,000	50	0.0	0.0
C- / 4.0	14.6	0.86	17.20	3	0	100	0	0	93	30.6	-31.0	50	11	1,000	50	0.0	0.0
C- / 4.0	14.6	0.86	17.53	28	0	100	0	0	93	32.2	-30.9	55	11	1,000,000	0	0.0	0.0
C- / 4.0	14.5	0.86	17.40	7	0	100	0	0	93	31.7	-31.0	54	11	1,000,000	0	0.0	0.0
C+ / 6.2	11.7	0.71	44.53	53	3	96	0	1	73	92.5	-23.8	97	5	1,000	50	5.5	0.0
C+ / 6.1	11.8	0.72	40.43	N/A	3	96	0	1	73	87.6	-24.0	96	5	1,000	50	0.0	0.0
C+ / 6.1	11.7	0.72	40.42	24	3	96	0	1	73	87.7	-24.0	96	5	1,000	50	0.0	0.0
C+ / 6.2	11.7	0.71	44.48	33	3	96	0	1	73	92.6	-23.8	97	5	1,000	50	0.0	0.0
C+ / 6.2	11.7	0.71	46.97	75	3	96	0	1	73	94.8	-23.6	97	5	1,000,000	0	0.0	0.0
C+ / 6.2	11.7	0.71	46.73	23	3	96	0	1	73	94.2	-23.7	97	5	1,000,000	0	0.0	0.0
C+ / 6.5	11.1	0.68	12.68	133	4	95	0	1	28	60.8	-19.8	89	7	1,000	50	5.5	0.0
C+ / 6.5	11.0	0.68	12.30	76	4	95	0	1	28	56.8	-20.2	85	7	1,000	50	0.0	0.0
C+ / 6.5	11.0	0.68	12.63	24	4	95	0	1	28	60.5	-19.9	88	7	1,000	50	0.0	0.0
C+ / 6.6	11.1	0.69	12.56	26	4	95	0	1	28	62.7	-19.8	90	7	1,000,000	0	0.0	0.0
C+ / 6.6	11.0	0.68	12.72	83	4	95	0	1	28	62.0	-19.8	89	7	1,000,000	0	0.0	0.0
C- / 3.4	11.0	0.80	36.48	40	4	95	0	1	119	131.5	-15.0	98	10	1,000	50	5.5	0.0
D+ / 2.8	11.0	0.80	31.00	1	4	95	0	1	119	125.6	-15.2	98	10	1,000	50	0.0	0.0
D+ / 2.8	11.0	0.80	31.03	19	4	95	0	1	119	125.6	-15.2	98	10	1,000	50	0.0	0.0
C- / 3.4	11.0	0.80	36.47	147	4	95	0	1	119	131.4	-14.9	98	10	1,000	50	0.0	0.0
B- / 7.2	6.9	0.69	12.34	869	3	37	31	29	114	54.7	-14.4	48	8	1,000	50	5.5	0.0
B- / 7.2	6.9	0.68	11.71	1,134	3	37	31	29	114	50.6	-14.6	38	8	1,000	50	0.0	0.0
B- / 7.2	6.9	0.69	12.40	63	3	37	31	29	114	54.6	-14.4	48	8	1,000	50	0.0	0.0
B- / 7.3	6.9	0.68	12.61	172	3	37	31	29	114	56.5	-14.3	54	8	1,000,000	0	0.0	0.0
B- / 7.3	6.9	0.69	12.53	633	3	37	31	29	114	55.9	-14.3	52	8	1,000,000	0	0.0	0.0
B- / 7.2	6.9	0.69	12.37	4	3	37	31	29	114	53.3	-14.4	45	8	0	0	0.0	0.0
C- / 3.8	12.1	0.84	35.29	7	2	97	0	1	77	63.4	-24.5	91	N/A	1,000	50	5.5	0.0
C- / 3.8	12.1	0.84	34.81	1	2	97	0	1	77	59.2	-24.8	89	N/A	1,000	50	0.0	0.0
C- / 3.6	12.1	0.84	35.74	2	2	97	0	1	77	63.3	-24.5	91	N/A	1,000	50	0.0	0.0
C- / 4.0	12.1	0.84	36.34	58	2	97	0	1	77	64.9	-24.4	91	N/A	1,000,000	0	0.0	0.0
C- / 3.8	12.1	0.84	35.19	32	2	97	0	1	77	64.3	-24.4	91	N/A	1,000,000	0	0.0	0.0
C- / 3.6	12.1	0.84	34.80	N/A	2	97	0	1	77	62.0	-24.6	90	N/A	0	0	0.0	0.0
C+ / 6.5	9.9	0.66	14.50	19	6	93	0	1	86	44.8	-24.5	87	9	1,000	50	5.5	0.0
C+ / 6.6	9.9	0.66	14.46	9	6	93	0	1	86	41.1	-24.7	82	9	1,000	50	0.0	0.0
C+ / 6.5	9.9	0.66	14.47	1	6	93	0	1	86	44.3	-24.4	86	9	1,000	50	0.0	0.0
C+ / 6.5	9.9	0.66	14.42	57	6	93	0	1	86	46.4	-24.3	88	9	1,000,000	0	0.0	0.0
C+ / 6.5	9.9	0.66	14.37	1	6	93	0	1	86	46.0	-24.4	88	9	1,000,000	0	0.0	0.0
C+ / 6.5	10.0	0.66	14.30	N/A	6	93	0	1	86	43.5	-24.5	85	9	0	0	0.0	0.0
C- / 3.7	17.5	1.24	15.36	6	2	97	0	1	48	122.5	-35.5	31	20	1,000	50	5.5	0.0
C- / 3.8	17.5	1.24	15.48	35	2	97	0	1	48	124.1	-35.4	33	20	1,000,000	0	0.0	0.0
C- / 3.8	17.5	1.24	15.41	3	2	97	0	1	48	123.5	-35.5	32	20	1,000,000	0	0.0	0.0
C / 4.5	12.7	1.06	3.67	103	0	99	0	1	88	85.7	-22.7	16	10	1,000	50	5.5	0.0
C / 4.6	12.7	1.06	3.83	1	0	99	0	1	88	87.0	-22.9	17	10	1,000,000	0	0.0	0.0
C- / 4.1	12.8	1.06	3.26	1	0	99	0	1	88	81.8	-23.2	11	10	1,000	50	0.0	0.0

					PERFORMANCE							Incl. in Returns	
	99 Pct = Best *0 Pct = Worst*		**Overall**		**Perfor-**		Total Return % through 3/31/15						
			Investment		**mance**					Annualized		Dividend	Expense
Fund Type	Fund Name	Ticker Symbol	**Rating**	Phone	**Rating/Pts**	3 Mo	6 Mo	1Yr / Pct	3Yr / Pct	5Yr / Pct		Yield	Ratio
MC	AllianzGI Mid-Cap C	RMDCX	**C-**	(800) 988-8380	**C+ / 6.4**	5.52	9.83	10.15 /75	12.59 /57	11.87 /60		0.00	1.88
MC	AllianzGI Mid-Cap D	DMCNX	**C**	(800) 988-8380	**B- / 7.0**	5.93	10.32	11.17 /79	13.47 /63	12.73 /66		0.00	1.13
MC	AllianzGI Mid-Cap Institutional	DRMCX	**C+**	(800) 988-8380	**B- / 7.3**	5.76	10.39	11.45 /80	13.81 /66	13.02 /68		0.00	0.78
MC	AllianzGI Mid-Cap P	ARMPX	**B-**	(800) 988-8380	**B- / 7.2**	5.77	10.42	11.48 /80	13.73 /65	12.97 /68		0.00	0.88
MC	AllianzGI Mid-Cap R	PRMRX	**C**	(800) 988-8380	**C+ / 6.8**	5.80	10.24	10.82 /78	13.22 /61	12.42 /63		0.00	1.38
GR	AllianzGI NFJ All-Cap Value A	PNFAX	**C+**	(800) 988-8380	**C / 5.3**	0.25	3.63	8.93 /69	13.52 /64	12.95 /68		1.01	1.31
GR	● AllianzGI NFJ All-Cap Value B	PNFBX	**B-**	(800) 988-8380	**C+ / 5.6**	0.06	3.25	8.13 /64	12.68 /57	12.10 /61		0.00	2.06
GR	AllianzGI NFJ All-Cap Value C	PNFCX	**B-**	(800) 988-8380	**C+ / 5.6**	0.07	3.26	8.12 /64	12.65 /57	12.09 /61		0.65	2.06
GR	AllianzGI NFJ All-Cap Value D	PNFDX	**B-**	(800) 988-8380	**C+ / 6.2**	0.25	3.65	8.93 /69	13.52 /64	12.94 /68		1.19	1.31
GR	AllianzGI NFJ All-Cap Value Inst	PNFIX	**B-**	(800) 988-8380	**C+ / 6.4**	0.30	3.84	9.29 /71	13.89 /66	13.31 /71		1.49	0.96
GR	AllianzGI NFJ All-Cap Value P	ANFPX	**B-**	(800) 988-8380	**C+ / 6.4**	0.31	3.76	9.24 /71	13.81 /66	13.22 /70		1.56	1.06
IN	AllianzGI NFJ Dividend Value A	PNEAX	**C+**	(800) 988-8380	**C / 4.4**	-1.76	-0.09	5.14 /40	12.95 /59	12.32 /63		1.79	1.05
IN	AllianzGI NFJ Dividend Value Admn	ANDAX	**C+**	(800) 988-8380	**C / 5.3**	-1.71	0.02	5.25 /40	13.07 /60	12.44 /64		1.98	0.95
IN	● AllianzGI NFJ Dividend Value B	PNEBX	**C+**	(800) 988-8380	**C / 4.7**	-1.93	-0.43	4.36 /34	12.11 /53	11.47 /57		1.01	1.80
IN	AllianzGI NFJ Dividend Value C	PNECX	**C+**	(800) 988-8380	**C / 4.7**	-1.99	-0.46	4.33 /34	12.12 /53	11.47 /57		1.13	1.80
IN	AllianzGI NFJ Dividend Value D	PEIDX	**C+**	(800) 988-8380	**C / 5.3**	-1.75	-0.02	5.12 /39	12.96 /59	12.29 /62		1.90	1.05
IN	AllianzGI NFJ Dividend Value Inst	NFJEX	**B-**	(800) 988-8380	**C / 5.5**	-1.66	0.15	5.49 /42	13.35 /62	12.70 /66		2.26	0.70
IN	AllianzGI NFJ Dividend Value P	ADJPX	**B-**	(800) 988-8380	**C / 5.5**	-1.69	0.10	5.39 /41	13.26 /61	12.59 /65		2.16	0.80
IN	AllianzGI NFJ Dividend Value R	PNERX	**C+**	(800) 988-8380	**C / 5.1**	-1.82	-0.21	4.84 /37	12.68 /57	12.02 /61		1.66	1.30
IN	AllianzGI NFJ Dividend Value R6	ANDVX	**B-**	(800) 988-8380	**C / 5.5**	-1.65	0.15	5.53 /43	13.36 /62	12.71 /66		2.42	0.65
GL	AllianzGI NFJ Global Div Val A	ANUAX	**D-**	(800) 988-8380	**D- / 1.2**	-0.91	-2.56	-0.79 /14	7.19 /22	7.22 /24		3.57	1.51
GL	AllianzGI NFJ Global Div Val C	ANUCX	**D-**	(800) 988-8380	**D- / 1.4**	-1.14	-3.00	-1.63 /11	6.33 /18	6.39 /19		3.04	2.27
GL	AllianzGI NFJ Global Div Val D	ANUDX	**D-**	(800) 988-8380	**D / 1.7**	-0.94	-2.63	-0.87 /13	7.08 /22	7.17 /24		3.79	1.55
GL	AllianzGI NFJ Global Div Val Inst	ANUIX	**D-**	(800) 988-8380	**D / 1.9**	-0.89	-2.47	-0.58 /14	7.45 /24	7.52 /27		3.81	1.21
GL	AllianzGI NFJ Global Div Val P	ANUPX	**D-**	(800) 988-8380	**D / 1.9**	-0.87	-2.48	-0.64 /14	7.35 /23	7.43 /26		3.90	1.32
FO	AllianzGI NFJ Internatl Value A	AFJAX	**E+**	(800) 988-8380	**E+ / 0.6**	0.70	-4.18	-5.32 / 5	3.97 /10	4.45 /10		2.44	1.29
FO	AllianzGI NFJ Internatl Value Admn	AIVAX	**E+**	(800) 988-8380	**E+ / 0.8**	0.73	-4.09	-5.21 / 5	4.08 /10	4.57 /10		2.73	1.19
FO	AllianzGI NFJ Internatl Value C	AFJCX	**E+**	(800) 988-8380	**E+ / 0.7**	0.51	-4.53	-6.02 / 4	3.19 / 8	3.68 / 7		1.85	2.04
FO	AllianzGI NFJ Internatl Value D	AFJDX	**E+**	(800) 988-8380	**E+ / 0.8**	0.70	-4.16	-5.33 / 5	3.97 /10	4.45 /10		2.64	1.29
FO	AllianzGI NFJ Internatl Value Inst	ANJIX	**D-**	(800) 988-8380	**E+ / 0.9**	0.79	-4.01	-5.01 / 5	4.33 /11	4.82 /11		2.99	0.94
FO	AllianzGI NFJ Internatl Value P	AFVPX	**D-**	(800) 988-8380	**E+ / 0.8**	0.77	-4.04	-5.07 / 5	4.23 /11	4.71 /11		2.93	1.04
FO	AllianzGI NFJ Internatl Value R	ANJRX	**E+**	(800) 988-8380	**E+ / 0.8**	0.69	-4.27	-5.55 / 5	3.71 / 9	4.19 / 9		2.36	1.54
FO	AllianzGI NFJ Internatl Value R6	ANAVX	**D**	(800) 988-8380	**E+ / 0.9**	0.80	-3.99	-4.97 / 6	4.34 /11	4.82 /11		3.18	0.89
FO	AllianzGI NFJ Intl Value II A	NFJAX	**D**	(800) 988-8380	**D- / 1.3**	3.83	-1.42	-1.02 /13	6.91 /21	--		1.66	7.16
FO	AllianzGI NFJ Intl Value II C	NFJCX	**D**	(800) 988-8380	**D- / 1.5**	3.57	-1.83	-1.80 /11	6.09 /17	--		1.20	8.26
FO	AllianzGI NFJ Intl Value II D	NFJDX	**D+**	(800) 988-8380	**D / 1.9**	3.82	-1.42	-1.04 /13	6.90 /21	--		1.74	7.04
FO	AllianzGI NFJ Intl Value II Inst	NFJIX	**D+**	(800) 988-8380	**D / 2.1**	3.85	-1.31	-0.78 /14	7.20 /22	--		2.17	6.77
FO	AllianzGI NFJ Intl Value II P	NFJPX	**D+**	(800) 988-8380	**D / 2.0**	3.86	-1.32	-0.81 /14	7.12 /22	--		2.39	6.87
GR	AllianzGI NFJ Large Cap Value A	PNBAX	**B-**	(800) 988-8380	**C+ / 5.8**	-0.93	2.74	8.37 /65	14.69 /72	12.56 /65		1.38	1.11
GR	AllianzGI NFJ Large Cap Value Admn	ALNFX	**B-**	(800) 988-8380	**C+ / 6.7**	-0.94	2.74	8.45 /66	14.79 /73	12.66 /65		0.86	1.01
GR	● AllianzGI NFJ Large Cap Value B	PNBBX	**B-**	(800) 988-8380	**C+ / 6.1**	-1.12	2.31	7.50 /59	13.82 /66	11.71 /58		0.39	1.86
GR	AllianzGI NFJ Large Cap Value C	PNBCX	**B-**	(800) 988-8380	**C+ / 6.1**	-1.11	2.35	7.54 /59	13.81 /66	11.71 /58		0.52	1.86
GR	AllianzGI NFJ Large Cap Value D	PNBDX	**B-**	(800) 988-8380	**C+ / 6.7**	-0.92	2.74	8.37 /65	14.68 /72	12.55 /64		1.47	1.11
GR	AllianzGI NFJ Large Cap Value Inst	ANVIX	**B-**	(800) 988-8380	**C+ / 6.9**	-0.89	2.86	8.68 /67	15.07 /75	12.95 /68		2.08	0.76
GR	AllianzGI NFJ Large Cap Value P	ALCPX	**B-**	(800) 988-8380	**C+ / 6.9**	-0.90	2.83	8.60 /67	14.95 /74	12.82 /66		1.99	0.86
GR	AllianzGI NFJ Large Cap Value R	ANLRX	**B-**	(800) 988-8380	**C+ / 6.5**	-0.98	2.61	8.09 /63	14.40 /70	12.26 /62		1.09	1.36
GL	AllianzGI NFJ Mid-Cap Value A	PQNAX	**B-**	(800) 988-8380	**C+ / 6.0**	1.73	4.29	7.67 /60	14.93 /74	13.55 /73		1.35	1.35
GL	AllianzGI NFJ Mid-Cap Value Admn	PRAAX	**B+**	(800) 988-8380	**B- / 7.1**	1.80	4.36	7.82 /61	15.06 /75	13.67 /75		1.53	1.25
GL	● AllianzGI NFJ Mid-Cap Value B	PQNBX	**B-**	(800) 988-8380	**C+ / 6.4**	1.54	3.90	6.86 /54	14.05 /67	12.69 /66		0.56	2.10
GL	AllianzGI NFJ Mid-Cap Value C	PQNCX	**B-**	(800) 988-8380	**C+ / 6.4**	1.53	3.93	6.89 /54	14.07 /68	12.71 /66		1.06	2.10
GL	AllianzGI NFJ Mid-Cap Value D	PREDX	**B+**	(800) 988-8380	**B- / 7.0**	1.75	4.31	7.69 /60	14.92 /74	13.55 /73		1.44	1.35
GL	AllianzGI NFJ Mid-Cap Value Inst	PRNIX	**B+**	(800) 988-8380	**B- / 7.3**	1.82	4.48	8.06 /63	15.33 /77	13.94 /77		1.69	1.00

● Denotes fund is closed to new investors

★ Denotes fund is included in Section II

RISK			NET ASSETS		ASSET				Portfolio	BULL / BEAR		FUND MANAGER		MINIMUMS		LOADS	
	3 Year		NAV							Last Bull	Last Bear	Manager	Manager	Initial	Additional	Front	Back
Risk	Standard		As of	Total	Cash	Stocks	Bonds	Other	Turnover	Market	Market	Quality	Tenure	Purch.	Purch.	End	End
Rating/Pts	Deviation	Beta	3/31/15	$(Mil)	%	%	%	%	Ratio	Return	Return	Pct	(Years)	$	$	Load	Load
C- /4.1	12.8	1.07	3.25	190	0	99	0	1	88	81.4	-22.9	10	10	1,000	50	0.0	0.0
C /4.5	12.9	1.08	3.75	2	0	99	0	1	88	86.8	-22.9	14	10	1,000	50	0.0	0.0
C /4.7	12.7	1.06	4.04	35	0	99	0	1	88	88.7	-22.7	19	10	1,000,000	0	0.0	0.0
C+ /6.1	12.7	1.06	4.03	2	0	99	0	1	88	88.3	-22.7	18	10	1,000,000	0	0.0	0.0
C /4.4	12.8	1.07	3.65	3	0	99	0	1	88	84.8	-22.9	14	10	0	0	0.0	0.0
B- /7.5	10.5	1.08	15.80	10	1	98	0	1	23	81.6	-17.1	21	8	1,000	50	5.5	0.0
B- /7.4	10.5	1.08	15.57	N/A	1	98	0	1	23	77.0	-17.4	15	8	0	0	0.0	0.0
B- /7.4	10.6	1.08	15.04	8	1	98	0	1	23	77.1	-17.4	14	8	1,000	50	0.0	0.0
B- /7.5	10.5	1.08	16.04	2	1	98	0	1	23	81.6	-17.1	21	8	1,000	50	0.0	0.0
B- /7.5	10.5	1.08	16.84	2	1	98	0	1	23	83.7	-17.0	24	8	1,000,000	0	0.0	0.0
B- /7.5	10.5	1.08	16.08	7	1	98	0	1	23	83.2	-17.1	23	8	1,000,000	0	0.0	0.0
B- /7.5	10.5	1.06	16.74	1,471	1	98	0	1	26	83.0	-16.8	19	15	1,000	50	5.5	0.0
B- /7.5	10.5	1.06	16.93	700	1	98	0	1	26	83.5	-16.7	19	15	1,000,000	0	0.0	0.0
B- /7.5	10.5	1.06	17.05	5	1	98	0	1	26	78.4	-17.1	13	15	1,000	50	0.0	0.0
B- /7.5	10.5	1.06	16.89	461	1	98	0	1	26	78.3	-17.0	13	15	1,000	50	0.0	0.0
B- /7.5	10.5	1.06	16.84	225	1	98	0	1	26	82.7	-16.7	18	15	1,000	50	0.0	0.0
B- /7.5	10.6	1.07	16.82	3,914	1	98	0	1	26	85.1	-16.6	21	15	1,000,000	0	0.0	0.0
B- /7.5	10.5	1.06	16.83	1,618	1	98	0	1	26	84.5	-16.7	21	15	1,000,000	0	0.0	0.0
B- /7.5	10.5	1.06	16.71	239	1	98	0	1	26	81.3	-16.8	16	15	0	0	0.0	0.0
B- /7.7	10.6	1.06	16.80	108	1	98	0	1	26	85.1	-16.6	21	15	0	0	0.0	0.0
C+ /5.9	11.8	0.83	19.48	12	2	97	0	1	49	57.1	-20.9	58	6	1,000	50	5.5	0.0
C+ /5.9	11.8	0.83	19.23	6	2	97	0	1	49	52.9	-21.2	45	6	1,000	50	0.0	0.0
C+ /5.9	11.8	0.83	19.67	3	2	97	0	1	49	56.7	-20.9	56	6	1,000	50	0.0	0.0
C+ /5.9	11.8	0.83	19.41	17	2	97	0	1	49	58.5	-20.8	61	6	1,000,000	0	0.0	0.0
C+ /5.9	11.8	0.83	19.60	2	2	97	0	1	49	58.0	-20.9	60	6	1,000,000	0	0.0	0.0
C+ /6.1	12.6	0.92	21.46	495	1	98	0	1	33	39.1	-23.1	13	12	1,000	50	5.5	0.0
C+ /6.1	12.6	0.92	21.53	19	1	98	0	1	33	39.6	-23.0	14	12	1,000,000	0	0.0	0.0
C+ /6.1	12.6	0.92	21.23	160	1	98	0	1	33	35.6	-23.3	9	12	1,000	50	0.0	0.0
C+ /6.1	12.6	0.92	21.43	90	1	98	0	1	33	39.1	-23.1	13	12	1,000	50	0.0	0.0
C+ /6.1	12.6	0.92	21.56	1,124	1	98	0	1	33	40.8	-23.0	15	12	1,000,000	0	0.0	0.0
C+ /6.1	12.6	0.92	21.55	748	1	98	0	1	33	40.3	-23.0	15	12	1,000,000	0	0.0	0.0
C+ /6.1	12.6	0.92	21.52	22	1	98	0	1	33	38.0	-23.2	12	12	0	0	0.0	0.0
B- /7.3	12.5	0.91	21.53	63	1	98	0	1	33	40.9	-23.0	15	12	0	0	0.0	0.0
B- /7.4	12.2	0.90	17.89	N/A	5	94	0	1	34	N/A	N/A	44	4	1,000	50	5.5	0.0
B- /7.4	12.2	0.90	17.73	N/A	5	94	0	1	34	N/A	N/A	33	4	1,000	50	0.0	0.0
B- /7.4	12.2	0.90	17.91	N/A	5	94	0	1	34	N/A	N/A	44	4	1,000	50	0.0	0.0
B- /7.4	12.2	0.90	17.92	47	5	94	0	1	34	N/A	N/A	48	4	1,000,000	0	0.0	0.0
B- /7.4	12.2	0.90	17.88	1	5	94	0	1	34	N/A	N/A	47	4	1,000,000	0	0.0	0.0
B- /7.5	10.5	1.08	21.48	153	0	99	0	1	22	89.4	-16.8	32	15	1,000	50	5.5	0.0
B- /7.5	10.6	1.08	21.76	2	0	99	0	1	22	90.1	-16.7	33	15	1,000,000	0	0.0	0.0
B- /7.5	10.5	1.07	21.77	1	0	99	0	1	22	84.6	-17.0	24	15	0	0	0.0	0.0
B- /7.5	10.5	1.08	21.61	97	0	99	0	1	22	84.6	-17.0	24	15	1,000	50	0.0	0.0
B- /7.5	10.6	1.08	21.68	38	0	99	0	1	22	89.4	-16.8	32	15	1,000	50	0.0	0.0
B- /7.5	10.6	1.08	21.42	400	0	99	0	1	22	91.8	-16.6	36	15	1,000,000	0	0.0	0.0
B- /7.5	10.5	1.08	21.71	18	0	99	0	1	22	91.1	-16.7	35	15	1,000,000	0	0.0	0.0
B- /7.5	10.5	1.08	21.64	9	0	99	0	1	22	87.9	-16.9	29	15	0	0	0.0	0.0
B- /7.3	10.6	0.66	25.85	419	7	92	0	1	40	87.7	-19.9	97	6	1,000	50	5.5	0.0
B- /7.3	10.6	0.66	26.57	5	7	92	0	1	40	88.4	-19.8	97	6	1,000,000	0	0.0	0.0
B- /7.3	10.6	0.66	23.11	2	7	92	0	1	40	83.0	-20.1	96	6	0	0	0.0	0.0
B- /7.3	10.6	0.66	21.90	204	7	92	0	1	40	83.1	-20.2	96	6	1,000	50	0.0	0.0
B- /7.3	10.6	0.65	26.16	11	7	92	0	1	40	87.8	-19.9	97	6	1,000	50	0.0	0.0
B- /7.3	10.6	0.66	27.34	90	7	92	0	1	40	90.1	-19.8	97	6	1,000,000	0	0.0	0.0

			99 Pct = Best / 0 Pct = Worst		PERFORMANCE						Incl. in Returns	
			Overall		Perfor-	Total Return % through 3/31/15						
			Investment		mance				Annualized		Dividend	Expense
Fund Type	Fund Name	Ticker Symbol	Rating	Phone	Rating/Pts	3 Mo	6 Mo	1Yr / Pct	3Yr / Pct	5Yr / Pct	Yield	Ratio
GL	AllianzGI NFJ Mid-Cap Value P	ANRPX	B+	(800) 988-8380	B- / 7.2	1.83	4.47	7.97 /63	15.23 /77	13.64 /74	2.25	1.10
GL	AllianzGI NFJ Mid-Cap Value R	PRNRX	B-	(800) 988-8380	C+ / 6.8	1.66	4.19	7.39 /58	14.65 /72	13.26 /71	1.49	1.60
SC	● AllianzGI NFJ Small Cap Value A	PCVAX	E+	(800) 988-8380	C / 4.4	2.68	4.26	3.82 /31	12.32 /55	12.19 /62	1.90	1.21
SC	● AllianzGI NFJ Small Cap Value Admn	PVADX	D-	(800) 988-8380	C / 5.4	2.73	4.32	3.98 /32	12.49 /56	12.35 /63	2.09	1.11
SC	● AllianzGI NFJ Small Cap Value B	PCVBX	E+	(800) 988-8380	C / 4.7	2.50	3.84	3.01 /26	11.48 /49	11.35 /56	1.36	1.96
SC	● AllianzGI NFJ Small Cap Value C	PCVCX	E+	(800) 988-8380	C / 4.7	2.51	3.86	3.04 /27	11.48 /49	11.34 /55	1.51	1.96
SC	● AllianzGI NFJ Small Cap Value D	PNVDX	D-	(800) 988-8380	C / 5.3	2.68	4.21	3.79 /30	12.31 /55	12.18 /62	1.90	1.21
SC	● AllianzGI NFJ Small Cap Value Inst	PSVIX	D-	(800) 988-8380	C+ / 5.6	2.77	4.42	4.21 /33	12.76 /58	12.63 /65	2.19	0.86
SC	● AllianzGI NFJ Small Cap Value P	ASVPX	D-	(800) 988-8380	C / 5.5	2.74	4.35	4.06 /32	12.60 /57	12.47 /64	2.13	0.96
SC	● AllianzGI NFJ Small Cap Value R	PNVRX	D-	(800) 988-8380	C / 5.1	2.61	4.09	3.51 /29	12.04 /53	11.90 /60	1.68	1.46
SC	AllianzGI NFJ Small Cap Value R6	ANFVX	B-	(800) 988-8380	C+ / 5.6	2.81	4.45	4.28 /34	12.78 /58	12.65 /65	2.33	0.81
GI	AllianzGI Retirement 2015 A	AZGAX	D-	(800) 988-8380	E+ / 0.8	1.59	0.89	2.13 /22	4.20 /11	5.50 /14	2.67	1.16
GI	AllianzGI Retirement 2015 Admn	AZAMX	D-	(800) 988-8380	D- / 1.2	1.52	0.82	2.10 /22	4.21 /11	5.52 /14	2.74	1.01
GI	AllianzGI Retirement 2015 C	AZGCX	D-	(800) 988-8380	D- / 1.0	1.44	0.53	1.42 /20	3.42 / 9	4.70 /11	1.75	1.91
GI	AllianzGI Retirement 2015 D	AZGDX	D	(800) 988-8380	D- / 1.1	1.62	0.86	2.09 /22	4.09 /10	5.41 /14	2.26	1.16
GI	AllianzGI Retirement 2015 P	AZGPX	D-	(800) 988-8380	D- / 1.3	1.73	1.05	2.48 /24	4.53 /12	5.79 /16	3.05	0.76
GI	AllianzGI Retirement 2015 R	AZGRX	D-	(800) 988-8380	D- / 1.1	1.52	0.69	1.81 /21	3.85 /10	5.15 /13	2.35	1.41
GI	AllianzGI Retirement 2015 R6	AZGIX	D-	(800) 988-8380	D- / 1.3	1.68	1.08	2.56 /24	4.60 /12	5.87 /16	3.13	0.66
GI	AllianzGI Retirement 2020 A	AGLAX	D-	(800) 988-8380	E+ / 0.8	1.44	0.38	1.63 /20	4.21 /11	5.48 /14	2.76	1.17
GI	AllianzGI Retirement 2020 Admn	AGLMX	D-	(800) 988-8380	D- / 1.1	1.43	0.39	1.68 /21	4.23 /11	5.51 /14	2.86	1.02
GI	AllianzGI Retirement 2020 C	ABSCX	D-	(800) 988-8380	E+ / 0.9	1.28	0.00	0.88 /18	3.41 / 9	4.67 /11	2.07	1.92
GI	AllianzGI Retirement 2020 D	AGLDX	D-	(800) 988-8380	D- / 1.1	1.43	0.38	1.52 /20	4.10 /10	5.39 /14	2.59	1.17
GI	AllianzGI Retirement 2020 P	AGLPX	D	(800) 988-8380	D- / 1.2	1.48	0.56	1.90 /21	4.51 /11	5.75 /15	3.12	0.77
GI	AllianzGI Retirement 2020 R	AGLRX	D-	(800) 988-8380	D- / 1.0	1.33	0.21	1.25 /19	3.84 /10	5.13 /12	2.49	1.42
GI	AllianzGI Retirement 2020 R6	AGNIX	D	(800) 988-8380	D- / 1.3	1.53	0.58	2.02 /22	4.61 /12	5.86 /16	3.19	0.67
GL	AllianzGI Retirement 2025 A	GVSAX	D	(800) 988-8380	E+ / 0.9	1.76	0.64	1.88 /21	4.52 /12	--	2.83	1.19
GL	AllianzGI Retirement 2025 Admn	GVDAX	D	(800) 988-8380	D- / 1.3	1.75	0.64	1.88 /21	4.55 /12	--	3.00	1.04
GL	AllianzGI Retirement 2025 P	GVSPX	D	(800) 988-8380	D- / 1.3	1.81	0.73	2.15 /22	4.83 /13	--	3.25	0.79
GL	AllianzGI Retirement 2025 R	GVSRX	D	(800) 988-8380	D- / 1.1	1.70	0.46	1.53 /20	4.16 /11	--	2.53	1.44
GL	AllianzGI Retirement 2025 R6	GVSIX	D	(800) 988-8380	D- / 1.4	1.87	0.86	2.27 /23	4.94 /13	--	3.32	0.69
GR	AllianzGI Retirement 2030 A	ABLAX	D-	(800) 988-8380	D- / 1.0	1.93	0.62	1.74 /21	5.29 /14	6.16 /18	3.19	1.24
GR	AllianzGI Retirement 2030 Admn	ABAMX	D-	(800) 988-8380	D- / 1.5	1.95	0.68	1.79 /21	5.34 /14	6.23 /18	3.36	1.09
GR	AllianzGI Retirement 2030 C	ABLCX	D-	(800) 988-8380	D- / 1.2	1.73	0.23	0.91 /18	4.48 /11	5.38 /14	2.46	1.99
GR	AllianzGI Retirement 2030 D	ABDIX	D-	(800) 988-8380	D- / 1.4	1.91	0.58	1.60 /20	5.18 /14	6.09 /17	3.18	1.24
GR	AllianzGI Retirement 2030 P	ABLPX	D-	(800) 988-8380	D / 1.6	2.05	0.78	2.03 /22	5.61 /15	6.46 /20	3.59	0.84
GR	AllianzGI Retirement 2030 R	ABLRX	D-	(800) 988-8380	D- / 1.3	1.87	0.42	1.33 /19	4.91 /13	5.83 /16	2.97	1.49
GR	AllianzGI Retirement 2030 R6	ABLIX	D-	(800) 988-8380	D / 1.6	2.05	0.82	2.11 /22	5.70 /16	6.57 /20	3.67	0.74
GL	AllianzGI Retirement 2035 A	GVRAX	D	(800) 988-8380	D- / 1.2	2.13	0.89	1.89 /21	6.05 /17	--	3.31	1.27
GL	AllianzGI Retirement 2035 Admn	GVLAX	D	(800) 988-8380	D / 1.8	2.06	0.87	1.86 /21	6.08 /17	--	3.46	1.12
GL	AllianzGI Retirement 2035 P	GVPAX	D+	(800) 988-8380	D / 1.9	2.18	1.02	2.18 /23	6.37 /18	--	3.71	0.87
GL	AllianzGI Retirement 2035 R	GVRRX	D	(800) 988-8380	D / 1.6	2.02	0.71	1.49 /20	5.68 /15	--	3.10	1.52
GL	AllianzGI Retirement 2035 R6	GVLIX	D+	(800) 988-8380	D / 2.0	2.23	1.09	2.31 /23	6.47 /19	--	3.78	0.77
GR	AllianzGI Retirement 2040 A	AVSAX	D-	(800) 988-8380	D- / 1.4	2.34	1.14	1.95 /22	6.53 /19	6.93 /23	3.74	1.30
GR	AllianzGI Retirement 2040 Admn	AVAMX	D-	(800) 988-8380	D / 2.0	2.27	1.08	1.94 /22	6.55 /19	6.97 /23	3.94	1.15
GR	AllianzGI Retirement 2040 C	AVSCX	D-	(800) 988-8380	D / 1.6	2.19	0.75	1.19 /19	5.75 /16	6.13 /18	2.82	2.05
GR	AllianzGI Retirement 2040 D	AVSDX	D-	(800) 988-8380	D / 1.9	2.33	1.10	1.86 /21	6.40 /18	6.85 /22	3.77	1.30
GR	AllianzGI Retirement 2040 P	AVSPX	D-	(800) 988-8380	D+ / 2.2	2.41	1.30	2.29 /23	6.87 /21	7.24 /25	4.17	0.90
GR	AllianzGI Retirement 2040 R	AVSRX	D-	(800) 988-8380	D / 1.8	2.29	0.97	1.60 /20	6.18 /17	6.61 /21	3.56	1.55
GR	AllianzGI Retirement 2040 R6	AVTIX	D-	(800) 988-8380	D+ / 2.2	2.46	1.33	2.32 /23	6.94 /21	7.32 /25	4.25	0.80
GL	AllianzGI Retirement 2045 A	GBVAX	D	(800) 988-8380	D- / 1.5	2.59	1.48	2.24 /23	7.05 /22	--	3.69	1.33
GL	AllianzGI Retirement 2045 Admn	GBMAX	D+	(800) 988-8380	D+ / 2.3	2.59	1.43	2.24 /23	7.06 /22	--	3.91	1.18
GL	AllianzGI Retirement 2045 P	GBVPX	D+	(800) 988-8380	D+ / 2.5	2.69	1.63	2.60 /25	7.37 /23	--	4.14	0.93

● Denotes fund is closed to new investors
* Denotes fund is included in Section II

Risk Rating/Pts	3 Year Standard Deviation	Beta	NAV As of 3/31/15	Total $(Mil)	Cash %	Stocks %	Bonds %	Other %	Portfolio Turnover Ratio	Last Bull Market Return	Last Bear Market Return	Manager Quality Pct	Manager Tenure (Years)	Initial Purch. $	Additional Purch. $	Front End Load	Back End Load
B- /7.3	10.6	0.66	21.72	15	7	92	0	1	40	89.4	-19.8	97	6	1,000,000	0	0.0	0.0
B- /7.3	10.6	0.65	22.72	12	7	92	0	1	40	86.2	-20.0	97	6	0	0	0.0	0.0
D /1.9	11.8	0.79	26.43	1,815	7	92	0	1	29	69.7	-18.5	62	24	1,000	50	5.5	0.0
D /1.9	11.8	0.79	26.38	888	7	92	0	1	29	70.6	-18.4	65	24	1,000,000	0	0.0	0.0
D /1.9	11.8	0.79	25.41	7	7	92	0	1	29	65.5	-18.8	50	24	1,000	50	0.0	0.0
D /1.8	11.8	0.79	24.52	281	7	92	0	1	29	65.4	-18.8	51	24	1,000	50	0.0	0.0
D /2.1	11.8	0.79	27.54	96	7	92	0	1	29	69.8	-18.5	62	24	1,000	50	0.0	0.0
D /2.1	11.8	0.79	28.58	3,193	7	92	0	1	29	72.1	-18.4	68	24	1,000,000	0	0.0	0.0
D /2.1	11.8	0.79	28.47	113	7	92	0	1	29	71.2	-18.4	66	24	1,000,000	0	0.0	0.0
D /2.1	11.8	0.79	27.55	109	7	92	0	1	29	68.3	-18.6	58	24	0	0	0.0	0.0
B- /7.5	11.8	0.79	28.55	124	7	92	0	1	29	72.2	-18.4	68	24		0	0.0	0.0
C+ /6.8	4.2	0.30	19.17	12	1	26	71	2	114	24.3	-7.6	62	7	1,000	50	5.5	0.0
C+ /6.8	4.2	0.30	19.32	N/A	1	26	71	2	114	24.5	-7.7	63	7	1,000,000	0	0.0	0.0
B- /7.0	4.2	0.30	19.07	1	1	26	71	2	114	21.2	-8.1	50	7	1,000	50	0.0	0.0
C+ /6.9	4.2	0.30	19.40	N/A	1	26	71	2	114	23.9	-7.8	61	7	1,000	50	0.0	0.0
C+ /6.8	4.2	0.30	19.37	10	1	26	71	2	114	25.7	-7.6	67	7	1,000,000	0	0.0	0.0
C+ /6.9	4.2	0.30	19.34	N/A	1	26	71	2	114	23.0	-7.9	57	7	0	0	0.0	0.0
C+ /6.7	4.2	0.30	19.38	13	1	26	71	2	114	26.1	-7.6	67	7	0	0	0.0	0.0
C+ /6.9	4.6	0.35	19.03	33	1	29	67	3	89	25.8	-9.3	50	7	1,000	50	5.5	0.0
C+ /6.9	4.6	0.35	19.16	2	1	29	67	3	89	25.8	-9.3	51	7	1,000,000	0	0.0	0.0
B- /7.0	4.6	0.35	19.03	N/A	1	29	67	3	89	22.4	-9.6	39	7	1,000	50	0.0	0.0
C+ /6.9	4.6	0.35	19.17	N/A	1	29	67	3	89	25.2	-9.3	49	7	1,000	0	0.0	0.0
C+ /6.9	4.6	0.35	19.26	23	1	29	67	3	89	27.0	-9.3	55	7	1,000,000	0	0.0	0.0
C+ /6.9	4.6	0.35	19.07	1	1	29	67	3	89	24.2	-9.4	45	7	0	0	0.0	0.0
C+ /6.8	4.6	0.35	19.29	5	1	29	67	3	89	27.4	-9.2	56	7	0	0	0.0	0.0
B- /7.6	5.0	0.32	16.78	31	2	35	61	2	93	N/A	N/A	80	4	1,000	50	5.5	0.0
B- /7.6	5.0	0.32	16.85	1	2	35	61	2	93	N/A	N/A	81	4	1,000,000	0	0.0	0.0
B- /7.6	5.0	0.33	16.88	30	2	35	61	2	93	N/A	N/A	82	4	1,000,000	0	0.0	0.0
B- /7.6	5.0	0.32	16.75	1	2	35	61	2	93	N/A	N/A	78	4	0	0	0.0	0.0
B- /7.6	5.0	0.32	16.90	5	2	35	61	2	93	N/A	N/A	83	4	0	0	0.0	0.0
C+ /6.4	5.7	0.50	20.11	24	3	42	52	3	93	32.9	-13.9	33	7	1,000	50	5.5	0.0
C+ /6.4	5.7	0.50	20.34	2	3	42	52	3	93	33.2	-13.9	33	7	1,000,000	0	0.0	0.0
C+ /6.5	5.7	0.50	20.03	1	3	42	52	3	93	29.5	-14.1	24	7	1,000	50	0.0	0.0
C+ /6.4	5.7	0.50	20.25	1	3	42	52	3	93	32.5	-13.9	32	7	1,000	50	0.0	0.0
C+ /6.3	5.7	0.50	20.40	29	3	42	52	3	93	34.3	-13.8	37	7	1,000,000	0	0.0	0.0
C+ /6.4	5.7	0.50	20.19	2	3	42	52	3	93	31.4	-14.0	29	7	0	0	0.0	0.0
C+ /6.3	5.7	0.50	20.44	9	3	42	52	3	93	34.8	-13.8	38	7	0	0	0.0	0.0
B- /7.2	6.6	0.47	17.72	20	4	51	42	3	90	N/A	N/A	82	4	1,000	50	5.5	0.0
B- /7.2	6.6	0.47	17.80	1	4	51	42	3	90	N/A	N/A	82	4	1,000,000	0	0.0	0.0
B- /7.2	6.6	0.47	17.85	29	4	51	42	3	90	N/A	N/A	84	4	1,000,000	0	0.0	0.0
B- /7.2	6.6	0.47	17.71	2	4	51	42	3	90	N/A	N/A	79	4	0	0	0.0	0.0
B- /7.2	6.6	0.47	17.88	3	4	51	42	3	90	N/A	N/A	84	4	0	0	0.0	0.0
C+ /5.7	7.3	0.68	20.58	16	5	58	34	3	84	42.3	-19.3	17	7	1,000	50	5.5	0.0
C+ /5.7	7.3	0.68	20.68	1	5	58	34	3	84	42.3	-19.2	17	7	1,000,000	0	0.0	0.0
C+ /5.8	7.3	0.68	20.55	N/A	5	58	34	3	84	38.7	-19.5	13	7	1,000	50	0.0	0.0
C+ /5.7	7.4	0.68	20.64	N/A	5	58	34	3	84	41.7	-19.2	16	7	1,000	50	0.0	0.0
C+ /5.7	7.3	0.68	20.79	17	5	58	34	3	84	43.8	-19.2	20	7	1,000,000	0	0.0	0.0
C+ /5.7	7.3	0.68	20.54	1	5	58	34	3	84	40.7	-19.3	15	7	0	0	0.0	0.0
C+ /5.6	7.3	0.68	20.82	9	5	58	34	3	84	44.2	-19.1	20	7	0	0	0.0	0.0
C+ /6.9	7.9	0.56	18.19	11	6	65	27	2	69	N/A	N/A	82	4	1,000	50	5.5	0.0
C+ /6.9	7.9	0.56	18.24	N/A	6	65	27	2	69	N/A	N/A	82	4	1,000,000	0	0.0	0.0
C+ /6.9	7.9	0.56	18.31	11	6	65	27	2	69	N/A	N/A	84	4	1,000,000	0	0.0	0.0

99 Pct = Best
0 Pct = Worst

Fund Type	Fund Name	Ticker Symbol	Overall Investment Rating	Phone	Performance Rating/Pts	3 Mo	6 Mo	1Yr / Pct	3Yr / Pct	5Yr / Pct	Dividend Yield	Expense Ratio
					PERFORMANCE			Total Return % through 3/31/15	Annualized		Incl. in Returns	
GL	AllianzGI Retirement 2045 R	GBVRX	D	(800) 988-8380	D / 2.1	2.54	1.36	1.90 /21	6.67 /20	--	3.57	1.58
GL	AllianzGI Retirement 2045 R6	GBVIX	D+	(800) 988-8380	D+ / 2.5	2.69	1.69	2.66 /25	7.45 /24	--	4.20	0.83
GR	AllianzGI Retirement 2050 A	ASNAX	E+	(800) 988-8380	D / 1.6	2.71	1.42	2.19 /23	7.18 /22	7.54 /27	3.88	1.35
GR	AllianzGI Retirement 2050 Admn	ANAMX	D-	(800) 988-8380	D+ / 2.3	2.69	1.42	2.19 /23	7.18 /22	7.58 /27	4.04	1.20
GR	AllianzGI Retirement 2050 C	ASNCX	D-	(800) 988-8380	D / 1.9	2.47	1.05	1.40 /20	6.33 /18	6.72 /21	3.34	2.10
GR	AllianzGI Retirement 2050 D	ASNDX	D-	(800) 988-8380	D / 2.2	2.64	1.35	2.07 /22	7.03 /21	7.45 /26	3.74	1.35
GR	AllianzGI Retirement 2050 P	ASNPX	D-	(800) 988-8380	D+ / 2.5	2.78	1.55	2.50 /24	7.48 /24	7.83 /29	4.29	0.95
GR	AllianzGI Retirement 2050 R	ASNRX	D-	(800) 988-8380	D / 2.1	2.61	1.24	1.82 /21	6.80 /20	7.21 /24	3.69	1.60
GR	AllianzGI Retirement 2050 R6	ASNIX	D-	(800) 988-8380	D+ / 2.5	2.77	1.59	2.54 /24	7.56 /24	7.92 /29	4.32	0.85
GL	AllianzGI Retirement 2055 A	GLIAX	D	(800) 988-8380	D / 1.6	2.69	1.45	2.21 /23	7.23 /23	--	4.04	1.35
GL	AllianzGI Retirement 2055 Admn	GLRAX	D+	(800) 988-8380	D+ / 2.4	2.68	1.41	2.23 /23	7.28 /23	--	4.23	1.20
GL	AllianzGI Retirement 2055 P	GLIPX	D+	(800) 988-8380	D+ / 2.5	2.73	1.56	2.48 /24	7.58 /25	--	4.41	0.95
GL	AllianzGI Retirement 2055 R	GLLRX	D	(800) 988-8380	D / 2.2	2.63	1.29	1.88 /21	6.90 /21	--	3.95	1.60
GL	AllianzGI Retirement 2055 R6	GBLIX	D+	(800) 988-8380	D+ / 2.6	2.78	1.66	2.58 /24	7.66 /25	--	4.45	0.85
GI	AllianzGI Retirement Income A	AGRAX	D-	(800) 988-8380	E+ / 0.8	1.58	0.87	2.10 /22	4.00 /10	5.32 /13	3.36	1.15
GI	AllianzGI Retirement Income Admn	ARAMX	D-	(800) 988-8380	D- / 1.1	1.29	0.65	1.90 /21	3.98 /10	5.32 /13	3.19	1.00
GI	AllianzGI Retirement Income C	ARTCX	D-	(800) 988-8380	E+ / 0.9	1.36	0.49	1.32 /19	3.23 / 8	4.53 /10	2.85	1.90
GI	AllianzGI Retirement Income D	ARTDX	D-	(800) 988-8380	D- / 1.1	1.49	0.80	1.99 /22	3.90 /10	5.25 /13	3.44	1.15
GI	AllianzGI Retirement Income P	AGRPX	D-	(800) 988-8380	D- / 1.2	1.62	1.04	2.42 /24	4.33 /11	5.62 /15	3.80	0.75
GI	AllianzGI Retirement Income R	ASRRX	D-	(800) 988-8380	D- / 1.0	1.44	0.71	1.74 /21	3.65 / 9	4.98 /12	3.10	1.40
GI	AllianzGI Retirement Income R6	AVRIX	D-	(800) 988-8380	D- / 1.3	1.68	1.12	2.52 /24	4.43 /11	5.72 /15	3.98	0.65
SC	AllianzGI Small Cap Blend A	AZBAX	U	(800) 988-8380	U /	5.19	12.35	6.73 /53	--	--	0.23	1.32
SC	AllianzGI Small Cap Blend C	AZBCX	U	(800) 988-8380	U /	5.00	11.92	5.91 /46	--	--	0.00	2.07
TC	AllianzGI Technology A	RAGTX	C-	(800) 988-8380	B- / 7.4	2.18	5.35	13.01 /87	16.34 /86	15.90 /92	0.00	1.58
TC	AllianzGI Technology Administrative	DGTAX	C+	(800) 988-8380	B+ / 8.6	2.21	5.41	13.13 /87	16.49 /87	16.03 /93	0.00	1.48
TC	● AllianzGI Technology B	RBGTX	C-	(800) 988-8380	B / 7.8	1.99	4.96	12.17 /83	15.46 /79	15.03 /87	0.00	2.33
TC	AllianzGI Technology C	RCGTX	C-	(800) 988-8380	B / 7.8	1.99	4.96	12.16 /83	15.46 /79	15.03 /87	0.00	2.33
TC	AllianzGI Technology D	DGTNX	C	(800) 988-8380	B+ / 8.4	2.18	5.34	13.01 /87	16.33 /86	15.90 /92	0.00	1.58
TC	AllianzGI Technology Institutional	DRGTX	C+	(800) 988-8380	B+ / 8.7	2.27	5.54	13.42 /88	16.78 /89	16.33 /94	0.00	1.23
TC	AllianzGI Technology P	ARTPX	C+	(800) 988-8380	B+ / 8.7	2.24	5.49	13.30 /88	16.65 /88	16.20 /94	0.00	1.33
SC	● AllianzGI Ultra Micro Cap A	GUCAX	B-	(800) 988-8380	A- / 9.0	7.41	16.11	2.73 /25	19.18 /97	21.09 /99	0.00	2.30
SC	● AllianzGI Ultra Micro Cap Inst	AUMIX	B	(800) 988-8380	A+ / 9.6	7.40	16.18	2.87 /26	19.43 /97	21.38 /99	0.00	2.00
SC	● AllianzGI Ultra Micro Cap P	AAUPX	B	(800) 988-8380	A+ / 9.6	7.46	16.32	3.00 /26	19.44 /97	21.33 /99	0.00	2.07
GR	AllianzGI US Mgd Volatility A	NGWAX	D+	(800) 988-8380	C / 4.8	0.84	4.25	9.55 /72	12.51 /56	10.44 /48	1.16	0.97
GR	● AllianzGI US Mgd Volatility B	NGWBX	C-	(800) 988-8380	C / 5.2	0.68	3.84	8.74 /68	11.69 /50	9.62 /41	0.00	1.72
GR	AllianzGI US Mgd Volatility C	NGWCX	C-	(800) 988-8380	C / 5.2	0.68	3.90	8.74 /68	11.69 /50	9.61 /41	0.72	1.72
GR	AllianzGI US Mgd Volatility D	NGWDX	C-	(800) 988-8380	C+ / 5.8	0.84	4.23	9.58 /72	12.53 /56	10.43 /48	1.15	0.97
GR	AllianzGI US Mgd Volatility Inst	NGFIX	C	(800) 988-8380	C+ / 6.0	0.94	4.50	9.97 /74	12.93 /59	10.83 /51	1.56	0.62
GR	AllianzGI US Mgd Volatility P	ANCPX	C	(800) 988-8380	C+ / 6.0	0.95	4.46	9.88 /74	12.84 /58	10.73 /50	1.52	0.72
SC	AllianzGI US Small-Cap Growth A	AEGAX	C-	(800) 988-8380	C+ / 6.6	6.23	10.99	5.22 /40	15.11 /76	14.44 /82	0.00	1.91
SC	AllianzGI US Small-Cap Growth C	AEGCX	C	(800) 988-8380	C+ / 6.9	6.00	10.50	4.42 /34	14.26 /69	13.61 /74	0.00	2.73
SC	AllianzGI US Small-Cap Growth D	AEGDX	C	(800) 988-8380	B / 7.6	6.22	10.91	5.21 /40	15.12 /76	14.46 /82	0.00	2.00
SC	AllianzGI US Small-Cap Growth Inst	AEMIX	C+	(800) 988-8380	B / 7.8	6.31	11.13	5.49 /42	15.48 /79	14.81 /85	0.00	1.69
SC	AllianzGI US Small-Cap Growth P	AEGPX	C+	(800) 988-8380	B / 7.7	6.22	10.98	5.39 /41	15.36 /78	14.71 /84	0.00	1.74
SC	AllianzGI US Small-Cap Growth R	AEGRX	C	(800) 988-8380	B- / 7.4	6.17	10.83	4.97 /38	14.88 /74	14.20 /79	0.00	2.16
GL	Alpha Defensive Alternatives I	ACDEX	D	(877) 925-7422	E+ / 0.6	-0.41	-2.20	0.13 /16	1.25 / 5	--	2.71	2.44
GL	Alpha Opportunistic Alternatives I	ACOPX	D+	(877) 925-7422	E+ / 0.9	0.00	-2.76	-1.85 /11	3.77 /10	--	2.37	2.51
AA	AlphaCentric Asset Rotation A	ROTAX	U	(844) 223-8637	U /	-3.80	2.58	--	--	--	0.00	N/A
GR	AlphaMark Large Cap Growth Fund	AMLCX	B	(866) 420-3350	B+ / 8.6	3.09	7.31	13.85 /89	16.75 /88	12.75 /66	0.03	1.94
SC	AlphaMark Small Cap Growth Fund	AMSCX	E+	(866) 420-3350	C / 5.1	7.98	6.66	7.52 /59	11.26 /47	14.60 /83	0.00	2.04
SC	AlphaOne Micro Cap Equity I	AOMCX	B	(855) 425-7426	B+ / 8.4	5.57	16.56	10.86 /78	15.71 /81	--	0.00	1.44
SC	AlphaOne Micro Cap Equity Inv	AOMAX	B	(855) 425-7426	B / 8.2	5.53	16.39	10.58 /77	15.45 /79	--	0.00	1.69

● Denotes fund is closed to new investors
* Denotes fund is included in Section II

www.thestreetratings.com

RISK Risk Rating/Pts	3 Year Standard Deviation	Beta	NET ASSETS NAV As of 3/31/15	Total $(Mil)	ASSET Cash %	Stocks %	Bonds %	Other %	Portfolio Turnover Ratio	BULL/BEAR Last Bull Market Return	Last Bear Market Return	FUND MANAGER Manager Quality Pct	Manager Tenure (Years)	MINIMUMS Initial Purch. $	Additional Purch. $	LOADS Front End Load	Back End Load
C+ / 6.9	7.9	0.56	18.16	1	6	65	27	2	69	N/A	N/A	80	4	0	0	0.0	0.0
C+ / 6.9	7.9	0.56	18.34	5	6	65	27	2	69	N/A	N/A	85	4	0	0	0.0	0.0
C / 5.2	8.3	0.78	20.48	5	6	68	23	3	78	47.1	-20.5	11	7	1,000	50	5.5	0.0
C / 5.2	8.3	0.78	20.64	1	6	68	23	3	78	47.3	-20.5	11	7	1,000,000	0	0.0	0.0
C / 5.3	8.3	0.78	20.34	N/A	6	68	23	3	78	43.2	-20.8	8	7	1,000	50	0.0	0.0
C / 5.3	8.3	0.78	20.59	N/A	6	68	23	3	78	46.5	-20.5	11	7	1,000	50	0.0	0.0
C / 5.2	8.3	0.78	20.72	8	6	68	23	3	78	48.6	-20.4	13	7	1,000,000	0	0.0	0.0
C / 5.3	8.3	0.78	20.48	1	6	68	23	3	78	45.4	-20.7	10	7	0	0	0.0	0.0
C / 5.2	8.3	0.78	20.77	8	6	68	23	3	78	49.1	-20.5	13	7	0	0	0.0	0.0
C+ / 6.7	8.4	0.60	17.57	1	6	68	23	3	74	N/A	N/A	81	4	1,000	50	5.5	0.0
C+ / 6.7	8.4	0.60	17.63	N/A	6	68	23	3	74	N/A	N/A	81	4	1,000,000	0	0.0	0.0
C+ / 6.7	8.3	0.60	17.70	2	6	68	23	3	74	N/A	N/A	83	4	1,000,000	0	0.0	0.0
C+ / 6.7	8.4	0.60	17.54	N/A	6	68	23	3	74	N/A	N/A	79	4	0	0	0.0	0.0
C+ / 6.7	8.4	0.60	17.75	5	6	68	23	3	74	N/A	N/A	84	4	0	0	0.0	0.0
C+ / 6.7	4.0	0.28	18.42	6	1	23	73	3	101	22.9	-6.4	64	N/A	1,000	50	5.5	0.0
C+ / 6.7	4.0	0.27	18.65	N/A	1	23	73	3	101	22.8	-6.4	65	N/A	1,000,000	0	0.0	0.0
C+ / 6.7	4.0	0.27	18.23	4	1	23	73	3	101	19.8	-6.7	53	N/A	1,000	50	0.0	0.0
C+ / 6.7	4.0	0.28	18.52	1	1	23	73	3	101	22.5	-6.5	62	N/A	1,000	50	0.0	0.0
C+ / 6.7	4.0	0.28	18.67	7	1	23	73	3	101	24.2	-6.3	68	N/A	1,000,000	0	0.0	0.0
C+ / 6.8	4.0	0.28	19.03	N/A	1	23	73	3	101	21.5	-6.6	59	N/A	0	0	0.0	0.0
C+ / 6.7	4.0	0.28	18.29	9	1	23	73	3	101	24.6	-6.3	69	N/A	0	0	0.0	0.0
U /	N/A	N/A	18.23	40	13	86	0	1	119	N/A	N/A	N/A	2	1,000	50	5.5	0.0
U /	N/A	N/A	18.05	46	13	86	0	1	119	N/A	N/A	N/A	2	1,000	50	0.0	0.0
C- / 3.3	14.0	1.09	56.63	336	9	90	0	1	152	91.4	-22.2	49	N/A	1,000	50	5.5	0.0
C- / 3.4	14.0	1.09	58.73	70	9	90	0	1	152	92.2	-22.2	52	N/A	1,000,000	0	0.0	0.0
D+ / 2.7	14.0	1.09	48.78	1	9	90	0	1	152	86.6	-22.4	38	N/A	1,000	50	0.0	0.0
D+ / 2.7	14.0	1.09	48.76	129	9	90	0	1	152	86.5	-22.4	38	N/A	1,000	50	0.0	0.0
C- / 3.3	14.0	1.09	55.77	164	9	90	0	1	152	91.4	-22.2	49	N/A	1,000	50	0.0	0.0
C- / 3.6	14.0	1.09	60.81	599	9	90	0	1	152	93.9	-22.1	55	N/A	1,000,000	0	0.0	0.0
C- / 3.5	14.0	1.09	60.25	52	9	90	0	1	152	93.2	-22.1	53	N/A	1,000,000	0	0.0	0.0
C / 4.3	16.6	1.18	25.79	50	0	99	0	1	66	132.4	-29.5	63	9	1,000	50	5.5	0.0
C / 4.3	16.6	1.18	25.99	46	0	99	0	1	66	134.3	-29.4	67	9	1,000,000	0	0.0	0.0
C / 4.3	16.6	1.18	25.93	9	0	99	0	1	66	134.0	-29.4	66	9	1,000,000	0	0.0	0.0
C / 4.9	8.3	0.62	14.42	15	1	98	0	1	122	66.6	-15.2	87	6	1,000	50	5.5	0.0
C / 5.0	8.4	0.63	13.42	N/A	1	98	0	1	122	62.3	-15.5	82	6	1,000	50	0.0	0.0
C / 4.9	8.4	0.62	13.24	2	1	98	0	1	122	62.3	-15.5	82	6	1,000	50	0.0	0.0
C / 5.0	8.4	0.63	14.49	1	1	98	0	1	122	66.6	-15.2	86	6	1,000	50	0.0	0.0
C / 5.0	8.4	0.63	15.00	66	1	98	0	1	122	68.6	-15.1	88	6	1,000,000	0	0.0	0.0
C / 5.0	8.3	0.62	14.95	N/A	1	98	0	1	122	68.0	-15.1	88	6	1,000,000	0	0.0	0.0
C / 4.3	14.3	1.02	17.05	4	2	97	0	1	69	102.5	-30.4	48	5	1,000	50	5.5	0.0
C- / 4.1	14.3	1.02	16.42	1	2	97	0	1	69	97.3	-30.6	37	5	1,000	50	0.0	0.0
C / 4.3	14.4	1.02	17.07	N/A	2	97	0	1	69	102.5	-30.4	48	5	1,000	50	0.0	0.0
C / 4.3	14.3	1.02	17.35	35	2	97	0	1	69	104.6	-30.3	52	22	1,000,000	0	0.0	0.0
C / 4.3	14.3	1.02	17.26	N/A	2	97	0	1	69	104.0	-30.3	51	5	1,000,000	0	0.0	0.0
C- / 4.2	14.3	1.02	16.87	N/A	2	97	0	1	69	100.9	-30.5	45	5	0	0	0.0	0.0
B / 8.4	2.9	0.33	9.79	34	24	20	52	4	103	8.7	-4.1	42	4	10,000	100	0.0	0.0
B / 8.7	4.1	0.54	10.15	62	32	40	26	2	72	17.6	-11.1	53	4	10,000	100	0.0	0.0
U /	N/A	N/A	10.12	43	0	0	0	100	0	N/A	N/A	N/A	1	2,500	50	5.8	0.0
C / 4.8	11.0	1.08	16.33	24	0	99	0	1	30	101.8	-19.9	57	7	1,000	100	0.0	1.5
E+ / 0.8	12.9	0.81	12.32	26	6	93	0	1	99	76.4	-24.6	45	7	1,000	100	0.0	1.5
C / 5.5	13.0	0.86	12.13	137	2	97	0	1	75	83.9	-20.7	81	4	250,000	10,000	0.0	2.0
C / 5.5	13.0	0.86	12.03	1	2	97	0	1	75	82.5	-20.8	80	4	2,500	100	0.0	2.0

						PERFORMANCE							
							Total Return % through 3/31/15					Incl. in Returns	
						Perfor-				Annualized			
Fund		Ticker	Overall Investment		Performance	3 Mo	6 Mo	1Yr / Pct	3Yr / Pct	5Yr / Pct	Dividend	Expense
Type	Fund Name	Symbol	Rating	Phone	Rating/Pts						Yield	Ratio
RE	Alpine Cyclical Advantage Proprty I	EUEYX	D+	(888) 785-5578	C- / 3.9	5.16	3.61	4.14 /33	9.75 /38	7.12 /24	2.94	1.53
GL	Alpine Dynamic Dividend A	ADAVX	C	(888) 785-5578	C- / 4.1	5.14	7.83	10.47 /76	10.04 /40	--	5.43	1.69
IN	Alpine Dynamic Dividend Inst	ADVDX	C	(888) 785-5578	C / 5.2	5.20	8.24	10.74 /77	10.39 /42	6.12 /17	5.99	1.44
RE	Alpine Emg Mkts Real Estate A	AEAMX	E+	(888) 785-5578	E / 0.5	0.31	-2.98	3.54 /29	1.41 / 6	--	3.52	2.63
RE	Alpine Emg Mkts Real Estate Inst	AEMEX	E-	(888) 785-5578	E+ / 0.6	0.38	-2.84	3.81 /31	1.66 / 6	2.74 / 5	3.98	2.38
BA	Alpine Equity Income A	ADABX	C-	(888) 785-5578	C- / 3.0	0.51	6.29	10.21 /75	9.09 /34	--	1.30	1.55
BA	Alpine Equity Income Institutional	ADBYX	C+	(888) 785-5578	C- / 4.2	0.85	6.72	10.79 /77	9.47 /36	9.06 /37	1.75	1.30
FS	Alpine Financial Services A	ADAFX	B-	(888) 785-5578	C+ / 6.9	1.89	2.84	0.87 /18	17.98 /94	--	0.00	1.74
FS	Alpine Financial Services Inst	ADFSX	A+	(888) 785-5578	B+ / 8.3	1.95	2.91	1.09 /19	18.28 /95	10.71 /50	0.15	1.49
OT	Alpine Global Infrastructure Fd A	AIAFX	C	(888) 785-5578	C / 4.4	2.37	1.53	4.80 /37	12.83 /58	--	3.21	1.46
GL	Alpine Global Infrastructure Inst	AIFRX	C+	(888) 785-5578	C / 5.5	2.48	1.66	5.05 /39	13.12 /60	12.52 /64	3.63	1.21
RE	Alpine Intl Real Estate A	EGALX	E+	(888) 785-5578	E / 0.3	0.41	-5.82	-5.09 / 5	0.62 / 5	--	0.00	1.87
RE	Alpine Intl Real Estate Inst	EGLRX	E	(888) 785-5578	E / 0.5	0.45	-5.67	-4.83 / 6	0.91 / 5	1.41 / 4	0.00	1.62
RE	Alpine Realty Inc and Growth A	AIAGX	B	(888) 785-5578	A- / 9.2	5.56	21.42	25.74 /98	14.31 /69	--	2.86	1.72
RE	Alpine Realty Inc and Growth Inst	AIGYX	B-	(888) 785-5578	A+ / 9.6	5.62	21.54	26.09 /98	14.59 /72	16.26 /94	3.25	1.47
GR	Alpine Small Cap A	ADIAX	E+	(888) 785-5578	D- / 1.5	8.06	9.96	-1.51 /11	6.34 /18	--	0.00	1.87
GR	Alpine Small Cap Institutional	ADINX	E+	(888) 785-5578	D+ / 2.3	8.14	10.02	-1.24 /12	6.62 /20	9.49 /40	0.00	1.62
GR	Alpine Transformations A	ADATX	C-	(888) 785-5578	C- / 4.1	4.09	10.43	6.95 /55	10.85 /45	--	0.00	2.14
MC	Alpine Transformations Inst	ADTRX	C-	(888) 785-5578	C / 5.1	4.12	10.64	7.25 /57	11.14 /46	13.19 /70	0.00	1.89
OT	ALPS CoreComm Mgt CompComm	JCRAX	E-	(866) 759-5679	E- / 0.1	-5.48	-19.72	-25.38 / 0	-11.24 / 1	--	0.00	1.46
OT	ALPS CoreComm Mgt CompComm	JCRCX	E-	(866) 759-5679	E- / 0.1	-5.58	-19.96	-25.83 / 0	-11.79 / 1	--	0.00	2.07
OT	ALPS CoreComm Mgt CompComm	JCRIX	E-	(866) 759-5679	E- / 0.1	-5.38	-19.57	-25.09 / 0	-10.99 / 1	--	0.58	1.16
FO	ALPS/Kotak India Growth A	INDAX	C	(866) 759-5679	A+ / 9.8	5.42	13.10	40.04 /99	17.84 /94	--	1.19	5.02
FO	ALPS/Kotak India Growth C	INFCX	C	(866) 759-5679	A+ / 9.8	5.31	12.77	39.04 /99	17.09 /90	--	0.81	5.57
FO	ALPS/Kotak India Growth I	INDIX	C	(866) 759-5679	A+ / 9.8	5.43	13.35	40.56 /99	18.21 /95	--	0.91	4.49
FS	ALPS/Red Rocks Listed Priv Eq A	LPEFX	C+	(866) 759-5679	C+ / 6.5	3.49	5.34	0.26 /16	17.18 /91	12.44 /64	3.01	2.35
FS	ALPS/Red Rocks Listed Priv Eq C	LPFCX	C+	(866) 759-5679	C+ / 6.9	3.28	4.77	-0.40 /14	16.38 /86	--	3.06	2.85
FS	ALPS/Red Rocks Listed Priv Eq I	LPEIX	B+	(866) 759-5679	B / 7.8	3.46	5.32	0.58 /17	17.53 /92	12.72 /66	3.33	1.95
FS	ALPS/Red Rocks Listed Priv Eq R	LPERX	B+	(866) 759-5679	B / 7.6	3.44	5.30	0.25 /16	17.37 /92	12.30 /62	3.73	2.33
GI	ALPS/WMC Research Value A	AMWYX	B	(866) 759-5679	B- / 7.1	1.12	5.41	10.23 /75	16.39 /86	13.19 /70	0.44	1.48
GI	ALPS/WMC Research Value C	AMWCX	B	(866) 759-5679	B / 7.6	1.05	5.12	9.52 /72	15.59 /80	--	0.36	2.24
GI	ALPS/WMC Research Value I	AMWIX	B+	(866) 759-5679	B+ / 8.4	1.19	5.57	10.53 /76	16.68 /88	13.46 /72	0.49	1.23
GL	Altegris Equity Long Short I	ELSIX	U	(877) 772-5838	U /	3.71	5.43	6.70 /53	--	--	0.00	3.79
GL	Altegris Futures Evolution Strat C	EVOCX	A	(877) 772-5838	B+ / 8.8	7.53	21.47	33.41 /99	9.41 /36	--	9.80	2.83
IN	Altegris Macro Strategy A	MCRAX	D-	(877) 772-5838	E / 0.4	4.33	11.24	11.79 /82	-2.32 / 3	--	0.00	2.41
IN	Altegris Macro Strategy C	MCRCX	D-	(877) 772-5838	E / 0.5	4.07	10.84	10.98 /78	-3.03 / 2	--	0.00	3.16
IN	Altegris Macro Strategy I	MCRIX	D-	(877) 772-5838	E+ / 0.6	4.41	11.39	12.08 /83	-2.06 / 3	--	0.00	2.16
IN	Altegris Macro Strategy N	MCRNX	D-	(877) 772-5838	E+ / 0.6	4.33	11.38	11.79 /82	-2.29 / 3	--	0.00	2.41
IN	Altegris Managed Futures Strategy A	MFTAX	D	(877) 772-5838	D- / 1.5	5.19	10.46	15.75 /93	2.41 / 7	--	0.00	2.01
IN	Altegris Managed Futures Strategy C	MFTCX	D+	(877) 772-5838	D / 1.8	4.91	9.96	14.84 /91	1.61 / 6	--	0.00	2.76
IN	Altegris Managed Futures Strategy I	MFTIX	C-	(877) 772-5838	D+ / 2.4	5.24	10.57	16.08 /93	2.64 / 7	--	0.00	1.76
GL	Altegris Multi Strat Alternative N	MULNX	U	(877) 772-5838	U /	3.24	5.34	7.79 /61	--	--	1.56	21.22
RE	Altegris/AACA RE Lng Sh I	RAAIX	U	(877) 772-5838	U /	4.73	15.66	24.76 /98	--	--	0.59	N/A
SC	Am Beacon Stephens Small Cap Gro	SPWAX	D+	(800) 658-5811	C / 4.6	3.84	8.58	2.10 /22	12.54 /56	--	0.00	1.51
SC	Am Beacon Stephens Small Cap Gro	SPWCX	D+	(800) 658-5811	C / 5.0	3.60	8.15	1.32 /19	11.71 /50	--	0.00	2.26
SC	Am Beacon Stephens Small Cap Gro	SPWYX	C-	(800) 658-5811	C+ / 5.9	3.87	8.73	2.45 /24	13.00 /60	15.13 /88	0.00	1.21
EM	Amana Developing World Investor	AMDWX	E+	(800) 732-6262	E / 0.3	-3.67	-6.39	-3.39 / 8	-0.99 / 3	0.03 / 2	0.20	1.59
GR	Amana Growth Institutional	AMIGX	U	(800) 732-6262	U /	1.60	8.34	12.27 /84	--	--	0.49	0.87
GR	Amana Growth Investor	AMAGX	C+	(800) 732-6262	C+ / 6.0	1.58	8.25	12.04 /83	12.26 /54	11.44 /56	0.34	1.10
IN	Amana Income Institutional	AMINX	U	(800) 732-6262	U /	-0.13	4.45	7.82 /61	--	--	1.74	0.90
IN	Amana Income Investor	AMANX	B-	(800) 732-6262	C+ / 6.0	-0.19	4.32	7.54 /59	13.40 /63	11.55 /57	1.49	1.15
GR	Amer Beacon Bridgeway LC Val A	BWLAX	A+	(800) 658-5811	B+ / 8.9	1.73	6.27	12.04 /83	19.18 /97	--	0.45	1.29

● Denotes fund is closed to new investors
* Denotes fund is included in Section II

www.thestreetratings.com

RISK Risk Rating/Pts	3 Year Standard Deviation	Beta	NET ASSETS NAV As of 3/31/15	Total $(Mil)	ASSET Cash %	Stocks %	Bonds %	Other %	Portfolio Turnover Ratio	BULL / BEAR Last Bull Market Return	Last Bear Market Return	FUND MANAGER Manager Quality Pct	Manager Tenure (Years)	MINIMUMS Initial Purch. $	Additional Purch. $	LOADS Front End Load	Back End Load
C /5.3	14.3	0.58	25.66	58	0	100	0	0	42	69.2	-28.0	82	22	1,000,000	0	0.0	1.0
B- /7.3	10.6	0.71	4.01	4	0	100	0	0	81	N/A	N/A	89	4	2,500	0	5.5	1.0
C+ /6.3	10.5	1.02	4.01	200	0	100	0	0	81	58.7	-29.1	9	4	1,000,000	0	0.0	1.0
C+ /6.0	16.9	0.65	16.03	1	1	97	0	2	117	N/A	N/A	4	7	2,500	0	5.5	1.0
D+ /2.9	17.0	0.65	16.05	5	1	97	0	2	117	37.2	-27.9	5	7	1,000,000	0	0.0	1.0
B- /7.8	7.6	1.29	14.14	N/A	10	68	20	2	59	N/A	N/A	13	14	2,500	0	5.5	1.0
B /8.2	7.5	1.27	14.17	80	10	68	20	2	59	57.0	-13.4	16	14	1,000,000	0	0.0	1.0
B- /7.5	10.8	0.80	13.51	7	11	87	0	2	131	N/A	N/A	91	10	2,500	0	5.5	1.0
B- /7.4	10.7	0.80	13.59	22	11	87	0	2	131	103.9	-28.2	91	10	1,000,000	0	0.0	1.0
B- /7.3	10.3	0.84	19.59	26	5	94	0	1	109	N/A	N/A	61	7	2,500	0	5.5	1.0
C+ /6.6	10.3	0.70	19.62	189	5	94	0	1	109	77.4	-20.7	95	7	1,000,000	0	0.0	1.0
C+ /5.6	16.5	0.66	22.17	N/A	1	98	0	1	23	N/A	N/A	3	26	2,500	0	5.5	1.0
C /4.6	16.5	0.66	22.28	141	1	98	0	1	23	29.7	-31.6	3	26	1,000,000	0	0.0	1.0
C /4.9	13.4	1.07	23.04	3	0	100	0	0	32	N/A	N/A	56	16	2,500	0	5.5	1.0
C- /3.6	13.4	1.07	23.06	118	0	100	0	0	32	90.9	-18.0	60	16	1,000,000	0	0.0	1.0
C /4.7	16.2	1.25	15.02	1	0	99	0	1	171	N/A	N/A	1	1	2,500	0	5.5	1.0
C- /3.5	16.1	1.24	15.15	14	0	99	0	1	171	53.9	-21.2	1	1	1,000,000	0	0.0	1.0
C+ /6.2	13.4	1.20	15.00	N/A	10	89	0	1	50	N/A	N/A	3	8	2,500	0	5.5	1.0
C /5.1	13.5	1.09	15.15	8	10	89	0	1	50	74.8	-20.5	5	8	1,000,000	0	0.0	1.0
C- /3.4	13.4	0.93	7.94	35	10	38	51	1	28	-17.5	-22.5	0	5	2,500	0	5.5	2.0
C- /3.4	13.4	0.93	7.78	9	10	38	51	1	28	-19.2	-22.6	0	5	2,500	0	0.0	2.0
C- /3.4	13.3	0.93	7.92	372	10	38	51	1	28	-16.7	-22.3	0	5	1,000,000	0	0.0	2.0
D /1.9	23.0	1.01	13.41	8	1	98	0	1	65	76.0	-20.6	96	4	2,500	0	5.5	2.0
D /1.9	23.0	1.01	13.10	2	1	98	0	1	65	72.3	-20.9	96	4	2,500	0	0.0	2.0
D /1.9	23.0	1.01	13.58	13	1	98	0	1	65	78.3	-20.6	97	4	1,000,000	0	0.0	2.0
C+ /6.7	12.5	0.85	6.82	215	16	83	0	1	40	93.4	-30.8	86	8	2,500	0	5.5	2.0
C+ /6.7	12.4	0.84	6.62	18	16	83	0	1	40	88.9	-31.0	82	8	2,500	0	0.0	2.0
C+ /6.7	12.5	0.85	6.88	271	16	83	0	1	40	95.5	-30.8	87	8	1,000,000	0	0.0	2.0
C+ /6.7	12.6	0.85	6.02	2	16	83	0	1	40	93.4	-30.9	86	8	0	0	0.0	2.0
C+ /6.2	10.4	1.07	11.71	59	0	99	0	1	19	99.3	-20.5	56	6	2,500	0	5.5	0.0
C+ /6.2	10.4	1.07	11.51	2	0	99	0	1	19	94.5	-20.8	44	6	2,500	0	0.0	0.0
C+ /6.3	10.4	1.07	11.87	45	0	99	0	1	19	101.0	-20.4	60	6	1,000,000	0	0.0	0.0
U /	N/A	N/A	11.18	120	63	36	0	1	432	N/A	N/A	N/A	3	1,000,000	250	0.0	1.0
C+ /6.7	9.9	0.09	11.67	19	28	0	71	1	97	N/A	N/A	97	4	5,000	250	0.0	1.0
B- /7.0	5.9	-0.23	8.91	5	34	0	65	1	178	-12.4	N/A	77	4	2,500	250	5.8	1.0
C+ /6.8	6.0	-0.23	8.69	2	34	0	65	1	178	N/A	N/A	70	4	5,000	250	0.0	1.0
B- /7.1	6.0	-0.23	9.00	51	34	0	65	1	178	-11.6	N/A	79	4	1,000,000	250	0.0	1.0
B- /7.0	6.0	-0.23	8.91	30	34	0	65	1	178	-12.4	N/A	77	4	2,500	250	0.0	1.0
B- /7.6	7.4	0.09	10.14	101	32	0	67	1	346	1.0	-4.2	76	5	2,500	250	5.8	1.0
B- /7.5	7.4	0.10	9.83	19	32	0	67	1	346	-1.5	-4.5	69	5	5,000	250	0.0	1.0
B- /7.6	7.4	0.10	10.25	134	32	0	67	1	346	1.9	-4.1	78	5	1,000,000	250	0.0	1.0
U /	N/A	N/A	10.50	34	36	18	37	9	21	N/A	N/A	N/A	2	2,500	250	0.0	1.0
U /	N/A	N/A	12.77	97	0	100	0	0	0	N/A	N/A	N/A	N/A	1,000,000	250	0.0	1.0
C /4.8	14.0	0.95	16.21	9	0	100	0	0	39	N/A	N/A	30	10	2,500	50	5.8	0.0
C /4.8	14.1	0.95	15.81	3	0	100	0	0	39	N/A	N/A	22	10	1,000	50	0.0	0.0
C /4.8	14.0	0.95	17.19	176	0	100	0	0	39	84.8	-21.9	35	10	100,000	50	0.0	0.0
C+ /6.0	10.0	0.65	10.24	21	0	98	1	1	11	10.0	-12.3	45	6	250	25	0.0	0.0
U /	N/A	N/A	34.82	161	0	100	0	0	1	N/A	N/A	N/A	21	100,000	25	0.0	0.0
C+ /6.7	9.9	0.97	34.80	1,916	0	100	0	0	1	76.4	-15.6	25	21	250	25	0.0	0.0
U /	N/A	N/A	46.54	139	0	100	0	0	1	N/A	N/A	N/A	25	100,000	25	0.0	0.0
B- /7.4	9.5	0.95	46.55	1,405	0	100	0	0	1	75.6	-15.5	42	25	250	25	0.0	0.0
B- /7.9	9.8	0.99	24.07	115	3	96	0	1	38	N/A	N/A	88	12	2,500	50	5.8	0.0

					PERFORMANCE						
	99 Pct = Best					Total Return % through 3/31/15					Incl. in Returns
	0 Pct = Worst		**Overall**		**Perfor-**				Annualized		Dividend / Expense
Fund		Ticker	**Investment**		**mance**						
Type	Fund Name	Symbol	**Rating**	Phone	**Rating/Pts**	3 Mo	6 Mo	1Yr / Pct	3Yr / Pct	5Yr / Pct	Yield	Ratio
GR	Amer Beacon Bridgeway LC Val C	BWLCX	A+	(800) 658-5811	A- / 9.2	1.55	5.85	11.18 /79	18.37 /95	--	0.29	2.04
GR	Amer Beacon Bridgeway LC Val Inst	BRLVX	A+	(800) 658-5811	A+ / 9.6	1.80	6.43	12.45 /85	19.75 /98	15.85 /92	0.68	1.02
GR	Amer Beacon Bridgeway LC Val Inv	BWLIX	A+	(800) 658-5811	A / 9.5	1.72	6.26	12.11 /83	19.35 /97	--	0.41	1.10
GR	Amer Beacon Bridgeway LC Val Y	BWLYX	A+	(800) 658-5811	A+ / 9.6	1.80	6.44	12.42 /84	19.65 /97	--	0.68	0.95
IN	AmericaFirst Absolute Return A	ABRFX	D	(877) 217-8363	D- / 1.5	0.00	4.82	5.09 /39	6.59 /19	4.45 /10	0.00	3.09
IN	AmericaFirst Absolute Return I	ABRWX	D+	(877) 217-8363	D+ / 2.5	0.24	5.24	5.95 /46	7.23 /23	--	0.00	2.60
IN	AmericaFirst Absolute Return U	ABRUX	D	(877) 217-8363	D- / 1.5	-0.08	4.57	4.57 /36	6.06 /17	3.92 / 8	0.00	3.59
GL	AmericaFirst Defensive Growth A	DGQAX	C	(877) 217-8363	C+ / 5.6	4.01	7.04	9.85 /74	13.49 /63	--	0.00	3.60
GL	AmericaFirst Defensive Growth I	DGQIX	B-	(877) 217-8363	B- / 7.3	4.30	7.76	11.49 /80	14.50 /71	--	0.00	3.10
GL	AmericaFirst Defensive Growth U	DGQUX	C	(877) 217-8363	C+ / 5.6	3.83	6.75	9.24 /71	12.89 /59	--	0.00	4.10
GI	AmericaFirst Income Trends A	AFPAX	D-	(877) 217-8363	E+ / 0.9	2.40	0.55	-0.52 /14	4.87 /13	--	7.18	2.47
GI	AmericaFirst Income Trends I	AFPIX	D-	(877) 217-8363	D- / 1.4	2.63	0.92	0.32 /17	5.55 /15	--	7.95	1.98
GI	AmericaFirst Income Trends U	AFPUX	D-	(877) 217-8363	E+ / 0.9	2.27	0.30	-1.00 /13	4.40 /11	--	6.82	2.97
GI	AmericaFirst Quantitative Strgy A	AFIAX	D	(877) 217-8363	D / 2.2	-0.64	-0.22	-1.41 /12	9.51 /36	9.27 /39	1.93	1.82
GI	AmericaFirst Quantitative Strgy C	AFISX	D	(877) 217-8363	D / 2.2	-0.69	-0.42	-1.95 /10	8.72 /31	8.50 /33	1.45	2.56
BA	American Beacon Balanced A	ABFAX	C+	(800) 658-5811	C- / 3.8	1.15	3.50	7.11 /56	11.13 /46	--	2.18	0.97
BA	American Beacon Balanced Adv	ABLSX	B-	(800) 658-5811	C / 4.7	1.16	3.48	7.04 /55	11.12 /46	10.03 /45	2.02	1.08
BA	American Beacon Balanced AMR	AABNX	B	(800) 658-5811	C / 5.3	1.38	3.86	7.86 /62	11.96 /52	10.88 /52	2.81	0.33
BA	American Beacon Balanced C	ABCCX	C+	(800) 658-5811	C- / 4.2	1.01	3.17	6.31 /49	10.31 /41	--	1.51	1.73
BA	American Beacon Balanced Inst	AADBX	B	(800) 658-5811	C / 5.1	1.29	3.73	7.51 /59	11.65 /50	10.57 /49	2.36	0.59
BA	American Beacon Balanced Inv	AABPX	B-	(800) 658-5811	C / 4.9	1.22	3.51	7.17 /56	11.28 /47	10.21 /46	2.31	0.93
BA	American Beacon Balanced Y	ACBYX	B-	(800) 658-5811	C / 5.0	1.29	3.64	7.41 /58	11.54 /49	10.46 /48	2.34	0.68
EM	American Beacon Emerg Mkts A	AEMAX	E-	(800) 658-5811	E- / 0.2	-0.98	-9.92	-5.25 / 5	-0.98 / 3	--	0.18	1.80
EM	American Beacon Emerg Mkts AMR	AAMRX	E	(800) 658-5811	E / 0.3	-0.86	-9.76	-4.90 / 6	-0.53 / 4	0.40 / 3	0.42	1.39
EM	American Beacon Emerg Mkts C	AEMCX	E-	(800) 658-5811	E / 0.3	-1.09	-10.19	-5.91 / 5	-1.71 / 3	--	0.00	2.55
EM	American Beacon Emerg Mkts Inst	AEMFX	E	(800) 658-5811	E / 0.3	-0.86	-9.72	-4.89 / 6	-0.57 / 4	0.40 / 3	0.38	1.44
EM	American Beacon Emerg Mkts	AAEPX	E	(800) 658-5811	E / 0.3	-0.98	-9.92	-5.34 / 5	-1.01 / 3	-0.03 / 2	0.27	1.89
EM	American Beacon Emerg Mkts Y	ACEYX	E	(800) 658-5811	E / 0.3	-0.95	-9.84	-5.04 / 5	-0.72 / 4	0.24 / 3	0.29	1.55
EM	American Beacon Glb Ev FM Inc Y	AGEYX	U	(800) 658-5811	U /	0.26	-2.20	1.88 /21	--	--	6.87	1.95
GR	American Beacon Holland LC Gr A	LHGAX	C-	(800) 658-5811	C / 5.5	4.02	6.04	11.81 /82	12.99 /60	13.38 /72	0.00	1.30
GR	American Beacon Holland LC Gr C	LHGCX	C+	(800) 658-5811	C+ / 5.9	3.84	5.62	10.94 /78	12.14 /53	--	0.00	2.05
GR	American Beacon Holland LC Gr Inst	LHGIX	C+	(800) 658-5811	C+ / 6.8	4.13	6.23	12.26 /84	13.52 /64	13.79 /76	0.00	0.89
GI	American Beacon Holland LC Gr Inv	LHGFX	C	(800) 658-5811	C+ / 6.5	4.03	6.03	11.85 /82	13.11 /60	13.47 /73	0.00	1.27
GR	American Beacon Holland LC Gr Y	LHGYX	C+	(800) 658-5811	C+ / 6.7	4.07	6.06	12.00 /82	13.34 /62	--	0.00	0.99
FO	American Beacon Intl Eq A	AIEAX	D-	(800) 658-5811	D / 2.2	5.20	-0.20	-2.71 / 9	9.26 /35	--	2.23	1.09
FO	American Beacon Intl Eq Adv	AAISX	D	(800) 658-5811	C- / 3.0	5.19	-0.26	-2.81 / 9	9.25 /35	6.16 /18	2.30	1.20
FO	American Beacon Intl Eq AMR	AAIAX	D	(800) 658-5811	C- / 3.3	5.32	0.10	-2.06 /10	10.11 /40	7.00 /23	2.98	0.43
FO	American Beacon Intl Eq C	AILCX	D	(800) 658-5811	D+ / 2.6	4.98	-0.60	-3.46 / 8	8.47 /30	--	1.82	1.84
FO	American Beacon Intl Eq Index Inst	AIIIX	D	(800) 658-5811	D+ / 2.8	5.24	0.48	-1.88 /11	8.53 /30	5.88 /16	3.86	0.21
FO	American Beacon Intl Eq Inst	AAIEX	D	(800) 658-5811	C- / 3.4	5.27	-0.04	-2.34 /10	9.80 /38	6.72 /21	2.70	0.73
FO	American Beacon Intl Eq Inv	AAIPX	D	(800) 658-5811	C- / 3.1	5.26	-0.18	-2.64 / 9	9.42 /36	6.35 /19	2.38	1.06
FO	American Beacon Intl Eq Ret	ABIRX	D	(800) 658-5811	D+ / 2.9	5.14	-0.41	-3.07 / 9	9.00 /33	5.98 /17	1.89	1.47
FO	American Beacon Intl Eq Y	ABEYX	D	(800) 658-5811	C- / 3.3	5.30	-0.09	-2.40 /10	9.68 /37	6.60 /21	2.65	0.83
GR	American Beacon Lg Cap Val A	ALVAX	C+	(800) 658-5811	C+ / 6.1	0.48	3.42	7.41 /58	15.41 /78	--	1.98	0.98
GR	American Beacon Lg Cap Val AMR	AAGAX	B+	(800) 658-5811	B / 7.8	0.63	3.75	8.14 /64	16.27 /85	13.68 /75	2.44	0.33
GR	American Beacon Lg Cap Val C	ALVCX	C+	(800) 658-5811	C+ / 6.5	0.30	3.03	6.59 /52	14.51 /71	--	1.43	1.73
GR	American Beacon Lg Cap Val Inst	AADEX	B+	(800) 658-5811	B / 7.6	0.58	3.62	7.89 /62	15.97 /83	13.38 /72	2.14	0.59
GR	American Beacon Lg Cap Val	AAGPX	B	(800) 658-5811	B- / 7.2	0.47	3.46	7.47 /59	15.55 /80	12.97 /68	1.94	0.94
GR	American Beacon Lg Cap Val Ret	ALCRX	C+	(800) 658-5811	C+ / 6.9	0.41	3.25	7.10 /56	15.08 /75	12.51 /64	1.84	1.33
GR	American Beacon Lg Cap Val Svc	AVASX	B	(800) 658-5811	B- / 7.1	0.44	3.38	7.35 /58	15.40 /78	12.82 /67	1.95	1.08
GR	American Beacon Lg Cap Val Y	ABLYX	B+	(800) 658-5811	B- / 7.5	0.55	3.60	7.78 /61	15.87 /82	13.28 /71	2.11	0.68
IN	American Beacon London Co I Eq A	ABCAX	U	(800) 658-5811	U /	1.71	7.62	15.05 /92	--	--	1.60	1.29

RISK			NET ASSETS		ASSET					BULL / BEAR		FUND MANAGER		MINIMUMS		LOADS	
	3 Year		NAV						Portfolio	Last Bull	Last Bear	Manager	Manager	Initial	Additional	Front	Back
Risk Rating/Pts	Standard Deviation	Beta	As of 3/31/15	Total $(Mil)	Cash %	Stocks %	Bonds %	Other %	Turnover Ratio	Market Return	Market Return	Quality Pct	Tenure (Years)	Purch. $	Purch. $	End Load	End Load
B- / 7.9	9.8	0.99	23.63	50	3	96	0	1	38	N/A	N/A	85	12	1,000	50	0.0	0.0
B- / 7.9	9.8	0.99	24.32	400	3	96	0	1	38	114.4	-18.4	89	12	250,000	50	0.0	0.0
B- / 7.9	9.8	0.99	24.18	766	3	96	0	1	38	N/A	N/A	88	12	2,500	50	0.0	0.0
B- / 7.9	9.8	0.99	24.27	192	3	96	0	1	38	N/A	N/A	89	12	100,000	50	0.0	0.0
C+ / 6.7	12.3	0.94	12.18	8	1	98	0	1	375	40.8	-19.8	3	5	1,000	50	5.0	1.0
C+ / 6.7	12.3	0.94	12.46	1	1	98	0	1	375	43.5	-19.6	4	5	1,000,000	50	0.0	1.0
C+ / 6.6	12.3	0.94	11.90	7	1	98	0	1	375	38.3	-20.0	3	5	1,000	50	2.5	1.0
C+ / 5.9	9.8	0.39	11.94	18	16	81	1	2	587	62.6	N/A	98	4	1,000	50	5.0	1.0
C+ / 6.0	9.8	0.39	12.38	35	16	81	1	2	587	67.5	N/A	98	4	1,000,000	50	0.0	1.0
C+ / 5.8	9.8	0.39	11.65	13	16	81	1	2	587	59.7	N/A	97	4	1,000	50	2.5	1.0
C+ / 6.2	5.9	0.45	8.53	13	20	23	55	2	336	27.9	-16.3	36	5	1,000	50	4.0	1.0
C+ / 6.3	5.8	0.45	8.58	7	20	23	55	2	336	30.4	-16.0	47	5	1,000,000	50	0.0	1.0
C+ / 6.2	5.9	0.45	8.53	12	20	23	55	2	336	25.9	-16.4	31	5	1,000	50	2.0	1.0
C+ / 6.9	8.5	0.72	6.10	35	13	77	9	1	307	50.3	-12.7	41	8	1,000	50	4.0	1.0
C+ / 6.8	8.5	0.71	6.05	35	13	77	9	1	307	46.4	-13.0	33	8	1,000	50	1.0	1.0
B / 8.2	6.5	1.10	14.90	31	7	57	34	2	34	64.1	-11.2	55	28	2,500	50	5.8	0.0
B / 8.3	6.5	1.10	15.67	16	7	57	34	2	34	64.2	-11.2	55	28	2,500	50	0.0	0.0
B / 8.3	6.5	1.10	15.48	719	7	57	34	2	34	68.3	-11.0	66	28	0	0	0.0	0.0
B / 8.2	6.6	1.11	15.05	43	7	57	34	2	34	60.1	-11.5	42	28	1,000	50	0.0	0.0
B / 8.3	6.5	1.11	16.47	82	7	57	34	2	34	66.9	-11.1	62	28	250,000	50	0.0	0.0
B / 8.2	6.5	1.10	14.93	169	7	57	34	2	34	65.0	-11.2	57	28	2,500	50	0.0	0.0
B / 8.3	6.5	1.10	16.51	46	7	57	34	2	34	66.2	-11.0	61	28	100,000	50	0.0	0.0
C- / 3.5	14.6	1.04	10.14	1	7	92	0	1	51	19.3	-27.5	42	15	2,500	50	5.8	2.0
C- / 3.6	14.7	1.05	10.43	103	7	92	0	1	51	21.1	-27.4	49	15	0	0	0.0	2.0
C- / 3.5	14.7	1.05	10.02	N/A	7	92	0	1	51	16.3	-27.7	31	15	1,000	50	0.0	2.0
C- / 3.6	14.6	1.04	10.34	10	7	92	0	1	51	21.0	-27.3	48	15	250,000	50	0.0	2.0
C- / 3.5	14.7	1.05	10.13	7	7	92	0	1	51	19.2	-27.4	41	15	2,500	50	0.0	2.0
C- / 3.6	14.6	1.04	10.39	1	7	92	0	1	51	20.2	-27.3	46	15	100,000	50	0.0	2.0
U /	N/A	N/A	9.60	140	0	0	0	100	0	N/A	N/A	N/A	1	100,000	50	0.0	2.0
C / 5.3	11.0	1.07	26.41	1	2	97	0	1	29	82.6	-14.3	18	19	2,500	50	5.8	0.0
C+ / 6.5	11.0	1.06	25.70	1	2	97	0	1	29	N/A	N/A	13	19	1,000	50	0.0	0.0
C / 5.3	11.0	1.07	26.95	19	2	97	0	1	29	85.3	-14.2	23	19	250,000	50	0.0	0.0
C / 5.3	11.0	1.06	26.60	82	2	97	0	1	29	83.3	-14.3	19	19	2,500	50	0.0	0.0
C+ / 6.5	11.0	1.06	26.84	N/A	2	97	0	1	29	N/A	N/A	21	19	100,000	50	0.0	0.0
C+ / 5.7	13.5	1.01	19.22	10	6	93	0	1	23	55.1	-25.2	63	14	2,500	50	5.8	0.0
C+ / 5.7	13.5	1.01	19.66	11	6	93	0	1	23	54.8	-25.2	63	14	2,500	50	0.0	0.0
C+ / 5.7	13.5	1.01	19.40	446	6	93	0	1	23	59.2	-25.0	72	14	0	0	0.0	2.0
C+ / 5.7	13.6	1.01	18.77	3	6	93	0	1	23	51.3	-25.5	51	14	1,000	50	0.0	0.0
C / 5.5	13.3	1.01	10.85	589	3	96	0	1	8	50.5	-23.4	53	4	250,000	0	0.0	0.0
C+ / 5.7	13.5	1.01	19.37	1,024	6	93	0	1	23	57.8	-25.1	69	14	250,000	50	0.0	0.0
C+ / 5.7	13.6	1.01	19.22	374	6	93	0	1	23	55.8	-25.2	65	14	2,500	50	0.0	0.0
C+ / 5.8	13.6	1.01	20.66	1	6	93	0	1	23	53.9	-25.3	59	14	2,500	50	0.0	0.0
C+ / 5.7	13.5	1.01	20.07	572	6	93	0	1	23	57.2	-25.1	68	14	100,000	50	0.0	0.0
C+ / 6.6	10.6	1.08	27.42	38	5	94	0	1	29	100.1	-19.7	41	28	2,500	50	5.8	0.0
C+ / 6.6	10.6	1.07	28.92	791	5	94	0	1	29	105.5	-19.5	53	28	0	0	0.0	0.0
C+ / 6.7	10.6	1.07	27.18	12	5	94	0	1	29	94.9	-19.9	31	28	1,000	50	0.0	0.0
C+ / 6.7	10.6	1.07	29.29	6,188	5	94	0	1	29	103.5	-19.5	49	28	250,000	50	0.0	0.0
C+ / 6.6	10.6	1.08	27.60	3,877	5	94	0	1	29	101.1	-19.7	43	28	2,500	50	0.0	0.0
C+ / 6.6	10.6	1.08	26.82	11	5	94	0	1	29	98.2	-19.8	37	28	2,500	50	0.0	0.0
C+ / 6.6	10.6	1.08	27.32	158	5	94	0	1	29	100.3	-19.7	40	28	2,500	50	0.0	0.0
C+ / 6.7	10.6	1.07	29.12	444	5	94	0	1	29	103.0	-19.6	48	28	100,000	50	0.0	0.0
U /	N/A	N/A	14.68	67	3	96	0	1	10	N/A	N/A	N/A	3	2,500	50	5.8	0.0

Fund Type	Fund Name	Ticker Symbol	Overall Investment Rating	Phone	Performance Rating/Pts	3 Mo	6 Mo	1Yr / Pct	3Yr / Pct	5Yr / Pct	Dividend Yield	Expense Ratio
						Total Return % through 3/31/15			Annualized		**Incl. in Returns**	
IN	American Beacon London Co I Eq C	ABECX	U	(800) 658-5811	U /	1.55	7.23	14.21 /90	--	--	1.09	2.03
IN	American Beacon London Co I Eq	ABCIX	U	(800) 658-5811	U /	1.78	7.82	15.54 /93	--	--	2.06	0.83
IN	American Beacon London Co I Eq Y	ABCYX	U	(800) 658-5811	U /	1.84	7.82	15.52 /93	--	--	1.99	0.90
MC	American Beacon MidCap Val A	ABMAX	B+	(800) 658-5811	B- / 7.5	2.86	8.04	8.27 /65	16.93 /89	--	0.35	1.29
MC	American Beacon MidCap Val AMR	AMDIX	A	(800) 658-5811	B+ / 8.8	3.00	8.43	9.03 /69	17.78 /93	15.29 /89	0.81	0.67
MC	American Beacon MidCap Val C	AMCCX	B+	(800) 658-5811	B / 8.0	2.71	7.67	7.44 /59	16.07 /84	--	0.00	2.08
MC	American Beacon MidCap Val F	AMCSX	A	(800) 658-5811	B+ / 8.5	2.79	7.93	8.09 /63	16.86 /89	14.46 /82	0.48	1.42
MC	American Beacon MidCap Val Inst	AACIX	A+	(800) 658-5811	B+ / 8.9	2.94	8.24	8.69 /67	17.47 /92	15.04 /87	0.63	0.91
MC	American Beacon MidCap Val	AMPAX	A	(800) 658-5811	B+ / 8.7	2.84	8.12	8.49 /66	17.19 /91	14.92 /86	0.58	1.15
MC	American Beacon MidCap Val Y	ACMYX	A+	(800) 658-5811	B+ / 8.9	2.96	8.23	8.69 /67	17.42 /92	14.97 /87	0.64	1.00
IX	American Beacon S&P 500 Idx Inv	AAFPX	A+	(800) 658-5811	B / 7.7	0.79	5.59	12.03 /83	15.43 /78	13.78 /76	1.33	0.60
IX	American Beacon S&P 500 Inst	AASPX	A+	(800) 658-5811	B / 8.1	0.89	5.83	12.54 /85	15.90 /82	14.28 /80	1.72	0.14
GL	American Beacon SGA Global Gro	SGAGX	D+	(800) 658-5811	C- / 3.5	4.12	6.52	7.38 /58	8.13 /28	--	0.23	5.29
SC	● American Beacon Sm Cap Index Inst	ASCIX	B+	(800) 658-5811	B+ / 8.7	4.41	14.61	8.32 /65	16.33 /86	14.58 /83	1.57	0.23
SC	American Beacon Sm Cap Val A	ABSAX	C	(800) 658-5811	C+ / 6.6	3.04	10.80	5.75 /44	15.57 /80	--	0.20	1.23
SC	American Beacon Sm Cap Val Adv	AASSX	C+	(800) 658-5811	B / 7.7	3.04	10.78	5.71 /44	15.57 /80	13.48 /73	0.18	1.30
SC	American Beacon Sm Cap Val AMR	AASVX	B	(800) 658-5811	B+ / 8.4	3.21	11.19	6.51 /51	16.43 /86	14.35 /81	0.90	0.55
SC	American Beacon Sm Cap Val C	ASVCX	C+	(800) 658-5811	B- / 7.0	2.82	10.36	4.94 /38	14.70 /72	--	0.00	1.98
SC	American Beacon Sm Cap Val II Inv	ABBVX	B-	(800) 658-5811	C+ / 6.3	2.41	10.08	4.71 /36	13.52 /64	--	0.00	2.29
SC	American Beacon Sm Cap Val II Y	ABBYX	B-	(800) 658-5811	C+ / 6.5	2.46	10.21	5.03 /39	13.85 /66	--	0.00	2.01
SC	American Beacon Sm Cap Val Inst	AVFIX	B-	(800) 658-5811	B / 8.1	3.11	11.00	6.22 /48	16.13 /84	14.04 /78	0.66	0.81
SC	American Beacon Sm Cap Val Inv	AVPAX	C+	(800) 658-5811	B / 7.8	3.05	10.86	5.86 /45	15.72 /81	13.64 /74	0.30	1.17
SC	American Beacon Sm Cap Val Ret	ASCVX	C+	(800) 658-5811	B- / 7.4	2.93	10.58	5.38 /41	15.21 /76	13.17 /70	0.02	1.58
SC	American Beacon Sm Cap Val Y	ABSYX	B-	(800) 658-5811	B / 8.0	3.10	10.99	6.12 /47	16.02 /83	13.92 /77	0.60	0.90
MC	American Beacon Stephens MC Gr A	SMFAX	C-	(800) 658-5811	C / 4.8	4.31	7.23	7.23 /57	12.34 /55	--	0.00	1.46
MC	American Beacon Stephens MC Gr C	SMFCX	C	(800) 658-5811	C / 5.3	4.10	6.83	6.46 /50	11.56 /49	--	0.00	2.18
MC	American Beacon Stephens MC Gr	SFMIX	C	(800) 658-5811	C+ / 6.1	4.42	7.49	7.71 /60	12.86 /59	15.00 /87	0.00	1.11
MC	American Beacon Stephens MC Gr	STMGX	C	(800) 658-5811	C+ / 5.9	4.36	7.27	7.27 /57	12.45 /56	14.63 /83	0.00	1.38
MC	American Beacon Stephens MC Gr Y	SMFYX	C+	(800) 658-5811	C+ / 6.1	4.37	7.44	7.61 /60	12.80 /58	--	0.00	1.14
SC	American Beacon Stephens SC Gr	STSIX	C-	(800) 658-5811	C+ / 5.9	3.86	8.71	2.44 /24	13.06 /60	15.27 /89	0.00	1.13
SC	American Beacon Stephens SC Gr	STSGX	D+	(800) 658-5811	C+ / 5.7	3.82	8.52	2.21 /23	12.75 /58	14.97 /87	0.00	1.41
GR	American Beacon Zebra Global Eq A	AZLAX	E+	(800) 658-5811	C- / 3.5	1.54	3.46	4.22 /33	10.92 /45	--	0.90	3.03
GR	American Beacon Zebra Global Eq C	AZLCX	E+	(800) 658-5811	C- / 3.9	1.38	2.96	3.39 /28	10.08 /40	--	0.96	3.72
GR	American Beacon Zebra Global Eq	AZLIX	D-	(800) 658-5811	C / 4.7	1.64	3.58	4.60 /36	11.43 /48	--	0.95	2.56
GR	American Beacon Zebra Global Eq	AZLPX	D-	(800) 658-5811	C / 4.5	1.56	3.41	4.26 /33	11.00 /45	--	0.95	2.88
GR	American Beacon Zebra Global Eq Y	AZLYX	D-	(800) 658-5811	C / 4.7	1.63	3.55	4.48 /35	11.30 /48	--	0.95	2.51
SC	American Beacon Zebra Sm Cap Eq	AZSAX	C+	(800) 658-5811	B- / 7.2	3.27	13.36	8.34 /65	15.86 /82	--	0.12	2.06
SC	American Beacon Zebra Sm Cap Eq	AZSCX	C+	(800) 658-5811	B / 7.6	3.07	13.01	7.50 /59	14.97 /75	--	0.00	2.82
SC	American Beacon Zebra Sm Cap Eq	AZSIX	B	(800) 658-5811	B+ / 8.7	3.41	13.68	8.86 /68	16.41 /86	--	0.29	1.65
SC	American Beacon Zebra Sm Cap Eq	AZSPX	B	(800) 658-5811	B+ / 8.4	3.27	13.45	8.42 /66	15.96 /83	--	0.05	1.87
SC	American Beacon Zebra Sm Cap Eq	AZSYX	B	(800) 658-5811	B+ / 8.6	3.38	13.62	8.77 /68	16.31 /86	--	0.29	1.66
SC	American Century All Cap Gro A	ACAQX	D+	(800) 345-6488	C+ / 6.1	4.84	9.66	14.24 /90	12.81 /58	13.65 /74	0.00	1.25
SC	American Century All Cap Gro C	ACAHX	C-	(800) 345-6488	C+ / 6.5	4.64	9.28	13.41 /88	11.96 /52	12.79 /66	0.00	2.00
SC	American Century All Cap Gro Inst	ACAJX	C	(800) 345-6488	B- / 7.5	4.96	9.94	14.78 /91	13.31 /62	14.09 /78	0.00	0.80
SC	American Century All Cap Gro Inv	TWGTX	C	(800) 345-6488	B- / 7.3	4.89	9.84	14.53 /91	13.09 /60	13.93 /77	0.00	1.00
SC	American Century All Cap Gro R	ACAWX	C-	(800) 345-6488	C+ / 6.9	4.79	9.55	13.98 /89	12.53 /56	13.36 /72	15.59	1.50
BA	American Century Balanced Inst	ABINX	C+	(800) 345-6488	C / 4.4	0.49	4.13	8.35 /65	10.34 /41	10.54 /49	1.63	0.70
BA	American Century Balanced Inv	TWBIX	C	(800) 345-6488	C / 4.3	0.45	4.03	8.08 /63	10.10 /40	10.31 /47	1.44	0.90
GI	American Century Capital Val A	ACCVX	B-	(800) 345-6488	C+ / 6.4	0.11	4.85	10.07 /75	15.46 /79	12.86 /67	1.05	1.35
GI	American Century Capital Val Inst	ACPIX	A-	(800) 345-6488	B / 7.9	0.32	5.21	10.66 /77	16.00 /83	13.37 /72	1.54	0.90
GI	American Century Capital Val Inv	ACTIX	B+	(800) 345-6488	B / 7.8	0.22	5.11	10.46 /76	15.80 /82	13.17 /70	1.35	1.10
GR	American Century Core Eq Plus A	ACPQX	C+	(800) 345-6488	C+ / 6.5	-0.71	3.74	9.64 /73	15.89 /82	--	0.40	2.02

● Denotes fund is closed to new investors
* Denotes fund is included in Section II

www.thestreetratings.com

RISK			NET ASSETS		ASSET					BULL / BEAR		FUND MANAGER		MINIMUMS		LOADS	
	3 Year		NAV						Portfolio	Last Bull	Last Bear	Manager	Manager	Initial	Additional	Front	Back
Risk Rating/Pts	Standard Deviation	Beta	As of 3/31/15	Total $(Mil)	Cash %	Stocks %	Bonds %	Other %	Turnover Ratio	Market Return	Market Return	Quality Pct	Tenure (Years)	Purch. $	Purch. $	End Load	End Load
U /	N/A	N/A	14.60	105	3	96	0	1	10	N/A	N/A	N/A	3	1,000	50	0.0	0.0
U /	N/A	N/A	14.81	117	3	96	0	1	10	N/A	N/A	N/A	3	250,000	50	0.0	0.0
U /	N/A	N/A	14.75	283	3	96	0	1	10	N/A	N/A	N/A	3	100,000	50	0.0	0.0
C+ / 6.9	11.1	0.96	14.75	20	5	94	0	1	24	109.3	-22.3	72	11	2,500	50	5.8	0.0
C+ / 6.9	11.1	0.97	15.10	123	5	94	0	1	24	114.4	-22.1	78	11	0	0	0.0	2.0
C+ / 6.8	11.1	0.97	14.39	6	5	94	0	1	24	104.0	-22.5	63	11	1,000	50	0.0	0.0
C+ / 6.9	11.1	0.96	14.75	9	5	94	0	1	24	109.0	-22.2	72	11	2,500	50	0.0	0.0
C+ / 6.9	11.2	0.97	15.07	242	5	94	0	1	24	112.7	-22.1	76	11	250,000	50	0.0	0.0
C+ / 6.9	11.2	0.97	15.20	294	5	94	0	1	24	111.1	-22.2	74	11	2,500	50	0.0	0.0
C+ / 6.9	11.1	0.97	14.97	54	5	94	0	1	24	112.3	-22.2	76	11	100,000	50	0.0	0.0
B / 8.0	9.6	1.00	27.96	38	0	0	0	100	4	96.6	-16.6	58	11	2,500	500	0.0	0.0
B / 8.0	9.5	1.00	28.24	1,305	0	0	0	100	4	99.3	-16.4	65	11	250,000	0	0.0	0.0
C+ / 5.7	11.4	0.74	14.14	6	7	92	0	1	39	60.7	-14.2	78	5	250,000	50	0.0	0.0
C+ / 5.7	13.4	1.00	18.47	304	2	97	0	1	22	100.7	-25.2	68	4	250,000	0	0.0	0.0
C / 5.0	13.5	0.98	24.71	34	4	95	0	1	73	102.2	-26.6	63	12	2,500	50	5.8	0.0
C / 5.0	13.5	0.98	24.78	105	4	95	0	1	73	102.3	-26.5	62	12	2,500	50	0.0	0.0
C / 5.0	13.5	0.98	25.76	391	4	95	0	1	73	107.5	-26.3	72	12	0	0	0.0	0.0
C / 4.9	13.5	0.98	24.08	11	4	95	0	1	73	97.0	-26.8	51	12	1,000	50	0.0	0.0
B- / 7.2	12.5	0.90	12.34	3	0	0	0	100	107	N/A	N/A	53	4	2,500	50	0.0	0.0
B- / 7.2	12.6	0.90	12.49	3	0	0	0	100	107	N/A	N/A	58	4	100,000	50	0.0	0.0
C / 5.1	13.5	0.98	25.85	4,336	4	95	0	1	73	105.8	-26.4	69	12	250,000	50	0.0	0.0
C / 5.1	13.5	0.98	25.04	837	4	95	0	1	73	103.3	-26.5	64	12	2,500	50	0.0	0.0
C / 5.0	13.5	0.98	24.26	12	4	95	0	1	73	100.3	-26.6	58	12	2,500	50	0.0	0.0
C / 5.1	13.5	0.98	25.57	210	4	95	0	1	73	105.1	-26.4	67	12	100,000	50	0.0	0.0
C+ / 5.8	11.6	0.97	17.67	16	0	99	0	1	25	N/A	N/A	19	11	2,500	50	5.8	0.0
C+ / 5.7	11.6	0.97	17.25	2	0	99	0	1	25	N/A	N/A	14	11	1,000	50	0.0	0.0
C+ / 5.6	11.6	0.97	20.09	94	0	99	0	1	25	86.0	-16.9	23	11	250,000	50	0.0	0.0
C / 5.5	11.6	0.98	17.71	18	0	99	0	1	25	83.9	-17.1	19	11	2,500	50	0.0	0.0
C+ / 5.8	11.6	0.97	20.06	3	0	99	0	1	25	N/A	N/A	22	11	100,000	50	0.0	0.0
C- / 4.2	14.0	0.95	17.22	376	0	100	0	0	39	85.2	-21.8	36	10	250,000	50	0.0	0.0
C- / 4.1	14.1	0.96	16.31	143	0	100	0	0	39	83.7	-21.9	32	10	2,500	50	0.0	0.0
D+ / 2.9	9.6	0.92	11.20	4	6	93	0	1	63	68.4	-17.9	21	5	2,500	50	5.8	0.0
C- / 3.0	9.6	0.92	11.05	1	6	93	0	1	63	63.8	-18.0	15	5	1,000	50	0.0	0.0
D+ / 2.9	9.6	0.92	11.13	1	6	93	0	1	63	70.9	-17.6	25	5	250,000	50	0.0	0.0
D+ / 2.7	9.6	0.93	11.10	1	6	93	0	1	63	68.8	-17.8	21	5	2,500	50	0.0	0.0
D+ / 2.9	9.6	0.93	11.21	1	6	93	0	1	63	70.1	-17.7	24	5	100,000	50	0.0	0.0
C / 5.0	14.3	1.03	15.18	5	7	92	0	1	76	94.2	-20.7	56	5	2,500	50	5.8	0.0
C / 5.0	14.3	1.03	14.79	2	7	92	0	1	76	89.2	-21.0	43	5	1,000	50	0.0	0.0
C / 5.0	14.2	1.02	15.15	2	7	92	0	1	76	97.5	-20.6	64	5	250,000	50	0.0	0.0
C / 5.0	14.3	1.03	15.18	3	7	92	0	1	76	94.8	-20.7	57	5	2,500	50	0.0	0.0
C / 5.0	14.3	1.03	15.29	10	7	92	0	1	76	96.8	-20.6	62	5	100,000	50	0.0	0.0
C- / 3.6	10.9	0.65	31.39	9	0	99	0	1	56	84.3	-18.0	85	14	2,500	50	5.8	0.0
C- / 3.4	10.9	0.65	30.42	4	0	99	0	1	56	79.6	-18.3	80	14	2,500	50	0.0	0.0
C- / 3.7	10.9	0.65	31.97	N/A	0	99	0	1	56	87.0	-17.9	87	14	5,000,000	50	0.0	0.0
C- / 3.7	10.9	0.65	31.72	1,111	0	99	0	1	56	85.8	-17.9	86	14	2,500	50	0.0	0.0
C- / 3.6	10.9	0.65	31.07	12	0	99	0	1	56	82.7	-18.1	84	14	2,500	50	0.0	0.0
B- / 7.5	5.9	1.04	18.33	52	1	60	38	1	64	58.3	-8.1	53	18	5,000,000	50	0.0	0.0
B- / 7.5	5.9	1.04	18.32	838	1	60	38	1	64	57.2	-8.2	50	18	2,500	50	0.0	0.0
B- / 7.1	10.3	1.05	9.23	5	0	99	0	1	31	96.8	-17.5	48	15	2,500	50	5.8	0.0
B- / 7.0	10.3	1.05	9.28	3	0	99	0	1	31	99.5	-17.4	56	15	5,000,000	50	0.0	0.0
B- / 7.0	10.2	1.04	9.26	151	0	99	0	1	31	98.0	-17.4	54	15	2,500	50	0.0	0.0
C+ / 5.7	9.9	1.01	13.95	1	1	98	0	1	104	N/A	N/A	62	4	2,500	50	5.8	0.0

					PERFORMANCE							
						Total Return % through 3/31/15					Incl. in Returns	
99 Pct = Best					Perfor-				Annualized		Dividend	Expense
0 Pct = Worst			Ticker	Overall Investment	mance							
Fund Type	Fund Name	Symbol	Rating	Phone	Rating/Pts	3 Mo	6 Mo	1Yr / Pct	3Yr / Pct	5Yr / Pct	Yield	Ratio
GR	American Century Core Eq Plus C	ACPHX	C+	(800) 345-6488	C+ / 6.9	-0.86	3.36	8.88 /69	15.04 /75	--	0.00	2.77
GR	American Century Core Eq Plus Inst	ACPKX	B	(800) 345-6488	B / 8.0	-0.64	3.98	10.11 /75	16.42 /86	--	0.83	1.57
GR	American Century Core Eq Plus Inv	ACPVX	B	(800) 345-6488	B / 7.8	-0.64	3.88	9.98 /74	16.20 /85	--	0.65	1.77
GR	American Century Core Eq Plus R	ACPWX	B-	(800) 345-6488	B- / 7.4	-0.78	3.61	9.40 /71	15.60 /80	--	0.19	2.27
GR	American Century Discpl Gr A	ADCVX	C+	(800) 345-6488	C+ / 6.5	1.48	5.92	12.52 /85	14.92 /74	15.89 /92	0.16	1.27
GR	American Century Discpl Gr C	ADCCX	C+	(800) 345-6488	C+ / 6.9	1.31	5.55	11.70 /81	14.06 /68	15.03 /87	0.00	2.02
GR	American Century Discpl Gr Inst	ADCIX	B+	(800) 345-6488	B / 7.9	1.57	6.20	13.06 /87	15.45 /79	16.41 /94	0.60	0.82
GR	American Century Discpl Gr Inv	ADSIX	B+	(800) 345-6488	B / 7.8	1.52	6.04	12.75 /86	15.22 /77	16.19 /94	0.41	1.02
GR	American Century Discpl Gr R	ADRRX	B+	(800) 345-6488	B- / 7.3	1.44	5.80	12.21 /83	14.65 /72	15.61 /91	0.01	1.52
GR	American Century Disp Gr Plus A	ACDQX	A-	(800) 345-6488	B+ / 8.5	3.92	10.22	17.63 /95	16.65 /88	--	0.00	2.06
GR	American Century Disp Gr Plus C	ACDHX	A	(800) 345-6488	B+ / 8.8	3.75	9.83	16.72 /94	15.79 /82	--	0.00	2.81
GR	American Century Disp Gr Plus Inst	ACDKX	A+	(800) 345-6488	A / 9.4	4.03	10.40	18.09 /96	17.18 /91	--	0.26	1.61
GR	American Century Disp Gr Plus Inv	ACDJX	A+	(800) 345-6488	A / 9.3	3.97	10.33	17.88 /95	16.96 /90	--	0.07	1.81
GR	American Century Disp Gr Plus R	ACDWX	A+	(800) 345-6488	A- / 9.1	3.82	10.07	17.35 /95	16.37 /86	--	0.00	2.31
EM	American Century Emerging Mkt A	AEMMX	E+	(800) 345-6488	E+ / 0.8	4.45	1.76	4.70 /36	3.20 / 8	2.91 / 6	0.00	1.97
EM	American Century Emerging Mkt C	ACECX	E+	(800) 345-6488	E+ / 0.9	4.36	1.37	4.10 /32	2.44 / 7	2.14 / 5	0.00	2.72
EM	American Century Emerging Mkt Inst	AMKIX	E+	(800) 345-6488	D- / 1.2	4.58	2.04	5.29 /41	3.66 / 9	3.38 / 7	0.26	1.52
EM	American Century Emerging Mkt Inv	TWMIX	E+	(800) 345-6488	D- / 1.2	4.61	1.88	5.09 /39	3.47 / 9	3.17 / 6	0.07	1.72
EM	American Century Emerging Mkt R	AEMRX	E+	(800) 345-6488	D- / 1.0	4.51	1.73	4.63 /36	2.96 / 8	2.67 / 5	0.00	2.22
EM	American Century Emerging Mkt R6	AEDMX	U	(800) 345-6488	U /	4.61	2.07	5.44 /42	--	--	0.40	1.37
GR	American Century Eqty Mkt Ntrl A	ALIAX	C-	(800) 345-6488	E / 0.5	-0.63	-0.18	-0.72 /14	1.62 / 6	2.27 / 5	0.00	3.17
GR	American Century Eqty Mkt Ntrl C	ALICX	C-	(800) 345-6488	E / 0.5	-0.77	-0.58	-1.52 /11	0.85 / 5	1.49 / 4	0.00	3.92
GR	American Century Eqty Mkt Ntrl I	ALISX	C-	(800) 345-6488	E+ / 0.7	-0.43	0.09	-0.26 /15	2.09 / 6	2.72 / 5	0.00	2.72
GR	American Century Eqty Mkt Ntrl Inv	ALHIX	C-	(800) 345-6488	E+ / 0.7	-0.53	0.00	-0.44 /14	1.87 / 6	2.53 / 5	0.00	2.92
GR	American Century Eqty Mkt Ntrl R	ALIRX	C-	(800) 345-6488	E+ / 0.6	-0.73	-0.37	-1.01 /13	1.36 / 6	2.00 / 4	0.00	3.42
GR	American Century Equity Growth A	BEQAX	C+	(800) 345-6488	C+ / 6.3	-0.28	4.66	10.34 /76	15.27 /77	14.31 /80	1.01	0.92
GR	American Century Equity Growth C	AEYCX	C+	(800) 345-6488	C+ / 6.7	-0.46	4.25	9.50 /72	14.41 /70	13.45 /72	0.36	1.67
GR	American Century Equity Growth Inst	AMEIX	B	(800) 345-6488	B / 7.7	-0.19	4.88	10.81 /78	15.77 /81	14.82 /85	1.48	0.47
GR	American Century Equity Growth Inv	BEQGX	B	(800) 345-6488	B / 7.6	-0.23	4.78	10.60 /77	15.55 /80	14.60 /83	1.30	0.67
GR	American Century Equity Growth R	AEYRX	B-	(800) 345-6488	B- / 7.1	-0.33	4.53	10.06 /75	14.98 /75	14.03 /78	0.83	1.17
IN	American Century Equity Income A	TWEAX	C	(800) 345-6488	C / 4.3	-0.18	3.90	8.27 /65	11.86 /51	10.87 /52	1.97	1.18
IN	American Century Equity Income B	AEKBX	C+	(800) 345-6488	C / 4.6	-0.32	3.52	7.47 /59	11.03 /46	10.04 /45	1.36	1.93
IN	American Century Equity Income C	AEYIX	C+	(800) 345-6488	C / 4.6	-0.32	3.53	7.47 /59	11.04 /46	10.06 /45	1.36	1.93
IN	American Century Equity Income Inst	ACIIX	C+	(800) 345-6488	C / 5.5	-0.09	4.13	8.63 /67	12.36 /55	11.37 /56	2.51	0.73
IN	American Century Equity Income Inv	TWEIX	C+	(800) 345-6488	C / 5.4	-0.13	4.03	8.54 /67	12.14 /53	11.15 /54	2.32	0.93
IN	American Century Equity Income R	AEURX	C+	(800) 345-6488	C / 5.0	-0.22	3.79	8.03 /63	11.62 /50	10.60 /49	1.85	1.43
IN	American Century Equity Income R6	AEUDX	U	(800) 345-6488	U /	-0.06	4.20	8.90 /69	--	--	2.65	0.58
IN	American Century Fdmtl Equity A	AFDAX	B-	(800) 345-6488	C+ / 6.7	0.74	6.65	12.95 /86	15.29 /77	14.26 /80	0.92	1.25
IN	● American Century Fdmtl Equity B	AFDBX	B+	(800) 345-6488	B- / 7.1	0.56	6.30	12.11 /83	14.42 /70	13.43 /72	0.25	2.00
IN	American Century Fdmtl Equity C	AFDCX	B+	(800) 345-6488	B- / 7.1	0.56	6.29	12.10 /83	14.44 /70	13.42 /72	0.25	2.00
IN	American Century Fdmtl Equity Inst	AFEIX	A	(800) 345-6488	B / 8.2	0.88	6.90	13.46 /88	15.81 /82	14.80 /85	1.40	0.80
IN	American Century Fdmtl Equity Inv	AFDIX	A	(800) 345-6488	B / 8.0	0.78	6.80	13.26 /87	15.59 /80	14.56 /83	1.21	1.00
IN	American Century Fdmtl Equity R	AFDRX	A-	(800) 345-6488	B / 7.6	0.70	6.56	12.71 /86	15.01 /75	14.00 /78	0.73	1.50
GR	American Century Focused Growth A	AFGAX	D	(800) 345-6488	C+ / 5.6	2.46	8.52	11.89 /82	13.04 /60	12.81 /66	0.10	1.25
GR	American Century Focused Growth C	AFGCX	D	(800) 345-6488	C+ / 6.0	2.31	8.13	11.12 /79	12.17 /54	11.97 /60	0.00	2.00
GR	American Century Focused Growth I	AFGNX	D+	(800) 345-6488	C+ / 6.9	2.62	8.81	12.42 /84	13.54 /64	13.32 /71	0.54	0.80
GR	American Century Focused Growth	AFSIX	D+	(800) 345-6488	C+ / 6.7	2.54	8.71	12.17 /83	13.29 /62	13.07 /69	0.35	1.00
GR	American Century Focused Growth R	AFGRX	D+	(800) 345-6488	C+ / 6.3	2.39	8.35	11.59 /81	12.70 /57	12.51 /64	0.00	1.50
RE	American Century Gl Real Estate A	ARYMX	C	(800) 345-6488	C+ / 6.3	4.76	11.56	14.37 /90	12.87 /59	--	3.24	1.45
RE	American Century Gl Real Estate C	ARYTX	C	(800) 345-6488	C+ / 6.7	4.58	11.10	13.50 /88	12.03 /53	--	2.70	2.20
RE	American Century Gl Real Estate Ins	ARYNX	C+	(800) 345-6488	B / 7.8	4.94	11.88	14.90 /91	13.42 /63	--	3.88	1.00
RE	American Century Gl Real Estate Inv	ARYVX	C+	(800) 345-6488	B / 7.6	4.85	11.75	14.66 /91	13.15 /61	--	3.68	1.20

● Denotes fund is closed to new investors
* Denotes fund is included in Section II

www.thestreetratings.com

Risk Rating/Pts	Standard Deviation	Beta	NAV As of 3/31/15	Total $(Mil)	Cash %	Stocks %	Bonds %	Other %	Portfolio Turnover Ratio	Last Bull Market Return	Last Bear Market Return	Manager Quality Pct	Manager Tenure (Years)	Initial Purch. $	Additional Purch. $	Front End Load	Back End Load
C+ / 5.7	9.9	1.01	13.79	1	1	98	0	1	104	N/A	N/A	51	4	2,500	50	0.0	0.0
C+ / 5.7	9.9	1.01	13.97	3	1	98	0	1	104	N/A	N/A	69	4	5,000,000	0	0.0	0.0
C+ / 5.7	9.9	1.01	13.96	167	1	98	0	1	104	N/A	N/A	67	4	2,500	50	0.0	0.0
C+ / 5.7	9.9	1.01	13.93	N/A	1	98	0	1	104	N/A	N/A	59	4	2,500	50	0.0	0.0
C+ / 6.8	10.2	1.03	19.24	162	1	98	0	1	102	99.2	-16.4	44	10	2,500	50	5.8	0.0
C+ / 6.7	10.2	1.03	18.55	46	1	98	0	1	102	94.3	-16.7	33	10	2,500	50	0.0	0.0
C+ / 6.8	10.1	1.03	19.37	293	1	98	0	1	102	102.3	-16.3	52	10	5,000,000	0	0.0	0.0
C+ / 6.8	10.1	1.03	19.31	509	1	98	0	1	102	100.9	-16.3	48	10	2,500	50	0.0	0.0
C+ / 6.8	10.1	1.03	19.04	13	1	98	0	1	102	97.6	-16.5	41	10	2,500	50	0.0	0.0
C+ / 6.8	10.2	1.01	16.69	5	0	100	0	0	96	N/A	N/A	71	4	2,500	50	5.8	0.0
C+ / 6.7	10.2	1.01	16.31	2	0	100	0	0	96	N/A	N/A	62	4	2,500	50	0.0	0.0
C+ / 6.8	10.2	1.00	16.77	1	0	100	0	0	96	N/A	N/A	76	4	5,000,000	0	0.0	0.0
C+ / 6.8	10.2	1.01	16.76	39	0	100	0	0	96	N/A	N/A	74	4	2,500	50	0.0	0.0
C+ / 6.7	10.2	1.01	16.59	1	0	100	0	0	96	N/A	N/A	69	4	2,500	50	0.0	0.0
C / 5.3	14.4	1.01	8.69	9	1	98	0	1	74	33.9	-30.3	87	9	2,500	50	5.8	0.0
C / 5.3	14.4	1.01	8.13	3	1	98	0	1	74	30.5	-30.5	83	9	2,500	50	0.0	0.0
C / 5.3	14.4	1.01	9.22	4	1	98	0	1	74	36.0	-30.1	88	9	5,000,000	50	0.0	2.0
C / 5.3	14.4	1.01	9.00	390	1	98	0	1	74	35.0	-30.1	88	9	2,500	50	0.0	2.0
C / 5.3	14.4	1.00	8.81	2	1	98	0	1	74	32.9	-30.4	86	9	2,500	50	0.0	2.0
U /	N/A	N/A	9.22	28	1	98	0	1	74	N/A	N/A	N/A	9	0	0	0.0	2.0
B+ / 9.9	2.5	0.06	11.04	21	100	0	0	0	226	8.2	0.7	74	10	2,500	50	5.8	0.0
B+ / 9.9	2.4	0.07	10.36	6	100	0	0	0	226	5.4	0.4	65	10	2,500	50	0.0	0.0
B+ / 9.9	2.5	0.06	11.45	18	100	0	0	0	226	9.8	0.9	78	10	5,000,000	0	0.0	0.0
B+ / 9.9	2.5	0.07	11.26	62	100	0	0	0	226	9.0	0.8	76	10	2,500	50	0.0	0.0
B+ / 9.9	2.4	0.06	10.81	2	100	0	0	0	226	7.3	0.6	71	10	2,500	50	0.0	0.0
C+ / 6.1	10.0	1.04	30.53	334	1	98	0	1	80	98.6	-15.8	47	18	2,500	50	5.8	0.0
C+ / 6.1	10.0	1.04	30.29	16	1	98	0	1	80	93.6	-16.1	36	18	2,500	50	0.0	0.0
C+ / 6.1	10.0	1.04	30.58	485	1	98	0	1	80	101.7	-15.7	53	18	5,000,000	0	0.0	0.0
C+ / 6.1	10.0	1.04	30.56	2,693	1	98	0	1	80	100.3	-15.8	51	18	2,500	50	0.0	0.0
C+ / 6.1	10.0	1.04	30.55	31	1	98	0	1	80	96.9	-15.9	43	18	2,500	50	0.0	0.0
B- / 7.2	7.0	0.69	8.71	2,174	6	84	5	5	57	65.9	-12.3	76	21	2,500	50	5.8	0.0
B- / 7.2	7.1	0.69	8.72	6	6	84	5	5	57	61.6	-12.6	69	21	2,500	50	0.0	0.0
B- / 7.2	7.0	0.69	8.71	549	6	84	5	5	57	61.5	-12.5	69	21	2,500	50	0.0	0.0
B- / 7.2	7.1	0.69	8.71	1,323	6	84	5	5	57	68.2	-12.0	80	21	5,000,000	50	0.0	0.0
B- / 7.2	7.1	0.69	8.71	5,467	6	84	5	5	57	67.3	-12.2	78	21	2,500	50	0.0	0.0
B- / 7.2	7.1	0.69	8.69	129	6	84	5	5	57	64.3	-12.3	74	21	2,500	50	0.0	0.0
U /	N/A	N/A	8.72	118	6	84	5	5	57	N/A	N/A	N/A	21	0	0	0.0	0.0
B- / 7.4	9.5	0.98	21.78	124	0	99	0	1	41	98.6	-16.2	60	7	2,500	50	5.8	0.0
B- / 7.3	9.5	0.98	21.47	3	0	99	0	1	41	93.4	-16.4	49	7	2,500	50	0.0	0.0
B- / 7.3	9.5	0.98	21.48	19	0	99	0	1	41	93.5	-16.4	49	7	2,500	50	0.0	0.0
B- / 7.4	9.4	0.98	21.87	13	0	99	0	1	41	101.5	-16.0	67	7	5,000,000	50	0.0	0.0
B- / 7.4	9.4	0.98	21.83	96	0	99	0	1	41	100.2	-16.1	65	7	2,500	50	0.0	0.0
B- / 7.4	9.5	0.98	21.70	6	0	99	0	1	41	96.8	-16.3	57	7	2,500	50	0.0	0.0
C- / 3.0	10.2	1.02	12.50	1	1	98	0	1	97	89.3	-18.3	25	10	2,500	50	5.8	0.0
D+ / 2.8	10.2	1.02	11.95	N/A	1	98	0	1	97	84.4	-18.6	18	10	2,500	50	0.0	0.0
D+ / 2.9	10.2	1.02	12.53	N/A	1	98	0	1	97	92.1	-18.1	30	10	5,000,000	50	0.0	0.0
C- / 3.0	10.2	1.02	12.53	16	1	98	0	1	97	90.6	-18.1	28	10	2,500	50	0.0	0.0
C- / 3.0	10.2	1.02	12.40	N/A	1	98	0	1	97	87.6	-18.3	22	10	2,500	50	0.0	0.0
C / 4.9	11.7	0.84	12.11	19	6	93	0	1	275	70.7	-17.3	77	4	2,500	50	5.8	0.0
C / 4.9	11.6	0.84	12.10	6	6	93	0	1	275	66.5	-17.6	71	4	2,500	50	0.0	0.0
C / 4.8	11.6	0.84	12.11	6	6	93	0	1	275	73.3	-17.1	81	4	5,000,000	50	0.0	0.0
C / 4.9	11.7	0.84	12.11	75	6	93	0	1	275	72.1	-17.2	79	4	2,500	50	0.0	0.0

						PERFORMANCE							
	99 Pct = Best						Total Return % through 3/31/15					Incl. in Returns	
	0 Pct = Worst		Overall		Perfor-					Annualized		Dividend	Expense
Fund		Ticker	Investment		mance								
Type	Fund Name	Symbol	Rating	Phone	Rating/Pts	3 Mo	6 Mo	1Yr / Pct	3Yr / Pct	5Yr / Pct	Yield	Ratio
RE	American Century Gl Real Estate R	ARYWX	C+	(800) 345-6488	B- / 7.1	4.75	11.46	14.06 / 90	12.61 / 57	--	3.19	1.70
GL	American Century Global Alloc A	AGAEX	D	(800) 345-6488	E+ / 0.6	0.61	-1.24	-2.29 / 10	3.21 / 8	--	1.01	2.43
GL	American Century Global Alloc C	AGAGX	D	(800) 345-6488	E+ / 0.7	0.42	-1.65	-2.96 / 9	2.46 / 7	--	0.31	3.18
GL	American Century Global Alloc Inst	AGANX	D	(800) 345-6488	E+ / 0.9	0.70	-1.05	-1.84 / 11	3.69 / 9	--	1.52	1.98
GL	American Century Global Alloc Inv	AGAVX	D	(800) 345-6488	E+ / 0.8	0.70	-1.07	-1.94 / 10	3.50 / 9	--	1.32	2.18
GL	American Century Global Alloc R	AGAFX	D	(800) 345-6488	E+ / 0.8	0.61	-1.32	-2.45 / 9	2.98 / 8	--	0.81	2.68
PM	American Century Global Gold A	ACGGX	E-	(800) 345-6488	E- / 0.0	-2.04	-16.28	-22.95 / 1	-26.63 / 0	-14.43 / 0	3.02	0.92
PM	American Century Global Gold C	AGYCX	E-	(800) 345-6488	E- / 0.0	-2.23	-16.63	-23.62 / 1	-27.19 / 0	-15.08 / 0	2.51	1.67
PM	American Century Global Gold I	AGGNX	E-	(800) 345-6488	E- / 0.0	-2.00	-16.13	-22.61 / 1	-26.30 / 0	-14.04 / 0	3.59	0.47
PM	American Century Global Gold Inv	BGEIX	E-	(800) 345-6488	E- / 0.0	-2.01	-16.28	-22.86 / 1	-26.46 / 0	-14.23 / 0	3.41	0.67
PM	American Century Global Gold R	AGGWX	E-	(800) 345-6488	E- / 0.0	-2.18	-16.46	-23.22 / 1	-26.80 / 0	-14.64 / 0	2.96	1.17
GL	American Century Global Growth A	AGGRX	D+	(800) 345-6488	C / 4.4	4.06	5.29	6.68 / 52	11.73 / 51	10.81 / 51	0.00	1.34
GL	American Century Global Growth C	AGLCX	C-	(800) 345-6488	C / 4.7	3.88	4.84	5.87 / 45	10.88 / 45	9.97 / 44	0.00	2.09
GL	American Century Global Growth Inst	AGGIX	C	(800) 345-6488	C / 5.3	4.27	5.55	7.17 / 56	12.25 / 54	11.34 / 55	0.00	0.89
GL	American Century Global Growth Inv	TWGGX	C-	(800) 345-6488	C / 5.1	4.15	5.36	6.90 / 54	11.99 / 52	11.10 / 53	0.00	1.09
GL	American Century Global Growth R	AGORX	C-	(800) 345-6488	C / 4.8	3.99	5.14	6.45 / 50	11.45 / 49	10.55 / 49	0.00	1.59
GR	American Century Growth A	TCRAX	D	(800) 345-6488	C+ / 5.8	3.24	8.92	13.01 / 87	13.18 / 61	13.24 / 70	0.03	1.22
GR	American Century Growth C	TWRCX	D+	(800) 345-6488	C+ / 6.2	3.04	8.49	12.13 / 83	12.33 / 55	12.39 / 63	0.00	1.97
GR	American Century Growth Inst	TWGIX	C-	(800) 345-6488	B- / 7.2	3.36	9.14	13.51 / 88	13.69 / 65	13.75 / 75	0.46	0.77
GR	American Century Growth Inv	TWCGX	C-	(800) 345-6488	B- / 7.0	3.27	9.02	13.26 / 87	13.45 / 63	13.52 / 73	0.27	0.97
GR	American Century Growth R	AGWRX	D+	(800) 345-6488	C+ / 6.6	3.18	8.75	12.70 / 86	12.89 / 59	12.95 / 68	0.00	1.47
GR	American Century Growth R6	AGRDX	U	(800) 345-6488	U /	3.40	9.23	13.66 / 89	--	--	0.60	0.62
MC	American Century Heritage A	ATHAX	C-	(800) 345-6488	B- / 7.0	7.96	13.68	13.55 / 88	14.36 / 70	14.67 / 84	0.00	1.25
MC	● American Century Heritage B	ATHBX	C-	(800) 345-6488	B- / 7.5	7.72	13.22	12.67 / 85	13.50 / 63	13.81 / 76	0.00	2.00
MC	American Century Heritage C	AHGCX	D+	(800) 345-6488	B- / 7.5	7.76	13.26	12.71 / 86	13.51 / 63	13.82 / 76	0.00	2.00
MC	American Century Heritage Inst	ATHIX	C+	(800) 345-6488	B+ / 8.5	8.09	13.96	14.05 / 89	14.89 / 74	15.19 / 88	0.00	0.80
MC	American Century Heritage Inv	TWHIX	C	(800) 345-6488	B+ / 8.4	7.99	13.77	13.81 / 89	14.65 / 72	14.95 / 86	0.00	1.00
MC	American Century Heritage R	ATHWX	C	(800) 345-6488	B / 7.9	7.85	13.52	13.25 / 87	14.07 / 68	14.38 / 81	0.00	1.50
GR	American Century Heritage R6	ATHDX	B+	(800) 345-6488	B+ / 8.5	8.11	14.02	14.23 / 90	14.87 / 74	15.09 / 87	0.00	0.65
GI	American Century Inc and Gr A	AMADX	B-	(800) 345-6488	C+ / 6.1	-0.78	3.92	8.88 / 69	15.28 / 77	13.78 / 76	1.67	0.92
GI	American Century Inc and Gr C	ACGCX	B-	(800) 345-6488	C+ / 6.5	-0.98	3.52	8.06 / 63	14.42 / 70	12.92 / 67	1.04	1.67
GI	American Century Inc and Gr Inst	AMGIX	B+	(800) 345-6488	B- / 7.5	-0.67	4.17	9.38 / 71	15.80 / 82	14.29 / 80	2.20	0.47
GI	American Century Inc and Gr Inv	BIGRX	B+	(800) 345-6488	B- / 7.4	-0.73	4.04	9.14 / 70	15.58 / 80	14.06 / 78	2.01	0.67
GI	American Century Inc and Gr R	AICRX	B-	(800) 345-6488	C+ / 6.9	-0.83	3.79	8.61 / 67	15.00 / 75	13.50 / 73	1.52	1.17
FO	American Century Intl Core Eq A	ACIQX	D	(800) 345-6488	D+ / 2.6	4.62	-0.43	-2.15 / 10	10.22 / 41	7.11 / 24	2.74	1.41
FO	American Century Intl Core Eq C	ACIKX	D	(800) 345-6488	C- / 3.1	4.39	-0.88	-2.91 / 9	9.43 / 36	6.26 / 18	2.17	2.16
FO	American Century Intl Core Eq Inst	ACIUX	D+	(800) 345-6488	C- / 3.5	4.74	-0.30	-1.80 / 11	10.70 / 44	7.55 / 27	3.36	0.96
FO	American Century Intl Core Eq Inv	ACIMX	D+	(800) 345-6488	C- / 3.3	4.50	-0.51	-2.11 / 10	10.45 / 42	7.32 / 25	3.16	1.16
FO	American Century Intl Core Eq R	ACIRX	D	(800) 345-6488	C- / 3.0	4.51	-0.69	-2.51 / 9	9.91 / 39	6.79 / 22	2.67	1.66
FO	American Century Intl Disc A	ACIDX	D-	(800) 345-6488	C- / 3.0	6.77	3.10	-3.96 / 7	10.55 / 43	7.66 / 28	0.00	1.81
FO	American Century Intl Disc C	TWECX	D	(800) 345-6488	C- / 3.4	6.53	2.70	-4.70 / 6	9.73 / 38	6.87 / 22	0.00	2.56
FO	American Century Intl Disc Inst	TIDIX	D	(800) 345-6488	C- / 3.9	6.79	3.26	-3.56 / 8	11.03 / 46	8.13 / 31	0.42	1.36
FO	American Century Intl Disc Inv	TWEGX	D	(800) 345-6488	C- / 3.7	6.83	3.26	-3.72 / 7	10.82 / 44	7.93 / 29	0.22	1.56
FO	American Century Intl Disc R	TWERX	D	(800) 345-6488	C- / 3.4	6.66	2.97	-4.19 / 7	10.27 / 41	7.40 / 26	0.00	2.06
FO	American Century Intl Gr A	TWGAX	D-	(800) 345-6488	D+ / 2.3	4.32	1.68	-1.36 / 12	9.19 / 34	7.59 / 27	0.40	1.47
FO	American Century Intl Gr C	AIWCX	D-	(800) 345-6488	D+ / 2.7	4.23	1.40	-1.98 / 10	8.39 / 29	6.80 / 22	0.00	2.22
FO	American Century Intl Gr Inst	TGRIX	D	(800) 345-6488	C- / 3.2	4.47	2.00	-0.87 / 13	9.70 / 37	8.09 / 30	0.77	1.02
FO	American Century Intl Gr Inv	TWIEX	D-	(800) 345-6488	C- / 3.0	4.36	1.82	-1.10 / 13	9.47 / 36	7.86 / 29	0.61	1.22
FO	American Century Intl Gr R	ATGRX	D-	(800) 345-6488	D+ / 2.7	4.28	1.62	-1.54 / 11	8.93 / 32	7.33 / 25	0.24	1.72
FO	American Century Intl Gr R6	ATGDX	U	(800) 345-6488	U /	4.47	2.04	-0.76 / 14	--	--	0.88	0.87
FO	American Century Intl Opps A	AIVOX	D	(800) 345-6488	C- / 3.8	6.70	3.19	-4.30 / 6	12.15 / 53	9.76 / 43	0.15	2.05
FO	American Century Intl Opps C	AIOCX	D	(800) 345-6488	C- / 4.2	6.54	2.85	-5.03 / 5	11.32 / 48	8.97 / 36	0.01	2.80

RISK			NET ASSETS		ASSET				Portfolio Turnover Ratio	BULL / BEAR		FUND MANAGER		MINIMUMS		LOADS	
Risk Rating/Pts	3 Year		NAV As of 3/31/15	Total $(Mil)	Cash %	Stocks %	Bonds %	Other %		Last Bull Market Return	Last Bear Market Return	Manager Quality Pct	Manager Tenure (Years)	Initial Purch. $	Additional Purch. $	Front End Load	Back End Load
	Standard Deviation	Beta															
C /4.9	11.6	0.84	12.12	1	6	93	0	1	275	69.3	-17.4	76	4	2,500	50	0.0	0.0
B- /7.6	7.5	1.13	10.57	11	8	59	32	1	47	N/A	N/A	5	3	2,500	50	5.8	0.0
B- /7.5	7.5	1.14	10.50	11	8	59	32	1	47	N/A	N/A	4	3	2,500	50	0.0	0.0
B- /7.7	7.5	1.13	10.61	4	8	59	32	1	47	N/A	N/A	6	3	5,000,000	50	0.0	0.0
B- /7.6	7.5	1.13	10.60	16	8	59	32	1	47	N/A	N/A	6	3	2,500	50	0.0	0.0
B- /7.5	7.4	1.13	10.55	N/A	8	59	32	1	47	N/A	N/A	5	3	2,500	50	0.0	0.0
E- /0.2	37.2	1.70	7.21	9	1	98	0	1	29	-58.2	-15.0	1	23	2,500	50	5.8	0.0
E- /0.2	37.1	1.70	7.02	2	1	98	0	1	29	-59.2	-15.3	1	23	2,500	50	0.0	0.0
E- /0.2	37.1	1.70	7.34	10	1	98	0	1	29	-57.6	-14.9	1	23	5,000,000	0	0.0	1.0
E- /0.2	37.1	1.70	7.30	300	1	98	0	1	29	-57.9	-14.9	1	23	2,500	50	0.0	1.0
E- /0.2	37.2	1.70	7.18	3	1	98	0	1	29	-58.5	-15.1	1	23	2,500	50	0.0	1.0
C /5.5	10.8	0.73	11.79	54	0	99	0	1	46	75.0	-20.6	92	14	2,500	50	5.8	0.0
C /5.3	10.8	0.73	10.71	8	0	99	0	1	46	70.6	-20.9	91	14	2,500	50	0.0	0.0
C /5.5	10.9	0.73	12.19	36	0	99	0	1	46	77.9	-20.6	93	14	5,000,000	50	0.0	2.0
C /5.5	10.9	0.73	12.02	457	0	99	0	1	46	76.6	-20.6	93	14	2,500	50	0.0	2.0
C /5.4	10.8	0.73	11.72	6	0	99	0	1	46	73.6	-20.8	92	14	2,500	50	0.0	2.0
C- /3.1	9.9	0.98	29.00	652	0	99	0	1	103	87.2	-17.3	33	18	2,500	50	5.8	0.0
C- /3.1	9.9	0.98	28.43	13	0	99	0	1	103	82.4	-17.6	25	18	2,500	50	0.0	0.0
C- /3.2	9.9	0.98	30.13	2,084	0	99	0	1	103	90.0	-17.2	39	18	5,000,000	50	0.0	0.0
C- /3.2	9.9	0.98	29.71	5,944	0	99	0	1	103	88.7	-17.2	36	18	2,500	50	0.0	0.0
C- /3.1	9.9	0.98	28.58	132	0	99	0	1	103	85.5	-17.4	30	18	2,500	50	0.0	0.0
U /	N/A	N/A	30.11	310	0	99	0	1	103	N/A	N/A	N/A	18	0	0	0.0	0.0
C- /3.0	11.7	0.97	24.14	877	1	98	0	1	73	88.1	-21.5	40	12	2,500	50	5.8	0.0
D+ /2.8	11.6	0.97	23.30	3	1	98	0	1	73	83.3	-21.7	30	12	2,500	50	0.0	0.0
D+ /2.3	11.6	0.97	21.11	135	1	98	0	1	73	83.4	-21.7	30	12	2,500	50	0.0	0.0
C- /3.5	11.6	0.97	26.45	161	1	98	0	1	73	90.9	-21.3	48	12	5,000,000	50	0.0	0.0
C- /3.3	11.7	0.97	25.40	4,593	1	98	0	1	73	89.7	-21.4	44	12	2,500	50	0.0	0.0
C- /3.0	11.7	0.97	24.33	63	1	98	0	1	73	86.5	-21.5	37	12	2,500	50	0.0	0.0
C+ /6.1	11.6	1.03	26.52	104	1	98	0	1	73	90.7	-21.4	44	12	0	0	0.0	0.0
B- /7.3	10.0	1.03	37.38	241	1	98	0	1	76	97.0	-16.2	50	5	2,500	50	5.8	0.0
B- /7.3	10.0	1.03	37.31	8	1	98	0	1	76	92.1	-16.4	39	5	2,500	50	0.0	0.0
B- /7.3	10.0	1.03	37.46	127	1	98	0	1	76	100.1	-16.0	58	5	5,000,000	0	0.0	0.0
B- /7.3	10.0	1.03	37.42	1,732	1	98	0	1	76	98.8	-16.1	55	5	2,500	50	0.0	0.0
B- /7.3	10.0	1.03	37.41	7	1	98	0	1	76	95.4	-16.2	46	5	2,500	50	0.0	0.0
C+ /5.9	13.1	0.98	8.83	6	2	97	0	1	125	55.0	-23.9	75	5	2,500	50	5.8	0.0
C+ /6.0	13.1	0.98	8.80	1	2	97	0	1	125	50.9	-24.2	68	5	2,500	50	0.0	0.0
C+ /5.9	13.1	0.98	8.84	1	2	97	0	1	125	57.3	-23.8	79	5	5,000,000	0	0.0	2.0
C+ /5.9	13.2	0.99	8.82	19	2	97	0	1	125	55.9	-23.9	77	5	2,500	50	0.0	2.0
C+ /6.0	13.1	0.98	8.81	N/A	2	97	0	1	125	53.6	-24.0	73	5	2,500	50	0.0	2.0
C /4.8	13.3	0.91	12.62	6	1	98	0	1	134	60.0	-29.3	83	21	10,000	50	5.8	0.0
C /4.8	13.3	0.91	12.57	1	1	98	0	1	134	55.8	-29.5	77	21	10,000	50	0.0	0.0
C /4.9	13.3	0.90	13.08	23	1	98	0	1	134	62.3	-29.2	86	21	5,000,000	50	0.0	2.0
C /4.9	13.3	0.91	12.94	537	1	98	0	1	134	61.3	-29.3	84	21	10,000	50	0.0	2.0
C /4.8	13.2	0.90	12.81	N/A	1	98	0	1	134	58.5	-29.3	81	21	10,000	50	0.0	2.0
C /5.0	12.6	0.93	12.62	290	0	99	0	1	75	57.0	-24.4	70	13	2,500	50	5.8	0.0
C /5.0	12.6	0.93	12.40	10	0	99	0	1	75	53.0	-24.7	61	13	2,500	50	0.0	0.0
C /5.0	12.6	0.93	12.45	84	0	99	0	1	75	59.4	-24.3	75	13	5,000,000	50	0.0	2.0
C /5.0	12.6	0.93	12.52	1,372	0	99	0	1	75	58.2	-24.3	73	13	2,500	50	0.0	2.0
C /5.0	12.6	0.93	12.75	3	0	99	0	1	75	55.6	-24.5	68	13	2,500	50	0.0	2.0
U /	N/A	N/A	12.44	42	0	99	0	1	75	N/A	N/A	N/A	13	0	0	0.0	2.0
C /4.8	13.3	0.89	8.82	15	2	97	0	1	128	66.9	-25.8	90	14	10,000	50	5.8	0.0
C /4.7	13.3	0.89	8.65	1	2	97	0	1	128	63.0	-26.2	87	14	10,000	50	0.0	0.0

I. Index of Stock Mutual Funds — Spring 2015

99 Pct = Best
0 Pct = Worst

Fund Type	Fund Name	Ticker Symbol	Overall Investment Rating	Phone	Performance Rating/Pts	Total Return % through 3/31/15			Annualized		Incl. in Returns	
						3 Mo	6 Mo	1Yr / Pct	3Yr / Pct	5Yr / Pct	Dividend Yield	Expense Ratio
FO	American Century Intl Opps Inst	ACIOX	D+	(800) 345-6488	C / 4.6	6.83	3.34	-3.96 / 7	12.62 /57	10.26 /47	0.43	1.60
FO	American Century Intl Opps Inv	AIOIX	D+	(800) 345-6488	C / 4.5	6.85	3.39	-4.08 / 7	12.41 /55	10.04 /45	0.25	1.80
FO	American Century Intl Opps R	AIORX	D	(800) 345-6488	C- / 4.2	6.68	3.15	-4.56 / 6	11.90 /52	9.52 /41	0.11	2.30
FO	American Century Intl Value A	MEQAX	D-	(800) 345-6488	D / 2.0	3.24	-1.51	-2.37 /10	9.15 /34	6.44 /20	3.41	1.57
FO	American Century Intl Value C	ACCOX	D	(800) 345-6488	D+ / 2.4	3.14	-1.87	-3.17 / 8	8.34 /29	5.63 /15	2.95	2.32
FO	American Century Intl Value Inst	ACVUX	D	(800) 345-6488	D+ / 2.8	3.36	-1.30	-1.95 /10	9.63 /37	6.92 /22	4.08	1.12
FO	American Century Intl Value Inv	ACEVX	D	(800) 345-6488	D+ / 2.7	3.31	-1.49	-2.25 /10	9.41 /36	6.70 /21	3.88	1.32
FO	American Century Intl Value R	ACVRX	D	(800) 345-6488	D+ / 2.4	3.21	-1.65	-2.62 / 9	8.89 /32	6.18 /18	3.39	1.82
GR	American Century Leg Foc Lg Cp Adv	ACFDX	A	(800) 345-6488	B / 8.2	2.43	7.03	11.00 /78	16.01 /83	13.20 /70	1.06	1.35
GR	American Century Leg Foc Lg Cp Inst	ACFSX	A+	(800) 345-6488	B+ / 8.6	2.53	7.25	11.48 /80	16.52 /87	13.71 /75	1.48	0.90
GR	American Century Leg Foc Lg Cp Inv	ACFOX	A+	(800) 345-6488	B+ / 8.4	2.48	7.19	11.29 /80	16.28 /85	13.50 /73	1.29	1.10
GR	American Century Leg Foc Lg Cp R	ACFCX	A	(800) 345-6488	B / 8.0	2.32	6.86	10.72 /77	15.71 /81	12.93 /67	0.82	1.60
GR	American Century Leg Multi Cp Adv	ACMFX	A+	(800) 345-6488	A / 9.3	4.39	10.97	13.26 /87	17.70 /93	15.70 /91	0.22	1.40
GR	American Century Leg Multi Cp Inst	ACMHX	A+	(800) 345-6488	A / 9.5	4.49	11.28	13.81 /89	18.24 /95	16.23 /94	0.63	0.95
GR	American Century Leg Multi Cp Inv	ACMNX	A+	(800) 345-6488	A / 9.4	4.41	11.07	13.55 /88	17.98 /94	15.99 /93	0.45	1.15
GR	American Century Leg Multi Cp R	ACMEX	A+	(800) 345-6488	A- / 9.2	4.31	10.83	13.00 /86	17.40 /92	15.41 /90	0.00	1.65
GR	American Century Legacy Lg Cp Adv	ACGDX	B+	(800) 345-6488	B / 8.1	1.27	5.92	11.56 /81	16.03 /84	14.19 /79	0.05	1.35
GR	American Century Legacy Lg Cp Inst	ACGHX	A-	(800) 345-6488	B+ / 8.5	1.38	6.18	12.06 /83	16.59 /87	14.72 /84	0.49	0.90
GR	American Century Legacy Lg Cp Inv	ACGOX	A-	(800) 345-6488	B+ / 8.4	1.32	6.10	11.79 /82	16.34 /86	14.49 /82	0.30	1.10
GR	American Century Legacy Lg Cp R	ACGEX	B+	(800) 345-6488	B / 7.9	1.22	5.83	11.28 /80	15.76 /81	13.91 /77	0.00	1.60
GR	American Century Lrge Comp Val A	ALPAX	B-	(800) 345-6488	C+ / 6.7	0.52	5.14	10.65 /77	15.75 /81	13.14 /69	0.93	1.10
GR	● American Century Lrge Comp Val B	ALBVX	B+	(800) 345-6488	B- / 7.1	0.22	4.68	9.73 /73	14.87 /74	12.27 /62	0.31	1.85
GR	American Century Lrge Comp Val C	ALPCX	B+	(800) 345-6488	B- / 7.1	0.22	4.69	9.77 /73	14.87 /74	12.29 /62	0.31	1.85
GR	American Century Lrge Comp Val Inst	ALVSX	A	(800) 345-6488	B / 8.2	0.61	5.37	11.14 /79	16.24 /85	13.67 /75	1.42	0.65
GR	American Century Lrge Comp Val Inv	ALVIX	A	(800) 345-6488	B / 8.0	0.46	5.27	10.92 /78	16.03 /84	13.42 /72	1.23	0.85
GR	American Century Lrge Comp Val R	ALVRX	A-	(800) 345-6488	B- / 7.5	0.36	5.00	10.37 /76	15.39 /78	12.86 /67	0.74	1.35
GI	American Century Lrge Comp Val R6	ALVDX	U	(800) 345-6488	U /	0.64	5.45	11.30 /80	--	--	1.57	0.50
MC	● American Century Mid Cap Val A	ACLAX	B+	(800) 345-6488	B / 8.1	1.46	8.05	13.40 /88	17.28 /91	14.49 /82	0.77	1.26
MC	● American Century Mid Cap Val C	ACCLX	A-	(800) 345-6488	B+ / 8.5	1.28	7.66	12.53 /85	16.38 /86	13.63 /74	0.25	2.01
MC	● American Century Mid Cap Val Inst	AVUAX	A+	(800) 345-6488	A- / 9.2	1.56	8.29	13.83 /89	17.79 /94	15.00 /87	1.18	0.81
MC	● American Century Mid Cap Val Inv	ACMVX	A+	(800) 345-6488	A- / 9.1	1.52	8.19	13.62 /88	17.54 /92	14.76 /85	1.00	1.01
MC	● American Century Mid Cap Val R	AMVRX	A	(800) 345-6488	B+ / 8.9	1.34	7.92	13.07 /87	16.95 /90	14.20 /79	0.62	1.51
MC	● American Century Mid Cap Val R6	AMDVX	U	(800) 345-6488	U /	1.59	8.43	14.07 /90	--	--	1.32	0.66
GR	American Century Mkt Neut Val A	ACVQX	C-	(800) 345-6488	E+ / 0.7	1.77	2.02	3.93 /31	2.58 / 7	--	0.00	4.67
GR	American Century Mkt Neut Val C	ACVHX	C-	(800) 345-6488	E+ / 0.8	1.61	1.67	3.10 /27	1.78 / 6	--	0.00	5.42
GR	American Century Mkt Neut Val Inst	ACVKX	C	(800) 345-6488	D- / 1.0	1.84	2.19	4.28 /34	3.02 / 8	--	0.00	4.22
GR	American Century Mkt Neut Val Inv	ACVVX	C-	(800) 345-6488	D- / 1.0	1.85	2.11	4.10 /32	2.80 / 7	--	0.00	4.42
GR	American Century Mkt Neut Val R	ACVWX	C-	(800) 345-6488	E+ / 0.9	1.68	1.84	3.56 /29	2.29 / 7	--	0.00	4.92
SC	American Century New Opps A	TWNAX	B-	(800) 345-6488	B / 7.8	7.28	15.47	11.87 /82	15.79 /82	15.54 /90	0.00	1.76
SC	American Century New Opps C	TWNCX	B	(800) 345-6488	B+ / 8.3	7.21	15.07	11.07 /79	14.94 /74	14.71 /84	0.00	2.51
SC	American Century New Opps Inst	TWNIX	B+	(800) 345-6488	B+ / 8.9	7.47	15.78	12.43 /84	16.36 /86	16.08 /93	0.00	1.31
SC	American Century New Opps Inv	TWNOX	B	(800) 345-6488	B+ / 8.7	7.46	15.65	12.18 /83	16.11 /84	15.85 /92	0.00	1.51
SC	American Century New Opps R	TWNRX	B	(800) 345-6488	B+ / 8.4	7.29	15.37	11.64 /81	15.54 /79	15.26 /89	0.00	2.01
GR	American Century NT Core Eq Inst	ACNKX	A+	(800) 345-6488	B / 8.0	-0.62	3.97	10.06 /75	16.41 /86	--	0.82	1.57
EM	American Century NT Emg Market	ACLKX	E+	(800) 345-6488	D- / 1.3	4.56	1.80	5.17 /40	3.31 / 8	3.05 / 6	0.19	1.53
GR	American Century NT Equity Gr Inst	ACLEX	B	(800) 345-6488	B / 7.8	-0.19	4.84	10.72 /77	15.81 /82	14.71 /84	1.47	0.47
GR	American Century NT Growth Inst	ACLTX	C+	(800) 345-6488	B- / 7.2	3.27	9.08	13.45 /88	13.80 /66	13.76 /75	0.47	0.77
GR	American Century NT Growth R6	ACDTX	U	(800) 345-6488	U /	3.34	9.20	13.65 /89	--	--	0.61	0.62
GR	American Century NT Heritage Inst	ACLWX	B	(800) 345-6488	B+ / 8.5	8.05	13.88	13.97 /89	14.79 /73	13.80 /76	0.00	0.80
FO	American Century NT Intl Gr Inst	ACLNX	D	(800) 345-6488	C- / 3.5	4.39	2.04	-0.66 /14	9.65 /37	7.85 /29	0.47	1.02
FO	American Century NT Intl Gr R6	ACDNX	U	(800) 345-6488	U /	4.39	2.11	-0.51 /14	--	--	0.61	0.87
GR	American Century NT Lrg Co Val Inst	ACLLX	A-	(800) 345-6488	B / 8.1	0.65	5.42	11.01 /78	16.13 /84	13.48 /73	1.33	0.65

● Denotes fund is closed to new investors
* Denotes fund is included in Section II

www.thestreetratings.com

RISK			NET ASSETS		ASSET						BULL / BEAR		FUND MANAGER		MINIMUMS		LOADS	
	3 Year		NAV							Portfolio	Last Bull	Last Bear	Manager	Manager	Initial	Additional	Front	Back
Risk Rating/Pts	Standard Deviation	Beta	As of 3/31/15	Total $(Mil)	Cash %	Stocks %	Bonds %	Other %		Turnover Ratio	Market Return	Market Return	Quality Pct	Tenure (Years)	Purch. $	Purch. $	End Load	End Load
C /4.8	13.2	0.89	8.94	1	2	97	0	1		128	69.7	-25.8	91	14	5,000,000	50	0.0	2.0
C /4.8	13.3	0.89	8.86	119	2	97	0	1		128	68.6	-25.8	90	14	10,000	50	0.0	2.0
C /4.8	13.2	0.89	8.78	1	2	97	0	1		128	65.5	-25.9	89	14	10,000	50	0.0	2.0
C+ /5.8	13.9	1.03	8.57	17	2	97	0	1		89	53.1	-23.2	58	4	2,500	50	5.8	0.0
C+ /5.9	13.8	1.03	8.53	3	2	97	0	1		89	49.2	-23.4	46	4	2,500	50	0.0	0.0
C+ /5.7	13.9	1.03	8.53	16	2	97	0	1		89	55.6	-23.1	64	4	5,000,000	50	0.0	2.0
C+ /5.8	13.8	1.03	8.53	20	2	97	0	1		89	54.4	-23.1	62	4	2,500	50	0.0	2.0
C+ /5.8	13.9	1.03	8.53	1	2	97	0	1		89	51.8	-23.3	54	4	2,500	50	0.0	2.0
B- /7.4	9.7	0.94	16.84	1	2	97	0	1		228	87.3	-13.6	75	8	2,500	50	0.0	0.0
B- /7.4	9.7	0.94	16.99	N/A	2	97	0	1		228	90.3	-13.5	79	8	5,000,000	50	0.0	0.0
B- /7.4	9.7	0.94	16.94	12	2	97	0	1		228	88.8	-13.5	78	8	2,500	50	0.0	0.0
B- /7.4	9.7	0.94	16.74	1	2	97	0	1		228	85.8	-13.8	73	8	2,500	50	0.0	0.0
B- /7.3	9.5	0.95	18.08	2	3	96	0	1		175	89.6	-12.5	85	8	2,500	50	0.0	0.0
B- /7.3	9.5	0.94	18.38	N/A	3	96	0	1		175	92.5	-12.3	87	8	5,000,000	50	0.0	0.0
B- /7.4	9.5	0.94	18.25	22	3	96	0	1		175	91.1	-12.3	86	8	2,500	50	0.0	0.0
B- /7.3	9.5	0.95	17.91	N/A	3	96	0	1		175	87.9	-12.5	84	8	2,500	50	0.0	0.0
C+ /6.7	10.4	1.03	17.52	2	4	95	0	1		202	93.0	-12.7	59	8	2,500	50	0.0	0.0
C+ /6.7	10.4	1.03	17.63	N/A	4	95	0	1		202	96.0	-12.6	66	8	5,000,000	50	0.0	0.0
C+ /6.7	10.4	1.04	17.59	24	4	95	0	1		202	94.7	-12.6	63	8	2,500	50	0.0	0.0
C+ /6.7	10.4	1.03	17.43	N/A	4	95	0	1		202	91.4	-12.8	55	8	2,500	50	0.0	0.0
B- /7.5	10.3	1.05	9.07	70	0	99	0	1		35	97.4	-17.2	52	15	2,500	50	5.8	0.0
B- /7.4	10.4	1.06	9.09	1	0	99	0	1		35	92.8	-17.6	38	15	2,500	50	0.0	0.0
B- /7.4	10.3	1.05	9.06	12	0	99	0	1		35	92.6	-17.5	40	15	2,500	50	0.0	0.0
B- /7.5	10.3	1.05	9.08	49	0	99	0	1		35	100.5	-17.1	58	15	5,000,000	50	0.0	0.0
B- /7.5	10.4	1.05	9.07	588	0	99	0	1		35	99.2	-17.2	54	15	2,500	50	0.0	0.0
B- /7.5	10.4	1.05	9.07	6	0	99	0	1		35	95.8	-17.4	46	15	2,500	50	0.0	0.0
U /	N/A	N/A	9.08	38	0	99	0	1		35	N/A	N/A	N/A	15	0	0	0.0	0.0
C+ /6.6	8.9	0.76	16.68	1,465	3	96	0	1		67	98.7	-17.3	91	11	2,500	50	5.8	0.0
C+ /6.6	8.9	0.76	16.57	79	3	96	0	1		67	93.6	-17.4	89	11	2,500	50	0.0	0.0
C+ /6.6	8.8	0.76	16.71	1,018	3	96	0	1		67	101.8	-17.1	92	11	5,000,000	50	0.0	0.0
C+ /6.6	8.9	0.77	16.70	3,779	3	96	0	1		67	100.4	-17.2	92	11	2,500	50	0.0	0.0
C+ /6.6	8.9	0.77	16.64	131	3	96	0	1		67	96.9	-17.2	90	11	2,500	50	0.0	0.0
U /	N/A	N/A	16.71	219	3	96	0	1		67	N/A	N/A	N/A	11	0	0	0.0	0.0
B+ /9.8	2.0	0.02	10.36	9	99	0	0	1		521	N/A	N/A	86	4	2,500	50	5.8	0.0
B+ /9.5	2.0	0.01	10.08	8	99	0	0	1		521	N/A	N/A	81	4	2,500	50	0.0	0.0
B+ /9.8	2.0	0.02	10.52	6	99	0	0	1		521	N/A	N/A	87	4	5,000,000	50	0.0	0.0
B+ /9.8	2.0	0.02	10.44	49	99	0	0	1		521	N/A	N/A	86	4	2,500	50	0.0	0.0
B+ /9.7	2.0	0.02	10.26	N/A	99	0	0	1		521	N/A	N/A	84	4	2,500	50	0.0	0.0
C /5.2	13.2	0.92	12.08	1	2	97	0	1		76	100.2	-27.7	75	9	2,500	50	5.8	0.0
C /5.1	13.1	0.92	11.60	N/A	2	97	0	1		76	94.9	-27.8	68	9	2,500	50	0.0	0.0
C /5.2	13.2	0.92	12.38	N/A	2	97	0	1		76	103.2	-27.5	79	9	5,000,000	50	0.0	2.0
C /5.2	13.2	0.92	12.25	196	2	97	0	1		76	101.8	-27.6	77	9	2,500	50	0.0	2.0
C /5.2	13.2	0.92	11.92	N/A	2	97	0	1		76	98.6	-27.8	73	9	2,500	50	0.0	2.0
B /8.5	9.8	1.00	14.54	449	0	0	0	100		104	N/A	N/A	70	N/A	0	0	0.0	0.0
C /5.3	14.2	0.99	10.80	359	1	98	0	1		84	34.1	-29.9	87	9	0	0	0.0	0.0
C+ /6.1	9.9	1.03	12.31	1,311	0	99	0	1		77	100.6	-15.4	57	9	0	0	0.0	0.0
C /4.7	9.9	0.98	15.16	964	0	99	0	1		119	89.7	-16.9	41	9	5,000,000	50	0.0	0.0
U /	N/A	N/A	15.15	42	0	99	0	1		119	N/A	N/A	N/A	9	0	0	0.0	0.0
C /5.0	11.8	1.05	14.10	574	2	97	0	1		76	88.2	-21.7	39	9	5,000,000	50	0.0	0.0
C /5.5	12.5	0.92	11.17	727	4	95	0	1		67	58.7	-24.4	76	7	0	0	0.0	0.0
U /	N/A	N/A	11.17	31	4	95	0	1		67	N/A	N/A	N/A	7	0	0	0.0	0.0
B- /7.0	10.4	1.05	12.38	1,398	0	99	0	1		35	99.8	-17.3	57	9	0	0	0.0	0.0

Fund Type	Fund Name	Ticker Symbol	Overall Investment Rating	Phone	Performance Rating/Pts	3 Mo	6 Mo	1Yr / Pct	3Yr / Pct	5Yr / Pct	Dividend Yield	Expense Ratio
GI	American Century NT Lrg Co Val R6	ACDLX	U	(800) 345-6488	U /	0.68	5.49	11.17 /79	--	--	1.48	0.50
MC	American Century NT Md Cp Val Inst	ACLMX	A	(800) 345-6488	A /9.3	1.62	8.50	14.05 /89	17.82 /94	15.14 /88	1.17	0.81
MC	American Century NT Md Cp Val R6	ACDSX	U	(800) 345-6488	U /	1.57	8.49	14.14 /90	--	--	1.31	0.66
SC	American Century NT Sm Comp Inst	ACLOX	B	(800) 345-6488	A /9.4	5.85	13.65	10.40 /76	17.90 /94	16.44 /95	0.24	0.67
AA	American Century One Chc Agg Inv	AOGIX	B-	(800) 345-6488	C /5.3	3.13	6.41	8.81 /68	11.41 /48	10.97 /52	2.17	0.96
AA	American Century One Chc Conv Inv	AOCIX	C+	(800) 345-6488	D+ /2.8	1.36	3.94	6.00 /46	7.39 /23	7.88 /29	1.97	0.75
AA	American Century One Chc Mod Inv	AOMIX	C+	(800) 345-6488	C- /4.1	2.18	5.04	7.32 /58	9.62 /37	9.59 /41	2.07	0.86
AA	American Century One Chc VryAgg	AOVIX	C+	(800) 345-6488	C+ /6.4	3.39	7.19	9.78 /73	13.12 /60	12.03 /61	1.81	1.02
AA	American Century One Chc VryCon	AONIX	C-	(800) 345-6488	D- /1.4	0.82	2.69	4.42 /34	4.62 /12	5.47 /14	1.84	0.66
GI	American Century OneChoice 2020 A	ARBMX	C	(800) 345-6488	D /2.1	1.32	3.71	5.78 /45	7.83 /26	8.26 /32	1.80	1.04
GI	American Century OneChoice 2020 C	ARNCX	C	(800) 345-6488	D+ /2.5	1.15	3.34	5.06 /39	7.03 /21	7.46 /26	1.15	1.79
GI	American Century OneChoice 2020 I	ARBSX	C+	(800) 345-6488	C- /3.3	1.40	4.01	6.35 /49	8.34 /29	8.76 /35	2.36	0.59
GI	American Century OneChoice 2020	ARBVX	C+	(800) 345-6488	C- /3.2	1.40	3.89	6.13 /48	8.12 /28	8.55 /33	2.16	0.79
GI	American Century OneChoice 2020 R	ARBRX	C	(800) 345-6488	D+ /2.8	1.24	3.62	5.61 /43	7.55 /24	7.99 /30	1.66	1.29
GI	American Century OneChoice 2020	ARBDX	U	(800) 345-6488	U /	1.39	4.07	6.43 /50	--	--	2.19	0.53
BA	American Century OneChoice 2025 A	ARWAX	C	(800) 345-6488	D+ /2.5	1.67	4.22	6.41 /50	8.48 /30	8.76 /35	1.82	1.07
BA	American Century OneChoice 2025 C	ARWCX	C	(800) 345-6488	D+ /2.9	1.39	3.78	5.60 /43	7.66 /25	7.93 /29	1.17	1.82
BA	American Century OneChoice 2025 I	ARWFX	C+	(800) 345-6488	C- /3.7	1.74	4.47	6.89 /54	8.97 /33	9.24 /38	2.38	0.62
BA	American Century OneChoice 2025	ARWIX	C+	(800) 345-6488	C- /3.5	1.67	4.34	6.67 /52	8.73 /31	9.03 /37	2.18	0.82
BA	American Century OneChoice 2025 R	ARWRX	C+	(800) 345-6488	C- /3.2	1.53	4.03	6.07 /47	8.19 /28	8.47 /33	1.68	1.32
BA	American Century OneChoice 2025	ARWDX	U	(800) 345-6488	U /	1.74	4.57	7.13 /56	--	--	2.12	0.56
AA	American Century OneChoice 2030 A	ARCMX	C	(800) 345-6488	C- /3.0	1.95	4.84	7.08 /56	9.24 /34	9.30 /39	1.77	1.09
GI	American Century OneChoice 2030 C	ARWOX	C+	(800) 345-6488	C- /3.4	1.78	4.46	6.34 /49	8.43 /29	8.48 /33	1.11	1.84
AA	American Century OneChoice 2030 I	ARCSX	C+	(800) 345-6488	C- /4.2	2.11	5.06	7.55 /59	9.75 /38	9.80 /43	2.33	0.64
AA	American Century OneChoice 2030	ARCVX	C+	(800) 345-6488	C- /4.1	2.03	4.93	7.34 /58	9.53 /36	9.58 /41	2.12	0.84
AA	American Century OneChoice 2030 R	ARCRX	C+	(800) 345-6488	C- /3.7	1.95	4.74	6.89 /54	8.99 /33	9.02 /37	1.62	1.34
GI	American Century OneChoice 2030	ARCUX	U	(800) 345-6488	U /	2.01	5.17	7.74 /61	--	--	2.07	0.57
GI	American Century OneChoice 2035 A	ARYAX	C	(800) 345-6488	C- /3.5	2.27	5.44	7.86 /62	10.12 /40	9.96 /44	1.77	1.12
GI	American Century OneChoice 2035 C	ARLCX	C+	(800) 345-6488	C- /3.9	2.07	4.98	6.97 /55	9.29 /35	9.12 /38	1.13	1.87
GI	American Century OneChoice 2035 I	ARLIX	B-	(800) 345-6488	C /4.7	2.40	5.64	8.34 /65	10.61 /43	10.46 /48	2.33	0.67
GI	American Century OneChoice 2035	ARYIX	C+	(800) 345-6488	C /4.6	2.33	5.50	8.06 /63	10.37 /42	10.24 /46	2.13	0.87
GI	American Century OneChoice 2035 R	ARYRX	C+	(800) 345-6488	C /4.3	2.20	5.24	7.52 /59	9.85 /38	9.69 /42	1.63	1.37
GI	American Century OneChoice 2035	ARLDX	U	(800) 345-6488	U /	2.44	5.79	8.56 /67	--	--	2.01	0.60
GI	American Century OneChoice 2040 A	ARDMX	C+	(800) 345-6488	C- /4.0	2.43	5.83	8.36 /65	10.84 /44	10.54 /49	1.78	1.15
GI	American Century OneChoice 2040 C	ARNOX	C+	(800) 345-6488	C /4.4	2.19	5.36	7.54 /59	10.01 /39	9.68 /42	1.13	1.90
GI	American Century OneChoice 2040 I	ARDSX	B-	(800) 345-6488	C /5.2	2.51	5.98	8.84 /68	11.37 /48	11.03 /53	2.34	0.70
GI	American Century OneChoice 2040	ARDVX	B-	(800) 345-6488	C /5.1	2.51	5.93	8.71 /68	11.15 /47	10.80 /51	2.14	0.90
GI	American Century OneChoice 2040 R	ARDRX	C+	(800) 345-6488	C /4.7	2.35	5.65	8.17 /64	10.57 /43	10.27 /47	1.64	1.40
GI	American Century OneChoice 2040	ARDUX	U	(800) 345-6488	U /	2.52	6.10	9.06 /70	--	--	2.16	0.63
GI	American Century OneChoice 2045 A	AROAX	C+	(800) 345-6488	C /4.3	2.49	6.05	8.86 /68	11.45 /49	10.93 /52	1.84	1.19
GI	American Century OneChoice 2045 C	AROCX	C+	(800) 345-6488	C /4.7	2.30	5.69	8.02 /63	10.59 /43	10.10 /45	1.20	1.94
GI	American Century OneChoice 2045 I	AOOIX	B	(800) 345-6488	C+ /5.6	2.61	6.32	9.34 /71	11.93 /52	11.43 /56	2.40	0.74
GI	American Century OneChoice 2045	AROIX	B-	(800) 345-6488	C /5.5	2.61	6.25	9.13 /70	11.71 /50	11.21 /54	2.20	0.94
GI	American Century OneChoice 2045 R	ARORX	C+	(800) 345-6488	C /5.1	2.43	5.91	8.58 /67	11.16 /47	10.65 /50	1.70	1.44
GI	American Century OneChoice 2045	ARDOX	U	(800) 345-6488	U /	2.68	6.40	9.55 /72	--	--	2.23	0.66
GI	American Century OneChoice 2050 A	ARFMX	C+	(800) 345-6488	C /4.5	2.58	6.21	9.00 /69	11.66 /50	11.12 /54	1.78	1.20
GI	American Century OneChoice 2050 C	ARFDX	C+	(800) 345-6488	C /4.9	2.34	5.80	8.16 /64	10.84 /44	10.27 /47	1.13	1.95
GI	American Century OneChoice 2050 I	ARFSX	B-	(800) 345-6488	C+ /5.8	2.73	6.52	9.57 /72	12.17 /54	11.61 /58	2.33	0.75
GI	American Century OneChoice 2050	ARFVX	B-	(800) 345-6488	C+ /5.6	2.58	6.31	9.27 /71	11.93 /52	11.38 /56	2.14	0.95
GI	American Century OneChoice 2050 R	ARFWX	B-	(800) 345-6488	C /5.2	2.50	6.10	8.72 /68	11.37 /48	10.84 /51	1.63	1.45
GI	American Century OneChoice 2050	ARFEX	U	(800) 345-6488	U /	2.68	6.53	9.68 /73	--	--	2.21	0.68
AA	American Century OneChoice 2055 A	AREMX	C+	(800) 345-6488	C /4.7	2.63	6.43	9.32 /71	11.98 /52	--	1.67	1.21

99 Pct = Best
0 Pct = Worst

PERFORMANCE
Total Return % through 3/31/15
Annualized
Incl. in Returns

● Denotes fund is closed to new investors
* Denotes fund is included in Section II

www.thestreetratings.com

Risk Rating/Pts	Standard Deviation	Beta	NAV As of 3/31/15	Total $(Mil)	Cash %	Stocks %	Bonds %	Other %	Portfolio Turnover Ratio	Last Bull Market Return	Last Bear Market Return	Manager Quality Pct	Manager Tenure (Years)	Initial Purch. $	Additional Purch. $	Front End Load	Back End Load
U /	N/A	N/A	12.38	60	0	99	0	1	35	N/A	N/A	N/A	9	0	0	0.0	0.0
C+ / 6.4	8.9	0.77	12.82	763	3	96	0	1	69	102.0	-16.9	92	9	0	0	0.0	0.0
U /	N/A	N/A	12.81	33	3	96	0	1	69	N/A	N/A	N/A	9	0	0	0.0	0.0
C- / 4.2	13.6	0.99	10.31	338	1	98	0	1	96	109.3	-22.8	81	9	0	0	0.0	0.0
B- / 7.6	8.3	1.41	16.80	1,126	0	80	19	1	5	67.6	-15.8	18	N/A	2,500	50	0.0	0.0
B+ / 9.3	4.7	0.81	13.68	1,042	6	46	47	1	2	39.5	-7.0	49	N/A	2,500	50	0.0	0.0
B / 8.5	6.7	1.15	15.46	1,620	3	65	30	2	3	54.8	-12.0	29	N/A	2,500	50	0.0	0.0
C+ / 6.8	9.8	1.66	18.29	288	1	96	2	1	8	80.6	-19.2	11	N/A	2,500	50	0.0	0.0
B+ / 9.4	3.2	0.49	11.90	370	6	26	67	1	12	23.5	-2.8	59	11	2,500	50	0.0	0.0
B+ / 9.0	5.3	0.52	12.28	355	5	49	45	1	43	43.9	-9.3	63	7	2,500	50	5.8	0.0
B+ / 9.0	5.3	0.53	12.30	12	5	49	45	1	43	40.2	-9.6	50	7	2,500	50	0.0	0.0
B / 8.9	5.3	0.52	12.30	477	5	49	45	1	43	46.2	-9.2	69	7	5,000,000	0	0.0	0.0
B / 8.9	5.3	0.53	12.30	594	5	49	45	1	43	45.1	-9.3	66	7	2,500	50	0.0	0.0
B+ / 9.0	5.3	0.53	12.28	159	5	49	45	1	43	42.7	-9.5	58	7	2,500	50	0.0	0.0
U /	N/A	N/A	10.91	83	5	49	45	1	43	N/A	N/A	N/A	7	0	0	0.0	0.0
B / 8.7	5.8	1.00	14.61	558	2	53	43	2	18	48.0	-10.6	35	11	2,500	50	5.8	0.0
B / 8.8	5.8	1.00	14.61	8	2	53	43	2	18	44.3	-10.9	25	11	2,500	50	0.0	0.0
B / 8.7	5.8	1.00	14.62	579	2	53	43	2	18	50.3	-10.4	40	11	5,000,000	0	0.0	0.0
B / 8.7	5.8	1.01	14.61	1,077	2	53	43	2	18	49.4	-10.5	36	11	2,500	50	0.0	0.0
B / 8.8	5.8	1.00	14.59	236	2	53	43	2	18	46.7	-10.7	31	11	2,500	50	0.0	0.0
U /	N/A	N/A	11.09	101	2	53	43	2	18	N/A	N/A	N/A	9	0	0	0.0	0.0
B / 8.6	6.3	1.10	12.54	379	3	59	36	2	23	53.0	-12.0	30	7	2,500	50	5.8	0.0
B / 8.6	6.4	0.64	12.56	5	3	59	36	2	23	49.1	-12.2	45	N/A	2,500	50	0.0	0.0
B / 8.5	6.3	1.10	12.56	471	3	59	36	2	23	55.2	-11.7	36	7	5,000,000	0	0.0	0.0
B / 8.5	6.3	1.10	12.56	569	3	59	36	2	23	54.3	-11.9	34	7	2,500	50	0.0	0.0
B / 8.6	6.3	1.10	12.54	163	3	59	36	2	23	51.6	-12.0	28	7	2,500	50	0.0	0.0
U /	N/A	N/A	11.18	85	3	59	36	2	23	N/A	N/A	N/A	7	0	0	0.0	0.0
B / 8.3	6.9	0.70	15.78	455	3	65	30	2	12	58.5	-13.3	56	11	2,500	50	5.8	0.0
B / 8.3	6.9	0.69	15.77	6	3	65	30	2	12	54.6	-13.5	45	11	2,500	50	0.0	0.0
B / 8.3	6.9	0.69	15.80	457	3	65	30	2	12	61.0	-13.1	64	11	5,000,000	0	0.0	0.0
B / 8.3	6.9	0.69	15.78	834	3	65	30	2	12	59.8	-13.2	60	11	2,500	50	0.0	0.0
B / 8.3	6.9	0.69	15.77	205	3	65	30	2	12	57.2	-13.4	52	11	2,500	50	0.0	0.0
U /	N/A	N/A	11.32	79	3	65	30	2	12	N/A	N/A	N/A	9	0	0	0.0	0.0
B / 8.1	7.5	0.76	13.08	259	1	71	26	2	11	63.9	-14.6	52	7	2,500	50	5.8	0.0
B / 8.1	7.5	0.75	13.07	4	1	71	26	2	11	59.8	-14.9	41	7	2,500	50	0.0	0.0
B / 8.0	7.5	0.75	13.09	369	1	71	26	2	11	66.4	-14.4	60	7	5,000,000	0	0.0	0.0
B / 8.1	7.5	0.75	13.09	441	1	71	26	2	11	65.3	-14.5	58	7	2,500	50	0.0	0.0
B / 8.1	7.5	0.75	13.07	117	1	71	26	2	11	62.6	-14.7	49	7	2,500	50	0.0	0.0
U /	N/A	N/A	11.40	56	1	71	26	2	11	N/A	N/A	N/A	7	0	0	0.0	0.0
B- / 7.8	8.0	0.80	16.47	299	0	77	22	1	12	67.9	-15.4	50	N/A	2,500	50	5.8	0.0
B- / 7.8	8.0	0.81	16.48	2	0	77	22	1	12	63.7	-15.7	37	N/A	2,500	50	0.0	0.0
B- / 7.8	8.0	0.81	16.50	373	0	77	22	1	12	70.6	-15.3	55	N/A	5,000,000	0	0.0	0.0
B- / 7.8	8.0	0.80	16.49	596	0	77	22	1	12	69.5	-15.4	53	N/A	2,500	50	0.0	0.0
B- / 7.8	8.0	0.80	16.47	134	0	77	22	1	12	66.6	-15.6	45	N/A	2,500	50	0.0	0.0
U /	N/A	N/A	11.50	47	0	77	22	1	12	N/A	N/A	N/A	9	0	0	0.0	0.0
B- / 7.7	8.2	0.82	13.12	152	0	80	19	1	13	69.8	-16.0	47	7	2,500	50	5.8	0.0
B- / 7.7	8.2	0.83	13.13	2	0	80	19	1	13	65.6	-16.3	36	7	2,500	50	0.0	0.0
B- / 7.7	8.2	0.83	13.15	218	0	80	19	1	13	72.6	-15.9	53	7	5,000,000	0	0.0	0.0
B- / 7.7	8.2	0.83	13.13	245	0	80	19	1	13	71.5	-16.0	51	7	2,500	50	0.0	0.0
B- / 7.7	8.2	0.83	13.12	60	0	80	19	1	13	68.5	-16.2	43	7	2,500	50	0.0	0.0
U /	N/A	N/A	11.51	29	0	80	19	1	13	N/A	N/A	N/A	7	0	0	0.0	0.0
B- / 7.7	8.4	1.45	13.64	46	3	79	16	2	23	71.7	-16.2	19	4	2,500	50	5.8	0.0

I. Index of Stock Mutual Funds

99 Pct = Best
0 Pct = Worst

Fund Type	Fund Name	Ticker Symbol	Overall Investment Rating	Phone	Perfor-mance Rating/Pts	3 Mo	6 Mo	1Yr / Pct	3Yr / Pct	5Yr / Pct	Dividend Yield	Expense Ratio
AA	American Century OneChoice 2055 C	AREFX	C+	(800) 345-6488	C / 5.1	2.41	6.03	8.50 /66	11.12 /46	--	1.02	1.96
AA	American Century OneChoice 2055 I	ARENX	B-	(800) 345-6488	C+ / 6.0	2.71	6.74	9.80 /74	12.47 /56	--	2.22	0.76
AA	American Century OneChoice 2055	AREVX	B-	(800) 345-6488	C+ / 5.8	2.63	6.53	9.58 /72	12.22 /54	--	2.02	0.96
AA	American Century OneChoice 2055 R	AREOX	B-	(800) 345-6488	C / 5.5	2.56	6.32	9.04 /69	11.70 /50	--	1.52	1.46
GI	American Century OneChoice InRe A	ARTAX	C-	(800) 345-6488	D / 1.7	1.09	3.31	5.26 /41	7.11 /22	7.57 /27	1.79	1.01
GI	American Century OneChoice InRe C	ATTCX	C	(800) 345-6488	D / 2.0	0.90	2.91	4.46 /35	6.29 /18	6.78 /22	1.21	1.76
GI	American Century OneChoice InRe I	ATTIX	C	(800) 345-6488	D+ / 2.8	1.19	3.55	5.65 /44	7.56 /24	8.06 /30	2.34	0.56
GI	American Century OneChoice InRe	ARTOX	C	(800) 345-6488	D+ / 2.7	1.07	3.36	5.44 /42	7.35 /23	7.83 /29	2.14	0.76
GI	American Century OneChoice InRe R	ARSRX	C	(800) 345-6488	D+ / 2.3	1.03	3.19	4.92 /38	6.82 /20	7.29 /25	1.64	1.26
AA	American Century OneChoice InRe	ARDTX	U	(800) 345-6488	U /	1.21	3.64	5.92 /46	--	--	2.43	0.50
RE	American Century Real Estate A	AREEX	C+	(800) 345-6488	B+ / 8.7	5.25	20.20	24.55 /98	13.51 /63	16.07 /93	1.52	1.39
RE	American Century Real Estate C	ARYCX	B-	(800) 345-6488	A- / 9.0	5.02	19.71	23.59 /98	12.65 /57	15.20 /88	0.99	2.14
RE	American Century Real Estate Inst	REAIX	B	(800) 345-6488	A / 9.5	5.36	20.47	25.10 /98	14.01 /67	16.59 /95	2.03	0.94
RE	American Century Real Estate Inv	REACX	B	(800) 345-6488	A / 9.5	5.30	20.31	24.87 /98	13.79 /66	16.36 /94	1.85	1.14
RE	American Century Real Estate R	AREWX	B-	(800) 345-6488	A / 9.3	5.19	20.01	24.22 /98	13.22 /61	15.77 /92	1.39	1.64
RE	American Century Real Estate R6	AREDX	U	(800) 345-6488	U /	5.40	20.56	25.30 /98	--	--	2.17	0.79
GR	American Century Select A	TWCAX	C+	(800) 345-6488	B- / 7.0	5.39	10.17	17.01 /95	13.80 /66	13.83 /76	0.13	1.25
GR	American Century Select C	ACSLX	B-	(800) 345-6488	B- / 7.5	5.21	9.77	16.14 /93	12.97 /59	12.98 /68	0.00	2.00
GR	American Century Select Inst	TWSIX	B+	(800) 345-6488	B+ / 8.5	5.51	10.42	17.55 /95	14.33 /70	14.34 /81	0.55	0.80
GR	American Century Select Inv	TWCIX	B+	(800) 345-6488	B+ / 8.3	5.46	10.32	17.31 /95	14.10 /68	14.12 /79	0.37	1.00
GR	American Century Select R	ASERX	B	(800) 345-6488	B / 7.9	5.32	10.03	16.72 /94	13.53 /64	13.54 /73	0.00	1.50
GI	American Century Select R6	ASDEX	A	(800) 345-6488	B+ / 8.5	5.53	10.51	17.72 /95	14.31 /69	14.25 /80	0.69	0.65
SC	● American Century Sm Cap Val A	ACSCX	C-	(800) 345-6488	C+ / 6.3	3.18	13.22	5.96 /46	14.81 /73	12.06 /61	0.27	1.55
SC	● American Century Sm Cap Val C	ASVNX	C-	(800) 345-6488	C+ / 6.8	3.00	12.81	5.14 /40	13.93 /67	11.23 /55	0.08	2.30
SC	● American Century Sm Cap Val Inst	ACVIX	C	(800) 345-6488	B / 7.8	3.25	13.43	6.35 /49	15.34 /78	12.58 /65	0.69	1.10
SC	● American Century Sm Cap Val Inv	ASVIX	C	(800) 345-6488	B / 7.6	3.27	13.33	6.18 /48	15.12 /76	12.37 /63	0.51	1.30
SC	● American Century Sm Cap Val R	ASVRX	C-	(800) 345-6488	B- / 7.2	3.18	13.13	5.65 /44	14.54 /71	11.80 /59	0.21	1.80
SC	● American Century Sm Cap Val R6	ASVDX	U	(800) 345-6488	U /	3.36	13.60	6.62 /52	--	--	0.83	0.95
SC	American Century Small Cap Gro A	ANOAX	B-	(800) 345-6488	B / 8.1	6.51	17.38	11.55 /81	16.10 /84	15.46 /90	0.00	1.66
SC	● American Century Small Cap Gro B	ANOBX	B-	(800) 345-6488	B+ / 8.5	6.29	17.00	10.72 /77	15.24 /77	14.61 /83	0.00	2.41
SC	American Century Small Cap Gro C	ANOCX	B-	(800) 345-6488	B+ / 8.5	6.27	17.03	10.77 /77	15.26 /77	14.59 /83	0.00	2.41
SC	American Century Small Cap Gro Inst	ANONX	B	(800) 345-6488	A- / 9.0	6.64	17.75	12.09 /83	16.62 /88	15.97 /93	0.00	1.21
SC	American Century Small Cap Gro Inv	ANOIX	B	(800) 345-6488	B+ / 8.9	6.59	17.59	11.86 /82	16.39 /86	15.78 /92	0.00	1.41
SC	American Century Small Cap Gro R	ANORX	B	(800) 345-6488	B+ / 8.6	6.43	17.25	11.26 /79	15.84 /82	15.17 /88	0.00	1.91
SC	American Century Small Company A	ASQAX	B+	(800) 345-6488	B+ / 8.4	5.33	13.01	9.57 /72	17.39 /92	15.97 /93	0.01	1.12
SC	American Century Small Company C	ASQCX	B+	(800) 345-6488	B+ / 8.7	5.17	12.58	8.75 /68	16.53 /87	15.09 /87	0.00	1.87
SC	American Century Small Company	ASCQX	A	(800) 345-6488	A / 9.4	5.42	13.27	10.09 /75	17.93 /94	16.47 /95	0.31	0.67
SC	American Century Small Company	ASQIX	A	(800) 345-6488	A / 9.3	5.37	13.16	9.84 /74	17.67 /93	16.26 /94	0.13	0.87
SC	American Century Small Company R	ASCRX	A-	(800) 345-6488	A- / 9.1	5.32	12.93	9.35 /71	17.12 /90	15.68 /91	0.00	1.37
AA	American Century Str Alloc:Agg A	ACVAX	D+	(800) 345-6488	C- / 3.9	3.05	6.26	8.33 /65	10.65 /43	10.33 /47	0.08	1.40
AA	● American Century Str Alloc:Agg B	ALLBX	D+	(800) 345-6488	C / 4.3	2.84	5.87	7.46 /59	9.82 /38	9.50 /40	0.00	2.15
AA	American Century Str Alloc:Agg C	ASTAX	D+	(800) 345-6488	C / 4.3	2.85	5.90	7.50 /59	9.81 /38	9.49 /40	0.00	2.15
AA	American Century Str Alloc:Agg Inst	AAAIX	C-	(800) 345-6488	C / 5.2	3.21	6.59	8.81 /68	11.15 /47	10.86 /51	0.52	0.95
AA	American Century Str Alloc:Agg Inv	TWSAX	C-	(800) 345-6488	C / 5.0	3.19	6.46	8.55 /67	10.93 /45	10.62 /50	0.32	1.15
AA	American Century Str Alloc:Agg R	AAARX	C-	(800) 345-6488	C / 4.6	2.92	6.16	7.99 /63	10.36 /42	10.03 /45	0.00	1.65
GI	American Century Str Alloc:Con A	ACCAX	D+	(800) 345-6488	D / 1.6	1.22	3.70	5.46 /42	6.65 /20	7.22 /24	0.47	1.25
GI	● American Century Str Alloc:Con B	ACVBX	C-	(800) 345-6488	D / 1.9	1.05	3.36	4.58 /36	5.85 /16	6.43 /20	0.00	2.00
GI	American Century Str Alloc:Con C	AACCX	C-	(800) 345-6488	D / 1.9	1.05	3.36	4.58 /36	5.85 /16	6.43 /20	0.00	2.00
GI	American Century Str Alloc:Con Inst	ACCIX	C-	(800) 345-6488	D+ / 2.7	1.45	4.07	5.90 /46	7.17 /22	7.72 /28	0.91	0.80
GI	American Century Str Alloc:Con Inv	TWSCX	C-	(800) 345-6488	D+ / 2.5	1.41	3.97	5.69 /44	6.96 /21	7.51 /26	0.72	1.00
GI	American Century Str Alloc:Con R	AACRX	C-	(800) 345-6488	D / 2.2	1.22	3.62	5.25 /40	6.41 /19	7.01 /23	0.31	1.50
AA	American Century Str Alloc:Mod A	ACOAX	D+	(800) 345-6488	D+ / 2.8	2.01	4.80	6.87 /54	8.94 /32	9.03 /37	0.52	1.32

● Denotes fund is closed to new investors
* Denotes fund is included in Section II

www.thestreetratings.com

RISK Risk Rating/Pts	3 Year Standard Deviation	Beta	NAV As of 3/31/15	Total $(Mil)	Cash %	Stocks %	Bonds %	Other %	Portfolio Turnover Ratio	Last Bull Market Return	Last Bear Market Return	Manager Quality Pct	Manager Tenure (Years)	Initial Purch. $	Additional Purch. $	Front End Load	Back End Load
B- / 7.7	8.3	1.44	13.62	1	3	79	16	2	23	67.3	-16.4	14	4	2,500	50	0.0	0.0
B- / 7.7	8.4	1.45	13.66	69	3	79	16	2	23	74.3	-16.0	23	4	5,000,000	0	0.0	0.0
B- / 7.7	8.3	1.44	13.65	57	3	79	16	2	23	73.2	-16.1	22	4	2,500	50	0.0	0.0
B- / 7.7	8.4	1.45	13.64	21	3	79	16	2	23	70.4	-16.3	17	4	2,500	50	0.0	0.0
B / 8.9	4.7	0.46	12.67	444	7	44	48	1	34	38.6	-7.3	66	N/A	2,500	50	5.8	0.0
B+ / 9.0	4.7	0.46	12.65	8	7	44	48	1	34	35.1	-7.6	55	N/A	2,500	50	0.0	0.0
B / 8.9	4.7	0.46	12.67	410	7	44	48	1	34	40.7	-7.1	71	N/A	5,000,000	0	0.0	0.0
B / 8.9	4.7	0.46	12.66	843	7	44	48	1	34	39.8	-7.3	69	N/A	2,500	50	0.0	0.0
B+ / 9.0	4.7	0.46	12.66	252	7	44	48	1	34	37.4	-7.4	62	N/A	2,500	50	0.0	0.0
U /	N/A	N/A	10.50	66	7	44	48	1	34	N/A	N/A	N/A	9	0	0	0.0	0.0
C- / 3.9	12.9	1.03	31.22	200	1	98	0	1	127	84.4	-14.8	53	7	2,500	50	5.8	0.0
C- / 3.9	12.9	1.03	30.74	20	1	98	0	1	127	79.7	-15.1	41	7	2,500	50	0.0	0.0
C- / 3.9	12.9	1.03	31.28	163	1	98	0	1	127	87.2	-14.6	60	7	5,000,000	50	0.0	0.0
C- / 3.9	12.9	1.03	31.21	1,080	1	98	0	1	127	86.0	-14.7	57	7	2,500	50	0.0	0.0
C- / 3.9	12.9	1.03	31.08	13	1	98	0	1	127	82.7	-14.9	49	7	2,500	50	0.0	0.0
U /	N/A	N/A	31.27	54	1	98	0	1	127	N/A	N/A	N/A	7	0	0	0.0	0.0
C+ / 5.9	10.6	1.02	58.28	39	0	99	0	1	25	91.2	-15.9	32	14	2,500	50	5.8	0.0
C+ / 5.8	10.6	1.02	54.36	6	0	99	0	1	25	86.4	-16.1	24	14	2,500	50	0.0	0.0
C+ / 5.9	10.7	1.03	60.13	36	0	99	0	1	25	94.2	-15.7	38	14	5,000,000	50	0.0	0.0
C+ / 5.9	10.6	1.02	59.32	2,411	0	99	0	1	25	92.8	-15.8	36	14	2,500	50	0.0	0.0
C+ / 5.9	10.6	1.02	58.18	3	0	99	0	1	25	89.6	-15.9	29	14	2,500	50	0.0	0.0
C+ / 6.9	10.7	1.02	60.10	9	0	99	0	1	25	93.9	-15.8	38	14	0	0	0.0	0.0
C- / 3.7	12.4	0.90	9.09	385	2	97	0	1	111	91.5	-23.6	70	17	2,500	50	5.8	0.0
C- / 3.5	12.4	0.90	8.93	N/A	2	97	0	1	111	86.5	-23.8	60	17	2,500	50	0.0	0.0
C- / 3.7	12.4	0.90	9.22	599	2	97	0	1	111	94.3	-23.5	75	17	5,000,000	50	0.0	0.0
C- / 3.7	12.4	0.90	9.16	818	2	97	0	1	111	93.1	-23.6	73	17	2,500	50	0.0	0.0
C- / 3.6	12.4	0.90	9.09	2	2	97	0	1	111	89.8	-23.7	67	17	2,500	50	0.0	0.0
U /	N/A	N/A	9.23	40	2	97	0	1	111	N/A	N/A	N/A	17	0	0	0.0	0.0
C / 4.8	14.0	0.99	13.91	108	1	98	0	1	75	104.6	-28.8	67	9	2,500	50	5.8	0.0
C / 4.8	14.0	0.99	13.01	1	1	98	0	1	75	99.7	-29.1	56	9	2,500	50	0.0	0.0
C / 4.8	14.0	0.99	13.06	13	1	98	0	1	75	99.7	-29.1	56	9	2,500	50	0.0	0.0
C / 4.9	14.0	1.00	14.46	70	1	98	0	1	75	107.8	-28.7	71	9	5,000,000	50	0.0	2.0
C / 4.9	14.0	0.99	14.24	183	1	98	0	1	75	106.5	-28.7	70	9	2,500	50	0.0	2.0
C / 4.8	14.1	1.00	13.73	2	1	98	0	1	75	103.2	-28.9	63	9	2,500	50	0.0	2.0
C+ / 6.0	13.6	0.99	13.64	43	0	99	0	1	83	106.2	-23.2	78	10	2,500	50	5.8	0.0
C+ / 6.0	13.6	0.99	13.42	1	0	99	0	1	83	101.0	-23.3	71	10	2,500	50	0.0	0.0
C+ / 6.0	13.7	0.99	14.00	41	0	99	0	1	83	109.3	-22.9	81	10	5,000,000	0	0.0	0.0
C+ / 6.0	13.7	0.99	13.93	470	0	99	0	1	83	107.7	-23.0	79	10	2,500	50	0.0	0.0
C+ / 6.0	13.6	0.99	13.45	5	0	99	0	1	83	104.2	-23.1	76	10	2,500	50	0.0	0.0
C / 5.5	8.2	1.41	8.46	334	1	80	17	2	77	64.0	-16.0	14	6	2,500	50	5.8	0.0
C / 5.5	8.2	1.40	8.32	6	1	80	17	2	77	59.8	-16.3	10	6	2,500	50	0.0	0.0
C / 5.4	8.2	1.40	8.30	78	1	80	17	2	77	60.0	-16.3	10	6	2,500	50	0.0	0.0
C / 5.3	8.2	1.40	8.37	137	1	80	17	2	77	66.7	-15.9	17	6	5,000,000	50	0.0	0.0
C / 5.3	8.2	1.40	8.41	532	1	80	17	2	77	65.3	-15.9	16	6	2,500	50	0.0	0.0
C / 5.5	8.2	1.40	8.45	25	1	80	17	2	77	62.4	-16.0	12	6	2,500	50	0.0	0.0
B / 8.0	4.6	0.43	5.91	176	4	46	48	2	59	36.2	-7.2	66	6	2,500	50	5.8	0.0
B / 8.0	4.7	0.45	5.88	2	4	46	48	2	59	33.0	-7.4	52	6	2,500	50	0.0	0.0
B / 8.0	4.7	0.44	5.88	46	4	46	48	2	59	32.7	-7.3	53	6	2,500	50	0.0	0.0
B / 8.0	4.7	0.44	5.92	68	4	46	48	2	59	38.2	-6.8	71	6	5,000,000	50	0.0	0.0
B / 8.0	4.7	0.44	5.92	305	4	46	48	2	59	37.5	-7.1	68	6	2,500	50	0.0	0.0
B / 8.0	4.7	0.44	5.91	17	4	46	48	2	59	35.1	-7.1	62	6	2,500	50	0.0	0.0
C+ / 6.7	6.6	1.14	7.13	563	2	65	31	2	69	51.6	-12.0	23	6	2,500	50	5.8	0.0

Fund Type	Fund Name	Ticker Symbol	Overall Investment Rating	Phone	Perfor- mance Rating/Pts	3 Mo	6 Mo	1Yr / Pct	3Yr / Pct	5Yr / Pct	Dividend Yield	Expense Ratio
			99 Pct = Best / 0 Pct = Worst		PERFORMANCE / Total Return % through 3/31/15 (Annualized) / Incl. in Returns							
AA	● American Century Str Alloc:Mod B	ASTBX	C-	(800) 345-6488	C- / 3.2	1.87	4.57	6.15 /48	8.18 /28	8.22 /31	0.02	2.07
AA	American Century Str Alloc:Mod C	ASTCX	C-	(800) 345-6488	C- / 3.2	1.87	4.42	6.00 /46	8.17 /28	8.21 /31	0.02	2.07
AA	American Century Str Alloc:Mod Inst	ASAMX	C-	(800) 345-6488	C- / 4.1	2.20	5.13	7.44 /59	9.50 /36	9.52 /41	0.95	0.87
AA	American Century Str Alloc:Mod Inv	TWSMX	C-	(800) 345-6488	C- / 3.9	2.16	5.02	7.23 /57	9.28 /35	9.30 /39	0.76	1.07
AA	American Century Str Alloc:Mod R	ASMRX	C-	(800) 345-6488	C- / 3.5	2.01	4.73	6.67 /52	8.67 /31	8.75 /35	0.36	1.57
GR	American Century Ultra A	TWUAX	B-	(800) 345-6488	B- / 7.1	3.81	8.55	14.38 /90	15.31 /77	14.66 /84	0.07	1.26
GR	American Century Ultra C	TWCCX	B	(800) 345-6488	B / 7.6	3.63	8.17	13.54 /88	14.46 /71	13.81 /76	0.00	2.01
GR	American Century Ultra Inst	TWUIX	B+	(800) 345-6488	B+ / 8.6	3.91	8.77	14.88 /91	15.84 /82	15.18 /88	0.49	0.81
GR	American Century Ultra Inv	TWCUX	B+	(800) 345-6488	B+ / 8.5	3.88	8.68	14.68 /91	15.60 /80	14.96 /86	0.31	1.01
GR	American Century Ultra R	AULRX	B	(800) 345-6488	B / 8.0	3.77	8.41	14.11 /90	15.03 /75	14.39 /81	0.00	1.51
GR	American Century Ultra R6	AULDX	U	(800) 345-6488	U /	3.97	8.88	15.05 /92	--	--	0.63	0.66
UT	American Century Utilities Inv	BULIX	C	(800) 345-6488	C / 5.0	-5.10	3.98	6.40 /50	12.21 /54	12.15 /62	3.16	0.67
GI	American Century Value A	TWADX	B-	(800) 345-6488	C+ / 5.9	-0.76	3.18	8.64 /67	14.84 /74	12.55 /64	1.14	1.23
GI	● American Century Value B	ACBVX	B-	(800) 345-6488	C+ / 6.2	-0.93	2.78	7.83 /61	14.01 /67	11.75 /59	0.56	1.98
GI	American Century Value C	ACLCX	B-	(800) 345-6488	C+ / 6.3	-0.82	2.81	7.77 /61	14.03 /67	11.75 /59	0.56	1.98
GI	American Century Value Inst	AVLIX	B+	(800) 345-6488	B- / 7.2	-0.55	3.40	9.10 /70	15.37 /78	13.06 /69	1.63	0.78
GI	American Century Value Inv	TWVLX	B+	(800) 345-6488	B- / 7.1	-0.59	3.30	8.91 /69	15.17 /76	12.86 /67	1.44	0.98
GI	American Century Value R	AVURX	B-	(800) 345-6488	C+ / 6.7	-0.69	3.05	8.37 /65	14.60 /72	12.31 /63	0.96	1.48
GI	American Century Value R6	AVUDX	A-	(800) 345-6488	B- / 7.3	-0.53	3.47	9.27 /71	15.39 /78	12.99 /68	1.78	0.63
GR	American Century Veedot Inst	AVDIX	A+	(800) 345-6488	A / 9.4	5.29	10.90	14.87 /91	18.38 /95	15.80 /92	0.68	1.05
GR	American Century Veedot Inv	AMVIX	A+	(800) 345-6488	A / 9.4	5.30	10.90	14.72 /91	18.16 /95	15.60 /91	0.50	1.25
BA	American Century VP Balanced I	AVBIX	C	(800) 345-6488	C / 4.3	0.43	4.13	8.18 /64	10.15 /40	10.37 /47	1.62	0.91
GI	American Century VP Inc & Gro III	AIGTX	B	(800) 345-6488	B- / 7.3	-0.70	4.06	9.28 /71	15.65 /80	14.17 /79	2.01	0.70
GI	American Century VP Inc & Growth I	AVGIX	B+	(800) 345-6488	B- / 7.4	-0.70	4.06	9.28 /71	15.65 /80	14.18 /79	2.01	0.70
GI	American Century VP Inc & Growth II	AVPGX	B	(800) 345-6488	B- / 7.2	-0.85	3.93	8.89 /69	15.36 /78	13.85 /76	1.76	0.95
GL	American Century VP Intl I	AVIIX	D	(800) 345-6488	C- / 3.2	4.38	1.63	-1.17 /12	9.15 /34	7.51 /26	0.37	1.37
GL	American Century VP Intl II	ANVPX	D	(800) 345-6488	C- / 3.1	4.23	1.58	-1.32 /12	8.96 /33	7.32 /25	0.21	1.52
GL	American Century VP Intl III	AIVPX	D	(800) 345-6488	C- / 3.0	4.38	1.63	-1.17 /12	9.15 /34	7.51 /26	0.37	1.37
GR	American Century VP Large Co Val I	AVVIX	A	(800) 345-6488	B / 8.0	0.54	5.27	10.97 /78	16.08 /84	13.33 /71	1.45	0.91
MC	American Century VP Mid Cap Val I	AVIPX	A+	(800) 345-6488	A- / 9.2	1.54	8.42	13.80 /89	17.61 /93	14.74 /85	1.42	1.01
MC	American Century VP Mid Cap Val II	AVMTX	A+	(800) 345-6488	A- / 9.1	1.50	8.27	13.62 /88	17.42 /92	14.56 /83	1.28	1.16
GR	American Century VP Ultra I	AVPUX	B+	(800) 345-6488	B+ / 8.4	3.80	8.65	14.68 /91	15.57 /80	14.82 /85	0.44	1.01
GR	American Century VP Ultra II	AVPSX	B+	(800) 345-6488	B+ / 8.3	3.82	8.60	14.55 /91	15.43 /78	14.66 /84	0.29	1.16
GR	American Century VP Ultra III	AVUTX	B+	(800) 345-6488	B+ / 8.3	3.87	8.66	14.69 /91	15.58 /80	14.83 /85	Incl.	1.01
GI	American Century VP Value I	AVPIX	B+	(800) 345-6488	B- / 7.3	-0.54	3.37	9.05 /70	15.48 /79	13.11 /69	1.64	0.97
GI	American Century VP Value II	AVPVX	B+	(800) 345-6488	B- / 7.1	-0.57	3.29	9.00 /69	15.28 /77	12.93 /67	1.49	1.12
GI	American Century VP Value III	AVPTX	B+	(800) 345-6488	B- / 7.1	-0.54	3.37	9.05 /70	15.48 /79	13.07 /69	1.64	0.97
GR	American Funds AMCAP 529A	CAFAX	B+	(800) 421-0180	B / 7.7	2.37	5.82	11.38 /80	17.11 /90	14.39 /81	0.00	0.79
GR	● American Funds AMCAP 529B	CAFBX	B+	(800) 421-0180	B / 8.2	2.21	5.43	10.51 /76	16.21 /85	13.48 /73	0.00	1.59
GR	American Funds AMCAP 529C	CAFCX	B+	(800) 421-0180	B / 8.2	2.21	5.43	10.50 /76	16.21 /85	13.50 /73	0.00	1.58
GR	American Funds AMCAP 529E	CAFEX	A-	(800) 421-0180	B+ / 8.6	2.35	5.70	11.10 /79	16.83 /89	14.10 /79	0.00	1.04
GR	American Funds AMCAP 529F1	CAFFX	A	(800) 421-0180	B+ / 8.9	2.44	5.95	11.60 /81	17.37 /92	14.63 /83	0.12	0.58
★ GR	American Funds AMCAP A	AMCPX	B+	(800) 421-0180	B / 7.8	2.39	5.89	11.48 /80	17.23 /91	14.48 /82	0.02	0.70
GR	● American Funds AMCAP B	AMPBX	B+	(800) 421-0180	B+ / 8.3	2.24	5.52	10.66 /77	16.35 /86	13.62 /74	0.00	1.47
GR	American Funds AMCAP C	AMPCX	B+	(800) 421-0180	B / 8.2	2.22	5.46	10.57 /77	16.29 /85	13.58 /74	0.00	1.51
GR	American Funds AMCAP F1	AMPFX	A	(800) 421-0180	B+ / 8.8	2.41	5.86	11.41 /80	17.18 /91	14.46 /82	0.00	0.74
GR	American Funds AMCAP F2	AMCFX	A	(800) 421-0180	A- / 9.0	2.46	6.02	11.72 /81	17.48 /92	14.75 /85	0.21	0.49
GR	American Funds AMCAP R1	RAFAX	B+	(800) 421-0180	B+ / 8.3	2.25	5.50	10.63 /77	16.34 /86	13.62 /74	0.00	1.47
GR	American Funds AMCAP R2	RAFBX	B+	(800) 421-0180	B+ / 8.3	2.21	5.50	10.64 /77	16.36 /86	13.63 /74	0.00	1.46
GR	American Funds AMCAP R2E	RAEBX	B+	(800) 421-0180	B+ / 8.5	2.36	5.89	11.19 /79	16.64 /88	13.86 /76	0.00	1.18
GR	American Funds AMCAP R3	RAFCX	A-	(800) 421-0180	B+ / 8.6	2.33	5.75	11.13 /79	16.86 /89	14.12 /79	0.00	1.03
GR	American Funds AMCAP R4	RAFEX	A	(800) 421-0180	B+ / 8.8	2.45	5.89	11.45 /80	17.22 /91	14.47 /82	0.03	0.72

● Denotes fund is closed to new investors
★ Denotes fund is included in Section II

www.thestreetratings.com

RISK			NET ASSETS		ASSET						BULL / BEAR		FUND MANAGER		MINIMUMS		LOADS	
	3 Year		NAV							Portfolio	Last Bull	Last Bear	Manager	Manager	Initial	Additional	Front	Back
Risk	Standard		As of	Total	Cash	Stocks	Bonds	Other		Turnover	Market	Market	Quality	Tenure	Purch.	Purch.	End	End
Rating/Pts	Deviation	Beta	3/31/15	$(Mil)	%	%	%	%		Ratio	Return	Return	Pct	(Years)	$	$	Load	Load
C+ / 6.7	6.7	1.15	7.10	12	2	65	31	2		69	47.9	-12.4	16	6	2,500	50	0.0	0.0
C+ / 6.7	6.6	1.14	7.11	127	2	65	31	2		69	47.8	-12.3	17	6	2,500	50	0.0	0.0
C+ / 6.7	6.7	1.15	7.15	295	2	65	31	2		69	54.1	-12.0	27	6	5,000,000	50	0.0	0.0
C+ / 6.7	6.6	1.15	7.15	718	2	65	31	2		69	53.1	-12.1	26	6	2,500	50	0.0	0.0
C+ / 6.7	6.6	1.14	7.11	52	2	65	31	2		69	50.4	-12.3	20	6	2,500	50	0.0	0.0
C+ / 5.9	11.1	1.05	34.87	74	0	99	0	1		16	97.4	-15.7	46	7	2,500	50	5.8	0.0
C+ / 5.8	11.1	1.05	31.12	3	0	99	0	1		16	92.4	-15.9	35	7	2,500	50	0.0	0.0
C+ / 5.9	11.1	1.05	37.16	195	0	99	0	1		16	100.5	-15.5	53	7	5,000,000	50	0.0	0.0
C+ / 5.9	11.1	1.05	36.14	8,140	0	99	0	1		16	99.1	-15.6	50	7	2,500	50	0.0	0.0
C+ / 5.9	11.1	1.05	34.37	8	0	99	0	1		16	95.8	-15.7	42	7	2,500	50	0.0	0.0
U /	N/A	N/A	37.15	33	0	99	0	1		16	N/A	N/A	N/A	7	0	0	0.0	0.0
C+ / 6.4	11.1	0.74	17.03	382	1	98	0	1		45	54.3	-4.7	87	5	2,500	50	0.0	0.0
B- / 7.2	9.7	0.99	8.54	366	3	96	0	1		49	91.6	-16.9	53	22	2,500	50	5.8	0.0
B- / 7.2	9.7	0.99	8.50	1	3	96	0	1		49	86.6	-17.0	42	22	2,500	50	0.0	0.0
B- / 7.2	9.8	0.99	8.43	29	3	96	0	1		49	86.5	-17.0	41	22	2,500	50	0.0	0.0
B- / 7.2	9.7	0.99	8.56	1,215	3	96	0	1		49	94.4	-16.6	60	22	5,000,000	50	0.0	0.0
B- / 7.2	9.7	0.98	8.55	2,006	3	96	0	1		49	92.8	-16.6	59	22	2,500	50	0.0	0.0
B- / 7.2	9.7	0.99	8.55	53	3	96	0	1		49	89.7	-16.8	50	22	2,500	50	0.0	0.0
B- / 7.6	9.7	0.99	8.56	34	3	96	0	1		49	94.0	-16.6	60	22	0	0	0.0	0.0
B- / 7.2	10.3	1.03	11.14	3	3	96	0	1		184	100.9	-13.7	81	16	5,000,000	50	0.0	2.0
B- / 7.1	10.3	1.03	10.93	96	3	96	0	1		184	99.8	-13.9	80	16	2,500	50	0.0	2.0
C+ / 6.7	6.0	1.05	7.23	130	1	59	38	2		67	57.6	-8.1	49	18	0	0	0.0	0.0
C+ / 6.7	10.0	1.03	9.16	11	1	98	0	1		77	99.4	-16.1	55	5	0	0	0.0	1.0
C+ / 6.7	10.0	1.03	9.16	318	1	98	0	1		77	99.4	-16.1	54	5	0	0	0.0	0.0
C+ / 6.7	10.0	1.03	9.16	21	1	98	0	1		77	97.5	-16.1	50	5	0	0	0.0	0.0
C+ / 5.6	12.6	1.88	10.38	208	0	99	0	1		77	56.8	-24.7	4	18	0	0	0.0	0.0
C+ / 5.6	12.6	1.88	10.37	52	0	99	0	1		77	56.0	-24.7	3	18	0	0	0.0	0.0
C+ / 5.6	12.6	1.88	10.38	1	0	99	0	1		77	56.8	-24.7	4	18	0	0	0.0	1.0
B- / 7.5	10.4	1.05	15.22	9	0	99	0	1		70	98.7	-17.2	55	11	0	0	0.0	0.0
B- / 7.2	8.9	0.77	19.13	238	3	96	0	1		60	100.6	-17.1	92	11	0	0	0.0	0.0
B- / 7.2	8.9	0.77	19.14	537	3	96	0	1		60	99.5	-17.1	92	11	0	0	0.0	0.0
C+ / 5.8	11.2	1.06	15.11	40	0	99	0	1		35	99.0	-15.6	47	7	0	0	0.0	0.0
C+ / 5.8	11.1	1.05	14.91	155	0	99	0	1		35	98.0	-15.7	46	7	0	0	0.0	0.0
C+ / 5.8	11.1	1.05	15.10	1	0	99	0	1		35	99.0	-15.6	49	7	0	0	0.0	1.0
B- / 7.4	9.7	0.99	9.30	453	3	96	0	1		44	95.0	-16.6	62	19	0	0	0.0	0.0
B- / 7.4	9.8	0.99	9.31	452	3	96	0	1		44	93.8	-16.7	58	19	0	0	0.0	0.0
B- / 7.4	9.7	0.99	9.30	11	3	96	0	1		44	95.0	-16.6	62	19	0	0	0.0	1.0
C+ / 6.5	9.5	0.93	28.45	1,359	0	83	15	2		29	101.8	-15.8	83	19	250	50	5.8	0.0
C+ / 6.4	9.5	0.94	26.36	19	0	83	15	2		29	96.4	-16.1	77	19	250	50	0.0	0.0
C+ / 6.4	9.4	0.93	26.38	331	0	83	15	2		29	96.5	-16.1	78	19	250	50	0.0	0.0
C+ / 6.5	9.5	0.93	27.92	68	0	83	15	2		29	100.2	-15.9	81	19	250	50	0.0	0.0
C+ / 6.5	9.5	0.94	28.57	83	0	83	15	2		29	103.3	-15.7	84	19	250	50	0.0	0.0
C+ / 6.5	9.5	0.94	28.67	25,520	0	83	15	2		29	102.5	-15.8	84	19	250	50	5.8	0.0
C+ / 6.4	9.5	0.93	26.53	117	0	83	15	2		29	97.2	-16.0	78	19	250	50	0.0	0.0
C+ / 6.4	9.5	0.93	26.22	1,581	0	83	15	2		29	96.9	-16.0	78	19	250	50	0.0	0.0
C+ / 6.5	9.5	0.94	28.47	2,712	0	83	15	2		29	102.2	-15.8	83	19	250	50	0.0	0.0
C+ / 6.5	9.5	0.93	28.76	3,627	0	83	15	2		29	104.0	-15.7	85	19	250	50	0.0	0.0
C+ / 6.4	9.5	0.93	26.81	110	0	83	15	2		29	97.2	-16.1	78	19	250	50	0.0	0.0
C+ / 6.4	9.5	0.94	26.79	590	0	83	15	2		29	97.3	-16.0	78	19	250	50	0.0	0.0
C+ / 5.9	9.5	0.94	28.67	N/A	0	83	15	2		29	98.9	-16.0	80	19	250	50	0.0	0.0
C+ / 6.5	9.5	0.93	28.05	1,241	0	83	15	2		29	100.2	-15.9	82	19	250	50	0.0	0.0
C+ / 6.5	9.5	0.93	28.48	1,116	0	83	15	2		29	102.3	-15.8	84	19	250	50	0.0	0.0

Fund Type	Fund Name	Ticker Symbol	Overall Investment Rating	Phone	PERFORMANCE Perfor-mance Rating/Pts	Total Return % through 3/31/15 3 Mo	6 Mo	1Yr / Pct	Annualized 3Yr / Pct	5Yr / Pct	Incl. in Returns Dividend Yield	Expense Ratio
GR	American Funds AMCAP R5	RAFFX	A	(800) 421-0180	A- / 9.0	2.48	6.03	11.77 /82	17.56 /93	14.81 /85	0.23	0.42
GR	American Funds AMCAP R6	RAFGX	A	(800) 421-0180	A- / 9.0	2.49	6.08	11.81 /82	17.62 /93	14.87 /86	0.28	0.37
BA	American Funds Amer Balncd Fd	CLBAX	C+	(800) 421-0180	C / 4.3	0.71	3.86	7.95 /62	11.85 /51	11.32 /55	1.32	0.68
BA	● American Funds Amer Balncd Fd	CLBBX	C+	(800) 421-0180	C / 4.6	0.54	3.50	7.12 /56	10.97 /45	10.46 /48	0.59	1.46
BA	American Funds Amer Balncd Fd	CLBCX	C+	(800) 421-0180	C / 4.6	0.56	3.51	7.13 /56	10.98 /45	10.47 /48	0.66	1.46
BA	American Funds Amer Balncd Fd	CLBEX	B-	(800) 421-0180	C / 5.0	0.65	3.78	7.69 /60	11.57 /49	11.04 /53	1.16	0.93
BA	American Funds Amer Balncd Fd	CLBFX	B	(800) 421-0180	C / 5.4	0.77	4.02	8.24 /64	12.10 /53	11.57 /57	1.62	0.46
★ BA	American Funds Amer Balncd Fd A	ABALX	C+	(800) 421-0180	C / 4.3	0.77	3.94	8.08 /63	11.94 /52	11.42 /56	1.41	0.59
BA	● American Funds Amer Balncd Fd B	BALBX	C+	(800) 421-0180	C / 4.7	0.57	3.57	7.27 /57	11.12 /46	10.59 /49	0.71	1.34
BA	American Funds Amer Balncd Fd C	BALCX	C+	(800) 421-0180	C / 4.7	0.54	3.52	7.18 /56	11.05 /46	10.53 /49	0.73	1.39
BA	American Funds Amer Balncd Fd F1	BALFX	B-	(800) 421-0180	C / 5.2	0.72	3.88	7.98 /63	11.89 /52	11.39 /56	1.43	0.65
BA	American Funds Amer Balncd Fd F2	AMBFX	B	(800) 421-0180	C / 5.5	0.83	4.06	8.31 /65	12.18 /54	11.66 /58	1.69	0.39
BA	American Funds Amer Balncd Fd R1	RLBAX	C+	(800) 421-0180	C / 4.7	0.55	3.53	7.24 /57	11.08 /46	10.56 /49	0.74	1.38
BA	American Funds Amer Balncd Fd R2	RLBBX	C+	(800) 421-0180	C / 4.7	0.56	3.55	7.23 /57	11.12 /46	10.59 /49	0.77	1.36
BA	American Funds Amer Balncd Fd R3	RLBCX	B-	(800) 421-0180	C / 5.0	0.66	3.79	7.70 /60	11.58 /50	11.05 /53	1.16	0.94
BA	American Funds Amer Balncd Fd R4	RLBEX	B-	(800) 421-0180	C / 5.3	0.73	3.94	8.00 /63	11.91 /52	11.38 /56	1.45	0.64
BA	American Funds Amer Balncd Fd R5	RLBFX	B	(800) 421-0180	C / 5.5	0.84	4.08	8.34 /65	12.25 /54	11.72 /59	1.73	0.34
BA	American Funds Amer Balncd Fd R6	RLBGX	B	(800) 421-0180	C / 5.5	0.81	4.10	8.40 /66	12.29 /54	11.77 /59	1.78	0.29
BA	American Funds Amer Balncd R2E	RAMHX	C+	(800) 421-0180	C / 5.0	0.77	4.00	7.89 /62	11.42 /48	10.84 /51	1.46	1.09
GI	American Funds Amer Mutual Fd	CMLAX	B-	(800) 421-0180	C+ / 6.0	0.05	5.67	10.40 /76	14.54 /71	12.93 /67	1.79	0.69
GI	● American Funds Amer Mutual Fd	CMLBX	B-	(800) 421-0180	C+ / 6.4	-0.12	5.28	9.56 /72	13.66 /65	12.04 /61	1.08	1.48
GI	American Funds Amer Mutual Fd	CMLCX	B-	(800) 421-0180	C+ / 6.4	-0.14	5.26	9.55 /72	13.65 /64	12.05 /61	1.16	1.47
GI	American Funds Amer Mutual Fd	CMLEX	B-	(800) 421-0180	C+ / 6.8	-0.01	5.53	10.14 /75	14.26 /69	12.64 /65	1.66	0.94
GI	American Funds Amer Mutual Fd	CMLFX	B+	(800) 421-0180	B- / 7.2	0.13	5.80	10.66 /77	14.80 /73	13.18 /70	2.11	0.47
★ GI	American Funds Amer Mutual Fd A	AMRMX	B-	(800) 421-0180	C+ / 6.1	0.10	5.73	10.55 /77	14.67 /72	13.05 /69	1.88	0.59
GI	● American Funds Amer Mutual Fd B	AMFBX	B-	(800) 421-0180	C+ / 6.5	-0.08	5.34	9.70 /73	13.80 /66	12.18 /62	1.21	1.35
GI	American Funds Amer Mutual Fd C	AMFCX	B-	(800) 421-0180	C+ / 6.4	-0.10	5.30	9.65 /73	13.75 /65	12.13 /61	1.24	1.40
GI	American Funds Amer Mutual Fd F1	AMFFX	B+	(800) 421-0180	B- / 7.0	0.09	5.69	10.44 /76	14.58 /72	12.97 /68	1.91	0.67
GI	American Funds Amer Mutual Fd F2	AMRFX	A-	(800) 421-0180	B- / 7.2	0.15	5.83	10.72 /77	14.87 /74	13.26 /71	2.16	0.42
GI	American Funds Amer Mutual Fd R1	RMFAX	B-	(800) 421-0180	C+ / 6.4	-0.12	5.28	9.60 /72	13.72 /65	12.12 /61	1.22	1.42
GI	American Funds Amer Mutual Fd R2	RMFBX	B-	(800) 421-0180	C+ / 6.4	-0.09	5.33	9.66 /73	13.76 /65	12.13 /61	1.24	1.41
GI	American Funds Amer Mutual Fd	RMEBX	C+	(800) 421-0180	C+ / 6.7	0.04	5.72	10.25 /75	14.10 /68	12.43 /64	1.91	1.11
GI	American Funds Amer Mutual Fd R3	RMFCX	B-	(800) 421-0180	C+ / 6.8	0.01	5.55	10.13 /75	14.26 /69	12.65 /65	1.65	0.96
GI	American Funds Amer Mutual Fd R4	RMFEX	B+	(800) 421-0180	B- / 7.0	0.09	5.70	10.45 /76	14.60 /72	12.98 /68	1.94	0.66
GI	American Funds Amer Mutual Fd R5	RMFFX	A-	(800) 421-0180	B- / 7.3	0.14	5.83	10.78 /77	14.94 /74	13.32 /71	2.21	0.36
GI	American Funds Amer Mutual Fd R6	RMFGX	A-	(800) 421-0180	B- / 7.3	0.15	5.89	10.83 /78	15.00 /75	13.37 /72	2.26	0.30
BA	American Funds Balanced 529A	CBAAX	U	(800) 421-0180	U /	1.75	3.85	6.79 /53	--	--	1.34	0.91
BA	American Funds Balanced 529C	CBPCX	U	(800) 421-0180	U /	1.60	3.41	6.04 /47	--	--	0.71	1.70
BA	American Funds Balanced A	BLPAX	U	(800) 421-0180	U /	1.84	3.88	6.96 /55	--	--	1.42	0.82
BA	American Funds Balanced C	BLPCX	U	(800) 421-0180	U /	1.62	3.47	6.07 /47	--	--	0.82	1.61
BA	American Funds Balanced F1	BLPFX	U	(800) 421-0180	U /	1.84	3.87	6.90 /54	--	--	1.45	0.88
BA	American Funds Balanced F2	BLPEX	U	(800) 421-0180	U /	1.88	3.99	7.16 /56	--	--	1.70	0.62
BA	American Funds Balanced R2	RBABX	U	(800) 421-0180	U /	1.62	3.55	6.11 /47	--	--	0.78	1.67
BA	American Funds Balanced R3	RBACX	U	(800) 421-0180	U /	1.79	3.76	6.56 /51	--	--	1.21	1.20
BA	American Funds Balanced R4	RBAEX	U	(800) 421-0180	U /	1.84	3.87	6.92 /54	--	--	1.47	0.86
BA	American Funds Balanced R6	RBAGX	U	(800) 421-0180	U /	1.83	4.04	7.26 /57	--	--	1.79	0.52
★ IN	American Funds Cap Inc Builder A	CAIBX	C-	(800) 421-0180	D+ / 2.7	0.63	1.96	5.24 /40	9.40 /36	8.79 /35	3.78	0.59
IN	● American Funds Cap Inc Builder B	CIBBX	C	(800) 421-0180	C- / 3.1	0.43	1.57	4.45 /35	8.58 /30	7.97 /30	3.16	1.35
IN	American Funds Cap Inc Builder C	CIBCX	C	(800) 421-0180	C- / 3.1	0.43	1.55	4.40 /34	8.53 /30	7.92 /29	3.18	1.39
IN	American Funds Cap Inc Builder F1	CIBFX	C	(800) 421-0180	C- / 3.6	0.61	1.92	5.16 /40	9.34 /35	8.74 /35	3.93	0.66
IN	American Funds Cap Inc Builder F2	CAIFX	C	(800) 421-0180	C- / 3.7	0.67	2.05	5.44 /42	9.61 /37	9.01 /37	4.22	0.39
IN	American Funds Cap Inc Builder R1	RIRAX	C	(800) 421-0180	C- / 3.1	0.44	1.56	4.40 /34	8.53 /30	7.93 /29	3.19	1.39

RISK Rating/Pts	3 Year Standard Deviation	Beta	NAV As of 3/31/15	Total $(Mil)	Cash %	Stocks %	Bonds %	Other %	Portfolio Turnover Ratio	Last Bull Market Return	Last Bear Market Return	Manager Quality Pct	Manager Tenure (Years)	Initial Purch. $	Additional Purch. $	Front End Load	Back End Load
C+ / 6.5	9.4	0.93	28.90	1,400	0	83	15	2	29	104.4	-15.7	86	19	250	50	0.0	0.0
C+ / 6.5	9.5	0.93	28.83	6,469	0	83	15	2	29	104.7	-15.6	86	19	250	50	0.0	0.0
B / 8.0	6.9	1.19	24.71	2,871	0	64	35	1	68	66.4	-10.0	50	12	250	50	5.8	0.0
B / 8.0	6.9	1.20	24.76	64	0	64	35	1	68	62.0	-10.3	38	12	250	50	0.0	0.0
B / 8.0	6.9	1.20	24.70	916	0	64	35	1	68	62.0	-10.3	38	12	250	50	0.0	0.0
B+ / 8.0	6.9	1.20	24.70	145	0	64	35	1	68	65.0	-10.1	46	12	250	50	0.0	0.0
B / 8.0	6.9	1.20	24.70	114	0	64	35	1	68	67.6	-9.9	53	12	250	50	0.0	0.0
B / 8.0	6.9	1.20	24.75	47,852	0	64	35	1	68	66.9	-10.0	50	12	250	50	5.8	0.0
B / 8.0	6.9	1.20	24.71	463	0	64	35	1	68	62.6	-10.3	40	12	250	50	0.0	0.0
B / 8.0	6.9	1.20	24.62	5,735	0	64	35	1	68	62.4	-10.2	39	12	250	50	0.0	0.0
B / 8.0	6.9	1.20	24.73	3,037	0	64	35	1	68	66.6	-10.0	51	12	250	50	0.0	0.0
B / 8.0	6.9	1.20	24.74	2,098	0	64	35	1	68	68.2	-9.9	54	12	250	50	0.0	0.0
B / 8.0	6.8	1.19	24.60	157	0	64	35	1	68	62.5	-10.3	40	12	250	50	0.0	0.0
B / 8.0	6.9	1.20	24.61	1,297	0	64	35	1	68	62.7	-10.3	40	12	250	50	0.0	0.0
B / 8.0	6.9	1.20	24.64	3,310	0	64	35	1	68	65.0	-10.1	46	12	250	50	0.0	0.0
B / 8.0	6.9	1.20	24.71	4,572	0	64	35	1	68	66.7	-10.0	50	12	250	50	0.0	0.0
B / 8.0	6.9	1.20	24.77	2,712	0	64	35	1	68	68.4	-9.9	55	12	250	50	0.0	0.0
B / 8.0	6.9	1.20	24.75	6,016	0	64	35	1	68	68.7	-9.9	56	12	250	50	0.0	0.0
B- / 7.0	6.9	1.20	24.74	N/A	0	64	35	1	68	64.1	-10.2	44	12	250	50	0.0	0.0
B- / 7.7	8.1	0.81	36.91	730	0	91	7	2	16	81.6	-12.7	80	9	250	50	5.8	0.0
B- / 7.7	8.1	0.81	36.86	9	0	91	7	2	16	76.8	-13.0	74	9	250	50	0.0	0.0
B- / 7.7	8.1	0.81	36.74	183	0	91	7	2	16	76.8	-13.0	74	9	250	50	0.0	0.0
B- / 7.7	8.1	0.81	36.79	37	0	91	7	2	16	80.0	-12.8	79	9	250	50	0.0	0.0
B- / 7.7	8.0	0.81	36.96	55	0	91	7	2	16	83.0	-12.7	82	9	250	50	0.0	0.0
B- / 7.7	8.1	0.81	36.99	22,822	0	91	7	2	16	82.2	-12.7	81	9	250	50	5.8	0.0
B- / 7.7	8.1	0.81	36.74	83	0	91	7	2	16	77.6	-13.0	75	9	250	50	0.0	0.0
B- / 7.7	8.1	0.81	36.55	1,195	0	91	7	2	16	77.3	-13.0	75	9	250	50	0.0	0.0
B- / 7.7	8.1	0.81	36.85	1,403	0	91	7	2	16	81.9	-12.7	81	9	250	50	0.0	0.0
B- / 7.7	8.1	0.81	36.98	2,275	0	91	7	2	16	83.4	-12.6	83	9	250	50	0.0	0.0
B- / 7.7	8.1	0.81	36.66	76	0	91	7	2	16	77.2	-13.0	75	9	250	50	0.0	0.0
B- / 7.7	8.1	0.81	36.64	261	0	91	7	2	16	77.3	-13.0	75	9	250	50	0.0	0.0
C+ / 6.2	8.1	0.81	36.96	N/A	0	91	7	2	16	79.0	-12.9	78	9	250	50	0.0	0.0
B- / 7.7	8.1	0.81	36.75	659	0	91	7	2	16	80.1	-12.8	79	9	250	50	0.0	0.0
B- / 7.7	8.1	0.81	36.88	822	0	91	7	2	16	81.9	-12.7	81	9	250	50	0.0	0.0
B- / 7.7	8.1	0.81	36.98	312	0	91	7	2	16	83.8	-12.6	83	9	250	50	0.0	0.0
B- / 7.7	8.1	0.81	36.99	5,531	0	91	7	2	16	84.1	-12.6	83	9	250	50	0.0	0.0
U /	N/A	N/A	13.45	164	0	62	37	1	0	N/A	N/A	N/A	3	250	50	5.8	0.0
U /	N/A	N/A	13.41	84	0	62	37	1	0	N/A	N/A	N/A	3	250	50	0.0	0.0
U /	N/A	N/A	13.46	2,136	0	62	37	1	0	N/A	N/A	N/A	3	250	50	5.8	0.0
U /	N/A	N/A	13.40	517	0	62	37	1	0	N/A	N/A	N/A	3	250	50	0.0	0.0
U /	N/A	N/A	13.46	71	0	62	37	1	0	N/A	N/A	N/A	3	250	50	0.0	0.0
U /	N/A	N/A	13.47	84	0	62	37	1	0	N/A	N/A	N/A	3	250	50	0.0	0.0
U /	N/A	N/A	13.41	45	0	62	37	1	0	N/A	N/A	N/A	3	250	50	0.0	0.0
U /	N/A	N/A	13.44	50	0	62	37	1	0	N/A	N/A	N/A	3	250	50	0.0	0.0
U /	N/A	N/A	13.46	42	0	62	37	1	0	N/A	N/A	N/A	3	250	50	0.0	0.0
U /	N/A	N/A	13.47	70	0	62	37	1	0	N/A	N/A	N/A	3	250	50	0.0	0.0
B- / 7.8	7.7	0.65	59.45	70,612	1	78	20	1	55	50.2	-10.0	56	15	250	50	5.8	0.0
B- / 7.8	7.7	0.65	59.62	641	1	78	20	1	55	46.3	-10.3	44	15	250	50	0.0	0.0
B- / 7.8	7.7	0.65	59.50	6,768	1	78	20	1	55	46.1	-10.3	43	15	250	50	0.0	0.0
B- / 7.8	7.7	0.65	59.45	3,798	1	78	20	1	55	49.9	-10.0	55	15	250	50	0.0	0.0
B- / 7.8	7.7	0.65	59.41	4,912	1	78	20	1	55	51.2	-9.9	59	15	250	50	0.0	0.0
B- / 7.8	7.7	0.65	59.46	150	1	78	20	1	55	46.2	-10.3	44	15	250	50	0.0	0.0

Fund Type	Fund Name	Ticker Symbol	Overall Investment Rating	Phone	Performance Rating/Pts	3 Mo	6 Mo	1Yr / Pct	3Yr / Pct	5Yr / Pct	Dividend Yield	Expense Ratio
	99 Pct = Best				PERFORMANCE			Total Return % through 3/31/15	Annualized		Incl. in Returns	
	0 Pct = Worst											
IN	American Funds Cap Inc Builder R2	RIRBX	C	(800) 421-0180	C- / 3.1	0.44	1.57	4.41 /34	8.56 /30	7.94 /29	3.21	1.38
AA	American Funds Cap Inc Builder R2E	RCEEX	D+	(800) 421-0180	C- / 3.2	0.49	1.72	4.73 /37	8.78 /32	8.15 /31	3.75	1.11
IN	American Funds Cap Inc Builder R3	RIRCX	C	(800) 421-0180	C- / 3.4	0.55	1.79	4.86 /38	9.00 /33	8.40 /32	3.64	0.95
IN	American Funds Cap Inc Builder R4	RIREX	C	(800) 421-0180	C- / 3.6	0.63	1.95	5.18 /40	9.35 /35	8.74 /35	3.96	0.64
IN	American Funds Cap Inc Builder R5	RIRFX	C	(800) 421-0180	C- / 3.8	0.70	2.10	5.49 /42	9.68 /37	9.07 /37	4.26	0.35
IN	American Funds Cap Inc Builder R6	RIRGX	C	(800) 421-0180	C- / 3.8	0.71	2.10	5.55 /43	9.73 /38	9.12 /38	4.31	0.29
IN	American Funds Cap Inc Buildr 529A	CIRAX	C-	(800) 421-0180	D+ / 2.6	0.59	1.90	5.12 /39	9.29 /35	8.69 /34	3.69	0.69
IN	● American Funds Cap Inc Buildr 529B	CIRBX	C-	(800) 421-0180	C- / 3.0	0.42	1.51	4.31 /34	8.44 /30	7.84 /29	3.04	1.47
IN	American Funds Cap Inc Buildr 529C	CIRCX	C-	(800) 421-0180	C- / 3.0	0.42	1.52	4.32 /34	8.45 /30	7.85 /29	3.12	1.46
IN	American Funds Cap Inc Buildr 529E	CIREX	C	(800) 421-0180	C- / 3.4	0.55	1.78	4.89 /38	9.04 /33	8.42 /33	3.67	0.92
IN	American Funds Cap Inc Buildr	CIRFX	C	(800) 421-0180	C- / 3.7	0.67	2.02	5.37 /41	9.53 /36	8.93 /36	4.14	0.46
GL	American Funds Cap Wld Gr&Inc	CWIAX	C	(800) 421-0180	C / 4.4	2.64	2.56	4.98 /38	12.52 /56	9.48 /40	2.03	0.86
GL	● American Funds Cap Wld Gr&Inc	CWIBX	C	(800) 421-0180	C / 4.8	2.44	2.14	4.14 /33	11.63 /50	8.62 /34	1.31	1.65
GL	American Funds Cap Wld Gr&Inc	CWICX	C	(800) 421-0180	C / 4.8	2.43	2.14	4.14 /33	11.64 /50	8.62 /34	1.39	1.64
GL	American Funds Cap Wld Gr&Inc	CWIEX	C+	(800) 421-0180	C / 5.2	2.56	2.42	4.71 /36	12.25 /54	9.21 /38	1.92	1.09
GL	American Funds Cap Wld Gr&Inc	CWIFX	C+	(800) 421-0180	C+ / 5.6	2.70	2.67	5.21 /40	12.76 /58	9.72 /42	2.37	0.64
* GL	American Funds Cap Wld Gr&Inc A	CWGIX	C	(800) 421-0180	C / 4.5	2.65	2.59	5.05 /39	12.61 /57	9.57 /41	2.10	0.77
GL	● American Funds Cap Wld Gr&Inc B	CWGBX	C	(800) 421-0180	C / 4.9	2.47	2.19	4.28 /34	11.77 /51	8.73 /35	1.42	1.52
GL	American Funds Cap Wld Gr&Inc C	CWGCX	C	(800) 421-0180	C / 4.9	2.45	2.18	4.21 /33	11.72 /51	8.69 /34	1.44	1.57
GL	American Funds Cap Wld Gr&Inc F1	CWGFX	C+	(800) 421-0180	C / 5.4	2.65	2.57	5.01 /39	12.59 /57	9.54 /41	2.19	0.81
GL	American Funds Cap Wld Gr&Inc F2	WGIFX	C+	(800) 421-0180	C+ / 5.7	2.72	2.70	5.32 /41	12.91 /59	9.84 /43	2.48	0.53
GL	American Funds Cap Wld Gr&Inc R1	RWIAX	C	(800) 421-0180	C / 4.9	2.46	2.20	4.24 /33	11.76 /51	8.74 /35	1.48	1.54
GL	American Funds Cap Wld Gr&Inc R2	RWIBX	C	(800) 421-0180	C / 4.9	2.48	2.22	4.28 /34	11.79 /51	8.76 /35	1.51	1.52
GL	American Funds Cap Wld Gr&Inc	RWBEX	C-	(800) 421-0180	C / 5.0	2.54	2.40	4.62 /36	11.99 /52	8.94 /36	2.01	1.25
GL	American Funds Cap Wld Gr&Inc R3	RWICX	C+	(800) 421-0180	C / 5.2	2.57	2.41	4.71 /36	12.26 /54	9.23 /38	1.93	1.09
GL	American Funds Cap Wld Gr&Inc R4	RWIEX	C+	(800) 421-0180	C / 5.4	2.66	2.60	5.04 /39	12.61 /57	9.56 /41	2.21	0.79
GL	American Funds Cap Wld Gr&Inc R5	RWIFX	C+	(800) 421-0180	C+ / 5.7	2.73	2.72	5.35 /41	12.94 /59	9.89 /44	2.51	0.49
GL	American Funds Cap Wld Gr&Inc R6	RWIGX	C+	(800) 421-0180	C+ / 5.7	2.74	2.77	5.42 /42	13.01 /60	9.94 /44	2.56	0.44
AA	American Funds College 2015 529A	CFFAX	U	(800) 421-0180	U /	0.99	1.74	3.16 /27	--	--	1.18	0.90
AA	American Funds College 2015 529C	CFFCX	U	(800) 421-0180	U /	0.80	1.41	2.42 /24	--	--	0.60	1.67
AA	American Funds College 2015 529F1	CFIFX	U	(800) 421-0180	U /	0.99	1.87	3.39 /28	--	--	1.45	0.67
AA	American Funds College 2018 529A	CNEAX	U	(800) 421-0180	U /	1.18	2.94	5.24 /40	--	--	1.51	0.85
AA	American Funds College 2018 529C	CNECX	U	(800) 421-0180	U /	1.01	2.56	4.57 /36	--	--	1.01	1.63
AA	American Funds College 2018 529E	CNEEX	U	(800) 421-0180	U /	1.09	2.86	5.06 /39	--	--	1.40	1.11
AA	American Funds College 2018 529F1	CNEFX	U	(800) 421-0180	U /	1.27	3.14	5.63 /43	--	--	1.77	0.63
AA	American Funds College 2021 529A	CTOAX	U	(800) 421-0180	U /	0.79	2.19	4.75 /37	--	--	1.54	0.83
AA	American Funds College 2021 529C	CTOCX	U	(800) 421-0180	U /	0.62	1.77	3.87 /31	--	--	1.02	1.63
AA	American Funds College 2021 529F1	CTOFX	U	(800) 421-0180	U /	0.88	2.28	4.92 /38	--	--	1.79	0.63
AA	American Funds College 2024 529A	CFTAX	U	(800) 421-0180	U /	0.93	2.19	5.27 /41	--	--	1.38	0.89
AA	American Funds College 2024 529C	CTFCX	U	(800) 421-0180	U /	0.68	1.76	4.41 /34	--	--	0.85	1.69
AA	American Funds College 2024 529F1	CTFFX	U	(800) 421-0180	U /	0.93	2.27	5.43 /42	--	--	1.60	0.70
GI	American Funds College 2027 529A	CSTAX	U	(800) 421-0180	U /	1.40	2.25	5.30 /41	--	--	1.31	0.89
GI	American Funds College 2027 529C	CTSCX	U	(800) 421-0180	U /	1.16	1.79	4.43 /35	--	--	0.76	1.72
GI	American Funds College 2030 529A	CTHAX	U	(800) 421-0180	U /	1.75	2.27	5.31 /41	--	--	1.28	0.89
GI	American Funds College 2030 529C	CTYCX	U	(800) 421-0180	U /	1.53	1.83	4.39 /34	--	--	0.75	1.74
EM	American Funds DevWld G and I A	DWGAX	U	(800) 421-0180	U /	-0.75	-5.04	-3.59 / 8	--	--	1.29	1.39
EM	American Funds DevWld G and I C	DWGCX	U	(800) 421-0180	U /	-0.96	-5.34	-4.23 / 7	--	--	0.88	2.13
EM	American Funds DevWld G and I F1	DWGFX	U	(800) 421-0180	U /	-0.74	-5.03	-3.54 / 8	--	--	1.43	1.33
EM	American Funds DevWld G and I F2	DWGHX	U	(800) 421-0180	U /	-0.77	-4.90	-3.30 / 8	--	--	1.68	1.07
FO	American Funds EuroPacific Gr 529A	CEUAX	D	(800) 421-0180	D+ / 2.9	5.87	4.05	2.41 /24	9.51 /36	6.70 /21	1.20	0.90
FO	● American Funds EuroPacific Gr 529B	CEUBX	D+	(800) 421-0180	C- / 3.3	5.66	3.62	1.58 /20	8.63 /31	5.83 /16	0.17	1.70
FO	American Funds EuroPacific Gr 529C	CEUCX	D+	(800) 421-0180	C- / 3.3	5.68	3.63	1.62 /20	8.65 /31	5.85 /16	0.52	1.68

● Denotes fund is closed to new investors
* Denotes fund is included in Section II

www.thestreetratings.com

RISK			NET ASSETS		ASSET				Portfolio	BULL / BEAR		FUND MANAGER		MINIMUMS		LOADS	
	3 Year		NAV							Last Bull	Last Bear	Manager	Manager	Initial	Additional	Front	Back
Risk Rating/Pts	Standard Deviation	Beta	As of 3/31/15	Total $(Mil)	Cash %	Stocks %	Bonds %	Other %	Turnover Ratio	Market Return	Market Return	Quality Pct	Tenure (Years)	Purch. $	Purch. $	End Load	End Load
B- / 7.8	7.7	0.65	59.46	730	1	78	20	1	55	46.3	-10.3	44	15	250	50	0.0	0.0
C+ / 6.3	7.6	1.18	59.38	N/A	1	78	20	1	55	47.3	-10.2	18	15	250	50	0.0	0.0
B- / 7.8	7.7	0.65	59.45	1,037	1	78	20	1	55	48.4	-10.1	50	15	250	50	0.0	0.0
B- / 7.8	7.7	0.65	59.44	591	1	78	20	1	55	49.9	-10.0	55	15	250	50	0.0	0.0
B- / 7.8	7.7	0.65	59.46	395	1	78	20	1	55	51.5	-9.9	60	15	250	50	0.0	0.0
B- / 7.8	7.6	0.65	59.44	4,775	1	78	20	1	55	51.7	-9.9	61	15	250	50	0.0	0.0
B- / 7.8	7.7	0.65	59.43	2,225	1	78	20	1	55	49.7	-10.0	54	15	250	50	5.8	0.0
B- / 7.8	7.7	0.65	59.59	43	1	78	20	1	55	45.7	-10.3	42	15	250	50	0.0	0.0
B- / 7.8	7.7	0.65	59.44	722	1	78	20	1	55	45.8	-10.3	42	15	250	50	0.0	0.0
B- / 7.8	7.7	0.65	59.44	93	1	78	20	1	55	48.5	-10.1	51	15	250	50	0.0	0.0
B- / 7.8	7.7	0.65	59.44	71	1	78	20	1	55	50.8	-9.9	58	15	250	50	0.0	0.0
C+ / 6.9	10.0	0.73	47.01	3,064	0	92	6	2	36	72.1	-20.8	94	22	250	50	5.8	0.0
C+ / 6.9	10.0	0.73	46.95	63	0	92	6	2	36	67.5	-21.1	92	22	250	50	0.0	0.0
C+ / 6.9	10.0	0.73	46.83	742	0	92	6	2	36	67.5	-21.1	92	22	250	50	0.0	0.0
C+ / 6.9	10.0	0.73	46.95	127	0	92	6	2	36	70.6	-20.9	93	22	250	50	0.0	0.0
C+ / 6.9	10.0	0.73	47.04	115	0	92	6	2	36	73.4	-20.7	94	22	250	50	0.0	0.0
C+ / 6.9	10.0	0.73	47.14	56,439	0	92	6	2	36	72.5	-20.8	94	22	250	50	5.8	0.0
C+ / 6.9	10.0	0.73	46.96	618	0	92	6	2	36	68.1	-21.0	92	22	250	50	0.0	0.0
C+ / 6.9	10.0	0.73	46.68	4,282	0	92	6	2	36	67.9	-21.0	92	22	250	50	0.0	0.0
C+ / 6.9	10.0	0.73	47.05	4,031	0	92	6	2	36	72.4	-20.8	94	22	250	50	0.0	0.0
C+ / 6.9	10.0	0.73	47.10	4,281	0	92	6	2	36	74.1	-20.7	94	22	250	50	0.0	0.0
C+ / 6.9	10.0	0.73	46.75	290	0	92	6	2	36	68.1	-21.0	92	22	250	50	0.0	0.0
C+ / 6.9	10.0	0.73	46.65	1,182	0	92	6	2	36	68.3	-21.0	92	22	250	50	0.0	0.0
C+ / 5.7	10.0	0.73	47.10	N/A	0	92	6	2	36	69.3	-21.0	93	22	250	50	0.0	0.0
C+ / 6.9	10.0	0.73	46.86	2,522	0	92	6	2	36	70.8	-20.9	93	22	250	50	0.0	0.0
C+ / 6.9	10.0	0.73	47.04	2,182	0	92	6	2	36	72.5	-20.8	94	22	250	50	0.0	0.0
C+ / 6.9	10.0	0.73	47.14	1,486	0	92	6	2	36	74.3	-20.7	94	22	250	50	0.0	0.0
C+ / 6.9	10.0	0.73	47.14	6,821	0	92	6	2	36	74.6	-20.7	95	22	250	50	0.0	0.0
U /	N/A	N/A	10.20	194	0	5	94	1	2	N/A	N/A	N/A	3	250	50	4.3	0.0
U /	N/A	N/A	10.14	95	0	5	94	1	2	N/A	N/A	N/A	3	250	50	0.0	0.0
U /	N/A	N/A	10.21	30	0	5	94	1	2	N/A	N/A	N/A	3	250	50	0.0	0.0
U /	N/A	N/A	11.11	413	0	22	77	1	0	N/A	N/A	N/A	3	250	50	4.3	0.0
U /	N/A	N/A	11.03	170	0	22	77	1	0	N/A	N/A	N/A	3	250	50	0.0	0.0
U /	N/A	N/A	11.09	25	0	22	77	1	0	N/A	N/A	N/A	3	250	50	0.0	0.0
U /	N/A	N/A	11.14	41	0	22	77	1	0	N/A	N/A	N/A	3	250	50	0.0	0.0
U /	N/A	N/A	11.46	442	0	0	0	100	0	N/A	N/A	N/A	3	250	50	4.3	0.0
U /	N/A	N/A	11.37	134	0	0	0	100	0	N/A	N/A	N/A	3	250	50	0.0	0.0
U /	N/A	N/A	11.48	40	0	0	0	100	0	N/A	N/A	N/A	3	250	50	0.0	0.0
U /	N/A	N/A	11.89	398	0	0	0	100	0	N/A	N/A	N/A	3	250	50	4.3	0.0
U /	N/A	N/A	11.79	100	0	0	0	100	0	N/A	N/A	N/A	3	250	50	0.0	0.0
U /	N/A	N/A	11.91	30	0	0	0	100	0	N/A	N/A	N/A	3	250	50	0.0	0.0
U /	N/A	N/A	12.33	309	0	0	0	100	0	N/A	N/A	N/A	3	250	50	4.3	0.0
U /	N/A	N/A	12.23	76	0	0	0	100	0	N/A	N/A	N/A	3	250	50	0.0	0.0
U /	N/A	N/A	12.76	366	0	0	0	100	0	N/A	N/A	N/A	3	250	50	4.3	0.0
U /	N/A	N/A	12.64	77	0	0	0	100	0	N/A	N/A	N/A	3	250	50	0.0	0.0
U /	N/A	N/A	10.31	1,358	0	0	0	100	20	N/A	N/A	N/A	1	250	50	5.8	0.0
U /	N/A	N/A	10.28	127	0	0	0	100	20	N/A	N/A	N/A	1	250	50	0.0	0.0
U /	N/A	N/A	10.31	125	0	0	0	100	20	N/A	N/A	N/A	1	250	50	0.0	0.0
U /	N/A	N/A	10.31	630	0	0	0	100	20	N/A	N/A	N/A	1	250	50	0.0	0.0
C+ / 5.9	11.5	0.85	49.41	1,206	0	86	13	1	28	53.8	-24.1	80	9	250	50	5.8	0.0
C+ / 6.0	11.6	0.85	49.07	19	0	86	13	1	28	49.6	-24.3	73	9	250	50	0.0	0.0
C+ / 5.9	11.5	0.85	48.38	374	0	86	13	1	28	49.7	-24.3	73	9	250	50	0.0	0.0

						PERFORMANCE							
							Total Return % through 3/31/15					Incl. in Returns	
	99 Pct = Best 0 Pct = Worst			Overall		Perfor-				Annualized		Dividend	Expense
Fund Type	Fund Name	Ticker Symbol	Investment Rating		Phone	mance Rating/Pts	3 Mo	6 Mo	1Yr / Pct	3Yr / Pct	5Yr / Pct	Yield	Ratio
FO	American Funds EuroPacific Gr 529E	CEUEX	D+		(800) 421-0180	C- / 3.7	5.81	3.92	2.14 /22	9.24 /34	6.41 /19	1.03	1.15
FO	American Funds EuroPacific Gr	CEUFX	C-		(800) 421-0180	C- / 4.0	5.94	4.16	2.62 /25	9.74 /38	6.92 /22	1.49	0.68
* FO	American Funds EuroPacific Gr A	AEPGX	D		(800) 421-0180	C- / 3.0	5.90	4.08	2.47 /24	9.57 /37	6.75 /21	1.23	0.84
FO	● American Funds EuroPacific Gr B	AEGBX	D+		(800) 421-0180	C- / 3.4	5.70	3.68	1.72 /21	8.77 /31	5.96 /17	0.24	1.58
FO	American Funds EuroPacific Gr C	AEPCX	D+		(800) 421-0180	C- / 3.3	5.68	3.65	1.65 /21	8.72 /31	5.92 /16	0.52	1.62
FO	American Funds EuroPacific Gr F1	AEGFX	D+		(800) 421-0180	C- / 3.9	5.88	4.06	2.43 /24	9.55 /36	6.72 /21	1.20	0.87
FO	American Funds EuroPacific Gr F2	AEPFX	C-		(800) 421-0180	C- / 4.0	5.95	4.19	2.69 /25	9.85 /38	7.01 /23	1.58	0.59
FO	American Funds EuroPacific Gr R1	RERAX	D+		(800) 421-0180	C- / 3.3	5.69	3.67	1.67 /21	8.74 /31	5.93 /16	0.59	1.61
FO	American Funds EuroPacific Gr R2	RERBX	D+		(800) 421-0180	C- / 3.4	5.71	3.69	1.70 /21	8.77 /31	5.94 /16	0.56	1.57
FO	American Funds EuroPacific Gr R2E	REEBX	D		(800) 421-0180	C- / 3.5	5.77	3.87	2.01 /22	8.96 /33	6.13 /18	1.58	1.30
FO	American Funds EuroPacific Gr R3	RERCX	D+		(800) 421-0180	C- / 3.7	5.82	3.92	2.16 /22	9.25 /35	6.43 /20	1.01	1.14
FO	American Funds EuroPacific Gr R4	REREX	D+		(800) 421-0180	C- / 3.9	5.90	4.08	2.45 /24	9.57 /37	6.74 /21	1.32	0.84
FO	American Funds EuroPacific Gr R5	RERFX	C-		(800) 421-0180	C- / 4.1	5.97	4.23	2.77 /25	9.91 /39	7.06 /23	1.60	0.54
FO	American Funds EuroPacific Gr R6	RERGX	C-		(800) 421-0180	C- / 4.1	5.97	4.24	2.80 /25	9.95 /39	7.11 /24	1.65	0.49
GI	American Funds Fundamntl Invs	CFNAX	C+		(800) 421-0180	C+ / 6.3	1.58	4.54	10.20 /75	15.08 /75	12.75 /66	1.58	0.70
GI	● American Funds Fundamntl Invs	CFNBX	C+		(800) 421-0180	C+ / 6.7	1.38	4.11	9.33 /71	14.17 /68	11.84 /59	0.85	1.49
GI	American Funds Fundamntl Invs	CFNCX	C+		(800) 421-0180	C+ / 6.7	1.37	4.13	9.32 /71	14.18 /68	11.85 /60	0.92	1.49
GI	American Funds Fundamntl Invs	CFNEX	B		(800) 421-0180	B- / 7.1	1.52	4.42	9.95 /74	14.80 /73	12.46 /64	1.44	0.94
GI	American Funds Fundamntl Invs	CFNFX	B+		(800) 421-0180	B- / 7.5	1.62	4.64	10.43 /76	15.33 /77	12.98 /68	1.88	0.48
* GI	American Funds Fundamntl Invs A	ANCFX	C+		(800) 421-0180	C+ / 6.4	1.60	4.58	10.31 /76	15.19 /76	12.84 /67	1.66	0.61
GI	● American Funds Fundamntl Invs B	AFIBX	C+		(800) 421-0180	C+ / 6.8	1.42	4.19	9.47 /72	14.31 /69	11.98 /60	0.98	1.37
GI	American Funds Fundamntl Invs C	AFICX	C+		(800) 421-0180	C+ / 6.7	1.41	4.17	9.42 /72	14.27 /69	11.94 /60	1.00	1.41
GI	American Funds Fundamntl Invs F1	AFIFX	B+		(800) 421-0180	B- / 7.4	1.58	4.54	10.21 /75	15.13 /76	12.79 /67	1.69	0.66
GI	American Funds Fundamntl Invs F2	FINFX	B+		(800) 421-0180	B / 7.6	1.65	4.68	10.52 /76	15.44 /78	13.09 /69	1.96	0.40
GI	American Funds Fundamntl Invs R1	RFNAX	C+		(800) 421-0180	C+ / 6.7	1.39	4.16	9.43 /72	14.28 /69	11.95 /60	1.00	1.41
GI	American Funds Fundamntl Invs R2	RFNBX	C+		(800) 421-0180	C+ / 6.8	1.41	4.18	9.45 /72	14.32 /69	11.98 /60	1.04	1.38
GL	American Funds Fundamntl Invs R2E	RFEBX	C+		(800) 421-0180	B- / 7.0	1.62	4.62	10.07 /75	14.63 /72	12.23 /62	1.74	1.11
GI	American Funds Fundamntl Invs R3	RFNCX	B		(800) 421-0180	B- / 7.1	1.53	4.40	9.93 /74	14.80 /73	12.47 /64	1.43	0.96
GI	American Funds Fundamntl Invs R4	RFNEX	B+		(800) 421-0180	B- / 7.4	1.60	4.56	10.26 /75	15.15 /76	12.80 /66	1.71	0.66
GI	American Funds Fundamntl Invs R5	RFNFX	B+		(800) 421-0180	B / 7.6	1.67	4.72	10.58 /77	15.49 /79	13.14 /69	2.00	0.35
GI	American Funds Fundamntl Invs R6	RFNGX	B+		(800) 421-0180	B / 7.7	1.68	4.74	10.62 /77	15.54 /79	13.20 /70	2.05	0.31
FO	American Funds Glbl Balanced 529A	CBFAX	C-		(800) 421-0180	D / 2.0	0.61	-0.03	1.92 /22	8.61 /30	--	1.38	0.96
FO	● American Funds Glbl Balanced 529B	CBFBX	C-		(800) 421-0180	D+ / 2.3	0.37	-0.45	1.11 /19	7.73 /25	--	0.57	1.77
FO	American Funds Glbl Balanced 529C	CBFCX	C-		(800) 421-0180	D+ / 2.3	0.39	-0.46	1.10 /19	7.72 /25	--	0.69	1.76
FO	American Funds Glbl Balanced 529E	CBFEX	C-		(800) 421-0180	D+ / 2.7	0.55	-0.16	1.67 /21	8.33 /29	--	1.22	1.21
FO	American Funds Glbl Balanced	CBFFX	C		(800) 421-0180	C- / 3.0	0.63	0.04	2.13 /22	8.82 /32	--	1.68	0.76
FO	American Funds Glbl Balanced A	GBLAX	C-		(800) 421-0180	D / 2.0	0.60	-0.03	1.99 /22	8.68 /31	--	1.45	0.89
FO	● American Funds Glbl Balanced B	GBLBX	C-		(800) 421-0180	D+ / 2.4	0.45	-0.38	1.24 /19	7.86 /26	--	0.73	1.64
FO	American Funds Glbl Balanced C	GBLCX	C-		(800) 421-0180	D+ / 2.4	0.44	-0.39	1.21 /19	7.82 /26	--	0.76	1.69
FO	American Funds Glbl Balanced F1	GBLEX	C		(800) 421-0180	D+ / 2.9	0.61	-0.03	1.95 /22	8.64 /31	--	1.46	0.94
FO	American Funds Glbl Balanced F2	GBLFX	C		(800) 421-0180	C- / 3.0	0.65	0.08	2.21 /23	8.91 /32	--	1.76	0.68
FO	American Funds Glbl Balanced R1	RGBLX	C-		(800) 421-0180	D+ / 2.5	0.43	-0.36	1.31 /19	8.10 /27	--	0.90	1.65
FO	American Funds Glbl Balanced R2	RGBBX	C-		(800) 421-0180	D+ / 2.4	0.46	-0.37	1.24 /19	7.85 /26	--	0.79	1.69
GL	American Funds Glbl Balanced R2E	RGGHX	C-		(800) 421-0180	D+ / 2.6	0.62	0.02	1.79 /21	8.17 /28	--	1.48	1.38
FO	American Funds Glbl Balanced R3	RGBCX	C-		(800) 421-0180	D+ / 2.7	0.56	-0.15	1.67 /21	8.34 /29	--	1.22	1.22
FO	American Funds Glbl Balanced R4	RGBEX	C		(800) 421-0180	D+ / 2.9	0.63	-0.01	1.97 /22	8.68 /31	--	1.52	0.91
FO	American Funds Glbl Balanced R5	RGBFX	C		(800) 421-0180	C- / 3.1	0.69	0.13	2.27 /23	8.99 /33	--	1.75	0.62
FO	American Funds Glbl Balanced R6	RGBGX	C		(800) 421-0180	C- / 3.1	0.68	0.16	2.31 /23	9.04 /33	--	1.86	0.57
GL	American Funds Global Growth 529A	CPGAX	U		(800) 421-0180	U /	3.43	3.72	4.94 /38	--	--	0.83	1.00
GL	American Funds Global Growth 529C	CPGCX	U		(800) 421-0180	U /	3.25	3.28	4.07 /32	--	--	0.29	1.81
GL	American Funds Global Growth A	PGGAX	U		(800) 421-0180	U /	3.43	3.70	5.00 /38	--	--	0.88	0.93
GL	American Funds Global Growth C	GGPCX	U		(800) 421-0180	U /	3.32	3.29	4.15 /33	--	--	0.31	1.73

● Denotes fund is closed to new investors
* Denotes fund is included in Section II

RISK			NET ASSETS		ASSET				Portfolio	BULL / BEAR		FUND MANAGER		MINIMUMS		LOADS	
	3 Year		NAV							Last Bull	Last Bear	Manager	Manager	Initial	Additional	Front	Back
Risk Rating/Pts	Standard Deviation	Beta	As of 3/31/15	Total $(Mil)	Cash %	Stocks %	Bonds %	Other %	Turnover Ratio	Market Return	Market Return	Quality Pct	Tenure (Years)	Purch. $	Purch. $	End Load	End Load
C+ / 5.9	11.5	0.85	49.00	62	0	86	13	1	28	52.4	-24.2	78	9	250	50	0.0	0.0
C+ / 5.9	11.5	0.85	49.40	97	0	86	13	1	28	54.9	-24.0	81	9	250	50	0.0	0.0
C+ / 5.9	11.5	0.85	49.91	30,814	0	86	13	1	28	54.1	-24.0	80	9	250	50	5.8	0.0
C+ / 6.0	11.5	0.85	49.89	141	0	86	13	1	28	50.2	-24.3	74	9	250	50	0.0	0.0
C+ / 5.9	11.6	0.85	48.75	1,802	0	86	13	1	28	50.0	-24.3	73	9	250	50	0.0	0.0
C+ / 5.9	11.5	0.85	49.67	6,770	0	86	13	1	28	54.0	-24.1	80	9	250	50	0.0	0.0
C+ / 5.9	11.5	0.85	49.82	16,265	0	86	13	1	28	55.4	-24.0	82	9	250	50	0.0	0.0
C+ / 6.0	11.5	0.85	48.14	286	0	86	13	1	28	50.1	-24.3	74	9	250	50	0.0	0.0
C+ / 5.9	11.5	0.85	48.49	977	0	86	13	1	28	50.2	-24.3	74	9	250	50	0.0	0.0
C / 5.4	11.5	0.85	49.67	N/A	0	86	13	1	28	51.1	-24.2	76	9	250	50	0.0	0.0
C+ / 6.0	11.5	0.85	48.93	6,510	0	86	13	1	28	52.5	-24.1	78	9	250	50	0.0	0.0
C+ / 6.0	11.5	0.85	48.99	13,569	0	86	13	1	28	54.1	-24.1	80	9	250	50	0.0	0.0
C+ / 5.9	11.5	0.85	49.85	11,427	0	86	13	1	28	55.6	-23.9	82	9	250	50	0.0	0.0
C+ / 5.9	11.5	0.85	49.90	38,264	0	86	13	1	28	55.9	-23.9	82	9	250	50	0.0	0.0
C+ / 6.7	9.8	1.00	52.07	1,774	0	94	4	2	29	92.8	-19.7	54	22	250	50	5.8	0.0
C+ / 6.7	9.8	1.00	52.13	26	0	94	4	2	29	87.6	-20.0	42	22	250	50	0.0	0.0
C+ / 6.7	9.8	1.00	52.01	451	0	94	4	2	29	87.7	-20.0	42	22	250	50	0.0	0.0
C+ / 6.7	9.8	1.00	52.03	73	0	94	4	2	29	91.2	-19.8	50	22	250	50	0.0	0.0
C+ / 6.7	9.8	1.00	52.03	78	0	94	4	2	29	94.2	-19.6	57	22	250	50	0.0	0.0
C+ / 6.7	9.8	1.00	52.13	44,458	0	94	4	2	29	93.4	-19.7	56	22	250	50	5.8	0.0
C+ / 6.7	9.8	1.00	52.03	295	0	94	4	2	29	88.4	-19.9	44	22	250	50	0.0	0.0
C+ / 6.7	9.8	1.00	51.90	2,453	0	94	4	2	29	88.2	-20.0	43	22	250	50	0.0	0.0
C+ / 6.7	9.8	1.00	52.10	4,727	0	94	4	2	29	93.1	-19.7	55	22	250	50	0.0	0.0
C+ / 6.7	9.8	1.00	52.11	4,109	0	94	4	2	29	94.8	-19.6	59	22	250	50	0.0	0.0
C+ / 6.7	9.8	1.00	51.89	164	0	94	4	2	29	88.3	-19.9	43	22	250	50	0.0	0.0
C+ / 6.7	9.8	1.00	51.88	785	0	94	4	2	29	88.5	-19.9	44	22	250	50	0.0	0.0
C+ / 5.8	9.8	0.63	52.08	N/A	0	94	4	2	29	90.0	-19.9	97	22	250	50	0.0	0.0
C+ / 6.7	9.8	1.00	52.01	2,584	0	94	4	2	29	91.2	-19.8	51	22	250	50	0.0	0.0
C+ / 6.7	9.8	1.00	52.03	2,593	0	94	4	2	29	93.2	-19.7	55	22	250	50	0.0	0.0
C+ / 6.7	9.8	1.00	52.15	1,988	0	94	4	2	29	95.2	-19.6	60	22	250	50	0.0	0.0
C+ / 6.7	9.8	1.00	52.13	5,933	0	94	4	2	29	95.5	-19.6	60	22	250	50	0.0	0.0
B / 8.0	7.0	0.49	30.26	200	1	56	41	2	74	47.6	-12.2	91	4	250	50	5.8	0.0
B / 8.1	7.0	0.49	30.27	1	1	56	41	2	74	43.5	-12.5	88	4	250	50	0.0	0.0
B / 8.1	7.0	0.49	30.17	75	1	56	41	2	74	43.6	-12.5	89	4	250	50	0.0	0.0
B / 8.0	7.0	0.49	30.24	12	1	56	41	2	74	46.3	-12.3	90	4	250	50	0.0	0.0
B / 8.0	7.0	0.49	30.27	13	1	56	41	2	74	48.5	-12.1	91	4	250	50	0.0	0.0
B / 8.0	7.0	0.49	30.27	4,506	1	56	41	2	74	48.0	-12.2	91	4	250	50	5.8	0.0
B / 8.0	7.0	0.49	30.28	9	1	56	41	2	74	44.1	-12.5	89	4	250	50	0.0	0.0
B / 8.0	7.0	0.49	30.22	598	1	56	41	2	74	43.9	-12.5	89	4	250	50	0.0	0.0
B / 8.0	7.0	0.49	30.28	183	1	56	41	2	74	47.8	-12.2	91	4	250	50	0.0	0.0
B / 8.0	7.0	0.49	30.28	525	1	56	41	2	74	49.0	-12.1	92	4	250	50	0.0	0.0
B / 8.0	7.0	0.49	30.22	8	1	56	41	2	74	45.1	-12.5	90	4	250	50	0.0	0.0
B / 8.0	7.0	0.50	30.20	39	1	56	41	2	74	44.2	-12.4	89	4	250	50	0.0	0.0
B- / 7.2	7.0	1.07	30.26	N/A	1	56	41	2	74	45.4	-12.4	46	4	250	50	0.0	0.0
B / 8.0	7.0	0.49	30.24	40	1	56	41	2	74	46.4	-12.3	90	4	250	50	0.0	0.0
B / 8.0	7.0	0.49	30.28	23	1	56	41	2	74	48.0	-12.2	91	4	250	50	0.0	0.0
B / 8.0	7.0	0.49	30.31	5	1	56	41	2	74	49.4	-12.1	92	4	250	50	0.0	0.0
B / 8.0	7.0	0.49	30.29	2,453	1	56	41	2	74	49.6	-12.1	92	4	250	50	0.0	0.0
U /	N/A	N/A	14.77	109	0	89	9	2	0	N/A	N/A	N/A	3	250	50	5.8	0.0
U /	N/A	N/A	14.61	48	0	89	9	2	0	N/A	N/A	N/A	3	250	50	0.0	0.0
U /	N/A	N/A	14.78	828	0	89	9	2	0	N/A	N/A	N/A	3	250	50	5.8	0.0
U /	N/A	N/A	14.63	162	0	89	9	2	0	N/A	N/A	N/A	3	250	50	0.0	0.0

99 Pct = Best
0 Pct = Worst

Fund Type	Fund Name	Ticker Symbol	Overall Investment Rating	Phone	Perfor-mance Rating/Pts	3 Mo	6 Mo	1Yr / Pct	3Yr / Pct	5Yr / Pct	Dividend Yield	Expense Ratio
GL	American Funds Global Growth F1	PGGFX	U	(800) 421-0180	U /	3.43	3.70	4.92 /38	--	--	0.86	1.00
GL	American Funds Global Growth F2	PGWFX	U	(800) 421-0180	U /	3.49	3.86	5.15 /40	--	--	1.08	0.73
GL	American Funds Global Growth R2	RGGBX	U	(800) 421-0180	U /	3.32	3.32	4.11 /32	--	--	0.34	1.79
GL	American Funds Global Growth R6	RGGGX	U	(800) 421-0180	U /	3.55	3.85	5.28 /41	--	--	1.15	0.63
GR	American Funds Gr Fnd of Amer	CGFAX	B-	(800) 421-0180	B / 7.6	3.38	6.17	11.86 /82	16.63 /88	13.24 /70	0.27	0.74
GR ●	American Funds Gr Fnd of Amer	CGFBX	B	(800) 421-0180	B / 8.0	3.17	5.75	11.00 /78	15.72 /81	12.35 /63	0.00	1.53
GR	American Funds Gr Fnd of Amer	CGFCX	B	(800) 421-0180	B / 8.0	3.18	5.74	11.01 /78	15.73 /81	12.35 /63	0.05	1.52
GR	American Funds Gr Fnd of Amer	CGFEX	B+	(800) 421-0180	B+ / 8.4	3.31	6.02	11.57 /81	16.35 /86	12.95 /68	0.05	0.99
GR	American Funds Gr Fnd of Amer	CGFFX	B+	(800) 421-0180	B+ / 8.8	3.41	6.27	12.10 /83	16.89 /89	13.48 /73	0.49	0.52
* GR	American Funds Gr Fnd of Amer A	AGTHX	B	(800) 421-0180	B / 7.6	3.37	6.20	11.95 /82	16.72 /88	13.31 /71	0.33	0.66
GR ●	American Funds Gr Fnd of Amer B	AGRBX	B	(800) 421-0180	B / 8.1	3.21	5.81	11.12 /79	15.85 /82	12.46 /64	0.00	1.41
GR	American Funds Gr Fnd of Amer C	GFACX	B	(800) 421-0180	B / 8.0	3.17	5.77	11.06 /79	15.80 /82	12.43 /64	0.00	1.45
GR	American Funds Gr Fnd of Amer F1	GFAFX	B+	(800) 421-0180	B+ / 8.7	3.39	6.18	11.92 /82	16.71 /88	13.31 /71	0.21	0.69
GR	American Funds Gr Fnd of Amer F2	GFFFX	B+	(800) 421-0180	B+ / 8.9	3.45	6.34	12.22 /84	17.01 /90	13.60 /74	0.61	0.43
GR	American Funds Gr Fnd of Amer R1	RGAAX	B	(800) 421-0180	B / 8.1	3.20	5.80	11.11 /79	15.86 /88	12.47 /64	0.00	1.43
GR	American Funds Gr Fnd of Amer R2	RGABX	B	(800) 421-0180	B / 8.2	3.23	5.83	11.16 /79	15.92 /83	12.53 /64	0.00	1.38
GR	American Funds Gr Fnd of Amer R2E	RGEBX	B+	(800) 421-0180	B+ / 8.3	3.27	6.11	11.60 /81	16.13 /84	12.69 /66	0.62	1.15
GR	American Funds Gr Fnd of Amer R3	RGACX	B+	(800) 421-0180	B+ / 8.5	3.33	6.04	11.62 /81	16.39 /86	12.99 /68	0.03	0.98
GR	American Funds Gr Fnd of Amer R4	RGAEX	B+	(800) 421-0180	B+ / 8.7	3.38	6.18	11.92 /82	16.72 /88	13.32 /71	0.32	0.68
GR	American Funds Gr Fnd of Amer R5	RGAFX	B+	(800) 421-0180	B+ / 8.9	3.45	6.35	12.26 /84	17.07 /90	13.66 /75	0.60	0.38
GR	American Funds Gr Fnd of Amer R6	RGAGX	B+	(800) 421-0180	B+ / 8.9	3.47	6.38	12.31 /84	17.13 /90	13.71 /75	0.66	0.33
GL	American Funds Growth 529A	CGPAX	U	(800) 421-0180	U /	3.48	5.40	7.97 /63	--	--	0.67	0.92
GL	American Funds Growth 529C	CGPCX	U	(800) 421-0180	U /	3.30	5.04	7.12 /56	--	--	0.07	1.74
GL	American Funds Growth A	GWPAX	U	(800) 421-0180	U /	3.47	5.46	8.03 /63	--	--	0.72	0.85
GL	American Funds Growth and Inc	CGNAX	U	(800) 421-0180	U /	1.36	2.64	6.40 /50	--	--	2.04	0.88
GL	American Funds Growth and Inc	CGNCX	U	(800) 421-0180	U /	1.20	2.20	5.55 /43	--	--	1.43	1.68
GL	American Funds Growth and Inc A	GAIOX	U	(800) 421-0180	U /	1.37	2.61	6.49 /51	--	--	2.12	0.79
GL	American Funds Growth and Inc C	GAITX	U	(800) 421-0180	U /	1.15	2.19	5.59 /43	--	--	1.53	1.59
GL	American Funds Growth and Inc F1	GAIFX	U	(800) 421-0180	U /	1.36	2.58	6.42 /50	--	--	2.19	0.86
GL	American Funds Growth and Inc F2	GAIEX	U	(800) 421-0180	U /	1.49	2.78	6.75 /53	--	--	2.43	0.60
GL	American Funds Growth and Inc R2	RGNBX	U	(800) 421-0180	U /	1.23	2.26	5.64 /43	--	--	1.51	1.65
GL	American Funds Growth and Inc R3	RAICX	U	(800) 421-0180	U /	1.31	2.45	6.07 /47	--	--	1.92	1.17
GL	American Funds Growth and Inc R4	RGNEX	U	(800) 421-0180	U /	1.37	2.60	6.46 /50	--	--	2.22	0.84
GL	American Funds Growth and Inc R6	RGNGX	U	(800) 421-0180	U /	1.51	2.82	6.85 /54	--	--	2.52	0.49
GL	American Funds Growth C	GWPCX	U	(800) 421-0180	U /	3.30	5.02	7.17 /56	--	--	0.18	1.66
GL	American Funds Growth F1	GWPFX	U	(800) 421-0180	U /	3.48	5.40	7.97 /63	--	--	0.71	0.93
GL	American Funds Growth F2	GWPEX	U	(800) 421-0180	U /	3.53	5.52	8.22 /64	--	--	0.89	0.67
GL	American Funds Growth R2	RGWBX	U	(800) 421-0180	U /	3.30	5.05	7.13 /56	--	--	0.15	1.72
GL	American Funds Growth R3	RGPCX	U	(800) 421-0180	U /	3.35	5.26	7.61 /60	--	--	0.49	1.24
GL	American Funds Growth R6	RGWGX	U	(800) 421-0180	U /	3.60	5.60	8.38 /65	--	--	0.97	0.56
IN	American Funds Inc Fnd of Amr 529A	CIMAX	C	(800) 421-0180	C- / 3.7	0.93	2.85	6.46 /50	11.10 /46	10.60 /49	3.36	0.67
IN ●	American Funds Inc Fnd of Amr 529B	CIMBX	C+	(800) 421-0180	C- / 4.1	0.72	2.46	5.63 /43	10.23 /41	9.73 /42	2.72	1.45
IN	American Funds Inc Fnd of Amr 529C	CIMCX	C+	(800) 421-0180	C- / 4.1	0.74	2.47	5.67 /44	10.25 /41	9.74 /42	2.80	1.44
IN	American Funds Inc Fnd of Amr 529E	CIMEX	C+	(800) 421-0180	C / 4.5	0.88	2.74	6.22 /48	10.82 /44	10.31 /47	3.33	0.91
IN	American Funds Inc Fnd of Amr	CIMFX	C+	(800) 421-0180	C / 4.8	0.99	2.97	6.75 /53	11.35 /48	10.84 /51	3.79	0.44
* IN	American Funds Inc Fnd of Amr A	AMECX	C+	(800) 421-0180	C- / 3.8	0.96	2.94	6.60 /52	11.21 /47	10.70 /50	3.44	0.57
IN ●	American Funds Inc Fnd of Amr B	IFABX	C+	(800) 421-0180	C- / 4.2	0.75	2.53	5.78 /45	10.38 /42	9.87 /43	2.85	1.32
IN	American Funds Inc Fnd of Amr C	IFACX	C+	(800) 421-0180	C- / 4.2	0.77	2.52	5.73 /44	10.32 /41	9.82 /43	2.89	1.37
IN	American Funds Inc Fnd of Amr F1	IFAFX	C+	(800) 421-0180	C / 4.6	0.94	2.86	6.47 /50	11.12 /46	10.62 /50	3.57	0.65
IN	American Funds Inc Fnd of Amr F2	AMEFX	B-	(800) 421-0180	C / 4.8	0.96	2.99	6.75 /53	11.39 /48	10.89 /52	3.84	0.40
IN	American Funds Inc Fnd of Amr R1	RIDAX	C+	(800) 421-0180	C- / 4.1	0.72	2.50	5.69 /44	10.30 /41	9.80 /43	2.87	1.39
IN	American Funds Inc Fnd of Amr R2	RIDBX	C+	(800) 421-0180	C- / 4.2	0.78	2.53	5.73 /44	10.33 /41	9.81 /43	2.89	1.37

● Denotes fund is closed to new investors
* Denotes fund is included in Section II

www.thestreetratings.com

RISK			NET ASSETS		ASSET					BULL / BEAR		FUND MANAGER		MINIMUMS		LOADS	
	3 Year		NAV						Portfolio	Last Bull	Last Bear	Manager	Manager	Initial	Additional	Front	Back
Risk	Standard		As of	Total	Cash	Stocks	Bonds	Other	Turnover	Market	Market	Quality	Tenure	Purch.	Purch.	End	End
Rating/Pts	Deviation	Beta	3/31/15	$(Mil)	%	%	%	%	Ratio	Return	Return	Pct	(Years)	$	$	Load	Load
U /	N/A	N/A	14.78	50	0	89	9	2	0	N/A	N/A	N/A	3	250	50	0.0	0.0
U /	N/A	N/A	14.82	41	0	89	9	2	0	N/A	N/A	N/A	3	250	50	0.0	0.0
U /	N/A	N/A	14.62	26	0	89	9	2	0	N/A	N/A	N/A	3	250	50	0.0	0.0
U /	N/A	N/A	14.89	35	0	89	9	2	0	N/A	N/A	N/A	3	250	50	0.0	0.0
C+ / 5.7	9.7	0.95	43.77	6,033	0	90	9	1	26	99.0	-19.0	79	27	250	50	5.8	0.0
C+ / 5.7	9.7	0.95	42.01	123	0	90	9	1	26	93.7	-19.3	72	27	250	50	0.0	0.0
C+ / 5.7	9.7	0.95	41.88	1,478	0	90	9	1	26	93.8	-19.3	72	27	250	50	0.0	0.0
C+ / 5.8	9.7	0.95	43.40	269	0	90	9	1	26	97.3	-19.1	77	27	250	50	0.0	0.0
C+ / 5.7	9.7	0.95	43.70	212	0	90	9	1	26	100.4	-19.0	80	27	250	50	0.0	0.0
C+ / 5.7	9.7	0.95	44.12	74,756	0	90	9	1	26	99.5	-19.0	79	27	250	50	5.8	0.0
C+ / 5.7	9.7	0.95	42.17	654	0	90	9	1	26	94.4	-19.3	73	27	250	50	0.0	0.0
C+ / 5.7	9.7	0.95	41.71	5,915	0	90	9	1	26	94.2	-19.3	72	27	250	50	0.0	0.0
C+ / 5.8	9.7	0.95	43.88	8,752	0	90	9	1	26	99.4	-19.0	79	27	250	50	0.0	0.0
C+ / 5.7	9.7	0.95	44.07	10,798	0	90	9	1	26	101.2	-18.9	81	27	250	50	0.0	0.0
C+ / 5.7	9.7	0.95	42.21	522	0	90	9	1	26	94.5	-19.3	73	27	250	50	0.0	0.0
C+ / 5.7	9.7	0.95	42.53	2,425	0	90	9	1	26	94.8	-19.2	74	27	250	50	0.0	0.0
C+ / 5.8	9.7	0.95	43.96	N/A	0	90	9	1	26	95.9	-19.2	75	27	250	50	0.0	0.0
C+ / 5.8	9.7	0.95	43.42	7,961	0	90	9	1	26	97.5	-19.1	77	27	250	50	0.0	0.0
C+ / 5.7	9.7	0.95	43.80	7,652	0	90	9	1	26	99.5	-19.0	79	27	250	50	0.0	0.0
C+ / 5.7	9.7	0.95	44.10	5,214	0	90	9	1	26	101.6	-18.9	81	27	250	50	0.0	0.0
C+ / 5.7	9.7	0.95	44.16	13,443	0	90	9	1	26	101.9	-18.9	82	27	250	50	0.0	0.0
U /	N/A	N/A	15.48	230	0	90	8	2	0	N/A	N/A	N/A	3	250	50	5.8	0.0
U /	N/A	N/A	15.33	83	0	90	8	2	0	N/A	N/A	N/A	3	250	50	0.0	0.0
U /	N/A	N/A	15.49	1,655	0	90	8	2	0	N/A	N/A	N/A	3	250	50	5.8	0.0
U /	N/A	N/A	13.55	252	0	75	24	1	0	N/A	N/A	N/A	3	250	50	5.8	0.0
U /	N/A	N/A	13.50	104	0	75	24	1	0	N/A	N/A	N/A	3	250	50	0.0	0.0
U /	N/A	N/A	13.55	2,957	0	75	24	1	0	N/A	N/A	N/A	3	250	50	5.8	0.0
U /	N/A	N/A	13.49	606	0	75	24	1	0	N/A	N/A	N/A	3	250	50	0.0	0.0
U /	N/A	N/A	13.55	73	0	75	24	1	0	N/A	N/A	N/A	3	250	50	0.0	0.0
U /	N/A	N/A	13.57	100	0	75	24	1	0	N/A	N/A	N/A	3	250	50	0.0	0.0
U /	N/A	N/A	13.49	50	0	75	24	1	0	N/A	N/A	N/A	3	250	50	0.0	0.0
U /	N/A	N/A	13.52	33	0	75	24	1	0	N/A	N/A	N/A	3	250	50	0.0	0.0
U /	N/A	N/A	13.55	27	0	75	24	1	0	N/A	N/A	N/A	3	250	50	0.0	0.0
U /	N/A	N/A	13.57	38	0	75	24	1	0	N/A	N/A	N/A	3	250	50	0.0	0.0
U /	N/A	N/A	15.32	338	0	90	8	2	0	N/A	N/A	N/A	3	250	50	0.0	0.0
U /	N/A	N/A	15.48	47	0	90	8	2	0	N/A	N/A	N/A	3	250	50	0.0	0.0
U /	N/A	N/A	15.53	67	0	90	8	2	0	N/A	N/A	N/A	3	250	50	0.0	0.0
U /	N/A	N/A	15.33	46	0	90	8	2	0	N/A	N/A	N/A	3	250	50	0.0	0.0
U /	N/A	N/A	15.43	28	0	90	8	2	0	N/A	N/A	N/A	3	250	50	0.0	0.0
U /	N/A	N/A	15.55	37	0	90	8	2	0	N/A	N/A	N/A	3	250	50	0.0	0.0
B / 8.1	6.7	0.64	21.58	1,515	1	72	26	1	39	59.3	-10.1	76	23	250	50	5.8	0.0
B / 8.1	6.7	0.64	21.55	25	1	72	26	1	39	55.1	-10.4	68	23	250	50	0.0	0.0
B / 8.1	6.7	0.65	21.51	478	1	72	26	1	39	55.1	-10.4	68	23	250	50	0.0	0.0
B / 8.1	6.7	0.64	21.52	66	1	72	26	1	39	57.9	-10.2	74	23	250	50	0.0	0.0
B / 8.1	6.7	0.64	21.58	58	1	72	26	1	39	60.5	-10.0	78	23	250	50	0.0	0.0
B / 8.1	6.7	0.65	21.62	73,697	1	72	26	1	39	59.8	-10.1	76	23	250	50	5.8	0.0
B / 8.1	6.7	0.64	21.49	405	1	72	26	1	39	55.8	-10.4	70	23	250	50	0.0	0.0
B / 8.1	6.7	0.64	21.38	6,588	1	72	26	1	39	55.5	-10.3	69	23	250	50	0.0	0.0
B / 8.1	6.7	0.64	21.57	4,093	1	72	26	1	39	59.4	-10.1	76	23	250	50	0.0	0.0
B / 8.1	6.7	0.64	21.60	3,933	1	72	26	1	39	60.7	-10.0	78	23	250	50	0.0	0.0
B / 8.1	6.7	0.64	21.50	141	1	72	26	1	39	55.5	-10.4	69	23	250	50	0.0	0.0
B / 8.1	6.7	0.65	21.41	633	1	72	26	1	39	55.5	-10.4	69	23	250	50	0.0	0.0

					PERFORMANCE						Incl. in Returns	
	99 Pct = Best						Total Return % through 3/31/15					
	0 Pct = Worst		Overall		Perfor-				Annualized		Dividend	Expense
Fund		Ticker	Investment		mance						Yield	Ratio
Type	Fund Name	Symbol	Rating	Phone	Rating/Pts	3 Mo	6 Mo	1Yr / Pct	3Yr / Pct	5Yr / Pct		
AA	American Funds Inc Fnd of Amr R2E	RIEBX	C	(800) 421-0180	C / 4.4	0.86	2.85	6.25 /49	10.64 /43	10.09 /45	3.47	1.10
IN	American Funds Inc Fnd of Amr R3	RIDCX	C+	(800) 421-0180	C / 4.5	0.87	2.77	6.24 /48	10.80 /44	10.29 /47	3.30	0.94
IN	American Funds Inc Fnd of Amr R4	RIDEX	C+	(800) 421-0180	C / 4.7	0.95	2.92	6.54 /51	11.13 /46	10.63 /50	3.59	0.64
IN	American Funds Inc Fnd of Amr R5	RIDFX	B-	(800) 421-0180	C / 4.9	1.02	3.06	6.85 /54	11.47 /49	10.96 /52	3.88	0.34
IN	American Funds Inc Fnd of Amr R6	RIDGX	B-	(800) 421-0180	C / 4.9	1.03	3.08	6.89 /54	11.54 /49	11.01 /53	3.93	0.29
GL	American Funds Income 529A	CIPAX	U	(800) 421-0180	U /	1.11	2.87	5.41 /42	--	--	2.91	0.84
GL	American Funds Income 529C	CIPCX	U	(800) 421-0180	U /	0.95	2.42	4.57 /36	--	--	2.37	1.62
GL	American Funds Income A	INPAX	U	(800) 421-0180	U /	1.21	2.90	5.50 /42	--	--	2.99	0.76
GL	American Funds Income C	INPCX	U	(800) 421-0180	U /	0.98	2.48	4.70 /36	--	--	2.49	1.53
GL	American Funds Income F1	INPFX	U	(800) 421-0180	U /	1.12	2.89	5.46 /42	--	--	3.14	0.80
GL	American Funds Income F2	INPEX	U	(800) 421-0180	U /	1.25	3.01	5.72 /44	--	--	3.39	0.54
GI	American Funds Ins Ser Gr & Inc 4		U	(800) 421-0180	U /	1.60	4.26	10.69 /77	--	--	1.30	0.79
GR	American Funds Ins Ser Growth 4		U	(800) 421-0180	U /	4.08	7.44	12.31 /84	--	--	1.06	0.85
EM	American Funds Ins Ser New Wrld 4		U	(800) 421-0180	U /	2.82	-4.12	-4.78 / 6	--	--	1.05	1.28
FO	American Funds Intl Gr & Inc 529A	CGIAX	D-	(800) 421-0180	D- / 1.5	1.65	-2.35	-3.37 / 8	8.29 /29	6.58 /21	2.42	0.98
FO ●	American Funds Intl Gr & Inc 529B	CGIBX	D-	(800) 421-0180	D / 1.8	1.46	-2.75	-4.17 / 7	7.40 /24	5.70 /15	1.62	1.80
FO	American Funds Intl Gr & Inc 529C	CIICX	D-	(800) 421-0180	D / 1.8	1.46	-2.75	-4.16 / 7	7.41 /24	5.71 /15	1.71	1.78
FO	American Funds Intl Gr & Inc 529E	CGIEX	D-	(800) 421-0180	D / 2.1	1.59	-2.46	-3.62 / 8	8.01 /27	6.29 /19	2.30	1.23
FO	American Funds Intl Gr & Inc 529F1	CGIFX	D-	(800) 421-0180	D+ / 2.4	1.70	-2.24	-3.19 / 8	8.50 /30	6.79 /22	2.78	0.78
FO	American Funds Intl Gr & Inc A	IGAAX	D-	(800) 421-0180	D- / 1.5	1.67	-2.34	-3.33 / 8	8.36 /29	6.65 /21	2.49	0.91
FO ●	American Funds Intl Gr & Inc B	IGIBX	D-	(800) 421-0180	D / 1.8	1.49	-2.68	-4.05 / 7	7.55 /24	5.84 /16	1.77	1.66
FO	American Funds Intl Gr & Inc C	IGICX	D-	(800) 421-0180	D / 1.8	1.47	-2.71	-4.07 / 7	7.50 /24	5.79 /16	1.79	1.71
FO	American Funds Intl Gr & Inc F1	IGIFX	D-	(800) 421-0180	D / 2.2	1.69	-2.33	-3.35 / 8	8.32 /29	6.61 /21	2.58	0.96
FO	American Funds Intl Gr & Inc F2	IGFFX	D	(800) 421-0180	D+ / 2.4	1.72	-2.23	-3.11 / 8	8.59 /30	6.87 /22	2.87	0.70
FO	American Funds Intl Gr & Inc R1	RIGAX	D-	(800) 421-0180	D / 2.0	1.51	-2.62	-3.91 / 7	7.93 /27	6.13 /18	2.05	1.67
FO	American Funds Intl Gr & Inc R2	RIGBX	D-	(800) 421-0180	D / 1.8	1.46	-2.75	-4.15 / 7	7.45 /24	5.77 /15	1.72	1.75
FO	American Funds Intl Gr & Inc R2E	RIIEX	D-	(800) 421-0180	D / 2.0	1.72	-2.27	-3.52 / 8	7.85 /26	6.08 /17	2.60	1.41
FO	American Funds Intl Gr & Inc R3	RGICX	D-	(800) 421-0180	D / 2.1	1.59	-2.47	-3.64 / 8	7.99 /27	6.27 /19	2.28	1.26
FO	American Funds Intl Gr & Inc R4	RIGEX	D-	(800) 421-0180	D+ / 2.3	1.70	-2.31	-3.31 / 8	8.35 /29	6.63 /21	2.62	0.93
FO	American Funds Intl Gr & Inc R5	RIGFX	D	(800) 421-0180	D+ / 2.5	1.77	-2.16	-3.03 / 9	8.67 /31	6.93 /23	2.89	0.63
FO	American Funds Intl Gr & Inc R6	RIGGX	D	(800) 421-0180	D+ / 2.5	1.75	-2.18	-3.00 / 9	8.71 /31	6.98 /23	2.98	0.59
GI	American Funds Inv Co of Amer 529A	CICAX	C+	(800) 421-0180	C+ / 6.5	0.55	3.09	10.11 /75	15.70 /81	12.62 /65	1.62	0.69
GI ●	American Funds Inv Co of Amer 529B	CICBX	C+	(800) 421-0180	C+ / 6.9	0.33	2.68	9.22 /70	14.79 /73	11.72 /59	0.89	1.47
GI	American Funds Inv Co of Amer	CICCX	C+	(800) 421-0180	C+ / 6.9	0.33	2.68	9.24 /71	14.80 /73	11.74 /59	0.97	1.46
GI	American Funds Inv Co of Amer 529E	CICEX	B	(800) 421-0180	B- / 7.3	0.49	2.98	9.84 /74	15.41 /78	12.33 /63	1.48	0.93
GI	American Funds Inv Co of Amer	CICFX	B	(800) 421-0180	B / 7.8	0.61	3.22	10.37 /76	15.96 /83	12.87 /67	1.93	0.46
* GI	American Funds Inv Co of Amer A	AIVSX	C+	(800) 421-0180	C+ / 6.6	0.57	3.17	10.23 /75	15.82 /82	12.73 /66	1.71	0.59
GI ●	American Funds Inv Co of Amer B	AICBX	B-	(800) 421-0180	B- / 7.0	0.36	2.75	9.37 /71	14.94 /74	11.87 /60	1.02	1.34
GI	American Funds Inv Co of Amer C	AICCX	C+	(800) 421-0180	C+ / 6.9	0.38	2.72	9.35 /71	14.89 /74	11.81 /59	1.04	1.39
GI	American Funds Inv Co of Amer F1	AICFX	B	(800) 421-0180	B / 7.6	0.53	3.08	10.10 /75	15.72 /81	12.65 /65	1.73	0.67
GI	American Funds Inv Co of Amer F2	ICAFX	B	(800) 421-0180	B / 7.8	0.59	3.24	10.42 /76	16.04 /84	12.95 /68	2.00	0.39
GI	American Funds Inv Co of Amer R1	RICAX	C+	(800) 421-0180	C+ / 6.9	0.38	2.75	9.33 /71	14.90 /74	11.83 /59	1.05	1.40
GI	American Funds Inv Co of Amer R2	RICBX	B-	(800) 421-0180	B- / 7.0	0.39	2.74	9.35 /71	14.93 /74	11.84 /59	1.07	1.37
GI	American Funds Inv Co of Amer R2E	RIBEX	B-	(800) 421-0180	B- / 7.2	0.47	3.03	9.83 /74	15.20 /76	12.09 /61	1.62	1.11
GI	American Funds Inv Co of Amer R3	RICCX	B	(800) 421-0180	B- / 7.3	0.49	2.96	9.80 /74	15.39 /78	12.32 /63	1.46	0.96
GI	American Funds Inv Co of Amer R4	RICEX	B	(800) 421-0180	B / 7.6	0.56	3.13	10.16 /75	15.77 /81	12.68 /65	1.76	0.65
GI	American Funds Inv Co of Amer R5	RICFX	B	(800) 421-0180	B / 7.9	0.61	3.27	10.47 /76	16.11 /84	13.01 /68	2.04	0.35
GI	American Funds Inv Co of Amer R6	RICGX	B	(800) 421-0180	B / 7.9	0.65	3.29	10.52 /76	16.16 /85	13.07 /69	2.08	0.30
AA	American Funds Mgd Risk Asst All P2		U	(800) 421-0180	U /	0.33	1.20	3.24 /28	--	--	0.06	1.11
GR	American Funds New Economy 529A	CNGAX	B	(800) 421-0180	B / 8.0	3.54	5.86	7.02 /55	18.09 /95	14.62 /83	0.41	0.87
GR ●	American Funds New Economy 529B	CNGBX	B+	(800) 421-0180	B+ / 8.4	3.35	5.44	6.18 /48	17.15 /91	13.70 /75	0.00	1.67
GR	American Funds New Economy 529C	CNGCX	B+	(800) 421-0180	B+ / 8.4	3.35	5.44	6.16 /48	17.15 /91	13.70 /75	0.00	1.67

● Denotes fund is closed to new investors
* Denotes fund is included in Section II

RISK			NET ASSETS		ASSET					BULL / BEAR		FUND MANAGER		MINIMUMS		LOADS	
	3 Year		NAV						Portfolio	Last Bull	Last Bear	Manager	Manager	Initial	Additional	Front	Back
Risk	Standard		As of	Total	Cash	Stocks	Bonds	Other	Turnover	Market	Market	Quality	Tenure	Purch.	Purch.	End	End
Rating/Pts	Deviation	Beta	3/31/15	$(Mil)	%	%	%	%	Ratio	Return	Return	Pct	(Years)	$	$	Load	Load
C+ / 6.5	6.7	1.13	21.61	N/A	1	72	26	1	39	56.8	-10.3	43	23	250	50	0.0	0.0
B / 8.1	6.7	0.64	21.55	1,332	1	72	26	1	39	57.8	-10.2	74	23	250	50	0.0	0.0
B / 8.1	6.7	0.64	21.59	1,247	1	72	26	1	39	59.4	-10.1	77	23	250	50	0.0	0.0
B / 8.1	6.7	0.64	21.62	671	1	72	26	1	39	61.1	-10.0	79	23	250	50	0.0	0.0
B / 8.1	6.7	0.65	21.63	2,938	1	72	26	1	39	61.4	-10.0	79	23	250	50	0.0	0.0
U /	N/A	N/A	11.88	67	0	48	51	1	0	N/A	N/A	N/A	3	250	50	5.8	0.0
U /	N/A	N/A	11.84	44	0	48	51	1	0	N/A	N/A	N/A	3	250	50	0.0	0.0
U /	N/A	N/A	11.89	2,026	0	48	51	1	0	N/A	N/A	N/A	3	250	50	5.8	0.0
U /	N/A	N/A	11.84	458	0	48	51	1	0	N/A	N/A	N/A	3	250	50	0.0	0.0
U /	N/A	N/A	11.89	69	0	48	51	1	0	N/A	N/A	N/A	3	250	50	0.0	0.0
U /	N/A	N/A	11.90	72	0	48	51	1	0	N/A	N/A	N/A	3	250	50	0.0	0.0
U /	N/A	N/A	53.23	37	0	0	0	100	25	N/A	N/A	N/A	6	0	0	0.0	0.0
U /	N/A	N/A	82.99	29	0	0	0	100	19	N/A	N/A	N/A	3	0	0	0.0	0.0
U /	N/A	N/A	21.14	82	0	0	0	100	43	N/A	N/A	N/A	16	0	0	0.0	0.0
C+ / 5.7	11.6	0.86	32.16	126	1	91	6	2	29	48.4	-20.1	68	7	250	50	5.8	0.0
C+ / 5.8	11.6	0.86	32.16	1	1	91	6	2	29	44.4	-20.4	57	7	250	50	0.0	0.0
C+ / 5.7	11.6	0.86	32.01	31	1	91	6	2	29	44.4	-20.4	57	7	250	50	0.0	0.0
C+ / 5.7	11.6	0.86	32.16	5	1	91	6	2	29	47.2	-20.2	66	7	250	50	0.0	0.0
C+ / 5.7	11.6	0.86	32.20	11	1	91	6	2	29	49.5	-20.0	71	7	250	50	0.0	0.0
C+ / 5.7	11.6	0.86	32.19	4,870	1	91	6	2	29	48.9	-20.1	69	7	250	50	5.8	0.0
C+ / 5.7	11.6	0.86	32.19	11	1	91	6	2	29	45.0	-20.4	59	7	250	50	0.0	0.0
C+ / 5.7	11.6	0.86	32.11	306	1	91	6	2	29	44.8	-20.4	58	7	250	50	0.0	0.0
C+ / 5.7	11.6	0.86	32.19	1,634	1	91	6	2	29	48.6	-20.1	69	7	250	50	0.0	0.0
C+ / 5.7	11.6	0.86	32.20	1,954	1	91	6	2	29	49.9	-20.0	71	7	250	50	0.0	0.0
C+ / 5.7	11.6	0.86	32.11	13	1	91	6	2	29	46.7	-20.3	64	7	250	50	0.0	0.0
C+ / 5.7	11.6	0.86	32.05	51	1	91	6	2	29	44.6	-20.3	57	7	250	50	0.0	0.0
C / 5.4	11.6	0.86	32.16	N/A	1	91	6	2	29	46.2	-20.3	63	7	250	50	0.0	0.0
C+ / 5.7	11.6	0.86	32.14	56	1	91	6	2	29	47.0	-20.2	65	7	250	50	0.0	0.0
C+ / 5.7	11.6	0.86	32.18	67	1	91	6	2	29	48.8	-20.1	69	7	250	50	0.0	0.0
C+ / 5.7	11.6	0.86	32.35	25	1	91	6	2	29	50.2	-20.0	72	7	250	50	0.0	0.0
C+ / 5.7	11.6	0.86	32.19	1,204	1	91	6	2	29	50.5	-20.0	73	7	250	50	0.0	0.0
C+ / 6.1	9.1	0.93	36.81	2,247	0	91	7	2	29	94.2	-17.3	74	N/A	250	50	5.8	0.0
C+ / 6.1	9.1	0.93	36.79	42	0	91	7	2	29	89.0	-17.5	66	N/A	250	50	0.0	0.0
C+ / 6.1	9.1	0.93	36.69	510	0	91	7	2	29	89.1	-17.6	67	N/A	250	50	0.0	0.0
C+ / 6.1	9.1	0.93	36.71	83	0	91	7	2	29	92.6	-17.4	73	N/A	250	50	0.0	0.0
C+ / 6.1	9.1	0.92	36.78	62	0	91	7	2	29	95.6	-17.2	77	N/A	250	50	0.0	0.0
C+ / 6.1	9.1	0.93	36.88	58,368	0	91	7	2	29	94.9	-17.2	76	N/A	250	50	5.8	0.0
C+ / 6.1	9.1	0.92	36.77	262	0	91	7	2	29	89.8	-17.5	68	N/A	250	50	0.0	0.0
C+ / 6.1	9.1	0.93	36.57	1,770	0	91	7	2	29	89.5	-17.5	67	N/A	250	50	0.0	0.0
C+ / 6.1	9.1	0.93	36.80	2,556	0	91	7	2	29	94.4	-17.3	75	N/A	250	50	0.0	0.0
C+ / 6.1	9.1	0.93	36.86	1,852	0	91	7	2	29	96.2	-17.2	77	N/A	250	50	0.0	0.0
C+ / 6.1	9.1	0.93	36.64	95	0	91	7	2	29	89.5	-17.5	68	N/A	250	50	0.0	0.0
C+ / 6.1	9.1	0.92	36.68	719	0	91	7	2	29	89.7	-17.5	68	N/A	250	50	0.0	0.0
C+ / 5.9	9.1	0.93	36.86	N/A	0	91	7	2	29	91.3	-17.5	71	N/A	250	50	0.0	0.0
C+ / 6.1	9.1	0.93	36.77	946	0	91	7	2	29	92.4	-17.4	72	N/A	250	50	0.0	0.0
C+ / 6.1	9.1	0.93	36.80	1,032	0	91	7	2	29	94.5	-17.3	75	N/A	250	50	0.0	0.0
C+ / 6.1	9.1	0.93	36.86	819	0	91	7	2	29	96.5	-17.1	78	N/A	250	50	0.0	0.0
C+ / 6.1	9.1	0.92	36.87	4,437	0	91	7	2	29	96.9	-17.1	78	N/A	250	50	0.0	0.0
U /	N/A	N/A	12.31	111	0	0	0	100	3	N/A	N/A	N/A	N/A	0	0	0.0	0.0
C+ / 5.9	10.2	0.92	37.78	403	0	90	9	1	27	106.7	-18.7	88	24	250	50	5.8	0.0
C+ / 5.8	10.2	0.93	35.83	5	0	90	9	1	27	101.0	-19.0	84	24	250	50	0.0	0.0
C+ / 5.8	10.2	0.93	35.77	113	0	90	9	1	27	101.1	-19.0	84	24	250	50	0.0	0.0

99 Pct = Best
0 Pct = Worst

Fund Type	Fund Name	Ticker Symbol	Overall Investment Rating	Phone	Performance Rating/Pts	3 Mo	6 Mo	1Yr / Pct	3Yr / Pct	5Yr / Pct	Dividend Yield	Expense Ratio
					PERFORMANCE — Total Return % through 3/31/15 / Annualized / Incl. in Returns							
GR	American Funds New Economy 529E	CNGEX	B+	(800) 421-0180	B+ / 8.8	3.46	5.70	6.73 /53	17.78 /93	14.31 /80	0.20	1.12
GR	American Funds New Economy	CNGFX	A-	(800) 421-0180	A- / 9.1	3.60	5.97	7.24 /57	18.32 /95	14.86 /86	0.62	0.67
* GR	American Funds New Economy A	ANEFX	B	(800) 421-0180	B / 8.1	3.56	5.91	7.11 /56	18.19 /95	14.70 /84	0.46	0.79
GR ●	American Funds New Economy B	ANFBX	B+	(800) 421-0180	B+ / 8.5	3.38	5.50	6.31 /49	17.29 /91	13.83 /76	0.00	1.55
GR	American Funds New Economy C	ANFCX	B+	(800) 421-0180	B+ / 8.5	3.34	5.46	6.22 /48	17.23 /91	13.78 /76	0.00	1.60
GR	American Funds New Economy F1	ANFFX	A-	(800) 421-0180	A- / 9.0	3.56	5.87	7.05 /55	18.14 /95	14.68 /84	0.36	0.84
GR	American Funds New Economy F2	NEFFX	A-	(800) 421-0180	A- / 9.2	3.62	6.01	7.36 /58	18.48 /96	14.99 /87	0.73	0.57
GR	American Funds New Economy R1	RNGAX	B+	(800) 421-0180	B+ / 8.5	3.37	5.49	6.26 /49	17.28 /91	13.82 /76	0.00	1.56
GR	American Funds New Economy R2	RNGBX	B+	(800) 421-0180	B+ / 8.5	3.38	5.49	6.29 /49	17.29 /91	13.82 /76	0.00	1.57
GR	American Funds New Economy R2E	RNNEX	B+	(800) 421-0180	B+ / 8.8	3.60	5.96	6.92 /54	17.63 /93	14.09 /78	0.77	1.28
GR	American Funds New Economy R3	RNGCX	B+	(800) 421-0180	B+ / 8.8	3.49	5.74	6.74 /53	17.80 /94	14.33 /81	0.23	1.13
GR	American Funds New Economy R4	RNGEX	A-	(800) 421-0180	A- / 9.0	3.56	5.90	7.08 /56	18.18 /95	14.70 /84	0.51	0.81
GR	American Funds New Economy R5	RNGFX	A-	(800) 421-0180	A- / 9.2	3.63	6.05	7.39 /58	18.53 /96	15.05 /87	0.71	0.52
GR	American Funds New Economy R6	RNGGX	A-	(800) 421-0180	A- / 9.2	3.64	6.08	7.45 /59	18.59 /96	15.10 /88	0.80	0.46
GL	American Funds New Perspectve	CNPAX	C	(800) 421-0180	C / 5.3	4.68	6.47	7.69 /60	13.22 /61	10.90 /52	0.48	0.85
GL ●	American Funds New Perspectve	CNPBX	C+	(800) 421-0180	C+ / 5.7	4.45	6.04	6.84 /54	12.33 /55	10.02 /45	0.00	1.64
GL	American Funds New Perspectve	CNPCX	C+	(800) 421-0180	C+ / 5.7	4.46	6.04	6.85 /54	12.33 /55	10.03 /45	0.00	1.63
GL	American Funds New Perspectve	CNPEX	C+	(800) 421-0180	C+ / 6.1	4.57	6.32	7.41 /58	12.94 /59	10.60 /49	0.27	1.09
GL	American Funds New Perspectve	CNPFX	C+	(800) 421-0180	C+ / 6.5	4.71	6.55	7.92 /62	13.46 /63	11.13 /54	0.72	0.63
* GL	American Funds New Perspectve A	ANWPX	C	(800) 421-0180	C / 5.4	4.69	6.48	7.78 /61	13.31 /62	10.98 /52	0.54	0.76
GL ●	American Funds New Perspectve B	NPFBX	C+	(800) 421-0180	C+ / 5.8	4.46	6.09	6.97 /55	12.46 /56	10.15 /46	0.00	1.51
GL	American Funds New Perspectve C	NPFCX	C+	(800) 421-0180	C+ / 5.8	4.46	6.06	6.93 /54	12.42 /55	10.10 /45	0.00	1.55
GL	American Funds New Perspectve F1	NPFFX	C+	(800) 421-0180	C+ / 6.3	4.68	6.48	7.73 /61	13.27 /61	10.95 /52	0.49	0.82
GL	American Funds New Perspectve F2	ANWFX	C+	(800) 421-0180	C+ / 6.5	4.72	6.59	8.00 /63	13.58 /64	11.24 /55	0.81	0.54
GL	American Funds New Perspectve R1	RNPAX	C+	(800) 421-0180	C+ / 5.8	4.49	6.08	6.96 /55	12.44 /56	10.13 /46	0.00	1.55
GL	American Funds New Perspectve R2	RNPBX	C+	(800) 421-0180	C+ / 5.8	4.48	6.09	6.96 /55	12.47 /56	10.12 /46	0.00	1.54
GL	American Funds New Perspectve	RPEBX	C	(800) 421-0180	C+ / 6.0	4.70	6.53	7.56 /60	12.77 /58	10.39 /48	0.83	1.26
GL	American Funds New Perspectve R3	RNPCX	C+	(800) 421-0180	C+ / 6.1	4.61	6.32	7.42 /58	12.94 /59	10.61 /50	0.25	1.10
GL	American Funds New Perspectve R4	RNPEX	C+	(800) 421-0180	C+ / 6.3	4.68	6.50	7.76 /61	13.29 /62	10.96 /52	0.55	0.80
GL	American Funds New Perspectve R5	RNPFX	C+	(800) 421-0180	C+ / 6.6	4.75	6.65	8.06 /63	13.63 /64	11.30 /55	0.84	0.49
GL	American Funds New Perspectve R6	RNPGX	C+	(800) 421-0180	C+ / 6.6	4.74	6.65	8.12 /64	13.68 /65	11.34 /55	0.88	0.45
GL	American Funds New World 529A	CNWAX	E+	(800) 421-0180	E+ / 0.9	2.84	-0.87	-1.46 /12	5.05 /13	4.88 /11	0.75	1.10
GL ●	American Funds New World 529B	CNWBX	E+	(800) 421-0180	D- / 1.0	2.63	-1.27	-2.24 /10	4.21 /11	4.02 / 8	0.00	1.91
GL	American Funds New World 529C	CNWCX	E+	(800) 421-0180	D- / 1.0	2.65	-1.24	-2.23 /10	4.22 /11	4.03 / 8	0.00	1.90
GL	American Funds New World 529E	CNWEX	E+	(800) 421-0180	D- / 1.2	2.79	-0.98	-1.67 /11	4.81 /11	4.61 /11	0.57	1.33
GL	American Funds New World 529F1	CNWFX	E+	(800) 421-0180	D- / 1.3	2.88	-0.76	-1.25 /12	5.26 /14	5.08 /12	1.02	0.89
* GL	American Funds New World A	NEWFX	E+	(800) 421-0180	E+ / 0.9	2.86	-0.85	-1.39 /12	5.12 /13	4.93 /12	0.80	1.03
GL ●	American Funds New World B	NEWBX	E+	(800) 421-0180	D- / 1.0	2.66	-1.20	-2.14 /10	4.33 /11	4.13 / 9	0.00	1.79
GL ●	American Funds New World C	NEWCX	E+	(800) 421-0180	D- / 1.0	2.66	-1.23	-2.18 /10	4.28 /11	4.10 / 9	0.04	1.84
GL	American Funds New World F1	NWFFX	E+	(800) 421-0180	D- / 1.3	2.88	-0.80	-1.36 /12	5.15 /14	4.95 /12	0.74	1.02
GL	American Funds New World F2	NFFFX	E+	(800) 421-0180	D- / 1.4	2.94	-0.69	-1.10 /13	5.43 /15	5.23 /13	1.17	0.75
GL	American Funds New World R1	RNWAX	E+	(800) 421-0180	D- / 1.0	2.67	-1.21	-2.14 /10	4.34 /11	4.13 / 9	0.09	1.79
GL	American Funds New World R2	RNWBX	E+	(800) 421-0180	D- / 1.0	2.67	-1.20	-2.13 /10	4.34 /11	4.14 / 9	0.09	1.79
EM	American Funds New World R2E	RNEBX	E+	(800) 421-0180	D- / 1.1	2.76	-1.01	-1.81 /11	4.54 /12	4.32 / 9	1.16	1.46
GL	American Funds New World R3	RNWCX	E+	(800) 421-0180	D- / 1.2	2.80	-0.96	-1.66 /11	4.82 /13	4.62 /11	0.59	1.32
GL	American Funds New World R4	RNWEX	E+	(800) 421-0180	D- / 1.3	2.87	-0.82	-1.36 /12	5.17 /14	4.97 /12	0.92	1.00
GL	American Funds New World R5	RNWFX	E+	(800) 421-0180	D- / 1.4	2.95	-0.65	-1.05 /13	5.49 /15	5.28 /13	1.19	0.69
GL	American Funds New World R6	RNWGX	E+	(800) 421-0180	D- / 1.4	2.97	-0.63	-0.99 /13	5.55 /15	5.34 /13	1.26	0.65
SC	American Funds SMALLCAP World	CSPAX	C-	(800) 421-0180	C / 5.2	5.37	8.32	5.90 /46	13.03 /60	11.05 /53	0.00	1.15
SC ●	American Funds SMALLCAP World	CSPBX	C-	(800) 421-0180	C+ / 5.6	5.16	7.90	5.08 /39	12.12 /53	10.16 /46	0.00	1.95
SC	American Funds SMALLCAP World	CSPCX	C-	(800) 421-0180	C+ / 5.6	5.15	7.90	5.08 /39	12.14 /53	10.17 /46	0.00	1.94
SC	American Funds SMALLCAP World	CSPEX	C	(800) 421-0180	C+ / 6.0	5.30	8.21	5.67 /44	12.75 /58	10.76 /51	0.00	1.39

● Denotes fund is closed to new investors
* Denotes fund is included in Section II

RISK			NET ASSETS		ASSET					BULL / BEAR		FUND MANAGER		MINIMUMS		LOADS	
	3 Year		NAV						Portfolio	Last Bull	Last Bear	Manager	Manager	Initial	Additional	Front	Back
Risk	Standard		As of	Total	Cash	Stocks	Bonds	Other	Turnover	Market	Market	Quality	Tenure	Purch.	Purch.	End	End
Rating/Pts	Deviation	Beta	3/31/15	$(Mil)	%	%	%	%	Ratio	Return	Return	Pct	(Years)	$	$	Load	Load
C+ / 5.9	10.2	0.92	37.34	21	0	90	9	1	27	104.8	-18.8	87	24	250	50	0.0	0.0
C+ / 5.9	10.2	0.93	37.74	31	0	90	9	1	27	108.1	-18.6	89	24	250	50	0.0	0.0
C+ / 5.9	10.2	0.93	38.09	10,130	0	90	9	1	27	107.2	-18.7	88	24	250	50	5.8	0.0
C+ / 5.9	10.2	0.93	35.80	33	0	90	9	1	27	101.8	-18.9	85	24	250	50	0.0	0.0
C+ / 5.8	10.2	0.93	35.29	488	0	90	9	1	27	101.5	-18.9	85	24	250	50	0.0	0.0
C+ / 5.9	10.2	0.92	38.15	403	0	90	9	1	27	107.0	-18.7	88	24	250	50	0.0	0.0
C+ / 5.9	10.2	0.93	38.06	652	0	90	9	1	27	109.0	-18.6	89	24	250	50	0.0	0.0
C+ / 5.9	10.2	0.93	36.23	54	0	90	9	1	27	101.9	-18.9	85	24	250	50	0.0	0.0
C+ / 5.9	10.2	0.93	36.42	185	0	90	9	1	27	101.9	-19.0	85	24	250	50	0.0	0.0
C+ / 5.7	10.2	0.92	38.00	N/A	0	90	9	1	27	103.6	-18.9	86	24	250	50	0.0	0.0
C+ / 5.9	10.2	0.92	37.40	334	0	90	9	1	27	105.0	-18.8	87	24	250	50	0.0	0.0
C+ / 5.9	10.2	0.93	37.78	366	0	90	9	1	27	107.2	-18.7	88	24	250	50	0.0	0.0
C+ / 5.9	10.2	0.93	38.25	149	0	90	9	1	27	109.3	-18.6	89	24	250	50	0.0	0.0
C+ / 5.8	10.2	0.93	38.15	1,469	0	90	9	1	27	109.6	-18.6	89	24	250	50	0.0	0.0
C+ / 6.2	10.4	0.74	37.61	1,604	0	91	8	1	25	76.1	-19.8	95	23	250	50	5.8	0.0
C+ / 6.2	10.4	0.74	37.12	23	0	91	8	1	25	71.4	-20.0	93	23	250	50	0.0	0.0
C+ / 6.2	10.4	0.74	36.75	357	0	91	8	1	25	71.4	-20.0	93	23	250	50	0.0	0.0
C+ / 6.2	10.4	0.74	37.27	76	0	91	8	1	25	74.6	-19.9	94	23	250	50	0.0	0.0
C+ / 6.2	10.4	0.74	37.54	65	0	91	8	1	25	77.4	-19.7	95	23	250	50	0.0	0.0
C+ / 6.2	10.4	0.74	37.98	37,580	0	91	8	1	25	76.6	-19.7	95	23	250	50	5.8	0.0
C+ / 6.2	10.4	0.74	37.50	153	0	91	8	1	25	72.1	-20.0	94	23	250	50	0.0	0.0
C+ / 6.2	10.3	0.73	36.78	1,404	0	91	8	1	25	71.9	-20.0	94	23	250	50	0.0	0.0
C+ / 6.2	10.4	0.74	37.79	1,346	0	91	8	1	25	76.4	-19.8	95	23	250	50	0.0	0.0
C+ / 6.2	10.4	0.74	37.91	2,519	0	91	8	1	25	78.1	-19.7	95	23	250	50	0.0	0.0
C+ / 6.2	10.4	0.74	36.51	106	0	91	8	1	25	72.0	-20.0	94	23	250	50	0.0	0.0
C+ / 6.2	10.4	0.74	36.81	602	0	91	8	1	25	72.1	-20.0	94	23	250	50	0.0	0.0
C+ / 5.6	10.4	0.73	37.89	N/A	0	91	8	1	25	73.6	-20.0	94	23	250	50	0.0	0.0
C+ / 6.2	10.4	0.74	37.23	1,697	0	91	8	1	25	74.7	-19.9	94	23	250	50	0.0	0.0
C+ / 6.2	10.4	0.74	37.54	1,903	0	91	8	1	25	76.5	-19.8	95	23	250	50	0.0	0.0
C+ / 6.2	10.4	0.74	37.96	1,496	0	91	8	1	25	78.3	-19.7	95	23	250	50	0.0	0.0
C+ / 6.2	10.4	0.73	38.01	8,196	0	91	8	1	25	78.6	-19.6	95	23	250	50	0.0	0.0
C / 5.2	11.1	0.79	54.59	769	0	77	21	2	32	37.5	-22.0	33	16	250	50	5.8	0.0
C / 5.3	11.1	0.79	53.84	11	0	77	21	2	32	33.7	-22.2	24	16	250	50	0.0	0.0
C / 5.3	11.1	0.79	53.36	166	0	77	21	2	32	33.8	-22.2	24	16	250	50	0.0	0.0
C / 5.2	11.1	0.79	54.20	37	0	77	21	2	32	36.4	-22.0	30	16	250	50	0.0	0.0
C / 5.2	11.1	0.79	54.59	48	0	77	21	2	32	38.4	-21.9	36	16	250	50	0.0	0.0
C / 5.2	11.1	0.79	55.03	12,667	0	77	21	2	32	37.8	-21.9	34	16	250	50	5.8	0.0
C / 5.3	11.1	0.79	54.40	91	0	77	21	2	32	34.2	-22.2	25	16	250	50	0.0	0.0
C / 5.3	11.1	0.79	53.27	977	0	77	21	2	32	34.1	-22.2	25	16	250	50	0.0	0.0
C / 5.2	11.1	0.79	54.67	1,729	0	77	21	2	32	37.9	-21.9	35	16	250	50	0.0	0.0
C / 5.2	11.1	0.79	54.98	3,699	0	77	21	2	32	39.2	-21.9	38	16	250	50	0.0	0.0
C / 5.3	11.1	0.79	53.42	35	0	77	21	2	32	34.3	-22.2	26	16	250	50	0.0	0.0
C / 5.3	11.1	0.79	53.40	347	0	77	21	2	32	34.3	-22.2	26	16	250	50	0.0	0.0
C+ / 5.6	11.1	0.75	54.75	N/A	0	77	21	2	32	35.1	-22.1	91	16	250	50	0.0	0.0
C / 5.2	11.1	0.79	54.31	486	0	77	21	2	32	36.4	-22.0	31	16	250	50	0.0	0.0
C / 5.2	11.1	0.79	54.79	473	0	77	21	2	32	38.0	-21.9	35	16	250	50	0.0	0.0
C / 5.2	11.1	0.79	55.19	426	0	77	21	2	32	39.4	-21.8	39	16	250	50	0.0	0.0
C / 5.2	11.1	0.79	55.08	1,743	0	77	21	2	32	39.7	-21.8	40	16	250	50	0.0	0.0
C / 5.3	10.9	0.73	47.32	1,000	0	93	6	1	38	76.8	-24.4	79	24	250	50	5.8	0.0
C / 5.1	10.9	0.73	44.39	14	0	93	6	1	38	72.0	-24.7	72	24	250	50	0.0	0.0
C / 5.1	10.9	0.73	44.12	294	0	93	6	1	38	72.1	-24.7	72	24	250	50	0.0	0.0
C / 5.3	10.9	0.73	46.32	52	0	93	6	1	38	75.4	-24.5	77	24	250	50	0.0	0.0

Fund Type	Fund Name	Ticker Symbol	Overall Investment Rating	Phone	Performance Rating/Pts	Total Return % through 3/31/15					Incl. in Returns	
									Annualized		Dividend Yield	Expense Ratio
						3 Mo	6 Mo	1Yr / Pct	3Yr / Pct	5Yr / Pct		
SC	American Funds SMALLCAP World	CSPFX	C	(800) 421-0180	C+ / 6.4	5.44	8.47	6.15 /48	13.28 /62	11.29 /55	0.00	0.94
★ SC	American Funds SMALLCAP World A	SMCWX	C-	(800) 421-0180	C / 5.3	5.39	8.38	6.00 /46	13.11 /60	11.12 /54	0.00	1.07
SC ●	American Funds SMALLCAP World B	SCWBX	C-	(800) 421-0180	C+ / 5.7	5.17	7.96	5.19 /40	12.25 /54	10.27 /47	0.00	1.83
SC	American Funds SMALLCAP World C	SCWCX	C-	(800) 421-0180	C+ / 5.7	5.19	7.95	5.15 /40	12.21 /54	10.25 /46	0.00	1.87
SC	American Funds SMALLCAP World	SCWFX	C	(800) 421-0180	C+ / 6.2	5.39	8.37	5.98 /46	13.12 /60	11.13 /54	0.00	1.09
SC	American Funds SMALLCAP World	SMCFX	C	(800) 421-0180	C+ / 6.5	5.46	8.51	6.29 /49	13.44 /63	11.43 /56	0.00	0.81
SC	American Funds SMALLCAP World	RSLAX	C	(800) 421-0180	C+ / 5.7	5.20	7.98	5.20 /40	12.29 /54	10.30 /47	0.00	1.82
SC	American Funds SMALLCAP World	RSLBX	C	(800) 421-0180	C+ / 5.7	5.20	7.98	5.20 /40	12.28 /54	10.28 /47	0.00	1.83
GL	American Funds SMALLCAP World	RSEBX	C	(800) 421-0180	C+ / 6.0	5.43	8.46	5.84 /45	12.59 /57	10.54 /49	0.00	1.52
SC	American Funds SMALLCAP World	RSLCX	C	(800) 421-0180	C+ / 6.0	5.31	8.20	5.68 /44	12.77 /58	10.79 /51	0.00	1.39
SC	American Funds SMALLCAP World	RSLEX	C	(800) 421-0180	C+ / 6.3	5.40	8.40	6.03 /47	13.16 /61	11.16 /54	0.00	1.06
SC	American Funds SMALLCAP World	RSLFX	C+	(800) 421-0180	C+ / 6.5	5.47	8.55	6.35 /49	13.49 /63	11.50 /57	0.00	0.76
SC	American Funds SMALLCAP World	RLLGX	C+	(800) 421-0180	C+ / 6.5	5.48	8.57	6.39 /50	13.55 /64	11.55 /57	0.00	0.71
AA	American Funds Tax Adv Income A	TAIAX	U	(800) 421-0180	U /	1.37	3.18	7.79 /61	--	--	2.35	0.91
AA	American Funds Tax Adv Income C	TAICX	U	(800) 421-0180	U /	1.16	2.71	6.99 /55	--	--	1.84	1.61
AA	American Funds Tax Adv Income F2	TXIFX	U	(800) 421-0180	U /	1.43	3.31	8.18 /64	--	--	2.72	0.61
AA	American Funds Tgt Dte Ret 2010 A	AAATX	C-	(800) 421-0180	D / 2.1	1.07	2.62	5.50 /42	8.02 /27	7.97 /30	1.37	0.81
AA	American Funds Tgt Dte Ret 2010 B	BBATX	C-	(800) 421-0180	D+ / 2.5	0.88	2.28	4.75 /37	7.22 /23	7.15 /24	1.12	1.56
AA	American Funds Tgt Dte Ret 2010 C	CCATX	C-	(800) 421-0180	D+ / 2.5	0.88	2.27	4.75 /37	7.22 /23	7.15 /24	1.40	1.55
AA	American Funds Tgt Dte Ret 2010 F1	FAATX	C	(800) 421-0180	D+ / 2.9	1.07	2.60	5.48 /42	7.84 /26	7.74 /28	1.53	0.82
AA	American Funds Tgt Dte Ret 2010 F2	FBATX	C	(800) 421-0180	C- / 3.1	1.17	2.71	5.79 /45	8.12 /28	8.03 /30	1.73	0.57
AA	American Funds Tgt Dte Ret 2010 R1	RAATX	C	(800) 421-0180	D+ / 2.5	0.88	2.22	4.70 /36	7.22 /23	7.15 /24	0.77	1.59
AA	American Funds Tgt Dte Ret 2010 R2	RBATX	C	(800) 421-0180	D+ / 2.5	0.78	2.23	4.73 /37	7.29 /23	7.22 /24	0.77	1.51
AA	American Funds Tgt Dte Ret 2010	RBEAX	C-	(800) 421-0180	D+ / 2.7	1.07	2.69	5.31 /41	7.52 /24	7.40 /26	1.71	1.28
AA	American Funds Tgt Dte Ret 2010 R3	RCATX	C	(800) 421-0180	D+ / 2.7	0.88	2.40	5.09 /39	7.65 /25	7.62 /27	1.15	1.13
AA	American Funds Tgt Dte Ret 2010 R4	RDATX	C	(800) 421-0180	C- / 3.0	1.07	2.64	5.52 /43	8.05 /27	7.97 /30	1.47	0.81
AA	American Funds Tgt Dte Ret 2010 R5	REATX	C	(800) 421-0180	C- / 3.2	1.06	2.72	5.79 /45	8.35 /29	8.30 /32	1.74	0.51
AA	American Funds Tgt Dte Ret 2010 R6	RFTTX	C	(800) 421-0180	C- / 3.2	1.06	2.76	5.84 /45	8.41 /29	8.35 /32	1.78	0.46
AA	American Funds Tgt Dte Ret 2015 A	AABTX	C	(800) 421-0180	D+ / 2.6	1.09	2.78	5.69 /44	9.01 /33	8.51 /33	1.29	0.81
AA	American Funds Tgt Dte Ret 2015 B	BBBTX	C	(800) 421-0180	C- / 3.0	0.91	2.36	5.08 /39	8.23 /28	7.71 /28	1.31	1.56
AA	American Funds Tgt Dte Ret 2015 C	CCBTX	C	(800) 421-0180	C- / 3.0	0.91	2.42	4.95 /38	8.19 /28	7.69 /28	1.28	1.55
AA	American Funds Tgt Dte Ret 2015 F1	FAKTX	C	(800) 421-0180	C- / 3.4	1.18	2.80	5.71 /44	8.83 /32	8.29 /32	1.56	0.81
AA	American Funds Tgt Dte Ret 2015 F2	FBBTX	C	(800) 421-0180	C- / 3.6	1.18	2.89	5.99 /46	9.11 /34	8.57 /34	1.65	0.57
AA	American Funds Tgt Dte Ret 2015 R1	RAJTX	C	(800) 421-0180	C- / 3.0	0.92	2.35	4.92 /38	8.14 /28	7.69 /28	0.66	1.58
AA	American Funds Tgt Dte Ret 2015 R2	RBJTX	C	(800) 421-0180	C- / 3.0	0.92	2.37	4.93 /38	8.26 /28	7.78 /28	0.68	1.50
AA	American Funds Tgt Dte Ret 2015	RBEJX	C	(800) 421-0180	C- / 3.2	1.18	2.77	5.51 /42	8.50 /30	7.94 /29	1.62	1.28
AA	American Funds Tgt Dte Ret 2015 R3	RCJTX	C+	(800) 421-0180	C- / 3.3	1.01	2.57	5.31 /41	8.63 /31	8.15 /31	1.07	1.13
AA	American Funds Tgt Dte Ret 2015 R4	RDBTX	C+	(800) 421-0180	C- / 3.5	1.09	2.72	5.73 /44	9.00 /33	8.51 /33	1.39	0.81
AA	American Funds Tgt Dte Ret 2015 R5	REJTX	C+	(800) 421-0180	C- / 3.7	1.18	2.97	6.06 /47	9.35 /35	8.85 /36	1.64	0.50
AA	American Funds Tgt Dte Ret 2015 R6	RFJTX	C+	(800) 421-0180	C- / 3.7	1.18	2.93	6.03 /47	9.35 /35	8.88 /36	1.69	0.46
AA	American Funds Tgt Dte Ret 2020 A	AACTX	C+	(800) 421-0180	C- / 3.3	1.47	3.20	6.19 /48	10.18 /40	9.33 /39	1.14	0.81
AA	American Funds Tgt Dte Ret 2020 B	BBCTX	D+	(800) 421-0180	C- / 3.7	1.31	2.75	5.36 /41	9.32 /35	8.49 /33	0.85	1.57
AA	American Funds Tgt Dte Ret 2020 C	CCCTX	D+	(800) 421-0180	C- / 3.7	1.31	2.76	5.37 /41	9.33 /35	8.49 /33	1.11	1.57
AA	American Funds Tgt Dte Ret 2020 F1	FAOTX	C-	(800) 421-0180	C- / 4.1	1.48	3.16	6.14 /48	9.97 /39	9.09 /37	1.42	0.83
AA	American Funds Tgt Dte Ret 2020 F2	FBCTX	C	(800) 421-0180	C- / 4.2	1.48	3.23	6.39 /50	10.25 /41	9.37 /39	1.49	0.59
AA	American Funds Tgt Dte Ret 2020 R1	RACTX	C+	(800) 421-0180	C- / 3.6	1.23	2.74	5.29 /41	9.31 /35	8.49 /33	0.39	1.61
AA	American Funds Tgt Dte Ret 2020 R2	RBCTX	C+	(800) 421-0180	C- / 3.7	1.32	2.83	5.48 /42	9.41 /36	8.59 /34	0.56	1.52
AA	American Funds Tgt Dte Ret 2020	RBEHX	C-	(800) 421-0180	C- / 3.9	1.48	3.19	5.90 /46	9.62 /37	8.73 /35	1.45	1.29
AA	American Funds Tgt Dte Ret 2020 R3	RCCTX	C+	(800) 421-0180	C- / 4.0	1.40	3.00	5.82 /45	9.82 /38	8.98 /37	0.92	1.15
AA	American Funds Tgt Dte Ret 2020 R4	RDCTX	C+	(800) 421-0180	C- / 4.2	1.48	3.14	6.22 /48	10.17 /40	9.35 /39	1.23	0.83
AA	American Funds Tgt Dte Ret 2020 R5	RECTX	B-	(800) 421-0180	C / 4.4	1.55	3.30	6.45 /50	10.50 /42	9.66 /42	1.48	0.52
AA	American Funds Tgt Dte Ret 2020 R6	RRCTX	B-	(800) 421-0180	C / 4.4	1.56	3.34	6.50 /51	10.54 /42	9.70 /42	1.52	0.48

99 Pct = Best
0 Pct = Worst

● Denotes fund is closed to new investors
★ Denotes fund is included in Section II

www.thestreetratings.com

Risk Rating/Pts	3 Year Standard Deviation	Beta	NAV As of 3/31/15	Total $(Mil)	Cash %	Stocks %	Bonds %	Other %	Portfolio Turnover Ratio	Last Bull Market Return	Last Bear Market Return	Manager Quality Pct	Manager Tenure (Years)	Initial Purch. $	Additional Purch. $	Front End Load	Back End Load
C / 5.3	10.9	0.73	47.65	86	0	93	6	1	38	78.1	-24.4	81	24	250	50	0.0	0.0
C / 5.3	10.9	0.73	47.75	17,744	0	93	6	1	38	77.2	-24.4	79	24	250	50	5.8	0.0
C / 5.1	10.9	0.73	43.96	98	0	93	6	1	38	72.6	-24.7	73	24	250	50	0.0	0.0
C / 5.1	10.9	0.73	43.35	904	0	93	6	1	38	72.5	-24.7	73	24	250	50	0.0	0.0
C / 5.3	10.9	0.73	47.28	655	0	93	6	1	38	77.3	-24.4	80	24	250	50	0.0	0.0
C / 5.4	10.9	0.73	48.09	1,393	0	93	6	1	38	79.0	-24.4	82	24	250	50	0.0	0.0
C / 5.2	10.9	0.73	44.53	40	0	93	6	1	38	72.8	-24.7	74	24	250	50	0.0	0.0
C / 5.2	10.9	0.73	44.52	697	0	93	6	1	38	72.8	-24.7	73	24	250	50	0.0	0.0
C / 5.5	10.9	0.67	47.80	N/A	0	93	6	1	38	74.2	-24.6	95	24	250	50	0.0	0.0
C / 5.3	10.9	0.73	46.24	829	0	93	6	1	38	75.5	-24.5	77	24	250	50	0.0	0.0
C / 5.3	10.9	0.73	47.40	757	0	93	6	1	38	77.5	-24.4	80	24	250	50	0.0	0.0
C / 5.4	10.9	0.73	48.62	494	0	93	6	1	38	79.4	-24.3	82	24	250	50	0.0	0.0
C / 5.4	10.9	0.73	48.13	2,112	0	93	6	1	38	79.6	-24.3	82	24	250	50	0.0	0.0
U /	N/A	N/A	12.55	527	0	47	51	2	1	N/A	N/A	N/A	3	250	50	3.8	0.0
U /	N/A	N/A	12.49	77	0	47	51	2	1	N/A	N/A	N/A	3	250	50	0.0	0.0
U /	N/A	N/A	12.56	27	0	47	51	2	1	N/A	N/A	N/A	3	250	50	0.0	0.0
B / 8.4	4.8	0.81	10.42	592	0	45	54	1	17	41.2	-6.9	58	8	250	50	5.8	0.0
B / 8.1	4.8	0.81	10.37	N/A	0	45	54	1	17	37.7	-7.2	45	8	250	50	0.0	0.0
B / 8.1	4.8	0.80	10.34	11	0	45	54	1	17	37.5	-7.2	47	8	250	50	0.0	0.0
B / 8.1	4.8	0.80	10.41	1	0	45	54	1	17	40.3	-7.0	56	8	250	50	0.0	0.0
B / 8.1	4.8	0.81	10.42	1	0	45	54	1	17	41.6	-6.9	59	8	250	50	0.0	0.0
B / 8.6	4.8	0.81	10.36	5	0	45	54	1	17	37.6	-7.2	46	8	250	50	0.0	0.0
B / 8.6	4.8	0.82	10.29	145	0	45	54	1	17	38.0	-7.3	46	8	250	50	0.0	0.0
B / 8.1	4.8	0.80	10.40	N/A	0	45	54	1	17	38.8	-7.1	51	8	250	50	0.0	0.0
B / 8.5	4.9	0.82	10.36	215	0	45	54	1	17	39.7	-7.0	50	8	250	50	0.0	0.0
B / 8.4	4.8	0.81	10.41	192	0	45	54	1	17	41.2	-6.9	58	8	250	50	0.0	0.0
B / 8.3	4.8	0.81	10.47	84	0	45	54	1	17	42.7	-6.7	62	8	250	50	0.0	0.0
B / 8.3	4.8	0.81	10.44	376	0	45	54	1	17	42.9	-6.8	62	8	250	50	0.0	0.0
B / 8.6	5.5	0.94	11.13	897	0	46	53	1	6	47.0	-9.0	51	8	250	50	5.8	0.0
B / 8.0	5.5	0.94	11.06	N/A	0	46	53	1	6	43.5	-9.3	40	8	250	50	0.0	0.0
B / 8.0	5.5	0.94	11.05	17	0	46	53	1	6	43.3	-9.3	39	8	250	50	0.0	0.0
B / 8.0	5.5	0.94	11.11	2	0	46	53	1	6	46.1	-9.1	48	8	250	50	0.0	0.0
B / 8.0	5.5	0.94	11.13	1	0	46	53	1	6	47.4	-9.0	52	8	250	50	0.0	0.0
B / 8.8	5.5	0.94	10.95	15	0	46	53	1	6	43.2	-9.3	38	8	250	50	0.0	0.0
B / 8.8	5.5	0.94	10.97	354	0	46	53	1	6	43.7	-9.3	41	8	250	50	0.0	0.0
B / 8.0	5.5	0.94	11.11	N/A	0	46	53	1	6	44.5	-9.2	44	8	250	50	0.0	0.0
B / 8.7	5.5	0.94	11.05	496	0	46	53	1	6	45.6	-9.2	45	8	250	50	0.0	0.0
B / 8.6	5.5	0.93	11.12	303	0	46	53	1	6	47.1	-9.1	52	8	250	50	0.0	0.0
B / 8.6	5.5	0.94	11.19	127	0	46	53	1	6	48.6	-8.9	55	8	250	50	0.0	0.0
B / 8.6	5.6	0.95	11.15	530	0	46	53	1	6	48.9	-9.0	54	8	250	50	0.0	0.0
B / 8.7	6.3	1.07	11.70	1,403	0	54	45	1	4	54.5	-11.3	47	8	250	50	5.8	0.0
C+ / 5.9	6.3	1.07	11.64	1	0	54	45	1	4	50.5	-11.6	35	8	250	50	0.0	0.0
C+ / 5.9	6.3	1.07	11.61	27	0	54	45	1	4	50.5	-11.6	36	8	250	50	0.0	0.0
C+ / 6.4	6.3	1.07	11.67	5	0	54	45	1	4	53.6	-11.4	44	8	250	50	0.0	0.0
C+ / 6.7	6.3	1.07	11.69	2	0	54	45	1	4	55.0	-11.3	47	8	250	50	0.0	0.0
B / 8.7	6.3	1.08	11.55	19	0	54	45	1	4	50.4	-11.5	34	8	250	50	0.0	0.0
B / 8.7	6.3	1.08	11.53	689	0	54	45	1	4	51.0	-11.6	35	8	250	50	0.0	0.0
C+ / 6.1	6.3	1.07	11.67	N/A	0	54	45	1	4	51.9	-11.5	39	8	250	50	0.0	0.0
B / 8.7	6.3	1.08	11.62	901	0	54	45	1	4	53.0	-11.4	40	8	250	50	0.0	0.0
B / 8.7	6.3	1.08	11.69	704	0	54	45	1	4	54.5	-11.3	46	8	250	50	0.0	0.0
B / 8.6	6.3	1.08	11.76	280	0	54	45	1	4	56.2	-11.1	49	8	250	50	0.0	0.0
B / 8.7	6.3	1.08	11.73	1,153	0	54	45	1	4	56.5	-11.2	50	8	250	50	0.0	0.0

Fund Type	Fund Name	Ticker Symbol	Overall Investment Rating	Phone	PERFORMANCE Perfor-mance Rating/Pts	Total Return % through 3/31/15			Annualized		Incl. in Returns	
						3 Mo	6 Mo	1Yr / Pct	3Yr / Pct	5Yr / Pct	Dividend Yield	Expense Ratio
AA	American Funds Tgt Dte Ret 2025 A	AADTX	C+	(800) 421-0180	C- / 4.2	1.47	3.25	6.32 /49	11.83 /51	10.48 /48	1.05	0.83
AA	American Funds Tgt Dte Ret 2025 B	BBDTX	C	(800) 421-0180	C / 4.5	1.31	2.90	5.54 /43	10.98 /45	9.63 /41	0.93	1.60
AA	American Funds Tgt Dte Ret 2025 C	CCDTX	C	(800) 421-0180	C / 4.5	1.32	2.84	5.47 /42	10.96 /45	9.61 /41	1.02	1.59
AA	American Funds Tgt Dte Ret 2025 F1	FAPTX	C	(800) 421-0180	C / 5.0	1.56	3.32	6.31 /49	11.63 /50	10.23 /46	1.33	0.85
AA	American Funds Tgt Dte Ret 2025 F2	FBDTX	C+	(800) 421-0180	C / 5.1	1.55	3.37	6.53 /51	11.91 /52	10.52 /49	1.39	0.61
AA	American Funds Tgt Dte Ret 2025 R1	RADTX	C+	(800) 421-0180	C / 4.5	1.32	2.85	5.43 /42	10.97 /45	9.63 /41	0.38	1.63
AA	American Funds Tgt Dte Ret 2025 R2	RBDTX	C+	(800) 421-0180	C / 4.6	1.33	2.95	5.54 /43	11.07 /46	9.72 /42	0.46	1.55
AA	American Funds Tgt Dte Ret 2025	RBEDX	C	(800) 421-0180	C / 4.8	1.56	3.32	6.12 /47	11.30 /48	9.88 /44	1.34	1.31
AA	American Funds Tgt Dte Ret 2025 R3	RCDTX	B-	(800) 421-0180	C / 4.9	1.48	3.13	5.96 /46	11.50 /49	10.15 /46	0.82	1.17
AA	American Funds Tgt Dte Ret 2025 R4	RDDTX	B-	(800) 421-0180	C / 5.1	1.55	3.34	6.33 /49	11.86 /51	10.50 /49	1.12	0.85
AA	American Funds Tgt Dte Ret 2025 R5	REDTX	B	(800) 421-0180	C / 5.3	1.63	3.42	6.65 /52	12.17 /54	10.81 /51	1.37	0.54
AA	American Funds Tgt Dte Ret 2025 R6	RFDTX	B	(800) 421-0180	C / 5.3	1.63	3.47	6.71 /53	12.21 /54	10.88 /52	1.41	0.50
AA	American Funds Tgt Dte Ret 2030 A	AAETX	C+	(800) 421-0180	C / 4.8	2.05	4.06	7.21 /57	12.75 /58	11.05 /53	0.93	0.85
AA	American Funds Tgt Dte Ret 2030 B	BBETX	C	(800) 421-0180	C / 5.2	1.82	3.59	6.40 /50	11.89 /52	10.20 /46	0.83	1.62
AA	American Funds Tgt Dte Ret 2030 C	CCETX	C	(800) 421-0180	C / 5.1	1.82	3.59	6.31 /49	11.86 /51	10.18 /46	0.90	1.61
AA	American Funds Tgt Dte Ret 2030 F1	FAETX	C+	(800) 421-0180	C+ / 5.6	2.05	4.03	7.18 /56	12.55 /56	10.81 /51	1.18	0.87
AA	American Funds Tgt Dte Ret 2030 F2	FBETX	C+	(800) 421-0180	C+ / 5.8	2.05	4.11	7.42 /58	12.83 /58	11.10 /53	1.25	0.63
AA	American Funds Tgt Dte Ret 2030 R1	RAETX	C+	(800) 421-0180	C / 5.1	1.83	3.57	6.32 /49	11.89 /52	10.22 /46	0.25	1.65
AA	American Funds Tgt Dte Ret 2030 R2	RBETX	B-	(800) 421-0180	C / 5.2	1.92	3.67	6.44 /50	11.97 /52	10.29 /47	0.33	1.57
AA	American Funds Tgt Dte Ret 2030	RBEEX	C	(800) 421-0180	C / 5.4	1.97	3.98	6.93 /54	12.19 /54	10.44 /48	1.20	1.33
AA	American Funds Tgt Dte Ret 2030 R3	RCETX	B-	(800) 421-0180	C / 5.5	1.98	3.85	6.85 /54	12.39 /55	10.70 /50	0.68	1.19
AA	American Funds Tgt Dte Ret 2030 R4	RDETX	B	(800) 421-0180	C+ / 5.7	2.05	4.00	7.15 /56	12.75 /58	11.06 /53	1.00	0.87
AA	American Funds Tgt Dte Ret 2030 R5	REETX	B-	(800) 421-0180	C+ / 6.0	2.12	4.15	7.45 /59	13.09 /60	11.38 /56	1.23	0.56
AA	American Funds Tgt Dte Ret 2030 R6	RFETX	B-	(800) 421-0180	C+ / 6.0	2.12	4.20	7.60 /60	13.14 /61	11.44 /56	1.28	0.52
AA	American Funds Tgt Dte Ret 2035 A	AAFTX	C+	(800) 421-0180	C / 4.9	2.20	4.18	7.41 /58	12.92 /59	11.11 /53	0.96	0.86
AA	American Funds Tgt Dte Ret 2035 B	BBFTX	C	(800) 421-0180	C / 5.3	1.97	3.83	6.56 /51	12.07 /53	10.26 /47	0.83	1.62
AA	American Funds Tgt Dte Ret 2035 C	CCFTX	C	(800) 421-0180	C / 5.3	1.89	3.75	6.47 /50	12.04 /53	10.24 /46	0.97	1.62
AA	American Funds Tgt Dte Ret 2035 F1	FAQTX	C+	(800) 421-0180	C+ / 5.8	2.12	4.13	7.28 /57	12.71 /57	10.85 /51	1.12	0.89
AA	American Funds Tgt Dte Ret 2035 F2	FBFTX	C+	(800) 421-0180	C+ / 5.9	2.20	4.22	7.54 /59	13.00 /60	11.15 /54	1.29	0.64
AA	American Funds Tgt Dte Ret 2035 R1	RAFTX	C+	(800) 421-0180	C / 5.3	1.99	3.75	6.52 /51	12.04 /53	10.25 /46	0.24	1.66
AA	American Funds Tgt Dte Ret 2035 R2	RBFTX	C+	(800) 421-0180	C / 5.3	1.99	3.88	6.65 /52	12.15 /53	10.32 /47	0.38	1.58
AA	American Funds Tgt Dte Ret 2035	RBEFX	C	(800) 421-0180	C / 5.5	2.12	4.17	7.13 /56	12.35 /55	10.49 /49	1.24	1.35
AA	American Funds Tgt Dte Ret 2035 R3	RCFTX	B-	(800) 421-0180	C+ / 5.6	2.13	4.06	7.06 /55	12.56 /56	10.74 /51	0.73	1.20
AA	American Funds Tgt Dte Ret 2035 R4	RDFTX	B-	(800) 421-0180	C+ / 5.9	2.20	4.20	7.35 /58	12.92 /59	11.09 /53	1.03	0.88
AA	American Funds Tgt Dte Ret 2035 R5	REFTX	B-	(800) 421-0180	C+ / 6.1	2.18	4.35	7.65 /60	13.25 /61	11.43 /56	1.27	0.58
AA	American Funds Tgt Dte Ret 2035 R6	RFFTX	B-	(800) 421-0180	C+ / 6.1	2.27	4.32	7.71 /60	13.30 /62	11.49 /57	1.31	0.53
AA	American Funds Tgt Dte Ret 2040 A	AAGTX	C+	(800) 421-0180	C / 5.0	2.17	4.09	7.36 /58	13.09 /60	11.18 /54	0.86	0.86
AA	American Funds Tgt Dte Ret 2040 B	BBGTX	C	(800) 421-0180	C / 5.4	2.02	3.83	6.60 /52	12.26 /54	10.34 /47	0.65	1.63
AA	American Funds Tgt Dte Ret 2040 C	CCGTX	C	(800) 421-0180	C / 5.4	2.03	3.76	6.53 /51	12.24 /54	10.33 /47	0.80	1.62
AA	American Funds Tgt Dte Ret 2040 F1	FAUTX	C+	(800) 421-0180	C+ / 5.9	2.25	4.14	7.33 /58	12.91 /59	10.94 /52	1.03	0.90
AA	American Funds Tgt Dte Ret 2040 F2	FBGTX	C+	(800) 421-0180	C+ / 6.1	2.33	4.28	7.64 /60	13.22 /61	11.25 /55	1.17	0.65
AA	American Funds Tgt Dte Ret 2040 R1	RAKTX	C+	(800) 421-0180	C / 5.4	2.05	3.76	6.57 /51	12.21 /54	10.33 /47	0.17	1.66
AA	American Funds Tgt Dte Ret 2040 R2	RBKTX	B-	(800) 421-0180	C / 5.5	2.05	3.88	6.61 /52	12.32 /55	10.42 /48	0.27	1.58
AA	American Funds Tgt Dte Ret 2040	RBEKX	C+	(800) 421-0180	C+ / 5.7	2.25	4.24	7.24 /57	12.57 /56	10.59 /49	1.13	1.35
AA	American Funds Tgt Dte Ret 2040 R3	RCKTX	B-	(800) 421-0180	C+ / 5.7	2.11	3.96	7.00 /55	12.71 /57	10.81 /51	0.61	1.20
AA	American Funds Tgt Dte Ret 2040 R4	RDGTX	B-	(800) 421-0180	C+ / 5.9	2.25	4.19	7.38 /58	13.07 /60	11.20 /54	0.92	0.88
AA	American Funds Tgt Dte Ret 2040 R5	REGTX	B-	(800) 421-0180	C+ / 6.2	2.31	4.34	7.67 /60	13.43 /63	11.52 /57	1.16	0.58
AA	American Funds Tgt Dte Ret 2040 R6	RFGTX	B-	(800) 421-0180	C+ / 6.2	2.32	4.39	7.74 /61	13.48 /63	11.58 /58	1.20	0.53
AA	American Funds Tgt Dte Ret 2045 A	AAHTX	C+	(800) 421-0180	C / 5.0	2.24	4.22	7.49 /59	13.15 /61	11.21 /54	0.85	0.86
AA	American Funds Tgt Dte Ret 2045 B	BBHTX	C	(800) 421-0180	C / 5.5	2.09	3.90	6.75 /53	12.30 /55	10.37 /47	0.66	1.63
AA	American Funds Tgt Dte Ret 2045 C	CCHTX	C	(800) 421-0180	C / 5.4	1.94	3.80	6.57 /51	12.24 /54	10.33 /47	0.79	1.62
AA	American Funds Tgt Dte Ret 2045 F1	FATTX	C+	(800) 421-0180	C+ / 5.9	2.17	4.22	7.41 /58	12.92 /59	10.95 /52	1.05	0.89

RISK			NET ASSETS		ASSET				Portfolio Turnover Ratio	BULL / BEAR		FUND MANAGER		MINIMUMS		LOADS	
	3 Year		NAV							Last Bull	Last Bear	Manager	Manager	Initial	Additional	Front	Back
Risk Rating/Pts	Standard Deviation	Beta	As of 3/31/15	Total $(Mil)	Cash %	Stocks %	Bonds %	Other %		Market Return	Market Return	Quality Pct	Tenure (Years)	Purch. $	Purch. $	End Load	End Load
B / 8.2	7.6	1.29	12.42	1,316	0	65	34	1	3	66.4	-14.4	35	8	250	50	5.8	0.0
C+ / 6.8	7.6	1.30	12.34	N/A	0	65	34	1	3	62.1	-14.7	25	8	250	50	0.0	0.0
C+ / 6.8	7.6	1.30	12.32	25	0	65	34	1	3	62.0	-14.7	25	8	250	50	0.0	0.0
C+ / 6.8	7.6	1.30	12.39	3	0	65	34	1	3	65.1	-14.5	32	8	250	50	0.0	0.0
C+ / 6.9	7.6	1.30	12.41	3	0	65	34	1	3	66.7	-14.4	35	8	250	50	0.0	0.0
B / 8.2	7.6	1.29	12.25	23	0	65	34	1	3	62.2	-14.8	26	8	250	50	0.0	0.0
B / 8.2	7.5	1.29	12.22	791	0	65	34	1	3	62.5	-14.7	28	8	250	50	0.0	0.0
C+ / 6.8	7.6	1.29	12.40	N/A	0	65	34	1	3	63.5	-14.7	29	8	250	50	0.0	0.0
B / 8.2	7.6	1.29	12.33	906	0	65	34	1	3	64.6	-14.6	32	8	250	50	0.0	0.0
B / 8.2	7.6	1.29	12.41	626	0	65	34	1	3	66.4	-14.5	36	8	250	50	0.0	0.0
B / 8.2	7.6	1.29	12.49	284	0	65	34	1	3	68.3	-14.5	39	8	250	50	0.0	0.0
B / 8.1	7.6	1.29	12.46	998	0	65	34	1	3	68.5	-14.4	41	8	250	50	0.0	0.0
B- / 7.7	8.2	1.39	12.96	1,189	0	77	22	1	2	72.5	-15.8	32	8	250	50	5.8	0.0
C+ / 6.4	8.2	1.39	12.87	N/A	0	77	22	1	2	68.0	-16.1	24	8	250	50	0.0	0.0
C+ / 6.4	8.2	1.39	12.85	21	0	77	22	1	2	67.9	-16.1	23	8	250	50	0.0	0.0
C+ / 6.5	8.2	1.39	12.93	2	0	77	22	1	2	71.3	-15.9	30	8	250	50	0.0	0.0
C+ / 6.5	8.2	1.39	12.95	3	0	77	22	1	2	72.8	-15.8	33	8	250	50	0.0	0.0
B- / 7.7	8.2	1.39	12.80	30	0	77	22	1	2	67.7	-16.0	24	8	250	50	0.0	0.0
B- / 7.7	8.2	1.39	12.75	779	0	77	22	1	2	68.2	-16.0	25	8	250	50	0.0	0.0
C+ / 6.4	8.1	1.39	12.93	N/A	0	77	22	1	2	69.4	-16.1	27	8	250		0.0	0.0
B- / 7.7	8.2	1.40	12.86	912	0	77	22	1	2	70.5	-15.9	28	8	250	50	0.0	0.0
B- / 7.7	8.2	1.40	12.94	678	0	77	22	1	2	72.4	-15.7	32	8	250	50	0.0	0.0
B- / 7.7	8.2	1.39	13.03	293	0	77	22	1	2	74.2	-15.7	36	8	250	50	0.0	0.0
B- / 7.7	8.2	1.40	12.99	1,072	0	77	22	1	2	74.3	-15.6	36	8	250	50	0.0	0.0
B- / 7.5	8.4	1.42	13.03	881	0	81	17	2	1	73.6	-16.2	30	8	250	50	5.8	0.0
C+ / 6.2	8.4	1.43	12.95	N/A	0	81	17	2	1	69.1	-16.5	21	8	250	50	0.0	0.0
C+ / 6.2	8.4	1.43	12.92	18	0	81	17	2	1	69.1	-16.5	21	8	250	50	0.0	0.0
C+ / 6.3	8.4	1.43	13.01	1	0	81	17	2	1	72.5	-16.3	27	8	250	50	0.0	0.0
C+ / 6.3	8.4	1.43	13.02	1	0	81	17	2	1	74.0	-16.2	30	8	250	50	0.0	0.0
B- / 7.5	8.4	1.43	12.79	17	0	81	17	2	1	68.9	-16.4	21	8	250	50	0.0	0.0
B- / 7.5	8.4	1.43	12.82	628	0	81	17	2	1	69.5	-16.4	23	8	250	50	0.0	0.0
C+ / 6.3	8.4	1.43	13.00	N/A	0	81	17	2	1	70.5	-16.4	24	8	250	50	0.0	0.0
B- / 7.5	8.3	1.42	12.93	641	0	81	17	2	1	71.6	-16.3	27	8	250	50	0.0	0.0
B- / 7.5	8.4	1.43	13.01	456	0	81	17	2	1	73.4	-16.1	29	8	250	50	0.0	0.0
B- / 7.5	8.4	1.43	13.10	232	0	81	17	2	1	75.2	-16.0	33	8	250	50	0.0	0.0
B- / 7.5	8.4	1.43	13.06	651	0	81	17	2	1	75.4	-16.0	34	8	250	50	0.0	0.0
B- / 7.5	8.5	1.45	13.17	798	0	83	16	1	1	74.7	-16.5	29	8	250	50	5.8	0.0
C+ / 6.2	8.5	1.45	13.11	N/A	0	83	16	1	1	70.3	-16.8	21	8	250	50	0.0	0.0
C+ / 6.2	8.5	1.45	13.08	12	0	83	16	1	1	70.2	-16.8	21	8	250	50	0.0	0.0
C+ / 6.2	8.5	1.44	13.16	1	0	83	16	1	1	73.5	-16.6	28	8	250	50	0.0	0.0
C+ / 6.3	8.5	1.45	13.18	1	0	83	16	1	1	75.2	-16.5	30	8	250	50	0.0	0.0
B- / 7.5	8.5	1.45	12.97	17	0	83	16	1	1	70.2	-16.8	20	8	250	50	0.0	0.0
B- / 7.5	8.5	1.45	12.96	505	0	83	16	1	1	70.7	-16.7	21	8	250	50	0.0	0.0
C+ / 6.2	8.5	1.44	13.16	N/A	0	83	16	1	1	71.7	-16.7	25	8	250	50	0.0	0.0
B- / 7.5	8.5	1.45	13.08	518	0	83	16	1	1	72.8	-16.6	25	8	250	50	0.0	0.0
B- / 7.5	8.5	1.46	13.16	415	0	83	16	1	1	74.7	-16.5	28	8	250	50	0.0	0.0
B- / 7.5	8.5	1.45	13.26	216	0	83	16	1	1	76.5	-16.4	32	8	250	50	0.0	0.0
B- / 7.5	8.5	1.45	13.22	649	0	83	16	1	1	76.7	-16.3	33	8	250	50	0.0	0.0
B- / 7.5	8.5	1.46	13.24	493	0	84	15	1	1	75.1	-16.5	28	8	250	50	5.8	0.0
C+ / 6.2	8.5	1.46	13.17	N/A	0	84	15	1	1	70.5	-16.8	21	8	250	50	0.0	0.0
C+ / 6.1	8.6	1.46	13.13	9	0	84	15	1	1	70.3	-16.8	20	8	250	50	0.0	0.0
C+ / 6.2	8.5	1.45	13.21	N/A	0	84	15	1	1	73.8	-16.6	27	8	250	50	0.0	0.0

						PERFORMANCE							
	99 Pct = Best 0 Pct = Worst						Total Return % through 3/31/15					Incl. in Returns	
				Overall		Perfor- mance				Annualized		Dividend	Expense
Fund Type	Fund Name		Ticker Symbol	Investment Rating	Phone	Rating/Pts	3 Mo	6 Mo	1Yr / Pct	3Yr / Pct	5Yr / Pct	Yield	Ratio
AA	American Funds Tgt Dte Ret 2045 F2		FBHTX	C+	(800) 421-0180	C+ / 6.1	2.32	4.34	7.70 /60	13.22 /61	11.26 /55	1.02	0.69
AA	American Funds Tgt Dte Ret 2045 R1		RAHTX	B-	(800) 421-0180	C / 5.4	2.03	3.90	6.71 /53	12.23 /54	10.35 /47	0.33	1.67
AA	American Funds Tgt Dte Ret 2045 R2		RBHTX	B-	(800) 421-0180	C / 5.5	2.04	3.85	6.75 /53	12.34 /55	10.44 /48	0.27	1.59
AA	American Funds Tgt Dte Ret 2045		RBHHX	C+	(800) 421-0180	C+ / 5.7	2.24	4.27	7.27 /57	12.60 /57	10.60 /49	1.10	1.35
AA	American Funds Tgt Dte Ret 2045 R3		RCHTX	B-	(800) 421-0180	C+ / 5.8	2.18	4.08	7.12 /56	12.76 /58	10.85 /51	0.60	1.21
AA	American Funds Tgt Dte Ret 2045 R4		RDHTX	B-	(800) 421-0180	C+ / 6.0	2.16	4.22	7.41 /58	13.10 /60	11.18 /54	0.90	0.89
AA	American Funds Tgt Dte Ret 2045 R5		REHTX	B-	(800) 421-0180	C+ / 6.2	2.30	4.45	7.78 /61	13.47 /63	11.55 /57	1.14	0.58
AA	American Funds Tgt Dte Ret 2045 R6		RFHTX	B-	(800) 421-0180	C+ / 6.2	2.31	4.42	7.85 /62	13.50 /63	11.59 /58	1.18	0.53
AA	American Funds Tgt Dte Ret 2050 A		AALTX	C+	(800) 421-0180	C / 5.0	2.21	4.18	7.43 /59	13.12 /61	11.20 /54	0.80	0.87
AA	American Funds Tgt Dte Ret 2050 B		BBITX	C	(800) 421-0180	C / 5.5	2.06	3.89	6.88 /54	12.32 /55	10.37 /47	0.64	1.63
AA	American Funds Tgt Dte Ret 2050 C		CCITX	C	(800) 421-0180	C / 5.4	1.99	3.84	6.66 /52	12.24 /54	10.33 /47	0.81	1.62
AA	American Funds Tgt Dte Ret 2050 F1		FAITX	C+	(800) 421-0180	C+ / 5.9	2.29	4.31	7.56 /60	12.94 /59	10.96 /52	1.04	0.89
AA	American Funds Tgt Dte Ret 2050 F2		FBITX	C+	(800) 421-0180	C+ / 6.1	2.29	4.35	7.68 /60	13.21 /61	11.25 /55	1.08	0.65
AA	American Funds Tgt Dte Ret 2050 R1		RAITX	C+	(800) 421-0180	C / 5.4	2.00	3.82	6.60 /52	12.23 /54	10.36 /47	0.15	1.67
AA	American Funds Tgt Dte Ret 2050 R2		RBITX	B-	(800) 421-0180	C / 5.5	2.08	3.88	6.74 /53	12.33 /55	10.43 /48	0.21	1.59
AA	American Funds Tgt Dte Ret 2050		RBHEX	C+	(800) 421-0180	C+ / 5.7	2.21	4.26	7.23 /57	12.58 /57	10.60 /49	1.07	1.36
AA	American Funds Tgt Dte Ret 2050 R3		RCITX	B-	(800) 421-0180	C+ / 5.7	2.15	4.06	7.16 /56	12.73 /58	10.84 /51	0.56	1.21
AA	American Funds Tgt Dte Ret 2050 R4		RDITX	B-	(800) 421-0180	C+ / 6.0	2.29	4.26	7.52 /59	13.11 /60	11.22 /55	0.85	0.89
AA	American Funds Tgt Dte Ret 2050 R5		REITX	B-	(800) 421-0180	C+ / 6.2	2.28	4.34	7.74 /61	13.44 /63	11.54 /57	1.10	0.59
AA	American Funds Tgt Dte Ret 2050 R6		RFITX	B-	(800) 421-0180	C+ / 6.2	2.28	4.39	7.81 /61	13.49 /63	11.57 /57	1.14	0.54
AA	American Funds Tgt Dte Ret 2055 A		AAMTX	C+	(800) 421-0180	C / 5.0	2.18	4.21	7.48 /59	13.12 /61	11.23 /55	0.77	0.89
AA	American Funds Tgt Dte Ret 2055 B		BBJTX	C	(800) 421-0180	C / 5.5	2.05	3.89	6.81 /53	12.29 /54	10.38 /48	0.13	1.68
AA	American Funds Tgt Dte Ret 2055 C		CCJTX	C	(800) 421-0180	C / 5.4	2.00	3.78	6.64 /52	12.23 /54	10.34 /47	0.70	1.63
AA	American Funds Tgt Dte Ret 2055 F1		FAJTX	C+	(800) 421-0180	C+ / 5.9	2.19	4.23	7.51 /59	12.91 /59	10.97 /52	0.96	0.94
AA	American Funds Tgt Dte Ret 2055 F2		FBJTX	C+	(800) 421-0180	C+ / 6.0	2.25	4.30	7.64 /60	13.20 /61	11.28 /55	1.02	0.71
AA	American Funds Tgt Dte Ret 2055 R1		RAMTX	B-	(800) 421-0180	C / 5.4	2.02	3.84	6.66 /52	12.25 /54	10.36 /47	0.16	1.71
AA	American Funds Tgt Dte Ret 2055 R2		RBMTX	B-	(800) 421-0180	C / 5.5	2.08	3.91	6.73 /53	12.31 /55	10.44 /48	0.23	1.64
AA	American Funds Tgt Dte Ret 2055		RBEMX	C	(800) 421-0180	C+ / 5.7	2.25	4.32	7.31 /57	12.57 /56	10.61 /50	0.98	1.39
AA	American Funds Tgt Dte Ret 2055 R3		RCMTX	B-	(800) 421-0180	C+ / 5.7	2.07	4.00	7.08 /56	12.69 /57	10.82 /51	0.53	1.26
AA	American Funds Tgt Dte Ret 2055 R4		RDJTX	B-	(800) 421-0180	C+ / 5.9	2.18	4.18	7.46 /59	13.06 /60	11.19 /54	0.78	0.94
AA	American Funds Tgt Dte Ret 2055 R5		REKTX	B-	(800) 421-0180	C+ / 6.2	2.30	4.41	7.81 /61	13.43 /63	11.52 /57	1.02	0.64
AA	American Funds Tgt Dte Ret 2055 R6		RFKTX	B-	(800) 421-0180	C+ / 6.2	2.30	4.37	7.83 /62	13.46 /63	11.57 /57	1.05	0.57
GI	American Funds Wash Mutl Invs		CWMAX	B-	(800) 421-0180	C+ / 6.2	0.22	3.60	9.30 /71	15.27 /77	13.97 /77	1.78	0.69
GI	● American Funds Wash Mutl Invs		CWMBX	B-	(800) 421-0180	C+ / 6.6	0.01	3.21	8.46 /66	14.36 /70	13.07 /69	1.06	1.48
GI	American Funds Wash Mutl Invs		CWMCX	B-	(800) 421-0180	C+ / 6.6	0.02	3.20	8.46 /66	14.37 /70	13.09 /69	1.15	1.47
GI	American Funds Wash Mutl Invs		CWMEX	B+	(800) 421-0180	B- / 7.0	0.14	3.49	9.03 /69	14.98 /75	13.67 /75	1.65	0.94
GI	American Funds Wash Mutl Invs		CWMFX	B+	(800) 421-0180	B- / 7.4	0.26	3.72	9.56 /72	15.52 /79	14.22 /80	2.11	0.47
* GI	American Funds Wash Mutl Invs A		AWSHX	B-	(800) 421-0180	C+ / 6.3	0.22	3.66	9.41 /71	15.38 /78	14.07 /78	1.86	0.60
GI	● American Funds Wash Mutl Invs B		WSHBX	B-	(800) 421-0180	C+ / 6.7	0.06	3.26	8.59 /67	14.51 /71	13.22 /70	1.19	1.35
GI	American Funds Wash Mutl Invs C		WSHCX	B-	(800) 421-0180	C+ / 6.6	0.06	3.24	8.57 /67	14.46 /71	13.17 /70	1.21	1.39
GI	American Funds Wash Mutl Invs F1		WSHFX	B+	(800) 421-0180	B- / 7.3	0.23	3.61	9.34 /71	15.30 /77	14.01 /78	1.88	0.67
GI	American Funds Wash Mutl Invs F2		WMFFX	B+	(800) 421-0180	B- / 7.5	0.30	3.77	9.63 /73	15.59 /80	14.31 /80	2.17	0.41
GI	American Funds Wash Mutl Invs R1		RWMAX	B-	(800) 421-0180	C+ / 6.6	0.04	3.25	8.54 /67	14.46 /71	13.17 /70	1.22	1.39
GI	American Funds Wash Mutl Invs R2		RWMBX	B-	(800) 421-0180	C+ / 6.7	0.07	3.28	8.60 /67	14.51 /71	13.21 /70	1.26	1.35
GI	American Funds Wash Mutl Invs R2E		RWEBX	C+	(800) 421-0180	C+ / 6.9	0.19	3.63	9.11 /70	14.80 /73	13.45 /72	1.96	1.11
GI	American Funds Wash Mutl Invs R3		RWMCX	B+	(800) 421-0180	B- / 7.0	0.14	3.47	9.02 /69	14.97 /75	13.67 /75	1.64	0.95
GI	American Funds Wash Mutl Invs R4		RWMEX	B+	(800) 421-0180	B- / 7.3	0.22	3.63	9.34 /71	15.32 /77	14.02 /78	1.93	0.65
GI	American Funds Wash Mutl Invs R5		RWMFX	B+	(800) 421-0180	B- / 7.5	0.29	3.77	9.68 /73	15.66 /80	14.36 /81	2.21	0.35
GI	American Funds Wash Mutl Invs R6		RWMGX	B+	(800) 421-0180	B / 7.6	0.30	3.79	9.72 /73	15.72 /81	14.42 /82	2.25	0.30
GR	American Growth Fund Series One A		AMRAX	C+	(800) 525-2406	C+ / 6.2	0.70	6.45	9.44 /72	14.87 /74	8.52 /33	0.00	4.96
GR	American Growth Fund Series One B		AMRBX	C+	(800) 525-2406	C+ / 6.6	0.54	5.95	8.72 /68	14.07 /68	7.79 /29	0.00	5.69
GR	American Growth Fund Series One C		AMRCX	C+	(800) 525-2406	C+ / 6.5	0.27	5.98	8.45 /66	14.01 /67	7.76 /28	0.00	5.66

RISK	3 Year		NET ASSETS		ASSET				Portfolio	BULL / BEAR		FUND MANAGER		MINIMUMS		LOADS	
Risk Rating/Pts	Standard Deviation	Beta	NAV As of 3/31/15	Total $(Mil)	Cash %	Stocks %	Bonds %	Other %	Turnover Ratio	Last Bull Market Return	Last Bear Market Return	Manager Quality Pct	Manager Tenure (Years)	Initial Purch. $	Additional Purch. $	Front End Load	Back End Load
C+ / 6.2	8.5	1.46	13.25	N/A	0	84	15	1	1	75.3	-16.5	30	8	250	50	0.0	0.0
B- / 7.5	8.5	1.45	13.05	9	0	84	15	1	1	70.3	-16.7	21	8	250	50	0.0	0.0
B- / 7.5	8.5	1.45	13.00	335	0	84	15	1	1	70.8	-16.7	21	8	250	50	0.0	0.0
C+ / 6.2	8.5	1.46	13.22	N/A	0	84	15	1	1	72.0	-16.7	23	8	250	50	0.0	0.0
B- / 7.5	8.5	1.45	13.13	347	0	84	15	1	1	73.1	-16.6	25	8	250	50	0.0	0.0
B- / 7.5	8.5	1.45	13.22	252	0	84	15	1	1	74.8	-16.4	29	8	250	50	0.0	0.0
B- / 7.5	8.5	1.46	13.33	126	0	84	15	1	1	76.7	-16.4	32	8	250	50	0.0	0.0
B- / 7.5	8.5	1.45	13.28	307	0	84	15	1	1	77.0	-16.4	33	8	250	50	0.0	0.0
B- / 7.5	8.5	1.46	12.95	441	0	84	15	1	1	74.9	-16.4	28	8	250	50	5.8	0.0
C+ / 6.2	8.5	1.46	12.89	N/A	0	84	15	1	1	70.5	-16.7	21	8	250	50	0.0	0.0
C+ / 6.1	8.6	1.46	12.84	8	0	84	15	1	1	70.3	-16.7	20	8	250	50	0.0	0.0
C+ / 6.2	8.5	1.46	12.93	1	0	84	15	1	1	73.7	-16.5	27	8	250	50	0.0	0.0
C+ / 6.2	8.5	1.45	12.95	N/A	0	84	15	1	1	75.2	-16.4	30	8	250	50	0.0	0.0
B- / 7.5	8.5	1.45	12.76	7	0	84	15	1	1	70.3	-16.7	21	8	250	50	0.0	0.0
B- / 7.5	8.5	1.45	12.76	262	0	84	15	1	1	70.8	-16.7	22	8	250	50	0.0	0.0
C+ / 6.2	8.5	1.45	12.93	N/A	0	84	15	1	1	71.7	-16.6	24	8	250	50	0.0	0.0
B- / 7.5	8.6	1.46	12.85	269	0	84	15	1	1	73.1	-16.6	24	8	250	50	0.0	0.0
B- / 7.5	8.5	1.46	12.94	208	0	84	15	1	1	74.9	-16.4	28	8	250	50	0.0	0.0
B- / 7.5	8.5	1.45	13.03	103	0	84	15	1	1	76.7	-16.4	32	8	250	50	0.0	0.0
B- / 7.5	8.6	1.46	12.99	247	0	84	15	1	1	77.1	-16.4	32	8	250	50	0.0	0.0
B- / 7.5	8.5	1.46	15.92	167	0	85	14	1	2	75.0	-16.5	29	N/A	250	50	5.8	0.0
C+ / 6.1	8.5	1.45	15.92	N/A	0	85	14	1	2	70.6	-16.8	21	5	250	50	0.0	0.0
C+ / 6.1	8.5	1.45	15.80	6	0	85	14	1	2	70.3	-16.8	20	5	250	50	0.0	0.0
C+ / 6.2	8.5	1.45	15.90	N/A	0	85	14	1	2	73.8	-16.6	27	5	250	50	0.0	0.0
C+ / 6.2	8.5	1.46	15.92	N/A	0	85	14	1	2	75.4	-16.5	29	5	250	50	0.0	0.0
B- / 7.5	8.5	1.45	15.69	2	0	85	14	1	2	70.4	-16.8	21	N/A	250	50	0.0	0.0
B- / 7.5	8.5	1.45	15.71	103	0	85	14	1	2	70.8	-16.8	21	N/A	250	50	0.0	0.0
C+ / 6.1	8.5	1.45	15.91	N/A	0	85	14	1	2	71.8	-16.7	23	5	250	50	0.0	0.0
B- / 7.5	8.6	1.46	15.81	99	0	85	14	1	2	72.9	-16.6	24	N/A	250	50	0.0	0.0
B- / 7.5	8.5	1.45	15.91	67	0	85	14	1	2	74.9	-16.6	28	N/A	250	50	0.0	0.0
B- / 7.5	8.5	1.46	16.01	29	0	85	14	1	2	76.6	-16.4	31	N/A	250	50	0.0	0.0
B- / 7.5	8.6	1.46	16.02	66	0	85	14	1	2	77.0	-16.5	31	N/A	250	50	0.0	0.0
B- / 7.3	8.8	0.91	40.79	1,823	0	96	3	1	19	87.2	-12.6	74	18	250	50	5.8	0.0
B- / 7.3	8.9	0.91	40.70	27	0	96	3	1	19	82.3	-12.9	65	18	250	50	0.0	0.0
B- / 7.3	8.8	0.91	40.54	462	0	96	3	1	19	82.3	-12.9	65	18	250	50	0.0	0.0
B- / 7.3	8.9	0.91	40.60	94	0	96	3	1	19	85.7	-12.7	71	18	250	50	0.0	0.0
B- / 7.3	8.9	0.91	40.71	107	0	96	3	1	19	88.6	-12.5	76	18	250	50	0.0	0.0
B- / 7.3	8.8	0.91	40.86	52,290	0	96	3	1	19	87.8	-12.5	75	18	250	50	5.8	0.0
B- / 7.3	8.8	0.91	40.66	152	0	96	3	1	19	83.1	-12.8	67	18	250	50	0.0	0.0
B- / 7.3	8.9	0.91	40.44	1,713	0	96	3	1	19	82.8	-12.8	66	18	250	50	0.0	0.0
B- / 7.3	8.8	0.91	40.74	2,895	0	96	3	1	19	87.4	-12.6	74	18	250	50	0.0	0.0
B- / 7.3	8.8	0.91	40.84	4,620	0	96	3	1	19	89.1	-12.5	77	18	250	50	0.0	0.0
B- / 7.3	8.9	0.91	40.51	102	0	96	3	1	19	82.8	-12.8	66	18	250	50	0.0	0.0
B- / 7.3	8.9	0.91	40.40	807	0	96	3	1	19	83.1	-12.8	67	18	250	50	0.0	0.0
C+ / 6.0	8.8	0.91	40.82	N/A	0	96	3	1	19	84.5	-12.7	70	18	250	50	0.0	0.0
B- / 7.3	8.8	0.91	40.58	1,937	0	96	3	1	19	85.6	-12.7	72	18	250	50	0.0	0.0
B- / 7.3	8.8	0.91	40.69	2,357	0	96	3	1	19	87.6	-12.5	74	18	250	50	0.0	0.0
B- / 7.3	8.9	0.91	40.84	1,933	0	96	3	1	19	89.5	-12.5	77	18	250	50	0.0	0.0
B- / 7.3	8.9	0.91	40.87	6,149	0	96	3	1	19	89.8	-12.4	77	18	250	50	0.0	0.0
C+ / 6.6	12.6	1.22	4.29	6	0	100	0	0	8	100.0	-24.0	13	4	0	0	5.8	0.0
C+ / 6.6	12.6	1.21	3.74	N/A	0	100	0	0	8	96.4	-24.5	10	4	0	0	0.0	0.0
C+ / 6.6	12.6	1.22	3.72	3	0	100	0	0	8	95.4	-24.2	10	4	0	0	0.0	0.0

99 Pct = Best
0 Pct = Worst

Fund Type	Fund Name	Ticker Symbol	Overall Investment Rating	Phone	Perfor-mance Rating/Pts	PERFORMANCE Total Return % through 3/31/15 3 Mo	6 Mo	1Yr / Pct	Annualized 3Yr / Pct	5Yr / Pct	Incl. in Returns Dividend Yield	Expense Ratio
GR	American Growth Fund Series One D	AMRGX	C+	(800) 525-2406	C+ / 6.4	0.67	6.37	9.73 /73	15.20 /76	8.86 /36	0.00	4.65
GR	American Growth Fund Series Two E	AMREX	C-		C- / 3.1	4.78	5.33	7.78 /61	9.14 /34	--	0.00	6.16
GR	American Growth Fund Series Two F	AMRHX	C-		C- / 3.6	4.55	5.02	7.03 /55	8.40 /29	--	0.00	6.86
FO	American Ind Itl Alpha Strategies A	IIESX	E+	(866) 410-2006	D- / 1.1	3.44	-0.74	-4.11 / 7	6.55 /19	4.24 / 9	1.87	1.80
EM	American Ind Itl Alpha Strategies I	IMSSX	E+	(866) 410-2006	D / 1.8	3.55	-0.55	-3.65 / 8	7.07 /22	4.75 /11	2.02	1.30
GL	American Ind Risk-Mgd Alloc A	AARMX	U	(866) 410-2006	U /	4.73	7.16	8.62 /67	--	--	2.40	2.55
GR	American Ind Stock Fund A	IFCSX	E	(866) 410-2006	C- / 4.0	0.28	2.97	3.99 /32	12.08 /53	10.58 /49	0.62	1.85
GR	American Ind Stock Fund C	ISFSX	E+	(866) 410-2006	C / 4.5	0.14	2.63	3.35 /28	11.34 /48	9.82 /43	0.59	2.46
GR	American Ind Stock Fund I	ISISX	E+	(866) 410-2006	C / 5.2	0.27	3.06	4.27 /33	12.44 /56	10.90 /52	0.66	1.46
GR	American Trust Allegiance Fd	ATAFX	C	(800) 385-7003	C / 5.1	4.54	5.01	6.70 /53	11.41 /48	11.51 /57	0.11	1.88
GI	AMF Large Cap Equity H	IICHX	C	(800) 527-3713	C / 4.5	-2.12	1.22	4.50 /35	11.46 /49	11.07 /53	1.29	1.11
GI	AMF Large Cap Equity Inst	IICAX	C	(800) 527-3713	C / 4.4	-2.15	1.22	4.33 /34	11.34 /48	10.93 /52	1.13	1.36
BA	AMG CEP Balanced Inst	MBEYX	C+	(800) 835-3879	C / 5.4	3.43	6.23	11.17 /79	11.07 /46	10.83 /51	0.91	1.27
BA	AMG CEP Balanced Inv	MBEAX	C+	(800) 835-3879	C / 5.2	3.39	6.12	10.90 /78	10.81 /44	10.55 /49	0.68	1.52
FO	AMG FQ Global Alternatives Inst	MGAIX	E	(800) 835-3879	E- / 0.2	-6.02	-9.15	-10.37 / 3	-4.95 / 2	-4.45 / 1	0.00	2.17
FO	AMG FQ Global Alternatives Inv	MGAAX	E	(800) 835-3879	E- / 0.2	-6.05	-9.33	-10.66 / 3	-5.36 / 2	-4.86 / 1	0.00	2.62
FO	AMG FQ Global Alternatives Svc	MGASX	E	(800) 835-3879	E- / 0.2	-6.04	-9.18	-10.40 / 3	-5.10 / 2	-4.58 / 1	0.00	2.32
GL	AMG FQ Global Risk-Balanced Inst	MMAFX	D	(800) 835-3879	D+ / 2.3	5.29	5.08	6.69 /53	5.25 /14	7.26 /25	3.05	1.28
GL	AMG FQ Global Risk-Balanced Inv	MMAVX	D	(800) 835-3879	D / 2.0	5.09	4.73	6.13 /48	4.69 /12	6.73 /21	2.30	1.78
GL	AMG FQ Global Risk-Balanced Svc	MMASX	D	(800) 835-3879	D / 2.2	5.22	4.96	6.50 /51	5.17 /14	7.13 /24	2.95	1.36
GI	AMG FQ Tax-Managed US Equity	MFQTX	A+	(800) 835-3879	A / 9.3	2.34	9.29	12.69 /86	18.00 /94	16.77 /95	0.37	1.04
GR	AMG FQ Tax-Managed US Equity Inv	MFQAX	A+	(800) 835-3879	A- / 9.2	2.30	9.11	12.35 /84	17.70 /93	16.48 /95	0.22	1.29
GR	AMG FQ US Equity Inst	MEQFX	B-	(800) 835-3879	C+ / 6.0	0.27	3.69	7.33 /58	13.52 /64	13.54 /73	1.31	0.80
GR	AMG FQ US Equity Inv	FQUAX	B-	(800) 835-3879	C+ / 5.9	0.20	3.56	7.13 /56	13.21 /61	13.25 /71	0.88	1.05
SC	● AMG Frontier Small Cap Growth Inst	MSSYX	C-	(800) 835-3879	A / 9.4	7.36	19.82	10.91 /78	17.20 /91	15.45 /90	0.00	1.24
SC	● AMG Frontier Small Cap Growth Inv	MSSVX	D+	(800) 835-3879	A- / 9.2	7.19	19.54	10.34 /76	16.61 /87	14.90 /86	0.00	1.74
SC	● AMG Frontier Small Cap Growth Svc	MSSCX	D+	(800) 835-3879	A / 9.3	7.24	19.67	10.64 /77	16.90 /89	15.17 /88	0.00	1.47
SC	● AMG GW&K Small Cap Core Inst	GWEIX	B+	(800) 835-3879	B+ / 8.3	3.18	12.98	6.15 /48	16.30 /85	16.40 /94	0.15	1.08
SC	● AMG GW&K Small Cap Core Inv	GWETX	B	(800) 835-3879	B / 7.9	3.08	12.66	5.61 /43	15.79 /82	15.87 /92	0.00	1.48
SC	● AMG GW&K Small Cap Core Svc	GWESX	B+	(800) 835-3879	B / 8.2	3.14	12.88	5.98 /46	16.11 /84	16.16 /94	0.04	1.24
GR	AMG Mgrs Brandywine	BRWIX	B-	(800) 656-3017	B / 8.1	6.79	12.60	15.31 /92	13.33 /62	10.14 /46	0.00	1.09
MC	AMG Mgrs Brandywine Adv MCG	BWAFX	D	(800) 656-3017	C- / 3.9	6.97	8.76	4.93 /38	8.73 /31	6.92 /22	0.00	1.12
GR	AMG Mgrs Brandywine Blue	BLUEX	C	(800) 656-3017	C+ / 6.3	4.17	10.24	14.90 /91	11.12 /46	10.02 /45	0.00	1.19
GR	AMG Mgrs Cadence Cap Appr Inst	MPCIX	C+	(800) 835-3879	C+ / 6.9	3.78	9.08	13.65 /89	13.00 /60	12.46 /64	0.95	0.82
GR	AMG Mgrs Cadence Cap Appr Inv	MPAFX	C+	(800) 835-3879	C+ / 6.6	3.64	8.82	13.17 /87	12.57 /56	12.01 /61	0.54	1.22
GR	AMG Mgrs Cadence Cap Appr Svc	MCFYX	C+	(800) 835-3879	C+ / 6.7	3.71	8.90	13.41 /88	12.73 /58	12.17 /62	0.16	1.07
SC	AMG Mgrs Cadence Em Comp Inst	MECIX	B+	(800) 835-3879	A- / 9.2	7.12	20.31	9.75 /73	16.51 /87	19.64 /99	0.00	1.66
SC	AMG Mgrs Cadence Em Comp Svc	MECAX	B	(800) 835-3879	A- / 9.1	7.07	20.17	9.49 /72	16.24 /85	19.35 /98	0.00	1.89
MC	AMG Mgrs Cadence Mid Cap Inst	MCMFX	C	(800) 835-3879	B / 8.2	5.66	12.51	15.18 /92	13.85 /66	14.59 /83	0.00	0.77
MC	AMG Mgrs Cadence Mid Cap Inv	MCMAX	C	(800) 835-3879	B / 7.9	5.59	12.31	14.75 /91	13.41 /63	14.14 /79	0.00	1.17
MC	AMG Mgrs Cadence Mid Cap Svc	MCMYX	C	(800) 835-3879	B / 8.0	5.63	12.41	14.92 /91	13.58 /64	14.31 /80	0.00	1.02
SC	AMG Mgrs Emerging Opptys Inst	MIMFX	C+	(800) 835-3879	A- / 9.1	3.69	16.36	3.91 /31	17.89 /94	17.14 /96	0.00	1.36
SC	AMG Mgrs Emerging Opptys Svc	MMCFX	C+	(800) 835-3879	A- / 9.0	3.59	16.20	3.64 /30	17.55 /93	16.97 /96	0.00	1.61
SC	AMG Mgrs Essex SM Cap Gro Inv	MBRSX	B	(800) 835-3879	A+ / 9.7	4.49	15.78	4.70 /36	20.91 /98	17.17 /96	0.00	1.49
RE	AMG Mgrs Real Estate Securities	MRESX	B-	(800) 835-3879	A / 9.5	5.07	21.14	25.49 /98	13.93 /67	16.04 /93	1.25	1.19
SC	● AMG Mgrs Skyline Special Eqty	SKSEX	A	(800) 835-3879	A / 9.4	3.06	12.59	6.99 /55	19.42 /97	17.10 /96	0.00	1.47
SC	AMG Mgrs Special Equity Inst	MSEIX	B	(800) 835-3879	B+ / 8.5	7.88	14.81	9.36 /71	15.39 /78	17.64 /97	0.00	1.25
SC	AMG Mgrs Special Equity Svc	MGSEX	B	(800) 835-3879	B+ / 8.3	7.81	14.66	9.09 /70	15.24 /77	17.40 /97	0.00	1.50
GR	AMG Renaissance Large Cap Gro	MRLIX	C	(800) 835-3879	A+ / 9.7	2.10	11.82	18.83 /96	18.74 /96	15.75 /92	0.47	1.13
GR	AMG Renaissance Large Cap Gro Inv	MRLTX	C	(800) 835-3879	A / 9.5	2.00	11.50	18.18 /96	18.14 /95	15.19 /88	0.21	1.63
GR	AMG Renaissance Large Cap Gro	MRLSX	C	(800) 835-3879	A+ / 9.6	1.98	11.65	18.57 /96	18.57 /96	15.56 /90	0.35	1.23
SC	AMG SouthernSun Small Cap Inst	SSSIX	D+	(800) 835-3879	C+ / 5.9	5.11	0.61	-2.75 / 9	15.14 /76	18.73 /98	0.04	0.95

● Denotes fund is closed to new investors
* Denotes fund is included in Section II

98

RISK			NET ASSETS		ASSET				Portfolio Turnover Ratio	BULL / BEAR		FUND MANAGER		MINIMUMS		LOADS	
	3 Year		NAV							Last Bull	Last Bear	Manager	Manager	Initial	Additional	Front	Back
Risk Rating/Pts	Standard Deviation	Beta	As of 3/31/15	Total $(Mil)	Cash %	Stocks %	Bonds %	Other %		Market Return	Market Return	Quality Pct	Tenure (Years)	Purch. $	Purch. $	End Load	End Load
C+ / 6.6	12.6	1.21	4.51	6	0	100	0	0	8	102.2	-24.1	16	4	0	0	5.8	0.0
C+ / 6.7	10.3	0.97	12.05	2	0	99	0	1	4	58.5	-23.3	7	57	0	0	5.8	0.0
C+ / 6.7	10.3	0.97	11.72	1	0	99	0	1	4	54.8	-23.5	5	57	0	0	0.0	0.0
C / 4.5	12.4	0.91	11.13	N/A	1	98	0	1	77	39.7	-20.9	37	1	5,000	250	5.8	0.0
C / 4.6	12.4	0.70	11.37	54	1	98	0	1	77	42.0	-20.8	96	1	3,000,000	5,000	0.0	0.0
U /	N/A	N/A	10.90	26	4	80	15	1	166	N/A	N/A	N/A	2	5,000	250	5.8	0.0
D- / 1.4	11.4	1.08	7.04	5	3	96	0	1	226	79.7	-19.3	12	9	5,000	250	5.8	0.0
D- / 1.4	11.4	1.08	7.14	6	3	96	0	1	226	75.7	-19.5	8	9	5,000	250	0.0	0.0
D- / 1.4	11.4	1.08	7.32	20	3	96	0	1	226	81.8	-19.1	13	9	250,000	5,000	0.0	0.0
C+ / 6.5	11.3	1.09	28.08	25	0	95	3	2	48	77.8	-18.6	8	18	2,500	250	0.0	0.0
C+ / 6.7	9.3	0.92	10.55	7	4	95	0	1	7	70.2	-8.8	26	24	50,000,000	0	0.0	0.0
C+ / 6.7	9.3	0.92	10.56	42	4	95	0	1	7	69.5	-8.8	25	24	2,500	100	0.0	0.0
C+ / 6.8	6.0	1.00	15.70	13	1	64	34	1	90	57.3	-7.1	70	15	1,000,000	1,000	0.0	0.0
C+ / 6.8	6.0	1.00	15.57	48	1	64	34	1	90	56.0	-7.1	66	15	2,000	100	0.0	0.0
C / 4.7	6.9	-0.20	6.87	4	18	30	51	1	0	-12.9	-8.0	22	9	1,000,000	1,000	0.0	0.0
C / 4.7	6.9	-0.21	6.83	11	18	30	51	1	0	-14.3	-8.1	19	9	2,000	100	0.0	0.0
C / 4.7	6.9	-0.20	6.85	28	18	30	51	1	0	-13.3	-8.1	20	9	100,000	100	0.0	0.0
C+ / 6.7	9.0	0.44	14.13	73	36	11	52	1	5	28.2	-3.5	78	6	1,000,000	1,000	0.0	0.0
C+ / 6.7	9.0	0.44	14.03	2	36	11	52	1	5	26.0	-3.7	73	6	2,000	100	0.0	0.0
C+ / 6.7	8.9	0.44	14.10	2	36	11	52	1	5	27.8	-3.6	77	6	100,000	100	0.0	0.0
B- / 7.4	10.6	1.07	24.88	59	0	100	0	0	45	112.2	-18.7	73	7	1,000,000	1,000	0.0	0.0
B- / 7.4	10.6	1.07	24.91	16	0	100	0	0	45	110.3	-18.8	70	7	2,000	100	0.0	0.0
B- / 7.5	8.7	0.87	17.52	44	3	96	0	1	87	86.2	-16.4	62	7	1,000,000	1,000	0.0	0.0
B- / 7.5	8.7	0.87	17.54	27	3	96	0	1	87	84.6	-16.5	58	7	2,000	100	0.0	0.0
E / 0.5	13.9	1.00	16.05	21	1	98	0	1	63	103.6	-26.7	76	6	100,000	1,000	0.0	0.0
E / 0.5	13.9	1.00	15.66	N/A	1	98	0	1	63	100.1	-26.9	71	6	2,000	100	0.0	0.0
E / 0.5	13.9	1.00	15.85	16	1	98	0	1	63	102.0	-26.8	73	6	25,000	100	0.0	0.0
C+ / 6.0	12.1	0.87	24.36	301	3	96	0	1	19	96.0	-20.2	84	6	1,000,000	1,000	0.0	0.0
C+ / 5.9	12.1	0.87	24.11	39	3	96	0	1	19	93.3	-20.4	81	6	2,000	100	0.0	0.0
C+ / 5.9	12.1	0.87	24.27	45	3	96	0	1	19	94.8	-20.3	83	6	100,000	100	0.0	0.0
C / 5.2	13.8	1.22	37.44	852	0	98	1	1	219	72.8	-28.9	7	5	2,000	100	0.0	0.0
C / 4.6	14.3	1.17	10.43	162	0	94	5	1	249	50.9	-29.2	2	5	2,000	100	0.0	0.0
C / 5.4	12.3	1.07	36.94	205	3	96	0	1	182	72.1	-21.5	8	5	2,000	100	0.0	0.0
C+ / 6.2	10.9	1.07	26.90	46	0	99	0	1	52	80.3	-16.0	18	23	1,000,000	1,000	0.0	0.0
C+ / 6.2	10.9	1.08	25.92	76	0	99	0	1	52	77.9	-16.1	14	23	2,000	100	0.0	0.0
C+ / 6.2	10.9	1.07	26.29	10	0	99	0	1	52	78.8	-16.0	16	23	100,000	100	0.0	0.0
C / 4.9	15.7	1.10	38.51	36	3	96	0	1	127	107.8	-25.0	47	22	1,000,000	1,000	0.0	0.0
C / 4.9	15.6	1.10	35.75	3	3	96	0	1	127	106.0	-25.1	44	22	2,000	100	0.0	0.0
C- / 3.3	12.3	1.01	34.16	34	0	100	0	0	203	86.5	-19.8	26	23	1,000,000	1,000	0.0	0.0
C- / 3.3	12.3	1.01	31.91	118	0	100	0	0	203	84.0	-19.9	22	23	2,000	100	0.0	0.0
C- / 3.3	12.3	1.01	32.81	15	0	100	0	0	203	84.9	-19.8	24	23	100,000	100	0.0	0.0
C- / 3.4	15.4	1.08	45.58	36	0	0	0	100	98	114.9	-25.2	70	8	1,000,000	1,000	0.0	0.0
C- / 3.3	15.4	1.08	45.32	174	0	0	0	100	98	113.4	-25.2	66	8	2,000	100	0.0	0.0
C- / 3.8	15.1	1.02	28.41	39	2	97	0	1	130	113.8	-28.0	91	13	2,000	100	0.0	0.0
C- / 3.6	13.3	1.06	12.65	361	0	99	0	1	49	84.8	-16.1	52	11	2,000	100	0.0	0.0
C+ / 6.2	14.6	1.05	41.10	1,429	4	95	0	1	39	126.9	-25.2	84	14	2,000	100	0.0	2.0
C / 5.4	14.0	1.00	97.29	20	3	96	0	1	129	98.6	-23.4	57	9	2,500,000	1,000	0.0	0.0
C / 5.4	14.1	1.00	95.20	216	3	96	0	1	129	97.4	-23.5	54	9	2,000	100	0.0	0.0
D / 1.7	10.6	1.05	11.69	10	1	98	0	1	53	122.8	-22.0	80	N/A	1,000,000	1,000	0.0	0.0
D / 1.8	10.6	1.05	11.74	3	1	98	0	1	53	119.0	-22.1	77	N/A	2,000	100	0.0	0.0
D / 1.8	10.6	1.05	11.82	20	1	98	0	1	53	121.5	-22.0	80	N/A	100,000	100	0.0	0.0
C- / 3.7	15.1	0.89	26.53	384	8	91	0	1	24	105.4	-23.6	75	12	1,000,000	1,000	0.0	2.0

						99 Pct = Best / 0 Pct = Worst PERFORMANCE							

99 Pct = Best
0 Pct = Worst

						Total Return % through 3/31/15					Incl. in Returns	
Fund Type	Fund Name	Ticker Symbol	Overall Investment Rating	Phone	Perfor-mance Rating/Pts	3 Mo	6 Mo	1Yr / Pct	Annualized 3Yr / Pct	5Yr / Pct	Dividend Yield	Expense Ratio
SC	AMG SouthernSun Small Cap Inv	SSSFX	D+	(800) 835-3879	C+ / 5.7	5.02	0.47	-3.03 / 9	14.86 /74	18.40 /98	0.00	1.20
MC	AMG SouthernSun US Equity C	SSECX	U	(800) 835-3879	U /	5.82	2.06	4.97 /38	--	--	0.00	1.98
MC	AMG SouthernSun US Equity Inst	SSEIX	U	(800) 835-3879	U /	6.01	2.54	6.04 /47	--	--	0.10	0.98
MC	AMG SouthernSun US Equity Inv	SSEFX	U	(800) 835-3879	U /	5.95	2.36	5.79 /45	--	--	0.00	1.23
GR	AMG Systematic Large Cap Value	MSYSX	C	(800) 835-3879	B- / 7.0	0.26	3.98	8.05 /63	15.11 /76	12.14 /62	1.10	0.88
GR	AMG Systematic Large Cap Value Inv	MSYAX	C	(800) 835-3879	C+ / 6.9	0.35	3.93	7.92 /62	14.85 /74	11.86 /60	0.85	1.13
MC	AMG Systematic Mid Cap Value Inst	SYIMX	C+	(800) 835-3879	C+ / 6.5	3.12	5.82	5.60 /43	14.15 /68	12.67 /65	0.73	0.82
MC	AMG Systematic Mid Cap Value Inv	SYAMX	C+	(800) 835-3879	C+ / 6.3	3.06	5.59	5.30 /41	13.84 /66	12.36 /63	0.30	1.07
GR	AMG TimesSquare All Cap Growth	MTGIX	B+	(800) 835-3879	A / 9.4	6.76	13.77	15.84 /93	17.01 /90	--	0.15	1.30
GR	AMG TimesSquare All Cap Growth	MTGVX	B+	(800) 835-3879	A- / 9.2	6.66	13.53	15.32 /92	16.51 /87	--	0.00	1.79
GR	AMG TimesSquare All Cap Growth	MTGSX	B+	(800) 835-3879	A / 9.3	6.75	13.71	15.70 /93	16.88 /89	--	0.06	1.40
GL	AMG TimesSquare Intl Small Cap	TCMIX	U	(800) 835-3879	U /	5.67	5.47	3.37 /28	--	--	1.13	8.03
MC	● AMG TimesSquare Mid Cap Growth	TMDIX	B+	(800) 835-3879	B+ / 8.9	6.53	10.30	10.66 /77	16.56 /87	14.75 /85	0.00	1.03
MC	● AMG TimesSquare Mid Cap Growth	TMDPX	B+	(800) 835-3879	B+ / 8.7	6.52	10.22	10.46 /76	16.36 /86	14.52 /82	0.00	1.23
SC	● AMG TimesSquare Small Cap Gro	TSCIX	B	(800) 835-3879	A / 9.3	7.22	17.57	9.34 /71	17.24 /91	16.76 /95	0.00	1.05
SC	● AMG TimesSquare Small Cap Gro	TSCPX	B	(800) 835-3879	A- / 9.2	7.18	17.39	9.10 /70	17.00 /90	16.58 /95	0.00	1.18
EM	AMG Trilogy Emerging Mkts Eqty Inst	TLEIX	E	(800) 835-3879	E / 0.3	-0.49	-5.96	-3.86 / 7	-2.85 / 2	--	1.64	0.92
EM	AMG Trilogy Emerging Mkts Eqty Inv	TLEVX	D-	(800) 835-3879	E- / 0.2	-0.61	-6.13	-4.36 / 6	-3.26 / 2	--	0.00	1.42
EM	AMG Trilogy Emerging Mkts Eqty Svc	TLESX	E	(800) 835-3879	E / 0.3	-0.49	-5.98	-3.99 / 7	-3.01 / 2	--	1.51	1.04
GL	AMG Trilogy Global Equity Inst	TLGIX	D+	(800) 835-3879	C- / 4.0	3.17	3.62	4.16 /33	9.80 /38	--	1.50	0.73
GL	AMG Trilogy Global Equity Inv	TLGVX	C	(800) 835-3879	C- / 3.7	3.04	3.34	3.70 /30	9.36 /35	--	0.00	1.23
GL	AMG Trilogy Global Equity Svc	TLGSX	D+	(800) 835-3879	C- / 3.9	3.16	3.51	4.05 /32	9.68 /37	--	1.39	0.83
GR	AMG Trilogy Intl Small Cap Inst	TLSIX	E+	(800) 835-3879	D- / 1.3	4.83	0.62	-7.32 / 4	6.53 /19	--	0.00	1.49
GR	AMG Trilogy Intl Small Cap Inv	TLSVX	E	(800) 835-3879	D- / 1.2	4.76	0.29	-7.82 / 3	6.07 /17	--	0.00	1.99
GR	AMG Trilogy Intl Small Cap Svc	TLSSX	E+	(800) 835-3879	D- / 1.3	4.84	0.71	-7.34 / 4	6.45 /19	--	0.00	1.60
GI	● AMG Yacktman Focused Inst	YAFIX	B	(800) 835-3879	C / 4.8	-2.86	2.11	6.94 /55	12.40 /55	11.65 /58	0.84	1.10
* GI	● AMG Yacktman Focused Svc	YAFFX	C+	(800) 835-3879	C / 4.7	-2.90	2.02	6.78 /53	12.23 /54	11.55 /57	0.66	1.26
* GI	● AMG Yacktman Svc	YACKX	C+	(800) 835-3879	C / 4.9	-3.30	2.02	6.84 /54	12.56 /56	11.83 /59	1.06	0.76
FO	Amidex 35 Israel Mutual A	AMDAX	E	(888) 876-3566	E+ / 0.9	5.29	2.53	0.17 /16	4.56 /12	-1.00 / 2	0.00	3.37
FO	Amidex 35 Israel Mutual C	AMDCX	E+	(888) 876-3566	D- / 1.1	5.11	2.11	-0.60 /14	3.75 /10	-1.76 / 2	0.00	4.12
FO	Amidex 35 Israel Mutual Fd	AMDEX	E+	(888) 876-3566	D- / 1.2	5.28	2.54	0.20 /16	4.56 /12	-0.95 / 2	0.00	3.37
GI	Ancora Equity Fund Class C	ANQCX	D+	(866) 626-2672	C- / 3.7	-1.74	-1.38	3.09 /27	10.98 /45	8.70 /35	0.00	2.72
GI	Ancora Equity Fund I	ANQIX	C-	(866) 626-2672	C- / 4.2	-1.51	-0.98	3.92 /31	11.75 /51	9.37 /39	0.00	1.97
GI	Ancora Income Fund Class C	ANICX	D	(866) 626-2672	D- / 1.4	2.10	3.13	6.24 /48	4.45 /11	5.37 /14	6.72	2.21
GI	Ancora Income Fund Class I	AAIIX	D	(866) 626-2672	D / 1.6	2.29	3.66	7.07 /55	5.08 /13	5.83 /16	7.01	1.71
SC	Ancora Microcap Fund Class C	ANCCX	B-	(866) 626-2672	B / 8.0	-0.30	9.41	8.87 /69	16.72 /88	13.60 /74	0.00	2.59
SC	Ancora Microcap Fund I	ANCIX	B	(866) 626-2672	B+ / 8.7	-0.14	9.92	9.77 /73	17.69 /93	14.37 /81	0.00	1.84
SC	Ancora Special Opportunity Fund C	ANSCX	D+	(866) 626-2672	C+ / 5.6	-0.33	0.35	0.21 /16	14.76 /73	9.31 /39	0.00	3.05
SC	Ancora Special Opportunity Fund I	ANSIX	C-	(866) 626-2672	C+ / 6.2	-0.15	0.74	0.88 /18	15.59 /80	10.03 /45	0.00	2.30
MC	Ancora Thelen Small Mid Cap I	AATIX	U	(866) 626-2672	U /	2.46	10.42	6.73 /53	--		0.96	1.47
AA	Angel Oak Multi Strategy Income A	ANGLX	C+	(877) 625-3042	D+ / 2.5	1.78	2.33	5.07 /39	7.89 /26	--	5.01	1.92
MC	APEXcm Small/Mid Cap Growth	APSGX	U	(888) 575-4800	U /	4.03	6.01	9.04 /69	--		0.00	1.49
GI	API Efficient Frontier Cap Inc A	APIGX	D+	(800) 544-6060	D+ / 2.3	1.47	2.17	2.74 /25	8.90 /32	8.74 /35	1.78	1.87
GI	API Efficient Frontier Cap Inc Inst	AFAAX	C-	(800) 544-6060	C- / 3.5	1.58	2.40	3.25 /28	9.44 /36	9.28 /39	2.30	1.37
GI	API Efficient Frontier Cap Inc L	AFDDX	C-	(800) 544-6060	D+ / 2.9	1.34	1.90	2.23 /23	8.36 /29	8.20 /31	1.50	2.37
GL	API Efficient Frontier Core Inc A	APIMX	D	(800) 544-6060	E+ / 0.6	1.96	-1.32	-0.66 /14	3.01 / 8	3.30 / 7	4.17	1.85
GL	API Efficient Frontier Core Inc L	AFMMX	D	(800) 544-6060	E+ / 0.7	1.70	-1.73	-1.61 /11	1.98 / 6	2.26 / 5	3.84	2.85
GL	API Efficient Frontier Growth A	AFGGX	C	(800) 544-6060	C / 5.5	4.64	8.56	5.87 /45	13.54 /64	12.75 /66	0.00	1.48
GL	API Efficient Frontier Growth L	APITX	C+	(800) 544-6060	C+ / 5.7	4.37	8.02	4.86 /38	12.39 /55	11.62 /58	0.00	2.48
AA	API Efficient Frontier Income Fd I	APIIX	D-	(800) 544-6060	D / 1.6	2.41	-2.11	-1.93 /10	6.47 /19	--	7.62	1.48
GR	API Efficient Frontier Value A	ADVAX	C-	(800) 544-6060	C / 4.3	3.15	4.01	4.54 /35	12.17 /54	9.24 /38	0.00	1.62
GR	API Efficient Frontier Value L	YCVTX	C	(800) 544-6060	C / 4.6	2.86	3.49	3.56 /29	11.16 /47	8.26 /32	0.00	2.52

● Denotes fund is closed to new investors
* Denotes fund is included in Section II

www.thestreetratings.com

RISK			NET ASSETS		ASSET				Portfolio	BULL / BEAR		FUND MANAGER		MINIMUMS		LOADS	
	3 Year		NAV							Last Bull	Last Bear	Manager	Manager	Initial	Additional	Front	Back
Risk Rating/Pts	Standard Deviation	Beta	As of 3/31/15	Total $(Mil)	Cash %	Stocks %	Bonds %	Other %	Turnover Ratio	Market Return	Market Return	Quality Pct	Tenure (Years)	Purch. $	Purch. $	End Load	End Load
C- /3.7	15.1	0.89	26.14	291	8	91	0	1	24	103.7	-23.7	73	12	2,000	100	0.0	2.0
U /	N/A	N/A	13.64	38	8	91	0	1	20	N/A	N/A	N/A	3	1,000	250	0.0	2.0
U /	N/A	N/A	13.94	724	8	91	0	1	20	N/A	N/A	N/A	3	1,000,000	0	0.0	2.0
U /	N/A	N/A	13.88	108	8	91	0	1	20	N/A	N/A	N/A	3	1,000	250	0.0	2.0
C /4.3	10.7	1.07	11.50	31	1	98	0	1	103	97.9	-24.9	38	13	2,500,000	1,000	0.0	0.0
C /4.4	10.7	1.07	11.50	20	1	98	0	1	103	96.1	-25.0	35	13	2,000	100	0.0	0.0
C+/5.7	10.9	0.96	14.19	629	0	99	0	1	153	90.7	-24.8	39	9	1,000,000	1,000	0.0	0.0
C+/5.7	10.9	0.96	14.16	37	0	99	0	1	153	89.0	-24.8	35	9	2,000	100	0.0	0.0
C /5.1	11.9	1.11	16.74	19	4	95	0	1	94	110.2	-22.7	54	5	1,000,000	1,000	0.0	0.0
C /5.1	11.8	1.11	16.50	N/A	4	95	0	1	94	107.1	-22.8	48	5	2,000	100	0.0	0.0
C /5.2	11.8	1.11	16.77	32	4	95	0	1	94	109.3	-22.8	53	5	100,000	100	0.0	0.0
U /	N/A	N/A	12.49	31	1	98	0	1	19	N/A	N/A	N/A	2	5,000,000	100,000	0.0	2.0
C+/5.6	11.3	0.97	19.75	1,527	3	96	0	1	54	104.5	-21.0	68	10	3,000,000	100,000	0.0	0.0
C+/5.6	11.3	0.97	19.43	1,031	3	96	0	1	54	103.2	-21.1	67	10	1,000,000	10,000	0.0	0.0
C /4.3	13.4	0.95	17.96	858	3	96	0	1	61	99.4	-21.5	81	15	5,000,000	100,000	0.0	0.0
C /4.3	13.4	0.95	17.62	299	3	96	0	1	61	98.1	-21.5	80	15	1,000,000	10,000	0.0	0.0
C /5.1	14.2	1.02	8.05	100	4	95	0	1	35	12.1	-27.8	19	4	1,000,000	1,000	0.0	2.0
C+/6.7	14.2	1.02	8.11	N/A	4	95	0	1	35	N/A	N/A	16	4	2,000	100	0.0	2.0
C /5.1	14.2	1.02	8.05	24	4	95	0	1	35	11.7	-27.8	18	4	100,000	100	0.0	2.0
C+/5.6	10.8	0.76	11.07	13	6	93	0	1	49	67.8	-21.5	86	4	1,000,000	1,000	0.0	0.0
B- /7.2	10.8	0.77	11.17	N/A	6	93	0	1	49	N/A	N/A	84	4	2,000	100	0.0	2.0
C+/5.7	10.8	0.76	11.10	59	6	93	0	1	49	67.4	-21.5	86	4	100,000	100	0.0	0.0
C /4.3	14.1	1.11	9.98	11	2	97	0	1	65	51.7	-29.5	2	4	1,000,000	1,000	0.0	2.0
C /4.3	14.1	1.11	9.90	N/A	2	97	0	1	65	49.7	N/A	2	4	2,000	100	0.0	2.0
C /4.3	14.1	1.11	9.97	11	2	97	0	1	65	51.1	-29.5	2	4	100,000	100	0.0	2.0
B /8.7	8.2	0.79	25.14	3,136	0	0	0	100	17	68.7	-9.4	65	18	1,000,000	1,000	0.0	0.0
B- /7.2	8.2	0.79	25.13	7,072	0	0	0	100	17	68.0	-9.4	62	18	2,500	100	0.0	2.0
B- /7.6	8.3	0.81	24.29	13,053	17	82	0	1	17	71.6	-10.2	63	23	2,500	100	0.0	2.0
C /4.7	13.7	0.67	11.75	1	1	98	0	1	12	17.2	-28.8	42	14	500	250	5.5	0.0
C /4.6	13.7	0.67	8.23	1	1	98	0	1	12	14.2	-29.0	32	14	500	250	0.0	0.0
C /4.6	13.7	0.67	15.34	11	1	98	0	1	12	17.3	-28.7	42	14	500	250	0.0	0.0
C+/6.1	11.1	1.11	13.58	6	7	91	0	2	29	72.2	-20.4	6	11	5,000	1,000	0.0	2.0
C+/6.2	11.2	1.11	14.36	2	7	91	0	2	29	76.1	-20.2	8	11	5,000	1,000	0.0	2.0
B- /7.1	3.7	0.08	8.41	14	2	64	32	2	122	19.6	-0.4	89	11	5,000	1,000	0.0	2.0
B- /7.1	3.6	0.08	8.49	14	2	64	32	2	122	21.6	-0.2	91	11	5,000	1,000	0.0	2.0
C /5.0	13.4	0.91	13.37	1	6	93	0	1	23	94.2	-23.1	83	7	5,000	1,000	0.0	2.0
C /5.2	13.4	0.91	14.13	16	6	93	0	1	23	99.3	-22.9	87	7	5,000	1,000	0.0	2.0
C- /3.9	11.0	0.64	6.02	8	5	84	9	2	114	72.2	-18.8	92	11	5,000	1,000	0.0	2.0
C- /4.2	11.0	0.64	6.47	3	5	84	9	2	114	76.3	-18.5	93	11	5,000	1,000	0.0	2.0
U /	N/A	N/A	13.76	56	0	99	0	1	47	N/A	N/A	N/A	2	5,000	1,000	0.0	2.0
B+ /9.5	3.7	0.16	12.13	415	0	0	99	1	62	37.1	N/A	95	4	1,000	0	2.3	0.0
U /	N/A	N/A	16.76	200	5	94	0	1	47	N/A	N/A	N/A	3	2,500	100	0.0	0.0
B- /7.2	9.0	0.85	45.45	6	4	93	1	2	16	54.7	-15.8	14	27	1,000	100	5.8	0.0
B- /7.2	9.0	0.85	46.29	20	4	93	1	2	16	57.4	-15.6	18	27	1,000,000	100,000	0.0	0.0
B- /7.2	9.0	0.85	44.24	13	4	93	1	2	16	52.1	-16.0	12	27	1,000	100	0.0	0.0
B /8.3	4.5	0.22	12.20	5	6	20	73	1	103	13.1	-9.9	77	18	1,000	100	5.8	0.0
B /8.2	4.5	0.21	11.29	16	6	20	73	1	103	9.2	-10.2	67	18	1,000	100	0.0	0.0
C+/6.3	11.5	0.71	15.34	31	2	97	0	1	50	83.5	-21.5	95	30	1,000	100	5.8	0.0
C+/6.2	11.5	0.71	13.60	37	2	97	0	1	50	77.3	-21.9	94	30	1,000	100	0.0	0.0
C+/6.1	7.4	0.96	11.34	201	3	51	44	2	59	36.4	-12.4	19	18	1,000,000	100,000	0.0	0.0
C+/6.5	11.1	1.09	18.67	19	3	96	0	1	25	74.5	-23.7	11	23	1,000	100	5.8	0.0
C+/6.5	11.1	1.09	16.88	10	3	96	0	1	25	69.3	-24.0	7	23	1,000	100	0.0	0.0

Fund Type	Fund Name	Ticker Symbol	Overall Investment Rating	Phone	Performance Rating/Pts	3 Mo	6 Mo	1Yr / Pct	3Yr / Pct	5Yr / Pct	Dividend Yield	Expense Ratio
AA	API Master Allocation Fund A	APIFX	C-	(800) 544-6060	C- / 3.3	2.90	4.36	3.31 /28	10.31 /41	8.95 /36	0.00	2.63
AA	API Master Allocation Fund L	APILX	C-	(800) 544-6060	C- / 3.8	2.79	4.14	2.81 /25	9.77 /38	8.41 /33	0.00	3.13
GL	Appleseed Fund Institutional	APPIX	D-	(800) 408-4682	D / 2.1	2.67	1.11	-0.94 /13	7.75 /26	--	0.10	1.18
GL	Appleseed Fund Investor	APPLX	E+	(800) 408-4682	D / 1.9	2.60	1.01	-1.11 /13	7.51 /24	6.19 /18	0.00	1.43
GR	Appleton Equity Growth		C	(866) 993-7767	C / 5.3	4.37	5.33	7.86 /62	11.49 /49	11.62 /58	0.00	2.67
GR	Appleton Group PLUS	AGPLX	D+	(866) 993-7767	D- / 1.5	1.53	0.83	2.67 /25	5.26 /14	2.09 / 5	0.44	2.02
GR	● AQR Diversified Arbitrage I	ADAIX	D	(866) 290-2688	E / 0.4	0.10	-3.74	-6.01 / 4	-0.99 / 3	0.83 / 3	1.94	1.71
GR	● AQR Diversified Arbitrage N	ADANX	D	(866) 290-2688	E / 0.3	0.00	-3.82	-6.19 / 4	-1.23 / 3	0.55 / 3	1.69	1.95
EM	AQR Emerging Defensive Style I	AZEIX	U	(866) 290-2688	U /	-1.55	-7.22	-4.38 / 6	--	--	1.86	1.22
GL	AQR Global Equity Fund I	AQGIX	D-	(866) 290-2688	C+ / 6.8	5.11	6.43	7.15 /56	14.15 /68	11.37 /56	1.60	1.14
GL	AQR Global Equity Fund N	AQGNX	D-	(866) 290-2688	C+ / 6.6	5.02	6.27	6.87 /54	13.79 /66	11.02 /53	1.53	1.59
GL	AQR Global Equity Fund R6	AQGRX	U	(866) 290-2688	U /	5.21	6.56	7.40 /58	--	--	1.72	0.73
GL	AQR Global Equity Fund Y	AQGYX	D	(866) 290-2688	B- / 7.1	5.21	6.49	7.57 /60	14.59 /72	11.79 /59	1.89	0.54
GL	AQR Global Macro I	QGMIX	U	(866) 290-2688	U /	2.82	3.95	--	--	--	0.00	1.84
GR	AQR International Def Style I	ANDIX	U	(866) 290-2688	U /	2.61	0.42	1.99 /22	--	--	2.62	1.22
FO	AQR International Equity Fund I	AQIIX	D-	(866) 290-2688	C- / 3.5	5.59	2.94	-2.39 /10	9.76 /38	6.76 /22	3.04	0.90
FO	AQR International Equity N	AQINX	D-	(866) 290-2688	C- / 3.3	5.59	2.88	-2.62 / 9	9.42 /36	6.39 /19	2.71	1.23
FO	AQR International Equity R6	AQIRX	U	(866) 290-2688	U /	5.68	3.12	-2.13 /10	--	--	3.01	0.74
FO	AQR International Equity Y	AQIYX	D	(866) 290-2688	C- / 3.8	5.77	3.26	-1.91 /11	10.19 /40	7.17 /24	3.22	0.54
FO	AQR International Momentum Style I	AIMOX	D	(866) 290-2688	D+ / 2.5	4.41	-0.17	-2.96 / 9	8.33 /29	5.55 /14	2.14	0.71
FO	AQR International Momentum Style N	AIONX	U	(866) 290-2688	U /	4.35	-0.30	-3.23 / 8	--	--	1.88	1.00
FO	AQR International Momentum Style	QIORX	U	(866) 290-2688	U /	4.50	-0.06	--	--	--	0.00	0.64
GR	AQR International Multi-Style I	QICLX	U	(866) 290-2688	U /	3.65	-1.09	-2.28 /10	--	--	1.70	1.40
GR	AQR International Multi-Style R6	QICRX	U	(866) 290-2688	U /	3.75	-0.98	--	--	--	0.00	1.36
GI	AQR Large Cap Defensive Style I	AUEIX	U	(866) 290-2688	U /	3.04	11.15	16.53 /94	--	--	1.87	0.57
GR	AQR Large Cap Momentum Style I	AMOMX	B+	(866) 290-2688	B+ / 8.8	3.14	7.05	11.48 /80	16.94 /89	14.62 /83	0.58	0.55
GR	AQR Large Cap Momentum Style N	AMONX	U	(866) 290-2688	U /	3.05	6.87	11.14 /79	--	--	0.32	0.83
GR	AQR Large Cap Momentum Style R6	QMORX	U	(866) 290-2688	U /	3.10	7.07	--	--	--	0.00	0.48
GR	AQR Large Cap Multi-Style I	QCELX	U	(866) 290-2688	U /	1.51	6.52	12.22 /84	--	--	0.40	0.73
GR	AQR Large Cap Multi-Style N	QCENX	U	(866) 290-2688	U /	1.44	6.41	12.03 /83	--	--	0.35	1.16
GR	AQR Large Cap Multi-Style R6	QCERX	U	(866) 290-2688	U /	1.51	6.57	--	--	--	0.00	0.63
GR	AQR Long Short Equity I	QLEIX	U	(866) 290-2688	U /	3.68	10.08	16.73 /94	--	--	6.81	3.65
GL	AQR Managed Futures Strat HV I	QMHIX	U	(866) 290-2688	U /	13.00	29.71	42.81 /99	--	--	6.66	2.58
GL	AQR Managed Futures Strat HV R6	QMHRX	U	(866) 290-2688	U /	13.00	29.76	--	--	--	0.00	2.52
IN	AQR Managed Futures Strategy I	AQMIX	A+	(866) 290-2688	B+ / 8.8	8.56	19.19	26.74 /99	10.56 /43	5.97 /17	3.97	1.34
IN	AQR Managed Futures Strategy N	AQMNX	A+	(866) 290-2688	B+ / 8.6	8.54	19.01	26.37 /99	10.28 /41	5.70 /15	3.72	1.61
GL	AQR Multi-Strategy Alternative R6	QSARX	U	(866) 290-2688	U /	2.15	7.39	--	--	--	0.00	3.30
OT	AQR Risk Bal Commodities Strat I	ARCIX	U	(866) 290-2688	U /	-8.02	-17.48	-30.07 / 0	--	--	0.00	1.40
AA	● AQR Risk Parity I	AQRIX	D	(866) 290-2688	C- / 3.3	4.73	4.71	8.97 /69	7.02 /21	--	3.76	0.95
GL	AQR Risk Parity II HV I	QRHIX	U	(866) 290-2688	U /	5.45	5.07	10.05 /74	--	--	0.49	1.91
GL	AQR Risk Parity II MV I	QRMIX	U	(866) 290-2688	U /	3.54	3.38	6.48 /50	--	--	0.16	1.23
AA	● AQR Risk Parity N	AQRNX	D	(866) 290-2688	C- / 3.0	4.64	4.45	8.51 /66	6.70 /20	--	3.35	1.26
SC	AQR Small Cap Momentum Style I	ASMOX	B+	(866) 290-2688	A / 9.3	4.91	14.41	6.86 /54	18.30 /95	16.34 /94	0.15	0.72
GL	AQR Style Premia Alternative I	QSPIX	U	(866) 290-2688	U /	-2.54	4.63	7.84 /62	--	--	12.95	2.15
GL	AQR Style Premia Alternative N	QSPNX	U	(866) 290-2688	U /	-2.63	4.52	7.52 /59	--	--	12.62	2.74
GL	AQR Style Premia Alternative R6	QSPRX	U	(866) 290-2688	U /	-2.53	4.74	--	--	--	0.00	2.15
FO	AQR TM Intl Momentum Style I	ATIMX	D+	(866) 290-2688	D+ / 2.7	3.92	-0.45	-3.26 / 8	8.82 /32	--	1.99	0.88
FO	AQR TM Intl Momentum Style R6	QTIRX	U	(866) 290-2688	U /	4.01	-0.32	--	--	--	0.00	0.91
GR	AQR TM Lg Cap Momentum Style I	ATMOX	A+	(866) 290-2688	B+ / 8.8	2.79	6.53	12.17 /83	16.98 /90	--	0.48	0.64
GR	AQR TM Lg Cap Momentum Style R6	QTMRX	U	(866) 290-2688	U /	2.73	6.54	--	--	--	0.00	0.62
SC	AQR TM SC Momentum Style I	ATSMX	B+	(866) 290-2688	A- / 9.2	4.91	14.24	5.89 /45	17.77 /93	--	0.09	1.61
IN	Aquila Three Peaks Oppty Gro A	ATGAX	A+	(800) 437-1020	A+ / 9.8	8.01	12.35	20.73 /97	23.71 /99	18.49 /98	0.00	1.91

● Denotes fund is closed to new investors
* Denotes fund is included in Section II

RISK			NET ASSETS		ASSET					BULL / BEAR		FUND MANAGER		MINIMUMS		LOADS	
	3 Year		NAV						Portfolio	Last Bull	Last Bear	Manager	Manager	Initial	Additional	Front	Back
Risk Rating/Pts	Standard Deviation	Beta	As of 3/31/15	Total $(Mil)	Cash %	Stocks %	Bonds %	Other %	Turnover Ratio	Market Return	Market Return	Quality Pct	Tenure (Years)	Purch. $	Purch. $	End Load	End Load
C+ / 6.7	10.2	1.68	38.02	10	3	96	0	1	3	64.0	-20.7	4	6	1,000	100	5.8	0.0
C+ / 6.7	10.3	1.69	36.90	30	3	96	0	1	3	61.2	-20.8	3	6	1,000	100	0.0	0.0
C / 4.8	9.9	0.59	12.70	113	10	73	16	1	53	41.1	-11.7	85	9	100,000	0	0.0	2.0
C / 4.8	10.0	0.59	12.64	144	10	73	16	1	53	40.1	-11.8	83	9	2,500	0	0.0	2.0
C+ / 6.2	10.4	1.02	11.45	19	1	98	0	1	34	73.1	-18.0	14	15	1,000	0	0.0	0.0
B- / 7.7	7.2	0.61	10.60	35	10	89	0	1	191	29.9	-17.1	16	10	2,500	0	0.0	0.0
B- / 7.7	2.3	0.05	10.16	1,463	15	22	33	30	349	-0.5	-0.5	40	6	5,000,000	0	0.0	0.0
B- / 7.8	2.3	0.05	10.12	351	15	22	33	30	349	-1.4	-0.7	37	6	1,000,000	0	0.0	0.0
U /	N/A	N/A	9.53	88	0	98	1	1	181	N/A	N/A	N/A	3	5,000,000	0	0.0	0.0
D- / 1.2	11.5	0.82	8.44	1	8	85	6	1	71	82.6	-23.7	95	6	5,000,000	0	0.0	0.0
D- / 1.2	11.4	0.82	8.37	1	8	85	6	1	71	80.7	-23.8	94	6	1,000,000	0	0.0	0.0
U /	N/A	N/A	8.48	81	8	85	6	1	71	N/A	N/A	N/A	6	50,000,000	0	0.0	0.0
D- / 1.2	11.4	0.82	8.48	226	8	85	6	1	71	85.0	-23.6	95	6	10,000,000	0	0.0	0.1
U /	N/A	N/A	10.22	38	0	0	0	100	0	N/A	N/A	N/A	1	5,000,000	0	0.0	0.0
U /	N/A	N/A	11.81	31	1	98	0	1	115	N/A	N/A	N/A	3	5,000,000	0	0.0	0.0
C- / 4.2	14.4	1.07	10.39	318	11	81	7	1	59	57.5	-28.0	62	6	5,000,000	0	0.0	0.0
C- / 4.2	14.3	1.06	10.58	40	11	81	7	1	59	55.4	-28.1	57	6	1,000,000	0	0.0	0.0
U /	N/A	N/A	10.98	41	11	81	7	1	59	N/A	N/A	N/A	6	50,000,000	0	0.0	0.0
C / 4.3	14.3	1.07	10.99	412	11	81	7	1	59	59.4	-27.9	67	6	10,000,000	0	0.0	0.1
C+ / 5.7	12.2	0.87	14.43	266	2	95	2	1	76	47.3	-26.9	68	6	5,000,000	0	0.0	0.0
U /	N/A	N/A	14.39	42	2	95	2	1	76	N/A	N/A	N/A	6	1,000,000	0	0.0	0.0
U /	N/A	N/A	14.41	30	2	95	2	1	76	N/A	N/A	N/A	6	50,000,000	0	0.0	0.0
U /	N/A	N/A	11.07	31	1	98	0	1	218	N/A	N/A	N/A	2	5,000,000	0	0.0	0.0
U /	N/A	N/A	11.06	59	1	98	0	1	218	N/A	N/A	N/A	2	50,000,000	0	0.0	0.0
U /	N/A	N/A	14.91	139	3	92	4	1	106	N/A	N/A	N/A	3	5,000,000	0	0.0	0.0
C+ / 6.1	9.9	0.93	21.33	969	0	98	1	1	62	102.9	-20.7	83	6	5,000,000	0	0.0	0.0
U /	N/A	N/A	21.31	85	0	98	1	1	62	N/A	N/A	N/A	6	1,000,000	0	0.0	0.0
U /	N/A	N/A	21.29	51	0	98	1	1	62	N/A	N/A	N/A	6	50,000,000	0	0.0	0.0
U /	N/A	N/A	14.12	428	0	99	0	1	233	N/A	N/A	N/A	2	5,000,000	0	0.0	0.0
U /	N/A	N/A	14.08	55	0	99	0	1	233	N/A	N/A	N/A	2	1,000,000	0	0.0	0.0
U /	N/A	N/A	14.11	134	0	99	0	1	233	N/A	N/A	N/A	2	50,000,000	0	0.0	0.0
U /	N/A	N/A	11.27	65	0	0	0	100	0	N/A	N/A	N/A	2	5,000,000	0	0.0	0.0
U /	N/A	N/A	12.69	192	0	0	0	100	0	N/A	N/A	N/A	2	5,000,000	0	0.0	0.0
U /	N/A	N/A	12.69	52	0	0	0	100	0	N/A	N/A	N/A	2	50,000,000	0	0.0	0.0
B / 8.3	9.3	-0.16	11.54	6,834	76	0	23	1	0	25.2	-5.4	99	5	5,000,000	0	0.0	0.0
B / 8.2	9.3	-0.16	11.44	1,471	76	0	23	1	0	24.0	-5.4	99	5	1,000,000	0	0.0	0.0
U /	N/A	N/A	9.97	56	76	0	3	21	137	N/A	N/A	N/A	4	50,000,000	0	0.0	0.0
U /	N/A	N/A	6.42	46	100	0	0	0	0	N/A	N/A	N/A	3	5,000,000	0	0.0	0.0
C / 5.5	9.0	1.03	10.62	635	44	0	56	0	167	34.2	-6.5	17	5	5,000,000	0	0.0	0.0
U /	N/A	N/A	10.07	53	10	0	89	1	257	N/A	N/A	N/A	5	5,000,000	0	0.0	0.0
U /	N/A	N/A	10.25	93	35	0	64	1	234	N/A	N/A	N/A	3	5,000,000	0	0.0	0.0
C+ / 5.6	9.1	1.03	10.61	38	44	0	56	0	167	33.0	-6.6	15	5	1,000,000	0	0.0	0.0
C / 4.8	14.0	1.02	21.60	424	0	97	2	1	49	115.6	-26.2	80	6	5,000,000	0	0.0	0.0
U /	N/A	N/A	9.61	535	0	0	0	100	0	N/A	N/A	N/A	2	5,000,000	0	0.0	0.0
U /	N/A	N/A	9.61	32	0	0	0	100	0	N/A	N/A	N/A	2	1,000,000	0	0.0	0.0
U /	N/A	N/A	9.62	114	0	0	0	100	0	N/A	N/A	N/A	2	50,000,000	0	0.0	0.0
C+ / 6.7	12.3	0.88	12.71	22	0	98	0	2	154	N/A	N/A	72	3	5,000,000	0	0.0	0.0
U /	N/A	N/A	12.71	43	0	98	0	2	154	N/A	N/A	N/A	3	50,000,000	0	0.0	0.0
B- / 7.1	9.8	0.93	16.58	51	0	99	0	1	178	N/A	N/A	83	3	5,000,000	0	0.0	0.0
U /	N/A	N/A	16.57	80	0	99	0	1	178	N/A	N/A	N/A	3	50,000,000	0	0.0	0.0
C / 5.5	14.0	1.02	16.23	20	0	98	1	1	81	N/A	N/A	77	3	5,000,000	0	0.0	0.0
C+ / 6.3	10.1	0.96	47.19	91	5	94	0	1	33	129.9	-21.0	96	12	1,000	0	4.3	2.0

					PERFORMANCE							
					Perfor-mance Rating/Pts	Total Return % through 3/31/15					Incl. in Returns	
			Overall						Annualized		Dividend	Expense
Fund Type	Fund Name	Ticker Symbol	Investment Rating	Phone		3 Mo	6 Mo	1Yr / Pct	3Yr / Pct	5Yr / Pct	Yield	Ratio
IN	Aquila Three Peaks Oppty Gro C	ATGCX	A+	(800) 437-1020	A+ / 9.9	7.84	11.97	19.85 /97	22.82 /98	17.63 /97	0.00	2.53
IN	Aquila Three Peaks Oppty Gro I	ATRIX	A+	(800) 437-1020	A+ / 9.9	8.03	12.43	20.90 /97	24.03 /99	18.85 /98	0.00	1.81
IN	Aquila Three Peaks Oppty Gro Y	ATGYX	A+	(800) 437-1020	A+ / 9.9	8.10	12.52	21.10 /97	24.10 /99	18.85 /98	0.00	1.55
AA	AR 529 Gift College Inv Csv Gr		C	(800) 662-7447	D / 1.7	1.75	3.62	5.71 /44	4.97 /13	5.73 /15	0.00	0.75
AA	AR 529 Gift College Inv Gr		C+	(800) 662-7447	C / 4.3	2.11	4.26	6.92 /54	10.16 /40	9.52 /41	0.00	0.75
BA	AR 529 Gift College Inv Mod Gr		C+	(800) 662-7447	D+ / 2.9	1.94	3.95	6.37 /50	7.56 /24	7.70 /28	0.00	0.75
GR	Arbitrage Event-Driven I	AEDNX	D	(800) 295-4485	E / 0.5	0.31	-1.82	-1.72 /11	1.25 / 5	--	0.92	2.11
GR	Arbitrage Event-Driven R	AEDFX	D	(800) 295-4485	E / 0.5	0.21	-1.97	-1.97 /10	1.00 / 5	--	0.78	2.36
GR	Arbitrage Fund (The) - C	ARBCX	U	(800) 295-4485	U /	0.88	1.62	2.28 /23	--	--	0.00	2.92
GI	Arbitrage Fund (The) - Instl	ARBNX	D+	(800) 295-4485	E+ / 0.7	1.15	2.17	3.37 /28	1.21 / 5	1.81 / 4	0.00	1.92
GI	Arbitrage Fund (The) - Retail	ARBFX	D+	(800) 295-4485	E+ / 0.6	1.02	1.98	3.12 /27	0.96 / 5	1.55 / 4	0.00	2.17
BA	Archer Balanced Fund	ARCHX	B	(800) 494-2755	C+ / 5.8	2.41	7.71	14.51 /91	11.25 /47	8.45 /33	1.42	1.93
IN	Archer Stock Fund	ARSKX	B+	(800) 494-2755	B / 8.2	6.30	9.63	12.41 /84	15.50 /79	--	0.00	2.00
AA	Arden Alternative Strategies I	ARDNX	U	(866) 773-7145	U /	3.02	3.02	2.12 /22	--	--	0.00	3.85
GL	Arden Alternative Strategies II I	IARDX	U	(866) 773-7145	U /	2.76	3.27	1.66 /21	--	--	0.00	6.43
MC	Ariel Appreciation Fund Inst	CAAIX	A+	(800) 292-7435	A+ / 9.7	4.41	12.25	14.32 /90	19.56 /97	--	0.90	0.79
MC	Ariel Appreciation Fund Investor	CAAPX	A-	(800) 292-7435	A+ / 9.7	4.34	12.05	13.93 /89	19.21 /97	15.28 /89	0.60	1.12
SC	Ariel Discovery Institutional	ADYIX	E+	(800) 292-7435	D- / 1.4	-4.15	4.42	-10.77 / 3	7.17 /22	--	0.00	1.25
GL	Ariel Discovery Investor	ARDFX	E	(800) 292-7435	D- / 1.3	-4.18	4.37	-10.93 / 3	6.92 /21	--	0.00	1.93
SC	Ariel Focus Institutional	AFOYX	B-	(800) 292-7435	C+ / 5.8	-2.13	1.40	5.59 /43	13.75 /65	--	0.98	1.06
GR	Ariel Focus Investor	ARFFX	C	(800) 292-7435	C+ / 5.6	-2.20	1.31	5.28 /41	13.47 /63	10.77 /51	0.70	1.40
SC	Ariel Fund Institutional	ARAIX	A+	(800) 292-7435	A+ / 9.8	6.77	15.94	19.89 /97	21.99 /98	--	0.72	0.72
SC	Ariel Fund Investor	ARGFX	A+	(800) 292-7435	A+ / 9.8	6.67	15.76	19.54 /96	21.60 /98	16.12 /94	0.46	1.03
GL	Ariel Global Institutional	AGLYX	B-	(800) 292-7435	C / 5.1	2.98	2.54	6.00 /46	11.86 /51	--	1.32	1.51
GL	Ariel Global Investor	AGLOX	B-	(800) 292-7435	C / 4.9	2.91	2.38	5.71 /44	11.56 /49	--	0.00	3.70
FO	Ariel International Institutional	AINIX	C-	(800) 292-7435	C- / 3.4	5.57	3.05	0.99 /18	9.08 /33	--	1.82	3.17
FO	Ariel International Investor	AINTX	C-	(800) 292-7435	C- / 3.3	5.55	2.89	0.78 /18	8.81 /32	--	1.02	4.24
GL	Aristotle/Saul Glbl Opportunities I	ARSOX	D-	(888) 661-6691	E+ / 0.8	1.32	-2.24	-6.59 / 4	4.33 /11	--	1.93	2.54
GR	Arrow Alter Soltns A	ASFFX	D-	(877) 277-6933	E / 0.4	1.31	2.88	3.54 /29	-0.73 / 4	-0.99 / 2	0.45	2.60
GR	Arrow Alter Soltns C	ASFTX	D-	(877) 277-6933	E / 0.4	1.11	2.49	2.76 /25	-1.48 / 3	-1.74 / 2	0.26	3.35
IN	Arrow Alter Soltns Institutional	ASFNX	D	(877) 277-6933	E / 0.5	1.34	2.95	3.73 /30	-0.50 / 4	--	0.55	2.35
IN	Arrow Commodity Strategy A	CSFFX	E-	(877) 277-6933	E- / 0.0	-5.96	-18.30	-25.54 / 0	-12.98 / 1	--	2.44	2.45
IN	Arrow Commodity Strategy C	CSFTX	E-	(877) 277-6933	E- / 0.1	-6.12	-18.70	-26.16 / 0	-13.66 / 1	--	2.40	3.20
OT	Arrow Commodity Strategy Inst	CSFNX	D-	(877) 277-6933	E- / 0.1	-5.82	-18.21	-25.33 / 0	-12.73 / 1	--	3.56	2.20
AA	Arrow DWA Balanced A	DWAFX	D	(877) 277-6933	D / 1.8	2.79	5.56	4.91 /38	7.20 /22	7.10 /24	1.49	1.81
AA	Arrow DWA Balanced C	DWATX	D	(877) 277-6933	D / 2.1	2.58	5.19	4.08 /32	6.40 /18	6.30 /19	0.90	2.56
BA	Arrow DWA Balanced Institutional	DWANX	C-	(877) 277-6933	D+ / 2.7	2.85	5.71	5.13 /40	7.45 /24	--	1.85	1.56
AA	Arrow DWA Tactical A	DWTFX	C	(877) 277-6933	C- / 3.9	1.47	7.01	6.60 /52	11.25 /47	8.00 /30	0.19	1.86
AA	Arrow DWA Tactical C	DWTTX	C	(877) 277-6933	C / 4.3	1.24	6.55	5.71 /44	10.42 /42	7.21 /24	0.00	2.61
AA	Arrow DWA Tactical Inst	DWTNX	C+	(877) 277-6933	C / 5.0	1.56	7.10	6.79 /53	11.53 /49	--	0.49	1.62
GI	Arrow Managed Futures Strategy A	MFTFX	D	(877) 277-6933	E+ / 0.6	3.63	13.40	9.59 /72	0.15 / 4	--	0.00	2.22
GI	Arrow Managed Futures Strategy C	MFTTX	D	(877) 277-6933	E+ / 0.7	3.51	13.03	8.86 /68	-0.63 / 4	--	0.00	2.97
GL	Arrow Managed Futures Strategy Inst	MFTNX	C-	(877) 277-6933	E+ / 0.9	3.71	13.55	9.76 /73	0.44 / 5	--	0.00	1.97
EM	Artisan Emerging Markets Inst	APHEX	E	(800) 344-1770	E / 0.3	0.42	-3.34	-2.33 /10	-2.21 / 3	-2.31 / 2	1.48	1.21
EM	Artisan Emerging Markets Inv	ARTZX	E	(800) 344-1770	E / 0.3	0.50	-3.32	-2.47 / 9	-2.47 / 3	-2.58 / 1	0.80	1.53
GL	Artisan Global Equity Inv	ARTHX	A-	(800) 344-1770	B+ / 8.5	5.18	8.60	8.67 /67	17.03 /90	14.76 /85	0.00	1.46
GR	Artisan Global Opportunities Fd Inv	ARTRX	B-	(800) 344-1770	C+ / 5.7	5.20	4.21	7.80 /61	12.85 /58	14.70 /84	0.29	1.20
GR	Artisan Global Opportunities Inst	APHRX	B-	(800) 344-1770	C+ / 5.9	5.29	4.31	8.00 /63	13.12 /61	--	0.56	0.97
GL	Artisan Global Small Cap Investor	ARTWX	U	(800) 344-1770	U /	5.59	2.12	-8.91 / 3	--	--	0.15	1.55
GL	● Artisan Global Value Inst	APHGX	U	(800) 344-1770	U /	0.52	3.11	3.91 /31	--	--	0.70	1.06
GL	● Artisan Global Value Inv	ARTGX	B-	(800) 344-1770	C+ / 5.9	0.52	3.09	3.69 /30	14.50 /71	12.97 /68	0.49	1.32
FO	Artisan International Fund Inst	APHIX	C+	(800) 344-1770	C / 5.1	4.28	4.84	5.36 /41	12.19 /54	10.55 /49	0.91	0.95

RISK Rating/Pts	3 Year Standard Deviation	Beta	NAV As of 3/31/15	Total $(Mil)	Cash %	Stocks %	Bonds %	Other %	Portfolio Turnover Ratio	Last Bull Market Return	Last Bear Market Return	Manager Quality Pct	Manager Tenure (Years)	Initial Purch. $	Additional Purch. $	Front End Load	Back End Load
C+ / 6.3	10.1	0.96	40.30	30	5	94	0	1	33	124.2	-21.2	95	12	1,000	0	0.0	0.0
C+ / 6.3	10.1	0.96	48.55	7	5	94	0	1	33	132.1	-20.8	96	12	0	0	0.0	2.0
C+ / 6.3	10.1	0.96	49.76	141	5	94	0	1	33	132.4	-20.9	96	12	0	0	0.0	2.0
B+ / 9.7	3.2	0.44	15.74	53	0	24	74	2	0	22.9	-1.9	70	10	25	10	0.0	0.0
B / 8.3	7.5	1.29	18.86	55	0	74	24	2	0	58.4	-14.2	19	10	25	10	0.0	0.0
B+ / 9.3	5.1	0.86	17.36	82	0	49	49	2	0	39.9	-8.3	42	10	25	10	0.0	0.0
B / 8.2	2.8	0.18	9.81	408	34	39	24	3	340	13.6	-4.3	46	5	100,000	0	0.0	2.0
B / 8.2	2.8	0.17	9.73	203	34	39	24	3	340	12.5	-4.2	42	5	2,000	0	0.0	2.0
U /	N/A	N/A	12.58	32	50	49	0	1	462	N/A	N/A	N/A	15	2,000	0	0.0	0.0
B / 8.7	2.5	0.06	13.19	1,509	50	49	0	1	462	5.6	1.7	70	15	100,000	0	0.0	2.0
B / 8.7	2.5	0.06	12.88	505	50	49	0	1	462	4.6	1.7	67	15	2,000	0	0.0	2.0
B / 8.0	6.9	1.18	11.88	26	7	71	21	1	35	57.4	-10.7	45	10	2,500	100	0.0	0.5
C+ / 6.6	11.6	1.09	43.36	13	2	97	0	1	68	89.8	-23.5	38	4	2,500	100	0.0	1.0
U /	N/A	N/A	9.88	1,003	65	21	12	2	404	N/A	N/A	N/A	3	1,000	500	0.0	0.0
U /	N/A	N/A	10.04	77	0	0	0	100	251	N/A	N/A	N/A	1	100,000	1,000	0.0	0.0
C+ / 6.9	13.4	1.12	56.06	206	5	94	0	1	24	N/A	N/A	70	13	1,000,000	100	0.0	0.0
C / 5.4	13.4	1.12	55.97	1,907	5	94	0	1	24	122.0	-24.9	66	13	1,000	100	0.0	0.0
C / 4.8	16.3	1.08	11.56	33	7	92	0	1	36	N/A	N/A	2	4	1,000,000	100	0.0	0.0
C- / 3.8	16.3	0.56	11.45	8	7	92	0	1	36	62.5	-24.3	81	4	1,000	100	0.0	0.0
B- / 7.3	12.3	0.75	13.77	13	0	99	0	1	40	N/A	N/A	82	10	1,000,000	100	0.0	0.0
C+ / 6.2	12.3	1.18	13.78	53	0	99	0	1	40	82.4	-17.3	10	10	1,000	100	0.0	0.0
C+ / 6.6	13.9	0.96	76.68	634	7	92	0	1	29	N/A	N/A	94	29	1,000,000	100	0.0	0.0
C+ / 5.9	13.9	0.96	76.61	1,942	7	92	0	1	29	138.1	-31.1	94	29	1,000	100	0.0	0.0
B / 8.0	10.4	0.71	13.81	55	0	0	0	100	20	N/A	N/A	93	4	1,000,000	100	0.0	0.0
B / 8.0	10.3	0.71	14.15	5	0	0	0	100	20	N/A	N/A	92	4	1,000	100	0.0	0.0
B- / 7.0	12.2	0.88	12.51	9	10	89	0	1	19	N/A	N/A	74	4	1,000,000	100	0.0	0.0
B- / 7.0	12.3	0.89	12.75	5	10	89	0	1	19	N/A	N/A	71	4	1,000	100	0.0	0.0
B- / 7.1	10.6	0.76	10.70	52	9	81	9	1	24	N/A	N/A	29	3	2,500	100	0.0	1.0
B- / 7.2	4.6	0.29	8.11	8	16	0	83	1	800	2.6	-7.3	9	8	5,000	250	5.8	1.0
B- / 7.1	4.5	0.28	7.82	1	16	0	83	1	800	N/A	-7.6	7	8	5,000	250	0.0	1.0
B- / 7.8	4.5	0.29	8.16	18	16	0	83	1	800	N/A	N/A	11	8	1,000,000	0	0.0	1.0
C- / 3.6	12.5	0.66	6.15	2	27	0	72	1	834	-27.3	-20.3	0	5	5,000	250	5.8	1.0
C- / 3.6	12.5	0.66	5.98	N/A	27	0	72	1	834	-29.2	-20.5	0	5	5,000	250	0.0	1.0
C+ / 6.8	12.5	0.66	6.15	4	27	0	72	1	834	N/A	N/A	0	5	1,000,000	0	0.0	1.0
C+ / 6.5	7.3	1.22	13.63	105	0	72	27	1	106	37.7	-13.0	7	9	5,000	250	5.8	1.0
C+ / 6.6	7.2	1.22	13.10	108	0	72	27	1	106	34.3	-13.3	6	9	5,000	250	0.0	1.0
B- / 7.6	7.3	1.22	13.69	40	0	72	27	1	106	N/A	N/A	8	9	1,000,000	0	0.0	1.0
B- / 7.3	9.0	1.48	11.07	79	0	99	0	1	123	46.9	-18.4	12	7	5,000	250	5.8	1.0
B- / 7.3	9.1	1.50	10.63	69	0	99	0	1	123	43.2	-18.6	8	7	5,000	250	0.0	1.0
B- / 7.1	9.0	1.49	11.08	106	0	99	0	1	123	N/A	N/A	13	7	1,000,000	0	0.0	1.0
B- / 7.9	7.6	-0.13	9.14	3	28	0	71	1	175	-11.3	-9.6	84	5	5,000	250	5.8	1.0
B- / 7.7	7.5	-0.12	8.85	1	28	0	71	1	175	-13.5	-9.9	78	5	5,000	250	0.0	1.0
B+ / 9.0	7.5	-0.10	9.22	3	28	0	71	1	175	N/A	N/A	79	5	1,000,000	0	0.0	1.0
C / 4.9	14.8	1.07	11.94	168	1	98	0	1	32	12.5	-30.9	26	9	1,000,000	0	0.0	2.0
C / 4.8	14.8	1.07	12.03	40	1	98	0	1	32	11.3	-31.0	23	9	1,000	0	0.0	2.0
C+ / 6.6	11.2	0.72	17.05	262	0	95	3	2	89	99.5	-20.0	98	5	1,000	0	0.0	2.0
B- / 7.3	11.6	0.96	19.21	664	0	0	0	100	45	83.4	-19.9	34	7	1,000	0	0.0	2.0
B- / 7.3	11.5	0.95	19.30	509	0	0	0	100	45	84.9	N/A	39	7	1,000,000	0	0.0	2.0
U /	N/A	N/A	11.14	126	4	90	5	1	72	N/A	N/A	N/A	2	1,000	0	0.0	2.0
U /	N/A	N/A	15.60	609	0	0	0	100	25	N/A	N/A	N/A	8	1,000,000	0	0.0	2.0
B- / 7.8	9.7	0.65	15.59	1,286	0	0	0	100	25	85.2	-14.8	97	8	1,000	0	0.0	2.0
C+ / 6.9	11.7	0.84	31.44	4,149	0	0	0	100	46	80.0	-24.1	91	20	1,000,000	0	0.0	2.0

	99 Pct = Best 0 Pct = Worst				**PERFORMANCE**								
					Perfor-mance	Total Return % through 3/31/15						Incl. in Returns	
										Annualized		Dividend	Expense
Fund Type	Fund Name	Ticker Symbol	Overall Investment Rating	Phone	Rating/Pts	3 Mo	6 Mo	1Yr / Pct	3Yr / Pct	5Yr / Pct		Yield	Ratio
* FO	Artisan International Fund Inv	ARTIX	C	(800) 344-1770	C / 4.9	4.24	4.74	5.16 /40	11.95 /52	10.30 /47		0.73	1.17
FO ●	Artisan International Small Cap Inv	ARTJX	D-	(800) 344-1770	C- / 3.2	4.76	2.72	-9.92 / 3	10.89 /45	9.68 /42		0.00	1.50
FO ●	Artisan International Value Inst	APHKX	C+	(800) 344-1770	C+ / 6.0	3.73	3.75	3.05 /27	14.29 /69	12.07 /61		1.67	1.00
* FO ●	Artisan International Value Inv	ARTKX	C+	(800) 344-1770	C+ / 5.8	3.65	3.63	2.84 /26	14.06 /68	11.85 /60		1.47	1.20
MC ●	Artisan Mid Cap Fund Inst	APHMX	C+	(800) 344-1770	B- / 7.2	3.86	9.72	7.31 /57	14.52 /71	17.18 /96		0.00	0.95
MC ●	Artisan Mid Cap Fund Inv	ARTMX	C+	(800) 344-1770	B- / 7.0	3.81	9.59	7.06 /55	14.24 /69	16.87 /96		0.00	1.20
MC ●	Artisan Mid Cap Value Institutional	APHQX	B-	(800) 344-1770	C / 5.4	2.11	3.71	2.02 /22	12.99 /60	--		0.88	0.95
* MC ●	Artisan Mid Cap Value Inv	ARTQX	C	(800) 344-1770	C / 5.3	2.03	3.58	1.77 /21	12.72 /58	13.07 /69		0.61	1.19
SC ●	Artisan Small Cap Fund Inst	APHSX	U	(800) 344-1770	U /	2.41	12.55	1.89 /21	--	--		0.00	1.00
SC ●	Artisan Small Cap Fund Inv	ARTSX	D+	(800) 344-1770	C+ / 6.1	2.35	12.41	1.69 /21	13.47 /63	16.48 /95		0.00	1.21
SC ●	Artisan Small Cap Value Inst	APHVX	D-	(800) 344-1770	E+ / 0.8	-1.62	0.81	-8.77 / 3	3.99 /10	--		0.00	0.99
SC ●	Artisan Small Cap Value Inv	ARTVX	E-	(800) 344-1770	E+ / 0.7	-1.63	0.70	-9.00 / 3	3.74 /10	5.75 /15		0.00	1.23
GR	Artisan Value Institutional	APHLX	C-	(800) 344-1770	C / 4.8	2.44	2.17	4.75 /37	11.52 /49	--		1.04	0.74
GR	Artisan Value Investor	ARTLX	C-	(800) 344-1770	C / 4.6	2.45	2.12	4.56 /35	11.25 /47	11.42 /56		0.79	0.98
GL	Ascendant Balanced A	ATBAX	D+	(855) 527-2363	D / 1.6	0.43	0.69	2.01 /22	7.55 /24	--		0.32	2.36
GL	Ascendant Balanced C	ATBTX	D+	(855) 527-2363	D / 1.9	0.29	0.34	1.32 /19	6.73 /20	--		0.00	3.11
GL	Ascendant Balanced I	ATBIX	C-	(855) 527-2363	D+ / 2.5	0.50	0.80	2.26 /23	7.81 /26	--		0.59	2.11
GL	Ascendant Deep Value Convertibles	AEQAX	D-	(855) 527-2363	E+ / 0.6	-0.58	-4.33	-4.47 / 6	4.16 /11	--		0.77	2.44
GL	Ascendant Deep Value Convertibles	AEQCX	D-	(855) 527-2363	E+ / 0.7	-0.77	-4.70	-5.07 / 5	3.44 / 9	--		0.25	3.19
GL	Ascendant Deep Value Convertibles I	AEQIX	D	(855) 527-2363	E+ / 0.9	-0.52	-4.18	-4.14 / 7	4.41 /11	--		1.01	2.19
EM	Ashmore Em Mkts Frontier Eq Inst	EFEIX	U	(866) 876-8294	U /	-1.29	-11.63	-1.55 /11	--	--		1.60	5.13
EM	Ashmore Emerg Mkts Eqty A	EMEAX	D-	(866) 876-8294	E- / 0.2	-4.84	-7.51	-8.67 / 3	-3.61 / 2	--		1.09	3.62
EM	Ashmore Emerg Mkts Eqty Inst	EMFIX	E	(866) 876-8294	E- / 0.2	-4.68	-7.37	-8.37 / 3	-2.96 / 2	--		1.20	3.37
EM	Ashmore Emerg Mkts Sm-Cap Eqty A	ESSAX	D-	(866) 876-8294	E / 0.4	4.46	-3.15	-4.98 / 5	0.62 / 5	--		0.27	2.64
EM	Ashmore Emerg Mkts Sm-Cap Eqty	ESCIX	E	(866) 876-8294	E / 0.5	4.51	-2.96	-4.69 / 6	0.97 / 5	--		0.23	2.39
GI	Aspen Managed Futures Strategy A	MFBPX	C+	(855) 845-9444	C- / 3.1	5.47	10.77	18.28 /96	5.83 /16	--		0.00	1.88
GI	Aspen Managed Futures Strategy I	MFBTX	B-	(855) 845-9444	C- / 4.2	5.48	11.05	18.74 /96	6.28 /18	--		0.00	1.31
GL	Aspiriant Risk Managed Glbl Eq Adv	RMEAX	U	(877) 997-9971	U /	2.70	0.18	2.33 /23	--	--		0.26	1.66
IN	ASTON/Anchor Cap Enhanced Equity	AMDSX	D+	(800) 992-8151	D- / 1.4	-0.66	2.38	4.88 /38	4.87 /13	6.36 /19		1.82	0.95
IN	ASTON/Anchor Cap Enhanced Equity	AMBEX	D+	(800) 992-8151	D- / 1.4	-0.72	2.26	4.62 /36	4.62 /12	6.08 /17		1.57	1.20
FO	ASTON/Barings International Fund N	ABARX	E-	(800) 992-8151	D- / 1.3	5.50	1.55	-0.14 /15	5.01 /13	4.56 /10		1.97	1.95
FO	ASTON/Barings International Inst	ABIIX	E	(800) 992-8151	D- / 1.4	5.85	1.71	0.30 /16	5.33 /14	4.83 /11		2.23	1.70
GI	ASTON/Cornerstone Large Cap	AAVIX	C-	(800) 992-8151	C- / 3.7	-5.68	-1.71	0.40 /17	11.20 /47	11.22 /55		0.94	1.06
GI	ASTON/Cornerstone Large Cap	RVALX	C-	(800) 992-8151	C- / 3.5	-5.75	-1.86	0.12 /16	10.95 /45	10.93 /52		0.78	1.31
MC ●	ASTON/Fairpointe Mid Cap Fund I	ABMIX	B-	(800) 992-8151	A / 9.3	2.33	6.90	7.29 /57	18.95 /97	15.22 /88		0.13	0.86
MC ●	ASTON/Fairpointe Mid Cap Fund N	CHTTX	B-	(800) 992-8151	A- / 9.2	2.29	6.77	7.03 /55	18.66 /96	14.93 /86		0.09	1.11
RE	ASTON/Harrison Street Real Estate I	AARIX	C-	(800) 992-8151	C+ / 6.7	2.82	15.24	16.96 /94	11.56 /49	14.92 /86		1.42	1.91
RE	ASTON/Harrison Street Real Estate	ARFCX	C-	(800) 992-8151	C+ / 6.5	2.73	15.15	16.66 /94	11.25 /47	14.64 /84		1.17	2.16
GR	ASTON/Herndon Large Cap Value I	AHRNX	C-	(800) 992-8151	C- / 3.6	1.54	-0.68	1.62 /20	10.14 /40	--		0.95	1.06
GR	ASTON/Herndon Large Cap Value N	AALIX	C-	(800) 992-8151	C- / 3.4	1.46	-0.83	1.33 /19	9.85 /38	11.02 /53		0.33	1.31
GR	ASTON/Lake Partners LASSO Altern	ALSOX	C-	(800) 992-8151	D- / 1.2	0.61	0.43	1.16 /19	4.62 /12	4.46 /10		0.28	3.00
GR	ASTON/Lake Partners LASSO Altern	ALSNX	C-	(800) 992-8151	D- / 1.1	0.53	0.33	0.92 /18	4.35 /11	4.21 / 9		0.03	3.25
IN	ASTON/LMCG Small Cap Growth I	ACWIX	B+	(800) 992-8151	A+ / 9.8	8.52	16.91	16.74 /94	21.55 /98	--		0.00	1.43
IN	ASTON/LMCG Small Cap Growth N	ACWDX	B+	(800) 992-8151	A+ / 9.8	8.46	16.83	16.50 /94	21.27 /98	--		0.00	1.68
BA	ASTON/Montag & Caldwell Balanced	MOBIX	C	(800) 992-8151	C- / 3.7	1.96	5.55	8.90 /69	8.49 /30	8.13 /31		0.92	1.34
BA	ASTON/Montag & Caldwell Balanced	MOBAX	C	(800) 992-8151	C- / 3.6	1.93	5.48	8.76 /68	8.38 /29	7.99 /30		0.82	1.59
GR	ASTON/Montag & Caldwell Gr I	MCGIX	C-	(800) 992-8151	C+ / 6.4	2.40	7.08	11.79 /82	12.92 /59	11.54 /57		0.58	0.79
GR	ASTON/Montag & Caldwell Gr N	MCGFX	C-	(800) 992-8151	C+ / 6.2	2.33	6.97	11.52 /80	12.65 /57	11.27 /55		0.16	1.04
GR	ASTON/Montag & Caldwell Gr R	MCRGX	C-	(800) 992-8151	C+ / 6.0	2.25	6.81	11.20 /79	12.36 /55	10.98 /52		0.04	1.29
MC	ASTON/Montag & Caldwell MdCp Gr	AMCMX	C-	(800) 992-8151	C+ / 6.0	4.22	13.10	10.57 /77	11.71 /50	14.23 /80		0.00	2.17
FO	ASTON/Pictet International I	APCTX	U	(800) 992-8151	U /	7.35	1.27	--	--	--		0.00	3.01
IN ●	ASTON/River Road Div All Cap Val I	ARIDX	B	(800) 992-8151	B- / 7.0	0.68	5.61	9.68 /73	14.58 /72	13.60 /74		2.69	0.84

● Denotes fund is closed to new investors

* Denotes fund is included in Section II

RISK			NET ASSETS		ASSET					BULL / BEAR		FUND MANAGER		MINIMUMS		LOADS	
Risk Rating/Pts	3 Year Standard Deviation	Beta	NAV As of 3/31/15	Total $(Mil)	Cash %	Stocks %	Bonds %	Other %	Portfolio Turnover Ratio	Last Bull Market Return	Last Bear Market Return	Manager Quality Pct	Manager Tenure (Years)	Initial Purch. $	Additional Purch. $	Front End Load	Back End Load
C+ / 6.9	11.7	0.84	31.23	15,064	0	0	0	100	46	78.6	-24.2	91	20	1,000	0	0.0	2.0
C / 4.4	12.6	0.79	23.53	988	1	98	0	1	58	62.5	-23.8	89	14	1,000	0	0.0	2.0
C+ / 6.0	11.0	0.78	35.58	2,740	0	0	0	100	20	80.2	-19.8	95	13	1,000,000	0	0.0	2.0
C+ / 6.0	11.0	0.78	35.46	8,894	0	0	0	100	20	79.0	-19.9	95	13	1,000	0	0.0	2.0
C+ / 5.6	13.6	1.08	49.76	4,714	0	0	0	100	55	92.3	-16.4	21	9	1,000,000	0	0.0	0.0
C / 5.4	13.6	1.08	47.17	5,090	0	0	0	100	55	90.6	-16.5	19	9	1,000	0	0.0	0.0
B- / 7.6	11.0	0.95	25.15	1,711	0	0	0	100	26	N/A	N/A	29	14	1,000,000	0	0.0	0.0
C+ / 5.7	11.0	0.95	25.14	8,048	0	0	0	100	26	78.8	-17.0	26	14	1,000	0	0.0	0.0
U /	N/A	N/A	30.22	265	4	95	0	1	39	N/A	N/A	N/A	11	1,000,000	0	0.0	0.0
C- / 3.0	16.2	1.02	30.08	1,272	4	95	0	1	39	85.5	-16.9	28	11	1,000	0	0.0	0.0
C+ / 6.4	13.2	0.91	13.98	221	12	86	0	2	31	N/A	N/A	2	18	1,000,000	0	0.0	0.0
D / 2.2	13.2	0.91	13.91	737	12	86	0	2	31	41.1	-23.2	2	18	1,000	0	0.0	0.0
C+ / 5.7	10.4	0.92	13.42	264	0	0	0	100	53	75.6	N/A	26	9	1,000,000	0	0.0	0.0
C+ / 5.7	10.4	0.93	13.40	1,088	0	0	0	100	53	74.1	-14.6	23	9	1,000	0	0.0	0.0
B- / 7.6	6.8	1.00	14.03	2	3	54	11	32	59	N/A	N/A	47	4	1,000	100	5.8	0.0
B- / 7.5	6.8	1.00	13.77	1	3	54	11	32	59	N/A	N/A	35	4	1,000	100	0.0	0.0
B- / 7.5	6.9	1.00	14.07	19	3	54	11	32	59	N/A	N/A	50	4	1,000,000	25,000	0.0	0.0
B- / 7.3	7.7	0.45	12.64	25	3	0	6	91	112	N/A	N/A	67	4	1,000	100	5.8	0.0
B- / 7.1	7.7	0.45	12.46	N/A	3	0	6	91	112	N/A	N/A	57	4	1,000	100	0.0	0.0
B- / 7.2	7.7	0.45	12.69	4	3	0	6	91	112	N/A	N/A	69	4	1,000,000	25,000	0.0	0.0
U /	N/A	N/A	9.29	27	0	0	0	100	157	N/A	N/A	N/A	1	1,000,000	5,000	0.0	0.0
C+ / 6.8	14.2	0.97	8.46	N/A	1	97	0	2	130	N/A	N/A	14	3	1,000	50	5.3	0.0
C / 5.2	14.3	0.98	8.14	9	1	97	0	2	130	13.9	N/A	19	4	1,000,000	5,000	0.0	0.0
C+ / 6.7	14.0	0.86	8.66	N/A	0	98	0	2	104	N/A	N/A	67	4	1,000	50	5.3	0.0
C / 4.4	14.0	0.87	10.89	44	0	98	0	2	104	N/A	N/A	71	4	1,000,000	5,000	0.0	0.0
B / 8.9	7.4	-0.10	10.42	17	16	15	68	1	90	5.4	N/A	96	N/A	2,500	0	5.5	2.0
B+ / 9.0	7.3	-0.09	10.58	245	16	15	68	1	90	7.0	N/A	96	N/A	100,000	0	0.0	2.0
U /	N/A	N/A	11.43	310	10	89	0	1	43	N/A	N/A	N/A	2	0	0	0.0	0.0
B / 8.0	6.0	0.55	9.61	117	0	100	0	0	41	33.0	-5.9	20	7	1,000,000	50	0.0	0.0
B / 8.1	6.0	0.55	9.60	100	0	100	0	0	41	31.8	-5.9	18	7	2,500	50	0.0	0.0
D+ / 2.5	12.0	0.88	6.14	N/A	1	98	0	1	53	36.4	-20.4	24	7	2,500	50	0.0	2.0
D+ / 2.5	11.9	0.87	6.15	20	1	98	0	1	53	37.5	-20.2	28	7	1,000,000	50	0.0	2.0
B- / 7.0	11.9	1.17	14.79	97	4	95	0	1	30	74.5	-14.3	5	4	1,000,000	50	0.0	0.0
C+ / 6.9	11.9	1.16	14.76	56	4	95	0	1	30	73.3	-14.5	4	4	2,500	50	0.0	0.0
C- / 4.0	13.9	1.14	42.54	3,310	0	99	0	1	50	124.4	-25.7	59	16	1,000,000	50	0.0	0.0
C- / 3.9	13.8	1.14	41.62	2,431	0	99	0	1	50	122.5	-25.7	56	16	2,500	50	0.0	0.0
C- / 3.9	12.5	1.00	13.11	1	0	99	0	1	163	76.5	-16.9	33	4	1,000,000	50	0.0	2.0
C- / 3.9	12.6	1.01	13.19	13	0	99	0	1	163	75.0	-16.9	29	4	2,500	50	0.0	2.0
C+ / 6.3	10.6	1.04	13.89	130	4	95	0	1	30	71.3	-16.0	7	5	1,000,000	50	0.0	0.0
C+ / 6.4	10.6	1.04	13.93	10	4	95	0	1	30	69.9	-16.1	6	5	2,500	50	0.0	0.0
B+ / 9.0	3.9	0.38	13.21	247	36	42	19	3	46	25.3	-9.5	49	N/A	100,000	50	0.0	0.0
B+ / 9.0	3.9	0.38	13.18	44	36	42	19	3	46	24.2	-9.6	45	N/A	2,500	50	0.0	0.0
C / 4.3	13.6	1.02	15.79	37	3	96	0	1	144	125.6	N/A	92	5	1,000,000	50	0.0	0.0
C / 4.3	13.6	1.02	15.64	66	3	96	0	1	144	123.6	-30.2	92	5	2,500	50	0.0	0.0
B- / 7.2	5.6	0.93	23.32	2	3	61	35	1	27	44.0	-5.9	44	21	1,000,000	50	0.0	0.0
B- / 7.3	5.6	0.93	23.40	21	3	61	35	1	27	43.5	-6.0	43	21	2,500	50	0.0	0.0
C- / 4.0	9.1	0.88	25.98	2,385	4	96	0	0	47	75.3	-11.6	51	21	1,000,000	50	0.0	0.0
C- / 4.1	9.1	0.88	25.87	911	4	96	0	0	47	73.8	-11.7	48	21	2,500	50	0.0	0.0
C- / 4.1	9.1	0.88	25.47	7	4	96	0	0	47	72.3	-11.8	44	21	2,500	50	0.0	0.0
C / 4.7	10.5	0.89	11.86	5	4	95	0	1	33	75.9	-18.0	26	8	2,500	50	0.0	0.0
U /	N/A	N/A	9.49	32	0	99	0	1	26	N/A	N/A	N/A	N/A	1,000,000	50	0.0	2.0
C+ / 6.5	9.4	0.92	13.22	748	7	92	0	1	32	79.8	-11.6	64	10	100,000	50	0.0	0.0

Fund Type	Fund Name	Ticker Symbol	Overall Investment Rating	Phone	Performance Rating/Pts	3 Mo	6 Mo	1Yr / Pct	3Yr / Pct	5Yr / Pct	Dividend Yield	Expense Ratio
IN	● ASTON/River Road Div All Cap Val N	ARDEX	C+	(800) 992-8151	C+ / 6.8	0.62	5.47	9.39 /71	14.28 /69	13.31 /71	2.44	1.09
GL	● ASTON/River Road Independent Val I	ARVIX	D	(800) 992-8151	E+ / 0.7	-0.96	-2.34	-3.38 / 8	2.85 / 8	--	0.00	1.21
GL	● ASTON/River Road Independent Val	ARIVX	D-	(800) 992-8151	E+ / 0.7	-0.97	-2.36	-3.58 / 8	2.61 / 7	--	0.00	1.46
GL	ASTON/River Road Long-Short Fund	ALSIX	U	(800) 992-8151	U /	0.26	0.07	1.89 /21	--	--	0.00	2.37
AA	ASTON/River Road Long-Short Fund	ARLSX	D+	(800) 992-8151	D / 1.7	0.18	-0.11	1.63 /20	6.27 /18	--	0.00	2.62
MC	ASTON/River Road Select Value I	ARIMX	D-	(800) 992-8151	C / 5.4	3.39	7.80	2.28 /23	12.28 /54	11.57 /57	0.00	1.21
MC	ASTON/River Road Select Value N	ARSMX	D-	(800) 992-8151	C / 5.1	3.31	7.64	1.96 /22	11.96 /52	11.25 /55	0.00	1.46
SC	ASTON/River Road Sm Cap Value I	ARSIX	D-	(800) 992-8151	C / 5.0	2.50	8.63	0.26 /16	12.00 /52	10.65 /50	0.00	1.10
SC	ASTON/River Road Sm Cap Value N	ARSVX	E+	(800) 992-8151	C / 4.8	2.43	8.52	-0.03 /15	11.71 /50	10.38 /48	0.00	1.35
IN	ASTON/RiverRoad Div AC Val II I	ADIVX	U	(800) 992-8151	U /	-0.01	4.81	9.65 /73	--	--	2.27	0.93
SC	ASTON/Silvercrest Small Cap I	ACRTX	B+	(877) 738-0333	B+ / 8.3	4.35	14.88	8.41 /66	15.63 /80	--	0.19	1.36
SC	ASTON/Silvercrest Small Cap N	ASCTX	B+	(877) 738-0333	B / 8.1	4.31	14.75	8.19 /64	15.34 /78	--	0.15	1.61
GR	ASTON/TAMRO Diversified Fund I	ATDEX	B	(800) 992-8151	B- / 7.0	1.11	7.25	10.86 /78	14.21 /69	--	0.00	1.12
GR	ASTON/TAMRO Diversified Fund N	ATLVX	C+	(800) 992-8151	C+ / 6.8	1.01	7.10	10.53 /76	13.92 /66	12.67 /65	0.00	1.37
SC	● ASTON/TAMRO Small Cap Fund I	ATSIX	D	(800) 992-8151	C / 4.8	2.83	13.02	3.61 /29	10.66 /43	12.59 /65	0.00	1.06
SC	● ASTON/TAMRO Small Cap Fund N	ATASX	D-	(800) 992-8151	C / 4.6	2.78	12.87	3.35 /28	10.39 /42	12.31 /63	0.00	1.31
GL	Astor Active Income ETF A	AXAIX	D	(877) 738-0333	E+ / 0.7	0.50	1.10	2.39 /24	3.05 / 8	--	2.36	11.95
GL	Astor Active Income ETF C	CXAIX	D	(877) 738-0333	E+ / 0.7	0.29	0.80	1.40 /20	2.16 / 6	--	1.89	12.70
GR	Astor Long/Short ETF A	ASTLX	E	(877) 738-0333	D+ / 2.5	1.76	5.64	7.88 /62	7.64 /25	--	0.46	2.18
GR	Astor Long/Short ETF C	ASTZX	C	(877) 738-0333	D+ / 2.7	1.55	5.26	7.02 /55	6.83 /20	3.46 / 7	0.12	2.93
GR	Astor Long/Short ETF I	ASTIX	C+	(877) 738-0333	C- / 3.4	1.74	5.76	8.07 /63	7.91 /26	4.48 /10	0.74	1.93
GR	Astor Long/Short ETF R	ASTRX	C	(877) 738-0333	C- / 3.2	1.76	5.63	7.89 /62	7.62 /25	4.24 / 9	0.48	2.18
GL	Astor STAR ETF A	ASPGX	B-	(877) 738-0333	C+ / 6.2	2.84	7.91	8.59 /67	14.36 /70	--	0.00	2.50
GL	Astor STAR ETF C	CSPGX	B-	(877) 738-0333	C+ / 6.4	2.69	7.49	7.79 /61	13.43 /63	--	0.00	3.25
GL	Astor STAR ETF I	STARX	U	(877) 738-0333	U /	2.90	8.04	8.87 /69	--	--	0.00	2.25
IN	AT Disciplined Equity Institutional	AWEIX	A	(800) 338-2550	B+ / 8.7	2.38	8.06	14.94 /91	16.15 /84	14.72 /84	0.76	0.81
AA	AT Income Opportunities Instl	AWIIX	U	(866) 777-7818	U /	2.56	5.81	--	--	--	0.00	1.01
MC	AT Mid Cap Equity Instl	AWMIX	U	(866) 777-7818	U /	8.67	17.38	--	--	--	0.00	1.67
GL	ATAC Inflation Rotation Investor	ATACX	U	(855) 282-2386	U /	9.16	7.16	1.35 /20	--	--	0.34	2.17
GL	Aurora Horizons Y	AHFYX	U	(800) 443-2862	U /	1.17	0.75	-0.21 /15	--	--	0.24	2.85
GR	Auxier Focus A	AUXAX	C	(877) 328-9437	C- / 3.5	0.63	5.09	7.76 /61	10.88 /45	9.86 /43	0.65	1.62
GR	Auxier Focus Institutional	AUXIX	U	(877) 328-9437	U /	0.72	5.23	8.05 /63	--	--	0.79	1.47
GR	Auxier Focus Inv	AUXFX	C+	(877) 328-9437	C / 4.4	0.68	5.11	7.80 /61	10.90 /45	9.88 /44	0.92	1.26
GR	Ave Maria Catholic Values	AVEMX	D+	(866) 283-6274	C- / 3.4	0.35	5.11	1.22 /19	9.39 /35	10.98 /52	0.00	1.43
GR	Ave Maria Growth Fund	AVEGX	C+	(866) 283-6274	C+ / 6.9	3.19	11.78	11.08 /79	13.36 /66	14.61 /83	0.00	1.44
SC	Ave Maria Opportunity Fund	AVESX	E	(866) 283-6274	E- / 0.2	-9.26	-11.88	-19.49 / 1	-0.12 / 4	4.46 /10	0.00	1.42
GI	Ave Maria Rising Dividend Fd	AVEDX	B+	(866) 283-6274	B- / 7.3	0.34	4.06	8.16 /64	15.42 /78	13.90 /77	1.10	0.98
GL	Ave Maria World Equity Fund	AVEWX	C-	(866) 283-6274	C- / 3.4	2.04	2.49	2.78 /25	9.14 /34	--	0.27	1.51
AA	AZ 529 Fidelity CSP 100% Eq Ptf		C+	(800) 544-8544	C+ / 6.3	3.42	6.04	8.41 /66	13.31 /62	10.91 /52	0.00	1.00
AA	AZ 529 Fidelity CSP 70% Eq Ptf		C+	(800) 544-8544	C / 4.6	2.91	5.03	7.18 /56	10.60 /43	9.41 /40	0.00	0.93
AA	AZ 529 Fidelity CSP College Ptf		C	(800) 544-8544	D- / 1.2	1.47	2.47	3.65 /30	3.92 /10	4.22 / 9	0.00	0.67
AA	AZ 529 Fidelity CSP Consv Ptf		C-	(800) 544-8544	E+ / 0.7	0.84	1.38	2.32 /23	1.61 / 6	2.40 / 5	0.00	0.59
AA	AZ 529 Fidelity CSP Idx 100% Eq Ptf		B-	(800) 544-8544	C+ / 6.0	2.66	4.62	6.88 /54	13.15 /61	11.52 /57	0.00	0.27
AA	AZ 529 Fidelity CSP Idx 70% Eq Ptf		C+	(800) 544-8544	C- / 4.2	2.40	4.07	6.12 /47	10.12 /40	10.00 /44	0.00	0.30
AA	AZ 529 Fidelity CSP Index Clg Ptf		C	(800) 544-8544	D- / 1.0	1.08	2.04	3.10 /27	3.39 / 9	4.38 /10	0.00	0.33
AA	AZ 529 Fidelity CSP Index Ptf 2015		C	(800) 544-8544	D- / 1.3	1.22	2.17	3.36 /28	4.44 /11	5.85 /16	0.00	0.32
AA	AZ 529 Fidelity CSP Index Ptf 2018		C	(800) 544-8544	D / 2.1	1.52	2.73	4.27 /33	6.35 /18	7.36 /25	0.00	0.31
AA	AZ 529 Fidelity CSP Index Ptf 2021		C+	(800) 544-8544	C- / 3.1	1.83	3.29	5.17 /40	8.14 /28	8.62 /34	0.00	0.30
AA	AZ 529 Fidelity CSP Index Ptf 2024		C+	(800) 544-8544	C- / 4.0	2.12	3.84	5.83 /45	9.79 /38	9.66 /42	0.00	0.29
AA	AZ 529 Fidelity CSP Index Ptf 2027		C+	(800) 544-8544	C / 4.7	2.38	4.19	6.37 /50	11.09 /46	10.41 /48	0.00	0.28
AA	AZ 529 Fidelity CSP Portfolio 2015		C	(800) 544-8544	D- / 1.5	1.56	2.64	4.01 /32	5.02 /13	5.50 /14	0.00	0.80
AA	AZ 529 Fidelity CSP Portfolio 2018		C	(800) 544-8544	D+ / 2.5	2.05	3.52	5.25 /40	6.99 /21	6.96 /23	0.00	0.86

PERFORMANCE — Total Return % through 3/31/15 (Annualized for 3Yr/Pct and 5Yr/Pct); Incl. in Returns

99 Pct = Best
0 Pct = Worst

● Denotes fund is closed to new investors
* Denotes fund is included in Section II

www.thestreetratings.com

RISK			NET ASSETS		ASSET					BULL / BEAR		FUND MANAGER		MINIMUMS		LOADS	
	3 Year		NAV						Portfolio	Last Bull	Last Bear	Manager	Manager	Initial	Additional	Front	Back
Risk Rating/Pts	Standard Deviation	Beta	As of 3/31/15	Total $(Mil)	Cash %	Stocks %	Bonds %	Other %	Turnover Ratio	Market Return	Market Return	Quality Pct	Tenure (Years)	Purch. $	Purch. $	End Load	End Load
C+ / 6.5	9.4	0.92	13.23	247	7	92	0	1	32	78.1	-11.7	61	10	2,500	50	0.0	0.0
B- / 7.4	5.6	0.20	10.27	200	71	28	0	1	91	22.2	N/A	76	5	1,000,000	50	0.0	0.0
B- / 7.4	5.6	0.20	10.17	263	71	28	0	1	91	21.2	-7.4	75	5	2,500	50	0.0	0.0
U /	N/A	N/A	11.46	83	48	51	0	1	303	N/A	N/A	N/A	5	1,000,000	50	0.0	0.0
B / 8.1	7.3	0.92	11.39	101	48	51	0	1	303	33.9	N/A	21	5	2,500	50	0.0	0.0
D+ / 2.3	11.5	0.92	7.92	131	0	99	0	1	64	77.2	-17.5	27	8	1,000,000	50	0.0	0.0
D+ / 2.3	11.5	0.92	7.80	8	0	99	0	1	64	75.6	-17.7	24	8	2,500	50	0.0	0.0
D / 1.9	11.5	0.80	12.29	249	9	90	0	1	66	75.3	-18.0	56	10	1,000,000	50	0.0	0.0
D / 1.9	11.5	0.80	12.20	27	9	90	0	1	66	74.0	-18.1	52	10	2,500	50	0.0	0.0
U /	N/A	N/A	13.54	135	9	90	0	1	29	N/A	N/A	N/A	3	1,000,000	50	0.0	0.0
C+ / 6.2	13.8	0.99	15.82	122	2	97	0	1	37	N/A	N/A	62	4	1,000,000	50	0.0	0.0
C+ / 6.2	13.8	0.99	15.74	6	2	97	0	1	37	N/A	N/A	58	4	2,500	50	0.0	0.0
C+ / 6.7	11.1	1.10	18.14	23	1	98	0	1	40	N/A	N/A	23	15	1,000,000	50	0.0	0.0
C+ / 6.4	11.1	1.11	18.04	22	1	98	0	1	40	87.8	-20.4	20	15	2,500	50	0.0	0.0
C- / 3.5	14.2	1.01	21.08	438	1	98	0	1	70	75.1	-24.3	10	15	1,000,000	50	0.0	0.0
C- / 3.3	14.2	1.01	20.34	296	1	98	0	1	70	73.7	-24.4	9	15	2,500	50	0.0	0.0
B / 8.1	3.2	0.31	10.24	2	15	12	72	1	36	N/A	N/A	71	4	5,000	100	4.8	0.0
B / 8.1	3.2	0.31	10.16	1	15	12	72	1	36	N/A	N/A	59	4	5,000	100	0.0	0.0
D- / 1.4	6.0	0.59	12.13	16	8	66	24	2	55	N/A	N/A	46	4	1,000	100	4.8	0.0
B / 8.6	6.0	0.58	11.80	22	8	66	24	2	55	23.8	-11.9	35	4	1,000	100	0.0	0.0
B / 8.6	6.0	0.58	12.14	86	8	66	24	2	55	27.9	-11.4	50	4	50,000	100	0.0	0.0
B / 8.6	6.0	0.58	12.11	3	8	66	24	2	55	26.8	-11.5	46	4	1,000	100	0.0	0.0
B- / 7.6	9.7	1.33	15.58	51	4	93	2	1	25	N/A	N/A	84	N/A	5,000	100	4.8	0.0
B- / 7.6	9.7	1.32	15.25	44	4	93	2	1	25	N/A	N/A	79	N/A	5,000	100	0.0	0.0
U /	N/A	N/A	15.62	57	4	93	2	1	25	N/A	N/A	N/A	N/A	5,000	100	0.0	0.0
B- / 7.0	9.4	0.97	15.92	628	1	98	0	1	22	98.7	-13.6	72	5	250,000	0	0.0	0.0
U /	N/A	N/A	10.26	172	0	0	0	100	0	N/A	N/A	N/A	N/A	250,000	0	0.0	0.0
U /	N/A	N/A	11.78	137	0	0	0	100	0	N/A	N/A	N/A	N/A	250,000	0	0.0	0.0
U /	N/A	N/A	27.16	75	3	96	0	1	2,431	N/A	N/A	N/A	3	2,500	100	0.0	2.0
U /	N/A	N/A	10.35	188	25	59	15	1	262	N/A	N/A	N/A	2	100,000	100	0.0	2.0
B- / 7.7	8.9	0.90	20.84	6	8	91	0	1	9	61.6	-11.6	24	16	2,000	50	5.8	2.0
U /	N/A	N/A	20.93	28	8	91	0	1	9	N/A	N/A	N/A	16	100,000	0	0.0	2.0
B- / 7.7	8.9	0.90	20.70	251	8	91	0	1	9	61.6	-11.6	24	16	5,000	50	0.0	2.0
C+ / 5.9	11.3	1.08	20.04	243	2	97	0	1	29	65.8	-19.9	4	13	2,500	0	0.0	0.0
C / 5.5	10.5	1.01	29.14	314	4	95	0	1	18	86.7	-19.0	30	2	2,500	0	0.0	0.0
C- / 4.1	13.1	0.82	10.98	43	8	91	0	1	58	26.6	-16.8	1	9	2,500	0	0.0	0.0
C+ / 6.9	9.4	0.95	17.72	850	4	95	0	1	14	89.7	-16.1	69	10	2,500	0	0.0	0.0
C+ / 6.6	11.2	0.75	13.49	45	12	87	0	1	31	58.3	-23.8	84	5	2,500	0	0.0	0.0
C+ / 6.7	10.2	1.72	18.43	14	4	94	0	2	24	82.9	-23.1	9	10	50	25	0.0	0.0
B / 8.1	7.6	1.29	18.36	8	4	67	27	2	24	61.5	-17.3	23	10	50	25	0.0	0.0
B+ / 9.9	2.6	0.40	14.50	9	22	21	55	2	43	18.6	-4.4	62	10	50	25	0.0	0.0
B+ / 9.7	1.4	0.05	13.23	3	48	0	51	1	34	6.4	0.7	78	10	50	25	0.0	0.0
B- / 7.0	10.1	1.71	15.85	10	4	95	0	1	24	80.0	-19.3	9	9	50	25	0.0	0.0
B / 8.6	7.3	1.24	16.64	8	3	67	28	2	33	56.1	-11.2	23	9	50	25	0.0	0.0
B+ / 9.9	2.2	0.34	13.99	7	36	18	45	1	36	15.6	-0.3	64	9	50	25	0.0	0.0
B+ / 9.9	3.1	0.50	14.15	10	33	20	45	2	32	23.6	-4.0	55	9	50	25	0.0	0.0
B+ / 9.6	4.4	0.74	14.65	13	22	33	43	2	33	34.5	-7.2	45	9	50	25	0.0	0.0
B+ / 9.1	5.8	0.98	15.06	17	14	46	39	1	25	45.5	-10.5	33	9	50	25	0.0	0.0
B / 8.6	7.1	1.21	15.43	21	9	58	32	1	18	56.5	-13.6	23	9	50	25	0.0	0.0
B / 8.1	8.2	1.39	14.19	18	4	70	24	2	11	65.2	-15.9	17	8	50	25	0.0	0.5
B+ / 9.6	3.6	0.58	15.58	18	21	23	54	2	22	27.4	-9.0	51	10	50	25	0.0	0.0
B+ / 9.2	4.9	0.82	16.45	23	13	37	48	2	24	39.0	-12.4	41	10	50	25	0.0	0.0

Fund Type	Fund Name	Ticker Symbol	Overall Investment Rating	Phone	Performance Rating/Pts	3 Mo	6 Mo	1Yr / Pct	3Yr / Pct	5Yr / Pct	Dividend Yield	Expense Ratio
AA	AZ 529 Fidelity CSP Portfolio 2021		C+	(800) 544-8544	C- / 3.5	2.45	4.32	6.27 /49	8.72 /31	8.15 /31	0.00	0.92
AA	AZ 529 Fidelity CSP Portfolio 2024		C+	(800) 544-8544	C / 4.4	2.69	4.78	6.82 /54	10.27 /41	9.08 /37	0.00	0.97
AA	AZ 529 Fidelity CSP Portfolio 2027		C+	(800) 544-8544	C / 5.2	2.88	5.19	7.35 /58	11.60 /50	9.82 /43	0.00	0.99
MC	Azzad Ethical Fund	ADJEX	C	(888) 350-3369	C+ / 6.1	4.63	7.69	10.26 /75	12.90 /59	14.32 /81	0.00	1.19
GL	Azzad Wise Capital	WISEX	C-	(888) 350-3369	E+ / 0.8	0.50	1.02	1.91 /22	3.14 / 8	--	0.54	1.55
GR	● Baird Large Cap Inst	BHGIX	D	(866) 442-2473	C+ / 6.8	-0.22	5.76	11.46 /80	14.07 /68	13.94 /77	0.92	1.24
GR	● Baird Large Cap Inv	BHGSX	D-	(866) 442-2473	C+ / 6.6	-0.34	5.52	11.25 /79	13.78 /65	13.65 /74	0.78	1.49
MC	Baird MidCap Inst	BMDIX	C+	(866) 442-2473	C+ / 6.5	4.37	8.28	7.50 /59	13.48 /63	15.78 /92	0.00	0.88
MC	Baird MidCap Inv	BMDSX	C+	(866) 442-2473	C+ / 6.3	4.34	8.27	7.31 /57	13.23 /61	15.53 /90	0.00	1.13
GR	Balter Long/Short Equity Inst	BEQIX	U	(855) 854-7258	U /	1.59	2.61	3.13 /27	--	--	0.00	N/A
MC	Baron Asset Fd Retail	BARAX	B+	(800) 992-2766	B+ / 8.9	3.44	10.29	12.57 /85	16.63 /88	14.98 /87	0.00	1.31
MC	Baron Asset Inst	BARIX	B+	(800) 992-2766	A- / 9.0	3.52	10.45	12.88 /86	16.96 /90	15.30 /89	0.00	1.04
SC	Baron Discovery Fd Inst	BDFIX	U	(800) 992-2766	U /	6.78	21.09	11.39 /80	--	--	0.00	1.91
EM	Baron Emerging Markets Inst	BEXIX	D	(800) 992-2766	D+ / 2.6	-0.34	-0.06	1.55 /20	8.28 /29	--	0.46	1.80
EM	Baron Emerging Markets Retail	BEXFX	D	(800) 992-2766	D+ / 2.4	-0.42	-0.17	1.28 /19	8.02 /27	--	0.26	1.90
EN	Baron Energy and Res Inst	BENIX	E	(800) 992-2766	E / 0.3	1.73	-19.47	-16.42 / 2	1.79 / 6	--	0.00	2.84
EN	Baron Energy and Res Retail	BENFX	E	(800) 992-2766	E / 0.3	1.65	-19.54	-16.67 / 2	1.55 / 6	--	0.00	2.25
GR	Baron Fifth Avenue Growth Fd	BFTHX	B-	(800) 992-2766	B / 7.9	4.95	8.44	13.14 /87	14.81 /73	13.89 /77	0.00	1.37
GR	Baron Fifth Avenue Growth Inst	BFTIX	B	(800) 992-2766	B / 8.1	5.01	8.55	13.35 /88	15.11 /76	14.17 /79	0.13	1.08
GR	Baron Growth Fd Retail	BGRFX	A-	(800) 992-2766	A- / 9.1	4.68	12.25	9.07 /70	17.31 /91	15.69 /91	0.00	1.29
GR	Baron Growth Inst	BGRIX	A-	(800) 992-2766	A- / 9.2	4.75	12.38	9.35 /71	17.62 /93	15.99 /93	0.00	1.04
FO	Baron International Growth Fd Rtl	BIGFX	D-	(800) 992-2766	D+ / 2.3	2.84	2.35	-1.07 /13	7.48 /24	7.41 /26	0.02	1.74
FO	Baron International Growth Inst	BINIX	D-	(800) 992-2766	D+ / 2.4	2.87	2.44	-0.87 /13	7.75 /26	7.69 /28	0.21	1.37
TC	Baron Opportunity Inst	BIOIX	D	(800) 992-2766	C / 4.9	4.10	7.92	3.48 /29	11.30 /48	12.76 /66	0.00	1.08
TC	Baron Opportunity Retail	BIOPX	D-	(800) 992-2766	C / 4.8	4.06	7.76	3.21 /27	11.03 /46	12.46 /64	0.00	1.35
MC	Baron Partners Retail	BPTRX	A-	(800) 992-2766	A / 9.4	2.56	8.03	7.32 /58	19.50 /97	16.98 /96	0.00	1.67
RE	Baron Real Estate Institutional	BREIX	A+	(800) 992-2766	A+ / 9.9	4.55	14.39	16.48 /94	24.39 /99	21.63 /99	0.31	1.09
RE	Baron Real Estate Retail	BREFX	A+	(800) 992-2766	A+ / 9.9	4.51	14.28	16.19 /94	24.10 /99	21.34 /99	0.10	1.35
GI	Baron Select Focused Growth Inst	BFGIX	C	(800) 992-2766	C+ / 5.8	3.48	8.17	6.57 /51	12.45 /56	12.80 /66	0.00	1.12
GI	Baron Select Focused Growth Rtl	BFGFX	C	(800) 992-2766	C+ / 5.6	3.38	8.04	6.27 /49	12.17 /54	12.52 /64	0.00	1.42
MC	Baron Select Partners Inst	BPTIX	A-	(800) 992-2766	A / 9.5	2.63	8.14	7.59 /60	19.80 /98	17.30 /97	0.00	1.41
SC	Baron Small Cap Fd Retail	BSCFX	B	(800) 992-2766	B / 8.1	5.64	10.97	8.49 /66	15.48 /79	15.02 /87	0.00	1.30
SC	Baron Small Cap Inst	BSFIX	B	(800) 992-2766	B+ / 8.3	5.70	11.11	8.76 /68	15.77 /81	15.31 /89	0.00	1.04
GR	Barrett Growth	BGRWX	C+	(800) 451-2010	C+ / 6.8	2.34	7.60	14.40 /90	13.16 /61	10.19 /46	0.20	2.43
GR	Barrett Opportunity Fund	SAOPX	C-	(800) 451-2010	C / 4.8	-1.01	1.65	4.74 /37	11.99 /52	8.56 /33	1.15	1.16
GR	Barrow All-Cap Core Institutional	BALIX	A+	(877) 767-6633	A / 9.4	6.14	11.16	10.23 /75	18.07 /94	16.08 /93	0.68	1.86
GR	Barrow All-Cap Core Investor	BALAX	A+	(877) 767-6633	A / 9.3	6.07	10.99	9.93 /74	17.91 /94	15.99 /93	0.52	16.03
GR	● BBH Core Select Fund Class N	BBTEX	B-	(800) 625-5759	C / 5.2	-1.19	2.39	5.16 /40	13.21 /61	13.00 /68	0.63	1.07
GR	● BBH Core Select Fund Class Retail	BBTRX	B-	(800) 625-5759	C / 5.0	-1.23	2.29	4.88 /38	12.92 /59	--	0.71	1.40
GL	BBH Global Core Select N	BBGNX	U	(800) 625-5759	U /	0.09	0.22	-0.22 /15	--	--	1.10	1.32
FO	BBH International Equity I	BBHLX	D	(800) 625-5759	D / 2.1	4.17	0.77	0.57 /17	7.38 /23	6.14 /18	2.59	0.90
FO	BBH International Equity N	BBHEX	D	(800) 625-5759	D / 1.9	4.11	0.67	0.34 /17	7.11 /22	5.87 /16	2.38	1.12
GR	BearlyBullish Fund Investor	BRBLX	C+	(877) 337-3707	C+ / 6.4	2.03	3.99	4.72 /37	14.70 /72	--	0.00	2.10
GL	Beck Mack & Oliver International	BMGEX	E	(800) 943-6786	E+ / 0.8	1.42	-2.72	-0.67 /14	3.82 /10	4.36 /10	2.71	2.22
FO	Beck Mack & Oliver Partners	BMPEX	E+	(800) 943-6786	E+ / 0.8	-4.46	-8.22	-10.70 / 3	6.17 /17	10.02 /45	0.66	1.29
GR	Becker Value Equity Inst	BVEIX	A-	(800) 551-3998	B+ / 8.3	0.80	5.11	9.76 /73	17.00 /90	--	1.75	0.72
GR	Becker Value Equity Retail	BVEFX	A-	(800) 551-3998	B / 8.1	0.74	5.02	9.52 /72	16.73 /88	13.54 /73	1.55	0.97
GR	Beech Hill Total Return A	BHTAX	D	(877) 760-0005	D / 2.2	3.65	0.21	3.28 /28	8.40 /29	--	0.16	3.20
GR	Beech Hill Total Return C	BHTCX	D	(877) 760-0005	D+ / 2.3	3.46	-0.21	2.55 /24	7.58 /25	--	0.01	3.94
GR	Beehive Fund	BEEHX	C+	(866) 684-4915	C+ / 5.9	-0.07	4.53	7.33 /58	13.18 /61	11.37 /56	0.47	1.01
GR	Berkshire Focus Fund	BFOCX	E+	(877) 526-0707	C / 4.6	4.72	5.07	3.65 /30	11.48 /49	18.28 /98	0.00	2.04
GR	Berwyn Cornerstone Fund	BERCX	D-	(800) 992-6757	D / 2.1	-3.73	-3.24	-6.10 / 4	9.40 /36	8.57 /34	0.73	1.77

● Denotes fund is closed to new investors
* Denotes fund is included in Section II

www.thestreetratings.com

RISK Risk Rating/Pts	3 Year Standard Deviation	Beta	NET ASSETS NAV As of 3/31/15	Total $(Mil)	ASSET Cash %	Stocks %	Bonds %	Other %	Portfolio Turnover Ratio	BULL / BEAR Last Bull Market Return	Last Bear Market Return	FUND MANAGER Manager Quality Pct	Manager Tenure (Years)	MINIMUMS Initial Purch. $	Additional Purch. $	LOADS Front End Load	Back End Load
B /8.7	6.3	1.06	17.13	28	8	50	41	1	19	50.7	-16.1	30	10	50	25	0.0	0.0
B /8.1	7.6	1.28	17.54	37	5	62	31	2	17	61.3	-19.1	21	10	50	25	0.0	0.0
B- /7.6	8.7	1.47	13.58	22	5	74	19	2	16	70.5	-21.2	15	8	50	25	0.0	0.0
C /5.2	12.5	1.04	13.57	62	1	98	0	1	57	82.4	-17.0	15	15	1,000	50	0.0	2.0
B+ /9.6	2.3	0.11	10.42	87	38	7	54	1	27	10.8	-0.6	85	5	4,000	300	0.0	2.0
D- /1.3	10.8	1.06	8.91	40	5	94	0	1	128	97.1	-18.4	29	10	25,000	0	0.0	0.0
D- /1.3	10.8	1.06	8.84	1	5	94	0	1	128	95.6	-18.6	26	10	2,500	100	0.0	0.0
C+ /6.3	11.0	0.94	16.25	1,096	3	96	0	1	36	91.4	-16.8	36	15	25,000	0	0.0	0.0
C+ /6.3	11.0	0.94	15.61	207	3	96	0	1	36	89.8	-16.9	33	15	2,500	100	0.0	0.0
U /	N/A	N/A	10.21	138	72	27	0	1	248	N/A	N/A	N/A	2	50,000	500	0.0	1.0
C /5.4	11.6	0.98	65.94	2,090	2	96	0	2	11	96.6	-19.8	67	12	2,000	0	0.0	0.0
C /5.4	11.6	0.98	67.27	769	2	96	0	2	11	98.4	-19.7	70	12	1,000,000	0	0.0	0.0
U /	N/A	N/A	14.18	68	13	86	0	1	109	N/A	N/A	N/A	2	1,000,000	0	0.0	0.0
C+ /6.0	12.1	0.77	11.90	793	10	88	0	2	15	47.1	-18.5	96	5	1,000,000	0	0.0	0.0
C+ /6.0	12.1	0.77	11.86	721	10	88	0	2	15	46.0	-18.6	96	5	2,000	0	0.0	0.0
C- /3.7	17.9	1.01	10.59	35	26	73	0	1	26	N/A	N/A	37	4	1,000,000	0	0.0	0.0
C- /3.7	17.9	1.01	10.50	44	26	73	0	1	26	N/A	N/A	33	4	2,000	0	0.0	0.0
C /5.4	12.2	1.02	18.25	70	4	95	0	1	17	106.2	-16.7	45	4	2,000	0	0.0	0.0
C /5.4	12.2	1.02	18.43	67	4	95	0	1	17	108.1	-16.7	49	4	1,000,000	0	0.0	0.0
C+ /6.0	10.6	0.91	75.65	4,184	6	93	0	1	13	94.5	-19.3	86	21	2,000	0	0.0	0.0
C+ /6.0	10.6	0.91	76.72	4,062	6	93	0	1	13	96.2	-19.2	87	21	1,000,000	0	0.0	0.0
C+ /5.6	12.6	0.85	18.45	53	5	94	0	1	41	47.7	-22.9	59	14	2,000	0	0.0	0.0
C+ /5.6	12.6	0.85	18.61	54	5	94	0	1	41	49.0	-22.9	63	14	1,000,000	0	0.0	0.0
C- /3.3	15.5	1.14	19.29	108	0	99	0	1	63	71.3	-19.9	6	9	1,000,000	0	0.0	0.0
C- /3.3	15.5	1.14	18.96	286	0	99	0	1	63	69.7	-20.0	5	9	2,000	0	0.0	0.0
C /5.5	13.8	1.17	37.68	1,284	0	100	0	0	19	120.3	-25.1	58	23	2,000	0	0.0	0.0
C+ /6.2	11.6	0.44	27.33	977	6	93	0	1	19	158.1	-23.1	99	6	1,000,000	0	0.0	0.0
C+ /6.2	11.6	0.44	27.09	864	6	93	0	1	19	155.8	-23.1	99	6	2,000	0	0.0	0.0
C+ /5.7	12.0	1.05	14.87	154	2	93	0	5	34	76.4	-20.8	16	19	1,000,000	0	0.0	0.0
C+ /5.7	12.0	1.05	14.69	46	2	93	0	5	34	75.0	-20.9	15	19	2,000	0	0.0	0.0
C /5.5	13.8	1.17	38.26	736	0	100	0	0	19	122.4	-25.0	62	23	1,000,000	0	0.0	0.0
C /5.4	12.2	0.85	35.19	3,271	5	94	0	1	16	93.5	-22.6	82	18	2,000	0	0.0	0.0
C /5.4	12.2	0.85	35.77	2,206	5	94	0	1	16	95.3	-22.5	83	18	1,000,000	0	0.0	0.0
C+ /6.7	10.2	1.02	15.72	19	6	93	0	1	30	81.4	-17.8	26	11	2,500	50	0.0	0.0
C /5.5	11.4	1.09	32.44	63	0	99	0	1	1	73.9	-24.6	10	9	1,000	50	0.0	0.0
B- /7.4	11.6	1.09	26.44	26	3	96	0	1	45	107.0	-20.2	72	2	250,000	0	0.0	0.0
B- /7.4	11.6	1.09	26.39	N/A	3	96	0	1	45	106.2	-20.2	70	2	2,500	100	0.0	0.0
B- /7.9	8.2	0.82	22.42	5,506	5	89	4	2	8	78.9	-11.5	69	10	10,000	10,000	0.0	2.0
B- /7.9	8.1	0.82	14.44	354	5	89	4	2	8	77.5	-11.6	67	10	5,000	250	0.0	2.0
U /	N/A	N/A	11.24	133	8	91	0	1	40	N/A	N/A	N/A	2	10,000	1,000	0.0	2.0
C+ /6.2	11.7	0.87	14.99	81	2	97	0	1	15	42.0	-16.6	56	11	5,000,000	25,000	0.0	2.0
C+ /6.2	11.7	0.87	14.96	760	2	97	0	1	15	40.7	-16.7	52	11	10,000	10,000	0.0	2.0
C+ /6.5	11.9	1.12	15.11	32	2	97	0	1	51	85.6	N/A	24	4	1,000	1	0.0	1.0
C- /4.2	8.2	0.50	17.12	68	27	70	1	2	39	31.3	-21.6	55	10	2,500	1,000	0.0	2.0
C /5.3	11.6	0.67	12.42	124	12	87	0	1	32	56.2	-15.5	66	6	2,500	1,000	0.0	2.0
C+ /6.9	10.0	1.02	19.01	218	5	94	0	1	41	102.2	N/A	72	12	250,000	100	0.0	1.0
C+ /6.9	10.0	1.02	18.95	162	5	94	0	1	41	100.7	-18.5	69	12	2,500	100	0.0	1.0
C+ /6.1	8.6	0.77	11.32	1	23	76	0	1	100	45.9	-13.0	21	4	500	250	4.0	1.0
C+ /6.1	8.6	0.77	11.09	12	23	76	0	1	100	42.2	-13.3	15	4	500	250	0.0	1.0
C+ /6.4	11.9	1.18	14.12	117	3	96	0	1	28	81.8	-21.6	9	7	2,500	500	0.0	0.0
D- /1.2	20.5	1.16	18.41	63	0	99	0	1	464	78.4	-13.3	5	18	5,000	500	0.0	2.0
C /5.0	11.8	1.08	15.24	21	15	84	0	1	32	73.2	-18.7	4	13	1,000	250	0.0	1.0

I. Index of Stock Mutual Funds

						PERFORMANCE					Incl. in Returns	
								Total Return % through 3/31/15				
			Overall		Perfor-				Annualized		Dividend	Expense
Fund Type	Fund Name	Ticker Symbol	Investment Rating	Phone	mance Rating/Pts	3 Mo	6 Mo	1Yr / Pct	3Yr / Pct	5Yr / Pct	Yield	Ratio
GR	Berwyn Fund	BERWX	E+	(800) 992-6757	C- / 3.6	1.38	3.48	-3.64 / 8	10.71 / 44	12.80 / 66	0.00	1.20
GR	Biondo Focus Inv	BFONX	D-	(800) 672-9152	C+ / 5.8	-1.73	0.57	10.65 / 77	13.62 / 64	10.01 / 45	0.00	3.59
GR	Biondo Growth Inv	BIONX	D+	(800) 672-9152	C- / 3.9	0.08	1.07	6.98 / 55	10.42 / 42	7.62 / 27	0.00	1.75
GR	Bishop Street Dividend Value I	BSLIX	B-	(800) 262-9565	C+ / 6.5	-0.30	4.13	9.78 / 73	13.91 / 66	13.03 / 68	1.79	1.38
GR	Bishop Street Strategic Growth Inst	BSRIX	C	(800) 262-9565	B / 8.0	5.74	9.99	14.45 / 90	14.13 / 68	13.98 / 77	0.00	1.40
FS	BlackRock ACWI ex US Id Fd Inst	BDOIX	E+	(800) 441-7762	D- / 1.4	3.68	-0.81	-1.52 / 11	5.58 / 15	--	2.59	1.09
FS	BlackRock ACWI ex US Id Fd Inv A	BDOAX	E+	(800) 441-7762	D- / 1.3	3.77	-0.98	-1.79 / 11	5.33 / 14	--	2.41	1.75
FS	BlackRock ACWI ex US Id Fd K	BDOKX	E+	(800) 441-7762	D / 1.7	3.71	-0.87	-1.55 / 11	6.36 / 18	--	2.56	1.20
AG	BlackRock Aggr Pre Inst	BIAPX	C	(800) 441-7762	C+ / 6.4	2.70	6.19	9.18 / 70	13.43 / 63	11.65 / 58	3.24	1.23
AG	BlackRock Aggr Pre Inv A	BAAPX	C-	(800) 441-7762	C / 5.3	2.56	5.99	8.78 / 68	13.04 / 60	11.25 / 55	2.75	1.53
AG	BlackRock Aggr Pre Inv C	BCAPX	C	(800) 441-7762	C+ / 5.6	2.45	5.63	7.99 / 63	12.21 / 54	10.43 / 48	1.97	2.28
AG	BlackRock Aggr Pre R	BRAPX	C	(800) 441-7762	C+ / 6.1	2.58	5.94	8.67 / 67	12.89 / 59	11.08 / 53	2.67	1.78
EN	BlackRock AllCap Energy & Res Inst	BACIX	E-	(800) 441-7762	E- / 0.2	-4.71	-18.91	-17.18 / 1	-2.34 / 3	-0.41 / 2	1.87	1.00
EN	BlackRock AllCap Energy & Res Inv	BACAX	E-	(800) 441-7762	E- / 0.2	-4.83	-19.04	-17.52 / 1	-2.75 / 2	-0.83 / 2	1.21	1.40
EN	● BlackRock AllCap Energy & Res Inv	BACBX	E-	(800) 441-7762	E- / 0.2	-4.98	-19.38	-18.12 / 1	-3.46 / 2	-1.57 / 2	0.00	2.34
EN	BlackRock AllCap Energy & Res Inv	BACCX	E-	(800) 441-7762	E- / 0.2	-4.99	-19.38	-18.12 / 1	-3.45 / 2	-1.55 / 2	0.38	2.12
EN	BlackRock AllCap Energy & Res Svc	BACSX	E-	(800) 441-7762	E- / 0.2	-4.82	-19.08	-17.46 / 1	-2.72 / 2	-0.80 / 2	1.34	1.35
BA	BlackRock Bal Capital Inst	MACPX	C+	(800) 441-7762	C / 5.5	0.92	5.39	9.35 / 71	11.89 / 52	10.67 / 50	1.91	0.95
BA	BlackRock Bal Capital Inv A	MDCPX	C	(800) 441-7762	C / 4.4	0.88	5.24	9.05 / 70	11.55 / 49	10.32 / 47	1.56	1.25
BA	● BlackRock Bal Capital Inv B	MBCPX	C	(800) 441-7762	C / 4.5	0.60	4.64	7.94 / 62	10.43 / 42	9.22 / 38	0.56	2.26
BA	BlackRock Bal Capital Inv C	MCCPX	C	(800) 441-7762	C / 4.6	0.69	4.85	8.21 / 64	10.69 / 44	9.46 / 40	1.13	2.02
BA	BlackRock Bal Capital R	MRBPX	C	(800) 441-7762	C / 5.0	0.80	5.07	8.68 / 68	11.18 / 47	9.91 / 44	1.38	1.59
GI	BlackRock Basic Value Inst	MABAX	C	(800) 441-7762	B+ / 8.4	2.66	5.38	9.92 / 74	16.61 / 87	13.08 / 69	1.49	0.54
GI	BlackRock Basic Value Inv A	MDBAX	C-	(800) 441-7762	B- / 7.1	2.61	5.26	9.66 / 73	16.30 / 85	12.76 / 66	1.20	0.81
GI	● BlackRock Basic Value Inv B	MBBAX	C-	(800) 441-7762	B- / 7.3	2.35	4.72	8.56 / 67	15.11 / 76	11.62 / 58	0.00	1.89
GI	BlackRock Basic Value Inv C	MCBAX	C-	(800) 441-7762	B- / 7.5	2.39	4.83	8.79 / 68	15.39 / 78	11.86 / 60	0.62	1.60
GI	BlackRock Basic Value R	MRBVX	C-	(800) 441-7762	B / 7.9	2.54	5.08	9.29 / 71	15.92 / 83	12.38 / 63	0.96	1.12
GR	BlackRock Capital Appr BlackRock	BFGBX	C-	(800) 441-7762	B / 8.2	4.08	9.88	15.83 / 93	14.53 / 71	12.79 / 66	0.00	0.76
GR	BlackRock Capital Appr Inst	MAFGX	C-	(800) 441-7762	B / 8.1	4.01	9.80	15.68 / 93	14.41 / 70	12.68 / 66	0.00	0.79
GR	BlackRock Capital Appr Inv A	MDFGX	D+	(800) 441-7762	C+ / 6.9	3.97	9.68	15.40 / 92	14.11 / 68	12.38 / 63	0.00	1.07
GR	● BlackRock Capital Appr Inv B	MBFGX	D	(800) 441-7762	C+ / 6.9	3.66	9.06	14.25 / 90	12.95 / 59	11.28 / 55	0.00	2.10
GR	BlackRock Capital Appr Inv C	MCFGX	D	(800) 441-7762	B- / 7.2	3.74	9.24	14.48 / 91	13.21 / 61	11.47 / 57	0.00	1.86
GR	BlackRock Capital Appr R	MRFGX	D+	(800) 441-7762	B / 7.6	3.91	9.55	15.11 / 92	13.80 / 66	12.06 / 61	0.00	1.33
AA	BlackRock Cmdty Strat Ptf Inst	BICSX	E-	(800) 441-7762	E- / 0.1	-5.68	-16.12	-21.70 / 1	-10.07 / 1	--	0.03	1.33
AA	BlackRock Cmdty Strat Ptf Inv A	BCSAX	E-	(800) 441-7762	E- / 0.1	-5.71	-16.21	-21.81 / 1	-10.24 / 1	--	0.00	1.78
AA	BlackRock Cmdty Strat Ptf Inv C	BCSCX	E-	(800) 441-7762	E- / 0.1	-5.97	-16.57	-22.43 / 1	-10.92 / 1	--	0.00	2.43
GI	BlackRock Cons Prepared Inst	BICPX	C	(800) 441-7762	C- / 3.9	2.89	5.18	7.93 / 62	9.00 / 33	8.92 / 36	3.21	0.84
GI	BlackRock Cons Prepared Inv A	BACPX	C-	(800) 441-7762	D+ / 2.8	2.83	5.03	7.44 / 59	8.57 / 30	8.47 / 33	2.74	1.16
GI	BlackRock Cons Prepared Inv C	BCCPX	C	(800) 441-7762	C- / 3.1	2.58	4.63	6.69 / 53	7.79 / 26	7.68 / 28	2.26	1.91
GI	BlackRock Cons Prepared R	BRCPX	C	(800) 441-7762	C- / 3.5	2.75	4.95	7.28 / 57	8.36 / 29	8.24 / 31	2.64	1.50
EM	BlackRock Emerg Mkt Alloc Inst	BEEIX	U	(800) 441-7762	U /	2.99	-0.02	5.39 / 42	--	--	0.67	2.00
EM	BlackRock Emerg Mkt Institutional	MADCX	E+	(800) 441-7762	E / 0.5	-0.15	-3.35	0.52 / 17	0.06 / 4	1.96 / 4	0.56	1.17
EM	BlackRock Emerg Mkt Inv A	MDDCX	E+	(800) 441-7762	E / 0.4	-0.27	-3.59	0.10 / 16	-0.31 / 4	1.61 / 4	0.14	1.58
EM	● BlackRock Emerg Mkt Inv B	MBDCX	E+	(800) 441-7762	E / 0.4	-0.54	-4.07	-0.96 / 13	-1.36 / 3	0.62 / 3	0.00	2.66
EM	BlackRock Emerg Mkt Inv C	MCDCX	E+	(800) 441-7762	E / 0.4	-0.44	-3.96	-0.74 / 14	-1.15 / 3	0.77 / 3	0.00	2.41
FO	BlackRock Emerging Mkts Div Inst	BICHX	E	(800) 441-7762	E+ / 0.7	0.00	-3.65	-1.99 / 10	2.59 / 7	--	2.57	6.99
FO	BlackRock Emerging Mkts Div Inv A	BACHX	E	(800) 441-7762	E / 0.5	-0.12	-3.80	-2.24 / 10	2.29 / 7	--	2.20	7.44
FO	BlackRock Emerging Mkts Div Inv C	BCCHX	E	(800) 441-7762	E+ / 0.6	-0.24	-4.08	-2.92 / 9	1.62 / 6	--	1.76	8.38
EM	BlackRock Emg Mkt LS Eqty Inst	BLSIX	D+	(800) 441-7762	E+ / 0.6	1.07	0.00	3.18 / 27	0.49 / 5	--	0.00	2.03
EM	BlackRock Emg Mkt LS Eqty Inv A	BLSAX	D+	(800) 441-7762	E / 0.5	1.08	0.00	3.09 / 27	0.30 / 5	--	0.00	2.19
EM	BlackRock Emg Mkt LS Eqty Inv C	BLSCX	D+	(800) 441-7762	E / 0.5	0.80	-0.39	2.23 / 23	-0.48 / 4	--	0.00	2.97
EN	BlackRock Energy & Resources Inst	SGLSX	E-	(800) 441-7762	E- / 0.1	-4.49	-28.71	-31.79 / 0	-10.10 / 1	-5.17 / 1	0.00	1.04

● Denotes fund is closed to new investors
* Denotes fund is included in Section II

RISK			NET ASSETS		ASSET					BULL / BEAR		FUND MANAGER		MINIMUMS		LOADS	
	3 Year		NAV						Portfolio	Last Bull	Last Bear	Manager	Manager	Initial	Additional	Front	Back
Risk	Standard		As of	Total	Cash	Stocks	Bonds	Other	Turnover	Market	Market	Quality	Tenure	Purch.	Purch.	End	End
Rating/Pts	Deviation	Beta	3/31/15	$(Mil)	%	%	%	%	Ratio	Return	Return	Pct	(Years)	$	$	Load	Load
D+ / 2.4	14.3	1.21	32.23	311	0	100	0	0	29	87.0	-24.9	3	31	1,000	250	0.0	1.0
D / 1.9	22.6	1.77	15.90	31	0	0	0	100	81	94.9	-28.8	1	5	1,000	100	0.0	2.0
C / 5.2	13.6	1.23	13.18	37	5	94	0	1	46	72.2	-22.0	3	9	1,000	100	0.0	2.0
B- / 7.9	9.1	0.92	13.52	55	2	97	0	1	13	84.2	-13.0	56	5	1,000	0	0.0	0.0
C- / 3.1	13.5	1.16	15.10	46	25	74	0	1	130	94.3	-21.0	16	2	1,000	0	0.0	0.0
C / 4.3	13.0	0.81	8.69	18	2	97	0	1	36	38.2	N/A	4	N/A	2,000,000	0	0.0	0.0
C / 4.3	13.0	0.80	8.68	2	2	97	0	1	36	36.9	N/A	3	N/A	1,000	50	0.0	0.0
C / 4.3	13.2	0.81	8.92	7	2	97	0	1	36	41.4	N/A	5	N/A	1	1	0.0	0.0
C / 5.3	10.4	1.06	12.56	2	17	82	0	1	56	82.7	-20.4	23	8	2,000,000	0	0.0	0.0
C / 5.3	10.4	1.06	12.40	22	17	82	0	1	56	80.3	-20.4	20	8	1,000	50	5.3	0.0
C / 5.4	10.4	1.06	12.11	15	17	82	0	1	56	75.7	-20.7	14	8	1,000	50	0.0	0.0
C / 5.3	10.4	1.06	12.31	7	17	82	0	1	56	79.5	-20.5	18	8	100	0	0.0	0.0
D+ / 2.7	17.7	1.06	12.95	31	1	98	0	1	71	13.2	-33.6	6	2	2,000,000	0	0.0	0.0
D+ / 2.7	17.7	1.06	12.61	70	1	98	0	1	71	11.5	-33.7	5	2	1,000	50	5.3	0.0
D+ / 2.7	17.7	1.06	12.02	2	1	98	0	1	71	8.7	-33.9	4	2	1,000	50	0.0	0.0
D+ / 2.7	17.7	1.06	12.00	46	1	98	0	1	71	8.8	-33.9	4	2	1,000	50	0.0	0.0
D+ / 2.7	17.7	1.06	12.63	1	1	98	0	1	71	11.7	-33.7	5	2	5,000	0	0.0	0.0
C+ / 6.6	6.8	1.15	24.26	385	2	64	32	2	40	65.0	-12.8	58	9	2,000,000	0	0.0	0.0
C+ / 6.6	6.8	1.15	24.19	507	2	64	32	2	40	63.4	-13.0	53	9	1,000	50	5.3	0.0
C+ / 6.7	6.8	1.15	23.47	3	2	64	32	2	40	57.8	-13.3	38	9	1,000	50	0.0	0.0
C+ / 6.4	6.8	1.15	21.87	91	2	64	32	2	40	59.0	-13.2	41	9	1,000	50	0.0	0.0
C+ / 6.4	6.8	1.15	22.81	10	2	64	32	2	40	61.4	-13.1	48	9	100	0	0.0	0.0
C- / 3.0	11.8	1.16	27.76	1,952	0	99	0	1	47	102.4	-21.1	37	6	2,000,000	0	0.0	0.0
C- / 3.0	11.8	1.16	27.49	1,784	0	99	0	1	47	100.5	-21.2	33	6	1,000	50	5.3	0.0
C- / 3.4	11.8	1.16	27.46	9	0	99	0	1	47	93.5	-21.5	22	6	0	0	0.0	0.0
D+ / 2.6	11.8	1.17	24.80	438	0	99	0	1	47	95.2	-21.4	24	6	1,000	50	0.0	0.0
D+ / 2.8	11.8	1.17	26.22	16	0	99	0	1	47	98.2	-21.3	29	6	100	0	0.0	0.0
D+ / 2.6	12.0	1.08	26.27	455	0	99	0	1	100	87.9	-20.4	30	2	5,000,000	0	0.0	0.0
D+ / 2.7	12.0	1.08	26.21	769	0	99	0	1	100	87.3	-20.4	29	2	2,000,000	0	0.0	0.0
D+ / 2.4	12.0	1.08	24.87	1,730	0	99	0	1	100	85.6	-20.5	27	2	1,000	50	5.3	0.0
D- / 1.4	12.0	1.08	20.10	15	0	99	0	1	100	79.2	-20.8	17	2	1,000	50	0.0	0.0
D- / 1.3	12.0	1.08	20.26	639	0	99	0	1	100	80.5	-20.8	19	2	1,000	50	0.0	0.0
D / 1.7	12.0	1.07	21.80	76	0	99	0	1	100	83.8	-20.6	24	2	100	0	0.0	0.0
D+ / 2.5	12.9	1.49	7.64	396	2	48	48	2	71	N/A	N/A	0	4	2,000,000	0	0.0	0.0
D+ / 2.4	12.9	1.48	7.60	11	2	48	48	2	71	N/A	N/A	0	4	1,000	50	5.3	0.0
D+ / 2.3	12.9	1.48	7.40	6	2	48	48	2	71	N/A	N/A	0	4	1,000	50	0.0	0.0
B- / 7.9	4.5	0.43	11.73	15	19	34	46	1	46	44.6	-8.2	85	8	2,000,000	0	0.0	0.0
B- / 7.9	4.6	0.43	11.62	56	19	34	46	1	46	42.7	-8.4	82	8	1,000	50	5.3	0.0
B / 8.1	4.6	0.43	11.53	46	19	34	46	1	46	39.2	-8.7	77	8	1,000	50	0.0	0.0
B / 8.0	4.6	0.43	11.57	10	19	34	46	1	46	41.5	-8.4	81	8	100	0	0.0	0.0
U /	N/A	N/A	9.66	55	0	54	45	1	37	N/A	N/A	N/A	2	2,000,000	0	0.0	0.0
C / 5.4	14.0	1.00	19.46	529	6	93	0	1	94	24.9	-24.8	58	6	2,000,000	0	0.0	0.0
C / 5.4	14.0	1.00	18.79	221	6	93	0	1	94	23.3	-24.8	52	6	1,000	50	5.3	0.0
C / 5.3	14.1	1.00	16.48	1	6	93	0	1	94	19.0	-25.1	37	6	1,000	50	0.0	0.0
C / 5.3	14.0	1.00	16.02	124	6	93	0	1	94	19.8	-25.1	40	6	1,000	50	0.0	0.0
C / 4.9	14.9	0.81	8.29	3	2	97	0	1	71	32.7	-31.0	11	2	2,000,000	0	0.0	0.0
C / 4.9	14.9	0.81	8.25	1	2	97	0	1	71	31.5	-31.1	9	2	1,000	50	5.3	0.0
C / 4.8	14.9	0.81	8.19	N/A	2	97	0	1	71	28.4	-31.3	7	2	1,000	0	0.0	0.0
B / 8.9	4.5	0.12	10.39	494	79	20	0	1	0	N/A	N/A	71	N/A	2,000,000	0	0.0	0.0
B / 8.9	4.5	0.12	10.33	29	79	20	0	1	0	N/A	N/A	69	N/A	1,000	50	5.3	0.0
B / 8.8	4.5	0.12	10.10	11	79	20	0	1	0	N/A	N/A	58	N/A	1,000	50	0.0	0.0
D- / 1.4	21.9	1.23	27.01	120	1	98	0	1	56	-8.6	-37.2	0	2	2,000,000	0	0.0	0.0

Fund Type	Fund Name	Ticker Symbol	Overall Investment Rating	Phone	Perfor-mance Rating/Pts	3 Mo	6 Mo	1Yr / Pct	3Yr / Pct	5Yr / Pct	Dividend Yield	Expense Ratio
								Total Return % through 3/31/15			Incl. in Returns	
									Annualized			
EN	BlackRock Energy & Resources Inv A	SSGRX	E-	(800) 441-7762	E- / 0.1	-4.58	-28.82	-31.99 / 0	-10.37 / 1	-5.48 / 1	0.00	1.32
EN	● BlackRock Energy & Resources Inv B	SSGPX	E-	(800) 441-7762	E- / 0.1	-4.75	-29.12	-32.56 / 0	-11.07 / 1	-6.20 / 1	0.00	2.33
EN	BlackRock Energy & Resources Inv C	SSGDX	E-	(800) 441-7762	E- / 0.1	-4.73	-29.07	-32.48 / 0	-11.04 / 1	-6.18 / 1	0.00	2.07
IN	BlackRock Eq Dividend Inst	MADVX	C+	(800) 441-7762	C / 5.0	-1.00	3.20	6.93 / 54	11.91 / 52	11.92 / 60	1.90	0.70
* IN	BlackRock Eq Dividend Inv A	MDDVX	C	(800) 441-7762	C- / 4.0	-1.08	3.04	6.65 / 52	11.61 / 50	11.61 / 58	1.55	0.95
IN	● BlackRock Eq Dividend Inv B	MBDVX	C	(800) 441-7762	C / 4.3	-1.23	2.66	5.84 / 45	10.77 / 44	10.76 / 51	0.84	1.71
IN	BlackRock Eq Dividend Inv C	MCDVX	C	(800) 441-7762	C / 4.3	-1.23	2.70	5.89 / 45	10.82 / 44	10.82 / 51	1.01	1.67
IN	BlackRock Eq Dividend Inv C1	BEDCX	C+	(800) 441-7762	C / 4.5	-1.19	2.81	6.10 / 47	11.03 / 46	--	1.19	1.49
IN	BlackRock Eq Dividend R	MRDVX	C+	(800) 441-7762	C / 4.6	-1.12	2.91	6.32 / 49	11.27 / 47	11.27 / 55	1.33	1.27
IN	BlackRock Eq Dividend Svc	MSDVX	C+	(800) 441-7762	C / 4.8	-1.05	3.06	6.58 / 52	11.56 / 49	11.61 / 58	1.57	1.01
FO	BlackRock Eurofund Inst	MAEFX	D-	(800) 441-7762	C- / 3.1	4.99	2.13	-7.15 / 4	9.68 / 37	6.13 / 18	2.97	1.02
FO	BlackRock Eurofund Inv A	MDEFX	D-	(800) 441-7762	D / 2.1	4.86	1.97	-7.40 / 4	9.44 / 36	5.90 / 16	2.57	1.23
FO	BlackRock Eurofund Inv C	MCEFX	D-	(800) 441-7762	D+ / 2.4	4.74	1.62	-8.12 / 3	8.55 / 30	5.01 / 12	2.99	2.07
FO	BlackRock Eurofund R	MREFX	D-	(800) 441-7762	D+ / 2.5	4.78	1.68	-7.90 / 3	8.87 / 32	5.30 / 13	2.69	1.79
GR	● BlackRock Exchange Port BlkRk	STSEX	C	(800) 441-7762	C / 4.3	-2.28	-0.04	5.04 / 39	11.26 / 47	9.96 / 44	2.49	0.68
MC	BlackRock Flexible Equity Inst	CMVIX	D-	(800) 441-7762	C- / 3.1	1.50	4.42	4.06 / 32	8.21 / 28	8.44 / 33	2.78	1.09
MC	BlackRock Flexible Equity Inv A	BMCAX	E+	(800) 441-7762	D / 2.1	1.47	4.26	3.75 / 30	7.84 / 26	8.10 / 31	2.48	1.40
MC	● BlackRock Flexible Equity Inv B	BMCVX	E+	(800) 441-7762	D+ / 2.3	1.19	3.82	2.93 / 26	7.01 / 21	7.26 / 25	2.02	2.41
MC	BlackRock Flexible Equity Inv C	BMCCX	E+	(800) 441-7762	D+ / 2.3	1.21	3.79	2.89 / 26	6.99 / 21	7.25 / 25	2.29	2.14
MC	BlackRock Flexible Equity R	BMCRX	D-	(800) 441-7762	D+ / 2.6	1.35	4.05	3.41 / 29	7.45 / 24	--	2.38	1.68
MC	BlackRock Flexible Equity Svc	CMVSX	D-	(800) 441-7762	D+ / 2.8	1.36	4.17	3.73 / 30	7.85 / 26	8.09 / 30	2.46	1.30
GR	BlackRock Focus Growth Fd Inst	MAFOX	C+	(800) 441-7762	B+ / 8.9	4.55	11.13	17.33 / 95	15.26 / 77	13.89 / 77	0.00	1.30
GR	BlackRock Focus Growth Fd Inv A	MDFOX	C-	(800) 441-7762	B / 7.7	4.50	11.08	16.89 / 94	14.91 / 74	13.44 / 72	0.00	1.69
GR	BlackRock Focus Growth Fd Inv C	MCFOX	C-	(800) 441-7762	B / 8.2	4.45	10.68	16.03 / 93	14.22 / 69	12.64 / 65	0.00	2.44
GI	BlackRock Glbl Long/Short Eqty Inst	BDMIX	U	(800) 441-7762	U /	0.93	-1.29	4.38 / 34	--	--	0.00	1.89
GI	BlackRock Glbl Long/Short Eqty InvA	BDMAX	U	(800) 441-7762	U /	0.85	-1.46	4.04 / 32	--	--	0.00	2.15
GI	BlackRock Glbl Long/Short Eqty InvC	BDMCX	U	(800) 441-7762	U /	0.69	-1.82	3.28 / 28	--	--	0.00	2.90
GL	BlackRock Global Allocation Inst	MALOX	D+	(800) 441-7762	D+ / 2.5	2.77	2.20	4.34 / 34	7.09 / 22	6.80 / 22	2.40	0.87
* GL	BlackRock Global Allocation Inv A	MDLOX	D	(800) 441-7762	D / 1.6	2.68	2.05	4.02 / 32	6.80 / 20	6.51 / 20	2.03	1.13
GL	● BlackRock Global Allocation Inv B	MBLOX	D	(800) 441-7762	D / 1.8	2.54	1.68	3.26 / 28	5.98 / 17	5.66 / 15	1.28	1.93
GL	BlackRock Global Allocation Inv C	MCLOX	D	(800) 441-7762	D / 1.9	2.53	1.68	3.28 / 28	6.02 / 17	5.72 / 15	1.60	1.87
GL	BlackRock Global Allocation R	MRLOX	D	(800) 441-7762	D / 2.1	2.63	1.91	3.73 / 30	6.43 / 19	6.14 / 18	1.89	1.47
AA	BlackRock Global Dividend Inst	BIBDX	C-	(800) 441-7762	C- / 3.0	0.42	-0.78	0.97 / 18	9.20 / 34	9.27 / 39	3.35	0.76
AA	BlackRock Global Dividend Inv A	BABDX	D	(800) 441-7762	D / 2.0	0.34	-0.94	0.59 / 17	8.88 / 32	8.97 / 36	2.91	1.04
AA	BlackRock Global Dividend Inv C	BCBDX	D+	(800) 441-7762	D+ / 2.3	0.17	-1.25	-0.06 / 15	8.08 / 27	8.18 / 31	2.35	1.78
GL	BlackRock Global Opps Port Inst	BROIX	C-	(800) 441-7762	C / 4.4	4.96	4.77	1.75 / 21	10.75 / 44	7.59 / 27	1.71	1.20
GL	BlackRock Global Opps Port Inv A	BROAX	D+	(800) 441-7762	C- / 3.4	4.93	4.63	1.52 / 20	10.48 / 42	7.29 / 25	1.36	1.46
GL	● BlackRock Global Opps Port Inv B	BROBX	D+	(800) 441-7762	C- / 3.6	4.66	4.12	0.64 / 17	9.53 / 36	6.37 / 19	0.00	2.21
GL	● BlackRock Global Opps Port Inv C	BROCX	D+	(800) 441-7762	C- / 3.7	4.71	4.19	0.76 / 18	9.59 / 37	6.39 / 19	0.58	2.24
GL	● BlackRock Global Opps Port Inv R	BGORX	C-	(800) 441-7762	C- / 4.0	4.80	4.40	1.14 / 19	10.04 / 40	--	0.93	1.81
GL	BlackRock Global Small Cap Inst	MAGCX	D	(800) 441-7762	C / 5.4	2.57	3.44	0.54 / 17	13.13 / 61	10.91 / 52	0.37	1.03
GL	BlackRock Global Small Cap Inv A	MDGCX	D-	(800) 441-7762	C / 4.3	2.48	3.28	0.19 / 16	12.75 / 58	10.55 / 49	0.21	1.37
GL	● BlackRock Global Small Cap Inv B	MBGCX	D-	(800) 441-7762	C / 4.5	2.26	2.81	-0.64 / 14	11.72 / 51	9.54 / 41	0.00	2.22
GL	BlackRock Global Small Cap Inv C	MCGCX	D-	(800) 441-7762	C / 4.6	2.29	2.85	-0.60 / 14	11.84 / 51	9.64 / 42	0.00	2.16
GL	BlackRock Global SmallCap R	MRGSX	D-	(800) 441-7762	C / 4.9	2.38	3.07	-0.15 / 15	12.33 / 55	10.11 / 46	0.02	1.72
GR	BlackRock Gr Prepared Inst	BIGPX	C+	(800) 441-7762	C+ / 5.7	2.84	5.86	8.81 / 68	12.11 / 53	10.95 / 52	3.44	1.05
GR	BlackRock Gr Prepared Inv A	BAGPX	C	(800) 441-7762	C / 4.5	2.71	5.57	8.30 / 65	11.65 / 50	10.51 / 49	2.85	1.30
GR	BlackRock Gr Prepared Inv C	BCGPX	C+	(800) 441-7762	C / 4.8	2.50	5.25	7.53 / 59	10.88 / 45	9.74 / 42	2.29	2.06
GR	BlackRock Gr Prepared R	BRGPX	C+	(800) 441-7762	C / 5.2	2.63	5.50	8.16 / 64	11.47 / 49	10.34 / 47	2.77	1.61
HL	BlackRock Health Sci Opps Inst	SHSSX	A	(800) 441-7762	A+ / 9.9	10.26	20.60	34.91 / 99	30.38 / 99	21.38 / 99	0.26	0.91
HL	BlackRock Health Sci Opps Inv A	SHSAX	A	(800) 441-7762	A+ / 9.9	10.20	20.43	34.56 / 99	30.02 / 99	21.02 / 99	0.04	1.19
HL	● BlackRock Health Sci Opps Inv B	SHSPX	A	(800) 441-7762	A+ / 9.9	9.98	19.95	33.49 / 99	28.98 / 99	20.08 / 99	0.00	1.98

99 Pct = Best
0 Pct = Worst

RISK			NET ASSETS		ASSET					BULL / BEAR		FUND MANAGER		MINIMUMS		LOADS	
	3 Year		NAV						Portfolio	Last Bull	Last Bear	Manager	Manager	Initial	Additional	Front	Back
Risk Rating/Pts	Standard Deviation	Beta	As of 3/31/15	Total $(Mil)	Cash %	Stocks %	Bonds %	Other %	Turnover Ratio	Market Return	Market Return	Quality Pct	Tenure (Years)	Purch. $	Purch. $	End Load	End Load
D- / 1.4	21.9	1.23	23.34	230	1	98	0	1	56	-9.6	-37.3	0	2	1,000	50	5.3	0.0
D- / 1.4	21.9	1.23	16.84	2	1	98	0	1	56	-11.9	-37.5	0	2	1,000	50	0.0	0.0
D- / 1.4	21.9	1.23	16.71	57	1	98	0	1	56	-11.8	-37.5	0	2	1,000	50	0.0	0.0
B- / 7.4	9.1	0.92	24.70	14,435	0	99	0	1	6	72.4	-13.7	30	14	2,000,000	0	0.0	0.0
B- / 7.5	9.1	0.92	24.63	7,825	0	99	0	1	6	70.9	-13.8	27	14	1,000	50	5.3	0.0
B- / 7.5	9.1	0.92	24.82	26	0	99	0	1	6	66.5	-14.1	20	14	1,000	50	0.0	0.0
B- / 7.4	9.1	0.92	24.01	3,469	0	99	0	1	6	66.8	-14.1	20	14	1,000	50	0.0	0.0
B- / 7.4	9.1	0.92	23.99	7	0	99	0	1	6	67.8	N/A	22	14	0	0	0.0	0.0
B- / 7.5	9.1	0.92	24.74	1,078	0	99	0	1	6	69.2	-14.0	24	14	100	0	0.0	0.0
B- / 7.5	9.1	0.92	24.61	262	0	99	0	1	6	70.8	-13.8	27	14	5,000	0	0.0	0.0
C / 4.9	14.6	1.04	15.16	270	1	98	0	1	129	63.2	-28.9	64	5	2,000,000	0	0.0	0.0
C / 5.0	14.6	1.04	14.88	153	1	98	0	1	129	62.0	-29.0	61	5	1,000	50	5.3	0.0
C / 4.8	14.6	1.04	10.60	17	1	98	0	1	129	57.5	-29.2	48	5	1,000	50	0.0	0.0
C / 4.9	14.5	1.04	11.40	1	1	98	0	1	129	59.0	-29.1	53	5	100	0	0.0	0.0
B- / 7.3	10.1	1.01	849.54	180	0	99	0	1	2	71.0	-15.1	13	2	1,000	50	0.0	0.0
C / 4.5	9.3	0.74	12.88	50	1	97	0	2	102	63.9	-24.3	18	N/A	2,000,000	0	0.0	0.0
C / 4.4	9.3	0.74	12.41	416	1	97	0	2	102	62.0	-24.4	15	N/A	1,000	50	5.3	0.0
C- / 4.1	9.3	0.74	11.03	6	1	97	0	2	102	57.9	-24.7	11	N/A	1,000	50	0.0	0.0
C- / 4.0	9.3	0.75	10.90	85	1	97	0	2	102	57.8	-24.7	10	N/A	1,000	50	0.0	0.0
C / 4.5	9.3	0.74	12.79	1	1	97	0	2	102	60.0	-24.5	13	N/A	100	0	0.0	0.0
C / 4.5	9.3	0.75	12.67	N/A	1	97	0	2	102	62.1	-24.4	15	N/A	5,000	0	0.0	0.0
C- / 3.0	12.3	1.07	3.22	17	0	99	0	1	130	90.0	-21.2	41	2	2,000,000	0	0.0	0.0
D+ / 2.8	12.3	1.07	3.02	38	0	99	0	1	130	87.3	-21.4	36	2	1,000	50	5.3	0.0
D / 2.1	12.4	1.07	2.58	26	0	99	0	1	130	82.5	-21.4	28	2	1,000	50	0.0	0.0
U /	N/A	N/A	11.97	1,410	95	4	0	1	0	N/A	N/A	N/A	N/A	2,000,000	0	0.0	0.0
U /	N/A	N/A	11.90	235	95	4	0	1	0	N/A	N/A	N/A	N/A	1,000	50	5.3	0.0
U /	N/A	N/A	11.72	102	95	4	0	1	0	N/A	N/A	N/A	N/A	1,000	50	0.0	0.0
C+ / 6.9	6.7	1.04	20.42	20,828	2	58	35	5	75	39.8	-13.6	36	26	2,000,000	0	0.0	0.0
C+ / 6.9	6.6	1.03	20.30	17,135	2	58	35	5	75	38.6	-13.7	33	26	1,000	50	5.3	0.0
C+ / 6.9	6.7	1.04	19.80	275	2	58	35	5	75	34.9	-14.0	24	26	1,000	50	0.0	0.0
C+ / 6.8	6.6	1.03	18.63	15,217	2	58	35	5	75	35.1	-14.0	24	26	1,000	50	0.0	0.0
C+ / 6.8	6.7	1.04	19.50	1,232	2	58	35	5	75	36.9	-13.8	28	26	100	0	0.0	0.0
B- / 7.0	9.9	1.52	11.82	1,126	1	98	0	1	14	52.9	-9.7	5	5	2,000,000	0	0.0	0.0
B- / 7.0	9.9	1.53	11.77	644	1	98	0	1	14	51.6	-9.8	4	5	1,000	50	5.3	0.0
B- / 7.0	9.9	1.53	11.70	411	1	98	0	1	14	47.7	-10.1	3	5	1,000	50	0.0	0.0
C+ / 6.0	11.6	0.80	14.60	66	1	98	0	1	99	62.6	-23.8	88	9	2,000,000	0	0.0	0.0
C+ / 6.0	11.6	0.80	14.47	187	1	98	0	1	99	61.2	-23.9	87	9	1,000	50	5.3	0.0
C+ / 6.0	11.6	0.80	14.15	1	1	98	0	1	99	56.7	-24.2	83	9	1,000	50	0.0	0.0
C+ / 6.0	11.7	0.80	14.02	49	1	98	0	1	99	56.8	-24.1	83	9	1,000	50	0.0	0.0
C+ / 6.0	11.6	0.80	14.41	10	1	98	0	1	99	59.1	N/A	86	9	100	0	0.0	0.0
C- / 3.4	12.5	0.77	25.19	253	0	98	0	2	77	76.8	-23.7	94	10	2,000,000	0	0.0	0.0
C- / 3.3	12.5	0.77	24.35	469	0	98	0	2	77	74.7	-23.8	93	10	1,000	50	5.3	0.0
C- / 3.0	12.5	0.77	22.66	3	0	98	0	2	77	69.3	-24.1	92	10	1,000	50	0.0	0.0
D+ / 2.7	12.5	0.77	21.42	316	0	98	0	2	77	70.1	-24.1	92	10	1,000	50	0.0	0.0
C- / 3.0	12.5	0.77	22.77	26	0	98	0	2	77	72.5	-23.9	93	10	100	0	0.0	0.0
C+ / 6.9	8.6	0.87	13.05	5	17	66	16	1	69	69.5	-16.1	43	8	2,000,000	0	0.0	0.0
B- / 7.0	8.6	0.87	12.90	48	17	66	16	1	69	67.4	-16.4	37	8	1,000	50	5.3	0.0
B- / 7.1	8.6	0.88	12.70	39	17	66	16	1	69	63.3	-16.6	27	8	1,000	50	0.0	0.0
B- / 7.0	8.6	0.87	12.86	8	17	66	16	1	69	66.4	-16.4	35	8	100	0	0.0	0.0
C / 5.4	11.0	0.83	56.42	1,518	1	98	0	1	57	156.1	-12.5	99	12	2,000,000	0	0.0	0.0
C / 5.4	11.0	0.83	54.46	2,800	1	98	0	1	57	153.6	-12.6	99	12	1,000	50	5.3	0.0
C / 5.5	11.0	0.83	50.57	20	1	98	0	1	57	146.8	-12.9	99	12	1,000	50	0.0	0.0

					PERFORMANCE							
	99 Pct = Best					Total Return % through 3/31/15					Incl. in Returns	
	0 Pct = Worst		Overall		Perfor-					Annualized	Dividend	Expense
Fund		Ticker	Investment		mance						Yield	Ratio
Type	Fund Name	Symbol	Rating	Phone	Rating/Pts	3 Mo	6 Mo	1Yr / Pct	3Yr / Pct	5Yr / Pct		
HL	BlackRock Health Sci Opps Inv C	SHSCX	A	(800) 441-7762	A+ / 9.9	9.98	20.00	33.58 /99	29.07 /99	20.15 /99	0.00	1.91
HL	● BlackRock Health Sci Opps R	BHSRX	A	(800) 441-7762	A+ / 9.9	10.11	20.25	34.15 /99	29.59 /99	--	0.00	1.49
HL	BlackRock Health Sci Opps Svc	SHISX	A	(800) 441-7762	A+ / 9.9	10.19	20.42	34.53 /99	30.00 /99	21.01 /99	0.02	1.21
FO	BlackRock International Inst	MAILX	D-	(800) 441-7762	D- / 1.3	0.91	-2.91	-2.46 / 9	5.92 /16	5.68 /15	2.22	1.23
FO	BlackRock International Inv A	MDILX	E+	(800) 441-7762	E+ / 0.8	0.71	-3.16	-2.89 / 9	5.48 /15	5.29 /13	1.78	1.57
FO	● BlackRock International Inv B	MBILX	E+	(800) 441-7762	E+ / 0.9	0.53	-3.56	-3.77 / 7	4.47 /11	4.21 / 9	0.00	2.65
FO	BlackRock International Inv C	MCILX	E+	(800) 441-7762	E+ / 0.9	0.53	-3.61	-3.82 / 7	4.45 /11	4.33 / 9	0.96	2.43
FO	BlackRock International R	BIFRX	E+	(800) 441-7762	D- / 1.1	0.71	-3.26	-3.13 / 8	5.17 /14	--	1.43	1.84
FO	BlackRock Intl Index Inst	MAIIX	D	(800) 441-7762	D+ / 2.8	5.28	0.60	-1.77 /11	8.52 /30	5.79 /16	0.80	0.19
FO	BlackRock Intl Index Inv A	MDIIX	D	(800) 441-7762	D+ / 2.6	5.24	0.39	-2.07 /10	8.23 /28	5.51 /14	0.52	0.48
FO	BlackRock Intl Index K	BTMKX	D	(800) 441-7762	D+ / 2.8	5.36	0.61	-1.76 /11	8.56 /30	--	0.80	0.15
FO	BlackRock Intl Opps Inst	BISIX	E	(800) 441-7762	D / 1.9	5.27	1.50	-5.33 / 5	7.07 /22	5.22 /13	2.44	1.22
FO	BlackRock Intl Opps Inv A	BREAX	E	(800) 441-7762	D- / 1.2	5.21	1.34	-5.63 / 5	6.74 /20	4.92 /12	2.17	1.53
FO	● BlackRock Intl Opps Inv B	BREBX	E	(800) 441-7762	D- / 1.4	4.99	0.91	-6.36 / 4	5.85 /16	4.06 / 9	1.66	2.39
FO	BlackRock Intl Opps Inv C	BRECX	E	(800) 441-7762	D- / 1.4	5.02	0.99	-6.30 / 4	5.94 /16	4.13 / 9	1.91	2.27
FO	BlackRock Intl Opps Svc	BRESX	E	(800) 441-7762	D / 1.7	5.21	1.34	-5.62 / 5	6.65 /20	4.80 /11	2.26	1.51
GR	BlackRock Large Cap Core Inst	MALRX	B+	(800) 441-7762	B- / 7.3	0.22	5.41	9.69 /73	15.16 /76	12.56 /65	0.55	0.88
GR	BlackRock Large Cap Core Inv A	MDLRX	B-	(800) 441-7762	C+ / 6.1	0.17	5.28	9.41 /71	14.79 /73	12.29 /62	0.31	1.24
GR	● BlackRock Large Cap Core Inv B	MBLRX	B-	(800) 441-7762	C+ / 6.4	-0.06	4.83	8.51 /66	13.86 /66	11.36 /56	0.00	2.29
GR	BlackRock Large Cap Core Inv C	MCLRX	B-	(800) 441-7762	C+ / 6.4	-0.06	4.91	8.58 /67	13.83 /66	11.34 /56	0.00	1.97
GR	● BlackRock Large Cap Core Plus Inst	BILPX	B-	(800) 441-7762	C+ / 6.6	-0.99	5.55	8.23 /64	14.23 /69	13.44 /72	0.00	2.35
GR	● BlackRock Large Cap Core Plus Inv	BALPX	C+	(800) 441-7762	C / 5.5	-1.07	5.36	7.92 /62	13.91 /66	13.09 /69	0.00	2.64
GR	● BlackRock Large Cap Core Plus Inv	BCLPX	C+	(800) 441-7762	C+ / 5.8	-1.26	5.01	7.12 /56	13.08 /60	12.29 /62	0.00	3.44
GR	BlackRock Large Cap Core R	MRLRX	B-	(800) 441-7762	C+ / 6.8	0.12	5.16	9.14 /70	14.41 /70	11.91 /60	0.00	1.43
GR	BlackRock Large Cap Core Ret Port	MKLRX	D	(800) 441-7762	B- / 7.5	0.16	5.50	9.96 /74	15.35 /78	12.84 /67	0.22	0.59
GR	BlackRock Large Cap Core Service	MSLRX	B	(800) 441-7762	B- / 7.0	0.16	5.25	9.36 /71	14.71 /73	12.21 /62	0.27	1.20
GR	BlackRock Large Cap Gro Ret Port K	MKLHX	D+	(800) 441-7762	B+ / 8.4	1.48	8.12	14.55 /91	15.87 /82	14.60 /83	0.57	2.84
GR	BlackRock Large Cap Growth Inst	MALHX	B	(800) 441-7762	B / 8.0	1.41	8.05	14.29 /90	15.15 /76	13.59 /74	0.24	0.95
GR	BlackRock Large Cap Growth Inv A	MDLHX	C+	(800) 441-7762	C+ / 6.7	1.40	7.96	13.97 /89	14.82 /73	13.23 /70	0.06	1.24
GR	● BlackRock Large Cap Growth Inv B	MBLHX	C+	(800) 441-7762	B- / 7.0	1.16	7.47	13.06 /87	13.85 /66	12.31 /63	0.00	2.05
GR	BlackRock Large Cap Growth Inv C	MCLHX	C+	(800) 441-7762	B- / 7.0	1.18	7.50	13.04 /87	13.92 /66	12.36 /63	0.00	2.01
GR	BlackRock Large Cap Growth R	MRLHX	B-	(800) 441-7762	B- / 7.5	1.33	7.78	13.65 /89	14.51 /71	12.92 /67	0.00	1.49
GR	BlackRock Large Cap Growth Svc	MSLHX	B	(800) 441-7762	B / 7.7	1.35	7.89	13.99 /89	14.80 /73	13.26 /71	0.09	1.25
GR	BlackRock Large Cap Value Inst	MALVX	C+	(800) 441-7762	C+ / 6.5	-1.03	4.46	8.16 /64	14.27 /69	11.27 /55	1.07	0.89
GR	BlackRock Large Cap Value Inv A	MDLVX	C+	(800) 441-7762	C / 5.4	-1.10	4.34	7.85 /62	13.92 /66	10.98 /52	0.72	1.22
GR	● BlackRock Large Cap Value Inv B	MBLVX	C+	(800) 441-7762	C+ / 5.6	-1.31	3.83	6.98 /55	12.92 /59	10.00 /44	0.00	2.01
GR	BlackRock Large Cap Value Inv C	MCLVX	C+	(800) 441-7762	C+ / 5.7	-1.32	3.89	6.96 /55	12.99 /60	10.06 /45	0.07	2.01
GR	BlackRock Large Cap Value R	MRLVX	C+	(800) 441-7762	C+ / 6.1	-1.14	4.20	7.59 /60	13.61 /64	10.65 /50	0.49	1.48
GR	BlackRock Large Cap Value Retire K	MKLVX	C+	(800) 441-7762	C+ / 6.7	-0.95	4.58	8.38 /65	14.52 /71	11.60 /58	1.16	0.68
GR	BlackRock Large Cap Value Svc	MSLVX	C+	(800) 441-7762	C+ / 6.3	-1.08	4.31	7.83 /62	13.91 /66	10.98 /52	0.77	1.20
FO	BlackRock Latin America Inst	MALTX	E-	(800) 441-7762	E- / 0.1	-8.96	-19.91	-17.61 / 1	-11.93 / 1	-6.77 / 1	2.70	1.25
FO	BlackRock Latin America Inv A	MDLTX	E-	(800) 441-7762	E- / 0.1	-9.01	-20.02	-17.84 / 1	-12.16 / 1	-7.02 / 1	2.21	1.53
FO	● BlackRock Latin America Inv B	MBLTX	E-	(800) 441-7762	E- / 0.1	-9.25	-20.40	-18.62 / 1	-12.98 / 1	-7.85 / 1	0.68	2.51
FO	BlackRock Latin America Inv C	MCLTX	E-	(800) 441-7762	E- / 0.1	-9.19	-20.34	-18.50 / 1	-12.88 / 1	-7.76 / 1	1.31	2.36
AA	BlackRock LifePath 2020 Inst	STLCX	D+	(800) 441-7762	D+ / 2.4	1.93	3.48	5.30 /41	6.81 /20	7.26 /25	1.48	1.16
AA	BlackRock LifePath 2020 Inv A	LPRCX	D	(800) 441-7762	D / 1.6	1.89	3.35	5.06 /39	6.54 /19	6.99 /23	1.33	1.41
AA	BlackRock LifePath 2020 Inv C	LPCMX	D+	(800) 441-7762	D / 1.8	1.72	2.96	4.29 /34	5.75 /16	--	0.64	2.16
AA	BlackRock LifePath 2020 K	LPSCX	C-	(800) 441-7762	D+ / 2.6	2.03	3.62	5.66 /44	7.17 /22	7.62 /27	1.86	0.81
AA	BlackRock LifePath 2020 R	LPRMX	D+	(800) 441-7762	D / 2.1	1.79	3.19	4.73 /37	6.27 /18	--	1.01	1.66
GI	BlackRock LifePath 2025 Inst	LPBIX	C	(800) 441-7762	D+ / 2.9	2.07	3.71	5.63 /43	7.61 /25	--	1.45	1.25
GI	BlackRock LifePath 2025 Inv A	LPBAX	C-	(800) 441-7762	D / 1.9	2.04	3.57	5.39 /42	7.35 /23	--	1.23	1.50
GI	BlackRock LifePath 2025 Inv C	LPBCX	C-	(800) 441-7762	D / 2.2	1.83	3.15	4.52 /35	6.51 /19	--	0.62	2.25

● Denotes fund is closed to new investors
* Denotes fund is included in Section II

www.thestreetratings.com

Risk Rating/Pts	3 Year Standard Deviation	Beta	NAV As of 3/31/15	Total $(Mil)	Cash %	Stocks %	Bonds %	Other %	Portfolio Turnover Ratio	Last Bull Market Return	Last Bear Market Return	Manager Quality Pct	Manager Tenure (Years)	Initial Purch. $	Additional Purch. $	Front End Load	Back End Load
C /5.4	11.0	0.83	49.72	1,123	1	98	0	1	57	147.4	-12.9	99	12	1,000	50	0.0	0.0
C /5.4	11.0	0.83	53.92	120	1	98	0	1	57	150.7	N/A	99	12	100	0	0.0	0.0
C /5.4	11.0	0.83	54.62	36	1	98	0	1	57	153.6	-12.6	99	12	5,000	0	0.0	0.0
C+ /5.7	12.5	0.92	14.44	180	5	94	0	1	128	40.1	-24.3	30	8	2,000,000	0	0.0	0.0
C+ /5.6	12.6	0.92	14.13	284	5	94	0	1	128	38.3	-24.4	25	8	1,000	50	5.3	0.0
C+ /5.7	12.6	0.92	13.26	1	5	94	0	1	128	33.7	-24.8	16	8	1,000	50	0.0	0.0
C+ /5.6	12.6	0.92	13.24	143	5	94	0	1	128	33.7	-24.7	16	8	1,000	50	0.0	0.0
C+ /5.7	12.6	0.92	14.14	22	5	94	0	1	128	36.8	N/A	22	8	100	0	0.0	0.0
C+ /5.9	13.4	1.01	12.85	1,999	3	96	0	1	8	50.3	-23.4	52	4	2,000,000	0	0.0	0.0
C+ /5.9	13.4	1.01	12.75	281	3	96	0	1	8	48.9	-23.5	48	4	1,000	50	0.0	0.0
C+ /5.9	13.3	1.01	12.86	24	3	96	0	1	8	50.3	-23.4	53	4	1	1	0.0	0.0
C- /3.2	12.4	0.90	34.16	509	2	97	0	1	138	43.8	-25.1	47	17	2,000,000	0	0.0	0.0
C- /3.1	12.4	0.89	32.32	483	2	97	0	1	138	42.3	-25.2	43	17	1,000	50	5.3	0.0
D+ /2.9	12.4	0.89	29.68	2	2	97	0	1	138	38.3	-25.4	31	17	1,000	50	0.0	0.0
D+ /2.8	12.4	0.90	29.29	115	2	97	0	1	138	38.7	-25.5	32	17	1,000	50	0.0	0.0
C- /3.1	12.4	0.90	32.69	26	2	97	0	1	138	41.8	-25.2	41	17	5,000	0	0.0	0.0
B- /7.0	10.9	1.10	18.53	481	3	96	0	1	40	98.0	-22.5	33	5	2,000,000	0	0.0	0.0
B- /7.0	10.9	1.10	18.09	837	3	96	0	1	40	95.9	-22.5	29	5	1,000	50	5.3	0.0
B- /7.0	10.9	1.10	16.70	10	3	96	0	1	40	90.5	-22.8	21	5	1,000	50	0.0	0.0
B- /7.0	10.9	1.10	16.46	403	3	96	0	1	40	90.2	-22.8	20	5	1,000	50	0.0	0.0
B- /7.0	11.5	1.13	15.02	12	1	98	0	1	44	92.5	-22.1	20	5	2,000,000	0	0.0	0.0
B- /7.0	11.5	1.13	14.74	12	1	98	0	1	44	90.6	-22.2	17	5	1,000	50	5.3	0.0
C+ /6.9	11.5	1.13	14.05	8	1	98	0	1	44	85.9	-22.4	12	5	1,000	50	0.0	0.0
B- /7.0	10.9	1.10	17.32	40	3	96	0	1	40	93.7	-22.6	25	5	100	0	0.0	0.0
D- /1.2	11.0	1.10	6.14	2	3	96	0	1	40	99.2	-22.3	35	5	1	1	0.0	0.0
B- /7.0	11.0	1.10	18.42	1	3	96	0	1	40	95.4	-22.6	28	5	5,000	0	0.0	0.0
D- /1.2	10.7	1.08	2.06	1	4	95	0	1	49	109.2	-20.4	46	16	1	1	0.0	0.0
C+ /5.6	10.6	1.07	14.35	403	4	95	0	1	49	100.5	-20.5	38	16	2,000,000	0	0.0	0.0
C+ /5.6	10.7	1.07	13.72	574	4	95	0	1	49	98.4	-20.6	34	16	1,000	50	5.3	0.0
C /5.4	10.6	1.07	12.17	3	4	95	0	1	49	92.9	-20.9	25	16	1,000	50	0.0	0.0
C /5.3	10.7	1.07	12.04	214	4	95	0	1	49	93.3	-20.9	25	16	1,000	50	0.0	0.0
C /5.5	10.6	1.07	12.99	24	4	95	0	1	49	96.7	-20.6	32	16	100	0	0.0	0.0
C+ /5.7	10.7	1.08	14.29	2	4	95	0	1	49	98.4	-20.5	33	16	5,000	0	0.0	0.0
C+ /6.9	11.4	1.12	22.99	185	1	98	0	1	32	91.4	-24.3	21	16	2,000,000	0	0.0	0.0
C+ /6.9	11.4	1.12	22.56	336	1	98	0	1	32	89.4	-24.3	18	16	1,000	50	5.3	0.0
C+ /6.8	11.4	1.12	21.14	5	1	98	0	1	32	83.8	-24.6	12	16	1,000	50	0.0	0.0
C+ /6.8	11.5	1.12	20.96	201	1	98	0	1	32	84.2	-24.5	12	16	1,000	50	0.0	0.0
C+ /6.8	11.4	1.12	21.73	40	1	98	0	1	32	87.5	-24.4	16	16	100	0	0.0	0.0
C+ /5.8	11.4	1.12	19.84	169	1	98	0	1	32	93.0	-24.1	23	16	1	1	0.0	0.0
C+ /6.9	11.4	1.12	22.84	13	1	98	0	1	32	89.4	-24.3	18	16	5,000	0	0.0	0.0
D- /1.5	20.9	1.13	42.39	63	5	94	0	1	42	-9.3	-29.0	0	13	2,000,000	0	0.0	0.0
D- /1.5	20.9	1.13	41.82	124	5	94	0	1	42	-10.0	-29.0	0	13	1,000	50	5.3	0.0
D- /1.5	20.9	1.13	39.35	2	5	94	0	1	42	-12.8	-29.3	0	13	1,000	50	0.0	0.0
D- /1.5	20.9	1.13	38.33	34	5	94	0	1	42	-12.5	-29.3	0	13	1,000	50	0.0	0.0
B- /7.3	5.6	0.92	15.89	445	6	40	52	2	19	39.1	-9.8	26	N/A	2,000,000	0	0.0	0.0
B- /7.1	5.5	0.91	14.83	361	6	40	52	2	19	37.9	-10.0	24	N/A	1,000	50	5.3	0.0
B- /7.4	5.6	0.92	15.73	3	6	40	52	2	19	34.3	-10.2	17	5	1,000	50	0.0	0.0
B- /7.3	5.6	0.91	15.85	10	6	40	52	2	19	40.6	-9.7	30	N/A	1	1	0.0	0.0
B- /7.4	5.6	0.92	15.82	3	6	40	52	2	19	36.6	-10.0	21	5	100	0	0.0	0.0
B /8.3	6.3	0.60	13.02	19	10	45	44	1	30	44.6	-11.9	43	5	2,000,000	0	0.0	0.0
B /8.3	6.4	0.60	13.00	36	10	45	44	1	30	43.5	-12.1	39	5	1,000	50	5.3	0.0
B /8.4	6.3	0.60	12.93	4	10	45	44	1	30	39.7	-12.3	29	5	1,000	50	0.0	0.0

Fund Type	Fund Name	Ticker Symbol	Overall Investment Rating	Phone	Performance Rating/Pts	3 Mo	6 Mo	1Yr / Pct	3Yr / Pct	5Yr / Pct	Dividend Yield	Expense Ratio
	99 Pct = Best 0 Pct = Worst				PERFORMANCE — Total Return % through 3/31/15 (Annualized) / Incl. in Returns							
GI	BlackRock LifePath 2025 K	LPBKX	C	(800) 441-7762	C- / 3.0	2.19	3.88	5.95 /46	7.73 /25	--	1.81	0.82
GI	BlackRock LifePath 2025 R	LPBRX	C	(800) 441-7762	D+ / 2.5	2.00	3.40	5.12 /39	7.08 /22	--	1.05	1.75
AA	BlackRock LifePath 2030 Inst	STLDX	D+	(800) 441-7762	C- / 3.2	2.19	3.82	5.85 /45	8.27 /29	8.21 /31	1.46	1.17
AA	BlackRock LifePath 2030 Inv A	LPRDX	D	(800) 441-7762	D+ / 2.3	2.14	3.68	5.60 /43	7.99 /27	7.94 /29	1.25	1.42
AA	BlackRock LifePath 2030 Inv C	LPCNX	D+	(800) 441-7762	D+ / 2.6	1.92	3.30	4.82 /37	7.20 /22	--	0.61	2.17
AA	BlackRock LifePath 2030 K	LPSDX	C-	(800) 441-7762	C- / 3.5	2.28	4.02	6.19 /48	8.65 /31	8.60 /34	1.83	0.93
AA	BlackRock LifePath 2030 R	LPRNX	D+	(800) 441-7762	D+ / 2.9	2.09	3.57	5.33 /41	7.73 /26	--	1.02	1.67
GL	BlackRock LifePath 2035 Inst	LPJIX	C	(800) 441-7762	C- / 3.6	2.31	4.01	6.16 /48	8.88 /32	--	1.41	1.28
GL	BlackRock LifePath 2035 Inv A	LPJAX	C-	(800) 441-7762	D+ / 2.6	2.27	3.93	5.91 /46	8.61 /30	--	1.18	1.53
GL	BlackRock LifePath 2035 Inv C	LPJCX	C-	(800) 441-7762	D+ / 2.9	2.08	3.54	5.12 /39	7.78 /26	--	0.56	2.28
GL	BlackRock LifePath 2035 K	LPJKX	C	(800) 441-7762	C- / 3.9	2.44	4.25	6.47 /50	9.41 /36	--	1.67	0.93
GL	BlackRock LifePath 2035 R	LPJRX	C	(800) 441-7762	C- / 3.3	2.21	3.79	5.66 /44	8.33 /29	--	0.95	1.78
AA	BlackRock LifePath 2040 Inst	STLEX	C-	(800) 441-7762	C- / 3.9	2.46	4.13	6.34 /49	9.46 /36	8.96 /36	1.39	1.18
AA	BlackRock LifePath 2040 Inv A	LPREX	D	(800) 441-7762	D+ / 2.9	2.35	4.00	6.03 /47	9.17 /34	8.69 /34	1.24	1.43
AA	BlackRock LifePath 2040 Inv C	LPCKX	D+	(800) 441-7762	C- / 3.2	2.17	3.58	5.29 /41	8.37 /29	--	0.51	2.18
AA	BlackRock LifePath 2040 K	LPSFX	C-	(800) 441-7762	C- / 4.2	2.53	4.35	6.70 /53	9.84 /38	9.37 /39	1.74	0.83
AA	BlackRock LifePath 2040 R	LPRKX	D+	(800) 441-7762	C- / 3.6	2.32	3.88	5.78 /45	8.90 /32	--	0.93	1.68
GL	BlackRock LifePath 2045 Inst	LPHIX	C	(800) 441-7762	C- / 4.2	2.46	4.22	6.53 /51	9.93 /39	--	1.38	1.41
GL	BlackRock LifePath 2045 Inv A	LPHAX	C-	(800) 441-7762	C- / 3.2	2.42	4.07	6.27 /49	9.68 /37	--	1.15	1.66
GL	BlackRock LifePath 2045 Inv C	LPHCX	C	(800) 441-7762	C- / 3.5	2.21	3.77	5.46 /42	8.86 /32	--	0.55	2.41
GL	BlackRock LifePath 2045 K	LPHKX	C	(800) 441-7762	C / 4.4	2.54	4.40	6.62 /52	10.31 /41	--	1.44	1.06
GL	BlackRock LifePath 2045 R	LPHRX	C	(800) 441-7762	C- / 3.9	2.38	4.01	6.01 /46	9.39 /35	--	0.90	1.91
AA	BlackRock LifePath 2050 Inst	STLFX	C-	(800) 441-7762	C / 4.5	2.50	4.38	6.68 /52	10.40 /42	9.57 /41	1.38	1.19
AA	BlackRock LifePath 2050 Inv A	LPRFX	D+	(800) 441-7762	C- / 3.5	2.50	4.27	6.46 /50	10.14 /40	9.30 /39	1.12	1.44
AA	BlackRock LifePath 2050 Inv C	LPCPX	C-	(800) 441-7762	C- / 3.8	2.26	3.84	5.62 /43	9.30 /35	--	0.53	2.19
AA	BlackRock LifePath 2050 K	LPSGX	C	(800) 441-7762	C / 4.7	2.62	4.60	7.10 /56	10.78 /44	9.97 /44	1.72	0.84
AA	BlackRock LifePath 2050 R	LPRPX	C-	(800) 441-7762	C- / 4.1	2.39	4.14	6.15 /48	9.87 /39	--	0.85	1.69
GL	BlackRock LifePath 2055 Inst	LPVIX	C	(800) 441-7762	C / 4.6	2.46	4.46	6.81 /53	10.76 /44	--	1.36	1.93
GL	BlackRock LifePath 2055 Inv A	LPVAX	C-	(800) 441-7762	C- / 3.7	2.43	4.32	6.54 /51	10.49 /42	--	1.11	2.18
GL	BlackRock LifePath 2055 Inv C	LPVCX	C	(800) 441-7762	C- / 4.0	2.20	3.97	5.68 /44	9.66 /37	--	0.48	2.93
GL	BlackRock LifePath 2055 K	LPVKX	C+	(800) 441-7762	C / 5.0	2.60	4.70	7.19 /57	11.27 /47	--	1.56	1.58
GL	BlackRock LifePath 2055 R	LPVRX	C	(800) 441-7762	C / 4.3	2.34	4.21	6.26 /49	10.21 /40	--	0.86	2.43
AA	BlackRock LifePath Active 2020 A	BAPCX	D+	(800) 441-7762	D / 2.2	2.41	3.68	5.31 /41	7.83 /26	8.16 /31	2.46	1.69
AA	BlackRock LifePath Active 2020 K	BIPCX	C-	(800) 441-7762	C- / 3.2	2.49	3.88	5.69 /44	8.23 /28	8.58 /34	2.88	1.31
AA	BlackRock LifePath Active 2020 R	BRPCX	C-	(800) 441-7762	D+ / 2.8	2.33	3.48	4.92 /38	7.56 /24	7.86 /29	2.39	1.91
AA	BlackRock LifePath Active 2025 A	BAPDX	C-	(800) 441-7762	D+ / 2.6	2.37	3.77	5.83 /45	8.59 /30	8.66 /34	2.40	1.74
AA	BlackRock LifePath Active 2025 K	BIPDX	C	(800) 441-7762	C- / 3.6	2.36	3.92	6.17 /48	8.96 /33	9.09 /37	2.86	1.40
AA	BlackRock LifePath Active 2025 R	BRPDX	C-	(800) 441-7762	C- / 3.2	2.20	3.63	5.52 /43	8.32 /29	8.39 /32	2.39	1.98
AA	BlackRock LifePath Active 2030 A	BAPEX	D+	(800) 441-7762	D+ / 2.7	2.58	3.91	5.68 /44	8.78 /32	8.76 /35	1.96	1.73
AA	BlackRock LifePath Active 2030 K	BIPEX	C-	(800) 441-7762	C- / 3.8	2.56	4.04	5.98 /46	9.18 /34	9.20 /38	2.38	1.38
AA	BlackRock LifePath Active 2030 R	BRPEX	C-	(800) 441-7762	C- / 3.3	2.49	3.75	5.42 /42	8.53 /30	8.47 /33	1.81	1.98
AA	BlackRock LifePath Active 2035 A	BAPGX	D+	(800) 441-7762	D+ / 2.6	2.10	3.48	5.30 /41	8.72 /31	8.77 /35	1.52	2.07
AA	BlackRock LifePath Active 2035 K	BIPGX	C-	(800) 441-7762	C- / 3.7	2.18	3.60	5.60 /43	9.13 /34	9.21 /38	1.90	1.69
AA	BlackRock LifePath Active 2035 R	BRPGX	C-	(800) 441-7762	C- / 3.3	2.02	3.28	5.01 /39	8.47 /30	8.47 /33	1.48	2.32
AA	BlackRock LifePath Active 2040 A	BAPHX	D+	(800) 441-7762	C- / 3.0	2.41	3.94	5.83 /45	9.30 /35	9.10 /37	1.67	2.03
AA	BlackRock LifePath Active 2040 K	BIPHX	C-	(800) 441-7762	C- / 4.1	2.48	4.07	6.22 /48	9.72 /38	9.56 /41	2.07	1.63
AA	BlackRock LifePath Active 2040 R	BRPHX	C-	(800) 441-7762	C- / 3.6	2.41	3.73	5.53 /43	9.04 /33	8.85 /36	1.56	2.29
AA	BlackRock LifePath Active 2045 A	BAPJX	C-	(800) 441-7762	C- / 3.3	2.58	3.98	5.67 /44	9.95 /39	9.47 /40	1.51	2.70
AA	BlackRock LifePath Active 2045 K	BIPJX	C	(800) 441-7762	C / 4.4	2.63	4.10	6.04 /47	10.37 /42	9.95 /44	1.90	2.30
AA	BlackRock LifePath Active 2045 R	BRPJX	C	(800) 441-7762	C- / 4.0	2.50	3.84	5.45 /42	9.68 /37	9.23 /38	1.52	2.90
AA	BlackRock LifePath Active 2050 A	BAPKX	C-	(800) 441-7762	C- / 3.4	2.58	3.84	5.67 /44	10.14 /40	9.63 /41	1.39	2.95
AA	BlackRock LifePath Active 2050 K	BIPKX	C	(800) 441-7762	C / 4.5	2.55	4.05	5.95 /46	10.58 /43	10.10 /45	1.77	2.41

RISK			NET ASSETS		ASSET					BULL / BEAR		FUND MANAGER		MINIMUMS		LOADS	
Risk Rating/Pts	3 Year		NAV As of 3/31/15	Total $(Mil)	Cash %	Stocks %	Bonds %	Other %	Portfolio Turnover Ratio	Last Bull Market Return	Last Bear Market Return	Manager Quality Pct	Manager Tenure (Years)	Initial Purch. $	Additional Purch. $	Front End Load	Back End Load
	Standard Deviation	Beta															
B /8.3	6.4	0.60	13.00	1	10	45	44	1	30	45.3	-11.8	44	5	1	1	0.0	0.0
B /8.3	6.3	0.60	13.01	2	10	45	44	1	30	42.1	-12.1	36	5	100	0	0.0	0.0
C+ /6.5	7.1	1.18	14.98	424	13	57	28	2	22	49.5	-13.6	14	8	2,000,000	0	0.0	0.0
C+ /6.4	7.1	1.18	14.54	350	13	57	28	2	22	48.1	-13.7	13	8	1,000	50	5.3	0.0
C+ /6.5	7.1	1.19	14.78	3	13	57	28	2	22	44.4	-13.9	9	8	1,000	50	0.0	0.0
C+ /6.5	7.1	1.18	14.97	10	13	57	28	2	22	51.3	-13.4	17	8	1	1	0.0	0.0
C+ /6.5	7.1	1.18	14.87	3	13	57	28	2	22	46.9	-13.8	12	8	100	0	0.0	0.0
B- /7.9	7.8	1.22	13.70	20	14	55	29	2	39	54.2	-15.1	37	5	2,000,000	0	0.0	0.0
B- /7.9	7.8	1.22	13.68	33	14	55	29	2	39	53.0	-15.2	33	5	1,000	50	5.3	0.0
B- /7.9	7.8	1.22	13.59	2	14	55	29	2	39	49.0	-15.5	25	5	1,000	50	0.0	0.0
B- /7.9	7.8	1.22	13.88	N/A	14	55	29	2	39	56.7	-15.0	45	5	1	1	0.0	0.0
B- /7.9	7.8	1.22	13.71	1	14	55	29	2	39	51.6	-15.3	31	5	100	0	0.0	0.0
C+ /6.1	8.3	1.39	18.77	422	19	71	8	2	26	58.4	-16.6	9	21	2,000,000	0	0.0	0.0
C+ /5.8	8.3	1.39	17.58	268	19	71	8	2	26	57.0	-16.6	8	21	1,000	50	5.3	0.0
C+ /6.1	8.3	1.39	18.57	3	19	71	8	2	26	53.2	-16.9	6	21	1,000	50	0.0	0.0
C+ /6.1	8.3	1.39	18.87	5	19	71	8	2	26	60.4	-16.4	10	21	1	1	0.0	0.0
C+ /6.1	8.3	1.39	18.68	1	19	71	8	2	26	55.8	-16.8	7	21	100	0	0.0	0.0
B- /7.4	8.9	1.39	14.36	13	17	64	17	2	38	62.4	-17.8	31	5	2,000,000	0	0.0	0.0
B- /7.4	8.9	1.39	14.35	18	17	64	17	2	38	61.1	-17.9	28	5	1,000	50	5.3	0.0
B- /7.4	8.9	1.40	14.20	2	17	64	17	2	38	56.9	-18.1	20	5	1,000	50	0.0	0.0
B- /7.4	8.9	1.40	14.49	N/A	17	64	17	2	38	64.6	-17.8	34	5	1	1	0.0	0.0
B- /7.4	8.9	1.40	14.35	1	17	64	17	2	38	59.8	-18.0	25	5	100	0	0.0	0.0
C+ /6.3	9.3	1.55	20.03	118	54	42	3	1	28	66.1	-19.0	6	7	2,000,000	0	0.0	0.0
C+ /6.3	9.3	1.55	20.01	74	54	42	3	1	28	64.6	-19.1	6	7	1,000	50	5.3	0.0
C+ /6.3	9.3	1.55	19.86	1	54	42	3	1	28	60.5	-19.4	4	7	1,000	50	0.0	0.0
C+ /6.3	9.4	1.55	20.11	1	54	42	3	1	28	68.1	-18.9	7	7	1	1	0.0	0.0
C+ /6.3	9.3	1.55	19.97	1	54	42	3	1	28	63.4	-19.2	5	7	100	0	0.0	0.0
B- /7.1	9.8	1.54	14.65	6	20	72	6	2	67	68.8	-19.6	25	5	2,000,000	0	0.0	0.0
B- /7.1	9.8	1.52	14.62	7	20	72	6	2	67	67.3	-19.7	24	5	1,000	50	5.3	0.0
B- /7.0	9.8	1.53	14.49	1	20	72	6	2	67	63.0	-20.0	16	5	1,000	50	0.0	0.0
B- /7.1	9.8	1.53	14.82	N/A	20	72	6	2	67	71.2	-19.4	31	5	1	1	0.0	0.0
B- /7.1	9.8	1.53	14.63	N/A	20	72	6	2	67	65.8	-19.7	21	5	100	0	0.0	0.0
B- /7.3	6.0	1.00	10.63	24	13	43	42	2	41	45.2	-12.2	27	8	1,000	50	5.3	0.0
B- /7.3	5.9	0.99	10.71	2	13	43	42	2	41	47.0	-11.9	33	8	1	1	0.0	0.0
B- /7.4	5.9	0.99	10.54	12	13	43	42	2	41	43.9	-12.3	25	8	100	0	0.0	0.0
B- /7.5	6.7	1.13	10.78	18	15	48	35	2	49	50.1	-13.5	21	8	1,000	50	5.3	0.0
B- /7.4	6.7	1.13	10.85	2	15	48	35	2	49	52.0	-13.2	24	8	1	1	0.0	0.0
B- /7.5	6.7	1.12	10.70	12	15	48	35	2	49	48.8	-13.5	19	8	100	0	0.0	0.0
C+ /6.9	7.5	1.26	10.34	19	17	54	28	1	66	53.5	-15.4	12	8	1,000	50	5.3	0.0
C+ /6.9	7.5	1.26	10.43	2	17	54	28	1	66	55.4	-15.2	14	8	1	1	0.0	0.0
B- /7.0	7.5	1.26	10.30	10	17	54	28	1	66	52.2	-15.5	11	8	100	0	0.0	0.0
B- /7.1	8.6	1.43	10.71	13	21	55	22	2	61	57.9	-18.4	6	8	1,000	50	5.3	0.0
B- /7.1	8.7	1.44	10.80	1	21	55	22	2	61	60.0	-18.2	6	8	1	1	0.0	0.0
B- /7.1	8.6	1.43	10.63	8	21	55	22	2	61	56.6	-18.5	5	8	100	0	0.0	0.0
C+ /6.6	9.0	1.51	10.64	14	19	62	17	2	57	60.2	-18.2	5	8	1,000	50	5.3	0.0
C+ /6.5	9.0	1.50	10.75	1	19	62	17	2	57	62.4	-18.0	6	8	1	1	0.0	0.0
C+ /6.6	9.0	1.49	10.61	8	19	62	17	2	57	58.9	-18.3	5	8	100	0	0.0	0.0
B- /7.1	9.2	1.54	11.55	7	22	64	12	2	72	63.2	-18.2	6	8	1,000	50	5.3	0.0
B- /7.1	9.2	1.53	11.72	1	22	64	12	2	72	65.5	-18.0	7	8	1	1	0.0	0.0
B- /7.1	9.2	1.53	11.46	6	22	64	12	2	72	61.7	-18.2	5	8	100	0	0.0	0.0
B- /7.2	9.4	1.57	10.72	7	24	66	8	2	68	64.1	-18.3	5	8	1,000	50	5.3	0.0
B- /7.1	9.5	1.58	10.84	1	24	66	8	2	68	66.5	-18.2	6	8	1	1	0.0	0.0

Fund Type	Fund Name	Ticker Symbol	Overall Investment Rating	Phone	Performance Rating/Pts	3 Mo	6 Mo	1Yr / Pct	3Yr / Pct	5Yr / Pct	Dividend Yield	Expense Ratio
	99 Pct = Best				PERFORMANCE			Total Return % through 3/31/15			Incl. in Returns	
	0 Pct = Worst								Annualized			
AA	BlackRock LifePath Active 2050 R	BRPKX	C	(800) 441-7762	C- / 4.1	2.40	3.67	5.30 /41	9.90 /39	9.36 /39	1.38	3.13
AA	BlackRock LifePath Active Ret A	BAPBX	D	(800) 441-7762	D / 1.9	2.53	3.50	5.20 /40	7.21 /22	7.75 /28	3.04	1.76
AA	BlackRock LifePath Active Ret K	BIPBX	C-	(800) 441-7762	D+ / 2.9	2.61	3.57	5.55 /43	7.57 /24	8.15 /31	3.54	1.41
AA	BlackRock LifePath Active Ret R	BRPBX	D+	(800) 441-7762	D+ / 2.5	2.43	3.36	4.96 /38	6.92 /21	7.47 /26	3.07	2.05
AA	BlackRock LifePath Idx 2020 Inst	LIQIX	C+	(800) 441-7762	C- / 3.1	2.26	4.22	6.64 /52	7.89 /26	--	1.81	0.30
AA	BlackRock LifePath Idx 2020 Inv A	LIQAX	C+	(800) 441-7762	C- / 3.0	2.21	4.10	6.41 /50	7.62 /25	--	1.59	0.55
AA	BlackRock LifePath Idx 2020 K	LIMKX	C+	(800) 441-7762	C- / 3.2	2.27	4.25	6.69 /53	7.96 /27	--	1.86	0.25
AA	BlackRock LifePath Idx 2025 Inst	LIBIX	C+	(800) 441-7762	C- / 3.6	2.40	4.47	6.96 /55	8.69 /31	--	1.84	0.33
IX	BlackRock LifePath Idx 2025 Inv A	LILAX	C+	(800) 441-7762	C- / 3.4	2.34	4.35	6.72 /53	8.43 /29	--	1.62	0.58
IX	BlackRock LifePath Idx 2025 K	LIBKX	C+	(800) 441-7762	C- / 3.6	2.41	4.49	7.10 /56	8.75 /31	--	1.89	0.29
AA	BlackRock LifePath Idx 2030 Inst	LINIX	C+	(800) 441-7762	C- / 4.0	2.48	4.58	7.27 /57	9.39 /35	--	1.91	0.32
AA	BlackRock LifePath Idx 2030 Inv A	LINAX	C+	(800) 441-7762	C- / 3.8	2.51	4.55	7.12 /56	9.14 /34	--	1.69	0.57
AA	BlackRock LifePath Idx 2030 K	LINKX	C+	(800) 441-7762	C- / 4.0	2.49	4.70	7.42 /58	9.44 /36	--	1.96	0.27
AA	BlackRock LifePath Idx 2035 Inst	LIJIX	C+	(800) 441-7762	C / 4.4	2.71	4.82	7.65 /60	10.03 /39	--	1.94	0.36
AA	BlackRock LifePath Idx 2035 Inv A	LIJAX	C+	(800) 441-7762	C- / 4.2	2.57	4.62	7.34 /58	9.75 /38	--	1.73	0.62
AA	BlackRock LifePath Idx 2035 K	LIJKX	C+	(800) 441-7762	C / 4.4	2.64	4.85	7.70 /60	10.03 /39	--	1.98	0.33
AA	BlackRock LifePath Idx 2040 Inst	LIKIX	C+	(800) 441-7762	C / 4.7	2.69	4.96	7.86 /62	10.59 /43	--	1.99	0.36
AA	BlackRock LifePath Idx 2040 Inv A	LIKAX	C+	(800) 441-7762	C / 4.5	2.72	4.84	7.63 /60	10.36 /42	--	1.78	0.60
AA	BlackRock LifePath Idx 2040 K	LIKKX	C+	(800) 441-7762	C / 4.7	2.79	4.99	7.91 /62	10.67 /43	--	2.04	0.31
AA	BlackRock LifePath Idx 2045 Inst	LIHIX	C+	(800) 441-7762	C / 5.0	2.82	5.18	8.16 /64	11.15 /47	--	2.02	0.45
AA	BlackRock LifePath Idx 2045 Inv A	LIHAX	C+	(800) 441-7762	C / 4.8	2.77	5.07	7.84 /62	10.87 /45	--	1.80	0.69
AA	BlackRock LifePath Idx 2045 K	LIHKX	C+	(800) 441-7762	C / 5.1	2.83	5.20	8.20 /64	11.22 /47	--	2.05	0.42
AA	BlackRock LifePath Idx 2050 Inst	LIPIX	C+	(800) 441-7762	C / 5.3	2.87	5.32	8.39 /65	11.65 /50	--	2.02	0.46
AA	BlackRock LifePath Idx 2050 Inv A	LIPAX	C+	(800) 441-7762	C / 5.2	2.82	5.21	8.16 /64	11.40 /48	--	1.81	0.71
AA	BlackRock LifePath Idx 2050 K	LIPKX	C+	(800) 441-7762	C / 5.4	2.88	5.34	8.44 /66	11.69 /50	--	2.07	0.45
AA	BlackRock LifePath Idx 2055 Inst	LIVIX	C+	(800) 441-7762	C+ / 5.6	2.81	5.37	8.50 /66	12.14 /53	--	2.05	1.07
AA	BlackRock LifePath Idx 2055 Inv A	LIVAX	C+	(800) 441-7762	C / 5.5	2.84	5.34	8.35 /65	11.88 /52	--	1.82	1.24
AA	BlackRock LifePath Idx 2055 K	LIVKX	C+	(800) 441-7762	C+ / 5.7	2.82	5.39	8.55 /67	12.19 /54	--	2.08	1.04
GL	BlackRock LifePath Idx Ret Inv A	LIRAX	C	(800) 441-7762	D / 2.2	1.98	3.84	5.90 /46	6.28 /18	--	1.52	0.55
GL	BlackRock LifePath Idx Ret Ptf Inst	LIRIX	C	(800) 441-7762	D+ / 2.4	2.12	3.95	6.12 /47	6.55 /19	--	1.74	0.30
GL	BlackRock LifePath Idx Ret Ptf K	LIRKX	C	(800) 441-7762	D+ / 2.4	2.04	3.89	6.18 /48	6.56 /19	--	1.79	0.26
AA	BlackRock LifePath Retirement Inst	STLAX	D+	(800) 441-7762	D / 1.8	1.79	3.20	4.84 /37	5.50 /15	6.35 /19	1.52	1.14
AA	BlackRock LifePath Retirement Inv A	LPRAX	D	(800) 441-7762	D- / 1.2	1.65	3.05	4.57 /36	5.25 /14	6.08 /17	1.44	1.39
AA	BlackRock LifePath Retirement Inv C	LPCRX	D+	(800) 441-7762	D- / 1.4	1.61	2.76	3.86 /31	4.46 /11	--	0.67	2.14
AA	BlackRock LifePath Retirement K	LPSAX	D+	(800) 441-7762	D / 2.0	1.89	3.41	5.25 /40	5.93 /16	6.75 /21	1.89	0.79
AA	BlackRock LifePath Retirement R	LPRRX	D+	(800) 441-7762	D- / 1.5	1.69	2.97	4.34 /34	5.00 /13	--	0.96	1.64
GL	BlackRock Long-Horizon Eq Inst	MAEGX	D	(800) 441-7762	C / 4.5	2.75	4.59	4.87 /38	10.64 /43	9.11 /37	1.22	0.95
GL	BlackRock Long-Horizon Eq Inv A	MDEGX	D-	(800) 441-7762	C- / 3.4	2.67	4.49	4.56 /35	10.30 /41	8.80 /35	0.95	1.22
GL	● BlackRock Long-Horizon Eq Inv B	MBEGX	D-	(800) 441-7762	C- / 3.7	2.45	3.96	3.61 /29	9.36 /35	7.87 /29	0.00	2.14
GL	BlackRock Long-Horizon Eq Inv C	MCEGX	D-	(800) 441-7762	C- / 3.7	2.43	4.01	3.80 /30	9.45 /36	7.97 /30	0.32	1.99
GL	BlackRock Long-Horizon Eq R	MREGX	D-	(800) 441-7762	C- / 4.0	2.50	4.19	4.12 /33	9.82 /38	8.32 /32	0.49	1.79
AA	BlackRock Managed Volatility Inst	PBAIX	D+	(800) 441-7762	D+ / 2.9	4.50	4.92	6.66 /52	7.23 /23	7.36 /25	2.20	0.96
AA	BlackRock Managed Volatility Inv A	PCBAX	D	(800) 441-7762	D / 2.0	4.45	4.73	6.32 /49	6.89 /21	7.03 /23	1.84	1.27
AA	● BlackRock Managed Volatility Inv B	CBIBX	D	(800) 441-7762	D / 2.1	4.16	4.24	5.28 /41	5.87 /16	6.08 /17	0.99	2.27
AA	BlackRock Managed Volatility Inv C	BRBCX	D	(800) 441-7762	D+ / 2.3	4.27	4.42	5.62 /43	6.17 /17	6.29 /19	1.47	1.95
AA	BlackRock Managed Volatility Svc	PCBSX	D+	(800) 441-7762	D+ / 2.7	4.45	4.76	6.28 /49	6.86 /21	7.04 /23	1.90	1.32
MC	BlackRock Mid Cap Growth Eq Inst	CMGIX	C+	(800) 441-7762	A+ / 9.8	11.48	14.16	16.53 /94	18.94 /97	15.28 /89	0.00	1.10
MC	BlackRock Mid Cap Growth Eq Inv A	BMGAX	C+	(800) 441-7762	A / 9.5	11.42	13.96	16.17 /93	18.57 /96	14.90 /86	0.00	1.47
MC	● BlackRock Mid Cap Growth Eq Inv B	BMGBX	C	(800) 441-7762	A+ / 9.6	11.17	13.49	15.23 /92	17.67 /93	14.01 /78	0.00	2.65
MC	BlackRock Mid Cap Growth Eq Inv C	BMGCX	C	(800) 441-7762	A+ / 9.6	11.16	13.57	15.32 /92	17.67 /93	14.01 /78	0.00	2.16
MC	BlackRock Mid Cap Growth Eq R	BMRRX	C+	(800) 441-7762	A+ / 9.7	11.31	13.82	15.90 /93	18.27 /95	14.65 /84	0.00	1.73
MC	BlackRock Mid Cap Growth Eq Svc	CMGSX	C+	(800) 441-7762	A+ / 9.7	11.38	13.85	15.98 /93	18.35 /95	14.75 /85	0.00	1.57

● Denotes fund is closed to new investors
* Denotes fund is included in Section II

www.thestreetratings.com

RISK			NET ASSETS		ASSET						BULL / BEAR		FUND MANAGER		MINIMUMS		LOADS	
	3 Year		NAV							Portfolio	Last Bull	Last Bear	Manager	Manager	Initial	Additional	Front	Back
Risk	Standard		As of	Total	Cash	Stocks	Bonds	Other		Turnover	Market	Market	Quality	Tenure	Purch.	Purch.	End	End
Rating/Pts	Deviation	Beta	3/31/15	$(Mil)	%	%	%	%		Ratio	Return	Return	Pct	(Years)	$	$	Load	Load
B- / 7.2	9.5	1.59	10.67	6	24	66	8	2		68	62.9	-18.4	4	8	100	0	0.0	0.0
B- / 7.1	5.3	0.86	10.54	16	0	0	0	100		42	40.9	-11.1	39	8	1,000	50	5.3	0.0
B- / 7.0	5.3	0.85	10.62	1	0	0	0	100		42	42.7	-11.0	45	8	1	1	0.0	0.0
B- / 7.2	5.3	0.85	10.54	7	0	0	0	100		42	39.9	-11.2	35	8	100	0	0.0	0.0
B+ / 9.1	5.5	0.91	11.79	88	2	49	48	1		12	43.6	N/A	39	4	2,000,000	0	0.0	0.0
B+ / 9.1	5.5	0.90	11.77	128	2	49	48	1		12	42.3	N/A	37	4	1,000	50	0.0	0.0
B+ / 9.1	5.5	0.91	11.79	775	2	49	48	1		12	43.7	N/A	41	4	1	1	0.0	0.0
B / 8.7	6.3	1.05	11.98	69	2	57	39	2		13	49.3	N/A	30	11	2,000,000	0	0.0	0.0
B / 8.7	6.3	0.59	11.97	98	2	57	39	2		13	48.2	N/A	55	11	1,000	50	0.0	0.0
B / 8.7	6.2	0.59	11.99	441	2	57	39	2		13	49.6	N/A	61	11	1	1	0.0	0.0
B / 8.3	7.0	1.18	12.11	86	2	64	32	2		12	54.8	N/A	23	4	2,000,000	0	0.0	0.0
B / 8.3	7.0	1.18	12.11	142	2	64	32	2		12	53.5	N/A	21	4	1,000	50	0.0	0.0
B / 8.3	7.0	1.18	12.10	713	2	64	32	2		12	54.8	N/A	23	4	1	1	0.0	0.0
B- / 7.9	7.6	1.29	12.26	50	3	70	25	2		12	59.5	N/A	18	4	2,000,000	0	0.0	0.0
B- / 7.9	7.6	1.28	12.23	92	3	70	25	2		12	58.0	N/A	16	4	1,000	50	0.0	0.0
B- / 7.9	7.6	1.29	12.25	331	3	70	25	2		12	59.5	N/A	18	4	1	1	0.0	0.0
B- / 7.6	8.3	1.39	12.39	61	3	76	19	2		12	64.4	N/A	14	4	2,000,000	0	0.0	0.0
B- / 7.6	8.2	1.38	12.38	79	3	76	19	2		12	62.8	N/A	13	4	1,000	50	0.0	0.0
B- / 7.6	8.2	1.39	12.39	497	3	76	19	2		12	64.5	N/A	15	4	1	1	0.0	0.0
B- / 7.2	8.8	1.48	12.55	42	3	82	14	1		12	68.3	N/A	12	4	2,000,000	0	0.0	0.0
B- / 7.2	8.8	1.47	12.53	39	3	82	14	1		12	66.8	N/A	11	4	1,000	50	0.0	0.0
B- / 7.2	8.8	1.48	12.56	191	3	82	14	1		12	68.6	N/A	12	4	1	1	0.0	0.0
B- / 7.0	9.2	1.55	12.72	34	3	86	9	2		12	72.6	N/A	10	4	2,000,000	0	0.0	0.0
B- / 7.0	9.2	1.55	12.70	28	3	86	9	2		12	71.0	N/A	9	4	1,000	50	0.0	0.0
B- / 7.0	9.3	1.55	12.72	220	3	86	9	2		12	72.8	N/A	10	4	1	1	0.0	0.0
C+ / 6.8	9.7	1.63	12.91	15	3	91	4	2		15	75.7	N/A	9	4	2,000,000	0	0.0	0.0
C+ / 6.8	9.7	1.61	12.90	11	3	91	4	2		15	74.2	N/A	8	4	1,000	50	0.0	0.0
C+ / 6.8	9.8	1.63	12.91	56	3	91	4	2		15	76.1	N/A	9	4	1	1	0.0	0.0
B+ / 9.4	4.3	0.28	11.52	67	2	37	60	1		18	32.2	N/A	90	4	1,000	50	0.0	0.0
B+ / 9.4	4.2	0.27	11.53	73	2	37	60	1		18	33.3	N/A	91	4	2,000,000	0	0.0	0.0
B+ / 9.4	4.2	0.27	11.52	328	2	37	60	1		18	33.5	N/A	91	4	1	1	0.0	0.0
B- / 7.7	4.3	0.68	11.22	207	2	29	67	2		17	29.5	-5.3	42	8	2,000,000	0	0.0	0.0
B- / 7.4	4.3	0.68	10.11	135	2	29	67	2		17	28.4	-5.4	38	8	1,000	50	5.3	0.0
B- / 7.8	4.3	0.68	11.12	1	2	29	67	2		17	25.0	-5.6	28	8	1,000	50	0.0	0.0
B- / 7.7	4.3	0.67	11.20	3	2	29	67	2		17	31.0	-5.1	49	8	1	1	0.0	0.0
B- / 7.8	4.3	0.67	11.16	1	2	29	67	2		17	27.3	-5.5	36	8	100	0	0.0	0.0
C- / 3.8	10.9	0.74	13.10	76	0	99	0	1		45	63.8	-19.5	90	3	2,000,000	0	0.0	0.0
C- / 3.9	10.8	0.74	13.08	307	0	99	0	1		45	62.2	-19.6	89	3	1,000	50	5.3	0.0
C / 4.3	10.9	0.74	13.39	2	0	99	0	1		45	57.5	-19.9	85	3	1,000	50	0.0	0.0
C- / 4.0	10.8	0.74	13.05	112	0	99	0	1		45	58.0	-19.8	86	3	1,000	50	0.0	0.0
C- / 4.0	10.8	0.74	13.11	4	0	99	0	1		45	59.8	-19.7	87	3	100	0	0.0	0.0
C+ / 6.8	5.7	0.85	15.09	318	40	28	30	2		181	39.3	-13.0	40	9	2,000,000	0	0.0	0.0
C+ / 6.8	5.7	0.85	15.02	346	40	28	30	2		181	37.9	-13.1	35	9	1,000	50	5.3	0.0
C+ / 6.8	5.6	0.84	14.77	6	40	28	30	2		181	33.5	-13.4	25	9	1,000	50	0.0	0.0
C+ / 6.7	5.6	0.84	14.66	72	40	28	30	2		181	34.6	-13.4	28	9	1,000	0	0.0	0.0
C+ / 6.8	5.7	0.85	15.03	2	40	28	30	2		181	37.8	-13.1	36	9	5,000	0	0.0	0.0
D+ / 2.9	14.1	1.07	17.96	33	0	99	0	1		123	112.1	-21.1	72	2	2,000,000	0	0.0	0.0
D+ / 2.4	14.0	1.07	15.81	354	0	99	0	1		123	110.0	-21.2	69	2	1,000	50	5.3	0.0
D / 1.7	14.1	1.08	12.94	3	0	99	0	1		123	104.4	-21.4	58	2	1,000	50	0.0	0.0
D / 1.6	14.1	1.08	12.85	35	0	99	0	1		123	104.3	-21.4	58	2	1,000	50	0.0	0.0
D+ / 2.4	14.1	1.07	15.65	8	0	99	0	1		123	108.0	-21.2	66	2	100	0	0.0	0.0
D+ / 2.6	14.1	1.07	16.44	2	0	99	0	1		123	108.6	-21.2	67	2	5,000	0	0.0	0.0

					PERFORMANCE						Incl. in Returns	
	99 Pct = Best					Total Return % through 3/31/15						
	0 Pct = Worst		Overall		Perfor-				Annualized		Dividend	Expense
Fund		Ticker	Investment		mance						Yield	Ratio
Type	Fund Name	Symbol	Rating	Phone	Rating/Pts	3 Mo	6 Mo	1Yr / Pct	3Yr / Pct	5Yr / Pct		
MC	BlackRock Mid Cap Val Opps Inst	MARFX	C	(800) 441-7762	C+ / 6.4	2.32	5.19	5.27 /41	14.12 /68	13.71 /75	0.67	0.88
MC	BlackRock Mid Cap Val Opps Inv A	MDRFX	C-	(800) 441-7762	C / 5.3	2.25	5.06	5.00 /38	13.77 /65	13.35 /71	0.43	1.18
MC	● BlackRock Mid Cap Val Opps Inv B	MBRFX	C-	(800) 441-7762	C / 5.5	1.98	4.51	3.92 /31	12.71 /58	12.31 /63	0.00	2.08
MC	BlackRock Mid Cap Val Opps Inv C	MCRFX	C-	(800) 441-7762	C+ / 5.6	2.05	4.63	4.10 /32	12.80 /58	12.34 /63	0.00	2.02
MC	BlackRock Mid Cap Value Opp R	MRRFX	C-	(800) 441-7762	C+ / 5.9	2.15	4.84	4.61 /36	13.39 /62	12.94 /68	0.22	1.50
GI	BlackRock Mod Prepared Inst	BIMPX	C	(800) 441-7762	C / 4.7	2.75	5.36	8.27 /65	10.61 /43	9.95 /44	2.63	0.88
GI	BlackRock Mod Prepared Inv A	BAMPX	C	(800) 441-7762	C- / 3.7	2.76	5.22	7.97 /63	10.24 /41	9.56 /41	2.22	1.16
GI	BlackRock Mod Prepared Inv C	BCMPX	C	(800) 441-7762	C- / 4.0	2.52	4.84	7.08 /56	9.36 /35	8.72 /35	1.64	1.93
GI	BlackRock Mod Prepared R	BRMPX	C	(800) 441-7762	C / 4.4	2.69	5.17	7.85 /62	10.07 /40	9.43 /40	2.12	1.44
BA	BlackRock Multi Asset Inc Ptf C	BCICX	C-	(800) 441-7762	D / 2.2	1.50	2.01	3.45 /29	6.92 /21	7.58 /27	4.02	1.75
BA	BlackRock Multi Asset Inc Ptf Inst	BIICX	C-	(800) 441-7762	D+ / 2.9	1.75	2.52	4.59 /36	8.00 /27	8.67 /34	5.03	0.74
BA	BlackRock Multi Asset Income Ptf A	BAICX	D+	(800) 441-7762	D / 2.0	1.69	2.39	4.33 /34	7.77 /26	8.38 /32	4.53	0.99
SC	BlackRock Multi-Asst Real Rtn Inst	BRRIX	U	(800) 441-7762	U /	0.62	-3.21	-3.67 / 7	--	--	1.72	1.53
GL	BlackRock Multi-Mgr Alt Str Inst	BMMNX	U	(800) 441-7762	U /	1.92	1.57		--	--	0.00	3.14
EN	BlackRock Natural Resource Inst	MAGRX	E-	(800) 441-7762	E- / 0.2	-2.80	-19.31	-18.27 / 1	-1.49 / 3	1.64 / 4	0.64	0.80
EN	BlackRock Natural Resource Inv A	MDGRX	E-	(800) 441-7762	E- / 0.2	-2.86	-19.42	-18.48 / 1	-1.75 / 3	1.37 / 4	0.49	1.06
EN	● BlackRock Natural Resource Inv B	MBGRX	E-	(800) 441-7762	E- / 0.2	-3.08	-19.77	-19.16 / 1	-2.54 / 3	0.56 / 3	0.11	1.88
EN	BlackRock Natural Resource Inv C	MCGRX	E-	(800) 441-7762	E- / 0.2	-3.03	-19.73	-19.11 / 1	-2.51 / 3	0.58 / 3	0.21	1.84
FO	BlackRock Pacific Inst	MAPCX	C-	(800) 441-7762	C+ / 5.9	8.05	6.15	10.53 /76	11.82 /51	7.01 /23	1.04	0.90
FO	BlackRock Pacific Inv A	MDPCX	D+	(800) 441-7762	C / 4.9	8.08	6.11	10.29 /75	11.57 /49	6.77 /22	0.76	1.13
FO	● BlackRock Pacific Inv B	MBPCX	D+	(800) 441-7762	C / 5.1	7.77	5.54	9.23 /71	10.56 /43	5.84 /16	0.68	1.96
FO	BlackRock Pacific Inv C	MCPCX	D	(800) 441-7762	C / 5.2	7.78	5.65	9.40 /71	10.70 /44	5.93 /16	0.76	1.91
FO	BlackRock Pacific R	MRPCX	D+	(800) 441-7762	C / 5.4	7.95	5.87	9.80 /74	11.02 /46	6.21 /18	0.70	1.61
GR	BlackRock Russell 1000 Index Inst	BRGNX	A	(800) 441-7762	B+ / 8.4	1.51	6.44	12.56 /85	16.34 /86	--	1.71	0.50
GR	BlackRock Russell 1000 Index Inv A	BRGAX	A	(800) 441-7762	B / 8.2	1.51	6.41	12.33 /84	15.92 /83	--	1.47	0.60
GR	BlackRock Russell 1000 Index K	BRGKX	A	(800) 441-7762	B+ / 8.4	1.52	6.49	12.65 /85	16.27 /85	--	1.75	0.27
IX	BlackRock S&P 500 Stock Inst	BSPIX	A	(800) 441-7762	B / 8.2	0.93	5.88	12.62 /85	15.94 /83	14.30 /80	1.77	0.12
IX	BlackRock S&P 500 Stock Investor A	BSPAX	A	(800) 441-7762	B / 7.9	0.87	5.75	12.34 /84	15.65 /80	14.01 /78	1.53	0.37
IX	BlackRock S&P 500 Stock Investor	BSPZX	B+	(800) 441-7762	B- / 7.3	0.69	5.37	11.53 /81	14.84 /74	13.24 /70	0.82	1.09
IX	BlackRock S&P 500 Stock K	WFSPX	A	(800) 441-7762	B / 8.2	0.95	5.92	12.70 /86	15.99 /83	14.33 /81	1.84	0.05
IX	BlackRock S&P 500 Stock Service	BSPSX	A	(800) 441-7762	B / 8.0	0.90	5.82	12.48 /85	15.79 /82	14.14 /79	1.65	0.24
TC	BlackRock Sci & Tech Opp Inst	BGSIX	B-	(800) 441-7762	B / 8.1	5.29	12.25	12.88 /86	14.73 /73	13.01 /68	0.00	1.36
TC	BlackRock Sci & Tech Opp Inv A	BGSAX	C	(800) 441-7762	C+ / 6.8	5.19	12.10	12.52 /85	14.38 /70	12.61 /65	0.00	1.64
TC	● BlackRock Sci & Tech Opp Inv B	BGSBX	C+	(800) 441-7762	B- / 7.1	4.99	11.61	11.61 /81	13.44 /63	11.67 /58	0.00	2.42
TC	BlackRock Sci & Tech Opp Inv C	BGSCX	C+	(800) 441-7762	B- / 7.0	5.01	11.55	11.55 /81	13.37 /61	11.64 /58	0.00	2.46
TC	BlackRock Sci & Tech Opp R	BGSRX	C+	(800) 441-7762	B- / 7.5	5.10	11.88	12.20 /83	14.03 /67	12.30 /62	0.00	1.91
TC	BlackRock Sci & Tech Opp Svc	BSTSX	C+	(800) 441-7762	B / 7.9	5.17	12.10	12.59 /85	14.48 /71	12.78 /66	0.00	1.50
SC	BlackRock Small Cap Gr Equity Inst	PSGIX	D	(800) 441-7762	B- / 7.4	5.30	11.82	7.99 /63	14.50 /71	14.07 /78	0.00	0.86
SC	BlackRock Small Cap Gr Equity Inv A	CSGEX	D-	(800) 441-7762	C+ / 6.2	5.21	11.65	7.67 /60	14.14 /68	13.69 /75	0.00	1.14
SC	● BlackRock Small Cap Gr Equity Inv B	CSGBX	D-	(800) 441-7762	C+ / 6.5	5.00	11.12	6.75 /53	13.15 /61	12.72 /66	0.00	1.98
SC	BlackRock Small Cap Gr Equity Inv C	CGICX	D-	(800) 441-7762	C+ / 6.5	4.99	11.23	6.80 /53	13.23 /61	12.76 /66	0.00	1.92
SC	BlackRock Small Cap Gr Equity Svc	PCGEX	D-	(800) 441-7762	B- / 7.2	5.26	11.65	7.67 /60	14.16 /68	13.74 /75	0.00	1.11
SC	BlackRock Small Cap Growth II Inst	MASWX	C-	(800) 441-7762	B- / 7.2	5.22	11.76	7.72 /61	14.19 /68	13.49 /73	0.00	1.30
SC	BlackRock Small Cap Growth II Inv A	MDSWX	D	(800) 441-7762	C+ / 6.1	5.12	11.68	7.48 /59	13.86 /66	13.13 /69	0.00	1.78
SC	● BlackRock Small Cap Growth II Inv B	MBSWX	D-	(800) 441-7762	C+ / 6.2	4.92	11.09	6.45 /50	12.73 /58	11.95 /60	0.00	2.56
SC	BlackRock Small Cap Growth II Inv C	MCSWX	D-	(800) 441-7762	C+ / 6.3	4.86	11.17	6.58 /52	12.87 /59	12.13 /61	0.00	2.46
SC	BlackRock Small Cap Growth II R	MRUSX	D	(800) 441-7762	C+ / 6.8	5.08	11.46	7.22 /57	13.58 /64	12.83 /67	0.00	1.83
SC	BlackRock Small Cap Index Class K	BDBKX	B+	(800) 441-7762	B+ / 8.7	4.45	14.63	8.36 /65	16.39 /86	--	1.44	0.34
SC	BlackRock Small Cap Index Inst	MASKX	B+	(800) 441-7762	B+ / 8.7	4.40	14.58	8.31 /65	16.34 /86	14.49 /82	1.39	0.36
SC	BlackRock Small Cap Index Inv A	MDSKX	B	(800) 441-7762	B+ / 8.5	4.39	14.49	8.03 /63	16.05 /84	14.23 /80	1.16	0.62
GL	BlackRock Strat Risk Alloc Inst	BSTIX	U	(800) 441-7762	U /	4.26	6.58	9.99 /74	--	--	3.39	1.66
AA	BlackRock Strategic Inc Opps Inst	BSIIX	C-	(800) 441-7762	D- / 1.5	1.57	2.20	3.79 /30	4.91 /13	5.50 /14	2.26	0.92

● Denotes fund is closed to new investors
* Denotes fund is included in Section II

Risk Rating/Pts	3 Year Standard Deviation	Beta	NAV As of 3/31/15	Total $(Mil)	Cash %	Stocks %	Bonds %	Other %	Portfolio Turnover Ratio	Last Bull Market Return	Last Bear Market Return	Manager Quality Pct	Manager Tenure (Years)	Initial Purch. $	Additional Purch. $	Front End Load	Back End Load
C /4.8	11.8	1.04	22.54	160	0	99	0	1	57	90.2	-21.8	24	6	2,000,000	0	0.0	0.0
C /4.7	11.8	1.04	21.84	316	0	99	0	1	57	88.0	-21.9	20	6	1,000	50	5.3	0.0
C /4.7	11.9	1.04	19.58	1	0	99	0	1	57	82.2	-22.2	13	6	1,000	50	0.0	0.0
C /4.4	11.8	1.04	18.90	71	0	99	0	1	57	82.7	-22.3	14	6	1,000	50	0.0	0.0
C /4.5	11.8	1.04	19.94	63	0	99	0	1	57	85.9	-22.0	18	6	100	0	0.0	0.0
B- /7.1	6.5	0.66	11.96	16	19	52	28	1	60	56.8	-12.3	70	8	2,000,000	0	0.0	0.0
B- /7.2	6.5	0.66	11.90	76	19	52	28	1	60	55.1	-12.5	66	8	1,000	50	5.3	0.0
B- /7.3	6.5	0.66	11.79	57	19	52	28	1	60	51.1	-12.7	54	8	1,000	50	0.0	0.0
B- /7.2	6.5	0.66	11.85	17	19	52	28	1	60	54.5	-12.5	64	8	100	0	0.0	0.0
B- /7.7	4.7	0.74	11.27	2,917	21	24	52	3	146	36.8	-7.5	53	4	1,000	50	0.0	0.0
B- /7.7	4.7	0.73	11.30	5,103	21	24	52	3	146	41.5	-7.0	68	4	2,000,000	0	0.0	0.0
B- /7.7	4.6	0.73	11.29	3,244	21	24	52	3	146	40.2	-7.1	66	4	1,000	50	5.3	0.0
U /	N/A	N/A	9.73	62	28	24	47	1	140	N/A	N/A	N/A	3	2,000,000	0	0.0	0.0
U /	N/A	N/A	10.11	102	0	0	0	100	0	N/A	N/A	N/A	1	2,000,000	0	0.0	0.0
D+ /2.4	16.9	1.03	52.84	95	1	98	0	1	5	20.1	-30.7	8	18	2,000,000	0	0.0	0.0
D+ /2.3	16.9	1.03	51.28	228	1	98	0	1	5	19.0	-30.8	7	18	1,000	50	5.3	0.0
D+ /2.3	16.9	1.03	45.35	2	1	98	0	1	5	15.7	-31.0	5	18	1,000	50	0.0	0.0
D /2.2	16.9	1.03	44.52	67	1	98	0	1	5	15.8	-31.0	5	18	1,000	50	0.0	0.0
C /4.4	13.8	0.91	18.52	142	4	95	0	1	121	60.8	-23.7	88	4	2,000,000	0	0.0	0.0
C /4.4	13.8	0.91	18.33	134	4	95	0	1	121	59.5	-23.8	88	4	1,000	50	5.3	0.0
C- /4.1	13.8	0.91	15.53	1	4	95	0	1	121	54.8	-24.1	83	4	1,000	50	0.0	0.0
C- /3.5	13.8	0.91	13.72	30	4	95	0	1	121	55.3	-24.0	84	4	1,000	50	0.0	0.0
C- /3.8	13.9	0.91	15.08	5	4	95	0	1	121	56.9	-24.0	85	4	100	0	0.0	0.0
B- /7.2	9.6	1.00	14.88	2	1	98	0	1	14	101.2	-17.2	69	4	2,000,000	0	0.0	0.0
B- /7.2	9.6	1.00	14.82	15	1	98	0	1	14	98.9	-17.3	65	4	1,000	50	0.0	0.0
B- /7.2	9.6	1.00	14.83	76	1	98	0	1	14	100.9	-17.2	68	4	1	1	0.0	0.0
B- /7.5	9.5	1.00	248.65	2,764	1	98	0	1	3	99.2	-16.3	65	7	2,000,000	0	0.0	0.0
B- /7.4	9.5	1.00	248.64	1,190	1	98	0	1	3	97.5	-16.4	61	7	1,000	50	0.0	0.0
B- /7.4	9.6	1.00	248.65	79	1	98	0	1	3	92.9	-16.6	51	7	0	0	0.0	0.0
B- /7.3	9.5	1.00	248.69	950	1	98	0	1	3	99.5	-16.3	66	7	1,000,000	0	0.0	0.0
B- /7.5	9.5	1.00	248.65	289	1	98	0	1	3	98.3	-16.4	63	7	5,000	0	0.0	0.0
C /5.0	14.9	1.10	16.13	60	2	97	0	1	99	87.8	-21.4	28	15	2,000,000	0	0.0	0.0
C /5.0	14.9	1.10	15.19	135	2	97	0	1	99	85.5	-21.4	26	15	1,000	50	5.3	0.0
C /4.9	14.9	1.10	13.46	1	2	97	0	1	99	80.6	-21.8	17	15	1,000	50	0.0	0.0
C /4.9	14.9	1.09	13.42	37	2	97	0	1	99	80.3	-21.8	18	15	1,000	50	0.0	0.0
C /4.9	14.9	1.10	15.45	5	2	97	0	1	99	83.9	-21.5	22	15	100	0	0.0	0.0
C /5.0	14.9	1.10	15.47	1	2	97	0	1	99	86.4	-21.4	26	15	5,000	0	0.0	0.0
E+ /0.7	15.9	1.10	19.47	487	1	98	0	1	132	106.0	-26.9	25	2	2,000,000	0	0.0	0.0
E+ /0.7	15.9	1.10	15.74	303	1	98	0	1	132	103.7	-27.0	21	2	1,000	50	5.3	0.0
E+ /0.7	15.9	1.10	10.51	1	1	98	0	1	132	97.9	-27.2	15	2	1,000	50	0.0	0.0
E+ /0.7	15.9	1.10	10.30	33	1	98	0	1	132	98.4	-27.2	15	2	1,000	50	0.0	0.0
E+ /0.7	15.9	1.10	17.02	21	1	98	0	1	132	103.8	-26.9	22	2	5,000	0	0.0	0.0
D+ /2.7	16.0	1.11	14.31	80	0	99	0	1	152	103.3	-27.3	21	2	2,000,000	0	0.0	0.0
D+ /2.5	15.9	1.10	13.54	76	0	99	0	1	152	101.2	-27.4	19	2	1,000	50	5.3	0.0
D- /1.4	15.9	1.10	11.09	1	0	99	0	1	152	94.3	-27.8	12	2	1,000	50	0.0	0.0
D- /1.4	16.0	1.11	11.01	44	0	99	0	1	152	95.3	-27.7	13	2	1,000	50	0.0	0.0
D /2.1	16.0	1.10	12.41	25	0	99	0	1	152	99.5	-27.5	17	2	100	0	0.0	0.0
C /5.5	13.4	1.00	17.36	5	2	97	0	1	22	101.1	-25.3	69	4	1	1	0.0	0.0
C /5.5	13.4	1.00	17.33	82	2	97	0	1	22	100.7	-25.3	68	4	2,000,000	0	0.0	0.0
C /5.5	13.4	1.00	17.34	99	2	97	0	1	22	99.0	-25.3	65	4	1,000	50	0.0	0.0
U /	N/A	N/A	10.28	36	59	0	40	1	77	N/A	N/A	N/A	3	2,000,000	0	0.0	0.0
B /8.6	2.0	0.19	10.22	22,171	25	0	72	3	1,413	20.1	-2.7	88	4	2,000,000	0	0.0	0.0

Fund Type	Fund Name	Ticker Symbol	Overall Investment Rating	Phone	Performance Rating/Pts	Total Return % through 3/31/15			Annualized		Incl. in Returns	
						3 Mo	6 Mo	1Yr / Pct	3Yr / Pct	5Yr / Pct	Dividend Yield	Expense Ratio
★ AA	BlackRock Strategic Inc Opps Inv A	BASIX	D+	(800) 441-7762	D- / 1.0	1.49	2.05	3.47 /29	4.62 /12	5.22 /13	1.88	1.18
AA	BlackRock Strategic Inc Opps Inv C	BSICX	D+	(800) 441-7762	D- / 1.1	1.31	1.57	2.70 /25	3.84 /10	4.43 /10	1.21	1.96
MC	BlackRock US Opportunities Inst	BMCIX	C+	(800) 441-7762	A+ / 9.6	5.16	12.16	15.58 /93	18.17 /95	14.40 /81	0.00	1.34
MC	BlackRock US Opportunities Inv A	BMEAX	C	(800) 441-7762	B+ / 8.9	5.03	11.93	15.10 /92	17.67 /93	13.88 /77	0.00	1.61
MC ●	BlackRock US Opportunities Inv B	BRMBX	C	(800) 441-7762	A- / 9.1	4.83	11.50	14.22 /90	16.74 /88	12.99 /68	0.00	2.39
MC	BlackRock US Opportunities Inv C	BMECX	C	(800) 441-7762	A- / 9.1	4.86	11.51	14.27 /90	16.79 /89	13.04 /69	0.00	2.33
MC	BlackRock US Opportunities Svc	BMCSX	C+	(800) 441-7762	A / 9.4	5.04	11.93	15.11 /92	17.67 /93	13.90 /77	0.00	1.59
SC	BlackRock Value Opportunities Inst	MASPX	B-	(800) 441-7762	B- / 7.4	2.48	9.85	4.79 /37	15.33 /78	14.66 /84	0.00	0.97
SC	BlackRock Value Opportunities Inv A	MDSPX	C	(800) 441-7762	C+ / 6.2	2.39	9.71	4.53 /35	15.04 /75	14.36 /81	0.00	1.25
SC ●	BlackRock Value Opportunities Inv B	MBSPX	C+	(800) 441-7762	C+ / 6.4	2.21	9.30	3.57 /29	13.89 /66	13.23 /70	0.00	2.37
SC	BlackRock Value Opportunities Inv C	MCSPX	C+	(800) 441-7762	C+ / 6.4	2.19	9.24	3.65 /30	14.03 /67	13.32 /71	0.00	2.11
SC	BlackRock Value Opportunities R	MRSPX	C+	(800) 441-7762	C+ / 6.9	2.30	9.50	4.21 /33	14.68 /72	13.98 /77	0.00	1.54
GL	Blackstone Alternative Mlt Mngr I	BXMMX	U	(800) 831-5776	U /	3.82	3.08	5.24 /40	--	--	0.68	3.41
GL	Blackstone Alternative Multi Str I	BXMIX	U	(800) 831-5776	U /	3.59	3.09		--	--	0.00	3.32
GR	Blue Chip Investor Fund	BCIFX	A-	(800) 710-5777	B- / 7.0	-1.66	3.86	8.12 /64	15.21 /76	11.32 /55	0.00	1.57
GL	Blue Current Global Dividend Instl	BCGDX	U		U /	1.05	2.91	--	--	--	0.00	N/A
GR	BMO Aggressive Allocation I	BDSHX	C+	(800) 236-3863	C+ / 6.4	2.86	5.63	8.79 /68	13.52 /64	11.74 /59	1.84	0.97
GR	BMO Aggressive Allocation R3	BDSRX	C+	(800) 236-3863	C+ / 6.3	2.76	5.43	8.37 /65	13.37 /62	11.66 /58	1.56	1.47
GR	BMO Aggressive Allocation R-6	BDSQX	C+	(800) 236-3863	C+ / 6.5	2.96	5.83	8.99 /69	13.59 /64	11.79 /59	1.93	0.82
GI	BMO Balanced Allocation I	BGRHX	C	(800) 236-3863	C- / 4.1	2.40	4.47	6.87 /54	9.74 /38	9.13 /38	1.82	0.79
GI	BMO Balanced Allocation R3	BGRRX	C	(800) 236-3863	C- / 4.0	2.20	4.08	6.36 /50	9.56 /36	9.03 /37	1.54	1.29
GI	BMO Balanced Allocation R6	BGRQX	C	(800) 236-3863	C- / 4.2	2.40	4.48	6.96 /55	9.77 /38	9.15 /38	1.91	0.64
GI	BMO Balanced Allocation Y	BGRYX	C	(800) 236-3863	C- / 4.0	2.20	4.11	6.50 /51	9.61 /37	9.06 /37	1.67	1.04
AA	BMO Conservative Allocation Fund	BDVSX	C-	(800) 236-3863	D / 1.8	1.83	3.01	5.02 /39	5.63 /15	6.18 /18	1.80	0.70
AA	BMO Conservative Allocation I	BDVIX	C-	(800) 236-3863	D / 1.8	1.73	2.82	4.82 /37	5.56 /15	6.14 /18	1.72	0.85
AA	BMO Conservative Allocation R3	BDVRX	C-	(800) 236-3863	D / 1.7	1.62	2.62	4.41 /34	5.42 /15	6.06 /17	1.42	1.35
AA	BMO Conservative Allocation Y	BDVYX	C-	(800) 236-3863	D / 1.8	1.73	2.78	4.67 /36	5.51 /15	6.11 /17	1.57	1.10
IN	BMO Dividend Income A	BADIX	C	(800) 236-3863	C+ / 5.9	-0.69	3.65	10.60 /77	14.31 /69	--	2.12	1.05
IN	BMO Dividend Income I	MDIVX	A-	(800) 236-3863	B- / 7.0	-0.63	3.76	10.89 /78	14.80 /73	--	2.46	0.80
IN	BMO Dividend Income Y	MDIYX	B	(800) 236-3863	C+ / 6.8	-0.69	3.65	10.64 /77	14.52 /71	--	2.22	1.05
GI	BMO Growth Allocation I	BABHX	C	(800) 236-3863	C / 5.3	2.68	5.17	7.78 /61	11.77 /51	10.60 /49	1.68	0.96
GI	BMO Growth Allocation R3	BABRX	C	(800) 236-3863	C / 5.2	2.48	4.88	7.26 /57	11.59 /50	10.49 /49	1.40	1.46
GI	BMO Growth Allocation R6	BABQX	C	(800) 236-3863	C / 5.4	2.68	5.28	7.88 /62	11.80 /51	10.62 /50	1.78	0.81
GI	BMO Growth Allocation Y	BABYX	C	(800) 236-3863	C / 5.3	2.58	5.04	7.53 /59	11.68 /50	10.55 /49	1.55	1.21
GI	BMO Large Cap Value A	BALVX	B-	(800) 236-3863	B / 7.6	1.34	6.39	10.86 /78	16.70 /88	12.91 /67	0.85	1.23
GI	BMO Large Cap Value I	MLVIX	A	(800) 236-3863	B+ / 8.8	1.40	6.51	11.16 /79	17.19 /91	13.41 /72	1.17	0.98
GI	BMO Large Cap Value Y	MREIX	A-	(800) 236-3863	B+ / 8.6	1.34	6.39	10.90 /78	16.91 /89	13.14 /69	0.89	1.23
GR	BMO Large-Cap Growth A	BALGX	B+	(800) 236-3863	B+ / 8.7	3.63	8.74	17.59 /95	17.12 /90	14.69 /84	0.04	1.24
GR	BMO Large-Cap Growth I	MLCIX	B+	(800) 236-3863	A / 9.4	3.67	8.86	17.91 /95	17.60 /93	15.20 /88	0.23	0.99
GR	BMO Large-Cap Growth Y	MASTX	B+	(800) 236-3863	A / 9.3	3.63	8.74	17.63 /95	17.33 /91	14.93 /86	0.04	1.24
EM	BMO LGM Emg Mkts Eqty A	BAEMX	E+	(800) 236-3863	E+ / 0.6	2.24	0.59	6.66 /52	1.97 / 6	1.30 / 4	1.16	1.55
EM	BMO LGM Emg Mkts Eqty I	MIEMX	E+	(800) 236-3863	E+ / 0.9	2.31	0.75	7.02 /55	2.43 / 7	1.77 / 4	1.44	1.30
EM	BMO LGM Emg Mkts Eqty Y	MEMYX	E+	(800) 236-3863	E+ / 0.8	2.24	0.59	6.70 /53	2.16 / 6	1.52 / 4	1.22	1.55
GR	BMO Low Volatility Equity I	MLVEX	U	(800) 236-3863	U /	2.88	10.93	15.72 /93	--	--	1.55	0.89
MC	BMO Mid-Cap Growth A	BGMAX	C-	(800) 236-3863	C+ / 5.6	4.18	8.43	8.67 /67	13.10 /60	13.78 /76	0.00	1.22
MC	BMO Mid-Cap Growth I	MRMIX	C-	(800) 236-3863	C+ / 6.7	4.28	8.59	9.01 /69	13.60 /64	14.31 /80	0.00	0.97
MC	BMO Mid-Cap Growth R-3	BMGDX	C	(800) 236-3863	C+ / 6.2	4.15	8.32	8.43 /66	12.83 /58	13.50 /73	0.00	1.47
MC	BMO Mid-Cap Growth R-6	BMGGX	C	(800) 236-3863	C+ / 6.6	4.33	8.68	9.10 /70	13.44 /63	14.09 /78	0.00	0.82
MC	BMO Mid-Cap Growth Y	MRMSX	D+	(800) 236-3863	C+ / 6.5	4.18	8.43	8.72 /68	13.30 /62	14.01 /78	0.00	1.22
MC	BMO Mid-Cap Value A	BAMCX	B+	(800) 236-3863	B+ / 8.7	2.27	8.14	11.65 /81	18.23 /95	14.16 /79	0.11	1.21
MC	BMO Mid-Cap Value I	MRVIX	B+	(800) 236-3863	A / 9.4	2.34	8.31	11.94 /82	18.74 /96	14.67 /84	0.41	0.96
MC	BMO Mid-Cap Value R-3	BMVDX	B+	(800) 236-3863	A- / 9.2	2.21	8.03	11.37 /80	17.93 /94	13.87 /76	0.00	1.46

● Denotes fund is closed to new investors
★ Denotes fund is included in Section II

www.thestreetratings.com

RISK	3 Year		NET ASSETS		ASSET				Portfolio	BULL / BEAR		FUND MANAGER		MINIMUMS		LOADS	
Risk Rating/Pts	Standard Deviation	Beta	NAV As of 3/31/15	Total $(Mil)	Cash %	Stocks %	Bonds %	Other %	Portfolio Turnover Ratio	Last Bull Market Return	Last Bear Market Return	Manager Quality Pct	Manager Tenure (Years)	Initial Purch. $	Additional Purch. $	Front End Load	Back End Load
B / 8.6	2.0	0.19	10.22	5,995	25	0	72	3	1,413	19.0	-2.8	87	4	1,000	50	4.0	0.0
B / 8.6	2.0	0.19	10.21	1,140	25	0	72	3	1,413	16.0	-3.2	83	4	1,000	50	0.0	0.0
C- / 3.2	11.5	1.01	41.38	919	2	97	0	1	66	100.7	-24.7	76	17	2,000,000	0	0.0	0.0
D+ / 2.8	11.5	1.00	38.19	435	2	97	0	1	66	97.7	-24.9	72	17	1,000	50	5.3	0.0
D / 2.0	11.5	1.00	32.12	10	2	97	0	1	66	92.4	-25.1	63	17	1,000	50	0.0	0.0
D / 1.9	11.5	1.00	32.12	226	2	97	0	1	66	92.7	-25.1	63	17	1,000	50	0.0	0.0
C- / 3.2	11.5	1.01	39.36	32	2	97	0	1	66	97.7	-24.9	72	17	5,000	0	0.0	0.0
C+ / 5.6	13.9	1.00	33.01	167	0	99	0	1	61	96.3	-24.3	55	6	2,000,000	0	0.0	0.0
C+ / 5.6	13.9	1.00	32.09	459	0	99	0	1	61	94.5	-24.4	50	6	1,000	50	5.3	0.0
C+ / 5.6	13.9	1.00	25.85	7	0	99	0	1	61	87.9	-24.8	36	6	1,000	50	0.0	0.0
C+ / 5.6	13.9	1.00	24.72	181	0	99	0	1	61	88.8	-24.8	37	6	1,000	50	0.0	0.0
C+ / 5.6	13.9	1.00	26.74	26	0	99	0	1	61	92.4	-24.6	46	6	100	0	0.0	0.0
U /	N/A	N/A	10.33	1,329	47	19	32	2	135	N/A	N/A	N/A	2	0	0	0.0	0.0
U /	N/A	N/A	10.38	1,101	0	0	0	100	0	N/A	N/A	N/A	1	1,000,000	200,000	0.0	0.0
B / 8.2	9.3	0.89	158.43	27	9	90	0	1	23	88.9	-16.0	76	13	5,000	100	0.0	0.0
U /	N/A	N/A	9.89	28	0	0	0	100	0	N/A	N/A	N/A	1	100,000	0	0.0	0.0
C+ / 5.7	9.8	1.00	10.42	34	2	97	0	1	0	83.1	-20.6	34	1	2,000,000	0	0.0	0.0
C+ / 5.6	9.8	1.00	10.41	30	2	97	0	1	0	82.4	-20.6	32	1	0	0	0.0	0.0
C+ / 5.7	9.8	1.00	10.43	120	2	97	0	1	0	83.5	-20.6	35	1	0	0	0.0	0.0
B- / 7.2	6.5	0.65	10.22	79	5	64	29	2	0	54.3	-13.8	61	1	2,000,000	0	0.0	0.0
B- / 7.1	6.5	0.65	10.20	46	5	64	29	2	0	53.7	-13.8	58	1	0	0	0.0	0.0
B- / 7.2	6.5	0.65	10.22	292	5	64	29	2	0	54.5	-13.8	62	1	0	0	0.0	0.0
B- / 7.1	6.5	0.65	10.20	173	5	64	29	2	0	54.1	-13.8	59	1	1,000	50	0.0	0.0
B / 8.4	3.6	0.52	10.03	90	9	23	67	1	0	28.4	-5.4	68	1	0	0	0.0	0.0
B / 8.4	3.6	0.53	10.02	30	9	23	67	1	0	28.2	-5.4	67	1	2,000,000	0	0.0	0.0
B / 8.4	3.6	0.52	10.01	11	9	23	67	1	0	27.7	-5.4	66	1	0	0	0.0	0.0
B / 8.4	3.6	0.52	10.02	24	9	23	67	1	0	27.9	-5.4	N/A	1	1,000	50	0.0	0.0
C+ / 6.0	9.0	0.90	13.45	N/A	2	97	0	1	45	N/A	N/A	66	2	1,000	50	5.0	0.0
B / 8.0	9.0	0.90	13.47	57	2	97	0	1	45	N/A	N/A	71	2	2,000,000	0	0.0	0.0
B / 8.0	9.0	0.90	13.45	72	2	97	0	1	45	N/A	N/A	69	2	1,000	50	0.0	0.0
C+ / 6.3	8.3	0.84	10.36	16	3	85	11	1	0	68.8	-17.5	45	1	2,000,000	0	0.0	0.0
C+ / 6.3	8.3	0.85	10.34	31	3	85	11	1	0	68.2	-17.5	41	1	0	0	0.0	0.0
C+ / 6.3	8.3	0.84	10.36	63	3	85	11	1	0	69.0	-17.5	45	1	0	0	0.0	0.0
C+ / 6.3	8.3	0.85	10.35	45	3	85	11	1	0	68.5	-17.5	43	1	1,000	50	0.0	0.0
C+ / 5.7	10.1	1.02	16.02	N/A	2	97	0	1	68	100.9	-19.0	69	3	1,000	50	5.0	0.0
C+ / 6.5	10.1	1.02	16.03	131	2	97	0	1	68	104.0	-18.8	73	3	2,000,000	0	0.0	0.0
C+ / 6.6	10.1	1.02	16.02	157	2	97	0	1	68	102.2	-18.9	71	3	1,000	50	0.0	0.0
C+ / 5.7	9.8	0.98	16.54	N/A	1	98	0	1	67	107.0	-18.6	79	3	1,000	50	5.0	0.0
C / 4.8	9.9	0.98	16.65	140	1	98	0	1	67	110.3	-18.4	81	3	2,000,000	0	0.0	0.0
C / 4.8	9.8	0.98	16.54	169	1	98	0	1	67	108.3	-18.5	80	3	1,000	50	0.0	0.0
C / 5.3	11.8	0.78	13.70	N/A	0	99	0	1	38	26.2	-27.5	80	4	1,000	50	5.0	2.0
C / 4.8	11.8	0.78	13.73	105	0	99	0	1	38	28.0	-27.3	83	4	2,000,000	0	0.0	2.0
C / 4.8	11.8	0.78	13.70	66	0	99	0	1	38	27.0	-27.4	81	4	1,000	50	0.0	2.0
U /	N/A	N/A	13.40	74	1	98	0	1	47	N/A	N/A	N/A	3	2,000,000	0	0.0	0.0
C / 5.0	12.3	1.03	21.42	N/A	2	97	0	1	57	87.9	-25.9	16	11	1,000	50	5.0	0.0
C- / 3.4	12.3	1.03	21.92	139	2	97	0	1	57	90.8	-25.7	20	11	2,000,000	0	0.0	0.0
C / 5.0	12.3	1.03	21.82	N/A	2	97	0	1	57	86.3	-25.9	15	11	0	0	0.0	0.0
C / 5.1	12.3	1.03	21.95	N/A	2	97	0	1	57	89.7	-25.8	19	11	0	0	0.0	0.0
C- / 3.3	12.3	1.03	21.42	130	2	97	0	1	57	89.2	-25.8	18	11	1,000	50	0.0	0.0
C / 5.5	11.3	0.98	16.22	N/A	3	96	0	1	30	112.2	-24.3	80	22	1,000	50	5.0	0.0
C / 5.0	11.4	0.98	16.19	136	3	96	0	1	30	115.3	-24.1	83	22	2,000,000	0	0.0	0.0
C / 5.5	11.3	0.98	16.17	N/A	3	96	0	1	30	110.3	-24.4	78	22	0	0	0.0	0.0

www.thestreetratings.com
125
Data as of March 31, 2015

					PERFORMANCE						Incl. in Returns	
	99 Pct = Best 0 Pct = Worst		Overall		Perfor-	Total Return % through 3/31/15						
		Ticker	Investment		mance				Annualized		Dividend	Expense
Fund Type	Fund Name	Symbol	Rating	Phone	Rating/Pts	3 Mo	6 Mo	1Yr / Pct	3Yr / Pct	5Yr / Pct	Yield	Ratio
MC	BMO Mid-Cap Value R-6	BMVGX	B+	(800) 236-3863	A / 9.4	2.40	8.40	12.10 /83	18.59 /96	14.48 /82	0.32	0.81
MC	BMO Mid-Cap Value Y	MRVEX	B+	(800) 236-3863	A / 9.3	2.27	8.14	11.69 /81	18.44 /95	14.40 /81	0.18	1.21
GI	BMO Moderate Allocation Fund Y	BMBYX	C	(800) 236-3863	D+ / 2.8	2.01	3.55	5.71 /44	7.58 /25	7.63 /27	1.64	1.14
GI	BMO Moderate Allocation I	BMBHX	C	(800) 236-3863	D+ / 2.9	2.11	3.69	5.96 /46	7.67 /25	7.68 /28	1.77	0.89
GI	BMO Moderate Allocation R3	BMBQX	C	(800) 236-3863	D+ / 2.8	1.91	3.41	5.46 /42	7.50 /24	7.58 /27	1.50	1.39
GI	BMO Moderate Allocation R6	BMBTX	C	(800) 236-3863	C- / 3.0	2.11	3.68	6.06 /47	7.70 /25	7.70 /28	1.87	0.74
AA	BMO Multi-Asset Income I	BMANX	U	(800) 236-3863	U /	-0.26	-1.75	-1.09 /13	--	--	2.81	1.80
FO	BMO Pyrford International Stock A	BPIAX	D-	(800) 236-3863	D / 1.9	2.92	0.50	1.38 /20	8.65 /31	--	0.61	1.27
FO	BMO Pyrford International Stock I	MISNX	C-	(800) 236-3863	D+ / 2.9	3.00	0.64	1.66 /21	9.13 /34	--	3.22	1.02
FO	BMO Pyrford International Stock R3	BISDX	D	(800) 236-3863	D+ / 2.8	2.84	0.36	1.12 /19	8.38 /29	--	0.50	1.52
FO	BMO Pyrford International Stock R6	BISGX	D	(800) 236-3863	C- / 3.2	3.00	0.72	1.80 /21	8.98 /33	--	0.85	0.87
FO	BMO Pyrford International Stock Y	MISYX	C-	(800) 236-3863	D+ / 2.8	2.92	0.50	1.42 /20	8.85 /32	--	2.98	1.27
SC	● BMO Small-Cap Growth I	MSGIX	D+	(800) 236-3863	B / 8.0	8.56	14.64	3.65 /30	15.40 /78	15.20 /88	0.00	1.16
SC	● BMO Small-Cap Growth Y	MRSCX	D+	(800) 236-3863	B / 7.8	8.50	14.49	3.41 /29	15.13 /76	14.93 /86	0.00	1.41
SC	BMO Small-Cap Value A	BACVX	C+	(800) 236-3863	B- / 7.0	1.26	7.87	2.78 /25	16.86 /89	--	0.00	1.41
SC	BMO Small-Cap Value I	MRSNX	B+	(800) 236-3863	B+ / 8.3	1.32	8.04	3.10 /27	17.37 /92	--	0.00	1.16
SC	BMO Small-Cap Value R3	BSVDX	C+	(800) 236-3863	B / 7.7	1.18	7.67	2.51 /24	16.56 /87	--	0.00	1.66
SC	BMO Small-Cap Value R6	BSVGX	B-	(800) 236-3863	B / 8.2	1.32	8.04	3.16 /27	17.20 /91	--	0.00	1.01
SC	BMO Small-Cap Value Y	MRSYX	B	(800) 236-3863	B / 8.1	1.26	7.87	2.82 /26	17.08 /90	--	0.00	1.41
GI	BMO Target Retirement 2010 I	BTRIX	C+	(800) 236-3863	D+ / 2.7	1.87	2.97	5.10 /39	7.47 /24	7.61 /27	2.81	1.36
GI	BMO Target Retirement 2010 R3	BTRRX	C	(800) 236-3863	D+ / 2.5	1.77	2.75	4.59 /36	7.20 /22	7.45 /26	2.32	1.86
GI	BMO Target Retirement 2010 R6	BTRTX	C+	(800) 236-3863	D+ / 2.8	1.97	3.08	5.30 /41	7.58 /25	7.68 /28	3.09	1.21
GI	BMO Target Retirement 2010 Y	BTRYX	C	(800) 236-3863	D+ / 2.6	1.77	2.86	4.79 /37	7.33 /23	7.53 /27	2.70	1.61
GI	BMO Target Retirement 2020 I	BTREX	C+	(800) 236-3863	C- / 4.1	2.43	4.05	6.34 /49	9.72 /38	9.26 /39	2.47	0.97
GI	BMO Target Retirement 2020 R3	BTRFX	C+	(800) 236-3863	C- / 3.8	2.15	3.67	5.67 /44	9.39 /35	9.07 /37	1.94	1.47
GI	BMO Target Retirement 2020 R6	BTRGX	C+	(800) 236-3863	C- / 4.1	2.33	4.09	6.39 /50	9.78 /38	9.30 /39	2.62	0.82
GI	BMO Target Retirement 2020 Y	BTRDX	C+	(800) 236-3863	C- / 4.0	2.34	3.89	6.09 /47	9.57 /37	9.17 /38	2.24	1.22
GI	BMO Target Retirement 2025 R6	BRTHX	U	(800) 236-3863	U /	2.53	4.24	7.49 /59	--	--	0.59	24.80
GI	BMO Target Retirement 2030 I	BTRJX	B-	(800) 236-3863	C / 5.1	2.61	4.67	6.94 /55	11.47 /49	10.47 /48	1.62	1.04
GI	BMO Target Retirement 2030 R3	BTRKX	C+	(800) 236-3863	C / 4.8	2.43	4.31	6.29 /49	11.16 /47	10.29 /47	1.19	1.54
GI	BMO Target Retirement 2030 R6	BTRLX	B-	(800) 236-3863	C / 5.1	2.61	4.65	7.01 /55	11.55 /49	10.52 /49	1.86	0.89
GI	BMO Target Retirement 2030 Y	BTRHX	B-	(800) 236-3863	C / 5.0	2.61	4.55	6.62 /52	11.33 /48	10.39 /48	1.50	1.29
GI	BMO Target Retirement 2035 R6	BRTLX	U	(800) 236-3863	U /	2.73	4.79	8.20 /64	--	--	0.25	23.85
GI	BMO Target Retirement 2040 I	BTRNX	B-	(800) 236-3863	C+ / 5.7	2.85	5.12	7.37 /58	12.46 /56	11.14 /54	1.94	1.15
GI	BMO Target Retirement 2040 R3	BTRPX	B-	(800) 236-3863	C / 5.5	2.67	4.78	6.84 /54	12.16 /53	10.96 /52	1.45	1.65
GI	BMO Target Retirement 2040 R6	BTRQX	B-	(800) 236-3863	C+ / 5.8	2.94	5.19	7.63 /60	12.57 /56	11.20 /54	2.10	1.00
GI	BMO Target Retirement 2040 Y	BTRMX	B-	(800) 236-3863	C+ / 5.6	2.76	4.97	7.13 /56	12.32 /55	11.05 /53	1.72	1.40
GI	BMO Target Retirement 2050 I	BTRVX	B-	(800) 236-3863	C+ / 5.7	2.84	5.08	7.42 /58	12.39 /55	11.11 /53	1.78	1.47
GI	BMO Target Retirement 2050 R3	BTRWX	B-	(800) 236-3863	C / 5.5	2.75	4.93	6.99 /55	12.12 /53	10.95 /52	1.29	1.97
GI	BMO Target Retirement 2050 R6	BTRZX	B-	(800) 236-3863	C+ / 5.8	2.93	5.24	7.58 /60	12.50 /56	11.18 /54	1.94	1.32
GI	BMO Target Retirement 2050 Y	BTRUX	B-	(800) 236-3863	C+ / 5.6	2.84	4.95	7.20 /57	12.25 /54	11.03 /53	1.58	1.72
BA	BNY Mellon Asset Allocation Fund M	MPBLX	C-	(800) 645-6561	C- / 3.7	2.65	5.00	7.63 /60	8.81 /32	7.74 /28	2.40	1.00
BA	BNY Mellon Asset Allocation Inv	MIBLX	C-	(800) 645-6561	C- / 3.5	2.57	4.83	7.31 /57	8.51 /30	7.46 /26	2.14	1.26
EM	BNY Mellon Emerging Markets Inv	MIEGX	E	(800) 645-6561	E / 0.3	-0.63	-6.79	-3.63 / 8	-1.96 / 3	-0.51 / 2	1.21	1.67
EM	BNY Mellon Emerging Markets M	MEMKX	E	(800) 645-6561	E / 0.3	-0.53	-6.60	-3.34 / 8	-1.68 / 3	-0.24 / 2	1.41	1.42
GR	BNY Mellon Focused Eqty Opps Inv	MFOIX	C+	(800) 645-6561	B / 8.2	4.00	6.80	12.65 /85	15.66 /80	12.49 /64	0.39	1.11
GR	BNY Mellon Focused Eqty Opps M	MFOMX	C+	(800) 645-6561	B+ / 8.5	4.04	6.97	12.93 /86	16.01 /83	12.76 /66	0.51	0.85
GI	BNY Mellon Income Stock Inv	MIISX	B+	(800) 645-6561	B+ / 8.6	2.68	5.11	10.37 /76	16.98 /90	14.06 /78	1.86	1.07
GI	BNY Mellon Income Stock M	MPISX	B+	(800) 645-6561	B+ / 8.8	2.66	5.19	10.75 /77	17.33 /91	14.36 /81	2.12	0.80
FO	BNY Mellon International App Fd Inv	MARIX	D	(800) 645-6561	D+ / 2.8	5.98	1.93	-0.47 /14	8.17 /28	5.39 /14	2.76	1.06
FO	BNY Mellon International App Fd M	MPPMX	D	(800) 645-6561	C- / 3.0	6.00	2.03	-0.28 /15	8.43 /29	5.64 /15	2.98	0.81
FO	BNY Mellon International Inv	MIINX	D	(800) 645-6561	D+ / 2.9	5.45	-0.89	-3.54 / 8	9.09 /34	4.96 /12	1.35	1.28

● Denotes fund is closed to new investors

* Denotes fund is included in Section II

www.thestreetratings.com

RISK			NET ASSETS		ASSET					BULL / BEAR		FUND MANAGER		MINIMUMS		LOADS	
	3 Year		NAV						Portfolio	Last Bull	Last Bear	Manager	Manager	Initial	Additional	Front	Back
Risk Rating/Pts	Standard Deviation	Beta	As of 3/31/15	Total $(Mil)	Cash %	Stocks %	Bonds %	Other %	Turnover Ratio	Market Return	Market Return	Quality Pct	Tenure (Years)	Purch. $	Purch. $	End Load	End Load
C / 5.5	11.3	0.98	16.21	9	3	96	0	1	30	114.2	-24.2	82	22	0	0	0.0	0.0
C / 5.1	11.3	0.98	16.22	195	3	96	0	1	30	113.6	-24.2	81	22	1,000	50	0.0	0.0
B / 8.1	4.9	0.46	10.13	24	8	43	47	2	0	40.5	-9.6	72	1	1,000	50	0.0	0.0
B / 8.1	4.9	0.46	10.14	16	8	43	47	2	0	40.7	-9.6	73	1	2,000,000	0	0.0	0.0
B / 8.1	4.9	0.46	10.12	21	8	43	47	2	0	40.1	-9.6	71	1	0	0	0.0	0.0
B / 8.1	4.9	0.46	10.14	96	8	43	47	2	0	40.9	-9.6	73	1	0	0	0.0	0.0
U /	N/A	N/A	9.73	58	13	32	48	7	0	N/A	N/A	N/A	N/A	2,000,000	0	0.0	0.0
C+ / 5.9	9.6	0.70	12.68	N/A	3	96	0	1	6	N/A	N/A	83	4	1,000	50	5.0	2.0
B- / 7.8	9.6	0.71	12.71	347	3	96	0	1	6	N/A	N/A	86	4	2,000,000	0	0.0	2.0
C+ / 5.9	9.6	0.70	12.69	N/A	3	96	0	1	6	N/A	N/A	82	4	0	0	0.0	0.0
C+ / 5.9	9.5	0.70	12.72	3	3	96	0	1	6	N/A	N/A	85	4	0	0	0.0	0.0
B- / 7.8	9.6	0.71	12.68	87	3	96	0	1	6	N/A	N/A	84	4	1,000	50	0.0	2.0
D / 1.8	15.8	1.09	20.42	361	2	97	0	1	82	104.0	-29.2	36	11	2,000,000	0	0.0	0.0
D / 1.6	15.8	1.09	19.91	391	2	97	0	1	82	102.3	-29.3	32	11	1,000	50	0.0	0.0
C / 5.0	13.1	0.91	13.67	N/A	2	97	0	1	43	99.8	-22.2	83	4	1,000	50	5.0	0.0
C+ / 5.8	13.1	0.91	13.79	11	2	97	0	1	43	102.8	-22.1	86	4	2,000,000	0	0.0	0.0
C / 5.0	13.1	0.91	13.72	N/A	2	97	0	1	43	98.1	-22.3	81	4	0	0	0.0	0.0
C / 5.0	13.1	0.91	13.80	N/A	2	97	0	1	43	101.7	-22.1	85	4	0	0	0.0	0.0
C+ / 5.7	13.1	0.91	13.67	76	2	97	0	1	43	101.1	-22.1	84	4	1,000	50	0.0	0.0
B+ / 9.2	4.9	0.45	10.35	N/A	6	37	56	1	45	42.1	-11.0	72	2	2,000,000	0	0.0	0.0
B+ / 9.2	4.9	0.45	10.34	3	6	37	56	1	45	41.1	-11.0	70	2	0	0	0.0	0.0
B+ / 9.2	4.9	0.45	10.35	19	6	37	56	1	45	42.5	-11.0	73	2	0	0	0.0	0.0
B+ / 9.2	4.9	0.45	10.33	7	6	37	56	1	45	41.6	-11.0	71	2	1,000	50	0.0	0.0
B / 8.6	6.7	0.65	10.96	6	4	60	34	2	35	57.0	-15.1	60	2	2,000,000	0	0.0	0.0
B / 8.5	6.7	0.66	10.94	22	4	60	34	2	35	55.7	-15.1	54	2	0	0	0.0	0.0
B / 8.6	6.7	0.65	10.96	53	4	60	34	2	35	57.3	-15.1	61	2	0	0	0.0	0.0
B / 8.6	6.6	0.65	10.95	33	4	60	34	2	35	56.3	-15.1	58	2	1,000	50	0.0	0.0
U /	N/A	N/A	10.95	25	3	69	27	1	22	N/A	N/A	N/A	2	0	0	0.0	0.0
B / 8.1	8.2	0.82	11.41	4	4	76	19	1	29	69.2	-18.0	46	2	2,000,000	0	0.0	0.0
B / 8.0	8.2	0.82	11.38	19	4	76	19	1	29	67.9	-18.0	42	2	0	0	0.0	0.0
B / 8.1	8.2	0.82	11.40	60	4	76	19	1	29	69.5	-18.0	47	2	0	0	0.0	0.0
B / 8.1	8.2	0.82	11.39	35	4	76	19	1	29	68.5	-18.0	45	2	1,000	50	0.0	0.0
U /	N/A	N/A	10.92	26	4	83	11	2	29	N/A	N/A	N/A	2	0	0	0.0	0.0
B- / 7.6	9.1	0.91	11.55	4	3	89	7	1	22	76.0	-19.2	39	2	2,000,000	0	0.0	0.0
B- / 7.6	9.0	0.90	11.53	12	3	89	7	1	22	74.7	-19.2	37	2	0	0	0.0	0.0
B- / 7.6	9.0	0.91	11.56	39	3	89	7	1	22	76.5	-19.2	41	2	0	0	0.0	0.0
B- / 7.6	9.1	0.91	11.54	20	3	89	7	1	22	75.3	-19.2	38	2	1,000	50	0.0	0.0
B- / 7.6	9.0	0.91	11.59	3	3	89	6	2	28	75.5	-19.2	39	2	2,000,000	0	0.0	0.0
B- / 7.5	9.1	0.91	11.58	7	3	89	6	2	28	74.2	-19.2	35	2	0	0	0.0	0.0
B- / 7.6	9.1	0.91	11.60	21	3	89	6	2	28	76.0	-19.2	40	2	0	0	0.0	0.0
B- / 7.6	9.0	0.90	11.58	13	3	89	6	2	28	74.9	-19.2	38	2	1,000	50	0.0	0.0
C+ / 6.8	7.0	1.20	12.14	499	8	63	27	2	48	48.8	-15.0	17	2	10,000	100	0.0	0.0
C+ / 6.8	7.0	1.19	12.22	7	8	63	27	2	48	47.4	-15.1	15	2	10,000	100	0.0	0.0
C / 5.1	14.8	1.07	9.53	23	1	98	0	1	71	16.1	-28.4	28	15	10,000	100	0.0	0.0
C / 5.1	14.7	1.07	9.30	1,434	1	98	0	1	71	17.3	-28.4	32	15	10,000	100	0.0	0.0
C- / 3.7	12.1	1.18	15.60	8	0	99	0	1	76	99.6	-23.1	25	6	10,000	100	0.0	0.0
C- / 3.7	12.0	1.17	15.70	626	0	99	0	1	76	101.4	-23.1	29	6	10,000	100	0.0	0.0
C+ / 6.1	10.1	1.02	9.22	14	2	97	0	1	58	98.3	-16.2	71	4	10,000	100	0.0	0.0
C+ / 6.0	10.0	1.02	9.14	1,233	2	97	0	1	58	100.2	-16.1	75	4	10,000	100	0.0	0.0
C+ / 5.7	13.2	1.00	13.11	5	1	98	0	1	4	48.5	-24.4	49	6	10,000	100	0.0	0.0
C+ / 5.7	13.2	1.00	13.25	109	1	98	0	1	4	49.8	-24.3	53	6	10,000	100	0.0	0.0
C+ / 5.7	13.8	1.04	12.78	15	2	97	0	1	93	51.2	-25.1	57	13	10,000	100	0.0	0.0

					PERFORMANCE								
			99 Pct = Best 0 Pct = Worst				Total Return % through 3/31/15					Incl. in Returns	
			Overall		Perfor-					Annualized		Dividend	Expense
Fund Type	Fund Name	Ticker Symbol	Investment Rating	Phone	mance Rating/Pts	3 Mo	6 Mo	1Yr / Pct	3Yr / Pct	5Yr / Pct		Yield	Ratio
FO	BNY Mellon International M	MPITX	D	(800) 645-6561	C- / 3.1	5.53	-0.80	-3.31 / 8	9.37 /35	5.23 /13		1.56	1.03
FO	BNY Mellon Internatl Eqty Inc Inv	MLIIX	D-	(800) 645-6561	E+ / 0.6	0.29	-4.77	-6.02 / 4	2.52 / 7	--		4.48	1.36
FO	BNY Mellon Internatl Eqty Inc M	MLIMX	D-	(800) 645-6561	E+ / 0.7	0.33	-4.67	-5.78 / 5	2.87 / 8	--		4.72	1.08
GR	BNY Mellon Large Cap Mkt Opps Inv	MMOIX	C-	(800) 645-6561	C+ / 6.7	2.69	6.03	10.10 /75	13.85 /66	--		1.35	1.21
GR	BNY Mellon Large Cap Mkt Opps M	MMOMX	C-	(800) 645-6561	C+ / 6.9	2.71	6.14	10.24 /75	14.12 /68	--		1.49	0.93
GR	BNY Mellon Large Cap Stock Inv	MILCX	D	(800) 645-6561	B- / 7.4	1.31	6.36	14.11 /90	14.48 /71	12.27 /62		0.97	1.06
GR	BNY Mellon Large Cap Stock M	MPLCX	D	(800) 645-6561	B / 7.6	1.37	6.49	14.39 /90	14.76 /73	12.56 /65		1.20	0.81
MC	BNY Mellon MC Multi-Strategy Inv	MIMSX	B+	(800) 645-6561	B / 8.2	3.38	9.72	10.69 /77	15.73 /81	13.07 /69		0.05	1.15
MC	BNY Mellon MC Mutli-Strategy M	MPMCX	B+	(800) 645-6561	B+ / 8.4	3.40	9.83	10.93 /78	16.01 /83	13.34 /71		0.25	0.90
SC	BNY Mellon SC Multi-Strategy Inv	MISCX	B-	(800) 645-6561	B / 7.6	3.76	12.68	3.91 /31	15.45 /79	12.84 /67		0.00	1.28
SC	BNY Mellon SC Multi-Strategy M	MPSSX	B-	(800) 645-6561	B / 7.8	3.82	12.86	4.20 /33	15.76 /81	13.12 /69		0.00	1.03
GR	BNY Mellon Sm/Mid Cap Mlti-Str Inv	MMCIX	D-	(800) 645-6561	C+ / 5.9	4.83	12.02	8.38 /65	11.90 /52	10.65 /50		0.00	1.17
GR	BNY Mellon Sm/Mid Cap Mlti-Str M	MMCMX	D-	(800) 645-6561	C+ / 6.1	4.87	12.09	8.60 /67	12.18 /54	10.95 /52		0.00	0.91
GR	BNY Mellon Tx Sens LC Mulit-Str Inv	MTSIX	C	(800) 645-6561	B- / 7.1	1.94	5.78	10.70 /77	14.43 /70	--		1.28	1.16
GR	BNY Mellon Tx Sens LC Mulit-Str M	MTSMX	C	(800) 645-6561	B- / 7.0	1.98	5.97	10.98 /78	14.22 /69	--		1.49	0.90
SC	Bogle Inv Mgt Small Cap Gr Inst	BOGIX	B	(877) 264-5346	A / 9.5	6.24	6.58	6.46 /50	19.86 /98	18.31 /98		0.00	1.39
SC	Bogle Inv Mgt Small Cap Gr Inv	BOGLX	B	(877) 264-5346	A / 9.5	6.24	6.55	6.40 /50	19.75 /98	18.19 /98		0.00	1.49
FO	Boston Common International	BCAIX	D-	(877) 777-6944	D / 1.6	5.12	1.81	-1.48 /11	6.36 /18	--		1.89	1.17
GR	Boston Common US Equity	BCAMX	U	(877) 777-6944	U /	1.73	4.55	8.92 /69	--	--		0.76	1.66
BA	Boston Trust Asset Management	BTBFX	C+	(800) 282-8782	C / 4.3	-0.14	5.04	8.21 /64	10.02 /39	10.01 /45		1.10	0.93
IN	Boston Trust Equity	BTEFX	C+	(800) 282-8782	C / 5.1	-1.01	4.71	8.01 /63	11.79 /51	11.85 /60		0.89	0.96
MC	Boston Trust Mid Cap	BTMFX	B-	(800) 282-8782	C+ / 6.8	3.14	9.88	12.65 /85	13.23 /61	15.02 /87		0.32	1.01
SC	● Boston Trust Small Cap	BOSOX	C-	(800) 282-8782	C / 5.1	2.98	11.54	3.81 /31	11.22 /47	12.11 /61		0.08	1.07
GL	Boston Trust SMID Cap	BTSMX	C+	(800) 282-8782	C+ / 6.2	4.65	12.44	7.69 /60	12.46 /56	--		0.03	1.59
MC	Boyar Value Fund	BOYAX	A+	(800) 266-5566	B / 8.1	2.14	9.99	16.23 /94	16.95 /90	14.07 /78		0.00	2.35
EN	BP Capital TwinLine Energy I	BPEIX	U	(855) 402-7227	U /	5.23	-8.91	-3.92 / 7	--	--		0.00	1.74
GL	BPV Core Diversification Inst	BPVDX	D+	(855) 784-2399	E+ / 0.8	0.85	-0.22	1.96 /22	3.08 / 8	--		0.98	1.66
GR	BPV Large Cap Value Instl	BPVAX	U	(855) 784-2399	U /	2.46	4.90	8.26 /65	--	--		0.14	N/A
GL	BPV Low Volatility	BPVLX	U	(855) 784-2399	U /	0.39	2.26	3.68 /30	--	--		0.45	1.84
GL	BPV Wealth Preservation Inst	BPVPX	C-	(855) 784-2399	E+ / 0.8	0.28	2.02	3.30 /28	2.79 / 7	--		0.01	1.54
EM	Brandes Emerging Markets Value A	BEMAX	E-	(800) 237-7119	E- / 0.2	-5.91	-17.84	-14.14 / 2	-3.12 / 2	-0.02 / 2		1.35	1.37
EM	Brandes Emerging Markets Value I	BEMIX	E-	(800) 237-7119	E- / 0.2	-5.85	-17.72	-13.83 / 2	-2.87 / 2	0.18 / 3		1.66	1.17
GL	Brandes Global Equity A	BGEAX	D+	(800) 237-7119	C- / 3.4	2.89	0.39	1.08 /19	11.21 /47	--		1.45	1.73
GL	Brandes Global Equity E	BGVEX	C-	(800) 237-7119	C / 4.3	2.87	0.38	1.09 /19	11.23 /47	8.23 /31		1.78	1.73
GL	Brandes Global Equity I	BGVIX	C-	(800) 237-7119	C / 4.5	2.93	0.52	1.34 /20	11.50 /49	8.51 /33		1.70	1.53
FO	Brandes Intl Equity Fund A	BIEAX	D-	(800) 237-7119	D / 2.2	6.66	1.03	-1.27 /12	8.74 /31	--		1.75	1.19
FO	Brandes Intl Equity Fund E	BIEEX	D	(800) 237-7119	C- / 3.0	6.67	0.84	-1.47 /12	8.69 /31	5.25 /13		1.60	1.19
FO	Brandes Intl Equity Fund I	BIIEX	D	(800) 237-7119	C- / 3.2	6.72	1.09	-1.12 /13	8.94 /32	5.44 /14		2.01	1.00
FO	Brandes Intl Small Cap Equity A	BISAX	D+	(800) 237-7119	C- / 4.1	5.94	-0.39	-2.00 /10	12.80 /58	10.81 /51		1.19	1.40
FO	Brandes Intl Small Cap Equity I	BISMX	C-	(800) 237-7119	C / 5.2	6.01	-0.30	-1.81 /11	13.10 /60	10.96 /52		1.45	1.18
GR	Braver Tactical Opportunity N	BRAVX	U	(855) 294-7539	U /	0.00	1.94	0.56 /17	--	--		0.00	2.10
GR	Bread & Butter Fund Inc	BABFX	D	(888) 476-8585	D- / 1.1	-3.93	-3.58	-3.51 / 8	5.55 /15	5.61 /15		0.00	2.89
GL	Bretton	BRTNX	B	(800) 231-2901	C+ / 5.6	-0.97	5.88	7.53 /59	12.53 /56	--		0.06	1.50
GI	Bridges Investment Fund	BRGIX	C+	(866) 934-4700	C+ / 6.5	1.84	5.00	10.33 /76	13.68 /65	12.32 /63		0.51	0.87
AG	Bridgeway Aggressive Investor 1 Fd	BRAGX	A+	(800) 661-3550	A+ / 9.7	1.25	7.88	11.61 /81	20.83 /98	15.35 /89		0.20	1.01
GR	Bridgeway Blue Chip 35 Index Fund	BRLIX	B-	(800) 661-3550	C+ / 6.7	-0.43	2.71	9.71 /73	14.48 /71	13.04 /69		1.94	0.25
GR	Bridgeway Large-Cap Growth	BRLGX	A+	(800) 661-3550	A+ / 9.8	5.75	14.87	22.54 /97	20.83 /98	16.24 /94		0.46	0.87
BA	Bridgeway Managed Volatility Fund	BRBPX	C	(800) 661-3550	D / 2.1	1.57	2.80	4.77 /37	6.31 /18	5.83 /16		0.12	1.15
GR	Bridgeway Omni SCV	BOSVX	C+	(800) 661-3550	C+ / 6.7	1.90	7.22	0.78 /18	15.18 /76	--		0.55	0.73
SC	Bridgeway Omni Tax-Mgd SCV	BOTSX	C+	(800) 661-3550	C+ / 6.5	2.44	8.02	0.66 /17	14.58 /72	--		0.19	0.72
SC	Bridgeway Small-Cap Growth	BRSGX	B+	(800) 661-3550	A / 9.5	7.02	13.52	13.40 /88	17.77 /93	14.78 /85		0.06	1.07
SC	Bridgeway Small-Cap Momentum	BRSMX	D+	(800) 661-3550	C+ / 5.9	4.65	12.42	3.43 /29	13.11 /60	--		0.51	3.13

● Denotes fund is closed to new investors
★ Denotes fund is included in Section II

www.thestreetratings.com

I. Index of Stock Mutual Funds

RISK Risk Rating/Pts	3 Year Standard Deviation	Beta	NET ASSETS NAV As of 3/31/15	Total $(Mil)	ASSET Cash %	Stocks %	Bonds %	Other %	Portfolio Turnover Ratio	BULL / BEAR Last Bull Market Return	Last Bear Market Return	FUND MANAGER Manager Quality Pct	Manager Tenure (Years)	MINIMUMS Initial Purch. $	Additional Purch. $	LOADS Front End Load	Back End Load
C+ / 5.7	13.8	1.03	12.03	964	2	97	0	1	93	52.6	-25.0	61	13	10,000	100	0.0	0.0
C+ / 6.8	13.1	0.95	13.13	3	2	97	0	1	83	N/A	N/A	6	4	10,000	100	0.0	0.0
C+ / 6.8	13.1	0.95	13.07	315	2	97	0	1	83	N/A	N/A	7	4	10,000	100	0.0	0.0
C- / 3.2	10.3	1.03	14.10	1	2	97	0	1	26	87.3	-19.6	31	N/A	10,000	100	0.0	0.0
C- / 3.1	10.3	1.03	14.01	158	2	97	0	1	26	87.4	-19.5	34	N/A	10,000	100	0.0	0.0
D- / 1.2	9.8	1.01	6.24	12	0	99	0	1	142	91.6	-21.3	44	2	10,000	100	0.0	0.0
D- / 1.2	9.8	1.00	6.24	449	0	99	0	1	142	93.2	-21.2	48	2	10,000	100	0.0	0.0
C+ / 6.1	10.9	0.96	15.31	59	3	96	0	1	54	93.9	-26.8	59	3	10,000	100	0.0	0.0
C+ / 6.1	10.9	0.96	15.51	2,158	3	96	0	1	54	95.5	-26.7	63	3	10,000	100	0.0	0.0
C / 5.3	14.0	1.02	16.82	13	1	98	0	1	93	95.6	-28.0	53	3	10,000	100	0.0	0.0
C / 5.4	14.0	1.01	17.40	385	1	98	0	1	93	97.2	-27.9	58	3	10,000	100	0.0	0.0
D- / 1.5	12.7	1.18	13.23	2	0	99	0	1	145	68.9	-27.7	6	1	10,000	100	0.0	0.0
D- / 1.5	12.8	1.18	13.35	373	0	99	0	1	145	70.2	-27.6	6	1	10,000	100	0.0	0.0
C / 4.7	10.3	1.05	15.76	5	1	98	0	1	13	89.2	-19.2	34	5	10,000	100	0.0	0.0
C / 4.6	9.9	1.02	15.46	440	1	98	0	1	13	88.2	-18.5	38	5	10,000	100	0.0	0.0
C- / 4.0	14.5	1.00	33.01	101	1	98	0	1	175	125.1	-26.8	89	16	1,000,000	0	0.0	0.0
C- / 3.9	14.5	1.00	32.37	104	1	98	0	1	175	124.4	-26.8	89	16	10,000	0	0.0	0.0
C+ / 5.6	12.3	0.91	27.33	202	2	97	0	1	24	43.5	-22.8	36	5	100,000	1,000	0.0	2.0
U /	N/A	N/A	34.65	28	2	97	0	1	21	N/A	N/A	N/A	3	100,000	1,000	0.0	2.0
B / 8.2	7.2	1.24	41.80	354	1	77	21	1	9	57.8	-10.2	23	20	100,000	1,000	0.0	0.0
B- / 7.3	9.6	0.99	20.66	111	3	96	0	1	6	76.3	-15.7	19	12	100,000	1,000	0.0	0.0
B- / 7.2	9.6	0.84	16.12	48	3	96	0	1	16	82.3	-18.0	56	8	100,000	1,000	0.0	0.0
C / 5.2	12.9	0.92	15.20	440	1	98	0	1	35	73.8	-21.9	22	10	100,000	1,000	0.0	0.0
C+ / 6.7	11.9	0.57	13.72	5	0	99	0	1	36	N/A	N/A	96	4	100,000	1,000	0.0	0.0
B / 8.1	8.6	0.65	23.34	25	16	83	0	1	7	102.9	-16.9	94	17	5,000	1,000	5.0	2.0
U /	N/A	N/A	20.13	102	17	80	0	3	72	N/A	N/A	N/A	2	250,000	0	0.0	0.0
B / 8.3	4.8	0.68	10.68	40	11	43	44	2	47	N/A	N/A	27	5	100,000	100	0.0	1.0
U /	N/A	N/A	10.81	73	4	95	0	1	0	N/A	N/A	N/A	N/A	100,000	100	0.0	1.0
U /	N/A	N/A	10.38	64	50	49	0	1	0	N/A	N/A	N/A	1	5,000,000	1,000	0.0	1.0
B+ / 9.7	2.0	0.24	10.65	72	48	51	0	1	51	N/A	N/A	74	5	100,000	100	0.0	1.0
C- / 3.0	16.6	1.11	7.60	232	8	91	0	1	23	17.5	-26.2	17	4	2,500	500	5.8	0.0
C- / 3.0	16.6	1.11	7.62	907	8	91	0	1	23	18.6	-26.1	19	4	100,000	500	0.0	0.0
C+ / 6.0	11.7	0.83	23.82	3	5	94	0	1	30	64.8	-19.1	89	2	2,500	500	5.8	0.0
C+ / 5.9	11.7	0.83	23.52	N/A	5	94	0	1	30	64.8	-19.2	89	2	2,500	500	0.0	0.0
C+ / 6.0	11.7	0.83	23.92	47	5	94	0	1	30	66.2	-19.0	90	2	100,000	500	0.0	0.0
C+ / 5.8	14.4	1.04	16.69	13	7	92	0	1	40	49.8	-20.6	51	18	2,500	500	5.8	0.0
C+ / 5.8	14.4	1.04	16.68	2	7	92	0	1	40	49.7	-20.8	49	18	2,500	500	0.0	0.0
C+ / 5.8	14.4	1.04	16.72	534	7	92	0	1	40	50.8	-20.7	53	18	100,000	500	0.0	0.0
C / 5.4	13.1	0.88	12.92	59	10	89	0	1	24	64.5	-20.1	92	N/A	2,500	500	5.8	0.0
C / 5.4	13.2	0.88	12.95	641	10	89	0	1	24	65.7	-20.1	92	N/A	100,000	0	0.0	0.0
U /	N/A	N/A	11.02	32	35	44	19	2	1,000	N/A	N/A	N/A	N/A	1,000	50	0.0	0.0
B- / 7.8	9.4	0.87	13.93	2	37	62	0	1	20	33.8	-13.1	3	10	3,000	500	0.0	0.0
B- / 7.8	9.1	0.35	25.47	11	18	81	0	1	7	86.9	-11.7	97	5	5,000	100	0.0	0.0
C+ / 6.3	10.4	1.05	50.41	124	3	95	0	2	12	93.2	-16.1	26	18	1,000	0	0.0	0.0
C+ / 6.2	12.6	1.24	60.13	262	0	99	0	1	125	129.1	-31.0	72	21	2,000	100	0.0	0.0
B- / 7.5	9.6	0.99	11.68	655	0	99	0	1	28	93.7	-13.2	49	18	2,000	100	0.0	0.0
B- / 7.0	10.6	1.04	23.91	135	2	97	0	1	74	124.2	-20.0	90	12	2,000	100	0.0	0.0
B+ / 9.2	3.7	0.52	14.23	53	0	52	47	1	39	37.2	-10.6	75	14	2,000	100	0.0	0.0
C / 5.5	15.2	1.31	15.54	467	1	98	0	1	31	100.8	N/A	8	5	0	0	0.0	0.0
C+ / 5.9	14.9	1.06	14.71	440	1	98	0	1	25	94.7	-26.1	33	5	0	0	0.0	0.0
C / 5.2	15.4	1.06	20.42	36	0	99	0	1	121	119.9	-27.8	72	12	2,000	100	0.0	0.0
C- / 3.6	13.3	0.97	12.16	5	0	99	0	1	242	87.8	-25.1	33	5	2,000	100	0.0	2.0

Fund Type	Fund Name	Ticker Symbol	Overall Investment Rating	Phone	Performance Rating/Pts	3 Mo	6 Mo	1Yr / Pct	3Yr / Pct	5Yr / Pct	Dividend Yield	Expense Ratio
SC	Bridgeway Small-Cap Value	BRSVX	C+	(800) 661-3550	C+ / 6.9	1.03	8.77	0.12 /16	15.59 /80	14.04 /78	0.73	1.06
SC	● Bridgeway Ultra-SmCo	BRUSX	D+	(800) 661-3550	B / 8.0	1.99	7.14	-1.64 /11	17.58 /93	14.40 /81	0.74	1.13
SC	Bridgeway Ultra-SmCo Market Fund	BRSIX	C+	(800) 661-3550	B+ / 8.8	1.89	10.69	4.26 /33	18.44 /95	15.76 /92	0.80	0.83
GL	Bright Rock Mid Cap Growth Inst	BQMGX	C+	(800) 273-7223	C+ / 6.5	7.31	15.81	15.20 /92	11.22 /47	--	0.00	1.34
GL	Bright Rock Qual Lrg Cap Inst	BQLCX	C+	(800) 273-7223	C+ / 6.4	-0.15	2.66	8.22 /64	14.14 /68	--	1.41	0.92
SC	Broadview Opportunity	BVAOX	C+	(855) 846-1463	B / 7.6	3.94	11.15	6.00 /46	15.28 /77	14.56 /83	0.00	1.25
OT	Brookfield Global Listed Infr A	BGLAX	D+	(855) 244-4859	D+ / 2.7	-3.45	-8.36	-1.14 /13	12.02 /53	--	1.45	1.51
OT	Brookfield Global Listed Infr C	BGLCX	U	(855) 244-4859	U /	-3.73	-8.79	-1.97 /10	--	--	1.04	2.26
OT	Brookfield Global Listed Infr I	BGLIX	C-	(855) 244-4859	C- / 3.6	-3.45	-8.35	-0.95 /13	12.23 /54	--	1.72	1.26
OT	Brookfield Global Listed Infr Y	BGLYX	C-	(855) 244-4859	C- / 3.6	-3.38	-8.22	-0.88 /13	12.23 /54	--	1.72	1.26
RE	Brookfield Global Listed Rl Est I	BLRIX	A	(855) 244-4859	A- / 9.1	5.05	13.40	19.09 /96	15.56 /80	--	3.54	1.41
RE	Brookfield Global Listed Rl Est Y	BLRYX	A	(855) 244-4859	A- / 9.1	5.12	13.39	19.07 /96	15.58 /80	--	3.54	1.41
RE	Brookfield US Listed Real Est I	BRUIX	U	(855) 244-4859	U /	4.12	18.31	24.27 /98	--	--	2.95	2.27
EM	Brown Adv - Somerset Em Mkts Inst	BAFQX	U	(800) 540-6807	U /	3.68	1.86	4.85 /37	--	--	1.49	1.28
EM	Brown Adv - Somerset Em Mkts Inv	BIAQX	U	(800) 540-6807	U /	3.69	1.85	4.63 /36	--	--	1.39	1.43
IN	Brown Advisory Eqty Inc Adv	BADAX	B-	(800) 540-6807	C+ / 6.2	0.15	4.39	9.00 /69	13.46 /63	--	1.81	1.18
IN	Brown Advisory Eqty Inc Inv	BIADX	B-	(800) 540-6807	C+ / 6.4	0.21	4.52	9.35 /71	13.75 /65	--	2.05	0.93
GR	Brown Advisory Flexible Equity Adv	BAFAX	A+	(800) 540-6807	B+ / 8.8	0.56	6.80	12.87 /86	17.00 /90	14.31 /80	0.15	1.21
GR	Brown Advisory Flexible Equity Inv	BIAFX	A+	(800) 540-6807	B+ / 8.9	0.63	6.90	13.19 /87	17.26 /91	14.56 /83	0.45	0.96
GR	Brown Advisory Growth Equity Adv	BAGAX	C	(800) 540-6807	C+ / 5.7	3.90	8.85	10.35 /76	11.53 /49	13.60 /74	0.00	1.14
GR	Brown Advisory Growth Equity Inst	BAFGX	U	(800) 540-6807	U /	3.97	9.04	10.73 /77	--	--	0.00	0.74
GR	Brown Advisory Growth Equity Inv	BIAGX	C+	(800) 540-6807	C+ / 5.9	3.98	9.01	10.58 /77	11.79 /51	13.91 /77	0.00	0.89
GR	Brown Advisory Opportunity Inv	BIAOX	C+	(800) 540-6807	B- / 7.0	2.30	8.61	7.99 /63	14.41 /70	14.25 /80	0.00	1.56
SC	Brown Advisory Small-Cap Gr Adv	BASAX	C+	(800) 540-6807	B+ / 8.3	7.36	16.83	8.60 /67	15.23 /77	14.24 /80	0.00	1.41
SC	Brown Advisory Small-Cap Gr Inst	BAFSX	C+	(800) 540-6807	B+ / 8.7	7.46	17.04	8.96 /69	15.66 /80	14.71 /84	0.00	1.01
SC	Brown Advisory Small-Cap Gr Inv	BIASX	C+	(800) 540-6807	B+ / 8.6	7.45	17.02	8.87 /69	15.51 /79	14.60 /83	0.00	1.16
GR	Brown Advisory SmCP Fund Val Adv	BAUAX	A+	(800) 540-6807	A / 9.4	2.13	11.56	9.72 /73	18.73 /96	--	0.32	1.48
GR	Brown Advisory SmCP Fund Val Inst	BAUUX	U	(800) 540-6807	U /	2.20	11.79	10.14 /75	--	--	0.56	1.08
GL	Brown Advisory SmCP Fund Val Inv	BIAUX	A+	(800) 540-6807	A / 9.5	2.16	11.69	10.00 /74	19.04 /97	17.44 /97	0.43	1.23
GR	Brown Advisory Sustain Gro Adv	BAWAX	U	(800) 540-6807	U /	6.29	11.53	13.79 /89	--	--	0.00	1.17
GR	Brown Advisory Sustain Gro Inst	BAFWX	U	(800) 540-6807	U /	6.43	11.78	14.35 /90	--	--	0.00	0.77
GR	Brown Advisory Sustain Gro Inv	BIAWX	U	(800) 540-6807	U /	6.39	11.68	14.18 /90	--	--	0.00	0.92
GR	Brown Advisory Value Equity Adv	BAVAX	C	(800) 540-6807	C / 4.5	-0.17	-1.13	1.24 /19	12.01 /53	11.14 /54	1.12	1.17
GR	Brown Advisory Value Equity Inv	BIAVX	C	(800) 540-6807	C / 4.6	-0.06	-1.02	1.53 /20	12.30 /55	11.46 /56	1.41	0.92
FO	Brown Advisory WCMJpn Alp Opps	BAFJX	U	(800) 540-6807	U /	11.60	15.64	28.55 /99	--	--	4.20	1.21
FO	Brown Advisory WMC Str Euro Eq	BAFHX	U	(800) 540-6807	U /	4.69	4.85	-1.36 /12	--	--	1.06	1.23
FO	Brown Capital Mgmt Intl Eq Investor	BCIIX	C	(877) 892-4226	C / 5.0	7.40	3.61	0.40 /17	12.51 /56	6.87 /22	0.08	3.37
MC	Brown Capital Mgmt-Mid Cap Inst	BCMIX	C+	(877) 892-4226	C+ / 5.6	4.49	8.38	5.90 /46	12.06 /53	--	0.00	1.02
MC	Brown Capital Mgmt-Mid Cap	BCMSX	C	(877) 892-4226	C / 5.4	4.46	8.25	5.60 /43	11.71 /50	13.11 /69	0.00	1.27
FO	● Brown Capital Mgmt-Small Co Ins	BCSSX	B+	(877) 892-4226	A / 9.5	4.81	14.23	9.81 /74	18.71 /96	--	0.00	1.06
SC	● Brown Capital Mgmt-Small Co Inv	BCSIX	B+	(877) 892-4226	A / 9.5	4.75	14.12	9.59 /72	18.47 /96	17.71 /97	0.00	1.26
GR	Bruce Fund	BRUFX	B	(800) 872-7823	C+ / 6.1	3.10	3.66	10.56 /77	12.94 /59	13.66 /75	1.67	0.73
TC	Buffalo Discovery Fund	BUFTX	A-	(800) 492-8332	A / 9.4	7.50	13.68	15.56 /93	17.53 /92	16.94 /96	0.00	1.01
IN	Buffalo Dividend Focus	BUFDX	U	(800) 492-8332	U /	1.93	8.25	18.86 /96	--	--	0.92	0.94
SC	● Buffalo Emerging Opportunities	BUFOX	C	(800) 492-8332	B+ / 8.5	3.66	14.06	-0.71 /14	17.96 /94	18.63 /98	0.00	1.49
BA	Buffalo Flexible Income Fund	BUFBX	C	(800) 492-8332	D+ / 2.6	0.86	-0.29	3.33 /28	8.54 /30	9.79 /43	2.02	1.03
GL	Buffalo Growth Fund	BUFGX	C+	(800) 492-8332	B- / 7.3	4.00	8.33	11.32 /80	14.80 /73	14.56 /83	0.46	0.91
FO	Buffalo International Fund	BUFIX	D	(800) 492-8332	D+ / 2.8	4.37	4.64	2.32 /23	8.25 /28	7.01 /23	0.59	1.08
GR	Buffalo Large Cap Fund	BUFEX	B+	(800) 492-8332	A+ / 9.6	6.27	14.40	20.29 /97	17.37 /92	13.67 /75	0.17	0.97
MC	Buffalo Mid Cap Fund	BUFMX	C-	(800) 492-8332	C+ / 6.6	7.05	11.18	10.43 /76	13.19 /61	12.28 /62	0.00	1.01
SC	● Buffalo Small Cap Fund	BUFSX	D	(800) 492-8332	C+ / 5.7	3.86	9.14	0.56 /17	13.59 /64	10.98 /52	0.00	1.00
GR	Bullfinch Unrestricted Series	BUNRX	B+	(888) 285-5346	B / 7.9	3.82	12.89	16.47 /94	13.35 /62	12.82 /67	0.21	1.89

99 Pct = Best
0 Pct = Worst

● Denotes fund is closed to new investors
* Denotes fund is included in Section II

Risk Rating/Pts	3 Year Standard Deviation	Beta	NAV As of 3/31/15	Total $(Mil)	Cash %	Stocks %	Bonds %	Other %	Portfolio Turnover Ratio	Last Bull Market Return	Last Bear Market Return	Manager Quality Pct	Manager Tenure (Years)	Initial Purch. $	Additional Purch. $	Front End Load	Back End Load
C+ / 5.6	15.3	1.06	22.63	77	0	99	0	1	83	96.3	-24.0	45	12	2,000	100	0.0	0.0
D / 1.6	16.1	1.12	32.35	139	0	100	0	0	99	125.3	-30.0	58	21	2,000	100	0.0	0.0
C- / 3.5	14.0	1.00	16.19	407	0	99	0	1	29	119.4	-26.0	83	18	2,000	100	0.0	2.0
C / 5.5	11.7	0.64	14.10	48	4	95	0	1	31	67.2	-23.4	93	3	100,000	5,000	0.0	0.0
C+ / 6.3	8.6	0.50	14.35	178	0	99	0	1	53	94.7	-15.8	97	5	100,000	5,000	0.0	0.0
C / 5.0	13.4	0.94	38.55	973	9	90	0	1	56	98.5	-24.5	67	18	1,000	100	0.0	0.0
C+ / 6.8	10.4	0.78	13.59	71	18	81	0	1	64	N/A	N/A	62	4	1,000	100	4.8	2.0
U /	N/A	N/A	13.42	33	18	81	0	1	64	N/A	N/A	N/A	4	1,000	100	0.0	2.0
C+ / 6.9	10.4	0.78	13.62	286	18	81	0	1	64	N/A	N/A	65	4	1,000,000	0	0.0	2.0
C+ / 6.9	10.4	0.78	13.62	162	18	81	0	1	64	N/A	N/A	65	4	1,000	100	0.0	2.0
C+ / 6.3	12.1	0.87	13.93	274	14	85	0	1	147	N/A	N/A	88	4	1,000,000	0	0.0	2.0
C+ / 6.3	12.1	0.87	13.94	190	14	85	0	1	147	N/A	N/A	89	4	1,000	100	0.0	2.0
U /	N/A	N/A	12.20	34	0	99	0	1	0	N/A	N/A	N/A	4	1,000,000	0	0.0	2.0
U /	N/A	N/A	9.85	240	16	83	0	1	19	N/A	N/A	N/A	3	1,000,000	100	0.0	0.0
U /	N/A	N/A	9.84	45	16	83	0	1	19	N/A	N/A	N/A	3	5,000	100	0.0	0.0
B- / 7.6	8.7	0.84	13.37	3	5	94	0	1	32	N/A	N/A	68	4	2,000	100	0.0	0.0
B- / 7.6	8.7	0.84	13.39	188	5	94	0	1	32	N/A	N/A	71	4	5,000	100	0.0	0.0
B- / 7.3	10.0	1.00	16.07	14	6	93	0	1	15	106.0	-15.5	75	7	2,000	100	0.0	0.0
B- / 7.3	9.9	1.00	16.07	256	6	93	0	1	15	107.7	-15.4	77	7	5,000	100	0.0	0.0
C+ / 6.1	11.0	1.02	19.46	46	2	97	0	1	25	81.6	-18.5	14	16	2,000	100	0.0	0.0
U /	N/A	N/A	20.16	248	2	97	0	1	25	N/A	N/A	N/A	16	1,000,000	100	0.0	0.0
C+ / 6.1	11.0	1.02	20.10	2,216	2	97	0	1	25	83.1	-18.4	15	16	5,000	100	0.0	0.0
C+ / 5.7	12.0	1.12	24.47	12	3	96	0	1	41	94.1	-17.8	23	5	5,000	100	0.0	0.0
C- / 4.2	12.3	0.86	17.07	6	3	96	0	1	19	91.9	-24.5	79	16	2,000	100	0.0	0.5
C- / 4.2	12.4	0.86	35.28	14	3	96	0	1	19	94.2	-24.3	81	16	2,000	100	0.0	0.0
C- / 4.2	12.4	0.86	17.74	259	3	96	0	1	19	93.5	-24.3	80	16	5,000	100	0.0	0.0
C+ / 6.8	11.0	0.98	24.02	57	3	96	0	1	30	104.5	N/A	87	7	2,000	100	0.0	0.0
U /	N/A	N/A	24.12	64	3	96	0	1	30	N/A	N/A	N/A	7	1,000,000	100	0.0	0.0
C+ / 6.7	11.0	0.56	24.11	720	3	96	0	1	30	106.3	-20.6	99	7	5,000	100	0.0	0.0
U /	N/A	N/A	15.37	135	3	96	0	1	30	N/A	N/A	N/A	3	2,000	100	0.0	0.0
U /	N/A	N/A	15.55	30	3	96	0	1	30	N/A	N/A	N/A	3	1,000,000	100	0.0	0.0
U /	N/A	N/A	15.48	49	3	96	0	1	30	N/A	N/A	N/A	3	5,000	100	0.0	0.0
C+ / 6.6	11.8	1.14	17.48	1	1	98	0	1	37	79.7	-18.3	8	12	2,000	100	0.0	0.0
C+ / 6.5	11.8	1.14	17.37	187	1	98	0	1	37	81.2	-18.3	8	12	5,000	100	0.0	0.0
U /	N/A	N/A	12.03	1,499	6	93	0	1	0	N/A	N/A	N/A	1	1,000,000	100	0.0	0.0
U /	N/A	N/A	10.05	221	1	98	0	1	25	N/A	N/A	N/A	2	1,000,000	100	0.0	0.0
C+ / 6.7	11.7	0.83	12.63	2	0	0	0	100	9	63.8	-25.2	92	10	5,000	500	0.0	2.0
C+ / 6.4	12.2	1.01	26.77	56	2	97	0	1	16	N/A	N/A	13	13	500,000	500	0.0	0.0
C+ / 5.9	12.2	1.01	26.49	23	2	97	0	1	16	76.7	-20.8	11	13	5,000	500	0.0	0.0
C / 5.1	14.2	0.56	75.66	660	5	94	0	1	5	N/A	N/A	99	23	500,000	500	0.0	0.0
C / 5.0	14.2	0.94	75.13	2,068	5	94	0	1	5	102.0	-18.8	88	23	5,000	500	0.0	0.0
B / 8.4	7.8	0.56	520.51	551	23	50	20	7	11	60.5	-10.4	91	32	1,000	500	0.0	0.0
C / 5.5	12.6	1.07	21.50	772	5	94	0	1	48	114.6	-19.1	68	N/A	2,500	100	0.0	2.0
U /	N/A	N/A	13.76	41	16	83	0	1	77	N/A	N/A	N/A	3	2,500	100	0.0	2.0
D+ / 2.7	17.5	1.14	17.85	239	1	98	0	1	23	126.5	-20.9	58	4	2,500	100	0.0	2.0
B / 8.5	5.8	0.92	14.53	1,352	16	59	18	7	13	47.9	-6.7	47	12	2,500	100	0.0	2.0
C / 5.2	11.1	0.70	34.60	464	2	97	0	1	37	96.0	-18.1	96	4	2,500	100	0.0	2.0
C+ / 6.2	11.0	0.79	11.93	257	9	90	0	1	15	55.5	-23.5	74	7	2,500	100	0.0	2.0
C / 5.1	10.6	0.97	25.09	44	8	91	0	1	45	102.6	-19.6	81	11	2,500	100	0.0	2.0
C- / 3.4	12.2	1.01	18.68	567	3	96	0	1	45	82.1	-20.0	20	N/A	2,500	100	0.0	2.0
C- / 3.0	13.4	0.92	32.83	3,009	2	97	0	1	22	96.3	-25.5	50	17	2,500	100	0.0	2.0
C+ / 6.8	9.8	0.95	20.92	7	9	90	0	1	12	83.8	-14.8	41	18	2,500	250	0.0	0.0

99 Pct = Best 0 Pct = Worst					**PERFORMANCE**								
						Total Return % through 3/31/15					Incl. in Returns		
			Overall Investment Rating		Perfor-mance				Annualized		Dividend	Expense
Fund Type	Fund Name	Ticker Symbol		Phone	Rating/Pts	3 Mo	6 Mo	1Yr / Pct	3Yr / Pct	5Yr / Pct	Yield	Ratio
FS	Burnham Financial Long/Short A	BURFX	A-	(800) 462-2392	B / 8.2	3.82	13.58	10.40 /76	17.43 /92	8.04 /30	0.00	2.41
FS	Burnham Financial Long/Short C	BURCX	A	(800) 462-2392	B+ / 8.5	3.60	13.21	9.65 /73	16.62 /88	7.28 /25	0.00	3.11
FS	Burnham Financial Services A	BURKX	A+	(800) 462-2392	B+ / 8.9	1.69	10.71	7.44 /59	19.65 /97	9.95 /44	0.00	1.81
FS	Burnham Financial Services C	BURNX	A+	(800) 462-2392	A- / 9.1	1.52	10.28	6.65 /52	18.74 /96	9.12 /38	0.00	2.56
GI	Burnham Fund A	BURHX	C	(800) 462-2392	C / 5.0	5.37	6.89	14.21 /90	11.54 /49	14.25 /80	0.33	1.33
GI	Burnham Fund C	BURJX	C	(800) 462-2392	C / 5.3	5.17	6.49	13.35 /88	10.70 /44	13.41 /72	0.00	2.08
CV	Calamos Convertible A	CCVIX	D	(800) 582-6959	D / 2.2	1.32	2.85	4.60 /36	8.12 /28	6.98 /23	2.03	1.11
CV	● Calamos Convertible B	CALBX	D+	(800) 582-6959	D+ / 2.5	1.14	2.45	3.81 /31	7.32 /23	6.18 /18	0.89	1.86
CV	● Calamos Convertible C	CCVCX	D	(800) 582-6959	D+ / 2.5	1.08	2.43	3.80 /30	7.32 /23	6.17 /18	1.40	1.86
CV	Calamos Convertible I	CICVX	D+	(800) 582-6959	C- / 3.2	1.40	2.95	4.89 /38	8.41 /29	7.25 /25	2.60	0.86
CV	Calamos Convertible R	CCVRX	D+	(800) 582-6959	D+ / 2.8	1.26	2.70	4.32 /34	7.85 /26	6.71 /21	1.86	1.36
GR	Calamos Discovery Growth A	CADGX	D	(800) 582-6959	C / 4.8	4.06	12.62	9.63 /73	11.14 /46	--	0.00	1.63
GR	● Calamos Discovery Growth B	CBDGX	D	(800) 582-6959	C / 5.0	3.83	12.12	8.80 /68	10.30 /41	--	0.00	2.38
GR	Calamos Discovery Growth C	CCDGX	D	(800) 582-6959	C / 5.0	3.92	12.21	8.88 /69	10.28 /41	--	0.00	2.38
GR	Calamos Discovery Growth I	CIDGX	C-	(800) 582-6959	C+ / 5.8	4.08	12.77	9.96 /74	11.40 /48	--	0.00	1.38
GR	Calamos Discovery Growth R	CRDGX	D+	(800) 582-6959	C / 5.5	4.03	12.53	9.43 /72	10.88 /45	--	0.00	1.88
GL	Calamos Evolving World Growth A	CNWGX	E+	(800) 582-6959	E / 0.5	3.04	-0.62	-2.96 / 9	1.22 / 5	4.15 / 9	0.19	1.62
GL	● Calamos Evolving World Growth B	CNWZX	E+	(800) 582-6959	E / 0.5	2.82	-1.00	-3.71 / 7	0.43 / 5	3.37 / 7	0.00	2.36
GL	Calamos Evolving World Growth C	CNWDX	E+	(800) 582-6959	E / 0.5	2.91	-1.00	-3.71 / 7	0.46 / 5	3.37 / 7	0.00	2.37
GL	Calamos Evolving World Growth I	CNWIX	E+	(800) 582-6959	E+ / 0.6	3.10	-0.52	-2.71 / 9	1.45 / 6	4.41 /10	0.50	1.37
GL	Calamos Evolving World Growth R	CNWRX	E+	(800) 582-6959	E+ / 0.6	2.98	-0.75	-3.18 / 8	0.93 / 5	3.88 / 8	0.00	1.86
GR	Calamos Focus Growth A	CBCAX	C	(800) 582-6959	C+ / 5.8	4.28	8.80	11.07 /79	12.98 /60	11.78 /59	0.00	1.56
GR	● Calamos Focus Growth B	CBCBX	C	(800) 582-6959	C+ / 6.0	4.10	8.42	10.24 /75	12.20 /54	10.96 /52	0.00	2.31
GR	Calamos Focus Growth C	CBXCX	C	(800) 582-6959	C+ / 6.0	4.10	8.42	10.24 /75	12.19 /54	10.98 /52	0.00	2.31
GR	Calamos Focus Growth I	CBCIX	C+	(800) 582-6959	C+ / 6.8	4.35	8.95	11.32 /80	13.32 /62	12.08 /61	0.00	1.31
GR	Calamos Focus Growth R	CBCRX	C+	(800) 582-6959	C+ / 6.4	4.22	8.69	10.79 /77	12.74 /58	11.54 /57	0.00	1.81
GL	Calamos Global Equity A	CAGEX	E+	(800) 582-6959	C- / 3.2	6.65	6.99	7.97 /63	8.56 /30	10.35 /47	0.00	1.40
GL	● Calamos Global Equity B	CBGEX	E+	(800) 582-6959	C- / 3.4	6.42	6.55	7.20 /57	7.77 /26	9.53 /41	0.00	2.15
GL	Calamos Global Equity C	CCGEX	E+	(800) 582-6959	C- / 3.4	6.43	6.57	7.22 /57	7.76 /26	9.53 /41	0.00	2.14
GL	Calamos Global Equity I	CIGEX	E+	(800) 582-6959	C- / 4.1	6.73	7.13	8.25 /65	8.82 /32	10.63 /50	0.00	1.15
GL	Calamos Global Equity R	CRGEX	E+	(800) 582-6959	C- / 3.8	6.54	6.81	7.66 /60	8.27 /29	10.05 /45	0.00	1.64
GL	Calamos Global Growth and Income	CVLOX	E-	(800) 582-6959	D- / 1.4	3.44	3.47	3.78 /30	5.89 /16	6.68 /21	0.37	1.44
GL	● Calamos Global Growth and Income	CVLDX	E	(800) 582-6959	D / 1.6	3.26	3.06	2.96 /26	5.11 /13	5.87 /16	0.00	2.19
GL	Calamos Global Growth and Income	CVLCX	E-	(800) 582-6959	D / 1.6	3.23	3.15	2.93 /26	5.12 /13	5.88 /16	0.00	2.19
GL	Calamos Global Growth and Income I	CGCIX	E	(800) 582-6959	D / 2.1	3.48	3.64	3.94 /31	6.15 /17	6.92 /22	0.59	1.19
GL	Calamos Global Growth and Income	CVLRX	E-	(800) 582-6959	D / 1.8	3.36	3.31	3.41 /29	5.62 /15	6.37 /19	0.24	1.69
MC	Calamos Growth A	CVGRX	E+	(800) 582-6959	C+ / 5.9	4.61	9.88	13.20 /87	12.28 /54	11.79 /59	0.00	1.29
GI	Calamos Growth and Income A	CVTRX	D-	(800) 582-6959	D+ / 2.4	0.62	3.56	7.32 /58	7.94 /27	8.37 /32	1.10	1.09
GI	● Calamos Growth and Income B	CVTYX	D	(800) 582-6959	D+ / 2.8	0.43	3.17	6.72 /53	7.55 /24	7.80 /29	0.33	1.85
GI	Calamos Growth and Income C	CVTCX	D	(800) 582-6959	D+ / 2.6	0.39	3.15	6.52 /51	7.13 /22	7.55 /27	0.53	1.84
GI	Calamos Growth and Income I	CGIIX	D	(800) 582-6959	C- / 3.3	0.64	3.67	7.59 /60	8.21 /28	8.63 /34	1.44	0.84
GI	Calamos Growth and Income R	CGNRX	D	(800) 582-6959	D+ / 2.9	0.56	3.43	7.08 /56	7.68 /25	8.10 /31	0.93	1.34
MC	● Calamos Growth B	CVGBX	D-	(800) 582-6959	C+ / 6.1	4.40	9.46	12.32 /84	11.44 /48	10.96 /52	0.00	2.04
MC	Calamos Growth C	CVGCX	D-	(800) 582-6959	C+ / 6.1	4.42	9.48	12.35 /84	11.44 /48	10.96 /52	0.00	2.04
MC	Calamos Growth I	CGRIX	D-	(800) 582-6959	C+ / 6.9	4.65	10.00	13.47 /88	12.56 /56	12.07 /61	0.00	1.04
MC	Calamos Growth R	CGRRX	D-	(800) 582-6959	C+ / 6.5	4.55	9.74	12.93 /86	12.00 /52	11.52 /57	0.00	1.54
FO	Calamos International Growth A	CIGRX	E	(800) 582-6959	D- / 1.1	7.05	3.16	-0.38 /15	4.83 /13	7.35 /25	0.00	1.39
FO	● Calamos International Growth B	CIGBX	E	(800) 582-6959	D- / 1.2	6.83	2.78	-1.16 /12	4.04 /10	6.54 /20	0.00	2.15
FO	Calamos International Growth C	CIGCX	E	(800) 582-6959	D- / 1.2	6.83	2.78	-1.11 /13	4.04 /10	6.54 /20	0.00	2.14
FO	Calamos International Growth I	CIGIX	E	(800) 582-6959	D / 1.6	7.07	3.29	-0.12 /15	5.10 /13	7.63 /27	0.00	1.14
FO	Calamos International Growth R	CIGFX	E	(800) 582-6959	D- / 1.4	6.99	3.04	-0.65 /14	4.58 /12	7.08 /24	0.00	1.64
GL	Calamos Long/Short A	CALSX	U	(800) 582-6959	U /	0.56	3.90	1.40 /20	--	--	0.00	2.61

● Denotes fund is closed to new investors
* Denotes fund is included in Section II

Risk Rating/Pts	3 Year Standard Deviation	Beta	NAV As of 3/31/15	Total $(Mil)	Cash %	Stocks %	Bonds %	Other %	Portfolio Turnover Ratio	Last Bull Market Return	Last Bear Market Return	Manager Quality Pct	Manager Tenure (Years)	Initial Purch. $	Additional Purch. $	Front End Load	Back End Load
C+ / 6.9	10.7	0.79	15.49	81	24	75	0	1	172	96.3	-24.0	90	11	2,500	500	5.0	2.0
C+ / 6.8	10.7	0.79	14.68	12	24	75	0	1	172	91.5	-24.2	88	11	2,500	500	0.0	2.0
B- / 7.0	10.6	0.68	28.35	76	0	99	0	1	126	97.2	-20.1	96	16	2,500	500	5.0	2.0
B- / 7.0	10.6	0.68	26.76	13	0	99	0	1	126	92.3	-20.4	95	16	2,500	500	0.0	2.0
C+ / 6.1	9.6	0.90	39.66	123	10	89	0	1	45	79.5	-13.4	31	20	2,500	500	5.0	2.0
C+ / 6.0	9.6	0.90	37.05	14	10	89	0	1	45	75.0	-13.7	22	20	2,500	500	0.0	2.0
C+ / 6.4	7.8	1.02	17.63	473	13	9	5	73	68	41.6	-13.9	9	30	2,500	50	4.8	0.0
B- / 7.0	7.8	1.02	22.40	9	13	9	5	73	68	38.0	-14.1	6	30	2,500	50	0.0	0.0
C+ / 6.5	7.8	1.02	17.48	310	13	9	5	73	68	38.0	-14.1	6	30	2,500	50	0.0	0.0
C+ / 6.0	7.8	1.01	16.04	515	13	9	5	73	68	42.8	-13.7	11	30	1,000,000	0	0.0	0.0
C+ / 6.5	7.8	1.02	17.57	2	13	9	5	73	68	40.4	-14.0	8	30	0	0	0.0	0.0
C- / 4.2	13.9	1.17	13.84	31	4	95	0	1	153	66.3	-32.1	5	5	2,500	50	4.8	0.0
C- / 4.0	13.8	1.16	13.27	2	4	95	0	1	153	62.2	-32.3	3	5	2,500	50	0.0	0.0
C- / 4.0	13.9	1.17	13.27	3	4	95	0	1	153	62.1	-32.3	3	5	2,500	50	0.0	0.0
C / 4.3	13.9	1.17	14.04	11	4	95	0	1	153	67.8	-32.1	5	5	1,000,000	0	0.0	0.0
C- / 4.2	13.9	1.17	13.67	2	4	95	0	1	153	65.0	-32.3	4	5	0	0	0.0	0.0
C+ / 5.8	10.3	0.69	13.23	144	4	77	1	18	100	20.0	-21.5	10	7	2,500	50	4.8	0.0
C+ / 5.8	10.3	0.69	12.75	1	4	77	1	18	100	16.9	-21.7	7	7	2,500	50	0.0	0.0
C+ / 5.8	10.3	0.69	12.75	42	4	77	1	18	100	17.0	-21.7	7	7	2,500	50	0.0	0.0
C+ / 5.8	10.3	0.69	13.30	403	4	77	1	18	100	21.0	-21.4	11	7	1,000,000	0	0.0	0.0
C+ / 5.8	10.3	0.69	13.13	2	4	77	1	18	100	19.0	-21.5	8	7	0	0	0.0	0.0
C+ / 5.6	12.1	1.08	17.79	20	5	94	0	1	61	78.7	-19.9	16	12	2,500	50	4.8	0.0
C / 5.5	12.0	1.08	16.50	1	5	94	0	1	61	74.3	-20.2	12	12	2,500	50	0.0	0.0
C / 5.5	12.1	1.08	16.51	15	5	94	0	1	61	74.3	-20.2	12	12	2,500	50	0.0	0.0
C+ / 5.7	12.1	1.08	18.00	32	5	94	0	1	61	80.3	-19.8	19	12	1,000,000	0	0.0	0.0
C+ / 5.6	12.1	1.08	17.52	N/A	5	94	0	1	61	77.4	-20.1	15	12	0	0	0.0	0.0
D+ / 2.7	11.2	0.70	13.15	82	3	96	0	1	53	54.0	-17.7	83	8	2,500	50	4.8	0.0
D+ / 2.4	11.1	0.69	12.44	1	3	96	0	1	53	50.1	-17.9	78	8	2,500	50	0.0	0.0
D+ / 2.4	11.1	0.69	12.41	25	3	96	0	1	53	50.2	-17.9	78	8	2,500	50	0.0	0.0
D+ / 2.7	11.1	0.69	13.32	99	3	96	0	1	53	55.3	-17.5	85	8	1,000,000	0	0.0	0.0
D+ / 2.6	11.1	0.69	12.87	8	3	96	0	1	53	52.7	-17.7	82	8	0	0	0.0	0.0
D / 2.0	8.3	0.54	8.71	131	4	51	6	39	73	33.0	-12.5	75	19	2,500	50	4.8	0.0
D / 2.2	8.3	0.54	8.87	4	4	51	6	39	73	29.7	-12.8	67	19	2,500	50	0.0	0.0
D / 1.8	8.3	0.55	7.98	137	4	51	6	39	73	29.7	-12.8	67	19	2,500	50	0.0	0.0
D / 2.0	8.3	0.54	8.91	161	4	51	6	39	73	34.1	-12.4	77	19	1,000,000	0	0.0	0.0
D / 2.0	8.3	0.54	8.61	2	4	51	6	39	73	31.9	-12.6	73	19	0	0	0.0	0.0
E+ / 0.9	12.6	0.97	42.67	1,645	7	92	0	1	42	77.6	-22.6	18	25	2,500	50	4.8	0.0
C+ / 5.6	8.7	0.87	31.61	1,244	11	59	6	24	33	46.0	-13.7	9	27	2,500	50	4.8	0.0
C+ / 6.3	8.7	0.87	37.56	16	11	59	6	24	33	43.9	-14.0	7	27	2,500	50	0.0	0.0
C+ / 5.7	8.7	0.87	31.75	983	11	59	6	24	33	42.4	-14.0	6	27	2,500	50	0.0	0.0
C / 5.4	8.7	0.87	30.65	647	11	59	6	24	33	47.3	-13.6	10	27	1,000,000	0	0.0	0.0
C+ / 5.6	8.7	0.87	31.39	19	11	59	6	24	33	44.8	-13.8	8	27	0	0	0.0	0.0
E+ / 0.9	12.6	0.97	40.07	31	7	92	0	1	42	73.1	-22.9	13	25	2,500	50	0.0	0.0
E+ / 0.9	12.6	0.97	33.53	911	7	92	0	1	42	73.1	-22.9	13	25	2,500	50	0.0	0.0
D- / 1.1	12.6	0.97	50.61	722	7	92	0	1	42	79.1	-22.6	20	25	1,000,000	0	0.0	0.0
E+ / 0.9	12.6	0.97	41.16	10	7	92	0	1	42	76.1	-22.7	16	25	0	0	0.0	0.0
C- / 3.9	11.7	0.82	17.76	237	1	98	0	1	82	35.6	-20.0	28	10	2,500	50	4.8	0.0
C- / 3.7	11.7	0.82	16.59	2	1	98	0	1	82	32.1	-20.2	20	10	2,500	50	0.0	0.0
C- / 3.7	11.8	0.82	16.57	54	1	98	0	1	82	32.2	-20.2	20	10	2,500	50	0.0	0.0
C- / 4.0	11.8	0.82	18.02	387	1	98	0	1	82	36.7	-19.9	31	10	1,000,000	0	0.0	0.0
C- / 3.9	11.8	0.82	17.46	15	1	98	0	1	82	34.4	-20.0	25	10	0	0	0.0	0.0
U /	N/A	N/A	10.81	38	0	0	0	100	260	N/A	N/A	N/A	2	2,500	50	4.8	0.0

Fund Type	Fund Name	Ticker Symbol	Overall Investment Rating	Phone	Performance Rating/Pts	3 Mo	6 Mo	1Yr / Pct	3Yr / Pct	5Yr / Pct	Dividend Yield	Expense Ratio
GL	Calamos Long/Short I	CILSX	U	(800) 582-6959	U /	0.65	3.98	1.58 /20	--	--	0.00	2.14
IN	Calamos Market Neutral Income A	CVSIX	D+	(800) 582-6959	E+ / 0.7	0.53	0.92	2.07 /22	3.41 / 9	4.00 / 8	0.80	1.22
IN	● Calamos Market Neutral Income B	CAMNX	D+	(800) 582-6959	E+ / 0.8	0.43	0.62	1.28 /19	2.66 / 7	3.24 / 6	0.06	1.96
IN	Calamos Market Neutral Income C	CVSCX	D+	(800) 582-6959	E+ / 0.8	0.40	0.61	1.30 /19	2.65 / 7	3.24 / 6	0.18	1.96
IN	Calamos Market Neutral Income I	CMNIX	C-	(800) 582-6959	D- / 1.0	0.60	1.06	2.28 /23	3.65 / 9	4.26 / 9	1.11	0.97
IN	Calamos Market Neutral Income R	CVSRX	C-	(800) 582-6959	E+ / 0.9	0.46	0.79	1.76 /21	3.16 / 8	3.73 / 7	0.61	1.47
GL	Calamos Mid Cap Growth A	CMXAX	U	(800) 582-6959	U /	4.67	9.80	7.56 /60	--	--	0.00	1.69
GR	Calamos Opportunistic A	CVAAX	D+	(800) 582-6959	C- / 3.1	-0.43	-0.51	1.31 /19	10.80 /44	7.72 /28	0.90	1.50
GR	● Calamos Opportunistic B	CVABX	D+	(800) 582-6959	C- / 3.3	-0.62	-0.92	0.53 /17	9.98 /39	6.92 /22	0.00	2.25
GR	Calamos Opportunistic C	CVACX	D+	(800) 582-6959	C- / 3.3	-0.63	-0.94	0.52 /17	9.98 /39	6.91 /22	0.20	2.25
GR	Calamos Opportunistic I	CVAIX	C-	(800) 582-6959	C- / 4.0	-0.42	-0.45	1.54 /20	11.06 /46	7.97 /30	1.23	1.25
GR	Calamos Opportunistic R	CVARX	C-	(800) 582-6959	C- / 3.7	-0.58	-0.73	0.97 /18	10.53 /42	7.44 /26	0.80	1.75
AA	Caldwell & Orkin Mkt Opportunity	COAGX	C	(800) 467-7903	C- / 3.2	3.89	7.59	12.92 /86	6.44 /19	4.86 /11	0.00	1.78
AA	Calvert Aggressive Allocation A	CAAAX	C	(800) 368-2745	C / 4.9	3.46	7.16	8.63 /67	12.60 /57	10.65 /50	0.90	1.59
AA	Calvert Aggressive Allocation C	CAACX	C	(800) 368-2745	C / 4.8	3.18	6.55	7.47 /59	11.30 /48	9.31 /39	0.70	2.36
BA	Calvert Balanced Portfolio A	CSIFX	C-	(800) 368-2745	C- / 3.4	1.65	5.59	9.66 /73	9.94 /39	9.78 /43	1.06	1.18
BA	● Calvert Balanced Portfolio B	CSLBX	C-	(800) 368-2745	C- / 3.4	1.32	4.96	8.44 /66	8.74 /31	8.62 /34	0.09	2.33
BA	Calvert Balanced Portfolio C	CSGCX	C-	(800) 368-2745	C- / 3.6	1.45	5.18	8.80 /68	9.07 /33	8.88 /36	0.37	1.96
BA	Calvert Balanced Portfolio I	CBAIX	C	(800) 368-2745	C / 4.8	1.76	5.85	10.21 /75	10.49 /42	10.33 /47	1.62	0.67
BA	Calvert Balanced Portfolio Y	CBAYX	B-	(800) 368-2745	C- / 4.2	1.67	5.67	9.86 /74	10.06 /40	9.85 /43	1.14	3.33
MC	Calvert Capital Accumulation A	CCAFX	B	(800) 368-2745	B+ / 8.3	8.50	14.63	15.44 /92	15.29 /77	16.22 /94	0.00	1.43
MC	● Calvert Capital Accumulation B	CWCBX	C	(800) 368-2745	B- / 7.4	8.09	13.83	13.83 /89	13.70 /65	14.73 /85	0.00	2.93
MC	Calvert Capital Accumulation C	CCACX	C+	(800) 368-2745	B+ / 8.5	8.28	14.20	14.59 /91	14.42 /70	15.30 /89	0.00	2.19
MC	Calvert Capital Accumulation I	CCPIX	A-	(800) 368-2745	A / 9.5	8.65	14.98	16.17 /93	16.01 /83	17.00 /96	0.00	0.82
MC	Calvert Capital Accumulation Y	CCAYX	B+	(800) 368-2745	A- / 9.1	8.57	14.78	15.61 /93	15.52 /79	16.40 /94	0.00	1.26
AA	Calvert Conservative Allocation A	CCLAX	C	(800) 368-2745	D / 2.2	2.72	5.46	7.49 /59	7.80 /26	7.66 /28	1.57	1.29
AA	Calvert Conservative Allocation C	CALCX	C	(800) 368-2745	D+ / 2.3	2.45	4.97	6.44 /50	6.75 /20	6.53 /20	0.75	2.01
EM	Calvert Emerging Markets Equity A	CVMAX	U	(800) 368-2745	U /	3.77	1.88	4.83 /37	--	--	0.22	2.22
EM	Calvert Emerging Markets Equity I	CVMIX	U	(800) 368-2745	U /	3.90	2.14	5.23 /40	--	--	0.56	1.42
IN	Calvert Equity Income A	CEIAX	C	(800) 368-2745	C- / 4.2	-1.13	0.31	4.91 /38	13.07 /60	--	1.96	1.66
IN	Calvert Equity Income C	CEICX	C	(800) 368-2745	C- / 4.2	-1.41	-0.24	3.69 /30	11.81 /51	--	0.94	2.41
IN	Calvert Equity Income Y	CEIYX	C+	(800) 368-2745	C / 5.2	-1.11	0.42	5.15 /40	13.31 /62	--	2.21	1.42
GR	Calvert Equity Portfolio A	CSIEX	C+	(800) 368-2745	C+ / 6.2	2.62	8.70	14.03 /89	14.11 /68	13.24 /70	0.03	1.17
GR	● Calvert Equity Portfolio B	CSEBX	C+	(800) 368-2745	C+ / 6.3	2.38	8.15	12.90 /86	13.08 /60	12.22 /62	0.00	2.11
GR	Calvert Equity Portfolio C	CSECX	C+	(800) 368-2745	C+ / 6.4	2.44	8.33	13.17 /87	13.31 /62	12.42 /63	0.00	1.90
GR	Calvert Equity Portfolio I	CEYIX	B+	(800) 368-2745	B / 7.8	2.77	8.97	14.57 /91	14.72 /73	13.85 /76	0.33	0.66
GR	Calvert Equity Portfolio Y	CIEYX	B	(800) 368-2745	B- / 7.3	2.73	8.90	14.35 /90	14.53 /71	13.64 /74	0.23	0.85
EN	Calvert Global Energy Solutions A	CGAEX	E	(800) 368-2745	D- / 1.1	6.31	-0.28	-7.45 / 4	6.93 /21	-4.17 / 1	0.00	2.13
EN	Calvert Global Energy Solutions C	CGACX	E	(800) 368-2745	D- / 1.1	6.01	-0.74	-8.34 / 3	5.91 /16	-5.12 / 1	0.00	2.93
EN	Calvert Global Energy Solutions I	CAEIX	E+	(800) 368-2745	D / 2.0	6.50	0.00	-7.09 / 4	7.52 /24	-3.71 / 1	0.00	2.88
EN	Calvert Global Energy Solutions Y	CGAYX	E+	(800) 368-2745	D / 1.6	6.21	-0.14	-7.31 / 4	7.18 /22	-3.97 / 1	0.00	1.85
GL	Calvert Global Water A	CFWAX	E+	(800) 368-2745	D / 1.9	-0.23	-3.91	-7.23 / 4	10.56 /43	9.16 /38	0.00	1.83
GL	Calvert Global Water C	CFWCX	E+	(800) 368-2745	D / 2.1	-0.37	-4.22	-7.82 / 3	9.65 /37	8.19 /31	0.00	2.51
EN	Calvert Global Water I	CFWIX	D+	(800) 368-2745	C- / 3.1	-0.11	-3.67	-6.67 / 4	10.72 /44	9.25 /39	0.00	4.85
GL	Calvert Global Water Y	CFWYX	D-	(800) 368-2745	D+ / 2.8	-0.17	-3.76	-6.88 / 4	10.91 /45	9.47 /40	0.00	1.47
FO	Calvert International Equity A	CWVGX	D-	(800) 368-2745	D- / 1.5	4.71	1.56	-2.06 /10	7.55 /24	4.70 /11	0.59	1.68
FO	● Calvert International Equity B	CWVBX	D-	(800) 368-2745	D- / 1.4	4.37	0.90	-3.38 / 8	6.21 /18	3.43 / 7	0.00	3.21
FO	Calvert International Equity C	CWVCX	D-	(800) 368-2745	D- / 1.5	4.49	1.05	-2.96 / 9	6.58 /19	3.78 / 8	0.00	2.59
FO	Calvert International Equity I	CWVIX	D	(800) 368-2745	D+ / 2.7	4.89	1.92	-1.43 /12	8.30 /29	5.45 /14	1.13	1.04
FO	Calvert International Equity Y	CWEYX	D	(800) 368-2745	D / 2.2	4.82	1.72	-1.72 /11	7.96 /27	5.12 /12	0.71	1.33
FO	Calvert International Opp A	CIOAX	D	(800) 368-2745	C- / 3.5	5.85	2.18	-1.77 /11	11.69 /50	7.67 /28	1.05	1.85
FO	Calvert International Opp C	COICX	D	(800) 368-2745	C- / 3.6	5.59	1.76	-2.66 / 9	10.71 /44	6.75 /21	0.23	2.81

● Denotes fund is closed to new investors
* Denotes fund is included in Section II

www.thestreetratings.com

RISK			NET ASSETS		ASSET						BULL / BEAR		FUND MANAGER		MINIMUMS		LOADS	
	3 Year		NAV							Portfolio	Last Bull	Last Bear	Manager	Manager	Initial	Additional	Front	Back
Risk Rating/Pts	Standard Deviation	Beta	As of 3/31/15	Total $(Mil)	Cash %	Stocks %	Bonds %	Other %		Turnover Ratio	Market Return	Market Return	Quality Pct	Tenure (Years)	Purch. $	Purch. $	End Load	End Load
U /	N/A	N/A	10.85	60	0	0	0	100		260	N/A	N/A	N/A	2	1,000,000	0	0.0	0.0
B+ / 9.0	3.1	0.31	12.99	1,200	23	27	13	37		71	20.0	-4.5	47	25	2,500	50	4.8	0.0
B+ / 9.0	3.1	0.31	13.76	4	23	27	13	37		71	17.0	-4.9	37	25	2,500	50	0.0	0.0
B+ / 9.0	3.1	0.31	13.20	344	23	27	13	37		71	17.0	-4.8	37	25	2,500	50	0.0	0.0
B+ / 9.0	3.1	0.31	12.85	2,563	23	27	13	37		71	21.0	-4.4	51	25	1,000,000	0	0.0	0.0
B+ / 9.0	3.0	0.30	12.94	8	23	27	13	37		71	19.0	-4.6	45	25	0	0	0.0	0.0
U /	N/A	N/A	12.10	33	3	96	0	1		69	N/A	N/A	N/A	2	2,500	50	4.8	0.0
C+ / 6.2	9.8	0.95	13.77	48	6	93	0	1		165	63.6	-17.4	17	13	2,500	50	4.8	0.0
C+ / 6.2	9.8	0.95	12.76	N/A	6	93	0	1		165	59.4	-17.7	12	13	2,500	50	0.0	0.0
C+ / 6.0	9.8	0.95	12.58	8	6	93	0	1		165	59.5	-17.7	12	13	2,500	50	0.0	0.0
C+ / 6.2	9.8	0.95	14.10	25	6	93	0	1		165	65.0	-17.3	18	13	1,000,000	0	0.0	0.0
C+ / 6.2	9.8	0.95	13.62	N/A	6	93	0	1		165	62.2	-17.5	15	13	0	0	0.0	0.0
B / 8.2	6.1	0.39	23.75	134	77	22	0	1		657	21.7	0.4	85	23	25,000	100	0.0	2.0
C+ / 6.9	9.6	1.61	20.62	93	3	91	5	1		15	72.9	-17.5	11	8	2,000	250	4.8	2.0
C+ / 6.8	9.7	1.62	18.47	16	3	91	5	1		15	66.3	-18.0	6	8	2,000	250	0.0	2.0
C+ / 6.9	5.9	1.00	34.33	606	3	60	35	2		124	55.0	-8.2	54	13	2,000	250	4.8	2.0
C+ / 6.8	5.9	1.00	33.69	3	3	60	35	2		124	49.4	-8.6	37	13	2,000	250	0.0	2.0
C+ / 6.9	5.9	1.00	33.53	56	3	60	35	2		124	50.8	-8.6	42	13	2,000	250	0.0	2.0
C+ / 6.9	5.9	1.01	34.82	47	3	60	35	2		124	57.7	-8.0	61	13	1,000,000	0	0.0	0.0
B / 8.9	5.9	1.00	34.56	5	3	60	35	2		124	55.5	-8.2	55	13	2,000	250	0.0	2.0
C / 5.0	11.9	1.01	36.51	243	1	98	0	1		81	96.3	-24.0	42	10	2,000	250	4.8	2.0
C- / 3.7	11.9	1.01	28.18	1	1	98	0	1		81	87.4	-24.3	25	10	2,000	250	0.0	2.0
C- / 3.8	11.9	1.01	28.11	31	1	98	0	1		81	91.2	-24.3	32	10	2,000	250	0.0	2.0
C / 5.5	11.9	1.01	41.46	175	1	98	0	1		81	100.5	-23.7	52	10	1,000,000	0	0.0	0.0
C / 5.1	11.9	1.01	36.87	12	1	98	0	1		81	97.5	-23.9	46	10	2,000	250	0.0	2.0
B / 8.8	4.2	0.69	17.25	107	5	38	55	2		17	35.9	-3.1	71	8	2,000	250	4.8	2.0
B / 8.8	4.2	0.69	17.08	29	5	38	55	2		17	31.4	-3.6	58	8	2,000	250	0.0	2.0
U /	N/A	N/A	12.94	26	2	97	0	1		95	N/A	N/A	N/A	3	2,000	250	4.8	2.0
U /	N/A	N/A	13.04	41	2	97	0	1		95	N/A	N/A	N/A	3	1,000,000	0	0.0	0.0
B- / 7.3	9.2	0.93	20.07	27	3	96	0	1		57	N/A	N/A	42	4	2,000	250	4.8	2.0
B- / 7.3	9.2	0.93	20.07	5	3	96	0	1		57	N/A	N/A	27	4	2,000	250	0.0	2.0
B- / 7.3	9.2	0.93	20.25	3	3	96	0	1		57	N/A	N/A	46	4	2,000	250	0.0	2.0
C+ / 6.1	10.3	1.03	49.68	1,554	0	99	0	1		24	85.2	-16.0	35	9	2,000	250	4.8	2.0
C+ / 5.7	10.3	1.03	40.04	12	0	99	0	1		24	79.5	-16.3	25	9	2,000	250	0.0	2.0
C / 5.5	10.3	1.03	36.50	181	0	99	0	1		24	80.7	-16.3	27	9	2,000	250	0.0	2.0
C+ / 6.3	10.2	1.02	54.61	1,004	0	99	0	1		24	88.6	-15.8	43	9	1,000,000	0	0.0	0.0
C+ / 6.2	10.3	1.02	50.77	152	0	99	0	1		24	87.6	-15.9	41	9	2,000	250	0.0	2.0
C / 4.4	17.0	0.75	7.08	73	1	98	0	1		62	31.2	-38.7	91	8	2,000	250	4.8	2.0
C / 4.3	16.9	0.74	6.70	17	1	98	0	1		62	26.8	-38.9	88	8	2,000	250	0.0	2.0
C / 4.4	16.9	0.74	7.21	N/A	1	98	0	1		62	33.4	-38.5	92	8	1,000,000	0	0.0	0.0
C / 4.4	17.0	0.75	7.35	9	1	98	0	1		62	32.4	-38.6	92	8	2,000	250	0.0	2.0
C / 4.4	13.5	0.83	17.50	361	3	96	0	1		77	67.9	-19.0	87	6	2,000	250	4.8	2.0
C / 4.3	13.5	0.83	16.35	92	3	96	0	1		77	63.1	-19.4	82	6	2,000	250	0.0	2.0
C+ / 6.5	13.4	0.69	17.63	N/A	3	96	0	1		77	68.6	-19.0	97	6	1,000,000	0	0.0	0.0
C / 4.5	13.5	0.83	17.70	116	3	96	0	1		77	69.8	-19.0	88	6	2,000	250	0.0	2.0
C+ / 6.0	11.7	0.87	16.66	230	2	95	1	2		82	48.2	-23.3	58	6	2,000	250	4.8	2.0
C+ / 5.9	11.8	0.87	14.58	1	2	95	1	2		82	42.1	-23.7	38	6	2,000	250	0.0	2.0
C+ / 5.9	11.8	0.87	14.43	17	2	95	1	2		82	43.7	-23.6	43	6	2,000	250	0.0	2.0
C+ / 6.0	11.7	0.87	17.81	99	2	95	1	2		82	51.7	-23.1	68	6	1,000,000	0	0.0	0.0
C+ / 6.0	11.8	0.87	17.62	20	2	95	1	2		82	50.2	-23.2	63	6	2,000	250	0.0	2.0
C / 5.2	12.5	0.90	15.57	100	6	93	0	1		56	64.6	-23.5	88	4	2,000	250	4.8	2.0
C / 5.3	12.5	0.90	15.31	5	6	93	0	1		56	59.8	-23.7	84	4	2,000	250	0.0	2.0

Fund Type	Fund Name	Ticker Symbol	Overall Investment Rating	Phone	Performance Rating/Pts	3 Mo	6 Mo	1Yr / Pct	3Yr / Pct	5Yr / Pct	Dividend Yield	Expense Ratio
FO	Calvert International Opp I	COIIX	C-	(800) 368-2745	C / 4.9	5.95	2.42	-1.35 /12	12.19 /54	8.15 /31	1.43	1.18
FO	Calvert International Opp Y	CWVYX	D+	(800) 368-2745	C / 4.4	5.96	2.33	-1.50 /11	11.96 /52	7.92 /29	0.59	1.48
GR	Calvert Large Cap Core A	CMIFX	C+	(800) 368-2745	C+ / 5.9	1.47	6.93	11.37 /80	14.25 /69	12.65 /65	0.61	1.30
GR	● Calvert Large Cap Core B	CDXBX	C+	(800) 368-2745	C+ / 5.6	1.05	6.09	9.73 /73	12.56 /56	11.07 /53	0.00	3.32
GR	Calvert Large Cap Core C	CMICX	C+	(800) 368-2745	C+ / 6.1	1.25	6.50	10.50 /76	13.32 /62	11.69 /58	0.00	2.09
GR	Calvert Large Cap Core I	CMIIX	B+	(800) 368-2745	B- / 7.5	1.53	7.12	11.91 /82	14.80 /73	13.22 /70	0.94	0.81
GR	Calvert Large Cap Core Y	CLYCX	B-	(800) 368-2745	C+ / 6.8	1.45	6.97	11.52 /81	14.32 /66	12.69 /66	0.00	2.96
GR	Calvert Large Cap Val A	CLVAX	C	(800) 368-2745	C / 4.7	-1.00	0.49	4.99 /38	13.89 /66	11.11 /54	0.66	1.55
GR	Calvert Large Cap Val C	CLVCX	C	(800) 368-2745	C / 4.7	-1.25	-0.03	3.85 /31	12.64 /57	9.88 /44	0.00	2.46
GR	Calvert Large Cap Val Y	CLVYX	C+	(800) 368-2745	C+ / 5.7	-0.94	0.61	5.24 /40	14.18 /68	11.39 /56	1.00	1.10
AA	Calvert Moderate Allocation A	CMAAX	C	(800) 368-2745	C- / 3.5	3.08	6.47	8.18 /64	10.19 /40	9.14 /38	0.95	1.38
AA	Calvert Moderate Allocation C	CMACX	C+	(800) 368-2745	C- / 3.8	2.89	6.10	7.39 /58	9.38 /35	8.34 /32	0.67	2.12
SC	Calvert Small Cap A	CCVAX	B	(800) 368-2745	B+ / 8.5	4.63	14.37	10.75 /77	17.67 /93	13.86 /76	0.01	1.61
SC	● Calvert Small Cap B	CSCBX	C+	(800) 368-2745	B / 8.0	4.19	13.39	8.86 /68	15.79 /82	--	0.00	3.44
SC	Calvert Small Cap C	CSCCX	B-	(800) 368-2745	B+ / 8.7	4.40	13.97	9.92 /74	16.72 /88	12.85 /67	0.00	2.38
SC	Calvert Small Cap I	CSVIX	A-	(800) 368-2745	A / 9.5	4.72	14.69	11.32 /80	18.46 /96	14.66 /84	0.29	0.95
SC	Calvert Small Cap Y	CSCYX	A+	(800) 368-2745	A- / 9.2	4.69	14.56	11.04 /78	17.87 /94	13.98 /77	0.02	2.20
GR	Calvert Social Index A	CSXAX	B+	(800) 368-2745	B- / 7.3	1.76	7.78	13.94 /89	16.27 /85	14.14 /79	0.64	0.87
GR	● Calvert Social Index B	CSXBX	B+	(800) 368-2745	B- / 7.4	1.46	7.15	12.73 /86	15.10 /76	13.00 /68	0.01	2.32
GR	Calvert Social Index C	CSXCX	B+	(800) 368-2745	B- / 7.5	1.57	7.34	13.05 /87	15.26 /77	13.12 /69	0.14	1.61
GR	Calvert Social Index I	CISIX	A+	(800) 368-2745	A- / 9.0	1.83	8.02	14.52 /91	16.90 /89	14.77 /85	0.93	0.37
GR	Calvert Social Index Y	CISYX	A	(800) 368-2745	B+ / 8.3	1.76	7.84	13.72 /89	16.31 /86	14.17 /79	1.12	0.65
GR	Cambiar Agg Value fund Investor Shs	CAMAX	C+	(866) 777-8227	B+ / 8.3	7.87	5.90	6.82 /54	16.95 /90	14.01 /78	1.40	1.39
GL	Cambiar Global Select Investor	CAMGX	C	(866) 777-8227	C / 4.8	4.09	3.64	4.64 /36	11.84 /51	--	1.40	5.68
FO	Cambiar International Equity Inst	CAMYX	U	(866) 777-8227	U /	7.12	3.32	1.40 /20	--	--	1.63	1.17
FO	Cambiar International Equity Inv	CAMIX	D+	(866) 777-8227	C- / 3.2	7.13	3.28	1.27 /19	9.09 /34	8.01 /30	1.43	1.45
GR	Cambiar Opportunity Fund Inst	CAMWX	C+	(866) 777-8227	C+ / 6.2	2.42	4.88	8.28 /65	13.42 /63	10.85 /51	1.08	1.01
GR	Cambiar Opportunity Fund Inv	CAMOX	C+	(866) 777-8227	C+ / 6.1	2.34	4.73	7.99 /63	13.15 /61	10.57 /49	0.78	1.26
SC	Cambiar Small Cap Fund Inst	CAMZX	D	(866) 777-8227	C / 5.2	4.45	8.05	2.82 /26	12.44 /56	14.56 /83	0.00	1.11
SC	● Cambiar Small Cap Fund Inv	CAMSX	D	(866) 777-8227	C / 5.0	4.38	7.94	2.59 /24	12.16 /53	14.32 /81	0.00	1.36
GR	Cambiar SMID Investor	CAMMX	B	(866) 777-8227	B / 8.1	3.53	4.99	7.79 /61	16.95 /90	--	0.33	4.37
IN	Camelot Premium Return A	CPRFX	C-	(866) 447-4228	C- / 3.5	2.44	0.45	4.68 /36	10.93 /45	--	1.26	2.25
IN	Camelot Premium Return C	CPRCX	C	(866) 447-4228	C- / 3.8	2.17	0.14	4.00 /32	9.99 /39	--	0.68	3.00
AG	CAN SLIM Select Growth	CANGX	C	(800) 558-9105	C+ / 6.2	1.72	5.86	7.99 /63	13.94 /67	11.57 /57	0.00	1.63
EM	Capital Group Emg Mkts Total Oppty	ETOPX	D	(800) 421-0180	E / 0.5	0.28	-3.89	-3.37 / 8	0.28 / 4	--	0.40	1.10
GL	Capital Group Global Equity Fund	CGLOX	B-	(800) 421-0180	C+ / 5.8	3.46	5.07	7.11 /56	12.59 /57	--	1.01	0.85
FO	Capital Group Non-U.S. Equity	CNUSX	C-	(800) 421-0180	C- / 3.3	5.46	3.91	2.33 /23	8.59 /30	--	1.16	0.85
IN	Capital Group U.S. Equity Fund	CUSEX	B	(800) 421-0180	B- / 7.1	2.97	6.43	10.75 /77	14.33 /70	--	1.18	0.66
MC	Capital Management Mid-Cap Inst	CMEIX	B	(888) 626-3863	B- / 7.0	3.76	6.39	9.13 /70	14.33 /70	11.87 /60	0.00	1.77
MC	Capital Management Mid-Cap Inv	CMCIX	C+	(888) 626-3863	C+ / 6.0	3.55	6.02	8.59 /67	13.56 /64	11.09 /53	0.00	2.52
SC	Capital Management Sm-Cap Inst	CMSSX	D	(888) 626-3863	C- / 3.8	0.61	4.01	-6.85 / 4	11.40 /48	12.28 /62	0.07	1.87
SC	Capital Management Sm-Cap Inv	CMSVX	D-	(888) 626-3863	C- / 3.1	0.50	3.82	-7.22 / 4	11.01 /45	11.89 /60	0.00	2.62
GL	Carlyle Core Allocation I	CCAIX	U	(888) 207-9542	U /	1.04	0.07	--	--	--	0.00	N/A
GR	Carne Hedged Equity Institutional	CARNX	E	(877) 356-9055	D+ / 2.5	3.03	7.77	-4.77 / 6	7.97 /27	10.22 /46	0.15	1.70
GR	Carne Hedged Equity Investor	CRNEX	E	(877) 356-9055	D / 2.2	2.92	7.50	-5.25 / 5	7.30 /23	9.73 /42	0.00	2.42
GL	Castle Focus Fund C	CASTX	D	(877) 743-7820	D / 1.6	-0.68	0.62	3.80 /31	6.31 /18	--	0.00	2.60
GL	Castle Focus Fund Inv	MOATX	D+	(877) 743-7820	D / 2.1	-0.45	1.12	4.84 /37	7.37 /23	--	0.03	1.60
GR	Catalyst Dynamic Alpha A	CPEAX	A+	(866) 447-4228	A+ / 9.8	6.92	14.52	23.53 /98	22.76 /98	--	0.00	1.56
GR	Catalyst Dynamic Alpha C	CPECX	A+	(866) 447-4228	A+ / 9.9	6.77	14.03	22.61 /98	21.84 /98	--	0.00	2.31
IN	Catalyst Hedged Futures Strategy A	HFXAX	D+	(866) 447-4228	D- / 1.0	4.11	-1.96	1.66 /21	5.16 /14	8.23 /31	0.00	2.35
IN	Catalyst Hedged Futures Strategy I	HFXIX	U	(866) 447-4228	U /	4.20	-1.86	1.94 /22	--	--	0.00	2.10
GR	Catalyst Hedged Insider Buying A	STVAX	E-	(866) 447-4228	E / 0.5	-4.25	-9.50	-12.34 / 2	5.33 /14	--	0.00	2.10

● Denotes fund is closed to new investors
* Denotes fund is included in Section II

RISK			NET ASSETS		ASSET					BULL / BEAR		FUND MANAGER		MINIMUMS		LOADS	
	3 Year		NAV						Portfolio	Last Bull	Last Bear	Manager	Manager	Initial	Additional	Front	Back
Risk Rating/Pts	Standard Deviation	Beta	As of 3/31/15	Total $(Mil)	Cash %	Stocks %	Bonds %	Other %	Turnover Ratio	Market Return	Market Return	Quality Pct	Tenure (Years)	Purch. $	Purch. $	End Load	End Load
C / 5.2	12.5	0.90	15.32	39	6	93	0	1	56	67.1	-23.3	90	4	1,000,000	0	0.0	0.0
C / 5.3	12.5	0.90	14.93	21	6	93	0	1	56	65.8	-23.4	89	4	2,000	250	0.0	2.0
C+ / 6.9	9.9	1.00	23.45	76	5	94	0	1	68	84.1	-14.1	44	6	5,000	250	4.8	2.0
C+ / 6.7	9.9	1.00	20.12	1	5	94	0	1	68	75.2	-14.7	24	6	5,000	250	0.0	2.0
C+ / 6.8	9.9	1.00	21.04	14	5	94	0	1	68	79.0	-14.5	32	6	5,000	250	0.0	2.0
C+ / 6.9	9.9	1.00	23.96	106	5	94	0	1	68	87.3	-14.0	51	6	1,000,000	0	0.0	0.0
B- / 7.8	9.9	1.00	23.83	3	5	94	0	1	68	84.4	-14.1	44	6	5,000	250	0.0	2.0
B- / 7.0	10.3	1.03	68.20	57	4	95	0	1	64	86.2	-18.6	32	15	2,000	250	4.8	2.0
B- / 7.0	10.3	1.03	67.75	5	4	95	0	1	64	79.3	-18.9	20	15	2,000	250	0.0	2.0
C+ / 6.9	10.3	1.03	67.58	72	4	95	0	1	64	87.8	-18.5	36	15	2,000	250	0.0	2.0
B / 8.2	7.0	1.20	19.91	191	3	69	26	2	10	54.8	-11.6	28	7	2,000	250	4.8	2.0
B / 8.2	7.1	1.21	19.25	41	3	69	26	2	10	50.9	-11.9	20	7	2,000	250	0.0	2.0
C / 5.2	12.6	0.89	23.30	155	3	96	0	1	103	100.9	-23.7	88	5	2,000	250	4.8	2.0
C / 4.7	12.6	0.89	21.88	1	3	96	0	1	103	90.1	-24.1	79	5	2,000	250	0.0	2.0
C / 4.7	12.6	0.89	21.10	16	3	96	0	1	103	95.1	-24.0	85	5	2,000	250	0.0	2.0
C / 5.4	12.6	0.89	24.62	81	3	96	0	1	103	105.6	-23.4	90	5	1,000,000	0	0.0	0.0
B- / 7.1	12.6	0.89	23.43	8	3	96	0	1	103	101.8	-23.7	89	5	2,000	250	0.0	2.0
B- / 7.1	10.0	1.03	19.09	264	1	98	0	1	8	102.9	-15.9	64	3	2,000	250	4.8	2.0
B- / 7.0	10.0	1.03	18.12	1	1	98	0	1	8	96.1	-16.3	48	3	2,000	250	0.0	2.0
B- / 7.0	10.0	1.03	18.16	34	1	98	0	1	8	96.9	-16.2	49	3	2,000	250	0.0	2.0
B- / 7.1	10.0	1.03	19.50	163	1	98	0	1	8	106.7	-15.7	70	3	1,000,000	0	0.0	0.0
B- / 7.3	10.0	1.03	19.12	12	1	98	0	1	8	103.0	-15.9	63	3	2,000	250	0.0	2.0
C- / 4.1	18.5	1.60	18.09	143	13	86	0	1	167	105.0	-39.9	3	8	2,500	100	0.0	2.0
C+ / 6.9	11.5	0.78	12.48	2	5	94	0	1	67	N/A	N/A	92	4	2,500	100	0.0	2.0
U /	N/A	N/A	24.68	230	4	95	0	1	58	N/A	N/A	N/A	18	5,000,000	0	0.0	2.0
C+ / 5.9	12.4	0.91	24.65	138	4	95	0	1	58	57.8	-24.1	72	18	2,500	100	0.0	2.0
C+ / 6.6	10.9	1.06	25.78	406	2	97	0	1	58	82.4	-26.6	23	17	5,000,000	0	0.0	0.0
C+ / 6.6	10.9	1.06	25.82	328	2	97	0	1	58	80.8	-26.6	20	17	2,500	100	0.0	0.0
C- / 3.5	14.4	0.97	20.91	734	5	94	0	1	67	93.8	-26.8	26	11	5,000,000	0	0.0	2.0
C- / 3.4	14.4	0.97	20.51	506	5	94	0	1	67	92.2	-26.9	23	11	2,500	100	0.0	2.0
C+ / 5.8	13.5	1.22	14.38	35	3	96	0	1	71	118.1	N/A	30	4	2,500	100	0.0	2.0
B- / 7.4	8.3	0.75	10.77	67	19	61	18	2	21	71.8	-17.2	53	5	2,500	50	5.8	0.0
B- / 7.4	8.2	0.75	10.72	2	19	61	18	2	21	67.0	-17.4	42	5	2,500	50	0.0	0.0
C / 5.2	9.9	0.97	14.19	128	0	88	10	2	269	65.8	-15.8	46	7	2,500	100	0.0	0.0
B / 8.4	9.1	0.63	10.73	479	11	51	36	2	56	N/A	N/A	65	4	25,000	0	0.0	0.0
B- / 7.3	10.0	0.71	13.47	522	0	94	5	1	29	71.2	-18.9	94	4	25,000	0	0.0	0.0
B- / 7.1	10.6	0.79	11.97	1,309	0	89	10	1	33	48.6	-20.0	78	4	25,000	0	0.0	0.0
C+ / 6.9	9.9	1.01	20.10	203	0	95	3	2	27	84.4	-17.6	41	4	25,000	0	0.0	0.0
C+ / 6.4	11.0	0.93	23.45	20	4	95	0	1	22	86.7	-21.5	48	8	25,000	500	0.0	0.0
C+ / 6.1	11.1	0.93	19.56	1	4	95	0	1	22	82.4	-21.7	37	8	1,000	500	3.0	0.0
C / 4.8	13.7	0.95	21.48	16	4	95	0	1	29	64.5	-17.6	20	8	25,000	500	0.0	0.0
C / 4.7	13.7	0.95	20.20	N/A	4	95	0	1	29	62.6	-17.7	17	8	1,000	500	3.0	0.0
U /	N/A	N/A	9.73	50	0	0	0	100	0	N/A	N/A	N/A	1	1,000,000	0	0.0	0.0
D / 1.9	10.6	0.78	12.37	34	0	0	0	100	172	63.4	-14.9	16	6	100,000	25,000	0.0	0.0
D / 1.9	10.6	0.78	12.32	N/A	0	0	0	100	172	60.3	-15.1	12	6	2,500	100	0.0	0.0
B- / 7.1	6.5	0.37	19.12	13	28	71	0	1	51	34.9	-6.1	88	5	2,000	100	0.0	2.0
B- / 7.2	6.5	0.37	19.79	139	28	71	0	1	51	39.6	-5.7	91	5	4,000	100	0.0	2.0
C+ / 6.6	11.0	0.90	16.69	94	6	93	0	1	108	N/A	N/A	96	4	2,500	50	5.8	0.0
C+ / 6.6	10.9	0.89	16.25	6	6	93	0	1	108	N/A	N/A	96	4	2,500	50	0.0	0.0
B / 8.7	9.0	-0.45	10.63	274	0	0	0	100	0	23.5	8.5	99	2	2,500	50	5.8	0.0
U /	N/A	N/A	10.67	398	0	0	0	100	0	N/A	N/A	N/A	2	2,500	50	0.0	0.0
C- / 3.1	13.0	0.86	10.36	13	12	87	0	1	255	27.9	-11.4	3	5	2,500	50	5.8	0.0

| | | | | | | Total Return % through 3/31/15 | | | | | Incl. in Returns | |
Fund Type	Fund Name	Ticker Symbol	Overall Investment Rating	Phone	Perfor-mance Rating/Pts	3 Mo	6 Mo	1Yr / Pct	Annualized 3Yr / Pct	5Yr / Pct	Dividend Yield	Expense Ratio
GR	Catalyst Hedged Insider Buying C	STVCX	E-	(866) 447-4228	E+ / 0.6	-4.43	-9.83	-13.04 / 2	4.68 /12	--	0.00	2.85
IN	Catalyst Insider Buying A	INSAX	C+	(866) 447-4228	C+ / 6.3	-0.40	1.37	4.41 /34	16.37 /86	--	0.30	1.50
IN	Catalyst Insider Buying C	INSCX	B	(866) 447-4228	B- / 7.2	-0.59	0.97	3.63 /30	16.39 /86	--	0.00	2.25
GR	Catalyst Insider Buying I	INSIX	U	(866) 447-4228	U /	-0.40	1.47	--	--	--	0.00	1.25
SC	Catalyst Small Cap Insider Buying A	CTVAX	E	(866) 447-4228	D- / 1.5	-2.60	-6.17	-7.39 / 4	9.54 /36	4.39 /10	0.09	2.06
SC	Catalyst Small Cap Insider Buying C	CTVCX	E+	(866) 447-4228	D / 1.7	-2.76	-6.55	-8.14 / 3	8.70 /31	3.60 / 7	0.00	2.81
SC	Catalyst Small Cap Insider Buying I	CTVIX	E+	(866) 447-4228	D+ / 2.3	-2.52	-6.03	-7.13 / 4	9.81 /38	4.67 /11	0.25	1.81
IN	Catalyst/Groesbeck Growth of Inc A	CGGAX	C+	(866) 447-4228	C / 5.2	-0.03	7.22	12.52 /85	12.62 /57	12.18 /62	0.61	1.69
IN	Catalyst/Groesbeck Growth of Inc C	CGGCX	C+	(866) 447-4228	C+ / 5.6	-0.21	6.87	11.71 /81	11.81 /51	11.29 /55	0.06	2.44
IN	Catalyst/Groesbeck Growth of Inc I	CGGIX	B-	(866) 447-4228	C+ / 6.3	0.03	7.35	12.80 /86	12.93 /59	--	0.88	1.44
AA	Catalyst/Lyons Tactical Alloc A	CLTAX	U	(866) 447-4228	U /	2.74	9.19	13.62 /88	--	--	0.76	1.78
AA	Catalyst/Lyons Tactical Alloc C	CLTCX	U	(866) 447-4228	U /	2.56	8.78	12.76 /86	--	--	0.22	2.53
GL	Catalyst/MAP Global Capital Appr A	CAXAX	D	(866) 447-4228	D / 1.9	-0.97	-3.15	-1.14 /13	9.29 /35	--	0.94	1.78
GL	Catalyst/MAP Global Capital Appr C	CAXCX	D+	(866) 447-4228	D+ / 2.3	-1.06	-3.47	-1.89 /11	8.49 /30	--	0.00	2.53
GL	Catalyst/MAP Global Total Ret Inc A	TRXAX	D	(866) 447-4228	D- / 1.5	0.76	0.41	2.15 /22	7.23 /23	--	1.37	1.84
GL	Catalyst/MAP Global Total Ret Inc C	TRXCX	D	(866) 447-4228	D / 1.8	0.58	0.03	1.34 /20	6.43 /19	--	0.83	2.59
GI	Catalyst/SMH Total Return Income A	TRIFX	E	(866) 447-4228	E / 0.3	-0.02	-7.31	-13.54 / 2	0.62 / 5	2.32 / 5	6.75	3.00
GI	Catalyst/SMH Total Return Income C	TRICX	E	(866) 447-4228	E / 0.3	-0.20	-7.49	-14.18 / 2	-0.13 / 4	1.56 / 4	6.32	3.75
EM	Causeway Emerging Mkt Instl	CEMIX	E+	(866) 947-7000	D- / 1.0	3.02	-0.74	4.61 /36	3.63 / 9	5.44 /14	2.32	1.22
EM	Causeway Emerging Mkt Inv	CEMVX	E+	(866) 947-7000	E+ / 0.9	2.91	-0.87	4.35 /34	3.38 / 9	5.23 /13	2.01	1.47
FO	Causeway Global Absolute Rtn Inst	CGAIX	D-	(866) 947-7000	E / 0.4	-3.59	-4.04	-4.39 / 6	1.00 / 5	--	0.00	1.92
FO	Causeway Global Absolute Rtn Inv	CGAVX	D-	(866) 947-7000	E / 0.4	-3.62	-4.24	-4.68 / 6	0.68 / 5	--	0.00	2.17
GL	Causeway Global Value Institutional	CGVIX	C-	(866) 947-7000	C- / 3.9	0.00	-0.12	2.42 /24	11.26 /47	11.60 /58	1.82	1.19
GL	Causeway Global Value Investor	CGVVX	D+	(866) 947-7000	C- / 3.7	-0.09	-0.25	2.13 /22	11.00 /45	--	1.63	1.44
FO	Causeway International Oppty Instl	CIOIX	D	(866) 947-7000	D+ / 2.4	3.97	0.00	--	8.37 /29	7.49 /26	0.00	1.32
FO	Causeway International Oppty Inv	CIOVX	D	(866) 947-7000	D+ / 2.3	3.91	-0.15	-0.30 /15	8.10 /27	6.59 /21	0.00	1.57
FO	Causeway International Value Instl	CIVIX	D	(866) 947-7000	D+ / 2.8	4.33	-0.81	-2.22 /10	9.39 /35	7.93 /29	2.46	0.92
FO	Causeway International Value Inv	CIVVX	D	(866) 947-7000	D+ / 2.6	4.29	-0.89	-2.49 / 9	9.10 /34	7.66 /28	2.22	1.17
BA	Cavanal Hill Balanced A	AABAX	C	(800) 762-7085	C- / 3.6	2.33	5.82	8.64 /67	9.32 /35	--	1.35	1.57
BA	Cavanal Hill Balanced Instl	AIBLX	C	(800) 762-7085	C / 4.3	2.46	5.99	8.88 /69	9.60 /37	9.55 /41	1.63	1.47
BA	Cavanal Hill Balanced NL Inv	APBAX	C	(800) 762-7085	C- / 4.1	2.33	5.81	8.56 /67	9.32 /35	9.27 /39	1.40	1.72
GL	Cavanal Hill Opportunistic A	AAOPX	C	(800) 762-7085	C- / 4.2	2.71	5.84	4.05 /32	11.14 /46	--	0.05	2.47
GL	Cavanal Hill Opportunistic Inst	AIOPX	C	(800) 762-7085	C / 4.9	2.85	5.97	4.31 /34	11.41 /48	--	0.23	2.37
GL	Cavanal Hill Opportunistic Investor	APOPX	C	(800) 762-7085	C / 4.6	2.72	5.78	4.03 /32	11.03 /46	--	0.01	2.62
GI	Cavanal Hill US Lg Cp Eq A	AAEQX	C	(800) 762-7085	C+ / 6.0	1.23	7.01	10.45 /76	13.66 /65	--	0.33	1.41
GR	Cavanal Hill US Lg Cp Eq Instl	AIEQX	C+	(800) 762-7085	C+ / 6.8	1.31	7.12	10.74 /77	13.93 /67	11.23 /55	0.56	1.31
GR	Cavanal Hill US Lg Cp Eq NL Inv	APEQX	C+	(800) 762-7085	C+ / 6.6	1.33	7.03	10.45 /76	13.66 /65	10.95 /52	0.34	1.56
EN	Cavanal Hill World Energy Instl	AIWEX	U	(800) 762-7085	U /	0.79	-11.76	-8.93 / 3	--	--	0.95	1.28
* AG	CB Aggressive Growth A	SHRAX	A+	(877) 534-4627	A / 9.4	3.01	4.75	11.38 /80	20.93 /98	18.65 /98	0.00	1.15
AG	● CB Aggressive Growth B	SAGBX	A+	(877) 534-4627	A / 9.5	2.74	4.17	10.23 /75	19.73 /98	17.62 /97	0.00	2.14
AG	CB Aggressive Growth C	SAGCX	A+	(877) 534-4627	A+ / 9.6	2.84	4.39	10.60 /77	20.13 /98	17.93 /97	0.00	1.84
AG	CB Aggressive Growth FI	LMPFX	A+	(877) 534-4627	A+ / 9.7	3.03	4.77	11.42 /80	20.91 /98	18.61 /98	0.00	1.19
AG	CB Aggressive Growth I	SAGYX	A+	(877) 534-4627	A+ / 9.8	3.09	4.92	11.73 /81	21.35 /98	19.08 /98	0.00	0.83
AG	CB Aggressive Growth IS	LSIFX	A+	(877) 534-4627	A+ / 9.8	3.12	4.97	11.85 /82	21.49 /98	19.22 /98	0.00	0.72
AG	CB Aggressive Growth R	LMPRX	A+	(877) 534-4627	A+ / 9.7	2.95	4.62	11.08 /79	20.65 /98	18.37 /98	0.00	1.42
GR	CB All Cap Value A	SHFVX	C-	(877) 534-4627	C / 4.9	0.31	2.95	6.58 /52	13.41 /63	10.40 /48	2.39	1.29
GR	● CB All Cap Value B	SFVBX	C	(877) 534-4627	C / 5.1	0.00	2.30	5.35 /41	12.18 /54	9.37 /39	1.31	2.40
GR	CB All Cap Value C	SFVCX	C	(877) 534-4627	C / 5.4	0.14	2.64	5.86 /45	12.71 /58	9.79 /43	2.07	1.98
GR	CB All Cap Value I	SFVYX	C+	(877) 534-4627	C+ / 6.2	0.42	3.20	7.06 /55	13.91 /66	10.87 /52	2.82	0.90
GR	CB Appreciation A	SHAPX	B-	(877) 534-4627	C+ / 6.0	0.73	5.44	10.57 /77	14.55 /71	12.83 /67	0.79	1.00
GR	● CB Appreciation B	SAPBX	B-	(877) 534-4627	C+ / 6.1	0.41	4.81	9.26 /71	13.28 /62	11.70 /58	0.00	2.13
GR	CB Appreciation C	SAPCX	B-	(877) 534-4627	C+ / 6.5	0.55	5.04	9.75 /73	13.74 /65	12.06 /61	0.21	1.71

● Denotes fund is closed to new investors
* Denotes fund is included in Section II

RISK			NET ASSETS		ASSET					BULL / BEAR		FUND MANAGER		MINIMUMS		LOADS	
	3 Year		NAV						Portfolio	Last Bull	Last Bear	Manager	Manager	Initial	Additional	Front	Back
Risk Rating/Pts	Standard Deviation	Beta	As of 3/31/15	Total $(Mil)	Cash %	Stocks %	Bonds %	Other %	Turnover Ratio	Market Return	Market Return	Quality Pct	Tenure (Years)	Purch. $	Purch. $	End Load	End Load
C- / 3.1	13.1	0.86	10.13	3	12	87	0	1	255	25.2	-11.7	3	5	2,500	50	0.0	0.0
C+ / 6.4	11.6	1.10	15.06	266	6	93	0	1	185	102.8	N/A	48	4	2,500	50	5.8	0.0
C+ / 6.5	11.8	1.13	15.21	67	6	93	0	1	185	102.6	N/A	43	4	2,500	50	0.0	0.0
U /	N/A	N/A	15.07	65	6	93	0	1	185	N/A	N/A	N/A	4	2,500	50	0.0	0.0
C- / 4.1	17.7	1.05	15.72	51	4	95	0	1	231	65.8	-32.9	5	9	2,500	50	5.8	0.0
C- / 4.0	17.7	1.04	15.13	16	4	95	0	1	231	61.4	-33.1	4	9	2,500	50	0.0	0.0
C- / 4.1	17.7	1.05	15.87	21	4	95	0	1	231	67.1	-32.8	6	9	2,500	50	0.0	0.0
B- / 7.3	9.3	0.93	15.67	17	3	96	0	1	25	76.2	-11.1	37	6	2,500	50	5.8	0.0
B- / 7.3	9.3	0.93	15.45	1	3	96	0	1	25	71.8	-11.4	28	6	2,500	50	0.0	0.0
B- / 7.3	9.3	0.93	15.67	4	3	96	0	1	25	77.7	-11.0	41	6	2,500	50	0.0	0.0
U /	N/A	N/A	15.02	96	2	97	0	1	165	N/A	N/A	N/A	3	2,500	50	5.8	0.0
U /	N/A	N/A	14.84	38	2	97	0	1	165	N/A	N/A	N/A	3	2,500	50	0.0	0.0
C+ / 6.8	9.7	0.66	12.20	25	10	89	0	1	50	55.0	N/A	88	4	2,500	50	5.8	0.0
C+ / 6.9	9.6	0.65	12.10	7	10	89	0	1	50	51.1	N/A	85	4	2,500	50	0.0	0.0
B- / 7.2	6.4	0.44	11.47	15	7	58	32	3	42	37.8	N/A	89	4	2,500	50	5.8	0.0
B- / 7.2	6.4	0.44	11.41	4	7	58	32	3	42	34.5	N/A	85	4	2,500	50	0.0	0.0
C / 4.7	9.6	0.66	5.02	11	17	39	37	7	72	20.5	-19.6	2	7	2,500	50	5.8	0.0
C / 4.7	9.6	0.67	5.02	16	17	39	37	7	72	17.5	-19.9	2	7	2,500	50	0.0	0.0
C+ / 5.6	14.2	1.02	11.95	1,217	3	96	0	1	112	36.9	-27.4	88	8	1,000,000	0	0.0	2.0
C+ / 5.6	14.2	1.02	12.04	141	3	96	0	1	112	35.8	-27.4	87	8	5,000	0	0.0	2.0
B- / 7.3	6.9	-0.04	10.46	113	100	0	0	0	0	15.1	-0.7	79	4	1,000,000	0	0.0	2.0
B- / 7.4	7.0	-0.04	10.38	31	100	0	0	0	0	14.0	-0.8	77	4	5,000	0	0.0	2.0
C+ / 5.9	11.0	0.74	11.28	94	1	98	0	1	69	79.6	-22.8	91	7	1,000,000	0	0.0	2.0
C+ / 6.0	11.0	0.75	11.24	2	1	98	0	1	69	78.4	-22.9	91	7	5,000	0	0.0	2.0
C+ / 6.0	12.4	0.92	13.10	83	4	95	0	1	33	57.6	-26.2	63	N/A	1,000,000	0	0.0	2.0
C+ / 6.0	12.4	0.92	13.03	2	4	95	0	1	33	51.8	-26.3	59	N/A	5,000	0	0.0	2.0
C+ / 6.0	12.6	0.92	15.43	5,756	1	98	0	1	27	62.8	-25.8	74	14	1,000,000	0	0.0	2.0
C+ / 6.1	12.6	0.92	15.32	873	1	98	0	1	27	61.5	-25.9	71	14	5,000	0	0.0	2.0
B- / 7.5	5.2	0.89	13.86	N/A	1	54	43	2	62	48.8	N/A	63	10	0	0	3.5	0.0
B- / 7.5	5.2	0.90	13.92	56	1	54	43	2	62	50.2	-9.3	66	10	100,000	100	0.0	0.0
B- / 7.5	5.2	0.90	13.88	12	1	54	43	2	62	48.9	-9.3	62	10	1,000	100	0.0	0.0
C+ / 6.8	10.1	0.62	14.01	5	6	80	3	11	276	72.1	N/A	93	3	0	0	3.5	0.0
C+ / 6.8	10.1	0.62	14.08	13	6	80	3	11	276	73.5	N/A	94	3	100,000	100	0.0	0.0
C+ / 6.8	10.1	0.62	13.97	1	6	80	3	11	276	71.6	N/A	93	3	1,000	100	0.0	0.0
C+ / 5.7	10.3	1.03	13.99	N/A	2	97	0	1	94	86.9	N/A	30	9	0	0	3.5	0.0
C+ / 5.7	10.2	1.03	14.07	36	2	97	0	1	94	88.2	-18.8	33	9	100,000	100	0.0	0.0
C+ / 5.7	10.2	1.03	14.00	2	2	97	0	1	94	86.7	-18.9	30	9	1,000	100	0.0	0.0
U /	N/A	N/A	9.57	28	0	0	0	100	71	N/A	N/A	N/A	N/A	100,000	100	0.0	0.0
C+ / 6.6	11.3	1.06	209.82	6,034	2	90	7	1	5	131.9	-19.7	89	32	1,000	50	5.8	0.0
C+ / 6.5	11.3	1.06	170.31	217	2	90	7	1	5	124.2	-20.0	86	32	1,000	50	0.0	0.0
C+ / 6.6	11.3	1.06	176.20	1,689	2	90	7	1	5	126.7	-19.9	87	32	1,000	50	0.0	0.0
C+ / 6.6	11.3	1.05	210.42	54	2	90	7	1	5	131.8	-19.7	89	32	0	0	0.0	0.0
C+ / 6.6	11.3	1.05	227.64	5,574	2	90	7	1	5	134.7	-19.5	90	32	1,000,000	0	0.0	0.0
C+ / 6.6	11.3	1.05	229.50	1,265	2	90	7	1	5	135.7	-19.5	91	32	0	0	0.0	0.0
C+ / 6.6	11.3	1.05	206.63	98	2	90	7	1	5	130.1	-19.7	89	32	0	0	0.0	0.0
C+ / 5.9	10.8	1.10	16.11	1,623	0	99	0	1	12	86.0	-24.3	17	25	1,000	50	5.8	0.0
C+ / 5.8	10.8	1.10	14.42	78	0	99	0	1	12	79.3	-24.7	11	25	1,000	50	0.0	0.0
C+ / 5.7	10.8	1.10	14.56	186	0	99	0	1	12	82.1	-24.6	13	25	1,000	50	0.0	0.0
C+ / 5.9	10.8	1.10	16.81	30	0	99	0	1	12	88.9	-24.2	21	25	1,000,000	0	0.0	0.0
B- / 7.5	9.2	0.95	20.66	3,697	4	95	0	1	10	88.5	-15.3	58	20	1,000	50	5.8	0.0
B- / 7.6	9.1	0.95	19.82	87	4	95	0	1	10	81.5	-15.8	41	20	1,000	50	0.0	0.0
B- / 7.6	9.1	0.95	20.01	441	4	95	0	1	10	83.9	-15.5	47	20	1,000	50	0.0	0.0

Data as of March 31, 2015

99 Pct = Best
0 Pct = Worst

Fund Type	Fund Name	Ticker Symbol	Overall Investment Rating	Phone	PERFORMANCE Performance Rating/Pts	Total Return % through 3/31/15			Annualized		Incl. in Returns	
						3 Mo	6 Mo	1Yr / Pct	3Yr / Pct	5Yr / Pct	Dividend Yield	Expense Ratio
GR	CB Appreciation FI	LMPIX	B+	(877) 534-4627	B- / 7.0	0.73	5.39	10.53 /76	14.56 /71	12.85 /67	0.59	1.12
GR	CB Appreciation I	SAPYX	B+	(877) 534-4627	B- / 7.3	0.79	5.58	10.91 /78	14.94 /74	13.20 /70	1.13	0.68
GR	CB Appreciation IS	LMESX	B+	(877) 534-4627	B- / 7.4	0.83	5.60	11.03 /78	15.04 /75	13.30 /71	1.22	0.59
GR	CB Appreciation R	LMPPX	B-	(877) 534-4627	C+ / 6.8	0.64	5.28	10.21 /75	14.23 /69	12.49 /64	0.51	1.31
IN	● CB Equity Income 1	LCBOX	B	(877) 534-4627	C+ / 6.5	-1.06	4.42	9.90 /74	13.93 /67	--	1.67	0.91
GI	CB Equity Income A	SOPAX	B	(877) 534-4627	C / 5.3	-1.12	4.28	9.61 /73	13.63 /64	13.26 /71	1.32	1.18
GI	● CB Equity Income B	SOPTX	B	(877) 534-4627	C+ / 5.7	-1.32	3.88	8.73 /68	12.81 /58	12.63 /65	0.59	1.88
GI	CB Equity Income C	SBPLX	B	(877) 534-4627	C+ / 5.7	-1.30	3.87	8.81 /68	12.81 /58	12.40 /63	0.74	1.86
GI	CB Equity Income I	SOPYX	B	(877) 534-4627	C+ / 6.5	-1.02	4.45	9.97 /74	14.01 /67	13.62 /74	1.69	0.86
IN	CB Equity Income R	LMMRX	B	(877) 534-4627	C+ / 6.0	-1.19	4.08	9.26 /71	13.29 /62	--	1.17	1.71
GR	CB Global Growth A	LGGAX	C	(877) 534-4627	C / 5.0	3.09	6.32	8.18 /64	12.76 /58	12.32 /63	0.00	1.29
GR	CB Global Growth C	LMGTX	C	(877) 534-4627	C / 5.4	2.89	5.91	7.35 /58	11.90 /52	11.48 /57	0.00	2.06
GR	CB Global Growth FI	LMGFX	C+	(877) 534-4627	C+ / 6.0	3.09	6.31	8.16 /64	12.77 /58	12.33 /63	0.00	1.39
GR	CB Global Growth I	LMGNX	C+	(877) 534-4627	C+ / 6.2	3.13	6.44	8.43 /66	13.03 /60	12.62 /65	0.00	1.02
GR	CB Global Growth R	LMGRX	C	(877) 534-4627	C+ / 5.8	3.01	6.17	7.82 /61	12.45 /56	12.04 /61	0.00	1.83
FO	CB International Small Cap A	LCOAX	C-	(877) 534-4627	C- / 4.2	7.25	0.74	-4.85 / 6	13.33 /62	--	0.64	1.66
FO	CB International Small Cap C	LCOCX	C-	(877) 534-4627	C / 4.6	7.10	0.40	-5.54 / 5	12.51 /56	--	0.37	2.54
FO	CB International Small Cap I	LCOIX	C	(877) 534-4627	C / 5.4	7.34	0.89	-4.61 / 6	13.60 /64	--	0.81	1.30
GR	CB Large Cap Growth A	SBLGX	A	(877) 534-4627	A- / 9.2	3.10	8.22	15.82 /93	18.85 /96	14.67 /84	0.00	1.23
GR	● CB Large Cap Growth B	SBLBX	A-	(877) 534-4627	A / 9.3	2.84	7.61	14.57 /91	17.68 /93	14.30 /80	0.00	2.36
GR	CB Large Cap Growth C	SLCCX	A	(877) 534-4627	A / 9.4	2.91	7.82	14.93 /91	17.98 /94	13.97 /77	0.00	2.00
GR	CB Large Cap Growth I	SBLYX	A+	(877) 534-4627	A+ / 9.7	3.22	8.42	16.21 /94	19.35 /97	15.13 /88	0.00	0.91
GR	CB Large Cap Growth R	LMPLX	A+	(877) 534-4627	A / 9.5	3.06	8.07	15.46 /92	18.46 /96	14.31 /80	0.00	1.72
GI	CB Large Cap Value 1	LCLIX	U	(877) 534-4627	U /	-0.40	4.11	9.14 /70	--	--	1.71	0.78
GR	CB Large Cap Value A	SINAX	B-	(877) 534-4627	C+ / 6.1	-0.44	4.00	8.94 /69	15.19 /76	13.30 /71	1.44	0.93
GI	CB Large Cap Value A2	LIVVX	U	(877) 534-4627	U /	-0.49	3.93	8.71 /68	--	--	1.27	1.15
GR	CB Large Cap Value C	SINOX	B-	(877) 534-4627	C+ / 6.5	-0.62	3.59	8.07 /63	14.28 /69	12.44 /64	0.77	1.74
GR	CB Large Cap Value I	SAIFX	B+	(877) 534-4627	B- / 7.4	-0.36	4.18	9.28 /71	15.54 /79	13.64 /74	1.86	0.60
MC	● CB Mid Cap Core 1	SMCPX	A-	(877) 534-4627	A- / 9.0	4.73	12.07	10.03 /74	16.96 /90	15.72 /91	0.00	1.09
MC	CB Mid Cap Core A	SBMAX	B+	(877) 534-4627	B / 7.9	4.65	11.91	9.78 /73	16.77 /89	15.51 /90	0.00	1.25
MC	● CB Mid Cap Core B	SBMDX	B+	(877) 534-4627	B / 8.2	4.41	11.36	8.68 /67	15.67 /81	14.64 /84	0.00	2.29
MC	CB Mid Cap Core C	SBMLX	B+	(877) 534-4627	B+ / 8.4	4.48	11.52	9.03 /69	15.95 /83	14.75 /85	0.00	1.96
MC	CB Mid Cap Core I	SMBYX	A	(877) 534-4627	A- / 9.1	4.72	12.08	10.18 /75	17.20 /91	15.93 /93	0.00	0.88
MC	CB Mid Cap Core IS	LSIRX	A	(877) 534-4627	A- / 9.1	4.79	12.17	10.28 /75	17.30 /91	16.04 /93	0.00	0.79
MC	CB Mid Cap Core R	LMREX	B+	(877) 534-4627	B+ / 8.7	4.59	11.77	9.50 /72	16.46 /87	15.19 /88	0.00	1.54
GL	CB Mid Cap Growth A	LBGAX	B-	(877) 534-4627	B- / 7.0	3.20	9.73	8.55 /67	15.86 /82	--	0.00	1.49
GL	CB Mid Cap Growth C	LBGCX	B	(877) 534-4627	B- / 7.5	3.04	9.33	7.83 /62	15.02 /75	--	0.00	2.41
GL	CB Mid Cap Growth I	LBGIX	B+	(877) 534-4627	B+ / 8.3	3.29	9.90	8.88 /69	16.15 /84	--	0.00	1.24
SC	● CB Small Cap Growth 1	LMPMX	C+	(877) 534-4627	B- / 7.3	1.26	10.53	4.90 /38	15.22 /77	16.76 /95	0.00	1.20
SC	CB Small Cap Growth A	SASMX	C	(877) 534-4627	C+ / 6.2	1.21	10.45	4.83 /37	15.11 /76	16.58 /95	0.00	1.26
SC	● CB Small Cap Growth B	SBSMX	C	(877) 534-4627	C+ / 6.4	0.95	9.91	3.73 /30	13.95 /67	15.51 /90	0.00	2.27
SC	CB Small Cap Growth C	SCSMX	C	(877) 534-4627	C+ / 6.6	1.06	10.07	4.04 /32	14.25 /69	15.66 /91	0.00	1.99
SC	CB Small Cap Growth FI	LMPSX	C+	(877) 534-4627	B- / 7.2	1.24	10.48	4.85 /37	15.10 /76	16.58 /95	0.00	1.26
SC	CB Small Cap Growth I	SBPYX	C+	(877) 534-4627	B- / 7.5	1.28	10.59	5.13 /40	15.53 /79	17.07 /96	0.00	0.91
SC	CB Small Cap Growth IS	LMOIX	C+	(877) 534-4627	B / 7.6	1.31	10.69	5.28 /41	15.65 /80	17.17 /96	0.00	0.78
SC	● CB Small Cap Growth R	LMPOX	C	(877) 534-4627	B- / 7.0	1.15	10.33	4.53 /35	14.85 /74	16.35 /94	0.00	1.51
SC	CB Small Cap Value A	SBVAX	D	(877) 534-4627	C- / 4.0	0.74	6.23	-1.17 /12	12.30 /55	11.34 /56	0.00	1.35
SC	CB Small Cap Value C	SBVLX	D	(877) 534-4627	C / 4.3	0.59	5.88	-1.92 /10	11.46 /49	10.47 /48	0.00	2.09
SC	CB Small Cap Value I	SMCYX	C-	(877) 534-4627	C / 5.1	0.87	6.46	-0.84 /13	12.64 /57	11.71 /58	0.00	1.01
MC	CB Special Inv A	LMSAX	C-	(877) 534-4627	C+ / 6.9	2.46	11.14	9.33 /71	15.51 /79	10.08 /45	0.00	1.10
MC	CB Special Inv C	LMASX	C	(877) 534-4627	B- / 7.3	2.28	10.68	8.46 /66	14.62 /72	9.21 /38	0.00	1.90
MC	CB Special Inv FI	LGASX	C+	(877) 534-4627	B / 7.8	2.45	10.99	9.03 /69	15.24 /77	9.87 /43	0.00	1.44

● Denotes fund is closed to new investors
* Denotes fund is included in Section II

www.thestreetratings.com

Risk Rating/Pts	Standard Deviation	Beta	NAV As of 3/31/15	Total $(Mil)	Cash %	Stocks %	Bonds %	Other %	Portfolio Turnover Ratio	Last Bull Market Return	Last Bear Market Return	Manager Quality Pct	Manager Tenure (Years)	Initial Purch. $	Additional Purch. $	Front End Load	Back End Load
B- /7.5	9.1	0.95	20.66	4	4	95	0	1	10	88.5	-15.3	59	20	0	0	0.0	0.0
B- /7.5	9.1	0.95	20.54	840	4	95	0	1	10	90.7	-15.2	64	20	1,000,000	0	0.0	0.0
B- /7.5	9.1	0.95	20.59	536	4	95	0	1	10	91.3	-15.2	66	20	0	0	0.0	0.0
B- /7.6	9.2	0.95	20.57	75	4	95	0	1	10	86.8	-15.5	54	20	0	0	0.0	0.0
B /8.1	8.2	0.82	19.96	1,413	10	89	0	1	32	83.2	-11.4	75	6	0	0	0.0	0.0
B /8.1	8.2	0.83	19.95	3,330	10	89	0	1	32	81.6	-11.5	72	6	1,000	50	5.8	0.0
B /8.1	8.2	0.83	19.65	80	10	89	0	1	32	77.2	-11.7	63	6	1,000	50	0.0	0.0
B /8.1	8.2	0.83	19.70	390	10	89	0	1	32	77.1	-11.7	63	6	1,000	50	0.0	0.0
B /8.1	8.2	0.83	20.41	951	10	89	0	1	32	83.7	-11.4	75	6	1,000,000	0	0.0	0.0
B /8.0	8.2	0.83	19.89	2	10	89	0	1	32	N/A	N/A	69	6	0	0	0.0	0.0
C+ /6.0	10.9	1.02	33.99	11	2	97	0	1	45	82.9	-17.6	23	3	1,000	50	5.8	0.0
C+ /5.9	11.0	1.02	32.44	104	2	97	0	1	45	78.2	-17.8	16	3	1,000	50	0.0	0.0
C+ /6.0	11.0	1.02	35.39	12	2	97	0	1	45	83.0	-17.6	23	3	0	0	0.0	0.0
C+ /6.0	11.0	1.02	36.52	20	2	97	0	1	45	84.5	-17.5	25	3	1,000,000	0	0.0	0.0
C+ /6.0	11.0	1.02	34.60	N/A	2	97	0	1	45	81.3	-17.7	20	3	0	0	0.0	0.0
C+ /5.7	11.9	0.77	15.68	20	7	92	0	1	45	66.7	-20.9	94	5	1,000	50	5.8	0.0
C+ /5.6	11.9	0.77	15.53	2	7	92	0	1	45	62.3	-21.1	93	5	1,000	50	0.0	0.0
C+ /5.7	11.9	0.77	15.79	75	7	92	0	1	45	68.0	-20.8	95	5	1,000,000	0	0.0	0.0
C+ /6.3	10.7	1.05	31.56	708	4	95	0	1	18	113.5	-15.5	81	6	1,000	50	5.8	0.0
C+ /6.0	10.7	1.05	27.16	12	4	95	0	1	18	106.5	-15.9	73	6	1,000	50	0.0	0.0
C+ /6.0	10.7	1.05	26.49	240	4	95	0	1	18	108.3	-15.8	76	6	1,000	50	0.0	0.0
C+ /6.4	10.6	1.05	34.60	297	4	95	0	1	18	116.4	-15.4	84	6	1,000,000	0	0.0	0.0
C+ /6.2	10.7	1.05	30.67	4	4	95	0	1	18	111.0	-15.6	79	6	0	0	0.0	0.0
U /	N/A	N/A	28.59	195	1	98	0	1	16	N/A	N/A	N/A	11	0	0	0.0	0.0
B- /7.4	10.0	1.01	28.60	426	1	98	0	1	16	96.2	-16.7	52	11	1,000	50	5.8	0.0
U /	N/A	N/A	28.58	170	1	98	0	1	16	N/A	N/A	N/A	11	1,000	50	0.0	0.0
B- /7.4	10.0	1.02	27.85	111	1	98	0	1	16	91.0	-17.0	39	11	1,000	50	0.0	0.0
B- /7.4	10.0	1.02	28.55	659	1	98	0	1	16	98.3	-16.6	57	11	1,000,000	0	0.0	0.0
C+ /6.2	11.9	1.03	32.76	4	2	97	0	1	30	111.7	-24.5	59	10	0	0	0.0	0.0
C+ /6.2	11.9	1.03	31.74	915	2	97	0	1	30	110.4	-24.5	57	10	1,000	50	5.8	0.0
C+ /6.0	11.9	1.03	26.27	27	2	97	0	1	30	103.8	-24.8	42	10	1,000	50	0.0	0.0
C+ /6.1	11.9	1.03	26.61	210	2	97	0	1	30	105.3	-24.7	45	10	1,000	50	0.0	0.0
C+ /6.3	11.9	1.03	34.58	330	2	97	0	1	30	113.1	-24.4	62	10	1,000,000	0	0.0	0.0
C+ /6.3	11.9	1.03	34.80	111	2	97	0	1	30	113.6	-24.4	63	10	0	0	0.0	0.0
C+ /6.2	11.9	1.03	31.24	27	2	97	0	1	30	108.3	-24.6	52	10	0	0	0.0	0.0
C+ /6.0	12.7	0.73	23.90	40	5	94	0	1	44	121.7	-25.1	97	5	1,000	50	5.8	0.0
C+ /6.0	12.7	0.73	23.07	7	5	94	0	1	44	116.3	-25.4	96	5	1,000	50	0.0	0.0
C+ /6.0	12.8	0.73	24.18	36	5	94	0	1	44	123.6	-25.1	97	5	1,000,000	0	0.0	0.0
C /4.7	13.8	0.93	28.96	4	0	99	0	1	16	111.9	-22.6	68	8	0	0	0.0	0.0
C /4.7	13.8	0.94	28.52	1,357	0	99	0	1	16	111.1	-22.7	67	8	1,000	50	5.8	0.0
C /4.7	13.8	0.93	23.40	15	0	99	0	1	16	103.8	-23.0	52	8	1,000	50	0.0	0.0
C /4.7	13.8	0.93	23.94	65	0	99	0	1	16	105.5	-23.0	56	8	1,000	50	0.0	0.0
C /4.7	13.8	0.94	28.65	16	0	99	0	1	16	110.9	-22.7	67	8	0	0	0.0	0.0
C /4.8	13.8	0.93	29.96	1,678	0	99	0	1	16	113.8	-22.5	71	8	1,000,000	0	0.0	0.0
C /4.8	13.8	0.93	30.12	582	0	99	0	1	16	114.6	-22.6	72	8	0	0	0.0	0.0
C /4.7	13.8	0.93	28.09	109	0	99	0	1	16	109.4	-22.7	64	8	0	0	0.0	0.0
C /4.8	13.1	0.93	21.89	128	1	98	0	1	27	81.2	-27.0	31	16	1,000	50	5.8	0.0
C- /4.1	13.1	0.94	18.66	61	1	98	0	1	27	76.6	-27.2	22	16	1,000	50	0.0	0.0
C /5.0	13.1	0.94	23.11	19	1	98	0	1	27	83.0	-26.8	34	16	1,000,000	0	0.0	0.0
C- /3.8	12.9	1.08	35.41	39	0	0	0	100	52	92.9	-30.3	30	N/A	1,000	50	5.8	0.0
C- /3.6	12.9	1.08	34.52	551	0	0	0	100	52	87.8	-30.5	21	N/A	1,000	50	0.0	0.0
C /5.0	12.9	1.08	48.56	1	0	0	0	100	52	91.4	-30.3	27	N/A	0	0	0.0	0.0

Fund Type	Fund Name	Ticker Symbol	Overall Investment Rating	Phone	Performance Rating/Pts	3 Mo	6 Mo	1Yr / Pct	3Yr / Pct	5Yr / Pct	Dividend Yield	Expense Ratio
MC	CB Special Inv I	LMNSX	B	(877) 534-4627	B / 8.2	2.51	11.24	9.55 /72	15.77 /81	10.33 /47	0.00	0.89
MC	CB Special Inv R	LMARX	C+	(877) 534-4627	B / 7.6	2.40	10.93	8.84 /68	14.98 /75	9.59 /41	0.00	1.58
GR	CB Tactical Dividend Income A	CFLGX	C+	(877) 534-4627	C / 5.0	0.43	1.38	6.26 /49	13.68 /65	9.21 /38	4.58	1.71
IN	CB Tactical Dividend Income A2	LBDAX	C+	(877) 534-4627	C / 4.9	0.41	1.34	6.12 /47	13.61 /64	9.17 /38	4.50	1.85
GR	CB Tactical Dividend Income C	SMDLX	C+	(877) 534-4627	C / 5.4	0.28	1.04	5.53 /43	12.88 /59	8.41 /33	4.37	2.44
GR	CB Tactical Dividend Income I	LADIX	B-	(877) 534-4627	C+ / 6.1	0.49	1.50	6.54 /51	13.98 /67	9.46 /40	5.08	1.45
GR	CB Value A	LGVAX	B+	(877) 534-4627	B- / 7.4	0.40	4.35	9.91 /74	17.03 /90	12.54 /64	0.33	1.02
GR	CB Value C	LMVTX	B+	(877) 534-4627	B / 7.8	0.23	3.97	9.09 /70	16.15 /84	11.68 /58	0.00	1.77
GR	CB Value FI	LMVFX	A-	(877) 534-4627	B+ / 8.4	0.34	4.25	9.75 /73	16.96 /90	12.44 /64	0.00	1.09
GR	CB Value I	LMNVX	A	(877) 534-4627	B+ / 8.6	0.46	4.46	10.13 /75	17.28 /91	12.77 /66	0.44	0.82
GR	CB Value R	LMVRX	A-	(877) 534-4627	B / 8.1	0.32	4.17	9.45 /72	16.55 /87	12.07 /61	0.00	1.46
OT	CBRE Clarion Gbl Infras Val Inst	CGIVX	U	(866) 777-7818	U /	0.58	0.82	7.48 /59	--	--	1.62	1.54
RE	CBRE Clarion Long/Short Inst	CLSIX	D-	(855) 520-4227	D / 1.9	2.15	11.34	11.13 /79	4.71 /12	--	0.11	3.73
RE	CBRE Clarion Long/Short Investor	CLSVX	D-	(855) 520-4227	D / 1.8	2.06	11.34	10.91 /78	4.46 /11	--	0.00	3.92
GL	CCM Alternative Income Inst	CCMNX	U	(877) 272-1977	U /	0.59	1.59	3.26 /28	--	--	3.25	3.35
FS	Cedar Ridge Uncons Credit Inst	CRUMX	U	(855) 550-5090	U /	0.61	1.07	4.44 /35	--	--	2.22	2.26
GI	Centaur Total Return	TILDX	D	(888) 484-5766	C- / 4.0	0.23	4.31	4.08 /32	10.68 /43	9.96 /44	0.00	2.39
EN	Center Coast MLP Focus A	CCCAX	D	(877) 766-0066	E+ / 0.9	-2.24	-8.02	3.77 /30	6.00 /17	--	6.34	8.98
EN	Center Coast MLP Focus C	CCCCX	D	(877) 766-0066	D- / 1.1	-2.42	-8.31	3.03 /27	5.19 /14	--	7.00	9.73
EN	Center Coast MLP Focus Inst	CCCNX	D	(877) 766-0066	E+ / 0.9	-2.13	-7.80	4.03 /32	4.12 /11	--	6.67	8.73
GR	Centre American Select Equity Inv	DHAMX	C	(855) 298-4236	C- / 4.1	-0.49	1.45	6.75 /53	10.91 /45	--	1.38	1.43
GL	Centre Global Select Equity Inst	DHGLX	D	(855) 298-4236	E+ / 0.9	3.51	-0.32	-3.65 / 8	4.59 /12	--	1.23	1.95
AA	Centre Multi-Asset Real Return Inst	DHMUX	U	(855) 298-4236	U /	0.95	0.02	0.12 /16	--	--	2.02	1.77
GR	Century Growth Opportunities Instl	CGOIX	C-	(800) 321-1928	B / 7.6	7.56	14.63	13.10 /87	13.86 /66	--	0.00	1.10
FS	Century Shares Trust Inst	CENSX	C-	(800) 321-1928	A- / 9.0	5.17	11.27	17.29 /95	15.79 /82	14.80 /85	0.00	1.09
SC	Century Small Cap Select Instl	CSMCX	C	(800) 321-1928	B / 7.8	10.54	16.10	8.67 /67	14.27 /69	16.16 /94	0.02	1.11
SC	Century Small Cap Select Inv	CSMVX	C-	(800) 321-1928	B- / 7.5	10.40	15.91	8.31 /65	13.90 /66	15.77 /92	0.02	1.40
EM	CGCM Emerging Mkts Eqty Invest	TEMUX	E-	(800) 444-4273	E / 0.3	-0.72	-5.88	-3.20 / 8	-2.37 / 3	-0.13 / 2	1.59	1.09
FO	CGCM Intl Equity Invest	TIEUX	D-	(800) 444-4273	D- / 1.5	4.57	0.56	-2.46 / 9	5.86 /16	5.14 /13	1.76	0.81
GR	CGCM Large Cap Gro Invest	TLGUX	B	(800) 444-4273	B+ / 8.5	3.21	8.99	13.84 /89	15.80 /82	14.65 /84	0.30	0.67
GR	CGCM Large Cap Val Eq Invest	TLVUX	B-	(800) 444-4273	C+ / 5.7	-1.13	1.19	5.35 /41	13.43 /63	12.04 /61	1.67	0.67
SC	CGCM Small Cap Growth Invest	TSGUX	C	(800) 444-4273	A / 9.3	6.69	17.01	10.10 /75	17.28 /91	15.39 /89	0.00	0.92
SC	CGCM Small Cap Val Eq Invest	TSVUX	D+	(800) 444-4273	C / 5.5	0.51	6.32	1.45 /20	13.08 /60	13.56 /73	1.07	0.92
AG	CGM Focus	CGMFX	C-	(800) 345-4048	C / 5.3	2.23	6.01	6.09 /47	11.86 /51	6.35 /19	0.00	2.00
BA	CGM Mutual	LOMMX	C	(800) 345-4048	C / 5.4	3.56	9.41	12.39 /84	10.14 /40	7.61 /27	0.00	1.11
RE	CGM Realty	CGMRX	B	(800) 345-4048	B / 7.9	3.56	17.74	22.54 /97	11.25 /47	12.33 /63	0.64	0.92
GL	Chadwick & D'Amato	CDFFX	D+		D- / 1.2	-1.10	-1.55	1.50 /20	4.73 /12	--	0.00	1.98
MC	Champlain Mid Cap Fd Institutional	CIPIX	B	(866) 777-7818	B / 8.2	3.76	8.80	10.77 /77	15.69 /81	--	0.00	1.05
MC	Champlain Mid Cap Fund	CIPMX	B	(866) 777-7818	B / 8.0	3.73	8.66	10.50 /76	15.42 /78	14.76 /85	0.00	1.30
SC	Chartwell Small Cap Value A	CWSVX	C+	(866) 585-6552	C+ / 5.8	0.62	11.44	5.56 /43	14.77 /73	--	0.00	1.95
SC	Chartwell Small Cap Value I	CWSIX	C+	(866) 585-6552	C+ / 6.9	0.62	11.57	5.92 /46	15.11 /76	--	0.30	1.61
GR	Chase Growth Fund	CHASX	D+	(888) 861-7556	B+ / 8.8	5.72	11.27	15.91 /93	16.33 /86	14.53 /83	0.00	1.33
GR	Chase Growth Fund Institutional	CHAIX	C-	(888) 861-7556	A- / 9.0	5.73	11.46	16.16 /93	16.64 /88	14.81 /85	0.00	1.08
MC	Chase Mid-Cap Growth Fund Inst	CHIMX	B+	(888) 861-7556	B / 7.6	8.08	11.62	11.89 /82	14.59 /72	--	0.00	1.44
MC	Chase Mid-Cap Growth Fund N	CHAMX	C+	(888) 861-7556	B- / 7.4	8.06	11.49	11.62 /81	14.32 /69	16.87 /96	0.00	1.69
GR	Chesapeake Core Growth Fund	CHCGX	B-	(800) 430-3863	B- / 7.1	4.34	6.78	12.63 /85	13.85 /66	10.64 /50	0.00	1.94
MC	Chesapeake Growth Inst	CHESX	C+	(800) 430-3863	B / 8.0	5.13	6.61	11.20 /79	15.50 /79	12.37 /63	0.00	2.47
MC	Chesapeake Growth Investor	CHEAX	C	(800) 430-3863	B / 7.8	5.12	6.58	11.16 /79	15.08 /75	11.91 /60	0.00	2.93
GI	● Chestnut Street Exchange	CHNTX	B-	(800) 441-7762	C+ / 6.4	-1.92	1.57	8.28 /65	14.48 /71	12.91 /67	1.88	N/A
EM	Cheswold Lane Intl High Div Inst	CLIDX	E+	(800) 771-4701	E+ / 0.6	0.61	-7.60	-9.80 / 3	3.87 /10	2.38 / 5	2.82	1.56
GL	Chou Opportunity	CHOEX	C+	(877) 682-6352	B- / 7.4	1.53	12.83	-1.12 /13	16.59 /87	--	0.00	1.50
GR	Christopher Weil & Co Core Inv	CWCFX	B+	(888) 550-9266	B / 7.6	4.33	8.21	11.70 /81	15.21 /77	--	0.00	1.51

● Denotes fund is closed to new investors
* Denotes fund is included in Section II

Risk Rating/Pts	3 Year Standard Deviation	3 Year Beta	NAV As of 3/31/15	Total $(Mil)	Cash %	Stocks %	Bonds %	Other %	Portfolio Turnover Ratio	Last Bull Market Return	Last Bear Market Return	Manager Quality Pct	Manager Tenure (Years)	Initial Purch. $	Additional Purch. $	Front End Load	Back End Load
C /5.2	12.9	1.08	50.14	74	0	0	0	100	52	94.4	-30.2	32	N/A	1,000,000	0	0.0	0.0
C /5.0	12.9	1.08	47.87	5	0	0	0	100	52	89.8	-30.4	25	N/A	0	0	0.0	0.0
B- /7.1	9.4	0.82	19.02	384	31	67	0	2	45	76.7	-21.5	74	3	1,000	50	5.8	0.0
B- /7.7	9.4	0.81	18.98	48	31	67	0	2	45	76.4	-21.5	74	3	1,000	50	5.8	0.0
B- /7.1	9.4	0.82	18.21	376	31	67	0	2	45	72.5	-21.7	66	3	1,000	50	0.0	0.0
B- /7.1	9.4	0.81	19.14	365	31	67	0	2	45	78.4	-21.4	76	3	1,000,000	0	0.0	0.0
C+ /6.8	11.4	1.13	67.05	132	3	96	0	1	37	104.9	-18.1	51	5	1,000	50	5.8	0.0
C+ /6.8	11.4	1.13	66.00	1,932	3	96	0	1	37	99.7	-18.4	39	5	1,000	50	0.0	0.0
C+ /6.8	11.4	1.13	75.84	19	3	96	0	1	37	104.6	-18.2	50	5	0	0	0.0	0.0
C+ /6.8	11.4	1.13	78.37	596	3	96	0	1	37	106.4	-18.0	54	5	1,000,000	0	0.0	0.0
C+ /6.8	11.4	1.13	74.96	11	3	96	0	1	37	102.0	-18.3	45	5	0	0	0.0	0.0
U /	N/A	N/A	11.02	41	16	83	0	1	93	N/A	N/A	N/A	2	1,000,000	0	0.0	2.0
C+ /5.9	8.9	0.64	11.40	801	11	88	0	1	131	N/A	N/A	17	N/A	1,000,000	0	0.0	2.0
C+ /5.9	8.9	0.64	11.39	18	11	88	0	1	131	N/A	N/A	15	N/A	5,000	100	0.0	2.0
U /	N/A	N/A	10.25	29	24	38	36	2	109	N/A	N/A	N/A	2	1,000		0.0	0.0
U /	N/A	N/A	10.92	48	0	0	0	100	95	N/A	N/A	N/A	2	50,000	5,000	0.0	1.0
C /4.5	9.4	0.83	13.24	42	35	62	0	3	135	60.0	-15.4	33	10	1,500	100	0.0	2.0
B- /7.6	8.8	0.36	10.76	546	86	13	0	1	55	30.3	-6.9	92	5	2,500	100	5.8	0.0
B- /7.5	8.7	0.36	10.34	1,049	86	13	0	1	55	26.8	-7.2	91	5	2,500	100	0.0	0.0
B- /7.6	8.5	0.34	10.85	1,599	86	13	0	1	55	23.5	-6.8	88	5	1,000,000	100,000	0.0	0.0
B- /7.2	9.3	0.94	12.09	196	2	97	0	1	72	N/A	N/A	19	N/A	5,000	1,000	0.0	2.0
B- /7.1	12.1	0.88	10.31	21	2	97	0	1	156	N/A	N/A	20	4	1,000,000	10,000	0.0	2.0
U /	N/A	N/A	9.59	58	16	59	24	1	199	N/A	N/A	N/A	N/A	1,000,000	10,000	0.0	0.0
C- /3.0	13.2	1.18	13.52	90	3	96	0	1	165	79.1	-18.6	12	5	100,000	0	0.0	1.0
D /1.7	11.8	0.81	20.53	228	1	98	0	1	126	101.6	-17.3	82	16	100,000	0	0.0	1.0
C- /3.4	13.9	0.96	32.41	182	0	100	0	0	97	89.9	-24.2	50	16	100,000	0	0.0	1.0
C- /3.3	13.9	0.96	30.88	118	0	100	0	0	97	87.7	-24.3	45	16	2,500	50	0.0	1.0
C- /3.1	15.0	1.08	12.42	323	3	96	0	1	29	15.7	-27.0	24	6	100	0	0.0	0.0
C+ /6.0	12.3	0.92	11.45	1,094	4	95	0	1	95	43.1	-25.5	29	13	100	0	0.0	0.0
C /5.1	10.6	1.02	21.19	1,795	1	98	0	1	56	99.4	-18.4	59	11	100	0	0.0	0.0
B- /7.4	10.3	1.05	13.12	1,387	5	94	0	1	24	83.9	-18.4	25	18	100	0	0.0	0.0
D+ /2.5	14.1	0.99	25.68	316	3	96	0	1	80	109.6	-28.1	77	18	100	0	0.0	0.0
C- /4.2	12.9	0.91	13.71	277	5	94	0	1	31	87.9	-24.1	46	15	100	0	0.0	0.0
C /4.7	17.2	1.48	41.79	1,281	1	98	0	1	291	70.7	-27.5	1	18	2,500	50	0.0	0.0
C+ /5.8	11.7	1.65	31.39	453	1	71	27	1	374	61.1	-18.9	4	34	2,500	50	0.0	0.0
C /5.5	12.9	0.75	34.06	1,254	2	97	0	1	146	77.1	-22.5	75	21	2,500	50	0.0	0.0
B /8.2	6.5	0.88	11.74	101	41	33	25	1	149	26.4	-14.6	26	5	250	50	0.0	0.0
C+ /5.7	11.1	0.95	14.90	140	3	96	0	1	52	90.9	-18.3	63	11	1,000,000	0	0.0	0.0
C+ /5.7	11.1	0.94	14.74	553	3	96	0	1	52	89.5	-18.5	60	11	10,000	0	0.0	0.0
C+ /6.4	12.9	0.92	16.21	N/A	3	96	0	1	157	N/A	N/A	66	4	1,000	100	5.8	2.0
C+ /6.4	12.9	0.92	16.30	148	3	96	0	1	157	N/A	N/A	70	4	1,000,000	0	0.0	2.0
D- /1.0	10.4	0.97	13.67	69	2	97	0	1	78	95.0	-15.9	73	18	2,000	250	0.0	2.0
D- /1.0	10.4	0.98	14.03	32	2	97	0	1	78	96.7	-15.8	75	18	1,000,000	1,000	0.0	2.0
C+ /6.5	11.6	0.93	45.46	9	1	98	0	1	111	N/A	N/A	52	13	1,000,000	1,000	0.0	2.0
C /4.5	11.6	0.93	45.07	23	1	98	0	1	111	79.7	-15.1	48	13	2,000	250	0.0	2.0
C+ /6.0	12.0	1.11	24.26	27	4	95	0	1	49	95.4	-22.9	19	21	2,500	500	0.0	0.0
C /4.4	12.4	0.96	18.65	10	2	97	0	1	64	99.6	-26.0	57	21	250,000	5,000	0.0	0.0
C- /3.9	12.4	0.96	16.63	2	2	97	0	1	64	96.8	-26.2	51	21	2,500	500	0.0	0.0
B- /7.5	10.1	1.03	546.28	210	1	98	0	1	0	92.8	-15.4	40	2	0	0	0.0	0.0
C /5.0	13.3	0.79	13.29	30	0	99	0	1	38	39.9	-22.6	90	10	500,000	1,000	0.0	2.0
C /4.7	19.8	0.83	13.92	102	28	71	0	1	56	93.3	-25.7	97	5	5,000	500	0.0	2.0
B- /7.0	9.6	0.82	14.93	39	6	93	0	1	56	N/A	N/A	84	4	3,500	100	0.0	2.0

					PERFORMANCE							
							Total Return % through 3/31/15				Incl. in Returns	
										Annualized		
Fund Type	Fund Name	Ticker Symbol	Overall Investment Rating	Phone	Performance Rating/Pts	3 Mo	6 Mo	1Yr / Pct	3Yr / Pct	5Yr / Pct	Dividend Yield	Expense Ratio
GL	Christopher Weil & Co Global Div	CWGDX	C-	(888) 550-9266	D+ / 2.8	-1.20	-1.36	-0.99 /13	9.94 /39	--	3.38	1.76
GR	Clark Fork Tarkio	TARKX	B+	(866) 738-3629	A- / 9.1	5.91	17.97	13.05 /87	16.16 /85	--	0.00	1.00
GI	Clear River Fund Inv	CLRVX	D	(866) 777-7818	C / 4.3	1.33	2.73	5.20 /40	11.20 /47	9.47 /40	0.78	1.53
FO	ClearBridge International Value A	SBIEX	D-	(877) 534-4627	D- / 1.3	3.57	-2.68	-8.20 / 3	8.15 /28	5.23 /13	0.80	1.52
FO	ClearBridge International Value C	SBICX	D-	(877) 534-4627	D- / 1.5	3.35	-3.07	-8.87 / 3	7.35 /23	4.56 /10	0.29	2.26
FO	ClearBridge International Value I	SBIYX	D-	(877) 534-4627	D / 2.2	3.73	-2.39	-7.74 / 3	8.59 /30	5.55 /14	1.28	1.08
FO	ClearBridge International Value IS	LSIUX	D-	(877) 534-4627	D / 2.2	3.76	-2.39	-7.74 / 3	8.70 /31	5.66 /15	1.30	0.97
GI	Clearwater Core Equity	QWVPX	B+	(888) 228-0935	B- / 7.3	1.47	6.06	9.13 /70	15.02 /75	12.31 /63	1.52	0.90
FO	Clearwater International	QCVAX	C-	(888) 228-0935	C- / 3.0	4.58	1.07	-0.84 /13	8.87 /32	6.43 /20	2.32	1.00
SC	Clearwater Small Companies	QWVOX	A	(888) 228-0935	B+ / 8.8	4.88	13.61	10.06 /75	16.27 /85	15.61 /91	0.18	1.35
GR	Clipper	CFIMX	B+	(800) 279-0279	B- / 7.1	2.00	4.60	8.29 /65	14.97 /75	12.81 /66	0.41	0.75
IX	Cloud Capital Strat All Cap Inst	CCILX	D-	(877) 670-2227	B / 7.7	2.12	6.35	10.53 /76	15.44 /78	--	1.16	1.51
FO	Clough China A	CHNAX	C	(866) 759-5679	C / 5.4	4.29	12.31	15.88 /93	11.31 /48	6.77 /22	1.93	2.06
FO	Clough China C	CHNCX	C+	(866) 759-5679	C+ / 5.8	4.07	11.89	15.00 /92	10.44 /42	5.96 /17	1.78	2.87
FO	Clough China I	CHNIX	C+	(866) 759-5679	C+ / 6.5	4.33	12.48	16.20 /94	11.61 /50	7.09 /24	2.12	1.82
GR	CM Advisors	CMAFX	E	(800) 664-4888	E / 0.3	-5.77	-10.71	-19.00 / 1	1.22 / 5	3.79 / 8	0.27	1.30
AA	CM Advisors Small Cap Value Fd I	CMOVX	E	(800) 664-4888	E / 0.3	-8.80	-12.19	-20.81 / 1	3.07 / 8	--	0.00	2.56
AA	CMG Tactical Futures Strategy A	SCOTX	D-	(866) 264-9456	E- / 0.1	-3.25	-7.87	-12.66 / 2	-7.22 / 1	--	0.00	2.50
AA	CMG Tactical Futures Strategy I	SCOIX	D-	(866) 264-9456	E- / 0.2	-3.23	-7.80	-12.36 / 2	-6.94 / 1	--	0.00	2.20
IN	CNR Dividend and Income N	RIMHX	C+	(888) 889-0799	C / 5.0	0.17	4.98	8.44 /66	11.32 /48	11.65 /58	2.98	1.14
EM	CNR Emerging Markets N	RIMIX	B	(888) 889-0799	B- / 7.0	5.45	6.83	13.27 /87	13.26 /61	--	0.31	1.64
AA	CNR Multi-Asset N	CNIAX	C-	(888) 889-0799	D- / 1.1	1.28	2.52	2.21 /23	3.85 /10	3.51 / 7	1.01	1.87
AA	CNR Multi-Asset Servicing	CNIIX	C-	(888) 889-0799	D- / 1.2	1.33	2.65	2.47 /24	4.07 /10	3.77 / 8	1.27	1.63
GR	CNR Socially Responsible Eqty Inst	AHSRX	D+	(800) 445-1341	C / 4.6	-1.32	1.42	1.88 /21	12.03 /53	10.27 /47	0.89	0.96
GR	CNR Socially Responsible Eqty N	AHRAX	D+	(800) 445-1341	C / 4.5	-1.29	1.39	1.72 /21	11.78 /51	10.00 /44	0.64	1.46
GR	CNR US Core Equity N	CNRWX	U	(888) 889-0799	U /	2.51	5.96	13.40 /88	--	--	0.16	1.04
GR	CNR US Core Equity Servicing	CNRVX	U	(888) 889-0799	U /	2.56	6.07	13.74 /89	--	--	0.38	0.79
GR	CO 529 CollegeInvest Agg Gro Port		B-	(800) 662-7447	C+ / 6.7	2.15	5.43	9.21 /70	14.04 /67	12.39 /63	0.00	0.52
GI	CO 529 CollegeInvest Csv Growth		C	(800) 662-7447	D / 2.1	1.80	4.09	6.81 /54	5.68 /15	6.35 /19	0.00	0.52
GI	CO 529 CollegeInvest Growth Port		B	(800) 662-7447	C / 5.1	2.06	5.07	8.49 /66	11.29 /48	10.54 /49	0.00	0.52
GI	CO 529 CollegeInvest Mod Growth		B-	(800) 662-7447	C- / 3.6	1.98	4.66	7.79 /61	8.53 /30	8.52 /33	0.00	0.52
GR	CO 529 CollegeInvest Stock Idx Port		A	(800) 662-7447	B / 8.2	1.73	6.96	11.95 /82	15.98 /83	14.34 /81	0.00	0.52
GI	Cohen & Steers Dividend Value A	DVFAX	C+	(800) 330-7348	C+ / 6.8	0.43	5.05	11.41 /80	15.53 /79	12.55 /64	0.64	1.34
GI	Cohen & Steers Dividend Value C	DVFCX	B-	(800) 330-7348	B- / 7.1	0.26	4.73	10.70 /77	14.78 /73	11.83 /59	0.09	1.99
GI	Cohen & Steers Dividend Value I	DVFIX	B+	(800) 330-7348	B / 8.0	0.51	5.23	11.76 /82	15.94 /83	12.96 /68	0.96	1.09
UT	Cohen & Steers Glbl Infr A	CSUAX	C+	(800) 330-7348	C / 5.1	1.72	2.82	6.61 /52	13.30 /62	10.64 /50	1.25	1.50
UT	● Cohen & Steers Glbl Infr B	CSUBX	C+	(800) 330-7348	C / 5.4	1.55	2.45	5.85 /45	12.50 /56	9.89 /44	0.41	2.15
UT	Cohen & Steers Glbl Infr C	CSUCX	C+	(800) 330-7348	C / 5.4	1.51	2.46	5.83 /45	12.52 /56	9.91 /44	0.72	2.15
UT	Cohen & Steers Glbl Infr I	CSUIX	C+	(800) 330-7348	C+ / 6.0	1.77	2.93	6.80 /53	13.41 /63	10.88 /52	1.56	1.21
GL	Cohen & Steers Inst Glbl Realty Shs	GRSIX	C+	(800) 330-7348	B- / 7.0	4.60	12.28	15.08 /92	12.01 /53	9.94 /44	2.57	1.01
RE	Cohen & Steers Inst Realty Shrs	CSRIX	B-	(800) 330-7348	A / 9.5	5.16	20.50	24.85 /98	14.15 /68	15.20 /88	2.31	0.77
FO	Cohen & Steers Intl Realty A	IRFAX	D+	(800) 330-7348	C- / 3.9	3.95	5.27	7.57 /60	10.28 /41	6.96 /23	3.90	1.53
FO	Cohen & Steers Intl Realty C	IRFCX	D+	(800) 330-7348	C- / 4.1	3.81	4.94	6.90 /54	9.57 /37	6.27 /19	3.43	2.18
FO	Cohen & Steers Intl Realty I	IRFIX	C-	(800) 330-7348	C / 4.9	4.11	5.53	8.08 /63	10.68 /43	7.34 /25	4.40	1.27
EN	Cohen & Steers MLP & Energy Oppty	MLOIX	U	(800) 330-7348	U /	-2.21	-10.90	4.29 /34	--	--	3.47	N/A
★ RE	Cohen & Steers Realty Shares	CSRSX	B-	(800) 330-7348	A / 9.5	5.14	20.57	24.77 /98	13.93 /67	14.97 /87	2.11	0.97
RE	Cohen and Steers Global Rlty Shs A	CSFAX	C	(800) 330-7348	C+ / 5.9	4.51	11.97	14.56 /91	11.55 /49	9.52 /41	1.90	1.46
RE	● Cohen and Steers Global Rlty Shs B	CSFBX	C	(800) 330-7348	C+ / 6.1	4.34	11.60	13.80 /89	10.82 /44	8.81 /35	1.16	2.11
RE	Cohen and Steers Global Rlty Shs C	CSFCX	C	(800) 330-7348	C+ / 6.2	4.36	11.62	13.83 /89	10.83 /44	8.81 /35	1.43	2.11
RE	Cohen and Steers Global Rlty Shs I	CSSPX	C+	(800) 330-7348	C+ / 6.9	4.61	12.19	14.97 /92	11.92 /52	9.89 /44	2.32	1.18
GL	Cohen and Steers Real Assets A	RAPAX	D-	(800) 330-7348	E / 0.3	-0.64	-4.42	-5.15 / 5	-0.94 / 3	--	1.03	2.16
OT	Cohen and Steers Real Assets C	RAPCX	D-	(800) 330-7348	E / 0.3	-0.75	-4.70	-5.71 / 5	-1.55 / 3	--	0.59	2.81

● Denotes fund is closed to new investors
★ Denotes fund is included in Section II

99 Pct = Best
0 Pct = Worst

| RISK | 3 Year | | NET ASSETS | | ASSET | | | | Portfolio | BULL / BEAR | | FUND MANAGER | | MINIMUMS | | LOADS | |
Risk Rating/Pts	Standard Deviation	Beta	NAV As of 3/31/15	Total $(Mil)	Cash %	Stocks %	Bonds %	Other %	Turnover Ratio	Last Bull Market Return	Last Bear Market Return	Manager Quality Pct	Manager Tenure (Years)	Initial Purch. $	Additional Purch. $	Front End Load	Back End Load
B- /7.6	10.1	0.68	12.35	33	3	96	0	1	23	N/A	N/A	90	N/A	3,500	100	0.0	2.0
C /5.3	15.0	1.22	15.41	30	0	99	0	1	19	109.9	N/A	23	4	2,500	100	0.0	0.0
C /4.8	10.4	1.06	15.33	36	1	98	0	1	11	67.6	-17.0	9	6	5,000	500	0.0	2.0
C+ /5.7	13.1	0.95	10.43	120	8	91	0	1	33	49.4	-21.5	56	9	1,000	50	5.8	0.0
C+ /5.7	13.1	0.94	8.65	16	8	91	0	1	33	45.6	-21.7	45	9	1,000	50	0.0	0.0
C+ /5.7	13.1	0.94	10.29	45	8	91	0	1	33	51.4	-21.4	63	9	1,000,000	0	0.0	0.0
C+ /5.7	13.0	0.94	10.48	153	8	91	0	1	33	51.9	-21.3	65	9	0	0	0.0	0.0
B- /7.5	9.9	1.02	39.99	533	4	95	0	1	21	91.4	-19.5	48	5	1,000	1,000	0.0	0.0
B- /7.1	12.0	0.90	15.07	510	4	95	0	1	23	52.1	-23.4	71	6	1,000	1,000	0.0	0.0
C+ /6.6	11.9	0.86	21.29	337	1	98	0	1	60	97.8	-23.9	85	9	1,000	1,000	0.0	0.0
B- /7.3	10.0	1.00	100.77	1,115	4	95	0	1	38	82.6	-14.0	53	9	2,500	25	0.0	0.0
E- /0.0	9.4	0.95	8.66	26	0	0	0	100	90	91.8	N/A	69	4	1,000,000	0	0.0	0.0
C+ /6.3	13.1	0.61	24.06	32	9	90	0	1	232	55.7	-24.2	94	10	2,500	0	5.5	2.0
C+ /6.3	13.1	0.61	23.04	12	9	90	0	1	232	51.6	-24.4	92	10	2,500	0	0.0	2.0
C+ /6.3	13.0	0.61	24.56	42	9	90	0	1	232	57.1	-24.1	94	10	1,000,000	0	0.0	2.0
C /4.8	12.6	0.96	11.26	104	7	92	0	1	34	36.7	-16.8	1	12	2,500	0	0.0	1.0
C- /3.5	13.9	1.63	9.74	49	15	84	0	1	42	51.0	-22.2	1	4	2,500	0	0.0	1.0
B- /7.1	12.4	0.71	7.73	2	25	0	74	1	11	N/A	N/A	1	N/A	25,000	1,000	5.8	0.0
B- /7.1	12.4	0.73	7.80	13	25	0	74	1	11	N/A	N/A	1	N/A	100,000	1,000	0.0	0.0
B- /7.8	8.4	0.68	36.29	199	10	89	0	1	16	58.8	-8.6	74	12	0	0	0.0	0.0
B- /7.0	12.0	0.74	41.42	720	10	89	0	1	42	N/A	N/A	99	4	0	0	0.0	0.0
B /8.9	4.5	0.72	11.22	17	7	49	42	2	75	19.5	-12.0	18	5	0	0	0.0	0.0
B /8.9	4.4	0.72	11.23	5	7	49	42	2	75	20.6	-12.0	20	5	0	0	0.0	0.0
C /5.1	9.9	0.99	11.25	238	3	96	0	1	34	73.5	-19.0	21	11	1,000,000	0	0.0	0.0
C /5.1	9.9	0.99	11.23	27	3	96	0	1	34	72.0	-19.1	19	11	1,000	0	0.0	0.0
U /	N/A	N/A	13.53	105	3	96	0	1	60	N/A	N/A	N/A	3	0	0	0.0	0.0
U /	N/A	N/A	13.55	108	3	96	0	1	60	N/A	N/A	N/A	3	0	0	0.0	0.0
B- /7.0	9.9	1.02	21.34	419	0	99	0	1	0	86.6	-19.2	36	11	25	15	0.0	0.0
B+ /9.7	3.0	0.21	17.56	365	0	25	74	1	0	25.7	-1.6	86	11	25	15	0.0	0.0
B /8.4	7.3	0.75	20.32	454	0	74	24	2	0	64.5	-13.5	60	11	25	15	0.0	0.0
B+ /9.4	5.0	0.48	19.10	431	0	49	49	2	0	44.3	-7.8	77	11	25	15	0.0	0.0
B- /7.2	9.7	1.01	23.51	218	0	99	0	1	0	99.3	-17.8	63	11	25	15	0.0	0.0
C+ /6.1	10.0	1.02	16.17	23	1	98	0	1	83	93.9	-16.8	55	11	1,000	250	4.5	0.0
C+ /6.1	10.0	1.02	16.08	35	1	98	0	1	83	89.6	-17.0	45	11	1,000	250	0.0	0.0
C+ /6.1	10.0	1.02	16.19	192	1	98	0	1	83	96.2	-16.7	61	11	100,000	0	0.0	0.0
C+ /6.8	10.2	0.44	18.91	53	9	90	0	1	68	61.8	-8.1	96	11	1,000	250	4.5	0.0
C+ /6.8	10.2	0.45	19.06	N/A	9	90	0	1	68	58.0	-8.4	96	11	1,000	250	0.0	0.0
C+ /6.8	10.2	0.45	18.82	27	9	90	0	1	68	58.1	-8.4	96	11	1,000	250	0.0	0.0
C+ /6.8	10.2	0.45	18.97	182	9	90	0	1	68	62.5	-8.0	96	11	100,000	0	0.0	0.0
C /5.3	12.2	0.64	26.24	552	10	89	0	1	126	70.1	-22.1	94	9	3,000,000	10,000	0.0	0.0
C- /3.6	13.0	1.04	52.37	3,212	2	97	0	1	75	84.7	-17.7	60	10	3,000,000	10,000	0.0	0.0
C+ /5.6	13.7	0.82	11.57	125	18	81	0	1	93	57.0	-23.0	86	11	1,000	250	4.5	0.0
C+ /5.7	13.7	0.82	11.44	82	18	81	0	1	93	53.5	-23.2	82	11	1,000	250	0.0	0.0
C+ /5.7	13.6	0.81	11.65	702	18	81	0	1	93	58.8	-22.9	88	11	100,000	0	0.0	0.0
U /	N/A	N/A	10.95	59	0	0	0	100	26	N/A	N/A	N/A	2	100,000	0	0.0	0.0
C- /3.7	13.1	1.05	80.43	6,506	2	97	0	1	73	83.7	-17.7	56	10	10,000	500	0.0	0.0
C /5.3	12.1	0.87	52.39	75	11	88	0	1	119	67.8	-22.3	58	18	1,000	250	4.5	0.0
C /5.3	12.1	0.87	52.44	N/A	11	88	0	1	119	64.1	-22.5	48	18	1,000	250	0.0	0.0
C /5.3	12.1	0.87	51.97	83	11	88	0	1	119	64.2	-22.5	48	18	1,000	250	0.0	0.0
C /5.3	12.1	0.87	52.65	304	11	88	0	1	119	69.7	-22.1	63	18	100,000	0	0.0	0.0
C+ /6.9	9.8	1.30	9.36	24	13	56	30	1	145	N/A	N/A	1	3	1,000	250	4.5	0.0
C+ /6.9	9.8	0.69	9.31	16	13	56	30	1	145	N/A	N/A	1	3	1,000	250	0.0	0.0

					PERFORMANCE							
						Total Return % through 3/31/15					Incl. in Returns	
									Annualized		Dividend	Expense
Fund Type	Fund Name	Ticker Symbol	Overall Investment Rating	Phone	Perfor-mance Rating/Pts	3 Mo	6 Mo	1Yr / Pct	3Yr / Pct	5Yr / Pct	Yield	Ratio
	99 Pct = Best											
	0 Pct = Worst											
TC	Cohen and Steers Real Assets I	RAPIX	D-	(800) 330-7348	E / 0.4	-0.63	-4.32	-4.85 / 6	-0.60 / 4	--	1.40	1.86
GL	Cohen and Steers Real Assets R	RAPRX	D-	(800) 330-7348	E / 0.3	-0.74	-4.54	-5.37 / 5	-1.05 / 3	--	0.92	2.31
GL	Cohen and Steers Real Assets Z	RAPZX	D-	(800) 330-7348	E / 0.4	-0.53	-4.27	-4.86 / 6	-0.75 / 4	--	1.28	1.81
RE	Cohen and Steers Real Estate Sec A	CSEIX	B	(800) 330-7348	A+ / 9.7	5.61	22.21	27.35 /99	15.60 /80	15.76 /92	1.89	1.23
RE	● Cohen and Steers Real Estate Sec B	CSBIX	B	(800) 330-7348	A+ / 9.7	5.42	21.86	26.52 /99	14.84 /74	15.04 /87	1.44	1.87
RE	Cohen and Steers Real Estate Sec C	CSCIX	B	(800) 330-7348	A+ / 9.7	5.39	21.85	26.50 /99	14.86 /74	15.02 /87	1.59	1.87
RE	Cohen and Steers Real Estate Sec I	CSDIX	B	(800) 330-7348	A+ / 9.8	5.64	22.35	27.61 /99	15.91 /83	16.13 /94	2.15	0.96
IN	Coho Relative Value Equity Adv	COHOX	U		U /	0.57	7.12	12.45 /85	--	--	0.81	1.78
IN	Coho Relative Value Equity Inst	COHIX	U		U /	0.66	7.18	--	--	--	0.00	1.36
GR	Coldstream Dividend Growth Fund	CMDGX	B+	(888) 263-6443	B / 7.8	1.89	5.80	12.27 /84	15.39 /78	--	1.22	1.18
RE	Cole Real Estate Income Strategy		A+	(866) 907-2653	C+ / 6.5	4.64	8.68	12.57 /85	12.39 /55	--	5.41	N/A
IN	Collins Alternative Solutions Inst	CLLIX	U	(855) 552-5863	U /	0.37	3.38	3.76 /30	--	--	1.28	3.20
IN	Columbia Abs Rtn Currency & Inc R4	CARCX	B	(800) 345-6611	C+ / 5.7	17.51	16.92	19.32 /96	4.66 /12	3.22 / 6	0.00	1.50
IN	Columbia Abs Rtn Currency & Inc R5	COUIX	B	(800) 345-6611	C+ / 5.6	17.42	16.83	19.22 /96	4.52 /12	3.14 / 6	0.00	1.38
IN	Columbia Abs Rtn Currency & Inc Y	CABYX	B	(800) 345-6611	C+ / 5.7	17.44	16.97	19.49 /96	4.75 /12	3.27 / 7	0.00	1.33
MC	Columbia Acorn A	LACAX	D	(800) 345-6611	C- / 4.2	3.89	7.87	4.55 /35	11.58 /50	12.31 /63	0.00	1.08
MC	● Columbia Acorn B	LACBX	D	(800) 345-6611	C / 4.7	3.69	7.44	3.79 /30	10.86 /45	11.63 /58	0.00	1.74
MC	Columbia Acorn C	LIACX	D	(800) 345-6611	C / 4.6	3.70	7.45	3.80 /31	10.79 /44	11.49 /57	0.00	1.78
EM	Columbia Acorn Emg Mkts A	CAGAX	E+	(800) 345-6611	E+ / 0.8	-0.86	-3.21	-4.17 / 7	5.57 /15	--	0.59	1.08
EM	Columbia Acorn Emg Mkts C	CGMCX	E+	(800) 345-6611	E+ / 0.9	-1.03	-3.62	-4.94 / 6	4.79 /12	--	0.00	1.78
EM	Columbia Acorn Emg Mkts I	CATIX	D-	(800) 345-6611	D- / 1.2	-0.78	-3.09	-3.90 / 7	5.93 /16	--	0.97	0.70
EM	Columbia Acorn Emg Mkts R4	CAERX	D-	(800) 345-6611	D- / 1.2	-0.86	-3.12	-3.93 / 7	5.89 /16	--	0.91	0.79
EM	Columbia Acorn Emg Mkts R5	CANRX	D-	(800) 345-6611	D- / 1.2	-0.86	-3.18	-3.91 / 7	5.90 /16	--	0.93	0.75
EM	Columbia Acorn Emg Mkts Y	CPHRX	D-	(800) 345-6611	D- / 1.2	-0.87	-3.10	-3.92 / 7	5.97 /17	--	0.97	0.70
EM	Columbia Acorn Emg Mkts Z	CEFZX	D-	(800) 345-6611	D- / 1.2	-0.78	-3.13	-3.94 / 7	5.83 /16	--	0.85	0.79
FO	Columbia Acorn European A	CAEAX	D	(800) 345-6611	C- / 3.1	4.39	3.59	-5.17 / 5	11.11 /46	--	0.34	3.66
FO	Columbia Acorn European C	CAECX	D+	(800) 345-6611	C- / 3.5	4.24	3.22	-5.90 / 5	10.27 /41	--	0.00	4.50
FO	Columbia Acorn European I	CAFIX	C-	(800) 345-6611	C- / 4.2	4.47	3.77	-4.94 / 6	11.40 /48	--	0.66	3.29
FO	Columbia Acorn European R4	CLOFX	D+	(800) 345-6611	C- / 4.2	4.44	3.70	-4.90 / 6	11.39 /48	--	0.62	N/A
FO	Columbia Acorn European R5	CAEEX	C	(800) 345-6611	C- / 4.1	4.42	3.66	-5.01 / 5	11.36 /48	--	0.59	3.34
FO	Columbia Acorn European Z	CAEZX	C-	(800) 345-6611	C- / 4.2	4.44	3.72	-4.91 / 6	11.39 /48	--	0.62	3.33
SC	Columbia Acorn I	CANIX	D+	(800) 345-6611	C / 5.5	4.00	8.06	4.94 /38	11.98 /52	12.71 /66	0.00	0.70
FO	Columbia Acorn International A	LAIAX	D-	(800) 345-6611	D / 2.0	4.29	1.49	-1.60 /11	8.57 /30	8.30 /32	1.13	1.29
FO	● Columbia Acorn International B	LIABX	D-	(800) 345-6611	D+ / 2.3	4.09	1.07	-2.35 /10	7.76 /26	7.53 /27	0.45	2.02
FO	Columbia Acorn International C	LAICX	D-	(800) 345-6611	D+ / 2.3	4.08	1.10	-2.34 /10	7.76 /26	7.48 /26	0.46	2.03
FO	Columbia Acorn International I	CARIX	D	(800) 345-6611	C- / 3.1	4.38	1.68	-1.21 /12	8.97 /33	8.72 /35	1.56	0.86
FO	Columbia Acorn International R	CACRX	D	(800) 345-6611	D+ / 2.6	4.18	1.27	-2.01 /10	8.16 /28	7.97 /30	0.78	1.64
FO	Columbia Acorn International R4	CCIRX	C-	(800) 345-6611	C- / 3.0	4.33	1.57	-1.41 /12	8.83 /32	8.61 /34	1.38	1.02
FO	Columbia Acorn International R5	CAIRX	D	(800) 345-6611	C- / 3.0	4.36	1.66	-1.28 /12	8.92 /32	8.66 /34	1.52	0.91
FO	Columbia Acorn International Sel A	LAFAX	E-	(800) 345-6611	E+ / 0.7	1.41	-6.98	-8.44 / 3	5.75 /16	7.13 /24	0.37	1.29
FO	● Columbia Acorn International Sel B	LFFBX	E-	(800) 345-6611	E+ / 0.8	1.26	-7.34	-9.05 / 3	5.05 /13	6.45 /20	0.00	2.02
FO	Columbia Acorn International Sel C	LFFCX	E-	(800) 345-6611	E+ / 0.8	1.27	-7.35	-9.14 / 3	4.95 /13	6.30 /19	0.00	2.03
FO	Columbia Acorn International Sel I	CRSIX	E-	(800) 345-6611	D- / 1.1	1.48	-6.87	-8.15 / 3	6.11 /17	7.55 /27	0.78	0.86
FO	Columbia Acorn International Sel R4	CILRX	D	(800) 345-6611	D- / 1.1	1.51	-6.84	-8.17 / 3	6.04 /17	7.47 /26	0.66	1.02
FO	Columbia Acorn International Sel R5	CRIRX	D	(800) 345-6611	D- / 1.1	1.52	-6.85	-8.12 / 3	6.09 /17	7.50 /26	0.72	0.91
FO	Columbia Acorn International Sel Y	CSIRX	D	(800) 345-6611	D- / 1.1	1.52	-6.79	-8.09 / 3	6.12 /17	7.52 /27	0.79	0.86
FO	Columbia Acorn International Sel Z	ACFFX	E-	(800) 345-6611	D- / 1.1	1.48	-6.87	-8.18 / 3	6.06 /17	7.49 /26	0.71	0.94
FO	Columbia Acorn International Y	CCYIX	C-	(800) 345-6611	C- / 3.1	4.38	1.66	-1.24 /12	8.96 /33	8.68 /34	1.56	0.86
FO	Columbia Acorn International Z	ACINX	D	(800) 345-6611	C- / 3.0	4.36	1.65	-1.31 /12	8.90 /32	8.65 /34	1.49	0.94
SC	Columbia Acorn R4	CEARX	C+	(800) 345-6611	C / 5.4	3.97	8.01	4.81 /37	11.88 /52	12.62 /65	0.00	0.79
SC	Columbia Acorn R5	CRBRX	C+	(800) 345-6611	C / 5.4	3.96	8.03	4.89 /38	11.94 /52	12.66 /65	0.00	0.75
MC	Columbia Acorn Select A	LTFAX	E+	(800) 345-6611	C- / 4.2	2.76	5.62	5.40 /42	11.74 /51	9.06 /37	0.00	1.31

● Denotes fund is closed to new investors
* Denotes fund is included in Section II

www.thestreetratings.com

RISK	3 Year		NET ASSETS		ASSET					BULL / BEAR		FUND MANAGER		MINIMUMS		LOADS	
Risk Rating/Pts	Standard Deviation	Beta	NAV As of 3/31/15	Total $(Mil)	Cash %	Stocks %	Bonds %	Other %	Portfolio Turnover Ratio	Last Bull Market Return	Last Bear Market Return	Manager Quality Pct	Manager Tenure (Years)	Initial Purch. $	Additional Purch. $	Front End Load	Back End Load
C+ / 6.9	9.7	0.68	9.39	167	13	56	30	1	145	N/A	N/A	2	3	100,000	0	0.0	0.0
C+ / 6.8	9.8	1.31	9.38	1	13	56	30	1	145	N/A	N/A	1	3	100	0	0.0	0.0
C+ / 6.9	9.8	1.30	9.38	10	13	56	30	1	145	N/A	N/A	1	3	250	25	0.0	0.0
C- / 3.8	12.9	1.03	17.00	324	2	97	0	1	101	90.2	-17.2	77	11	1,000	250	4.5	0.0
C- / 3.7	12.8	1.03	15.98	N/A	2	97	0	1	101	86.0	-17.4	70	11	1,000	250	0.0	0.0
C- / 3.7	12.8	1.02	15.84	330	2	97	0	1	101	86.2	-17.4	71	11	1,000	250	0.0	0.0
C- / 3.8	12.8	1.03	17.65	659	2	97	0	1	101	92.3	-17.1	79	11	100,000	0	0.0	0.0
U /	N/A	N/A	12.27	152	3	96	0	1	17	N/A	N/A	N/A	2	100,000	100	0.0	2.0
U /	N/A	N/A	12.28	70	3	96	0	1	17	N/A	N/A	N/A	2	1,000,000	100	0.0	0.0
C+ / 6.5	10.0	1.02	14.52	69	10	89	0	1	38	85.2	-15.4	54	5	1,000	0	0.0	0.0
B+ / 9.9	2.3	0.01	18.08	110	0	0	0	100	0	N/A	N/A	99	4	0	0	0.0	0.0
U /	N/A	N/A	10.76	124	63	17	13	7	103	N/A	N/A	N/A	N/A	1,000,000	1,000	0.0	0.0
B / 8.1	10.0	-0.09	11.61	N/A	98	0	1	1	0	16.2	-3.2	95	9	0	0	0.0	0.0
B / 8.5	10.0	-0.09	11.66	N/A	98	0	1	1	0	15.8	-3.2	95	9	0	0	0.0	0.0
B / 8.1	10.0	-0.09	11.65	N/A	98	0	1	1	0	16.5	-3.2	95	9	0	0	0.0	0.0
C- / 4.1	11.7	1.03	31.48	2,477	3	96	0	1	18	76.4	-22.2	9	37	2,000	0	5.8	0.0
C- / 3.5	11.7	1.03	27.51	5	3	96	0	1	18	73.0	-22.5	7	37	2,000	0	0.0	0.0
C- / 3.4	11.7	1.03	26.88	749	3	96	0	1	18	72.2	-22.5	7	37	2,000	0	0.0	0.0
C+ / 6.0	12.1	0.82	12.61	150	6	93	0	1	36	48.9	N/A	93	4	2,000	0	5.8	0.0
C+ / 5.9	12.2	0.82	12.52	39	6	93	0	1	36	45.4	N/A	92	4	2,000	0	0.0	0.0
C+ / 5.9	12.2	0.82	12.65	N/A	6	93	0	1	36	51.0	N/A	94	4	0	0	0.0	0.0
C+ / 6.8	12.2	0.82	12.72	15	6	93	0	1	36	50.8	N/A	94	4	0	0	0.0	0.0
C+ / 6.8	12.2	0.82	12.71	20	6	93	0	1	36	50.8	N/A	94	4	0	0	0.0	0.0
C+ / 6.8	12.2	0.82	12.60	N/A	6	93	0	1	36	51.1	N/A	94	4	0	0	0.0	0.0
C+ / 5.9	12.2	0.82	12.64	226	6	93	0	1	36	50.4	N/A	94	4	2,000	0	0.0	0.0
C+ / 5.9	12.2	0.84	14.97	25	6	93	0	1	42	65.7	N/A	88	4	2,000	0	5.8	0.0
C+ / 5.8	12.1	0.83	14.76	6	6	93	0	1	42	61.7	N/A	85	4	2,000	0	0.0	0.0
C+ / 5.9	12.1	0.84	14.97	N/A	6	93	0	1	42	67.3	N/A	89	4	0	0	0.0	0.0
C / 5.4	12.2	0.84	15.04	1	6	93	0	1	42	67.2	N/A	89	4	0	0	0.0	0.0
C+ / 6.8	12.1	0.83	15.11	2	6	93	0	1	42	67.1	N/A	89	4	0	0	0.0	0.0
C+ / 5.9	12.2	0.84	14.98	9	6	93	0	1	42	67.2	N/A	89	4	2,000	0	0.0	0.0
C / 4.3	11.7	0.84	33.31	18	3	96	0	1	18	78.5	-22.1	48	37	0	0	0.0	0.0
C / 5.5	11.2	0.81	43.47	970	8	91	0	1	45	51.1	-21.5	76	16	2,000	0	5.8	0.0
C / 5.5	11.3	0.81	42.03	5	8	91	0	1	45	47.4	-21.7	68	16	2,000	0	0.0	0.0
C / 5.5	11.2	0.81	41.84	105	8	91	0	1	45	47.3	-21.7	68	16	2,000	0	0.0	0.0
C / 5.4	11.2	0.81	43.59	25	8	91	0	1	45	53.1	-21.3	79	16	0	0	0.0	0.0
C / 5.5	11.3	0.81	43.41	5	8	91	0	1	45	49.3	-21.5	72	16	0	0	0.0	0.0
B- / 7.1	11.2	0.81	43.84	475	8	91	0	1	45	52.5	-21.3	78	16	0	0	0.0	0.0
C / 5.4	11.2	0.81	43.53	412	8	91	0	1	45	52.9	-21.3	78	16	0	0	0.0	0.0
D+ / 2.6	10.7	0.61	22.35	50	11	88	0	1	72	35.0	-18.6	67	14	2,000	0	5.8	0.0
D+ / 2.4	10.7	0.61	20.95	N/A	11	88	0	1	72	32.1	-18.8	58	14	2,000	0	0.0	0.0
D+ / 2.3	10.7	0.61	20.80	8	11	88	0	1	72	31.5	-18.9	56	14	2,000	0	0.0	0.0
D+ / 2.5	10.7	0.61	22.62	N/A	11	88	0	1	72	36.7	-18.4	71	14	0	0	0.0	0.0
B- / 7.2	10.7	0.61	22.79	1	11	88	0	1	72	36.3	-18.5	71	14	0	0	0.0	0.0
B- / 7.2	10.7	0.61	22.77	3	11	88	0	1	72	36.5	-18.5	71	14	0	0	0.0	0.0
B- / 7.2	10.7	0.61	22.76	12	11	88	0	1	72	36.6	-18.5	72	14	0	0	0.0	0.0
D+ / 2.5	10.7	0.61	22.63	169	11	88	0	1	72	36.4	-18.5	71	14	2,000	0	0.0	0.0
B- / 7.1	11.3	0.81	43.86	241	8	91	0	1	45	53.0	-21.3	79	16	0	0	0.0	0.0
C / 5.4	11.3	0.81	43.55	5,681	8	91	0	1	45	52.8	-21.3	78	16	2,000	0	0.0	0.0
C+ / 6.5	11.7	0.84	33.80	245	3	96	0	1	18	78.0	-22.1	46	37	0	0	0.0	0.0
C+ / 6.5	11.7	0.84	33.84	254	3	96	0	1	18	78.3	-22.1	47	37	0	0	0.0	0.0
D / 1.9	11.1	0.93	21.61	256	1	98	0	1	20	77.6	-27.3	20	15	2,000	0	5.8	0.0

					PERFORMANCE							
						Total Return % through 3/31/15					Incl. in Returns	
			Overall		**Perfor-**				Annualized		Dividend	Expense
Fund		Ticker	**Investment**		**mance**						Yield	Ratio
Type	Fund Name	Symbol	**Rating**	Phone	**Rating/Pts**	3 Mo	6 Mo	1Yr / Pct	3Yr / Pct	5Yr / Pct		

99 Pct = Best
0 Pct = Worst

Fund Type	Fund Name	Ticker Symbol	Overall Investment Rating	Phone	Performance Rating/Pts	3 Mo	6 Mo	1Yr / Pct	3Yr / Pct	5Yr / Pct	Dividend Yield	Expense Ratio
MC	● Columbia Acorn Select B	LTFBX	E+	(800) 345-6611	C / 4.6	2.55	5.21	4.58 /36	10.91 /45	8.33 /32	0.00	2.05
MC	Columbia Acorn Select C	LTFCX	E+	(800) 345-6611	C / 4.6	2.60	5.31	4.71 /36	10.93 /45	8.26 /32	0.00	2.04
MC	Columbia Acorn Select I	CACIX	D-	(800) 345-6611	C / 5.4	2.90	5.87	5.82 /45	12.15 /53	9.49 /40	0.00	0.93
MC	Columbia Acorn Select R4	CSSRX	C+	(800) 345-6611	C / 5.3	2.81	5.78	5.66 /44	12.01 /53	9.36 /39	0.00	1.03
MC	Columbia Acorn Select R5	CSLRX	C+	(800) 345-6611	C / 5.4	2.85	5.86	5.78 /45	12.09 /53	9.40 /40	0.00	0.98
MC	Columbia Acorn Select Y	CSLYX	C+	(800) 345-6611	C / 5.4	2.89	5.89	5.84 /45	12.14 /53	9.43 /40	0.00	0.93
MC	Columbia Acorn Select Z	ACTWX	D-	(800) 345-6611	C / 5.4	2.83	5.81	5.72 /44	12.06 /53	9.38 /40	0.00	1.03
SC	Columbia Acorn USA A	LAUAX	D+	(800) 345-6611	C+/ 6.0	5.08	13.16	7.97 /63	13.63 /64	13.24 /70	0.00	1.33
SC	● Columbia Acorn USA B	LAUBX	D	(800) 345-6611	C+/ 6.2	4.75	12.50	6.85 /54	12.66 /57	12.40 /63	0.00	2.16
SC	Columbia Acorn USA C	LAUCX	D	(800) 345-6611	C+/ 6.4	4.88	12.77	7.23 /57	12.85 /58	12.44 /64	0.00	2.00
SC	Columbia Acorn USA I	CAUIX	C	(800) 345-6611	B- / 7.3	5.16	13.36	8.40 /66	14.08 /68	13.67 /75	0.00	0.93
SC	Columbia Acorn USA R4	CUSAX	B-	(800) 345-6611	B- / 7.2	5.14	13.28	8.24 /64	13.93 /67	13.56 /73	0.00	1.01
SC	Columbia Acorn USA R5	CYSRX	B-	(800) 345-6611	B- / 7.2	5.17	13.31	8.33 /65	13.97 /67	13.59 /74	0.00	0.98
SC	Columbia Acorn USA Y	CUSYX	B	(800) 345-6611	B- / 7.3	5.16	13.34	8.37 /65	14.02 /67	13.61 /74	0.00	0.93
SC	Columbia Acorn USA Z	AUSAX	C	(800) 345-6611	B- / 7.2	5.12	13.26	8.22 /64	13.90 /66	13.54 /73	0.00	1.07
SC	Columbia Acorn Y	CRBYX	C+	(800) 345-6611	C / 5.5	3.99	8.07	4.94 /38	11.98 /52	12.69 /66	0.00	0.70
MC	Columbia Acorn Z	ACRNX	D+	(800) 345-6611	C / 5.4	3.97	8.01	4.86 /38	11.90 /52	12.64 /65	0.00	0.79
GL	Columbia Act Ptf Mlti-Mgr Growth A	CSLGX	U	(800) 345-6611	U /	4.71	9.04	13.23 /87	--	--	0.00	1.19
GL	Columbia Act Ptf Mlti-Mgr Value A	CDEIX	U	(800) 345-6611	U /	-0.62	0.99	6.47 /50	--	--	2.13	1.20
IN	Columbia Act Ptf MMrg Alt Strat A	CPASX	U	(800) 345-6611	U /	2.86	4.97	7.35 /58	--	--	0.91	1.81
GL	Columbia Act Ptf MMrg SC Eqty A	CSCEX	U	(800) 345-6611	U /	4.60	13.03	4.55 /35	--	--	0.00	1.60
AA	Columbia Adaptive Risk Alloc A	CRAAX	U	(800) 345-6611	U /	1.09	3.24	6.19 /48	--	--	0.06	2.26
AA	Columbia Adaptive Risk Alloc C	CRACX	U	(800) 345-6611	U /	0.90	2.92	5.25 /40	--	--	0.00	3.01
AA	Columbia Adaptive Risk Alloc W	CRAWX	U	(800) 345-6611	U /	1.09	3.24	6.29 /49	--	--	0.06	2.26
FO	Columbia Asia Pacific ex-Japan A	CAJAX	D	(800) 345-6611	D+/ 2.7	5.22	5.13	8.83 /68	7.55 /24	5.63 /15	0.87	1.38
FO	Columbia Asia Pacific ex-Japan C	CAJCX	D	(800) 345-6611	C- / 3.0	4.97	4.73	7.99 /63	6.72 /20	4.78 /11	0.19	2.13
FO	Columbia Asia Pacific ex-Japan I	CAPIX	C-	(800) 345-6611	C- / 3.9	5.36	5.42	9.34 /71	8.00 /27	6.03 /17	1.39	0.92
FO	Columbia Asia Pacific ex-Japan R	CAJRX	D+	(800) 345-6611	C- / 3.3	5.11	4.96	8.52 /66	7.21 /22	5.29 /13	0.67	1.63
FO	Columbia Asia Pacific ex-Japan R5	TAPRX	C-	(800) 345-6611	C- / 3.8	5.28	5.37	9.22 /70	7.92 /26	5.99 /17	1.29	0.97
FO	Columbia Asia Pacific ex-Japan Z	CAJZX	D+	(800) 345-6611	C- / 3.7	5.29	5.30	9.07 /70	7.78 /26	5.84 /16	1.15	1.13
BA	Columbia Balanced A	CBLAX	B-	(800) 345-6611	C / 4.5	1.29	4.63	9.97 /74	11.84 /51	10.80 /51	0.68	1.09
BA	● Columbia Balanced B	CBLBX	B-	(800) 345-6611	C / 4.9	1.10	4.25	9.15 /70	10.99 /45	9.98 /44	0.08	1.84
BA	Columbia Balanced C	CBLCX	B-	(800) 345-6611	C / 4.9	1.07	4.22	9.14 /70	11.00 /45	9.97 /44	0.08	1.84
BA	● Columbia Balanced K	CLRFX	B	(800) 345-6611	C / 5.5	1.31	4.70	10.08 /75	11.95 /52	10.93 /52	0.83	0.98
BA	Columbia Balanced R	CBLRX	B	(800) 345-6611	C / 5.3	1.23	4.51	9.73 /73	11.57 /49	10.54 /49	0.48	1.34
BA	Columbia Balanced R4	CBDRX	B+	(800) 345-6611	C+/ 5.7	1.34	4.76	10.27 /75	12.13 /53	11.08 /53	0.95	0.84
BA	Columbia Balanced R5	CLREX	B+	(800) 345-6611	C+/ 5.7	1.35	4.79	10.37 /76	12.25 /54	11.17 /54	1.06	0.73
BA	Columbia Balanced Y	CBDYX	B+	(800) 345-6611	C+/ 5.8	1.38	4.84	10.46 /76	12.28 /54	11.17 /54	1.10	0.68
BA	Columbia Balanced Z	CBALX	B+	(800) 345-6611	C+/ 5.7	1.35	4.77	10.23 /75	12.12 /53	11.07 /53	0.96	0.84
BA	Columbia Capital Alloc Mod Aggr A	NBIAX	C-	(800) 345-6611	C- / 3.2	2.80	5.28	7.37 /58	9.59 /37	9.46 /40	1.63	1.20
BA	● Columbia Capital Alloc Mod Aggr B	NLBBX	C-	(800) 345-6611	C- / 3.6	2.50	4.88	6.52 /51	8.76 /31	8.62 /34	1.14	1.95
BA	Columbia Capital Alloc Mod Aggr C	NBICX	C-	(800) 345-6611	C- / 3.6	2.54	4.88	6.50 /51	8.77 /31	8.62 /34	1.12	1.95
GL	● Columbia Capital Alloc Mod Aggr K	CAMKX	C+	(800) 345-6611	C- / 4.2	2.76	5.36	7.43 /59	9.69 /37	9.52 /41	1.83	1.08
BA	Columbia Capital Alloc Mod Aggr R	CLBRX	C	(800) 345-6611	C- / 4.0	2.66	5.16	7.04 /55	9.30 /35	9.18 /38	1.49	1.45
GL	Columbia Capital Alloc Mod Aggr R4	CGBRX	C+	(800) 345-6611	C / 4.3	2.77	5.37	7.58 /60	9.81 /38	9.59 /41	1.93	0.95
GL	Columbia Capital Alloc Mod Aggr R5	CLHRX	C+	(800) 345-6611	C / 4.4	2.88	5.52	7.80 /61	9.92 /39	9.66 /42	2.04	0.83
BA	● Columbia Capital Alloc Mod Aggr T	CGGTX	C-	(800) 345-6611	C- / 3.2	2.72	5.28	7.35 /58	9.57 /37	9.42 /40	1.60	1.25
GL	Columbia Capital Alloc Mod Aggr Y	CPHNX	C+	(800) 345-6611	C / 4.3	2.85	5.57	7.85 /62	9.74 /38	9.55 /41	2.14	0.78
BA	Columbia Capital Alloc Mod Aggr Z	NBGPX	C	(800) 345-6611	C / 4.3	2.87	5.43	7.66 /60	9.88 /39	9.75 /43	1.95	0.95
GI	Columbia Capital Alloc Mod Consv A	NLGAX	C-	(800) 345-6611	D / 1.7	2.17	3.84	5.84 /45	6.87 /21	7.42 /26	1.89	1.09
GI	● Columbia Capital Alloc Mod Consv B	NLIBX	C-	(800) 345-6611	D / 2.1	2.00	3.47	5.08 /39	6.07 /17	6.63 /21	1.30	1.84
GI	Columbia Capital Alloc Mod Consv C	NIICX	C-	(800) 345-6611	D / 2.0	1.92	3.40	5.02 /39	6.04 /17	6.61 /21	1.31	1.84

Risk Rating/Pts	Standard Deviation	Beta	NAV As of 3/31/15	Total $(Mil)	Cash %	Stocks %	Bonds %	Other %	Portfolio Turnover Ratio	Last Bull Market Return	Last Bear Market Return	Manager Quality Pct	Manager Tenure (Years)	Initial Purch. $	Additional Purch. $	Front End Load	Back End Load
D- / 1.5	11.1	0.94	18.49	1	1	98	0	1	20	73.4	-27.5	14	15	2,000	0	0.0	0.0
D- / 1.4	11.1	0.93	18.15	46	1	98	0	1	20	73.2	-27.5	14	15	2,000	0	0.0	0.0
D / 2.0	11.1	0.93	23.03	12	1	98	0	1	20	79.8	-27.1	23	15	0	0	0.0	0.0
C+ / 6.6	11.1	0.93	23.39	1	1	98	0	1	20	79.2	-27.2	21	15	0	0	0.0	0.0
C+ / 6.6	11.1	0.93	23.43	11	1	98	0	1	20	79.5	-27.2	22	15	0	0	0.0	0.0
C+ / 6.6	11.1	0.93	23.52	4	1	98	0	1	20	79.7	-27.2	22	15	0	0	0.0	0.0
D / 2.0	11.1	0.93	22.91	294	1	98	0	1	20	79.4	-27.2	22	15	2,000	0	0.0	0.0
C- / 3.5	13.1	0.94	30.61	143	1	98	0	1	17	89.1	-24.8	46	19	2,000	0	5.8	0.0
D+ / 2.7	13.1	0.94	26.47	N/A	1	98	0	1	17	84.3	-25.0	33	19	2,000	0	0.0	0.0
D+ / 2.7	13.1	0.94	26.20	37	1	98	0	1	17	84.7	-25.1	36	19	2,000	0	0.0	0.0
C- / 3.8	13.1	0.94	32.80	N/A	1	98	0	1	17	91.8	-24.7	52	19		0	0.0	0.0
C+ / 6.1	13.1	0.94	33.33	11	1	98	0	1	17	90.9	-24.7	50	19	0	0	0.0	0.0
C+ / 6.1	13.1	0.94	33.35	39	1	98	0	1	17	91.2	-24.7	50	19	0	0	0.0	0.0
C+ / 6.1	13.1	0.94	33.44	37	1	98	0	1	17	91.4	-24.7	51	19	0	0	0.0	0.0
C- / 3.8	13.1	0.94	32.62	1,080	1	98	0	1	17	90.8	-24.7	49	19	2,000	0	0.0	0.0
C+ / 6.5	11.7	0.84	33.91	242	3	96	0	1	18	78.5	-22.1	47	37	0	0	0.0	0.0
C / 4.3	11.7	1.03	33.22	10,327	3	96	0	1	18	78.1	-22.1	11	37	2,000	0	0.0	0.0
U /	N/A	N/A	13.79	1,833	2	97	0	1	64	N/A	N/A	N/A	3	500	0	0.0	0.0
U /	N/A	N/A	12.04	1,760	3	95	0	2	99	N/A	N/A	N/A	3	500	0	0.0	0.0
U /	N/A	N/A	10.78	783	48	33	16	3	246	N/A	N/A	N/A	3	500	0	0.0	0.0
U /	N/A	N/A	13.42	691	3	96	0	1	73	N/A	N/A	N/A	N/A	500	0	0.0	0.0
U /	N/A	N/A	10.23	110	64	8	27	1	303	N/A	N/A	N/A	3	2,000	0	5.8	0.0
U /	N/A	N/A	10.05	34	64	8	27	1	303	N/A	N/A	N/A	3	2,000	0	0.0	0.0
U /	N/A	N/A	10.24	178	64	8	27	1	303	N/A	N/A	N/A	3	500	0	0.0	0.0
C+ / 6.0	12.7	0.82	14.71	1	4	95	0	1	39	48.1	-27.2	65	6	2,000	0	5.8	0.0
C+ / 6.0	12.7	0.82	14.56	N/A	4	95	0	1	39	44.3	-27.5	52	6	2,000	0	0.0	0.0
C+ / 6.0	12.8	0.83	14.75	N/A	4	95	0	1	39	50.3	-27.1	69	6	0	0	0.0	0.0
C+ / 6.0	12.7	0.82	14.61	N/A	4	95	0	1	39	46.6	-27.3	59	6	0	0	0.0	0.0
C+ / 6.0	12.7	0.82	14.76	1,499	4	95	0	1	39	49.9	-27.0	69	6	0	0	0.0	0.0
C+ / 6.0	12.7	0.82	14.73	1	4	95	0	1	39	49.2	-27.2	67	6	2,000	0	0.0	0.0
B / 8.4	6.5	1.13	36.75	1,650	11	57	31	1	109	66.5	-10.9	61	18	2,000	0	5.8	0.0
B / 8.4	6.5	1.13	36.66	11	11	57	31	1	109	62.3	-11.2	49	18	2,000	0	0.0	0.0
B / 8.4	6.5	1.13	36.67	471	11	57	31	1	109	62.4	-11.2	49	18	2,000	0	0.0	0.0
B / 8.4	6.5	1.13	36.69	24	11	57	31	1	109	67.1	-10.9	62	18	0	0	0.0	0.0
B / 8.4	6.5	1.13	36.76	26	11	57	31	1	109	65.3	-11.0	57	18	0	0	0.0	0.0
B / 8.6	6.5	1.13	36.99	34	11	57	31	1	109	68.0	-10.9	64	18	0	0	0.0	0.0
B / 8.4	6.5	1.13	36.70	102	11	57	31	1	109	68.6	-10.8	66	18	0	0	0.0	0.0
B / 8.6	6.5	1.13	37.00	33	11	57	31	1	109	68.7	-10.9	66	18	0	0	0.0	0.0
B / 8.4	6.5	1.13	36.68	428	11	57	31	1	109	68.0	-10.9	64	18	0	0	0.0	0.0
B- / 7.2	7.0	1.21	12.87	1,858	17	55	27	1	22	54.1	-13.4	22	N/A	2,000	0	5.8	0.0
B- / 7.2	7.1	1.22	12.73	57	17	55	27	1	22	50.2	-13.7	14	N/A	2,000	0	0.0	0.0
B- / 7.2	7.1	1.22	12.93	220	17	55	27	1	22	50.2	-13.7	15	N/A	2,000	0	0.0	0.0
B / 8.2	7.0	1.08	12.83	N/A	17	55	27	1	22	54.5	-13.4	66	6	0	0	0.0	0.0
B- / 7.2	7.1	1.22	12.85	4	17	55	27	1	22	52.9	-13.6	19	N/A	0	0	0.0	0.0
B / 8.2	7.1	1.09	12.95	1	17	55	27	1	22	55.1	-13.4	67	6	0	0	0.0	0.0
B / 8.2	7.1	1.08	12.95	1	17	55	27	1	22	55.4	-13.4	68	6	0	0	0.0	0.0
B- / 7.2	7.1	1.22	12.87	99	17	55	27	1	22	53.9	-13.5	20	4	2,000	0	5.8	0.0
B / 8.2	7.1	1.10	12.72	N/A	17	55	27	1	22	54.7	-13.4	65	6	0	0	0.0	0.0
B- / 7.2	7.1	1.21	12.85	131	17	55	27	1	22	55.4	-13.3	24	N/A	2,000	0	0.0	0.0
B / 8.2	4.2	0.38	11.15	550	14	29	56	1	30	35.0	-6.4	76	N/A	2,000	0	5.8	0.0
B / 8.2	4.2	0.39	11.10	16	14	29	56	1	30	31.7	-6.6	68	N/A	2,000	0	0.0	0.0
B / 8.2	4.2	0.38	11.01	92	14	29	56	1	30	31.5	-6.6	68	N/A	2,000	0	0.0	0.0

Fund Type	Fund Name	Ticker Symbol	Overall Investment Rating	Phone	Performance Rating/Pts	3 Mo	6 Mo	1Yr / Pct	3Yr / Pct	5Yr / Pct	Dividend Yield	Expense Ratio
AA	● Columbia Capital Alloc Mod Consv K	CCAKX	C+	(800) 345-6611	D+ / 2.6	2.23	3.94	6.02 /47	6.94 /21	7.47 /26	2.11	0.99
GI	Columbia Capital Alloc Mod Consv R	CLIRX	C-	(800) 345-6611	D+ / 2.4	2.11	3.70	5.57 /43	6.61 /19	7.18 /24	1.76	1.34
AA	Columbia Capital Alloc Mod Consv	CHWRX	C+	(800) 345-6611	D+ / 2.7	2.25	4.00	6.15 /48	7.08 /22	7.55 /27	2.24	0.84
AA	Columbia Capital Alloc Mod Consv	CLRRX	C+	(800) 345-6611	D+ / 2.7	2.27	4.04	6.24 /48	7.16 /22	7.60 /27	2.33	0.74
AA	Columbia Capital Alloc Mod Consv Y	CPDGX	C+	(800) 345-6611	D+ / 2.8	2.30	4.11	6.33 /49	7.23 /23	7.64 /27	2.46	0.69
GI	Columbia Capital Alloc Mod Consv Z	NIPAX	C-	(800) 345-6611	D+ / 2.7	2.26	4.01	6.17 /48	7.14 /22	7.71 /28	2.26	0.84
AA	Columbia Capital Allocation Aggr A	AXBAX	C	(800) 345-6611	C- / 4.1	2.84	5.50	7.75 /61	11.16 /47	10.36 /47	2.01	1.27
AA	● Columbia Capital Allocation Aggr B	AXPBX	C+	(800) 345-6611	C / 4.5	2.68	5.19	6.97 /55	10.34 /41	9.55 /41	1.41	2.02
AA	Columbia Capital Allocation Aggr C	RBGCX	C+	(800) 345-6611	C / 4.5	2.64	5.12	6.92 /54	10.35 /41	9.53 /41	1.44	2.02
AA	● Columbia Capital Allocation Aggr K	CAGRX	C+	(800) 345-6611	C / 5.1	2.83	5.59	7.85 /62	11.29 /48	10.49 /49	2.23	1.14
GR	Columbia Capital Allocation Aggr R	CPARX	C+	(800) 345-6611	C / 4.9	2.85	5.46	7.53 /59	10.95 /45	10.12 /46	1.90	1.52
GR	Columbia Capital Allocation Aggr R4	CPDAX	B	(800) 345-6611	C / 5.2	2.88	5.74	8.04 /63	11.38 /48	10.49 /49	2.39	1.02
GR	Columbia Capital Allocation Aggr R5	CPANX	B	(800) 345-6611	C / 5.3	2.96	5.78	8.18 /64	11.49 /49	10.55 /49	2.50	0.89
GI	Columbia Capital Allocation Aggr Y	CPDIX	B	(800) 345-6611	C / 5.3	2.97	5.74	8.15 /64	11.50 /49	10.56 /49	2.55	0.84
GR	Columbia Capital Allocation Aggr Z	CPAZX	C+	(800) 345-6611	C / 5.2	2.93	5.68	8.04 /63	11.47 /49	10.63 /50	2.37	1.02
AA	Columbia Capital Allocation Consv Y	CPDHX	C	(800) 345-6611	D / 1.8	1.77	3.16	5.09 /39	5.40 /15	5.79 /16	2.28	0.67
AA	Columbia Capital Allocation Csv A	ABDAX	D+	(800) 345-6611	D- / 1.2	1.75	3.06	4.90 /38	5.11 /13	5.61 /15	1.85	1.06
AA	● Columbia Capital Allocation Csv B	ABBDX	D+	(800) 345-6611	D- / 1.3	1.57	2.59	4.03 /32	4.29 /11	4.81 /11	1.22	1.81
AA	Columbia Capital Allocation Csv C	RPCCX	D+	(800) 345-6611	D- / 1.3	1.57	2.59	4.03 /32	4.32 /11	4.82 /11	1.22	1.81
AA	● Columbia Capital Allocation Csv K	CPVRX	C-	(800) 345-6611	D / 1.7	1.79	3.03	4.93 /38	5.22 /14	5.71 /15	2.04	0.97
AA	Columbia Capital Allocation Csv R	CBVRX	D+	(800) 345-6611	D- / 1.5	1.59	2.83	4.54 /35	4.84 /13	5.35 /13	1.70	1.31
AA	Columbia Capital Allocation Csv R4	CPCYX	C	(800) 345-6611	D / 1.7	1.73	3.00	4.96 /38	5.30 /14	5.73 /15	2.17	0.81
AA	Columbia Capital Allocation Csv R5	CPAOX	C	(800) 345-6611	D / 1.7	1.75	3.13	5.02 /39	5.36 /14	5.77 /15	2.22	0.72
AA	Columbia Capital Allocation Csv Z	CBVZX	C-	(800) 345-6611	D / 1.7	1.82	3.09	5.06 /39	5.34 /14	5.84 /16	2.18	0.81
AA	Columbia Capital Allocation Modt A	ABUAX	C-	(800) 345-6611	D+ / 2.6	2.59	4.57	6.65 /52	8.48 /30	8.49 /33	1.86	1.14
AA	● Columbia Capital Allocation Modt B	AURBX	C	(800) 345-6611	C- / 3.0	2.41	4.21	5.88 /45	7.67 /25	7.67 /28	1.27	1.89
AA	Columbia Capital Allocation Modt C	AMTCX	C	(800) 345-6611	C- / 3.0	2.41	4.30	5.90 /46	7.70 /25	7.70 /28	1.27	1.89
AA	● Columbia Capital Allocation Modt K	CBRRX	C	(800) 345-6611	C- / 3.5	2.61	4.62	6.74 /53	8.59 /30	8.59 /34	2.05	1.04
AA	Columbia Capital Allocation Modt R	CBMRX	C	(800) 345-6611	C- / 3.3	2.53	4.54	6.40 /50	8.21 /28	8.22 /31	1.74	1.39
BA	Columbia Capital Allocation Modt R4	CPCZX	C+	(800) 345-6611	C- / 3.6	2.67	4.75	6.99 /55	8.73 /31	8.64 /34	2.23	0.89
BA	Columbia Capital Allocation Modt R5	CPAMX	C+	(800) 345-6611	C- / 3.7	2.69	4.79	7.13 /56	8.82 /32	8.69 /34	2.35	0.79
BA	Columbia Capital Allocation Modt Y	CPDMX	C+	(800) 345-6611	C- / 3.7	2.70	4.83	7.10 /56	8.83 /32	8.69 /34	2.40	0.74
AA	Columbia Capital Allocation Modt Z	CBMZX	C	(800) 345-6611	C- / 3.7	2.65	4.79	7.01 /55	8.77 /31	8.74 /35	2.20	0.89
OT	Columbia Commodity Strategy A	CCSAX	E+	(800) 345-6611	E- / 0.0	-6.17	-20.00	-28.81 / 0	-13.97 / 0	--	0.00	1.33
OT	Columbia Commodity Strategy C	CCSCX	E+	(800) 345-6611	E- / 0.0	-6.30	-20.35	-29.34 / 0	-14.64 / 0	--	0.00	2.08
OT	Columbia Commodity Strategy I	CCIYX	E-	(800) 345-6611	E- / 0.1	-5.95	-19.87	-28.51 / 0	-13.64 / 1	--	0.00	0.95
OT	Columbia Commodity Strategy R	CCSRX	E+	(800) 345-6611	E- / 0.0	-6.07	-20.11	-28.94 / 0	-14.18 / 0	--	0.00	1.58
OT	Columbia Commodity Strategy R4	CCOMX	E+	(800) 345-6611	E- / 0.0	-5.95	-19.79	-28.62 / 0	-13.82 / 0	--	0.00	1.08
OT	Columbia Commodity Strategy R5	CADLX	E+	(800) 345-6611	E- / 0.0	-6.09	-19.87	-28.59 / 0	-13.87 / 0	--	0.00	1.00
OT	Columbia Commodity Strategy W	CCSWX	E-	(800) 345-6611	E- / 0.0	-6.03	-20.00	-28.72 / 0	-13.97 / 0	--	0.00	1.33
OT	Columbia Commodity Strategy Y	CCFYX	E+	(800) 345-6611	E- / 0.0	-6.08	-19.85	-28.58 / 0	-13.92 / 0	--	0.00	0.95
OT	Columbia Commodity Strategy Z	CCSZX	E+	(800) 345-6611	E- / 0.0	-5.98	-19.87	-28.55 / 0	-13.74 / 1	--	0.00	1.08
GR	Columbia Contrarian Core A	LCCAX	B+	(800) 345-6611	B / 7.6	1.16	5.81	12.86 /86	16.83 /89	14.65 /84	0.43	1.12
GR	● Columbia Contrarian Core B	LCCBX	B+	(800) 345-6611	B / 8.1	0.96	5.42	11.99 /82	15.94 /83	13.79 /76	0.00	1.87
GR	Columbia Contrarian Core C	LCCCX	B+	(800) 345-6611	B / 8.1	1.01	5.46	12.02 /83	15.96 /83	13.79 /76	0.00	1.87
GR	Columbia Contrarian Core I	CCCIX	A	(800) 345-6611	A- / 9.0	1.25	6.04	13.32 /88	17.33 /91	15.12 /88	0.85	0.68
GR	● Columbia Contrarian Core K	CCRFX	A	(800) 345-6611	B+ / 8.8	1.20	5.92	13.05 /87	16.99 /90	14.83 /85	0.58	0.98
GR	Columbia Contrarian Core R	CCCRX	A	(800) 345-6611	B+ / 8.5	1.11	5.69	12.58 /85	16.54 /87	14.39 /81	0.22	1.37
GI	Columbia Contrarian Core R4	CORRX	A+	(800) 345-6611	B+ / 8.9	1.23	5.99	13.12 /87	17.15 /91	14.96 /86	0.67	0.87
GI	Columbia Contrarian Core R5	COFRX	A+	(800) 345-6611	B+ / 8.9	1.23	6.04	13.28 /88	17.26 /91	15.02 /87	0.79	0.73
GR	● Columbia Contrarian Core T	SGIEX	B+	(800) 345-6611	B / 7.6	1.17	5.82	12.77 /86	16.76 /88	14.58 /83	0.39	1.12
GR	Columbia Contrarian Core W	CTRWX	A	(800) 345-6611	B+ / 8.7	1.16	5.81	12.81 /86	16.81 /89	14.66 /84	0.45	1.12

● Denotes fund is closed to new investors
* Denotes fund is included in Section II

www.thestreetratings.com

99 Pct = Best
0 Pct = Worst

RISK			NET ASSETS		ASSET				Portfolio Turnover Ratio	BULL / BEAR		FUND MANAGER		MINIMUMS		LOADS	
	3 Year		NAV							Last Bull Market Return	Last Bear Market Return	Manager Quality Pct	Manager Tenure (Years)	Initial Purch. $	Additional Purch. $	Front End Load	Back End Load
Risk Rating/Pts	Standard Deviation	Beta	As of 3/31/15	Total $(Mil)	Cash %	Stocks %	Bonds %	Other %									
B+ / 9.4	4.3	0.72	11.00	N/A	14	29	56	1	30	35.3	-6.4	57	6	0	0	0.0	0.0
B / 8.2	4.3	0.39	11.17	2	14	29	56	1	30	33.9	-6.5	73	N/A	0	0	0.0	0.0
B+ / 9.4	4.2	0.70	11.06	1	14	29	56	1	30	35.8	-6.4	61	6	0	0	0.0	0.0
B+ / 9.4	4.2	0.70	11.06	N/A	14	29	56	1	30	36.0	-6.4	62	6	0	0	0.0	0.0
B+ / 9.4	4.2	0.70	10.94	N/A	14	29	56	1	30	36.3	-6.4	63	6	0	0	0.0	0.0
B / 8.2	4.2	0.39	11.02	27	14	29	56	1	30	36.1	-6.2	78	N/A	2,000	0	0.0	0.0
B- / 7.5	8.6	1.46	13.05	598	16	70	13	1	29	65.0	-16.5	13	11	2,000	0	5.8	0.0
B- / 7.6	8.6	1.46	13.03	21	16	70	13	1	29	60.8	-16.7	9	11	2,000	0	0.0	0.0
B- / 7.6	8.6	1.46	12.81	67	16	70	13	1	29	60.9	-16.7	9	11	2,000	0	0.0	0.0
B- / 7.5	8.7	1.47	13.08	N/A	16	70	13	1	29	65.6	-16.3	13	11	0	0	0.0	0.0
B- / 7.5	8.6	0.87	12.98	1	16	70	13	1	29	63.6	-16.4	30	5	0	0	0.0	0.0
B / 8.2	8.6	0.87	12.85	1	16	70	13	1	29	66.1	-16.5	35	5	0	0	0.0	0.0
B / 8.2	8.6	0.87	12.85	N/A	16	70	13	1	29	66.4	-16.5	36	5	0	0	0.0	0.0
B / 8.2	8.6	0.87	12.84	N/A	16	70	13	1	29	66.5	-16.5	36	5	0	0	0.0	0.0
B- / 7.5	8.6	0.86	13.01	2	16	70	13	1	29	66.5	-16.3	36	5	2,000	0	0.0	0.0
B+ / 9.2	3.1	0.47	10.11	N/A	14	16	69	1	22	25.7	-4.2	71	5	0	0	0.0	0.0
B / 8.3	3.2	0.47	10.18	246	14	16	69	1	22	24.7	-4.2	68	11	2,000	0	4.8	0.0
B / 8.4	3.2	0.47	10.15	7	14	16	69	1	22	21.6	-4.6	57	11	2,000	0	0.0	0.0
B / 8.4	3.2	0.48	10.13	49	14	16	69	1	22	21.6	-4.5	57	11	2,000	0	0.0	0.0
B / 8.3	3.2	0.48	10.08	N/A	14	16	69	1	22	25.1	-4.2	68	11	0	0	0.0	0.0
B / 8.3	3.2	0.48	10.17	N/A	14	16	69	1	22	23.6	-4.4	64	5	0	0	0.0	0.0
B+ / 9.2	3.1	0.47	10.11	N/A	14	16	69	1	22	25.4	-4.2	71	5	0	0	0.0	0.0
B+ / 9.2	3.2	0.47	10.11	N/A	14	16	69	1	22	25.6	-4.2	71	5	0	0	0.0	0.0
B / 8.3	3.2	0.48	10.17	3	14	16	69	1	22	25.7	-4.1	70	5	2,000	0	0.0	0.0
B- / 7.9	5.7	0.97	11.77	1,457	14	44	41	1	23	45.5	-10.5	39	11	2,000	0	5.8	0.0
B / 8.0	5.7	0.98	11.72	46	14	44	41	1	23	41.8	-10.8	28	11	2,000	0	0.0	0.0
B / 8.0	5.7	0.97	11.70	185	14	44	41	1	23	41.9	-10.8	29	11	2,000	0	0.0	0.0
B- / 7.9	5.6	0.97	11.76	N/A	14	44	41	1	23	45.9	-10.4	41	11	0	0	0.0	0.0
B- / 7.9	5.7	0.97	11.75	2	14	44	41	1	23	44.2	-10.5	35	5	0	0	0.0	0.0
B+ / 9.1	5.7	0.97	11.66	N/A	14	44	41	1	23	46.4	-10.5	42	5	0	0	0.0	0.0
B+ / 9.1	5.7	0.97	11.66	N/A	14	44	41	1	23	46.8	-10.5	43	5	0	0	0.0	0.0
B+ / 9.1	5.7	0.98	11.65	N/A	14	44	41	1	23	46.8	-10.5	42	5	0	0	0.0	0.0
B- / 7.9	5.6	0.97	11.76	3	14	44	41	1	23	46.6	-10.3	43	5	2,000	0	0.0	0.0
C+ / 5.8	13.7	0.82	6.08	3	0	0	0	100	0	-26.0	N/A	0	4	2,000	0	5.8	0.0
C+ / 5.8	13.7	0.81	5.95	N/A	0	0	0	100	0	-27.9	N/A	0	4	2,000	0	0.0	0.0
D / 2.0	13.7	0.81	6.17	25	0	0	0	100	0	-25.1	N/A	0	4	0	0	0.0	0.0
C+ / 5.8	13.7	0.80	6.04	N/A	0	0	0	100	0	-26.6	N/A	0	4	0	0	0.0	0.0
C+ / 5.9	13.7	0.81	6.16	N/A	0	0	0	100	0	-25.7	N/A	0	4	0	0	0.0	0.0
C+ / 5.9	13.7	0.81	6.17	N/A	0	0	0	100	0	-25.8	N/A	0	4	100,000	0	0.0	0.0
D / 2.0	13.7	0.81	6.08	N/A	0	0	0	100	0	-26.0	N/A	0	4	500	0	0.0	0.0
C+ / 6.7	13.6	0.81	6.18	N/A	0	0	0	100	0	-26.0	N/A	0	4	0	0	0.0	0.0
C+ / 5.8	13.7	0.82	6.13	1	0	0	0	100	0	-25.5	N/A	0	4	2,000	0	0.0	0.0
C+ / 6.8	10.3	1.06	21.78	2,069	4	95	0	1	65	107.5	-18.2	63	10	2,000	0	5.8	0.0
C+ / 6.7	10.3	1.07	19.93	12	4	95	0	1	65	102.3	-18.5	50	10	2,000	0	0.0	0.0
C+ / 6.7	10.3	1.06	19.97	342	4	95	0	1	65	102.3	-18.5	51	10	2,000	0	0.0	0.0
C+ / 6.7	10.3	1.07	21.90	551	4	95	0	1	65	110.6	-18.1	68	10	0	0	0.0	0.0
C+ / 6.8	10.3	1.06	21.91	N/A	4	95	0	1	65	108.4	-18.1	65	10	0	0	0.0	0.0
C+ / 6.8	10.3	1.06	21.80	41	4	95	0	1	65	105.8	-18.3	59	10	0	0	0.0	0.0
B- / 7.3	10.3	1.06	22.24	212	4	95	0	1	65	109.4	-18.1	66	10	0	0	0.0	0.0
B- / 7.3	10.3	1.06	22.22	291	4	95	0	1	65	110.0	-18.1	68	10	0	0	0.0	0.0
C+ / 6.8	10.3	1.06	21.59	151	4	95	0	1	65	107.1	-18.2	62	10	2,000	0	5.8	0.0
C+ / 6.8	10.3	1.06	21.78	117	4	95	0	1	65	107.4	-18.1	62	10	500	0	0.0	0.0

					PERFORMANCE							
						Total Return % through 3/31/15					Incl. in Returns	
									Annualized		Dividend	Expense
Fund Type	Fund Name	Ticker Symbol	Overall Investment Rating	Phone	Performance Rating/Pts	3 Mo	6 Mo	1Yr / Pct	3Yr / Pct	5Yr / Pct	Yield	Ratio
GI	Columbia Contrarian Core Y	COFYX	A+	(800) 345-6611	A- / 9.0	1.28	6.09	13.38 /88	17.32 /91	15.06 /87	0.84	0.68
GR	Columbia Contrarian Core Z	SMGIX	A	(800) 345-6611	B+ / 8.8	1.20	5.94	13.12 /87	17.12 /90	14.94 /86	0.69	0.87
CV	Columbia Convertible Securities A	PACIX	C+	(800) 345-6611	C / 4.7	3.54	3.90	7.50 /59	12.46 /56	11.25 /55	2.21	1.35
CV	● Columbia Convertible Securities B	NCVBX	C+	(800) 345-6611	C / 5.1	3.31	3.53	6.66 /52	11.63 /50	10.41 /48	1.65	2.10
CV	Columbia Convertible Securities C	PHIKX	C+	(800) 345-6611	C / 5.1	3.36	3.53	6.72 /53	11.63 /50	10.42 /48	1.62	2.10
CV	Columbia Convertible Securities I	CCSIX	B-	(800) 345-6611	C+ / 6.0	3.64	4.11	7.94 /62	12.94 /59	11.65 /58	2.75	0.85
CV	Columbia Convertible Securities R	CVBRX	B-	(800) 345-6611	C / 5.5	3.48	3.77	7.24 /57	12.19 /54	10.98 /53	2.10	1.60
CV	Columbia Convertible Securities R4	COVRX	B-	(800) 345-6611	C+ / 5.9	3.63	4.05	7.81 /61	12.72 /58	11.40 /56	2.57	1.10
CV	Columbia Convertible Securities R5	COCRX	B-	(800) 345-6611	C+ / 5.9	3.60	4.11	7.90 /62	12.81 /58	11.45 /58	2.69	0.90
CV	Columbia Convertible Securities W	CVBWX	B	(800) 345-6611	C+ / 5.7	3.51	3.88	7.46 /59	12.44 /56	11.24 /55	2.40	1.35
CV	Columbia Convertible Securities Y	CSFYX	B-	(800) 345-6611	C+ / 5.8	3.70	4.15	7.75 /61	12.55 /56	11.30 /55	2.52	N/A
CV	Columbia Convertible Securities Z	NCIAX	B-	(800) 345-6611	C+ / 5.9	3.60	4.02	7.76 /61	12.75 /58	11.53 /57	2.58	1.10
IN	Columbia Diversified Equity Inc A	INDZX	C+	(800) 345-6611	C / 5.4	-0.75	3.28	8.01 /63	14.14 /68	11.68 /58	1.07	1.08
IN	● Columbia Diversified Equity Inc B	IDEBX	C+	(800) 345-6611	C+ / 5.8	-1.00	2.82	7.19 /57	13.27 /62	10.83 /51	0.41	1.83
IN	Columbia Diversified Equity Inc C	ADECX	C+	(800) 345-6611	C+ / 5.8	-0.93	2.90	7.23 /57	13.29 /62	10.84 /51	0.42	1.83
IN	Columbia Diversified Equity Inc I	ADIIX	C+	(800) 345-6611	C+ / 6.7	-0.72	3.44	8.42 /66	14.61 /72	12.17 /62	1.57	0.64
IN	● Columbia Diversified Equity Inc K	IDQYX	C+	(800) 345-6611	C+ / 6.5	-0.73	3.34	8.14 /64	14.28 /69	11.84 /59	1.25	0.94
IN	Columbia Diversified Equity Inc R	RDEIX	C+	(800) 345-6611	C+ / 6.2	-0.82	3.09	7.70 /60	13.83 /66	11.41 /56	0.90	1.33
IN	Columbia Diversified Equity Inc R4	RDERX	C+	(800) 345-6611	C+ / 6.5	-0.69	3.41	8.28 /65	14.36 /70	11.75 /59	1.37	0.83
IN	Columbia Diversified Equity Inc R5	RSEDX	C+	(800) 345-6611	C+ / 6.6	-0.67	3.47	8.40 /66	14.54 /71	12.13 /61	1.49	0.69
IN	Columbia Diversified Equity Inc W	CDEWX	C+	(800) 345-6611	C+ / 6.3	-0.83	3.19	7.91 /62	14.11 /68	11.69 /58	1.13	1.08
IN	Columbia Diversified Equity Inc Y	CDEYX	B-	(800) 345-6611	C+ / 6.7	-0.72	3.46	8.47 /66	14.55 /71	11.92 /60	1.53	0.64
IN	Columbia Diversified Equity Inc Z	CDVZX	C+	(800) 345-6611	C+ / 6.6	-0.69	3.41	8.28 /65	14.42 /70	11.94 /60	1.37	0.83
GI	Columbia Dividend Income A	LBSAX	C+	(800) 345-6611	C / 5.4	-0.44	4.03	9.79 /73	13.76 /65	12.90 /67	1.87	1.02
GI	● Columbia Dividend Income B	LBSBX	B-	(800) 345-6611	C+ / 5.8	-0.59	3.68	8.97 /69	12.91 /59	12.06 /61	1.29	1.77
GI	Columbia Dividend Income C	LBSCX	B-	(800) 345-6611	C+ / 5.8	-0.59	3.68	8.98 /69	12.92 /59	12.07 /61	1.29	1.77
IN	Columbia Dividend Income I	CDVIX	B-	(800) 345-6611	C+ / 6.7	-0.33	4.31	10.25 /75	14.24 /69	13.37 /72	2.39	0.59
GI	Columbia Dividend Income R	CDIRX	B-	(800) 345-6611	C+ / 6.2	-0.50	3.90	9.51 /72	13.47 /63	12.63 /65	1.74	1.27
IN	Columbia Dividend Income R4	CVIRX	B-	(800) 345-6611	C+ / 6.6	-0.32	4.21	10.09 /75	14.06 /68	13.20 /70	2.19	0.77
IN	Columbia Dividend Income R5	CDDRX	B-	(800) 345-6611	C+ / 6.6	-0.34	4.23	10.19 /75	14.16 /68	13.27 /71	2.32	0.64
GI	● Columbia Dividend Income T	GEQAX	C+	(800) 345-6611	C / 5.4	-0.45	4.07	9.74 /73	13.73 /65	12.86 /67	1.84	1.02
IN	Columbia Dividend Income W	CDVWX	B-	(800) 345-6611	C+ / 6.3	-0.44	4.03	9.74 /73	13.75 /65	12.92 /67	1.98	1.02
IN	Columbia Dividend Income Y	CDDYX	B-	(800) 345-6611	C+ / 6.7	-0.28	4.31	10.29 /75	14.22 /69	13.30 /71	2.36	0.59
GI	Columbia Dividend Income Z	GSFTX	B-	(800) 345-6611	C+ / 6.5	-0.38	4.16	10.05 /75	14.03 /67	13.19 /70	2.22	0.77
IN	Columbia Dividend Opportunity A	INUTX	D+	(800) 345-6611	C- / 4.2	-1.01	0.46	6.43 /50	12.47 /56	13.12 /69	2.62	1.01
IN	● Columbia Dividend Opportunity B	IUTBX	C-	(800) 345-6611	C / 4.6	-1.21	0.06	5.56 /43	11.61 /50	12.28 /62	2.04	1.76
IN	Columbia Dividend Opportunity C	ACUIX	C-	(800) 345-6611	C / 4.6	-1.22	0.07	5.61 /43	11.62 /50	12.26 /62	2.06	1.76
IN	Columbia Dividend Opportunity I	RSOIX	C-	(800) 345-6611	C / 5.5	-0.91	0.75	6.83 /54	12.92 /59	13.62 /74	3.14	0.60
IN	● Columbia Dividend Opportunity K	RSORX	C-	(800) 345-6611	C / 5.2	-0.99	0.50	6.51 /51	12.60 /57	13.30 /71	2.85	0.90
IN	Columbia Dividend Opportunity R	RSOOX	C-	(800) 345-6611	C / 4.9	-1.18	0.31	6.05 /47	12.14 /53	12.84 /67	2.52	1.26
IN	Columbia Dividend Opportunity R4	CDORX	B-	(800) 345-6611	C / 5.3	-1.04	0.57	6.60 /52	12.67 /57	13.24 /70	2.97	0.76
IN	Columbia Dividend Opportunity R5	RSDFX	C-	(800) 345-6611	C / 5.4	-0.93	0.63	6.77 /53	12.87 /59	13.55 /73	3.10	0.65
IN	Columbia Dividend Opportunity W	CDOWX	C-	(800) 345-6611	C / 5.1	-1.01	0.45	6.42 /50	12.43 /55	13.11 /69	2.76	1.01
IN	Columbia Dividend Opportunity Y	CDOYX	B-	(800) 345-6611	C / 5.4	-0.90	0.75	6.87 /54	12.82 /58	13.33 /71	3.11	0.60
IN	Columbia Dividend Opportunity Z	CDOZX	C-	(800) 345-6611	C / 5.3	-0.95	0.58	6.67 /52	12.75 /58	13.37 /72	3.00	0.76
EM	Columbia Emerging Markets A	EEMAX	E+	(800) 345-6611	E+ / 0.7	4.46	0.49	1.48 /20	2.83 / 8	3.14 / 6	0.00	1.67
EM	● Columbia Emerging Markets B	CEBMX	D-	(800) 345-6611	E+ / 0.8	4.31	0.10	0.71 /18	2.07 / 6	2.36 / 5	0.00	2.42
EM	Columbia Emerging Markets C	EEMCX	E+	(800) 345-6611	E+ / 0.8	4.19	0.10	0.61 /17	2.05 / 6	2.34 / 5	0.00	2.42
EM	Columbia Emerging Markets I	CEHIX	E+	(800) 345-6611	D- / 1.0	4.54	0.71	1.90 /21	3.31 / 8	3.55 / 7	0.49	1.18
EM	● Columbia Emerging Markets K	CEKMX	D-	(800) 345-6611	E+ / 0.9	4.55	0.60	1.59 /20	3.04 / 8	3.36 / 7	0.20	1.48
EM	Columbia Emerging Markets R	CEMRX	E+	(800) 345-6611	E+ / 0.9	4.38	0.39	1.19 /19	2.58 / 7	2.90 / 6	0.00	1.92
EM	Columbia Emerging Markets R4	CEMHX	D-	(800) 345-6611	D- / 1.0	4.51	0.57	1.64 /21	3.09 / 8	3.39 / 7	0.26	1.42

99 Pct = Best
0 Pct = Worst

● Denotes fund is closed to new investors
* Denotes fund is included in Section II

www.thestreetratings.com

RISK			NET ASSETS		ASSET					BULL / BEAR		FUND MANAGER		MINIMUMS		LOADS	
	3 Year		NAV						Portfolio	Last Bull	Last Bear	Manager	Manager	Initial	Additional	Front	Back
Risk	Standard		As of	Total	Cash	Stocks	Bonds	Other	Turnover	Market	Market	Quality	Tenure	Purch.	Purch.	End	End
Rating/Pts	Deviation	Beta	3/31/15	$(Mil)	%	%	%	%	Ratio	Return	Return	Pct	(Years)	$	$	Load	Load
B- / 7.3	10.3	1.07	22.23	25	4	95	0	1	65	110.3	-18.1	68	10	0	0	0.0	0.0
C+ / 6.7	10.3	1.06	21.91	2,050	4	95	0	1	65	109.3	-18.1	66	10	0	0	0.0	0.0
B- / 7.4	7.6	1.01	19.36	402	5	14	0	81	76	66.9	-16.7	48	9	2,000	0	5.8	0.0
B- / 7.4	7.6	1.02	19.00	1	5	14	0	81	76	62.7	-17.0	37	9	2,000	0	0.0	0.0
B- / 7.4	7.6	1.01	19.32	56	5	14	0	81	76	62.7	-17.0	37	9	2,000	0	0.0	0.0
B- / 7.4	7.6	1.01	19.40	95	5	14	0	81	76	69.2	-16.6	55	9	0	0	0.0	0.0
B- / 7.7	7.6	1.02	19.35	2	5	14	0	81	76	65.5	-16.8	44	9	0	0	0.0	0.0
B- / 7.8	7.6	1.02	19.52	3	5	14	0	81	76	67.9	-16.7	51	9	0	0	0.0	0.0
B- / 7.8	7.6	1.02	19.50	41	5	14	0	81	76	68.4	-16.7	52	9	0	0	0.0	0.0
B- / 7.7	7.6	1.02	19.31	N/A	5	14	0	81	76	66.8	-16.7	48	9	500	0	0.0	0.0
B- / 7.4	7.6	1.01	19.63	N/A	5	14	0	81	76	67.2	-16.7	49	9	0	0	0.0	0.0
B- / 7.4	7.7	1.02	19.38	806	5	14	0	81	76	68.4	-16.7	51	9	2,000	0	0.0	0.0
C+ / 6.7	9.8	1.01	13.83	2,407	2	96	0	2	74	88.0	-21.6	40	2	2,000	0	5.8	0.0
C+ / 6.8	9.8	1.00	13.88	47	2	96	0	2	74	83.3	-21.8	30	2	2,000	0	0.0	0.0
C+ / 6.7	9.9	1.01	13.81	71	2	96	0	2	74	83.4	-21.9	30	2	2,000	0	0.0	0.0
C+ / 6.7	9.9	1.01	13.80	N/A	2	96	0	2	74	90.9	-21.4	46	2	0	0	0.0	0.0
C+ / 6.7	9.8	1.00	13.84	62	2	96	0	2	74	89.0	-21.5	42	2	0	0	0.0	0.0
C+ / 6.7	9.8	1.01	13.76	7	2	96	0	2	74	86.4	-21.6	36	2	0	0	0.0	0.0
C+ / 6.7	9.8	1.01	13.82	10	2	96	0	2	74	89.0	-21.7	43	2	0	0	0.0	0.0
C+ / 6.7	9.8	1.00	13.83	30	2	96	0	2	74	90.5	-21.4	46	2	0	0	0.0	0.0
C+ / 6.8	9.9	1.01	13.85	N/A	2	96	0	2	74	88.0	-21.5	39	2	500	0	0.0	0.0
B- / 7.5	9.8	1.01	13.94	21	2	96	0	2	74	90.1	-21.6	45	2	0	0	0.0	0.0
C+ / 6.7	9.8	1.01	13.81	20	2	96	0	2	74	89.7	-21.5	44	2	2,000	0	0.0	0.0
B- / 7.2	9.0	0.91	18.75	2,595	2	97	0	1	19	83.2	-12.6	57	14	2,000	0	5.8	0.0
B- / 7.2	9.0	0.91	18.27	9	2	97	0	1	19	78.6	-12.8	45	14	2,000	0	0.0	0.0
B- / 7.2	9.0	0.91	18.26	659	2	97	0	1	19	78.5	-12.9	46	14	2,000	0	0.0	0.0
B- / 7.2	8.9	0.91	18.78	213	2	97	0	1	19	85.8	-12.4	64	14	0	0	0.0	0.0
B- / 7.2	9.0	0.91	18.76	89	2	97	0	1	19	81.6	-12.7	52	14	0	0	0.0	0.0
B- / 7.8	9.0	0.91	19.02	186	2	97	0	1	19	84.7	-12.4	61	14	0	0	0.0	0.0
B- / 7.8	9.0	0.91	19.00	292	2	97	0	1	19	85.3	-12.4	62	14	0	0	0.0	0.0
B- / 7.2	9.0	0.91	18.76	82	2	97	0	1	19	82.8	-12.5	56	14	2,000	0	5.8	0.0
B- / 7.2	8.9	0.91	18.74	N/A	2	97	0	1	19	83.1	-12.6	58	14	500	0	0.0	0.0
B- / 7.9	9.0	0.91	19.02	136	2	97	0	1	19	85.4	-12.4	63	14	0	0	0.0	0.0
B- / 7.2	9.0	0.91	18.76	4,818	2	97	0	1	19	84.7	-12.4	60	14	2,000	0	0.0	0.0
C / 5.3	8.8	0.87	9.31	3,771	6	93	0	1	73	78.2	-14.3	49	11	2,000	0	5.8	0.0
C / 5.3	8.7	0.87	9.23	28	6	93	0	1	73	73.9	-14.6	38	11	2,000	0	0.0	0.0
C / 5.3	8.8	0.87	9.14	466	6	93	0	1	73	73.9	-14.6	36	11	2,000	0	0.0	0.0
C / 5.3	8.8	0.87	9.35	172	6	93	0	1	73	80.8	-14.1	53	11	0	0	0.0	0.0
C / 5.3	8.8	0.87	9.35	4	6	93	0	1	73	79.1	-14.2	50	11	0	0	0.0	0.0
C / 5.3	8.8	0.87	9.30	37	6	93	0	1	73	76.9	-14.3	44	11	0	0	0.0	0.0
B- / 7.8	8.8	0.87	9.44	113	6	93	0	1	73	79.4	-14.3	51	11	0	0	0.0	0.0
C / 5.3	8.8	0.87	9.35	256	6	93	0	1	73	80.8	-14.2	54	11	0	0	0.0	0.0
C / 5.3	8.8	0.87	9.32	N/A	6	93	0	1	73	78.3	-14.3	48	11	500	0	0.0	0.0
B- / 7.8	8.8	0.87	9.46	55	6	93	0	1	73	79.8	-14.3	53	11	0	0	0.0	0.0
C / 5.3	8.8	0.87	9.34	977	6	93	0	1	73	80.0	-14.2	52	11	2,000	0	0.0	0.0
C / 5.2	13.1	0.91	10.31	286	2	97	0	1	80	29.6	-25.8	85	7	2,000	0	5.8	0.0
C+ / 6.5	13.1	0.91	9.93	4	2	97	0	1	80	26.4	-26.0	80	7	2,000	0	0.0	0.0
C / 5.2	13.1	0.91	9.94	25	2	97	0	1	80	26.2	-26.0	80	7	2,000	0	0.0	0.0
C / 5.2	13.1	0.91	10.37	149	2	97	0	1	80	31.7	-25.7	87	7	0	0	0.0	0.0
C+ / 6.5	13.1	0.91	10.33	N/A	2	97	0	1	80	30.5	-25.7	86	7	0	0	0.0	0.0
C / 5.2	13.1	0.91	10.24	7	2	97	0	1	80	28.7	-25.8	84	7	0	0	0.0	0.0
C+ / 6.5	13.1	0.91	10.42	N/A	2	97	0	1	80	30.7	-25.7	86	7	0	0	0.0	0.0

Fund Type	Fund Name	Ticker Symbol	Overall Investment Rating	Phone	Performance Rating/Pts	3 Mo	6 Mo	1Yr / Pct	3Yr / Pct	5Yr / Pct	Dividend Yield	Expense Ratio
EM	Columbia Emerging Markets R5	CEKRX	D-	(800) 345-6611	D- / 1.0	4.53	0.67	1.85 /21	3.22 / 8	3.47 / 7	0.45	1.23
EM	Columbia Emerging Markets W	CEMWX	E+	(800) 345-6611	E+ / 0.9	4.46	0.49	1.38 /20	2.82 / 8	3.12 / 6	0.00	1.67
EM	Columbia Emerging Markets Y	CEKYX	D-	(800) 345-6611	D- / 1.0	4.62	0.70	1.88 /21	3.29 / 8	3.51 / 7	0.48	1.18
EM	Columbia Emerging Markets Z	UMEMX	E+	(800) 345-6611	D- / 1.0	4.55	0.57	1.65 /21	3.09 / 8	3.39 / 7	0.26	1.42
FO	Columbia European Equity A	AXEAX	D-	(800) 345-6611	D+ / 2.6	5.11	3.47	-4.96 / 6	10.03 /39	9.21 /38	1.60	1.36
FO ●	Columbia European Equity B	AEEBX	D-	(800) 345-6611	C- / 3.0	4.83	3.11	-5.75 / 5	9.23 /34	8.39 /32	0.93	2.11
FO	Columbia European Equity C	REECX	D-	(800) 345-6611	D+ / 2.9	4.92	3.00	-5.73 / 5	9.19 /34	8.39 /32	0.94	2.11
FO	Columbia European Equity I	CEEIX	D	(800) 345-6611	C- / 3.8	5.26	3.66	-4.63 / 6	10.57 /43	9.84 /43	2.16	0.92
FO ●	Columbia European Equity K	CEQRX	D	(800) 345-6611	C- / 3.6	5.13	3.50	-4.96 / 6	10.21 /41	9.39 /40	1.86	1.22
FO	Columbia European Equity R4	CADJX	D+	(800) 345-6611	C- / 3.5	5.13	3.61	-4.73 / 6	10.12 /40	9.26 /39	1.96	1.11
FO	Columbia European Equity R5	CADKX	C-	(800) 345-6611	C- / 3.6	5.10	3.60	-4.57 / 6	10.18 /40	9.30 /39	2.10	0.97
FO	Columbia European Equity W	CEEWX	D+	(800) 345-6611	C- / 3.4	5.13	3.51	-4.96 / 6	9.99 /39	9.18 /38	1.72	1.36
FO	Columbia European Equity Z	CEEZX	D	(800) 345-6611	C- / 3.7	5.13	3.61	-4.73 / 6	10.35 /41	9.52 /41	1.96	1.11
AA	Columbia Flexible Cap Inc A	CFIAX	C-	(800) 345-6611	D+ / 2.8	2.34	2.42	3.86 /31	9.68 /37	--	3.23	1.29
AA	Columbia Flexible Cap Inc C	CFIGX	C	(800) 345-6611	C- / 3.3	2.24	2.05	3.10 /27	8.85 /32	--	2.68	2.04
AA	Columbia Flexible Cap Inc I	CFIIX	C	(800) 345-6611	C- / 4.0	2.52	2.70	4.32 /34	10.06 /40	--	3.79	0.88
AA	Columbia Flexible Cap Inc R	CFIRX	C	(800) 345-6611	C- / 3.6	2.36	2.38	3.60 /29	9.39 /35	--	3.17	1.54
GL	Columbia Flexible Cap Inc R4	CFCRX	C+	(800) 345-6611	C- / 3.9	2.47	2.53	4.18 /33	9.90 /39	--	3.66	1.04
GL	Columbia Flexible Cap Inc R5	CFXRX	C+	(800) 345-6611	C- / 3.9	2.41	2.57	4.15 /33	9.93 /39	--	3.71	0.93
AA	Columbia Flexible Cap Inc W	CFIWX	C	(800) 345-6611	C- / 3.8	2.42	2.49	3.90 /31	9.66 /37	--	3.39	1.29
AA	Columbia Flexible Cap Inc Z	CFIZX	C	(800) 345-6611	C- / 3.9	2.48	2.63	4.21 /33	9.94 /39	--	3.68	1.04
GR	Columbia FS Lrg Cap Idx Port Dir		A	(800) 345-6611	B / 8.1	0.90	5.83	12.50 /85	15.84 /82	14.14 /79	0.00	0.34
MC	Columbia FS Mid Cap Indx Port Dir		A+	(800) 345-6611	A- / 9.0	5.29	11.88	11.96 /82	16.75 /88	15.37 /89	0.00	0.34
SC	Columbia FS Sm Cap Indx Port Dir		A-	(800) 345-6611	A- / 9.0	3.91	14.05	8.44 /66	17.02 /90	15.90 /92	0.00	0.41
EN	Columbia Gl Energy and Nat Res A	EENAX	E-	(800) 345-6611	E- / 0.2	-2.54	-14.97	-15.64 / 2	-1.40 / 3	0.33 / 3	0.00	1.29
EN ●	Columbia Gl Energy and Nat Res B	CEGBX	E-	(800) 345-6611	E- / 0.2	-2.71	-15.28	-16.26 / 2	-2.15 / 3	-0.43 / 2	0.00	2.04
EN	Columbia Gl Energy and Nat Res C	EENCX	E-	(800) 345-6611	E- / 0.2	-2.70	-15.27	-16.26 / 2	-2.14 / 3	-0.42 / 2	0.00	2.04
EN	Columbia Gl Energy and Nat Res I	CERIX	E-	(800) 345-6611	E / 0.3	-2.41	-14.79	-15.23 / 2	-0.93 / 3	0.79 / 3	0.00	0.82
EN ●	Columbia Gl Energy and Nat Res K	CEGFX	E-	(800) 345-6611	E- / 0.2	-2.47	-14.89	-15.48 / 2	-1.24 / 3	0.51 / 3	0.00	1.12
EN	Columbia Gl Energy and Nat Res R	CETRX	E-	(800) 345-6611	E- / 0.2	-2.60	-15.09	-15.87 / 2	-1.66 / 3	0.08 / 3	0.00	1.54
EN	Columbia Gl Energy and Nat Res R4	CENRX	E+	(800) 345-6611	E- / 0.2	-2.43	-14.86	-15.40 / 2	-1.16 / 3	0.58 / 3	0.00	1.04
EN	Columbia Gl Energy and Nat Res R5	CNRRX	E+	(800) 345-6611	E / 0.3	-2.42	-14.76	-15.27 / 2	-1.02 / 3	0.66 / 3	0.00	0.87
EN	Columbia Gl Energy and Nat Res Z	UMESX	E-	(800) 345-6611	E- / 0.2	-2.47	-14.88	-15.43 / 2	-1.16 / 3	0.58 / 3	0.00	1.04
GR ●	Columbia Globa Equity Value K	AEVYX	C	(800) 345-6611	C / 5.1	0.05	0.34	5.44 /42	12.51 /56	10.71 /50	1.17	1.04
MC	Columbia Global Dividend Opp A	CSVAX	E+	(800) 345-6611	D- / 1.1	-0.46	-3.09	-2.29 /10	7.10 /22	7.26 /25	3.38	1.37
MC ●	Columbia Global Dividend Opp B	CSVBX	E+	(800) 345-6611	D- / 1.3	-0.68	-3.50	-3.09 / 8	6.29 /18	6.45 /20	2.95	2.12
MC	Columbia Global Dividend Opp C	CSRCX	E+	(800) 345-6611	D- / 1.4	-0.68	-3.45	-3.04 / 9	6.30 /18	6.45 /20	2.95	2.12
MC	Columbia Global Dividend Opp I	CEVIX	E+	(800) 345-6611	D / 1.9	-0.39	-2.84	-1.87 /11	7.58 /25	7.71 /28	4.05	0.79
MC	Columbia Global Dividend Opp R	CSGRX	E+	(800) 345-6611	D- / 1.5	-0.57	-3.21	-2.59 / 9	6.83 /20	6.98 /23	3.32	1.62
GR	Columbia Global Dividend Opp R4	CGOLX	D+	(800) 345-6611	D / 1.8	-0.39	-2.94	-2.03 /10	7.37 /23	7.53 /27	3.81	1.12
GR	Columbia Global Dividend Opp R5	CADPX	D+	(800) 345-6611	D / 1.9	-0.40	-2.87	-1.86 /11	7.46 /24	7.58 /27	4.02	0.84
MC	Columbia Global Dividend Opp W	CTVWX	E+	(800) 345-6611	D / 1.7	-0.46	-3.06	-2.21 /10	7.15 /22	7.30 /25	3.60	1.37
MC	Columbia Global Dividend Opp Y	CLSYX	E+	(800) 345-6611	D / 1.9	-0.38	-2.85	-1.81 /11	7.59 /25	7.72 /28	4.11	0.79
MC	Columbia Global Dividend Opp Z	CSVFX	E+	(800) 345-6611	D / 1.8	-0.40	-2.96	-2.04 /10	7.37 /23	7.53 /27	3.82	1.12
GR	Columbia Global Equity Value A	IEVAX	C-	(800) 345-6611	C- / 4.1	0.02	0.26	5.24 /40	12.34 /55	10.54 /49	0.99	1.19
GR ●	Columbia Global Equity Value B	INEGX	C-	(800) 345-6611	C / 4.5	-0.16	-0.10	4.51 /35	11.50 /49	9.72 /42	0.35	1.94
GR	Columbia Global Equity Value C	REVCX	C-	(800) 345-6611	C / 4.5	-0.17	-0.11	4.51 /35	11.49 /49	9.73 /42	0.35	1.94
GR	Columbia Global Equity Value I	CEQIX	C	(800) 345-6611	C / 5.4	0.14	0.52	5.80 /45	12.88 /59	11.02 /53	1.51	0.74
GR	Columbia Global Equity Value R	REVRX	C	(800) 345-6611	C / 4.9	-0.05	0.14	4.99 /38	12.06 /53	10.26 /47	0.81	1.44
GR	Columbia Global Equity Value R4	RSEVX	C	(800) 345-6611	C / 5.2	0.08	0.39	5.48 /42	12.53 /56	10.69 /50	1.27	0.94
GR	Columbia Global Equity Value R5	RSEYX	C	(800) 345-6611	C / 5.3	0.11	0.46	5.64 /43	12.74 /58	10.97 /52	1.40	0.79
GR	Columbia Global Equity Value W	CEVWX	C	(800) 345-6611	C / 5.0	0.02	0.27	5.29 /41	12.36 /55	10.50 /49	1.04	1.19

● Denotes fund is closed to new investors
* Denotes fund is included in Section II

www.thestreetratings.com

I. Index of Stock Mutual Funds

RISK			NET ASSETS		ASSET					BULL / BEAR		FUND MANAGER		MINIMUMS		LOADS	
Risk Rating/Pts	3 Year		NAV		Cash	Stocks	Bonds	Other	Portfolio	Last Bull	Last Bear	Manager	Manager	Initial	Additional	Front	Back
	Standard Deviation	Beta	As of 3/31/15	Total $(Mil)	%	%	%	%	Turnover Ratio	Market Return	Market Return	Quality Pct	Tenure (Years)	Purch. $	Purch. $	End Load	End Load
C+ / 6.5	13.1	0.91	10.38	14	2	97	0	1	80	31.2	-25.7	87	7	0	0	0.0	0.0
C / 5.2	13.1	0.91	10.30	N/A	2	97	0	1	80	29.5	-25.8	85	7	500	0	0.0	0.0
C+ / 6.5	13.1	0.91	10.42	4	2	97	0	1	80	31.5	-25.7	87	7	0	0	0.0	0.0
C / 5.2	13.1	0.91	10.35	1,045	2	97	0	1	80	30.7	-25.7	86	7	0	0	0.0	0.0
C / 4.9	14.2	1.01	7.00	161	0	99	0	1	64	62.8	-25.6	71	6	2,000	0	5.8	0.0
C / 4.9	14.4	1.02	6.95	1	0	99	0	1	64	58.7	-25.8	61	6	2,000	0	0.0	0.0
C / 4.9	14.3	1.01	6.83	25	0	99	0	1	64	58.5	-25.7	61	6	2,000	0	0.0	0.0
C / 4.8	14.4	1.02	7.01	250	0	99	0	1	64	65.5	-25.4	75	6	0	0	0.0	0.0
C / 4.8	14.4	1.02	6.97	N/A	0	99	0	1	64	63.9	-25.5	72	6	0	0	0.0	0.0
C+ / 6.3	14.3	1.01	6.97	3	0	99	0	1	64	63.2	-25.6	72	6	0	0	0.0	0.0
C+ / 6.3	14.2	1.01	7.01	N/A	0	99	0	1	64	63.4	-25.6	72	6	0	0	0.0	0.0
C+ / 6.3	14.3	1.01	6.97	N/A	0	99	0	1	64	62.6	-25.6	71	6	500	0	0.0	0.0
C / 4.9	14.3	1.01	6.97	71	0	99	0	1	64	63.9	-25.4	74	6	2,000	0	0.0	0.0
B- / 7.6	6.6	1.08	12.25	356	6	52	22	20	48	58.1	N/A	38	4	2,000	0	5.8	0.0
B- / 7.7	6.6	1.08	12.20	152	6	52	22	20	48	54.2	N/A	29	4	2,000	0	0.0	0.0
B- / 7.6	6.6	1.08	12.26	49	6	52	22	20	48	60.2	N/A	44	4	0	0	0.0	0.0
B- / 7.6	6.6	1.08	12.25	1	6	52	22	20	48	56.8	N/A	34	4	0	0	0.0	0.0
B / 8.3	6.5	0.97	12.33	22	6	52	22	20	48	59.1	N/A	77	4	0	0	0.0	0.0
B / 8.3	6.6	0.98	12.33	5	6	52	22	20	48	59.2	N/A	77	4	0	0	0.0	0.0
B- / 7.6	6.5	1.08	12.26	N/A	6	52	22	20	48	58.2	N/A	38	4	500	0	0.0	0.0
B- / 7.6	6.6	1.08	12.25	138	6	52	22	20	48	59.5	N/A	42	4	0	0	0.0	0.0
B- / 7.4	9.5	1.00	22.32	32	1	98	0	1	12	98.6	-16.4	64	N/A	250	50	0.0	0.0
C+ / 6.7	11.0	1.00	32.86	26	2	97	0	1	24	101.0	-22.7	63	N/A	250	50	0.0	0.0
C+ / 6.3	12.8	0.94	23.38	10	2	97	0	1	0	106.7	-22.1	81	N/A	250	50	0.0	0.0
D+ / 2.8	15.7	0.96	18.03	101	3	96	0	1	34	20.6	-30.5	10	4	2,000	0	5.8	0.0
D+ / 2.8	15.8	0.96	17.26	1	3	96	0	1	34	17.5	-30.7	7	4	2,000	0	0.0	0.0
D+ / 2.8	15.7	0.96	17.27	16	3	96	0	1	34	17.6	-30.7	7	4	2,000	0	0.0	0.0
D+ / 2.9	15.8	0.96	18.24	33	3	96	0	1	34	22.7	-30.4	13	4	0	0	0.0	0.0
D+ / 2.8	15.8	0.96	18.15	N/A	3	96	0	1	34	21.4	-30.5	11	4	0	0	0.0	0.0
D+ / 2.8	15.8	0.96	17.97	2	3	96	0	1	34	19.7	-30.6	9	4	0	0	0.0	0.0
C+ / 6.2	15.8	0.96	18.48	9	3	96	0	1	34	21.7	-30.4	11	4	0	0	0.0	0.0
C+ / 6.2	15.8	0.96	18.52	5	3	96	0	1	34	22.1	-30.4	12	4	0	0	0.0	0.0
D+ / 2.9	15.8	0.96	18.17	121	3	96	0	1	34	21.7	-30.4	11	4	0	0	0.0	0.0
C+ / 6.1	10.1	1.02	12.69	5	2	97	0	1	61	83.8	-22.3	20	12	0	0	0.0	0.0
C / 4.8	9.6	0.70	17.78	134	3	96	0	1	75	58.9	-24.5	15	3	2,000	0	5.8	0.0
C / 4.6	9.6	0.70	16.72	1	3	96	0	1	75	54.8	-24.7	11	3	2,000	0	0.0	0.0
C / 4.6	9.6	0.70	16.74	14	3	96	0	1	75	54.9	-24.8	11	3	2,000	0	0.0	0.0
C / 4.7	9.6	0.70	17.79	149	3	96	0	1	75	61.3	-24.4	19	3	0	0	0.0	0.0
C / 4.8	9.6	0.70	17.76	1	3	96	0	1	75	57.5	-24.6	14	3	0	0	0.0	0.0
B- / 7.4	9.6	0.91	17.91	1	3	96	0	1	75	60.3	-24.4	5	3	0	0	0.0	0.0
B- / 7.4	9.6	0.90	17.79	N/A	3	96	0	1	75	60.6	-24.4	6	3	100,000	0	0.0	0.0
C / 4.8	9.6	0.70	17.78	N/A	3	96	0	1	75	59.0	-24.4	16	3	500	0	0.0	0.0
C / 4.7	9.6	0.70	17.81	N/A	3	96	0	1	75	61.4	-24.4	19	3	0	0	0.0	0.0
C / 4.8	9.6	0.70	17.83	523	3	96	0	1	75	60.3	-24.4	17	3	0	0	0.0	0.0
C+ / 6.1	10.1	1.03	12.64	865	2	97	0	1	61	82.9	-22.3	18	12	2,000	0	5.8	0.0
C+ / 6.1	10.1	1.02	12.74	9	2	97	0	1	61	78.3	-22.6	14	12	2,000	0	0.0	0.0
C+ / 6.1	10.0	1.02	12.52	28	2	97	0	1	61	78.4	-22.6	14	12	2,000	0	0.0	0.0
C+ / 6.0	10.1	1.03	12.31	N/A	2	97	0	1	61	85.7	-22.2	23	12	0	0	0.0	0.0
C+ / 6.1	10.1	1.03	12.62	1	2	97	0	1	61	81.5	-22.4	16	12	0	0	0.0	0.0
C+ / 6.1	10.1	1.03	12.68	N/A	2	97	0	1	61	83.8	-22.4	20	12	0	0	0.0	0.0
C+ / 6.1	10.1	1.03	12.63	N/A	2	97	0	1	61	85.2	-22.2	22	12	0	0	0.0	0.0
C+ / 6.1	10.1	1.03	12.73	N/A	2	97	0	1	61	82.6	-22.4	19	12	500	0	0.0	0.0

99 Pct = Best
0 Pct = Worst

Fund Type	Fund Name	Ticker Symbol	Overall Investment Rating	Phone	Performance Rating/Pts	3 Mo	6 Mo	1Yr / Pct	3Yr / Pct	5Yr / Pct	Dividend Yield	Expense Ratio
GI	Columbia Global Equity Value Y	CEVYX	C+	(800) 345-6611	C / 5.3	0.13	0.50	5.74 /44	12.68 /57	10.74 /51	1.48	0.74
GI	Columbia Global Equity Value Z	CEVZX	C	(800) 345-6611	C / 5.2	0.08	0.39	5.50 /42	12.62 /57	10.81 /51	1.28	0.94
GR	Columbia Global Infrastructure A	RRIAX	E+	(800) 345-6611	C+ / 5.6	0.99	2.00	3.59 /29	15.00 /75	12.04 /61	1.31	1.17
GR	● Columbia Global Infrastructure B	RRIBX	D-	(800) 345-6611	C+ / 6.3	0.91	1.97	3.57 /29	14.56 /71	11.45 /56	1.33	1.92
GR	Columbia Global Infrastructure C	RRICX	E+	(800) 345-6611	C+ / 5.9	0.78	1.58	2.78 /25	14.12 /68	11.20 /54	0.66	1.92
GR	Columbia Global Infrastructure I	RRIIX	D-	(800) 345-6611	C+ / 6.8	1.03	2.18	3.95 /31	15.44 /78	12.48 /64	1.73	0.77
GR	● Columbia Global Infrastructure K	RRIYX	D-	(800) 345-6611	C+ / 6.6	0.98	1.97	3.61 /29	15.10 /76	12.14 /62	1.45	1.07
GR	Columbia Global Infrastructure R	RRIRX	D-	(800) 345-6611	C+ / 6.3	0.88	1.85	3.32 /28	14.69 /72	11.75 /59	1.15	1.42
OT	Columbia Global Infrastructure R4	CRRIX	C+	(800) 345-6611	C+ / 6.7	1.03	2.07	3.83 /31	15.19 /76	12.15 /62	1.59	0.92
GR	Columbia Global Infrastructure R5	RRIZX	D-	(800) 345-6611	C+ / 6.8	1.04	2.18	3.91 /31	15.41 /78	12.43 /64	1.68	0.82
GR	Columbia Global Infrastructure Z	CRIZX	D-	(800) 345-6611	C+ / 6.7	1.04	2.11	3.88 /31	15.28 /77	12.31 /63	1.60	0.92
AA	Columbia Global Opportunities A	IMRFX	D+	(800) 345-6611	D- / 1.2	2.01	1.74	1.45 /20	6.10 /17	7.07 /23	0.31	1.19
AA	● Columbia Global Opportunities B	IMRBX	D+	(800) 345-6611	D- / 1.4	1.86	1.32	0.75 /18	5.29 /14	6.27 /19	0.14	1.94
AA	Columbia Global Opportunities C	RSSCX	D+	(800) 345-6611	D- / 1.4	1.87	1.42	0.76 /18	5.31 /14	6.29 /19	0.14	1.94
AA	● Columbia Global Opportunities K	IDRYX	C-	(800) 345-6611	D / 1.8	2.09	1.74	1.57 /20	6.24 /18	7.22 /24	0.36	1.09
AA	Columbia Global Opportunities R	CSARX	D+	(800) 345-6611	D / 1.6	2.02	1.57	1.05 /19	5.81 /16	6.78 /22	0.27	1.44
AA	Columbia Global Opportunities R4	CSDRX	D+	(800) 345-6611	D / 1.9	2.09	1.82	1.59 /20	6.27 /18	7.17 /24	0.38	0.94
AA	Columbia Global Opportunities R5	CLNRX	D+	(800) 345-6611	D / 1.9	2.18	1.91	1.82 /21	6.43 /19	7.27 /25	0.44	0.84
AA	Columbia Global Opportunities W	CGOPX	D-	(800) 345-6611	D / 1.8	2.01	1.66	1.36 /20	6.07 /17	7.05 /23	0.33	1.19
AA	Columbia Global Opportunities Z	CSAZX	C-	(800) 345-6611	D / 1.9	2.10	1.83	1.69 /21	6.37 /18	7.34 /25	0.39	0.94
TC	Columbia Global Technology Gro 5	CTHRX	A	(800) 345-6611	A+ / 9.8	4.14	9.68	17.67 /95	19.86 /98	16.99 /96	0.52	1.03
TC	Columbia Global Technology Gro A	CTCAX	B+	(800) 345-6611	A / 9.4	4.06	9.52	17.18 /95	19.40 /97	16.60 /95	0.40	1.44
TC	● Columbia Global Technology Gro B	CTCBX	A-	(800) 345-6611	A+ / 9.6	3.87	9.11	16.30 /94	18.52 /96	15.72 /91	0.21	2.19
TC	Columbia Global Technology Gro C	CTHCX	A-	(800) 345-6611	A+ / 9.6	3.86	9.16	16.41 /94	18.54 /96	15.75 /92	0.21	2.19
TC	Columbia Global Technology Gro R4	CTYRX	A	(800) 345-6611	A+ / 9.7	4.10	9.66	17.48 /95	19.73 /98	16.91 /96	0.48	1.19
TC	Columbia Global Technology Gro Z	CMTFX	A-	(800) 345-6611	A+ / 9.7	4.10	9.60	17.51 /95	19.70 /97	16.89 /96	0.48	1.19
FO	Columbia Greater China A	NGCAX	D-	(800) 345-6611	C+ / 6.5	7.70	11.75	17.38 /95	11.89 /52	6.20 /18	0.60	1.59
FO	● Columbia Greater China B	NGCBX	D-	(800) 345-6611	C+ / 6.9	7.49	11.35	16.49 /94	11.05 /46	5.40 /14	0.00	2.34
FO	Columbia Greater China C	NGCCX	D-	(800) 345-6611	C+ / 6.9	7.48	11.35	16.49 /94	11.06 /46	5.41 /14	0.00	2.34
FO	Columbia Greater China I	CCINX	D	(800) 345-6611	B / 7.9	7.80	12.02	17.90 /95	12.40 /55	6.56 /20	1.04	1.13
FO	Columbia Greater China R4	CGCHX	B+	(800) 345-6611	B / 7.7	7.73	11.87	17.65 /95	12.07 /53	6.30 /19	0.80	1.34
FO	Columbia Greater China R5	CGCRX	B+	(800) 345-6611	B / 7.8	7.78	11.98	17.83 /95	12.24 /54	6.40 /19	0.93	1.18
FO	Columbia Greater China W	CGCWX	B	(800) 345-6611	B / 7.6	7.67	11.76	17.41 /95	11.95 /52	6.23 /18	0.68	1.59
FO	Columbia Greater China Z	LNGZX	D	(800) 345-6611	B / 7.7	7.74	11.90	17.66 /95	12.17 /54	6.47 /20	0.82	1.34
GI	Columbia Income Builder A	RBBAX	D+	(800) 345-6611	D- / 1.3	1.27	1.85	3.59 /29	5.99 /17	7.12 /24	3.01	1.07
GI	● Columbia Income Builder B	RBBBX	D+	(800) 345-6611	D- / 1.5	1.17	1.56	2.81 /25	5.20 /14	6.32 /19	2.41	1.82
GI	Columbia Income Builder C	RBBCX	D+	(800) 345-6611	D- / 1.5	1.09	1.48	2.82 /26	5.19 /14	6.32 /19	2.41	1.82
GI	● Columbia Income Builder K	CIPRX	C-	(800) 345-6611	D / 1.9	1.37	1.97	3.74 /30	6.08 /17	7.19 /24	3.23	1.00
AA	Columbia Income Builder R	CBURX	D+	(800) 345-6611	D / 1.7	1.20	1.72	3.32 /28	5.70 /16	6.96 /23	2.90	1.32
AA	Columbia Income Builder R4	CNMRX	C-	(800) 345-6611	D / 1.9	1.41	1.97	3.84 /31	6.19 /18	7.24 /25	3.40	0.82
AA	Columbia Income Builder R5	CKKRX	C-	(800) 345-6611	D / 2.0	1.42	2.00	3.89 /31	6.27 /18	7.29 /25	3.46	0.75
AA	Columbia Income Builder W	CINDX	D+	(800) 345-6611	D / 1.8	1.26	1.84	3.57 /29	5.98 /17	7.11 /24	3.14	N/A
AA	Columbia Income Builder Z	CBUZX	C-	(800) 345-6611	D / 2.0	1.32	1.98	3.84 /31	6.22 /18	7.37 /26	3.41	0.82
FO	Columbia International Value A	NIVLX	D-	(800) 345-6611	D / 1.6	5.79	1.18	-1.75 /11	7.49 /24	4.32 / 9	3.79	1.42
FO	● Columbia International Value B	NBIVX	D-	(800) 345-6611	D / 1.9	5.49	0.73	-2.56 / 9	6.66 /20	3.55 / 7	3.38	2.17
FO	Columbia International Value C	NVICX	D-	(800) 345-6611	D / 1.9	5.51	0.73	-2.57 / 9	6.65 /20	3.52 / 7	3.39	2.17
FO	Columbia International Value I	CVLIX	D	(800) 345-6611	D+ / 2.6	5.83	1.29	-1.45 /12	7.89 /26	3.92 / 8	4.58	0.98
FO	Columbia International Value R	CIVRX	D	(800) 345-6611	D / 2.2	5.71	1.02	-2.01 /10	7.23 /23	4.04 / 8	3.76	1.67
FO	Columbia International Value R4	CVFRX	D+	(800) 345-6611	D+ / 2.5	5.81	1.24	-1.59 /11	7.71 /25	4.45 /10	4.19	1.17
FO	Columbia International Value R5	CLVRX	D+	(800) 345-6611	D+ / 2.5	5.81	1.34	-1.41 /12	7.79 /26	4.50 /10	4.31	1.03
FO	Columbia International Value Z	EMIEX	D	(800) 345-6611	D+ / 2.5	5.80	1.25	-1.54 /11	7.73 /26	4.57 /10	4.23	1.17
GR	Columbia Large Cap Enh Core A	NMIAX	A+	(800) 345-6611	B+ / 8.9	1.26	6.44	14.68 /91	16.99 /90	15.38 /89	0.94	1.25

● Denotes fund is closed to new investors
* Denotes fund is included in Section II

www.thestreetratings.com

RISK Rating/Pts	3 Year Standard Deviation	Beta	NAV As of 3/31/15	Total $(Mil)	Cash %	Stocks %	Bonds %	Other %	Portfolio Turnover Ratio	Last Bull Market Return	Last Bear Market Return	Manager Quality Pct	Manager Tenure (Years)	Initial Purch. $	Additional Purch. $	Front End Load	Back End Load
B- /7.5	10.1	1.03	12.35	N/A	2	97	0	1	61	84.5	-22.3	21	12	0	0	0.0	0.0
C+ /6.1	10.1	1.02	12.65	108	2	97	0	1	61	84.7	-22.2	21	12	2,000	0	0.0	0.0
E+ /0.9	13.3	1.15	16.36	269	3	91	3	3	51	107.4	-32.8	23	8	2,000	0	5.8	0.0
E+ /0.9	13.3	1.15	15.60	10	3	91	3	3	51	104.4	-33.0	19	8	2,000	0	0.0	0.0
E+ /0.9	13.3	1.15	15.51	38	3	91	3	3	51	102.2	-33.0	16	8	2,000	0	0.0	0.0
E+ /0.9	13.3	1.15	16.64	36	3	91	3	3	51	110.3	-32.7	27	8	0	0	0.0	0.0
E+ /0.9	13.3	1.15	16.43	N/A	3	91	3	3	51	108.3	-32.7	24	8	0	0	0.0	0.0
E+ /0.9	13.3	1.15	16.02	1	3	91	3	3	51	105.7	-32.8	20	8	0	0	0.0	0.0
C+ /6.3	13.3	1.15	16.68	N/A	3	91	3	3	51	108.5	-32.8	25	2	0	0	0.0	0.0
E+ /0.9	13.3	1.15	16.59	N/A	3	91	3	3	51	110.0	-32.7	27	8	0	0	0.0	0.0
E+ /0.9	13.3	1.15	16.59	38	3	91	3	3	51	109.1	-32.7	26	2	2,000	0	0.0	0.0
B /8.1	7.1	1.17	11.68	683	14	62	20	4	104	41.3	-11.8	6	5	2,000	0	5.8	0.0
B /8.1	7.1	1.17	11.50	18	14	62	20	4	104	37.6	-12.1	4	5	2,000	0	0.0	0.0
B /8.1	7.1	1.17	11.43	30	14	62	20	4	104	37.8	-12.2	4	5	2,000	0	0.0	0.0
B /8.1	7.2	1.18	11.72	N/A	14	62	20	4	104	41.9	-11.7	6	5	0	0	0.0	0.0
B /8.1	7.1	1.17	11.63	N/A	14	62	20	4	104	39.9	-11.9	6	5	0	0	0.0	0.0
B- /7.2	7.1	1.16	11.72	N/A	14	62	20	4	104	41.8	-11.8	7	5	0	0	0.0	0.0
B- /7.3	7.1	1.17	11.74	N/A	14	62	20	4	104	42.5	-11.8	7	5	0	0	0.0	0.0
C+ /6.0	7.0	1.15	11.65	N/A	14	62	20	4	104	41.2	-11.8	6	5	500	0	0.0	0.0
B /8.1	7.1	1.17	11.69	6	14	62	20	4	104	42.6	-11.7	7	5	2,000	0	0.0	0.0
C+ /5.9	13.5	1.13	19.60	6	0	99	0	1	68	116.1	-24.7	79	13	0	0	0.0	0.0
C /5.4	13.5	1.13	18.72	109	0	99	0	1	68	113.4	-24.8	76	13	2,000	0	5.8	0.0
C /5.3	13.5	1.13	17.19	2	0	99	0	1	68	108.0	-25.0	68	13	2,000	0	0.0	0.0
C /5.4	13.5	1.13	17.23	33	0	99	0	1	68	107.9	-25.0	68	13	2,000	0	0.0	0.0
C+ /5.9	13.5	1.13	19.54	6	0	99	0	1	68	115.4	-24.7	78	13	0	0	0.0	0.0
C /5.4	13.5	1.13	19.30	156	0	99	0	1	68	115.3	-24.7	78	13	0	0	0.0	0.0
D- /1.0	13.8	0.68	39.44	77	4	95	0	1	61	58.7	-32.2	93	10	2,000	0	5.8	0.0
D- /1.0	13.8	0.68	36.30	2	4	95	0	1	61	54.6	-32.4	92	10	2,000	0	0.0	0.0
D- /1.0	13.8	0.68	37.21	15	4	95	0	1	61	54.6	-32.4	92	10	2,000	0	0.0	0.0
D- /1.0	13.8	0.69	42.57	N/A	4	95	0	1	61	61.1	-32.1	94	10	0	0	0.0	0.0
C+ /6.4	13.8	0.68	43.18	N/A	4	95	0	1	61	59.4	-32.2	94	10	0	0	0.0	0.0
C+ /6.4	13.8	0.68	43.21	N/A	4	95	0	1	61	60.1	-32.2	94	10	0	0	0.0	0.0
C+ /6.4	13.8	0.68	39.44	N/A	4	95	0	1	61	58.9	-32.2	94	10	500	0	0.0	0.0
D- /1.0	13.8	0.69	42.44	41	4	95	0	1	61	60.0	-32.1	94	10	0	0	0.0	0.0
B /8.0	4.4	0.39	11.89	1,052	0	26	71	3	28	33.1	-5.9	67	9	2,000	0	4.8	0.0
B /8.0	4.5	0.39	11.95	17	0	26	71	3	28	29.8	-6.2	56	9	2,000	0	0.0	0.0
B /8.0	4.4	0.39	11.93	246	0	26	71	3	28	29.8	-6.2	55	9	2,000	0	0.0	0.0
B /8.0	4.5	0.39	11.91	N/A	0	26	71	3	28	33.5	-5.9	68	9	0	0	0.0	0.0
B /8.0	4.5	0.72	11.95	1	0	26	71	3	28	32.0	-6.0	39	5	0	0	0.0	0.0
B /8.3	4.5	0.71	11.92	5	0	26	71	3	28	33.9	-5.9	47	9	0	0	0.0	0.0
B /8.3	4.5	0.71	11.93	1	0	26	71	3	28	34.1	-5.9	48	9	0	0	0.0	0.0
B- /7.5	4.4	0.71	11.88	N/A	0	26	71	3	28	33.1	-5.9	44	9	500	0	0.0	0.0
B /8.0	4.5	0.72	11.89	50	0	26	71	3	28	34.2	-5.8	46	5	2,000	0	0.0	0.0
C+ /5.9	13.7	0.99	14.43	79	0	99	0	1	14	41.1	-20.5	41	20	2,000	0	5.8	0.0
C+ /5.9	13.7	0.99	13.84	N/A	0	99	0	1	14	37.6	-20.7	30	20	2,000	0	0.0	0.0
C+ /5.9	13.7	0.99	13.79	22	0	99	0	1	14	37.5	-20.7	30	20	2,000	0	0.0	0.0
C+ /5.9	13.7	0.99	13.98	N/A	0	99	0	1	14	37.9	-20.4	46	20	0	0	0.0	0.0
C+ /5.9	13.7	0.99	14.44	N/A	0	99	0	1	14	39.8	-20.6	37	20	0	0	0.0	0.0
C+ /6.9	13.7	0.99	14.75	2	0	99	0	1	14	42.0	-20.5	44	20	0	0	0.0	0.0
C+ /6.9	13.7	0.99	14.74	4	0	99	0	1	14	42.3	-20.5	45	20	0	0	0.0	0.0
C+ /5.9	13.7	0.99	14.60	78	0	99	0	1	14	42.3	-20.4	44	20	2,000	0	0.0	0.0
B- /7.4	10.2	1.05	21.65	83	2	97	0	1	101	107.1	-15.2	66	6	2,000	0	0.0	0.0

Fund Type	Fund Name	Ticker Symbol	Overall Investment Rating	Phone	Perfor-mance Rating/Pts	3 Mo	6 Mo	1Yr / Pct	3Yr / Pct	5Yr / Pct	Dividend Yield	Expense Ratio
	99 Pct = Best							Total Return % through 3/31/15	Annualized		Incl. in Returns	
GI	Columbia Large Cap Enh Core I	CCEIX	A+	(800) 345-6611	A- / 9.1	1.31	6.63	15.14 /92	17.44 /92	15.75 /92	1.31	0.80
GR	Columbia Large Cap Enh Core R	CCERX	A+	(800) 345-6611	B+ / 8.7	1.17	6.30	14.39 /90	16.70 /88	15.09 /87	0.72	1.50
GI	Columbia Large Cap Enh Core R5	CLNCX	B+	(800) 345-6611	A- / 9.0	1.36	6.66	15.04 /92	17.11 /90	15.45 /90	1.22	N/A
GR	Columbia Large Cap Enh Core Y	CECYX	A+	(800) 345-6611	A- / 9.2	1.36	6.68	15.19 /92	17.47 /92	15.80 /92	1.31	0.80
GR	Columbia Large Cap Enh Core Z	NMIMX	A+	(800) 345-6611	A- / 9.1	1.31	6.56	14.97 /92	17.30 /91	15.67 /91	1.17	1.00
GR	Columbia Large Cap Growth A	LEGAX	A-	(800) 345-6611	A / 9.4	6.86	13.68	20.91 /97	17.55 /93	15.71 /91	0.22	1.14
GR ●	Columbia Large Cap Growth B	LEGBX	B+	(800) 345-6611	A+ / 9.6	6.68	13.24	20.01 /97	16.68 /88	14.85 /86	0.00	1.89
GR	Columbia Large Cap Growth C	LEGCX	B+	(800) 345-6611	A+ / 9.6	6.67	13.26	19.99 /97	16.67 /88	14.84 /85	0.00	1.89
GR ●	Columbia Large Cap Growth E	CLGEX	A-	(800) 345-6611	A / 9.5	6.84	13.60	20.76 /97	17.43 /92	15.59 /91	0.14	1.24
GR ●	Columbia Large Cap Growth F	CLGFX	B+	(800) 345-6611	A+ / 9.6	6.64	13.24	19.98 /97	16.66 /88	14.84 /86	0.00	1.89
GR	Columbia Large Cap Growth I	CLGIX	A-	(800) 345-6611	A+ / 9.8	6.97	13.88	21.40 /97	18.06 /94	16.20 /94	0.59	0.70
GR ●	Columbia Large Cap Growth K	CLRUX	A	(800) 345-6611	A+ / 9.7	6.89	13.72	21.05 /97	17.71 /93	15.90 /92	0.34	1.00
GR	Columbia Large Cap Growth R	CGWRX	A-	(800) 345-6611	A+ / 9.7	6.81	13.53	20.62 /97	17.26 /91	15.42 /90	0.02	1.39
GR	Columbia Large Cap Growth R4	CCGRX	A+	(800) 345-6611	A+ / 9.8	6.92	13.81	21.28 /97	17.85 /94	16.00 /93	0.43	0.89
GR	Columbia Large Cap Growth R5	CLWFX	A-	(800) 345-6611	A+ / 9.8	6.97	13.86	21.35 /97	18.02 /94	16.15 /94	0.54	0.75
GR ●	Columbia Large Cap Growth T	GAEGX	A-	(800) 345-6611	A / 9.4	6.85	13.64	20.84 /97	17.50 /92	15.65 /91	0.18	1.14
GR	Columbia Large Cap Growth W	CLGWX	A-	(800) 345-6611	A+ / 9.7	6.85	13.66	20.97 /97	17.58 /93	15.74 /91	0.24	1.14
GR	Columbia Large Cap Growth Y	CGFYX	A-	(800) 345-6611	A+ / 9.8	6.96	13.88	21.40 /97	18.09 /95	16.23 /94	0.60	0.70
GR	Columbia Large Cap Growth Z	GEGTX	A-	(800) 345-6611	A+ / 9.7	6.90	13.78	21.20 /97	17.83 /94	15.99 /93	0.44	0.89
IX	Columbia Large Cap Index A	NEIAX	A-	(800) 345-6611	B / 7.9	0.83	5.69	12.20 /83	15.59 /80	13.97 /77	1.47	0.45
IX ●	Columbia Large Cap Index B	CLIBX	B+	(800) 345-6611	B- / 7.2	0.68	5.30	11.46 /80	14.74 /73	13.13 /69	0.77	1.20
GR	Columbia Large Cap Index I	CCXIX	A	(800) 345-6611	B / 8.1	0.88	5.82	12.50 /85	15.89 / 82	14.26 /80	1.73	0.20
GI	Columbia Large Cap Index R5	CLXRX	A	(800) 345-6611	B / 8.1	0.89	5.82	12.48 /85	15.88 /82	14.26 /80	1.68	0.20
IX	Columbia Large Cap Index Z	NINDX	A	(800) 345-6611	B / 8.1	0.91	5.81	12.50 /85	15.88 /82	14.26 /80	1.70	0.20
GI	Columbia Large Core Quant A	AQEAX	A-	(800) 345-6611	B / 7.8	1.87	7.61	15.62 /93	16.48 /87	15.78 /92	0.96	1.08
GI ●	Columbia Large Core Quant B	AQEBX	A	(800) 345-6611	B+ / 8.3	1.66	7.25	14.90 /91	15.61 /80	14.93 /86	0.34	1.83
GI	Columbia Large Core Quant C	RDCEX	A	(800) 345-6611	B+ / 8.3	1.68	7.24	14.86 /91	15.64 /80	14.93 /86	0.35	1.83
GI	Columbia Large Core Quant I	ALEIX	A+	(800) 345-6611	A- / 9.1	2.06	7.87	16.24 /94	17.07 /90	16.34 /94	1.42	0.66
GI ●	Columbia Large Core Quant K	RQEYX	A+	(800) 345-6611	B+ / 8.9	1.85	7.70	15.94 /93	16.70 /88	16.00 /93	1.15	0.96
GI	Columbia Large Core Quant R	CLQRX	A+	(800) 345-6611	B+ / 8.7	1.76	7.47	15.49 /92	16.23 /85	15.50 /90	0.79	1.33
GR	Columbia Large Core Quant R4	CLCQX	A+	(800) 345-6611	B+ / 8.9	1.95	7.77	16.00 /93	16.68 /88	15.89 /92	1.23	0.83
GI	Columbia Large Core Quant R5	RSIPX	A+	(800) 345-6611	A- / 9.1	1.97	7.75	16.14 /93	16.95 /90	16.28 /94	1.38	0.71
GI	Columbia Large Core Quant W	RDEWX	A+	(800) 345-6611	B+ / 8.8	1.85	7.55	15.65 /93	16.48 /87	15.77 /92	1.01	1.08
GR	Columbia Large Core Quant Z	CCRZX	A+	(800) 345-6611	A- / 9.0	1.96	7.80	16.06 /93	16.83 /89	16.08 /93	1.24	0.83
GR	Columbia Large Growth Quant A	RDLAX	C+	(800) 345-6611	B+ / 8.9	4.44	10.15	20.06 /97	16.96 /90	15.46 /90	0.32	1.28
GR ●	Columbia Large Growth Quant B	CGQBX	B-	(800) 345-6611	A- / 9.2	4.28	9.78	19.12 /96	16.11 /84	14.57 /83	0.00	2.03
GR	Columbia Large Growth Quant C	RDLCX	C+	(800) 345-6611	A- / 9.2	4.31	9.73	19.12 /96	16.09 /84	14.58 /83	0.00	2.03
GR	Columbia Large Growth Quant I	RDLIX	B-	(800) 345-6611	A+ / 9.6	4.60	10.46	20.65 /97	17.52 /92	16.00 /93	0.74	0.80
GR ●	Columbia Large Growth Quant K	RDLFX	B-	(800) 345-6611	A / 9.5	4.61	10.30	20.35 /97	17.18 /91	15.67 /91	0.49	1.10
GR	Columbia Large Growth Quant R	CGQRX	B-	(800) 345-6611	A / 9.4	4.31	9.97	19.72 /97	16.65 /88	15.13 /88	0.12	1.53
GR	Columbia Large Growth Quant R5	CQURX	A+	(800) 345-6611	A+ / 9.6	4.54	10.37	20.54 /97	17.38 /92	15.71 /91	0.69	0.85
GR	Columbia Large Growth Quant W	RDLWX	B-	(800) 345-6611	A / 9.4	4.54	10.08	20.07 /97	16.91 /89	15.41 /90	0.33	1.28
GR	Columbia Large Growth Quant Z	CLQZX	B-	(800) 345-6611	A / 9.5	4.53	10.21	20.32 /97	17.28 /91	15.66 /91	0.55	1.03
GR	Columbia Large Value Quant A	RLCAX	B+	(800) 345-6611	B- / 7.3	-0.52	4.59	11.37 /80	16.84 /89	14.77 /85	1.01	1.27
GR ●	Columbia Large Value Quant B	CVQBX	B+	(800) 345-6611	B / 7.8	-0.63	4.31	10.53 /76	15.93 /83	13.91 /77	0.37	2.02
GR	Columbia Large Value Quant C	RDCCX	B+	(800) 345-6611	B / 7.8	-0.64	4.26	10.45 /76	15.96 /83	13.89 /77	0.37	2.02
GR	Columbia Large Value Quant I	CLQIX	A	(800) 345-6611	B+ / 8.7	-0.41	4.86	11.83 /82	17.29 /91	15.25 /88	1.45	0.82
GR ●	Columbia Large Value Quant K	RLCYX	A	(800) 345-6611	B+ / 8.5	-0.41	4.71	11.46 /80	16.97 /90	14.91 /86	1.20	1.12
GR	Columbia Large Value Quant R	RLCOX	A-	(800) 345-6611	B / 8.2	-0.52	4.55	11.09 /79	16.53 /87	14.47 /82	0.84	1.52
GR ●	Columbia Large Value Quant T	CVQTX	B+	(800) 345-6611	B- / 7.3	-0.52	4.66	11.34 /80	16.76 /88	14.70 /84	0.97	1.27
GR	Columbia Large Value Quant W	RLCWX	A-	(800) 345-6611	B+ / 8.4	-0.41	4.67	11.42 /80	16.83 /89	14.75 /85	1.07	1.27
GR	Columbia Large Value Quant Z	CVQZX	A	(800) 345-6611	B+ / 8.6	-0.41	4.80	11.66 /81	17.11 /90	15.05 /87	1.30	1.02

● Denotes fund is closed to new investors
* Denotes fund is included in Section II

www.thestreetratings.com

RISK Rating/Pts	Standard Deviation	Beta	NAV As of 3/31/15	Total $(Mil)	Cash %	Stocks %	Bonds %	Other %	Portfolio Turnover Ratio	Last Bull Market Return	Last Bear Market Return	Manager Quality Pct	Manager Tenure (Years)	Initial Purch. $	Additional Purch. $	Front End Load	Back End Load
B- / 7.4	10.2	1.06	21.60	12	2	97	0	1	101	109.7	-15.1	70	6	0	0	0.0	0.0
B- / 7.4	10.2	1.06	21.61	27	2	97	0	1	101	105.3	-15.4	62	6	0	0	0.0	0.0
C+ / 5.7	10.2	1.06	21.54	N/A	2	97	0	1	101	107.6	-15.2	67	6	0	0	0.0	0.0
B- / 7.4	10.2	1.06	21.62	3	2	97	0	1	101	109.8	-15.1	71	6	1,000,000	0	0.0	0.0
B- / 7.4	10.2	1.05	21.61	341	2	97	0	1	101	109.0	-15.2	69	6	2,000	0	0.0	0.0
C / 5.5	10.5	1.00	36.14	1,780	3	96	0	1	88	105.6	-18.6	78	10	2,000	0	5.8	0.0
C / 5.2	10.5	1.00	31.80	20	3	96	0	1	88	100.4	-18.9	72	10	2,000	0	0.0	0.0
C / 5.2	10.5	1.00	31.83	76	3	96	0	1	88	100.4	-18.8	72	10	2,000	0	0.0	0.0
C / 5.5	10.5	1.00	36.07	16	3	96	0	1	88	104.8	-18.6	78	10	0	0	4.5	0.0
C / 5.2	10.5	1.00	31.79	1	3	96	0	1	88	100.3	-18.8	72	10	0	0	0.0	0.0
C / 5.5	10.5	1.00	37.16	163	3	96	0	1	88	108.7	-18.4	82	10	0	0	0.0	0.0
C / 5.5	10.5	1.00	37.07	N/A	3	96	0	1	88	106.6	-18.5	80	10	0	0	0.0	0.0
C / 5.5	10.5	1.00	36.08	2	3	96	0	1	88	103.8	-18.7	76	10	0	0	0.0	0.0
C+ / 6.8	10.5	1.00	37.83	3	3	96	0	1	88	107.4	-18.5	80	10	0	0	0.0	0.0
C / 5.5	10.5	1.00	37.13	N/A	3	96	0	1	88	108.4	-18.4	81	10	0	0	0.0	0.0
C / 5.5	10.5	1.00	35.87	193	3	96	0	1	88	105.2	-18.6	78	10	2,000	0	5.8	0.0
C / 5.5	10.5	1.00	36.20	142	3	96	0	1	88	105.7	-18.6	79	10	500	0	0.0	0.0
C / 5.5	10.5	1.00	37.18	N/A	3	96	0	1	88	108.8	-18.4	82	10	1,000,000	0	0.0	0.0
C / 5.5	10.5	1.00	37.16	992	3	96	0	1	88	107.3	-18.5	80	10	2,000	0	0.0	0.0
B- / 7.3	9.5	1.00	39.94	1,118	3	96	0	1	3	97.2	-16.4	61	6	2,000	0	0.0	0.0
B- / 7.3	9.6	1.00	40.01	N/A	3	96	0	1	3	92.2	-16.7	49	6	2,000	0	0.0	0.0
B- / 7.5	9.6	1.00	40.12	N/A	3	96	0	1	3	99.0	-16.3	64	6	0	0	0.0	0.0
B- / 7.5	9.5	1.00	40.63	169	3	96	0	1	3	98.9	-16.3	64	6	0	0	0.0	0.0
B- / 7.3	9.5	1.00	40.13	2,411	3	96	0	1	3	98.9	-16.3	65	6	2,000	0	0.0	0.0
B- / 7.2	10.5	1.08	9.83	3,605	0	99	0	1	73	106.1	-14.6	54	5	2,000	0	5.8	0.0
B- / 7.2	10.5	1.08	9.79	51	0	99	0	1	73	100.8	-14.9	43	5	2,000	0	0.0	0.0
B- / 7.2	10.5	1.08	9.66	49	0	99	0	1	73	100.8	-14.9	43	5	2,000	0	0.0	0.0
B- / 7.2	10.5	1.08	9.90	330	0	99	0	1	73	109.2	-14.5	63	5	0	0	0.0	0.0
B- / 7.2	10.5	1.08	9.89	30	0	99	0	1	73	107.4	-14.7	57	5	0	0	0.0	0.0
B- / 7.2	10.5	1.08	9.83	3	0	99	0	1	73	104.5	-14.8	52	5	0	0	0.0	0.0
B- / 7.5	10.5	1.08	9.91	1	0	99	0	1	73	107.1	-14.6	57	5	0	0	0.0	0.0
B- / 7.2	10.4	1.07	9.85	70	0	99	0	1	73	109.0	-14.4	62	5	0	0	0.0	0.0
B- / 7.2	10.5	1.08	9.89	77	0	99	0	1	73	105.8	-14.6	54	5	500	0	0.0	0.0
B- / 7.2	10.5	1.08	9.88	44	0	99	0	1	73	108.0	-14.7	59	5	2,000	0	0.0	0.0
C- / 3.6	10.1	1.01	9.17	276	1	98	0	1	105	107.3	-15.9	73	5	2,000	0	5.8	0.0
C- / 3.7	10.1	1.01	9.01	1	1	98	0	1	105	101.8	-16.1	65	5	2,000	0	0.0	0.0
C- / 3.7	10.1	1.01	8.95	9	1	98	0	1	105	102.1	-16.2	64	5	2,000	0	0.0	0.0
C- / 3.6	10.1	1.02	9.32	289	1	98	0	1	105	110.2	-15.7	76	5	0	0	0.0	0.0
C- / 3.6	10.0	1.01	9.31	N/A	1	98	0	1	105	108.6	-15.9	75	5	0	0	0.0	0.0
C- / 3.7	10.1	1.02	9.19	N/A	1	98	0	1	105	105.6	-16.0	70	5	0	0	0.0	0.0
B- / 7.4	10.1	1.01	9.45	N/A	1	98	0	1	105	109.4	-15.9	76	5	0	0	0.0	0.0
C- / 3.6	10.1	1.01	9.22	113	1	98	0	1	105	106.9	-15.9	73	5	500	0	0.0	0.0
C- / 3.6	10.1	1.01	9.23	9	1	98	0	1	105	108.9	-15.8	75	5	2,000	0	0.0	0.0
C+ / 6.8	10.8	1.10	9.56	90	1	98	0	1	90	105.1	-18.6	55	5	2,000	0	5.8	0.0
C+ / 6.9	10.9	1.10	9.50	1	1	98	0	1	90	100.1	-18.9	41	5	2,000	0	0.0	0.0
C+ / 6.9	10.8	1.10	9.37	16	1	98	0	1	90	100.1	-18.9	43	5	2,000	0	0.0	0.0
C+ / 6.8	10.8	1.10	9.64	414	1	98	0	1	90	108.2	-18.5	61	5	0	0	0.0	0.0
C+ / 6.8	10.9	1.10	9.61	N/A	1	98	0	1	90	106.1	-18.5	56	5	0	0	0.0	0.0
C+ / 6.8	10.8	1.10	9.58	1	1	98	0	1	90	103.3	-18.7	51	5	0	0	0.0	0.0
C+ / 6.8	10.9	1.10	9.54	86	1	98	0	1	90	104.8	-18.6	53	5	2,000	0	5.8	0.0
C+ / 6.8	10.9	1.11	9.62	236	1	98	0	1	90	105.0	-18.5	52	5	500	0	0.0	0.0
C+ / 6.8	10.8	1.10	9.64	143	1	98	0	1	90	106.9	-18.5	58	5	2,000	0	0.0	0.0

Fund Type	Fund Name	Ticker Symbol	Overall Investment Rating	Phone	Performance Rating/Pts	3 Mo	6 Mo	1Yr / Pct	3Yr / Pct	5Yr / Pct	Dividend Yield	Expense Ratio
GR	Columbia Life Goal Growth A	NLGIX	C	(800) 345-6611	C / 4.6	2.53	5.00	8.33 /65	12.12 /53	11.28 /55	1.91	1.25
GR	● Columbia Life Goal Growth B	NLGBX	C	(800) 345-6611	C / 5.0	2.38	4.60	7.52 /59	11.26 /47	10.45 /48	1.45	2.00
GR	Columbia Life Goal Growth C	NLGCX	C	(800) 345-6611	C / 5.0	2.33	4.64	7.51 /59	11.28 /47	10.45 /48	1.46	2.00
GR	● Columbia Life Goal Growth K	CGRUX	C+	(800) 345-6611	C+ / 5.7	2.58	5.09	8.44 /66	12.26 /54	11.38 /56	2.11	1.11
GR	Columbia Life Goal Growth R	CLGRX	C+	(800) 345-6611	C / 5.4	2.50	4.86	8.09 /63	11.84 /51	11.00 /53	1.81	1.50
GR	Columbia Life Goal Growth R4	CWPRX	C+	(800) 345-6611	C+ / 5.7	2.64	5.16	8.60 /67	12.35 /55	11.42 /56	2.20	1.00
GR	Columbia Life Goal Growth R5	CGPRX	B-	(800) 345-6611	C+ / 5.8	2.60	5.15	8.72 /68	12.48 /56	11.50 /57	2.31	0.86
GR	Columbia Life Goal Growth Z	NGPAX	C+	(800) 345-6611	C+ / 5.8	2.61	5.16	8.56 /67	12.38 /55	11.57 /57	2.22	1.00
GR	Columbia Marsico 21st Century A	NMTAX	C+	(800) 345-6611	C+ / 6.9	3.94	7.28	12.53 /85	15.39 /78	11.73 /59	0.00	1.23
GR	● Columbia Marsico 21st Century B	NMTBX	B-	(800) 345-6611	B- / 7.4	3.76	6.86	11.68 /81	14.51 /71	10.90 /52	0.00	1.98
GR	Columbia Marsico 21st Century C	NMYCX	B-	(800) 345-6611	B- / 7.4	3.76	6.86	11.68 /81	14.51 /71	10.90 /52	0.00	1.98
GR	Columbia Marsico 21st Century R	CMTRX	B	(800) 345-6611	B / 7.8	3.86	7.09	12.24 /84	15.08 /75	11.46 /56	0.00	1.48
GR	Columbia Marsico 21st Century R4	CTFRX	B+	(800) 345-6611	B+ / 8.3	3.99	7.38	12.79 /86	15.62 /80	11.87 /60	0.00	0.98
GR	Columbia Marsico 21st Century R5	CADQX	B+	(800) 345-6611	B+ / 8.3	4.05	7.50	13.01 /87	15.57 /80	11.84 /60	0.00	0.83
GR	Columbia Marsico 21st Century Z	NMYAX	B+	(800) 345-6611	B+ / 8.3	4.01	7.41	12.80 /86	15.69 /81	12.02 /61	0.00	0.98
GR	Columbia Marsico Flex Cap A	CCMAX	C	(800) 345-6611	C+ / 6.4	2.26	6.36	9.52 /72	15.16 /76	--	0.25	1.29
GR	Columbia Marsico Flex Cap C	CCFCX	C+	(800) 345-6611	C+ / 6.8	1.97	5.87	8.66 /67	14.26 /69	--	0.00	2.04
GR	Columbia Marsico Flex Cap I	CFCIX	B-	(800) 345-6611	B / 7.8	2.33	6.48	9.85 /74	15.58 /80	--	0.64	0.87
GR	Columbia Marsico Flex Cap R	CCFRX	C+	(800) 345-6611	B- / 7.2	2.16	6.19	9.25 /71	14.84 /74	--	0.04	1.54
AA	Columbia Marsico Flex Cap R4	CMECX	B	(800) 345-6611	B- / 7.5	2.27	6.40	9.71 /73	15.22 /77	--	0.48	1.04
AA	Columbia Marsico Flex Cap R5	CTXRX	B+	(800) 345-6611	B / 7.7	2.30	6.48	9.88 /74	15.48 /79	--	0.59	0.92
GR	Columbia Marsico Flex Cap Z	CCMZX	B-	(800) 345-6611	B / 7.6	2.25	6.43	9.78 /73	15.39 /78	--	0.50	1.04
GR	Columbia Marsico Focused Eq A	NFEAX	D	(800) 345-6611	C+ / 6.6	2.60	4.45	16.11 /93	14.94 /74	13.85 /76	0.00	1.21
GR	● Columbia Marsico Focused Eq B	NFEBX	D-	(800) 345-6611	B- / 7.0	2.43	4.06	15.23 /92	14.08 /68	13.00 /68	0.00	1.96
GR	Columbia Marsico Focused Eq C	NFECX	D-	(800) 345-6611	B- / 7.0	2.42	4.09	15.20 /92	14.09 /68	13.00 /68	0.00	1.96
GR	Columbia Marsico Focused Eq I	CMRIX	C-	(800) 345-6611	B / 8.1	2.70	4.72	16.71 /94	15.49 /79	14.41 /81	0.00	0.76
GR	Columbia Marsico Focused Eq R4	CSFRX	B+	(800) 345-6611	B / 7.9	2.67	4.61	16.40 /94	15.17 /76	13.99 /78	0.00	0.96
GR	Columbia Marsico Focused Eq R5	CADRX	B	(800) 345-6611	B / 7.9	2.66	4.66	16.57 /94	15.14 /76	13.97 /77	0.00	0.81
GR	Columbia Marsico Focused Eq Z	NFEPX	C-	(800) 345-6611	B / 7.9	2.68	4.60	16.40 /94	15.23 /77	14.14 /79	0.00	0.96
GL	Columbia Marsico Global A	COGAX	C	(800) 345-6611	C+ / 5.9	4.42	5.60	9.46 /72	14.12 /68	13.63 /74	0.00	1.80
GL	Columbia Marsico Global C	COGCX	C+	(800) 345-6611	C+ / 6.3	4.27	5.23	8.71 /68	13.27 /62	12.81 /66	0.00	2.55
GL	Columbia Marsico Global R	COGRX	C+	(800) 345-6611	C+ / 6.7	4.32	5.50	9.16 /70	13.83 /66	13.36 /72	0.00	2.05
GL	Columbia Marsico Global R4	CADHX	B	(800) 345-6611	B- / 7.0	4.44	5.68	9.67 /73	14.22 /69	13.70 /75	0.00	N/A
GL	Columbia Marsico Global R5	CADIX	B	(800) 345-6611	B- / 7.0	4.44	5.76	9.75 /73	14.25 /69	13.71 /75	0.00	N/A
GL	Columbia Marsico Global Z	COGZX	B-	(800) 345-6611	B- / 7.1	4.44	5.68	9.75 /73	14.37 /70	13.93 /77	0.00	1.55
GR	Columbia Marsico Growth A	NMGIX	C-	(800) 345-6611	C / 5.5	1.85	3.68	12.29 /84	13.44 /63	13.43 /72	0.00	1.18
GR	● Columbia Marsico Growth B	NGIBX	D+	(800) 345-6611	C+ / 5.9	1.66	3.29	11.42 /80	12.59 /57	12.58 /65	0.00	1.93
GR	Columbia Marsico Growth C	NMICX	D+	(800) 345-6611	C+ / 5.9	1.66	3.28	11.40 /80	12.60 /57	12.58 /65	0.00	1.93
GI	Columbia Marsico Growth I	CMWIX	C	(800) 345-6611	C+ / 6.8	1.96	3.90	12.72 /86	13.92 /66	13.91 /77	0.00	0.72
GR	Columbia Marsico Growth R	CMWRX	C-	(800) 345-6611	C+ / 6.3	1.76	3.54	11.94 /82	13.14 /61	13.14 /69	0.00	1.43
GI	Columbia Marsico Growth R4	CWSRX	C+	(800) 345-6611	C+ / 6.7	1.93	3.81	12.55 /85	13.66 /65	13.56 /73	0.00	0.93
GI	Columbia Marsico Growth R5	CTGRX	C+	(800) 345-6611	C+ / 6.8	1.93	3.88	12.71 /86	13.79 /66	13.64 /74	0.00	0.77
GI	Columbia Marsico Growth W	CMSWX	C-	(800) 345-6611	C+ / 6.5	1.89	3.72	12.32 /84	13.46 /63	13.46 /72	0.00	1.18
GR	Columbia Marsico Growth Z	NGIPX	C	(800) 345-6611	C+ / 6.7	1.92	3.80	12.55 /85	13.72 /65	13.71 /75	0.00	0.93
FO	Columbia Marsico Intl Opps A	MAIOX	D-	(800) 345-6611	D / 2.1	5.17	7.62	4.90 /38	7.25 /23	6.01 /17	0.18	1.41
FO	● Columbia Marsico Intl Opps B	MBIOX	D-	(800) 345-6611	D+ / 2.5	5.11	7.32	4.16 /33	6.46 /19	5.25 /13	0.08	2.16
FO	Columbia Marsico Intl Opps C	MCIOX	D-	(800) 345-6611	D+ / 2.5	5.02	7.23	4.16 /33	6.42 /19	5.23 /13	0.08	2.16
FO	Columbia Marsico Intl Opps I	CMOIX	D	(800) 345-6611	C- / 3.3	5.36	7.97	5.39 /42	7.70 /25	6.53 /20	0.25	0.98
FO	Columbia Marsico Intl Opps R	CMORX	D-	(800) 345-6611	D+ / 2.8	5.15	7.54	4.67 /36	6.99 /21	5.76 /15	0.15	1.66
FO	Columbia Marsico Intl Opps R4	CLFRX	D	(800) 345-6611	C- / 3.2	5.31	7.85	5.24 /40	7.48 /24	6.15 /18	0.22	1.16
FO	Columbia Marsico Intl Opps Z	NMOAX	D-	(800) 345-6611	C- / 3.2	5.34	7.82	5.20 /40	7.53 /24	6.29 /19	0.23	1.16
MC	Columbia Mid Cap Growth A	CBSAX	C-	(800) 345-6611	C+ / 6.2	6.54	10.71	12.94 /86	12.76 /58	13.63 /74	0.00	1.18

● Denotes fund is closed to new investors
* Denotes fund is included in Section II

www.thestreetratings.com

RISK	3 Year		NET ASSETS		ASSET					BULL / BEAR		FUND MANAGER		MINIMUMS		LOADS	
Risk Rating/Pts	Standard Deviation	Beta	NAV As of 3/31/15	Total $(Mil)	Cash %	Stocks %	Bonds %	Other %	Portfolio Turnover Ratio	Last Bull Market Return	Last Bear Market Return	Manager Quality Pct	Manager Tenure (Years)	Initial Purch. $	Additional Purch. $	Front End Load	Back End Load
C+ / 6.8	9.5	0.96	15.90	639	3	88	1	8	18	75.7	-20.0	26	N/A	2,000	0	5.8	0.0
C+ / 6.7	9.6	0.96	14.38	26	3	88	1	8	18	71.3	-20.3	18	N/A	2,000	0	0.0	0.0
C+ / 6.7	9.5	0.96	14.25	100	3	88	1	8	18	71.3	-20.3	19	N/A	2,000	0	0.0	0.0
C+ / 6.8	9.5	0.96	16.20	N/A	3	88	1	8	18	76.4	-20.1	27	4	0	0	0.0	0.0
C+ / 6.8	9.5	0.96	15.73	3	3	88	1	8	18	74.2	-20.1	24	N/A	0	0	0.0	0.0
B- / 7.1	9.5	0.96	16.41	N/A	3	88	1	8	18	76.7	-20.0	28	6	0	0	0.0	0.0
B- / 7.1	9.6	0.96	16.41	N/A	3	88	1	8	18	77.4	-20.0	29	6	0	0	0.0	0.0
C+ / 6.8	9.5	0.96	16.21	52	3	88	1	8	18	77.2	-20.0	29	N/A	2,000	0	0.0	0.0
C+ / 5.9	11.2	0.99	21.38	477	0	99	0	1	99	98.7	-25.5	61	4	2,000	0	5.8	0.0
C+ / 5.9	11.2	0.99	19.31	26	0	99	0	1	99	93.5	-25.7	48	4	2,000	0	0.0	0.0
C+ / 5.8	11.2	0.99	19.31	247	0	99	0	1	99	93.5	-25.7	48	4	2,000	0	0.0	0.0
C+ / 5.9	11.2	0.99	21.00	21	0	99	0	1	99	96.8	-25.5	56	4	0	0	0.0	0.0
C+ / 6.2	11.2	0.99	22.40	1	0	99	0	1	99	99.9	-25.5	63	4	0	0	0.0	0.0
C+ / 6.2	11.2	0.99	22.07	N/A	0	99	0	1	99	99.6	-25.5	63	4	100,000	0	0.0	0.0
C+ / 5.9	11.2	0.99	22.03	237	0	99	0	1	99	100.3	-25.4	64	4	2,000	0	0.0	0.0
C / 5.4	10.1	0.90	14.91	90	6	89	4	1	119	95.0	-17.5	74	3	2,000	0	5.8	0.0
C / 5.3	10.1	0.91	14.46	27	6	89	4	1	119	90.1	-17.8	64	3	2,000	0	0.0	0.0
C / 5.4	10.2	0.90	14.95	N/A	6	89	4	1	119	97.7	-17.7	77	3	0	0	0.0	0.0
C / 5.4	10.2	0.90	14.68	1	6	89	4	1	119	93.3	-17.6	71	3	0	0	0.0	0.0
C+ / 5.8	10.1	1.53	14.86	2	6	89	4	1	119	95.4	-17.5	43	3	0	0	0.0	0.0
C+ / 6.9	10.1	1.53	15.15	2	6	89	4	1	119	96.6	-17.5	46	3	0	0	0.0	0.0
C / 5.5	10.1	0.90	15.02	80	6	89	4	1	119	96.5	-17.4	76	3	0	0	0.0	0.0
D / 2.2	10.9	0.95	20.16	526	2	97	0	1	95	97.3	-17.6	63	18	2,000	0	5.8	0.0
E+ / 0.9	10.9	0.96	16.41	6	2	97	0	1	95	92.3	-17.9	51	18	2,000	0	0.0	0.0
D- / 1.0	10.9	0.95	16.52	221	2	97	0	1	95	92.4	-17.9	52	18	2,000	0	0.0	0.0
D+ / 2.5	10.9	0.95	21.27	N/A	2	97	0	1	95	100.6	-17.4	69	18	0	0	0.0	0.0
C+ / 6.6	10.9	0.96	21.52	18	2	97	0	1	95	98.5	-17.6	65	18	0	0	0.0	0.0
C / 5.5	10.9	0.95	21.60	9	2	97	0	1	95	98.3	-17.6	65	18	100,000	0	0.0	0.0
D+ / 2.5	10.9	0.95	21.09	277	2	97	0	1	95	99.1	-17.5	66	18	2,000	0	0.0	0.0
C+ / 5.8	11.1	0.68	13.46	34	9	90	0	1	149	94.5	-23.6	96	7	2,000	0	5.8	0.0
C+ / 5.7	11.2	0.68	12.95	10	9	90	0	1	149	89.8	-23.9	95	7	2,000	0	0.0	0.0
C+ / 5.8	11.1	0.68	13.29	1	9	90	0	1	149	92.7	-23.7	96	7	0	0	0.0	0.0
C+ / 6.5	11.1	0.68	13.63	4	9	90	0	1	149	95.0	-23.6	96	7	0	0	0.0	0.0
C+ / 6.5	11.1	0.68	13.64	N/A	9	90	0	1	149	95.1	-23.6	96	7	100,000	0	0.0	0.0
C+ / 5.8	11.1	0.68	13.63	10	9	90	0	1	149	96.3	-23.6	96	7	2,000	0	0.0	0.0
C / 4.3	10.8	0.97	24.25	418	1	98	0	1	97	90.3	-18.1	38	17	2,000	0	5.8	0.0
C- / 3.8	10.9	0.97	20.84	4	1	98	0	1	97	85.4	-18.4	28	17	2,000	0	0.0	0.0
C- / 3.8	10.9	0.97	20.88	287	1	98	0	1	97	85.5	-18.4	29	17	2,000	0	0.0	0.0
C / 4.4	10.9	0.97	24.99	N/A	1	98	0	1	97	93.5	-18.0	44	17	0	0	0.0	0.0
C / 4.3	10.9	0.97	23.74	23	1	98	0	1	97	88.6	-18.2	34	17	0	0	0.0	0.0
C+ / 6.5	10.9	0.97	25.35	27	1	98	0	1	97	91.4	-18.1	41	17	0	0	0.0	0.0
C+ / 6.6	10.9	0.97	25.36	12	1	98	0	1	97	92.0	-18.1	43	17	0	0	0.0	0.0
C / 4.3	10.9	0.97	24.26	N/A	1	98	0	1	97	90.4	-18.1	38	17	500	0	0.0	0.0
C / 4.4	10.9	0.97	24.91	814	1	98	0	1	97	91.9	-18.1	42	17	2,000	0	0.0	0.0
C / 4.8	12.9	0.87	13.84	40	1	98	0	1	141	51.7	-25.3	53	5	2,000	0	5.8	0.0
C / 4.8	12.9	0.87	12.76	1	1	98	0	1	141	48.0	-25.6	42	5	2,000	0	0.0	0.0
C / 4.8	12.9	0.87	12.76	12	1	98	0	1	141	47.8	-25.6	41	5	2,000	0	0.0	0.0
C / 4.8	12.9	0.87	14.36	N/A	1	98	0	1	141	53.9	-25.2	60	5	2,000	0	0.0	0.0
C / 4.8	13.0	0.87	13.69	1	1	98	0	1	141	50.4	-25.3	49	5	0	0	0.0	0.0
C+ / 5.8	12.9	0.87	14.28	1	1	98	0	1	141	52.5	-25.3	56	5	0	0	0.0	0.0
C / 4.8	12.9	0.87	14.20	29	1	98	0	1	141	53.0	-25.2	57	5	2,000	0	0.0	0.0
C- / 4.0	11.6	0.97	29.48	1,005	2	97	0	1	100	78.3	-23.1	23	9	2,000	0	5.8	0.0

					PERFORMANCE							
						Total Return % through 3/31/15					Incl. in Returns	
					Perfor-				Annualized		Dividend	Expense
Fund		Ticker	Overall Investment		mance						Yield	Ratio
Type	Fund Name	Symbol	Rating	Phone	Rating/Pts	3 Mo	6 Mo	1Yr / Pct	3Yr / Pct	5Yr / Pct		
MC	● Columbia Mid Cap Growth B	CBSBX	C-	(800) 345-6611	C+ / 6.6	6.30	10.25	12.08 /83	11.90 /52	12.77 /66	0.00	1.93
MC	Columbia Mid Cap Growth C	CMCCX	C-	(800) 345-6611	C+ / 6.6	6.31	10.29	12.07 /83	11.90 /52	12.78 /66	0.00	1.93
MC	Columbia Mid Cap Growth I	CMTIX	C	(800) 345-6611	B / 7.6	6.62	10.95	13.43 /88	13.25 /61	14.10 /79	0.00	0.75
MC	● Columbia Mid Cap Growth K	CMCKX	B	(800) 345-6611	B- / 7.4	6.54	10.79	13.08 /87	12.95 /59	13.86 /76	0.00	1.05
MC	Columbia Mid Cap Growth R	CMGRX	C	(800) 345-6611	B- / 7.0	6.46	10.58	12.67 /85	12.47 /56	13.35 /71	0.00	1.43
MC	Columbia Mid Cap Growth R4	CPGRX	B	(800) 345-6611	B- / 7.4	6.60	10.84	13.23 /87	13.00 /60	13.89 /77	0.00	0.93
MC	Columbia Mid Cap Growth R5	CMGVX	C	(800) 345-6611	B- / 7.5	6.61	10.90	13.35 /88	13.17 /61	14.04 /78	0.00	0.80
MC	● Columbia Mid Cap Growth T	CBSTX	C-	(800) 345-6611	C+ / 6.1	6.49	10.70	12.89 /86	12.70 /57	13.57 /74	0.00	1.18
MC	Columbia Mid Cap Growth W	CMRWX	C	(800) 345-6611	B- / 7.2	6.50	10.70	12.93 /86	12.74 /58	13.63 /74	0.00	1.18
MC	Columbia Mid Cap Growth Y	CMGYX	C	(800) 345-6611	B / 7.6	6.65	10.91	13.40 /88	13.21 /61	14.06 /78	0.00	0.75
MC	Columbia Mid Cap Growth Z	CLSPX	C	(800) 345-6611	B- / 7.4	6.60	10.85	13.25 /87	13.04 /60	13.91 /77	0.00	0.93
MC	Columbia Mid Cap Index A	NTIAX	A	(800) 345-6611	B+ / 8.9	5.21	11.72	11.66 /81	16.49 /87	15.20 /88	0.83	0.67
MC	Columbia Mid Cap Index I	CIDIX	A	(800) 345-6611	A- / 9.1	5.30	11.96	12.09 /83	16.84 /89	15.52 /90	1.10	0.23
MC	Columbia Mid Cap Index R5	CPXRX	A+	(800) 345-6611	A- / 9.1	5.28	11.86	11.99 /82	16.83 /89	15.51 /90	1.05	0.28
MC	Columbia Mid Cap Index Z	NMPAX	A	(800) 345-6611	A- / 9.0	5.30	11.91	11.97 /82	16.80 /89	15.49 /90	1.06	0.42
MC	Columbia Mid Cap Value A	CMUAX	C+	(800) 345-6611	B- / 7.3	1.53	4.84	8.33 /65	17.04 /90	14.28 /80	0.38	1.17
MC	● Columbia Mid Cap Value B	CMUBX	B-	(800) 345-6611	B / 7.7	1.29	4.42	7.50 /59	16.15 /84	13.41 /72	0.11	1.92
MC	Columbia Mid Cap Value C	CMUCX	B-	(800) 345-6611	B / 7.7	1.29	4.39	7.47 /59	16.15 /84	13.41 /72	0.11	1.92
MC	Columbia Mid Cap Value I	CMVUX	B+	(800) 345-6611	B+ / 8.7	1.64	5.07	8.80 /68	17.56 /93	14.77 /85	0.80	0.73
MC	● Columbia Mid Cap Value K	CMUFX	B+	(800) 345-6611	B+ / 8.5	1.50	4.90	8.46 /66	17.22 /91	14.47 /82	0.54	1.03
MC	Columbia Mid Cap Value R	CMVRX	B	(800) 345-6611	B / 8.2	1.41	4.66	8.00 /63	16.75 /88	13.97 /77	0.22	1.42
MC	Columbia Mid Cap Value R4	CFDRX	A+	(800) 345-6611	B+ / 8.6	1.56	4.99	8.62 /67	17.37 /92	14.58 /83	0.62	0.92
MC	Columbia Mid Cap Value R5	CVERX	A+	(800) 345-6611	B+ / 8.7	1.59	5.00	8.76 /68	17.49 /92	14.65 /84	0.74	0.78
MC	Columbia Mid Cap Value W	CMUWX	B	(800) 345-6611	B+ / 8.4	1.47	4.78	8.27 /65	17.02 /90	14.27 /80	0.41	1.17
MC	Columbia Mid Cap Value Y	CMVYX	B+	(800) 345-6611	B+ / 8.7	1.63	5.06	8.79 /68	17.53 /92	14.71 /84	0.79	0.73
MC	Columbia Mid Cap Value Z	NAMAX	B+	(800) 345-6611	B+ / 8.6	1.53	4.96	8.58 /67	17.34 /92	14.56 /83	0.63	0.92
IN	Columbia Mortgage Opportunities I	CLMIX	U	(800) 345-6611	U /	0.99	2.26	--	--	--	0.00	0.85
FO	Columbia Multi-Adv Intl Equity A	NIIAX	D-	(800) 345-6611	D- / 1.2	5.09	2.76	-1.61 /11	6.03 /17	4.54 /10	0.00	1.42
FO	● Columbia Multi-Adv Intl Equity B	NIENX	D-	(800) 345-6611	D- / 1.4	4.90	2.31	-2.36 /10	5.22 /14	3.73 / 7	0.00	2.17
FO	Columbia Multi-Adv Intl Equity C	NITRX	D-	(800) 345-6611	D- / 1.4	4.88	2.25	-2.39 /10	5.22 /14	3.74 / 7	0.00	2.17
FO	Columbia Multi-Adv Intl Equity I	CUAIX	D-	(800) 345-6611	D / 2.0	5.28	2.99	-1.08 /13	6.57 /19	5.02 /12	0.00	0.94
FO	● Columbia Multi-Adv Intl Equity K	CMEFX	D-	(800) 345-6611	D / 1.8	5.15	2.86	-1.37 /12	6.23 /18	4.74 /11	0.00	1.24
FO	Columbia Multi-Adv Intl Equity R	CIERX	D-	(800) 345-6611	D / 1.6	5.12	2.69	-1.77 /11	5.81 /16	4.29 / 9	0.00	1.67
FO	Columbia Multi-Adv Intl Equity R4	CQYRX	D	(800) 345-6611	D / 1.8	5.12	2.84	-1.36 /12	6.26 /18	4.79 /11	0.00	1.17
FO	Columbia Multi-Adv Intl Equity R5	CQQRX	D	(800) 345-6611	D / 1.9	5.26	2.98	-1.15 /13	6.43 /19	4.89 /11	0.00	0.99
FO	Columbia Multi-Adv Intl Equity W	CMAWX	D-	(800) 345-6611	D / 1.7	5.09	2.68	-1.61 /11	6.03 /17	4.54 /10	0.00	1.42
FO	Columbia Multi-Adv Intl Equity Y	CMIYX	D-	(800) 345-6611	D / 2.0	5.19	2.99	-1.08 /13	6.55 /19	4.99 /12	0.00	0.94
FO	Columbia Multi-Adv Intl Equity Z	NIEQX	D-	(800) 345-6611	D / 1.9	5.15	2.86	-1.37 /12	6.28 /18	4.80 /11	0.00	1.17
SC	Columbia Multi-Adv Sm Cp Val A	ASVAX	C-	(800) 345-6611	C / 5.2	1.90	8.96	3.41 /29	13.70 /65	11.78 /59	0.07	1.64
SC	● Columbia Multi-Adv Sm Cp Val B	ASVBX	D+	(800) 345-6611	C+ / 5.7	1.68	8.58	2.53 /24	12.88 /59	10.94 /52	0.00	2.39
SC	Columbia Multi-Adv Sm Cp Val C	APVCX	D+	(800) 345-6611	C+ / 5.7	1.67	8.56	2.69 /25	12.90 /59	10.99 /53	0.00	2.39
SC	Columbia Multi-Adv Sm Cp Val I	CAVIX	C	(800) 345-6611	C+ / 6.5	1.92	9.18	3.78 /30	14.19 /69	12.27 /62	0.23	1.13
SC	● Columbia Multi-Adv Sm Cp Val K	RSGLX	C	(800) 345-6611	C+ / 6.3	1.84	9.03	3.49 /29	13.88 /66	11.97 /60	0.13	1.43
SC	Columbia Multi-Adv Sm Cp Val R	RSVTX	C-	(800) 345-6611	C+ / 6.1	1.78	8.84	3.23 /28	13.48 /63	11.51 /57	0.00	1.89
SC	Columbia Multi-Adv Sm Cp Val R4	RSVRX	C	(800) 345-6611	C+ / 6.3	1.87	9.07	3.60 /29	13.90 /66	11.85 /60	0.17	1.39
SC	Columbia Multi-Adv Sm Cp Val R5	RSCVX	C	(800) 345-6611	C+ / 6.5	1.95	9.15	3.81 /31	14.16 /68	12.22 /62	0.22	1.18
SC	Columbia Multi-Adv Sm Cp Val Z	CMAZX	C	(800) 345-6611	C+ / 6.4	1.93	9.16	3.59 /29	14.02 /67	11.99 /60	0.16	1.39
FO	Columbia Overseas Value A	COAVX	D+	(800) 345-6611	D / 2.1	6.02	1.34	-1.43 /12	8.77 /31	5.81 /16	2.89	1.71
FO	● Columbia Overseas Value B	COBVX	D+	(800) 345-6611	D+ / 2.5	5.90	1.11	-2.01 /10	7.98 /27	5.03 /12	2.30	2.46
FO	Columbia Overseas Value C	COCVX	D+	(800) 345-6611	D+ / 2.5	5.90	1.11	-2.01 /10	7.98 /27	5.03 /12	2.30	2.46
FO	Columbia Overseas Value I	COVIX	D+	(800) 345-6611	C- / 3.3	6.27	1.67	-0.82 /14	9.22 /34	6.22 /18	3.55	1.04
FO	● Columbia Overseas Value K	COKVX	C-	(800) 345-6611	C- / 3.1	6.02	1.51	-1.24 /12	8.96 /33	6.03 /17	3.26	1.34

● Denotes fund is closed to new investors
* Denotes fund is included in Section II

www.thestreetratings.com

RISK			NET ASSETS		ASSET					BULL / BEAR		FUND MANAGER		MINIMUMS		LOADS	
	3 Year		NAV						Portfolio	Last Bull	Last Bear	Manager	Manager	Initial	Additional	Front	Back
Risk Rating/Pts	Standard Deviation	Beta	As of 3/31/15	Total $(Mil)	Cash %	Stocks %	Bonds %	Other %	Turnover Ratio	Market Return	Market Return	Quality Pct	Tenure (Years)	Purch. $	Purch. $	End Load	End Load
C- / 3.6	11.6	0.97	25.99	10	2	97	0	1	100	73.7	-23.4	16	9	2,000	0	0.0	0.0
C- / 3.6	11.6	0.97	26.11	53	2	97	0	1	100	73.7	-23.4	16	9	2,000	0	0.0	0.0
C- / 4.1	11.6	0.97	31.07	50	2	97	0	1	100	80.9	-23.0	28	9	0	0	0.0	0.0
C+ / 6.4	11.6	0.97	30.78	1	2	97	0	1	100	79.4	-23.0	25	9	0	0	0.0	0.0
C- / 3.9	11.6	0.97	28.68	20	2	97	0	1	100	76.7	-23.2	21	9	0	0	0.0	0.0
C+ / 6.4	11.6	0.97	31.48	1	2	97	0	1	100	79.6	-23.0	25	9	0	0	0.0	0.0
C- / 4.1	11.6	0.97	30.98	40	2	97	0	1	100	80.6	-23.0	27	9	0	0	0.0	0.0
C- / 4.0	11.6	0.96	29.39	25	2	97	0	1	100	77.9	-23.1	23	9	2,000	0	5.8	0.0
C- / 4.0	11.6	0.97	29.48	N/A	2	97	0	1	100	78.3	-23.1	23	9	500	0	0.0	0.0
C- / 4.1	11.6	0.96	30.97	N/A	2	97	0	1	100	80.7	-23.0	27	9	0	0	0.0	0.0
C- / 4.1	11.6	0.97	30.83	1,042	2	97	0	1	100	79.8	-23.0	26	9	0	0	0.0	0.0
C+ / 6.4	11.0	1.00	16.35	1,086	3	96	0	1	14	99.6	-22.7	60	6	2,000	0	0.0	0.0
C+ / 6.4	11.0	1.00	16.30	N/A	3	96	0	1	14	101.7	-22.6	65	6	0	0	0.0	0.0
C+ / 6.8	11.1	1.01	16.55	633	3	96	0	1	14	101.6	-22.6	63	6	0	0	0.0	0.0
C+ / 6.4	11.0	1.00	16.30	2,305	3	96	0	1	14	101.4	-22.6	64	6	2,000	0	0.0	0.0
C / 5.5	10.2	0.89	17.27	1,109	5	94	0	1	48	101.7	-23.2	82	11	2,000	0	5.8	0.0
C / 5.4	10.2	0.89	16.46	9	5	94	0	1	48	96.6	-23.5	77	11	2,000	0	0.0	0.0
C / 5.4	10.2	0.89	16.54	139	5	94	0	1	48	96.7	-23.4	77	11	2,000	0	0.0	0.0
C / 5.5	10.2	0.89	17.26	N/A	5	94	0	1	48	104.9	-23.1	85	11	0	0	0.0	0.0
C+ / 5.6	10.2	0.89	17.32	N/A	5	94	0	1	48	103.0	-23.2	83	11	0	0	0.0	0.0
C+ / 5.6	10.2	0.89	17.22	78	5	94	0	1	48	100.2	-23.3	81	11	0	0	0.0	0.0
B- / 7.3	10.2	0.89	17.60	36	5	94	0	1	48	103.6	-23.1	84	11	0	0	0.0	0.0
B- / 7.3	10.2	0.89	17.60	74	5	94	0	1	48	104.2	-23.1	85	11	0	0	0.0	0.0
C / 5.5	10.2	0.89	17.26	1	5	94	0	1	48	101.7	-23.2	82	11	500	0	0.0	0.0
C / 5.5	10.2	0.89	17.26	28	5	94	0	1	48	104.6	-23.1	85	11	1,000,000	0	0.0	0.0
C+ / 5.6	10.2	0.89	17.29	2,321	5	94	0	1	48	103.4	-23.1	84	11	2,000	0	0.0	0.0
U /	N/A	N/A	9.93	225	0	0	0	100	0	N/A	N/A	N/A	1	0	0	0.0	0.0
C+ / 5.8	13.2	0.96	13.42	267	2	97	0	1	125	45.9	-25.2	26	6	2,000	0	5.8	0.0
C+ / 5.7	13.1	0.96	11.98	2	2	97	0	1	125	42.2	-25.5	19	6	2,000	0	0.0	0.0
C+ / 5.7	13.1	0.96	11.83	11	2	97	0	1	125	42.2	-25.4	19	6	2,000	0	0.0	0.0
C+ / 5.8	13.1	0.96	13.76	N/A	2	97	0	1	125	48.3	-25.0	32	6	0	0	0.0	0.0
C+ / 5.8	13.2	0.96	13.67	N/A	2	97	0	1	125	46.9	-25.1	28	6	0	0	0.0	0.0
C+ / 5.8	13.1	0.96	13.35	1	2	97	0	1	125	44.8	-25.3	24	6	0	0	0.0	0.0
C+ / 6.6	13.1	0.96	13.76	N/A	2	97	0	1	125	47.2	-25.1	28	6	0	0	0.0	0.0
C+ / 6.6	13.1	0.96	13.81	N/A	2	97	0	1	125	47.8	-25.1	31	6	0	0	0.0	0.0
C+ / 5.8	13.2	0.96	13.42	200	2	97	0	1	125	46.0	-25.2	26	6	500	0	0.0	0.0
C+ / 5.8	13.1	0.96	13.77	15	2	97	0	1	125	48.3	-25.0	31	6	0	0	0.0	0.0
C+ / 5.8	13.1	0.96	13.68	134	2	97	0	1	125	47.3	-25.1	29	6	2,000	0	0.0	0.0
C / 4.7	12.9	0.93	6.97	284	10	89	0	1	74	93.8	-27.2	50	11	2,000	0	5.8	0.0
C- / 4.1	12.9	0.93	6.06	6	10	89	0	1	74	89.0	-27.4	38	11	2,000	0	0.0	0.0
C- / 4.1	12.9	0.93	6.09	11	10	89	0	1	74	89.0	-27.4	39	11	2,000	0	0.0	0.0
C / 4.9	12.9	0.93	7.44	23	10	89	0	1	74	96.8	-27.0	56	11	0	0	0.0	0.0
C / 4.8	12.9	0.93	7.20	3	10	89	0	1	74	94.6	-27.0	52	11	0	0	0.0	0.0
C / 4.6	12.9	0.93	6.87	6	10	89	0	1	74	92.3	-27.2	47	11	0	0	0.0	0.0
C / 4.7	12.9	0.93	7.10	10	10	89	0	1	74	94.5	-27.0	53	11	0	0	0.0	0.0
C / 4.8	12.9	0.93	7.32	24	10	89	0	1	74	96.2	-26.9	56	11	0	0	0.0	0.0
C / 4.8	12.9	0.93	7.38	10	10	89	0	1	74	95.4	-27.0	53	11	2,000	0	0.0	0.0
B- / 7.0	13.3	0.98	8.63	186	0	99	0	1	63	49.1	-22.6	60	7	2,000	100	5.8	0.0
B- / 7.0	13.3	0.98	8.62	5	0	99	0	1	63	45.3	-22.8	49	7	2,000	100	0.0	0.0
B- / 7.0	13.3	0.98	8.62	5	0	99	0	1	63	45.3	-22.8	49	7	2,000	100	0.0	0.0
C+ / 5.9	13.3	0.98	8.64	278	0	99	0	1	63	51.1	-22.5	66	7	0	0	0.0	0.0
B- / 7.0	13.2	0.98	8.63	N/A	0	99	0	1	63	50.1	-22.5	63	7	0	0	0.0	0.0

						Total Return % through 3/31/15					Incl. in Returns	
	99 Pct = Best 0 Pct = Worst		Overall		Perfor-				Annualized		Dividend	Expense
Fund Type	Fund Name	Ticker Symbol	Investment Rating	Phone	mance Rating/Pts	3 Mo	6 Mo	1Yr / Pct	3Yr / Pct	5Yr / Pct	Yield	Ratio
FO	Columbia Overseas Value W	COVWX	D	(800) 345-6611	C- / 3.0	6.02	1.46	-1.32 /12	8.78 /32	5.86 /16	3.07	1.71
FO	Columbia Overseas Value Z	COSZX	D+	(800) 345-6611	C- / 3.2	6.14	1.45	-1.18 /12	9.01 /33	6.06 /17	3.32	1.46
FO	Columbia Pacific/Asia A	CASAX	C-	(800) 345-6611	C / 4.3	9.14	8.29	12.17 /83	8.94 /32	7.18 /24	0.82	1.49
FO	Columbia Pacific/Asia C	CASCX	C	(800) 345-6611	C / 4.7	8.86	7.83	11.36 /80	8.13 /28	6.41 /19	0.33	2.24
FO	Columbia Pacific/Asia I	CPCIX	C+	(800) 345-6611	C / 5.5	9.11	8.38	12.61 /85	9.38 /35	7.57 /27	1.25	1.05
FO	Columbia Pacific/Asia R4	CPRAX	C+	(800) 345-6611	C / 5.4	9.09	8.26	12.42 /84	9.20 /34	7.41 /26	1.02	1.24
FO	Columbia Pacific/Asia W	CPAWX	C+	(800) 345-6611	C / 5.2	9.03	8.16	12.16 /83	8.89 /32	7.13 /24	0.85	1.49
FO	Columbia Pacific/Asia Z	USPAX	C	(800) 345-6611	C / 5.4	9.10	8.34	12.51 /85	9.22 /34	7.42 /26	1.08	1.24
RE	Columbia Real Estate Equity A	CREAX	C-	(800) 345-6611	B- / 7.5	3.89	18.68	22.07 /97	12.22 /54	13.77 /76	1.51	1.28
RE	● Columbia Real Estate Equity B	CREBX	C-	(800) 345-6611	B / 7.9	3.69	18.19	21.11 /97	11.40 /48	12.91 /67	0.91	2.03
RE	Columbia Real Estate Equity C	CRECX	C-	(800) 345-6611	B / 7.9	3.69	18.25	21.16 /97	11.40 /48	12.91 /67	0.92	2.03
RE	Columbia Real Estate Equity I	CREIX	C	(800) 345-6611	B+ / 8.9	3.99	18.94	22.59 /97	12.74 /58	14.28 /80	1.99	0.80
RE	● Columbia Real Estate Equity K	CRRFX	C	(800) 345-6611	B+ / 8.7	3.98	18.78	22.25 /97	12.43 /55	13.97 /77	1.72	1.10
RE	Columbia Real Estate Equity R	CRSRX	C	(800) 345-6611	B+ / 8.4	3.83	18.55	21.78 /97	11.95 /52	13.47 /73	1.37	1.53
RE	Columbia Real Estate Equity R4	CRERX	B	(800) 345-6611	B+ / 8.7	4.01	18.88	22.37 /97	12.51 /56	14.04 /78	1.79	1.03
RE	Columbia Real Estate Equity R5	CRRVX	C	(800) 345-6611	B+ / 8.8	3.99	18.83	22.47 /97	12.59 /57	14.15 /79	1.96	0.85
RE	Columbia Real Estate Equity W	CREWX	C	(800) 345-6611	B+ / 8.5	3.89	18.67	22.05 /97	12.21 /54	13.77 /76	1.60	1.28
RE	Columbia Real Estate Equity Z	CREEX	C	(800) 345-6611	B+ / 8.7	3.95	18.79	22.33 /97	12.51 /56	14.04 /78	1.82	1.03
GL	Columbia Select Global Equity A	IGLGX	D	(800) 345-6611	D+ / 2.8	1.95	2.32	3.71 /30	9.63 /37	8.48 /33	0.24	1.41
GL	● Columbia Select Global Equity B	IDGBX	D+	(800) 345-6611	C- / 3.2	1.78	2.00	3.04 /27	8.84 /32	7.68 /28	0.00	2.16
GL	Columbia Select Global Equity C	RGCEX	D+	(800) 345-6611	C- / 3.2	1.69	1.92	2.96 /26	8.82 /32	7.67 /28	0.00	2.16
GL	Columbia Select Global Equity I	CGEIX	C-	(800) 345-6611	C- / 4.0	2.04	2.56	4.26 /33	10.14 /40	9.01 /37	0.70	0.95
GL	● Columbia Select Global Equity K	IDGYX	C-	(800) 345-6611	C- / 3.8	1.94	2.39	3.98 /32	9.83 /38	8.70 /35	0.44	1.25
GL	Columbia Select Global Equity R	CGERX	D+	(800) 345-6611	C- / 3.5	1.84	2.16	3.43 /29	9.36 /35	8.21 /31	0.01	1.66
GL	Columbia Select Global Equity R5	RGERX	C-	(800) 345-6611	C- / 4.0	2.04	2.65	4.24 /33	10.15 /40	8.99 /37	0.68	1.00
GL	Columbia Select Global Equity W	CGEWX	C-	(800) 345-6611	C- / 3.7	1.94	2.28	3.77 /30	9.62 /37	8.51 /33	0.23	1.41
GL	Columbia Select Global Equity Z	CGEZX	C-	(800) 345-6611	C- / 3.9	1.94	2.44	4.04 /32	9.87 /39	8.72 /35	0.48	1.16
GR	Columbia Select Large Cap Equity A	NSGAX	D	(800) 345-6611	C+ / 6.7	2.00	6.79	13.10 /87	15.07 /75	13.11 /69	0.66	1.25
GR	● Columbia Select Large Cap Equity B	NSIBX	D+	(800) 345-6611	B- / 7.1	1.79	6.36	12.24 /84	14.19 /69	12.25 /62	0.08	2.00
GR	Columbia Select Large Cap Equity C	NSGCX	D	(800) 345-6611	B- / 7.0	1.71	6.37	12.15 /83	14.17 /68	12.24 /62	0.08	2.00
GR	Columbia Select Large Cap Equity I	CLPIX	C-	(800) 345-6611	B / 8.1	2.10	7.00	13.52 /88	15.51 /79	13.55 /73	1.05	0.81
GR	Columbia Select Large Cap Equity R5	CLCRX	A+	(800) 345-6611	B / 8.0	2.05	6.98	13.44 /88	15.43 /78	13.44 /72	0.98	0.86
GR	Columbia Select Large Cap Equity W	CLCWX	C-	(800) 345-6611	B / 7.8	2.00	6.90	13.13 /87	15.07 /75	13.15 /69	0.71	1.25
GR	Columbia Select Large Cap Equity Z	NSEPX	C-	(800) 345-6611	B / 7.9	2.02	6.89	13.37 /88	15.32 /77	13.38 /72	0.92	1.00
GR	Columbia Select Large Cap Gr A	ELGAX	C	(800) 345-6611	B / 8.0	5.60	9.96	14.42 /90	16.39 /86	16.62 /95	0.00	1.10
GR	Columbia Select Large Cap Gr C	ELGCX	C	(800) 345-6611	B+ / 8.5	5.42	9.60	13.62 /88	15.54 /79	15.77 /92	0.00	1.85
GR	Columbia Select Large Cap Gr I	CSPIX	C+	(800) 345-6611	A- / 9.2	5.73	10.23	14.96 /92	16.94 /89	17.14 /96	0.00	0.65
GR	Columbia Select Large Cap Gr R	URLGX	C+	(800) 345-6611	B+ / 8.8	5.53	9.88	14.16 /90	16.13 /84	16.35 /94	0.00	1.35
GR	Columbia Select Large Cap Gr R4	CSRRX	B	(800) 345-6611	A- / 9.1	5.66	10.17	14.76 /91	16.69 /88	16.93 /96	0.00	0.85
GR	Columbia Select Large Cap Gr R5	CGTRX	B	(800) 345-6611	A- / 9.2	5.71	10.21	14.89 /91	16.82 /89	17.01 /96	0.00	0.70
GR	Columbia Select Large Cap Gr W	CSLWX	C+	(800) 345-6611	A- / 9.0	5.60	9.96	14.41 /90	16.38 /86	16.62 /95	0.00	1.10
GR	Columbia Select Large Cap Gr Y	CCWRX	B	(800) 345-6611	A- / 9.2	5.67	10.20	14.91 /91	16.87 /89	17.04 /96	0.00	0.65
GR	Columbia Select Large Cap Gr Z	UMLGX	C+	(800) 345-6611	A- / 9.1	5.66	10.14	14.74 /91	16.68 /88	16.92 /96	0.00	0.85
GR	Columbia Select Large-Cap Value A	SLVAX	C+	(800) 345-6611	C+ / 6.1	-0.61	2.28	6.93 /54	15.56 /80	13.79 /76	0.76	1.25
GR	● Columbia Select Large-Cap Value B	SLVBX	C+	(800) 345-6611	C+ / 6.4	-0.85	1.90	6.12 /48	14.68 /72	12.92 /67	0.09	2.00
GR	Columbia Select Large-Cap Value C	SVLCX	C+	(800) 345-6611	C+ / 6.4	-0.85	1.90	6.13 /48	14.68 /72	12.94 /68	0.09	2.00
GR	Columbia Select Large-Cap Value I	CLVIX	B	(800) 345-6611	B- / 7.4	-0.51	2.51	7.41 /58	16.02 /84	14.27 /80	1.16	0.80
GR	● Columbia Select Large-Cap Value K	SLVTX	B	(800) 345-6611	B- / 7.2	-0.64	2.32	7.04 /55	15.69 /81	13.92 /77	0.89	1.10
GR	Columbia Select Large-Cap Value R	SLVRX	C+	(800) 345-6611	C+ / 6.8	-0.71	2.15	6.67 /52	15.26 /77	13.50 /73	0.58	1.50
GI	Columbia Select Large-Cap Value R4	CSERX	B+	(800) 345-6611	B- / 7.3	-0.59	2.43	7.22 /57	15.80 /82	13.93 /77	1.01	1.00
GR	Columbia Select Large-Cap Value R5	SLVIX	B	(800) 345-6611	B- / 7.4	-0.59	2.47	7.31 /57	15.96 /83	14.20 /79	1.12	0.85
GR	Columbia Select Large-Cap Value W	CSVWX	B-	(800) 345-6611	B- / 7.0	-0.66	2.29	6.92 /54	15.51 /79	13.77 /76	0.81	1.25

● Denotes fund is closed to new investors
* Denotes fund is included in Section II

www.thestreetratings.com

RISK			NET ASSETS		ASSET				Portfolio	BULL / BEAR		FUND MANAGER		MINIMUMS		LOADS	
	3 Year		NAV							Last Bull	Last Bear	Manager	Manager	Initial	Additional	Front	Back
Risk Rating/Pts	Standard Deviation	Beta	As of 3/31/15	Total $(Mil)	Cash %	Stocks %	Bonds %	Other %	Turnover Ratio	Market Return	Market Return	Quality Pct	Tenure (Years)	Purch. $	Purch. $	End Load	End Load
C+ / 6.0	13.2	0.98	8.63	207	0	99	0	1	63	49.1	-22.6	60	7	500	0	0.0	0.0
C+ / 5.9	13.2	0.98	8.64	N/A	0	99	0	1	63	50.1	-22.5	64	7	2,000	0	0.0	0.0
C+ / 6.4	11.9	0.75	9.91	2	3	96	0	1	88	43.3	-18.9	82	7	2,000	0	5.8	0.0
C+ / 6.4	11.9	0.74	9.83	N/A	3	96	0	1	88	39.8	-19.0	77	7	2,000	0	0.0	0.0
C+ / 6.4	11.9	0.75	9.94	179	3	96	0	1	88	45.6	-18.7	85	7	0	0	0.0	0.0
B- / 7.3	11.9	0.75	9.96	N/A	3	96	0	1	88	44.6	-18.7	84	7	0	0	0.0	0.0
B- / 7.3	11.9	0.75	9.90	N/A	3	96	0	1	88	43.2	-18.8	82	7	500	0	0.0	0.0
C+ / 6.4	11.9	0.75	9.95	78	3	96	0	1	88	44.7	-18.7	84	7	2,000	0	0.0	0.0
D+ / 2.7	13.4	1.07	16.51	137	1	98	0	1	80	77.2	-16.4	29	9	2,000	0	5.8	0.0
D+ / 2.7	13.4	1.07	16.55	2	1	98	0	1	80	72.8	-16.8	22	9	2,000	0	0.0	0.0
D+ / 2.7	13.4	1.07	16.51	22	1	98	0	1	80	72.7	-16.7	21	9	2,000	0	0.0	0.0
D+ / 2.7	13.5	1.07	16.57	59	1	98	0	1	80	80.2	-16.2	35	9	0	0	0.0	0.0
D+ / 2.7	13.5	1.07	16.56	N/A	1	98	0	1	80	78.3	-16.4	31	9	0	0	0.0	0.0
D+ / 2.7	13.5	1.07	16.50	10	1	98	0	1	80	75.8	-16.6	26	9	0	0	0.0	0.0
C / 4.8	13.4	1.07	16.78	N/A	1	98	0	1	80	78.8	-16.6	33	9	0	0	0.0	0.0
D+ / 2.7	13.5	1.07	16.50	N/A	1	98	0	1	80	79.4	-16.3	33	9	0	0	0.0	0.0
D+ / 2.7	13.5	1.07	16.52	N/A	1	98	0	1	80	77.2	-16.4	29	9	500	0	0.0	0.0
D+ / 2.7	13.4	1.07	16.54	368	1	98	0	1	80	78.8	-16.6	33	9	2,000	0	0.0	0.0
C+ / 6.3	11.1	0.77	9.91	343	1	98	0	1	63	64.4	-23.0	85	2	2,000	0	5.8	0.0
C+ / 6.2	11.0	0.76	9.16	5	1	98	0	1	63	60.3	-23.4	81	2	2,000	0	0.0	0.0
C+ / 6.2	11.0	0.76	9.04	16	1	98	0	1	63	60.2	-23.3	81	2	2,000	0	0.0	0.0
C+ / 6.3	11.0	0.76	9.99	N/A	1	98	0	1	63	67.1	-23.0	88	2	0	0	0.0	0.0
C+ / 6.2	11.0	0.76	10.00	7	1	98	0	1	63	65.5	-23.1	87	2	0	0	0.0	0.0
C+ / 6.2	11.0	0.76	9.96	N/A	1	98	0	1	63	63.0	-23.2	84	2	0	0	0.0	0.0
C+ / 6.3	11.0	0.76	9.99	N/A	1	98	0	1	63	66.8	-23.1	88	2	0	0	0.0	0.0
C+ / 6.3	11.0	0.76	9.97	N/A	1	98	0	1	63	64.3	-23.1	86	2	500	0	0.0	0.0
C+ / 6.3	11.0	0.76	9.97	3	1	98	0	1	63	65.8	-23.1	87	2	2,000	0	0.0	0.0
D+ / 2.3	9.2	0.94	12.72	137	3	95	0	2	184	95.1	-18.1	66	11	2,000	0	5.8	0.0
D / 2.0	9.2	0.94	11.91	N/A	3	95	0	2	184	90.2	-18.5	55	11	2,000	0	0.0	0.0
D / 2.0	9.2	0.95	11.90	6	3	95	0	2	184	90.1	-18.4	54	11	2,000	0	0.0	0.0
D / 2.2	9.2	0.95	12.65	129	3	95	0	2	184	97.8	-18.1	70	11	0	0	0.0	0.0
B- / 7.6	9.2	0.95	12.93	N/A	3	95	0	2	184	97.3	-18.1	69	11	0	0	0.0	0.0
D+ / 2.3	9.3	0.95	12.72	N/A	3	95	0	2	184	95.2	-18.2	65	11	500	0	0.0	0.0
D+ / 2.3	9.2	0.95	12.64	206	3	95	0	2	184	96.8	-18.1	68	11	2,000	0	0.0	0.0
C- / 3.4	16.1	1.32	18.49	1,466	0	100	0	0	53	103.6	-18.6	12	12	2,000	0	5.8	0.0
C- / 3.2	16.1	1.33	17.32	227	0	100	0	0	53	98.5	-18.9	9	12	2,000	0	0.0	0.0
C- / 3.5	16.1	1.32	19.01	256	0	100	0	0	53	106.8	-18.5	16	12	0	0	0.0	0.0
C- / 3.3	16.1	1.32	17.74	23	0	100	0	0	53	102.0	-18.7	11	12	0	0	0.0	0.0
C / 4.3	16.1	1.32	19.22	18	0	100	0	0	53	105.4	-18.6	14	12	0	0	0.0	0.0
C / 4.3	16.1	1.32	19.26	755	0	100	0	0	53	106.1	-18.6	15	12	0	0	0.0	0.0
C- / 3.4	16.1	1.32	18.49	42	0	100	0	0	53	103.6	-18.6	12	12	500	0	0.0	0.0
C / 4.3	16.1	1.32	19.39	28	0	100	0	0	53	106.4	-18.6	15	12	0	0	0.0	0.0
C- / 3.4	16.1	1.32	18.84	4,278	0	100	0	0	53	105.4	-18.6	14	12	2,000	0	0.0	0.0
C+ / 6.3	12.4	1.20	22.72	327	3	96	0	1	8	109.6	-22.6	21	18	2,000	0	5.8	0.0
C+ / 6.2	12.4	1.20	21.11	2	3	96	0	1	8	104.2	-22.8	15	18	2,000	0	0.0	0.0
C+ / 6.2	12.5	1.20	21.10	94	3	96	0	1	8	104.3	-22.9	14	18	2,000	0	0.0	0.0
C+ / 6.3	12.4	1.20	23.41	140	3	96	0	1	8	112.6	-22.5	25	18	0	0	0.0	0.0
C+ / 6.3	12.4	1.20	23.34	N/A	3	96	0	1	8	110.4	-22.6	22	18	0	0	0.0	0.0
C+ / 6.3	12.4	1.20	22.42	21	3	96	0	1	8	107.8	-22.7	18	18	0	0	0.0	0.0
C+ / 6.9	12.4	1.20	23.68	30	3	96	0	1	8	110.9	-22.6	23	18	0	0	0.0	0.0
C+ / 6.3	12.4	1.20	23.43	19	3	96	0	1	8	112.2	-22.5	24	18	0	0	0.0	0.0
C+ / 6.3	12.4	1.20	22.60	41	3	96	0	1	8	109.4	-22.6	21	18	500	0	0.0	0.0

Fund Type	Fund Name	Ticker Symbol	Overall Investment Rating	Phone	Perfor- mance Rating/Pts	3 Mo	6 Mo	1Yr / Pct	3Yr / Pct	5Yr / Pct	Dividend Yield	Expense Ratio
GI	Columbia Select Large-Cap Value Y	CSRYX	C+	(800) 345-6611	B- / 7.2	-0.54	2.53	7.19 /57	15.66 /80	13.84 /76	1.17	0.80
GR	Columbia Select Large-Cap Value Z	CSVZX	B	(800) 345-6611	B- / 7.3	-0.55	2.45	7.25 /57	15.84 /82	14.06 /78	1.02	1.00
SC	Columbia Select Smaller-Cap Val A	SSCVX	B+	(800) 345-6611	A- / 9.1	6.89	13.85	11.73 /81	18.39 /95	15.15 /88	0.00	1.41
SC	● Columbia Select Smaller-Cap Val B	SSCBX	B	(800) 345-6611	A / 9.3	6.77	13.46	10.93 /78	17.51 /92	14.30 /80	0.00	2.16
SC	Columbia Select Smaller-Cap Val C	SVMCX	B	(800) 345-6611	A / 9.3	6.76	13.51	10.92 /78	17.51 /92	14.31 /80	0.00	2.16
SC	Columbia Select Smaller-Cap Val I	CSSIX	A-	(800) 345-6611	A+ / 9.7	7.06	14.16	12.27 /84	18.95 /97	15.72 /91	0.00	0.93
SC	● Columbia Select Smaller-Cap Val K	SSLRX	B+	(800) 345-6611	A+ / 9.6	6.97	13.94	11.92 /82	18.58 /96	15.37 /89	0.00	1.23
SC	Columbia Select Smaller-Cap Val R	SSVRX	B+	(800) 345-6611	A / 9.5	6.87	13.77	11.47 /80	18.09 /95	14.87 /86	0.00	1.66
SC	Columbia Select Smaller-Cap Val R4	CSPRX	A+	(800) 345-6611	A+ / 9.6	6.96	14.00	12.01 /83	18.63 /96	15.29 /89	0.00	1.16
SC	Columbia Select Smaller-Cap Val R5	SSVIX	B+	(800) 345-6611	A+ / 9.6	7.05	14.12	12.22 /84	18.83 /96	15.63 /91	0.00	0.98
SC	Columbia Select Smaller-Cap Val Y	CSSYX	B+	(800) 345-6611	A+ / 9.6	7.06	14.00	11.88 /82	18.44 /96	15.18 /88	0.00	0.93
SC	Columbia Select Smaller-Cap Val Z	CSSZX	B+	(800) 345-6611	A+ / 9.6	7.00	14.07	12.07 /83	18.70 /96	15.43 /90	0.00	1.16
TC	Columbia Seligman Comm & Info A	SLMCX	C	(800) 345-6611	B- / 7.1	4.22	11.72	24.12 /98	12.46 /56	13.25 /71	0.00	1.36
TC	● Columbia Seligman Comm & Info B	SLMBX	C+	(800) 345-6611	B / 8.1	4.21	11.71	24.11 /98	12.25 /54	12.78 /66	0.00	2.11
TC	Columbia Seligman Comm & Info C	SCICX	C	(800) 345-6611	B / 7.6	4.03	11.30	23.20 /98	11.62 /50	12.41 /63	0.00	2.11
TC	Columbia Seligman Comm & Info I	CSFIX	B-	(800) 345-6611	B+ / 8.6	4.33	11.97	24.67 /98	12.94 /59	13.73 /75	0.00	0.93
TC	● Columbia Seligman Comm & Info K	SCIFX	C+	(800) 345-6611	B+ / 8.4	4.26	11.80	24.29 /98	12.61 /57	13.39 /72	0.00	1.23
TC	Columbia Seligman Comm & Info R	SCIRX	C+	(800) 345-6611	B / 8.0	4.15	11.59	23.83 /98	12.18 /54	12.96 /68	0.00	1.61
TC	Columbia Seligman Comm & Info R4	SCIOX	C+	(800) 345-6611	B+ / 8.4	4.28	11.86	24.45 /98	12.65 /57	13.31 /71	0.00	1.11
TC	Columbia Seligman Comm & Info R5	SCMIX	B-	(800) 345-6611	B+ / 8.6	4.30	11.92	24.59 /98	12.89 /59	13.67 /75	0.00	0.98
TC	Columbia Seligman Comm & Info Z	CCIZX	C+	(800) 345-6611	B+ / 8.5	4.28	11.87	24.45 /98	12.74 /58	13.54 /73	0.00	1.11
TC	Columbia Seligman Global Tech A	SHGTX	C+	(800) 345-6611	B / 8.0	5.06	12.82	24.46 /98	13.48 /63	13.19 /70	0.00	1.47
TC	● Columbia Seligman Global Tech B	SHTBX	B-	(800) 345-6611	B+ / 8.4	4.86	12.43	23.56 /98	12.63 /57	12.34 /63	0.00	2.22
TC	Columbia Seligman Global Tech C	SHTCX	B-	(800) 345-6611	B+ / 8.4	4.86	12.43	23.51 /98	12.64 /57	12.35 /63	0.00	2.22
TC	Columbia Seligman Global Tech I	CSYIX	B	(800) 345-6611	A- / 9.2	5.20	13.11	25.05 /98	14.00 /67	13.73 /75	0.00	0.99
TC	● Columbia Seligman Global Tech K	SGTSX	B	(800) 345-6611	A- / 9.0	5.12	12.95	24.66 /98	13.67 /65	13.41 /72	0.00	1.29
TC	Columbia Seligman Global Tech R	SGTRX	B	(800) 345-6611	B+ / 8.8	5.03	12.72	24.18 /98	13.20 /61	12.91 /67	0.00	1.72
TC	Columbia Seligman Global Tech R4	CCHRX	A-	(800) 345-6611	A- / 9.1	5.14	12.99	24.74 /98	13.72 /65	13.33 /71	0.00	1.22
TC	Columbia Seligman Global Tech R5	SGTTX	B	(800) 345-6611	A- / 9.2	5.19	13.08	24.97 /98	13.97 /67	13.66 /75	0.00	1.04
TC	Columbia Seligman Global Tech Z	CSGZX	B	(800) 345-6611	A- / 9.1	5.14	12.99	24.80 /98	13.76 /65	13.47 /73	0.00	1.22
SC	Columbia Small Cap Core A	LSMAX	D	(800) 345-6611	C- / 3.9	1.79	8.48	0.32 /17	11.69 /50	12.26 /62	0.07	1.38
SC	● Columbia Small Cap Core B	LSMBX	D	(800) 345-6611	C / 4.3	1.60	8.11	-0.46 /14	10.86 /45	11.42 /56	0.00	2.13
SC	Columbia Small Cap Core C	LSMCX	D	(800) 345-6611	C / 4.3	1.60	8.10	-0.46 /14	10.84 /44	11.43 /56	0.00	2.13
SC	Columbia Small Cap Core I	CPOIX	C-	(800) 345-6611	C / 5.2	1.92	8.77	0.82 /18	12.24 /54	12.76 /66	0.23	0.88
SC	Columbia Small Cap Core R4	CFFRX	C	(800) 345-6611	C / 5.0	1.86	8.65	0.59 /17	11.97 /52	12.55 /64	0.15	1.13
SC	Columbia Small Cap Core R5	CLLRX	C	(800) 345-6611	C / 5.1	1.91	8.70	0.74 /18	12.14 /53	12.64 /65	0.21	0.93
SC	● Columbia Small Cap Core T	SSCEX	D	(800) 345-6611	C- / 3.9	1.77	8.48	0.31 /16	11.65 /50	12.21 /62	0.06	1.38
SC	Columbia Small Cap Core W	CSCWX	D+	(800) 345-6611	C / 4.8	1.73	8.43	0.27 /16	11.67 /50	12.26 /62	0.08	1.38
SC	Columbia Small Cap Core Y	CPFRX	C	(800) 345-6611	C / 5.1	1.90	8.79	0.81 /18	12.17 /54	12.67 /65	0.22	0.88
SC	Columbia Small Cap Core Z	SMCEX	D+	(800) 345-6611	C / 5.0	1.82	8.62	0.54 /17	11.97 /52	12.54 /64	0.15	1.13
SC	● Columbia Small Cap Growth I A	CGOAX	E+	(800) 345-6611	C / 5.1	8.01	18.36	3.19 /27	11.98 /52	12.40 /63	0.00	1.32
SC	● Columbia Small Cap Growth I B	CGOBX	E+	(800) 345-6611	C / 5.5	7.82	17.91	2.42 /24	11.14 /46	11.56 /57	0.00	2.07
SC	● Columbia Small Cap Growth I C	CGOCX	E+	(800) 345-6611	C / 5.5	7.82	17.91	2.42 /24	11.14 /46	11.56 /57	0.00	2.07
SC	● Columbia Small Cap Growth I I	CSWIX	D-	(800) 345-6611	C+ / 6.4	8.16	18.62	3.65 /30	12.47 /56	12.88 /67	0.00	0.86
SC	● Columbia Small Cap Growth I K	CSCKX	C	(800) 345-6611	C+ / 6.2	8.06	18.45	3.32 /28	12.19 /54	12.64 /65	0.00	1.16
SC	● Columbia Small Cap Growth I R	CCRIX	E+	(800) 345-6611	C+ / 5.9	7.94	18.18	2.93 /26	11.69 /50	12.12 /61	0.00	1.57
SC	● Columbia Small Cap Growth I R4	CHHRX	C	(800) 345-6611	C+ / 6.3	8.10	18.53	3.44 /29	12.28 /54	12.70 /66	0.00	1.07
SC	● Columbia Small Cap Growth I R5	CSCRX	C	(800) 345-6611	C+ / 6.4	8.12	18.59	3.89 /31	12.49 /56	12.82 /67	0.00	0.91
SC	● Columbia Small Cap Growth I Y	CSGYX	D-	(800) 345-6611	C+ / 6.4	8.12	18.63	3.62 /30	12.46 /56	12.89 /67	0.00	0.86
SC	● Columbia Small Cap Growth I Z	CMSCX	D-	(800) 345-6611	C+ / 6.3	8.07	18.48	3.41 /29	12.26 /54	12.68 /66	0.00	1.07
SC	Columbia Small Cap Index A	NMSAX	B+	(800) 345-6611	B+ / 8.8	3.86	13.98	8.21 /64	16.79 /89	15.74 /91	0.71	0.50
SC	● Columbia Small Cap Index B	CIDBX	B+	(800) 345-6611	B+ / 8.3	3.66	13.56	7.41 /58	15.90 /83	14.86 /86	0.10	1.25

● Denotes fund is closed to new investors
* Denotes fund is included in Section II

RISK			NET ASSETS		ASSET						BULL / BEAR		FUND MANAGER		MINIMUMS		LOADS	
	3 Year		NAV															
Risk Rating/Pts	Standard Deviation	Beta	As of 3/31/15	Total $(Mil)	Cash %	Stocks %	Bonds %	Other %		Portfolio Turnover Ratio	Last Bull Market Return	Last Bear Market Return	Manager Quality Pct	Manager Tenure (Years)	Initial Purch. $	Additional Purch. $	Front End Load	Back End Load
C / 5.1	12.4	1.19	23.73	N/A	3	96	0	1		8	110.0	-22.6	22	18	0	0	0.0	0.0
C+ / 6.3	12.4	1.20	23.43	353	3	96	0	1		8	111.4	-22.5	23	18	2,000	0	0.0	0.0
C / 5.0	13.8	0.98	21.41	401	3	96	0	1		22	116.5	-27.7	85	18	2,000	0	5.8	0.0
C / 4.5	13.8	0.98	17.34	4	3	96	0	1		22	111.1	-27.9	80	18	2,000	0	0.0	0.0
C / 4.5	13.8	0.98	17.37	44	3	96	0	1		22	111.2	-28.0	80	18	2,000	0	0.0	0.0
C / 5.2	13.8	0.98	23.80	23	3	96	0	1		22	120.2	-27.6	87	18	0	0	0.0	0.0
C / 5.2	13.8	0.98	23.32	7	3	96	0	1		22	117.9	-27.6	86	18	0	0	0.0	0.0
C / 4.9	13.8	0.98	20.53	12	3	96	0	1		22	114.6	-27.7	83	18	0	0	0.0	0.0
C+ / 6.1	13.8	0.98	23.81	1	3	96	0	1		22	117.8	-27.7	86	18	0	0	0.0	0.0
C / 5.2	13.8	0.98	23.70	2	3	96	0	1		22	119.5	-27.6	87	18	0	0	0.0	0.0
C / 4.9	13.8	0.98	24.25	N/A	3	96	0	1		22	116.7	-27.7	85	18	0	0	0.0	0.0
C / 5.2	13.8	0.98	23.53	15	3	96	0	1		22	118.4	-27.6	86	18	2,000	0	0.0	0.0
C / 4.3	13.1	1.08	58.08	2,771	1	98	0	1		48	92.9	-17.5	13	25	2,000	0	5.8	0.0
C- / 3.8	13.1	1.09	44.57	22	1	98	0	1		48	91.1	-17.7	12	25	2,000	0	0.0	0.0
C- / 3.9	13.1	1.08	44.39	760	1	98	0	1		48	88.0	-17.7	9	25	2,000	0	0.0	0.0
C / 4.4	13.1	1.08	62.22	N/A	1	98	0	1		48	95.8	-17.3	16	25	0	0	0.0	0.0
C / 4.4	13.1	1.08	61.22	N/A	1	98	0	1		48	93.8	-17.4	14	25	0	0	0.0	0.0
C / 4.3	13.1	1.08	56.01	50	1	98	0	1		48	91.3	-17.6	12	25	0	0	0.0	0.0
C / 4.3	13.1	1.08	56.74	18	1	98	0	1		48	93.8	-17.5	14	25	0	0	0.0	0.0
C / 4.4	13.1	1.08	62.06	33	1	98	0	1		48	95.5	-17.3	16	25	0	0	0.0	0.0
C / 4.4	13.1	1.08	61.88	308	1	98	0	1		48	94.6	-17.4	15	25	2,000	0	0.0	0.0
C / 4.8	12.7	1.05	30.08	429	1	98	0	1		89	95.6	-17.8	25	21	2,000	0	5.8	0.0
C / 4.6	12.7	1.05	24.59	4	1	98	0	1		89	90.7	-18.0	18	21	2,000	0	0.0	0.0
C / 4.6	12.7	1.05	24.58	87	1	98	0	1		89	90.7	-18.1	18	21	2,000	0	0.0	0.0
C / 4.8	12.7	1.05	30.74	N/A	1	98	0	1		89	98.8	-17.6	30	21	0	0	0.0	0.0
C / 4.8	12.7	1.05	30.36	N/A	1	98	0	1		89	96.9	-17.7	27	21	0	0	0.0	0.0
C / 4.7	12.7	1.05	29.23	9	1	98	0	1		89	94.0	-17.9	22	21	0	0	0.0	0.0
C+ / 6.0	12.7	1.05	30.87	N/A	1	98	0	1		89	96.8	-17.8	27	21	0	0	0.0	0.0
C / 4.8	12.7	1.05	30.62	N/A	1	98	0	1		89	98.2	-17.6	30	21	0	0	0.0	0.0
C / 4.8	12.7	1.05	30.50	36	1	98	0	1		89	97.4	-17.7	27	21	2,000	0	0.0	0.0
C / 4.7	13.7	0.98	18.22	357	1	98	0	1		19	75.8	-23.6	19	10	2,000	0	5.8	0.0
C- / 4.1	13.6	0.97	15.21	N/A	1	98	0	1		19	71.6	-23.9	14	10	2,000	0	0.0	0.0
C- / 4.1	13.7	0.98	15.23	28	1	98	0	1		19	71.5	-23.9	13	10	2,000	0	0.0	0.0
C / 4.8	13.6	0.97	19.12	63	1	98	0	1		19	78.9	-23.5	24	10	0	0	0.0	0.0
C+ / 6.1	13.7	0.98	19.19	7	1	98	0	1		19	77.5	-23.6	21	10	0	0	0.0	0.0
C+ / 6.1	13.7	0.98	19.23	26	1	98	0	1		19	78.3	-23.6	22	10	0	0	0.0	0.0
C / 4.6	13.7	0.98	17.80	74	1	98	0	1		19	75.6	-23.7	18	10	2,000	0	5.8	0.0
C / 4.7	13.7	0.97	18.21	N/A	1	98	0	1		19	75.8	-23.6	19	10	500	0	0.0	0.0
C+ / 6.1	13.7	0.98	19.32	14	1	98	0	1		19	78.4	-23.6	23	10	0	0	0.0	0.0
C / 4.8	13.6	0.97	19.00	358	1	98	0	1		19	77.5	-23.6	21	10	0	0	0.0	0.0
D- / 1.0	15.9	1.09	27.25	211	3	96	0	1		148	76.9	-28.5	9	9	2,000	0	5.8	0.0
E+ / 0.8	15.9	1.09	24.97	2	3	96	0	1		148	72.5	-28.7	7	9	2,000	0	0.0	0.0
E+ / 0.8	15.9	1.09	24.97	18	3	96	0	1		148	72.5	-28.7	7	9	2,000	0	0.0	0.0
D- / 1.0	15.9	1.09	28.24	57	3	96	0	1		148	79.7	-28.4	12	9	0	0	0.0	0.0
C / 4.7	15.9	1.09	27.90	N/A	3	96	0	1		148	78.1	-28.4	10	9	0	0	0.0	0.0
D- / 1.0	15.9	1.09	27.04	2	3	96	0	1		148	75.4	-28.6	8	9	0	0	0.0	0.0
C / 4.7	15.9	1.09	28.69	N/A	3	96	0	1		148	78.5	-28.4	11	9	0	0	0.0	0.0
C / 4.7	15.9	1.10	28.09	9	3	96	0	1		148	79.5	-28.4	11	9	0	0	0.0	0.0
D- / 1.0	15.9	1.09	28.22	2	3	96	0	1		148	79.6	-28.3	11	9	0	0	0.0	0.0
D- / 1.0	15.9	1.09	27.98	283	3	96	0	1		148	78.4	-28.4	10	9	0	0	0.0	0.0
C+ / 5.9	12.8	0.94	23.66	1,249	3	96	0	1		15	105.4	-22.2	79	6	2,000	0	0.0	0.0
C+ / 5.9	12.8	0.94	23.51	5	3	96	0	1		15	100.1	-22.4	73	6	2,000	0	0.0	0.0

Fund Type	Fund Name	Ticker Symbol	Overall Investment Rating	Phone	Perfor-mance Rating/Pts	3 Mo	6 Mo	1Yr / Pct	3Yr / Pct	5Yr / Pct	Dividend Yield	Expense Ratio
SC	Columbia Small Cap Index I	CSIIX	A-	(800) 345-6611	A- / 9.0	3.95	14.13	8.55 /67	17.10 /90	15.95 /93	0.96	0.25
SC	● Columbia Small Cap Index K	CIDUX	B+	(800) 345-6611	B+ / 8.8	3.89	13.98	8.23 /64	16.79 /89	15.73 /91	0.71	0.50
SC	Columbia Small Cap Index R5	CXXRX	A-	(800) 345-6611	A- / 9.0	3.96	14.15	8.48 /66	17.03 /90	15.89 /92	0.92	0.25
SC	Columbia Small Cap Index W	CSMWX	B	(800) 345-6611	B+ / 8.8	3.85	13.96	8.19 /64	16.78 /89	15.74 /91	0.74	N/A
SC	Columbia Small Cap Index Z	NMSCX	A-	(800) 345-6611	A- / 9.0	3.94	14.10	8.48 /66	17.07 /90	16.02 /93	0.93	0.25
SC	Columbia Small Cap Value I A	CSMIX	D-	(800) 345-6611	C / 4.6	2.76	8.88	3.35 /28	12.58 /57	11.28 /55	0.34	1.31
SC	● Columbia Small Cap Value I B	CSSBX	D-	(800) 345-6611	C / 5.1	2.58	8.47	2.60 /25	11.74 /51	10.45 /48	0.00	2.06
SC	Columbia Small Cap Value I C	CSSCX	D-	(800) 345-6611	C / 5.0	2.53	8.44	2.55 /24	11.73 /51	10.44 /48	0.00	2.06
SC	Columbia Small Cap Value I I	CVUIX	D+	(800) 345-6611	C+ / 6.0	2.88	9.13	3.83 /31	13.09 /60	11.73 /59	0.75	0.86
SC	Columbia Small Cap Value I R	CSVRX	D	(800) 345-6611	C / 5.5	2.69	8.74	3.09 /27	12.31 /55	11.02 /53	0.10	1.56
SC	Columbia Small Cap Value I R4	CVVRX	C+	(800) 345-6611	C+ / 5.8	2.80	9.00	3.59 /29	12.83 /58	11.42 /56	0.55	1.06
SC	Columbia Small Cap Value I R5	CUURX	C+	(800) 345-6611	C+ / 5.9	2.84	9.09	3.77 /30	12.95 /59	11.50 /57	0.69	0.91
SC	Columbia Small Cap Value I Y	CSVYX	D+	(800) 345-6611	C+ / 6.0	2.85	9.12	3.82 /31	13.09 /60	11.77 /59	0.75	0.86
SC	Columbia Small Cap Value I Z	CSCZX	D+	(800) 345-6611	C+ / 5.8	2.81	9.01	3.60 /29	12.86 /59	11.56 /57	0.56	1.06
SC	● Columbia Small Cap Value II A	COVAX	C+	(800) 345-6611	C+ / 6.8	3.91	10.89	6.08 /47	15.77 /81	14.41 /81	0.17	1.33
SC	● Columbia Small Cap Value II B	COVBX	C+	(800) 345-6611	B- / 7.3	3.73	10.48	5.28 /41	14.90 /74	13.54 /73	0.00	2.08
SC	● Columbia Small Cap Value II C	COVCX	C+	(800) 345-6611	B- / 7.3	3.67	10.42	5.28 /41	14.92 /74	13.54 /73	0.00	2.08
SC	Columbia Small Cap Value II I	CSLIX	B	(800) 345-6611	B+ / 8.3	3.98	11.08	6.54 /51	16.28 /85	14.89 /86	0.54	0.88
SC	● Columbia Small Cap Value II R	CCTRX	B	(800) 345-6611	B / 7.7	3.82	10.76	5.86 /45	15.50 /79	14.12 /79	0.00	1.58
SC	Columbia Small Cap Value II R4	CLURX	B+	(800) 345-6611	B / 8.1	3.92	11.02	6.32 /49	15.99 /83	14.54 /83	0.38	1.08
SC	Columbia Small Cap Value II R5	CRRRX	A-	(800) 345-6611	B / 8.2	3.97	11.09	6.50 /51	16.12 /84	14.61 /83	0.49	0.93
SC	Columbia Small Cap Value II Y	CRRYX	A-	(800) 345-6611	B+ / 8.3	4.02	11.10	6.57 /51	16.19 /85	14.65 /84	0.51	0.88
SC	● Columbia Small Cap Value II Z	NSVAX	B	(800) 345-6611	B / 8.2	3.93	10.95	6.36 /50	16.06 /84	14.68 /84	0.37	1.08
MC	Columbia Small/Mid Cap Value A	AMVAX	C+	(800) 345-6611	B- / 7.4	4.81	11.36	8.28 /65	16.27 /85	13.18 /70	0.00	1.26
MC	● Columbia Small/Mid Cap Value B	AMVBX	C+	(800) 345-6611	B / 7.8	4.61	10.91	7.45 /59	15.37 /78	12.32 /63	0.00	2.01
MC	Columbia Small/Mid Cap Value C	AMVCX	C+	(800) 345-6611	B / 7.8	4.62	10.92	7.45 /59	15.39 /78	12.30 /62	0.00	2.01
MC	Columbia Small/Mid Cap Value I	RMCIX	B	(800) 345-6611	B+ / 8.8	5.02	11.55	8.72 /68	16.79 /89	13.69 /75	0.19	0.80
MC	● Columbia Small/Mid Cap Value K	RMCVX	B	(800) 345-6611	B+ / 8.6	4.77	11.30	8.34 /65	16.39 /86	13.33 /71	0.03	1.10
MC	Columbia Small/Mid Cap Value R	RMVTX	B-	(800) 345-6611	B+ / 8.3	4.77	11.17	7.96 /63	15.95 /83	12.86 /67	0.00	1.51
MC	Columbia Small/Mid Cap Value R4	RMCRX	B	(800) 345-6611	B+ / 8.6	4.93	11.47	8.48 /66	16.45 /87	13.25 /71	0.09	1.01
MC	Columbia Small/Mid Cap Value R5	RSCMX	B	(800) 345-6611	B+ / 8.8	4.97	11.55	8.69 /67	16.72 /88	13.63 /74	0.16	0.85
MC	Columbia Small/Mid Cap Value W	CVOWX	B-	(800) 345-6611	B+ / 8.5	4.77	11.27	8.11 /64	16.24 /85	13.17 /70	0.00	1.26
MC	Columbia Small/Mid Cap Value Y	CPHPX	A	(800) 345-6611	B+ / 8.6	4.83	11.41	8.62 /67	16.47 /87	13.30 /71	0.19	0.80
MC	Columbia Small/Mid Cap Value Z	CMOZX	B	(800) 345-6611	B+ / 8.7	4.92	11.45	8.52 /66	16.57 /87	13.47 /73	0.08	1.01
GI	Columbia Thermostat A	CTFAX	D+	(800) 345-6611	D / 1.6	1.41	3.21	4.85 /37	6.86 /21	9.05 /37	1.75	1.07
GI	● Columbia Thermostat B	CTFBX	C-	(800) 345-6611	D / 2.1	1.27	2.96	4.31 /34	6.33 /18	8.51 /33	1.36	1.71
GI	Columbia Thermostat C	CTFDX	D+	(800) 345-6611	D / 1.9	1.27	2.85	4.06 /32	6.07 /17	8.25 /32	1.11	1.82
AA	Columbia Thermostat R4	CTORX	C	(800) 345-6611	D+ / 2.5	1.49	3.35	5.08 /39	7.13 /22	9.33 /39	2.11	0.83
AA	Columbia Thermostat R5	CQTRX	C	(800) 345-6611	D+ / 2.6	1.49	3.30	5.09 /39	7.16 /22	9.34 /39	2.13	0.79
AA	Columbia Thermostat Y	CYYYX	C	(800) 345-6611	D+ / 2.6	1.49	3.35	5.15 /40	7.20 /22	9.37 /39	2.18	0.74
GI	Columbia Thermostat Z	COTZX	C-	(800) 345-6611	D+ / 2.5	1.50	3.31	5.11 /39	7.13 /22	9.33 /39	2.13	0.81
GR	Columbia Value & Restructuring A	EVRAX	C-	(800) 345-6611	B- / 7.3	1.18	5.87	12.89 /86	16.30 /85	12.31 /63	0.37	1.22
GR	Columbia Value & Restructuring C	EVRCX	C-	(800) 345-6611	B / 7.8	0.98	5.48	12.05 /83	15.43 /78	11.47 /57	0.00	1.97
GI	Columbia Value & Restructuring I	CVRIX	C	(800) 345-6611	B+ / 8.7	1.29	6.12	13.41 /88	16.81 /89	12.74 /66	0.80	0.77
GR	Columbia Value & Restructuring R	URBIX	C	(800) 345-6611	B / 8.2	1.12	5.75	12.61 /85	16.01 /83	12.03 /61	0.17	1.47
GI	Columbia Value & Restructuring R4	CVRRX	A+	(800) 345-6611	B+ / 8.6	1.26	6.03	13.19 /87	16.61 /87	12.59 /65	0.61	0.97
GI	Columbia Value & Restructuring R5	CVCRX	A+	(800) 345-6611	B+ / 8.7	1.29	6.10	13.37 /88	16.73 /88	12.66 /65	0.73	0.82
GI	Columbia Value & Restructuring W	CVRWX	C	(800) 345-6611	B+ / 8.4	1.19	5.92	12.97 /86	16.36 /86	12.34 /63	0.43	1.22
GI	Columbia Value & Restructuring Y	CVRYX	A+	(800) 345-6611	B+ / 8.7	1.31	6.12	13.40 /88	16.77 /89	12.69 /66	0.78	0.77
GR	Columbia Value & Restructuring Z	UMBIX	C	(800) 345-6611	B+ / 8.6	1.24	6.01	13.18 /87	16.60 /87	12.59 /65	0.62	0.97
GR	Commerce Growth	CFGRX	C-	(800) 995-6365	B / 8.2	2.58	9.27	15.96 /93	14.89 /74	13.16 /70	0.68	1.08
MC	Commerce Mid Cap Growth	CFAGX	C+	(800) 995-6365	B / 7.7	3.64	11.27	13.05 /87	14.44 /70	14.19 /79	0.13	1.05

● Denotes fund is closed to new investors
* Denotes fund is included in Section II

99 Pct = Best
0 Pct = Worst

RISK			NET ASSETS		ASSET				Portfolio	BULL / BEAR		FUND MANAGER		MINIMUMS		LOADS	
	3 Year		NAV							Last Bull	Last Bear	Manager	Manager	Initial	Additional	Front	Back
Risk Rating/Pts	Standard Deviation	Beta	As of 3/31/15	Total $(Mil)	Cash %	Stocks %	Bonds %	Other %	Turnover Ratio	Market Return	Market Return	Quality Pct	Tenure (Years)	Purch. $	Purch. $	End Load	End Load
C+ / 6.2	12.8	0.94	23.69	N/A	3	96	0	1	15	107.2	-22.2	81	6	0	0	0.0	0.0
C+ / 5.9	12.8	0.94	23.74	13	3	96	0	1	15	105.3	-22.2	80	6	0	0	0.0	0.0
C+ / 6.2	12.8	0.94	24.16	181	3	96	0	1	15	106.6	-22.2	81	6	0	0	0.0	0.0
C / 5.1	12.8	0.94	23.48	68	3	96	0	1	15	105.4	-22.2	79	6	500	0	0.0	0.0
C+ / 5.9	12.8	0.94	23.76	1,811	3	96	0	1	15	107.1	-22.1	81	6	2,000	0	0.0	0.0
C- / 3.2	13.0	0.93	43.51	328	2	97	0	1	38	78.9	-24.0	34	10	2,000	0	5.8	0.0
D / 1.9	13.0	0.93	30.98	2	2	97	0	1	38	74.4	-24.3	25	10	2,000	0	0.0	0.0
D / 2.1	13.0	0.93	34.02	33	2	97	0	1	38	74.4	-24.3	25	10	2,000	0	0.0	0.0
C- / 3.5	13.0	0.93	46.84	69	2	97	0	1	38	81.8	-23.9	41	10	0	0	0.0	0.0
C- / 3.3	13.0	0.93	43.58	4	2	97	0	1	38	77.5	-24.1	31	10	0	0	0.0	0.0
C+ / 6.5	13.0	0.93	47.76	10	2	97	0	1	38	80.1	-24.0	37	10	0	0	0.0	0.0
C+ / 6.5	13.0	0.93	47.72	4	2	97	0	1	38	80.7	-24.0	39	10	0	0	0.0	0.0
C- / 3.5	13.0	0.93	46.87	12	2	97	0	1	38	81.8	-23.9	41	10	0	0	0.0	0.0
C- / 3.5	13.0	0.93	46.78	671	2	97	0	1	38	80.5	-23.9	38	10	2,000	0	0.0	0.0
C+ / 5.8	12.4	0.91	18.08	269	3	96	0	1	36	99.1	-26.8	77	13	2,000	0	5.8	0.0
C / 5.5	12.4	0.90	16.69	1	3	96	0	1	36	94.2	-27.1	70	13	2,000	0	0.0	0.0
C / 5.5	12.4	0.90	16.67	15	3	96	0	1	36	94.3	-27.1	70	13	2,000	0	0.0	0.0
C+ / 5.7	12.4	0.90	18.28	N/A	3	96	0	1	36	102.3	-26.7	80	13	0	0	0.0	0.0
C+ / 5.8	12.4	0.91	17.94	15	3	96	0	1	36	97.6	-26.9	75	13	0	0	0.0	0.0
C+ / 6.7	12.4	0.90	18.57	26	3	96	0	1	36	100.3	-26.8	79	13	0	0	0.0	0.0
C+ / 6.7	12.4	0.91	18.58	17	3	96	0	1	36	100.9	-26.8	79	13	0	0	0.0	0.0
C+ / 6.7	12.4	0.91	18.62	116	3	96	0	1	36	101.2	-26.8	80	13	0	0	0.0	0.0
C+ / 5.8	12.4	0.90	18.26	1,296	3	96	0	1	36	101.0	-26.8	79	13	2,000	0	0.0	0.0
C / 4.8	10.9	0.96	10.02	893	3	96	0	1	110	94.7	-25.4	67	2	2,000	0	5.8	0.0
C / 4.5	10.9	0.96	9.30	16	3	96	0	1	110	89.7	-25.6	55	2	2,000	0	0.0	0.0
C / 4.5	10.9	0.96	9.29	35	3	96	0	1	110	89.8	-25.6	55	2	2,000	0	0.0	0.0
C / 4.8	10.9	0.96	10.26	N/A	3	96	0	1	110	97.6	-25.2	72	2	0	0	0.0	0.0
C / 4.8	10.9	0.96	10.10	92	3	96	0	1	110	95.8	-25.4	69	2	0	0	0.0	0.0
C / 4.8	10.9	0.96	9.88	10	3	96	0	1	110	93.0	-25.4	63	2	0	0	0.0	0.0
C / 4.8	10.9	0.96	10.01	15	3	96	0	1	110	95.7	-25.4	69	2	0	0	0.0	0.0
C / 4.8	10.9	0.96	10.14	83	3	96	0	1	110	97.3	-25.2	71	2	0	0	0.0	0.0
C / 4.8	10.9	0.96	10.10	N/A	3	96	0	1	110	94.7	-25.3	N/A	2	500	0	0.0	0.0
B- / 7.0	10.9	0.96	9.99	N/A	3	96	0	1	110	95.7	-25.4	69	2	0	0	0.0	0.0
C / 4.8	10.9	0.95	10.23	30	3	96	0	1	110	96.3	-25.2	71	2	2,000	0	0.0	0.0
B- / 7.7	4.0	0.33	15.07	439	0	9	90	1	92	42.1	-8.1	81	N/A	2,000	0	5.8	0.0
B- / 7.8	4.0	0.33	15.16	1	0	9	90	1	92	39.7	-8.3	78	N/A	2,000	0	0.0	0.0
B- / 7.8	4.0	0.33	15.15	398	0	9	90	1	92	38.5	-8.4	76	N/A	2,000	0	0.0	0.0
B / 8.5	4.0	0.60	14.96	23	0	9	90	1	92	43.3	-8.0	74	12	0	0	0.0	0.0
B / 8.5	4.0	0.60	14.97	5	0	9	90	1	92	43.4	-8.0	74	12	0	0	0.0	0.0
B / 8.5	4.0	0.60	14.96	N/A	0	9	90	1	92	43.6	-8.0	75	12	0	0	0.0	0.0
B- / 7.6	4.0	0.33	14.89	369	0	9	90	1	92	43.3	-8.0	83	N/A	2,000	0	0.0	0.0
C- / 3.0	10.6	1.08	46.80	84	2	97	0	1	55	102.7	-26.9	51	6	2,000	0	5.8	0.0
C- / 3.0	10.6	1.08	46.19	28	2	97	0	1	55	97.6	-27.2	39	6	2,000	0	0.0	0.0
C- / 3.0	10.6	1.08	46.63	N/A	2	97	0	1	55	105.8	-26.8	58	6	0	0	0.0	0.0
C- / 3.0	10.6	1.08	46.74	10	2	97	0	1	55	101.0	-27.0	47	6	0	0	0.0	0.0
B- / 7.2	10.6	1.08	47.66	4	2	97	0	1	55	104.5	-26.9	55	6	0	0	0.0	0.0
B- / 7.2	10.6	1.08	47.66	16	2	97	0	1	55	105.0	-26.9	56	6	0	0	0.0	0.0
C- / 3.0	10.6	1.08	46.78	N/A	2	97	0	1	55	102.9	-27.0	52	6	500	0	0.0	0.0
B- / 7.2	10.6	1.09	47.56	1	2	97	0	1	55	105.3	-26.9	57	6	0	0	0.0	0.0
C- / 3.0	10.6	1.08	46.76	1,632	2	97	0	1	55	104.4	-26.9	55	6	0	0	0.0	0.0
D+ / 2.6	10.1	1.01	28.67	76	1	98	0	1	40	97.4	-18.0	48	21	1,000	250	0.0	0.0
C / 4.6	11.1	0.96	36.18	68	1	98	0	1	43	89.5	-22.1	43	9	1,000	250	0.0	0.0

Fund Type	Fund Name	Ticker Symbol	Overall Investment Rating	Phone	Performance Rating/Pts	3 Mo	6 Mo	1Yr / Pct	3Yr / Pct	5Yr / Pct	Dividend Yield	Expense Ratio
GI	Commerce Value	CFVLX	A-	(800) 995-6365	B- / 7.2	-0.35	4.00	8.08 /63	15.35 /78	14.33 /81	2.46	0.71
EM	Commonwealth Africa	CAFRX	D-	(888) 345-1898	E / 0.3	-0.52	-2.05	-5.07 / 5	-1.38 / 3	--	0.00	5.90
GL	Commonwealth Global	CNGLX	E+	(888) 345-1898	D / 1.7	2.30	1.75	-2.47 / 9	6.39 /18	5.47 /14	0.00	3.08
FO	Commonwealth Japan	CNJFX	C-	(888) 345-1898	C- / 4.0	10.63	8.12	11.00 /78	6.20 /18	3.45 / 7	0.00	4.25
FO	Commonwealth-Australia/New	CNZLX	E+	(888) 345-1898	E+ / 0.9	-2.84	-2.41	-5.96 / 4	4.62 /12	5.71 /15	0.88	3.08
RE	Commonwealth-Real Estate	CNREX	C+	(888) 345-1898	B- / 7.0	3.97	11.69	15.34 /92	12.15 /53	10.15 /46	0.00	3.22
GL	Compass EMP Alternative Strat A	CAIAX	D	(888) 944-4367	E / 0.5	0.29	2.28	1.59 /20	0.72 / 5	0.94 / 3	2.22	1.80
GL	Compass EMP Alternative Strat T	CAITX	D	(888) 944-4367	E / 0.5	0.30	2.18	1.38 /20	0.52 / 5	0.71 / 3	2.08	2.05
FO	Compass EMP Intl 500 Enh Vol Wtd I	CVHIX	U	(888) 944-4367	U /	2.85	0.79	-0.91 /13	--	--	1.17	1.73
GL	Compass EMP Multi-Asset Bal A	CTMAX	D+	(888) 944-4367	E+ / 0.8	0.58	2.43	2.68 /25	4.21 /11	3.76 / 8	1.93	1.51
GL	Compass EMP Multi-Asset Bal C	CTMCX	D+	(888) 944-4367	D- / 1.0	0.26	1.92	1.75 /21	3.40 / 9	2.99 / 6	1.30	2.26
GL	Compass EMP Multi-Asset Bal T	CTMTX	D+	(888) 944-4367	E+ / 0.9	0.42	2.13	2.30 /23	3.90 /10	3.48 / 7	1.70	1.76
GL	Compass EMP Multi-Asset Growth A	LTGAX	E+	(888) 944-4367	D / 1.6	1.03	3.52	4.03 /32	7.09 /22	4.99 /12	2.16	1.73
GL	Compass EMP Multi-Asset Growth C	LTGCX	D-	(888) 944-4367	D / 2.0	0.88	3.16	3.33 /28	6.28 /18	4.21 / 9	1.58	2.48
GL	Compass EMP Multi-Asset Growth T	LTGTX	E+	(888) 944-4367	D / 1.8	1.04	3.47	3.82 /31	6.83 /20	4.74 /11	2.00	2.06
GR	Compass EMP US 500 Enhanced	CUHAX	U	(888) 944-4367	U /	2.00	7.91	11.09 /79	--	--	0.16	1.68
GR	Compass EMP US 500 Enhanced	CUHCX	U	(888) 944-4367	U /	1.80	7.60	10.30 /76	--	--	0.00	2.43
GR	Compass EMP US 500 Enhanced	CUHIX	U	(888) 944-4367	U /	2.06	8.05	11.44 /80	--	--	0.39	1.43
IN	Comstock Capital Value A	DRCVX	E-	(800) 422-3554	E- / 0.0	-3.31	-9.31	-17.81 / 1	-18.92 / 0	-17.70 / 0	0.00	2.73
IN	Comstock Capital Value AAA	COMVX	E-	(800) 422-3554	E- / 0.0	-3.19	-9.20	-17.71 / 1	-18.88 / 0	-17.68 / 0	0.00	2.73
IN	Comstock Capital Value C	CPCCX	E-	(800) 422-3554	E- / 0.0	-3.46	-9.48	-18.95 / 1	-19.58 / 0	-18.34 / 0	0.00	3.48
IN	Comstock Capital Value R	CPCRX	E-	(800) 422-3554	E- / 0.0	-3.14	-8.98	-18.27 / 1	-18.87 / 0	-17.53 / 0	0.00	2.48
GR	Concorde Value	CONVX	C+	(800) 294-1699	C+ / 5.7	1.82	3.39	10.63 /77	12.29 /55	9.79 /43	0.00	2.07
GL	Conductor Global I	RAILX	U	(844) 467-2459	U /	4.67	5.32	2.49 /24	--	--	0.00	2.31
SC	Conestoga Small Cap Institutional	CCALX	U	(800) 344-2716	U /	5.16	15.42	--	--	--	0.00	1.09
SC	Conestoga Small Cap Investor	CCASX	C-	(800) 344-2716	C+ / 6.5	5.10	15.30	2.76 /25	13.36 /62	15.21 /88	0.00	1.24
GR	Congress Large Cap Growth I	CMLIX	B	(888) 688-1299	B- / 7.4	5.01	10.45	14.36 /90	13.46 /63	--	0.38	1.45
GR	Congress Large Cap Growth R	CAMLX	B	(888) 688-1299	B- / 7.2	4.96	10.36	14.06 /90	13.21 /61	12.76 /66	0.12	1.70
MC	Congress Mid Cap Growth Inst	IMIDX	U	(888) 688-1299	U /	4.32	13.39	14.70 /91	--	--	0.13	1.17
EM	Consilium Emerg Market Sm Cp Instl	CEMNX	U	(202) 551-8090	U /	-4.63	-8.43	-3.93 / 7	--	--	0.18	N/A
GI	Context Alternative Strategies Inv	CALTX	U	(855) 612-2257	U /	-0.71	-2.61	-1.35 /12	--	--	0.00	3.38
GR	Contravisory Strategic Equity Instl	CSSFX	C+	(855) 558-8818	C+ / 6.3	1.08	5.40	10.89 /78	13.84 /66	--	0.41	3.29
GR	Contravisory Strategic Equity Inv	CSEFX	C+	(855) 558-8818	C+ / 6.1	1.00	5.24	10.56 /77	13.56 /64	--	0.18	3.54
GL	Convergence Core Plus Fund Inst	MARNX	B+	(877) 677-9414	B / 7.6	1.16	6.40	10.72 /77	15.35 /78	15.60 /91	0.26	2.21
SC	Convergence Opportunities Instl	CIPOX	U	(877) 677-9414	U /	4.93	14.40	11.90 /82	--	--	0.00	1.59
GL	Cook & Bynum	COBYX	D+	(877) 839-2629	D- / 1.4	-3.34	-2.76	1.48 /20	6.45 /19	8.48 /33	0.00	1.76
GL	Copeland Risk Managed Div Gro A	CDGRX	B-	(888) 926-7352	C+ / 5.9	2.84	7.57	8.38 /65	14.53 /71	--	0.17	1.55
IN	Copeland Risk Managed Div Gro C	CDCRX	B-	(888) 926-7352	C+ / 6.3	2.73	7.15	7.60 /60	13.69 /65	--	0.00	2.30
IN	Copeland Risk Managed Div Gro I	CDIVX	U	(888) 926-7352	U /	2.98	7.73	8.69 /67	--	--	0.50	1.30
IN	Copley	COPLX	C+	(800) 424-8570	C / 4.4	-2.85	4.98	6.63 /52	10.78 /44	10.80 /51	0.00	6.18
BA	CornerCap Balanced	CBLFX	C-	(888) 813-8637	C- / 3.6	-0.54	2.09	5.12 /39	9.80 /38	8.08 /30	1.43	1.41
SC	CornerCap Large/Mid-Cap Value	CMCRX	C+	(888) 813-8637	C+ / 6.4	-1.29	3.15	7.46 /59	14.63 /72	10.81 /51	0.92	1.50
GR	CornerCap Sm Cap Value Fd	CSCVX	B+	(888) 813-8637	A- / 9.0	3.19	15.23	8.14 /64	17.52 /92	14.79 /85	0.11	1.50
GL	Cornerstone Advisors Glb Pb Eq Inst	CAGLX	U		U /	4.04	6.31	6.89 /54	--	--	1.00	0.99
AA	Cornerstone Advisors Pb Alt Inst	CAALX	U		U /	3.91	6.97	11.65 /81	--	--	4.51	2.01
AA	Cornerstone Advisors Real Asst Inst	CAREX	U		U /	-2.11	-11.11	-8.04 / 3	--	--	3.70	0.99
SC	Cortina Small Cap Growth Inst	CRSGX	E	(855) 612-3936	D- / 1.5	0.54	6.99	-8.87 / 3	7.26 /23	--	0.00	1.88
SC	Cortina Small Cap Value Inst	CRSVX	B	(855) 612-3936	B / 7.9	2.26	8.65	0.14 /16	17.58 /93	--	0.00	1.95
SC	Cove Street Capital Sm Cap Val Inst	CSCAX	C	(866) 497-0097	C+ / 6.5	2.64	7.54	5.43 /42	14.52 /71	14.33 /81	0.00	1.65
SC	Cove Street Capital Sm Cap Val Inv	CSCSX	C-	(866) 497-0097	C+ / 6.3	2.57	7.41	5.15 /40	14.23 /69	14.07 /78	0.00	1.40
SC	Cozad Small Cap Value I	COZIX	U	(800) 437-1686	U /	-1.85	7.47	--	--	--	0.00	N/A
GR	Crawford Dividend Growth C	CDGCX	C-	(800) 408-4682	C- / 3.6	-2.16	1.44	1.93 /22	10.13 /40	9.17 /38	0.84	1.98

● Denotes fund is closed to new investors
* Denotes fund is included in Section II

www.thestreetratings.com

RISK			NET ASSETS		ASSET					BULL / BEAR		FUND MANAGER		MINIMUMS		LOADS	
	3 Year		NAV						Portfolio	Last Bull	Last Bear	Manager	Manager	Initial	Additional	Front	Back
Risk Rating/Pts	Standard Deviation	Beta	As of 3/31/15	Total $(Mil)	Cash %	Stocks %	Bonds %	Other %	Turnover Ratio	Market Return	Market Return	Quality Pct	Tenure (Years)	Purch. $	Purch. $	End Load	End Load
B- / 7.8	9.3	0.90	31.82	227	0	99	0	1	18	88.3	-11.8	75	18	1,000	250	0.0	0.0
C+ / 6.8	13.1	0.75	9.55	2	10	88	0	2	4	N/A	N/A	38	4	200	0	0.0	0.0
C / 5.0	11.3	0.78	15.54	17	1	98	0	1	27	43.5	-23.2	54	13	200	0	0.0	0.0
C+ / 6.3	12.1	0.55	3.33	5	1	98	0	1	9	19.9	-0.4	77	18	200	0	0.0	0.0
C / 4.8	14.4	0.89	11.28	19	2	95	2	1	16	34.9	-13.1	20	24	200	0	0.0	0.0
C / 5.5	9.9	0.65	15.19	10	2	96	0	2	16	79.7	-22.5	88	N/A	200	0	0.0	0.0
B / 8.5	5.4	0.21	10.23	40	14	73	12	1	49	0.6	-8.9	49	N/A	1,000	50	5.8	0.0
B / 8.5	5.3	0.21	10.13	2	14	73	12	1	49	-0.1	-9.1	46	N/A	1,000	50	3.5	0.0
U /	N/A	N/A	11.35	41	4	95	0	1	81	N/A	N/A	N/A	N/A	100,000	50	0.0	0.0
B / 8.3	4.7	0.58	12.04	23	14	68	16	2	12	15.8	-5.0	54	7	1,000	50	5.8	0.0
B / 8.3	4.7	0.58	11.79	13	14	68	16	2	12	12.9	-5.3	42	7	1,000	50	0.0	0.0
B / 8.4	4.6	0.57	11.99	8	14	68	16	2	12	14.8	-5.1	51	7	1,000	50	3.5	0.0
C / 5.0	8.6	0.49	11.81	7	6	93	0	1	4	28.3	-14.1	86	N/A	1,000	50	5.8	0.0
C / 5.0	8.6	0.49	11.45	6	6	93	0	1	4	24.9	-14.4	81	N/A	1,000	50	0.0	0.0
C / 4.9	8.6	0.49	11.67	4	6	93	0	1	4	27.1	-14.2	85	N/A	1,000	50	3.5	0.0
U /	N/A	N/A	14.29	78	1	98	0	1	29	N/A	N/A	N/A	N/A	2,500	50	5.8	0.0
U /	N/A	N/A	14.11	53	1	98	0	1	29	N/A	N/A	N/A	N/A	2,500	50	0.0	0.0
U /	N/A	N/A	14.29	63	1	98	0	1	29	N/A	N/A	N/A	N/A	100,000	50	0.0	0.0
D+ / 2.3	11.1	-1.10	7.89	30	23	0	76	1	246	-61.1	22.6	12	28	1,000	0	5.8	0.0
D+ / 2.3	11.3	-1.13	7.90	4	23	0	76	1	246	-60.9	22.0	15	28	1,000	0	0.0	0.0
D+ / 2.3	11.0	-1.09	6.97	5	23	0	76	1	246	-62.2	22.8	8	28	1,000	0	5.8	0.0
D+ / 2.4	11.2	-1.11	8.01	N/A	23	0	76	1	246	-60.7	22.4	13	28	1,000	0	0.0	0.0
C+ / 6.4	9.2	0.90	15.65	11	2	97	0	1	32	73.5	-21.3	40	28	500	100	0.0	0.0
U /	N/A	N/A	10.30	35	2	94	3	1	99	N/A	N/A	N/A	2	100,000	1,000	0.0	0.0
U /	N/A	N/A	35.47	125	0	99	0	1	18	N/A	N/A	N/A	13	250,000	0	0.0	0.0
C- / 3.8	15.1	1.03	35.42	553	0	99	0	1	18	76.8	-18.0	25	13	2,500	0	0.0	0.0
C+ / 6.3	10.5	1.03	22.65	24	4	95	0	1	51	84.6	-15.3	28	6	500,000	250	0.0	1.0
C+ / 6.3	10.5	1.03	22.64	17	4	95	0	1	51	83.1	-15.4	26	6	2,000	250	0.0	1.0
U /	N/A	N/A	15.23	225	2	97	0	1	31	N/A	N/A	N/A	3	500,000	250	0.0	1.0
U /	N/A	N/A	9.89	63	6	85	7	2	0	N/A	N/A	N/A	2	1,000,000	100	0.0	1.0
U /	N/A	N/A	9.81	44	0	0	0	100	0	N/A	N/A	N/A	N/A	2,000	200	0.0	0.0
C+ / 6.1	9.8	0.93	12.14	8	2	97	0	1	64	80.5	N/A	52	4	1,000,000	250	0.0	2.0
C+ / 6.1	9.7	0.93	12.12	4	2	97	0	1	64	79.2	N/A	49	4	2,500	250	0.0	2.0
B- / 7.1	10.1	0.57	18.25	275	1	98	0	1	268	103.3	-19.6	98	6	100,000	5,000	0.0	0.0
U /	N/A	N/A	11.28	91	2	97	0	1	282	N/A	N/A	N/A	2	100,000	5,000	0.0	0.0
B / 8.2	6.2	0.20	15.06	132	0	62	36	2	6	37.9	-2.5	92	6	5,000	1,000	0.0	2.0
B- / 7.2	9.5	0.58	15.21	312	7	92	0	1	44	65.4	-7.8	97	5	1,000	500	5.8	1.0
B- / 7.6	9.5	0.92	15.05	98	7	92	0	1	44	N/A	N/A	52	5	1,000	500	0.0	1.0
U /	N/A	N/A	15.21	344	7	92	0	1	44	N/A	N/A	N/A	5	250,000	500	0.0	1.0
B / 8.0	8.4	0.50	69.14	73	2	97	0	1	0	51.1	-3.2	88	37	1,000	100	0.0	0.0
C+ / 6.9	7.1	1.14	14.62	27	9	58	32	1	43	53.6	-13.3	31	18	2,000	250	0.0	1.0
C+ / 6.6	11.6	0.70	13.75	12	2	97	0	1	60	89.5	-23.0	89	19	2,000	250	0.0	1.0
C / 5.0	14.7	1.22	15.55	85	3	96	0	1	109	107.5	-28.0	36	23	2,000	250	0.0	1.0
U /	N/A	N/A	12.62	839	1	98	0	1	75	N/A	N/A	N/A	3	2,000	0	0.0	0.0
U /	N/A	N/A	10.64	465	68	0	21	11	153	N/A	N/A	N/A	3	2,000	0	0.0	0.0
U /	N/A	N/A	8.82	155	37	9	53	1	81	N/A	N/A	N/A	3	2,000	0	0.0	0.0
D+ / 2.3	16.8	1.09	14.94	50	0	100	0	0	81	61.5	N/A	2	4	25,000	0	0.0	2.0
C+ / 6.1	11.7	0.83	18.56	48	2	97	0	1	78	110.7	N/A	91	4	25,000	0	0.0	2.0
C / 4.6	13.8	0.96	34.27	19	2	97	0	1	77	112.3	-19.8	54	17	10,000	100	0.0	2.0
C / 4.5	13.8	0.96	33.12	29	2	97	0	1	77	110.9	-19.9	50	17	1,000	100	0.0	2.0
U /	N/A	N/A	19.60	30	0	0	0	100	0	N/A	N/A	N/A	N/A	10,000	100	0.0	0.0
C+ / 6.7	9.6	0.96	12.30	8	0	100	0	0	34	64.8	-17.2	12	11	2,500	0	0.0	0.0

99 Pct = Best
0 Pct = Worst

Fund Type	Fund Name	Ticker Symbol	Overall Investment Rating	Phone	Performance Rating/Pts	3 Mo	6 Mo	1Yr / Pct	3Yr / Pct	5Yr / Pct	Dividend Yield	Expense Ratio
GR	Crawford Dividend Growth I	CDGIX	C	(800) 408-4682	C- / 4.2	-2.00	1.82	2.90 /26	11.21 /47	10.24 /46	1.79	0.98
IN	Crawford Dividend Opportunity	CDOFX	U	(800) 408-4682	U /	4.77	14.54	11.50 /80	--	--	1.11	1.67
OT	Credit Suisse Comdty ACCESS Strat	CRCIX	U	(877) 927-2874	U /	-9.12	-27.98	-34.42 / 0	--	--	0.00	1.52
IN	Credit Suisse Mgd Fut Str I	CSAIX	U	(877) 927-2874	U /	11.04	18.41	27.79 /99	--	--	0.30	1.60
AA	Credit Suisse Mltialtern Strategy A	CSQAX	C-	(877) 927-2874	D- / 1.0	2.55	4.17	4.57 /36	3.71 / 9	--	1.38	4.57
AA	Credit Suisse Mltialtern Strategy C	CSQCX	C-	(877) 927-2874	D- / 1.0	2.37	3.83	3.83 /31	2.93 / 8	--	0.72	5.32
AA	Credit Suisse Mltialtern Strategy I	CSQIX	C	(877) 927-2874	D- / 1.4	2.64	4.31	4.92 /38	3.97 /10	--	1.69	4.32
IX	Credit Suisse Volaris US Strat I	VAEIX	U	(800) 927-2874	U /	0.00	0.07	6.98 /55	--	--	0.00	2.42
GR	Crescent Large Cap Macro Advs	GCALX	C	(800) 773-3863	C / 4.5	0.29	4.44	7.68 /60	12.01 /53	--	0.31	1.71
GR	Crescent Large Cap Macro Inst	GCILX	C+	(800) 773-3863	C / 5.2	0.29	4.53	7.69 /60	12.19 /54	--	0.35	1.46
GR	CRM All Cap Value Inst	CRIEX	D+	(800) 276-2883	C+ / 6.4	3.79	7.64	7.81 /61	13.42 /63	11.38 /56	0.41	1.19
GR	CRM All Cap Value Inv	CRMEX	D	(800) 276-2883	C+ / 6.2	3.62	7.50	7.58 /60	13.12 /61	11.11 /54	0.18	1.46
GL	CRM Global Opportunity Inst	CRIWX	D+	(800) 276-2883	D+ / 2.6	3.08	2.99	3.05 /27	7.94 /27	6.65 /21	0.32	1.74
GL	CRM Global Opportunity Inv	CRMWX	D	(800) 276-2883	D+ / 2.5	3.05	2.85	2.85 /26	7.70 /25	6.40 /19	0.22	2.55
FO	CRM International Opportunity Inst	CRIIX	E	(800) 276-2883	E+ / 0.9	5.08	1.46	-1.73 /11	3.38 / 9	4.01 / 8	0.40	1.36
FO	CRM International Opportunity Inv	CRMIX	E	(800) 276-2883	E+ / 0.8	5.01	1.27	-1.86 /11	3.17 / 8	3.79 / 8	0.16	1.75
MC	CRM Large Cap Opportunity Inst	CRIGX	D	(800) 276-2883	B / 7.6	2.63	8.39	11.52 /81	14.79 /73	12.40 /63	0.67	1.11
MC	CRM Large Cap Opportunity Inv	CRMGX	D	(800) 276-2883	B- / 7.3	2.53	8.21	11.16 /79	14.48 /71	12.12 /61	0.45	1.36
MC	CRM Mid Cap Value Instl	CRIMX	D+	(800) 276-2883	B- / 7.2	2.86	8.05	7.62 /60	14.77 /73	12.52 /64	0.73	0.82
MC	CRM Mid Cap Value Inv	CRMMX	D	(800) 276-2883	B- / 7.0	2.82	7.94	7.37 /58	14.52 /71	12.28 /62	0.52	1.04
SC	CRM Small Cap Value Inst	CRISX	C	(800) 276-2883	B+ / 8.5	3.71	13.51	8.46 /66	16.15 /84	12.43 /64	0.47	0.86
SC	CRM Small Cap Value Inv	CRMSX	C-	(800) 276-2883	B+ / 8.3	3.65	13.40	8.21 /64	15.90 /83	12.18 /62	0.29	1.08
SC	CRM Small/Mid Cap Value Inst	CRIAX	D+	(800) 276-2883	B- / 7.1	4.44	7.18	7.24 /57	14.61 /72	13.35 /71	1.05	0.86
SC	CRM Small/Mid Cap Value Inv	CRMAX	D+	(800) 276-2883	C+ / 6.9	4.35	7.11	6.99 /55	14.37 /70	13.10 /69	0.52	1.08
GR	Croft Value R	CLVFX	D-	(800) 551-0990	C- / 3.8	-0.50	2.82	3.95 /31	10.59 /43	9.59 /41	0.45	1.42
FO	● CSTG&E Intl Social Core Equity	DFCCX	D-	(800) 984-9472	D / 1.9	3.81	-0.91	-5.24 / 5	7.41 /24	5.55 /14	2.59	0.53
AA	CT 529 CHET Adv AB Ptf 14-15 A		C-	(888) 843-7824	D- / 1.3	1.90	0.67	0.92 /18	6.43 /19	--	0.00	1.25
AA	CT 529 CHET Adv AB Ptf 14-15 C		C-	(888) 843-7824	D- / 1.5	1.73	0.31	0.18 /16	5.64 /15	--	0.00	2.00
AA	CT 529 CHET Adv AB Ptf 14-15 E		C-	(888) 843-7824	D / 2.0	2.02	0.84	1.22 /19	6.71 /20	--	0.00	1.00
AA	CT 529 CHET Adv AB Ptf 16-17 A		C-	(888) 843-7824	E+ / 0.8	1.19	0.42	0.95 /18	3.80 /10	--	0.00	1.20
AA	CT 529 CHET Adv AB Ptf 16-17 C		C-	(888) 843-7824	E+ / 0.8	0.95	0.00	0.15 /16	3.01 / 8	--	0.00	1.95
AA	CT 529 CHET Adv AB Ptf 16-17 E		C-	(888) 843-7824	D- / 1.1	1.23	0.54	1.20 /19	4.07 /10	--	0.00	0.95
AA	CT 529 CHET Adv AB Ptf 18+ A		C-	(888) 843-7824	E+ / 0.6	0.72	-0.06	0.26 /16	1.69 / 6	--	0.00	1.17
AA	CT 529 CHET Adv AB Ptf 18+ C		C-	(888) 843-7824	E+ / 0.6	0.51	-0.46	-0.52 /14	0.92 / 5	--	0.00	1.92
AA	CT 529 CHET Adv AB Ptf 18+ E		C-	(888) 843-7824	E+ / 0.7	0.79	0.07	0.51 /17	1.93 / 6	--	0.00	0.92
AA	CT 529 CHET Adv AB Ptf 9-13 A		C-	(888) 843-7824	D / 1.9	2.35	1.09	1.27 /19	8.03 /27	--	0.00	1.27
AA	CT 529 CHET Adv AB Ptf 9-13 C		C-	(888) 843-7824	D / 2.2	2.15	0.71	0.51 /17	7.22 /23	--	0.00	2.02
AA	CT 529 CHET Adv AB Ptf 9-13 E		C	(888) 843-7824	D+ / 2.8	2.35	1.16	1.46 /20	8.28 /29	--	0.00	1.02
AA	CT 529 CHET Adv Age-Based 0-8 A		C	(888) 843-7824	C- / 3.2	2.90	2.44	2.76 /25	10.39 /42	--	0.00	1.32
AA	CT 529 CHET Adv Age-Based 0-8 C		C	(888) 843-7824	C- / 3.6	2.71	2.06	1.99 /22	9.56 /36	--	0.00	2.07
AA	CT 529 CHET Adv Age-Based 0-8 E		C+	(888) 843-7824	C- / 4.2	2.95	2.55	2.99 /26	10.66 /43	--	0.00	1.07
AG	CT 529 CHET Adv Aggr Growth A		C+	(888) 843-7824	C / 5.4	3.25	3.08	3.48 /29	12.66 /57	--	0.00	1.37
AG	CT 529 CHET Adv Aggr Growth C		C	(888) 843-7824	C / 4.9	3.11	2.75	2.76 /25	11.84 /51	--	0.00	2.12
AG	CT 529 CHET Adv Aggr Growth E		C+	(888) 843-7824	C+ / 5.6	3.32	3.22	3.75 /30	12.95 /59	--	0.00	1.12
BA	CT 529 CHET Adv Balanced Ptf A		C-	(888) 843-7824	D / 2.1	2.30	1.04	1.22 /19	6.92 /21	--	0.00	N/A
BA	CT 529 CHET Adv Balanced Ptf C		C-	(888) 843-7824	D / 1.7	2.12	0.66	0.47 /17	6.12 /17	--	0.00	N/A
AA	CT 529 CHET Adv Checks & Bals Ptf		C+	(888) 843-7824	C / 4.3	1.48	4.22	8.02 /63	11.71 /50	--	0.00	1.23
AA	CT 529 CHET Adv Checks & Bals Ptf		B-	(888) 843-7824	C / 4.6	1.32	3.86	7.23 /57	10.88 /45	--	0.00	1.98
AA	CT 529 CHET Adv Checks & Bals Ptf		B	(888) 843-7824	C / 5.4	1.55	4.35	8.29 /65	11.99 /52	--	0.00	0.98
AA	CT 529 CHET Adv Consv Ptf A		C-	(888) 843-7824	D- / 1.0	1.16	0.39	0.91 /18	3.81 /10	--	0.00	N/A
AA	CT 529 CHET Adv Consv Ptf C		C-	(888) 843-7824	E+ / 0.8	0.98	0.03	0.18 /16	3.04 / 8	--	0.00	N/A
AA	CT 529 CHET Adv Consv Ptf E		C-	(888) 843-7824	D- / 1.1	1.22	0.53	1.18 /19	4.08 /10	--	0.00	N/A

RISK			NET ASSETS		ASSET					BULL / BEAR		FUND MANAGER		MINIMUMS		LOADS	
	3 Year		NAV						Portfolio	Last Bull	Last Bear	Manager	Manager	Initial	Additional	Front	Back
Risk Rating/Pts	Standard Deviation	Beta	As of 3/31/15	Total $(Mil)	Cash %	Stocks %	Bonds %	Other %	Turnover Ratio	Market Return	Market Return	Quality Pct	Tenure (Years)	Purch. $	Purch. $	End Load	End Load
C+ / 6.6	9.6	0.96	12.37	86	0	100	0	0	34	70.5	-16.8	19	11	10,000	0	0.0	0.0
U /	N/A	N/A	36.15	94	4	95	0	1	34	N/A	N/A	N/A	3	10,000	0	0.0	0.0
U /	N/A	N/A	6.38	41	0	0	0	100	117	N/A	N/A	N/A	N/A	250,000	100,000	0.0	0.0
U /	N/A	N/A	12.57	77	0	0	0	100	0	N/A	N/A	N/A	N/A	250,000	100,000	0.0	0.0
B+ / 9.8	3.4	0.57	10.47	N/A	88	9	1	2	431	N/A	N/A	34	3	2,500	100	5.3	0.0
B+ / 9.8	3.5	0.57	10.35	1	88	9	1	2	431	N/A	N/A	24	3	2,500	100	0.0	0.0
B+ / 9.8	3.4	0.56	10.51	12	88	9	1	2	431	N/A	N/A	38	3	250,000	100,000	0.0	0.0
U /	N/A	N/A	9.92	26	0	0	0	100	0	N/A	N/A	N/A	N/A	250,000	100,000	0.0	0.0
B- / 7.1	10.1	1.04	13.99	2	2	97	0	1	72	N/A	N/A	15	N/A	1,000	100	4.0	1.0
B- / 7.1	10.1	1.04	14.03	16	2	97	0	1	72	N/A	N/A	16	N/A	10,000	1,000	0.0	1.0
D+ / 2.8	10.8	1.05	10.69	6	2	97	0	1	76	80.6	-24.5	23	5	1,000,000	0	0.0	0.0
D+ / 2.8	10.9	1.06	10.58	26	2	97	0	1	76	79.1	-24.7	20	5	2,500	100	0.0	0.0
C+ / 6.6	11.3	0.77	17.08	1	15	84	0	1	82	51.6	-28.2	74	N/A	1,000,000	0	0.0	1.5
C+ / 6.6	11.3	0.77	16.88	3	15	84	0	1	82	50.4	-28.2	72	N/A	2,500	100	0.0	1.5
C- / 4.0	12.0	0.88	13.04	3	16	83	0	1	102	35.2	-27.5	12	N/A	1,000,000	0	0.0	1.5
C- / 4.1	12.1	0.88	12.99	8	16	83	0	1	102	34.2	-27.6	11	N/A	2,500	100	0.0	1.5
D- / 1.1	10.3	0.84	9.35	21	4	95	0	1	89	88.6	-19.5	73	10	1,000,000	0	0.0	0.0
D- / 1.1	10.3	0.84	9.33	14	4	95	0	1	89	86.8	-19.6	71	10	2,500	100	0.0	0.0
D / 2.0	10.3	0.87	29.09	1,242	2	97	0	1	77	86.7	-23.1	68	17	1,000,000	0	0.0	0.0
D / 2.0	10.3	0.87	28.44	505	2	97	0	1	77	85.4	-23.2	66	17	2,500	100	0.0	0.0
D+ / 2.7	12.9	0.92	21.82	444	3	96	0	1	66	91.1	-28.1	77	7	1,000,000	0	0.0	0.0
D / 2.2	12.8	0.92	19.88	76	3	96	0	1	66	89.6	-28.1	76	7	2,500	100	0.0	0.0
D+ / 2.7	10.6	0.72	15.54	830	3	96	0	1	86	95.1	-24.3	88	11	1,000,000	0	0.0	0.0
D+ / 2.7	10.7	0.73	15.34	81	3	96	0	1	86	93.7	-24.3	87	11	2,500	100	0.0	0.0
C- / 3.5	11.4	1.14	23.87	62	13	86	0	1	17	76.5	-25.6	5	20	2,000	100	0.0	2.0
C+ / 5.6	13.8	1.03	8.72	100	0	99	0	1	18	46.6	-24.6	34	6	0	0	0.0	0.0
B / 8.8	5.8	0.95	13.74	17	11	48	39	2	0	39.3	-10.6	19	5	50	25	5.5	0.0
B / 8.7	5.8	0.95	13.29	8	11	48	39	2	0	35.8	-10.9	14	5	50	25	0.0	0.0
B / 8.8	5.8	0.95	13.91	3	11	48	39	2	0	40.5	-10.5	22	5	50	25	0.0	0.0
B+ / 9.2	3.7	0.56	12.33	11	23	24	51	2	0	21.7	-4.3	36	5	50	25	3.0	0.0
B+ / 9.2	3.7	0.56	11.91	9	23	24	51	2	0	18.6	-4.6	27	5	50	25	0.0	0.0
B+ / 9.2	3.7	0.56	12.47	1	23	24	51	2	0	22.8	-4.2	39	5	50	25	0.0	0.0
B+ / 9.9	2.3	0.30	11.12	8	38	9	51	2	0	10.1	-1.6	45	5	50	25	3.0	0.0
B+ / 9.9	2.3	0.30	10.75	6	38	9	51	2	0	7.3	-2.0	34	5	50	25	0.0	0.0
B+ / 9.9	2.3	0.30	11.24	2	38	9	51	2	0	11.0	-1.6	49	5	50	25	0.0	0.0
B / 8.4	7.1	1.16	14.51	44	12	63	23	2	0	48.9	-13.5	14	5	50	25	5.5	0.0
B / 8.4	7.0	1.16	14.03	14	12	63	23	2	0	45.1	-13.7	10	5	50	25	0.0	0.0
B / 8.4	7.1	1.16	14.66	6	12	63	23	2	0	50.1	-13.4	16	5	50	25	0.0	0.0
B- / 7.9	8.5	1.40	15.69	42	10	77	11	2	0	64.0	-17.7	13	5	50	25	5.5	0.0
B- / 7.8	8.5	1.40	15.17	15	10	77	11	2	0	59.9	-17.9	9	5	50	25	0.0	0.0
B- / 7.9	8.5	1.40	15.86	7	10	77	11	2	0	65.4	-17.6	14	5	50	25	0.0	0.0
C+ / 6.8	10.3	1.01	16.96	6	3	95	1	1	0	82.0	-22.6	23	5	50	25	0.0	0.0
C+ / 6.8	10.3	1.01	16.41	3	3	95	1	1	0	77.4	-22.9	16	5	50	25	0.0	0.0
C+ / 6.8	10.3	1.01	17.15	3	3	95	1	1	0	83.6	-22.6	26	5	50	25	0.0	0.0
B / 8.5	6.5	1.06	13.96	9	13	63	23	1	0	41.1	-10.3	14	5	50	25	0.0	0.0
B / 8.4	6.5	1.06	13.50	6	13	63	23	1	0	37.5	-10.6	10	5	50	25	0.0	0.0
B / 8.5	6.7	1.16	15.79	3	0	62	37	1	0	64.0	-14.0	54	5	50	25	5.5	0.0
B / 8.5	6.7	1.16	15.27	2	0	62	37	1	0	59.8	-14.2	43	5	50	25	0.0	0.0
B / 8.5	6.7	1.15	15.97	N/A	0	62	37	1	0	65.3	-13.9	58	5	50	25	0.0	0.0
B+ / 9.2	3.7	0.56	12.35	3	23	24	51	2	0	21.9	-4.2	36	5	50	25	0.0	0.0
B+ / 9.2	3.7	0.56	11.95	3	23	24	51	2	0	18.9	-4.5	27	5	50	25	0.0	0.0
B+ / 9.2	3.7	0.56	12.49	N/A	23	24	51	2	0	23.0	-4.1	40	5	50	25	0.0	0.0

Fund Type	Fund Name	Ticker Symbol	Overall Investment Rating	Phone	Performance Rating/Pts	3 Mo	6 Mo	1Yr / Pct	3Yr / Pct	5Yr / Pct	Dividend Yield	Expense Ratio
GR	CT 529 CHET Adv Growth A		C+	(888) 843-7824	C- / 4.1	2.88	2.43	2.74 /25	10.39 /42	--	0.00	N/A
GR	CT 529 CHET Adv Growth C		C	(888) 843-7824	C- / 3.6	2.72	2.07	2.00 /22	9.58 /37	--	0.00	N/A
GR	CT 529 CHET Adv Growth E		C+	(888) 843-7824	C- / 4.2	2.94	2.55	2.99 /26	10.67 /43	--	0.00	N/A
BA	CT 529 CHET Advisor Balanced Ptf E		C-	(888) 843-7824	D+ / 2.3	2.39	1.19	1.50 /20	7.20 /22	--	0.00	N/A
GR	CT 529 Hartford Cap App 529 Ptf A		B+	(888) 843-7824	B / 7.9	3.35	6.03	10.32 /76	17.36 /92	--	0.00	1.29
GR	CT 529 Hartford Cap App 529 Ptf C		B+	(888) 843-7824	B+ / 8.3	3.15	5.63	9.49 /72	16.48 /87	--	0.00	2.04
GR	CT 529 Hartford Cap App 529 Ptf E		A	(888) 843-7824	A- / 9.0	3.37	6.13	10.56 /77	17.64 /93	--	0.00	1.04
GI	'CT 529 Hartford Eqty Inc 529 Ptf A		B-	(888) 843-7824	C+ / 5.8	-0.16	3.92	9.14 /70	14.54 /71	--	0.00	1.26
GI	'CT 529 Hartford Eqty Inc 529 Ptf C		B-	(888) 843-7824	C+ / 6.2	-0.29	3.58	8.38 /65	13.71 /65	--	0.00	2.01
GI	'CT 529 Hartford Eqty Inc 529 Ptf E		B+	(888) 843-7824	B- / 7.0	-0.06	4.09	9.45 /72	14.84 /74	--	0.00	1.01
GR	CT 529 Hartford Gro Oppty 529 Ptf A		A	(888) 843-7824	A+ / 9.6	6.35	13.42	19.39 /96	19.03 /97	--	0.00	1.36
GR	CT 529 Hartford Gro Oppty 529 Ptf C		A+	(888) 843-7824	A+ / 9.7	6.17	13.01	18.52 /96	18.14 /95	--	0.00	2.11
GR	CT 529 Hartford Gro Oppty 529 Ptf E		A+	(888) 843-7824	A+ / 9.8	6.46	13.61	19.74 /97	19.34 /97	--	0.00	1.11
FO	CT 529 Hartford Itl Oppty 529 Ptf A		D	(888) 843-7824	D / 2.1	4.88	2.63	1.77 /21	8.08 /27	--	0.00	1.42
FO	CT 529 Hartford Itl Oppty 529 Ptf C		D	(888) 843-7824	D+ / 2.4	4.65	2.20	0.97 /18	7.26 /23	--	0.00	2.17
FO	CT 529 Hartford Itl Oppty 529 Ptf E		D+	(888) 843-7824	C- / 3.1	4.91	2.72	1.99 /22	8.33 /29	--	0.00	1.17
MC	CT 529 Hartford MidCap 529 Ptf A		A	(888) 843-7824	A- / 9.0	5.77	11.04	12.75 /86	18.30 /95	--	0.00	1.38
MC	CT 529 Hartford MidCap 529 Ptf C		A	(888) 843-7824	A- / 9.2	5.58	10.63	11.92 /82	17.42 /92	--	0.00	2.13
MC	CT 529 Hartford MidCap 529 Ptf E		A+	(888) 843-7824	A+ / 9.6	5.83	11.18	13.03 /87	18.59 /96	--	0.00	1.13
SC	CT 529 Hartford SmCap Gr 529 Ptf A		B+	(888) 843-7824	B+ / 8.8	6.85	19.00	12.54 /85	17.01 /90	--	0.00	1.47
SC	CT 529 Hartford SmCap Gr 529 Ptf C		B+	(888) 843-7824	A- / 9.1	6.65	18.55	11.70 /81	16.14 /84	--	0.00	2.22
SC	CT 529 Hartford SmCap Gr 529 Ptf E		A-	(888) 843-7824	A / 9.5	6.94	19.18	12.85 /86	17.32 /91	--	0.00	1.22
GR	CT 529 Hartford Value 529 Ptf A		C+	(888) 843-7824	C / 5.2	-0.09	3.73	6.75 /53	13.74 /65	--	0.00	1.30
GR	CT 529 Hartford Value 529 Ptf C		C+	(888) 843-7824	C+ / 5.6	-0.27	3.35	5.96 /46	12.90 /59	--	0.00	2.05
GR	CT 529 Hartford Value 529 Ptf E		B-	(888) 843-7824	C+ / 6.3	0.00	3.89	7.05 /55	14.03 /67	--	0.00	1.05
EM	Cullen Emerging Mrkts High Div I	CEMFX	U	(877) 485-8586	U /	2.08	-3.28	1.58 /20	--	--	3.17	1.07
EM	Cullen Emerging Mrkts High Div Rtl	CEMDX	U	(877) 485-8586	U /	1.99	-3.45	1.23 /19	--	--	3.01	1.32
GI	Cullen High Dividend Equity C	CHVCX	C+	(877) 485-8586	C / 4.5	-2.79	0.50	5.56 /43	11.47 /49	10.83 /51	1.59	2.07
GI	Cullen High Dividend Equity I	CHDVX	C+	(877) 485-8586	C / 5.2	-2.51	1.02	6.67 /52	12.59 /57	11.92 /60	2.48	1.07
GI	Cullen High Dividend Equity Retail	CHDEX	C+	(877) 485-8586	C / 5.0	-2.63	0.83	6.34 /49	12.29 /55	11.64 /58	2.23	1.32
FO	Cullen Intl High Dividend C	CIHCX	E+	(877) 485-8586	E+ / 0.9	1.93	-5.26	-5.95 / 4	4.83 /13	3.69 / 7	1.88	2.14
FO	Cullen Intl High Dividend I	CIHIX	D-	(877) 485-8586	D- / 1.2	2.16	-4.77	-4.98 / 6	5.89 /16	4.72 /11	2.87	1.14
FO	Cullen Intl High Dividend Retail	CIHDX	D-	(877) 485-8586	D- / 1.1	2.11	-4.92	-5.25 / 5	5.63 /15	4.43 /10	2.63	1.39
SC	Cullen Small Cap Value C	CUSCX	E	(877) 485-8586	D- / 1.0	3.50	-1.14	-6.87 / 4	4.94 /13	7.16 /24	0.00	4.29
SC	Cullen Small Cap Value I	CUSIX	E	(877) 485-8586	D- / 1.3	3.80	-0.87	-6.18 / 4	5.89 /16	8.17 /31	0.00	3.29
SC	Cullen Small Cap Value Retail	CUSRX	E	(877) 485-8586	D- / 1.2	3.61	-0.84	-6.26 / 4	5.69 /15	7.92 /29	0.00	3.54
GI	Cullen Value Fund I	CVLVX	U	(877) 485-8586	U /	1.54	3.10	6.20 /48	--	--	1.28	1.85
GI	Cutler Equity	CALEX	B-	(888) 288-5374	C / 5.3	-1.45	2.16	6.29 /49	12.61 /57	13.40 /72	1.37	1.15
SC	CWC Small Cap Aggressive Value	CWCIX	D	(855) 881-2381	C- / 4.2	1.63	4.62	5.87 /45	10.45 /42	--	0.00	1.98
SC	CWC Small Cap Aggressive Value Rtl	CWCRX	D	(855) 881-2381	C- / 4.1	1.65	4.58	5.67 /44	10.18 /40	--	0.00	2.23
GR	Dana Large Cap Equity A	DLCAX	B+		B- / 7.1	2.92	8.41	13.72 /89	15.78 /82	--	0.78	1.93
GR	Dana Large Cap Equity Institutional	DLCIX	U		U /	2.97	8.55	14.07 /90	--	--	1.02	1.68
GR	Dana Large Cap Equity N	DLCEX	A		B / 8.2	2.93	8.40	13.77 /89	15.98 /83	15.37 /89	0.84	1.93
GR	Davenport Core	DAVPX	B+	(800) 281-2317	B / 8.0	2.22	8.82	12.42 /84	15.33 /78	14.10 /79	0.45	0.94
GR	Davenport Equity Opportunities	DEOPX	A+	(800) 281-2317	A+ / 9.7	5.59	16.07	16.67 /94	18.99 /97	--	1.45	0.98
IN	Davenport Value and Income Fund	DVIPX	A+	(800) 281-2317	B+ / 8.5	1.76	8.39	11.92 /82	16.24 /85	--	1.55	1.07
GR	Davidson Multi Cap Equity Fund A	DFMAX	B+	(888) 263-6443	B- / 7.4	1.96	8.26	11.79 /82	16.12 /84	14.37 /81	0.84	1.38
GR	Davidson Multi Cap Equity Fund C	DFMCX	A-	(888) 263-6443	B / 7.7	1.77	7.84	10.97 /78	15.26 /77	13.51 /73	0.27	2.13
GI	Davis Appreciation & Income A	RPFCX	D+	(800) 279-0279	D+ / 2.7	1.17	-2.09	2.34 /23	9.96 /39	8.89 /36	0.97	0.93
GI	Davis Appreciation & Income B	DCSBX	D+	(800) 279-0279	D+ / 2.8	0.93	-2.57	1.31 /19	8.91 /32	7.86 /29	0.15	1.88
GI	Davis Appreciation & Income C	DCSCX	D+	(800) 279-0279	D+ / 2.9	0.97	-2.49	1.46 /20	9.05 /33	8.01 /30	0.27	1.74
GI	Davis Appreciation & Income Y	DCSYX	C-	(800) 279-0279	C- / 3.6	1.19	-2.01	2.46 /24	10.13 /40	9.08 /37	1.14	0.75

99 Pct = Best
0 Pct = Worst

● Denotes fund is closed to new investors
* Denotes fund is included in Section II

www.thestreetratings.com

RISK	3 Year		NET ASSETS		ASSET				Portfolio	BULL / BEAR		FUND MANAGER		MINIMUMS		LOADS	
Risk Rating/Pts	Standard Deviation	Beta	NAV As of 3/31/15	Total $(Mil)	Cash %	Stocks %	Bonds %	Other %	Turnover Ratio	Last Bull Market Return	Last Bear Market Return	Manager Quality Pct	Manager Tenure (Years)	Initial Purch. $	Additional Purch. $	Front End Load	Back End Load
B- /7.9	8.5	0.83	15.66	14	10	77	11	2	0	63.8	-17.7	30	5	50	25	0.0	0.0
B- /7.8	8.5	0.83	15.15	5	10	77	11	2	0	59.8	-17.9	22	5	50	25	0.0	0.0
B- /7.9	8.5	0.83	15.84	2	10	77	11	2	0	65.2	-17.6	33	5	50	25	0.0	0.0
B /8.5	6.5	1.06	14.12	2	13	63	23	1	0	42.3	-10.2	16	5	50	25	0.0	0.0
C+ /6.3	11.3	1.10	17.85	3	0	99	0	1	0	104.5	-25.7	61	5	50	25	5.5	0.0
C+ /6.3	11.3	1.10	17.26	3	0	99	0	1	0	99.4	-25.9	50	5	50	25	0.0	0.0
C+ /6.3	11.3	1.10	18.05	2	0	99	0	1	0	106.2	-25.6	65	5	50	25	0.0	0.0
B- /7.6	9.4	0.96	18.26	6	3	96	0	1	0	87.8	-17.4	55	5	50	25	5.5	0.0
B- /7.5	9.4	0.96	17.66	8	3	96	0	1	0	83.2	-17.7	43	5	50	25	0.0	0.0
B- /7.6	9.3	0.96	18.46	2	3	96	0	1	0	89.4	-17.3	59	5	50	25	0.0	0.0
C+ /6.0	11.5	1.02	21.08	3	1	98	0	1	0	115.9	-23.1	85	N/A	50	25	5.5	0.0
C+ /6.0	11.5	1.03	20.39	1	1	98	0	1	0	110.5	-23.3	80	N/A	50	25	0.0	0.0
C+ /6.1	11.5	1.02	21.33	1	1	98	0	1	0	117.8	-23.0	86	N/A	50	25	0.0	0.0
C+ /6.2	11.0	0.81	13.22	3	2	97	0	1	0	51.7	-23.2	71	5	50	25	5.5	0.0
C+ /6.1	11.0	0.81	12.77	2	2	97	0	1	0	47.8	-23.5	62	5	50	25	0.0	0.0
C+ /6.2	11.0	0.81	13.36	1	2	97	0	1	0	52.9	-23.2	74	5	50	25	0.0	0.0
C+ /6.4	11.5	1.00	19.91	3	0	99	0	1	0	115.4	-25.7	78	5	50	25	5.5	0.0
C+ /6.4	11.5	1.00	19.26	2	0	99	0	1	0	109.9	-25.9	71	5	50	25	0.0	0.0
C+ /6.4	11.5	1.00	20.13	1	0	99	0	1	0	117.2	-25.6	79	5	50	25	0.0	0.0
C+ /5.7	13.3	0.96	20.56	2	1	98	0	1	0	99.3	-24.9	79	5	50	25	5.5	0.0
C+ /5.6	13.3	0.96	19.87	1	1	98	0	1	0	94.3	-25.1	73	5	50	25	0.0	0.0
C+ /5.7	13.3	0.96	20.79	1	1	98	0	1	0	101.1	-24.8	81	5	50	25	0.0	0.0
B- /7.2	10.1	1.02	17.98	2	2	97	0	1	0	89.7	-20.4	32	5	50	25	5.5	0.0
B- /7.1	10.1	1.02	17.39	1	2	97	0	1	0	85.0	-20.7	23	5	50	25	0.0	0.0
B- /7.2	10.0	1.02	18.19	N/A	2	97	0	1	0	91.3	-20.4	35	5	50	25	0.0	0.0
U /	N/A	N/A	10.81	134	6	93	0	1	60	N/A	N/A	N/A	3	1,000,000	100	0.0	0.0
U /	N/A	N/A	10.77	29	6	93	0	1	60	N/A	N/A	N/A	3	1,000	100	0.0	0.0
B- /7.6	8.4	0.79	16.75	94	2	97	0	1	6	64.0	-8.8	53	12	1,000	100	0.0	0.0
B- /7.6	8.4	0.79	16.85	1,754	2	97	0	1	6	69.7	-8.4	67	12	1,000,000	100	0.0	0.0
B- /7.6	8.4	0.79	16.84	436	2	97	0	1	6	68.3	-8.5	64	12	1,000	100	0.0	0.0
C+ /5.8	11.6	0.85	10.17	4	2	97	0	1	45	32.3	-21.0	25	10	1,000	100	0.0	0.0
C+ /5.8	11.6	0.85	10.27	337	2	97	0	1	45	37.0	-20.7	37	10	1,000,000	100	0.0	0.0
C+ /5.8	11.6	0.85	10.20	58	2	97	0	1	45	35.5	-20.7	34	10	1,000	100	0.0	0.0
D+ /2.9	13.9	0.86	13.02	N/A	5	94	0	1	27	48.2	-23.5	3	N/A	1,000	100	0.0	0.0
C- /3.1	13.9	0.86	13.66	5	5	94	0	1	27	52.8	-23.1	4	N/A	1,000,000	100	0.0	0.0
C- /3.1	13.9	0.86	13.50	1	5	94	0	1	27	51.6	-23.2	4	N/A	1,000	100	0.0	0.0
U /	N/A	N/A	13.83	28	7	92	0	1	8	N/A	N/A	N/A	3	1,000,000	100	0.0	0.0
B- /7.8	9.2	0.93	17.32	124	3	96	0	1	8	76.4	-13.0	36	12	2,500	0	0.0	0.0
C /4.9	13.7	0.94	11.85	12	2	97	0	1	44	65.7	-27.2	15	5	250,000	0	0.0	1.0
C /4.8	13.8	0.94	11.72	N/A	2	97	0	1	44	64.2	-27.2	13	5	10,000	1,000	0.0	1.0
B- /7.3	9.5	0.97	18.80	1	2	97	0	1	57	94.9	-18.0	69	7	1,000	250	5.0	2.0
U /	N/A	N/A	18.82	51	2	97	0	1	57	N/A	N/A	N/A	7	1,000,000	1,000	0.0	2.0
B- /7.3	9.5	0.97	18.84	47	2	97	0	1	57	96.0	-18.0	71	7	1,000	250	0.0	2.0
C+ /6.8	9.7	1.00	20.02	330	4	95	0	1	29	97.0	-16.2	58	17	5,000	0	0.0	0.0
C+ /6.4	9.7	0.86	16.61	277	1	98	0	1	49	114.4	-17.1	93	5	5,000	0	0.0	0.0
B- /7.4	9.1	0.92	15.46	408	4	95	0	1	32	96.8	-12.7	80	5	5,000	0	0.0	0.0
B- /7.2	10.2	1.02	22.91	53	1	98	0	1	12	100.2	-19.3	62	7	2,500	0	5.0	0.0
B- /7.2	10.2	1.02	22.40	23	1	98	0	1	12	95.1	-19.5	51	7	2,500	0	0.0	0.0
C+ /6.6	11.9	1.08	36.44	213	10	73	1	16	20	61.6	-21.6	5	22	1,000	25	4.8	0.0
C+ /6.6	11.9	1.08	35.90	4	10	73	1	16	20	56.4	-21.9	3	22	1,000	25	0.0	0.0
C+ /6.6	11.9	1.08	36.50	65	10	73	1	16	20	57.1	-21.9	4	22	1,000	25	0.0	0.0
C+ /6.6	11.9	1.08	36.61	62	10	73	1	16	20	62.5	-21.5	5	22	5,000,000	25	0.0	0.0

99 Pct = Best
0 Pct = Worst

Fund Type	Fund Name	Ticker Symbol	Overall Investment Rating	Phone	Performance Rating/Pts	Total Return % through 3/31/15			Annualized		Incl. in Returns	
						3 Mo	6 Mo	1Yr / Pct	3Yr / Pct	5Yr / Pct	Dividend Yield	Expense Ratio
FS	Davis Financial A	RPFGX	C+	(800) 279-0279	C+ / 6.7	-0.25	6.32	12.18 /83	15.28 /77	11.21 /54	0.61	0.88
FS	Davis Financial B	DFIBX	C+	(800) 279-0279	C+ / 6.7	-0.53	5.77	10.98 /78	14.00 /67	9.97 /44	0.00	1.99
FS	Davis Financial C	DFFCX	C+	(800) 279-0279	C+ / 6.9	-0.48	5.85	11.17 /79	14.23 /69	10.20 /46	0.00	1.79
FS	Davis Financial Y	DVFYX	B	(800) 279-0279	B / 7.8	-0.22	6.41	12.34 /84	15.47 /79	11.38 /56	0.79	0.71
GL	Davis Global Fund A	DGFAX	C-	(800) 279-0279	C / 4.6	3.91	3.99	1.42 /20	13.51 /63	9.60 /41	0.10	0.96
GL	Davis Global Fund B	DGFBX	C-	(800) 279-0279	C / 4.5	3.58	3.30	0.10 /16	12.04 /53	8.21 /31	0.00	2.26
GL	Davis Global Fund C	DGFCX	C-	(800) 279-0279	C / 4.8	3.71	3.55	0.53 /17	12.45 /56	8.58 /34	0.00	1.83
GL	Davis Global Fund Y	DGFYX	C	(800) 279-0279	C+ / 5.7	3.97	4.12	1.71 /21	13.82 /66	9.89 /44	0.37	0.69
FO	Davis International Fund A	DILAX	E+	(800) 279-0279	D- / 1.2	1.98	-1.70	-3.89 / 7	7.52 /24	3.99 / 8	0.38	1.17
FO	Davis International Fund B	DILBX	E+	(800) 279-0279	D- / 1.2	1.74	-2.36	-5.16 / 5	6.36 /18	2.49 / 5	0.00	4.27
FO	Davis International Fund C	DILCX	E+	(800) 279-0279	D- / 1.2	1.74	-2.26	-5.07 / 5	6.40 /18	2.49 / 5	0.00	2.55
FO	Davis International Fund Y	DILYX	D-	(800) 279-0279	D / 1.8	2.10	-1.57	-3.60 / 8	7.93 /27	3.95 / 8	0.74	0.82
* GR	Davis New York Venture Fund A	NYVTX	C-	(800) 279-0279	C+ / 5.6	1.98	5.42	6.55 /51	13.89 /66	11.11 /54	0.40	0.86
GR	Davis New York Venture Fund B	NYVBX	C-	(800) 279-0279	C+ / 5.7	1.75	4.93	5.55 /43	12.83 /58	10.08 /45	0.00	1.79
GR	Davis New York Venture Fund C	NYVCX	C-	(800) 279-0279	C+ / 5.8	1.78	5.00	5.72 /44	13.00 /60	10.24 /46	0.00	1.64
GR	Davis New York Venture Fund R	NYVRX	C	(800) 279-0279	C+ / 6.1	1.89	5.26	6.22 /48	13.55 /64	10.76 /51	0.15	1.16
GR	Davis New York Venture Fund Y	DNVYX	C	(800) 279-0279	C+ / 6.6	2.03	5.54	6.80 /53	14.16 /68	11.38 /56	0.63	0.62
MC	Davis Opportunity A	RPEAX	C+	(800) 279-0279	C+ / 6.8	2.55	4.45	3.35 /28	16.54 /87	13.29 /71	0.06	0.98
MC	Davis Opportunity B	RPFEX	C	(800) 279-0279	C+ / 6.8	2.34	3.98	2.38 /23	15.41 /78	12.20 /62	0.00	1.95
MC	Davis Opportunity C	DGOCX	C	(800) 279-0279	B- / 7.0	2.37	4.06	2.58 /24	15.63 /80	12.41 /63	0.00	1.78
MC	Davis Opportunity Y	DGOYX	B-	(800) 279-0279	B / 7.9	2.62	4.59	3.64 /30	16.84 /89	13.59 /74	0.30	0.74
RE	Davis Real Estate A	RPFRX	C+	(800) 279-0279	B / 7.6	5.06	18.82	23.56 /98	11.61 /50	13.34 /71	1.12	0.98
RE	Davis Real Estate B	DREBX	C+	(800) 279-0279	B / 7.6	4.78	18.17	22.23 /97	10.40 /42	12.10 /61	0.23	2.06
RE	Davis Real Estate C	DRECX	C+	(800) 279-0279	B / 7.8	4.83	18.32	22.48 /97	10.64 /43	12.39 /63	0.41	1.85
RE	Davis Real Estate Y	DREYX	B	(800) 279-0279	B+ / 8.7	5.13	18.95	23.85 /98	11.86 /51	13.62 /74	1.36	0.76
OT	Davis Research Fund Class A	DRFAX	B-	(800) 279-0279	C+ / 6.2	1.23	7.61	9.47 /72	14.47 /71	12.50 /64	0.72	0.70
GR	Davlin Philanthropic Fund	DPFDX	B+	(877) 328-5468	B / 7.7	1.42	10.65	10.45 /76	15.42 /78	12.56 /65	1.18	1.55
AA	Day Hagan Tact Alloc Fd of ETFs A	DHAAX	D+	(877) 329-4246	D- / 1.2	0.61	3.09	3.09 /27	5.90 /16	5.12 /12	0.09	1.91
AA	Day Hagan Tact Alloc Fd of ETFs C	DHACX	D+	(877) 329-4246	D- / 1.4	0.45	2.64	2.28 /23	5.10 /13	4.33 / 9	0.00	2.66
AA	DE 529 Fidelity CIP 100% Eq Ptf		C+	(800) 544-8544	C+ / 6.3	3.44	6.05	8.42 /66	13.33 /62	10.92 /52	0.00	1.00
AA	DE 529 Fidelity CIP 70% Eq Ptf		C+	(800) 544-8544	C / 4.6	2.90	5.01	7.14 /56	10.59 /43	9.42 /40	0.00	0.93
AA	DE 529 Fidelity CIP College Ptf		C	(800) 544-8544	D- / 1.2	1.50	2.46	3.65 /30	3.91 /10	4.22 / 9	0.00	0.67
AA	DE 529 Fidelity CIP Consv Ptf		C-	(800) 544-8544	E+ / 0.7	0.87	1.41	2.38 /23	1.62 / 6	2.41 / 5	0.00	0.59
AA	DE 529 Fidelity CIP Idx 100% Eq Ptf		B-	(800) 544-8544	C+ / 6.0	2.64	4.66	6.90 /54	13.14 /61	11.53 /57	0.00	0.27
AA	DE 529 Fidelity CIP Idx 70% Eq Ptf		C+	(800) 544-8544	C- / 4.2	2.36	4.03	6.04 /47	10.10 /40	9.98 /44	0.00	0.30
AA	DE 529 Fidelity CIP Idx Consv Ptf		C-	(800) 544-8544	E+ / 0.7	0.69	1.47	2.43 /24	1.25 / 5	2.45 / 5	0.00	0.34
AA	DE 529 Fidelity CIP Index Clg Ptf		C	(800) 544-8544	D- / 1.0	1.17	2.06	3.12 /27	3.41 / 9	4.38 /10	0.00	0.33
AA	DE 529 Fidelity CIP Index Ptf 2015		C	(800) 544-8544	D- / 1.3	1.15	2.10	3.29 /28	4.45 /11	5.84 /16	0.00	0.32
AA	DE 529 Fidelity CIP Index Ptf 2018		C	(800) 544-8544	D / 2.1	1.59	2.81	4.34 /34	6.37 /18	7.36 /25	0.00	0.31
AA	DE 529 Fidelity CIP Index Ptf 2021		C+	(800) 544-8544	C- / 3.1	1.90	3.37	5.17 /40	8.15 /28	8.61 /34	0.00	0.30
AA	DE 529 Fidelity CIP Index Ptf 2024		C+	(800) 544-8544	C- / 4.0	2.13	3.86	5.86 /45	9.79 /38	9.66 /42	0.00	0.29
AA	DE 529 Fidelity CIP Index Ptf 2027		B-	(800) 544-8544	C / 4.8	2.38	4.18	6.37 /50	11.12 /46	10.42 /48	0.00	0.28
AA	DE 529 Fidelity CIP Portfolio 2015		C	(800) 544-8544	D- / 1.5	1.56	2.63	3.99 /32	5.04 /13	5.50 /14	0.00	0.80
GL	DE 529 Fidelity CIP Portfolio 2018		C	(800) 544-8544	D+ / 2.5	2.04	3.52	5.26 /41	6.98 /21	6.98 /23	0.00	0.86
AA	DE 529 Fidelity CIP Portfolio 2021		C+	(800) 544-8544	C- / 3.5	2.46	4.28	6.27 /49	8.73 /31	8.15 /31	0.00	0.92
AA	DE 529 Fidelity CIP Portfolio 2024		C+	(800) 544-8544	C / 4.4	2.75	4.84	6.88 /54	10.27 /41	9.09 /37	0.00	0.97
AA	DE 529 Fidelity CIP Portfolio 2027		C+	(800) 544-8544	C / 5.2	2.88	5.10	7.26 /57	11.55 /49	9.84 /43	0.00	0.99
GR	Dean Mid Cap Value No load	DALCX	C+	(888) 899-8343	C+ / 6.6	0.51	7.64	7.50 /59	14.10 /68	10.50 /49	0.61	2.01
SC	Dean Small Cap Value No Load	DASCX	B	(888) 899-8343	B- / 7.5	1.75	9.09	7.25 /57	15.37 /78	13.44 /72	0.52	1.22
IN	Dearborn Partners Rising Dividend A	DRDAX	U	(888) 983-3380	U /	-0.25	6.25	11.96 /82	--	--	1.51	2.11
IN	Dearborn Partners Rising Dividend C	DRDCX	U	(888) 983-3380	U /	-0.41	5.93	11.15 /79	--	--	0.93	2.87
IN	Dearborn Partners Rising Dividend I	DRDIX	U	(888) 983-3380	U /	-0.19	6.37	12.20 /83	--	--	1.81	1.92

● Denotes fund is closed to new investors
* Denotes fund is included in Section II

www.thestreetratings.com

| RISK | 3 Year | | NET ASSETS | | ASSET | | | | Portfolio | BULL / BEAR | | FUND MANAGER | | MINIMUMS | | LOADS | |
Risk Rating/Pts	Standard Deviation	Beta	NAV As of 3/31/15	Total $(Mil)	Cash %	Stocks %	Bonds %	Other %	Turnover Ratio	Last Bull Market Return	Last Bear Market Return	Manager Quality Pct	Manager Tenure (Years)	Initial Purch. $	Additional Purch. $	Front End Load	Back End Load
C+ / 5.9	10.7	0.88	39.49	545	3	96	0	1	32	87.6	-19.8	69	24	1,000	25	4.8	0.0
C / 5.5	10.7	0.88	32.11	4	3	96	0	1	32	80.6	-20.1	52	24	1,000	25	0.0	0.0
C+ / 5.6	10.7	0.88	33.47	78	3	96	0	1	32	81.8	-20.1	56	24	1,000	25	0.0	0.0
C+ / 5.9	10.7	0.88	40.61	96	3	96	0	1	32	88.7	-19.7	70	24	5,000,000	25	0.0	0.0
C+ / 5.9	12.0	0.77	19.15	79	3	96	0	1	33	77.7	-26.0	95	11	1,000	25	4.8	2.0
C+ / 5.9	12.0	0.77	18.24	1	3	96	0	1	33	70.1	-26.4	92	11	1,000	25	0.0	2.0
C+ / 5.9	12.0	0.77	18.46	46	3	96	0	1	33	72.3	-26.3	93	11	1,000	25	0.0	2.0
C+ / 5.9	12.0	0.77	19.11	178	3	96	0	1	33	79.3	-25.9	95	11	5,000,000	25	0.0	2.0
C+ / 5.6	12.9	0.87	10.31	7	2	97	0	1	44	50.4	-31.5	57	9	1,000	25	4.8	2.0
C / 5.5	12.9	0.87	9.93	N/A	2	97	0	1	44	45.2	-32.9	40	9	1,000	25	0.0	2.0
C / 5.5	12.9	0.87	9.93	1	2	97	0	1	44	45.4	-33.0	41	9	1,000	25	0.0	2.0
C / 5.5	12.8	0.87	10.19	87	2	97	0	1	44	52.7	-32.5	63	9	5,000,000	25	0.0	2.0
C / 5.0	10.6	1.07	37.57	9,588	2	97	0	1	20	86.0	-20.2	25	20	1,000	25	4.8	0.0
C / 4.8	10.6	1.07	34.84	102	2	97	0	1	20	80.2	-20.6	16	20	1,000	25	0.0	0.0
C / 4.8	10.6	1.07	35.41	3,120	2	97	0	1	20	81.1	-20.5	17	20	1,000	25	0.0	0.0
C / 5.0	10.6	1.07	37.65	269	2	97	0	1	20	84.1	-20.3	22	20	500,000	25	0.0	0.0
C / 5.0	10.6	1.07	38.13	4,478	2	97	0	1	20	87.5	-20.2	28	20	5,000,000	25	0.0	0.0
C / 5.2	11.1	0.86	32.54	299	4	95	0	1	40	93.8	-18.3	82	16	1,000	25	4.8	0.0
C / 4.7	11.1	0.87	26.72	4	4	95	0	1	40	87.5	-18.7	74	16	1,000	25	0.0	0.0
C / 4.8	11.1	0.86	28.45	102	4	95	0	1	40	88.7	-18.7	76	16	1,000	25	0.0	0.0
C / 5.2	11.1	0.87	33.63	160	4	95	0	1	40	95.5	-18.3	84	16	5,000,000	25	0.0	0.0
C / 4.7	11.5	0.91	37.60	206	11	87	0	2	53	73.3	-14.3	51	13	1,000	25	4.8	0.0
C / 4.7	11.5	0.91	37.01	2	11	87	0	2	53	66.9	-14.7	35	13	1,000	25	0.0	0.0
C / 4.7	11.5	0.91	37.52	28	11	87	0	2	53	68.3	-14.6	38	13	1,000	25	0.0	0.0
C / 4.7	11.5	0.91	38.12	40	11	87	0	2	53	74.6	-14.2	55	13	5,000,000	25	0.0	0.0
B- / 7.1	10.5	1.06	18.89	54	10	89	0	1	27	87.8	-16.1	32	N/A	1,000	25	4.8	0.0
B- / 7.0	10.9	1.03	17.89	12	4	93	1	2	18	87.2	-19.8	50	7	2,500	100	0.0	1.0
B / 8.2	7.0	1.13	11.52	45	20	57	21	2	206	35.9	-14.0	7	6	1,000	50	5.8	0.0
B / 8.2	7.0	1.13	11.07	10	20	57	21	2	206	32.5	-14.2	5	6	1,000	50	0.0	0.0
C+ / 6.7	10.2	1.71	18.92	46	4	94	0	2	42	82.9	-23.0	9	10	50	25	0.0	0.0
B / 8.1	7.6	1.29	20.56	22	4	67	27	2	44	61.4	-17.3	22	10	50	25	0.0	0.0
B+ / 9.9	2.6	0.40	19.60	61	23	21	54	2	145	18.6	-4.4	62	10	50	25	0.0	0.0
B+ / 9.6	1.5	0.06	15.06	8	40	0	59	1	131	6.4	0.6	77	10	50	25	0.0	0.0
B- / 7.0	10.1	1.71	15.96	9	4	95	0	1	42	80.0	-19.3	9	9	50	25	0.0	0.0
B / 8.6	7.2	1.24	16.51	6	3	67	28	2	21	56.0	-11.3	24	9	50	25	0.0	0.0
B+ / 9.9	1.3	N/A	13.09	2	55	0	44	1	219	3.9	4.4	78	9	50	25	0.0	0.0
B+ / 9.9	2.2	0.34	13.89	4	35	18	45	2	297	15.6	-0.3	65	9	50	25	0.0	0.0
B+ / 9.9	3.1	0.49	14.13	9	33	20	45	2	49	23.5	-4.0	56	9	50	25	0.0	0.0
B+ / 9.6	4.5	0.74	14.66	10	21	33	44	2	28	34.5	-7.2	44	9	50	25	0.0	0.0
B+ / 9.1	5.8	0.98	15.04	10	14	46	39	1	21	45.6	-10.6	33	9	50	25	0.0	0.0
B / 8.6	7.1	1.21	15.35	11	8	59	32	1	9	56.4	-13.6	23	9	50	25	0.0	0.0
B / 8.1	8.2	1.39	14.20	7	3	70	25	2	3	65.1	-15.8	18	8	50	25	0.0	0.0
B+ / 9.6	3.6	0.57	19.54	102	22	23	53	2	60	27.4	-9.0	52	10	50	25	0.0	0.0
B+ / 9.2	4.9	0.77	20.02	131	13	37	48	2	43	39.1	-12.4	68	10	50	25	0.0	0.0
B / 8.7	6.3	1.06	19.99	91	8	50	40	2	34	50.7	-16.1	30	10	50	25	0.0	0.0
B / 8.1	7.6	1.28	17.55	38	6	62	31	1	38	61.3	-19.1	20	10	50	25	0.0	0.0
B- / 7.6	8.7	1.47	13.59	12	5	74	19	2	0	70.4	-21.2	15	8	50	25	0.0	0.0
C+ / 6.7	10.8	1.04	15.83	16	3	96	0	1	43	98.0	-23.9	32	7	1,000	0	0.0	0.0
C+ / 6.1	12.9	0.92	15.71	143	4	95	0	1	96	104.0	-25.8	72	7	1,000	0	0.0	0.0
U /	N/A	N/A	12.15	54	7	92	0	1	13	N/A	N/A	N/A	2	5,000	500	5.0	0.0
U /	N/A	N/A	12.11	59	7	92	0	1	13	N/A	N/A	N/A	2	5,000	500	0.0	0.0
U /	N/A	N/A	12.16	26	7	92	0	1	13	N/A	N/A	N/A	2	500,000	500	0.0	0.0

| | | | | | | | Total Return % through 3/31/15 | | | | | Incl. in Returns | |
| | | | | | | | | | | Annualized | | | |
Fund Type	Fund Name	Ticker Symbol	Overall Investment Rating	Phone	Performance Rating/Pts	3 Mo	6 Mo	1Yr / Pct	3Yr / Pct	5Yr / Pct	Dividend Yield	Expense Ratio
SC	Delafield	DEFIX	E	(800) 697-3863	D- / 1.4	-2.17	-1.91	-7.00 / 4	7.71 /25	9.09 /37	0.00	1.22
BA	Delaware Dividend Income A	DDIAX	C+	(800) 523-1918	C- / 4.0	1.48	2.99	6.69 /53	11.47 /49	10.65 /50	2.24	1.12
BA	Delaware Dividend Income C	DDICX	C+	(800) 523-1918	C / 4.4	1.28	2.60	5.88 /45	10.65 /43	9.83 /43	1.63	1.87
BA	Delaware Dividend Income I	DDIIX	B	(800) 523-1918	C / 5.1	1.46	3.11	6.95 /55	11.75 /51	10.92 /52	2.62	0.87
BA	Delaware Dividend Income R	DDDRX	B-	(800) 523-1918	C / 4.7	1.41	2.87	6.42 /50	11.19 /47	10.40 /48	2.12	1.37
EM	● Delaware Emerging Markets	DPEMX	E	(800) 523-1918	E / 0.4	-0.24	-4.31	-2.15 /10	-0.86 / 4	2.46 / 5	2.47	1.16
EM	Delaware Emerging Markets A	DEMAX	E	(800) 523-1918	E / 0.3	-3.96	-14.33	-10.78 / 3	1.27 / 6	1.26 / 4	0.43	1.70
EM	Delaware Emerging Markets C	DEMCX	E	(800) 523-1918	E / 0.3	-4.12	-14.64	-11.41 / 2	0.52 / 5	0.50 / 3	0.00	2.45
EM	Delaware Emerging Markets I	DEMIX	E	(800) 523-1918	E / 0.4	-3.93	-14.17	-10.53 / 3	1.54 / 6	1.50 / 4	0.74	1.45
EM	Delaware Emerging Markets II	DPEGX	E-	(800) 523-1918	E / 0.4	-3.08	-13.86	-7.74 / 3	0.82 / 5	--	1.65	1.32
EM	Delaware Emerging Markets R	DEMRX	E	(800) 523-1918	E / 0.3	-3.99	-14.34	-10.94 / 2	1.03 / 5	1.01 / 3	0.16	1.95
GL	Delaware Focus Global Growth A	DGGAX	D	(800) 523-1918	D+ / 2.4	1.12	4.42	4.53 /35	8.66 /31	11.36 /56	0.36	1.51
GL	Delaware Focus Global Growth C	DGGCX	D	(800) 523-1918	D+ / 2.8	0.94	4.03	3.75 /30	7.88 /26	--	0.00	2.26
GL	Delaware Focus Global Growth Inst	DGGIX	D+	(800) 523-1918	C- / 3.5	1.16	4.52	4.79 /37	8.95 /33	11.59 /58	0.62	1.26
GL	Delaware Focus Global Growth R	DGGRX	D	(800) 523-1918	C- / 3.1	1.02	4.26	4.26 /33	8.39 /29	--	0.14	1.76
AA	Delaware Foundation Consv All A	DFIAX	D	(800) 523-1918	D- / 1.5	2.18	2.86	5.11 /39	6.49 /19	6.65 /21	2.04	1.33
AA	Delaware Foundation Consv All C	DFICX	D	(800) 523-1918	D / 1.8	1.88	2.37	4.21 /33	5.68 /15	5.84 /16	1.41	2.08
AA	Delaware Foundation Consv All Inst	DFIIX	D+	(800) 523-1918	D+ / 2.4	2.24	2.98	5.36 /41	6.74 /20	6.93 /23	2.38	1.08
AA	Delaware Foundation Consv All R	DFIRX	D	(800) 523-1918	D / 2.1	2.02	2.63	4.74 /37	6.19 /18	6.36 /19	1.90	1.58
AA	Delaware Foundation Growth All A	DFGAX	D	(800) 523-1918	D+ / 2.9	2.41	3.15	5.60 /43	9.39 /36	8.67 /34	1.61	1.44
AA	Delaware Foundation Growth All C	DFGCX	D	(800) 523-1918	C- / 3.3	2.17	2.72	4.76 /37	8.57 /30	7.84 /29	1.01	2.19
AA	Delaware Foundation Growth All Inst	DFGIX	D+	(800) 523-1918	C- / 4.0	2.39	3.21	5.83 /45	9.67 /37	8.93 /36	1.93	1.19
AA	Delaware Foundation Growth All R	DFGRX	D+	(800) 523-1918	C- / 3.6	2.23	2.91	5.28 /41	9.11 /34	8.39 /32	1.47	1.69
AA	Delaware Foundation Modt All A	DFBAX	D	(800) 523-1918	D / 2.2	2.24	2.88	5.28 /41	8.03 /27	7.77 /28	1.67	1.17
AA	Delaware Foundation Modt All C	DFBCX	D+	(800) 523-1918	D+ / 2.5	2.06	2.50	4.49 /35	7.21 /22	6.94 /23	1.03	1.94
AA	Delaware Foundation Modt All Inst	DFFIX	C-	(800) 523-1918	C- / 3.2	2.39	3.01	5.61 /43	8.28 /29	8.03 /30	1.99	0.94
AA	Delaware Foundation Modt All R	DFBRX	D+	(800) 523-1918	D+ / 2.8	2.19	2.76	5.03 /39	7.73 /26	7.47 /26	1.52	1.44
RE	Delaware Global RE Opps A	DGRPX	C	(800) 523-1918	C+ / 6.3	3.60	11.66	14.60 /91	13.02 /60	12.28 /62	2.00	1.78
RE	Delaware Global RE Opps Inst	DGROX	C+	(800) 523-1918	B- / 7.5	3.67	11.80	15.07 /92	13.25 /61	12.57 /65	2.37	1.53
GL	Delaware Global Value A	DABAX	C-	(800) 523-1918	C- / 3.1	3.06	1.92	4.34 /34	10.09 /40	8.20 /31	0.42	1.78
GL	Delaware Global Value C	DABCX	C-	(800) 523-1918	C- / 3.5	2.75	1.49	3.49 /29	9.24 /34	7.38 /26	0.00	2.53
GL	Delaware Global Value I	DABIX	C	(800) 523-1918	C- / 4.2	3.05	1.99	4.59 /36	10.36 /42	8.46 /33	0.69	1.53
HL	Delaware Healthcare Fund A	DLHAX	A	(800) 523-1918	A+ / 9.8	6.76	9.31	16.37 /94	23.61 /99	19.82 /99	0.05	1.35
HL	Delaware Healthcare Fund C	DLHCX	A	(800) 523-1918	A+ / 9.8	6.52	8.92	15.51 /92	22.71 /98	18.95 /98	0.00	2.10
HL	Delaware Healthcare Fund I	DLHIX	A	(800) 523-1918	A+ / 9.9	6.85	9.48	16.70 /94	23.95 /99	20.14 /99	0.28	1.10
HL	Delaware Healthcare Fund R	DLRHX	A	(800) 523-1918	A+ / 9.8	6.72	9.17	16.10 /93	23.34 /99	19.53 /99	0.00	1.60
FO	Delaware Intl Value Equity A	DEGIX	D-	(800) 523-1918	D- / 1.2	5.73	-1.58	-3.04 / 9	6.81 /20	4.55 /10	1.87	1.47
FO	Delaware Intl Value Equity C	DEGCX	D-	(800) 523-1918	D- / 1.5	5.48	-1.90	-3.79 / 7	6.02 /17	3.78 / 8	1.23	2.22
FO	Delaware Intl Value Equity Inst	DEQIX	D-	(800) 523-1918	D / 2.0	5.79	-1.39	-2.77 / 9	7.08 /22	4.85 /11	2.24	1.22
FO	Delaware Intl Value Equity R	DIVRX	D-	(800) 523-1918	D / 1.7	5.66	-1.64	-3.24 / 8	6.54 /19	4.32 / 9	1.73	1.72
GR	Delaware Large Cap Growth Eqty	DPLGX	B+	(800) 523-1918	B+ / 8.8	2.81	9.67	15.93 /93	16.19 /85	16.99 /96	0.61	0.64
GI	Delaware Large Cap Value Eqty Port	DPDEX	A+	(800) 523-1918	A- / 9.2	1.77	5.31	13.11 /87	18.13 /95	17.07 /96	1.50	0.68
MC	Delaware Mid Cap Value A	DLMAX	E+	(800) 523-1918	C / 4.7	2.57	5.68	6.03 /47	12.60 /57	11.97 /60	0.25	4.34
MC	Delaware Mid Cap Value C	DLMCX	E+	(800) 523-1918	C / 5.2	2.50	5.44	5.44 /42	11.81 /51	11.19 /54	0.00	5.09
MC	Delaware Mid Cap Value Inst	DLMIX	D-	(800) 523-1918	C+ / 5.9	2.57	5.79	6.31 /49	12.90 /59	12.28 /62	0.50	4.09
MC	Delaware Mid Cap Value R	DLMRX	E+	(800) 523-1918	C / 5.5	2.57	5.58	5.93 /46	12.35 /55	11.72 /59	0.02	4.59
FO	● Delaware Pooled Tr-Intl Equity Orig	DPIEX	D	(800) 523-1918	D+ / 2.9	5.41	-0.08	-1.10 /13	8.70 /31	6.61 /21	4.58	0.86
FO	Delaware Pooled Tr-Labor Sel Itl Eq	DELPX	D-	(800) 523-1918	D+ / 2.3	4.72	-0.99	-2.60 / 9	7.79 /26	5.81 /16	5.64	0.86
RE	Delaware RE Inv A	DPREX	C+	(800) 523-1918	B / 8.1	4.49	19.19	22.76 /98	12.95 /59	15.36 /89	1.46	1.34
RE	Delaware RE Inv C	DPRCX	C+	(800) 523-1918	B+ / 8.5	4.25	18.71	21.81 /97	12.10 /53	14.49 /82	0.94	2.09
RE	Delaware RE Inv Inst	DPRSX	B-	(800) 523-1918	A- / 9.1	4.54	19.27	22.99 /98	13.23 /61	15.64 /91	1.76	1.09
RE	Delaware RE Inv R	DPRRX	C+	(800) 523-1918	B+ / 8.9	4.43	18.99	22.49 /97	12.68 /57	15.08 /87	1.35	1.59

99 Pct = Best
0 Pct = Worst

● Denotes fund is closed to new investors
★ Denotes fund is included in Section II

www.thestreetratings.com

Risk Rating/Pts	Standard Deviation	Beta	NAV As of 3/31/15	Total $(Mil)	Cash %	Stocks %	Bonds %	Other %	Portfolio Turnover Ratio	Last Bull Market Return	Last Bear Market Return	Manager Quality Pct	Manager Tenure (Years)	Initial Purch. $	Additional Purch. $	Front End Load	Back End Load
C- / 3.8	13.8	0.88	31.97	1,012	7	85	6	2	34	71.8	-27.4	7	N/A	1,000	100	0.0	2.0
B / 8.3	6.2	1.04	13.75	326	11	59	19	11	56	61.9	-13.3	68	9	1,000	100	5.8	0.0
B / 8.3	6.1	1.03	13.77	321	11	59	19	11	56	57.9	-13.6	59	9	1,000	100	0.0	0.0
B / 8.3	6.2	1.04	13.75	163	11	59	19	11	56	63.5	-13.3	71	9	0	0	0.0	0.0
B / 8.3	6.2	1.05	13.75	4	11	59	19	11	56	60.7	-13.4	65	9	0	0	0.0	0.0
C- / 3.6	14.5	1.02	8.42	253	1	98	0	1	30	23.1	-20.6	44	18	1,000,000	0	0.6	0.6
C- / 3.5	16.5	1.14	13.83	348	0	100	0	0	26	30.8	-30.4	73	9	1,000	100	5.8	0.0
C- / 3.5	16.4	1.13	13.03	168	0	100	0	0	26	27.5	-30.7	64	9	1,000	100	0.0	0.0
C- / 3.5	16.4	1.14	13.92	1,960	0	100	0	0	26	31.9	-30.3	75	9	0	0	0.0	0.0
C- / 3.4	15.6	1.08	8.18	37	0	99	0	1	11	26.7	-28.8	68	5	1,000,000	0	0.0	0.0
C- / 3.6	16.4	1.13	13.97	18	0	100	0	0	26	29.6	-30.5	70	9	0	0	0.0	0.0
C+ / 5.7	11.7	0.80	19.92	29	2	97	0	1	26	63.6	-16.8	77	7	1,000	100	5.8	0.0
C+ / 5.6	11.7	0.80	19.36	6	2	97	0	1	26	59.4	-17.0	70	7	1,000	100	0.0	0.0
C+ / 5.7	11.7	0.80	20.07	97	2	97	0	1	26	64.9	-16.7	79	7	0	0	0.0	0.0
C+ / 5.7	11.7	0.80	19.74	N/A	2	97	0	1	26	62.1	-16.9	75	7	0	0	0.0	0.0
C+ / 6.9	4.8	0.76	10.16	52	1	40	56	3	163	33.5	-7.7	43	11	1,000	100	5.8	0.0
C+ / 6.9	4.8	0.77	10.18	35	1	40	56	3	163	30.2	-7.9	32	11	1,000	100	0.0	0.0
C+ / 6.9	4.9	0.77	10.18	18	1	40	56	3	163	34.7	-7.6	45	11	0	0	0.0	0.0
C+ / 6.9	4.8	0.77	10.15	4	1	40	56	3	163	32.4	-7.7	38	11	0	0	0.0	0.0
C+ / 5.6	8.1	1.34	10.64	45	1	79	18	2	77	55.5	-16.4	11	11	1,000	100	5.8	0.0
C+ / 5.7	8.1	1.35	10.36	11	1	79	18	2	77	51.6	-16.7	7	11	1,000	100	0.0	0.0
C+ / 5.6	8.0	1.34	10.70	20	1	79	18	2	77	56.8	-16.3	13	11	0	0	0.0	0.0
C+ / 5.7	8.1	1.35	10.56	4	1	79	18	2	77	54.2	-16.5	9	11	0	0	0.0	0.0
C+ / 6.8	6.4	1.07	11.97	196	1	60	37	2	115	44.8	-12.3	22	N/A	1,000	100	5.8	0.0
C+ / 6.8	6.5	1.07	11.97	29	1	60	37	2	115	40.9	-12.5	15	N/A	1,000	100	0.0	0.0
C+ / 6.8	6.4	1.07	11.98	63	1	60	37	2	115	45.9	-12.2	24	N/A	0	0	0.0	0.0
C+ / 6.8	6.4	1.06	11.93	3	1	60	37	2	115	43.4	-12.4	20	N/A	0	0	0.0	0.0
C / 5.3	12.2	0.91	7.40	9	15	84	0	1	107	73.9	-18.1	69	8	1,000	100	5.8	0.0
C / 5.3	12.1	0.91	7.40	47	15	84	0	1	107	74.7	-17.9	72	8	0	0	0.0	0.0
C+ / 6.8	11.5	0.79	11.80	17	1	98	0	1	43	59.6	-23.7	86	9	1,000	100	5.8	0.0
C+ / 6.8	11.5	0.79	11.58	5	1	98	0	1	43	55.6	-23.9	82	9	1,000	100	0.0	0.0
C+ / 6.8	11.5	0.79	11.83	2	1	98	0	1	43	61.0	-23.6	87	9	0	0	0.0	0.0
C+ / 5.6	12.8	0.95	20.36	219	0	100	0	0	60	137.5	-17.5	96	8	1,000	100	5.8	0.0
C / 5.5	12.8	0.95	19.60	76	0	100	0	0	60	131.5	-17.8	95	8	1,000	100	0.0	0.0
C / 5.5	12.8	0.95	20.44	180	0	100	0	0	60	139.6	-17.4	96	8	0	0	0.0	0.0
C+ / 5.6	12.8	0.95	20.17	6	0	100	0	0	60	135.5	-17.6	96	8	0	0	0.0	0.0
C+ / 5.7	12.7	0.93	13.46	73	0	99	0	1	26	44.9	-28.1	38	9	1,000	100	5.8	0.0
C+ / 5.7	12.8	0.93	13.27	28	0	99	0	1	26	41.2	-28.3	29	9	1,000	100	0.0	0.0
C+ / 5.7	12.7	0.93	13.51	152	0	99	0	1	26	46.3	-28.0	42	9	0	0	0.0	0.0
C+ / 5.7	12.7	0.93	13.43	2	0	99	0	1	26	43.6	-28.1	35	9	0	0	0.0	0.0
C / 5.5	10.6	1.02	16.49	295	2	97	0	1	30	105.6	-12.4	63	10	1,000,000	0	0.0	0.0
B- / 7.8	8.4	0.84	27.65	233	3	96	0	1	19	104.6	-13.6	92	9	1,000,000	0	0.0	0.0
D- / 1.1	11.0	0.95	5.18	4	0	99	0	1	28	83.7	-25.2	24	7	1,000	100	5.8	0.0
D- / 1.1	11.1	0.96	4.92	1	0	99	0	1	28	78.8	-25.4	17	7	1,000	100	0.0	0.0
D- / 1.1	11.0	0.95	5.19	1	0	99	0	1	28	85.0	-25.0	27	7	0	0	0.0	0.0
D- / 1.1	11.0	0.95	5.19	N/A	0	99	0	1	28	81.1	-25.2	22	7	0	0	0.0	0.0
C / 5.4	13.0	0.95	14.81	385	1	98	0	1	21	45.5	-17.1	62	16	1,000,000	0	0.0	0.0
C / 5.0	13.2	0.96	14.19	376	1	98	0	1	23	40.4	-16.2	48	20	1,000,000	0	0.0	0.0
C- / 4.0	13.0	1.04	16.08	104	5	94	0	1	83	80.8	-15.4	44	18	1,000	100	5.8	0.0
C- / 4.0	13.0	1.04	16.05	25	5	94	0	1	83	76.2	-15.6	34	18	1,000	100	0.0	0.0
C- / 4.0	13.0	1.04	16.11	118	5	94	0	1	83	82.4	-15.2	48	18	0	0	0.0	0.0
C- / 4.0	13.0	1.04	16.08	15	5	94	0	1	83	79.2	-15.4	41	18	0	0	0.0	0.0

Fund Type	Fund Name	Ticker Symbol	Overall Investment Rating	Phone	Performance Rating/Pts	3 Mo	6 Mo	1Yr / Pct	3Yr / Pct	5Yr / Pct	Dividend Yield	Expense Ratio
	99 Pct = Best 0 Pct = Worst				PERFORMANCE		Total Return % through 3/31/15		Annualized		Incl. in Returns	
AG	Delaware Select 20 Port	DPCEX	D	(800) 523-1918	B- / 7.2	1.90	10.00	15.54 /93	13.27 /62	16.26 /94	0.11	0.87
AG	● Delaware Select Growth A	DVEAX	C-	(800) 523-1918	C / 5.5	3.48	11.68	11.88 /82	12.51 /56	16.44 /95	0.15	1.25
AG	● Delaware Select Growth C	DVECX	C-	(800) 523-1918	C+ / 5.9	3.27	11.26	11.03 /78	11.67 /50	15.57 /91	0.00	2.00
AG	● Delaware Select Growth I	VAGGX	C+	(800) 523-1918	C+ / 6.7	3.54	11.81	12.15 /83	12.79 /58	16.73 /95	0.37	1.00
AG	● Delaware Select Growth R	DFSRX	C	(800) 523-1918	C+ / 6.3	3.40	11.54	11.59 /81	12.22 /54	16.15 /94	0.00	1.50
SC	Delaware Small Cap Core A	DCCAX	A-	(800) 523-1918	B+ / 8.6	3.05	12.88	10.36 /76	17.89 /94	16.84 /96	0.00	1.31
SC	Delaware Small Cap Core C	DCCCX	A-	(800) 523-1918	B+ / 8.9	2.90	12.46	9.60 /72	17.03 /90	15.95 /93	0.00	2.06
SC	Delaware Small Cap Core I	DCCIX	A+	(800) 523-1918	A / 9.4	3.11	13.04	10.65 /77	18.20 /95	17.12 /96	0.00	1.06
SC	Delaware Small Cap Core R	DCCRX	A	(800) 523-1918	A- / 9.2	3.01	12.75	10.13 /75	17.59 /93	16.54 /95	0.00	1.56
SC	Delaware Small Cap Value A	DEVLX	C	(800) 523-1918	C / 5.3	3.01	7.44	5.49 /42	13.57 /64	13.90 /77	0.30	1.25
SC	Delaware Small Cap Value C	DEVCX	C+	(800) 523-1918	C+ / 5.7	2.81	7.05	4.70 /36	12.72 /58	13.04 /69	0.00	2.00
SC	Delaware Small Cap Value I	DEVIX	C+	(800) 523-1918	C+ / 6.5	3.07	7.59	5.76 /44	13.86 /66	14.18 /79	0.53	1.00
SC	Delaware Small Cap Value R	DVLRX	C+	(800) 523-1918	C+ / 6.1	2.95	7.32	5.22 /40	13.29 /62	13.61 /74	0.09	1.50
MC	● Delaware Smid Cap Growth A	DFCIX	C	(800) 523-1918	C+ / 6.4	5.91	16.02	13.87 /89	13.12 /61	18.69 /98	0.00	1.19
MC	● Delaware Smid Cap Growth C	DEEVX	C-	(800) 523-1918	C+ / 6.8	5.66	15.60	13.02 /87	12.28 /54	17.82 /97	0.00	1.94
MC	● Delaware Smid Cap Growth I	DFDIX	C+	(800) 523-1918	B / 7.6	5.94	16.13	14.15 /90	13.40 /63	19.00 /98	0.00	0.94
MC	● Delaware Smid Cap Growth R	DFRIX	C+	(800) 523-1918	B- / 7.2	5.81	15.85	13.59 /88	12.84 /58	18.40 /98	0.00	1.44
SC	Delaware Smid-Cap Growth Equity	DCGTX	C-	(800) 523-1918	B- / 7.2	5.84	15.69	13.77 /89	12.88 /59	18.29 /98	0.33	0.91
IN	Delaware US Growth A	DUGAX	B	(800) 523-1918	B- / 7.4	2.72	9.41	15.60 /93	15.59 /80	16.48 /95	0.20	1.06
IN	Delaware US Growth C	DEUCX	B	(800) 523-1918	B / 7.8	2.50	8.97	14.75 /91	14.72 /73	15.61 /91	0.00	1.81
IN	Delaware US Growth I	DEUIX	B+	(800) 523-1918	B+ / 8.7	2.78	9.55	15.88 /93	15.85 /82	16.78 /95	0.41	0.81
IN	Delaware US Growth R	DEURX	B+	(800) 523-1918	B+ / 8.3	2.64	9.26	15.32 /92	15.28 /77	16.18 /94	0.00	1.31
GR	Delaware Value A	DDVAX	A+	(800) 523-1918	B / 8.0	1.83	4.87	12.43 /84	17.53 /92	16.36 /94	1.26	1.02
GR	Delaware Value C	DDVCX	A+	(800) 523-1918	B+ / 8.4	1.64	4.42	11.54 /81	16.63 /88	15.47 /90	0.60	1.77
GR	Delaware Value Institutional	DDVIX	A+	(800) 523-1918	A- / 9.1	1.83	4.94	12.64 /85	17.78 /93	16.64 /95	1.57	0.77
GR	Delaware Value R	DDVRX	A+	(800) 523-1918	B+ / 8.8	1.76	4.74	12.14 /83	17.22 /91	16.05 /93	1.08	1.27
GL	Destra Dividend Total Return A	DHDAX	C	(877) 287-9646	C- / 4.0	0.35	-0.48	7.49 /59	11.74 /51	--	1.31	2.19
GL	Destra Dividend Total Return C	DHDCX	C+	(877) 287-9646	C / 4.4	0.16	-0.86	6.74 /53	10.92 /45	--	0.79	2.75
GL	Destra Dividend Total Return I	DHDIX	C+	(877) 287-9646	C / 4.8	0.42	-0.25	7.94 /62	12.15 /53	--	1.67	1.72
GL	Destra Focused Equity A	DFOAX	B+	(877) 287-9646	B- / 7.2	2.72	10.61	19.73 /97	14.14 /68	--	0.00	1.83
GR	Destra Focused Equity C	DFOCX	B+	(877) 287-9646	B / 7.7	2.54	10.19	18.85 /96	13.28 /62	--	0.00	3.00
GL	Destra Focused Equity I	DFOIX	A-	(877) 287-9646	B+ / 8.3	2.78	10.76	20.11 /97	14.51 /71	--	0.00	1.41
GL	Destra Preferred & Income Sec A	DPIAX	C	(877) 287-9646	D+ / 2.9	3.23	5.38	9.52 /72	7.96 /27	--	4.25	2.26
AA	Destra Preferred & Income Sec C	DPICX	B-	(877) 287-9646	C- / 3.3	3.02	5.09	8.80 /68	7.59 /25	--	3.70	3.10
GL	Destra Preferred & Income Sec I	DPIIX	C+	(877) 287-9646	C- / 3.8	3.31	5.61	10.01 /74	8.76 /31	--	4.75	1.64
AA	Deutsche Alt Asset Allocation A	AAAAX	D+	(800) 728-3337	E+ / 0.6	0.21	-0.02	0.76 /18	2.97 / 8	3.81 / 8	2.77	1.98
AA	Deutsche Alt Asset Allocation C	AAAPX	D+	(800) 728-3337	E+ / 0.7	0.00	-0.39	-0.01 /16	2.21 / 7	3.04 / 6	2.15	2.73
AA	Deutsche Alt Asset Allocation Inst	AAAZX	D+	(800) 728-3337	E+ / 0.9	0.22	0.12	1.10 /19	3.30 / 8	4.14 / 9	3.30	1.65
AA	Deutsche Alt Asset Allocation R	AAAQX	D+	(800) 728-3337	E+ / 0.8	0.11	-0.17	0.55 /17	2.79 / 7	--	2.71	2.35
AA	Deutsche Alt Asset Allocation S	AAASX	D+	(800) 728-3337	E+ / 0.9	0.22	0.11	0.92 /18	3.15 / 8	4.03 / 8	3.12	1.84
GR	Deutsche Capital Growth A	SDGAX	B	(800) 728-3337	B+ / 8.8	5.56	10.82	19.54 /96	16.41 /86	13.88 /77	0.11	0.98
GR	● Deutsche Capital Growth B	SDGBX	B-	(800) 728-3337	A- / 9.0	5.32	10.30	18.40 /96	15.30 /77	12.82 /67	0.00	1.97
GR	Deutsche Capital Growth C	SDGCX	B	(800) 728-3337	A- / 9.1	5.35	10.37	18.58 /96	15.49 /79	13.00 /68	0.00	1.78
GR	Deutsche Capital Growth Inst	SDGTX	B	(800) 728-3337	A / 9.5	5.63	10.97	19.87 /97	16.75 /88	14.24 /80	0.37	0.71
GR	Deutsche Capital Growth R	SDGRX	B	(800) 728-3337	A / 9.3	5.46	10.59	19.05 /96	15.95 /83	13.50 /73	0.00	1.38
GR	Deutsche Capital Growth S	SCGSX	B	(800) 728-3337	A / 9.5	5.63	10.95	19.86 /97	16.71 /88	14.18 /79	0.36	0.72
TC	Deutsche Communication A	TISHX	C	(800) 728-3337	C- / 3.9	1.22	1.18	3.31 /28	11.97 /52	11.99 /60	1.62	1.67
TC	● Deutsche Communication B	FTEBX	C	(800) 728-3337	C / 4.3	1.05	0.76	2.51 /24	11.11 /46	11.14 /54	0.99	2.67
TC	Deutsche Communication C	FTICX	C	(800) 728-3337	C / 4.3	1.05	0.81	2.52 /24	11.14 /46	11.16 /54	0.99	2.51
TC	Deutsche Communication Inst	FLICX	C+	(800) 728-3337	C / 5.0	1.28	1.31	3.57 /29	12.28 /54	12.27 /62	1.97	1.28
GI	Deutsche Core Equity A	SUWAX	B+	(800) 728-3337	B+ / 8.4	3.72	7.86	15.67 /93	17.20 /91	14.35 /81	0.36	0.89
GI	● Deutsche Core Equity B	SUWBX	B+	(800) 728-3337	B+ / 8.7	3.45	7.32	14.61 /91	16.17 /85	13.30 /71	0.00	1.77

● Denotes fund is closed to new investors
* Denotes fund is included in Section II

RISK			NET ASSETS		ASSET					BULL / BEAR		FUND MANAGER		MINIMUMS		LOADS	
	3 Year		NAV						Portfolio	Last Bull	Last Bear	Manager	Manager	Initial	Additional	Front	Back
Risk Rating/Pts	Standard Deviation	Beta	As of 3/31/15	Total $(Mil)	Cash %	Stocks %	Bonds %	Other %	Turnover Ratio	Market Return	Market Return	Quality Pct	Tenure (Years)	Purch. $	Purch. $	End Load	End Load
D /1.6	10.3	0.97	8.58	93	3	96	0	1	21	92.3	-8.7	36	10	1,000,000	0	0.0	0.0
C /5.2	11.3	1.03	50.28	399	0	99	0	1	41	80.6	-12.0	19	10	1,000	100	5.8	0.0
C /4.8	11.3	1.03	41.33	102	0	99	0	1	41	76.0	-12.2	14	10	1,000	100	0.0	0.0
C /5.3	11.2	1.03	52.87	502	0	99	0	1	41	82.1	-11.9	22	10	0	0	0.0	0.0
C /5.2	11.3	1.03	48.59	20	0	99	0	1	41	79.0	-12.1	17	10	0	0	0.0	0.0
C+ /6.4	12.5	0.91	20.60	180	3	96	0	1	30	114.6	-24.2	88	11	1,000	100	5.8	0.0
C+ /6.3	12.5	0.91	19.16	75	3	96	0	1	30	109.1	-24.5	84	11	1,000	100	0.0	0.0
C+ /6.4	12.5	0.91	20.90	402	3	96	0	1	30	116.3	-24.1	89	11	0	0	0.0	0.0
C+ /6.4	12.5	0.91	20.17	25	3	96	0	1	30	112.6	-24.3	87	11	0	0	0.0	0.0
C+ /6.4	11.7	0.83	54.08	823	3	96	0	1	17	86.4	-22.4	70	18	1,000	100	5.8	0.0
C+ /6.2	11.7	0.83	45.76	115	3	96	0	1	17	81.7	-22.7	59	18	1,000	100	0.0	0.0
C+ /6.4	11.7	0.83	56.74	1,934	3	96	0	1	17	88.0	-22.4	72	18	0	0	0.0	0.0
C+ /6.4	11.7	0.83	52.63	88	3	96	0	1	17	84.8	-22.5	67	18	0	0	0.0	0.0
C /4.8	11.7	0.90	29.41	839	2	97	0	1	26	81.6	-15.7	39	5	1,000	100	5.8	0.0
C- /3.9	11.7	0.90	21.46	80	2	97	0	1	26	77.1	-16.0	30	5	1,000	100	0.0	0.0
C /5.2	11.7	0.90	34.98	365	2	97	0	1	26	83.1	-15.6	43	5	0	0	0.0	0.0
C /4.7	11.7	0.90	28.24	17	2	97	0	1	26	80.1	-15.8	36	5	0	0	0.0	0.0
D+ /2.9	11.7	0.75	18.68	48	4	95	0	1	40	81.3	-16.0	75	10	1,000,000	0	0.0	0.0
C+ /6.0	10.5	1.02	26.40	399	1	98	0	1	25	101.9	-12.4	56	10	1,000	100	5.8	0.0
C+ /6.0	10.5	1.02	24.16	100	1	98	0	1	25	96.8	-12.7	44	10	1,000	100	0.0	0.0
C+ /6.0	10.6	1.02	28.06	3,190	1	98	0	1	25	103.6	-12.3	59	10	0	0	0.0	0.0
C+ /6.0	10.6	1.02	25.69	25	1	98	0	1	25	100.2	-12.5	52	10	0	0	0.0	0.0
B- /7.8	8.4	0.84	18.50	2,706	4	95	0	1	7	100.9	-14.5	90	11	1,000	100	5.8	0.0
B- /7.8	8.4	0.84	18.47	524	4	95	0	1	7	95.8	-14.7	88	11	1,000	100	0.0	0.0
B- /7.8	8.4	0.84	18.49	4,777	4	95	0	1	7	102.5	-14.4	91	11	0	0	0.0	0.0
B- /7.8	8.4	0.84	18.49	54	4	95	0	1	7	99.2	-14.6	90	11	0	0	0.0	0.0
B- /7.3	8.6	0.49	22.17	15	20	79	0	1	24	65.0	N/A	96	4	2,500	0	5.8	0.0
B- /7.7	8.7	0.49	19.89	20	20	79	0	1	24	N/A	N/A	95	4	2,500	0	0.0	0.0
B- /7.3	8.6	0.49	22.20	48	20	79	0	1	24	66.7	N/A	96	4	1,000,000	0	0.0	2.0
C+ /6.9	10.1	0.55	23.43	13	1	98	0	1	58	88.1	-13.1	97	4	2,500	0	5.8	0.0
B- /7.0	10.1	0.96	22.61	6	1	98	0	1	58	N/A	N/A	40	4	2,500	0	0.0	0.0
C+ /6.9	10.1	0.55	23.63	58	1	98	0	1	58	89.7	-12.9	97	4	1,000,000	0	0.0	2.0
B /8.7	3.9	0.22	17.47	17	2	69	28	1	27	36.0	-1.1	95	4	2,500	0	4.5	0.0
B+ /9.9	3.8	0.27	17.54	6	2	69	28	1	27	N/A	N/A	93	4	2,500	0	0.0	0.0
B /8.7	3.8	0.25	17.39	28	2	69	28	1	27	39.2	-1.0	95	4	1,000,000	0	0.0	2.0
B /8.7	4.8	0.63	9.36	158	34	37	20	9	41	18.5	-11.2	19	2	1,000	50	5.8	0.0
B /8.8	4.8	0.63	9.33	103	34	37	20	9	41	15.6	-11.5	14	2	1,000	50	0.0	0.0
B /8.7	4.8	0.63	9.29	113	34	37	20	9	41	19.9	-11.1	22	2	1,000,000	0	0.0	0.0
B /8.7	4.9	0.64	9.42	3	34	37	20	9	41	17.9	N/A	17	2	0	0	0.0	0.0
B /8.7	4.8	0.63	9.29	154	34	37	20	9	41	19.2	-11.0	21	2	2,500	50	0.0	0.0
C /4.6	10.5	1.01	75.76	641	0	98	0	2	41	102.9	-19.5	68	6	1,000	50	5.8	0.0
C /4.4	10.5	1.01	68.87	1	0	98	0	2	41	96.3	-19.8	55	6	1,000	50	0.0	0.0
C /4.4	10.5	1.01	68.74	29	0	98	0	2	41	97.5	-19.8	57	6	1,000	50	0.0	0.0
C /4.6	10.5	1.01	76.31	220	0	98	0	2	41	105.0	-19.4	72	6	1,000,000	0	0.0	0.0
C /4.6	10.5	1.01	75.18	7	0	98	0	2	41	100.5	-19.4	63	6	0	0	0.0	0.0
C /4.6	10.5	1.01	76.36	757	0	98	0	2	41	104.7	-19.4	71	6	2,500	50	0.0	0.0
B- /7.0	10.7	0.83	24.12	113	7	92	0	1	23	69.0	-15.3	50	5	1,000	50	5.8	0.0
B- /7.0	10.7	0.83	22.19	N/A	7	92	0	1	23	64.6	-15.5	38	5	1,000	50	0.0	0.0
B- /7.0	10.7	0.83	22.11	6	7	92	0	1	23	64.7	-15.5	39	5	1,000	50	0.0	0.0
B- /7.0	10.7	0.83	24.64	1	7	92	0	1	23	70.3	-15.3	55	5	1,000,000	0	0.0	0.0
C+ /6.0	11.2	1.12	24.84	340	0	98	0	2	44	103.3	-19.3	55	2	1,000	50	5.8	0.0
C+ /5.9	11.2	1.12	23.69	1	0	98	0	2	44	97.3	-19.6	41	2	1,000	50	0.0	0.0

Fund Type	Fund Name	Ticker Symbol	Overall Investment Rating	Phone	Performance Rating/Pts	Total Return % through 3/31/15			Annualized		Incl. in Returns	
						3 Mo	6 Mo	1Yr / Pct	3Yr / Pct	5Yr / Pct	Dividend Yield	Expense Ratio
GI	Deutsche Core Equity C	SUWCX	B+	(800) 728-3337	B+ / 8.7	3.54	7.46	14.79 /91	16.30 /85	13.49 /73	0.00	1.66
GI	Deutsche Core Equity Inst	SUWIX	A	(800) 728-3337	A / 9.3	3.82	8.07	16.11 /93	17.67 /93	14.84 /86	0.72	0.53
GI	Deutsche Core Equity S	SCDGX	A	(800) 728-3337	A / 9.3	3.77	8.00	15.97 /93	17.55 /93	14.71 /84	0.67	0.59
GR	Deutsche CROCI Equity Dividend A	KDHAX	C	(800) 728-3337	C- / 4.2	0.12	3.26	7.15 /56	11.87 /52	10.10 /45	1.76	1.17
GR	● Deutsche CROCI Equity Dividend B	KDHBX	C+	(800) 728-3337	C / 4.5	-0.06	2.86	6.35 /49	11.00 /45	9.22 /38	1.11	2.15
GR	Deutsche CROCI Equity Dividend C	KDHCX	C+	(800) 728-3337	C / 4.5	-0.06	2.85	6.35 /49	11.03 /46	9.27 /39	1.12	1.93
GR	Deutsche CROCI Equity Dividend Inst	KDHIX	C+	(800) 728-3337	C / 5.3	0.21	3.39	7.43 /59	12.20 /54	10.46 /48	2.13	0.89
GR	Deutsche CROCI Equity Dividend R	KDHRX	C+	(800) 728-3337	C / 4.9	0.06	3.11	6.86 /54	11.58 /50	9.78 /43	1.62	1.54
GR	Deutsche CROCI Equity Dividend S	KDHSX	C+	(800) 728-3337	C / 5.3	0.19	3.37	7.41 /58	12.14 /53	10.35 /47	2.12	0.92
FO	Deutsche CROCI International A	SUIAX	C-	(800) 728-3337	C / 4.6	8.63	6.20	8.45 /66	11.52 /49	5.96 /17	9.25	1.18
FO	● Deutsche CROCI International B	SUIBX	C-	(800) 728-3337	C / 4.9	8.34	5.69	7.42 /58	10.51 /42	5.04 /12	8.83	2.12
FO	Deutsche CROCI International C	SUICX	C	(800) 728-3337	C / 5.0	8.44	5.83	7.65 /60	10.66 /43	5.15 /13	8.94	1.97
FO	Deutsche CROCI International Inst	SUIIX	C	(800) 728-3337	C+ / 5.9	8.70	6.39	8.81 /68	11.97 /52	6.42 /20	10.19	0.84
FO	Deutsche CROCI International S	SCINX	C	(800) 728-3337	C+ / 5.9	8.69	6.34	8.72 /68	11.84 /51	6.28 /19	10.12	0.90
GL	Deutsche CROCI Sector Opps A	DSOAX	U	(800) 728-3337	U /	3.62	-4.50	--	--	--	0.00	1.75
GL	Deutsche CROCI Sector Opps C	DSOCX	U	(800) 728-3337	U /	3.42	-4.91	--	--	--	0.00	2.55
GL	Deutsche CROCI Sector Opps S	DSOSX	U	(800) 728-3337	U /	3.62	-4.52	--	--	--	0.00	1.54
GR	Deutsche Diversified Mkt Neut A	DDMAX	D-	(800) 728-3337	E / 0.3	-0.72	-1.42	-2.23 /10	-0.36 / 4	0.51 / 3	0.00	3.70
GR	Deutsche Diversified Mkt Neut C	DDMCX	D-	(800) 728-3337	E / 0.4	-1.01	-1.76	-2.97 / 9	-1.15 / 3	-0.24 / 2	0.00	4.44
GR	Deutsche Diversified Mkt Neut Inst	DDMIX	D-	(800) 728-3337	E / 0.5	-0.70	-1.28	-1.96 /10	-0.07 / 4	0.84 / 3	0.00	3.33
GR	Deutsche Diversified Mkt Neut S	DDMSX	D-	(800) 728-3337	E / 0.4	-0.71	-1.29	-2.09 /10	-0.25 / 4	0.68 / 3	0.00	3.60
FO	Deutsche EAFE Equity Index Inst	BTAEX	D	(800) 728-3337	D+ / 2.9	5.34	0.99	-1.41 /12	8.60 /30	5.89 /16	3.06	0.50
EM	Deutsche Emerging Markets Eqty A	SEKAX	E+	(800) 728-3337	E / 0.4	1.15	-0.43	1.78 /21	-0.19 / 4	-0.67 / 2	0.87	1.98
EM	● Deutsche Emerging Markets Eqty B	SEKBX	E+	(800) 728-3337	E / 0.4	0.99	-0.72	1.10 /19	-0.95 / 3	-1.46 / 2	0.18	3.03
EM	Deutsche Emerging Markets Eqty C	SEKCX	E+	(800) 728-3337	E / 0.4	0.98	-0.78	1.03 /19	-0.95 / 3	-1.45 / 2	0.18	2.76
EM	Deutsche Emerging Markets Eqty Inst	SEKIX	E+	(800) 728-3337	E+ / 0.6	1.26	-0.22	2.10 /22	0.07 / 4	-0.35 / 2	1.18	1.54
EM	Deutsche Emerging Markets Eqty S	SEMGX	E+	(800) 728-3337	E+ / 0.6	1.26	-0.28	2.03 /22	0.06 / 4	-0.44 / 2	1.18	1.74
EN	Deutsche Enhanced Comdty Strat A	SKNRX	E+	(800) 728-3337	E- / 0.1	-3.38	-5.96	-14.07 / 2	-6.80 / 1	-2.25 / 2	3.34	1.50
EN	● Deutsche Enhanced Comdty Strat B	SKBRX	E+	(800) 728-3337	E- / 0.1	-3.63	-6.34	-14.75 / 2	-7.55 / 1	-3.04 / 1	2.98	2.39
EN	Deutsche Enhanced Comdty Strat C	SKCRX	E+	(800) 728-3337	E- / 0.1	-3.63	-6.39	-14.78 / 2	-7.57 / 1	-2.99 / 1	3.00	2.28
EN	Deutsche Enhanced Comdty Strat	SKIRX	E+	(800) 728-3337	E- / 0.2	-3.33	-5.83	-13.77 / 2	-6.50 / 1	-1.92 / 1	3.84	1.16
EN	Deutsche Enhanced Comdty Strat S	SKSRX	E+	(800) 728-3337	E- / 0.2	-3.35	-5.89	-13.87 / 2	-6.60 / 1	-2.07 / 1	3.72	1.30
IX	Deutsche Equity 500 Index Inst	BTIIX	A-	(800) 728-3337	B / 8.0	0.86	5.74	12.37 /84	15.76 /81	14.20 /79	1.86	0.25
IX	Deutsche Equity 500 Index S	BTIEX	A-	(800) 728-3337	B / 7.9	0.84	5.71	12.31 /84	15.70 /81	14.13 /79	1.80	0.31
RE	Deutsche Gl Real Est Sec A	RRGAX	C	(800) 728-3337	C+ / 6.2	4.00	12.22	16.13 /93	12.28 /54	10.79 /51	2.71	1.55
RE	Deutsche Gl Real Est Sec C	RRGCX	C	(800) 728-3337	C+ / 6.5	3.75	11.82	15.17 /92	11.38 /48	9.91 /44	2.10	2.34
RE	Deutsche Gl Real Est Sec Inst	RRGIX	C+	(800) 728-3337	B- / 7.5	4.12	12.38	16.44 /94	12.71 /58	11.21 /54	3.23	1.19
RE	Deutsche Gl Real Est Sec S	RRGTX	C+	(800) 728-3337	B- / 7.4	4.10	12.41	16.32 /94	12.54 /56	11.04 /53	3.05	1.36
GL	Deutsche Glb Infrastructure A	TOLLX	C+	(800) 728-3337	C+ / 6.1	-1.58	0.75	9.71 /73	15.48 /79	15.55 /90	1.04	1.42
GL	Deutsche Glb Infrastructure C	TOLCX	C+	(800) 728-3337	C+ / 6.5	-1.68	0.47	8.93 /69	14.64 /72	14.68 /84	0.70	2.19
GL	Deutsche Glb Infrastructure Inst	TOLIX	B	(800) 728-3337	B- / 7.4	-1.46	0.96	9.99 /74	15.85 /82	15.90 /92	1.39	1.10
GL	Deutsche Glb Infrastructure S	TOLSX	B	(800) 728-3337	B- / 7.3	-1.48	0.92	9.94 /74	15.70 /81	15.79 /92	1.28	1.25
FO	Deutsche Global Equity A	DBISX	D	(800) 728-3337	D+ / 2.4	2.73	2.73	2.13 /22	9.07 /33	6.43 /20	0.00	1.80
FO	● Deutsche Global Equity B	DBIBX	D	(800) 728-3337	D+ / 2.8	2.60	2.34	1.34 /20	8.25 /28	5.63 /15	0.00	2.80
FO	Deutsche Global Equity C	DBICX	D	(800) 728-3337	D+ / 2.9	2.59	2.47	1.47 /20	8.29 /29	5.65 /15	0.00	2.54
FO	Deutsche Global Equity Inst	MGINX	D+	(800) 728-3337	C- / 3.5	2.81	2.81	2.44 /24	9.32 /35	6.75 /22	0.00	1.37
FO	Deutsche Global Equity R	DBITX	D	(800) 728-3337	C- / 3.2	2.69	2.69	1.94 /22	8.83 /32	6.16 /18	0.00	2.08
FO	Deutsche Global Equity S	DBIVX	D+	(800) 728-3337	C- / 3.5	2.82	2.82	2.31 /23	9.27 /35	6.63 /21	0.00	1.58
GL	Deutsche Global Growth A	SGQAX	D	(800) 728-3337	D+ / 2.9	4.21	3.33	0.64 /17	9.90 /39	7.20 /24	0.58	1.50
GL	● Deutsche Global Growth B	SGQBX	D+	(800) 728-3337	C- / 3.3	4.04	2.95	-0.14 /15	9.06 /33	6.38 /19	0.00	2.28
GL	Deutsche Global Growth C	SGQCX	D+	(800) 728-3337	C- / 3.3	4.04	2.97	-0.10 /15	9.08 /33	6.41 /19	0.00	2.23
GL	Deutsche Global Growth Inst	SGQIX	C-	(800) 728-3337	C- / 4.0	4.30	3.47	0.91 /18	10.20 /40	7.52 /27	0.87	1.17

● Denotes fund is closed to new investors
* Denotes fund is included in Section II

www.thestreetratings.com

RISK			NET ASSETS		ASSET				Portfolio Turnover Ratio	BULL / BEAR		FUND MANAGER		MINIMUMS		LOADS	
Risk Rating/Pts	3 Year		NAV		Cash %	Stocks %	Bonds %	Other %		Last Bull Market Return	Last Bear Market Return	Manager Quality Pct	Manager Tenure (Years)	Initial Purch. $	Additional Purch. $	Front End Load	Back End Load
	Standard Deviation	Beta	As of 3/31/15	Total $(Mil)													
C+ / 6.0	11.2	1.12	23.98	32	0	98	0	2	44	98.1	-19.6	43	2	1,000	50	0.0	0.0
C+ / 6.0	11.2	1.12	25.10	73	0	98	0	2	44	106.1	-19.2	61	2	1,000,000	0	0.0	0.0
C+ / 6.0	11.2	1.12	25.05	2,902	0	98	0	2	44	105.4	-19.2	60	2	2,500	50	0.0	0.0
B- / 7.5	10.4	1.05	46.00	963	0	99	0	1	132	80.7	-19.5	13	1	1,000	50	5.8	0.0
B- / 7.5	10.4	1.05	45.82	3	0	99	0	1	132	75.9	-19.8	9	1	1,000	50	0.0	0.0
B- / 7.5	10.4	1.05	45.88	153	0	99	0	1	132	76.1	-19.7	9	1	1,000	50	0.0	0.0
B- / 7.5	10.4	1.05	46.01	21	0	99	0	1	132	82.6	-19.4	15	1	1,000,000	0	0.0	0.0
B- / 7.5	10.4	1.05	45.90	4	0	99	0	1	132	79.1	-19.5	12	1	0	0	0.0	0.0
B- / 7.5	10.4	1.05	45.99	48	0	99	0	1	132	82.3	-19.4	14	1	2,500	50	0.0	0.0
C+ / 5.8	12.2	0.88	49.60	334	5	94	0	1	167	64.4	-26.3	88	1	1,000	50	5.8	0.0
C+ / 5.9	12.1	0.88	49.24	N/A	5	94	0	1	167	59.1	-26.4	84	1	1,000	50	0.0	0.0
C+ / 5.9	12.2	0.88	49.23	69	5	94	0	1	167	60.1	-26.5	85	1	1,000	50	0.0	0.0
C+ / 5.7	12.2	0.88	49.58	185	5	94	0	1	167	66.7	-26.1	90	1	1,000,000	0	0.0	0.0
C+ / 5.7	12.1	0.88	49.80	1,287	5	94	0	1	167	66.0	-26.2	89	1	2,500	50	0.0	0.0
U /	N/A	N/A	9.72	65	0	0	0	100	0	N/A	N/A	N/A	1	1,000	50	5.8	0.0
U /	N/A	N/A	9.69	27	0	0	0	100	0	N/A	N/A	N/A	1	1,000	50	0.0	0.0
U /	N/A	N/A	9.72	78	0	0	0	100	0	N/A	N/A	N/A	1	2,500	50	0.0	0.0
B- / 7.3	2.2	0.02	8.33	8	52	18	29	1	347	1.2	0.1	56	9	1,000	50	5.8	0.0
B- / 7.0	2.2	0.03	7.83	7	52	18	29	1	347	-1.4	-0.2	41	9	1,000	50	0.0	0.0
B- / 7.4	2.2	0.03	8.51	115	52	18	29	1	347	2.2	0.3	59	9	1,000,000	0	0.0	0.0
B- / 7.4	2.2	0.03	8.43	41	52	18	29	1	347	1.7	0.2	57	9	2,500	50	0.0	0.0
C+ / 5.7	13.3	1.00	14.04	267	2	97	0	1	10	50.5	-23.4	54	2	1,000,000	0	0.0	0.0
C / 5.4	14.1	1.01	15.88	12	3	96	0	1	65	20.1	-30.0	54	1	1,000	50	5.8	0.0
C / 5.4	14.1	1.01	14.29	N/A	3	96	0	1	65	16.9	-30.2	43	1	1,000	50	0.0	0.0
C / 5.4	14.1	1.01	14.40	2	3	96	0	1	65	16.9	-30.2	43	1	1,000	50	0.0	0.0
C / 5.4	14.1	1.01	16.08	9	3	96	0	1	65	21.1	-29.8	58	1	1,000,000	0	0.0	0.0
C / 5.4	14.0	1.01	16.09	54	3	96	0	1	65	20.9	-29.9	58	1	2,500	50	0.0	0.0
C+ / 5.9	8.0	0.33	13.13	119	7	0	92	1	93	-14.1	-20.1	3	5	1,000	50	5.8	0.0
C+ / 5.8	7.9	0.33	11.94	N/A	7	0	92	1	93	-16.6	-20.2	2	5	1,000	50	0.0	0.0
C+ / 5.8	8.0	0.33	11.96	31	7	0	92	1	93	-16.3	-20.4	2	5	1,000	50	0.0	0.0
C+ / 5.9	8.0	0.33	13.34	280	7	0	92	1	93	-13.2	-19.9	3	5	1,000,000	0	0.0	0.0
C+ / 5.9	8.0	0.33	13.29	250	7	0	92	1	93	-13.5	-19.9	3	5	2,500	50	0.0	0.0
B- / 7.2	9.5	1.00	223.58	519	2	96	0	2	3	98.4	-16.3	63	8	1,000,000	0	0.0	0.0
B- / 7.2	9.5	1.00	221.30	446	2	96	0	2	3	98.0	-16.4	62	8	2,500	50	0.0	0.0
C / 5.2	12.3	0.92	9.37	735	9	90	0	1	107	72.2	-20.4	59	9	1,000	50	5.8	0.0
C / 5.2	12.5	0.93	9.40	20	9	90	0	1	107	67.8	-20.7	45	9	1,000	50	0.0	0.0
C / 5.2	12.3	0.92	9.36	109	9	90	0	1	107	74.2	-20.3	65	9	1,000,000	0	0.0	0.0
C / 5.2	12.4	0.92	9.39	107	9	90	0	1	107	73.8	-20.4	62	9	2,500	50	0.0	0.0
C+ / 6.5	8.7	0.47	14.73	1,783	9	90	0	1	132	74.6	-3.7	98	N/A	1,000	50	5.8	0.0
C+ / 6.5	8.8	0.47	14.63	964	9	90	0	1	132	70.1	-4.1	98	N/A	1,000	50	0.0	0.0
C+ / 6.5	8.8	0.47	14.67	1,121	9	90	0	1	132	76.5	-3.6	98	N/A	1,000,000	0	0.0	0.0
C+ / 6.5	8.8	0.47	14.68	2,630	9	90	0	1	132	75.8	-3.7	98	N/A	2,500	50	0.0	0.0
C+ / 5.8	12.6	0.92	8.65	17	1	98	0	1	70	50.7	-23.1	71	2	1,000	50	5.8	0.0
C+ / 5.7	12.7	0.93	8.30	N/A	1	98	0	1	70	46.8	-23.4	60	2	1,000	50	0.0	0.0
C+ / 5.7	12.6	0.92	8.31	3	1	98	0	1	70	46.8	-23.4	61	2	1,000	50	0.0	0.0
C+ / 5.8	12.7	0.92	8.41	8	1	98	0	1	70	52.0	-23.0	73	2	1,000,000	0	0.0	0.0
C+ / 5.7	12.7	0.93	8.40	1	1	98	0	1	70	49.5	-23.3	68	2	0	0	0.0	0.0
C+ / 5.7	12.6	0.92	8.40	4	1	98	0	1	70	51.6	-23.1	73	2	2,500	50	0.0	0.0
C+ / 6.0	12.2	0.83	29.93	73	4	95	0	1	45	61.5	-26.1	84	2	1,000	50	5.8	0.0
C+ / 5.9	12.2	0.83	28.60	1	4	95	0	1	45	57.4	-26.3	78	2	1,000	50	0.0	0.0
C+ / 5.9	12.2	0.83	28.81	27	4	95	0	1	45	57.5	-26.3	78	2	1,000	50	0.0	0.0
C+ / 6.0	12.2	0.83	29.81	46	4	95	0	1	45	63.1	-26.0	85	2	1,000,000	0	0.0	0.0

					PERFORMANCE						Incl. in Returns	
								Total Return % through 3/31/15				
									Annualized		Dividend	Expense
Fund Type	Fund Name	Ticker Symbol	Overall Investment Rating	Phone	Performance Rating/Pts	3 Mo	6 Mo	1Yr / Pct	3Yr / Pct	5Yr / Pct	Yield	Ratio
GL	Deutsche Global Growth R	SGQRX	D+	(800) 728-3337	C- / 3.6	4.18	3.22	0.39 /17	9.61 /37	6.89 /22	0.38	1.86
GL	Deutsche Global Growth S	SCOBX	C-	(800) 728-3337	C- / 4.0	4.30	3.46	0.90 /18	10.18 /40	7.49 /26	0.86	1.20
BA	Deutsche Global Income Builder A	KTRAX	D-	(800) 728-3337	D- / 1.4	0.63	-1.14	0.38 /17	7.33 /23	6.72 /21	3.40	0.90
BA	● Deutsche Global Income Builder B	KTRBX	D-	(800) 728-3337	D- / 1.5	0.37	-1.56	-0.56 /14	6.28 /18	5.69 /15	2.54	1.93
BA	Deutsche Global Income Builder C	KTRCX	D-	(800) 728-3337	D / 1.6	0.43	-1.44	-0.32 /15	6.49 /19	5.87 /16	2.79	1.69
BA	Deutsche Global Income Builder Inst	KTRIX	D-	(800) 728-3337	D / 2.2	0.70	-1.02	0.64 /17	7.62 /25	7.03 /23	3.86	0.64
BA	Deutsche Global Income Builder S	KTRSX	D-	(800) 728-3337	D / 2.2	0.68	-1.04	0.58 /17	7.54 /24	6.94 /23	3.80	0.69
GL	Deutsche Global Small Cap A	KGDAX	D	(800) 728-3337	C- / 3.8	6.17	5.13	-1.16 /12	11.54 /49	10.75 /51	0.63	1.53
GL	● Deutsche Global Small Cap B	KGDBX	D	(800) 728-3337	C- / 4.2	5.96	4.75	-1.91 /11	10.71 /44	9.89 /44	0.00	2.34
GL	Deutsche Global Small Cap C	KGDCX	D	(800) 728-3337	C- / 4.2	5.99	4.76	-1.87 /11	10.73 /44	9.92 /44	0.00	2.26
GL	Deutsche Global Small Cap Inst	KGDIX	D+	(800) 728-3337	C / 4.9	6.25	5.29	-0.84 /13	11.93 /52	11.16 /54	1.01	1.17
GL	Deutsche Global Small Cap S	SGSCX	D+	(800) 728-3337	C / 4.9	6.25	5.29	-0.89 /13	11.85 /51	11.06 /53	0.94	1.25
PM	Deutsche Gold & Prec Metals Fund A	SGDAX	E-	(800) 728-3337	E- / 0.0	-4.40	-17.16	-25.36 / 0	-27.39 / 0	-16.45 / 0	0.00	1.67
PM	● Deutsche Gold & Prec Metals Fund B	SGDBX	E-	(800) 728-3337	E- / 0.0	-4.60	-17.46	-25.96 / 0	-27.95 / 0	-17.10 / 0	0.00	2.54
PM	Deutsche Gold & Prec Metals Fund C	SGDCX	E-	(800) 728-3337	E- / 0.0	-4.61	-17.48	-26.00 / 0	-27.94 / 0	-17.07 / 0	0.00	2.38
PM	Deutsche Gold & Prec Metals Fund I	SGDIX	E-	(800) 728-3337	E- / 0.0	-4.20	-17.03	-25.20 / 0	-27.21 / 0	-16.22 / 0	0.00	1.32
PM	Deutsche Gold & Prec Metals Fund S	SCGDX	E-	(800) 728-3337	E- / 0.0	-4.37	-17.06	-25.23 / 0	-27.24 / 0	-16.26 / 0	0.00	1.39
HL	Deutsche Health and Wellness A	SUHAX	A-	(800) 728-3337	A+ / 9.9	9.20	18.23	30.43 /99	28.59 /99	21.23 /99	0.00	1.37
HL	● Deutsche Health and Wellness B	SUHBX	B+	(800) 728-3337	A+ / 9.9	9.02	17.79	29.47 /99	27.62 /99	20.29 /99	0.00	2.27
HL	Deutsche Health and Wellness C	SUHCX	B+	(800) 728-3337	A+ / 9.9	9.02	17.82	29.47 /99	27.64 /99	20.35 /99	0.00	2.11
HL	Deutsche Health and Wellness Inst	SUHIX	A-	(800) 728-3337	A+ / 9.9	9.26	18.35	30.72 /99	28.92 /99	21.62 /99	0.02	1.12
HL	Deutsche Health and Wellness S	SCHLX	A-	(800) 728-3337	A+ / 9.9	9.27	18.38	30.74 /99	28.92 /99	21.56 /99	0.02	1.12
EM	Deutsche International Value A	DNVAX	E	(800) 728-3337	E / 0.5	2.70	-7.24	-7.67 / 3	3.69 / 9	2.63 / 5	2.77	1.42
EM	Deutsche International Value C	DNVCX	E	(800) 728-3337	E+ / 0.6	2.50	-7.52	-8.32 / 3	2.90 / 8	1.86 / 4	2.30	2.17
EM	Deutsche International Value Inst	DNVIX	E	(800) 728-3337	E+ / 0.7	2.80	-7.04	-7.36 / 4	3.96 /10	2.87 / 6	3.14	1.15
EM	Deutsche International Value S	DNVSX	E	(800) 728-3337	E+ / 0.7	2.81	-7.06	-7.47 / 4	3.89 /10	2.86 / 6	3.13	1.20
GR	Deutsche Large Cap Focus Gro A	SGGAX	C+	(800) 728-3337	B / 7.9	5.18	11.74	19.31 /96	14.70 /72	13.49 /73	0.00	1.26
GR	● Deutsche Large Cap Focus Gro B	SGGBX	C+	(800) 728-3337	B+ / 8.4	4.99	11.32	18.43 /96	13.82 /66	12.60 /65	0.00	2.15
GR	Deutsche Large Cap Focus Gro C	SGGCX	C+	(800) 728-3337	B+ / 8.4	5.00	11.33	18.44 /96	13.85 /66	12.66 /65	0.00	1.99
GR	Deutsche Large Cap Focus Gro Inst	SGGIX	B	(800) 728-3337	A- / 9.1	5.24	11.88	19.62 /96	15.02 /75	13.86 /76	0.00	0.96
GR	Deutsche Large Cap Focus Gro S	SCQGX	B	(800) 728-3337	A- / 9.0	5.22	11.87	19.60 /96	14.98 /75	13.76 /75	0.00	1.01
GR	Deutsche Large Cap Value A	KDCAX	D	(800) 728-3337	C+ / 6.0	2.94	5.17	10.24 /75	14.33 /70	11.44 /56	0.96	0.99
GR	● Deutsche Large Cap Value B	KDCBX	D	(800) 728-3337	C+ / 6.4	2.74	4.77	9.36 /71	13.44 /63	10.58 /49	0.37	1.75
GR	Deutsche Large Cap Value C	KDCCX	D	(800) 728-3337	C+ / 6.4	2.74	4.81	9.47 /72	13.54 /64	10.67 /50	0.44	1.69
GR	Deutsche Large Cap Value Inst	KDCIX	D+	(800) 728-3337	B- / 7.3	3.02	5.38	10.58 /77	14.69 /72	11.80 /59	1.28	0.68
GI	Deutsche Large Cap Value R	KDCQX	D	(800) 728-3337	C+ / 6.7	2.87	5.01	9.91 /74	13.97 /67	--	0.72	1.30
GR	Deutsche Large Cap Value S	KDCSX	D+	(800) 728-3337	B- / 7.3	2.97	5.30	10.56 /77	14.69 /72	11.80 /59	1.31	0.66
FO	Deutsche Latin America Equity A	SLANX	E-	(800) 728-3337	E- / 0.1	-9.31	-18.83	-19.29 / 1	-9.39 / 1	-6.33 / 1	1.71	1.84
FO	● Deutsche Latin America Equity B	SLAOX	E-	(800) 728-3337	E- / 0.1	-9.46	-19.04	-19.79 / 1	-10.03 / 1	-7.02 / 1	0.97	2.72
FO	Deutsche Latin America Equity C	SLAPX	E-	(800) 728-3337	E- / 0.1	-9.47	-19.12	-19.87 / 1	-10.05 / 1	-7.03 / 1	0.97	2.57
FO	Deutsche Latin America Equity S	SLAFX	E-	(800) 728-3337	E- / 0.1	-9.26	-18.76	-19.11 / 1	-9.17 / 1	-6.08 / 1	2.09	1.53
AA	Deutsche LifeCompass 2015 A	SPDAX	C-	(800) 728-3337	D- / 1.5	1.73	3.11	4.34 /34	6.70 /20	6.70 /21	2.74	1.31
AA	● Deutsche LifeCompass 2015 B	SPDBX	C-	(800) 728-3337	D / 1.8	1.55	2.73	3.55 /29	5.89 /16	5.88 /16	2.14	2.30
AA	Deutsche LifeCompass 2015 C	SPDCX	C-	(800) 728-3337	D / 1.8	1.55	2.73	3.55 /29	5.89 /16	5.88 /16	2.14	2.03
AA	Deutsche LifeCompass 2015 S	SPBAX	C	(800) 728-3337	D+ / 2.4	1.80	3.25	4.60 /36	6.97 /21	6.96 /23	3.16	1.07
GI	Deutsche LifeCompass 2020 A	SUPAX	C-	(800) 728-3337	D / 2.0	2.01	3.63	5.10 /39	7.77 /26	7.45 /26	2.82	1.27
GI	● Deutsche LifeCompass 2020 B	SUPBX	C-	(800) 728-3337	D+ / 2.4	1.76	3.16	4.31 /34	7.02 /21	6.67 /21	2.21	2.16
GI	Deutsche LifeCompass 2020 C	SUPCX	C-	(800) 728-3337	D+ / 2.4	1.76	3.17	4.31 /34	6.95 /21	6.65 /21	2.22	1.99
GI	Deutsche LifeCompass 2020 S	SPGRX	C	(800) 728-3337	C- / 3.1	2.01	3.70	5.31 /41	8.02 /27	7.70 /28	3.25	1.04
GR	Deutsche LifeCompass 2030 A	PLUSX	D+	(800) 728-3337	C- / 3.0	2.37	4.31	6.30 /49	9.49 /36	8.56 /33	2.22	1.44
GR	● Deutsche LifeCompass 2030 B	PLSBX	C-	(800) 728-3337	C- / 3.4	2.17	3.86	5.58 /43	8.69 /31	7.74 /28	1.58	2.27
GR	Deutsche LifeCompass 2030 C	PLSCX	C-	(800) 728-3337	C- / 3.4	2.08	3.85	5.48 /42	8.66 /31	7.74 /28	1.58	2.10

● Denotes fund is closed to new investors
* Denotes fund is included in Section II

www.thestreetratings.com

RISK	3 Year		NET ASSETS		ASSET				Portfolio Turnover Ratio	BULL / BEAR		FUND MANAGER		MINIMUMS		LOADS	
Risk Rating/Pts	Standard Deviation	Beta	NAV As of 3/31/15	Total $(Mil)	Cash %	Stocks %	Bonds %	Other %		Last Bull Market Return	Last Bear Market Return	Manager Quality Pct	Manager Tenure (Years)	Initial Purch. $	Additional Purch. $	Front End Load	Back End Load
C+ / 6.0	12.2	0.83	29.89	5	4	95	0	1	45	60.1	-26.2	82	2	0	0	0.0	0.0
C+ / 6.0	12.2	0.83	29.81	622	4	95	0	1	45	63.0	-25.9	85	2	2,500	50	0.0	0.0
C+ / 5.8	7.1	1.13	9.32	705	5	52	42	1	100	43.2	-12.5	12	10	1,000	50	5.8	0.0
C+ / 5.9	7.1	1.13	9.34	2	5	52	42	1	100	38.2	-12.8	8	10	1,000	50	0.0	0.0
C+ / 5.8	7.1	1.13	9.32	26	5	52	42	1	100	39.3	-12.9	8	10	1,000	50	0.0	0.0
C+ / 5.8	7.1	1.13	9.31	4	5	52	42	1	100	44.4	-12.5	14	10	1,000,000	0	0.0	0.0
C+ / 5.8	7.1	1.13	9.32	230	5	52	42	1	100	44.1	-12.5	13	10	2,500	50	0.0	0.0
C / 4.4	12.7	0.79	41.28	116	2	97	0	1	38	61.9	-21.0	91	13	1,000	50	5.8	0.0
C- / 4.1	12.7	0.79	35.58	1	2	97	0	1	38	57.8	-21.3	89	13	1,000	50	0.0	0.0
C- / 4.1	12.7	0.79	35.90	18	2	97	0	1	38	57.8	-21.3	89	13	1,000	50	0.0	0.0
C / 4.5	12.7	0.79	42.83	29	2	97	0	1	38	63.8	-20.9	92	13	1,000,000	0	0.0	0.0
C / 4.5	12.7	0.79	42.84	373	2	97	0	1	38	63.3	-21.0	92	13	2,500	50	0.0	0.0
E / 0.4	34.9	1.64	5.65	22	0	99	0	1	26	-58.6	-17.0	1	4	1,000	50	5.8	0.0
E / 0.4	35.0	1.65	5.39	N/A	0	99	0	1	26	-59.7	-17.3	1	4	1,000	50	0.0	0.0
E / 0.4	34.9	1.64	5.38	9	0	99	0	1	26	-59.7	-17.3	1	4	1,000	50	0.0	2.0
E / 0.4	34.9	1.65	5.70	1	0	99	0	1	26	-58.4	-16.9	1	4	1,000,000	0	0.0	0.0
E / 0.4	34.9	1.64	5.69	67	0	99	0	1	26	-58.3	-16.9	1	4	2,500	50	0.0	0.0
C / 5.2	10.7	0.84	43.69	95	2	97	0	1	33	156.5	-13.8	99	14	1,000	50	5.8	0.0
C / 4.9	10.7	0.84	36.76	N/A	2	97	0	1	33	149.7	-14.1	99	14	1,000	50	0.0	0.0
C / 4.9	10.7	0.84	37.11	21	2	97	0	1	33	150.2	-14.1	99	14	1,000	50	0.0	0.0
C / 5.3	10.7	0.84	47.44	4	2	97	0	1	33	158.7	-13.6	99	14	1,000,000	0	0.0	0.0
C / 5.3	10.7	0.84	45.96	274	2	97	0	1	33	158.8	-13.6	99	14	2,500	50	0.0	0.0
C / 4.5	15.6	0.98	9.12	28	1	98	0	1	25	35.6	-25.5	89	5	1,000	50	5.8	0.0
C / 4.6	15.6	0.98	9.01	12	1	98	0	1	25	32.1	-25.8	85	5	1,000	50	0.0	0.0
C / 4.5	15.6	0.98	9.17	2	1	98	0	1	25	36.8	-25.5	89	5	1,000,000	0	0.0	0.0
C / 4.5	15.6	0.98	9.16	56	1	98	0	1	25	36.6	-25.4	89	5	2,500	50	0.0	0.0
C / 4.6	11.0	1.01	41.86	28	0	99	0	1	84	94.0	-20.1	46	8	1,000	50	5.8	0.0
C / 4.3	11.0	1.01	37.44	N/A	0	99	0	1	84	88.9	-20.3	35	8	1,000	50	0.0	0.0
C / 4.3	11.0	1.01	37.61	5	0	99	0	1	84	89.1	-20.3	36	8	1,000	50	0.0	0.0
C / 4.7	11.0	1.01	43.56	4	0	99	0	1	84	95.9	-20.0	51	8	1,000,000	0	0.0	0.0
C / 4.7	11.0	1.01	43.11	195	0	99	0	1	84	95.6	-20.0	50	8	2,500	50	0.0	0.0
D / 2.2	9.8	0.99	18.47	313	1	98	0	1	129	77.7	-15.7	46	1	1,000	50	5.8	0.0
D+ / 2.3	9.8	0.99	18.59	2	1	98	0	1	129	73.2	-16.0	34	1	1,000	50	0.0	0.0
D+ / 2.3	9.8	0.99	18.53	37	1	98	0	1	129	73.6	-16.0	35	1	1,000	50	0.0	0.0
D / 2.2	9.8	0.99	18.48	139	1	98	0	1	129	79.8	-15.7	51	1	1,000,000	0	0.0	0.0
D / 2.2	9.8	0.99	18.47	3	1	98	0	1	129	76.0	-15.8	41	1	0	0	0.0	0.0
D / 2.2	9.8	0.99	18.46	1,028	1	98	0	1	129	79.9	-15.7	50	1	2,500	50	0.0	0.0
D- / 1.0	22.5	1.22	21.04	11	0	99	0	1	195	-2.0	-27.7	0	2	1,000	50	5.8	0.0
D- / 1.0	22.5	1.22	20.11	N/A	0	99	0	1	195	-4.3	-28.0	0	2	1,000	50	0.0	0.0
D- / 1.0	22.5	1.21	20.08	2	0	99	0	1	195	-4.5	-28.0	0	2	1,000	50	0.0	0.0
D- / 1.0	22.5	1.21	20.96	283	0	99	0	1	195	-1.1	-27.7	0	2	2,500	50	0.0	0.0
B / 8.7	5.7	0.96	12.62	35	7	48	41	4	61	38.5	-12.3	21	13	1,000	50	5.8	0.0
B / 8.7	5.7	0.96	12.62	N/A	7	48	41	4	61	35.0	-12.5	15	13	1,000	50	0.0	0.0
B / 8.7	5.8	0.96	12.62	9	7	48	41	4	61	34.9	-12.5	15	13	1,000	50	0.0	0.0
B / 8.7	5.7	0.95	12.60	29	7	48	41	4	61	39.7	-12.2	24	13	2,500	50	0.0	0.0
B / 8.3	6.7	0.65	15.74	63	8	58	31	3	60	45.3	-14.2	33	2	1,000	50	5.8	0.0
B / 8.3	6.7	0.65	15.65	N/A	8	58	31	3	60	41.8	-14.4	26	2	1,000	50	0.0	0.0
B / 8.3	6.7	0.65	15.65	12	8	58	31	3	60	41.7	-14.5	25	2	1,000	50	0.0	0.0
B / 8.3	6.7	0.65	15.74	76	8	58	31	3	60	46.6	-14.1	37	2	2,500	50	0.0	0.0
C+ / 6.3	8.2	0.81	10.81	31	0	74	23	3	60	57.7	-18.5	25	11	1,000	50	5.8	0.0
C+ / 6.5	8.1	0.80	10.81	N/A	0	74	23	3	60	53.7	-18.8	19	11	1,000	50	0.0	0.0
C+ / 6.5	8.2	0.81	10.80	6	0	74	23	3	60	53.7	-18.7	18	11	1,000	50	0.0	0.0

					PERFORMANCE							
	99 Pct = Best					Total Return % through 3/31/15					Incl. in Returns	
	0 Pct = Worst								Annualized		Dividend	Expense
Fund		Ticker	Overall Investment		Perfor- mance							
Type	Fund Name	Symbol	Rating	Phone	Rating/Pts	3 Mo	6 Mo	1Yr / Pct	3Yr / Pct	5Yr / Pct	Yield	Ratio
GR	Deutsche LifeCompass 2030 S	PPLSX	C-	(800) 728-3337	C- / 4.1	2.27	4.31	6.49 /51	9.75 /38	8.82 /35	2.60	1.18
AA	Deutsche LifeCompass 2040 A	TGTAX	D-	(800) 728-3337	C- / 3.6	2.67	4.73	6.70 /53	10.39 /42	9.11 /37	1.93	1.73
AA	Deutsche LifeCompass 2040 C	TGTCX	D-	(800) 728-3337	C- / 4.0	2.54	4.37	5.99 /46	9.59 /37	8.29 /32	1.26	2.49
AA	Deutsche LifeCompass 2040 S	TGTSX	D	(800) 728-3337	C / 4.6	2.80	4.90	6.99 /55	10.67 /43	9.36 /39	2.28	1.47
AA	Deutsche LifeCompass Retirement A	SUCAX	C-	(800) 728-3337	D- / 1.2	1.52	2.86	4.06 /32	5.77 /16	5.80 /16	2.49	1.34
AA	● Deutsche LifeCompass Retirement B	SUCBX	C-	(800) 728-3337	D- / 1.5	1.33	2.47	3.28 /28	4.97 /13	5.02 /12	1.88	2.26
AA	Deutsche LifeCompass Retirement C	SUCCX	C-	(800) 728-3337	D- / 1.5	1.33	2.47	3.28 /28	4.97 /13	5.02 /12	1.88	2.05
AA	Deutsche LifeCompass Retirement S	SCPCX	C	(800) 728-3337	D / 2.0	1.58	2.99	4.32 /34	6.04 /17	6.07 /17	2.89	1.04
MC	Deutsche Mid Cap Growth A	SMCAX	B	(800) 728-3337	B+ / 8.3	6.74	13.31	16.03 /93	15.32 /77	15.44 /90	0.00	1.26
MC	● Deutsche Mid Cap Growth B	SMCBX	B	(800) 728-3337	B+ / 8.6	6.58	12.95	15.14 /92	14.39 /70	14.49 /82	0.00	2.15
MC	Deutsche Mid Cap Growth C	SMCCX	B	(800) 728-3337	B+ / 8.6	6.58	12.90	15.15 /92	14.40 /70	14.53 /83	0.00	2.07
MC	Deutsche Mid Cap Growth Inst	BTEAX	B+	(800) 728-3337	A- / 9.2	6.83	13.48	16.34 /94	15.68 /81	15.85 /92	0.00	0.97
MC	Deutsche Mid Cap Growth S	SMCSX	B+	(800) 728-3337	A- / 9.2	6.82	13.46	16.41 /94	15.65 /80	15.78 /92	0.00	0.98
MC	Deutsche Mid Cap Value A	MIDVX	A-	(800) 728-3337	B+ / 8.5	4.65	9.79	11.61 /81	17.66 /93	14.32 /81	0.01	1.28
MC	● Deutsche Mid Cap Value B	MIDYX	A-	(800) 728-3337	B+ / 8.8	4.47	9.38	10.82 /78	16.79 /89	13.42 /72	0.00	2.17
MC	Deutsche Mid Cap Value C	MIDZX	A-	(800) 728-3337	B+ / 8.8	4.48	9.40	10.84 /78	16.77 /89	13.46 /72	0.00	2.04
MC	Deutsche Mid Cap Value Inst	MIDIX	A+	(800) 728-3337	A / 9.3	4.78	9.94	11.97 /82	17.98 /94	14.64 /84	0.24	1.00
MC	Deutsche Mid Cap Value R	MIDQX	A	(800) 728-3337	A- / 9.2	4.65	9.70	11.39 /80	17.42 /92	--	0.00	1.59
MC	Deutsche Mid Cap Value S	MIDTX	A+	(800) 728-3337	A / 9.3	4.72	9.88	11.90 /82	17.95 /94	14.58 /83	0.24	1.05
RE	Deutsche Real Est Secs A	RRRAX	C	(800) 728-3337	B+ / 8.4	4.22	19.49	24.20 /98	13.27 /62	15.45 /90	1.42	0.96
RE	● Deutsche Real Est Secs B	RRRBX	C+	(800) 728-3337	B+ / 8.8	4.02	19.05	23.29 /98	12.36 /55	14.53 /83	0.74	1.79
RE	Deutsche Real Est Secs C	RRRCX	C+	(800) 728-3337	B+ / 8.8	4.04	19.07	23.39 /98	12.49 /56	14.65 /84	0.85	1.68
RE	● Deutsche Real Est Secs Inst	RRRRX	C+	(800) 728-3337	A / 9.3	4.31	19.70	24.63 /98	13.67 /65	15.88 /92	1.80	0.62
RE	Deutsche Real Est Secs R	RRRSX	C+	(800) 728-3337	A- / 9.1	4.14	19.29	23.85 /98	12.93 /59	15.10 /88	1.22	1.26
RE	Deutsche Real Est Secs R6	RRRZX	U	(800) 728-3337	U /	4.33	19.76	--	--	--	0.00	N/A
RE	Deutsche Real Est Secs S	RRREX	C+	(800) 728-3337	A / 9.3	4.31	19.63	24.57 /98	13.52 /64	15.75 /92	1.71	0.77
IX	Deutsche S&P 500 Index A	SXPAX	B-	(800) 728-3337	C+ / 6.8	0.78	5.54	11.95 /82	15.32 /77	13.74 /75	1.35	0.67
IX	● Deutsche S&P 500 Index B	SXPBX	B+	(800) 728-3337	B- / 7.0	0.60	5.15	11.13 /79	14.48 /71	12.90 /67	0.69	1.40
IX	Deutsche S&P 500 Index C	SXPCX	B+	(800) 728-3337	B- / 7.1	0.61	5.19	11.16 /79	14.55 /71	12.95 /68	0.76	1.34
IX	Deutsche S&P 500 Index S	SCPIX	A-	(800) 728-3337	B / 7.9	0.86	5.70	12.28 /84	15.67 /81	14.08 /78	1.72	0.36
TC	Deutsche Science and Tech A	KTCAX	D-	(800) 728-3337	C / 4.5	3.07	9.14	11.71 /81	10.50 /42	12.85 /67	0.00	0.99
TC	● Deutsche Science and Tech B	KTCBX	E+	(800) 728-3337	C / 4.5	2.74	8.49	10.41 /76	9.22 /34	11.59 /58	0.00	2.18
TC	Deutsche Science and Tech C	KTCCX	E+	(800) 728-3337	C / 4.7	2.81	8.71	10.75 /77	9.52 /36	11.86 /60	0.00	1.87
TC	Deutsche Science and Tech Inst	KTCIX	D	(800) 728-3337	C+ / 5.6	3.15	9.31	12.02 /83	10.83 /44	13.22 /70	0.00	0.76
TC	Deutsche Science and Tech S	KTCSX	D	(800) 728-3337	C / 5.5	3.11	9.26	11.88 /82	10.62 /43	12.96 /68	0.00	0.85
GR	Deutsche Select Alt Allocation Inst	SELIX	D+	(800) 728-3337	E+ / 0.9	0.36	0.15	1.47 /20	3.37 / 9	4.45 /10	3.37	1.45
GR	Deutsche Select Alternative Alloc A	SELAX	D+	(800) 728-3337	E+ / 0.6	0.27	0.02	1.16 /19	3.03 / 8	4.13 / 9	2.88	1.74
GR	Deutsche Select Alternative Alloc C	SELEX	D+	(800) 728-3337	E+ / 0.7	0.09	-0.42	0.36 /17	2.26 / 7	3.35 / 7	2.26	2.50
GR	Deutsche Select Alternative Alloc S	SELSX	D+	(800) 728-3337	E+ / 0.9	0.36	0.10	1.32 /19	3.23 / 8	4.34 / 9	3.22	1.58
SC	Deutsche Small Cap Core A	SZCAX	B	(800) 728-3337	B / 7.6	5.13	16.19	8.12 /64	16.16 /85	14.71 /84	0.00	1.43
SC	● Deutsche Small Cap Core B	SZCBX	B	(800) 728-3337	B / 8.1	4.92	15.73	7.30 /57	15.29 /77	13.85 /76	0.00	2.17
SC	Deutsche Small Cap Core C	SZCCX	B	(800) 728-3337	B / 8.1	4.96	15.74	7.33 /58	15.30 /77	13.84 /76	0.00	2.20
SC	Deutsche Small Cap Core S	SSLCX	B+	(800) 728-3337	B+ / 8.9	5.22	16.31	8.43 /66	16.45 /87	15.03 /87	0.00	1.13
SC	Deutsche Small Cap Growth A	SSDAX	B-	(800) 728-3337	B+ / 8.6	9.69	17.82	12.51 /85	16.47 /87	17.61 /97	0.00	1.41
SC	● Deutsche Small Cap Growth B	SSDBX	C+	(800) 728-3337	B+ / 8.9	9.47	17.35	11.65 /81	15.59 /80	16.64 /95	0.00	2.26
SC	Deutsche Small Cap Growth C	SSDCX	C+	(800) 728-3337	B+ / 8.9	9.47	17.36	11.68 /81	15.61 /80	16.72 /95	0.00	2.19
SC	Deutsche Small Cap Growth Inst	SSDIX	B	(800) 728-3337	A / 9.4	9.78	18.04	12.87 /86	16.92 /89	18.09 /97	0.00	1.11
SC	Deutsche Small Cap Growth S	SSDSX	B	(800) 728-3337	A / 9.4	9.78	17.98	12.84 /86	16.77 /89	17.88 /97	0.00	1.16
SC	Deutsche Small Cap Value A	KDSAX	E+	(800) 728-3337	C / 5.1	2.91	13.15	4.95 /38	12.64 /57	10.16 /46	0.00	1.19
SC	● Deutsche Small Cap Value B	KDSBX	E+	(800) 728-3337	C / 5.4	2.71	12.73	4.09 /32	11.71 /50	9.26 /39	0.00	2.04
SC	Deutsche Small Cap Value C	KDSCX	E+	(800) 728-3337	C / 5.5	2.70	12.71	4.12 /33	11.81 /51	9.36 /39	0.00	1.93
SC	Deutsche Small Cap Value Inst	KDSIX	D-	(800) 728-3337	C+ / 6.3	3.02	13.37	5.31 /41	13.06 /60	10.60 /49	0.22	0.82

● Denotes fund is closed to new investors
* Denotes fund is included in Section II

RISK			NET ASSETS		ASSET				BULL / BEAR			FUND MANAGER		MINIMUMS		LOADS	
	3 Year		NAV						Last Bull	Last Bear		Manager	Manager	Initial	Additional	Front	Back
Risk	Standard		As of	Total	Cash	Stocks	Bonds	Other	Portfolio	Market	Market	Quality	Tenure	Purch.	Purch.	End	End
Rating/Pts	Deviation	Beta	3/31/15	$(Mil)	%	%	%	%	Turnover Ratio	Return	Return	Pct	(Years)	$	$	Load	Load
C+ / 6.2	8.2	0.81	10.80	9	0	74	23	3	60	59.0	-18.4	28	11	2,500	50	0.0	0.0
C- / 3.5	9.1	1.53	8.07	11	0	82	16	2	69	64.0	-20.1	7	2	1,000	50	5.8	0.0
C- / 3.7	9.2	1.54	8.06	N/A	0	82	16	2	69	59.9	-20.4	5	2	1,000	50	0.0	0.0
C- / 3.5	9.1	1.54	8.08	4	0	82	16	2	69	65.4	-20.0	7	2	2,500	50	0.0	0.0
B+ / 9.0	4.8	0.78	12.68	14	7	43	45	5	64	29.9	-7.9	31	2	1,000	50	5.8	0.0
B+ / 9.0	4.8	0.78	12.70	N/A	7	43	45	5	64	26.8	-8.2	23	2	1,000	50	0.0	0.0
B+ / 9.0	4.8	0.78	12.69	4	7	43	45	5	64	26.6	-8.1	23	2	1,000	50	0.0	0.0
B+ / 9.0	4.7	0.78	12.67	38	7	43	45	5	64	31.1	-7.9	35	2	2,500	50	0.0	0.0
C / 5.4	12.2	1.04	21.22	213	3	96	0	1	46	88.0	-22.1	35	9	1,000	50	5.8	0.0
C / 5.2	12.2	1.04	18.96	1	3	96	0	1	46	82.9	-22.4	26	9	1,000	50	0.0	0.0
C / 5.2	12.2	1.04	18.95	12	3	96	0	1	46	83.1	-22.4	26	9	1,000	50	0.0	0.0
C / 5.4	12.2	1.04	22.06	3	3	96	0	1	46	90.2	-22.1	40	9	1,000,000	0	0.0	0.0
C / 5.4	12.2	1.04	21.76	181	3	96	0	1	46	89.9	-22.0	40	9	2,500	50	0.0	0.0
C+ / 6.5	11.8	1.02	18.05	54	5	94	0	1	34	103.5	-23.7	69	2	1,000	50	5.8	0.0
C+ / 6.4	11.9	1.03	17.82	N/A	5	94	0	1	34	98.2	-23.9	58	2	1,000	50	0.0	0.0
C+ / 6.4	11.8	1.02	17.80	19	5	94	0	1	34	98.2	-23.9	58	2	1,000	50	0.0	0.0
C+ / 6.5	11.8	1.03	18.04	7	5	94	0	1	34	105.4	-23.6	71	2	1,000,000	0	0.0	0.0
C+ / 6.4	11.8	1.03	18.07	13	5	94	0	1	34	102.2	-23.8	66	2	0	0	0.0	0.0
C+ / 6.5	11.8	1.02	18.03	138	5	94	0	1	34	105.0	-23.6	72	2	2,500	50	0.0	0.0
C- / 3.2	13.4	1.07	24.55	424	0	99	0	1	108	83.3	-17.3	42	16	1,000	50	5.8	0.0
C- / 3.3	13.4	1.07	24.81	N/A	0	99	0	1	108	78.3	-17.5	32	16	1,000	50	0.0	0.0
C- / 3.2	13.4	1.07	24.80	56	0	99	0	1	108	79.0	-17.5	33	16	1,000	50	0.0	0.0
C- / 3.2	13.4	1.07	24.53	706	0	99	0	1	108	85.5	-17.1	48	16	1,000,000	0	0.0	0.0
C- / 3.2	13.4	1.06	24.57	35	0	99	0	1	108	81.1	-17.2	38	16	0	0	0.0	0.0
U /	N/A	N/A	24.53	155	0	99	0	1	108	N/A	N/A	N/A	16	0	0	0.0	0.0
C- / 3.2	13.4	1.07	24.68	356	0	99	0	1	108	84.7	-17.1	46	16	2,500	50	0.0	0.0
B- / 7.1	9.5	1.00	26.00	229	2	96	0	2	3	95.9	-16.5	58	8	1,000	50	4.5	0.0
B- / 7.1	9.5	1.00	25.97	1	2	96	0	2	3	90.9	-16.7	46	8	1,000	50	0.0	0.0
B- / 7.1	9.5	1.00	25.96	54	2	96	0	2	3	91.3	-16.7	47	8	1,000	50	0.0	0.0
B- / 7.1	9.5	1.00	26.06	657	2	96	0	2	3	97.8	-16.3	62	8	2,500	50	0.0	0.0
C- / 3.2	12.7	1.05	17.44	570	2	97	0	1	174	79.4	-16.8	8	7	1,000	50	5.8	0.0
D / 1.7	12.7	1.05	12.39	1	2	97	0	1	174	72.6	-17.1	5	7	1,000	50	0.0	0.0
D / 2.0	12.8	1.05	13.18	18	2	97	0	1	174	74.2	-17.1	5	7	1,000	50	0.0	0.0
C- / 3.4	12.8	1.05	18.67	5	2	97	0	1	174	81.3	-16.6	8	7	1,000,000	0	0.0	0.0
C- / 3.2	12.7	1.05	17.57	100	2	97	0	1	174	80.1	-16.7	8	7	2,500	50	0.0	0.0
B / 8.5	4.4	0.30	11.21	16	14	26	47	13	29	19.1	-8.5	49	2	1,000,000	0	0.0	0.0
B / 8.6	4.4	0.30	11.21	364	14	26	47	13	29	17.9	-8.7	44	2	1,000	50	5.8	0.0
B / 8.7	4.5	0.30	11.20	39	14	26	47	13	29	14.7	-8.9	33	2	1,000	50	0.0	0.0
B / 8.6	4.4	0.29	11.21	81	14	26	47	13	29	18.4	-8.5	49	2	2,500	50	0.0	0.0
C+ / 5.8	14.2	1.02	26.65	13	4	94	0	2	69	101.0	-25.4	61	2	1,000	50	5.8	0.0
C+ / 5.8	14.3	1.02	23.23	N/A	4	94	0	2	69	95.9	-25.6	49	2	1,000	50	0.0	0.0
C+ / 5.8	14.2	1.02	23.28	1	4	94	0	2	69	95.9	-25.7	50	2	1,000	50	0.0	0.0
C+ / 5.9	14.2	1.02	27.63	79	4	94	0	2	69	102.7	-25.3	66	2	2,500	50	0.0	0.0
C / 4.3	14.2	1.01	31.92	36	2	97	0	1	72	98.3	-21.3	68	9	1,000	50	5.8	0.0
C- / 3.8	14.2	1.01	27.97	N/A	2	97	0	1	72	93.2	-21.6	57	9	1,000	50	0.0	0.0
C- / 3.8	14.2	1.01	28.09	6	2	97	0	1	72	93.2	-21.5	56	9	1,000	50	0.0	0.0
C / 4.5	14.2	1.01	33.35	2	2	97	0	1	72	100.9	-21.1	72	9	1,000,000	0	0.0	0.0
C / 4.4	14.2	1.01	32.99	110	2	97	0	1	72	99.9	-21.2	71	9	2,500	50	0.0	0.0
E+ / 0.9	13.7	0.97	26.48	411	2	97	0	1	17	80.0	-27.1	28	2	1,000	50	5.8	0.0
E+ / 0.9	13.8	0.97	21.26	1	2	97	0	1	17	74.9	-27.3	19	2	1,000	50	0.0	0.0
E+ / 0.9	13.7	0.97	22.08	83	2	97	0	1	17	75.5	-27.3	20	2	1,000	50	0.0	0.0
E+ / 0.9	13.8	0.97	27.07	346	2	97	0	1	17	82.3	-27.0	31	2	1,000,000	0	0.0	0.0

Fund Type	Fund Name	Ticker Symbol	Overall Investment Rating	Phone	Performance Rating/Pts	3 Mo	6 Mo	1Yr / Pct	3Yr / Pct	5Yr / Pct	Dividend Yield	Expense Ratio
	99 Pct = Best 0 Pct = Worst				**PERFORMANCE** Total Return % through 3/31/15 Annualized / Incl. in Returns							
SC	Deutsche Small Cap Value S	KDSSX	D-	(800) 728-3337	C+ / 6.2	3.01	13.35	5.24 /40	12.89 /59	10.37 /48	0.13	0.92
GL	Deutsche Strat Equity Lng Sht Instl	DSLIX	U	(800) 728-3337	U /	2.50	1.48	--	--	--	0.00	N/A
FO	Deutsche World Dividend A	SERAX	D+	(800) 728-3337	D / 2.2	0.64	-1.30	0.43 /17	9.39 /36	7.52 /27	2.14	1.25
FO	● Deutsche World Dividend B	SERBX	D+	(800) 728-3337	D+ / 2.5	0.44	-1.68	-0.35 /15	8.51 /30	6.60 /21	1.44	2.57
FO	Deutsche World Dividend C	SERCX	D+	(800) 728-3337	D+ / 2.6	0.50	-1.64	-0.27 /15	8.61 /30	6.71 /21	1.52	1.98
FO	Deutsche World Dividend Inst	SERNX	C-	(800) 728-3337	C- / 3.3	0.71	-1.13	0.72 /18	9.72 /38	7.89 /29	2.58	0.95
FO	Deutsche World Dividend S	SCGEX	C-	(800) 728-3337	C- / 3.2	0.69	-1.16	0.64 /17	9.62 /38	7.73 /28	2.48	1.06
GR	DF Dent MidCap Growth	DFDMX	B	(800) 754-8757	B / 7.9	2.09	9.03	6.13 /48	16.71 /88	--	0.00	2.08
GR	DF Dent Premier Growth	DFDPX	C+	(866) 233-3368	C+ / 6.4	0.73	7.77	7.89 /62	13.60 /64	14.39 /81	0.00	1.20
FO	DFA Asia Pacif Sm Comp Ptf Inst	DFRSX	E	(800) 984-9472	E / 0.4	0.89	-4.64	-9.38 / 3	-0.03 / 4	3.00 / 6	5.20	0.55
IN	DFA Commodity Strategy Port	DCMSX	E-	(800) 984-9472	E- / 0.1	-5.28	-16.52	-25.52 / 0	-9.87 / 1	--	1.10	0.33
FO	DFA Continental Small Co Inst	DFCSX	D	(800) 984-9472	C / 4.7	7.00	2.88	-9.14 / 3	12.85 /58	7.68 /28	2.14	0.56
GR	DFA CSTG&E US Soc Core Eq 2	DFCUX	B+	(800) 984-9472	B- / 7.3	1.11	5.58	7.11 /56	15.39 /78	14.02 /78	1.52	0.32
EM	DFA Emerging Markets II Inst	DFETX	E+	(800) 984-9472	E+ / 0.6	1.53	-3.00	0.19 /16	0.67 / 5	2.47 / 5	2.52	0.34
EM	DFA Emerging Markets Inst	DFEMX	E+	(800) 984-9472	E / 0.5	1.48	-3.08	0.01 /16	0.44 / 5	2.25 / 5	2.00	0.56
★ FO	DFA Emerging Markets Sm Cap Inst	DEMSX	E+	(800) 984-9472	D- / 1.1	3.42	-1.81	3.04 /27	3.70 / 9	4.53 /10	2.04	0.72
EM	DFA Emerging Markets Val Inst	DFEVX	E	(800) 984-9472	E / 0.3	-0.19	-6.51	-3.94 / 7	-1.78 / 3	-0.78 / 2	2.63	0.55
EM	DFA Emerging Markets Val R2	DFEPX	E	(800) 984-9472	E / 0.3	-0.23	-6.63	-4.14 / 7	-2.02 / 3	-1.01 / 2	2.40	0.80
★ EM	DFA Emerging Markts Core Eqty Inst	DFCEX	E+	(800) 984-9472	E+ / 0.6	1.96	-2.82	0.40 /17	0.98 / 5	2.29 / 5	2.00	0.61
EM	DFA Emerging Mkts Socl Core Eq	DFESX	E+	(800) 984-9472	E / 0.5	1.49	-3.08	-0.02 /15	0.42 / 5	1.76 / 4	2.02	0.63
GR	DFA Enhanced US Large Co Inst	DFELX	B	(800) 984-9472	B+ / 8.4	1.23	6.11	12.87 /86	16.28 /85	14.75 /85	0.38	0.23
RE	DFA Gl Real Estate Securities Port	DFGEX	B-	(800) 984-9472	B / 8.2	4.02	14.47	18.68 /96	12.97 /59	13.86 /76	3.61	0.47
GL	DFA Global Allocation 25/75 Inst	DGTSX	C	(800) 984-9472	D- / 1.3	1.45	2.06	2.97 /26	4.32 /11	4.84 /11	2.57	0.44
GL	DFA Global Allocation 25/75 R2	DFGPX	C-	(800) 984-9472	D- / 1.1	1.40	2.00	2.37 /23	3.91 /10	4.37 /10	2.14	0.69
GL	DFA Global Allocation 60/40 Inst	DGSIX	C	(800) 984-9472	C- / 3.2	1.93	2.83	3.75 /30	8.54 /30	8.18 /31	2.07	0.52
GL	DFA Global Allocation 60/40 R2	DFPRX	C	(800) 984-9472	C- / 3.0	1.87	2.72	3.57 /29	8.29 /29	7.90 /29	1.54	0.77
GL	DFA Global Equity Inst	DGEIX	C+	(800) 984-9472	C+ / 5.9	2.72	4.27	5.30 /41	13.27 /62	11.30 /55	1.95	0.60
GL	DFA Global Equity R2	DGERX	C+	(800) 984-9472	C+ / 5.8	2.64	4.16	5.03 /39	12.99 /60	11.03 /53	1.68	0.85
FO	DFA International Large Cap Gr Inst	DILRX	U	(800) 984-9472	U /	4.21	0.99	-1.24 /12	--	--	2.44	0.37
★ FO	DFA International Sm Cap Val Inst	DISVX	D+	(800) 984-9472	C- / 3.9	4.68	0.53	-6.26 / 4	11.31 /48	8.36 /32	1.96	0.68
FO	DFA International Small Cap Gr Inst	DISMX	U	(800) 984-9472	U /	5.12	2.89	-2.66 / 9	--	--	1.99	0.72
★ FO	DFA International Small Co Inst	DFISX	D-	(800) 984-9472	D+ / 2.5	3.89	-0.50	-6.60 / 4	8.81 /32	7.98 /30	2.45	0.53
EM	DFA International Value II Inst	DIVTX	D-	(800) 984-9472	D / 2.1	4.14	-1.42	-3.97 / 7	7.85 /26	4.78 /11	3.18	0.28
EM	DFA International Value III Inst	DFVIX	D-	(800) 984-9472	D / 2.2	4.26	-1.37	-3.92 / 7	7.91 /26	4.83 /11	3.14	0.24
EM	DFA International Value Inst	DFIVX	D-	(800) 984-9472	D / 2.1	4.14	-1.47	-4.18 / 7	7.69 /26	4.62 /11	2.98	0.43
EM	DFA International Value IV Inst	DFVFX	D-	(800) 984-9472	D / 2.2	4.16	-1.43	-3.99 / 7	7.87 /26	4.79 /11	5.19	0.27
EM	DFA International Value R2	DFIPX	D-	(800) 984-9472	D / 1.9	4.13	-1.56	-4.37 / 6	7.42 /24	4.35 /10	2.77	0.68
FO	DFA International Vector Eq Inst	DFVQX	D-	(800) 984-9472	D / 2.2	4.09	-0.78	-5.31 / 5	8.18 /28	6.21 /18	2.50	0.49
GR	DFA Internatl Soc Cre Eqty Ptf Inst	DSCLX	U	(800) 984-9472	U /	3.62	-1.49	-5.64 / 5	--	--	2.51	0.53
★ FO	DFA Intl Core Equity Port Inst	DFIEX	D	(800) 984-9472	D+ / 2.4	4.13	-0.49	-4.14 / 7	8.34 /29	6.13 /18	2.63	0.38
RE	DFA Intl Real Estate Sec Port Inst	DFITX	C	(800) 984-9472	C / 5.5	2.67	5.65	9.91 /74	11.64 /50	11.14 /54	6.15	0.31
FO	DFA Intl Sustainability Core 1	DFSPX	D	(800) 984-9472	D+ / 2.5	4.50	-0.18	-3.28 / 8	8.29 /29	5.85 /16	2.38	0.49
FO	DFA Intl Value ex Tobacco Portfolio	DFVLX	D-	(800) 984-9472	D / 1.7	4.00	-2.01	-4.91 / 6	7.14 /22	4.24 / 9	2.86	0.55
FO	DFA Japanese Small Co Inst	DFJSX	C-	(800) 984-9472	C- / 3.5	8.59	2.81	8.02 /63	7.97 /27	8.11 /31	1.51	0.55
FO	DFA Large Cap International Inst	DFALX	D	(800) 984-9472	D+ / 2.5	4.22	-0.23	-2.09 /10	8.14 /28	5.80 /16	2.79	0.28
FO	DFA LWAS Intl Hi Bk to Mkt Port	DFHBX	D-	(800) 984-9472	D / 2.1	4.17	-1.41	-4.17 / 7	7.68 /25	4.59 /10	2.94	0.50
GR	DFA LWAS US High Bk to Mkt Port	DFBMX	A+	(800) 984-9472	B+ / 8.9	-0.26	2.44	8.00 /63	18.40 /95	14.71 /84	1.78	0.34
★ RE	DFA Real Estate Securities Ptf Inst	DFREX	B-	(800) 984-9472	A / 9.4	4.76	20.18	24.59 /98	13.94 /67	15.80 /92	3.01	0.19
GL	DFA Select Hedged Global Eq Inst	DSHGX	B-	(800) 984-9472	C / 5.5	3.84	4.68	6.19 /48	12.27 /54	--	2.93	0.69
★ GR	DFA TA US Core Equity 2 Inst	DFTCX	A+	(800) 984-9472	B+ / 8.8	2.21	7.21	9.80 /74	17.24 /91	14.94 /86	1.47	0.24
FO	DFA TA World ex US Core Eq Inst	DFTWX	D-	(800) 984-9472	D / 1.6	3.67	-0.81	-3.04 / 9	6.50 /19	5.04 /12	2.42	0.45
FO	DFA Tax Managed Intl Val Inst	DTMIX	D-	(800) 984-9472	D / 1.8	4.10	-1.64	-4.72 / 6	7.17 /22	4.43 /10	2.73	0.53

● Denotes fund is closed to new investors
★ Denotes fund is included in Section II

www.thestreetratings.com

RISK			NET ASSETS		ASSET					BULL / BEAR		FUND MANAGER		MINIMUMS		LOADS	
	3 Year		NAV						Portfolio	Last Bull	Last Bear	Manager	Manager	Initial	Additional	Front	Back
Risk Rating/Pts	Standard Deviation	Beta	As of 3/31/15	Total $(Mil)	Cash %	Stocks %	Bonds %	Other %	Turnover Ratio	Market Return	Market Return	Quality Pct	Tenure (Years)	Purch. $	Purch. $	End Load	End Load
E+ / 0.9	13.7	0.97	26.89	122	2	97	0	1	17	81.1	-27.1	30	2	2,500	50	0.0	0.0
U /	N/A	N/A	9.83	74	0	0	0	100	0	N/A	N/A	N/A	N/A	1,000,000	0	0.0	0.0
B- / 7.1	9.8	0.67	28.63	98	1	98	0	1	51	54.2	-15.6	88	5	1,000	50	5.8	0.0
B- / 7.1	9.9	0.67	28.38	N/A	1	98	0	1	51	50.0	-16.0	84	5	1,000	50	0.0	0.0
B- / 7.1	9.8	0.67	28.44	37	1	98	0	1	51	50.4	-15.9	85	5	1,000	50	0.0	0.0
B- / 7.1	9.8	0.67	28.91	12	1	98	0	1	51	55.8	-15.5	89	5	1,000,000	0	0.0	0.0
B- / 7.1	9.9	0.67	28.67	187	1	98	0	1	51	55.2	-15.6	89	5	2,500	50	0.0	0.0
C+ / 5.7	12.0	0.97	15.63	22	0	99	0	1	32	103.8	N/A	77	4	2,500	500	0.0	2.0
C+ / 5.8	11.5	1.02	27.75	178	0	99	0	1	25	89.6	-18.9	31	14	2,500	500	0.0	0.0
C- / 3.9	15.6	0.95	20.41	247	1	98	0	1	7	25.4	-28.0	2	17	2,000,000	0	0.0	0.0
C- / 3.5	12.8	0.69	6.64	1,198	3	0	96	1	104	-21.6	-19.7	0	5	0	0	0.0	0.0
C / 4.4	16.4	1.13	20.47	238	0	99	0	1	13	66.6	-32.9	83	17	2,000,000	0	0.0	0.0
C+ / 6.9	11.3	1.13	14.71	93	0	99	0	1	11	99.2	-22.4	30	3	0	0	0.0	0.0
C / 5.1	13.9	1.01	24.63	100	0	99	0	1	5	24.9	-25.7	N/A	17	0	0	0.0	0.0
C / 5.2	13.9	1.01	25.41	3,968	0	99	0	1	5	23.9	-25.7	64	17	2,000,000	0	0.0	0.0
C / 5.4	13.0	0.80	20.57	5,189	0	99	0	1	9	35.4	-27.1	19	17	5,000,000	0	0.0	0.0
C / 4.6	15.2	1.09	25.70	17,507	0	99	0	1	12	16.7	-31.1	31	17	2,000,000	0	0.0	0.0
C / 4.7	15.2	1.09	25.68	94	0	99	0	1	12	15.7	-31.2	28	17	0	0	0.0	0.0
C / 5.4	13.7	0.99	19.29	16,162	0	99	0	1	2	26.0	-27.4	71	N/A	0	0	0.0	0.0
C / 5.4	13.9	1.00	12.27	982	0	99	0	1	10	25.0	-28.1	64	N/A	0	0	0.0	0.0
C / 5.5	9.5	1.00	12.35	219	1	4	93	2	202	101.1	-16.1	69	14	2,000,000	0	0.0	0.0
C / 4.9	12.5	0.99	10.87	3,857	15	84	0	1	17	75.4	-17.2	54	N/A	0	0	0.0	0.0
B+ / 9.7	3.0	0.20	12.80	707	1	24	73	2	0	21.4	-4.7	86	N/A	0	0	0.0	0.0
B+ / 9.7	3.0	0.20	12.84	1	1	24	73	2	0	19.7	-4.9	84	N/A	0	0	0.0	0.0
B / 8.6	7.0	0.49	15.97	2,858	3	58	38	1	54	48.0	-13.8	91	N/A	0	0	0.0	0.0
B / 8.6	7.0	0.49	16.11	5	3	58	38	1	54	46.9	-14.0	90	N/A	0	0	0.0	0.0
C+ / 6.6	10.9	0.75	18.86	4,185	1	98	0	1	15	81.9	-23.1	95	N/A	0	0	0.0	0.0
C+ / 6.6	10.9	0.75	19.02	13	1	98	0	1	15	80.3	-23.1	94	N/A	0	0	0.0	0.0
U /	N/A	N/A	11.65	183	0	99	0	1	20	N/A	N/A	N/A	N/A	0	0	0.0	0.0
C / 5.3	14.9	1.06	19.47	12,311	0	99	0	1	8	66.4	-26.1	78	17	2,000,000	0	0.0	0.0
U /	N/A	N/A	12.22	80	0	99	0	1	29	N/A	N/A	N/A	N/A	0	0	0.0	0.0
C / 5.3	13.3	0.95	17.64	8,805	14	85	0	1	18	51.6	-23.3	65	17	2,000,000	0	0.0	0.0
C / 5.0	14.5	0.85	5.28	109	0	99	0	1	17	47.3	-26.8	96	17	0	0	0.0	0.0
C / 5.3	14.5	0.85	15.91	1,936	0	99	0	1	17	47.5	-26.8	96	17	0	0	0.0	0.0
C / 5.5	14.5	0.85	18.38	7,194	0	99	0	1	17	46.5	-26.9	96	17	0	0	0.0	0.0
C / 5.0	14.4	0.84	14.02	251	0	99	0	1	17	47.3	-26.8	96	17	0	0	0.0	0.0
C / 5.5	14.5	0.85	18.39	12	0	99	0	1	17	45.2	-27.0	96	17	0	0	0.0	0.0
C / 5.5	13.9	1.03	11.19	1,487	0	99	0	1	8	50.0	-25.8	45	N/A	0	0	0.0	0.0
U /	N/A	N/A	11.63	381	1	98	0	1	5	N/A	N/A	N/A	3	0	0	0.0	0.0
C+ / 5.8	13.5	1.01	12.17	13,369	0	99	0	1	7	50.8	-25.1	49	N/A	0	0	0.0	0.0
C / 5.5	13.2	0.86	5.38	3,296	40	59	0	1	1	63.2	-18.8	63	N/A	0	0	0.0	0.0
C+ / 5.9	13.1	0.98	9.51	370	1	98	0	1	3	49.7	-24.4	52	N/A	0	0	0.0	0.0
C / 5.4	14.7	1.09	9.01	71	0	99	0	1	23	44.7	-26.5	25	N/A	0	0	0.0	0.0
C+ / 6.5	13.6	0.68	19.73	485	0	99	0	1	9	30.5	3.5	80	17	2,000,000	0	0.0	0.0
C+ / 5.9	13.0	0.98	21.56	3,146	0	99	0	1	4	49.2	-23.5	51	17	2,000,000	0	0.0	0.0
C / 5.1	14.4	1.07	8.37	67	0	99	0	1	17	46.2	-26.9	32	17	2,000,000	0	0.0	0.0
C+ / 6.8	11.5	1.13	18.98	65	0	99	0	1	15	117.6	-24.0	N/A	14	0	0	0.0	0.0
C- / 3.7	13.5	1.08	34.34	7,216	0	99	0	1	1	85.1	-16.1	49	3	2,000,000	0	0.0	0.0
B- / 7.4	10.9	0.77	14.05	187	3	96	0	1	0	N/A	N/A	93	4	0	0	0.0	0.0
C+ / 6.9	10.9	1.10	14.53	5,462	0	99	0	1	7	107.5	-22.0	59	3	0	0	0.0	0.0
C+ / 5.8	13.1	0.97	9.89	2,141	0	99	0	1	8	44.3	-26.0	30	N/A	2,000,000	0	0.0	0.0
C / 5.5	14.6	1.08	15.05	3,143	0	99	0	1	13	45.2	-27.0	26	16	2,000,000	0	0.0	0.0

99 Pct = Best					**PERFORMANCE**					
0 Pct = Worst						Total Return % through 3/31/15				Incl. in Returns
		Ticker	Overall Investment Rating	Phone	Perfor-mance Rating/Pts				Annualized	Dividend Expense
Fund Type	Fund Name	Symbol				3 Mo	6 Mo	1Yr / Pct	3Yr / Pct	5Yr / Pct	Yield	Ratio

Fund Type	Fund Name	Ticker	Rating	Phone	Perf/Pts	3 Mo	6 Mo	1Yr/Pct	3Yr/Pct	5Yr/Pct	Yield	Ratio
SC	DFA Tax Managed US Sm Cap Inst	DFTSX	A-	(800) 984-9472	A- / 9.1	3.80	13.09	7.18 /57	17.66 /93	15.94 /93	0.75	0.52
MC	DFA Tax Mgd US MktWide Val Inst	DTMMX	A+	(800) 984-9472	A / 9.3	0.87	4.94	9.77 /73	18.90 /96	15.36 /89	1.46	0.37
SC	DFA Tax Mgd US Target Val Inst	DTMVX	A	(800) 984-9472	A / 9.4	4.31	9.81	7.40 /58	18.83 /96	15.82 /92	0.85	0.46
IN	DFA Tax-Managed US Eq Inst	DTMEX	A	(800) 984-9472	B+ / 8.4	1.59	6.58	11.85 /82	16.26 /85	14.61 /83	1.60	0.22
IN	DFA U.S. Vector Equity Port Inst	DFVEX	A-	(800) 984-9472	B+ / 8.5	2.31	6.88	7.15 /56	17.10 /90	14.65 /84	1.29	0.32
FO	DFA United Kingdom Small Co Inst	DFUKX	C-	(800) 984-9472	C+ / 5.8	1.27	1.79	-7.48 / 4	15.27 /77	15.45 /90	2.82	0.62
* IN	DFA US Core Equity 1 Ptf Inst	DFEOX	A+	(800) 984-9472	B+ / 8.7	2.23	7.08	10.75 /77	16.93 /89	14.97 /87	1.53	0.19
* IN	DFA US Core Equity 2 Ptf Inst	DFQTX	A+	(800) 984-9472	B+ / 8.7	2.14	6.91	9.51 /72	17.22 /91	14.89 /86	1.52	0.22
GR	DFA US Large Cap Equity Inst	DUSQX	U	(800) 984-9472	U /	1.64	5.82	11.73 /81	--	--	1.53	0.20
GR	DFA US Large Cap Growth Inst	DUSLX	U	(800) 984-9472	U /	2.32	7.98	14.12 /90	--	--	1.55	0.22
GR	DFA US Large Cap Value I Inst	DFLVX	A+	(800) 984-9472	B+ / 8.9	-0.21	2.48	8.10 /64	18.49 /96	14.80 /85	1.82	0.27
GR	DFA US Large Cap Value II Inst	DFCVX	A+	(800) 984-9472	A- / 9.0	-0.20	2.54	8.25 /65	18.62 /96	14.93 /86	1.97	0.16
GR	DFA US Large Cap Value III Inst	DFUVX	A+	(800) 984-9472	A- / 9.0	-0.15	2.55	8.26 /65	18.67 /96	14.95 /86	1.97	0.13
* GR	DFA US Large Company Portfolio	DFUSX	A	(800) 984-9472	B / 8.2	0.96	5.88	12.61 /85	16.00 /83	14.36 /81	1.90	0.08
* SC	DFA US Micro Cap Portfolio Inst	DFSCX	B+	(800) 984-9472	B+ / 8.9	3.13	12.71	5.54 /43	17.49 /92	16.12 /94	0.71	0.53
SC	DFA US Small Cap Growth Inst	DSCGX	U	(800) 984-9472	U /	5.84	15.23	10.96 /78	--	--	0.62	0.41
* SC	DFA US Small Cap Port Inst	DFSTX	A-	(800) 984-9472	A- / 9.1	3.99	13.10	7.71 /60	17.52 /92	16.04 /93	0.91	0.37
* SC	DFA US Small Cap Value I Inst	DFSVX	B+	(800) 984-9472	B+ / 8.6	2.44	9.32	4.74 /37	17.46 /92	14.72 /84	0.69	0.53
GR	DFA US Social Core Eq 2 Inst	DFUEX	B+	(800) 984-9472	B / 7.7	1.25	5.64	7.74 /61	15.99 /83	14.23 /80	1.48	0.28
GR	DFA US Sustainability Core 1 Inst	DFSIX	A	(800) 984-9472	B+ / 8.6	2.04	6.73	10.60 /77	16.85 /89	14.68 /84	1.40	0.32
GR	DFA US Targeted Value Port Inst	DFFVX	B+	(800) 984-9472	B+ / 8.7	3.91	7.91	4.70 /36	17.65 /93	14.56 /83	0.99	0.40
GR	DFA US Targeted Value Portfolio R1	DFTVX	B+	(800) 984-9472	B+ / 8.7	3.89	7.90	4.60 /36	17.57 /93	14.47 /82	0.90	0.50
GR	DFA US Targeted Value Portfolio R2	DFTPX	B+	(800) 984-9472	B+ / 8.6	3.82	7.78	4.44 /35	17.37 /92	14.27 /80	0.75	0.65
FO	DFA Wld ex US Val Institutional	DFWVX	E+	(800) 984-9472	D- / 1.3	3.22	-2.43	-4.32 / 6	5.74 /16	--	2.88	0.76
GL	DFA World Core Eqty Inst	DREIX	B-	(800) 984-9472	C / 5.5	3.03	3.12	3.97 /32	12.69 /57	--	1.75	0.97
FO	DFA World ex US Core Eqty Port Inst	DFWIX	U	(800) 984-9472	U /	3.82	-0.94	-3.02 / 9	--	--	2.08	0.88
GR	DFA World ex US Tgtd Val Port Inst	DWUSX	U	(800) 984-9472	U /	3.39	-1.53	-5.17 / 5	--	--	2.10	1.17
GR	DGHM All-Cap Value C	DGACX	C-	(800) 653-2839	C+ / 6.3	1.55	7.36	5.85 /45	13.73 /65	10.81 /51	0.62	2.34
GR	DGHM All-Cap Value Inst	DGAIX	C	(800) 653-2839	B- / 7.1	1.47	7.73	6.74 /53	14.88 /74	--	1.36	1.27
GR	DGHM All-Cap Value Investor	DGHMX	C	(800) 653-2839	C+ / 6.9	1.64	7.67	6.52 /51	14.54 /71	11.63 /58	1.07	1.60
SC	DGHM V2000 Small Cap Value Inst	DGIVX	C+	(800) 653-2839	C+ / 6.7	3.18	10.99	5.14 /40	13.93 /67	--	0.44	4.62
SC	DGHM V2000 Small Cap Value	DGSMX	C+	(800) 653-2839	C+ / 6.4	3.09	10.76	4.66 /36	13.56 /64	--	0.00	7.59
FS	Diamond Hill Financial Lng-Sht A	BANCX	C+	(614) 255-3333	C+ / 6.5	-0.97	5.14	7.17 /56	15.77 /81	10.69 /50	0.00	1.75
FS	Diamond Hill Financial Lng-Sht C	BSGCX	C+	(614) 255-3333	C+ / 6.7	-1.15	4.70	6.43 /50	14.90 /74	9.88 /44	0.00	2.50
FS	Diamond Hill Financial Lng-Sht I	DHFSX	B+		B / 7.6	-0.92	5.22	7.43 /59	16.04 /84	11.00 /53	0.28	1.50
GR	Diamond Hill Large Cap A	DHLAX	B-	(614) 255-3333	C+ / 6.6	0.04	5.61	8.70 /68	15.64 /80	12.62 /65	0.78	1.04
GR	Diamond Hill Large Cap C	DHLCX	B-	(614) 255-3333	C+ / 6.9	-0.14	5.23	7.89 /62	14.79 /73	11.79 /59	0.30	1.79
GR	Diamond Hill Large Cap I	DHLRX	B+	(614) 255-3333	B / 7.7	0.09	5.74	8.97 /69	15.92 /83	12.94 /68	1.01	0.79
GR	Diamond Hill Large Cap Y	DHLYX	A-		B / 7.9	0.13	5.84	9.12 /70	16.10 /84	12.93 /68	1.16	0.65
GR	Diamond Hill Long-Short Fd Cl A	DIAMX	C	(614) 255-3333	C- / 3.1	-0.21	2.67	5.21 /40	10.03 /39	8.18 /31	0.00	1.84
GR	Diamond Hill Long-Short Fd Cl C	DHFCX	C	(614) 255-3333	C- / 3.4	-0.41	2.29	4.44 /35	9.20 /34	7.37 /26	0.00	2.59
GR	Diamond Hill Long-Short Fd Cl I	DHLSX	C+	(614) 255-3333	C- / 4.1	-0.17	2.81	5.50 /42	10.30 /41	8.48 /33	0.00	1.59
GR	Diamond Hill Long-Short Fd Cl Y	DIAYX	C+		C- / 4.2	-0.12	2.89	5.63 /43	10.46 /42	8.47 /33	0.00	1.45
GR	Diamond Hill Rsrch Opptys A	DHROX	C+		C / 5.1	2.40	7.31	7.82 /61	12.66 /57	13.11 /69	0.05	1.75
GR	Diamond Hill Rsrch Opptys C	DROCX	B-		C / 5.4	2.18	6.86	7.01 /55	11.82 /51	12.57 /65	0.00	2.50
GR	Diamond Hill Rsrch Opptys I	DROIX	B-		C+ / 6.1	2.43	7.42	8.06 /63	12.94 /59	13.29 /71	0.25	1.50
GR	Diamond Hill Rsrch Opptys Y	DROYX	B-		C+ / 6.2	2.47	7.49	8.23 /64	13.13 /61	13.40 /72	0.37	1.36
GR	Diamond Hill Select Fund A	DHTAX	A-	(614) 255-3333	A / 9.4	5.48	11.97	13.98 /89	19.26 /97	14.37 /81	0.35	1.19
GR	Diamond Hill Select Fund C	DHTCX	A-	(614) 255-3333	A / 9.5	5.26	11.52	13.14 /87	18.39 /95	13.52 /73	0.00	1.94
GR	Diamond Hill Select Fund I	DHLTX	A-	(614) 255-3333	A+ / 9.7	5.56	12.07	14.25 /90	19.56 /97	14.69 /84	0.45	0.94
GR	Diamond Hill Select Fund Y	DHTYX	A+		A+ / 9.7	5.56	12.16	14.42 /90	19.73 /98	14.67 /84	0.66	0.80
SC	Diamond Hill Small Cap A	DHSCX	C+	(614) 255-3333	C+ / 6.5	2.73	5.58	5.39 /42	15.66 /80	12.46 /64	0.00	1.32

● Denotes fund is closed to new investors
* Denotes fund is included in Section II

www.thestreetratings.com

RISK			NET ASSETS		ASSET					BULL / BEAR		FUND MANAGER		MINIMUMS		LOADS	
	3 Year		NAV						Portfolio	Last Bull	Last Bear	Manager	Manager	Initial	Additional	Front	Back
Risk	Standard		As of	Total	Cash	Stocks	Bonds	Other	Turnover	Market	Market	Quality	Tenure	Purch.	Purch.	End	End
Rating/Pts	Deviation	Beta	3/31/15	$(Mil)	%	%	%	%	Ratio	Return	Return	Pct	(Years)	$	$	Load	Load
C+ / 6.1	13.4	0.98	38.50	2,241	1	98	0	1	7	108.2	-24.6	80	3	2,000,000	0	0.0	0.0
B- / 7.0	11.3	0.90	25.92	3,844	0	99	0	1	2	119.1	-23.8	89	N/A	2,000,000	0	0.0	0.0
C+ / 6.2	13.4	0.96	33.76	3,749	0	99	0	1	7	116.7	-26.6	88	3	2,000,000	0	0.0	0.0
B- / 7.2	9.9	1.03	22.56	2,418	0	99	0	1	2	100.5	-17.4	62	3	5,000,000	0	0.0	0.0
C+ / 6.6	12.1	1.17	17.01	3,719	0	99	0	1	10	108.2	-24.8	41	3	0	0	0.0	0.0
C / 4.4	14.9	0.94	33.53	35	0	99	0	1	8	101.6	-22.8	95	17	2,000,000	0	0.0	0.0
B- / 7.0	10.4	1.06	18.26	12,357	0	99	0	1	5	105.3	-20.2	64	3	0	0	0.0	0.0
B- / 7.0	10.9	1.10	17.82	14,374	0	99	0	1	6	107.8	-22.0	59	3	0	0	0.0	0.0
U /	N/A	N/A	13.01	536	0	99	0	1	1	N/A	N/A	N/A	2	0	0	0.0	0.0
U /	N/A	N/A	14.83	641	0	99	0	1	8	N/A	N/A	N/A	3	0	0	0.0	0.0
B- / 7.1	11.4	1.13	33.78	15,688	0	99	0	1	15	118.1	-24.0	68	14	2,000,000	0	0.0	0.0
B- / 7.1	11.4	1.13	16.15	171	0	99	0	1	15	119.0	-23.9	70	14	0	0	0.0	0.0
B- / 7.0	11.4	1.13	24.26	2,997	0	99	0	1	15	119.2	-24.0	70	14	0	0	0.0	0.0
B- / 7.3	9.6	1.00	16.31	5,775	0	99	0	1	3	99.7	-16.3	65	3	0	0	0.0	0.0
C+ / 5.8	14.1	1.03	19.96	5,263	0	99	0	1	12	106.0	-24.0	74	3	2,000,000	0	0.0	0.0
U /	N/A	N/A	15.43	220	0	99	0	1	19	N/A	N/A	N/A	3	0	0	0.0	0.0
C+ / 5.9	13.3	0.98	32.33	10,590	0	99	0	1	9	107.6	-24.7	80	3	2,000,000	0	0.0	0.0
C+ / 5.8	14.2	1.02	35.82	12,330	0	99	0	1	9	109.8	-27.8	75	3	2,000,000	0	0.0	0.0
C+ / 6.8	11.3	1.13	13.24	577	0	99	0	1	11	102.7	-22.9	37	3	0	0	0.0	0.0
B- / 7.0	10.5	1.08	16.94	475	0	99	0	1	7	105.4	-20.1	60	3	0	0	0.0	0.0
C+ / 6.0	13.5	1.25	22.98	6,162	0	99	0	1	10	111.0	-27.4	32	3	0	0	0.0	0.0
C+ / 6.0	13.5	1.25	23.01	31	0	99	0	1	10	110.4	-27.5	31	3	0	0	0.0	0.0
C+ / 6.0	13.5	1.25	22.94	94	0	99	0	1	10	109.2	-27.5	29	3	0	0	0.0	0.0
C / 5.5	14.1	1.04	11.21	117	0	99	0	1	0	40.4	-27.8	17	5	0	0	0.0	0.0
B- / 7.5	10.1	0.68	13.49	134	2	97	0	1	0	N/A	N/A	95	N/A	0	0	0.0	0.0
U /	N/A	N/A	10.46	764	1	98	0	1	0	N/A	N/A	N/A	N/A	0	0	0.0	0.0
U /	N/A	N/A	11.91	204	0	99	0	1	0	N/A	N/A	N/A	N/A	0	0	0.0	0.0
C- / 4.2	11.6	1.14	11.82	6	5	94	0	1	40	78.6	-21.8	15	8	1,000	500	0.0	0.0
C / 4.3	11.6	1.14	12.40	22	5	94	0	1	40	85.1	-21.4	24	8	100,000	500	0.0	0.0
C / 4.3	11.6	1.14	12.42	23	5	94	0	1	40	83.1	-21.5	20	8	2,500	500	0.0	0.0
C+ / 6.7	11.6	0.83	11.69	14	0	0	0	100	41	80.9	-22.3	73	5	100,000	500	0.0	0.0
C+ / 6.6	11.6	0.83	11.00	N/A	0	0	0	100	41	78.9	-22.2	70	5	2,500	500	0.0	0.0
C+ / 6.9	12.3	1.02	19.42	11	18	81	0	1	66	104.1	-23.6	43	14	2,500	100	5.0	0.0
C+ / 6.8	12.3	1.02	18.05	2	18	81	0	1	66	99.1	-23.9	32	14	2,500	100	0.0	0.0
C+ / 6.9	12.3	1.02	19.39	16	18	81	0	1	66	106.0	-23.5	47	14	2,500	100	0.0	0.0
B- / 7.1	10.8	1.08	22.72	1,210	0	99	0	1	21	95.1	-17.1	42	13	2,500	100	5.0	0.0
B- / 7.1	10.8	1.08	21.74	84	0	99	0	1	21	90.1	-17.3	32	13	2,500	100	0.0	0.0
B- / 7.1	10.8	1.08	22.85	1,637	0	99	0	1	21	96.8	-17.0	46	13	2,500	100	0.0	0.0
B- / 7.4	10.8	1.08	22.87	421	0	99	0	1	21	97.6	-17.1	48	13	500,000	100	0.0	0.0
B / 8.2	7.7	0.74	23.82	726	34	65	0	1	30	58.4	-12.1	45	15	2,500	100	5.0	0.0
B / 8.2	7.7	0.73	21.89	174	34	65	0	1	30	54.4	-12.4	34	15	2,500	100	0.0	0.0
B / 8.2	7.8	0.74	24.18	2,836	34	65	0	1	30	59.8	-12.1	49	15	2,500	100	0.0	0.0
B / 8.3	7.7	0.73	24.22	294	34	65	0	1	30	60.5	-12.1	52	15	500,000	100	0.0	0.0
B- / 7.8	9.2	0.85	23.06	10	27	72	0	1	72	78.4	-12.5	56	N/A	2,500	100	5.0	0.0
B- / 7.7	9.2	0.84	22.48	1	27	72	0	1	72	74.3	-12.5	45	N/A	2,500	100	0.0	0.0
B- / 7.8	9.2	0.85	23.16	52	27	72	0	1	72	79.8	-12.5	60	N/A	2,500	100	0.0	0.0
B- / 7.8	9.2	0.85	23.20	17	27	72	0	1	72	80.6	-12.5	63	N/A	500,000	100	0.0	0.0
C / 5.5	11.5	1.10	13.67	14	4	95	0	1	70	110.4	-18.5	78	2	2,500	100	5.0	0.0
C / 5.5	11.5	1.10	13.20	9	4	95	0	1	70	105.1	-18.8	72	2	2,500	100	0.0	0.0
C / 5.4	11.5	1.10	13.67	43	4	95	0	1	70	112.0	-18.4	80	2	2,500	100	0.0	0.0
B- / 7.0	11.5	1.10	13.68	10	4	95	0	1	70	113.0	-18.5	81	2	500,000	100	0.0	0.0
C+ / 6.8	10.7	0.73	33.50	591	19	80	0	1	43	84.3	-21.7	90	15	5,000	100	5.0	0.0

Fund Type	Fund Name	Ticker Symbol	Overall Investment Rating	Phone	Performance Rating/Pts	Total Return % through 3/31/15 3 Mo	6 Mo	1Yr / Pct	Annualized 3Yr / Pct	5Yr / Pct	Incl. in Returns Dividend Yield	Expense Ratio
SC	Diamond Hill Small Cap C	DHSMX	C+	(614) 255-3333	C+ / 6.8	2.50	5.18	4.58 /36	14.80 /73	11.61 /58	0.00	2.07
SC	Diamond Hill Small Cap I	DHSIX	B+	(614) 255-3333	B / 7.6	2.78	5.71	5.65 /44	15.96 /83	12.76 /66	0.15	1.07
SC	Diamond Hill Small Cap Y	DHSYX	B+		B / 7.7	2.81	5.77	5.81 /45	16.13 /84	12.76 /66	0.28	0.93
SC	Diamond Hill Small-Mid Cap Fd A	DHMAX	A-	(614) 255-3333	B+ / 8.6	4.20	10.61	9.45 /72	18.02 /94	15.01 /87	0.09	1.25
SC	Diamond Hill Small-Mid Cap Fd C	DHMCX	A	(614) 255-3333	B+ / 8.9	4.01	10.14	8.59 /67	17.13 /90	14.17 /79	0.00	2.00
SC	Diamond Hill Small-Mid Cap Fd I	DHMIX	A+	(614) 255-3333	A / 9.4	4.33	10.77	9.74 /73	18.35 /95	15.34 /89	0.31	1.00
MC	Diamond Hill Small-Mid Cap Fd Y	DHMYX	A+		A / 9.4	4.33	10.83	9.92 /74	18.50 /96	15.32 /89	0.43	0.86
AA	Direxion Hilton Tactical Inc Instl	HCYIX	U	(800) 851-0511	U /	1.13	0.91	4.86 /38	--	--	2.86	1.22
IN	Direxion Idx Managed Futrs Stg Inst	DXMIX	C-	(800) 851-0511	D / 1.9	-1.66	10.76	20.54 /97	1.85 / 6	--	0.00	1.20
IN	Direxion Idx Managed Futures Stg A	DXMAX	D+	(800) 851-0511	D- / 1.2	-1.70	10.64	20.24 /97	1.60 / 6	--	0.00	1.45
IN	Direxion Idx Managed Futures Stg C	DXMCX	D+	(800) 851-0511	D- / 1.5	-1.93	10.16	19.31 /96	0.83 / 5	--	0.00	2.20
OT	Direxion Indexed Commodity Stg A	DXCTX	E	(800) 851-0511	E- / 0.1	-4.14	-5.14	-12.74 / 2	-7.95 / 1	-8.93 / 1	0.00	1.26
OT	Direxion Indexed Commodity Stg C	DXSCX	E	(800) 851-0511	E- / 0.1	-4.39	-5.53	-13.46 / 2	-8.66 / 1	-9.56 / 0	0.00	2.01
OT	Direxion Indexed Commodity Stg Inst	DXCIX	E	(800) 851-0511	E- / 0.1	-4.09	-5.03	-12.57 / 2	-7.75 / 1	-8.72 / 1	0.00	1.01
CV	Direxion Indexed CVT Strategy	DXCBX	U	(800) 851-0511	U /	2.55	7.49	7.65 /60	--	--	0.78	1.51
FO	Direxion Mo China Bull 2X Inv	DXHLX	D+	(800) 851-0511	A+ / 9.9	13.31	36.49	57.81 /99	15.03 /75	0.37 / 3	0.00	1.35
FO	Direxion Mo Emerg Mkts Bull 2X Inv	DXELX	E-	(800) 851-0511	E- / 0.2	2.85	-6.81	-5.58 / 5	-6.66 / 1	-6.60 / 1	0.00	1.35
FO	Direxion Mo Latin America Bl 2X Inv	DXZLX	E-	(800) 851-0511	E- / 0.0	-16.80	-38.20	-39.14 / 0	-29.99 / 0	-21.45 / 0	0.00	1.35
GR	Direxion Mo NASDAQ-100 Bull 2X	DXQLX	C-	(800) 851-0511	A+ / 9.9	4.12	13.60	43.73 /99	33.97 /99	34.51 /99	0.00	1.35
GR	Direxion Mo Natural Res Bull 2X Inv	DXCLX	E-	(800) 851-0511	E- / 0.1	-4.04	-30.13	-31.90 / 0	-7.80 / 1	-3.71 / 1	0.00	1.35
GR	Direxion Mo S&P 500 Bear 2X Inv	DXSSX	E-	(800) 851-0511	E- / 0.0	-3.54	-13.04	-24.53 / 0	-29.46 / 0	-29.11 / 0	0.00	1.35
GR	Direxion Mo S&P 500 Bull 2X Inv	DXSLX	B	(800) 851-0511	A+ / 9.9	0.91	10.44	23.59 /98	30.47 /99	25.55 /99	0.00	1.35
SC	Direxion Mo Small Cap Bear 2X Inv	DXRSX	E-	(800) 851-0511	E- / 0.0	-10.20	-27.16	-23.07 / 1	-32.50 / 0	-33.42 / 0	0.00	1.35
SC	Direxion Mo Small Cap Bull 2X Inv	DXRLX	C-	(800) 851-0511	A+ / 9.9	7.91	28.99	13.04 /87	30.96 /99	25.33 /99	0.00	1.35
BA	Disciplined Growth Investors I	DGIFX	B-	(855) 344-3863	C+ / 6.0	1.46	9.53	12.15 /83	12.67 /57	--	0.52	0.79
IN	Discretionary Mngd Futures Strat A	FUTEX	U		U /	0.96	0.89	4.07 /32	--	--	0.64	10.75
BA	Dividend Plus Income Fund Inst	MAIPX	C-	(877) 414-7884	D / 1.9	1.25	2.01	4.46 /35	6.10 /17	--	0.30	1.25
BA	Dividend Plus Income Fund Inv	DIVPX	C-	(877) 414-7884	D / 1.8	1.21	1.91	4.19 /33	5.91 /16	--	0.00	3.48
* GL	Dodge & Cox Global Stock	DODWX	C+	(800) 621-3979	C+ / 6.8	1.44	0.11	4.57 /36	15.42 /78	10.81 /51	1.25	0.65
* FO ●	Dodge & Cox International Stock	DODFX	C-	(800) 621-3979	C / 4.9	4.20	-0.66	1.48 /20	12.25 /54	7.99 /30	2.21	0.64
* GI	Dodge & Cox Stk Fund	DODGX	A	(800) 621-3979	B+ / 8.5	-1.19	0.99	6.50 /51	18.20 /95	13.81 /76	1.39	0.52
FO	Domini International Social Eq A	DOMAX	C-	(800) 498-1351	C- / 4.2	5.95	4.36	2.05 /22	12.29 /55	8.42 /33	0.99	1.82
FO	Domini International Social Eq Inst	DOMOX	U	(800) 498-1351	U /	6.11	4.58	2.54 /24	--	--	1.44	1.16
FO	Domini International Social Eq Inv	DOMIX	C-	(800) 498-1351	C / 4.9	5.83	4.29	2.00 /22	12.24 /54	8.40 /32	1.05	1.62
GR	Domini Social Equity A	DSEPX	D-	(800) 498-1351	C+ / 5.7	1.12	4.46	12.09 /83	13.96 /67	13.42 /72	5.12	1.54
GR	Domini Social Equity Inst	DIEQX	C+	(800) 498-1351	C+ / 6.7	1.18	4.59	12.45 /85	14.39 /70	13.82 /76	2.79	0.81
GR	Domini Social Equity Inv	DSEFX	C+	(800) 498-1351	C+ / 6.4	1.11	4.41	12.02 /83	13.92 /66	13.35 /72	1.11	1.20
GR	Domini Social Equity R	DSFRX	D-	(800) 498-1351	C+ / 6.7	1.23	4.60	12.40 /84	14.31 /69	13.74 /75	6.33	0.90
AA	DoubleLine Multi-Asset Growth A	DMLAX	D	(877) 354-6311	D- / 1.1	3.74	5.86	5.96 /46	3.80 /10	--	3.52	1.93
AA	DoubleLine Multi-Asset Growth I	DMLIX	D	(877) 354-6311	D / 1.7	3.90	6.09	6.22 /48	4.11 /10	--	3.91	1.68
IN	DoubleLine Shiller Enhanced CAPE I	DSEEX	U	(877) 354-6311	U /	2.70	8.91	16.96 /94	--	--	2.80	1.38
IN	DoubleLine Shiller Enhanced CAPE	DSENX	U	(877) 354-6311	U /	2.56	8.70	16.60 /94	--	--	2.58	1.63
SC	Dreman Contrarian Small Cp Val A	DRSAX	C+	(800) 408-4682	C+ / 6.5	3.94	9.54	5.71 /44	15.45 /79	11.93 /60	0.66	1.41
SC	Dreman Contrarian Small Cp Val Inst	DRISX	B-	(800) 408-4682	B / 7.7	3.96	9.56	5.94 /46	15.59 /80	12.12 /61	0.97	1.16
SC	Dreman Contrarian Small Cp Val Rtl	DRSVX	C+	(800) 408-4682	B- / 7.4	3.93	9.48	5.71 /44	15.38 /78	11.90 /60	0.75	1.41
MC	Dreyfus Active MidCap A	DNLDX	A+	(800) 782-6620	A+ / 9.6	5.86	12.40	18.36 /96	19.57 /97	14.96 /86	0.23	1.15
MC	Dreyfus Active MidCap C	DNLCX	A+	(800) 782-6620	A+ / 9.7	5.63	11.93	17.36 /95	18.55 /96	13.99 /78	0.00	2.04
MC	Dreyfus Active MidCap I	DNLRX	A+	(800) 782-6620	A+ / 9.8	5.89	12.51	18.60 /96	19.80 /98	15.12 /88	0.68	0.95
GI	Dreyfus Alternative Dvfsr Strat Y	DRYNX	U	(800) 645-6561	U /	3.65	5.16	6.08 /47	--	--	1.37	2.19
GR	Dreyfus Appreciation Inv	DGAGX	C-	(800) 645-6561	C- / 3.9	-0.15	1.92	7.46 /59	9.63 /37	11.45 /56	1.64	0.94
BA	Dreyfus Balanced Opport A	DBOAX	C	(800) 645-6561	C- / 4.0	1.90	4.83	7.83 /62	11.14 /46	9.79 /43	0.75	1.32
BA	Dreyfus Balanced Opport C	DBOCX	C+	(800) 645-6561	C / 4.4	1.76	4.47	7.08 /56	10.32 /41	8.97 /36	0.07	2.05

RISK			NET ASSETS		ASSET				Portfolio	BULL / BEAR		FUND MANAGER		MINIMUMS		LOADS	
Risk Rating/Pts	3 Year		NAV As of 3/31/15	Total $(Mil)	Cash %	Stocks %	Bonds %	Other %	Portfolio Turnover Ratio	Last Bull Market Return	Last Bear Market Return	Manager Quality Pct	Manager Tenure (Years)	Initial Purch. $	Additional Purch. $	Front End Load	Back End Load
	Standard Deviation	Beta															
C+ / 6.6	10.7	0.73	29.96	57	19	80	0	1	43	79.7	-22.0	88	15	5,000	100	0.0	0.0
C+ / 6.8	10.7	0.73	33.96	764	19	80	0	1	43	85.9	-21.6	91	15	5,000	100	0.0	0.0
C+ / 6.8	10.6	0.73	33.98	140	19	80	0	1	43	86.7	-21.7	91	15	500,000	100	0.0	0.0
C+ / 6.6	11.3	0.78	19.10	105	7	92	0	1	35	102.4	-21.4	93	10	2,500	100	5.0	0.0
C+ / 6.6	11.3	0.78	17.90	26	7	92	0	1	35	97.1	-21.6	92	10	2,500	100	0.0	0.0
C+ / 6.6	11.3	0.78	19.27	366	7	92	0	1	35	103.9	-21.2	94	10	2,500	100	0.0	0.0
B- / 7.0	11.4	0.98	19.29	440	7	92	0	1	35	104.9	-21.4	82	10	500,000	100	0.0	0.0
U /	N/A	N/A	15.80	46	0	0	0	100	58	N/A	N/A	N/A	N/A	250,000	100	0.0	1.0
B / 8.2	9.8	-0.18	42.54	63	100	0	0	0	0	N/A	N/A	93	3	5,000,000	0	0.0	1.0
B / 8.2	9.8	-0.19	42.23	35	100	0	0	0	0	N/A	N/A	92	3	2,500	0	5.5	1.0
B / 8.2	9.8	-0.19	41.21	9	100	0	0	0	0	N/A	N/A	90	3	2,500	0	0.0	0.0
C / 5.0	7.4	0.40	16.44	11	100	0	0	0	0	-26.7	-25.4	1	7	2,500	0	5.5	1.0
C / 4.7	7.4	0.40	15.88	3	100	0	0	0	0	-28.5	-25.7	1	7	2,500	0	0.0	0.0
C / 5.1	7.4	0.40	16.63	46	100	0	0	0	0	-26.1	-25.4	1	7	5,000,000	0	0.0	1.0
U /	N/A	N/A	45.85	71	50	0	49	1	0	N/A	N/A	N/A	1	25,000	500	0.0	0.0
E- / 0.0	37.5	1.64	49.79	6	100	0	0	0	0	98.3	-56.1	55	8	25,000	500	0.0	0.0
E- / 0.0	30.1	1.84	44.35	4	100	0	0	0	0	20.7	-53.8	0	10	25,000	500	0.0	0.0
E- / 0.0	44.4	2.37	16.84	7	100	0	0	0	0	-40.4	-50.6	0	9	25,000	500	0.0	0.0
E- / 0.0	23.5	2.12	56.64	137	100	0	0	0	0	310.1	-21.3	33	9	25,000	500	0.0	0.0
E- / 0.0	30.9	1.99	44.17	7	100	0	0	0	0	9.0	-51.8	0	10	25,000	500	0.0	0.0
E- / 0.0	19.7	-2.03	29.20	13	100	0	0	0	0	-79.8	37.8	12	9	25,000	500	0.0	0.0
C- / 4.0	19.3	2.00	90.97	56	100	0	0	0	0	253.6	-31.5	23	9	25,000	500	0.0	0.0
E- / 0.0	27.9	-2.04	30.75	9	100	0	0	0	0	-83.1	64.8	2	11	25,000	500	0.0	0.0
E- / 0.0	27.3	2.00	53.18	92	100	0	0	0	0	255.3	-45.8	24	11	25,000	500	0.0	0.0
B- / 7.8	8.8	1.36	16.91	112	4	72	23	1	10	79.8	N/A	35	4	10,000	0	0.0	2.0
U /	N/A	N/A	10.49	27	27	0	72	1	48	N/A	N/A	N/A	2	2,500	500	5.8	1.0
B / 8.0	4.8	0.80	10.75	108	52	47	0	1	203	35.3	-7.3	32	5	50,000	5,000	0.0	0.0
B / 8.0	4.9	0.81	10.87	1	52	47	0	1	203	34.3	-7.4	29	5	2,500	100	0.0	0.0
C+ / 6.1	12.0	0.83	12.00	6,260	3	96	0	1	24	89.9	-24.3	96	N/A	2,500	100	0.0	0.0
C / 5.4	13.8	1.01	43.88	68,696	1	98	0	1	13	67.2	-25.7	86	11	2,500	100	0.0	0.0
B- / 7.0	10.9	1.08	176.55	60,672	1	98	0	1	15	111.5	-21.6	73	N/A	2,500	100	0.0	0.0
C+ / 5.8	13.0	0.97	8.19	37	0	99	0	1	232	65.7	-24.4	88	6	2,500	100	4.8	2.0
U /	N/A	N/A	7.82	51	0	99	0	1	232	N/A	N/A	N/A	6	1,000,000	0	0.0	2.0
C+ / 5.8	13.0	0.97	7.80	260	0	99	0	1	232	65.5	-24.5	88	6	2,500	100	0.0	2.0
D / 1.8	10.3	1.05	10.67	10	0	99	0	1	86	88.2	-16.1	30	6	2,500	100	4.8	2.0
C / 5.4	10.4	1.05	26.23	260	0	99	0	1	86	90.6	-15.9	34	6	1,000,000	0	0.0	2.0
C+ / 6.6	10.4	1.05	45.92	784	0	99	0	1	86	87.9	-16.1	28	6	2,500	100	0.0	2.0
D- / 1.2	10.4	1.05	9.50	57	0	99	0	1	86	90.0	-15.9	33	6	0	0	0.0	2.0
B- / 7.4	4.9	0.67	9.78	84	28	16	54	2	150	14.6	-0.1	23	5	2,000	100	4.3	1.0
B- / 7.4	4.9	0.67	9.81	43	28	16	54	2	150	15.6	N/A	27	5	100,000	100	0.0	1.0
U /	N/A	N/A	12.13	301	7	0	91	2	0	N/A	N/A	N/A	2	100,000	100	0.0	0.0
U /	N/A	N/A	12.12	78	7	0	91	2	0	N/A	N/A	N/A	2	2,000	100	0.0	0.0
C / 5.5	12.5	0.89	22.44	4	5	94	0	1	37	94.6	-27.1	76	9	2,500	1,000	5.8	0.0
C / 5.5	12.4	0.88	22.56	88	5	94	0	1	37	95.2	-26.8	78	9	100,000	1,000	0.0	0.0
C / 5.5	12.4	0.88	22.48	65	5	94	0	1	37	94.1	-27.0	77	9	2,500	1,000	0.0	0.0
C+ / 6.9	11.6	1.02	59.40	517	0	99	0	1	75	115.6	-24.0	83	3	1,000	100	5.8	0.0
C+ / 6.9	11.6	1.02	55.90	6	0	99	0	1	75	109.3	-24.3	77	3	1,000	100	0.0	0.0
B- / 7.0	11.6	1.02	59.86	10	0	99	0	1	75	116.9	-24.0	85	3	1,000	100	0.0	0.0
U /	N/A	N/A	13.07	428	26	44	28	2	0	N/A	N/A	N/A	1	1,000,000	0	0.0	0.0
B- / 7.0	10.5	1.06	52.53	4,555	0	99	0	1	6	65.9	-12.5	5	25	2,500	100	0.0	0.0
B- / 7.4	7.0	1.20	21.41	187	4	62	33	1	110	62.5	-14.4	40	8	1,000	100	5.8	0.0
B- / 7.5	7.0	1.19	21.44	34	4	62	33	1	110	58.4	-14.7	31	8	1,000	100	0.0	0.0

99 Pct = Best
0 Pct = Worst

Fund Type	Fund Name	Ticker Symbol	Overall Investment Rating	Phone	Performance Rating/Pts	3 Mo	6 Mo	1Yr / Pct	3Yr / Pct	5Yr / Pct	Dividend Yield	Expense Ratio
								Total Return % through 3/31/15	Annualized		Incl. in Returns	
BA	Dreyfus Balanced Opport I	DBORX	C+	(800) 645-6561	C / 5.1	1.95	4.96	8.10 /64	11.41 /48	10.07 /45	1.05	1.05
BA	● Dreyfus Balanced Opport J	THPBX	C+	(800) 645-6561	C / 5.1	1.95	4.95	8.10 /64	11.37 /48	10.01 /45	1.04	1.03
BA	Dreyfus Balanced Opport Z	DBOZX	C+	(800) 645-6561	C / 5.0	1.96	4.96	8.03 /63	11.25 /47	9.86 /43	0.99	1.17
IX	Dreyfus Basic S&P 500 Stock Idx	DSPIX	A	(800) 645-6561	B / 8.1	0.90	5.82	12.51 /85	15.90 /83	14.27 /80	1.68	0.21
GI	Dreyfus Conservative Allocation Fd	SCALX	C-	(800) 645-6561	D / 2.1	1.61	2.60	4.37 /34	6.35 /18	6.59 /21	2.15	1.20
GR	Dreyfus Core Equity A	DLTSX	D+	(800) 645-6561	D+ / 2.4	-0.66	1.04	6.56 /51	8.86 /32	10.82 /51	1.10	1.36
GR	Dreyfus Core Equity C	DPECX	D+	(800) 645-6561	D+ / 2.8	-0.86	0.63	5.75 /44	8.04 /27	10.00 /44	0.44	2.11
GR	Dreyfus Core Equity I	DPERX	C-	(800) 645-6561	C- / 3.5	-0.63	1.14	6.79 /53	9.13 /34	11.10 /53	1.39	1.11
GI	Dreyfus Disciplined Stock Fund	DDSTX	C-	(800) 645-6561	C+ / 6.2	1.97	6.23	9.92 /74	13.07 /60	11.56 /57	0.68	1.01
FO	Dreyfus Divers Intl A	DFPAX	D-	(800) 782-6620	D- / 1.5	4.66	0.18	0.35 /17	7.17 /22	4.81 /11	1.66	1.88
FO	Dreyfus Divers Intl C	DFPCX	D-	(800) 782-6620	D / 1.8	4.47	-0.19	-0.36 /15	6.38 /18	4.04 / 8	1.07	2.36
FO	Dreyfus Divers Intl I	DFPIX	D	(800) 782-6620	D+ / 2.4	4.84	0.41	0.76 /18	7.54 /24	5.09 /12	2.06	0.95
EM	Dreyfus Diversified Emerg Mkt A	DBEAX	E	(800) 645-6561	E / 0.4	1.43	-2.28	1.82 /21	0.53 / 5	1.17 / 3	0.58	5.27
EM	Dreyfus Diversified Emerg Mkt C	DBECX	E	(800) 645-6561	E / 0.4	1.34	-2.58	1.13 /19	-0.19 / 4	0.43 / 3	0.00	6.57
EM	Dreyfus Diversified Emerg Mkt I	SBCEX	E	(800) 645-6561	E+ / 0.6	1.65	-1.88	2.38 /23	0.94 / 5	1.71 / 4	0.85	4.04
EM	Dreyfus Diversified Emerg Mkt Y	SBYEX	U	(800) 645-6561	U /	1.64	-1.93	2.42 /24	--	--	0.85	1.76
GL	Dreyfus Dynamic Total Return A	AVGAX	B	(800) 782-6620	C / 4.8	5.33	8.53	14.67 /91	10.30 /41	9.15 /38	0.00	1.54
GL	Dreyfus Dynamic Total Return C	AVGCX	B	(800) 782-6620	C / 5.3	5.17	8.15	13.81 /89	9.46 /36	8.34 /32	0.00	2.30
GL	Dreyfus Dynamic Total Return I	AVGRX	B	(800) 782-6620	C+ / 6.0	5.43	8.72	14.93 /91	10.62 /43	9.51 /41	0.00	1.21
GL	Dreyfus Dynamic Total Return Y	AVGYX	U	(800) 782-6620	U /	5.50	8.74	15.11 /92	--	--	0.00	1.16
EM	Dreyfus Emerging Markets A	DRFMX	E	(800) 782-6620	E- / 0.2	-0.97	-9.51	-3.78 / 7	-2.70 / 2	-2.02 / 2	0.88	1.87
EM	Dreyfus Emerging Markets C	DCPEX	E	(800) 782-6620	E- / 0.2	-1.10	-9.89	-4.44 / 6	-3.43 / 2	-2.79 / 1	0.13	2.65
EM	Dreyfus Emerging Markets I	DRPEX	E	(800) 782-6620	E / 0.3	-0.86	-9.43	-3.43 / 8	-2.44 / 3	-1.79 / 2	1.41	1.60
EM	Dreyfus Emerging Markets Y	DYPEX	U	(800) 782-6620	U /	-0.86	-9.32	-2.82 / 9	--	--	1.62	1.42
IN	Dreyfus Equity Income A	DQIAX	C+	(800) 782-6620	C / 5.2	-0.53	3.43	8.72 /68	13.56 /64	13.54 /73	2.40	1.21
IN	Dreyfus Equity Income C	DQICX	B-	(800) 782-6620	C+ / 5.6	-0.79	3.03	7.85 /62	12.70 /57	12.68 /66	1.93	2.00
IN	Dreyfus Equity Income I	DQIRX	B-	(800) 782-6620	C+ / 6.3	-0.49	3.54	8.97 /69	13.84 /66	13.81 /76	2.79	0.96
GI	Dreyfus Fund Incorporated	DREVX	C+	(800) 645-6561	C+ / 6.9	1.68	4.99	9.95 /74	14.45 /70	12.35 /63	0.59	0.74
EM	Dreyfus Global Emerging Markets Y	DGEYX	U	(800) 645-6561	U /	2.00	-1.29	6.17 /48	--	--	0.33	1.70
GL	Dreyfus Global Equity Income A	DEQAX	D	(800) 782-6620	D / 2.1	1.38	0.05	1.10 /19	8.78 /32	9.46 /40	2.94	1.30
GL	Dreyfus Global Equity Income C	DEQCX	D+	(800) 782-6620	D+ / 2.4	1.24	-0.35	0.38 /17	7.96 /27	8.66 /34	2.29	2.04
GL	Dreyfus Global Equity Income I	DQEIX	C-	(800) 782-6620	C- / 3.1	1.41	0.18	1.33 /19	9.05 /33	9.72 /42	3.51	1.04
GL	Dreyfus Global Equity Income Y	DEQYX	U	(800) 782-6620	U /	1.51	0.21	1.48 /20	--	--	3.57	0.96
RE	Dreyfus Global Real Estate Sec A	DRLAX	C	(800) 645-6561	C+ / 5.9	4.59	12.87	16.34 /94	11.52 /49	10.79 /51	2.08	1.45
RE	Dreyfus Global Real Estate Sec C	DGBCX	C	(800) 645-6561	C+ / 6.3	4.32	12.32	15.43 /92	10.71 /44	9.97 /44	1.43	2.24
RE	Dreyfus Global Real Estate Sec I	DRLIX	C+	(800) 645-6561	B- / 7.2	4.64	13.05	16.56 /94	11.85 /51	11.15 /54	2.47	1.02
RE	Dreyfus Global Real Estate Sec Y	DRLYX	U	(800) 645-6561	U /	4.64	12.93	16.57 /94	--	--	2.48	1.02
GL	Dreyfus Global Real Return A	DRRAX	D+	(800) 782-6620	D- / 1.1	2.27	2.75	4.76 /37	5.05 /13	--	4.34	1.20
GL	Dreyfus Global Real Return C	DRRCX	D+	(800) 782-6620	D- / 1.3	2.10	2.33	4.01 /32	4.29 /11	--	4.16	1.96
GL	Dreyfus Global Real Return I	DRRIX	C-	(800) 782-6620	D / 1.8	2.34	2.87	5.02 /39	5.38 /14	--	4.85	0.90
GL	Dreyfus Global Real Return Y	DRRYX	U	(800) 782-6620	U /	2.34	2.89	5.03 /39	--	--	4.87	0.88
GL	● Dreyfus Global Stock CL A	DGLAX	D+	(800) 782-6620	D+ / 2.5	1.36	1.59	4.75 /37	9.06 /33	8.61 /34	0.63	1.24
GL	● Dreyfus Global Stock CL C	DGLCX	D+	(800) 782-6620	D+ / 2.9	1.17	1.20	3.96 /31	8.23 /28	7.78 /28	0.00	2.01
GL	● Dreyfus Global Stock CL I	DGLRX	C-	(800) 782-6620	C- / 3.6	1.40	1.74	5.09 /39	9.42 /36	8.98 /37	1.09	0.91
GL	● Dreyfus Global Stock CL Y	DGLYX	U	(800) 782-6620	U /	1.46	1.75	5.10 /39	--	--	1.10	0.90
FO	● Dreyfus Greater China A	DPCAX	E+	(800) 782-6620	D- / 1.4	4.31	0.38	2.81 /25	6.98 /21	-0.78 / 2	0.00	1.83
FO	● Dreyfus Greater China C	DPCCX	E+	(800) 782-6620	D / 1.6	4.09	-0.03	2.02 /22	6.16 /17	-1.53 / 2	0.00	2.59
FO	● Dreyfus Greater China I	DPCRX	D-	(800) 782-6620	D / 2.2	4.37	0.48	3.07 /27	7.26 /23	-0.52 / 2	0.00	1.55
GI	Dreyfus Growth Allocation Fund	SGALX	C	(800) 645-6561	C- / 4.0	2.10	3.92	6.19 /48	9.66 /37	8.84 /36	1.58	1.55
GI	Dreyfus Growth and Income	DGRIX	B+	(800) 645-6561	B+ / 8.4	2.29	6.20	10.08 /75	16.53 /87	14.54 /83	0.60	0.92
FO	Dreyfus Intl Equity A	DIEAX	D	(800) 782-6620	D+ / 2.9	5.40	-0.66	-2.51 / 9	10.76 /44	7.76 /28	1.29	1.40
FO	Dreyfus Intl Equity C	DIECX	D+	(800) 782-6620	C- / 3.3	5.20	-1.02	-3.26 / 8	9.91 /39	6.92 /22	0.62	2.17

● Denotes fund is closed to new investors
* Denotes fund is included in Section II

www.thestreetratings.com

Risk Rating/Pts	Standard Deviation (3 Year)	Beta	NAV As of 3/31/15	Total $(Mil)	Cash %	Stocks %	Bonds %	Other %	Portfolio Turnover Ratio	Last Bull Market Return	Last Bear Market Return	Manager Quality Pct	Manager Tenure (Years)	Initial Purch. $	Additional Purch. $	Front End Load	Back End Load
B- / 7.4	7.0	1.19	21.44	4	4	62	33	1	110	63.9	-14.4	44	8	1,000	100	0.0	0.0
B- / 7.4	7.0	1.20	21.44	19	4	62	33	1	110	63.7	-14.4	43	8	1,000	100	0.0	0.0
B- / 7.4	7.0	1.20	21.33	40	4	62	33	1	110	62.8	-14.4	41	8	1,000	100	0.0	0.0
B- / 7.2	9.5	1.00	42.57	2,294	1	97	0	2	5	99.0	-16.3	65	13	10,000	1,000	0.0	0.0
B / 8.6	5.1	0.48	15.76	38	0	42	57	1	20	33.6	-8.6	51	6	2,500	100	0.0	0.0
C+ / 7.0	10.6	1.07	21.66	107	0	99	0	1	1	62.6	-12.7	4	17	1,000	100	5.8	0.0
C+ / 6.9	10.6	1.07	21.24	127	0	99	0	1	1	58.5	-13.0	3	17	1,000	100	0.0	0.0
C+ / 7.0	10.6	1.07	22.13	85	0	99	0	1	1	64.0	-12.6	4	17	1,000	100	0.0	0.0
C / 4.5	10.7	1.09	35.17	591	0	99	0	1	69	84.2	-21.0	16	11	2,500	100	0.0	0.0
C+ / 6.2	12.0	0.90	11.46	12	2	97	0	1	9	44.3	-23.3	48	6	1,000	100	5.8	0.0
C+ / 6.2	12.0	0.90	11.45	N/A	2	97	0	1	9	40.6	-23.4	37	6	1,000	100	0.0	0.0
C+ / 6.2	12.1	0.91	11.48	653	2	97	0	1	9	45.8	-23.2	53	6	1,000	100	0.0	0.0
C / 4.8	14.1	1.02	20.52	N/A	4	95	0	1	129	22.4	-29.1	65	1	1,000	100	5.8	2.0
C / 4.8	14.1	1.01	19.71	N/A	4	95	0	1	129	19.4	-29.3	54	1	1,000	100	0.0	2.0
C / 4.8	14.1	1.02	20.38	2	4	95	0	1	129	24.3	-28.9	70	1	1,000	100	0.0	2.0
U /	N/A	N/A	20.41	199	4	95	0	1	129	N/A	N/A	N/A	1	1,000,000	0	0.0	2.0
B / 8.8	7.0	0.99	16.41	127	22	3	73	2	124	49.1	-11.4	79	5	1,000	100	5.8	0.0
B / 8.8	7.0	0.99	15.66	63	22	3	73	2	124	45.2	-11.6	73	5	1,000	100	0.0	0.0
B / 8.8	7.0	0.99	16.70	231	22	3	73	2	124	50.6	-11.2	81	5	1,000	100	0.0	0.0
U /	N/A	N/A	16.68	458	22	3	73	2	124	N/A	N/A	N/A	5	1,000,000	0	0.0	0.0
C / 4.9	15.7	1.11	9.19	82	2	97	0	1	52	12.2	-28.1	20	19	1,000	100	5.8	2.0
C / 4.9	15.7	1.11	8.99	11	2	97	0	1	52	9.3	-28.4	14	19	1,000	100	0.0	2.0
C / 4.9	15.7	1.10	9.21	384	2	97	0	1	52	13.2	-28.0	23	19	1,000	100	0.0	2.0
U /	N/A	N/A	9.21	60	2	97	0	1	52	N/A	N/A	N/A	19	1,000,000	0	0.0	2.0
B- / 7.7	9.5	0.93	17.70	214	0	99	0	1	20	79.3	-10.3	50	4	1,000	100	5.8	0.0
B- / 7.7	9.4	0.92	17.47	18	0	99	0	1	20	74.7	-10.5	39	4	1,000	100	0.0	0.0
B- / 7.7	9.4	0.92	17.76	30	0	99	0	1	20	80.8	-10.1	55	4	1,000	100	0.0	0.0
C+ / 5.8	10.3	1.04	11.71	1,507	0	99	0	1	73	90.6	-20.2	37	10	2,500	100	0.0	0.0
U /	N/A	N/A	14.30	101	3	96	0	1	31	N/A	N/A	N/A	1	1,000,000	0	0.0	2.0
B- / 7.0	9.2	0.65	12.31	90	4	95	0	1	33	52.4	-13.3	87	8	1,000	100	5.8	0.0
B- / 7.0	9.2	0.65	12.52	47	4	95	0	1	33	48.7	-13.5	83	8	1,000	100	0.0	0.0
B- / 7.0	9.2	0.65	11.89	113	4	95	0	1	33	53.8	-13.2	88	8	1,000	100	0.0	0.0
U /	N/A	N/A	11.89	25	4	95	0	1	33	N/A	N/A	N/A	8	1,000,000	0	0.0	0.0
C / 5.2	12.4	0.92	9.58	14	11	88	0	1	50	68.4	-19.2	48	9	1,000	100	5.8	0.0
C / 5.2	12.3	0.91	9.41	1	11	88	0	1	50	64.3	-19.3	38	9	1,000	100	0.0	0.0
C / 5.2	12.4	0.92	9.47	159	11	88	0	1	50	70.0	-18.9	52	9	1,000,000	0	0.0	0.0
U /	N/A	N/A	9.47	613	11	88	0	1	50	N/A	N/A	N/A	9	1,000,000	0	0.0	0.0
B / 8.4	4.5	0.22	14.85	64	8	55	34	3	47	21.2	-7.2	88	5	1,000	100	5.8	0.0
B / 8.5	4.5	0.22	14.56	15	8	55	34	3	47	18.2	-7.5	85	5	1,000	100	0.0	0.0
B / 8.4	4.5	0.22	14.90	80	8	55	34	3	47	22.5	-7.1	89	5	1,000	100	0.0	0.0
U /	N/A	N/A	14.90	309	8	55	34	3	47	N/A	N/A	N/A	5	1,000,000	0	0.0	0.0
C+ / 6.8	9.7	0.70	18.62	51	1	98	0	1	7	57.6	-14.1	86	9	1,000	100	5.8	0.0
C+ / 6.8	9.7	0.70	18.23	18	1	98	0	1	7	53.4	-14.4	81	9	1,000	100	0.0	0.0
C+ / 6.8	9.7	0.70	18.84	1,442	1	98	0	1	7	59.3	-14.0	87	9	1,000	100	0.0	0.0
U /	N/A	N/A	18.82	380	1	98	0	1	7	N/A	N/A	N/A	9	1,000,000	0	0.0	0.0
C / 5.3	16.0	0.63	39.91	109	0	100	0	0	157	35.7	-42.3	77	17	1,000	100	5.8	2.0
C / 5.2	16.0	0.63	34.89	58	0	100	0	0	157	32.1	-42.5	70	17	1,000	100	0.0	2.0
C / 5.3	16.1	0.63	41.57	35	0	100	0	0	157	36.8	-42.2	79	17	1,000	100	0.0	2.0
B- / 7.7	7.9	0.79	17.98	25	0	75	23	2	27	55.7	-15.7	30	6	2,500	100	0.0	0.0
C+ / 6.2	10.8	1.09	21.14	941	0	99	0	1	50	104.4	-20.4	53	7	2,500	100	0.0	0.0
C+ / 6.0	13.7	1.02	34.96	69	3	96	0	1	89	62.7	-24.9	76	5	1,000	100	5.8	0.0
C+ / 6.0	13.6	1.02	35.20	9	3	96	0	1	89	58.5	-25.1	69	5	1,000	100	0.0	0.0

	99 Pct = Best 0 Pct = Worst				PERFORMANCE						Incl. in Returns	
						Total Return % through 3/31/15						
			Overall		Perfor-				Annualized		Dividend	Expense
Fund		Ticker	Investment		mance							
Type	Fund Name	Symbol	Rating	Phone	Rating/Pts	3 Mo	6 Mo	1Yr / Pct	3Yr / Pct	5Yr / Pct	Yield	Ratio
FO	Dreyfus Intl Equity I	DIERX	C-	(800) 782-6620	C- / 4.0	5.47	-0.52	-2.23 /10	11.08 /46	8.05 /30	1.45	1.04
FO	● Dreyfus Intl Stk CL A	DISAX	D-	(800) 782-6620	E+ / 0.9	3.70	0.60	1.54 /20	4.82 /13	4.98 /12	0.91	1.30
FO	● Dreyfus Intl Stk CL C	DISCX	D-	(800) 782-6620	D- / 1.1	3.54	0.28	0.82 /18	4.03 /10	4.21 / 9	0.20	2.04
FO	● Dreyfus Intl Stk CL I	DISRX	D-	(800) 782-6620	D- / 1.5	3.75	0.75	1.88 /21	5.18 /14	5.34 /13	1.49	0.92
FO	● Dreyfus Intl Stk CL Y	DISYX	U	(800) 782-6620	U /	3.79	0.79	1.66 /21	--	--	1.54	0.91
FO	Dreyfus Intl Stock Index	DIISX	D	(800) 645-6561	D+ / 2.8	5.29	0.67	-1.57 /11	8.47 /30	5.65 /15	2.66	0.61
FO	Dreyfus Intl Value A	DVLAX	E+	(800) 782-6620	D- / 1.0	5.73	-1.56	-5.18 / 5	6.32 /18	2.39 / 5	1.06	1.59
FO	Dreyfus Intl Value C	DICVX	E+	(800) 782-6620	D- / 1.2	5.59	-1.98	-5.85 / 5	5.49 /15	1.61 / 4	0.24	2.37
FO	Dreyfus Intl Value I	DIRVX	D-	(800) 782-6620	D / 1.7	5.87	-1.40	-4.82 / 6	6.74 /20	2.81 / 6	1.71	1.20
GR	Dreyfus Inv Core Value I		B+	(800) 645-6561	B+ / 8.9	1.66	5.87	9.57 /72	17.70 /93	13.01 /68	0.80	1.02
GR	Dreyfus Inv Core Value S		B+	(800) 645-6561	B+ / 8.7	1.58	5.76	9.26 /71	17.42 /92	12.73 /66	0.53	1.27
MC	Dreyfus Inv MidCap Stock I		B+	(800) 645-6561	A+ / 9.6	4.47	9.51	14.24 /90	18.86 /96	16.83 /96	0.58	0.86
MC	Dreyfus Inv MidCap Stock S		B+	(800) 645-6561	A / 9.5	4.40	9.40	13.98 /89	18.56 /96	16.57 /95	0.43	1.11
GR	Dreyfus Inv Tech Growth Fund I		D+	(800) 645-6561	C+ / 5.6	3.41	6.85	8.72 /68	11.88 /52	14.99 /87	0.00	0.85
GR	Dreyfus Inv Tech Growth Fund S		D+	(800) 645-6561	C / 5.4	3.31	6.68	8.42 /66	11.59 /50	14.68 /84	0.00	1.10
GR	Dreyfus LgCap Eq A	DLQAX	B	(800) 782-6620	B- / 7.1	4.03	7.12	13.00 /87	15.54 /79	13.06 /69	0.65	1.19
GR	Dreyfus LgCap Eq C	DEYCX	B+	(800) 782-6620	B- / 7.5	3.85	6.69	12.12 /83	14.70 /72	12.25 /62	0.13	2.03
GR	Dreyfus LgCap Eq I	DLQIX	A	(800) 782-6620	B+ / 8.5	4.17	7.35	13.44 /88	16.00 /83	13.54 /73	0.96	0.78
GR	Dreyfus Lrg Cap Gr A	DAPAX	B	(800) 645-6561	B+ / 8.9	4.77	9.11	18.53 /96	17.51 /92	14.47 /82	0.06	1.50
GR	Dreyfus Lrg Cap Gr C	DGTCX	B	(800) 645-6561	A- / 9.2	4.62	8.69	17.76 /95	16.70 /88	13.65 /74	0.00	2.31
GR	Dreyfus Lrg Cap Gr Inst	DAPIX	B+	(800) 645-6561	A+ / 9.6	4.85	9.35	18.95 /96	17.91 /94	14.93 /86	0.26	1.14
MC	Dreyfus Mid Cap Growth A	FRSDX	C	(800) 645-6561	C+ / 5.9	3.89	6.98	8.92 /69	14.03 /67	15.35 /89	0.00	1.36
MC	Dreyfus Mid Cap Growth C	FRSCX	C+	(800) 645-6561	C+ / 6.3	3.76	6.70	8.16 /64	13.15 /61	14.51 /82	0.00	2.14
MC	● Dreyfus Mid Cap Growth F	FRSPX	C+	(800) 645-6561	B- / 7.0	3.97	7.19	9.20 /70	14.25 /69	15.56 /90	0.00	1.19
MC	Dreyfus Mid Cap Growth I	FRSRX	C+	(800) 645-6561	B- / 7.1	4.10	7.21	9.34 /71	14.34 /70	15.69 /91	0.00	1.13
MC	Dreyfus MidCap Index Fund	PESPX	A	(800) 645-6561	B+ / 8.9	5.18	11.75	11.75 /81	16.49 /87	15.18 /88	0.96	0.51
BA	Dreyfus Moderate Allocation Fund	SMDAX	C	(800) 645-6561	C- / 3.0	1.86	3.16	5.24 /40	7.89 /26	7.62 /27	1.90	1.19
EN	Dreyfus Natural Resources A	DNLAX	E	(800) 782-6620	E+ / 0.6	-0.95	-6.86	-7.53 / 4	4.29 /11	5.29 /13	0.70	1.58
EN	Dreyfus Natural Resources C	DLDCX	E	(800) 782-6620	E+ / 0.6	-1.14	-7.22	-8.21 / 3	3.49 / 9	4.50 /10	0.17	2.39
EN	Dreyfus Natural Resources I	DLDRX	E+	(800) 782-6620	E+ / 0.8	-0.93	-6.76	-7.30 / 4	4.54 /12	5.57 /15	0.95	1.35
FO	Dreyfus Newton Intl Equity Fd A	NIEAX	D	(800) 645-6561	D+ / 2.8	5.83	2.67	3.28 /28	9.38 /35	6.32 /19	1.77	1.30
FO	Dreyfus Newton Intl Equity Fd C	NIECX	D+	(800) 645-6561	C- / 3.2	5.44	2.19	2.50 /24	8.52 /30	5.49 /14	1.86	2.04
FO	Dreyfus Newton Intl Equity Fd I	SNIEX	C-	(800) 645-6561	C- / 3.9	5.72	2.76	3.52 /29	9.70 /37	6.63 /21	2.66	0.96
FO	Dreyfus Newton Intl Equity Fd Y	NIEYX	U	(800) 645-6561	U /	5.74	2.80	3.66 /30	--	--	3.16	0.91
MC	Dreyfus Opportunistic Midcap Val A	DMCVX	B	(800) 645-6561	B / 7.7	1.04	8.22	6.43 /50	17.61 /93	14.94 /86	0.10	1.15
MC	Dreyfus Opportunistic Midcap Val C	DVLCX	B	(800) 645-6561	B / 8.1	0.84	7.82	5.65 /44	16.70 /88	14.03 /78	0.00	1.92
MC	Dreyfus Opportunistic Midcap Val I	DVLIX	A-	(800) 645-6561	B+ / 8.9	1.10	8.36	6.73 /53	17.87 /94	15.21 /88	0.33	0.90
MC	Dreyfus Opportunistic Midcap Val Y	DMCYX	U	(800) 645-6561	U /	1.15	8.44	7.08 /56	--	--	0.45	0.83
SC	● Dreyfus Opportunistic Small Cap	DSCVX	C-	(800) 645-6561	B / 7.7	2.45	11.58	2.51 /24	16.07 /84	13.60 /74	0.00	1.10
GR	Dreyfus Opportunistic US Stock A	DOSAX	B+	(800) 645-6561	B / 8.1	2.85	6.21	5.63 /43	18.41 /95	--	0.00	1.86
GR	Dreyfus Opportunistic US Stock C	DOSCX	A-	(800) 645-6561	B+ / 8.5	2.65	5.85	4.84 /37	17.50 /92	--	0.00	2.75
GR	Dreyfus Opportunistic US Stock I	DOSIX	A	(800) 645-6561	A- / 9.1	2.83	6.33	5.91 /46	18.68 /96	--	0.00	1.61
GR	Dreyfus Research Growth A	DWOAX	C+	(800) 645-6561	C+ / 6.4	2.87	6.28	9.67 /73	15.03 /75	14.84 /86	0.00	1.18
GR	Dreyfus Research Growth C	DWOCX	C+	(800) 645-6561	C+ / 6.8	2.62	5.86	8.82 /68	14.14 /68	13.93 /77	0.00	1.95
GR	Dreyfus Research Growth I	DWOIX	B+	(800) 645-6561	B / 7.6	2.85	6.37	9.91 /74	15.31 /77	15.16 /88	0.05	0.86
GR	Dreyfus Research Growth Y	DRYQX	U	(800) 645-6561	U /	2.92	6.44	10.06 /75	--	--	0.11	0.92
GR	● Dreyfus Research Growth Z	DREQX	B+	(800) 645-6561	B / 7.6	2.89	6.40	9.90 /74	15.24 /77	15.09 /87	0.01	0.95
GL	Dreyfus Research LngSht Equity A	DLSAX	U	(800) 645-6561	U /	0.86	1.10	-0.39 /14	--	--	0.00	3.56
GL	Dreyfus Research LngSht Equity Y	DLYYX	U	(800) 645-6561	U /	0.94	1.25	-0.08 /15	--	--	0.00	3.32
IX	Dreyfus S&P 500 Index Fund	PEOPX	B+	(800) 645-6561	B / 7.8	0.81	5.66	12.16 /83	15.55 /80	13.92 /77	1.52	0.51
GR	Dreyfus Select Managers L/S Y	DBNYX	U	(800) 645-6561	U /	3.44	2.85	0.96 /18	--	--	0.00	2.75
GR	Dreyfus Select Managers SmCap Gro	DSGAX	C-	(800) 782-6620	C+ / 6.1	4.83	13.69	3.99 /32	14.44 /70	--	0.00	1.38

● Denotes fund is closed to new investors
* Denotes fund is included in Section II

196

RISK Risk Rating/Pts	Standard Deviation (3 Year)	Beta	NAV As of 3/31/15	Total $(Mil)	Cash %	Stocks %	Bonds %	Other %	Portfolio Turnover Ratio	Last Bull Market Return	Last Bear Market Return	Manager Quality Pct	Manager Tenure (Years)	Initial Purch. $	Additional Purch. $	Front End Load	Back End Load
C+ / 6.0	13.6	1.02	35.31	242	3	96	0	1	89	64.3	-24.8	79	5	1,000	100	0.0	0.0
C+ / 6.5	11.3	0.81	15.13	124	1	98	0	1	12	35.2	-18.5	29	9	1,000	100	5.8	0.0
C+ / 6.5	11.4	0.82	14.90	22	1	98	0	1	12	31.8	-18.8	20	9	1,000	100	0.0	0.0
C+ / 6.5	11.4	0.81	15.22	1,618	1	98	0	1	12	37.0	-18.4	32	9	1,000	100	0.0	0.0
U /	N/A	N/A	15.06	1,619	1	98	0	1	12	N/A	N/A	N/A	9	1,000,000	0	0.0	0.0
C+ / 5.7	13.3	1.00	16.32	595	2	97	0	1	10	49.7	-23.4	52	8	2,500	100	0.0	0.0
C / 5.5	14.3	1.05	12.00	41	1	98	0	1	65	39.2	-25.3	20	13	1,000	100	5.8	0.0
C / 5.5	14.2	1.05	11.90	6	1	98	0	1	65	35.6	-25.5	15	13	1,000	100	0.0	0.0
C / 5.4	14.2	1.05	11.90	41	1	98	0	1	65	41.2	-25.2	25	13	1,000	100	0.0	0.0
C+ / 5.9	11.2	1.12	18.31	22	0	100	0	0	67	112.0	-24.5	61	14	0	0	0.0	0.0
C+ / 6.0	11.2	1.12	18.45	13	0	100	0	0	67	110.4	-24.7	57	14	0	0	0.0	0.0
C / 5.1	11.9	1.04	20.26	164	0	99	0	1	83	116.2	-23.1	76	3	0	0	0.0	0.0
C / 5.1	11.8	1.04	20.22	43	0	99	0	1	83	114.4	-23.1	74	3	0	0	0.0	0.0
C- / 4.0	15.2	1.23	17.32	89	2	97	0	1	72	85.4	-19.3	4	8	0	0	0.0	0.0
C- / 3.9	15.2	1.23	16.64	195	2	97	0	1	72	83.8	-19.4	4	8	0	0	0.0	0.0
C+ / 6.7	10.4	1.06	16.77	3	0	98	0	2	67	96.4	-20.4	47	12	1,000	100	5.8	0.0
C+ / 6.7	10.4	1.05	16.98	1	0	98	0	2	67	91.2	-20.6	37	12	1,000	100	0.0	0.0
C+ / 6.7	10.4	1.06	17.62	463	0	98	0	2	67	98.9	-20.2	53	12	1,000	100	0.0	0.0
C / 4.8	11.2	1.06	9.18	10	1	98	0	1	77	103.5	-18.8	71	10	1,000	100	5.8	0.0
C / 4.7	11.2	1.06	8.92	1	1	98	0	1	77	98.9	-19.3	62	10	1,000	100	0.0	0.0
C / 4.9	11.2	1.06	9.42	29	1	98	0	1	77	106.0	-18.7	74	10	1,000	100	0.0	0.0
C+ / 5.7	11.9	0.99	8.63	25	1	98	0	1	166	83.8	-16.7	31	5	1,000	100	5.8	0.0
C+ / 5.7	11.9	1.00	7.54	13	1	98	0	1	166	79.3	-17.1	21	5	1,000	100	0.0	0.0
C+ / 5.7	11.8	0.99	8.98	102	1	98	0	1	166	85.1	-16.9	33	5	1,000	100	0.0	0.0
C+ / 5.8	11.8	0.99	8.97	14	1	98	0	1	166	85.5	-16.8	35	5	1,000	100	0.0	0.0
C+ / 6.4	11.0	1.00	39.52	3,732	2	97	0	1	16	99.6	-22.7	61	15	2,500	100	0.0	0.0
B / 8.4	6.5	1.10	16.99	77	0	59	40	1	18	43.7	-12.0	18	6	2,500	100	0.0	0.0
C / 4.9	14.1	0.79	29.08	54	3	96	0	1	103	39.7	-27.2	79	6	1,000	100	5.8	0.0
C / 4.9	14.1	0.79	26.99	9	3	96	0	1	103	36.1	-27.5	72	6	1,000	100	0.0	0.0
C / 4.9	14.1	0.79	29.85	37	3	96	0	1	103	40.9	-27.2	80	6	1,000	100	0.0	0.0
C+ / 6.1	11.2	0.82	20.16	4	2	97	0	1	39	51.2	-21.9	81	10	1,000	100	5.8	0.0
C+ / 6.1	11.2	0.83	19.76	1	2	97	0	1	39	47.2	-22.2	74	10	1,000	100	0.0	0.0
C+ / 6.0	11.2	0.83	19.97	32	2	97	0	1	39	52.8	-21.9	83	10	1,000	100	0.0	0.0
U /	N/A	N/A	19.88	809	2	97	0	1	39	N/A	N/A	N/A	10	1,000,000	0	0.0	0.0
C+ / 6.0	12.6	1.05	39.85	1,296	1	98	0	1	67	118.2	-27.9	63	12	1,000	100	5.8	0.0
C+ / 5.9	12.6	1.05	37.04	125	1	98	0	1	67	112.5	-28.1	51	12	1,000	100	0.0	0.0
C+ / 6.0	12.6	1.05	39.65	1,062	1	98	0	1	67	119.8	-27.8	66	12	1,000	100	0.0	0.0
U /	N/A	N/A	39.75	87	1	98	0	1	67	N/A	N/A	N/A	12	1,000,000	0	0.0	0.0
D+ / 2.9	16.1	1.13	31.42	890	1	98	0	1	89	118.3	-34.1	34	10	2,500	100	0.0	0.0
C+ / 6.5	12.4	1.11	20.22	13	0	99	0	1	111	N/A	N/A	71	4	1,000	100	5.8	0.0
C+ / 6.5	12.4	1.10	19.78	1	0	99	0	1	111	N/A	N/A	62	4	1,000	100	0.0	0.0
C+ / 6.5	12.4	1.11	20.33	7	0	99	0	1	111	N/A	N/A	73	4	1,000	100	0.0	0.0
C+ / 6.5	10.7	1.01	14.35	566	2	97	0	1	46	94.8	-19.3	50	10	1,000	100	5.8	0.0
C+ / 6.5	10.7	1.01	13.69	134	2	97	0	1	46	89.7	-19.6	39	10	1,000	100	0.0	0.0
C+ / 6.5	10.7	1.02	14.43	306	2	97	0	1	46	96.6	-19.2	53	10	1,000	100	0.0	0.0
U /	N/A	N/A	14.44	264	2	97	0	1	46	N/A	N/A	N/A	10	1,000,000	0	0.0	0.0
C+ / 6.5	10.7	1.01	14.60	436	2	97	0	1	46	95.8	-19.1	52	10	1,000	100	0.0	0.0
U /	N/A	N/A	12.86	28	78	21	0	1	205	N/A	N/A	N/A	2	1,000	100	5.8	0.0
U /	N/A	N/A	12.92	70	78	21	0	1	205	N/A	N/A	N/A	2	1,000,000	0	0.0	0.0
C+ / 6.9	9.5	1.00	52.11	2,876	1	97	0	2	4	97.0	-16.4	61	15	2,500	100	0.0	0.0
U /	N/A	N/A	12.62	300	34	65	0	1	313	N/A	N/A	N/A	1	1,000,000	0	0.0	0.0
C- / 4.0	14.4	1.08	24.74	5	1	98	0	1	121	86.4	-20.4	29	5	1,000	100	5.8	0.0

					PERFORMANCE								
	99 Pct = Best			Overall		Perfor-	Total Return % through 3/31/15					Incl. in Returns	
	0 Pct = Worst			Investment		mance				Annualized		Dividend	Expense
Fund Type	Fund Name	Ticker Symbol	Rating	Phone	Rating/Pts	3 Mo	6 Mo	1Yr / Pct	3Yr / Pct	5Yr / Pct	Yield	Ratio
GR	Dreyfus Select Managers SmCap Gro	DSGCX	C-	(800) 782-6620	C+ / 6.5	4.66	13.30	3.26 /28	13.60 /64	--	0.00	2.34
GR	Dreyfus Select Managers SmCap Gro	DSGIX	C	(800) 782-6620	B- / 7.4	4.97	13.90	4.38 /34	14.80 /73	--	0.00	0.98
SC	Dreyfus Select Managers SmCap Gro	DSGYX	U	(800) 782-6620	U /	4.97	13.91	4.34 /34	--	--	0.00	1.16
SC	Dreyfus Select Managers SmCap Val	DMVAX	C	(800) 645-6561	C+ / 6.5	3.11	10.41	4.32 /34	15.52 /79	13.86 /76	0.02	1.33
SC	Dreyfus Select Managers SmCap Val	DMECX	C	(800) 645-6561	C+ / 6.9	2.94	10.04	3.61 /29	14.69 /72	13.02 /68	0.00	2.16
SC	Dreyfus Select Managers SmCap Val	DMVIX	C+	(800) 645-6561	B / 7.8	3.16	10.58	4.64 /36	15.94 /83	14.24 /80	0.21	0.95
SC	Dreyfus Select Managers SmCap Val	DMVYX	U	(800) 645-6561	U /	3.16	10.59	4.68 /36	--	--	0.24	1.01
SC	Dreyfus Small Cap Eqty A	DSEAX	C-	(800) 782-6620	B- / 7.0	5.80	11.41	9.73 /73	15.24 /77	12.36 /63	0.00	1.40
SC	Dreyfus Small Cap Eqty C	DSECX	C-	(800) 782-6620	B- / 7.4	5.58	10.97	8.87 /69	14.30 /69	11.44 /56	0.00	2.17
SC	Dreyfus Small Cap Eqty I	DSERX	C+	(800) 782-6620	B+ / 8.3	5.86	11.56	10.00 /74	15.55 /80	12.65 /65	0.00	1.04
SC	Dreyfus Small Cap Stock Index Fd	DISSX	A-	(800) 645-6561	B+ / 8.9	4.01	14.22	8.53 /66	16.93 /89	15.95 /93	0.75	0.51
GR	Dreyfus Socially Resp Growth I		C+	(800) 645-6561	B- / 7.4	1.55	5.31	11.90 /82	14.89 /74	14.00 /78	1.01	0.86
GR	Dreyfus Socially Resp Growth S		C+	(800) 645-6561	B- / 7.2	1.49	5.16	11.60 /81	14.60 /72	13.72 /75	0.79	1.11
GI	Dreyfus Stock Index Fund I		A-	(800) 645-6561	B / 8.0	0.87	5.80	12.43 /84	15.82 /82	14.19 /79	1.72	0.29
GI	Dreyfus Stock Index Fund S		A-	(800) 645-6561	B / 7.8	0.83	5.66	12.16 /83	15.53 /79	13.90 /77	1.47	0.54
GR	Dreyfus Strategic Value A	DAGVX	B	(800) 782-6620	B / 7.8	1.63	5.86	9.64 /73	17.58 /93	13.12 /69	0.77	1.12
GR	Dreyfus Strategic Value C	DCGVX	B+	(800) 782-6620	B+ / 8.3	1.43	5.47	8.80 /68	16.69 /88	12.28 /62	0.16	1.88
GR	Dreyfus Strategic Value I	DRGVX	A-	(800) 782-6620	A- / 9.0	1.68	5.99	9.90 /74	17.88 /94	13.41 /72	1.07	0.84
GR	Dreyfus Strategic Value Y	DRGYX	U	(800) 782-6620	U /	1.68	5.99	9.90 /74	--	--	1.07	0.78
MC	Dreyfus Structure Midcap A	DPSAX	B+	(800) 782-6620	A- / 9.1	5.14	10.21	14.30 /90	18.63 /96	16.49 /95	0.39	1.25
MC	Dreyfus Structure Midcap C	DPSCX	B+	(800) 782-6620	A / 9.3	4.97	9.81	13.44 /88	17.76 /93	15.67 /91	0.00	1.98
MC	Dreyfus Structure Midcap I	DPSRX	A-	(800) 782-6620	A+ / 9.6	5.23	10.35	14.56 /91	18.95 /97	16.74 /95	0.63	1.16
GR	Dreyfus Tax Mgd Growth A	DTMGX	D+	(800) 782-6620	D+ / 2.3	-0.73	1.04	6.53 /51	8.55 /30	11.09 /53	1.04	1.36
GR	Dreyfus Tax Mgd Growth C	DPTAX	D+	(800) 782-6620	D+ / 2.6	-0.93	0.64	5.74 /44	7.74 /26	10.26 /47	0.46	2.11
GR	Dreyfus Tax Mgd Growth I	DPTRX	C-	(800) 782-6620	C- / 3.3	-0.69	1.17	6.82 /54	8.81 /32	11.36 /56	1.37	1.11
TC	Dreyfus Tech Growth A	DTGRX	D-	(800) 782-6620	C / 4.4	3.20	6.56	8.24 /64	11.51 /49	14.65 /84	0.00	1.26
TC	Dreyfus Tech Growth C	DTGCX	D-	(800) 782-6620	C / 4.7	2.97	6.10	7.35 /58	10.58 /43	13.69 /75	0.00	2.10
TC	Dreyfus Tech Growth I	DGVRX	D	(800) 782-6620	C / 5.5	3.24	6.68	8.49 /66	11.80 /51	15.00 /87	0.00	1.05
GR	Dreyfus Third Century A	DTCAX	C+	(800) 782-6620	C+ / 6.0	1.50	5.11	11.52 /81	14.40 /70	13.45 /72	0.62	1.22
GR	Dreyfus Third Century C	DTCCX	C+	(800) 782-6620	C+ / 6.4	1.27	4.73	10.68 /77	13.51 /63	12.64 /65	0.16	1.99
GR	Dreyfus Third Century I	DRTCX	B	(800) 782-6620	B- / 7.3	1.55	5.25	11.87 /82	14.76 /73	13.88 /77	0.90	0.91
GR	● Dreyfus Third Century Z	DRTHX	B	(800) 782-6620	B- / 7.2	1.55	5.21	11.76 /82	14.64 /72	13.75 /75	0.80	1.01
EM	Dreyfus TOBAM Emerging Markets Y	DABNX	U	(800) 645-6561	U /	2.40	-4.73	-3.81 / 7	--	--	1.40	1.84
EM	Dreyfus Total Emerging Markets A	DTMAX	E+	(800) 645-6561	E / 0.3	-0.36	-6.46	-2.81 / 9	-1.32 / 3	--	1.76	1.71
EM	Dreyfus Total Emerging Markets C	DTMCX	E+	(800) 645-6561	E / 0.3	-0.64	-6.84	-3.58 / 8	-2.07 / 3	--	1.12	2.44
EM	Dreyfus Total Emerging Markets I	DTEIX	E+	(800) 645-6561	E / 0.3	-0.36	-6.34	-2.61 / 9	-1.10 / 3	--	2.18	1.35
IN	● Dreyfus US Equity Fd A	DPUAX	C-	(800) 782-6620	C- / 3.9	1.42	5.07	6.56 /51	11.13 /46	11.36 /56	0.38	1.15
IN	● Dreyfus US Equity Fd C	DPUCX	C	(800) 782-6620	C / 4.3	1.26	4.65	5.80 /45	10.26 /41	10.47 /48	0.00	2.02
IN	● Dreyfus US Equity Fd I	DPUIX	C+	(800) 782-6620	C / 5.1	1.52	5.23	6.98 /55	11.55 /49	11.77 /59	0.81	0.79
GR	● Dreyfus US Equity Fd Y	DPUYX	U	(800) 782-6620	U /	1.52	5.24	6.62 /52	--	--	0.83	0.76
GL	Dreyfus Wrldwde Growth A	PGROX	D+	(800) 782-6620	D+ / 2.3	0.80	1.76	5.16 /40	8.68 /31	10.79 /51	1.53	1.17
GL	Dreyfus Wrldwde Growth C	PGRCX	D+	(800) 782-6620	D+ / 2.7	0.62	1.38	4.39 /34	7.88 /26	9.98 /44	1.09	1.91
GL	Dreyfus Wrldwde Growth I	DPWRX	C-	(800) 782-6620	C- / 3.4	0.87	1.88	5.44 /42	8.97 /33	11.09 /53	1.87	0.91
FS	Dreyfus Yield Enhancement Strat Y	DABJX	U	(800) 645-6561	U /	1.71	2.12	4.25 /33	--	--	3.36	0.76
SC	Dreyfus/Boston Co Sm Cap Growth I	SSETX	D+	(800) 221-4795	A / 9.4	7.78	18.77	9.15 /70	17.40 /92	15.41 /90	0.00	1.15
SC	● Dreyfus/Boston Co Sm Cap Value I	STSVX	D-	(800) 221-4795	C+ / 6.3	1.45	9.02	1.84 /21	14.22 /69	12.44 /64	0.44	0.96
SC	Dreyfus/Boston Co Sm/Mid Cap Gro	DBMAX	C	(800) 645-6561	B- / 7.3	6.58	12.10	10.10 /75	15.49 /79	16.27 /94	0.00	1.04
SC	Dreyfus/Boston Co Sm/Mid Cap Gro	DBMCX	C	(800) 645-6561	B / 7.6	6.30	11.65	9.15 /70	14.50 /71	15.26 /89	0.00	1.83
SC	Dreyfus/Boston Co Sm/Mid Cap Gro I	SDSCX	B-	(800) 645-6561	B+ / 8.6	6.62	12.23	10.33 /76	15.78 /82	16.59 /95	0.00	0.80
SC	Dreyfus/Boston Co Sm/Mid Cap Gro	DBMYX	U	(800) 645-6561	U /	6.67	12.34	10.44 /76	--	--	0.00	0.72
GI	● Driehaus Active Income Fund	LCMAX	D	(800) 560-6111	E+ / 0.7	1.40	0.81	0.08 /16	2.03 / 6	1.88 / 4	2.95	1.14
EM	Driehaus Emerging Markets Growth	DREGX	E+	(800) 560-6111	E+ / 0.8	3.21	-2.73	-2.49 / 9	3.88 /10	5.11 /12	0.00	1.66

● Denotes fund is closed to new investors
* Denotes fund is included in Section II

www.thestreetratings.com

RISK			NET ASSETS		ASSET						BULL / BEAR		FUND MANAGER		MINIMUMS		LOADS	
	3 Year		NAV							Portfolio	Last Bull	Last Bear	Manager	Manager	Initial	Additional	Front	Back
Risk Rating/Pts	Standard Deviation	Beta	As of 3/31/15	Total $(Mil)	Cash %	Stocks %	Bonds %	Other %		Turnover Ratio	Market Return	Market Return	Quality Pct	Tenure (Years)	Purch. $	Purch. $	End Load	End Load
C- / 3.9	14.4	1.08	23.79	N/A	1	98	0	1		121	81.9	-20.7	21	5	1,000	100	0.0	0.0
C- / 4.0	14.4	1.08	25.14	24	1	98	0	1		121	88.3	-20.3	33	5	1,000	100	0.0	0.0
U /	N/A	N/A	25.12	573	1	98	0	1		121	N/A	N/A	N/A	5	1,000,000	0	0.0	0.0
C / 4.6	13.3	0.97	23.10	3	3	96	0	1		104	98.4	-25.6	65	7	1,000	100	5.8	0.0
C / 4.3	13.4	0.97	21.80	N/A	3	96	0	1		104	93.4	-25.8	53	7	1,000	100	0.0	0.0
C / 4.6	13.4	0.97	23.41	21	3	96	0	1		104	100.8	-25.4	69	7	1,000	100	0.0	0.0
U /	N/A	N/A	23.39	791	3	96	0	1		104	N/A	N/A	N/A	7	1,000,000	0	0.0	0.0
C- / 3.9	11.8	0.83	28.36	45	1	98	0	1		67	98.4	-26.3	82	15	1,000	100	5.8	0.0
C- / 3.2	11.8	0.83	24.51	10	1	98	0	1		67	92.9	-26.5	75	15	1,000	100	0.0	0.0
C- / 4.1	11.8	0.83	29.54	7	1	98	0	1		67	100.2	-26.2	83	15	1,000	100	0.0	0.0
C+ / 6.0	12.8	0.94	30.09	1,882	1	98	0	1		18	106.5	-22.2	81	15	2,500	100	0.0	0.0
C / 5.3	10.4	1.06	40.45	268	1	98	0	1		45	93.5	-16.6	37	4	0	0	0.0	0.0
C / 5.3	10.4	1.06	40.13	11	1	98	0	1		45	91.8	-16.7	34	4	0	0	0.0	0.0
B- / 7.2	9.6	1.00	43.94	1,902	0	99	0	1		2	98.6	-16.4	63	15	0	0	0.0	0.0
B- / 7.2	9.5	1.00	43.99	216	0	99	0	1		2	96.9	-16.5	60	15	0	0	0.0	0.0
C+ / 6.1	11.2	1.12	40.44	949	0	99	0	1		67	110.9	-24.5	59	14	1,000	100	5.8	0.0
C+ / 6.1	11.2	1.12	38.31	58	0	99	0	1		67	105.6	-24.8	47	14	1,000	100	0.0	0.0
C+ / 6.0	11.2	1.12	40.49	411	0	99	0	1		67	112.7	-24.4	63	14	1,000	100	0.0	0.0
U /	N/A	N/A	40.49	233	0	99	0	1		67	N/A	N/A	N/A	14	1,000,000	0	0.0	0.0
C / 5.3	12.1	1.06	30.66	130	0	99	0	1		75	113.6	-23.2	71	4	1,000	100	5.8	0.0
C / 5.1	12.1	1.06	27.86	34	0	99	0	1		75	108.4	-23.4	62	4	1,000	100	0.0	0.0
C / 5.3	12.1	1.07	31.20	78	0	99	0	1		75	115.1	-23.1	74	4	1,000	100	0.0	0.0
B- / 7.0	10.5	1.05	25.71	79	0	99	0	1		2	61.2	-11.0	4	18	1,000	100	5.8	0.0
B- / 7.0	10.5	1.05	24.38	34	0	99	0	1		2	57.1	-11.4	3	18	1,000	100	0.0	0.0
B- / 7.0	10.5	1.05	25.76	70	0	99	0	1		2	62.6	-11.0	4	18	1,000	100	0.0	0.0
C- / 3.1	15.4	1.24	41.22	233	3	96	0	1		70	85.1	-19.6	3	8	1,000	100	5.8	0.0
D+ / 2.5	15.4	1.24	34.65	27	3	96	0	1		70	79.9	-19.8	3	8	1,000	100	0.0	0.0
C- / 3.4	15.4	1.24	44.27	17	3	96	0	1		70	86.9	-19.4	4	8	1,000	100	0.0	0.0
C+ / 6.7	10.4	1.06	14.21	23	0	99	0	1		34	90.5	-16.7	32	3	1,000	100	5.8	0.0
C+ / 6.6	10.4	1.07	12.80	7	0	99	0	1		34	85.6	-17.0	22	3	1,000	100	0.0	0.0
C+ / 6.7	10.4	1.06	14.45	12	0	99	0	1		34	92.5	-16.5	36	3	1,000	100	0.0	0.0
C+ / 6.7	10.4	1.06	14.45	291	0	99	0	1		34	91.9	-16.6	34	3	1,000	100	0.0	0.0
U /	N/A	N/A	11.53	27	0	99	0	1		45	N/A	N/A	N/A	N/A	1,000,000	0	0.0	2.0
C / 5.4	11.9	0.85	11.01	1	3	71	24	2		97	14.7	-21.1	39	4	1,000	100	5.8	2.0
C / 5.5	11.9	0.85	10.90	1	3	71	24	2		97	11.9	-21.3	29	4	1,000	100	0.0	2.0
C / 5.3	11.9	0.85	11.01	73	3	71	24	2		97	15.8	-21.0	42	4	1,000	100	0.0	2.0
C+ / 6.9	9.0	0.88	19.98	2	1	98	0	1		12	71.9	-14.2	29	7	1,000	100	5.8	0.0
C+ / 6.9	9.0	0.88	19.24	N/A	1	98	0	1		12	67.3	-14.5	20	7	1,000	100	0.0	0.0
C+ / 6.9	9.1	0.89	20.04	31	1	98	0	1		12	74.2	-14.0	33	7	1,000	100	0.0	0.0
U /	N/A	N/A	20.04	711	1	98	0	1		12	N/A	N/A	N/A	7	1,000,000	0	0.0	0.0
C+ / 6.8	11.0	0.74	53.89	461	0	99	0	1		2	61.5	-14.2	81	22	1,000	100	5.8	0.0
C+ / 6.8	11.0	0.74	48.89	69	0	99	0	1		2	57.4	-14.5	76	22	1,000	100	0.0	0.0
C+ / 6.8	11.0	0.74	54.32	140	0	99	0	1		2	62.9	-14.1	83	22	1,000	100	0.0	0.0
U /	N/A	N/A	12.63	385	46	0	53	1		14	N/A	N/A	N/A	1	1,000,000	0	0.0	0.0
E / 0.4	14.0	0.98	39.21	28	2	97	0	1		138	98.8	-22.9	79	N/A	1,000	100	0.0	0.0
E+ / 0.8	13.4	0.98	24.43	307	0	0	0	100		68	98.9	-24.8	44	15	1,000	100	0.0	0.0
C / 4.3	11.8	0.82	17.82	248	0	99	0	1		139	98.3	-18.1	85	10	1,000	100	5.8	0.0
C- / 4.0	11.8	0.82	16.54	36	0	99	0	1		139	92.6	-18.5	78	10	1,000	100	0.0	0.0
C / 4.4	11.8	0.82	18.19	556	0	99	0	1		139	100.1	-18.1	86	10	1,000	100	0.0	0.0
U /	N/A	N/A	18.22	111	0	99	0	1		139	N/A	N/A	N/A	10	1,000,000	0	0.0	0.0
B- / 7.6	1.8	0.10	10.45	3,659	16	6	74	4		48	14.5	-9.1	73	10	25,000	5,000	0.0	0.0
C / 5.2	12.9	0.90	30.59	1,760	8	91	0	1		264	31.1	-22.2	89	7	10,000	2,000	0.0	2.0

Fund Type	Fund Name	Ticker Symbol	Overall Investment Rating	Phone	Performance Rating/Pts	3 Mo	6 Mo	1Yr / Pct	3Yr / Pct	5Yr / Pct	Dividend Yield	Expense Ratio
EM	Driehaus Emg Mkts Sm Cap Growth	DRESX	C-	(800) 560-6111	C / 4.6	4.24	2.15	3.30 / 28	11.79 / 51	10.35 / 47	0.00	1.85
IN	Driehaus Event Driven	DEVDX	U	(800) 560-6111	U /	4.44	1.01	-5.02 / 5	--	--	0.62	1.56
FO	● Driehaus Intl SmCap Gr Fd	DRIOX	D-	(800) 560-6111	C- / 3.9	6.09	3.90	-0.60 / 14	10.62 / 43	9.77 / 43	0.57	1.73
SC	Driehaus Micro Cap Growth	DMCRX	B	(800) 560-6111	A+ / 9.9	6.76	24.57	8.64 / 67	23.98 / 99	17.54 / 97	0.00	1.49
GL	DSM Global Growth Institutional	DSMGX	A-	(877) 862-9555	B / 7.7	6.29	9.54	12.01 / 83	14.81 / 73	--	0.27	5.92
GR	DSM Large Cap Growth Inst	DSMLX	B+	(877) 862-9555	A- / 9.0	4.53	11.92	15.84 / 93	16.47 / 87	16.11 / 93	0.00	1.07
GR	Dunham Alternative Strategy A	DAASX	D+	(888) 338-6426	E+ / 0.6	1.48	5.30	6.30 / 49	0.64 / 5	1.45 / 4	0.00	2.35
GR	Dunham Alternative Strategy C	DCASX	D	(888) 338-6426	E+ / 0.6	1.30	4.92	5.49 / 42	-0.10 / 4	0.70 / 3	0.00	3.10
GR	Dunham Alternative Strategy N	DNASX	D+	(888) 338-6426	E+ / 0.9	1.58	5.48	6.60 / 52	0.91 / 5	1.73 / 4	0.00	2.10
GI	Dunham Appreciation & Income A	DAAIX	D-	(888) 338-6426	D+ / 2.8	4.15	3.96	7.55 / 59	8.72 / 31	8.52 / 33	1.22	1.63
GI	Dunham Appreciation & Income C	DCAIX	D-	(888) 338-6426	C- / 3.2	3.98	3.49	6.71 / 53	7.88 / 26	7.69 / 28	0.56	2.38
GI	Dunham Appreciation & Income N	DNAIX	D	(888) 338-6426	C- / 3.9	4.15	4.01	7.69 / 60	8.98 / 33	8.77 / 35	1.51	1.38
GR	Dunham Dynamic Macro A	DAAVX	D+	(888) 338-6426	E+ / 0.7	3.69	6.64	6.45 / 50	2.16 / 6	--	0.50	4.30
GR	Dunham Dynamic Macro C	DCAVX	D+	(888) 338-6426	E+ / 0.9	3.55	6.32	5.70 / 44	1.42 / 6	--	0.36	5.05
GR	Dunham Dynamic Macro N	DNAVX	D+	(888) 338-6426	D- / 1.1	3.80	6.77	6.76 / 53	2.45 / 7	--	0.69	4.05
EM	Dunham Emerging Markets Stock A	DAEMX	E+	(888) 338-6426	E / 0.4	0.15	-2.68	1.87 / 21	-0.26 / 4	-0.17 / 2	1.12	1.58
EM	Dunham Emerging Markets Stock C	DCEMX	E+	(888) 338-6426	E / 0.4	-0.08	-3.04	1.01 / 18	-1.02 / 3	-0.94 / 2	0.55	2.33
EM	Dunham Emerging Markets Stock N	DNEMX	E+	(888) 338-6426	E / 0.5	0.22	-2.57	2.03 / 22	-0.05 / 4	0.06 / 2	1.37	1.33
GR	Dunham Focused Large Cap Growth	DAFGX	C-	(888) 338-6426	C+ / 5.9	7.48	10.16	12.02 / 83	12.85 / 58	--	0.00	1.29
GR	Dunham Focused Large Cap Growth	DCFGX	C	(888) 338-6426	C+ / 6.2	7.31	9.81	11.22 / 79	11.98 / 52	--	0.00	2.04
GR	Dunham Focused Large Cap Growth	DNFGX	C+	(888) 338-6426	B- / 7.0	7.63	10.36	12.37 / 84	13.11 / 60	--	0.00	1.04
FO	Dunham International Stock A	DAINX	D	(888) 338-6426	D+ / 2.9	6.44	2.47	2.01 / 22	9.58 / 37	6.84 / 22	1.57	2.29
FO	Dunham International Stock C	DCINX	D	(888) 338-6426	C- / 3.3	6.27	2.13	1.24 / 19	8.79 / 32	6.04 / 17	1.06	3.04
FO	Dunham International Stock N	DNINX	D+	(888) 338-6426	C- / 4.0	6.58	2.64	2.30 / 23	9.89 / 39	7.12 / 24	1.94	2.04
GI	Dunham Large Cap Value A	DALVX	C	(888) 338-6426	C / 4.4	-0.55	1.40	6.08 / 47	12.71 / 58	11.22 / 55	0.51	1.51
GI	Dunham Large Cap Value C	DCLVX	C+	(888) 338-6426	C / 4.8	-0.75	1.09	5.34 / 41	11.88 / 52	10.40 / 48	0.00	2.26
GI	Dunham Large Cap Value N	DNLVX	C+	(888) 338-6426	C+ / 5.6	-0.49	1.60	6.41 / 50	13.02 / 60	11.50 / 57	0.74	1.26
IN	Dunham Monthly Distribution Class A	DAMDX	D+	(888) 338-6426	E+ / 0.9	1.66	1.27	3.41 / 29	4.67 / 12	5.22 / 13	2.87	2.80
IN	Dunham Monthly Distribution Class C	DCMDX	D	(888) 338-6426	D- / 1.1	1.51	0.92	2.67 / 25	3.87 / 10	4.42 / 10	3.58	3.55
IN	Dunham Monthly Distribution Class N	DNMDX	D+	(888) 338-6426	D- / 1.4	1.74	1.40	3.68 / 30	4.94 / 13	5.48 / 14	2.99	2.55
RE	Dunham Real Estate Stock A	DAREX	B-	(888) 338-6426	A- / 9.2	4.90	21.34	25.21 / 98	14.39 / 70	14.93 / 86	0.41	1.84
RE	Dunham Real Estate Stock C	DCREX	B-	(888) 338-6426	A / 9.4	4.70	20.88	24.27 / 98	13.54 / 64	14.07 / 78	0.00	2.59
RE	Dunham Real Estate Stock N	DNREX	B	(888) 338-6426	A+ / 9.6	4.92	21.47	25.44 / 98	14.67 / 72	15.22 / 88	0.53	1.59
SC	Dunham Small Cap Growth A	DADGX	D+	(888) 338-6426	B- / 7.2	7.13	15.61	5.49 / 42	15.62 / 80	13.53 / 73	0.00	2.09
SC	Dunham Small Cap Growth C	DCDGX	D+	(888) 338-6426	B / 7.6	6.97	15.21	4.69 / 36	14.76 / 73	12.68 / 66	0.00	2.84
SC	Dunham Small Cap Growth N	DNDGX	C-	(888) 338-6426	B+ / 8.5	7.19	15.74	5.75 / 44	15.90 / 83	13.81 / 76	0.00	1.84
SC	Dunham Small Cap Value A	DASVX	C+	(888) 338-6426	C / 5.5	1.62	11.23	5.71 / 44	13.65 / 64	12.00 / 60	0.00	1.70
SC	Dunham Small Cap Value C	DCSVX	C+	(888) 338-6426	C+ / 5.9	1.53	10.91	4.95 / 38	12.71 / 58	11.14 / 54	0.00	2.45
SC	Dunham Small Cap Value N	DNSVX	C+	(888) 338-6426	C+ / 6.6	1.68	11.41	5.98 / 46	13.83 / 66	12.26 / 62	0.22	1.45
EM	Dupont Capital Emerging Mkts I	DCMEX	E	(888) 739-1390	E- / 0.2	1.70	-9.69	-10.51 / 3	-4.88 / 2	--	1.93	1.33
GR	Eagle Capital Appreciation A	HRCPX	B	(800) 421-4184	B+ / 8.5	3.98	8.72	18.09 / 96	16.55 / 87	14.09 / 78	0.00	1.23
GR	Eagle Capital Appreciation C	HRCCX	B-	(800) 421-4184	B+ / 8.7	3.79	8.31	17.17 / 95	15.67 / 81	13.27 / 71	0.00	1.97
GR	Eagle Capital Appreciation I	HRCIX	B+	(800) 421-4184	A / 9.3	4.06	8.87	18.40 / 96	16.89 / 89	14.46 / 82	0.12	0.93
GR	Eagle Capital Appreciation R3	HRCLX	B	(800) 421-4184	A- / 9.0	3.88	8.52	17.64 / 95	16.15 / 84	13.74 / 75	0.00	1.56
GR	Eagle Capital Appreciation R5	HRCMX	B+	(800) 421-4184	A / 9.3	4.04	8.85	18.37 / 96	16.87 / 89	14.45 / 82	0.03	0.94
GI	Eagle Growth and Income A	HRCVX	C+	(800) 421-4184	C / 5.2	-0.78	1.95	6.60 / 52	13.79 / 66	11.71 / 58	1.64	1.02
GI	Eagle Growth and Income C	HIGCX	C+	(800) 421-4184	C / 5.4	-0.99	1.53	5.71 / 44	12.94 / 59	10.90 / 52	1.06	1.79
GI	Eagle Growth and Income I	HIGJX	B-	(800) 421-4184	C+ / 6.2	-0.72	2.09	6.84 / 54	14.10 / 68	12.04 / 61	1.99	0.77
GI	Eagle Growth and Income R3	HIGRX	B-	(800) 421-4184	C+ / 5.7	-0.90	1.72	6.11 / 47	13.39 / 62	11.35 / 56	1.30	1.40
GI	Eagle Growth and Income R5	HIGSX	B-	(800) 421-4184	C+ / 6.2	-0.72	2.10	6.84 / 54	14.15 / 68	12.02 / 61	1.99	0.76
GI	Eagle Growth and Income R6	HIGUX	B-	(800) 421-4184	C+ / 6.2	-0.75	2.08	6.94 / 55	14.19 / 69	--	2.10	0.66
GR	Eagle Mid Cap Growth A	HAGAX	B+	(800) 421-4184	A- / 9.0	7.78	11.06	15.20 / 92	17.45 / 92	15.79 / 92	0.00	1.19

● Denotes fund is closed to new investors
* Denotes fund is included in Section II

www.thestreetratings.com

Risk Rating/Pts	3 Year Standard Deviation	Beta	NAV As of 3/31/15	Total $(Mil)	Cash %	Stocks %	Bonds %	Other %	Portfolio Turnover Ratio	Last Bull Market Return	Last Bear Market Return	Manager Quality Pct	Manager Tenure (Years)	Initial Purch. $	Additional Purch. $	Front End Load	Back End Load
C+ / 5.9	11.4	0.56	13.77	580	20	79	0	1	223	51.3	-18.0	98	4	10,000	2,000	0.0	2.0
U /	N/A	N/A	10.40	216	50	22	22	6	0	N/A	N/A	N/A	2	10,000	2,000	0.0	0.0
C- / 3.5	11.8	0.76	9.76	312	2	97	0	1	320	49.1	-22.4	89	8	10,000	2,000	0.0	2.0
C- / 4.0	19.3	1.25	12.01	122	0	0	0	100	0	146.0	-35.0	87	N/A	10,000	2,000	0.0	2.0
B- / 7.2	12.7	0.76	19.60	6	0	0	0	100	82	N/A	N/A	96	3	100,000	25,000	0.0	1.0
C+ / 5.7	12.0	1.08	32.57	184	0	99	0	1	56	105.3	-16.2	54	6	100,000	25,000	0.0	1.0
B / 8.6	5.8	0.49	24.62	2	29	61	9	1	4,686	9.1	-9.5	5	6	5,000	100	5.8	0.0
B / 8.5	5.8	0.49	23.44	1	29	61	9	1	4,686	6.4	-9.9	4	6	5,000	100	0.0	0.0
B / 8.7	5.7	0.49	25.04	18	29	61	9	1	4,686	10.0	-9.4	5	6	100,000	0	0.0	0.0
C / 4.3	8.5	0.82	9.28	4	6	11	0	83	129	44.0	-14.5	16	11	5,000	100	5.8	0.0
C / 4.3	8.6	0.83	9.14	4	6	11	0	83	129	40.5	-14.9	11	11	5,000	100	0.0	0.0
C- / 4.2	8.6	0.83	9.29	21	6	11	0	83	129	45.2	-14.5	18	11	100,000	0	0.0	0.0
B / 8.5	4.7	0.27	10.12	2	19	72	8	1	238	18.6	-7.9	39	5	5,000	100	5.8	0.0
B / 8.5	4.7	0.27	9.93	2	19	72	8	1	238	15.7	-8.1	29	5	5,000	100	0.0	0.0
B / 8.5	4.8	0.28	10.10	16	19	72	8	1	238	19.7	-7.7	41	5	100,000	0	0.0	0.0
C / 5.5	13.5	0.94	13.58	4	1	98	0	1	108	22.2	-30.6	54	N/A	5,000	100	5.8	0.0
C / 5.5	13.5	0.94	12.98	3	1	98	0	1	108	19.0	-30.9	42	N/A	5,000	100	0.0	0.0
C / 5.5	13.5	0.95	13.86	34	1	98	0	1	108	23.2	-30.6	57	N/A	100,000	0	0.0	0.0
C / 4.8	14.2	1.06	15.94	15	0	99	0	1	29	N/A	N/A	17	4	5,000	100	5.8	0.0
C / 4.8	14.2	1.06	15.56	5	0	99	0	1	29	N/A	N/A	12	4	5,000	100	0.0	0.0
C / 4.8	14.2	1.06	16.08	42	0	99	0	1	29	N/A	N/A	19	4	100,000	0	0.0	0.0
C+ / 5.8	13.7	1.02	15.36	8	2	97	0	1	117	51.7	-23.6	66	7	5,000	100	5.8	0.0
C+ / 5.8	13.7	1.02	14.91	7	2	97	0	1	117	48.0	-23.8	55	7	5,000	100	0.0	0.0
C+ / 5.8	13.7	1.02	15.38	63	2	97	0	1	117	53.1	-23.4	69	7	100,000	0	0.0	0.0
B- / 7.2	10.2	1.03	16.24	6	2	97	0	1	22	78.5	-18.4	20	11	5,000	100	5.8	0.0
B- / 7.2	10.2	1.03	15.79	6	2	97	0	1	22	74.0	-18.7	15	11	5,000	100	0.0	0.0
B- / 7.2	10.2	1.03	16.28	45	2	97	0	1	22	80.1	-18.4	23	11	100,000	0	0.0	0.0
B / 8.2	3.4	0.26	37.84	72	17	73	9	1	229	24.6	-6.3	73	7	5,000	100	5.8	0.0
B / 8.0	3.4	0.26	32.11	53	17	73	9	1	229	21.3	-6.6	65	7	5,000	100	0.0	0.0
B / 8.2	3.4	0.26	38.54	166	17	73	9	1	229	25.7	-6.2	76	7	100,000	0	0.0	0.0
C- / 3.9	13.1	1.05	20.11	11	0	99	0	1	97	87.8	-17.9	62	3	5,000	100	5.8	0.0
C- / 3.9	13.0	1.04	19.40	5	0	99	0	1	97	83.1	-18.1	52	3	5,000	100	0.0	0.0
C- / 3.9	13.1	1.04	20.04	39	0	99	0	1	97	89.5	-17.8	66	3	100,000	0	0.0	0.0
D / 2.2	14.9	0.99	17.72	7	4	95	0	1	192	93.1	-27.8	61	11	5,000	100	5.8	0.0
D / 1.7	15.0	0.99	15.65	4	4	95	0	1	192	88.2	-28.0	49	11	5,000	100	0.0	0.0
D+ / 2.3	14.9	0.99	18.18	23	4	95	0	1	192	94.8	-27.7	65	11	100,000	0	0.0	0.0
C+ / 6.4	12.2	0.87	15.02	4	1	98	0	1	106	79.3	-20.5	62	N/A	5,000	100	5.8	0.0
C+ / 6.3	12.3	0.87	13.90	2	1	98	0	1	106	74.3	-20.7	49	N/A	5,000	100	0.0	0.0
C+ / 6.4	12.3	0.87	15.10	25	1	98	0	1	106	80.4	-20.4	65	N/A	100,000	0	0.0	0.0
C- / 4.2	13.9	0.95	7.76	194	0	99	0	1	70	5.5	-24.5	8	N/A	1,000,000	100,000	0.0	2.0
C / 5.1	10.2	0.98	38.65	167	0	100	0	0	33	104.6	-17.6	74	2	1,000	0	4.8	0.0
C / 4.3	10.1	0.98	31.18	70	0	100	0	0	33	99.5	-17.9	66	2	1,000	0	0.0	0.0
C / 5.2	10.1	0.98	40.03	94	0	100	0	0	33	106.7	-17.5	77	2	2,500,000	0	0.0	0.0
C / 5.0	10.1	0.98	37.77	1	0	100	0	0	33	102.2	-17.7	71	2	0	0	0.0	0.0
C / 5.2	10.1	0.98	39.92	6	0	100	0	0	33	106.6	-17.5	77	2	0	0	0.0	0.0
B- / 7.4	9.6	0.96	18.10	219	0	100	0	0	10	81.3	-14.3	44	4	1,000	0	4.8	0.0
B- / 7.4	9.6	0.96	17.43	216	0	100	0	0	10	76.7	-14.5	34	4	1,000	0	0.0	0.0
B- / 7.4	9.6	0.96	18.06	216	0	100	0	0	10	83.0	-14.1	49	4	2,500,000	0	0.0	0.0
B- / 7.4	9.6	0.96	18.03	3	0	100	0	0	10	79.0	-14.4	40	4	0	0	0.0	0.0
B- / 7.4	9.5	0.96	18.04	4	0	100	0	0	10	83.0	-14.3	51	4	0	0	0.0	0.0
B- / 7.4	9.6	0.96	18.08	N/A	0	100	0	0	10	83.4	N/A	51	4	0	0	0.0	0.0
C / 5.1	12.4	1.11	44.88	343	0	100	0	0	60	104.4	-24.1	59	17	1,000	0	4.8	0.0

99 Pct = Best
0 Pct = Worst

Fund Type	Fund Name	Ticker Symbol	Overall Investment Rating	Phone	Perfor-mance Rating/Pts	3 Mo	6 Mo	1Yr / Pct	3Yr / Pct	5Yr / Pct	Dividend Yield	Expense Ratio
								Total Return % through 3/31/15 — Annualized			**Incl. in Returns**	
GR	Eagle Mid Cap Growth C	HAGCX	B	(800) 421-4184	A- / 9.2	7.62	10.69	14.39 /90	16.63 /88	14.98 /87	0.00	1.89
GR	Eagle Mid Cap Growth I	HAGIX	B+	(800) 421-4184	A / 9.5	7.89	11.28	15.62 /93	17.85 /94	16.20 /94	0.00	0.85
GR	Eagle Mid Cap Growth R3	HAREX	B+	(800) 421-4184	A / 9.3	7.74	10.93	14.89 /91	17.13 /90	15.49 /90	0.00	1.48
GR	Eagle Mid Cap Growth R5	HARSX	B+	(800) 421-4184	A / 9.5	7.88	11.25	15.56 /93	17.82 /94	16.17 /94	0.00	0.87
GR	Eagle Mid Cap Growth R6	HRAUX	B+	(800) 421-4184	A+ / 9.6	7.92	11.32	15.70 /93	17.96 /94	--	0.00	0.77
MC	Eagle Mid Cap Stock A	HMCAX	D+	(800) 421-4184	C / 4.9	4.19	8.77	8.55 /67	11.89 /52	10.79 /51	0.00	1.22
MC	Eagle Mid Cap Stock C	HMCCX	D+	(800) 421-4184	C / 5.2	4.03	8.40	7.78 /61	11.07 /46	10.00 /44	0.00	1.96
MC	Eagle Mid Cap Stock I	HMCJX	C-	(800) 421-4184	C+ / 5.9	4.27	8.95	8.84 /68	12.19 /54	11.13 /54	0.00	1.10
MC	Eagle Mid Cap Stock R3	HMRRX	C-	(800) 421-4184	C / 5.5	4.12	8.62	8.21 /64	11.55 /49	10.48 /48	0.00	1.53
MC	Eagle Mid Cap Stock R5	HMRSX	C-	(800) 421-4184	C+ / 6.0	4.25	8.94	8.83 /68	12.32 /55	11.20 /54	0.00	0.94
MC	Eagle Mid Cap Stock R6	HMRUX	C	(800) 421-4184	C+ / 6.0	4.28	9.00	8.97 /69	12.33 /55	--	0.00	0.82
EN	Eagle MLP Strategy A	EGLAX	U	(800) 421-4184	U /	0.53	-13.79	2.10 /22	--	--	4.36	1.74
EN	Eagle MLP Strategy C	EGLCX	U	(800) 421-4184	U /	0.35	-14.15	1.23 /19	--	--	3.98	2.49
EN	Eagle MLP Strategy I	EGLIX	U	(800) 421-4184	U /	0.60	-13.66	2.35 /23	--	--	4.88	1.49
SC	Eagle Small Cap Gr A	HRSCX	C	(800) 421-4184	C+ / 6.7	5.99	13.93	11.09 /79	14.08 /68	16.14 /94	0.00	1.11
SC	Eagle Small Cap Gr C	HSCCX	C	(800) 421-4184	B- / 7.0	5.82	13.56	10.31 /76	13.28 /62	15.33 /89	0.00	1.82
SC	Eagle Small Cap Gr I	HSIIX	B-	(800) 421-4184	B / 7.9	6.05	14.11	11.43 /80	14.44 /70	16.46 /95	0.00	0.78
SC	Eagle Small Cap Gr R3	HSRRX	C+	(800) 421-4184	B- / 7.4	5.91	13.80	10.75 /77	13.77 /65	15.89 /92	0.00	1.42
SC	Eagle Small Cap Gr R5	HSRSX	B-	(800) 421-4184	B / 7.9	6.07	14.14	11.45 /80	14.46 /71	16.54 /95	0.00	0.77
SC	Eagle Small Cap Gr R6	HSRUX	B-	(800) 421-4184	B / 8.0	6.08	14.19	11.60 /81	14.60 /72	--	0.00	0.66
SC	Eagle Smaller Company A	EGEAX	E+	(800) 421-4184	C / 5.1	3.37	8.95	3.10 /27	13.10 /60	12.90 /67	0.00	1.40
SC	Eagle Smaller Company C	EGECX	E+	(800) 421-4184	C / 5.4	3.16	8.59	2.38 /24	12.27 /54	12.03 /61	0.00	2.13
SC	Eagle Smaller Company I	EGEIX	D-	(800) 421-4184	C+ / 6.5	4.09	9.88	4.28 /34	13.84 /66	13.56 /73	0.00	1.12
SC	Eagle Smaller Company R3	EGERX	E+	(800) 421-4184	C+ / 5.7	3.31	8.93	2.86 /26	12.77 /58	12.58 /65	0.00	1.79
SC	Eagle Smaller Company R5	EGESX	E+	(800) 421-4184	C+ / 6.3	3.57	9.34	3.63 /30	13.64 /64	13.42 /72	0.00	1.06
SC	Eagle Smaller Company R6	EGEUX	E+	(800) 421-4184	C+ / 6.3	3.50	9.33	3.54 /29	13.65 /64	--	0.00	0.96
GR	EAS Crow Point Alternatives A	EASAX	D+		E+ / 0.7	0.47	1.18	2.32 /23	3.38 / 9	2.22 / 5	0.90	2.80
GR	EAS Crow Point Alternatives C	EASYX	D+		E+ / 0.7	0.30	0.86	1.56 /20	2.63 / 7	1.48 / 4	0.41	3.55
GR	EAS Crow Point Alternatives I	EASIX	C-		E+ / 0.9	0.54	1.37	2.62 /25	3.63 / 9	2.48 / 5	1.14	2.55
GR	Eaton Vance Atlanta Cap Focusd Gr	EAALX	D+	(800) 262-1122	C- / 3.9	1.35	6.19	10.32 /76	10.50 /42	11.64 /58	0.05	1.08
GR	Eaton Vance Atlanta Cap Focusd Gr	EAGCX	C-	(800) 262-1122	C / 4.3	1.10	5.80	9.40 /71	9.65 /37	10.80 /51	0.00	1.83
GR	Eaton Vance Atlanta Cap Focusd Gr I	EILGX	C-	(800) 262-1122	C / 5.0	1.36	6.30	10.51 /76	10.79 /44	11.90 /60	0.30	0.83
GR	Eaton Vance Atlanta Cap Sel Eq A	ESEAX	A-	(800) 262-1122	B / 7.6	2.15	12.06	14.50 /91	15.82 /82	--	0.00	1.29
GR	Eaton Vance Atlanta Cap Sel Eq C	ESECX	A	(800) 262-1122	B / 8.0	1.94	11.61	13.62 /88	14.93 /74	--	0.00	2.04
GR	Eaton Vance Atlanta Cap Sel Eq I	ESEIX	A+	(800) 262-1122	B+ / 8.8	2.26	12.20	14.79 /91	16.11 /84	--	0.00	1.04
SC	● Eaton Vance Atlanta Cap SMID Cap	EAASX	B+	(800) 262-1122	B / 7.9	6.00	14.34	13.27 /87	15.84 /82	16.10 /93	0.00	1.23
SC	● Eaton Vance Atlanta Cap SMID Cap	ECASX	A	(800) 262-1122	B+ / 8.3	5.81	13.91	12.44 /84	14.97 /75	15.25 /88	0.00	1.98
SC	● Eaton Vance Atlanta Cap SMID Cap I	EISMX	A+	(800) 262-1122	A- / 9.0	6.03	14.43	13.53 /88	16.12 /84	16.39 /94	0.00	0.98
SC	● Eaton Vance Atlanta Cap SMID Cap	ERSMX	A	(800) 262-1122	B+ / 8.7	5.91	14.15	13.02 /87	15.54 /79	15.82 /92	0.00	1.48
SC	● Eaton Vance Atlanta Cap SMID Cap	ERASX	B+	(800) 262-1122	A- / 9.0	6.07	14.51	13.66 /89	16.16 /85	16.41 /94	0.00	0.90
MC	Eaton Vance Atlanta Cp Horizon Gr A	EXMCX	D-	(800) 262-1122	D+ / 2.5	1.76	6.60	5.57 /43	8.29 /29	11.00 /53	0.00	1.73
MC	● Eaton Vance Atlanta Cp Horizon Gr B	EBMCX	D-	(800) 262-1122	D+ / 2.8	1.56	6.16	4.76 /37	7.48 /24	10.17 /46	0.00	2.48
MC	Eaton Vance Atlanta Cp Horizon Gr C	ECMCX	D-	(800) 262-1122	D+ / 2.8	1.56	6.17	4.76 /37	7.48 /24	10.18 /46	0.00	2.48
MC	Eaton Vance Atlanta Cp Horizon Gr I	EIMCX	D	(800) 262-1122	C- / 3.5	1.87	6.74	5.85 /45	8.58 /30	11.22 /55	0.00	1.48
BA	Eaton Vance Balanced A	EVIFX	C+	(800) 262-1122	C / 4.6	2.87	5.27	10.22 /75	11.88 /52	10.10 /45	0.98	1.14
BA	● Eaton Vance Balanced B	EMIFX	C+	(800) 262-1122	C / 5.0	2.61	4.78	9.30 /71	11.05 /46	9.23 /38	0.36	1.89
BA	Eaton Vance Balanced C	ECIFX	C+	(800) 262-1122	C / 5.0	2.73	4.79	9.42 /72	11.02 /46	9.24 /38	0.39	1.89
BA	Eaton Vance Balanced I	EIIFX	B+	(800) 262-1122	C+ / 5.8	2.92	5.38	10.48 /76	12.11 /53	10.23 /46	1.26	0.89
OT	Eaton Vance Commodity Strategy A	EACSX	E-	(800) 262-1122	E- / 0.1	-5.72	-16.97	-26.62 / 0	-12.19 / 1	--	0.85	1.48
OT	Eaton Vance Commodity Strategy C	ECCSX	E-	(800) 262-1122	E- / 0.1	-5.88	-17.17	-27.10 / 0	-12.82 / 1	--	0.00	2.23
OT	Eaton Vance Commodity Strategy I	EICSX	E-	(800) 262-1122	E- / 0.1	-5.71	-16.88	-26.41 / 0	-11.98 / 1	--	1.56	1.23
UT	Eaton Vance Dividend Builder Fd A	EVTMX	B-	(800) 262-1122	C+ / 6.0	2.85	6.38	12.93 /86	13.77 /65	11.79 /59	1.27	1.06

● Denotes fund is closed to new investors
* Denotes fund is included in Section II

www.thestreetratings.com

| RISK | 3 Year | | NET ASSETS | | ASSET | | | | Portfolio | BULL / BEAR | | FUND MANAGER | | MINIMUMS | | LOADS | |
Risk Rating/Pts	Standard Deviation	Beta	NAV As of 3/31/15	Total $(Mil)	Cash %	Stocks %	Bonds %	Other %	Turnover Ratio	Last Bull Market Return	Last Bear Market Return	Manager Quality Pct	Manager Tenure (Years)	Initial Purch. $	Additional Purch. $	Front End Load	Back End Load
C /4.7	12.4	1.11	37.16	114	0	100	0	0	60	99.6	-24.3	48	17	1,000	0	0.0	0.0
C /5.1	12.4	1.11	46.74	252	0	100	0	0	60	106.8	-23.9	64	17	2,500,000	0	0.0	0.0
C /5.0	12.4	1.11	43.99	21	0	100	0	0	60	102.5	-24.1	55	17	0	0	0.0	0.0
C /5.1	12.4	1.11	46.67	68	0	100	0	0	60	106.6	-23.9	64	17	0	0	0.0	0.0
C /5.1	12.4	1.11	46.87	78	0	100	0	0	60	107.4	N/A	66	17	0	0	0.0	0.0
C /4.7	10.6	0.93	29.60	168	0	100	0	0	32	74.9	-23.0	22	3	1,000	0	4.8	0.0
C- /4.0	10.6	0.93	23.75	123	0	100	0	0	32	70.6	-23.2	16	3	1,000	0	0.0	0.0
C /4.8	10.6	0.92	30.75	89	0	100	0	0	32	76.6	-22.9	25	3	2,500,000	0	0.0	0.0
C /4.6	10.6	0.92	28.83	2	0	100	0	0	32	73.1	-23.0	19	3	0	0	0.0	0.0
C /4.8	10.7	0.93	30.90	N/A	0	100	0	0	32	77.1	-22.9	25	3	0	0	0.0	0.0
C /4.8	10.6	0.92	30.93	1	0	100	0	0	32	77.1	N/A	26	3	0	0	0.0	0.0
U /	N/A	N/A	12.70	122	45	54	0	1	7	N/A	N/A	N/A	3	2,500	100	5.8	0.0
U /	N/A	N/A	12.65	60	45	54	0	1	7	N/A	N/A	N/A	3	2,500	100	0.0	0.0
U /	N/A	N/A	12.72	720	45	54	0	1	7	N/A	N/A	N/A	3	100,000	100	0.0	0.0
C /5.0	13.8	0.96	56.30	811	0	100	0	0	37	87.0	-21.9	48	22	1,000	0	4.8	0.0
C /4.4	13.8	0.96	44.94	202	0	100	0	0	37	82.5	-22.1	37	22	1,000	0	0.0	0.0
C /5.0	13.8	0.96	58.16	1,913	0	100	0	0	37	88.5	-21.7	52	22	2,500,000	0	0.0	0.0
C /4.9	13.8	0.96	55.17	126	0	100	0	0	37	85.3	-21.8	43	22	0	0	0.0	0.0
C /5.0	13.8	0.96	58.36	387	0	100	0	0	37	89.0	-21.7	53	22	0	0	0.0	0.0
C /5.0	13.8	0.96	58.58	652	0	100	0	0	37	89.8	N/A	54	22	0	0	0.0	0.0
E+ /0.6	12.6	0.90	13.24	28	0	100	0	0	68	80.2	-21.7	47	N/A	1,000	0	4.8	0.0
E+ /0.6	12.6	0.90	11.93	23	0	100	0	0	68	75.8	-22.0	36	N/A	1,000	0	0.0	0.0
E+ /0.6	12.7	0.91	14.02	20	0	100	0	0	68	84.0	-21.5	57	N/A	2,500,000	0	0.0	0.0
E+ /0.6	12.7	0.91	12.88	N/A	0	100	0	0	68	78.5	-21.8	42	N/A	0	0	0.0	0.0
E+ /0.6	12.6	0.90	13.86	N/A	0	100	0	0	68	83.0	-21.6	54	N/A	0	0	0.0	0.0
E+ /0.6	12.6	0.90	13.88	25	0	100	0	0	68	83.2	N/A	55	N/A	0	0	0.0	0.0
B+ /9.0	4.6	0.38	9.01	11	57	22	19	2	219	17.0	-11.4	32	6	2,500	500	5.5	2.0
B+ /9.0	4.6	0.37	8.84	2	57	22	19	2	219	14.0	-11.7	25	6	2,500	500	0.0	2.0
B /8.9	4.6	0.38	9.07	18	57	22	19	2	219	17.9	-11.4	36	6	500,000	0	0.0	2.0
C+ /5.7	11.5	1.11	14.98	86	1	98	0	1	46	73.9	-18.2	5	13	1,000	0	5.8	0.0
C+ /5.7	11.5	1.11	14.72	4	1	98	0	1	46	69.4	-18.4	4	13	1,000	0	0.0	0.0
C+ /5.7	11.5	1.11	14.13	67	1	98	0	1	46	75.3	-18.2	6	13	250,000	0	0.0	0.0
B- /7.5	9.2	0.87	17.09	58	4	95	0	1	45	N/A	N/A	82	3	1,000	0	5.8	0.0
B- /7.5	9.2	0.88	16.82	11	4	95	0	1	45	N/A	N/A	75	3	1,000	0	0.0	0.0
B- /7.5	9.2	0.88	17.19	41	4	95	0	1	45	N/A	N/A	83	3	250,000	0	0.0	0.0
B- /7.0	10.2	0.66	24.72	1,403	1	98	0	1	11	99.8	-19.2	93	13	1,000	0	5.8	0.0
B- /7.0	10.2	0.66	23.68	240	1	98	0	1	11	94.7	-19.4	91	13	1,000	0	0.0	0.0
B- /7.0	10.2	0.67	26.72	4,164	1	98	0	1	11	101.5	-19.0	93	13	250,000	0	0.0	0.0
B- /7.0	10.2	0.66	24.37	190	1	98	0	1	11	98.1	-19.2	92	13	1,000	0	0.0	0.0
C+ /5.7	10.2	0.67	26.75	42	1	98	0	1	11	101.6	-19.0	93	13	1,000,000	0	0.0	0.0
C /5.3	11.7	0.99	15.05	23	1	98	0	1	26	58.6	-21.0	3	13	1,000	0	5.8	0.0
C /5.2	11.8	0.99	12.99	2	1	98	0	1	26	54.4	-21.2	3	13	1,000	0	0.0	0.0
C /5.2	11.7	0.99	12.98	8	1	98	0	1	26	54.5	-21.2	3	13	1,000	0	0.0	0.0
C /5.3	11.7	0.99	15.22	2	1	98	0	1	26	60.0	-20.9	4	4	250,000	0	0.0	0.0
B- /7.4	6.5	1.12	8.68	210	0	59	40	1	2	62.5	-10.6	62	6	1,000	0	5.8	0.0
B- /7.4	6.5	1.12	8.68	10	0	59	40	1	2	58.5	-11.0	50	6	1,000	0	0.0	0.0
B- /7.4	6.6	1.14	8.72	70	0	59	40	1	2	58.5	-10.9	48	6	1,000	0	0.0	0.0
B /8.4	6.5	1.13	8.68	30	0	59	40	1	2	63.6	-10.6	64	6	250,000	0	0.0	0.0
C- /3.6	12.4	0.68	6.26	14	12	3	84	1	264	-28.3	-20.2	0	5	1,000	0	4.8	0.0
C- /3.6	12.4	0.68	6.08	5	12	3	84	1	264	-30.1	-20.5	0	5	1,000	0	0.0	0.0
C- /3.5	12.5	0.69	6.27	310	12	3	84	1	264	-27.7	-20.1	0	5	250,000	0	0.0	0.0
B- /7.1	9.5	0.12	14.54	769	2	97	0	1	59	82.3	-14.6	99	8	1,000	0	5.8	0.0

99 Pct = Best
0 Pct = Worst

Fund Type	Fund Name	Ticker Symbol	Overall Investment Rating	Phone	PERFORMANCE							
					Perfor-mance Rating/Pts	Total Return % through 3/31/15			Annualized		Incl. in Returns	
						3 Mo	6 Mo	1Yr / Pct	3Yr / Pct	5Yr / Pct	Dividend Yield	Expense Ratio
UT	Eaton Vance Dividend Builder Fd C	ECTMX	B-	(800) 262-1122	C+ / 6.3	2.59	5.96	12.03 /83	12.89 /59	10.95 /52	0.64	1.81
UT	Eaton Vance Dividend Builder Fd I	EIUTX	B+	(800) 262-1122	B- / 7.1	2.84	6.52	13.22 /87	14.03 /67	12.06 /61	1.59	0.81
FO	Eaton Vance Focused Growth Oppty	EAFGX	A+	(800) 262-1122	A / 9.4	5.80	10.63	19.16 /96	18.29 /95	--	0.00	1.72
FO	Eaton Vance Focused Growth Oppty	ECFGX	A+	(800) 262-1122	A / 9.5	5.61	10.18	18.28 /96	17.39 /92	--	0.00	2.47
FO	Eaton Vance Focused Growth Oppty I	EIFGX	A+	(800) 262-1122	A+ / 9.7	5.83	10.70	19.44 /96	18.56 /96	--	0.00	1.47
FO	Eaton Vance Focused Value Oppty A	EAFVX	B-	(800) 262-1122	C+ / 6.6	1.49	3.36	9.03 /69	15.92 /83	--	0.42	1.70
FO	Eaton Vance Focused Value Oppty C	ECFVX	B+	(800) 262-1122	B- / 7.0	1.29	3.03	8.20 /64	15.03 /75	--	0.19	2.45
FO	Eaton Vance Focused Value Oppty I	EIFVX	A-	(800) 262-1122	B / 7.9	1.56	3.53	9.27 /71	16.19 /85	--	0.74	1.45
GL	Eaton Vance Glb Mac Abs Ret Adv A	EGRAX	D-	(800) 262-1122	D- / 1.2	3.04	4.01	9.08 /70	3.55 / 9	--	3.21	1.74
GL	Eaton Vance Glb Mac Abs Ret Adv C	EGRCX	D-	(800) 262-1122	D- / 1.3	2.88	3.70	8.30 /65	2.85 / 8	--	2.37	2.47
GL	Eaton Vance Glb Mac Abs Ret Adv I	EGRIX	D-	(800) 262-1122	D / 1.7	3.12	4.13	9.37 /71	3.85 /10	--	3.58	1.45
GL	Eaton Vance Glb Mac Abs Ret Adv R	EGRRX	D-	(800) 262-1122	D- / 1.5	2.96	3.94	8.82 /68	3.36 / 9	--	3.20	1.95
IN	Eaton Vance Global Dividend Inc A	EDIAX	D+	(800) 262-1122	C- / 3.5	3.67	2.93	5.51 /42	10.44 /42	8.06 /30	3.81	1.24
IN	Eaton Vance Global Dividend Inc C	EDICX	C-	(800) 262-1122	C- / 3.9	3.58	2.58	4.80 /37	9.67 /37	7.24 /25	3.36	1.99
IN	Eaton Vance Global Dividend Inc I	EDIIX	C	(800) 262-1122	C / 4.6	3.73	3.08	5.95 /46	10.76 /44	8.33 /32	4.33	0.99
IN	Eaton Vance Global Dividend Inc R	EDIRX	C-	(800) 262-1122	C- / 4.2	3.64	2.79	5.36 /41	10.18 /40	7.79 /29	3.78	1.48
FO	Eaton Vance Greater China Gr A	EVCGX	C-	(800) 262-1122	C- / 3.7	5.84	6.91	9.11 /70	9.69 /37	4.92 /12	0.00	1.94
FO	● Eaton Vance Greater China Gr B	EMCGX	C-	(800) 262-1122	C- / 4.1	5.66	6.55	8.32 /65	8.93 /32	4.18 / 9	0.00	2.64
FO	Eaton Vance Greater China Gr C	ECCGX	C-	(800) 262-1122	C- / 4.1	5.67	6.57	8.40 /66	8.93 /32	4.19 / 9	0.00	2.64
FO	Eaton Vance Greater China Gr I	EICGX	C	(800) 262-1122	C / 4.8	5.92	7.09	9.45 /72	10.01 /39	5.21 /13	0.00	1.64
EM	Eaton Vance Greater India A	ETGIX	C-	(800) 262-1122	B+ / 8.9	7.14	12.25	35.09 /99	12.73 /58	4.34 / 9	1.64	2.02
EM	● Eaton Vance Greater India B	EMGIX	C	(800) 262-1122	A- / 9.2	6.99	11.87	34.20 /99	11.95 /52	3.62 / 7	0.98	2.72
EM	Eaton Vance Greater India C	ECGIX	C-	(800) 262-1122	A- / 9.2	7.01	11.89	34.16 /99	11.96 /52	3.62 / 7	1.45	2.72
EM	Eaton Vance Greater India I	EGIIX	C	(800) 262-1122	A+ / 9.6	7.22	12.43	35.51 /99	13.07 /60	4.66 /11	1.96	1.72
GR	Eaton Vance Growth A	EALCX	B	(800) 262-1122	B+ / 8.5	4.61	9.17	17.98 /95	16.61 /87	13.63 /74	0.00	1.20
GR	Eaton Vance Growth C	ECLCX	B	(800) 262-1122	B+ / 8.8	4.42	8.82	17.12 /95	15.74 /81	12.79 /66	0.00	1.95
GR	Eaton Vance Growth I	ELCIX	B+	(800) 262-1122	A / 9.3	4.66	9.32	18.30 /96	16.90 /89	13.92 /77	0.00	0.95
GR	Eaton Vance Growth R	ELCRX	B+	(800) 262-1122	A- / 9.1	4.50	9.03	17.69 /95	16.31 /86	13.34 /71	0.00	1.45
IN	Eaton Vance Hedged Stock A	EROAX	D+	(800) 262-1122	D- / 1.4	2.72	3.23	6.59 /52	5.72 /16	2.98 / 6	1.30	1.84
IN	Eaton Vance Hedged Stock C	EROCX	C-	(800) 262-1122	D / 1.9	2.48	2.74	5.69 /44	5.58 /15	2.62 / 5	1.02	2.59
IN	Eaton Vance Hedged Stock I	EROIX	C-	(800) 262-1122	D / 2.1	2.71	3.22	6.73 /53	5.70 /16	3.07 / 6	1.51	1.59
GL	Eaton Vance Hexavest Global Eq I	EHGIX	U	(800) 262-1122	U /	2.04	2.90	5.84 /45	--	--	1.70	1.19
GI	Eaton Vance Large-Cap Value A	EHSTX	D-	(800) 262-1122	C+ / 6.2	1.29	4.10	9.41 /71	15.07 /75	10.83 /51	1.18	0.99
GI	Eaton Vance Large-Cap Value C	ECSTX	D	(800) 262-1122	C+ / 6.6	1.09	3.69	8.58 /67	14.20 /69	9.99 /44	0.58	1.74
GI	Eaton Vance Large-Cap Value I	EILVX	D	(800) 262-1122	B- / 7.4	1.33	4.21	9.66 /73	15.34 /78	11.09 /53	1.46	0.74
GI	Eaton Vance Large-Cap Value R	ERSTX	D	(800) 262-1122	B- / 7.0	1.19	3.93	9.11 /70	14.76 /73	10.54 /49	1.02	1.24
GI	Eaton Vance Large-Cap Value R6	ERLVX	B-	(800) 262-1122	B- / 7.3	1.30	4.23	9.63 /73	15.15 /76	10.87 /52	1.41	N/A
AA	Eaton Vance Multi-Strat All Mkt A	EAAMX	D+	(800) 262-1122	D- / 1.0	3.24	3.74	4.97 /38	3.66 / 9	--	2.86	1.62
AA	Eaton Vance Multi-Strat All Mkt C	ECAMX	D+	(800) 262-1122	D- / 1.1	3.01	3.36	4.21 /33	2.88 / 8	--	2.47	2.37
AA	Eaton Vance Multi-Strat All Mkt I	EIAMX	D+	(800) 262-1122	D- / 1.5	3.31	3.88	5.25 /40	3.90 /10	--	3.26	1.37
RE	Eaton Vance Real Estate Fund A	EAREX	B-	(800) 262-1122	B+ / 8.9	5.81	20.97	25.88 /98	13.29 /62	15.65 /91	1.64	1.52
RE	Eaton Vance Real Estate Fund I	EIREX	B	(800) 262-1122	A / 9.5	5.93	21.09	26.16 /99	13.58 /64	15.93 /93	1.95	1.27
AA	Eaton Vance Richard B A Asst Str A	EARAX	C-	(800) 262-1122	D / 1.8	1.74	2.48	2.88 /26	7.54 /24	--	0.39	1.40
AA	Eaton Vance Richard B A Asst Str C	ECRAX	C-	(800) 262-1122	D / 2.1	1.60	2.08	2.08 /22	6.73 /20	--	0.00	2.15
AA	Eaton Vance Richard B A Asst Str I	EIRAX	C	(800) 262-1122	D+ / 2.7	1.73	2.54	3.11 /27	7.77 /26	--	0.64	1.16
IN	Eaton Vance Richard Bern Eq St A	ERBAX	C+	(800) 262-1122	C / 4.3	2.70	3.88	3.38 /28	12.42 /55	--	0.53	1.26
IN	Eaton Vance Richard Bern Eq St C	ERBCX	C+	(800) 262-1122	C / 4.7	2.51	3.47	2.61 /25	11.60 /50	--	0.00	2.01
IN	Eaton Vance Richard Bern Eq St I	ERBIX	B-	(800) 262-1122	C / 5.5	2.76	3.99	3.63 /30	12.71 /58	--	0.81	1.01
GL	Eaton Vance Richard Bern Mkt Opps	ERMIX	U	(800) 262-1122	U /	1.09	4.88	--	--	--	0.00	N/A
GL	Eaton Vance Small Cap A	ETEGX	C	(800) 262-1122	B- / 7.3	7.18	13.87	10.48 /76	15.26 /77	13.49 /73	0.00	1.36
GL	● Eaton Vance Small Cap B	EBSMX	C	(800) 262-1122	B / 7.7	6.96	13.42	9.62 /73	14.38 /70	12.62 /65	0.00	2.11
GL	Eaton Vance Small Cap C	ECSMX	C	(800) 262-1122	B / 7.8	6.98	13.49	9.69 /73	14.41 /70	12.63 /65	0.00	2.11

● Denotes fund is closed to new investors
* Denotes fund is included in Section II

www.thestreetratings.com

RISK			NET ASSETS		ASSET					BULL / BEAR		FUND MANAGER		MINIMUMS		LOADS	
Risk Rating/Pts	3 Year		NAV As of 3/31/15	Total $(Mil)	Cash %	Stocks %	Bonds %	Other %	Portfolio Turnover Ratio	Last Bull Market Return	Last Bear Market Return	Manager Quality Pct	Manager Tenure (Years)	Initial Purch. $	Additional Purch. $	Front End Load	Back End Load
	Standard Deviation	Beta															
B- / 7.1	9.5	0.12	14.59	179	2	97	0	1	59	77.6	-14.9	98	8	1,000	0	0.0	0.0
B- / 7.1	9.5	0.12	14.53	105	2	97	0	1	59	84.0	-14.6	99	8	250,000	0	0.0	0.0
C+ / 6.6	11.1	0.59	15.87	9	2	97	0	1	66	107.8	-20.7	99	4	1,000	0	5.8	0.0
C+ / 6.5	11.1	0.59	15.43	3	2	97	0	1	66	102.5	-21.0	98	4	1,000	0	0.0	0.0
C+ / 6.6	11.1	0.59	15.98	66	2	97	0	1	66	109.7	-20.6	99	4	250,000	0	0.0	0.0
B- / 7.3	9.6	0.58	14.30	2	5	94	0	1	44	95.6	-19.9	98	4	1,000	0	5.8	0.0
B- / 7.3	9.6	0.58	14.15	1	5	94	0	1	44	90.7	-20.1	97	4	1,000	0	0.0	0.0
B- / 7.3	9.6	0.58	14.31	54	5	94	0	1	44	97.5	-19.9	98	4	250,000	0	0.0	0.0
C+ / 6.1	4.0	0.14	10.17	427	7	0	91	2	116	16.4	-4.2	85	5	1,000	0	4.8	0.0
C+ / 6.1	4.0	0.14	10.01	48	7	0	91	2	116	13.7	-4.5	81	5	1,000	0	0.0	0.0
C+ / 6.1	4.0	0.14	10.26	900	7	0	91	2	116	17.7	-4.1	87	5	250,000	0	0.0	0.0
C+ / 6.1	4.0	0.15	10.09	3	7	0	91	2	116	15.7	-4.3	84	5	1,000	0	0.0	0.0
C+ / 6.3	10.2	0.99	8.53	202	2	92	5	1	119	60.8	-18.8	11	3	1,000	0	5.8	0.0
C+ / 6.3	10.1	0.98	8.46	150	2	92	5	1	119	56.8	-19.1	9	3	1,000	0	0.0	0.0
C+ / 6.3	10.1	0.97	8.52	65	2	92	5	1	119	62.2	-18.7	14	3	250,000	0	0.0	0.0
C+ / 6.3	10.2	0.98	8.52	1	2	92	5	1	119	59.6	-18.9	10	3	1,000	0	0.0	0.0
C+ / 6.4	12.1	0.68	22.28	88	4	95	0	1	78	56.2	-28.3	89	2	1,000	0	5.8	0.0
C+ / 6.4	12.0	0.67	21.48	5	4	95	0	1	78	52.6	-28.5	86	2	1,000	0	0.0	0.0
C+ / 6.4	12.0	0.68	21.42	19	4	95	0	1	78	52.6	-28.5	86	2	1,000	0	0.0	0.0
C+ / 6.4	12.0	0.68	22.36	12	4	95	0	1	78	57.8	-28.2	90	2	250,000	0	0.0	0.0
D / 1.6	23.4	1.25	29.26	218	1	98	0	1	42	53.9	-23.3	98	8	1,000	0	5.8	0.0
D / 1.6	23.4	1.25	25.88	14	1	98	0	1	42	50.3	-23.5	98	8	1,000	0	0.0	0.0
D / 1.6	23.4	1.25	25.81	36	1	98	0	1	42	50.2	-23.6	98	8	1,000	0	0.0	0.0
D / 1.6	23.4	1.25	29.72	38	1	98	0	1	42	55.5	-23.2	99	8	250,000	0	0.0	0.0
C / 5.5	10.6	1.04	22.67	210	4	95	0	1	42	99.3	-17.8	64	13	1,000	0	5.8	0.0
C / 5.2	10.6	1.04	20.08	51	4	95	0	1	42	94.2	-18.0	53	13	1,000	0	0.0	0.0
C / 5.5	10.6	1.04	23.15	56	4	95	0	1	42	101.1	-17.7	67	13	250,000	0	0.0	0.0
C / 5.4	10.6	1.04	22.28	3	4	95	0	1	42	97.6	-17.8	60	13	1,000	0	0.0	0.0
B / 8.0	6.2	0.58	8.32	14	1	98	0	1	106	24.6	-7.5	24	7	1,000	0	5.8	0.0
B / 8.1	6.0	0.56	8.25	8	1	98	0	1	106	23.9	-7.8	26	7	1,000	0	0.0	0.0
B / 8.0	6.3	0.59	8.33	11	1	98	0	1	106	24.7	-7.4	23	7	250,000	0	0.0	0.0
U /	N/A	N/A	12.02	57	11	88	0	1	84	N/A	N/A	N/A	3	250,000	0	0.0	0.0
D- / 1.5	9.3	0.95	18.89	1,425	2	97	0	1	49	89.0	-19.0	65	6	1,000	0	5.8	0.0
D- / 1.5	9.3	0.95	18.89	409	2	97	0	1	49	84.2	-19.2	53	6	1,000	0	0.0	0.0
D- / 1.5	9.3	0.95	18.95	1,907	2	97	0	1	49	90.6	-18.9	68	6	250,000	0	0.0	0.0
D- / 1.5	9.3	0.95	18.84	138	2	97	0	1	49	87.4	-19.1	61	6	1,000	0	0.0	0.0
C+ / 5.9	9.3	0.95	18.96	36	2	97	0	1	49	89.4	-19.0	66	6	1,000,000	0	0.0	0.0
B / 8.2	2.6	0.31	10.23	47	15	28	56	1	100	N/A	N/A	71	4	1,000	0	4.8	0.0
B / 8.2	2.6	0.32	10.20	1	15	28	56	1	100	N/A	N/A	60	4	1,000	0	0.0	0.0
B / 8.2	2.6	0.32	10.22	23	15	28	56	1	100	N/A	N/A	73	4	250,000	0	0.0	0.0
C- / 4.2	12.4	0.99	14.79	13	1	98	0	1	22	80.4	-15.1	59	9	1,000	0	5.8	0.0
C- / 4.2	12.4	0.99	14.80	27	1	98	0	1	22	81.9	-15.0	63	9	250,000	0	0.0	0.0
B / 8.7	5.6	0.91	12.87	114	20	49	29	2	42	34.8	N/A	35	4	1,000	0	5.8	0.0
B / 8.7	5.6	0.91	12.68	145	20	49	29	2	42	31.4	N/A	26	4	1,000	0	0.0	0.0
B / 8.7	5.6	0.92	12.91	213	20	49	29	2	42	35.9	N/A	37	4	250,000	0	0.0	0.0
B- / 7.6	9.3	0.92	14.85	251	12	87	0	1	49	65.5	-19.6	36	5	1,000	0	5.8	0.0
B- / 7.5	9.3	0.92	14.70	230	12	87	0	1	49	61.3	-19.9	27	5	1,000	0	0.0	0.0
B- / 7.6	9.3	0.92	14.87	600	12	87	0	1	49	66.7	-19.5	39	5	250,000	0	0.0	0.0
U /	N/A	N/A	10.23	27	0	0	0	100	0	N/A	N/A	N/A	1	250,000	0	0.0	0.0
C- / 3.6	12.8	0.64	16.42	31	4	95	0	1	44	86.3	-25.3	97	9	1,000	0	5.8	0.0
C- / 3.4	12.7	0.64	15.68	3	4	95	0	1	44	81.6	-25.5	97	9	1,000	0	0.0	0.0
C- / 3.2	12.8	0.64	15.02	11	4	95	0	1	44	81.4	-25.5	97	9	1,000	0	0.0	0.0

99 Pct = Best
0 Pct = Worst

Fund Type	Fund Name	Ticker Symbol	Overall Investment Rating	Phone	Perfor-mance Rating/Pts	3 Mo	6 Mo	1Yr / Pct	3Yr / Pct	5Yr / Pct	Dividend Yield	Expense Ratio
									Annualized		Incl. in Returns	
GL	Eaton Vance Small Cap Inst	EISGX	C+	(800) 262-1122	B+ / 8.6	7.23	13.98	10.74 /77	15.52 /79	13.76 /75	0.00	1.12
GL	Eaton Vance Small Cap R	ERSGX	C	(800) 262-1122	B / 8.2	7.11	13.77	10.22 /75	14.96 /75	13.20 /70	0.00	1.61
SC	Eaton Vance Small Cap Value A	EAVSX	C-	(800) 262-1122	C / 4.4	2.57	7.38	1.81 /21	12.47 /56	10.45 /48	0.00	1.75
SC	● Eaton Vance Small Cap Value B	EBVSX	C	(800) 262-1122	C / 4.8	2.39	6.97	1.04 /19	11.65 /50	9.63 /42	0.00	2.50
SC	Eaton Vance Small Cap Value C	ECVSX	C	(800) 262-1122	C / 4.8	2.34	6.93	1.04 /19	11.63 /50	9.62 /41	0.00	2.50
SC	Eaton Vance Small Cap Value I	EIVSX	C+	(800) 262-1122	C+ / 5.6	2.65	7.52	2.06 /22	12.76 /58	10.73 /50	0.00	1.50
SC	Eaton Vance Special Eq A	EVSEX	C	(800) 262-1122	C / 5.2	6.19	9.71	6.85 /54	12.57 /56	11.86 /60	0.00	1.31
SC	Eaton Vance Special Eq C	ECSEX	C	(800) 262-1122	C+ / 5.6	5.96	9.30	6.06 /47	11.74 /51	11.02 /53	0.00	2.06
SC	Eaton Vance Special Eq I	EISEX	C+	(800) 262-1122	C+ / 6.3	6.26	9.85	7.16 /56	12.87 /59	12.08 /61	0.00	1.06
GR	Eaton Vance Stock A	EAERX	B-	(800) 262-1122	B / 7.6	3.76	7.20	13.41 /88	16.31 /86	12.96 /68	0.38	1.29
GR	Eaton Vance Stock C	ECERX	B	(800) 262-1122	B / 8.0	3.57	6.79	12.54 /85	15.42 /78	12.13 /61	0.00	2.04
GR	Eaton Vance Stock I	EIERX	B+	(800) 262-1122	B+ / 8.8	3.83	7.32	13.66 /89	16.58 /87	13.24 /70	0.61	1.04
SC	Eaton Vance Tax Mgd SmCap A	ETMGX	C+	(800) 262-1122	C+ / 6.9	6.85	12.72	9.43 /72	14.93 /74	13.40 /72	0.00	1.19
SC	● Eaton Vance Tax Mgd SmCap B	EMMGX	B-	(800) 262-1122	B- / 7.4	6.66	12.32	8.61 /67	14.08 /68	12.54 /64	0.00	1.95
SC	Eaton Vance Tax Mgd SmCap C	ECMGX	B-	(800) 262-1122	B- / 7.4	6.69	12.32	8.65 /67	14.08 /68	12.55 /64	0.00	1.94
SC	Eaton Vance Tax Mgd SmCap I	EIMGX	B+	(800) 262-1122	B / 8.2	6.92	12.86	9.70 /73	15.23 /77	13.69 /75	0.00	0.94
AA	Eaton Vance Tax-Mgd Eqty A-Alloc A	EAEAX	C+	(800) 262-1122	C / 5.3	2.38	5.21	7.63 /60	13.50 /63	11.06 /53	0.53	1.95
AA	● Eaton Vance Tax-Mgd Eqty A-Alloc B	EBEAX	C+	(800) 262-1122	C+ / 5.7	2.21	4.79	6.83 /54	12.65 /57	10.23 /46	0.00	2.70
AA	Eaton Vance Tax-Mgd Eqty A-Alloc C	ECEAX	C+	(800) 262-1122	C+ / 5.7	2.23	4.85	6.84 /54	12.66 /57	10.24 /46	0.00	2.70
IN	Eaton Vance Tax-Mgd Gl Div Inc A	EADIX	C-	(800) 262-1122	C- / 3.5	3.63	2.88	5.34 /41	10.57 /43	8.94 /36	3.58	1.17
IN	● Eaton Vance Tax-Mgd Gl Div Inc B	EBDIX	C-	(800) 262-1122	C- / 3.9	3.34	2.50	4.56 /35	9.77 /38	8.12 /31	3.06	1.92
IN	Eaton Vance Tax-Mgd Gl Div Inc C	ECDIX	C-	(800) 262-1122	C- / 3.9	3.34	2.42	4.57 /36	9.78 /38	8.12 /31	3.07	1.92
IN	Eaton Vance Tax-Mgd Gl Div Inc I	EIDIX	C	(800) 262-1122	C / 4.6	3.58	2.92	5.51 /42	10.84 /44	9.18 /38	4.05	0.92
IN	● Eaton Vance Tax-Mgd Growth 1.0	CAPEX	A-	(800) 262-1122	B / 7.9	1.21	5.55	12.61 /85	15.59 /80	13.35 /72	1.37	0.45
GR	● Eaton Vance Tax-Mgd Growth 1.1 A	ETTGX	B-	(800) 262-1122	C+ / 6.6	1.13	5.38	12.22 /84	15.23 /77	12.98 /68	0.98	0.83
GR	● Eaton Vance Tax-Mgd Growth 1.1 B	EMTGX	B+	(800) 262-1122	B- / 7.0	0.94	4.99	11.42 /80	14.36 /70	12.14 /62	0.19	1.59
GR	● Eaton Vance Tax-Mgd Growth 1.1 C	ECTGX	B+	(800) 262-1122	B- / 7.0	0.97	4.99	11.40 /80	14.38 /70	12.13 /61	0.46	1.58
GR	● Eaton Vance Tax-Mgd Growth 1.1 I	EITMX	A-	(800) 262-1122	B / 7.8	1.18	5.49	12.51 /85	15.51 /79	13.27 /71	1.36	0.59
GR	Eaton Vance Tax-Mgd Growth 1.2 A	EXTGX	B-	(800) 262-1122	C+ / 6.4	1.09	5.24	12.04 /83	15.03 /75	12.77 /66	0.84	1.00
GR	● Eaton Vance Tax-Mgd Growth 1.2 B	EYTGX	B-	(800) 262-1122	C+ / 6.8	0.92	4.88	11.21 /79	14.16 /68	11.95 /60	0.02	1.75
GR	Eaton Vance Tax-Mgd Growth 1.2 C	EZTGX	B-	(800) 262-1122	C+ / 6.8	0.88	4.85	11.20 /79	14.15 /68	11.94 /60	0.22	1.75
GR	Eaton Vance Tax-Mgd Growth 1.2 I	EITGX	A-	(800) 262-1122	B / 7.7	1.14	5.41	12.27 /84	15.29 /77	13.05 /69	1.12	0.75
GR	Eaton Vance Tax-Mgd MultiCap Gr A	EACPX	C	(800) 262-1122	C / 5.3	4.01	7.19	10.80 /78	12.65 /57	11.57 /57	0.00	1.42
GR	● Eaton Vance Tax-Mgd MultiCap Gr B	EBCPX	C	(800) 262-1122	C+ / 5.7	3.85	6.81	9.95 /74	11.80 /51	10.74 /51	0.00	2.17
GR	Eaton Vance Tax-Mgd MultiCap Gr C	ECCPX	C	(800) 262-1122	C+ / 5.7	3.84	6.80	9.99 /74	11.81 /51	10.75 /51	0.00	2.17
SC	Eaton Vance Tax-Mgd Small-Cap Val	ESVAX	C	(800) 262-1122	C+ / 5.9	3.34	8.41	4.01 /32	14.77 /73	12.52 /64	0.00	1.61
SC	Eaton Vance Tax-Mgd Small-Cap Val	ESVCX	C	(800) 262-1122	C+ / 6.3	3.19	7.97	3.20 /27	13.92 /66	11.67 /58	0.00	2.36
SC	Eaton Vance Tax-Mgd Small-Cap Val	ESVIX	C+	(800) 262-1122	B- / 7.1	3.46	8.51	4.23 /33	15.06 /75	12.79 /66	0.00	1.36
GR	Eaton Vance Tax-Mgd Value A	EATVX	C+	(800) 262-1122	C+ / 6.0	0.34	3.35	8.55 /67	15.10 /76	11.01 /53	1.01	1.21
GR	Eaton Vance Tax-Mgd Value C	ECTVX	C+	(800) 262-1122	C+ / 6.5	0.18	2.97	7.74 /61	14.26 /69	10.18 /46	0.39	1.96
GR	Eaton Vance Tax-Mgd Value Cl I	EITVX	B	(800) 262-1122	B- / 7.3	0.35	3.37	8.77 /68	15.39 /78	11.28 /55	1.32	0.96
HL	Eaton Vance WW Health Sciences A	ETHSX	C+	(800) 262-1122	A+ / 9.9	8.98	16.88	29.82 /99	28.19 /99	19.67 /99	0.00	1.46
HL	● Eaton Vance WW Health Sciences B	EMHSX	B-	(800) 262-1122	A+ / 9.9	8.73	16.45	28.87 /99	27.23 /99	18.78 /98	0.00	2.21
HL	Eaton Vance WW Health Sciences C	ECHSX	B-	(800) 262-1122	A+ / 9.9	8.72	16.40	28.80 /99	27.22 /99	18.75 /98	0.00	2.21
HL	Eaton Vance WW Health Sciences I	EIHSX	C+	(800) 262-1122	A+ / 9.9	8.94	16.93	30.15 /99	28.47 /99	19.95 /99	0.00	1.21
HL	Eaton Vance WW Health Sciences R	ERHSX	B-	(800) 262-1122	A+ / 9.9	8.86	16.68	29.50 /99	27.87 /99	19.38 /98	0.00	1.71
GR	Edgar Lomax Value Fund	LOMAX	C+	(888) 263-6443	C+ / 6.6	-1.79	2.53	9.58 /72	14.41 /70	13.39 /72	1.64	1.33
GR	Edgewood Growth Fund Inst	EGFIX	B+	(866) 777-7818	A- / 9.1	1.92	6.43	16.43 /94	17.17 /91	16.83 /96	0.00	1.10
GR	Edgewood Growth Fund Retail	EGFFX	B+	(866) 777-7818	A- / 9.0	1.87	6.26	16.03 /93	16.98 /90	16.69 /95	0.00	1.45
IN	EIC Value A	EICVX	C	(888) 739-1390	C- / 3.6	-0.79	4.25	7.78 /61	11.23 /47	--	0.66	1.29
IN	EIC Value C	EICCX	C+	(888) 739-1390	C+ / 4.0	-1.02	3.88	7.04 /55	10.44 /42	--	0.16	2.04
IN	EIC Value Fund Inst	EICIX	C+	(888) 739-1390	C / 4.7	-0.79	4.41	8.09 /63	11.54 /49	--	1.01	1.04

● Denotes fund is closed to new investors
* Denotes fund is included in Section II

www.thestreetratings.com

| RISK | | | NET ASSETS | | ASSET | | | | | BULL / BEAR | | FUND MANAGER | | MINIMUMS | | LOADS | |
| Risk Rating/Pts | 3 Year | | NAV | | | | | | Portfolio | Last Bull | Last Bear | Manager | Manager | Initial | Additional | Front | Back |
	Standard Deviation	Beta	As of 3/31/15	Total $(Mil)	Cash %	Stocks %	Bonds %	Other %	Turnover Ratio	Market Return	Market Return	Quality Pct	Tenure (Years)	Purch. $	Purch. $	End Load	End Load
C- / 3.8	12.8	0.64	17.36	72	4	95	0	1	44	87.8	-25.2	97	9	250,000	0	0.0	0.0
C- / 3.5	12.7	0.64	16.12	N/A	4	95	0	1	44	84.6	-25.4	97	9	1,000	0	0.0	0.0
C+ / 6.3	11.1	0.79	17.56	20	5	94	0	1	52	76.3	-23.0	65	10	1,000	0	5.8	0.0
C+ / 6.1	11.1	0.79	16.26	2	5	94	0	1	52	71.9	-23.2	53	10	1,000	0	0.0	0.0
C+ / 6.1	11.1	0.79	16.19	9	5	94	0	1	52	71.9	-23.2	54	10	1,000	0	0.0	0.0
C+ / 6.3	11.1	0.79	17.84	13	5	94	0	1	52	77.8	-22.9	68	10	250,000	0	0.0	0.0
C+ / 6.1	12.8	0.88	23.85	37	3	96	0	1	61	69.6	-21.2	45	9	1,000	0	5.8	0.0
C+ / 6.0	12.8	0.88	22.22	3	3	96	0	1	61	65.3	-21.5	34	9	1,000	0	0.0	0.0
C+ / 6.1	12.8	0.88	24.09	10	3	96	0	1	61	71.2	-21.2	49	9	250,000	0	0.0	0.0
C / 5.4	9.8	1.00	16.27	52	2	97	0	1	90	98.0	-17.9	70	8	1,000	0	5.8	0.0
C / 5.5	9.7	0.99	15.97	12	2	97	0	1	90	92.8	-18.0	60	8	1,000	0	0.0	0.0
C / 5.3	9.7	0.99	16.28	14	2	97	0	1	90	99.6	-17.7	73	8	250,000	0	0.0	0.0
C+ / 5.9	12.8	0.90	25.43	76	5	94	0	1	58	85.6	-25.1	70	9	1,000	0	5.8	0.0
C+ / 5.8	12.8	0.91	22.25	1	5	94	0	1	58	80.8	-25.4	60	9	1,000	0	0.0	0.0
C+ / 5.8	12.8	0.90	22.16	25	5	94	0	1	58	80.8	-25.4	60	9	1,000	0	0.0	0.0
C+ / 5.9	12.8	0.91	25.80	24	5	94	0	1	58	87.2	-25.1	73	9	250,000	0	0.0	0.0
C+ / 6.7	9.8	1.66	17.65	265	2	97	0	1	1	83.0	-20.2	13	2	1,000	0	5.8	0.0
C+ / 6.7	9.8	1.66	16.68	10	2	97	0	1	1	78.4	-20.5	9	2	1,000	0	0.0	0.0
C+ / 6.7	9.8	1.66	16.53	178	2	97	0	1	1	78.4	-20.5	9	2	1,000	0	0.0	0.0
C+ / 6.9	9.1	0.89	11.68	464	1	93	4	2	118	59.6	-16.7	23	5	1,000	0	5.8	0.0
C+ / 6.9	9.1	0.88	11.65	25	1	93	4	2	118	55.6	-16.9	17	5	1,000	0	0.0	0.0
C+ / 6.9	9.1	0.89	11.65	322	1	93	4	2	118	55.6	-17.0	17	5	1,000	0	0.0	0.0
C+ / 6.9	9.1	0.88	11.68	116	1	93	4	2	118	61.1	-16.6	26	5	250,000	0	0.0	0.0
B- / 7.3	9.6	1.00	879.20	828	1	98	0	1	3	96.5	-16.1	61	9	0	0	0.0	0.0
B- / 7.3	9.6	1.00	39.35	1,096	1	98	0	1	3	94.4	-16.2	57	9	1,000	0	5.8	0.0
B- / 7.3	9.6	1.00	38.49	7	1	98	0	1	3	89.5	-16.5	44	9	1,000	0	0.0	0.0
B- / 7.3	9.6	1.00	35.44	279	1	98	0	1	3	89.5	-16.4	44	9	1,000	0	0.0	0.0
B- / 7.3	9.6	1.00	36.86	47	1	98	0	1	3	96.1	-16.1	60	9	250,000	0	0.0	0.0
B- / 7.3	9.6	1.00	17.69	380	1	98	0	1	3	93.2	-16.2	54	9	1,000	0	5.8	0.0
B- / 7.3	9.6	1.00	17.49	5	1	98	0	1	3	88.3	-16.5	43	9	1,000	0	0.0	0.0
B- / 7.3	9.6	1.00	17.22	171	1	98	0	1	3	88.4	-16.5	42	9	1,000	0	0.0	0.0
B- / 7.3	9.6	1.00	17.73	55	1	98	0	1	3	94.9	-16.2	57	9	250,000	0	0.0	0.0
C+ / 6.1	11.5	1.09	20.73	45	0	99	0	1	29	85.7	-20.7	14	2	1,000	0	5.8	0.0
C+ / 6.0	11.5	1.09	18.35	2	0	99	0	1	29	80.9	-20.9	10	2	1,000	0	0.0	0.0
C+ / 6.0	11.5	1.09	18.38	21	0	99	0	1	29	80.9	-20.9	10	2	1,000	0	0.0	0.0
C / 5.4	11.3	0.81	17.95	30	5	94	0	1	48	86.0	-21.3	82	10	1,000	0	5.8	0.0
C / 4.7	11.4	0.81	15.52	10	5	94	0	1	48	81.4	-21.5	76	10	1,000	0	0.0	0.0
C / 5.5	11.3	0.80	18.26	5	5	94	0	1	48	87.5	-21.1	83	10	250,000	0	0.0	0.0
C+ / 6.8	9.4	0.96	23.31	364	2	97	0	1	19	90.3	-18.3	64	16	1,000	0	5.8	0.0
C+ / 6.8	9.4	0.95	22.47	158	2	97	0	1	19	85.4	-18.5	53	16	1,000	0	0.0	0.0
C+ / 6.7	9.4	0.95	23.22	100	2	97	0	1	19	91.8	-18.2	68	16	250,000	0	0.0	0.0
D+ / 2.9	12.4	0.88	13.35	1,098	1	98	0	1	57	136.8	-9.7	99	26	1,000	0	5.8	0.0
C- / 3.2	12.3	0.87	13.82	21	1	98	0	1	57	131.2	-10.1	98	26	1,000	0	0.0	0.0
C- / 3.1	12.4	0.87	13.71	357	1	98	0	1	57	131.1	-10.1	98	26	1,000	0	0.0	0.0
D+ / 2.9	12.4	0.88	13.52	220	1	98	0	1	57	139.0	-9.6	99	26	250,000	0	0.0	0.0
C- / 3.1	12.4	0.87	14.13	77	1	98	0	1	57	134.9	-9.8	99	26	1,000	0	0.0	0.0
C+ / 6.3	9.2	0.92	14.24	71	3	96	0	1	43	80.0	-10.3	64	18	2,500	100	0.0	0.0
C+ / 5.6	10.9	0.96	20.67	3,625	2	97	0	1	41	109.0	-11.9	81	9	100,000	0	0.0	0.0
C+ / 5.6	11.1	0.97	20.19	231	2	97	0	1	41	108.9	-12.4	78	9	3,000	0	0.0	0.0
B / 8.1	8.4	0.84	13.77	85	12	87	0	1	19	65.6	N/A	39	4	2,500	250	5.5	2.0
B / 8.0	8.5	0.84	13.62	62	12	87	0	1	19	61.4	N/A	29	4	2,500	250	0.0	2.0
B / 8.1	8.5	0.85	13.81	187	12	87	0	1	19	67.0	-8.5	41	4	100,000	0	0.0	2.0

Fund Type	Fund Name	Ticker Symbol	Overall Investment Rating	Phone	Performance Rating/Pts	3 Mo	6 Mo	1Yr / Pct	3Yr / Pct	5Yr / Pct	Dividend Yield	Expense Ratio
	99 Pct = Best							Total Return % through 3/31/15			Incl. in Returns	
	0 Pct = Worst								Annualized			
RE	Ell Global Property Inst	EIIGX	E+	(888) 323-8912	C / 5.3	4.62	11.21	11.72 /81	9.63 /37	10.15 /46	5.13	0.99
RE	Ell International Property I	EIIPX	E	(888) 323-8912	C- / 3.2	4.76	5.68	2.78 /25	8.23 /28	7.29 /25	26.65	1.00
RE	Ell Realty Sec Inst	EIIRX	C	(888) 323-8912	A / 9.5	4.22	20.04	24.16 /98	14.37 /70	16.69 /95	2.03	1.27
AA	Elfun Diversified	ELDFX	C-	(800) 242-0134	C- / 3.8	2.40	3.81	6.45 /50	9.21 /34	8.06 /30	1.84	0.36
FO	Elfun International	EGLBX	D+	(800) 242-0134	C- / 3.6	7.41	4.07	1.26 /19	9.10 /34	5.35 /13	2.68	0.31
GI	Elfun Trusts	ELFNX	B+	(800) 242-0134	A- / 9.2	1.60	6.63	15.19 /92	17.54 /92	15.34 /89	1.17	0.15
FS	Emerald Banking and Finance A	HSSAX	A+	(855) 828-9909	A- / 9.2	2.48	10.72	4.37 /34	20.00 /98	14.27 /80	0.00	1.72
FS	Emerald Banking and Finance C	HSSCX	A+	(855) 828-9909	A / 9.3	2.30	10.34	3.63 /30	19.22 /97	13.56 /73	0.00	2.38
FS	Emerald Banking and Finance Inst	HSSIX	A+	(855) 828-9909	A+ / 9.6	2.53	10.86	4.66 /36	20.39 /98	--	0.00	1.37
FS	Emerald Banking and Finance Inv	FFBFX	A+	(855) 828-9909	A / 9.5	2.48	10.72	4.33 /34	20.01 /98	13.29 /71	0.00	1.69
SC	Emerald Growth A	HSPGX	B-	(855) 828-9909	A+ / 9.6	8.67	20.82	11.90 /82	19.12 /97	19.41 /98	0.00	1.31
SC	Emerald Growth C	HSPCX	B-	(855) 828-9909	A+ / 9.7	8.53	20.43	11.24 /79	18.35 /95	18.65 /98	0.00	1.96
SC	Emerald Growth Institutional	FGROX	B	(855) 828-9909	A+ / 9.8	8.76	21.06	12.31 /84	19.50 /97	19.78 /99	0.00	1.00
GR	Emerald Growth Investor	FFGRX	B	(855) 828-9909	A+ / 9.7	8.69	20.81	11.94 /82	19.09 /97	--	0.00	1.34
*EM	Emerging Markets Growth	EMRGX	E	(800) 421-0180	E / 0.4	1.77	-3.65	-3.53 / 8	-1.58 / 3	-0.66 / 2	1.96	0.77
GL	Empiric 2500 A	EMCAX	B-	(800) 880-0324	B- / 7.4	3.74	8.86	10.71 /77	16.17 /85	8.52 /33	0.00	1.79
GL	Empiric 2500 C	EMCCX	B	(800) 880-0324	B / 7.8	3.54	8.47	9.88 /74	15.30 /77	7.70 /28	0.00	2.54
GL	Encompass	ENCPX	E-	(888) 263-6443	E- / 0.0	-5.18	-29.48	-39.40 / 0	-32.76 / 0	-17.80 / 0	0.00	1.50
GR	EntrepreneurShares AllCp Impct Inst	IMPAX	U	(877) 271-8811	U /	4.52	9.61	8.56 /67	--	--	0.04	N/A
GL	EntrepreneurShares Global Inst	ENTIX	D+	(877) 271-8811	C- / 3.9	4.59	6.93	2.48 /24	9.55 /36	--	0.00	2.42
GR	EntrepreneurShares US Lg Cap Inst	IMPLX	U	(877) 271-8811	U /	2.69	5.08	--	--	--	0.00	0.82
FO	EP Asia Small Companies Fund A	EPASX	E+	(888) 558-5851	D+ / 2.5	3.31	-3.85	-2.76 / 9	10.69 /44	--	0.00	2.48
FO	EP China Fund A	EPHCX	D+	(888) 558-5851	C- / 3.1	4.46	5.66	6.51 /51	9.43 /36	3.22 / 6	0.31	2.14
FO	EP Latin America A	EPLAX	E	(888) 558-5851	E- / 0.2	-4.36	-17.41	-10.44 / 3	-2.27 / 3	--	0.01	2.83
GR	Epiphany FFV A	EPVAX	C		C / 5.4	-1.19	5.79	7.97 /63	14.29 /69	12.59 /65	0.10	1.60
FO	Epiphany FFV Latin America A	ELAAX	E		E- / 0.1	-7.01	-19.02	-18.83 / 1	-8.87 / 1	--	1.11	3.58
FO	● Epiphany FFV Latin America C	ELACX	E		E- / 0.1	-7.14	-19.29	-19.29 / 1	-9.62 / 1	--	0.00	4.28
FO	Epiphany FFV Latin America N	ELANX	E		E- / 0.1	-7.02	-19.05	-18.77 / 1	-9.00 / 1	--	1.15	3.54
GR	Epiphany FFV N	EPVNX	C+		C+ / 6.2	-1.20	5.72	7.99 /63	14.32 /69	12.55 /64	0.11	1.60
AA	Epiphany FFV Strat Income A	EPIAX	C-		E+ / 0.6	1.09	1.80	3.42 /29	2.82 / 8	--	2.36	1.77
AA	Epiphany FFV Strat Income C	EPICX	C-		E+ / 0.7	0.82	1.32	2.69 /25	2.03 / 6	--	1.81	2.53
AA	Epiphany FFV Strat Income N	EPINX	C-		E+ / 0.8	1.09	1.82	3.38 /28	2.70 / 7	3.98 / 8	2.53	1.77
IN	Equinox BlueCrest Sys Macro I	EBCIX	U	(888) 643-3431	U /	7.25	11.17	--	--	--	0.00	0.94
AA	Equinox Campbell Strategy A	EBSAX	U	(888) 643-3431	U /	7.50	19.99	42.36 /99	--	--	5.14	1.30
AA	Equinox Campbell Strategy C	EBSCX	U	(888) 643-3431	U /	7.29	19.59	41.40 /99	--	--	5.57	2.17
AA	Equinox Campbell Strategy I	EBSIX	U	(888) 643-3431	U /	7.56	20.20	42.82 /99	--	--	5.59	1.05
AA	Equinox Campbell Strategy P	EBSPX	U	(888) 643-3431	U /	7.65	20.20	42.82 /99	--	--	5.59	1.06
IN	Equinox Chesapeake Strat I	EQCHX	U	(888) 643-3431	U /	18.35	29.71	49.80 /99	--	--	16.49	2.62
GR	Equinox MutualHedge Futures Str A	MHFAX	C-	(866) 643-3431	C- / 3.9	8.98	17.04	23.16 /98	4.22 /11	3.73 / 7	7.98	2.49
GR	Equinox MutualHedge Futures Str C	MHFCX	C	(866) 643-3431	C- / 4.2	8.67	16.54	22.28 /97	3.46 / 9	2.95 / 6	7.96	3.24
GR	Equinox MutualHedge Futures Str I	MHFIX	C	(866) 643-3431	C / 4.9	8.92	17.15	23.50 /98	4.51 /12	--	8.70	2.24
GI	ESG Managers Balanced A	PMPAX	D	(800) 767-1729	C- / 3.0	1.76	4.34	7.13 /56	9.25 /35	8.21 /31	1.13	2.88
GI	ESG Managers Balanced C	PWPCX	D+	(800) 767-1729	C- / 3.3	1.53	4.02	6.39 /50	8.44 /30	7.41 /26	0.62	3.63
GI	ESG Managers Balanced Institutional	PWPIX	C-	(800) 767-1729	C- / 4.0	1.76	4.45	7.44 /59	9.53 /36	8.46 /33	1.41	2.63
AG	ESG Managers Growth A	PAGAX	D	(800) 767-1729	C / 4.9	1.69	5.53	8.58 /67	12.71 /58	10.05 /45	0.48	3.00
GR	ESG Managers Growth and Income A	PGPAX	D	(800) 767-1729	C- / 4.0	1.44	4.15	7.48 /59	11.28 /47	9.39 /40	1.19	3.38
GR	ESG Managers Growth and Income C	PWCCX	D+	(800) 767-1729	C / 4.4	1.29	3.71	6.68 /52	10.43 /42	8.51 /33	0.49	4.13
GR	ESG Managers Growth and Income	PMIIX	C-	(800) 767-1729	C / 5.2	1.60	4.26	7.78 /61	11.64 /50	9.66 /42	1.46	3.13
AG	ESG Managers Growth C	PAGCX	D+	(800) 767-1729	C / 5.3	1.48	5.10	7.71 /61	11.82 /51	9.23 /38	0.49	3.75
AG	ESG Managers Growth Institutional	PAGIX	C-	(800) 767-1729	C+ / 6.0	1.69	5.65	8.73 /68	12.85 /58	10.30 /47	0.73	2.75
GI	ESG Managers Income A	PWMAX	D	(800) 767-1729	D / 1.9	1.63	3.62	6.80 /53	6.87 /21	6.61 /21	1.81	4.66
GI	ESG Managers Income C	PWMCX	D	(800) 767-1729	D / 2.1	1.38	3.22	5.91 /46	6.04 /17	5.80 /16	1.28	5.41

● Denotes fund is closed to new investors
* Denotes fund is included in Section II

RISK			NET ASSETS		ASSET					Portfolio	BULL / BEAR		FUND MANAGER		MINIMUMS		LOADS	
	3 Year		NAV								Last Bull	Last Bear	Manager	Manager	Initial	Additional	Front	Back
Risk	Standard		As of	Total	Cash	Stocks	Bonds	Other		Turnover	Market	Market	Quality	Tenure	Purch.	Purch.	End	End
Rating/Pts	Deviation	Beta	3/31/15	$(Mil)	%	%	%	%		Ratio	Return	Return	Pct	(Years)	$	$	Load	Load
E+ / 0.6	11.1	0.80	9.74	67	5	94	0	1		18	58.0	-18.5	47	9	100,000	0	0.0	0.0
D / 2.1	13.4	0.66	15.18	53	12	87	0	1		9	49.4	-22.3	55	5	100,000	0	0.0	0.0
D / 2.2	12.4	0.98	5.19	19	5	94	0	1		112	89.3	-15.1	72	11	100,000	0	0.0	0.0
C+ / 6.7	6.5	1.12	19.23	233	18	54	26	2		144	51.6	-13.8	28	4	500	100	0.0	0.0
C+ / 5.9	12.5	0.92	21.16	267	2	97	0	1		49	53.4	-25.9	71	24	500	100	0.0	0.0
C / 5.5	10.5	1.05	58.95	2,483	2	97	0	1		12	112.3	-17.0	73	27	500	100	0.0	0.0
B- / 7.0	11.9	0.84	28.91	48	1	98	0	1		34	116.2	-20.2	93	18	2,000	100	4.8	0.0
B- / 7.0	11.9	0.84	26.25	32	1	98	0	1		34	111.4	-20.3	92	18	2,000	100	0.0	0.0
C+ / 6.9	11.9	0.84	29.19	24	1	98	0	1		34	N/A	N/A	94	18	1,000,000	0	0.0	0.0
B- / 7.0	11.9	0.84	27.69	27	1	98	0	1		34	116.6	-20.0	93	18	2,000	100	0.0	0.0
C- / 3.7	16.2	1.05	20.68	125	1	98	0	1		70	128.6	-26.9	82	23	2,000	100	4.8	0.0
C- / 3.5	16.2	1.04	18.07	14	1	98	0	1		70	123.4	-27.1	78	23	2,000	100	0.0	0.0
C- / 3.7	16.2	1.05	21.22	177	1	98	0	1		70	130.8	-26.8	84	23	1,000,000	0	0.0	0.0
C- / 3.7	16.2	1.11	20.63	22	1	98	0	1		70	128.2	N/A	76	23	2,000	100	0.0	0.0
C / 4.4	13.2	0.94	6.90	7,195	7	89	2	2		41	13.5	-28.2	34	N/A	100,000	25,000	0.0	0.0
C+ / 5.8	12.0	0.57	34.70	31	0	100	0	0		622	88.4	-24.0	98	20	2,500	100	5.8	0.0
C+ / 5.6	12.0	0.58	32.15	2	0	100	0	0		622	83.6	-24.2	98	20	2,500	100	0.0	0.0
D- / 1.1	27.0	0.91	3.66	2	4	89	5	2		24	-63.5	-32.8	0	9	5,000	100	0.0	2.0
U /	N/A	N/A	11.34	142	6	93	0	1		55	N/A	N/A	N/A	2	2,500	0	0.0	0.0
C / 5.2	11.1	0.70	12.08	5	0	0	0	100		64	61.7	-24.8	88	5	2,500	0	0.0	0.0
U /	N/A	N/A	10.68	82	0	0	0	100		0	N/A	N/A	N/A	1	2,500	0	0.0	0.0
C- / 3.6	16.1	0.67	12.50	29	2	97	0	1		82	68.7	-25.1	92	5	2,500	250	4.5	2.0
C+ / 6.1	11.9	0.66	13.11	33	1	98	0	1		28	42.5	-32.5	89	6	2,500	250	4.5	2.0
C / 5.3	16.8	0.93	9.86	18	1	98	0	1		65	N/A	N/A	2	4	2,500	250	4.5	2.0
C+ / 5.8	10.4	1.04	12.31	5	4	95	0	1		70	89.2	-18.0	35	7	1,000	250	5.0	2.0
C / 5.5	16.8	1.00	7.28	1	4	93	1	2		17	N/A	N/A	0	3	1,000	250	5.0	2.0
C / 5.5	16.7	1.00	7.28	N/A	4	93	1	2		17	N/A	N/A	0	3	1,000	250	0.0	2.0
C / 5.5	16.9	1.00	7.27	3	4	93	1	2		17	N/A	N/A	0	3	1,000	250	0.0	2.0
C+ / 5.8	10.5	1.04	12.28	19	4	95	0	1		70	89.2	-17.8	34	7	1,000	250	0.0	2.0
B+ / 9.9	2.2	0.23	10.58	6	5	23	70	2		27	13.2	-1.8	71	5	1,000	250	5.0	2.0
B+ / 9.9	2.1	0.22	10.51	1	5	23	70	2		27	10.5	-2.1	63	5	1,000	250	0.0	2.0
B+ / 9.9	2.1	0.22	10.52	13	5	23	70	2		27	13.0	-1.6	71	5	1,000	250	0.0	2.0
U /	N/A	N/A	10.95	56	0	0	0	100		0	N/A	N/A	N/A	N/A	25,000	0	0.0	0.0
U /	N/A	N/A	12.47	73	46	14	39	1		871	N/A	N/A	N/A	N/A	2,500	500	5.8	Back End Load
U /	N/A	N/A	12.36	41	46	14	39	1		871	N/A	N/A	N/A	N/A	2,500	500	0.0	Back End Load
U /	N/A	N/A	12.52	977	46	14	39	1		871	N/A	N/A	N/A	N/A	100,000	0	0.0	0.0
U /	N/A	N/A	12.52	73	46	14	39	1		871	N/A	N/A	N/A	N/A	2,500	0	0.0	0.0
U /	N/A	N/A	13.80	27	49	0	50	1		298	N/A	N/A	N/A	N/A	25,000	0	0.0	0.0
C+ / 6.8	8.2	0.06	10.07	128	29	0	70	1		0	6.4	-0.2	89	4	2,500	500	5.8	1.0
C+ / 6.7	8.2	0.07	9.78	43	29	0	70	1		0	3.7	-0.6	86	4	2,500	500	0.0	1.0
C+ / 6.8	8.2	0.07	10.13	136	29	0	70	1		0	7.3	N/A	90	4	1,000,000	0	0.0	1.0
C+ / 6.0	6.5	0.66	12.12	13	0	63	35	2		106	48.1	-10.9	52	6	1,000	50	5.5	0.0
C+ / 6.0	6.5	0.66	11.98	7	0	63	35	2		106	44.4	-11.1	40	6	1,000	50	0.0	0.0
C+ / 6.0	6.5	0.66	12.15	6	0	63	35	2		106	49.3	-10.7	56	6	250,000	0	0.0	0.0
C- / 4.1	10.0	1.02	13.20	11	2	97	0	1		126	73.2	-20.7	23	6	1,000	50	5.5	0.0
C / 5.0	8.4	0.85	12.68	12	2	81	16	1		140	62.2	-16.4	37	6	1,000	50	5.5	0.0
C / 5.1	8.4	0.85	12.60	4	2	81	16	1		140	58.0	-16.6	28	6	1,000	50	0.0	0.0
C / 5.0	8.4	0.85	12.72	3	2	81	16	1		140	63.8	-16.3	42	6	250,000	0	0.0	0.0
C- / 4.1	10.1	1.02	13.01	2	2	97	0	1		126	68.7	-20.8	15	6	1,000	50	0.0	0.0
C- / 4.1	10.1	1.03	13.23	4	2	97	0	1		126	74.2	-20.4	22	6	250,000	0	0.0	0.0
B- / 7.0	4.2	0.40	11.22	5	0	36	63	1		97	32.6	-6.7	74	6	1,000	50	4.5	0.0
B- / 7.0	4.2	0.40	11.05	2	0	36	63	1		97	29.3	-7.0	65	6	1,000	50	0.0	0.0

Fund Type	Fund Name	Ticker Symbol	Overall Investment Rating	Phone	Performance Rating/Pts	3 Mo	6 Mo	1Yr / Pct	3Yr / Pct	5Yr / Pct	Dividend Yield	Expense Ratio
								Total Return % through 3/31/15	Annualized		Incl. in Returns	
GI	ESG Managers Income Institutional	PWMIX	D+	(800) 767-1729	D+ / 2.7	1.72	3.75	7.04 /55	7.11 /22	6.87 /22	2.13	4.41
EN	EuroPac Gold A	EPGFX	U	(888) 558-5851	U /	-5.01	-17.15	-25.08 / 0	--	--	0.00	2.03
FO	EuroPac International Div Inc A	EPDPX	U	(888) 558-5851	U /	-1.66	-5.91	-6.82 / 4	--	--	3.59	2.06
FO	EuroPac International Value A	EPIVX	E	(888) 558-5851	E- / 0.2	-0.85	-12.48	-14.12 / 2	-3.71 / 2	--	2.25	1.90
EM	European Equity A	VEEEX	E	(800) 527-9525	E / 0.5	1.89	0.72	-5.87 / 5	2.45 / 7	-1.85 / 2	0.00	2.96
EM	European Equity C	VEECX	E	(800) 527-9525	E+ / 0.6	1.73	0.37	-6.57 / 4	1.68 / 6	-2.64 / 1	0.00	3.71
FO	European Gro and Inc Direct	EUGIX	D-	(800) 955-9988	D / 2.0	4.25	-2.58	-5.30 / 5	7.77 /26	3.96 / 8	2.58	1.29
FO	European Gro and Inc K	EUGKX	D-	(800) 955-9988	D / 1.7	4.01	-2.86	-5.88 / 5	7.22 /23	3.43 / 7	1.90	1.79
GL	Even Keel Multi-Asset Mgd Risk I	EKAIX	U	(800) 595-9111	U /	0.76	1.10	2.73 /25	--	--	0.80	0.95
GR	Eventide Gilead A	ETAGX	A+	(877) 453-7877	A+ / 9.9	5.16	16.29	16.24 /94	24.76 /99	20.37 /99	0.00	1.50
GR	Eventide Gilead C	ETCGX	A+	(877) 453-7877	A+ / 9.9	4.94	15.82	15.32 /92	23.80 /99	19.43 /98	0.00	2.25
GR	Eventide Gilead I	ETILX	A+	(877) 453-7877	A+ / 9.9	5.25	16.40	16.50 /94	25.09 /99	20.63 /99	0.00	1.25
GR	Eventide Gilead N	ETGLX	A+	(877) 453-7877	A+ / 9.9	5.19	16.30	16.30 /94	24.85 /99	20.42 /99	0.00	1.45
HL	Eventide Healthcare & Life Sci A	ETAHX	U	(877) 453-7877	U /	11.84	38.01	32.54 /99	--	--	0.00	1.75
HL	Eventide Healthcare & Life Sci C	ETCHX	U	(877) 453-7877	U /	11.68	37.61	31.64 /99	--	--	0.00	2.50
HL	Eventide Healthcare & Life Sci I	ETIHX	U	(877) 453-7877	U /	11.92	38.26	32.88 /99	--	--	0.00	1.50
HL	Eventide Healthcare & Life Sci N	ETNHX	U	(877) 453-7877	U /	11.92	38.12	32.66 /99	--	--	0.00	1.70
GL	Evermore Global Value A	EVGBX	D+	(866) 383-7667	C- / 3.5	10.27	10.38	0.78 /18	10.23 /41	5.12 /12	4.17	1.84
GL	Evermore Global Value I	EVGIX	C-	(866) 383-7667	C / 4.5	10.31	10.48	1.02 /18	10.49 /42	5.39 /14	4.59	1.59
* GR	Fairholme	FAIRX	E	(866) 202-2263	D / 2.2	-1.97	-7.01	-7.81 / 3	10.21 /41	5.69 /15	0.00	1.02
AA ●	Fairholme Allocation	FAAFX	E	(866) 202-2263	D / 1.9	4.89	-2.50	-9.94 / 3	8.72 /31	--	0.00	1.02
IN	Fallen Angels Income Fund	FAINX	C	(888) 999-1395	C- / 3.7	2.00	2.78	3.55 /29	9.54 /36	8.52 /33	1.50	2.34
GR	Fallen Angels Value Fund	FAVLX	C	(888) 999-1395	C- / 4.0	-1.89	1.24	4.77 /37	10.58 /43	6.76 /22	0.00	2.30
IN	FAM Equity-Income Inv	FAMEX	C+	(800) 932-3271	C+ / 6.6	2.11	8.36	8.47 /66	13.75 /65	12.87 /67	1.25	1.29
GR	FAM Small Cap Investor	FAMFX	A	(800) 932-3271	B+ / 8.8	1.31	13.82	7.25 /57	17.18 /91	--	0.50	1.58
SC	FAM Value Inv	FAMVX	A+	(800) 932-3271	B+ / 8.9	3.00	12.71	13.55 /88	16.28 /85	13.52 /73	0.00	1.20
BA	FBP Appreciation and Income Opps	FBPBX	C	(800) 443-4249	C- / 3.6	-1.78	-0.36	2.36 /23	10.29 /41	7.33 /25	1.37	1.05
GR	FBP Equity and Dividend Plus	FBPEX	C+	(800) 443-4249	C / 4.7	-2.22	-0.26	4.23 /33	12.13 /53	7.20 /24	2.00	1.22
GR	FDP Marsico Growth A	MDDDX	C	(800) 441-7762	C / 5.0	1.48	3.18	11.29 /80	12.56 /56	12.88 /67	0.00	1.32
GR	FDP Marsico Growth C	MCDDX	C	(800) 441-7762	C / 5.3	1.34	2.78	10.45 /76	11.71 /50	12.02 /61	0.00	2.08
GR	FDP Marsico Growth Inst	MADDX	C+	(800) 441-7762	C+ / 6.1	1.57	3.28	11.55 /81	12.82 /58	13.15 /70	0.00	1.07
FO	FDP MFS Res Inter FDP Fd A	MDIQX	D-	(800) 441-7762	D- / 1.3	5.43	1.14	-1.73 /11	6.60 /19	5.64 /15	1.80	1.48
FO	FDP MFS Res Inter FDP Fd C	MCIQX	D-	(800) 441-7762	D- / 1.5	5.31	0.82	-2.45 / 9	5.81 /16	4.86 /11	1.17	2.24
FO	FDP MFS Res Inter FDP Fd I	MAIQX	D-	(800) 441-7762	D / 2.0	5.57	1.30	-1.44 /12	6.86 /21	5.91 /16	2.10	1.23
AA	Federated Absolute Return A	FMAAX	D	(800) 341-7400	E+ / 0.8	1.99	2.84	6.52 /51	2.36 / 7	1.57 / 4	1.23	1.66
AA	Federated Absolute Return B	FMBBX	D	(800) 341-7400	E+ / 0.9	1.70	2.41	5.60 /43	1.57 / 6	0.77 / 3	0.00	2.43
AA	Federated Absolute Return C	FMRCX	D	(800) 341-7400	E+ / 0.9	1.81	2.42	5.73 /44	1.57 / 6	0.79 / 3	0.00	2.44
AA	Federated Absolute Return Inst	FMIIX	D	(800) 341-7400	D- / 1.1	1.98	2.88	6.65 /52	2.58 / 7	1.78 / 4	1.55	1.43
GI	Federated Capital Income A	CAPAX	D	(800) 341-7400	D- / 1.4	0.71	-1.10	0.75 /18	7.29 /23	7.74 /28	5.14	1.08
GI	Federated Capital Income B	CAPBX	D	(800) 341-7400	D / 1.6	0.41	-1.59	-0.11 /15	6.44 /19	6.93 /23	4.66	1.86
GI	Federated Capital Income C	CAPCX	D	(800) 341-7400	D / 1.7	0.53	-1.47	0.01 /16	6.51 /19	6.95 /23	4.68	1.83
GI	Federated Capital Income F	CAPFX	D	(800) 341-7400	D / 1.9	0.59	-1.11	0.74 /18	7.25 /23	7.75 /28	5.39	1.08
AA	Federated Capital Income Inst	CAPSX	D+	(800) 341-7400	D / 2.2	0.65	-1.10	0.87 /18	7.54 /24	7.89 /29	5.70	0.82
AA	Federated Capital Income R	CAPRX	E+	(800) 341-7400	D / 1.9	0.55	-1.31	0.43 /17	6.98 /21	7.35 /25	5.23	1.52
SC	Federated Clover Small Value A	VSFAX	C-	(800) 341-7400	C / 5.2	1.33	6.85	4.43 /35	13.66 /65	11.84 /60	0.37	1.45
SC	Federated Clover Small Value C	VSFCX	C	(800) 341-7400	C+ / 5.6	1.12	6.44	3.64 /30	12.80 /58	11.00 /53	0.00	2.21
SC	Federated Clover Small Value Inst	VSFIX	C	(800) 341-7400	C+ / 6.3	1.36	6.96	4.66 /36	13.93 /67	12.12 /61	0.62	1.14
SC	Federated Clover Small Value R	VSFRX	C	(800) 341-7400	C+ / 6.0	1.30	6.79	4.26 /33	13.43 /63	11.57 /57	0.26	1.78
GR	Federated Clover Value Fund A	VFCAX	C+	(800) 341-7400	C+ / 6.0	1.72	4.95	5.80 /45	15.05 /75	12.09 /61	0.88	1.28
GR	Federated Clover Value Fund B	VFCBX	C+	(800) 341-7400	C+ / 6.4	1.57	4.63	5.10 /39	14.22 /69	11.29 /55	0.41	2.10
GR	Federated Clover Value Fund C	VFCCX	C+	(800) 341-7400	C+ / 6.4	1.57	4.57	5.04 /39	14.21 /69	11.28 /55	0.40	2.06
GR	Federated Clover Value Fund I	VFCIX	B	(800) 341-7400	B- / 7.2	1.83	5.07	6.06 /47	15.34 /78	12.37 /63	1.18	0.98

● Denotes fund is closed to new investors
* Denotes fund is included in Section II

www.thestreetratings.com

RISK Risk Rating/Pts	3 Year Standard Deviation	Beta	NET ASSETS NAV As of 3/31/15	Total $(Mil)	ASSET Cash %	Stocks %	Bonds %	Other %	Portfolio Turnover Ratio	BULL / BEAR Last Bull Market Return	Last Bear Market Return	FUND MANAGER Manager Quality Pct	Manager Tenure (Years)	MINIMUMS Initial Purch. $	Additional Purch. $	LOADS Front End Load	Back End Load
C+ / 6.9	4.2	0.40	11.24	3	0	36	63	1	97	33.6	-6.6	76	6	250,000	0	0.0	0.0
U /	N/A	N/A	7.20	48	10	89	0	1	14	N/A	N/A	N/A	2	2,500	250	4.5	2.0
U /	N/A	N/A	9.18	60	20	79	0	1	28	N/A	N/A	N/A	2	2,500	250	4.5	2.0
C- / 3.7	13.5	0.85	8.13	61	9	90	0	1	29	11.3	-23.6	1	5	2,500	250	4.5	2.0
C / 4.3	15.9	0.89	23.74	17	0	99	0	1	61	18.6	-29.5	83	3	2,500	50	5.8	0.0
C / 4.3	15.9	0.89	21.77	N/A	0	99	0	1	61	15.6	-29.8	78	3	2,500	50	0.0	0.0
C / 5.4	14.8	1.08	8.99	7	0	99	0	1	15	48.4	-26.9	32	12	1,000	250	0.0	0.0
C / 5.4	14.7	1.07	9.04	5	0	99	0	1	15	45.9	-27.1	28	12	1,000	250	0.0	0.0
U /	N/A	N/A	11.96	307	0	0	0	100	12	N/A	N/A	N/A	3	20,000	0	0.0	1.0
C+ / 6.1	13.0	0.93	27.72	517	11	87	0	2	17	166.2	-25.5	97	7	1,000	0	5.8	0.0
C+ / 6.0	12.9	0.93	26.53	125	11	87	0	2	17	159.4	-25.7	96	7	1,000	0	0.0	0.0
C+ / 6.1	12.9	0.93	28.06	281	11	87	0	2	17	168.4	-25.4	97	7	100,000	0	0.0	0.0
C+ / 6.1	13.0	0.93	27.78	494	11	87	0	2	17	166.6	-25.4	97	7	1,000	0	0.0	0.0
U /	N/A	N/A	23.42	109	4	95	0	1	33	N/A	N/A	N/A	3	1,000	0	5.8	1.0
U /	N/A	N/A	23.05	26	4	95	0	1	33	N/A	N/A	N/A	3	1,000	0	0.0	1.0
U /	N/A	N/A	23.56	50	4	95	0	1	33	N/A	N/A	N/A	3	100,000	0	0.0	1.0
U /	N/A	N/A	23.48	29	4	95	0	1	33	N/A	N/A	N/A	3	1,000	0	0.0	1.0
C+ / 6.3	11.4	0.65	11.60	37	7	92	0	1	54	55.9	-30.1	91	6	5,000	100	5.0	2.0
C+ / 6.3	11.4	0.65	11.66	237	7	92	0	1	54	57.3	-30.0	92	6	1,000,000	100	0.0	2.0
C- / 3.2	17.8	1.33	34.39	5,750	0	94	4	2	2	77.1	-30.6	2	16	10,000	1,000	0.0	2.0
D+ / 2.5	19.7	2.25	11.80	359	8	80	10	2	33	77.2	-25.6	1	5	25,000	2,500	0.0	2.0
B / 8.1	7.4	0.74	10.15	10	5	78	16	1	66	52.8	-11.4	38	9	10,000	1,000	0.0	0.0
C+ / 6.9	11.1	1.08	11.41	10	9	90	0	1	22	70.1	-23.0	6	9	10,000	1,000	0.0	0.0
C+ / 6.7	10.1	0.96	26.01	156	3	96	0	1	10	84.7	-14.4	45	19	500	50	0.0	0.0
C+ / 6.5	12.6	0.96	15.52	65	14	85	0	1	20	N/A	N/A	81	3	5,000	50	0.0	0.0
B- / 7.2	9.8	0.66	68.58	975	4	95	0	1	8	95.9	-18.4	94	28	500	50	0.0	0.0
B- / 7.5	9.3	1.45	18.53	39	16	76	6	2	10	62.7	-18.1	9	26	5,000	0	0.0	0.0
B- / 7.5	10.0	0.98	24.89	29	7	92	0	1	24	77.4	-25.3	22	22	5,000	0	0.0	0.0
C+ / 6.3	10.7	0.96	17.09	61	4	95	0	1	101	85.7	-18.3	31	10	1,000	50	5.3	0.0
C+ / 6.2	10.7	0.96	15.83	93	4	95	0	1	101	81.0	-18.5	22	10	1,000	50	0.0	0.0
C+ / 6.3	10.7	0.96	17.51	6	4	95	0	1	101	87.4	-18.2	33	10	2,000,000	0	0.0	0.0
C+ / 5.9	12.9	0.96	12.43	69	1	98	0	1	29	41.6	-22.1	32	10	1,000	50	5.3	0.0
C+ / 5.9	12.9	0.96	12.30	106	1	98	0	1	29	38.0	-22.4	24	10	1,000	50	0.0	0.0
C+ / 5.9	12.9	0.97	12.51	6	1	98	0	1	29	42.9	-22.0	35	10	2,000,000	0	0.0	0.0
B / 8.0	4.0	0.42	10.26	87	21	77	0	2	117	6.8	-0.5	36	6	1,500	100	5.5	0.0
B / 8.0	3.9	0.42	10.19	10	21	77	0	2	117	4.1	-0.8	27	6	1,500	100	0.0	0.0
B / 8.0	4.0	0.42	10.15	66	21	77	0	2	117	4.1	-0.8	27	6	1,500	100	0.0	0.0
B / 8.0	4.0	0.43	10.31	46	21	77	0	2	117	7.7	-0.4	39	6	1,000,000	0	0.0	0.0
B- / 7.1	6.2	0.54	8.31	1,100	12	40	45	3	41	39.5	-7.2	51	15	1,500	100	5.5	0.0
B- / 7.1	6.3	0.56	8.32	97	12	40	45	3	41	35.9	-7.5	36	15	1,500	100	0.0	0.0
B- / 7.1	6.2	0.55	8.31	1,114	12	40	45	3	41	36.0	-7.5	39	15	1,500	100	0.0	0.0
B- / 7.1	6.2	0.55	8.30	223	12	40	45	3	41	39.5	-7.2	47	15	1,500	100	1.0	0.0
B- / 7.1	6.3	1.00	8.31	502	12	40	45	3	41	40.6	-7.2	25	15	1,000,000	0	0.0	0.0
C- / 3.7	6.2	0.98	8.31	N/A	12	40	45	3	41	38.1	-7.4	21	15	0	0	0.0	0.0
C / 5.4	11.9	0.85	25.17	175	0	99	0	1	73	84.7	-24.9	66	N/A	1,500	100	5.5	0.0
C / 5.3	11.9	0.86	24.39	27	0	99	0	1	73	80.1	-25.1	54	N/A	1,500	100	0.0	0.0
C / 5.4	11.9	0.86	25.25	557	0	99	0	1	73	86.3	-24.8	69	N/A	1,000,000	0	0.0	0.0
C / 5.4	11.9	0.86	24.87	10	0	99	0	1	73	83.4	-25.0	63	5	0	0	0.0	0.0
C+ / 6.7	11.2	1.11	23.50	709	2	97	0	1	98	93.9	-20.0	30	6	1,500	100	5.5	0.0
C+ / 6.7	11.2	1.11	23.32	32	2	97	0	1	98	89.1	-20.2	22	6	1,500	100	0.0	0.0
C+ / 6.7	11.2	1.11	23.34	46	2	97	0	1	98	89.0	-20.2	22	6	1,500	100	0.0	0.0
C+ / 6.7	11.2	1.11	23.53	177	2	97	0	1	98	95.6	-19.9	34	6	1,000,000	0	0.0	0.0

99 Pct = Best
0 Pct = Worst

Fund Type	Fund Name	Ticker Symbol	Overall Investment Rating	Phone	Perfor-mance Rating/Pts	3 Mo	6 Mo	1Yr / Pct	3Yr / Pct	5Yr / Pct	Dividend Yield	Expense Ratio
								Total Return % through 3/31/15	(Annualized)		Incl. in Returns	
GR	Federated Clover Value Fund R	VFCKX	C+	(800) 341-7400	C+ / 6.8	1.69	4.87	5.62 /43	14.83 /73	11.82 /59	0.80	1.67
GL	Federated Emerging Markets Eq Inst	FGLEX	E-	(800) 341-7400	D- / 1.3	1.80	-1.60	-4.15 / 7	5.97 /17	--	0.75	3.38
IN	Federated Equity Income A	LEIFX	C+	(800) 341-7400	C / 4.8	0.32	3.58	6.34 /49	13.14 /61	12.79 /66	1.18	1.13
IN	Federated Equity Income B	LEIBX	C+	(800) 341-7400	C / 5.2	0.17	3.18	5.52 /43	12.27 /54	11.91 /60	0.59	1.94
IN	Federated Equity Income C	LEICX	C+	(800) 341-7400	C / 5.2	0.17	3.19	5.54 /43	12.29 /55	11.92 /60	0.61	1.90
IN	Federated Equity Income F	LFEIX	C+	(800) 341-7400	C / 5.4	0.26	3.45	6.09 /47	12.86 /59	12.48 /64	1.00	1.37
IN	Federated Equity Income Inst	LEISX	B-	(800) 341-7400	C+ / 5.9	0.38	3.72	6.63 /52	13.41 /63	12.95 /68	1.50	0.86
BA	Federated Global Allocation A	FSTBX	D	(800) 341-7400	D+ / 2.9	3.40	5.53	6.34 /49	8.89 /32	8.42 /33	0.71	1.34
BA	Federated Global Allocation B	FSBBX	D	(800) 341-7400	C- / 3.2	3.19	5.09	5.44 /42	7.99 /27	7.55 /27	0.28	2.15
BA	Federated Global Allocation C	FSBCX	D	(800) 341-7400	C- / 3.2	3.20	5.08	5.55 /43	8.06 /27	7.60 /27	0.31	2.12
BA	Federated Global Allocation Inst	SBFIX	D+	(800) 341-7400	C- / 3.9	3.45	5.65	6.64 /52	9.19 /34	8.75 /35	0.94	1.07
BA	Federated Global Allocation R	FSBKX	D	(800) 341-7400	C- / 3.5	3.31	5.29	5.87 /45	8.44 /30	7.97 /30	0.44	1.76
FO	Federated Intercontinental Fund A	RIMAX	E+	(800) 341-7400	E+ / 0.9	7.65	3.34	-1.33 /12	4.37 /11	4.56 /10	0.36	1.51
FO	Federated Intercontinental Fund B	ICFBX	E+	(800) 341-7400	D- / 1.0	7.46	2.93	-2.11 /10	3.54 / 9	3.74 / 7	0.00	2.39
FO	Federated Intercontinental Fund C	ICFFX	E+	(800) 341-7400	D- / 1.1	7.45	2.94	-2.10 /10	3.55 / 9	3.75 / 8	0.00	2.28
FO	Federated Intercontinental Fund I	ICFIX	D-	(800) 341-7400	D- / 1.4	7.74	3.50	-1.03 /13	4.69 /12	4.90 /11	0.88	1.20
FO	Federated Intercontinental Fund R	ICFKX	D-	(800) 341-7400	D- / 1.3	7.61	3.27	-1.39 /12	4.22 /11	4.37 /10	0.00	1.76
FO	Federated Intercontinental Fund R6	ICRSX	D	(800) 341-7400	D- / 1.4	7.74	3.52	-0.98 /13	4.50 /11	4.64 /11	0.92	1.17
FO	Federated International Sm-Mid A	ISCAX	E	(800) 341-7400	D / 1.9	8.14	6.49	-1.12 /13	8.02 /27	8.02 /30	0.00	1.95
FO	Federated International Sm-Mid B	ISCBX	E	(800) 341-7400	D / 2.2	7.92	6.04	-1.91 /11	7.09 /22	7.12 /24	0.00	2.70
FO	Federated International Sm-Mid C	ISCCX	E	(800) 341-7400	D / 2.2	7.96	6.08	-1.88 /11	7.10 /22	7.13 /24	0.00	2.70
FO	Federated International Sm-Mid Inst	ISCIX	E+	(800) 341-7400	D+ / 2.8	8.22	6.62	-0.90 /13	8.25 /28	8.25 /32	0.00	1.70
FO	Federated International Str VI Dv A	IVFAX	E+	(800) 341-7400	E+ / 0.6	-1.70	-7.75	-7.72 / 3	4.58 /12	5.59 /15	3.50	1.25
FO	Federated International Str VI Dv C	IVFCX	E+	(800) 341-7400	E+ / 0.7	-1.89	-8.06	-8.37 / 3	3.82 /10	4.78 /11	2.98	2.00
FO	Federated International Str VI Dv I	IVFIX	E+	(800) 341-7400	E+ / 0.8	-1.39	-7.41	-7.27 / 4	4.92 /13	5.89 /16	3.94	1.00
FO	Federated Intl Leaders A	FGFAX	D+	(800) 341-7400	C- / 4.2	6.44	5.78	-0.51 /14	12.05 /53	10.03 /45	0.73	1.45
FO	Federated Intl Leaders B	FGFBX	C-	(800) 341-7400	C / 4.5	6.23	5.38	-1.26 /12	11.20 /47	9.19 /38	0.13	2.24
FO	Federated Intl Leaders C	FGFCX	C-	(800) 341-7400	C / 4.5	6.21	5.35	-1.27 /12	11.20 /47	9.20 /38	0.24	2.25
FO	Federated Intl Leaders Instl	FGFLX	C-	(800) 341-7400	C / 5.2	6.49	5.91	-0.28 /15	12.31 /55	10.29 /47	1.02	1.18
FO	Federated Intl Leaders R	FGFRX	C	(800) 341-7400	C / 4.8	6.37	5.68	-0.70 /14	11.71 /50	9.61 /41	0.90	1.90
FO	Federated Intl Leaders R6	FGRSX	C	(800) 341-7400	C / 5.2	6.50	5.92	-0.21 /15	12.23 /54	10.14 /46	1.06	1.11
GR	Federated Kaufman Large Cap IS	KLCIX	A	(800) 341-7400	A+ / 9.8	7.50	11.55	20.03 /97	20.01 /98	17.69 /97	0.00	1.05
GR	Federated Kaufman Large Cap R	KLCKX	A	(800) 341-7400	A+ / 9.8	7.34	11.18	19.22 /96	19.25 /97	16.89 /96	0.00	1.75
GR	Federated Kaufman Large Cap R6	KLCSX	A	(800) 341-7400	A+ / 9.8	7.55	11.60	20.08 /97	20.05 /98	17.72 /97	0.00	0.90
MC	Federated Kaufmann A	KAUAX	C+	(800) 341-7400	B+ / 8.9	7.28	12.36	14.31 /90	17.55 /93	13.52 /73	0.00	2.11
MC	Federated Kaufmann B	KAUBX	C+	(800) 341-7400	A- / 9.2	6.96	12.18	13.73 /89	16.89 /89	12.89 /67	0.00	2.62
MC	Federated Kaufmann C	KAUCX	C+	(800) 341-7400	A / 9.3	7.17	12.21	13.97 /89	16.90 /89	12.91 /67	0.00	2.62
GR	Federated Kaufmann Large Cap A	KLCAX	A	(800) 341-7400	A+ / 9.7	7.44	11.43	19.73 /97	19.75 /98	17.40 /97	0.00	1.33
GR	Federated Kaufmann Large Cap C	KLCCX	A	(800) 341-7400	A+ / 9.7	7.26	11.00	18.82 /96	18.78 /96	16.46 /95	0.00	2.08
MC	Federated Kaufmann R	KAUFX	B-	(800) 341-7400	A / 9.4	7.27	12.33	14.47 /90	17.52 /92	13.50 /73	0.00	2.34
SC	Federated Kaufmann Sm Cap A	FKASX	C-	(800) 341-7400	B+ / 8.3	9.50	16.15	12.27 /84	16.03 /84	15.54 /90	0.00	2.19
SC	Federated Kaufmann Sm Cap B	FKBSX	C-	(800) 341-7400	B+ / 8.7	9.34	15.80	11.60 /81	15.39 /78	14.89 /86	0.00	2.76
SC	Federated Kaufmann Sm Cap C	FKCSX	C-	(800) 341-7400	B+ / 8.7	9.34	15.80	11.60 /81	15.39 /78	14.89 /86	0.00	2.70
SC	Federated Kaufmann Sm Cap R	FKKSX	C	(800) 341-7400	A- / 9.1	9.52	16.16	12.29 /84	16.08 /84	15.56 /90	0.00	2.29
GR	Federated Max-Cap Index C	MXCCX	B-	(800) 341-7400	B- / 7.1	0.59	5.09	11.00 /78	14.72 /73	13.05 /69	0.54	1.47
GR	Federated Max-Cap Index Inst	FISPX	B	(800) 341-7400	B / 8.1	0.82	5.67	12.18 /83	15.95 /83	14.27 /80	1.50	0.43
GR	Federated Max-Cap Index R	FMXKX	B-	(800) 341-7400	B- / 7.4	0.66	5.27	11.38 /80	15.10 /76	13.44 /72	0.82	1.15
GR	Federated Max-Cap Index Svc	FMXSX	B	(800) 341-7400	B / 7.8	0.76	5.49	11.86 /82	15.62 /80	13.93 /77	1.23	1.01
GR	Federated MDT All Cap Core Fd A	QAACX	A+	(800) 341-7400	B+ / 8.4	1.24	5.86	10.21 /75	18.35 /95	14.30 /80	0.12	1.44
GR	Federated MDT All Cap Core Fd C	QCACX	A+	(800) 341-7400	B+ / 8.7	1.06	5.49	9.41 /71	17.42 /92	13.40 /72	0.00	2.22
GR	Federated MDT All Cap Core Fd Inst	QIACX	A+	(800) 341-7400	A / 9.3	1.28	5.98	10.55 /77	18.66 /96	14.59 /83	0.40	1.11
GR	Federated MDT All Cap Core Fd R	QKACX	A+	(800) 341-7400	B+ / 8.9	1.12	5.60	9.76 /73	17.79 /94	13.75 /75	0.00	1.82

● Denotes fund is closed to new investors
* Denotes fund is included in Section II

www.thestreetratings.com

RISK			NET ASSETS		ASSET				Portfolio	BULL / BEAR		FUND MANAGER		MINIMUMS		LOADS	
	3 Year		NAV							Last Bull	Last Bear	Manager	Manager	Initial	Additional	Front	Back
Risk	Standard		As of	Total	Cash	Stocks	Bonds	Other	Turnover	Market	Market	Quality	Tenure	Purch.	Purch.	End	End
Rating/Pts	Deviation	Beta	3/31/15	$(Mil)	%	%	%	%	Ratio	Return	Return	Pct	(Years)	$	$	Load	Load
C+ / 6.7	11.2	1.11	23.49	27	2	97	0	1	98	92.6	-20.1	28	6	0	0	0.0	0.0
D / 1.7	12.6	0.83	9.62	14	1	98	0	1	118	50.0	-23.7	41	5	1,000,000	0	0.0	0.0
B- / 7.1	10.6	1.08	23.86	1,095	2	97	0	1	118	79.4	-12.2	18	N/A	1,500	100	5.5	0.0
B- / 7.1	10.6	1.07	23.79	66	2	97	0	1	118	74.6	-12.5	13	N/A	1,500	100	0.0	0.0
B- / 7.1	10.6	1.07	23.82	120	2	97	0	1	118	74.7	-12.5	13	N/A	1,500	100	0.0	0.0
B- / 7.1	10.6	1.08	23.87	56	2	97	0	1	118	77.7	-12.3	16	N/A	1,500	100	1.0	0.0
B- / 7.1	10.6	1.08	23.85	222	2	97	0	1	118	80.6	-12.2	20	N/A	1,000,000	0	0.0	0.0
C+ / 5.7	7.8	1.32	18.85	197	29	60	9	2	100	50.2	-13.4	10	8	1,500	100	5.5	0.0
C+ / 5.6	7.8	1.32	18.42	25	29	60	9	2	100	46.1	-13.7	7	8	1,500	100	0.0	0.0
C / 5.5	7.8	1.32	18.36	84	29	60	9	2	100	46.4	-13.7	7	8	1,500	100	0.0	0.0
C+ / 5.7	7.8	1.32	18.95	72	29	60	9	2	100	51.7	-13.3	11	8	1,000,000	0	0.0	0.0
C+ / 5.6	7.8	1.31	18.73	66	29	60	9	2	100	48.0	-13.6	8	8	0	0	0.0	0.0
C+ / 5.8	13.4	0.97	52.18	95	3	96	0	1	64	34.9	-27.9	13	N/A	1,500	100	5.5	0.0
C+ / 5.7	13.4	0.97	52.02	7	3	96	0	1	64	31.3	-28.2	9	N/A	1,500	100	0.0	0.0
C+ / 5.7	13.4	0.97	51.81	31	3	96	0	1	64	31.3	-28.2	9	N/A	1,500	100	0.0	0.0
C+ / 5.8	13.4	0.97	51.93	125	3	96	0	1	64	36.3	-27.8	14	N/A	1,000,000	0	0.0	0.0
C+ / 5.8	13.4	0.97	51.73	2	3	96	0	1	64	34.2	-28.0	12	N/A	0	0	0.0	0.0
C+ / 6.7	13.4	0.97	52.08	7	3	96	0	1	64	35.3	-27.9	13	N/A	0	0	0.0	0.0
D+ / 2.9	12.6	0.88	38.52	128	5	94	0	1	49	59.4	-29.4	63	16	1,500	100	5.5	2.0
D+ / 2.3	12.6	0.88	31.90	4	5	94	0	1	49	54.9	-29.6	50	16	1,500	100	0.0	2.0
D+ / 2.3	12.6	0.88	31.87	23	5	94	0	1	49	54.8	-29.6	50	16	1,500	100	0.0	2.0
D+ / 2.9	12.6	0.88	39.08	34	5	94	0	1	49	60.4	-29.3	66	16	1,000,000	0	0.0	2.0
C+ / 5.6	12.6	0.86	3.84	298	1	98	0	1	11	35.6	-15.9	21	N/A	1,500	100	5.5	0.0
C+ / 5.6	12.6	0.87	3.82	129	1	98	0	1	11	32.4	-16.3	15	N/A	1,500	100	0.0	0.0
C+ / 5.6	12.7	0.87	3.85	536	1	98	0	1	11	36.6	-15.8	24	N/A	1,000,000	0	0.0	0.0
C / 5.5	14.9	1.06	34.06	689	17	82	0	1	4	78.3	-29.5	82	17	1,500	100	5.5	0.0
C / 5.5	14.9	1.06	31.91	26	17	82	0	1	4	73.8	-29.7	77	17	1,500	100	0.0	0.0
C / 5.5	14.9	1.06	31.81	110	17	82	0	1	4	73.7	-29.7	77	17	1,500	100	0.0	0.0
C / 5.5	14.9	1.06	34.11	971	17	82	0	1	4	79.8	-29.4	84	17	1,000,000	0	0.0	0.0
C+ / 6.4	14.9	1.06	33.89	51	17	82	0	1	4	76.3	-29.6	80	17	0	0	0.0	0.0
C+ / 6.4	14.9	1.06	34.06	84	17	82	0	1	4	79.1	-29.5	83	17	0	0	0.0	0.0
C+ / 5.8	11.7	0.97	19.63	1,077	6	93	0	1	68	131.3	-20.3	91	8	1,000,000	0	0.0	0.0
C+ / 5.8	11.7	0.98	18.73	78	6	93	0	1	68	126.2	-20.5	89	8	250	100	0.0	0.0
C / 5.5	11.7	0.97	19.65	160	6	93	0	1	68	131.4	-20.3	91	8	0	0	0.0	0.0
C- / 3.5	11.7	0.96	6.19	1,644	5	94	0	1	52	107.1	-25.6	77	29	1,500	100	5.5	0.0
C- / 3.0	11.8	0.97	5.53	120	5	94	0	1	52	103.5	-25.7	71	29	1,500	100	0.0	0.0
D+ / 2.9	11.9	0.98	5.53	440	5	94	0	1	52	103.5	-25.7	69	29	1,500	100	0.0	0.0
C+ / 5.8	11.7	0.98	19.34	693	6	93	0	1	68	129.2	-20.4	90	8	1,500	100	5.5	0.0
C+ / 5.8	11.7	0.98	18.31	364	6	93	0	1	68	123.2	-20.7	87	8	1,500	100	0.0	0.0
C- / 3.5	11.8	0.97	6.20	3,683	5	94	0	1	52	107.3	-25.6	76	29	1,500	100	0.0	0.2
D / 1.8	15.7	1.04	26.86	498	0	99	0	1	65	113.8	-29.2	55	N/A	1,500	100	5.5	0.0
D- / 1.1	15.7	1.04	24.12	24	0	99	0	1	65	109.8	-29.3	46	N/A	1,500	100	0.0	0.0
D- / 1.1	15.7	1.04	24.12	193	0	99	0	1	65	109.8	-29.3	46	N/A	1,500	100	0.0	0.0
D / 1.8	15.8	1.04	26.92	40	0	99	0	1	65	114.1	-29.2	55	N/A	250	100	0.0	0.0
C+ / 5.8	9.6	1.01	15.96	41	3	96	0	1	28	92.0	-16.7	47	3	1,500	100	0.0	0.0
C+ / 5.8	9.6	1.01	16.19	272	3	96	0	1	28	99.0	-16.3	64	3	1,000,000	0	0.0	0.0
C+ / 5.8	9.6	1.01	16.09	46	3	96	0	1	28	94.1	-16.6	52	3	250	100	0.0	0.0
C+ / 5.8	9.6	1.01	16.09	252	3	96	0	1	28	97.1	-16.5	60	3	1,000,000	0	0.0	0.0
B- / 7.4	10.5	1.05	21.97	44	2	97	0	1	31	113.4	-23.0	78	7	1,500	100	5.5	0.0
B- / 7.3	10.5	1.06	20.93	42	2	97	0	1	31	107.7	-23.3	70	7	1,500	100	0.0	0.0
B- / 7.4	10.6	1.06	22.21	75	2	97	0	1	31	115.4	-23.0	79	7	1,000,000	0	0.0	0.0
B- / 7.3	10.6	1.06	21.70	6	2	97	0	1	31	110.1	-23.2	73	7	250	100	0.0	0.0

Fund Type	Fund Name	Ticker Symbol	Overall Investment Rating	Phone	Performance Rating/Pts	3 Mo	6 Mo	1Yr / Pct	Annualized 3Yr / Pct	Annualized 5Yr / Pct	Dividend Yield	Expense Ratio
BA	Federated MDT Balanced Fund A	QABGX	C+	(800) 341-7400	C / 4.4	2.13	5.23	8.04 /63	11.68 /50	9.59 /41	1.03	1.46
BA	Federated MDT Balanced Fund C	QCBGX	B-	(800) 341-7400	C / 4.7	1.90	4.79	7.28 /57	10.82 /44	8.76 /35	0.37	2.18
BA	Federated MDT Balanced Fund Inst	QIBGX	B	(800) 341-7400	C / 5.5	2.18	5.35	8.35 /65	11.95 /52	9.86 /43	1.33	1.16
BA	Federated MDT Balanced Fund R	QKBGX	B-	(800) 341-7400	C / 5.0	2.06	5.09	7.83 /62	11.32 /48	9.16 /38	0.89	1.79
GR	Federated MDT Large Cap Gr Fd A	QALGX	B+	(800) 341-7400	B / 7.7	2.43	8.19	12.30 /84	16.54 /87	14.35 /81	0.00	1.62
GR	Federated MDT Large Cap Gr Fd B	QBLGX	A-	(800) 341-7400	B / 8.1	2.25	7.76	11.47 /80	15.68 /81	13.49 /73	0.00	2.37
GR	Federated MDT Large Cap Gr Fd C	QCLGX	A-	(800) 341-7400	B / 8.1	2.30	7.80	11.53 /81	15.67 /81	13.51 /73	0.00	2.37
GR	Federated MDT Large Cap Gr Fd Inst	QILGX	A+	(800) 341-7400	B+ / 8.8	2.54	8.34	12.57 /85	16.83 /89	14.62 /83	0.00	1.36
MC	Federated MDT MidCap Gr Strat A	FGSAX	C+	(800) 341-7400	B / 7.9	3.28	10.45	14.54 /91	16.21 /85	13.93 /77	0.12	1.29
MC	Federated MDT MidCap Gr Strat B	FGSBX	C+	(800) 341-7400	B+ / 8.3	3.11	10.04	13.66 /89	15.34 /78	13.08 /69	0.00	2.12
MC	Federated MDT MidCap Gr Strat C	FGSCX	C+	(800) 341-7400	B+ / 8.3	3.09	10.04	13.67 /89	15.35 /78	13.08 /69	0.00	2.08
MC	Federated MDT MidCap Gr Strat Inst	FGSIX	B	(800) 341-7400	B+ / 8.9	3.36	10.57	14.81 /91	16.42 /86	14.17 /79	0.36	1.05
MC	Federated MDT MidCap Gr Strat R	FGSKX	B-	(800) 341-7400	B+ / 8.5	3.17	10.19	13.97 /89	15.65 /80	13.39 /72	0.00	1.81
SC	Federated MDT Small Cap Gr Fd A	QASGX	B	(800) 341-7400	B- / 7.5	7.53	14.74	10.19 /75	15.50 /79	17.29 /96	0.00	2.19
SC	Federated MDT Small Cap Gr Fd B	QBSGX	B	(800) 341-7400	B / 7.9	7.31	14.31	9.34 /71	14.61 /72	16.41 /94	0.00	2.94
SC	Federated MDT Small Cap Gr Fd C	QCSGX	B	(800) 341-7400	B / 7.9	7.26	14.24	9.34 /71	14.62 /72	16.40 /94	0.00	2.94
SC	Federated MDT Small Cap Gr Fd Inst	QISGX	B+	(800) 341-7400	B+ / 8.7	7.56	14.92	10.46 /76	15.79 /82	17.57 /97	0.00	1.94
SC	Federated MDT Small Cp Core Fd A	QASCX	B+	(800) 341-7400	B+ / 8.6	3.68	12.03	7.50 /59	18.30 /95	16.47 /95	0.00	2.23
SC	Federated MDT Small Cp Core Fd C	QCSCX	B+	(800) 341-7400	B+ / 8.9	3.47	11.57	6.68 /52	17.42 /92	15.61 /91	0.00	3.00
SC	Federated MDT Small Cp Core Fd	QISCX	A-	(800) 341-7400	A / 9.4	3.73	12.11	7.80 /61	18.58 /96	16.77 /95	0.00	1.98
GI	Federated MDT Stock Tr A	FSTRX	B	(800) 341-7400	B+ / 8.4	0.30	4.77	8.50 /66	18.73 /96	15.23 /88	1.02	1.26
GI	Federated MDT Stock Tr IS	FMSTX	A	(800) 341-7400	A / 9.3	0.38	4.91	8.75 /68	19.04 /97	15.54 /90	1.23	1.01
GI	Federated MDT Stock Tr Svc	FSTKX	A	(800) 341-7400	A- / 9.2	0.32	4.80	8.51 /66	18.78 /96	15.28 /89	1.02	1.26
MC	Federated Mid-Cap Index Inst	FMCRX	A-	(800) 341-7400	A- / 9.1	5.29	11.82	11.90 /82	16.91 /89	15.41 /90	1.09	0.41
MC	Federated Mid-Cap Index Svc	FMDCX	B+	(800) 341-7400	B+ / 8.9	5.27	11.68	11.67 /81	16.61 /87	15.24 /88	0.87	0.66
AA	Federated Muni & Stock Advtd Inst	FMUIX	C	(800) 341-7400	D+ / 2.5	0.22	-0.42	4.25 /33	7.65 /25	7.85 /29	3.59	0.84
GR	Federated Prudent Bear Fund A	BEARX	E-	(800) 341-7400	E- / 0.0	-2.68	-8.79	-15.18 / 2	-17.41 / 0	-15.63 / 0	0.00	3.04
GR	Federated Prudent Bear Fund C	PBRCX	E-	(800) 341-7400	E- / 0.0	-2.96	-9.22	-15.81 / 2	-17.98 / 0	-16.25 / 0	0.00	3.79
GR	Federated Prudent Bear Fund IS	PBRIX	E-	(800) 341-7400	E- / 0.1	-2.63	-8.64	-14.94 / 2	-17.12 / 0	-15.39 / 0	0.00	2.77
IN	Federated Strategic Value Div A	SVAAX	C	(800) 341-7400	C / 4.6	0.25	1.81	7.45 /59	12.75 /58	12.84 /67	2.97	1.19
IN	Federated Strategic Value Div C	SVACX	C+	(800) 341-7400	C / 5.0	0.07	1.43	6.83 /54	11.90 /52	12.04 /61	2.40	1.94
IN	Federated Strategic Value Div Inst	SVAIX	C+	(800) 341-7400	C+ / 5.7	0.31	1.92	7.69 /60	12.98 /60	13.12 /69	3.38	0.94
AA	Federated Unconstrained Bond Inst	FUBDX	E	(800) 341-7400	E- / 0.2	-3.47	-7.98	-7.94 / 3	-3.64 / 2	--	5.09	2.24
GR	Fidelity 100 Index F	FOHJX	B+	(800) 544-8544	B- / 7.0	-0.15	3.52	11.43 /80	14.60 /72	13.46 /72	2.05	0.05
GR	Fidelity 100 Index FD	FOHIX	B	(800) 544-8544	B- / 7.0	-0.15	3.47	11.38 /80	14.59 /72	13.45 /72	2.01	0.10
AA	Fidelity Adv 529 100% Equity A	FFAGX	C	(800) 522-7297	C / 4.9	2.86	4.83	6.81 /54	12.80 /58	10.85 /51	0.00	1.26
AA	Fidelity Adv 529 100% Equity B		C+	(800) 522-7297	C / 5.3	2.69	4.49	6.03 /47	11.95 /52	10.01 /45	0.00	2.01
AA	Fidelity Adv 529 100% Equity C	FFCGX	C+	(800) 522-7297	C / 5.3	2.69	4.49	6.09 /47	11.98 /52	10.03 /45	0.00	2.01
AA	Fidelity Adv 529 100% Equity D	FFRGX	C+	(800) 522-7297	C+ / 5.6	2.77	4.72	6.57 /51	12.52 /56	10.57 /49	0.00	1.51
AA	Fidelity Adv 529 100% Equity Old-A	FFOGX	C+	(800) 522-7297	C / 5.2	2.92	4.89	6.88 /54	12.80 /58	10.85 /51	0.00	1.26
AA	Fidelity Adv 529 100% Equity Old-B		C+	(800) 522-7297	C / 5.5	2.78	4.65	6.34 /49	12.23 /54	10.29 /47	0.00	1.76
AA	Fidelity Adv 529 100% Equity P	FFPGX	C+	(800) 522-7297	C / 5.5	2.74	4.58	6.30 /49	12.23 /54	10.30 /47	0.00	1.76
AA	Fidelity Adv 529 2016 A	FPCAX	C-	(800) 522-7297	D- / 1.1	1.56	2.51	3.85 /31	5.38 /14	5.85 /16	0.00	1.10
AA	Fidelity Adv 529 2016 B	FPCBX	C-	(800) 522-7297	D- / 1.3	1.39	2.17	3.02 /27	4.60 /12	5.05 /12	0.00	1.85
AA	Fidelity Adv 529 2016 C	FPJCX	C-	(800) 522-7297	D- / 1.3	1.39	2.17	3.02 /27	4.59 /12	5.07 /12	0.00	1.85
AA	Fidelity Adv 529 2016 D	FPCDX	C	(800) 522-7297	D- / 1.5	1.49	2.41	3.53 /29	5.11 /13	5.60 /15	0.00	1.35
AA	Fidelity Adv 529 2016 Old-A	FPCOX	C-	(800) 522-7297	D- / 1.3	1.56	2.51	3.84 /31	5.39 /14	5.86 /16	0.00	1.10
AA	Fidelity Adv 529 2016 Old-B	FPBBX	C	(800) 522-7297	D- / 1.4	1.35	2.23	3.26 /28	4.84 /13	5.32 /13	0.00	1.60
AA	Fidelity Adv 529 2016 P	FPCPX	C	(800) 522-7297	D- / 1.4	1.42	2.24	3.27 /28	4.86 /13	5.31 /13	0.00	1.60
AA	Fidelity Adv 529 2019 A		C-	(800) 522-7297	D / 1.8	1.93	3.25	4.83 /37	7.22 /23	7.26 /25	0.00	1.16
AA	Fidelity Adv 529 2019 B	FPBDX	C	(800) 522-7297	D / 2.1	1.76	2.82	4.02 /32	6.42 /19	6.45 /20	0.00	1.91
AA	Fidelity Adv 529 2019 C	FPLCX	C	(800) 522-7297	D / 2.1	1.76	2.81	4.02 /32	6.41 /19	6.46 /20	0.00	1.91

• Denotes fund is closed to new investors
* Denotes fund is included in Section II

www.thestreetratings.com

RISK			NET ASSETS		ASSET					BULL / BEAR		FUND MANAGER		MINIMUMS		LOADS	
	3 Year		NAV						Portfolio	Last Bull	Last Bear	Manager	Manager	Initial	Additional	Front	Back
Risk Rating/Pts	Standard Deviation	Beta	As of 3/31/15	Total $(Mil)	Cash %	Stocks %	Bonds %	Other %	Turnover Ratio	Market Return	Market Return	Quality Pct	Tenure (Years)	Purch. $	Purch. $	End Load	End Load
B /8.2	6.9	1.18	16.82	61	9	67	23	1	34	62.4	-14.8	50	N/A	1,500	100	5.5	0.0
B /8.2	6.9	1.18	16.62	32	9	67	23	1	34	58.2	-15.0	39	N/A	1,500	100	0.0	0.0
B /8.3	6.9	1.18	16.86	55	9	67	23	1	34	63.7	-14.7	54	N/A	1,000,000	0	0.0	0.0
B /8.2	6.9	1.18	16.81	1	9	67	23	1	34	60.4	-15.0	44	N/A	250	100	0.0	0.0
B- /7.2	10.2	1.03	17.71	56	2	97	0	1	51	103.4	-18.8	66	7	1,500	100	5.5	0.0
B- /7.1	10.3	1.04	16.81	16	2	97	0	1	51	98.3	-18.9	53	7	1,500	100	0.0	0.0
B- /7.1	10.2	1.03	16.45	13	2	97	0	1	51	98.2	-19.1	55	7	1,500	100	0.0	0.0
B- /7.2	10.2	1.03	18.18	8	2	97	0	1	51	105.0	-18.7	68	7	1,000,000	0	0.0	0.0
C /4.9	11.7	0.98	44.97	277	1	98	0	1	41	92.1	-22.7	62	2	1,500	100	5.5	0.0
C- /4.0	11.7	0.98	35.86	4	1	98	0	1	41	87.3	-23.0	50	2	1,500	100	0.0	0.0
C- /4.1	11.7	0.98	36.42	13	1	98	0	1	41	87.3	-22.9	50	2	1,500	100	0.0	0.0
C /4.9	11.7	0.98	45.58	59	1	98	0	1	41	93.4	-22.6	65	2	1,000,000	0	0.0	0.0
C /4.8	11.7	0.98	43.23	2	1	98	0	1	41	89.0	-22.9	54	2	250	100	0.0	0.0
C+ /6.0	13.1	0.93	20.00	31	1	98	0	1	61	105.9	-27.2	71	7	1,500	100	5.5	0.0
C+ /5.9	13.1	0.93	19.09	2	1	98	0	1	61	100.7	-27.4	61	7	1,500	100	0.0	0.0
C+ /5.9	13.1	0.93	18.61	4	1	98	0	1	61	100.7	-27.4	61	7	1,500	100	0.0	0.0
C+ /6.0	13.1	0.93	20.49	36	1	98	0	1	61	107.6	-27.1	74	7	1,000,000	0	0.0	0.0
C+ /5.9	14.0	1.01	15.78	6	1	98	0	1	174	113.8	-29.3	81	7	1,500	100	5.5	0.0
C+ /5.8	14.0	1.01	14.62	4	1	98	0	1	174	108.4	-29.5	76	7	1,500	100	0.0	0.0
C+ /5.9	14.0	1.01	16.15	21	1	98	0	1	174	115.6	-29.2	83	7	1,000,000	0	0.0	0.0
C /5.3	12.0	1.16	28.60	8	2	97	0	1	34	123.8	-22.3	65	6	1,500	100	5.5	0.0
C+ /6.2	12.0	1.16	28.61	201	2	97	0	1	34	125.8	-22.2	68	6	1,000,000	0	0.0	0.0
C+ /6.2	12.0	1.16	28.62	306	2	97	0	1	34	124.1	-22.3	66	6	1,000,000	0	0.0	0.0
C+ /5.8	11.0	1.00	28.66	150	4	95	0	1	37	101.7	-22.7	65	5	1,000,000	0	0.0	0.0
C+ /5.8	11.0	1.00	28.68	931	4	95	0	1	37	100.2	-22.7	61	5	1,000,000	0	0.0	0.0
B /8.8	4.9	0.68	12.50	155	0	44	54	2	18	38.2	-0.4	70	12	1,000,000	0	0.0	0.0
D+ /2.8	9.1	-0.92	2.18	143	55	0	44	1	465	-56.8	16.1	8	16	1,500	100	5.5	0.0
D+ /2.7	9.3	-0.94	1.97	37	55	0	44	1	465	-57.7	15.5	7	16	1,500	100	0.0	0.0
D+ /2.7	9.5	-0.96	2.22	125	55	0	44	1	465	-56.3	16.0	13	16	1,000,000	0	0.0	0.0
B- /7.1	8.9	0.67	5.87	2,323	1	98	0	1	17	61.4	-4.1	84	N/A	1,500	100	5.5	0.0
B- /7.1	9.0	0.67	5.88	1,492	1	98	0	1	17	57.3	-4.4	79	N/A	1,500	100	0.0	0.0
B- /7.1	8.9	0.67	5.89	5,887	1	98	0	1	17	62.9	-4.2	85	N/A	1,000,000	0	0.0	0.0
C /5.3	5.4	0.49	8.48	5	81	0	18	1	149	-7.5	2.8	2	2	1,000,000	0	0.0	0.0
B- /7.5	9.7	1.00	13.29	1,729	1	98	0	1	8	94.8	-14.9	47	8	0	0	0.0	0.0
C+ /6.7	9.6	1.00	13.29	1,750	1	98	0	1	8	94.7	-14.9	48	8	0	0	0.0	0.0
C+ /6.6	10.3	1.72	19.75	108	3	95	0	2	21	79.8	-21.4	7	10	1,000	50	5.8	0.0
C+ /6.6	10.3	1.72	17.93	5	3	95	0	2	21	75.1	-21.7	5	10	1,000	50	0.0	0.0
C+ /6.6	10.3	1.72	17.93	43	3	95	0	2	21	75.2	-21.7	5	10	1,000	50	0.0	0.0
C+ /6.7	10.2	1.71	19.29	15	3	95	0	2	21	78.1	-21.5	7	10	1,000	50	0.0	0.0
C+ /6.7	10.3	1.72	19.72	29	3	95	0	2	21	79.7	-21.5	7	10	1,000	50	3.5	0.0
C+ /6.6	10.3	1.72	18.46	1	3	95	0	2	21	76.5	-21.6	6	10	1,000	50	0.0	0.0
C+ /6.6	10.3	1.72	18.73	1	3	95	0	2	21	76.7	-21.6	6	10	1,000	50	0.0	0.0
B+ /9.5	4.1	0.66	17.53	334	18	28	53	1	21	29.9	-9.4	42	10	1,000	50	5.8	0.0
B+ /9.5	4.0	0.66	16.02	14	18	28	53	1	21	26.6	-9.7	33	10	1,000	50	0.0	0.0
B+ /9.5	4.1	0.66	16.03	133	18	28	53	1	21	26.6	-9.7	32	10	1,000	50	0.0	0.0
B+ /9.5	4.1	0.67	16.99	30	18	28	53	1	21	28.8	-9.6	37	10	1,000	50	0.0	0.0
B+ /9.5	4.0	0.66	17.56	95	18	28	53	1	21	29.8	-9.4	43	10	1,000	50	3.5	0.0
B+ /9.5	4.1	0.66	16.48	3	18	28	53	1	21	27.7	-9.6	35	10	1,000	50	0.0	0.0
B+ /9.5	4.0	0.66	16.44	11	18	28	53	1	21	27.7	-9.7	35	10	1,000	50	0.0	0.0
B+ /9.0	5.4	0.90	18.44	426	10	41	46	3	22	41.3	-12.9	33	10	1,000	50	5.8	0.0
B+ /9.0	5.4	0.90	16.80	20	10	41	46	3	22	37.7	-13.1	24	10	1,000	50	0.0	0.0
B+ /9.0	5.4	0.91	16.81	141	10	41	46	3	22	37.7	-13.1	23	10	1,000	50	0.0	0.0

Fund Type	Fund Name	Ticker Symbol	Overall Investment Rating	Phone	Performance Rating/Pts	3 Mo	6 Mo	1Yr / Pct	3Yr / Pct	5Yr / Pct	Dividend Yield	Expense Ratio
AA	Fidelity Adv 529 2019 D	FPDDX	C	(800) 522-7297	D+ / 2.4	1.83	3.07	4.52 /35	6.93 /21	6.99 /23	0.00	1.41
AA	Fidelity Adv 529 2019 Old-A	FAAPX	C	(800) 522-7297	D / 2.1	1.93	3.19	4.77 /37	7.22 /23	7.25 /25	0.00	1.16
AA	Fidelity Adv 529 2019 Old-B	FABPX	C	(800) 522-7297	D+ / 2.3	1.82	2.98	4.28 /34	6.68 /20	6.73 /21	0.00	1.66
AA	Fidelity Adv 529 2019 P	FPPCX	C	(800) 522-7297	D+ / 2.3	1.83	2.98	4.29 /34	6.70 /20	6.73 /21	0.00	1.66
AA	Fidelity Adv 529 2022 A	FPIAX	C	(800) 522-7297	D+ / 2.6	2.27	3.77	5.50 /42	8.87 /32	8.41 /33	0.00	1.21
AA	Fidelity Adv 529 2022 B	FPIBX	C	(800) 522-7297	C- / 3.0	2.05	3.38	4.69 /36	8.05 /27	7.60 /27	0.00	1.96
AA	Fidelity Adv 529 2022 C	FPICX	C	(800) 522-7297	C- / 3.0	2.05	3.38	4.74 /37	8.06 /27	7.61 /27	0.00	1.96
AA	Fidelity Adv 529 2022 D	FADPX	C+	(800) 522-7297	C- / 3.3	2.20	3.65	5.23 /40	8.59 /30	8.14 /31	0.00	1.46
AA	Fidelity Adv 529 2022 Old-A	FPKAX	C	(800) 522-7297	C- / 3.0	2.23	3.76	5.49 /42	8.84 /32	8.41 /33	0.00	1.21
AA	Fidelity Adv 529 2022 Old-B	FPGBX	C	(800) 522-7297	C- / 3.2	2.13	3.52	4.95 /38	8.32 /29	7.86 /29	0.00	1.71
AA	Fidelity Adv 529 2022 P	FAEPX	C	(800) 522-7297	C- / 3.2	2.13	3.56	4.99 /38	8.34 /29	7.88 /29	0.00	1.71
AA	Fidelity Adv 529 2025 A	FPGAX	C	(800) 522-7297	C- / 3.4	2.37	4.04	5.83 /45	10.27 /41	9.27 /39	0.00	1.25
AA	Fidelity Adv 529 2025 B	FPHBX	C	(800) 522-7297	C- / 3.8	2.12	3.62	5.00 /38	9.46 /36	8.45 /33	0.00	2.00
AA	Fidelity Adv 529 2025 C	FPHCX	C	(800) 522-7297	C- / 3.8	2.12	3.61	5.00 /38	9.46 /36	8.45 /33	0.00	2.00
AA	Fidelity Adv 529 2025 P	FPFPX	C+	(800) 522-7297	C- / 4.0	2.21	3.75	5.25 /40	9.72 /38	8.71 /35	0.00	1.75
AA	Fidelity Adv 529 70% Equity A	FMAFX	C	(800) 522-7297	C- / 3.4	2.58	4.20	6.03 /47	10.17 /40	9.29 /39	0.00	1.21
AA	Fidelity Adv 529 70% Equity B	FMGBX	C+	(800) 522-7297	C- / 3.8	2.37	3.82	5.19 /40	9.33 /35	8.47 /33	0.00	1.96
AA	Fidelity Adv 529 70% Equity C	FMCGX	C+	(800) 522-7297	C- / 3.8	2.37	3.76	5.25 /40	9.35 /35	8.49 /33	0.00	1.96
AA	Fidelity Adv 529 70% Equity D	FMGDX	C+	(800) 522-7297	C- / 4.1	2.46	4.03	5.70 /44	9.88 /39	9.02 /37	0.00	1.46
AA	Fidelity Adv 529 70% Equity Old-A	FMGOX	C+	(800) 522-7297	C- / 3.7	2.57	4.19	6.02 /47	10.15 /40	9.29 /39	0.00	1.21
AA	Fidelity Adv 529 70% Equity Old-B	FMGMX	C+	(800) 522-7297	C- / 3.9	2.40	3.92	5.49 /42	9.61 /37	8.75 /35	0.00	1.71
AA	Fidelity Adv 529 70% Equity P	FBBBX	C+	(800) 522-7297	C- / 3.9	2.43	3.88	5.49 /42	9.60 /37	8.75 /35	0.00	1.71
AA	Fidelity Adv 529 College A	FACAX	C-	(800) 522-7297	E+ / 0.8	1.38	2.14	3.12 /27	3.57 / 9	3.98 / 8	0.00	0.98
AA	Fidelity Adv 529 College B	FACBX	C-	(800) 522-7297	E+ / 0.9	1.11	1.68	2.32 /23	2.79 / 7	3.19 / 6	0.00	1.73
AA	Fidelity Adv 529 College C	FCCLX	C-	(800) 522-7297	E+ / 0.9	1.11	1.68	2.33 /23	2.79 / 7	3.19 / 6	0.00	1.73
AA	Fidelity Adv 529 College D	FCDLX	C	(800) 522-7297	D- / 1.0	1.23	1.96	2.83 /26	3.30 / 8	3.71 / 7	0.00	1.23
AA	Fidelity Adv 529 College Old-A	FCPOX	C-	(800) 522-7297	E+ / 0.9	1.31	2.08	3.12 /27	3.57 / 9	3.96 / 8	0.00	0.98
AA	Fidelity Adv 529 College Old-B	FCOPX	C	(800) 522-7297	E+ / 0.9	1.22	1.84	2.61 /25	3.05 / 8	3.46 / 7	0.00	1.48
AA	Fidelity Adv 529 College P	FCPLX	C	(800) 522-7297	E+ / 0.9	1.21	1.89	2.58 /24	3.07 / 8	3.45 / 7	0.00	1.48
FO	Fidelity Adv 529 Diversified Intl A	FDAPX	C-	(800) 522-7297	C- / 4.1	6.74	5.62	3.54 /29	11.47 /49	7.90 /29	0.00	1.44
FO	Fidelity Adv 529 Diversified Intl B	FDBPX	C-	(800) 522-7297	C / 4.5	6.53	5.25	2.73 /25	10.64 /43	7.09 /24	0.00	2.19
FO	Fidelity Adv 529 Diversified Intl C	FDIIX	C-	(800) 522-7297	C / 4.5	6.57	5.29	2.78 /25	10.67 /43	7.10 /24	0.00	2.19
FO	Fidelity Adv 529 Diversified Intl D	FDIPX	C	(800) 522-7297	C / 4.9	6.71	5.56	3.32 /28	11.21 /47	7.65 /27	0.00	1.69
FO	Fidelity Adv 529 Diversified Intl P	FDPPX	C-	(800) 522-7297	C / 4.7	6.62	5.38	3.03 /27	10.93 /45	7.35 /25	0.00	1.94
GR	Fidelity Adv 529 Dividend Growth A	FDGAX	C+	(800) 522-7297	C+ / 6.0	1.07	5.02	11.08 /79	14.42 /70	12.46 /64	0.00	1.21
GR	Fidelity Adv 529 Dividend Growth B	FDGBX	C+	(800) 522-7297	C+ / 6.4	0.87	4.65	10.24 /75	13.55 /64	11.63 /58	0.00	1.96
GR	Fidelity Adv 529 Dividend Growth C	FDGGX	C+	(800) 522-7297	C+ / 6.4	0.86	4.64	10.23 /75	13.56 /64	11.63 /58	0.00	1.96
GR	Fidelity Adv 529 Dividend Growth D	FDGDX	C+	(800) 522-7297	C+ / 6.8	0.96	4.88	10.77 /77	14.13 /68	12.19 /62	0.00	1.46
GR	Fidelity Adv 529 Dividend Growth P	FDGPX	C+	(800) 522-7297	C+ / 6.6	0.94	4.77	10.49 /76	13.86 /66	11.93 /60	0.00	1.71
GR	Fidelity Adv 529 Equity Growth A	FEGAX	C+	(800) 522-7297	C+ / 6.8	4.58	6.01	11.38 /80	15.43 /78	15.70 /91	0.00	1.25
GR	Fidelity Adv 529 Equity Growth B	FEGBX	B	(800) 522-7297	B- / 7.3	4.32	5.53	10.47 /76	14.55 /71	14.80 /85	0.00	2.00
GR	Fidelity Adv 529 Equity Growth C	FEGCX	B	(800) 522-7297	B- / 7.3	4.35	5.55	10.46 /76	14.55 /71	14.83 /85	0.00	2.00
GR	Fidelity Adv 529 Equity Growth D	FEGDX	B+	(800) 522-7297	B / 7.7	4.50	5.88	11.10 /79	15.17 /76	15.41 /90	0.00	1.50
GR	Fidelity Adv 529 Equity Growth P	FEGPX	B	(800) 522-7297	B- / 7.5	4.40	5.71	10.76 /77	14.85 /74	15.11 /88	0.00	1.75
IN	Fidelity Adv 529 Equity Income A	FEIZX	C+	(800) 522-7297	C / 4.8	0.09	1.84	5.98 /46	13.41 /63	11.47 /57	0.00	1.17
IN	Fidelity Adv 529 Equity Income B	FEPBX	B-	(800) 522-7297	C / 5.2	-0.10	1.48	5.22 /40	12.54 /56	10.63 /50	0.00	1.92
IN	Fidelity Adv 529 Equity Income C	FEPCX	C+	(800) 522-7297	C / 5.2	-0.10	1.43	5.16 /40	12.54 /56	10.63 /50	0.00	1.92
IN	Fidelity Adv 529 Equity Income D	FEIDX	B-	(800) 522-7297	C+ / 5.6	0.00	1.69	5.70 /44	13.10 /60	11.18 /54	0.00	1.42
IN	Fidelity Adv 529 Equity Income P	FEIPX	B-	(800) 522-7297	C / 5.4	-0.05	1.59	5.43 /42	12.83 /58	10.89 /52	0.00	1.67
GR	Fidelity Adv 529 New Insights B	FNPBX	B-	(800) 522-7297	C+ / 6.3	2.50	5.24	8.38 /65	13.40 /63	12.75 /66	0.00	2.06
GR	Fidelity Adv 529 New Insights C	FNPCX	B-	(800) 522-7297	C+ / 6.3	2.50	5.23	8.43 /66	13.44 /63	12.75 /66	0.00	2.06
GR	Fidelity Adv 529 New Insights P	FNPPX	B-	(800) 522-7297	C+ / 6.5	2.60	5.39	8.69 /67	13.71 /65	13.03 /68	0.00	1.81

• Denotes fund is closed to new investors
* Denotes fund is included in Section II

www.thestreetratings.com

RISK			NET ASSETS		ASSET					BULL / BEAR		FUND MANAGER		MINIMUMS		LOADS	
	3 Year		NAV						Portfolio	Last Bull	Last Bear	Manager	Manager	Initial	Additional	Front	Back
Risk	Standard		As of	Total	Cash	Stocks	Bonds	Other	Turnover	Market	Market	Quality	Tenure	Purch.	Purch.	End	End
Rating/Pts	Deviation	Beta	3/31/15	$(Mil)	%	%	%	%	Ratio	Return	Return	Pct	(Years)	$	$	Load	Load
B+ / 9.0	5.5	0.91	17.80	34	10	41	46	3	22	40.1	-12.8	28	10	1,000	50	0.0	0.0
B+ / 9.0	5.4	0.90	18.45	112	10	41	46	3	22	41.4	-12.8	32	10	1,000	50	3.5	0.0
B+ / 9.0	5.4	0.91	17.30	4	10	41	46	3	22	39.0	-13.0	26	10	1,000	50	0.0	0.0
B+ / 9.0	5.4	0.91	17.26	12	10	41	46	3	22	39.0	-13.0	26	10	1,000	50	0.0	0.0
B / 8.5	6.8	1.14	23.41	488	6	54	38	2	22	52.4	-16.0	23	10	1,000	50	5.8	0.0
B / 8.5	6.8	1.14	21.42	25	6	54	38	2	22	48.5	-16.2	16	10	1,000	50	0.0	0.0
B / 8.5	6.7	1.14	21.44	140	6	54	38	2	22	48.5	-16.2	16	10	1,000	50	0.0	0.0
B / 8.5	6.8	1.14	22.74	3	6	54	38	2	22	51.1	-16.1	20	10	1,000	50	0.0	0.0
B / 8.5	6.8	1.14	23.43	12	6	54	38	2	22	52.2	-16.0	22	10	1,000	50	3.5	0.0
B / 8.5	6.8	1.14	22.04	N/A	6	54	38	2	22	49.7	-16.2	18	10	1,000		0.0	0.0
B / 8.5	6.8	1.14	22.09	9	6	54	38	2	22	49.8	-16.1	18	10	1,000	50	0.0	0.0
B / 8.0	8.0	1.35	15.97	276	4	67	27	2	20	62.0	-18.6	15	10	1,000	50	5.8	0.0
B- / 7.9	8.0	1.35	14.90	12	4	67	27	2	20	58.0	-18.8	10	10	1,000	50	0.0	0.0
B- / 7.9	8.1	1.36	14.91	79	4	67	27	2	20	57.9	-18.8	10	10	1,000	50	0.0	0.0
B / 8.0	8.0	1.34	15.23	4	4	67	27	2	20	59.3	-18.7	12	10	1,000	50	0.0	0.0
B / 8.1	7.6	1.29	21.10	75	3	68	27	2	28	59.0	-16.1	19	10	1,000	50	5.8	0.0
B / 8.1	7.6	1.29	19.04	2	3	68	27	2	28	54.9	-16.4	13	10	1,000	50	0.0	0.0
B / 8.1	7.6	1.29	19.04	46	3	68	27	2	28	54.9	-16.3	14	10	1,000	50	0.0	0.0
B / 8.1	7.7	1.30	20.39	12	3	68	27	2	28	57.6	-16.2	16	10	1,000	50	0.0	0.0
B / 8.1	7.6	1.29	21.13	23	3	68	27	2	28	59.0	-16.1	19	10	1,000	50	3.5	0.0
B / 8.1	7.7	1.29	19.61	1	3	68	27	2	28	56.3	-16.2	15	10	1,000	50	0.0	0.0
B / 8.1	7.7	1.30	19.79	1	3	68	27	2	28	56.4	-16.3	15	10	1,000	50	0.0	0.0
B+ / 9.9	2.6	0.41	16.20	223	26	21	51	2	20	17.3	-4.2	57	10	1,000	50	5.8	0.0
B+ / 9.9	2.7	0.41	14.53	6	26	21	51	2	20	14.4	-4.5	44	10	1,000	50	0.0	0.0
B+ / 9.9	2.7	0.41	14.51	118	26	21	51	2	20	14.4	-4.4	44	10	1,000	50	0.0	0.0
B+ / 9.9	2.6	0.41	15.62	40	26	21	51	2	20	16.3	-4.2	51	10	1,000	50	0.0	0.0
B+ / 9.9	2.6	0.41	16.20	84	26	21	51	2	20	17.2	-4.1	56	10	1,000	50	3.5	0.0
B+ / 9.9	2.6	0.41	14.96	1	26	21	51	2	20	15.3	-4.3	48	10	1,000	50	0.0	0.0
B+ / 9.9	2.6	0.41	15.11	7	26	21	51	2	20	15.3	-4.3	48	10	1,000	50	0.0	0.0
C+ / 6.2	12.1	0.90	23.12	65	3	96	0	1	0	64.3	-24.7	87	10	1,000	50	5.8	0.0
C+ / 6.1	12.1	0.90	21.06	3	3	96	0	1	0	60.2	-25.0	84	10	1,000	50	0.0	0.0
C+ / 6.1	12.2	0.90	21.08	25	3	96	0	1	0	60.2	-25.0	84	10	1,000	50	0.0	0.0
C+ / 6.1	12.2	0.90	22.42	1	3	96	0	1	0	63.0	-24.8	86	10	1,000	50	0.0	0.0
C+ / 6.1	12.1	0.90	21.73	1	3	96	0	1	0	61.6	-24.9	85	10	1,000	50	0.0	0.0
C+ / 6.8	10.5	1.08	21.75	43	5	94	0	1	10	96.4	-24.8	30	10	1,000	50	5.8	0.0
C+ / 6.8	10.5	1.07	19.81	2	5	94	0	1	10	91.4	-25.0	22	10	1,000	50	0.0	0.0
C+ / 6.8	10.5	1.08	19.83	18	5	94	0	1	10	91.4	-25.0	21	10	1,000	50	0.0	0.0
C+ / 6.8	10.5	1.07	21.08	1	5	94	0	1	10	94.6	-24.8	27	10	1,000	50	0.0	0.0
C+ / 6.8	10.5	1.07	20.43	1	5	94	0	1	10	93.1	-24.9	24	10	1,000	50	0.0	0.0
C+ / 6.4	10.9	0.93	23.30	40	6	93	0	1	5	97.3	-18.2	72	10	1,000	50	5.8	0.0
C+ / 6.4	10.9	0.93	21.00	2	6	93	0	1	5	92.3	-18.5	63	10	1,000	50	0.0	0.0
C+ / 6.4	10.9	0.93	21.12	14	6	93	0	1	5	92.3	-18.5	63	10	1,000	50	0.0	0.0
C+ / 6.4	10.9	0.93	22.52	2	6	93	0	1	5	95.9	-18.4	70	10	1,000	50	0.0	0.0
C+ / 6.4	10.9	0.93	21.83	1	6	93	0	1	5	93.9	-18.4	67	10	1,000	50	0.0	0.0
B- / 7.7	9.2	0.93	21.08	41	11	84	0	5	4	81.8	-17.9	48	10	1,000	50	5.8	0.0
B- / 7.7	9.2	0.93	19.14	2	11	84	0	5	4	77.3	-18.2	36	10	1,000	50	0.0	0.0
B- / 7.7	9.2	0.93	19.17	18	11	84	0	5	4	77.2	-18.2	36	10	1,000	50	0.0	0.0
B- / 7.7	9.2	0.93	20.40	1	11	84	0	5	4	80.3	-18.1	44	10	1,000	50	0.0	0.0
B- / 7.7	9.2	0.93	19.82	1	11	84	0	5	4	78.7	-18.1	39	10	1,000	50	0.0	0.0
B- / 7.0	9.6	0.92	19.28	5	3	96	0	1	0	80.3	-14.9	50	10	1,000	50	0.0	0.0
B- / 7.0	9.6	0.92	19.30	70	3	96	0	1	0	80.3	-14.8	50	10	1,000	50	0.0	0.0
B- / 7.0	9.6	0.92	19.76	1	3	96	0	1	0	81.7	-14.7	54	10	1,000	50	0.0	0.0

99 Pct = Best
0 Pct = Worst

Fund Type	Fund Name	Ticker Symbol	Overall Investment Rating	Phone	Performance Rating/Pts	3 Mo	6 Mo	1Yr / Pct	3Yr / Pct	5Yr / Pct	Dividend Yield	Expense Ratio
SC	Fidelity Adv 529 Small Cap A	FSLAX	B-	(800) 522-7297	B- / 7.1	5.83	12.88	13.88 /89	14.72 /73	12.64 /65	0.00	1.48
SC	Fidelity Adv 529 Small Cap B	FSPBX	B	(800) 522-7297	B- / 7.5	5.64	12.44	12.99 /86	13.84 /66	11.79 /59	0.00	2.23
SC	Fidelity Adv 529 Small Cap C	FSZPX	B	(800) 522-7297	B- / 7.5	5.60	12.44	12.98 /86	13.85 /66	11.79 /59	0.00	2.23
SC	Fidelity Adv 529 Small Cap D	FSPDX	B	(800) 522-7297	B / 8.0	5.76	12.73	13.59 /88	14.42 /70	12.35 /63	0.00	1.73
SC	Fidelity Adv 529 Small Cap P	FSPPX	B	(800) 522-7297	B / 7.8	5.68	12.59	13.28 /88	14.15 /68	12.07 /61	0.00	1.98
MC	Fidelity Adv 529 Stock Select MC A	FBBEX	B	(800) 522-7297	B- / 7.3	4.51	11.22	11.22 /79	15.70 /81	13.76 /75	0.00	1.24
MC	Fidelity Adv 529 Stock Select MC B	FSSBX	B+	(800) 522-7297	B / 7.7	4.28	10.78	10.34 /76	14.82 /73	12.90 /67	0.00	1.99
MC	Fidelity Adv 529 Stock Select MC C	FBBFX	B+	(800) 522-7297	B / 7.8	4.32	10.86	10.42 /76	14.85 /74	12.91 /67	0.00	1.99
MC	Fidelity Adv 529 Stock Select MC D	FSSDX	B+	(800) 522-7297	B / 8.2	4.43	11.09	10.90 /78	15.40 /78	13.48 /73	0.00	1.49
MC	Fidelity Adv 529 Stock Select MC P	FSMPX	B+	(800) 522-7297	B / 8.0	4.39	10.94	10.66 /77	15.14 /76	13.21 /70	0.00	1.74
AA	Fidelity Adv 529 Value Strat A	FVASX	B+	(800) 522-7297	B- / 7.3	4.36	6.05	9.68 /73	16.43 /86	13.23 /70	0.00	1.25
AA	Fidelity Adv 529 Value Strat B	FVSBX	A-	(800) 522-7297	B / 7.7	4.17	5.67	8.82 /68	15.54 /79	12.38 /63	0.00	2.00
AA	Fidelity Adv 529 Value Strat C	FVSCX	A-	(800) 522-7297	B / 7.8	4.18	5.64	8.85 /68	15.57 /80	12.40 /63	0.00	2.00
AA	Fidelity Adv 529 Value Strat D	FVSDX	A	(800) 522-7297	B / 8.2	4.27	5.90	9.38 /71	16.11 /84	12.94 /68	0.00	1.50
AA	Fidelity Adv 529 Value Strat P	FVSPX	A-	(800) 522-7297	B / 7.9	4.20	5.79	9.12 /70	15.84 /82	12.67 /65	0.00	1.75
AA	Fidelity Adv Asset Manager 20% A	FTAWX	D+	(800) 522-7297	E+ / 0.9	1.63	2.64	3.86 /31	4.45 /11	5.04 /12	1.14	0.82
AA	● Fidelity Adv Asset Manager 20% B	FTBWX	C-	(800) 522-7297	D- / 1.1	1.43	2.26	3.08 /27	3.64 / 9	4.22 / 9	0.46	1.60
AA	Fidelity Adv Asset Manager 20% C	FTCWX	C-	(800) 522-7297	D- / 1.1	1.43	2.34	3.09 /27	3.67 / 9	4.25 / 9	0.47	1.60
AA	Fidelity Adv Asset Manager 20% I	FTIWX	C-	(800) 522-7297	D- / 1.4	1.74	2.84	4.19 /33	4.73 /12	5.33 /13	1.45	0.56
AA	Fidelity Adv Asset Manager 20% T	FTDWX	C-	(800) 522-7297	D- / 1.0	1.58	2.59	3.67 /30	4.18 /11	4.77 /11	0.92	1.10
GI	Fidelity Adv Asset Manager 30% A	FTAAX	C-	(800) 522-7297	D- / 1.3	2.01	3.28	4.75 /37	5.86 /16	6.27 /19	1.25	0.86
GI	● Fidelity Adv Asset Manager 30% B	FTBNX	C-	(800) 522-7297	D- / 1.5	1.78	2.88	3.94 /31	5.05 /13	5.46 /14	0.56	1.63
GI	Fidelity Adv Asset Manager 30% C	FCANX	C-	(800) 522-7297	D / 1.6	1.80	2.92	4.01 /32	5.07 /13	5.46 /14	0.61	1.62
GI	Fidelity Adv Asset Manager 30% I	FTINX	C-	(800) 522-7297	D / 2.1	2.05	3.40	5.02 /39	6.13 /17	6.52 /20	1.57	0.62
GI	Fidelity Adv Asset Manager 30% T	FTTNX	C-	(800) 522-7297	D- / 1.4	1.88	3.16	4.50 /35	5.58 /15	5.98 /17	1.05	1.13
GI	Fidelity Adv Asset Manager 40% A	FFNAX	C-	(800) 522-7297	D / 1.8	2.23	3.68	5.30 /41	7.12 /22	7.22 /24	1.19	0.86
GI	● Fidelity Adv Asset Manager 40% B	FFNBX	C-	(800) 522-7297	D / 2.1	2.04	3.37	4.58 /36	6.32 /18	6.40 /19	0.51	1.61
GI	Fidelity Adv Asset Manager 40% C	FFNCX	C-	(800) 522-7297	D / 2.1	2.05	3.30	4.54 /35	6.32 /18	6.40 /19	0.54	1.63
GI	Fidelity Adv Asset Manager 40% I	FFNIX	C	(800) 522-7297	D+ / 2.8	2.42	3.92	5.76 /44	7.42 /24	7.49 /26	1.51	0.58
GI	Fidelity Adv Asset Manager 40% T	FFNTX	C-	(800) 522-7297	D / 2.0	2.14	3.55	5.11 /39	6.86 /21	6.94 /23	0.96	1.13
AA	Fidelity Adv Asset Manager 50% A	FFAMX	D+	(800) 544-8544	D+ / 2.4	2.59	4.20	5.91 /46	8.28 /29	8.07 /30	1.17	0.96
AA	● Fidelity Adv Asset Manager 50% B	FFBMX	C-	(800) 544-8544	D+ / 2.8	2.36	3.79	5.10 /39	7.47 /24	7.26 /25	0.50	1.71
AA	Fidelity Adv Asset Manager 50% C	FFCMX	C-	(800) 544-8544	D+ / 2.8	2.37	3.74	5.07 /39	7.45 /24	7.26 /25	0.50	1.73
AA	Fidelity Adv Asset Manager 50% I	FFIMX	C-	(800) 544-8544	C- / 3.5	2.64	4.32	6.17 /48	8.57 /30	8.37 /32	1.47	0.71
AA	Fidelity Adv Asset Manager 50% T	FFTMX	C-	(800) 544-8544	D+ / 2.6	2.53	4.05	5.63 /43	8.00 /27	7.81 /29	0.94	1.23
GI	Fidelity Adv Asset Manager 60% A	FSAAX	C-	(800) 522-7297	C- / 3.0	2.81	4.55	6.30 /49	9.35 /35	8.73 /35	0.95	1.04
GI	● Fidelity Adv Asset Manager 60% B	FSABX	C	(800) 522-7297	C- / 3.3	2.62	4.16	5.44 /42	8.47 /30	7.89 /29	0.15	1.83
GI	Fidelity Adv Asset Manager 60% C	FSCNX	C-	(800) 522-7297	C- / 3.4	2.66	4.18	5.48 /42	8.49 /30	7.91 /29	0.37	1.80
GI	Fidelity Adv Asset Manager 60% I	FSNIX	C	(800) 522-7297	C- / 4.1	2.89	4.63	6.47 /50	9.60 /37	9.01 /37	1.26	0.79
GI	Fidelity Adv Asset Manager 60% T	FSATX	C-	(800) 522-7297	C- / 3.1	2.73	4.29	5.96 /46	9.03 /33	8.44 /33	0.73	1.31
AA	Fidelity Adv Asset Manager 85% A	FEYAX	C-	(800) 522-7297	C / 4.5	3.37	5.24	7.06 /55	12.11 /53	10.45 /48	0.86	1.05
AA	● Fidelity Adv Asset Manager 85% B	FEYBX	C	(800) 522-7297	C / 4.9	3.18	4.78	6.17 /48	11.20 /47	9.55 /41	0.02	1.84
AA	Fidelity Adv Asset Manager 85% C	FEYCX	C	(800) 522-7297	C / 4.9	3.23	4.82	6.23 /48	11.26 /47	9.62 /41	0.33	1.82
AA	Fidelity Adv Asset Manager 85% I	FEYIX	C	(800) 522-7297	C+ / 5.7	3.42	5.37	7.31 /58	12.42 /55	10.76 /51	1.26	0.77
AA	Fidelity Adv Asset Manager 85% T	FEYTX	C-	(800) 522-7297	C / 4.7	3.32	4.98	6.68 /52	11.77 /51	10.13 /46	0.70	1.34
GI	Fidelity Adv Asset Mang 70% A	FAASX	C-	(800) 522-7297	C- / 3.6	3.04	4.77	6.47 /50	10.38 /42	9.49 /40	0.94	1.04
GI	● Fidelity Adv Asset Mang 70% B	FBASX	C	(800) 522-7297	C- / 3.9	2.80	4.32	5.60 /43	9.47 /36	8.59 /34	0.00	1.88
GI	Fidelity Adv Asset Mang 70% C	FCASX	C	(800) 522-7297	C- / 4.0	2.79	4.35	5.65 /44	9.55 /36	8.66 /34	0.30	1.80
GI	Fidelity Adv Asset Mang 70% I	FTASX	C-	(800) 522-7297	C- / 3.7	2.94	4.57	6.17 /48	10.07 /40	9.19 /38	0.71	1.30
GI	Fidelity Adv Asset Mang 70% T	FAAIX	C	(800) 522-7297	C / 4.6	3.09	4.88	6.79 /53	10.68 /43	9.79 /43	1.24	0.78
BA	Fidelity Adv Balanced A	FABLX	C+	(800) 522-7297	C / 4.4	2.09	5.27	10.07 /75	11.57 /49	10.82 /51	0.99	0.92
BA	● Fidelity Adv Balanced B	FAISX	C+	(800) 522-7297	C / 4.8	1.88	4.81	9.18 /70	10.65 /43	9.93 /44	0.25	1.76

● Denotes fund is closed to new investors
* Denotes fund is included in Section II

Risk Rating/Pts	Standard Deviation	Beta	NAV As of 3/31/15	Total $(Mil)	Cash %	Stocks %	Bonds %	Other %	Portfolio Turnover Ratio	Last Bull Market Return	Last Bear Market Return	Manager Quality Pct	Manager Tenure (Years)	Initial Purch. $	Additional Purch. $	Front End Load	Back End Load
C+ / 5.9	13.0	0.90	33.56	42	2	97	0	1	3	84.1	-24.0	69	10	1,000	50	5.8	0.0
C+ / 5.9	13.0	0.90	30.54	2	2	97	0	1	3	79.5	-24.2	58	10	1,000	50	0.0	0.0
C+ / 5.9	12.9	0.90	30.55	15	2	97	0	1	3	79.5	-24.2	59	10	1,000	50	0.0	0.0
C+ / 5.9	12.9	0.90	32.51	1	2	97	0	1	3	82.5	-24.0	66	10	1,000	50	0.0	0.0
C+ / 5.9	12.9	0.90	31.65	1	2	97	0	1	3	81.0	-24.1	62	10	1,000	50	0.0	0.0
C+ / 6.7	10.4	0.93	27.55	53	4	95	0	1	2	97.3	-21.2	66	10	1,000	50	5.8	0.0
C+ / 6.6	10.4	0.93	25.08	2	4	95	0	1	2	92.4	-21.5	55	10	1,000	50	0.0	0.0
C+ / 6.6	10.4	0.93	25.12	21	4	95	0	1	2	92.4	-21.4	55	10	1,000	50	0.0	0.0
C+ / 6.6	10.4	0.93	26.85	1	4	95	0	1	2	95.8	-21.3	63	10	1,000	50	0.0	0.0
C+ / 6.6	10.4	0.93	26.16	1	4	95	0	1	2	94.0	-21.3	59	10	1,000	50	0.0	0.0
B- / 7.3	9.9	1.59	29.45	24	4	95	0	1	7	105.0	-26.9	49	10	1,000	50	5.8	0.0
B- / 7.2	10.0	1.59	27.01	1	4	95	0	1	7	99.9	-27.2	37	10	1,000	50	0.0	0.0
B- / 7.2	9.9	1.59	27.18	8	4	95	0	1	7	99.9	-27.1	38	10	1,000	50	0.0	0.0
B- / 7.2	10.0	1.59	28.35	N/A	4	95	0	1	7	103.1	-27.0	45	10	1,000	50	0.0	0.0
B- / 7.2	9.9	1.59	27.76	1	4	95	0	1	7	101.5	-27.1	42	10	1,000	50	0.0	0.0
B / 8.9	2.6	0.40	13.41	39	25	21	53	1	13	20.7	-3.4	69	6	2,500	0	5.8	0.0
B / 8.9	2.7	0.40	13.36	2	25	21	53	1	13	17.5	-3.6	59	6	2,500	0	0.0	0.0
B / 8.9	2.7	0.40	13.34	28	25	21	53	1	13	17.5	-3.6	59	6	2,500	0	0.0	0.0
B / 8.9	2.7	0.40	13.43	15	25	21	53	1	13	21.7	-3.2	72	6	2,500	0	0.0	0.0
B / 8.9	2.7	0.40	13.39	20	25	21	53	1	13	19.6	-3.5	66	6	2,500	0	3.5	0.0
B / 8.7	3.6	0.31	10.69	22	15	31	52	2	13	28.4	-5.7	77	6	2,500	0	5.8	0.0
B / 8.7	3.5	0.31	10.67	1	15	31	52	2	13	25.1	-6.0	71	6	2,500	0	0.0	0.0
B / 8.7	3.5	0.31	10.64	19	15	31	52	2	13	25.2	-6.0	71	6	2,500	0	0.0	0.0
B / 8.7	3.5	0.30	10.69	8	15	31	52	2	13	29.5	-5.6	80	6	2,500	0	0.0	0.0
B / 8.7	3.5	0.30	10.68	11	15	31	52	2	13	27.2	-5.8	76	6	2,500	0	3.5	0.0
B / 8.5	4.4	0.41	10.98	29	10	42	46	2	11	35.9	-8.2	75	6	2,500	0	5.8	0.0
B / 8.5	4.5	0.42	10.98	1	10	42	46	2	11	32.5	-8.5	66	6	2,500	0	0.0	0.0
B / 8.5	4.4	0.41	10.93	19	10	42	46	2	11	32.4	-8.5	67	6	2,500	0	0.0	0.0
B / 8.4	4.4	0.41	10.99	6	10	42	46	2	11	37.1	-8.1	77	6	2,500	0	0.0	0.0
B / 8.5	4.5	0.41	10.96	10	10	42	46	2	11	34.8	-8.3	72	6	2,500	0	3.5	0.0
B- / 7.3	5.4	0.91	17.43	74	6	51	42	1	10	42.9	-10.7	45	6	2,500	0	5.8	0.0
B- / 7.4	5.4	0.91	17.38	3	6	51	42	1	10	39.4	-11.0	34	6	2,500	0	0.0	0.0
B- / 7.4	5.4	0.90	17.31	41	6	51	42	1	10	39.4	-11.0	35	6	2,500	0	0.0	0.0
B- / 7.3	5.4	0.91	17.47	31	6	51	42	1	10	44.3	-10.6	50	6	2,500	0	0.0	0.0
B- / 7.4	5.4	0.91	17.41	36	6	51	42	1	10	41.8	-10.8	40	6	2,500	0	3.5	0.0
B- / 7.4	6.3	0.61	11.35	57	3	61	35	1	11	50.1	-13.2	64	6	2,500	0	5.8	0.0
B- / 7.5	6.3	0.62	11.36	2	3	61	35	1	11	46.3	-13.5	51	6	2,500	0	0.0	0.0
B- / 7.5	6.4	0.62	11.20	30	3	61	35	1	11	46.4	-13.5	50	6	2,500	0	0.0	0.0
B- / 7.3	6.3	0.61	11.39	17	3	61	35	1	11	51.5	-13.1	67	6	2,500	0	0.0	0.0
B- / 7.4	6.3	0.61	11.30	17	3	61	35	1	11	48.9	-13.3	59	6	2,500	0	3.5	0.0
C+ / 6.0	8.9	1.49	16.88	72	4	84	10	2	14	70.1	-19.4	16	6	2,500	0	5.8	0.0
C+ / 6.1	8.9	1.49	16.88	2	4	84	10	2	14	65.3	-19.7	12	6	2,500	0	0.0	0.0
C+ / 6.0	8.8	1.48	16.64	35	4	84	10	2	14	65.6	-19.7	12	6	2,500	0	0.0	0.0
C+ / 5.9	8.9	1.49	16.94	41	4	84	10	2	14	71.5	-19.3	19	6	2,500	0	0.0	0.0
C+ / 6.0	8.8	1.48	16.79	21	4	84	10	2	14	68.1	-19.4	15	6	2,500	0	3.5	0.0
C+ / 6.8	7.4	0.72	20.34	153	5	68	26	1	13	57.8	-15.8	53	6	2,500	0	5.8	0.0
B- / 7.1	7.4	0.72	20.56	3	5	68	26	1	13	53.3	-16.1	41	6	2,500	0	0.0	0.0
B- / 7.0	7.4	0.72	20.25	57	5	68	26	1	13	53.7	-16.1	42	6	2,500	0	0.0	0.0
C+ / 6.9	7.3	0.72	20.34	51	5	68	26	1	13	56.3	-15.9	50	6	2,500	0	3.5	0.0
C+ / 6.8	7.4	0.72	20.38	42	5	68	26	1	13	59.2	-15.7	58	6	2,500	0	0.0	0.0
B- / 7.8	6.6	1.15	19.55	419	8	64	27	1	79	61.7	-10.5	53	7	2,500	0	5.8	0.0
B- / 7.8	6.6	1.15	19.55	9	8	64	27	1	79	57.3	-10.8	41	7	2,500	0	0.0	0.0

					PERFORMANCE							
99 Pct = Best 0 Pct = Worst						Total Return % through 3/31/15					Incl. in Returns	
			Overall Investment Rating		Perfor-mance Rating/Pts				Annualized		Dividend Yield	Expense Ratio
Fund Type	Fund Name	Ticker Symbol		Phone		3 Mo	6 Mo	1Yr / Pct	3Yr / Pct	5Yr / Pct		
BA	Fidelity Adv Balanced C	FABCX	C+	(800) 522-7297	C / 4.8	1.94	4.91	9.29 /71	10.75 /44	10.01 /45	0.39	1.68
BA	Fidelity Adv Balanced Inst	FAIOX	B	(800) 522-7297	C+ / 5.6	2.21	5.45	10.42 /76	11.89 /52	11.13 /54	1.27	0.68
BA	Fidelity Adv Balanced T	FAIGX	C+	(800) 522-7297	C / 4.6	2.02	5.14	9.82 /74	11.31 /48	10.58 /49	0.79	1.15
BA	Fidelity Adv Balanced Z	FZAAX	U	(800) 522-7297	U /	2.21	5.52	10.58 /77	--	--	1.41	0.53
HL	Fidelity Adv Biotechnology A	FBTAX	B-	(800) 522-7297	A+ / 9.9	14.66	29.47	45.91 /99	42.13 /99	32.61 /99	0.00	1.08
HL	● Fidelity Adv Biotechnology B	FBTBX	B-	(800) 522-7297	A+ / 9.9	14.39	28.97	44.74 /99	41.00 /99	31.58 /99	0.00	1.89
HL	Fidelity Adv Biotechnology C	FBTCX	B-	(800) 522-7297	A+ / 9.9	14.41	28.96	44.78 /99	41.04 /99	31.63 /99	0.00	1.83
HL	Fidelity Adv Biotechnology I	FBTIX	B-	(800) 522-7297	A+ / 9.9	14.69	29.66	46.25 /99	42.54 /99	32.99 /99	0.01	0.81
HL	Fidelity Adv Biotechnology T	FBTTX	B-	(800) 522-7297	A+ / 9.9	14.54	29.26	45.37 /99	41.64 /99	32.18 /99	0.00	1.41
FO	Fidelity Adv Canada A	FACNX	E-	(800) 522-7297	E / 0.4	-5.69	-7.89	-3.40 / 8	3.04 / 8	2.86 / 6	0.84	1.29
FO	● Fidelity Adv Canada B	FBCNX	E	(800) 522-7297	E / 0.5	-5.88	-8.25	-4.16 / 7	2.24 / 7	2.06 / 4	0.00	2.09
FO	Fidelity Adv Canada C	FCCNX	E	(800) 522-7297	E / 0.5	-5.87	-8.25	-4.13 / 7	2.28 / 7	2.10 / 5	0.04	2.03
FO	Fidelity Adv Canada I	FICCX	E	(800) 522-7297	E+ / 0.6	-5.62	-7.76	-3.12 / 8	3.36 / 9	3.17 / 6	1.21	1.00
FO	Fidelity Adv Canada T	FTCNX	E	(800) 522-7297	E / 0.4	-5.77	-8.04	-3.69 / 7	2.74 / 7	2.56 / 5	0.52	1.59
GR	Fidelity Adv Capital Devp Class A	FDTTX	C-	(800) 522-7297	C / 5.5	1.21	3.89	8.40 /66	13.98 /67	12.92 /67	0.96	0.89
GR	● Fidelity Adv Capital Devp Class B	FDEBX	C-	(800) 522-7297	C+ / 5.7	0.97	3.32	7.36 /58	12.85 /58	11.82 /59	0.00	1.89
GR	Fidelity Adv Capital Devp Class C	FDECX	C-	(800) 522-7297	C+ / 5.7	0.97	3.30	7.28 /57	12.85 /58	11.84 /60	0.08	1.89
GR	Fidelity Adv Capital Devp Class I	FDEIX	C	(800) 522-7297	C+ / 6.5	1.17	3.88	8.52 /66	14.09 /68	13.01 /68	1.14	0.74
GR	Fidelity Adv Capital Devp Class O	FDETX	C	(800) 522-7297	C+ / 6.7	1.25	3.97	8.71 /68	14.32 /69	13.26 /71	1.27	0.60
GR	Fidelity Adv Capital Devp Class T	FDTZX	C-	(800) 522-7297	C / 5.4	1.02	3.53	7.76 /61	13.33 /62	12.30 /62	0.58	1.43
FO	Fidelity Adv China Region Fd A	FHKAX	C	(800) 522-7297	B- / 7.1	6.35	12.10	14.70 /91	14.45 /70	9.12 /38	0.58	1.35
FO	● Fidelity Adv China Region Fd B	FHKBX	C+	(800) 522-7297	B / 7.6	6.12	11.64	13.83 /89	13.59 /64	8.30 /32	0.00	2.11
FO	Fidelity Adv China Region Fd C	FCHKX	C+	(800) 522-7297	B / 7.6	6.15	11.69	13.89 /89	13.61 /64	8.31 /32	0.12	2.07
FO	Fidelity Adv China Region Fd I	FHKIX	C+	(800) 522-7297	B+ / 8.5	6.42	12.27	15.14 /92	14.87 /74	9.49 /40	0.98	0.98
FO	Fidelity Adv China Region Fd T	FHKTX	C	(800) 522-7297	B- / 7.3	6.26	11.90	14.36 /90	14.13 /68	8.82 /35	0.32	1.65
TC	Fidelity Adv Commu Equipment A	FDMAX	D-	(800) 522-7297	C- / 3.1	-0.71	5.58	8.01 /63	9.73 /38	7.99 /30	0.23	1.96
TC	● Fidelity Adv Commu Equipment B	FDMBX	D-	(800) 522-7297	C- / 3.5	-0.78	5.17	7.24 /57	8.93 /32	7.20 /24	0.00	2.74
TC	Fidelity Adv Commu Equipment C	FDMCX	D-	(800) 522-7297	C- / 3.5	-0.87	5.17	7.25 /57	8.94 /32	7.21 /24	0.00	2.73
TC	Fidelity Adv Commu Equipment I	FDMIX	D	(800) 522-7297	C- / 4.2	-0.61	5.65	8.22 /64	10.01 /39	8.26 /32	0.44	1.45
TC	Fidelity Adv Commu Equipment T	FDMTX	D-	(800) 522-7297	C- / 3.3	-0.73	5.42	7.78 /61	9.51 /36	7.73 /28	0.04	2.25
GR	Fidelity Adv Consumer Discre A	FCNAX	B+	(800) 522-7297	B+ / 8.9	4.05	14.36	14.48 /91	17.96 /94	17.36 /97	0.00	1.20
GR	● Fidelity Adv Consumer Discre B	FCIBX	B	(800) 522-7297	A- / 9.2	3.83	13.88	13.54 /88	17.01 /90	16.44 /95	0.00	2.01
GR	Fidelity Adv Consumer Discre C	FCECX	B	(800) 522-7297	A- / 9.2	3.90	13.94	13.63 /89	17.10 /90	16.50 /95	0.00	1.97
GR	Fidelity Adv Consumer Discre I	FCNIX	B+	(800) 522-7297	A+ / 9.6	4.12	14.52	14.84 /91	18.33 /95	17.75 /97	0.00	0.91
GR	Fidelity Adv Consumer Discre T	FACPX	B+	(800) 522-7297	A- / 9.0	3.97	14.21	14.13 /90	17.60 /93	17.04 /96	0.00	1.50
GR	Fidelity Adv Consumer Staples A	FDAGX	C+	(800) 522-7297	C+ / 6.4	1.62	8.00	15.61 /93	14.53 /71	14.08 /78	1.17	1.06
GR	● Fidelity Adv Consumer Staples B	FDBGX	C+	(800) 522-7297	C+ / 6.8	1.42	7.57	14.71 /91	13.63 /64	13.17 /70	0.47	1.86
GR	Fidelity Adv Consumer Staples C	FDCGX	C+	(800) 522-7297	C+ / 6.9	1.43	7.58	14.75 /91	13.67 /65	13.23 /70	0.65	1.82
GR	Fidelity Adv Consumer Staples I	FDIGX	B	(800) 522-7297	B / 7.7	1.68	8.13	15.90 /93	14.81 /73	14.36 /81	1.39	0.82
GR	Fidelity Adv Consumer Staples T	FDTGX	C+	(800) 522-7297	C+ / 6.6	1.54	7.84	15.29 /92	14.22 /69	13.76 /75	0.98	1.33
GR	Fidelity Adv Divers Stk A	FDTOX	C+	(800) 522-7297	C+ / 6.4	0.04	3.38	8.39 /65	15.78 /82	14.10 /79	0.93	0.81
GR	● Fidelity Adv Divers Stk B	FDTBX	C+	(800) 522-7297	C+ / 6.6	-0.18	2.90	7.35 /58	14.68 /72	13.04 /69	0.04	1.77
GR	Fidelity Adv Divers Stk C	FDTCX	C+	(800) 522-7297	C+ / 6.6	-0.23	2.89	7.35 /58	14.68 /72	13.05 /69	0.33	1.76
GR	Fidelity Adv Divers Stk I	FDTIX	B+	(800) 522-7297	B / 7.6	0.08	3.50	8.63 /67	15.94 /83	14.25 /80	0.54	0.68
GR	Fidelity Adv Divers Stk O	FDESX	B	(800) 522-7297	B / 7.7	0.13	3.56	8.70 /68	16.13 /84	14.47 /82	1.23	0.51
GR	Fidelity Adv Divers Stk T	FDTEX	C+	(800) 522-7297	C+ / 6.4	-0.04	3.14	7.89 /62	15.25 /77	13.60 /74	0.65	1.27
FO	Fidelity Adv Diversified Intl A	FDVAX	C-	(800) 522-7297	C- / 4.1	6.76	5.70	3.73 /30	11.64 /50	8.05 /30	0.92	1.24
FO	● Fidelity Adv Diversified Intl B	FDIBX	C-	(800) 522-7297	C / 4.4	6.55	5.25	2.89 /26	10.76 /44	7.20 /24	0.00	2.05
FO	Fidelity Adv Diversified Intl C	FADCX	C-	(800) 522-7297	C / 4.5	6.54	5.32	2.94 /26	10.82 /44	7.25 /25	0.28	1.98
FO	Fidelity Adv Diversified Intl I	FDVIX	C	(800) 522-7297	C / 5.2	6.86	5.88	4.00 /32	11.98 /52	8.38 /32	1.27	0.95
FO	Fidelity Adv Diversified Intl T	FADIX	C-	(800) 522-7297	C / 4.3	6.70	5.56	3.47 /29	11.35 /48	7.77 /28	0.69	1.49
FO	Fidelity Adv Diversified Intl Z	FZABX	U	(800) 522-7297	U /	6.92	5.98	4.20 /33	--	--	1.46	0.79

● Denotes fund is closed to new investors
* Denotes fund is included in Section II

www.thestreetratings.com

RISK			NET ASSETS		ASSET					BULL / BEAR		FUND MANAGER		MINIMUMS		LOADS	
	3 Year		NAV						Portfolio	Last Bull	Last Bear	Manager	Manager	Initial	Additional	Front	Back
Risk	Standard		As of	Total	Cash	Stocks	Bonds	Other	Turnover	Market	Market	Quality	Tenure	Purch.	Purch.	End	End
Rating/Pts	Deviation	Beta	3/31/15	$(Mil)	%	%	%	%	Ratio	Return	Return	Pct	(Years)	$	$	Load	Load
B- / 7.8	6.5	1.14	19.43	231	8	64	27	1	79	57.6	-10.8	43	7	2,500	0	0.0	0.0
B- / 7.8	6.5	1.14	19.89	198	8	64	27	1	79	63.1	-10.4	60	7	2,500	0	0.0	0.0
B- / 7.8	6.6	1.15	19.73	1,026	8	64	27	1	79	60.5	-10.6	50	7	2,500	0	3.5	0.0
U /	N/A	N/A	19.89	33	8	64	27	1	79	N/A	N/A	N/A	7	5,000,000	0	0.0	0.0
C- / 3.2	19.8	0.83	28.31	1,172	0	98	0	2	50	282.1	-12.0	99	10	2,500	0	5.8	0.8
C- / 3.1	19.8	0.83	25.04	8	0	98	0	2	50	271.9	-12.2	99	10	2,500	0	0.0	0.8
C- / 3.1	19.8	0.82	25.09	718	0	98	0	2	50	272.6	-12.2	99	10	2,500	0	0.0	0.8
C- / 3.2	19.7	0.82	29.66	1,053	0	98	0	2	50	285.8	-11.9	99	10	2,500	0	0.0	0.8
C- / 3.2	19.8	0.83	27.10	160	0	98	0	2	50	277.8	-12.0	99	10	2,500	0	3.5	0.8
C- / 3.4	12.0	0.69	49.39	79	2	97	0	1	85	25.0	-23.9	22	7	2,500	0	5.8	1.5
C- / 3.4	12.0	0.69	48.50	5	2	97	0	1	85	21.8	-24.1	16	7	2,500	0	0.0	1.5
C- / 3.4	12.0	0.69	48.26	31	2	97	0	1	85	21.9	-24.1	16	7	2,500	0	0.0	1.5
C- / 3.3	12.0	0.69	49.51	22	2	97	0	1	85	26.4	-23.8	25	7	2,500	0	0.0	1.5
C- / 3.4	12.0	0.69	49.20	17	2	97	0	1	85	23.8	-24.0	19	7	2,500	0	3.5	1.5
C / 4.6	10.5	1.06	14.17	391	1	98	0	1	115	83.5	-19.6	28	2	2,500	0	5.8	0.0
C / 4.7	10.5	1.05	13.55	N/A	1	98	0	1	115	77.5	-19.9	19	2	2,500	0	0.0	0.0
C / 4.6	10.5	1.05	13.48	2	1	98	0	1	115	77.4	-19.8	19	2	2,500	0	0.0	0.0
C / 4.7	10.6	1.06	14.64	2	1	98	0	1	115	84.1	-19.5	29	2	2,500	0	0.0	0.0
C / 4.7	10.5	1.06	14.58	2,619	1	98	0	1	115	85.4	-19.4	32	2	0	0	0.0	0.0
C / 4.6	10.5	1.06	13.86	2	1	98	0	1	115	80.2	-19.7	22	2	2,500	0	3.5	0.0
C / 4.4	12.3	0.63	32.34	31	3	96	0	1	87	67.4	-27.2	97	4	2,500	0	5.8	1.5
C / 4.6	12.3	0.63	32.07	1	3	96	0	1	87	63.2	-27.4	96	4	2,500	0	0.0	1.5
C / 4.4	12.3	0.63	31.76	11	3	96	0	1	87	63.3	-27.4	96	4	2,500	0	0.0	1.5
C / 4.4	12.3	0.63	32.47	30	3	96	0	1	87	69.5	-27.1	97	4	2,500	0	0.0	1.5
C / 4.5	12.3	0.63	32.23	6	3	96	0	1	87	65.9	-27.2	96	4	2,500	0	3.5	1.5
C- / 3.9	17.1	1.32	12.67	5	1	98	0	1	160	68.1	-32.4	2	1	2,500	0	5.8	0.8
C- / 3.8	17.1	1.32	11.40	N/A	1	98	0	1	160	63.9	-32.6	1	1	2,500	0	0.0	0.8
C- / 3.8	17.0	1.32	11.39	3	1	98	0	1	160	63.7	-32.6	1	1	2,500	0	0.0	0.8
C- / 3.9	17.0	1.32	13.10	3	1	98	0	1	160	69.6	-32.4	2	1	2,500	0	0.0	0.8
C- / 3.9	17.0	1.32	12.26	4	1	98	0	1	160	66.8	-32.5	2	1	2,500	0	3.5	0.8
C / 5.2	11.4	1.07	20.53	81	3	96	0	1	171	114.1	-16.6	74	3	2,500	0	5.8	0.8
C / 4.9	11.5	1.07	17.06	1	3	96	0	1	171	108.4	-16.8	64	3	2,500	0	0.0	0.8
C / 4.8	11.4	1.06	17.07	31	3	96	0	1	171	108.9	-16.9	66	3	2,500	0	0.0	0.8
C / 5.3	11.4	1.06	21.99	49	3	96	0	1	171	116.6	-16.5	77	3	2,500	0	0.0	0.8
C / 5.1	11.4	1.07	19.36	23	3	96	0	1	171	112.0	-16.7	70	3	2,500	0	3.5	0.8
C+ / 6.2	11.2	0.95	98.66	412	0	99	0	1	31	81.3	-6.7	59	11	2,500	0	5.8	0.8
C+ / 6.3	11.2	0.95	97.43	15	0	99	0	1	31	76.4	-7.0	47	11	2,500	0	0.0	0.8
C+ / 6.3	11.2	0.95	96.60	226	0	99	0	1	31	76.7	-7.0	47	11	2,500	0	0.0	0.8
C+ / 6.2	11.2	0.95	99.24	199	0	99	0	1	31	82.8	-6.7	62	11	2,500	0	0.0	0.8
C+ / 6.2	11.2	0.95	97.94	80	0	99	0	1	31	79.6	-6.8	54	11	2,500	0	3.5	0.8
C+ / 6.3	10.4	1.06	22.66	226	6	93	0	1	55	102.5	-18.3	50	9	2,500	0	5.8	0.0
C+ / 6.5	10.5	1.06	22.42	1	6	93	0	1	55	96.0	-18.7	34	9	2,500	0	0.0	0.0
C+ / 6.4	10.5	1.07	22.07	26	6	93	0	1	55	96.2	-18.7	34	9	2,500	0	0.0	0.0
C+ / 6.5	10.4	1.06	23.81	48	6	93	0	1	55	103.4	-18.2	51	9	2,500	0	0.0	0.0
C+ / 6.3	10.4	1.06	23.16	1,865	6	93	0	1	55	104.7	-18.2	53	9	0	0	0.0	0.0
C+ / 6.4	10.4	1.06	22.51	32	6	93	0	1	55	99.4	-18.5	41	9	2,500	0	3.5	0.0
C+ / 6.0	12.2	0.90	20.38	656	2	97	0	1	40	65.1	-24.7	88	6	2,500	0	5.8	1.0
C+ / 6.0	12.2	0.90	19.67	16	2	97	0	1	40	60.7	-24.9	84	6	2,500	0	0.0	1.0
C+ / 6.0	12.2	0.90	19.54	247	2	97	0	1	40	60.9	-24.9	85	6	2,500	0	0.0	1.0
C+ / 6.0	12.1	0.90	20.71	691	2	97	0	1	40	66.8	-24.6	89	6	2,500	0	0.0	1.0
C+ / 6.0	12.1	0.90	20.23	282	2	97	0	1	40	63.6	-24.7	87	6	2,500	0	3.5	1.0
U /	N/A	N/A	20.70	72	2	97	0	1	40	N/A	N/A	N/A	6	5,000,000	0	0.0	1.0

						PERFORMANCE							
							Total Return % through 3/31/15					Incl. in Returns	
										Annualized		Dividend	Expense
Fund Type	Fund Name	Ticker Symbol	Overall Investment Rating	Phone	Performance Rating/Pts	3 Mo	6 Mo	1Yr / Pct	3Yr / Pct	5Yr / Pct		Yield	Ratio
GR	Fidelity Adv Dividend Growth A	FADAX	C+	(800) 522-7297	C+ / 6.1	1.03	5.10	11.20 /79	14.61 /72	12.64 /65		0.94	0.98
GR ●	Fidelity Adv Dividend Growth B	FADBX	C+	(800) 522-7297	C+ / 6.5	0.88	4.67	10.36 /76	13.68 /65	11.76 /59		0.05	1.79
GR	Fidelity Adv Dividend Growth C	FDGCX	C+	(800) 522-7297	C+ / 6.5	0.89	4.72	10.42 /76	13.77 /65	11.82 /59		0.34	1.72
GR	Fidelity Adv Dividend Growth I	FDGIX	B	(800) 522-7297	B- / 7.4	1.15	5.26	11.56 /81	14.92 /74	12.97 /68		1.18	0.70
GR	Fidelity Adv Dividend Growth T	FDGTX	C+	(800) 522-7297	C+ / 6.3	1.03	4.98	10.99 /78	14.34 /70	12.39 /63		0.75	1.21
TC	Fidelity Adv Electronics A	FELAX	B	(800) 522-7297	A+ / 9.6	3.68	14.35	27.30 /99	17.83 /94	15.57 /91		0.04	1.84
TC ●	Fidelity Adv Electronics B	FELBX	B	(800) 522-7297	A+ / 9.7	3.42	13.86	26.28 /99	16.94 /89	14.69 /84		0.00	2.68
TC	Fidelity Adv Electronics C	FELCX	B	(800) 522-7297	A+ / 9.7	3.43	13.87	26.30 /99	16.96 /90	14.71 /84		0.00	2.60
TC	Fidelity Adv Electronics I	FELIX	B	(800) 522-7297	A+ / 9.8	3.73	14.52	27.55 /99	18.16 /95	15.84 /92		0.11	1.34
TC	Fidelity Adv Electronics T	FELTX	B	(800) 522-7297	A+ / 9.6	3.53	14.17	26.84 /99	17.53 /92	15.27 /89		0.00	2.19
EM	Fidelity Adv Emerg Mkts Discv A	FEDAX	D-	(800) 522-7297	E+ / 0.6	1.73	-5.53	--	3.47 / 9	--		0.00	1.82
EM	Fidelity Adv Emerg Mkts Discv C	FEDGX	D-	(800) 522-7297	E+ / 0.7	1.49	-5.85	-0.77 /14	2.73 / 7	--		0.00	2.58
EM	Fidelity Adv Emerg Mkts Discv Inst	FEDIX	D	(800) 522-7297	E+ / 0.8	1.80	-5.34	0.25 /16	3.75 /10	--		0.00	1.56
EM	Fidelity Adv Emerg Mkts Discv T	FEDTX	D-	(800) 522-7297	E+ / 0.6	1.65	-5.63	-0.25 /15	3.22 / 8	--		0.00	2.10
EM	Fidelity Adv Emerging Asia A	FEAAX	D+	(800) 522-7297	C- / 3.3	5.15	7.07	13.16 /87	8.11 /28	7.39 /26		0.52	1.42
EM ●	Fidelity Adv Emerging Asia B	FERBX	D+	(800) 522-7297	C- / 3.5	4.93	6.65	12.26 /84	6.99 /21	6.38 /19		0.00	2.22
EM	Fidelity Adv Emerging Asia C	FERCX	D+	(800) 522-7297	C- / 3.6	4.93	6.66	12.29 /84	7.05 /22	6.45 /20		0.00	2.17
EM	Fidelity Adv Emerging Asia I	FERIX	C-	(800) 522-7297	C / 4.3	5.24	7.22	13.47 /88	8.14 /28	7.54 /27		0.90	1.12
EM	Fidelity Adv Emerging Asia T	FEATX	D+	(800) 522-7297	C- / 3.4	5.05	6.86	12.77 /86	7.68 /25	7.01 /23		0.23	1.73
EM	Fidelity Adv Emerging EMEA A	FMEAX	E	(800) 522-7297	E- / 0.2	1.50	-8.72	-9.42 / 3	-1.19 / 3	1.70 / 4		1.56	1.60
EM ●	Fidelity Adv Emerging EMEA B	FEMBX	E	(800) 522-7297	E / 0.3	1.36	-9.07	-10.06 / 3	-1.93 / 3	0.94 / 3		0.72	2.40
EM	Fidelity Adv Emerging EMEA C	FEMCX	E	(800) 522-7297	E / 0.3	1.39	-9.10	-10.10 / 3	-1.94 / 3	0.93 / 3		0.97	2.40
EM	Fidelity Adv Emerging EMEA Fd	FEMEX	E	(800) 522-7297	E / 0.3	1.63	-8.63	-9.13 / 3	-0.95 / 3	1.96 / 4		2.08	1.37
EM	Fidelity Adv Emerging EMEA I	FIEMX	E	(800) 522-7297	E / 0.3	1.75	-8.52	-9.02 / 3	-0.83 / 4	2.06 / 4		2.21	1.26
EM	Fidelity Adv Emerging EMEA T	FEMTX	E	(800) 522-7297	E- / 0.2	1.51	-8.86	-9.66 / 3	-1.45 / 3	1.45 / 4		1.49	1.92
EM	Fidelity Adv Emerging Markets A	FAMKX	E+	(800) 522-7297	E+ / 0.7	2.76	1.50	3.83 /31	2.97 / 8	2.10 / 5		0.08	1.52
EM ●	Fidelity Adv Emerging Markets B	FBMKX	E+	(800) 522-7297	E+ / 0.8	2.56	1.13	3.03 /27	2.21 / 7	1.34 / 4		0.00	2.28
EM ●	Fidelity Adv Emerging Markets C	FMCKX	E+	(800) 522-7297	E+ / 0.8	2.57	1.13	3.04 /27	2.21 / 7	1.34 / 4		0.00	2.27
EM	Fidelity Adv Emerging Markets I	FIMKX	E+	(800) 522-7297	D- / 1.0	2.85	1.66	4.16 /33	3.31 / 8	2.44 / 5		0.46	1.18
EM	Fidelity Adv Emerging Markets T	FTMKX	E+	(800) 522-7297	E+ / 0.7	2.63	1.32	3.51 /29	2.70 / 7	1.84 / 4		0.00	1.78
EN	Fidelity Adv Energy A	FANAX	E-	(800) 522-7297	E / 0.3	1.19	-15.08	-13.85 / 2	2.31 / 7	5.12 /12		0.31	1.12
EN ●	Fidelity Adv Energy B	FANRX	E-	(800) 522-7297	E / 0.4	0.98	-15.43	-14.54 / 2	1.51 / 6	4.31 / 9		0.00	1.91
EN	Fidelity Adv Energy C	FNRCX	E-	(800) 522-7297	E / 0.4	0.97	-15.40	-14.48 / 2	1.55 / 6	4.34 /10		0.08	1.86
EN	Fidelity Adv Energy I	FANIX	E-	(800) 522-7297	E / 0.4	1.24	-14.98	-13.62 / 2	2.59 / 7	5.42 /14		0.49	0.85
EN	Fidelity Adv Energy T	FAGNX	E-	(800) 522-7297	E / 0.3	1.11	-15.18	-14.05 / 2	2.08 / 6	4.88 /11		0.20	1.34
GR	Fidelity Adv Equity Growth A	EPGAX	C+	(800) 522-7297	C+ / 6.9	4.58	6.06	11.51 /80	15.58 /80	15.82 /92		0.00	1.12
GR ●	Fidelity Adv Equity Growth B	EPGBX	B	(800) 522-7297	B- / 7.3	4.36	5.61	10.58 /77	14.66 /72	14.92 /86		0.00	1.90
GR	Fidelity Adv Equity Growth C	EPGCX	B	(800) 522-7297	B- / 7.4	4.39	5.66	10.67 /77	14.73 /73	14.97 /87		0.00	1.85
GR	Fidelity Adv Equity Growth Inst	EQPGX	B+	(800) 522-7297	B+ / 8.3	4.66	6.21	11.83 /82	15.95 /83	16.20 /94		0.00	0.79
GR	Fidelity Adv Equity Growth T	FAEGX	B	(800) 522-7297	B- / 7.2	4.53	5.95	11.27 /79	15.36 /78	15.61 /91		0.00	1.30
IN	Fidelity Adv Equity Income A	FEIAX	C+	(800) 522-7297	C / 4.9	0.10	1.93	6.18 /48	13.61 /64	11.67 /58		2.16	1.00
IN ●	Fidelity Adv Equity Income B	FEIBX	C+	(800) 522-7297	C / 5.3	-0.09	1.50	5.28 /41	12.67 /57	10.77 /51		1.46	1.82
IN	Fidelity Adv Equity Income C	FEICX	C+	(800) 522-7297	C / 5.3	-0.09	1.54	5.38 /41	12.74 /58	10.82 /51		1.57	1.76
IN	Fidelity Adv Equity Income Inst	EQPIX	B-	(800) 522-7297	C+ / 6.1	0.18	2.05	6.45 /50	13.90 /66	11.96 /60		2.45	0.74
IN	Fidelity Adv Equity Income T	FEIRX	C+	(800) 522-7297	C / 5.1	0.04	1.80	5.92 /46	13.35 /62	11.44 /56		1.95	1.21
GR	Fidelity Adv Equity Value A	FAVAX	A+	(800) 522-7297	B / 7.9	1.13	7.58	11.54 /81	17.29 /91	13.72 /75		1.12	1.22
GR ●	Fidelity Adv Equity Value B	FAVBX	A+	(800) 522-7297	B+ / 8.3	0.94	7.13	10.74 /77	16.38 /86	12.87 /67		0.37	1.99
GR	Fidelity Adv Equity Value C	FAVCX	A+	(800) 522-7297	B+ / 8.3	0.89	7.15	10.65 /77	16.38 /86	12.86 /67		0.61	1.97
GR	Fidelity Adv Equity Value I	FAIVX	A+	(800) 522-7297	A- / 9.1	1.17	7.71	11.91 /82	17.62 /93	14.06 /78		1.45	0.89
GR	Fidelity Adv Equity Value T	FAVTX	A+	(800) 522-7297	B / 8.1	1.00	7.35	11.24 /79	16.96 /90	13.44 /72		0.89	1.48
FS	Fidelity Adv Financial Serv A	FAFDX	C+	(800) 522-7297	C+ / 6.2	-0.19	6.01	9.40 /71	15.23 /77	7.33 /25		0.73	1.23
FS ●	Fidelity Adv Financial Serv B	FAFBX	C+	(800) 522-7297	C+ / 6.6	-0.32	5.60	8.56 /67	14.39 /70	6.52 /20		0.15	1.99

● Denotes fund is closed to new investors
* Denotes fund is included in Section II

RISK			NET ASSETS		ASSET					BULL / BEAR		FUND MANAGER		MINIMUMS		LOADS	
	3 Year		NAV						Portfolio	Last Bull	Last Bear	Manager	Manager	Initial	Additional	Front	Back
Risk	Standard		As of	Total	Cash	Stocks	Bonds	Other	Turnover	Market	Market	Quality	Tenure	Purch.	Purch.	End	End
Rating/Pts	Deviation	Beta	3/31/15	$(Mil)	%	%	%	%	Ratio	Return	Return	Pct	(Years)	$	$	Load	Load
C+ / 6.0	10.5	1.08	17.49	375	4	95	0	1	106	97.4	-24.7	31	1	2,500	0	5.8	0.0
C+ / 6.1	10.5	1.07	16.83	10	4	95	0	1	106	92.0	-24.9	23	1	2,500	0	0.0	0.0
C+ / 6.0	10.5	1.07	16.75	177	4	95	0	1	106	92.4	-24.9	24	1	2,500	0	0.0	0.0
C+ / 6.0	10.5	1.07	18.24	132	4	95	0	1	106	99.3	-24.6	35	1	2,500	0	0.0	0.0
C+ / 6.0	10.5	1.08	17.42	407	4	95	0	1	106	95.8	-24.7	28	1	2,500	0	3.5	0.0
C- / 4.2	15.5	1.18	16.33	40	7	92	0	1	156	118.6	-23.5	49	6	2,500	0	5.8	0.8
C- / 4.1	15.5	1.18	14.80	N/A	7	92	0	1	156	112.9	-23.7	38	6	2,500	0	0.0	0.8
C- / 4.1	15.5	1.17	14.77	20	7	92	0	1	156	112.7	-23.6	39	6	2,500	0	0.0	0.8
C- / 4.2	15.5	1.17	16.95	59	7	92	0	1	156	120.3	-23.4	55	6	2,500	0	0.0	0.8
C- / 4.2	15.5	1.18	15.83	11	7	92	0	1	156	116.6	-23.6	46	6	2,500	0	3.5	0.8
B- / 7.3	11.8	0.80	11.79	5	4	95	0	1	148	N/A	N/A	88	1	2,500	0	5.8	2.0
B- / 7.3	11.8	0.80	11.59	1	4	95	0	1	148	N/A	N/A	85	1	2,500	0	0.0	2.0
B- / 7.3	11.7	0.80	11.88	1	4	95	0	1	148	N/A	N/A	89	1	2,500	0	0.0	2.0
B- / 7.3	11.7	0.80	11.74	2	4	95	0	1	148	N/A	N/A	87	1	2,500	0	3.5	2.0
C+ / 6.0	12.4	0.86	31.64	146	2	97	0	1	91	47.1	-25.5	96	5	2,500	0	5.8	1.5
C+ / 6.0	12.4	0.86	29.36	6	2	97	0	1	91	42.0	-25.8	95	5	2,500	0	0.0	1.5
C+ / 6.0	12.4	0.86	28.92	62	2	97	0	1	91	42.4	-25.8	95	5	2,500	0	0.0	1.5
C+ / 5.9	12.4	0.86	32.55	58	2	97	0	1	91	47.4	-25.4	96	5	2,500	0	0.0	1.5
C+ / 6.0	12.4	0.86	30.79	44	2	97	0	1	91	45.2	-25.6	96	5	2,500	0	3.5	1.5
C- / 4.0	14.2	0.97	8.11	7	2	96	1	1	38	20.6	-26.8	39	7	2,500	0	5.8	1.5
C- / 4.1	14.2	0.96	8.17	N/A	2	96	1	1	38	17.4	-27.0	30	7	2,500	0	0.0	1.5
C- / 4.1	14.3	0.97	8.04	6	2	96	1	1	38	17.4	-27.0	30	7	2,500	0	0.0	1.5
C- / 4.0	14.2	0.96	8.12	80	2	96	1	1	38	21.6	-26.7	43	7	2,500	0	0.0	1.5
C- / 3.9	14.3	0.97	8.12	4	2	96	1	1	38	22.1	-26.7	45	7	2,500	0	0.0	1.5
C- / 4.0	14.3	0.97	8.08	2	2	96	1	1	38	19.4	-26.8	36	7	2,500	0	3.5	1.5
C / 5.1	13.9	0.98	23.05	134	1	98	0	1	97	29.4	-28.5	86	3	2,500	0	5.8	1.5
C / 5.1	13.9	0.98	22.41	6	1	98	0	1	97	26.2	-28.7	81	3	2,500	0	0.0	1.5
C / 5.1	13.9	0.99	22.36	58	1	98	0	1	97	26.2	-28.7	81	3	2,500	0	0.0	1.5
C / 5.1	13.9	0.98	23.11	212	1	98	0	1	97	30.9	-28.4	87	3	2,500	0	0.0	1.5
C / 5.1	13.9	0.99	22.99	52	1	98	0	1	97	28.4	-28.6	84	3	2,500	0	3.5	1.5
D+ / 2.5	17.2	1.07	34.85	318	8	91	0	1	112	33.5	-31.0	40	9	2,500	0	5.8	0.8
D+ / 2.5	17.2	1.07	32.06	11	8	91	0	1	112	30.0	-31.2	30	9	2,500	0	0.0	0.8
D+ / 2.5	17.2	1.07	32.25	165	8	91	0	1	112	30.1	-31.2	31	9	2,500	0	0.0	0.8
D+ / 2.5	17.2	1.07	36.68	128	8	91	0	1	112	34.8	-30.9	45	9	2,500	0	0.0	0.8
D+ / 2.5	17.2	1.07	35.63	189	8	91	0	1	112	32.5	-31.1	37	9	2,500	0	3.5	0.8
C+ / 6.5	10.9	0.93	96.72	859	5	93	0	2	49	98.2	-18.2	73	9	2,500	0	5.8	0.0
C+ / 6.4	10.9	0.93	85.06	15	5	93	0	2	49	92.9	-18.5	64	9	2,500	0	0.0	0.0
C+ / 6.4	10.9	0.93	86.60	180	5	93	0	2	49	93.3	-18.5	65	9	2,500	0	0.0	0.0
C+ / 6.5	12.2	0.85	103.64	431	5	93	0	2	49	100.4	-18.1	85	9	2,500	0	0.0	0.0
C+ / 6.4	10.9	0.93	95.78	1,371	5	93	0	2	49	96.9	-18.3	71	9	2,500	0	3.5	0.0
B- / 7.5	9.2	0.93	32.70	763	8	87	0	5	33	82.9	-17.9	51	4	2,500	0	5.8	0.0
B- / 7.5	9.2	0.93	32.90	16	8	87	0	5	33	77.9	-18.1	38	4	2,500	0	0.0	0.0
B- / 7.5	9.2	0.93	32.82	204	8	87	0	5	33	78.3	-18.1	39	4	2,500	0	0.0	0.0
B- / 7.5	9.2	0.93	33.85	471	8	87	0	5	33	84.6	-17.8	54	4	2,500	0	0.0	0.0
B- / 7.5	9.2	0.93	33.24	923	8	87	0	5	33	81.6	-17.9	47	4	2,500	0	3.5	0.0
B- / 7.8	9.9	1.00	16.14	56	7	92	0	1	68	106.8	-21.2	77	3	2,500	0	5.8	0.0
B- / 7.8	9.9	1.00	16.04	2	7	92	0	1	68	101.5	-21.4	70	3	2,500	0	0.0	0.0
B- / 7.8	9.9	1.00	15.81	27	7	92	0	1	68	101.5	-21.4	70	3	2,500	0	0.0	0.0
B- / 7.9	9.9	1.00	16.38	11	7	92	0	1	68	108.9	-21.1	79	3	2,500	0	0.0	0.0
B- / 7.8	9.9	1.00	16.12	33	7	92	0	1	68	104.8	-21.2	75	3	2,500	0	3.5	0.0
C+ / 6.7	11.7	0.98	16.13	91	7	92	0	1	49	105.9	-28.2	43	2	2,500	0	5.8	0.8
C+ / 6.6	11.7	0.98	15.48	5	7	92	0	1	49	100.6	-28.3	33	2	2,500	0	0.0	0.8

Fund Type	Fund Name	Ticker Symbol	Overall Investment Rating	Phone	Performance Rating/Pts	3 Mo	6 Mo	1Yr / Pct	3Yr / Pct	5Yr / Pct	Dividend Yield	Expense Ratio
	99 Pct = Best						Total Return % through 3/31/15		Annualized		Incl. in Returns	
FS	Fidelity Adv Financial Serv C	FAFCX	C+	(800) 522-7297	C+ / 6.6	-0.33	5.68	8.67 /67	14.42 /70	6.54 /20	0.24	1.95
FS	Fidelity Adv Financial Serv I	FFSIX	B+	(800) 522-7297	B- / 7.5	-0.12	6.15	9.78 /73	15.63 /80	7.66 /28	1.05	0.88
FS	Fidelity Adv Financial Serv T	FAFSX	C+	(800) 522-7297	C+ / 6.4	-0.25	5.85	9.15 /70	14.96 /75	7.05 /23	0.48	1.49
AA	Fidelity Adv Freedom 2005 A	FFAVX	C-	(800) 522-7297	D- / 1.2	1.77	2.90	4.60 /36	5.45 /15	5.89 /16	1.46	0.83
AA	● Fidelity Adv Freedom 2005 B	FFBVX	C-	(800) 522-7297	D- / 1.4	1.59	2.51	3.75 /30	4.65 /12	5.09 /12	0.67	1.58
AA	Fidelity Adv Freedom 2005 C	FCFVX	C-	(800) 522-7297	D- / 1.4	1.60	2.48	3.73 /30	4.67 /12	5.08 /12	0.80	1.58
AA	Fidelity Adv Freedom 2005 I	FFIVX	C	(800) 522-7297	D / 1.9	1.84	3.08	4.85 /37	5.74 /16	6.15 /18	1.79	0.58
AA	Fidelity Adv Freedom 2005 T	FFTVX	C-	(800) 522-7297	D- / 1.3	1.68	2.78	4.33 /34	5.19 /14	5.62 /15	1.24	1.08
AA	Fidelity Adv Freedom 2010 A	FACFX	C-	(800) 522-7297	D / 1.6	2.00	3.29	5.08 /39	6.75 /20	6.98 /23	1.54	0.87
AA	● Fidelity Adv Freedom 2010 B	FCFBX	C-	(800) 522-7297	D / 1.9	1.76	2.83	4.30 /34	5.93 /16	6.17 /18	0.76	1.62
AA	Fidelity Adv Freedom 2010 C	FCFCX	C-	(800) 522-7297	D / 1.9	1.78	2.81	4.33 /34	5.95 /17	6.17 /18	0.91	1.62
AA	Fidelity Adv Freedom 2010 I	FCIFX	C	(800) 522-7297	D+ / 2.5	2.00	3.32	5.34 /41	6.99 /21	7.25 /25	1.88	0.62
AA	Fidelity Adv Freedom 2010 T	FCFTX	C-	(800) 522-7297	D / 1.7	1.93	3.09	4.81 /37	6.47 /19	6.71 /21	1.32	1.12
AA	Fidelity Adv Freedom 2015 A	FFVAX	C-	(800) 522-7297	D / 1.8	2.17	3.54	5.51 /42	7.16 /22	7.27 /25	1.52	0.90
AA	● Fidelity Adv Freedom 2015 B	FFVBX	C-	(800) 522-7297	D / 2.2	2.01	3.16	4.81 /37	6.37 /18	6.47 /20	0.74	1.65
AA	Fidelity Adv Freedom 2015 C	FFVCX	C-	(800) 522-7297	D / 2.2	1.94	3.14	4.75 /37	6.36 /18	6.47 /20	0.88	1.65
AA	Fidelity Adv Freedom 2015 I	FFVIX	C	(800) 522-7297	D+ / 2.8	2.24	3.72	5.83 /45	7.43 /24	7.55 /27	1.85	0.65
AA	Fidelity Adv Freedom 2015 T	FFVTX	C-	(800) 522-7297	D / 2.0	2.09	3.44	5.26 /41	6.90 /21	7.00 /23	1.32	1.15
AA	Fidelity Adv Freedom 2020 A	FDAFX	C-	(800) 522-7297	D / 2.1	2.21	3.73	5.82 /45	7.69 /25	7.75 /28	1.51	0.93
AA	● Fidelity Adv Freedom 2020 B	FDBFX	C	(800) 522-7297	D+ / 2.4	2.05	3.27	5.04 /39	6.90 /21	6.93 /23	0.77	1.68
AA	Fidelity Adv Freedom 2020 C	FDCFX	C	(800) 522-7297	D+ / 2.5	2.06	3.33	5.07 /39	6.92 /21	6.95 /23	0.89	1.68
AA	Fidelity Adv Freedom 2020 I	FDIFX	C	(800) 522-7297	C- / 3.1	2.34	3.83	6.13 /48	7.99 /27	8.02 /30	1.83	0.68
AA	Fidelity Adv Freedom 2020 T	FDTFX	C-	(800) 522-7297	D+ / 2.3	2.21	3.62	5.56 /43	7.46 /24	7.48 /26	1.32	1.18
AA	Fidelity Adv Freedom 2025 A	FATWX	C-	(800) 522-7297	D+ / 2.7	2.40	4.01	6.26 /49	8.91 /32	8.58 /34	1.47	0.97
AA	● Fidelity Adv Freedom 2025 B	FBTWX	C	(800) 522-7297	C- / 3.1	2.17	3.55	5.42 /42	8.11 /28	7.75 /28	0.75	1.72
AA	Fidelity Adv Freedom 2025 C	FCTWX	C	(800) 522-7297	C- / 3.1	2.19	3.58	5.42 /42	8.10 /27	7.75 /28	0.90	1.72
AA	Fidelity Adv Freedom 2025 I	FITWX	C	(800) 522-7297	C- / 3.8	2.38	4.02	6.48 /50	9.17 /34	8.83 /35	1.79	0.72
AA	Fidelity Adv Freedom 2025 T	FTTWX	C	(800) 522-7297	D+ / 2.9	2.31	3.82	6.00 /46	8.65 /31	8.30 /32	1.28	1.22
AA	Fidelity Adv Freedom 2030 A	FAFEX	C-	(800) 522-7297	C- / 3.0	2.54	4.16	6.54 /51	9.43 /36	8.87 /36	1.34	1.02
AA	● Fidelity Adv Freedom 2030 B	FBFEX	C	(800) 522-7297	C- / 3.4	2.33	3.83	5.82 /45	8.62 /31	8.06 /30	0.69	1.77
AA	Fidelity Adv Freedom 2030 C	FCFEX	C	(800) 522-7297	C- / 3.4	2.34	3.78	5.76 /44	8.61 /30	8.06 /30	0.83	1.77
AA	Fidelity Adv Freedom 2030 I	FEFIX	C	(800) 522-7297	C- / 4.1	2.60	4.34	6.85 /54	9.71 /37	9.16 /38	1.66	0.77
AA	Fidelity Adv Freedom 2030 T	FTFEX	C-	(800) 522-7297	C- / 3.3	2.55	4.13	6.37 /50	9.20 /34	8.62 /34	1.15	1.27
AA	Fidelity Adv Freedom 2035 A	FATHX	C-	(800) 522-7297	C- / 3.5	2.66	4.33	6.81 /54	10.24 /41	9.35 /39	1.29	1.03
AA	● Fidelity Adv Freedom 2035 B	FBTHX	C	(800) 522-7297	C- / 3.9	2.46	3.92	6.00 /46	9.40 /36	8.54 /33	0.68	1.78
AA	Fidelity Adv Freedom 2035 C	FCTHX	C	(800) 522-7297	C- / 3.9	2.39	3.92	6.01 /46	9.40 /36	8.53 /33	0.81	1.78
AA	Fidelity Adv Freedom 2035 I	FITHX	C	(800) 522-7297	C / 4.6	2.72	4.50	7.11 /56	10.51 /42	9.63 /42	1.59	0.78
AA	Fidelity Adv Freedom 2035 T	FTTHX	C-	(800) 522-7297	B- / 3.7	2.52	4.17	6.52 /51	9.97 /39	9.07 /37	1.11	1.28
AA	Fidelity Adv Freedom 2040 A	FAFFX	C-	(800) 522-7297	C- / 3.5	2.62	4.29	6.76 /53	10.31 /41	9.42 /40	1.27	1.03
AA	● Fidelity Adv Freedom 2040 B	FBFFX	C	(800) 522-7297	C- / 3.9	2.43	3.85	5.97 /46	9.49 /36	8.58 /34	0.66	1.78
AA	Fidelity Adv Freedom 2040 C	FCFFX	C	(800) 522-7297	C- / 3.9	2.44	3.93	6.01 /46	9.52 /36	8.60 /34	0.79	1.78
AA	Fidelity Adv Freedom 2040 I	FIFFX	C	(800) 522-7297	C / 4.6	2.68	4.40	6.99 /55	10.61 /43	9.68 /42	1.58	0.78
AA	Fidelity Adv Freedom 2040 T	FTFFX	C-	(800) 522-7297	C- / 3.7	2.56	4.18	6.51 /51	10.04 /40	9.14 /38	1.08	1.28
AA	Fidelity Adv Freedom 2045 A	FFFZX	C-	(800) 522-7297	C- / 3.6	2.58	4.34	6.80 /53	10.54 /42	9.55 /41	1.26	1.03
AA	● Fidelity Adv Freedom 2045 B	FFFKX	C	(800) 522-7297	C- / 4.0	2.40	3.96	6.04 /47	9.74 /38	8.73 /35	0.66	1.78
AA	Fidelity Adv Freedom 2045 C	FFFJX	C	(800) 522-7297	C- / 4.0	2.42	3.94	5.96 /46	9.73 /38	8.74 /35	0.79	1.78
AA	Fidelity Adv Freedom 2045 I	FFFIX	C	(800) 522-7297	C / 4.7	2.66	4.41	7.03 /55	10.82 /44	9.82 /43	1.56	0.78
AA	Fidelity Adv Freedom 2045 T	FFFTX	C-	(800) 522-7297	C- / 3.8	2.50	4.17	6.50 /51	10.27 /41	9.27 /39	1.08	1.28
AA	Fidelity Adv Freedom 2050 A	FFFLX	C-	(800) 522-7297	C- / 3.7	2.60	4.25	6.77 /53	10.59 /43	9.56 /41	1.24	1.03
AA	● Fidelity Adv Freedom 2050 B	FFFWX	C	(800) 522-7297	C- / 4.1	2.43	3.95	5.99 /46	9.79 /38	8.75 /35	0.62	1.78
AA	Fidelity Adv Freedom 2050 C	FFFYX	C	(800) 522-7297	C- / 4.1	2.43	3.94	6.01 /46	9.81 /38	8.76 /35	0.78	1.78
AA	Fidelity Adv Freedom 2050 I	FFFPX	C	(800) 522-7297	C / 4.8	2.77	4.52	7.10 /56	10.90 /45	9.84 /43	1.55	0.78

● Denotes fund is closed to new investors
* Denotes fund is included in Section II

www.thestreetratings.com

RISK			NET ASSETS		ASSET				BULL / BEAR			FUND MANAGER		MINIMUMS		LOADS	
	3 Year		NAV								Portfolio	Last Bull	Last Bear	Manager	Manager	Initial	Additional	Front	Back
Risk Rating/Pts	Standard Deviation	Beta	As of 3/31/15	Total $(Mil)	Cash %	Stocks %	Bonds %	Other %	Turnover Ratio	Market Return	Market Return	Quality Pct	Tenure (Years)	Purch. $	Purch. $	End Load	End Load
C+ / 6.6	11.6	0.98	15.33	42	7	92	0	1	49	100.7	-28.3	35	2	2,500	0	0.0	0.8
C+ / 6.7	11.7	0.98	16.51	27	7	92	0	1	49	108.3	-28.0	50	2	2,500	0	0.0	0.8
C+ / 6.7	11.7	0.98	16.03	33	7	92	0	1	49	104.2	-28.3	41	2	2,500	0	3.5	0.8
B+ / 9.1	4.1	0.68	12.10	162	13	39	46	2	49	28.9	-8.5	40	12	2,500	0	5.8	0.0
B+ / 9.3	4.0	0.68	12.14	1	13	39	46	2	49	25.6	-8.8	31	12	2,500	0	0.0	0.0
B+ / 9.2	4.1	0.68	12.06	7	13	39	46	2	49	25.7	-8.8	31	12	2,500	0	0.0	0.0
B+ / 9.1	4.1	0.68	12.18	66	13	39	46	2	49	30.1	-8.4	45	12	2,500	0	0.0	0.0
B+ / 9.1	4.1	0.69	12.09	29	13	39	46	2	49	27.9	-8.6	36	12	2,500	0	3.5	0.0
B / 8.7	5.1	0.87	12.72	432	10	48	41	1	39	36.5	-10.4	31	12	2,500	0	5.8	0.0
B / 8.8	5.1	0.86	12.74	2	10	48	41	1	39	32.9	-10.6	24	12	2,500	0	0.0	0.0
B / 8.8	5.1	0.87	12.60	35	10	48	41	1	39	33.0	-10.6	23	12	2,500	0	0.0	0.0
B / 8.6	5.1	0.87	12.77	158	10	48	41	1	39	37.7	-10.4	34	12	2,500	0	0.0	0.0
B / 8.7	5.1	0.87	12.68	106	10	48	41	1	39	35.3	-10.5	28	12	2,500	0	3.5	0.0
B / 8.5	5.5	0.94	12.70	969	7	55	36	2	37	38.5	-10.6	27	12	2,500	0	5.8	0.0
B / 8.6	5.5	0.94	12.70	8	7	55	36	2	37	35.0	-10.9	20	12	2,500	0	0.0	0.0
B / 8.6	5.5	0.94	12.60	73	7	55	36	2	37	35.0	-10.9	20	12	2,500	0	0.0	0.0
B / 8.5	5.5	0.93	12.80	425	7	55	36	2	37	39.7	-10.6	31	12	2,500	0	0.0	0.0
B / 8.5	5.5	0.93	12.68	209	7	55	36	2	37	37.4	-10.7	26	12	2,500	0	3.5	0.0
B / 8.3	6.1	1.03	13.44	1,779	6	61	32	1	40	42.9	-12.6	22	12	2,500	0	5.8	0.0
B / 8.5	6.1	1.04	13.45	16	6	61	32	1	40	39.3	-12.9	16	12	2,500	0	0.0	0.0
B / 8.4	6.0	1.03	13.35	113	6	61	32	1	40	39.2	-12.9	17	12	2,500	0	0.0	0.0
B / 8.3	6.1	1.03	13.54	839	6	61	32	1	40	44.2	-12.6	26	12	2,500	0	0.0	0.0
B / 8.4	6.1	1.03	13.44	442	6	61	32	1	40	41.6	-12.7	21	12	2,500	0	3.5	0.0
B / 8.0	7.1	1.21	13.25	1,857	6	70	23	1	41	50.7	-15.0	16	12	2,500	0	5.8	0.0
B / 8.0	7.2	1.22	13.20	11	6	70	23	1	41	47.0	-15.3	11	12	2,500	0	0.0	0.0
B / 8.0	7.2	1.22	13.09	95	6	70	23	1	41	46.9	-15.2	11	12	2,500	0	0.0	0.0
B / 8.0	7.1	1.21	13.35	840	6	70	23	1	41	52.0	-14.9	18	12	2,500	0	0.0	0.0
B / 8.0	7.1	1.21	13.27	408	6	70	23	1	41	49.5	-15.1	15	12	2,500	0	3.5	0.0
B- / 7.5	7.9	1.33	14.13	1,706	5	82	11	2	53	54.3	-15.8	12	12	2,500	0	5.8	0.0
B- / 7.6	7.9	1.34	14.08	14	5	82	11	2	53	50.4	-16.1	8	12	2,500	0	0.0	0.0
B- / 7.6	7.9	1.34	13.97	91	5	82	11	2	53	50.4	-16.1	8	12	2,500	0	0.0	0.0
B- / 7.5	7.9	1.33	14.21	921	5	82	11	2	53	55.5	-15.7	13	12	2,500	0	0.0	0.0
B- / 7.5	7.8	1.33	14.09	454	5	82	11	2	53	52.8	-15.9	11	12	2,500	0	3.5	0.0
B- / 7.1	8.7	1.47	13.51	1,317	6	88	5	1	48	60.5	-18.1	8	12	2,500	0	5.8	0.0
B- / 7.2	8.7	1.47	13.34	10	6	88	5	1	48	56.4	-18.3	6	12	2,500	0	0.0	0.0
B- / 7.2	8.7	1.47	13.27	56	6	88	5	1	48	56.3	-18.3	6	12	2,500	0	0.0	0.0
B- / 7.1	8.7	1.46	13.59	712	6	88	5	1	48	61.7	-17.9	10	12	2,500	0	0.0	0.0
B- / 7.2	8.7	1.46	13.42	304	6	88	5	1	48	59.0	-18.1	8	12	2,500	0	3.5	0.0
B- / 7.1	8.7	1.48	14.49	1,155	6	88	5	1	47	61.1	-18.3	8	12	2,500	0	5.8	0.0
B- / 7.2	8.7	1.48	14.35	12	6	88	5	1	47	57.1	-18.6	6	12	2,500	0	0.0	0.0
B- / 7.2	8.7	1.47	14.27	77	6	88	5	1	47	57.0	-18.6	6	12	2,500	0	0.0	0.0
B- / 7.1	8.7	1.47	14.57	690	6	88	5	1	47	62.5	-18.3	10	12	2,500	0	0.0	0.0
B- / 7.2	8.7	1.47	14.45	334	6	88	5	1	47	59.9	-18.4	8	12	2,500	0	3.5	0.0
C+ / 6.9	8.9	1.50	11.15	624	6	88	5	1	46	62.9	-18.9	8	9	2,500	0	5.8	0.0
C+ / 6.9	8.9	1.51	11.08	3	6	88	5	1	46	58.9	-19.2	6	9	2,500	0	0.0	0.0
C+ / 6.9	8.9	1.50	11.01	22	6	88	5	1	46	58.8	-19.2	6	9	2,500	0	0.0	0.0
C+ / 6.9	8.9	1.50	11.21	401	6	88	5	1	46	64.3	-18.8	9	9	2,500	0	0.0	0.0
C+ / 6.9	8.9	1.51	11.09	154	6	88	5	1	46	61.4	-18.9	7	9	2,500	0	3.5	0.0
B- / 7.0	9.0	1.52	11.06	416	6	88	5	1	47	64.1	-19.7	8	9	2,500	0	5.8	0.0
B- / 7.0	9.1	1.53	10.98	3	6	88	5	1	47	60.1	-20.1	5	9	2,500	0	0.0	0.0
B- / 7.0	9.0	1.52	10.95	25	6	88	5	1	47	59.9	-20.0	6	9	2,500	0	0.0	0.0
B- / 7.0	9.0	1.51	11.13	303	6	88	5	1	47	65.4	-19.7	9	9	2,500	0	0.0	0.0

						PERFORMANCE						
	99 Pct = Best *0 Pct = Worst*						Total Return % through 3/31/15				Incl. in Returns	
				Overall		Perfor- mance				Annualized		Dividend Expense
Fund Type	Fund Name	Ticker Symbol	Investment Rating	Phone		Rating/Pts	3 Mo	6 Mo	1Yr / Pct	3Yr / Pct	5Yr / Pct	Yield	Ratio
AA	Fidelity Adv Freedom 2050 T	FFFQX	C	(800) 522-7297		C- / 3.8	2.51	4.16	6.54 / 51	10.33 / 41	9.29 / 39	1.05	1.28
GL	Fidelity Adv Freedom 2055 A	FHFAX	C-	(800) 522-7297		C- / 3.8	2.67	4.33	6.85 / 54	10.88 / 45	--	1.18	1.03
GL	Fidelity Adv Freedom 2055 C	FHFCX	C	(800) 522-7297		C- / 4.2	2.41	3.95	6.01 / 46	10.00 / 39	--	0.75	1.78
GL	Fidelity Adv Freedom 2055 I	FHFIX	C+	(800) 522-7297		C / 4.9	2.75	4.49	7.15 / 56	11.15 / 47	--	1.45	0.78
GL	Fidelity Adv Freedom 2055 T	FHFTX	C	(800) 522-7297		C- / 4.0	2.50	4.18	6.55 / 51	10.56 / 43	--	1.01	1.28
AA	Fidelity Adv Freedom Income A	FAFAX	C-	(800) 522-7297		E+ / 0.8	1.43	2.30	3.63 / 30	3.94 / 10	4.44 / 10	1.38	0.76
AA	● Fidelity Adv Freedom Income B	FBFAX	C-	(800) 522-7297		D- / 1.0	1.31	2.03	2.96 / 26	3.20 / 8	3.69 / 7	0.74	1.51
AA	Fidelity Adv Freedom Income C	FCAFX	C-	(800) 522-7297		D- / 1.0	1.23	1.95	2.89 / 26	3.16 / 8	3.67 / 7	0.75	1.51
AA	Fidelity Adv Freedom Income I	FIAFX	C-	(800) 522-7297		D- / 1.3	1.46	2.51	3.87 / 31	4.20 / 11	4.70 / 11	1.69	0.51
AA	Fidelity Adv Freedom Income T	FTAFX	C-	(800) 522-7297		E+ / 0.9	1.39	2.27	3.37 / 28	3.71 / 9	4.19 / 9	1.18	1.01
GL	Fidelity Adv Glb Commodity Stk A	FFGAX	E-	(800) 522-7297		E- / 0.1	-3.46	-12.92	-14.45 / 2	-6.13 / 1	-3.30 / 1	1.09	1.35
GL	● Fidelity Adv Glb Commodity Stk B	FFGBX	E	(800) 522-7297		E- / 0.1	-3.63	-13.23	-15.02 / 2	-6.82 / 1	-4.04 / 1	0.13	2.11
GL	Fidelity Adv Glb Commodity Stk C	FCGCX	E	(800) 522-7297		E- / 0.1	-3.64	-13.23	-15.08 / 2	-6.81 / 1	-4.03 / 1	0.21	2.11
GL	Fidelity Adv Glb Commodity Stk Fd	FFGCX	E-	(800) 544-8544		E- / 0.2	-3.37	-12.82	-14.22 / 2	-5.89 / 2	-3.06 / 1	1.48	1.11
GL	Fidelity Adv Glb Commodity Stk I	FFGIX	E-	(800) 522-7297		E- / 0.2	-3.37	-12.76	-14.17 / 2	-5.83 / 2	-3.01 / 1	1.54	1.06
GL	Fidelity Adv Glb Commodity Stk T	FFGTX	E	(800) 522-7297		E- / 0.1	-3.54	-13.02	-14.67 / 2	-6.36 / 1	-3.55 / 1	0.80	1.62
GL	Fidelity Adv Global Cap App-Cl A	FGEAX	B+	(800) 522-7297		B / 7.7	5.32	6.14	8.63 / 67	17.40 / 92	10.81 / 51	0.00	1.62
GL	● Fidelity Adv Global Cap App-Cl B	FGEBX	B+	(800) 522-7297		B / 8.1	5.13	5.82	7.86 / 62	16.50 / 87	9.96 / 44	0.00	2.44
GL	Fidelity Adv Global Cap App-Cl C	FEUCX	B+	(800) 522-7297		B / 8.1	5.15	5.84	7.89 / 62	16.49 / 87	9.97 / 44	0.00	2.40
GL	Fidelity Adv Global Cap App-Cl I	FEUIX	A	(800) 522-7297		B+ / 8.9	5.36	6.29	8.90 / 69	17.76 / 93	11.14 / 54	0.00	1.29
GL	Fidelity Adv Global Cap App-Cl T	FGETX	B+	(800) 522-7297		B / 7.9	5.23	6.02	8.36 / 65	17.05 / 90	10.51 / 49	0.00	1.93
AA	Fidelity Adv Global Strat A	FDASX	D-	(800) 522-7297		D- / 1.3	2.43	3.05	4.18 / 33	5.90 / 16	6.15 / 18	1.55	1.09
AA	● Fidelity Adv Global Strat B	FDBSX	D	(800) 522-7297		D / 1.6	2.32	2.66	3.49 / 29	5.12 / 14	5.35 / 13	0.99	1.85
AA	Fidelity Adv Global Strat C	FDCSX	D	(800) 522-7297		D / 1.6	2.23	2.69	3.42 / 29	5.12 / 14	5.36 / 14	1.00	1.85
AA	Fidelity Adv Global Strat Inst	FDYIX	D	(800) 522-7297		D / 2.1	2.54	3.10	4.47 / 35	6.16 / 17	6.42 / 20	1.92	0.85
AA	Fidelity Adv Global Strat T	FDTSX	D-	(800) 522-7297		D- / 1.4	2.32	2.90	3.94 / 31	5.62 / 15	5.88 / 16	1.36	1.35
PM	Fidelity Adv Gold A	FGDAX	E-	(800) 522-7297		E- / 0.0	-1.12	-14.59	-21.15 / 1	-26.59 / 0	-15.06 / 0	0.00	1.21
PM	● Fidelity Adv Gold B	FGDBX	E-	(800) 522-7297		E- / 0.0	-1.30	-14.92	-21.72 / 1	-27.13 / 0	-15.70 / 0	0.00	1.95
PM	Fidelity Adv Gold C	FGDCX	E-	(800) 522-7297		E- / 0.0	-1.31	-14.87	-21.71 / 1	-27.13 / 0	-15.68 / 0	0.00	1.96
PM	Fidelity Adv Gold I	FGDIX	E-	(800) 522-7297		E- / 0.0	-1.09	-14.47	-20.91 / 1	-26.35 / 0	-14.78 / 0	0.00	0.87
PM	Fidelity Adv Gold T	FGDTX	E-	(800) 522-7297		E- / 0.0	-1.20	-14.70	-21.37 / 1	-26.79 / 0	-15.29 / 0	0.00	1.49
GR	Fidelity Adv Gr Opportunity A	FAGAX	B-	(800) 522-7297		B- / 7.0	2.68	9.66	12.65 / 85	15.34 / 78	16.93 / 96	0.00	1.23
GR	● Fidelity Adv Gr Opportunity B	FABGX	B-	(800) 522-7297		B- / 7.4	2.48	9.21	11.71 / 81	14.42 / 70	16.01 / 93	0.00	2.03
GR	Fidelity Adv Gr Opportunity C	FACGX	B	(800) 522-7297		B- / 7.5	2.50	9.26	11.81 / 82	14.49 / 71	16.07 / 93	0.00	1.96
GR	Fidelity Adv Gr Opportunity Inst	FAGCX	B+	(800) 522-7297		B+ / 8.4	2.76	9.82	12.95 / 86	15.69 / 81	17.29 / 97	0.00	0.93
GR	Fidelity Adv Gr Opportunity T	FAGOX	B-	(800) 522-7297		B- / 7.3	2.63	9.55	12.40 / 84	15.10 / 76	16.69 / 95	0.00	1.43
GI	Fidelity Adv Growth and Income A	FGIRX	C+	(800) 522-7297		C+ / 6.1	0.33	3.46	9.15 / 70	15.20 / 76	13.80 / 76	1.21	1.03
GI	● Fidelity Adv Growth and Income B	FGISX	C+	(800) 522-7297		C+ / 6.5	0.11	3.04	8.26 / 65	14.27 / 69	12.91 / 67	0.33	1.82
GI	Fidelity Adv Growth and Income C	FGIUX	C+	(800) 522-7297		C+ / 6.6	0.15	3.11	8.35 / 65	14.36 / 70	12.98 / 68	0.68	1.75
GI	Fidelity Adv Growth and Income I	FGIOX	B	(800) 522-7297		B- / 7.4	0.36	3.60	9.48 / 72	15.58 / 80	14.18 / 79	1.58	0.70
GI	Fidelity Adv Growth and Income T	FGITX	C+	(800) 522-7297		C+ / 6.3	0.25	3.34	8.91 / 69	14.92 / 74	13.53 / 73	1.00	1.25
HL	Fidelity Adv Health Care A	FACDX	A-	(800) 522-7297		A+ / 9.9	11.75	20.69	34.53 / 99	35.23 / 99	26.32 / 99	0.00	1.08
HL	● Fidelity Adv Health Care B	FAHTX	B+	(800) 522-7297		A+ / 9.9	11.52	20.19	33.42 / 99	34.14 / 99	25.34 / 99	0.00	1.91
HL	Fidelity Adv Health Care C	FHCCX	B+	(800) 522-7297		A+ / 9.9	11.53	20.22	33.51 / 99	34.22 / 99	25.40 / 99	0.00	1.83
HL	Fidelity Adv Health Care I	FHCIX	A-	(800) 522-7297		A+ / 9.9	11.83	20.85	34.90 / 99	35.59 / 99	26.68 / 99	0.00	0.81
HL	Fidelity Adv Health Care T	FACTX	A-	(800) 522-7297		A+ / 9.9	11.68	20.54	34.16 / 99	34.89 / 99	26.00 / 99	0.00	1.34
AA	● Fidelity Adv Inc Replacement 2016 A	FRJAX	C-	(800) 522-7297		E+ / 0.6	0.35	0.66	1.29 / 19	2.56 / 7	3.72 / 7	0.29	0.60
AA	● Fidelity Adv Inc Replacement 2016 C	FRJCX	C-	(800) 522-7297		E+ / 0.7	0.16	0.27	0.52 / 17	1.80 / 6	2.94 / 6	0.00	1.35
AA	● Fidelity Adv Inc Replacement 2016 I	FRJIX	C-	(800) 522-7297		E+ / 0.8	0.41	0.79	1.53 / 20	2.82 / 8	3.98 / 8	0.56	0.35
AA	● Fidelity Adv Inc Replacement 2016 T	FRJTX	C-	(800) 522-7297		E+ / 0.6	0.27	0.53	1.01 / 18	2.31 / 7	3.45 / 7	0.12	0.85
AA	● Fidelity Adv Inc Replacement 2018 A	FRKAX	C-	(800) 522-7297		E+ / 0.9	0.91	1.73	2.99 / 26	4.51 / 12	5.13 / 12	0.81	0.71
AA	● Fidelity Adv Inc Replacement 2018 C	FRKCX	C-	(800) 522-7297		D- / 1.0	0.71	1.34	2.22 / 23	3.72 / 9	4.34 / 10	0.25	1.46

● Denotes fund is closed to new investors
* Denotes fund is included in Section II

www.thestreetratings.com

RISK			NET ASSETS		ASSET					BULL / BEAR		FUND MANAGER		MINIMUMS		LOADS	
	3 Year		NAV						Portfolio	Last Bull	Last Bear	Manager	Manager	Initial	Additional	Front	Back
Risk Rating/Pts	Standard Deviation	Beta	As of 3/31/15	Total $(Mil)	Cash %	Stocks %	Bonds %	Other %	Turnover Ratio	Market Return	Market Return	Quality Pct	Tenure (Years)	Purch. $	Purch. $	End Load	End Load
B- / 7.0	9.0	1.52	11.02	127	6	88	5	1	47	62.7	-19.9	7	9	2,500	0	3.5	0.0
B- / 7.0	9.2	0.63	11.92	116	4	88	7	1	43	65.7	N/A	93	4	2,500	0	5.8	0.0
B- / 7.0	9.2	0.63	11.88	4	4	88	7	1	43	61.5	N/A	91	4	2,500	0	0.0	0.0
B- / 7.0	9.2	0.63	11.96	88	4	88	7	1	43	67.1	N/A	93	4	2,500	0	0.0	0.0
B- / 7.0	9.2	0.63	11.88	33	4	88	7	1	43	64.1	N/A	92	4	2,500	0	3.5	0.0
B+ / 9.4	2.7	0.42	11.07	125	19	25	55	1	36	19.0	-3.9	59	12	2,500	0	5.8	0.0
B+ / 9.4	2.7	0.43	11.06	1	19	25	55	1	36	16.0	-4.2	47	12	2,500	0	0.0	0.0
B+ / 9.4	2.7	0.42	11.04	16	19	25	55	1	36	16.1	-4.2	48	12	2,500	0	0.0	0.0
B+ / 9.4	2.7	0.43	11.10	83	19	25	55	1	36	20.0	-3.8	63	12	2,500	0	0.0	0.0
B+ / 9.4	2.7	0.43	11.06	48	19	25	55	1	36	18.0	-4.0	56	12	2,500	0	3.5	0.0
C- / 3.7	16.0	0.98	12.00	42	0	99	0	1	75	3.8	-29.7	0	6	2,500	0	5.8	1.0
C- / 3.7	16.0	0.98	11.96	1	0	99	0	1	75	1.1	-29.9	0	6	2,500	0	0.0	1.0
C- / 3.7	16.0	0.98	11.90	15	0	99	0	1	75	1.1	-29.9	0	6	2,500	0	0.0	1.0
C- / 3.7	15.9	0.98	12.03	198	0	99	0	1	75	4.6	-29.6	1	6	2,500	0	0.0	1.0
C- / 3.6	16.0	0.98	12.03	23	0	99	0	1	75	4.8	-29.6	1	6	2,500	0	0.0	1.0
C- / 3.7	16.0	0.98	11.99	9	0	99	0	1	75	2.8	-29.8	0	6	2,500	0	3.5	1.0
C+ / 6.5	11.5	0.79	16.24	38	5	94	0	1	249	86.5	-23.0	97	5	2,500	0	5.8	1.0
C+ / 6.5	11.5	0.79	14.54	1	5	94	0	1	249	81.7	-23.3	97	5	2,500	0	0.0	1.0
C+ / 6.5	11.5	0.79	14.50	17	5	94	0	1	249	81.7	-23.3	97	5	2,500	0	0.0	1.0
C+ / 6.5	11.5	0.79	16.89	44	5	94	0	1	249	88.4	-22.9	98	5	2,500	0	0.0	1.0
C+ / 6.5	11.5	0.79	15.68	23	5	94	0	1	249	84.6	-23.1	97	5	2,500	0	3.5	1.0
C+ / 6.6	6.0	0.94	8.86	37	1	62	35	2	106	35.4	-16.1	16	8	2,500	0	5.8	0.0
C+ / 6.7	5.9	0.93	8.82	2	1	62	35	2	106	31.8	-16.4	12	8	2,500	0	0.0	0.0
C+ / 6.6	6.0	0.94	8.72	36	1	62	35	2	106	31.9	-16.4	12	8	2,500	0	0.0	0.0
C+ / 6.5	5.9	0.92	8.89	19	1	62	35	2	106	36.5	-16.1	20	8	2,500	0	0.0	0.0
C+ / 6.6	5.9	0.93	8.82	25	1	62	35	2	106	34.0	-16.1	15	8	2,500	0	3.5	0.0
E / 0.4	37.3	1.80	15.92	41	10	88	0	2	56	-59.2	-13.7	2	8	2,500	0	5.8	0.8
E / 0.4	37.3	1.80	15.17	2	10	88	0	2	56	-60.3	-14.0	1	8	2,500	0	0.0	0.8
E / 0.4	37.3	1.80	15.11	35	10	88	0	2	56	-60.3	-14.0	1	8	2,500	0	0.0	0.8
E / 0.4	37.3	1.80	16.26	20	10	88	0	2	56	-58.8	-13.6	2	8	2,500	0	0.0	0.8
E / 0.4	37.3	1.80	15.67	14	10	88	0	2	56	-59.6	-13.8	1	8	2,500	0	3.5	0.8
C+ / 5.9	12.6	1.10	64.82	661	1	98	0	1	13	105.5	-16.3	35	6	2,500	0	5.8	0.0
C+ / 5.9	12.6	1.10	59.42	7	1	98	0	1	13	100.0	-16.5	26	6	2,500	0	0.0	0.0
C+ / 5.9	12.6	1.10	59.84	229	1	98	0	1	13	100.4	-16.5	26	6	2,500	0	0.0	0.0
C+ / 6.0	12.6	1.10	67.77	1,361	1	98	0	1	13	107.6	-16.1	39	6	2,500	0	0.0	0.0
C+ / 5.9	12.6	1.10	64.81	1,495	1	98	0	1	13	104.1	-16.3	33	6	2,500	0	3.5	0.0
C+ / 6.4	10.2	1.05	26.47	271	2	97	0	1	44	99.1	-16.9	44	4	2,500	0	5.8	0.0
C+ / 6.5	10.3	1.05	25.31	7	2	97	0	1	44	93.8	-17.2	32	4	2,500	0	0.0	0.0
C+ / 6.4	10.3	1.05	25.16	83	2	97	0	1	44	94.3	-17.2	33	4	2,500	0	0.0	0.0
C+ / 6.4	10.2	1.05	26.91	29	2	97	0	1	44	101.5	-16.8	48	4	2,500	0	0.0	0.0
C+ / 6.5	10.3	1.05	26.48	207	2	97	0	1	44	97.6	-17.0	40	4	2,500	0	3.5	0.0
C / 5.2	12.4	0.85	43.08	1,098	2	97	0	1	111	192.8	-14.9	99	7	2,500	0	5.8	0.8
C / 4.9	12.4	0.85	36.11	14	2	97	0	1	111	184.8	-15.1	99	7	2,500	0	0.0	0.8
C / 4.9	12.4	0.85	35.80	557	2	97	0	1	111	185.4	-15.1	99	7	2,500	0	0.0	0.8
C / 5.3	12.4	0.85	46.24	674	2	97	0	1	111	195.5	-14.8	99	7	2,500	0	0.0	0.8
C / 5.1	12.3	0.85	40.74	311	2	97	0	1	111	190.2	-15.0	99	7	2,500	0	3.5	0.8
B+ / 9.9	1.6	0.25	51.26	N/A	63	6	30	1	31	14.7	-4.5	66	8	25,000	0	5.8	0.0
B+ / 9.9	1.6	0.25	50.86	N/A	63	6	30	1	31	11.8	-4.8	55	8	25,000	0	0.0	0.0
B+ / 9.9	1.6	0.25	51.25	N/A	63	6	30	1	31	15.7	-4.4	69	8	25,000	0	0.0	0.0
B+ / 9.9	1.6	0.25	51.23	N/A	63	6	30	1	31	13.7	-4.6	62	8	25,000	0	3.5	0.0
B+ / 9.8	2.7	0.44	55.15	1	37	15	47	1	56	23.6	-6.4	65	8	25,000	0	5.8	0.0
B+ / 9.8	2.7	0.44	54.98	1	37	15	47	1	56	20.4	-6.7	53	8	25,000	0	0.0	0.0

Fund Type	Fund Name	Ticker Symbol	Overall Investment Rating	Phone	Perfor-mance Rating/Pts	3 Mo	6 Mo	1Yr / Pct	3Yr / Pct	5Yr / Pct	Dividend Yield	Expense Ratio
								99 Pct = Best 0 Pct = Worst				
AA	● Fidelity Adv Inc Replacement 2018 I	FRKIX	C	(800) 522-7297	D- / 1.4	0.95	1.84	3.24 /28	4.76 /12	5.39 /14	1.10	0.46
AA	● Fidelity Adv Inc Replacement 2018 T	FRKTX	C-	(800) 522-7297	D- / 1.0	0.83	1.60	2.73 /25	4.24 /11	4.86 /11	0.58	0.96
AA	Fidelity Adv Inc Replacement 2020 A	FILAX	C	(800) 522-7297	D- / 1.2	1.37	2.53	4.07 /32	5.83 /16	6.11 /17	1.09	0.77
AA	Fidelity Adv Inc Replacement 2020 C	FILCX	C	(800) 522-7297	D- / 1.5	1.19	2.15	3.31 /28	5.04 /13	5.32 /13	0.45	1.52
AA	Fidelity Adv Inc Replacement 2020 I	FILIX	C	(800) 522-7297	D / 2.0	1.45	2.67	4.34 /34	6.10 /17	6.38 /19	1.40	0.52
AA	Fidelity Adv Inc Replacement 2020 T	FILTX	C	(800) 522-7297	D- / 1.3	1.31	2.40	3.81 /31	5.56 /15	5.84 /16	0.88	1.02
AA	Fidelity Adv Inc Replacement 2022 A	FRAMX	C	(800) 522-7297	D / 1.6	1.61	2.97	4.76 /37	6.82 /20	6.83 /22	1.06	0.81
AA	Fidelity Adv Inc Replacement 2022 C	FRCMX	C	(800) 522-7297	D / 1.9	1.42	2.58	3.97 /32	6.02 /17	6.03 /17	0.42	1.56
AA	Fidelity Adv Inc Replacement 2022 I	FRIMX	C+	(800) 522-7297	D+ / 2.5	1.67	3.10	5.01 /39	7.08 /22	7.10 /24	1.37	0.56
AA	Fidelity Adv Inc Replacement 2022 T	FRTMX	C	(800) 522-7297	D / 1.7	1.53	2.83	4.47 /35	6.57 /19	6.58 /21	0.90	1.06
AA	Fidelity Adv Inc Replacement 2024 A	FRNAX	C	(800) 522-7297	D / 1.9	1.78	3.30	5.23 /40	7.56 /24	7.36 /25	1.09	0.83
AA	Fidelity Adv Inc Replacement 2024 C	FRNCX	C	(800) 522-7297	D+ / 2.3	1.58	2.91	4.45 /35	6.76 /20	6.56 /20	0.49	1.58
AA	Fidelity Adv Inc Replacement 2024 I	FRNIX	C+	(800) 522-7297	C- / 3.0	1.84	3.43	5.49 /42	7.84 /26	7.63 /27	1.41	0.58
AA	Fidelity Adv Inc Replacement 2024 T	FRNTX	C	(800) 522-7297	D / 2.1	1.71	3.16	4.96 /38	7.30 /23	7.09 /24	0.89	1.08
AA	Fidelity Adv Inc Replacement 2026 A	FIOAX	C	(800) 522-7297	D / 2.2	1.91	3.52	5.56 /43	8.08 /27	7.71 /28	1.08	0.85
AA	Fidelity Adv Inc Replacement 2026 C	FIOCX	C	(800) 522-7297	D+ / 2.6	1.72	3.14	4.79 /37	7.29 /23	6.92 /23	0.52	1.60
AA	Fidelity Adv Inc Replacement 2026 I	FIOIX	C+	(800) 522-7297	C- / 3.3	1.97	3.67	5.84 /45	8.36 /29	7.98 /30	1.39	0.60
AA	Fidelity Adv Inc Replacement 2026 T	FIOTX	C	(800) 522-7297	D+ / 2.4	1.84	3.40	5.30 /41	7.81 /26	7.44 /26	0.83	1.10
AA	Fidelity Adv Inc Replacement 2028 A	FARPX	C	(800) 522-7297	D+ / 2.4	2.00	3.68	5.77 /44	8.45 /30	7.97 /30	1.09	0.86
AA	Fidelity Adv Inc Replacement 2028 C	FCRPX	C+	(800) 522-7297	D+ / 2.8	1.81	3.30	4.99 /38	7.64 /25	7.16 /24	0.52	1.61
AA	Fidelity Adv Inc Replacement 2028 I	FRAPX	C+	(800) 522-7297	C- / 3.5	2.07	3.83	6.05 /47	8.72 /31	8.24 /31	1.40	0.61
AA	Fidelity Adv Inc Replacement 2028 T	FTRPX	C	(800) 522-7297	D+ / 2.6	1.95	3.56	5.52 /43	8.18 /28	7.70 /28	0.88	1.11
AA	Fidelity Adv Inc Replacement 2030 A	FRQAX	C	(800) 522-7297	D+ / 2.6	2.07	3.80	5.90 /46	8.73 /31	8.17 /31	1.12	0.87
AA	Fidelity Adv Inc Replacement 2030 C	FRQCX	C+	(800) 522-7297	C- / 3.0	1.89	3.42	5.14 /40	7.91 /26	7.37 /26	0.55	1.62
AA	Fidelity Adv Inc Replacement 2030 I	FRQIX	C+	(800) 522-7297	C- / 3.7	2.14	3.94	6.18 /48	9.00 /33	8.45 /33	1.43	0.62
AA	Fidelity Adv Inc Replacement 2030 T	FRQTX	C	(800) 522-7297	D+ / 2.8	2.01	3.67	5.66 /44	8.48 /30	7.91 /29	0.90	1.12
AA	Fidelity Adv Inc Replacement 2032 A	FIARX	C	(800) 522-7297	D+ / 2.7	2.15	3.91	6.08 /47	8.98 /33	8.35 /32	1.16	0.88
AA	Fidelity Adv Inc Replacement 2032 C	FICRX	C	(800) 522-7297	C- / 3.1	1.97	3.52	5.30 /41	8.17 /28	7.54 /27	0.60	1.63
AA	Fidelity Adv Inc Replacement 2032 I	FIIRX	C+	(800) 522-7297	C- / 3.8	2.20	4.03	6.35 /49	9.25 /35	8.62 /34	1.48	0.63
AA	Fidelity Adv Inc Replacement 2032 T	FTIRX	C	(800) 522-7297	D+ / 2.9	2.08	3.77	5.81 /45	8.70 /31	8.07 /30	0.95	1.13
AA	Fidelity Adv Inc Replacement 2034 A	FARSX	C	(800) 522-7297	D+ / 2.8	2.22	3.98	6.12 /48	9.17 /34	8.47 /33	1.11	0.89
AA	Fidelity Adv Inc Replacement 2034 C	FCRSX	C+	(800) 522-7297	C- / 3.2	2.01	3.58	5.33 /41	8.35 /29	7.66 /28	0.56	1.64
AA	Fidelity Adv Inc Replacement 2034 I	FRASX	C+	(800) 522-7297	C- / 3.9	2.28	4.11	6.39 /50	9.44 /36	8.75 /35	1.41	0.64
AA	Fidelity Adv Inc Replacement 2034 T	FTRSX	C+	(800) 522-7297	C- / 3.0	2.14	3.85	5.86 /45	8.90 /32	8.20 /31	Incl.	1.14
AA	Fidelity Adv Inc Replacement 2036 A	FURAX	C	(800) 522-7297	C- / 3.0	2.27	4.05	6.20 /48	9.38 /35	8.62 /34	1.11	0.90
AA	Fidelity Adv Inc Replacement 2036 C	FURCX	C+	(800) 522-7297	C- / 3.3	2.06	3.65	5.40 /42	8.56 /30	7.81 /29	0.56	1.65
AA	Fidelity Adv Inc Replacement 2036 I	FURIX	C+	(800) 522-7297	C- / 4.1	2.34	4.20	6.52 /51	9.69 /37	8.91 /36	1.40	0.65
AA	Fidelity Adv Inc Replacement 2036 T	FURTX	C+	(800) 522-7297	C- / 3.1	2.19	3.91	5.93 /46	9.11 /34	8.35 /32	0.91	1.15
AA	Fidelity Adv Inc Replacement 2038 A	FARVX	C	(800) 522-7297	C- / 3.1	2.33	4.13	6.28 /49	9.59 /37	8.78 /35	1.08	0.91
AA	Fidelity Adv Inc Replacement 2038 C	FCRVX	C+	(800) 522-7297	C- / 3.5	2.13	3.74	5.47 /42	8.77 /31	7.98 /30	0.53	1.66
AA	Fidelity Adv Inc Replacement 2038 I	FIIVX	C+	(800) 522-7297	C- / 4.2	2.39	4.25	6.53 /51	9.86 /39	9.06 /37	1.39	0.66
AA	Fidelity Adv Inc Replacement 2038 T	FTRVX	C+	(800) 522-7297	C- / 3.3	2.28	3.99	6.00 /46	9.31 /35	8.52 /33	0.87	1.16
AA	Fidelity Adv Inc Replacement 2040 A	FARWX	C+	(800) 522-7297	C- / 3.3	2.40	4.22	6.38 /50	9.90 /39	9.05 /37	1.09	0.92
AA	Fidelity Adv Inc Replacement 2040 C	FCRWX	C+	(800) 522-7297	C- / 3.6	2.21	3.83	5.58 /43	9.06 /33	8.23 /31	0.58	1.67
AA	Fidelity Adv Inc Replacement 2040 I	FIIWX	B-	(800) 522-7297	C / 4.3	2.48	4.35	6.64 /52	10.15 /40	9.32 /39	1.40	0.67
AA	Fidelity Adv Inc Replacement 2040 T	FTRWX	C+	(800) 522-7297	C- / 3.4	2.33	4.08	6.10 /47	9.60 /37	8.77 /35	0.92	1.17
AA	Fidelity Adv Inc Replacement 2042 A	FARFX	C+	(800) 522-7297	C- / 3.4	2.47	4.33	6.50 /51	10.22 /41	9.26 /39	1.12	0.93
AA	Fidelity Adv Inc Replacement 2042 C	FCRFX	C+	(800) 522-7297	C- / 3.8	2.29	3.94	5.71 /44	9.40 /36	8.45 /33	0.59	1.68
AA	Fidelity Adv Inc Replacement 2042 I	FIRFX	B-	(800) 522-7297	C / 4.5	2.55	4.46	6.78 /53	10.50 /42	9.54 /41	1.42	0.68
AA	Fidelity Adv Inc Replacement 2042 T	FITTX	C+	(800) 522-7297	C- / 3.6	2.43	4.20	6.24 /48	9.95 /39	8.99 /37	0.90	1.18
GR	Fidelity Adv Industrials A	FCLAX	C+	(800) 522-7297	C+ / 6.7	1.73	9.22	7.79 /61	15.91 /83	14.95 /86	0.25	1.09
GR	● Fidelity Adv Industrials B	FCLBX	C+	(800) 522-7297	B- / 7.1	1.51	8.80	6.94 /55	14.98 /75	14.04 /78	0.09	1.33

● Denotes fund is closed to new investors
* Denotes fund is included in Section II

www.thestreetratings.com

RISK			NET ASSETS		ASSET					BULL / BEAR		FUND MANAGER		MINIMUMS		LOADS	
	3 Year		NAV						Portfolio	Last Bull	Last Bear	Manager	Manager	Initial	Additional	Front	Back
Risk Rating/Pts	Standard Deviation	Beta	As of 3/31/15	Total $(Mil)	Cash %	Stocks %	Bonds %	Other %	Turnover Ratio	Market Return	Market Return	Quality Pct	Tenure (Years)	Purch. $	Purch. $	End Load	End Load
B+ / 9.8	2.7	0.44	55.16	N/A	37	15	47	1	56	24.6	-6.3	68	8	25,000	0	0.0	0.0
B+ / 9.8	2.7	0.44	55.16	N/A	37	15	47	1	56	22.5	-6.5	61	8	25,000	0	3.5	0.0
B+ / 9.6	3.5	0.59	56.35	1	20	25	53	2	25	30.4	-8.0	60	8	25,000	0	5.8	0.0
B+ / 9.6	3.5	0.59	56.24	1	20	25	53	2	25	27.1	-8.3	49	8	25,000	0	0.0	0.0
B+ / 9.6	3.5	0.59	56.36	N/A	20	25	53	2	25	31.5	-7.9	64	8	25,000	0	0.0	0.0
B+ / 9.6	3.5	0.59	56.36	N/A	20	25	53	2	25	29.3	-8.1	56	8	25,000	0	3.5	0.0
B+ / 9.5	4.2	0.71	58.70	N/A	17	33	48	2	26	35.6	-9.2	56	8	25,000	0	5.8	0.0
B+ / 9.5	4.2	0.71	58.60	N/A	17	33	48	2	26	32.2	-9.5	44	8	25,000	0	0.0	0.0
B+ / 9.5	4.2	0.71	58.68	N/A	17	33	48	2	26	36.8	-9.1	60	8	25,000	0	0.0	0.0
B+ / 9.5	4.2	0.71	58.72	N/A	17	33	48	2	26	34.5	-9.3	52	8	25,000	0	3.5	0.0
B+ / 9.3	4.7	0.80	59.25	N/A	15	39	44	2	30	39.7	-10.0	52	8	25,000	0	5.8	0.0
B+ / 9.3	4.6	0.80	59.05	N/A	15	39	44	2	30	36.1	-10.3	41	8	25,000	0	0.0	0.0
B+ / 9.3	4.7	0.80	59.24	N/A	15	39	44	2	30	40.8	-9.9	56	8	25,000	0	0.0	0.0
B+ / 9.3	4.6	0.80	59.24	N/A	15	39	44	2	30	38.5	-10.1	48	8	25,000	0	3.5	0.0
B+ / 9.2	5.0	0.86	60.45	1	13	44	41	2	27	42.4	-10.6	50	8	25,000	0	5.8	0.0
B+ / 9.2	5.0	0.87	60.30	N/A	13	44	41	2	27	38.9	-10.9	38	8	25,000	0	0.0	0.0
B+ / 9.2	5.0	0.86	60.46	N/A	13	44	41	2	27	43.7	-10.5	53	8	25,000	0	0.0	0.0
B+ / 9.2	5.0	0.87	60.48	N/A	13	44	41	2	27	41.2	-10.7	46	8	25,000	0	3.5	0.0
B+ / 9.1	5.3	0.91	61.52	1	12	47	39	2	18	44.5	-11.1	47	8	25,000	0	5.8	0.0
B+ / 9.1	5.3	0.91	61.35	N/A	12	47	39	2	18	40.9	-11.4	36	8	25,000	0	0.0	0.0
B+ / 9.1	5.3	0.91	61.52	N/A	12	47	39	2	18	45.8	-11.0	51	8	25,000	0	0.0	0.0
B+ / 9.1	5.3	0.91	61.53	N/A	12	47	39	2	18	43.3	-11.2	43	8	25,000	0	3.5	0.0
B+ / 9.0	5.5	0.95	61.08	N/A	11	50	37	2	27	46.2	-11.6	46	8	25,000	0	5.8	0.0
B+ / 9.0	5.5	0.95	60.83	N/A	11	50	37	2	27	42.6	-11.8	34	8	25,000	0	0.0	0.0
B+ / 9.0	5.5	0.95	61.09	N/A	11	50	37	2	27	47.5	-11.5	49	8	25,000	0	0.0	0.0
B+ / 9.0	5.5	0.95	61.20	N/A	11	50	37	2	27	45.0	-11.6	42	8	25,000	0	3.5	0.0
B / 8.2	5.7	0.98	58.24	1	11	52	36	1	29	47.7	-11.9	44	8	25,000	0	5.8	0.0
B / 8.2	5.7	0.98	58.09	N/A	11	52	36	1	29	44.0	-12.2	33	8	25,000	0	0.0	0.0
B / 8.2	5.7	0.98	58.25	N/A	11	52	36	1	29	49.0	-11.8	47	8	25,000	0	0.0	0.0
B / 8.2	5.7	0.98	58.28	N/A	11	52	36	1	29	46.4	-12.0	40	8	25,000	0	3.5	0.0
B / 8.9	5.9	1.01	61.10	N/A	10	53	35	2	19	48.9	-12.3	42	8	25,000	0	5.8	0.0
B / 8.8	5.9	1.01	60.91	N/A	10	53	35	2	19	45.2	-12.6	31	8	25,000	0	0.0	0.0
B / 8.9	5.9	1.01	61.09	N/A	10	53	35	2	19	50.2	-12.2	45	8	25,000	0	0.0	0.0
B / 8.9	5.9	1.01	61.11	N/A	10	53	35	2	19	47.6	-12.4	38	8	25,000	0	3.5	0.0
B / 8.8	6.0	1.04	61.62	N/A	10	55	34	1	25	50.3	-12.7	40	8	25,000	0	5.8	0.0
B / 8.8	6.0	1.04	61.34	1	10	55	34	1	25	46.5	-13.0	30	8	25,000	0	0.0	0.0
B / 8.8	6.0	1.04	61.68	N/A	10	55	34	1	25	51.7	-12.6	45	8	25,000	0	0.0	0.0
B / 8.8	6.0	1.04	61.58	1	10	55	34	1	25	49.0	-12.8	37	8	25,000	0	3.5	0.0
B / 8.7	6.2	1.07	59.18	N/A	9	56	33	2	39	51.8	-13.2	38	8	25,000	0	5.8	0.0
B / 8.7	6.2	1.07	58.92	N/A	9	56	33	2	39	48.0	-13.5	28	8	25,000	0	0.0	0.0
B / 8.7	6.2	1.07	59.18	N/A	9	56	33	2	39	53.1	-13.1	41	8	25,000	0	0.0	0.0
B / 8.7	6.2	1.07	59.17	N/A	9	56	33	2	39	50.5	-13.3	34	8	25,000	0	3.5	0.0
B / 8.6	6.5	1.11	60.49	N/A	8	58	32	2	34	53.8	-13.8	37	8	25,000	0	5.8	0.0
B / 8.6	6.5	1.11	60.15	N/A	8	58	32	2	34	49.9	-14.1	27	8	25,000	0	0.0	0.0
B / 8.6	6.5	1.11	60.45	N/A	8	58	32	2	34	55.1	-13.7	40	8	25,000	0	0.0	0.0
B / 8.6	6.5	1.11	60.55	1	8	58	32	2	34	52.4	-13.9	33	8	25,000	0	3.5	0.0
B / 8.5	6.7	1.15	60.55	1	7	60	30	3	16	55.7	-14.1	34	8	25,000	0	5.8	0.0
B / 8.5	6.7	1.15	60.32	N/A	7	60	30	3	16	51.8	-14.4	26	8	25,000	0	0.0	0.0
B / 8.5	6.7	1.15	60.57	N/A	7	60	30	3	16	57.1	-14.0	39	8	25,000	0	0.0	0.0
B / 8.5	6.7	1.15	60.57	1	7	60	30	3	16	54.4	-14.2	32	8	25,000	0	3.5	0.0
C+ / 5.7	11.5	1.07	37.66	364	0	99	0	1	57	107.7	-26.1	50	8	2,500	0	5.8	0.8
C / 5.5	11.5	1.06	34.36	9	0	99	0	1	57	102.2	-26.4	38	8	2,500	0	0.0	0.8

						PERFORMANCE						Incl. in Returns	
	99 Pct = Best 0 Pct = Worst			Overall		Perfor-	Total Return % through 3/31/15						
				Investment		mance				Annualized		Dividend	Expense
Fund Type	Fund Name	Ticker Symbol	Rating	Phone		Rating/Pts	3 Mo	6 Mo	1Yr / Pct	3Yr / Pct	5Yr / Pct	Yield	Ratio
GR	Fidelity Adv Industrials C	FCLCX	C+	(800) 522-7297		B- / 7.1	1.52	8.82	6.99 /55	15.05 /75	14.09 /79	0.00	1.83
GR	Fidelity Adv Industrials I	FCLIX	B	(800) 522-7297		B / 8.0	1.76	9.35	8.06 /63	16.22 /85	15.27 /89	0.53	0.81
GR	Fidelity Adv Industrials T	FCLTX	C+	(800) 522-7297		C+/ 6.9	1.65	9.10	7.52 /59	15.61 /80	14.66 /84	0.11	1.33
FO	Fidelity Adv International Disc A	FAIDX	D+	(800) 522-7297		C- / 3.1	5.88	4.39	1.07 /19	10.38 /42	6.93 /23	0.27	1.26
FO ●	Fidelity Adv International Disc B	FADDX	D+	(800) 522-7297		C- / 3.5	5.68	3.99	0.30 /16	9.56 /36	6.13 /18	0.00	2.04
FO	Fidelity Adv International Disc C	FCADX	D+	(800) 522-7297		C- / 3.5	5.67	4.00	0.30 /16	9.56 /37	6.14 /18	0.00	2.01
FO	Fidelity Adv International Disc I	FIADX	C-	(800) 522-7297		C / 4.3	5.96	4.58	1.41 /20	10.76 /44	7.31 /25	0.66	0.91
FO	Fidelity Adv International Disc T	FTADX	D+	(800) 522-7297		C- / 3.3	5.83	4.27	0.83 /18	10.12 /40	6.68 /21	0.05	1.49
FO	Fidelity Adv International Disc Z	FZAIX	U	(800) 522-7297		U /	5.99	4.64	1.55 /20	--	--	0.79	0.78
FO	Fidelity Adv International Gr A	FIAGX	D+	(800) 522-7297		C- / 3.2	6.42	5.73	4.10 /32	9.81 /38	9.21 /38	0.50	1.35
FO ●	Fidelity Adv International Gr B	FBIGX	C-	(800) 522-7297		C- / 3.5	6.27	5.29	3.28 /28	8.96 /33	8.41 /33	0.00	2.14
FO	Fidelity Adv International Gr C	FIGCX	C-	(800) 522-7297		C- / 3.5	6.20	5.31	3.29 /28	8.95 /33	8.40 /32	0.00	2.12
FO	Fidelity Adv International Gr Inst	FIIIX	C-	(800) 522-7297		C- / 4.2	6.49	5.84	4.41 /34	10.10 /40	9.54 /41	0.84	1.04
FO	Fidelity Adv International Gr T	FITGX	D+	(800) 522-7297		C- / 3.3	6.33	5.56	3.84 /31	9.50 /36	8.94 /36	0.10	1.65
FO	Fidelity Adv International Sm Cap A	FIASX	D-	(800) 522-7297		C- / 3.3	5.38	3.63	-0.49 /14	11.28 /47	10.08 /45	0.58	1.51
FO ●	Fidelity Adv International Sm Cap B	FIBSX	D-	(800) 522-7297		C- / 3.6	5.18	3.25	-1.26 /12	10.44 /42	9.25 /39	0.00	2.29
FO	Fidelity Adv International Sm Cap C	FICSX	D-	(800) 522-7297		C- / 3.6	5.14	3.24	-1.24 /12	10.46 /42	9.28 /39	0.00	2.24
FO	Fidelity Adv International Sm Cap I	FIXIX	D	(800) 522-7297		C / 4.4	5.46	3.82	-0.14 /15	11.73 /51	10.49 /49	0.31	1.09
FO	Fidelity Adv International Sm Cap T	FTISX	D-	(800) 522-7297		C- / 3.4	5.26	3.48	-0.81 /14	10.98 /45	9.79 /43	0.21	1.78
FO	Fidelity Adv International Val A	FIVMX	D-	(800) 522-7297		D / 2.0	4.83	0.19	-2.49 / 9	9.12 /34	4.28 / 9	3.15	1.32
FO ●	Fidelity Adv International Val B	FIVNX	D	(800) 522-7297		D+/ 2.3	4.65	-0.31	-3.40 / 8	8.28 /29	3.48 / 7	2.11	2.08
FO	Fidelity Adv International Val C	FIVOX	D-	(800) 522-7297		D+/ 2.3	4.58	-0.23	-3.34 / 8	8.26 /28	3.49 / 7	2.70	2.07
FO	Fidelity Adv International Val I	FIVQX	D	(800) 522-7297		C- / 3.0	4.96	0.35	-2.33 /10	9.43 /36	4.62 /11	3.75	1.05
FO	Fidelity Adv International Val T	FIVPX	D-	(800) 522-7297		D / 2.1	4.71	0.03	-2.87 / 9	8.82 /32	3.99 / 8	2.97	1.59
FO	Fidelity Adv Intl Cap Apprec A	FCPAX	C-	(800) 522-7297		C- / 4.1	4.01	6.09	6.31 /49	11.53 /49	9.42 /40	0.19	1.73
FO ●	Fidelity Adv Intl Cap Apprec B	FCPBX	C-	(800) 522-7297		C / 4.5	3.74	5.72	5.48 /42	10.65 /43	8.59 /34	0.00	2.50
FO	Fidelity Adv Intl Cap Apprec C	FCPCX	C-	(800) 522-7297		C / 4.5	3.83	5.74	5.50 /42	10.66 /43	8.61 /34	0.00	2.47
FO	Fidelity Adv Intl Cap Apprec I	FCPIX	C	(800) 522-7297		C / 5.2	4.08	6.21	6.62 /52	11.78 /51	9.68 /42	0.41	1.38
FO	Fidelity Adv Intl Cap Apprec T	FIATX	C-	(800) 522-7297		C / 4.3	3.87	5.92	6.07 /47	11.21 /47	9.14 /38	0.00	1.94
FO	Fidelity Adv Intl Real Estate A	FIRAX	C+	(800) 522-7297		C+/ 6.0	5.68	6.92	8.24 /64	14.74 /73	9.64 /42	1.20	1.38
FO ●	Fidelity Adv Intl Real Estate B	FIRBX	C+	(800) 522-7297		C+/ 6.4	5.45	6.45	7.37 /58	13.89 /66	8.80 /35	0.75	2.14
FO	Fidelity Adv Intl Real Estate C	FIRCX	C+	(800) 522-7297		C+/ 6.5	5.49	6.52	7.43 /59	13.92 /66	8.80 /35	0.65	2.13
FO	Fidelity Adv Intl Real Estate Inst	FIRIX	B	(800) 522-7297		B- / 7.3	5.75	7.13	8.56 /67	15.09 /76	9.94 /44	1.50	1.12
FO	Fidelity Adv Intl Real Estate T	FIRTX	C+	(800) 522-7297		C+/ 6.2	5.51	6.73	7.89 /62	14.42 /70	9.33 /39	0.89	1.66
FO	Fidelity Adv Japan A	FPJAX	D-	(800) 544-8544		D / 1.7	9.52	3.71	6.18 /48	6.58 /19	3.47 / 7	0.37	1.23
FO ●	Fidelity Adv Japan B	FJPBX	D	(800) 544-8544		D / 2.0	9.22	3.19	5.28 /41	5.73 /16	2.71 / 5	0.00	2.02
FO	Fidelity Adv Japan C	FJPCX	D	(800) 544-8544		D / 2.1	9.27	3.30	5.40 /42	5.81 /16	2.76 / 6	0.00	1.93
FO	Fidelity Adv Japan I	FJPIX	D	(800) 544-8544		D+/ 2.7	9.52	3.86	6.43 /50	6.94 /21	3.87 / 8	0.78	0.89
FO	Fidelity Adv Japan T	FJPTX	D	(800) 544-8544		D / 1.8	9.32	3.46	5.75 /44	6.22 /18	3.20 / 6	0.00	1.54
GR	Fidelity Adv Large Cap Fund A	FALAX	B	(800) 522-7297		B- / 7.3	0.88	3.61	7.91 /62	17.19 /91	14.75 /85	0.46	1.26
GR ●	Fidelity Adv Large Cap Fund B	FALHX	B+	(800) 522-7297		B / 7.7	0.64	3.16	7.10 /56	16.28 /85	13.87 /76	0.00	2.06
GR	Fidelity Adv Large Cap Fund C	FLCCX	B+	(800) 522-7297		B / 7.7	0.65	3.17	7.08 /56	16.29 /85	13.88 /77	0.05	2.00
GR	Fidelity Adv Large Cap Fund I	FALIX	A-	(800) 522-7297		B+/ 8.6	0.92	3.73	8.17 /64	17.52 /92	15.10 /88	0.64	0.95
GR	Fidelity Adv Large Cap Fund T	FALGX	B	(800) 522-7297		B- / 7.5	0.81	3.45	7.64 /60	16.90 /89	14.47 /82	0.23	1.51
GR	Fidelity Adv Leveraged Co Stk A	FLSAX	B+	(800) 522-7297		B / 8.1	4.10	4.68	8.07 /63	18.05 /94	14.81 /85	0.47	1.07
GR ●	Fidelity Adv Leveraged Co Stk B	FLCBX	A-	(800) 522-7297		B+/ 8.4	3.89	4.26	7.22 /57	17.11 /90	13.90 /77	0.00	1.87
GR	Fidelity Adv Leveraged Co Stk C	FLSCX	A-	(800) 522-7297		B+/ 8.5	3.91	4.28	7.27 /57	17.17 /91	13.97 /77	0.00	1.82
GR	Fidelity Adv Leveraged Co Stk I	FLVIX	A+	(800) 522-7297		A- / 9.1	4.15	4.79	8.35 /65	18.36 /95	15.13 /88	0.76	0.82
GR	Fidelity Adv Leveraged Co Stk T	FLSTX	A-	(800) 522-7297		B+/ 8.3	4.03	4.53	7.82 /61	17.77 /93	14.55 /83	0.27	1.32
GR	Fidelity Adv Leveraged Co Stk Z	FZAKX	U	(800) 522-7297		U /	4.20	4.87	8.51 /66	--	--	0.88	0.68
PM	Fidelity Adv Materials A	FMFAX	D-	(800) 522-7297		D / 1.7	0.60	-2.48	-2.51 / 9	9.05 /33	10.25 /46	0.48	1.10
PM ●	Fidelity Adv Materials B	FMFBX	D-	(800) 522-7297		D / 2.0	0.40	-2.87	-3.32 / 8	8.17 /28	9.37 /39	0.00	1.90

● Denotes fund is closed to new investors
* Denotes fund is included in Section II

www.thestreetratings.com

RISK			NET ASSETS		ASSET					BULL / BEAR		FUND MANAGER		MINIMUMS		LOADS	
	3 Year		NAV						Portfolio	Last Bull	Last Bear	Manager	Manager	Initial	Additional	Front	Back
Risk Rating/Pts	Standard Deviation	Beta	As of 3/31/15	Total $(Mil)	Cash %	Stocks %	Bonds %	Other %	Turnover Ratio	Market Return	Market Return	Quality Pct	Tenure (Years)	Purch. $	Purch. $	End Load	End Load
C+ / 5.6	11.5	1.06	34.66	154	0	99	0	1	57	102.5	-26.4	39	8	2,500	0	0.0	0.8
C+ / 5.7	11.5	1.06	39.26	234	0	99	0	1	57	109.7	-26.0	54	8	2,500	0	0.0	0.8
C+ / 5.7	11.5	1.06	36.97	94	0	99	0	1	57	106.0	-26.2	46	8	2,500	0	3.5	0.8
C+ / 6.1	12.6	0.93	40.00	293	5	94	0	1	57	57.3	-24.6	80	10	2,500	0	5.8	1.0
C+ / 6.1	12.6	0.93	39.60	4	5	94	0	1	57	53.2	-24.8	74	10	2,500	0	0.0	1.0
C+ / 6.1	12.6	0.93	39.52	36	5	94	0	1	57	53.3	-24.8	74	10	2,500	0	0.0	1.0
C+ / 6.1	12.6	0.93	40.17	867	5	94	0	1	57	59.1	-24.5	83	10	2,500	0	0.0	1.0
C+ / 6.1	12.6	0.93	39.78	46	5	94	0	1	57	55.9	-24.7	78	10	2,500	0	3.5	1.0
U /	N/A	N/A	40.14	36	5	94	0	1	57	N/A	N/A	N/A	10	5,000,000	0	0.0	1.0
C+ / 6.4	11.2	0.82	11.43	143	4	95	0	1	27	61.3	-22.0	84	8	2,500	0	5.8	1.0
C+ / 6.4	11.2	0.82	11.35	1	4	95	0	1	27	57.2	-22.4	78	8	2,500	0	0.0	1.0
C+ / 6.4	11.1	0.81	11.31	38	4	95	0	1	27	57.1	-22.3	78	8	2,500	0	0.0	1.0
C+ / 6.4	11.2	0.81	11.48	160	4	95	0	1	27	62.9	-22.0	85	8	2,500	0	0.0	1.0
C+ / 6.4	11.1	0.81	11.42	28	4	95	0	1	27	59.8	-22.2	82	8	2,500	0	3.5	1.0
C- / 4.1	12.9	0.89	22.51	24	4	95	0	1	102	56.6	-21.7	87	1	2,500	0	5.8	2.0
C- / 4.1	12.9	0.89	22.14	N/A	4	95	0	1	102	52.6	-22.0	83	1	2,500	0	0.0	2.0
C- / 4.1	12.9	0.89	21.88	9	4	95	0	1	102	52.6	-21.9	83	1	2,500	0	0.0	2.0
C- / 4.2	12.9	0.89	23.00	9	4	95	0	1	102	58.8	-21.6	89	1	2,500	0	0.0	2.0
C- / 4.1	12.9	0.89	22.40	11	4	95	0	1	102	55.2	-21.8	86	1	2,500	0	3.5	2.0
C+ / 5.7	13.3	0.99	8.46	7	1	98	0	1	69	48.5	-27.7	63	4	2,500	0	5.8	1.0
C+ / 5.8	13.3	0.99	8.56	N/A	1	98	0	1	69	44.7	-28.0	52	4	2,500	0	0.0	1.0
C+ / 5.7	13.4	0.99	8.45	4	1	98	0	1	69	44.7	-28.0	51	4	2,500	0	0.0	1.0
C+ / 5.6	13.4	0.99	8.46	4	1	98	0	1	69	50.1	-27.7	67	4	2,500	0	0.0	1.0
C+ / 5.7	13.4	1.00	8.45	4	1	98	0	1	69	47.4	-27.9	58	4	2,500	0	3.5	1.0
C+ / 5.9	12.0	0.86	15.32	68	3	96	0	1	197	78.6	-26.0	89	7	2,500	0	5.8	1.0
C+ / 5.8	12.0	0.86	13.86	1	3	96	0	1	197	74.1	-26.3	86	7	2,500	0	0.0	1.0
C+ / 5.8	12.0	0.86	13.81	27	3	96	0	1	197	74.1	-26.3	86	7	2,500	0	0.0	1.0
C+ / 5.9	12.0	0.86	16.32	59	3	96	0	1	197	80.2	-26.0	90	7	2,500	0	0.0	1.0
C+ / 5.9	12.0	0.86	15.02	61	3	96	0	1	197	77.2	-26.1	88	7	2,500	0	3.5	1.0
C+ / 6.3	12.8	0.82	10.60	14	18	81	0	1	138	82.7	-25.3	95	5	2,500	0	5.8	1.5
C+ / 6.4	12.7	0.82	10.44	N/A	18	81	0	1	138	78.1	-25.5	95	5	2,500	0	0.0	1.5
C+ / 6.4	12.7	0.82	10.38	6	18	81	0	1	138	77.9	-25.5	95	5	2,500	0	0.0	1.5
C+ / 6.3	12.7	0.82	10.67	18	18	81	0	1	138	84.2	-25.2	96	5	2,500	0	0.0	1.5
C+ / 6.4	12.7	0.82	10.53	5	18	81	0	1	138	80.8	-25.3	95	5	2,500	0	3.5	1.5
C+ / 6.3	13.9	0.75	11.97	17	0	99	0	1	112	30.3	-10.4	61	1	2,500	0	5.8	1.5
C+ / 6.2	13.9	0.75	11.97	N/A	0	99	0	1	112	27.1	-10.7	48	1	2,500	0	0.0	1.5
C+ / 6.2	13.9	0.75	11.91	13	0	99	0	1	112	27.2	-10.7	49	1	2,500	0	0.0	1.5
C+ / 6.3	13.9	0.75	11.96	9	0	99	0	1	112	32.0	-10.3	65	1	2,500	0	0.0	1.5
C+ / 6.3	13.9	0.75	11.96	4	0	99	0	1	112	29.0	-10.5	55	1	2,500	0	3.5	1.5
C+ / 6.6	11.2	1.13	28.59	461	2	97	0	1	28	112.5	-19.3	51	10	2,500	0	5.8	0.0
C+ / 6.6	11.2	1.13	26.69	7	2	97	0	1	28	107.0	-19.6	39	10	2,500	0	0.0	0.0
C+ / 6.6	11.2	1.13	26.25	184	2	97	0	1	28	107.2	-19.6	39	10	2,500	0	0.0	0.0
C+ / 6.6	11.2	1.13	29.73	513	2	97	0	1	28	114.7	-19.2	56	10	2,500	0	0.0	0.0
C+ / 6.6	11.2	1.13	28.54	181	2	97	0	1	28	110.7	-19.4	47	10	2,500	0	3.5	0.0
C+ / 6.7	11.2	1.04	58.34	1,577	5	93	0	2	9	121.5	-30.1	78	12	10,000	0	5.8	0.0
C+ / 6.7	11.2	1.04	54.43	36	5	93	0	2	9	115.6	-30.4	70	12	10,000	0	0.0	0.0
C+ / 6.7	11.2	1.04	54.53	603	5	93	0	2	9	116.1	-30.4	71	12	10,000	0	0.0	0.0
C+ / 6.7	11.2	1.04	59.20	1,389	5	93	0	2	9	123.6	-30.1	80	12	10,000	0	0.0	0.0
C+ / 6.7	11.2	1.04	57.11	941	5	93	0	2	9	119.9	-30.2	76	12	10,000	0	3.5	0.0
U /	N/A	N/A	59.23	52	5	93	0	2	9	N/A	N/A	N/A	12	5,000,000	0	0.0	0.0
C+ / 5.8	11.9	0.26	77.21	306	0	99	0	1	53	77.2	-28.4	99	7	2,500	0	5.8	0.8
C+ / 5.8	11.9	0.26	75.12	6	0	99	0	1	53	72.4	-28.6	98	7	2,500	0	0.0	0.8

						PERFORMANCE							
	99 Pct = Best								Total Return % through 3/31/15			Incl. in Returns	
	0 Pct = Worst			Overall		Perfor-				Annualized		Dividend	Expense
Fund			Ticker	Investment		mance						Yield	Ratio
Type	Fund Name		Symbol	Rating	Phone	Rating/Pts	3 Mo	6 Mo	1Yr / Pct	3Yr / Pct	5Yr / Pct		
PM	Fidelity Adv Materials C		FMFCX	D-	(800) 522-7297	D / 2.0	0.42	-2.84	-3.25 / 8	8.23 /28	9.42 /40	0.00	1.85
PM	Fidelity Adv Materials I		FMFEX	D	(800) 522-7297	D+ / 2.7	0.68	-2.34	-2.25 /10	9.36 /35	10.57 /49	0.81	0.81
PM	Fidelity Adv Materials T		FMFTX	D-	(800) 522-7297	D / 1.8	0.52	-2.63	-2.82 / 9	8.72 /31	9.93 /44	0.21	1.40
MC	Fidelity Adv Mid Cap II A		FIIAX	C	(800) 522-7297	C+ / 6.7	5.15	9.66	9.87 /74	14.96 /75	12.97 /68	0.00	1.07
MC	● Fidelity Adv Mid Cap II B		FIIBX	C	(800) 522-7297	B- / 7.1	4.93	9.18	8.96 /69	14.06 /68	12.09 /61	0.00	1.90
MC	Fidelity Adv Mid Cap II C		FIICX	C	(800) 522-7297	B- / 7.1	4.93	9.19	9.02 /69	14.10 /68	12.13 /61	0.00	1.83
MC	Fidelity Adv Mid Cap II I		FIIMX	C+	(800) 522-7297	B / 8.0	5.24	9.81	10.12 /75	15.23 /77	13.24 /70	0.00	0.85
MC	Fidelity Adv Mid Cap II T		FITIX	C	(800) 522-7297	C+ / 6.9	5.08	9.49	9.60 /72	14.72 /73	12.72 /66	0.00	1.30
MC	Fidelity Adv Mid Cap Value A		FMPAX	A+	(800) 522-7297	A / 9.5	2.51	10.74	15.38 /92	20.25 /98	16.35 /94	0.62	1.15
MC	● Fidelity Adv Mid Cap Value B		FMPBX	A+	(800) 522-7297	A+ / 9.6	2.30	10.28	14.42 /90	19.31 /97	15.45 /90	0.00	1.91
MC	Fidelity Adv Mid Cap Value C		FMPEX	A+	(800) 522-7297	A+ / 9.6	2.32	10.33	14.51 /91	19.33 /97	15.48 /90	0.23	1.89
MC	Fidelity Adv Mid Cap Value I		FMPOX	A+	(800) 522-7297	A+ / 9.8	2.57	10.91	15.69 /93	20.57 /98	16.66 /95	0.88	0.85
MC	Fidelity Adv Mid Cap Value T		FMPTX	A+	(800) 522-7297	A+ / 9.6	2.42	10.59	15.05 /92	19.91 /98	16.03 /93	0.37	1.42
★ GR	Fidelity Adv New Insights A		FNIAX	C	(800) 522-7297	C+ / 6.0	2.76	5.71	9.41 /71	14.49 /71	13.81 /76	0.00	0.92
GR	● Fidelity Adv New Insights B		FNIBX	C	(800) 522-7297	C+ / 6.4	2.58	5.31	8.58 /67	13.58 /64	12.91 /67	0.00	1.71
GR	Fidelity Adv New Insights C		FNICX	C	(800) 522-7297	C+ / 6.4	2.56	5.35	8.64 /67	13.64 /64	12.97 /68	0.00	1.67
GR	Fidelity Adv New Insights I		FINSX	B-	(800) 522-7297	B- / 7.3	2.82	5.87	9.70 /73	14.79 /73	14.11 /79	0.22	0.67
GR	Fidelity Adv New Insights T		FNITX	C	(800) 522-7297	C+ / 6.2	2.67	5.56	9.16 /70	14.20 /69	13.53 /73	0.00	1.17
GR	Fidelity Adv New Insights Z		FZANX	U	(800) 522-7297	U /	2.85	5.94	9.88 /74	--	--	0.35	0.54
FO	Fidelity Adv Overseas Fund A		FAOAX	D-	(800) 522-7297	D+ / 2.4	5.14	2.41	-0.78 /14	9.53 /36	6.85 /22	0.08	1.28
FO	● Fidelity Adv Overseas Fund B		FAOBX	D	(800) 522-7297	D+ / 2.8	4.90	1.99	-1.55 /11	8.69 /31	6.03 /17	0.00	2.07
FO	Fidelity Adv Overseas Fund C		FAOCX	D	(800) 522-7297	D+ / 2.8	4.91	1.98	-1.54 /11	8.68 /31	6.03 /17	0.00	2.06
FO	Fidelity Adv Overseas Fund I		FAOIX	D	(800) 522-7297	C- / 3.5	5.19	2.58	-0.46 /14	9.88 /39	7.21 /24	0.43	0.94
FO	Fidelity Adv Overseas Fund T		FAERX	D	(800) 522-7297	D+ / 2.6	5.06	2.30	-0.94 /13	9.34 /35	6.66 /21	0.00	1.46
RE	Fidelity Adv Real Estate A		FHEAX	C+	(800) 522-7297	B+ / 8.9	5.48	20.38	24.68 /98	13.81 /66	15.34 /89	1.17	1.16
RE	● Fidelity Adv Real Estate B		FHEBX	C+	(800) 522-7297	A- / 9.2	5.29	19.91	23.69 /98	12.94 /59	14.48 /82	0.56	1.92
RE	Fidelity Adv Real Estate C		FHECX	C+	(800) 522-7297	A- / 9.2	5.26	19.93	23.69 /98	12.98 /60	14.49 /82	0.63	1.90
RE	Fidelity Adv Real Estate I		FHEIX	B-	(800) 522-7297	A / 9.5	5.57	20.56	25.01 /98	14.12 /68	15.66 /91	1.42	0.89
RE	Fidelity Adv Real Estate Income A		FRINX	C	(800) 522-7297	C- / 3.8	2.57	6.65	9.38 /71	9.96 /39	10.57 /49	4.09	1.06
RE	Fidelity Adv Real Estate Income C		FRIOX	C+	(800) 522-7297	C- / 3.9	2.25	6.27	8.45 /66	9.15 /34	9.74 /42	3.64	1.79
RE	Fidelity Adv Real Estate Income I		FRIRX	C+	(800) 522-7297	C / 4.6	2.61	6.78	9.65 /73	10.27 /41	10.85 /51	4.51	0.78
RE	Fidelity Adv Real Estate Income T		FRIQX	C	(800) 522-7297	C- / 3.8	2.47	6.63	9.25 /71	9.94 /39	10.56 /49	4.06	1.08
RE	Fidelity Adv Real Estate T		FHETX	C+	(800) 522-7297	A- / 9.1	5.44	20.25	24.37 /98	13.57 /64	15.08 /87	1.01	1.37
GR	Fidelity Adv Series Growth and Inc		FMALX	U	(800) 522-7297	U /	0.37	3.53	9.27 /71	--	--	1.66	0.69
SC	Fidelity Adv Small Cap A		FSCDX	C+	(800) 522-7297	B- / 7.3	5.87	12.98	14.07 /90	14.89 /74	12.80 /66	0.00	1.01
SC	● Fidelity Adv Small Cap B		FSCBX	C	(800) 522-7297	B / 7.6	5.61	12.50	13.13 /87	13.96 /67	11.90 /60	0.00	1.81
SC	Fidelity Adv Small Cap C		FSCEX	C	(800) 522-7297	B / 7.7	5.66	12.53	13.19 /87	14.04 /67	11.95 /60	0.00	1.76
SC	Fidelity Adv Small Cap Growth A		FCAGX	C+	(800) 522-7297	B+ / 8.9	8.61	19.04	11.83 /82	17.61 /93	15.62 /91	0.00	1.22
SC	● Fidelity Adv Small Cap Growth B		FCBGX	C+	(800) 522-7297	A- / 9.2	8.49	18.63	11.05 /78	16.71 /88	14.75 /85	0.00	2.01
SC	Fidelity Adv Small Cap Growth C		FCCGX	C+	(800) 522-7297	A- / 9.2	8.41	18.59	10.98 /78	16.70 /88	14.74 /85	0.00	2.01
SC	Fidelity Adv Small Cap Growth I		FCIGX	B	(800) 522-7297	A / 9.5	8.73	19.24	12.21 /84	17.96 /94	15.97 /93	0.00	0.92
SC	Fidelity Adv Small Cap Growth T		FCTGX	B-	(800) 522-7297	A- / 9.0	8.57	18.94	11.55 /81	17.30 /91	15.33 /89	0.00	1.50
SC	Fidelity Adv Small Cap I		FSCIX	B	(800) 522-7297	B+ / 8.6	5.94	13.12	14.37 /90	15.22 /77	13.14 /69	0.24	0.71
SC	Fidelity Adv Small Cap T		FSCTX	C+	(800) 522-7297	B- / 7.5	5.82	12.85	13.82 /89	14.65 /72	12.57 /65	0.00	1.22
SC	Fidelity Adv Small Cap Value A		FCVAX	C	(800) 522-7297	B- / 7.4	2.09	13.68	8.35 /65	16.67 /88	14.32 /81	0.07	1.37
SC	● Fidelity Adv Small Cap Value B		FCVBX	C+	(800) 522-7297	B / 7.8	1.84	13.20	7.44 /59	15.74 /81	13.42 /72	0.00	2.19
SC	Fidelity Adv Small Cap Value C		FCVCX	C+	(800) 522-7297	B / 7.8	1.89	13.24	7.55 /59	15.78 /82	13.47 /73	0.00	2.13
SC	Fidelity Adv Small Cap Value I		FCVIX	B-	(800) 522-7297	B+ / 8.7	2.11	13.84	8.65 /67	17.00 /90	14.65 /84	0.33	1.10
SC	Fidelity Adv Small Cap Value T		FCVTX	C+	(800) 522-7297	B / 7.6	2.07	13.57	8.15 /64	16.40 /86	14.06 /78	0.00	1.61
SC	Fidelity Adv Small Cap Z		FZAOX	U	(800) 522-7297	U /	5.95	13.20	14.54 /91	--	--	0.40	0.56
GR	Fidelity Adv Srs Stock Selector LCV		FMMLX	U	(800) 544-8544	U /	0.80	6.55	12.69 /86	--	--	1.31	0.78
MC	Fidelity Adv Stk Selector Mid Cap		FSSMX	A	(800) 522-7297	B+ / 8.7	4.66	11.55	11.79 /82	16.18 /85	14.01 /78	0.29	0.72

● Denotes fund is closed to new investors
★ Denotes fund is included in Section II

www.thestreetratings.com

RISK	3 Year		NET ASSETS		ASSET				Portfolio Turnover Ratio	BULL / BEAR		FUND MANAGER		MINIMUMS		LOADS	
Risk Rating/Pts	Standard Deviation	Beta	NAV As of 3/31/15	Total $(Mil)	Cash %	Stocks %	Bonds %	Other %		Last Bull Market Return	Last Bear Market Return	Manager Quality Pct	Manager Tenure (Years)	Initial Purch. $	Additional Purch. $	Front End Load	Back End Load
C+ / 5.8	11.9	0.26	74.94	103	0	99	0	1	53	72.7	-28.6	98	7	2,500	0	0.0	0.8
C+ / 5.8	11.9	0.26	77.39	454	0	99	0	1	53	78.9	-28.3	99	7	2,500	0	0.0	0.8
C+ / 5.8	11.9	0.26	76.72	42	0	99	0	1	53	75.4	-28.5	99	7	2,500	0	3.5	0.8
C / 4.5	11.5	1.01	19.80	962	0	99	0	1	134	79.3	-20.5	39	11	2,500	0	5.8	0.0
C- / 4.2	11.5	1.01	18.30	21	0	99	0	1	134	74.5	-20.8	29	11	2,500	0	0.0	0.0
C- / 4.1	11.5	1.00	18.29	284	0	99	0	1	134	74.9	-20.8	29	11	2,500	0	0.0	0.0
C / 4.6	11.5	1.01	20.28	1,354	0	99	0	1	134	80.8	-20.4	42	11	2,500	0	0.0	0.0
C / 4.4	11.5	1.01	19.44	439	0	99	0	1	134	78.0	-20.6	36	11	2,500	0	3.5	0.0
B- / 7.1	10.5	0.91	24.81	224	4	95	0	1	169	121.5	-23.2	92	2	2,500	0	5.8	0.8
B- / 7.1	10.5	0.91	24.46	2	4	95	0	1	169	115.7	-23.4	90	2	2,500	0	0.0	0.8
B- / 7.1	10.5	0.91	24.16	97	4	95	0	1	169	115.9	-23.5	90	2	2,500	0	0.0	0.8
B- / 7.1	10.5	0.91	24.91	212	4	95	0	1	169	123.7	-23.1	92	2	2,500	0	0.0	0.8
B- / 7.1	10.5	0.91	24.71	51	4	95	0	1	169	119.4	-23.3	91	2	2,500	0	3.5	0.8
C+ / 5.6	9.6	0.92	27.25	8,519	1	98	0	1	79	86.0	-14.5	65	12	2,500	0	5.8	0.0
C / 5.3	9.6	0.92	24.71	165	1	98	0	1	79	81.0	-14.8	52	12	2,500	0	0.0	0.0
C / 5.4	9.6	0.92	24.92	3,970	1	98	0	1	79	81.4	-14.8	53	12	2,500	0	0.0	0.0
C+ / 5.7	9.6	0.92	27.76	13,262	1	98	0	1	79	87.7	-14.4	68	12	2,500	0	0.0	0.0
C+ / 5.6	9.6	0.92	26.64	2,234	1	98	0	1	79	84.5	-14.6	61	12	2,500	0	3.5	0.0
U /	N/A	N/A	27.79	480	1	98	0	1	79	N/A	N/A	N/A	12	5,000,000	0	0.0	0.0
C / 5.4	12.9	0.95	21.67	66	0	99	0	1	39	57.6	-27.6	73	10	2,500	0	5.8	1.0
C / 5.4	12.9	0.95	20.97	2	0	99	0	1	39	53.5	-27.8	63	10	2,500	0	0.0	1.0
C / 5.4	12.9	0.95	21.15	18	0	99	0	1	39	53.5	-27.8	63	10	2,500	0	0.0	1.0
C / 5.4	13.0	0.95	22.10	316	0	99	0	1	39	59.4	-27.5	75	10	2,500	0	0.0	1.0
C / 5.4	12.9	0.95	22.22	286	0	99	0	1	39	56.6	-27.7	71	10	2,500	0	3.5	1.0
C- / 3.5	13.2	1.05	24.24	370	1	98	0	1	83	88.0	-18.9	52	11	2,500	0	5.8	0.0
C- / 3.5	13.2	1.05	23.90	5	1	98	0	1	83	83.2	-19.2	41	11	2,500	0	0.0	0.0
C- / 3.5	13.2	1.05	23.82	92	1	98	0	1	83	83.3	-19.2	41	11	2,500	0	0.0	0.0
C- / 3.5	13.2	1.05	24.45	384	1	98	0	1	83	89.7	-18.8	57	11	2,500	0	0.0	0.0
B- / 7.9	5.0	0.37	11.91	517	9	46	40	5	29	49.2	-6.5	93	12	2,500	0	4.0	0.8
B / 8.0	5.0	0.38	11.81	298	9	46	40	5	29	45.5	-6.8	91	12	2,500	0	0.0	0.8
B- / 7.9	5.0	0.37	11.93	1,005	9	46	40	5	29	50.7	-6.4	93	12	2,500	0	0.0	0.8
B / 8.0	5.0	0.37	11.91	57	9	46	40	5	29	49.2	-6.5	93	12	2,500	0	4.0	0.8
C- / 3.5	13.2	1.05	24.22	180	1	98	0	1	83	86.5	-19.0	50	11	2,500	0	3.5	0.0
U /	N/A	N/A	13.59	1,294	3	96	0	1	60	N/A	N/A	N/A	3	0	0	0.0	0.0
C / 5.0	12.9	0.90	28.31	1,109	2	97	0	1	39	85.1	-23.9	71	10	2,500	0	5.8	0.0
C- / 3.9	12.9	0.90	22.76	30	2	97	0	1	39	80.0	-24.1	60	10	2,500	0	0.0	0.0
C- / 4.0	12.9	0.90	23.16	331	2	97	0	1	39	80.4	-24.1	61	10	2,500	0	0.0	0.0
C- / 4.0	13.2	0.93	19.43	97	3	96	0	1	148	100.6	-24.6	85	4	2,500	0	5.8	1.5
C- / 3.7	13.2	0.93	18.01	2	3	96	0	1	148	95.5	-24.9	80	4	2,500	0	0.0	1.5
C- / 3.7	13.2	0.93	17.91	44	3	96	0	1	148	95.5	-24.9	80	4	2,500	0	0.0	1.5
C- / 4.1	13.2	0.93	20.06	67	3	96	0	1	148	102.8	-24.5	87	4	2,500	0	0.0	1.5
C- / 3.9	13.2	0.93	19.01	47	3	96	0	1	148	98.9	-24.7	84	4	2,500	0	3.5	1.5
C / 5.1	12.9	0.90	30.34	660	2	97	0	1	39	86.9	-23.8	73	10	2,500	0	0.0	0.0
C / 4.7	13.0	0.90	26.74	969	2	97	0	1	39	83.7	-23.9	68	10	2,500	0	3.5	0.0
C / 4.4	12.8	0.89	19.05	247	0	99	0	1	26	107.3	-23.8	84	7	2,500	0	5.8	1.5
C- / 4.2	12.8	0.89	17.75	4	0	99	0	1	26	101.8	-24.0	78	7	2,500	0	0.0	1.5
C / 4.3	12.8	0.89	17.78	68	0	99	0	1	26	102.1	-24.0	78	7	2,500	0	0.0	1.5
C / 4.4	12.8	0.90	19.34	370	0	99	0	1	26	109.3	-23.6	85	7	2,500	0	0.0	1.5
C / 4.4	12.8	0.89	18.71	97	0	99	0	1	26	105.6	-23.8	83	7	2,500	0	3.5	1.5
U /	N/A	N/A	30.25	44	2	97	0	1	39	N/A	N/A	N/A	10	5,000,000	0	0.0	0.0
U /	N/A	N/A	13.16	1,257	3	96	0	1	61	N/A	N/A	N/A	3	0	0	0.0	0.0
C+ / 6.8	10.4	0.93	35.01	578	2	97	0	1	89	99.7	-21.2	71	4	2,500	0	0.0	0.0

I. Index of Stock Mutual Funds

Fund Type	Fund Name	Ticker Symbol	Overall Investment Rating	Phone	Performance Rating/Pts	3 Mo	6 Mo	1Yr / Pct	3Yr / Pct	5Yr / Pct	Dividend Yield	Expense Ratio
MC	Fidelity Adv Stk Selector Mid Cap A	FMCDX	B+	(800) 522-7297	B- / 7.5	4.60	11.42	11.53 /81	15.93 /83	13.96 /77	0.00	0.95
MC	● Fidelity Adv Stk Selector Mid Cap B	FMCBX	B+	(800) 522-7297	B / 7.9	4.36	10.91	10.55 /77	14.97 /75	13.03 /68	0.00	1.76
MC	Fidelity Adv Stk Selector Mid Cap C	FMCEX	B+	(800) 522-7297	B / 7.9	4.39	10.97	10.65 /77	15.06 /75	13.10 /69	0.00	1.69
MC	Fidelity Adv Stk Selector Mid Cap I	FMCCX	A	(800) 522-7297	B+ / 8.7	4.62	11.47	11.72 /81	16.22 /85	14.27 /80	0.27	0.68
MC	Fidelity Adv Stk Selector Mid Cap T	FMCAX	B+	(800) 522-7297	B / 7.7	4.54	11.27	11.23 /79	15.68 /81	13.71 /75	0.00	1.16
GR	Fidelity Adv Stock Sel Lg Cap Val A	FLUAX	B-	(800) 522-7297	C+ / 6.9	0.47	5.05	10.02 /74	16.30 /85	12.25 /62	0.63	1.00
GR	● Fidelity Adv Stock Sel Lg Cap Val B	FLUBX	B+	(800) 522-7297	B- / 7.3	0.23	4.66	9.07 /70	15.37 /78	11.36 /56	0.00	1.81
GR	Fidelity Adv Stock Sel Lg Cap Val C	FLUEX	B+	(800) 522-7297	B- / 7.3	0.24	4.66	9.06 /70	15.34 /78	11.37 /56	0.00	1.81
GR	Fidelity Adv Stock Sel Lg Cap Val I	FLUIX	A+	(800) 522-7297	B+ / 8.3	0.49	5.19	10.22 /75	16.59 /87	12.54 /64	0.92	0.73
GR	Fidelity Adv Stock Sel Lg Cap Val T	FLUTX	B+	(800) 522-7297	B- / 7.1	0.41	4.89	9.65 /73	15.93 /83	11.92 /60	0.38	1.32
SC	Fidelity Adv Stock Select Sm Cap A	FCDAX	C	(800) 522-7297	C+ / 5.9	5.26	14.19	7.50 /59	13.90 /66	14.48 /82	0.11	0.99
SC	● Fidelity Adv Stock Select Sm Cap B	FCDBX	C+	(800) 522-7297	C+ / 6.3	5.07	13.77	6.63 /52	13.01 /60	13.60 /74	0.00	1.81
SC	Fidelity Adv Stock Select Sm Cap C	FCDCX	C	(800) 522-7297	C+ / 6.2	5.05	13.73	6.62 /52	13.00 /60	13.60 /74	0.00	1.79
SC	Fidelity Adv Stock Select Sm Cap I	FCDIX	C+	(800) 522-7297	B- / 7.2	5.34	14.36	7.81 /61	14.37 /70	14.87 /86	0.35	0.70
SC	Fidelity Adv Stock Select Sm Cap T	FCDTX	C	(800) 522-7297	C+ / 6.0	5.19	14.02	7.14 /56	13.55 /64	14.14 /79	0.00	1.32
GR	Fidelity Adv Stock Selector AC A	FMAMX	B+	(800) 544-8544	B- / 7.4	3.48	7.28	11.69 /81	16.28 /85	13.84 /76	0.22	1.01
GR	Fidelity Adv Stock Selector AC B	FHRLX	B+	(800) 544-8544	B / 7.8	3.27	6.83	10.78 /77	15.34 /78	12.95 /68	0.00	1.84
GR	Fidelity Adv Stock Selector AC C	FLACX	B+	(800) 544-8544	B / 7.8	3.29	6.86	10.83 /78	15.38 /78	12.97 /68	0.00	1.78
GR	Fidelity Adv Stock Selector AC Inst	FBRNX	A+	(800) 544-8544	B+ / 8.7	3.54	7.40	11.99 /82	16.58 /87	14.13 /79	0.57	0.74
GR	Fidelity Adv Stock Selector AC T	FSJHX	B+	(800) 544-8544	B / 7.6	3.39	7.12	11.38 /80	15.97 /83	13.54 /73	0.00	1.27
GI	Fidelity Adv Strat Div and Inc A	FASDX	B-	(800) 522-7297	C / 4.8	0.95	5.30	10.20 /75	12.36 /55	11.76 /59	2.33	1.05
GI	● Fidelity Adv Strat Div and Inc B	FBSDX	B	(800) 522-7297	C / 5.1	0.74	4.86	9.34 /71	11.42 /48	10.86 /51	1.58	1.89
GI	Fidelity Adv Strat Div and Inc C	FCSDX	B	(800) 522-7297	C / 5.2	0.68	4.84	9.37 /71	11.48 /49	10.92 /52	1.78	1.81
GI	Fidelity Adv Strat Div and Inc I	FSIDX	B	(800) 522-7297	C+ / 6.0	0.95	5.43	10.46 /76	12.64 /57	12.07 /61	2.70	0.78
GI	Fidelity Adv Strat Div and Inc T	FTSDX	B-	(800) 522-7297	C / 5.0	0.88	5.16	9.93 /74	12.08 /53	11.48 /57	2.15	1.31
GL	Fidelity Adv Strat Real Return A	FSRAX	D	(800) 522-7297	E / 0.4	0.11	-1.23	-3.09 / 8	1.00 / 5	3.76 / 8	1.80	1.06
GL	● Fidelity Adv Strat Real Return B	FSBRX	D	(800) 522-7297	E / 0.5	0.00	-1.60	-3.73 / 7	0.31 / 5	3.05 / 6	1.21	1.74
GL	Fidelity Adv Strat Real Return C	FCSRX	D	(800) 522-7297	E / 0.4	-0.11	-1.66	-3.81 / 7	0.22 / 4	2.97 / 6	1.15	1.82
GL	Fidelity Adv Strat Real Return I	FSIRX	D	(800) 522-7297	E / 0.5	0.11	-1.19	-2.84 / 9	1.22 / 5	3.99 / 8	2.13	0.83
GL	Fidelity Adv Strat Real Return T	FSRTX	D	(800) 522-7297	E / 0.4	0.11	-1.33	-3.09 / 8	0.97 / 5	3.74 / 7	1.79	1.07
TC	Fidelity Adv Technology A	FADTX	C	(800) 522-7297	C+ / 6.0	5.26	7.55	14.11 /90	13.33 /62	14.44 /82	0.06	1.14
TC	● Fidelity Adv Technology B	FABTX	C	(800) 522-7297	C+ / 6.4	5.04	7.11	13.17 /87	12.45 /56	13.57 /74	0.00	1.92
TC	Fidelity Adv Technology C	FTHCX	C	(800) 522-7297	C+ / 6.4	5.06	7.15	13.26 /87	12.49 /56	13.60 /74	0.00	1.87
TC	Fidelity Adv Technology I	FATIX	C+	(800) 522-7297	B- / 7.3	5.33	7.70	14.45 /90	13.69 /65	14.80 /85	0.18	0.83
TC	Fidelity Adv Technology T	FATEX	C	(800) 522-7297	C+ / 6.2	5.16	7.40	13.80 /89	13.05 /60	14.16 /79	0.00	1.38
TC	Fidelity Adv Telecom A	FTUAX	C	(800) 522-7297	C / 4.5	2.49	3.86	5.73 /44	12.57 /56	11.36 /56	3.11	1.18
TC	● Fidelity Adv Telecom B	FTUBX	C	(800) 522-7297	C / 4.8	2.28	3.47	4.90 /38	11.71 /50	10.52 /49	2.35	1.93
TC	Fidelity Adv Telecom C	FTUCX	C	(800) 522-7297	C / 4.9	2.30	3.50	4.98 /38	11.78 /51	10.56 /49	2.67	1.88
TC	Fidelity Adv Telecom I	FTUIX	C+	(800) 522-7297	C+ / 5.6	2.59	4.05	6.04 /47	12.90 /59	11.69 /58	3.54	0.91
TC	Fidelity Adv Telecom T	FTUTX	C	(800) 522-7297	C / 4.6	2.42	3.71	5.40 /42	12.23 /54	11.03 /53	2.89	1.48
EM	Fidelity Adv Total Emerg Mkts A	FTEDX	D-	(800) 522-7297	E / 0.5	1.87	-3.99	-0.10 /15	2.26 / 7	--	1.47	1.98
EM	Fidelity Adv Total Emerg Mkts C	FTEFX	D-	(800) 522-7297	E+ / 0.6	1.59	-4.38	-0.84 /13	1.49 / 6	--	0.90	2.72
EM	Fidelity Adv Total Emerg Mkts Inst	FTEJX	D	(800) 522-7297	E+ / 0.7	1.87	-3.90	0.07 /16	2.49 / 7	--	1.82	1.71
EM	Fidelity Adv Total Emerg Mkts T	FTEHX	D-	(800) 522-7297	E / 0.5	1.77	-4.08	-0.37 /15	2.01 / 6	--	1.24	2.32
FO	Fidelity Adv Total Intl Eq A	FTAEX	D	(800) 522-7297	D / 1.9	5.37	2.93	1.15 /19	8.13 /28	6.03 /17	1.17	1.44
FO	● Fidelity Adv Total Intl Eq B	FTBEX	D	(800) 522-7297	D+ / 2.3	5.04	2.53	0.40 /17	7.28 /23	5.22 /13	0.50	2.22
FO	Fidelity Adv Total Intl Eq C	FTCEX	D	(800) 522-7297	D+ / 2.3	5.08	2.58	0.31 /16	7.33 /23	5.22 /13	0.65	2.22
FO	Fidelity Adv Total Intl Eq Inst	FTEIX	D	(800) 522-7297	C- / 3.0	5.38	3.07	1.41 /20	8.42 /29	6.30 /19	1.49	1.15
FO	Fidelity Adv Total Intl Eq T	FTTEX	D	(800) 522-7297	D / 2.1	5.34	2.92	0.90 /18	7.85 /26	5.74 /15	1.07	1.68
UT	Fidelity Adv Utilities A	FUGAX	C	(800) 522-7297	C / 5.4	-2.88	2.84	6.77 /53	14.79 /73	13.99 /78	1.30	1.16
UT	● Fidelity Adv Utilities B	FAUBX	C+	(800) 522-7297	C+ / 5.8	-3.08	2.46	5.96 /46	13.89 /66	13.11 /69	0.51	1.95
UT	Fidelity Adv Utilities C	FUGCX	C+	(800) 522-7297	C+ / 5.8	-3.05	2.45	6.00 /46	13.95 /67	13.15 /70	0.79	1.89

● Denotes fund is closed to new investors
* Denotes fund is included in Section II

234

RISK			NET ASSETS		ASSET					Portfolio	BULL / BEAR		FUND MANAGER		MINIMUMS		LOADS	
	3 Year		NAV								Last Bull	Last Bear	Manager	Manager	Initial	Additional	Front	Back
Risk	Standard		As of	Total	Cash	Stocks	Bonds	Other		Turnover	Market	Market	Quality	Tenure	Purch.	Purch.	End	End
Rating/Pts	Deviation	Beta	3/31/15	$(Mil)	%	%	%	%		Ratio	Return	Return	Pct	(Years)	$	$	Load	Load
C+ / 6.6	10.4	0.93	33.67	669	2	97	0	1		89	98.5	-21.1	69	4	2,500	0	5.8	0.0
C+ / 6.6	10.4	0.93	31.11	15	2	97	0	1		89	93.1	-21.3	58	4	2,500	0	0.0	0.0
C+ / 6.6	10.4	0.93	31.16	176	2	97	0	1		89	93.7	-21.4	58	4	2,500	0	0.0	0.0
C+ / 6.6	10.4	0.93	35.08	417	2	97	0	1		89	100.4	-21.0	72	4	2,500	0	0.0	0.0
C+ / 6.6	10.4	0.93	33.87	799	2	97	0	1		89	97.2	-21.2	66	4	2,500	0	3.5	0.0
B- / 7.4	9.7	0.99	17.11	27	4	95	0	1		64	100.4	-20.3	71	3	2,500	0	5.8	0.0
B- / 7.4	9.8	0.99	17.07	1	4	95	0	1		64	95.1	-20.5	60	3	2,500	0	0.0	0.0
B- / 7.4	9.8	0.99	16.85	11	4	95	0	1		64	95.1	-20.5	59	3	2,500	0	0.0	0.0
B- / 7.4	9.7	0.99	17.14	10	4	95	0	1		64	102.2	-20.2	73	3	2,500	0	0.0	0.0
B- / 7.4	9.7	0.99	17.09	11	4	95	0	1		64	98.2	-20.3	67	3	2,500	0	3.5	0.0
C+ / 5.6	12.7	0.92	25.60	11	3	96	0	1		73	88.0	-25.5	54	10	2,500	0	5.8	1.5
C+ / 5.6	12.6	0.92	24.46	N/A	3	96	0	1		73	83.1	-25.8	42	10	2,500	0	0.0	1.5
C+ / 5.6	12.7	0.92	24.33	5	3	96	0	1		73	83.1	-25.7	41	10	2,500	0	0.0	1.5
C+ / 5.7	12.7	0.92	26.05	49	3	96	0	1		73	90.4	-25.5	61	10	2,500	0	0.0	1.5
C+ / 5.6	12.7	0.92	25.14	3	3	96	0	1		73	86.2	-25.6	49	10	2,500	0	3.5	1.5
B- / 7.1	9.9	1.00	36.58	226	3	96	0	1		10	98.5	-21.2	69	6	2,500	0	5.8	0.0
B- / 7.0	9.9	1.00	36.68	7	3	96	0	1		10	93.2	-21.5	58	6	2,500	0	0.0	0.0
B- / 7.0	9.9	1.00	36.45	75	3	96	0	1		10	93.3	-21.5	59	6	2,500	0	0.0	0.0
B- / 7.1	9.9	1.00	36.58	330	3	96	0	1		10	100.3	-21.1	72	6	2,500	0	0.0	0.0
B- / 7.1	9.9	1.00	36.55	142	3	96	0	1		10	96.7	-21.3	66	6	2,500	0	3.5	0.0
B / 8.2	6.6	0.62	14.51	691	11	70	9	10		58	69.6	-11.7	86	12	2,500	0	5.8	0.0
B / 8.3	6.6	0.62	14.50	7	11	70	9	10		58	64.8	-11.9	81	12	2,500	0	0.0	0.0
B / 8.3	6.6	0.62	14.43	384	11	70	9	10		58	65.2	-12.0	81	12	2,500	0	0.0	0.0
B / 8.3	6.6	0.62	14.56	368	11	70	9	10		58	71.2	-11.5	87	12	2,500	0	0.0	0.0
B / 8.3	6.6	0.62	14.50	239	11	70	9	10		58	68.2	-11.7	85	12	2,500	0	3.5	0.0
B- / 7.7	5.0	0.24	9.01	105	27	15	56	2		18	11.4	-7.8	49	10	2,500	0	4.0	0.8
B- / 7.7	4.9	0.23	8.98	3	27	15	56	2		18	8.9	-8.1	40	10	2,500	0	0.0	0.8
B- / 7.7	4.9	0.24	8.92	55	27	15	56	2		18	8.6	-8.2	38	10	2,500	0	0.0	0.8
B- / 7.7	5.0	0.24	9.03	411	27	15	56	2		18	12.3	-7.8	52	10	2,500	0	0.0	0.8
B- / 7.7	4.9	0.23	9.02	19	27	15	56	2		18	11.4	-7.9	49	10	2,500	0	4.0	0.8
C / 5.2	12.4	0.98	36.40	447	1	98	0	1		186	87.2	-21.7	36	10	2,500	0	5.8	0.8
C / 5.1	12.4	0.98	31.86	10	1	98	0	1		186	82.3	-22.0	27	10	2,500	0	0.0	0.8
C / 5.1	12.5	0.98	31.98	125	1	98	0	1		186	82.6	-22.0	27	10	2,500	0	0.0	0.8
C / 5.2	12.5	0.98	38.53	765	1	98	0	1		186	89.3	-21.7	41	10	2,500	0	0.0	0.8
C / 5.1	12.5	0.98	34.88	207	1	98	0	1		186	85.7	-21.8	33	10	2,500	0	3.5	0.8
C+ / 6.8	10.7	0.69	61.65	11	0	99	0	1		111	65.0	-16.7	81	2	2,500	0	5.8	0.8
C+ / 6.8	10.7	0.68	61.79	N/A	0	99	0	1		111	60.8	-16.9	76	2	2,500	0	0.0	0.8
C+ / 6.8	10.6	0.68	61.40	7	0	99	0	1		111	61.0	-16.9	76	2	2,500	0	0.0	0.8
C+ / 6.8	10.7	0.69	61.79	3	0	99	0	1		111	66.6	-16.6	83	2	2,500	0	0.0	0.8
C+ / 6.8	10.7	0.69	61.42	5	0	99	0	1		111	63.3	-16.8	79	2	2,500	0	3.5	0.8
B- / 7.4	12.0	0.86	10.91	13	4	73	22	1		102	N/A	N/A	82	4	2,500	0	5.8	1.5
B- / 7.4	12.0	0.86	10.86	10	4	73	22	1		102	N/A	N/A	76	4	2,500	0	0.0	1.5
B- / 7.4	12.0	0.86	10.92	7	4	73	22	1		102	N/A	N/A	83	4	2,500	0	0.0	1.5
B- / 7.4	12.1	0.86	10.91	5	4	73	22	1		102	N/A	N/A	80	4	2,500	0	3.5	1.5
C+ / 6.1	11.8	0.87	8.05	9	1	98	0	1		85	49.7	-25.3	66	8	2,500	0	5.8	1.0
C+ / 6.2	11.7	0.87	8.13	N/A	1	98	0	1		85	46.0	-25.6	54	8	2,500	0	0.0	1.0
C+ / 6.2	11.8	0.88	8.06	4	1	98	0	1		85	45.9	-25.6	54	8	2,500	0	0.0	1.0
C+ / 6.1	11.7	0.87	8.03	2	1	98	0	1		85	51.1	-25.3	70	8	2,500	0	0.0	1.0
C+ / 6.1	11.8	0.87	8.09	12	1	98	0	1		85	48.5	-25.3	62	8	2,500	0	3.5	1.0
C+ / 6.0	12.0	0.81	26.32	157	6	93	0	1		112	61.0	-2.6	92	9	2,500	0	5.8	0.8
C+ / 6.1	12.0	0.81	26.15	4	6	93	0	1		112	56.8	-2.9	90	9	2,500	0	0.0	0.8
C+ / 6.0	12.1	0.81	25.79	59	6	93	0	1		112	57.0	-2.9	90	9	2,500	0	0.0	0.8

Fund Type	Fund Name	Ticker Symbol	Overall Investment Rating	Phone	Performance Rating/Pts	3 Mo	6 Mo	1Yr / Pct	3Yr / Pct	5Yr / Pct	Dividend Yield	Expense Ratio
	99 Pct = Best				PERFORMANCE			Total Return % through 3/31/15			Incl. in Returns	
	0 Pct = Worst								Annualized			
UT	Fidelity Adv Utilities I	FUGIX	C+	(800) 522-7297	C+ / 6.6	-2.83	2.99	7.08 /56	15.13 /76	14.32 /81	1.64	0.85
UT	Fidelity Adv Utilities T	FAUFX	C	(800) 522-7297	C+ / 5.6	-2.95	2.72	6.47 /50	14.46 /71	13.68 /75	1.06	1.45
GR	Fidelity Adv Value A	FAVFX	A	(800) 522-7297	B+ / 8.6	2.97	8.58	10.48 /76	18.34 /95	14.46 /82	0.20	1.32
GR	● Fidelity Adv Value B	FBVFX	A+	(800) 522-7297	B+ / 8.9	2.76	8.14	9.62 /73	17.44 /92	13.60 /74	0.00	2.16
GR	Fidelity Adv Value C	FCVFX	A+	(800) 522-7297	B+ / 8.9	2.72	8.11	9.59 /72	17.43 /92	13.59 /74	0.00	2.09
GR	Fidelity Adv Value I	FVIFX	A+	(800) 522-7297	A / 9.4	3.03	8.71	10.77 /77	18.67 /96	14.77 /85	0.49	1.00
GR	Fidelity Adv Value Leaders A	FVLAX	A-	(800) 522-7297	B / 7.8	2.51	10.42	13.92 /89	16.29 /85	10.92 /52	0.66	1.38
GR	● Fidelity Adv Value Leaders B	FVLBX	A	(800) 522-7297	B / 8.2	2.29	10.05	13.06 /87	15.44 /78	10.10 /45	0.00	2.20
GR	Fidelity Adv Value Leaders C	FVLCX	A	(800) 522-7297	B / 8.2	2.38	10.11	13.07 /87	15.46 /79	10.10 /45	0.00	2.17
GR	Fidelity Adv Value Leaders I	FVLIX	A+	(800) 522-7297	A- / 9.0	2.61	10.59	14.22 /90	16.66 /88	11.26 /55	0.98	1.09
GR	Fidelity Adv Value Leaders T	FVLTX	A-	(800) 522-7297	B / 8.0	2.50	10.34	13.68 /89	16.03 /84	10.67 /50	0.43	1.66
MC	Fidelity Adv Value Strategies A	FSOAX	B+	(800) 522-7297	B- / 7.4	4.40	6.16	9.89 /74	16.62 /88	13.40 /72	0.71	1.04
MC	● Fidelity Adv Value Strategies B	FASBX	A-	(800) 522-7297	B / 7.8	4.18	5.70	8.97 /69	15.68 /81	12.53 /64	0.00	1.83
MC	Fidelity Adv Value Strategies C	FVCSX	A-	(800) 522-7297	B / 7.9	4.20	5.73	9.04 /69	15.74 /81	12.55 /64	0.16	1.78
MC	Fidelity Adv Value Strategies Fd	FSLSX	A+	(800) 522-7297	B+ / 8.7	4.47	6.30	10.16 /75	16.95 /90	13.74 /75	0.91	0.73
MC	Fidelity Adv Value Strategies I	FASOX	A+	(800) 522-7297	B+ / 8.7	4.47	6.28	10.16 /75	16.94 /89	13.74 /75	0.96	0.76
MC	Fidelity Adv Value Strategies T	FASPX	A-	(800) 522-7297	B / 7.7	4.34	6.04	9.66 /73	16.39 /86	13.19 /70	0.50	1.23
GR	Fidelity Adv Value T	FTVFX	A	(800) 522-7297	B+ / 8.8	2.90	8.42	10.18 /75	18.02 /94	14.17 /79	0.00	1.60
CV	Fidelity Advisor Convertible Sec A	FACVX	C+	(800) 522-7297	C / 4.6	1.03	4.78	7.80 /61	12.37 /55	10.72 /50	1.50	0.86
CV	● Fidelity Advisor Convertible Sec B	FCBVX	C+	(800) 522-7297	C / 4.9	0.84	4.33	6.94 /55	11.44 /48	9.79 /43	0.76	1.69
CV	Fidelity Advisor Convertible Sec C	FCCVX	C+	(800) 522-7297	C / 5.0	0.84	4.36	7.01 /55	11.52 /49	9.86 /43	0.89	1.62
CV	Fidelity Advisor Convertible Sec I	FICVX	B-	(800) 522-7297	C+ / 5.8	1.12	4.92	8.09 /64	12.66 /57	11.00 /53	1.81	0.61
CV	Fidelity Advisor Convertible Sec T	FTCVX	C+	(800) 522-7297	C / 4.8	0.96	4.63	7.53 /59	12.04 /53	10.39 /48	1.25	1.14
FO	Fidelity Advisor Europe A	FHJUX	D-	(800) 544-8544	D+ / 2.7	5.14	2.43	-4.37 / 6	10.60 /43	6.93 /23	2.14	1.35
FO	● Fidelity Advisor Europe B	FHJWX	D-	(800) 544-8544	C- / 3.1	4.94	2.02	-5.08 / 5	9.77 /38	6.12 /17	1.77	2.10
FO	Fidelity Advisor Europe C	FHJTX	D-	(800) 544-8544	C- / 3.1	4.97	2.04	-5.07 / 5	9.77 /38	6.13 /18	1.67	2.11
FO	Fidelity Advisor Europe Inst	FHJMX	D	(800) 544-8544	C- / 4.0	5.27	2.64	-3.99 / 7	10.93 /45	7.23 /25	2.45	0.97
FO	Fidelity Advisor Europe T	FHJVX	D-	(800) 544-8544	D+ / 2.9	5.09	2.30	-4.62 / 6	10.31 /41	6.65 /21	2.07	1.62
GL	Fidelity Advisor Global Balanced A	FGLAX	D-	(800) 522-7297	D- / 1.2	1.76	1.07	-0.27 /15	6.60 /19	6.78 /22	0.04	1.28
GL	● Fidelity Advisor Global Balanced B	FGLBX	D-	(800) 522-7297	D- / 1.4	1.54	0.64	-1.06 /13	5.76 /16	5.95 /17	0.00	2.07
GL	Fidelity Advisor Global Balanced C	FGLCX	D-	(800) 522-7297	D- / 1.4	1.57	0.65	-1.07 /13	5.74 /16	5.95 /17	0.00	2.08
GL	Fidelity Advisor Global Balanced I	FGLIX	D-	(800) 522-7297	D / 1.9	1.84	1.16	-0.01 /16	6.89 /21	7.07 /23	0.30	1.03
GL	Fidelity Advisor Global Balanced T	FGLTX	D-	(800) 522-7297	D- / 1.3	1.68	0.93	-0.53 /14	6.31 /18	6.52 /20	0.00	1.55
FO	Fidelity Advisor Intl SC Opp A	FOPAX	C-	(800) 522-7297	C- / 4.1	6.71	5.48	0.45 /17	12.54 /56	11.68 /58	0.33	1.63
FO	● Fidelity Advisor Intl SC Opp B	FOPBX	C	(800) 522-7297	C / 4.5	6.48	5.05	-0.42 /14	11.68 /50	10.83 /51	0.00	2.38
FO	Fidelity Advisor Intl SC Opp C	FOPCX	C	(800) 522-7297	C / 4.5	6.44	5.01	-0.43 /14	11.69 /50	10.82 /51	0.00	2.38
FO	Fidelity Advisor Intl SC Opp I	FOPIX	C	(800) 522-7297	C / 5.3	6.80	5.64	0.66 /17	12.86 /59	11.97 /60	0.73	1.36
FO	Fidelity Advisor Intl SC Opp T	FOPTX	C-	(800) 522-7297	C / 4.3	6.60	5.33	0.13 /16	12.23 /54	11.37 /56	0.04	1.89
EM	Fidelity Advisor Latin America Fd A	FLFAX	E-	(800) 544-8544	E- / 0.0	-9.35	-23.06	-22.78 / 1	-16.96 / 0	-8.78 / 1	1.22	1.38
EM	● Fidelity Advisor Latin America Fd B	FLFBX	E-	(800) 544-8544	E- / 0.0	-9.53	-23.35	-23.37 / 1	-17.58 / 0	-9.41 / 1	0.00	2.14
EM	Fidelity Advisor Latin America Fd C	FLFCX	E-	(800) 544-8544	E- / 0.0	-9.54	-23.34	-23.36 / 1	-17.58 / 0	-9.41 / 1	0.21	2.13
EM	Fidelity Advisor Latin America Fd I	FLFIX	E-	(800) 544-8544	E- / 0.0	-9.29	-22.93	-22.55 / 1	-16.68 / 0	-8.44 / 1	1.79	1.04
EM	Fidelity Advisor Latin America Fd T	FLFTX	E-	(800) 544-8544	E- / 0.0	-9.44	-23.18	-23.03 / 1	-17.19 / 0	-8.98 / 1	0.92	1.65
GI	Fidelity Advisor Mega Cap Stock A	FGTAX	B-	(800) 544-8544	C+ / 6.1	-0.37	2.96	9.18 /70	15.23 /77	14.13 /79	0.98	0.96
GI	● Fidelity Advisor Mega Cap Stock B	FGRBX	B-	(800) 544-8544	C+ / 6.5	-0.61	2.52	8.39 /65	14.29 /69	13.23 /70	0.11	1.78
GI	Fidelity Advisor Mega Cap Stock C	FGRCX	B-	(800) 544-8544	C+ / 6.5	-0.55	2.57	8.48 /66	14.37 /70	13.29 /71	0.46	1.71
GI	Fidelity Advisor Mega Cap Stock I	FTRIX	B+	(800) 544-8544	B- / 7.4	-0.30	3.09	9.55 /72	15.53 /79	14.42 /82	0.87	0.71
GI	Fidelity Advisor Mega Cap Stock T	FTGRX	B-	(800) 544-8544	C+ / 6.3	-0.49	2.82	8.95 /69	14.92 /74	13.81 /76	0.75	1.22
GL	Fidelity Advisor Series Equity Gro	FMFMX	U	(800) 522-7297	U /	4.68	5.75	--	--	--	0.00	N/A
GR	Fidelity Advisor Series Equity Inc	FLMLX	U	(800) 544-8544	U /	-0.40	2.50	7.81 /61	--	--	2.13	0.72
GL	Fidelity Advisor Series Growth Opp	FAOFX	U	(800) 522-7297	U /	2.92	8.64	12.30 /84	--	--	0.13	0.80
GL	Fidelity Advisor Series Small Cap	FSSFX	U	(800) 522-7297	U /	5.99	13.50	13.72 /89	--	--	0.16	0.98

● Denotes fund is closed to new investors
★ Denotes fund is included in Section II

www.thestreetratings.com

RISK			NET ASSETS		ASSET					BULL / BEAR		FUND MANAGER		MINIMUMS		LOADS	
	3 Year		NAV						Portfolio	Last Bull	Last Bear	Manager	Manager	Initial	Additional	Front	Back
Risk Rating/Pts	Standard Deviation	Beta	As of 3/31/15	Total $(Mil)	Cash %	Stocks %	Bonds %	Other %	Turnover Ratio	Market Return	Market Return	Quality Pct	Tenure (Years)	Purch. $	Purch. $	End Load	End Load
C+ / 6.0	12.1	0.81	26.79	44	6	93	0	1	112	62.7	-2.5	92	9	2,500	0	0.0	0.8
C+ / 6.1	12.0	0.81	26.36	52	6	93	0	1	112	59.5	-2.7	91	9	2,500	0	3.5	0.8
C+ / 6.9	10.8	1.05	22.57	52	7	92	0	1	78	112.0	-24.8	79	5	2,500	0	5.8	0.0
C+ / 6.9	10.8	1.05	21.63	1	7	92	0	1	78	106.4	-25.0	72	5	2,500	0	0.0	0.0
C+ / 6.9	10.8	1.05	21.56	19	7	92	0	1	78	106.5	-25.0	72	5	2,500	0	0.0	0.0
C+ / 6.9	10.7	1.05	22.76	11	7	92	0	1	78	113.8	-24.7	81	5	2,500	0	0.0	0.0
B- / 7.2	10.9	1.08	16.76	17	7	92	0	1	182	94.6	-23.9	52	N/A	2,500	0	5.8	0.0
B- / 7.2	10.9	1.08	16.55	N/A	7	92	0	1	182	89.7	-24.1	40	N/A	2,500	0	0.0	0.0
B- / 7.2	10.9	1.08	16.36	5	7	92	0	1	182	89.8	-24.1	41	N/A	2,500	0	0.0	0.0
B- / 7.2	10.9	1.08	16.88	2	7	92	0	1	182	96.6	-23.8	56	N/A	2,500	0	0.0	0.0
B- / 7.2	11.0	1.08	16.78	8	7	92	0	1	182	92.8	-23.9	48	N/A	2,500	0	3.5	0.0
B- / 7.2	9.9	0.82	40.32	238	4	94	0	2	6	106.1	-26.8	87	5	2,500	0	5.8	0.0
B- / 7.2	9.9	0.82	36.92	6	4	94	0	2	6	100.5	-27.1	82	5	2,500	0	0.0	0.0
B- / 7.2	9.9	0.82	36.47	54	4	94	0	2	6	100.9	-27.1	82	5	2,500	0	0.0	0.0
B- / 7.3	9.9	0.82	45.10	727	4	94	0	2	6	108.2	-26.8	88	5	2,500	0	0.0	0.0
B- / 7.2	9.9	0.82	43.03	86	4	94	0	2	6	108.1	-26.8	88	5	2,500	0	0.0	0.0
B- / 7.2	10.0	0.82	41.81	328	4	94	0	2	6	104.7	-26.9	86	5	2,500	0	3.5	0.0
C+ / 6.9	10.8	1.05	22.37	19	7	92	0	1	78	110.1	-24.9	76	5	2,500	0	3.5	0.0
B- / 7.3	8.4	1.04	32.43	145	15	31	0	54	23	70.4	-19.9	42	10	2,500	0	5.8	0.0
B- / 7.4	8.4	1.04	32.37	1	15	31	0	54	23	65.7	-20.2	31	10	2,500	0	0.0	0.0
B- / 7.4	8.4	1.04	32.22	50	15	31	0	54	23	65.9	-20.1	32	10	2,500	0	0.0	0.0
B- / 7.3	8.4	1.04	32.53	205	15	31	0	54	23	71.8	-19.8	46	10	2,500	0	0.0	0.0
B- / 7.4	8.4	1.04	32.44	14	15	31	0	54	23	68.6	-20.0	38	10	2,500	0	3.5	0.0
C / 4.8	13.8	1.00	37.05	26	0	100	0	0	80	65.6	-29.4	77	2	2,500	0	5.8	1.0
C / 4.8	13.8	1.00	36.94	1	0	100	0	0	80	61.3	-29.6	69	2	2,500	0	0.0	1.0
C / 4.8	13.8	1.00	36.98	8	0	100	0	0	80	61.3	-29.6	69	2	2,500	0	0.0	1.0
C / 4.8	13.8	1.00	37.13	6	0	100	0	0	80	67.2	-29.3	79	2	2,500	0	0.0	0.0
C / 4.8	13.8	1.00	36.99	14	0	100	0	0	80	64.1	-29.5	74	2	2,500	0	3.5	1.0
C+ / 6.2	7.4	1.10	23.09	44	6	57	36	1	157	35.7	-13.0	24	9	2,500	0	5.8	1.0
C+ / 6.4	7.4	1.10	23.01	2	6	57	36	1	157	32.1	-13.3	17	9	2,500	0	0.0	1.0
C+ / 6.3	7.4	1.10	22.71	29	6	57	36	1	157	32.0	-13.3	17	9	2,500	0	0.0	1.0
C+ / 6.1	7.4	1.10	23.20	6	6	57	36	1	157	37.0	-12.9	27	9	2,500	0	0.0	1.0
C+ / 6.2	7.4	1.10	22.99	18	6	57	36	1	157	34.5	-13.1	21	9	2,500	0	3.5	1.0
C+ / 6.5	10.9	0.75	14.48	26	3	96	0	1	18	67.5	-20.5	94	7	2,500	0	5.8	2.0
C+ / 6.5	10.9	0.75	14.14	1	3	96	0	1	18	63.2	-20.7	92	7	2,500	0	0.0	2.0
C+ / 6.5	10.9	0.75	14.05	8	3	96	0	1	18	63.2	-20.7	92	7	2,500	0	0.0	2.0
C+ / 6.5	10.8	0.74	14.60	80	3	96	0	1	18	69.0	-20.4	94	7	2,500	0	0.0	2.0
C+ / 6.5	10.9	0.75	14.37	10	3	96	0	1	18	66.0	-20.6	93	7	2,500	0	3.5	2.0
D- / 1.2	19.3	1.25	21.62	23	2	97	0	1	30	-22.8	-24.9	0	6	2,500	0	5.8	1.5
D- / 1.2	19.3	1.25	21.93	1	2	97	0	1	30	-24.7	-25.1	0	6	2,500	0	0.0	1.5
D- / 1.2	19.3	1.25	21.82	8	2	97	0	1	30	-24.7	-25.1	0	6	2,500	0	0.0	1.5
D- / 1.2	19.3	1.25	21.57	2	2	97	0	1	30	-21.9	-24.8	0	6	2,500	0	0.0	1.5
D- / 1.2	19.3	1.25	21.67	7	2	97	0	1	30	-23.5	-25.0	0	6	2,500	0	3.5	1.5
B- / 7.0	10.7	1.09	16.31	113	0	99	0	1	28	102.5	-16.1	36	6	2,500	0	5.8	0.0
B- / 7.0	10.6	1.08	16.28	1	0	99	0	1	28	97.0	-16.3	27	6	2,500	0	0.0	0.0
B- / 7.0	10.7	1.09	16.13	34	0	99	0	1	28	97.5	-16.4	27	6	2,500	0	0.0	0.0
B- / 7.0	10.7	1.09	16.46	189	0	99	0	1	28	104.4	-16.0	39	6	2,500	0	0.0	0.0
B- / 7.0	10.7	1.09	16.32	23	0	99	0	1	28	100.7	-16.2	32	6	2,500	0	3.5	0.0
U /	N/A	N/A	10.97	943	0	0	0	100	0	N/A	N/A	N/A	1	0	0	0.0	0.0
U /	N/A	N/A	12.68	1,868	5	94	0	1	44	N/A	N/A	N/A	3	0	0	0.0	0.0
U /	N/A	N/A	11.77	989	2	97	0	1	16	N/A	N/A	N/A	6	0	0	0.0	0.0
U /	N/A	N/A	11.64	531	13	85	0	2	58	N/A	N/A	N/A	2	0	0	0.0	0.0

	99 Pct = Best 0 Pct = Worst				**PERFORMANCE**							
			Overall		**Perfor-**	Total Return % through 3/31/15					Incl. in Returns	
		Ticker	**Investment**		**mance**				Annualized		Dividend	Expense
Fund Type	Fund Name	Symbol	**Rating**	Phone	**Rating/Pts**	3 Mo	6 Mo	1Yr / Pct	3Yr / Pct	5Yr / Pct	Yield	Ratio
GR	Fidelity Advisor Srs Opp Insights	FAMGX	**U**	(800) 522-7297	**U /**	4.05	7.55	14.70 /91	--	--	0.00	0.88
FO	Fidelity Advisor Worldwide A	FWAFX	**C-**	(800) 522-7297	**C / 5.0**	5.16	5.98	5.07 /39	13.25 /61	11.47 /57	0.00	1.29
FO	● Fidelity Advisor Worldwide B	FWBFX	**C-**	(800) 522-7297	**C / 5.4**	4.92	5.52	4.26 /33	12.37 /55	10.62 /50	0.00	2.07
FO	Fidelity Advisor Worldwide C	FWCFX	**C-**	(800) 522-7297	**C / 5.4**	4.94	5.56	4.28 /34	12.42 /55	10.64 /50	0.00	2.02
FO	Fidelity Advisor Worldwide I	FWIFX	**C**	(800) 522-7297	**C+ / 6.1**	5.23	6.06	5.37 /41	13.56 /64	11.76 /59	0.29	0.99
FO	Fidelity Advisor Worldwide T	FWTFX	**C-**	(800) 522-7297	**C / 5.1**	5.09	5.81	4.76 /37	12.93 /59	11.16 /54	0.00	1.56
AA	Fidelity Asset Manager 20%	FASIX	**C-**	(800) 544-8544	**D- / 1.5**	1.68	2.86	4.17 /33	4.77 /12	5.35 /13	1.51	0.53
GI	Fidelity Asset Manager 30%	FTANX	**C-**	(800) 544-8544	**D / 2.1**	2.06	3.43	5.09 /39	6.20 /18	6.57 /20	1.63	0.55
GI	Fidelity Asset Manager 40%	FFANX	**C**	(800) 544-8544	**D+ / 2.8**	2.33	3.84	5.60 /43	7.44 /24	7.51 /26	1.53	0.56
AA	Fidelity Asset Manager 50%	FASMX	**C-**	(800) 544-8544	**C- / 3.5**	2.64	4.28	6.15 /48	8.61 /30	8.40 /32	1.51	0.66
GI	Fidelity Asset Manager 60%	FSANX	**C**	(800) 544-8544	**C- / 4.1**	2.80	4.59	6.52 /51	9.66 /37	9.06 /37	1.30	0.73
AA	Fidelity Asset Manager 70%	FASGX	**C**	(800) 544-8544	**C / 4.7**	3.09	4.88	6.79 /53	10.71 /44	9.82 /43	1.28	0.73
AG	Fidelity Asset Manager 85%	FAMRX	**C**	(800) 544-8544	**C+ / 5.7**	3.47	5.38	7.37 /58	12.43 /56	10.77 /51	1.22	0.75
AA	Fidelity AZ Conservative Index		**C-**	(800) 544-8544	**E+ / 0.7**	0.69	1.48	2.43 /24	1.26 / 5	2.43 / 5	0.00	0.34
GL	Fidelity AZ International Index		**D**	(800) 544-8544	**D+ / 2.8**	5.30	1.02	-1.24 /12	8.77 /31	6.04 /17	0.00	0.35
AA	Fidelity AZ Spartan 500 Index		**A**	(800) 544-8544	**B / 8.1**	0.91	5.85	12.51 /85	15.87 /82	14.23 /80	0.00	0.25
AA	Fidelity AZ Ttl Mkt Index		**A**	(800) 544-8544	**B+ / 8.3**	1.78	7.02	12.07 /83	16.12 /84	14.51 /82	0.00	0.25
★ BA	Fidelity Balanced Fd	FBALX	**B-**	(800) 544-8544	**C+ / 5.7**	2.24	5.48	10.60 /77	12.05 /53	11.26 /55	1.46	0.56
BA	Fidelity Balanced K	FBAKX	**B-**	(800) 544-8544	**C+ / 5.8**	2.24	5.49	10.71 /77	12.17 /54	11.38 /56	1.54	0.46
★ GR	Fidelity Blue Chip Growth Fd	FBGRX	**A**	(800) 544-8544	**A+ / 9.7**	5.47	11.13	18.66 /96	18.79 /96	16.98 /96	0.11	0.80
GR	Fidelity Blue Chip Growth K	FBGKX	**A**	(800) 544-8544	**A+ / 9.7**	5.51	11.20	18.81 /96	18.96 /97	17.15 /96	0.22	0.68
GR	Fidelity Blue Chip Value	FBCVX	**A+**	(800) 544-8544	**A- / 9.0**	2.52	10.56	14.24 /90	16.86 /89	11.29 /55	1.35	0.73
FO	Fidelity Canada Fund	FICDX	**E**	(800) 544-8544	**E+ / 0.6**	-5.63	-7.78	-3.11 / 8	3.35 / 9	3.17 / 6	1.21	0.98
★ GI	Fidelity Capital and Income	FAGIX	**C-**	(800) 544-8544	**C- / 3.9**	4.01	4.49	7.02 /55	9.37 /35	9.05 /37	3.94	0.71
★ GR	Fidelity Capital Appreciation Fd	FDCAX	**A-**	(800) 544-8544	**A / 9.3**	4.16	7.74	14.57 /91	17.88 /94	15.29 /89	0.25	0.82
GR	Fidelity Capital Appreciation K	FCAKX	**A-**	(800) 544-8544	**A / 9.4**	4.19	7.80	14.68 /91	18.03 /94	15.46 /90	0.36	0.70
FO	Fidelity China Region Fund	FHKCX	**C+**	(800) 544-8544	**B+ / 8.5**	6.43	12.24	15.06 /92	14.83 /73	9.48 /40	0.89	1.01
★ GR	Fidelity Contrafund Fd	FCNTX	**B+**	(800) 544-8544	**B+ / 8.3**	4.05	7.30	13.46 /88	15.64 /80	14.91 /86	0.23	0.64
GR	Fidelity Contrafund K	FCNKX	**A-**	(800) 544-8544	**B+ / 8.4**	4.08	7.35	13.57 /88	15.77 /81	15.05 /87	0.33	0.54
CV	Fidelity Convertible Securities	FCVSX	**B-**	(800) 544-8544	**C+ / 5.8**	1.11	4.92	8.13 /64	12.69 /57	11.03 /53	1.82	0.58
GL	Fidelity DE International Index		**D**	(800) 544-8544	**C- / 3.0**	5.26	1.03	-1.17 /12	8.81 /32	6.07 /17	0.00	0.35
AA	Fidelity DE Spartan 500 Index		**A**	(800) 544-8544	**B / 8.1**	0.92	5.83	12.52 /85	15.89 /82	14.20 /79	0.00	0.25
AA	Fidelity DE Total Market Index		**A**	(800) 544-8544	**B+ / 8.3**	1.78	7.01	12.06 /83	16.13 /84	14.51 /82	0.00	0.25
GR	Fidelity Disciplined Equity Fd	FDEQX	**A**	(800) 544-8544	**A- / 9.0**	2.50	7.72	12.42 /84	17.28 /91	12.77 /66	1.03	0.50
GR	Fidelity Disciplined Equity K	FDEKX	**A**	(800) 544-8544	**A- / 9.1**	2.53	7.75	12.56 /85	17.42 /92	12.93 /68	1.14	0.39
★ FO	Fidelity Diversified Intl Fd	FDIVX	**C-**	(800) 544-8544	**C / 4.6**	6.36	5.18	3.80 /31	10.97 /45	7.66 /28	1.06	0.91
FO	Fidelity Diversified Intl K	FDIKX	**C-**	(800) 544-8544	**C / 4.7**	6.40	5.27	3.95 /31	11.14 /46	7.83 /29	1.19	0.78
★ GR	Fidelity Dividend Growth Fd	FDGFX	**C+**	(800) 544-8544	**B- / 7.4**	1.17	5.19	11.51 /80	14.97 /75	12.95 /68	1.30	0.56
GR	Fidelity Dividend Growth K	FDGKX	**C+**	(800) 544-8544	**B- / 7.5**	1.20	5.22	11.63 /81	15.11 /76	13.11 /69	1.42	0.44
EM	Fidelity Emerg Mkts Discv	FEDDX	**D**	(800) 522-7297	**E+ / 0.8**	1.72	-5.43	0.17 /16	3.72 / 9	--	0.00	1.48
FO	Fidelity Emerging Asia Fund	FSEAX	**C-**	(800) 544-8544	**C- / 4.2**	5.21	7.17	13.75 /89	8.07 /27	7.52 /27	0.86	1.04
EM	Fidelity Emerging Markets Fd	FEMKX	**E+**	(800) 544-8544	**D- / 1.0**	2.80	1.65	4.26 /33	3.41 / 9	2.60 / 5	0.57	1.07
EM	Fidelity Emerging Markets K	FKEMX	**E+**	(800) 544-8544	**D- / 1.1**	2.84	1.74	4.48 /35	3.63 / 9	2.81 / 6	0.78	0.86
IN	Fidelity Equity Dividend Income	FEQTX	**B+**	(800) 544-8544	**B- / 7.1**	0.13	5.11	10.28 /75	14.73 /73	11.54 /57	2.53	0.63
IN	Fidelity Equity Dividend Income K	FETKX	**B+**	(800) 544-8544	**B- / 7.2**	0.13	5.16	10.38 /76	14.85 /74	11.68 /58	2.62	0.52
IN	Fidelity Equity Income I	FEQIX	**B-**	(800) 544-8544	**C+ / 6.1**	0.19	2.15	6.49 /51	13.91 /66	11.00 /53	2.58	0.66
IN	Fidelity Equity Income K	FEIKX	**B-**	(800) 544-8544	**C+ / 6.2**	0.21	2.21	6.62 /52	14.05 /67	11.15 /54	2.69	0.54
FO	Fidelity Europe	FIEUX	**D+**	(800) 544-8544	**C- / 3.8**	5.22	2.60	-4.05 / 7	10.91 /45	7.22 /24	2.46	0.97
FS	Fidelity Event Driven Opportunities	FARNX	**U**	(800) 544-8544	**U /**	3.44	10.90	7.37 /58	--	--	0.51	1.42
GR	Fidelity Export and Multination	FEXPX	**C-**	(800) 544-8544	**C+ / 6.5**	2.72	7.98	11.99 /82	13.24 /61	11.33 /55	1.59	0.78
GR	Fidelity Export and Multination K	FEXKX	**C-**	(800) 544-8544	**C+ / 6.6**	2.78	8.05	12.17 /83	13.40 /63	11.51 /57	1.72	0.64
AG	● Fidelity Fifty Fund	FFTYX	**B**	(800) 544-8544	**B / 7.7**	4.29	5.98	7.21 /57	15.66 /80	14.10 /79	0.06	0.83

● Denotes fund is closed to new investors
★ Denotes fund is included in Section II

www.thestreetratings.com

RISK			NET ASSETS		ASSET					BULL / BEAR		FUND MANAGER		MINIMUMS		LOADS	
	3 Year		NAV						Portfolio	Last Bull	Last Bear	Manager	Manager	Initial	Additional	Front	Back
Risk Rating/Pts	Standard Deviation	Beta	As of 3/31/15	Total $(Mil)	Cash %	Stocks %	Bonds %	Other %	Turnover Ratio	Market Return	Market Return	Quality Pct	Tenure (Years)	Purch. $	Purch. $	End Load	End Load
U /	N/A	N/A	15.58	867	5	94	0	1	52	N/A	N/A	N/A	3	0	0	0.0	0.0
C / 5.0	11.4	0.78	23.24	29	2	97	0	1	163	73.0	-20.1	94	9	2,500	0	5.8	1.0
C / 5.1	11.4	0.78	23.01	1	2	97	0	1	163	68.5	-20.3	93	9	2,500	0	0.0	1.0
C / 5.1	11.4	0.78	22.94	10	2	97	0	1	163	68.7	-20.3	93	9	2,500	0	0.0	1.0
C / 5.0	11.4	0.78	23.35	21	2	97	0	1	163	74.6	-19.9	95	9	2,500	0	0.0	1.0
C / 5.0	11.4	0.78	23.12	13	2	97	0	1	163	71.5	-20.2	94	9	2,500	0	3.5	1.0
B / 8.9	2.7	0.40	13.43	5,014	25	21	53	1	13	21.9	-3.2	73	6	2,500	0	0.0	0.0
B / 8.7	3.5	0.31	10.69	833	15	31	52	2	13	29.8	-5.6	80	6	2,500	0	0.0	0.0
B / 8.4	4.5	0.41	10.98	908	10	42	46	2	11	37.3	-8.0	77	6	2,500	0	0.0	0.0
B- / 7.3	5.4	0.91	17.49	8,167	6	51	42	1	10	44.5	-10.6	50	6	2,500	0	0.0	0.0
B- / 7.3	6.3	0.61	11.38	1,368	3	61	35	1	11	51.8	-13.0	68	6	2,500	0	0.0	0.0
C+ / 6.8	7.4	1.24	20.36	3,999	5	68	26	1	13	59.4	-15.7	29	6	2,500	0	0.0	0.0
C+ / 5.9	8.8	0.87	17.00	1,428	4	84	10	2	14	71.5	-19.2	47	6	2,500	0	0.0	0.0
B+ / 9.9	1.4	0.01	13.07	3	55	0	44	1	46	3.8	4.5	78	9	50	25	0.0	0.0
C+ / 6.0	13.3	1.97	11.93	6	4	95	0	1	3	50.7	-23.0	3	9	50	25	0.0	1.0
B- / 7.4	9.5	1.66	17.72	15	1	98	0	1	2	98.7	-16.3	32	9	50	25	0.0	0.0
B- / 7.2	9.8	1.68	18.29	11	2	97	0	1	0	100.0	-17.7	31	9	50	25	0.0	0.0
B- / 7.5	6.6	1.15	23.28	20,775	6	65	28	1	176	64.0	-10.4	60	7	2,500	0	0.0	0.0
B- / 7.4	6.6	1.15	23.28	7,954	6	65	28	1	176	64.6	-10.3	62	7	0	0	0.0	0.0
C+ / 5.9	11.6	1.08	72.16	14,299	0	99	0	1	57	114.0	-17.2	78	6	2,500	0	0.0	0.0
C+ / 5.9	11.6	1.08	72.25	6,019	0	99	0	1	57	114.9	-17.1	79	6	0	0	0.0	0.0
B- / 7.2	11.0	1.09	16.71	375	8	91	0	1	102	97.5	-23.9	58	1	2,500	0	0.0	0.0
C- / 3.3	12.0	0.69	49.64	1,669	2	97	0	1	85	26.4	-23.8	25	7	2,500	0	0.0	1.5
C+ / 6.5	5.0	0.40	9.97	10,985	7	18	74	1	47	47.5	-12.8	89	12	2,500	0	0.0	1.0
C+ / 5.7	9.6	0.87	37.53	6,285	4	95	0	1	112	110.9	-17.0	90	10	2,500	0	0.0	0.0
C+ / 5.7	9.5	0.87	37.59	2,659	4	95	0	1	112	111.9	-16.9	90	10	0	0	0.0	0.0
C / 4.4	12.3	0.63	32.63	1,426	3	96	0	1	87	69.4	-27.1	97	4	2,500	0	0.0	1.5
C+ / 6.5	9.7	0.93	100.96	77,111	1	98	0	1	46	93.5	-14.4	74	25	2,500	0	0.0	0.0
C+ / 6.5	9.7	0.93	100.91	34,734	1	98	0	1	46	94.2	-14.4	75	25	0	0	0.0	0.0
B- / 7.3	8.4	1.04	32.58	2,233	15	31	0	54	23	72.0	-19.8	47	10	2,500	0	0.0	0.0
C+ / 6.0	13.2	1.96	11.80	4	4	95	0	1	8	51.0	-23.1	3	9	50	25	0.0	0.0
B- / 7.4	9.5	1.66	17.62	9	1	98	0	1	22	98.9	-16.5	33	9	50	25	0.0	0.0
B- / 7.2	9.8	1.69	18.31	8	2	97	0	1	24	100.1	-17.7	31	9	50	25	0.0	0.0
C+ / 6.6	10.3	1.06	34.47	1,261	1	98	0	1	184	105.0	-21.9	68	2	2,500	0	0.0	0.0
C+ / 6.6	10.3	1.06	34.42	163	1	98	0	1	184	105.9	-21.9	69	2	0	0	0.0	0.0
C+ / 6.0	12.0	0.89	36.64	14,143	5	94	0	1	39	62.3	-24.5	86	14	2,500	0	0.0	1.0
C+ / 6.0	12.0	0.89	36.59	11,276	5	94	0	1	39	63.1	-24.5	87	14	0	0	0.0	1.0
C / 5.0	10.5	1.08	33.81	6,529	3	96	0	1	99	99.5	-24.6	35	1	2,500	0	0.0	0.0
C / 4.9	10.6	1.08	33.78	2,129	3	96	0	1	99	100.5	-24.5	37	1	0	0	0.0	0.0
B- / 7.3	11.7	0.80	11.84	67	4	95	0	1	148	N/A	N/A	89	1	2,500	0	0.0	2.0
C+ / 6.2	12.4	0.76	34.35	1,141	3	96	0	1	90	47.2	-25.4	75	6	2,500	0	0.0	1.5
C / 5.1	13.9	0.98	24.99	2,365	1	98	0	1	94	31.1	-28.3	88	3	2,500	0	0.0	1.5
C / 5.1	13.9	0.99	25.00	593	1	98	0	1	94	32.1	-28.2	88	3	0	0	0.0	1.5
B- / 7.7	9.1	0.93	26.72	5,122	7	92	0	1	52	92.3	-22.3	66	4	2,500	0	0.0	0.0
B- / 7.7	9.1	0.93	26.72	375	7	92	0	1	52	93.2	-22.3	66	4	0	0	0.0	0.0
B- / 7.2	9.2	0.93	57.70	6,834	8	87	0	5	43	85.9	-22.3	54	4	2,500	0	0.0	0.0
B- / 7.2	9.2	0.93	57.69	2,252	8	87	0	5	43	86.7	-22.2	56	4	0	0	0.0	0.0
C / 5.5	13.8	1.00	37.11	1,319	0	100	0	0	80	67.2	-29.3	79	2	2,500	0	0.0	1.0
U /	N/A	N/A	11.42	188	1	98	0	1	0	N/A	N/A	N/A	2	2,500	0	0.0	0.0
C- / 3.7	9.4	0.96	21.88	1,584	1	98	0	1	124	80.8	-18.5	38	5	2,500	0	0.0	0.8
C- / 3.7	9.4	0.96	21.85	199	1	98	0	1	124	81.5	-18.4	39	5	0	0	0.0	0.8
C+ / 6.2	11.3	1.00	30.41	749	1	98	0	1	197	89.0	-16.3	61	4	2,500	0	0.0	0.0

					PERFORMANCE							
	99 Pct = Best 0 Pct = Worst					Total Return % through 3/31/15					Incl. in Returns	
			Overall		Perfor-				Annualized		Dividend	Expense
Fund Type	Fund Name	Ticker Symbol	Investment Rating	Phone	mance Rating/Pts	3 Mo	6 Mo	1Yr / Pct	3Yr / Pct	5Yr / Pct	Yield	Ratio
GR	Fidelity Focused Stock Fund	FTQGX	B-	(800) 544-8544	B / 7.9	4.80	6.57	7.79 /61	15.90 /83	15.95 /93	0.08	0.78
AA	Fidelity Four In One Index	FFNOX	B-	(800) 544-8544	C+ / 5.7	2.64	5.05	7.74 /61	12.40 /55	11.04 /53	2.03	0.24
AA	Fidelity Freedom 2005	FFFVX	C	(800) 544-8544	D / 2.0	2.09	3.42	5.26 /41	5.89 /16	6.18 /18	1.81	0.57
AA	Fidelity Freedom 2010	FFFCX	C	(800) 544-8544	D+ / 2.7	2.27	3.78	5.84 /45	7.19 /22	7.28 /25	1.83	0.61
* AA	Fidelity Freedom 2015	FFVFX	C	(800) 544-8544	C- / 3.0	2.46	4.23	6.42 /50	7.65 /25	7.59 /27	1.83	0.64
* AA	Fidelity Freedom 2020	FFFDX	C	(800) 544-8544	C- / 3.3	2.60	4.41	6.71 /53	8.21 /28	8.05 /30	1.78	0.67
* AA	Fidelity Freedom 2025	FFTWX	C+	(800) 544-8544	C- / 4.0	2.82	4.71	7.23 /57	9.43 /36	8.88 /36	1.74	0.72
* AA	Fidelity Freedom 2030	FFFEX	C+	(800) 544-8544	C / 4.4	3.04	5.08	7.76 /61	10.02 /39	9.19 /38	1.61	0.77
* AA	Fidelity Freedom 2035	FFTHX	C+	(800) 544-8544	C / 4.8	3.09	5.20	7.90 /62	10.80 /44	9.62 /41	1.57	0.78
* AA	Fidelity Freedom 2040	FFFFX	C+	(800) 544-8544	C / 4.9	3.10	5.17	7.86 /62	10.92 /45	9.68 /42	1.56	0.78
AA	Fidelity Freedom 2045	FFFGX	C+	(800) 544-8544	C / 5.0	3.14	5.17	7.93 /62	11.11 /46	9.79 /43	1.52	0.78
AA	Fidelity Freedom 2050	FFFHX	C+	(800) 544-8544	C / 5.0	3.12	5.21	7.91 /62	11.16 /47	9.78 /43	1.50	0.78
GL	Fidelity Freedom 2055	FDEEX	C+	(800) 544-8544	C / 5.2	3.17	5.21	7.98 /63	11.41 /48	--	1.48	0.78
BA	Fidelity Freedom Income	FFFAX	C-	(800) 544-8544	D- / 1.3	1.68	2.81	4.31 /34	4.35 /11	4.76 /11	1.67	0.49
GI	Fidelity Freedom Index 2005	FJIFX	C	(800) 544-8544	D / 1.6	1.60	2.86	4.87 /38	5.10 /13	5.60 /15	2.59	0.25
GI	Fidelity Freedom Index 2010	FKIFX	C	(800) 544-8544	D / 2.2	1.67	3.14	5.36 /41	6.40 /18	6.76 /22	2.63	0.25
GL	Fidelity Freedom Index 2015	FLIFX	C	(800) 544-8544	D+ / 2.5	1.87	3.48	5.87 /45	6.87 /21	7.09 /24	2.96	0.24
GL	Fidelity Freedom Index 2020	FPIFX	C	(800) 544-8544	D+ / 2.8	1.95	3.68	6.18 /48	7.36 /23	7.58 /27	2.91	0.24
GL	Fidelity Freedom Index 2025	FQIFX	C+	(800) 544-8544	C- / 3.5	2.14	4.00	6.73 /53	8.65 /31	8.54 /33	3.17	0.25
GL	Fidelity Freedom Index 2030	FXIFX	C+	(800) 544-8544	C- / 3.9	2.23	4.23	7.16 /56	9.24 /34	8.87 /36	3.18	0.25
GL	Fidelity Freedom Index 2035	FIHFX	C+	(800) 544-8544	C / 4.3	2.28	4.32	7.25 /57	10.05 /40	9.44 /40	3.25	0.26
GL	Fidelity Freedom Index 2040	FBIFX	C+	(800) 544-8544	C / 4.4	2.27	4.31	7.27 /57	10.16 /40	9.51 /41	3.19	0.26
GL	Fidelity Freedom Index 2045	FIOFX	C+	(800) 544-8544	C / 4.4	2.25	4.32	7.22 /57	10.31 /41	9.62 /41	3.22	0.26
GL	Fidelity Freedom Index 2050	FIPFX	C+	(800) 544-8544	C / 4.5	2.30	4.37	7.25 /57	10.37 /42	9.63 /42	3.15	0.26
GL	Fidelity Freedom Index 2055	FDEWX	C+	(800) 544-8544	C / 4.6	2.25	4.37	7.27 /57	10.65 /43	--	1.85	0.26
GL	Fidelity Freedom Index Income	FIKFX	C	(800) 544-8544	D- / 1.1	1.25	2.27	3.83 /31	3.52 / 9	3.99 / 8	1.38	0.25
GI	Fidelity Freedom K 2005	FFKVX	C	(800) 544-8544	D / 2.0	2.08	3.43	5.33 /41	5.95 /17	6.25 /18	2.92	0.50
GI	Fidelity Freedom K 2010	FFKCX	C	(800) 544-8544	D+ / 2.7	2.27	3.82	5.96 /46	7.27 /23	7.37 /26	3.19	0.53
* GI	Fidelity Freedom K 2015	FKVFX	C	(800) 544-8544	C- / 3.1	2.50	4.19	6.54 /51	7.74 /26	7.69 /28	3.14	0.55
* GI	Fidelity Freedom K 2020	FFKDX	C	(800) 544-8544	C- / 3.4	2.67	4.46	6.84 /54	8.31 /29	8.16 /31	3.17	0.57
* GI	Fidelity Freedom K 2025	FKTWX	C	(800) 544-8544	C- / 4.1	2.76	4.74	7.35 /58	9.53 /36	8.99 /37	3.00	0.61
* GL	Fidelity Freedom K 2030	FFKEX	C	(800) 544-8544	C / 4.5	2.97	5.07	7.78 /61	10.12 /40	9.30 /39	2.98	0.65
* GI	Fidelity Freedom K 2035	FKTHX	C	(800) 544-8544	C / 4.9	3.14	5.25	8.08 /63	10.94 /45	9.76 /43	2.80	0.66
* GI	Fidelity Freedom K 2040	FFKFX	C+	(800) 544-8544	C / 5.0	3.13	5.21	8.01 /63	11.04 /46	9.81 /43	2.80	0.66
* GI	Fidelity Freedom K 2045	FFKGX	C+	(800) 544-8544	C / 5.1	3.18	5.26	8.10 /64	11.26 /47	9.94 /44	2.72	0.66
GL	Fidelity Freedom K 2050	FFKHX	C+	(800) 544-8544	C / 5.1	3.09	5.28	8.09 /64	11.27 /47	9.92 /44	2.71	0.65
GL	Fidelity Freedom K 2055	FDENX	C+	(800) 544-8544	C / 5.2	3.11	5.18	8.03 /63	11.50 /49	--	2.31	0.66
GI	Fidelity Freedom K Income	FFKAX	C-	(800) 544-8544	D- / 1.3	1.63	2.74	4.28 /34	4.37 /11	4.79 /11	1.70	0.44
GR	Fidelity Fund Fd	FFIDX	B+	(800) 544-8544	B+ / 8.3	3.36	8.96	14.31 /90	15.38 /78	13.50 /73	0.61	0.53
GR	Fidelity Fund K	FFDKX	B+	(800) 544-8544	B+ / 8.4	3.39	9.02	14.45 /90	15.53 /79	13.66 /75	0.71	0.41
GL	Fidelity Global Balanced Fund	FGBLX	D-	(800) 544-8544	D / 1.9	1.84	1.21	--	6.91 /21	7.11 /24	0.30	0.99
GL	Fidelity Global Equity Income	FGILX	U	(800) 522-7297	U /	2.84	5.15	6.36 /50	--	--	1.96	1.16
AA	Fidelity Global Strategies	FDYSX	D	(800) 544-8544	D / 2.1	2.54	3.21	4.47 /35	6.16 /17	6.42 /20	1.92	0.85
* GI	Fidelity Growth and Income	FGRIX	B+	(800) 544-8544	B / 7.6	0.36	3.65	9.49 /72	15.77 /81	14.09 /79	1.72	0.66
GI	Fidelity Growth and Income K	FGIKX	B+	(800) 544-8544	B / 7.7	0.40	3.75	9.63 /73	15.94 /83	14.28 /80	1.83	0.53
* GR ●	Fidelity Growth Company Fd	FDGRX	A-	(800) 544-8544	A / 9.4	4.86	12.00	16.98 /95	17.33 /91	17.51 /97	0.09	0.82
GR ●	Fidelity Growth Company K	FGCKX	A-	(800) 544-8544	A / 9.5	4.89	12.06	17.11 /95	17.47 /92	17.66 /97	0.18	0.71
GR	Fidelity Growth Discovery Fd	FDSVX	A-	(800) 544-8544	B+ / 8.4	4.70	6.15	12.11 /83	16.11 /84	16.34 /94	0.09	0.82
GR	Fidelity Growth Discovery K	FGDKX	A-	(800) 544-8544	B+ / 8.5	4.70	6.17	12.23 /84	16.26 /85	16.52 /95	0.27	0.68
AG	Fidelity Growth Strategies Fd	FDEGX	A+	(800) 544-8544	A+ / 9.7	6.53	14.87	19.73 /97	17.82 /94	14.50 /82	0.26	0.72
AG	Fidelity Growth Strategies K	FAGKX	A+	(800) 544-8544	A+ / 9.7	6.58	14.99	19.98 /97	18.08 /94	14.76 /85	0.42	0.53
AA	Fidelity Inc Replacement 2016	FIRJX	C-	(800) 544-8544	E+ / 0.8	0.41	0.79	1.53 /20	2.82 / 8	3.98 / 8	0.56	0.35

● Denotes fund is closed to new investors

* Denotes fund is included in Section II

Risk Rating/Pts	3 Year Standard Deviation	Beta	NAV As of 3/31/15	Total $(Mil)	Cash %	Stocks %	Bonds %	Other %	Portfolio Turnover Ratio	Last Bull Market Return	Last Bear Market Return	Manager Quality Pct	Manager Tenure (Years)	Initial Purch. $	Additional Purch. $	Front End Load	Back End Load
C /5.1	11.7	1.03	19.64	1,505	0	99	0	1	223	90.7	-17.3	58	8	2,500	0	0.0	0.0
B- /7.4	8.6	1.47	38.10	4,211	2	83	14	1	9	71.7	-16.0	20	16	2,500	0	0.0	0.0
B+ /9.3	4.1	0.68	12.24	639	11	39	48	2	44	30.6	-8.5	47	10	2,500	0	0.0	0.0
B+ /9.0	5.2	0.87	15.74	4,943	8	48	42	2	35	38.3	-10.3	36	10	2,500	0	0.0	0.0
B /8.8	5.5	0.94	12.92	6,063	6	56	37	1	39	40.4	-10.5	33	10	2,500	0	0.0	0.0
B /8.5	6.1	1.04	15.76	12,880	5	61	32	2	39	45.0	-12.6	26	10	2,500	0	0.0	0.0
B /8.1	7.2	1.22	13.51	9,056	5	70	24	1	46	53.0	-14.9	19	10	2,500	0	0.0	0.0
B- /7.7	7.9	1.34	16.62	10,889	4	83	12	1	54	56.6	-15.8	14	10	2,500	0	0.0	0.0
B- /7.3	8.8	1.48	13.67	6,295	4	89	6	1	54	62.9	-18.1	10	10	2,500	0	0.0	0.0
B- /7.3	8.8	1.49	9.63	6,903	4	89	6	1	49	63.8	-18.4	10	10	2,500	0	0.0	0.0
C+ /6.9	9.0	1.52	10.84	3,000	4	89	6	1	53	65.4	-19.0	9	8	2,500	0	0.0	0.0
C+ /6.9	9.2	1.55	10.90	2,376	4	89	6	1	57	66.6	-19.9	9	9	2,500	0	0.0	0.0
B- /7.1	9.3	0.64	12.06	527	4	88	7	1	47	68.0	N/A	94	4	2,500	0	0.0	0.0
B+ /9.4	2.7	0.43	11.75	2,485	16	25	58	1	31	20.5	-3.9	64	10	2,500	0	0.0	0.0
B+ /9.7	3.8	0.36	12.71	74	22	37	39	2	49	26.5	-6.9	61	N/A	0	0	0.0	0.0
B+ /9.4	4.9	0.47	13.36	481	17	46	36	1	39	33.9	-8.6	55	N/A	0	0	0.0	0.0
B+ /9.2	5.2	0.82	13.62	909	13	53	33	1	29	36.2	-8.8	61	6	0	0	0.0	0.0
B+ /9.0	5.8	0.91	14.10	2,458	10	59	30	1	25	40.2	-10.6	57	6	0	0	0.0	0.0
B /8.5	6.8	1.06	14.80	1,723	5	68	26	1	21	48.1	-12.7	54	6	0	0	0.0	0.0
B /8.1	7.5	1.16	15.15	2,223	4	80	15	1	32	51.5	-13.5	50	6	0	0	0.0	0.0
B- /7.7	8.4	1.30	15.67	1,281	3	86	9	2	25	57.9	-15.7	43	6	0	0	0.0	0.0
B- /7.7	8.4	1.30	15.76	1,509	3	86	9	2	26	58.7	-15.9	44	6	0	0	0.0	0.0
B- /7.6	8.5	1.32	15.89	749	4	85	9	2	22	59.8	-16.3	44	6	0	0	0.0	0.0
B- /7.6	8.7	1.34	16.01	729	4	85	9	2	24	60.9	-17.2	42	6	0	0	0.0	0.0
B- /7.5	8.8	0.61	12.71	183	4	85	9	2	21	62.5	N/A	93	4	0	0	0.0	0.0
B+ /9.9	2.4	0.35	11.52	244	32	22	45	1	43	16.5	-2.6	71	6	0	0	0.0	0.0
B /8.9	4.1	0.38	13.24	471	13	39	46	2	55	31.0	-8.5	N/A	N/A	0	0	0.0	0.0
B /8.1	5.2	0.50	13.50	3,675	10	48	40	2	39	38.8	-10.4	61	N/A	0	0	0.0	0.0
B /8.3	5.5	0.54	13.94	6,739	8	55	35	2	43	40.9	-10.6	59	N/A	0	0	0.0	0.0
B /8.1	6.1	0.60	14.62	17,529	7	61	31	1	43	45.5	-12.6	53	N/A	0	0	0.0	0.0
B- /7.7	7.2	0.71	15.27	12,953	4	70	24	2	44	53.5	-15.0	44	N/A	0	0	0.0	0.0
B- /7.3	7.9	1.22	15.62	16,027	4	83	12	1	56	57.4	-15.9	55	6	0	0	0.0	0.0
C+ /6.9	8.7	0.87	16.10	10,139	4	88	7	1	50	63.6	-18.0	28	N/A	0	0	0.0	0.0
C+ /6.9	8.8	0.88	16.14	10,934	4	88	7	1	50	64.5	-18.4	28	N/A	0	0	0.0	0.0
C+ /6.9	9.0	0.90	16.57	5,971	4	88	7	1	47	66.2	-18.9	28	N/A	0	0	0.0	0.0
C+ /6.8	9.1	1.39	16.67	4,859	4	88	7	1	48	67.2	-19.8	47	6	0	0	0.0	0.0
B- /7.0	9.2	0.63	12.27	972	4	88	7	1	45	68.8	N/A	94	4	0	0	0.0	0.0
B+ /9.5	2.8	0.23	12.01	2,013	18	23	57	2	40	20.6	-3.9	75	N/A	0	0	0.0	0.0
C+ /6.1	10.0	1.01	44.29	4,172	7	92	0	1	93	90.4	-18.4	55	13	2,500	0	0.0	0.0
C+ /6.1	10.0	1.01	44.28	957	7	92	0	1	93	91.2	-18.4	57	13	0	0	0.0	0.0
C+ /6.1	7.4	1.10	23.27	506	6	57	36	1	157	37.1	-12.9	27	9	2,500	0	0.0	1.0
U /	N/A	N/A	12.30	63	4	95	0	1	92	N/A	N/A	N/A	3	2,500	0	0.0	1.0
C+ /6.5	6.0	0.94	8.89	115	1	62	35	2	106	36.6	-16.1	18	8	2,500	0	0.0	0.0
B- /7.2	10.3	1.05	30.32	6,587	2	97	0	1	41	102.5	-16.9	51	4	2,500	0	0.0	0.0
B- /7.2	10.3	1.06	30.31	973	2	97	0	1	41	103.5	-16.9	52	4	0	0	0.0	0.0
C+ /5.8	12.2	1.09	138.08	23,244	0	99	0	1	12	113.7	-16.9	64	18	2,500	0	0.0	0.0
C+ /5.8	12.2	1.09	137.94	19,249	0	99	0	1	12	114.6	-16.9	66	18	0	0	0.0	0.0
C+ /6.5	10.8	0.92	24.73	1,081	6	92	0	2	70	100.4	-17.6	78	8	2,500	0	0.0	0.0
C+ /6.5	10.8	0.92	24.72	212	6	92	0	2	70	101.3	-17.5	79	8	0	0	0.0	0.0
C+ /6.3	11.1	1.07	34.41	2,485	1	98	0	1	58	102.7	-23.7	71	2	2,500	0	0.0	1.5
C+ /6.3	11.1	1.08	34.65	576	1	98	0	1	58	104.2	-23.6	73	2	0	0	0.0	1.5
B+ /9.9	1.6	0.25	51.25	4	63	6	30	1	31	15.7	-4.4	69	8	25,000	0	0.0	0.0

Fund Type	Fund Name	Ticker Symbol	Overall Investment Rating	Phone	Performance Rating/Pts	3 Mo	6 Mo	1Yr / Pct	3Yr / Pct	5Yr / Pct	Dividend Yield	Expense Ratio
	99 Pct = Best							Total Return % through 3/31/15			Incl. in Returns	
	0 Pct = Worst								Annualized			
AA	Fidelity Inc Replacement 2018	FIRKX	C	(800) 544-8544	D- / 1.4	0.96	1.86	3.24 /28	4.77 /12	5.39 /14	1.10	0.46
AA	Fidelity Inc Replacement 2020	FIRLX	C	(800) 544-8544	D / 2.0	1.45	2.67	4.34 /34	6.10 /17	6.38 /19	1.40	0.52
AA	Fidelity Inc Replacement 2022	FIRMX	C+	(800) 544-8544	D+ / 2.5	1.65	3.08	5.00 /38	7.09 /22	7.10 /24	1.37	0.56
AA	Fidelity Inc Replacement 2024	FIRNX	C+	(800) 544-8544	C- / 3.0	1.83	3.41	5.49 /42	7.83 /26	7.63 /27	1.41	0.58
AA	Fidelity Inc Replacement 2026	FIROX	C+	(800) 544-8544	C- / 3.3	1.97	3.65	5.84 /45	8.36 /29	7.98 /30	1.39	0.60
AA	Fidelity Inc Replacement 2028	FIRPX	C+	(800) 544-8544	C- / 3.5	2.07	3.83	6.05 /47	8.72 /31	8.24 /31	1.40	0.61
AA	Fidelity Inc Replacement 2030	FIRQX	C+	(800) 544-8544	C- / 3.7	2.14	3.94	6.18 /48	9.00 /33	8.45 /33	1.43	0.62
AA	Fidelity Inc Replacement 2032	FIRRX	C+	(800) 544-8544	C- / 3.8	2.20	4.03	6.35 /49	9.25 /35	8.62 /34	1.48	0.63
AA	Fidelity Inc Replacement 2034	FIRSX	C+	(800) 544-8544	C- / 3.9	2.26	4.11	6.37 /50	9.44 /36	8.75 /35	1.41	0.64
AA	Fidelity Inc Replacement 2036	FIRUX	C+	(800) 544-8544	C- / 4.0	2.33	4.18	6.47 /50	9.66 /37	8.90 /36	1.41	0.65
AA	Fidelity Income Replacement 2038 Fd	FIRVX	C+	(800) 544-8544	C- / 4.2	2.41	4.27	6.55 /51	9.87 /39	9.06 /37	1.39	0.66
AA	Fidelity Income Replacement 2040 Fd	FIRWX	B-	(800) 544-8544	C / 4.3	2.46	4.33	6.64 /52	10.16 /40	9.32 /39	1.40	0.67
AA	Fidelity Income Replacement 2042 Fd	FIXRX	B-	(800) 544-8544	C / 4.5	2.55	4.46	6.78 /53	10.50 /42	9.54 /41	1.42	0.68
GR	Fidelity Independence Fd	FDFFX	A	(800) 544-8544	A+ / 9.6	6.95	8.68	13.50 /88	19.18 /97	15.29 /89	0.10	0.73
GR	Fidelity Independence K	FDFKX	A	(800) 544-8544	A+ / 9.7	6.98	8.73	13.58 /88	19.28 /97	15.41 /90	0.19	0.64
FO	Fidelity International Cap App Fd	FIVFX	C	(800) 544-8544	C / 5.3	4.10	6.49	6.87 /54	11.86 /51	9.72 /42	0.52	1.14
FO	Fidelity International Discovery Fd	FIGRX	C-	(800) 522-7297	C / 4.3	5.95	4.55	1.41 /20	10.77 /44	7.29 /25	0.64	0.91
FO	Fidelity International Discovery K	FIDKX	C-	(800) 522-7297	C / 4.4	6.02	4.65	1.55 /20	10.95 /45	7.48 /26	0.77	0.78
FO	Fidelity International Growth Fund	FIGFX	C-	(800) 522-7297	C- / 4.2	6.48	5.88	4.36 /34	10.11 /40	9.52 /41	0.79	1.04
GL	Fidelity International Real Estate	FIREX	B	(800) 544-8544	B- / 7.3	5.73	7.07	8.47 /66	15.05 /75	9.90 /44	1.44	1.14
FO	Fidelity International Small Cap	FISMX	D	(800) 544-8544	C / 4.4	5.45	3.78	-0.24 /15	11.60 /50	10.39 /48	0.90	1.22
FO	Fidelity International Value Fund	FIVLX	D	(800) 522-7297	C- / 3.1	4.97	0.35	-2.22 /10	9.44 /36	4.63 /11	3.75	0.96
FO	Fidelity Intl Enhanced Index Fd	FIENX	C-	(800) 544-8544	C- / 3.9	5.99	2.36	0.66 /17	10.31 /41	7.16 /24	1.88	0.62
FO	Fidelity Intl Sm Cp Opp Fd	FSCOX	C	(800) 522-7297	C / 5.3	6.80	5.66	0.74 /18	12.87 /59	11.97 /60	0.62	1.30
FO	Fidelity Japan Fund	FJPNX	D	(800) 544-8544	D+ / 2.7	9.51	3.80	6.45 /50	6.89 /21	3.84 / 8	0.73	0.90
FO	Fidelity Japan Small Companies	FJSCX	B+	(800) 544-8544	B+ / 8.4	8.61	3.59	8.71 /68	16.85 /89	11.03 /53	0.24	1.00
GR	Fidelity Large Cap Stock Fund	FLCSX	A-	(800) 544-8544	B+ / 8.5	1.06	3.94	8.43 /66	17.40 /92	14.99 /87	0.88	0.88
EM	Fidelity Latin American Fund	FLATX	E-	(800) 544-8544	E- / 0.0	-9.29	-22.95	-22.58 / 1	-16.71 / 0	-8.45 / 1	1.71	1.08
GR	Fidelity Leveraged Company Stock	FLVCX	A	(800) 544-8544	B+ / 8.7	4.17	4.84	8.31 /65	17.81 /94	14.65 /84	0.73	0.79
GR	Fidelity Leveraged Company Stock K	FLCKX	A	(800) 544-8544	B+ / 8.8	4.21	4.93	8.46 /66	17.97 /94	14.82 /85	0.85	0.67
GR	Fidelity LgCp Core Enh Idx Fd	FLCEX	B+	(800) 544-8544	B+ / 8.4	0.92	5.27	12.86 /86	16.42 /86	14.69 /84	1.24	0.46
GR	Fidelity LgCp Gr Enh Idx Fd	FLGEX	A+	(800) 544-8544	A- / 9.0	3.26	7.97	16.35 /94	16.55 /87	15.52 /90	0.94	0.45
GR	Fidelity LgCp Val Enh Idx Fd	FLVEX	A+	(800) 544-8544	B+ / 8.6	-0.27	4.28	10.50 /76	17.37 /92	14.40 /81	1.08	0.47
★ MC	Fidelity Low-Priced Stock Fd	FLPSX	B	(800) 544-8544	B- / 7.0	1.77	6.03	7.39 /58	15.23 /77	14.19 /79	0.97	0.82
MC	Fidelity Low-Priced Stock K	FLPKX	B+	(800) 544-8544	B- / 7.1	1.81	6.08	7.51 /59	15.36 /78	14.32 /81	1.07	0.72
GL	Fidelity MA Intl Index		D	(800) 544-8544	D+ / 2.9	5.34	1.02	-1.17 /12	8.82 /32	6.05 /17	0.00	0.35
AA	Fidelity MA Spart 500 Index		A	(800) 544-8544	B / 8.1	0.86	5.80	12.52 /85	15.88 /82	14.23 /80	0.00	0.25
★ GR	Fidelity Magellan Fund	FMAGX	A	(800) 544-8544	A- / 9.1	2.83	8.13	14.97 /92	17.18 /91	12.13 /61	0.66	0.53
GR	Fidelity Magellan Fund K	FMGKX	A	(800) 544-8544	A- / 9.2	2.86	8.17	15.07 /92	17.30 /91	12.26 /62	0.75	0.42
GI	Fidelity Mega Cap Stock Fund	FGRTX	B+	(800) 544-8544	B- / 7.4	-0.30	3.15	9.54 /72	15.56 /80	14.46 /82	1.23	0.54
MC	Fidelity Mid Cap Enhanced Index Fd	FMEIX	A+	(800) 544-8544	A+ / 9.7	4.42	11.08	14.79 /91	19.63 /97	16.75 /95	0.68	0.62
MC	Fidelity Mid Cap Value	FSMVX	A+	(800) 544-8544	A+ / 9.8	2.59	10.89	15.74 /93	20.63 /98	16.71 /95	0.84	0.80
★ MC	Fidelity Mid-Cap Stock Fund	FMCSX	B+	(800) 544-8544	B / 8.2	4.40	8.68	7.53 /59	16.35 /86	14.15 /79	0.21	0.81
MC	Fidelity Mid-Cap Stock Fund K	FKMCX	B+	(800) 544-8544	B+ / 8.3	4.43	8.71	7.64 /60	16.52 /87	14.32 /81	0.29	0.68
GR	Fidelity NASDAQ Composite Index	FNCMX	A+	(800) 544-8544	A / 9.4	3.72	9.64	18.00 /95	17.88 /94	16.53 /95	0.80	0.55
MC	Fidelity New Millennium	FMILX	C+	(800) 544-8544	C+ / 6.7	1.42	3.56	3.99 /32	15.03 /75	14.24 /80	0.66	0.84
AA	Fidelity NH International Index		D	(800) 544-8544	D+ / 2.9	5.31	1.04	-1.18 /12	8.82 /32	6.06 /17	0.00	0.35
AA	Fidelity NH Spart 500 Index		A	(800) 544-8544	B / 8.1	0.92	5.85	12.50 /85	15.87 /82	14.21 /80	0.00	0.25
AA	Fidelity NH Ttl Mkt Index		A	(800) 544-8544	B / 8.2	1.74	7.02	12.05 /83	16.12 /84	14.51 /82	0.00	0.25
FO	Fidelity Nordic Fund	FNORX	C	(800) 544-8544	C+ / 6.2	4.77	0.79	-3.21 / 8	15.58 /80	11.45 /56	0.00	0.99
★ SC	Fidelity OTC Portfolio Fd	FOCPX	B+	(800) 544-8544	A+ / 9.7	4.83	10.92	18.43 /96	19.32 /97	17.62 /97	0.00	0.77
SC	Fidelity OTC Portfolio K	FOCKX	B+	(800) 544-8544	A+ / 9.8	4.87	10.99	18.57 /96	19.47 /97	17.79 /97	0.00	0.65

● Denotes fund is closed to new investors
★ Denotes fund is included in Section II

www.thestreetratings.com

RISK			NET ASSETS		ASSET				Portfolio Turnover Ratio	BULL / BEAR		FUND MANAGER		MINIMUMS		LOADS	
	3 Year		NAV							Last Bull	Last Bear	Manager	Manager	Initial	Additional	Front	Back
Risk Rating/Pts	Standard Deviation	Beta	As of 3/31/15	Total $(Mil)	Cash %	Stocks %	Bonds %	Other %		Market Return	Market Return	Quality Pct	Tenure (Years)	Purch. $	Purch. $	End Load	End Load
B+ / 9.8	2.7	0.44	55.16	5	37	15	47	1	56	24.6	-6.3	68	8	25,000	0	0.0	0.0
B+ / 9.6	3.5	0.59	56.36	7	20	25	53	2	25	31.5	-7.9	64	8	25,000	0	0.0	0.0
B+ / 9.5	4.1	0.71	58.69	14	17	33	48	2	26	36.8	-9.1	60	8	25,000	0	0.0	0.0
B+ / 9.3	4.6	0.80	59.24	8	15	39	44	2	30	40.8	-9.9	56	8	25,000	0	0.0	0.0
B+ / 9.2	5.0	0.86	60.46	6	13	44	41	2	27	43.7	-10.5	53	8	25,000	0	0.0	0.0
B+ / 9.1	5.3	0.91	61.52	25	12	47	39	2	18	45.8	-11.0	51	8	25,000	0	0.0	0.0
B+ / 9.0	5.5	0.95	61.09	17	11	50	37	2	27	47.5	-11.5	49	8	25,000	0	0.0	0.0
B / 8.2	5.7	0.98	58.25	8	11	52	36	1	29	49.0	-11.8	47	8	25,000	0	0.0	0.0
B / 8.9	5.9	1.01	61.08	9	10	53	35	2	19	50.2	-12.2	46	8	25,000	0	0.0	0.0
B / 8.8	6.0	1.04	61.63	8	10	55	34	1	25	51.6	-12.6	44	8	25,000	0	0.0	0.0
B / 8.7	6.2	1.07	59.19	7	9	56	33	2	39	53.1	-13.1	42	8	25,000	0	0.0	0.0
B / 8.6	6.5	1.11	60.44	9	8	58	32	2	34	55.1	-13.7	40	8	25,000	0	0.0	0.0
B / 8.5	6.7	1.15	60.57	37	7	60	30	3	16	57.1	-14.1	38	8	25,000	0	0.0	0.0
C+ / 5.7	12.2	1.03	41.03	4,351	1	98	0	1	53	115.5	-25.5	85	9	2,500	0	0.0	0.0
C+ / 5.8	12.2	1.03	41.04	671	1	98	0	1	53	116.2	-25.4	85	9	0	0	0.0	0.0
C+ / 5.7	12.0	0.85	17.03	1,349	2	97	0	1	178	80.5	-25.9	90	7	2,500	0	0.0	1.0
C+ / 6.1	12.6	0.93	40.25	7,358	5	94	0	1	57	59.1	-24.5	83	11	2,500	0	0.0	1.0
C+ / 6.1	12.6	0.93	40.17	2,490	5	94	0	1	57	60.0	-24.4	84	11	0	0	0.0	1.0
C+ / 6.4	11.2	0.82	11.50	729	4	95	0	1	27	62.7	-21.9	85	8	2,500	0	0.0	1.0
C+ / 6.3	12.7	0.82	10.71	334	18	81	0	1	138	84.0	-25.2	96	5	2,500	0	0.0	1.5
C- / 4.1	12.9	0.89	22.83	737	4	95	0	1	102	58.1	-21.6	88	1	2,500	0	0.0	2.0
C+ / 5.6	13.4	0.99	8.45	192	1	98	0	1	69	50.3	-27.7	67	4	2,500	0	0.0	1.0
C+ / 6.2	13.0	0.99	8.67	114	7	92	0	1	63	56.0	-22.4	76	8	2,500	0	0.0	1.0
C+ / 6.5	10.9	0.74	14.61	558	3	96	0	1	18	68.9	-20.4	94	7	2,500	0	0.0	2.0
C+ / 6.3	13.9	0.75	11.98	409	0	99	0	1	112	31.9	-10.3	65	1	2,500	0	0.0	1.5
C+ / 6.0	19.2	0.86	13.37	401	2	97	0	1	112	64.5	-6.4	97	7	2,500	0	0.0	1.5
C+ / 6.7	11.2	1.13	28.55	3,131	1	98	0	1	31	113.9	-19.3	54	10	2,500	0	0.0	0.0
D- / 1.2	19.3	1.25	21.58	637	2	97	0	1	30	-22.0	-24.8	0	6	2,500	0	0.0	1.5
C+ / 6.6	11.1	1.02	47.21	3,881	2	97	0	1	10	119.2	-30.1	78	12	10,000	0	0.0	1.5
C+ / 6.6	11.1	1.02	47.29	1,155	2	97	0	1	10	120.3	-30.1	79	12	0	0	0.0	1.5
C+ / 6.3	9.7	1.01	12.08	393	8	91	0	1	125	101.6	-15.1	69	8	2,500	0	0.0	0.0
B- / 7.1	9.8	1.00	15.22	413	6	93	0	1	83	103.6	-15.1	72	8	2,500	0	0.0	0.0
B- / 7.4	10.0	1.02	11.22	1,169	4	95	0	1	85	105.2	-17.5	75	8	2,500	0	0.0	0.0
B- / 7.0	10.4	0.86	51.14	30,086	11	88	0	1	12	92.6	-17.6	74	26	2,500	0	0.0	1.5
B- / 7.0	10.4	0.86	51.11	15,697	11	88	0	1	12	93.3	-17.6	75	26	0	0	0.0	1.5
C+ / 6.0	13.3	1.97	11.83	46	6	93	0	1	0	50.8	-23.1	3	9	50	25	0.0	1.0
B- / 7.3	9.6	1.66	17.52	104	1	98	0	1	0	98.8	-16.3	32	9	50	25	0.0	0.0
C+ / 6.3	10.4	1.05	95.14	14,225	2	97	0	1	77	104.3	-24.3	69	4	2,500	0	0.0	0.0
C+ / 6.3	10.4	1.05	95.03	2,528	2	97	0	1	77	105.0	-24.2	71	4	0	0	0.0	0.0
B- / 7.1	10.7	1.09	16.45	3,212	0	99	0	1	28	104.6	-16.0	40	6	2,500	0	0.0	0.0
C+ / 6.8	10.4	0.92	14.17	680	8	91	0	1	128	115.7	-21.5	90	8	2,500	0	0.0	0.8
B- / 7.1	10.5	0.91	25.07	3,018	4	95	0	1	169	123.9	-23.1	92	2	2,500	0	0.0	0.8
C+ / 6.1	10.9	0.95	40.08	5,904	3	96	0	1	27	93.5	-18.8	70	4	2,500	0	0.0	0.8
C+ / 6.1	10.9	0.95	40.09	3,220	3	96	0	1	27	94.4	-18.7	71	4	0	0	0.0	0.8
C+ / 6.6	11.3	1.08	64.65	1,723	3	95	0	2	5	113.4	-15.6	71	11	2,500	0	0.0	0.8
C+ / 6.2	10.6	0.88	39.30	3,909	0	98	0	2	44	89.1	-15.4	70	9	2,500	0	0.0	0.0
C+ / 5.9	13.3	1.85	11.70	92	6	93	0	1	0	50.8	-23.1	2	9	50	25	0.0	1.0
B- / 7.4	9.6	1.66	17.55	221	1	98	0	1	0	98.8	-16.3	32	9	50	25	0.0	0.0
B- / 7.2	9.7	1.68	18.13	179	2	97	0	1	0	100.0	-17.7	32	9	50	25	0.0	0.5
C / 5.1	15.6	1.10	44.62	432	3	96	0	1	103	91.2	-31.8	93	11	2,500	0	0.0	1.5
C / 4.8	14.1	0.81	83.40	9,198	0	99	0	1	106	115.0	-17.4	94	6	2,500	0	0.0	0.0
C / 4.8	14.1	0.81	84.22	3,910	0	99	0	1	106	116.0	-17.4	95	6	0	0	0.0	0.0

Fund Type	Fund Name	Ticker Symbol	Overall Investment Rating	Phone	Performance Rating/Pts	3 Mo	6 Mo	1Yr / Pct	3Yr / Pct	5Yr / Pct	Dividend Yield	Expense Ratio
	99 Pct = Best				PERFORMANCE			Total Return % through 3/31/15			Incl. in Returns	
	0 Pct = Worst								Annualized			
FO	Fidelity Overseas Fd	FOSFX	C	(800) 544-8544	C / 5.4	7.16	6.38	2.52 / 24	12.32 / 55	8.15 / 31	1.64	1.02
FO	Fidelity Overseas K	FOSKX	C	(800) 544-8544	C / 5.5	7.20	6.45	2.66 / 25	12.49 / 56	8.33 / 32	1.77	0.88
FO	Fidelity Pacific Basin	FPBFX	C	(800) 544-8544	C+ / 6.6	8.06	6.72	9.60 / 72	13.48 / 63	10.90 / 52	0.61	1.18
* GI	Fidelity Puritan Fd	FPURX	B-	(800) 544-8544	C+ / 5.9	2.65	5.78	11.12 / 79	12.15 / 53	11.35 / 56	1.50	0.56
GI	Fidelity Puritan K	FPUKX	B-	(800) 544-8544	C+ / 5.9	2.65	5.79	11.24 / 79	12.27 / 54	11.47 / 57	1.59	0.46
RE	Fidelity Real Estate High Income Fd		B+	(800) 544-8544	C / 4.6	2.65	4.56	8.77 / 68	10.28 / 41	11.88 / 60	5.44	0.81
RE	Fidelity Real Estate Income	FRIFX	C+	(800) 544-8544	C / 4.6	2.59	6.82	9.56 / 72	10.21 / 41	10.82 / 51	4.43	0.83
RE	Fidelity Real Estate Investment	FRESX	B-	(800) 544-8544	A- / 9.2	4.46	18.84	24.19 / 98	13.37 / 62	15.52 / 90	1.59	0.80
GR	Fidelity Sel Defense and Aerospace	FSDAX	A+	(800) 544-8888	A+ / 9.8	9.86	16.31	13.61 / 88	19.85 / 98	17.08 / 96	0.71	0.81
GR	Fidelity Select Air Transport	FSAIX	A+	(800) 544-8888	A+ / 9.9	-1.81	14.79	21.54 / 97	26.07 / 99	18.41 / 98	0.11	0.87
GR	Fidelity Select Automotive Fund	FSAVX	B	(800) 544-8888	A- / 9.2	6.14	12.46	8.96 / 69	17.83 / 94	15.16 / 88	0.63	0.84
FS	Fidelity Select Banking Port	FSRBX	C+	(800) 544-8888	C+ / 6.0	-2.05	3.77	1.31 / 19	14.70 / 72	9.65 / 42	1.25	0.81
* HL	Fidelity Select Biotech Port	FBIOX	C+	(800) 544-8888	A+ / 9.9	16.02	31.81	46.13 / 99	43.52 / 99	33.30 / 99	0.00	0.76
FS	Fidelity Select Brkg and Inv Mgmt	FSLBX	B+	(800) 544-8888	B / 8.2	-1.31	3.57	6.33 / 49	17.61 / 93	9.16 / 38	1.09	1.42
GR	Fidelity Select Chemicals Port	FSCHX	C+	(800) 544-8888	C+ / 5.7	0.41	-3.54	2.31 / 23	14.48 / 71	16.93 / 96	0.94	0.81
TC	Fidelity Select Commun Equip Port	FSDCX	D	(800) 544-8888	C / 4.4	-0.57	5.71	8.34 / 65	10.48 / 42	8.88 / 36	0.91	0.92
TC	Fidelity Select Computers Port	FDCPX	D	(800) 544-8888	C- / 3.3	-4.44	1.79	5.49 / 42	9.44 / 36	13.78 / 76	0.59	0.82
GR	Fidelity Select Constn and Housing	FSHOX	A	(800) 544-8888	A+ / 9.9	8.58	19.86	21.85 / 97	21.09 / 98	19.13 / 98	0.43	0.81
GR	Fidelity Select Consu Staples Port	FDFAX	B	(800) 544-8888	B / 7.7	1.68	8.14	15.93 / 93	14.84 / 74	14.38 / 81	1.49	0.79
GR	Fidelity Select Consumer Discr	FSCPX	A-	(800) 544-8888	A+ / 9.6	4.22	14.67	15.14 / 92	18.53 / 96	17.90 / 97	0.28	0.82
FS	Fidelity Select Consumer Finance	FSVLX	C	(800) 544-8888	B+ / 8.3	1.13	8.10	8.34 / 65	16.72 / 88	12.18 / 62	1.71	0.85
TC	Fidelity Select Electronics Port	FSELX	B	(800) 544-8888	A+ / 9.8	3.36	14.25	27.76 / 99	18.59 / 96	16.37 / 94	0.51	0.82
EN	Fidelity Select Energy	FSENX	E-	(800) 544-8888	E / 0.4	1.16	-15.17	-13.80 / 2	2.48 / 7	5.31 / 13	0.93	0.80
EN	Fidelity Select Energy Svcs	FSESX	E-	(800) 544-8888	E- / 0.1	-5.92	-31.34	-31.53 / 0	-3.81 / 2	0.71 / 3	0.63	0.80
EN	Fidelity Select Envir and Alt Ener	FSLEX	C	(800) 544-8888	C+ / 5.7	1.96	5.58	1.03 / 19	13.67 / 65	9.70 / 42	0.61	0.97
FS	Fidelity Select Financial Services	FIDSX	B	(800) 544-8888	B- / 7.3	-0.06	5.97	9.51 / 72	15.37 / 78	7.43 / 26	1.00	0.86
PM	Fidelity Select Gold	FSAGX	E-	(800) 544-8888	E- / 0.0	-1.09	-14.47	-20.91 / 1	-26.39 / 0	-14.84 / 0	0.00	0.94
* HL	Fidelity Select Health Care	FSPHX	B	(800) 544-8888	A+ / 9.9	11.77	20.95	35.12 / 99	36.11 / 99	26.96 / 99	0.00	0.77
GR	Fidelity Select Ind Equipment	FSCGX	D	(800) 544-8888	C / 4.7	2.34	6.65	2.53 / 24	11.56 / 49	12.67 / 65	0.78	0.79
GR	Fidelity Select Industrials Port	FCYIX	B	(800) 544-8888	B / 7.8	1.67	9.12	7.51 / 59	16.07 / 84	15.18 / 88	0.63	0.81
FS	Fidelity Select Insurance	FSPCX	A+	(800) 544-8888	A / 9.4	-0.61	6.55	11.31 / 80	19.52 / 97	13.49 / 73	1.30	0.83
GR	Fidelity Select IT Serv Portfolio	FBSOX	A	(800) 544-8888	A+ / 9.8	5.82	18.14	15.74 / 93	20.31 / 98	19.63 / 99	0.01	0.84
GR	Fidelity Select Leisure	FDLSX	B	(800) 544-8888	B+ / 8.6	5.30	12.56	12.85 / 86	15.83 / 82	17.99 / 97	0.99	0.82
GR	Fidelity Select Materials Port	FSDPX	D	(800) 544-8888	D+ / 2.7	0.66	-2.35	-2.26 / 10	9.35 / 35	10.55 / 49	0.77	0.82
HL	Fidelity Select Medical Delivery	FSHCX	A+	(800) 544-8888	A+ / 9.9	9.99	21.00	29.21 / 99	20.44 / 98	18.89 / 98	0.00	0.82
GR	Fidelity Select Medical Eqpmnt Sys	FSMEX	A-	(800) 544-8888	A+ / 9.9	10.77	26.77	30.83 / 99	25.97 / 99	18.18 / 98	0.10	0.80
GR	Fidelity Select Multimedia	FBMPX	A+	(800) 544-8888	A+ / 9.8	2.34	8.72	13.61 / 88	23.14 / 99	20.52 / 99	0.23	0.81
EN	Fidelity Select Natural Gas	FSNGX	E-	(800) 544-8888	E- / 0.2	-3.80	-23.90	-21.74 / 1	0.96 / 5	1.00 / 3	1.23	0.84
EN	Fidelity Select Natural Resources	FNARX	E-	(800) 544-8888	E / 0.3	2.17	-14.82	-13.93 / 2	0.72 / 5	3.93 / 8	0.46	0.84
HL	Fidelity Select Pharmaceuticals	FPHAX	A-	(800) 544-8888	A+ / 9.9	10.71	14.67	26.48 / 99	27.58 / 99	22.55 / 99	0.68	0.82
GR	Fidelity Select Retailing	FSRPX	A+	(800) 544-8888	A+ / 9.8	5.79	19.01	21.98 / 97	20.99 / 98	20.01 / 99	0.16	0.83
TC	Fidelity Select Sware and Comp Svcs	FSCSX	B	(800) 544-8888	B+ / 8.6	1.07	7.37	8.22 / 64	17.45 / 92	18.59 / 98	0.00	0.79
TC	Fidelity Select Technology	FSPTX	C	(800) 544-8888	B- / 7.3	5.28	7.63	14.23 / 90	13.76 / 65	14.86 / 86	0.12	0.80
TC	Fidelity Select Telecommunications	FSTCX	C+	(800) 544-8888	C+ / 5.7	2.58	4.04	6.07 / 47	12.93 / 59	11.71 / 58	3.57	0.85
GR	Fidelity Select Transportation	FSRFX	A+	(800) 544-8888	A+ / 9.8	-5.25	9.43	19.69 / 97	24.36 / 99	18.33 / 98	0.36	0.85
UT	Fidelity Select Utilities	FSUTX	C+	(800) 544-8888	C+ / 6.6	-2.83	3.03	7.22 / 57	15.19 / 76	14.33 / 81	1.55	0.82
TC	Fidelity Select Wireless Fund	FWRLX	D+	(800) 544-8888	C+ / 5.6	1.76	4.09	4.69 / 36	13.02 / 60	11.87 / 60	6.00	0.88
GR	Fidelity Series 1000 Value Index	FIOOX	U	(800) 544-8544	U /	-0.67	4.21	9.28 / 71	--	--	2.11	0.10
GR	Fidelity Series 1000 Value Index F	FSIOX	U	(800) 544-8544	U /	-0.74	4.26	9.34 / 71	--	--	2.16	0.05
GR	Fidelity Series Blue Chip Growth	FSBDX	U	(800) 544-8544	U /	5.62	11.54	19.14 / 96	--	--	0.18	0.74
GR	Fidelity Series Blue Chip Growth F	FSBEX	U	(800) 544-8544	U /	5.62	11.52	19.32 / 96	--	--	0.32	0.57
GR	Fidelity Series Equity Income	FNKLX	U	(800) 544-8544	U /	-0.40	2.46	7.73 / 61	--	--	2.13	0.69

● Denotes fund is closed to new investors
* Denotes fund is included in Section II

www.thestreetratings.com

RISK			NET ASSETS		ASSET					BULL / BEAR		FUND MANAGER		MINIMUMS		LOADS	
	3 Year		NAV						Portfolio	Last Bull	Last Bear	Manager	Manager	Initial	Additional	Front	Back
Risk	Standard		As of	Total	Cash	Stocks	Bonds	Other	Turnover	Market	Market	Quality	Tenure	Purch.	Purch.	End	End
Rating/Pts	Deviation	Beta	3/31/15	$(Mil)	%	%	%	%	Ratio	Return	Return	Pct	(Years)	$	$	Load	Load
C+ / 6.1	12.1	0.90	40.87	2,951	3	96	0	1	41	75.4	-27.5	90	3	2,500	0	0.0	1.0
C+ / 6.1	12.1	0.90	40.77	702	3	96	0	1	41	76.3	-27.5	90	3	0	0	0.0	1.0
C / 4.5	12.4	0.80	28.17	698	3	96	0	1	30	65.1	-21.3	94	2	2,500	0	0.0	1.5
B- / 7.2	6.7	0.67	22.06	19,514	4	65	29	2	160	65.9	-11.8	81	8	2,500	0	0.0	0.0
B- / 7.2	6.7	0.67	22.05	6,453	4	65	29	2	160	66.5	-11.8	81	8	0	0	0.0	0.0
B+ / 9.7	3.0	0.13	9.03	940	4	6	88	2	20	44.5	-1.5	97	15	1,000,000	0	0.0	0.0
B- / 7.9	5.0	0.38	11.96	2,743	9	46	40	5	29	50.5	-6.4	93	12	2,500	0	0.0	0.8
C- / 3.9	13.3	1.06	42.67	4,964	1	98	0	1	24	86.7	-16.9	45	18	2,500	0	0.0	0.8
C+ / 6.5	11.4	0.92	129.39	1,003	4	95	0	1	48	113.5	-15.4	92	3	2,500	0	0.0	0.8
C+ / 6.8	12.2	0.82	73.26	649	1	98	0	1	125	146.1	-18.1	98	3	2,500	0	0.0	0.8
C- / 4.2	14.4	0.99	48.76	136	2	97	0	1	148	118.7	-33.1	81	2	2,500	0	0.0	0.8
C+ / 6.8	12.3	0.95	26.32	578	0	99	0	1	91	110.6	-25.9	45	3	2,500	0	0.0	0.8
D+ / 2.6	20.5	0.85	256.71	14,209	0	99	0	1	35	291.5	-12.5	99	10	2,500	0	0.0	0.8
C+ / 5.9	15.2	1.23	74.56	572	9	90	0	1	182	115.8	-30.1	21	2	2,500	0	0.0	0.8
C+ / 6.7	11.6	1.01	147.34	1,536	3	96	0	1	109	117.0	-26.7	44	5	2,500	0	0.0	0.8
C- / 3.8	17.3	1.32	31.66	249	1	98	0	1	65	73.6	-31.9	2	1	2,500	0	0.0	0.8
C / 5.1	14.3	1.26	79.11	753	1	98	0	1	35	88.4	-20.4	2	2	2,500	0	0.0	0.8
C+ / 5.7	13.6	1.10	60.87	436	2	95	1	2	53	157.3	-23.4	88	3	2,500	0	0.0	0.8
C+ / 6.2	11.1	0.94	99.37	2,070	0	99	0	1	31	83.0	-6.6	64	11	2,500	0	0.0	0.8
C+ / 5.7	11.5	1.08	35.06	1,086	2	97	0	1	138	117.8	-16.2	76	3	2,500	0	0.0	0.8
C- / 3.4	11.5	0.92	14.26	132	0	100	0	0	89	105.4	-15.9	74	3	2,500	0	0.0	0.8
C- / 4.2	15.5	1.17	87.63	2,332	5	94	0	1	186	123.1	-22.9	61	6	2,500	0	0.0	0.8
D+ / 2.4	17.2	1.07	45.33	2,162	7	92	0	1	98	34.3	-30.9	43	9	2,500	0	0.0	0.8
D / 1.9	21.6	1.24	52.94	681	2	97	0	1	34	12.1	-36.4	2	2	2,500	0	0.0	0.8
C / 5.2	11.6	0.53	20.80	87	3	96	0	1	28	71.2	-29.0	98	5	2,500	0	0.0	0.8
C+ / 6.6	11.7	0.98	88.84	1,405	7	92	0	1	197	106.6	-28.3	47	2	2,500	0	0.0	0.8
E / 0.4	37.3	1.80	16.26	865	10	88	0	2	56	-58.9	-13.6	2	8	2,500	0	0.0	0.8
C- / 4.1	12.3	0.85	243.32	10,328	1	98	0	1	99	200.1	-14.9	99	7	2,500	0	0.0	0.8
C- / 4.1	12.8	1.18	38.48	220	1	98	0	1	100	92.9	-28.5	5	3	2,500	0	0.0	0.8
C+ / 6.1	11.6	1.07	32.32	1,137	0	99	0	1	58	108.6	-26.1	51	8	2,500	0	0.0	0.8
C+ / 6.7	12.3	0.98	67.08	402	1	98	0	1	126	113.0	-22.5	85	2	2,500	0	0.0	0.8
C+ / 5.7	14.4	1.26	38.89	988	2	97	0	1	74	127.8	-17.3	64	6	2,500	0	0.0	0.8
C / 5.2	12.6	0.97	139.59	449	3	96	0	1	65	109.1	-12.1	69	2	2,500	0	0.0	0.8
C+ / 5.8	11.9	1.09	77.55	1,043	0	99	0	1	53	78.9	-28.3	4	7	2,500	0	0.0	0.8
C+ / 6.0	11.1	0.68	90.32	929	0	99	0	1	65	119.7	-17.6	97	3	2,500	0	0.0	0.8
C / 5.0	12.9	0.94	43.00	2,189	0	99	0	1	75	123.8	-15.9	98	8	2,500	0	0.0	0.8
C+ / 6.5	12.8	1.16	82.20	797	0	100	0	0	111	147.3	-22.5	90	2	2,500	0	0.0	0.8
D+ / 2.9	17.0	0.99	31.14	501	7	90	0	3	135	25.7	-28.0	28	3	2,500	0	0.0	0.8
D+ / 2.4	17.3	1.03	31.07	738	5	94	0	1	99	25.2	-31.0	23	9	2,500	0	0.0	0.8
C / 5.1	10.5	0.83	23.67	1,997	1	98	0	1	95	140.0	-10.4	99	2	2,500	0	0.0	0.8
C+ / 5.9	13.8	1.15	95.25	956	2	96	0	2	72	123.2	-8.4	83	1	2,500	0	0.0	0.8
C / 4.9	13.6	1.13	117.15	2,921	2	97	0	1	87	119.2	-15.4	55	1	2,500	0	0.0	0.8
C- / 4.1	12.4	0.97	120.51	2,795	1	98	0	1	181	89.6	-21.6	42	8	2,500	0	0.0	0.8
C+ / 6.8	10.7	0.68	61.94	326	0	99	0	1	111	66.8	-16.6	84	2	2,500	0	0.0	0.8
C+ / 6.9	11.8	0.86	91.17	1,027	0	99	0	1	78	150.8	-23.3	98	3	2,500	0	0.0	0.8
C+ / 6.2	12.1	0.81	73.01	915	5	94	0	1	160	62.9	-2.4	92	9	2,500	0	0.0	0.8
C- / 4.2	10.5	0.88	9.26	261	0	99	0	1	120	70.8	-15.6	53	6	2,500	0	0.0	0.8
U /	N/A	N/A	11.20	877	2	97	0	1	0	N/A	N/A	N/A	2	0	0	0.0	0.0
U /	N/A	N/A	11.20	982	2	97	0	1	0	N/A	N/A	N/A	2	0	0	0.0	0.0
U /	N/A	N/A	12.77	3,064	1	98	0	1	67	N/A	N/A	N/A	2	0	0	0.0	0.0
U /	N/A	N/A	12.77	4,481	1	98	0	1	67	N/A	N/A	N/A	2	0	0	0.0	0.0
U /	N/A	N/A	12.62	5,047	6	93	0	1	42	N/A	N/A	N/A	3	0	0	0.0	0.0

						PERFORMANCE							
	99 Pct = Best							Total Return % through 3/31/15				Incl. in Returns	
	0 Pct = Worst			Overall		Perfor-					Annualized	Dividend	Expense
Fund		Ticker	Investment			mance							
Type	Fund Name	Symbol	Rating	Phone		Rating/Pts	3 Mo	6 Mo	1Yr / Pct	3Yr / Pct	5Yr / Pct	Yield	Ratio
GR	Fidelity Series Equity Income F	FRLLX	U	(800) 544-8544		U /	-0.32	2.54	7.92 /62	--	--	2.31	0.51
FO	Fidelity Series Global ex US Idx Fd	FSGEX	D-	(800) 544-8544		D / 1.7	3.87	-0.52	-1.08 /13	6.26 /18	4.64 /11	2.97	0.20
GR	Fidelity Series Growth and Income	FGLGX	U	(800) 522-7297		U /	0.37	3.47	9.23 /71	--	--	1.64	0.66
GR	Fidelity Series Growth and Income F	FTBTX	U	(800) 522-7297		U /	0.37	3.56	9.42 /72	--	--	1.81	0.48
GR	Fidelity Series Growth Company	FCGSX	U	(800) 544-8544		U /	5.03	12.00	17.07 /95	--	--	0.18	0.74
GR	Fidelity Series Growth Company F	FFGSX	U	(800) 544-8544		U /	5.03	11.98	17.15 /95	--	--	0.33	0.57
CV	Fidelity Series High Income	FSHNX	C-	(800) 544-8544		D / 1.9	1.90	1.18	1.02 /18	6.51 /19	--	5.44	0.70
CV	Fidelity Series High Income F	FSHFX	C-	(800) 544-8544		D / 2.0	1.93	1.23	1.13 /19	6.64 /20	--	5.55	0.58
FO	Fidelity Series International Gr	FIGSX	C-	(800) 544-8544		C / 4.4	6.59	5.95	4.52 /35	9.96 /39	9.24 /38	1.27	0.97
*FO	Fidelity Series International Gr F	FFIGX	C-	(800) 544-8544		C / 4.5	6.65	6.12	4.78 /37	10.19 /40	9.48 /40	1.45	0.80
FO	Fidelity Series International SC	FSTSX	C	(800) 544-8544		C / 5.3	6.72	5.57	0.28 /16	12.37 /55	11.27 /55	0.87	1.18
FO	Fidelity Series International SC F	FFSTX	C	(800) 544-8544		C / 5.4	6.78	5.64	0.43 /17	12.58 /57	11.47 /57	1.07	1.01
FO	Fidelity Series International Val	FINVX	D	(800) 544-8544		C- / 3.3	4.97	0.43	-2.01 /10	9.63 /37	4.56 /10	4.18	0.82
*FO	Fidelity Series International Val F	FFVNX	D	(800) 544-8544		C- / 3.4	4.96	0.43	-1.91 /11	9.80 /38	4.76 /11	4.37	0.65
GR	Fidelity Series Intrinsic Opp	FDMLX	U	(800) 522-7297		U /	5.22	8.08	13.43 /88	--	--	1.33	0.81
GR	Fidelity Series Intrinsic Opp F	FGLLX	U	(800) 522-7297		U /	5.29	8.22	13.68 /89	--	--	1.48	0.64
GR	Fidelity Series Opp Insights	FVWSX	U	(800) 522-7297		U /	4.07	7.52	14.83 /91	--	--	0.00	0.84
GR	Fidelity Series Opp Insights F	FWWEX	U	(800) 522-7297		U /	4.06	7.66	15.06 /92	--	--	0.08	0.67
SC	Fidelity Series Sm Cap Discovery	FJACX	U	(800) 544-8544		U /	4.63	16.26	11.76 /82	--	--	0.17	1.01
SC	Fidelity Series Sm Cap Discovery F	FJAKX	U	(800) 544-8544		U /	4.73	16.37	11.92 /82	--	--	0.31	0.83
SC	Fidelity Sm Cap Enhanced Index Fd	FCPEX	A	(800) 544-8544		A / 9.4	6.78	16.63	11.86 /82	17.90 /94	16.70 /95	0.41	0.73
*SC ●	Fidelity Small Cap Discovery Fund	FSCRX	A-	(800) 544-8544		A- / 9.1	1.93	12.76	8.47 /66	18.23 /95	17.77 /97	0.25	1.01
SC	Fidelity Small Cap Growth Fund	FCPGX	B	(800) 544-8544		A / 9.5	8.75	19.22	12.18 /83	17.99 /94	15.99 /93	0.00	0.91
SC	Fidelity Small Cap Opp Fd	FSOPX	C	(800) 544-8544		C+ / 6.7	5.07	13.28	6.51 /51	13.34 /62	14.06 /78	0.29	0.82
SC	Fidelity Small Cap Stock Fund	FSLCX	C+	(800) 544-8544		B- / 7.5	7.08	14.96	14.23 /90	13.88 /66	9.99 /44	0.52	0.68
SC ●	Fidelity Small Cap Value Fund	FCPVX	B-	(800) 544-8544		B+ / 8.7	2.17	13.84	8.66 /67	17.02 /90	14.66 /84	0.34	1.09
IX	Fidelity Spartan 500 Index Adv	FUSVX	A	(800) 544-8544		B / 8.2	0.95	5.90	12.69 /86	16.06 /84	14.42 /82	1.82	0.07
IX	Fidelity Spartan 500 Index FAI	FXAIX	A	(800) 544-8544		B+ / 8.3	0.95	5.92	12.70 /86	16.09 /84	14.44 /82	1.85	0.03
IX	Fidelity Spartan 500 Index Inst	FXSIX	A	(800) 544-8544		B+ / 8.3	0.93	5.91	12.70 /86	16.08 /84	14.42 /82	1.83	0.05
*IX	Fidelity Spartan 500 Index Inv	FUSEX	A	(800) 544-8544		B / 8.2	0.92	5.88	12.62 /85	16.01 /83	14.37 /81	1.78	0.10
EM	Fidelity Spartan EM Index FA	FPMAX	E	(800) 544-8544		E+ / 0.6	2.02	-1.80	2.95 /26	0.44 / 5	--	1.89	0.35
EM	Fidelity Spartan EM Index FAI	FPADX	E	(800) 544-8544		E+ / 0.6	1.91	-1.80	3.05 /27	0.52 / 5	--	1.99	0.25
EM	Fidelity Spartan EM Index Inst	FPMIX	E	(800) 544-8544		E+ / 0.6	2.02	-1.73	3.02 /27	0.52 / 5	--	1.96	0.28
EM	Fidelity Spartan EM Index Inv	FPEMX	E	(800) 544-8544		E / 0.5	1.91	-1.92	2.73 /25	0.32 / 5	--	1.78	0.46
GR	Fidelity Spartan Ext Mkt Idx Adv	FSEVX	A-	(800) 544-8544		A- / 9.1	5.33	12.22	10.37 /76	17.40 /92	15.85 /92	1.20	0.07
GI	Fidelity Spartan Ext Mkt Idx FAI	FSMAX	A-	(800) 544-8544		A- / 9.1	5.33	12.21	10.37 /76	17.41 /92	15.85 /92	1.21	0.07
GR	Fidelity Spartan Ext Mkt Idx Inv	FSEMX	A-	(800) 544-8544		A- / 9.1	5.31	12.20	10.32 /76	17.36 /92	15.82 /92	1.17	0.10
FO	Fidelity Spartan Gl ex US Idx FA	FSGDX	D-	(800) 544-8544		D- / 1.5	3.82	-0.59	-1.15 /13	6.17 /17	--	2.35	0.28
FO	Fidelity Spartan Gl ex US Idx FAI	FSGGX	D-	(800) 544-8544		D- / 1.5	3.90	-0.59	-1.15 /13	6.23 /18	--	2.35	0.20
FO	Fidelity Spartan Gl ex US Idx Inst	FSGSX	D-	(800) 544-8544		D- / 1.5	3.90	-0.46	-1.10 /13	6.22 /18	--	2.40	0.23
FO	Fidelity Spartan Gl ex US Idx Inv	FSGUX	D-	(800) 544-8544		D- / 1.5	3.82	-0.55	-1.19 /12	6.11 /17	--	2.31	0.34
FO	Fidelity Spartan Intl Index Adv	FSIVX	D	(800) 544-8544		C- / 3.0	5.32	1.10	-1.04 /13	9.01 /33	6.25 /18	3.29	0.17
FO	Fidelity Spartan Intl Index FAI	FSPSX	D	(800) 544-8544		C- / 3.0	5.35	1.14	-0.96 /13	9.09 /34	6.28 /19	3.35	0.08
FO	Fidelity Spartan Intl Index Inst	FSPNX	D	(800) 544-8544		C- / 3.0	5.35	1.13	-0.97 /13	9.07 /33	6.27 /19	3.34	0.10
FO	Fidelity Spartan Intl Index Inv	FSIIX	D	(800) 544-8544		D+ / 2.9	5.32	1.06	-1.10 /13	8.94 /32	6.19 /18	3.21	0.20
MC	Fidelity Spartan Mid Cap Idx FA	FSCKX	A+	(800) 544-8544		A / 9.3	3.95	10.13	13.59 /88	18.01 /94	--	1.14	0.21
MC	Fidelity Spartan Mid Cap Idx FAI	FSMDX	A+	(800) 544-8544		A / 9.3	3.95	10.09	13.64 /89	18.03 /94	--	1.18	0.13
MC	Fidelity Spartan Mid Cap Idx Inst	FSTPX	A+	(800) 544-8544		A / 9.3	3.95	10.08	13.62 /88	18.00 /94	--	1.16	0.15
MC	Fidelity Spartan Mid Cap Idx Inv	FSCLX	A+	(800) 544-8544		A / 9.3	3.90	10.06	13.45 /88	17.85 /94	--	1.01	0.34
RE	Fidelity Spartan Real Est Idx FA	FSRVX	B-	(800) 544-8544		A / 9.4	4.75	20.44	25.12 /98	13.84 /66	--	2.02	0.19
RE	Fidelity Spartan Real Est Idx Inst	FSRNX	B-	(800) 544-8544		A / 9.4	4.82	20.53	25.23 /98	13.89 /66	--	2.03	0.15
RE	Fidelity Spartan Real Est Idx Inv	FRXIX	B-	(800) 544-8544		A / 9.4	4.80	20.37	25.06 /98	13.66 /65	--	1.89	0.33

● Denotes fund is closed to new investors
* Denotes fund is included in Section II

www.thestreetratings.com

I. Index of Stock Mutual Funds

RISK			NET ASSETS		ASSET					BULL / BEAR		FUND MANAGER		MINIMUMS		LOADS	
	3 Year		NAV						Portfolio	Last Bull	Last Bear	Manager	Manager	Initial	Additional	Front	Back
Risk	Standard		As of	Total	Cash	Stocks	Bonds	Other	Turnover	Market	Market	Quality	Tenure	Purch.	Purch.	End	End
Rating/Pts	Deviation	Beta	3/31/15	$(Mil)	%	%	%	%	Ratio	Return	Return	Pct	(Years)	$	$	Load	Load
U /	N/A	N/A	12.63	7,389	6	93	0	1	42	N/A	N/A	N/A	3	0	0	0.0	0.0
C+ / 5.7	12.8	0.95	11.80	2,798	5	94	0	1	2	41.8	-24.2	29	6	0	0	0.0	0.0
U /	N/A	N/A	13.56	3,857	3	96	0	1	53	N/A	N/A	N/A	3	0	0	0.0	0.0
U /	N/A	N/A	13.58	5,647	3	96	0	1	53	N/A	N/A	N/A	3	0	0	0.0	0.0
U /	N/A	N/A	12.58	4,479	0	99	0	1	14	N/A	N/A	N/A	2	0	0	0.0	0.0
U /	N/A	N/A	12.58	6,535	0	99	0	1	14	N/A	N/A	N/A	2	0	0	0.0	0.0
B / 8.0	4.5	0.47	9.80	3,043	8	2	88	2	54	37.6	-8.4	70	4	0	0	0.0	0.0
B / 8.0	4.5	0.47	9.80	3,305	8	2	88	2	54	38.1	-8.4	72	4	0	0	0.0	0.0
C+ / 6.2	11.3	0.82	14.39	6,052	2	97	0	1	33	62.2	-22.4	84	6	0	0	0.0	0.0
C+ / 6.2	11.3	0.83	14.43	6,784	2	97	0	1	33	63.4	-22.3	85	6	0	0	0.0	0.0
C+ / 6.4	11.0	0.75	15.87	1,386	1	98	0	1	18	67.0	-20.9	93	6	0	0	0.0	0.0
C+ / 6.4	10.9	0.75	15.90	1,557	1	98	0	1	18	68.1	-20.8	94	6	0	0	0.0	0.0
C / 4.8	13.3	0.99	10.13	5,970	1	98	0	1	70	51.0	-27.6	69	4	0	0	0.0	0.0
C / 4.8	13.3	0.99	10.15	6,690	1	98	0	1	70	52.1	-27.5	71	4	0	0	0.0	0.0
U /	N/A	N/A	15.11	2,577	0	98	0	2	16	N/A	N/A	N/A	3	0	0	0.0	0.0
U /	N/A	N/A	15.13	3,774	0	98	0	2	16	N/A	N/A	N/A	3	0	0	0.0	0.0
U /	N/A	N/A	15.43	2,522	3	96	0	1	52	N/A	N/A	N/A	3	0	0	0.0	0.0
U /	N/A	N/A	15.46	3,694	3	96	0	1	52	N/A	N/A	N/A	3	0	0	0.0	0.0
U /	N/A	N/A	11.29	666	0	99	0	1	0	N/A	N/A	N/A	2	0	0	0.0	0.0
U /	N/A	N/A	11.30	982	0	99	0	1	0	N/A	N/A	N/A	2	0	0	0.0	0.0
C+ / 6.0	13.1	0.96	13.38	504	3	96	0	1	107	110.7	-23.5	85	8	2,500	0	0.0	1.5
C+ / 6.1	12.6	0.88	30.67	6,115	0	99	0	1	17	121.9	-24.4	90	9	2,500	0	0.0	1.5
C- / 4.1	13.2	0.93	20.02	1,009	3	96	0	1	148	102.8	-24.5	87	4	2,500	0	0.0	1.5
C / 5.2	12.4	0.91	13.69	2,715	4	95	0	1	90	85.2	-25.4	50	8	0	0	0.0	0.0
C / 5.3	12.1	0.86	20.12	1,896	3	96	0	1	50	85.7	-32.4	67	4	2,500	0	0.0	2.0
C / 4.4	12.8	0.89	19.34	2,086	0	99	0	1	26	109.4	-23.6	86	7	2,500	0	0.0	1.5
B- / 7.3	9.5	1.00	73.54	49,391	1	98	0	1	4	100.0	-16.3	67	9	10,000	0	0.0	0.0
B- / 7.3	9.5	1.00	73.54	6,362	1	98	0	1	4	100.2	-16.3	67	9	0	0	0.0	0.0
B- / 7.3	9.5	1.00	73.54	25,139	1	98	0	1	4	100.0	-16.3	67	9	0	0	0.0	0.0
B- / 7.3	9.5	1.00	73.52	7,112	1	98	0	1	4	99.7	-16.3	66	9	2,500	0	0.0	0.0
C / 5.0	14.1	1.02	9.60	412	5	94	0	1	8	21.8	N/A	64	4	10,000	0	0.0	1.5
C / 5.0	14.1	1.02	9.60	N/A	5	94	0	1	8	22.3	N/A	65	4	0	0	0.0	1.5
C / 5.0	14.1	1.02	9.61	35	5	94	0	1	8	22.2	N/A	65	4	0	0	0.0	1.5
C / 5.1	14.1	1.02	9.59	19	5	94	0	1	8	21.3	N/A	62	4	2,500	0	0.0	1.5
C+ / 6.1	11.8	1.08	58.12	13,866	2	97	0	1	14	107.2	-23.6	67	11	10,000	0	0.0	0.8
C+ / 6.1	11.7	1.08	58.10	961	2	97	0	1	14	107.3	-23.6	67	11	0	0	0.0	0.8
C+ / 6.1	11.8	1.08	58.11	2,001	2	97	0	1	14	107.0	-23.6	66	11	2,500	0	0.0	0.8
C+ / 5.8	12.7	0.95	11.97	582	6	93	0	1	1	41.6	N/A	29	4	10,000	0	0.0	1.0
C+ / 5.8	12.7	0.95	11.98	80	6	93	0	1	1	41.9	N/A	30	4	0	0	0.0	1.0
C+ / 5.8	12.7	0.95	11.98	170	6	93	0	1	1	41.8	N/A	29	4	0	0	0.0	1.0
C+ / 5.8	12.7	0.95	11.97	17	6	93	0	1	1	41.4	N/A	28	4	2,500	0	0.0	1.0
C+ / 5.7	13.2	1.00	39.20	8,284	6	93	0	1	2	51.9	-23.0	60	11	10,000	0	0.0	1.0
C+ / 5.7	13.2	1.00	39.21	2,020	6	93	0	1	2	52.1	-23.0	61	11	0	0	0.0	1.0
C+ / 5.8	13.2	1.00	39.21	1,971	6	93	0	1	2	52.1	-23.0	61	11	0	0	0.0	1.0
C+ / 5.8	13.2	1.00	39.20	2,911	6	93	0	1	2	51.5	-23.0	59	11	2,500	0	0.0	1.0
C+ / 6.7	10.2	0.91	18.14	951	1	98	0	1	7	108.2	N/A	85	4	10,000	0	0.0	0.8
C+ / 6.7	10.2	0.91	18.14	26	1	98	0	1	7	108.5	N/A	85	4	0	0	0.0	0.8
C+ / 6.7	10.2	0.91	18.14	228	1	98	0	1	7	108.4	N/A	85	4	0	0	0.0	0.8
C+ / 6.7	10.2	0.91	18.12	35	1	98	0	1	7	107.2	N/A	85	4	2,500	200	0.0	0.8
C- / 3.9	13.4	1.07	15.50	533	1	98	0	1	14	84.7	N/A	49	4	10,000	0	0.0	0.8
C- / 3.9	13.5	1.08	15.51	36	1	98	0	1	14	84.8	N/A	49	4	0	0	0.0	0.8
C- / 3.9	13.4	1.07	15.49	33	1	98	0	1	14	83.7	N/A	47	4	2,500	0	0.0	0.8

Data as of March 31, 2015

Fund Type	Fund Name	Ticker Symbol	Overall Investment Rating	Phone	Performance Rating/Pts	3 Mo	6 Mo	1Yr / Pct	3Yr / Pct	5Yr / Pct	Dividend Yield	Expense Ratio
	99 Pct = Best											
	0 Pct = Worst											
SC	Fidelity Spartan Small Cap Idx FA	FSSVX	B+	(800) 544-8544	B+ / 8.5	4.41	14.65	8.48 /66	16.43 /86	--	1.11	0.34
SC	Fidelity Spartan Small Cap Idx FAI	FSSNX	B+	(800) 544-8544	B+ / 8.5	4.35	14.61	8.52 /66	16.48 /87	--	1.15	0.26
SC	Fidelity Spartan Small Cap Idx Inst	FSSSX	B+	(800) 544-8544	B+ / 8.5	4.35	14.59	8.50 /66	16.45 /87	--	1.13	0.28
SC	Fidelity Spartan Small Cap Idx Inv	FSSPX	B+	(800) 544-8544	B+ / 8.4	4.29	14.52	8.27 /65	16.25 /85	--	0.98	0.47
GI	Fidelity Spartan Total Mkt Idx Adv	FSTVX	A	(800) 544-8544	B+ / 8.4	1.82	7.15	12.26 /84	16.32 /86	14.71 /84	1.59	0.05
GI	Fidelity Spartan Total Mkt Idx F	FFSMX	A	(800) 544-8544	B+ / 8.4	1.80	7.14	12.27 /84	16.34 /86	14.72 /84	1.61	0.05
GI	Fidelity Spartan Total Mkt Idx FAI	FSKAX	A	(800) 544-8544	B+ / 8.4	1.82	7.16	12.28 /84	16.34 /86	14.71 /84	1.61	0.06
GI	Fidelity Spartan Total Mkt Idx Ins	FSKTX	A	(800) 544-8544	B+ / 8.4	1.82	7.14	12.27 /84	16.33 /86	14.70 /84	1.60	0.07
GI	Fidelity Spartan Total Mkt Idx Inv	FSTMX	A	(800) 544-8544	B+ / 8.3	1.80	7.11	12.21 /84	16.27 /85	14.66 /84	1.55	0.10
GR	Fidelity Srs All-Sector Equity Fd	FSAEX	B+	(800) 544-8544	B+ / 8.6	2.57	7.02	12.93 /86	16.48 /87	14.21 /80	0.87	0.65
GR	Fidelity Srs All-Sector Equity Fd F	FSFFX	B+	(800) 544-8544	B+ / 8.8	2.66	7.06	13.13 /87	16.70 /88	14.41 /81	1.03	0.47
GR	Fidelity Srs Broad Market Opps Fd	FBMAX	A-	(800) 544-8544	B+ / 8.6	3.42	7.45	11.74 /81	16.39 /86	13.96 /77	0.40	1.09
OT	Fidelity Srs Commodity Strat Fund	FCSSX	E-	(800) 544-8544	E- / 0.1	-6.28	-17.63	-27.57 / 0	-12.13 / 1	-6.36 / 1	0.00	0.64
OT	Fidelity Srs Commodity Strat Fund F	FCSFX	E-	(800) 544-8544	E- / 0.1	-6.23	-17.51	-27.41 / 0	-11.95 / 1	-6.18 / 1	0.00	0.44
* EM	Fidelity Srs Emerging Markets Fd	FEMSX	E+	(800) 544-8544	E+ / 0.7	2.04	-3.93	-0.07 /15	2.10 / 6	2.59 / 5	0.82	1.06
EM	Fidelity Srs Emerging Markets Fd F	FEMFX	E+	(800) 544-8544	E+ / 0.7	2.10	-3.88	0.09 /16	2.27 / 7	2.79 / 6	0.97	0.89
RE	Fidelity Srs Real Estate Equity	FREDX	B-	(800) 544-8544	A+ / 9.6	5.56	20.50	25.03 /98	14.19 /69	--	1.57	0.77
RE	Fidelity Srs Real Estate Equity F	FREFX	B-	(800) 544-8544	A+ / 9.6	5.63	20.64	25.28 /98	14.41 /70	--	1.70	0.59
AA	Fidelity Srs Real Estate Income	FSREX	C+	(800) 544-8544	C / 4.3	2.36	5.57	8.45 /66	9.76 /38	--	5.18	0.77
AA	Fidelity Srs Real Estate Income F	FSRWX	C+	(800) 544-8544	C / 4.4	2.38	5.65	8.63 /67	9.95 /39	--	5.35	0.61
SC	Fidelity Srs Small Cap Opp Fd F	FSOFX	C+	(800) 544-8544	C+ / 6.8	5.11	13.36	6.74 /53	13.53 /64	14.28 /80	0.46	0.65
GR	Fidelity Srs Stock Selector LCV	FBLEX	U	(800) 544-8544	U /	0.83	6.56	12.69 /86	--	--	1.30	0.75
GR	Fidelity Srs Stock Selector LCV F	FRGEX	U	(800) 544-8544	U /	0.76	6.57	12.78 /86	--	--	1.47	0.57
GR	Fidelity Stock Sel Lg Cap Val LCV	FSLVX	A+	(800) 544-8544	B+ / 8.3	0.48	5.19	10.25 /75	16.62 /88	12.56 /65	0.94	0.72
GR	Fidelity Stock Selector All Cap	FDSSX	B+	(800) 544-8544	B+ / 8.7	3.57	7.47	12.08 /83	16.66 /88	14.18 /79	0.68	0.67
GR	Fidelity Stock Selector All Cap K	FSSKX	B+	(800) 544-8544	B+ / 8.8	3.60	7.50	12.15 /83	16.77 /89	14.33 /81	0.76	0.58
SC	Fidelity Stock Selector Small Cap	FDSCX	C+	(800) 544-8544	B- / 7.1	5.35	14.36	7.80 /61	14.23 /69	14.80 /85	0.33	0.73
GL	Fidelity Strat Adv Core Mlt Mngr	FLAUX	B+	(800) 544-8544	B- / 7.4	1.18	5.76	11.63 /81	14.91 /74	--	0.78	1.22
GL	Fidelity Strat Adv Core Mlt Mngr F	FHJSX	B+	(800) 544-8544	B- / 7.2	1.26	5.84	11.79 /82	14.60 /72	--	0.78	1.12
GL	Fidelity Strat Adv Core Mlt Mngr L	FQAPX	B-	(800) 544-8544	B- / 7.4	1.18	5.76	11.63 /81	14.91 /74	--	0.78	1.20
GL	Fidelity Strat Adv Core Mlt Mngr N	FQAQX	B-	(800) 544-8544	B- / 7.1	1.10	5.61	11.37 /80	14.47 /71	--	0.56	1.46
GL	Fidelity Strat Adv Gro Mlt Mng	FMELX	A-	(800) 544-8544	B / 8.2	3.75	7.98	14.09 /90	15.35 /78	--	0.38	0.84
GL	Fidelity Strat Adv Gro Mlt Mng F	FFSPX	A-	(800) 544-8544	B / 8.2	3.83	8.04	14.21 /90	15.24 /77	--	0.48	0.74
GL	Fidelity Strat Adv Gro Mlt Mng L	FQACX	B	(800) 544-8544	B+ / 8.3	3.83	8.06	14.12 /90	15.37 /78	--	0.41	0.85
GL	Fidelity Strat Adv Gro Mlt Mng N	FQAEX	B	(800) 544-8544	B / 7.8	3.68	7.83	13.77 /89	14.74 /73	--	0.19	1.11
FO	Fidelity Strat Adv Intl M-M	FMJDX	U	(800) 544-8544	U /	5.61	2.81	1.28 /19	--	--	2.15	1.21
GR	Fidelity Strat Adv SmMid Cp MM	FNAPX	B	(800) 544-8544	B- / 7.1	4.89	10.65	7.71 /61	14.60 /72	--	0.00	1.30
GR	Fidelity Strat Adv SmMid Cp MM F	FARMX	C+	(800) 544-8544	C+ / 6.8	4.88	10.72	7.78 /61	14.15 /68	--	0.00	1.29
GR	Fidelity Strat Adv SmMid Cp MM L	FQAJX	C+	(800) 544-8544	B- / 7.0	4.81	10.57	7.63 /60	14.57 /71	--	0.00	1.50
GR	Fidelity Strat Adv SmMid Cp MM N	FQAKX	C+	(800) 544-8544	C+ / 6.7	4.81	10.52	7.45 /59	14.01 /67	--	0.00	1.75
GL	Fidelity Strat Adv Value Mlt Mngr	FKMOX	A-	(800) 544-8544	B- / 7.4	0.14	4.88	8.94 /69	15.45 /79	--	0.93	1.32
GL	Fidelity Strat Adv Value Mlt Mngr F	FGWBX	B-	(800) 544-8544	C+ / 6.9	0.14	4.87	8.99 /69	14.64 /72	--	0.93	1.26
GL	Fidelity Strat Adv Value Mlt Mngr L	FQALX	B-	(800) 544-8544	B- / 7.4	0.14	4.88	8.93 /69	15.45 /79	--	0.93	1.38
GL	Fidelity Strat Adv Value Mlt Mngr N	FQAMX	C+	(800) 544-8544	B- / 7.0	0.07	4.73	8.67 /67	14.85 /74	--	0.70	1.63
EM	Fidelity Strategic Adv Emerg Mkt	FSAMX	E	(800) 544-8544	E / 0.5	0.87	-3.60	-0.65 /14	0.40 / 5	--	1.59	1.38
* IN	Fidelity Strategic Advisers Core	FCSAX	B	(800) 544-8544	B / 8.0	1.41	6.08	11.74 /81	15.71 /81	13.63 /74	0.97	0.97
* GR	Fidelity Strategic Advisers Growth	FSGFX	B+	(800) 544-8544	B+ / 8.4	3.84	8.48	14.60 /91	15.57 /80	--	0.66	0.78
* FO	Fidelity Strategic Advisers Intl	FILFX	D	(800) 544-8544	C- / 3.5	5.72	3.11	0.73 /18	9.24 /34	7.13 /24	1.70	1.14
FO	Fidelity Strategic Advisers Intl II	FUSIX	D+	(800) 544-8544	C- / 4.1	5.55	3.69	1.69 /21	10.24 /41	7.01 /23	1.12	1.17
* GR	Fidelity Strategic Advisers Sm-Mid	FSCFX	C	(800) 544-8544	B- / 7.4	4.22	10.82	7.07 /56	14.73 /73	13.35 /72	0.17	1.17
* GR	Fidelity Strategic Advisers Val Fd	FVSAX	A-	(800) 544-8544	B / 7.9	0.48	5.42	9.66 /73	16.10 /84	13.01 /68	1.31	0.79
GI	Fidelity Strategic Div and Inc	FSDIX	B	(800) 544-8544	C+ / 6.0	1.02	5.43	10.52 /76	12.68 /57	12.08 /61	2.71	0.78

● Denotes fund is closed to new investors

* Denotes fund is included in Section II

www.thestreetratings.com

RISK			NET ASSETS		ASSET				BULL / BEAR		FUND MANAGER		MINIMUMS		LOADS	
	3 Year		NAV						Portfolio	Last Bull Last Bear		Manager Manager		Initial Additional		Front Back	
Risk Rating/Pts	Standard Deviation	Beta	As of 3/31/15	Total $(Mil)	Cash %	Stocks %	Bonds %	Other %	Turnover Ratio	Market Return	Market Return	Quality Pct	Tenure (Years)	Purch. $	Purch. $	End Load	End Load
C+ / 5.9	13.4	1.00	17.52	898	3	96	0	1	9	100.7	N/A	69	4	10,000	0	0.0	1.5
C+ / 5.9	13.4	1.00	17.52	5	3	96	0	1	9	101.0	N/A	69	4	0	0	0.0	1.5
C+ / 5.9	13.4	1.00	17.52	363	3	96	0	1	9	100.9	N/A	69	4	0	0	0.0	1.5
C+ / 5.9	13.4	1.00	17.49	31	3	96	0	1	9	100.0	N/A	67	4	2,500	0	0.0	1.5
B- / 7.2	9.8	1.02	60.96	18,885	2	97	0	1	2	101.3	-17.7	66	11	10,000	0	0.0	0.5
B- / 7.2	9.8	1.02	60.96	6,395	2	97	0	1	2	101.4	-17.7	67	11	0	0	0.0	0.5
B- / 7.2	9.8	1.02	60.95	871	2	97	0	1	2	101.4	-17.7	67	11	0	0	0.0	0.5
B- / 7.2	9.8	1.02	60.95	1,298	2	97	0	1	2	101.3	-17.7	67	11	0	0	0.0	0.5
B- / 7.2	9.8	1.02	60.95	1,954	2	97	0	1	2	101.0	-17.7	66	11	2,500	0	0.0	0.5
C+ / 5.9	9.7	1.00	14.16	5,129	4	95	0	1	72	98.8	-18.7	70	7	0	0	0.0	0.0
C+ / 5.8	9.7	1.00	14.15	5,676	4	95	0	1	72	100.0	-18.5	73	7	0	0	0.0	0.0
C+ / 6.5	10.0	1.01	15.71	17	3	96	0	1	18	99.8	-21.4	68	6	0	0	0.0	0.0
D+ / 2.3	12.9	0.73	6.12	801	99	0	0	1	23	-27.7	-20.5	0	6	0	0	0.0	0.0
D+ / 2.3	12.8	0.73	6.17	857	99	0	0	1	23	-27.2	-20.5	0	6	0	0	0.0	0.0
C / 5.3	14.1	1.00	17.00	5,418	2	97	0	1	93	30.3	-28.3	80	6	0	0	0.0	0.0
C / 5.3	14.1	1.00	17.04	6,035	2	97	0	1	93	31.2	-28.2	81	6	0	0	0.0	0.0
C- / 3.5	13.2	1.05	15.01	583	1	98	0	1	69	N/A	N/A	58	4	0	0	0.0	0.0
C- / 3.5	13.2	1.05	15.02	667	1	98	0	1	69	N/A	N/A	61	4	0	0	0.0	0.0
B / 8.3	3.7	0.34	11.31	411	3	37	52	8	33	N/A	N/A	95	4	0	0	0.0	0.0
B / 8.2	3.7	0.34	11.31	443	3	37	52	8	33	N/A	N/A	95	4	0	0	0.0	0.0
C / 5.2	12.5	0.91	13.77	3,043	4	95	0	1	90	86.3	-25.3	52	8	0	0	0.0	0.0
U /	N/A	N/A	12.99	3,371	5	94	0	1	66	N/A	N/A	N/A	3	0	0	0.0	0.0
U /	N/A	N/A	12.99	4,935	5	94	0	1	66	N/A	N/A	N/A	3	0	0	0.0	0.0
B- / 7.4	9.7	0.99	17.22	761	4	95	0	1	64	102.3	-20.1	74	3	2,500	0	0.0	0.0
C+ / 5.6	9.9	1.00	36.58	4,604	3	96	0	1	10	100.6	-21.1	73	6	2,500	0	0.0	0.0
C / 5.5	9.9	1.00	36.58	107	3	96	0	1	10	101.3	-21.1	74	6	0	0	0.0	0.0
C+ / 5.7	12.6	0.92	26.00	1,456	3	96	0	1	73	89.9	-25.4	59	10	2,500	0	0.0	1.5
B- / 7.5	9.7	0.59	12.83	59	6	93	0	1	134	N/A	N/A	97	2	0	0	0.0	0.0
B- / 7.4	9.8	0.59	12.86	3	6	93	0	1	134	N/A	N/A	97	2	0	0	0.0	0.0
C+ / 5.9	9.8	0.60	12.83	N/A	6	93	0	1	134	N/A	N/A	97	2	0	0	0.0	0.0
C+ / 5.9	9.7	0.60	12.82	N/A	6	93	0	1	134	N/A	N/A	97	2	0	0	0.0	0.0
C+ / 6.9	10.5	0.62	13.83	61	5	94	0	1	51	N/A	N/A	97	4	0	0	0.0	0.0
C+ / 6.9	10.5	0.62	13.83	2	5	94	0	1	51	N/A	N/A	97	4	0	0	0.0	0.0
C+ / 5.7	10.5	0.62	13.83	N/A	5	94	0	1	51	N/A	N/A	97	4	0	0	0.0	0.0
C+ / 5.7	10.5	0.62	13.81	N/A	5	94	0	1	51	N/A	N/A	97	4	0	0	0.0	0.0
U /	N/A	N/A	12.04	63	10	89	0	1	46	N/A	N/A	N/A	2	0	0	0.0	1.0
C+ / 6.5	11.6	1.05	11.58	34	5	94	0	1	117	N/A	N/A	36	4	0	0	0.0	1.5
C+ / 6.5	11.6	1.06	11.60	1	5	94	0	1	117	N/A	N/A	30	4	0	0	0.0	1.5
C / 5.4	11.6	1.05	11.56	N/A	5	94	0	1	117	N/A	N/A	35	4	0	0	0.0	1.5
C / 5.3	11.6	1.06	11.56	N/A	5	94	0	1	117	N/A	N/A	29	4	0	0	0.0	1.5
B- / 7.8	10.3	0.59	14.45	17	4	95	0	1	59	N/A	N/A	98	N/A	0	0	0.0	0.0
B- / 7.8	10.3	0.58	14.49	3	4	95	0	1	59	N/A	N/A	97	N/A	0	0	0.0	0.0
C+ / 5.7	10.3	0.59	14.45	N/A	4	95	0	1	59	N/A	N/A	98	N/A	0	0	0.0	0.0
C+ / 5.7	10.3	0.59	14.44	N/A	4	95	0	1	59	N/A	N/A	97	N/A	0	0	0.0	0.0
C / 4.8	14.1	1.02	9.27	1,561	8	91	0	1	21	23.3	-24.8	63	5	0	0	0.0	0.0
C+ / 6.0	9.7	1.01	15.79	23,744	3	96	0	1	109	98.0	-18.8	60	6	0	0	0.0	0.0
C+ / 6.1	10.5	1.03	17.32	12,814	6	93	0	1	39	98.6	-17.6	54	5	0	0	0.0	0.0
C / 5.2	11.9	0.90	10.35	21,571	15	83	0	2	11	54.7	-22.8	74	N/A	0	0	0.0	0.0
C / 5.2	12.4	0.93	9.32	1,614	16	83	0	1	27	58.6	-24.6	79	N/A	0	0	0.0	0.0
C- / 4.0	11.7	1.06	13.84	7,210	12	86	0	2	84	90.8	-24.1	36	5	0	0	0.0	0.0
B- / 7.0	10.1	1.04	18.82	12,858	10	89	0	1	42	99.0	-18.6	57	7	0	0	0.0	0.0
B / 8.2	6.6	0.62	14.59	3,267	11	70	9	10	58	71.2	-11.5	87	12	2,500	0	0.0	0.0

99 Pct = Best / 0 Pct = Worst

Fund Type	Fund Name	Ticker Symbol	Overall Investment Rating	Phone	Performance Rating/Pts	3 Mo	6 Mo	1Yr / Pct	3Yr / Pct	5Yr / Pct	Dividend Yield	Expense Ratio
GL	Fidelity Strategic Real Return Fund	FSRRX	D	(800) 544-8544	E / 0.5	0.11	-1.18	-2.90 / 9	1.28 / 6	4.06 / 9	2.17	0.77
UT	Fidelity Telecom and Utilities	FIUIX	C+	(800) 544-8544	C+ / 6.5	0.29	1.81	7.15 / 56	14.45 / 70	14.37 / 81	3.21	0.76
EM	Fidelity Total Emerg Mkts	FTEMX	D	(800) 522-7297	E+ / 0.7	1.86	-3.90	0.16 / 16	2.51 / 7	--	1.82	1.73
FO	Fidelity Total International Equity	FTIEX	D+	(800) 544-8544	C- / 3.0	5.36	3.18	1.53 / 20	8.50 / 30	6.35 / 19	1.61	1.04
GR	Fidelity Trend Fund	FTRNX	B	(800) 544-8544	A- / 9.2	3.97	9.13	15.10 / 92	17.12 / 90	16.22 / 94	0.77	0.75
GI	Fidelity Value Discovery Fd	FVDFX	A+	(800) 544-8544	A- / 9.1	1.22	7.81	12.11 / 83	17.78 / 93	14.25 / 80	1.27	0.80
GI	Fidelity Value Discovery K	FVDKX	A+	(800) 544-8544	A- / 9.2	1.26	7.87	12.24 / 84	17.94 / 94	14.44 / 82	1.37	0.66
* GI	Fidelity Value Fd	FDVLX	A+	(800) 544-8544	A / 9.5	3.05	8.80	10.90 / 78	18.97 / 97	15.02 / 87	0.77	0.76
GI	Fidelity Value K	FVLKX	A+	(800) 544-8544	A / 9.5	3.08	8.86	11.03 / 78	19.11 / 97	15.18 / 88	0.87	0.65
MC	Fidelity Value Strategies Fund K	FVSKX	A+	(800) 522-7297	B+ / 8.8	4.50	6.38	10.35 / 76	17.14 / 91	13.94 / 77	1.05	0.58
FO	Fidelity Worldwide Fund	FWWFX	C	(800) 544-8544	C+ / 6.2	5.20	6.10	5.37 / 41	13.61 / 64	11.82 / 59	0.31	0.96
MC	First Eagle Fund of America A	FEFAX	C+	(800) 334-2143	C+ / 6.9	0.75	4.36	7.03 / 55	16.42 / 86	15.14 / 88	0.28	1.38
MC	First Eagle Fund of America C	FEAMX	B	(800) 334-2143	B- / 7.2	0.57	3.97	6.25 / 49	15.54 / 79	14.27 / 80	0.00	2.13
GR	First Eagle Fund of America I	FEAIX	A-	(800) 334-2143	B / 8.0	0.84	4.51	7.33 / 58	16.63 / 88	15.26 / 89	0.53	1.06
MC	● First Eagle Fund of America Y	FEAFX	B+	(800) 334-2143	B / 7.8	0.74	4.33	7.01 / 55	16.42 / 86	15.13 / 88	0.28	1.38
* GL	First Eagle Global A	SGENX	D+	(800) 334-2143	D / 2.0	2.25	2.33	2.33 / 23	7.97 / 27	9.01 / 37	0.50	1.11
GL	First Eagle Global C	FESGX	D+	(800) 334-2143	D+ / 2.3	2.06	1.95	1.57 / 20	7.16 / 22	8.19 / 31	0.00	1.86
GL	First Eagle Global I	SGIIX	C-	(800) 334-2143	D+ / 2.9	2.34	2.48	2.61 / 25	8.25 / 28	9.28 / 39	0.79	0.83
GL	First Eagle Global Income Builder A	FEBAX	U	(800) 334-2143	U /	2.41	-0.90	-0.74 / 14	--	--	3.24	1.23
GL	First Eagle Global Income Builder C	FEBCX	U	(800) 334-2143	U /	2.22	-1.27	-1.49 / 11	--	--	2.64	1.99
GL	First Eagle Global Income Builder I	FEBIX	U	(800) 334-2143	U /	2.39	-0.88	-0.53 / 14	--	--	3.63	0.96
PM	First Eagle Gold A	SGGDX	E-	(800) 334-2143	E- / 0.0	-1.55	-9.89	-15.36 / 2	-20.76 / 0	-9.95 / 0	0.00	1.32
PM	First Eagle Gold C	FEGOX	E-	(800) 334-2143	E- / 0.0	-1.70	-10.22	-15.97 / 2	-21.35 / 0	-10.64 / 0	0.00	2.08
PM	First Eagle Gold I	FEGIX	E-	(800) 334-2143	E- / 0.0	-1.46	-9.74	-15.14 / 2	-20.55 / 0	-9.73 / 0	0.00	0.97
FO	● First Eagle Overseas A	SGOVX	D-	(800) 334-2143	D / 1.6	5.24	2.40	0.44 / 17	6.83 / 20	7.41 / 26	0.94	1.16
FO	● First Eagle Overseas C	FESOX	D	(800) 334-2143	D / 1.8	5.11	2.05	-0.28 / 15	6.06 / 17	6.60 / 21	0.33	1.90
FO	● First Eagle Overseas I	SGOIX	D	(800) 334-2143	D+ / 2.4	5.36	2.57	0.72 / 18	7.11 / 22	7.68 / 28	1.04	0.86
FO	First Eagle Overseas Variable Fund	FEOVX	D-	(800) 334-2143	D+ / 2.4	5.28	2.07	-0.36 / 15	7.44 / 24	7.76 / 28	2.86	1.26
SC	First Eagle US Value A	FEVAX	C-	(800) 334-2143	D+ / 2.3	-0.99	1.45	4.22 / 33	8.77 / 31	9.76 / 43	0.34	1.17
SC	First Eagle US Value C	FEVCX	C-	(800) 334-2143	D+ / 2.6	-1.15	1.09	3.48 / 29	7.96 / 27	8.94 / 36	0.00	1.92
SC	First Eagle US Value I	FEVIX	C	(800) 334-2143	C- / 3.3	-0.88	1.63	4.56 / 35	9.05 / 33	10.04 / 45	0.62	0.87
IN	First Inv Equity Income A	FIUTX	C+	(800) 423-4026	C / 4.9	1.23	4.05	8.13 / 64	13.02 / 60	11.29 / 55	1.33	1.22
IN	● First Inv Equity Income Adv	FIUUX	U	(800) 423-4026	U /	1.39	4.30	8.51 / 66	--	--	1.64	0.81
IN	First Inv Equity Income B	FIUBX	C+	(800) 423-4026	C / 5.3	0.96	3.59	7.22 / 57	12.11 / 53	10.43 / 48	0.67	2.06
GL	First Inv Global A	FIISX	D	(800) 423-4026	C / 5.0	4.43	8.09	11.44 / 80	11.91 / 52	9.31 / 39	0.00	1.54
GL	● First Inv Global Adv	FIITX	U	(800) 423-4026	U /	4.52	8.40	11.99 / 82	--	--	0.00	1.11
GL	First Inv Global B	FIBGX	D	(800) 423-4026	C / 5.4	4.26	7.70	10.55 / 77	11.02 / 46	8.52 / 33	0.00	2.36
GI	First Inv Growth & Income A	FGINX	C+	(800) 423-4026	C+ / 6.7	2.62	5.54	9.90 / 74	15.57 / 80	14.19 / 79	0.72	1.15
GI	● First Inv Growth & Income Adv	FGIPX	U	(800) 423-4026	U /	2.74	5.76	10.36 / 76	--	--	0.98	0.74
GI	First Inv Growth & Income B	FGIBX	B	(800) 423-4026	B- / 7.1	2.40	5.13	9.07 / 70	14.70 / 72	13.35 / 72	0.19	1.93
FO	First Inv International A	FIINX	D-	(800) 423-4026	D- / 1.1	1.94	1.14	-0.01 / 16	5.82 / 16	7.28 / 25	0.34	1.66
FO	● First Inv International Adv	FIIPX	U	(800) 423-4026	U /	2.08	1.30	0.38 / 17	--	--	0.37	1.27
FO	First Inv International B	FIIOX	D-	(800) 423-4026	D- / 1.3	1.71	0.73	-0.87 / 13	5.00 / 13	6.46 / 20	0.00	2.49
MC	First Inv Opportunity A	FIUSX	B+	(800) 423-4026	A- / 9.0	6.19	9.90	12.82 / 86	18.38 / 95	17.01 / 96	0.13	1.20
MC	● First Inv Opportunity Adv	FIVUX	U	(800) 423-4026	U /	6.27	10.06	13.19 / 87	--	--	0.19	0.90
MC	First Inv Opportunity B	FIMBX	A-	(800) 423-4026	A- / 9.2	5.96	9.46	11.96 / 82	17.50 / 92	16.15 / 94	0.00	1.99
AG	First Inv Select Growth A	FICGX	A-	(800) 423-4026	B / 8.0	4.58	12.50	15.99 / 93	15.56 / 80	16.35 / 94	0.01	1.27
GR	● First Inv Select Growth Advisor	FICHX	U	(800) 423-4026	U /	4.64	12.70	16.40 / 94	--	--	0.06	0.83
AG	First Inv Select Growth B	FIGBX	A-	(800) 423-4026	B+ / 8.4	4.36	12.02	15.06 / 92	14.65 / 72	15.51 / 90	0.00	2.06
SC	First Inv Special Situations A	FISSX	C-	(800) 423-4026	C+ / 5.6	7.10	11.13	11.30 / 80	12.52 / 56	13.82 / 76	0.12	1.35
SC	● First Inv Special Situations Adv	FISTX	U	(800) 423-4026	U /	7.16	11.31	11.73 / 81	--	--	0.26	1.03
SC	First Inv Special Situations B	FISBX	D+	(800) 423-4026	C+ / 6.0	6.88	10.67	10.41 / 76	11.61 / 50	12.95 / 68	0.00	2.18

● Denotes fund is closed to new investors
* Denotes fund is included in Section II

www.thestreetratings.com

Risk Rating/Pts	Standard Deviation	Beta	NAV As of 3/31/15	Total $(Mil)	Cash %	Stocks %	Bonds %	Other %	Portfolio Turnover Ratio	Last Bull Market Return	Last Bear Market Return	Manager Quality Pct	Manager Tenure (Years)	Initial Purch. $	Additional Purch. $	Front End Load	Back End Load
B- /7.7	5.0	0.23	9.05	597	27	15	56	2	18	12.5	-7.7	54	10	2,500	0	0.0	0.8
C+ /6.8	10.1	0.57	24.20	968	4	95	0	1	160	65.1	-5.8	96	10	2,500	0	0.0	0.0
B- /7.5	12.0	0.85	10.93	36	4	73	22	1	102	N/A	N/A	84	4	2,500	0	0.0	1.5
C+ /6.1	11.8	0.88	8.06	324	1	98	0	1	85	51.6	-25.2	69	8	2,500	0	0.0	1.0
C /4.9	10.4	1.01	87.83	1,518	1	98	0	1	152	101.8	-17.0	75	3	2,500	0	0.0	0.0
B- /7.8	9.8	1.00	24.95	1,103	7	92	0	1	58	109.9	-21.0	80	3	2,500	0	0.0	0.0
B- /7.8	9.8	1.00	24.94	147	7	92	0	1	58	111.1	-21.0	81	3	0	0	0.0	0.0
C+ /6.9	10.8	1.05	116.72	8,133	5	94	0	1	81	115.7	-24.7	82	5	2,500	0	0.0	0.0
C+ /6.9	10.8	1.05	116.83	1,623	5	94	0	1	81	116.6	-24.6	83	5	0	0	0.0	0.0
B- /7.3	10.0	0.82	45.07	86	4	94	0	2	6	109.3	-26.7	88	5	2,500	0	0.0	0.0
C /5.0	11.4	0.78	23.46	1,568	2	97	0	1	163	75.0	-19.9	95	9	2,500	0	0.0	1.0
C+ /6.5	10.3	0.82	37.45	1,371	5	93	0	2	35	102.1	-19.9	86	28	2,500	100	5.0	0.0
C+ /6.3	10.3	0.81	31.61	745	5	93	0	2	35	96.9	-20.1	82	28	2,500	100	0.0	0.0
B- /7.2	10.3	0.97	38.25	1,090	5	93	0	2	35	103.1	-19.9	76	28	1,000,000	100	0.0	0.0
C+ /6.5	10.3	0.81	38.26	551	5	93	0	2	35	102.1	-19.9	86	28	2,500	100	0.0	0.0
B- /7.4	7.7	0.55	53.62	17,476	25	72	2	1	15	46.0	-11.4	87	7	2,500	100	5.0	0.0
B- /7.4	7.7	0.55	52.40	12,253	25	72	2	1	15	42.3	-11.7	84	7	2,500	100	0.0	0.0
B- /7.3	7.7	0.55	53.87	20,544	25	72	2	1	15	47.2	-11.3	88	7	1,000,000	100	0.0	0.0
U /	N/A	N/A	11.09	425	11	51	37	1	18	N/A	N/A	N/A	3	2,500	100	5.0	0.0
U /	N/A	N/A	11.06	391	11	51	37	1	18	N/A	N/A	N/A	3	2,500	100	0.0	0.0
U /	N/A	N/A	11.06	462	11	51	37	1	18	N/A	N/A	N/A	3	1,000,000	100	0.0	0.0
E- /0.0	30.4	1.51	13.94	470	26	70	2	2	13	-48.5	-11.3	6	2	2,500	100	5.0	2.0
E- /0.0	30.4	1.51	13.26	177	26	70	2	2	13	-49.8	-11.6	4	2	2,500	100	0.0	2.0
E- /0.0	30.4	1.51	14.18	373	26	70	2	2	13	-48.0	-11.2	6	2	1,000,000	100	0.0	2.0
C+ /6.5	8.7	0.63	22.91	4,560	23	74	1	2	12	35.1	-11.7	76	7	2,500	100	5.0	0.0
C+ /6.6	8.8	0.63	22.22	1,074	23	74	1	2	12	31.7	-12.0	69	7	2,500	100	0.0	0.0
C+ /6.5	8.8	0.63	23.38	8,795	23	74	1	2	12	36.4	-11.6	78	7	1,000,000	100	0.0	0.0
C /5.0	9.3	0.67	27.70	544	22	75	1	2	15	38.2	-13.0	78	7	0	0	0.0	0.0
B- /7.6	7.5	0.45	20.10	1,166	24	75	0	1	16	54.8	-10.3	81	6	2,500	100	5.0	0.0
B- /7.7	7.6	0.45	19.79	681	24	75	0	1	16	50.9	-10.6	76	6	2,500	100	0.0	0.0
B- /7.6	7.6	0.45	20.37	1,137	24	75	0	1	16	56.1	-10.2	83	6	1,000,000	100	0.0	0.0
B- /7.2	9.1	0.93	9.84	532	0	93	6	1	27	80.2	-17.8	41	4	1,000	0	5.8	0.0
U /	N/A	N/A	9.85	38	0	93	6	1	27	N/A	N/A	N/A	4	1,000	0	0.0	0.0
B- /7.2	9.1	0.94	9.66	5	0	93	6	1	27	75.6	-18.0	30	4	1,000	0	0.0	0.0
C- /3.9	10.8	0.74	7.78	357	0	98	1	1	154	74.1	-22.6	92	15	1,000	0	5.8	0.0
U /	N/A	N/A	7.87	83	0	98	1	1	154	N/A	N/A	N/A	15	1,000	0	0.0	0.0
C- /3.1	10.7	0.74	6.37	4	0	98	1	1	154	69.7	-22.8	91	15	1,000	0	0.0	0.0
C+ /6.7	10.9	1.11	22.83	1,701	0	99	0	1	22	102.2	-18.8	35	13	1,000	0	5.8	0.0
U /	N/A	N/A	22.93	146	0	99	0	1	22	N/A	N/A	N/A	13	1,000	0	0.0	0.0
C+ /6.7	10.9	1.11	21.29	24	0	99	0	1	22	97.2	-19.1	26	13	1,000	0	0.0	0.0
C+ /6.3	11.4	0.79	13.16	200	1	95	3	1	34	44.7	-14.2	45	9	1,000	0	5.8	0.0
U /	N/A	N/A	13.25	42	1	95	3	1	34	N/A	N/A	N/A	9	1,000	0	0.0	0.0
C+ /6.2	11.4	0.78	12.49	2	1	95	3	1	34	41.1	-14.4	34	9	1,000	0	0.0	0.0
C+ /5.9	12.1	1.03	42.02	896	0	97	2	1	34	111.9	-20.9	75	11	1,000	0	5.8	0.0
U /	N/A	N/A	42.39	46	0	97	2	1	34	N/A	N/A	N/A	11	1,000	0	0.0	0.0
C+ /5.7	12.1	1.03	34.47	12	0	97	2	1	34	106.6	-21.1	N/A	11	1,000	0	0.0	0.0
C+ /6.9	10.9	1.07	12.34	371	0	97	2	1	33	96.3	-16.5	45	8	1,000	0	5.8	0.0
U /	N/A	N/A	12.40	39	0	97	2	1	33	N/A	N/A	N/A	8	1,000	0	0.0	0.0
C+ /6.8	10.9	1.06	11.00	5	0	97	2	1	33	91.3	-16.9	34	8	1,000	0	0.0	0.0
C /4.3	12.3	0.83	28.05	477	0	98	1	1	55	77.1	-19.7	57	2	1,000	0	5.8	0.0
U /	N/A	N/A	28.12	34	0	98	1	1	55	N/A	N/A	N/A	2	1,000	0	0.0	0.0
C- /3.5	12.2	0.83	22.05	4	0	98	1	1	55	72.4	-20.0	44	2	1,000	0	0.0	0.0

						PERFORMANCE							
							Total Return % through 3/31/15					Incl. in Returns	
	99 Pct = Best			Overall		Perfor-				Annualized		Dividend	Expense
	0 Pct = Worst		Ticker	Investment		mance						Yield	Ratio
Fund Type	Fund Name	Symbol	Rating	Phone	Rating/Pts	3 Mo	6 Mo	1Yr / Pct	3Yr / Pct	5Yr / Pct		
BA	First Inv Total Return A	FITRX	C	(800) 423-4026	C- / 3.4	2.14	4.22	7.23 /57	10.15 /40	10.23 /46	1.35	1.19
BA	First Inv Total Return B	FBTRX	C+	(800) 423-4026	C- / 3.8	1.94	3.86	6.41 /50	9.33 /35	9.41 /40	0.59	1.97
BA	First Inv Total Return Inst	FITVX	U	(800) 423-4026	U /	2.24	4.48	7.68 /60	--	--	1.50	0.78
AA	First Investors Strategic Inc A	FSIFX	U	(800) 423-4026	U /	1.16	0.96	1.60 /20	--	--	3.04	1.41
GI	First Trust Pref Sec and Inc A	FPEAX	D+	(800) 621-1675	D / 1.8	2.95	4.16	8.37 /65	5.96 /17	--	4.98	1.40
GI	First Trust Pref Sec and Inc C	FPECX	C-	(800) 621-1675	D / 2.1	3.00	4.01	7.81 /61	5.27 /14	--	4.70	2.18
GI	First Trust Pref Sec and Inc F	FPEFX	C-	(800) 621-1675	D+ / 2.5	3.00	4.23	8.46 /66	6.04 /17	--	5.27	1.81
GI	First Trust Pref Sec and Inc I	FPEIX	C-	(800) 621-1675	D+ / 2.6	3.00	4.28	8.61 /67	6.21 /18	--	5.44	1.15
GI	First Trust Pref Sec and Inc R3	FPERX	C-	(800) 621-1675	D+ / 2.3	2.88	4.08	8.11 /64	5.62 /15	--	4.97	5.74
IN	First Trust/Confluence SCV A	FOVAX	C+	(800) 621-1675	C+ / 6.0	3.01	10.01	9.60 /72	13.92 /66	--	0.00	8.88
IN	First Trust/Confluence SCV C	FOVCX	C+	(800) 621-1675	C+ / 6.5	3.01	9.77	8.99 /69	13.25 /61	--	0.00	9.04
IN	First Trust/Confluence SCV I	FOVIX	B+	(800) 621-1675	B- / 7.4	3.25	10.37	10.21 /75	14.49 /71	--	0.00	11.28
EN	Firsthand Alternative Energy Fd	ALTEX	D-	(888) 884-2675	C / 5.2	4.95	-1.88	-8.87 / 3	14.39 /70	-2.71 / 1	0.00	2.02
TC	Firsthand Technology Opportunities	TEFQX	B-	(888) 884-2675	B+ / 8.6	8.60	6.62	13.63 /89	15.84 /82	14.76 /85	0.00	1.86
GR	FMC Strategic Value Fund	FMSVX	E+	(866) 777-7818	D / 2.2	1.32	1.13	-5.30 / 5	8.19 /28	8.51 /33	0.00	1.20
SC	● FMI Common Stock	FMIMX	C	(800) 811-5311	C+ / 6.0	2.36	7.26	7.04 /55	12.93 /59	13.22 /70	0.07	1.18
FO	FMI International	FMIJX	A+	(800) 811-5311	B / 7.9	7.94	8.48	10.92 /78	14.85 /74	--	1.92	1.03
* GR	● FMI Large Cap	FMIHX	B+	(800) 811-5311	B / 8.0	1.79	7.42	11.59 /81	15.56 /80	12.90 /67	0.77	0.94
FO	Forester Discovery	INTLX	D	(800) 388-0365	E+ / 0.9	1.41	-1.61	-1.13 /13	3.56 / 9	2.39 / 5	0.63	1.37
IX	Forester Value I	FVILX	D+	(800) 388-0365	E+ / 0.7	-0.92	2.77	1.16 /19	2.08 / 6	2.11 / 5	0.46	1.00
IX	Forester Value N	FVALX	D+	(800) 388-0365	E+ / 0.7	-0.95	2.60	0.96 /18	1.87 / 6	1.84 / 4	0.64	1.26
GR	Forester Value R	FVRLX	D+	(800) 388-0365	E+ / 0.7	-1.08	2.44	0.60 /17	1.77 / 6	--	0.21	1.51
GI	Fort Pitt Capital Total Return Fd	FPCGX	B-	(800) 471-5827	C / 5.5	1.15	4.29	8.23 /64	12.84 /58	12.67 /65	0.75	1.45
BA	Forward Balanced Allocation A	AOBAX	D+	(800) 999-6809	E+ / 0.7	0.48	-0.63	0.29 /16	3.32 / 8	3.94 / 8	3.09	1.79
BA	Forward Balanced Allocation C	ABAFX	D+	(800) 999-6809	E+ / 0.8	0.31	-0.98	-0.35 /15	2.65 / 7	3.26 / 6	2.76	2.44
BA	Forward Balanced Allocation Inst	ABAAX	D+	(800) 999-6809	E+ / 0.9	0.60	-0.49	0.65 /17	3.68 / 9	4.30 / 9	3.57	1.44
BA	Forward Balanced Allocation Inv	ACBIX	D+	(800) 999-6809	E+ / 0.8	0.45	-0.68	0.17 /16	3.14 / 8	3.77 / 8	3.15	1.94
IN	Forward Commodity Lng/Sht Str Inst	FCMLX	E	(800) 999-6809	E- / 0.2	-2.49	4.00	1.02 /18	-5.59 / 2	--	0.00	1.42
IN	Forward Commodity Lng/Sht Str Inv	FCOMX	E	(800) 999-6809	E- / 0.2	-2.56	3.84	0.69 /18	-5.92 / 2	--	0.00	1.77
IN	Forward Commodity Long/Short Str	FCMSX	D-	(800) 999-6809	E- / 0.2	-2.45	3.97	0.98 /18	-5.64 / 2	--	0.00	1.45
IN	Forward Commodity Long/Short Str C	FFCCX	E	(800) 999-6809	E- / 0.2	-2.69	3.48	0.05 /16	-6.50 / 1	--	0.00	2.36
IN	Forward Commodity Long/Short Str Z	FTEZX	E	(800) 999-6809	E- / 0.2	-2.44	4.05	1.12 /19	-5.51 / 2	--	0.00	1.36
GI	Forward Credit Analysis Long/Sh C	FLSFX	E	(800) 999-6809	E+ / 0.6	0.84	2.07	4.91 /38	-0.43 / 4	1.90 / 4	1.69	2.45
GI	Forward Credit Analysis Long/Sh I	FLSIX	E	(800) 999-6809	E+ / 0.7	1.08	2.46	5.85 /45	0.54 / 5	2.88 / 6	2.69	1.50
GI	Forward Credit Analysis Long/Sh Inv	FLSRX	E	(800) 999-6809	E+ / 0.7	0.99	2.23	5.42 /42	0.13 / 4	2.50 / 5	2.31	1.85
AA	Forward Dynamic Income Inst	FDYTX	U	(800) 999-6809	U /	-0.93	1.75	11.13 /79	--	--	7.20	3.10
EM	Forward Emerg Markets Inst	PTEMX	E+	(800) 999-6809	E+ / 0.6	0.10	-4.50	-3.28 / 8	2.23 / 7	1.55 / 4	2.10	2.07
EM	Forward Emerg Markets Inv	PGERX	E+	(800) 999-6809	E+ / 0.6	0.00	-4.76	-3.70 / 7	1.82 / 6	1.18 / 4	1.83	2.42
EM	Forward Emerging Markets Adv	FEMMX	E+	(800) 999-6809	E+ / 0.6	0.00	-4.59	-3.41 / 8	2.13 / 6	1.57 / 4	2.00	2.12
GL	Forward Equity Long/Short Inst	FENIX	C-	(800) 999-6809	D / 2.2	2.03	1.43	8.48 /66	5.97 /17	--	0.00	3.07
GL	Forward Equity Long/Short Inv	FENRX	C-	(800) 999-6809	D / 2.0	1.93	1.22	8.08 /63	5.61 /15	--	0.00	3.42
EM	Forward Frontier Strategy Adv	FROMX	E-	(800) 999-6809	D- / 1.0	-3.33	-16.78	-6.61 / 4	7.08 /22	--	0.00	1.26
EM	Forward Frontier Strategy Inst	FRNMX	E-	(800) 999-6809	D- / 1.0	-3.24	-16.79	-6.62 / 4	7.05 /22	2.58 / 5	0.00	1.26
EM	Forward Frontier Strategy Inv	FRONX	E-	(800) 999-6809	E+ / 0.9	-3.45	-16.88	-6.89 / 4	6.76 /20	2.32 / 5	0.00	1.56
EM	Forward Frontier Strategy Z		E-	(800) 999-6809	D- / 1.0	-3.32	-16.74	-6.52 / 4	7.14 /22	2.43 / 5	0.00	1.16
GL	Forward Glb Infrastructure A	KGIAX	D-	(800) 999-6809	E+ / 0.9	2.32	-1.82	-1.18 /12	5.14 /14	6.06 /17	1.27	1.72
OT	Forward Glb Infrastructure Adv	FGIMX	D-	(800) 999-6809	D- / 1.4	2.41	-1.64	-0.82 /14	5.49 /15	6.39 /19	1.72	1.37
GL	Forward Glb Infrastructure B	KGIBX	D-	(800) 999-6809	D- / 1.1	2.21	-2.06	-1.72 /11	4.53 /12	5.38 /14	0.76	2.29
GL	Forward Glb Infrastructure C	KGICX	D-	(800) 999-6809	D- / 1.1	2.20	-2.10	-1.73 /11	4.51 /12	5.39 /14	0.79	2.29
GL	Forward Glb Infrastructure Inst	KGIYX	D-	(800) 999-6809	D- / 1.4	2.59	-1.48	-0.64 /14	5.59 /15	6.45 /20	1.77	1.32
OT	Forward Glb Infrastructure Inv	FGLRX	D-	(800) 999-6809	D- / 1.3	2.39	-1.76	-1.12 /13	5.16 /14	--	1.47	1.67
GR	Forward Global Dividend A	FFLAX	D-	(800) 999-6809	D- / 1.2	4.12	2.73	1.29 /19	5.70 /16	7.97 /30	3.20	1.94

● Denotes fund is closed to new investors
* Denotes fund is included in Section II

www.thestreetratings.com

RISK			NET ASSETS		ASSET					BULL / BEAR		FUND MANAGER		MINIMUMS		LOADS	
Risk Rating/Pts	3 Year		NAV As of 3/31/15	Total $(Mil)	Cash %	Stocks %	Bonds %	Other %	Portfolio Turnover Ratio	Last Bull Market Return	Last Bear Market Return	Manager Quality Pct	Manager Tenure (Years)	Initial Purch. $	Additional Purch. $	Front End Load	Back End Load
	Standard Deviation	Beta															
B / 8.2	6.5	1.12	19.63	824	0	59	40	1	44	59.6	-10.6	39	14	1,000	0	5.8	0.0
B / 8.2	6.5	1.12	19.29	10	0	59	40	1	44	55.5	-10.8	29	14	1,000	0	0.0	0.0
U /	N/A	N/A	19.71	32	0	59	40	1	44	N/A	N/A	N/A	14	2,000,000	0	0.0	0.0
U /	N/A	N/A	9.79	121	3	9	87	1	20	N/A	N/A	N/A	2	1,000	0	5.8	0.0
B- / 7.9	4.5	0.14	21.44	34	0	62	37	1	170	29.7	-0.6	91	4	2,500	50	4.5	0.0
B- / 7.9	4.5	0.14	21.48	45	0	62	37	1	170	26.8	-0.6	89	4	2,500	50	0.0	0.0
B- / 7.9	4.5	0.14	21.61	2	0	62	37	1	170	31.0	-0.7	91	4	2,500	50	0.0	0.0
B- / 7.9	4.5	0.14	21.51	82	0	62	37	1	170	30.9	-0.4	91	4	1,000,000	0	0.0	0.0
B- / 7.9	4.5	0.14	21.44	N/A	0	62	37	1	170	28.4	-1.1	90	4	0	0	0.0	0.0
C+ / 6.7	9.5	0.74	27.35	2	4	95	0	1	39	77.2	-19.3	84	4	2,500	50	5.5	0.0
C+ / 6.6	9.4	0.74	25.65	2	4	95	0	1	39	71.7	-19.3	80	4	2,500	50	0.0	0.0
C+ / 6.7	9.4	0.74	27.96	1	4	95	0	1	39	80.6	-18.8	87	4	1,000,000	0	0.0	0.0
D / 1.9	25.7	0.89	6.78	9	2	97	0	1	26	49.2	-40.8	98	8	2,000	50	0.0	0.0
C / 4.5	14.9	1.04	8.84	116	0	99	0	1	21	80.8	-18.0	54	16	2,000	50	0.0	0.0
C / 4.6	15.1	1.36	29.13	202	7	92	0	1	17	66.7	-30.2	1	17	10,000	1,000	0.0	0.0
C / 5.4	10.2	0.69	27.81	1,421	0	85	14	1	33	84.8	-17.6	83	18	1,000	100	0.0	0.0
B- / 7.8	7.4	0.46	30.03	1,675	1	83	15	1	22	78.7	-13.7	98	N/A	2,500	100	0.0	0.0
C+ / 6.5	9.0	0.91	21.60	9,559	0	92	7	1	31	91.1	-15.4	76	14	1,000	100	0.0	0.0
B / 8.0	5.7	0.40	13.67	7	11	40	47	2	17	19.2	-10.1	65	16	2,500	100	0.0	0.0
B / 8.5	4.6	0.30	12.86	77	8	77	14	1	7	8.8	-5.3	32	16	25,000	100	0.0	0.0
B / 8.5	4.5	0.29	12.54	50	8	77	14	1	7	7.9	-5.4	30	16	2,500	100	0.0	0.0
B / 8.6	4.5	0.29	12.85	2	8	77	14	1	7	8.2	-5.6	28	16	2,500	100	0.0	0.0
B- / 7.4	8.8	0.86	21.02	56	8	85	5	2	12	72.6	-11.8	56	14	2,500	100	0.0	2.0
B / 8.5	5.2	0.79	14.90	4	4	36	58	2	46	23.6	-12.8	11	N/A	4,000	100	5.8	0.0
B / 8.6	5.2	0.79	14.86	4	4	36	58	2	46	20.9	-13.1	8	N/A	4,000	100	0.0	0.0
B / 8.5	5.2	0.78	14.93	1	4	36	58	2	46	25.1	-12.7	13	N/A	100,000	0	0.0	0.0
B / 8.5	5.2	0.79	14.90	1	4	36	58	2	46	22.9	-12.9	10	N/A	4,000	100	0.0	0.0
C / 5.0	10.4	-0.06	20.79	14	0	0	100	0	59	-20.6	-6.8	10	5	100,000	0	0.0	0.0
C / 4.9	10.5	-0.06	20.57	19	0	0	100	0	59	-21.5	-6.9	9	5	4,000	100	0.0	0.0
B- / 7.8	10.4	-0.06	20.70	14	0	0	100	0	59	N/A	N/A	10	5	0	0	0.0	0.0
C / 4.8	10.4	-0.06	20.24	3	0	0	100	0	59	-23.1	N/A	7	5	4,000	100	0.0	0.0
C / 5.0	10.4	-0.06	20.79	3	0	0	100	0	59	-20.4	-6.8	11	5	0	0	0.0	0.0
C / 5.0	6.7	0.04	7.54	9	1	0	98	1	125	4.6	5.6	52	2	4,000	100	0.0	0.0
C / 4.9	6.7	0.03	7.47	35	1	0	98	1	125	8.1	6.0	68	2	100,000	0	0.0	0.0
C / 4.9	6.6	0.03	7.53	83	1	0	98	1	125	6.7	5.9	62	2	4,000	100	0.0	0.0
U /	N/A	N/A	25.88	39	0	0	0	100	0	N/A	N/A	N/A	2	100,000	0	0.0	0.0
C / 5.1	13.2	0.84	10.39	8	0	0	0	100	88	26.6	-29.6	82	3	100,000	0	0.0	0.0
C / 5.1	13.1	0.84	10.24	4	0	0	0	100	88	25.3	-29.7	79	3	4,000	100	0.0	0.0
C / 5.1	13.1	0.84	10.68	1	0	0	0	100	88	26.8	-29.6	81	3	0	0	0.0	0.0
B / 8.4	9.1	0.25	26.15	2	0	0	0	100	283	N/A	N/A	90	4	100,000	0	0.0	0.0
B / 8.4	9.1	0.25	25.84	N/A	0	0	0	100	283	N/A	N/A	89	4	4,000	100	0.0	0.0
D- / 1.2	11.9	0.46	9.86	2	0	0	0	100	57	30.5	N/A	96	7	0	0	0.0	0.0
D- / 1.2	11.9	0.46	9.85	94	0	0	0	100	57	30.3	-18.7	96	7	100,000	0	0.0	0.0
D- / 1.2	11.9	0.45	9.79	13	0	0	0	100	57	29.3	-18.8	95	7	4,000	100	0.0	0.0
D- / 1.2	11.9	0.46	9.89	2	0	0	0	100	57	30.6	-18.7	96	7	0	0	0.0	0.0
C+ / 6.5	11.4	0.76	23.47	16	15	84	0	1	101	42.3	-21.8	38	8	4,000	100	5.8	0.0
C+ / 6.5	11.4	0.93	23.50	N/A	15	84	0	1	101	43.9	-21.7	3	8	0	0	0.0	0.0
C+ / 6.5	11.4	0.76	23.37	1	15	84	0	1	101	39.4	-22.1	31	8	4,000	100	0.0	0.0
C+ / 6.5	11.4	0.76	23.40	6	15	84	0	1	101	39.5	-22.1	30	8	4,000	100	0.0	0.0
C+ / 6.5	11.4	0.76	23.55	14	15	84	0	1	101	44.3	-21.7	44	8	100,000	0	0.0	0.0
C+ / 6.5	11.4	0.93	23.34	17	15	84	0	1	101	42.4	N/A	2	8	4,000	100	0.0	0.0
C+ / 6.8	9.5	0.88	11.62	12	2	96	0	2	142	45.9	-15.1	4	6	4,000	100	5.8	0.0

						PERFORMANCE					Incl. in Returns	
99 Pct = Best / 0 Pct = Worst								Total Return % through 3/31/15				
			Overall		Perfor-				Annualized		Dividend	Expense
Fund Type	Fund Name	Ticker Symbol	Investment Rating	Phone	mance Rating/Pts	3 Mo	6 Mo	1Yr / Pct	3Yr / Pct	5Yr / Pct	Yield	Ratio
GR	Forward Global Dividend Inst	FFLSX	D	(800) 999-6809	D / 2.0	4.28	2.91	1.69 /21	6.22 /18	8.49 /33	3.91	1.44
GR	Forward Global Dividend Investor	FFLRX	D	(800) 999-6809	D / 1.8	4.15	2.71	1.42 /20	5.86 /16	--	3.52	1.79
GI	Forward Growth & Income Alloc A	AOIAX	D	(800) 999-6809	E+ / 0.7	0.88	-0.71	-0.01 /16	4.05 /10	4.43 /10	3.56	1.84
GI	Forward Growth & Income Alloc C	AGIGX	D+	(800) 999-6809	E+ / 0.9	0.72	-1.04	-0.69 /14	3.37 / 9	3.76 / 8	3.07	2.49
GI	Forward Growth & Income Alloc Inst	AGWAX	D+	(800) 999-6809	D- / 1.1	0.96	-0.53	0.35 /17	4.41 /11	4.81 /11	4.13	1.49
GI	Forward Growth & Income Alloc Inv	AGIIX	D+	(800) 999-6809	D- / 1.0	0.85	-0.85	-0.16 /15	3.89 /10	4.27 / 9	3.61	1.99
AA	Forward Growth Allocation A	AOGAX	D	(800) 999-6809	E+ / 0.8	1.28	-0.76	-0.04 /15	4.43 /11	4.55 /10	4.04	1.86
AA	Forward Growth Allocation C	AGGGX	D	(800) 999-6809	E+ / 0.9	1.14	-1.03	-0.65 /14	3.78 /10	3.89 / 8	3.62	2.51
AA	Forward Growth Allocation Inst	ACGAX	D	(800) 999-6809	D- / 1.2	1.37	-0.58	0.32 /17	4.80 /12	4.93 /12	4.66	1.51
AA	Forward Growth Allocation Inv	AGALX	D	(800) 999-6809	D- / 1.1	1.25	-0.83	-0.13 /15	4.27 /11	4.40 /10	4.13	2.01
GL	Forward Income & Growth Alloc A	AOLAX	E-	(800) 999-6809	E+ / 0.6	0.07	-0.45	0.78 /18	3.04 / 8	3.88 / 8	1.73	1.84
GL	Forward Income & Growth Alloc C	AIGMX	E-	(800) 999-6809	E+ / 0.7	-0.17	-0.78	0.16 /16	2.38 / 7	3.20 / 6	1.45	2.49
GL	Forward Income & Growth Alloc Inst	AIGAX	E-	(800) 999-6809	E+ / 0.9	0.10	-0.36	1.06 /19	3.38 / 9	4.21 / 9	2.01	1.49
GL	Forward Income & Growth Alloc Inv	ACIGX	E-	(800) 999-6809	E+ / 0.8	-0.04	-0.65	0.61 /17	2.88 / 8	3.72 / 7	1.74	1.99
AA	Forward Income Builder A	AILAX	D-	(800) 999-6809	D / 1.6	1.17	1.09	2.56 /24	6.82 /20	6.50 /20	5.02	1.90
AA	Forward Income Builder C	AIACX	D-	(800) 999-6809	D / 1.7	1.01	0.76	1.79 /21	6.04 /17	5.71 /15	4.58	2.65
AA	Forward Income Builder Inst	AIAAX	D	(800) 999-6809	D / 2.2	1.23	1.21	2.80 /25	7.09 /22	6.75 /22	5.44	1.65
AA	Forward Income Builder Inv	AIAIX	D-	(800) 999-6809	D / 2.0	1.12	1.02	2.33 /23	6.57 /19	6.23 /18	4.97	2.15
RE	Forward Int Real Estate A	KIRAX	D-	(800) 999-6809	D+ / 2.4	3.72	4.78	7.72 /61	7.55 /24	9.26 /39	7.59	1.83
RE	Forward Int Real Estate Adv	FINMX	D	(800) 999-6809	C- / 3.6	3.85	5.02	8.18 /64	7.98 /27	--	8.50	1.45
RE	Forward Int Real Estate C	KIRCX	D	(800) 999-6809	D+ / 2.9	3.60	4.50	7.19 /57	6.96 /21	8.58 /34	7.48	2.38
RE	Forward Int Real Estate Inst	KIRYX	D	(800) 999-6809	C- / 3.5	3.79	4.97	8.14 /64	7.98 /27	9.64 /42	8.53	1.41
RE	Forward Int Real Estate Inv	FFIRX	D	(800) 999-6809	C- / 3.3	3.76	4.82	7.83 /62	7.64 /25	--	8.02	1.75
FO	Forward International Dividend Adv	FIDMX	D-	(800) 999-6809	D / 1.7	3.74	-0.32	-2.49 / 9	6.51 /19	--	6.76	1.28
FO	Forward International Dividend Inst	FFIEX	D-	(800) 999-6809	D / 1.7	3.75	-0.29	-2.44 / 9	6.55 /19	6.69 /21	6.81	1.23
FO	Forward International Dividend Inv	FFINX	D-	(800) 999-6809	D / 1.6	3.71	-0.41	-2.78 / 9	6.20 /18	6.32 /19	5.27	1.58
FO	Forward Intl Small Comp Eq Adv	FNSMX	C-	(800) 999-6809	C- / 4.2	8.33	5.85	-1.90 /11	10.51 /42	7.65 /27	0.68	1.40
FO	Forward Intl Small Comp Eq Inst	PTSCX	C-	(800) 999-6809	C / 4.3	8.33	5.88	-1.87 /11	10.55 /43	7.91 /29	0.71	1.35
FO	Forward Intl Small Comp Eq Inv	PISRX	D+	(800) 999-6809	C- / 4.0	8.26	5.67	-2.25 /10	10.16 /40	7.34 /25	0.29	1.70
AG	Forward Multi-Strategy A	AGRRX	D	(800) 999-6809	E+ / 0.9	0.21	-0.55	1.76 /21	4.77 /12	4.41 /10	4.29	2.58
AG	Forward Multi-Strategy C	ACAGX	D	(800) 999-6809	D- / 1.0	0.06	-0.84	1.15 /19	4.10 /10	3.73 / 7	4.13	3.23
AG	Forward Multi-Strategy Inst	AAGRX	D	(800) 999-6809	D- / 1.4	0.29	-0.36	2.10 /22	5.14 /14	4.78 /11	4.85	2.23
AG	Forward Multi-Strategy Inv	ACAIX	D	(800) 999-6809	D- / 1.2	0.17	-0.64	1.63 /20	4.60 /12	4.22 / 9	4.47	2.73
RE	Forward Progressive Real Est A	KREAX	C+	(800) 999-6809	B+ / 8.5	4.30	18.99	23.13 /98	13.65 /65	14.75 /85	0.84	1.68
RE	Forward Progressive Real Est C	KRECX	B-	(800) 999-6809	B+ / 8.9	4.19	18.63	22.44 /97	12.98 /60	14.02 /78	0.48	2.23
RE	Forward Progressive Real Est Inst	FPREX	B	(800) 999-6809	A / 9.4	4.45	19.18	23.60 /98	14.08 /68	15.15 /88	1.41	1.28
RE	Forward Progressive Real Est Inv	FFREX	B	(800) 999-6809	A- / 9.2	4.33	19.05	23.15 /98	13.66 /65	14.69 /84	0.90	1.63
RE	Forward Real Estate Long/Short A	KSRAX	C	(800) 999-6809	C+ / 6.5	3.30	13.78	17.33 /95	12.60 /57	13.66 /75	0.67	2.48
RE	Forward Real Estate Long/Short Adv	FRLSX	B-	(800) 999-6809	B / 7.9	3.38	14.01	17.76 /95	13.03 /60	--	0.92	2.13
RE	Forward Real Estate Long/Short B	KSRBX	C+	(800) 999-6809	B- / 7.1	3.20	13.50	16.71 /94	11.98 /52	12.94 /68	0.29	3.03
RE	Forward Real Estate Long/Short C	KSRCX	C+	(800) 999-6809	B- / 7.1	3.15	13.47	16.66 /94	11.95 /52	12.92 /67	0.32	3.03
RE	Forward Real Estate Long/Short Inst	KSRYX	B-	(800) 999-6809	B / 7.9	3.39	13.99	17.79 /95	13.05 /60	14.06 /78	0.96	2.08
RE	Forward Real Estate Long/Short Inv	FFSRX	B-	(800) 999-6809	B / 7.6	3.34	13.82	17.45 /95	12.64 /57	--	0.75	2.43
GL	Forward Select EM Dividend Advisor	FSLMX	E-	(800) 999-6809	E / 0.4	-0.36	-8.44	-9.53 / 3	0.97 / 5	--	5.54	1.79
GL	Forward Select EM Dividend C	FSLDX	E-	(800) 999-6809	E / 0.3	-0.55	-8.84	-10.37 / 3	0.04 / 4	--	4.62	2.69
GL	Forward Select EM Dividend Inst	FSLIX	E-	(800) 999-6809	E / 0.4	-0.31	-8.42	-9.53 / 3	1.03 / 5	--	5.59	1.74
GL	Forward Select EM Dividend Inv	FSLRX	E-	(800) 999-6809	E / 0.4	-0.41	-8.56	-9.78 / 3	0.63 / 5	--	5.23	2.09
RE	Forward Select Income A	KIFAX	C+	(800) 999-6809	C / 4.9	2.94	7.84	11.95 /82	11.59 /50	11.86 /60	4.09	1.79
RE	Forward Select Income Adv	FSIMX	B-	(800) 999-6809	C+ / 6.1	3.04	8.00	12.38 /84	12.00 /52	12.23 /62	4.69	1.44
RE	Forward Select Income B	KIFBX	B-	(800) 999-6809	C / 5.4	2.77	7.53	11.36 /80	10.96 /45	11.15 /54	3.82	2.34
RE	Forward Select Income C	KIFCX	B-	(800) 999-6809	C / 5.4	2.78	7.51	11.35 /80	10.96 /45	11.14 /54	3.89	2.34
RE	Forward Select Income Inst	KIFYX	B-	(800) 999-6809	C+ / 6.1	3.04	8.06	12.42 /84	12.04 /53	12.25 /62	4.72	1.39

● Denotes fund is closed to new investors
* Denotes fund is included in Section II

www.thestreetratings.com

Risk Rating/Pts	Standard Deviation	Beta	NAV As of 3/31/15	Total $(Mil)	Cash %	Stocks %	Bonds %	Other %	Portfolio Turnover Ratio	Last Bull Market Return	Last Bear Market Return	Manager Quality Pct	Manager Tenure (Years)	Initial Purch. $	Additional Purch. $	Front End Load	Back End Load
C+ / 6.8	9.5	0.87	11.44	2	2	96	0	2	142	48.4	-15.0	4	6	100,000	0	0.0	0.0
C+ / 6.8	9.5	0.87	11.61	N/A	2	96	0	2	142	46.7	N/A	4	6	4,000	100	0.0	0.0
B / 8.3	6.3	0.54	15.17	8	5	47	47	1	62	28.2	-14.5	15	N/A	4,000	100	5.8	0.0
B / 8.3	6.3	0.54	15.17	8	5	47	47	1	62	25.5	-14.7	12	N/A	4,000	100	0.0	0.0
B / 8.3	6.2	0.53	15.22	4	5	47	47	1	62	29.8	-14.3	18	N/A	100,000	0	0.0	0.0
B / 8.3	6.3	0.53	15.20	4	5	47	47	1	62	27.6	-14.6	15	N/A	4,000	100	0.0	0.0
B- / 7.8	7.7	1.18	14.37	7	4	58	36	2	83	34.9	-18.3	3	N/A	4,000	100	5.8	0.0
B- / 7.8	7.7	1.18	14.25	7	4	58	36	2	83	31.9	-18.5	3	N/A	4,000	100	0.0	0.0
B- / 7.8	7.7	1.18	14.38	11	4	58	36	2	83	36.5	-18.1	4	N/A	100,000	0	0.0	0.0
B- / 7.8	7.7	1.19	14.38	3	4	58	36	2	83	34.2	-18.3	3	N/A	4,000	100	0.0	0.0
D+ / 2.8	4.0	0.55	11.10	1	7	27	65	1	38	19.8	-8.7	40	N/A	4,000	100	5.8	0.0
D+ / 2.7	4.0	0.55	11.02	1	7	27	65	1	38	17.1	-8.9	32	N/A	4,000	100	0.0	0.0
D+ / 2.8	4.0	0.55	11.12	1	7	27	65	1	38	21.0	-8.5	46	N/A	100,000	0	0.0	0.0
D+ / 2.7	4.0	0.55	11.10	N/A	7	27	65	1	38	19.2	-8.6	38	N/A	4,000	100	0.0	0.0
C+ / 6.1	5.6	0.75	14.61	2	6	27	66	1	95	25.8	0.5	49	N/A	4,000	100	3.8	0.0
C+ / 6.1	5.6	0.75	14.54	7	6	27	66	1	95	22.5	0.3	38	N/A	4,000	100	0.0	0.0
C+ / 6.1	5.6	0.75	14.62	4	6	27	66	1	95	26.7	0.6	53	N/A	100,000	0	0.0	0.0
C+ / 6.1	5.6	0.75	14.60	2	6	27	66	1	95	24.6	0.5	47	N/A	4,000	100	0.0	0.0
C+ / 5.6	10.8	0.54	15.05	19	22	77	0	1	202	67.1	-26.5	68	7	4,000	100	5.8	0.0
C / 5.5	10.8	0.54	14.97	5	22	77	0	1	202	69.6	N/A	73	7	0	0	0.0	0.0
C+ / 5.6	10.8	0.54	15.08	12	22	77	0	1	202	64.0	-26.8	61	7	4,000	100	0.0	0.0
C / 5.5	10.7	0.54	14.97	23	22	77	0	1	202	69.7	-26.5	73	7	100,000	0	0.0	0.0
C+ / 5.6	10.7	0.54	15.07	17	22	77	0	1	202	67.6	N/A	70	7	4,000	100	0.0	0.0
C+ / 5.6	12.2	0.87	7.43	78	9	86	3	2	115	44.1	N/A	43	7	0	0	0.0	0.0
C+ / 5.6	12.2	0.88	7.43	104	9	86	3	2	115	44.0	-20.3	43	7	100,000	0	0.0	0.0
C+ / 5.9	12.2	0.87	9.00	123	9	86	3	2	115	42.1	-20.3	38	7	4,000	100	0.0	0.0
C+ / 5.6	12.6	0.91	17.17	3	3	96	0	1	86	57.5	-26.7	82	14	0	0	0.0	0.0
C+ / 5.6	12.6	0.91	17.16	140	3	96	0	1	86	57.4	-26.7	83	14	100,000	0	0.0	0.0
C+ / 5.6	12.6	0.91	17.17	33	3	96	0	1	86	55.6	-26.8	80	14	4,000	100	0.0	0.0
B- / 7.4	7.7	0.62	14.66	3	24	63	11	2	109	39.6	-21.6	12	N/A	4,000	100	5.8	0.0
B- / 7.4	7.7	0.62	13.95	2	24	63	11	2	109	36.6	-21.9	9	N/A	4,000	100	0.0	0.0
B- / 7.5	7.7	0.62	14.89	9	24	63	11	2	109	41.3	-21.6	14	N/A	100,000	0	0.0	0.0
B- / 7.4	7.7	0.62	14.36	1	24	63	11	2	109	38.8	-21.7	11	N/A	4,000	100	0.0	0.0
C / 4.3	11.9	0.94	18.03	7	8	91	0	1	58	86.3	-19.6	71	5	4,000	100	5.8	0.0
C / 4.3	11.9	0.94	18.17	4	8	91	0	1	58	82.6	-19.8	64	5	4,000	100	0.0	0.0
C- / 4.2	11.9	0.94	15.95	6	8	91	0	1	58	88.8	-19.4	75	5	100,000	0	0.0	0.0
C / 4.3	11.9	0.94	18.19	46	8	91	0	1	58	86.3	-19.6	71	5	4,000	100	0.0	0.0
C / 5.3	10.4	0.82	34.70	36	18	80	1	1	63	85.5	-19.4	77	6	4,000	100	5.8	0.0
C / 5.3	10.4	0.82	35.75	1	18	80	1	1	63	87.9	N/A	80	6	0	0	0.0	0.0
C / 5.3	10.4	0.82	34.49	1	18	80	1	1	63	81.8	-19.6	72	6	4,000	100	0.0	0.0
C / 5.3	10.4	0.82	34.37	19	18	80	1	1	63	81.7	-19.6	72	6	4,000	100	0.0	0.0
C / 5.3	10.4	0.82	35.72	14	18	80	1	1	63	88.0	-19.3	80	6	100,000	0	0.0	0.0
C / 5.3	10.4	0.82	34.64	2	18	80	1	1	63	85.7	N/A	77	6	4,000	100	0.0	0.0
C- / 3.2	13.7	0.89	19.41	1	0	0	0	100	210	29.5	N/A	4	4	0	0	0.0	0.0
C- / 3.2	13.7	0.90	19.38	2	0	0	0	100	210	25.4	N/A	3	4	4,000	100	0.0	0.0
C- / 3.2	13.7	0.90	19.42	12	0	0	0	100	210	29.6	N/A	4	4	100,000	0	0.0	0.0
C- / 3.2	13.7	0.90	19.42	28	0	0	0	100	210	27.9	N/A	4	4	4,000	100	0.0	0.0
B- / 7.7	5.2	0.33	26.00	717	11	73	15	1	50	55.4	-5.4	96	14	4,000	100	5.8	0.0
B- / 7.7	5.2	0.33	25.95	49	11	73	15	1	50	57.2	-5.3	96	14	0	0	0.0	0.0
B- / 7.7	5.2	0.33	25.71	6	11	73	15	1	50	52.2	-5.7	95	14	4,000	100	0.0	0.0
B- / 7.7	5.2	0.33	25.44	273	11	73	15	1	50	52.2	-5.7	95	14	4,000	100	0.0	0.0
B- / 7.7	5.3	0.33	25.96	630	11	73	15	1	50	57.4	-5.3	96	14	100,000	0	0.0	0.0

					PERFORMANCE							
						Total Return % through 3/31/15					Incl. in Returns	
									Annualized			
Fund Type	Fund Name	Ticker Symbol	Overall Investment Rating	Phone	Performance Rating/Pts	3 Mo	6 Mo	1Yr / Pct	3Yr / Pct	5Yr / Pct	Dividend Yield	Expense Ratio
RE	Forward Select Income Inv	FFSLX	B-	(800) 999-6809	C+ / 5.9	2.92	7.84	12.02 /83	11.62 /50	--	4.37	1.74
SC	Forward Small Cap Equity Adv	FSCMX	C-	(800) 999-6809	C / 5.2	1.41	5.68	1.84 /21	12.38 /55	8.89 /36	0.00	1.47
SC	Forward Small Cap Equity Inst	FFHIX	C	(800) 999-6809	C / 5.2	1.40	5.70	1.92 /22	12.43 /56	8.99 /37	0.00	1.42
SC	Forward Small Cap Equity Inv	FFSCX	C-	(800) 999-6809	C / 5.0	1.34	5.55	1.57 /20	12.10 /53	8.60 /34	0.00	1.77
IX	Forward Tactical Enhanced A	FTEAX	E+	(800) 999-6809	E- / 0.2	-5.51	-6.34	-7.41 / 4	-1.03 / 3	--	0.00	1.97
IX	Forward Tactical Enhanced Advisor	FTENX	D-	(800) 999-6809	E / 0.3	-5.50	-6.28	-7.13 / 4	-0.59 / 4	--	0.00	1.52
IX	Forward Tactical Enhanced C	FTEGX	E+	(800) 999-6809	E / 0.3	-5.59	-6.55	-7.81 / 3	-1.47 / 3	--	0.00	2.42
IX	Forward Tactical Enhanced Inst	FTETX	D-	(800) 999-6809	E / 0.3	-5.41	-6.12	-6.97 / 4	-0.54 / 4	--	0.00	1.47
IX	Forward Tactical Enhanced Investor	FTEEX	E+	(800) 999-6809	E / 0.3	-5.47	-6.27	-7.26 / 4	-0.88 / 4	--	0.00	1.82
GR	Forward Tactical Growth A	FTAGX	D-	(800) 999-6809	E+ / 0.8	-1.07	0.62	1.69 /21	4.17 /11	2.56 / 5	0.00	1.92
GR	Forward Tactical Growth Adv	FTGMX	D	(800) 999-6809	D- / 1.2	-0.96	0.84	2.16 /22	4.66 /12	3.09 / 6	0.00	1.47
GR	Forward Tactical Growth C	FTGOX	D	(800) 999-6809	D- / 1.0	-1.18	0.35	1.20 /19	3.71 / 9	2.12 / 5	0.00	2.37
GR	Forward Tactical Growth Inst	FTGWX	D	(800) 999-6809	D- / 1.2	-0.96	0.84	2.16 /22	4.68 /12	3.09 / 6	0.00	1.42
GR	Forward Tactical Growth Invest	FFTGX	D	(800) 999-6809	D- / 1.1	-1.06	0.66	1.80 /21	4.33 /11	2.74 / 5	0.00	1.77
SC	Forward Total MarketPlus Inst	ASMCX	A-	(800) 999-6809	B / 7.9	1.83	7.00	11.56 /81	15.56 /80	13.46 /72	0.00	1.07
SC	Forward Total MarketPlus Inv	ACSIX	A-	(800) 999-6809	B / 7.6	1.75	6.83	11.18 /79	15.15 /76	13.01 /68	0.00	1.47
SC	Forward Total MarketPlus Z		A	(800) 999-6809	B / 8.0	1.87	7.08	11.71 /81	15.71 /81	13.59 /74	0.00	0.97
GR	● FPA Capital Inc	FPPTX	E	(800) 982-4372	E+ / 0.7	-4.92	-7.51	-11.49 / 2	5.23 /14	8.37 /32	0.00	0.83
★ BA	FPA Crescent	FPACX	C+	(800) 982-4372	C- / 3.8	0.15	2.67	4.67 /36	10.45 /42	9.73 /42	0.89	1.23
FO	FPA International Value	FPIVX	D+	(800) 982-4372	D- / 1.4	3.65	0.11	-6.84 / 4	6.78 /20	--	1.19	1.26
GR	FPA Perennial Inc	FPPFX	A-	(800) 982-4372	A- / 9.0	2.71	16.15	12.86 /86	17.08 /90	14.94 /86	0.00	0.96
GR	Frank Value C	FNKCX	C-	(866) 706-9790	C- / 3.4	-3.48	0.61	-0.79 /14	10.39 /42	--	0.00	2.27
GR	Frank Value Instl	FNKIX	C-	(866) 706-9790	C- / 4.1	-3.28	1.01	0.12 /16	11.49 /49	--	0.00	1.26
GR	Frank Value Investor	FRNKX	C-	(866) 706-9790	C- / 3.9	-3.36	0.95	-0.08 /15	11.20 /47	11.63 /58	0.00	1.52
GI	Franklin All Cap Value A	FRAVX	C	(800) 342-5236	C / 4.9	0.79	5.36	0.72 /18	13.99 /67	11.11 /54	0.07	1.42
GI	Franklin All Cap Value Adv		C+	(800) 321-8563	C+ / 6.1	0.78	5.43	0.97 /18	14.31 /69	11.41 /56	0.38	1.12
GI	Franklin All Cap Value C		C	(800) 342-5236	C / 5.4	0.56	4.97	-0.05 /15	13.21 /61	10.31 /47	0.00	2.12
GI	Franklin All Cap Value R		C+	(800) 342-5236	C+ / 5.8	0.71	5.20	0.42 /17	13.75 /65	10.85 /51	0.01	1.62
GI	Franklin Balance Sheet Investmt A	FRBSX	E+	(800) 342-5236	C- / 3.0	-3.69	-3.09	-2.71 / 9	11.98 /52	9.80 /43	0.32	0.91
GI	Franklin Balance Sheet Investmt Adv	FBSAX	D-	(800) 321-8563	C- / 4.1	-3.65	-2.98	-2.48 / 9	12.26 /54	10.07 /45	0.61	0.66
GI	Franklin Balance Sheet Investmt C	FCBSX	E+	(800) 342-5236	C- / 3.3	-3.89	-3.46	-3.44 / 8	11.15 /47	8.98 /37	0.00	1.66
GI	Franklin Balance Sheet Investmt R	FBSRX	D-	(800) 342-5236	C- / 3.7	-3.76	-3.21	-2.94 / 9	11.71 /50	9.53 /41	0.01	1.16
GR	Franklin Balance Sheet Investmt R6	FBSIX	C	(800) 342-5236	C- / 4.1	-3.61	-2.91	-2.33 /10	12.25 /54	9.96 /44	0.76	0.51
BA	Franklin Balanced A	FBLAX	C	(800) 342-5236	D+ / 2.6	1.20	2.52	6.14 /48	9.04 /33	9.67 /42	2.84	1.09
BA	Franklin Balanced Adv	FBFZX	C+	(800) 321-8563	C- / 3.8	1.27	2.67	6.45 /50	9.35 /35	10.01 /45	3.31	0.79
BA	Franklin Balanced C	FBMCX	C	(800) 342-5236	C- / 3.1	0.94	2.08	5.35 /41	8.25 /28	8.90 /36	2.34	1.79
BA	Franklin Balanced R		C	(800) 342-5236	C- / 3.4	1.06	2.32	5.83 /45	8.80 /32	9.44 /40	2.81	1.29
BA	Franklin Balanced R6	FBFRX	D+	(800) 342-5236	C- / 3.8	1.21	2.82	6.57 /51	9.43 /36	10.06 /45	3.41	0.68
HL	● Franklin Biotechnology Discvry A	FBDIX	B-	(800) 342-5236	A+ / 9.9	14.40	27.44	43.56 /99	41.68 /99	31.02 /99	0.00	1.10
HL	● Franklin Biotechnology Discvry Adv	FTDZX	B-	(800) 321-8563	A+ / 9.9	14.47	27.58	43.93 /99	42.09 /99	31.39 /99	0.00	0.80
HL	● Franklin Biotechnology Discvry R6	FRBRX	C	(800) 342-5236	A+ / 9.9	14.51	27.68	44.17 /99	42.24 /99	31.47 /99	0.00	1.80
GL	Franklin Conservative Alloc A	FTCIX	C-	(800) 342-5236	D- / 1.3	1.67	2.43	3.99 /32	5.97 /17	5.83 /16	2.56	1.22
GL	Franklin Conservative Alloc Adv	FTCZX	C-	(800) 321-8563	D / 2.0	1.79	2.62	4.31 /34	6.25 /18	6.09 /17	2.95	0.97
GL	Franklin Conservative Alloc C	FTCCX	C-	(800) 342-5236	D- / 1.5	1.48	2.06	3.26 /28	5.18 /14	5.04 /12	2.06	1.97
GL	Franklin Conservative Alloc R	FTCRX	C-	(800) 342-5236	D / 1.8	1.62	2.32	3.82 /31	5.72 /16	5.58 /15	2.48	1.47
GL	Franklin Conservative Alloc R6		C	(800) 342-5236	D / 2.0	1.74	2.60	4.41 /34	6.23 /18	5.99 /17	3.05	1.64
CV	Franklin Convertible Securities A	FISCX	C-	(800) 342-5236	C- / 3.7	2.69	2.90	3.85 /31	11.13 /46	10.20 /46	1.59	0.88
CV	Franklin Convertible Securities Adv	FCSZX	C	(800) 321-8563	C / 4.7	2.74	3.04	4.13 /33	11.41 /48	10.48 /48	1.95	0.63
CV	Franklin Convertible Securities C	FROTX	C	(800) 342-5236	C- / 4.0	2.50	2.50	3.08 /27	10.30 /41	9.37 /39	0.99	1.63
GI	Franklin Corefolio 529 Port A		C+	(800) 342-5236	C / 5.2	3.14	5.32	7.51 /59	13.33 /62	11.28 /55	0.00	1.44
GI	● Franklin Corefolio 529 Port B		B-	(800) 342-5236	C+ / 5.7	2.92	4.90	6.68 /52	12.48 /56	10.44 /48	0.00	2.19
GI	Franklin Corefolio 529 Port C		B-	(800) 342-5236	C+ / 5.7	2.94	4.93	6.73 /53	12.49 /56	10.45 /48	0.00	2.19

www.thestreetratings.com

RISK			NET ASSETS		ASSET					BULL / BEAR		FUND MANAGER		MINIMUMS		LOADS	
	3 Year		NAV						Portfolio	Last Bull	Last Bear	Manager	Manager	Initial	Additional	Front	Back
Risk	Standard		As of	Total	Cash	Stocks	Bonds	Other	Turnover	Market	Market	Quality	Tenure	Purch.	Purch.	End	End
Rating/Pts	Deviation	Beta	3/31/15	$(Mil)	%	%	%	%	Ratio	Return	Return	Pct	(Years)	$	$	Load	Load
B- / 7.7	5.2	0.33	25.92	159	11	73	15	1	50	N/A	N/A	96	14	4,000	100	0.0	0.0
C+ / 5.7	13.8	0.94	23.80	3	11	88	0	1	115	76.2	-30.1	31	4	0	0	0.0	0.0
C+ / 5.7	13.8	0.94	23.92	4	11	88	0	1	115	77.1	-30.1	31	4	100,000	0	0.0	0.0
C+ / 5.6	13.8	0.94	22.64	21	11	88	0	1	115	74.7	-30.2	27	4	4,000	100	0.0	0.0
C+ / 6.5	6.0	0.35	22.48	1	1	98	0	1	11,621	7.5	-9.3	6	3	4,000	100	5.8	0.0
C+ / 6.6	6.0	0.35	22.85	N/A	1	98	0	1	11,621	9.2	-9.1	7	3	0	0	0.0	0.0
C+ / 6.4	6.0	0.35	22.11	1	1	98	0	1	11,621	5.9	-9.5	5	3	4,000	100	0.0	0.0
C+ / 6.6	6.0	0.35	22.92	10	1	98	0	1	11,621	9.3	-9.1	7	3	100,000	0	0.0	0.0
C+ / 6.5	6.0	0.35	22.62	11	1	98	0	1	11,621	8.0	-9.3	6	3	4,000	100	0.0	0.0
B- / 7.3	6.2	0.59	25.03	58	13	41	44	2	1,797	19.9	-7.0	11	6	4,000	100	5.8	0.0
B- / 7.4	6.2	0.59	25.79	457	13	41	44	2	1,797	21.8	-6.8	14	6	0	0	0.0	0.0
B- / 7.1	6.2	0.59	24.34	76	13	41	44	2	1,797	18.1	-7.2	9	6	4,000	100	0.0	0.0
B- / 7.4	6.2	0.59	25.79	44	13	41	44	2	1,797	21.9	-6.8	14	6	100,000	0	0.0	0.0
B- / 7.3	6.2	0.59	25.28	122	13	41	44	2	1,797	20.5	-7.0	12	6	4,000	100	0.0	0.0
B- / 7.3	10.0	0.66	40.64	15	19	0	80	1	218	101.0	-26.7	93	5	100,000	0	0.0	0.0
B- / 7.3	10.1	0.66	37.72	2	19	0	80	1	218	98.4	-26.8	92	5	4,000	100	0.0	0.0
B- / 7.3	10.0	0.66	40.83	9	19	0	80	1	218	101.8	-26.7	93	5	0	0	0.0	0.0
C- / 3.2	13.3	1.06	37.66	1,084	12	73	14	1	17	48.7	-22.2	2	8	1,500	100	0.0	2.0
B / 8.5	6.4	1.04	33.79	19,966	6	52	40	2	22	58.6	-11.6	56	22	1,500	100	0.0	2.0
B / 8.1	10.0	0.66	13.34	510	37	62	0	1	44	N/A	N/A	73	4	1,500	100	0.0	2.0
C+ / 6.0	13.2	1.16	54.95	337	4	95	0	1	8	104.7	-24.8	44	20	1,500	100	0.0	2.0
C+ / 6.7	10.4	0.97	13.60	4	18	81	0	1	81	72.2	-14.7	12	11	1,500	100	0.0	0.0
C+ / 6.8	10.4	0.97	14.16	22	18	81	0	1	81	78.2	-14.4	19	11	1,000,000	500	0.0	0.0
C+ / 6.8	10.4	0.97	14.10	22	18	81	0	1	81	76.6	-14.4	17	11	1,500	100	0.0	0.0
C+ / 6.2	11.9	1.10	12.82	47	2	96	0	2	30	73.4	-20.4	22	8	1,000	0	5.8	0.0
C+ / 6.3	11.9	1.10	12.87	3	2	96	0	2	30	75.2	-20.3	25	8	1,000,000	0	0.0	0.0
C+ / 6.2	11.9	1.10	12.52	8	2	96	0	2	30	69.2	-20.5	16	8	1,000	0	0.0	0.0
C+ / 6.2	11.9	1.09	12.81	N/A	2	96	0	2	30	72.1	-20.4	21	8	1,000	0	0.0	0.0
C- / 3.4	12.0	1.13	41.97	1,135	9	90	0	1	25	77.0	-22.7	8	25	1,000	0	5.8	0.0
C- / 3.4	12.0	1.13	42.97	98	9	90	0	1	25	78.4	-22.6	9	25	1,000,000	0	0.0	0.0
C- / 3.3	12.0	1.13	40.72	89	9	90	0	1	25	72.5	-22.9	6	25	1,000	0	0.0	0.0
C- / 3.5	12.0	1.13	42.03	12	9	90	0	1	25	75.5	-22.8	7	25	1,000	0	0.0	0.0
B- / 7.0	12.0	1.13	42.94	8	9	90	0	1	25	78.2	-22.7	9	25	1,000,000	0	0.0	0.0
B / 8.4	6.1	1.02	11.79	2,298	13	52	30	5	41	53.3	-10.8	38	9	1,000	0	5.8	0.0
B / 8.4	6.1	1.02	11.81	51	13	52	30	5	41	54.9	-10.8	43	9	1,000,000	0	0.0	0.0
B / 8.4	6.1	1.02	11.69	567	13	52	30	5	41	49.8	-11.1	29	9	1,000	0	0.0	0.0
B / 8.4	6.1	1.02	11.81	5	13	52	30	5	41	52.4	-11.0	35	9	1,000	0	0.0	0.0
C+ / 5.7	6.1	1.03	11.81	1	13	52	30	5	41	55.3	-10.8	43	9	1,000,000	0	0.0	0.0
C- / 3.1	19.9	0.83	192.85	1,659	4	95	0	1	49	268.2	-15.6	99	18	1,000	0	5.8	0.0
C- / 3.1	19.9	0.83	195.80	174	4	95	0	1	49	271.8	-15.5	99	18	1,000	0	0.0	0.0
D / 1.8	19.9	0.83	196.46	79	4	95	0	1	49	273.0	-15.5	99	18	1,000,000	0	0.0	0.0
B / 8.8	5.2	0.82	14.74	928	7	41	50	2	17	30.6	-8.4	48	15	1,000	0	5.8	0.0
B / 8.8	5.2	0.82	14.74	91	7	41	50	2	17	31.8	-8.3	52	15	1,000	0	0.0	0.0
B / 8.8	5.2	0.82	14.47	556	7	41	50	2	17	27.4	-8.7	37	15	1,000	0	0.0	0.0
B / 8.8	5.2	0.82	14.69	162	7	41	50	2	17	29.6	-8.5	45	15	1,000	0	0.0	0.0
B+ / 9.3	5.2	0.36	14.73	2	7	41	50	2	17	31.5	-8.4	88	15	1,000,000	0	0.0	0.0
B- / 7.0	8.0	1.04	18.42	936	10	9	0	81	23	61.3	-18.4	27	13	1,000	0	5.8	0.0
B- / 7.0	8.0	1.04	18.42	875	10	9	0	81	23	62.8	-18.3	31	13	1,000,000	0	0.0	0.0
B- / 7.1	8.0	1.04	18.18	334	10	9	0	81	23	57.2	-18.7	20	13	1,000	0	0.0	0.0
B- / 7.5	10.0	1.00	27.92	90	0	0	0	100	0	81.2	-19.0	31	12	250	0	5.8	0.0
B- / 7.4	10.0	1.00	25.06	7	0	0	0	100	0	76.6	-19.2	23	12	250	0	0.0	0.0
B- / 7.4	10.0	1.00	25.54	40	0	0	0	100	0	76.6	-19.3	23	12	250	0	0.0	0.0

Fund Type	Fund Name	Ticker Symbol	Overall Investment Rating	Phone	Perfor-mance Rating/Pts	3 Mo	6 Mo	1Yr / Pct	3Yr / Pct	5Yr / Pct	Dividend Yield	Expense Ratio
	99 Pct = Best 0 Pct = Worst				**PERFORMANCE** Total Return % through 3/31/15 / Annualized / Incl. in Returns							
GI	Franklin Corefolio Allocation A	FTCOX	C+	(800) 342-5236	C / 5.4	3.22	5.42	7.71 /61	13.63 /64	11.60 /58	1.45	1.08
GI	Franklin Corefolio Allocation Adv	FCAZX	C+	(800) 321-8563	C+ / 6.6	3.27	5.55	8.02 /63	13.95 /67	11.92 /60	1.82	0.79
GI	Franklin Corefolio Allocation C	FTCLX	C+	(800) 342-5236	C+ / 5.9	3.03	5.04	6.93 /54	12.84 /58	10.82 /51	0.87	1.79
GI	Franklin Corefolio Allocation R		C+	(800) 342-5236	C+ / 6.2	3.11	5.29	7.47 /59	13.38 /62	11.36 /56	1.26	1.29
TC	Franklin DynaTech A	FKDNX	C+	(800) 342-5236	B- / 7.3	5.42	9.23	14.40 /90	15.36 /78	15.07 /87	0.00	0.89
TC	Franklin DynaTech Adv	FDYZX	B	(800) 321-8563	B+ / 8.6	5.49	9.36	14.69 /91	15.65 /80	15.36 /89	0.00	0.64
TC	Franklin DynaTech C	FDYNX	C+	(800) 342-5236	B / 7.8	5.21	8.84	13.54 /88	14.50 /71	14.21 /80	0.00	1.64
TC	Franklin DynaTech R	FDNRX	B-	(800) 342-5236	B / 8.2	5.34	9.07	14.10 /90	15.07 /75	14.78 /85	0.00	1.14
GR	Franklin DynaTech R6	FDTRX	B+	(800) 342-5236	B+ / 8.6	5.52	9.45	14.85 /91	15.65 /80	15.25 /88	0.00	0.49
IN	Franklin Equity Inc A	FISEX	C+	(800) 342-5236	C / 4.8	0.08	3.53	7.03 /55	13.13 /61	12.29 /62	2.71	0.87
IN	Franklin Equity Inc Adv	FEIFX	B-	(800) 321-8563	C+ / 6.0	0.18	3.66	7.34 /58	13.44 /63	12.58 /65	3.11	0.62
IN	Franklin Equity Inc C	FRETX	C+	(800) 342-5236	C / 5.3	-0.07	3.15	6.26 /49	12.29 /55	11.45 /56	2.15	1.62
IN	Franklin Equity Inc R	FREIX	B-	(800) 342-5236	C+ / 5.6	0.01	3.35	6.76 /53	12.85 /58	11.99 /60	2.63	1.12
IN	Franklin Equity Inc R6		B-	(800) 342-5236	C+ / 5.9	0.17	3.68	7.41 /58	13.31 /62	12.40 /63	3.22	1.78
GR	Franklin Flex Cap Growth A	FKCGX	D	(800) 342-5236	C+ / 5.9	5.65	9.57	11.60 /81	13.19 /61	12.59 /65	0.00	0.97
GR	Franklin Flex Cap Growth Adv	FKCAX	D+	(800) 321-8563	B- / 7.0	5.72	9.70	11.88 /82	13.48 /63	12.88 /67	0.00	0.72
GR	Franklin Flex Cap Growth C	FCIIX	D-	(800) 342-5236	C+ / 6.2	5.45	9.17	10.77 /77	12.34 /55	11.75 /59	0.00	1.72
GR	Franklin Flex Cap Growth R	FRCGX	D	(800) 342-5236	C+ / 6.6	5.58	9.42	11.33 /80	12.90 /59	12.31 /63	0.00	1.22
GL	Franklin Flex Cap Growth R6	FFCRX	B-	(800) 342-5236	B- / 7.1	5.77	9.81	12.11 /83	13.53 /64	12.80 /66	0.00	0.48
GR	Franklin Focused Core Equity A	FCEQX	B+	(800) 342-5236	A- / 9.0	4.71	8.64	17.47 /95	17.95 /94	13.56 /73	0.00	1.73
GR	Franklin Focused Core Equity Adv		A	(800) 342-5236	A+ / 9.6	4.74	8.78	17.80 /95	18.29 /95	13.87 /76	0.13	1.43
GR	Franklin Focused Core Equity C		A-	(800) 342-5236	A / 9.3	4.52	8.27	16.66 /94	17.15 /91	12.77 /66	0.00	2.43
GR	Franklin Focused Core Equity R		A-	(800) 342-5236	A / 9.4	4.68	8.57	17.30 /95	17.70 /93	13.32 /71	0.00	1.93
GR	Franklin Focused Core Equity R6	FEFCX	A+	(800) 342-5236	A+ / 9.6	4.80	8.90	18.10 /96	18.42 /95	13.95 /77	0.23	2.28
GI	Franklin Founding Funds 529 Port A		C	(800) 342-5236	C- / 3.3	1.51	0.36	1.26 /19	11.23 /47	9.36 /39	0.00	1.32
GI	● Franklin Founding Funds 529 Port B		C	(800) 342-5236	C- / 3.7	1.29	0.00	0.51 /17	10.40 /42	8.54 /33	0.00	2.07
GI	Franklin Founding Funds 529 Port C		C	(800) 342-5236	C- / 3.7	1.30	-0.06	0.51 /17	10.39 /42	8.55 /33	0.00	2.07
GI	Franklin Founding Funds Alloc A	FFALX	C-	(800) 342-5236	C- / 3.4	1.50	0.40	1.43 /20	11.46 /49	9.64 /42	3.18	1.02
GI	Franklin Founding Funds Alloc Adv	FFAAX	C+	(800) 321-8563	C / 4.5	1.57	0.54	1.69 /21	11.74 /51	9.92 /44	3.62	0.77
GI	Franklin Founding Funds Alloc C	FFACX	C	(800) 342-5236	C- / 3.9	1.37	0.02	0.70 /18	10.66 /43	8.82 /35	2.66	1.77
GI	Franklin Founding Funds Alloc R	FFARX	C	(800) 342-5236	C- / 4.2	1.50	0.36	1.27 /19	11.19 /47	9.39 /40	3.14	1.27
GL	Franklin Global Allocation A	FGAAX	D-	(800) 342-5236	D- / 1.0	3.62	1.13	2.58 /24	4.77 /12	--	2.73	2.04
GL	Franklin Global Allocation Adv	FGAZX	D-	(800) 342-5236	D- / 1.5	3.62	1.28	2.82 /26	4.95 /13	--	3.30	1.74
GL	Franklin Global Allocation C		D-	(800) 342-5236	D- / 1.1	3.33	0.75	1.75 /21	3.97 /10	--	1.69	2.74
GL	Franklin Global Allocation R		D-	(800) 342-5236	D- / 1.3	3.42	1.00	2.27 /23	4.44 /11	--	2.52	2.24
OT	Franklin Global Listed Infra A	FLGIX	U	(800) 342-5236	U /	0.50	1.99	7.14 /56	--	--	1.50	4.15
IX	Franklin Global Real Estate A	FGRRX	C	(800) 342-5236	C+ / 6.0	4.35	12.60	16.16 /93	11.71 /51	10.91 /52	1.43	1.61
IX	Franklin Global Real Estate Adv	FVGRX	C+	(800) 342-5236	B- / 7.2	4.44	12.82	16.42 /94	12.05 /53	11.27 /55	1.79	1.31
IX	Franklin Global Real Estate C	FCGRX	C	(800) 342-5236	C+ / 6.4	4.16	12.15	15.39 /92	10.92 /45	10.15 /46	0.99	2.31
RE	Franklin Global Real Estate R6		B-	(800) 342-5236	B- / 7.3	4.44	12.76	16.61 /94	12.15 /53	11.33 /55	1.93	1.15
PM	Franklin Gold & Precious Metals A	FKRCX	E-	(800) 342-5236	E- / 0.0	-4.16	-17.16	-24.82 / 0	-26.63 / 0	-16.05 / 0	1.08	1.07
PM	Franklin Gold & Precious Metals Adv	FGADX	E-	(800) 321-8563	E- / 0.0	-4.09	-17.05	-24.65 / 0	-26.44 / 0	-15.84 / 0	1.39	0.82
PM	Franklin Gold & Precious Metals C	FRGOX	E-	(800) 342-5236	E- / 0.0	-4.34	-17.42	-25.36 / 0	-27.17 / 0	-16.67 / 0	0.18	1.82
PM	Franklin Gold & Precious Metals R6		E-	(800) 342-5236	E- / 0.0	-4.01	-16.90	-24.44 / 0	-26.34 / 0	-15.85 / 0	1.77	0.67
GI	Franklin Gr and Inc 529 Port A		C	(800) 342-5236	D / 1.9	2.55	3.40	4.79 /37	7.49 /24	7.18 /24	0.00	1.34
GI	● Franklin Gr and Inc 529 Port B		C	(800) 342-5236	D+ / 2.3	2.35	3.01	4.01 /32	6.69 /20	6.39 /19	0.00	2.09
GI	Franklin Gr and Inc 529 Port C		C	(800) 342-5236	D+ / 2.3	2.38	3.06	4.01 /32	6.69 /20	6.38 /19	0.00	2.09
GI	Franklin Growth 529 Port A		A	(800) 342-5236	B- / 7.3	3.22	9.60	15.73 /93	15.26 /77	13.24 /70	0.00	1.29
GI	● Franklin Growth 529 Port B		A+	(800) 342-5236	B / 7.8	3.04	9.21	14.85 /91	14.38 /70	12.38 /63	0.00	2.04
GI	Franklin Growth 529 Port C		A+	(800) 342-5236	B / 7.7	3.05	9.13	14.80 /91	14.34 /70	12.37 /63	0.00	2.04
* GR	Franklin Growth A	FKGRX	A-	(800) 342-5236	B / 7.6	3.31	9.70	16.01 /93	15.61 /80	13.62 /74	0.23	0.90
GR	Franklin Growth Adv	FCGAX	A+	(800) 321-8563	B+ / 8.8	3.37	9.85	16.29 /94	15.90 /83	13.91 /77	0.46	0.65

● Denotes fund is closed to new investors
* Denotes fund is included in Section II

www.thestreetratings.com

RISK			NET ASSETS		ASSET					BULL / BEAR		FUND MANAGER		MINIMUMS		LOADS	
	3 Year		NAV						Portfolio	Last Bull	Last Bear	Manager	Manager	Initial	Additional	Front	Back
Risk Rating/Pts	Standard Deviation	Beta	As of 3/31/15	Total $(Mil)	Cash %	Stocks %	Bonds %	Other %	Turnover Ratio	Market Return	Market Return	Quality Pct	Tenure (Years)	Purch. $	Purch. $	End Load	End Load
C+ / 6.7	10.0	1.00	18.58	576	3	93	3	1	6	83.0	-18.9	34	12	1,000	0	5.8	0.0
C+ / 6.7	10.0	1.00	18.62	20	3	93	3	1	6	84.6	-18.8	38	12	1,000	0	0.0	0.0
C+ / 6.7	10.0	1.00	18.35	183	3	93	3	1	6	78.6	-19.2	26	12	1,000	0	0.0	0.0
C+ / 6.7	10.0	1.00	18.57	2	3	93	3	1	6	81.6	-19.0	32	12	1,000	0	0.0	0.0
C / 4.8	12.8	1.03	48.64	1,724	2	97	0	1	26	94.4	-16.8	50	11	1,000	0	5.8	0.0
C / 4.9	12.8	1.03	49.56	178	2	97	0	1	26	96.2	-16.8	54	11	1,000	0	0.0	0.0
C / 4.8	12.8	1.03	42.42	243	2	97	0	1	26	89.6	-17.1	39	11	1,000	0	0.0	0.0
C / 4.8	12.8	1.03	47.77	47	2	97	0	1	26	92.8	-16.9	46	11	1,000	0	0.0	0.0
C / 5.5	12.8	1.03	49.71	381	2	97	0	1	26	95.9	-16.8	54	11	1,000,000	0	0.0	0.0
B- / 7.3	9.2	0.95	22.97	1,842	5	92	0	3	20	80.3	-15.6	40	10	1,000	0	5.8	0.0
B- / 7.3	9.2	0.95	23.00	32	5	92	0	3	20	81.8	-15.5	44	10	1,000,000	0	0.0	0.0
B- / 7.3	9.2	0.95	22.84	259	5	92	0	3	20	75.7	-15.8	30	10	1,000	0	0.0	0.0
B- / 7.3	9.2	0.94	22.97	8	5	92	0	3	20	78.6	-15.6	37	10	1,000	0	0.0	0.0
B- / 7.7	9.2	0.94	22.99	N/A	5	92	0	3	20	81.1	-15.6	43	10	1,000,000	0	0.0	0.0
D+ / 2.6	11.9	1.07	52.32	2,297	0	99	0	1	41	84.2	-19.0	20	22	1,000	0	5.8	0.0
D+ / 2.8	11.9	1.06	54.16	407	0	99	0	1	41	85.8	-18.9	22	22	1,000	0	0.0	0.0
D / 1.6	11.9	1.06	43.75	374	0	99	0	1	41	79.6	-19.3	14	22	1,000	0	0.0	0.0
D+ / 2.4	11.9	1.07	49.95	48	0	99	0	1	41	82.6	-19.1	18	22	1,000	0	0.0	0.0
C+ / 5.9	11.9	0.66	54.44	305	0	99	0	1	41	85.8	-19.0	96	22	1,000,000	0	0.0	0.0
C+ / 5.7	12.5	1.16	15.12	81	5	94	0	1	43	107.2	-20.8	55	8	1,000	0	5.8	0.0
C+ / 5.7	12.5	1.16	15.26	10	5	94	0	1	43	109.4	-20.6	59	8	1,000	0	0.0	0.0
C+ / 5.7	12.4	1.16	14.57	17	5	94	0	1	43	102.6	-21.0	44	8	1,000	0	0.0	0.0
C+ / 5.7	12.4	1.16	14.98	N/A	5	94	0	1	43	106.0	-20.9	52	8	1,000	0	0.0	0.0
C+ / 6.3	12.5	1.16	15.28	25	5	94	0	1	43	109.9	-20.6	61	8	1,000,000	0	0.0	0.0
B- / 7.9	9.3	0.89	16.83	174	0	0	0	100	0	65.2	-17.6	28	10	250	0	5.8	0.0
B- / 7.9	9.2	0.89	15.65	15	0	0	0	100	0	60.9	-17.8	21	10	250	0	0.0	0.0
B- / 7.9	9.3	0.89	15.63	83	0	0	0	100	0	61.0	-17.8	20	10	250	0	0.0	0.0
B- / 7.4	9.2	0.89	13.51	4,014	2	78	16	4	4	66.4	-17.4	32	12	1,000	0	5.8	0.0
B- / 7.4	9.3	0.89	13.59	145	2	78	16	4	4	67.9	-17.4	34	12	1,000	0	0.0	0.0
B- / 7.4	9.2	0.88	13.29	1,770	2	78	16	4	4	62.2	-17.7	24	12	1,000	0	0.0	0.0
B- / 7.4	9.2	0.89	13.53	12	2	78	16	4	4	65.2	-17.6	29	12	1,000	0	0.0	0.0
C+ / 6.4	8.1	1.16	10.60	20	8	62	29	1	40	29.4	N/A	9	4	1,000	0	5.8	0.0
C+ / 6.3	8.1	1.17	10.60	11	8	62	29	1	40	30.2	N/A	9	4	1,000	0	0.0	0.0
C+ / 6.6	8.1	1.18	10.56	6	8	62	29	1	40	26.1	N/A	6	4	1,000	0	0.0	0.0
C+ / 6.5	8.1	1.17	10.58	2	8	62	29	1	40	27.8	N/A	7	4	1,000	0	0.0	0.0
U /	N/A	N/A	12.02	28	15	84	0	1	35	N/A	N/A	N/A	2	1,000	0	5.8	0.0
C / 5.2	12.2	0.49	9.19	102	10	89	0	1	22	67.8	-19.0	91	5	1,000	0	5.8	0.0
C / 5.2	12.2	0.50	9.23	49	10	89	0	1	22	69.3	-18.9	91	5	0	0	0.0	0.0
C / 5.2	12.2	0.49	9.09	24	10	89	0	1	22	63.7	-19.3	89	5	1,000	0	0.0	0.0
C+ / 6.0	12.1	0.90	9.23	1	10	89	0	1	22	69.8	-18.9	60	5	1,000,000	0	0.0	0.0
D- / 1.2	35.6	1.76	13.60	605	0	99	0	1	16	-58.4	-21.1	1	16	1,000	0	5.8	0.0
D- / 1.2	35.7	1.76	14.30	120	0	99	0	1	16	-58.1	-21.1	1	16	0	0	0.0	0.0
D- / 1.2	35.6	1.75	12.78	134	0	99	0	1	16	-59.4	-21.4	1	16	1,000	0	0.0	0.0
D- / 1.2	35.6	1.75	14.35	1	0	99	0	1	16	-57.9	-21.1	1	16	1,000,000	0	0.0	0.0
B+ / 9.1	5.7	0.55	22.53	76	0	0	0	100	0	39.5	-10.8	52	10	250	0	5.8	0.0
B+ / 9.1	5.7	0.55	20.51	5	0	0	0	100	0	36.0	-11.0	40	10	250	0	0.0	0.0
B+ / 9.1	5.7	0.55	20.23	43	0	0	0	100	0	36.0	-11.0	40	10	250	0	0.0	0.0
B / 8.1	8.8	0.88	26.26	49	0	0	0	100	0	93.6	-16.1	77	12	250	0	5.8	0.0
B / 8.1	8.8	0.88	23.36	3	0	0	0	100	0	88.7	-16.4	70	12	250	0	0.0	0.0
B / 8.1	8.8	0.88	24.98	16	0	0	0	100	0	88.5	-16.4	70	12	250	0	0.0	0.0
B- / 7.3	8.8	0.88	77.16	7,603	10	89	0	1	2	95.8	-16.0	80	24	1,000	0	5.8	0.0
B- / 7.3	8.8	0.88	77.35	1,600	10	89	0	1	2	97.4	-15.9	81	24	1,000	0	0.0	0.0

99 Pct = Best
0 Pct = Worst

Fund Type	Fund Name	Ticker Symbol	Overall Investment Rating	Phone	Performance Rating/Pts	3 Mo	6 Mo	1Yr / Pct	3Yr / Pct	5Yr / Pct	Dividend Yield	Expense Ratio
GI	Franklin Growth Allocation A	FGTIX	C	(800) 342-5236	C- / 3.4	2.87	4.72	6.71 /53	9.99 /39	9.04 /37	1.38	1.32
GI	Franklin Growth Allocation Adv	FGTZX	C+	(800) 321-8563	C / 4.4	2.91	4.83	6.98 /55	10.25 /41	9.32 /39	1.68	1.07
GI	Franklin Growth Allocation C	FTGTX	C	(800) 342-5236	C- / 3.8	2.66	4.33	5.89 /45	9.17 /34	8.21 /31	0.81	2.07
GI	Franklin Growth Allocation R	FGTRX	C	(800) 342-5236	C- / 4.1	2.80	4.60	6.44 /50	9.71 /38	8.76 /35	1.21	1.57
AA	Franklin Growth Allocation R6		C+	(800) 342-5236	C / 4.5	2.97	4.92	7.14 /56	10.26 /41	9.20 /38	1.82	1.58
GR	Franklin Growth C	FRGSX	A	(800) 342-5236	B / 8.1	3.13	9.29	15.14 /92	14.76 /73	12.77 /66	0.00	1.65
AG	Franklin Growth Opportunities A	FGRAX	B-	(800) 342-5236	B / 8.0	6.98	10.97	15.81 /93	15.36 /78	14.95 /86	0.00	1.17
AG	Franklin Growth Opportunities Adv	FRAAX	B+	(800) 321-8563	A- / 9.1	7.05	11.11	16.15 /93	15.69 /81	15.29 /89	0.00	0.87
AG	Franklin Growth Opportunities C	FKACX	B	(800) 342-5236	B+ / 8.5	6.80	10.60	14.99 /92	14.55 /71	14.15 /79	0.00	1.87
AG	Franklin Growth Opportunities R	FKARX	B	(800) 342-5236	B+ / 8.8	6.94	10.86	15.56 /93	15.13 /76	14.71 /84	0.00	1.37
GR	Franklin Growth Opportunities R6	FOPPX	B+	(800) 342-5236	A- / 9.2	7.12	11.23	16.39 /94	15.83 /82	15.38 /89	0.00	0.71
GR	Franklin Growth R	FGSRX	A+	(800) 342-5236	B+ / 8.5	3.26	9.58	15.71 /93	15.33 /78	13.34 /71	0.00	1.15
GR	Franklin Growth R6	FIFRX	A+	(800) 342-5236	B+ / 8.9	3.41	9.94	16.51 /94	15.94 /83	13.81 /76	0.60	0.47
GI	Franklin Income 529 Port A		C-	(800) 342-5236	D / 2.0	0.76	-1.41	0.40 /17	8.51 /30	8.37 /32	0.00	1.21
GI	● Franklin Income 529 Port B		C-	(800) 342-5236	D / 2.2	0.61	-1.73	-0.34 /15	7.71 /25	7.57 /27	0.00	1.96
GI	Franklin Income 529 Port C		C-	(800) 342-5236	D / 2.1	0.57	-1.78	-0.39 /14	7.70 /25	7.56 /27	0.00	1.96
* GL	Franklin Income A	FKINX	D	(800) 342-5236	D / 2.2	0.84	-1.21	0.75 /18	8.92 /32	8.92 /36	4.81	0.61
GL	Franklin Income Adv	FRIAX	D+	(800) 321-8563	C- / 3.0	0.88	-1.15	0.90 /18	9.16 /34	9.05 /37	5.22	0.46
GL	Franklin Income C	FCISX	D+	(800) 342-5236	D+ / 2.4	0.29	-1.46	-0.17 /15	8.29 /29	8.29 /32	4.46	1.11
GL	Franklin Income R	FISRX	D+	(800) 342-5236	D+ / 2.6	0.77	-1.40	0.41 /17	8.53 /30	8.57 /34	4.74	0.96
AA	Franklin Income R6	FNCFX	C-	(800) 342-5236	C- / 3.0	0.90	-1.11	0.98 /18	9.11 /34	9.03 /37	5.29	0.38
EM	Franklin India Growth Fund A	FINGX	B-	(800) 342-5236	A+ / 9.6	6.17	14.09	39.39 /99	14.10 /68	7.47 /26	0.56	2.25
EM	Franklin India Growth Fund Adv	FIGZX	B-	(800) 321-8563	A+ / 9.8	6.23	14.25	39.76 /99	14.41 /70	7.78 /28	0.71	1.95
EM	Franklin India Growth Fund C	FINDX	B-	(800) 342-5236	A+ / 9.7	6.04	13.70	38.37 /99	13.27 /62	6.70 /21	0.28	2.95
FO	Franklin India Growth Fund R6		B-	(800) 342-5236	A+ / 9.8	6.22	14.16	39.83 /99	14.51 /71	7.84 /29	0.81	1.80
FO	● Franklin Inter Small Cap Growth A	FINAX	D	(800) 342-5236	C / 4.7	6.99	1.85	-5.42 / 5	14.17 /68	11.01 /53	1.32	1.42
FO	● Franklin Inter Small Cap Growth Adv	FKSCX	C-	(800) 342-5236	C+ / 5.9	7.09	1.95	-5.21 / 5	14.45 /71	11.30 /55	1.57	1.12
FO	● Franklin Inter Small Cap Growth C	FCSMX	D+	(800) 342-5236	C / 5.1	6.80	1.52	-6.12 / 4	13.34 /62	10.21 /46	0.92	2.12
FO	● Franklin Inter Small Cap Growth R	FISDX	D+	(800) 342-5236	C / 5.5	6.94	1.71	-5.69 / 5	13.88 /66	10.74 /51	1.18	1.62
FO	● Franklin Inter Small Cap Growth R6	FCAPX	C+	(800) 342-5236	C+ / 5.9	7.14	2.03	-5.05 / 5	14.52 /71	11.35 /56	1.64	1.00
FO	Franklin International Growth A	FNGAX	E+	(800) 342-5236	D- / 1.0	3.95	2.86	-1.75 /11	5.45 /15	5.37 /14	0.30	1.70
FO	Franklin International Growth Adv	FNGZX	D-	(800) 321-8563	D / 1.6	3.93	2.94	-1.47 /12	5.74 /16	5.68 /15	0.57	1.40
FO	Franklin International Growth C		D-	(800) 342-5236	D- / 1.2	3.72	2.46	-2.38 /10	4.71 /12	4.62 /11	0.00	2.40
FO	Franklin International Growth R		D-	(800) 342-5236	D- / 1.4	3.85	2.67	-1.94 /10	5.23 /14	5.12 /12	0.06	1.90
FO	Franklin International Growth R6	FILRX	D	(800) 342-5236	D / 1.6	4.02	3.08	-1.25 /12	5.84 /16	5.74 /15	0.70	1.02
GL	Franklin K2 Alternative Strat A	FAAAX	U	(800) 342-5236	U /	2.68	4.67	5.36 /41	--	--	0.57	3.71
GL	Franklin K2 Alternative Strat Adv	FABZX	U	(800) 342-5236	U /	2.77	5.01	5.80 /45	--	--	0.84	3.41
GL	Franklin K2 Alternative Strat C	FASCX	U	(800) 342-5236	U /	2.50	4.40	4.69 /36	--	--	0.23	4.41
GL	Franklin K2 Alternative Strat R6	FASRX	U	(800) 342-5236	U /	2.77	4.93	5.72 /44	--	--	0.86	3.34
GI	Franklin Large Cap Equity A	FLCAX	C-	(800) 342-5236	C / 4.4	1.79	4.22	8.49 /66	11.89 /52	11.00 /53	0.05	1.36
GI	Franklin Large Cap Equity Adv	FLCIX	C	(800) 321-8563	C+ / 5.6	1.78	4.33	8.71 /68	12.29 /55	11.43 /56	0.29	1.06
GI	Franklin Large Cap Equity C		C	(800) 342-5236	C / 4.9	1.55	3.92	7.71 /61	11.21 /47	10.34 /47	0.00	2.06
GI	Franklin Large Cap Equity R		C	(800) 342-5236	C / 5.2	1.63	3.94	8.04 /63	11.75 /51	10.83 /51	0.00	1.56
GR	Franklin Large Cap Growth VIP 2		B+	(800) 342-5236	B+ / 8.8	6.28	10.02	16.97 /95	15.11 /76	12.61 /65	0.97	1.04
GI	Franklin Large Cap Value A	FLVAX	C+	(800) 342-5236	C / 5.2	-0.37	2.46	6.16 /48	14.08 /68	10.75 /51	0.52	1.30
GI	Franklin Large Cap Value Adv		B-	(800) 321-8563	C+ / 6.4	-0.27	2.67	6.51 /51	14.42 /70	11.10 /53	0.86	1.00
GI	Franklin Large Cap Value C	FLCVX	C+	(800) 342-5236	C+ / 5.7	-0.48	2.16	5.48 /42	13.29 /62	9.99 /44	0.00	2.00
GI	Franklin Large Cap Value R	FLCRX	B-	(800) 342-5236	C+ / 6.0	-0.43	2.40	5.95 /46	13.84 /66	10.52 /49	0.33	1.50
GI	Franklin Large Cap Value R6	FRLGX	B-	(800) 342-5236	C+ / 6.4	-0.27	2.72	6.69 /53	14.43 /70	10.95 /52	1.00	0.83
GL	Franklin LifeSmart 2015 Ret Tgt A	FTRAX	D+	(800) 342-5236	D- / 1.4	1.53	2.15	3.39 /28	6.51 /19	6.72 /21	2.96	1.45
GL	Franklin LifeSmart 2015 Ret Tgt Adv	FLRDX	C-	(800) 342-5236	D / 2.2	1.58	2.28	3.76 /30	6.83 /20	7.03 /23	3.40	1.15
GL	Franklin LifeSmart 2015 Ret Tgt C	FRTCX	D+	(800) 342-5236	D / 1.7	1.32	1.76	2.65 /25	5.74 /16	5.97 /17	2.50	2.15

● Denotes fund is closed to new investors
* Denotes fund is included in Section II

www.thestreetratings.com

RISK			NET ASSETS		ASSET					BULL / BEAR		FUND MANAGER		MINIMUMS		LOADS	
Risk Rating/Pts	Standard Deviation	Beta	NAV As of 3/31/15	Total $(Mil)	Cash %	Stocks %	Bonds %	Other %	Portfolio Turnover Ratio	Last Bull Market Return	Last Bear Market Return	Manager Quality Pct	Manager Tenure (Years)	Initial Purch. $	Additional Purch. $	Front End Load	Back End Load
B- / 7.6	7.9	0.77	19.10	924	8	78	12	2	18	54.7	-15.1	37	15	1,000	0	5.8	0.0
B- / 7.6	7.9	0.77	19.17	54	8	78	12	2	18	56.1	-15.0	40	15	1,000	0	0.0	0.0
B- / 7.6	8.0	0.78	18.63	347	8	78	12	2	18	50.8	-15.3	27	15	1,000	0	0.0	0.0
B- / 7.6	7.9	0.77	18.86	184	8	78	12	2	18	53.4	-15.1	33	15	1,000	0	0.0	0.0
B- / 7.7	7.9	1.32	19.17	2	8	78	12	2	18	55.8	-15.1	17	15	1,000,000	0	0.0	0.0
B- / 7.3	8.8	0.88	71.86	795	10	89	0	1	2	90.8	-16.2	74	24	1,000	0	0.0	0.0
C / 4.9	12.4	1.09	33.24	432	0	99	0	1	37	98.0	-20.0	38	16	1,000	0	5.8	0.0
C / 5.0	12.4	1.09	35.07	277	0	99	0	1	37	100.1	-19.9	42	16	1,000	0	0.0	0.0
C / 4.9	12.4	1.09	29.39	106	0	99	0	1	37	93.2	-20.2	29	16	1,000	0	0.0	0.0
C / 4.9	12.4	1.08	32.22	49	0	99	0	1	37	96.5	-20.0	36	16	1,000	0	0.0	0.0
C / 5.5	12.4	1.09	35.20	249	0	99	0	1	37	100.7	-19.9	44	16	1,000,000	0	0.0	0.0
B- / 7.3	8.8	0.88	76.76	599	10	89	0	1	2	94.1	-16.1	78	24	1,000	0	0.0	0.0
B- / 7.6	8.8	0.88	77.31	1,210	10	89	0	1	2	97.4	-16.0	81	24	1,000,000	0	0.0	0.0
B / 8.5	7.0	0.61	25.26	119	0	0	0	100	0	47.8	-11.9	53	10	250	0	4.3	0.0
B / 8.4	7.0	0.61	23.27	6	0	0	0	100	0	44.0	-12.1	42	10	250	0	0.0	0.0
B / 8.4	7.0	0.61	23.11	66	0	0	0	100	0	44.0	-12.2	42	10	250	0	0.0	0.0
C+ / 6.8	7.2	1.04	2.39	53,635	3	45	41	11	36	50.4	-11.7	61	13	1,000	0	4.3	0.0
C+ / 6.8	7.0	0.99	2.37	9,524	3	45	41	11	36	50.9	-11.7	69	13	1,000	0	0.0	0.0
C+ / 6.9	7.0	1.01	2.41	28,952	3	45	41	11	36	47.3	-11.7	57	13	1,000	0	0.0	0.0
C+ / 6.8	7.3	1.05	2.35	512	3	45	41	11	36	48.1	-11.5	54	13	1,000	0	0.0	0.0
B- / 7.1	7.2	1.10	2.37	2,065	3	45	41	11	36	51.2	-11.7	29	13	1,000,000	0	0.0	0.0
C- / 3.5	21.3	1.11	13.24	80	98	1	0	1	35	56.0	-18.5	99	N/A	1,000	0	5.8	0.0
C- / 3.5	21.3	1.11	13.48	53	98	1	0	1	35	57.4	-18.4	99	N/A	1,000,000	0	0.0	0.0
C- / 3.5	21.4	1.12	12.65	18	98	1	0	1	35	52.1	-18.7	99	N/A	1,000	0	0.0	0.0
C- / 3.2	21.3	0.94	13.50	1	98	1	0	1	35	57.8	-18.4	93	N/A	1,000,000	0	0.0	0.0
C- / 4.2	13.5	0.88	19.28	210	11	88	0	1	16	68.5	-20.3	94	9	1,000	0	5.8	0.0
C- / 4.2	13.5	0.89	19.34	1,175	11	88	0	1	16	70.1	-20.2	94	9	0	0	0.0	0.0
C- / 4.2	13.5	0.88	19.01	30	11	88	0	1	16	64.4	-20.5	92	9	1,000	0	0.0	0.0
C- / 4.2	13.5	0.89	19.25	7	11	88	0	1	16	67.1	-20.4	93	9	1,000	0	0.0	0.0
C+ / 6.8	13.5	0.89	19.36	365	11	88	0	1	16	70.3	-20.2	94	9	1,000,000	0	0.0	0.0
C+ / 5.8	12.5	0.89	11.06	182	2	97	0	1	30	46.2	-25.1	27	7	1,000	0	5.8	0.0
C+ / 5.8	12.5	0.89	11.12	96	2	97	0	1	30	47.7	-25.0	30	7	0	0	0.0	0.0
C+ / 5.7	12.4	0.89	10.87	6	2	97	0	1	30	42.7	-25.2	20	7	1,000	0	0.0	0.0
C+ / 5.8	12.4	0.89	11.05	N/A	2	97	0	1	30	45.1	-25.1	25	7	1,000	0	0.0	0.0
C+ / 6.6	12.5	0.89	11.13	32	2	97	0	1	30	48.0	-25.0	31	7	1,000,000	0	0.0	0.0
U /	N/A	N/A	11.11	126	33	34	14	19	181	N/A	N/A	N/A	2	1,000	0	5.8	0.0
U /	N/A	N/A	11.13	258	33	34	14	19	181	N/A	N/A	N/A	2	1,000,000	0	0.0	0.0
U /	N/A	N/A	11.05	39	33	34	14	19	181	N/A	N/A	N/A	2	1,000	0	0.0	0.0
U /	N/A	N/A	11.13	227	33	34	14	19	181	N/A	N/A	N/A	2	0	0	0.0	0.0
C+ / 6.0	11.0	1.11	8.11	18	1	98	0	1	50	79.2	-19.6	9	10	1,000	0	5.8	0.0
C+ / 6.1	10.9	1.10	8.16	190	1	98	0	1	50	81.7	-19.4	11	10	0	0	0.0	0.0
C+ / 6.0	11.0	1.11	7.88	4	1	98	0	1	50	75.8	-19.7	7	10	1,000	0	0.0	0.0
C+ / 6.0	10.9	1.10	8.09	N/A	1	98	0	1	50	78.4	-19.5	9	10	1,000	0	0.0	0.0
C+ / 5.8	9.8	0.98	24.38	264	0	99	0	1	94	93.3	-17.3	60	1	0	0	0.0	0.0
B- / 7.2	10.8	1.10	18.73	166	4	95	0	1	7	88.6	-22.3	23	15	1,000	0	5.8	0.0
B- / 7.2	10.8	1.09	18.66	7	4	95	0	1	7	90.5	-22.2	27	15	1,000,000	0	0.0	0.0
B- / 7.2	10.8	1.09	18.56	41	4	95	0	1	7	84.1	-22.5	17	15	1,000	0	0.0	0.0
B- / 7.2	10.8	1.10	18.61	5	4	95	0	1	7	87.4	-22.4	21	15	1,000	0	0.0	0.0
B- / 7.4	10.8	1.10	18.64	8	4	95	0	1	7	90.3	-22.3	26	15	1,000,000	0	0.0	0.0
B / 8.0	5.5	0.86	11.81	49	7	36	55	2	74	35.1	-10.5	51	15	1,000	0	5.8	0.0
B / 8.0	5.5	0.85	11.85	2	7	36	55	2	74	36.4	-10.3	57	15	1,000	0	0.0	0.0
B / 8.0	5.5	0.85	11.68	22	7	36	55	2	74	31.8	-10.7	40	15	1,000	0	0.0	0.0

	99 Pct = Best 0 Pct = Worst				PERFORMANCE							
						Total Return % through 3/31/15					Incl. in Returns	
			Overall		Perfor-				Annualized		Dividend	Expense
Fund Type	Fund Name	Ticker Symbol	Investment Rating	Phone	mance Rating/Pts	3 Mo	6 Mo	1Yr / Pct	3Yr / Pct	5Yr / Pct	Yield	Ratio
GL	Franklin LifeSmart 2015 Ret Tgt R	FBRLX	C-	(800) 342-5236	D / 1.9	1.41	1.98	3.13 /27	6.27 /18	6.48 /20	2.96	1.65
GL	Franklin LifeSmart 2015 Ret Tgt R6	FLMTX	C	(800) 342-5236	D+ / 2.3	1.59	2.30	3.80 /31	6.89 /21	7.06 /23	3.45	1.22
GL	Franklin LifeSmart 2025 Ret Tgt A	FTRTX	C	(800) 342-5236	C- / 3.1	2.73	4.54	5.84 /45	9.62 /37	8.71 /35	1.85	1.51
GL	Franklin LifeSmart 2025 Ret Tgt Adv	FLRFX	C+	(800) 342-5236	C- / 4.2	2.81	4.69	6.15 /48	9.93 /39	9.04 /37	2.17	1.21
GL	Franklin LifeSmart 2025 Ret Tgt C	FTTCX	C	(800) 342-5236	C- / 3.5	2.52	4.16	5.12 /39	8.84 /32	7.95 /30	1.47	2.21
GL	Franklin LifeSmart 2025 Ret Tgt R	FRELX	C	(800) 342-5236	C- / 3.9	2.66	4.42	5.62 /43	9.37 /35	8.48 /33	1.81	1.71
GL	Franklin LifeSmart 2025 Ret Tgt R6	FTLMX	C+	(800) 342-5236	C- / 4.2	2.80	4.70	6.27 /49	9.99 /39	9.07 /37	2.20	1.11
GL	Franklin LifeSmart 2035 Ret Tgt A	FRTAX	C	(800) 342-5236	C- / 3.6	2.90	5.03	6.57 /51	10.33 /41	9.32 /39	1.67	1.62
GL	Franklin LifeSmart 2035 Ret Tgt Adv	FLRHX	C+	(800) 342-5236	C / 4.7	3.04	5.21	6.90 /54	10.68 /43	9.66 /42	2.03	1.32
GL	Franklin LifeSmart 2035 Ret Tgt C	FTRCX	C	(800) 342-5236	C- / 4.0	2.72	4.63	5.86 /45	9.59 /37	8.57 /34	1.19	2.32
GL	Franklin LifeSmart 2035 Ret Tgt R	FLRGX	C+	(800) 342-5236	C / 4.3	2.83	4.90	6.35 /49	10.14 /40	9.11 /37	1.57	1.82
GL	Franklin LifeSmart 2035 Ret Tgt R6	FMTLX	C+	(800) 342-5236	C / 4.7	2.96	5.26	6.95 /55	10.68 /43	9.66 /42	2.07	1.17
GL	Franklin LifeSmart 2045 Ret Tgt A	FTTAX	C	(800) 342-5236	C- / 3.8	2.97	5.31	6.78 /53	10.68 /43	9.82 /43	1.57	1.86
GL	Franklin LifeSmart 2045 Ret Tgt Adv	FLRLX	C+	(800) 342-5236	C / 4.9	3.12	5.49	7.12 /56	11.00 /45	10.15 /46	1.92	1.56
GL	Franklin LifeSmart 2045 Ret Tgt C	FLRIX	C	(800) 342-5236	C- / 4.2	2.80	4.86	5.94 /46	9.91 /39	9.05 /37	1.09	2.56
GL	Franklin LifeSmart 2045 Ret Tgt R	FLRJX	C+	(800) 342-5236	C+ / 4.5	2.90	5.12	6.52 /51	10.44 /42	9.61 /41	1.32	2.06
GL	Franklin LifeSmart 2045 Ret Tgt R6	FMLTX	B-	(800) 342-5236	C / 4.9	3.04	5.46	7.08 /56	11.03 /46	10.16 /46	1.96	1.32
SC	Franklin MicroCap Value A	FRMCX	D	(800) 342-5236	C- / 3.9	-0.14	1.53	-2.61 / 9	12.91 /59	11.19 /54	0.00	1.18
SC	Franklin MicroCap Value Adv	FVRMX	D+	(800) 321-8563	C / 4.9	-0.06	1.64	-2.35 /10	13.17 /61	11.45 /56	0.00	0.94
SC	Franklin MicroCap Value R6	FMCVX	C+	(800) 342-5236	C / 5.0	-0.06	1.69	-2.23 /10	13.17 /61	11.35 /56	0.00	0.81
MC	Franklin MidCap Value A	FMVAX	C+	(800) 342-5236	C / 5.5	1.19	6.27	5.93 /46	14.05 /67	12.30 /63	0.62	1.57
MC	Franklin MidCap Value Adv		B-	(800) 321-8563	C+ / 6.7	1.25	6.42	6.22 /48	14.41 /70	12.67 /65	0.93	1.27
MC	Franklin MidCap Value C	FMVCX	B-	(800) 342-5236	C+ / 5.9	0.95	5.82	5.14 /40	13.24 /61	11.52 /57	0.00	2.27
MC	Franklin MidCap Value R		B-	(800) 342-5236	C+ / 6.2	1.07	6.11	5.71 /44	13.79 /66	12.07 /61	0.39	1.77
GL	Franklin Moderate Allocation A	FMTIX	C-	(800) 342-5236	D / 2.0	2.29	3.50	5.25 /40	7.70 /25	7.26 /25	2.11	1.25
GL	Franklin Moderate Allocation Adv	FMTZX	C	(800) 321-8563	C- / 3.1	2.33	3.61	5.56 /43	7.96 /27	7.53 /27	2.46	1.00
GL	Franklin Moderate Allocation C	FTMTX	C	(800) 342-5236	D+ / 2.4	2.07	3.10	4.51 /35	6.89 /21	6.45 /20	1.59	2.00
GL	Franklin Moderate Allocation R	FTMRX	C	(800) 342-5236	D+ / 2.7	2.18	3.38	5.02 /39	7.41 /24	6.99 /23	2.00	1.50
GL	Franklin Moderate Allocation R6		C	(800) 342-5236	C- / 3.1	2.29	3.67	5.63 /43	7.94 /27	7.40 /26	2.58	1.04
GL	Franklin Multi- Asset Real Rtn A	FTMAX	D+	(800) 342-5236	E / 0.4	1.33	-2.10	-3.66 / 8	1.46 / 6	--	2.40	1.96
GL	Franklin Multi- Asset Real Rtn Adv		C-	(800) 342-5236	E+ / 0.6	1.43	-1.88	-3.35 / 8	1.66 / 6	--	2.87	1.70
GL	Franklin Multi- Asset Real Rtn C		D+	(800) 342-5236	E / 0.5	1.13	-2.47	-4.41 / 6	0.65 / 5	--	1.84	2.70
GL	Franklin Multi- Asset Real Rtn R		C-	(800) 342-5236	E / 0.5	1.23	-2.19	-3.94 / 7	1.19 / 5	--	2.28	2.20
GI	Franklin Mutual Beacon A	TEBIX	C+	(800) 342-5236	C+ / 6.1	4.07	6.22	9.31 /71	14.43 /70	11.21 /55	3.34	1.10
GI	Franklin Mutual Beacon C	TEMEX	C+	(800) 342-5236	C+ / 6.5	3.85	5.82	8.49 /66	13.63 /64	10.43 /48	2.87	1.80
GI	Franklin Mutual Beacon R		C+	(800) 342-5236	C+ / 6.9	3.98	6.12	9.04 /69	14.21 /69	10.98 /53	3.43	1.30
GR	Franklin Mutual Beacon R6	FMBRX	A-	(800) 321-8563	B- / 7.4	4.16	6.42	9.74 /73	14.86 /74	11.57 /57	3.90	2.10
GI	Franklin Mutual Beacon Z	BEGRX	B	(800) 321-8563	B- / 7.4	4.10	6.38	9.64 /73	14.79 /73	11.53 /57	3.81	0.80
FO	Franklin Mutual European A	TEMIX	D	(800) 342-5236	C / 4.8	8.26	6.99	3.60 /29	12.41 /55	8.21 /31	2.34	1.37
FO	Franklin Mutual European C	TEURX	D+	(800) 342-5236	C / 5.2	8.05	6.63	2.85 /26	11.62 /50	7.45 /26	1.81	2.07
FO	Franklin Mutual European R		D+	(800) 342-5236	C+ / 5.6	8.24	6.90	3.39 /28	12.20 /54	7.99 /30	2.51	1.57
FO	Franklin Mutual European R6	FMEUX	B-	(800) 321-8563	C+ / 6.0	8.35	7.25	4.02 /32	12.87 /59	8.60 /34	2.86	0.90
FO	Franklin Mutual European Z	MEURX	C-	(800) 321-8563	C+ / 6.0	8.34	7.15	3.92 /31	12.76 /58	8.53 /33	2.70	1.07
FS	Franklin Mutual Financial Svcs A	TFSIX	A	(800) 342-5236	B- / 7.2	2.93	7.16	13.08 /87	15.86 /82	10.55 /49	1.56	1.46
FS	Franklin Mutual Financial Svcs C	TMFSX	A+	(800) 342-5236	B / 7.7	2.72	6.71	12.25 /84	15.06 /75	9.77 /43	1.00	2.16
FS	Franklin Mutual Financial Svcs R6		A+	(800) 321-8563	B+ / 8.6	3.03	7.32	13.59 /88	16.34 /86	10.95 /52	1.44	2.18
FS	Franklin Mutual Financial Svcs Z	TEFAX	A+	(800) 321-8563	B+ / 8.6	2.93	7.26	13.39 /88	16.19 /85	10.86 /51	1.95	1.16
* GL	Franklin Mutual Global Discovery A	TEDIX	C	(800) 342-5236	C / 4.7	3.14	4.10	6.07 /47	12.72 /58	9.63 /42	1.94	1.28
GL	Franklin Mutual Global Discovery C	TEDSX	C+	(800) 342-5236	C / 5.2	2.95	3.74	5.32 /41	11.94 /52	8.87 /36	1.40	1.98
GL	Franklin Mutual Global Discovery R	TEDRX	C+	(800) 342-5236	C+ / 5.6	3.11	4.01	5.85 /45	12.50 /56	9.42 /40	1.86	1.48
GL	Franklin Mutual Global Discovery R6	FMDRX	B-	(800) 321-8563	C+ / 6.0	3.24	4.33	6.51 /51	13.17 /61	10.03 /45	2.43	0.84
GL	Franklin Mutual Global Discovery Z	MDISX	C+	(800) 321-8563	C+ / 5.9	3.21	4.25	6.37 /50	13.05 /60	9.96 /44	2.30	0.98

● Denotes fund is closed to new investors
* Denotes fund is included in Section II

www.thestreetratings.com

RISK	3 Year		NET ASSETS		ASSET				Portfolio	BULL / BEAR		FUND MANAGER		MINIMUMS		LOADS	
Risk Rating/Pts	Standard Deviation	Beta	NAV As of 3/31/15	Total $(Mil)	Cash %	Stocks %	Bonds %	Other %	Turnover Ratio	Last Bull Market Return	Last Bear Market Return	Manager Quality Pct	Manager Tenure (Years)	Initial Purch. $	Additional Purch. $	Front End Load	Back End Load
B /8.0	5.5	0.86	11.77	3	7	36	55	2	74	34.0	-10.5	48	15	1,000	0	0.0	0.0
B+ /9.3	5.5	0.39	11.86	6	7	36	55	2	74	36.6	-10.3	89	15	1,000,000	0	0.0	0.0
B- /7.9	7.6	1.14	12.69	72	8	69	21	2	47	51.7	-14.4	58	9	1,000	0	5.8	0.0
B- /7.9	7.6	1.13	12.72	4	8	69	21	2	47	53.2	-14.2	63	9	1,000	0	0.0	0.0
B- /7.9	7.6	1.15	12.48	30	8	69	21	2	47	48.1	-14.7	46	9	1,000	0	0.0	0.0
B- /7.9	7.6	1.14	12.63	6	8	69	21	2	47	50.7	-14.5	54	9	1,000	0	0.0	0.0
B /8.5	7.6	0.51	12.73	15	8	69	21	2	47	53.4	-14.2	93	9	1,000,000	0	0.0	0.0
B- /7.6	8.1	1.21	13.03	53	8	77	13	2	50	56.1	-15.3	59	9	1,000	0	5.8	0.0
B- /7.6	8.1	1.20	13.13	3	8	77	13	2	50	57.8	-15.3	64	9	1,000	0	0.0	0.0
B- /7.6	8.1	1.21	12.76	21	8	77	13	2	50	52.5	-15.7	48	9	1,000	0	0.0	0.0
B- /7.6	8.0	1.20	13.01	5	8	77	13	2	50	55.1	-15.5	58	9	1,000	0	0.0	0.0
B /8.2	8.1	0.54	13.12	17	8	77	13	2	50	57.8	-15.3	94	9	1,000,000	0	0.0	0.0
B- /7.5	8.3	1.24	13.07	37	8	81	9	2	44	57.8	-15.6	59	9	1,000	0	5.8	0.0
B- /7.4	8.4	1.25	13.15	2	8	81	9	2	44	59.5	-15.5	63	9	1,000	0	0.0	0.0
B- /7.5	8.3	1.24	12.76	12	8	81	9	2	44	54.0	-15.9	49	9	1,000	0	0.0	0.0
B- /7.5	8.3	1.24	13.02	4	8	81	9	2	44	56.6	-15.7	56	9	1,000	0	0.0	0.0
B /8.0	8.4	0.56	13.15	10	8	81	9	2	44	59.6	-15.5	94	9	1,000,000	0	0.0	0.0
C /4.7	11.0	0.71	35.12	307	7	92	0	1	12	66.1	-15.9	80	20	1,000	0	5.8	0.0
C /4.7	11.0	0.71	35.18	77	7	92	0	1	12	67.5	-15.8	82	20	1,000,000	0	0.0	0.0
B- /7.0	11.0	0.71	35.23	22	7	92	0	1	12	67.2	-15.9	82	20	1,000,000	0	0.0	0.0
B- /7.2	9.8	0.85	16.15	137	4	95	0	1	24	86.1	-22.7	65	10	1,000	0	5.8	0.0
B- /7.2	9.8	0.85	16.22	5	4	95	0	1	24	88.0	-22.6	69	10	1,000,000	0	0.0	0.0
B- /7.1	9.8	0.84	15.94	26	4	95	0	1	24	81.7	-22.9	55	10	1,000	0	0.0	0.0
B- /7.2	9.8	0.85	16.13	1	4	95	0	1	24	84.8	-22.7	61	10	1,000	0	0.0	0.0
B /8.5	6.3	0.98	16.04	1,701	7	55	36	2	18	40.1	-10.9	52	15	1,000	0	5.8	0.0
B /8.5	6.2	0.98	16.05	87	7	55	36	2	18	41.4	-10.8	56	15	1,000	0	0.0	0.0
B /8.5	6.2	0.97	15.64	731	7	55	36	2	18	36.6	-11.2	42	15	1,000	0	0.0	0.0
B /8.5	6.2	0.97	15.98	260	7	55	36	2	18	39.1	-11.0	49	15	1,000	0	0.0	0.0
B /8.3	6.3	0.97	16.04	5	7	55	36	2	18	41.1	-10.9	56	15	1,000,000	0	0.0	0.0
B+ /9.3	5.1	0.73	9.92	8	28	32	39	1	40	N/A	N/A	11	4	1,000	0	5.8	0.0
B+ /9.3	5.1	0.74	9.93	3	28	32	39	1	40	N/A	N/A	12	4	1,000	0	0.0	0.0
B+ /9.3	5.1	0.73	9.81	4	28	32	39	1	40	N/A	N/A	7	4	1,000	0	0.0	0.0
B+ /9.3	5.1	0.73	9.90	N/A	28	32	39	1	40	N/A	N/A	9	4	1,000	0	0.0	0.0
C+ /6.7	8.9	0.86	17.14	1,139	3	87	8	2	40	82.9	-17.3	74	8	1,000	0	5.8	0.0
C+ /6.7	8.9	0.86	16.99	331	3	87	8	2	40	78.7	-17.5	66	8	1,000	0	0.0	0.0
C+ /6.7	8.9	0.86	16.98	2	3	87	8	2	40	81.7	-17.3	71	8	1,000	0	0.0	0.0
B- /7.6	8.9	0.86	17.27	53	3	87	8	2	40	85.1	-17.1	77	8	1,000,000	0	0.0	0.0
C+ /6.6	8.9	0.86	17.27	2,865	3	87	8	2	40	84.7	-17.1	77	8	1,000	0	0.0	0.0
C /4.3	10.1	0.66	22.01	929	4	89	5	2	54	63.6	-20.8	95	11	1,000	0	5.8	0.0
C /4.4	10.1	0.66	22.01	237	4	89	5	2	54	59.7	-21.0	93	11	1,000	0	0.0	0.0
C- /4.2	10.1	0.66	21.68	N/A	4	89	5	2	54	62.4	-20.8	94	11	1,000	0	0.0	0.0
B- /7.3	10.1	0.66	22.59	369	4	89	5	2	54	65.7	-20.7	95	11	1,000,000	0	0.0	0.0
C /4.3	10.1	0.66	22.60	1,250	4	89	5	2	54	65.2	-20.7	95	11	1,000	0	0.0	0.0
B /8.3	8.2	0.67	19.00	256	7	83	9	1	34	78.8	-19.8	92	6	1,000	0	5.8	0.0
B /8.2	8.3	0.67	18.91	90	7	83	9	1	34	74.7	-20.1	90	6	1,000	0	0.0	0.0
B /8.4	8.2	0.66	19.07	N/A	7	83	9	1	34	81.3	-19.7	92	6	1,000,000	0	0.0	0.0
B /8.3	8.2	0.67	18.94	113	7	83	9	1	34	80.7	-19.7	92	6	1,000	0	0.0	0.0
C+ /6.9	8.7	0.58	33.84	12,100	1	84	13	2	24	69.4	-17.3	96	10	1,000	0	5.8	0.0
B- /7.0	8.7	0.58	33.45	3,187	1	84	13	2	24	65.4	-17.5	95	10	1,000	0	0.0	0.0
C+ /6.9	8.7	0.58	33.44	547	1	84	13	2	24	68.3	-17.3	96	10	1,000	0	0.0	0.0
B- /7.8	8.7	0.59	34.41	169	1	84	13	2	24	71.7	-17.1	96	10	1,000,000	0	0.0	0.0
C+ /6.9	8.7	0.58	34.39	10,724	1	84	13	2	24	71.2	-17.1	96	10	1,000	0	0.0	0.0

					PERFORMANCE						Incl. in Returns	
							Total Return % through 3/31/15					
			Overall		Perfor-				Annualized		Dividend	Expense
Fund Type	Fund Name	Ticker Symbol	Investment Rating	Phone	mance Rating/Pts	3 Mo	6 Mo	1Yr / Pct	3Yr / Pct	5Yr / Pct	Yield	Ratio
FO	Franklin Mutual International A	FMIAX	D+	(800) 342-5236	D+ / 2.7	5.91	4.92	5.24 /40	8.64 /31	7.42 /26	2.27	1.79
FO	Franklin Mutual International C	FCMIX	C-	(800) 342-5236	C- / 3.2	5.77	4.66	4.58 /36	7.88 /26	6.68 /21	1.77	2.49
FO	Franklin Mutual International R	FRMIX	C-	(800) 342-5236	C- / 3.5	5.93	4.88	5.07 /39	8.40 /29	7.19 /24	2.30	1.99
FO	Franklin Mutual International R6	FIMFX	C+	(800) 342-5236	C- / 3.9	6.03	5.16	5.68 /44	9.05 /33	7.81 /29	2.81	2.89
FO	Franklin Mutual International Z	FMIZX	C-	(800) 342-5236	C- / 3.8	6.03	5.11	5.56 /43	8.96 /33	7.76 /28	2.70	1.49
GI	Franklin Mutual Quest A	TEQIX	D-	(800) 342-5236	C- / 3.7	2.25	3.47	2.96 /26	11.39 /48	9.05 /37	4.17	1.14
GI	Franklin Mutual Quest C	TEMQX	D	(800) 342-5236	C- / 4.1	2.03	3.05	2.25 /23	10.60 /43	8.28 /32	3.75	1.84
GI	Franklin Mutual Quest R		D	(800) 342-5236	C / 4.5	2.14	3.29	2.73 /25	11.17 /47	8.83 /36	4.20	1.34
GL	Franklin Mutual Quest R6	FMQRX	B	(800) 321-8563	C / 4.9	2.28	3.61	3.33 /28	11.76 /51	9.40 /40	4.74	2.00
GI	Franklin Mutual Quest Z	MQIFX	D	(800) 321-8563	C / 4.8	2.28	3.57	3.24 /28	11.72 /51	9.38 /40	4.66	0.84
GI	Franklin Mutual Shares 529 Port A		B	(800) 342-5236	C / 5.2	2.39	3.85	7.17 /56	13.51 /63	10.55 /49	0.00	1.41
GI	● Franklin Mutual Shares 529 Port B		B	(800) 342-5236	C+ / 5.6	2.17	3.43	6.38 /50	12.66 /57	9.72 /42	0.00	2.16
GI	Franklin Mutual Shares 529 Port C		B	(800) 342-5236	C+ / 5.6	2.16	3.42	6.35 /49	12.66 /57	9.73 /42	0.00	2.16
* GI	Franklin Mutual Shares A	TESIX	C+	(800) 342-5236	C / 5.4	2.39	3.90	7.38 /58	13.81 /66	10.89 /52	2.79	1.09
GI	Franklin Mutual Shares C	TEMTX	B-	(800) 342-5236	C+ / 5.8	2.24	3.58	6.65 /52	13.02 /60	10.11 /46	2.30	1.79
GI	Franklin Mutual Shares R	TESRX	B-	(800) 342-5236	C+ / 6.2	2.33	3.80	7.15 /56	13.58 /64	10.67 /50	2.76	1.29
GI	Franklin Mutual Shares R6	FMSHX	B-	(800) 321-8563	C+ / 6.6	2.51	4.13	7.80 /61	14.24 /69	11.27 /55	3.35	0.67
GI	Franklin Mutual Shares VIP 2		B-	(800) 342-5236	C+ / 6.3	2.21	3.49	7.07 /56	13.78 /65	10.89 /52	1.98	0.96
GI	Franklin Mutual Shares Z	MUTHX	B-	(800) 321-8563	C+ / 6.6	2.51	4.08	7.71 /61	14.17 /68	11.23 /55	3.24	0.79
EN	Franklin Natural Resources A	FRNRX	E-	(800) 342-5236	E- / 0.1	-1.05	-22.34	-24.43 / 1	-7.72 / 1	-1.81 / 2	0.95	1.07
EN	Franklin Natural Resources Adv	FNRAX	E-	(800) 321-8563	E- / 0.1	-0.98	-22.20	-24.20 / 1	-7.44 / 1	-1.52 / 2	1.28	0.77
EN	Franklin Natural Resources C	FNCRX	E-	(800) 342-5236	E- / 0.1	-1.23	-22.60	-24.98 / 0	-8.36 / 1	-2.49 / 1	0.03	1.76
OT	Franklin Pelagos Comdty Strat A	FLSQX	D-	(800) 342-5236	E- / 0.1	-4.72	-17.04	-25.76 / 0	-11.29 / 1	--	0.00	3.58
OT	Franklin Pelagos Comdty Strat Adv	FSLPX	D-	(800) 342-5236	E- / 0.1	-4.65	-16.90	-25.52 / 0	-10.63 / 1	--	0.00	3.28
OT	Franklin Pelagos Comdty Strat C	FLSVX	D-	(800) 342-5236	E- / 0.1	-4.90	-17.38	-26.34 / 0	-11.95 / 1	--	0.00	N/A
OT	Franklin Pelagos Comdty Strat R	FLSWX	D-	(800) 342-5236	E- / 0.1	-4.74	-17.18	-25.97 / 0	-11.48 / 1	--	0.00	N/A
OT	Franklin Pelagos Comdty Strat R6	FPELX	D-	(800) 342-5236	E- / 0.1	-4.58	-16.88	-25.53 / 0	-11.01 / 1	--	0.00	1.78
RE	Franklin Real Estate Sec A	FREEX	C+	(800) 342-5236	B+ / 8.7	4.76	20.34	24.15 /98	13.50 /63	15.29 /89	1.22	1.05
RE	Franklin Real Estate Sec Adv	FRLAX	B	(800) 321-8563	A / 9.4	4.81	20.54	24.49 /98	13.81 /66	15.60 /91	1.50	0.80
RE	Franklin Real Estate Sec C	FRRSX	B-	(800) 342-5236	A- / 9.0	4.51	19.87	23.22 /98	12.65 /57	14.44 /82	0.70	1.80
RE	Franklin Real Estate Sec R6	FSERX	B+	(800) 342-5236	A / 9.5	4.89	20.66	24.74 /98	13.84 /66	15.50 /90	1.69	0.58
* GI	Franklin Rising Dividends A	FRDPX	B-	(800) 342-5236	C / 5.3	0.10	6.29	8.45 /66	13.43 /63	13.35 /72	1.08	0.91
GI	Franklin Rising Dividends Adv	FRDAX	B-	(800) 321-8563	C+ / 6.4	0.16	6.43	8.72 /68	13.71 /65	13.63 /74	1.39	0.66
GI	Franklin Rising Dividends C	FRDTX	B-	(800) 342-5236	C+ / 5.7	-0.07	5.91	7.65 /60	12.59 /57	12.50 /64	0.45	1.66
GI	Franklin Rising Dividends R	FRDRX	B-	(800) 342-5236	C+ / 6.0	0.05	6.18	8.18 /64	13.15 /61	13.07 /69	0.91	1.16
GI	Franklin Rising Dividends R6	FRISX	B-	(800) 342-5236	C+ / 6.4	0.20	6.52	8.87 /69	13.72 /65	13.52 /73	1.52	0.52
GI	Franklin S&P 500 Index 529 Port A		B	(800) 342-5236	C+ / 6.6	0.82	5.62	12.05 /83	15.33 /78	13.72 /75	0.00	0.85
GI	● Franklin S&P 500 Index 529 Port B		A-	(800) 342-5236	B- / 7.0	0.60	5.22	11.16 /79	14.45 /71	12.86 /67	0.00	1.60
GI	Franklin S&P 500 Index 529 Port C		A-	(800) 342-5236	B- / 7.0	0.60	5.19	11.15 /79	14.44 /70	12.87 /67	0.00	1.60
SC	● Franklin Small Cap Growth A	FSGRX	B-	(800) 342-5236	B+ / 8.5	5.18	13.36	5.26 /41	18.23 /95	17.79 /97	0.00	1.22
SC	● Franklin Small Cap Growth Adv	FSSAX	B+	(800) 342-5236	A / 9.4	5.26	13.46	5.55 /43	18.57 /96	18.15 /98	0.00	0.92
SC	● Franklin Small Cap Growth C	FCSGX	B	(800) 342-5236	B+ / 8.9	5.01	12.96	4.54 /35	17.40 /92	16.97 /96	0.00	1.92
SC	● Franklin Small Cap Growth R	FSSRX	B	(800) 342-5236	A- / 9.2	5.16	13.26	5.07 /39	17.99 /94	17.55 /97	0.00	1.42
SC	● Franklin Small Cap Growth R6	FSMLX	B+	(800) 342-5236	A / 9.4	5.35	13.65	5.79 /45	18.72 /96	18.24 /98	0.00	0.74
SC	Franklin Small Cap Value A	FRVLX	D+	(800) 342-5236	C / 4.3	0.33	6.85	-1.19 /12	12.92 /59	12.43 /64	0.19	1.14
SC	Franklin Small Cap Value Adv	FVADX	C-	(800) 321-8563	C / 5.4	0.41	7.01	-0.90 /13	13.25 /61	12.76 /66	0.50	0.84
SC	Franklin Small Cap Value C	FRVFX	D+	(800) 342-5236	C / 4.7	0.16	6.46	-1.89 /11	12.13 /53	11.65 /58	0.00	1.84
SC	Franklin Small Cap Value R	FVFRX	C-	(800) 342-5236	C / 5.0	0.30	6.74	-1.38 /12	12.69 /57	12.20 /62	0.00	1.34
GI	Franklin Small Cap Value R6	FRCSX	C	(800) 342-5236	C / 5.5	0.47	7.14	-0.66 /14	13.30 /62	12.65 /65	0.72	0.61
GI	Franklin Small-Mid Cap Growth 529 A		B+	(800) 342-5236	B- / 7.3	7.18	12.42	13.25 /87	15.00 /75	14.60 /83	0.00	1.49
GI	● Franklin Small-Mid Cap Growth 529 B		B+	(800) 342-5236	B / 7.8	7.03	12.05	12.48 /85	14.16 /68	13.76 /75	0.00	2.24
GI	Franklin Small-Mid Cap Growth 529 C		B+	(800) 342-5236	B / 7.8	6.99	12.03	12.42 /84	14.15 /68	13.76 /75	0.00	2.24

99 Pct = Best
0 Pct = Worst

● Denotes fund is closed to new investors
* Denotes fund is included in Section II

www.thestreetratings.com

RISK			NET ASSETS		ASSET					BULL / BEAR		FUND MANAGER		MINIMUMS		LOADS	
	3 Year		NAV						Portfolio	Last Bull	Last Bear	Manager	Manager	Initial	Additional	Front	Back
Risk	Standard		As of	Total	Cash	Stocks	Bonds	Other	Turnover	Market	Market	Quality	Tenure	Purch.	Purch.	End	End
Rating/Pts	Deviation	Beta	3/31/15	$(Mil)	%	%	%	%	Ratio	Return	Return	Pct	(Years)	$	$	Load	Load
B- / 7.0	9.3	0.64	15.40	47	4	92	2	2	55	50.7	-21.2	86	6	1,000	0	5.8	0.0
B- / 7.0	9.3	0.64	15.21	17	4	92	2	2	55	47.1	-21.4	82	6	1,000	0	0.0	0.0
C+ / 6.9	9.3	0.64	15.37	N/A	4	92	2	2	55	49.4	-21.2	85	6	1,000	0	0.0	0.0
B / 8.0	9.3	0.64	15.47	22	4	92	2	2	55	52.6	-21.1	88	6	1,000,000	0	0.0	0.0
C+ / 6.9	9.3	0.64	15.47	22	4	92	2	2	55	52.2	-21.1	88	6	1,000	0	0.0	0.0
C- / 4.2	7.6	0.71	16.38	1,410	5	63	28	4	66	60.5	-14.9	69	12	1,000	0	5.8	0.0
C / 4.3	7.7	0.71	16.10	401	5	63	28	4	66	56.7	-15.2	59	12	1,000	0	0.0	0.0
C- / 4.1	7.7	0.71	16.21	1	5	63	28	4	66	59.5	-15.0	67	12	1,000	0	0.0	0.0
B / 8.9	7.7	0.50	16.57	47	5	63	28	4	66	62.4	-14.8	96	12	1,000,000	0	0.0	0.0
C- / 4.1	7.6	0.71	16.58	4,162	5	63	28	4	66	62.2	-14.8	73	12	1,000	0	0.0	0.0
B / 8.2	8.9	0.89	26.15	65	0	0	0	100	0	78.6	-17.8	57	10	250	0	5.8	0.0
B / 8.1	8.9	0.90	23.52	4	0	0	0	100	0	74.1	-18.0	44	10	250	0	0.0	0.0
B / 8.1	8.9	0.90	23.62	23	0	0	0	100	0	74.0	-18.0	44	10	250	0	0.0	0.0
B- / 7.5	8.9	0.90	29.99	5,539	1	86	12	1	19	80.5	-17.6	60	14	1,000	0	5.8	0.0
B- / 7.5	8.9	0.90	29.67	1,274	1	86	12	1	19	76.2	-17.9	50	14	1,000	0	0.0	0.0
B- / 7.5	8.9	0.90	29.83	169	1	86	12	1	19	79.3	-17.7	57	14	1,000	0	0.0	0.0
B- / 7.8	8.9	0.90	30.25	2,268	1	86	12	1	19	82.7	-17.5	66	14	1,000,000	0	0.0	0.0
B- / 7.0	9.0	0.91	23.10	4,269	1	83	14	2	21	80.7	-17.5	58	14	0	0	0.0	0.0
B- / 7.5	8.9	0.90	30.26	7,600	1	86	12	1	19	82.3	-17.5	65	14	1,000	0	0.0	0.0
D+ / 2.3	18.9	1.12	28.27	509	5	93	0	2	21	-0.6	-32.6	1	16	1,000	0	5.8	0.0
D+ / 2.3	18.9	1.12	30.21	74	5	93	0	2	21	0.4	-32.5	1	16	1,000	0	0.0	0.0
D+ / 2.3	19.0	1.12	27.39	108	5	93	0	2	21	-3.0	-32.8	1	16	1,000	0	0.0	0.0
C+ / 6.9	12.7	0.72	7.06	2	0	0	0	100	34	N/A	N/A	0	4	1,000	0	5.8	0.0
B- / 7.0	12.7	0.70	7.18	N/A	0	0	0	100	34	N/A	N/A	0	4	0	0	0.0	0.0
C+ / 6.9	12.7	0.72	6.99	N/A	0	0	0	100	34	N/A	N/A	0	4	1,000	0	0.0	0.0
C+ / 6.9	12.7	0.72	7.04	N/A	0	0	0	100	34	N/A	N/A	0	4	1,000	0	0.0	0.0
B- / 7.0	12.7	0.72	7.09	55	0	0	0	100	34	N/A	N/A	0	4	1,000,000	0	0.0	0.0
C- / 4.0	13.3	1.06	22.86	401	1	98	0	1	17	82.5	-15.5	47	5	1,000	0	5.8	0.0
C- / 4.0	13.3	1.06	23.04	22	1	98	0	1	17	84.1	-15.4	51	5	1,000	0	0.0	0.0
C- / 3.9	13.3	1.06	22.08	95	1	98	0	1	17	77.8	-15.8	35	5	1,000	0	0.0	0.0
C / 4.9	13.3	1.06	23.04	112	1	98	0	1	17	84.1	-15.5	51	5	1,000,000	0	0.0	0.0
B- / 7.7	9.2	0.92	52.04	11,609	1	98	0	1	4	77.8	-11.9	51	28	1,000	0	5.8	0.0
B- / 7.7	9.2	0.92	52.00	1,981	1	98	0	1	4	79.3	-11.9	54	28	1,000	0	0.0	0.0
B- / 7.6	9.2	0.92	51.21	3,038	1	98	0	1	4	73.3	-12.2	39	28	1,000	0	0.0	0.0
B- / 7.7	9.2	0.92	51.88	340	1	98	0	1	4	76.3	-12.0	47	28	1,000	0	0.0	0.0
B- / 7.5	9.2	0.92	52.00	663	1	98	0	1	4	79.1	-11.9	55	28	1,000,000	0	0.0	0.0
B / 8.0	9.5	1.00	27.06	32	0	0	0	100	0	95.7	-16.6	58	12	250	0	5.8	0.0
B / 8.0	9.5	1.00	23.40	3	0	0	0	100	0	90.6	-16.8	46	12	250	0	0.0	0.0
B / 8.0	9.5	1.00	25.33	14	0	0	0	100	0	90.5	-16.8	46	12	250	0	0.0	0.0
C / 4.8	14.8	1.01	19.28	1,186	5	94	0	1	40	112.7	-22.6	81	15	1,000	0	5.8	0.0
C / 4.8	14.8	1.01	20.41	1,089	5	94	0	1	40	114.8	-22.4	83	15	1,000	0	0.0	0.0
C / 4.7	14.8	1.01	16.76	234	5	94	0	1	40	107.6	-22.7	75	15	1,000	0	0.0	0.0
C / 4.8	14.8	1.01	18.55	89	5	94	0	1	40	111.2	-22.6	79	15	1,000	0	0.0	0.0
C / 5.3	14.8	1.01	20.49	572	5	94	0	1	40	115.6	-22.4	83	15	1,000,000	0	0.0	0.0
C / 4.8	14.2	0.98	54.17	1,252	4	94	0	2	21	91.2	-25.7	29	19	1,000	0	5.8	0.0
C / 4.9	14.2	0.98	56.12	807	4	94	0	2	21	93.1	-25.6	32	19	1,000,000	0	0.0	0.0
C / 4.7	14.2	0.98	49.66	260	4	94	0	2	21	86.6	-25.9	21	19	1,000	0	0.0	0.0
C / 4.8	14.2	0.98	53.68	267	4	94	0	2	21	89.9	-25.7	26	19	1,000	0	0.0	0.0
C+ / 6.3	14.2	1.21	56.11	46	4	94	0	2	21	93.0	-25.7	8	19	1,000,000	0	0.0	0.0
C+ / 6.8	12.1	1.08	35.22	43	0	0	0	100	0	94.2	-24.1	36	12	250	0	5.8	0.0
C+ / 6.7	12.1	1.08	32.27	3	0	0	0	100	0	89.4	-24.4	27	12	250	0	0.0	0.0
C+ / 6.8	12.1	1.08	32.14	12	0	0	0	100	0	89.3	-24.4	27	12	250	0	0.0	0.0

Fund Type	Fund Name	Ticker Symbol	Overall Investment Rating	Phone	Performance Rating/Pts	3 Mo	6 Mo	1Yr / Pct	3Yr / Pct	5Yr / Pct	Dividend Yield	Expense Ratio
	99 Pct = Best				PERFORMANCE			Total Return % through 3/31/15		Incl. in Returns		
	0 Pct = Worst								Annualized			
MC	Franklin Small-Mid Cap Growth A	FRSGX	C-	(800) 342-5236	B / 7.6	7.28	12.61	13.58 /88	15.43 /78	15.05 /87	0.00	0.96
MC	Franklin Small-Mid Cap Growth Adv	FSGAX	C	(800) 321-8563	B+ / 8.8	7.34	12.74	13.87 /89	15.71 /81	15.33 /89	0.00	0.71
MC	Franklin Small-Mid Cap Growth C	FRSIX	D+	(800) 342-5236	B / 8.1	7.06	12.23	12.81 /86	14.57 /71	14.18 /79	0.00	1.71
MC	Franklin Small-Mid Cap Growth R	FSMRX	C-	(800) 342-5236	B+ / 8.5	7.21	12.51	13.33 /88	15.14 /76	14.76 /85	0.00	1.21
SC	Franklin Small-Mid Cap Growth R6	FMGGX	B+	(800) 342-5236	B+ / 8.9	7.41	12.87	14.13 /90	15.78 /82	15.25 /88	0.00	0.47
FO	Franklin Templeton Growth 529 A		D+	(800) 342-5236	C- / 3.0	1.35	-1.35	-3.54 / 8	11.58 /50	9.00 /37	0.00	1.43
FO	● Franklin Templeton Growth 529 B		D+	(800) 342-5236	C- / 3.4	1.13	-1.75	-4.26 / 7	10.74 /44	8.18 /31	0.00	2.18
FO	Franklin Templeton Growth 529 C		D+	(800) 342-5236	C- / 3.4	1.14	-1.77	-4.27 / 7	10.73 /44	8.17 /31	0.00	2.18
UT	Franklin Utilities A	FKUTX	C+	(800) 342-5236	C / 5.2	-3.86	6.19	10.80 /78	12.96 /59	13.61 /74	2.62	0.75
UT	Franklin Utilities Adv	FRUAX	C+	(800) 321-8563	C+ / 6.0	-3.84	6.31	10.97 /78	13.12 /61	13.80 /76	2.88	0.60
UT	Franklin Utilities C	FRUSX	C+	(800) 342-5236	C+ / 5.6	-3.98	5.97	10.25 /75	12.39 /55	13.05 /69	2.22	1.25
UT	Franklin Utilities R	FRURX	C+	(800) 342-5236	C+ / 5.7	-3.93	6.05	10.41 /76	12.57 /56	13.22 /70	2.37	1.10
UT	Franklin Utilities R6	FUFRX	B-	(800) 342-5236	C+ / 6.1	-3.75	6.38	11.10 /79	13.15 /61	13.72 /75	2.99	0.48
GL	Franklin World Perspectives A	FWPAX	D	(800) 342-5236	C- / 3.7	3.64	5.01	4.45 /35	10.77 /44	--	0.77	2.11
GL	Franklin World Perspectives Advisor	FWPZX	C-	(800) 342-5236	C / 4.6	3.64	5.15	4.67 /36	10.91 /45	--	1.01	1.81
GL	Franklin World Perspectives C		D+	(800) 342-5236	C- / 4.1	3.49	4.72	3.76 /30	10.03 /39	--	0.12	2.81
GL	Franklin World Perspectives R		D+	(800) 342-5236	C / 4.3	3.56	4.85	4.12 /33	10.33 /41	--	0.45	2.31
OT	Frontier MFG Core Infra Inst	FMGIX	C+	(888) 825-2100	C / 4.7	-2.49	3.09	5.49 /42	12.20 /54	--	2.41	1.46
GL	Frontier MFG Global Equity Inst	FMGEX	B+	(888) 825-2100	B- / 7.1	2.27	6.86	7.43 /59	15.42 /78	--	0.77	0.89
SC	Frontier Netols Small Cap Val Fd	FNSVX	D-	(888) 825-2100	B- / 7.1	1.95	10.51	5.27 /41	14.89 /74	12.87 /67	0.00	1.17
SC	Frontier Netols Small Cap Value Y	FNSYX	D-	(888) 825-2100	C+ / 6.9	1.95	10.60	5.16 /40	14.43 /70	12.42 /63	0.00	1.57
SC	Frontier Phocas Sm Cap Val Fd Inst	FPSVX	B+	(888) 825-2100	A- / 9.0	3.83	11.67	9.48 /72	17.22 /91	14.33 /81	0.08	2.00
IN	Frontier Timpani SCG Instl	FTSGX	C+	(888) 825-2100	A+ / 9.6	6.95	18.26	7.54 /59	18.81 /96	--	0.00	2.46
GI	Frost Cinque LC Buy-Write Eq Inst	FCBWX	U	(866) 777-7818	U /	1.56	3.89	8.55 /67	--	--	1.20	1.17
GR	Frost Growth Equity Inst	FICEX	B+	(866) 777-7818	B / 8.0	4.16	7.82	17.43 /95	14.17 /68	13.39 /72	0.17	0.80
GR	Frost Growth Equity Inv	FACEX	B	(866) 777-7818	B- / 7.1	4.11	7.74	17.22 /95	13.91 /66	13.13 /69	0.00	1.05
FO	Frost International Equity Inst	FITNX	E-	(866) 777-7818	D / 1.6	5.52	5.69	1.91 /22	5.52 /15	4.82 /11	3.37	1.00
FO	Frost International Equity Inv	FANTX	E-	(866) 777-7818	D- / 1.2	5.67	5.59	1.57 /20	5.28 /14	4.54 /10	2.84	1.24
GI	Frost Kempner MC Deep Val Eqty	FIKDX	C	(866) 777-7818	C- / 3.9	-1.05	0.28	1.86 /21	10.76 /44	8.98 /37	1.72	0.77
GI	Frost Kempner MC Deep Val Eqty Inv	FAKDX	C-	(866) 777-7818	C- / 3.2	-1.03	0.25	1.63 /20	10.51 /42	8.72 /35	1.45	1.02
SC	Frost Mid Cap Equity Inst	FIKSX	D+	(866) 777-7818	C+ / 6.3	6.79	6.93	6.85 /54	13.17 /61	14.05 /78	0.00	1.33
GR	Frost Mid Cap Equity Inv	FAKSX	C+	(866) 777-7818	C+ / 5.7	6.74	6.81	6.66 /52	13.01 /60	--	0.00	1.58
GL	● Frost Moderate Allocation Inst	FIBTX	C+	(866) 777-7818	C- / 3.5	1.74	3.76	6.78 /53	8.69 /31	7.71 /28	2.42	1.57
GL	Frost Moderate Allocation Inv	FASTX	C+	(866) 777-7818	D+ / 2.8	1.69	3.56	6.53 /51	8.41 /29	7.43 /26	2.12	1.77
EN	Frost Natural Resources Inst	FNRFX	E-	(866) 777-7818	E- / 0.1	-1.46	-19.62	-21.15 / 1	-4.88 / 2	--	1.09	1.07
EN	Frost Natural Resources Inv	FNATX	E-	(866) 777-7818	E- / 0.1	-1.57	-19.71	-21.37 / 1	-5.15 / 2	--	0.72	1.32
GI	Frost Value Equity Inst	FIDVX	B-	(866) 777-7818	B- / 7.1	2.24	7.34	11.47 /80	14.14 /68	11.06 /53	1.41	0.81
GI	Frost Value Equity Inv	FADVX	C+	(866) 777-7818	C+ / 6.3	2.27	7.31	11.30 /80	13.86 /66	10.79 /51	1.15	1.06
AA	FT 529 Age-Based Csv AA Age		C-	(800) 342-5236	E / 0.5	0.51	0.26	1.82 /21	1.70 / 6	--	0.00	1.21
AA	● FT 529 Age-Based Csv AA Age		C-	(800) 342-5236	E+ / 0.6	0.35	-0.18	1.07 /19	0.93 / 5	--	0.00	1.96
AA	FT 529 Age-Based Csv AA Age		C-	(800) 342-5236	E+ / 0.6	0.44	-0.09	1.16 /19	0.96 / 5	--	0.00	1.96
AA	FT 529 Age-Based Csv AA Age 17+		C-	(800) 342-5236	E / 0.4	0.20	0.00	0.70 /18	0.57 / 5	--	0.00	1.04
AA	● FT 529 Age-Based Csv AA Age 17+		C-	(800) 342-5236	E / 0.5	0.00	-0.41	-0.10 /15	-0.17 / 4	--	0.00	1.79
AA	FT 529 Age-Based Csv AA Age 17+		C-	(800) 342-5236	E / 0.5	0.10	-0.31	-0.10 /15	-0.17 / 4	--	0.00	1.79
AA	FT 529 Age-Based Csv AA Age 9-12		C	(800) 342-5236	D- / 1.1	1.84	2.71	4.33 /34	4.98 /13	--	0.00	1.29
AA	● FT 529 Age-Based Csv AA Age 9-12		C	(800) 342-5236	D- / 1.3	1.67	2.32	3.65 /30	4.22 /11	--	0.00	2.04
AA	FT 529 Age-Based Csv AA Age 9-12		C	(800) 342-5236	D- / 1.3	1.67	2.32	3.65 /30	4.22 /11	--	0.00	2.04
AA	FT 529 Age-Based Csv AA Age		C	(800) 342-5236	D / 2.0	2.72	3.59	5.22 /40	7.69 /25	--	0.00	1.37
AA	● FT 529 Age-Based Csv AA Age		C	(800) 342-5236	D+ / 2.4	2.60	3.28	4.50 /35	6.92 /21	--	0.00	2.12
AA	FT 529 Age-Based Csv AA Age		C	(800) 342-5236	D+ / 2.4	2.53	3.20	4.50 /35	6.90 /21	--	0.00	2.12
GL	FT 529 Age-Based Gro AA Age 13-16		C	(800) 342-5236	D / 1.9	2.59	3.42	4.78 /37	7.47 /24	7.17 /24	0.00	1.37
GL	● FT 529 Age-Based Gro AA Age 13-16		C	(800) 342-5236	D+ / 2.3	2.37	2.98	3.97 /32	6.66 /20	6.35 /19	0.00	2.12

● Denotes fund is closed to new investors
* Denotes fund is included in Section II

www.thestreetratings.com

RISK			NET ASSETS		ASSET				Portfolio Turnover Ratio	BULL / BEAR		FUND MANAGER		MINIMUMS		LOADS	
	3 Year		NAV							Last Bull	Last Bear	Manager	Manager	Initial	Additional	Front	Back
Risk Rating/Pts	Standard Deviation	Beta	As of 3/31/15	Total $(Mil)	Cash %	Stocks %	Bonds %	Other %		Market Return	Market Return	Quality Pct	Tenure (Years)	Purch. $	Purch. $	End Load	End Load
D+ / 2.5	12.1	1.04	38.78	2,523	2	97	0	1	41	96.7	-23.9	38	23	1,000	0	5.8	0.0
D+ / 2.8	12.1	1.04	41.24	689	2	97	0	1	41	98.4	-23.8	41	23	1,000	0	0.0	0.0
D- / 1.1	12.1	1.04	30.77	446	2	97	0	1	41	91.7	-24.2	28	23	1,000	0	0.0	0.0
D / 2.2	12.1	1.04	36.57	99	2	97	0	1	41	95.1	-24.0	34	23	1,000	0	0.0	0.0
C+ / 5.9	12.1	0.83	41.45	204	2	97	0	1	41	98.4	-23.9	85	23	1,000,000	0	0.0	0.0
C+ / 6.2	13.1	0.94	24.80	60	0	0	0	100	0	70.2	-23.0	86	12	250	0	5.8	0.0
C+ / 6.2	13.1	0.94	22.46	4	0	0	0	100	0	65.9	-23.3	82	12	250	0	0.0	0.0
C+ / 6.1	13.1	0.94	22.21	19	0	0	0	100	0	65.9	-23.3	82	12	250	0	0.0	0.0
C+ / 6.7	11.9	0.85	16.95	4,102	2	96	1	1	8	58.8	1.6	84	17	1,000	0	4.3	0.0
C+ / 6.7	11.9	0.85	17.06	644	2	96	1	1	8	59.6	1.7	85	17	1,000	0	0.0	0.0
C+ / 6.8	11.9	0.85	16.88	1,082	2	96	1	1	8	56.0	1.5	80	17	1,000	0	0.0	0.0
C+ / 6.8	11.9	0.85	16.90	105	2	96	1	1	8	56.8	1.5	82	17	1,000	0	0.0	0.0
B- / 7.1	11.9	0.85	17.06	238	2	96	1	1	8	59.5	1.6	85	17	1,000,000	0	0.0	0.0
C / 5.3	10.9	0.77	12.53	15	3	96	0	1	79	65.0	-19.9	90	5	1,000	0	5.8	0.0
C / 5.2	10.8	0.76	12.54	10	3	96	0	1	79	65.8	-20.0	90	5	1,000,000	0	0.0	0.0
C / 5.3	10.8	0.76	12.47	3	3	96	0	1	79	61.3	-20.1	87	5	1,000	0	0.0	0.0
C / 5.3	10.8	0.76	12.50	3	3	96	0	1	79	62.9	-20.1	88	5	1,000	0	0.0	0.0
B- / 7.5	10.3	0.63	13.65	101	8	91	0	1	16	N/A	N/A	85	3	100,000	1,000	0.0	2.0
B- / 7.6	9.1	0.55	15.78	1,062	2	97	0	1	20	N/A	N/A	98	4	1,000,000	1,000	0.0	2.0
E+ / 0.7	14.0	1.00	11.52	85	0	99	0	1	24	98.9	-28.8	48	10	100,000	1,000	0.0	0.0
E+ / 0.7	14.1	1.01	10.99	1	0	99	0	1	24	96.1	-29.0	41	10	1,000	50	0.0	0.0
C+ / 5.7	12.9	0.92	35.47	31	2	97	0	1	53	101.4	-24.5	84	5	100,000	1,000	0.0	0.0
C- / 3.1	16.5	1.24	17.55	41	4	95	0	1	173	125.8	-27.9	48	4	100,000	1,000	0.0	0.0
U /	N/A	N/A	13.16	58	0	0	0	100	20	N/A	N/A	N/A	N/A	1,000,000	0	0.0	0.0
C+ / 6.8	10.9	1.02	15.01	396	3	96	0	1	28	91.9	-17.1	37	13	1,000,000	0	0.0	0.0
C+ / 6.8	10.8	1.02	14.95	65	3	96	0	1	28	90.1	-17.1	34	13	2,500	500	3.3	0.0
E+ / 0.9	12.2	0.87	7.26	46	4	95	0	1	120	40.0	-25.7	30	13	1,000,000	0	0.0	2.0
D- / 1.0	12.2	0.87	7.27	11	4	95	0	1	120	38.7	-25.7	27	13	2,500	500	3.3	2.0
B- / 7.0	8.8	0.86	10.64	103	10	89	0	1	22	65.6	-18.2	29	13	1,000,000	0	0.0	0.0
B- / 7.0	8.8	0.86	10.64	15	10	89	0	1	22	64.1	-18.3	27	13	2,500	500	3.3	0.0
C- / 3.5	13.1	0.83	13.06	16	4	95	0	1	53	79.6	-24.2	65	7	1,000,000	0	0.0	0.0
C+ / 6.5	13.1	1.19	12.99	1	4	95	0	1	53	N/A	N/A	8	7	2,500	500	3.3	0.0
B+ / 9.1	6.1	0.41	12.85	2	0	0	0	100	103	47.2	-12.9	93	9	1,000,000	0	0.0	0.0
B+ / 9.1	6.1	0.41	12.84	20	0	0	0	100	103	45.8	-13.0	92	9	2,500	500	3.3	0.0
D / 1.7	16.8	1.02	9.44	34	0	0	0	100	35	2.1	N/A	2	4	1,000,000	0	0.0	0.0
D / 1.6	16.8	1.03	9.43	5	0	0	0	100	35	1.2	N/A	2	4	2,500	500	3.3	0.0
C+ / 5.9	11.2	1.14	10.95	282	1	98	0	1	52	76.1	-17.9	18	13	1,000,000	0	0.0	0.0
C+ / 5.9	11.1	1.13	10.95	58	1	98	0	1	52	74.5	-18.0	17	13	2,500	500	3.3	0.0
B+ / 9.9	2.0	0.20	11.74	8	0	0	0	100	0	8.3	0.5	61	5	250	0	5.8	0.0
B+ / 9.9	2.0	0.21	11.31	N/A	0	0	0	100	0	5.6	0.2	48	5	250	0	0.0	0.0
B+ / 9.9	2.0	0.20	11.32	6	0	0	0	100	0	5.5	0.2	50	5	250	0	0.0	0.0
B+ / 9.9	1.0	0.11	10.05	12	0	0	0	100	0	1.5	-0.3	59	5	250	0	5.8	0.0
B+ / 9.9	1.0	0.11	9.68	N/A	0	0	0	100	0	-1.0	-0.6	47	5	250	0	0.0	0.0
B+ / 9.9	1.1	0.10	9.68	10	0	0	0	100	0	-1.1	-0.6	48	5	250	0	0.0	0.0
B+ / 9.9	3.6	0.59	13.26	8	0	0	0	100	0	24.6	-5.5	48	5	250	0	5.8	0.0
B+ / 9.9	3.6	0.60	12.79	N/A	0	0	0	100	0	21.4	-5.8	35	5	250	0	0.0	0.0
B+ / 9.9	3.6	0.59	12.77	4	0	0	0	100	0	21.4	-5.8	37	5	250	0	0.0	0.0
B+ / 9.2	5.7	0.94	14.71	14	0	0	0	100	0	39.9	-10.8	33	5	250	0	5.8	0.0
B+ / 9.1	5.7	0.94	14.18	N/A	0	0	0	100	0	36.4	-11.1	25	5	250	0	0.0	0.0
B+ / 9.1	5.8	0.95	14.17	4	0	0	0	100	0	36.3	-11.0	24	5	250	0	0.0	0.0
B+ / 9.1	5.7	0.87	23.00	264	0	0	0	100	0	39.4	-10.9	63	10	250	0	5.8	0.0
B+ / 9.1	5.7	0.87	20.71	27	0	0	0	100	0	35.9	-11.2	52	12	250	0	0.0	0.0

I. Index of Stock Mutual Funds

Fund Type	Fund Name	Ticker Symbol	Overall Investment Rating	Phone	Performance Rating/Pts	3 Mo	6 Mo	1Yr / Pct	3Yr / Pct	5Yr / Pct	Dividend Yield	Expense Ratio
GL	FT 529 Age-Based Gro AA Age 13-16		C	(800) 342-5236	D / 2.2	2.37	2.98	3.96 /31	6.65 /20	6.36 /19	0.00	2.12
GL	FT 529 Age-Based Gro AA Age 17 +		C	(800) 342-5236	E+ / 0.9	1.61	1.95	3.50 /29	4.62 /12	5.13 /12	0.00	1.29
GL	● FT 529 Age-Based Gro AA Age 17 +		C	(800) 342-5236	D- / 1.1	1.44	1.63	2.81 /26	3.86 /10	4.35 /10	0.00	2.04
GL	FT 529 Age-Based Gro AA Age 17 +		C	(800) 342-5236	D- / 1.1	1.42	1.60	2.76 /25	3.86 /10	4.35 /10	0.00	2.04
GI	FT 529 Age-Based Gro AA Age 9-12		C	(800) 342-5236	C- / 3.4	3.50	4.88	6.11 /47	10.09 /40	9.07 /37	0.00	1.44
GI	● FT 529 Age-Based Gro AA Age 9-12		C+	(800) 342-5236	C- / 3.8	3.32	4.51	5.35 /41	9.26 /35	8.26 /32	0.00	2.19
GI	FT 529 Age-Based Gro AA Age 9-12		C+	(800) 342-5236	C- / 3.8	3.32	4.49	5.36 /41	9.28 /35	8.26 /32	0.00	2.19
GL	FT 529 Age-Based Gro AA Age		C+	(800) 342-5236	C / 5.1	4.61	6.41	7.56 /60	12.89 /59	11.02 /53	0.00	1.55
GL	● FT 529 Age-Based Gro AA Age		C+	(800) 342-5236	C+ / 5.6	4.43	6.02	6.77 /53	12.05 /53	10.18 /46	0.00	2.30
GL	FT 529 Age-Based Gro AA Age		C+	(800) 342-5236	C+ / 5.6	4.45	6.06	6.80 /53	12.05 /53	10.21 /46	0.00	2.30
AA	FT 529 Age-Based Mdt AA Age 13-16		C	(800) 342-5236	E+ / 0.9	1.63	1.94	3.39 /28	4.62 /12	--	0.00	1.30
AA	● FT 529 Age-Based Mdt AA Age 13-16		C	(800) 342-5236	D- / 1.1	1.44	1.53	2.60 /25	3.84 /10	--	0.00	2.05
AA	FT 529 Age-Based Mdt AA Age 13-16		C	(800) 342-5236	D- / 1.1	1.45	1.53	2.68 /25	3.84 /10	--	0.00	2.05
AA	FT 529 Age-Based Mdt AA Age 17+		C-	(800) 342-5236	E / 0.5	0.60	0.34	1.99 /22	1.82 / 6	--	0.00	1.21
AA	● FT 529 Age-Based Mdt AA Age 17+		C-	(800) 342-5236	E+ / 0.6	0.35	-0.18	1.16 /19	1.05 / 5	--	0.00	1.96
AA	FT 529 Age-Based Mdt AA Age 17+		C-	(800) 342-5236	E+ / 0.6	0.35	-0.18	1.16 /19	1.05 / 5	--	0.00	1.96
AA	FT 529 Age-Based Mdt AA Age 9-12		C	(800) 342-5236	D / 1.9	2.70	3.65	5.01 /39	7.31 /23	--	0.00	1.38
AA	● FT 529 Age-Based Mdt AA Age 9-12		C	(800) 342-5236	D / 2.2	2.50	3.26	4.19 /33	6.50 /19	--	0.00	2.13
AA	FT 529 Age-Based Mdt AA Age 9-12		C	(800) 342-5236	D / 2.2	2.50	3.25	4.18 /33	6.49 /19	--	0.00	2.13
AA	FT 529 Age-Based Mdt AA Age		C	(800) 342-5236	C- / 3.4	3.57	4.93	6.18 /48	10.12 /40	--	0.00	1.46
AA	● FT 529 Age-Based Mdt AA Age		C+	(800) 342-5236	C- / 3.9	3.43	4.62	5.41 /42	9.32 /35	--	0.00	2.21
AA	FT 529 Age-Based Mdt AA Age		C+	(800) 342-5236	C- / 3.9	3.43	4.56	5.42 /42	9.31 /35	--	0.00	2.21
AG	Fund *X Aggressive Upgrader	HOTFX	C+	(866) 455-3863	C+ / 6.7	4.55	9.62	9.05 /70	13.49 /63	10.50 /49	0.26	2.18
GR	Fund *X Conservative Upgrader	RELAX	C-	(866) 455-3863	C- / 4.1	1.77	4.39	6.31 /49	9.79 /38	7.74 /28	1.46	2.09
BA	Fund *X Flexible Income	INCMX	D+	(866) 455-3863	D- / 1.3	1.42	1.82	2.87 /26	4.63 /12	4.45 /10	3.57	1.66
GR	Fund *X Upgrader	FUNDX	B	(866) 455-3863	B- / 7.0	3.24	7.95	10.46 /76	14.08 /68	10.64 /50	0.37	1.99
AA	FundX Flexible Total Return	TOTLX	D+	(866) 455-3863	E+ / 0.9	1.49	3.11	1.88 /21	2.75 / 7	3.73 / 7	1.70	3.12
GR	FundX Tactical Upgrader	TACTX	D	(866) 455-3863	D- / 1.2	2.69	6.44	2.50 /24	3.51 / 9	5.11 /12	0.21	1.73
AA	Gabelli ABC Fund AAA	GABCX	D+	(800) 422-3554	E+ / 0.9	0.89	1.26	1.75 /21	2.99 / 8	3.47 / 7	0.47	0.58
AA	Gabelli ABC Fund Advisor	GADVX	D+	(800) 422-3554	E+ / 0.8	0.80	1.09	1.49 /20	2.71 / 7	3.21 / 6	0.21	0.83
GR	Gabelli Asset A	GATAX	C+	(800) 422-3554	C / 5.3	0.82	4.89	4.81 /37	14.03 /67	13.22 /70	0.24	1.35
GR	Gabelli Asset AAA	GABAX	C+	(800) 422-3554	C+ / 6.2	0.81	4.87	4.81 /37	14.03 /67	13.21 /70	0.26	1.35
GR	Gabelli Asset C	GATCX	C+	(800) 422-3554	C+ / 5.7	0.61	4.47	4.01 /32	13.17 /61	12.37 /63	0.00	2.10
GR	Gabelli Asset I	GABIX	C+	(800) 422-3554	C+ / 6.4	0.87	5.02	5.08 /39	14.31 /69	13.49 /73	0.51	1.10
GR	Gabelli Capital Asset Fund		C	(800) 422-3554	C+ / 6.1	0.65	4.08	1.02 /18	14.50 /71	14.52 /82	0.46	1.13
GL	Gabelli Dividend Growth A	GBCAX	C-	(800) 422-3554	C / 4.6	1.18	1.00	6.78 /53	12.85 /58	11.28 /55	1.28	2.00
GL	Gabelli Dividend Growth AAA	GABBX	C	(800) 422-3554	C / 5.5	1.12	0.97	6.74 /53	12.83 /58	11.28 /55	1.32	2.00
GL	Gabelli Dividend Growth C	GBCCX	C	(800) 422-3554	C / 4.9	0.91	0.59	5.94 /46	11.94 /52	10.43 /48	0.76	2.75
GL	Gabelli Dividend Growth I	GBCIX	C+	(800) 422-3554	C+ / 5.7	1.17	1.08	6.98 /55	13.09 /60	11.55 /57	1.57	1.75
GR	Gabelli Enterprise Mrgrs & Acq A	EMAAX	D	(800) 422-3554	D- / 1.3	1.23	3.39	2.26 /23	6.12 /17	5.79 /16	0.00	1.66
GR	Gabelli Enterprise Mrgrs & Acq AAA	EAAAX	D+	(800) 422-3554	D / 2.0	1.30	3.52	2.47 /24	6.34 /18	6.02 /17	0.00	1.46
GR	Gabelli Enterprise Mrgrs & Acq C	EMACX	D+	(800) 422-3554	D / 1.6	1.16	3.12	1.75 /21	5.55 /15	5.23 /13	0.00	2.21
GR	Gabelli Enterprise Mrgrs & Acq Y	EMAYX	D+	(800) 422-3554	D / 2.1	1.39	3.60	2.75 /25	6.62 /20	6.28 /19	0.00	1.21
IN	Gabelli Equity Income A	GCAEX	C+	(800) 422-3554	C / 5.1	1.35	4.31	6.37 /50	13.44 /63	12.37 /63	3.52	1.37
IN	Gabelli Equity Income AAA	GABEX	B-	(800) 422-3554	C+ / 6.0	1.31	4.26	6.35 /49	13.43 /63	12.37 /63	3.72	1.37
IN	Gabelli Equity Income C	GCCEX	C+	(800) 422-3554	C / 5.5	1.14	3.91	5.55 /43	12.59 /57	11.53 /57	4.11	2.12
IN	Gabelli Equity Income I	GCIEX	B-	(800) 422-3554	C+ / 6.2	1.39	4.42	6.62 /52	13.73 /65	12.65 /65	3.65	1.12
SC	Gabelli Focus Five A	GWSAX	C+	(800) 422-3554	B- / 7.3	2.76	5.45	7.62 /60	16.97 /90	13.77 /76	0.00	1.38
SC	Gabelli Focus Five AAA	GWSVX	B	(800) 422-3554	B+ / 8.4	2.72	5.43	7.62 /60	16.95 /90	13.75 /75	0.00	1.38
SC	Gabelli Focus Five C	GWSCX	C+	(800) 422-3554	B / 7.7	2.50	5.05	6.76 /53	16.09 /84	12.92 /67	0.00	2.13
SC	Gabelli Focus Five I	GWSIX	B	(800) 422-3554	B+ / 8.6	2.80	5.53	7.83 /62	17.23 /91	14.04 /78	0.00	1.13
CV	Gabelli Global Rising Inc & Div A	GAGAX	D+	(800) 422-3554	D- / 1.3	1.40	3.55	2.20 /23	6.16 /17	4.97 /12	1.09	2.31

● Denotes fund is closed to new investors
* Denotes fund is included in Section II

Risk Rating/Pts	Standard Deviation	Beta	NAV As of 3/31/15	Total $(Mil)	Cash %	Stocks %	Bonds %	Other %	Portfolio Turnover Ratio	Last Bull Market Return	Last Bear Market Return	Manager Quality Pct	Manager Tenure (Years)	Initial Purch. $	Additional Purch. $	Front End Load	Back End Load
B+ / 9.1	5.7	0.87	20.73	105	0	0	0	100	0	35.8	-11.1	51	12	250	0	0.0	0.0
B+ / 9.9	3.6	0.56	18.31	182	0	0	0	100	0	23.6	-5.2	63	10	250	0	5.8	0.0
B+ / 9.9	3.6	0.56	16.85	17	0	0	0	100	0	20.5	-5.5	52	12	250	0	0.0	0.0
B+ / 9.9	3.6	0.55	17.15	102	0	0	0	100	0	20.4	-5.5	52	12	250	0	0.0	0.0
B / 8.2	7.9	0.77	26.03	304	0	0	0	100	0	56.8	-16.1	39	10	250	0	5.8	0.0
B / 8.1	7.9	0.77	23.62	35	0	0	0	100	0	52.8	-16.4	29	12	250	0	0.0	0.0
B / 8.1	7.9	0.77	23.96	91	0	0	0	100	0	52.8	-16.4	30	12	250	0	0.0	0.0
B- / 7.2	10.2	1.48	29.72	303	0	0	0	100	0	76.9	-21.3	58	12	250	0	5.8	0.0
B- / 7.2	10.2	1.49	27.12	28	0	0	0	100	0	72.3	-21.6	46	12	250	0	0.0	0.0
B- / 7.2	10.2	1.48	27.49	81	0	0	0	100	0	72.4	-21.6	47	12	250	0	0.0	0.0
B+ / 9.9	3.5	0.58	13.11	57	0	0	0	100	0	23.1	-5.5	44	5	250	0	5.8	0.0
B+ / 9.9	3.6	0.59	12.64	2	0	0	0	100	0	20.0	-5.9	32	5	250	0	0.0	0.0
B+ / 9.9	3.5	0.58	12.63	36	0	0	0	100	0	19.9	-5.8	33	5	250	0	0.0	0.0
B+ / 9.9	2.0	0.22	11.76	23	0	0	0	100	0	8.6	0.5	60	5	250	0	5.8	0.0
B+ / 9.9	2.0	0.21	11.33	1	0	0	0	100	0	6.0	0.1	50	5	250	0	0.0	0.0
B+ / 9.9	2.0	0.21	11.33	25	0	0	0	100	0	6.0	0.1	49	5	250	0	0.0	0.0
B+ / 9.1	5.6	0.93	14.47	56	0	0	0	100	0	38.3	-10.8	30	5	250	0	5.8	0.0
B+ / 9.1	5.6	0.92	13.94	2	0	0	0	100	0	34.9	-11.1	22	5	250	0	0.0	0.0
B+ / 9.1	5.6	0.93	13.96	20	0	0	0	100	0	34.8	-11.0	22	5	250	0	0.0	0.0
B / 8.2	7.9	1.27	15.97	86	0	0	0	100	0	56.1	-15.9	20	5	250	0	5.8	0.0
B / 8.2	7.8	1.26	15.39	2	0	0	0	100	0	52.2	-16.2	15	5	250	0	0.0	0.0
B / 8.2	7.8	1.26	15.36	24	0	0	0	100	0	52.0	-16.2	15	5	250	0	0.0	0.0
C+ / 6.2	11.0	1.02	58.64	69	1	98	0	1	168	78.7	-22.2	29	13	1,000	100	0.0	0.0
C+ / 6.7	6.6	0.66	37.69	60	3	64	32	1	127	50.6	-14.3	60	13	1,000	100	0.0	0.0
B / 8.1	2.8	0.31	29.09	149	0	14	85	1	54	18.5	-4.4	79	13	1,000	100	0.0	0.0
B- / 7.0	10.2	1.00	51.19	286	4	94	1	1	164	81.4	-21.0	41	14	1,000	100	0.0	0.0
B / 8.6	4.0	0.56	25.78	13	8	48	41	3	155	14.3	-3.9	24	6	1,000	100	0.0	0.0
B- / 7.4	6.6	0.55	21.57	37	10	87	2	1	202	19.7	-3.7	12	7	1,000	100	0.0	0.0
B / 8.4	2.0	0.28	10.22	670	0	60	39	1	324	14.6	-3.1	68	22	10,000	0	0.0	0.0
B / 8.5	2.1	0.29	10.13	635	0	60	39	1	324	13.7	-3.4	63	22	10,000	0	0.0	0.0
C+ / 6.7	10.6	1.06	65.41	107	0	99	0	1	8	83.2	-19.0	28	29	1,000	0	5.8	0.0
C+ / 6.7	10.6	1.06	65.92	2,850	0	99	0	1	8	83.1	-19.0	28	29	1,000	0	0.0	0.0
C+ / 6.7	10.6	1.06	62.59	124	0	99	0	1	8	78.6	-19.3	20	29	1,000	0	0.0	0.0
C+ / 6.7	10.6	1.06	65.90	406	0	99	0	1	8	84.7	-18.9	31	29	500,000	0	0.0	0.0
C / 5.2	11.7	1.14	23.24	125	0	99	0	1	10	88.9	-21.1	21	20	0	0	0.0	0.0
C+ / 6.3	10.8	0.65	18.92	4	3	96	0	1	45	84.4	-19.3	95	16	1,000	0	5.8	0.0
C+ / 6.3	10.9	0.65	18.95	23	3	96	0	1	45	84.5	-19.4	95	16	1,000	0	0.0	0.0
C+ / 6.3	10.9	0.65	17.83	2	3	96	0	1	45	79.7	-19.6	94	16	1,000	0	0.0	0.0
C+ / 6.2	10.9	0.65	19.04	6	3	96	0	1	45	86.0	-19.3	96	16	500,000	0	0.0	0.0
B- / 7.6	5.0	0.47	13.12	90	0	93	6	1	181	29.1	-6.7	51	14	1,000	0	5.8	0.0
B- / 7.6	5.0	0.47	13.25	5	0	93	6	1	181	30.0	-6.5	54	14	1,000	0	0.0	0.0
B- / 7.6	5.0	0.47	12.23	55	0	93	6	1	181	26.6	-6.8	43	14	1,000	0	0.0	0.0
B- / 7.6	5.0	0.47	13.83	65	0	93	6	1	181	31.0	-6.4	59	14	500,000	0	0.0	0.0
B- / 7.1	9.8	1.00	29.07	215	0	98	0	2	14	78.4	-16.3	32	23	1,000	0	5.8	0.0
B- / 7.1	9.8	1.00	29.16	1,264	0	98	0	2	14	78.5	-16.3	32	23	1,000	0	0.0	0.0
B- / 7.0	9.8	1.00	26.40	362	0	98	0	2	14	74.0	-16.6	24	23	1,000	0	0.0	0.0
B- / 7.1	9.8	1.00	29.79	782	0	98	0	2	14	80.1	-16.3	36	23	500,000	0	0.0	0.0
C / 5.4	11.5	0.68	14.88	94	0	96	3	1	94	107.9	-27.8	94	3	1,000	0	5.8	0.0
C / 5.4	11.5	0.68	14.73	56	0	96	3	1	94	107.9	-27.8	94	3	1,000	0	0.0	0.0
C / 5.1	11.5	0.68	13.11	92	0	96	3	1	94	102.8	-28.1	93	3	1,000	0	0.0	0.0
C / 5.4	11.5	0.68	15.04	270	0	96	3	1	94	109.7	-27.8	95	3	500,000	0	0.0	0.0
B / 8.4	6.2	0.66	22.41	1	0	39	56	5	80	24.9	-11.3	31	21	1,000	0	5.8	0.0

99 Pct = Best
0 Pct = Worst

Fund Type	Fund Name	Ticker Symbol	Overall Investment Rating	Phone	Performance Rating/Pts	3 Mo	6 Mo	1Yr / Pct	3Yr / Pct	5Yr / Pct	Dividend Yield	Expense Ratio
CV	Gabelli Global Rising Inc & Div AAA	GAGCX	C-	(800) 422-3554	D / 1.9	1.41	3.54	2.19 /23	6.21 /18	4.95 /12	1.13	2.31
CV	Gabelli Global Rising Inc & Div C	GACCX	D+	(800) 422-3554	D- / 1.2	1.21	3.22	1.51 /20	4.30 /11	3.43 / 7	1.24	3.06
CV	Gabelli Global Rising Inc & Div I	GAGIX	C-	(800) 422-3554	D / 2.0	1.45	3.71	2.50 /24	6.45 /19	5.20 /13	1.40	2.06
PM	Gabelli Gold A	GLDAX	E-	(800) 422-3554	E- / 0.0	-2.17	-11.22	-17.70 / 1	-22.74 / 0	-12.33 / 0	0.00	1.57
PM	Gabelli Gold AAA	GOLDX	E-	(800) 422-3554	E- / 0.0	-2.18	-11.24	-17.74 / 1	-22.75 / 0	-12.39 / 0	0.00	1.57
PM	Gabelli Gold C	GLDCX	E-	(800) 422-3554	E- / 0.0	-2.42	-11.62	-18.41 / 1	-23.33 / 0	-13.04 / 0	0.00	2.32
PM	Gabelli Gold I	GLDIX	E-	(800) 422-3554	E- / 0.0	-2.14	-11.16	-17.57 / 1	-22.57 / 0	-12.17 / 0	0.00	1.32
SC	Gabelli Small Cap Growth A	GCASX	B	(800) 422-3554	B- / 7.1	3.81	10.64	6.33 /49	16.19 /85	14.56 /83	0.00	1.38
SC	Gabelli Small Cap Growth AAA	GABSX	B+	(800) 422-3554	B / 8.2	3.81	10.63	6.33 /49	16.18 /85	14.56 /83	0.00	1.38
SC	Gabelli Small Cap Growth C	GCCSX	B	(800) 422-3554	B- / 7.5	3.64	10.24	5.53 /43	15.33 /78	13.70 /75	0.00	2.13
SC	Gabelli Small Cap Growth I	GACIX	B+	(800) 422-3554	B+ / 8.4	3.86	10.77	6.58 /52	16.48 /87	14.85 /86	0.00	1.13
GR	Gabelli SRI Inc A	SRIAX	C	(800) 422-3554	C / 4.4	0.88	8.48	10.09 /75	11.28 /48	9.13 /38	0.00	1.74
GR	Gabelli SRI Inc AAA	SRIGX	C+	(800) 422-3554	C / 5.3	0.88	8.47	10.08 /75	11.27 /47	9.10 /37	0.00	1.74
GR	Gabelli SRI Inc C	SRICX	C	(800) 422-3554	C / 4.8	0.71	8.11	9.37 /71	10.47 /42	8.29 /32	0.00	2.49
GR	Gabelli SRI Inc I	SRIDX	C+	(800) 422-3554	C / 5.5	1.01	8.58	10.41 /76	11.58 /50	9.38 /40	0.00	1.49
UT	Gabelli Utilities A	GAUAX	D	(800) 422-3554	D+ / 2.4	-2.97	2.42	2.41 /24	9.53 /36	9.71 /42	15.21	1.37
UT	Gabelli Utilities AAA	GABUX	D+	(800) 422-3554	C- / 3.3	-2.82	2.44	2.44 /24	9.49 /36	9.72 /42	16.33	1.37
UT	Gabelli Utilities C	GAUCX	D-	(800) 422-3554	D+ / 2.8	-3.05	2.06	1.82 /21	8.72 /31	8.92 /36	20.64	2.12
UT	Gabelli Utilities I	GAUIX	D+	(800) 422-3554	C- / 3.5	-2.84	2.67	2.66 /25	9.79 /38	10.01 /45	15.86	1.12
AG	Gabelli Value 25 A	GABVX	C-	(800) 422-3554	C / 4.9	0.60	4.62	3.71 /30	13.49 /63	13.49 /73	0.13	1.39
GR	Gabelli Value 25 AAA	GVCAX	C	(800) 422-3554	C+ / 5.8	0.55	4.59	3.68 /30	13.47 /63	--	0.15	1.39
AG	Gabelli Value 25 C	GVCCX	C-	(800) 422-3554	C / 5.2	0.39	4.20	2.90 /26	12.63 /57	12.65 /65	0.00	2.14
AG	Gabelli Value 25 I	GVCIX	C	(800) 422-3554	C+ / 6.0	0.60	4.74	3.93 /31	13.76 /65	13.79 /76	0.41	1.14
GL	GAMCO Global Growth A	GGGAX	C-	(800) 422-3554	C / 4.7	2.45	4.01	6.14 /48	12.73 /58	11.56 /57	0.40	1.77
GL	GAMCO Global Growth AAA	GICPX	C	(800) 422-3554	C+ / 5.7	2.45	4.01	6.11 /47	12.71 /58	11.56 /57	0.36	1.77
GL	GAMCO Global Growth C	GGGCX	C	(800) 422-3554	C / 5.1	2.26	3.65	5.34 /41	11.88 /52	10.72 /50	0.00	2.52
GL	GAMCO Global Growth I	GGGIX	C+	(800) 422-3554	C+ / 5.9	2.63	4.39	6.69 /53	13.10 /60	11.90 /60	0.74	1.52
GL	GAMCO Global Opportunity A	GOCAX	D	(800) 422-3554	D / 1.7	1.82	0.29	-0.66 /14	8.23 /28	7.58 /27	0.00	2.74
GL	GAMCO Global Opportunity AAA	GABOX	D+	(800) 422-3554	D+ / 2.5	1.86	0.29	-0.66 /14	8.24 /28	7.59 /27	0.00	2.74
GL	GAMCO Global Opportunity C	GGLCX	D	(800) 422-3554	D / 2.1	1.66	-0.13	-1.44 /12	7.41 /24	6.77 /22	0.00	3.49
GL	GAMCO Global Opportunity I	GLOIX	D+	(800) 422-3554	D+ / 2.9	2.09	0.79	0.04 /16	8.69 /31	7.95 /30	0.00	2.49
TC	GAMCO Global Telecom A	GTCAX	D	(800) 422-3554	D+ / 2.4	1.52	2.22	2.14 /22	9.06 /33	7.39 /26	1.44	1.64
TC	GAMCO Global Telecom AAA	GABTX	D+	(800) 422-3554	C- / 3.3	1.52	2.24	2.16 /22	9.07 /33	7.39 /26	1.54	1.64
TC	GAMCO Global Telecom C	GTCCX	D+	(800) 422-3554	D+ / 2.7	1.35	1.86	1.38 /20	8.25 /28	6.60 /21	0.72	2.39
TC	GAMCO Global Telecom I	GTTIX	D+	(800) 422-3554	C- / 3.4	1.61	2.38	2.43 /24	9.35 /35	7.68 /28	1.80	1.39
GR	GAMCO Growth A	GGCAX	C+	(800) 422-3554	C+ / 6.6	2.88	7.75	12.47 /85	14.82 /73	12.84 /67	0.00	1.45
GR	GAMCO Growth AAA	GABGX	B+	(800) 422-3554	B / 7.6	2.86	7.76	12.47 /85	14.82 /73	12.84 /67	0.00	1.45
GR	GAMCO Growth C	GGCCX	B	(800) 422-3554	B- / 7.0	2.69	7.35	11.64 /81	13.96 /67	12.00 /60	0.00	2.20
GR	GAMCO Growth I	GGCIX	B+	(800) 422-3554	B / 7.9	2.92	7.88	12.73 /86	15.11 /76	13.11 /69	0.00	1.20
FO	GAMCO International Growth A	GAIGX	E+	(800) 422-3554	D- / 1.3	6.05	3.42	0.72 /18	5.92 /16	6.36 /19	0.00	2.24
FO	GAMCO International Growth AAA	GIGRX	D-	(800) 422-3554	D / 1.9	6.08	3.44	0.78 /18	5.90 /16	6.35 /19	0.00	2.24
FO	GAMCO International Growth C	GCIGX	D-	(800) 422-3554	D- / 1.5	5.86	3.07	-0.01 /16	5.14 /14	5.56 /14	0.00	2.99
FO	GAMCO International Growth I	GIIGX	D-	(800) 422-3554	D / 2.2	6.38	4.04	1.56 /20	6.38 /18	6.75 /22	0.00	1.99
GR	GAMCO Mathers Fund	MATRX	E	(800) 422-3554	E- / 0.1	-2.58	-6.85	-9.93 / 3	-10.04 / 1	-8.11 / 1	0.00	3.80
GI	Gateway A	GATEX	D+	(800) 225-5478	D- / 1.0	1.09	1.53	3.93 /31	4.78 /12	4.72 /11	1.17	1.03
GI	Gateway C	GTECX	D+	(800) 225-5478	D- / 1.1	0.88	1.14	3.12 /27	3.99 /10	3.93 / 8	0.48	1.78
GR	Gateway Equity Call Premium Y	GCPYX	U	(800) 225-5478	U /	1.96	2.10	--	--	--	0.00	N/A
FO	Gateway International A	GAIAX	D-	(800) 225-5478	E / 0.3	0.67	-3.03	-3.73 / 7	-1.01 / 3	--	3.19	2.17
FO	Gateway International C	GAICX	D-	(800) 225-5478	E / 0.3	0.45	-3.31	-4.41 / 6	-1.69 / 3	--	2.62	2.78
FO	Gateway International Y	GAIYX	D-	(800) 225-5478	E / 0.4	0.77	-2.82	-3.41 / 8	-0.66 / 4	--	3.69	1.93
GI	Gateway Y	GTEYX	C-	(800) 225-5478	D- / 1.5	1.15	1.66	4.16 /33	5.04 /13	4.97 /12	1.49	0.78
GL	GaveKal Knowledge Leaders Adv	GAVAX	C+	(888) 998-9890	C / 4.4	4.84	8.54	9.03 /69	10.00 /39	--	0.27	1.50

• Denotes fund is closed to new investors
* Denotes fund is included in Section II

www.thestreetratings.com

RISK			NET ASSETS		ASSET						BULL / BEAR		FUND MANAGER		MINIMUMS		LOADS	
	3 Year		NAV						Portfolio		Last Bull	Last Bear	Manager	Manager	Initial	Additional	Front	Back
Risk Rating/Pts	Standard Deviation	Beta	As of 3/31/15	Total $(Mil)	Cash %	Stocks %	Bonds %	Other %	Turnover Ratio		Market Return	Market Return	Quality Pct	Tenure (Years)	Purch. $	Purch. $	End Load	End Load
B /8.3	6.2	0.66	22.32	13	0	39	56	5	80		24.8	-11.1	32	21	1,000	0	0.0	0.0
B /8.3	6.2	0.65	19.20	N/A	0	39	56	5	80		17.8	-11.6	15	21	1,000	0	0.0	0.0
B /8.3	6.2	0.66	22.45	32	0	39	56	5	80		26.0	-11.2	34	21	500,000	0	0.0	0.0
E /0.4	37.9	1.86	10.37	13	0	100	0	0	4		-51.8	-12.2	11	21	1,000	0	5.8	0.0
E /0.4	37.9	1.86	10.34	123	0	100	0	0	4		-51.9	-12.3	11	21	1,000	0	0.0	0.0
E /0.4	37.9	1.86	9.66	6	0	100	0	0	4		-53.1	-12.5	7	21	1,000	0	0.0	0.0
E /0.4	37.9	1.86	10.51	45	0	100	0	0	4		-51.5	-12.2	12	21	500,000	0	0.0	0.0
C+ /6.5	11.3	0.81	50.92	316	0	90	8	2	14		90.9	-21.0	88	24	1,000	0	5.8	0.0
C+ /6.5	11.4	0.81	50.94	2,183	0	90	8	2	14		90.8	-21.0	88	24	1,000	0	0.0	0.0
C+ /6.4	11.4	0.81	46.46	248	0	90	8	2	14		86.1	-21.2	84	24	1,000	0	0.0	0.0
C+ /6.5	11.3	0.81	51.68	1,152	0	90	8	2	14		92.5	-20.9	89	24	500,000	0	0.0	0.0
C+ /6.5	10.8	1.04	14.84	21	0	98	1	1	47		55.8	-28.5	11	8	1,000	0	5.8	0.0
C+ /6.6	10.8	1.04	14.85	21	0	98	1	1	47		55.9	-28.5	11	8	1,000	0	0.0	0.0
C+ /6.5	10.8	1.04	14.13	11	0	98	1	1	47		52.1	-28.8	8	8	1,000	0	0.0	0.0
C+ /6.6	10.8	1.04	15.06	23	0	98	1	1	47		57.3	-28.4	12	8	100,000	0	0.0	0.0
C+ /6.2	9.1	0.52	9.98	919	1	89	8	2	11		47.0	-8.7	88	16	1,000	0	5.8	0.0
C+ /6.1	9.0	0.51	9.86	555	1	89	8	2	11		47.0	-8.7	88	16	1,000	0	0.0	0.0
C /4.9	9.0	0.50	7.80	921	1	89	8	2	11		43.4	-9.0	86	16	1,000	0	0.0	0.0
C+ /6.3	9.1	0.51	10.15	190	1	89	8	2	11		48.3	-8.6	89	16	500,000	0	0.0	0.0
C+ /5.8	11.1	1.08	18.40	557	1	98	0	1	9		81.0	-19.7	21	26	1,000	0	5.8	0.0
C+ /5.8	11.1	1.08	18.33	7	1	98	0	1	9		81.0	-19.7	21	26	1,000	0	0.0	0.0
C /5.5	11.1	1.07	15.61	18	1	98	0	1	9		76.4	-19.9	15	26	1,000	0	0.0	0.0
C+ /5.8	11.1	1.07	18.39	132	1	98	0	1	9		82.7	-19.6	24	26	500,000	0	0.0	0.0
C+ /6.1	10.5	0.72	30.96	4	0	100	0	0	34		88.7	-22.5	94	21	1,000	0	5.8	0.0
C+ /6.1	10.4	0.72	30.97	79	0	100	0	0	34		88.6	-22.4	94	21	1,000	0	0.0	0.0
C+ /5.8	10.5	0.72	27.62	2	0	100	0	0	34		83.9	-22.7	93	21	1,000	0	0.0	0.0
C+ /6.1	10.5	0.72	31.22	3	0	100	0	0	34		90.7	-22.3	95	21	500,000	0	0.0	0.0
C+ /6.8	10.6	0.75	24.05	N/A	0	99	0	1	5		54.6	-22.7	78	17	1,000	0	5.8	0.0
C+ /6.8	10.6	0.75	24.15	10	0	99	0	1	5		54.5	-22.6	78	17	1,000	0	0.0	0.0
C+ /6.8	10.6	0.75	23.32	N/A	0	99	0	1	5		50.7	-22.9	70	17	1,000	0	0.0	0.0
C+ /6.9	10.6	0.75	24.38	1	0	99	0	1	5		56.6	-22.6	81	17	500,000	0	0.0	0.0
C+ /6.3	12.7	1.09	23.97	1	0	96	3	1	3		48.3	-18.6	3	22	1,000	0	5.8	0.0
C+ /6.3	12.7	1.09	23.99	117	0	96	3	1	3		48.3	-18.6	3	22	1,000	0	0.0	0.0
C+ /6.4	12.7	1.09	23.29	1	0	96	3	1	3		44.6	-18.9	3	22	1,000	0	0.0	0.0
C+ /6.3	12.7	1.09	23.98	2	0	96	3	1	3		49.6	-18.5	4	22	500,000	0	0.0	0.0
C+ /6.6	10.3	1.03	50.34	2	0	99	0	1	67		100.0	-19.9	42	20	1,000	0	5.8	0.0
C+ /6.6	10.4	1.03	50.33	520	0	99	0	1	67		100.0	-19.9	42	20	1,000	0	0.0	0.0
C+ /6.5	10.3	1.03	46.27	2	0	99	0	1	67		95.0	-20.2	32	20	1,000	0	0.0	0.0
C+ /6.6	10.3	1.03	50.83	17	0	99	0	1	67		101.7	-19.8	47	20	500,000	0	0.0	0.0
C+ /5.6	12.1	0.88	22.77	1	0	100	0	0	14		41.7	-20.9	33	20	1,000	0	5.8	0.0
C+ /5.6	12.1	0.88	22.35	24	0	100	0	0	14		41.5	-20.9	33	20	1,000	0	0.0	0.0
C /5.4	12.2	0.88	20.61	1	0	100	0	0	14		38.1	-21.1	25	20	1,000	0	0.0	0.0
C+ /5.6	12.1	0.88	22.67	3	0	100	0	0	14		43.6	-20.8	39	20	500,000	0	0.0	0.0
C /4.5	5.4	-0.47	6.80	15	0	0	100	0	0		-31.8	0.6	19	41	1,000	0	0.0	0.0
B /8.7	3.7	0.36	29.80	1,906	2	97	0	1	10		25.2	-6.0	56	9	2,500	100	5.8	0.0
B /8.7	3.8	0.37	29.69	353	2	97	0	1	10		21.9	-6.3	43	9	2,500	100	0.0	0.0
U /	N/A	N/A	10.14	25	0	0	0	100	0		N/A	N/A	N/A	1	100,000	100	0.0	0.0
B- /7.1	7.6	0.54	9.08	7	1	98	0	1	35		N/A	N/A	7	3	2,500	100	5.8	0.0
B- /7.0	7.5	0.53	8.99	4	1	98	0	1	35		N/A	N/A	5	3	2,500	100	0.0	0.0
B- /7.2	7.6	0.53	9.12	5	1	98	0	1	35		N/A	N/A	8	3	100,000	100	0.0	0.0
B /8.7	3.7	0.37	29.79	5,819	2	97	0	1	10		26.2	-5.9	59	9	100,000	100	0.0	0.0
B- /7.8	6.8	0.38	14.29	34	25	74	0	1	66		53.1	-2.3	95	5	2,500	250	0.0	2.0

Fund Type	Fund Name	Ticker Symbol	Overall Investment Rating	Phone	Perfor-mance Rating/Pts	3 Mo	6 Mo	1Yr / Pct	3Yr / Pct	5Yr / Pct	Dividend Yield	Expense Ratio
GL	GaveKal Knowledge Leaders Inst	GAVIX	C+	(888) 998-9890	C / 4.6	4.88	8.66	9.22 /70	10.26 /41	--	0.51	1.25
FO	GE Institutional Intl Equity Inv	GIEIX	D+	(800) 242-0134	C- / 3.2	7.34	4.00	1.14 /19	9.01 /33	5.24 /13	2.63	0.56
FO	GE Institutional Intl Equity Svc	GIESX	D	(800) 242-0134	C- / 3.0	7.30	3.91	0.88 /18	8.70 /31	4.96 /12	2.39	0.81
GR	GE Institutional Premier Gro Eq Inv	GEIPX	A	(800) 242-0134	A / 9.5	2.29	8.02	17.52 /95	18.26 /95	15.40 /90	0.80	0.37
GR	GE Institutional Premier Gro Eq Svc	GEPSX	A-	(800) 242-0134	A / 9.4	2.17	7.78	17.19 /95	17.92 /94	15.13 /88	0.60	0.62
IX	GE Institutional S&P 500 Index Inv	GIDIX	A	(800) 242-0134	B / 8.1	0.88	5.71	12.39 /84	15.88 /82	14.29 /80	2.01	0.15
IX	GE Institutional S&P 500 Index Svc	GIDSX	A-	(800) 242-0134	B / 7.9	0.86	5.62	12.16 /83	15.62 /80	14.01 /78	1.74	0.40
SC	GE Institutional Sm-Cp Eq Inv	GSVIX	C+	(800) 242-0134	B / 7.6	4.06	10.87	7.53 /59	15.09 /76	15.92 /93	0.10	0.88
SC	GE Institutional Sm-Cp Eq Svc	GSQSX	C+	(800) 242-0134	B- / 7.4	4.05	10.77	7.28 /57	14.81 /73	15.64 /91	0.00	1.13
AA	GE Institutional Strat Invest Inv	GSIVX	C-	(800) 242-0134	C- / 3.8	2.42	3.85	6.44 /50	9.23 /34	8.05 /30	1.84	0.36
AA	GE Institutional Strat Invest Svc	GSRVX	C-	(800) 242-0134	C- / 3.6	2.36	3.70	6.15 /48	8.94 /32	7.78 /28	1.61	0.61
GR	GE Institutional US Equity Inv	GUSIX	B-	(800) 242-0134	B / 7.9	0.58	4.64	11.25 /79	15.91 /83	12.86 /67	1.39	0.36
GR	GE Institutional US Equity Svc	GUSSX	B-	(800) 242-0134	B / 7.8	0.49	4.47	10.96 /78	15.85 /82	12.73 /66	1.13	0.61
GR	GE Investment US Equities 1	GEUSX	B	(800) 242-0134	B- / 7.5	0.47	4.48	10.88 /78	15.44 /78	12.43 /64	0.89	0.80
GR	GE Investments Premier Growth Eq 1	GEPGX	B+	(800) 242-0134	A / 9.4	2.24	7.88	17.14 /95	17.86 /94	14.99 /87	0.46	0.83
RE	GE Investments Real Est Sec 1	GEIRX	C+	(800) 242-0134	A+/ 9.6	4.88	20.98	25.47 /98	14.34 /70	16.51 /95	1.70	0.96
GR	GE Investments S&P 500 Index 1	GESPX	A	(800) 242-0134	B / 8.0	0.85	5.74	12.29 /84	15.74 /81	14.10 /79	1.61	0.40
SC	GE Investments Small-Cap Equity 1	GESEX	C-	(800) 242-0134	B- / 7.4	3.96	10.81	7.22 /57	14.77 /73	15.68 /91	0.00	1.29
GL	GE Investments Total Return 3	GETTX	C	(800) 242-0134	C- / 3.1	1.76	3.16	5.56 /43	8.21 /28	7.26 /25	1.49	0.86
* GI	GE RSP US Equity	GESSX	B	(800) 242-0134	B / 8.2	0.79	4.77	11.48 /80	16.30 /85	13.23 /70	1.49	0.17
GR	Geneva Advisors All Cap Gr- Retail	GNVRX	D-	(800) 242-0134	C- / 3.3	4.50	7.00	8.32 /65	7.64 /25	11.96 /60	0.00	1.70
GR	Geneva Advisors All Cap Growth Inst	GNVIX	D-	(800) 242-0134	C- / 3.6	4.59	7.22	8.75 /68	8.04 /27	12.31 /63	0.00	1.35
GR	Geneva Advisors Equity Income I	GNEIX	C+	(800) 242-0134	C / 5.3	1.67	5.46	8.59 /67	12.33 /55	--	1.40	1.40
GR	Geneva Advisors Equity Income R	GNERX	C+	(800) 242-0134	C / 5.1	1.58	5.26	8.24 /64	11.93 /52	--	1.09	1.75
AA	George Putnam Balanced A	PGEOX	C+	(800) 225-1581	C / 4.4	1.86	5.38	10.02 /74	11.45 /49	10.34 /47	1.12	0.99
AA	George Putnam Balanced B	PGEBX	B-	(800) 225-1581	C / 4.8	1.69	5.06	9.26 /71	10.61 /43	9.54 /41	0.48	1.74
AA	George Putnam Balanced C	PGPCX	B-	(800) 225-1581	C / 4.8	1.70	5.04	9.24 /71	10.61 /43	9.56 /41	0.51	1.74
AA	George Putnam Balanced M	PGEMX	C+	(800) 225-1581	C / 4.4	1.76	5.13	9.49 /72	10.88 /45	9.82 /43	0.71	1.49
AA	George Putnam Balanced R	PGPRX	B	(800) 225-1581	C / 5.1	1.82	5.28	9.80 /74	11.16 /47	10.10 /45	0.97	1.24
BA	George Putnam Balanced R5	PGELX	U	(800) 225-1581	U /	1.99	5.62	10.39 /76	--	--	1.43	0.73
AA	George Putnam Balanced Y	PGEYX	B	(800) 225-1581	C / 5.5	1.92	5.55	10.32 /76	11.71 /51	10.65 /50	1.42	0.74
RE	Gerstein Fisher Mlt-Fac Gl RE Sec	GFMRX	U	(800) 473-1155	U /	4.31	14.61	18.27 /96	--	--	2.68	1.73
GL	Gerstein Fisher Mlt-Fac Intl Gr Ety	GFIGX	C	(800) 473-1155	C / 5.2	7.51	6.32	0.07 /16	12.33 /55	--	1.97	1.03
GL	GF Multi-Factor Growth Equity Fd I	GFMGX	A	(800) 473-1155	A / 9.3	3.83	9.99	17.14 /95	17.44 /92	15.85 /92	0.38	1.08
AA	Ginkgo Multi-Strategy Inv	GNKIX	D	(855) 289-4656	D- / 1.4	-3.78	-0.32	2.56 /24	6.01 /17	--	0.00	2.02
GL	● Giralda Manager	GDAMX	B	(855) 417-2532	C+/ 5.6	1.28	4.20	10.58 /77	12.40 /55	--	0.00	1.40
FO	Glenmede International Port	GTCIX	E+	(800) 442-8299	D- / 1.3	4.94	-1.53	-4.05 / 7	5.34 /14	3.78 / 8	1.74	1.25
FO	Glenmede Intl Sec Opt Ptfl	NOVIX	U	(800) 442-8299	U /	2.96	-1.56	-2.83 / 9	--	--	1.34	0.98
GR	Glenmede Large Cap core	GTLOX	A+	(800) 442-8299	A+/ 9.7	3.64	10.20	15.24 /92	19.61 /97	17.30 /97	0.84	0.87
GR	Glenmede Large Cap Growth Port	GTLLX	A+	(800) 442-8299	A+/ 9.8	4.52	12.85	20.97 /97	19.99 /98	18.37 /98	0.50	0.88
GR	Glenmede Large Cap Value Port	GTMEX	C+	(800) 442-8299	B / 7.9	0.44	5.06	10.28 /75	16.11 /84	12.58 /65	0.31	0.92
IN	Glenmede Long/Short Portfolio	GTAPX	C	(800) 442-8299	D+/ 2.4	0.71	5.80	4.72 /37	6.70 /20	6.10 /17	0.00	2.48
FO	● Glenmede Philadelphia Intl	GTIIX	E+	(800) 442-8299	D- / 1.2	3.85	-1.71	-4.35 / 6	5.32 /14	3.80 / 8	2.01	1.21
EM	Glenmede Philadelphia Intl EM IV	GPEMX	E-	(800) 442-8299	E / 0.3	0.65	-7.28	-5.09 / 5	-0.76 / 4	--	1.83	1.14
FO	Glenmede Philadelphia Intl SC IV	GPISX	C	(800) 442-8299	C+/ 5.7	6.70	3.11	-2.21 /10	13.81 /66	--	2.13	0.97
IN	Glenmede Secured Options Portfolio	GTSOX	D+	(800) 442-8299	D+/ 2.5	0.92	0.91	3.63 /30	7.62 /25	--	0.00	0.87
SC	Glenmede Small Cap Equity Adv	GTCSX	A-	(800) 442-8299	A / 9.3	5.17	14.70	6.92 /54	18.07 /94	17.17 /96	0.07	0.94
SC	Glenmede Small Cap Equity Inst	GTSCX	A-	(800) 442-8299	A / 9.4	5.20	14.82	7.14 /56	18.29 /95	17.42 /97	0.11	0.74
GR	Glenmede Strategic Equity	GTCEX	C+	(800) 442-8299	C+/ 6.8	1.20	7.55	13.38 /88	13.54 /64	12.56 /65	0.99	0.86
FO	Glenmede Total Market Port	GTTMX	A+	(800) 442-8299	A / 9.3	4.18	10.59	11.23 /79	17.78 /93	15.32 /89	0.32	2.23
SC	Glenmede US Emerging Growth Port	GTGSX	B-	(800) 442-8299	B / 7.7	6.95	16.26	9.90 /74	14.10 /68	15.13 /88	0.01	0.96
GL	GMG Defensive Beta	MPDAX	D+	(877) 464-3111	D / 1.9	0.74	2.71	3.25 /28	6.11 /17	6.50 /20	0.24	1.92

● Denotes fund is closed to new investors

* Denotes fund is included in Section II

www.thestreetratings.com

Risk Rating/Pts	Standard Deviation	Beta	NAV As of 3/31/15	Total $(Mil)	Cash %	Stocks %	Bonds %	Other %	Portfolio Turnover Ratio	Last Bull Market Return	Last Bear Market Return	Manager Quality Pct	Manager Tenure (Years)	Initial Purch. $	Additional Purch. $	Front End Load	Back End Load
B- /7.8	6.8	0.38	14.41	160	25	74	0	1	66	54.6	-2.2	95	5	500,000	25,000	0.0	2.0
C+ /5.9	12.5	0.92	12.87	1,521	1	98	0	1	39	52.7	-25.8	70	18	5,000,000	0	0.0	2.0
C+ /5.9	12.5	0.92	12.79	41	1	98	0	1	39	51.5	-25.9	67	18	5,000,000	0	0.0	2.0
C+ /5.8	10.6	1.04	14.77	371	2	97	0	1	21	115.6	-16.8	79	16	5,000,000	0	0.0	0.0
C+ /5.9	10.7	1.04	14.62	4	2	97	0	1	21	113.8	-16.8	77	16	5,000,000	0	0.0	0.0
B- /7.3	9.6	1.00	19.52	21	5	94	0	1	16	99.0	-16.3	64	N/A	5,000,000	0	0.0	0.0
B- /7.3	9.6	1.00	19.93	8	5	94	0	1	16	97.3	-16.4	61	N/A	5,000,000	0	0.0	0.0
C /4.7	12.0	0.87	19.22	1,347	4	95	0	1	37	96.0	-21.7	76	5	5,000,000	0	0.0	0.0
C /4.7	12.0	0.87	19.28	N/A	4	95	0	1	37	94.2	-21.7	74	5	5,000,000	0	0.0	0.0
C+ /6.8	6.5	1.11	12.68	818	14	59	25	2	185	51.6	-13.7	29	N/A	5,000,000	0	0.0	0.0
C+ /6.9	6.5	1.12	12.59	N/A	14	59	25	2	185	50.3	-13.8	25	N/A	5,000,000	0	0.0	0.0
C /5.1	10.3	1.05	15.69	703	4	95	0	1	38	100.5	-18.7	52	14	5,000,000	0	0.0	0.0
C /5.3	10.4	1.07	16.36	N/A	4	95	0	1	38	100.0	-18.7	49	14	5,000,000	0	0.0	0.0
C+ /6.4	10.3	1.06	48.67	35	5	94	0	1	40	98.1	-18.8	45	14	0	0	0.0	0.0
C /4.7	10.7	1.04	108.97	40	1	98	0	1	21	113.2	-17.0	76	18	0	0	0.0	0.0
C- /3.2	13.4	1.07	15.46	90	0	99	0	1	82	87.8	-16.2	56	9	0	0	0.0	0.0
B- /7.3	9.6	1.00	36.91	198	2	97	0	1	3	98.1	-16.5	62	8	0	0	0.0	0.0
C- /3.3	12.0	0.87	14.96	43	5	94	0	1	39	94.5	-21.8	74	N/A	0	0	0.0	0.0
B- /7.8	6.5	1.03	19.08	1,826	6	63	30	1	175	47.8	-14.0	52	2	0	0	0.0	0.0
C /5.3	10.4	1.06	54.74	5,412	2	97	0	1	40	103.4	-18.6	56	14	0	0	0.0	0.0
C- /3.7	12.9	1.03	26.46	31	0	99	0	1	74	52.3	-18.8	3	8	1,000	100	0.0	2.0
C- /3.7	12.9	1.03	27.14	132	0	99	0	1	74	54.1	-18.7	3	8	100,000	1,000	0.0	2.0
B- /7.2	10.2	0.98	33.42	246	14	85	0	1	68	76.8	-13.1	24	12	100,000	1,000	0.0	2.0
B- /7.2	10.2	0.99	33.33	8	14	85	0	1	68	74.8	-13.3	20	12	1,000	100	0.0	2.0
B /8.4	6.0	1.04	17.15	1,032	4	62	32	2	98	61.0	-10.5	68	7	500	0	5.8	0.0
B /8.4	6.0	1.04	16.97	25	4	62	32	2	98	57.0	-10.9	57	7	500	0	0.0	0.0
B /8.4	6.0	1.04	17.05	35	4	62	32	2	98	57.0	-10.9	58	7	500	0	0.0	0.0
B /8.4	6.0	1.04	16.93	79	4	62	32	2	98	58.3	-10.7	62	7	500	0	3.5	0.0
B /8.4	6.0	1.04	17.10	1	4	62	32	2	98	59.6	-10.7	65	7	500	0	0.0	0.0
U /	N/A	N/A	17.22	71	4	62	32	2	98	N/A	N/A	N/A	7	500	0	0.0	0.0
B /8.4	6.0	1.04	17.21	118	4	62	32	2	98	62.5	-10.5	71	7	500	0	0.0	0.0
U /	N/A	N/A	10.80	88	14	85	0	1	80	N/A	N/A	N/A	1	2,500	100	0.0	1.0
C+ /6.4	13.7	1.01	13.60	130	1	98	0	1	51	N/A	N/A	87	3	2,500	100	0.0	1.0
C+ /6.4	11.0	0.66	17.89	233	0	100	0	0	59	108.1	-16.8	98	6	2,500	100	0.0	1.0
B- /7.2	8.6	1.39	11.21	52	0	0	0	100	304	29.7	N/A	3	4	250	50	0.0	1.0
B /8.3	9.4	0.54	13.48	217	0	0	0	100	28	66.6	N/A	96	4	0	0	0.0	1.0
C /5.4	14.5	1.08	13.82	71	1	98	0	1	47	40.6	-27.6	12	21	1,000	0	0.0	0.0
U /	N/A	N/A	10.44	96	46	53	0	1	81	N/A	N/A	N/A	3	1,000	0	0.0	0.0
B- /7.0	10.9	1.10	22.52	1,064	0	99	0	1	73	120.7	-18.4	81	11	1,000	0	0.0	0.0
C+ /6.8	11.0	1.09	24.53	1,554	0	99	0	1	76	125.2	-18.4	84	11	1,000	0	0.0	0.0
C /4.8	10.6	1.06	11.51	93	0	99	0	1	106	100.4	-26.6	53	7	1,000	0	0.0	0.0
B+ /9.4	4.4	0.38	11.31	171	69	30	0	1	150	34.0	-5.1	76	9	1,000	0	0.0	0.0
C /5.4	14.4	1.07	12.42	14	2	97	0	1	57	39.8	-27.6	13	23	1,000,000	1,000	0.0	0.0
C- /3.1	15.1	1.09	7.79	6	0	0	0	100	131	25.6	N/A	45	4	10,000,000	1,000	0.8	0.0
C /5.3	13.4	0.95	11.47	46	0	0	0	100	101	75.2	N/A	92	7	10,000,000	1,000	0.5	0.0
C+ /6.6	5.1	0.45	12.01	359	97	2	0	1	1,108	49.3	-10.4	73	N/A	1,000	0	0.0	0.0
C+ /5.8	13.6	0.98	27.26	1,299	1	98	0	1	45	106.4	-23.6	83	19	1,000	0	0.0	0.0
C+ /5.8	13.6	0.98	28.32	724	1	98	0	1	45	107.8	-23.6	84	19	10,000,000	0	0.0	0.0
C+ /5.6	9.8	1.00	21.93	181	0	99	0	1	22	90.5	-18.3	34	11	1,000	0	0.0	0.0
C+ /6.5	11.6	0.70	15.22	90	2	97	0	1	117	106.8	-21.0	98	9	1,000	0	0.0	0.0
C /5.3	13.6	0.97	10.15	41	0	99	0	1	127	91.5	-24.6	45	10	1,000	0	0.0	0.0
B- /7.2	8.4	0.51	13.70	27	6	91	1	2	24	43.4	-16.9	79	6	1,000	250	0.0	0.0

					PERFORMANCE							
	99 Pct = Best					Total Return % through 3/31/15					Incl. in Returns	
	0 Pct = Worst								Annualized		Dividend	Expense
Fund Type	Fund Name	Ticker Symbol	Overall Investment Rating	Phone	Performance Rating/Pts	3 Mo	6 Mo	1Yr / Pct	3Yr / Pct	5Yr / Pct	Yield	Ratio
GL	GMO Alpha Only III	GGHEX	D		E / 0.4	-0.53	-2.68	-4.38 / 6	-1.37 / 3	-0.67 / 2	1.88	1.01
GL	GMO Alpha Only IV	GAPOX	D		E / 0.4	-0.48	-2.64	-4.29 / 6	-1.31 / 3	-0.62 / 2	1.93	0.96
AA	GMO Asset Allocation Bond III	GMOBX	D+		E+ / 0.7	-1.96	0.29	5.13 / 40	1.87 / 6	2.86 / 6	2.70	0.42
AA	GMO Asset Allocation Bond VI	GABFX	D+		E+ / 0.7	-1.95	0.32	5.22 / 40	1.97 / 6	2.97 / 6	2.79	0.33
IN	GMO Benchmark-Free Alloca Srs R6	GBMRX	U		U /	1.47	0.60	1.27 / 19	--	--	3.03	0.91
* AA	GMO Benchmark-Free Allocation III	GBMFX	D+		D- / 1.5	1.42	0.61	1.37 / 20	5.70 / 16	6.02 / 17	1.91	1.08
AA	GMO Benchmark-Free Allocation IV	GBMBX	U		U /	1.42	0.63	1.41 / 20	--	--	1.94	1.03
IN	GMO Developed World Stock III	GDWTX	C		C / 4.8	3.71	1.93	1.80 / 21	12.01 / 53	9.76 / 43	2.76	0.71
IN	GMO Developed World Stock IV	GDWFX	C		C / 4.8	3.71	1.96	1.85 / 21	12.07 / 53	9.82 / 43	2.81	0.66
EM	● GMO Emerging Countries III	GMCEX	E		E / 0.3	1.72	-5.10	-2.46 / 9	-3.34 / 2	-0.21 / 2	3.90	1.70
EM	GMO Emerging Markets II	GMEMX	E		E / 0.3	0.41	-4.86	-3.04 / 9	-3.19 / 2	-0.12 / 2	3.22	1.11
EM	● GMO Emerging Markets III	GMOEX	E		E / 0.3	0.41	-4.86	-2.96 / 9	-3.14 / 2	-0.06 / 2	3.28	1.04
EM	● GMO Emerging Markets IV	GMEFX	E		E / 0.3	0.41	-4.86	-2.94 / 9	-3.08 / 2	-0.03 / 2	3.36	1.00
EM	● GMO Emerging Markets V	GEMVX	E		E / 0.3	0.41	-4.83	-2.91 / 9	-3.06 / 2	0.01 / 2	3.41	0.98
EM	● GMO Emerging Markets VI	GEMMX	E		E / 0.3	0.41	-4.88	-2.88 / 9	-3.02 / 2	0.04 / 2	3.43	0.95
EM	GMO Emg Domestic Opportunities II	GEDTX	E+		D / 1.9	3.86	4.59	5.79 / 45	5.80 / 16	--	0.95	1.16
EM	GMO Emg Domestic Opportunities III	GEDSX	U		U /	3.86	4.63	5.89 / 45	--	--	1.00	1.09
EM	GMO Emg Domestic Opportunities IV	GEDIX	U		U /	3.86	4.67	5.90 / 46	--	--	1.05	1.05
EM	GMO Emg Domestic Opportunities VI	GEDFX	E+		D / 1.9	3.89	4.69	5.99 / 46	5.31 / 14	--	1.10	1.00
FO	GMO Foreign II	GMFRX	E+		D- / 1.5	5.97	-0.04	-5.58 / 5	6.32 / 18	4.23 / 9	3.14	0.94
FO	GMO Foreign III	GMOFX	E+		D / 1.6	6.02	0.02	-5.46 / 5	6.41 / 19	4.31 / 9	3.21	0.88
FO	GMO Foreign IV	GMFFX	E+		D / 1.6	6.03	0.01	-5.46 / 5	6.43 / 19	4.35 / 10	3.14	0.81
FO	GMO Foreign Small Companies Fund	GFSFX	D-		C- / 3.1	7.02	2.58	-6.65 / 4	9.84 / 38	8.94 / 36	1.47	0.88
FO	● GMO Foreign Small Companies III	GMFSX	D-		C- / 3.1	7.00	2.54	-6.74 / 4	9.77 / 38	8.87 / 36	1.42	0.93
GL	GMO Global Asset Allocation III	GMWAX	D		D / 1.7	1.30	0.09	0.89 / 18	6.33 / 18	6.50 / 20	3.67	0.56
GL	GMO Global Asset Allocation Srs R6	GATRX	U		U /	1.24	0.08	0.80 / 18	--	--	3.78	0.60
AA	GMO Global Develope Eqty Alloc III	GWOAX	D		C- / 3.7	2.77	0.47	-0.30 / 15	10.39 / 42	9.50 / 41	3.36	0.57
GL	GMO Global Eq Allocation III	GMGEX	D-		D+ / 2.8	2.53	0.20	-0.39 / 15	8.78 / 32	8.32 / 32	3.28	0.58
GL	GMO Global Focused Equity III	GGFEX	C		C / 4.5	2.93	0.31	-1.33 / 12	11.93 / 52	--	1.19	2.53
GL	● GMO International Eq Alloc III	GIEAX	E+		D- / 1.4	3.53	-2.09	-4.69 / 6	6.41 / 19	5.41 / 14	4.33	0.71
FO	GMO International Eq Alloc Srs R6	GEARX	D		D- / 1.4	3.44	-2.14	-4.74 / 6	6.19 / 18	--	4.08	0.75
FO	GMO International Equity II	GMICX	E+		D+ / 2.7	4.83	-1.09	-5.17 / 5	9.07 / 33	5.84 / 16	4.50	0.76
FO	GMO International Equity III	GMOIX	D-		D+ / 2.7	4.82	-1.07	-5.13 / 5	9.15 / 34	5.91 / 16	4.52	0.69
FO	GMO International Equity IV	GMCFX	D-		D+ / 2.8	4.83	-1.03	-5.03 / 5	9.22 / 34	5.97 / 17	4.60	0.63
FO	● GMO International Small Co III	GMISX	E+		C- / 3.9	4.77	1.22	-7.29 / 4	11.81 / 51	9.50 / 41	2.31	0.92
GL	GMO Intl Developed Equity Alloc III	GIOTX	D-		D+ / 2.9	4.39	-1.39	-4.74 / 6	9.53 / 36	7.13 / 24	4.49	0.67
FO	GMO Intl Large/Mid Cap Eqty III	GMIEX	E+		D+ / 2.7	4.71	-1.50	-5.80 / 5	9.15 / 34	6.77 / 22	4.62	0.59
FO	GMO Intl Large/Mid Cap Eqty IV	GMIRX	E+		D+ / 2.7	4.71	-1.46	-5.72 / 5	9.22 / 34	6.84 / 22	4.69	0.53
FO	GMO Intl Large/Mid Cap Eqty VI	GCEFX	E+		D+ / 2.7	4.72	-1.44	-5.71 / 5	9.23 / 34	6.86 / 22	4.73	0.50
* IN	GMO Quality Equity III	GQETX	C-		C+ / 6.2	0.49	5.61	10.79 / 78	13.15 / 61	13.04 / 69	1.79	0.49
IN	GMO Quality Equity IV	GQEFX	C-		C+ / 6.3	0.45	5.60	10.82 / 78	13.19 / 61	13.09 / 69	1.83	0.45
IN	GMO Quality Equity V	GQLFX	C-		C+ / 6.3	0.49	5.65	10.87 / 78	13.24 / 61	13.12 / 69	1.86	0.43
IN	GMO Quality Equity VI	GQLOX	C-		C+ / 6.3	0.49	5.67	10.93 / 78	13.26 / 61	13.15 / 70	1.87	0.40
EN	GMO Resources III	GOFIX	E		E- / 0.2	-0.96	-19.72	-19.02 / 1	-4.83 / 2	--	6.03	0.86
EN	GMO Resources IV	GOVIX	U		U /	-0.97	-19.69	-18.96 / 1	--	--	6.23	0.81
GL	GMO Risk Premium VI	GMOKX	U		U /	4.39	-0.73	2.74 / 25	--	--	0.00	0.57
GL	GMO Special Opportunities VI	GSOFX	U		U /	1.17	2.28	--	--	--	0.00	1.38
AA	GMO Strategic Opps Alloc III	GBATX	D		C- / 3.1	1.29	-0.07	1.07 / 19	9.20 / 34	8.74 / 35	3.80	0.60
FO	GMO Taiwan	GMOTX	D-		D- / 1.3	2.32	0.31	5.39 / 42	4.39 / 11	7.72 / 28	2.27	1.42
FO	GMO Tax-Managed Intl Equities III	GTMIX	D-		D+ / 2.9	5.53	-1.37	-5.35 / 5	9.42 / 36	6.78 / 22	3.95	0.76
IN	GMO US Equity Allocation III	GMUEX	C		C+ / 6.1	0.62	4.05	7.82 / 61	13.41 / 63	12.90 / 67	1.68	0.48
IN	GMO US Equity Allocation IV	GMRTX	C		C+ / 6.1	0.62	4.10	7.90 / 62	13.50 / 63	12.98 / 68	1.75	0.43

● Denotes fund is closed to new investors
* Denotes fund is included in Section II

www.thestreetratings.com

RISK			NET ASSETS		ASSET				Portfolio	BULL / BEAR		FUND MANAGER		MINIMUMS		LOADS	
	3 Year		NAV							Last Bull	Last Bear	Manager	Manager	Initial	Additional	Front	Back
Risk Rating/Pts	Standard Deviation	Beta	As of 3/31/15	Total $(Mil)	Cash %	Stocks %	Bonds %	Other %	Turnover Ratio	Market Return	Market Return	Quality Pct	Tenure (Years)	Purch. $	Purch. $	End Load	End Load
B /8.3	2.0	-0.04	22.68	27	1	90	8	1	66	-5.8	6.1	51	19	0	0	0.0	0.0
B /8.3	2.0	-0.04	22.70	3,300	1	90	8	1	66	-5.7	6.1	51	19	125,000,000	0	0.0	0.0
B /8.5	5.9	0.12	24.57	383	0	0	99	1	32	14.8	0.5	73	6	0	0	0.0	0.0
B /8.5	5.9	0.12	24.61	4,309	0	0	99	1	32	15.2	0.5	74	6	300,000,000	0	0.0	0.0
U /	N/A	N/A	10.36	278	20	51	28	1	8	N/A	N/A	N/A	2	10,000,000	0	0.0	0.0
B /8.0	5.5	0.84	26.39	6,036	10	52	36	2	52	32.8	-4.0	23	N/A	0	0	0.1	0.1
U /	N/A	N/A	26.38	3,243	10	52	36	2	52	N/A	N/A	N/A	12	125,000,000	0	0.1	0.1
C+ /6.6	11.0	1.02	24.32	155	0	98	1	1	64	70.5	-18.9	17	10	0	0	0.3	0.3
C+ /6.6	10.9	1.02	24.34	283	0	98	1	1	64	70.7	-18.8	17	10	125,000,000	0	0.3	0.3
C /4.5	15.2	1.09	8.86	37	0	98	0	2	122	10.5	-27.2	15	18	0	0	0.0	0.0
C /4.8	15.2	1.09	9.86	943	1	97	0	2	98	10.3	-26.5	16	22	0	0	0.8	0.8
C /4.7	15.3	1.09	9.89	275	1	97	0	2	98	10.5	-26.5	17	22	50,000,000	0	0.8	0.8
C /4.7	15.3	1.09	9.80	819	1	97	0	2	98	10.8	-26.5	17	22	125,000,000	0	0.8	0.8
C /4.7	15.3	1.09	9.78	171	1	97	0	2	98	10.9	-26.5	17	22	250,000,000	0	0.8	0.8
C /4.7	15.2	1.09	9.80	5,260	1	97	0	2	98	11.0	-26.5	18	22	300,000,000	0	0.8	0.8
C /4.9	11.9	0.76	23.94	736	3	92	4	1	274	40.7	-17.9	94	4	0	0	0.8	0.8
U /	N/A	N/A	23.94	336	3	92	4	1	274	N/A	N/A	N/A	4	50,000,000	0	0.8	0.8
U /	N/A	N/A	23.95	685	3	92	4	1	274	N/A	N/A	N/A	4	125,000,000	0	0.8	0.8
C /4.9	12.0	0.77	24.01	604	3	92	4	1	274	38.9	N/A	93	4	300,000,000	0	0.8	0.8
C /4.4	14.0	1.04	11.90	92	0	97	2	1	98	40.8	-23.2	21	31	0	0	0.0	0.0
C /4.4	14.0	1.04	11.98	160	0	97	2	1	98	41.1	-23.2	22	31	0	0	0.0	0.0
C /4.4	14.0	1.04	12.30	25	0	97	2	1	98	41.3	-23.1	23	31	125,000,000	0	0.0	0.0
C /4.9	12.5	0.90	15.10	752	2	94	3	1	57	55.3	-24.2	79	4	125,000,000	0	0.5	0.5
C /4.9	12.5	0.90	15.13	329	2	94	3	1	57	55.0	-24.2	78	4	0	0	0.5	0.5
B- /7.2	6.8	1.03	10.95	4,708	5	58	36	1	46	36.4	-7.9	28	N/A	0	0	0.1	0.1
U /	N/A	N/A	10.59	790	12	59	27	2	2	N/A	N/A	N/A	19	10,000,000	0	0.0	0.0
C /4.9	10.4	1.66	22.27	1,725	0	98	1	1	36	61.1	-14.2	4	10	0	0	0.1	0.1
C /5.0	10.7	1.64	8.52	3,687	0	98	1	1	51	54.0	-15.6	7	N/A	0	0	0.1	0.1
C+ /6.7	14.5	1.01	21.81	11	2	96	1	1	225	N/A	N/A	85	N/A	0	0	0.0	0.0
C /4.8	13.4	1.98	10.27	1,553	1	97	1	1	40	41.4	-21.9	2	N/A	0	0	0.2	0.2
C+ /6.9	13.3	0.99	10.21	245	2	96	1	1	6	N/A	N/A	25	3	10,000,000	0	0.0	0.0
C- /4.2	14.5	1.07	22.79	113	0	98	1	1	48	48.0	-21.8	52	17	0	0	0.0	0.0
C- /4.2	14.5	1.07	23.05	1,265	0	98	1	1	48	48.4	-21.8	53	17	0	0	0.0	0.0
C- /4.2	14.5	1.07	23.02	10,927	0	98	1	1	48	48.6	-21.8	54	17	125,000,000	0	0.0	0.0
D+ /2.4	14.6	1.05	7.47	279	0	98	0	2	79	64.1	-22.9	82	17	0	0	0.5	0.5
C /5.1	13.5	1.96	16.42	1,165	0	97	1	2	52	52.1	-20.3	3	N/A	0	0	0.1	0.1
C- /3.5	14.1	1.05	29.34	572	0	98	0	2	54	50.9	-21.2	56	13	0	0	0.0	0.0
C- /3.5	14.1	1.05	29.32	1,313	0	98	0	2	54	51.3	-21.2	57	13	125,000,000	0	0.0	0.0
C- /3.5	14.1	1.05	29.29	1	0	98	0	2	54	51.4	-21.2	57	13	300,000,000	0	0.0	0.0
C /4.3	9.1	0.92	22.50	5,144	0	98	1	1	48	78.9	-6.9	47	11	0	0	0.0	0.0
C- /4.2	9.1	0.92	22.52	2,107	0	98	1	1	48	79.2	-6.8	47	11	125,000,000	0	0.0	0.0
C- /4.2	9.1	0.92	22.52	252	0	98	1	1	48	79.4	-6.8	47	11	250,000,000	0	0.0	0.0
C- /4.2	9.1	0.92	22.51	2,381	0	98	1	1	48	79.5	-6.8	48	11	300,000,000	0	0.0	0.0
C- /4.0	17.8	0.96	15.41	22	0	98	1	1	40	N/A	N/A	2	4	0	0	0.3	0.3
U /	N/A	N/A	15.37	151	0	98	1	1	40	N/A	N/A	N/A	4	125,000,000	0	0.3	0.3
U /	N/A	N/A	9.98	433	63	0	36	1	0	N/A	N/A	N/A	3	300,000,000	0	0.2	0.2
U /	N/A	N/A	19.81	845	0	0	0	100	0	N/A	N/A	N/A	1	300,000,000	0	0.5	0.5
C+ /5.9	8.5	1.33	21.16	2,368	4	66	28	2	53	52.9	-9.8	10	10	0	0	0.1	0.1
C+ /6.5	11.7	0.45	22.45	102	0	99	0	1	201	27.1	-18.9	70	13	0	0	0.2	0.5
C /4.9	13.9	1.03	16.41	407	0	96	3	1	49	50.6	-21.3	63	17	0	0	0.0	0.0
C /5.5	9.1	0.92	16.27	237	0	98	0	2	74	82.0	-10.3	49	30	0	0	0.0	0.0
C /5.5	9.1	0.92	16.24	419	0	98	0	2	74	82.5	-10.3	50	30	125,000,000	0	0.0	0.0

					PERFORMANCE							
							Total Return % through 3/31/15				Incl. in Returns	
									Annualized			
Fund Type	Fund Name	Ticker Symbol	Overall Investment Rating	Phone	Perfor-mance Rating/Pts	3 Mo	6 Mo	1Yr / Pct	3Yr / Pct	5Yr / Pct	Dividend Yield	Expense Ratio
IN	GMO US Equity Allocation VI	GMCQX	C		C+ / 6.1	0.62	4.14	7.97 /63	13.53 /64	13.01 /68	1.80	0.39
PM	Gold Bullion Strategy Fund Investor	QGLDX	U	(855) 747-9555	U /	-0.39	-3.57	-9.92 / 3	--	--	0.00	1.66
GR	Golden Large Cap Core Inst	GLDLX	A	(800) 754-8757	A+ / 9.6	3.53	8.43	15.90 /93	18.76 /96	15.42 /90	0.56	0.70
SC	Golden Small Cap Core Inst	GLDSX	A+	(800) 754-8757	A+ / 9.7	5.43	16.28	14.27 /90	18.60 /96	16.66 /95	0.14	1.10
GI	Goldman Sachs Abslt Ret Tracker A	GARTX	D+	(800) 526-7384	E+ / 0.9	1.11	3.41	3.98 /32	3.73 / 9	2.52 / 5	0.00	1.68
GI	Goldman Sachs Abslt Ret Tracker C	GCRTX	D+	(800) 526-7384	D- / 1.0	0.82	3.00	3.11 /27	2.95 / 8	1.74 / 4	0.00	2.43
GI	Goldman Sachs Abslt Ret Tracker I	GJRTX	C-	(800) 526-7384	D- / 1.3	1.08	3.54	4.21 /33	4.13 /11	2.91 / 6	0.42	1.28
GI	Goldman Sachs Abslt Ret Tracker IR	GSRTX	C-	(800) 526-7384	D- / 1.3	1.20	3.53	4.20 /33	3.96 /10	2.77 / 6	0.06	1.43
GI	Goldman Sachs Abslt Ret Tracker R	GRRTX	D+	(800) 526-7384	D- / 1.1	1.02	3.35	3.58 /29	3.48 / 9	2.25 / 5	0.00	1.93
FO	Goldman Sachs Asia Equity A	GSAGX	D-	(800) 526-7384	D / 2.1	7.20	6.18	7.37 /58	5.82 /16	5.32 /13	0.00	2.23
FO	Goldman Sachs Asia Equity C	GSACX	D-	(800) 526-7384	D / 2.0	7.01	5.80	6.61 /52	5.05 /13	4.53 /10	0.00	2.99
FO	Goldman Sachs Asia Equity Inst	GSAIX	D	(800) 526-7384	C- / 3.2	7.33	6.42	7.77 /61	6.25 /18	5.74 /15	0.29	1.86
AA	Goldman Sachs Balanced Strat A	GIPAX	D+	(800) 526-7384	D- / 1.1	1.61	1.01	2.65 /25	5.44 /15	5.07 /12	2.82	1.42
AA	Goldman Sachs Balanced Strat C	GIPCX	C-	(800) 526-7384	D- / 1.3	1.42	0.72	1.96 /22	4.65 /12	4.29 / 9	2.21	2.17
AA	Goldman Sachs Balanced Strat Inst	GIPIX	C-	(800) 526-7384	D / 1.7	1.71	1.30	3.06 /27	5.87 /16	5.50 /14	3.39	1.02
AA	Goldman Sachs Balanced Strat IR	GIPTX	C-	(800) 526-7384	D / 1.7	1.59	1.14	2.82 /26	5.70 /16	5.30 /13	3.25	1.17
AA	Goldman Sachs Balanced Strat R	GIPRX	C-	(800) 526-7384	D- / 1.5	1.56	0.99	2.41 /24	5.21 /14	4.82 /11	2.75	1.67
AA	Goldman Sachs Balanced Strat Svc	GIPSX	C-	(800) 526-7384	D- / 1.5	1.59	1.05	2.54 /24	5.35 /14	4.97 /12	2.87	1.52
EM	Goldman Sachs BRIC A	GBRAX	E	(800) 526-7384	E+ / 0.6	6.59	2.50	4.92 /38	0.98 / 5	-1.45 / 2	0.30	2.04
EM	Goldman Sachs BRIC C	GBRCX	E	(800) 526-7384	E+ / 0.7	6.39	2.10	4.11 /33	0.22 / 4	-2.20 / 2	0.00	2.79
EM	Goldman Sachs BRIC Inst	GBRIX	E	(800) 526-7384	E+ / 0.8	6.71	2.68	5.38 /41	1.38 / 6	-1.05 / 2	0.81	1.63
EM	Goldman Sachs BRIC IR	GIRBX	E	(800) 526-7384	E+ / 0.8	6.65	2.66	5.18 /40	1.23 / 5	--	0.53	1.79
GR	Goldman Sachs Capital Growth A	GSCGX	C-	(800) 526-7384	B / 7.9	3.03	9.55	16.36 /94	16.06 /84	14.07 /78	0.00	1.51
GR	Goldman Sachs Capital Growth C	GSPCX	D+	(800) 526-7384	B+ / 8.3	2.83	9.14	15.50 /92	15.20 /76	13.23 /70	0.00	2.26
GR	Goldman Sachs Capital Growth Inst	GSPIX	C+	(800) 526-7384	A- / 9.1	3.14	9.76	16.84 /94	16.51 /87	14.54 /83	0.00	1.11
GR	Goldman Sachs Capital Growth IR	GSPTX	C	(800) 526-7384	A- / 9.0	3.08	9.67	16.61 /94	16.34 /86	14.37 /81	0.00	1.26
GR	Goldman Sachs Capital Growth R	GSPRX	C	(800) 526-7384	B+ / 8.6	2.93	9.39	16.05 /93	15.76 /81	13.79 /76	0.00	1.76
GR	Goldman Sachs Capital Growth Svc	GSPSX	C	(800) 526-7384	B+ / 8.8	2.99	9.52	16.26 /94	15.94 /83	13.97 /77	0.00	1.61
GI	Goldman Sachs Commodity Strat A	GSCAX	E-	(800) 526-7384	E- / 0.0	-6.68	-29.92	-36.76 / 0	-16.12 / 0	-7.47 / 1	0.00	1.10
GI	Goldman Sachs Commodity Strat C	GSCCX	E-	(800) 526-7384	E- / 0.0	-6.93	-30.20	-37.12 / 0	-16.76 / 0	-8.14 / 1	0.00	1.85
GI	Goldman Sachs Commodity Strat I	GCCIX	E-	(800) 526-7384	E- / 0.0	-6.62	-29.79	-36.45 / 0	-15.81 / 0	-7.14 / 1	0.12	0.76
GI	Goldman Sachs Commodity Strat IR	GCCTX	E-	(800) 526-7384	E- / 0.0	-6.62	-29.83	-36.60 / 0	-15.93 / 0	-7.25 / 1	0.03	0.85
GI	Goldman Sachs Commodity Strat R	GCCRX	E-	(800) 526-7384	E- / 0.0	-7.01	-30.08	-36.97 / 0	-16.37 / 0	-7.73 / 1	0.00	1.35
GR	Goldman Sachs Concentrated Gr A	GCGAX	C-	(800) 526-7384	B- / 7.0	2.99	9.38	15.32 /92	14.84 /74	13.20 /70	0.00	1.59
GR	Goldman Sachs Concentrated Gr C	GCGCX	C-	(800) 526-7384	B- / 7.4	2.78	8.93	14.44 /90	13.98 /67	12.35 /63	0.00	2.34
GR	Goldman Sachs Concentrated Gr Inst	GCRIX	C+	(800) 526-7384	B+ / 8.4	3.03	9.52	15.72 /93	15.31 /77	13.65 /74	0.21	1.19
GR	Goldman Sachs Concentrated Gr IR	GGCTX	C	(800) 526-7384	B+ / 8.3	3.08	9.50	15.58 /93	15.14 /76	13.47 /73	0.07	1.34
GR	Goldman Sachs Concentrated Gr R	GGCRX	C	(800) 526-7384	B / 7.9	2.93	9.25	15.02 /92	14.57 /72	12.93 /68	0.00	1.83
OT	Goldman Sachs Dyn Comm Strat Inst	GDCIX	U	(800) 526-7384	U /	-5.84	-17.09	--	--	--	0.00	N/A
GL	Goldman Sachs Dynamic Alloc A	GDAFX	D	(800) 526-7384	D- / 1.0	2.29	1.82	4.82 /37	4.56 /12	4.73 /11	0.43	1.53
GL	Goldman Sachs Dynamic Alloc C	GDCFX	D	(800) 526-7384	D- / 1.2	2.17	1.48	3.98 /32	3.79 /10	3.97 / 8	0.00	2.28
GL	Goldman Sachs Dynamic Alloc Inst	GDIFX	D	(800) 526-7384	D / 1.6	2.36	1.97	5.22 /40	4.98 /13	5.15 /13	0.96	1.13
GL	Goldman Sachs Dynamic Alloc IR	GDHFX	D	(800) 526-7384	D- / 1.5	2.37	1.88	5.04 /39	4.80 /12	4.98 /12	0.78	1.28
GL	Goldman Sachs Dynamic Alloc R	GDRFX	D	(800) 526-7384	D- / 1.3	2.21	1.66	4.49 /35	4.27 /11	4.47 /10	0.39	1.78
EM	Goldman Sachs EM Eqty Insights A	GERAX	E+	(800) 526-7384	E+ / 0.6	3.86	0.47	4.03 /32	1.62 / 6	2.76 / 6	1.38	1.66
EM	Goldman Sachs EM Eqty Insights C	GERCX	E+	(800) 526-7384	E+ / 0.7	3.63	0.08	3.30 /28	0.85 / 5	1.99 / 4	0.52	2.41
EM	Goldman Sachs EM Eqty Insights Inst	GERIX	E+	(800) 526-7384	E+ / 0.9	3.99	0.73	4.54 /35	2.00 / 6	3.18 / 6	1.83	1.26
EM	Goldman Sachs EM Eqty Insights IR	GIRPX	E+	(800) 526-7384	E+ / 0.9	3.99	0.61	4.42 /35	1.86 / 6	--	1.60	1.39
EM	Goldman Sachs Emerg Mkts Eq A	GEMAX	E	(800) 526-7384	E+ / 0.7	4.37	0.44	5.19 /40	2.06 / 6	1.54 / 4	0.00	1.94
EM	Goldman Sachs Emerg Mkts Eq C	GEMCX	E	(800) 526-7384	E+ / 0.8	4.24	0.14	4.47 /35	1.30 / 6	0.79 / 3	0.00	2.69
EM	Goldman Sachs Emerg Mkts Eq Inst	GEMIX	E+	(800) 526-7384	D- / 1.1	4.54	0.68	5.65 /44	2.47 / 7	1.95 / 4	0.32	1.54
EM	Goldman Sachs Emerg Mkts Eq IR	GIRMX	E+	(800) 526-7384	D- / 1.0	4.43	0.57	5.44 /42	2.31 / 7	--	0.15	1.69

● Denotes fund is closed to new investors
* Denotes fund is included in Section II

www.thestreetratings.com

Risk Rating/Pts	3 Year Standard Deviation	Beta	NAV As of 3/31/15	Total $(Mil)	Cash %	Stocks %	Bonds %	Other %	Portfolio Turnover Ratio	Last Bull Market Return	Last Bear Market Return	Manager Quality Pct	Manager Tenure (Years)	Initial Purch. $	Additional Purch. $	Front End Load	Back End Load
C /5.5	9.1	0.92	16.21	5,736	0	98	0	2	74	82.5	-10.2	50	30	300,000,000	0	0.0	0.0
U /	N/A	N/A	23.24	40	0	0	0	100	0	N/A	N/A	N/A	2	5,000	1,000	0.0	0.0
C+ /5.9	10.2	1.02	14.67	89	1	98	0	1	70	117.4	-20.0	84	20	2,500	1,000	0.0	0.0
C+ /6.4	12.1	0.86	18.45	56	1	98	0	1	68	111.6	-24.8	92	10	2,500	1,000	0.0	0.0
B /8.7	4.3	0.43	9.11	61	88	11	0	1	163	16.8	-8.3	28	N/A	1,000	50	5.5	0.0
B /8.5	4.3	0.43	8.61	28	88	11	0	1	163	13.8	-8.6	20	N/A	1,000	50	0.0	0.0
B /8.7	4.3	0.43	9.32	1,972	88	11	0	1	163	18.2	-8.1	32	N/A	1,000,000	0	0.0	0.0
B /8.7	4.3	0.42	9.26	8	88	11	0	1	163	17.5	-8.2	31	N/A	0	0	0.0	0.0
B /8.6	4.3	0.42	8.94	2	88	11	0	1	163	15.7	-8.5	26	N/A	0	0	0.0	0.0
C+ /5.9	12.0	0.75	21.13	14	0	100	0	0	169	36.4	-24.6	50	4	1,000	50	5.5	0.0
C+ /5.9	12.0	0.74	19.69	2	0	100	0	0	169	33.0	-24.8	39	4	1,000	50	0.0	0.0
C+ /5.9	12.0	0.74	22.11	63	0	100	0	0	169	38.3	-24.5	57	4	1,000,000	0	0.0	0.0
B /8.6	5.4	0.86	11.21	172	14	38	47	1	63	28.8	-10.0	19	N/A	1,000	50	5.5	0.0
B /8.6	5.4	0.85	11.22	61	14	38	47	1	63	25.5	-10.3	14	N/A	1,000	50	0.0	0.0
B /8.6	5.4	0.86	11.22	238	14	38	47	1	63	30.5	-9.9	23	N/A	1,000,000	0	0.0	0.0
B /8.6	5.4	0.86	11.17	5	14	38	47	1	63	29.8	-9.9	22	8	0	0	0.0	0.0
B /8.6	5.4	0.85	11.17	6	14	38	47	1	63	27.6	-10.1	18	8	0	0	0.0	0.0
B /8.6	5.4	0.86	11.25	1	14	38	47	1	63	28.3	-10.1	19	N/A	0	0	0.0	0.0
C- /3.8	17.4	1.20	13.27	52	0	99	0	1	64	20.0	-30.2	69	5	1,000	50	5.5	0.0
C- /3.8	17.4	1.20	12.66	37	0	99	0	1	64	17.0	-30.4	59	5	1,000	50	0.0	0.0
C- /3.8	17.4	1.20	13.51	51	0	99	0	1	64	21.7	-30.1	73	5	1,000,000	0	0.0	0.0
C- /3.8	17.4	1.20	13.64	1	0	99	0	1	64	21.0	-30.2	72	5	0	0	0.0	0.0
D+ /2.8	10.6	1.04	25.87	727	1	98	0	1	75	105.8	-16.7	59	15	1,000	50	5.5	0.0
D- /1.3	10.6	1.03	20.69	83	1	98	0	1	75	100.5	-17.0	47	15	1,000	50	0.0	0.0
C- /3.2	10.6	1.04	27.93	180	1	98	0	1	75	108.5	-16.6	65	15	1,000,000	0	0.0	0.0
D+ /2.8	10.6	1.03	26.12	3	1	98	0	1	75	107.5	-16.6	63	15	0	0	0.0	0.0
D+ /2.6	10.6	1.03	25.26	4	1	98	0	1	75	103.9	-16.8	55	15	0	0	0.0	0.0
D+ /2.6	10.6	1.03	25.17	2	1	98	0	1	75	104.9	-16.7	57	15	0	0	0.0	0.0
D- /1.1	17.0	0.94	3.63	91	54	14	30	2	266	-27.8	-22.9	0	8	1,000	50	4.5	0.0
D- /1.1	16.9	0.94	3.49	7	54	14	30	2	266	-29.5	-23.2	0	8	1,000	50	0.0	0.0
D- /1.2	16.9	0.93	3.67	818	54	14	30	2	266	-26.9	-22.8	0	8	1,000,000	0	0.0	0.0
D- /1.1	17.0	0.95	3.67	8	54	14	30	2	266	-27.2	-22.8	0	8	0	0	0.0	0.0
D- /1.1	17.0	0.95	3.58	2	54	14	30	2	266	-28.4	-23.0	0	8	0	0	0.0	0.0
C- /3.5	10.6	1.02	16.87	8	0	99	0	1	60	97.6	-16.9	47	13	1,000	50	5.5	0.0
D+ /2.9	10.6	1.02	14.80	4	0	99	0	1	60	92.7	-17.1	35	13	1,000	50	0.0	0.0
C- /3.6	10.7	1.02	17.69	170	0	99	0	1	60	100.4	-16.7	52	13	1,000,000	0	0.0	0.0
C- /3.5	10.6	1.02	17.06	N/A	0	99	0	1	60	99.3	-16.7	51	13	0	0	0.0	0.0
C- /3.4	10.7	1.02	16.52	N/A	0	99	0	1	60	96.1	-17.0	42	13	0	0	0.0	0.0
U /	N/A	N/A	7.42	29	0	0	0	100	0	N/A	N/A	N/A	N/A	1,000,000	0	0.0	0.0
B- /7.3	6.6	0.92	10.73	75	65	29	4	2	311	21.2	-9.8	20	5	1,000	50	5.5	0.0
B- /7.1	6.6	0.92	10.37	39	65	29	4	2	311	18.1	-10.2	15	5	1,000	50	0.0	0.0
B- /7.3	6.6	0.91	10.86	628	65	29	4	2	311	22.9	-9.7	25	5	1,000,000	0	0.0	0.0
B- /7.3	6.7	0.92	10.82	18	65	29	4	2	311	22.2	-9.7	22	5	0	0	0.0	0.0
B- /7.2	6.6	0.92	10.63	N/A	65	29	4	2	311	20.1	-9.9	18	5	0	0	0.0	0.0
C /5.2	15.0	1.08	8.62	37	0	99	0	1	180	28.9	-26.8	76	7	1,000	50	5.5	0.0
C /5.2	15.0	1.08	8.57	1	0	99	0	1	180	25.5	-27.0	69	7	1,000	50	0.0	0.0
C /5.2	15.0	1.08	8.60	596	0	99	0	1	180	30.5	-26.7	79	7	1,000,000	0	0.0	0.0
C /5.2	15.0	1.08	8.60	1	0	99	0	1	180	29.9	-26.8	78	7	0	0	0.0	0.0
C /4.6	14.3	1.02	16.00	42	0	99	0	1	114	24.5	-26.4	80	5	1,000	50	5.5	0.0
C /4.6	14.4	1.02	14.50	10	0	99	0	1	114	21.3	-26.6	74	5	1,000	50	0.0	0.0
C /4.6	14.4	1.02	17.05	294	0	99	0	1	114	26.2	-26.3	83	5	1,000,000	0	0.0	0.0
C /4.6	14.4	1.02	16.98	N/A	0	99	0	1	114	25.5	-26.3	82	5	0	0	0.0	0.0

						PERFORMANCE						
	99 Pct = Best			Overall		Perfor-	Total Return % through 3/31/15				Incl. in Returns	
	0 Pct = Worst			Investment		mance				Annualized	Dividend	Expense
Fund		Ticker		Rating	Phone	Rating/Pts	3 Mo	6 Mo	1Yr / Pct	3Yr / Pct	5Yr / Pct	Yield	Ratio
Type	Fund Name	Symbol										

Fund Type	Fund Name	Ticker Symbol	Overall Investment Rating	Phone	Performance Rating/Pts	3 Mo	6 Mo	1Yr / Pct	3Yr / Pct	5Yr / Pct	Dividend Yield	Expense Ratio
EM	Goldman Sachs Emerg Mkts Eq Svc	GEMSX	E	(800) 526-7384	E+ / 0.9	4.44	0.45	5.15 /40	1.96 / 6	1.44 / 4	0.00	2.04
GL	Goldman Sachs Enhanced Div GE A	GADGX	D+	(800) 526-7384	C- / 3.3	3.05	3.52	6.04 /47	9.89 /39	9.39 /40	1.97	1.57
GL	Goldman Sachs Enhanced Div GE	GIDGX	C-	(800) 526-7384	C / 4.4	3.29	3.77	6.49 /51	10.37 /42	9.83 /43	2.43	1.17
AA	Goldman Sachs Equity Gr Strat A	GAPAX	C-	(800) 526-7384	C- / 3.6	2.97	3.11	4.39 /34	10.82 /44	9.02 /37	1.66	1.49
AA	Goldman Sachs Equity Gr Strat C	GAXCX	C-	(800) 526-7384	C- / 4.0	2.82	2.74	3.62 /30	9.99 /39	8.20 /31	1.05	2.24
AA	Goldman Sachs Equity Gr Strat Inst	GAPIX	C	(800) 526-7384	C / 4.8	3.16	3.42	4.83 /37	11.26 /47	9.46 /40	2.13	1.09
AA	Goldman Sachs Equity Gr Strat IR	GAPTX	C	(800) 526-7384	C / 4.6	3.08	3.30	4.67 /36	11.13 /46	9.31 /39	2.06	1.24
AA	Goldman Sachs Equity Gr Strat R	GAPRX	C	(800) 526-7384	C / 4.3	2.99	3.08	4.15 /33	10.56 /43	8.76 /35	1.31	1.74
AA	Goldman Sachs Equity Gr Strat Svc	GAPSX	C	(800) 526-7384	C / 4.4	2.99	3.11	4.25 /33	10.73 /44	8.91 /36	1.61	1.59
FS	Goldman Sachs FI Mac Str Inst	GAAOX	U	(800) 526-7384	U /	-2.82	-7.83	-7.89 / 3	--	--	0.26	2.85
GR	Goldman Sachs Flexible Cap Gr A	GALLX	C+	(800) 526-7384	B+ / 8.5	3.89	9.93	17.05 /95	16.72 /88	14.23 /80	0.00	3.28
GR	Goldman Sachs Flexible Cap Gr C	GCLLX	C+	(800) 526-7384	B+ / 8.8	3.64	9.54	16.11 /93	15.83 /82	13.39 /72	0.00	4.05
GR	Goldman Sachs Flexible Cap Gr I	GILLX	B	(800) 526-7384	A / 9.3	3.89	10.13	17.47 /95	17.16 /91	14.68 /84	0.00	2.88
GR	Goldman Sachs Flexible Cap Gr IR	GSLLX	B-	(800) 526-7384	A / 9.3	3.94	10.08	17.32 /95	17.01 /90	14.51 /82	0.00	3.00
GR	Goldman Sachs Flexible Cap Gr R	GRLLX	B-	(800) 526-7384	A- / 9.1	3.80	9.88	16.75 /94	16.45 /87	13.98 /78	0.00	3.52
GL	Goldman Sachs Focused Growth A	GFGAX	C+	(800) 526-7384	C+ / 6.8	1.45	8.20	13.01 /87	15.11 /76	--	0.00	2.81
GL	Goldman Sachs Focused Growth C	GFGCX	B	(800) 526-7384	B- / 7.2	1.26	7.83	12.14 /83	14.28 /69	--	0.00	3.47
GL	Goldman Sachs Focused Growth Inst	GFGSX	B+	(800) 526-7384	B / 8.2	1.50	8.42	13.44 /88	15.59 /80	--	0.25	2.29
GL	Goldman Sachs Focused Growth IR	GFGIX	B+	(800) 526-7384	B / 8.1	1.50	8.34	13.28 /88	15.42 /78	--	0.11	2.49
GL	Goldman Sachs Focused Growth R	GFGRX	B	(800) 526-7384	B / 7.6	1.38	8.08	12.74 /86	14.84 /74	--	0.00	2.99
FO	Goldman Sachs Focused Intl Eqty A	GSIFX	E+	(800) 526-7384	D- / 1.4	4.47	-2.60	-6.85 / 4	8.01 /27	4.70 /11	2.96	1.63
FO	Goldman Sachs Focused Intl Eqty C	GSICX	D-	(800) 526-7384	D / 1.6	4.29	-2.93	-7.57 / 4	7.23 /23	3.92 / 8	2.59	2.38
FO	Goldman Sachs Focused Intl Eqty I	GSIEX	D-	(800) 526-7384	D / 2.2	4.56	-2.37	-6.50 / 4	8.48 /30	5.13 /13	3.54	1.23
FO	Goldman Sachs Focused Intl Eqty IR	GIRNX	D-	(800) 526-7384	D / 2.2	4.58	-2.46	-6.61 / 4	8.32 /29	--	3.31	1.38
FO	Goldman Sachs Focused Intl Eqty	GSISX	D-	(800) 526-7384	D / 1.9	4.44	-2.62	-6.95 / 4	7.93 /27	4.61 /11	3.03	1.73
AA	Goldman Sachs Gr and Inc Strat A	GOIAX	C-	(800) 526-7384	D / 1.6	2.21	1.80	3.20 /27	7.15 /22	6.44 /20	2.43	1.42
AA	Goldman Sachs Gr and Inc Strat C	GOICX	C-	(800) 526-7384	D / 1.9	2.02	1.39	2.40 /24	6.34 /18	5.64 /15	2.11	2.17
AA	Goldman Sachs Gr and Inc Strat Inst	GOIIX	C	(800) 526-7384	D+ / 2.6	2.31	1.99	3.60 /29	7.56 /24	6.85 /22	2.97	1.02
AA	Goldman Sachs Gr and Inc Strat IR	GPITX	C	(800) 526-7384	D+ / 2.5	2.29	1.93	3.47 /29	7.43 /24	6.69 /21	2.84	1.17
AA	Goldman Sachs Gr and Inc Strat R	GPIRX	C-	(800) 526-7384	D / 2.2	2.17	1.60	2.87 /26	6.87 /21	6.17 /18	2.34	1.67
AA	Goldman Sachs Gr and Inc Strat Svc	GOISX	C-	(800) 526-7384	D+ / 2.3	2.19	1.66	3.01 /26	7.02 /21	6.32 /19	2.48	1.52
GI	Goldman Sachs Growth & Income A	GSGRX	B-	(800) 526-7384	C+ / 6.7	0.59	4.40	9.55 /72	15.92 /83	11.44 /56	1.29	1.23
GI	Goldman Sachs Growth & Income C	GSGCX	B+	(800) 526-7384	B- / 7.1	0.38	4.02	8.71 /68	15.06 /75	10.61 /50	0.72	1.98
GI	Goldman Sachs Growth & Income	GSIIX	A	(800) 526-7384	B / 8.1	0.68	4.63	9.99 /74	16.39 /86	11.88 /60	1.72	0.83
GI	Goldman Sachs Growth & Income IR	GRGTX	A	(800) 526-7384	B / 8.0	0.66	4.57	9.85 /74	16.22 /85	11.73 /59	1.62	0.97
GI	Goldman Sachs Growth & Income R	GRGRX	A-	(800) 526-7384	B- / 7.5	0.54	4.29	9.29 /71	15.65 /80	11.17 /54	1.16	1.48
GI	Goldman Sachs Growth & Income	GSGSX	A-	(800) 526-7384	B / 7.6	0.58	4.38	9.46 /72	15.82 /82	11.34 /56	1.25	1.33
MC	Goldman Sachs Growth Opps A	GGOAX	D+	(800) 526-7384	C+ / 6.6	2.05	7.57	11.36 /80	15.01 /75	14.08 /78	0.00	1.40
MC	Goldman Sachs Growth Opps C	GGOCX	D	(800) 526-7384	C+ / 6.9	1.86	7.18	10.53 /76	14.14 /68	13.23 /70	0.00	2.15
MC	Goldman Sachs Growth Opps Inst	GGOIX	C	(800) 526-7384	B / 8.0	2.16	7.80	11.83 /82	15.46 /79	14.54 /83	0.00	1.00
MC	Goldman Sachs Growth Opps IR	GGOTX	C-	(800) 526-7384	B / 7.8	2.12	7.70	11.64 /81	15.29 /77	14.36 /81	0.00	1.15
MC	Goldman Sachs Growth Opps R	GGORX	C-	(800) 526-7384	B- / 7.4	1.98	7.47	11.09 /79	14.72 /73	13.80 /76	0.00	1.65
MC	Goldman Sachs Growth Opps Svc	GGOSX	C-	(800) 526-7384	B- / 7.5	2.03	7.51	11.23 /79	14.88 /74	13.97 /77	0.00	1.50
AA	Goldman Sachs Growth Strategy A	GGSAX	C-	(800) 526-7384	D+ / 2.5	2.87	2.67	4.01 /32	8.91 /32	7.58 /27	2.04	1.45
AA	Goldman Sachs Growth Strategy C	GGSCX	C-	(800) 526-7384	D+ / 2.9	2.64	2.28	3.22 /28	8.08 /27	6.78 /22	1.32	2.20
AA	Goldman Sachs Growth Strategy Inst	GGSIX	C	(800) 526-7384	C- / 3.7	2.95	2.84	4.41 /34	9.33 /35	8.00 /30	2.54	1.05
AA	Goldman Sachs Growth Strategy IR	GGSTX	C	(800) 526-7384	C- / 3.6	2.99	2.81	4.33 /34	9.19 /34	7.86 /29	2.44	1.20
AA	Goldman Sachs Growth Strategy R	GGSRX	C-	(800) 526-7384	C- / 3.2	2.77	2.45	3.66 /30	8.63 /31	7.31 /25	1.78	1.70
AA	Goldman Sachs Growth Strategy Svc	GGSSX	C	(800) 526-7384	C- / 3.3	2.80	2.62	3.88 /31	8.80 /32	7.49 /26	1.96	1.55
BA	Goldman Sachs Income Builder A	GSBFX	D+	(800) 526-7384	D+ / 2.5	1.89	1.34	3.03 /27	9.14 /34	9.52 /41	4.03	1.13
BA	Goldman Sachs Income Builder C	GSBCX	C-	(800) 526-7384	D+ / 2.8	1.73	0.99	2.28 /23	8.34 /29	8.70 /35	3.59	1.88
BA	Goldman Sachs Income Builder Inst	GSBIX	C-	(800) 526-7384	C- / 3.6	1.99	1.56	3.42 /29	9.58 /37	9.95 /44	4.58	0.73

www.thestreetratings.com

RISK			NET ASSETS		ASSET					BULL / BEAR		FUND MANAGER		MINIMUMS		LOADS	
	3 Year		NAV						Portfolio	Last Bull	Last Bear	Manager	Manager	Initial	Additional	Front	Back
Risk Rating/Pts	Standard Deviation	Beta	As of 3/31/15	Total $(Mil)	Cash %	Stocks %	Bonds %	Other %	Turnover Ratio	Market Return	Market Return	Quality Pct	Tenure (Years)	Purch. $	Purch. $	End Load	End Load
C /4.6	14.4	1.02	15.52	16	0	99	0	1	114	24.1	-26.4	79	5	0	0	0.0	0.0
C+/5.9	9.1	0.65	11.34	1	0	91	8	1	14	60.3	-17.2	90	11	1,000	50	5.5	0.0
C+/6.0	9.0	0.64	11.40	390	0	91	8	1	14	62.5	-16.9	91	11	1,000,000	0	0.0	0.0
C+/6.9	10.7	1.74	14.89	148	2	97	0	1	23	67.6	-22.2	3	N/A	1,000	50	5.5	0.0
C+/6.9	10.6	1.74	14.22	95	2	97	0	1	23	63.4	-22.4	3	N/A	1,000	50	0.0	0.0
C+/6.9	10.7	1.74	15.04	122	2	97	0	1	23	70.0	-22.1	4	N/A	1,000,000	0	0.0	0.0
C+/6.9	10.6	1.73	14.71	6	2	97	0	1	23	69.0	-22.0	4	N/A	0	0	0.0	0.0
C+/6.9	10.7	1.74	14.80	2	2	97	0	1	23	66.3	-22.3	3	N/A	0	0	0.0	0.0
C+/6.9	10.6	1.73	14.83	1	2	97	0	1	23	67.0	-22.2	3	N/A	0	0	0.0	0.0
U /	N/A	N/A	9.05	72	0	0	0	100	0	N/A	N/A	N/A	2	1,000,000	0	0.0	0.0
C- /3.9	10.6	1.03	12.29	7	4	95	0	1	56	107.5	-19.1	68	7	1,000	50	5.5	0.0
C- /3.6	10.7	1.04	11.39	2	4	95	0	1	56	102.2	-19.4	56	7	1,000	50	0.0	0.0
C- /4.0	10.6	1.03	12.82	9	4	95	0	1	56	110.3	-19.0	72	7	1,000,000	0	0.0	0.0
C- /4.0	10.6	1.04	12.66	N/A	4	95	0	1	56	109.2	-19.0	70	7	0	0	0.0	0.0
C- /3.8	10.6	1.03	12.02	N/A	4	95	0	1	56	105.7	-19.2	65	7	0	0	0.0	0.0
C+/6.4	10.4	0.61	14.73	N/A	2	97	0	1	97	N/A	N/A	97	3	1,000	50	5.5	0.0
C+/6.4	10.5	0.61	14.42	N/A	2	97	0	1	97	N/A	N/A	97	3	1,000	50	0.0	0.0
C+/6.4	10.5	0.61	14.85	31	2	97	0	1	97	N/A	N/A	97	3	1,000,000	0	0.0	0.0
C+/6.4	10.4	0.61	14.84	N/A	2	97	0	1	97	N/A	N/A	97	3	0	0	0.0	0.0
C+/6.4	10.4	0.61	14.67	N/A	2	97	0	1	97	N/A	N/A	97	3	0	0	0.0	0.0
C /5.3	13.5	0.98	18.01	52	0	100	0	0	121	48.6	-24.9	49	3	1,000	50	5.5	0.0
C /5.3	13.5	0.98	16.77	18	0	100	0	0	121	44.9	-25.2	38	3	1,000	50	0.0	0.0
C /5.3	13.5	0.98	18.33	142	0	100	0	0	121	50.7	-24.8	56	3	1,000,000	0	0.0	0.0
C /5.3	13.5	0.98	18.26	2	0	100	0	0	121	50.0	-24.9	54	3	0	0	0.0	0.0
C /5.3	13.5	0.98	18.10	N/A	0	100	0	0	121	48.0	-25.0	48	3	0	0	0.0	0.0
B /8.3	7.2	1.18	12.35	396	12	59	27	2	50	40.0	-14.2	9	N/A	1,000	50	5.5	0.0
B /8.3	7.2	1.18	12.15	166	12	59	27	2	50	36.6	-14.5	6	N/A	1,000	50	0.0	0.0
B /8.3	7.3	1.19	12.39	416	12	59	27	2	50	42.0	-14.1	10	N/A	1,000,000	0	0.0	0.0
B /8.3	7.2	1.18	12.30	3	12	59	27	2	50	41.1	-14.1	10	8	0	0	0.0	0.0
B /8.3	7.2	1.18	12.28	3	12	59	27	2	50	38.9	-14.3	8	8	0	0	0.0	0.0
B /8.3	7.2	1.18	12.32	4	12	59	27	2	50	39.6	-14.3	8	N/A	0	0	0.0	0.0
B- /7.4	10.1	1.02	32.62	411	4	95	0	1	40	97.9	-21.8	60	14	1,000	50	5.5	0.0
B- /7.3	10.1	1.02	31.18	26	4	95	0	1	40	93.0	-22.1	48	14	1,000	50	0.0	0.0
B- /7.4	10.1	1.02	33.13	30	4	95	0	1	40	100.7	-21.7	66	14	1,000,000	0	0.0	0.0
B- /7.4	10.1	1.02	32.55	4	4	95	0	1	40	99.7	-21.7	64	14	0	0	0.0	0.0
B- /7.4	10.1	1.02	32.48	2	4	95	0	1	40	96.2	-21.9	56	14	0	0	0.0	0.0
B- /7.4	10.1	1.02	32.62	N/A	4	95	0	1	40	97.2	-21.8	59	14	0	0	0.0	0.0
D+/2.8	11.1	0.92	25.34	1,059	1	98	0	1	59	105.2	-23.3	60	16	1,000	50	5.5	0.0
D /1.7	11.1	0.92	20.21	187	1	98	0	1	59	100.0	-23.5	48	16	1,000	50	0.0	0.0
C- /3.3	11.1	0.92	28.35	3,689	1	98	0	1	59	107.9	-23.1	66	16	1,000,000	0	0.0	0.0
D+/2.9	11.1	0.92	26.04	172	1	98	0	1	59	106.9	-23.2	63	16	0	0	0.0	0.0
D+/2.7	11.1	0.92	24.70	87	1	98	0	1	59	103.4	-23.3	56	16	0	0	0.0	0.0
D+/2.7	11.1	0.92	24.58	56	1	98	0	1	59	104.5	-23.3	58	16	0	0	0.0	0.0
B- /7.6	9.2	1.51	13.28	382	11	80	8	1	32	52.9	-18.9	4	N/A	1,000	50	5.5	0.0
B- /7.6	9.2	1.51	13.22	187	11	80	8	1	32	49.1	-19.2	3	N/A	1,000	50	0.0	0.0
B- /7.6	9.2	1.51	13.28	296	11	80	8	1	32	55.1	-18.9	5	N/A	1,000,000	0	0.0	0.0
B- /7.6	9.2	1.51	13.11	4	11	80	8	1	32	54.2	-18.9	5	8	0	0	0.0	0.0
B- /7.6	9.2	1.50	12.97	3	11	80	8	1	32	51.6	-19.1	4	8	0	0	0.0	0.0
B- /7.6	9.2	1.51	13.24	2	11	80	8	1	32	52.5	-18.9	4	N/A	0	0	0.0	0.0
B- /7.2	5.9	0.98	22.70	693	9	41	48	2	52	50.6	-8.4	46	3	1,000	50	5.5	0.0
B- /7.2	5.9	0.98	22.38	621	9	41	48	2	52	46.8	-8.7	36	3	1,000	50	0.0	0.0
B- /7.2	5.9	0.98	23.13	692	9	41	48	2	52	52.7	-8.2	53	3	1,000,000	0	0.0	0.0

Fund Type	Fund Name	Ticker Symbol	Overall Investment Rating	Phone	PERFORMANCE							Incl. in Returns	
					Performance Rating/Pts	Total Return % through 3/31/15			Annualized			Dividend Yield	Expense Ratio
						3 Mo	6 Mo	1Yr / Pct	3Yr / Pct	5Yr / Pct			
BA	Goldman Sachs Income Builder IR	GKIRX	C-	(800) 526-7384	C- / 3.5	1.96	1.49	3.32 / 28	9.42 / 36	--	4.44	0.88
FO	Goldman Sachs Intl Eq Div and Prm	GIDAX	E+	(800) 526-7384	E+ / 0.7	0.96	-4.38	-6.25 / 4	4.72 / 12	3.42 / 7	2.65	1.36
FO	Goldman Sachs Intl Eq Div and Prm	GIDCX	E+	(800) 526-7384	E+ / 0.7	0.67	-4.77	-7.00 / 4	3.90 / 10	2.64 / 5	2.22	2.11
FO	Goldman Sachs Intl Eq Div and Prm I	GIDHX	E+	(800) 526-7384	D- / 1.0	1.07	-4.12	-5.83 / 5	5.16 / 14	3.85 / 8	3.27	0.96
FO	Goldman Sachs Intl Eq Dv and Prm	GIRVX	E+	(800) 526-7384	E+ / 0.9	1.03	-4.21	-5.99 / 4	4.93 / 13	--	3.10	1.11
FO	Goldman Sachs Intl Eq Insights A	GCIAX	D-	(800) 526-7384	D / 1.8	5.92	0.09	-3.15 / 8	8.25 / 28	4.66 / 11	3.70	1.36
FO	Goldman Sachs Intl Eq Insights C	GCICX	D-	(800) 526-7384	D / 2.1	5.89	-0.30	-3.83 / 7	7.45 / 24	3.90 / 8	3.20	2.11
FO	Goldman Sachs Intl Eq Insights Inst	GCIIX	D	(800) 526-7384	D+ / 2.8	6.08	0.33	-2.74 / 9	8.70 / 31	5.09 / 12	4.24	0.96
FO	Goldman Sachs Intl Eq Insights IR	GCITX	D	(800) 526-7384	D+ / 2.7	6.02	0.21	-2.89 / 9	8.51 / 30	4.92 / 12	4.20	1.10
FO	Goldman Sachs Intl Eq Insights R	GCIRX	D-	(800) 526-7384	D+ / 2.4	5.93	-0.11	-3.39 / 8	7.95 / 27	4.44 / 10	3.98	1.61
FO	Goldman Sachs Intl Eq Insights Svc	GCISX	D	(800) 526-7384	D+ / 2.5	5.97	0.01	-3.20 / 8	8.12 / 28	4.56 / 10	3.52	1.45
RE	Goldman Sachs Intl Rel Est Sec A	GIRAX	C-	(800) 526-7384	C- / 4.1	4.39	5.54	7.12 / 56	10.95 / 45	7.62 / 27	3.30	1.60
RE	Goldman Sachs Intl Rel Est Sec C	GIRCX	C-	(800) 526-7384	C / 4.4	4.08	4.98	6.16 / 48	10.15 / 40	6.82 / 22	2.74	2.35
RE	Goldman Sachs Intl Rel Est Sec Inst	GIRIX	C	(800) 526-7384	C / 5.2	4.52	5.62	7.47 / 59	11.38 / 48	8.01 / 30	4.04	1.20
RE	Goldman Sachs Intl Rel Est Sec IR	GIRTX	C	(800) 526-7384	C / 5.1	4.42	5.62	7.36 / 58	11.25 / 47	7.89 / 29	3.69	1.35
FO	Goldman Sachs Intl SC Insights A	GICAX	D+	(800) 526-7384	C- / 3.5	6.00	3.82	-2.62 / 9	11.34 / 48	10.10 / 45	1.50	1.39
FO	Goldman Sachs Intl SC Insights C	GICCX	C-	(800) 526-7384	C- / 3.9	5.83	3.43	-3.24 / 8	10.54 / 43	9.30 / 39	1.17	2.15
FO	Goldman Sachs Intl SC Insights Inst	GICIX	C-	(800) 526-7384	C / 4.6	6.12	4.02	-2.24 / 10	11.77 / 51	10.54 / 49	1.96	0.99
FO	Goldman Sachs Intl SC Insights IR	GIRLX	C-	(800) 526-7384	C / 4.5	6.03	3.90	-2.37 / 10	11.62 / 50	--	1.84	1.14
FO	Goldman Sachs Intl Sm Cap A	GISAX	D	(800) 526-7384	D+ / 2.8	4.63	2.62	-2.41 / 10	10.24 / 41	9.54 / 41	1.31	1.77
FO	Goldman Sachs Intl Sm Cap C	GISCX	D+	(800) 526-7384	C- / 3.2	4.47	2.22	-3.14 / 8	9.42 / 36	8.73 / 35	0.86	2.52
FO	Goldman Sachs Intl Sm Cap Inst	GISIX	C-	(800) 526-7384	C- / 4.0	4.72	2.78	-2.03 / 10	10.67 / 43	10.02 / 45	1.77	1.37
FO	Goldman Sachs Intl Sm Cap IR	GIRSX	C-	(800) 526-7384	C- / 3.9	4.68	2.71	-2.20 / 10	10.49 / 42	--	1.70	1.52
FO	Goldman Sachs Intl Sm Cap Svc	GISSX	D+	(800) 526-7384	C- / 3.6	4.58	2.54	-2.50 / 9	10.11 / 40	9.44 / 40	1.35	1.86
FO	Goldman Sachs Intl Tax Mgd Eq A	GATMX	D-	(800) 526-7384	D / 2.1	5.44	1.10	-1.94 / 10	8.72 / 31	5.65 / 15	2.15	1.48
FO	Goldman Sachs Intl Tax Mgd Eq C	GCTMX	D	(800) 526-7384	D+ / 2.5	5.32	0.77	-2.55 / 9	7.95 / 27	4.86 / 11	1.98	2.23
FO	Goldman Sachs Intl Tax Mgd Eq Inst	GHTMX	D+	(800) 526-7384	C- / 3.2	5.62	1.39	-1.46 / 12	9.18 / 34	6.06 / 17	2.80	1.08
FO	Goldman Sachs Intl Tax Mgd Eq IR	GITRX	D	(800) 526-7384	C- / 3.1	5.58	1.22	-1.62 / 11	9.01 / 33	--	2.61	1.23
GR	Goldman Sachs Large Cap Value A	GSLAX	C+	(800) 526-7384	C+ / 6.4	-0.28	3.10	8.49 / 66	15.79 / 82	11.34 / 56	0.72	1.20
GR	Goldman Sachs Large Cap Value C	GSVCX	C+	(800) 526-7384	C+ / 6.8	-0.47	2.71	7.71 / 61	14.92 / 74	10.50 / 49	0.09	1.95
GR	Goldman Sachs Large Cap Value Inst	GSLIX	B+	(800) 526-7384	B / 7.8	-0.23	3.31	8.91 / 69	16.26 / 85	11.77 / 59	1.14	0.80
GR	Goldman Sachs Large Cap Value IR	GSVTX	B+	(800) 526-7384	B / 7.6	-0.23	3.24	8.81 / 68	16.10 / 84	11.61 / 58	0.00	0.95
GR	Goldman Sachs Large Cap Value R	GSVRX	B	(800) 526-7384	B- / 7.2	-0.35	2.93	8.22 / 64	15.50 / 79	11.05 / 53	0.62	1.45
GR	Goldman Sachs Large Cap Value Svc	GSVSX	B+	(800) 526-7384	B- / 7.4	-0.29	3.07	8.43 / 66	15.69 / 81	11.24 / 55	0.73	1.30
GR	Goldman Sachs LC Gro Insights A	GLCGX	A+	(800) 526-7384	B+ / 8.8	2.80	8.92	17.89 / 95	17.82 / 94	16.06 / 93	0.63	1.20
GR	Goldman Sachs LC Gro Insights C	GLCCX	A+	(800) 526-7384	A- / 9.1	2.57	8.50	16.98 / 95	16.95 / 90	15.21 / 88	0.24	1.95
GR	Goldman Sachs LC Gro Insights Inst	GCGIX	A+	(800) 526-7384	A / 9.5	2.90	9.16	18.34 / 96	18.28 / 95	16.53 / 95	0.93	0.80
GR	Goldman Sachs LC Gro Insights IR	GLCTX	A+	(800) 526-7384	A / 9.5	2.84	9.03	18.11 / 96	18.11 / 95	16.35 / 94	1.00	0.97
GR	Goldman Sachs LC Gro Insights R	GLCRX	A+	(800) 526-7384	A / 9.3	2.71	8.78	17.57 / 95	17.53 / 92	15.77 / 92	0.78	1.45
GR	Goldman Sachs LC Gro Insights Svc	GSCLX	A+	(800) 526-7384	A / 9.4	2.78	8.88	17.74 / 95	17.71 / 93	15.95 / 93	0.89	1.30
GI	Goldman Sachs LC Val Insights A	GCVAX	B-	(800) 526-7384	C+ / 6.9	-0.26	5.24	9.51 / 72	16.26 / 85	14.01 / 78	1.15	1.14
GI	Goldman Sachs LC Val Insights C	GCVCX	B+	(800) 526-7384	B- / 7.3	-0.44	4.83	8.79 / 68	15.41 / 78	13.17 / 70	0.50	1.89
GI	Goldman Sachs LC Val Insights Inst	GCVIX	A+	(800) 526-7384	B+ / 8.3	-0.16	5.45	10.02 / 74	16.75 / 88	14.49 / 82	1.60	0.74
GI	Goldman Sachs LC Val Insights IR	GCVTX	A+	(800) 526-7384	B / 8.2	-0.20	5.32	9.77 / 73	16.53 / 87	14.31 / 80	1.48	0.88
GI	Goldman Sachs LC Val Insights R	GCVRX	A-	(800) 526-7384	B / 7.7	-0.31	5.08	9.23 / 71	15.97 / 83	13.74 / 75	1.06	1.39
GI	Goldman Sachs LC Val Insights Svc	GCLSX	A	(800) 526-7384	B / 7.9	-0.28	5.16	9.43 / 72	16.14 / 84	13.90 / 77	1.11	1.24
GL	Goldman Sachs Long Short Instl	GSLSX	U	(800) 526-7384	U /	3.54	5.40	--	--	--	0.00	N/A
IN	Goldman Sachs Mgd Fut Strat A	GMSAX	C-	(800) 526-7384	D / 1.8	9.82	10.33	11.59 / 81	2.77 / 7	--	0.00	2.62
IN	Goldman Sachs Mgd Fut Strat C	GMSCX	C-	(800) 526-7384	D / 2.1	9.63	9.91	10.72 / 77	1.93 / 6	--	0.00	3.37
IN	Goldman Sachs Mgd Fut Strat Inst	GMSSX	C	(800) 526-7384	D+ / 2.8	9.93	10.54	12.02 / 83	3.12 / 8	--	0.00	2.22
IN	Goldman Sachs Mgd Fut Strat IR	GFIRX	C	(800) 526-7384	D+ / 2.7	9.87	10.36	11.85 / 82	2.96 / 8	--	0.00	2.37
IN	Goldman Sachs Mgd Fut Strat R	GFFRX	C	(800) 526-7384	D+ / 2.4	9.80	10.19	11.35 / 80	2.48 / 7	--	0.00	2.87

• Denotes fund is closed to new investors
* Denotes fund is included in Section II

www.thestreetratings.com

RISK			NET ASSETS		ASSET					BULL / BEAR		FUND MANAGER		MINIMUMS		LOADS	
	3 Year		NAV						Portfolio	Last Bull	Last Bear	Manager	Manager	Initial	Additional	Front	Back
Risk	Standard		As of	Total	Cash	Stocks	Bonds	Other	Turnover	Market	Market	Quality	Tenure	Purch.	Purch.	End	End
Rating/Pts	Deviation	Beta	3/31/15	$(Mil)	%	%	%	%	Ratio	Return	Return	Pct	(Years)	$	$	Load	Load
B- /7.2	5.9	0.97	23.08	111	9	41	48	2	52	51.9	-8.3	51	3	0	0	0.0	0.0
C /5.3	12.8	0.95	7.16	10	0	100	0	0	97	34.0	-22.2	16	5	1,000	50	5.5	0.0
C /5.3	12.8	0.95	6.95	3	0	100	0	0	97	30.7	-22.4	11	5	1,000	50	0.0	0.0
C /5.3	12.8	0.95	7.05	365	0	100	0	0	97	35.9	-22.1	19	5	1,000,000	0	0.0	0.0
C /5.3	12.9	0.96	7.04	1	0	100	0	0	97	35.1	-22.1	17	5	0	0	0.0	0.0
C /5.5	13.1	0.97	10.38	79	0	99	0	1	142	48.0	-26.5	53	18	1,000	50	5.5	0.0
C+ /5.6	13.0	0.97	10.25	3	0	99	0	1	142	44.2	-26.7	42	18	1,000	50	0.0	0.0
C /5.5	13.1	0.97	10.64	642	0	99	0	1	142	50.0	-26.4	60	18	1,000,000	0	0.0	0.0
C /5.5	13.0	0.97	10.21	N/A	0	99	0	1	142	49.2	-26.4	57	18	0	0	0.0	0.0
C /5.5	13.0	0.97	10.19	N/A	0	99	0	1	142	46.7	-26.6	50	18	0	0	0.0	0.0
C+ /5.6	13.0	0.97	10.48	2	0	99	0	1	142	47.4	-26.5	52	18	0	0	0.0	0.0
C+ /5.9	13.5	0.75	6.66	10	19	80	0	1	45	63.6	-24.4	73	N/A	1,000	50	5.5	0.0
C+ /5.9	13.5	0.74	6.64	2	19	80	0	1	45	59.3	-24.4	65	N/A	1,000	50	0.0	0.0
C+ /5.8	13.4	0.74	6.47	390	19	80	0	1	45	65.6	-24.2	77	N/A	1,000,000	0	0.0	0.0
C+ /5.8	13.6	0.75	6.61	N/A	19	80	0	1	45	65.0	-24.2	74	N/A	0	0	0.0	0.0
C+ /6.1	13.3	0.94	10.24	152	1	98	0	1	129	59.7	-21.9	85	8	1,000	50	5.5	0.0
C+ /6.0	13.3	0.95	9.98	22	1	98	0	1	129	55.7	-22.1	80	8	1,000	50	0.0	0.0
C+ /6.0	13.3	0.95	10.23	672	1	98	0	1	129	62.0	-21.8	87	8	1,000,000	0	0.0	0.0
C+ /6.1	13.3	0.95	10.20	24	1	98	0	1	129	61.2	-21.8	86	8	0	0	0.0	0.0
C+ /6.1	12.5	0.88	19.21	15	0	99	0	1	100	58.4	-23.5	82	7	1,000	50	5.5	0.0
C+ /6.1	12.5	0.88	18.48	4	0	99	0	1	100	54.5	-23.7	77	7	1,000	50	0.0	0.0
C+ /6.1	12.5	0.88	19.75	154	0	99	0	1	100	60.9	-23.4	85	7	1,000,000	0	0.0	0.0
C+ /6.1	12.5	0.89	19.69	5	0	99	0	1	100	59.7	-23.4	84	7	0	0	0.0	0.0
C+ /6.1	12.5	0.88	18.95	1	0	99	0	1	100	57.9	-23.5	81	7	0	0	0.0	0.0
C+ /5.9	13.4	1.00	8.91	2	0	100	0	0	95	50.8	-23.8	56	5	1,000	50	5.5	0.0
C+ /5.9	13.4	1.00	8.71	N/A	0	100	0	0	95	46.8	-24.0	45	5	1,000	50	0.0	0.0
C+ /5.9	13.4	1.00	8.83	376	0	100	0	0	95	52.6	-23.6	63	5	1,000,000	0	0.0	0.0
C+ /5.9	13.3	1.00	8.90	N/A	0	100	0	0	95	51.8	-23.7	61	5	0	0	0.0	0.0
C+ /6.8	10.8	1.08	17.57	258	1	98	0	1	67	99.3	-22.6	45	14	1,000	50	5.5	0.0
C+ /6.8	10.8	1.08	16.97	46	1	98	0	1	67	94.4	-22.9	34	14	1,000	50	0.0	0.0
C+ /6.8	10.8	1.09	17.71	1,198	1	98	0	1	67	102.1	-22.5	50	14	1,000,000	0	0.0	0.0
C+ /6.9	10.8	1.08	17.58	7	1	98	0	1	67	101.1	-22.6	49	14	0	0	0.0	0.0
C+ /6.8	10.8	1.08	17.24	8	1	98	0	1	67	97.6	-22.7	41	14	0	0	0.0	0.0
C+ /6.8	10.8	1.08	17.49	4	1	98	0	1	67	98.7	-22.7	44	14	0	0	0.0	0.0
B- /7.3	10.3	1.04	22.74	131	4	95	0	1	234	112.6	-15.1	75	4	1,000	50	5.5	0.0
B- /7.3	10.4	1.05	20.76	34	4	95	0	1	234	107.3	-15.4	67	4	1,000	50	0.0	0.0
B- /7.3	10.3	1.05	23.41	440	4	95	0	1	234	115.6	-15.0	78	4	1,000,000	0	0.0	0.0
B- /7.3	10.3	1.04	22.46	19	4	95	0	1	234	114.5	-15.1	77	4	0	0	0.0	0.0
B- /7.3	10.3	1.04	22.36	3	4	95	0	1	234	110.9	-15.2	73	4	0	0	0.0	0.0
B- /7.3	10.3	1.04	22.52	1	4	95	0	1	234	111.9	-15.1	75	4	0	0	0.0	0.0
B- /7.5	10.2	1.04	17.19	67	2	97	0	1	222	100.1	-17.4	60	4	1,000	50	5.5	0.0
B- /7.5	10.3	1.05	17.06	17	2	97	0	1	222	95.1	-17.7	47	4	1,000	50	0.0	0.0
B- /7.5	10.2	1.04	17.18	395	2	97	0	1	222	102.9	-17.3	66	4	1,000,000	0	0.0	0.0
B- /7.5	10.2	1.04	17.14	7	2	97	0	1	222	101.8	-17.3	64	4	0	0	0.0	0.0
B- /7.5	10.2	1.04	17.12	1	2	97	0	1	222	98.4	-17.5	56	4	0	0	0.0	0.0
B- /7.5	10.3	1.04	17.26	7	2	97	0	1	222	99.5	-17.5	58	4	0	0	0.0	0.0
U /	N/A	N/A	10.54	73	0	0	0	100	0	N/A	N/A	N/A	1	1,000,000	0	0.0	0.0
B /8.6	8.6	0.08	10.62	3	0	0	0	100	0	N/A	N/A	81	3	1,000	0	5.5	0.0
B /8.6	8.6	0.08	10.36	1	0	0	0	100	0	N/A	N/A	75	3	1,000	50	0.0	0.0
B /8.6	8.6	0.08	10.74	94	0	0	0	100	0	N/A	N/A	83	3	1,000,000	0	0.0	0.0
B /8.6	8.6	0.08	10.69	1	0	0	0	100	0	N/A	N/A	82	3	0	0	0.0	0.0
B /8.6	8.7	0.08	10.53	N/A	0	0	0	100	0	N/A	N/A	78	3	0	0	0.0	0.0

Fund Type	Fund Name	Ticker Symbol	Overall Investment Rating	Phone	PERFORMANCE Performance Rating/Pts	Total Return % through 3/31/15 3 Mo	6 Mo	1Yr / Pct	Annualized 3Yr / Pct	5Yr / Pct	Incl. in Returns Dividend Yield	Expense Ratio
MC	Goldman Sachs Mid Cap Value A	GCMAX	C	(800) 526-7384	B / 7.8	1.84	7.55	11.25 /79	16.96 /90	14.04 /78	0.25	1.14
MC	Goldman Sachs Mid Cap Value C	GCMCX	C	(800) 526-7384	B / 8.2	1.65	7.12	10.41 /76	16.09 /84	13.18 /70	0.00	1.89
MC	Goldman Sachs Mid Cap Value Inst	GSMCX	C+	(800) 526-7384	A- / 9.0	1.92	7.75	11.68 /81	17.43 /92	14.49 /82	0.79	0.74
MC	Goldman Sachs Mid Cap Value IR	GCMTX	C+	(800) 526-7384	B+ / 8.9	1.87	7.67	11.53 /81	17.25 /91	14.32 /81	0.68	0.89
MC	Goldman Sachs Mid Cap Value Svc	GSMSX	C+	(800) 526-7384	B+ / 8.7	1.80	7.48	11.12 /79	16.85 /89	13.93 /77	0.17	1.24
MC	Goldman Sachs MidCap Val R	GCMRX	C+	(800) 526-7384	B+ / 8.6	1.75	7.39	10.97 /78	16.67 /88	13.75 /75	0.24	1.39
EN	Goldman Sachs MLP Energy Infr A	GLPAX	U	(800) 526-7384	U /	-2.35	-11.19	-0.62 /14	--	--	4.47	9.78
EN	Goldman Sachs MLP Energy Infr C	GLPCX	U	(800) 526-7384	U /	-2.47	-11.47	-1.32 /12	--	--	4.80	10.53
EN	Goldman Sachs MLP Energy Infr Inst	GMLPX	U	(800) 526-7384	U /	-2.16	-10.96	-0.18 /15	--	--	4.69	9.38
EN	Goldman Sachs MLP Energy Infr IR	GLPIX	U	(800) 526-7384	U /	-2.25	-11.05	-0.27 /15	--	--	4.70	9.53
GL	Goldman Sachs Multi-Mgr Alt A	GMAMX	U	(800) 526-7384	U /	3.31	4.31	5.80 /45	--	--	0.31	4.12
GL	Goldman Sachs Multi-Mgr Alt C	GMCMX	U	(800) 526-7384	U /	3.15	3.95	5.05 /39	--	--	0.05	4.87
GL	Goldman Sachs Multi-Mgr Alt Inst	GSMMX	U	(800) 526-7384	U /	3.49	4.50	6.19 /48	--	--	0.61	3.72
GL	Goldman Sachs Multi-Mgr Alt IR	GIMMX	U	(800) 526-7384	U /	3.40	4.45	6.04 /47	--	--	0.56	3.86
GL	● Goldman Sachs N-11 Equity A	GSYAX	E+	(800) 526-7384	E / 0.4	-2.17	-8.88	-5.47 / 5	1.73 / 6	--	0.01	2.07
GL	● Goldman Sachs N-11 Equity C	GSYCX	E+	(800) 526-7384	E / 0.4	-2.42	-9.27	-6.23 / 4	0.97 / 5	--	0.00	2.82
GL	● Goldman Sachs N-11 Equity Inst	GSYIX	E+	(800) 526-7384	E / 0.5	-2.16	-8.75	-5.19 / 5	2.11 / 6	--	0.48	1.67
GL	● Goldman Sachs N-11 Equity IR	GSYRX	E+	(800) 526-7384	E / 0.5	-2.17	-8.76	-5.27 / 5	1.96 / 6	--	0.30	1.81
RE	Goldman Sachs Real Estate Sec A	GREAX	C+	(800) 526-7384	B / 8.2	4.02	18.55	23.16 /98	13.16 /61	15.46 /90	1.38	1.51
RE	Goldman Sachs Real Estate Sec C	GRECX	C+	(800) 526-7384	B+ / 8.6	3.84	18.15	22.19 /97	12.31 /55	14.60 /83	1.00	2.26
RE	Goldman Sachs Real Estate Sec Inst	GREIX	B-	(800) 526-7384	A- / 9.2	4.15	18.81	23.60 /98	13.61 /64	15.94 /93	1.71	1.11
RE	Goldman Sachs Real Estate Sec IR	GRETX	B-	(800) 526-7384	A- / 9.2	4.12	18.67	23.46 /98	13.45 /63	15.74 /91	1.65	1.26
RE	Goldman Sachs Real Estate Sec R	GRERX	B-	(800) 526-7384	B+ / 8.9	3.94	18.41	22.84 /98	12.88 /59	15.19 /88	1.34	1.76
RE	Goldman Sachs Real Estate Sec Svc	GRESX	B-	(800) 526-7384	A- / 9.0	4.01	18.52	22.97 /98	13.02 /60	15.34 /89	1.38	1.61
GI	Goldman Sachs Rising Div Gr A	GSRAX	B-	(800) 526-7384	C+ / 5.7	0.91	3.85	10.81 /78	13.98 /67	12.92 /67	0.77	1.16
IN	Goldman Sachs Rising Div Gr C	GSRCX	B-	(800) 526-7384	C+ / 6.1	0.73	3.45	9.94 /74	13.13 /61	12.30 /63	0.12	1.91
GI	Goldman Sachs Rising Div Gr Inst	GSRLX	B-	(800) 526-7384	C+ / 6.9	0.99	4.06	11.26 /79	14.43 /70	13.42 /72	1.17	0.76
IN	Goldman Sachs Rising Div Gr IR	GSRIX	B-	(800) 526-7384	C+ / 6.8	0.95	3.94	11.06 /79	14.25 /69	--	1.04	0.91
IN	Goldman Sachs Rising Div Gr R	GSRRX	B-	(800) 526-7384	C+ / 6.4	0.85	3.73	10.51 /76	13.70 /65	--	0.58	1.41
GL	Goldman Sachs Satellite Strat A	GXSAX	D-	(800) 526-7384	E+ / 0.8	2.42	0.41	-0.11 /15	4.05 /10	5.47 /14	2.68	1.50
GL	Goldman Sachs Satellite Strat C	GXSCX	D-	(800) 526-7384	E+ / 0.9	2.24	0.03	-0.87 /13	3.25 / 8	4.67 /11	2.08	2.25
GL	Goldman Sachs Satellite Strat I	GXSIX	D	(800) 526-7384	D- / 1.2	2.53	0.49	0.30 /16	4.44 /11	5.85 /16	3.27	1.10
GL	Goldman Sachs Satellite Strat IR	GXSTX	D	(800) 526-7384	D- / 1.1	2.49	0.54	0.14 /16	4.28 /11	5.70 /15	3.11	1.25
GL	Goldman Sachs Satellite Strat R	GXSRX	D	(800) 526-7384	D- / 1.0	2.37	0.27	-0.25 /15	3.81 /10	5.22 /13	2.58	1.75
GL	Goldman Sachs Satellite Strat Svc	GXSSX	D	(800) 526-7384	D- / 1.1	2.50	0.46	-0.12 /15	4.00 /10	5.36 /14	2.84	1.60
SC	Goldman Sachs SC Eqty Insights A	GCSAX	B	(800) 526-7384	B / 7.7	6.83	18.43	13.05 /87	15.10 /76	14.87 /86	0.00	1.51
SC	Goldman Sachs SC Eqty Insights C	GCSCX	B	(800) 526-7384	B / 8.1	6.64	18.00	12.21 /84	14.23 /69	14.03 /78	0.00	2.26
SC	Goldman Sachs SC Eqty Insights Inst	GCSIX	B+	(800) 526-7384	A- / 9.0	6.91	18.64	13.50 /88	15.57 /80	15.34 /89	0.33	1.11
SC	Goldman Sachs SC Eqty Insights IR	GDSTX	B+	(800) 526-7384	B+ / 8.9	6.88	18.52	13.30 /88	15.38 /78	15.15 /88	0.12	1.24
SC	Goldman Sachs SC Eqty Insights R	GDSRX	B+	(800) 526-7384	B+ / 8.6	6.77	18.28	12.78 /86	14.83 /74	14.59 /83	0.00	1.76
SC	Goldman Sachs SC Eqty Insights Svc	GCSSX	B+	(800) 526-7384	B+ / 8.6	6.82	18.32	12.95 /86	14.99 /75	14.75 /85	0.00	1.60
SC	Goldman Sachs SC Gro Insights A	GSAOX	B+	(800) 526-7384	B+ / 8.8	7.82	17.94	14.04 /89	16.81 /89	17.14 /96	0.00	1.87
SC	Goldman Sachs SC Gro Insights C	GSCOX	B	(800) 526-7384	A- / 9.1	7.58	17.50	13.15 /87	15.93 /83	16.25 /94	0.00	2.62
SC	Goldman Sachs SC Gro Insights Inst	GSIOX	A-	(800) 526-7384	A / 9.5	7.90	18.17	14.45 /90	17.28 /91	17.59 /97	0.00	1.48
SC	Goldman Sachs SC Gro Insights IR	GSTOX	B+	(800) 526-7384	A / 9.5	7.86	18.08	14.29 /90	17.09 /90	17.43 /97	0.00	1.63
SC	Goldman Sachs SC Gro Insights R	GSROX	B+	(800) 526-7384	A / 9.3	7.73	17.76	13.71 /89	16.52 /87	16.83 /96	0.00	2.10
SC	Goldman Sachs SC Val Insights A	GSATX	C+	(800) 526-7384	C+ / 6.0	4.17	15.74	9.17 /70	13.32 /62	13.06 /69	0.32	1.60
SC	Goldman Sachs SC Val Insights C	GSCTX	C+	(800) 526-7384	C+ / 6.4	3.94	15.30	8.32 /65	12.47 /56	12.20 /62	0.00	2.35
SC	Goldman Sachs SC Val Insights Inst	GSITX	B	(800) 526-7384	B- / 7.3	4.28	15.99	9.60 /72	13.78 /65	13.51 /73	0.56	1.21
SC	Goldman Sachs SC Val Insights IR	GTTTX	B-	(800) 526-7384	B- / 7.2	4.24	15.89	9.44 /72	13.60 /64	13.34 /71	0.57	1.36
SC	Goldman Sachs SC Val Insights R	GTTRX	C+	(800) 526-7384	C+ / 6.8	4.07	15.58	8.87 /69	13.03 /60	12.77 /66	0.06	1.85
SC	● Goldman Sachs Small Cap Value A	GSSMX	B-	(800) 526-7384	B- / 7.5	2.85	11.03	7.87 /62	16.57 /87	15.34 /89	0.17	1.40

● Denotes fund is closed to new investors
* Denotes fund is included in Section II

www.thestreetratings.com

RISK			NET ASSETS		ASSET						BULL / BEAR		FUND MANAGER		MINIMUMS		LOADS	
	3 Year		NAV							Portfolio	Last Bull	Last Bear	Manager	Manager	Initial	Additional	Front	Back
Risk	Standard		As of	Total	Cash	Stocks	Bonds	Other		Turnover	Market	Market	Quality	Tenure	Purch.	Purch.	End	End
Rating/Pts	Deviation	Beta	3/31/15	$(Mil)	%	%	%	%		Ratio	Return	Return	Pct	(Years)	$	$	Load	Load
C- / 3.8	9.8	0.85	42.01	2,227	2	97	0	1		87	99.5	-22.3	86	14	1,000	50	5.5	0.0
C- / 3.4	9.8	0.85	38.87	201	2	97	0	1		87	94.4	-22.5	81	14	1,000	50	0.0	0.0
C- / 3.7	9.8	0.85	42.38	6,410	2	97	0	1		87	102.1	-22.1	87	14	1,000,000	0	0.0	0.0
C- / 3.6	9.8	0.85	41.33	371	2	97	0	1		87	101.2	-22.2	87	14	0	0	0.0	0.0
C- / 3.7	9.8	0.85	41.37	271	2	97	0	1		87	98.8	-22.3	85	14	0	0	0.0	0.0
C- / 3.7	9.8	0.85	41.17	44	2	97	0	1		87	97.7	-22.3	84	14	0	0	0.0	0.0
U /	N/A	N/A	11.15	477	0	0	0	100		25	N/A	N/A	N/A	2	1,000	50	5.5	0.0
U /	N/A	N/A	10.99	251	0	0	0	100		25	N/A	N/A	N/A	2	1,000	50	0.0	0.0
U /	N/A	N/A	11.25	1,548	0	0	0	100		25	N/A	N/A	N/A	2	1,000,000	0	0.0	0.0
U /	N/A	N/A	11.22	152	0	0	0	100		25	N/A	N/A	N/A	2	0	0	0.0	0.0
U /	N/A	N/A	10.93	138	31	28	38	3		102	N/A	N/A	N/A	N/A	1,000	50	5.5	0.0
U /	N/A	N/A	10.80	50	31	28	38	3		102	N/A	N/A	N/A	N/A	1,000	50	0.0	0.0
U /	N/A	N/A	10.98	772	31	28	38	3		102	N/A	N/A	N/A	N/A	1,000,000	0	0.0	0.0
U /	N/A	N/A	10.96	71	31	28	38	3		102	N/A	N/A	N/A	N/A	0	0	0.0	0.0
C+ / 5.7	12.4	0.71	10.35	78	1	98	0	1		41	18.1	-19.9	11	3	1,000	50	5.5	0.0
C+ / 5.6	12.5	0.72	10.08	12	1	98	0	1		41	15.1	-20.2	8	3	1,000	50	0.0	0.0
C+ / 5.7	12.5	0.72	10.40	252	1	98	0	1		41	19.8	-19.8	13	3	1,000,000	0	0.0	0.0
C+ / 5.7	12.4	0.72	10.38	22	1	98	0	1		41	19.1	-19.8	12	3	0	0	0.0	0.0
C- / 4.1	12.6	1.00	20.50	70	0	100	0	0		61	83.6	-16.2	54	5	1,000	50	5.5	0.0
C- / 4.1	12.5	1.00	19.97	18	0	100	0	0		61	79.0	-16.4	43	5	1,000	50	0.0	0.0
C- / 4.1	12.5	1.00	20.87	513	0	100	0	0		61	86.1	-16.0	60	5	1,000,000	0	0.0	0.0
C- / 4.1	12.5	1.00	20.58	7	0	100	0	0		61	85.1	-16.1	58	5	0	0	0.0	0.0
C- / 4.1	12.5	1.00	20.39	2	0	100	0	0		61	82.2	-16.3	50	5	0	0	0.0	0.0
C- / 4.1	12.6	1.01	20.62	3	0	100	0	0		61	82.9	-16.2	52	5	0	0	0.0	0.0
B- / 7.5	9.2	0.91	21.66	1,164	20	79	0	1		12	76.6	-12.4	60	11	1,000	50	5.5	0.0
B- / 7.5	9.2	0.91	21.83	753	20	79	0	1		12	72.3	-12.5	48	11	1,000	50	0.0	0.0
B- / 7.5	9.2	0.91	22.11	1,720	20	79	0	1		12	79.1	-12.1	66	11	1,000,000	0	0.0	0.0
B- / 7.5	9.2	0.91	22.09	510	20	79	0	1		12	N/A	N/A	64	11	0	0	0.0	0.0
B- / 7.5	9.2	0.91	21.61	8	20	79	0	1		12	N/A	N/A	56	11	0	0	0.0	0.0
B- / 7.1	8.0	1.13	8.02	165	6	53	40	1		36	28.8	-13.6	7	8	1,000	50	5.5	0.0
B- / 7.1	8.1	1.15	7.97	96	6	53	40	1		36	25.7	-14.0	5	8	1,000	50	0.0	0.0
B- / 7.1	8.1	1.14	8.00	842	6	53	40	1		36	30.7	-13.5	8	8	1,000,000	0	0.0	0.0
B- / 7.1	8.1	1.14	8.00	88	6	53	40	1		36	29.9	-13.6	8	8	0	0	0.0	0.0
B- / 7.1	8.0	1.14	7.99	4	6	53	40	1		36	27.9	-13.7	6	8	0	0	0.0	0.0
B- / 7.1	8.1	1.13	7.98	8	6	53	40	1		36	28.5	-13.7	7	8	0	0	0.0	0.0
C+ / 5.8	13.1	0.95	20.18	41	2	97	0	1		130	93.8	-22.8	63	4	1,000	50	5.5	0.0
C+ / 5.8	13.1	0.95	17.83	16	2	97	0	1		130	89.1	-23.1	51	4	1,000	50	0.0	0.0
C+ / 5.8	13.1	0.95	20.90	109	2	97	0	1		130	96.7	-22.7	68	4	1,000,000	0	0.0	0.0
C+ / 5.8	13.1	0.95	20.05	1	2	97	0	1		130	95.5	-22.7	66	4	0	0	0.0	0.0
C+ / 5.8	13.1	0.96	19.86	9	2	97	0	1		130	92.4	-23.0	59	4	0	0	0.0	0.0
C+ / 5.8	13.1	0.96	19.89	1	2	97	0	1		130	93.2	-22.9	61	4	0	0	0.0	0.0
C / 5.3	13.1	0.96	32.83	40	4	95	0	1		162	107.6	-23.4	78	4	1,000	50	5.5	0.0
C / 5.0	13.2	0.96	27.10	8	4	95	0	1		162	102.5	-23.6	71	4	1,000	50	0.0	0.0
C / 5.5	13.2	0.96	37.28	38	4	95	0	1		162	110.4	-23.2	81	4	1,000,000	0	0.0	0.0
C / 5.4	13.2	0.96	33.33	2	4	95	0	1		162	109.4	-23.3	79	4	0	0	0.0	0.0
C / 5.3	13.1	0.96	32.05	1	4	95	0	1		162	105.9	-23.5	76	4	0	0	0.0	0.0
C+ / 6.1	12.8	0.93	40.97	105	2	97	0	1		114	83.2	-21.9	45	4	1,000	50	5.5	0.0
C+ / 6.1	12.8	0.93	31.90	19	2	97	0	1		114	78.6	-22.1	34	4	1,000	50	0.0	0.0
C+ / 6.1	12.8	0.93	51.20	19	2	97	0	1		114	85.7	-21.8	51	4	1,000,000	0	0.0	0.0
C+ / 6.1	12.8	0.93	40.85	2	2	97	0	1		114	84.7	-21.8	48	4	0	0	0.0	0.0
C+ / 6.1	12.8	0.93	40.62	1	2	97	0	1		114	81.6	-22.0	40	4	0	0	0.0	0.0
C+ / 5.6	12.2	0.89	53.81	1,085	2	97	0	1		46	105.7	-22.8	84	9	1,000	50	5.5	0.0

							PERFORMANCE						
99 Pct = Best								Total Return % through 3/31/15					Incl. in Returns
0 Pct = Worst				Overall		Perfor-					Annualized		Dividend Expense
Fund			Ticker	Investment		mance							
Type	Fund Name		Symbol	Rating	Phone	Rating/Pts	3 Mo	6 Mo	1Yr / Pct	3Yr / Pct	5Yr / Pct	Yield	Ratio
SC	● Goldman Sachs Small Cap Value C	GSSCX		C+	(800) 526-7384	B / 7.9	2.66	10.61	7.07 /56	15.70 /81	14.48 /82	0.00	2.15
SC	● Goldman Sachs Small Cap Value Inst	GSSIX		B+	(800) 526-7384	B+ / 8.8	2.95	11.23	8.29 /65	17.03 /90	15.80 /92	0.53	1.00
SC	● Goldman Sachs Small Cap Value IR	GSQTX		B+	(800) 526-7384	B+ / 8.7	2.90	11.16	8.15 /64	16.86 /89	15.63 /91	0.43	1.15
SC	● Goldman Sachs Small Cap Value R	GSQRX		B	(800) 526-7384	B+ / 8.3	2.79	10.88	7.61 /60	16.27 /85	15.05 /87	0.00	1.65
SC	● Goldman Sachs Small Cap Value Svc	GSSSX		B	(800) 526-7384	B+ / 8.4	2.82	10.98	7.75 /61	16.45 /87	15.22 /88	0.07	1.50
MC	Goldman Sachs Small/Mid-Cap Gr A	GSMAX		B+	(800) 526-7384	B+ / 8.7	4.43	12.92	11.66 /81	17.79 /94	15.66 /91	0.00	1.47
MC	Goldman Sachs Small/Mid-Cap Gr C	GSMGX		B+	(800) 526-7384	A- / 9.0	4.17	12.51	10.79 /78	16.90 /89	14.78 /85	0.00	2.22
MC	Goldman Sachs Small/Mid-Cap Gr	GSMYX		A	(800) 526-7384	A / 9.5	4.53	13.15	12.09 /83	18.26 /95	16.11 /93	0.00	1.07
MC	Goldman Sachs Small/Mid-Cap Gr IR	GTMTX		A	(800) 526-7384	A / 9.4	4.48	13.06	11.93 /82	18.09 /95	15.95 /93	0.00	1.22
MC	Goldman Sachs Small/Mid-Cap Gr R	GTMRX		A-	(800) 526-7384	A / 9.3	4.32	12.76	11.37 /80	17.48 /92	15.37 /89	0.00	1.72
MC	Goldman Sachs Small/Mid-Cap Gr	GSMQX		A-	(800) 526-7384	A / 9.3	4.36	12.87	11.54 /81	17.66 /93	15.53 /90	0.00	1.57
GR	Goldman Sachs Strategic Gr A	GGRAX		C	(800) 526-7384	B / 8.0	3.10	8.44	16.30 /94	16.35 /86	13.86 /76	0.00	1.53
GR	Goldman Sachs Strategic Gr C	GGRCX		C	(800) 526-7384	B+ / 8.4	2.83	8.10	15.39 /92	15.50 /79	13.00 /68	0.00	2.28
GR	Goldman Sachs Strategic Gr Inst	GSTIX		B-	(800) 526-7384	A- / 9.1	3.18	8.68	16.80 /94	16.85 /89	14.33 /81	0.29	1.13
GR	Goldman Sachs Strategic Gr IR	GSTTX		B-	(800) 526-7384	A- / 9.1	3.10	8.59	16.62 /94	16.67 /88	14.13 /79	0.14	1.28
GR	Goldman Sachs Strategic Gr R	GSTRX		C+	(800) 526-7384	B+ / 8.8	3.04	8.33	16.06 /93	16.15 /84	13.64 /74	0.00	1.75
GR	Goldman Sachs Strategic Gr Svc	GSTSX		C+	(800) 526-7384	B+ / 8.9	3.11	8.47	16.17 /93	16.27 /85	13.79 /76	0.00	1.63
FO	Goldman Sachs Strategic Intl Eq A	GSAKX		D-	(800) 526-7384	D / 2.1	6.18	0.31	-2.05 /10	8.77 /31	5.71 /15	3.50	1.79
FO	Goldman Sachs Strategic Intl Eq C	GSCKX		D-	(800) 526-7384	D+ / 2.4	6.04	-0.01	-2.77 / 9	7.98 /27	4.93 /12	3.25	2.54
FO	Goldman Sachs Strategic Intl Eq I	GSIKX		D	(800) 526-7384	C- / 3.2	6.31	0.48	-1.71 /11	9.20 /34	6.11 /17	3.93	1.39
FO	Goldman Sachs Strategic Intl Eq IR	GSTKX		D	(800) 526-7384	C- / 3.1	6.27	0.41	-1.87 /11	9.05 /33	6.07 /17	4.02	1.54
FO	Goldman Sachs Strategic Intl Eq R	GSRKX		D-	(800) 526-7384	D+ / 2.8	6.15	0.19	-2.37 /10	8.51 /30	5.44 /14	3.41	2.04
GL	Goldman Sachs Tax-Advtg GE A	TAGGX		C-	(800) 526-7384	C / 5.0	3.34	4.56	6.77 /53	13.05 /60	11.26 /55	0.72	1.52
GL	Goldman Sachs Tax-Advtg GE Inst	TIGGX		C+	(800) 526-7384	C+ / 6.2	3.44	4.75	7.21 /57	13.48 /63	11.71 /58	1.37	1.12
TC	Goldman Sachs Tech Tollkeeper A	GITAX		C-	(800) 526-7384	C / 5.5	3.37	7.48	12.71 /86	12.67 /57	13.13 /69	0.00	1.54
TC	Goldman Sachs Tech Tollkeeper C	GITCX		C-	(800) 526-7384	C+ / 5.9	3.26	7.11	11.92 /82	11.86 /51	12.29 /62	0.00	2.29
TC	Goldman Sachs Tech Tollkeeper Inst	GITIX		C	(800) 526-7384	C+ / 6.8	3.52	7.71	13.16 /87	13.12 /61	13.59 /74	0.00	1.14
TC	Goldman Sachs Tech Tollkeeper IR	GISTX		C	(800) 526-7384	C+ / 6.6	3.44	7.65	12.96 /86	12.96 /59	--	0.00	1.29
TC	Goldman Sachs Tech Tollkeeper Svc	GITSX		C	(800) 526-7384	C+ / 6.4	3.36	7.46	12.63 /85	12.56 /56	13.02 /68	0.00	1.64
IN	Goldman Sachs US Eqty Divi & Pre A	GSPAX		C+	(800) 526-7384	C / 5.0	1.80	5.37	11.64 /81	12.38 /55	12.26 /62	1.64	1.21
IN	Goldman Sachs US Eqty Divi & Pre C	GSPQX		C+	(800) 526-7384	C / 5.4	1.54	4.91	10.76 /77	11.53 /49	11.40 /56	1.03	1.96
IN	Goldman Sachs US Eqty Divi & Pre I	GSPKX		B-	(800) 526-7384	C+ / 6.2	1.91	5.50	12.12 /83	12.82 /58	12.71 /66	2.13	0.81
IN	Goldman Sachs US Eqty Divi & Pre	GVIRX		B-	(800) 526-7384	C+ / 6.1	1.78	5.42	11.84 /82	12.65 /57	--	1.98	0.96
GI	Goldman Sachs US Eqty Insights A	GSSQX		A	(800) 526-7384	B / 7.9	1.09	6.96	13.64 /89	17.00 /90	15.00 /87	0.66	1.21
GI	Goldman Sachs US Eqty Insights C	GSUSX		A+	(800) 526-7384	B+ / 8.3	0.90	6.55	12.76 /86	16.13 /84	14.14 /79	0.09	1.96
GI	Goldman Sachs US Eqty Insights Inst	GSELX		A+	(800) 526-7384	A- / 9.1	1.18	7.18	14.08 /90	17.46 /92	15.45 /90	1.06	0.81
GI	Goldman Sachs US Eqty Insights IR	GSUTX		A+	(800) 526-7384	A- / 9.0	1.15	7.07	13.92 /89	17.29 /91	15.28 /89	0.98	0.96
GI	Goldman Sachs US Eqty Insights R	GSURX		A+	(800) 526-7384	B+ / 8.7	1.00	6.81	13.34 /88	16.71 /88	14.71 /84	0.79	1.46
GI	Goldman Sachs US Eqty Insights Svc	GSESX		A+	(800) 526-7384	B+ / 8.8	1.04	6.88	13.51 /88	16.88 /89	14.88 /86	0.62	1.31
GR	Goldman Sachs US Equity A	GAGVX		C	(800) 526-7384	C+ / 6.8	0.62	5.75	11.46 /80	15.64 /80	12.53 /64	0.43	3.00
GR	Goldman Sachs US Equity C	GCGVX		C	(800) 526-7384	B- / 7.2	0.42	5.36	10.66 /77	14.78 /73	11.68 /58	0.00	3.74
GR	Goldman Sachs US Equity Inst	GINGX		C+	(800) 526-7384	B / 8.2	0.68	5.93	11.90 /82	16.12 /84	12.99 /68	0.80	2.61
GR	Goldman Sachs US Equity IR	GIRGX		C+	(800) 526-7384	B / 8.0	0.62	5.85	11.75 /81	15.93 /83	12.82 /67	0.67	2.76
GR	Goldman Sachs US Equity R	GRGVX		C+	(800) 526-7384	B / 7.6	0.48	5.57	11.14 /79	15.33 /78	12.25 /62	0.22	3.26
GR	Goldman Sachs US Tax Mgd Eq A	GCTAX		A-	(800) 526-7384	B / 8.1	1.38	7.44	11.77 /82	17.39 /92	15.34 /89	0.36	1.21
GR	Goldman Sachs US Tax Mgd Eq C	GCTCX		A	(800) 526-7384	B+ / 8.4	1.20	7.04	10.91 /78	16.51 /87	14.49 /82	0.00	1.96
GR	Goldman Sachs US Tax Mgd Eq Inst	GCTIX		A+	(800) 526-7384	A- / 9.2	1.47	7.62	12.16 /83	17.85 /94	15.81 /92	0.72	0.81
GR	Goldman Sachs US Tax Mgd Eq IR	GQIRX		A+	(800) 526-7384	A- / 9.1	1.41	7.49	11.96 /82	17.68 /93	--	0.60	0.96
GR	Goldman Sachs US Tax Mgd Eq Svc	GCTSX		A+	(800) 526-7384	B+ / 8.9	1.37	7.37	11.69 /81	17.26 /91	15.23 /88	0.00	1.31
GL	Golub Group Equity Fund	GGEFX		C+	(866) 954-6682	C+ / 6.2	-0.63	2.27	8.55 /67	13.82 /66	12.21 /62	0.33	1.46
AA	Good Harbor Tactical Core US A	GHUAX		U	(877) 270-2848	U /	-1.17	-3.60	-14.56 / 2	--	--	0.00	1.48
AA	Good Harbor Tactical Core US C	GHUCX		U	(877) 270-2848	U /	-1.40	-3.96	-15.16 / 2	--	--	0.00	2.23

● Denotes fund is closed to new investors
* Denotes fund is included in Section II

www.thestreetratings.com

| RISK | 3 Year | | NET ASSETS | | ASSET | | | | Portfolio | BULL / BEAR | | FUND MANAGER | | MINIMUMS | | LOADS | |
Risk Rating/Pts	Standard Deviation	Beta	NAV As of 3/31/15	Total $(Mil)	Cash %	Stocks %	Bonds %	Other %	Turnover Ratio	Last Bull Market Return	Last Bear Market Return	Manager Quality Pct	Manager Tenure (Years)	Initial Purch. $	Additional Purch. $	Front End Load	Back End Load
C /5.0	12.2	0.89	43.62	69	2	97	0	1	46	100.5	-23.1	78	9	1,000	50	0.0	0.0
C+ /5.7	12.2	0.89	57.29	4,789	2	97	0	1	46	108.5	-22.7	86	9	1,000,000	0	0.0	0.0
C /5.5	12.2	0.89	53.50	137	2	97	0	1	46	107.5	-22.8	85	9	0	0	0.0	0.0
C+ /5.6	12.2	0.89	52.97	153	2	97	0	1	46	104.0	-22.9	82	9	0	0	0.0	0.0
C /5.5	12.3	0.89	52.44	156	2	97	0	1	46	105.1	-22.9	83	9	0	0	0.0	0.0
C+ /5.8	11.6	0.96	21.21	841	1	98	0	1	43	114.8	-22.9	79	10	1,000	50	5.5	0.0
C+ /5.6	11.6	0.96	19.24	251	1	98	0	1	43	109.2	-23.1	72	10	1,000	50	0.0	0.0
C+ /5.9	11.6	0.96	22.16	1,271	1	98	0	1	43	117.8	-22.8	82	10	1,000,000	0	0.0	0.0
C+ /5.9	11.6	0.96	21.69	194	1	98	0	1	43	116.5	-22.7	81	10	0	0	0.0	0.0
C+ /5.8	11.6	0.96	20.75	37	1	98	0	1	43	112.9	-22.9	77	10	0	0	0.0	0.0
C+ /5.8	11.7	0.96	20.84	11	1	98	0	1	43	114.1	-22.9	78	10	0	0	0.0	0.0
C- /3.8	10.5	1.02	12.30	47	1	98	0	1	64	104.4	-15.7	66	15	1,000	50	5.5	0.0
C- /3.1	10.5	1.02	10.53	12	1	98	0	1	64	99.2	-15.9	55	15	1,000	50	0.0	0.0
C- /3.9	10.5	1.02	12.98	350	1	98	0	1	64	107.1	-15.5	71	15	1,000,000	0	0.0	0.0
C- /3.9	10.5	1.02	12.98	1	1	98	0	1	64	106.1	-15.7	70	15	0	0	0.0	0.0
C- /3.8	10.5	1.01	12.19	N/A	1	98	0	1	64	103.0	-15.7	65	15	0	0	0.0	0.0
C- /3.8	10.5	1.02	12.26	N/A	1	98	0	1	64	103.9	-15.7	66	15	0	0	0.0	0.0
C /5.2	13.1	0.98	13.23	23	0	99	0	1	89	50.2	-23.8	61	3	1,000	50	5.5	0.0
C /5.2	13.1	0.97	11.93	5	0	99	0	1	89	46.4	-24.0	50	3	1,000	50	0.0	0.0
C /5.2	13.1	0.97	13.82	38	0	99	0	1	89	52.3	-23.6	67	3	1,000,000	0	0.0	0.0
C /5.1	13.1	0.98	13.23	N/A	0	99	0	1	89	51.5	-23.6	64	3	0	0	0.0	0.0
C /5.2	13.1	0.97	13.30	N/A	0	99	0	1	89	49.0	-23.9	57	3	0	0	0.0	0.0
C+ /5.7	10.2	0.72	13.32	N/A	0	90	8	2	9	78.4	-18.5	95	7	1,000	50	5.5	0.0
C+ /5.7	10.1	0.72	13.24	1,604	0	90	8	2	9	80.9	-18.4	95	7	1,000,000	0	0.0	0.0
C /4.8	13.5	1.09	18.40	272	3	96	0	1	39	96.5	-23.6	14	16	1,000	50	5.5	0.0
C /4.6	13.4	1.08	16.17	58	3	96	0	1	39	91.5	-23.9	10	16	1,000	50	0.0	0.0
C /4.9	13.5	1.09	19.70	96	3	96	0	1	39	99.1	-23.5	17	16	1,000,000	0	0.0	0.0
C /4.9	13.4	1.08	19.55	7	3	96	0	1	39	98.1	-23.6	16	16	0	0	0.0	0.0
C /4.8	13.5	1.08	18.16	11	3	96	0	1	39	95.9	-23.6	14	16	0	0	0.0	0.0
B- /7.0	8.0	0.82	11.90	168	0	100	0	0	69	75.0	-13.0	58	5	1,000	50	5.5	0.0
B- /7.1	8.0	0.82	11.87	74	0	100	0	0	69	70.9	-13.4	47	5	1,000	50	0.0	0.0
B- /7.0	8.1	0.82	11.87	1,172	0	100	0	0	69	77.5	-12.9	64	5	1,000,000	0	0.0	0.0
B- /7.0	8.0	0.82	11.88	40	0	100	0	0	69	76.7	-13.0	62	5	0	0	0.0	0.0
B- /7.4	10.1	1.05	41.71	286	2	97	0	1	222	104.1	-15.3	67	4	1,000	50	5.5	0.0
B- /7.4	10.1	1.05	38.27	40	2	97	0	1	222	99.0	-15.6	57	4	1,000	50	0.0	0.0
B- /7.4	10.1	1.05	42.76	151	2	97	0	1	222	106.9	-15.2	72	4	1,000,000	0	0.0	0.0
B- /7.4	10.1	1.05	41.31	6	2	97	0	1	222	105.8	-15.3	70	4	0	0	0.0	0.0
B- /7.4	10.1	1.05	41.21	27	2	97	0	1	222	102.4	-15.4	64	4	0	0	0.0	0.0
B- /7.4	10.1	1.05	41.64	3	2	97	0	1	222	103.4	-15.4	67	4	0	0	0.0	0.0
C /4.4	10.1	1.04	14.67	3	1	98	0	1	67	98.9	-19.9	53	6	1,000	50	5.5	0.0
C /4.5	10.1	1.04	14.34	N/A	1	98	0	1	67	93.8	-20.1	41	6	1,000	50	0.0	0.0
C /4.4	10.1	1.04	14.74	9	1	98	0	1	67	101.7	-19.7	60	6	1,000,000	0	0.0	0.0
C /4.4	10.1	1.04	14.72	N/A	1	98	0	1	67	100.4	-19.7	56	6	0	0	0.0	0.0
C /4.5	10.1	1.04	14.64	N/A	1	98	0	1	67	97.2	-19.9	49	6	0	0	0.0	0.0
B- /7.2	10.6	1.09	17.68	55	0	100	0	0	95	108.0	-16.7	63	5	1,000	50	5.5	0.0
B- /7.2	10.6	1.09	16.87	18	0	100	0	0	95	102.5	-17.0	52	5	1,000	50	0.0	0.0
B- /7.2	10.6	1.09	17.95	881	0	100	0	0	95	110.7	-16.5	68	5	1,000,000	0	0.0	0.0
B- /7.2	10.6	1.09	17.95	6	0	100	0	0	95	109.4	-16.5	67	5	0	0	0.0	0.0
B- /7.2	10.6	1.09	17.77	1	0	100	0	0	95	107.2	-16.7	63	5	0	0	0.0	0.0
C+ /6.4	10.1	0.57	18.89	48	7	92	0	1	30	89.7	-13.5	97	6	1,000	0	0.0	0.0
U /	N/A	N/A	9.31	101	32	17	50	1	773	N/A	N/A	N/A	3	2,500	250	5.8	1.0
U /	N/A	N/A	9.16	141	32	17	50	1	773	N/A	N/A	N/A	3	2,500	250	0.0	1.0

Fund Type	Fund Name	Ticker Symbol	Overall Investment Rating	Phone	Performance Rating/Pts	3 Mo	6 Mo	1Yr / Pct	3Yr / Pct	5Yr / Pct	Dividend Yield	Expense Ratio
	99 Pct = Best / 0 Pct = Worst				PERFORMANCE — Total Return % through 3/31/15 / Annualized / Incl. in Returns							
AA	Good Harbor Tactical Core US I	GHUIX	U	(877) 270-2848	U /	-1.16	-3.48	-14.34 / 2	--	--	0.00	1.23
IN	Good Harbor Tactical Equity Inc A	GHTAX	U	(877) 270-2848	U /	1.59	-3.85	-7.92 / 3	--	--	1.54	1.53
IN	Good Harbor Tactical Equity Inc C	GHTCX	U	(877) 270-2848	U /	1.48	-4.15	-8.55 / 3	--	--	1.14	2.28
IN	Good Harbor Tactical Equity Inc I	GHTIX	U	(877) 270-2848	U /	1.82	-3.67	-7.58 / 4	--	--	1.78	1.28
GL	GoodHaven	GOODX	E	(855) 654-6639	E / 0.4	-4.76	-12.92	-15.16 / 2	3.06 / 8	--	0.00	1.10
GR	Goodwood SMID Cap Discovery A	GAMAX	E	(800) 773-3863	C- / 3.3	3.76	0.09	-0.30 /15	11.48 /49	10.90 /52	0.00	3.97
IN	Gotham Absolute Return Inst	GARIX	U	(888) 739-1390	U /	-2.01	1.61	4.52 /35	--	--	0.00	2.98
GR	Gotham Enhanced Return Inst	GENIX	U	(888) 739-1390	U /	-1.64	4.59	10.77 /77	--	--	0.00	3.54
GR	Gotham Neutral Inst	GONIX	U	(888) 739-1390	U /	-4.47	-4.87	-1.73 /11	--	--	0.00	3.57
GI	Gottex Endowment Strategy I	GTEIX	U	(888) 946-8839	U /	3.34	5.34	4.28 /34	--	--	1.67	5.76
GR	Government Street Equity Fund	GVEQX	B-	(866) 738-1125	C+ / 6.5	2.34	5.74	11.88 /82	13.33 /62	13.00 /68	0.92	0.88
MC	Government Street Mid-Cap Fund	GVMCX	B	(866) 738-1125	B- / 7.2	3.75	9.56	10.14 /75	14.24 /69	13.62 /74	0.30	1.12
GL	Grand Prix Investors		C	(800) 453-6556	C / 4.4	6.16	11.64	8.43 /66	9.22 /34	--	0.56	2.24
EM	● Grandeur Peak Em Mkts Opptys Inst	GPEIX	U	(855) 377-7325	U /	1.04	-1.48	4.64 /36	--	--	0.29	1.75
EM	● Grandeur Peak Em Mkts Opptys Inv	GPEOX	U	(855) 377-7325	U /	1.04	-1.54	4.47 /35	--	--	0.14	2.00
GL	● Grandeur Peak Global Oppts Inst	GPGIX	A-	(855) 377-7325	B / 8.2	3.12	4.79	4.18 /33	17.72 /93	--	0.37	1.46
GL	● Grandeur Peak Global Oppts Investor	GPGOX	B+	(855) 377-7325	B / 7.9	3.14	4.95	4.02 /32	17.34 /92	--	0.20	1.70
GL	● Grandeur Peak Global Reach Inst	GPRIX	U	(855) 377-7325	U /	2.37	4.03	4.36 /34	--	--	0.17	1.72
GL	● Grandeur Peak Global Reach Inv	GPROX	U	(855) 377-7325	U /	2.21	3.89	4.06 /32	--	--	0.05	1.88
FO	● Grandeur Peak Internatl Oppts Inst	GPIIX	C+	(855) 377-7325	C+ / 6.6	1.91	-0.66	0.50 /17	16.40 /86	--	0.51	1.44
FO	● Grandeur Peak Internatl Oppts Inv	GPIOX	C+	(855) 377-7325	C+ / 6.3	1.60	-1.15	0.02 /16	16.01 /83	--	0.34	1.68
GL	Granite Harbor Alternative Investor	GHAFX	C-	(855) 282-1100	E+ / 0.9	1.45	1.85	1.95 /22	2.88 / 8	--	0.12	3.15
AA	Granite Harbor Tactical Investor	GHTFX	D+	(855) 282-1100	D / 1.6	1.50	2.79	3.07 /27	5.36 /14	--	0.00	3.23
GL	Granite Value Fund	GVFIX	C	(888) 442-9893	C- / 3.6	1.47	1.44	2.74 /25	10.26 /41	--	0.24	2.39
GI	Grant Park Mgd Future Strategy A	GPFAX	D	(855) 501-4758	D / 1.9	6.89	13.67	19.41 /96	1.71 / 6	--	0.80	2.23
GI	Grant Park Mgd Future Strategy C	GPFCX	D+	(855) 501-4758	D / 2.2	6.73	13.21	18.52 /96	0.97 / 5	--	0.39	2.99
GI	Grant Park Mgd Future Strategy I	GPFIX	C-	(855) 501-4758	D+ / 2.9	6.95	13.83	19.66 /96	1.99 / 6	--	1.07	1.99
GI	Grant Park Mgd Future Strategy N	GPFNX	C-	(855) 501-4758	D+ / 2.7	6.89	13.68	19.42 /96	1.71 / 6	--	0.86	2.23
GI	Grant Park Mgd Future Strategy W	GPFWX	D+	(855) 501-4758	D+ / 2.6	6.78	13.39	19.15 /96	1.50 / 6	--	0.00	2.47
GL	Grant Park Multi Alt Strat I	GPAIX	U	(855) 501-4758	U /	4.03	10.55	17.65 /95	--	--	3.12	4.85
GR	Great Lakes Disciplined Eq Inst	GLDNX	C+	(855) 278-2020	B+ / 8.7	2.26	7.06	12.01 /83	16.80 /89	14.43 /82	1.29	1.36
GR	Great Lakes Disciplined Eq Inv	GLDEX	C+	(855) 278-2020	B+ / 8.5	2.11	6.90	11.69 /81	16.52 /87	14.08 /78	1.05	1.61
FO	Great Lakes Large Cap Value Inst	GLLIX	U	(855) 278-2020	U /	-0.42	4.50	9.08 /70	--	--	1.52	1.57
SC	Great Lakes Small Cap Oppty Inst	GLSIX	D+	(855) 278-2020	C+ / 5.7	-1.83	5.00	1.01 /18	13.84 /66	14.57 /83	0.28	0.99
SC	Great Lakes Small Cap Oppty Inv	GLSCX	D	(855) 278-2020	C / 5.5	-1.91	4.82	0.74 /18	13.57 /64	14.28 /80	0.07	1.24
RE	Great West Real Estate Idx Initial	MXREX	U	(866) 831-7129	U /	4.56	20.00	24.37 /98	--	--	1.73	0.70
MC	Greater Western New York Series	BWNYX	C+	(888) 285-5346	C+ / 6.9	2.16	9.88	8.61 /67	13.96 /67	13.38 /72	0.00	2.28
GR	Great-West Aggressive Prof I Init	MXPPX	B+	(866) 831-7129	B- / 7.0	3.24	7.57	9.66 /73	14.14 /68	11.92 /60	3.01	1.33
GR	Great-West Aggressive Prof II Init	MXAPX	B+	(866) 831-7129	B- / 7.1	3.22	7.53	9.70 /73	14.29 /69	12.08 /61	3.15	1.18
GR	Great-West Aggressive Prof II L	MXEPX	B-	(866) 831-7129	C+ / 6.9	3.27	7.44	9.54 /72	14.04 /67	--	1.76	1.43
GR	Great-West American Century Gr Init	MXGRX	B-	(866) 831-7129	C+ / 6.9	3.30	9.04	13.25 /87	13.43 /63	--	2.93	1.00
MC	Great-West Ariel Mid Cap Val Init	MXMCX	A+	(866) 831-7129	A+ / 9.7	4.32	12.07	13.79 /89	19.60 /97	15.78 /92	1.68	1.25
GL	Great-West Consv Prof I Init	MXVPX	C	(866) 831-7129	D / 1.9	1.43	3.18	4.60 /36	5.88 /16	5.88 /16	2.76	0.98
AA	Great-West Consv Prof II Init	MXCPX	C-	(866) 831-7129	D / 2.0	1.54	3.27	4.84 /37	6.03 /17	6.05 /17	3.01	0.83
AA	Great-West Consv Prof II L	MXIPX	C	(866) 831-7129	D / 1.9	1.47	3.14	4.59 /36	5.79 /16	--	2.34	1.08
MC	Great-West Goldman Sachs MC V	MXMVX	A+	(866) 831-7129	A / 9.4	2.98	10.11	14.42 /90	18.08 /94	15.95 /93	12.32	1.25
FO	Great-West International Index Init	MXINX	D+	(866) 831-7129	D+ / 2.7	5.25	0.74	-1.78 /11	8.30 /29	--	1.65	0.70
SC	Great-West Invesco SC Value Init	MXSVX	A-	(866) 831-7129	B / 8.2	2.28	8.55	5.77 /44	16.63 /88	14.85 /86	4.21	1.40
GL	Great-West Lifetime 2015 I T	MXLTX	C	(866) 831-7129	D / 2.1	1.78	3.55	5.26 /41	6.16 /17	6.79 /22	2.56	0.83
GL	Great-West Lifetime 2015 I T1	MXLUX	C	(866) 831-7129	D / 2.1	1.85	3.59	5.25 /40	6.08 /17	6.70 /21	2.48	0.93
GI	Great-West Lifetime 2015 II L	MXLQX	C	(866) 831-7129	D+ / 2.6	1.92	4.02	5.74 /44	7.02 /21	--	3.31	1.11
GI	Great-West Lifetime 2015 II T	MXLVX	C+	(866) 831-7129	D+ / 2.8	2.11	4.17	6.04 /47	7.31 /23	7.65 /27	2.37	0.86

● Denotes fund is closed to new investors
* Denotes fund is included in Section II

www.thestreetratings.com

RISK			NET ASSETS		ASSET					Portfolio	BULL / BEAR		FUND MANAGER		MINIMUMS		LOADS	
Risk Rating/Pts	3 Year		NAV As of 3/31/15	Total $(Mil)	Cash %	Stocks %	Bonds %	Other %	Portfolio Turnover Ratio	Last Bull Market Return	Last Bear Market Return	Manager Quality Pct	Manager Tenure (Years)	Initial Purch. $	Additional Purch. $	Front End Load	Back End Load
	Standard Deviation	Beta															
U /	N/A	N/A	9.36	178	32	17	50	1	773	N/A	N/A	N/A	3	5,000,000	10,000	0.0	1.0
U /	N/A	N/A	8.95	45	11	88	0	1	90	N/A	N/A	N/A	N/A	2,500	250	5.8	1.0
U /	N/A	N/A	8.92	40	11	88	0	1	90	N/A	N/A	N/A	N/A	2,500	250	0.0	1.0
U /	N/A	N/A	8.97	89	11	88	0	1	90	N/A	N/A	N/A	N/A	5,000,000	10,000	0.0	1.0
C- / 3.9	10.6	0.44	22.62	306	11	71	16	2	37	34.4	-6.1	52	4	10,000	2,500	0.0	2.0
D- / 1.0	14.2	1.14	10.20	12	0	98	0	2	289	61.3	-15.8	6	N/A	2,500	100	4.5	2.0
U /	N/A	N/A	13.62	3,718	39	60	0	1	399	N/A	N/A	N/A	3	250,000	5,000	0.0	1.0
U /	N/A	N/A	12.56	1,611	0	99	0	1	365	N/A	N/A	N/A	2	250,000	5,000	0.0	1.0
U /	N/A	N/A	10.48	963	76	24	0	0	192	N/A	N/A	N/A	2	250,000	5,000	0.0	1.0
U /	N/A	N/A	10.20	48	40	55	4	1	0	N/A	N/A	N/A	N/A	1,000	1,000	0.0	0.0
B- / 7.3	9.1	0.93	65.95	94	1	98	0	1	36	81.6	-16.3	47	24	5,000	0	0.0	0.0
C+ / 6.8	9.9	0.89	22.96	52	2	97	0	1	10	82.7	-18.8	58	12	5,000	0	0.0	0.0
B- / 7.0	10.1	1.32	12.59	2	13	86	0	1	222	39.2	-13.4	31	5	1,000	100	0.0	1.0
U /	N/A	N/A	10.68	397	4	95	0	1	0	N/A	N/A	N/A	2	100,000	0	0.0	2.0
U /	N/A	N/A	10.67	38	4	95	0	1	0	N/A	N/A	N/A	2	2,000	50	0.0	2.0
C+ / 6.7	10.3	0.66	3.30	504	3	96	0	1	26	N/A	N/A	98	4	100,000	0	0.0	2.0
C+ / 6.7	10.5	0.66	3.28	195	3	96	0	1	26	N/A	N/A	98	4	2,000	50	0.0	2.0
U /	N/A	N/A	12.95	246	4	95	0	1	39	N/A	N/A	N/A	2	100,000	0	0.0	2.0
U /	N/A	N/A	12.94	83	4	95	0	1	39	N/A	N/A	N/A	2	2,000	50	0.0	2.0
C+ / 6.5	10.9	0.76	3.20	636	10	89	0	1	37	N/A	N/A	97	4	100,000	0	0.0	2.0
C+ / 6.5	10.9	0.76	3.18	162	10	89	0	1	37	N/A	N/A	97	4	2,000	50	0.0	2.0
B+ / 9.2	4.1	0.27	10.53	44	0	0	0	100	132	14.9	N/A	71	4	2,500	100	0.0	0.0
B- / 7.7	5.7	0.94	10.83	38	34	37	25	4	129	27.1	N/A	13	4	2,500	100	0.0	0.0
B- / 7.4	11.5	0.70	13.79	13	1	98	0	1	30	N/A	N/A	90	N/A	10,000	0	0.0	2.0
B- / 7.2	6.3	N/A	10.08	19	52	0	47	1	99	0.3	-2.8	82	4	2,500	100	5.8	1.0
C+ / 6.9	6.4	N/A	9.83	6	52	0	47	1	99	-2.3	-3.0	76	4	5,000	100	0.0	1.0
B- / 7.3	6.4	N/A	10.16	36	52	0	47	1	99	1.2	-2.7	83	4	100,000	1,000	0.0	1.0
B- / 7.2	6.3	N/A	10.08	5	52	0	47	1	99	0.3	-2.8	81	4	5,000	100	0.0	1.0
B- / 7.1	6.4	N/A	10.08	N/A	52	0	47	1	99	-0.4	-2.9	80	4	5,000	100	0.0	1.0
U /	N/A	N/A	11.35	44	62	37	0	1	0	N/A	N/A	N/A	2	100,000	1,000	0.0	1.0
C- / 3.9	9.5	0.96	14.94	51	2	97	0	1	95	100.1	-15.1	78	N/A	100,000	100	0.0	0.0
C- / 3.9	9.5	0.96	15.00	N/A	2	97	0	1	95	98.2	-15.1	76	N/A	1,000	200	0.0	0.0
U /	N/A	N/A	14.11	42	3	96	0	1	5	N/A	N/A	N/A	3	100,000	100	0.0	0.0
C- / 3.4	14.2	0.97	16.65	80	6	93	0	1	86	103.4	-25.2	41	5	100,000	100	0.0	0.0
C- / 3.4	14.1	0.97	16.44	16	6	93	0	1	86	101.6	-25.2	38	5	1,000	200	0.0	0.0
U /	N/A	N/A	13.08	354	0	100	0	0	83	N/A	N/A	N/A	3	0	0	0.0	0.0
C+ / 6.5	9.8	0.72	21.24	2	10	89	0	1	14	79.7	-15.8	83	18	2,500	250	0.0	0.0
B- / 7.2	10.0	0.99	10.82	95	0	97	2	1	27	85.7	-20.6	43	18	0	0	0.0	0.0
B- / 7.2	10.0	0.99	8.01	665	0	97	2	1	26	86.9	-20.6	45	16	0	0	0.0	0.0
B- / 7.2	9.9	0.98	12.63	37	0	97	2	1	26	84.9	N/A	43	16	0	0	0.0	0.0
B- / 7.2	9.9	0.98	11.59	497	0	98	0	2	83	88.4	N/A	36	4	0	0	0.0	0.0
C+ / 6.8	13.4	1.12	1.69	139	2	93	3	2	41	126.4	-25.2	70	16	0	0	0.0	0.0
B+ / 9.5	4.0	0.27	8.54	45	23	30	45	2	39	30.1	-6.7	89	18	0	0	0.0	0.0
B / 8.6	3.9	0.64	8.59	327	23	30	45	2	36	30.5	-6.5	56	16	0	0	0.0	0.0
B+ / 9.5	3.8	0.63	9.68	113	23	30	45	2	36	29.5	N/A	54	16	0	0	0.0	0.0
B- / 7.3	10.2	0.88	12.44	626	1	98	0	1	225	109.4	-20.5	88	4	0	0	0.0	0.0
C+ / 6.7	13.4	1.02	11.03	658	1	96	1	2	6	48.7	-23.4	48	4	0	0	0.0	0.0
C+ / 6.8	12.9	0.91	11.23	70	0	98	1	1	100	100.7	-24.5	81	7	0	0	0.0	0.0
B+ / 9.2	4.5	0.29	12.59	16	6	32	60	2	50	33.2	-7.7	90	6	0	0	0.0	0.0
B+ / 9.2	4.5	0.29	12.64	167	6	32	60	2	50	32.9	-7.8	89	6	0	0	0.0	0.0
B+ / 9.1	5.3	0.46	9.56	66	0	41	57	2	29	39.2	-10.0	66	6	0	0	0.0	0.0
B+ / 9.1	5.2	0.45	14.03	140	0	41	57	2	29	40.4	-9.8	70	6	0	0	0.0	0.0

					PERFORMANCE						Incl. in Returns	
						Total Return % through 3/31/15						
									Annualized			
Fund Type	Fund Name	Ticker Symbol	Overall Investment Rating	Phone	Performance Rating/Pts	3 Mo	6 Mo	1Yr / Pct	3Yr / Pct	5Yr / Pct	Dividend Yield	Expense Ratio
GI	Great-West Lifetime 2015 II T1	MXLWX	C	(866) 831-7129	D+ / 2.7	2.04	4.12	5.93 /46	7.19 /22	7.52 /27	2.27	0.96
GI	Great-West Lifetime 2015 III T	MXLYX	C+	(866) 831-7129	C- / 3.3	2.18	4.54	6.50 /51	8.32 /29	8.37 /32	1.84	0.88
GI	Great-West Lifetime 2015 III T1	MXLZX	C+	(866) 831-7129	C- / 3.3	2.19	4.63	6.50 /51	8.25 /28	8.29 /32	2.38	0.98
GI	Great-West Lifetime 2025 I T	MXALX	C+	(866) 831-7129	C- / 3.0	2.16	4.16	5.90 /46	7.73 /26	7.84 /29	2.44	0.89
GI	Great-West Lifetime 2025 I T1	MXBLX	C+	(866) 831-7129	D+ / 2.9	2.08	4.09	5.79 /45	7.63 /25	7.73 /28	2.33	0.99
GI	Great-West Lifetime 2025 II L	MXCDX	C+	(866) 831-7129	C- / 3.7	2.29	4.73	6.47 /50	8.95 /33	--	3.32	1.17
GI	Great-West Lifetime 2025 II T	MXCLX	C+	(866) 831-7129	C- / 3.8	2.34	4.79	6.64 /52	9.20 /34	8.87 /36	2.20	0.92
GI	Great-West Lifetime 2025 II T1	MXDLX	C+	(866) 831-7129	C- / 3.8	2.29	4.76	6.57 /51	9.08 /33	8.77 /35	2.11	1.02
GI	Great-West Lifetime 2025 III T	MXELX	B-	(866) 831-7129	C / 4.7	2.57	5.59	7.54 /59	10.65 /43	9.86 /43	1.96	0.95
GI	Great-West Lifetime 2025 III T1	MXFLX	C+	(866) 831-7129	C / 4.6	2.52	5.36	7.28 /57	10.49 /42	9.72 /42	2.44	1.05
GI	Great-West Lifetime 2035 I T	MXGLX	C+	(866) 831-7129	C- / 4.2	2.42	4.91	6.64 /52	9.84 /38	9.27 /39	2.18	0.94
GI	Great-West Lifetime 2035 I T1	MXHLX	C+	(866) 831-7129	C- / 4.1	2.42	4.85	6.54 /51	9.73 /38	9.17 /38	2.09	1.04
GI	Great-West Lifetime 2035 II L	MXLRX	C+	(866) 831-7129	C / 4.9	2.72	5.45	7.08 /56	10.96 /45	--	3.14	1.22
GI	Great-West Lifetime 2035 II T	MXILX	C+	(866) 831-7129	C / 5.0	2.71	5.57	7.35 /58	11.22 /47	10.18 /46	1.95	0.97
GI	Great-West Lifetime 2035 II T1	MXJLX	C+	(866) 831-7129	C / 4.9	2.66	5.46	7.26 /57	11.10 /46	10.07 /45	1.85	1.07
GL	Great-West Lifetime 2035 III T	MXKLX	B-	(866) 831-7129	C+ / 5.6	2.85	6.04	7.87 /62	12.07 /53	10.80 /51	1.48	0.99
GL	Great-West Lifetime 2035 III T1	MXLLX	B-	(866) 831-7129	C / 5.5	2.82	5.89	7.68 /60	11.93 /52	10.66 /50	2.34	1.09
GI	Great-West Lifetime 2045 I T	MXMLX	C+	(866) 831-7129	C / 4.8	2.73	5.28	6.89 /54	10.89 /45	9.93 /44	1.98	0.98
GI	Great-West Lifetime 2045 I T1	MXNLX	C+	(866) 831-7129	C / 4.7	2.67	5.17	6.74 /53	10.75 /44	9.80 /43	1.91	1.08
GI	Great-West Lifetime 2045 II L	MXYLX	C+	(866) 831-7129	C / 5.1	2.78	5.35	6.88 /54	11.37 /48	--	3.03	1.24
GI	Great-West Lifetime 2045 II T	MXOLX	C+	(866) 831-7129	C / 5.3	2.86	5.58	7.26 /57	11.66 /50	10.44 /48	1.81	0.99
GI	Great-West Lifetime 2045 II T1	MXPLX	C+	(866) 831-7129	C / 5.2	2.88	5.52	7.10 /56	11.53 /49	10.34 /47	1.74	1.09
GR	Great-West Lifetime 2045 III T	MXQLX	C+	(866) 831-7129	C / 5.4	2.91	5.41	7.08 /56	11.89 /52	10.60 /49	0.28	1.00
GR	Great-West Lifetime 2045 III T1	MXRLX	C+	(866) 831-7129	C / 5.4	2.92	5.65	7.24 /57	11.89 /52	10.55 /49	2.49	1.10
GI	Great-West Lifetime 2055 I T	MXSLX	C+	(866) 831-7129	C / 4.7	2.70	5.00	6.45 /50	10.77 /44	9.81 /43	1.89	0.99
GI	Great-West Lifetime 2055 I T1	MXTLX	C+	(866) 831-7129	C / 4.6	2.70	4.89	6.31 /49	10.65 /43	9.70 /42	1.81	1.09
GI	Great-West Lifetime 2055 II L	MXZLX	C+	(866) 831-7129	C / 4.9	2.82	5.08	6.44 /50	11.12 /46	--	2.89	1.25
GI	Great-West Lifetime 2055 II T	MXULX	C+	(866) 831-7129	C / 5.0	2.84	5.22	6.66 /52	11.39 /48	10.21 /46	1.78	1.00
GI	Great-West Lifetime 2055 II T1	MXVLX	C+	(866) 831-7129	C / 5.0	2.79	5.18	6.58 /52	11.30 /48	10.11 /46	1.69	1.10
GR	Great-West Lifetime 2055 III T	MXWLX	C+	(866) 831-7129	C / 5.2	2.92	5.36	6.89 /54	11.68 /50	10.40 /48	0.36	1.01
GR	Great-West Lifetime 2055 III T1	MXXLX	C+	(866) 831-7129	C / 5.1	2.87	5.25	6.64 /52	11.54 /49	10.29 /47	2.01	1.11
SC	Great-West Loomis Sayles SCV Init	MXLSX	B+	(866) 831-7129	B / 8.0	4.74	13.30	8.97 /69	15.19 /76	14.65 /84	0.89	1.08
FO	Great-West MFS Internatl Gro Init	MXIGX	C-	(866) 831-7129	C- / 3.1	5.88	2.79	1.57 /20	8.27 /29	7.33 /25	1.27	1.20
FO	Great-West MFS Internatl Value Init	MXIVX	C-	(866) 831-7129	C- / 3.6	6.68	6.68	6.87 /54	8.10 /27	9.80 /43	0.90	1.11
GR	Great-West Mlti-Mgr Lg Cap Gro Init	MXLGX	A	(866) 831-7129	B+ / 8.5	3.53	9.23	17.46 /95	15.09 /76	11.26 /55	0.66	1.00
GR	Great-West Mod Aggr Prof I Init	MXRPX	B-	(866) 831-7129	C / 5.0	2.66	5.85	7.76 /61	11.04 /46	9.73 /42	2.94	1.20
GR	Great-West Mod Aggr Prof II Init	MXBPX	B	(866) 831-7129	C / 5.1	2.69	5.94	7.97 /63	11.18 /47	9.85 /43	3.03	1.05
GR	Great-West Mod Aggr Prof II L	MXFPX	B-	(866) 831-7129	C / 4.9	2.48	5.77	7.63 /60	10.88 /45	--	2.33	1.30
BA	Great-West Mod Consv Prof I Init	MXTPX	C+	(866) 831-7129	D+ / 2.9	1.90	4.10	5.74 /44	7.62 /25	7.17 /24	2.77	1.03
BA	Great-West Mod Consv Prof II Init	MXDPX	C+	(866) 831-7129	C- / 3.0	1.90	4.27	5.94 /46	7.81 /26	7.32 /25	2.93	0.88
BA	Great-West Mod Consv Prof II L	MXHPX	C+	(866) 831-7129	D+ / 2.8	1.84	4.05	5.68 /44	7.53 /24	--	2.42	1.13
GL	Great-West Moderate Prof I Init	MXOPX	B-	(866) 831-7129	C- / 4.0	2.21	5.09	6.92 /54	9.38 /35	8.46 /33	2.89	1.11
AA	Great-West Moderate Prof II Init	MXMPX	C+	(866) 831-7129	C- / 4.1	2.34	5.21	7.05 /55	9.55 /36	8.65 /34	3.07	0.96
AA	Great-West Moderate Prof II L	MXGPX	C	(866) 831-7129	C- / 3.9	2.29	5.06	6.73 /53	9.27 /35	--	1.99	1.21
GI	Great-West Putnam Equity Inc Init	MXQIX	A+	(866) 831-7129	B+ / 8.4	1.22	6.02	10.78 /77	16.64 /88	--	2.26	1.10
IX	Great-West S&P 500 Index Init	MXVIX	A-	(866) 831-7129	B / 7.7	0.78	5.59	12.03 /83	15.42 /78	13.81 /76	1.45	0.60
IX	Great-West S&P 500 Index L	MXVJX	A-	(866) 831-7129	B / 7.6	0.75	5.53	11.83 /82	15.18 /76	--	1.99	0.85
MC	Great-West S&P MC 400 Index Init	MXMDX	A	(866) 831-7129	B+ / 8.8	5.11	11.67	11.54 /81	16.36 /86	--	1.31	0.60
SC	Great-West S&P SC 600 Index Init	MXISX	A-	(866) 831-7129	B+ / 8.8	3.79	13.92	8.10 /64	16.72 /88	15.63 /91	1.11	0.60
SC	Great-West S&P SC 600 Index L	MXNSX	A-	(866) 831-7129	B+ / 8.6	3.72	13.81	7.87 /62	16.42 /86	--	0.70	0.85
GL	Great-West SecureFndtn Bal ETF A	SFBPX	C+	(866) 831-7129	C- / 3.3	2.42	5.38	7.22 /57	9.53 /36	--	1.49	1.12
GL	Great-West SecureFndtn Balanced G	MXSBX	B-	(866) 831-7129	C- / 4.0	2.35	5.25	7.01 /55	9.43 /36	8.87 /36	1.56	0.65

• Denotes fund is closed to new investors
* Denotes fund is included in Section II

I. Index of Stock Mutual Funds

RISK			NET ASSETS		ASSET					BULL / BEAR		FUND MANAGER		MINIMUMS		LOADS	
	3 Year		NAV						Portfolio	Last Bull	Last Bear	Manager	Manager	Initial	Additional	Front	Back
Risk	Standard		As of	Total	Cash	Stocks	Bonds	Other	Turnover	Market	Market	Quality	Tenure	Purch.	Purch.	End	End
Rating/Pts	Deviation	Beta	3/31/15	$(Mil)	%	%	%	%	Ratio	Return	Return	Pct	(Years)	$	$	Load	Load
B+ / 9.1	5.2	0.46	14.00	812	0	41	57	2	29	40.0	-9.9	68	6	0	0	0.0	0.0
B+ / 9.0	6.0	0.55	14.08	4	4	51	43	2	60	47.6	-12.4	64	6	0	0	0.0	0.0
B+ / 9.0	6.0	0.55	13.98	45	4	51	43	2	60	47.3	-12.4	64	6	0	0	0.0	0.0
B+ / 9.0	5.7	0.51	13.72	34	0	44	54	2	42	43.1	-11.4	65	6	0	0	0.0	0.0
B+ / 9.0	5.7	0.51	13.71	256	0	44	54	2	42	42.7	-11.5	64	6	0	0	0.0	0.0
B / 8.5	6.7	0.63	9.82	62	3	58	37	2	22	51.8	-14.4	54	6	0	0	0.0	0.0
B / 8.5	6.7	0.64	15.73	202	3	58	37	2	22	53.2	-14.3	57	6	0	0	0.0	0.0
B / 8.5	6.8	0.64	15.64	1,412	3	58	37	2	22	52.6	-14.3	54	6	0	0	0.0	0.0
B / 8.2	7.9	0.76	15.97	11	2	71	25	2	30	63.2	-16.9	48	6	0	0	0.0	0.0
B / 8.2	7.9	0.76	15.89	64	2	71	25	2	30	62.5	-17.0	46	6	0	0	0.0	0.0
B / 8.3	7.4	0.71	15.23	22	1	65	31	3	36	57.5	-15.6	48	6	0	0	0.0	0.0
B / 8.3	7.5	0.72	15.22	215	1	65	31	3	36	57.1	-15.6	46	6	0	0	0.0	0.0
B- / 7.9	8.6	0.84	10.21	56	1	80	17	2	14	65.6	-18.0	35	6	0	0	0.0	0.0
B- / 7.9	8.6	0.84	17.43	162	1	80	17	2	14	67.2	-18.0	38	6	0	0	0.0	0.0
B- / 7.9	8.6	0.84	17.37	1,140	1	80	17	2	14	66.5	-18.0	36	6	0	0	0.0	0.0
B- / 7.7	9.3	0.65	16.98	7	1	89	9	1	22	73.4	-19.2	94	6	0	0	0.0	0.0
B- / 7.7	9.3	0.64	16.80	53	1	89	9	1	22	72.5	-19.2	94	6	0	0	0.0	0.0
B- / 7.9	8.6	0.84	16.16	13	2	79	18	1	33	64.8	-17.5	34	6	0	0	0.0	0.0
B- / 7.9	8.6	0.84	16.13	114	2	79	18	1	33	64.0	-17.5	33	6	0	0	0.0	0.0
B- / 7.5	9.3	0.91	10.37	24	2	87	9	2	12	69.0	-19.0	27	6	0	0	0.0	0.0
B- / 7.5	9.3	0.91	18.01	82	2	87	9	2	12	70.6	-19.0	29	6	0	0	0.0	0.0
B- / 7.5	9.4	0.92	17.89	598	2	87	9	2	12	69.9	-19.0	28	6	0	0	0.0	0.0
B- / 7.3	9.7	0.95	17.68	2	2	91	5	2	24	72.7	-19.7	26	6	0	0	0.0	0.0
B- / 7.3	9.6	0.95	17.27	29	2	91	5	2	24	72.5	-19.7	26	6	0	0	0.0	0.0
B- / 7.7	8.9	0.86	15.62	5	2	81	15	2	46	64.5	-17.9	29	6	0	0	0.0	0.0
B- / 7.7	8.9	0.87	15.59	36	2	81	15	2	46	63.9	-17.9	27	6	0	0	0.0	0.0
B- / 7.4	9.5	0.92	10.20	4	1	89	9	1	13	67.8	-19.3	22	6	0	0	0.0	0.0
B- / 7.4	9.5	0.93	17.75	28	1	89	9	1	13	69.3	-19.2	24	6	0	0	0.0	0.0
B- / 7.4	9.5	0.93	17.68	173	1	89	9	1	13	68.8	-19.3	23	6	0	0	0.0	0.0
B- / 7.3	9.8	0.95	17.96	N/A	2	91	5	2	40	71.5	-19.8	23	6	0	0	0.0	0.0
B- / 7.3	9.8	0.96	17.54	7	2	91	5	2	40	70.7	-19.8	21	6	0	0	0.0	0.0
C+ / 6.5	12.1	0.87	25.63	238	0	97	1	2	27	96.0	-23.7	77	15	0	0	0.0	0.0
C+ / 6.8	12.7	0.93	11.88	314	0	100	0	0	26	54.9	-23.2	59	12	0	0	0.0	0.0
B- / 7.0	11.6	0.67	11.82	679	0	96	3	1	28	61.7	-22.5	82	6	0	0	0.0	0.0
C+ / 6.9	9.9	0.92	9.67	323	0	97	2	1	230	96.1	-20.3	71	N/A	0	0	0.0	0.0
B / 8.4	7.6	0.75	10.03	172	9	71	18	2	29	62.7	-15.4	55	18	0	0	0.0	0.0
B / 8.5	7.5	0.74	8.77	355	11	71	17	1	21	63.4	-15.3	60	9	0	0	0.0	0.0
B / 8.4	7.6	0.75	9.90	48	11	71	17	1	21	62.1	N/A	54	9	0	0	0.0	0.0
B+ / 9.4	5.1	0.86	9.10	85	22	44	32	2	39	40.5	-9.7	44	18	0	0	0.0	0.0
B+ / 9.4	5.2	0.87	9.14	123	22	44	32	2	30	41.1	-9.6	45	16	0	0	0.0	0.0
B+ / 9.4	5.1	0.86	9.95	41	22	44	32	2	30	40.0	N/A	43	18	0	0	0.0	0.0
B+ / 9.0	6.4	0.44	9.26	198	16	59	24	1	31	51.3	-12.6	93	18	0	0	0.0	0.0
B- / 7.8	6.5	1.09	7.87	1,078	16	59	24	1	26	52.2	-12.5	35	16	0	0	0.0	0.0
B- / 7.6	6.4	1.08	10.74	103	16	59	24	1	26	50.9	N/A	33	16	0	0	0.0	0.0
B- / 7.6	10.5	1.05	14.12	585	0	97	0	3	39	104.7	N/A	62	3	0	0	0.0	0.0
B- / 7.5	9.6	1.00	18.17	2,245	0	97	2	1	4	96.5	-16.4	58	6	0	0	0.0	0.0
B- / 7.4	9.6	1.00	14.74	43	0	97	2	1	4	94.7	N/A	54	6	0	0	0.0	0.0
C+ / 6.8	11.0	1.00	15.43	601	0	96	2	2	13	98.7	-22.7	59	4	0	0	0.0	0.0
C+ / 6.3	12.8	0.94	13.13	751	0	98	1	1	17	104.8	-22.2	79	6	0	0	0.0	0.0
C+ / 6.3	12.8	0.94	16.16	18	0	98	1	1	17	103.1	N/A	77	6	0	0	0.0	0.0
B+ / 9.1	6.3	0.96	13.12	49	2	60	37	1	13	N/A	N/A	75	3	10,000	500	5.0	0.0
B+ / 9.2	6.2	0.96	13.06	95	6	58	34	2	26	51.1	-11.2	75	6	0	0	0.0	0.0

Data as of March 31, 2015

						PERFORMANCE							
							Total Return % through 3/31/15					Incl. in Returns	
			Overall			Perfor-				Annualized		Dividend	Expense
Fund		Ticker	Investment			mance						Yield	Ratio
Type	Fund Name	Symbol	Rating	Phone		Rating/Pts	3 Mo	6 Mo	1Yr / Pct	3Yr / Pct	5Yr / Pct		
GL	Great-West SecureFndtn Balanced	MXSHX	B-	(866) 831-7129		C- / 3.9	2.33	5.16	6.86 /54	9.32 /35	8.74 /35	1.39	0.75
GL	Great-West SecureFndtn Balanced L	MXLDX	B-	(866) 831-7129		C- / 3.9	2.26	5.14	6.80 /53	9.16 /34	--	1.41	0.90
GI	Great-West SecureFndtn LT 2015 G	MXSJX	B-	(866) 831-7129		C- / 3.6	2.36	4.85	6.60 /52	8.78 /32	8.17 /31	1.66	0.66
GI	Great-West SecureFndtn LT 2015 G1	MXSKX	C+	(866) 831-7129		C- / 3.5	2.33	4.72	6.49 /51	8.66 /31	8.05 /30	1.43	0.76
GI	Great-West SecureFndtn LT 2015 L	MXLEX	C+	(866) 831-7129		C- / 3.4	2.31	4.69	6.31 /49	8.51 /30	--	1.49	0.91
GI	Great-West SecureFndtn LT 2020 G	MXSMX	B-	(866) 831-7129		C- / 3.6	2.35	4.76	6.60 /52	8.78 /32	--	1.62	0.65
GI	Great-West SecureFndtn LT 2020 G1	MXSPX	C+	(866) 831-7129		C- / 3.6	2.35	4.78	6.57 /51	8.65 /31	--	1.42	0.75
GI	Great-West SecureFndtn LT 2020 L	MXLFX	C+	(866) 831-7129		C- / 3.4	2.26	4.64	6.28 /49	8.47 /30	--	1.34	0.90
GI	Great-West SecureFndtn LT 2025 G	MXSNX	B-	(866) 831-7129		C- / 4.0	2.45	4.90	6.66 /52	9.40 /36	8.34 /32	1.63	0.67
GI	Great-West SecureFndtn LT 2025 G1	MXSOX	C+	(866) 831-7129		C- / 3.9	2.43	4.87	6.57 /51	9.25 /35	8.25 /32	1.41	0.77
GI	Great-West SecureFndtn LT 2025 L	MXLHX	C+	(866) 831-7129		C- / 3.8	2.33	4.80	6.40 /50	9.14 /34	--	1.27	0.92
GI	Great-West SecureFndtn LT 2030 G	MXSQX	B-	(866) 831-7129		C / 4.5	2.59	5.09	6.80 /53	10.40 /42	--	1.52	0.69
GI	Great-West SecureFndtn LT 2030 G1	MXASX	B-	(866) 831-7129		C / 4.5	2.59	5.09	6.66 /52	10.34 /41	--	1.32	0.79
GI	Great-West SecureFndtn LT 2030 L	MXLIX	C+	(866) 831-7129		C / 4.4	2.57	5.02	6.53 /51	10.24 /41	--	1.22	0.94
GI	Great-West SecureFndtn LT 2035 G	MXSRX	B-	(866) 831-7129		C / 5.0	2.85	5.34	6.90 /54	11.27 /47	9.65 /42	1.54	0.70
GI	Great-West SecureFndtn LT 2035 G1	MXSSX	B-	(866) 831-7129		C / 4.9	2.75	5.30	6.72 /53	11.15 /47	9.70 /42	1.32	0.80
GI	Great-West SecureFndtn LT 2035 L	MXLJX	C+	(866) 831-7129		C / 4.9	2.80	5.29	6.74 /53	11.06 /46	--	1.62	0.95
GI	Great-West SecureFndtn LT 2040 G	MXDSX	C+	(866) 831-7129		C / 5.1	2.88	5.34	6.67 /52	11.54 /49	--	1.49	0.71
GI	Great-West SecureFndtn LT 2040 G1	MXESX	C+	(866) 831-7129		C / 5.1	2.89	5.34	6.62 /52	11.48 /49	--	1.28	0.81
GI	Great-West SecureFndtn LT 2040 L	MXLKX	C+	(866) 831-7129		C / 5.2	2.94	5.38	6.70 /53	11.58 /50	--	1.24	0.96
GI	Great-West SecureFndtn LT 2045 G	MXSTX	C+	(866) 831-7129		C / 5.2	3.02	5.32	6.52 /51	11.58 /50	9.84 /43	1.53	0.71
GI	Great-West SecureFndtn LT 2045 G1	MXSWX	C+	(866) 831-7129		C / 5.1	3.02	5.32	6.47 /50	11.45 /49	9.74 / 42	1.32	0.81
GI	Great-West SecureFndtn LT 2045 L	MXLNX	C+	(866) 831-7129		C / 5.1	3.04	5.34	6.52 /51	11.51 /49	--	0.76	0.96
GI	Great-West SecureFndtn LT 2050 G	MXFSX	C+	(866) 831-7129		C / 5.1	3.03	5.20	6.34 /49	11.44 /48	--	1.50	0.71
GI	Great-West SecureFndtn LT 2050 G1	MXHSX	C+	(866) 831-7129		C / 5.0	3.04	5.21	6.22 /48	11.33 /48	--	1.30	0.81
GI	Great-West SecureFndtn LT 2050 L	MXLOX	C+	(866) 831-7129		C / 5.1	3.02	5.26	6.30 /49	11.44 /48	--	1.40	0.96
GI	Great-West SecureFndtn LT 2055 G	MXSYX	C+	(866) 831-7129		C / 4.9	3.04	5.12	6.17 /48	11.24 /47	9.54 /41	1.53	0.70
GI	Great-West SecureFndtn LT 2055 G1	MXSZX	C+	(866) 831-7129		C / 4.8	3.05	5.06	5.99 /46	11.10 /46	9.42 /40	1.36	0.80
GI	Great-West SecureFndtn LT 2055 L	MXLPX	C+	(866) 831-7129		C / 4.9	3.07	5.16	6.26 /49	11.25 /47	--	1.67	0.95
SC	Great-West Small Cap Growth Init	MXSGX	C+	(866) 831-7129		B- / 7.0	5.53	13.86	3.61 /30	14.31 /69	13.86 /76	2.24	1.15
IN	Great-West T Rowe Price Eq Inc Init	MXEQX	B-	(866) 831-7129		C / 5.5	-1.14	1.84	4.57 /36	13.27 /62	11.58 /58	1.87	0.82
IN	Great-West T Rowe Price Eq Inc L	MXTQX	C+	(866) 831-7129		C / 5.3	-1.28	1.60	4.18 /33	12.88 /59	--	2.91	3.40
MC	Great-West T Rowe Price MC Gr Init	MXMGX	A+	(866) 831-7129		A+ / 9.7	6.70	15.83	17.14 /95	18.10 /95	16.65 /95	0.68	1.03
MC	Great-West T Rowe Price MC Gr L	MXTMX	A+	(866) 831-7129		A+ / 9.6	6.55	15.68	16.83 /94	17.78 /93	--	1.83	2.65
BA	Green Century Balanced	GCBLX	B-	(800) 221-5519		C / 5.3	3.39	7.44	9.34 /71	11.82 /51	10.29 /47	0.33	1.48
GR	Green Century Equity	GCEQX	B+	(800) 221-5519		B- / 7.5	1.12	6.92	12.17 /83	15.47 /79	12.77 /66	0.47	1.25
GL	Green Owl Intrinsic Value	GOWLX	A-	(888) 695-3729		B- / 7.5	1.48	6.31	8.39 /65	15.38 /78	--	1.22	1.38
BA	Greenspring	GRSPX	D-	(800) 366-3863		D- / 1.1	-0.32	-1.32	-3.62 / 8	5.75 /16	5.95 /17	2.79	0.94
GR	Growth 529 Port A		C+	(800) 342-5236		C / 5.1	4.47	6.31	7.46 /59	12.85 /58	11.00 /53	0.00	1.48
GR	● Growth 529 Port B		C+	(800) 342-5236		C / 5.5	4.30	5.93	6.68 /52	12.03 /53	10.19 /46	0.00	2.23
GR	Growth 529 Port C		C+	(800) 342-5236		C / 5.5	4.29	5.91	6.66 /52	12.04 /53	10.20 /46	0.00	2.23
IN	GRT Absolute Return Fund Adv	GRTHX	E+	(866) 777-7818		E- / 0.2	-1.26	-7.84	-7.94 / 3	-3.64 / 2	--	0.70	2.94
GL	GRT Value Fund Adv	GRTVX	D-	(866) 777-7818		C- / 3.0	1.53	2.76	-0.86 /13	9.00 /33	11.26 /55	0.41	1.61
IN	Guggenheim Alpha Opportunity A	SAOAX	C+	(800) 820-0888		C / 4.7	-2.05	4.03	6.22 /48	12.88 /59	14.27 /80	0.02	3.25
IN	Guggenheim Alpha Opportunity C	SAOCX	C+	(800) 820-0888		C / 4.9	-2.21	3.67	5.43 /42	12.01 /53	13.39 /72	0.03	4.11
IN	Guggenheim Alpha Opportunity Instl	SAOIX	B-	(800) 820-0888		C+/ 5.8	-1.99	4.17	6.46 /50	13.36 /62	14.66 /84	0.02	2.90
IX	Guggenheim Capital Stewardship Inst	GFCIX	U	(800) 820-0888		U /	0.43	3.70	--	--	--	0.00	N/A
GL	Guggenheim Event Dr Distr Strat A	RYDOX	D-	(800) 820-0888		D- / 1.1	2.88	1.61	-1.18 /12	5.56 /15	--	0.20	2.03
GL	Guggenheim Event Dr Distr Strat C	RYDQX	D-	(800) 820-0888		D- / 1.2	2.67	1.21	-1.92 /11	4.79 /12	--	0.22	2.78
GL	Guggenheim Event Dr Distr Strat H	RYDSX	D-	(800) 820-0888		D- / 1.5	2.88	1.57	-1.18 /12	5.56 /15	--	0.21	2.03
GL	Guggenheim Event Dr Distr Strat I	RYDTX	D	(800) 820-0888		D / 1.6	2.92	1.70	-0.96 /13	5.81 /16	--	0.21	1.78
GI	Guggenheim Large Cap Value A	SECIX	C+	(800) 820-0888		C / 5.2	0.21	2.18	5.73 /44	13.72 /65	10.86 /51	0.76	1.48

99 Pct = Best
0 Pct = Worst

● Denotes fund is closed to new investors
* Denotes fund is included in Section II

www.thestreetratings.com

RISK			NET ASSETS		ASSET				Portfolio Turnover Ratio	BULL / BEAR		FUND MANAGER		MINIMUMS		LOADS	
Risk Rating/Pts	3 Year		NAV As of 3/31/15	Total $(Mil)	Cash %	Stocks %	Bonds %	Other %		Last Bull Market Return	Last Bear Market Return	Manager Quality Pct	Manager Tenure (Years)	Initial Purch. $	Additional Purch. $	Front End Load	Back End Load
	Standard Deviation	Beta															
B+ / 9.2	6.2	0.96	13.16	62	6	58	34	2	26	50.6	-11.2	74	6	0	0	0.0	0.0
B+ / 9.2	6.2	0.96	11.76	26	6	58	34	2	26	49.8	-11.2	73	6	0	0	0.0	0.0
B+ / 9.3	5.8	0.56	11.72	28	6	54	38	2	31	46.7	-10.7	67	6	0	0	0.0	0.0
B+ / 9.3	5.8	0.56	11.84	45	6	54	38	2	31	46.2	-10.8	66	6	0	0	0.0	0.0
B+ / 9.3	5.8	0.56	10.65	6	6	54	38	2	31	45.4	-10.9	64	6	0	0	0.0	0.0
B+ / 9.3	5.9	0.57	12.17	19	5	55	38	2	18	46.9	-10.7	66	4	0	0	0.0	0.0
B+ / 9.3	5.8	0.56	12.18	9	5	55	38	2	18	46.3	-10.7	65	4	0	0	0.0	0.0
B+ / 9.3	5.8	0.57	12.21	1	5	55	38	2	18	45.8	-10.7	62	4	0	0	0.0	0.0
B+ / 9.0	6.4	0.62	12.14	26	4	59	35	2	33	51.2	-13.4	63	6	0	0	0.0	0.0
B / 8.9	6.4	0.62	12.22	46	4	59	35	2	33	50.8	-13.4	61	6	0	0	0.0	0.0
B / 8.8	6.4	0.63	11.00	N/A	4	59	35	2	33	50.0	-13.5	58	6	0	0	0.0	0.0
B / 8.5	7.6	0.75	12.67	27	3	70	26	1	18	59.3	-15.8	47	4	0	0	0.0	0.0
B / 8.5	7.6	0.74	12.69	8	3	70	26	1	18	58.9	-15.8	48	4	0	0	0.0	0.0
B / 8.5	7.6	0.75	12.75	N/A	3	70	26	1	18	58.6	-15.8	45	4	0	0	0.0	0.0
B / 8.0	8.6	0.85	13.00	34	2	80	17	1	31	65.9	-17.7	36	6	0	0	0.0	0.0
B / 8.0	8.6	0.85	13.07	32	2	80	17	1	31	65.3	-17.2	34	6	0	0	0.0	0.0
B / 8.0	8.6	0.85	11.73	N/A	2	80	17	1	31	65.0	-17.7	34	6	0	0	0.0	0.0
B- / 7.7	9.3	0.92	12.84	15	1	86	11	2	19	68.9	-18.6	28	4	0	0	0.0	0.0
B- / 7.7	9.3	0.92	12.83	6	1	86	11	2	19	68.4	-18.6	27	4	0	0	0.0	0.0
B- / 7.7	9.3	0.92	12.94	N/A	1	86	11	2	19	68.9	-18.5	28	4	0	0	0.0	0.0
B- / 7.5	9.5	0.94	12.98	11	1	88	9	2	26	69.3	-19.0	24	6	0	0	0.0	0.0
B- / 7.5	9.5	0.94	12.97	15	1	88	9	2	26	68.8	-19.0	23	6	0	0	0.0	0.0
B- / 7.5	9.5	0.94	11.52	N/A	1	88	9	2	26	69.1	-19.0	24	6	0	0	0.0	0.0
B- / 7.5	9.6	0.95	12.93	8	1	89	8	2	12	68.9	-19.3	22	4	0	0	0.0	0.0
B- / 7.5	9.7	0.95	12.90	2	1	89	8	2	12	68.3	-19.3	20	4	0	0	0.0	0.0
B- / 7.5	9.6	0.95	12.98	N/A	1	89	8	2	12	68.7	-19.2	22	4	0	0	0.0	0.0
B- / 7.4	9.7	0.95	12.86	2	1	89	8	2	20	68.0	-19.4	19	6	0	0	0.0	0.0
B- / 7.4	9.7	0.95	12.85	2	1	89	8	2	20	67.3	-19.5	19	6	0	0	0.0	0.0
B- / 7.5	9.7	0.95	11.42	N/A	1	89	8	2	20	67.9	-19.5	20	6	0	0	0.0	0.0
C / 5.3	14.5	1.01	19.27	74	0	100	0	0	94	89.3	-25.7	38	8	0	0	0.0	0.0
B- / 7.5	9.6	0.97	19.03	921	0	92	7	1	18	85.2	-18.3	37	21	0	0	0.0	0.0
B- / 7.5	9.6	0.97	10.80	2	0	92	7	1	18	83.2	N/A	32	21	0	0	0.0	0.0
C+ / 6.5	10.9	0.94	23.42	912	0	94	5	1	29	104.3	-20.3	83	18	0	0	0.0	0.0
C+ / 6.5	10.9	0.94	8.95	10	0	94	5	1	29	102.5	N/A	81	18	0	0	0.0	0.0
B- / 7.8	8.0	1.31	24.70	153	1	69	28	2	42	64.2	-11.7	32	10	2,500	100	0.0	2.0
B- / 7.2	9.6	0.99	32.43	128	0	99	0	1	32	91.9	-15.2	62	5	2,500	100	0.0	2.0
B- / 7.5	10.8	0.59	15.78	64	5	94	0	1	35	N/A	N/A	97	N/A	2,500	0	0.0	2.0
C+ / 6.6	6.9	0.92	24.72	543	4	62	33	1	68	34.7	-10.0	17	28	5,000	100	0.0	2.0
B- / 7.2	10.3	0.98	29.66	87	0	0	0	100	0	76.7	-21.2	30	12	250	0	5.8	0.0
B- / 7.2	10.2	0.98	27.14	5	0	0	0	100	0	72.2	-21.5	22	12	250	0	0.0	0.0
B- / 7.2	10.3	0.98	27.24	34	0	0	0	100	0	72.3	-21.4	22	12	250	0	0.0	0.0
C+ / 6.5	7.4	0.44	8.64	10	13	85	1	1	19	4.1	-9.6	2	14	2,500	250	0.0	0.0
C / 4.5	12.9	0.73	13.91	71	8	80	10	2	43	71.2	-25.9	84	N/A	2,500	250	0.0	0.0
B- / 7.3	11.6	1.06	18.68	10	9	0	90	1	488	94.6	-24.5	18	N/A	2,500	100	4.8	0.0
B- / 7.3	11.7	1.07	16.79	1	9	0	90	1	488	89.5	-24.7	12	N/A	2,500	100	0.0	0.0
B- / 7.4	11.5	1.05	26.10	2	9	0	90	1	488	97.3	-24.4	23	N/A	2,000,000	0	0.0	0.0
U /	N/A	N/A	25.63	212	0	0	0	100	0	N/A	N/A	N/A	1	2,000,000	0	0.0	0.0
C+ / 6.6	6.2	0.42	26.82	1	98	0	1	1	161	30.2	-12.9	81	N/A	2,500	0	4.8	0.0
C+ / 6.4	6.2	0.42	25.74	1	98	0	1	1	161	26.9	-13.1	76	N/A	2,500	0	0.0	0.0
C+ / 6.6	6.2	0.42	26.82	3	98	0	1	1	161	30.2	-12.9	81	N/A	2,500	0	0.0	0.0
C+ / 6.7	6.2	0.42	27.17	4	98	0	1	1	161	31.2	-12.7	83	N/A	2,000,000	0	0.0	0.0
B- / 7.1	10.1	1.00	43.06	52	2	97	0	1	40	87.7	-22.2	35	10	2,500	100	4.8	0.0

						PERFORMANCE						
							Total Return % through 3/31/15				Incl. in Returns	
				Overall		Perfor-				Annualized		Dividend	Expense
Fund Type	Fund Name	Ticker Symbol	Investment Rating	Phone	mance Rating/Pts	3 Mo	6 Mo	1Yr / Pct	3Yr / Pct	5Yr / Pct	Yield	Ratio
GI	● Guggenheim Large Cap Value B	SECBX	B-	(800) 820-0888	C+ / 6.2	0.28	2.34	6.04 /47	14.03 /67	11.11 /54	1.20	2.78
GI	Guggenheim Large Cap Value C	SEGIX	C+	(800) 820-0888	C / 5.4	0.05	1.84	4.99 /38	12.89 /59	10.03 /45	0.25	2.33
FS	Guggenheim Limited Duration A	GILDX	U	(800) 820-0888	U /	1.26	1.51	2.75 /25	--	--	3.18	1.16
FS	Guggenheim Limited Duration Inst	GILHX	U	(800) 820-0888	U /	1.28	1.63	3.00 /26	--	--	3.50	0.98
AG	Guggenheim Long Short Equity A	RYAMX	C-	(800) 820-0888	D+ / 2.3	3.39	10.38	7.23 /57	6.89 /21	5.20 /13	0.00	2.39
AG	Guggenheim Long Short Equity C	RYISX	C-	(800) 820-0888	D+ / 2.5	3.17	9.99	6.40 /50	6.09 /17	4.40 /10	0.00	3.16
AG	Guggenheim Long Short Equity H	RYSRX	C	(800) 820-0888	C- / 3.0	3.38	10.42	7.21 /57	6.87 /21	5.20 /13	0.00	2.41
GR	Guggenheim Long Short Equity Inst	RYQTX	C	(800) 820-0888	C- / 3.2	3.47	10.53	7.48 /59	7.15 /22	--	0.00	2.16
OT	Guggenheim Managed Futures Strat	RYMTX	C+	(800) 820-0888	C / 4.5	8.22	15.71	26.29 /99	4.79 /12	0.44 / 3	1.02	1.78
OT	Guggenheim Managed Futures Strat	RYMZX	C+	(800) 820-0888	C / 4.8	8.02	15.29	25.37 /98	4.01 /10	-0.31 / 2	1.14	2.53
OT	Guggenheim Managed Futures Strat	RYMFX	B-	(800) 820-0888	C / 5.3	8.22	15.77	26.29 /99	4.79 /12	0.44 / 3	1.07	1.79
OT	Guggenheim Managed Futures Strat I	RYIFX	B	(800) 820-0888	C / 5.5	8.33	15.89	26.59 /99	5.05 /13	--	1.06	1.56
OT	Guggenheim Managed Futures Strat	RYYMX	B	(800) 820-0888	C+ / 5.6	8.31	15.89	26.64 /99	5.10 /13	0.74 / 3	1.06	1.55
MC	Guggenheim Mid Cap Value A	SEVAX	D-	(800) 820-0888	C- / 3.9	1.69	3.82	-0.88 /13	11.94 /52	10.38 /48	0.00	1.39
MC	● Guggenheim Mid Cap Value B	SVSBX	D-	(800) 820-0888	C- / 4.0	1.48	3.34	-1.76 /11	10.98 /45	9.48 /40	0.00	2.23
MC	Guggenheim Mid Cap Value C	SEVSX	D-	(800) 820-0888	C- / 4.1	1.52	3.48	-1.58 /11	11.14 /46	9.58 /41	0.00	2.12
MC	Guggenheim Mid Cap Value Inst Fd	SVUIX	D	(800) 820-0888	C / 4.9	1.77	4.28	-0.27 /15	12.29 /55	10.62 /50	0.49	1.05
GL	Guggenheim Multi-Hedge Strat A	RYMQX	C-	(800) 820-0888	D- / 1.2	2.76	5.96	8.79 /68	3.40 / 9	4.03 / 8	0.72	2.86
GL	Guggenheim Multi-Hedge Strat C	RYMRX	C-	(800) 820-0888	D- / 1.3	2.56	5.56	7.98 /63	2.62 / 7	3.25 / 6	0.81	3.62
GL	Guggenheim Multi-Hedge Strat H	RYMSX	C	(800) 820-0888	D / 1.6	2.76	5.95	8.79 /68	3.41 / 9	4.04 / 8	0.76	2.88
GL	Guggenheim Multi-Hedge Strat I	RYIMX	C	(800) 820-0888	D / 1.7	2.81	6.10	9.05 /70	3.66 / 9	--	0.75	2.68
OT	Guggenheim Municipal Income C	GIJCX	C	(800) 820-0888	D / 1.6	1.02	2.57	8.61 /67	4.54 /12	--	1.72	2.08
EN	Guggenheim Municipal Income Inst	GIJIX	C	(800) 820-0888	D / 2.2	1.27	3.08	9.68 /73	5.60 /15	--	2.70	0.97
RE	Guggenheim Risk Managed Rl Est	GURIX	U	(800) 820-0888	U /	5.31	19.56	28.61 /99	--	--	0.43	2.69
SC	Guggenheim Small Cap Value A	SSUAX	E+	(800) 820-0888	C- / 3.8	1.75	7.68	-1.57 /11	11.54 /49	11.85 /60	0.49	1.85
SC	Guggenheim Small Cap Value C	SSVCX	E+	(800) 820-0888	C- / 4.1	1.64	7.32	-2.29 /10	10.72 /44	11.01 /53	0.00	2.51
SC	Guggenheim Small Cap Value Inst	SSUIX	E+	(800) 820-0888	C / 4.7	1.82	7.85	-1.36 /12	11.79 /51	12.11 /61	8.37	1.33
GR	Guggenheim StylePlus - Lg Cre A	SECEX	C-	(800) 820-0888	C+ / 6.1	1.25	6.15	13.31 /88	13.81 /66	11.65 /58	0.82	1.48
GR	● Guggenheim StylePlus - Lg Cre B	SEQBX	D-	(800) 820-0888	C+ / 5.9	0.93	5.44	11.89 /82	12.28 /54	10.39 /48	0.00	2.88
GR	Guggenheim StylePlus - Lg Cre C	SFECX	D	(800) 820-0888	C+ / 6.2	1.04	5.66	12.27 /84	12.72 /58	10.65 /50	0.36	2.43
GR	Guggenheim StylePlus - Lg Cre Inst	GILIX	A-	(800) 820-0888	B- / 7.0	1.31	6.25	13.45 /88	13.92 /66	--	1.08	1.46
MC	Guggenheim StylePlus - Mid Gro A	SECUX	B	(800) 820-0888	B / 8.0	5.38	11.54	15.63 /93	15.21 /77	14.00 /78	0.00	1.74
MC	● Guggenheim StylePlus - Mid Gro B	SEUBX	C	(800) 820-0888	B / 7.6	5.03	10.76	14.03 /89	13.49 /63	12.60 /65	0.00	3.20
MC	Guggenheim StylePlus - Mid Gro C	SUFCX	B-	(800) 820-0888	B / 8.1	5.18	11.05	14.63 /91	14.15 /68	13.05 /69	0.00	2.64
MC	Guggenheim StylePlus - Mid Gro Inst	GIUIX	A+	(800) 820-0888	B+ / 8.8	5.41	11.60	15.65 /93	15.33 /78	--	0.00	1.88
FO	Guggenheim World Equity Income A	SEQAX	D	(800) 820-0888	D+ / 2.7	1.78	0.43	3.21 /27	9.44 /36	6.41 /20	2.93	1.66
FO	● Guggenheim World Equity Income B	SGOBX	D+	(800) 820-0888	C- / 3.6	1.79	0.52	3.47 /29	9.72 /38	6.69 /21	3.48	3.24
FO	Guggenheim World Equity Income C	SFGCX	D	(800) 820-0888	D+ / 2.9	1.60	0.04	2.40 /24	8.61 /30	5.63 /15	2.34	2.62
FO	Guggenheim World Equity Income	SEWIX	D+	(800) 820-0888	C- / 3.6	1.83	0.55	3.46 /29	9.72 /38	--	2.92	1.33
GL	GuideMark Global Real Return Inst	GIGLX	E+	(800) 664-5345	E- / 0.2	-1.55	-7.01	-9.43 / 3	-2.91 / 2	--	1.50	1.31
GL	GuideMark Global Real Return Svc	GMGLX	E+	(800) 664-5345	E- / 0.2	-1.67	-7.24	-9.95 / 3	-3.48 / 2	--	1.01	1.88
GR	GuideMark Large Cap Growth Inst	GILGX	C+	(800) 664-5345	C+ / 6.7	2.21	7.26	12.51 /85	13.40 /63	--	0.59	0.92
GR	GuideMark Large Cap Growth Svc	GMLGX	C+	(800) 664-5345	C+ / 6.3	2.09	6.98	11.87 /82	12.76 /58	12.78 /66	0.20	1.52
GR	GuideMark Large Cap Value Inst	GILVX	A-	(800) 664-5345	B / 7.9	1.38	5.92	8.08 /63	16.15 /84	--	1.75	0.92
GR	GuideMark Large Cap Value Svc	GMLVX	B+	(800) 664-5345	B- / 7.3	1.21	5.50	7.46 /59	15.44 /78	12.36 /63	1.22	1.49
IN	GuideMark Opportunistic Equity Inst	GIOEX	B	(800) 664-5345	A / 9.4	3.80	9.92	13.26 /87	18.00 /94	--	0.94	1.07
IN	GuideMark Opportunistic Equity Svc	GMOPX	B	(800) 664-5345	A- / 9.1	3.66	9.59	12.61 /85	17.33 /91	--	0.42	1.64
MC	GuideMark Small/Mid Cap Core Inst	GISMX	A	(800) 664-5345	A / 9.4	4.94	13.13	11.99 /82	17.94 /94	--	0.00	1.09
MC	GuideMark Small/Mid Cap Core Svc	GMSMX	A-	(800) 664-5345	A- / 9.2	4.72	12.68	11.19 /79	17.23 /91	14.39 /81	0.00	1.66
FO	GuideMark World ex-US Inst	GIWEX	D-	(800) 664-5345	D / 1.9	4.17	0.58	-0.10 /15	6.57 /19	--	2.01	1.10
FO	GuideMark World ex-US Svc	GMWEX	D-	(800) 664-5345	D / 1.6	3.94	0.33	-0.68 /14	5.98 /17	2.92 / 6	1.45	1.67
AA	GuidePath Abs Ret Asst Alloc Svc	GPARX	D	(800) 664-5345	E+ / 0.8	1.11	1.26	2.47 /24	1.86 / 6	--	2.14	1.78

● Denotes fund is closed to new investors
* Denotes fund is included in Section II

www.thestreetratings.com

RISK			NET ASSETS		ASSET					BULL / BEAR		FUND MANAGER		MINIMUMS		LOADS	
	3 Year		NAV						Portfolio	Last Bull	Last Bear	Manager	Manager	Initial	Additional	Front	Back
Risk	Standard		As of	Total	Cash	Stocks	Bonds	Other	Turnover	Market	Market	Quality	Tenure	Purch.	Purch.	End	End
Rating/Pts	Deviation	Beta	3/31/15	$(Mil)	%	%	%	%	Ratio	Return	Return	Pct	(Years)	$	$	Load	Load
B- / 7.1	10.2	1.01	39.51	1	2	97	0	1	40	89.3	-22.1	39	10	100	100	0.0	0.0
B- / 7.1	10.1	1.01	40.22	4	2	97	0	1	40	83.0	-22.4	26	10	2,500	100	0.0	0.0
U /	N/A	N/A	24.87	49	3	0	95	2	40	N/A	N/A	N/A	N/A	2,500	100	2.3	0.0
U /	N/A	N/A	24.86	102	3	0	95	2	40	N/A	N/A	N/A	N/A	2,000,000	0	0.0	0.0
B / 8.0	6.5	0.50	16.16	6	39	60	0	1	256	35.8	-19.1	54	13	2,500	0	4.8	0.0
B- / 7.9	6.5	0.50	14.64	20	39	60	0	1	256	32.4	-19.3	43	13	2,500	0	0.0	0.0
B / 8.0	6.5	0.50	16.21	20	39	60	0	1	256	35.7	-19.1	54	13	2,500	0	0.0	0.0
B / 8.2	6.5	0.51	16.38	N/A	39	60	0	1	256	N/A	N/A	57	13	2,000,000	0	0.0	0.0
B- / 7.8	7.9	0.06	26.07	31	86	0	13	1	102	3.9	-7.8	91	8	2,500	0	4.8	0.0
B- / 7.5	7.9	0.07	24.51	26	86	0	13	1	102	1.2	-8.1	88	8	2,500	0	0.0	0.0
B- / 7.8	7.9	0.07	26.07	201	86	0	13	1	102	3.9	-7.8	91	8	2,500	0	0.0	0.0
B- / 7.9	7.9	0.06	26.41	12	86	0	13	1	102	4.8	-7.7	91	8	2,000,000	0	0.0	0.0
B- / 7.9	7.9	0.06	26.47	1	86	0	13	1	102	4.9	-7.7	91	8	25,000,000	0	0.0	0.0
C- / 4.1	12.5	1.08	34.39	722	0	99	0	1	41	75.5	-24.2	8	18	2,500	100	4.8	0.0
C- / 3.1	12.5	1.08	26.10	10	0	99	0	1	41	70.4	-24.4	5	18	100	100	0.0	0.0
C- / 3.3	12.5	1.08	27.45	172	0	99	0	1	41	71.3	-24.4	6	18	2,500	100	0.0	0.0
C- / 3.7	12.3	1.06	11.53	548	0	99	0	1	41	77.2	-24.4	10	18	2,000,000	0	0.0	0.0
B+ / 9.5	2.7	0.04	24.59	15	68	28	3	1	302	9.8	1.5	88	10	2,500	0	4.8	0.0
B+ / 9.5	2.7	0.04	22.85	10	68	28	3	1	302	7.0	1.2	85	10	2,500	0	0.0	0.0
B+ / 9.5	2.7	0.04	24.61	46	68	28	3	1	302	9.8	1.5	88	10	2,500	0	0.0	0.0
B+ / 9.5	2.7	0.04	24.91	41	68	28	3	1	302	10.7	1.6	89	10	2,000,000	0	0.0	0.0
B+ / 9.3	5.6	-0.04	12.73	2	4	0	95	1	173	N/A	N/A	93	3	2,500	100	0.0	0.0
B+ / 9.3	5.6	-0.03	12.74	8	4	0	95	1	173	N/A	N/A	94	3	2,000,000	0	0.0	0.0
U /	N/A	N/A	32.10	117	33	66	0	1	57	N/A	N/A	N/A	N/A	2,000,000	0	0.0	0.0
D+ / 2.3	13.6	0.96	14.52	16	1	98	0	1	45	82.7	-25.9	19	7	2,500	100	4.8	0.0
D / 2.1	13.5	0.96	13.64	7	1	98	0	1	45	78.1	-26.1	14	7	2,500	100	0.0	0.0
D- / 1.2	13.6	0.97	13.42	1	1	98	0	1	45	84.2	-25.8	21	7	2,000,000	0	0.0	0.0
C- / 3.9	9.7	1.00	22.63	196	63	14	21	2	107	90.1	-20.7	36	2	2,500	100	4.8	0.0
D / 1.7	9.8	1.01	16.22	3	63	14	21	2	107	81.9	-20.9	20	2	100	100	0.0	0.0
D+ / 2.7	9.8	1.01	18.46	3	63	14	21	2	107	84.1	-20.9	24	2	2,500	100	0.0	0.0
B / 8.0	9.7	1.00	22.48	N/A	63	14	21	2	107	N/A	N/A	38	2	2,000,000	0	0.0	0.0
C+ / 5.9	10.8	0.93	45.80	83	63	14	21	2	112	95.2	-20.6	61	2	2,500	100	4.8	0.0
C- / 4.1	10.8	0.93	29.44	1	63	14	21	2	112	85.8	-20.8	37	2	100	100	0.0	0.0
C / 5.1	10.8	0.93	36.33	5	63	14	21	2	112	89.3	-20.8	47	2	2,500	100	0.0	0.0
B- / 7.8	10.8	0.93	45.97	N/A	63	14	21	2	112	N/A	N/A	63	2	2,000,000	0	0.0	0.0
C+ / 6.0	12.1	0.87	13.39	83	3	96	0	1	131	50.2	-21.2	78	2	2,500	100	4.8	0.0
C+ / 6.0	12.1	0.87	11.63	2	3	96	0	1	131	51.6	-21.1	80	2	100	100	0.0	0.0
C+ / 6.0	12.1	0.88	11.50	6	3	96	0	1	131	46.5	-21.5	70	2	2,500	100	0.0	0.0
C+ / 6.0	12.1	0.88	13.33	4	3	96	0	1	131	50.6	N/A	79	2	2,000,000	0	0.0	0.0
C+ / 6.3	9.9	1.37	8.23	11	0	58	41	1	37	7.1	-18.0	1	4	0	0	0.0	0.0
C+ / 6.3	9.9	1.36	8.24	54	0	58	41	1	37	5.0	-18.3	0	4	0	0	0.0	0.0
C+ / 6.7	10.7	1.05	15.29	45	1	98	0	1	56	95.7	-20.1	24	4	0	0	0.0	0.0
C+ / 6.7	10.8	1.05	15.14	169	1	98	0	1	56	89.6	-20.4	18	4	0	0	0.0	0.0
B- / 7.3	10.3	1.04	12.46	61	1	98	0	1	29	100.0	-20.5	59	4	0	0	0.0	0.0
B- / 7.3	10.3	1.04	12.57	162	1	98	0	1	29	96.4	-20.7	48	4	0	0	0.0	0.0
C / 4.6	11.0	1.11	12.83	64	4	96	0	0	59	107.5	-22.5	67	4	0	0	0.0	0.0
C / 4.7	11.0	1.11	12.75	74	4	96	0	0	59	103.6	-22.7	59	4	0	0	0.0	0.0
C+ / 6.1	11.9	1.04	17.62	40	1	98	0	1	242	113.2	-26.9	69	1	0	0	0.0	0.0
C+ / 6.0	11.9	1.04	17.31	38	1	98	0	1	242	109.1	-27.1	61	1	0	0	0.0	0.0
C+ / 6.0	12.6	0.94	8.75	114	5	94	0	1	75	44.4	-25.5	34	4	0	0	0.0	0.0
C+ / 6.0	12.6	0.94	8.70	229	5	94	0	1	75	41.7	-25.6	28	4	0	0	0.0	0.0
B / 8.1	2.6	0.32	10.04	367	8	9	81	2	134	8.9	-2.0	45	4	0	0	0.0	0.0

Fund Type	Fund Name	Ticker Symbol	Overall Investment Rating	Phone	Performance Rating/Pts	3 Mo	6 Mo	1Yr / Pct	3Yr / Pct	5Yr / Pct	Dividend Yield	Expense Ratio
								Total Return % through 3/31/15	Annualized		Incl. in Returns	
GL	GuidePath Altegris Div Alt All Svc	GPAMX	U	(800) 664-5345	U /	3.35	5.56	7.91 /62	--	--	1.77	3.57
GL	GuidePath MultAsst Inc Asst All Svc	GPMIX	U	(800) 664-5345	U /	1.59	1.72	3.01 /26	--	--	3.53	1.83
GL	GuidePath Strat Asset Alloc Svc	GPSTX	C-	(800) 664-5345	C- / 3.7	2.83	3.56	4.47 /35	9.25 /35	--	1.13	1.65
GL	GuidePath Tct Cons Asst Alloc Svc	GPTCX	C-	(800) 664-5345	C- / 3.1	2.26	3.87	5.42 /42	8.01 /27	--	1.31	1.76
GL	GuidePath Tct Uncons Ast Alloc Svc	GPTUX	D+	(800) 664-5345	D / 2.1	2.08	2.42	3.08 /27	6.47 /19	--	1.39	1.91
GL	GuideStone Aggressive Alloc I Inst	GGBYX	C	(888) 984-8433	C / 5.1	2.56	3.62	5.38 /41	11.88 /52	10.84 /51	5.35	1.14
GL	GuideStone Aggressive Alloc Inv	GGBZX	C	(888) 984-8433	C / 5.0	2.49	3.50	5.17 /40	11.67 /50	10.68 /50	1.48	1.35
GL	GuideStone Balanced Alloc I Inst	GGIYX	C-	(888) 984-8433	D / 2.1	1.63	1.82	3.31 /28	6.71 /20	7.34 /25	5.00	0.92
GL	GuideStone Balanced Alloc Inv	GGIZX	C-	(888) 984-8433	D / 2.0	1.55	1.73	3.17 /27	6.52 /19	7.17 /24	2.01	1.08
GL	GuideStone Conservative All I Inst	GFIYX	D+	(888) 984-8433	D- / 1.0	1.37	1.01	1.72 /21	3.34 / 9	4.11 / 9	2.42	0.79
AA	GuideStone Defnsv Market Str Inst	GDMYX	C+	(888) 984-8433	C / 5.0	1.64	5.43	8.65 /67	11.12 /46	--	1.21	0.93
AA	GuideStone Defnsv Market Str Inv	GDMZX	C+	(888) 984-8433	C / 4.8	1.55	5.32	8.45 /66	10.85 /45	--	1.03	1.14
EM	GuideStone Em Mkts Eq Inst	GEMYX	U	(888) 984-8433	U /	0.11	-5.01	-4.04 / 7	--	--	0.73	1.56
EM	GuideStone Em Mkts Eq Inv	GEMZX	U	(888) 984-8433	U /	0.00	-5.15	-4.28 / 6	--	--	0.48	1.79
IX	GuideStone Equity Index Inst	GEQYX	A-	(888) 984-8433	B / 8.1	0.77	5.84	12.44 /84	15.88 /82	14.44 /82	2.98	0.25
IX	GuideStone Equity Index Inv	GEQZX	A-	(888) 984-8433	B / 7.9	0.70	5.67	12.20 /83	15.69 /81	14.25 /80	1.05	0.49
EN	GuideStone Global Natural Res Eq nv	GNRZX	U	(888) 984-8433	U /	-3.07	-20.36	-24.39 / 1	--	--	0.31	1.44
GL	GuideStone Growth Alloc I Inst	GCOYX	C-	(888) 984-8433	C- / 3.4	1.97	2.14	3.53 /29	9.05 /33	9.00 /37	3.74	1.02
GL	Guidestone Growth Equity Inst	GGEYX	D	(888) 984-8433	B / 7.6	2.53	6.50	13.28 /88	14.78 /73	14.96 /86	0.00	0.89
GL	GuideStone Growth Equity Inv	GGEZX	C+	(888) 984-8433	B- / 7.4	2.40	6.31	12.96 /86	14.51 /71	14.75 /85	0.00	1.13
FO	GuideStone International Eqty Inv	GIEZX	D-	(888) 984-8433	D / 2.2	5.13	1.35	-1.56 /11	7.25 /23	5.16 /13	2.04	1.50
GL	GuideStone My Destination 2015 Inv	GMTZX	C-	(888) 984-8433	D / 2.2	1.57	2.20	3.66 /30	6.68 /20	7.68 /28	1.95	1.10
GL	GuideStone My Destination 2025 Inv	GMWZX	C	(888) 984-8433	C- / 3.0	1.69	2.32	3.62 /30	8.26 /28	8.91 /36	1.97	1.19
GI	GuideStone My Destination 2055 Inv	GMGZX	C	(888) 984-8433	C- / 3.9	2.06	2.31	3.01 /26	10.10 /40	--	1.60	2.21
AA	GuideStone Real Assets Inv	GRAZX	U	(888) 984-8433	U /	-0.11	-4.44	-6.23 / 4	--	--	2.14	1.84
IN	GuideStone Small Cap Equity Inv	GSCZX	C	(888) 984-8433	B / 7.8	4.04	11.65	6.97 /55	15.29 /77	15.47 /90	0.10	1.26
IN	GuideStone Value Equity Inv	GVEZX	B+	(888) 984-8433	B / 7.6	0.05	4.33	8.13 /64	15.90 /83	13.59 /74	0.84	0.92
EN	Guinness Atkinson Alt Energy Fd	GAAEX	E-	(800) 915-6565	E+ / 0.7	3.80	-11.25	-15.88 / 2	5.05 /13	-9.42 / 0	0.00	2.13
FO	Guinness Atkinson Asia Focus	IASMX	E	(800) 915-6565	E / 0.5	2.31	1.41	6.28 /49	-0.70 / 4	0.35 / 3	1.02	1.88
FO	Guinness Atkinson Asia Pac Div Bldr	GAADX	D+	(800) 915-6565	C- / 3.4	4.05	6.05	13.45 /88	6.85 /20	7.20 /24	2.04	3.56
FO	Guinness Atkinson China & HK	ICHKX	E	(800) 915-6565	D / 1.9	4.82	6.84	10.92 /78	3.82 /10	0.17 / 3	1.45	1.54
GL	Guinness Atkinson Dividend Builder	GAINX	C+	(800) 915-6565	C / 5.1	0.12	0.50	3.53 /29	12.71 /58	--	3.04	5.47
EN	Guinness Atkinson Glob Energy	GAGEX	E-	(800) 915-6565	E- / 0.2	-2.68	-25.83	-25.81 / 0	-2.10 / 3	0.30 / 3	0.89	1.35
TC	Guinness Atkinson Glob Innov	IWIRX	A+	(800) 915-6565	A / 9.3	1.12	4.10	10.77 /77	18.90 /96	14.86 /86	0.77	1.47
GL	Guinness Atkinson Renminbi Yuan &	GARBX	D+	(800) 915-6565	E+ / 0.7	-0.40	-0.95	0.86 /18	2.32 / 7	--	3.50	0.97
IN	Hamlin High Dividend Eqty Inst	HHDFX	A+	(855) 443-3863	B+ / 8.6	2.94	7.33	10.65 /77	16.67 /88	--	2.50	1.31
IN	Hamlin High Dividend Eqty Inv	HHDVX	A+	(855) 443-3863	B / 8.2	2.79	7.01	10.08 /75	16.09 /84	--	1.68	1.81
SC	Hancock Horizon Burkenroad SC A	HHBUX	C+	(888) 346-6300	C+ / 6.3	6.09	7.78	2.09 /22	15.44 /79	16.81 /95	0.00	1.40
SC	Hancock Horizon Burkenroad SC D	HYBUX	B-	(888) 346-6300	B- / 7.1	6.02	7.64	1.81 /21	15.15 /76	16.52 /95	0.00	1.65
FO	Hancock Horizon Diversified Intl A	HHDAX	E+	(888) 346-6300	E+ / 0.6	0.56	-4.91	-5.54 / 5	4.12 /11	3.98 / 8	0.53	1.49
FO	Hancock Horizon Diversified Intl C	HHDCX	E+	(888) 346-6300	E+ / 0.7	0.39	-5.23	-6.21 / 4	3.35 / 9	3.21 / 6	0.00	2.24
GL	Hancock Horizon Dvsfd Income Inst	HHIIX	U	(888) 346-6300	U /	0.09	-3.85	-1.01 /13	--	--	5.69	1.32
FO	Hancock Horizon Dvsfd Intl Inst	HHDTX	E+	(888) 346-6300	E+ / 0.9	0.66	-4.77	-5.27 / 5	4.39 /11	4.25 / 9	0.82	1.24
GR	Hancock Horizon Growth A	HHRAX	C+	(888) 346-6300	B / 8.2	4.13	11.68	14.81 /91	16.43 /86	15.00 /87	0.00	1.26
GR	Hancock Horizon Growth C	HHRCX	C+	(888) 346-6300	B+ / 8.5	3.91	11.22	13.86 /89	15.54 /79	14.13 /79	0.00	2.01
GR	Hancock Horizon Growth Inst	HHRTX	B	(888) 346-6300	A- / 9.2	4.21	11.84	15.18 /92	16.76 /88	15.30 /89	0.05	1.01
GR	Hancock Horizon Quant Lg/Short Inst	HHQTX	C-	(888) 346-6300	C / 5.5	2.45	8.47	9.88 /74	11.47 /49	11.39 /56	0.00	1.67
GR	Hancock Horizon Quant Long/Short A	HHQAX	D+	(888) 346-6300	C / 4.5	2.44	8.37	9.68 /73	11.20 /47	11.12 /54	0.00	1.92
GR	Hancock Horizon Quant Long/Short C	HHQCX	D+	(888) 346-6300	C / 4.8	2.22	7.91	8.82 /68	10.39 /42	10.30 /47	0.00	2.67
IN	Hancock Horizon Value A	HHGAX	C-	(888) 346-6300	C+ / 5.6	0.14	3.93	4.19 /33	14.73 /73	12.78 /66	0.60	1.24
IN	Hancock Horizon Value C	HHGCX	C	(888) 346-6300	C+ / 5.9	-0.08	3.49	3.39 /28	13.86 /66	11.92 /60	0.14	1.99
IN	Hancock Horizon Value Inst	HHGTX	C	(888) 346-6300	C+ / 6.7	0.20	4.05	4.44 /35	15.01 /75	13.06 /69	0.81	0.99

Risk Rating/Pts	Standard Deviation	Beta	NAV As of 3/31/15	Total $(Mil)	Cash %	Stocks %	Bonds %	Other %	Portfolio Turnover Ratio	Last Bull Market Return	Last Bear Market Return	Manager Quality Pct	Manager Tenure (Years)	Initial Purch. $	Additional Purch. $	Front End Load	Back End Load
U /	N/A	N/A	10.48	100	40	21	29	10	40	N/A	N/A	N/A	3	0	0	0.0	0.0
U /	N/A	N/A	10.62	141	6	52	40	2	100	N/A	N/A	N/A	3	0	0	0.0	0.0
C+ / 6.7	10.1	1.56	11.62	260	4	92	3	1	30	60.1	-21.3	12	4	0	0	0.0	0.0
B- / 7.5	8.1	1.27	11.29	174	5	76	18	1	69	48.9	-15.9	23	4	0	0	0.0	0.0
B- / 7.7	6.2	0.90	10.32	481	34	50	15	1	245	34.7	-13.5	44	4	0	0	0.0	0.0
C+ / 6.2	10.9	0.76	13.60	188	10	89	0	1	17	76.1	-20.6	92	12	100,000	0	0.0	0.0
C+ / 6.2	10.9	0.76	14.41	877	10	89	0	1	12	74.9	-20.6	92	14	1,000	100	0.0	0.0
B / 8.0	5.3	0.82	10.58	374	7	44	46	3	31	37.7	-9.1	59	12	100,000	0	0.0	0.0
B / 8.0	5.3	0.83	13.09	1,302	7	44	46	3	27	37.0	-9.1	55	14	1,000	100	0.0	0.0
B / 8.7	2.8	0.18	9.61	78	9	21	67	3	21	17.7	-3.9	81	12	100,000	0	0.0	0.0
B- / 7.3	5.5	0.95	11.80	100	5	52	20	23	208	54.5	N/A	75	4	100,000	0	0.0	0.0
B- / 7.3	5.5	0.95	11.78	493	5	52	20	23	208	53.2	N/A	72	4	1,000	100	0.0	0.0
U /	N/A	N/A	9.10	45	0	0	0	100	0	N/A	N/A	N/A	N/A	100,000	0	0.0	0.0
U /	N/A	N/A	9.09	264	0	0	0	100	0	N/A	N/A	N/A	N/A	1,000	100	0.0	0.0
B- / 7.1	9.6	1.00	9.14	99	3	96	0	1	4	98.5	-15.2	64	14	100,000	0	0.0	0.0
B- / 7.3	9.6	1.01	23.06	341	3	96	0	1	4	97.5	-15.3	61	14	1,000	100	0.0	0.0
U /	N/A	N/A	7.57	282	5	94	0	1	18	N/A	N/A	N/A	2	1,000	100	0.0	0.0
B- / 7.1	8.2	0.59	11.91	272	7	70	21	2	28	55.9	-15.4	90	12	100,000	0	0.0	0.0
D- / 1.0	11.3	0.63	11.33	249	18	81	0	1	83	97.6	-15.8	97	12	100,000	0	0.0	0.0
C / 4.6	11.3	0.63	23.47	1,274	18	81	0	1	83	96.2	-15.9	97	12	1,000	100	0.0	0.0
C+ / 5.7	13.1	0.98	14.75	1,198	0	0	0	100	51	45.1	-25.0	38	14	1,000	100	0.0	0.0
B / 8.5	5.2	0.82	11.01	491	7	42	45	6	15	38.5	-10.2	58	9	1,000	100	0.0	0.0
B / 8.0	6.9	1.09	10.84	685	7	56	31	6	16	50.3	-14.0	45	9	1,000	100	0.0	0.0
B- / 7.5	9.9	0.97	12.86	31	7	85	6	2	30	N/A	N/A	11	4	1,000	100	0.0	0.0
U /	N/A	N/A	9.25	52	10	29	59	2	1	N/A	N/A	N/A	2	1,000	100	0.0	0.0
C- / 3.1	12.8	1.14	17.77	479	0	0	0	100	161	96.7	-23.8	28	14	1,000	100	0.0	0.0
C+ / 6.9	10.8	1.11	21.32	1,150	0	0	0	100	45	101.5	-19.9	40	14	1,000	100	0.0	0.0
D / 2.1	27.2	1.02	3.55	16	1	98	0	1	60	14.1	-48.3	78	9	5,000	250	0.0	0.0
C / 5.0	13.9	0.69	16.85	20	1	98	0	1	7	15.4	-31.5	4	12	5,000	250	0.0	2.0
C+ / 6.4	10.1	0.56	14.33	4	9	90	0	1	57	44.7	-22.5	81	9	5,000	250	0.0	2.0
D+ / 2.6	14.0	0.64	24.79	89	0	100	0	0	7	34.4	-34.4	35	17	5,000	250	0.0	2.0
B- / 7.6	10.2	0.68	15.73	10	1	98	0	1	25	N/A	N/A	95	3	10,000	1,000	0.0	0.0
D+ / 2.3	20.0	1.20	25.04	63	1	98	0	1	8	18.2	-34.1	5	11	5,000	250	0.0	0.0
C+ / 6.9	11.5	1.13	34.38	204	5	94	0	1	30	121.0	-21.0	71	5	5,000	250	0.0	0.0
B / 8.9	2.9	0.07	12.27	81	10	0	89	1	12	8.5	N/A	82	4	10,000	1,000	0.0	2.0
B- / 7.7	9.0	0.86	20.98	475	11	88	0	1	35	N/A	N/A	87	3	100,000	0	0.0	0.0
B- / 7.7	9.0	0.86	20.97	18	11	88	0	1	35	N/A	N/A	84	3	2,500	0	0.0	0.0
C+ / 6.0	12.3	0.86	59.60	727	1	98	0	1	28	94.7	-19.7	80	14	1,000	100	5.3	0.0
C+ / 6.0	12.3	0.86	57.94	53	1	98	0	1	28	93.1	-19.8	79	14	1,000	100	0.0	0.0
C+ / 5.8	13.2	0.95	21.40	46	1	98	0	1	19	34.3	-24.8	12	7	1,000	100	5.3	0.0
C+ / 5.7	13.1	0.95	20.84	N/A	1	98	0	1	19	30.9	-25.1	9	7	1,000	100	0.0	0.0
U /	N/A	N/A	14.71	52	30	29	40	1	74	N/A	N/A	N/A	N/A	1,000	100	0.0	0.0
C+ / 5.8	13.1	0.95	21.49	454	1	98	0	1	19	35.5	-24.8	14	7	1,000	100	0.0	0.0
C / 4.3	10.1	1.00	20.15	31	1	98	0	1	94	103.4	-19.7	70	14	1,000	100	5.3	0.0
C- / 3.6	10.1	1.00	17.28	1	1	98	0	1	94	98.3	-20.0	59	14	1,000	100	0.0	0.0
C / 4.5	10.1	1.00	21.06	124	1	98	0	1	94	105.3	-19.7	72	14	1,000	100	0.0	0.0
C / 5.2	8.3	0.77	18.39	69	33	66	0	1	223	69.9	-20.1	58	7	1,000	100	0.0	0.0
C / 5.1	8.3	0.77	18.08	46	33	66	0	1	223	68.4	-20.2	54	7	1,000	100	5.3	0.0
C / 4.9	8.2	0.77	17.03	2	33	66	0	1	223	64.3	-20.4	43	7	1,000	100	0.0	0.0
C / 5.1	11.8	1.16	26.33	49	0	99	0	1	65	88.2	-20.5	19	15	1,000	100	5.3	0.0
C / 5.0	11.8	1.16	25.46	1	0	99	0	1	65	83.5	-20.8	14	15	1,000	100	0.0	0.0
C / 5.2	11.8	1.16	26.47	128	0	99	0	1	65	89.8	-20.5	22	15	1,000	100	0.0	0.0

						PERFORMANCE							
	99 Pct = Best 0 Pct = Worst							Total Return % through 3/31/15				Incl. in Returns	
				Overall		Perfor- mance					Annualized	Dividend	Expense
Fund Type	Fund Name	Ticker Symbol	Investment Rating		Phone	Rating/Pts	3 Mo	6 Mo	1Yr / Pct	3Yr / Pct	5Yr / Pct	Yield	Ratio
GR	Harbor Capital Appreciation Admin	HRCAX	B		(800) 422-1050	B+ / 8.7	5.49	8.86	15.88 /93	15.48 /79	14.79 /85	0.00	0.93
GR	Harbor Capital Appreciation Inst	HACAX	B+		(800) 422-1050	B+ / 8.9	5.55	9.00	16.18 /94	15.78 /82	15.08 /87	0.07	0.68
GR	Harbor Capital Appreciation Inv	HCAIX	B		(800) 422-1050	B+ / 8.6	5.46	8.80	15.74 /93	15.35 /78	14.66 /84	0.00	1.05
IN	Harbor Commodity Real Rtn Str Adm	HCMRX	E-		(800) 422-1050	E- / 0.1	-5.22	-18.85	-28.38 / 0	-12.68 / 1	-4.22 / 1	4.55	1.30
IN	Harbor Commodity Real Rtn Str Inst	HACMX	E-		(800) 422-1050	E- / 0.1	-4.98	-18.69	-28.03 / 0	-12.39 / 1	-3.93 / 1	4.69	1.05
CV	Harbor Convertible Sec Adm	HRCSX	C-		(800) 422-1050	D / 2.1	3.32	2.71	2.21 /23	6.75 /20	--	1.76	1.00
CV	Harbor Convertible Sec Inst	HACSX	C-		(800) 422-1050	D / 2.2	3.27	2.74	2.36 /23	7.01 /21	--	1.99	0.75
CV	Harbor Convertible Sec Inv	HICSX	C-		(800) 422-1050	D / 2.0	3.18	2.55	1.98 /22	6.60 /19	--	1.62	1.12
EM	Harbor Emerging Markets Eqty Inst	HAEMX	U		(800) 422-1050	U /	-0.43	-6.27	-5.51 / 5	--	--	0.49	2.35
GL	Harbor Global Growth Admin	HRGAX	C		(800) 422-1050	B- / 7.2	4.51	5.75	9.40 /71	14.62 /72	13.81 /76	0.00	1.34
GL	Harbor Global Growth Inst	HGGAX	C+		(800) 422-1050	B- / 7.4	4.58	5.87	9.65 /73	14.90 /74	14.10 /79	0.14	1.09
GL	Harbor Global Growth Inv	HGGIX	C		(800) 422-1050	B- / 7.1	4.54	5.73	9.26 /71	14.48 /71	13.67 /75	0.00	1.46
FO	Harbor International Admin	HRINX	D-		(800) 422-1050	D / 1.8	5.71	1.37	-2.67 / 9	6.48 /19	6.33 /19	1.46	1.02
FO	Harbor International Growth Admin	HRIGX	D-		(800) 422-1050	D / 1.8	6.81	4.99	-0.11 /15	5.67 /15	5.21 /13	1.13	1.14
FO	Harbor International Growth Inst	HAIGX	D-		(800) 422-1050	D / 2.0	6.86	5.07	0.16 /16	5.93 /16	5.47 /14	1.45	0.89
FO	Harbor International Growth Inv	HIIGX	D-		(800) 422-1050	D / 1.8	6.82	4.93	-0.17 /15	5.55 /15	5.07 /12	1.07	1.26
FO	Harbor International Inst	HAINX	D-		(800) 422-1050	D / 2.0	5.77	1.49	-2.43 /10	6.76 /20	6.60 /21	2.07	0.77
FO	Harbor International Inv	HIINX	D-		(800) 422-1050	D / 1.8	5.69	1.30	-2.78 / 9	6.36 /18	6.21 /18	1.68	1.14
GI	Harbor Large Cap Value Admin	HRLVX	A-		(800) 422-1050	B+ / 8.5	3.27	7.02	9.69 /73	16.68 /88	13.31 /71	0.83	0.96
GI	Harbor Large Cap Value Inst	HAVLX	A-		(800) 422-1050	B+ / 8.7	3.27	7.07	9.85 /74	16.96 /90	13.58 /74	1.05	0.71
GI	Harbor Large Cap Value Inv	HILVX	A-		(800) 422-1050	B+ / 8.4	3.16	6.83	9.44 /72	16.53 /87	13.14 /69	0.76	1.08
MC	Harbor Mid Cap Growth Admin	HRMGX	C-		(800) 422-1050	B / 8.2	5.43	9.35	9.75 /73	15.62 /80	13.91 /77	0.00	1.10
MC	Harbor Mid Cap Growth Inst	HAMGX	C		(800) 422-1050	B+ / 8.4	5.48	9.49	10.08 /75	15.90 /83	14.20 /79	0.00	0.85
MC	Harbor Mid Cap Growth Inv	HIMGX	C-		(800) 422-1050	B / 8.1	5.44	9.33	9.74 /73	15.51 /79	13.78 /76	0.00	1.22
MC	Harbor Mid Cap Value Admin	HRMVX	A+		(800) 422-1050	A+ / 9.8	3.21	10.70	12.41 /84	21.13 /98	16.22 /94	0.74	1.15
MC	Harbor Mid Cap Value Inst	HAMVX	A+		(800) 422-1050	A+ / 9.8	3.29	10.80	12.70 /86	21.41 /98	16.53 /95	0.90	0.90
MC	Harbor Mid Cap Value Inv	HIMVX	A+		(800) 422-1050	A+ / 9.8	3.19	10.66	12.33 /84	20.98 /98	16.10 /93	0.67	1.27
SC	● Harbor Small Cap Growth Admin	HRSGX	B-		(800) 422-1050	A+ / 9.8	8.25	17.50	14.62 /91	20.04 /98	16.35 /94	0.00	1.09
SC	● Harbor Small Cap Growth Inst	HASGX	B		(800) 422-1050	A+ / 9.8	8.32	17.69	14.91 /91	20.36 /98	16.62 /95	0.00	0.84
SC	● Harbor Small Cap Growth Inv	HISGX	B-		(800) 422-1050	A+ / 9.8	8.22	17.51	14.47 /90	19.90 /98	16.19 /94	0.00	1.21
SC	Harbor Small Cap Growth Opps Instl	HASOX	U		(800) 422-1050	U /	3.69	11.30	5.58 /43	--	--	0.00	1.61
SC	Harbor Small Cap Value Admin	HSVRX	B		(800) 422-1050	A- / 9.0	4.32	13.61	10.50 /76	16.72 /88	14.42 /82	0.00	1.10
SC	Harbor Small Cap Value Inst	HASCX	B		(800) 422-1050	A- / 9.1	4.42	13.76	10.79 /78	17.03 /90	14.72 /84	0.21	0.85
SC	Harbor Small Cap Value Inv	HISVX	B		(800) 422-1050	B+ / 8.9	4.31	13.54	10.39 /76	16.59 /87	14.28 /80	0.00	1.22
AA	Harbor Target Ret 2015 Adm	HARHX	D		(800) 422-1050	D / 2.0	2.62	3.24	3.87 /31	6.06 /17	6.77 /22	3.38	0.90
AA	Harbor Target Ret 2015 Inst	HARGX	D		(800) 422-1050	D / 2.0	2.62	3.23	3.86 /31	6.06 /17	6.77 /22	3.38	0.65
AA	Harbor Target Ret 2015 Inv	HARIX	D		(800) 422-1050	D / 2.0	2.62	3.23	3.86 /31	6.06 /17	6.77 /22	3.38	1.02
AA	Harbor Target Ret 2020 Adm	HARKX	D+		(800) 422-1050	D+ / 2.3	3.05	3.68	4.18 /33	6.70 /20	7.29 /25	3.25	0.93
AA	Harbor Target Ret 2020 Inst	HARJX	D+		(800) 422-1050	D+ / 2.4	3.15	3.68	4.18 /33	6.70 /20	7.29 /25	3.24	0.68
AA	Harbor Target Ret 2020 Inv	HARLX	D+		(800) 422-1050	D+ / 2.3	3.05	3.68	4.08 /32	6.70 /20	7.29 /25	3.25	1.05
AA	Harbor Target Ret 2025 Adm	HARNX	D+		(800) 422-1050	D+ / 2.6	3.28	3.78	3.93 /31	7.24 /23	7.60 /27	3.06	0.95
AA	Harbor Target Ret 2025 Inst	HARMX	D+		(800) 422-1050	D+ / 2.6	3.28	3.69	3.93 /31	7.20 /22	7.60 /27	3.06	0.70
AA	Harbor Target Ret 2025 Inv	HAROX	D+		(800) 422-1050	D+ / 2.6	3.28	3.78	3.93 /31	7.24 /23	7.60 /27	3.06	1.07
AA	Harbor Target Ret 2030 Adm	HARQX	D+		(800) 422-1050	C- / 3.0	3.41	3.87	3.77 /30	8.01 /27	8.20 /31	2.76	0.97
AA	Harbor Target Ret 2030 Inst	HARPX	D+		(800) 422-1050	C- / 3.0	3.41	3.86	3.76 /30	8.00 /27	8.18 /31	2.76	0.72
AA	Harbor Target Ret 2030 Inv	HARTX	D+		(800) 422-1050	C- / 3.0	3.41	3.87	3.77 /30	8.01 /27	8.20 /31	2.76	1.09
AA	Harbor Target Ret 2035 Adm	HARVX	C-		(800) 422-1050	C- / 3.6	3.66	4.25	3.97 /32	9.02 /33	8.83 /36	2.44	0.98
AA	Harbor Target Ret 2035 Inst	HARUX	C-		(800) 422-1050	C- / 3.6	3.66	4.32	3.96 /31	9.02 /33	8.84 /36	2.43	0.73
AA	Harbor Target Ret 2035 Inv	HARWX	C-		(800) 422-1050	C- / 3.6	3.66	4.25	3.97 /32	9.02 /33	8.83 /36	2.44	1.10
AA	Harbor Target Ret 2040 Adm	HARZX	C-		(800) 422-1050	C / 4.3	4.04	4.98	4.66 /36	10.13 /40	9.45 /40	2.20	1.00
AA	Harbor Target Ret 2040 Inst	HARYX	C-		(800) 422-1050	C / 4.3	4.04	4.99	4.67 /36	10.13 /40	9.45 /40	2.20	0.75
AA	Harbor Target Ret 2040 Inv	HABBX	C-		(800) 422-1050	C / 4.3	4.04	4.98	4.66 /36	10.13 /40	9.45 /40	2.20	1.12

● Denotes fund is closed to new investors

★ Denotes fund is included in Section II

Risk Rating/Pts	Standard Deviation	Beta	NAV As of 3/31/15	Total $(Mil)	Cash %	Stocks %	Bonds %	Other %	Portfolio Turnover Ratio	Last Bull Market Return	Last Bear Market Return	Manager Quality Pct	Manager Tenure (Years)	Initial Purch. $	Additional Purch. $	Front End Load	Back End Load
C / 5.3	11.8	1.03	61.13	651	0	99	0	1	34	98.6	-13.9	52	25	50,000	0	0.0	0.0
C / 5.3	11.8	1.03	61.77	23,614	0	99	0	1	34	100.3	-13.8	56	25	50,000	0	0.0	0.0
C / 5.3	11.8	1.03	60.44	1,961	0	99	0	1	34	97.8	-13.9	50	25	2,500	0	0.0	0.0
D+ / 2.6	14.5	0.77	4.36	1	0	10	89	1	635	-25.6	-19.9	0	7	50,000	0	0.0	0.0
D+ / 2.6	14.5	0.77	4.39	145	0	10	89	1	635	-24.8	-19.8	0	7	1,000	0	0.0	0.0
B / 8.2	4.6	0.58	10.86	N/A	4	0	5	91	54	32.7	N/A	53	4	50,000	0	0.0	1.0
B / 8.3	4.6	0.58	10.86	365	4	0	5	91	54	33.7	N/A	57	4	1,000	0	0.0	1.0
B / 8.3	4.5	0.57	10.85	2	4	0	5	91	54	32.1	N/A	53	4	2,500	0	0.0	1.0
U /	N/A	N/A	9.27	43	6	93	0	1	50	N/A	N/A	N/A	2	50,000	0	0.0	0.0
C / 4.5	11.4	0.70	22.02	1	3	96	0	1	141	97.9	-24.4	96	6	50,000	0	0.0	0.0
C / 4.5	11.4	0.70	22.17	35	3	96	0	1	141	99.6	-24.3	96	6	50,000	0	0.0	0.0
C / 4.5	11.4	0.71	21.88	12	3	96	0	1	141	97.1	-24.4	96	6	2,500	0	0.0	0.0
C+ / 5.6	12.6	0.92	68.26	874	0	98	1	1	11	49.4	-25.7	35	6	50,000	0	0.0	0.0
C+ / 5.7	13.0	0.92	13.02	1	8	91	0	1	30	44.1	-24.5	26	2	50,000	0	0.0	0.0
C+ / 5.7	12.9	0.92	13.08	227	8	91	0	1	30	45.3	-24.4	29	2	50,000	0	0.0	0.0
C+ / 5.7	12.9	0.92	13.00	17	8	91	0	1	30	43.5	-24.6	26	2	2,500	0	0.0	0.0
C+ / 5.6	12.6	0.92	68.52	43,125	0	98	1	1	11	50.7	-25.7	39	6	50,000	0	0.0	0.0
C+ / 5.6	12.6	0.92	67.82	4,474	0	98	1	1	11	48.8	-25.8	34	6	2,500	0	0.0	0.0
C+ / 6.6	11.3	1.12	11.99	23	4	95	0	1	32	101.1	-17.1	48	3	50,000	0	0.0	0.0
C+ / 6.6	11.3	1.12	11.99	213	4	95	0	1	32	102.7	-17.0	50	3	50,000	0	0.0	0.0
C+ / 6.6	11.3	1.12	12.09	20	4	95	0	1	32	100.4	-17.2	45	3	2,500	0	0.0	0.0
D+ / 2.3	12.6	1.01	9.90	386	3	96	0	1	95	91.8	-24.1	46	10	50,000	0	0.0	0.0
D+ / 2.5	12.6	1.01	10.21	312	3	96	0	1	95	93.3	-24.0	50	10	50,000	0	0.0	0.0
D / 2.2	12.6	1.01	9.69	35	3	96	0	1	95	90.8	-24.1	45	10	2,500	0	0.0	0.0
B- / 7.3	11.3	0.98	21.54	24	1	98	0	1	13	131.8	-25.2	91	11	50,000	0	0.0	0.0
B- / 7.3	11.3	0.98	21.37	350	1	98	0	1	13	133.8	-25.1	92	11	50,000	0	0.0	0.0
B- / 7.3	11.3	0.98	21.34	145	1	98	0	1	13	130.8	-25.2	91	11	2,500	0	0.0	0.0
C- / 3.5	13.3	0.92	14.31	1	2	97	0	1	76	118.6	-28.7	92	15	50,000	0	0.0	0.0
C- / 3.8	13.3	0.92	14.97	644	2	97	0	1	76	120.2	-28.6	93	15	50,000	0	0.0	0.0
C- / 3.4	13.3	0.92	13.83	16	2	97	0	1	76	117.4	-28.7	92	15	2,500	0	0.0	0.0
U /	N/A	N/A	11.24	154	0	0	0	100	55	N/A	N/A	N/A	1	50,000	0	0.0	0.0
C / 4.6	12.9	0.92	27.78	1	3	96	0	1	13	100.3	-22.6	81	14	50,000	0	0.0	0.0
C / 4.6	12.9	0.92	27.88	798	3	96	0	1	13	102.2	-22.5	83	14	50,000	0	0.0	0.0
C / 4.5	12.9	0.93	27.32	19	3	96	0	1	13	99.6	-22.6	80	14	2,500	0	0.0	0.0
C+ / 6.9	4.8	0.74	10.97	N/A	5	29	64	2	38	33.8	-9.0	41	6	50,000	0	0.0	0.0
C+ / 6.9	4.8	0.72	10.97	11	5	29	64	2	38	33.8	-9.0	43	6	1,000	0	0.0	0.0
C+ / 6.9	4.8	0.73	10.97	N/A	5	29	64	2	38	33.8	-9.0	42	6	2,500	0	0.0	0.0
B- / 7.0	5.4	0.84	10.14	N/A	1	34	64	1	19	37.9	-10.4	34	6	50,000	0	0.0	0.0
B- / 7.0	5.4	0.85	10.15	29	1	34	64	1	19	37.9	-10.4	34	6	1,000	0	0.0	0.0
B- / 7.0	5.4	0.84	10.14	N/A	1	34	64	1	19	38.0	-10.5	34	6	2,500	0	0.0	0.0
C+ / 6.7	6.1	0.97	12.60	N/A	0	40	59	1	33	41.8	-12.6	25	6	50,000	0	0.0	0.0
C+ / 6.7	6.0	0.96	12.60	11	0	40	59	1	33	41.8	-12.6	26	6	1,000	0	0.0	0.0
C+ / 6.7	6.1	0.97	12.60	N/A	0	40	59	1	33	41.8	-12.6	25	6	2,500	0	0.0	0.0
C+ / 6.4	6.9	1.12	9.40	N/A	0	50	48	2	22	47.9	-14.8	17	6	50,000	0	0.0	0.0
C+ / 6.4	7.0	1.13	9.40	27	0	50	48	2	22	47.8	-14.8	16	6	1,000	0	0.0	0.0
C+ / 6.4	6.9	1.12	9.40	N/A	0	50	48	2	22	47.9	-14.8	17	6	2,500	0	0.0	0.0
C+ / 6.4	7.9	1.28	13.88	N/A	0	60	39	1	39	54.8	-16.8	13	6	50,000	0	0.0	0.0
C+ / 6.4	7.8	1.27	13.89	9	0	60	39	1	39	54.9	-16.8	13	6	1,000	0	0.0	0.0
C+ / 6.4	7.8	1.27	13.88	N/A	0	60	39	1	39	54.8	-16.8	13	6	2,500	0	0.0	0.0
C+ / 6.0	8.8	1.43	9.28	N/A	1	69	29	1	22	62.2	-19.0	10	6	50,000	0	0.0	0.0
C+ / 6.0	8.7	1.41	9.27	20	1	69	29	1	22	62.2	-19.0	11	6	1,000	0	0.0	0.0
C+ / 6.0	8.8	1.43	9.28	N/A	1	69	29	1	22	62.2	-19.0	10	6	2,500	0	0.0	0.0

Fund Type	Fund Name	Ticker Symbol	Overall Investment Rating	Phone	Performance Rating/Pts	3 Mo	6 Mo	1Yr / Pct	3Yr / Pct	5Yr / Pct	Dividend Yield	Expense Ratio
AA	Harbor Target Ret 2045 Adm	HADDX	C	(800) 422-1050	C / 4.8	4.29	5.31	4.82 /37	11.03 /46	9.97 /44	1.87	1.01
AA	Harbor Target Ret 2045 Inst	HACCX	C	(800) 422-1050	C / 4.8	4.29	5.31	4.82 /37	11.03 /46	9.97 /44	1.87	0.76
AA	Harbor Target Ret 2045 Inv	HAEEX	C	(800) 422-1050	C / 4.8	4.29	5.39	4.82 /37	11.03 /46	9.97 /44	1.87	1.13
AA	Harbor Target Ret 2050 Adm	HAGGX	C-	(800) 422-1050	C / 5.4	4.62	5.95	5.48 /42	11.94 /52	10.52 /49	1.65	1.03
AA	Harbor Target Ret 2050 Inst	HAFFX	C-	(800) 422-1050	C / 5.4	4.62	5.95	5.48 /42	11.91 /52	10.51 /49	1.65	0.78
AA	Harbor Target Ret 2050 Inv	HAHHX	C-	(800) 422-1050	C / 5.4	4.62	5.95	5.48 /42	11.94 /52	10.52 /49	1.65	1.15
AA	Harbor Target Ret Inc Adm	HARBX	D	(800) 422-1050	D / 1.6	2.46	3.26	4.43 /35	5.09 /13	5.92 /16	3.43	0.88
AA	Harbor Target Ret Inc Inst	HARAX	D	(800) 422-1050	D / 1.6	2.46	3.26	4.32 /34	5.09 /13	5.90 /16	3.43	0.63
AA	Harbor Target Ret Inc Inv	HARCX	D	(800) 422-1050	D / 1.6	2.46	3.26	4.43 /35	5.09 /13	5.92 /16	3.43	1.00
EM	Harding Loevner Emerg Mrkt Advisor	HLEMX	E+	(877) 435-8105	E+ / 0.7	1.42	-2.50	-0.97 /13	3.24 / 8	4.19 / 9	0.80	1.45
EM	Harding Loevner Frontier EM Inst	HLFMX	D-	(877) 435-8105	D- / 1.4	-4.95	-12.58	-5.16 / 5	8.61 /30	4.47 /10	0.62	1.77
EM	Harding Loevner Frontier EM Inv	HLMOX	D-	(877) 435-8105	D- / 1.3	-5.09	-12.74	-5.47 / 5	8.26 /28	--	0.22	2.22
GL	Harding Loevner Global Equity Adv	HLMGX	C-	(877) 435-8105	C- / 3.9	3.14	4.08	8.46 /66	9.64 /37	9.11 /37	0.10	1.15
GL	Harding Loevner Global Equity Inst	HLMVX	C-	(877) 435-8105	C- / 4.1	3.23	4.22	8.73 /68	9.92 /39	9.37 /39	0.35	0.92
FO	Harding Loevner Intl Equity Inst	HLMIX	D	(877) 435-8105	C- / 3.0	5.18	3.72	4.36 /34	8.29 /29	7.73 /28	0.98	0.86
FO	Harding Loevner Intl Equity Inv	HLMNX	D	(877) 435-8105	D+ / 2.8	5.13	3.64	4.11 /33	7.97 /27	7.39 /26	0.64	1.16
FO	Harding Loevner Intl Small Co Inst	HLMRX	D+	(877) 435-8105	C- / 3.2	4.66	0.65	-3.71 / 7	10.17 /40	--	0.35	1.59
FO	Harding Loevner Intl Small Co Inv	HLMSX	D	(877) 435-8105	C- / 3.0	4.60	0.50	-3.93 / 7	9.89 /39	9.74 /42	0.21	1.88
AA	Hartford Balanced A	ITTAX	C+	(888) 843-7824	C- / 4.0	1.35	4.73	9.20 /70	10.91 /45	10.04 /45	1.03	1.17
AA	● Hartford Balanced B	IHABX	C+	(888) 843-7824	C / 4.3	1.11	4.26	8.21 /64	9.95 /39	9.10 /37	0.16	2.27
AA	Hartford Balanced C	HAFCX	C+	(888) 843-7824	C / 4.4	1.19	4.40	8.49 /66	10.15 /40	9.27 /39	0.45	1.86
GL	Hartford Balanced HLS IA		B	(888) 843-7824	C / 5.3	1.51	4.95	9.49 /72	11.50 /49	10.59 /49	1.74	0.65
GL	Hartford Balanced HLS IB		B-	(888) 843-7824	C / 5.1	1.46	4.82	9.21 /70	11.22 /47	10.31 /47	1.47	0.90
BA	Hartford Balanced Income A	HBLAX	C	(888) 843-7824	D+ / 2.8	1.00	3.00	5.90 /46	9.24 /34	10.10 /45	2.24	0.97
BA	● Hartford Balanced Income B	HBLBX	C+	(888) 843-7824	C- / 3.6	0.99	2.97	5.85 /45	9.17 /34	9.71 /42	2.32	1.82
BA	Hartford Balanced Income C	HBLCX	C	(888) 843-7824	C- / 3.1	0.85	2.61	5.09 /39	8.42 /29	9.30 /39	1.72	1.70
BA	Hartford Balanced Income I	HBLIX	C+	(888) 843-7824	C- / 3.8	1.07	3.20	6.17 /48	9.51 /36	10.39 /48	2.62	0.70
BA	Hartford Balanced Income R3	HBLRX	C	(888) 843-7824	C- / 3.4	0.93	2.85	5.53 /43	8.93 /32	9.78 /43	2.10	1.32
BA	Hartford Balanced Income R4	HBLSX	C+	(888) 843-7824	C- / 3.7	1.08	3.07	5.89 /45	9.29 /35	10.11 /46	2.38	1.02
BA	Hartford Balanced Income R5	HBLTX	C+	(888) 843-7824	C- / 3.8	1.14	3.19	6.15 /48	9.54 /36	10.39 /48	2.62	0.73
BA	Hartford Balanced Income Y	HBLYX	C+	(888) 843-7824	C- / 3.9	1.15	3.21	6.27 /49	9.69 /37	10.60 /49	2.67	0.62
AA	Hartford Balanced R3	ITTRX	B-	(888) 843-7824	C / 4.7	1.33	4.61	8.96 /69	10.67 /43	9.80 /43	0.86	1.50
AA	Hartford Balanced R4	ITTSX	B-	(888) 843-7824	C / 4.9	1.33	4.74	9.25 /71	10.98 /45	10.12 /46	1.12	1.16
AA	Hartford Balanced R5	ITTTX	B	(888) 843-7824	C / 5.1	1.41	4.90	9.56 /72	11.31 /48	10.45 /48	1.41	0.86
AA	Hartford Balanced Y	IHAYX	B	(888) 843-7824	C / 5.2	1.48	4.93	9.68 /73	11.39 /48	10.53 /49	1.48	0.74
* GR	Hartford Capital Apprec A	ITHAX	D+	(888) 843-7824	B / 8.0	3.34	6.06	10.42 /76	17.46 /92	11.68 /58	0.27	1.10
GR	● Hartford Capital Apprec B	IHCAX	D+	(888) 843-7824	B+ / 8.3	3.13	5.61	9.47 /72	16.49 /87	10.76 /51	0.00	1.95
GR	Hartford Capital Apprec C	HCACX	D+	(888) 843-7824	B+ / 8.4	3.18	5.71	9.65 /73	16.64 /88	10.90 /52	0.00	1.81
GL	Hartford Capital Apprec HLS IA		B-	(888) 843-7824	B+ / 8.3	3.62	6.34	9.61 /73	16.39 /86	12.40 /63	0.77	0.67
GL	Hartford Capital Apprec HLS IB		B-	(888) 843-7824	B / 8.1	3.56	6.20	9.33 /71	16.09 /84	12.12 /61	0.55	0.92
GR	Hartford Capital Apprec HLS IC	HCPCX	B	(888) 843-7824	B / 8.0	3.48	6.07	9.09 /70	16.01 /83	12.07 /61	0.66	N/A
GR	Hartford Capital Apprec I	ITHIX	C-	(888) 843-7824	A- / 9.1	3.42	6.24	10.80 /78	17.83 /94	12.01 /61	0.53	0.76
GR	Hartford Capital Apprec R3	ITHRX	C-	(888) 843-7824	B+ / 8.7	3.27	5.90	10.07 /75	17.13 /90	11.38 /56	0.00	1.40
GR	Hartford Capital Apprec R4	ITHSX	C	(888) 843-7824	B+ / 8.9	3.33	6.07	10.42 /76	17.48 /92	11.72 /59	0.24	1.10
GR	Hartford Capital Apprec R5	ITHTX	C	(888) 843-7824	A- / 9.1	3.42	6.20	10.73 /77	17.83 /94	12.05 /61	0.45	0.80
GR	Hartford Capital Apprec Y	HCAYX	C	(888) 843-7824	A- / 9.2	3.45	6.28	10.86 /78	17.96 /94	12.16 /62	0.53	0.70
GI	Hartford Checks and Balances A	HCKAX	C	(888) 843-7824	C / 4.4	1.50	4.30	8.22 /64	11.89 /52	9.79 /43	3.50	1.00
GI	● Hartford Checks and Balances B	HCKBX	C	(888) 843-7824	C / 4.7	1.40	3.92	7.40 /58	10.99 /45	8.91 /36	2.92	1.80
GI	Hartford Checks and Balances C	HCKCX	C	(888) 843-7824	C / 4.8	1.32	3.86	7.39 /58	11.04 /46	8.95 /36	3.00	1.75
GI	Hartford Checks and Balances I	HCKIX	C+	(888) 843-7824	C / 5.5	1.53	4.48	8.45 /66	12.18 /54	10.05 /45	3.90	0.75
GI	Hartford Checks and Balances R3	HCKRX	C+	(888) 843-7824	C / 5.1	1.42	4.14	7.77 /61	11.50 /49	9.40 /40	3.36	1.36
GI	Hartford Checks and Balances R4	HCKSX	C+	(888) 843-7824	C / 5.3	1.58	4.37	8.22 /64	11.84 /51	9.75 /43	3.68	1.06

● Denotes fund is closed to new investors
* Denotes fund is included in Section II

www.thestreetratings.com

RISK	3 Year		NET ASSETS		ASSET				Portfolio	BULL / BEAR		FUND MANAGER		MINIMUMS		LOADS	
Risk Rating/Pts	Standard Deviation	Beta	NAV As of 3/31/15	Total $(Mil)	Cash %	Stocks %	Bonds %	Other %	Turnover Ratio	Last Bull Market Return	Last Bear Market Return	Manager Quality Pct	Manager Tenure (Years)	Initial Purch. $	Additional Purch. $	Front End Load	Back End Load
C+ / 6.6	9.7	1.57	14.60	N/A	1	79	19	1	21	68.9	-20.8	7	6	50,000	0	0.0	0.0
C+ / 6.6	9.7	1.57	14.60	5	1	79	19	1	21	68.9	-20.8	7	6	1,000	0	0.0	0.0
C+ / 6.6	9.7	1.58	14.60	N/A	1	79	19	1	21	68.9	-20.8	7	6	2,500	0	0.0	0.0
C / 5.2	10.4	1.69	10.65	N/A	1	87	10	2	23	74.4	-21.5	6	6	50,000	0	0.0	0.0
C / 5.2	10.4	1.69	10.64	21	1	87	10	2	23	74.5	-21.5	6	6	1,000	0	0.0	0.0
C / 5.2	10.4	1.69	10.65	N/A	1	87	10	2	23	74.4	-21.5	6	6	2,500	0	0.0	0.0
B- / 7.3	4.0	0.53	9.43	N/A	5	19	74	2	20	26.6	-5.1	60	6	50,000	0	0.0	0.0
B- / 7.3	4.0	0.52	9.43	17	5	19	74	2	20	26.6	-5.1	61	6	1,000	0	0.0	0.0
B- / 7.3	3.9	0.52	9.43	N/A	5	19	74	2	20	26.6	-5.1	61	6	2,500	0	0.0	0.0
C / 4.9	13.4	0.95	46.27	2,481	0	96	3	1	28	37.5	-24.1	87	10	5,000	0	0.0	2.0
C+ / 6.6	10.2	0.40	8.45	507	9	89	1	1	37	45.0	-19.7	97	7	100,000	0	0.0	2.0
C+ / 6.6	10.2	0.41	8.39	56	9	89	1	1	37	43.2	-19.8	97	7	5,000	0	0.0	2.0
C+ / 6.3	10.5	0.72	32.24	69	3	96	0	1	30	62.6	-18.5	87	14	5,000	0	0.0	2.0
C+ / 6.3	10.5	0.72	32.26	787	3	96	0	1	30	64.1	-18.4	88	14	100,000	0	0.0	2.0
C+ / 5.9	12.1	0.86	18.47	4,185	2	97	0	1	10	51.8	-22.2	69	14	100,000	0	0.0	2.0
C+ / 5.9	12.1	0.86	18.45	407	2	97	0	1	10	50.2	-22.3	65	14	5,000	0	0.0	2.0
C+ / 6.1	11.6	0.81	13.69	32	6	92	0	2	36	57.3	N/A	86	8	100,000	0	0.0	2.0
C+ / 6.1	11.7	0.81	13.65	65	6	92	0	2	36	56.0	-23.2	84	8	5,000	0	0.0	2.0
B / 8.3	6.7	1.18	21.08	605	2	68	28	2	39	62.7	-12.2	40	11	2,000	50	5.5	0.0
B / 8.2	6.8	1.18	20.97	7	2	68	28	2	39	58.0	-12.5	29	11	0	0	0.0	0.0
B / 8.2	6.7	1.18	21.09	147	2	68	28	2	39	58.7	-12.4	31	11	2,000	50	0.0	0.0
B / 8.3	6.8	1.01	27.50	2,507	1	66	32	1	31	66.0	-12.1	85	11	0	0	0.0	0.0
B / 8.3	6.7	1.00	27.85	353	1	66	32	1	31	64.5	-12.2	84	11	0	0	0.0	0.0
B / 8.3	5.2	0.85	13.57	2,550	3	45	50	2	40	48.2	-5.4	68	9	2,000	50	5.5	0.0
B / 8.3	5.2	0.85	13.53	16	3	45	50	2	40	47.5	-5.8	67	9	0	0	0.0	0.0
B / 8.3	5.2	0.85	13.41	2,213	3	45	50	2	40	44.5	-5.8	57	9	2,000	50	0.0	0.0
B / 8.3	5.2	0.86	13.57	1,251	3	45	50	2	40	49.5	-5.4	70	9	2,000	50	0.0	0.0
B / 8.3	5.2	0.85	13.61	119	3	45	50	2	40	46.9	-5.6	63	9	0	0	0.0	0.0
B / 8.3	5.2	0.85	13.62	62	3	45	50	2	40	48.4	-5.5	68	9	0	0	0.0	0.0
B / 8.3	5.2	0.85	13.63	22	3	45	50	2	40	49.6	-5.3	71	9	0	0	0.0	0.0
B / 8.3	5.2	0.85	13.69	31	3	45	50	2	40	50.5	-5.3	73	9	250,000	0	0.0	0.0
B / 8.3	6.8	1.18	21.30	1	2	68	28	2	39	61.4	-12.3	37	11	0	0	0.0	0.0
B / 8.3	6.8	1.18	21.32	1	2	68	28	2	39	63.0	-12.2	41	11	0	0	0.0	0.0
B / 8.3	6.7	1.18	21.34	N/A	2	68	28	2	39	64.7	-12.0	46	11	0	0	0.0	0.0
B / 8.3	6.7	1.17	21.36	4	2	68	28	2	39	65.1	-12.0	47	11	250,000	0	0.0	0.0
D / 1.6	11.3	1.10	38.33	5,744	2	96	0	2	111	105.2	-25.6	63	19	2,000	50	5.5	0.0
E+ / 0.9	11.3	1.10	31.30	218	2	96	0	2	111	99.5	-25.9	50	19	0	0	0.0	0.0
E+ / 0.9	11.3	1.10	31.76	1,935	2	96	0	2	111	100.3	-25.8	52	19	2,000	50	0.0	0.0
C / 4.9	11.2	0.69	56.69	6,426	1	98	0	1	86	100.3	-24.7	97	24	0	0	0.0	0.0
C / 4.9	11.2	0.69	56.13	756	1	98	0	1	86	98.6	-24.8	97	24	0	0	0.0	0.0
C / 5.3	11.2	1.10	56.49	4	1	98	0	1	86	98.2	-24.8	42	24	0	0	0.0	0.0
D / 1.6	11.3	1.10	38.42	1,856	2	96	0	2	111	107.4	-25.6	N/A	19	2,000	50	0.0	0.0
D / 2.0	11.3	1.10	41.33	134	2	96	0	2	111	103.3	-25.7	59	19	0	0	0.0	0.0
D / 2.1	11.3	1.10	42.26	185	2	96	0	2	111	105.4	-25.6	63	19	0	0	0.0	0.0
D / 2.1	11.3	1.10	42.96	57	2	96	0	2	111	107.5	-25.5	67	19	0	0	0.0	0.0
D / 2.2	11.3	1.10	43.15	1,300	2	96	0	2	111	108.2	-25.5	68	19	250,000	0	0.0	0.0
C+ / 6.8	6.7	0.68	10.93	1,442	0	64	35	1	15	64.8	-13.8	77	8	2,000	50	5.5	0.0
C+ / 6.8	6.7	0.69	10.88	104	0	64	35	1	15	60.5	-14.2	69	8	0	0	0.0	0.0
C+ / 6.8	6.7	0.69	10.87	348	0	64	35	1	15	60.7	-14.1	69	8	2,000	50	0.0	0.0
C+ / 6.8	6.7	0.68	10.94	36	0	64	35	1	15	66.4	-13.8	79	7	2,000	50	0.0	0.0
C+ / 6.8	6.7	0.69	10.90	13	0	64	35	1	15	63.0	-14.1	73	7	0	0	0.0	0.0
C+ / 6.8	6.7	0.68	10.91	4	0	64	35	1	15	64.7	-14.0	77	7	0	0	0.0	0.0

99 Pct = Best
0 Pct = Worst

Fund Type	Fund Name	Ticker Symbol	Overall Investment Rating	Phone	PERFORMANCE Perfor-mance Rating/Pts	Total Return % through 3/31/15 3 Mo	6 Mo	1Yr / Pct	Annualized 3Yr / Pct	5Yr / Pct	Incl. in Returns Dividend Yield	Expense Ratio
GI	Hartford Checks and Balances R5	HCKTX	C+	(888) 843-7824	C / 5.5	1.65	4.51	8.48 /66	12.19 /54	10.07 /45	3.92	0.76
AA	Hartford Conservative Alloc A	HCVAX	D-	(888) 843-7824	E / 0.5	1.40	-0.24	0.04 /16	1.85 / 6	4.05 / 8	1.53	1.30
AA	● Hartford Conservative Alloc B	HCVBX	D-	(888) 843-7824	E+ / 0.6	1.31	-0.56	-0.74 /14	1.07 / 5	3.23 / 6	1.21	2.14
AA	Hartford Conservative Alloc C	HCVCX	D-	(888) 843-7824	E+ / 0.6	1.31	-0.52	-0.61 /14	1.13 / 5	3.30 / 7	1.25	2.05
AA	Hartford Conservative Alloc I	HCVIX	D	(888) 843-7824	E+ / 0.7	1.50	-0.16	0.27 /16	2.14 / 6	4.34 /10	1.84	1.03
AA	Hartford Conservative Alloc R3	HCVRX	D	(888) 843-7824	E+ / 0.7	1.40	-0.41	-0.22 /15	1.53 / 6	3.70 / 7	1.34	1.65
AA	Hartford Conservative Alloc R4	HCVSX	D	(888) 843-7824	E+ / 0.7	1.40	-0.26	--	1.84 / 6	4.03 / 8	1.57	1.35
AA	Hartford Conservative Alloc R5	HCVTX	D	(888) 843-7824	E+ / 0.7	1.50	-0.07	0.36 /17	2.15 / 6	4.33 / 9	1.84	1.05
GR	Hartford Core Equity A	HAIAX	A+	(888) 843-7824	A- / 9.1	3.37	10.77	16.98 /95	18.20 /95	15.65 /91	0.00	1.07
GR	● Hartford Core Equity B	HGIBX	A+	(888) 843-7824	A / 9.3	3.18	10.34	16.03 /93	17.28 /91	14.77 /85	0.00	2.19
GR	Hartford Core Equity C	HGICX	A+	(888) 843-7824	A / 9.3	3.24	10.42	16.20 /94	17.37 /92	14.83 /85	0.00	1.76
GR	Hartford Core Equity R3	HGIRX	A+	(888) 843-7824	A / 9.5	3.31	10.61	16.69 /94	17.98 /94	15.46 /90	0.00	1.40
GR	Hartford Core Equity R4	HGISX	A+	(888) 843-7824	A+ / 9.6	3.36	10.80	17.05 /95	18.34 /95	15.80 /92	0.00	1.04
GR	Hartford Core Equity R5	HGITX	A+	(888) 843-7824	A+ / 9.6	3.44	10.94	17.40 /95	18.69 /96	16.16 /94	2.69	0.74
GR	Hartford Core Equity Y	HGIYX	A+	(888) 843-7824	A+ / 9.6	3.47	10.95	17.44 /95	18.73 /96	16.20 /94	2.72	0.61
IN	Hartford Div & Growth HLS IA		B-	(888) 843-7824	B- / 7.3	-0.08	4.28	9.87 /74	15.29 /77	13.08 /69	1.65	0.67
IN	Hartford Div & Growth HLS IB		B-	(888) 843-7824	B- / 7.1	-0.15	4.14	9.55 /72	15.00 /75	12.79 /66	1.42	0.92
GI	Hartford Dividend & Gr HLS Fd IA	HIADX	B-	(888) 843-7824	B- / 7.3	-0.08	4.28	9.87 /74	15.29 /77	13.08 /69	1.65	0.67
GI	Hartford Dividend & Gr HLS Fd IB	HDGBX	B-	(888) 843-7824	B- / 7.1	-0.15	4.14	9.55 /72	15.00 /75	12.79 /66	1.42	0.92
GI	Hartford Dividend & Growth A	IHGIX	C+	(888) 843-7824	C+ / 5.9	-0.14	4.02	9.28 /71	14.66 /72	12.46 /64	1.26	1.02
GI	● Hartford Dividend & Growth B	ITDGX	C+	(888) 843-7824	C+ / 6.1	-0.35	3.55	8.30 /65	13.63 /64	11.47 /57	0.40	1.96
GI	Hartford Dividend & Growth C	HDGCX	C+	(888) 843-7824	C+ / 6.3	-0.32	3.60	8.49 /66	13.82 /66	11.63 /58	0.68	1.77
GI	Hartford Dividend & Growth I	HDGIX	B	(888) 843-7824	B- / 7.0	-0.09	4.09	9.50 /72	14.90 /74	12.73 /66	1.53	0.81
GI	Hartford Dividend & Growth R3	HDGRX	C+	(888) 843-7824	C+ / 6.6	-0.22	3.81	8.91 /69	14.30 /69	12.13 /61	0.99	1.35
GI	Hartford Dividend & Growth R4	HDGSX	C+	(888) 843-7824	C+ / 6.9	-0.14	4.02	9.28 /71	14.65 /72	12.48 /64	1.27	1.04
GI	Hartford Dividend & Growth R5	HDGTX	B	(888) 843-7824	B- / 7.1	-0.03	4.16	9.62 /73	15.02 /75	12.83 /67	1.56	0.74
GI	Hartford Dividend & Growth Y	HDGYX	B	(888) 843-7824	B- / 7.2	-0.01	4.20	9.72 /73	15.12 /76	12.93 /68	1.64	0.64
GI	Hartford Dscpld Equity HLS IA		A+	(888) 843-7824	A+ / 9.7	3.67	11.29	17.87 /95	19.02 /97	16.22 /94	0.65	0.76
GI	Hartford Dscpld Equity HLS IB		A+	(888) 843-7824	A+ / 9.6	3.59	11.15	17.58 /95	18.70 /96	15.92 /93	0.41	1.01
EM	Hartford Emg Markets Research A	HERAX	E	(888) 843-7824	E / 0.4	3.18	-3.16	-0.70 /14	0.85 / 5	--	0.60	1.86
EM	Hartford Emg Markets Research C	HERCX	E	(888) 843-7824	E / 0.5	2.97	-3.57	-1.48 /11	0.12 / 4	--	0.00	2.50
EM	Hartford Emg Markets Research I	HERIX	E	(888) 843-7824	E+ / 0.6	3.32	-2.88	-0.18 /15	1.24 / 5	--	1.02	1.37
EM	Hartford Emg Markets Research R3	HERRX	E	(888) 843-7824	E / 0.5	3.20	-3.18	-0.81 /14	0.64 / 5	--	0.42	2.05
EM	Hartford Emg Markets Research R4	HERSX	E	(888) 843-7824	E+ / 0.6	3.19	-3.10	-0.63 /14	0.92 / 5	--	0.70	1.75
EM	Hartford Emg Markets Research R5	HERTX	E	(888) 843-7824	E+ / 0.6	3.32	-3.02	-0.33 /15	1.21 / 5	--	0.99	1.45
EM	Hartford Emg Markets Research Y	HERYX	E	(888) 843-7824	E+ / 0.6	3.32	-2.97	-0.28 /15	1.30 / 6	--	1.04	1.34
IN	Hartford Equity Income A	HQIAX	C+	(888) 843-7824	C / 5.2	-0.09	3.80	6.92 /54	13.76 /65	13.40 /72	1.66	1.03
IN	● Hartford Equity Income B	HQIBX	B-	(888) 843-7824	C+ / 5.9	-0.07	3.78	6.82 /54	13.32 /62	12.76 /66	1.61	1.91
IN	Hartford Equity Income C	HQICX	B-	(888) 843-7824	C+ / 5.6	-0.26	3.41	6.16 /48	12.93 /59	12.58 /65	1.08	1.76
IN	Hartford Equity Income I	HQIIX	B-	(888) 843-7824	C+ / 6.3	-0.03	3.89	7.17 /56	14.08 /68	13.69 /75	2.02	0.76
IN	Hartford Equity Income R3	HQIRX	B-	(888) 843-7824	C+ / 5.9	-0.11	3.63	6.57 /51	13.40 /63	13.03 /68	1.44	1.37
IN	Hartford Equity Income R4	HQISX	B-	(888) 843-7824	C+ / 6.1	-0.04	3.83	6.93 /54	13.74 /65	13.40 /72	1.72	1.06
IN	Hartford Equity Income R5	HQITX	B-	(888) 843-7824	C+ / 6.3	-0.02	3.91	7.16 /56	14.10 /68	13.74 /75	2.00	0.76
IN	Hartford Equity Income Y	HQIYX	B-	(888) 843-7824	C+ / 6.4	0.06	4.01	7.31 /58	14.20 /69	13.84 /76	2.10	0.66
GL	Hartford Global All Asset A	HLAAX	E+	(888) 843-7824	D- / 1.4	3.34	2.57	2.41 /24	6.48 /19	--	2.35	1.45
GL	Hartford Global All Asset C	HLACX	E+	(888) 843-7824	D / 1.7	3.07	2.22	1.65 /21	5.69 /15	--	1.77	2.18
GL	Hartford Global All Asset I	HLAIX	D-	(888) 843-7824	D+ / 2.3	3.43	2.72	2.72 /25	6.79 /20	--	2.77	1.15
GL	Hartford Global All Asset R3	HLARX	D-	(888) 843-7824	D / 2.0	3.23	2.41	2.16 /22	6.24 /18	--	2.09	1.78
GL	Hartford Global All Asset R4	HLASX	D-	(888) 843-7824	D / 2.1	3.30	2.64	2.47 /24	6.57 /19	--	2.54	1.49
GL	Hartford Global All Asset R5	HLATX	D-	(888) 843-7824	D / 2.2	3.33	2.67	2.67 /25	6.77 /20	--	2.80	1.17
GL	Hartford Global All Asset Y	HLAYX	D-	(888) 843-7824	D+ / 2.3	3.43	2.72	2.72 /25	6.85 /21	--	2.85	1.07
GR	Hartford Global Capital Apprec A	HCTAX	D+	(888) 843-7824	C+ / 5.7	4.00	4.35	5.54 /43	14.36 /70	11.29 /55	0.28	1.26

● Denotes fund is closed to new investors
* Denotes fund is included in Section II

RISK			NET ASSETS		ASSET					BULL / BEAR		FUND MANAGER		MINIMUMS		LOADS	
	3 Year		NAV						Portfolio	Last Bull	Last Bear	Manager	Manager	Initial	Additional	Front	Back
Risk Rating/Pts	Standard Deviation	Beta	As of 3/31/15	Total $(Mil)	Cash %	Stocks %	Bonds %	Other %	Turnover Ratio	Market Return	Market Return	Quality Pct	Tenure (Years)	Purch. $	Purch. $	End Load	End Load
C+ / 6.8	6.7	0.69	10.94	2	0	64	35	1	15	66.4	-13.8	79	7	0	0	0.0	0.0
B- / 7.4	4.4	0.61	10.15	122	6	29	63	2	27	18.2	-8.2	13	N/A	2,000	50	5.5	0.0
B- / 7.4	4.4	0.61	10.08	5	6	29	63	2	27	14.9	-8.5	9	N/A	0	0	0.0	0.0
B- / 7.4	4.5	0.62	10.07	43	6	29	63	2	27	15.2	-8.4	9	N/A	2,000	50	0.0	0.0
B- / 7.4	4.4	0.61	10.14	1	6	29	63	2	27	19.3	-8.1	14	N/A	2,000	50	0.0	0.0
B- / 7.4	4.5	0.61	10.17	9	6	29	63	2	27	16.9	-8.3	11	N/A	0	0	0.0	0.0
B- / 7.5	4.5	0.62	10.16	3	6	29	63	2	27	17.9	-8.1	12	N/A	0	0	0.0	0.0
B- / 7.4	4.4	0.61	10.16	3	6	29	63	2	27	19.1	-8.0	15	N/A	0	0	0.0	0.0
B- / 7.3	9.9	1.01	23.30	167	7	92	0	1	60	106.7	-16.2	81	17	2,000	50	5.5	0.0
B- / 7.3	9.9	1.02	21.73	2	7	92	0	1	60	101.5	-16.5	75	17	0	0	0.0	0.0
B- / 7.3	9.9	1.02	21.68	31	7	92	0	1	60	101.8	-16.5	75	17	2,000	50	0.0	0.0
B- / 7.3	9.9	1.02	23.72	1	7	92	0	1	60	105.5	-16.3	80	17	0	0	0.0	0.0
B- / 7.3	9.9	1.01	23.96	2	7	92	0	1	60	107.7	-16.2	82	17	0	0	0.0	0.0
B- / 7.2	9.9	1.02	23.46	1	7	92	0	1	60	109.8	-16.1	84	17	0	0	0.0	0.0
B- / 7.3	9.9	1.01	23.53	8	7	92	0	1	60	110.1	-16.0	84	17	250,000	0	0.0	0.0
C+ / 5.9	9.5	0.98	26.43	3,371	1	98	0	1	25	92.8	-17.5	61	15	0	0	0.0	0.0
C+ / 5.8	9.5	0.98	26.34	524	1	98	0	1	25	91.1	-17.6	57	15	0	0	0.0	0.0
C+ / 5.9	9.5	0.98	26.43	3,371	1	98	0	1	25	92.8	-17.5	61	15	0	0	0.0	0.0
C+ / 5.8	9.5	0.98	26.34	524	1	98	0	1	25	91.1	-17.6	57	15	0	0	0.0	0.0
C+ / 6.4	9.4	0.97	25.10	3,807	2	96	0	2	23	88.6	-17.4	56	15	2,000	50	5.5	0.0
C+ / 6.4	9.4	0.97	24.66	62	2	96	0	2	23	82.9	-17.7	42	15	0	0	0.0	0.0
C+ / 6.4	9.4	0.97	24.46	478	2	96	0	2	23	83.8	-17.6	44	15	2,000	50	0.0	0.0
C+ / 6.4	9.4	0.97	24.99	1,881	2	96	0	2	23	90.1	-17.3	59	15	2,000	50	0.0	0.0
C+ / 6.4	9.4	0.97	25.35	92	2	96	0	2	23	86.7	-17.5	51	15	0	0	0.0	0.0
C+ / 6.4	9.4	0.97	25.48	157	2	96	0	2	23	88.6	-17.3	56	15	0	0	0.0	0.0
C+ / 6.4	9.4	0.96	25.55	239	2	96	0	2	23	90.6	-17.3	61	15	0	0	0.0	0.0
C+ / 6.4	9.4	0.97	25.56	1,333	2	96	0	2	23	91.2	-17.2	62	15	250,000	0	0.0	0.0
B / 8.1	9.9	1.02	21.76	718	0	0	0	100	23	111.8	-16.4	85	17	0	0	0.0	0.0
B / 8.1	9.9	1.02	21.63	103	0	0	0	100	23	109.9	-16.5	84	17	0	0	0.0	0.0
C- / 3.9	14.1	1.01	8.11	11	1	98	0	1	106	25.8	N/A	69	4	2,000	50	5.5	0.0
C- / 3.9	14.0	1.00	7.97	3	1	98	0	1	106	22.7	N/A	59	4	2,000	50	0.0	0.0
C- / 3.8	14.0	1.00	8.09	3	1	98	0	1	106	27.3	N/A	73	4	2,000	50	0.0	0.0
C- / 3.9	14.0	1.00	8.06	2	1	98	0	1	106	24.7	N/A	67	4	0	0	0.0	0.0
C- / 3.9	14.1	1.01	8.08	2	1	98	0	1	106	26.0	N/A	70	4	0	0	0.0	0.0
C- / 3.8	14.0	1.00	8.09	2	1	98	0	1	106	27.1	N/A	73	4	0	0	0.0	0.0
C- / 3.9	14.1	1.01	8.08	179	1	98	0	1	106	27.5	N/A	74	4	250,000	0	0.0	0.0
B- / 7.5	9.3	0.95	18.73	1,923	0	99	0	1	13	84.7	-14.1	48	12	2,000	50	5.5	0.0
B- / 7.5	9.3	0.94	18.75	18	0	99	0	1	13	81.7	-14.4	43	12	0	0	0.0	0.0
B- / 7.5	9.3	0.94	18.66	481	0	99	0	1	13	80.2	-14.3	38	12	2,000	0	0.0	0.0
B- / 7.5	9.3	0.94	18.65	920	0	99	0	1	13	86.5	-14.0	53	12	2,000	50	0.0	0.0
B- / 7.5	9.3	0.94	18.76	62	0	99	0	1	13	82.8	-14.2	44	12	0	0	0.0	0.0
B- / 7.5	9.3	0.94	18.78	79	0	99	0	1	13	84.5	-14.0	49	12	0	0	0.0	0.0
B- / 7.5	9.3	0.94	18.84	95	0	99	0	1	13	86.6	-14.0	54	12	0	0	0.0	0.0
B- / 7.5	9.3	0.94	18.88	252	0	99	0	1	13	87.2	-13.9	55	12	250,000	0	0.0	0.0
C / 5.1	8.0	1.25	11.15	186	15	59	24	2	75	36.2	-15.6	13	5	5,000	50	5.5	0.0
C / 5.2	8.0	1.25	11.09	115	15	59	24	2	75	32.9	-15.9	9	5	5,000	50	0.0	0.0
C / 5.1	8.0	1.25	11.17	76	15	59	24	2	75	37.4	-15.5	15	5	5,000	50	0.0	0.0
C / 5.2	8.1	1.25	11.18	3	15	59	24	2	75	35.1	-15.8	12	5	0	0	0.0	0.0
C / 5.1	8.1	1.25	11.27	2	15	59	24	2	75	36.6	-15.7	13	5	0	0	0.0	0.0
C / 5.1	8.0	1.25	11.16	3	15	59	24	2	75	37.5	-15.5	15	5	0	0	0.0	0.0
C / 5.0	8.1	1.25	11.16	30	15	59	24	2	75	37.8	-15.5	15	5	250,000	0	0.0	0.0
C- / 3.9	11.0	1.06	17.43	729	3	96	0	1	144	89.7	-25.5	31	10	2,000	50	5.5	0.0

Fund Type	Fund Name	Ticker Symbol	Overall Investment Rating	Phone	Perfor- mance Rating/Pts	3 Mo	6 Mo	1Yr / Pct	3Yr / Pct	5Yr / Pct	Dividend Yield	Expense Ratio
	99 Pct = Best				**PERFORMANCE**			Total Return % through 3/31/15	Annualized		Incl. in Returns	
GR	● Hartford Global Capital Apprec B	HCTBX	D+	(888) 843-7824	C+ / 6.0	3.78	3.99	4.75 /37	13.51 /63	10.42 /48	0.00	2.09
GR	Hartford Global Capital Apprec C	HFCCX	D+	(888) 843-7824	C+ / 6.1	3.81	4.03	4.84 /37	13.56 /64	10.49 /49	0.00	1.96
GR	Hartford Global Capital Apprec I	HCTIX	C-	(888) 843-7824	C+ / 6.9	4.07	4.59	5.90 /46	14.71 /73	11.63 /58	0.53	0.93
GR	Hartford Global Capital Apprec R3	HCTRX	C-	(888) 843-7824	C+ / 6.5	3.99	4.36	5.45 /42	14.24 /69	11.11 /54	0.20	1.55
GR	Hartford Global Capital Apprec R4	HCTSX	C-	(888) 843-7824	C+ / 6.8	4.06	4.51	5.79 /45	14.60 /72	11.44 /56	0.42	1.24
GR	Hartford Global Capital Apprec R5	HCTTX	C-	(888) 843-7824	C+ / 6.9	4.10	4.55	5.86 /45	14.73 /73	11.64 /58	0.52	0.95
GR	Hartford Global Capital Apprec Y	HCTYX	C	(888) 843-7824	C+ / 6.9	4.12	4.60	6.02 /47	14.80 /73	11.75 /59	0.66	0.84
GL	Hartford Global Equtiy Income A	HLEAX	C-	(888) 843-7824	C- / 3.8	2.80	2.03	2.91 /26	11.47 /49	9.79 /43	0.96	1.53
GL	● Hartford Global Equtiy Income B	HLEBX	C-	(888) 843-7824	C- / 4.1	2.54	1.66	2.10 /22	10.64 /43	8.98 /37	0.28	2.48
GL	Hartford Global Equtiy Income C	HLECX	C-	(888) 843-7824	C- / 4.1	2.49	1.63	2.07 /22	10.61 /43	8.96 /36	0.34	2.27
GL	Hartford Global Equtiy Income I	HLEJX	C	(888) 843-7824	C / 4.8	2.85	2.16	3.16 /27	11.72 /51	10.11 /46	1.34	1.13
GL	Hartford Global Equtiy Income R3	HLERX	C-	(888) 843-7824	C / 4.5	2.75	1.92	2.71 /25	11.24 /47	9.56 /41	0.72	1.73
GL	Hartford Global Equtiy Income R4	HLESX	C-	(888) 843-7824	C / 4.7	2.81	2.08	3.01 /26	11.57 /49	9.89 /44	1.10	1.41
GL	Hartford Global Equtiy Income R5	HLETX	C	(888) 843-7824	C / 4.9	2.88	2.21	3.29 /28	11.88 /52	10.23 /46	1.46	1.09
GL	Hartford Global Equtiy Income Y	HLEYX	C	(888) 843-7824	C / 5.0	2.90	2.24	3.37 /28	11.99 /52	10.30 /47	1.53	0.83
GL	Hartford Global Growth HLS IA		B+	(888) 843-7824	B+ / 8.3	4.17	7.01	11.14 /79	15.91 /83	12.40 /63	0.43	0.82
GL	Hartford Global Growth HLS IB		B	(888) 843-7824	B / 8.0	4.07	6.89	10.87 /78	15.62 /80	12.11 /61	0.24	1.07
OT	Hartford Global Real Asset A	HRLAX	E	(888) 843-7824	E- / 0.1	-2.09	-12.77	-14.28 / 2	-5.87 / 2	--	0.06	1.58
OT	Hartford Global Real Asset C	HRLCX	E	(888) 843-7824	E- / 0.1	-2.35	-13.21	-14.98 / 2	-6.58 / 1	--	0.00	2.31
OT	Hartford Global Real Asset I	HRLIX	E	(888) 843-7824	E- / 0.2	-2.09	-12.73	-14.07 / 2	-5.64 / 2	--	0.43	1.21
OT	Hartford Global Real Asset R3	HRLRX	E	(888) 843-7824	E- / 0.2	-2.19	-12.87	-14.45 / 2	-6.06 / 1	--	0.00	1.93
OT	Hartford Global Real Asset R4	HRLSX	E	(888) 843-7824	E- / 0.2	-2.19	-12.84	-14.26 / 2	-5.83 / 2	--	0.16	1.55
OT	Hartford Global Real Asset R5	HRLTX	E	(888) 843-7824	E- / 0.2	-2.09	-12.72	-14.06 / 2	-5.59 / 2	--	0.52	1.26
OT	Hartford Global Real Asset Y	HRLYX	E	(888) 843-7824	E- / 0.2	-1.98	-12.68	-13.94 / 2	-5.53 / 2	--	0.57	1.15
AA	Hartford Growth Alloc A	HRAAX	E	(888) 843-7824	C- / 3.1	3.62	3.82	4.73 /37	9.71 /38	9.00 /37	2.19	1.40
AA	● Hartford Growth Alloc B	HRABX	E+	(888) 843-7824	C- / 3.4	3.28	3.34	3.76 /30	8.80 /32	8.10 /31	1.36	2.25
AA	Hartford Growth Alloc C	HRACX	E+	(888) 843-7824	C- / 3.5	3.39	3.47	3.96 /32	8.92 /32	8.21 /31	1.71	2.13
AA	Hartford Growth Alloc I	HRAIX	E+	(888) 843-7824	C- / 4.2	3.64	3.99	5.05 /39	10.05 /40	9.35 /39	2.56	1.08
AA	Hartford Growth Alloc R3	HRARX	E+	(888) 843-7824	C- / 3.8	3.52	3.67	4.39 /34	9.39 /36	8.68 /34	2.09	1.70
AA	Hartford Growth Alloc R4	HRASX	E+	(888) 843-7824	C- / 4.0	3.55	3.72	4.63 /36	9.72 /38	9.00 /37	2.28	1.40
AA	Hartford Growth Alloc R5	HRATX	E+	(888) 843-7824	C- / 4.2	3.62	3.94	4.99 /38	10.03 /39	9.34 /39	2.53	1.10
GR	Hartford Growth Opportunities A	HGOAX	C+	(888) 843-7824	A+ / 9.7	6.41	13.53	19.56 /96	19.17 /97	15.74 /91	0.00	1.15
GR	● Hartford Growth Opportunities B	HGOBX	C	(888) 843-7824	A+ / 9.7	6.13	12.98	18.48 /96	18.19 /95	14.81 /85	0.00	2.07
GR	Hartford Growth Opportunities C	HGOCX	C	(888) 843-7824	A+ / 9.7	6.19	13.10	18.69 /96	18.32 /95	14.93 /86	0.00	1.88
GR	Hartford Growth Opportunities I	HGOIX	B-	(888) 843-7824	A+ / 9.8	6.46	13.66	19.84 /97	19.47 /97	16.06 /93	0.00	0.91
GR	Hartford Growth Opportunities R3	HGORX	B-	(888) 843-7824	A+ / 9.8	6.30	13.35	19.19 /96	18.83 /96	15.45 /90	0.00	1.46
GR	Hartford Growth Opportunities R4	HGOSX	B-	(888) 843-7824	A+ / 9.8	6.39	13.52	19.56 /96	19.19 /97	15.80 /92	0.00	1.15
GR	Hartford Growth Opportunities R5	HGOTX	B-	(888) 843-7824	A+ / 9.8	6.45	13.65	19.88 /97	19.54 /97	16.14 /94	0.00	0.85
GR	Hartford Growth Opportunities Y	HGOYX	B-	(888) 843-7824	A+ / 9.8	6.50	13.72	20.01 /97	19.66 /97	16.25 /94	0.00	0.75
GR	Hartford Growth Opps HLS Fd IA	HAGOX	B	(888) 843-7824	A+ / 9.8	6.58	13.94	20.06 /97	19.93 /98	16.41 /94	0.15	0.65
GR	Hartford Growth Opps HLS Fd IB	HBGOX	B	(888) 843-7824	A+ / 9.8	6.51	13.77	19.73 /97	19.62 /97	16.11 /93	0.01	0.90
GL	Hartford Growth Oppty HLS IA		B	(888) 843-7824	A+ / 9.8	6.58	13.94	20.06 /97	19.93 /98	16.41 /94	0.15	0.65
GL	Hartford Growth Oppty HLS IB		B	(888) 843-7824	A+ / 9.8	6.51	13.77	19.73 /97	19.62 /97	16.11 /93	0.01	0.90
MC	Hartford Growth Oppty HLS IC	HCGOX	A-	(888) 843-7824	A+ / 9.8	6.43	13.64	19.49 /96	19.54 /97	16.07 /93	0.15	N/A
HL	Hartford Healthcare A	HGHAX	A+	(888) 843-7824	A+ / 9.9	9.49	22.15	29.12 /99	29.34 /99	21.36 /99	0.00	1.33
HL	● Hartford Healthcare B	HGHBX	A+	(888) 843-7824	A+ / 9.9	9.23	21.64	27.96 /99	28.24 /99	20.36 /99	0.00	2.20
HL	Hartford Healthcare C	HGHCX	A+	(888) 843-7824	A+ / 9.9	9.29	21.71	28.16 /99	28.42 /99	20.51 /99	0.00	2.06
HL	Hartford Healthcare HLS IA		A	(888) 843-7824	A+ / 9.9	9.63	22.48	29.89 /99	30.54 /99	22.46 /99	0.21	0.89
HL	Hartford Healthcare HLS IB		A	(888) 843-7824	A+ / 9.9	9.58	22.35	29.55 /99	30.20 /99	22.15 /99	0.03	1.14
HL	Hartford Healthcare I	HGHIX	A+	(888) 843-7824	A+ / 9.9	9.55	22.36	29.49 /99	29.75 /99	21.75 /99	0.00	1.05
HL	Hartford Healthcare R3	HGHRX	A+	(888) 843-7824	A+ / 9.9	9.39	21.96	28.68 /99	29.00 /99	21.09 /99	0.00	1.64
HL	Hartford Healthcare R4	HGHSX	A+	(888) 843-7824	A+ / 9.9	9.45	22.14	29.06 /99	29.37 /99	21.46 /99	0.00	1.34

99 Pct = Best
0 Pct = Worst

● Denotes fund is closed to new investors

* Denotes fund is included in Section II

www.thestreetratings.com

RISK			NET ASSETS		ASSET				Portfolio	BULL / BEAR		FUND MANAGER		MINIMUMS		LOADS	
Risk Rating/Pts	3 Year		NAV As of 3/31/15	Total $(Mil)	Cash %	Stocks %	Bonds %	Other %	Turnover Ratio	Last Bull Market Return	Last Bear Market Return	Manager Quality Pct	Manager Tenure (Years)	Initial Purch. $	Additional Purch. $	Front End Load	Back End Load
	Standard Deviation	Beta															
C- / 3.5	11.0	1.07	15.94	37	3	96	0	1	144	84.8	-25.7	22	10	0	0	0.0	0.0
C- / 3.6	11.0	1.07	16.08	280	3	96	0	1	144	85.0	-25.7	23	10	2,000	50	0.0	0.0
C- / 3.9	11.0	1.07	17.92	112	3	96	0	1	144	91.6	-25.4	34	10	2,000	50	0.0	0.0
C- / 3.8	11.1	1.07	17.19	32	3	96	0	1	144	89.0	-25.6	29	10	0	0	0.0	0.0
C- / 3.9	11.0	1.07	17.68	10	3	96	0	1	144	90.7	-25.4	33	10	0	0	0.0	0.0
C- / 4.0	11.0	1.07	18.01	N/A	3	96	0	1	144	91.7	-25.4	34	10	0	0	0.0	0.0
C- / 4.0	11.0	1.07	18.19	207	3	96	0	1	144	92.3	-25.3	35	10	250,000	0	0.0	0.0
C+ / 6.1	10.9	0.78	11.31	90	2	97	0	1	90	72.5	-22.9	91	N/A	2,000	50	5.5	0.0
C+ / 6.1	10.8	0.78	11.08	2	2	97	0	1	90	68.2	-23.2	89	N/A	0	0	0.0	0.0
C+ / 6.1	10.9	0.78	11.05	11	2	97	0	1	90	68.2	-23.2	89	N/A	2,000	50	0.0	0.0
C+ / 6.1	10.9	0.78	11.32	2	2	97	0	1	90	73.9	-22.9	91	N/A	2,000	50	0.0	0.0
C+ / 6.1	10.9	0.78	11.28	N/A	2	97	0	1	90	71.5	-23.1	90	N/A	0	0	0.0	0.0
C+ / 6.1	10.8	0.78	11.32	1	2	97	0	1	90	73.2	-22.9	91	N/A	0	0	0.0	0.0
C+ / 6.1	10.9	0.78	11.33	1	2	97	0	1	90	75.0	-22.9	92	N/A	0	0	0.0	0.0
C+ / 6.1	10.9	0.78	11.32	186	2	97	0	1	90	75.4	-22.8	92	N/A	250,000	0	0.0	0.0
C+ / 5.9	12.1	0.80	24.73	396	1	98	0	1	71	97.4	-24.8	96	10	0	0	0.0	0.0
C+ / 5.9	12.1	0.80	24.52	92	1	98	0	1	71	95.7	-24.9	96	10	0	0	0.0	0.0
C / 5.3	10.8	0.79	8.91	31	15	59	24	2	162	-5.7	-20.2	0	5	5,000	50	5.5	0.0
C / 5.1	10.8	0.79	8.74	13	15	59	24	2	162	-8.1	-20.5	0	5	5,000	50	0.0	0.0
C / 5.2	10.8	0.79	8.90	26	15	59	24	2	162	-4.8	-20.1	0	5	5,000	50	0.0	0.0
C / 5.3	10.8	0.79	8.94	N/A	15	59	24	2	162	-6.4	-20.3	0	5	0	0	0.0	0.0
C / 5.3	10.8	0.79	8.92	3	15	59	24	2	162	-5.6	-20.2	0	5	0	0	0.0	0.0
C / 5.2	10.8	0.79	8.91	1	15	59	24	2	162	-4.8	-20.1	0	5	0	0	0.0	0.0
C / 5.2	10.8	0.79	8.91	298	15	59	24	2	162	-4.6	-20.1	0	5	250,000	0	0.0	0.0
D+ / 2.3	8.7	1.41	11.74	623	4	76	18	2	103	58.0	-17.6	9	3	2,000	50	5.5	0.0
D+ / 2.4	8.7	1.41	11.64	32	4	76	18	2	103	53.7	-17.9	6	3	0	0	0.0	0.0
D+ / 2.3	8.7	1.41	11.59	202	4	76	18	2	103	54.2	-17.9	6	3	2,000	50	0.0	0.0
D+ / 2.3	8.7	1.42	11.67	6	4	76	18	2	103	59.9	-17.5	10	3	2,000	50	0.0	0.0
D / 2.2	8.7	1.42	11.48	18	4	76	18	2	103	56.5	-17.7	8	3	0	0	0.0	0.0
D+ / 2.3	8.7	1.41	11.67	16	4	76	18	2	103	58.1	-17.6	9	3	0	0	0.0	0.0
D+ / 2.3	8.7	1.41	11.74	7	4	76	18	2	103	59.8	-17.5	10	3	0	0	0.0	0.0
C- / 3.2	11.5	1.02	39.50	1,640	1	98	0	1	136	116.7	-23.1	86	14	2,000	50	5.5	0.0
D / 1.9	11.5	1.02	28.38	21	1	98	0	1	136	110.9	-23.3	80	14	0	0	0.0	0.0
D / 2.0	11.5	1.02	28.63	285	1	98	0	1	136	111.6	-23.3	81	14	2,000	50	0.0	0.0
C- / 3.3	11.5	1.03	40.71	1,906	1	98	0	1	136	118.6	-22.9	87	14	0	0	0.0	0.0
C- / 3.2	11.5	1.02	39.99	34	1	98	0	1	136	114.7	-23.1	84	14	0	0	0.0	0.0
C- / 3.3	11.5	1.02	41.28	58	1	98	0	1	136	116.9	-23.0	86	14	0	0	0.0	0.0
C- / 3.4	11.5	1.03	42.39	113	1	98	0	1	136	119.2	-22.9	87	14	0	0	0.0	0.0
C- / 3.5	11.5	1.02	42.79	79	1	98	0	1	136	119.9	-22.9	87	14	250,000	0	0.0	0.0
C- / 3.7	11.6	1.03	41.44	1,239	0	99	0	1	119	121.2	-22.9	88	14	0	0	0.0	0.0
C- / 3.7	11.6	1.03	40.40	168	0	99	0	1	119	119.3	-23.0	87	14	0	0	0.0	0.0
C- / 3.8	11.6	0.65	41.44	1,239	0	99	0	1	119	121.2	-22.9	99	14	0	0	0.0	0.0
C- / 3.7	11.6	0.65	40.40	168	0	99	0	1	119	119.3	-23.0	99	14	0	0	0.0	0.0
C / 5.3	11.6	0.92	41.24	2	0	99	0	1	119	118.9	-23.0	90	14	0	0	0.0	0.0
C+ / 6.2	10.9	0.81	39.13	772	4	94	1	1	28	160.8	-12.9	99	15	2,000	50	5.5	0.0
C+ / 6.1	10.9	0.81	33.95	10	4	94	1	1	28	153.5	-13.2	99	15	0	0	0.0	0.0
C+ / 6.1	10.9	0.81	34.25	241	4	94	1	1	28	154.6	-13.2	99	15	2,000	50	0.0	0.0
C+ / 5.7	11.1	0.82	32.91	349	2	97	0	1	33	169.7	-12.5	99	15	0	0	0.0	0.0
C+ / 5.7	11.1	0.83	32.03	68	2	97	0	1	33	167.4	-12.6	99	15	0	0	0.0	0.0
C+ / 6.2	10.9	0.81	40.36	198	4	94	1	1	28	163.7	-12.8	99	15	2,000	50	0.0	0.0
C+ / 6.2	10.9	0.81	40.20	54	4	94	1	1	28	158.7	-13.0	99	15	0	0	0.0	0.0
C+ / 6.2	10.9	0.81	41.46	41	4	94	1	1	28	161.2	-12.9	99	15	0	0	0.0	0.0

Fund Type	Fund Name	Ticker Symbol	Overall Investment Rating	Phone	Performance Rating/Pts	3 Mo	6 Mo	1Yr / Pct	3Yr / Pct	5Yr / Pct	Dividend Yield	Expense Ratio
	99 Pct = Best / 0 Pct = Worst				PERFORMANCE Total Return % through 3/31/15 — Annualized						Incl. in Returns	
HL	Hartford Healthcare R5	HGHTX	A+	(888) 843-7824	A+ / 9.9	9.56	22.35	29.47 /99	29.78 /99	21.81 /99	0.00	1.05
HL	Hartford Healthcare Y	HGHYX	A+	(888) 843-7824	A+ / 9.9	9.57	22.40	29.59 /99	29.90 /99	21.92 /99	0.00	0.94
FO	Hartford International Growth A	HNCAX	D+	(888) 843-7824	C- / 3.2	4.82	2.93	1.79 /21	10.19 /40	8.53 /33	0.18	1.58
FO	● Hartford International Growth B	HNCBX	D+	(888) 843-7824	C- / 3.5	4.58	2.59	0.94 /18	9.35 /35	7.71 /28	0.00	2.64
FO	Hartford International Growth C	HNCCX	D+	(888) 843-7824	C- / 3.5	4.59	2.60	1.02 /18	9.37 /35	7.72 /28	0.00	2.30
FO	Hartford International Growth I	HNCJX	C-	(888) 843-7824	C / 4.3	4.86	3.15	2.16 /23	10.58 /43	8.91 /36	0.68	1.18
FO	Hartford International Growth R3	HNCRX	C-	(888) 843-7824	C- / 3.9	4.68	2.86	1.65 /21	10.05 /40	8.39 /32	0.00	1.83
FO	Hartford International Growth R4	HNCSX	C-	(888) 843-7824	C- / 4.2	4.86	3.12	2.01 /22	10.41 /42	8.76 /35	0.44	1.44
FO	Hartford International Growth R5	HNCTX	C-	(888) 843-7824	C / 4.4	4.91	3.21	2.34 /23	10.74 /44	9.12 /38	0.69	1.13
FO	Hartford International Growth Y	HNCYX	C-	(888) 843-7824	C / 4.4	4.90	3.24	2.29 /23	10.78 /44	9.13 /38	0.72	1.01
FO	Hartford International Value A	HILAX	D	(888) 843-7824	D+ / 2.8	5.18	-1.12	-3.33 / 8	10.67 /43	--	0.45	1.37
FO	Hartford International Value C	HILCX	D+	(888) 843-7824	C- / 3.2	5.03	-1.49	-4.05 / 7	9.92 /39	--	0.14	2.05
FO	Hartford International Value I	HILIX	C-	(888) 843-7824	C- / 4.0	5.29	-0.95	-3.02 / 9	11.11 /46	--	0.70	1.02
FO	Hartford International Value R3	HILRX	D+	(888) 843-7824	C- / 3.5	5.11	-1.28	-3.62 / 8	10.42 /42	--	0.19	1.70
FO	Hartford International Value R4	HILSX	D+	(888) 843-7824	C- / 3.7	5.16	-1.12	-3.33 / 8	10.75 /44	--	0.47	1.39
FO	Hartford International Value R5	HILTX	C-	(888) 843-7824	C- / 4.0	5.28	-0.94	-3.01 / 9	11.11 /46	--	0.65	1.08
FO	Hartford International Value Y	HILYX	C-	(888) 843-7824	C / 4.3	5.34	-0.90	-2.94 / 9	11.77 /51	--	0.72	0.96
FO	Hartford Intl Capital Apprec A	HDVAX	E+	(888) 843-7824	D- / 1.2	4.34	0.04	-2.12 /10	6.43 /19	6.01 /17	0.80	1.84
FO	● Hartford Intl Capital Apprec B	HDVBX	D-	(888) 843-7824	D- / 1.4	4.12	-0.34	-2.79 / 9	5.69 /15	5.29 /13	0.00	2.53
FO	Hartford Intl Capital Apprec C	HDVCX	D-	(888) 843-7824	D- / 1.4	4.15	-0.37	-2.83 / 9	5.63 /15	5.24 /13	0.17	2.59
FO	Hartford Intl Capital Apprec I	HDVIX	D-	(888) 843-7824	D / 2.0	4.54	0.29	-1.68 /11	6.89 /21	6.47 /20	1.17	1.44
FO	Hartford Intl Capital Apprec R3	HDVRX	D-	(888) 843-7824	D / 1.6	4.33	-0.05	-2.30 /10	6.21 /18	5.80 /16	0.57	2.12
FO	Hartford Intl Capital Apprec R4	HDVSX	D-	(888) 843-7824	D / 1.8	4.43	0.17	-1.89 /11	6.54 /19	6.11 /17	0.87	1.81
FO	Hartford Intl Capital Apprec R5	HDVTX	D-	(888) 843-7824	D / 2.0	4.43	0.28	-1.68 /11	6.88 /21	6.44 /20	1.17	1.50
FO	Hartford Intl Capital Apprec Y	HDVYX	D-	(888) 843-7824	D / 2.0	4.54	0.33	-1.63 /11	6.93 /21	6.49 /20	1.22	1.40
FO	Hartford Intl Opportunities A	IHOAX	E+	(888) 843-7824	D / 2.1	4.88	2.60	1.77 /21	8.10 /27	6.48 /20	0.92	1.20
FO	● Hartford Intl Opportunities B	HIOBX	E+	(888) 843-7824	D+ / 2.4	4.67	2.14	0.91 /18	7.21 /22	5.63 /15	0.11	2.30
FO	Hartford Intl Opportunities C	HIOCX	E+	(888) 843-7824	D+ / 2.4	4.73	2.21	1.02 /18	7.32 /23	5.70 /15	0.51	1.93
FO	Hartford Intl Opportunities HLS IA		D+	(888) 843-7824	C- / 3.5	5.17	3.05	2.52 /24	9.05 /33	7.15 /24	2.26	0.74
FO	Hartford Intl Opportunities HLS IB		D+	(888) 843-7824	C- / 3.3	5.11	2.95	2.24 /23	8.77 /31	6.88 /22	1.97	0.99
FO	Hartford Intl Opportunities I	IHOIX	D-	(888) 843-7824	C- / 3.2	4.97	2.84	2.18 /23	8.49 /30	6.86 /22	1.29	0.84
FO	Hartford Intl Opportunities R3	IHORX	E+	(888) 843-7824	D+ / 2.8	4.79	2.50	1.56 /20	7.87 /26	6.26 /18	0.78	1.44
FO	Hartford Intl Opportunities R4	IHOSX	D-	(888) 843-7824	C- / 3.0	4.86	2.60	1.79 /21	8.18 /28	6.57 /20	1.01	1.14
FO	Hartford Intl Opportunities R5	IHOTX	D-	(888) 843-7824	C- / 3.2	5.03	2.79	2.15 /22	8.53 /30	6.90 /22	1.23	0.84
FO	Hartford Intl Opportunities Y	HAOYX	D-	(888) 843-7824	C- / 3.3	5.00	2.87	2.23 /23	8.62 /31	7.00 /23	1.31	0.74
FO	Hartford Intl Opps HLS Fd IA	HIAOX	D+	(888) 843-7824	C- / 3.5	5.17	3.05	2.52 /24	9.05 /33	7.15 /24	2.26	0.74
FO	Hartford Intl Opps HLS Fd IB	HBIOX	D+	(888) 843-7824	C- / 3.3	5.11	2.95	2.24 /23	8.77 /31	6.88 /22	1.97	0.99
FO	Hartford Intl Small Company A	HNSAX	E+	(888) 843-7824	C- / 3.5	6.63	2.41	-3.68 / 7	11.62 /50	10.00 /44	1.34	1.49
FO	● Hartford Intl Small Company B	HNSBX	E+	(888) 843-7824	C- / 3.9	6.41	2.06	-4.47 / 6	10.76 /44	9.16 /38	0.42	2.52
FO	Hartford Intl Small Company C	HNSCX	E+	(888) 843-7824	C- / 3.9	6.43	2.11	-4.36 / 6	10.81 /44	9.21 /38	0.90	2.19
FO	Hartford Intl Small Company I	HNSJX	E+	(888) 843-7824	C / 4.7	6.69	2.59	-3.38 / 8	12.04 /53	10.47 /48	1.67	1.19
FO	Hartford Intl Small Company R3	HNSRX	E+	(888) 843-7824	C / 4.3	6.58	2.34	-3.87 / 7	11.45 /49	9.88 /44	1.35	1.70
FO	Hartford Intl Small Company R4	HNSSX	E+	(888) 843-7824	C / 4.5	6.63	2.57	-3.47 / 8	11.84 /51	10.22 /46	1.60	1.40
FO	Hartford Intl Small Company R5	HNSTX	E+	(888) 843-7824	C / 4.7	6.76	2.70	-3.28 / 8	12.14 /53	10.53 /49	1.77	1.10
FO	Hartford Intl Small Company Y	HNSYX	E+	(888) 843-7824	C / 4.8	6.76	2.67	-3.25 / 8	12.20 /54	10.58 /49	1.85	0.99
GL	Hartford MidCap A	HFMCX	B+	(888) 843-7824	A- / 9.1	5.79	11.05	12.88 /86	18.43 /95	15.10 /88	0.00	1.15
GL	● Hartford MidCap B	HAMBX	B	(888) 843-7824	A- / 9.2	5.57	10.59	11.87 /82	17.38 /92	14.11 /79	0.00	2.05
GL	Hartford MidCap C	HMDCX	B+	(888) 843-7824	A / 9.3	5.57	10.67	12.08 /83	17.58 /93	14.30 /80	0.00	1.88
GL	Hartford MidCap HLS Fd IA	HIMCX	B+	(888) 843-7824	A+ / 9.7	5.93	11.34	13.48 /88	19.15 /97	15.61 /91	0.09	0.71
GL	Hartford MidCap HLS Fd IB	HBMCX	B+	(888) 843-7824	A+ / 9.6	5.86	11.22	13.20 /87	18.85 /96	15.32 /89	0.00	0.96
MC	Hartford MidCap HLS IA		B+	(888) 843-7824	A+ / 9.7	5.93	11.34	13.48 /88	19.15 /97	15.61 /91	0.09	0.71
MC	Hartford MidCap HLS IB		B+	(888) 843-7824	A+ / 9.6	5.86	11.22	13.20 /87	18.85 /96	15.32 /89	0.00	0.96

RISK			NET ASSETS		ASSET					BULL / BEAR		FUND MANAGER		MINIMUMS		LOADS	
	3 Year		NAV						Portfolio	Last Bull	Last Bear	Manager	Manager	Initial	Additional	Front	Back
Risk	Standard		As of	Total	Cash	Stocks	Bonds	Other	Turnover	Market	Market	Quality	Tenure	Purch.	Purch.	End	End
Rating/Pts	Deviation	Beta	3/31/15	$(Mil)	%	%	%	%	Ratio	Return	Return	Pct	(Years)	$	$	Load	Load
C+ / 6.3	10.9	0.81	42.62	4	4	94	1	1	28	164.1	-12.8	99	15	0	0	0.0	0.0
C+ / 6.3	10.9	0.81	42.92	8	4	94	1	1	28	164.7	-12.7	99	15	250,000	0	0.0	0.0
C+ / 6.1	11.8	0.84	12.82	108	3	96	0	1	84	57.8	-24.2	85	14	2,000	50	5.5	0.0
C+ / 6.1	11.8	0.84	11.87	4	3	96	0	1	84	53.8	-24.4	79	14	0	0	0.0	0.0
C+ / 6.1	11.8	0.84	11.86	16	3	96	0	1	84	53.9	-24.5	80	14	2,000	50	0.0	0.0
C+ / 6.1	11.8	0.84	12.72	28	3	96	0	1	84	59.7	-24.1	86	14	2,000	50	0.0	0.0
C+ / 6.1	11.8	0.84	12.96	1	3	96	0	1	84	57.2	-24.3	84	14	0	0	0.0	0.0
C+ / 6.1	11.8	0.84	13.17	2	3	96	0	1	84	59.0	-24.2	86	14	0	0	0.0	0.0
C+ / 6.1	11.8	0.84	13.24	4	3	96	0	1	84	60.6	-24.1	87	14	0	0	0.0	0.0
C+ / 6.1	11.8	0.84	13.28	38	3	96	0	1	84	60.8	-24.0	87	14	250,000	0	0.0	0.0
C+ / 5.9	13.1	0.96	14.62	264	9	90	0	1	31	58.4	-22.8	80	2	2,000	50	5.5	0.0
C+ / 5.9	13.1	0.96	14.42	56	9	90	0	1	31	54.7	-22.9	75	2	2,000	50	0.0	0.0
C+ / 5.9	13.1	0.96	14.74	490	9	90	0	1	31	60.4	-22.6	83	2	2,000	50	0.0	0.0
C+ / 6.0	13.1	0.96	14.61	1	9	90	0	1	31	57.2	-22.8	79	2	0	0	0.0	0.0
C+ / 5.9	13.1	0.96	14.67	3	9	90	0	1	31	58.9	-22.8	81	2	0	0	0.0	0.0
C+ / 5.9	13.1	0.96	14.75	1	9	90	0	1	31	60.4	-22.6	83	2	0	0	0.0	0.0
C+ / 5.9	13.2	0.97	15.00	99	9	90	0	1	31	63.3	-22.5	86	2	250,000	0	0.0	0.0
C+ / 5.6	12.0	0.90	9.62	13	4	95	0	1	69	43.2	-23.5	38	7	2,000	50	5.5	0.0
C+ / 5.7	12.0	0.90	9.60	1	4	95	0	1	69	40.0	-23.7	29	7	0	0	0.0	0.0
C+ / 5.7	12.0	0.90	9.54	2	4	95	0	1	69	39.8	-23.7	29	7	2,000	50	0.0	0.0
C+ / 5.6	12.0	0.89	9.67	3	4	95	0	1	69	45.1	-23.4	45	7	2,000	50	0.0	0.0
C+ / 5.7	12.0	0.90	9.64	1	4	95	0	1	69	42.1	-23.6	35	7	0	0	0.0	0.0
C+ / 5.7	12.0	0.89	9.66	1	4	95	0	1	69	43.8	-23.5	40	7	0	0	0.0	0.0
C+ / 5.6	12.0	0.89	9.67	1	4	95	0	1	69	45.2	-23.4	45	7	0	0	0.0	0.0
C+ / 5.6	12.0	0.89	9.67	11	4	95	0	1	69	45.3	-23.4	46	7	250,000	0	0.0	0.0
C- / 4.0	11.0	0.81	15.27	505	1	97	0	2	104	51.8	-23.2	72	15	2,000	50	5.5	0.0
C- / 3.9	11.0	0.81	13.90	6	1	97	0	2	104	47.8	-23.5	61	15	0	0	0.0	0.0
C- / 3.7	11.0	0.81	13.52	55	1	97	0	2	104	48.1	-23.5	63	15	2,000	50	0.0	0.0
C+ / 5.8	11.3	0.83	14.86	1,278	1	98	0	1	100	56.1	-23.5	78	15	0	0	0.0	0.0
C+ / 5.9	11.3	0.83	15.02	193	1	98	0	1	100	54.9	-23.6	76	15	0	0	0.0	0.0
C- / 3.9	11.0	0.81	15.20	90	1	97	0	2	104	53.6	-23.1	75	15	2,000	50	0.0	0.0
C- / 4.0	11.0	0.81	15.52	47	1	97	0	2	104	50.7	-23.2	70	15	0	0	0.0	0.0
C- / 4.1	11.0	0.81	15.75	115	1	97	0	2	104	52.3	-23.2	72	15	0	0	0.0	0.0
C- / 4.0	11.1	0.81	15.88	91	1	97	0	2	104	53.8	-23.1	75	15	0	0	0.0	0.0
C- / 4.0	11.1	0.81	15.95	591	1	97	0	2	104	54.4	-23.0	76	15	250,000	0	0.0	0.0
C+ / 5.8	11.3	0.83	14.86	1,278	1	98	0	1	100	56.1	-23.5	78	15	0	0	0.0	0.0
C+ / 5.9	11.3	0.83	15.02	193	1	98	0	1	100	54.9	-23.6	76	15	0	0	0.0	0.0
D / 2.1	13.1	0.94	14.15	69	2	97	0	1	66	62.8	-21.4	86	13	2,000	50	5.5	0.0
D / 2.0	13.1	0.94	13.28	2	2	97	0	1	66	58.4	-21.7	82	13	0	0	0.0	0.0
D / 1.9	13.1	0.94	12.92	15	2	97	0	1	66	58.8	-21.7	82	13	2,000	50	0.0	0.0
D / 2.0	13.1	0.94	14.04	48	2	97	0	1	66	64.9	-21.3	88	13	2,000	50	0.0	0.0
D / 2.1	13.1	0.94	14.25	10	2	97	0	1	66	61.9	-21.4	86	13	0	0	0.0	0.0
D / 2.1	13.1	0.94	14.31	7	2	97	0	1	66	63.8	-21.4	87	13	0	0	0.0	0.0
D / 2.1	13.1	0.94	14.38	N/A	2	97	0	1	66	65.3	-21.2	88	13	0	0	0.0	0.0
D / 2.1	13.1	0.94	14.38	157	2	97	0	1	66	65.6	-21.3	89	13	250,000	0	0.0	0.0
C / 5.4	11.5	0.65	26.51	2,036	0	99	0	1	34	116.1	-25.6	98	11	2,000	50	5.5	0.0
C / 4.7	11.5	0.65	20.27	29	0	99	0	1	34	109.8	-25.9	98	11	0	0	0.0	0.0
C / 4.8	11.5	0.65	20.85	596	0	99	0	1	34	110.9	-25.8	98	11	2,000	50	0.0	0.0
C / 4.8	11.5	0.65	39.49	1,778	0	99	0	1	34	120.2	-25.6	99	11	0	0	0.0	0.0
C / 4.8	11.5	0.65	38.99	133	0	99	0	1	34	118.3	-25.7	99	11	0	0	0.0	0.0
C / 4.8	11.5	1.00	39.49	1,778	0	99	0	1	34	120.2	-25.6	83	11	0	0	0.0	0.0
C / 4.8	11.5	1.00	38.99	133	0	99	0	1	34	118.3	-25.7	81	11	0	0	0.0	0.0

Fund Type	Fund Name	Ticker Symbol	Overall Investment Rating	Phone	Perfor-mance Rating/Pts	Total Return % through 3/31/15			Annualized		Incl. in Returns	
	99 Pct = Best / 0 Pct = Worst					3 Mo	6 Mo	1Yr / Pct	3Yr / Pct	5Yr / Pct	Dividend Yield	Expense Ratio
GL	Hartford MidCap I	HFMIX	A-	(888) 843-7824	A+ / 9.6	5.81	11.20	13.18 /87	18.72 /96	15.39 /89	0.00	0.90
GL	Hartford MidCap R3	HFMRX	A-	(888) 843-7824	A / 9.4	5.70	10.89	12.52 /85	18.07 /94	14.78 /85	0.00	1.47
GL	Hartford MidCap R4	HFMSX	A-	(888) 843-7824	A / 9.5	5.79	11.06	12.86 /86	18.44 /96	15.14 /88	0.00	1.16
GL	Hartford MidCap R5	HFMTX	A	(888) 843-7824	A+ / 9.6	5.85	11.22	13.18 /87	18.79 /96	15.48 /90	0.00	0.86
MC	Hartford MidCap Value A	HMVAX	B-	(888) 843-7824	B / 8.1	5.81	10.59	9.04 /69	17.15 /91	14.27 /80	0.12	1.27
MC	● Hartford MidCap Value B	HMVBX	B-	(888) 843-7824	B+ / 8.4	5.56	10.09	8.07 /63	16.20 /85	13.38 /72	0.00	2.28
MC	Hartford MidCap Value C	HMVCX	B-	(888) 843-7824	B+ / 8.5	5.67	10.22	8.26 /65	16.35 /86	13.45 /72	0.00	1.99
GL	Hartford MidCap Value HLS IA		B	(888) 843-7824	A / 9.3	5.96	10.90	9.58 /72	17.94 /94	14.91 /86	0.63	0.84
GL	Hartford MidCap Value HLS IB		B	(888) 843-7824	A- / 9.2	5.93	10.74	9.34 /71	17.65 /93	14.62 /83	0.39	1.09
MC	Hartford MidCap Value I	HMVJX	B+	(888) 843-7824	A- / 9.2	5.92	10.84	9.43 /72	17.58 /93	14.68 /84	0.44	0.92
MC	Hartford MidCap Value R3	HMVRX	B	(888) 843-7824	B+ / 8.8	5.80	10.49	8.75 /68	16.88 /89	14.04 /78	0.00	1.53
MC	Hartford MidCap Value R4	HMVSX	B+	(888) 843-7824	A- / 9.0	5.81	10.64	9.04 /69	17.24 /91	--	0.21	1.22
MC	Hartford MidCap Value R5	HMVTX	B+	(888) 843-7824	A- / 9.2	5.96	10.82	9.42 /72	17.58 /93	14.73 /85	0.43	0.93
MC	Hartford MidCap Value Y	HMVYX	B+	(888) 843-7824	A- / 9.2	5.94	10.86	9.52 /72	17.73 /93	14.82 /85	0.47	0.82
GL	Hartford MidCap Y	HMDYX	A	(888) 843-7824	A+ / 9.6	5.89	11.31	13.31 /88	18.92 /96	15.60 /91	0.00	0.76
AA	Hartford Moderate Allocation A	HBAAX	D-	(888) 843-7824	D- / 1.0	2.29	1.21	1.80 /21	5.13 /14	6.23 /18	1.82	1.30
AA	● Hartford Moderate Allocation B	HBABX	D-	(888) 843-7824	D- / 1.2	2.05	0.82	0.97 /18	4.28 /11	5.36 /14	1.59	2.14
AA	Hartford Moderate Allocation C	HBACX	D-	(888) 843-7824	D- / 1.2	2.06	0.86	1.02 /18	4.36 /11	5.45 /14	1.64	2.03
AA	Hartford Moderate Allocation I	HBAIX	D	(888) 843-7824	D / 1.6	2.29	1.36	2.11 /22	5.43 /15	6.54 /20	2.15	0.99
AA	Hartford Moderate Allocation R3	HBARX	D-	(888) 843-7824	D- / 1.3	2.14	1.05	1.43 /20	4.78 /12	5.86 /16	1.73	1.63
AA	Hartford Moderate Allocation R4	HBASX	D	(888) 843-7824	D- / 1.4	2.21	1.18	1.78 /21	5.10 /13	6.18 /18	1.83	1.33
AA	Hartford Moderate Allocation R5	HBATX	D	(888) 843-7824	D / 1.6	2.38	1.43	2.08 /22	5.42 /15	6.51 /20	2.11	1.03
GI	Hartford Multi-Asset Income Y	HAFYX	U	(888) 843-7824	U /	2.01	0.93	--	--	--	0.00	0.88
GL	Hartford Real Total Return Y	HABPX	U	(888) 843-7824	U /	6.00	3.31	0.28 /16	--	--	0.00	1.37
SC	Hartford Small Company A	IHSAX	C-	(888) 843-7824	B / 7.9	5.15	12.56	11.10 /79	16.42 /86	15.04 /87	0.00	1.34
SC	● Hartford Small Company B	HSCBX	D+	(888) 843-7824	B+ / 8.3	4.92	12.13	10.25 /75	15.54 /79	14.17 /79	0.00	2.29
SC	Hartford Small Company C	HSMCX	D+	(888) 843-7824	B+ / 8.4	5.00	12.22	10.39 /76	15.62 /80	14.25 /80	0.00	2.05
GL	Hartford Small Company HLS IA		C	(888) 843-7824	A / 9.3	5.36	12.86	11.92 /82	17.38 /92	16.07 /93	0.00	0.71
GL	Hartford Small Company HLS IB		C	(888) 843-7824	A- / 9.2	5.26	12.66	11.64 /81	17.08 /90	15.77 /92	0.00	0.96
SC	Hartford Small Company I	IHSIX	C	(888) 843-7824	A- / 9.0	5.21	12.70	11.37 /80	16.73 /88	15.35 /89	0.00	1.10
SC	Hartford Small Company R3	IHSRX	C	(888) 843-7824	B+ / 8.7	5.10	12.49	10.90 /78	16.23 /85	14.86 /86	0.00	1.55
SC	Hartford Small Company R4	IHSSX	C+	(888) 843-7824	B+ / 8.9	5.22	12.68	11.26 /79	16.58 /87	15.20 /88	0.00	1.25
SC	Hartford Small Company R5	IHSUX	C+	(888) 843-7824	A- / 9.1	5.30	12.81	11.59 /81	16.93 /89	15.54 /90	0.00	0.97
SC	● Hartford Small Company Y	HSCYX	C+	(888) 843-7824	A- / 9.2	5.31	12.86	11.69 /81	17.04 /90	15.65 /91	Incl.	0.85
GL	Hartford Small/Mid Cap Eq HLS Fd IB	HMCVX	C-	(888) 843-7824	B+ / 8.6	5.10	12.13	8.43 /66	16.23 /85	15.00 /87	1.20	1.10
GL	Hartford Small/Mid Cap Eqty HLS IA		C-	(888) 843-7824	B+ / 8.7	5.17	12.29	8.74 /68	16.53 /87	15.29 /89	1.49	0.85
GL	Hartford Small/Mid Cap Eqty HLS IB		C-	(888) 843-7824	B+ / 8.6	5.10	12.13	8.43 /66	16.23 /85	15.00 /87	1.20	1.10
MC	Hartford Small/Mid Cap Equity A	HSMAX	C+	(888) 843-7824	B- / 7.3	5.10	12.33	8.72 /68	15.85 /82	14.74 /85	0.54	1.41
MC	● Hartford Small/Mid Cap Equity B	HSMBX	C+	(888) 843-7824	B / 7.7	4.90	11.92	7.87 /62	14.99 /75	13.88 /77	0.00	2.32
MC	Hartford Small/Mid Cap Equity C	HTSCX	C+	(888) 843-7824	B / 7.7	4.89	11.91	7.90 /62	14.96 /75	13.89 /77	0.00	2.16
MC	Hartford Small/Mid Cap Equity R3	HSMRX	C+	(888) 843-7824	B / 8.2	5.04	12.17	8.49 /66	15.61 /80	14.56 /83	0.42	1.70
MC	Hartford Small/Mid Cap Equity R4	HSMSX	B-	(888) 843-7824	B+ / 8.5	5.19	12.40	8.88 /69	15.97 /83	14.90 /86	0.70	1.37
MC	Hartford Small/Mid Cap Equity R5	HSMTX	B-	(888) 843-7824	B+ / 8.7	5.17	12.51	9.15 /70	16.29 /85	15.22 /88	0.89	1.05
MC	Hartford Small/Mid Cap Equity Y	HSMYX	B-	(888) 843-7824	B+ / 8.7	5.26	12.65	9.21 /70	16.33 /86	15.24 /88	0.93	0.96
SC	● Hartford SmallCap Growth A	HSLAX	A-	(888) 843-7824	A / 9.4	6.87	19.02	12.60 /85	18.53 /96	18.79 /98	0.00	1.28
SC	● Hartford SmallCap Growth B	HSLBX	B+	(888) 843-7824	A / 9.5	6.63	18.56	11.67 /81	17.61 /93	17.87 /97	0.00	2.26
SC	● Hartford SmallCap Growth C	HSLCX	B+	(888) 843-7824	A / 9.5	6.70	18.61	11.83 /82	17.72 /93	17.94 /97	0.00	1.97
GL	● Hartford SmallCap Growth HLS IA		C	(888) 843-7824	A+ / 9.7	7.08	19.67	13.05 /87	18.80 /96	19.61 /99	0.06	0.67
GL	● Hartford SmallCap Growth HLS IB		C	(888) 843-7824	A+ / 9.7	7.03	19.54	12.79 /86	18.50 /96	19.31 /98	0.00	0.92
SC	● Hartford SmallCap Growth I	HSLIX	A	(888) 843-7824	A+ / 9.7	6.95	19.21	12.96 /86	18.92 /96	19.16 /98	0.00	0.97
SC	● Hartford SmallCap Growth R3	HSLRX	A-	(888) 843-7824	A+ / 9.6	6.82	18.88	12.32 /84	18.28 /95	18.54 /98	0.00	1.53
SC	● Hartford SmallCap Growth R4	HSLSX	A	(888) 843-7824	A+ / 9.7	6.89	19.09	12.70 /86	18.65 /96	18.90 /98	0.00	1.22

● Denotes fund is closed to new investors
* Denotes fund is included in Section II

www.thestreetratings.com

| RISK | 3 Year | | NET ASSETS | | ASSET | | | | Portfolio | BULL / BEAR | | FUND MANAGER | | MINIMUMS | | LOADS | |
Risk Rating/Pts	Standard Deviation	Beta	NAV As of 3/31/15	Total $(Mil)	Cash %	Stocks %	Bonds %	Other %	Turnover Ratio	Last Bull Market Return	Last Bear Market Return	Manager Quality Pct	Manager Tenure (Years)	Initial Purch. $	Additional Purch. $	Front End Load	Back End Load
C / 5.5	11.5	0.64	26.96	652	0	99	0	1	34	118.0	-25.6	99	11	2,000	50	0.0	0.0
C+ / 5.6	11.5	0.65	29.30	69	0	99	0	1	34	114.1	-25.7	98	11	0	0	0.0	0.0
C+ / 5.7	11.5	0.65	29.98	132	0	99	0	1	34	116.3	-25.6	98	11	0	0	0.0	0.0
C+ / 5.7	11.5	0.65	30.39	143	0	99	0	1	34	118.6	-25.5	99	11	0	0	0.0	0.0
C / 5.1	11.3	1.00	15.84	239	1	98	0	1	43	109.1	-25.6	69	14	2,000	50	5.5	0.0
C / 4.6	11.3	1.00	13.85	2	1	98	0	1	43	103.5	-25.8	58	14	0	0	0.0	0.0
C / 4.6	11.3	1.00	13.79	44	1	98	0	1	43	104.1	-25.8	60	14	2,000	50	0.0	0.0
C / 4.6	11.3	0.64	15.47	354	1	98	0	1	49	113.1	-25.2	98	14	0	0	0.0	0.0
C / 4.6	11.3	0.64	15.36	114	1	98	0	1	49	111.3	-25.3	98	14	0	0	0.0	0.0
C / 5.1	11.4	1.00	15.93	35	1	98	0	1	43	111.7	-25.5	72	14	2,000	50	0.0	0.0
C / 5.2	11.3	1.00	16.61	9	1	98	0	1	43	107.4	-25.6	66	14	0	0	0.0	0.0
C / 5.2	11.4	1.00	16.76	12	1	98	0	1	43	109.6	-25.5	70	14	0	0	0.0	0.0
C / 5.2	11.4	1.00	16.90	7	1	98	0	1	43	111.9	-25.4	73	14	0	0	0.0	0.0
C / 5.2	11.4	1.00	16.93	167	1	98	0	1	43	112.5	-25.4	74	14	250,000	0	0.0	0.0
C+ / 5.7	11.5	0.65	30.55	1,114	0	99	0	1	34	119.3	-25.5	99	11	250,000	0	0.0	0.0
C+ / 6.7	6.2	0.99	12.04	446	6	53	39	2	28	34.9	-13.0	9	N/A	2,000	50	5.5	0.0
C+ / 6.7	6.2	0.99	11.93	20	6	53	39	2	28	31.3	-13.3	6	N/A	0	0	0.0	0.0
C+ / 6.7	6.2	0.99	11.91	153	6	53	39	2	28	31.6	-13.3	6	N/A	2,000	50	0.0	0.0
C+ / 6.7	6.2	0.99	12.04	11	6	53	39	2	28	36.3	-12.9	10	N/A	2,000	50	0.0	0.0
C+ / 6.7	6.2	0.99	11.92	29	6	53	39	2	28	33.4	-13.1	8	N/A	0	0	0.0	0.0
C+ / 6.8	6.2	0.99	12.04	18	6	53	39	2	28	34.8	-13.0	9	N/A	0	0	0.0	0.0
C+ / 6.7	6.2	0.99	12.06	9	6	53	39	2	28	36.1	-12.9	10	N/A	0	0	0.0	0.0
U /	N/A	N/A	9.73	118	11	21	66	2	26	N/A	N/A	N/A	1	250,000	0	0.0	0.0
U /	N/A	N/A	10.25	103	9	53	34	4	305	N/A	N/A	N/A	2	250,000	0	0.0	0.0
D+ / 2.5	13.5	0.95	22.05	383	2	96	0	2	92	98.8	-24.9	76	16	2,000	50	5.5	0.0
D- / 1.3	13.5	0.95	17.26	4	2	96	0	2	92	93.6	-25.1	69	16	0	0	0.0	0.0
D- / 1.3	13.5	0.95	17.23	41	2	96	0	2	92	94.1	-25.1	70	16	2,000	50	0.0	0.0
D+ / 2.4	13.5	0.64	24.58	1,320	0	99	0	1	96	104.8	-24.5	98	16	0	0	0.0	0.0
D / 2.2	13.5	0.64	23.41	128	0	99	0	1	96	103.2	-24.6	98	16	0	0	0.0	0.0
D+ / 2.7	13.5	0.95	22.80	69	2	96	0	2	92	100.4	-24.8	78	16	2,000	50	0.0	0.0
D+ / 2.8	13.5	0.95	23.70	41	2	96	0	2	92	97.5	-25.0	75	16	0	0	0.0	0.0
C- / 3.0	13.5	0.95	24.61	71	2	96	0	2	92	99.6	-24.8	77	16	0	0	0.0	0.0
C- / 3.2	13.5	0.95	25.43	10	2	96	0	2	92	101.7	-24.7	80	16	0	0	0.0	0.0
C- / 3.2	13.5	0.95	25.78	357	2	96	0	2	92	102.4	-24.7	80	16	250,000	0	0.0	0.0
D / 1.6	12.0	0.66	9.89	23	0	0	0	100	128	95.3	-22.4	98	3	0	0	0.0	0.0
D / 1.6	12.0	0.66	9.96	100	0	0	0	100	128	96.9	-22.3	98	3	0	0	0.0	0.0
D / 1.6	12.0	0.66	9.89	23	0	0	0	100	128	95.3	-22.4	98	3	0	0	0.0	0.0
C / 4.6	12.0	1.05	13.40	58	1	98	0	1	116	93.4	-22.4	40	3	2,000	50	5.5	0.0
C / 4.4	12.0	1.05	12.62	3	1	98	0	1	116	88.6	-22.6	30	3	0	0	0.0	0.0
C / 4.3	12.0	1.05	12.45	14	1	98	0	1	116	88.7	-22.7	30	3	2,000	50	0.0	0.0
C / 4.6	12.0	1.05	13.75	1	1	98	0	1	116	92.1	-22.4	37	3	0	0	0.0	0.0
C / 4.7	11.9	1.05	13.79	1	1	98	0	1	116	94.2	-22.3	41	3	0	0	0.0	0.0
C / 4.7	12.0	1.05	13.83	N/A	1	98	0	1	116	96.1	-22.2	45	3	0	0	0.0	0.0
C / 4.6	12.0	1.05	13.82	1	1	98	0	1	116	96.3	-22.2	46	3	250,000	0	0.0	0.0
C+ / 5.6	13.7	0.99	52.12	289	1	98	0	1	61	113.8	-24.1	85	6	2,000	50	5.5	0.0
C / 5.3	13.7	0.99	42.43	3	1	98	0	1	61	108.1	-24.3	79	6	0	0	0.0	0.0
C / 5.3	13.7	0.99	42.07	55	1	98	0	1	61	108.7	-24.3	80	6	2,000	50	0.0	0.0
D / 2.1	13.6	0.67	29.93	715	1	98	0	1	81	115.6	-23.5	98	14	0	0	0.0	0.0
D / 2.1	13.6	0.67	29.37	136	1	98	0	1	81	113.8	-23.6	98	14	0	0	0.0	0.0
C+ / 5.7	13.7	0.99	53.23	209	1	98	0	1	61	116.1	-24.0	86	6	0	0	0.0	0.0
C+ / 5.6	13.7	0.99	52.19	16	1	98	0	1	61	112.2	-24.1	83	6	0	0	0.0	0.0
C+ / 5.6	13.7	0.99	53.52	72	1	98	0	1	61	114.5	-24.1	85	6	0	0	0.0	0.0

						PERFORMANCE						
						Perfor-	Total Return % through 3/31/15					Incl. in Returns	
	99 Pct = Best			Overall		mance				Annualized		Dividend	Expense
	0 Pct = Worst		Ticker	Investment		Rating/Pts	3 Mo	6 Mo	1Yr / Pct	3Yr / Pct	5Yr / Pct	Yield	Ratio
Fund Type	Fund Name	Symbol	Rating	Phone									

Fund Type	Fund Name	Ticker Symbol	Overall Investment Rating	Phone	Performance Rating/Pts	3 Mo	6 Mo	1Yr / Pct	3Yr / Pct	5Yr / Pct	Dividend Yield	Expense Ratio
SC	● Hartford SmallCap Growth R5	HSLTX	A	(888) 843-7824	A+ / 9.7	6.96	19.25	13.02 /87	19.00 /97	19.25 /98	0.00	0.91
SC	Hartford SmallCap Growth Y	HSLYX	A	(888) 843-7824	A+ / 9.7	6.99	19.30	13.11 /87	19.11 /97	19.36 /98	0.00	0.81
GI	Hartford SMART529 Advisers 529 A		B-	(888) 843-7824	C / 4.4	1.53	4.32	8.15 /64	11.79 /51	9.69 /42	0.00	1.85
GI	Hartford SMART529 Advisers 529 B		B	(888) 843-7824	C / 4.9	1.39	4.02	7.54 /59	11.18 /47	9.09 /37	0.00	2.40
GI	Hartford SMART529 Advisers 529 C		B-	(888) 843-7824	C / 4.7	1.31	3.89	7.31 /58	10.95 /45	8.88 /36	0.00	2.59
GI	Hartford SMART529 Advisers 529 E		B	(888) 843-7824	C / 5.5	1.56	4.41	8.38 /65	12.06 /53	9.96 /44	0.00	1.19
GR	Hartford SMART529 Age Bsd 0-8 A		C-	(888) 843-7824	D+ / 2.7	2.84	2.67	3.14 /27	9.44 /36	8.68 /34	0.00	1.85
GR	Hartford SMART529 Age Bsd 0-8 B		C	(888) 843-7824	C- / 3.3	2.73	2.41	2.60 /25	8.85 /32	8.09 /30	0.00	2.40
GR	Hartford SMART529 Age Bsd 0-8 C		C	(888) 843-7824	C- / 3.1	2.66	2.31	2.40 /24	8.64 /31	7.88 /29	0.00	2.59
GR	Hartford SMART529 Age Bsd 0-8 E		C	(888) 843-7824	C- / 3.8	2.90	2.80	3.40 /28	9.72 /38	8.95 /36	0.00	1.19
BA	Hartford SMART529 Age Bsd 14-18		C-	(888) 843-7824	D- / 1.1	1.83	0.73	0.97 /18	5.56 /15	6.25 /18	0.00	1.85
BA	Hartford SMART529 Age Bsd 14-18		C-	(888) 843-7824	D- / 1.3	1.68	0.44	0.40 /17	4.97 /13	5.67 /15	0.00	2.40
BA	Hartford SMART529 Age Bsd 14-18		C-	(888) 843-7824	D- / 1.2	1.61	0.33	0.19 /16	4.77 /12	5.45 /14	0.00	2.59
BA	Hartford SMART529 Age Bsd 14-18		C-	(888) 843-7824	D / 1.6	1.88	0.84	1.21 /19	5.82 /16	6.51 /20	0.00	1.19
AA	Hartford SMART529 Age Bsd 19+ A		C-	(888) 843-7824	E+ / 0.6	0.49	0.00	0.39 /17	1.99 / 6	2.92 / 6	0.00	1.85
AA	Hartford SMART529 Age Bsd 19+ B		C-	(888) 843-7824	E+ / 0.6	0.32	-0.30	-0.18 /15	1.42 / 6	2.35 / 5	0.00	2.40
AA	Hartford SMART529 Age Bsd 19+ C		C-	(888) 843-7824	E+ / 0.6	0.26	-0.41	-0.39 /15	1.22 / 5	2.15 / 5	0.00	2.59
AA	Hartford SMART529 Age Bsd 19+ E		C-	(888) 843-7824	E+ / 0.7	0.52	0.09	0.61 /17	2.23 / 7	3.16 / 6	0.00	1.19
AA	Hartford SMART529 Age Bsd 9-13 A		C-	(888) 843-7824	D- / 1.5	2.20	1.14	1.40 /20	7.03 /21	7.25 /25	0.00	1.85
AA	Hartford SMART529 Age Bsd 9-13 B		C-	(888) 843-7824	D / 1.9	2.08	0.88	0.86 /18	6.45 /19	6.66 /21	0.00	2.40
AA	Hartford SMART529 Age Bsd 9-13 C		C-	(888) 843-7824	D / 1.7	2.01	0.76	0.64 /17	6.24 /18	6.46 /20	0.00	2.59
AA	Hartford SMART529 Age Bsd 9-13 E		C-	(888) 843-7824	D+ / 2.3	2.27	1.27	1.66 /21	7.30 /23	7.52 /27	0.00	1.19
GR	Hartford SMART529 Cptl Appr 529 A		B+	(888) 843-7824	B / 7.9	3.34	6.03	10.33 /76	17.38 /92	11.61 /58	0.00	1.85
GR	Hartford SMART529 Cptl Appr 529 B		B+	(888) 843-7824	B+ / 8.5	3.19	5.73	9.71 /73	16.73 /88	11.00 /53	0.00	2.40
GR	Hartford SMART529 Cptl Appr 529 C		B+	(888) 843-7824	B+ / 8.3	3.13	5.61	9.49 /72	16.50 /87	10.78 /51	0.00	2.59
GR	Hartford SMART529 Cptl Appr 529 E		A	(888) 843-7824	A- / 9.0	3.37	6.13	10.57 /77	17.66 /93	11.88 /60	0.00	1.19
GI	Hartford SMART529 Div & Gr 529 A		B-	(888) 843-7824	C+ / 5.9	-0.12	3.96	9.18 /70	14.55 /71	12.37 /63	0.00	1.85
GI	Hartford SMART529 Div & Gr 529 B		B-	(888) 843-7824	C+ / 6.3	-0.25	3.68	8.59 /67	13.93 /67	11.75 /59	0.00	2.40
GI	Hartford SMART529 Div & Gr 529 C		B-	(888) 843-7824	C+ / 6.2	-0.30	3.58	8.38 /65	13.71 /65	11.54 /57	0.00	2.59
GI	Hartford SMART529 Div & Gr 529 E		B+	(888) 843-7824	B- / 7.0	-0.09	4.06	9.43 /72	14.83 /74	12.64 /65	0.00	1.19
GL	Hartford SMART529 Glb Gr 529 A		C	(888) 843-7824	C / 5.0	2.83	6.06	5.70 /44	13.05 /60	10.66 /50	0.00	1.85
GL	Hartford SMART529 Glb Gr 529 B		C+	(888) 843-7824	C / 5.5	2.65	5.73	5.08 /39	12.41 /55	10.05 /45	0.00	2.40
GL	Hartford SMART529 Glb Gr 529 C		C+	(888) 843-7824	C / 5.4	2.63	5.66	4.91 /38	12.21 /54	9.84 /43	0.00	2.59
GL	Hartford SMART529 Glb Gr 529 E		C+	(888) 843-7824	C+ / 6.1	2.85	6.15	5.92 /46	13.31 /62	10.93 /52	0.00	1.19
GR	Hartford SMART529 Gr Opp 529 A		A	(888) 843-7824	A+ / 9.6	6.35	13.42	19.39 /96	19.05 /97	15.66 /91	0.00	1.85
GR	Hartford SMART529 Gr Opp 529 B		A+	(888) 843-7824	A+ / 9.7	6.19	13.10	18.73 /96	18.39 /95	15.03 /87	0.00	2.40
GR	Hartford SMART529 Gr Opp 529 C		A+	(888) 843-7824	A+ / 9.7	6.15	13.00	18.51 /96	18.17 /95	14.81 /85	0.00	2.59
GR	Hartford SMART529 Gr Opp 529 E		A+	(888) 843-7824	A+ / 9.8	6.39	13.53	19.67 /97	19.34 /97	15.95 /93	0.00	1.19
FO	Hartford SMART529 Intl Gr 529 A		D	(888) 843-7824	D / 2.1	4.88	2.63	1.74 /21	8.09 /27	6.47 /20	0.00	1.85
FO	Hartford SMART529 Intl Gr 529 B		D	(888) 843-7824	D+ / 2.5	4.75	2.36	1.19 /19	7.50 /24	5.88 /16	0.00	2.40
FO	Hartford SMART529 Intl Gr 529 C		D	(888) 843-7824	D+ / 2.4	4.69	2.25	0.98 /18	7.29 /23	5.68 /15	0.00	2.59
FO	Hartford SMART529 Intl Gr 529 E		D+	(888) 843-7824	C- / 3.1	4.97	2.78	2.02 /22	8.37 /29	6.74 /21	0.00	1.19
MC	Hartford SMART529 MidCap 529 A		A	(888) 843-7824	A- / 9.0	5.77	11.04	12.76 /86	18.34 /95	15.03 /87	0.00	1.85
MC	Hartford SMART529 MidCap 529 B		A+	(888) 843-7824	A / 9.3	5.61	10.72	12.12 /83	17.68 /93	14.39 /81	0.00	2.40
MC	Hartford SMART529 MidCap 529 C		A	(888) 843-7824	A / 9.3	5.58	10.63	11.93 /82	17.46 /92	14.18 /79	0.00	2.59
MC	Hartford SMART529 MidCap 529 E		A+	(888) 843-7824	A+ / 9.6	5.81	11.16	13.02 /87	18.63 /96	15.31 /89	0.00	1.19
SC	Hartford SMART529 Sm Com 529 A		B-	(888) 843-7824	B / 8.0	5.20	12.61	11.16 /79	16.46 /87	15.08 /87	0.00	1.85
SC	Hartford SMART529 Sm Com 529 B		B	(888) 843-7824	B+ / 8.5	5.02	12.26	10.52 /76	15.81 /82	14.42 /82	0.00	2.40
SC	Hartford SMART529 Sm Com 529 C		B	(888) 843-7824	B+ / 8.3	4.99	12.17	10.33 /76	15.60 /80	14.22 /80	0.00	2.59
SC	Hartford SMART529 Sm Com 529 E		B+	(888) 843-7824	A- / 9.0	5.25	12.73	11.43 /80	16.75 /88	15.35 /89	0.00	1.19
GR	Hartford SMART529 Stable Val A		E+	(888) 843-7824	E+ / 0.6	0.27	0.52	0.98 /18	1.35 / 6	2.05 / 4	0.00	1.83
GR	Hartford SMART529 Stable Val B		E+	(888) 843-7824	E+ / 0.6	0.13	0.24	0.43 /17	0.80 / 5	1.49 / 4	0.00	2.38

● Denotes fund is closed to new investors
* Denotes fund is included in Section II

www.thestreetratings.com

| RISK | | | NET ASSETS | | ASSET | | | | Portfolio | BULL / BEAR | | FUND MANAGER | | MINIMUMS | | LOADS | |
Risk Rating/Pts	3 Year Standard Deviation	Beta	NAV As of 3/31/15	Total $(Mil)	Cash %	Stocks %	Bonds %	Other %	Turnover Ratio	Last Bull Market Return	Last Bear Market Return	Manager Quality Pct	Manager Tenure (Years)	Initial Purch. $	Additional Purch. $	Front End Load	Back End Load
C+ / 5.7	13.7	0.99	55.00	104	1	98	0	1	61	116.6	-23.9	86	6	0	0	0.0	0.0
C+ / 5.7	13.7	0.99	55.43	311	1	98	0	1	61	117.3	-23.9	87	6	250,000	0	0.0	0.0
B / 8.5	6.7	0.69	18.95	31	0	63	36	1	7	64.3	-13.9	76	13	250	25	5.5	0.0
B / 8.5	6.7	0.69	17.72	1	0	63	36	1	7	61.3	-14.1	71	13	250	25	0.0	0.0
B / 8.5	6.7	0.69	17.30	5	0	63	36	1	7	60.2	-14.2	69	13	250	25	0.0	0.0
B / 8.6	6.7	0.69	19.66	2	0	63	36	1	7	65.8	-13.8	78	13	250	25	0.0	0.0
B- / 7.8	8.4	0.82	23.22	107	10	78	11	1	59	59.4	-17.9	22	N/A	250	25	5.5	0.0
B- / 7.8	8.4	0.82	21.75	12	10	78	11	1	59	56.5	-18.1	17	N/A	250	25	0.0	0.0
B- / 7.7	8.4	0.82	21.26	22	10	78	11	1	59	55.5	-18.2	16	N/A	250	25	0.0	0.0
B- / 7.8	8.4	0.82	24.04	7	10	78	11	1	59	60.8	-17.9	25	N/A	250	25	0.0	0.0
B / 8.9	5.8	0.94	19.54	99	24	48	26	2	57	35.2	-11.0	14	N/A	250	25	5.5	0.0
B / 8.9	5.8	0.94	18.27	9	24	48	26	2	57	32.6	-11.2	11	N/A	250	25	0.0	0.0
B / 8.9	5.8	0.94	17.84	18	24	48	26	2	57	31.7	-11.3	10	N/A	250	25	0.0	0.0
B / 8.9	5.8	0.94	20.22	7	24	48	26	2	57	36.3	-10.9	16	N/A	250	25	0.0	0.0
B+ / 9.9	1.6	0.24	14.11	100	79	9	10	2	88	11.9	-2.9	60	N/A	250	25	4.5	0.0
B+ / 9.9	1.6	0.24	13.18	8	79	9	10	2	88	9.8	-3.1	51	N/A	250	25	0.0	0.0
B+ / 9.9	1.6	0.24	12.88	29	79	9	10	2	88	9.2	-3.2	48	N/A	250	25	0.0	0.0
B+ / 9.9	1.6	0.24	14.60	6	79	9	10	2	88	12.9	-2.8	63	N/A	250	25	0.0	0.0
B / 8.4	7.1	1.16	20.23	216	18	63	17	2	58	45.1	-14.6	9	N/A	250	25	5.5	0.0
B / 8.4	7.1	1.16	18.93	25	18	63	17	2	58	42.5	-14.8	7	N/A	250	25	0.0	0.0
B / 8.3	7.1	1.16	18.50	33	18	63	17	2	58	41.5	-14.9	6	N/A	250	25	0.0	0.0
B / 8.4	7.1	1.16	20.94	18	18	63	17	2	58	46.4	-14.5	10	N/A	250	25	0.0	0.0
C+ / 6.3	11.3	1.10	29.11	87	1	98	0	1	2	104.7	-25.6	62	13	250	25	5.5	0.0
C+ / 6.3	11.3	1.10	27.28	9	1	98	0	1	2	100.9	-25.8	53	13	250	25	0.0	0.0
C+ / 6.3	11.3	1.10	26.67	20	1	98	0	1	2	99.6	-25.9	50	13	250	25	0.0	0.0
C+ / 6.3	11.3	1.10	30.10	16	1	98	0	1	2	106.5	-25.5	65	13	250	25	0.0	0.0
B- / 7.5	9.4	0.97	25.19	67	2	96	0	2	4	87.9	-17.4	55	13	250	25	5.5	0.0
B- / 7.5	9.4	0.97	23.58	4	2	96	0	2	4	84.4	-17.6	46	13	250	25	0.0	0.0
B- / 7.5	9.4	0.97	23.04	11	2	96	0	2	4	83.3	-17.7	43	13	250	25	0.0	0.0
B- / 7.5	9.4	0.97	26.07	5	2	96	0	2	4	89.6	-17.3	58	13	250	25	0.0	0.0
C+ / 6.8	11.0	0.77	20.68	9	1	98	0	1	7	80.6	-19.9	94	13	250	25	5.5	0.0
C+ / 6.7	11.0	0.77	19.35	1	1	98	0	1	7	77.3	-20.1	93	13	250	25	0.0	0.0
C+ / 6.7	11.0	0.77	18.92	3	1	98	0	1	7	76.1	-20.2	93	13	250	25	0.0	0.0
C+ / 6.8	11.0	0.77	21.38	2	1	98	0	1	7	82.1	-19.8	94	13	250	25	0.0	0.0
C+ / 6.0	11.5	1.02	20.65	9	1	97	0	2	19	116.2	-23.0	85	N/A	250	25	5.5	0.0
C+ / 6.0	11.5	1.02	19.72	1	1	97	0	2	19	112.2	-23.2	81	N/A	250	25	0.0	0.0
C+ / 6.0	11.5	1.02	19.41	2	1	97	0	2	19	110.8	-23.3	80	N/A	250	25	0.0	0.0
C+ / 6.1	11.5	1.02	21.09	2	1	97	0	2	19	118.0	-23.0	86	N/A	250	25	0.0	0.0
C+ / 6.2	11.1	0.81	10.52	9	2	96	0	2	4	51.8	-23.2	71	N/A	250	25	5.5	0.0
C+ / 6.1	11.0	0.81	10.04	1	2	96	0	2	4	49.0	-23.4	65	N/A	250	25	0.0	0.0
C+ / 6.1	11.0	0.81	9.88	2	2	96	0	2	4	48.0	-23.4	62	N/A	250	25	0.0	0.0
C+ / 6.2	11.1	0.81	10.74	2	2	96	0	2	4	53.2	-23.1	74	N/A	250	25	0.0	0.0
C+ / 6.4	11.5	1.00	36.13	41	0	99	0	1	8	115.7	-25.6	78	13	250	25	5.5	0.0
C+ / 6.4	11.5	1.00	33.86	3	0	99	0	1	8	111.7	-25.8	73	13	250	25	0.0	0.0
C+ / 6.4	11.5	1.00	33.11	10	0	99	0	1	8	110.3	-25.9	71	13	250	25	0.0	0.0
C+ / 6.4	11.5	1.00	37.42	10	0	99	0	1	8	117.5	-25.6	80	13	250	25	0.0	0.0
C / 5.2	13.5	0.95	19.52	6	2	97	0	1	7	98.9	-24.9	76	N/A	250	25	5.5	0.0
C / 5.1	13.5	0.95	18.58	N/A	2	97	0	1	7	95.2	-25.0	71	N/A	250	25	0.0	0.0
C / 5.1	13.5	0.95	18.31	1	2	97	0	1	7	93.9	-25.1	69	N/A	250	25	0.0	0.0
C / 5.2	13.5	0.95	19.89	1	2	97	0	1	7	100.6	-24.8	78	N/A	250	25	0.0	0.0
C+ / 5.9	0.2	N/A	14.01	35	100	0	0	0	20	5.3	1.2	80	13	250	25	3.0	0.0
C+ / 5.9	0.2	N/A	13.12	3	100	0	0	0	20	3.3	1.0	75	13	250	25	0.0	0.0

Fund Type	Fund Name	Ticker Symbol	Overall Investment Rating	Phone	Performance Rating/Pts	PERFORMANCE Total Return % through 3/31/15			Annualized		Incl. in Returns	
						3 Mo	6 Mo	1Yr / Pct	3Yr / Pct	5Yr / Pct	Dividend Yield	Expense Ratio
GR	Hartford SMART529 Stable Val C		E+	(888) 843-7824	E+ / 0.6	0.09	0.15	0.24 /16	0.61 / 5	1.30 / 4	0.00	2.57
GR	Hartford SMART529 Stable Val E		E+	(888) 843-7824	E+ / 0.7	0.35	0.66	1.25 /19	1.61 / 6	2.31 / 5	0.00	1.17
AG	Hartford SMART529 Static Agg Gr A		C-	(888) 843-7824	C- / 4.0	3.23	3.48	4.09 /32	11.47 /49	10.18 /46	0.00	1.85
AG	Hartford SMART529 Static Agg Gr B		C	(888) 843-7824	C / 4.4	3.09	3.20	3.52 /29	10.86 /45	9.58 /41	0.00	2.40
AG	Hartford SMART529 Static Agg Gr C		C	(888) 843-7824	C / 4.3	3.04	3.10	3.32 /28	10.65 /43	9.37 /39	0.00	2.59
AG	Hartford SMART529 Static Agg Gr E		C	(888) 843-7824	C / 5.0	3.31	3.63	4.36 /34	11.76 /51	10.46 /48	0.00	1.19
BA	Hartford SMART529 Static Bal A		C-	(888) 843-7824	D- / 1.5	2.25	1.21	1.46 /20	7.07 /22	7.27 /25	0.00	1.85
BA	Hartford SMART529 Static Bal B		C-	(888) 843-7824	D / 1.9	2.06	0.88	0.86 /18	6.47 /19	6.67 /21	0.00	2.40
BA	Hartford SMART529 Static Bal C		C-	(888) 843-7824	D / 1.8	2.05	0.82	0.70 /18	6.28 /18	6.48 /20	0.00	2.59
BA	Hartford SMART529 Static Bal E		C-	(888) 843-7824	D+ / 2.3	2.31	1.34	1.71 /21	7.34 /23	7.54 /27	0.00	1.19
GR	Hartford SMART529 Static Gr A		C-	(888) 843-7824	D+ / 2.7	2.81	2.65	3.12 /27	9.46 /36	8.69 /34	0.00	1.85
GR	Hartford SMART529 Static Gr B		C	(888) 843-7824	C- / 3.3	2.67	2.36	2.55 /24	8.86 /32	8.09 /30	0.00	2.40
GR	Hartford SMART529 Static Gr C		C	(888) 843-7824	C- / 3.1	2.61	2.25	2.34 /23	8.65 /31	7.89 /29	0.00	2.59
GR	Hartford SMART529 Static Gr E		C	(888) 843-7824	C- / 3.8	2.87	2.77	3.37 /28	9.74 /38	8.96 /36	0.00	1.19
GR	Hartford SMART529 Stock 529 A		C+	(888) 843-7824	C / 5.1	-0.09	3.73	6.75 /53	13.62 /64	13.26 /71	0.00	1.85
GR	Hartford SMART529 Stock 529 B		B-	(888) 843-7824	C+ / 5.7	-0.20	3.48	6.20 /48	13.01 /60	12.64 /65	0.00	2.40
GR	Hartford SMART529 Stock 529 C		B-	(888) 843-7824	C / 5.5	-0.24	3.38	6.00 /46	12.80 /58	12.44 /64	0.00	2.59
GR	Hartford SMART529 Stock 529 E		B-	(888) 843-7824	C+ / 6.2	-0.01	3.88	7.04 /55	13.92 /67	13.55 /73	0.00	1.19
GL	Hartford Stock HLS IA		B+	(888) 843-7824	B- / 7.0	0.79	6.72	10.47 /76	14.42 /70	12.75 /66	1.81	0.51
GL	Hartford Stock HLS IB		B-	(888) 843-7824	C+ / 6.8	0.72	6.60	10.21 /75	14.13 /68	12.47 /64	1.56	0.76
GI	Hartford Value HLS Fd IA	HIAVX	B+	(888) 843-7824	B / 7.7	1.12	5.87	10.68 /77	15.45 /79	12.95 /68	1.47	0.76
GI	Hartford Value HLS Fd IB	HBVLX	B+	(888) 843-7824	B- / 7.5	1.07	5.74	10.42 /76	15.17 /76	12.68 /66	1.22	1.01
GR	Hartford Value HLS IA		B+	(888) 843-7824	B / 7.7	1.12	5.87	10.68 /77	15.45 /79	12.95 /68	1.47	0.76
GR	Hartford Value HLS IB		B+	(888) 843-7824	B- / 7.5	1.07	5.74	10.42 /76	15.17 /76	12.68 /66	1.22	1.01
GR	Hartford Value Opportunities A	HVOAX	C	(888) 843-7824	C / 5.5	1.74	3.19	4.95 /38	14.44 /70	12.22 /62	0.60	1.24
GR	● Hartford Value Opportunities B	HVOBX	C+	(888) 843-7824	C+ / 5.9	1.55	2.77	4.21 /33	13.57 /64	11.37 /56	0.00	2.26
GR	Hartford Value Opportunities C	HVOCX	C+	(888) 843-7824	C+ / 5.9	1.62	2.84	4.23 /33	13.61 /64	11.39 /56	0.22	1.94
GR	Hartford Value Opportunities I	HVOIX	C+	(888) 843-7824	C+ / 6.7	1.87	3.40	5.41 /42	14.81 /73	12.56 /65	0.96	0.86
GR	Hartford Value Opportunities R3	HVORX	C+	(888) 843-7824	C+ / 6.2	1.67	3.05	4.69 /36	14.18 /68	11.98 /60	0.38	1.52
GR	Hartford Value Opportunities R4	HVOSX	C+	(888) 843-7824	C+ / 6.5	1.76	3.25	5.09 /39	14.55 /71	12.32 /63	0.64	1.20
GR	Hartford Value Opportunities R5	HVOTX	C+	(888) 843-7824	C+ / 6.7	1.85	3.37	5.35 /41	14.85 /74	12.64 /65	0.77	0.87
GR	Hartford Value Opportunities Y	HVOYX	C+	(888) 843-7824	C+ / 6.7	1.90	3.41	5.44 /42	14.86 /74	12.66 /65	0.95	0.82
GR	Hatteras Alpha Hedged Strat A	APHAX	C-	(877) 569-2382	E+ / 0.6	1.32	0.26	-0.35 /15	2.32 / 7	--	0.24	4.74
AA	Hatteras Alpha Hedged Strat C	APHCX	C-	(877) 569-2382	E+ / 0.6	1.19	-0.09	-1.07 /13	1.56 / 6	1.79 / 4	0.00	5.49
GR	Hatteras Alpha Hedged Strat Inst	ALPIX	C-	(877) 569-2382	E+ / 0.9	1.46	0.54	0.11 /16	3.12 / 8	--	0.70	3.74
AA	Hatteras Alpha Hedged Strat NL	ALPHX	C-	(877) 569-2382	E+ / 0.8	1.48	0.52	0.17 /16	2.53 / 7	2.72 / 5	0.00	4.74
GR	Hatteras Disciplined Oppty Inst	HDOIX	U		U /	1.17	3.11	5.47 /42	--	--	0.00	2.67
IX	● Hatteras Hedged Strategies Inst	HHSIX	C-	(877) 569-2382	D- / 1.0	1.96	0.97	0.97 /18	3.66 / 9	--	1.49	3.06
GL	Hatteras Long/Short Debt A	HFIAX	D	(877) 569-2382	E / 0.5	1.22	-2.39	-3.16 / 8	1.49 / 6	--	2.60	3.39
FS	Hatteras Long/Short Debt C	HFICX	U	(877) 569-2382	U /	1.08	-2.71	-3.87 / 7	--	--	2.35	4.11
GL	Hatteras Long/Short Debt Inst	HFINX	D	(877) 569-2382	E+ / 0.6	1.34	-2.18	-2.64 / 9	2.00 / 6	--	3.25	2.89
IN	Hatteras Long/Short Equity A	HLSAX	D-	(877) 569-2382	D- / 1.1	2.90	3.21	4.61 /36	4.22 /11	--	0.00	3.95
IN	Hatteras Long/Short Equity Inst	HLSIX	D-	(877) 569-2382	D / 1.6	2.98	3.38	4.95 /38	4.67 /12	--	0.64	3.45
GR	Haverford Quality Gr Stk Fd	HAVGX	B-	(800) 307-4880	C+ / 6.4	-0.35	6.37	10.48 /76	13.46 /63	11.93 /60	1.11	0.84
GL	Heartland International Value	HINVX	E+	(800) 432-7856	E+ / 0.9	-0.72	-6.41	-4.54 / 6	5.58 /15	--	6.70	2.00
GR	Heartland Select Value Inst	HNSVX	C-	(800) 432-7856	C+ / 6.0	1.25	6.21	4.22 /33	13.56 /64	10.71 /50	0.72	0.88
GR	Heartland Select Value Inv	HRSVX	C-	(800) 432-7856	C+ / 5.8	1.18	6.05	3.92 /31	13.22 /61	10.37 /48	0.38	1.20
SC	Heartland Value Inst	HNTVX	D+	(800) 432-7856	C / 4.8	0.74	5.34	-0.83 /13	12.26 /54	11.07 /53	0.61	0.91
SC	Heartland Value Inv	HRTVX	D	(800) 432-7856	C / 4.7	0.69	5.28	-0.99 /13	12.06 /53	10.87 /52	0.45	1.08
GI	● Heartland Value Plus Inst	HNVIX	E	(800) 432-7856	D+ / 2.3	-2.57	0.51	-7.84 / 3	9.21 /34	9.76 /43	0.54	0.84
GI	● Heartland Value Plus Inv	HRVIX	E	(800) 432-7856	D / 2.1	-2.62	0.41	-8.07 / 3	8.92 /32	9.45 /40	0.20	1.14
GL	Henderson All Asset A	HGAAX	C	(866) 443-6337	D- / 1.1	3.01	2.81	4.46 /35	5.10 /13	--	1.18	1.33

● Denotes fund is closed to new investors
* Denotes fund is included in Section II

www.thestreetratings.com

RISK			NET ASSETS		ASSET					BULL / BEAR		FUND MANAGER		MINIMUMS		LOADS	
	3 Year		NAV						Portfolio	Last Bull	Last Bear	Manager	Manager	Initial	Additional	Front	Back
Risk Rating/Pts	Standard Deviation	Beta	As of 3/31/15	Total $(Mil)	Cash %	Stocks %	Bonds %	Other %	Turnover Ratio	Market Return	Market Return	Quality Pct	Tenure (Years)	Purch. $	Purch. $	End Load	End Load
C+ / 5.9	0.2	N/A	12.82	13	100	0	0	0	20	2.7	0.9	73	13	250	25	0.0	0.0
C+ / 5.9	0.2	N/A	14.49	6	100	0	0	0	20	6.2	1.4	81	13	250	25	0.0	0.0
C+ / 6.7	10.2	1.00	22.63	45	2	95	1	2	58	76.1	-22.9	16	N/A	250	25	5.5	0.0
C+ / 6.7	10.2	1.00	21.21	6	2	95	1	2	58	72.8	-23.0	12	N/A	250	25	0.0	0.0
C+ / 6.7	10.2	1.00	20.73	10	2	95	1	2	58	71.7	-23.1	11	N/A	250	25	0.0	0.0
C+ / 6.7	10.2	1.00	23.42	12	2	95	1	2	58	77.6	-22.8	17	N/A	250	25	0.0	0.0
B / 8.4	7.1	1.16	19.70	43	19	63	17	1	50	45.2	-14.7	9	N/A	250	25	5.5	0.0
B / 8.4	7.1	1.16	18.42	3	19	63	17	1	50	42.5	-14.9	7	N/A	250	25	0.0	0.0
B / 8.3	7.1	1.16	18.00	12	19	63	17	1	50	41.6	-14.9	7	N/A	250	25	0.0	0.0
B / 8.4	7.1	1.16	20.39	3	19	63	17	1	50	46.5	-14.6	11	N/A	250	25	0.0	0.0
B- / 7.8	8.4	0.82	22.03	72	10	78	11	1	55	59.5	-17.9	22	N/A	250	25	5.5	0.0
B- / 7.8	8.4	0.82	20.62	5	10	78	11	1	55	56.6	-18.1	17	N/A	250	25	0.0	0.0
B- / 7.8	8.4	0.82	20.15	16	10	78	11	1	55	55.6	-18.2	16	N/A	250	25	0.0	0.0
B- / 7.8	8.4	0.82	22.79	6	10	78	11	1	55	60.9	-17.9	25	N/A	250	25	0.0	0.0
B- / 7.6	9.3	0.94	19.41	21	0	98	0	2	8	84.0	-14.1	47	13	250	25	5.5	0.0
B- / 7.6	9.3	0.94	18.17	1	0	98	0	2	8	80.6	-14.3	39	13	250	25	0.0	0.0
B- / 7.6	9.3	0.94	17.76	5	0	98	0	2	8	79.5	-14.4	36	13	250	25	0.0	0.0
B- / 7.6	9.3	0.94	20.11	4	0	98	0	2	8	85.6	-14.0	51	13	250	25	0.0	0.0
B- / 7.5	9.2	0.54	63.99	1,509	1	98	0	1	27	94.5	-19.4	97	3	0	0	0.0	0.0
B- / 7.5	9.2	0.54	63.92	175	1	98	0	1	27	92.8	-19.5	97	3	0	0	0.0	0.0
B- / 7.1	10.3	1.05	17.08	507	0	99	0	1	19	99.2	-20.5	47	14	0	0	0.0	0.0
B- / 7.1	10.3	1.05	17.06	96	0	99	0	1	19	97.5	-20.6	44	14	0	0	0.0	0.0
B- / 7.1	10.3	1.05	17.08	507	0	99	0	1	19	99.2	-20.5	47	14	0	0	0.0	0.0
B- / 7.1	10.3	1.05	17.06	96	0	99	0	1	19	97.5	-20.6	44	14	0	0	0.0	0.0
C+ / 6.2	11.3	1.11	19.26	224	1	98	0	1	74	92.1	-22.1	25	19	2,000	50	5.5	0.0
C+ / 6.1	11.3	1.11	17.06	3	1	98	0	1	74	87.4	-22.4	17	19	0	0	0.0	0.0
C+ / 6.0	11.3	1.11	16.95	30	1	98	0	1	74	87.4	-22.4	18	19	2,000	50	0.0	0.0
C+ / 6.2	11.3	1.11	19.03	34	1	98	0	1	74	94.1	-22.0	28	19	0	0	0.0	0.0
C+ / 6.2	11.3	1.10	19.47	4	1	98	0	1	74	90.6	-22.2	22	19	0	0	0.0	0.0
C+ / 6.2	11.2	1.10	19.65	13	1	98	0	1	74	92.8	-22.1	26	19	0	0	0.0	0.0
C+ / 6.2	11.3	1.11	19.77	3	1	98	0	1	74	94.7	-22.0	29	19	0	0	0.0	0.0
C+ / 6.2	11.2	1.10	19.82	2	1	98	0	1	74	94.6	-22.0	30	19	250,000	0	0.0	0.0
B+ / 9.7	3.4	0.29	11.54	11	89	10	0	1	52	12.6	N/A	37	N/A	1,000	250	4.8	0.0
B+ / 9.6	3.5	0.48	11.05	31	89	10	0	1	52	9.8	-5.4	21	N/A	1,000	250	0.0	0.0
B+ / 9.7	3.5	0.29	11.82	470	89	10	0	1	52	19.1	N/A	48	N/A	1,000,000	0	0.0	0.0
B+ / 9.7	3.4	0.47	11.64	32	89	10	0	1	52	13.2	-5.0	32	N/A	1,000	250	0.0	0.0
U /	N/A	N/A	10.35	37	0	0	0	100	0	N/A	N/A	N/A	N/A	1,000,000	0	0.0	0.0
B+ / 9.0	3.7	0.31	10.91	196	100	0	0	0	35	18.9	N/A	51	4	150,000,000	0	0.0	0.0
B- / 7.8	2.7	0.28	9.11	45	100	0	0	0	4	9.1	N/A	52	4	1,000	250	4.8	0.0
U /	N/A	N/A	9.04	36	100	0	0	0	4	N/A	N/A	N/A	4	1,000	250	0.0	0.0
B / 8.3	2.8	0.28	9.33	298	100	0	0	0	4	10.9	N/A	61	4	1,000,000	0	0.0	0.0
C+ / 5.9	5.3	0.42	9.57	5	100	0	0	0	61	22.8	N/A	34	4	1,000	250	4.8	0.0
C+ / 5.8	5.3	0.43	9.69	33	100	0	0	0	61	24.6	N/A	39	4	1,000,000	0	0.0	0.0
B- / 7.1	10.8	1.10	14.44	173	1	98	0	1	16	85.7	-17.1	18	11	2,500	0	0.0	0.0
C / 5.1	11.4	0.71	9.70	29	3	94	2	1	31	25.2	-20.0	52	5	1,000	100	0.0	2.0
C- / 4.0	12.0	1.09	31.64	99	0	99	0	1	42	76.0	-21.9	20	11	500,000	100	0.0	0.0
C- / 4.1	12.0	1.09	31.69	322	0	99	0	1	42	74.1	-22.0	17	11	1,000	100	0.0	0.0
C / 4.4	13.5	0.91	44.72	81	0	95	4	1	38	73.1	-24.1	34	31	500,000	100	0.0	0.0
C / 4.3	13.5	0.91	44.03	1,041	0	95	4	1	38	72.1	-24.1	32	31	1,000	100	0.0	0.0
C- / 3.3	15.7	1.31	30.76	1,186	0	98	1	1	26	67.8	-25.0	2	9	500,000	100	0.0	0.0
C- / 3.3	15.7	1.31	30.83	1,063	0	98	1	1	26	66.2	-25.1	1	9	1,000	100	0.0	0.0
B+ / 9.8	4.3	0.65	10.62	7	40	33	25	2	52	N/A	N/A	58	3	500	0	5.8	0.0

www.thestreetratings.com
311
Data as of March 31, 2015

Fund Type	Fund Name	Ticker Symbol	Overall Investment Rating	Phone	Performance Rating/Pts	3 Mo	6 Mo	1Yr / Pct	3Yr / Pct	5Yr / Pct	Dividend Yield	Expense Ratio
	99 Pct = Best							Total Return % through 3/31/15	Annualized		Incl. in Returns	
GL	Henderson All Asset C	HGACX	C	(866) 443-6337	D- / 1.3	2.84	2.40	3.67 /30	4.30 /11	--	0.76	2.07
GL	Henderson All Asset I	HGAIX	C	(866) 443-6337	D / 1.8	3.11	2.88	4.73 /37	5.36 /14	--	1.59	1.02
EM	Henderson Emerging Markets Oppty	HEMAX	E+	(866) 443-6337	E / 0.4	1.92	-2.17	0.67 /17	-0.28 / 4	--	0.00	1.97
EM	Henderson Emerging Markets Oppty	HEMCX	E+	(866) 443-6337	E / 0.4	1.74	-2.56	-0.11 /15	-1.04 / 3	--	0.00	2.74
EM	Henderson Emerging Markets Oppty I	HEMIX	E+	(866) 443-6337	E / 0.5	2.03	-2.02	0.82 /18	-0.01 / 4	--	0.15	1.66
FO	Henderson European Focus A	HFEAX	D	(866) 443-6337	C- / 3.4	6.64	3.98	-1.17 /12	10.93 /45	9.97 /44	1.41	1.37
FO	● Henderson European Focus B	HFEBX	D	(866) 443-6337	C- / 3.8	6.43	3.53	-2.02 /10	10.01 /39	9.08 /37	0.06	2.19
FO	Henderson European Focus C	HFECX	D	(866) 443-6337	C- / 3.8	6.42	3.54	-1.95 /10	10.07 /40	9.12 /38	1.25	2.14
FO	Henderson European Focus I	HFEIX	D+	(866) 443-6337	C / 4.5	6.68	4.06	-0.95 /13	11.23 /47	10.27 /47	1.91	1.11
GL	Henderson Global Equity Income A	HFQAX	D+	(866) 443-6337	D+ / 2.9	3.65	2.65	1.41 /20	9.99 /39	7.94 /29	5.68	1.18
GL	Henderson Global Equity Income C	HFQCX	C-	(866) 443-6337	C- / 3.3	3.62	2.28	0.66 /17	9.19 /34	7.15 /24	5.29	1.93
GL	Henderson Global Equity Income I	HFQIX	C-	(866) 443-6337	C- / 4.0	3.71	2.76	1.54 /20	10.26 /41	8.21 /31	6.28	0.92
TC	Henderson Global Technology A	HFGAX	D-	(866) 443-6337	C- / 3.3	1.90	4.75	8.65 /67	9.58 /37	11.47 /57	0.00	1.35
TC	● Henderson Global Technology B	HFGBX	D	(866) 443-6337	C- / 3.6	1.72	4.35	7.80 /61	8.71 /31	10.57 /49	0.00	2.16
TC	Henderson Global Technology C	HFGCX	D	(866) 443-6337	C- / 3.6	1.68	4.36	7.80 /61	8.75 /31	10.61 /50	0.00	2.12
TC	Henderson Global Technology I	HFGIX	D+	(866) 443-6337	C / 4.4	1.95	4.86	8.91 /69	9.87 /39	11.76 /59	0.00	1.10
FO	Henderson Internatl Oppty A	HFOAX	C-	(866) 443-6337	C- / 4.2	6.54	7.39	5.39 /42	11.22 /47	7.46 /26	0.82	1.39
FO	● Henderson Internatl Oppty B	HFOBX	C-	(866) 443-6337	C / 4.6	6.30	6.94	4.52 /35	10.30 /41	6.59 /21	0.00	2.20
FO	Henderson Internatl Oppty C	HFOCX	C-	(866) 443-6337	C / 4.6	6.31	6.96	4.58 /36	10.35 /41	6.63 /21	0.34	2.16
FO	Henderson Internatl Oppty I	HFOIX	C	(866) 443-6337	C / 5.4	6.59	7.54	5.69 /44	11.52 /49	7.75 /28	1.25	1.11
FO	Henderson Internatl Oppty R	HFORX	C	(866) 443-6337	C / 4.9	6.45	7.23	5.09 /39	10.85 /45	7.12 /24	0.78	1.67
BA	Hennessy Balanced Investor	HBFBX	D+	(800) 966-4354	D- / 1.3	-0.44	-0.43	1.76 /21	5.01 /13	6.36 /19	0.18	1.68
SC	Hennessy Cornerstone Growth Inst	HICGX	A+	(800) 966-4354	A+ / 9.8	4.86	14.28	17.45 /95	19.99 /98	14.90 /86	0.00	0.95
SC	Hennessy Cornerstone Growth Inv	HFCGX	A+	(800) 966-4354	A+ / 9.8	4.81	14.19	17.23 /95	19.68 /97	14.56 /83	0.00	1.15
GR	Hennessy Cornerstone Large Gro	HILGX	B+	(800) 966-4354	B+ / 8.8	2.38	8.51	14.13 /90	16.56 /87	15.49 /90	1.03	0.99
GR	Hennessy Cornerstone Large Gro Inv	HFLGX	B+	(800) 966-4354	B+ / 8.7	2.32	8.48	14.00 /89	16.34 /86	15.20 /88	0.89	1.08
MC	Hennessy Cornerstone Mid Cap 30	HIMDX	A+	(800) 966-4354	A+ / 9.8	5.30	12.49	15.66 /93	19.92 /98	17.64 /97	0.00	0.99
MC	Hennessy Cornerstone Mid Cap 30	HFMDX	A+	(800) 966-4354	A+ / 9.7	5.29	12.44	15.42 /92	19.55 /97	17.26 /96	0.00	1.17
GL	Hennessy Cornerstone Val Investor	HFCVX	C+	(800) 966-4354	C / 5.1	-1.54	0.16	5.10 /39	12.61 /57	11.47 /57	2.26	1.09
GL	Hennessy Cornerstone Value Inst	HICVX	C+	(800) 966-4354	C / 5.2	-1.54	0.16	5.22 /40	12.85 /58	11.75 /59	2.44	0.95
BA	Hennessy Equity and Income Inst	HEIIX	B-	(800) 966-4354	C / 4.5	0.49	5.28	9.71 /73	10.20 /40	11.02 /53	1.19	1.07
BA	Hennessy Equity and Income Investor	HEIFX	C+	(800) 966-4354	C / 4.3	0.39	5.11	9.41 /71	9.89 /39	10.74 /51	0.85	1.40
SC	Hennessy Focus Institutional	HFCIX	A+	(800) 966-4354	A+ / 9.8	5.34	15.97	18.61 /96	19.40 /97	17.72 /97	0.06	1.10
SC	Hennessy Focus Investor	HFCSX	A+	(800) 966-4354	A+ / 9.8	5.26	15.77	18.24 /96	19.04 /97	17.35 /97	0.02	1.46
EN	Hennessy Gas Utility Investor	GASFX	A-	(800) 966-4354	B / 8.2	-1.84	2.50	10.89 /78	16.85 /87	17.40 /97	2.19	0.94
FO	Hennessy Japan Fund Institutional	HJPIX	A+	(800) 966-4354	A / 9.5	11.18	10.51	19.10 /96	15.76 /81	13.87 /76	0.00	1.44
FO	Hennessy Japan Fund Investor	HJPNX	A+	(800) 966-4354	A / 9.4	11.14	10.41	18.84 /96	15.52 /79	13.59 /74	0.00	1.64
FO	Hennessy Japan Small Cap Inv	HJPSX	C	(800) 966-4354	B / 8.1	5.07	1.03	10.33 /76	16.22 /85	13.07 /69	0.00	2.18
FS	Hennessy Large Cap Financial Inv	HLFNX	C	(800) 966-4354	C+ / 6.0	-3.92	2.20	2.30 /23	14.81 /73	8.31 /32	0.00	1.55
GI	Hennessy Large Value Institutional	HLVIX	A-	(800) 966-4354	B / 7.8	1.32	6.10	11.16 /79	15.49 /79	12.63 /65	1.01	1.11
GI	Hennessy Large Value Investor	HLVFX	B+	(800) 966-4354	B- / 7.5	1.29	6.01	10.92 /78	15.11 /76	12.21 /62	0.76	1.21
FS	Hennessy Small Cap Financial Inst	HISFX	D+	(800) 966-4354	C+ / 6.2	2.58	10.87	-0.58 /14	14.01 /67	7.19 /24	0.00	1.12
FS	Hennessy Small Cap Financial Inv	HSFNX	D+	(800) 966-4354	C+ / 6.0	2.45	10.70	-0.92 /13	13.67 /65	6.92 /23	0.00	1.49
TC	Hennessy Technology Inst	HTCIX	D-	(800) 966-4354	D+ / 2.9	2.75	2.14	4.65 /36	7.84 /26	7.72 /28	0.00	2.66
TC	Hennessy Technology Investor	HTECX	D-	(800) 966-4354	D+ / 2.7	2.65	2.02	4.35 /34	7.56 /24	7.46 /26	0.00	3.03
GR	Hennessy Total Return Investor	HDOGX	C-	(800) 966-4354	C- / 3.1	-0.17	-0.10	4.30 /34	8.84 /32	10.28 /47	1.30	1.26
GR	Henssler Equity Institutional	HEQCX	D-	(800) 936-3863	C+ / 6.4	0.00	4.76	9.43 /72	13.78 /65	--	1.08	0.81
GR	Henssler Equity Investor	HEQFX	D-	(800) 936-3863	C+ / 6.0	-0.10	4.49	8.87 /69	13.11 /60	11.17 /54	0.70	1.31
GI	HI 529 CSP Vanguard Csv Growth		C	(800) 662-7447	D / 1.9	1.78	3.85	6.01 /47	5.33 /14	6.04 /17	0.00	0.75
GI	HI 529 CSP Vanguard Growth Port		B	(800) 662-7447	C / 5.0	2.18	5.05	8.00 /63	11.27 /47	10.42 /48	0.00	0.75
GI	HI 529 CSP Vanguard Income Port		C-	(800) 662-7447	E+ / 0.7	0.98	1.72	2.90 /26	1.01 / 5	2.57 / 5	0.00	0.75
GI	HI 529 CSP Vanguard Mod Growth		C+	(800) 662-7447	C- / 3.4	1.93	4.45	7.02 /55	8.29 /29	8.24 /31	0.00	0.75

● Denotes fund is closed to new investors
* Denotes fund is included in Section II

www.thestreetratings.com

RISK			NET ASSETS		ASSET					BULL / BEAR		FUND MANAGER		MINIMUMS		LOADS	
Risk Rating/Pts	3 Year Standard Deviation	Beta	NAV As of 3/31/15	Total $(Mil)	Cash %	Stocks %	Bonds %	Other %	Portfolio Turnover Ratio	Last Bull Market Return	Last Bear Market Return	Manager Quality Pct	Manager Tenure (Years)	Initial Purch. $	Additional Purch. $	Front End Load	Back End Load
B+ / 9.8	4.3	0.64	10.49	12	40	33	25	2	52	N/A	N/A	47	3	500	0	0.0	0.0
B+ / 9.8	4.3	0.63	10.61	44	40	33	25	2	52	N/A	N/A	64	3	0	0	0.0	0.0
C+ / 5.6	13.7	0.95	9.01	8	2	97	0	1	97	30.7	-28.8	53	5	500	0	5.8	0.0
C+ / 5.6	13.7	0.96	8.77	3	2	97	0	1	97	27.3	-29.0	42	5	500	0	0.0	0.0
C+ / 5.6	13.7	0.96	9.04	16	2	97	0	1	97	31.8	-28.7	58	5	0	0	0.0	0.0
C / 4.8	15.6	1.02	35.15	739	2	97	0	1	90	81.5	-33.2	78	14	500	0	5.8	0.0
C / 4.8	15.7	1.02	33.45	8	2	97	0	1	90	76.4	-33.4	70	14	500	0	0.0	0.0
C / 4.8	15.7	1.02	33.00	298	2	97	0	1	90	76.8	-33.4	71	14	500	0	0.0	0.0
C / 4.8	15.6	1.02	35.11	1,733	2	97	0	1	90	83.3	-33.2	80	14	0	0	0.0	0.0
C+ / 6.8	10.5	0.76	7.97	642	4	95	0	1	103	54.7	-16.1	87	9	500	0	5.8	0.0
C+ / 6.8	10.5	0.77	7.93	1,033	4	95	0	1	103	50.9	-16.5	83	9	500	0	0.0	0.0
C+ / 6.8	10.5	0.77	7.98	1,636	4	95	0	1	103	56.2	-16.0	88	9	0	0	0.0	0.0
C / 4.7	12.9	1.14	25.20	100	2	97	0	1	65	68.7	-21.7	3	14	500	0	5.8	0.0
C / 4.5	12.9	1.14	22.43	7	2	97	0	1	65	64.1	-22.0	2	14	500	0	0.0	0.0
C / 4.5	12.9	1.14	22.41	79	2	97	0	1	65	64.2	-21.9	2	14	500	0	0.0	0.0
C / 4.8	12.9	1.14	25.66	97	2	97	0	1	65	70.1	-21.6	3	14	0	0	0.0	0.0
C+ / 6.0	12.3	0.88	28.01	1,538	4	95	0	1	74	62.8	-24.7	87	14	500	0	5.8	0.0
C+ / 6.0	12.3	0.88	26.34	22	4	95	0	1	74	58.3	-25.0	83	14	500	0	0.0	0.0
C+ / 6.0	12.3	0.88	26.27	519	4	95	0	1	74	58.5	-25.0	83	14	500	0	0.0	0.0
C+ / 6.0	12.3	0.88	28.00	2,019	4	95	0	1	74	64.5	-24.6	88	14	0	0	0.0	0.0
C+ / 6.0	12.3	0.88	27.57	12	4	95	0	1	74	61.0	-24.8	86	14	0	0	0.0	0.0
B / 8.4	4.9	0.72	12.34	12	1	50	48	1	23	27.6	-3.7	30	19	2,500	0	0.0	0.0
C+ / 6.8	11.1	0.73	20.73	44	4	95	0	1	84	144.4	-32.6	96	15	250,000	0	0.0	0.0
C+ / 6.8	11.1	0.73	20.28	259	4	95	0	1	84	142.1	-32.7	96	15	2,500	0	0.0	0.0
C / 5.4	10.2	1.01	13.79	15	5	94	0	1	57	96.7	-16.5	70	11	250,000	0	0.0	0.0
C / 5.4	10.1	1.01	13.68	109	5	94	0	1	57	95.1	-16.5	68	11	2,500	0	0.0	0.0
C+ / 6.1	12.5	0.99	20.08	104	3	96	0	1	132	107.9	-20.2	87	12	250,000	0	0.0	0.0
C+ / 6.1	12.4	0.99	19.69	368	3	96	0	1	132	105.6	-20.3	86	12	2,500	0	0.0	0.0
B- / 7.3	9.3	0.58	17.93	138	0	100	0	0	34	71.2	-11.2	96	19	2,500	0	0.0	0.0
B- / 7.3	9.3	0.58	17.91	3	0	100	0	0	34	72.6	-11.2	96	19	250,000	0	0.0	0.0
B / 8.4	5.5	0.91	15.63	155	3	60	35	2	28	55.0	-5.1	71	8	250,000	0	0.0	0.0
B / 8.5	5.5	0.91	16.51	364	3	60	35	2	28	53.7	-5.2	67	8	2,500	0	0.0	0.0
C+ / 6.6	10.3	0.66	72.01	349	11	88	0	1	18	117.1	-15.4	97	6	250,000	0	0.0	0.0
C+ / 6.6	10.3	0.66	70.89	1,361	11	88	0	1	18	114.9	-15.5	97	6	2,500	0	0.0	0.0
C+ / 6.9	11.0	0.40	29.77	2,159	0	99	0	1	20	81.7	-3.8	99	14	2,500	0	0.0	0.0
B- / 7.3	11.3	0.59	23.76	36	16	83	0	1	22	59.9	-2.6	98	9	250,000	0	0.0	0.0
B- / 7.3	11.3	0.59	23.34	61	16	83	0	1	22	58.7	-2.7	98	9	2,500	0	0.0	0.0
C- / 3.1	12.6	0.57	9.94	15	3	96	0	1	63	64.6	-0.4	98	8	2,500	0	0.0	0.0
C+ / 5.8	13.6	1.14	18.88	98	6	93	0	1	58	105.8	-25.1	13	18	2,500	0	0.0	0.0
B- / 7.2	10.1	1.03	34.53	N/A	1	98	0	1	85	96.7	-18.3	53	8	250,000	0	0.0	0.0
B- / 7.2	10.1	1.02	34.44	153	1	98	0	1	85	94.4	-18.5	49	8	2,500	0	0.0	0.0
C- / 3.2	14.1	1.07	13.11	16	0	99	0	1	47	83.7	-27.5	15	18	250,000	0	0.0	0.0
C- / 3.8	14.2	1.08	21.73	178	0	99	0	1	47	82.2	-27.7	13	18	2,500	0	0.0	0.0
C / 4.6	15.3	1.15	15.30	1	3	96	0	1	204	62.7	-23.1	2	13	250,000	0	0.0	0.0
C / 4.6	15.3	1.15	15.12	4	3	96	0	1	204	61.3	-23.2	2	13	2,500	0	0.0	0.0
B- / 7.4	6.9	0.60	14.14	77	0	53	46	1	23	49.8	-5.7	60	17	2,500	0	0.0	0.0
D- / 1.2	10.0	1.01	10.06	14	0	99	0	1	48	82.2	N/A	34	17	1,000,000	0	0.0	0.0
D- / 1.2	10.1	1.01	9.77	52	0	99	0	1	48	78.8	-15.9	27	17	2,000	200	0.0	0.0
B+ / 9.7	3.1	0.21	14.28	18	0	25	74	1	0	24.4	-1.6	84	8	15	15	0.0	0.0
B / 8.4	7.4	0.75	14.99	9	0	74	24	2	0	64.1	-13.6	59	8	15	15	0.0	0.0
B+ / 9.6	2.8	-0.05	12.41	11	25	0	74	1	0	4.1	3.7	83	8	15	15	0.0	0.0
B+ / 9.4	5.0	0.48	14.78	16	0	49	49	2	0	42.9	-7.7	75	8	15	15	0.0	0.0

					PERFORMANCE						
						Total Return % through 3/31/15				Incl. in Returns	
					Perfor-mance				Annualized		Dividend	Expense
Fund Type	Fund Name	Ticker Symbol	Overall Investment Rating	Phone	Rating/Pts	3 Mo	6 Mo	1Yr / Pct	3Yr / Pct	5Yr / Pct	Yield	Ratio
GI	HI 529 CSP Vanguard Tot Stk Mkt Idx		A-	(800) 662-7447	B / 7.9	1.67	6.74	11.52 /81	15.58 /80	13.97 /77	0.00	0.75
IN	Highland Dividend Equity A	HDFAX	C	(877) 665-1287	C- / 3.4	-0.13	1.82	1.75 /21	11.41 /48	--	1.41	1.95
IN	Highland Dividend Equity C	HDFCX	C	(877) 665-1287	C- / 3.9	-0.29	1.46	1.04 /19	10.64 /43	--	0.93	2.60
IN	Highland Dividend Equity Y	HDFYX	C+	(877) 665-1287	C / 4.6	-0.04	1.96	2.07 /22	11.77 /51	--	1.94	1.60
EN	Highland Energy MLP A	HEFAX	C-	(877) 665-1287	D / 2.1	-1.32	-9.00	1.92 /22	9.89 /39	--	4.34	10.54
EN	Highland Energy MLP C	HEFCX	C	(877) 665-1287	D+ / 2.5	-1.44	-9.25	1.28 /19	9.18 /34	--	4.15	11.29
EN	Highland Energy MLP R	HEFRX	C	(877) 665-1287	D+ / 2.8	-1.35	-9.06	1.75 /21	9.70 /37	--	4.33	10.79
EN	Highland Energy MLP Y	HEFYX	C+	(877) 665-1287	C- / 3.2	-1.27	-8.94	2.22 /23	10.26 /41	--	4.81	10.29
GR	Highland Global Allocation A	HCOAX	C	(877) 665-1287	B / 7.7	4.20	8.86	12.93 /86	16.33 /86	13.14 /69	2.23	1.00
GR	Highland Global Allocation C	HCOCX	C	(877) 665-1287	B / 8.1	4.03	8.47	12.02 /83	15.44 /79	12.29 /62	2.13	1.75
GR	Highland Global Allocation R	HCORX	C+	(877) 665-1287	B+ / 8.6	4.18	8.69	12.52 /85	16.08 /84	12.98 /68	2.15	1.25
GR	Highland Global Allocation Y	HCOYX	B-	(877) 665-1287	B+ / 8.9	4.33	9.02	13.14 /87	16.59 /87	13.41 /72	2.24	0.75
GR	Highland Long/Short Equity A	HEOAX	D+	(877) 665-1287	D / 2.2	4.95	6.41	6.59 /52	7.30 /23	6.33 /19	0.00	3.77
GR	Highland Long/Short Equity C	HEOCX	D+	(877) 665-1287	D+ / 2.6	4.77	6.11	5.84 /45	6.63 /20	5.70 /15	0.00	4.41
GR	Highland Long/Short Equity Z	HEOZX	C-	(877) 665-1287	C- / 3.3	4.98	6.57	6.83 /54	7.65 /25	6.66 /21	0.00	3.41
HL	Highland Long/Short Healthcare A	HHCAX	C+	(877) 665-1287	C+ / 6.4	10.34	11.85	9.62 /73	13.66 /65	11.50 /57	0.00	2.55
HL	Highland Long/Short Healthcare C	HHCCX	C+	(877) 665-1287	C+ / 6.8	10.17	11.51	8.91 /69	12.95 /59	10.84 /51	0.00	3.25
HL	Highland Long/Short Healthcare Z	HHCZX	B+	(877) 665-1287	B / 7.7	10.49	12.10	10.06 /75	14.12 /68	11.88 /60	0.00	2.26
FS	Highland Opportunistic Credit Z	HNRZX	C	(877) 665-1287	C / 4.8	-3.12	-10.40	-13.72 / 2	16.01 /83	6.64 /21	0.85	N/A
GR	Highland Premier Growth Equity A	HPEAX	B+	(877) 665-1287	B+ / 8.6	2.15	7.65	16.80 /94	17.47 /92	14.59 /83	0.00	1.16
GR	Highland Premier Growth Equity C	HPECX	B+	(877) 665-1287	B+ / 8.9	1.99	7.28	15.94 /93	16.61 /87	13.74 /75	0.00	1.91
GR	Highland Premier Growth Equity R	HPERX	A	(877) 665-1287	A- / 9.2	2.09	7.52	16.49 /94	17.17 /91	14.30 /80	0.00	1.41
GR	Highland Premier Growth Equity Y	HPEYX	A	(877) 665-1287	A / 9.4	2.20	7.77	17.07 /95	17.77 /93	14.87 /86	0.00	0.91
SC	Highland Small-Cap Equity A	HSZAX	C	(877) 665-1287	C+ / 6.2	4.02	11.08	9.31 /71	14.13 /68	15.06 /87	0.00	1.62
SC	Highland Small-Cap Equity C	HSZCX	C	(877) 665-1287	C+ / 6.6	3.77	10.58	8.51 /66	13.23 /61	14.20 /79	0.00	2.37
SC	Highland Small-Cap Equity R	HSZRX	C+	(877) 665-1287	B- / 7.1	3.93	10.99	9.14 /70	14.01 /68	14.93 /86	0.00	1.87
SC	Highland Small-Cap Equity Y	HSZYX	C+	(877) 665-1287	B- / 7.4	4.03	11.15	9.56 /72	14.39 /70	15.34 /89	0.00	1.37
AA	Highland Total Return A	HTAAX	D+	(877) 665-1287	D / 1.7	0.60	1.74	3.73 /30	7.49 /24	6.69 /21	0.94	1.39
AA	Highland Total Return C	HTACX	D+	(877) 665-1287	D / 2.0	0.42	1.35	2.94 /26	6.68 /20	5.90 /16	0.91	2.14
AA	Highland Total Return R	HTARX	C-	(877) 665-1287	D+ / 2.4	0.51	1.60	3.50 /29	7.26 /23	6.45 /20	0.91	1.64
AA	Highland Total Return Y	HTAYX	C-	(877) 665-1287	D+ / 2.7	0.63	1.86	4.00 /32	7.74 /26	6.94 /23	1.04	1.14
AG	Hillman Focused Advantage NL	HCMAX	C+	(800) 773-3863	C+ / 6.2	0.95	4.64	11.35 /80	13.03 /60	11.10 /53	0.44	1.52
GR	Hodges Blue Chip 25 Retail	HDPBX	B	(877) 232-1222	B / 8.1	5.78	-0.18	8.56 /67	16.87 /89	12.83 /67	0.19	2.47
IN	Hodges Equity Income Retail	HDPEX	C	(877) 232-1222	C / 4.8	3.05	4.02	10.09 /75	10.92 /45	11.72 /59	2.04	1.68
GL	Hodges Inst	HDPIX	A+	(877) 232-1222	A+ / 9.6	2.06	-2.56	4.00 /32	22.02 /98	14.64 /84	0.00	1.14
GR	Hodges Pure Contrarian Retail	HDPCX	E	(877) 232-1222	C- / 3.0	-6.60	-5.64	-8.86 / 3	12.00 /52	7.67 /28	3.85	2.54
GL	Hodges Retail	HDPMX	A	(877) 232-1222	A / 9.5	1.96	-2.84	3.53 /29	21.71 /98	14.33 /81	0.00	1.43
SC	Hodges Small Cap Inst	HDSIX	A	(877) 232-1222	A / 9.5	4.65	6.49	9.17 /70	19.57 /97	20.82 /99	0.00	1.05
SC	Hodges Small Cap Retail	HDPSX	A	(877) 232-1222	A / 9.4	4.55	6.27	8.78 /68	19.16 /97	20.30 /99	0.00	1.39
SC	Hodges Small Intrinsic Val Retail	HDSVX	U	(877) 232-1222	U /	11.20	18.18	19.66 /96	--	--	0.00	11.41
BA	Holland Balanced	HOLBX	C		C- / 3.5	-2.57	-0.18	4.88 /38	9.79 /38	9.00 /37	0.00	1.93
GR	Homestead Growth	HNASX	A-	(800) 258-3030	A / 9.3	5.39	10.02	14.23 /90	17.23 /91	16.03 /93	0.00	1.04
FO	Homestead International Value	HISIX	E+	(800) 258-3030	D / 1.6	4.88	0.76	-6.97 / 4	6.77 /20	4.26 / 9	3.15	0.96
SC	Homestead Small Company Stock	HSCSX	A+	(800) 258-3030	A / 9.5	4.25	15.22	11.30 /80	18.17 /95	17.71 /97	0.33	0.94
IX	Homestead Stock Index	HSTIX	A-	(800) 258-3030	B / 7.8	0.78	5.65	12.16 /83	15.49 /79	13.87 /76	1.40	0.56
GI	Homestead Value	HOVLX	A+	(800) 258-3030	B+ / 8.9	1.46	7.12	12.96 /86	17.19 /91	14.09 /79	1.52	0.64
GL	Horizon Spin-off and Corp Res A	LSHAX	C+	(800) 207-7108	C+ / 5.8	5.06	0.39	-0.76 /14	15.53 /79	11.94 /60	0.00	1.94
GL	Horizon Spin-off and Corp Res C	LSHCX	C+	(800) 754-8757	C+ / 6.1	4.87	0.00	-1.46 /12	14.80 /73	11.31 /55	0.00	2.69
GL	Horizon Spin-off and Corp Res Inst	LSHUX	C+	(800) 426-3750	C+ / 6.8	5.18	0.48	-0.48 /14	15.79 /82	12.26 /62	0.00	1.69
IN	Hotchkis and Wiley Capital Income A	HWIAX	C+	(866) 493-8637	C / 5.2	1.23	3.14	5.19 /40	13.63 /64	--	3.91	1.51
IN	Hotchkis and Wiley Capital Income I	HWIIX	B-	(866) 493-8637	C+ / 5.7	1.09	2.96	5.29 /41	13.10 /60	--	4.50	1.34
GR	Hotchkis and Wiley Divsfd Val A	HWCAX	B	(866) 493-8637	B- / 7.0	0.38	4.62	7.77 /61	16.67 /88	13.36 /72	2.08	1.26

• Denotes fund is closed to new investors
* Denotes fund is included in Section II

99 Pct = Best
0 Pct = Worst

RISK			NET ASSETS		ASSET				Portfolio	BULL / BEAR		FUND MANAGER		MINIMUMS		LOADS	
Risk Rating/Pts	3 Year		NAV As of 3/31/15	Total $(Mil)	Cash %	Stocks %	Bonds %	Other %	Turnover Ratio	Last Bull Market Return	Last Bear Market Return	Manager Quality Pct	Manager Tenure (Years)	Initial Purch. $	Additional Purch. $	Front End Load	Back End Load
	Standard Deviation	Beta															
B- / 7.2	9.7	1.01	16.46	10	0	99	0	1	0	96.9	-18.0	58	8	15	15	0.0	0.0
B- / 7.5	9.6	0.94	14.52	4	0	99	0	1	15	N/A	N/A	22	4	500	100	5.8	0.0
B- / 7.5	9.6	0.95	13.75	2	0	99	0	1	15	N/A	N/A	16	4	500	100	0.0	0.0
B- / 7.5	9.6	0.95	13.76	10	0	99	0	1	15	N/A	N/A	25	4	1,000,000	0	0.0	0.0
B / 8.7	8.3	0.41	10.84	11	86	13	0	1	40	N/A	N/A	97	4	500	100	5.8	0.0
B / 8.7	8.2	0.41	10.82	1	86	13	0	1	40	N/A	N/A	96	4	500	100	0.0	0.0
B / 8.7	8.2	0.41	10.86	N/A	86	13	0	1	40	N/A	N/A	97	4	0	0	0.0	0.0
B / 8.7	8.2	0.41	10.87	45	86	13	0	1	40	N/A	N/A	97	4	1,000,000	0	0.0	0.0
C- / 3.9	9.7	0.84	10.94	531	0	58	41	1	195	97.5	-19.3	87	13	500	100	5.8	0.0
C- / 3.4	9.7	0.84	9.79	357	0	58	41	1	195	92.3	-19.5	83	13	500	100	0.0	0.0
C- / 3.9	9.7	0.83	11.11	1	0	58	41	1	195	96.3	-19.3	87	13	0	0	0.0	0.0
C / 4.5	9.7	0.83	12.72	804	0	58	41	1	195	99.1	-19.3	89	13	1,000,000	0	0.0	0.0
B- / 7.2	6.6	0.46	12.29	74	41	58	0	1	349	34.2	-6.8	69	7	2,500	50	5.5	0.0
B- / 7.0	6.6	0.46	11.64	54	41	58	0	1	349	31.5	-7.1	61	7	2,500	50	0.0	0.0
B- / 7.3	6.7	0.47	12.66	741	41	58	0	1	349	35.6	-6.5	71	7	2,500	50	0.0	0.0
C+ / 6.5	14.8	0.46	16.32	154	56	42	1	1	538	45.2	N/A	95	N/A	2,500	50	5.5	0.0
C+ / 6.4	14.8	0.46	15.60	68	56	42	1	1	538	42.1	-0.2	94	N/A	2,500	50	0.0	0.0
C+ / 6.5	14.8	0.46	16.75	353	56	42	1	1	538	47.0	0.2	95	N/A	2,500	50	0.0	0.0
B- / 7.0	15.5	0.30	5.28	72	0	0	0	100	0	69.6	-11.7	98	N/A	2,500	50	0.0	0.0
C+ / 6.2	10.7	1.04	35.18	182	2	97	0	1	20	110.7	-17.2	73	19	500	100	5.8	0.0
C+ / 5.9	10.7	1.04	29.24	19	2	97	0	1	20	105.4	-17.4	65	19	500	100	0.0	0.0
C+ / 6.2	10.7	1.04	34.63	N/A	2	97	0	1	20	108.9	-17.3	71	19	0	0	0.0	0.0
C+ / 6.3	10.7	1.04	36.19	37	2	97	0	1	20	112.4	-17.1	76	19	1,000,000	0	0.0	0.0
C / 5.2	11.6	0.84	14.76	35	1	98	0	1	26	89.3	-20.7	73	3	500	100	5.8	0.0
C / 4.4	11.6	0.84	11.55	3	1	98	0	1	26	84.4	-20.9	63	3	500	100	0.0	0.0
C / 5.2	11.7	0.84	14.56	N/A	1	98	0	1	26	88.9	-20.7	71	3	0	0	0.0	0.0
C / 5.4	11.6	0.84	15.76	6	1	98	0	1	26	90.9	-20.6	75	3	1,000,000	0	0.0	0.0
B- / 7.7	6.6	1.13	23.49	66	11	57	30	2	121	45.1	-14.5	13	1	500	100	5.8	0.0
B- / 7.6	6.6	1.13	21.47	6	11	57	30	2	121	41.4	-14.7	9	1	500	100	0.0	0.0
B- / 7.7	6.6	1.14	23.58	N/A	11	57	30	2	121	43.9	-14.5	12	1	0	0	0.0	0.0
B- / 7.7	6.6	1.13	23.81	N/A	11	57	30	2	121	46.4	-14.4	14	1	1,000,000	0	0.0	0.0
C+ / 6.8	10.5	1.02	17.98	36	10	89	0	1	56	89.6	-21.8	25	15	5,000	500	0.0	0.0
C+ / 5.9	9.8	0.86	15.56	14	13	86	0	1	71	89.2	-14.6	87	6	1,000	50	0.0	1.0
B- / 7.0	9.8	0.90	15.03	19	0	100	0	0	41	62.6	-9.7	23	6	1,000	50	0.0	1.0
C+ / 6.1	14.7	0.76	39.55	10	5	94	0	1	105	117.5	-24.7	99	16	1,000,000	50	0.0	1.0
D+ / 2.5	16.1	1.36	12.60	9	1	98	0	1	131	77.4	-28.3	2	6	1,000	50	0.0	1.0
C+ / 6.1	14.7	0.76	38.98	332	5	94	0	1	105	115.6	-24.8	99	16	250	50	0.0	1.0
C+ / 6.0	13.4	0.90	20.93	447	8	91	0	1	58	118.2	-19.0	92	8	1,000,000	50	0.0	1.0
C+ / 6.0	13.4	0.90	20.43	1,624	8	91	0	1	58	115.9	-19.1	91	8	1,000	50	0.0	1.0
U /	N/A	N/A	12.41	29	11	88	0	1	0	N/A	N/A	N/A	2	1,000	50	0.0	1.0
B- / 7.9	7.7	1.23	19.30	31	21	71	6	2	0	58.0	-10.1	22	20	1,000	500	0.0	0.0
C+ / 5.9	12.1	1.07	8.21	104	1	98	0	1	39	111.9	-16.9	66	7	500	0	0.0	0.0
C / 5.2	15.1	1.11	7.52	219	2	97	0	1	19	41.2	-24.3	20	9	500	0	0.0	0.0
C+ / 6.5	12.2	0.85	40.95	1,181	3	96	0	1	1	111.2	-24.4	91	16	500	0	0.0	0.0
B- / 7.3	9.5	1.00	15.45	117	1	98	0	1	3	96.8	-16.5	59	7	500	0	0.0	0.0
B- / 7.5	10.5	1.05	51.53	949	2	97	0	1	2	106.5	-20.7	69	25	500	0	0.0	0.0
C+ / 6.1	14.1	0.90	10.38	15	18	81	0	1	18	87.4	-23.9	95	8	2,500	100	4.8	0.0
C+ / 6.0	14.1	0.89	10.13	12	18	81	0	1	18	83.8	-24.0	95	8	2,500	100	0.0	0.0
C+ / 6.1	14.1	0.89	10.36	52	18	81	0	1	18	89.2	-23.9	96	8	1,000,000	100,000	0.0	0.0
B- / 7.3	6.9	0.67	12.81	45	2	59	36	3	53	76.0	-10.1	88	5	2,500	100	4.8	0.0
B- / 7.2	6.8	0.66	12.38	36	2	59	36	3	53	73.1	-10.0	86	5	1,000,000	100	0.0	0.0
B- / 7.0	11.2	1.10	15.75	55	1	98	0	1	33	108.4	-21.5	52	11	2,500	100	5.3	0.0

www.thestreetratings.com
315
Data as of March 31, 2015

Fund Type	Fund Name	Ticker Symbol	Overall Investment Rating	Phone	Performance Rating/Pts	3 Mo	6 Mo	1Yr / Pct	3Yr / Pct	5Yr / Pct	Dividend Yield	Expense Ratio
GR	Hotchkis and Wiley Divsfd Val C	HWCCX	B+	(866) 493-8637	B- / 7.4	0.13	4.24	6.94 /55	15.78 /82	12.51 /64	0.55	2.01
GR	Hotchkis and Wiley Divsfd Val I	HWCIX	A-	(866) 493-8637	B+ / 8.3	0.38	4.78	8.02 /63	16.94 /89	13.65 /74	2.41	1.01
GI	Hotchkis and Wiley Large Cap Val A	HWLAX	B+	(866) 493-8637	B / 7.6	-0.19	4.40	7.67 /60	17.74 /93	14.01 /78	2.48	1.26
GI	Hotchkis and Wiley Large Cap Val C	HWLCX	A-	(866) 493-8637	B / 8.0	-0.38	3.98	6.85 /54	16.84 /89	13.15 /70	2.66	2.01
GI	Hotchkis and Wiley Large Cap Val I	HWLIX	A+	(866) 493-8637	B+ / 8.8	-0.15	4.52	7.94 /62	18.05 /94	14.29 /80	2.89	1.01
GI	Hotchkis and Wiley Large Cap Val R	HWLRX	A	(866) 493-8637	B+ / 8.4	-0.30	4.25	7.39 /58	17.44 /92	13.72 /75	2.46	1.51
MC	● Hotchkis and Wiley Mid-Cap Val A	HWMAX	A-	(866) 493-8637	B+ / 8.6	0.22	4.94	6.45 /50	19.33 /97	17.15 /96	0.31	1.26
MC	● Hotchkis and Wiley Mid-Cap Val C	HWMCX	A-	(866) 493-8637	B+ / 8.8	0.03	4.55	5.65 /44	18.44 /96	16.28 /94	0.00	2.01
MC	● Hotchkis and Wiley Mid-Cap Val I	HWMIX	A+	(866) 493-8637	A / 9.3	0.29	5.08	6.73 /53	19.64 /97	17.45 /97	0.59	1.01
MC	● Hotchkis and Wiley Mid-Cap Val R	HWMRX	A+	(866) 493-8637	A- / 9.1	0.17	4.82	6.20 /48	19.07 /97	16.87 /96	0.16	1.51
SC	● Hotchkis and Wiley Small Cap Val A	HWSAX	A	(866) 493-8637	A / 9.5	1.59	11.08	10.76 /77	20.75 /98	17.24 /96	0.00	1.25
SC	● Hotchkis and Wiley Small Cap Val C	HWSCX	A-	(866) 493-8637	A+ / 9.6	1.39	10.64	9.91 /74	19.84 /98	16.37 /94	0.00	2.00
SC	● Hotchkis and Wiley Small Cap Val I	HWSIX	A+	(866) 493-8637	A+ / 9.8	1.65	11.20	11.03 /78	21.05 /98	17.53 /97	0.18	1.00
GR	Hotchkis and Wiley Value Opptys A	HWAAX	B+	(866) 493-8637	B / 8.1	1.12	3.74	7.71 /61	18.33 /95	16.62 /95	1.13	1.25
GR	Hotchkis and Wiley Value Opptys C	HWACX	B+	(866) 493-8637	B+ / 8.4	0.95	3.35	6.90 /54	17.45 /92	15.73 /91	0.71	2.00
GR	Hotchkis and Wiley Value Opptys I	HWAIX	A	(866) 493-8637	A- / 9.1	1.19	3.91	7.99 /63	18.64 /96	16.90 /96	1.40	1.00
GL	● HSBC Frontier Markets A	HSFAX	D	(800) 728-8183	D+ / 2.7	-2.26	-11.77	-4.50 / 6	12.18 /54	--	0.66	2.30
GL	● HSBC Frontier Markets I	HSFIX	D	(800) 728-8183	C- / 3.7	-2.09	-11.52	-4.10 / 7	12.59 /57	--	1.23	1.95
CV	HSBC Global Emerging Markets Debt	HCGAX	E+	(800) 728-8183	E+ / 0.9	2.22	0.94	3.40 /28	3.98 /10	--	3.52	1.55
CV	HSBC Global Emerging Markets Debt	HCGIX	E+	(800) 728-8183	D- / 1.3	2.20	1.01	3.66 /30	4.31 /11	--	4.05	1.20
CV	HSBC Global Emerging Markets Debt	HBESX	E+	(800) 728-8183	D- / 1.3	2.32	1.16	3.87 /31	4.44 /11	--	4.15	1.10
MC	HSBC Growth A	HOTAX	C-	(800) 728-8183	C+ / 6.7	3.15	8.73	15.22 /92	14.20 /69	14.37 /81	0.00	1.33
MC	● HSBC Growth B	HOTBX	D+	(800) 728-8183	B- / 7.0	2.98	8.31	14.35 /90	13.36 /62	13.52 /73	0.00	2.08
MC	HSBC Growth C	HOTCX	D+	(800) 728-8183	B- / 7.0	2.95	8.30	14.35 /90	13.34 /62	13.52 /73	0.00	2.08
MC	HSBC Growth I	HOTYX	C	(800) 728-8183	B / 7.9	3.22	8.81	15.47 /92	14.49 /71	14.66 /84	0.00	1.08
SC	HSBC Opportunity A	HSOAX	C	(800) 728-8183	B / 7.8	5.83	9.81	9.55 /72	16.48 /87	16.35 /94	0.00	1.86
SC	● HSBC Opportunity B	HOPBX	D+	(800) 728-8183	B / 8.1	5.54	9.33	8.63 /67	15.61 /80	15.48 /90	0.00	2.61
SC	HSBC Opportunity C	HOPCX	D+	(800) 728-8183	B / 8.1	5.72	9.37	8.70 /68	15.60 /80	15.47 /90	0.00	2.61
SC	HSBC Opportunity I	RESCX	C+	(800) 728-8183	A- / 9.0	6.03	10.10	10.16 /75	17.07 /90	16.92 /96	0.21	1.00
EM	HSBC Total Return A	HTRAX	C-	(800) 728-8183	E+ / 0.7	0.86	1.47	3.54 /29	2.60 / 7	--	1.55	1.67
EM	HSBC Total Return I	HTRIX	C	(800) 728-8183	E+ / 0.9	0.83	1.63	3.79 /30	2.93 / 8	--	1.97	1.32
EM	HSBC Total Return S	HTRSX	C	(800) 728-8183	D- / 1.0	0.95	1.78	3.99 /32	3.06 / 8	--	2.06	1.22
AG	HSBC World Selection Aggr Strat A	HAAGX	E	(800) 728-8183	D+ / 2.6	1.82	1.96	3.37 /28	9.22 /34	8.26 /32	0.57	1.65
AG	● HSBC World Selection Aggr Strat B	HBAGX	E	(800) 728-8183	D+ / 2.9	1.57	1.51	2.50 /24	8.37 /29	7.43 /26	0.04	2.40
AG	HSBC World Selection Aggr Strat C	HCAGX	E	(800) 728-8183	D+ / 2.9	1.58	1.54	2.53 /24	8.37 /29	7.45 /26	0.05	2.40
GR	HSBC World Selection Bal Strat A	HAGRX	E+	(800) 728-8183	D / 1.9	1.78	1.78	2.82 /26	7.77 /26	7.78 /28	1.32	1.37
GR	● HSBC World Selection Bal Strat B	HSBGX	E+	(800) 728-8183	D / 2.1	1.60	1.32	2.06 /22	6.94 /21	6.96 /23	0.68	2.12
GR	HSBC World Selection Bal Strat C	HCGRX	E+	(800) 728-8183	D / 2.1	1.59	1.33	2.06 /22	6.93 /21	6.96 /23	0.76	2.12
GI	HSBC World Selection Csv Strat A	HACGX	D	(800) 728-8183	D- / 1.1	1.59	2.29	3.32 /28	5.10 /13	5.79 /16	1.19	1.58
GI	● HSBC World Selection Csv Strat B	HBCGX	D	(800) 728-8183	D- / 1.2	1.42	2.02	2.57 /24	4.31 /11	5.02 /12	0.69	2.33
GI	HSBC World Selection Csv Strat C	HCCGX	D	(800) 728-8183	D- / 1.2	1.37	1.95	2.50 /24	4.29 /11	5.00 /12	0.68	2.33
AA	HSBC World Selection Income Strat	HINAX	D	(800) 728-8183	E+ / 0.9	1.35	1.89	3.19 /27	3.88 /10	--	1.37	10.41
AA	● HSBC World Selection Income Strat	HINBX	D+	(800) 728-8183	E+ / 0.9	1.19	1.52	2.43 /24	3.14 / 8	--	0.69	11.16
AA	HSBC World Selection Income Strat	HINCX	D+	(800) 728-8183	E+ / 0.9	1.19	1.62	2.44 /24	3.14 / 8	--	0.71	11.16
GI	HSBC World Selection Modt Strat A	HSAMX	D-	(800) 728-8183	D- / 1.5	1.89	2.35	3.31 /28	6.45 /19	6.88 /22	1.56	1.39
GI	● HSBC World Selection Modt Strat B	HSBMX	D-	(800) 728-8183	D / 1.7	1.71	1.97	2.52 /24	5.67 /15	6.08 /17	0.89	2.14
GI	HSBC World Selection Modt Strat C	HSCMX	D-	(800) 728-8183	D / 1.6	1.60	1.90	2.51 /24	5.65 /15	6.07 /17	1.00	2.14
IN	Huber Capital Equity Income Inst	HULEX	D+	(888) 263-6443	D+ / 2.9	-4.21	-3.19	-6.40 / 4	11.10 /46	--	2.10	1.32
IN	Huber Capital Equity Income Inv	HULIX	D	(888) 263-6443	D+ / 2.6	-4.29	-3.45	-6.80 / 4	10.60 /43	11.41 /56	1.54	1.82
SC	Huber Capital Small Cap Value Inst	HUSEX	D-	(888) 263-6443	D+ / 2.4	-0.97	-1.89	-7.65 / 4	9.69 /37	--	0.14	1.61
SC	Huber Capital Small Cap Value Inv	HUSIX	D-	(888) 263-6443	D / 2.1	-0.99	-2.12	-8.10 / 3	9.17 /34	13.28 /71	0.00	2.11
GR	Hundredfold Select Alternative Inv	HFSAX	U	(855) 582-8006	U /	2.15	2.62	3.13 /27	--	--	0.00	2.37

99 Pct = Best
0 Pct = Worst

● Denotes fund is closed to new investors
* Denotes fund is included in Section II

RISK			NET ASSETS		ASSET				Portfolio	BULL / BEAR		FUND MANAGER		MINIMUMS		LOADS	
	3 Year		NAV							Last Bull	Last Bear	Manager	Manager	Initial	Additional	Front	Back
Risk	Standard		As of	Total	Cash	Stocks	Bonds	Other	Turnover	Market	Market	Quality	Tenure	Purch.	Purch.	End	End
Rating/Pts	Deviation	Beta	3/31/15	$(Mil)	%	%	%	%	Ratio	Return	Return	Pct	(Years)	$	$	Load	Load
B- / 7.0	11.2	1.11	15.62	5	1	98	0	1	33	103.2	-21.8	39	11	2,500	100	0.0	0.0
B- / 7.0	11.3	1.10	15.71	490	1	98	0	1	33	110.3	-21.5	54	11	1,000,000	100	0.0	0.0
B- / 7.1	11.2	1.09	26.76	199	1	98	0	1	57	111.6	-20.5	68	27	2,500	100	5.3	0.0
B- / 7.1	11.2	1.09	26.09	41	1	98	0	1	57	106.2	-20.7	56	27	2,500	100	0.0	0.0
B- / 7.1	11.2	1.09	26.93	528	1	98	0	1	57	113.4	-20.4	71	27	1,000,000	100	0.0	0.0
B- / 7.1	11.2	1.09	26.91	13	1	98	0	1	57	109.9	-20.6	64	27	2,500	100	0.0	0.0
C+ / 6.5	12.2	0.97	40.69	683	1	98	0	1	55	153.3	-31.1	86	18	2,500	100	5.3	0.0
C+ / 6.3	12.2	0.98	37.02	137	1	98	0	1	55	147.0	-31.4	81	18	2,500	100	0.0	0.0
C+ / 6.5	12.2	0.98	41.20	2,556	1	98	0	1	55	155.7	-31.1	87	18	1,000,000	100	0.0	0.0
C+ / 6.6	12.2	0.97	40.86	21	1	98	0	1	55	151.5	-31.2	85	18	2,500	100	0.0	0.0
C+ / 6.0	13.4	0.93	61.24	199	6	93	0	1	43	134.5	-29.2	93	20	2,500	100	5.3	0.0
C+ / 5.6	13.4	0.93	53.32	37	6	93	0	1	43	128.6	-29.4	92	20	2,500	100	0.0	0.0
C+ / 6.0	13.4	0.93	61.60	919	6	93	0	1	43	136.5	-29.1	94	20	1,000,000	100	0.0	0.0
C+ / 6.5	10.7	0.98	28.08	177	4	85	8	3	45	122.7	-23.7	85	13	2,500	100	5.3	0.0
C+ / 6.4	10.7	0.98	26.47	70	4	85	8	3	45	117.2	-23.9	80	13	2,500	100	0.0	0.0
C+ / 6.4	10.7	0.98	28.07	339	4	85	8	3	45	124.6	-23.6	86	13	1,000,000	100	0.0	0.0
C / 5.4	10.9	0.47	12.55	25	11	87	1	1	64	62.1	N/A	96	4	1,000	100	5.0	0.0
C / 5.3	10.9	0.47	12.62	170	11	87	1	1	64	64.1	N/A	97	4	1,000,000	0	0.0	0.0
C / 4.9	7.6	0.46	10.16	1	11	0	88	1	51	24.7	-1.1	37	N/A	1,000	100	4.8	0.0
C / 4.9	7.6	0.46	10.18	43	11	0	88	1	51	26.2	-0.9	41	N/A	1,000,000	0	0.0	0.0
C / 4.9	7.6	0.46	10.19	N/A	11	0	88	1	51	26.6	-0.9	43	N/A	25,000,000	0	0.0	0.0
C- / 3.5	12.1	0.94	19.64	13	0	99	0	1	68	94.9	-17.9	45	7	1,000	100	5.0	0.0
D+ / 2.7	12.1	0.94	16.59	N/A	0	99	0	1	68	89.9	-18.1	34	7	1,000	100	0.0	0.0
D+ / 2.7	12.1	0.94	16.74	1	0	99	0	1	68	90.0	-18.1	34	7	1,000	100	0.0	0.0
C- / 3.6	12.1	0.94	20.22	62	0	99	0	1	68	96.5	-17.8	48	7	5,000,000	0	0.0	0.0
C- / 3.4	13.1	0.86	11.43	19	4	95	0	1	66	106.3	-24.9	86	12	1,000	100	5.0	0.0
D- / 1.2	13.1	0.86	7.81	N/A	4	95	0	1	66	100.9	-25.1	81	12	1,000	100	0.0	0.0
D- / 1.4	13.0	0.85	8.13	1	4	95	0	1	66	100.9	-25.1	82	12	1,000	100	0.0	0.0
D+ / 2.9	13.0	0.86	15.12	218	4	95	0	1	66	109.7	-24.7	88	12	5,000,000	0	0.0	0.0
B+ / 9.9	3.5	0.17	10.31	1	56	0	43	1	77	N/A	N/A	86	3	1,000	100	4.8	0.0
B+ / 9.9	3.6	0.17	10.32	1,262	56	0	43	1	77	N/A	N/A	88	3	1,000,000	0	0.0	0.0
B+ / 9.9	3.6	0.17	10.33	26	56	0	43	1	77	N/A	N/A	88	3	25,000,000	0	0.0	0.0
D / 1.9	9.8	0.97	11.77	11	3	96	0	1	116	61.3	-21.9	8	N/A	1,000	100	5.0	0.0
D / 1.7	9.8	0.97	11.02	5	3	96	0	1	116	57.3	-22.2	6	N/A	1,000	100	0.0	0.0
D / 1.6	9.8	0.97	10.95	1	3	96	0	1	116	57.3	-22.2	6	N/A	1,000	100	0.0	0.0
C- / 3.8	8.2	0.79	11.46	27	5	75	18	2	35	49.5	-17.4	14	N/A	1,000	100	5.0	0.0
C- / 3.9	8.2	0.78	11.46	12	5	75	18	2	35	45.7	-17.7	10	N/A	1,000	100	0.0	0.0
C- / 3.9	8.2	0.79	11.47	5	5	75	18	2	35	45.8	-17.7	10	N/A	1,000	100	0.0	0.0
B- / 7.3	5.0	0.38	10.92	9	4	29	66	1	104	28.0	-8.4	56	N/A	1,000	100	5.0	0.0
B- / 7.3	5.0	0.38	10.74	7	4	29	66	1	104	24.8	-8.8	44	N/A	1,000	100	0.0	0.0
B- / 7.4	5.0	0.38	11.09	4	4	29	66	1	104	24.8	-8.8	43	N/A	1,000	100	0.0	0.0
B / 8.2	3.9	0.46	10.23	N/A	5	19	74	2	118	N/A	N/A	52	N/A	1,000	100	4.8	0.0
B / 8.2	3.9	0.47	10.21	N/A	5	19	74	2	118	N/A	N/A	40	N/A	1,000	100	0.0	0.0
B / 8.2	3.9	0.46	10.21	1	5	19	74	2	118	N/A	N/A	42	N/A	1,000	100	0.0	0.0
C+ / 6.0	6.6	0.59	11.28	26	5	51	43	1	102	38.7	-13.4	29	N/A	1,000	100	5.0	0.0
C+ / 6.1	6.6	0.59	11.27	10	5	51	43	1	102	35.4	-13.8	21	N/A	1,000	100	0.0	0.0
C+ / 6.0	6.6	0.59	10.87	4	5	51	43	1	102	35.3	-13.7	21	N/A	1,000	100	0.0	0.0
C+ / 6.4	11.4	1.09	12.98	87	1	98	0	1	29	N/A	N/A	7	8	1,000,000	5,000	0.0	1.0
C+ / 6.4	11.4	1.09	12.95	26	1	98	0	1	29	72.1	-16.1	6	8	5,000	100	0.0	1.0
C / 5.2	14.8	1.00	16.31	185	4	95	0	1	24	N/A	N/A	7	8	1,000,000	5,000	0.0	1.0
C / 5.2	14.8	1.00	16.08	89	4	95	0	1	24	80.8	-24.1	6	8	5,000	100	0.0	1.0
U /	N/A	N/A	22.81	28	42	8	47	3	367	N/A	N/A	N/A	11	1,000,000	0	0.0	0.0

					PERFORMANCE						Incl. in Returns	
						Total Return % through 3/31/15						
			Overall		Perfor-				Annualized		Dividend	Expense
Fund Type	Fund Name	Ticker Symbol	Investment Rating	Phone	mance Rating/Pts	3 Mo	6 Mo	1Yr / Pct	3Yr / Pct	5Yr / Pct	Yield	Ratio
GI	Hundredfold Select Equity Service	SFEOX	D-	(855) 582-8006	E+ / 0.8	1.13	2.96	-3.88 / 7	3.20 / 8	1.68 / 4	0.00	3.28
AA	Huntington Balanced Allocation A	HBAFX	D	(800) 253-0412	D- / 1.3	1.40	2.14	2.57 /24	5.82 /16	6.03 /17	1.89	2.13
MC	Huntington Dividend Capture A	HDCAX	D+	(800) 253-0412	C- / 3.7	0.13	3.42	5.81 /45	10.85 /45	10.71 /50	3.03	1.60
MC	Huntington Dividend Capture Instl	HDCTX	C-	(800) 253-0412	C / 4.6	0.29	3.53	6.06 /47	11.15 /47	10.99 /53	3.39	1.35
FO	Huntington Glbl Select Mkts A	HGSAX	E	(800) 253-0412	D- / 1.2	5.45	1.00	5.95 /46	4.22 /11	3.45 / 7	0.00	2.35
FO	Huntington Glbl Select Mkts Instl	HGSIX	E	(800) 253-0412	D / 1.7	5.54	1.09	6.24 /48	4.44 /11	3.74 / 7	0.00	2.10
GI	Huntington Real Strategies Invst A	HRSAX	E-	(800) 253-0412	E- / 0.2	-1.04	-15.40	-19.53 / 1	-3.53 / 2	0.46 / 3	1.27	1.67
GI	Huntington Real Strategies Invst I	HRSTX	E-	(800) 253-0412	E- / 0.2	-0.89	-15.20	-19.34 / 1	-3.31 / 2	0.69 / 3	1.56	1.42
SC	Huntington Situs A	HSUAX	E	(800) 253-0412	C- / 3.0	-0.05	3.99	-2.95 / 9	10.75 /44	12.07 /61	0.00	1.58
SC	Huntington Situs Institutional	HSUTX	E	(800) 253-0412	C- / 3.9	0.05	4.14	-2.72 / 9	11.02 /46	12.35 /63	0.06	1.33
IN	Hussman Strategic Dividend Value	HSDVX	D+	(800) 487-7626	E+ / 0.6	-1.97	-1.36	-1.82 /11	1.98 / 6	--	1.95	2.12
GR	Hussman Strategic Growth	HSGFX	E	(800) 487-7626	E- / 0.2	-0.11	-3.84	-9.61 / 3	-7.20 / 1	-6.03 / 1	0.78	1.15
FO	Hussman Strategic International	HSIEX	E+	(800) 487-7626	E- / 0.2	-7.93	-10.79	-15.76 / 2	-4.85 / 2	-2.70 / 1	1.10	1.53
GR	IA 529 CSI Aggressive Growth Port		C+	(800) 662-7447	C+ / 6.1	2.46	4.80	7.97 /63	13.22 /61	11.94 /60	0.00	0.34
GI	IA 529 CSI Conservative Growth Port		C+	(800) 662-7447	D+ / 2.8	2.03	4.19	6.95 /55	7.21 /22	7.54 /27	0.00	0.34
GI	IA 529 CSI Growth Port		B-	(800) 662-7447	C / 5.0	2.35	4.61	7.72 /61	11.29 /48	10.61 /50	0.00	0.34
AA	IA 529 CSI Income Port		C	(800) 662-7447	D / 1.8	1.86	3.90	6.54 /51	5.11 /13	6.05 /17	0.00	0.34
GI	IA 529 CSI Moderate Growth Port		C+	(800) 662-7447	C- / 3.9	2.17	4.33	7.35 /58	9.21 /34	9.13 /38	0.00	0.34
GL	Ibbotson Agg Gr ETF Asset Alloc I		C	(866) 432-2926	C- / 4.2	2.88	5.19	5.64 /43	9.96 /39	9.03 /37	1.14	0.71
GL	Ibbotson Agg Gr ETF Asset Alloc II	AGTFX	C	(866) 432-2926	C- / 4.0	2.82	5.02	5.29 /41	9.66 /37	8.75 /35	0.95	0.96
GL	Ibbotson Bal ETF Asset Alloc I		C	(866) 432-2926	D+ / 2.9	2.20	4.02	5.12 /39	7.66 /25	7.53 /27	1.38	0.67
GL	Ibbotson Bal ETF Asset Alloc II	BETFX	C	(866) 432-2926	D+ / 2.7	2.18	3.93	4.93 /38	7.41 /24	7.26 /25	1.14	0.92
GL	Ibbotson Consv ETF Asset Alloc I		C-	(866) 432-2926	D- / 1.0	1.33	2.02	3.10 /27	3.37 / 9	4.26 / 9	1.26	0.73
GL	Ibbotson Consv ETF Asset Alloc II	CETFX	C-	(866) 432-2926	D- / 1.0	1.25	1.87	2.77 /25	3.10 / 8	4.00 / 8	1.03	0.98
GL	Ibbotson Growth ETF Asset Alloc I		C	(866) 432-2926	C- / 3.8	2.66	4.85	5.60 /43	9.29 /35	8.57 /34	1.21	0.67
GL	Ibbotson Growth ETF Asset Alloc II	GETFX	C	(866) 432-2926	C- / 3.7	2.61	4.76	5.43 /42	9.03 /33	8.31 /32	0.99	0.92
GL	Ibbotson Inc & Gr ETF Asset All I		C-	(866) 432-2926	D / 1.7	1.65	2.60	3.72 /30	5.42 /15	5.80 /16	1.46	0.69
GL	Ibbotson Inc & Gr ETF Asset All II	IETFX	C-	(866) 432-2926	D- / 1.5	1.58	2.50	3.39 /28	5.13 /14	5.51 /14	1.14	0.94
GR	ICON A	ICNAX	C	(800) 764-0442	C / 5.3	2.17	12.28	9.36 /71	12.63 /57	10.85 /51	0.00	1.56
GR	ICON C	ICNCX	C+	(800) 764-0442	C+ / 5.8	2.01	11.86	8.56 /67	11.79 /51	10.52 /49	0.00	2.26
OT	ICON Consumer Discretionary A	ICCAX	C	(800) 764-0442	C+ / 6.3	2.02	10.96	8.96 /69	14.65 /72	--	0.00	1.76
OT	ICON Consumer Discretionary C	ICCEX	C	(800) 764-0442	C+ / 6.8	1.80	10.38	7.84 /62	13.88 /66	--	0.00	3.78
OT	ICON Consumer Discretionary S	ICCCX	B-	(800) 764-0442	B / 7.9	2.11	11.14	9.24 /71	15.36 /78	17.53 /97	0.00	1.46
OT	ICON Consumer Staples A	ICRAX	D	(800) 764-0442	C+ / 6.2	1.08	10.13	15.62 /93	13.53 /64	--	1.62	2.04
OT	ICON Consumer Staples C	ICLCX	D	(800) 764-0442	C+ / 6.7	0.89	9.71	14.69 /91	12.79 /58	--	1.36	2.76
GR	ICON Consumer Staples S	ICLEX	D+	(800) 764-0442	B- / 7.5	1.08	10.28	15.79 /93	13.91 /66	12.83 /67	1.49	1.45
FO	ICON Emerging Markets A	IPCAX	D-	(800) 764-0442	D- / 1.0	5.26	2.19	3.85 /31	4.59 /12	4.25 / 9	0.00	4.32
FO	ICON Emerging Markets C	ICPCX	D-	(800) 764-0442	D- / 1.2	4.85	1.67	2.92 /26	3.76 /10	3.44 / 7	0.00	4.65
FO	ICON Emerging Markets S	ICARX	D	(800) 764-0442	D- / 1.5	5.25	2.26	4.00 /32	4.76 /12	4.43 /10	0.00	2.11
EN	ICON Energy A	ICEAX	E-	(800) 764-0442	E- / 0.2	-1.63	-20.56	-22.68 / 1	-0.98 / 3	--	0.22	1.55
EN	ICON Energy C	ICEEX	E-	(800) 764-0442	E- / 0.2	-1.74	-20.79	-23.26 / 1	-1.75 / 3	--	0.00	2.38
EN	ICON Energy S	ICENX	E-	(800) 764-0442	E- / 0.2	-1.55	-20.42	-22.47 / 1	-0.71 / 4	2.76 / 6	0.50	1.28
IN	ICON Equity Income A	IEQAX	C+	(800) 764-0442	C / 5.2	1.66	7.14	10.95 /78	12.67 /57	11.14 /54	2.78	1.70
IN	ICON Equity Income C	IOECX	B-	(800) 764-0442	C+ / 5.6	1.47	6.69	10.04 /74	11.83 /51	10.31 /47	2.22	2.56
IN	ICON Equity Income S	IOEZX	B-	(800) 764-0442	C+ / 6.3	1.73	7.26	11.20 /79	12.96 /59	11.43 /56	3.21	1.49
FS	ICON Financial A	ICFAX	C-	(800) 764-0442	C- / 4.0	0.00	6.84	7.25 /57	11.13 /46	--	0.00	2.45
FS	ICON Financial C	ICOCX	C-	(800) 764-0442	C / 4.5	-0.12	6.44	6.44 /50	10.68 /43	--	0.00	7.45
FS	ICON Financial S	ICFSX	C	(800) 764-0442	C / 5.1	0.12	7.02	7.57 /60	11.48 /49	7.15 /24	0.00	1.74
HL	ICON Healthcare A	ICHAX	C	(800) 764-0442	A+ / 9.9	8.28	15.52	29.33 /99	27.83 /99	--	0.00	1.62
HL	ICON Healthcare C	ICHEX	C	(800) 764-0442	A+ / 9.9	8.06	15.00	28.28 /99	26.89 /99	--	0.00	4.31
HL	ICON Healthcare S	ICHCX	C	(800) 764-0442	A+ / 9.9	8.35	15.66	29.72 /99	28.32 /99	20.75 /99	0.00	1.36
OT	ICON Industrials A	ICIAX	C	(800) 764-0442	C / 4.5	-0.33	5.23	3.62 /30	12.90 /59	--	0.04	2.02

● Denotes fund is closed to new investors
* Denotes fund is included in Section II

www.thestreetratings.com

RISK			NET ASSETS		ASSET						BULL / BEAR		FUND MANAGER		MINIMUMS		LOADS	
	3 Year		NAV							Portfolio	Last Bull	Last Bear	Manager	Manager	Initial	Additional	Front	Back
Risk	Standard		As of	Total	Cash	Stocks	Bonds	Other		Turnover	Market	Market	Quality	Tenure	Purch.	Purch.	End	End
Rating/Pts	Deviation	Beta	3/31/15	$(Mil)	%	%	%	%		Ratio	Return	Return	Pct	(Years)	$	$	Load	Load
B- / 7.1	10.1	0.83	20.54	10	57	35	6	2		1,063	10.4	-13.9	2	11	5,000	1,000	0.0	0.0
B- / 7.3	5.7	0.97	11.51	20	4	60	35	1		44	34.4	-11.1	13	2	1,000	50	4.8	0.0
C+ / 6.1	7.4	0.59	9.94	64	6	93	0	1		130	62.4	-11.9	77	14	1,000	50	4.8	0.0
C+ / 6.1	7.5	0.59	9.95	118	6	93	0	1		130	63.9	-11.8	79	14	1,000	500	0.0	0.0
D+ / 2.9	13.2	0.83	9.86	6	6	92	0	2		156	29.5	-23.7	21	6	1,000	50	4.8	0.0
C- / 3.0	13.2	0.83	9.90	10	6	92	0	2		156	30.4	-23.6	23	6	1,000	500	0.0	0.0
C- / 3.1	12.7	0.87	6.65	2	31	67	0	2		43	6.5	-24.3	0	8	1,000	50	4.8	0.0
C- / 3.1	12.8	0.88	6.65	19	31	67	0	2		43	7.2	-24.2	0	8	1,000	500	0.0	0.0
D- / 1.1	12.3	0.84	19.88	41	0	99	0	1		22	77.6	-23.1	30	13	1,000	50	4.8	0.0
D- / 1.2	12.3	0.84	20.76	117	0	99	0	1		22	79.1	-23.0	33	13	1,000	500	0.0	0.0
B / 8.8	3.7	0.26	9.40	9	10	89	0	1		100	N/A	N/A	37	3	1,000	100	0.0	1.5
C / 5.2	4.8	-0.37	8.97	839	0	100	0	0		141	-29.5	9.0	37	15	1,000	100	0.0	1.5
C+ / 6.4	5.8	0.12	8.24	44	26	73	0	1		59	-14.0	-2.0	6	6	1,000	100	0.0	1.5
C+ / 6.9	10.1	1.02	27.10	891	0	99	0	1		0	82.7	-19.0	27	14	25	25	0.0	0.0
B+ / 9.6	4.2	0.37	20.63	398	0	39	59	2		0	35.8	-5.2	80	14	25	25	0.0	0.0
B / 8.1	8.0	0.80	21.34	1,010	0	79	19	2		0	66.1	-14.5	47	14	25	25	0.0	0.0
B+ / 9.6	2.9	0.34	19.72	323	0	19	79	2		0	22.7	N/A	80	14	25	25	0.0	0.0
B+ / 9.0	6.0	0.59	21.19	807	0	60	39	1		0	50.3	-9.9	67	14	25	25	0.0	0.0
B- / 7.2	9.0	0.63	12.13	27	4	88	7	1		8	59.5	-19.1	91	8	0	0	0.0	0.0
B- / 7.1	9.0	0.63	12.02	55	4	88	7	1		8	58.1	-19.1	90	8	0	0	0.0	0.0
B / 8.5	6.2	0.97	11.62	21	3	59	37	1		11	42.8	-12.2	53	8	0	0	0.0	0.0
B / 8.5	6.2	0.97	11.70	211	3	59	37	1		11	41.5	-12.2	48	8	0	0	0.0	0.0
B+ / 9.0	2.8	0.40	11.42	3	2	19	77	2		19	16.7	-2.6	66	8	0	0	0.0	0.0
B+ / 9.0	2.8	0.40	11.36	39	2	19	77	2		19	15.6	-2.7	62	8	0	0	0.0	0.0
B- / 7.5	8.0	0.56	11.57	67	3	78	17	2		6	54.2	-16.8	91	8	0	0	0.0	0.0
B- / 7.5	8.0	1.25	11.41	151	3	78	17	2		6	52.7	-16.8	36	8	0	0	0.0	0.0
B / 8.9	4.4	0.30	11.11	5	3	39	57	1		12	28.7	-7.5	87	8	0	0	0.0	0.0
B+ / 9.0	4.5	0.31	11.55	106	3	39	57	1		12	27.7	-7.6	85	8	0	0	0.0	0.0
C+ / 6.2	11.0	1.01	15.54	9	0	100	0	0		65	83.6	-21.4	23	4	1,000	100	5.8	0.0
C+ / 6.2	11.0	1.01	14.71	18	0	100	0	0		65	79.3	-21.3	17	4	1,000	100	0.0	0.0
C / 5.0	11.4	1.00	14.62	5	7	92	0	1		202	90.9	-9.1	49	4	1,000	100	5.8	0.0
C / 4.9	11.3	0.99	14.14	1	7	92	0	1		202	86.2	-9.4	39	4	1,000	100	0.0	0.0
C / 5.1	11.3	0.99	14.99	56	7	92	0	1		202	94.5	-8.7	60	4	1,000	100	0.0	0.0
D / 2.1	9.0	0.70	9.36	3	1	98	0	1		52	71.2	-6.7	85	1	1,000	100	5.8	0.0
D / 2.0	9.0	0.70	9.04	2	1	98	0	1		52	67.3	-7.8	81	1	1,000	100	0.0	0.0
D / 2.1	9.0	0.71	9.37	10	1	98	0	1		52	73.1	-7.5	86	1	1,000	100	0.0	0.0
C+ / 6.6	11.2	0.71	14.01	1	10	89	0	1		92	40.1	-26.5	38	6	1,000	100	5.8	0.0
C+ / 6.6	11.2	0.71	13.40	1	10	89	0	1		92	36.4	-26.7	28	6	1,000	100	0.0	0.0
C+ / 6.6	11.2	0.71	14.03	9	10	89	0	1		92	41.1	-26.5	40	6	1,000	100	0.0	0.0
D- / 1.5	17.9	1.10	13.91	21	5	94	0	1		97	16.9	-28.2	10	8	1,000	100	5.8	0.0
D- / 1.5	17.9	1.10	13.54	13	5	94	0	1		97	13.7	-28.4	7	8	1,000	100	0.0	0.0
D- / 1.5	18.0	1.10	13.97	424	5	94	0	1		97	18.1	-28.0	11	8	1,000	100	0.0	0.0
B- / 7.4	9.0	0.89	15.62	14	0	91	7	2		148	75.4	-16.7	47	13	1,000	100	5.8	0.0
B- / 7.4	9.0	0.89	15.79	7	0	91	7	2		148	71.1	-17.0	36	13	1,000	100	0.0	0.0
B- / 7.4	9.0	0.89	15.70	24	0	91	7	2		148	76.9	-16.6	51	13	1,000	100	0.0	0.0
C+ / 6.0	12.7	1.05	8.43	1	11	88	0	1		79	81.1	-25.5	6	12	1,000	100	5.8	0.0
C+ / 6.0	12.7	1.06	8.26	N/A	11	88	0	1		79	78.8	-25.8	5	12	1,000	100	0.0	0.0
C+ / 6.0	12.7	1.05	8.38	40	11	88	0	1		79	83.4	-25.4	6	12	1,000	100	0.0	0.0
D- / 1.4	9.6	0.80	19.61	15	22	77	0	1		188	150.2	-11.7	99	2	1,000	100	5.8	0.0
D- / 1.1	9.6	0.80	18.76	2	22	77	0	1		188	144.0	-12.1	99	2	1,000	100	0.0	0.0
D- / 1.5	9.6	0.80	20.11	133	22	77	0	1		188	153.6	-11.6	99	2	1,000	100	0.0	0.0
B- / 7.0	11.2	1.01	12.18	1	4	95	0	1		30	86.5	-26.2	26	8	1,000	100	5.8	0.0

Fund Type	Fund Name	Ticker Symbol	Overall Investment Rating	Phone	Performance Rating/Pts	3 Mo	6 Mo	1Yr / Pct	3Yr / Pct	5Yr / Pct	Dividend Yield	Expense Ratio
OT	ICON Industrials C	ICICX	C	(800) 764-0442	C / 4.8	-0.58	4.66	2.67 /25	11.94 /52	--	0.00	5.01
SC	ICON Industrials S	ICTRX	C+	(800) 764-0442	C+ / 5.7	-0.24	5.27	3.85 /31	13.19 /61	11.63 /58	0.04	1.41
TC	ICON Information Technology A	ICTTX	C+	(800) 764-0442	C+ / 6.9	5.36	13.66	22.49 /97	11.78 /51	--	0.00	1.94
TC	ICON Information Technology C	ICTFX	B	(800) 764-0442	B- / 7.4	5.16	13.19	21.54 /97	11.02 /46	--	0.00	4.20
TC	ICON Information Technology S	ICTEX	B+	(800) 764-0442	B+ / 8.4	5.47	13.80	22.87 /98	12.29 /55	12.84 /67	0.00	1.40
FO	ICON Intl Equity A	IIQAX	E+	(800) 764-0442	E+ / 0.7	4.99	3.00	-4.31 / 6	3.29 / 8	0.65 / 3	0.00	2.12
FO	ICON Intl Equity C	IIQCX	E+	(800) 764-0442	E+ / 0.8	4.86	2.81	-4.83 / 6	2.61 / 7	-0.05 / 2	0.10	2.82
FO	ICON Intl Equity S	ICNEX	E+	(800) 764-0442	D- / 1.0	5.03	3.24	-3.87 / 7	3.68 / 9	1.01 / 3	0.09	1.41
GR	ICON Long/Short A	ISTAX	C	(800) 764-0442	C / 5.4	3.22	14.06	11.40 /80	12.14 /53	11.33 /55	0.00	1.81
GR	ICON Long/Short C	IOLCX	C	(800) 764-0442	C+ / 5.8	2.98	13.62	10.52 /76	11.31 /48	10.49 /49	0.00	2.57
GR	ICON Long/Short S	IOLZX	C+	(800) 764-0442	C+ / 6.6	3.29	14.29	11.74 /81	12.49 /56	11.68 /58	0.00	1.45
OT	ICON Materials A	ICBAX	D+	(800) 764-0442	C- / 3.1	3.29	0.85	2.56 /24	10.36 /42	--	0.22	1.72
OT	ICON Materials C	ICBCX	C-	(800) 764-0442	C- / 3.4	3.14	0.20	1.44 /20	9.40 /36	--	0.00	4.17
OT	ICON Materials S	ICBMX	C-	(800) 764-0442	C- / 4.1	3.41	0.77	2.61 /25	10.64 /43	10.41 /48	0.23	1.36
GR	ICON Risk-Managed Balanced A	IOCAX	C	(800) 764-0442	D+ / 2.7	2.58	5.88	8.27 /65	8.12 /28	6.50 /20	1.09	1.69
GR	ICON Risk-Managed Balanced C	IOCCX	C+	(800) 764-0442	C- / 3.1	2.41	5.47	7.48 /59	7.32 /23	5.68 /15	0.49	2.37
GR	ICON Risk-Managed Balanced S	IOCZX	C+	(800) 764-0442	C- / 3.7	2.64	6.06	8.45 /66	8.37 /29	6.74 /21	1.06	1.26
GR	ICON S	ICNZX	C+	(800) 764-0442	C+ / 6.6	2.25	12.53	9.89 /74	13.06 /60	11.23 /55	0.00	1.10
UT	ICON Utilities A	ICTVX	C	(800) 764-0442	C / 4.5	-4.21	8.10	10.20 /75	11.97 /52	--	3.07	1.81
UT	ICON Utilities C	ICTZX	C	(800) 764-0442	C / 4.9	-4.29	7.74	9.40 /71	11.16 /47	--	2.13	2.55
UT	ICON Utilities S	ICTUX	C+	(800) 764-0442	C+ / 5.7	-3.99	8.38	10.55 /77	12.26 /54	11.97 /60	3.28	1.52
GR	ID 529 IDeal CSP Aggr Growth Port		C+	(800) 662-7447	C+ / 5.8	2.39	4.57	7.52 /59	12.71 /58	11.10 /53	0.00	0.86
GI	ID 529 IDeal CSP Csv Growth Port		C	(800) 662-7447	D / 1.8	1.82	3.71	5.90 /46	5.04 /13	5.73 /15	0.00	0.83
GI	ID 529 IDeal CSP Growth Port		C+	(800) 662-7447	C / 4.3	2.18	4.38	7.08 /56	10.14 /40	9.45 /40	0.00	0.85
GI	ID 529 IDeal CSP Mod Growth Port		C+	(800) 662-7447	C- / 3.0	2.02	4.04	6.46 /50	7.61 /25	7.70 /28	0.00	0.84
GR	Iman Fund	IMANX	C	(877) 417-6161	C+ / 5.9	2.48	7.16	9.41 /71	12.32 /55	11.54 /57	0.00	1.48
GR	IMS Capital Value Inst	IMSCX	C+	(800) 934-5550	C+ / 6.0	5.74	10.64	11.46 /80	11.02 /46	8.92 /36	0.00	2.05
AA	IMS Dividend Growth Inst	IMSAX	C+		C / 5.3	0.30	7.37	10.76 /77	11.46 /49	10.55 /49	0.53	2.50
IN	Income 529 Port A		C-	(800) 342-5236	E+ / 0.6	0.52	0.26	1.91 /22	1.76 / 6	2.88 / 6	0.00	1.21
IN	● Income 529 Port B		C-	(800) 342-5236	E+ / 0.6	0.36	-0.14	1.15 /19	0.99 / 5	2.11 / 5	0.00	1.96
IN	Income 529 Port C		C-	(800) 342-5236	E+ / 0.6	0.35	-0.14	1.14 /19	0.98 / 5	2.12 / 5	0.00	1.96
GR	Independent Franch Partners US Eq	IFPUX	B+	(855) 233-0437	B- / 7.2	2.64	6.81	12.98 /86	14.13 /68	--	1.15	0.81
GL	Infinity Q Diversified Alpha Fund I	IQDNX	U	(844) 473-8631	U /	2.53	-1.14	--	--	--	0.00	2.45
AA	Innealta Capital Country Rotation I	ICCIX	D+	(855) 873-3837	E+ / 0.7	1.60	-2.32	-0.88 /13	2.88 / 8	--	2.17	1.89
AA	Innealta Capital Country Rotation N	ICCNX	D+	(855) 873-3837	E+ / 0.7	1.65	-2.34	-1.09 /13	2.60 / 7	--	1.85	2.14
GR	Innealta Captl Sector Rotation I	ICSIX	D	(855) 873-3837	E+ / 0.7	0.84	-0.55	-0.12 /15	2.61 / 7	--	2.06	2.14
GR	Innealta Captl Sector Rotation N	ICSNX	D	(855) 873-3837	E+ / 0.7	0.88	-0.58	-0.27 /15	2.43 / 7	--	1.80	2.39
AA	Innovator Matrix Income A	IMIFX	D	(877) 386-3890	E+ / 0.8	7.68	-0.74	-1.55 /11	4.55 /12	--	5.82	3.00
GL	Insignia Macro I	IGMLX	U	(866) 759-5679	U /	4.82	7.00	12.16 /83	--	--	0.44	3.62
GR	Institutional Advisors LargeCap	IALFX	C+	(800) 344-2716	C+ / 6.8	-0.60	5.02	9.59 /72	14.44 /70	13.38 /72	0.74	1.29
EM	Institutional Emerging Markets I	HLMEX	E+	(877) 435-8105	E+ / 0.7	1.32	-2.64	-1.23 /12	3.14 / 8	4.22 / 9	0.71	1.31
EM	Institutional Emerging Markets II	HLEEX	U	(877) 435-8105	U /	1.41	-2.53	-1.02 /13	--	--	1.30	1.30
IX	Institutional Sector Alloc Model	SAMSX	D	(800) 338-9476	C- / 3.8	-4.19	-3.16	1.23 /19	11.26 /47	--	1.67	1.15
GL	INTECH Global Income Managed Vol	JGDAX	C-	(800) 295-2687	D+ / 2.5	3.52	1.69	0.34 /17	9.49 /36	--	3.73	1.96
GL	INTECH Global Income Managed Vol	JGDCX	C-	(800) 295-2687	D+ / 2.9	3.35	1.23	-0.45 /14	8.61 /30	--	3.24	2.70
GL	● INTECH Global Income Managed Vol	JGDDX	C-	(800) 295-2687	C- / 3.5	3.58	1.79	0.53 /17	9.57 /37	--	4.15	1.78
GL	INTECH Global Income Managed Vol	JGDIX	C	(800) 295-2687	C- / 3.6	3.59	1.75	0.64 /17	9.78 /38	--	4.25	1.67
GL	INTECH Global Income Managed Vol	JGDSX	C-	(800) 295-2687	C- / 3.4	3.49	1.61	0.19 /16	9.47 /36	--	3.80	2.13
GL	INTECH Global Income Managed Vol	JDGTX	C-	(800) 295-2687	C- / 3.5	3.55	1.74	0.45 /17	9.58 /37	--	4.06	1.83
FO	INTECH International Managed Vol A	JMIAX	D-	(800) 295-2687	D+ / 2.9	5.69	2.55	-2.86 / 9	10.40 /42	6.76 /22	1.61	1.21
FO	INTECH International Managed Vol C	JMICX	D-	(800) 295-2687	C- / 3.7	5.46	2.17	-3.48 / 8	10.30 /41	6.70 /21	1.12	1.93
FO	INTECH International Managed Vol I	JMIIX	D-	(800) 295-2687	C- / 4.0	5.72	2.64	-2.58 / 9	10.76 /44	6.90 /22	1.99	0.81

● Denotes fund is closed to new investors
* Denotes fund is included in Section II

www.thestreetratings.com

RISK			NET ASSETS		ASSET					BULL / BEAR		FUND MANAGER		MINIMUMS		LOADS	
Risk Rating/Pts	3 Year		NAV		Cash	Stocks	Bonds	Other	Portfolio	Last Bull	Last Bear	Manager	Manager	Initial	Additional	Front	Back
	Standard Deviation	Beta	As of 3/31/15	Total $(Mil)	%	%	%	%	Turnover Ratio	Market Return	Market Return	Quality Pct	Tenure (Years)	Purch. $	Purch. $	End Load	End Load
C+ / 6.9	11.2	1.01	11.91	N/A	4	95	0	1	30	83.3	-26.4	18	8	1,000	100	0.0	0.0
B- / 7.0	11.1	0.70	12.28	41	4	95	0	1	30	90.3	-25.9	83	8	1,000	100	0.0	0.0
C+ / 6.0	12.5	1.11	15.14	1	5	94	0	1	48	83.8	-13.6	8	6	1,000	100	5.8	0.0
C+ / 6.0	12.6	1.11	14.67	1	5	94	0	1	48	79.8	-14.0	6	6	1,000	100	0.0	0.0
C+ / 6.1	12.6	1.12	15.42	54	5	94	0	1	48	86.7	-13.5	10	6	1,000	100	0.0	0.0
C+ / 5.7	12.4	0.79	12.00	5	8	91	0	1	193	33.5	-33.2	16	10	1,000	100	5.8	0.0
C+ / 5.7	12.3	0.79	11.01	4	8	91	0	1	193	30.4	-33.4	12	10	1,000	100	0.0	0.0
C+ / 5.8	12.3	0.79	12.12	80	8	91	0	1	193	35.3	-33.1	20	10	1,000	100	0.0	0.0
C+ / 6.1	10.8	0.99	20.52	11	3	96	0	1	65	76.7	-16.3	22	4	1,000	100	5.8	0.0
C+ / 6.0	10.9	1.00	19.02	7	3	96	0	1	65	72.2	-16.5	15	4	1,000	100	0.0	0.0
C+ / 6.1	10.9	1.00	21.04	23	3	96	0	1	65	78.4	-16.1	24	4	1,000	100	0.0	0.0
C+ / 6.6	11.6	1.09	15.05	5	4	95	0	1	33	75.1	-27.1	5	8	1,000	100	5.8	0.0
C+ / 6.6	11.6	1.09	14.80	1	4	95	0	1	33	70.0	-27.3	4	8	1,000	100	0.0	0.0
C+ / 6.6	11.6	1.09	15.17	85	4	95	0	1	33	76.8	-27.0	6	8	1,000	100	0.0	0.0
B / 8.8	5.8	0.55	14.41	10	5	61	33	1	137	41.2	-10.7	61	13	1,000	100	5.8	0.0
B / 8.8	5.9	0.56	13.58	11	5	61	33	1	137	37.6	-11.0	48	13	1,000	100	0.0	0.0
B / 8.8	5.9	0.56	14.76	13	5	61	33	1	137	42.4	-10.6	63	13	1,000	100	0.0	0.0
C+ / 6.2	11.0	1.01	16.34	45	0	100	0	0	65	85.6	-20.8	27	4	1,000	100	0.0	0.0
C+ / 6.9	13.1	0.89	8.31	3	2	97	0	1	107	51.6	-0.2	73	1	1,000	100	5.8	0.0
C+ / 6.9	13.1	0.89	8.32	2	2	97	0	1	107	48.6	-0.4	64	1	1,000	100	0.0	0.0
C+ / 6.9	13.1	0.89	8.43	15	2	97	0	1	107	52.9	N/A	75	1	1,000	100	0.0	0.0
C+ / 6.9	10.1	1.02	13.73	80	0	99	0	1	0	78.4	-19.9	22	8	25	25	0.0	0.0
B+ / 9.7	3.1	0.21	13.99	58	0	25	74	1	0	23.1	-2.0	83	8	25	25	0.0	0.0
B / 8.3	7.5	0.75	14.07	47	0	74	24	2	0	58.3	-14.3	43	8	25	25	0.0	0.0
B+ / 9.3	5.1	0.48	14.17	53	0	49	49	2	0	40.1	-8.3	68	8	25	25	0.0	0.0
C+ / 5.7	11.0	1.06	11.16	67	0	99	0	1	72	77.9	-20.3	14	15	250	50	0.0	0.0
C+ / 6.4	10.6	1.00	22.66	39	1	98	0	1	110	83.3	-29.3	13	19	5,000	100	0.0	0.5
B- / 7.1	10.9	1.70	13.24	10	1	98	0	1	241	72.9	-14.7	5	13	5,000	100	0.0	0.5
B+ / 9.9	2.0	0.10	15.47	30	0	0	0	100	0	8.4	0.4	70	10	250	0	4.3	0.0
B+ / 9.9	2.0	0.10	14.13	2	0	0	0	100	0	5.6	0.2	59	10	250	0	0.0	0.0
B+ / 9.9	2.0	0.10	14.18	17	0	0	0	100	0	5.7	0.2	60	10	250	0	0.0	0.0
B- / 7.6	9.7	0.93	15.18	951	4	95	0	1	29	N/A	N/A	58	4	3,000,000	250,000	0.0	0.0
U /	N/A	N/A	9.74	51	0	0	0	100	0	N/A	N/A	N/A	1	100,000	10,000	0.0	1.0
B / 8.8	4.6	0.43	10.09	43	4	26	69	1	143	N/A	N/A	43	4	100,000	0	0.0	2.0
B / 8.8	4.6	0.43	10.09	16	4	26	69	1	143	N/A	N/A	39	4	5,000	1,000	0.0	2.0
B / 8.3	4.3	0.16	10.12	19	7	9	83	1	94	N/A	N/A	69	4	100,000	0	0.0	2.0
B / 8.3	4.3	0.16	10.13	10	7	9	83	1	94	N/A	N/A	67	4	5,000	1,000	0.0	2.0
B- / 7.5	10.7	1.26	19.40	77	33	50	16	1	91	N/A	N/A	3	N/A	2,000	1,000	5.8	2.0
U /	N/A	N/A	11.09	55	0	0	0	100	43	N/A	N/A	N/A	2	250,000	0	0.0	1.0
C+ / 6.7	9.3	0.93	21.36	67	0	99	0	1	20	83.6	-12.3	61	6	2,500	0	0.0	0.0
C / 5.5	13.3	0.94	17.63	1,763	1	95	3	1	26	38.0	-24.1	87	10	500,000	0	0.0	2.0
U /	N/A	N/A	10.09	214	1	95	3	1	26	N/A	N/A	N/A	10	25,000,000	0	0.0	2.0
C / 4.9	8.7	0.82	11.65	77	1	98	0	1	126	55.9	-10.9	44	5	250,000	0	0.0	0.0
B- / 7.3	10.6	1.50	11.74	3	1	98	0	1	51	N/A	N/A	17	4	2,500	0	5.8	0.0
B- / 7.3	10.6	1.50	11.68	1	1	98	0	1	51	N/A	N/A	12	4	2,500	0	0.0	0.0
B- / 7.4	10.5	1.50	11.71	8	1	98	0	1	51	N/A	N/A	18	4	2,500	100	0.0	0.0
B- / 7.4	10.6	1.50	11.76	3	1	98	0	1	51	N/A	N/A	19	4	1,000,000	0	0.0	0.0
B- / 7.3	10.6	1.50	11.72	N/A	1	98	0	1	51	N/A	N/A	17	4	2,500	0	0.0	0.0
B- / 7.3	10.6	1.50	11.73	4	1	98	0	1	51	N/A	N/A	18	4	2,500	0	0.0	0.0
C- / 4.0	12.6	0.90	7.99	6	5	94	0	1	160	53.2	-24.8	82	8	2,500	0	5.8	0.0
C- / 4.0	12.6	0.90	7.92	1	5	94	0	1	160	53.3	-24.9	81	8	2,500	0	0.0	0.0
C- / 3.9	12.6	0.90	7.95	64	5	94	0	1	160	54.7	-24.7	84	8	1,000,000	0	0.0	0.0

Fund Type	Fund Name	Ticker Symbol	Overall Investment Rating	Phone	Performance Rating/Pts	3 Mo	6 Mo	1Yr / Pct	3Yr / Pct	5Yr / Pct	Dividend Yield	Expense Ratio
FO	INTECH International Managed Vol S	JMISX	D-	(800) 295-2687	C- / 3.8	5.64	2.49	-2.97 / 9	10.43 /42	6.78 /22	1.76	1.33
FO	INTECH International Managed Vol T	JRMTX	D-	(800) 295-2687	C- / 3.8	5.59	2.59	-2.86 / 9	10.36 /42	6.74 /21	1.62	1.12
GR	INTECH US Core A	JDOAX	B+	(800) 295-2687	B+ / 8.3	2.90	7.91	14.27 /90	17.28 /91	15.84 /92	1.09	0.97
GR	INTECH US Core C	JLCCX	A-	(800) 295-2687	B+ / 8.6	2.67	7.45	13.40 /88	16.36 /86	14.95 /86	0.62	1.75
GR	● INTECH US Core D	JIRMX	A	(800) 295-2687	A- / 9.2	2.90	8.01	14.48 /91	17.47 /92	16.04 /93	1.29	0.80
GR	INTECH US Core I	JRMCX	A	(800) 295-2687	A / 9.3	2.95	8.08	14.60 /91	17.59 /93	16.17 /94	1.40	0.68
GR	INTECH US Core S	JLCIX	A	(800) 295-2687	A- / 9.0	2.86	7.84	14.11 /90	17.08 /90	15.67 /91	1.08	1.14
GR	INTECH US Core T	JRMSX	A	(800) 295-2687	A- / 9.2	2.90	7.93	14.34 /90	17.38 /92	15.94 /93	1.22	0.89
GR	INTECH US Managed Volatility A	JRSAX	C-	(800) 295-2687	B+ / 8.5	4.73	9.36	11.36 /80	17.84 /94	14.44 /82	0.99	1.04
GR	INTECH US Managed Volatility C	JRSCX	C-	(800) 295-2687	B+ / 8.9	4.61	8.98	10.54 /76	17.01 /90	13.60 /74	1.25	1.75
GR	INTECH US Managed Volatility I	JRSIX	C	(800) 295-2687	A / 9.4	4.85	9.48	11.64 /81	18.20 /95	14.77 /85	2.09	0.67
GR	● INTECH US Managed Volatility II A	JDRAX	B+	(800) 295-2687	B / 7.8	5.20	8.97	13.60 /88	16.25 /85	15.32 /89	0.56	0.95
GR	● INTECH US Managed Volatility II C	JCGCX	A	(800) 295-2687	B+ / 8.3	5.06	8.62	12.86 /86	15.52 /79	14.44 /82	0.04	1.59
GR	● INTECH US Managed Volatility II I	JRMGX	A+	(800) 295-2687	A- / 9.0	5.33	9.17	14.00 /89	16.68 /88	15.65 /91	0.86	0.61
GR	● INTECH US Managed Volatility II S	JCGIX	A+	(800) 295-2687	B+ / 8.7	5.21	8.90	13.43 /88	16.13 /84	15.13 /88	0.34	1.06
GR	● INTECH US Managed Volatility II T	JDRTX	A+	(800) 295-2687	B+ / 8.9	5.26	9.04	13.72 /89	16.42 /86	15.42 /90	0.71	0.81
GR	INTECH US Managed Volatility S	JRSSX	C	(800) 295-2687	A / 9.3	4.65	9.27	11.16 /79	17.84 /94	14.34 /81	2.02	1.24
GR	INTECH US Managed Volatility T	JRSTX	C	(800) 295-2687	A / 9.3	4.79	9.52	11.51 /80	17.95 /94	14.53 /83	2.16	0.91
IN	Integrity Dividend Harvest A	IDIVX	U	(800) 601-5593	U /	-0.74	2.17	8.38 /65	--	--	2.63	1.77
GI	Integrity Growth & Income A	IGIAX	D	(800) 601-5593	C- / 3.3	0.94	-1.36	4.09 /32	10.82 /44	12.48 /64	0.58	1.83
AA	Intrepid Capital Institutional	ICMVX	D+	(866) 996-3863	D+ / 2.6	1.09	1.07	2.09 /22	8.51 /30	--	1.48	1.16
GI	Intrepid Capital Investor	ICMBX	D	(866) 996-3863	D+ / 2.4	1.03	0.95	1.84 /21	8.26 /28	8.49 /33	1.23	1.41
GR	Intrepid Disciplined Value Investor	ICMCX	C-	(866) 996-3863	C- / 3.6	1.52	3.75	6.50 /51	9.53 /36	9.12 /38	0.00	1.57
SC	Intrepid Small Cap Institutional	ICMZX	D	(866) 996-3863	D- / 1.1	-0.27	-1.02	-1.26 /12	5.58 /15	7.23 /25	0.00	1.15
SC	Intrepid Small Cap Investor	ICMAX	D-	(866) 996-3863	D- / 1.1	-0.28	-1.16	-1.47 /12	5.32 /14	6.98 /23	0.00	1.40
* IN	Invesco American Franchise A	VAFAX	C+	(800) 959-4246	C+ / 6.5	3.54	6.31	13.02 /87	14.64 /72	13.53 /73	0.00	1.08
IN	● Invesco American Franchise B	VAFBX	C+	(800) 959-4246	B- / 7.5	3.57	6.28	13.02 /87	14.62 /72	13.31 /71	0.00	1.08
IN	Invesco American Franchise C	VAFCX	C+	(800) 959-4246	C+ / 6.9	3.34	5.91	12.13 /83	13.76 /65	12.72 /66	0.00	1.83
GR	Invesco American Franchise R	VAFRX	C+	(800) 959-4246	B- / 7.3	3.45	6.18	12.67 /85	14.33 /70	13.23 /70	0.00	1.33
GR	Invesco American Franchise R5	VAFNX	B-	(800) 959-4246	B / 7.8	3.62	6.49	13.43 /88	15.03 /75	13.89 /77	0.00	0.70
GR	Invesco American Franchise R6	VAFFX	B+	(800) 959-4246	B / 7.9	3.68	6.54	13.54 /88	15.05 /75	13.78 /76	0.00	0.63
IN	Invesco American Franchise Y	VAFIX	B-	(800) 959-4246	B / 7.7	3.56	6.42	13.28 /88	14.90 /74	13.78 /76	0.00	0.83
GR	Invesco American Value A	MSAVX	B	(800) 959-4246	B / 7.6	3.52	8.97	10.50 /76	16.59 /87	14.90 /86	0.05	1.20
GR	● Invesco American Value B	MGAVX	B+	(800) 959-4246	B+ / 8.6	3.51	8.94	10.48 /76	16.57 /87	14.85 /86	0.05	1.20
GR	Invesco American Value C	MSVCX	B	(800) 959-4246	B / 8.1	3.33	8.55	9.67 /73	15.72 /81	14.05 /78	0.00	1.92
GR	Invesco American Value R	MSARX	B+	(800) 959-4246	B+ / 8.5	3.45	8.83	10.22 /75	16.29 /85	14.61 /83	0.00	1.45
GR	Invesco American Value R5	MSAJX	A-	(800) 959-4246	B+ / 8.9	3.62	9.15	10.91 /78	17.01 /90	15.34 /89	0.37	0.86
MC	Invesco American Value R6	MSAFX	A+	(800) 959-4246	B+ / 8.9	3.64	9.20	11.00 /78	17.02 /90	15.15 /88	0.44	0.77
GR	Invesco American Value Y	MSAIX	A-	(800) 959-4246	B+ / 8.8	3.56	9.08	10.75 /77	16.87 /89	15.17 /88	0.25	0.95
FO	Invesco Asia Pacific Growth A	ASIAX	D	(800) 959-4246	D+ / 2.7	2.68	2.86	8.19 /64	8.54 /30	9.74 /42	1.19	1.50
FO	● Invesco Asia Pacific Growth B	ASIBX	D+	(800) 959-4246	C- / 3.0	2.49	2.48	7.35 /58	7.74 /26	8.92 /36	0.59	2.25
FO	Invesco Asia Pacific Growth C	ASICX	D+	(800) 959-4246	C- / 3.0	2.51	2.50	7.40 /58	7.75 /26	8.92 /36	0.59	2.25
FO	Invesco Asia Pacific Growth Y	ASIYX	C-	(800) 959-4246	C- / 3.7	2.74	2.98	8.44 /66	8.81 /32	10.01 /45	1.50	1.25
AA	Invesco Balanced Risk Alloc A	ABRZX	D-	(800) 959-4246	D- / 1.5	3.30	5.22	7.52 /59	5.27 /14	8.57 /34	1.85	1.29
AA	● Invesco Balanced Risk Alloc B	ABRBX	D	(800) 959-4246	D / 1.8	3.05	4.85	6.67 /52	4.49 /11	7.76 /28	1.19	2.04
AA	Invesco Balanced Risk Alloc C	ABRCX	D	(800) 959-4246	D / 1.8	3.05	4.85	6.67 /52	4.49 /11	7.76 /28	1.19	2.04
AA	Invesco Balanced Risk Alloc R	ABRRX	D	(800) 959-4246	D / 2.1	3.16	5.08	7.22 /57	5.01 /13	8.29 /32	1.71	1.54
AA	Invesco Balanced Risk Alloc R5	ABRIX	D	(800) 959-4246	D+ / 2.4	3.35	5.40	7.76 /61	5.56 /15	8.88 /36	2.23	1.02
GL	Invesco Balanced Risk Alloc R6	ALLFX	C+	(800) 959-4246	D+ / 2.4	3.35	5.44	7.88 /62	5.59 /15	8.77 /35	2.34	0.92
AA	Invesco Balanced Risk Alloc Y	ABRYX	D	(800) 959-4246	D+ / 2.4	3.35	5.39	7.74 /61	5.55 /15	8.87 /36	2.21	1.04
BA	Invesco Balanced-Risk Com Str A	BRCAX	E-	(800) 959-4246	E- / 0.1	-2.85	-10.15	-19.17 / 1	-13.11 / 1	--	0.00	1.62
BA	● Invesco Balanced-Risk Com Str B	BRCBX	E-	(800) 959-4246	E- / 0.1	-3.06	-10.51	-19.77 / 1	-13.72 / 1	--	0.00	2.37

● Denotes fund is closed to new investors
* Denotes fund is included in Section II

322

www.thestreetratings.com

RISK			NET ASSETS		ASSET				Portfolio	BULL / BEAR		FUND MANAGER		MINIMUMS		LOADS	
	3 Year		NAV							Last Bull	Last Bear	Manager	Manager	Initial	Additional	Front	Back
Risk	Standard		As of	Total	Cash	Stocks	Bonds	Other	Turnover	Market	Market	Quality	Tenure	Purch.	Purch.	End	End
Rating/Pts	Deviation	Beta	3/31/15	$(Mil)	%	%	%	%	Ratio	Return	Return	Pct	(Years)	$	$	Load	Load
C- /4.0	12.6	0.90	8.05	N/A	5	94	0	1	160	53.3	-24.7	82	8	2,500	0	0.0	0.0
C- /4.0	12.6	0.91	7.94	1	5	94	0	1	160	53.1	-24.8	81	8	2,500	0	0.0	0.0
C+ /6.3	9.5	0.97	20.91	27	0	99	0	1	59	103.3	-15.6	80	12	2,500	0	5.8	0.0
C+ /6.3	9.5	0.97	20.76	20	0	99	0	1	59	97.9	-15.9	74	12	2,500	0	0.0	0.0
C+ /6.2	9.5	0.97	20.93	320	0	99	0	1	59	104.4	-15.5	81	12	2,500	100	0.0	0.0
C+ /6.2	9.5	0.97	20.94	188	0	99	0	1	59	105.2	-15.4	82	12	1,000,000	0	0.0	0.0
C+ /6.3	9.5	0.97	20.86	41	0	99	0	1	59	102.2	-15.6	79	12	2,500	0	0.0	0.0
C+ /6.2	9.5	0.97	20.92	170	0	99	0	1	59	104.0	-15.6	81	12	2,500	0	0.0	0.0
D /1.9	9.7	0.93	10.62	2	0	99	0	1	150	100.7	-18.1	87	10	2,500	0	5.8	0.0
D /1.7	9.7	0.93	10.44	1	0	99	0	1	150	95.8	-18.4	83	10	2,500	0	0.0	0.0
D /1.6	9.8	0.94	10.59	5	0	99	0	1	150	102.8	-18.0	88	10	1,000,000	0	0.0	0.0
B- /7.0	9.5	0.89	22.86	7	0	99	0	1	110	93.3	-15.9	82	12	2,500	0	5.8	0.0
B- /7.0	9.5	0.90	22.01	4	0	99	0	1	110	88.9	-16.1	77	12	2,500	0	0.0	0.0
B- /7.0	9.5	0.90	22.71	177	0	99	0	1	110	95.6	-15.9	84	12	1,000,000	0	0.0	0.0
B- /7.0	9.4	0.89	22.81	12	0	99	0	1	110	92.5	-16.0	82	12	2,500	0	0.0	0.0
B- /7.0	9.5	0.90	22.60	68	0	99	0	1	110	94.2	-16.0	83	12	2,500	0	0.0	0.0
D /1.7	9.8	0.94	10.58	2	0	99	0	1	150	100.4	-18.1	86	10	2,500	0	0.0	0.0
D /1.6	9.8	0.94	10.50	21	0	99	0	1	150	101.2	-18.1	86	10	2,500	0	0.0	0.0
U /	N/A	N/A	12.46	32	1	98	0	1	26	N/A	N/A	N/A	3	1,000	50	5.0	0.0
C /5.3	11.6	1.10	47.47	36	0	100	0	0	116	77.9	-20.9	6	5	1,000	50	5.0	0.0
C+ /6.5	6.6	0.97	11.59	223	28	42	26	4	73	47.5	-9.5	39	N/A	250,000	100	0.0	2.0
C+ /6.5	6.6	0.59	11.59	188	28	42	26	4	73	46.2	-9.6	54	N/A	2,500	100	0.0	2.0
B- /7.2	6.6	0.58	10.71	48	48	51	0	1	66	59.9	-14.7	71	N/A	2,500	100	0.0	2.0
B- /7.0	5.0	0.29	14.66	126	74	25	0	1	38	36.2	-10.6	77	N/A	250,000	100	0.0	2.0
C+ /6.9	5.0	0.29	14.41	322	74	25	0	1	38	35.1	-10.6	76	N/A	2,500	100	0.0	2.0
C /5.4	11.9	1.11	17.26	9,012	2	97	0	1	77	92.3	-19.3	26	5	1,000	50	5.5	0.0
C /5.3	11.9	1.11	16.83	206	2	97	0	1	77	92.3	-19.5	26	5	1,000	50	0.0	0.0
C /5.3	11.9	1.11	16.42	414	2	97	0	1	77	87.5	-19.6	19	5	1,000	50	0.0	0.0
C /5.3	11.9	1.11	17.09	33	2	97	0	1	77	90.6	-19.4	24	5	0	0	0.0	0.0
C /5.4	11.9	1.10	17.44	50	2	97	0	1	77	94.6	-19.2	31	5	10,000,000	0	0.0	0.0
C+ /6.3	11.9	1.11	17.47	94	2	97	0	1	77	94.3	-19.3	31	5	10,000,000	0	0.0	0.0
C /5.4	11.9	1.11	17.45	161	2	97	0	1	77	93.8	-19.3	29	5	1,000	50	0.0	0.0
C+ /6.2	10.0	0.93	40.58	1,243	3	96	0	1	46	107.0	-21.8	80	12	1,000	50	5.5	0.0
C+ /5.9	10.0	0.93	36.30	26	3	96	0	1	46	107.1	-21.8	80	12	1,000	50	0.0	0.0
C+ /5.8	10.0	0.93	35.09	126	3	96	0	1	46	101.9	-22.0	74	12	1,000	50	0.0	0.0
C+ /6.1	10.0	0.93	40.44	78	3	96	0	1	46	105.3	-21.9	79	12	0	0	0.0	0.0
C+ /6.2	9.9	0.93	40.76	91	3	96	0	1	46	109.7	-21.6	83	12	10,000,000	0	0.0	0.0
B- /7.4	10.0	0.86	40.76	141	3	96	0	1	46	109.2	-21.8	85	12	10,000,000	0	0.0	0.0
C+ /6.2	10.0	0.93	40.75	541	3	96	0	1	46	108.7	-21.7	82	12	1,000	50	0.0	0.0
C+ /6.4	9.9	0.58	32.16	560	13	86	0	1	15	55.6	-19.8	88	16	1,000	50	5.5	0.0
C+ /6.4	9.9	0.58	30.02	11	13	86	0	1	15	51.7	-20.1	85	16	1,000	50	0.0	0.0
C+ /6.4	9.9	0.58	29.84	96	13	86	0	1	15	51.7	-20.1	85	16	1,000	50	0.0	0.0
C+ /6.4	9.9	0.58	32.23	395	13	86	0	1	15	57.0	-19.7	89	16	1,000	50	0.0	0.0
C+ /6.4	5.9	0.71	11.90	2,857	98	0	1	1	72	29.8	1.4	34	6	1,000	50	5.5	0.0
C+ /6.3	6.0	0.71	11.50	18	98	0	1	1	72	26.5	1.1	26	6	1,000	50	0.0	0.0
C+ /6.3	6.0	0.71	11.50	1,866	98	0	1	1	72	26.6	1.1	26	6	1,000	50	0.0	0.0
C+ /6.4	6.0	0.72	11.75	30	98	0	1	1	72	28.7	1.3	30	6	0	0	0.0	0.0
C+ /6.5	6.0	0.71	12.03	185	98	0	1	1	72	31.0	1.6	37	6	10,000,000	0	0.0	0.0
B+ /9.5	5.9	0.72	12.04	468	98	0	1	1	72	31.0	1.4	56	6	10,000,000	0	0.0	0.0
C+ /6.5	6.0	0.72	12.03	3,573	98	0	1	1	72	31.0	1.6	37	6	1,000	50	0.0	0.0
D /2.1	13.1	1.12	7.17	40	92	0	7	1	21	-22.4	-17.2	0	5	1,000	50	5.5	0.0
D /2.1	13.1	1.12	6.98	N/A	92	0	7	1	21	-24.3	-17.5	0	5	0	0	0.0	0.0

								PERFORMANCE						

99 Pct = Best
0 Pct = Worst

Fund Type	Fund Name	Ticker Symbol	Overall Investment Rating	Phone	Perfor-mance Rating/Pts	Total Return % through 3/31/15					Incl. in Returns	
						3 Mo	6 Mo	1Yr / Pct	3Yr / Pct (Annualized)	5Yr / Pct	Dividend Yield	Expense Ratio
BA	Invesco Balanced-Risk Com Str C	BRCCX	E-	(800) 959-4246	E- / 0.1	-3.06	-10.53	-19.79 / 1	-13.73 / 1	--	0.00	2.37
BA	Invesco Balanced-Risk Com Str R	BRCRX	E-	(800) 959-4246	E- / 0.1	-3.00	-10.33	-19.46 / 1	-13.33 / 1	--	0.00	1.87
BA	Invesco Balanced-Risk Com Str R5	BRCNX	E-	(800) 959-4246	E- / 0.1	-2.68	-9.91	-18.86 / 1	-12.81 / 1	--	0.00	1.24
OT	Invesco Balanced-Risk Com Str R6	IBRFX	E+	(800) 959-4246	E- / 0.1	-2.81	-10.02	-18.86 / 1	-12.89 / 1	--	0.00	1.15
BA	Invesco Balanced-Risk Com Str Y	BRCYX	E-	(800) 959-4246	E- / 0.1	-2.81	-10.04	-18.97 / 1	-12.88 / 1	--	0.00	1.37
AA	● Invesco Balanced-Risk Ret 2020 A	AFTAX	D	(800) 959-4246	D- / 1.2	2.52	4.21	6.20 /48	4.65 /12	8.05 /30	3.67	1.37
AA	Invesco Balanced-Risk Ret 2020 AX	VRCAX	D	(800) 959-4246	D- / 1.2	2.64	4.21	6.20 /48	4.65 /12	8.05 /30	3.67	1.37
AA	● Invesco Balanced-Risk Ret 2020 B	AFTBX	D+	(800) 959-4246	D- / 1.4	2.44	3.87	5.43 /42	3.89 /10	7.25 /25	3.13	2.12
AA	Invesco Balanced-Risk Ret 2020 C	AFTCX	D+	(800) 959-4246	D- / 1.4	2.45	3.88	5.44 /42	3.86 /10	7.24 /25	3.14	2.12
AA	● Invesco Balanced-Risk Ret 2020 CX	VRCCX	D+	(800) 959-4246	D- / 1.4	2.34	3.88	5.44 /42	3.86 /10	7.24 /25	3.14	2.12
AA	Invesco Balanced-Risk Ret 2020 R	ATFRX	D+	(800) 959-4246	D / 1.6	2.54	4.17	5.94 /46	4.41 /11	7.77 /28	3.62	1.62
AA	Invesco Balanced-Risk Ret 2020 R5	AFTSX	D+	(800) 959-4246	D / 1.9	2.73	4.48	6.57 /51	4.93 /13	8.34 /32	4.12	1.03
GI	Invesco Balanced-Risk Ret 2020 R6	VRCFX	C	(800) 959-4246	D / 1.9	2.73	4.47	6.57 /51	4.93 /13	8.22 /31	4.12	0.94
AA	● Invesco Balanced-Risk Ret 2020 RX	VRCRX	D+	(800) 959-4246	D / 1.6	2.54	4.17	6.05 /47	4.41 /11	7.78 /28	3.62	1.62
AA	Invesco Balanced-Risk Ret 2020 Y	AFTYX	D+	(800) 959-4246	D / 1.9	2.75	4.39	6.60 /52	4.91 /13	8.31 /32	4.14	1.12
AA	Invesco Balanced-Risk Ret 2030 A	TNAAX	D	(800) 959-4246	D / 1.7	3.41	5.67	8.20 /64	5.64 /15	8.81 /35	5.07	1.55
AA	● Invesco Balanced-Risk Ret 2030 AX	VREAX	D	(800) 959-4246	D / 1.7	3.41	5.67	8.20 /64	5.67 /15	8.83 /36	5.06	1.55
AA	● Invesco Balanced-Risk Ret 2030 B	TNABX	D+	(800) 959-4246	D / 2.0	3.22	5.26	7.35 /58	4.86 /13	8.00 /30	4.65	2.30
AA	Invesco Balanced-Risk Ret 2030 C	TNACX	D+	(800) 959-4246	D / 2.0	3.22	5.26	7.35 /58	4.86 /13	7.98 /30	4.66	2.30
AA	● Invesco Balanced-Risk Ret 2030 CX	VRECX	D+	(800) 959-4246	D / 2.0	3.22	5.26	7.35 /58	4.86 /13	8.00 /30	4.66	2.30
AA	Invesco Balanced-Risk Ret 2030 R	TNARX	D+	(800) 959-4246	D+ / 2.4	3.43	5.55	7.97 /63	5.42 /15	8.55 /33	5.12	1.80
AA	Invesco Balanced-Risk Ret 2030 R5	TNAIX	D+	(800) 959-4246	D+ / 2.7	3.51	5.81	8.45 /66	5.90 /16	9.08 /37	5.59	1.20
GI	Invesco Balanced-Risk Ret 2030 R6	TNAFX	C+	(800) 959-4246	D+ / 2.6	3.51	5.81	8.45 /66	5.87 /16	8.95 /36	5.59	1.11
AA	● Invesco Balanced-Risk Ret 2030 RX	VRERX	D+	(800) 959-4246	D+ / 2.3	3.44	5.54	7.85 /62	5.38 /14	8.55 /33	5.13	1.80
AA	Invesco Balanced-Risk Ret 2030 Y	TNAYX	D+	(800) 959-4246	D+ / 2.7	3.52	5.82	8.47 /66	5.92 /16	9.07 /37	5.60	1.30
AA	Invesco Balanced-Risk Ret 2040 A	TNDAX	D	(800) 959-4246	D / 2.2	3.97	6.62	9.51 /72	6.17 /17	9.14 /38	6.46	1.86
AA	● Invesco Balanced-Risk Ret 2040 AX	VRGAX	D	(800) 959-4246	D / 2.2	3.97	6.51	9.52 /72	6.17 /17	9.12 /38	6.47	1.86
AA	● Invesco Balanced-Risk Ret 2040 B	TNDBX	D	(800) 959-4246	D+ / 2.5	3.76	6.02	8.54 /67	5.34 /14	8.30 /32	6.17	2.61
AA	Invesco Balanced-Risk Ret 2040 C	TNDCX	D	(800) 959-4246	D+ / 2.5	3.77	6.15	8.55 /67	5.35 /14	8.29 /32	6.18	2.61
AA	● Invesco Balanced-Risk Ret 2040 CX	VRGCX	D	(800) 959-4246	D+ / 2.5	3.77	6.03	8.56 /67	5.35 /14	8.30 /32	6.18	2.61
AA	Invesco Balanced-Risk Ret 2040 R	TNDRX	D	(800) 959-4246	D+ / 2.8	3.99	6.39	9.29 /71	5.91 /16	8.88 /36	6.61	2.11
AA	Invesco Balanced-Risk Ret 2040 R5	TNDIX	D+	(800) 959-4246	C- / 3.2	4.07	6.74	9.87 /74	6.48 /19	9.42 /40	7.05	1.46
GI	Invesco Balanced-Risk Ret 2040 R6	TNDFX	C+	(800) 959-4246	C- / 3.1	3.95	6.62	9.74 /73	6.40 /18	9.28 /39	7.06	1.36
AA	● Invesco Balanced-Risk Ret 2040 RX	VRGRX	D	(800) 959-4246	D+ / 2.8	3.86	6.38	9.15 /70	5.90 /16	8.86 /36	6.61	2.11
AA	Invesco Balanced-Risk Ret 2040 Y	TNDYX	D+	(800) 959-4246	C- / 3.1	3.96	6.64	9.77 /73	6.41 /19	9.41 /40	7.06	1.61
AA	Invesco Balanced-Risk Ret 2050 A	TNEAX	D+	(800) 959-4246	D+ / 2.7	4.51	7.55	10.89 /78	6.72 /20	9.49 /40	6.94	2.42
AA	● Invesco Balanced-Risk Ret 2050 AX	VRIAX	D+	(800) 959-4246	D+ / 2.6	4.51	7.43	10.75 /77	6.72 /20	9.45 /40	6.94	2.42
AA	● Invesco Balanced-Risk Ret 2050 B	TNEBX	D+	(800) 959-4246	C- / 3.0	4.33	7.05	10.03 /74	5.95 /17	8.66 /34	6.76	3.17
AA	Invesco Balanced-Risk Ret 2050 C	TNECX	D+	(800) 959-4246	C- / 3.0	4.32	7.04	9.88 /74	5.90 /16	8.65 /34	6.75	3.17
AA	● Invesco Balanced-Risk Ret 2050 CX	VRICX	D+	(800) 959-4246	C- / 3.0	4.32	7.04	10.02 /74	5.94 /16	8.65 /34	6.75	3.17
AA	Invesco Balanced-Risk Ret 2050 R	TNERX	D+	(800) 959-4246	C- / 3.3	4.41	7.22	10.43 /76	6.43 /19	9.18 /38	7.15	2.67
AA	Invesco Balanced-Risk Ret 2050 R5	TNEIX	C-	(800) 959-4246	C- / 3.7	4.63	7.66	11.12 /79	6.99 /21	9.76 /43	7.55	1.92
GI	Invesco Balanced-Risk Ret 2050 R6	TNEFX	C+	(800) 959-4246	C- / 3.7	4.62	7.65	11.10 /79	6.95 /21	9.63 /42	7.54	1.83
AA	● Invesco Balanced-Risk Ret 2050 RX	VRIRX	C-	(800) 959-4246	C- / 3.3	4.41	7.33	10.55 /77	6.43 /19	9.20 /38	7.14	2.67
AA	Invesco Balanced-Risk Ret 2050 Y	TNEYX	C-	(800) 959-4246	C- / 3.7	4.37	7.55	11.00 /78	7.00 /21	9.71 /42	7.56	2.17
AA	Invesco Balanced-Risk Ret Now A	IANAX	D+	(800) 959-4246	E+ / 0.8	1.92	3.10	4.36 /34	3.15 / 8	5.14 /13	2.66	1.39
AA	● Invesco Balanced-Risk Ret Now AX	VIRAX	D+	(800) 959-4246	E+ / 0.8	1.92	3.10	4.36 /34	3.16 / 8	5.12 /12	2.66	1.39
AA	● Invesco Balanced-Risk Ret Now B	IANBX	D+	(800) 959-4246	E+ / 0.9	1.76	2.71	3.65 /30	2.41 / 7	4.34 /10	2.43	2.14
AA	Invesco Balanced-Risk Ret Now C	IANCX	D+	(800) 959-4246	E+ / 0.9	1.65	2.71	3.64 /30	2.41 / 7	4.34 /10	2.43	2.14
AA	● Invesco Balanced-Risk Ret Now CX	VIRCX	D+	(800) 959-4246	E+ / 0.9	1.76	2.71	3.65 /30	2.41 / 7	4.34 /10	2.43	2.14
AA	Invesco Balanced-Risk Ret Now R	IANRX	D+	(800) 959-4246	D- / 1.1	1.86	2.97	4.12 /33	2.91 / 8	4.87 /11	2.68	1.64
AA	Invesco Balanced-Risk Ret Now R5	IANIX	C-	(800) 959-4246	D- / 1.2	1.85	3.12	4.60 /36	3.39 / 9	5.39 /14	2.94	1.08

● Denotes fund is closed to new investors
* Denotes fund is included in Section II

www.thestreetratings.com

RISK	3 Year		NET ASSETS		ASSET				Portfolio	BULL / BEAR		FUND MANAGER		MINIMUMS		LOADS	
Risk Rating/Pts	Standard Deviation	Beta	NAV As of 3/31/15	Total $(Mil)	Cash %	Stocks %	Bonds %	Other %	Turnover Ratio	Last Bull Market Return	Last Bear Market Return	Manager Quality Pct	Manager Tenure (Years)	Initial Purch. $	Additional Purch. $	Front End Load	Back End Load
D / 2.1	13.1	1.13	6.97	3	92	0	7	1	21	-24.4	-17.5	0	5	1,000	50	0.0	0.0
D / 2.1	13.0	1.11	7.12	N/A	92	0	7	1	21	-23.0	-17.3	0	5	0	0	0.0	0.0
D / 2.1	13.1	1.12	7.27	276	92	0	7	1	21	-21.6	-17.2	0	5	10,000,000	0	0.0	0.0
C+ / 6.1	13.0	0.66	7.27	128	92	0	7	1	21	-21.9	-17.2	0	5	10,000,000	0	0.0	0.0
D / 2.1	13.1	1.13	7.26	245	92	0	7	1	21	-21.7	-17.1	0	5	1,000	50	0.0	0.0
B- / 7.7	5.2	0.64	9.34	49	85	0	14	1	7	26.8	1.5	36	8	1,000	50	5.5	0.0
B- / 7.7	5.2	0.63	9.34	10	85	0	14	1	7	26.8	1.5	37	5	1,000	50	5.5	0.0
B- / 7.9	5.1	0.61	9.22	2	85	0	14	1	7	23.6	1.2	30	8	1,000	50	0.0	0.0
B- / 7.9	5.2	0.63	9.20	10	85	0	14	1	7	23.7	1.0	28	8	1,000	50	0.0	0.0
B- / 7.8	5.2	0.63	9.20	3	85	0	14	1	7	23.5	1.2	27	5	1,000	50	0.0	0.0
B- / 7.7	5.2	0.64	9.30	8	85	0	14	1	7	25.7	1.3	33	8	0	0	0.0	0.0
B- / 7.6	5.2	0.63	9.40	30	85	0	14	1	7	27.9	1.6	41	8	10,000,000	0	0.0	0.0
B+ / 9.7	5.2	0.31	9.41	1	85	0	14	1	7	27.7	1.5	69	6	10,000,000	0	0.0	0.0
B- / 7.7	5.2	0.63	9.30	1	85	0	14	1	7	25.7	1.3	34	5	0	0	0.0	0.0
B- / 7.6	5.2	0.63	9.35	7	85	0	14	1	7	27.9	1.5	41	7	1,000	50	0.0	0.0
C+ / 6.9	6.4	0.76	9.09	50	75	0	24	1	9	31.1	1.4	31	8	1,000	50	5.5	0.0
C+ / 6.9	6.4	0.77	9.10	7	75	0	24	1	9	31.2	1.4	32	5	1,000	50	5.5	0.0
B- / 7.1	6.4	0.76	8.98	2	75	0	24	1	9	27.9	1.1	24	8	1,000	50	0.0	0.0
B- / 7.1	6.4	0.76	8.97	14	75	0	24	1	9	27.9	1.1	23	8	1,000	50	0.0	0.0
B- / 7.1	6.4	0.77	8.97	2	75	0	24	1	9	27.9	1.1	23	5	1,000	50	0.0	0.0
B- / 7.0	6.4	0.77	9.04	12	75	0	24	1	9	30.0	1.3	29	8	0	0	0.0	0.0
C+ / 6.9	6.4	0.76	9.14	31	75	0	24	1	9	32.3	1.6	35	8	10,000,000	0	0.0	0.0
B+ / 9.3	6.5	0.37	9.14	1	75	0	24	1	9	32.0	1.4	69	6	10,000,000	0	0.0	0.0
B- / 7.0	6.4	0.76	9.03	1	75	0	24	1	9	29.9	1.4	29	5	0	0	0.0	0.0
C+ / 6.9	6.5	0.77	9.12	6	75	0	24	1	9	32.4	1.4	34	7	1,000	50	0.0	0.0
C+ / 6.1	7.2	0.85	8.39	35	61	0	38	1	8	33.1	1.4	28	8	1,000	50	5.5	0.0
C+ / 6.1	7.2	0.84	8.38	3	61	0	38	1	8	33.1	1.4	28	5	1,000	50	5.5	0.0
C+ / 6.2	7.2	0.85	8.27	1	61	0	38	1	8	29.7	1.1	19	8	1,000	50	0.0	0.0
C+ / 6.2	7.2	0.85	8.26	7	61	0	38	1	8	29.8	1.1	19	8	1,000	50	0.0	0.0
C+ / 6.2	7.2	0.84	8.25	1	61	0	38	1	8	29.6	1.1	20	5	1,000	50	0.0	0.0
C+ / 6.1	7.2	0.84	8.34	9	61	0	38	1	8	32.0	1.3	26	8	0	0	0.0	0.0
C+ / 6.1	7.2	0.84	8.43	27	61	0	38	1	8	34.4	1.5	32	8	10,000,000	0	0.0	0.0
B+ / 9.0	7.3	0.41	8.42	1	61	0	38	1	8	34.0	1.4	68	6	10,000,000	0	0.0	0.0
C+ / 6.1	7.3	0.85	8.34	1	61	0	38	1	8	32.2	1.3	25	5	0	0	0.0	0.0
C+ / 6.0	7.2	0.84	8.41	3	61	0	38	1	8	34.1	1.6	31	7	1,000	50	0.0	0.0
C+ / 6.5	8.1	0.93	8.34	16	48	0	51	1	8	35.1	1.5	24	8	1,000	50	5.5	0.0
C+ / 6.5	8.1	0.92	8.34	1	48	0	51	1	8	35.2	1.4	25	5	1,000	50	5.5	0.0
C+ / 6.6	8.0	0.91	8.20	N/A	48	0	51	1	8	31.6	1.2	19	8	1,000	50	0.0	0.0
C+ / 6.6	8.0	0.93	8.21	5	48	0	51	1	8	31.7	1.2	17	8	1,000	50	0.0	0.0
C+ / 6.6	8.0	0.92	8.21	N/A	48	0	51	1	8	31.6	1.2	18	5	1,000	50	0.0	0.0
C+ / 6.5	8.1	0.92	8.28	5	48	0	51	1	8	33.9	1.4	22	8	0	0	0.0	0.0
C+ / 6.5	8.1	0.93	8.37	9	48	0	51	1	8	36.3	1.5	27	8	10,000,000	0	0.0	0.0
B / 8.9	8.1	0.44	8.38	1	48	0	51	1	8	35.9	1.5	69	6	10,000,000	0	0.0	0.0
C+ / 6.5	8.1	0.92	8.29	N/A	48	0	51	1	8	33.9	1.3	22	5	0	0	0.0	0.0
C+ / 6.5	8.0	0.92	8.36	3	48	0	51	1	8	36.2	1.5	28	7	1,000	50	0.0	0.0
B / 8.6	3.6	0.42	8.92	14	89	0	10	1	9	17.2	0.9	48	8	1,000	50	5.5	0.0
B / 8.6	3.5	0.43	8.91	11	89	0	10	1	9	17.2	0.8	47	5	1,000	50	5.5	0.0
B / 8.5	3.5	0.42	8.72	N/A	89	0	10	1	9	14.1	0.6	37	8	1,000	50	0.0	0.0
B / 8.4	3.6	0.44	8.72	4	89	0	10	1	9	14.2	0.6	35	8	1,000	50	0.0	0.0
B / 8.4	3.5	0.42	8.72	3	89	0	10	1	9	14.1	0.6	38	5	1,000	50	0.0	0.0
B / 8.6	3.6	0.44	8.87	2	89	0	10	1	9	16.0	0.8	42	8	0	0	0.0	0.0
B / 8.7	3.5	0.43	8.98	4	89	0	10	1	9	18.2	1.0	50	8	10,000,000	0	0.0	0.0

Fund Type	Fund Name	Ticker Symbol	Overall Investment Rating	Phone	Perfor-mance Rating/Pts	Total Return % through 3/31/15			Annualized		Incl. in Returns	
	99 Pct = Best 0 Pct = Worst					3 Mo	6 Mo	1Yr / Pct	3Yr / Pct	5Yr / Pct	Dividend Yield	Expense Ratio
AA	Invesco Balanced-Risk Ret Now R6	IANFX	C	(800) 959-4246	D- / 1.2	1.85	3.12	4.60 /36	3.35 / 9	5.27 /13	2.94	0.99
AA	● Invesco Balanced-Risk Ret Now RX	VIRRX	D+	(800) 959-4246	D- / 1.0	1.75	2.86	4.12 /33	2.88 / 8	4.84 /11	2.68	1.64
AA	Invesco Balanced-Risk Ret Now Y	IANYX	C-	(800) 959-4246	D- / 1.2	1.97	3.23	4.72 /37	3.43 / 9	5.41 /14	2.93	1.14
GI	Invesco Charter A	CHTRX	C-	(800) 959-4246	C- / 4.2	0.19	1.32	4.83 /37	12.32 /55	10.15 /46	0.51	1.09
GI	● Invesco Charter B	BCHTX	C-	(800) 959-4246	C / 4.5	0.05	0.96	4.05 /32	11.49 /49	9.34 /39	0.00	1.84
GI	Invesco Charter C	CHTCX	C-	(800) 959-4246	C / 4.5	0.05	0.96	4.04 /32	11.50 /49	9.34 /39	0.00	1.84
GI	Invesco Charter R	CHRRX	C	(800) 959-4246	C / 4.9	0.14	1.20	4.55 /35	12.04 /53	9.88 /44	0.26	1.34
GI	Invesco Charter R5	CHTVX	C	(800) 959-4246	C / 5.3	0.28	1.50	5.17 /40	12.72 /58	10.56 /49	0.84	0.76
GI	Invesco Charter R6	CHFTX	B-	(800) 959-4246	C / 5.3	0.32	1.56	5.28 /41	12.74 /58	10.39 /48	0.94	0.67
GI	Invesco Charter S	CHRSX	C	(800) 959-4246	C / 5.1	0.24	1.38	4.94 /38	12.43 /56	10.27 /47	0.64	0.99
GI	Invesco Charter Y	CHTYX	C	(800) 959-4246	C / 5.3	0.24	1.45	5.09 /39	12.61 /57	10.43 /48	0.79	0.84
FO	Invesco China A	AACFX	D-	(800) 959-4246	D / 1.8	4.66	10.88	4.78 /37	6.23 /18	2.07 / 4	0.40	1.85
FO	● Invesco China B	ABCFX	D-	(800) 959-4246	D / 2.1	4.43	10.45	4.00 /32	5.43 /15	1.30 / 4	0.00	2.60
FO	Invesco China C	CACFX	D-	(800) 959-4246	D / 2.1	4.43	10.47	4.00 /32	5.44 /15	1.30 / 4	0.00	2.60
FO	Invesco China R5	IACFX	D-	(800) 959-4246	D+ / 2.9	4.77	11.14	5.26 /41	6.71 /20	2.53 / 5	0.94	1.39
FO	Invesco China Y	AMCYX	D-	(800) 959-4246	D+ / 2.7	4.71	11.03	5.05 /39	6.49 /19	2.33 / 5	0.70	1.60
* GI	Invesco Comstock A	ACSTX	B-	(800) 959-4246	C+ / 6.2	-0.12	1.83	7.10 /56	15.81 /82	13.30 /71	1.54	0.83
GI	● Invesco Comstock B	ACSWX	B+	(800) 959-4246	B- / 7.1	-0.12	1.83	7.05 /55	15.65 /80	13.20 /70	1.63	0.83
GI	Invesco Comstock C	ACSYX	B-	(800) 959-4246	C+ / 6.6	-0.31	1.44	6.25 /49	14.93 /74	12.44 /64	0.88	1.58
GI	Invesco Comstock R	ACSRX	B+	(800) 959-4246	B- / 7.0	-0.18	1.70	6.83 /54	15.53 /79	13.01 /68	1.38	1.08
GI	Invesco Comstock R5	ACSHX	B+	(800) 959-4246	B- / 7.5	-0.03	2.00	7.46 /59	16.22 /85	13.70 /75	1.97	0.51
GI	Invesco Comstock R6	ICSFX	A-	(800) 959-4246	B / 7.6	-0.01	2.05	7.52 /59	16.24 /85	13.55 /73	2.06	0.42
GI	Invesco Comstock Y	ACSDX	B+	(800) 959-4246	B- / 7.5	-0.06	1.96	7.36 /58	16.10 /84	13.58 /74	1.88	0.58
AA	Invesco Cons Alloc A	CAAMX	C-	(800) 959-4246	D- / 1.4	1.91	2.86	4.75 /37	6.01 /17	6.77 /22	2.46	1.10
AA	● Invesco Cons Alloc B	CMBAX	C-	(800) 959-4246	D / 1.6	1.64	2.49	3.99 /32	5.20 /14	5.97 /17	1.84	1.85
AA	Invesco Cons Alloc C	CACMX	C-	(800) 959-4246	D / 1.6	1.64	2.49	3.89 /31	5.19 /14	5.96 /17	1.84	1.85
AA	Invesco Cons Alloc R	CMARX	C-	(800) 959-4246	D / 1.8	1.85	2.74	4.49 /35	5.75 /16	6.51 /20	2.35	1.35
AA	Invesco Cons Alloc R5	CMAIX	C-	(800) 959-4246	D / 2.1	1.89	3.02	4.97 /38	6.31 /18	7.05 /23	2.91	0.80
AA	Invesco Cons Alloc S	CMASX	C-	(800) 959-4246	D / 2.0	1.84	2.91	4.76 /37	6.10 /17	6.86 /22	2.70	1.00
AA	Invesco Cons Alloc Y	CAAYX	C-	(800) 959-4246	D / 2.1	1.97	3.08	5.02 /39	6.29 /18	7.01 /23	2.85	0.85
CV	Invesco Convertible Securities A	CNSAX	C-	(800) 959-4246	C- / 3.1	1.88	2.26	2.25 /23	10.27 /41	9.55 /41	2.02	0.90
CV	● Invesco Convertible Securities B	CNSBX	C-	(800) 959-4246	C- / 3.4	1.64	1.82	1.43 /20	9.44 /36	8.71 /35	1.37	1.66
CV	Invesco Convertible Securities C	CNSCX	C-	(800) 959-4246	C- / 3.5	1.77	2.07	1.67 /21	9.57 /37	8.80 /35	1.48	1.66
CV	Invesco Convertible Securities R5	CNSIX	C	(800) 959-4246	C- / 4.1	1.95	2.42	2.56 /24	10.63 /43	9.83 /43	2.44	0.59
CV	Invesco Convertible Securities R6	CNSFX	C	(800) 959-4246	C- / 4.1	1.93	2.41	2.57 /24	10.58 /42	9.73 /42	2.49	0.57
CV	Invesco Convertible Securities Y	CNSDX	C	(800) 959-4246	C- / 4.1	1.90	2.34	2.46 /24	10.53 /42	9.81 /43	2.37	0.66
EM	● Invesco Developing Markets A	GTDDX	E	(800) 959-4246	E- / 0.2	-3.39	-9.17	-7.25 / 4	-1.45 / 3	2.13 / 5	1.05	1.43
EM	● Invesco Developing Markets B	GTDBX	E	(800) 959-4246	E / 0.3	-3.57	-9.50	-7.93 / 3	-2.19 / 3	1.37 / 4	0.19	2.18
EM	● Invesco Developing Markets C	GTDCX	E	(800) 959-4246	E / 0.3	-3.57	-9.48	-7.94 / 3	-2.18 / 3	1.37 / 4	0.19	2.18
EM	● Invesco Developing Markets R5	GTDIX	E	(800) 959-4246	E / 0.3	-3.32	-9.00	-6.88 / 4	-1.07 / 3	2.54 / 5	1.61	1.03
EM	● Invesco Developing Markets R6	GTDFX	D-	(800) 959-4246	E / 0.3	-3.32	-8.98	-6.86 / 4	-1.10 / 3	2.35 / 5	1.64	1.01
EM	● Invesco Developing Markets Y	GTDYX	E	(800) 959-4246	E / 0.3	-3.35	-9.08	-7.02 / 4	-1.21 / 3	2.39 / 5	1.44	1.18
GI	Invesco Diversified Dividend A	LCEAX	A-	(800) 959-4246	B- / 7.2	2.06	7.68	10.18 /75	16.19 /85	13.10 /69	1.39	0.85
GI	● Invesco Diversified Dividend B	LCEDX	A	(800) 959-4246	B / 7.6	1.88	7.29	9.33 /71	15.33 /78	12.26 /62	0.75	1.60
GI	Invesco Diversified Dividend C	LCEVX	A	(800) 959-4246	B / 7.6	1.89	7.30	9.34 /71	15.32 /77	12.26 /62	0.74	1.60
GI	Invesco Diversified Dividend Inv	LCEIX	A+	(800) 959-4246	B+ / 8.3	2.02	7.72	10.23 /75	16.22 /85	13.16 /70	1.51	0.78
GI	Invesco Diversified Dividend R	DDFRX	A+	(800) 959-4246	B / 8.0	1.99	7.58	9.88 /74	15.90 /83	12.85 /67	1.23	1.10
GI	Invesco Diversified Dividend R5	DDFIX	A+	(800) 959-4246	B+ / 8.5	2.14	7.91	10.51 /76	16.57 /87	13.49 /73	1.75	0.56
GR	Invesco Diversified Dividend R6	LCEFX	A+	(800) 959-4246	B+ / 8.5	2.16	7.90	10.62 /77	16.56 /87	13.32 /71	1.85	0.46
GI	Invesco Diversified Dividend Y	LCEYX	A+	(800) 959-4246	B+ / 8.5	2.12	7.87	10.45 /76	16.49 /87	13.39 /72	1.71	0.60
UT	Invesco Dividend Income A	IAUTX	B-	(800) 959-4246	C+ / 6.4	1.55	7.92	12.88 /86	14.48 /71	13.31 /71	1.84	1.30
UT	● Invesco Dividend Income B	IBUTX	B-	(800) 959-4246	C+ / 6.8	1.36	7.50	12.01 /83	13.62 /64	12.46 /64	1.24	2.05

● Denotes fund is closed to new investors
* Denotes fund is included in Section II

www.thestreetratings.com

RISK			NET ASSETS		ASSET				Portfolio Turnover Ratio	BULL / BEAR		FUND MANAGER		MINIMUMS		LOADS	
Risk Rating/Pts	3 Year		NAV As of 3/31/15	Total $(Mil)	Cash %	Stocks %	Bonds %	Other %		Last Bull Market Return	Last Bear Market Return	Manager Quality Pct	Manager Tenure (Years)	Initial Purch. $	Additional Purch. $	Front End Load	Back End Load
	Standard Deviation	Beta															
B+ / 9.9	3.5	0.43	8.98	N/A	89	0	10	1	9	17.9	0.9	49	6	10,000,000	0	0.0	0.0
B / 8.6	3.5	0.43	8.85	N/A	89	0	10	1	9	16.2	0.7	43	5	0	0	0.0	0.0
B / 8.7	3.5	0.42	8.99	2	89	0	10	1	9	18.2	1.0	52	7	1,000	50	0.0	0.0
C+ / 6.2	8.8	0.88	21.11	4,315	11	88	0	1	23	71.3	-15.1	43	13	1,000	50	5.5	0.0
C+ / 6.2	8.8	0.88	20.10	65	11	88	0	1	23	67.0	-15.4	33	13	1,000	50	0.0	0.0
C+ / 6.2	8.8	0.88	20.16	272	11	88	0	1	23	67.1	-15.5	33	13	1,000	50	0.0	0.0
C+ / 6.3	8.8	0.88	20.95	53	11	88	0	1	23	69.9	-15.3	40	13	0	0	0.0	0.0
C+ / 6.3	8.8	0.88	21.83	324	11	88	0	1	23	73.4	-15.0	49	13	10,000,000	0	0.0	0.0
B- / 7.8	8.8	0.88	21.83	134	11	88	0	1	23	73.0	-15.1	49	13	10,000,000	0	0.0	0.0
C+ / 6.2	8.8	0.88	21.12	22	11	88	0	1	23	71.9	-15.1	45	13	0	0	0.0	0.0
C+ / 6.2	8.8	0.88	21.18	384	11	88	0	1	23	72.9	-15.1	48	13	1,000	50	0.0	0.0
C / 5.1	16.2	0.69	20.87	60	1	98	0	1	124	32.5	-29.9	65	3	1,000	50	5.5	0.0
C / 5.0	16.3	0.69	20.29	4	1	98	0	1	124	29.2	-30.1	53	3	1,000	50	0.0	0.0
C / 5.0	16.3	0.68	20.26	16	1	98	0	1	124	29.2	-30.2	53	3	1,000	50	0.0	0.0
C / 5.1	16.3	0.69	20.88	N/A	1	98	0	1	124	34.6	-29.8	70	3	10,000,000	0	0.0	0.0
C / 5.1	16.3	0.69	20.88	3	1	98	0	1	124	33.6	-29.9	68	3	1,000	50	0.0	0.0
B- / 7.1	10.4	1.04	25.41	7,541	5	94	0	1	11	98.5	-20.2	55	20	1,000	50	5.5	0.0
B- / 7.1	10.4	1.04	25.40	133	5	94	0	1	11	97.7	-20.2	52	20	1,000	50	0.0	0.0
B- / 7.1	10.5	1.04	25.41	625	5	94	0	1	11	93.5	-20.5	42	20	1,000	50	0.0	0.0
B- / 7.1	10.4	1.04	25.41	479	5	94	0	1	11	96.8	-20.3	51	20	0	0	0.0	0.0
B- / 7.1	10.5	1.04	25.40	802	5	94	0	1	11	101.1	-20.0	59	20	10,000,000	0	0.0	0.0
B- / 7.4	10.4	1.04	25.39	580	5	94	0	1	11	100.7	-20.2	60	20	10,000,000	0	0.0	0.0
B- / 7.2	10.4	1.04	25.41	3,342	5	94	0	1	11	100.2	-20.1	59	20	1,000	50	0.0	0.0
B / 8.6	4.7	0.70	11.50	261	9	30	59	2	7	31.7	-4.9	46	N/A	1,000	50	5.5	0.0
B / 8.6	4.7	0.71	11.36	16	9	30	59	2	7	28.5	-5.2	33	N/A	1,000	50	0.0	0.0
B / 8.6	4.7	0.71	11.38	80	9	30	59	2	7	28.4	-5.3	33	N/A	1,000	50	0.0	0.0
B / 8.6	4.7	0.70	11.46	11	9	30	59	2	7	30.5	-4.9	42	N/A	0	0	0.0	0.0
B / 8.6	4.7	0.71	11.55	N/A	9	30	59	2	7	32.9	-4.7	49	N/A	10,000,000	0	0.0	0.0
B / 8.6	4.7	0.71	11.51	3	9	30	59	2	7	32.2	-4.8	46	N/A	0	0	0.0	0.0
B / 8.6	4.7	0.70	11.49	4	9	30	59	2	7	32.7	-4.8	49	N/A	1,000	50	0.0	0.0
B- / 7.2	7.1	0.93	24.19	941	10	10	0	80	56	53.2	-14.8	34	17	1,000	50	5.5	0.0
B- / 7.2	7.1	0.93	24.25	5	10	10	0	80	56	49.2	-15.0	26	17	1,000	50	0.0	0.0
B- / 7.2	7.1	0.93	24.08	225	10	10	0	80	56	49.7	-15.0	27	17	1,000	50	0.0	0.0
B- / 7.2	7.1	0.93	24.20	5	10	10	0	80	56	54.8	-14.7	39	17	10,000,000	0	0.0	0.0
B- / 7.4	7.1	0.93	24.20	17	10	10	0	80	56	54.4	-14.8	38	17	10,000,000	0	0.0	0.0
B- / 7.2	7.0	0.93	24.21	1,147	10	10	0	80	56	54.4	-14.7	38	17	1,000	50	0.0	0.0
C / 4.6	13.0	0.90	29.39	991	8	91	0	1	13	17.4	-20.3	36	12	1,000	50	5.5	0.0
C / 4.7	13.0	0.89	28.63	20	8	91	0	1	13	14.5	-20.6	27	12	1,000	50	0.0	0.0
C / 4.7	13.0	0.90	28.60	111	8	91	0	1	13	14.5	-20.6	27	12	1,000	50	0.0	0.0
C / 4.6	13.0	0.90	29.38	617	8	91	0	1	13	19.0	-20.1	42	12	10,000,000	0	0.0	0.0
B- / 7.0	13.0	0.90	29.37	174	8	91	0	1	13	18.7	-20.3	41	12	10,000,000	0	0.0	0.0
C / 4.6	13.0	0.90	29.43	1,342	8	91	0	1	13	18.5	-20.2	40	12	1,000	50	0.0	0.0
B- / 7.8	8.3	0.82	18.61	4,436	9	90	0	1	6	90.1	-15.9	88	13	1,000	50	5.5	0.0
B- / 7.8	8.3	0.81	18.42	28	9	90	0	1	6	85.3	-16.2	85	13	1,000	50	0.0	0.0
B- / 7.8	8.3	0.81	18.40	382	9	90	0	1	6	85.3	-16.2	85	13	1,000	50	0.0	0.0
B- / 7.8	8.3	0.81	18.60	2,012	9	90	0	1	6	90.3	-15.9	88	13	1,000	50	0.0	0.0
B- / 7.8	8.3	0.81	18.67	147	9	90	0	1	6	88.5	-16.0	87	13	0	0	0.0	0.0
B- / 7.8	8.3	0.82	18.61	2,238	9	90	0	1	6	92.2	-15.8	89	13	10,000,000	0	0.0	0.0
B- / 7.9	8.3	0.81	18.61	796	9	90	0	1	6	91.8	-15.9	89	13	10,000,000	0	0.0	0.0
B- / 7.8	8.3	0.82	18.63	901	9	90	0	1	6	91.6	-15.8	89	13	1,000	50	0.0	0.0
B- / 7.5	8.4	0.45	21.16	410	9	90	0	1	4	56.7	0.2	97	6	1,000	50	5.5	0.0
B- / 7.5	8.3	0.45	21.22	10	9	90	0	1	4	52.7	N/A	96	6	1,000	50	0.0	0.0

Fund Type	Fund Name	Ticker Symbol	Overall Investment Rating	Phone	Performance Rating/Pts	3 Mo	6 Mo	1Yr / Pct	3Yr / Pct	5Yr / Pct	Dividend Yield	Expense Ratio
UT	Invesco Dividend Income C	IUTCX	B-	(800) 959-4246	C+ / 6.8	1.35	7.48	12.02 /83	13.61 /64	12.45 /64	1.24	2.05
UT	● Invesco Dividend Income Investor	FSTUX	A-	(800) 959-4246	B- / 7.4	1.54	7.91	12.90 /86	14.48 /71	13.30 /71	1.95	1.30
UT	Invesco Dividend Income R5	FSIUX	A-	(800) 959-4246	B / 7.7	1.62	8.08	13.20 /87	14.84 /74	13.75 /75	2.22	0.88
UT	Invesco Dividend Income R6	IFUTX	A	(800) 959-4246	B / 7.6	1.64	8.11	13.24 /87	14.78 /73	13.48 /73	2.26	0.84
UT	Invesco Dividend Income Y	IAUYX	A-	(800) 959-4246	B / 7.6	1.60	8.04	13.12 /87	14.79 /73	13.58 /74	2.19	1.05
GL	Invesco Em Mkt Equity Y	IEMYX	E	(800) 959-4246	E / 0.3	3.85	-2.16	1.35 /20	-3.25 / 2	--	0.75	2.34
GL	Invesco Em Mkts Equity A	IEMAX	E	(800) 959-4246	E / 0.3	3.85	-2.22	1.16 /19	-3.44 / 2	--	0.41	2.59
GL	Invesco Em Mkts Equity C	IEMCX	E	(800) 959-4246	E / 0.3	3.59	-2.70	0.28 /16	-4.22 / 2	--	0.00	3.34
GL	Invesco Em Mkts Equity R	IEMRX	E	(800) 959-4246	E / 0.3	3.86	-2.32	0.79 /18	-3.72 / 2	--	0.22	2.84
GL	Invesco Em Mkts Equity R5	IEMIX	E	(800) 959-4246	E / 0.3	3.85	-2.16	1.35 /20	-3.26 / 2	--	0.75	2.04
EM	Invesco Em Mkts Equity R6	EMEFX	E+	(800) 959-4246	E / 0.3	3.85	-2.16	1.35 /20	-3.25 / 2	--	0.75	2.02
MC	Invesco Endeavor A	ATDAX	C	(800) 959-4246	C / 5.0	0.44	2.69	4.23 /33	13.75 /65	12.35 /63	0.00	1.33
MC	● Invesco Endeavor B	ATDBX	C	(800) 959-4246	C / 5.3	0.26	2.31	3.46 /29	12.92 /59	11.52 /57	0.00	2.08
MC	Invesco Endeavor C	ATDCX	C	(800) 959-4246	C / 5.3	0.26	2.31	3.46 /29	12.91 /59	11.50 /57	0.00	2.08
MC	Invesco Endeavor R	ATDRX	C	(800) 959-4246	C+ / 5.7	0.40	2.56	3.99 /32	13.47 /63	12.09 /61	0.00	1.58
MC	Invesco Endeavor R5	ATDIX	C+	(800) 959-4246	C+ / 6.2	0.56	2.87	4.65 /36	14.18 /68	12.84 /67	0.00	0.97
MC	Invesco Endeavor R6	ATDFX	B-	(800) 959-4246	C+ / 6.2	0.61	2.92	4.74 /37	14.20 /69	12.62 /65	0.00	0.88
MC	Invesco Endeavor Y	ATDYX	C+	(800) 959-4246	C+ / 6.1	0.52	2.84	4.50 /35	14.05 /67	12.64 /65	0.00	1.08
EN	Invesco Energy A	IENAX	E-	(800) 959-4246	E- / 0.1	-4.67	-24.49	-24.16 / 1	-2.94 / 2	0.46 / 3	0.34	1.15
EN	● Invesco Energy B	IENBX	E-	(800) 959-4246	E- / 0.1	-4.83	-24.76	-24.72 / 0	-3.66 / 2	-0.29 / 2	0.00	1.90
EN	Invesco Energy C	IEFCX	E-	(800) 959-4246	E- / 0.1	-4.83	-24.75	-24.71 / 0	-3.66 / 2	-0.29 / 2	0.00	1.90
EN	● Invesco Energy Inv	FSTEX	E-	(800) 959-4246	E- / 0.2	-4.63	-24.47	-24.14 / 1	-2.93 / 2	0.46 / 3	0.36	1.15
EN	Invesco Energy R5	IENIX	E-	(800) 959-4246	E- / 0.2	-4.54	-24.33	-23.86 / 1	-2.58 / 3	0.83 / 3	0.85	0.79
EN	Invesco Energy Y	IENYX	E-	(800) 959-4246	E- / 0.2	-4.58	-24.37	-23.95 / 1	-2.69 / 2	0.71 / 3	0.71	0.90
GI	Invesco Equally-Weighted S&P 500 A	VADAX	A-	(800) 959-4246	B+ / 8.3	1.68	7.69	12.55 /85	17.63 /93	15.36 /89	0.92	0.56
GI	● Invesco Equally-Weighted S&P 500 B	VADBX	A	(800) 959-4246	B+ / 8.6	1.47	7.27	11.68 /81	16.74 /88	14.50 /82	0.52	1.31
GI	Invesco Equally-Weighted S&P 500 C	VADCX	A	(800) 959-4246	B+ / 8.6	1.48	7.27	11.70 /81	16.75 /88	14.51 /82	0.53	1.31
GI	Invesco Equally-Weighted S&P 500 R	VADRX	A+	(800) 959-4246	A- / 9.0	1.60	7.55	12.24 /84	17.33 /91	15.07 /87	0.82	0.81
GI	Invesco Equally-Weighted S&P 500	VADFX	A+	(800) 959-4246	A- / 9.2	1.74	7.88	12.95 /86	17.94 /94	15.54 /90	1.22	0.22
GI	Invesco Equally-Weighted S&P 500 Y	VADDX	A+	(800) 959-4246	A- / 9.2	1.72	7.79	12.81 /86	17.91 /94	15.65 /91	1.16	0.31
* GI	Invesco Equity and Income A	ACEIX	C	(800) 959-4246	C / 4.4	0.01	2.03	6.53 /51	12.51 /56	10.06 /45	2.42	0.81
GI	● Invesco Equity and Income B	ACEQX	C	(800) 959-4246	C / 4.8	-0.18	1.64	5.71 /44	11.75 /51	9.54 /41	1.81	1.56
GI	Invesco Equity and Income C	ACERX	C	(800) 959-4246	C / 4.8	-0.08	1.74	5.80 /45	11.72 /51	9.25 /39	1.80	1.56
GI	Invesco Equity and Income R	ACESX	C+	(800) 959-4246	C / 5.2	0.05	2.00	6.35 /49	12.26 /54	9.79 /43	2.30	1.06
GI	Invesco Equity and Income R5	ACEKX	C+	(800) 959-4246	C+ / 5.6	0.20	2.30	6.99 /55	12.91 /59	10.08 /45	2.87	0.50
GI	Invesco Equity and Income R6	IEIFX	B	(800) 959-4246	C+ / 5.6	0.12	2.25	6.98 /55	12.90 /59	10.28 /47	2.95	0.41
GI	Invesco Equity and Income Y	ACETX	C+	(800) 959-4246	C / 5.5	0.08	2.16	6.80 /53	12.79 /58	10.34 /47	2.79	0.56
FO	Invesco European Growth A	AEDAX	D-	(800) 959-4246	D / 1.7	2.94	-0.09	-4.66 / 6	8.63 /31	8.81 /35	1.74	1.38
FO	● Invesco European Growth B	AEDBX	D-	(800) 959-4246	D / 2.0	2.74	-0.47	-5.38 / 5	7.81 /26	7.99 /30	1.20	2.13
FO	Invesco European Growth C	AEDCX	D-	(800) 959-4246	D / 2.0	2.77	-0.44	-5.38 / 5	7.82 /26	8.00 /30	1.20	2.13
FO	● Invesco European Growth Inv	EGINX	D-	(800) 959-4246	D+ / 2.5	2.95	-0.07	-4.64 / 6	8.67 /31	8.85 /36	1.88	1.35
FO	Invesco European Growth R	AEDRX	D-	(800) 959-4246	D+ / 2.3	2.89	-0.21	-4.92 / 6	8.36 /29	8.53 /33	1.60	1.63
FO	Invesco European Growth Y	AEDYX	D-	(800) 959-4246	D+ / 2.6	2.99	0.05	-4.45 / 6	8.89 /32	9.08 /37	2.12	1.13
FO	● Invesco European Small Company A	ESMAX	E+	(800) 959-4246	D / 2.0	0.16	-3.22	-12.80 / 2	11.07 /46	10.76 /51	1.97	1.52
FO	● Invesco European Small Company B	ESMBX	E+	(800) 959-4246	D+ / 2.4	0.00	-3.52	-13.44 / 2	10.28 /41	9.94 /44	1.18	2.27
FO	● Invesco European Small Company C	ESMCX	E+	(800) 959-4246	D+ / 2.3	-0.09	-3.60	-13.50 / 2	10.23 /41	9.92 /44	1.18	2.27
FO	● Invesco European Small Company Y	ESMYX	D-	(800) 959-4246	C- / 3.0	0.16	-3.14	-12.62 / 2	11.33 /48	11.03 /53	2.43	1.27
GI	● Invesco Exchange	ACEHX	C-	(800) 959-4246	C- / 3.6	1.03	-2.69	1.97 /22	10.35 /41	10.36 /47	1.02	0.49
GL	Invesco Global Core Equity A	AWSAX	D-	(800) 959-4246	D+ / 2.6	3.15	2.08	2.08 /22	9.40 /36	5.80 /16	1.02	1.30
GL	● Invesco Global Core Equity B	AWSBX	D-	(800) 959-4246	C- / 3.1	2.91	1.75	1.34 /20	8.79 /32	5.22 /13	0.30	2.05
GL	Invesco Global Core Equity C	AWSCX	D-	(800) 959-4246	C- / 3.0	2.91	1.75	1.34 /20	8.59 /30	5.01 /12	0.29	2.05
GL	Invesco Global Core Equity R	AWSRX	D	(800) 959-4246	C- / 3.3	3.00	1.92	1.86 /21	9.13 /34	5.54 /14	0.81	1.55

● Denotes fund is closed to new investors
* Denotes fund is included in Section II

www.thestreetratings.com

Risk Rating/Pts	3 Year Standard Deviation	Beta	NAV As of 3/31/15	Total $(Mil)	Cash %	Stocks %	Bonds %	Other %	Portfolio Turnover Ratio	Last Bull Market Return	Last Bear Market Return	Manager Quality Pct	Manager Tenure (Years)	Initial Purch. $	Additional Purch. $	Front End Load	Back End Load
B- / 7.5	8.4	0.46	21.41	62	9	90	0	1	4	52.7	-0.1	96	6	1,000	50	0.0	0.0
B- / 7.6	8.4	0.45	21.35	76	9	90	0	1	4	56.7	0.3	97	6	1,000	50	0.0	0.0
B- / 7.6	8.3	0.45	21.17	N/A	9	90	0	1	4	58.5	0.5	97	6	10,000,000	0	0.0	0.0
B- / 7.9	8.4	0.45	21.18	49	9	90	0	1	4	57.9	0.3	97	6	10,000,000	0	0.0	0.0
B- / 7.6	8.4	0.45	21.35	58	9	90	0	1	4	58.1	0.4	97	6	1,000	50	0.0	0.0
C / 4.3	14.8	0.90	7.28	3	2	97	0	1	94	6.5	N/A	1	4	1,000	50	0.0	0.0
C / 4.3	14.9	0.90	7.29	13	2	97	0	1	94	5.8	N/A	1	4	1,000	50	5.5	0.0
C / 4.3	14.8	0.89	7.21	3	2	97	0	1	94	3.1	N/A	1	4	1,000	50	0.0	0.0
C / 4.3	14.9	0.90	7.27	1	2	97	0	1	94	4.8	N/A	1	4	0	0	0.0	0.0
C / 4.3	14.9	0.90	7.28	1	2	97	0	1	94	6.5	N/A	1	4	10,000,000	0	0.0	0.0
C+ / 6.2	14.9	1.06	7.29	8	2	97	0	1	94	6.5	N/A	16	4	10,000,000	0	0.0	0.0
C+ / 6.0	11.1	0.86	20.76	185	29	70	0	1	27	81.4	-18.2	57	8	1,000	50	5.5	0.0
C+ / 5.8	11.1	0.86	18.93	4	29	70	0	1	27	76.9	-18.4	46	8	1,000	50	0.0	0.0
C+ / 5.8	11.1	0.86	18.94	52	29	70	0	1	27	76.9	-18.4	46	8	1,000	50	0.0	0.0
C+ / 6.0	11.1	0.86	20.24	33	29	70	0	1	27	79.9	-18.2	53	8	0	0	0.0	0.0
C+ / 6.1	11.1	0.86	21.56	44	29	70	0	1	27	84.0	-18.0	63	8	10,000,000	0	0.0	0.0
B- / 7.5	11.1	0.86	21.60	102	29	70	0	1	27	83.5	-18.2	63	8	10,000,000	0	0.0	0.0
C+ / 6.1	11.1	0.86	21.13	67	29	70	0	1	27	83.1	-18.1	61	8	1,000	50	0.0	0.0
D / 2.0	18.0	1.12	31.22	540	4	95	0	1	14	16.2	-31.3	4	2	1,000	50	5.5	0.0
D / 1.9	18.0	1.12	27.60	18	4	95	0	1	14	13.2	-31.5	3	2	1,000	50	0.0	0.0
D / 1.8	18.0	1.12	26.82	167	4	95	0	1	14	13.2	-31.6	3	2	1,000	50	0.0	0.0
D / 2.0	18.0	1.12	31.10	260	4	95	0	1	14	16.1	-31.3	4	2	1,000	50	0.0	0.0
D / 2.0	18.0	1.12	31.95	28	4	95	0	1	14	17.6	-31.2	5	2	10,000,000	0	0.0	0.0
D / 2.0	18.0	1.12	31.27	70	4	95	0	1	14	17.1	-31.2	4	2	1,000	50	0.0	0.0
C+ / 6.9	10.2	1.05	49.73	1,892	3	96	0	1	17	107.6	-19.9	73	5	1,000	50	5.5	0.0
C+ / 6.9	10.2	1.05	49.55	12	3	96	0	1	17	102.3	-20.1	65	5	1,000	50	0.0	0.0
C+ / 6.9	10.3	1.05	47.92	663	3	96	0	1	17	102.3	-20.2	65	5	1,000	50	0.0	0.0
C+ / 6.9	10.3	1.05	49.54	89	3	96	0	1	17	105.7	-20.0	71	5	0	0	0.0	0.0
B- / 7.2	10.3	1.05	50.17	180	3	96	0	1	17	109.2	-19.9	76	5	10,000,000	0	0.0	0.0
C+ / 6.9	10.3	1.05	50.13	1,841	3	96	0	1	17	109.4	-19.8	75	5	1,000	50	0.0	0.0
C+ / 6.8	7.1	0.72	10.32	10,226	9	63	20	8	60	69.1	-15.4	77	16	1,000	50	5.5	0.0
C+ / 6.8	7.1	0.72	10.10	346	9	63	20	8	60	65.5	-15.4	71	16	1,000	50	0.0	0.0
C+ / 6.8	7.1	0.72	10.16	1,692	9	63	20	8	60	64.7	-15.6	71	16	1,000	50	0.0	0.0
C+ / 6.8	7.1	0.72	10.38	234	9	63	20	8	60	67.5	-15.4	75	16	0	0	0.0	0.0
C+ / 6.8	7.1	0.72	10.33	465	9	63	20	8	60	70.8	-15.2	80	16	10,000,000	0	0.0	0.0
B / 8.4	7.1	0.73	10.32	142	9	63	20	8	60	70.8	-15.4	79	16	10,000,000	0	0.0	0.0
C+ / 6.8	7.1	0.72	10.32	774	9	63	20	8	60	70.5	-15.3	79	16	1,000	50	0.0	0.0
C / 5.3	11.8	0.87	35.72	524	5	94	0	1	18	56.7	-20.6	71	18	1,000	50	5.5	0.0
C / 5.3	11.8	0.87	33.36	6	5	94	0	1	18	52.8	-20.9	62	18	1,000	50	0.0	0.0
C / 5.3	11.8	0.87	33.40	94	5	94	0	1	18	52.7	-20.9	62	18	1,000	50	0.0	0.0
C / 5.2	11.8	0.87	35.62	170	5	94	0	1	18	56.9	-20.7	72	18	1,000	50	0.0	0.0
C / 5.3	11.8	0.87	35.60	16	5	94	0	1	18	55.4	-20.7	69	18	0	0	0.0	0.0
C / 5.2	11.8	0.87	35.77	624	5	94	0	1	18	58.0	-20.6	74	18	1,000	50	0.0	0.0
C- / 4.2	12.8	0.84	12.38	155	4	95	0	1	14	57.0	-19.1	88	15	1,000	50	5.5	0.0
C- / 4.2	12.8	0.84	11.65	3	4	95	0	1	14	53.2	-19.5	85	15	1,000	50	0.0	0.0
C- / 4.2	12.8	0.84	11.66	30	4	95	0	1	14	53.1	-19.5	85	15	1,000	50	0.0	0.0
C- / 4.2	12.8	0.84	12.42	134	4	95	0	1	14	58.4	-19.1	89	15	1,000	50	0.0	0.0
C+ / 6.9	10.8	1.02	585.66	71	1	98	0	1	0	62.8	-18.6	9	5	1,000	25	0.0	0.0
C / 4.9	11.6	0.84	14.08	934	1	98	0	1	122	56.4	-24.0	80	7	1,000	50	5.5	0.0
C / 4.9	11.6	0.84	13.42	30	1	98	0	1	122	53.7	-24.1	75	7	1,000	50	0.0	0.0
C / 4.9	11.6	0.84	13.45	110	1	98	0	1	122	52.5	-24.2	74	7	1,000	50	0.0	0.0
C / 4.9	11.6	0.84	14.07	1	1	98	0	1	122	55.1	-24.0	78	7	0	0	0.0	0.0

Fund Type	Fund Name	Ticker Symbol	Overall Investment Rating	Phone	Performance Rating/Pts	3 Mo	6 Mo	1Yr / Pct	3Yr / Pct	5Yr / Pct	Dividend Yield	Expense Ratio
GL	Invesco Global Core Equity R5	AWSIX	D	(800) 959-4246	C- / 3.7	3.18	2.33	2.46 /24	9.76 /38	6.21 /18	1.43	0.95
GL	Invesco Global Core Equity Y	AWSYX	D	(800) 959-4246	C- / 3.7	3.15	2.23	2.37 /23	9.66 /37	6.05 /17	1.34	1.05
GL	Invesco Global Growth A	AGGAX	C-	(800) 959-4246	C / 4.4	2.87	3.65	6.05 /47	12.09 /53	10.17 /46	0.54	1.43
GL	● Invesco Global Growth B	AGGBX	C-	(800) 959-4246	C / 4.7	2.67	3.23	5.24 /40	11.25 /47	9.35 /39	0.00	2.18
GL	Invesco Global Growth C	AGGCX	C-	(800) 959-4246	C / 4.7	2.67	3.27	5.28 /41	11.25 /47	9.35 /39	0.00	2.18
GL	Invesco Global Growth R5	GGAIX	C	(800) 959-4246	C+ / 5.6	2.99	3.85	6.51 /51	12.57 /56	10.68 /50	0.99	0.94
GL	Invesco Global Growth R6	AGGFX	B-	(800) 959-4246	C+ / 5.6	2.99	3.85	6.54 /51	12.51 /56	10.42 /48	0.99	0.94
GL	Invesco Global Growth Y	AGGYX	C	(800) 959-4246	C / 5.5	2.94	3.74	6.31 /49	12.35 /55	10.44 /48	0.78	1.18
HL	Invesco Global Health Care A	GGHCX	A-	(800) 959-4246	A+ / 9.9	8.56	14.05	25.57 /98	25.87 /99	18.51 /98	0.00	1.09
HL	● Invesco Global Health Care B	GTHBX	B+	(800) 959-4246	A+ / 9.9	8.34	13.60	24.62 /98	24.93 /99	17.61 /97	0.00	1.84
HL	Invesco Global Health Care C	GTHCX	B+	(800) 959-4246	A+ / 9.9	8.36	13.61	24.62 /98	24.92 /99	17.62 /97	0.00	1.84
HL	Invesco Global Health Care Inv	GTHIX	A-	(800) 959-4246	A+ / 9.9	8.55	14.05	25.57 /98	25.86 /99	18.50 /98	0.00	1.09
HL	Invesco Global Health Care Y	GGHYX	A-	(800) 959-4246	A+ / 9.9	8.61	14.19	25.86 /98	26.18 /99	18.80 /98	0.03	0.84
GL	Invesco Global Low Vol Eq Yld A	GTNDX	D-	(800) 959-4246	D- / 1.5	-1.06	-6.36	-6.16 / 4	9.16 /34	8.79 /35	3.66	1.54
GL	● Invesco Global Low Vol Eq Yld B	GNDBX	D-	(800) 959-4246	D / 1.7	-1.22	-6.69	-6.92 / 4	8.34 /29	7.99 /30	3.05	2.29
GL	Invesco Global Low Vol Eq Yld C	GNDCX	D-	(800) 959-4246	D / 1.7	-1.22	-6.70	-6.87 / 4	8.37 /29	8.00 /30	3.05	2.29
GL	Invesco Global Low Vol Eq Yld R	GTNRX	D	(800) 959-4246	D / 2.0	-1.12	-6.47	-6.45 / 4	8.87 /32	8.54 /33	3.60	1.79
GL	Invesco Global Low Vol Eq Yld R5	GNDIX	D	(800) 959-4246	D+ / 2.5	-0.91	-6.10	-5.71 / 5	9.72 /38	9.42 /40	4.39	1.02
GL	Invesco Global Low Vol Eq Yld Y	GTNYX	D	(800) 959-4246	D+ / 2.3	-0.99	-6.23	-5.90 / 5	9.40 /36	9.05 /37	4.15	1.29
GL	Invesco Global Markets Strategy R6	GMSLX	U	(800) 959-4246	U /	1.27	7.06	10.14 /75	--	--	1.75	1.78
GL	Invesco Global Markets Strategy Y	GMSHX	U	(800) 959-4246	U /	1.27	7.06	10.14 /75	--	--	1.75	1.90
RE	Invesco Global Real Estate A	AGREX	C-	(800) 959-4246	C / 5.5	3.98	10.79	14.51 /91	11.34 /48	10.38 /48	2.24	1.46
RE	● Invesco Global Real Estate B	BGREX	C	(800) 959-4246	C+ / 5.9	3.86	10.42	13.69 /89	10.52 /42	9.56 /41	1.45	2.21
RE	Invesco Global Real Estate C	CGREX	C	(800) 959-4246	C+ / 5.8	3.85	10.41	13.68 /89	10.51 /42	9.57 /41	1.45	2.21
RE	Invesco Global Real Estate Inc A	ASRAX	C-	(800) 959-4246	C- / 3.5	2.55	7.49	11.29 /80	8.82 /32	9.90 /44	4.19	1.28
RE	● Invesco Global Real Estate Inc B	SARBX	C-	(800) 959-4246	C- / 3.9	2.47	7.21	10.57 /77	8.03 /27	9.10 /37	3.68	2.03
RE	Invesco Global Real Estate Inc C	ASRCX	C-	(800) 959-4246	C- / 3.8	2.36	7.09	10.45 /76	8.00 /27	9.08 /37	3.68	2.03
RE	Invesco Global Real Estate Inc R5	ASRIX	C	(800) 959-4246	C / 4.6	2.63	7.67	11.64 /81	9.21 /34	10.28 /47	4.74	0.92
RE	Invesco Global Real Estate Inc R6	ASRFX	B-	(800) 959-4246	C / 4.6	2.65	7.70	11.85 /82	9.27 /35	10.17 /46	4.82	0.88
RE	Invesco Global Real Estate Inc Y	ASRYX	C	(800) 959-4246	C / 4.5	2.62	7.65	11.59 /81	9.11 /34	10.17 /46	4.68	1.03
RE	Invesco Global Real Estate R	RGREX	C	(800) 959-4246	C+ / 6.2	3.99	10.66	14.23 /90	11.06 /46	10.10 /45	2.06	1.71
RE	Invesco Global Real Estate R5	IGREX	C+	(800) 959-4246	C+ / 6.8	4.13	11.09	15.15 /92	11.98 /52	11.02 /53	3.05	0.89
RE	Invesco Global Real Estate R6	FGREX	C+	(800) 959-4246	C+ / 6.8	4.23	11.14	15.23 /92	11.92 /52	10.72 /50	3.11	0.85
RE	Invesco Global Real Estate Y	ARGYX	C	(800) 959-4246	C+ / 6.6	4.04	10.91	14.77 /91	11.61 /50	10.67 /50	2.67	1.21
GL	Invesco Global Sm and Mid Cp Gro A	AGAAX	D-	(800) 959-4246	C- / 3.4	1.75	0.54	3.25 /28	10.98 /45	9.64 /42	0.52	1.37
GL	● Invesco Global Sm and Mid Cp Gro B	AGABX	D-	(800) 959-4246	C- / 3.8	1.58	0.16	2.48 /24	10.15 /40	8.81 /35	0.00	2.12
GL	Invesco Global Sm and Mid Cp Gro C	AGACX	D-	(800) 959-4246	C- / 3.8	1.58	0.11	2.48 /24	10.14 /40	8.82 /35	0.00	2.12
GL	Invesco Global Sm and Mid Cp Gro	GAIIX	D	(800) 959-4246	C / 4.5	1.87	0.69	3.61 /30	11.43 /48	10.12 /46	0.94	0.98
GL	Invesco Global Sm and Mid Cp Gro Y	AGAYX	D	(800) 959-4246	C / 4.4	1.80	0.62	3.47 /29	11.23 /47	9.91 /44	0.80	1.12
GL	Invesco Global Targeted Returns Y	GLTYX	U	(800) 959-4246	U /	0.38	3.16	4.68 /36	--	--	0.58	3.41
PM	Invesco Gold and Precious Mtls A	IGDAX	E-	(800) 959-4246	E- / 0.0	-5.01	-17.81	-21.40 / 1	-23.54 / 0	-12.23 / 0	0.00	1.50
PM	● Invesco Gold and Precious Mtls B	IGDBX	E-	(800) 959-4246	E- / 0.0	-5.28	-18.03	-21.97 / 1	-24.15 / 0	-12.91 / 0	0.00	2.25
PM	Invesco Gold and Precious Mtls C	IGDCX	E-	(800) 959-4246	E- / 0.0	-5.21	-18.20	-22.06 / 1	-24.19 / 0	-12.94 / 0	0.00	2.25
PM	● Invesco Gold and Precious Mtls Iv	FGLDX	E-	(800) 959-4246	E- / 0.0	-4.99	-17.73	-21.30 / 1	-23.59 / 0	-12.26 / 0	0.00	1.50
PM	Invesco Gold and Precious Mtls Y	IGDYX	E-	(800) 959-4246	E- / 0.0	-4.94	-17.75	-21.29 / 1	-23.41 / 0	-12.07 / 0	0.00	1.25
GR	Invesco Growth Allocation A	AADAX	C-	(800) 959-4246	D+ / 2.3	1.51	2.53	4.23 /33	8.48 /30	8.66 /34	1.65	1.25
GR	● Invesco Growth Allocation B	AAEBX	C-	(800) 959-4246	D+ / 2.6	1.38	2.25	3.45 /29	7.62 /25	7.82 /29	0.98	2.00
GR	Invesco Growth Allocation C	AADCX	C-	(800) 959-4246	D+ / 2.6	1.38	2.25	3.45 /29	7.65 /25	7.84 /29	0.98	2.00
GR	Invesco Growth Allocation R	AADRX	C	(800) 959-4246	C- / 3.0	1.51	2.48	3.97 /32	8.21 /28	8.38 /32	1.49	1.50
GR	Invesco Growth Allocation R5	AADIX	C	(800) 959-4246	C- / 3.4	1.64	2.75	4.60 /36	8.84 /32	9.01 /37	2.10	0.90
GR	Invesco Growth Allocation S	AADSX	C	(800) 959-4246	C- / 3.2	1.58	2.64	4.35 /34	8.56 /30	8.76 /35	1.85	1.15
GR	Invesco Growth Allocation Y	AADYX	C	(800) 959-4246	C- / 3.3	1.58	2.65	4.43 /35	8.72 /31	8.91 /36	2.01	1.00

99 Pct = Best
0 Pct = Worst

● Denotes fund is closed to new investors
* Denotes fund is included in Section II

www.thestreetratings.com

RISK	3 Year		NET ASSETS		ASSET					BULL / BEAR		FUND MANAGER		MINIMUMS		LOADS	
Risk Rating/Pts	Standard Deviation	Beta	NAV As of 3/31/15	Total $(Mil)	Cash %	Stocks %	Bonds %	Other %	Portfolio Turnover Ratio	Last Bull Market Return	Last Bear Market Return	Manager Quality Pct	Manager Tenure (Years)	Initial Purch. $	Additional Purch. $	Front End Load	Back End Load
C /4.9	11.6	0.84	14.26	N/A	1	98	0	1	122	58.2	-23.9	82	7	10,000,000	0	0.0	0.0
C /4.9	11.6	0.84	14.08	21	1	98	0	1	122	57.7	-23.9	82	7	1,000	50	0.0	0.0
C+ /5.9	11.0	0.77	29.41	317	4	95	0	1	27	71.6	-19.5	92	12	1,000	50	5.5	0.0
C+ /5.9	11.0	0.77	27.28	5	4	95	0	1	27	67.2	-19.7	91	12	1,000	50	0.0	0.0
C+ /5.9	11.0	0.78	27.29	26	4	95	0	1	27	67.2	-19.7	90	12	1,000	50	0.0	0.0
C+ /5.9	11.0	0.77	29.28	N/A	4	95	0	1	27	74.0	-19.3	93	12	10,000,000	0	0.0	0.0
B- /7.4	11.0	0.78	29.27	N/A	4	95	0	1	27	73.4	-19.5	93	12	10,000,000	0	0.0	0.0
C+ /5.9	11.0	0.77	29.46	6	4	95	0	1	27	73.0	-19.4	93	12	1,000	50	0.0	0.0
C /5.3	11.0	0.90	46.56	1,037	5	94	0	1	24	132.8	-13.8	98	N/A	1,000	50	5.5	0.0
C /4.5	11.0	0.90	35.86	14	5	94	0	1	24	127.0	-14.1	97	N/A	1,000	50	0.0	0.0
C /4.5	11.0	0.90	35.91	101	5	94	0	1	24	126.9	-14.1	97	N/A	1,000	50	0.0	0.0
C /5.3	11.0	0.90	46.57	786	5	94	0	1	24	132.9	-13.9	98	N/A	1,000	50	0.0	0.0
C /5.3	11.0	0.90	47.06	40	5	94	0	1	24	134.9	-13.8	98	N/A	1,000	50	0.0	0.0
C+ /6.1	11.8	0.81	13.61	133	6	93	0	1	64	60.2	-18.3	80	5	1,000	50	5.5	0.0
C+ /6.1	11.8	0.81	12.88	3	6	93	0	1	64	56.1	-18.6	74	5	1,000	50	0.0	0.0
C+ /6.1	11.8	0.81	12.87	17	6	93	0	1	64	56.0	-18.6	74	5	1,000	50	0.0	0.0
C+ /6.1	11.8	0.81	13.63	2	6	93	0	1	64	58.7	-18.4	78	5	0	0	0.0	0.0
C+ /6.1	11.8	0.81	13.80	14	6	93	0	1	64	63.0	-18.1	83	5	10,000,000	0	0.0	0.0
C+ /6.1	11.8	0.81	13.64	8	6	93	0	1	64	61.4	-18.3	81	5	1,000	50	0.0	0.0
U /	N/A	N/A	10.33	115	65	0	34	1	0	N/A	N/A	N/A	3	10,000,000	0	0.0	0.0
U /	N/A	N/A	10.33	58	65	0	34	1	0	N/A	N/A	N/A	3	1,000	50	0.0	0.0
C /5.3	12.2	0.90	13.50	302	13	86	0	1	45	67.4	-20.1	50	N/A	1,000	50	5.5	0.0
C /5.3	12.3	0.91	13.52	4	13	86	0	1	45	63.1	-20.3	38	N/A	1,000	50	0.0	0.0
C /5.3	12.2	0.90	13.53	46	13	86	0	1	45	63.1	-20.3	39	N/A	1,000	50	0.0	0.0
C+ /6.8	8.6	0.65	9.42	601	15	62	19	4	61	44.8	-8.2	65	N/A	1,000	50	5.5	0.0
C+ /6.9	8.6	0.65	9.42	1	15	62	19	4	61	41.3	-8.5	54	N/A	1,000	50	0.0	0.0
C+ /6.9	8.6	0.65	9.41	119	15	62	19	4	61	41.3	-8.5	53	N/A	1,000	50	0.0	0.0
C+ /6.8	8.6	0.65	9.41	23	15	62	19	4	61	46.8	-8.2	70	N/A	10,000,000	0	0.0	0.0
B /8.6	8.5	0.65	9.42	2	15	62	19	4	61	46.7	-8.2	70	N/A	10,000,000	0	0.0	0.0
C+ /6.8	8.5	0.65	9.39	461	15	62	19	4	61	46.3	-8.1	68	N/A	1,000	50	0.0	0.0
C /5.3	12.2	0.90	13.51	21	13	86	0	1	45	66.0	-20.2	46	N/A	0	0	0.0	0.0
C /5.2	12.2	0.90	13.47	340	13	86	0	1	45	70.7	-19.8	60	N/A	10,000,000	0	0.0	0.0
C+ /6.2	12.2	0.90	13.47	139	13	86	0	1	45	69.9	-20.1	58	N/A	10,000,000	0	0.0	0.0
C /5.3	12.2	0.90	13.50	838	13	86	0	1	45	68.8	-19.9	54	N/A	1,000	50	0.0	0.0
C /4.5	10.4	0.75	19.20	543	6	93	0	1	18	64.4	-21.9	91	16	1,000	50	5.5	0.0
C- /4.1	10.4	0.75	16.09	10	6	93	0	1	18	60.3	-22.2	88	16	1,000	50	0.0	0.0
C- /4.1	10.4	0.75	16.10	29	6	93	0	1	18	60.2	-22.2	88	16	1,000	50	0.0	0.0
C /4.5	10.4	0.75	19.10	14	6	93	0	1	18	66.7	-21.8	92	16	10,000,000	0	0.0	0.0
C /4.5	10.4	0.75	19.23	19	6	93	0	1	18	65.8	-21.9	91	16	1,000	50	0.0	0.0
U /	N/A	N/A	10.54	32	0	0	0	100	20	N/A	N/A	N/A	N/A	1,000	50	0.0	0.0
E+ /0.7	33.4	1.57	3.60	104	10	89	0	1	18	-52.1	-17.1	2	2	1,000	50	5.5	0.0
E+ /0.7	33.2	1.57	3.41	5	10	89	0	1	18	-53.4	-17.4	2	2	1,000	50	0.0	0.0
E+ /0.7	33.4	1.57	3.64	25	10	89	0	1	18	-53.3	-17.4	2	2	1,000	50	0.0	0.0
E+ /0.7	33.3	1.57	3.62	75	10	89	0	1	18	-52.1	-17.1	2	2	1,000	50	0.0	0.0
E+ /0.7	33.3	1.57	3.66	18	10	89	0	1	18	-51.9	-17.1	2	2	1,000	50	0.0	0.0
B /8.1	8.0	0.77	14.16	856	19	65	14	2	18	51.4	-13.6	22	N/A	1,000	50	5.5	0.0
B /8.1	8.0	0.77	13.99	83	19	65	14	2	18	47.4	-13.9	15	N/A	1,000	50	0.0	0.0
B /8.1	8.0	0.77	14.00	169	19	65	14	2	18	47.5	-13.9	15	N/A	1,000	50	0.0	0.0
B /8.1	8.0	0.76	14.12	26	19	65	14	2	18	50.0	-13.7	20	N/A	0	0	0.0	0.0
B /8.1	8.0	0.77	14.23	N/A	19	65	14	2	18	53.0	-13.4	25	N/A	10,000,000	0	0.0	0.0
B /8.1	8.0	0.77	14.15	27	19	65	14	2	18	51.8	-13.5	22	N/A	0	0	0.0	0.0
B /8.1	8.0	0.77	14.14	6	19	65	14	2	18	52.6	-13.5	24	N/A	1,000	50	0.0	0.0

Fund Type	Fund Name	Ticker Symbol	Overall Investment Rating	Phone	Performance Rating/Pts	3 Mo	6 Mo	1Yr / Pct	3Yr / Pct	5Yr / Pct	Dividend Yield	Expense Ratio
	99 Pct = Best 0 Pct = Worst				**PERFORMANCE** Total Return % through 3/31/15 Annualized						Incl. in Returns	
GI	Invesco Growth and Income A	ACGIX	C+	(800) 959-4246	C+ / 5.9	-0.61	1.59	6.95 /55	15.16 /76	11.56 /57	1.77	0.85
GI	● Invesco Growth and Income B	ACGJX	C+	(800) 959-4246	C+ / 6.8	-0.58	1.63	6.95 /55	15.19 /76	11.54 /57	1.86	0.85
GI	Invesco Growth and Income C	ACGKX	C+	(800) 959-4246	C+ / 6.2	-0.81	1.24	6.15 /48	14.31 /69	10.73 /50	1.13	1.60
GI	Invesco Growth and Income R	ACGLX	C+	(800) 959-4246	C+ / 6.6	-0.67	1.46	6.67 /52	14.88 /74	11.27 /55	1.62	1.10
GI	Invesco Growth and Income R5	ACGQX	B-	(800) 959-4246	B- / 7.1	-0.52	1.77	7.32 /58	15.57 /80	11.96 /60	2.21	0.49
GI	Invesco Growth and Income R6	GIFFX	B+	(800) 959-4246	B- / 7.1	-0.49	1.83	7.43 /59	15.59 /80	11.81 /59	2.31	0.40
GI	Invesco Growth and Income Y	ACGMX	B-	(800) 959-4246	B- / 7.0	-0.55	1.72	7.21 /57	15.46 /79	11.83 /59	2.11	0.60
FO	Invesco International Alloc A	AINAX	D-	(800) 959-4246	D- / 1.0	1.87	-0.93	-0.93 /13	5.91 /16	5.24 /13	1.56	1.52
FO	● Invesco International Alloc B	INABX	D-	(800) 959-4246	D- / 1.2	1.78	-1.32	-1.59 /11	5.14 /14	4.46 /10	0.83	2.27
FO	Invesco International Alloc C	INACX	D-	(800) 959-4246	D- / 1.2	1.78	-1.23	-1.59 /11	5.14 /14	4.46 /10	0.83	2.27
FO	Invesco International Alloc R	RINAX	D-	(800) 959-4246	D- / 1.4	1.87	-1.03	-1.11 /13	5.67 /15	5.01 /12	1.38	1.77
FO	Invesco International Alloc R5	INAIX	D-	(800) 959-4246	D / 1.7	2.06	-0.76	-0.40 /14	6.40 /18	5.64 /15	2.16	1.06
FO	Invesco International Alloc Y	AINYX	D-	(800) 959-4246	D / 1.6	1.97	-0.84	-0.66 /14	6.19 /18	5.52 /14	1.92	1.27
FO	Invesco International Growth A	AIIEX	D	(800) 959-4246	D+ / 2.4	3.48	2.80	2.86 /26	8.71 /31	7.83 /29	1.26	1.34
FO	● Invesco International Growth B	AIEBX	D	(800) 959-4246	D+ / 2.7	3.30	2.44	2.11 /22	7.90 /26	7.03 /23	0.83	2.09
FO	Invesco International Growth C	AIECX	D	(800) 959-4246	D+ / 2.8	3.30	2.43	2.11 /22	7.91 /26	7.03 /23	0.83	2.09
FO	Invesco International Growth R	AIERX	D+	(800) 959-4246	C- / 3.1	3.45	2.68	2.62 /25	8.45 /30	7.57 /27	1.16	1.59
FO	Invesco International Growth R5	AIEVX	D+	(800) 959-4246	C- / 3.5	3.58	2.96	3.23 /28	9.10 /34	8.23 /31	1.59	0.99
FO	Invesco International Growth R6	IGFRX	C	(800) 959-4246	C- / 3.5	3.58	3.03	3.29 /28	9.10 /34	8.06 /30	1.65	0.92
FO	Invesco International Growth Y	AIIYX	D+	(800) 959-4246	C- / 3.4	3.56	2.92	3.14 /27	8.98 /33	8.10 /31	1.54	1.09
EM	● Invesco International Small Co A	IEGAX	E	(800) 959-4246	E / 0.4	-2.55	-7.69	-10.41 / 3	3.40 / 9	7.05 /23	1.35	1.49
EM	● Invesco International Small Co B	IEGBX	E	(800) 959-4246	E / 0.5	-2.72	-8.07	-11.07 / 2	2.62 / 7	6.25 /18	0.56	2.24
EM	● Invesco International Small Co C	IEGCX	E	(800) 959-4246	E / 0.5	-2.72	-8.02	-11.06 / 2	2.64 / 7	6.26 /18	0.56	2.24
EM	● Invesco International Small Co R5	IEGIX	E	(800) 959-4246	E+ / 0.6	-2.46	-7.56	-10.13 / 3	3.73 / 9	7.45 /26	1.85	1.17
FO	● Invesco International Small Co R6	IEGFX	D-	(800) 959-4246	E+ / 0.6	-2.41	-7.50	-10.03 / 3	3.76 /10	7.28 /25	1.96	1.08
EM	● Invesco International Small Co Y	IEGYX	E	(800) 959-4246	E+ / 0.6	-2.44	-7.60	-10.19 / 3	3.65 / 9	7.32 /25	1.75	1.24
FO	Invesco Intl Core Equity A	IBVAX	D-	(800) 959-4246	D- / 1.5	4.61	3.80	1.82 /21	6.59 /19	3.14 / 6	0.86	1.59
FO	● Invesco Intl Core Equity B	IBVBX	D-	(800) 959-4246	D / 1.8	4.49	3.39	1.07 /19	5.81 /16	2.37 / 5	0.22	2.34
FO	Invesco Intl Core Equity C	IBVCX	D-	(800) 959-4246	D / 1.8	4.42	3.39	1.10 /19	5.81 /16	2.37 / 5	0.22	2.34
FO	● Invesco Intl Core Equity Inv	IIBCX	D-	(800) 959-4246	D / 2.2	4.63	3.74	1.80 /21	6.59 /19	3.12 / 6	0.90	1.59
FO	Invesco Intl Core Equity R	IIBRX	D-	(800) 959-4246	D / 2.1	4.60	3.63	1.57 /20	6.34 /18	2.88 / 6	0.68	1.84
FO	Invesco Intl Core Equity R5	IBVIX	D-	(800) 959-4246	D+ / 2.6	4.83	4.02	2.39 /24	7.22 /23	3.76 / 8	1.43	1.01
FO	Invesco Intl Core Equity R6	IBVFX	D+	(800) 959-4246	D+ / 2.5	4.83	4.03	2.40 /24	7.13 /22	3.44 / 7	1.44	1.00
FO	Invesco Intl Core Equity Y	IBVYX	D-	(800) 959-4246	D+ / 2.4	4.73	3.80	2.03 /22	6.85 /21	3.38 / 7	1.12	1.34
GR	Invesco Low Volatility Eq A	SCAUX	C	(800) 959-4246	C / 4.6	-0.40	3.00	6.54 /51	12.90 /59	11.62 /58	2.56	1.14
GR	● Invesco Low Volatility Eq B	SBCUX	C	(800) 959-4246	C / 5.0	-0.60	2.63	5.79 /45	12.08 /53	10.81 /51	1.95	1.89
GR	Invesco Low Volatility Eq C	SCCUX	C	(800) 959-4246	C / 5.0	-0.61	2.63	5.80 /45	12.05 /53	10.77 /51	1.95	1.89
GR	Invesco Low Volatility Eq Inv	SCNUX	C+	(800) 959-4246	C+ / 5.6	-0.39	3.09	6.63 /52	12.90 /59	11.64 /58	2.70	1.14
GR	Invesco Low Volatility Eq R	SCRUX	C	(800) 959-4246	C / 5.4	-0.47	2.87	6.29 /49	12.61 /57	11.35 /56	2.45	1.39
GR	Invesco Low Volatility Eq R5	SCIUX	C+	(800) 959-4246	C+ / 5.9	-0.29	3.29	7.06 /55	13.38 /62	12.01 /61	3.11	0.75
GR	Invesco Low Volatility Eq Y	SCAYX	C+	(800) 959-4246	C+ / 5.8	-0.33	3.22	6.90 /54	13.22 /61	11.92 /60	2.95	0.89
MC	Invesco Mid Cap Core Equity A	GTAGX	D	(800) 959-4246	C- / 3.6	2.30	1.82	4.22 /33	11.00 /45	8.92 /36	0.01	1.22
MC	● Invesco Mid Cap Core Equity B	GTABX	D-	(800) 959-4246	C- / 3.9	2.04	1.38	3.38 /28	10.15 /40	8.09 /30	0.00	1.97
MC	Invesco Mid Cap Core Equity C	GTACX	D-	(800) 959-4246	C- / 3.9	2.10	1.39	3.45 /29	10.18 /40	8.10 /31	0.00	1.97
MC	Invesco Mid Cap Core Equity R	GTARX	D+	(800) 959-4246	C / 4.3	2.23	1.65	3.95 /31	10.73 /44	8.64 /34	0.00	1.47
MC	Invesco Mid Cap Core Equity R5	GTAVX	C-	(800) 959-4246	C / 4.7	2.39	1.97	4.61 /36	11.40 /48	9.33 /39	0.37	0.86
MC	Invesco Mid Cap Core Equity R6	GTAFX	C+	(800) 959-4246	C / 4.7	2.43	2.03	4.74 /37	11.43 /48	9.17 /38	0.46	0.77
MC	Invesco Mid Cap Core Equity Y	GTAYX	C-	(800) 959-4246	C / 4.6	2.31	1.90	4.48 /35	11.27 /47	9.18 /38	0.28	0.97
MC	Invesco Mid Cap Growth A	VGRAX	B-	(800) 959-4246	B / 8.0	7.11	12.92	13.72 /89	15.91 /83	14.20 /79	0.00	1.21
MC	● Invesco Mid Cap Growth B	VGRBX	B	(800) 959-4246	B+ / 8.9	7.13	12.93	13.72 /89	15.91 /83	14.18 /79	0.00	1.21
MC	Invesco Mid Cap Growth C	VGRCX	B-	(800) 959-4246	B+ / 8.4	6.91	12.50	12.90 /86	15.07 /75	13.38 /72	0.00	1.93
MC	Invesco Mid Cap Growth R	VGRRX	B	(800) 959-4246	B+ / 8.7	7.05	12.78	13.44 /88	15.62 /80	13.92 /77	0.00	1.46

● Denotes fund is closed to new investors
* Denotes fund is included in Section II

RISK			NET ASSETS		ASSET				Portfolio	BULL / BEAR		FUND MANAGER		MINIMUMS		LOADS	
	3 Year		NAV							Last Bull	Last Bear	Manager	Manager	Initial	Additional	Front	Back
Risk	Standard		As of	Total	Cash	Stocks	Bonds	Other	Turnover	Market	Market	Quality	Tenure	Purch.	Purch.	End	End
Rating/Pts	Deviation	Beta	3/31/15	$(Mil)	%	%	%	%	Ratio	Return	Return	Pct	(Years)	$	$	Load	Load
C+ / 6.1	9.9	0.99	26.31	4,937	3	96	0	1	31	90.7	-19.7	57	16	1,000	50	5.5	0.0
C+ / 6.1	9.9	0.99	26.11	64	3	96	0	1	31	90.8	-19.7	57	16	1,000	50	0.0	0.0
C+ / 6.1	9.8	0.99	26.06	324	3	96	0	1	31	86.0	-20.0	46	16	1,000	50	0.0	0.0
C+ / 6.1	9.9	0.99	26.33	158	3	96	0	1	31	89.1	-19.8	54	16	0	0	0.0	0.0
C+ / 6.1	9.8	0.99	26.34	811	3	96	0	1	31	93.1	-19.6	63	16	10,000,000	0	0.0	0.0
B- / 7.5	9.9	0.99	26.35	706	3	96	0	1	31	92.7	-19.7	63	16	10,000,000	0	0.0	0.0
C+ / 6.1	9.8	0.99	26.32	2,206	3	96	0	1	31	92.4	-19.7	62	16	1,000	50	0.0	0.0
C+ / 6.3	11.9	0.88	10.89	130	8	91	0	1	12	38.7	-20.2	34	N/A	1,000	50	5.5	0.0
C+ / 6.3	11.9	0.88	10.88	4	8	91	0	1	12	35.2	-20.4	25	N/A	1,000	50	0.0	0.0
C+ / 6.3	11.9	0.88	10.88	28	8	91	0	1	12	35.2	-20.4	26	N/A	1,000	50	0.0	0.0
C+ / 6.3	11.9	0.88	10.89	7	8	91	0	1	12	37.6	-20.3	31	N/A	0	0	0.0	0.0
C+ / 6.3	11.9	0.88	10.90	8	8	91	0	1	12	40.8	-20.2	40	N/A	10,000,000	0	0.0	0.0
C+ / 6.3	11.9	0.88	10.86	7	8	91	0	1	12	40.0	-20.1	37	N/A	1,000	50	0.0	0.0
C+ / 6.2	11.4	0.83	33.34	2,765	7	92	0	1	18	51.9	-20.3	75	18	1,000	50	5.5	0.0
C+ / 6.2	11.4	0.83	30.67	24	7	92	0	1	18	48.1	-20.6	68	18	1,000	50	0.0	0.0
C+ / 6.2	11.4	0.83	30.70	196	7	92	0	1	18	48.0	-20.5	68	18	1,000	50	0.0	0.0
C+ / 6.3	11.3	0.83	32.96	115	7	92	0	1	18	50.5	-20.4	73	18	0	0	0.0	0.0
C+ / 6.2	11.4	0.83	33.86	2,013	7	92	0	1	18	53.7	-20.1	78	18	10,000,000	0	0.0	0.0
B- / 7.4	11.3	0.83	33.85	523	7	92	0	1	18	53.4	-20.3	79	18	10,000,000	0	0.0	0.0
C+ / 6.2	11.3	0.83	33.43	3,578	7	92	0	1	18	53.2	-20.2	78	18	1,000	50	0.0	0.0
C / 4.3	11.5	0.68	17.93	163	10	89	0	1	20	29.6	-17.6	88	15	1,000	50	5.5	0.0
C / 4.3	11.5	0.68	17.18	2	10	89	0	1	20	26.2	-17.8	85	15	1,000	50	0.0	0.0
C / 4.3	11.5	0.68	17.19	23	10	89	0	1	20	26.3	-17.9	85	15	1,000	50	0.0	0.0
C- / 4.2	11.5	0.68	17.82	49	10	89	0	1	20	31.0	-17.5	89	15	10,000,000	0	0.0	0.0
B- / 7.1	11.5	0.76	17.83	47	10	89	0	1	20	30.9	-17.6	23	15	10,000,000	0	0.0	0.0
C / 4.3	11.5	0.68	17.96	118	10	89	0	1	20	30.6	-17.5	89	15	1,000	50	0.0	0.0
C / 5.4	13.5	1.00	11.12	42	4	95	0	1	109	37.7	-22.5	28	17	1,000	50	5.5	0.0
C / 5.4	13.5	1.00	11.18	1	4	95	0	1	109	34.2	-22.7	21	17	1,000	50	0.0	0.0
C / 5.4	13.5	1.00	10.87	11	4	95	0	1	109	34.2	-22.8	21	17	1,000	50	0.0	0.0
C / 5.4	13.5	1.00	11.30	13	4	95	0	1	109	37.7	-22.5	28	17	1,000	50	0.0	0.0
C / 5.4	13.4	1.00	11.15	2	4	95	0	1	109	36.5	-22.5	26	17	0	0	0.0	0.0
C / 5.4	13.5	1.00	11.07	3	4	95	0	1	109	40.5	-22.3	36	17	10,000,000	0	0.0	0.0
C+ / 6.6	13.5	1.00	11.07	58	4	95	0	1	109	39.7	-22.5	35	17	10,000,000	0	0.0	0.0
C / 5.4	13.4	1.00	11.30	3	4	95	0	1	109	38.9	-22.5	31	17	1,000	50	0.0	0.0
C+ / 6.4	10.0	0.91	10.48	208	2	96	0	2	109	84.4	-17.7	45	4	1,000	50	5.5	0.0
C+ / 6.4	9.9	0.91	10.34	8	2	96	0	2	109	79.5	-17.8	35	4	1,000	50	0.0	0.0
C+ / 6.4	9.9	0.91	10.32	36	2	96	0	2	109	79.7	-17.8	35	4	1,000	50	0.0	0.0
C+ / 6.4	9.9	0.91	10.52	61	2	96	0	2	109	84.4	-17.7	45	4	1,000	50	0.0	0.0
C+ / 6.4	9.9	0.91	10.43	N/A	2	96	0	2	109	82.9	-17.7	42	4	0	0	0.0	0.0
C+ / 6.4	9.9	0.90	10.54	15	2	96	0	2	109	86.6	-17.5	53	4	10,000,000	0	0.0	0.0
C+ / 6.4	9.9	0.91	10.53	6	2	96	0	2	109	85.9	-17.5	50	4	1,000	50	0.0	0.0
C / 5.5	9.6	0.83	24.06	1,129	17	82	0	1	35	64.3	-20.8	30	17	1,000	50	5.5	0.0
C- / 4.0	9.6	0.83	17.04	23	17	82	0	1	35	60.0	-21.1	22	17	1,000	50	0.0	0.0
C- / 4.0	9.6	0.83	16.99	174	17	82	0	1	35	60.1	-21.1	22	17	1,000	50	0.0	0.0
C / 5.4	9.6	0.82	23.39	97	17	82	0	1	35	62.8	-20.9	27	17	0	0	0.0	0.0
C+ / 5.6	9.6	0.83	25.71	149	17	82	0	1	35	66.4	-20.7	34	17	10,000,000	0	0.0	0.0
B- / 7.5	9.6	0.83	25.75	4	17	82	0	1	35	66.1	-20.8	35	17	10,000,000	0	0.0	0.0
C / 5.4	9.6	0.82	24.31	811	17	82	0	1	35	65.7	-20.8	33	17	1,000	50	0.0	0.0
C / 5.2	12.0	1.01	39.31	2,516	0	99	0	1	95	93.1	-25.9	49	4	1,000	50	5.5	0.0
C / 4.9	12.0	1.02	33.52	79	0	99	0	1	95	93.3	-25.9	49	4	1,000	50	0.0	0.0
C / 4.8	12.0	1.02	31.71	179	0	99	0	1	95	88.3	-26.2	38	4	1,000	50	0.0	0.0
C / 5.2	12.0	1.02	38.57	35	0	99	0	1	95	91.4	-26.0	45	4	0	0	0.0	0.0

Fund Type	Fund Name	Ticker Symbol	Overall Investment Rating	Phone	Performance Rating/Pts	3 Mo	6 Mo	1Yr / Pct	3Yr / Pct	5Yr / Pct	Dividend Yield	Expense Ratio
	99 Pct = Best				PERFORMANCE			Total Return % through 3/31/15	Annualized		Incl. in Returns	
	0 Pct = Worst											
MC	Invesco Mid Cap Growth R5	VGRJX	B+	(800) 959-4246	A- / 9.1	7.21	13.10	14.11 /90	16.35 /86	14.59 /83	0.00	0.83
MC	Invesco Mid Cap Growth R6	VGRFX	U	(800) 959-4246	U /	7.23	13.14	14.21 /90	--	--	0.00	0.73
MC	Invesco Mid Cap Growth Y	VGRDX	B+	(800) 959-4246	A- / 9.0	7.17	13.06	14.01 /89	16.20 /85	14.50 /82	0.00	0.96
BA	Invesco Moderate Allocation A	AMKAX	C-	(800) 959-4246	D / 1.7	1.62	2.49	4.10 /32	7.20 /22	7.84 /29	1.91	1.15
BA	● Invesco Moderate Allocation B	AMKBX	C-	(800) 959-4246	D / 2.0	1.43	2.11	3.33 /28	6.40 /18	7.03 /23	1.26	1.90
BA	Invesco Moderate Allocation C	AMKCX	C-	(800) 959-4246	D / 2.0	1.44	2.11	3.33 /28	6.41 /19	7.04 /23	1.26	1.90
BA	Invesco Moderate Allocation R	AMKRX	C	(800) 959-4246	D+ / 2.3	1.56	2.36	3.84 /31	6.94 /21	7.55 /27	1.76	1.40
BA	Invesco Moderate Allocation R5	AMLIX	C	(800) 959-4246	D+ / 2.6	1.70	2.59	4.44 /35	7.49 /24	8.10 /31	2.35	0.86
BA	Invesco Moderate Allocation S	AMKSX	C	(800) 959-4246	D+ / 2.5	1.64	2.55	4.29 /34	7.33 /23	7.96 /30	2.12	1.05
BA	Invesco Moderate Allocation Y	ABKYX	C	(800) 959-4246	D+ / 2.6	1.68	2.62	4.36 /34	7.47 /24	8.12 /31	2.27	0.90
FO	Invesco Pacific Growth A	TGRAX	D	(800) 959-4246	D+ / 2.4	6.97	3.71	8.65 /67	6.80 /20	3.90 / 8	0.11	1.78
FO	● Invesco Pacific Growth B	TGRBX	D	(800) 959-4246	D+ / 2.7	6.82	3.32	7.86 /62	5.98 /17	3.11 / 6	0.00	2.54
FO	Invesco Pacific Growth C	TGRCX	D	(800) 959-4246	D+ / 2.7	6.81	3.27	7.84 /62	6.01 /17	3.14 / 6	0.00	2.54
FO	Invesco Pacific Growth R	TGRRX	D+	(800) 959-4246	C- / 3.1	6.93	3.57	8.39 /65	6.51 /19	3.62 / 7	0.00	2.04
FO	Invesco Pacific Growth R5	TGRSX	D+	(800) 959-4246	C- / 3.5	7.10	3.89	9.08 /70	7.22 /23	4.23 / 9	0.51	1.38
FO	Invesco Pacific Growth Y	TGRDX	D+	(800) 959-4246	C- / 3.4	7.09	3.84	8.94 /69	7.06 /22	4.16 / 9	0.36	1.54
RE	Invesco Real Estate A	IARAX	C-	(800) 959-4246	B / 7.6	3.48	16.79	22.35 /97	12.68 /57	14.09 /79	0.62	1.25
RE	● Invesco Real Estate B	AARBX	C-	(800) 959-4246	B / 7.9	3.29	16.36	21.42 /97	11.83 /51	13.24 /70	0.04	2.00
RE	Invesco Real Estate C	IARCX	C-	(800) 959-4246	B / 7.9	3.30	16.38	21.41 /97	11.83 /51	13.23 /70	0.04	2.00
RE	Invesco Real Estate Investor	REINX	C	(800) 959-4246	B+ / 8.6	3.48	16.83	22.34 /97	12.68 /57	14.08 /78	0.65	1.25
RE	Invesco Real Estate R	IARRX	C	(800) 959-4246	B+ / 8.4	3.41	16.67	22.06 /97	12.39 /55	13.80 /76	0.42	1.50
RE	Invesco Real Estate R5	IARIX	C	(800) 959-4246	B+ / 8.8	3.57	17.01	22.82 /98	13.10 /60	14.54 /83	1.00	0.88
RE	Invesco Real Estate R6	IARFX	B	(800) 959-4246	B+ / 8.9	3.59	17.07	22.93 /98	13.10 /60	14.35 /81	1.08	0.79
RE	Invesco Real Estate Y	IARYX	C	(800) 959-4246	B+ / 8.8	3.54	16.94	22.67 /98	12.96 /59	14.37 /81	0.89	1.00
IX	Invesco S&P 500 Index A	SPIAX	B-	(800) 959-4246	C+ / 6.7	0.81	5.61	12.06 /83	15.47 /79	13.81 /76	1.10	0.59
IX	● Invesco S&P 500 Index B	SPIBX	B+	(800) 959-4246	B- / 7.1	0.60	5.24	11.25 /79	14.60 /72	12.96 /68	0.55	1.35
IX	Invesco S&P 500 Index C	SPICX	B+	(800) 959-4246	B- / 7.1	0.60	5.25	11.22 /79	14.59 /72	12.98 /68	0.56	1.35
IX	Invesco S&P 500 Index Y	SPIDX	A	(800) 959-4246	B / 8.0	0.89	5.74	12.33 /84	15.75 /81	14.10 /79	1.37	0.35
SC	● Invesco Select Companies A	ATIAX	C-	(800) 959-4246	C / 5.0	2.93	7.11	7.19 /57	12.64 /57	14.50 /82	0.00	1.24
SC	● Invesco Select Companies B	ATIBX	C	(800) 959-4246	C / 5.3	2.73	6.72	6.44 /50	11.81 /51	13.65 /74	0.00	1.99
SC	● Invesco Select Companies C	ATICX	C	(800) 959-4246	C / 5.3	2.73	6.73	6.40 /50	11.81 /51	13.65 /74	0.00	1.99
SC	● Invesco Select Companies R	ATIRX	C	(800) 959-4246	C+ / 5.7	2.88	6.97	6.93 /54	12.36 /55	14.22 /80	0.00	1.49
SC	● Invesco Select Companies R5	ATIIX	C+	(800) 959-4246	C+ / 6.1	2.99	7.27	7.57 /60	13.01 /60	14.91 /86	0.00	0.92
SC	● Invesco Select Companies Y	ATIYX	C+	(800) 959-4246	C+ / 6.1	2.99	7.21	7.47 /59	12.93 /59	14.79 /85	0.00	0.99
GL	Invesco Select Opportunities Y	IZSYX	U	(800) 959-4246	U /	0.07	-1.31	-5.24 / 5	--	--	0.00	2.03
SC	Invesco Small Cap Discovery A	VASCX	C-	(800) 959-4246	B / 8.2	8.25	17.03	10.77 /77	16.20 /85	14.78 /85	0.00	1.32
SC	● Invesco Small Cap Discovery B	VBSCX	C	(800) 959-4246	A- / 9.1	8.28	16.98	10.74 /77	16.20 /85	14.74 /85	0.00	1.32
SC	Invesco Small Cap Discovery C	VCSCX	C-	(800) 959-4246	B+ / 8.6	7.92	16.53	9.88 /74	15.31 /77	13.93 /77	0.00	2.07
SC	Invesco Small Cap Discovery R6	VFSCX	A-	(800) 959-4246	A- / 9.2	8.27	17.21	11.24 /79	16.63 /88	15.04 /87	0.00	0.84
SC	Invesco Small Cap Discovery Y	VISCX	C	(800) 959-4246	A- / 9.2	8.23	17.11	11.02 /78	16.49 /87	15.07 /87	0.00	1.07
SC	Invesco Small Cap Equity A	SMEAX	C	(800) 959-4246	C+ / 6.3	4.75	13.00	7.34 /58	14.34 /70	14.40 /81	0.00	1.29
SC	● Invesco Small Cap Equity B	SMEBX	C-	(800) 959-4246	C+ / 6.7	4.57	12.50	6.44 /50	13.46 /63	13.52 /73	0.00	2.04
SC	Invesco Small Cap Equity C	SMECX	C-	(800) 959-4246	C+ / 6.7	4.57	12.59	6.53 /51	13.50 /63	13.55 /73	0.00	2.04
SC	Invesco Small Cap Equity R	SMERX	C	(800) 959-4246	B- / 7.1	4.69	12.86	7.05 /55	14.06 /68	14.10 /79	0.00	1.54
SC	Invesco Small Cap Equity R5	SMEIX	C+	(800) 959-4246	B / 7.7	4.86	13.14	7.72 /61	14.80 /73	14.90 /86	0.00	0.88
SC	Invesco Small Cap Equity R6	SMEFX	B	(800) 959-4246	B / 7.7	4.91	13.23	7.82 /61	14.80 /73	14.67 /84	0.00	0.80
SC	Invesco Small Cap Equity Y	SMEYX	C+	(800) 959-4246	B- / 7.5	4.85	13.09	7.58 /60	14.63 /72	14.68 /84	0.00	1.04
SC	● Invesco Small Cap Growth A	GTSAX	C+	(800) 959-4246	B+ / 8.6	5.51	11.71	10.64 /77	17.78 /94	17.11 /96	0.00	1.21
SC	● Invesco Small Cap Growth B	GTSBX	C	(800) 959-4246	A- / 9.0	5.33	11.29	9.85 /74	16.91 /89	16.25 /94	0.00	1.96
SC	● Invesco Small Cap Growth C	GTSDX	C	(800) 959-4246	B+ / 8.9	5.30	11.28	9.80 /74	16.90 /89	16.24 /94	0.00	1.96
SC	● Invesco Small Cap Growth Inv	GTSIX	B-	(800) 959-4246	A / 9.3	5.52	11.70	10.67 /77	17.79 /94	17.12 /96	0.00	1.21
SC	● Invesco Small Cap Growth R	GTSRX	C+	(800) 959-4246	A- / 9.2	5.44	11.55	10.38 /76	17.48 /92	16.82 /95	0.00	1.46

● Denotes fund is closed to new investors
* Denotes fund is included in Section II

www.thestreetratings.com

Risk Rating/Pts	3 Year Standard Deviation	Beta	NAV As of 3/31/15	Total $(Mil)	Cash %	Stocks %	Bonds %	Other %	Portfolio Turnover Ratio	Last Bull Market Return	Last Bear Market Return	Manager Quality Pct	Manager Tenure (Years)	Initial Purch. $	Additional Purch. $	Front End Load	Back End Load
C /5.3	12.0	1.02	40.72	86	0	99	0	1	95	95.6	-25.7	55	4	10,000,000	0	0.0	0.0
U /	N/A	N/A	40.78	62	0	99	0	1	95	N/A	N/A	N/A	4	10,000,000	0	0.0	0.0
C /5.3	12.0	1.02	40.50	82	0	99	0	1	95	94.7	-25.8	53	4	1,000	50	0.0	0.0
B /8.6	6.4	1.04	12.74	661	14	48	35	3	15	41.6	-9.6	18	N/A	1,000	50	5.5	0.0
B /8.6	6.4	1.04	12.65	45	14	48	35	3	15	38.0	-9.9	12	N/A	1,000	50	0.0	0.0
B /8.6	6.4	1.04	12.64	156	14	48	35	3	15	37.9	-9.9	13	N/A	1,000	50	0.0	0.0
B /8.6	6.4	1.05	12.71	22	14	48	35	3	15	40.3	-9.7	15	N/A	0	0	0.0	0.0
B /8.6	6.3	1.04	12.78	N/A	14	48	35	3	15	42.8	-9.5	20	N/A	10,000,000	0	0.0	0.0
B /8.6	6.4	1.04	12.74	31	14	48	35	3	15	42.0	-9.5	19	N/A	0	0	0.0	0.0
B /8.6	6.4	1.05	12.76	7	14	48	35	3	15	42.7	-9.4	19	N/A	1,000	50	0.0	0.0
C+ /6.2	12.2	0.80	24.85	71	0	99	0	1	63	36.2	-22.2	57	5	1,000	50	5.5	0.0
C+ /6.2	12.1	0.80	23.33	N/A	0	99	0	1	63	32.8	-22.5	46	5	1,000	50	0.0	0.0
C+ /6.2	12.1	0.80	23.37	5	0	99	0	1	63	33.0	-22.5	46	5	1,000	50	0.0	0.0
C+ /6.2	12.1	0.80	24.68	N/A	0	99	0	1	63	35.0	-22.3	53	5	0	0	0.0	0.0
C+ /6.2	12.1	0.80	25.20	N/A	0	99	0	1	63	38.1	-22.1	63	5	10,000,000	0	0.0	0.0
C+ /6.2	12.1	0.80	25.21	3	0	99	0	1	63	37.4	-22.2	61	5	1,000	50	0.0	0.0
D+ /2.5	12.3	0.99	27.33	1,344	2	97	0	1	50	78.8	-16.2	50	N/A	1,000	50	5.5	0.0
D+ /2.5	12.3	0.99	27.33	9	2	97	0	1	50	74.3	-16.5	39	N/A	1,000	50	0.0	0.0
D+ /2.5	12.3	0.99	27.23	167	2	97	0	1	50	74.4	-16.5	39	N/A	1,000	50	0.0	0.0
D+ /2.5	12.3	0.99	27.28	74	2	97	0	1	50	78.8	-16.2	51	N/A	1,000	50	0.0	0.0
D+ /2.5	12.3	0.99	27.36	146	2	97	0	1	50	77.3	-16.3	46	N/A	0	0	0.0	0.0
D+ /2.5	12.3	0.99	27.32	466	2	97	0	1	50	81.2	-16.1	57	N/A	10,000,000	0	0.0	0.0
C /5.2	12.3	0.99	27.31	111	2	97	0	1	50	80.8	-16.2	56	N/A	10,000,000	0	0.0	0.0
D+ /2.5	12.3	0.99	27.32	231	2	97	0	1	50	80.4	-16.2	54	N/A	1,000	50	0.0	0.0
B- /7.3	9.5	1.00	22.31	575	1	98	0	1	5	96.4	-16.5	59	5	1,000	50	5.5	0.0
B- /7.3	9.6	1.00	21.88	6	1	98	0	1	5	91.5	-16.8	47	5	1,000	50	0.0	0.0
B- /7.3	9.6	1.00	21.63	158	1	98	0	1	5	91.4	-16.8	47	5	1,000	50	0.0	0.0
B- /7.3	9.6	1.00	22.55	42	1	98	0	1	5	98.1	-16.4	62	5	1,000	50	0.0	0.0
C+ /5.9	10.2	0.68	23.51	703	25	74	0	1	10	75.8	-14.8	82	12	1,000	50	5.5	0.0
C+ /5.7	10.2	0.68	21.48	8	25	74	0	1	10	71.4	-15.1	77	12	1,000	50	0.0	0.0
C+ /5.7	10.2	0.68	21.45	175	25	74	0	1	10	71.3	-15.0	76	12	1,000	50	0.0	0.0
C+ /5.8	10.2	0.68	22.88	65	25	74	0	1	10	74.4	-14.9	80	12	0	0	0.0	0.0
C+ /6.0	10.2	0.68	24.48	68	25	74	0	1	10	77.8	-14.6	84	12	10,000,000	0	0.0	0.0
C+ /5.9	10.2	0.68	23.78	273	25	74	0	1	10	77.3	-14.7	84	12	1,000	50	0.0	0.0
U /	N/A	N/A	13.99	27	14	85	0	1	13	N/A	N/A	N/A	3	1,000	50	0.0	0.0
D+ /2.4	12.6	0.88	11.28	536	3	96	0	1	79	98.9	-25.0	82	15	1,000	50	5.5	0.0
D /1.8	12.6	0.88	10.07	9	3	96	0	1	79	99.0	-25.0	82	15	1,000	50	0.0	0.0
D- /1.4	12.6	0.88	9.40	61	3	96	0	1	79	93.8	-25.2	77	15	1,000	50	0.0	0.0
C+ /5.9	12.5	0.88	11.78	39	3	96	0	1	79	101.2	-25.0	85	15	10,000,000	0	0.0	0.0
D+ /2.6	12.6	0.88	11.71	110	3	96	0	1	79	100.5	-24.9	84	15	1,000	50	0.0	0.0
C /4.6	12.4	0.89	15.88	586	3	96	0	1	45	90.1	-24.9	66	N/A	1,000	50	5.5	0.0
C- /4.0	12.4	0.89	13.51	8	3	96	0	1	45	85.2	-25.1	55	N/A	1,000	50	0.0	0.0
C- /4.0	12.4	0.89	13.51	67	3	96	0	1	45	85.2	-25.0	55	N/A	1,000	50	0.0	0.0
C /4.4	12.4	0.89	15.18	101	3	96	0	1	45	88.3	-24.9	63	N/A	0	0	0.0	0.0
C /4.8	12.4	0.89	17.03	173	3	96	0	1	45	93.0	-24.7	71	N/A	10,000,000	0	0.0	0.0
C+ /6.3	12.4	0.89	17.08	117	3	96	0	1	45	92.4	-24.9	71	N/A	10,000,000	0	0.0	0.0
C /4.7	12.4	0.89	16.22	391	3	96	0	1	45	91.7	-24.8	69	N/A	1,000	50	0.0	0.0
C- /3.6	12.1	0.85	37.93	752	1	98	0	1	28	109.2	-23.7	91	N/A	1,000	50	5.5	0.0
D+ /2.7	12.1	0.85	29.24	4	1	98	0	1	28	103.9	-23.9	88	N/A	1,000	50	0.0	0.0
D+ /2.7	12.1	0.85	29.18	22	1	98	0	1	28	104.0	-23.9	88	N/A	1,000	50	0.0	0.0
C- /3.7	12.1	0.84	39.40	292	1	98	0	1	28	109.2	-23.6	91	N/A	1,000	50	0.0	0.0
C- /3.4	12.1	0.84	36.04	109	1	98	0	1	28	107.4	-23.7	90	N/A	0	0	0.0	0.0

Fund Type	Fund Name	Ticker Symbol	Overall Investment Rating	Phone	PERFORMANCE						Incl. in Returns	
					Perfor-mance Rating/Pts	Total Return % through 3/31/15					Dividend Yield	Expense Ratio
						3 Mo	6 Mo	1Yr / Pct	Annualized			
									3Yr / Pct	5Yr / Pct		
SC	● Invesco Small Cap Growth R5	GTSVX	B-	(800) 959-4246	A / 9.4	5.63	11.93	11.11 /79	18.25 /95	17.59 /97	0.00	0.83
SC	● Invesco Small Cap Growth R6	GTSFX	A	(800) 959-4246	A / 9.4	5.64	11.99	11.20 /79	18.25 /95	17.39 /97	0.00	0.74
SC	● Invesco Small Cap Growth Y	GTSYX	B-	(800) 959-4246	A / 9.4	5.57	11.85	10.93 /78	18.08 /94	17.41 /97	0.00	0.96
SC	● Invesco Small Cap Value A	VSCAX	C+	(800) 959-4246	B+/ 8.9	4.99	11.66	7.86 /62	18.72 /96	16.19 /94	0.00	1.12
SC	● Invesco Small Cap Value B	VSMBX	C+	(800) 959-4246	A- / 9.1	4.79	11.21	7.03 /55	17.87 /94	15.56 /90	0.00	1.87
SC	● Invesco Small Cap Value C	VSMCX	C+	(800) 959-4246	A- / 9.1	4.76	11.26	7.02 /55	17.84 /94	15.34 /89	0.00	1.87
SC	● Invesco Small Cap Value Y	VSMIX	B	(800) 959-4246	A / 9.5	5.04	11.78	8.11 /64	19.02 /97	16.49 /95	0.00	0.87
GR	Invesco Summit A	ASMMX	C+	(800) 959-4246	B / 7.9	5.17	9.90	15.05 /92	16.04 /84	13.75 /75	0.01	1.05
GR	● Invesco Summit B	BSMMX	C+	(800) 959-4246	B+/ 8.3	5.02	9.52	14.20 /90	15.16 /76	12.92 /67	0.00	1.80
GR	Invesco Summit C	CSMMX	C+	(800) 959-4246	B+/ 8.3	4.96	9.49	14.18 /90	15.16 /76	12.88 /67	0.00	1.80
GR	● Invesco Summit P	SMMIX	B	(800) 959-4246	B+/ 8.9	5.25	10.01	15.26 /92	16.22 /85	13.91 /77	0.01	0.90
GR	Invesco Summit R5	SMITX	B	(800) 959-4246	A- / 9.0	5.26	10.08	15.49 /92	16.44 /87	14.13 /79	0.01	0.69
GR	Invesco Summit S	SMMSX	B	(800) 959-4246	B+/ 8.9	5.22	10.00	15.21 /92	16.15 /84	13.85 /76	0.01	0.95
GR	Invesco Summit Y	ASMYX	B	(800) 959-4246	A- / 9.0	5.21	10.05	15.33 /92	16.31 /86	14.03 /78	0.01	0.80
TC	Invesco Technology A	ITYAX	D	(800) 959-4246	C- / 4.2	4.13	8.33	13.48 /88	9.30 /35	12.47 /64	0.00	1.45
TC	● Invesco Technology B	ITYBX	D	(800) 959-4246	C / 4.5	3.93	7.92	12.60 /85	8.49 /30	11.66 /58	0.00	2.20
TC	Invesco Technology C	ITHCX	D	(800) 959-4246	C / 4.5	3.95	7.92	12.62 /85	8.49 /30	11.65 /58	0.00	2.20
TC	Invesco Technology Inv	FTCHX	D	(800) 959-4246	C / 5.1	4.16	8.39	13.58 /88	9.39 /36	12.56 /65	0.00	1.36
TC	Invesco Technology R5	FTPIX	D+	(800) 959-4246	C / 5.5	4.29	8.63	14.13 /90	9.96 /39	13.20 /70	0.00	0.89
TC	● Invesco Technology Sector A	IFOAX	D+	(800) 959-4246	C / 4.4	4.33	8.57	14.00 /89	9.65 /37	10.74 /51	0.00	1.68
TC	● Invesco Technology Sector B	IFOBX	D+	(800) 959-4246	C / 4.7	4.14	8.08	13.11 /87	8.81 /32	9.89 /44	0.00	2.43
TC	● Invesco Technology Sector C	IFOCX	D+	(800) 959-4246	C / 4.8	4.14	8.16	13.10 /87	8.83 /32	9.93 /44	0.00	2.41
TC	● Invesco Technology Sector Y	IFODX	C-	(800) 959-4246	C / 5.5	4.38	8.70	14.27 /90	9.91 /39	11.02 /53	0.00	1.43
TC	Invesco Technology Y	ITYYX	D+	(800) 959-4246	C / 5.2	4.22	8.47	13.78 /89	9.59 /37	12.77 /66	0.00	1.20
GI	Invesco Value FDP Institutional	MAVVX	B+	(800) 441-7762	B- / 7.1	-0.25	1.59	6.83 /54	15.68 /81	13.19 /70	1.66	0.98
GI	Invesco Value FDP Investor A	MDVVX	B-	(800) 441-7762	C+/ 6.0	-0.25	1.52	6.59 /52	15.42 /78	12.93 /68	1.26	1.22
GI	Invesco Value FDP Investor C	MCVVX	B-	(800) 441-7762	C+/ 6.3	-0.50	1.14	5.78 /45	14.53 /71	12.07 /61	0.68	1.98
GI	Invesco Value Opportunities A	VVOAX	C	(800) 959-4246	C / 4.4	-0.96	0.89	3.73 /30	13.14 /61	11.15 /54	1.64	1.25
GI	● Invesco Value Opportunities B	VVOBX	C+	(800) 959-4246	C / 5.3	-0.97	0.90	3.71 /30	13.13 /61	11.02 /53	1.76	1.25
GI	Invesco Value Opportunities C	VVOCX	C+	(800) 959-4246	C / 4.8	-1.12	0.50	3.05 /27	12.32 /55	10.39 /48	1.04	1.96
GI	Invesco Value Opportunities R	VVORX	C+	(800) 959-4246	C / 5.1	-1.03	0.76	3.46 /29	12.83 /58	10.88 /52	1.48	1.50
GI	Invesco Value Opportunities R5	VVONX	B-	(800) 959-4246	C+/ 5.7	-0.82	1.06	4.19 /33	13.67 /65	11.60 /58	2.45	0.83
GI	Invesco Value Opportunities Y	VVOIX	C+	(800) 959-4246	C / 5.5	-0.89	0.99	3.98 /32	13.41 /63	11.41 /56	2.18	1.00
MC	Invesco VI American Value I	UMCVX	B+	(800) 959-4246	B+/ 8.8	3.66	9.32	10.98 /78	16.87 /89	15.25 /88	0.43	1.01
MC	Invesco VI American Value II	UMCCX	B+	(800) 959-4246	B+/ 8.7	3.59	9.18	10.72 /77	16.57 /87	15.03 /87	0.19	1.26
IN	Invesco VI Equity and Income II	UEIIX	C+	(800) 959-4246	C / 5.2	0.00	2.06	6.36 /50	12.33 /55	9.81 /43	1.55	0.93
GL	Invesco VI Gobal Core Equity I	UGEPX	C-	(800) 959-4246	C- / 3.8	3.36	2.44	2.48 /24	9.75 /38	6.66 /21	2.00	1.09
BA	InvestEd Balanced A	WBLAX	C-	(888) 923-3355	C- / 3.0	2.50	4.24	6.69 /53	9.27 /35	7.64 /27	1.46	1.05
GR	InvestEd Conservative A	WICAX	D+	(888) 923-3355	D / 1.6	0.79	1.05	3.62 /30	6.80 /20	5.31 /13	2.29	0.95
GR	InvestEd Growth A	WAGRX	C-	(888) 923-3355	C / 5.0	4.11	8.01	9.59 /72	12.15 /53	10.11 /46	0.86	1.17
GR	Investment House Growth	TIHGX	B+	(888) 309-1371	B / 8.1	2.03	4.63	11.72 /81	16.05 /84	15.87 /92	0.00	1.48
GI	Investment Partners Opportunities A	IPOFX	E	(866) 390-0440	E- / 0.2	0.64	-12.00	-10.17 / 3	-0.84 / 4	0.33 / 3	0.91	4.56
GI	IQ Alpha Hedge Strategy Inst	IQHIX	D	(888) 934-0777	E+/ 0.7	2.06	-3.43	-1.69 /11	2.67 / 7	1.90 / 4	0.00	1.39
GI	IQ Alpha Hedge Strategy Inv	IQHOX	D	(888) 934-0777	E+/ 0.7	1.93	-3.25	-1.69 /11	2.43 / 7	1.72 / 4	0.00	1.78
GI	Iron Horse A	IRHAX	D-	(855) 241-7514	D / 1.6	-0.60	-0.79	4.51 /35	7.33 /23	--	0.45	1.86
GI	Iron Horse I	IRHIX	D	(855) 241-7514	D+/ 2.5	-0.63	-0.67	4.78 /37	7.60 /25	--	0.72	1.61
GL	IronBridge Global	IBGFX	D	(888) 825-2100	C- / 4.1	3.07	3.89	5.79 /45	10.51 /42	9.00 /37	0.72	1.67
GR	IronBridge Large Cap	IBLCX	B+		B- / 7.1	2.57	6.72	11.30 /80	14.25 /69	--	0.54	1.27
SC	● IronBridge Small Cap	IBSCX	C-	(888) 825-2100	C+/ 6.7	3.97	11.53	7.05 /55	13.57 /64	13.00 /68	0.00	1.12
MC	IronBridge SMID Cap	IBSMX	D+	(888) 825-2100	C+/ 6.0	4.14	8.23	5.32 /41	12.88 /59	12.73 /66	0.04	0.94
GL	Ironclad Managed Risk	IRONX	D+	(888) 979-4766	D / 2.0	1.10	2.19	3.35 /28	7.09 /22	--	0.00	1.26
FO	● IVA Fiduciary Tr IVA Intl A	IVIOX	D+	(866) 941-4482	D / 1.7	3.23	0.96	2.46 /24	7.82 /26	7.85 /29	2.58	1.26

99 Pct = Best
0 Pct = Worst

● Denotes fund is closed to new investors
★ Denotes fund is included in Section II

www.thestreetratings.com

RISK Risk Rating/Pts	3 Year Standard Deviation	Beta	NET ASSETS NAV As of 3/31/15	Total $(Mil)	Cash %	Stocks %	Bonds %	Other %	Portfolio Turnover Ratio	Last Bull Market Return	Last Bear Market Return	Manager Quality Pct	Manager Tenure (Years)	Initial Purch. $	Additional Purch. $	Front End Load	Back End Load
C- / 3.9	12.1	0.85	41.30	1,014	1	98	0	1	28	112.1	-23.5	91	N/A	10,000,000	0	0.0	0.0
C+ / 6.0	12.1	0.85	41.38	164	1	98	0	1	28	111.7	-23.7	92	N/A	10,000,000	0	0.0	0.0
C- / 3.7	12.1	0.85	38.64	131	1	98	0	1	28	111.0	-23.6	91	N/A	1,000	50	0.0	0.0
C- / 3.9	15.4	1.02	20.62	1,781	4	95	0	1	33	132.3	-29.0	83	5	1,000	50	5.5	0.0
C- / 3.1	15.3	1.02	17.05	24	4	95	0	1	33	127.0	-29.1	78	5	1,000	50	0.0	0.0
D+ / 2.9	15.4	1.02	16.49	155	4	95	0	1	33	126.5	-29.2	78	5	1,000	50	0.0	0.0
C- / 4.0	15.4	1.02	21.27	1,616	4	95	0	1	33	134.2	-28.9	85	5	1,000	50	0.0	0.0
C / 4.7	11.5	1.10	17.29	38	0	99	0	1	52	98.8	-18.4	43	13	1,000	50	5.5	0.0
C / 4.5	11.4	1.10	16.33	1	0	99	0	1	52	94.0	-18.6	33	13	1,000	50	0.0	0.0
C / 4.5	11.4	1.10	16.28	3	0	99	0	1	52	93.7	-18.7	33	13	1,000	50	0.0	0.0
C / 4.7	11.5	1.10	17.44	1,884	0	99	0	1	52	99.8	-18.3	46	13	0	0	0.0	0.0
C / 4.7	11.5	1.10	17.41	N/A	0	99	0	1	52	101.4	-18.3	49	13	10,000,000	0	0.0	0.0
C / 4.7	11.5	1.10	17.34	4	0	99	0	1	52	99.5	-18.3	45	13	0	0	0.0	0.0
C / 4.7	11.5	1.10	17.37	2	0	99	0	1	52	100.6	-18.3	47	13	1,000	50	0.0	0.0
C- / 4.0	13.6	1.12	38.58	319	1	98	0	1	69	73.2	-17.4	3	7	1,000	50	5.5	0.0
C- / 3.7	13.6	1.12	34.39	10	1	98	0	1	69	68.8	-17.6	2	7	1,000	50	0.0	0.0
C- / 3.6	13.6	1.12	33.17	31	1	98	0	1	69	68.8	-17.6	2	7	1,000	50	0.0	0.0
C- / 4.0	13.6	1.12	38.31	394	1	98	0	1	69	73.7	-17.4	3	7	1,000	50	0.0	0.0
C / 4.3	13.6	1.12	43.56	1	1	98	0	1	69	76.8	-17.2	4	7	10,000,000	0	0.0	0.0
C / 5.1	13.3	1.10	17.10	90	4	95	0	1	69	76.9	-18.1	4	1	1,000	50	5.5	0.0
C / 5.0	13.4	1.10	14.84	1	4	95	0	1	69	72.7	-18.5	3	1	1,000	50	0.0	0.0
C / 5.0	13.4	1.10	14.85	8	4	95	0	1	69	72.7	-18.5	3	1	1,000	50	0.0	0.0
C / 5.1	13.4	1.10	17.86	1	4	95	0	1	69	78.7	-18.1	4	1	1,000	50	0.0	0.0
C- / 4.0	13.6	1.12	38.76	9	1	98	0	1	69	74.7	-17.3	3	7	1,000	50	0.0	0.0
B- / 7.1	10.5	1.05	16.22	6	5	94	0	1	14	97.5	-19.8	51	10	2,000,000	0	0.0	0.0
B- / 7.1	10.5	1.05	16.09	59	5	94	0	1	14	96.1	-19.9	47	10	1,000	50	5.3	0.0
B- / 7.1	10.6	1.05	15.82	91	5	94	0	1	14	91.0	-20.2	35	10	1,000	50	0.0	0.0
B- / 7.3	11.5	1.14	14.46	760	3	96	0	1	16	90.8	-20.8	12	5	1,000	50	5.5	0.0
B- / 7.3	11.5	1.14	14.25	30	3	96	0	1	16	90.9	-20.9	12	5	1,000	50	0.0	0.0
B- / 7.3	11.5	1.14	14.10	101	3	96	0	1	16	86.1	-21.0	9	5	1,000	50	0.0	0.0
B- / 7.3	11.5	1.14	14.43	21	3	96	0	1	16	89.3	-20.9	10	5	0	0	0.0	0.0
B- / 7.3	11.5	1.14	14.43	3	3	96	0	1	16	94.2	-20.7	15	5	10,000,000	0	0.0	0.0
B- / 7.3	11.5	1.14	14.40	23	3	96	0	1	16	92.5	-20.8	13	5	1,000	50	0.0	0.0
C / 5.5	10.0	0.86	20.65	154	3	96	0	1	48	108.6	-21.5	84	12	0	0	0.0	0.0
C / 5.5	10.0	0.87	20.46	281	3	96	0	1	48	107.1	-21.6	82	12	0	0	0.0	0.0
B- / 7.1	7.0	0.72	18.86	1,300	8	63	21	8	85	67.4	-15.3	76	12	0	0	0.0	0.0
C+ / 6.2	11.7	0.84	9.24	75	1	98	0	1	123	58.1	-23.8	82	5	0	0	0.0	0.0
C+ / 6.9	6.9	1.14	12.69	168	16	63	20	1	42	51.5	-13.7	26	13	750	0	5.8	0.0
B- / 7.5	4.5	0.43	11.55	101	21	39	38	2	42	28.9	-0.3	69	13	750	0	4.3	0.0
C+ / 5.7	8.8	0.83	13.67	152	15	81	3	1	37	68.0	-18.1	53	N/A	750	0	5.8	0.0
C+ / 6.1	11.4	1.05	26.11	67	0	100	0	0	9	111.5	-15.7	55	14	1,000	100	0.0	0.0
C / 5.1	11.0	0.75	9.42	8	23	71	5	1	67	7.4	-16.1	1	5	2,500	100	5.8	0.0
B / 8.1	6.8	0.46	10.79	209	0	30	61	9	174	12.7	-6.7	15	N/A	250,000	0	0.0	0.0
B / 8.2	6.7	0.46	10.76	19	0	30	61	9	174	12.3	-7.0	13	N/A	2,500	100	0.0	0.0
C+ / 5.9	6.2	0.62	10.21	12	4	95	0	1	114	46.4	N/A	34	4	5,000	500	5.8	0.0
C+ / 6.3	6.2	0.62	10.19	28	4	95	0	1	114	N/A	N/A	38	4	100,000	500	0.0	0.0
C / 4.6	10.3	0.71	9.06	16	1	98	0	1	55	64.2	-19.7	90	6	100,000	1,000	0.0	2.0
B- / 7.3	9.4	0.97	12.77	26	2	97	0	1	41	N/A	N/A	50	3	100,000	1,000	0.0	0.0
C- / 3.8	12.0	0.87	19.91	456	4	95	0	1	31	84.9	-23.2	62	13	100,000	1,000	0.0	0.0
C- / 3.5	11.3	1.00	13.59	840	3	96	0	1	56	79.4	-23.0	19	11	100,000	1,000	0.0	0.0
B- / 7.7	3.4	0.14	10.99	329	100	0	0	0	0	34.2	-3.7	94	5	2,500	500	0.0	2.0
B- / 7.5	6.8	0.49	16.95	456	13	54	31	2	23	35.5	-9.7	89	7	5,000	100	5.0	2.0

Fund Type	Fund Name	Ticker Symbol	Overall Investment Rating	Phone	Performance Rating/Pts	3 Mo	6 Mo	1Yr / Pct	3Yr / Pct	5Yr / Pct	Dividend Yield	Expense Ratio
	99 Pct = Best / 0 Pct = Worst							Total Return % through 3/31/15	Annualized		Incl. in Returns	
FO	● IVA Fiduciary Tr IVA Intl C	IVICX	D+	(866) 941-4482	D / 1.9	3.08	0.59	1.68 /21	7.04 /21	7.04 /23	1.98	2.01
FO	● IVA Fiduciary Tr IVA Intl I	IVIQX	C-	(866) 941-4482	D+ / 2.5	3.29	1.06	2.66 /25	8.11 /28	8.12 /31	2.96	1.01
FO	● IVA Fiduciary Tr IVA Worldwide A	IVWAX	D+	(866) 941-4482	D- / 1.4	1.49	0.67	2.27 /23	7.14 /22	7.45 /26	1.07	1.26
FO	● IVA Fiduciary Tr IVA Worldwide C	IVWCX	D+	(866) 941-4482	D / 1.6	1.27	0.29	1.50 /20	6.33 /18	6.66 /21	0.38	2.01
FO	● IVA Fiduciary Tr IVA Worldwide I	IVWIX	D+	(866) 941-4482	D / 2.1	1.55	0.82	2.53 /24	7.40 /24	7.73 /28	1.37	1.01
* GL	Ivy Asset Strategy A	WASAX	E	(800) 777-6472	D- / 1.5	1.57	1.25	-2.28 /10	7.79 /26	7.58 /27	0.38	0.96
GL	● Ivy Asset Strategy B	WASBX	E	(800) 777-6472	D / 1.8	1.35	0.86	-3.01 / 9	6.98 /21	6.76 /22	0.09	1.71
GL	Ivy Asset Strategy C	WASCX	E	(800) 777-6472	D / 1.8	1.34	0.86	-2.99 / 9	7.01 /21	6.80 /22	0.10	1.68
GL	Ivy Asset Strategy E	IASEX	E	(800) 777-6472	D- / 1.5	1.53	1.22	-2.29 /10	7.75 /26	7.56 /27	0.34	1.12
GL	Ivy Asset Strategy I	IVAEX	E+	(800) 777-6472	D+ / 2.4	1.59	1.34	-2.06 /10	8.02 /27	7.83 /29	0.63	0.73
GL	Ivy Asset Strategy R	IASRX	E+	(800) 777-6472	D / 2.0	1.46	1.02	-2.67 / 9	7.38 /23	7.20 /24	0.19	1.33
GL	Ivy Asset Strategy Y	WASYX	E+	(800) 777-6472	D / 2.2	1.53	1.21	-2.31 /10	7.77 /26	7.58 /27	0.40	0.98
BA	Ivy Balanced A	IBNAX	C+	(800) 777-6472	C / 4.4	2.56	5.86	9.06 /70	11.46 /49	11.18 /54	0.59	1.15
BA	● Ivy Balanced B	IBNBX	C+	(800) 777-6472	C / 4.8	2.41	5.49	8.28 /65	10.63 /43	10.34 /47	0.00	1.89
BA	Ivy Balanced C	IBNCX	C+	(800) 777-6472	C / 4.8	2.41	5.56	8.34 /65	10.69 /44	10.45 /48	0.01	1.84
BA	● Ivy Balanced E	IVYEX	C+	(800) 777-6472	C / 4.5	2.62	6.00	9.22 /70	11.78 /51	11.46 /57	0.72	1.16
BA	Ivy Balanced I	IYBIX	B	(800) 777-6472	C / 5.5	2.66	6.00	9.34 /71	11.75 /51	11.51 /57	0.87	0.88
BA	Ivy Balanced Y	IBNYX	B-	(800) 777-6472	C / 5.3	2.60	5.90	9.10 /70	11.48 /49	11.23 /55	0.63	1.13
GR	Ivy Core Equity A	WCEAX	C+	(800) 777-6472	C+ / 6.2	1.64	4.50	9.86 /74	14.96 /75	14.50 /82	0.00	1.20
GR	● Ivy Core Equity B	WCEBX	C+	(800) 777-6472	C+ / 6.4	1.39	4.07	8.80 /68	13.84 /66	13.35 /72	0.00	2.12
GR	Ivy Core Equity C	WTRCX	C+	(800) 777-6472	C+ / 6.6	1.44	4.17	9.04 /70	14.07 /68	13.63 /74	0.00	1.94
GR	Ivy Core Equity E	ICFEX	C+	(800) 777-6472	C+ / 6.1	1.57	4.45	9.60 /72	14.77 /73	14.38 /81	0.00	1.51
GR	Ivy Core Equity I	ICIEX	B	(800) 777-6472	B- / 7.5	1.69	4.66	10.14 /75	15.34 /78	14.89 /86	0.16	0.91
GR	Ivy Core Equity Y	WCEYX	B	(800) 777-6472	B- / 7.4	1.66	4.65	10.18 /75	15.24 /77	14.71 /84	0.16	1.16
GL	Ivy Cundill Global Value A	ICDAX	E+	(800) 777-6472	E+ / 0.9	-1.31	-6.93	-8.02 / 3	7.14 /22	5.54 /14	0.00	1.75
GL	● Ivy Cundill Global Value B	ICDBX	E+	(800) 777-6472	E+ / 0.9	-1.62	-7.49	-9.09 / 3	5.95 /17	4.46 /10	0.00	2.86
GL	Ivy Cundill Global Value C	ICDCX	E+	(800) 777-6472	D- / 1.1	-1.52	-7.27	-8.63 / 3	6.50 /19	4.93 /12	0.00	2.36
GL	Ivy Cundill Global Value E	ICVEX	E+	(800) 777-6472	E+ / 0.9	-1.31	-6.95	-8.03 / 3	7.25 /23	5.71 /15	0.00	2.08
GL	Ivy Cundill Global Value I	ICVIX	E+	(800) 777-6472	D- / 1.4	-1.22	-6.72	-7.58 / 4	7.67 /25	6.12 /17	0.00	1.28
GL	Ivy Cundill Global Value Y	ICDYX	E+	(800) 777-6472	D- / 1.4	-1.24	-6.83	-7.86 / 3	7.42 /24	5.99 /17	0.00	1.49
GI	Ivy Dividend Opportunities A	IVDAX	C-	(800) 777-6472	C / 5.0	0.67	4.52	8.19 /64	13.19 /61	11.34 /56	0.98	1.27
GI	● Ivy Dividend Opportunities B	IVDBX	C	(800) 777-6472	C / 5.4	0.42	4.06	7.33 /58	12.25 /54	10.39 /48	0.32	2.05
GI	Ivy Dividend Opportunities C	IVDCX	C	(800) 777-6472	C / 5.5	0.47	4.12	7.46 /59	12.42 /55	10.59 /49	0.42	1.93
GI	Ivy Dividend Opportunities E	IDIEX	C-	(800) 777-6472	C / 4.9	0.58	4.42	8.01 /63	13.05 /60	11.24 /55	0.86	1.66
GI	Ivy Dividend Opportunities I	IVDIX	C+	(800) 777-6472	C+ / 6.2	0.74	4.67	8.50 /66	13.54 /64	11.72 /59	1.33	0.94
GI	Ivy Dividend Opportunities Y	IVDYX	C	(800) 777-6472	C+ / 6.1	0.68	4.54	8.24 /64	13.27 /62	11.44 /56	1.09	1.19
FO	Ivy Emerging Markets Equity A	IPOAX	D-	(800) 777-6472	D / 1.6	3.89	5.31	7.48 /59	5.39 /14	2.89 / 6	0.69	1.71
FO	● Ivy Emerging Markets Equity B	IPOBX	D-	(800) 777-6472	D / 1.7	3.69	4.90	6.48 /51	4.20 /11	1.73 / 4	0.00	2.98
FO	Ivy Emerging Markets Equity C	IPOCX	D-	(800) 777-6472	D / 1.9	3.69	4.89	6.55 /51	4.54 /12	2.08 / 5	0.10	2.45
FO	● Ivy Emerging Markets Equity E	IPOEX	D-	(800) 777-6472	D / 1.7	3.97	5.41	7.63 /60	5.72 /16	3.23 / 6	0.89	1.42
FO	Ivy Emerging Markets Equity I	IPOIX	D	(800) 777-6472	D+ / 2.6	3.98	5.53	7.78 /61	5.88 /16	3.38 / 7	1.04	1.20
FO	Ivy Emerging Markets Equity Y	IPOYX	D	(800) 777-6472	D+ / 2.4	3.88	5.34	7.41 /58	5.57 /15	3.09 / 6	0.78	1.45
EN	Ivy Energy A	IEYAX	E-	(800) 777-6472	E / 0.4	1.37	-16.83	-14.35 / 2	3.43 / 9	4.78 /11	0.00	1.60
EN	● Ivy Energy B	IEYBX	E-	(800) 777-6472	E / 0.4	1.16	-17.15	-15.05 / 2	2.55 / 7	3.90 / 8	0.00	2.38
EN	Ivy Energy C	IEYCX	E-	(800) 777-6472	E / 0.4	1.22	-17.09	-14.86 / 2	2.79 / 7	4.12 / 9	0.00	2.16
EN	● Ivy Energy E	IVEEX	E-	(800) 777-6472	E / 0.4	1.42	-16.72	-14.11 / 2	3.74 /10	5.08 /12	0.00	1.66
EN	Ivy Energy I	IVEIX	E-	(800) 777-6472	E / 0.5	1.48	-16.72	-14.05 / 2	3.83 /10	5.19 /13	0.00	1.14
EN	Ivy Energy Y	IEYYX	E-	(800) 777-6472	E / 0.5	1.36	-16.82	-14.26 / 2	3.58 / 9	4.92 /12	0.00	1.39
FO	Ivy European Opptys A	IEOAX	D	(800) 777-6472	D+ / 2.6	6.38	3.56	-0.13 /15	9.33 /35	7.01 /23	1.62	1.76
FO	● Ivy European Opptys B	IEOBX	D	(800) 777-6472	D+ / 2.8	6.12	2.97	-1.27 /12	8.10 /27	5.87 /16	0.34	2.91
FO	Ivy European Opptys C	IEOCX	D	(800) 777-6472	C- / 3.1	6.20	3.23	-0.75 /14	8.65 /31	6.35 /19	1.06	2.37
FO	● Ivy European Opptys E	IVEOX	D	(800) 777-6472	D+ / 2.9	6.49	3.77	0.30 /16	9.82 /38	7.53 /27	2.01	1.32

● Denotes fund is closed to new investors
* Denotes fund is included in Section II

338

RISK			NET ASSETS		ASSET				Portfolio	BULL / BEAR		FUND MANAGER		MINIMUMS		LOADS	
	3 Year		NAV							Last Bull	Last Bear	Manager	Manager	Initial	Additional	Front	Back
Risk	Standard		As of	Total	Cash	Stocks	Bonds	Other	Turnover	Market	Market	Quality	Tenure	Purch.	Purch.	End	End
Rating/Pts	Deviation	Beta	3/31/15	$(Mil)	%	%	%	%	Ratio	Return	Return	Pct	(Years)	$	$	Load	Load
B- / 7.6	6.8	0.49	16.76	80	13	54	31	2	23	32.1	-10.0	86	7	5,000	100	0.0	2.0
B- / 7.4	6.8	0.49	16.97	3,173	13	54	31	2	23	36.6	-9.6	90	7	1,000,000	100	0.0	2.0
B- / 7.7	6.9	0.49	17.73	1,999	14	51	34	1	23	36.8	-11.7	86	7	5,000	100	5.0	2.0
B- / 7.8	6.8	0.49	17.59	1,355	14	51	34	1	23	33.4	-12.1	82	7	5,000	100	0.0	2.0
B- / 7.7	6.9	0.49	17.74	6,661	14	51	34	1	23	38.0	-11.7	87	7	1,000,000	100	0.0	2.0
C- / 3.7	10.4	1.40	25.89	6,593	8	76	14	2	65	55.1	-22.1	13	18	750	0	5.8	0.0
C- / 3.6	10.4	1.40	24.73	595	8	76	14	2	65	51.2	-22.4	13	18	750	0	0.0	0.0
C- / 3.6	10.4	1.40	24.88	8,124	8	76	14	2	65	51.4	-22.3	9	18	750	0	0.0	0.0
C- / 3.7	10.4	1.40	25.96	74	8	76	14	2	65	55.0	-22.1	13	18	750	0	5.8	0.0
C- / 3.7	10.4	1.40	26.15	9,659	8	76	14	2	65	56.4	-22.0	14	18	0	0	0.0	0.0
C- / 3.7	10.4	1.40	25.68	164	8	76	14	2	65	53.2	-22.2	11	18	0	0	0.0	0.0
C- / 3.7	10.3	1.40	25.94	1,177	8	76	14	2	65	55.2	-22.1	13	18	10,000,000	0	0.0	0.0
B- / 7.9	7.8	1.31	25.65	1,190	0	65	33	2	34	65.3	-11.7	29	1	750	0	5.8	0.0
B- / 7.9	7.8	1.31	25.45	75	0	65	33	2	34	61.1	-12.0	21	1	750	0	0.0	0.0
B- / 7.9	7.8	1.31	25.53	728	0	65	33	2	34	61.4	-12.0	21	1	750	0	0.0	0.0
B- / 7.9	7.7	1.29	25.76	N/A	0	65	33	2	34	66.8	-11.7	35	1	0	0	5.8	0.0
B- / 7.8	7.8	1.31	25.63	312	0	65	33	2	34	66.8	-11.6	32	1	0	0	0.0	0.0
B- / 7.9	7.8	1.31	25.66	185	0	65	33	2	34	65.4	-11.7	30	1	10,000,000	0	0.0	0.0
C+ / 5.9	10.6	1.07	14.29	627	2	91	5	2	61	96.0	-17.3	37	9	750	0	5.8	0.0
C+ / 5.8	10.6	1.06	12.36	12	2	91	5	2	61	89.2	-17.6	26	9	750	0	0.0	0.0
C+ / 5.8	10.6	1.06	12.71	164	2	91	5	2	61	90.7	-17.4	28	9	750	0	0.0	0.0
C+ / 5.9	10.6	1.07	14.23	10	2	91	5	2	61	95.0	-17.3	35	9	750	0	5.8	0.0
C+ / 6.0	10.5	1.06	15.67	247	2	91	5	2	61	98.0	-17.1	44	9	0	0	0.0	0.0
C+ / 6.0	10.6	1.06	15.29	103	2	91	5	2	61	97.3	-17.1	42	9	10,000,000	0	0.0	0.0
C / 5.0	13.9	0.90	16.52	303	2	82	12	4	47	54.3	-23.5	48	8	750	0	5.8	0.0
C / 5.0	13.8	0.90	15.20	2	2	82	12	4	47	48.7	-23.8	32	8	750	0	0.0	0.0
C / 5.0	13.9	0.90	15.56	20	2	82	12	4	47	51.3	-23.7	39	8	750	0	0.0	0.0
C / 5.1	13.8	0.90	16.60	1	2	82	12	4	47	55.1	-23.5	49	8	750	0	5.8	0.0
C / 5.1	13.8	0.90	16.94	5	2	82	12	4	47	57.1	-23.4	55	8	0	0	0.0	0.0
C / 5.1	13.9	0.90	16.77	3	2	82	12	4	47	56.2	-23.4	52	8	10,000,000	0	0.0	0.0
C+ / 5.6	10.4	1.06	19.55	327	4	89	6	1	43	86.9	-23.5	21	1	750	0	5.8	0.0
C+ / 5.7	10.4	1.06	19.22	12	4	89	6	1	43	81.8	-23.8	14	1	750	0	0.0	0.0
C+ / 5.7	10.4	1.06	19.31	56	4	89	6	1	43	82.6	-23.7	15	1	750	0	0.0	0.0
C+ / 5.6	10.4	1.06	19.48	5	4	89	6	1	43	86.3	-23.5	19	1	750	0	5.8	0.0
C+ / 5.6	10.4	1.06	19.61	23	4	89	6	1	43	88.9	-23.3	24	1	0	0	0.0	0.0
C+ / 5.6	10.4	1.06	19.58	10	4	89	6	1	43	87.3	-23.4	21	1	10,000,000	0	0.0	0.0
C+ / 5.7	12.3	0.70	16.04	435	1	91	6	2	138	35.7	-30.0	50	11	750	0	5.8	0.0
C+ / 5.7	12.3	0.71	13.48	7	1	91	6	2	138	30.3	-30.3	33	11	750	0	0.0	0.0
C+ / 5.7	12.3	0.71	14.05	35	1	91	6	2	138	32.0	-30.2	37	11	750	0	0.0	0.0
C+ / 5.7	12.3	0.70	16.23	N/A	1	91	6	2	138	37.2	-29.9	54	11	0	0	5.8	0.0
C+ / 5.7	12.3	0.71	16.45	117	1	91	6	2	138	37.8	-29.8	56	11	0	0	0.0	0.0
C+ / 5.7	12.2	0.70	16.33	10	1	91	6	2	138	36.5	-29.9	52	11	0	0	0.0	0.0
D+ / 2.6	17.1	1.02	14.03	213	3	86	10	1	34	37.6	-31.7	60	9	750	0	5.8	0.0
D+ / 2.6	17.1	1.02	13.04	5	3	86	10	1	34	33.7	-31.9	47	9	750	0	0.0	0.0
D+ / 2.6	17.1	1.02	13.24	75	3	86	10	1	34	34.7	-31.8	51	9	750	0	0.0	0.0
D+ / 2.6	17.1	1.02	14.30	N/A	3	86	10	1	34	38.8	-31.6	65	9	0	0	5.8	0.0
D+ / 2.6	17.1	1.02	14.44	83	3	86	10	1	34	39.5	-31.5	66	9	0	0	0.0	0.0
D+ / 2.6	17.1	1.02	14.19	39	3	86	10	1	34	38.3	-31.6	62	9	10,000,000	0	0.0	0.0
C+ / 5.9	12.4	0.87	29.19	147	0	98	0	2	116	58.7	-26.7	77	2	750	0	5.8	0.0
C+ / 5.9	12.4	0.88	27.21	1	0	98	0	2	116	52.7	-27.0	65	2	750	0	0.0	0.0
C+ / 5.9	12.4	0.88	27.73	9	0	98	0	2	116	55.3	-26.9	71	2	750	0	0.0	0.0
C+ / 5.9	12.4	0.88	29.36	N/A	0	98	0	2	116	61.2	-26.6	80	2	0	0	5.8	0.0

					PERFORMANCE							
99 Pct = Best 0 Pct = Worst						Total Return % through 3/31/15					Incl. in Returns	
				Overall	Perfor- mance				Annualized		Dividend	Expense
Fund Type	Fund Name	Ticker Symbol	Investment Rating	Phone	Rating/Pts	3 Mo	6 Mo	1Yr / Pct	3Yr / Pct	5Yr / Pct	Yield	Ratio
FO	Ivy European Opptys I	IEOIX	D+	(800) 777-6472	C- / 3.9	6.52	3.81	0.38 /17	9.94 /39	7.66 /28	2.24	1.19
FO	Ivy EuropeanOpptys Y	IEOYX	D+	(800) 777-6472	C- / 3.8	6.45	3.68	0.15 /16	9.68 /37	7.39 /26	1.98	1.46
GL	Ivy Global Equity Income A	IBIAX	U	(800) 777-6472	U /	4.79	4.71	5.84 /45	--	--	3.08	1.48
FO	Ivy Global Growth A	IVINX	D+	(800) 777-6472	C- / 3.3	5.69	5.47	5.27 /41	9.73 /38	9.18 /38	0.06	1.49
FO ●	Ivy Global Growth B	IVIBX	D+	(800) 777-6472	C- / 3.5	5.41	4.94	4.25 /33	8.65 /31	8.11 /31	0.00	2.47
FO	Ivy Global Growth C	IVNCX	D+	(800) 777-6472	C- / 3.7	5.49	5.08	4.50 /35	8.82 /32	8.24 /31	0.00	2.31
FO ●	Ivy Global Growth E	IIGEX	D+	(800) 777-6472	C- / 3.5	5.75	5.62	5.54 /43	10.00 /39	9.44 /40	0.21	1.34
FO	Ivy Global Growth I	IGIIX	C-	(800) 777-6472	C / 4.5	5.77	5.65	5.65 /44	10.13 /40	9.58 /41	0.31	1.11
FO	Ivy Global Growth Y	IVIYX	C-	(800) 777-6472	C / 4.3	5.72	5.53	5.40 /42	9.85 /38	9.33 /39	0.13	1.38
GL	Ivy Global Income Allocation A	IVBAX	D	(800) 777-6472	D- / 1.4	3.68	1.54	2.87 /26	6.40 /18	6.61 /21	3.67	1.46
GL ●	Ivy Global Income Allocation B	IVBBX	D	(800) 777-6472	D / 1.6	3.39	1.06	1.95 /22	5.43 /15	5.62 /15	3.07	2.38
GL	Ivy Global Income Allocation C	IVBCX	D	(800) 777-6472	D / 1.7	3.50	1.18	2.18 /23	5.69 /16	5.93 /16	3.29	2.10
GL	Ivy Global Income Allocation E	IIBEX	D	(800) 777-6472	D- / 1.4	3.60	1.52	2.82 /26	6.40 /18	6.66 /21	3.63	1.81
GL	Ivy Global Income Allocation I	IIBIX	D+	(800) 777-6472	D+ / 2.3	3.73	1.71	3.22 /28	6.83 /20	7.07 /23	4.23	1.05
GL	Ivy Global Income Allocation Y	IVBYX	D	(800) 777-6472	D / 2.1	3.69	1.60	2.97 /26	6.57 /19	6.79 /22	3.99	1.30
EN	Ivy Global Nat Resource A	IGNAX	E-	(800) 777-6472	E- / 0.2	1.57	-15.95	-15.42 / 2	-3.10 / 2	-2.77 / 1	0.00	1.56
EN ●	Ivy Global Nat Resource B	IGNBX	E-	(800) 777-6472	E- / 0.2	1.38	-16.29	-16.14 / 2	-3.92 / 2	-3.57 / 1	0.00	2.41
EN	Ivy Global Nat Resource C	IGNCX	E-	(800) 777-6472	E- / 0.2	1.48	-16.19	-15.93 / 2	-3.71 / 2	-3.40 / 1	0.00	2.18
EN	Ivy Global Nat Resource E	IGNEX	E-	(800) 777-6472	E- / 0.2	1.73	-15.74	-15.13 / 2	-2.81 / 2	-2.55 / 1	0.00	2.12
EN	Ivy Global Nat Resource I	IGNIX	E-	(800) 777-6472	E- / 0.2	1.77	-15.66	-14.98 / 2	-2.62 / 3	-2.33 / 2	0.00	1.08
EN	Ivy Global Nat Resource R	IGNRX	E-	(800) 777-6472	E- / 0.2	1.59	-15.97	-15.53 / 2	-3.21 / 2	-2.90 / 1	0.00	1.67
EN	Ivy Global Nat Resource Y	IGNYX	E-	(800) 777-6472	E- / 0.2	1.73	-15.77	-15.16 / 2	-2.85 / 2	-2.54 / 1	0.00	1.33
RE	Ivy Global Real Estate A	IREAX	U	(800) 777-6472	U /	4.99	12.01	16.31 /94	--	--	1.61	1.88
RE	Ivy Global Risk-Managed Real Est A	IVRAX	U	(800) 777-6472	U /	4.44	12.14	16.77 /94	--	--	2.34	1.65
FO	Ivy International Core Eq A	IVIAX	D	(800) 777-6472	C- / 3.6	5.18	3.19	4.98 /38	10.66 /43	7.80 /29	1.13	1.40
FO ●	Ivy International Core Eq B	IIFBX	D	(800) 777-6472	C- / 3.9	4.86	2.71	4.02 /32	9.71 /38	6.86 /22	0.51	2.22
FO	Ivy International Core Eq C	IVIFX	D	(800) 777-6472	C- / 4.1	4.99	2.82	4.25 /33	9.92 /39	7.10 /24	0.67	2.07
FO	Ivy International Core Eq E	IICEX	D	(800) 777-6472	C- / 3.6	5.14	3.09	4.82 /37	10.56 /43	7.73 /28	0.96	1.85
FO	Ivy International Core Eq I	ICEIX	D+	(800) 777-6472	C / 4.8	5.27	3.38	5.32 /41	11.09 /46	8.22 /31	1.51	1.04
FO	Ivy International Core Eq Y	IVVYX	D+	(800) 777-6472	C / 4.6	5.20	3.26	5.04 /39	10.78 /44	7.94 /29	1.26	1.29
GR	Ivy Large Cap Growth A	WLGAX	B-	(800) 777-6472	B / 7.9	5.15	10.30	17.45 /95	15.29 /77	14.40 /81	0.00	1.19
GR ●	Ivy Large Cap Growth B	WLGBX	B-	(800) 777-6472	B / 8.2	4.98	9.90	16.49 /94	14.25 /69	13.29 /71	0.00	2.06
GR	Ivy Large Cap Growth C	WLGCX	B	(800) 777-6472	B+ / 8.3	4.94	9.92	16.67 /94	14.43 /70	13.53 /73	0.00	1.90
GR	Ivy Large Cap Growth E	ILCEX	B-	(800) 777-6472	B / 7.9	5.10	10.26	17.47 /95	15.28 /77	14.40 /81	0.00	1.46
GR	Ivy Large Cap Growth I	IYGIX	B+	(800) 777-6472	A- / 9.0	5.18	10.45	17.75 /95	15.60 /80	14.70 /84	0.00	0.88
GR	Ivy Large Cap Growth R	WLGRX	B+	(800) 777-6472	B+ / 8.7	5.10	10.13	17.16 /95	14.92 /74	14.04 /78	0.00	1.47
GR	Ivy Large Cap Growth Y	WLGYX	B+	(800) 777-6472	B+ / 8.9	5.22	10.40	17.62 /95	15.39 /78	14.51 /82	0.00	1.13
GL	Ivy Managed Intl Opp Class Y	IVTYX	D+	(800) 777-6472	C- / 3.2	4.68	4.33	5.26 /41	8.06 /27	5.88 /16	1.44	1.54
GL	Ivy Managed Intl Opps A	IVTAX	D	(800) 777-6472	D+ / 2.3	4.68	4.34	5.17 /40	7.96 /27	5.82 /16	1.28	1.63
GL ●	Ivy Managed Intl Opps B	IVTBX	D	(800) 777-6472	D+ / 2.6	4.45	3.86	4.28 /34	7.12 /22	4.96 /12	0.78	2.53
GL	Ivy Managed Intl Opps C	IVTCX	D	(800) 777-6472	D+ / 2.7	4.54	3.90	4.32 /34	7.21 /22	5.03 /12	0.83	2.40
GL ●	Ivy Managed Intl Opps E	IVTEX	D	(800) 777-6472	D+ / 2.4	4.78	4.42	5.25 /40	8.08 /27	5.89 /16	1.35	0.44
GL	Ivy Managed Intl Opps I	IVTIX	D+	(800) 777-6472	C- / 3.3	4.77	4.49	5.41 /42	8.18 /28	6.07 /17	1.58	1.30
SC	Ivy Micro Cap Growth A	IGWAX	D-	(800) 777-6472	C / 4.5	2.49	12.14	-3.92 / 7	12.95 /59	14.60 /83	0.00	1.64
SC ●	Ivy Micro Cap Growth B	IGWBX	D-	(800) 777-6472	C / 4.7	2.29	11.62	-4.80 / 6	11.83 /51	13.34 /71	0.00	2.59
SC	Ivy Micro Cap Growth C	IGWCX	D-	(800) 777-6472	C / 4.9	2.30	11.69	-4.63 / 6	12.12 /53	13.72 /75	0.00	2.35
SC	Ivy Micro Cap Growth I	IGWIX	D	(800) 777-6472	C+ / 5.7	2.57	12.33	-3.56 / 8	13.44 /63	15.10 /88	0.00	1.23
SC	Ivy Micro Cap Growth Y	IGWYX	D	(800) 777-6472	C+ / 6.0	2.54	12.21	-3.77 / 7	13.92 /67	15.29 /89	0.00	1.50
MC	Ivy Mid Cap Growth A	WMGAX	C	(800) 777-6472	C+ / 5.8	3.90	10.40	10.73 /77	13.27 /62	14.81 /85	0.00	1.34
MC ●	Ivy Mid Cap Growth B	WMGBX	C	(800) 777-6472	C+ / 6.1	3.77	10.00	9.94 /74	12.35 /55	13.82 /76	0.00	2.10
MC	Ivy Mid Cap Growth C	WMGCX	C	(800) 777-6472	C+ / 6.2	3.78	10.05	10.00 /74	12.47 /56	13.98 /78	0.00	2.01
MC	Ivy Mid Cap Growth E	IMCEX	C	(800) 777-6472	C+ / 5.6	3.85	10.27	10.46 /76	12.97 /59	14.55 /83	0.00	1.71

● Denotes fund is closed to new investors
* Denotes fund is included in Section II

www.thestreetratings.com

RISK			NET ASSETS		ASSET					BULL / BEAR		FUND MANAGER		MINIMUMS		LOADS	
	3 Year		NAV						Portfolio	Last Bull	Last Bear	Manager	Manager	Initial	Additional	Front	Back
Risk	Standard		As of	Total	Cash	Stocks	Bonds	Other	Turnover	Market	Market	Quality	Tenure	Purch.	Purch.	End	End
Rating/Pts	Deviation	Beta	3/31/15	$(Mil)	%	%	%	%	Ratio	Return	Return	Pct	(Years)	$	$	Load	Load
C+ / 5.9	12.4	0.88	29.39	26	0	98	0	2	116	61.8	-26.5	81	2	0	0	0.0	0.0
C+ / 5.9	12.4	0.87	29.38	2	0	98	0	2	116	60.4	-26.6	79	2	10,000,000	0	0.0	0.0
U /	N/A	N/A	13.32	252	3	96	0	1	98	N/A	N/A	N/A	3	750	0	5.8	0.0
C+ / 6.1	10.9	0.80	42.75	407	0	87	12	1	46	61.0	-22.0	84	1	750	0	5.8	0.0
C+ / 6.1	10.9	0.80	37.61	4	0	87	12	1	46	55.8	-22.3	77	1	750	0	0.0	0.0
C+ / 6.1	10.8	0.80	37.68	26	0	87	12	1	46	56.5	-22.3	79	1	750	0	0.0	0.0
C+ / 6.1	10.9	0.80	42.83	N/A	0	87	12	1	46	62.4	-21.9	86	1	0	0	5.8	0.0
C+ / 6.1	10.9	0.80	43.24	74	0	87	12	1	46	63.1	-21.9	86	1	0	0	0.0	0.0
C+ / 6.1	10.9	0.80	42.86	10	0	87	12	1	46	61.7	-21.9	85	1	10,000,000	0	0.0	0.0
C+ / 6.9	9.4	1.42	15.42	652	1	64	33	2	92	35.7	-14.1	6	3	750	0	5.8	0.0
C+ / 6.9	9.4	1.42	15.15	6	1	64	33	2	92	31.5	-14.5	5	3	750	0	0.0	0.0
C+ / 6.9	9.4	1.42	15.24	51	1	64	33	2	92	32.8	-14.4	5	3	750	0	0.0	0.0
C+ / 6.9	9.4	1.42	15.42	3	1	64	33	2	92	35.9	-14.1	6	3	750	0	5.8	0.0
C+ / 6.9	9.4	1.42	15.54	49	1	64	33	2	92	37.7	-14.0	8	3	0	0	0.0	0.0
C+ / 6.9	9.4	1.42	15.48	3	1	64	33	2	92	36.6	-14.1	7	3	10,000,000	0	0.0	0.0
D+ / 2.8	16.8	0.98	16.13	662	6	92	1	1	100	10.7	-40.1	5	2	750	0	5.8	0.0
D+ / 2.7	16.8	0.98	13.98	22	6	92	1	1	100	7.6	-40.3	3	2	750	0	0.0	0.0
D+ / 2.8	16.7	0.98	13.67	195	6	92	1	1	100	8.4	-40.3	4	2	750	0	0.0	0.0
D+ / 2.8	16.8	0.98	16.43	6	6	92	1	1	100	11.7	-40.1	5	2	750	0	5.8	0.0
D+ / 2.9	16.8	0.98	16.69	183	6	92	1	1	100	12.5	-40.0	6	2	0	0	0.0	0.0
D+ / 2.8	16.7	0.98	15.94	34	6	92	1	1	100	10.3	-40.1	4	2	0	0	0.0	0.0
D+ / 2.8	16.8	0.98	16.45	62	6	92	1	1	100	11.6	-40.0	5	2	10,000,000	0	0.0	0.0
U /	N/A	N/A	11.15	28	9	88	1	2	36	N/A	N/A	N/A	2	750	0	5.8	0.0
U /	N/A	N/A	11.06	41	19	80	0	1	38	N/A	N/A	N/A	2	750	0	5.8	0.0
C / 4.8	12.3	0.91	17.88	1,367	0	97	1	2	87	59.9	-24.6	83	9	750	0	5.8	0.0
C / 4.7	12.2	0.91	15.97	13	0	97	1	2	87	55.3	-24.9	77	9	750	0	0.0	0.0
C / 4.7	12.2	0.91	16.00	158	0	97	1	2	87	56.4	-24.8	79	9	750	0	0.0	0.0
C / 4.9	12.2	0.91	17.99	5	0	97	1	2	87	59.5	-24.6	83	9	750	0	5.8	0.0
C / 4.8	12.3	0.91	17.99	1,205	0	97	1	2	87	62.0	-24.5	86	9	0	0	0.0	0.0
C / 4.9	12.3	0.91	18.00	524	0	97	1	2	87	60.6	-24.5	84	9	10,000,000	0	0.0	0.0
C / 5.4	11.5	1.01	19.19	1,081	1	96	2	1	50	97.8	-14.8	54	15	750	0	5.8	0.0
C / 5.0	11.4	1.01	15.82	12	1	96	2	1	50	91.5	-15.2	40	15	750	0	0.0	0.0
C / 5.2	11.5	1.01	16.78	94	1	96	2	1	50	92.8	-15.1	42	15	750	0	0.0	0.0
C / 5.4	11.5	1.01	19.17	9	1	96	2	1	50	97.8	-14.8	53	15	750	0	5.8	0.0
C / 5.5	11.4	1.01	19.90	314	1	96	2	1	50	99.5	-14.7	59	15	0	0	0.0	0.0
C / 5.4	11.4	1.01	18.74	27	1	96	2	1	50	95.7	-15.0	50	15	0	0	0.0	0.0
C / 5.5	11.5	1.01	19.57	132	1	96	2	1	50	98.3	-14.8	55	15	10,000,000	0	0.0	0.0
C+ / 6.3	10.9	1.60	10.51	2	1	89	9	1	21	47.4	-24.5	6	8	10,000,000	0	0.0	0.0
C+ / 6.3	10.9	1.60	10.52	230	1	89	9	1	21	46.9	-24.5	6	8	750	0	5.8	0.0
C+ / 6.3	11.0	1.62	10.33	2	1	89	9	1	21	43.4	-25.1	4	8	750	0	0.0	0.0
C+ / 6.3	11.1	1.63	10.36	6	1	89	9	1	21	43.8	-25.1	4	8	750	0	0.0	0.0
C+ / 6.3	10.9	1.59	10.53	1	1	89	9	1	21	47.2	-24.5	7	8	0	0	5.8	0.0
C+ / 6.3	10.8	1.59	10.54	1	1	89	9	1	21	48.0	-24.3	7	8	0	0	0.0	0.0
C- / 3.1	17.0	1.14	24.73	198	0	96	2	2	67	99.8	-28.6	10	6	750	0	5.8	0.0
C- / 3.0	17.0	1.14	23.70	2	0	96	2	2	67	92.9	-29.0	6	6	750	0	0.0	0.0
C- / 3.0	17.0	1.14	24.00	11	0	96	2	2	67	94.7	-28.8	7	6	750	0	0.0	0.0
C- / 3.1	17.0	1.14	25.12	20	0	96	2	2	67	102.9	-28.5	12	6	0	0	0.0	0.0
C- / 3.1	16.9	1.11	25.44	2	0	96	2	2	67	105.1	-28.6	18	6	10,000,000	0	0.0	0.0
C+ / 5.6	10.6	0.90	23.43	1,024	0	97	1	2	43	85.6	-20.7	42	14	750	0	5.8	0.0
C / 5.3	10.6	0.90	19.84	24	0	97	1	2	43	80.5	-21.0	31	14	750	0	0.0	0.0
C / 5.4	10.6	0.90	20.88	340	0	97	1	2	43	81.0	-20.9	33	14	750	0	0.0	0.0
C / 5.5	10.6	0.90	22.92	7	0	97	1	2	43	83.8	-20.7	38	14	750	0	5.8	0.0

Fund Type	Fund Name	Ticker Symbol	Overall Investment Rating	Phone	Performance Rating/Pts	3 Mo	6 Mo	1Yr / Pct	3Yr / Pct	5Yr / Pct	Dividend Yield	Expense Ratio
MC	Ivy Mid Cap Growth I	IYMIX	C+	(800) 777-6472	B- / 7.0	3.99	10.60	11.09 /79	13.62 /64	15.21 /88	0.00	0.99
MC	Ivy Mid Cap Growth R	WMGRX	C+	(800) 777-6472	C+ / 6.5	3.82	10.25	10.39 /76	12.95 /59	14.54 /83	0.00	1.59
MC	Ivy Mid Cap Growth Y	WMGYX	C+	(800) 777-6472	C+ / 6.8	3.94	10.46	10.83 /78	13.36 /62	14.96 /86	0.00	1.23
RE	Ivy Real Estate Securities A	IRSAX	B-	(800) 777-6472	B+ / 8.8	5.34	20.55	25.19 /98	13.38 /62	14.52 /82	0.52	1.66
RE	● Ivy Real Estate Securities B	IRSBX	B-	(800) 777-6472	B+ / 8.9	5.11	20.01	23.94 /98	12.20 /54	13.27 /71	0.00	2.71
RE	Ivy Real Estate Securities C	IRSCX	B-	(800) 777-6472	A- / 9.1	5.13	20.12	24.27 /98	12.55 /56	13.67 /75	0.03	2.37
RE	Ivy Real Estate Securities E	IREEX	C+	(800) 777-6472	B+ / 8.7	5.27	20.41	24.88 /98	13.24 /61	14.46 /82	0.34	2.15
RE	Ivy Real Estate Securities I	IREIX	B	(800) 777-6472	A / 9.5	5.45	20.80	25.75 /98	13.96 /67	15.15 /88	1.05	1.12
RE	Ivy Real Estate Securities R	IRSRX	B	(800) 777-6472	A / 9.3	5.28	20.43	24.92 /98	13.24 /61	14.46 /82	0.39	1.76
RE	Ivy Real Estate Securities Y	IRSYX	B	(800) 777-6472	A / 9.5	5.37	20.67	25.42 /98	13.67 /65	14.87 /86	0.80	1.37
TC	Ivy Science and Technology A	WSTAX	A-	(800) 777-6472	A / 9.4	5.01	6.82	8.48 /66	20.73 /98	17.03 /96	0.00	1.26
TC	● Ivy Science and Technology B	WSTBX	A	(800) 777-6472	A / 9.5	4.83	6.41	7.67 /60	19.80 /98	16.08 /93	0.00	2.04
TC	Ivy Science and Technology C	WSTCX	A	(800) 777-6472	A+ / 9.6	4.84	6.44	7.73 /61	19.89 /98	16.19 /94	0.00	1.97
TC	Ivy Science and Technology E	ISTEX	A-	(800) 777-6472	A / 9.4	4.98	6.73	8.29 /65	20.61 /98	16.94 /96	0.00	1.63
TC	Ivy Science and Technology I	ISTIX	A	(800) 777-6472	A+ / 9.7	5.10	6.97	8.79 /68	21.10 /98	17.40 /97	0.00	0.99
TC	Ivy Science and Technology R	WSTRX	A	(800) 777-6472	A+ / 9.6	4.94	6.65	8.15 /64	20.37 /98	16.71 /95	0.00	1.59
TC	Ivy Science and Technology Y	WSTYX	A	(800) 777-6472	A+ / 9.7	5.03	6.85	8.53 /66	20.80 /98	17.10 /96	0.00	1.24
SC	Ivy Small Cap Growth A	WSGAX	C+	(800) 777-6472	B- / 7.5	5.59	16.33	8.03 /63	15.81 /82	15.50 /90	0.00	1.43
SC	● Ivy Small Cap Growth B	WSGBX	C+	(800) 777-6472	B / 7.8	5.38	15.83	7.07 /56	14.75 /73	14.37 /81	0.00	2.34
SC	Ivy Small Cap Growth C	WRGCX	C+	(800) 777-6472	B / 8.0	5.44	16.02	7.36 /58	15.08 /75	14.75 /85	0.00	2.08
SC	Ivy Small Cap Growth E	ISGEX	C+	(800) 777-6472	B- / 7.4	5.56	16.30	7.90 /62	15.69 /81	15.41 /90	0.00	1.87
SC	Ivy Small Cap Growth I	IYSIX	B	(800) 777-6472	B+ / 8.8	5.71	16.56	8.42 /66	16.25 /85	15.99 /93	0.00	1.06
SC	Ivy Small Cap Growth R	WSGRX	B-	(800) 777-6472	B+ / 8.4	5.52	16.20	7.74 /61	15.54 /79	15.29 /89	0.00	1.66
SC	Ivy Small Cap Growth Y	WSCYX	B	(800) 777-6472	B+ / 8.6	5.65	16.42	8.16 /64	15.97 /83	15.69 /91	0.00	1.30
SC	Ivy Small Cap Value A	IYSAX	C	(800) 777-6472	C+ / 6.3	1.98	8.77	5.74 /44	15.23 /77	11.20 /54	0.00	1.68
SC	● Ivy Small Cap Value B	IYSBX	C	(800) 777-6472	C+ / 6.5	1.69	8.24	4.68 /36	14.05 /67	10.00 /45	0.00	2.69
SC	Ivy Small Cap Value C	IYSCX	C	(800) 777-6472	C+ / 6.7	1.81	8.38	5.02 /39	14.46 /71	10.40 /48	0.00	2.36
SC	● Ivy Small Cap Value E	IYVIX	C	(800) 777-6472	C+ / 6.6	2.05	8.93	6.08 /47	15.67 /81	11.63 /58	0.00	1.32
SC	Ivy Small Cap Value I	IVVIX	C+	(800) 777-6472	B / 7.7	2.10	9.03	6.20 /48	15.80 /82	11.77 /59	0.00	1.21
SC	Ivy Small Cap Value Y	IYSYX	C+	(800) 777-6472	B- / 7.5	2.03	8.86	5.93 /46	15.50 /79	11.46 /57	0.00	1.44
GR	Ivy Tax-Managed Equity A	IYEAX	B+	(800) 777-6472	B / 7.8	4.60	8.38	17.00 /95	15.69 /81	13.57 /74	0.00	1.43
GR	● Ivy Tax-Managed Equity B	IYEBX	B+	(800) 777-6472	B+ / 8.3	4.40	7.98	16.25 /94	15.00 /75	12.88 /67	0.00	2.06
GR	Ivy Tax-Managed Equity C	IYECX	B+	(800) 777-6472	B+ / 8.3	4.41	7.99	16.22 /94	14.93 /74	12.83 /67	0.00	2.09
GR	● Ivy Tax-Managed Equity I	WYTMX	A-	(800) 777-6472	B+ / 8.9	4.62	8.49	17.33 /95	15.81 /82	13.78 /76	0.00	1.15
GR	Ivy Tax-Managed Equity Y	IYEYX	A	(800) 777-6472	B+ / 8.8	4.60	8.37	17.04 /95	15.75 /81	13.62 /74	0.00	1.41
GR	Ivy Value A	IYVAX	C	(800) 777-6472	C / 5.2	-2.21	-1.45	5.71 /44	14.70 /72	11.67 /58	0.21	1.31
GR	● Ivy Value B	IYVBX	C+	(800) 777-6472	C / 5.5	-2.43	-1.86	4.81 /37	13.64 /64	10.43 /48	0.00	2.17
GR	Ivy Value C	IYVCX	C+	(800) 777-6472	C+ / 5.7	-2.36	-1.78	5.00 /38	13.93 /67	10.87 /52	0.00	2.01
GR	● Ivy Value E	IVVEX	C	(800) 777-6472	C / 5.4	-2.13	-1.33	5.98 /46	15.00 /75	12.00 /60	0.36	1.22
GR	Ivy Value I	IYAIX	C+	(800) 777-6472	C+ / 6.4	-2.08	-1.27	6.12 /48	15.12 /76	12.12 /61	0.44	0.99
GR	Ivy Value Y	IYVYX	C+	(800) 777-6472	C+ / 6.3	-2.17	-1.39	5.84 /45	14.85 /74	11.85 /60	0.27	1.22
GL	J Hancock Alt Asst Alloc A	JAAAX	D	(800) 257-3336	E+ / 0.6	0.98	-0.76	-0.09 /15	3.04 / 8	4.25 / 9	1.85	1.80
GR	J Hancock Alt Asst Alloc C	JAACX	D	(800) 257-3336	E+ / 0.7	0.84	-1.06	-0.80 /14	2.33 / 7	3.54 / 7	1.22	2.50
GL	J Hancock Alt Asst Alloc I	JAAIX	D	(800) 257-3336	E+ / 0.9	1.12	-0.55	0.18 /16	3.41 / 9	4.57 /10	2.22	1.48
GR	J Hancock Alt Asst Alloc R2	JAAPX	D	(800) 257-3336	E+ / 0.8	0.98	-0.79	-0.26 /15	2.88 / 8	4.14 / 9	1.70	1.89
GR	J Hancock Alt Asst Alloc R6	JAARX	D	(800) 257-3336	E+ / 0.9	1.12	-0.50	0.37 /17	3.41 / 9	4.52 /10	2.40	1.39
BA	J Hancock Balanced A	SVBAX	C	(800) 257-3336	C- / 3.7	1.18	3.70	7.06 /55	10.56 /43	9.42 /40	1.94	1.23
BA	● J Hancock Balanced B	SVBBX	C+	(800) 257-3336	C- / 4.0	1.01	3.34	6.33 /49	9.79 /38	8.65 /34	1.36	1.93
BA	J Hancock Balanced C	SVBCX	C+	(800) 257-3336	C- / 4.0	1.01	3.34	6.38 /50	9.80 /38	8.67 /34	1.36	1.93
BA	J Hancock Balanced I	SVBIX	C+	(800) 257-3336	C / 4.7	1.26	3.87	7.46 /59	10.96 /45	9.83 /43	2.35	0.92
BA	J Hancock Balanced R1	JBAOX	C+	(800) 257-3336	C- / 4.2	1.09	3.51	6.74 /53	10.21 /41	9.10 /37	1.71	1.57
BA	J Hancock Balanced R2	JBATX	C+	(800) 257-3336	C / 4.5	1.16	3.61	7.09 /56	10.66 /43	9.49 /40	2.11	1.32

● Denotes fund is closed to new investors
★ Denotes fund is included in Section II

www.thestreetratings.com

RISK			NET ASSETS		ASSET				Portfolio	BULL / BEAR		FUND MANAGER		MINIMUMS		LOADS	
	3 Year		NAV							Last Bull	Last Bear	Manager	Manager	Initial	Additional	Front	Back
Risk Rating/Pts	Standard Deviation	Beta	As of 3/31/15	Total $(Mil)	Cash %	Stocks %	Bonds %	Other %	Turnover Ratio	Market Return	Market Return	Quality Pct	Tenure (Years)	Purch. $	Purch. $	End Load	End Load
C+ / 5.7	10.6	0.90	24.77	2,886	0	97	1	2	43	87.6	-20.5	47	14	0	0	0.0	0.0
C+ / 5.6	10.6	0.90	23.08	96	0	97	1	2	43	83.8	-20.7	38	14	0	0	0.0	0.0
C+ / 5.6	10.6	0.90	24.26	746	0	97	1	2	43	86.1	-20.6	43	14	10,000,000	0	0.0	0.0
C- / 4.1	12.7	1.01	29.38	534	0	99	0	1	73	82.1	-18.2	56	9	750	0	5.8	0.0
C- / 4.1	12.7	1.01	28.58	6	0	99	0	1	73	75.7	-18.6	40	9	750	0	0.0	0.0
C- / 4.1	12.7	1.01	28.92	21	0	99	0	1	73	77.7	-18.5	45	9	750	0	0.0	0.0
C- / 4.1	12.7	1.01	29.37	3	0	99	0	1	73	81.6	-18.2	54	9	750	0	5.8	0.0
C- / 4.1	12.7	1.01	29.53	12	0	99	0	1	73	85.5	-18.0	64	9	0	0	0.0	0.0
C- / 4.1	12.7	1.01	29.37	2	0	99	0	1	73	81.6	-18.2	54	9	0	0	0.0	0.0
C- / 4.1	12.7	1.01	29.40	179	0	99	0	1	73	83.9	-18.1	60	9	10,000,000	0	0.0	0.0
C+ / 5.8	12.0	1.00	55.95	2,173	0	94	5	1	35	122.4	-19.8	91	14	750	0	5.8	0.0
C+ / 5.8	12.0	1.00	48.01	71	0	94	5	1	35	116.5	-20.1	89	14	750	0	0.0	0.0
C+ / 5.8	12.0	1.00	49.63	982	0	94	5	1	35	117.0	-20.1	89	14	750	0	0.0	0.0
C+ / 5.8	12.0	1.00	55.70	21	0	94	5	1	35	121.7	-19.9	91	14	750	0	5.8	0.0
C+ / 5.9	12.0	1.00	60.64	1,838	0	94	5	1	35	124.6	-19.7	92	14	0	0	0.0	0.0
C+ / 5.8	12.0	1.00	55.05	112	0	94	5	1	35	120.1	-19.9	91	14	0	0	0.0	0.0
C+ / 5.8	12.0	1.00	58.68	1,021	0	94	5	1	35	122.8	-19.8	91	14	10,000,000	0	0.0	0.0
C / 4.8	13.6	0.96	18.71	381	0	96	3	1	45	90.8	-24.7	70	5	750	0	5.8	0.0
C / 4.4	13.6	0.95	15.28	11	0	96	3	1	45	84.8	-25.1	58	5	750	0	0.0	0.0
C / 4.6	13.6	0.96	16.27	205	0	96	3	1	45	86.7	-25.0	62	5	750	0	0.0	0.0
C / 4.8	13.5	0.95	18.60	6	0	96	3	1	45	90.1	-24.8	70	5	750	0	5.8	0.0
C / 5.1	13.6	0.96	22.77	211	0	96	3	1	45	93.4	-24.6	74	5	0	0	0.0	0.0
C / 4.8	13.6	0.95	18.55	45	0	96	3	1	45	89.4	-24.8	68	5	0	0	0.0	0.0
C / 5.0	13.6	0.95	21.88	259	0	96	3	1	45	91.8	-24.7	72	5	10,000,000	0	0.0	0.0
C / 5.0	12.0	0.85	17.47	239	2	97	0	1	61	89.7	-27.1	80	1	750	0	5.8	0.0
C / 4.6	12.0	0.85	15.01	3	2	97	0	1	61	83.0	-27.4	71	1	750	0	0.0	0.0
C / 4.7	12.0	0.85	15.74	18	2	97	0	1	61	85.2	-27.3	75	1	750	0	0.0	0.0
C / 5.0	12.0	0.85	17.93	N/A	2	97	0	1	61	92.2	-27.0	83	1	0	0	5.8	0.0
C / 5.1	12.0	0.85	18.49	29	2	97	0	1	61	93.0	-26.9	84	1	0	0	0.0	0.0
C / 5.1	12.0	0.85	18.12	10	2	97	0	1	61	91.2	-27.0	82	1	10,000,000	0	0.0	0.0
C+ / 6.5	10.8	1.00	19.31	72	0	95	4	1	32	94.7	-14.9	61	6	750	0	5.8	0.0
C+ / 6.4	10.8	1.00	18.73	2	0	95	4	1	32	90.7	-15.2	52	6	750	0	0.0	0.0
C+ / 6.4	10.8	1.00	18.69	3	0	95	4	1	32	90.4	-15.2	51	6	750	0	0.0	0.0
C+ / 6.4	10.9	1.02	19.47	3	0	95	4	1	32	95.5	-14.8	60	6	0	0	0.0	0.0
C+ / 6.5	10.8	1.00	19.34	1	0	95	4	1	32	95.2	-15.0	62	6	10,000,000	0	0.0	0.0
C+ / 6.4	10.8	1.03	23.40	311	8	82	8	2	58	94.6	-22.1	43	21	750	0	5.8	0.0
C+ / 6.5	10.8	1.02	22.04	5	8	82	8	2	58	88.3	-22.5	30	21	750	0	0.0	0.0
C+ / 6.5	10.8	1.03	22.73	23	8	82	8	2	58	90.0	-22.3	33	21	750	0	0.0	0.0
C+ / 6.4	10.8	1.02	23.49	N/A	8	82	8	2	58	96.3	-21.9	47	21	0	0	5.8	0.0
C+ / 6.4	10.8	1.02	23.50	18	8	82	8	2	58	97.0	-21.9	49	21	0	0	0.0	0.0
C+ / 6.4	10.8	1.02	23.45	3	8	82	8	2	58	95.5	-22.0	46	21	10,000,000	0	0.0	0.0
B / 8.2	3.1	0.42	14.38	451	14	33	51	2	26	17.4	-9.1	58	5	1,000	0	5.0	0.0
B / 8.4	3.1	0.23	14.43	153	14	33	51	2	26	14.6	-9.3	49	5	1,000	0	0.0	0.0
B / 8.2	3.1	0.42	14.39	566	14	33	51	2	26	18.7	-8.9	63	5	250,000	0	0.0	0.0
B / 8.3	3.1	0.23	14.38	2	14	33	51	2	26	16.7	-9.1	57	5	0	0	0.0	0.0
B / 8.2	3.1	0.23	14.39	9	14	33	51	2	26	18.8	-9.1	65	5	1,000,000	0	0.0	0.0
B / 8.0	6.8	1.18	18.97	761	3	60	36	1	39	63.7	-14.5	35	12	1,000	0	5.0	0.0
B / 8.0	6.8	1.19	18.94	76	3	60	36	1	39	59.9	-14.8	26	12	1,000	0	0.0	0.0
B / 8.0	6.8	1.18	18.96	471	3	60	36	1	39	59.9	-14.8	27	12	1,000	0	0.0	0.0
B / 8.0	6.8	1.19	18.96	178	3	60	36	1	39	65.8	-14.4	39	12	250,000	0	0.0	0.0
B / 8.0	6.8	1.18	19.04	4	3	60	36	1	39	62.0	-14.7	31	12	0	0	0.0	0.0
B / 8.0	6.8	1.18	18.95	2	3	60	36	1	39	64.3	-14.5	36	12	0	0	0.0	0.0

	99 Pct = Best 0 Pct = Worst				**PERFORMANCE**							
							Total Return % through 3/31/15					Incl. in Returns
			Overall		Perfor- mance					Annualized		Dividend Expense
Fund Type	Fund Name	Ticker Symbol	Investment Rating	Phone	Rating/Pts	3 Mo	6 Mo	1Yr / Pct	3Yr / Pct	5Yr / Pct	Yield	Ratio
BA	J Hancock Balanced R3	JBAHX	C+	(800) 257-3336	C / 4.3	1.12	3.57	6.80 /53	10.31 /41	9.20 /38	1.81	1.46
BA	J Hancock Balanced R4	JBAFX	C+	(800) 257-3336	C / 4.6	1.22	3.78	7.28 /57	10.76 /44	9.58 /41	2.20	1.17
BA	J Hancock Balanced R5	JBAVX	C+	(800) 257-3336	C / 4.7	1.27	3.83	7.44 /59	10.99 /45	9.84 /43	2.40	0.87
BA	J Hancock Balanced R6	JBAWX	C+	(800) 257-3336	C / 4.8	1.28	3.93	7.52 /59	11.05 /46	9.75 /43	2.47	0.82
GR	J Hancock Classic Value A	PZFVX	C+	(800) 257-3336	C+ / 5.8	-2.21	2.72	6.29 /49	15.00 /75	11.42 /56	0.80	1.19
GR	● J Hancock Classic Value B	JCVBX	C+	(800) 257-3336	C+ / 6.0	-2.43	2.36	5.46 /42	14.12 /68	10.59 /49	0.12	1.94
GR	J Hancock Classic Value C	JCVCX	C+	(800) 257-3336	C+ / 6.0	-2.43	2.36	5.46 /42	14.13 /68	10.58 /49	0.12	1.94
GR	J Hancock Classic Value I	JCVIX	C+	(800) 257-3336	C+ / 6.8	-2.17	2.87	6.53 /51	15.32 /77	11.78 /59	1.10	0.93
GR	J Hancock Classic Value R1	JCVRX	C+	(800) 257-3336	C+ / 6.3	-2.32	2.54	5.85 /45	14.57 /72	11.07 /53	0.49	1.57
GR	J Hancock Classic Value R2	JCVSX	C+	(800) 257-3336	C+ / 6.6	-2.21	2.70	6.22 /48	15.08 /75	11.48 /57	0.93	1.33
GR	J Hancock Classic Value R3	JCVHX	C+	(800) 257-3336	C+ / 6.4	-2.29	2.57	5.98 /46	14.71 /73	11.16 /54	0.58	1.47
GR	J Hancock Classic Value R4	JCVFX	C+	(800) 257-3336	C+ / 6.8	-2.17	2.86	6.51 /51	15.26 /77	11.61 /58	1.09	1.17
GR	J Hancock Classic Value R5	JCVVX	C+	(800) 257-3336	C+ / 6.9	-2.14	2.91	6.65 /52	15.43 /78	11.83 /59	1.22	0.88
GR	J Hancock Classic Value R6	JCVWX	C+	(800) 257-3336	C+ / 6.9	-2.14	2.93	6.67 /52	15.43 /78	11.73 /59	1.24	0.83
GI	J Hancock Diversified Strategies A	JDSTX	D-	(800) 257-3336	D- / 1.1	1.67	1.04	1.79 /21	5.58 /15	--	2.80	1.72
GI	J Hancock Diversified Strategies I	JDSIX	D-	(800) 257-3336	D / 1.7	1.76	1.18	2.21 /23	5.96 /17	--	3.26	1.40
FS	J Hancock Financial Indust A	FIDAX	C+	(800) 257-3336	C+ / 6.7	-0.17	4.06	2.01 /22	16.91 /89	11.20 /54	0.50	1.43
FS	● J Hancock Financial Indust B	FIDBX	C+	(800) 257-3336	C+ / 6.9	-0.37	3.67	1.26 /19	16.03 /84	10.39 /48	0.00	2.13
FS	J Hancock Financial Indust C	FIDCX	B	(800) 257-3336	B- / 7.0	-0.31	3.73	1.32 /19	16.10 /84	10.41 /48	0.00	2.13
GR	J Hancock Fndmntl Glbl Fran NAV		U	(800) 257-3336	U /	3.96	4.76	6.64 /52	--	--	0.93	0.90
GL	J Hancock Glbl Abs Rtn Strat A	JHAAX	C-	(800) 257-3336	D- / 1.3	3.66	4.04	7.72 /61	4.28 /11	--	4.56	1.71
GL	J Hancock Glbl Abs Rtn Strat C	JHACX	U	(800) 257-3336	U /	3.48	3.69	6.98 /55	--	--	4.11	2.41
GL	J Hancock Glbl Abs Rtn Strat I	JHAIX	C	(800) 257-3336	D / 2.0	3.75	4.18	8.05 /63	4.62 /12	--	5.10	1.39
GL	J Hancock Glbl Abs Rtn Strat NAV		C	(800) 257-3336	D / 2.0	3.75	4.22	8.18 /64	4.75 /12	--	5.23	1.27
GL	J Hancock Glbl Abs Rtn Strat R2	JHARX	C-	(800) 257-3336	D / 1.6	3.57	3.83	7.32 /58	3.99 /10	--	4.51	1.79
GL	J Hancock Glbl Abs Rtn Strat R6	JHASX	C	(800) 257-3336	D / 2.0	3.75	4.31	8.28 /65	4.66 /12	--	5.23	1.29
GL	J Hancock Global Opportunities A	JGPAX	E+	(800) 257-3336	E / 0.4	2.56	2.14	3.06 /27	-0.79 / 4	-0.26 / 2	0.00	1.52
GL	● J Hancock Global Opportunities B	JGPBX	E+	(800) 257-3336	E / 0.4	2.37	1.64	2.15 /22	-1.59 / 3	-1.05 / 2	0.00	2.22
GL	J Hancock Global Opportunities C	JGPCX	E+	(800) 257-3336	E / 0.4	2.37	1.71	2.29 /23	-1.50 / 3	-0.97 / 2	0.00	2.22
GL	J Hancock Global Opportunities I	JGPIX	E+	(800) 257-3336	E / 0.5	2.74	2.32	3.44 /29	-0.46 / 4	0.10 / 3	0.00	1.20
GL	J Hancock Global Opportunities NAV		E+	(800) 257-3336	E+ / 0.6	2.65	2.30	3.42 /29	-0.33 / 4	0.22 / 3	0.00	1.09
GL	J Hancock Global Opportunities R2	JGPSX	E+	(800) 257-3336	E / 0.5	2.54	2.05	2.90 /26	-0.93 / 3	-0.35 / 2	0.00	1.61
GL	J Hancock Global Opportunities R6	JGPRX	E+	(800) 257-3336	E / 0.5	2.65	2.24	3.36 /28	-0.44 / 4	--	0.00	1.11
FO	J Hancock Greater China Opp A	JCOAX	C-	(800) 257-3336	C / 5.1	7.12	10.15	8.65 /67	11.85 /51	5.95 /17	1.09	1.80
FO	● J Hancock Greater China Opp B	JCOBX	C-	(800) 257-3336	C / 5.3	6.93	9.73	7.78 /61	10.90 /45	5.07 /12	0.34	2.50
FO	J Hancock Greater China Opp C	JCOCX	C-	(800) 257-3336	C / 5.3	6.88	9.73	7.73 /61	10.91 /45	5.07 /12	0.30	2.50
FO	J Hancock Greater China Opp I	JCOIX	C	(800) 257-3336	C+ / 6.3	7.25	10.40	9.04 /70	12.37 /55	6.29 /19	1.49	1.49
FO	J Hancock Greater China Opp NAV		C	(800) 257-3336	C+ / 6.3	7.21	10.39	9.10 /70	12.39 /55	6.48 /20	1.53	1.36
IN	J Hancock Health Sciences NAV		C-	(800) 257-3336	A+ / 9.9	13.91	26.68	41.60 /99	36.24 /99	--	0.00	0.99
FS	J Hancock II Absolute Ret Curr R6	JCURX	E+	(800) 257-3336	E / 0.3	-6.12	-11.77	-7.64 / 4	0.31 / 5	--	0.00	0.96
GR	J Hancock II All Cap Core NAV		A+	(800) 257-3336	A- / 9.2	5.18	10.37	13.09 /87	17.07 /90	14.28 /80	0.64	0.82
GI	J Hancock II Alpha Opptys NAV		B-	(800) 257-3336	B+ / 8.3	3.22	7.76	9.51 /72	16.14 /84	13.39 /72	0.41	1.00
GR	J Hancock II Blue Chip Grwth 1	JIBCX	B+	(800) 257-3336	A / 9.5	5.91	10.38	16.87 /94	17.57 /93	16.84 /96	0.00	0.86
GR	J Hancock II Blue Chip Grwth NAV		B+	(800) 257-3336	A / 9.5	5.94	10.42	16.94 /94	17.63 /93	16.90 /96	0.00	0.81
GR	J Hancock II Capital Appr 1	JICPX	B	(800) 257-3336	B+ / 8.8	5.65	8.98	15.93 /93	15.61 /80	14.98 /87	0.00	0.78
GR	J Hancock II Capital Appr NAV	JHCPX	B	(800) 257-3336	B+ / 8.8	5.64	9.02	16.04 /93	15.68 /81	15.05 /87	0.00	0.73
GR	J Hancock II Capital Value Appr NAV		C+	(800) 257-3336	B- / 7.1	3.02	7.98	12.37 /84	13.88 /66	--	1.24	0.87
EM	J Hancock II Emerg Mkts A	JEVAX	E+	(800) 257-3336	E / 0.4	1.51	-3.21	-0.47 /14	0.03 / 4	0.24 / 3	0.94	1.53
EM	J Hancock II Emerg Mkts I	JEVIX	E+	(800) 257-3336	E / 0.5	1.61	-3.11	-0.18 /15	0.43 / 5	0.63 / 3	1.28	1.20
EM	J Hancock II Emerg Mkts NAV	JEVNX	E+	(800) 257-3336	E / 0.5	1.61	-3.03	--	0.55 / 5	0.74 / 3	1.46	1.08
EM	J Hancock II Emerg Mkts R6	JEVRX	E+	(800) 257-3336	E / 0.5	1.72	-3.03	-0.10 /15	0.46 / 5	0.59 / 3	1.46	1.10
IN	J Hancock II Eqty-Inc 1	JIEMX	C+	(800) 257-3336	C / 5.5	-1.07	1.88	4.67 /36	13.28 /62	11.63 /58	1.99	0.89

● Denotes fund is closed to new investors
* Denotes fund is included in Section II

RISK			NET ASSETS		ASSET				Portfolio	BULL / BEAR		FUND MANAGER		MINIMUMS		LOADS	
Risk Rating/Pts	3 Year		NAV As of 3/31/15	Total $(Mil)	Cash %	Stocks %	Bonds %	Other %	Portfolio Turnover Ratio	Last Bull Market Return	Last Bear Market Return	Manager Quality Pct	Manager Tenure (Years)	Initial Purch. $	Additional Purch. $	Front End Load	Back End Load
	Standard Deviation	Beta															
B / 8.0	6.9	1.19	19.01	20	3	60	36	1	39	62.6	-14.7	31	12	0	0	0.0	0.0
B / 8.0	6.8	1.19	19.04	15	3	60	36	1	39	64.8	-14.6	37	12	0	0	0.0	0.0
B / 8.0	6.8	1.19	19.01	3	3	60	36	1	39	66.0	-14.4	39	12	0	0	0.0	0.0
B / 8.0	6.8	1.19	18.97	4	3	60	36	1	39	66.3	-14.6	40	12	1,000,000	0	0.0	0.0
C+ / 6.6	12.7	1.23	26.07	375	1	98	0	1	24	100.8	-23.6	13	19	1,000	0	5.0	0.0
C+ / 6.5	12.8	1.24	25.72	10	1	98	0	1	24	95.7	-23.9	9	19	1,000	0	0.0	0.0
C+ / 6.6	12.7	1.23	25.71	97	1	98	0	1	24	95.7	-23.8	9	19	1,000	0	0.0	0.0
C+ / 6.6	12.7	1.23	26.10	2,007	1	98	0	1	24	102.9	-23.5	15	19	250,000	0	0.0	0.0
C+ / 6.6	12.7	1.23	26.13	7	1	98	0	1	24	98.4	-23.7	11	19	0	0	0.0	0.0
C+ / 6.6	12.7	1.23	26.06	N/A	1	98	0	1	24	101.3	-23.6	14	19	0	0	0.0	0.0
C+ / 6.6	12.7	1.23	26.03	1	1	98	0	1	24	99.3	-23.6	12	19	0	0	0.0	0.0
C+ / 6.6	12.7	1.23	26.10	N/A	1	98	0	1	24	102.4	-23.6	15	19	0	0	0.0	0.0
C+ / 6.6	12.7	1.23	26.11	N/A	1	98	0	1	24	103.4	-23.5	16	19	0	0	0.0	0.0
C+ / 6.6	12.8	1.23	26.12	1	1	98	0	1	24	103.5	-23.5	15	19	1,000,000	0	0.0	0.0
C+ / 6.4	4.2	0.31	10.37	31	4	42	52	2	119	28.0	N/A	75	4	1,000	0	5.0	0.0
C+ / 6.3	4.2	0.31	10.39	9	4	42	52	2	119	29.6	N/A	78	4	250,000	0	0.0	0.0
C+ / 6.9	11.8	1.00	17.50	322	14	85	0	1	21	121.6	-28.9	63	17	1,000	0	5.0	0.0
C+ / 6.9	11.8	0.99	16.12	10	14	85	0	1	21	115.9	-29.2	52	17	1,000	0	0.0	0.0
C+ / 6.9	11.8	1.00	16.15	37	14	85	0	1	21	116.3	-29.2	52	17	1,000	0	0.0	0.0
U /	N/A	N/A	12.85	462	6	93	0	1	13	N/A	N/A	N/A	3	0	0	0.0	0.0
B+ / 9.2	3.0	0.12	11.32	957	17	35	47	1	56	N/A	N/A	89	4	1,000	0	5.0	0.0
U /	N/A	N/A	11.31	247	17	35	47	1	56	N/A	N/A	N/A	4	1,000	0	0.0	0.0
B+ / 9.2	3.0	0.13	11.34	4,303	17	35	47	1	56	N/A	N/A	90	4	250,000	0	0.0	0.0
B+ / 9.2	3.0	0.13	11.33	870	17	35	47	1	56	N/A	N/A	90	4	0	0	0.0	0.0
B+ / 9.2	3.0	0.12	11.31	2	17	35	47	1	56	N/A	N/A	88	4	0	0	0.0	0.0
B+ / 9.2	3.0	0.12	11.34	455	17	35	47	1	56	N/A	N/A	90	4	1,000,000	0	0.0	0.0
C / 5.3	13.8	0.78	14.81	64	1	98	0	1	64	20.5	-33.5	3	2	1,000	0	5.0	0.0
C / 5.2	13.7	0.77	14.26	10	1	98	0	1	64	17.5	-33.7	2	2	1,000	0	0.0	0.0
C / 5.2	13.8	0.78	14.28	26	1	98	0	1	64	17.7	-33.7	2	2	1,000	0	0.0	0.0
C / 5.4	13.7	0.77	15.02	15	1	98	0	1	64	21.9	-33.4	4	2	250,000	0	0.0	0.0
C / 5.4	13.7	0.77	15.12	5	1	98	0	1	64	22.6	-33.3	4	2	0	0	0.0	0.0
C / 5.3	13.7	0.77	14.92	N/A	1	98	0	1	64	20.0	-33.5	3	2	0	0	0.0	0.0
C / 5.4	13.7	0.77	15.09	N/A	1	98	0	1	64	22.2	-33.5	4	2	1,000,000	0	0.0	0.0
C / 5.4	12.0	0.65	21.52	47	0	99	0	1	123	57.7	-29.9	94	4	1,000	0	5.0	0.0
C / 5.5	11.9	0.64	20.82	3	0	99	0	1	123	53.2	-30.1	92	4	1,000	0	0.0	0.0
C / 5.5	12.0	0.65	20.82	9	0	99	0	1	123	53.2	-30.1	92	4	1,000	0	0.0	0.0
C / 5.3	12.0	0.65	21.46	5	0	99	0	1	123	59.9	-29.8	95	4	250,000	0	0.0	0.0
C / 5.4	12.0	0.64	21.72	13	0	99	0	1	123	60.5	-29.7	95	4	0	0	0.0	0.0
E+ / 0.7	13.2	0.86	18.59	450	2	97	0	1	61	209.3	N/A	99	4	0	0	0.0	0.0
C+ / 6.4	7.8	-0.12	8.59	86	6	0	93	1	0	1.8	-1.0	86	4	1,000,000	0	0.0	0.0
C+ / 6.6	10.7	1.07	14.00	790	0	99	0	1	245	102.5	-19.5	65	N/A	0	0	0.0	0.0
C / 4.9	10.7	1.04	12.51	1,860	1	98	0	1	109	99.6	-23.2	59	7	0	0	0.0	0.0
C / 5.2	11.3	1.01	35.10	961	0	99	0	1	33	113.3	-14.9	78	10	0	0	0.0	0.0
C / 5.2	11.3	1.01	35.11	1,783	0	99	0	1	33	113.8	-14.9	78	10	0	0	0.0	0.0
C / 5.2	11.7	1.02	18.15	597	0	99	0	1	45	99.3	-13.8	55	10	0	0	0.0	0.0
C / 5.2	11.8	1.02	18.18	1,743	0	99	0	1	45	99.6	-13.8	56	10	0	0	0.0	0.0
C+ / 5.7	5.9	0.60	11.95	2,200	9	62	27	2	63	78.1	-12.9	92	4	0	0	0.0	0.0
C+ / 5.6	13.6	0.98	10.10	407	1	98	0	1	17	21.6	-31.0	58	8	1,000	0	5.0	0.0
C+ / 5.6	13.6	0.98	10.09	40	1	98	0	1	17	23.3	-30.9	64	8	250,000	0	0.0	0.0
C+ / 5.6	13.6	0.98	10.09	2,269	1	98	0	1	17	23.9	-30.9	66	8	0	0	0.0	0.0
C+ / 5.6	13.6	0.98	10.08	N/A	1	98	0	1	17	23.3	-31.1	65	8	1,000,000	0	0.0	0.0
B- / 7.1	9.5	0.96	19.89	346	4	95	0	1	17	85.2	-18.2	38	10	0	0	0.0	0.0

99 Pct = Best
0 Pct = Worst

Fund Type	Fund Name	Ticker Symbol	Overall Investment Rating	Phone	Performance Rating/Pts	3 Mo	6 Mo	1Yr / Pct	3Yr / Pct	5Yr / Pct	Dividend Yield	Expense Ratio
IN	J Hancock II Eqty-Inc NAV		C+	(800) 257-3336	C+ / 5.6	-1.06	1.94	4.73 /37	13.32 /62	11.68 /58	2.06	0.84
GI	J Hancock II Fdm All Cap Core A	JFCAX	B+	(800) 257-3336	B / 8.1	2.43	6.23	11.23 /79	17.39 /92	--	0.00	1.58
GI	J Hancock II Fdm All Cap Core I	JFCIX	A-	(800) 257-3336	A- / 9.1	2.48	6.40	11.55 /81	17.81 /94	--	0.12	1.26
GR	J Hancock II Fdm All Cap Core NAV		U	(800) 257-3336	U /	2.62	6.57	--	--	--	0.00	1.14
GR	J Hancock II Fdm Large Cap Core A	JFLAX	C+	(800) 257-3336	C+ / 5.7	0.74	3.22	8.49 /66	14.12 /68	--	0.07	1.54
GR	J Hancock II Fdm Large Cap Core I	JFLIX	C+	(800) 257-3336	C+ / 6.8	0.87	3.42	8.91 /69	14.58 /72	--	0.42	1.22
GR	J Hancock II Fdm Large Cap Val NAV		B	(800) 257-3336	B / 7.8	0.07	2.79	8.45 /66	16.39 /86	--	0.89	0.66
GR	J Hancock II Fdm Large Cap Value A	JFVAX	C+	(800) 257-3336	C+ / 6.4	0.00	2.51	7.86 /62	15.70 /81	--	0.45	1.10
GR	J Hancock II Fdm Large Cap Value I	JFVIX	B	(800) 257-3336	B / 7.6	0.07	2.66	8.23 /64	16.15 /84	--	0.62	0.77
RE	J Hancock II Glb Real Est Nav		C+	(800) 257-3336	B- / 7.5	4.08	12.34	16.28 /94	12.69 /57	11.19 /54	2.41	1.02
FO	J Hancock II Int Small Comp NAV		D-	(800) 257-3336	D+ / 2.3	3.77	-0.60	-6.94 / 4	8.58 /30	7.31 /25	1.74	1.11
FO	J Hancock II Intl Gro Stock NAV		D+	(800) 257-3336	C- / 3.5	3.57	3.04	3.27 /28	9.13 /34	--	1.85	0.93
FO	J Hancock II Intl Small Cap 1	JIIMX	D+	(800) 257-3336	C- / 3.2	5.59	2.13	-1.30 /12	9.05 /33	7.35 /25	0.52	1.15
FO	J Hancock II Intl Small Cap NAV		D+	(800) 257-3336	C- / 3.2	5.53	2.13	-1.30 /12	9.08 /33	7.41 /26	0.57	1.10
FO	J Hancock II Intl Value 1	JIVIX	E+	(800) 257-3336	D- / 1.4	4.51	-6.00	-8.40 / 3	7.09 /22	5.17 /13	2.68	0.97
FO	J Hancock II Intl Value NAV	JHVIX	E+	(800) 257-3336	D- / 1.4	4.52	-5.98	-8.33 / 3	7.15 /22	5.23 /13	2.72	0.92
AG	J Hancock II Lifestyle Agg 1	JILAX	C+	(800) 257-3336	C / 5.4	3.27	4.64	6.45 /50	12.04 /53	10.46 /48	2.46	1.03
AG	J Hancock II Lifestyle Agg A	JALAX	C	(800) 257-3336	C / 4.3	3.13	4.45	6.06 /47	11.58 /50	9.98 /44	2.00	1.44
AG	J Hancock II Lifestyle Agg B	JBLAX	C	(800) 257-3336	C / 4.5	2.88	4.02	5.24 /40	10.70 /44	9.12 /38	1.34	2.18
AG	J Hancock II Lifestyle Agg C	JCLAX	C	(800) 257-3336	C / 4.5	2.94	4.06	5.28 /41	10.78 /44	9.18 /38	1.37	2.14
AG	J Hancock II Lifestyle Agg R1	JPLAX	C	(800) 257-3336	C / 4.7	3.00	4.20	5.49 /42	11.06 /46	9.50 /41	1.63	1.88
GR	J Hancock II Lifestyle Agg R2	JQLAX	C	(800) 257-3336	C / 5.0	3.08	4.38	5.93 /46	11.47 /49	9.92 /44	1.97	2.56
AG	J Hancock II Lifestyle Agg R3	JRLAX	C	(800) 257-3336	C / 4.8	3.01	4.25	5.61 /43	11.18 /47	9.60 /41	1.67	1.77
AG	J Hancock II Lifestyle Agg R4	JSLAX	C	(800) 257-3336	C / 5.1	3.14	4.44	5.99 /46	11.58 /50	9.95 /44	2.03	1.51
AG	J Hancock II Lifestyle Agg R5	JTLAX	C+	(800) 257-3336	C / 5.3	3.20	4.61	6.30 /49	11.86 /51	10.29 /47	2.32	1.17
GR	J Hancock II Lifestyle Agg R6	JULAX	C+	(800) 257-3336	C / 5.4	3.27	4.69	6.50 /51	12.08 /53	10.48 /48	2.51	1.31
BA	J Hancock II Lifestyle Bal 1	JILBX	C	(800) 257-3336	C- / 3.6	2.47	3.19	5.04 /39	9.18 /34	8.65 /34	3.06	0.95
BA	J Hancock II Lifestyle Bal 5	JHLAX	C+	(800) 257-3336	C- / 3.7	2.48	3.28	5.09 /39	9.23 /34	8.72 /35	3.11	0.90
BA	J Hancock II Lifestyle Bal A	JALBX	C-	(800) 257-3336	D+ / 2.6	2.36	3.06	4.71 /36	8.74 /31	8.22 /31	2.55	1.35
BA	● J Hancock II Lifestyle Bal B	JBLBX	C	(800) 257-3336	D+ / 2.9	2.19	2.68	3.91 /31	7.95 /27	7.41 /26	1.92	2.10
BA	J Hancock II Lifestyle Bal C	JCLBX	C	(800) 257-3336	D+ / 2.9	2.19	2.62	3.88 /31	7.94 /27	7.44 /26	1.96	2.05
BA	J Hancock II Lifestyle Bal R1	JPLBX	C	(800) 257-3336	C- / 3.1	2.27	2.79	4.15 /33	8.32 /29	7.80 /29	2.27	1.74
BA	J Hancock II Lifestyle Bal R2	JQLBX	C	(800) 257-3336	C- / 3.3	2.34	3.00	4.51 /35	8.62 /31	8.14 /31	2.55	1.99
BA	J Hancock II Lifestyle Bal R3	JRLBX	C	(800) 257-3336	C- / 3.2	2.30	2.91	4.34 /34	8.45 /30	7.94 /29	2.40	1.61
BA	J Hancock II Lifestyle Bal R4	JSLBX	C	(800) 257-3336	C- / 3.5	2.40	3.12	4.77 /37	8.93 /34	8.33 /32	2.80	1.30
BA	J Hancock II Lifestyle Bal R5	JTSBX	C	(800) 257-3336	C- / 3.6	2.44	3.15	4.96 /38	9.09 /34	8.58 /34	2.99	1.01
BA	J Hancock II Lifestyle Bal R6	JULBX	C+	(800) 257-3336	C- / 3.7	2.48	3.28	5.09 /39	9.20 /34	8.68 /34	3.11	1.02
AA	J Hancock II Lifestyle Cons 1	JILCX	D	(800) 257-3336	D / 1.6	1.51	1.71	3.38 /28	5.42 /15	6.23 /18	3.28	0.86
AA	J Hancock II Lifestyle Cons A	JALRX	D	(800) 257-3336	D- / 1.0	1.41	1.53	3.07 /27	5.01 /13	5.79 /16	2.77	1.27
AA	● J Hancock II Lifestyle Cons B	JBLCX	D	(800) 257-3336	D- / 1.2	1.22	1.14	2.21 /23	4.22 /11	5.00 /12	2.14	1.99
AA	J Hancock II Lifestyle Cons C	JCLCX	D	(800) 257-3336	D- / 1.2	1.23	1.15	2.31 /23	4.25 /11	5.03 /12	2.16	1.97
AA	J Hancock II Lifestyle Cons R1	JPLCX	D	(800) 257-3336	D- / 1.3	1.31	1.28	2.50 /24	4.51 /12	5.30 /13	2.42	1.66
AA	J Hancock II Lifestyle Cons R2	JQLCX	D	(800) 257-3336	D- / 1.4	1.38	1.38	2.85 /26	4.89 /13	5.71 /15	2.77	3.37
AA	J Hancock II Lifestyle Cons R3	JRLCX	D	(800) 257-3336	D- / 1.3	1.33	1.34	2.56 /24	4.64 /12	5.43 /14	2.56	1.51
AA	J Hancock II Lifestyle Cons R4	JSLCX	D	(800) 257-3336	D- / 1.4	1.41	1.45	2.99 /26	5.01 /13	5.77 /15	2.91	1.33
AA	J Hancock II Lifestyle Cons R5	JTLRX	D	(800) 257-3336	D- / 1.5	1.49	1.59	3.20 /27	5.28 /14	6.09 /17	3.18	0.92
AA	J Hancock II Lifestyle Cons R6	JULCX	D	(800) 257-3336	D / 1.6	1.52	1.74	3.43 /29	5.45 /15	6.25 /18	3.33	1.19
GR	J Hancock II Lifestyle Gr 1	JILGX	C+	(800) 257-3336	C / 4.7	2.83	4.07	6.05 /47	10.99 /45	9.86 /43	2.79	0.99
GR	J Hancock II Lifestyle Gr 5	JHLGX	C+	(800) 257-3336	C / 4.7	2.83	4.06	6.04 /47	11.03 /46	9.91 /44	2.84	0.94
GR	J Hancock II Lifestyle Gr A	JALGX	C	(800) 257-3336	C- / 3.7	2.69	3.87	5.65 /44	10.54 /43	9.40 /40	2.31	1.39
GR	● J Hancock II Lifestyle Gr B	JBLGX	C	(800) 257-3336	C- / 3.9	2.50	3.42	4.81 /37	9.74 /38	8.58 /34	1.69	2.10
GR	J Hancock II Lifestyle Gr C	JCLGX	C	(800) 257-3336	C- / 4.0	2.57	3.49	4.89 /38	9.76 /38	8.64 /34	1.70	2.09

● Denotes fund is closed to new investors
* Denotes fund is included in Section II

www.thestreetratings.com

RISK			NET ASSETS		ASSET						BULL / BEAR		FUND MANAGER		MINIMUMS		LOADS	
	3 Year		NAV							Portfolio	Last Bull	Last Bear	Manager	Manager	Initial	Additional	Front	Back
Risk	Standard		As of	Total	Cash	Stocks	Bonds	Other		Turnover	Market	Market	Quality	Tenure	Purch.	Purch.	End	End
Rating/Pts	Deviation	Beta	3/31/15	$(Mil)	%	%	%	%		Ratio	Return	Return	Pct	(Years)	$	$	Load	Load
B- / 7.0	9.4	0.96	19.87	1,774	4	95	0	1		17	85.6	-18.2	39	10	0	0	0.0	0.0
C+ / 6.1	12.5	1.19	15.18	19	3	96	0	1		44	106.8	N/A	40	4	1,000	0	5.0	0.0
C+ / 6.1	12.5	1.20	15.26	6	3	96	0	1		44	109.8	N/A	45	4	250,000	0	0.0	0.0
U /	N/A	N/A	15.27	121	3	96	0	1		44	N/A	N/A	N/A	4	0	0	0.0	0.0
C+ / 6.5	11.5	1.14	14.95	9	3	96	0	1		23	93.0	N/A	17	4	1,000	0	5.0	0.0
C+ / 6.5	11.4	1.14	15.00	46	3	96	0	1		23	95.8	N/A	21	4	250,000	0	0.0	0.0
C+ / 6.1	11.9	1.18	13.52	1,378	4	95	0	1		24	111.7	N/A	32	4	0	0	0.0	0.0
C+ / 6.2	11.9	1.17	13.47	18	4	95	0	1		24	107.5	N/A	26	4	1,000	0	5.0	0.0
C+ / 6.2	11.9	1.18	13.54	3	4	95	0	1		24	110.1	N/A	29	4	250,000	0	0.0	0.0
C / 5.1	12.3	0.92	9.69	311	9	90	0	1		109	75.1	-20.5	64	9	0	0	0.0	0.0
C+ / 5.7	13.4	0.95	9.90	590	0	99	0	1		11	50.1	-23.6	61	9	0	0	0.0	0.0
C+ / 6.3	11.3	0.82	13.35	680	6	93	0	1		26	53.9	-20.1	79	5	0	0	0.0	0.0
C+ / 6.3	12.1	0.84	18.71	98	3	93	3	1		23	50.9	-24.6	77	4	0	0	0.0	0.0
C+ / 6.3	12.1	0.84	18.70	602	3	93	3	1		23	51.1	-24.6	77	4	0	0	0.0	0.0
C / 4.7	15.1	1.06	15.75	230	1	96	2	1		28	42.1	-24.1	27	10	0	0	0.0	0.0
C / 4.7	15.0	1.06	15.71	1,754	1	96	2	1		28	42.4	-24.1	28	10	0	0	0.0	0.0
C+ / 6.8	9.8	0.96	16.75	3,999	3	93	2	2		18	73.6	-20.9	26	N/A	0	0	0.0	0.0
C+ / 6.8	9.7	0.95	16.80	411	3	93	2	2		18	71.1	-21.0	22	N/A	1,000	0	5.0	0.0
C+ / 6.8	9.8	0.96	16.80	21	3	93	2	2		18	66.6	-21.3	15	N/A	1,000	0	0.0	0.0
C+ / 6.8	9.8	0.96	16.81	176	3	93	2	2		18	67.0	-21.3	16	N/A	1,000	0	0.0	0.0
C+ / 6.8	9.8	0.96	16.81	8	3	93	2	2		18	68.4	-21.2	17	N/A	0	0	0.0	0.0
C+ / 6.8	9.7	0.95	16.72	7	3	93	2	2		18	70.7	-21.0	21	10	0	0	0.0	0.0
C+ / 6.8	9.8	0.96	16.76	7	3	93	2	2		18	69.0	-21.2	18	N/A	0	0	0.0	0.0
C+ / 6.8	9.8	0.96	16.75	8	3	93	2	2		18	71.1	-21.1	21	N/A	0	0	0.0	0.0
C+ / 6.8	9.8	0.96	16.78	12	3	93	2	2		18	72.7	-21.0	24	N/A	0	0	0.0	0.0
C+ / 6.8	9.8	0.96	16.76	19	3	93	2	2		18	73.7	-20.9	26	4	1,000,000	0	0.0	0.0
B / 8.2	6.5	1.09	15.80	12,085	3	60	36	1		15	51.6	-13.9	31	N/A	0	0	0.0	0.0
B / 8.2	6.5	1.08	15.81	145	3	60	36	1		15	51.8	-13.8	32	N/A	0	0	0.0	0.0
B / 8.2	6.5	1.09	15.89	1,852	3	60	36	1		15	49.5	-14.1	27	N/A	1,000	0	5.0	0.0
B / 8.2	6.5	1.08	15.88	95	3	60	36	1		15	45.7	-14.3	20	N/A	1,000	0	0.0	0.0
B / 8.2	6.5	1.08	15.89	915	3	60	36	1		15	45.8	-14.3	20	N/A	1,000	0	0.0	0.0
B / 8.2	6.5	1.09	15.82	20	3	60	36	1		15	47.5	-14.2	23	N/A	0	0	0.0	0.0
B / 8.2	6.4	1.08	15.82	14	3	60	36	1		15	48.9	-14.1	26	10	0	0	0.0	0.0
B / 8.2	6.5	1.09	15.85	30	3	60	36	1		15	48.1	-14.1	24	N/A	0	0	0.0	0.0
B / 8.2	6.5	1.08	15.86	41	3	60	36	1		15	50.1	-14.0	30	N/A	0	0	0.0	0.0
B / 8.2	6.5	1.09	15.87	42	3	60	36	1		15	51.2	-14.0	31	N/A	0	0	0.0	0.0
B / 8.2	6.4	1.08	15.81	48	3	60	36	1		15	51.6	-13.9	32	4	1,000,000	0	0.0	0.0
B- / 7.5	3.3	0.48	13.41	2,531	0	22	76	2		22	27.2	-4.9	70	N/A	0	0	0.0	0.0
B- / 7.5	3.3	0.48	13.44	606	0	22	76	2		22	25.5	-5.0	66	N/A	1,000	0	5.0	0.0
B- / 7.5	3.3	0.49	13.44	37	0	22	76	2		22	22.4	-5.3	53	N/A	1,000	0	0.0	0.0
B- / 7.5	3.3	0.48	13.44	384	0	22	76	2		22	22.4	-5.3	55	N/A	1,000	0	0.0	0.0
B- / 7.5	3.3	0.48	13.43	10	0	22	76	2		22	23.4	-5.2	59	N/A	0	0	0.0	0.0
B- / 7.5	3.3	0.48	13.42	5	0	22	76	2		22	25.1	-5.0	64	10	0	0	0.0	0.0
B- / 7.5	3.3	0.49	13.40	11	0	22	76	2		22	24.1	-5.2	60	N/A	0	0	0.0	0.0
B- / 7.5	3.3	0.48	13.41	9	0	22	76	2		22	25.5	-5.0	66	N/A	0	0	0.0	0.0
B- / 7.5	3.3	0.48	13.42	11	0	22	76	2		22	26.7	-4.9	69	N/A	0	0	0.0	0.0
B- / 7.4	3.4	0.49	13.41	12	0	22	76	2		22	27.3	-4.9	70	4	1,000,000	0	0.0	0.0
B- / 7.5	8.4	0.82	16.74	11,725	3	78	17	2		16	65.1	-18.1	39	N/A	0	0	0.0	0.0
B- / 7.5	8.3	0.82	16.72	245	3	78	17	2		16	65.4	-18.1	40	N/A	0	0	0.0	0.0
B- / 7.5	8.3	0.82	16.79	1,608	3	78	17	2		16	62.7	-18.2	34	N/A	1,000	0	5.0	0.0
B- / 7.5	8.3	0.82	16.80	96	3	78	17	2		16	58.8	-18.4	26	N/A	1,000	0	0.0	0.0
B- / 7.5	8.4	0.82	16.79	762	3	78	17	2		16	58.8	-18.5	26	N/A	1,000	0	0.0	0.0

Fund Type	Fund Name	Ticker Symbol	Overall Investment Rating	Phone	Performance Rating/Pts	3 Mo	6 Mo	1Yr / Pct	3Yr / Pct	5Yr / Pct	Dividend Yield	Expense Ratio
	99 Pct = Best							Total Return % through 3/31/15			Incl. in Returns	
	0 Pct = Worst								Annualized			
GR	J Hancock II Lifestyle Gr R1	JPLGX	C	(800) 257-3336	C- / 4.2	2.62	3.62	5.20 /40	10.16 /40	9.03 /37	2.01	1.77
GI	J Hancock II Lifestyle Gr R2	JQLGX	C+	(800) 257-3336	C / 4.4	2.64	3.74	5.46 /42	10.43 /42	9.32 /39	2.30	1.82
GR	J Hancock II Lifestyle Gr R3	JRLGX	C	(800) 257-3336	C- / 4.2	2.63	3.67	5.26 /41	10.22 /41	9.11 /38	2.11	1.68
GR	J Hancock II Lifestyle Gr R4	JSLGX	C+	(800) 257-3336	C / 4.5	2.76	3.89	5.73 /44	10.68 /43	9.50 /41	2.50	1.38
GR	J Hancock II Lifestyle Gr R5	JTLGX	C+	(800) 257-3336	C / 4.7	2.81	4.04	5.95 /46	10.94 /45	9.78 /43	2.71	1.06
GR	J Hancock II Lifestyle Gr R6	JULGX	C+	(800) 257-3336	C / 4.8	2.83	4.05	6.10 /47	11.04 /46	9.89 /44	2.84	1.08
BA	J Hancock II Lifestyle II Bal 1	JIBOX	U	(800) 257-3336	U /	2.18	4.34	6.72 /53	--	--	1.69	6.18
GR	J Hancock II Lifestyle II Growth 1	JLGOX	U	(800) 257-3336	U /	2.27	4.90	7.69 /60	--	--	1.39	5.70
BA	J Hancock II Lifestyle Mod 1	JILMX	C-	(800) 257-3336	D+ / 2.5	1.96	2.34	4.02 /32	7.28 /23	7.64 /27	3.24	0.89
BA	J Hancock II Lifestyle Mod 5	JHLMX	C-	(800) 257-3336	D+ / 2.5	1.97	2.37	4.15 /33	7.34 /23	7.70 /28	3.30	0.84
BA	J Hancock II Lifestyle Mod A	JALMX	D+	(800) 257-3336	D / 1.6	1.86	2.16	3.71 /30	6.85 /21	7.18 /24	2.74	1.29
BA	● J Hancock II Lifestyle Mod B	JBLMX	D+	(800) 257-3336	D / 1.8	1.67	1.77	2.92 /26	6.08 /17	6.38 /19	2.11	2.02
BA	J Hancock II Lifestyle Mod C	JCLMX	D+	(800) 257-3336	D / 1.8	1.68	1.78	2.95 /26	6.08 /17	6.42 /20	2.14	1.99
BA	J Hancock II Lifestyle Mod R1	JPLMX	C-	(800) 257-3336	D / 2.0	1.75	1.85	3.15 /27	6.38 /18	6.70 /21	2.40	1.73
AA	J Hancock II Lifestyle Mod R2	JQLMX	C-	(800) 257-3336	D / 2.2	1.90	2.09	3.56 /29	6.77 /20	7.11 /24	2.73	2.55
BA	J Hancock II Lifestyle Mod R3	JRLMX	C-	(800) 257-3336	D / 2.1	1.77	1.97	3.25 /28	6.50 /19	6.82 /22	2.50	1.63
BA	J Hancock II Lifestyle Mod R4	JSLMX	C-	(800) 257-3336	D+ / 2.3	1.88	2.18	3.67 /30	6.93 /21	7.20 /24	2.91	1.33
BA	J Hancock II Lifestyle Mod R5	JTLMX	C-	(800) 257-3336	D+ / 2.4	1.92	2.27	3.87 /31	7.13 /22	7.48 /26	3.10	1.03
AA	J Hancock II Lifestyle Mod R6	JULMX	C-	(800) 257-3336	D+ / 2.6	2.05	2.37	4.15 /33	7.34 /23	7.66 /28	3.30	1.11
MC	J Hancock II Mid Cap Stock 1	JIMSX	C+	(800) 257-3336	B+ / 8.8	5.46	11.09	11.45 /80	16.35 /86	14.43 /82	0.00	0.92
MC	J Hancock II Mid Cap Stock NAV		C+	(800) 257-3336	B+ / 8.8	5.53	11.13	11.54 /81	16.42 /86	14.50 /82	0.00	0.87
EN	● J Hancock II Natural Resources 1	JINRX	E-	(800) 257-3336	E- / 0.1	-1.90	-24.02	-27.83 / 0	-9.54 / 1	-6.22 / 1	0.54	1.09
EN	● J Hancock II Natural Resources A	JNRAX	E-	(800) 257-3336	E- / 0.1	-1.92	-24.20	-28.16 / 0	-9.97 / 1	-6.67 / 1	0.00	1.47
EN	● J Hancock II Natural Resources I	JNRIX	E-	(800) 257-3336	E- / 0.1	-1.92	-24.16	-28.04 / 0	-9.80 / 1	-6.47 / 1	0.18	1.16
EN	● J Hancock II Natural Resources NAV		E-	(800) 257-3336	E- / 0.1	-1.84	-23.98	-27.74 / 0	-9.48 / 1	-6.16 / 1	0.59	1.04
EN	● J Hancock II Natural Resources R6	JRNRX	E-	(800) 257-3336	E- / 0.1	-1.84	-24.01	-27.88 / 0	-9.68 / 1	-6.30 / 1	0.53	1.05
RE	J Hancock II Real Est Eq Nav		B	(800) 257-3336	A / 9.4	5.57	20.65	24.64 /98	13.65 /65	15.71 /91	1.19	0.94
RE	J Hancock II Real Estate Sec 1	JIREX	C	(800) 257-3336	A / 9.3	4.34	19.64	24.49 /98	13.49 /63	15.76 /92	1.53	0.79
AA	J Hancock II Ret Choices at 2010 1	JRTOX	C-	(800) 257-3336	D- / 1.0	1.27	2.26	3.28 /28	3.13 / 8	--	1.45	0.76
AA	J Hancock II Ret Choices at 2015 1	JRFOX	C-	(800) 257-3336	D- / 1.2	1.42	2.48	3.85 /31	3.82 /10	--	1.69	0.74
AA	J Hancock II Ret Choices at 2020 1	JRWOX	C	(800) 257-3336	D / 2.0	1.58	3.04	5.03 /39	5.95 /17	--	1.78	0.71
AA	J Hancock II Ret Choices at 2025 1	JREOX	C	(800) 257-3336	C- / 3.0	1.80	3.60	5.92 /46	7.82 /26	--	1.82	0.71
AA	J Hancock II Ret Choices at 2030 1	JRHOX	C+	(800) 257-3336	C- / 3.8	1.96	3.90	6.54 /51	9.15 /34	--	1.89	0.70
AA	J Hancock II Ret Choices at 2035 1	JRYOX	C+	(800) 257-3336	C- / 4.2	1.99	4.09	6.75 /53	9.92 /39	--	1.92	0.70
AA	J Hancock II Ret Choices at 2040 1	JRROX	C+	(800) 257-3336	C / 4.4	2.04	4.19	6.91 /54	10.32 /41	--	1.93	0.71
AA	J Hancock II Ret Choices at 2045 1	JRVOX	C+	(800) 257-3336	C / 4.4	2.03	4.19	6.99 /55	10.34 /41	--	1.97	0.71
AA	J Hancock II Ret Choices at 2050 1	JRIOX	C+	(800) 257-3336	C / 4.4	2.04	4.24	7.02 /55	10.37 /42	--	1.96	0.72
GI	J Hancock II Ret Choices at 2055 1	JRIYX	U	(800) 257-3336	U /	2.01	4.37	7.16 /56	--	--	1.62	10.07
AA	J Hancock II Ret Liv thru 2010 1	JLAOX	D+	(800) 257-3336	D+ / 2.7	1.95	2.56	4.37 /34	7.56 /24	7.69 /28	3.22	0.91
AA	J Hancock II Ret Liv thru 2010 A	JLAAX	D	(800) 257-3336	D / 1.7	1.85	2.30	4.00 /32	7.08 /22	7.19 /24	2.64	1.30
AA	J Hancock II Ret Liv thru 2010 R1	JLADX	D+	(800) 257-3336	D+ / 2.3	1.86	2.24	3.75 /30	6.84 /20	6.96 /23	2.53	1.64
BA	J Hancock II Ret Liv thru 2010 R2	JLAEX	D+	(800) 257-3336	D+ / 2.4	1.85	2.19	3.90 /31	7.09 /22	7.17 /24	2.77	1.39
AA	J Hancock II Ret Liv thru 2010 R3	JLAFX	D+	(800) 257-3336	D+ / 2.3	1.85	2.24	3.85 /31	6.94 /21	7.04 /23	2.63	1.54
AA	J Hancock II Ret Liv thru 2010 R4	JLAGX	D+	(800) 257-3336	D+ / 2.6	1.96	2.45	4.26 /33	7.35 /23	7.44 /26	3.02	1.24
AA	J Hancock II Ret Liv thru 2010 R5	JLAHX	D+	(800) 257-3336	D+ / 2.7	1.96	2.46	4.37 /34	7.56 /24	7.69 /28	3.23	0.94
BA	J Hancock II Ret Liv thru 2010 R6	JLAIX	D+	(800) 257-3336	D+ / 2.7	1.95	2.51	4.52 /35	7.64 /25	7.57 /27	3.27	0.88
AA	J Hancock II Ret Liv thru 2015 1	JLBOX	C-	(800) 257-3336	C- / 3.2	2.12	2.90	4.89 /38	8.35 /29	8.20 /31	3.01	0.90
AA	J Hancock II Ret Liv thru 2015 A	JLBAX	D+	(800) 257-3336	D / 2.1	1.92	2.62	4.41 /34	7.84 /26	7.72 /28	2.44	1.29
AA	J Hancock II Ret Liv thru 2015 R1	JLBDX	C-	(800) 257-3336	D+ / 2.7	1.92	2.47	4.16 /33	7.59 /25	7.49 /26	2.32	1.61
BA	J Hancock II Ret Liv thru 2015 R2	JLBKX	C-	(800) 257-3336	D+ / 2.8	2.02	2.63	4.43 /35	7.85 /26	7.71 /28	2.57	1.37
AA	J Hancock II Ret Liv thru 2015 R3	JLBFX	C-	(800) 257-3336	D+ / 2.7	1.92	2.57	4.26 /33	7.69 /25	7.57 /27	2.42	1.51
AA	J Hancock II Ret Liv thru 2015 R4	JLBGX	C-	(800) 257-3336	C- / 3.0	2.02	2.70	4.59 /36	8.12 /28	7.95 /30	2.82	1.21

● Denotes fund is closed to new investors
* Denotes fund is included in Section II

www.thestreetratings.com

RISK			NET ASSETS		ASSET					BULL / BEAR		FUND MANAGER		MINIMUMS		LOADS	
	3 Year		NAV						Portfolio	Last Bull	Last Bear	Manager	Manager	Initial	Additional	Front	Back
Risk	Standard		As of	Total	Cash	Stocks	Bonds	Other	Turnover	Market	Market	Quality	Tenure	Purch.	Purch.	End	End
Rating/Pts	Deviation	Beta	3/31/15	$(Mil)	%	%	%	%	Ratio	Return	Return	Pct	(Years)	$	$	Load	Load
B- / 7.5	8.3	0.82	16.84	22	3	78	17	2	16	60.8	-18.4	30	N/A	0	0	0.0	0.0
B- / 7.5	8.3	0.82	16.70	14	3	78	17	2	16	62.2	-18.2	33	10	0	0	0.0	0.0
B- / 7.5	8.3	0.82	16.76	23	3	78	17	2	16	61.3	-18.3	30	N/A	0	0	0.0	0.0
B- / 7.5	8.3	0.82	16.78	26	3	78	17	2	16	63.3	-18.2	35	N/A	0	0	0.0	0.0
B- / 7.5	8.3	0.82	16.81	37	3	78	17	2	16	64.7	-18.1	39	N/A	0	0	0.0	0.0
B- / 7.5	8.3	0.82	16.74	41	3	78	17	2	16	65.3	-18.1	40	4	1,000,000	0	0.0	0.0
U /	N/A	N/A	10.67	64	2	58	38	2	2	N/A	N/A	N/A	5	0	0	0.0	0.0
U /	N/A	N/A	10.80	46	2	79	18	1	21	N/A	N/A	N/A	2	0	0	0.0	0.0
B- / 7.9	4.7	0.78	14.29	3,430	1	40	57	2	14	38.7	-8.7	51	N/A	0	0	0.0	0.0
B- / 7.9	4.7	0.78	14.28	53	1	40	57	2	14	39.0	-8.7	53	N/A	0	0	0.0	0.0
B- / 7.9	4.7	0.77	14.33	682	1	40	57	2	14	36.8	-8.9	46	N/A	1,000	0	5.0	0.0
B / 8.0	4.7	0.78	14.32	37	1	40	57	2	14	33.3	-9.2	35	N/A	1,000	0	0.0	0.0
B / 8.0	4.7	0.77	14.33	416	1	40	57	2	14	33.5	-9.2	36	N/A	1,000	0	0.0	0.0
B / 8.0	4.7	0.77	14.31	9	1	40	57	2	14	34.7	-9.1	40	N/A	1,000	0	0.0	0.0
B- / 7.9	4.7	0.78	14.29	6	1	40	57	2	14	36.3	-8.9	45	10	0	0	0.0	0.0
B- / 7.9	4.7	0.78	14.30	10	1	40	57	2	14	35.1	-9.0	41	N/A	0	0	0.0	0.0
B- / 7.9	4.7	0.78	14.28	14	1	40	57	2	14	37.0	-8.9	47	N/A	0	0	0.0	0.0
B- / 7.9	4.7	0.78	14.29	12	1	40	57	2	14	38.0	-8.8	49	N/A	0	0	0.0	0.0
B- / 7.9	4.7	0.77	14.28	25	1	40	57	2	14	38.9	-8.8	54	4	1,000,000	0	0.0	0.0
C- / 3.6	12.4	1.00	21.05	367	0	96	3	1	107	96.0	-24.4	59	10	0	0	0.0	0.0
C- / 3.6	12.4	1.00	21.19	1,309	0	96	3	1	107	96.4	-24.4	59	10	0	0	0.0	0.0
D+ / 2.3	17.9	1.03	12.88	94	4	95	0	1	193	-12.7	-32.5	1	10	0	0	0.0	0.0
D+ / 2.3	17.9	1.03	12.78	6	4	95	0	1	193	-14.1	-32.6	1	10	1,000	0	5.0	0.0
D+ / 2.3	17.9	1.03	12.78	N/A	4	95	0	1	193	-13.5	-32.5	1	10	250,000	0	0.0	0.0
D+ / 2.3	17.9	1.03	12.79	535	4	95	0	1	193	-12.5	-32.5	1	10	0	0	0.0	0.0
D+ / 2.3	17.9	1.03	12.80	N/A	4	95	0	1	193	-13.2	-32.5	1	10	1,000,000	0	0.0	0.0
C / 4.6	12.5	0.99	12.69	250	5	93	0	2	15	85.3	-16.4	64	9	0	0	0.0	0.0
D / 2.2	13.4	1.07	15.16	656	0	99	0	1	108	84.6	-17.1	46	10	0	0	0.0	0.0
B+ / 9.0	2.1	0.19	11.20	264	0	11	87	2	26	12.3	2.8	78	3	0	0	0.0	0.0
B / 8.9	2.6	0.31	11.39	430	1	13	84	2	22	17.8	-0.9	73	5	0	0	0.0	0.0
B+ / 9.0	4.1	0.65	12.24	962	1	32	65	2	16	31.4	-6.3	52	5	0	0	0.0	0.0
B / 8.8	5.7	0.97	13.00	1,363	2	50	46	2	13	44.4	-10.6	31	5	0	0	0.0	0.0
B / 8.4	7.1	1.22	13.53	1,261	3	65	31	1	9	53.5	-13.1	18	5	0	0	0.0	0.0
B / 8.1	7.8	1.35	13.84	1,031	3	73	23	1	9	59.2	-14.5	13	5	0	0	0.0	0.0
B- / 7.9	8.2	1.42	14.00	745	3	77	18	2	9	62.0	-15.2	11	5	0	0	0.0	0.0
B- / 7.8	8.3	1.43	14.05	554	3	78	17	2	9	62.4	-15.3	10	5	0	0	0.0	0.0
B- / 7.8	8.3	1.43	12.51	415	3	78	17	2	9	62.4	-15.2	11	5	0	0	0.0	0.0
U /	N/A	N/A	10.66	38	4	78	17	1	0	N/A	N/A	N/A	1	0	0	0.0	0.0
C+ / 6.9	5.1	0.86	9.91	316	2	42	55	1	23	42.3	-11.2	44	N/A	0	0	0.0	0.0
B- / 7.0	5.1	0.85	9.91	42	2	42	55	1	23	40.2	-11.4	37	N/A	1,000	0	5.0	0.0
B- / 7.0	5.1	0.85	9.88	1	2	42	55	1	23	39.0	-11.4	35	N/A	0	0	0.0	0.0
B- / 7.0	5.1	0.85	9.90	1	2	42	55	1	23	40.1	-11.4	37	7	0	0	0.0	0.0
B- / 7.0	5.0	0.84	9.89	1	2	42	55	1	23	39.4	-11.4	37	N/A	0	0	0.0	0.0
C+ / 6.9	5.1	0.85	9.90	1	2	42	55	1	23	41.2	-11.3	42	N/A	0	0	0.0	0.0
C+ / 6.9	5.1	0.85	9.90	N/A	2	42	55	1	23	42.4	-11.2	44	N/A	0	0	0.0	0.0
C+ / 6.9	5.1	0.85	9.91	1	2	42	55	1	23	42.6	-11.3	46	4	1,000,000	0	0.0	0.0
B- / 7.2	5.9	0.99	10.61	550	2	50	46	2	20	47.8	-13.1	34	N/A	0	0	0.0	0.0
B- / 7.3	5.9	0.99	10.61	64	2	50	46	2	20	45.5	-13.2	28	N/A	1,000	0	5.0	0.0
B- / 7.3	5.9	1.00	10.59	1	2	50	46	2	20	44.3	-13.3	25	N/A	0	0	0.0	0.0
B- / 7.3	5.9	0.99	10.59	N/A	2	50	46	2	20	45.4	-13.2	29	7	0	0	0.0	0.0
B- / 7.3	5.9	1.00	10.59	6	2	50	46	2	20	44.8	-13.3	26	N/A	0	0	0.0	0.0
B- / 7.2	5.8	0.99	10.59	N/A	2	50	46	2	20	46.8	-13.2	32	N/A	0	0	0.0	0.0

Fund Type	Fund Name	Ticker Symbol	Overall Investment Rating	Phone	Performance Rating/Pts	3 Mo	6 Mo	1Yr / Pct	3Yr / Pct	5Yr / Pct	Dividend Yield	Expense Ratio
									Annualized		Incl. in Returns	
								Total Return % through 3/31/15				
AA	J Hancock II Ret Liv thru 2015 R5	JLBHX	C-	(800) 257-3336	C- / 3.1	2.12	2.81	4.89 /38	8.31 /29	8.22 /31	3.01	0.92
AA	J Hancock II Ret Liv thru 2015 R6	JLBJX	C-	(800) 257-3336	C- / 3.2	2.12	2.86	4.84 /37	8.40 /29	8.12 /31	3.06	0.87
AA	J Hancock II Ret Liv thru 2020 1	JLDOX	C	(800) 257-3336	C- / 3.7	2.21	3.25	5.37 /41	9.29 /35	8.80 /35	2.75	0.90
AA	J Hancock II Ret Liv thru 2020 A	JLDAX	C-	(800) 257-3336	D+ / 2.6	2.11	2.97	4.90 /38	8.82 /32	8.32 /32	2.19	1.28
AA	J Hancock II Ret Liv thru 2020 R1	JLDDX	C	(800) 257-3336	C- / 3.2	2.03	2.90	4.65 /36	8.54 /30	8.10 /31	2.06	1.61
GI	J Hancock II Ret Liv thru 2020 R2	JLDEX	C	(800) 257-3336	C- / 3.4	2.03	2.97	4.91 /38	8.77 /31	8.31 /32	2.31	1.36
AA	J Hancock II Ret Liv thru 2020 R3	JLDFX	C	(800) 257-3336	C- / 3.3	2.02	2.91	4.75 /37	8.64 /31	8.18 /31	2.16	1.51
AA	J Hancock II Ret Liv thru 2020 R4	JLDGX	C	(800) 257-3336	C- / 3.6	2.21	3.14	5.17 /40	9.07 /33	8.56 /34	2.55	1.21
AA	J Hancock II Ret Liv thru 2020 R5	JLDHX	C	(800) 257-3336	C- / 3.7	2.12	3.16	5.37 /41	9.26 /35	8.82 /35	2.75	0.92
AA	J Hancock II Ret Liv thru 2020 R6	JLDIX	C	(800) 257-3336	C- / 3.7	2.21	3.21	5.43 /42	9.32 /35	8.69 /34	2.80	0.86
AA	J Hancock II Ret Liv thru 2025 1	JLEOX	C	(800) 257-3336	C / 4.3	2.32	3.65	5.91 /46	10.28 /41	9.46 /40	2.56	0.89
AA	J Hancock II Ret Liv thru 2025 A	JLEAX	C-	(800) 257-3336	C- / 3.2	2.22	3.45	5.52 /43	9.81 /38	9.00 /37	2.01	1.27
AA	J Hancock II Ret Liv thru 2025 R1	JLEDX	C	(800) 257-3336	C- / 3.8	2.14	3.30	5.19 /40	9.55 /36	8.75 /35	1.87	1.62
GI	J Hancock II Ret Liv thru 2025 R2	JLEEX	C	(800) 257-3336	C- / 4.0	2.14	3.37	5.45 /42	9.78 /38	8.98 /37	2.12	1.37
AA	J Hancock II Ret Liv thru 2025 R3	JLEFX	C	(800) 257-3336	C- / 3.9	2.14	3.31	5.29 /41	9.62 /37	8.83 /36	1.97	1.51
AA	J Hancock II Ret Liv thru 2025 R4	JLEGX	C	(800) 257-3336	C- / 4.2	2.32	3.54	5.70 /44	10.07 /40	9.22 /38	2.36	1.21
AA	J Hancock II Ret Liv thru 2025 R5	JLEHX	C	(800) 257-3336	C / 4.3	2.32	3.65	5.91 /46	10.29 /41	9.48 /40	2.56	0.91
GI	J Hancock II Ret Liv thru 2025 R6	JLEIX	C	(800) 257-3336	C / 4.3	2.32	3.62	5.97 /46	10.34 /41	9.37 /40	2.61	0.87
AA	J Hancock II Ret Liv thru 2030 1	JLFOX	C+	(800) 257-3336	C / 4.7	2.47	3.96	6.30 /49	11.01 /45	9.93 /44	2.47	0.91
AA	J Hancock II Ret Liv thru 2030 A	JLFAX	C	(800) 257-3336	C- / 3.6	2.37	3.76	5.90 /46	10.51 /42	9.46 /40	1.93	1.30
AA	J Hancock II Ret Liv thru 2030 R1	JLFDX	C	(800) 257-3336	C- / 4.2	2.29	3.60	5.58 /43	10.26 /41	9.21 /38	1.79	1.62
GI	J Hancock II Ret Liv thru 2030 R2	JLFEX	C	(800) 257-3336	C / 4.4	2.29	3.69	5.84 /45	10.49 /42	9.42 /40	2.03	1.37
AA	J Hancock II Ret Liv thru 2030 R3	JLFFX	C	(800) 257-3336	C / 4.3	2.29	3.71	5.68 /44	10.35 /41	9.28 /39	1.88	1.52
AA	J Hancock II Ret Liv thru 2030 R4	JLFGX	C	(800) 257-3336	C / 4.6	2.47	3.94	6.09 /47	10.78 /44	9.66 /42	2.28	1.23
AA	J Hancock II Ret Liv thru 2030 R5	JLFHX	C+	(800) 257-3336	C / 4.7	2.47	3.96	6.30 /49	11.02 /46	9.93 /44	2.47	0.93
GI	J Hancock II Ret Liv thru 2030 R6	JLFIX	C+	(800) 257-3336	C / 4.8	2.47	4.02	6.44 /50	11.07 /46	9.84 /43	2.52	0.88
AA	J Hancock II Ret Liv thru 2035 1	JLHOX	C+	(800) 257-3336	C / 5.0	2.49	4.21	6.50 /51	11.43 /48	10.23 /46	2.32	0.91
AA	J Hancock II Ret Liv thru 2035 A	JLHAX	C	(800) 257-3336	C- / 3.9	2.50	4.03	6.15 /48	10.97 /45	9.75 /43	1.80	1.29
AA	J Hancock II Ret Liv thru 2035 R1	JLHDX	C	(800) 257-3336	C / 4.5	2.41	3.87	5.80 /45	10.69 /44	9.52 /41	1.65	1.62
GI	J Hancock II Ret Liv thru 2035 R2	JLHEX	C	(800) 257-3336	C / 4.7	2.49	4.02	6.12 /48	10.97 /45	9.77 /43	1.89	1.37
AA	J Hancock II Ret Liv thru 2035 R3	JLHFX	C	(800) 257-3336	C / 4.6	2.41	3.88	5.90 /46	10.78 /44	9.59 /41	1.75	1.53
AA	J Hancock II Ret Liv thru 2035 R4		C	(800) 257-3336	C / 4.8	2.49	4.10	6.29 /49	11.19 /47	10.02 /45	2.13	1.23
AA	J Hancock II Ret Liv thru 2035 R5	JLHHX	C+	(800) 257-3336	C / 5.0	2.57	4.21	6.50 /51	11.43 /48	10.25 /46	2.32	0.92
GI	J Hancock II Ret Liv thru 2035 R6	JLHIX	C+	(800) 257-3336	C / 5.0	2.57	4.26	6.64 /52	11.48 /49	10.13 /46	2.37	0.88
AA	J Hancock II Ret Liv thru 2040 1	JLIOX	C+	(800) 257-3336	C / 5.0	2.59	4.23	6.53 /51	11.53 /49	10.29 /47	2.31	0.91
AA	J Hancock II Ret Liv thru 2040 A	JLIAX	C	(800) 257-3336	C- / 4.0	2.51	4.04	6.17 /48	11.06 /46	9.81 /43	1.79	1.28
AA	J Hancock II Ret Liv thru 2040 R1	JLIDX	C	(800) 257-3336	C / 4.5	2.43	3.88	5.83 /45	10.75 /44	9.56 /41	1.64	1.64
GI	J Hancock II Ret Liv thru 2040 R2	JLIEX	C	(800) 257-3336	C / 4.7	2.51	4.04	6.07 /47	11.04 /46	9.79 /43	1.88	1.38
AA	J Hancock II Ret Liv thru 2040 R3	JLIFX	C	(800) 257-3336	C / 4.6	2.43	3.90	5.94 /46	10.87 /45	9.68 /42	1.74	1.52
AA	J Hancock II Ret Liv thru 2040 R4	JLIGX	C	(800) 257-3336	C / 4.9	2.51	4.12	6.34 /49	11.29 /48	10.03 /45	2.13	1.23
AA	J Hancock II Ret Liv thru 2040 R5	JLIHX	C+	(800) 257-3336	C / 5.0	2.59	4.22	6.52 /51	11.53 /49	10.31 /47	2.31	0.93
AA	J Hancock II Ret Liv thru 2040 R6	JLIIX	C+	(800) 257-3336	C / 5.1	2.59	4.20	6.58 /52	11.60 /50	10.19 /46	2.37	0.88
AA	J Hancock II Ret Liv thru 2045 1	JLJOX	C+	(800) 257-3336	C / 5.1	2.61	4.28	6.59 /52	11.55 /49	10.30 /47	2.31	0.92
AA	J Hancock II Ret Liv thru 2045 A	JLJAX	C	(800) 257-3336	C- / 4.0	2.45	4.01	6.06 /47	11.06 /46	9.81 /43	1.79	1.30
AA	J Hancock II Ret Liv thru 2045 R1	JLJDX	C	(800) 257-3336	C / 4.5	2.45	3.94	5.81 /45	10.77 /44	9.55 /41	1.64	1.63
GI	J Hancock II Ret Liv thru 2045 R2	JLJEX	C	(800) 257-3336	C / 4.7	2.44	4.00	6.04 /47	11.03 /46	9.81 /43	1.88	1.40
AA	J Hancock II Ret Liv thru 2045 R3	JLJFX	C	(800) 257-3336	C / 4.6	2.36	3.86	5.92 /46	10.84 /44	9.66 /42	1.74	1.54
AA	J Hancock II Ret Liv thru 2045 R4	JLJGX	C	(800) 257-3336	C / 4.9	2.53	4.08	6.31 /49	11.30 /48	10.03 /45	2.13	1.24
AA	J Hancock II Ret Liv thru 2045 R5	JLJHX	C+	(800) 257-3336	C / 5.1	2.61	4.27	6.59 /52	11.58 /50	10.32 /47	2.31	0.94
GI	J Hancock II Ret Liv thru 2045 R6	JLJIX	C+	(800) 257-3336	C / 5.1	2.61	4.24	6.65 /52	11.61 /50	10.19 /46	2.36	0.89
AA	J Hancock II Ret Liv thru 2050 1	JLKOX	C+	(800) 257-3336	C / 5.1	2.47	4.19	6.48 /51	11.57 /49	--	2.27	0.99
AA	J Hancock II Ret Liv thru 2050 A	JLKAX	C	(800) 257-3336	C- / 4.0	2.47	4.08	6.11 /47	11.10 /46	--	1.74	1.37

● Denotes fund is closed to new investors
* Denotes fund is included in Section II

www.thestreetratings.com

RISK			NET ASSETS		ASSET						BULL / BEAR		FUND MANAGER		MINIMUMS		LOADS	
	3 Year		NAV							Portfolio	Last Bull	Last Bear	Manager	Manager	Initial	Additional	Front	Back
Risk Rating/Pts	Standard Deviation	Beta	As of 3/31/15	Total $(Mil)	Cash %	Stocks %	Bonds %	Other %		Turnover Ratio	Market Return	Market Return	Quality Pct	Tenure (Years)	Purch. $	Purch. $	End Load	End Load
B- / 7.2	5.9	0.99	10.61	2	2	50	46	2		20	47.7	-13.1	33	N/A	0	0	0.0	0.0
B- / 7.2	5.9	0.99	10.61	1	2	50	46	2		20	48.2	-13.2	34	4	1,000,000	0	0.0	0.0
B- / 7.5	6.8	1.15	11.10	1,136	3	59	36	2		17	54.7	-15.4	25	N/A	0	0	0.0	0.0
B- / 7.6	6.8	1.15	11.11	87	3	59	36	2		17	52.4	-15.6	21	N/A	1,000	0	5.0	0.0
B- / 7.6	6.8	1.15	11.08	4	3	59	36	2		17	51.1	-15.7	18	N/A	0	0	0.0	0.0
B- / 7.6	6.8	0.67	11.07	1	3	59	36	2		17	52.5	-15.6	42	7	0	0	0.0	0.0
B- / 7.6	6.8	1.16	11.09	4	3	59	36	2		17	51.6	-15.6	19	N/A	0	0	0.0	0.0
B- / 7.5	6.8	1.16	11.08	1	3	59	36	2		17	53.7	-15.6	22	N/A	0	0	0.0	0.0
B- / 7.5	6.8	1.16	11.10	4	3	59	36	2		17	54.6	-15.4	24	N/A	0	0	0.0	0.0
B- / 7.5	6.8	1.15	11.09	2	3	59	36	2		17	55.0	-15.6	26	4	1,000,000	0	0.0	0.0
B- / 7.5	7.8	1.32	11.46	1,404	3	70	25	2		15	61.8	-17.5	17	N/A	0	0	0.0	0.0
B- / 7.6	7.8	1.32	11.50	84	3	70	25	2		15	59.5	-17.6	14	N/A	1,000	0	5.0	0.0
B- / 7.6	7.7	1.31	11.45	5	3	70	25	2		15	58.1	-17.7	14	N/A	0	0	0.0	0.0
B- / 7.5	7.8	0.77	11.44	1	3	70	25	2		15	59.4	-17.6	34	7	0	0	0.0	0.0
B- / 7.6	7.8	1.32	11.45	4	3	70	25	2		15	58.4	-17.6	13	N/A	0	0	0.0	0.0
B- / 7.5	7.8	1.32	11.47	1	3	70	25	2		15	60.5	-17.5	16	N/A	0	0	0.0	0.0
B- / 7.5	7.8	1.32	11.46	2	3	70	25	2		15	61.9	-17.5	18	N/A	0	0	0.0	0.0
B- / 7.5	7.7	0.77	11.45	1	3	70	25	2		15	61.9	-17.6	42	4	1,000,000	0	0.0	0.0
B- / 7.2	8.5	1.45	11.62	1,233	3	80	14	3		15	67.1	-19.0	13	N/A	0	0	0.0	0.0
B- / 7.3	8.5	1.44	11.65	83	3	80	14	3		15	64.4	-19.0	11	N/A	1,000	0	5.0	0.0
B- / 7.3	8.5	1.44	11.60	3	3	80	14	3		15	63.1	-19.2	10	N/A	0	0	0.0	0.0
B- / 7.2	8.5	0.85	11.59	1	3	80	14	3		15	64.1	-19.0	28	7	0	0	0.0	0.0
B- / 7.3	8.6	1.45	11.61	3	3	80	14	3		15	63.6	-19.1	10	N/A	0	0	0.0	0.0
B- / 7.2	8.5	1.44	11.61	1	3	80	14	3		15	65.7	-19.0	12	N/A	0	0	0.0	0.0
B- / 7.2	8.6	1.45	11.62	3	3	80	14	3		15	67.0	-18.9	13	N/A	0	0	0.0	0.0
B- / 7.2	8.5	0.85	11.62	2	3	80	14	3		15	67.3	-19.1	35	4	1,000,000	0	0.0	0.0
B- / 7.0	9.1	1.53	11.96	1,028	3	87	8	2		14	70.3	-19.7	10	N/A	0	0	0.0	0.0
B- / 7.0	9.0	1.52	11.91	64	3	87	8	2		14	67.8	-19.9	9	N/A	1,000	0	5.0	0.0
B- / 7.0	9.1	1.53	11.89	4	3	87	8	2		14	66.2	-19.9	8	N/A	0	0	0.0	0.0
B- / 7.0	9.0	0.90	11.95	1	3	87	8	2		14	67.9	-19.9	24	7	0	0	0.0	0.0
B- / 7.0	9.0	1.52	11.90	3	3	87	8	2		14	66.7	-19.8	8	N/A	0	0	0.0	0.0
B- / 7.0	9.0	1.53	11.95	2	3	87	8	2		14	69.0	-19.8	9	N/A	0	0	0.0	0.0
B- / 7.0	9.1	1.54	11.96	1	3	87	8	2		14	70.2	-19.6	10	N/A	0	0	0.0	0.0
B- / 7.0	9.1	0.90	11.96	1	3	87	8	2		14	70.5	-19.8	29	4	1,000,000	0	0.0	0.0
C+ / 6.9	9.1	1.54	11.88	794	4	88	7	1		14	70.7	-19.7	10	N/A	0	0	0.0	0.0
B- / 7.0	9.1	1.54	11.84	54	4	88	7	1		14	68.1	-19.7	8	N/A	1,000	0	5.0	0.0
B- / 7.0	9.1	1.54	11.81	2	4	88	7	1		14	66.6	-19.9	8	N/A	0	0	0.0	0.0
C+ / 6.9	9.1	0.91	11.86	2	4	88	7	1		14	68.0	-19.7	24	7	0	0	0.0	0.0
B- / 7.0	9.1	1.54	11.80	3	4	88	7	1		14	67.2	-19.8	8	N/A	0	0	0.0	0.0
C+ / 6.9	9.1	1.54	11.84	1	4	88	7	1		14	69.4	-19.7	9	N/A	0	0	0.0	0.0
C+ / 6.9	9.2	1.55	11.89	2	4	88	7	1		14	70.7	-19.6	10	N/A	0	0	0.0	0.0
C+ / 6.9	9.1	1.54	11.87	1	4	88	7	1		14	70.9	-19.7	11	4	1,000,000	0	0.0	0.0
C+ / 6.9	9.1	1.53	11.79	757	4	88	7	1		14	70.6	-19.7	11	N/A	0	0	0.0	0.0
C+ / 6.9	9.1	1.53	11.73	52	4	88	7	1		14	68.1	-19.8	9	N/A	1,000	0	5.0	0.0
C+ / 6.9	9.1	1.54	11.71	2	4	88	7	1		14	66.6	-19.8	8	N/A	0	0	0.0	0.0
C+ / 6.9	9.1	0.91	11.76	1	4	88	7	1		14	68.1	-19.8	24	7	0	0	0.0	0.0
C+ / 6.9	9.1	1.53	11.71	2	4	88	7	1		14	67.2	-19.9	8	N/A	0	0	0.0	0.0
C+ / 6.9	9.1	1.54	11.75	1	4	88	7	1		14	69.5	-19.8	9	N/A	0	0	0.0	0.0
C+ / 6.9	9.1	1.54	11.80	2	4	88	7	1		14	70.7	-19.6	10	N/A	0	0	0.0	0.0
C+ / 6.9	9.1	0.90	11.78	1	4	88	7	1		14	70.8	-19.8	30	4	1,000,000	0	0.0	0.0
B- / 7.1	9.1	1.53	12.03	261	3	88	7	2		10	70.8	-19.6	11	4	0	0	0.0	0.0
B- / 7.3	9.1	1.54	12.03	12	3	88	7	2		10	N/A	N/A	9	N/A	1,000	0	5.0	0.0

Fund Type	Fund Name	Ticker Symbol	Overall Investment Rating	Phone	Performance Rating/Pts	3 Mo	6 Mo	1Yr / Pct	3Yr / Pct	5Yr / Pct	Dividend Yield	Expense Ratio
AA	J Hancock II Ret Liv thru 2050 R1	JLKDX	C	(800) 257-3336	C / 4.6	2.39	3.92	5.85 /45	10.81 /44	--	1.59	1.72
AA	J Hancock II Ret Liv thru 2050 R2	JLKEX	C+	(800) 257-3336	C / 4.7	2.38	4.00	6.02 /47	11.07 /46	--	1.83	1.47
AA	J Hancock II Ret Liv thru 2050 R3	JLKFX	C+	(800) 257-3336	C / 4.6	2.39	3.93	5.86 /45	10.91 /45	--	1.69	1.61
AA	J Hancock II Ret Liv thru 2050 R4	JLKGX	C+	(800) 257-3336	C / 4.9	2.47	4.16	6.36 /50	11.33 /48	--	2.08	1.31
GI	J Hancock II Ret Liv thru 2050 R5	JLKHX	C+	(800) 257-3336	C / 5.1	2.56	4.28	6.57 /51	11.57 /49	--	2.27	1.02
GI	J Hancock II Ret Liv thru 2050 R6	JLKRX	C+	(800) 257-3336	C / 5.1	2.56	4.24	6.62 /52	11.62 /50	--	2.32	0.96
GI	J Hancock II Ret Liv thru 2055 1	JLKUX	U	(800) 257-3336	U /	2.53	4.32	6.48 /51	--	--	2.21	10.67
GI	J Hancock II RetLiv thru II 2020 1	JRLOX	U	(800) 257-3336	U /	2.11	4.12	6.59 /52	--	--	1.37	16.35
GI	J Hancock II RetLiv thru II 2025 1	JRTBX	U	(800) 257-3336	U /	2.09	4.42	7.19 /57	--	--	1.48	11.35
GI	J Hancock II RetLiv thru II 2030 1	JRTGX	U	(800) 257-3336	U /	2.18	4.59	7.57 /60	--	--	1.57	12.64
GI	J Hancock II RetLiv thru II 2035 1	JRTKX	U	(800) 257-3336	U /	2.27	4.74	7.92 /62	--	--	1.63	16.08
GR	J Hancock II SC Growth NAV		B-	(800) 257-3336	A- / 9.0	5.13	12.25	11.83 /82	16.73 /88	14.77 /85	0.00	1.10
SC	J Hancock II Sm Cap Oppty 1	JISOX	C	(800) 257-3336	B / 7.7	3.37	9.45	4.91 /38	15.79 /82	14.70 /84	0.08	1.14
SC	J Hancock II Sm Cap Oppty NAV	JHSOX	C	(800) 257-3336	B / 7.7	3.35	9.44	4.95 /38	15.83 /82	14.74 /85	0.13	1.09
SC	J Hancock II Small Cap Value NAV		B	(800) 257-3336	B+ / 8.6	4.16	16.04	9.49 /72	15.95 /83	14.44 /82	0.49	1.16
SC	J Hancock II Small Company Grth		B+	(800) 257-3336	A / 9.4	5.58	11.76	10.68 /77	17.94 /94	17.23 /96	0.00	1.07
SC	J Hancock II Small Company Val 1	JISVX	C-	(800) 257-3336	C / 5.0	1.40	9.61	0.22 /16	11.95 /52	11.61 /58	0.60	1.31
SC	J Hancock II Small Company Val		C-	(800) 257-3336	C / 5.0	1.40	9.64	0.27 /16	12.01 /53	11.67 /58	0.65	1.26
GR	J Hancock II Spectrum Income Nav		C-	(800) 257-3336	D- / 1.2	0.78	0.80	2.30 /23	4.56 /12	5.61 /15	3.42	0.79
GL	J Hancock II Strat Equity Alloc NAV		U	(800) 257-3336	U /	2.33	4.91	7.85 /62	--	--	1.70	0.68
GL	J Hancock II Technical Opport A	JTCAX	B	(800) 257-3336	A / 9.4	5.69	9.99	11.34 /80	19.74 /98	9.81 /43	0.00	1.66
GL	J Hancock II Technical Opport I	JTCIX	B	(800) 257-3336	A+ / 9.7	5.79	10.08	11.64 /81	20.09 /98	10.17 /46	0.00	1.34
GL	J Hancock II Technical Opport NAV		B	(800) 257-3336	A+ / 9.8	5.87	10.27	11.90 /82	20.40 /98	10.39 /48	0.00	1.22
GI	J Hancock II Total Return 1	JITRX	C-	(800) 257-3336	D- / 1.4	2.19	3.72	5.50 /42	3.73 / 9	4.44 /10	3.28	0.75
GI	J Hancock II Total Return NAV	JHTRX	C-	(800) 257-3336	D- / 1.4	2.20	3.75	5.56 /43	3.76 /10	4.49 /10	3.33	0.70
GR	J Hancock II US Equity 1	JHUPX	U	(800) 257-3336	U /	0.42	4.38	8.69 /67	--	--	1.14	0.85
IN	J Hancock II US Equity A	JHUAX	D+	(800) 257-3336	C / 5.0	0.34	4.24	8.29 /65	12.96 /59	12.28 /62	0.69	1.24
IN	J Hancock II US Equity I	JHUIX	C-	(800) 257-3336	C+ / 6.1	0.42	4.40	8.70 /68	13.42 /63	12.72 /66	1.08	0.92
IN	J Hancock II US Equity NAV		C-	(800) 257-3336	C+ / 6.3	0.51	4.52	8.83 /68	13.57 /64	12.81 /66	1.18	0.80
GR	J Hancock II Value NAV		B+	(800) 257-3336	A- / 9.0	3.67	9.16	10.79 /78	17.23 /91	15.51 /90	0.54	0.76
GI	J Hancock III Disciplined Val 12	JVLTX	A-	(800) 257-3336	B / 7.9	-0.26	5.11	7.85 /62	16.43 /86	13.98 /78	0.74	0.88
GI	● J Hancock III Disciplined Val B	JVLBX	B-	(800) 257-3336	C+ / 6.9	-0.59	4.53	6.68 /52	15.11 /76	12.66 /65	0.00	1.95
GI	J Hancock III Disciplined Val C	JVLCX	B-	(800) 257-3336	C+ / 6.9	-0.54	4.58	6.78 /53	15.19 /76	12.72 /66	0.00	1.87
GI	J Hancock III Disciplined Val I	JVLIX	A-	(800) 257-3336	B / 7.9	-0.32	5.07	7.86 /62	16.40 /86	13.97 /77	0.75	0.84
GI	J Hancock III Disciplined Val NAV	JDVNX	A-	(800) 257-3336	B / 8.0	-0.26	5.19	7.98 /63	16.56 /87	14.10 /79	0.87	0.74
GI	J Hancock III Disciplined Val R1	JDVOX	B+	(800) 257-3336	B- / 7.3	-0.47	4.71	7.09 /56	15.58 /80	13.13 /69	0.06	1.66
GI	J Hancock III Disciplined Val R2	JDVPX	B+	(800) 257-3336	B- / 7.5	-0.42	4.84	7.39 /58	15.87 /82	13.49 /73	0.39	1.38
GI	J Hancock III Disciplined Val R3	JDVHX	B+	(800) 257-3336	B- / 7.3	-0.42	4.76	7.20 /57	15.70 /81	13.25 /71	0.21	1.59
GI	J Hancock III Disciplined Val R4	JDVFX	B+	(800) 257-3336	B / 7.7	-0.32	5.05	7.67 /60	16.20 /85	13.68 /75	0.58	1.12
GI	J Hancock III Disciplined Val R5	JDVVX	A-	(800) 257-3336	B / 8.0	-0.26	5.13	7.98 /63	16.52 /87	14.02 /78	0.86	0.79
GI	J Hancock III Disciplined Val R6	JDVWX	A-	(800) 257-3336	B / 8.0	-0.21	5.20	7.99 /63	16.55 /87	14.04 /78	0.87	0.74
GI	J Hancock III Disciplined Value A	JVLAX	B-	(800) 257-3336	C+ / 6.7	-0.36	4.93	7.53 /59	16.06 /84	13.60 /74	0.46	1.11
MC	● J Hancock III Dsp Val Mid Cap A	JVMAX	A+	(800) 257-3336	A / 9.5	4.40	12.79	13.78 /89	19.64 /97	17.18 /96	0.25	1.18
MC	● J Hancock III Dsp Val Mid Cap Adv	JVMVX	A+	(800) 257-3336	A+ / 9.7	4.35	12.74	13.67 /89	19.58 /97	--	0.20	3.45
MC	● J Hancock III Dsp Val Mid Cap C	JVMCX	A+	(800) 257-3336	A+ / 9.6	4.18	12.36	12.90 /86	18.69 /96	16.29 /94	0.00	1.94
MC	● J Hancock III Dsp Val Mid Cap Inst	JVMIX	A+	(800) 257-3336	A+ / 9.8	4.46	12.99	14.13 /90	19.99 /98	17.52 /97	0.50	0.90
MC	● J Hancock III Dsp Val Mid Cap R2	JVMSX	A+	(800) 257-3336	A+ / 9.7	4.31	12.70	13.66 /89	19.50 /97	17.09 /96	0.14	1.32
MC	● J Hancock III Dsp Val Mid Cap R4	JVMTX	U	(800) 257-3336	U /	4.41	12.91	13.93 /89	--	--	0.38	1.32
MC	● J Hancock III Dsp Val Mid Cap R6	JVMRX	A+	(800) 257-3336	A+ / 9.8	4.46	13.01	14.21 /90	20.08 /98	17.49 /97	0.61	0.81
GL	J Hancock III Glb Shrhldr Yld A	JGYAX	D+	(800) 257-3336	C- / 3.2	-0.42	0.25	2.32 /23	10.83 /44	10.80 /51	3.58	1.34
GL	● J Hancock III Glb Shrhldr Yld B	JGYBX	C-	(800) 257-3336	C- / 3.5	-0.62	-0.14	1.61 /20	9.99 /39	9.98 /44	2.96	2.15
GL	J Hancock III Glb Shrhldr Yld C	JGYCX	C-	(800) 257-3336	C- / 3.5	-0.60	-0.02	1.68 /21	10.06 /40	10.02 /45	3.03	2.05

● Denotes fund is closed to new investors
* Denotes fund is included in Section II

RISK			NET ASSETS		ASSET					BULL / BEAR		FUND MANAGER		MINIMUMS		LOADS	
	3 Year		NAV						Portfolio	Last Bull	Last Bear	Manager	Manager	Initial	Additional	Front	Back
Risk	Standard		As of	Total	Cash	Stocks	Bonds	Other	Turnover	Market	Market	Quality	Tenure	Purch.	Purch.	End	End
Rating/Pts	Deviation	Beta	3/31/15	$(Mil)	%	%	%	%	Ratio	Return	Return	Pct	(Years)	$	$	Load	Load
B- / 7.3	9.1	1.54	12.02	1	3	88	7	2	10	N/A	N/A	8	N/A	0	0	0.0	0.0
B- / 7.3	9.1	1.53	12.02	1	3	88	7	2	10	N/A	N/A	9	N/A	0	0	0.0	0.0
B- / 7.3	9.1	1.53	12.02	N/A	3	88	7	2	10	N/A	N/A	8	N/A	0	0	0.0	0.0
B- / 7.3	9.1	1.54	12.03	N/A	3	88	7	2	10	N/A	N/A	9	N/A	0	0	0.0	0.0
B- / 7.5	9.1	0.91	12.04	N/A	3	88	7	2	10	N/A	N/A	30	4	0	0	0.0	0.0
B- / 7.5	9.1	0.91	12.04	2	3	88	7	2	10	N/A	N/A	30	4	1,000,000	0	0.0	0.0
U /	N/A	N/A	10.55	27	4	88	7	1	0	N/A	N/A	N/A	1	0	0	0.0	0.0
U /	N/A	N/A	10.65	36	0	67	32	1	68	N/A	N/A	N/A	N/A	0	0	0.0	0.0
U /	N/A	N/A	10.73	47	0	78	21	1	9	N/A	N/A	N/A	2	0	0	0.0	0.0
U /	N/A	N/A	10.78	42	0	86	13	1	4	N/A	N/A	N/A	2	0	0	0.0	0.0
U /	N/A	N/A	10.83	30	0	93	6	1	6	N/A	N/A	N/A	2	0	0	0.0	0.0
C- / 4.0	13.6	1.12	10.65	239	2	97	0	1	100	98.7	-25.7	47	7	0	0	0.0	0.0
C- / 3.8	13.0	0.94	27.32	69	1	98	0	1	30	100.6	-25.8	72	7	0	0	0.0	0.0
C- / 3.7	13.0	0.94	27.16	170	1	98	0	1	30	100.9	-25.7	73	7	0	0	0.0	0.0
C / 5.4	12.6	0.92	20.27	258	4	95	0	1	20	97.2	-21.4	77	7	0	0	0.0	0.0
C / 5.0	12.0	0.84	20.61	203	2	97	0	1	33	109.7	-23.6	91	N/A	0	0	0.0	0.0
C+ / 5.7	12.9	0.93	34.86	98	2	97	0	1	20	79.0	-23.4	27	10	0	0	0.0	0.0
C+ / 5.7	12.9	0.93	34.83	258	2	97	0	1	20	79.4	-23.4	28	10	0	0	0.0	0.0
B / 8.6	3.7	0.25	10.59	921	0	0	0	100	59	24.1	-4.0	74	4	0	0	0.0	0.0
U /	N/A	N/A	13.63	6,191	3	96	0	1	19	N/A	N/A	N/A	3	0	0	0.0	0.0
C- / 4.2	11.9	0.63	13.38	54	5	94	0	1	306	81.2	-21.1	99	6	1,000	0	5.0	0.0
C- / 4.2	11.9	0.63	13.71	32	5	94	0	1	306	83.2	-21.0	99	6	250,000	0	0.0	0.0
C / 4.3	11.9	0.63	13.89	811	5	94	0	1	306	84.5	-20.9	99	6	0	0	0.0	0.0
B / 8.7	3.5	0.03	14.00	282	0	1	98	1	130	16.5	-1.2	89	N/A	0	0	0.0	0.0
B / 8.7	3.5	0.02	13.95	1,776	0	1	98	1	130	16.6	-1.2	90	N/A	0	0	0.0	0.0
U /	N/A	N/A	11.88	57	1	98	0	1	52	N/A	N/A	N/A	10	0	0	0.0	0.0
C / 4.4	8.8	0.90	11.92	48	1	98	0	1	52	77.5	-9.6	49	10	1,000	0	5.0	0.0
C / 4.3	8.8	0.90	11.89	110	1	98	0	1	52	80.1	-9.5	55	10	250,000	0	0.0	0.0
C / 4.3	8.8	0.89	11.89	992	1	98	0	1	52	80.7	-9.5	58	10	0	0	0.0	0.0
C+ / 5.8	10.2	0.95	12.44	413	1	98	0	1	45	111.1	-21.5	82	9	0	0	0.0	0.0
B- / 7.1	10.7	1.07	18.92	89	2	97	0	1	45	107.8	-19.8	55	18	250,000	0	0.0	0.0
B- / 7.1	10.7	1.07	18.38	19	2	97	0	1	45	99.8	-20.2	38	18	1,000	0	0.0	0.0
B- / 7.1	10.7	1.07	18.43	302	2	97	0	1	45	100.4	-20.2	39	18	1,000	0	0.0	0.0
B- / 7.0	10.7	1.07	18.91	7,026	2	97	0	1	45	107.8	-19.7	54	18	250,000	0	0.0	0.0
B- / 7.0	10.7	1.07	18.94	845	2	97	0	1	45	108.6	-19.7	57	18	0	0	0.0	0.0
B- / 7.1	10.7	1.07	18.90	22	2	97	0	1	45	102.7	-20.0	44	18	0	0	0.0	0.0
B- / 7.1	10.7	1.07	18.90	120	2	97	0	1	45	104.8	-19.9	47	18	0	0	0.0	0.0
B- / 7.1	10.7	1.07	18.89	28	2	97	0	1	45	103.3	-20.0	46	18	0	0	0.0	0.0
B- / 7.0	10.7	1.07	18.92	226	2	97	0	1	45	106.4	-19.9	52	18	0	0	0.0	0.0
B- / 7.0	10.7	1.07	18.94	375	2	97	0	1	45	108.2	-19.8	56	18	0	0	0.0	0.0
B- / 7.1	10.7	1.07	18.94	1,445	2	97	0	1	45	108.3	-19.7	57	18	1,000,000	0	0.0	0.0
B- / 7.1	10.7	1.07	19.44	2,711	2	97	0	1	45	105.7	-19.9	50	18	1,000	0	5.0	0.0
C+ / 6.9	10.5	0.91	20.19	2,152	2	97	0	1	39	120.5	-21.4	90	15	1,000	0	5.0	0.0
C+ / 6.9	10.4	0.91	20.15	1	2	97	0	1	39	120.2	-21.4	90	15	0	0	0.0	0.0
C+ / 6.9	10.5	0.91	20.43	366	2	97	0	1	39	114.8	-21.6	88	15	1,000	0	0.0	0.0
C+ / 6.9	10.5	0.91	20.86	7,119	2	97	0	1	39	122.7	-21.3	91	15	250,000	0	0.0	0.0
C+ / 6.9	10.5	0.91	20.81	250	2	97	0	1	39	119.7	-21.4	90	15	0	0	0.0	0.0
U /	N/A	N/A	20.85	119	2	97	0	1	39	N/A	N/A	N/A	15	0	0	0.0	0.0
C+ / 6.9	10.5	0.91	20.85	799	2	97	0	1	39	123.2	-21.4	91	15	1,000,000	0	0.0	0.0
C+ / 6.6	9.7	0.65	11.28	567	4	95	0	1	40	60.6	-12.3	92	8	1,000	0	5.0	0.0
C+ / 6.6	9.7	0.65	11.29	16	4	95	0	1	40	56.7	-12.6	90	8	1,000	0	0.0	0.0
C+ / 6.6	9.7	0.65	11.30	165	4	95	0	1	40	56.8	-12.5	91	8	1,000	0	0.0	0.0

Fund Type	Fund Name	Ticker Symbol	Overall Investment Rating	Phone	Performance Rating/Pts	3 Mo	6 Mo	1Yr / Pct	3Yr / Pct	5Yr / Pct	Dividend Yield	Expense Ratio
GL	J Hancock III Glb Shrhldr Yld I	JGYIX	C-	(800) 257-3336	C- / 4.2	-0.34	0.42	2.73 /25	11.24 /47	11.25 /55	4.06	1.02
GL	J Hancock III Glb Shrhldr Yld NAV		C	(800) 257-3336	C / 4.4	-0.31	0.49	2.87 /26	11.40 /48	11.36 /56	4.21	10.30
GL	J Hancock III Glb Shrhldr Yld R2	JGSRX	C-	(800) 257-3336	C- / 3.9	-0.45	0.19	2.27 /23	10.72 /44	10.75 /51	3.61	8.68
GL	J Hancock III Glb Shrhldr Yld R6	JGRSX	C-	(800) 257-3336	C / 4.3	-0.31	0.49	2.80 /25	11.32 /48	11.14 /54	4.23	10.37
FO	J Hancock III Internatl Val Eq A	JIEAX	E+	(800) 257-3336	D- / 1.1	3.75	-0.31	-2.45 / 9	6.20 /18	4.56 /10	2.08	1.62
FO	J Hancock III Internatl Val Eq I	JIEEX	E+	(800) 257-3336	D / 1.7	3.88	-0.17	-2.20 /10	6.55 /19	--	2.42	1.47
FO	J Hancock III Internatl Val Eq NAV		E+	(800) 257-3336	D / 1.8	3.88	-0.11	-2.03 /10	6.75 /20	4.91 /12	2.69	16.37
FO	J Hancock III Intl Core A	GIDEX	D-	(800) 257-3336	D / 1.9	5.19	-1.04	-4.40 / 6	8.70 /31	5.97 /17	3.07	1.46
FO	● J Hancock III Intl Core B	GOCBX	D-	(800) 257-3336	D / 2.1	5.01	-1.46	-5.21 / 5	7.84 /26	5.18 /13	2.33	2.64
FO	J Hancock III Intl Core C	GOCCX	D-	(800) 257-3336	D / 2.1	5.01	-1.45	-5.20 / 5	7.84 /26	5.18 /13	2.34	2.46
FO	J Hancock III Intl Core I	GOCIX	D-	(800) 257-3336	D+ / 2.8	5.31	-0.85	-4.09 / 7	9.09 /34	6.40 /19	3.54	1.16
FO	J Hancock III Intl Core NAV		D-	(800) 257-3336	D+ / 2.9	5.34	-0.80	-3.96 / 7	9.23 /34	6.53 /20	3.70	14.17
FO	J Hancock III Intl Core R	GOCRX	D-	(800) 257-3336	D+ / 2.3	5.10	-1.24	-4.82 / 6	8.28 /29	5.60 /15	2.77	5.93
FO	J Hancock III Intl Core R2	JICGX	D-	(800) 257-3336	D+ / 2.5	5.17	-1.13	-4.58 / 6	8.55 /30	5.89 /16	3.02	16.14
FO	J Hancock III Intl Core R3	JICHX	D-	(800) 257-3336	D+ / 2.4	5.14	-1.18	-4.71 / 6	8.40 /29	5.71 /15	2.86	19.03
FO	J Hancock III Intl Core R4	JICFX	D-	(800) 257-3336	D+ / 2.7	5.24	-0.97	-4.32 / 6	8.82 /32	6.08 /17	3.29	21.15
FO	J Hancock III Intl Core R5	JICWX	D-	(800) 257-3336	D+ / 2.8	5.28	-0.90	-4.16 / 7	9.03 /33	6.34 /19	3.50	16.17
FO	J Hancock III Intl Core R6	JICEX	D-	(800) 257-3336	D+ / 2.9	5.34	-0.80	-3.95 / 7	9.17 /34	6.31 /19	3.70	21.97
FO	J Hancock III Intl Gwth 1	GOIOX	D+	(800) 257-3336	C+ / 6.3	6.45	8.10	6.64 /52	13.04 /60	10.21 /46	2.30	1.12
FO	J Hancock III Intl Gwth A	GOIGX	D	(800) 257-3336	C / 5.1	6.35	7.88	6.19 /48	12.55 /56	9.74 /42	1.79	1.56
FO	● J Hancock III Intl Gwth B	GONBX	D+	(800) 257-3336	C / 5.4	6.17	7.42	5.34 /41	11.73 /51	8.92 /36	1.09	3.29
FO	J Hancock III Intl Gwth C	GONCX	D+	(800) 257-3336	C / 5.4	6.13	7.43	5.38 /41	11.73 /51	8.91 /36	1.16	2.62
FO	J Hancock III Intl Gwth I	GOGIX	D+	(800) 257-3336	C+ / 6.3	6.49	8.08	6.57 /51	12.97 /59	10.16 /46	2.20	1.22
GR	J Hancock III Select Growth A	RGROX	E	(800) 257-3336	C- / 4.1	3.90	9.26	5.13 /40	10.76 /44	11.13 /54	0.00	1.18
GR	J Hancock III Select Growth ADV	RGRDX	E+	(800) 257-3336	C / 4.9	3.89	9.21	5.20 /40	10.83 /44	11.23 /55	0.00	1.24
GR	● J Hancock III Select Growth B	RGRBX	E	(800) 257-3336	C / 4.3	3.66	8.75	4.27 /34	9.84 /38	10.22 /46	0.00	1.99
GR	J Hancock III Select Growth C	RGRCX	E	(800) 257-3336	C / 4.3	3.66	8.76	4.26 /33	9.83 /38	10.21 /46	0.00	2.02
GR	J Hancock III Select Growth I	RLGIX	E+	(800) 257-3336	C / 5.0	3.92	9.31	5.35 /41	11.05 /46	11.48 /57	0.00	0.93
GR	J Hancock III Select Growth NAV		E+	(800) 257-3336	C / 5.2	3.99	9.45	5.57 /43	11.24 /47	11.63 /58	0.00	1.09
GR	J Hancock III Select Growth R1	RGRWX	E+	(800) 257-3336	C / 4.5	3.74	8.94	4.59 /36	10.21 /41	10.61 /50	0.00	4.23
GR	J Hancock III Select Growth R2	RGRTX	E+	(800) 257-3336	C / 4.7	3.83	9.07	4.89 /38	10.50 /42	10.97 /52	0.00	15.75
GR	J Hancock III Select Growth R3	RGRHX	E+	(800) 257-3336	C / 4.5	3.75	8.96	4.71 /36	10.32 /41	10.73 /50	0.00	13.14
GR	J Hancock III Select Growth R4	RGRFX	E+	(800) 257-3336	C / 4.9	3.88	9.20	5.15 /40	10.78 /44	11.12 /54	0.00	11.01
GR	J Hancock III Select Growth R5	RGRVX	E+	(800) 257-3336	C / 5.0	3.94	9.37	5.39 /42	11.00 /45	11.40 /56	Incl.	12.43
GR	J Hancock III Select Growth R6	RGRUX	E+	(800) 257-3336	C / 5.1	4.00	9.47	5.58 /43	11.18 /46	11.44 /56	0.00	1.09
GR	J Hancock III Select Growth T	JRGTX	E	(800) 257-3336	C- / 4.0	3.90	9.22	5.10 /39	10.67 /43	11.02 /53	0.00	1.26
SC	J Hancock III Small Company A	JCSAX	C	(800) 257-3336	C+ / 6.4	4.44	11.76	7.28 /57	14.55 /71	11.96 /60	0.00	1.46
SC	J Hancock III Small Company ADV	JCSDX	C+	(800) 257-3336	B- / 7.5	4.46	11.82	7.39 /58	14.69 /72	12.07 /61	0.00	7.66
SC	J Hancock III Small Company I	JCSIX	B-	(800) 257-3336	B / 7.6	4.48	11.93	7.61 /60	14.94 /74	12.32 /63	0.00	1.17
SC	J Hancock III Small Company R1	JCSOX	C+	(800) 257-3336	B- / 7.0	4.29	11.52	6.86 /54	14.17 /68	11.57 /57	0.00	2.96
SC	J Hancock III Small Company R2	JCSPX	C+	(800) 257-3336	B- / 7.3	4.39	11.72	7.18 /57	14.46 /71	11.91 /60	0.00	8.12
SC	J Hancock III Small Company R3	JCSHX	C+	(800) 257-3336	B- / 7.1	4.34	11.62	7.02 /55	14.27 /69	11.68 /58	0.00	10.87
SC	J Hancock III Small Company R4	JCSFX	B-	(800) 257-3336	B- / 7.5	4.45	11.85	7.42 /58	14.74 /73	12.07 /61	0.00	19.03
SC	J Hancock III Small Company R5	JCSVX	B-	(800) 257-3336	B / 7.7	4.48	11.92	7.64 /60	14.96 /75	12.34 /63	0.00	6.04
SC	J Hancock III Small Company R6	JCSWX	B-	(800) 257-3336	B / 7.8	4.54	12.00	7.80 /61	15.07 /75	12.34 /63	0.00	18.63
GR	J Hancock III Strat Growth A	JSGAX	B	(800) 257-3336	B- / 7.2	4.05	9.86	14.68 /91	15.01 /75	--	0.00	1.51
GR	J Hancock III Strat Growth I	JSGIX	A-	(800) 257-3336	B+ / 8.5	4.16	10.06	15.07 /92	15.41 /78	--	0.32	2.63
GR	J Hancock III Strat Growth NAV		A	(800) 257-3336	B+ / 8.6	4.28	10.27	15.43 /92	15.65 /80	--	0.50	0.74
GL	J Hancock International Gr Opps NAV		U	(800) 257-3336	U /	5.73	3.48	-0.95 /13	--	--	0.81	0.96
GR	J Hancock Large Cap Equity A	TAGRX	C+	(800) 257-3336	C+ / 6.1	0.90	3.53	8.91 /69	14.83 /74	11.40 /56	0.30	1.06
GR	● J Hancock Large Cap Equity B	TSGWX	C+	(800) 257-3336	C+ / 6.4	0.71	3.15	8.11 /64	13.97 /67	10.56 /49	0.00	1.81
GR	J Hancock Large Cap Equity C	JHLVX	C+	(800) 257-3336	C+ / 6.4	0.71	3.12	8.11 /64	13.97 /67	10.57 /49	0.00	1.81

99 Pct = Best
0 Pct = Worst

● Denotes fund is closed to new investors
* Denotes fund is included in Section II

www.thestreetratings.com

RISK	3 Year		NET ASSETS		ASSET				Portfolio	BULL / BEAR		FUND MANAGER		MINIMUMS		LOADS	
Risk Rating/Pts	Standard Deviation	Beta	NAV As of 3/31/15	Total $(Mil)	Cash %	Stocks %	Bonds %	Other %	Turnover Ratio	Last Bull Market Return	Last Bear Market Return	Manager Quality Pct	Manager Tenure (Years)	Initial Purch. $	Additional Purch. $	Front End Load	Back End Load
C+ / 6.6	9.7	0.65	11.32	1,209	4	95	0	1	40	62.6	-12.0	93	8	250,000	0	0.0	0.0
C+ / 6.5	9.7	0.65	11.31	674	4	95	0	1	40	63.2	-12.0	93	8	0	0	0.0	0.0
C+ / 6.6	9.7	0.65	11.32	1	4	95	0	1	40	60.2	-12.3	92	8	0	0	0.0	0.0
C+ / 6.5	9.7	0.65	11.30	N/A	4	95	0	1	40	62.8	-12.2	93	8	1,000,000	0	0.0	0.0
C / 4.6	12.0	0.90	8.29	22	4	95	0	1	38	40.3	-23.5	34	17	1,000	0	5.0	0.0
C / 4.6	12.0	0.90	8.29	3	4	95	0	1	38	41.7	-23.4	39	17	250,000	0	0.0	0.0
C / 4.5	12.1	0.91	8.29	417	4	95	0	1	38	42.7	-23.5	41	17	0	0	0.0	0.0
C / 5.2	13.7	1.02	32.41	113	2	97	0	1	47	47.9	-22.2	53	10	1,000	0	5.0	0.0
C / 5.3	13.8	1.02	32.30	2	2	97	0	1	47	44.2	-22.4	41	10	1,000	0	0.0	0.0
C / 5.3	13.8	1.02	32.30	12	2	97	0	1	47	44.2	-22.4	41	10	1,000	0	0.0	0.0
C / 5.1	13.8	1.02	32.53	535	2	97	0	1	47	49.9	-22.0	58	10	250,000	0	0.0	0.0
C / 5.1	13.8	1.02	32.55	753	2	97	0	1	47	50.6	-22.0	60	10	0	0	0.0	0.0
C / 5.2	13.8	1.02	32.35	1	2	97	0	1	47	46.1	-22.3	47	10	0	0	0.0	0.0
C / 5.2	13.8	1.02	32.54	N/A	2	97	0	1	47	47.4	-22.2	51	10	0	0	0.0	0.0
C / 5.2	13.8	1.02	32.55	N/A	2	97	0	1	47	46.6	-22.2	48	10	0	0	0.0	0.0
C / 5.1	13.8	1.02	32.52	N/A	2	97	0	1	47	48.5	-22.1	55	10	0	0	0.0	0.0
C / 5.1	13.8	1.02	32.51	N/A	2	97	0	1	47	49.7	-22.1	58	10	0	0	0.0	0.0
C / 5.1	13.8	1.02	32.57	N/A	2	97	0	1	47	50.3	-22.1	60	10	1,000,000	0	0.0	0.0
C- / 3.5	11.4	0.82	21.47	20	2	97	0	1	42	69.3	-20.4	93	9	0	0	0.0	0.0
C- / 3.6	11.4	0.82	21.45	160	2	97	0	1	42	66.8	-20.6	92	9	1,000	0	5.0	0.0
C- / 3.7	11.4	0.83	21.35	2	2	97	0	1	42	62.6	-20.8	90	9	1,000	0	0.0	0.0
C- / 3.7	11.4	0.82	21.29	19	2	97	0	1	42	62.6	-20.8	91	9	1,000	0	0.0	0.0
C- / 3.5	11.4	0.82	21.49	198	2	97	0	1	42	68.8	-20.4	93	9	250,000	0	0.0	0.0
D- / 1.4	12.2	1.07	20.76	274	2	97	0	1	81	71.7	-17.2	7	1	1,000	0	5.0	0.0
D- / 1.4	12.2	1.06	21.10	2	2	97	0	1	81	72.2	-17.2	8	1	0	0	0.0	0.0
D- / 1.2	12.2	1.06	19.26	13	2	97	0	1	81	67.0	-17.5	5	1	1,000	0	0.0	0.0
D- / 1.2	12.2	1.06	19.24	18	2	97	0	1	81	66.9	-17.5	5	1	1,000	0	0.0	0.0
D- / 1.5	12.2	1.07	21.48	13	2	97	0	1	81	73.4	-17.1	8	1	250,000	0	0.0	0.0
D- / 1.5	12.2	1.06	21.64	12	2	97	0	1	81	74.3	-17.1	9	1	0	0	0.0	0.0
D- / 1.3	12.2	1.06	19.97	1	2	97	0	1	81	69.0	-17.4	6	1	0	0	0.0	0.0
D- / 1.4	12.2	1.06	21.15	N/A	2	97	0	1	81	70.4	-17.2	7	1	0	0	0.0	0.0
D- / 1.3	12.2	1.06	20.18	N/A	2	97	0	1	81	69.6	-17.4	6	1	0	0	0.0	0.0
D- / 1.4	12.2	1.06	20.87	N/A	2	97	0	1	81	71.7	-17.3	8	1	0	0	0.0	0.0
D- / 1.5	12.2	1.06	21.35	N/A	2	97	0	1	81	73.1	-17.2	8	1	0	0	0.0	0.0
D- / 1.5	12.2	1.06	21.60	3	2	97	0	1	81	74.0	-17.2	9	1	1,000,000	0	0.0	0.0
D- / 1.4	12.2	1.06	20.49	72	2	97	0	1	81	71.3	-17.3	7	1	1,000	0	5.0	0.0
C / 5.4	12.1	0.87	27.75	180	3	96	0	1	85	86.4	-25.8	72	10	1,000	0	5.0	0.0
C / 5.4	12.1	0.87	27.90	1	3	96	0	1	85	87.3	-25.8	73	10	0	0	0.0	0.0
C / 5.5	12.1	0.87	28.22	43	3	96	0	1	85	88.7	-25.7	75	10	250,000	0	0.0	0.0
C / 5.4	12.1	0.87	27.23	1	3	96	0	1	85	84.4	-26.0	68	10	0	0	0.0	0.0
C / 5.4	12.1	0.87	27.83	1	3	96	0	1	85	85.9	-25.8	71	10	0	0	0.0	0.0
C / 5.4	12.1	0.87	27.38	N/A	3	96	0	1	85	84.9	-25.9	69	10	0	0	0.0	0.0
C / 5.4	12.1	0.87	27.92	N/A	3	96	0	1	85	87.4	-25.8	74	10	0	0	0.0	0.0
C / 5.4	12.1	0.87	28.24	N/A	3	96	0	1	85	88.8	-25.7	75	10	0	0	0.0	0.0
C / 5.5	12.1	0.87	28.34	1	3	96	0	1	85	89.4	-25.8	76	10	1,000,000	0	0.0	0.0
C+ / 6.7	11.3	1.04	16.44	18	4	95	0	1	91	N/A	N/A	44	N/A	1,000	0	5.0	0.0
C+ / 6.8	11.3	1.04	16.53	12	4	95	0	1	91	N/A	N/A	49	N/A	250,000	0	0.0	0.0
C+ / 6.8	11.3	1.04	16.55	2,083	4	95	0	1	91	N/A	N/A	53	N/A	0	0	0.0	0.0
U /	N/A	N/A	13.28	843	1	98	0	1	14	N/A	N/A	N/A	3	0	0	0.0	0.0
C+ / 6.6	11.5	1.15	40.14	1,536	3	96	0	1	21	94.9	-23.4	21	4	1,000	0	5.0	0.0
C+ / 6.5	11.5	1.15	36.66	71	3	96	0	1	21	90.0	-23.6	15	4	1,000	0	0.0	0.0
C+ / 6.5	11.5	1.15	36.65	301	3	96	0	1	21	90.0	-23.6	15	4	1,000	0	0.0	0.0

99 Pct = Best
0 Pct = Worst

Fund Type	Fund Name	Ticker Symbol	Overall Investment Rating	Phone	Perfor-mance Rating/Pts	3 Mo	6 Mo	1Yr / Pct	3Yr / Pct	5Yr / Pct	Dividend Yield	Expense Ratio
								Total Return % through 3/31/15			Incl. in Returns	
									Annualized			
GR	J Hancock Large Cap Equity I	JLVIX	B	(800) 257-3336	B- / 7.2	0.97	3.65	9.22 /70	15.16 /76	11.76 /59	0.51	0.80
GR	J Hancock Large Cap Equity R1	JLCRX	C+	(800) 257-3336	C+ / 6.7	0.78	3.31	8.50 /66	14.41 /70	11.03 /53	0.00	1.45
GR	J Hancock Large Cap Equity R2	JLCYX	C+	(800) 257-3336	C+ / 6.9	0.85	3.45	8.76 /68	14.81 /73	11.40 /56	0.20	1.20
GR	J Hancock Large Cap Equity R3	JLCHX	C+	(800) 257-3336	C+ / 6.7	0.83	3.39	8.61 /67	14.52 /71	11.10 /53	0.08	1.35
GR	J Hancock Large Cap Equity R4	JLCFX	B	(800) 257-3336	B- / 7.1	0.92	3.57	9.04 /70	14.98 /75	11.49 /57	0.40	1.05
GR	J Hancock Large Cap Equity R5	JLCVX	B	(800) 257-3336	B- / 7.2	0.97	3.67	9.24 /71	15.20 /76	11.77 /59	0.56	0.75
GR	J Hancock Large Cap Equity R6	JLCWX	B	(800) 257-3336	B- / 7.3	0.99	3.72	9.34 /71	15.27 /77	11.71 /58	0.62	0.70
MC	J Hancock Mid Value Fund NAV		B+	(800) 257-3336	B+ / 8.7	2.95	6.66	9.74 /73	17.00 /90	13.09 /69	0.76	1.05
IN	J Hancock Redwood NAV		D+	(800) 257-3336	D- / 1.0	0.45	1.09	1.80 /21	3.48 / 9	--	0.00	1.19
FS	J Hancock Regional Bank A	FRBAX	C+	(800) 257-3336	C+ / 6.6	-0.46	7.79	3.74 /30	16.26 /85	11.03 /53	0.48	1.29
FS	● J Hancock Regional Bank B	FRBFX	C+	(800) 257-3336	C+ / 6.9	-0.67	7.39	2.99 /26	15.44 /79	10.25 /46	0.00	1.99
FS	J Hancock Regional Bank C	FRBCX	C+	(800) 257-3336	C+ / 6.9	-0.67	7.37	2.98 /26	15.44 /79	10.25 /47	0.00	1.99
TC	J Hancock Science and Tech NAV		U	(800) 257-3336	U /	2.83	6.10	14.02 /89	--	--	0.00	1.06
SC	J Hancock Small Cap Equity A	SPVAX	D	(800) 257-3336	C / 4.4	4.00	12.78	3.01 /26	11.37 /48	13.15 /70	0.00	1.23
SC	● J Hancock Small Cap Equity B	SPVBX	D	(800) 257-3336	C / 4.7	3.81	12.36	2.28 /23	10.60 /43	12.36 /63	0.00	1.93
SC	J Hancock Small Cap Equity C	SPVCX	D	(800) 257-3336	C / 4.7	3.80	12.39	2.27 /23	10.61 /43	12.35 /63	0.00	1.93
SC	J Hancock Small Cap Equity I	SPVIX	D+	(800) 257-3336	C / 5.5	4.07	12.95	3.31 /28	11.75 /51	13.58 /74	0.00	0.91
SC	J Hancock Small Cap Equity R6	SPVSX	D+	(800) 257-3336	C / 5.5	4.11	13.04	3.44 /29	11.86 /51	13.52 /73	0.00	0.82
GR	J Hancock US Glob Lead Gr A	USGLX	C	(800) 257-3336	C+ / 6.1	2.84	9.27	12.64 /85	13.51 /63	13.99 /78	0.20	1.19
GR	● J Hancock US Glob Lead Gr B	USLBX	C	(800) 257-3336	C+ / 6.3	2.65	8.87	11.79 /82	12.66 /57	13.14 /69	0.00	1.94
GR	J Hancock US Glob Lead Gr C	USLCX	C	(800) 257-3336	C+ / 6.3	2.65	8.84	11.76 /82	12.66 /57	13.14 /69	0.00	1.94
GR	J Hancock US Glob Lead Gr I	USLIX	C+	(800) 257-3336	B- / 7.2	2.91	9.40	12.92 /86	13.84 /66	14.39 /81	0.37	0.93
GL	J Hancock US Glob Lead Gr R2	USLYX	C+	(800) 257-3336	C+ / 6.9	2.81	9.19	12.44 /84	13.47 /63	13.98 /78	0.10	1.33
GR	J Hancock US Glob Lead Gr R6	UGLSX	C+	(800) 257-3336	B- / 7.3	2.93	9.46	13.04 /87	13.96 /67	14.32 /81	0.47	0.83
IX	J Hancock VIT 500 Index B Nav		A	(800) 257-3336	B / 8.1	0.90	5.83	12.47 /85	15.85 /82	14.20 /79	1.53	0.48
GR	J Hancock VIT All Cap Core I	JEACX	A+	(800) 257-3336	A- / 9.2	5.20	10.33	13.09 /87	17.04 /90	14.27 /80	0.88	0.88
GR	J Hancock VIT All Cap Core II		A+	(800) 257-3336	A- / 9.0	5.13	10.23	12.87 /86	16.82 /89	14.04 /78	0.70	1.08
GR	J Hancock VIT All Cap Core NAV		A+	(800) 257-3336	A- / 9.2	5.23	10.41	13.18 /87	17.12 /90	14.33 /81	0.92	0.83
AA	J Hancock VIT Amer Ast All I		C+	(800) 257-3336	C / 4.5	0.89	2.74	5.22 /40	11.09 /46	10.57 /49	1.51	0.93
GL	J Hancock VIT Amer Growth I		B	(800) 257-3336	B- / 7.4	4.03	7.37	12.19 /83	14.32 /69	12.89 /67	0.79	0.97
GR	J Hancock VIT Amer Growth II		B	(800) 257-3336	B- / 7.2	4.00	7.29	12.03 /83	14.16 /68	12.73 /66	0.65	1.12
GI	J Hancock VIT Amer Growth-Inc I		A	(800) 257-3336	B / 8.1	1.58	4.21	10.59 /77	16.29 /85	12.75 /66	0.88	0.91
GI	J Hancock VIT Amer Growth-Inc II		A-	(800) 257-3336	B / 8.0	1.54	4.16	10.46 /76	16.13 /84	12.58 /65	0.74	1.06
FO	J Hancock VIT Amer Intl I		D+	(800) 257-3336	C- / 3.5	5.26	3.66	1.99 /22	9.03 /33	5.93 /16	1.01	1.17
FO	J Hancock VIT Amer Intl II		D+	(800) 257-3336	C- / 3.4	5.21	3.62	1.84 /21	8.86 /32	5.78 /16	0.86	1.32
GL	J Hancock VIT Blue Chip Gr I		A	(800) 257-3336	A / 9.5	5.96	10.43	16.91 /94	17.63 /93	16.91 /96	0.00	0.87
GL	J Hancock VIT Blue Chip Gr II		A	(800) 257-3336	A / 9.4	5.89	10.30	16.67 /94	17.40 /92	16.68 /95	0.00	1.07
GL	J Hancock VIT Blue Chip Gr NAV		A	(800) 257-3336	A / 9.5	5.97	10.43	16.96 /95	17.69 /93	16.98 /96	0.00	0.82
IN	J Hancock VIT Capital App I		B	(800) 257-3336	B+ / 8.8	5.69	9.07	15.96 /93	15.61 /80	14.96 /86	0.04	0.79
IN	J Hancock VIT Capital App II		B	(800) 257-3336	B+ / 8.7	5.58	8.95	15.73 /93	15.37 /78	14.74 /85	0.00	0.99
IN	J Hancock VIT Capital App NAV		B	(800) 257-3336	B+ / 8.8	5.68	9.07	15.99 /93	15.67 /81	15.02 /87	0.08	0.74
EM	J Hancock VIT Emerg Mkts Val NAV		E	(800) 257-3336	E / 0.3	-0.34	-7.29	-4.91 / 6	-2.25 / 3	-1.47 / 2	2.07	1.08
GL	J Hancock VIT Equity Income I		C+	(800) 257-3336	C+ / 5.6	-1.10	1.88	4.71 /36	13.37 /62	11.70 /58	1.71	0.88
GL	J Hancock VIT Equity Income II		C+	(800) 257-3336	C / 5.4	-1.15	1.76	4.47 /35	13.14 /61	11.48 /57	1.53	1.08
GL	J Hancock VIT Equity Income NAV		C+	(800) 257-3336	C+ / 5.6	-1.10	1.92	4.72 /37	13.42 /63	11.77 /59	1.77	0.83
FS	J Hancock VIT Financial Indus I	JEFSX	B-	(800) 257-3336	C+ / 5.9	-0.58	4.38	7.74 /61	13.27 /62	10.19 /46	0.70	0.91
FS	J Hancock VIT Financial Indus II		B-	(800) 257-3336	C+ / 5.8	-0.59	4.30	7.51 /59	13.05 /60	9.98 /44	0.52	1.11
FS	J Hancock VIT Financial Indus NAV		B-	(800) 257-3336	C+ / 6.0	-0.53	4.42	7.80 /61	13.31 /62	10.26 /47	0.75	0.86
AA	J Hancock VIT Frk Tmp Fdg Al NAV		C	(800) 257-3336	C / 4.5	1.54	0.26	1.30 /19	11.67 /50	9.88 /44	3.28	0.97
GR	J Hancock VIT Fund AC Core I	JEQAX	A+	(800) 257-3336	A / 9.3	2.62	6.66	12.07 /83	18.21 /95	15.71 /91	0.38	0.76
GR	J Hancock VIT Fund AC Core II		A	(800) 257-3336	A- / 9.2	2.58	6.51	11.84 /82	17.99 /94	15.47 /90	0.20	0.96
GR	J Hancock VIT Fund AC Core NAV		A+	(800) 257-3336	A / 9.3	2.65	6.67	12.13 /83	18.28 /95	15.75 /92	0.42	0.71

● Denotes fund is closed to new investors
* Denotes fund is included in Section II

| RISK | 3 Year | | NET ASSETS | | ASSET | | | | Portfolio | BULL / BEAR | | FUND MANAGER | | MINIMUMS | | LOADS | |
Risk Rating/Pts	Standard Deviation	Beta	NAV As of 3/31/15	Total $(Mil)	Cash %	Stocks %	Bonds %	Other %	Turnover Ratio	Last Bull Market Return	Last Bear Market Return	Manager Quality Pct	Manager Tenure (Years)	Initial Purch. $	Additional Purch. $	Front End Load	Back End Load
C+ / 6.6	11.5	1.15	41.66	1,035	3	96	0	1	21	96.9	-23.3	25	4	250,000	0	0.0	0.0
C+ / 6.6	11.5	1.15	41.25	8	3	96	0	1	21	92.7	-23.5	18	4	0	0	0.0	0.0
C+ / 6.6	11.5	1.15	41.59	2	3	96	0	1	21	94.9	-23.4	21	4	0	0	0.0	0.0
C+ / 6.6	11.5	1.15	41.30	1	3	96	0	1	21	93.2	-23.5	19	4	0	0	0.0	0.0
C+ / 6.6	11.5	1.15	41.50	3	3	96	0	1	21	95.7	-23.4	23	4	0	0	0.0	0.0
C+ / 6.6	11.5	1.15	41.70	2	3	96	0	1	21	97.2	-23.3	25	4	0	0	0.0	0.0
C+ / 6.6	11.5	1.15	41.70	4	3	96	0	1	21	97.6	-23.4	26	4	1,000,000	0	0.0	0.0
C+ / 5.8	10.3	0.88	16.40	1,047	5	94	0	1	40	94.8	-19.6	83	6	0	0	0.0	0.0
B / 8.3	3.2	0.30	11.06	581	32	67	0	1	74	24.2	N/A	51	N/A	0	0	0.0	0.0
C+ / 6.4	13.1	0.98	18.60	658	0	99	0	1	16	115.3	-25.7	59	17	1,000	0	5.0	0.0
C+ / 6.3	13.1	0.98	17.76	15	0	99	0	1	16	110.1	-25.9	48	17	1,000	0	0.0	0.0
C+ / 6.3	13.1	0.98	17.79	66	0	99	0	1	16	110.0	-25.9	47	17	1,000	0	0.0	0.0
U /	N/A	N/A	13.09	994	4	95	0	1	97	N/A	N/A	N/A	2	0	0	0.0	0.0
C- / 3.7	15.9	1.05	35.92	379	0	99	0	1	115	85.7	-29.5	10	3	1,000	0	5.0	0.0
C- / 3.7	15.9	1.05	31.90	12	0	99	0	1	115	81.5	-29.8	7	3	1,000	0	0.0	0.0
C- / 3.7	15.9	1.05	31.92	28	0	99	0	1	115	81.3	-29.7	7	3	1,000	0	0.0	0.0
C- / 3.7	15.9	1.05	38.37	13	0	99	0	1	115	88.0	-29.4	12	3	250,000	0	0.0	0.0
C- / 3.7	15.9	1.05	38.50	2	0	99	0	1	115	88.6	-29.5	12	3	1,000,000	0	0.0	0.0
C / 4.8	9.9	0.95	41.25	616	2	97	0	1	43	90.6	-14.4	44	20	1,000	0	5.0	0.0
C / 4.5	9.9	0.95	36.74	26	2	97	0	1	43	85.8	-14.7	33	20	1,000	0	0.0	0.0
C / 4.5	9.9	0.95	36.75	130	2	97	0	1	43	85.8	-14.7	33	20	1,000	0	0.0	0.0
C / 4.9	9.9	0.95	43.44	298	2	97	0	1	43	92.7	-14.3	48	20	250,000	0	0.0	0.0
C / 5.0	9.9	0.57	43.19	30	2	97	0	1	43	90.5	-14.4	96	20	0	0	0.0	0.0
C / 4.9	9.9	0.95	43.52	4	2	97	0	1	43	93.3	-14.4	50	20	1,000,000	0	0.0	0.0
B- / 7.4	9.6	1.00	25.91	1,519	5	94	0	1	4	98.7	-16.3	64	19	0	0	0.0	0.0
C+ / 6.9	10.7	1.07	28.74	84	1	98	0	1	180	102.4	-19.5	65	5	0	0	0.0	0.0
C+ / 6.9	10.7	1.07	28.67	7	1	98	0	1	180	101.0	-19.6	61	5	0	0	0.0	0.0
C+ / 6.9	10.7	1.06	28.76	258	1	98	0	1	180	102.7	-19.5	66	5	0	0	0.0	0.0
B / 8.1	7.2	1.23	15.89	228	0	64	35	1	2	66.8	-13.6	35	15	0	0	0.0	0.0
C+ / 6.6	10.0	0.63	25.04	122	0	94	4	2	2	86.0	-19.4	97	N/A	0	0	0.0	0.0
C+ / 6.6	10.0	0.96	24.95	802	0	94	4	2	2	85.0	-19.5	51	N/A	0	0	0.0	0.0
B- / 7.2	9.2	0.94	24.38	265	0	90	8	2	2	95.6	-17.2	78	16	0	0	0.0	0.0
B- / 7.2	9.2	0.94	24.33	710	0	90	8	2	2	94.6	-17.3	77	16	0	0	0.0	0.0
C+ / 5.9	11.4	0.84	19.42	95	0	92	7	1	3	53.7	-25.5	77	12	0	0	0.0	0.0
C+ / 5.9	11.4	0.84	19.40	472	0	92	7	1	3	52.8	-25.5	76	12	0	0	0.0	0.0
C+ / 6.0	11.3	0.64	38.02	324	0	99	0	1	27	113.8	-14.8	98	16	0	0	0.0	0.0
C+ / 6.0	11.3	0.64	37.59	141	0	99	0	1	27	112.3	-14.9	98	16	0	0	0.0	0.0
C+ / 6.1	11.3	0.64	38.00	1,319	0	99	0	1	27	114.2	-14.8	98	16	0	0	0.0	0.0
C / 4.7	11.8	1.03	16.35	200	0	99	0	1	38	100.2	-14.2	55	15	0	0	0.0	0.0
C / 4.7	11.7	1.02	16.07	75	0	99	0	1	38	98.7	-14.2	53	15	0	0	0.0	0.0
C / 4.7	11.7	1.02	16.36	753	0	99	0	1	38	100.5	-14.2	57	15	0	0	0.0	0.0
C- / 3.9	14.9	1.07	8.87	824	0	99	0	1	9	16.1	-31.9	25	8	0	0	0.0	0.0
C+ / 6.4	9.5	0.57	18.95	312	5	94	0	1	9	85.8	-18.3	96	19	0	0	0.0	0.0
C+ / 6.4	9.5	0.56	18.88	165	5	94	0	1	9	84.5	-18.4	96	19	0	0	0.0	0.0
C+ / 6.4	9.5	0.57	18.89	1,452	5	94	0	1	9	86.1	-18.3	96	19	0	0	0.0	0.0
B- / 7.3	10.7	0.88	17.00	127	11	88	0	1	3	76.9	-19.7	43	1	0	0	0.0	0.0
B- / 7.3	10.7	0.88	16.92	21	11	88	0	1	3	75.8	-19.7	40	1	0	0	0.0	0.0
B- / 7.3	10.7	0.88	16.98	21	11	88	0	1	3	77.1	-19.6	44	1	0	0	0.0	0.0
B- / 7.3	9.3	1.50	13.21	46	3	78	16	3	3	67.4	-17.2	13	7	0	0	0.0	0.0
C+ / 6.4	12.6	1.20	23.12	160	4	95	0	1	41	112.3	-20.6	49	4	0	0	0.0	0.0
C+ / 6.4	12.6	1.20	23.08	59	4	95	0	1	41	110.9	-20.7	46	4	0	0	0.0	0.0
C+ / 6.4	12.5	1.20	23.21	1,460	4	95	0	1	41	112.8	-20.6	51	4	0	0	0.0	0.0

						PERFORMANCE							
	99 Pct = Best *0 Pct = Worst*			**Overall**		**Perfor-**	Total Return % through 3/31/15					Incl. in Returns	
				Investment		**mance**				Annualized		Dividend	Expense
Fund Type	Fund Name	Ticker Symbol	**Rating**	Phone	**Rating/Pts**	3 Mo	6 Mo	1Yr / Pct	3Yr / Pct	5Yr / Pct	Yield	Ratio
GR	J Hancock VIT Fund LC Val I		**A-**	(800) 257-3336	**B / 7.9**	0.00	2.67	8.44 /66	16.57 /87	14.91 /86	0.64	0.74
GR	J Hancock VIT Fund LC Val II		**B+**	(800) 257-3336	**B / 7.7**	-0.06	2.55	8.18 /64	16.36 /86	14.68 /84	0.45	0.94
GR	J Hancock VIT Fund LC Val NAV		**A-**	(800) 257-3336	**B / 7.9**	0.00	2.65	8.49 /66	16.63 /88	14.97 /87	0.69	0.69
GL	J Hancock VIT Global I	JEFGX	**C-**	(800) 257-3336	**C- / 4.1**	1.53	-1.60	-3.69 / 7	12.00 /52	9.49 /40	2.01	0.96
GL	J Hancock VIT Global NAV		**C-**	(800) 257-3336	**C- / 4.2**	1.58	-1.51	-3.64 / 8	12.09 /53	9.55 /41	2.06	0.91
HL	J Hancock VIT Hlth Sciences I	JEHSX	**B+**	(800) 257-3336	**A+ / 9.9**	13.92	26.68	41.68 /99	36.38 /99	28.66 /99	0.00	1.09
FO	J Hancock VIT Intl Core I		**D**	(800) 257-3336	**D+ / 2.9**	5.23	-1.07	-4.27 / 7	9.26 /35	6.60 /21	3.81	1.07
FO	J Hancock VIT Intl Core II		**D-**	(800) 257-3336	**D+ / 2.8**	5.18	-1.15	-4.44 / 6	9.05 /33	6.37 /19	3.57	1.27
FO	J Hancock VIT Intl Core NAV		**D**	(800) 257-3336	**C- / 3.0**	5.34	-0.95	-4.15 / 7	9.34 /35	6.65 /21	3.88	1.02
FO	J Hancock VIT Intl Eqty Index B NAV		**D-**	(800) 257-3336	**D / 1.6**	3.79	-0.58	-1.36 /12	6.20 /18	4.71 /11	3.27	0.56
FO	J Hancock VIT Intl Val I		**E+**	(800) 257-3336	**D- / 1.5**	4.78	-5.84	-8.32 / 3	7.29 /23	5.28 /13	3.18	0.97
FO	J Hancock VIT Intl Val II		**E+**	(800) 257-3336	**D- / 1.4**	4.71	-5.96	-8.53 / 3	7.07 /22	5.06 /12	2.96	1.17
FO	J Hancock VIT Intl Val NAV		**E+**	(800) 257-3336	**D- / 1.5**	4.82	-5.83	-8.32 / 3	7.33 /23	5.32 /13	3.25	0.92
AG	J Hancock VIT Lifestyle Aggr I		**C-**	(800) 257-3336	**C- / 3.6**	1.12	0.23	1.41 /20	10.08 /40	9.52 /41	2.91	1.01
AG	J Hancock VIT Lifestyle Aggr II		**C-**	(800) 257-3336	**C- / 3.5**	1.03	0.12	1.22 /19	9.86 /39	9.32 /39	2.71	1.21
AG	J Hancock VIT Lifestyle Aggr NAV		**C-**	(800) 257-3336	**C- / 3.7**	1.12	0.28	1.47 /20	10.17 /40	9.60 /41	2.96	0.96
BA	J Hancock VIT Lifestyle Bal I	JELBX	**C**	(800) 257-3336	**D+ / 2.9**	2.16	2.86	4.93 /38	7.78 /26	7.81 /29	2.89	0.79
BA	J Hancock VIT Lifestyle Bal NAV		**C+**	(800) 257-3336	**D+ / 2.9**	2.23	2.91	5.05 /39	7.85 /26	7.86 /29	2.94	0.74
AA	J Hancock VIT Lifestyle Csv I	JELCX	**C-**	(800) 257-3336	**D / 1.8**	2.06	3.31	5.34 /41	5.26 /14	5.94 /17	2.68	0.76
AA	J Hancock VIT Lifestyle Csv NAV		**C-**	(800) 257-3336	**D / 1.8**	2.06	3.27	5.38 /41	5.31 /14	5.98 /17	2.72	0.71
GR	J Hancock VIT Lifestyle Gr NAV		**C**	(800) 257-3336	**C- / 3.0**	1.27	0.75	2.29 /23	8.69 /31	8.54 /33	2.92	0.76
GR	J Hancock VIT Lifestyle Gro I	JELGX	**C**	(800) 257-3336	**D+ / 2.9**	1.27	0.70	2.24 /23	8.62 /31	8.48 /33	2.88	0.81
GR	J Hancock VIT Lifestyle Gro II		**C**	(800) 257-3336	**D+ / 2.8**	1.13	0.57	1.97 /22	8.38 /29	8.25 /32	2.68	1.01
BA	J Hancock VIT Lifestyle Modt I	JELMX	**C**	(800) 257-3336	**D+ / 2.7**	2.33	3.64	5.69 /44	7.28 /23	7.44 /26	2.76	0.78
GR	J Hancock VIT Lifestyle Modt NAV		**C**	(800) 257-3336	**D+ / 2.8**	2.33	3.69	5.74 /44	7.36 /23	7.49 /26	2.81	0.73
MC	● J Hancock VIT Mid Cap Index I	JECIX	**B+**	(800) 257-3336	**A- / 9.0**	5.20	11.74	11.76 /82	16.61 /87	15.25 /88	0.87	0.56
MC	J Hancock VIT Mid Cap Index II		**B+**	(800) 257-3336	**B+ / 8.8**	5.18	11.71	11.54 /81	16.39 /86	15.03 /87	0.70	0.76
MC	J Hancock VIT Mid Cap Index NAV		**B+**	(800) 257-3336	**A- / 9.0**	5.25	11.83	11.86 /82	16.68 /88	15.32 /89	0.92	0.51
MC	J Hancock VIT Mid Cap Stock I		**C**	(800) 257-3336	**A- / 9.0**	5.59	11.39	11.82 /82	16.76 /88	14.71 /84	0.10	0.92
MC	J Hancock VIT Mid Cap Stock II		**C**	(800) 257-3336	**B+ / 8.9**	5.50	11.25	11.58 /81	16.54 /87	14.49 /82	0.00	1.12
MC	J Hancock VIT Mid Cap Stock NAV		**C**	(800) 257-3336	**A- / 9.0**	5.55	11.37	11.89 /82	16.81 /89	14.76 /85	0.13	0.87
MC	J Hancock VIT Mid Value II		**B+**	(800) 257-3336	**B+ / 8.6**	2.86	6.63	9.56 /72	16.82 /89	13.00 /68	0.48	1.25
MC	J Hancock VIT Mid Value NAV		**B+**	(800) 257-3336	**B+ / 8.7**	2.95	6.80	9.86 /74	17.13 /90	13.29 /71	0.71	1.00
MC	J Hancock VIT Mid Value Trust I	JEMUX	**B+**	(800) 257-3336	**B+ / 8.7**	2.94	6.81	9.77 /73	17.07 /90	13.23 /70	0.66	1.05
RE	J Hancock VIT Real Est Sec I		**B-**	(800) 257-3336	**A / 9.3**	4.23	19.62	24.45 /98	13.55 /64	15.82 /92	1.43	0.80
RE	J Hancock VIT Real Est Sec II		**B-**	(800) 257-3336	**A- / 9.2**	4.17	19.49	24.20 /98	13.34 /62	15.59 /91	1.27	1.00
RE	J Hancock VIT Real Est Sec NAV		**B-**	(800) 257-3336	**A / 9.3**	4.26	19.65	24.52 /98	13.61 /64	15.87 /92	1.48	0.75
TC	J Hancock VIT Science & Tech I	JESTX	**B-**	(800) 257-3336	**B / 7.8**	2.70	6.02	13.46 /88	15.09 /76	15.20 /88	0.00	1.14
TC	J Hancock VIT Science & Tech II		**C+**	(800) 257-3336	**B / 7.6**	2.64	5.92	13.25 /87	14.85 /74	14.97 /87	0.00	1.34
TC	J Hancock VIT Science & Tech NAV		**B-**	(800) 257-3336	**B / 7.8**	2.72	6.07	13.56 /88	15.14 /76	15.27 /89	0.00	1.09
SC	J Hancock VIT Small Cap Gr NAV		**C**	(800) 257-3336	**A- / 9.2**	5.27	12.14	12.58 /85	17.13 /90	14.88 /86	0.00	1.10
SC	● J Hancock VIT Small Cap Idx I	JESIX	**C+**	(800) 257-3336	**B+ / 8.5**	4.29	14.28	7.98 /63	16.04 /84	14.25 /80	0.83	0.66
SC	J Hancock VIT Small Cap Idx II		**C**	(800) 257-3336	**B+ / 8.3**	4.24	14.23	7.74 /61	15.80 /82	14.03 /78	0.66	0.86
SC	J Hancock VIT Small Cap Idx NAV		**C+**	(800) 257-3336	**B+ / 8.5**	4.28	14.38	8.03 /63	16.11 /84	14.33 /81	0.88	0.61
SC	J Hancock VIT Small Cap Oppt NAV		**B+**	(800) 257-3336	**B / 8.1**	4.17	10.39	5.46 /42	16.08 /84	14.76 /85	0.08	1.09
SC	J Hancock VIT Small Cap Oppty I		**B+**	(800) 257-3336	**B / 8.0**	4.15	10.38	5.40 /42	16.04 /84	14.70 /84	0.05	1.14
SC	J Hancock VIT Small Cap Oppty II		**B**	(800) 257-3336	**B / 7.8**	4.11	10.23	5.15 /40	15.79 /82	14.47 /82	0.00	1.34
SC	J Hancock VIT Small Cap Val I	JESVX	**B**	(800) 257-3336	**B+ / 8.8**	4.10	16.03	10.02 /74	16.15 /84	14.83 /85	0.53	1.17
GR	J Hancock VIT Small Cap Val NAV		**B**	(800) 257-3336	**B+ / 8.8**	4.11	16.12	10.09 /75	16.20 /85	14.88 /86	0.58	1.12
SC	J Hancock VIT Small Co Val I		**C-**	(800) 257-3336	**C / 5.0**	1.37	9.62	0.26 /16	12.03 /53	11.68 /58	0.03	1.34
SC	J Hancock VIT Small Co Val NAV		**C**	(800) 257-3336	**C / 5.1**	1.42	9.68	0.33 /17	12.08 /53	11.74 /59	0.06	1.29
GR	● J Hancock VIT Tot Stk Mkt Id I	JETSX	**A-**	(800) 257-3336	**B / 8.0**	1.62	6.45	11.32 /80	15.73 /81	14.11 /79	1.12	0.56

● Denotes fund is closed to new investors
* Denotes fund is included in Section II

Risk Rating/Pts	3 Year Standard Deviation	Beta	NAV As of 3/31/15	Total $(Mil)	Cash %	Stocks %	Bonds %	Other %	Portfolio Turnover Ratio	Last Bull Market Return	Last Bear Market Return	Manager Quality Pct	Manager Tenure (Years)	Initial Purch. $	Additional Purch. $	Front End Load	Back End Load
B- / 7.1	12.0	1.19	17.52	607	3	96	0	1	40	112.5	-19.9	32	4	0	0	0.0	0.0
B- / 7.1	12.0	1.19	17.63	256	3	96	0	1	40	111.2	-20.0	30	4	0	0	0.0	0.0
B- / 7.2	11.9	1.18	17.52	885	3	96	0	1	40	113.2	-20.0	34	4	0	0	0.0	0.0
C+ / 6.2	13.0	0.94	19.88	177	0	98	1	1	14	73.2	-22.7	88	12	0	0	0.0	0.0
C+ / 6.3	13.0	0.94	19.87	463	0	98	1	1	14	73.5	-22.7	88	12	0	0	0.0	0.0
C / 4.8	12.9	0.84	38.22	157	2	97	0	1	57	218.9	-14.7	99	2	0	0	0.0	0.0
C / 5.3	13.9	1.03	11.07	45	0	99	0	1	47	50.7	-21.7	60	10	0	0	0.0	0.0
C / 5.3	13.8	1.03	11.16	18	0	99	0	1	47	49.6	-21.8	57	10	0	0	0.0	0.0
C / 5.2	13.9	1.03	11.04	670	0	99	0	1	47	50.9	-21.7	61	10	0	0	0.0	0.0
C+ / 5.8	13.0	0.97	16.44	333	3	96	0	1	3	42.2	-24.5	27	10	0	0	0.0	0.0
C / 4.7	15.2	1.08	13.14	96	0	97	2	1	31	42.6	-24.0	28	16	0	0	0.0	0.0
C / 4.7	15.2	1.07	13.11	75	0	97	2	1	31	41.6	-24.0	26	16	0	0	0.0	0.0
C / 4.7	15.2	1.07	13.05	876	0	97	2	1	31	42.7	-23.9	29	16	0	0	0.0	0.0
C+ / 6.5	10.1	0.99	10.87	101	3	95	1	1	21	67.9	-21.3	9	N/A	0	0	0.0	0.0
C+ / 6.5	10.1	0.99	10.84	128	3	95	1	1	21	66.6	-21.3	8	N/A	0	0	0.0	0.0
C+ / 6.5	10.1	0.99	10.88	212	3	95	1	1	21	68.0	-21.2	10	N/A	0	0	0.0	0.0
B+ / 9.0	5.5	0.93	14.17	766	2	50	47	1	9	42.3	-9.6	35	N/A	0	0	0.0	0.0
B+ / 9.0	5.5	0.93	14.20	1,299	2	50	47	1	9	42.6	-9.7	37	N/A	0	0	0.0	0.0
B / 8.1	3.2	0.42	12.37	190	2	19	77	2	5	24.1	-2.2	75	N/A	0	0	0.0	0.0
B / 8.1	3.2	0.43	12.39	51	2	19	77	2	5	24.3	-2.2	74	N/A	0	0	0.0	0.0
B / 8.3	7.5	0.73	14.33	708	3	68	27	2	11	52.3	-14.0	29	N/A	0	0	0.0	0.0
B / 8.3	7.5	0.73	14.31	826	3	68	27	2	11	52.1	-14.1	28	N/A	0	0	0.0	0.0
B / 8.4	7.5	0.74	14.26	10,821	3	68	27	2	11	50.9	-14.1	26	N/A	0	0	0.0	0.0
B / 8.6	4.6	0.76	13.61	282	2	39	58	1	7	37.2	-6.8	55	N/A	0	0	0.0	0.0
B / 8.6	4.6	0.42	13.62	120	2	39	58	1	7	37.4	-6.7	76	10	0	0	0.0	0.0
C+ / 5.7	11.0	1.00	23.45	727	4	95	0	1	14	100.3	-22.7	63	15	0	0	0.0	0.0
C+ / 5.6	11.0	1.00	23.37	74	4	95	0	1	14	98.9	-22.8	59	15	0	0	0.0	0.0
C+ / 5.7	11.0	1.00	23.46	112	4	95	0	1	14	100.7	-22.7	63	15	0	0	0.0	0.0
D+ / 2.5	12.5	1.00	19.65	191	0	96	3	1	116	98.0	-24.3	63	16	0	0	0.0	0.0
D+ / 2.4	12.5	1.00	18.98	102	0	96	3	1	116	96.7	-24.4	60	16	0	0	0.0	0.0
D+ / 2.6	12.5	1.01	19.79	559	0	96	3	1	116	98.4	-24.3	63	16	0	0	0.0	0.0
C+ / 5.8	10.3	0.89	14.37	74	5	93	0	2	37	94.1	-19.5	81	11	0	0	0.0	0.0
C+ / 5.8	10.3	0.88	14.32	479	5	93	0	2	37	95.7	-19.4	84	11	0	0	0.0	0.0
C+ / 5.8	10.3	0.89	14.37	347	5	93	0	2	37	95.6	-19.5	83	11	0	0	0.0	0.0
C- / 3.9	13.4	1.07	18.71	103	0	99	0	1	104	85.0	-17.1	47	28	0	0	0.0	0.0
C- / 3.9	13.4	1.07	18.73	67	0	99	0	1	104	83.6	-17.1	43	28	0	0	0.0	0.0
C- / 3.8	13.4	1.07	18.60	283	0	99	0	1	104	85.3	-17.1	47	28	0	0	0.0	0.0
C / 5.1	13.8	1.16	27.81	433	5	94	0	1	108	96.6	-20.6	22	6	0	0	0.0	0.0
C / 5.1	13.8	1.16	27.18	48	5	94	0	1	108	95.2	-20.6	20	6	0	0	0.0	0.0
C / 5.1	13.8	1.16	27.97	25	5	94	0	1	108	96.9	-20.5	22	6	0	0	0.0	0.0
D+ / 2.5	13.6	0.94	12.38	351	0	97	2	1	114	99.7	-25.5	82	12	0	0	0.0	0.0
C- / 3.4	13.4	1.00	16.06	314	2	97	0	1	17	99.3	-25.3	65	15	0	0	0.0	0.0
C- / 3.4	13.4	1.00	15.99	51	2	97	0	1	17	97.9	-25.4	61	15	0	0	0.0	0.0
C- / 3.4	13.5	1.00	16.08	95	2	97	0	1	17	99.6	-25.2	65	15	0	0	0.0	0.0
C+ / 6.1	12.9	0.93	32.73	123	1	98	0	1	22	101.2	-26.0	76	7	0	0	0.0	0.0
C+ / 6.1	12.9	0.94	32.87	113	1	98	0	1	22	100.9	-26.0	75	7	0	0	0.0	0.0
C+ / 6.1	12.9	0.94	32.44	46	1	98	0	1	22	99.5	-26.1	73	7	0	0	0.0	0.0
C / 5.0	12.5	0.91	25.62	357	3	96	0	1	24	99.0	-21.3	79	13	0	0	0.0	0.0
C / 5.0	12.5	1.08	25.57	332	3	96	0	1	24	99.3	-21.2	50	13	0	0	0.0	0.0
C+ / 5.8	12.9	0.93	25.07	71	2	97	0	1	7	79.5	-23.4	28	14	0	0	0.0	0.0
C+ / 5.8	12.9	0.93	25.04	221	2	97	0	1	7	79.9	-23.4	29	14	0	0	0.0	0.0
B- / 7.2	9.7	1.01	18.83	482	7	92	0	1	3	97.5	-17.8	61	15	0	0	0.0	0.0

	99 Pct = Best 0 Pct = Worst				**PERFORMANCE**							
			Overall		**Perfor-**	Total Return % through 3/31/15					Incl. in Returns	
			Investment		**mance**				Annualized		Dividend	Expense
Fund Type	Fund Name	Ticker Symbol	**Rating**	Phone	**Rating/Pts**	3 Mo	6 Mo	1Yr / Pct	3Yr / Pct	5Yr / Pct	Yield	Ratio
GR	J Hancock VIT Tot Stk Mkt Id II		A-	(800) 257-3336	B / 7.8	1.57	6.43	11.09 /79	15.49 /79	13.88 /77	0.94	0.76
GR	J Hancock VIT Tot Stk Mkt Id NAV		A-	(800) 257-3336	B / 8.0	1.67	6.56	11.37 /80	15.78 /82	14.16 /79	1.17	0.51
UT	J Hancock VIT Utilities I	JEUTX	C+	(800) 257-3336	C+ / 6.2	0.86	1.61	6.78 /53	13.94 /67	13.69 /75	3.00	0.95
UT	J Hancock VIT Utilities II		C+	(800) 257-3336	C+ / 6.0	0.74	1.46	6.57 /51	13.72 /65	13.46 /72	2.83	1.15
UT	J Hancock VIT Utilities NAV		C+	(800) 257-3336	C+ / 6.2	0.80	1.59	6.84 /54	13.98 /67	13.75 /75	3.05	0.90
TC	Jacob Internet Fund Investor	JAMFX	D	(888) 522-6239	C+ / 5.6	6.77	5.53	8.03 /63	12.38 /55	14.32 /81	0.00	2.42
SC	Jacob Micro Cap Growth Inst	JMIGX	E	(888) 522-6239	C- / 4.1	9.78	14.80	4.77 /37	8.36 /29	13.16 /70	0.00	2.79
SC	Jacob Micro Cap Growth Inv	JMCGX	E	(888) 522-6239	C- / 3.6	9.73	14.63	4.49 /35	8.03 /27	12.83 /67	0.00	3.14
SC	Jacob Small Cap Growth Inst	JSIGX	E-	(888) 522-6239	E / 0.4	15.31	19.41	12.00 /82	-6.48 / 1	2.39 / 5	0.00	2.25
SC	Jacob Small Cap Growth Investor	JSCGX	C	(888) 522-6239	B- / 7.5	15.30	19.36	11.80 /82	12.87 /59	13.57 /74	0.00	2.59
GI	Jacob Wisdom Investor	JWSFX	C+	(888) 522-6239	C / 4.8	1.82	6.79	10.55 /77	10.99 /45	10.92 /52	0.00	2.39
GR	JAG Large Cap Growth A	JLGAX	C+	(855) 552-4596	C+ / 6.7	5.59	10.31	14.37 /90	13.78 /65	--	0.00	1.76
GR	JAG Large Cap Growth C	JLGCX	B-	(855) 552-4596	B- / 7.2	5.39	9.93	13.53 /88	12.95 /59	--	0.00	2.51
GR	JAG Large Cap Growth I	JLGIX	B	(855) 552-4596	B / 8.1	5.68	10.44	14.71 /91	14.07 /68	--	0.00	1.51
BA	James Adv Bal Goldn Rainbow Retail	GLRBX	C+	(888) 426-7640	C- / 3.7	2.58	5.10	7.39 /58	8.74 /31	9.45 /40	0.84	1.01
BA	James Advantage Bal Goldn Rainbow	GLRIX	C+	(888) 426-7640	C- / 3.9	2.59	5.21	7.66 /60	9.00 /33	9.72 /42	1.15	0.76
GI	James Advantage Long-Short	JAZZX	C+	(888) 426-7640	C / 4.7	1.87	3.58	6.05 /47	11.09 /46	--	0.00	2.59
MC	James Advantage Mid-Cap	JAMDX	B+	(888) 426-7640	B / 8.1	5.78	9.55	8.84 /68	15.54 /79	13.85 /76	0.04	1.51
SC	James Advantage Small Cap Value	JASCX	C+	(888) 426-7640	C+ / 5.6	1.81	7.92	3.44 /29	12.59 /57	15.03 /87	0.00	1.51
GR	James Micro Cap	JMCRX	C+	(888) 426-7640	B+ / 8.3	3.74	14.56	11.07 /79	15.90 /83	--	0.13	1.51
BA	Jamestown Balanced	JAMBX	C+	(866) 738-1126	C / 4.5	1.38	3.25	7.31 /58	10.57 /43	9.69 /42	1.01	1.25
GR	Jamestown Equity	JAMEX	B+	(866) 738-1126	B- / 7.3	1.76	4.30	10.14 /75	15.02 /75	13.25 /71	0.65	1.07
GR	Janus Adviser Forty A	JDCAX	D+	(800) 295-2687	A / 9.3	7.71	14.79	19.89 /97	16.68 /88	12.55 /64	0.00	0.92
GR	Janus Adviser Forty C	JACCX	D+	(800) 295-2687	A / 9.5	7.54	14.29	18.96 /96	15.78 /82	11.67 /58	0.00	1.67
GR	Janus Adviser Forty I	JCAPX	C-	(800) 295-2687	A+ / 9.7	7.83	15.02	20.34 /97	17.05 /90	12.86 /67	0.00	0.60
GR	Janus Adviser Forty N	JFRNX	A	(800) 295-2687	A+ / 9.7	7.82	15.15	20.51 /97	17.14 /91	12.73 /66	0.00	0.52
GR	Janus Adviser Forty R	JDCRX	C-	(800) 295-2687	A+ / 9.6	7.65	14.66	19.53 /96	16.29 /85	12.12 /61	0.00	1.27
GR	Janus Adviser Forty S	JARTX	C-	(800) 295-2687	A+ / 9.7	7.69	14.85	19.91 /97	16.64 /88	12.43 /64	0.00	1.02
GR	Janus Adviser Forty T	JACTX	C-	(800) 295-2687	A+ / 9.7	7.78	15.04	20.21 /97	16.89 /89	12.70 /66	0.00	0.77
FO	Janus Asia Equity A	JAQAX	D	(800) 295-2687	C- / 3.3	5.15	8.32	14.15 /90	7.30 /23	--	1.57	2.49
FO	Janus Asia Equity C	JAQCX	D+	(800) 295-2687	C- / 3.7	5.03	7.91	13.27 /87	6.44 /19	--	0.47	3.24
FO	● Janus Asia Equity D	JAQDX	C-	(800) 295-2687	C / 4.4	5.34	8.44	14.37 /90	7.41 /24	--	1.79	2.31
FO	Janus Asia Equity I	JAQIX	C-	(800) 295-2687	C / 4.5	5.33	8.53	14.46 /90	7.60 /25	--	1.87	2.15
FO	Janus Asia Equity S	JAQSX	D+	(800) 295-2687	C- / 4.2	5.15	8.20	14.03 /89	7.16 /22	--	1.65	2.58
FO	Janus Asia Equity T	JAQTX	C-	(800) 295-2687	C / 4.4	5.30	8.46	14.29 /90	7.45 /24	--	2.60	2.44
BA	Janus Aspen Balanced Inst	JABLX	C	(800) 295-2687	C / 4.9	1.37	4.71	8.66 /67	11.09 /46	9.80 /43	1.67	0.58
BA	Janus Aspen Balanced Svc		C	(800) 295-2687	C / 4.8	1.33	4.59	8.42 /66	10.81 /44	9.53 /41	1.45	0.84
MC	Janus Aspen Enterprise Inst	JAAGX	A+	(800) 295-2687	A+ / 9.7	7.17	15.72	17.93 /95	17.84 /94	16.92 /96	0.14	0.69
MC	Janus Aspen Enterprise Svc		A+	(800) 295-2687	A+ / 9.7	7.10	15.55	17.63 /95	17.54 /92	16.63 /95	0.03	0.94
GR	Janus Aspen Forty Inst	JACAX	C-	(800) 295-2687	A+ / 9.7	7.85	15.05	20.22 /97	16.98 /90	12.83 /67	0.15	0.55
GR	Janus Aspen Forty Svc		C-	(800) 295-2687	A+ / 9.7	7.78	14.90	19.93 /97	16.68 /88	12.55 /64	0.03	0.81
GL	Janus Aspen Global Research Inst	JAWGX	B	(800) 295-2687	B / 8.0	5.50	8.63	12.66 /85	14.96 /75	10.64 /50	1.00	0.53
GL	Janus Aspen Global Research Svc		B	(800) 295-2687	B / 7.8	5.42	8.51	12.38 /84	14.68 /72	10.37 /48	0.90	0.78
TC	Janus Aspen Global Technology Inst	JGLTX	B+	(800) 295-2687	B+ / 8.4	3.56	9.67	14.10 /90	15.52 /79	14.65 /84	0.00	0.77
TC	Janus Aspen Global Technology Svc		B	(800) 295-2687	B / 8.2	3.50	9.38	13.73 /89	15.23 /77	14.34 /81	0.00	1.02
FO	Janus Aspen Overseas Inst	JAIGX	E-	(800) 295-2687	E / 0.3	-0.83	-9.42	-12.54 / 2	-1.64 / 3	-2.35 / 2	3.46	0.51
FO	Janus Aspen Overseas Svc		E-	(800) 295-2687	E / 0.3	-0.89	-9.55	-12.75 / 2	-1.89 / 3	-2.60 / 1	3.40	0.76
MC	Janus Aspen Perkins Mid Cp Val Inst	JAMVX	C	(800) 295-2687	C / 4.9	0.16	4.13	6.62 /52	11.54 /49	10.23 /46	1.29	0.58
MC	Janus Aspen Perkins Mid Cp Val Svc		C-	(800) 295-2687	C / 4.7	0.11	3.98	6.32 /49	11.23 /47	9.90 /44	1.18	0.83
BA	Janus Balanced A	JDBAX	C+	(800) 295-2687	C- / 3.7	1.40	4.64	8.47 /66	10.56 /43	9.27 /39	1.56	0.95
BA	Janus Balanced C	JABCX	C+	(800) 295-2687	C- / 4.1	1.18	4.27	7.65 /60	9.74 /38	8.47 /33	1.04	1.68
BA	● Janus Balanced D	JANBX	B-	(800) 295-2687	C / 4.8	1.44	4.76	8.69 /67	10.83 /44	9.51 /41	1.82	0.73

● Denotes fund is closed to new investors
* Denotes fund is included in Section II

www.thestreetratings.com

RISK			NET ASSETS		ASSET				BULL / BEAR		FUND MANAGER		MINIMUMS		LOADS	
	3 Year		NAV						Last Bull	Last Bear	Manager	Manager	Initial	Additional	Front	Back
Risk Rating/Pts	Standard Deviation	Beta	As of 3/31/15	Total $(Mil)	Cash %	Stocks %	Bonds %	Other %	Portfolio Turnover Ratio	Market Return	Market Return	Quality Pct	Tenure (Years)	Purch. $	Purch. $	End Load	End Load
B- / 7.2	9.7	1.01	18.77	41	7	92	0	1	3	96.2	-17.8	57	15	0	0	0.0	0.0
B- / 7.2	9.7	1.01	18.83	96	7	92	0	1	3	97.7	-17.8	61	15	0	0	0.0	0.0
C+ / 6.2	10.3	0.47	16.41	425	10	86	1	3	58	69.1	-12.2	96	14	0	0	0.0	0.0
C+ / 6.2	10.2	0.47	16.26	21	10	86	1	3	58	68.0	-12.3	96	14	0	0	0.0	0.0
C+ / 6.2	10.3	0.47	16.39	40	10	86	1	3	58	69.5	-12.2	96	14	0	0	0.0	0.0
C- / 3.1	14.7	0.92	4.10	42	0	99	0	1	56	72.0	-21.8	35	16	2,500	100	0.0	2.0
E+ / 0.7	16.5	0.93	18.30	10	8	91	0	1	66	85.8	-30.7	7	3	1,000,000	1,000	0.0	0.0
E+ / 0.6	16.5	0.93	17.25	3	8	91	0	1	66	84.0	-30.8	6	3	2,500	100	0.0	2.0
E / 0.4	42.3	1.03	21.84	11	0	99	0	1	86	6.1	-25.2	0	5	1,000,000	1,000	0.0	0.0
C- / 3.8	18.1	1.05	21.70	11	0	99	0	1	86	77.9	-31.9	19	5	2,500	100	0.0	2.0
B- / 7.5	9.7	0.91	12.89	12	0	99	0	1	23	64.9	-9.2	22	5	2,500	100	0.0	2.0
C+ / 5.9	12.0	1.06	15.87	10	1	98	0	1	88	N/A	N/A	25	4	2,500	50	5.8	0.0
C+ / 5.9	12.0	1.06	15.44	N/A	1	98	0	1	88	N/A	N/A	19	4	2,500	50	0.0	0.0
C+ / 6.0	12.0	1.06	16.00	18	1	98	0	1	88	N/A	N/A	29	4	250,000	50	0.0	0.0
B+ / 9.0	5.5	0.91	25.24	2,871	3	42	54	1	32	42.0	-5.4	51	24	2,000	0	0.0	0.0
B+ / 9.0	5.5	0.91	24.99	1,220	3	42	54	1	32	43.2	-5.3	56	24	50,000	0	0.0	0.0
B / 8.1	8.5	0.66	14.19	37	2	97	0	1	171	63.7	N/A	74	18	2,000	0	0.0	0.0
C+ / 6.2	11.5	0.98	15.38	21	4	95	0	1	31	86.4	-21.6	52	9	2,000	0	0.0	0.0
C+ / 6.8	12.4	0.85	34.32	136	2	97	0	1	62	75.5	-16.4	52	18	2,000	0	0.0	0.0
C- / 4.2	14.4	1.26	15.27	22	12	87	0	1	96	105.0	-24.3	16	5	10,000	0	0.0	2.0
B- / 7.6	7.1	1.19	14.65	18	4	65	29	2	21	60.0	-11.4	34	16	5,000	0	0.0	0.0
C+ / 6.9	10.3	1.05	21.91	30	3	96	0	1	21	93.0	-16.5	42	15	5,000	0	0.0	0.0
E / 0.3	11.2	1.00	32.41	233	1	98	0	1	51	107.2	-18.5	72	2	2,500	0	5.8	0.0
E / 0.3	11.2	1.00	28.94	289	1	98	0	1	51	101.8	-18.8	63	2	2,500	0	0.0	0.0
E / 0.3	11.2	1.00	32.93	1,012	1	98	0	1	51	109.4	-18.5	75	2	1,000,000	0	0.0	0.0
C+ / 5.9	11.2	1.00	32.95	79	1	98	0	1	51	109.5	-18.6	76	2	0	0	0.0	0.0
E / 0.3	11.2	1.00	30.41	138	1	98	0	1	51	104.8	-18.7	69	2	2,500	0	0.0	0.0
E / 0.3	11.2	1.00	31.64	686	1	98	0	1	51	106.9	-18.6	72	2	2,500	0	0.0	0.0
E / 0.3	11.2	1.00	31.85	28	1	98	0	1	51	108.4	-18.5	74	2	2,500	0	0.0	0.0
C / 5.5	12.9	0.72	10.01	N/A	4	95	0	1	72	50.2	N/A	73	4	2,500	0	5.8	0.0
C / 5.5	12.9	0.71	10.03	N/A	4	95	0	1	72	46.5	N/A	64	4	2,500	0	0.0	0.0
C / 5.5	12.9	0.71	10.06	6	4	95	0	1	72	51.1	N/A	74	4	2,500	0	0.0	0.0
C / 5.5	12.9	0.72	10.07	4	4	95	0	1	72	51.7	N/A	75	4	1,000,000	0	0.0	0.0
C / 5.5	12.8	0.71	10.00	N/A	4	95	0	1	72	49.5	N/A	72	4	2,500	0	0.0	0.0
C / 5.5	12.8	0.71	9.93	1	4	95	0	1	72	50.7	N/A	74	4	2,500	0	0.0	0.0
C+ / 6.8	6.0	1.04	31.86	485	4	56	39	1	76	63.5	-12.3	64	10	0	0	0.0	0.0
C+ / 6.9	6.0	1.04	33.41	1,432	4	56	39	1	76	62.1	-12.3	61	10	0	0	0.0	0.0
C+ / 6.2	9.4	0.79	66.19	438	3	96	0	1	15	105.3	-19.2	91	8	0	0	0.0	0.0
C+ / 6.2	9.4	0.79	63.47	296	3	96	0	1	15	103.5	-19.3	91	8	0	0	0.0	0.0
E / 0.5	10.9	0.97	43.43	318	2	97	0	1	61	108.5	-18.4	79	2	0	0	0.0	0.0
E / 0.4	10.9	0.97	42.26	518	2	97	0	1	61	106.7	-18.5	77	2	0	0	0.0	0.0
C+ / 5.6	11.9	0.84	43.73	593	5	94	0	1	101	84.1	-23.7	95	1	0	0	0.0	0.0
C+ / 5.6	11.9	0.84	42.98	224	5	94	0	1	101	82.4	-23.8	95	1	0	0	0.0	0.0
C+ / 5.8	12.2	1.14	8.73	9	4	95	0	1	39	97.1	-19.2	30	4	0	0	0.0	0.0
C+ / 5.8	12.1	1.13	8.86	164	4	95	0	1	39	95.5	-19.4	28	4	0	0	0.0	0.0
D / 1.8	17.3	1.09	32.29	352	1	98	0	1	30	17.3	-31.9	1	14	0	0	0.0	0.0
D / 1.8	17.3	1.09	31.27	773	1	98	0	1	30	16.3	-31.9	1	14	0	0	0.0	0.0
C+ / 6.1	9.3	0.81	18.80	43	5	94	0	1	71	69.5	-19.7	40	13	0	0	0.0	0.0
C+ / 6.1	9.3	0.81	18.41	96	5	94	0	1	71	67.8	-19.8	37	13	0	0	0.0	0.0
B / 8.1	6.0	1.03	30.87	952	4	53	42	1	72	61.0	-12.4	59	10	2,500	0	5.8	0.0
B / 8.2	6.0	1.03	30.69	1,170	4	53	42	1	72	57.0	-12.7	46	10	2,500	0	0.0	0.0
B / 8.1	6.0	1.03	30.92	1,483	4	53	42	1	72	62.2	-12.3	63	10	2,500	0	0.0	0.0

					PERFORMANCE								
	99 Pct = Best						Total Return % through 3/31/15					Incl. in Returns	
	0 Pct = Worst			Overall	Perfor-					Annualized		Dividend	Expense
Fund		Ticker		Investment	mance							Yield	Ratio
Type	Fund Name	Symbol	Phone	Rating	Rating/Pts	3 Mo	6 Mo	1Yr / Pct	3Yr / Pct	5Yr / Pct			
BA	Janus Balanced I	JBALX	(800) 295-2687	B-	C / 4.8	1.42	4.77	8.73 /68	10.87 /45	9.58 /41	1.89	0.64
BA	Janus Balanced N	JABNX	(800) 295-2687	B	C / 4.9	1.44	4.85	8.85 /68	10.96 /45	9.55 /41	1.96	0.58
BA	Janus Balanced R	JDBRX	(800) 295-2687	C+	C / 4.4	1.28	4.45	8.04 /63	10.16 /40	8.85 /36	1.31	1.33
BA	Janus Balanced S	JABRX	(800) 295-2687	C+	C / 4.5	1.33	4.56	8.29 /65	10.43 /42	9.12 /38	1.52	1.08
BA	Janus Balanced T	JABAX	(800) 295-2687	C+	C / 4.7	1.39	4.69	8.57 /67	10.71 /44	9.40 /40	1.74	0.83
GL	Janus Contrarian A	JCNAX	(800) 295-2687	A+	A / 9.4	1.09	7.03	12.63 /85	20.63 /98	11.78 /59	0.24	1.02
GL	Janus Contrarian C	JCNCX	(800) 295-2687	A+	A+ / 9.6	0.89	6.59	11.74 /81	19.64 /97	10.90 /52	0.00	1.80
GL	● Janus Contrarian D	JACNX	(800) 295-2687	A+	A+ / 9.7	1.09	7.11	12.85 /86	20.87 /98	12.00 /60	0.30	0.80
GL	Janus Contrarian I	JCONX	(800) 295-2687	A+	A+ / 9.7	1.13	7.09	12.88 /86	20.99 /98	12.08 /61	0.41	0.74
GL	Janus Contrarian R	JCNRX	(800) 295-2687	A+	A+ / 9.6	0.97	6.82	12.18 /83	20.16 /98	11.34 /56	0.00	1.39
GL	Janus Contrarian S	JCNIX	(800) 295-2687	A+	A+ / 9.7	1.04	6.94	12.44 /85	20.47 /98	11.62 /58	0.06	1.16
GL	Janus Contrarian T	JSVAX	(800) 295-2687	A+	A+ / 9.7	1.09	7.06	12.71 /86	20.78 /98	11.90 /60	0.22	0.89
IN	Janus Diversified Alternatives N	JDANX	(800) 295-2687	U	U /	1.18	3.83	6.28 /49	--	--	0.00	1.25
GL	Janus Enterprise A	JDMAX	(800) 295-2687	A	A- / 9.2	6.95	15.09	17.00 /95	16.95 /90	16.22 /94	0.00	1.16
GL	Janus Enterprise C	JGRCX	(800) 295-2687	A+	A / 9.4	6.79	14.73	16.27 /94	16.13 /84	15.39 /89	0.00	1.82
GL	● Janus Enterprise D	JANEX	(800) 295-2687	A+	A+ / 9.7	7.04	15.28	17.39 /95	17.30 /91	16.55 /95	0.03	0.84
GL	Janus Enterprise I	JMGRX	(800) 295-2687	A+	A+ / 9.7	7.07	15.30	17.46 /95	17.39 /92	16.66 /95	0.06	0.75
MC	Janus Enterprise N	JDMNX	(800) 295-2687	A+	A+ / 9.7	7.08	15.38	17.58 /95	17.47 /92	16.61 /95	0.09	0.68
GL	Janus Enterprise R	JDMRX	(800) 295-2687	A+	A / 9.5	6.89	14.95	16.71 /94	16.63 /88	15.87 /92	0.00	1.42
GL	Janus Enterprise S	JGRTX	(800) 295-2687	A+	A+ / 9.6	6.96	15.10	17.01 /95	16.93 /89	16.17 /94	0.00	1.17
GL	Janus Enterprise T	JAENX	(800) 295-2687	A+	A+ / 9.6	7.03	15.25	17.30 /95	17.22 /91	16.46 /95	0.01	0.92
GR	Janus Fund A	JDGAX	(800) 295-2687	C+	B+ / 8.9	6.23	13.08	20.12 /97	16.08 /84	12.98 /68	0.00	0.90
GR	Janus Fund C	JGOCX	(800) 295-2687	C+	A- / 9.2	6.02	12.55	19.01 /96	15.22 /77	12.16 /62	0.00	1.65
GR	● Janus Fund D	JANDX	(800) 295-2687	C+	A / 9.5	6.28	13.22	20.31 /97	16.40 /86	13.26 /71	0.12	0.66
GR	Janus Fund I	JGROX	(800) 295-2687	C+	A+ / 9.6	6.28	13.29	20.41 /97	16.46 /87	13.33 /71	0.22	0.61
GR	Janus Fund N	JDGNX	(800) 295-2687	A+	A+ / 9.6	6.32	13.34	20.52 /97	16.56 /87	13.31 /71	0.25	0.51
GR	Janus Fund R	JDGRX	(800) 295-2687	C+	A / 9.4	6.13	12.92	19.61 /96	15.71 /81	12.59 /65	0.00	1.26
GR	Janus Fund S	JGORX	(800) 295-2687	C+	A / 9.4	6.19	13.06	19.91 /97	16.03 /84	12.88 /67	0.00	1.01
GR	Janus Fund T	JANSX	(800) 295-2687	C+	A / 9.5	6.26	13.20	20.21 /97	16.31 /86	13.16 /70	0.03	0.76
AA	Janus Global Allocation - Consv A	JCAAX	(800) 295-2687	D+	D / 1.6	2.03	2.71	4.12 /33	6.96 /21	7.01 /23	2.82	1.18
AA	Janus Global Allocation - Consv C	JCACX	(800) 295-2687	C-	D / 1.9	1.82	2.27	3.30 /28	6.18 /17	6.24 /18	2.41	1.92
AA	● Janus Global Allocation - Consv D	JMSCX	(800) 295-2687	C-	D+ / 2.5	2.02	2.76	4.23 /33	7.14 /22	7.20 /24	3.18	0.97
AA	Janus Global Allocation - Consv I	JCAIX	(800) 295-2687	C-	D+ / 2.5	2.02	2.76	4.32 /34	7.20 /22	7.25 /25	3.27	0.93
AA	Janus Global Allocation - Consv S	JCASX	(800) 295-2687	C-	D+ / 2.3	1.96	2.60	3.93 /31	6.79 /20	6.83 /22	2.88	1.33
AA	Janus Global Allocation - Consv T	JSPCX	(800) 295-2687	C-	D+ / 2.4	2.02	2.66	4.14 /33	7.10 /22	7.13 /24	3.16	1.08
GL	Janus Global Allocation - Gr A	JGCAX	(800) 295-2687	C-	D+ / 2.9	2.97	3.83	4.68 /36	9.40 /36	7.93 /29	1.84	1.17
GL	Janus Global Allocation - Gr C	JGCCX	(800) 295-2687	C-	C- / 3.2	2.72	3.37	3.87 /31	8.52 /30	7.07 /23	1.28	1.96
GL	● Janus Global Allocation - Gr D	JNSGX	(800) 295-2687	C	C- / 3.9	3.02	3.89	4.88 /38	9.55 /36	8.11 /31	2.08	1.00
GL	Janus Global Allocation - Gr I	JGCIX	(800) 295-2687	C	C- / 3.9	3.02	3.91	4.89 /38	9.64 /37	8.18 /31	2.16	0.94
GL	Janus Global Allocation - Gr S	JGCSX	(800) 295-2687	C	C- / 3.7	2.91	3.70	4.48 /35	9.23 /34	7.76 /28	1.82	1.34
GL	Janus Global Allocation - Gr T	JSPGX	(800) 295-2687	C	C- / 3.8	2.96	3.80	4.71 /36	9.50 /36	8.03 /30	2.06	1.09
GL	Janus Global Allocation - Modt A	JMOAX	(800) 295-2687	C-	D / 2.1	2.32	3.12	4.25 /33	8.10 /27	7.44 /26	2.29	1.16
GL	Janus Global Allocation - Modt C	JMOCX	(800) 295-2687	C-	D+ / 2.5	2.20	2.75	3.43 /29	7.27 /23	6.65 /21	1.69	1.95
GL	● Janus Global Allocation - Modt D	JNSMX	(800) 295-2687	C	C- / 3.1	2.46	3.27	4.46 /35	8.28 /29	7.63 /27	2.49	0.99
GL	Janus Global Allocation - Modt I	JMOIX	(800) 295-2687	C	C- / 3.2	2.46	3.26	4.53 /35	8.35 /29	7.71 /28	2.56	0.95
GL	Janus Global Allocation - Modt S	JMOSX	(800) 295-2687	C	D+ / 2.9	2.34	3.06	4.12 /33	7.91 /26	7.25 /25	2.22	1.34
GL	Janus Global Allocation - Modt T	JSPMX	(800) 295-2687	C	C- / 3.4	2.39	3.10	4.30 /34	8.96 /33	8.00 /30	2.48	1.09
GL	Janus Global Life Sciences A	JFNAX	(800) 295-2687	B+	A+ / 9.9	13.15	25.01	42.25 /99	36.88 /99	26.86 /99	0.00	1.03
GL	Janus Global Life Sciences C	JFNCX	(800) 295-2687	B+	A+ / 9.9	12.94	22.25	38.56 /99	34.99 /99	25.42 /99	0.00	1.80
GL	● Janus Global Life Sciences D	JNGLX	(800) 295-2687	B+	A+ / 9.9	13.20	25.15	42.53 /99	37.13 /99	27.07 /99	0.00	0.84
GL	Janus Global Life Sciences I	JFNIX	(800) 295-2687	B+	A+ / 9.9	13.23	25.07	42.46 /99	37.20 /99	27.12 /99	0.00	0.77
GL	Janus Global Life Sciences S	JFNSX	(800) 295-2687	B+	A+ / 9.9	13.12	24.96	42.03 /99	36.69 /99	26.66 /99	0.00	1.18

● Denotes fund is closed to new investors
* Denotes fund is included in Section II

www.thestreetratings.com

Risk Rating/Pts	3 Year Standard Deviation	Beta	NAV As of 3/31/15	Total $(Mil)	Cash %	Stocks %	Bonds %	Other %	Portfolio Turnover Ratio	Last Bull Market Return	Last Bear Market Return	Manager Quality Pct	Manager Tenure (Years)	Initial Purch. $	Additional Purch. $	Front End Load	Back End Load
B /8.1	6.0	1.03	30.92	1,506	4	53	42	1	72	62.5	-12.3	62	10	1,000,000	0	0.0	0.0
B /8.7	6.0	1.03	30.89	1,762	4	53	42	1	72	62.7	-12.3	64	10	0	0	0.0	0.0
B /8.2	6.0	1.03	30.76	302	4	53	42	1	72	58.9	-12.5	53	10	2,500	0	0.0	0.0
B /8.2	6.0	1.03	30.86	853	4	53	42	1	72	60.3	-12.4	56	10	2,500	0	0.0	0.0
B /8.1	6.0	1.03	30.89	5,009	4	53	42	1	72	61.6	-12.3	60	10	2,500	0	0.0	0.0
C+ /6.3	10.3	0.51	22.26	127	5	94	0	1	61	118.7	-26.1	99	4	2,500	0	5.8	0.0
C+ /6.3	10.3	0.51	21.42	99	5	94	0	1	61	112.7	-26.3	99	4	2,500	0	0.0	0.0
C+ /6.3	10.3	0.50	22.34	2,500	5	94	0	1	61	120.4	-26.1	99	4	2,500	0	0.0	0.0
C+ /6.3	10.3	0.50	22.33	450	5	94	0	1	61	120.9	-26.1	99	4	1,000,000	0	0.0	0.0
C+ /6.3	10.3	0.51	21.96	2	5	94	0	1	61	116.0	-26.3	99	4	2,500	0	0.0	0.0
C+ /6.4	10.3	0.50	22.27	7	5	94	0	1	61	118.0	-26.2	99	4	2,500	0	0.0	0.0
C+ /6.3	10.3	0.50	22.32	1,403	5	94	0	1	61	119.8	-26.1	99	4	2,500	0	0.0	0.0
U /	N/A	N/A	10.25	54	92	7	0	1	59	N/A	N/A	N/A	3	0	0	0.0	0.0
C+ /6.3	9.3	0.52	91.22	162	2	97	0	1	17	99.5	-19.1	98	8	2,500	0	5.8	0.0
C+ /6.3	9.3	0.52	87.01	57	2	97	0	1	17	94.6	-19.3	98	8	2,500	0	0.0	0.0
C+ /6.4	9.3	0.52	92.63	1,319	2	97	0	1	17	101.4	-19.0	99	8	2,500	0	0.0	0.0
C+ /6.4	9.3	0.52	93.10	730	2	97	0	1	17	102.0	-19.0	99	8	1,000,000	0	0.0	0.0
C+ /6.8	9.3	0.79	93.27	195	2	97	0	1	17	102.2	-19.1	90	8	0	0	0.0	0.0
C+ /6.3	9.3	0.52	89.37	87	2	97	0	1	17	97.5	-19.2	98	8	2,500	0	0.0	0.0
C+ /6.4	9.3	0.52	90.86	249	2	97	0	1	17	99.3	-19.2	98	8	2,500	0	0.0	0.0
C+ /6.4	9.3	0.52	92.27	1,538	2	97	0	1	17	100.9	-19.1	98	8	2,500	0	0.0	0.0
C- /3.2	9.8	0.94	39.02	16	2	97	0	1	62	97.3	-18.6	76	4	2,500	0	5.8	0.0
C- /3.0	9.9	0.95	37.85	6	2	97	0	1	62	92.4	-18.8	N/A	4	2,500	0	0.0	0.0
C- /3.2	9.9	0.95	39.29	6,338	2	97	0	1	62	99.2	-18.5	77	4	2,500	0	0.0	0.0
C- /3.2	9.9	0.95	39.29	532	2	97	0	1	62	99.6	-18.5	78	4	1,000,000	0	0.0	0.0
C+ /6.6	9.9	0.95	39.35	21	2	97	0	1	62	99.8	-18.5	78	4	0	0	0.0	0.0
C- /3.2	9.9	0.95	38.63	4	2	97	0	1	62	95.1	-18.7	72	4	2,500	0	0.0	0.0
C- /3.2	9.9	0.95	39.28	33	2	97	0	1	62	96.9	-18.6	74	4	2,500	0	0.0	0.0
C- /3.2	9.9	0.95	39.40	1,813	2	97	0	1	62	98.5	-18.5	77	4	2,500	0	0.0	0.0
B- /7.9	4.8	0.77	13.06	13	6	42	50	2	13	35.2	-7.2	49	10	2,500	0	5.8	0.0
B /8.0	4.8	0.77	12.84	22	6	42	50	2	13	31.9	-7.6	38	10	2,500	0	0.0	0.0
B- /7.8	4.8	0.77	13.13	225	6	42	50	2	13	36.2	-7.2	51	10	2,500	100	0.0	0.0
B- /7.8	4.9	0.78	13.13	7	6	42	50	2	13	36.4	-7.2	51	10	1,000,000	0	0.0	0.0
B- /7.9	4.8	0.77	13.02	2	6	42	50	2	13	34.4	-7.3	47	10	2,500	0	0.0	0.0
B- /7.8	4.8	0.76	13.11	28	6	42	50	2	13	35.9	-7.2	52	10	2,500	0	0.0	0.0
B- /7.5	8.4	0.60	14.57	4	7	78	14	1	13	54.6	-17.5	90	10	2,500	0	5.8	0.0
B- /7.5	8.4	0.60	14.34	6	7	78	14	1	13	50.6	-17.8	88	10	2,500	0	0.0	0.0
B- /7.5	8.4	0.60	14.65	240	7	78	14	1	13	55.5	-17.4	91	10	2,500	100	0.0	0.0
B- /7.5	8.4	0.60	14.65	6	7	78	14	1	13	56.2	-17.5	91	10	1,000,000	0	0.0	0.0
B- /7.5	8.4	0.60	14.50	2	7	78	14	1	13	53.9	-17.5	90	10	2,500	0	0.0	0.0
B- /7.5	8.4	0.60	14.63	20	7	78	14	1	13	55.4	-17.5	90	10	2,500	0	0.0	0.0
B /8.1	6.5	0.46	13.66	15	9	61	29	1	11	44.5	-12.5	90	10	2,500	0	5.8	0.0
B /8.2	6.5	0.46	13.48	11	9	61	29	1	11	40.8	-12.8	88	10	2,500	0	0.0	0.0
B /8.1	6.6	0.46	13.74	263	9	61	29	1	11	45.4	-12.5	91	10	2,500	100	0.0	0.0
B /8.1	6.6	0.46	13.74	6	9	61	29	1	11	45.7	-12.5	91	10	1,000,000	0	0.0	0.0
B /8.1	6.5	0.46	13.58	3	9	61	29	1	11	43.7	-12.6	90	10	2,500	0	0.0	0.0
B /8.1	6.8	0.48	13.70	25	9	61	29	1	11	48.2	-12.5	92	10	2,500	0	0.0	0.0
C /4.9	12.6	0.48	58.93	201	1	97	0	2	52	215.3	-13.1	99	8	2,500	0	5.8	0.0
C /4.8	12.6	0.49	56.13	106	1	97	0	2	52	201.5	-13.3	99	8	2,500	0	0.0	0.0
C /4.9	12.5	0.48	59.61	1,647	1	97	0	2	52	217.4	-13.1	99	8	2,500	0	0.0	0.0
C /4.9	12.6	0.48	59.67	403	1	97	0	2	52	217.8	-13.0	99	8	1,000,000	0	0.0	0.0
C /4.9	12.6	0.48	58.39	8	1	97	0	2	52	213.7	-13.2	99	8	2,500	0	0.0	0.0

Fund Type	Fund Name	Ticker Symbol	Overall Investment Rating	Phone	Performance Rating/Pts	3 Mo	6 Mo	1Yr / Pct	3Yr / Pct	5Yr / Pct	Dividend Yield	Expense Ratio
GL	Janus Global Life Sciences T	JAGLX	B+	(800) 295-2687	A+ / 9.9	13.19	25.11	42.40 /99	37.04 /99	26.97 /99	0.00	0.93
RE	Janus Global Real Estate A	JERAX	C	(800) 295-2687	C / 5.4	3.26	8.39	12.46 /85	12.38 /55	10.16 /46	1.74	1.32
RE	Janus Global Real Estate C	JERCX	C	(800) 295-2687	C+ / 5.8	3.02	7.88	11.51 /80	11.50 /49	9.34 /39	1.21	2.08
RE	● Janus Global Real Estate D	JNGSX	C+	(800) 295-2687	C+ / 6.5	3.26	8.49	12.65 /85	12.60 /57	10.44 /48	1.99	1.15
RE	Janus Global Real Estate I	JERIX	C+	(800) 295-2687	C+ / 6.6	3.29	8.56	12.81 /86	12.73 /58	10.53 /49	2.12	1.01
RE	Janus Global Real Estate S	JERSX	C+	(800) 295-2687	C+ / 6.2	3.22	8.31	12.22 /84	12.26 /54	10.04 /45	1.73	1.45
RE	Janus Global Real Estate T	JERTX	C+	(800) 295-2687	C+ / 6.4	3.26	8.49	12.53 /85	12.57 /56	10.37 /48	1.97	1.18
FO	Janus Global Research A	JDWAX	C	(800) 295-2687	C / 5.5	5.44	8.54	12.39 /84	12.05 /53	11.65 /58	0.74	0.97
FO	Janus Global Research C	JWWCX	C+	(800) 295-2687	C+ / 5.9	5.23	8.10	11.53 /81	11.25 /47	10.83 /51	0.19	1.73
FO	● Janus Global Research D	JANWX	C+	(800) 295-2687	C+ / 6.6	5.49	8.63	12.61 /85	12.20 /54	11.81 /59	0.96	0.77
FO	Janus Global Research I	JWWFX	C+	(800) 295-2687	C+ / 6.6	5.51	8.69	12.69 /86	12.26 /54	11.88 /60	1.05	0.67
FO	Janus Global Research R	JDWRX	C+	(800) 295-2687	C+ / 6.2	5.33	8.31	11.93 /82	11.77 /51	11.50 /57	0.53	1.35
FO	Janus Global Research S	JWGRX	C+	(800) 295-2687	C+ / 6.3	5.39	8.44	12.21 /84	11.92 /52	11.48 /57	0.62	1.10
FO	Janus Global Research T	JAWWX	C+	(800) 295-2687	C+ / 6.5	5.46	8.59	12.51 /85	12.16 /54	11.73 /59	0.89	0.85
FO	Janus Global Select A	JORAX	D-	(800) 295-2687	D+ / 2.6	3.85	6.39	9.44 /72	7.36 /23	6.13 /18	0.50	1.05
FO	Janus Global Select C	JORCX	D-	(800) 295-2687	C- / 3.0	3.72	5.97	8.49 /66	6.46 /19	5.28 /13	0.00	1.88
FO	● Janus Global Select D	JANRX	D-	(800) 295-2687	C- / 3.6	3.95	6.46	9.53 /72	7.57 /24	6.35 /19	0.69	0.86
FO	Janus Global Select I	JORFX	D	(800) 295-2687	C- / 3.7	3.94	6.55	9.70 /73	7.70 /25	6.43 /20	0.79	0.73
FO	Janus Global Select R	JORRX	D-	(800) 295-2687	C- / 3.2	3.74	6.11	8.86 /69	6.93 /21	5.73 /15	0.07	1.44
FO	Janus Global Select S	JORIX	D-	(800) 295-2687	C- / 3.4	3.83	6.29	9.16 /70	7.23 /23	6.09 /17	0.46	1.19
FO	Janus Global Select T	JORNX	D-	(800) 295-2687	C- / 3.6	3.87	6.40	9.38 /71	7.47 /24	6.26 /18	0.64	0.93
TC	Janus Global Technology A	JATAX	C-	(800) 295-2687	C+ / 6.7	3.19	8.96	13.21 /87	14.84 /74	14.12 /79	0.67	1.11
TC	Janus Global Technology C	JAGCX	C	(800) 295-2687	B- / 7.2	3.02	8.55	12.37 /84	14.03 /67	13.31 /71	0.00	1.82
TC	● Janus Global Technology D	JNGTX	C+	(800) 295-2687	B / 8.0	3.20	9.06	13.42 /88	15.09 /76	14.36 /81	0.10	0.88
TC	Janus Global Technology I	JATIX	C+	(800) 295-2687	B / 8.1	3.27	9.12	13.55 /88	15.17 /76	14.44 /82	0.19	0.82
TC	Janus Global Technology S	JATSX	C	(800) 295-2687	B / 7.8	3.17	8.93	13.12 /87	14.74 /73	14.02 /78	0.00	1.20
TC	Janus Global Technology T	JAGTX	C+	(800) 295-2687	B / 8.0	3.21	9.08	13.35 /88	15.04 /75	14.31 /80	0.06	0.95
GL	Janus Growth and Income A	JDNAX	B-	(800) 295-2687	C+ / 6.1	1.17	5.16	10.51 /76	14.67 /72	12.22 /62	1.81	0.96
GL	Janus Growth and Income C	JGICX	B-	(800) 295-2687	C+ / 6.5	0.96	4.75	9.66 /73	13.75 /65	11.34 /56	1.25	1.76
GL	● Janus Growth and Income D	JNGIX	B+	(800) 295-2687	B- / 7.3	1.21	5.25	10.70 /77	14.87 /74	12.40 /63	2.07	0.79
GL	Janus Growth and Income I	JGINX	B+	(800) 295-2687	B- / 7.3	1.24	5.27	10.77 /77	14.94 /74	12.49 /64	2.13	0.73
GL	Janus Growth and Income R	JDNRX	B-	(800) 295-2687	C+ / 6.8	1.07	4.92	10.05 /75	14.18 /68	11.73 /59	1.52	1.38
GL	Janus Growth and Income S	JADGX	B+	(800) 295-2687	B- / 7.0	1.13	5.06	10.30 /76	14.47 /71	12.02 /61	1.73	1.13
GL	Janus Growth and Income T	JAGIX	B+	(800) 295-2687	B- / 7.2	1.19	5.17	10.58 /77	14.76 /73	12.29 /62	1.98	0.88
FO	Janus International Equity A	JAIEX	E+	(800) 295-2687	D / 1.9	4.90	1.43	0.09 /16	8.05 /27	6.13 /18	1.69	1.10
FO	Janus International Equity C	JCIEX	D-	(800) 295-2687	D / 2.2	4.66	1.00	-0.66 /14	7.16 /22	5.28 /13	1.03	1.90
FO	● Janus International Equity D	JNISX	D-	(800) 295-2687	D+ / 2.8	5.01	1.67	0.40 /17	8.24 /28	6.36 /19	2.00	0.91
FO	Janus International Equity I	JIIEX	D-	(800) 295-2687	D+ / 2.9	5.01	1.58	0.39 /17	8.38 /29	6.47 /20	2.14	0.80
FO	Janus International Equity N	JNIEX	D+	(800) 295-2687	C- / 3.0	4.93	1.64	0.44 /17	8.44 /30	6.50 /20	2.19	0.75
FO	Janus International Equity R	JRIEX	D-	(800) 295-2687	D+ / 2.4	4.73	1.27	-0.31 /15	7.62 /25	5.72 /15	1.72	1.50
FO	Janus International Equity S	JSIEX	D-	(800) 295-2687	D+ / 2.6	4.86	1.37	-0.07 /15	7.88 /26	6.28 /19	1.72	1.25
FO	Janus International Equity T	JAITX	D-	(800) 295-2687	D+ / 2.8	4.88	1.48	0.21 /16	8.15 /28	6.27 /19	1.91	1.00
FO	Janus Overseas A	JDIAX	E-	(800) 295-2687	E- / 0.2	-1.45	-11.04	-14.12 / 2	-3.88 / 2	-4.72 / 1	0.27	0.87
FO	Janus Overseas C	JIGCX	E-	(800) 295-2687	E- / 0.2	-1.67	-11.38	-14.77 / 2	-4.64 / 2	-5.45 / 1	0.00	1.65
FO	● Janus Overseas D	JNOSX	E-	(800) 295-2687	E- / 0.2	-1.43	-10.94	-13.90 / 2	-3.59 / 2	-4.47 / 1	1.13	0.58
FO	Janus Overseas I	JIGFX	E-	(800) 295-2687	E- / 0.2	-1.39	-10.89	-13.82 / 2	-3.54 / 2	-4.41 / 1	1.14	0.54
FO	Janus Overseas N	JDINX	E-	(800) 295-2687	E- / 0.2	-1.37	-10.84	-13.75 / 2	-3.46 / 2	-4.42 / 1	1.33	0.43
FO	Janus Overseas R	JDIRX	E-	(800) 295-2687	E- / 0.2	-1.54	-11.20	-14.41 / 2	-4.17 / 2	-5.03 / 1	0.26	1.18
FO	Janus Overseas S	JIGRX	E-	(800) 295-2687	E- / 0.2	-1.49	-11.06	-14.17 / 2	-3.92 / 2	-4.79 / 1	0.54	0.93
FO	Janus Overseas T	JAOSX	E-	(800) 295-2687	E- / 0.2	-1.43	-10.96	-13.97 / 2	-3.68 / 2	-4.55 / 1	0.96	0.68
GR	Janus Portfolio Institutional	JAGRX	A+	(800) 295-2687	A+ / 9.6	6.29	13.24	20.49 /97	16.78 /89	14.30 /80	0.32	0.54
GR	Janus Portfolio Service	JAGRX	A	(800) 295-2687	A+ / 9.6	6.22	13.09	20.21 /97	16.48 /87	14.02 /78	0.19	0.79

● Denotes fund is closed to new investors
* Denotes fund is included in Section II

www.thestreetratings.com

RISK			NET ASSETS		ASSET					BULL / BEAR		FUND MANAGER		MINIMUMS		LOADS	
	3 Year		NAV						Portfolio	Last Bull	Last Bear	Manager	Manager	Initial	Additional	Front	Back
Risk Rating/Pts	Standard Deviation	Beta	As of 3/31/15	Total $(Mil)	Cash %	Stocks %	Bonds %	Other %	Turnover Ratio	Market Return	Market Return	Quality Pct	Tenure (Years)	Purch. $	Purch. $	End Load	End Load
C / 4.9	12.5	0.48	59.45	1,669	1	97	0	2	52	216.4	-13.0	99	8	2,500	0	0.0	0.0
C+ / 6.0	10.3	0.71	11.54	28	13	86	0	1	24	75.6	-23.9	86	8	2,500	0	5.8	0.0
C+ / 6.0	10.3	0.71	11.44	10	13	86	0	1	24	71.3	-24.1	81	8	2,500	0	0.0	0.0
C+ / 6.0	10.3	0.71	11.63	50	13	86	0	1	24	76.9	-23.8	87	6	2,500	0	0.0	0.0
C+ / 6.0	10.2	0.71	11.62	130	13	86	0	1	24	77.7	-23.7	87	8	1,000,000	0	0.0	0.0
C+ / 6.0	10.3	0.71	11.55	3	13	86	0	1	24	75.1	-23.9	85	8	2,500	0	0.0	0.0
C+ / 6.0	10.3	0.71	11.62	72	13	86	0	1	24	76.8	-23.8	87	8	2,500	0	0.0	0.0
C+ / 6.1	10.4	0.70	68.06	14	4	95	0	1	43	75.6	-20.9	93	1	2,500	0	5.8	0.0
C+ / 6.1	10.4	0.70	67.06	8	4	95	0	1	43	71.3	-21.2	92	1	2,500	0	0.0	0.0
C+ / 6.1	10.4	0.70	67.24	1,533	4	95	0	1	43	76.4	-20.9	94	1	2,500	0	0.0	0.0
C+ / 6.1	10.4	0.70	68.15	166	4	95	0	1	43	76.7	-20.8	94	1	1,000,000	0	0.0	0.0
C+ / 6.9	10.4	0.70	67.58	4	4	95	0	1	43	74.3	-20.9	93	1	2,500	0	0.0	0.0
C+ / 6.1	10.4	0.70	68.22	46	4	95	0	1	43	74.8	-21.0	93	1	2,500	0	0.0	0.0
C+ / 6.1	10.4	0.70	67.18	1,055	4	95	0	1	43	76.0	-20.9	94	1	2,500	0	0.0	0.0
C / 4.4	14.2	0.89	14.04	6	2	97	0	1	55	55.7	-26.1	52	3	2,500	0	5.8	0.0
C / 4.3	14.3	0.89	13.67	4	2	97	0	1	55	51.2	-26.3	39	3	2,500	0	0.0	0.0
C / 4.4	14.2	0.89	13.95	1,655	2	97	0	1	55	56.6	-26.1	55	3	2,500	0	0.0	0.0
C / 4.4	14.3	0.89	13.99	37	2	97	0	1	55	57.2	-26.1	57	3	1,000,000	0	0.0	0.0
C / 4.3	14.2	0.89	13.88	N/A	2	97	0	1	55	53.7	-26.2	46	3	2,500	0	0.0	0.0
C / 4.3	14.2	0.89	14.09	1	2	97	0	1	55	55.6	-26.1	50	3	2,500	0	0.0	0.0
C / 4.4	14.2	0.89	13.96	576	2	97	0	1	55	56.4	-26.1	54	3	2,500	0	0.0	0.0
C- / 4.0	12.1	1.13	22.30	11	1	98	0	1	57	93.2	-19.1	24	4	2,500	0	5.8	0.0
C- / 3.8	12.1	1.13	21.18	4	1	98	0	1	57	88.9	-19.4	18	4	2,500	0	0.0	0.0
C- / 4.0	12.1	1.13	22.60	759	1	98	0	1	57	94.9	-19.0	27	4	2,500	0	0.0	0.0
C- / 4.0	12.1	1.13	22.73	20	1	98	0	1	57	95.2	-19.0	28	4	1,000,000	0	0.0	0.0
C- / 3.9	12.1	1.13	22.11	3	1	98	0	1	57	92.7	-19.1	24	4	2,500	0	0.0	0.0
C- / 4.0	12.1	1.13	22.53	345	1	98	0	1	57	94.4	-19.0	27	4	2,500	0	0.0	0.0
B- / 7.2	10.0	0.62	48.50	28	7	88	2	3	23	100.5	-21.6	97	8	2,500	0	5.8	0.0
B- / 7.1	10.0	0.62	48.13	21	7	88	2	3	23	95.1	-21.8	96	8	2,500	0	0.0	0.0
B- / 7.2	9.9	0.62	48.53	2,786	7	88	2	3	23	101.6	-21.5	97	8	2,500	0	0.0	0.0
B- / 7.2	9.9	0.62	48.54	56	7	88	2	3	23	102.1	-21.5	97	8	1,000,000	0	0.0	0.0
B- / 7.1	9.9	0.62	48.34	4	7	88	2	3	23	97.6	-21.7	97	8	2,500	0	0.0	0.0
B- / 7.1	10.0	0.62	48.49	31	7	88	2	3	23	99.3	-21.6	97	8	2,500	0	0.0	0.0
B- / 7.2	10.0	0.62	48.50	1,546	7	88	2	3	23	101.0	-21.5	97	8	2,500	0	0.0	0.0
C / 4.7	12.8	0.93	12.84	49	0	99	0	1	57	50.3	-23.9	56	5	2,500	0	5.8	0.0
C / 4.8	12.8	0.93	12.58	15	0	99	0	1	57	46.1	-24.2	43	5	2,500	0	0.0	0.0
C / 4.7	12.8	0.93	12.79	20	0	99	0	1	57	51.2	-23.8	59	5	2,500	0	0.0	0.0
C / 4.7	12.8	0.93	12.79	72	0	99	0	1	57	51.8	-23.8	61	5	1,000,000	0	0.0	0.0
C+ / 6.4	12.8	0.93	12.77	112	0	99	0	1	57	52.0	-23.8	62	5	0	0	0.0	0.0
C / 4.7	12.8	0.93	12.61	4	0	99	0	1	57	48.3	-24.1	51	5	2,500	0	0.0	0.0
C / 4.7	12.8	0.93	13.17	13	0	99	0	1	57	51.6	-24.0	54	5	2,500	0	0.0	0.0
C / 4.7	12.8	0.93	12.69	9	0	99	0	1	57	50.8	-23.9	58	5	2,500	0	0.0	0.0
C- / 3.3	18.2	1.14	31.24	54	2	97	0	1	30	10.1	-33.4	1	14	2,500	0	5.8	0.0
C- / 3.3	18.2	1.14	30.59	40	2	97	0	1	30	7.2	-33.6	1	14	2,500	0	0.0	0.0
C- / 3.3	18.2	1.14	31.03	958	2	97	0	1	30	11.2	-33.3	1	14	2,500	0	0.0	0.0
C- / 3.3	18.2	1.14	31.13	290	2	97	0	1	30	11.4	-33.3	1	14	1,000,000	0	0.0	0.0
C- / 3.1	18.2	1.14	31.03	132	2	97	0	1	30	11.6	-33.4	1	14	0	0	0.0	0.0
C- / 3.3	18.2	1.14	30.74	57	2	97	0	1	30	9.0	-33.5	1	14	2,500	0	0.0	0.0
C- / 3.3	18.2	1.14	30.97	303	2	97	0	1	30	10.0	-33.4	1	14	2,500	0	0.0	0.0
C- / 3.3	18.2	1.14	31.04	1,062	2	97	0	1	30	10.9	-33.4	1	14	2,500	0	0.0	0.0
C+ / 6.1	10.1	0.97	38.01	457	4	95	0	1	50	102.4	-18.5	78	4	0	0	0.0	0.0
C+ / 6.1	10.0	0.96	37.40	171	4	95	0	1	50	100.6	-18.6	76	4	0	0	0.0	0.0

Fund Type	Fund Name	Ticker Symbol	Overall Investment Rating	Phone	Performance Rating/Pts	3 Mo	6 Mo	1Yr / Pct	3Yr / Pct	5Yr / Pct	Dividend Yield	Expense Ratio
	99 Pct = Best				**PERFORMANCE**							
	0 Pct = Worst							Total Return % through 3/31/15			Incl. in Returns	
									Annualized			
GL	Janus Preservation Series-Global A	JGSAX	D	(800) 295-2687	D- / 1.3	3.36	4.83	6.30 /49	4.87 /13	--	0.00	3.08
GL	Janus Preservation Series-Global C	JGGCX	D	(800) 295-2687	D / 1.6	3.18	4.41	5.56 /43	4.09 /10	--	0.00	3.80
GL	● Janus Preservation Series-Global D	JGGDX	D+	(800) 295-2687	D / 2.0	3.36	4.82	6.46 /50	4.99 /13	--	0.00	3.09
GL	Janus Preservation Series-Global I	JGSIX	D+	(800) 295-2687	D / 2.1	3.42	4.96	6.60 /52	5.17 /14	--	0.00	2.76
GL	Janus Preservation Series-Global S	JGSSX	D	(800) 295-2687	D / 1.8	3.30	4.68	6.07 /47	4.72 /12	--	0.00	3.26
GL	Janus Preservation Series-Global T	JGSTX	D+	(800) 295-2687	D / 2.0	3.35	4.81	6.37 /50	4.98 /13	--	0.00	3.01
GR	Janus Preservation Series-Growth A	JPGAX	C-	(800) 295-2687	C- / 3.9	6.19	11.25	15.32 /92	7.32 /23	--	0.00	1.91
GR	Janus Preservation Series-Growth C	JPTCX	C-	(800) 295-2687	C / 4.3	5.97	10.82	14.51 /91	6.54 /19	--	0.00	2.65
GR	● Janus Preservation Series-Growth D	JPGDX	C	(800) 295-2687	C / 4.9	6.26	11.39	15.56 /93	7.55 /24	--	0.00	1.81
GR	Janus Preservation Series-Growth I	JPGIX	C	(800) 295-2687	C / 5.0	6.23	11.46	15.74 /93	7.63 /25	--	0.00	1.65
GR	Janus Preservation Series-Growth S	JPTSX	C	(800) 295-2687	C / 4.7	6.12	11.19	15.16 /92	7.24 /23	--	0.00	2.07
GR	Janus Preservation Series-Growth T	JPGTX	C	(800) 295-2687	C / 4.8	6.18	11.32	15.39 /92	7.42 /24	--	0.00	1.81
GL	Janus Real Return A	JURAX	D-	(800) 295-2687	E / 0.5	1.86	1.27	1.26 /19	1.43 / 6	--	3.47	2.15
GL	Janus Real Return C	JURCX	D-	(800) 295-2687	E+ / 0.6	1.68	0.89	0.50 /17	0.71 / 5	--	2.88	2.90
GL	● Janus Real Return D	JURDX	D-	(800) 295-2687	E+ / 0.7	1.88	1.31	1.36 /20	1.56 / 6	--	3.74	2.08
GL	Janus Real Return I	JURIX	D-	(800) 295-2687	E+ / 0.7	1.93	1.40	1.51 /20	1.71 / 6	--	3.90	1.88
GL	Janus Real Return S	JURSX	D-	(800) 295-2687	E+ / 0.7	1.80	1.05	1.02 /18	1.37 / 6	--	3.40	2.37
GL	Janus Real Return T	JURTX	D-	(800) 295-2687	E+ / 0.7	1.85	1.26	1.25 /19	1.58 / 6	--	3.64	2.16
GL	Janus Research A	JRAAX	B+	(800) 295-2687	A- / 9.2	5.27	11.94	18.38 /96	17.76 /93	15.55 /90	0.03	0.93
GL	Janus Research C	JRACX	B+	(800) 295-2687	A / 9.4	5.09	11.53	17.51 /95	16.89 /89	14.69 /84	0.00	1.67
GL	● Janus Research D	JNRFX	B+	(800) 295-2687	A+ / 9.7	5.31	12.05	18.63 /96	18.03 /94	15.80 /92	0.32	0.72
GL	Janus Research I	JRAIX	B+	(800) 295-2687	A+ / 9.7	5.36	12.10	18.72 /96	18.12 /95	15.89 /92	0.43	0.65
GR	Janus Research N	JRANX	A+	(800) 295-2687	A+ / 9.7	5.36	12.15	18.82 /96	18.21 /95	15.86 /92	0.50	0.55
GL	Janus Research S	JRASX	B+	(800) 295-2687	A+ / 9.6	5.24	11.86	18.24 /96	17.64 /93	15.39 /89	0.00	1.06
GL	Janus Research T	JAMRX	B+	(800) 295-2687	A+ / 9.6	5.28	11.99	18.49 /96	17.94 /94	15.69 /91	0.23	0.80
SC	Janus Triton A	JGMAX	A-	(800) 295-2687	A+ / 9.6	6.88	17.64	18.87 /96	17.84 /94	18.43 /98	0.00	1.15
SC	Janus Triton C	JGMCX	A-	(800) 295-2687	A+ / 9.7	6.73	17.27	18.11 /96	17.01 /90	17.56 /97	0.00	1.85
MC	● Janus Triton D	JANIX	A	(800) 295-2687	A+ / 9.8	7.01	17.93	19.30 /96	18.24 /95	18.76 /98	0.09	0.84
SC	Janus Triton I	JSMGX	A	(800) 295-2687	A+ / 9.8	7.02	17.92	19.38 /96	18.30 /95	18.84 /98	0.11	0.79
MC	Janus Triton N	JGMNX	A+	(800) 295-2687	A+ / 9.8	7.01	17.98	19.49 /96	18.38 /95	18.79 /98	0.17	0.68
SC	Janus Triton R	JGMRX	A	(800) 295-2687	A+ / 9.7	6.80	17.52	18.55 /96	17.52 /92	18.05 /97	0.00	1.43
SC	Janus Triton S	JGMIX	A	(800) 295-2687	A+ / 9.6	6.87	17.66	18.89 /96	16.43 /86	17.50 /97	0.00	1.18
SC	Janus Triton T	JATTX	A	(800) 295-2687	A+ / 9.8	6.95	17.81	19.18 /96	18.12 /95	18.63 /98	0.05	0.93
GR	● Janus Twenty D	JNTFX	D	(800) 295-2687	C+ / 6.8	0.33	6.22	11.02 /78	14.11 /68	11.09 /53	0.68	0.70
GR	● Janus Twenty T	JAVLX	D	(800) 295-2687	C+ / 6.8	0.31	6.18	10.92 /78	14.01 /67	10.97 /52	0.56	0.81
SC	Janus Venture A	JVTAX	B-	(800) 295-2687	A / 9.5	4.53	17.58	18.23 /96	18.68 /96	17.85 /97	0.00	1.17
SC	Janus Venture C	JVTCX	B-	(800) 295-2687	A+ / 9.6	4.36	17.12	17.39 /95	17.94 /94	16.98 /96	0.00	1.82
GL	● Janus Venture D	JANVX	B	(800) 295-2687	A+ / 9.8	4.59	17.67	18.51 /96	19.02 /97	18.19 /98	0.00	0.82
SC	Janus Venture I	JVTIX	B	(800) 295-2687	A+ / 9.8	4.62	17.71	18.61 /96	19.12 /97	18.23 /98	0.00	0.75
SC	Janus Venture N	JVTNX	A	(800) 295-2687	A+ / 9.8	4.64	17.78	18.71 /96	19.19 /97	18.23 /98	0.00	0.68
SC	Janus Venture S	JVTSX	B	(800) 295-2687	A+ / 9.7	4.51	17.48	18.11 /96	18.60 /96	17.78 /97	0.00	1.18
GL	Janus Venture T	JAVTX	B	(800) 295-2687	A+ / 9.8	4.58	17.61	18.41 /96	18.90 /96	18.06 /97	0.00	0.93
GR	Jensen Quality Growth I	JENIX	A+	(800) 992-4144	B+ / 8.4	1.65	11.00	13.39 /88	15.65 /80	12.91 /67	1.16	0.63
GR	Jensen Quality Growth J	JENSX	A	(800) 992-4144	B / 8.2	1.57	10.84	13.11 /87	15.35 /78	12.59 /65	0.94	0.88
GR	Jensen Quality Growth R	JENRX	A-	(800) 992-4144	B / 7.9	1.47	10.62	12.71 /86	14.97 /75	12.28 /62	0.61	1.25
GR	Jensen Quality Value I	JNVIX	B	(800) 992-4144	B / 8.1	0.54	7.63	9.02 /69	16.24 /85	12.61 /65	0.82	1.53
GR	Jensen Quality Value J	JNVSX	B	(800) 992-4144	B / 7.9	0.49	7.57	8.84 /68	16.06 /84	12.43 /64	0.60	1.75
FO	JOHCM Asia Ex-Japan Equity Inst	JOAMX	U	(866) 260-9549	U /	5.51	6.02	6.65 /52	--	--	0.17	1.73
EM	JOHCM Emerging Markets Opps Inst	JOEMX	U	(866) 260-9549	U /	5.48	4.90	7.27 /57	--	--	1.26	1.56
GL	JOHCM Global Equity I	JOGEX	U	(866) 260-9549	U /	8.37	7.37	15.24 /92	--	--	0.00	1.60
GL	JOHCM Global Equity Inst	JOGIX	U	(866) 260-9549	U /	8.36	7.39	15.34 /92	--	--	0.02	1.50
FO	JOHCM International Select I	JOHIX	B+	(866) 260-9549	A / 9.5	10.54	11.25	16.27 /94	17.45 /92	14.55 /83	0.65	1.09

● Denotes fund is closed to new investors
* Denotes fund is included in Section II

www.thestreetratings.com

RISK			NET ASSETS		ASSET					BULL / BEAR		FUND MANAGER		MINIMUMS		LOADS	
	3 Year		NAV						Portfolio	Last Bull	Last Bear	Manager	Manager	Initial	Additional	Front	Back
Risk Rating/Pts	Standard Deviation	Beta	As of 3/31/15	Total $(Mil)	Cash %	Stocks %	Bonds %	Other %	Turnover Ratio	Market Return	Market Return	Quality Pct	Tenure (Years)	Purch. $	Purch. $	End Load	End Load
B- / 7.2	8.9	0.56	11.98	3	3	96	0	1	82	N/A	N/A	63	4	2,500	0	5.8	0.0
B- / 7.1	8.9	0.56	11.67	3	3	96	0	1	82	N/A	N/A	51	4	2,500	0	0.0	0.0
B- / 7.2	8.9	0.56	12.01	3	3	96	0	1	82	N/A	N/A	64	4	2,500	0	0.0	0.0
B- / 7.2	8.9	0.56	12.09	3	3	96	0	1	82	N/A	N/A	67	4	1,000,000	0	0.0	0.0
B- / 7.2	8.9	0.56	11.91	2	3	96	0	1	82	N/A	N/A	60	4	2,500	0	0.0	0.0
B- / 7.2	8.9	0.55	12.02	2	3	96	0	1	82	N/A	N/A	65	4	2,500	0	0.0	0.0
C+ / 6.6	7.9	0.68	10.80	17	0	97	2	1	114	32.4	N/A	24	4	2,500	0	5.8	0.0
C+ / 6.5	7.9	0.68	10.47	19	0	97	2	1	114	29.1	N/A	18	4	2,500	0	0.0	0.0
C+ / 6.6	7.9	0.68	10.87	10	0	97	2	1	114	33.2	N/A	26	4	2,500	0	0.0	0.0
C+ / 6.6	7.9	0.68	10.91	9	0	97	2	1	114	33.7	N/A	27	4	1,000,000	0	0.0	0.0
C+ / 6.6	7.9	0.69	10.75	4	0	97	2	1	114	32.0	N/A	22	4	2,500	0	0.0	0.0
C+ / 6.6	7.9	0.69	10.83	6	0	97	2	1	114	32.7	N/A	24	4	2,500	0	0.0	0.0
C+ / 6.9	2.9	0.37	9.67	2	0	4	94	2	91	12.5	N/A	41	N/A	2,500	0	4.8	0.0
C+ / 6.9	2.9	0.37	9.63	2	0	4	94	2	91	9.7	N/A	31	N/A	2,500	0	0.0	0.0
C+ / 6.9	2.9	0.36	9.69	4	0	4	94	2	91	12.9	N/A	43	N/A	2,500	100	0.0	0.0
C+ / 6.8	2.9	0.36	9.62	2	0	4	94	2	91	13.4	N/A	45	N/A	1,000,000	0	0.0	0.0
C+ / 6.9	3.0	0.37	9.69	1	0	4	94	2	91	12.2	N/A	39	N/A	2,500	0	0.0	0.0
C+ / 6.8	3.0	0.37	9.65	3	0	4	94	2	91	13.0	N/A	43	N/A	2,500	0	0.0	0.0
C / 5.2	10.3	0.60	45.36	21	3	96	0	1	44	106.8	-18.6	98	1	2,500	0	5.8	0.0
C / 5.1	10.3	0.60	44.01	8	3	96	0	1	44	101.6	-18.8	98	1	2,500	0	0.0	0.0
C / 5.1	10.3	0.60	45.63	2,747	3	96	0	1	44	108.4	-18.5	98	1	2,500	0	0.0	0.0
C / 5.1	10.3	0.60	45.57	247	3	96	0	1	44	108.9	-18.5	99	1	1,000,000	0	0.0	0.0
C+ / 6.8	10.3	1.00	45.57	77	3	96	0	1	44	109.2	-18.5	83	1	0	0	0.0	0.0
C / 5.2	10.3	0.60	45.02	4	3	96	0	1	44	106.0	-18.6	98	1	2,500	0	0.0	0.0
C / 5.2	10.2	0.60	45.63	1,704	3	96	0	1	44	107.8	-18.5	98	1	2,500	0	0.0	0.0
C+ / 5.7	10.9	0.77	24.87	582	1	98	0	1	30	106.3	-20.0	93	N/A	2,500	0	5.8	0.0
C / 5.5	10.9	0.76	23.79	247	1	98	0	1	30	101.2	-20.3	92	N/A	2,500	0	0.0	0.0
C+ / 5.7	10.9	0.91	25.19	929	1	98	0	1	30	108.4	-19.9	86	N/A	2,500	0	0.0	0.0
C+ / 5.7	10.9	0.77	25.31	1,344	1	98	0	1	30	108.7	-19.9	94	N/A	1,000,000	0	0.0	0.0
C+ / 6.2	10.9	0.92	25.34	307	1	98	0	1	30	109.1	-20.0	87	N/A	0	0	0.0	0.0
C+ / 5.6	10.9	0.77	24.49	173	1	98	0	1	30	104.2	-20.2	93	N/A	2,500	0	0.0	0.0
C+ / 5.6	10.9	0.75	24.72	383	1	98	0	1	30	98.7	-20.1	91	N/A	2,500	0	0.0	0.0
C+ / 5.7	10.9	0.76	25.07	2,588	1	98	0	1	30	107.8	-20.0	94	N/A	2,500	0	0.0	0.0
D / 1.8	10.6	1.01	58.65	6,258	3	96	0	1	71	96.9	-19.1	38	2	2,500	0	0.0	0.0
D / 1.8	10.6	1.01	58.66	3,296	3	96	0	1	71	96.2	-19.1	37	2	2,500	0	0.0	0.0
C- / 3.8	12.1	0.84	67.43	44	3	96	0	1	47	111.3	-20.4	92	2	2,500	0	5.8	0.0
C- / 3.7	12.1	0.84	64.88	15	3	96	0	1	47	106.8	-20.9	91	2	2,500	0	0.0	0.0
C- / 3.9	12.1	0.57	68.52	1,520	3	96	0	1	47	113.4	-20.3	99	2	2,500	0	0.0	0.0
C- / 3.9	12.1	0.84	68.65	281	3	96	0	1	47	114.0	-20.3	93	2	1,000,000	0	0.0	0.0
C+ / 5.9	12.1	0.84	68.82	9	3	96	0	1	47	114.1	-20.3	93	2	0	0	0.0	0.0
C- / 3.8	12.1	0.84	67.18	11	3	96	0	1	47	111.0	-20.4	92	2	2,500	0	0.0	0.0
C- / 3.8	12.1	0.57	67.99	1,025	3	96	0	1	47	112.6	-20.3	99	2	2,500	0	0.0	0.0
B- / 7.3	9.7	0.97	40.71	3,020	2	97	0	1	14	90.1	-16.1	67	22	1,000,000	100	0.0	0.0
B- / 7.3	9.7	0.97	40.70	2,365	2	97	0	1	14	88.4	-16.2	63	22	2,500	100	0.0	0.0
B- / 7.3	9.7	0.97	40.53	39	2	97	0	1	14	86.4	-16.3	58	22	2,500	100	0.0	0.0
C+ / 5.8	11.2	1.11	13.16	11	1	98	0	1	96	91.3	-14.5	44	5	1,000,000	100	0.0	0.0
C+ / 5.8	11.2	1.11	13.19	22	1	98	0	1	96	90.3	-14.5	42	5	2,500	100	0.0	0.0
U /	N/A	N/A	10.72	92	4	93	2	1	21	N/A	N/A	N/A	N/A	1,000,000	0	0.0	0.0
U /	N/A	N/A	10.98	78	7	92	0	1	53	N/A	N/A	N/A	3	1,000,000	0	0.0	0.0
U /	N/A	N/A	14.76	69	8	91	0	1	68	N/A	N/A	N/A	2	25,000	0	0.0	0.0
U /	N/A	N/A	14.77	169	8	91	0	1	68	N/A	N/A	N/A	2	1,000,000	0	0.0	0.0
C / 5.3	12.6	0.85	20.55	2,073	7	92	0	1	61	92.5	-23.6	97	6	25,000	0	0.0	0.0

Fund Type	Fund Name	Ticker Symbol	Overall Investment Rating	Phone	PERFORMANCE Performance Rating/Pts	3 Mo	6 Mo	1Yr / Pct	3Yr / Pct	5Yr / Pct	Dividend Yield	Expense Ratio
FO	JOHCM International Select II	JOHAX	B+	(866) 260-9549	A / 9.4	10.45	11.10	15.97 /93	17.17 /91	14.34 /81	0.56	1.34
FO	JOHCM Intl Small Cap Equity I	JOISX	U	(866) 260-9549	U /	3.90	0.87	-4.65 / 6	--	--	0.94	1.83
FO	JOHCM Intl Small Cap Equity Inst	JOSMX	U	(866) 260-9549	U /	3.91	0.91	-4.61 / 6	--	--	0.98	1.73
GL	John Hancock Dscpld Val Intl I	JDVIX	D+	(800) 257-3336	D / 1.8	4.73	1.61	-1.29 /12	6.34 /18	--	0.84	1.24
GL	John Hancock Dscpld Val Intl R6	JDIUX	U	(800) 257-3336	U /	4.73	1.68	--	--	--	0.00	1.14
GL	John Hancock Enduring Equity NAV		U	(800) 257-3336	U /	-0.65	0.89	4.56 /35	--	--	2.23	1.41
GL	John Hancock Glbl Consv Abs Ret		U	(800) 257-3336	U /	1.33	0.18	0.28 /16	--	--	2.64	N/A
GL	John Hancock II Global Equity NAV		U	(800) 257-3336	U /	2.77	2.47	3.75 /30	--	--	2.71	0.94
GR	John Hancock Seaport NAV		U	(800) 257-3336	U /	4.88	8.15	6.33 /49	--	--	0.00	2.83
SC	John Hancock Small Cap Core NAV		U	(800) 257-3336	U /	5.55	9.87	3.79 /30	--	--	0.11	1.15
GR	John Hancock Value Equity NAV		U	(800) 257-3336	U /	1.46	5.84	--	--	--	0.00	0.88
IN	Johnson Enhanced Return	JENHX	C	(800) 541-0170	B+ / 8.7	1.33	6.03	13.26 /87	16.78 /89	15.50 /90	0.77	0.36
GI	Johnson Equity Income	JEQIX	C+	(800) 541-0170	C+ / 6.0	-0.57	2.46	5.39 /42	13.85 /66	12.31 /63	1.10	1.01
GR	Johnson Growth	JGRWX	B-	(800) 541-0170	B- / 7.3	1.49	6.44	9.98 /74	14.82 /73	11.47 /57	0.22	1.01
FO	Johnson International	JINTX	D	(800) 541-0170	D+ / 2.3	3.96	0.71	2.51 /24	7.07 /22	5.09 /12	2.19	1.00
MC	Johnson Opportunity	JOPPX	B	(800) 541-0170	B / 8.2	3.79	7.61	7.13 /56	16.39 /86	13.25 /71	0.25	1.00
RE	Johnson Realty	JRLTX	C	(800) 541-0170	B+ / 8.5	3.49	17.97	22.75 /98	12.17 /54	14.17 /79	2.35	1.00
GR	Jordan Opportunity	JORDX	C+	(800) 441-7013	C+ / 6.1	5.05	4.31	7.56 /60	13.63 /64	11.88 /60	0.00	1.51
FO	JPMorgan Asia Pacific A	JAPFX	D+	(800) 480-4111	D+ / 2.6	5.68	5.58	7.90 /62	7.24 /23	--	1.27	4.53
FO	JPMorgan Asia Pacific C	JACPX	D+	(800) 480-4111	C- / 3.1	5.57	5.31	7.33 /58	6.68 /20	--	0.94	5.11
FO	JPMorgan Asia Pacific Select	JASPX	C-	(800) 480-4111	C- / 3.6	5.72	5.70	8.14 /64	7.49 /24	--	1.56	4.26
FO	JPMorgan China Region A	JCHAX	C	(800) 480-4111	C / 5.5	5.41	11.06	14.82 /91	10.84 /45	6.24 /18	0.29	2.16
FO	JPMorgan China Region C	JCHCX	C+	(800) 480-4111	C+ / 6.0	5.29	10.80	14.24 /90	10.29 /41	5.71 /15	0.00	2.58
FO	JPMorgan China Region Sel	JCHSX	C+	(800) 480-4111	C+ / 6.5	5.47	11.18	15.14 /92	11.10 /46	6.51 /20	0.55	1.76
OT	JPMorgan Commodities Strategy Sel	CSFSX	U	(800) 480-4111	U /	-5.94	-17.40	-26.59 / 0	--	--	0.00	1.81
GI	JPMorgan Disciplined Equity A	JDEAX	A-	(800) 480-4111	B+ / 8.3	1.44	6.94	14.04 /89	17.32 /91	14.94 /86	0.80	0.95
GI	JPMorgan Disciplined Equity I	JPIEX	A+	(800) 480-4111	A- / 9.2	1.52	7.12	14.47 /91	17.80 /94	15.41 /90	1.15	0.50
GI	JPMorgan Disciplined Equity R6	JDEUX	A+	(800) 480-4111	A / 9.3	1.59	7.21	14.62 /91	17.93 /94	15.52 /90	1.24	0.35
GI	JPMorgan Disciplined Equity Sel	JDESX	A+	(800) 480-4111	A- / 9.2	1.53	7.04	14.30 /90	17.63 /93	15.22 /88	1.03	0.68
BA	JPMorgan Diversified A	JDVAX	C	(800) 480-4111	C- / 3.9	2.58	5.38	7.79 /61	10.46 /42	9.73 /42	1.46	1.38
BA	● JPMorgan Diversified B	JDVBX	C	(800) 480-4111	C / 4.3	2.43	5.14	7.26 /57	9.89 /39	9.17 /38	1.06	1.91
BA	JPMorgan Diversified C	JDVCX	C	(800) 480-4111	C / 4.3	2.52	5.15	7.33 /58	9.92 /39	9.17 /38	1.13	1.89
BA	JPMorgan Diversified Inst	JPDVX	C+	(800) 480-4111	C / 5.0	2.75	5.68	8.35 /65	11.02 /46	10.26 /47	1.98	0.95
BA	JPMorgan Diversified Sel	JDVSX	C+	(800) 480-4111	C / 4.8	2.63	5.54	8.06 /63	10.74 /44	10.01 /45	1.74	1.11
IX	JPMorgan Dvsfd Real Return A	JRNAX	D	(800) 480-4111	E / 0.4	0.54	-0.22	-0.60 /14	-0.10 / 4	--	1.49	1.85
IX	JPMorgan Dvsfd Real Return C	JRNCX	D	(800) 480-4111	E / 0.4	0.35	-0.48	-1.18 /12	-0.63 / 4	--	0.96	2.21
IX	JPMorgan Dvsfd Real Return R2	JRFRX	D	(800) 480-4111	E / 0.5	0.49	-0.33	-0.83 /14	-0.37 / 4	--	0.95	1.87
IX	JPMorgan Dvsfd Real Return R5	JRLRX	D	(800) 480-4111	E / 0.5	0.62	-0.04	-0.23 /15	0.24 / 4	--	1.86	1.22
IX	JPMorgan Dvsfd Real Return Sel	JRNSX	D	(800) 480-4111	E / 0.5	0.60	-0.10	-0.38 /15	0.13 / 4	--	1.78	1.44
EM	JPMorgan Dynamic Emerging Econs	JEEAX	E+	(800) 480-4111	E / 0.3	2.38	-2.64	-1.12 /13	-1.78 / 3	1.81 / 4	1.52	1.93
EM	JPMorgan Dynamic Emerging Econs	JEECX	E+	(800) 480-4111	E / 0.3	2.33	-2.84	-1.53 /11	-2.27 / 3	1.30 / 4	1.07	2.34
EM	JPMorgan Dynamic Emerging Econs	JEERX	E+	(800) 480-4111	E / 0.4	2.54	-2.35	-0.61 /14	-1.31 / 3	2.28 / 5	2.02	1.26
EM	JPMorgan Dynamic Emerging Econs	JEESX	E+	(800) 480-4111	E / 0.4	2.46	-2.57	-0.90 /13	-1.54 / 3	2.05 / 4	1.81	1.47
GR	JPMorgan Dynamic Growth A	DGAAX	C-	(800) 480-4111	C / 5.5	3.41	3.95	6.67 /52	13.87 /66	14.27 /80	0.00	1.41
GR	JPMorgan Dynamic Growth C	DGXCX	C	(800) 480-4111	C+ / 6.0	3.23	3.66	6.09 /47	13.28 /62	13.70 /75	0.00	1.86
GR	JPMorgan Dynamic Growth R5	DGFRX	C	(800) 480-4111	C+ / 6.7	3.50	4.15	7.14 /56	14.37 /70	14.78 /85	0.00	0.85
GR	JPMorgan Dynamic Growth Select	JDGSX	C	(800) 480-4111	C+ / 6.6	3.47	4.04	6.94 /55	14.16 /68	14.56 /83	0.00	1.05
SC	● JPMorgan Dynamic Small Cap Gr A	VSCOX	C-	(800) 480-4111	C+ / 6.9	5.98	15.94	5.10 /39	15.22 /77	15.48 /90	0.00	1.59
SC	● JPMorgan Dynamic Small Cap Gr B	VSCBX	C	(800) 480-4111	B- / 7.5	5.86	15.69	4.60 /36	14.66 /72	14.89 /86	0.00	2.08
SC	● JPMorgan Dynamic Small Cap Gr C	VSCCX	C	(800) 480-4111	B- / 7.5	5.88	15.68	4.57 /36	14.64 /72	14.88 /86	0.00	2.29
SC	● JPMorgan Dynamic Small Cap Gr Sel	JDSCX	C+	(800) 480-4111	B / 8.2	6.04	16.11	5.38 /41	15.55 /80	15.86 /92	0.00	1.26
EM	JPMorgan Emerg Mkt Eq A	JFAMX	E	(800) 480-4111	E / 0.4	1.78	-1.08	-0.43 /14	0.22 / 4	1.27 / 4	0.80	1.87

RISK	3 Year		NET ASSETS		ASSET				Portfolio Turnover Ratio	BULL / BEAR		FUND MANAGER		MINIMUMS		LOADS	
Risk Rating/Pts	Standard Deviation	Beta	NAV As of 3/31/15	Total $(Mil)	Cash %	Stocks %	Bonds %	Other %		Last Bull Market Return	Last Bear Market Return	Manager Quality Pct	Manager Tenure (Years)	Initial Purch. $	Additional Purch. $	Front End Load	Back End Load
C /5.3	12.6	0.85	20.61	103	7	92	0	1	61	90.8	-23.6	97	6	2,000	0	0.0	0.0
U /	N/A	N/A	10.12	52	5	94	0	1	7	N/A	N/A	N/A	2	25,000	0	0.0	0.0
U /	N/A	N/A	10.11	62	5	94	0	1	7	N/A	N/A	N/A	2	1,000,000	0	0.0	0.0
B- /7.6	13.2	0.86	12.41	16	0	0	0	100	0	N/A	N/A	42	4	250,000	0	0.0	0.0
U /	N/A	N/A	12.41	87	0	0	0	100	0	N/A	N/A	N/A	4	1,000,000	0	0.0	0.0
U /	N/A	N/A	10.69	144	4	95	0	1	17	N/A	N/A	N/A	2	0	0	0.0	0.0
U /	N/A	N/A	9.92	101	16	0	83	1	134	N/A	N/A	N/A	2	0	0	0.0	0.0
U /	N/A	N/A	10.76	485	3	96	0	1	70	N/A	N/A	N/A	2	0	0	0.0	0.0
U /	N/A	N/A	10.75	242	53	46	0	1	375	N/A	N/A	N/A	2	0	0	0.0	0.0
U /	N/A	N/A	10.46	170	0	99	0	1	59	N/A	N/A	N/A	N/A	0	0	0.0	0.0
U /	N/A	N/A	10.39	440	1	98	0	1	0	N/A	N/A	N/A	1	0	0	0.0	0.0
D+ /2.7	9.6	1.00	16.01	99	12	0	87	1	33	104.3	-15.8	73	10	1,000,000	100	0.0	0.0
C+ /6.6	10.2	1.03	22.80	150	5	94	0	1	34	84.7	-14.9	32	10	2,000	100	0.0	0.0
C+ /5.9	10.6	1.04	31.23	54	1	98	0	1	41	87.3	-17.9	41	9	2,000	100	0.0	0.0
C+ /5.9	13.0	0.95	25.19	20	1	98	0	1	5	49.8	-25.1	39	7	2,000	100	0.0	0.0
C+ /5.6	13.4	1.14	40.84	45	0	99	0	1	72	101.0	-30.1	28	21	2,000	100	0.0	0.0
C- /3.4	13.1	1.05	16.23	11	0	99	0	1	10	74.6	-15.1	32	17	2,000	100	0.0	0.0
C+ /6.6	11.8	1.07	18.93	46	9	90	0	1	139	91.0	-25.3	22	10	10,000	500	0.0	2.0
C+ /6.8	14.4	0.93	18.98	1	1	98	0	1	73	N/A	N/A	45	4	1,000	50	5.3	0.0
C+ /6.8	14.4	0.93	18.95	N/A	1	98	0	1	73	N/A	N/A	37	4	1,000	50	0.0	0.0
C+ /6.8	14.4	0.93	19.03	6	1	98	0	1	73	N/A	N/A	48	4	1,000,000	0	0.0	0.0
C+ /6.3	12.2	0.70	23.00	6	0	100	0	0	72	57.3	-30.7	91	8	1,000	50	5.3	0.0
C+ /6.3	12.2	0.70	22.48	2	0	100	0	0	72	54.6	-30.8	90	8	1,000	50	0.0	0.0
C+ /6.3	12.1	0.70	23.12	341	0	100	0	0	72	58.6	-30.6	92	8	1,000,000	0	0.0	0.0
U /	N/A	N/A	10.30	62	0	0	0	100	0	N/A	N/A	N/A	2	1,000,000	0	0.0	0.0
C+ /6.8	9.9	1.02	23.84	425	1	98	0	1	113	106.3	-16.3	74	13	1,000	50	5.3	0.0
C+ /6.8	9.9	1.02	23.99	614	1	98	0	1	113	109.2	-16.1	78	13	3,000,000	0	0.0	0.0
C+ /6.8	9.9	1.02	24.00	5,514	1	98	0	1	113	109.9	-16.1	79	13	15,000,000	0	0.0	0.0
C+ /6.8	9.9	1.02	24.02	347	1	98	0	1	113	108.1	-16.2	76	13	1,000,000	0	0.0	0.0
B- /7.3	7.1	1.20	16.79	150	6	62	30	2	58	60.2	-14.2	31	21	1,000	50	4.5	0.0
B- /7.4	7.1	1.20	16.83	2	6	62	30	2	58	57.4	-14.4	26	21	1,000	50	0.0	0.0
B- /7.4	7.2	1.21	16.69	35	6	62	30	2	58	57.5	-14.4	25	21	1,000	50	0.0	0.0
B- /7.3	7.1	1.20	16.85	1,083	6	62	30	2	58	62.9	-14.0	37	21	3,000,000	0	0.0	0.0
B- /7.4	7.1	1.20	16.87	87	6	62	30	2	58	61.6	-14.0	34	21	1,000,000	0	0.0	0.0
B /8.0	4.8	0.27	14.39	2	15	29	54	2	59	7.4	-7.2	15	4	1,000	50	4.5	0.0
B /8.0	4.8	0.27	14.34	N/A	15	29	54	2	59	5.6	-7.3	12	4	1,000	50	0.0	0.0
B /8.0	4.8	0.26	14.42	N/A	15	29	54	2	59	6.5	-7.3	14	4	0	0	0.0	0.0
B /8.0	4.8	0.26	14.45	29	15	29	54	2	59	8.7	-7.0	18	4	0	0	0.0	0.0
B /8.0	4.8	0.26	14.43	15	15	29	54	2	59	8.3	-7.0	17	4	1,000,000	0	0.0	0.0
C /5.3	14.4	1.03	12.47	32	1	98	0	1	79	18.7	-29.2	31	7	1,000	50	5.3	0.0
C /5.3	14.5	1.04	12.32	5	1	98	0	1	79	16.9	-29.5	25	7	1,000	50	0.0	0.0
C /5.4	14.4	1.03	12.53	464	1	98	0	1	79	20.7	-29.1	37	7	0	0	0.0	0.0
C /5.4	14.4	1.03	12.49	261	1	98	0	1	79	19.7	-29.2	34	7	1,000,000	0	0.0	0.0
C /4.9	12.8	1.15	24.90	33	1	98	0	1	55	98.0	-18.2	15	8	1,000	50	5.3	0.0
C /4.9	12.8	1.15	23.99	8	1	98	0	1	55	94.7	-18.4	12	8	1,000	50	0.0	0.0
C /4.9	12.8	1.14	25.73	N/A	1	98	0	1	55	101.0	-18.0	19	8	0	0	0.0	0.0
C /5.2	12.8	1.15	25.36	280	1	98	0	1	55	99.7	-18.1	17	8	1,000,000	0	0.0	0.0
C- /3.8	15.4	1.07	25.16	72	0	99	0	1	65	99.7	-28.0	37	11	1,000	50	5.3	0.0
C- /3.6	15.4	1.07	21.32	N/A	0	99	0	1	65	96.4	-28.2	31	11	1,000	50	0.0	0.0
C- /3.6	15.4	1.07	21.26	50	0	99	0	1	65	96.3	-28.1	31	11	1,000	50	0.0	0.0
C- /3.8	15.5	1.07	27.37	432	0	99	0	1	65	101.9	-27.9	41	11	1,000,000	0	0.0	0.0
C /5.0	14.8	1.03	22.31	278	1	98	0	1	33	25.0	-24.4	61	10	1,000	50	5.3	0.0

			99 Pct = Best 0 Pct = Worst			PERFORMANCE							
							Total Return % through 3/31/15					Incl. in Returns	
			Overall			Perfor-				Annualized		Dividend	Expense
Fund Type	Fund Name	Ticker Symbol	Investment Rating	Phone		mance Rating/Pts	3 Mo	6 Mo	1Yr / Pct	3Yr / Pct	5Yr / Pct	Yield	Ratio
EM	● JPMorgan Emerg Mkt Eq B	JFBMX	E	(800) 480-4111		E / 0.5	1.62	-1.36	-0.91 /13	-0.30 / 4	0.77 / 3	0.12	2.39
EM	JPMorgan Emerg Mkt Eq C	JEMCX	E	(800) 480-4111		E / 0.5	1.64	-1.37	-0.92 /13	-0.30 / 4	0.76 / 3	0.35	2.32
EM	JPMorgan Emerg Mkt Eq Inst	JMIEX	E+	(800) 480-4111		E+ / 0.6	1.82	-0.95	-0.06 /15	0.60 / 5	1.68 / 4	1.05	1.46
EM	JPMorgan Emerg Mkt Eq R6	JEMWX	U	(800) 480-4111		U /	1.87	-0.87	0.07 /16	--	--	1.30	1.23
EM	JPMorgan Emerg Mkt Eq Sel	JEMSX	E+	(800) 480-4111		E / 0.5	1.79	-0.98	-0.17 /15	0.46 / 5	1.52 / 4	1.04	1.53
GR	JPMorgan Equity Focus A	JPFAX	C+	(800) 480-4111		C+ / 6.2	1.86	3.57	8.64 /67	15.12 /76	--	0.09	2.19
GR	JPMorgan Equity Focus C	JPFCX	C+	(800) 480-4111		C+ / 6.8	1.76	3.31	8.06 /63	14.55 /71	--	0.00	2.86
GR	JPMorgan Equity Focus Select	JPFSX	B	(800) 480-4111		B- / 7.4	1.97	3.73	8.91 /69	15.43 /78	--	0.14	1.52
IN	JPMorgan Equity Income A	OIEIX	B-	(800) 480-4111		C+ / 6.7	-0.04	6.30	10.70 /77	15.47 /79	15.29 /89	1.69	1.09
IN	● JPMorgan Equity Income B	OGIBX	B+	(800) 480-4111		B- / 7.2	-0.26	5.97	10.12 /75	14.87 /74	14.72 /84	1.35	1.61
IN	JPMorgan Equity Income C	OINCX	B+	(800) 480-4111		B- / 7.2	-0.19	6.03	10.14 /75	14.89 /74	14.71 /84	1.40	1.57
IN	JPMorgan Equity Income R2	OIEFX	A-	(800) 480-4111		B- / 7.4	-0.15	6.14	10.42 /76	15.17 /76	15.00 /87	1.59	1.39
IN	JPMorgan Equity Income R5	OIERX	A	(800) 480-4111		B / 8.0	0.00	6.51	11.16 /79	15.94 /83	15.74 /91	2.16	0.59
IN	JPMorgan Equity Income R6	OIEJX	A+	(800) 480-4111		B / 8.1	0.09	6.56	11.32 /80	16.04 /84	15.74 /91	2.22	0.51
IN	JPMorgan Equity Income Sel	HLIEX	A	(800) 480-4111		B / 7.8	-0.05	6.41	10.96 /78	15.73 /81	15.56 /90	1.97	0.79
IX	JPMorgan Equity Index A	OGEAX	C+	(800) 480-4111		C+ / 6.8	0.83	5.69	12.21 /84	15.56 /80	13.94 /77	1.40	0.91
IX	● JPMorgan Equity Index B	OGEIX	B	(800) 480-4111		B- / 7.2	0.67	5.31	11.39 /80	14.70 /72	13.08 /69	0.73	1.46
IX	JPMorgan Equity Index C	OEICX	B	(800) 480-4111		B- / 7.2	0.66	5.28	11.36 /80	14.70 /72	13.08 /69	0.83	1.42
IX	JPMorgan Equity Index Sel	HLEIX	B+	(800) 480-4111		B / 8.1	0.90	5.84	12.52 /85	15.85 /82	14.23 /80	1.69	0.65
EN	JPMorgan Glbl Natural Resources A	JGNAX	E-	(800) 480-4111		E- / 0.0	-7.38	-23.55	-26.74 / 0	-17.79 / 0	--	0.05	2.12
EN	JPMorgan Glbl Natural Resources C	JGNCX	E-	(800) 480-4111		E- / 0.0	-7.45	-23.68	-27.04 / 0	-18.19 / 0	--	0.00	2.65
EN	JPMorgan Glbl Natural Resources R2	JGNZX	E-	(800) 480-4111		E- / 0.0	-7.50	-23.59	-26.92 / 0	-18.00 / 0	--	0.00	2.28
EN	JPMorgan Glbl Natural Resources R5	JGNRX	E-	(800) 480-4111		E- / 0.0	-7.22	-23.22	-26.27 / 0	-17.37 / 0	--	0.72	1.57
EN	JPMorgan Glbl Natural Resources R6	JGRMX	E-	(800) 480-4111		E- / 0.0	-7.37	-23.32	-26.35 / 0	-17.38 / 0	--	0.81	1.50
EN	JPMorgan Glbl Natural Resources	JGNSX	E-	(800) 480-4111		E- / 0.0	-7.25	-23.36	-26.46 / 0	-17.56 / 0	--	0.53	1.73
GL	JPMorgan Global Allocation A	GAOAX	C	(800) 480-4111		C- / 3.8	4.37	6.21	7.94 /62	9.87 /39	--	2.25	1.87
GL	JPMorgan Global Allocation C	GAOCX	C	(800) 480-4111		C- / 4.1	4.27	5.92	7.42 /58	9.34 /35	--	2.14	2.36
GL	JPMorgan Global Allocation R2	GAONX	C	(800) 480-4111		C / 4.3	4.35	6.07	7.72 /61	9.62 /37	--	2.15	2.16
GL	JPMorgan Global Allocation Sel	GAOSX	C+	(800) 480-4111		C / 4.6	4.46	6.33	8.24 /64	10.16 /40	--	2.52	1.65
GL	JPMorgan Global Rsrch Enh Index	JEITX	U	(800) 480-4111		U /	2.24	3.60	6.52 /51	--	--	1.44	0.57
GL	JPMorgan Global Uncon Eqty A	JFUAX	C+	(800) 480-4111		C / 4.3	2.52	3.34	7.07 /56	11.75 /51	--	1.00	4.22
GL	JPMorgan Global Uncon Eqty C	JFECX	B-	(800) 480-4111		C / 4.8	2.41	3.10	6.51 /51	11.19 /47	--	0.63	4.72
GL	JPMorgan Global Uncon Eqty R5	JFETX	D-	(800) 480-4111		E+ / 0.6	2.63	-10.47	-7.05 / 4	3.17 / 8	--	0.00	3.76
GL	JPMorgan Global Uncon Eqty R6	JFEUX	D-	(800) 480-4111		E+ / 0.6	2.63	-10.46	-7.05 / 4	3.21 / 8	--	0.00	3.71
GL	JPMorgan Global Uncon Eqty Select	JMESX	B	(800) 480-4111		C / 5.4	2.64	3.52	7.37 /58	12.05 /53	--	1.27	3.96
GR	JPMorgan Growth Advantage A	VHIAX	B+	(800) 480-4111		A- / 9.0	6.07	11.36	16.02 /93	17.53 /92	17.12 /96	0.00	1.36
GR	● JPMorgan Growth Advantage B	VHIBX	A-	(800) 480-4111		A / 9.3	5.94	11.09	15.38 /92	16.95 /90	16.52 /95	0.00	1.85
GR	JPMorgan Growth Advantage C	JGACX	A-	(800) 480-4111		A / 9.3	5.94	11.00	15.37 /92	16.94 /89	16.54 /95	0.00	1.84
GR	JPMorgan Growth Advantage R5	JGVRX	A	(800) 480-4111		A+ / 9.6	6.17	11.53	16.39 /94	17.98 /94	17.59 /97	0.00	0.82
GR	JPMorgan Growth Advantage R6	JGVVX	U	(800) 480-4111		U /	6.23	11.59	16.54 /94	--	--	0.00	0.78
GR	JPMorgan Growth Advantage Sel	JGASX	A	(800) 480-4111		A / 9.5	6.09	11.43	16.17 /93	17.77 /93	17.36 /97	0.00	1.07
GI	JPMorgan Growth and Income A	VGRIX	A-	(800) 480-4111		B / 7.7	0.03	5.93	11.43 /80	17.12 /90	14.60 /83	1.13	1.14
GI	● JPMorgan Growth and Income B	VINBX	A	(800) 480-4111		B+ / 8.3	-0.10	5.65	10.85 /78	16.53 /87	14.02 /78	0.70	1.66
GI	JPMorgan Growth and Income C	VGICX	A	(800) 480-4111		B+ / 8.3	-0.10	5.64	10.83 /78	16.52 /87	14.03 /78	0.93	1.67
GI	JPMorgan Growth and Income Sel	VGIIX	A+	(800) 480-4111		B+ / 8.8	0.09	6.06	11.68 /81	17.42 /92	14.91 /86	1.35	0.91
GR	JPMorgan Hedged Equity A	JHQAX	U	(800) 480-4111		U /	0.84	4.89	8.55 /67	--	--	1.16	16.65
GR	JPMorgan Hedged Equity Sel	JHEQX	U	(800) 480-4111		U /	0.89	4.97	8.74 /68	--	--	1.28	9.91
GL	JPMorgan Income Builder A	JNBAX	D+	(800) 480-4111		D+ / 2.3	2.37	2.57	3.81 /31	8.23 /28	8.21 /31	4.27	1.11
GL	JPMorgan Income Builder C	JNBCX	D+	(800) 480-4111		D+ / 2.7	2.15	2.24	3.33 /28	7.67 /25	7.66 /28	4.00	1.62
GL	JPMorgan Income Builder Select	JNBSX	C-	(800) 480-4111		C- / 3.1	2.39	2.63	3.96 /32	8.38 /29	8.36 /32	4.62	0.87
FO	JPMorgan International Eq A	JSEAX	D-	(800) 480-4111		D- / 1.4	5.16	1.30	-0.49 /14	6.64 /20	5.26 /13	2.09	1.59
FO	● JPMorgan International Eq B	JSEBX	D-	(800) 480-4111		D / 1.7	5.03	1.05	-1.01 /13	6.10 /17	4.73 /11	1.84	2.16

● Denotes fund is closed to new investors
* Denotes fund is included in Section II

www.thestreetratings.com

RISK			NET ASSETS		ASSET					BULL / BEAR		FUND MANAGER		MINIMUMS		LOADS	
	3 Year		NAV						Portfolio	Last Bull	Last Bear	Manager	Manager	Initial	Additional	Front	Back
Risk	Standard		As of	Total	Cash	Stocks	Bonds	Other	Turnover	Market	Market	Quality	Tenure	Purch.	Purch.	End	End
Rating/Pts	Deviation	Beta	3/31/15	$(Mil)	%	%	%	%	Ratio	Return	Return	Pct	(Years)	$	$	Load	Load
C / 5.1	14.8	1.03	21.93	2	1	98	0	1	33	22.9	-24.5	52	10	1,000	50	0.0	0.0
C / 5.0	14.8	1.03	21.72	54	1	98	0	1	33	22.9	-24.5	52	10	1,000	50	0.0	0.0
C / 5.0	14.8	1.03	22.95	408	1	98	0	1	33	26.7	-24.2	66	10	3,000,000	0	0.0	0.0
U /	N/A	N/A	22.92	714	1	98	0	1	33	N/A	N/A	N/A	10	15,000,000	0	0.0	0.0
C / 5.1	14.8	1.03	22.78	543	1	98	0	1	33	26.0	-24.3	64	10	1,000,000	0	0.0	0.0
C+ / 6.3	11.0	1.09	24.69	1	1	98	0	1	76	103.7	N/A	34	4	1,000	50	5.3	0.0
C+ / 6.3	11.0	1.09	24.28	1	1	98	0	1	76	100.2	N/A	28	4	1,000	50	0.0	0.0
C+ / 6.3	11.1	1.09	24.85	80	1	98	0	1	76	105.4	N/A	38	4	1,000,000	0	0.0	0.0
B- / 7.6	9.3	0.94	14.00	3,015	1	98	0	1	20	92.4	-13.2	70	11	1,000	50	5.3	0.0
B- / 7.6	9.3	0.94	13.88	3	1	98	0	1	20	89.2	-13.3	64	11	1,000	50	0.0	0.0
B- / 7.6	9.3	0.95	13.81	1,126	1	98	0	1	20	89.0	-13.2	63	11	1,000	50	0.0	0.0
B- / 7.6	9.3	0.94	13.97	49	1	98	0	1	20	90.8	-13.2	N/A	11	0	0	0.0	0.0
B- / 7.6	9.3	0.94	14.20	491	1	98	0	1	20	95.3	-13.0	74	11	0	0	0.0	0.0
B- / 7.8	9.2	0.93	14.20	788	1	98	0	1	20	95.4	-13.1	76	11	15,000,000	0	0.0	0.0
B- / 7.6	9.3	0.94	14.20	4,483	1	98	0	1	20	94.1	-13.1	73	11	1,000,000	0	0.0	0.0
C+ / 6.7	9.5	1.00	41.21	707	0	99	0	1	5	97.0	-16.4	61	20	1,000	50	5.3	0.0
C+ / 6.7	9.5	1.00	41.08	7	0	99	0	1	5	92.1	-16.7	49	20	1,000	50	0.0	0.0
C+ / 6.6	9.5	1.00	40.95	91	0	99	0	1	5	92.1	-16.7	49	20	1,000	50	0.0	0.0
C+ / 6.7	9.6	1.00	41.24	1,147	0	99	0	1	5	98.8	-16.3	64	20	1,000,000	0	0.0	0.0
D- / 1.0	22.5	1.00	7.03	3	4	95	0	1	30	-31.1	-32.2	0	5	1,000	50	5.3	0.0
D- / 1.0	22.4	1.00	6.96	1	4	95	0	1	30	-32.3	-32.3	0	5	1,000	50	0.0	0.0
D- / 1.0	22.5	1.00	7.03	N/A	4	95	0	1	30	-31.7	-32.3	0	5	0	0	0.0	0.0
D- / 1.0	22.4	1.00	7.20	N/A	4	95	0	1	30	-30.0	-32.1	0	5	0	0	0.0	0.0
D- / 1.2	22.4	1.00	7.04	N/A	4	95	0	1	30	N/A	N/A	0	5	15,000,000	0	0.0	0.0
D- / 1.0	22.4	1.00	7.04	36	4	95	0	1	30	-30.5	-32.1	0	5	1,000,000	0	0.0	0.0
B- / 7.5	7.4	1.14	16.95	69	11	45	42	2	87	51.1	N/A	61	4	1,000	50	4.5	0.0
B- / 7.4	7.4	1.15	16.82	37	11	45	42	2	87	48.5	N/A	53	4	1,000	50	0.0	0.0
B- / 7.5	7.4	1.14	16.94	N/A	11	45	42	2	87	49.8	N/A	58	4	0	0	0.0	0.0
B- / 7.5	7.4	1.14	17.00	50	11	45	42	2	87	52.4	N/A	66	4	1,000,000	0	0.0	0.0
U /	N/A	N/A	18.72	6,334	3	96	0	1	40	N/A	N/A	N/A	N/A	1,000,000	0	0.0	0.0
B / 8.2	11.0	0.77	17.47	N/A	0	0	0	100	0	N/A	N/A	92	N/A	1,000	50	5.3	0.0
B / 8.2	11.0	0.77	17.40	N/A	0	0	0	100	0	N/A	N/A	91	N/A	1,000	50	0.0	0.0
C+ / 6.8	15.8	0.88	17.53	N/A	0	0	0	100	0	N/A	N/A	11	N/A	0	0	0.0	0.0
C+ / 6.8	15.8	0.88	17.54	N/A	0	0	0	100	0	N/A	N/A	11	N/A	15,000,000	0	0.0	0.0
B / 8.2	11.0	0.77	17.51	4	0	0	0	100	0	N/A	N/A	92	N/A	1,000,000	0	0.0	0.0
C+ / 5.9	11.9	1.04	15.20	1,005	3	96	0	1	62	116.9	-19.1	73	13	1,000	50	5.3	0.0
C+ / 5.8	12.0	1.04	13.73	2	3	96	0	1	62	113.9	-19.3	68	13	1,000	50	0.0	0.0
C+ / 5.8	11.9	1.04	13.74	246	3	96	0	1	62	113.4	-19.3	68	13	1,000	50	0.0	0.0
C+ / 5.9	11.9	1.04	15.67	51	3	96	0	1	62	119.9	-19.0	77	13	0	0	0.0	0.0
U /	N/A	N/A	15.69	2,254	3	96	0	1	62	N/A	N/A	N/A	13	15,000,000	0	0.0	0.0
C+ / 5.9	11.9	1.04	15.50	1,145	3	96	0	1	62	118.3	-19.1	75	13	1,000,000	0	0.0	0.0
B- / 7.3	10.0	1.02	46.00	433	2	97	0	1	42	107.7	-17.9	73	13	1,000	50	5.3	0.0
B- / 7.3	10.0	1.03	44.89	2	2	97	0	1	42	104.1	-18.1	67	13	1,000	50	0.0	0.0
B- / 7.3	10.0	1.03	42.35	23	2	97	0	1	42	104.2	-18.1	67	13	1,000	50	0.0	0.0
B- / 7.3	10.0	1.02	48.01	36	2	97	0	1	42	109.6	-17.9	75	13	1,000,000	0	0.0	0.0
U /	N/A	N/A	16.55	89	0	0	0	100	36	N/A	N/A	N/A	2	1,000	50	5.3	0.0
U /	N/A	N/A	16.58	87	0	0	0	100	36	N/A	N/A	N/A	2	1,000,000	0	0.0	0.0
B- / 7.0	6.2	0.93	10.35	4,292	4	46	46	4	41	45.5	-11.9	66	8	1,000	50	4.5	0.0
B- / 7.0	6.1	0.92	10.32	5,024	4	46	46	4	41	42.9	-12.0	60	8	1,000	50	0.0	0.0
B- / 7.0	6.2	0.93	10.36	3,143	4	46	46	4	41	46.3	-11.8	68	8	1,000,000	0	0.0	0.0
C+ / 5.9	12.5	0.93	15.54	195	3	96	0	1	6	46.9	-23.7	37	16	1,000	50	5.3	0.0
C+ / 5.9	12.6	0.94	15.00	1	3	96	0	1	6	44.5	-23.9	30	16	1,000	50	0.0	0.0

	99 Pct = Best 0 Pct = Worst				**PERFORMANCE**							
			Overall				Total Return % through 3/31/15					Incl. in Returns	
					Perfor-					Annualized		Dividend	Expense
Fund		Ticker	**Investment**		**mance**								
Type	Fund Name	Symbol	**Rating**	Phone	**Rating/Pts**	3 Mo	6 Mo	1Yr / Pct	3Yr / Pct	5Yr / Pct	Yield	Ratio
FO	JPMorgan International Eq C	JIECX	D-	(800) 480-4111	D / 1.7	4.99	1.04	-1.02 /13	6.11 /17	4.72 /11	1.93	2.04
FO	JPMorgan International Eq R2	JIEZX	D-	(800) 480-4111	D / 1.9	5.11	1.19	-0.76 /14	6.38 /18	4.99 /12	2.00	1.93
FO	JPMorgan International Eq R5	JIERX	D	(800) 480-4111	D+ / 2.3	5.27	1.50	-0.09 /15	7.13 /22	5.73 /15	2.57	1.06
FO	JPMorgan International Eq R6	JNEMX	D	(800) 480-4111	D+ / 2.3	5.28	1.59	0.01 /16	7.17 /22	5.72 /15	2.61	0.93
FO	JPMorgan International Eq Sel	VSIEX	D	(800) 480-4111	D / 2.1	5.22	1.43	-0.26 /15	6.90 /21	5.51 /14	2.40	1.23
GL	JPMorgan International Eqty Inc A	JEIAX	D+	(800) 480-4111	D+ / 2.9	2.42	3.33	2.79 /25	9.67 /37	--	5.40	1.57
GL	JPMorgan International Eqty Inc C	JEICX	D+	(800) 480-4111	C- / 3.4	2.25	3.02	2.21 /23	9.11 /34	--	5.20	2.12
GL	JPMorgan International Eqty Inc R2	JGEZX	C-	(800) 480-4111	C- / 3.5	2.29	3.13	2.45 /24	9.39 /36	--	5.42	1.78
GL	JPMorgan International Eqty Inc R5	JEIRX	C-	(800) 480-4111	C- / 4.0	2.44	3.52	3.19 /27	10.14 /40	--	6.27	1.08
GL	JPMorgan International Eqty Inc Sel	JEISX	C-	(800) 480-4111	C- / 3.9	2.47	3.44	3.01 /26	9.94 /39	--	6.03	1.33
FO	JPMorgan International Value A	JFEAX	E+	(800) 480-4111	E+ / 0.9	3.83	-1.17	-4.99 / 5	5.68 /15	4.27 / 9	3.32	1.42
FO	● JPMorgan International Value B	JFEBX	E+	(800) 480-4111	D- / 1.1	3.75	-1.34	-5.44 / 5	5.18 /14	3.75 / 8	2.47	1.98
FO	JPMorgan International Value C	JIUCX	E+	(800) 480-4111	D- / 1.1	3.69	-1.31	-5.43 / 5	5.18 /14	3.77 / 8	2.97	1.89
FO	JPMorgan International Value Inst	JNUSX	E+	(800) 480-4111	D- / 1.4	4.00	-0.90	-4.60 / 6	6.14 /17	4.71 /11	3.75	0.97
FO	JPMorgan International Value R2	JPVZX	E+	(800) 480-4111	D- / 1.2	3.81	-1.26	-5.20 / 5	5.44 /15	4.02 / 8	3.25	1.93
FO	JPMorgan International Value R6	JNVMX	E+	(800) 480-4111	D- / 1.5	3.92	-0.85	-4.48 / 6	6.23 /18	--	3.88	0.73
FO	JPMorgan International Value Sel	JIESX	E+	(800) 480-4111	D- / 1.4	3.97	-0.97	-4.65 / 6	5.98 /17	4.55 /10	3.59	1.03
FO	JPMorgan International Value SMA	JTIVX	E+	(800) 480-4111	D- / 1.0	4.02	-0.13	-6.01 / 4	4.39 /11	4.24 / 9	2.62	0.17
FO	JPMorgan Intl Opps A	JIOAX	D-	(800) 480-4111	D- / 1.3	2.98	0.39	-2.90 / 9	6.78 /20	4.88 /11	1.92	1.48
FO	● JPMorgan Intl Opps B	JIOBX	D-	(800) 480-4111	D- / 1.5	2.89	0.09	-3.42 / 8	6.27 /18	4.35 /10	1.71	2.00
FO	JPMorgan Intl Opps C	JIOCX	D-	(800) 480-4111	D- / 1.5	2.92	0.14	-3.42 / 8	6.25 /18	4.35 /10	1.96	1.83
FO	JPMorgan Intl Opps Inst	JPIOX	D-	(800) 480-4111	D / 2.0	3.08	0.60	-2.57 / 9	7.21 /22	5.29 /13	2.80	0.85
FO	JPMorgan Intl Opps R6	JIOMX	D-	(800) 480-4111	D / 2.1	3.15	0.67	-2.44 /10	7.33 /23	5.38 /14	2.94	0.74
FO	JPMorgan Intl Opps Sel	JIOSX	D-	(800) 480-4111	D / 1.9	3.02	0.46	-2.71 / 9	7.04 /22	5.12 /12	2.68	1.02
FO	JPMorgan Intl Res Enh Eq A	OEIAX	E	(800) 480-4111	D / 2.1	5.79	1.72	-1.40 /12	8.53 /30	5.00 /12	1.87	1.02
FO	● JPMorgan Intl Res Enh Eq B	OGEBX	E	(800) 480-4111	D+ / 2.5	5.62	1.46	-1.91 /11	7.93 /27	4.33 / 9	1.56	1.75
FO	JPMorgan Intl Res Enh Eq C	OIICX	E	(800) 480-4111	D+ / 2.5	5.63	1.46	-1.90 /11	7.91 /26	4.34 /10	1.60	1.57
FO	JPMorgan Intl Res Enh Eq R2	JEIZX	E	(800) 480-4111	D+ / 2.7	5.71	1.56	-1.65 /11	8.27 /29	4.73 /11	1.92	1.59
FO	JPMorgan Intl Res Enh Eq Sel	OIEAX	E	(800) 480-4111	C- / 3.1	5.81	1.82	-1.14 /13	8.80 /32	5.25 /13	2.19	0.64
GL	JPMorgan Intl Uncons Eqty A	IUAEX	D	(800) 480-4111	D+ / 2.5	5.88	5.34	2.39 /24	8.49 /30	--	0.86	5.01
GL	JPMorgan Intl Uncons Eqty C	IUCEX	D+	(800) 480-4111	C- / 3.0	5.73	5.06	1.82 /21	7.94 /27	--	0.37	6.08
GL	JPMorgan Intl Uncons Eqty R2	IUERX	D+	(800) 480-4111	C- / 3.2	5.76	5.15	2.09 /22	8.19 /28	--	0.58	5.93
GL	JPMorgan Intl Uncons Eqty R5	IUEFX	C-	(800) 480-4111	C- / 3.7	5.97	5.55	2.83 /26	8.96 /33	--	1.21	5.22
GL	JPMorgan Intl Uncons Eqty R6	IUENX	C-	(800) 480-4111	C- / 3.7	5.97	5.54	2.82 /26	9.01 /33	--	1.26	5.17
GL	JPMorgan Intl Uncons Eqty Sel	IUESX	C-	(800) 480-4111	C- / 3.5	5.92	5.47	2.64 /25	8.74 /31	--	1.04	5.43
GR	JPMorgan Intrepid Advantage A	JICAX	B+	(800) 480-4111	B- / 7.5	0.39	5.20	12.23 /84	16.70 /88	14.46 /82	0.63	2.18
GR	JPMorgan Intrepid Advantage C	JICCX	A	(800) 480-4111	B / 8.1	0.24	4.91	11.65 /81	16.11 /84	13.89 /77	0.59	2.68
GR	JPMorgan Intrepid Advantage Sel	JIISX	A+	(800) 480-4111	B+ / 8.7	0.42	5.30	12.49 /85	16.99 /90	14.75 /85	0.76	1.87
GR	JPMorgan Intrepid America A	JIAAX	A	(800) 480-4111	B / 8.2	0.93	6.78	13.61 /88	17.31 /91	14.51 /82	0.90	1.14
GR	JPMorgan Intrepid America C	JIACX	A+	(800) 480-4111	B+ / 8.7	0.83	6.54	13.06 /87	16.75 /88	13.95 /77	0.52	1.60
GR	JPMorgan Intrepid America R2	JIAZX	A+	(800) 480-4111	B+ / 8.8	0.89	6.67	13.33 /88	17.04 /90	14.23 /80	1.06	1.30
GR	JPMorgan Intrepid America R5	JIARX	A+	(800) 480-4111	A- / 9.2	1.05	7.05	14.15 /90	17.86 /94	15.04 /87	1.26	0.55
GR	JPMorgan Intrepid America Sel	JPIAX	A+	(800) 480-4111	A- / 9.1	1.02	6.94	13.93 /89	17.63 /93	14.80 /85	1.07	0.76
FO	JPMorgan Intrepid Euro A	VEUAX	D+	(800) 480-4111	C- / 3.9	4.23	0.85	-6.65 / 4	13.08 /60	8.70 /35	3.15	1.43
FO	● JPMorgan Intrepid Euro B	VEUBX	D+	(800) 480-4111	C / 4.4	4.10	0.57	-7.16 / 4	12.52 /56	8.14 /31	2.86	2.01
FO	JPMorgan Intrepid Euro C	VEUCX	D+	(800) 480-4111	C / 4.4	4.06	0.59	-7.16 / 4	12.51 /56	8.14 /31	3.31	1.91
FO	JPMorgan Intrepid Euro Inst	JFEIX	C-	(800) 480-4111	C / 5.1	4.33	1.11	-6.26 / 4	13.60 /64	9.21 /38	3.67	0.91
FO	JPMorgan Intrepid Euro Sel	JFESX	C-	(800) 480-4111	C / 4.9	4.30	0.99	-6.41 / 4	13.37 /62	8.96 /36	3.62	1.08
GR	JPMorgan Intrepid Growth A	JIGAX	A-	(800) 480-4111	B / 7.9	1.12	6.62	15.32 /92	16.61 /87	15.07 /87	0.45	1.20
GR	JPMorgan Intrepid Growth C	JCICX	A+	(800) 480-4111	B+ / 8.4	1.01	6.36	14.78 /91	16.04 /84	14.51 /82	0.14	1.71
GR	JPMorgan Intrepid Growth R2	JIGZX	A+	(800) 480-4111	B+ / 8.6	1.08	6.51	15.06 /92	16.33 /86	14.79 /85	0.16	1.45
GR	JPMorgan Intrepid Growth R5	JGIRX	A+	(800) 480-4111	A- / 9.1	1.24	6.88	15.88 /93	17.14 /91	15.59 /91	0.71	0.72

● Denotes fund is closed to new investors
* Denotes fund is included in Section II

RISK			NET ASSETS		ASSET					BULL / BEAR		FUND MANAGER		MINIMUMS		LOADS	
Risk Rating/Pts	3 Year		NAV As of 3/31/15	Total $(Mil)	Cash %	Stocks %	Bonds %	Other %	Portfolio Turnover Ratio	Last Bull Market Return	Last Bear Market Return	Manager Quality Pct	Manager Tenure (Years)	Initial Purch. $	Additional Purch. $	Front End Load	Back End Load
	Standard Deviation	Beta															
C+ / 5.9	12.5	0.93	14.79	27	3	96	0	1	6	44.4	-23.8	30	16	1,000	50	0.0	0.0
C+ / 5.9	12.5	0.93	15.48	1	3	96	0	1	6	45.6	-23.7	33	16	0	0	0.0	0.0
C+ / 6.0	12.5	0.93	15.76	60	3	96	0	1	6	49.2	-23.6	43	16	0	0	0.0	0.0
C+ / 5.9	12.5	0.93	15.76	1,855	3	96	0	1	6	49.3	-23.5	44	16	15,000,000	0	0.0	0.0
C+ / 5.9	12.5	0.93	15.75	522	3	96	0	1	6	48.1	-23.6	40	16	1,000,000	0	0.0	0.0
C+ / 6.4	9.9	0.71	16.26	45	4	95	0	1	138	54.2	-19.4	88	4	1,000	50	5.3	0.0
C+ / 6.4	9.9	0.71	16.19	4	4	95	0	1	138	51.5	-19.6	86	4	1,000	50	0.0	0.0
C+ / 6.4	9.9	0.71	16.24	1	4	95	0	1	138	52.9	-19.6	87	4	0	0	0.0	0.0
C+ / 6.4	10.0	0.71	16.30	1	4	95	0	1	138	56.5	-19.3	89	4	0	0	0.0	0.0
C+ / 6.4	9.9	0.71	16.29	26	4	95	0	1	138	55.6	-19.4	89	4	1,000,000	0	0.0	0.0
C / 5.1	14.2	1.06	13.54	583	1	98	0	1	59	41.2	-25.4	15	13	1,000	50	5.3	0.0
C / 5.2	14.3	1.06	13.54	1	1	98	0	1	59	38.8	-25.5	12	13	1,000	50	0.0	0.0
C / 5.1	14.2	1.06	13.19	29	1	98	0	1	59	38.8	-25.5	12	13	1,000	50	0.0	0.0
C / 5.0	14.2	1.06	13.79	2,675	1	98	0	1	59	43.0	-25.2	19	13	3,000,000	0	0.0	0.0
C / 5.1	14.2	1.06	13.36	2	1	98	0	1	59	39.9	-25.4	14	13	0	0	0.0	0.0
C / 5.0	14.2	1.06	13.79	7	1	98	0	1	59	43.7	-25.2	19	13	15,000,000	0	0.0	0.0
C / 5.1	14.2	1.06	13.88	264	1	98	0	1	59	42.4	-25.3	17	13	1,000,000	0	0.0	0.0
C / 5.2	13.7	1.00	12.42	341	2	97	0	1	85	37.2	-25.4	11	8	0	0	0.0	0.0
C+ / 5.7	13.4	0.99	14.51	129	4	95	0	1	55	47.5	-24.8	31	15	1,000	50	5.3	0.0
C+ / 5.7	13.3	0.99	14.61	N/A	4	95	0	1	55	44.9	-24.9	26	15	1,000	50	0.0	0.0
C+ / 5.7	13.4	0.99	14.11	2	4	95	0	1	55	45.0	-25.0	26	15	1,000	50	0.0	0.0
C+ / 5.6	13.3	0.99	14.74	45	4	95	0	1	55	49.5	-24.6	36	15	3,000,000	0	0.0	0.0
C+ / 5.6	13.3	0.99	14.73	1,624	4	95	0	1	55	50.0	-24.6	38	15	15,000,000	0	0.0	0.0
C+ / 5.6	13.3	0.99	14.68	51	4	95	0	1	55	48.8	-24.7	35	15	1,000,000	0	0.0	0.0
D / 2.1	14.1	1.06	16.99	90	3	96	0	1	63	49.1	-25.7	46	1	1,000	50	5.3	0.0
D / 1.9	14.1	1.06	15.42	1	3	96	0	1	63	46.2	-25.9	37	1	1,000	50	0.0	0.0
D / 2.0	14.1	1.06	16.33	20	3	96	0	1	63	46.1	-25.9	37	1	1,000	50	0.0	0.0
D / 2.0	14.1	1.06	16.67	3	3	96	0	1	63	47.9	-25.8	42	1	0	0	0.0	0.0
D / 2.1	14.1	1.06	17.12	672	3	96	0	1	63	50.4	-25.6	49	1	1,000,000	0	0.0	0.0
C+ / 6.6	12.6	0.91	17.82	1	2	97	0	1	63	N/A	N/A	65	4	1,000	50	5.3	0.0
C+ / 6.5	12.7	0.92	17.72	N/A	2	97	0	1	63	N/A	N/A	57	4	1,000	50	0.0	0.0
C+ / 6.5	12.7	0.92	17.81	N/A	2	97	0	1	63	N/A	N/A	61	4	0	0	0.0	0.0
C+ / 6.5	12.7	0.92	17.92	N/A	2	97	0	1	63	N/A	N/A	70	4	0	0	0.0	0.0
C+ / 6.6	12.6	0.91	17.92	N/A	2	97	0	1	63	N/A	N/A	71	4	15,000,000	0	0.0	0.0
C+ / 6.6	12.6	0.92	17.89	13	2	97	0	1	63	N/A	N/A	68	4	1,000,000	0	0.0	0.0
B- / 7.3	10.3	1.06	33.68	11	2	97	0	1	49	108.9	-19.7	62	10	1,000	50	5.3	0.0
B- / 7.3	10.3	1.06	33.00	7	2	97	0	1	49	105.2	-19.8	54	10	0	0	0.0	0.0
B- / 7.3	10.3	1.06	33.86	5	2	97	0	1	49	110.6	-19.6	65	10	1,000,000	0	0.0	0.0
B- / 7.3	10.1	1.04	38.07	179	2	97	0	1	67	106.1	-18.5	72	10	1,000	50	5.3	0.0
B- / 7.2	10.1	1.04	37.79	14	2	97	0	1	67	102.5	-18.6	67	10	1,000	50	0.0	0.0
B- / 7.2	10.1	1.04	37.47	3	2	97	0	1	67	104.3	-18.6	69	10	0	0	0.0	0.0
B- / 7.2	10.0	1.04	38.36	1,883	2	97	0	1	67	109.3	-18.3	76	10	0	0	0.0	0.0
B- / 7.3	10.1	1.04	38.46	1,510	2	97	0	1	67	107.9	-18.4	74	10	1,000,000	0	0.0	0.0
C / 5.2	15.8	1.12	24.39	184	4	95	0	1	197	77.6	-27.5	85	10	1,000	50	5.3	0.0
C / 5.2	15.8	1.12	22.07	2	4	95	0	1	197	74.5	-27.7	81	10	1,000	50	0.0	0.0
C / 5.1	15.8	1.12	21.81	60	4	95	0	1	197	74.6	-27.7	82	10	1,000	50	0.0	0.0
C / 5.2	15.8	1.12	25.04	374	4	95	0	1	197	80.4	-27.4	87	10	3,000,000	0	0.0	0.0
C / 5.2	15.8	1.12	24.75	457	4	95	0	1	197	79.1	-27.4	86	10	1,000,000	0	0.0	0.0
B- / 7.4	10.1	1.02	40.64	85	3	96	0	1	67	102.6	-16.9	69	10	1,000	50	5.3	0.0
B- / 7.4	10.1	1.02	39.97	46	3	96	0	1	67	99.2	-17.1	63	10	1,000	50	0.0	0.0
B- / 7.4	10.1	1.02	40.08	1	3	96	0	1	67	100.8	-17.0	66	10	0	0	0.0	0.0
B- / 7.4	10.1	1.02	40.73	162	3	96	0	1	67	105.7	-16.7	74	10	0	0	0.0	0.0

Fund Type	Fund Name	Ticker Symbol	Overall Investment Rating	Phone	Performance Rating/Pts	3 Mo	6 Mo	1Yr / Pct	3Yr / Pct	5Yr / Pct	Dividend Yield	Expense Ratio
GR	JPMorgan Intrepid Growth Sel	JPGSX	A+	(800) 480-4111	A- / 9.0	1.21	6.76	15.62 /93	16.91 /89	15.37 /89	0.52	0.88
FO	JPMorgan Intrepid Int A	JFTAX	D	(800) 480-4111	D / 2.2	5.45	1.85	-1.37 /12	8.64 /31	6.14 /18	1.03	1.45
FO	JPMorgan Intrepid Int C	JIICX	D	(800) 480-4111	D+ / 2.6	5.27	1.58	-1.89 /11	8.08 /27	5.60 /15	0.50	1.87
FO	JPMorgan Intrepid Int Inst	JFTIX	D+	(800) 480-4111	C- / 3.3	5.49	2.05	-0.92 /13	9.15 /34	6.66 /21	1.48	0.84
FO	JPMorgan Intrepid Int R2	JIIZX	D	(800) 480-4111	D+ / 2.8	5.31	1.69	-1.65 /11	8.35 /29	5.87 /16	0.73	1.59
FO	JPMorgan Intrepid Int Sel	JISIX	D	(800) 480-4111	C- / 3.1	5.46	1.95	-1.16 /12	8.90 /32	6.40 /19	1.20	1.07
MC	JPMorgan Intrepid Mid Cap A	PECAX	B+	(800) 480-4111	A / 9.5	3.00	11.17	15.26 /92	19.61 /97	15.79 /92	0.38	1.39
MC	● JPMorgan Intrepid Mid Cap B	ODMBX	B+	(800) 480-4111	A+ / 9.6	2.86	10.82	14.49 /91	18.85 /96	15.06 /87	0.09	1.95
MC	JPMorgan Intrepid Mid Cap C	ODMCX	B+	(800) 480-4111	A+ / 9.6	2.86	10.85	14.49 /91	18.85 /96	15.07 /87	0.13	1.93
MC	JPMorgan Intrepid Mid Cap Sel	WOOPX	A-	(800) 480-4111	A+ / 9.7	3.10	11.37	15.58 /93	19.90 /98	16.10 /93	0.51	1.08
GR	JPMorgan Intrepid Value A	JIVAX	B+	(800) 480-4111	B / 7.7	-0.21	4.61	10.86 /78	17.27 /91	13.87 /77	1.10	1.10
GR	JPMorgan Intrepid Value C	JIVCX	A-	(800) 480-4111	B / 8.2	-0.35	4.34	10.30 /76	16.69 /88	13.30 /71	0.75	1.62
GR	JPMorgan Intrepid Value R2	JIVZX	A	(800) 480-4111	B+ / 8.4	-0.29	4.47	10.56 /77	16.97 /90	13.58 /74	1.11	1.43
GR	JPMorgan Intrepid Value R5	JIVRX	A+	(800) 480-4111	B+ / 8.9	-0.15	4.80	11.26 /79	17.69 /93	14.28 /80	1.44	0.59
GR	JPMorgan Intrepid Value R6	JIVMX	A+	(800) 480-4111	B+ / 8.9	-0.14	4.82	11.31 /80	17.74 /93	14.30 /80	1.49	0.53
GR	JPMorgan Intrepid Value Sel	JPIVX	A	(800) 480-4111	B+ / 8.7	-0.21	4.68	11.01 /78	17.45 /92	14.05 /78	1.27	0.88
AA	JPMorgan Investor Balanced A	OGIAX	C	(800) 480-4111	D+ / 2.6	1.49	3.78	6.32 /49	8.43 /29	7.82 /29	1.70	1.55
AA	● JPMorgan Investor Balanced B	OGBBX	C+	(800) 480-4111	C- / 3.0	1.33	3.57	5.80 /45	7.88 /26	7.26 /25	1.30	2.08
AA	JPMorgan Investor Balanced C	OGBCX	C+	(800) 480-4111	C- / 3.0	1.35	3.60	5.82 /45	7.88 /26	7.26 /25	1.33	2.05
AA	JPMorgan Investor Balanced Sel	OIBFX	C+	(800) 480-4111	C- / 3.5	1.55	3.91	6.57 /51	8.70 /31	8.07 /30	2.02	1.29
AA	JPMorgan Investor Conserv Gr A	OICAX	C-	(800) 480-4111	D- / 1.5	1.26	2.86	4.85 /37	6.06 /17	6.05 /17	1.62	1.50
AA	● JPMorgan Investor Conserv Gr B	OICGX	C	(800) 480-4111	D / 1.7	1.10	2.65	4.35 /34	5.53 /15	5.50 /14	1.22	2.03
AA	JPMorgan Investor Conserv Gr C	OCGCX	C	(800) 480-4111	D / 1.7	1.12	2.65	4.38 /34	5.54 /15	5.51 /14	1.24	2.00
AA	JPMorgan Investor Conserv Gr Sel	ONCFX	C	(800) 480-4111	D / 2.1	1.31	3.04	5.14 /40	6.36 /18	6.32 /19	1.90	1.24
GI	JPMorgan Investor Gr & Inc A	ONGIX	C+	(800) 480-4111	C- / 3.7	1.78	4.53	7.33 /58	10.33 /41	9.38 /40	1.78	1.62
GI	● JPMorgan Investor Gr & Inc B	ONEBX	C+	(800) 480-4111	C- / 4.1	1.62	4.31	6.89 /54	9.76 /38	8.83 /36	1.43	2.15
GI	JPMorgan Investor Gr & Inc C	ONECX	C+	(800) 480-4111	C- / 4.1	1.65	4.39	6.85 /54	9.78 /38	8.83 /36	1.48	2.12
GI	JPMorgan Investor Gr & Inc Sel	ONGFX	C+	(800) 480-4111	C / 4.6	1.81	4.67	7.57 /60	10.60 /43	9.66 /42	2.14	1.36
GR	JPMorgan Investor Growth A	ONGAX	C+	(800) 480-4111	C / 5.5	1.97	5.87	9.50 /72	13.08 /60	11.26 /55	1.86	1.61
GR	● JPMorgan Investor Growth B	OGIGX	B-	(800) 480-4111	C+ / 5.8	1.84	5.65	8.99 /69	12.46 /56	10.67 /50	1.77	2.15
GR	JPMorgan Investor Growth C	OGGCX	B-	(800) 480-4111	C+ / 5.8	1.82	5.65	8.99 /69	12.47 /56	10.66 /50	1.80	2.12
GR	JPMorgan Investor Growth Sel	ONIFX	B-	(800) 480-4111	C+ / 6.4	2.06	6.02	9.84 /74	13.36 /62	11.55 /57	2.16	1.33
GR	JPMorgan Large Cap Growth A	OLGAX	C+	(800) 480-4111	C+ / 6.8	4.37	9.26	17.14 /95	13.63 /64	15.91 /92	0.00	1.21
GR	● JPMorgan Large Cap Growth B	OGLGX	B-	(800) 480-4111	B- / 7.4	4.23	9.00	16.54 /94	13.07 /60	15.33 /89	0.00	1.69
GR	JPMorgan Large Cap Growth C	OLGCX	B-	(800) 480-4111	B- / 7.4	4.24	8.99	16.56 /94	13.07 /60	15.33 /89	0.00	1.69
GR	JPMorgan Large Cap Growth R2	JLGZX	B	(800) 480-4111	B / 7.6	4.29	9.14	16.83 /94	13.35 /62	15.62 /91	0.00	1.50
GR	JPMorgan Large Cap Growth R5	JLGRX	B	(800) 480-4111	B / 8.1	4.44	9.44	17.56 /95	14.05 /67	16.34 /94	0.00	0.71
GR	JPMorgan Large Cap Growth R6	JLGMX	B+	(800) 480-4111	B / 8.2	4.49	9.52	17.63 /95	14.11 /68	16.38 /94	0.00	0.61
GR	JPMorgan Large Cap Growth Sel	SEEGX	B	(800) 480-4111	B / 7.9	4.39	9.33	17.32 /95	13.83 /66	16.11 /93	0.00	0.91
GR	JPMorgan Large Cap Value A	OLVAX	C+	(800) 480-4111	B- / 7.4	0.16	6.44	11.74 /81	16.51 /87	12.67 /65	0.92	1.08
GR	● JPMorgan Large Cap Value B	OLVBX	C+	(800) 480-4111	B / 7.9	0.00	6.12	11.19 /79	15.89 /82	12.12 /61	0.48	1.64
GR	JPMorgan Large Cap Value C	OLVCX	C+	(800) 480-4111	B / 7.9	-0.03	6.18	11.20 /79	15.91 /83	12.10 /61	0.58	1.61
GR	JPMorgan Large Cap Value R2	JLVZX	B-	(800) 480-4111	B / 8.2	0.03	6.29	11.43 /80	16.20 /85	12.39 /63	0.79	1.55
GR	JPMorgan Large Cap Value R5	JLVRX	B	(800) 480-4111	B+ / 8.6	0.19	6.65	12.16 /83	16.90 /89	13.10 /69	1.26	0.58
GR	JPMorgan Large Cap Value R6	JLVMX	B	(800) 480-4111	B+ / 8.7	0.21	6.64	12.20 /83	16.93 /89	13.08 /69	1.31	0.53
GR	JPMorgan Large Cap Value Sel	HLQVX	B-	(800) 480-4111	B+ / 8.5	0.14	6.47	11.92 /82	16.64 /88	12.85 /67	1.10	0.78
FO	JPMorgan Latin America A	JLTAX	E-	(800) 480-4111	E- / 0.1	-10.33	-20.98	-20.06 / 1	-11.48 / 1	-5.32 / 1	0.22	1.99
FO	JPMorgan Latin America C	JLTCX	E-	(800) 480-4111	E- / 0.1	-10.46	-21.22	-20.48 / 1	-11.92 / 1	-5.80 / 1	0.11	2.48
FO	JPMorgan Latin America Sel	JLTSX	E-	(800) 480-4111	E- / 0.1	-10.27	-20.87	-19.83 / 1	-11.25 / 1	-5.08 / 1	0.60	1.61
MC	JPMorgan Market Expnsion En Idx A	OMEAX	B	(800) 480-4111	B+ / 8.6	5.12	12.59	12.30 /84	17.39 /92	15.35 /89	0.67	0.98
MC	● JPMorgan Market Expnsion En Idx B	OMEBX	B+	(800) 480-4111	A- / 9.0	4.97	12.26	11.59 /81	16.60 /87	14.56 /83	0.14	1.52
MC	JPMorgan Market Expnsion En Idx C	OMECX	B+	(800) 480-4111	A- / 9.0	4.92	12.30	11.64 /81	16.61 /87	14.56 /83	0.23	1.51

● Denotes fund is closed to new investors
* Denotes fund is included in Section II

RISK			NET ASSETS		ASSET					BULL / BEAR		FUND MANAGER		MINIMUMS		LOADS	
	3 Year		NAV						Portfolio	Last Bull	Last Bear	Manager	Manager	Initial	Additional	Front	Back
Risk Rating/Pts	Standard Deviation	Beta	As of 3/31/15	Total $(Mil)	Cash %	Stocks %	Bonds %	Other %	Turnover Ratio	Market Return	Market Return	Quality Pct	Tenure (Years)	Purch. $	Purch. $	End Load	End Load
B- /7.4	10.1	1.02	40.90	699	3	96	0	1	67	104.3	-16.8	72	10	1,000,000	0	0.0	0.0
C+ /5.9	13.3	1.00	19.75	124	4	95	0	1	48	52.7	-25.9	55	10	1,000	50	5.3	0.0
C+ /5.9	13.3	1.00	19.97	2	4	95	0	1	48	50.1	-26.1	48	10	1,000	50	0.0	0.0
C+ /5.9	13.4	1.00	20.17	1,689	4	95	0	1	48	55.4	-25.7	62	10	3,000,000	0	0.0	0.0
C+ /5.9	13.4	1.00	19.62	N/A	4	95	0	1	48	51.4	-26.0	51	10	0	0	0.0	0.0
C+ /5.9	13.4	1.00	20.49	17	4	95	0	1	48	54.0	-25.8	59	10	1,000,000	0	0.0	0.0
C /5.2	10.7	0.95	22.66	364	4	95	0	1	64	117.9	-23.1	89	7	1,000	50	5.3	0.0
C /4.8	10.7	0.94	19.81	4	4	95	0	1	64	113.3	-23.3	87	7	1,000	50	0.0	0.0
C /4.8	10.7	0.94	19.81	76	4	95	0	1	64	113.3	-23.3	86	7	1,000	50	0.0	0.0
C /5.3	10.7	0.94	23.64	513	4	95	0	1	64	119.7	-23.0	90	7	1,000,000	0	0.0	0.0
C+ /6.9	10.3	1.05	35.72	167	3	96	0	1	49	104.4	-19.3	71	10	1,000	50	5.3	0.0
C+ /6.9	10.3	1.04	35.35	50	3	96	0	1	49	100.9	-19.4	65	10	1,000	50	0.0	0.0
C+ /6.9	10.3	1.05	35.54	13	3	96	0	1	49	102.6	-19.3	67	10	0	0	0.0	0.0
C+ /6.9	10.3	1.04	35.94	85	3	96	0	1	49	106.8	-19.1	74	10	0	0	0.0	0.0
C+ /6.9	10.3	1.05	35.94	32	3	96	0	1	49	107.1	-19.1	75	10	15,000,000	0	0.0	0.0
C+ /6.9	10.3	1.05	35.85	1,422	3	96	0	1	49	105.5	-19.2	72	10	1,000,000	0	0.0	0.0
B /8.9	5.6	0.97	15.20	3,950	15	51	33	1	12	46.0	-10.4	37	19	1,000	50	4.5	0.0
B /8.9	5.6	0.98	15.20	68	15	51	33	1	12	43.5	-10.6	30	19	1,000	50	0.0	0.0
B /8.9	5.6	0.97	15.00	1,148	15	51	33	1	12	43.5	-10.6	31	18	1,000	50	0.0	0.0
B+ /9.0	5.6	0.98	15.22	345	15	51	33	1	12	47.2	-10.3	40	19	1,000,000	0	0.0	0.0
B+ /9.3	3.8	0.66	12.88	2,568	16	32	50	2	20	30.9	-6.1	54	19	1,000	50	4.5	0.0
B+ /9.3	3.8	0.65	12.89	36	16	32	50	2	20	28.6	-6.3	46	19	1,000	50	0.0	0.0
B+ /9.4	3.7	0.64	12.83	1,792	16	32	50	2	20	28.5	-6.3	48	18	1,000	50	0.0	0.0
B+ /9.4	3.8	0.65	12.95	129	16	32	50	2	20	32.1	-6.0	59	19	1,000,000	0	0.0	0.0
B /8.3	7.3	0.74	17.05	2,583	11	67	20	2	10	60.4	-14.1	48	19	1,000	50	4.5	0.0
B /8.3	7.3	0.75	16.97	70	11	67	20	2	10	57.7	-14.3	39	19	1,000	50	0.0	0.0
B /8.2	7.2	0.74	16.65	412	11	67	20	2	10	57.6	-14.3	40	18	1,000	50	0.0	0.0
B /8.3	7.3	0.75	16.82	248	11	67	20	2	10	61.8	-14.0	51	19	1,000,000	0	0.0	0.0
B- /7.3	9.4	0.96	19.91	1,916	5	87	5	3	8	80.4	-18.2	36	19	1,000	50	4.5	0.0
B- /7.3	9.4	0.96	19.34	66	5	87	5	3	8	77.2	-18.4	29	19	1,000	50	0.0	0.0
B- /7.3	9.4	0.96	18.98	259	5	87	5	3	8	77.3	-18.4	29	18	1,000	50	0.0	0.0
B- /7.3	9.4	0.96	20.25	242	5	87	5	3	8	82.0	-18.1	40	19	1,000,000	0	0.0	0.0
C+ /5.9	11.6	1.02	36.04	4,929	3	96	0	1	39	89.5	-13.1	32	11	1,000	50	5.3	0.0
C+ /5.9	11.6	1.02	31.53	6	3	96	0	1	39	86.4	-13.3	26	11	1,000	50	0.0	0.0
C+ /5.9	11.6	1.02	31.22	582	3	96	0	1	39	86.3	-13.2	26	11	1,000	50	0.0	0.0
C+ /5.9	11.6	1.02	35.50	246	3	96	0	1	39	87.9	-13.1	29	11	0	0	0.0	0.0
C+ /5.9	11.6	1.02	36.43	1,416	3	96	0	1	39	92.0	-12.9	36	11	0	0	0.0	0.0
C+ /5.9	11.6	1.02	36.51	3,068	3	96	0	1	39	92.3	-12.9	37	11	15,000,000	0	0.0	0.0
C+ /5.9	11.6	1.01	36.12	5,473	3	96	0	1	39	90.6	-13.0	34	11	1,000,000	0	0.0	0.0
C /4.8	11.7	1.15	14.92	93	1	98	0	1	168	105.0	-21.5	38	4	1,000	50	5.3	0.0
C /4.8	11.6	1.15	14.66	1	1	98	0	1	168	101.4	-21.6	31	4	1,000	50	0.0	0.0
C /4.8	11.6	1.15	14.50	14	1	98	0	1	168	101.4	-21.6	32	4	1,000	50	0.0	0.0
C /4.8	11.6	1.15	14.86	1	1	98	0	1	168	103.0	-21.5	35	4	0	0	0.0	0.0
C /4.8	11.6	1.15	14.83	4	1	98	0	1	168	107.4	-21.3	44	4	0	0	0.0	0.0
C /4.8	11.6	1.15	14.76	2	1	98	0	1	168	107.6	-21.3	44	4	15,000,000	0	0.0	0.0
C /4.8	11.6	1.15	14.69	638	1	98	0	1	168	105.9	-21.3	40	4	1,000,000	0	0.0	0.0
D /2.2	18.8	1.04	13.80	18	2	97	0	1	58	-7.3	-24.6	0	8	1,000	50	5.3	0.0
D /2.2	18.8	1.04	13.53	3	2	97	0	1	58	-8.8	-24.8	0	8	1,000	50	0.0	0.0
D /2.2	18.8	1.04	13.89	61	2	97	0	1	58	-6.5	-24.5	0	8	1,000,000	0	0.0	0.0
C /5.4	11.3	1.02	13.11	112	3	96	0	1	25	105.9	-23.3	68	2	1,000	50	5.3	0.0
C /5.3	11.4	1.02	12.46	1	3	96	0	1	25	101.3	-23.6	56	2	1,000	50	0.0	0.0
C /5.1	11.3	1.02	11.74	24	3	96	0	1	25	101.0	-23.5	58	2	1,000	50	0.0	0.0

Fund Type	Fund Name	Ticker Symbol	Overall Investment Rating	Phone	Performance Rating/Pts	3 Mo	6 Mo	1Yr / Pct	3Yr / Pct	5Yr / Pct	Dividend Yield	Expense Ratio
MC	JPMorgan Market Expnsion En Idx	JMEZX	B+	(800) 480-4111	A- / 9.2	5.11	12.59	12.09 /83	17.11 /90	15.01 /87	0.52	1.32
MC	JPMorgan Market Expnsion En Idx	PGMIX	B+	(800) 480-4111	A / 9.4	5.23	12.79	12.63 /85	17.70 /93	15.64 /91	0.90	0.67
IN	JPMorgan Market Neutral A	HSKAX	C-	(800) 480-4111	E / 0.3	-1.15	-0.61	1.32 /19	-0.77 / 4	-1.53 / 2	0.00	4.66
IN	JPMorgan Market Neutral C	HSKCX	C-	(800) 480-4111	E / 0.4	-1.26	-0.85	0.86 /18	-1.25 / 3	-2.02 / 2	0.00	5.02
IN	JPMorgan Market Neutral Sel	HSKSX	C-	(800) 480-4111	E / 0.5	-1.13	-0.54	1.57 /20	-0.51 / 4	-1.29 / 2	0.00	4.21
MC	● JPMorgan Mid Cap Equity A	JCMAX	A	(800) 480-4111	A- / 9.1	4.85	11.49	13.95 /89	18.20 /95	16.42 /94	0.10	1.41
MC	● JPMorgan Mid Cap Equity C	JMCCX	A+	(800) 480-4111	A / 9.3	4.73	11.22	13.40 /88	17.60 /93	15.84 /92	0.01	1.91
GI	JPMorgan Mid Cap Equity R6	JPPEX	U	(800) 480-4111	U /	4.97	11.76	14.52 /91	--	--	0.37	0.72
MC	● JPMorgan Mid Cap Equity Sel	VSNGX	A+	(800) 480-4111	A+ / 9.6	4.95	11.68	14.36 /90	18.60 /96	16.82 /95	0.26	1.18
MC	JPMorgan Mid Cap Gr A	OSGIX	B	(800) 480-4111	B+ / 8.8	6.25	11.02	13.00 /87	17.74 /93	16.36 /94	0.00	1.34
MC	● JPMorgan Mid Cap Gr B	OGOBX	C+	(800) 480-4111	A- / 9.2	6.05	10.74	12.41 /84	17.15 /91	15.77 /92	0.00	1.90
MC	JPMorgan Mid Cap Gr C	OMGCX	B	(800) 480-4111	A- / 9.2	6.09	10.73	12.46 /85	17.17 /91	15.77 /92	0.00	1.87
MC	JPMorgan Mid Cap Gr R2	JMGZX	B+	(800) 480-4111	A / 9.3	6.17	10.95	12.83 /86	17.57 /93	16.18 /94	0.00	1.65
MC	JPMorgan Mid Cap Gr R5	JMGFX	A	(800) 480-4111	A / 9.5	6.33	11.27	13.48 /88	18.28 /95	16.85 /96	0.00	0.89
MC	JPMorgan Mid Cap Gr R6	JMGMX	A	(800) 480-4111	A / 9.5	6.35	11.32	13.57 /88	18.34 /95	16.89 /96	0.00	0.78
MC	JPMorgan Mid Cap Gr Sel	HLGEX	B+	(800) 480-4111	A / 9.5	6.33	11.22	13.36 /88	18.11 /95	16.74 /95	0.00	1.11
MC	● JPMorgan Mid Cap Value A	JAMCX	A+	(800) 480-4111	A / 9.3	3.56	11.97	15.15 /92	18.96 /97	16.68 /95	0.47	1.40
MC	● JPMorgan Mid Cap Value B	JBMCX	A+	(800) 480-4111	A / 9.5	3.44	11.67	14.55 /91	18.37 /95	16.09 /93	0.00	1.89
MC	● JPMorgan Mid Cap Value C	JCMVX	A+	(800) 480-4111	A / 9.5	3.42	11.68	14.55 /91	18.35 /95	16.08 /93	0.15	1.84
MC	● JPMorgan Mid Cap Value Inst	FLMVX	A+	(800) 480-4111	A+ / 9.7	3.69	12.26	15.70 /93	19.55 /97	17.26 /96	0.97	0.93
MC	● JPMorgan Mid Cap Value R2	JMVZX	A+	(800) 480-4111	A+ / 9.6	3.51	11.83	14.84 /91	18.66 /95	16.37 /94	0.39	1.68
MC	● JPMorgan Mid Cap Value Sel	JMVSX	A+	(800) 480-4111	A+ / 9.7	3.64	12.11	15.42 /92	19.26 /97	16.97 /96	0.72	1.13
AA	JPMorgan Multi-Cap Mrkt Netral A	OGNAX	C-	(800) 480-4111	E / 0.4	-1.79	-0.10	0.61 /17	0.51 / 5	-0.22 / 2	0.00	3.31
AA	● JPMorgan Multi-Cap Mrkt Netral B	OGNBX	C-	(800) 480-4111	E / 0.5	-1.89	-0.21	0.21 /16	-0.04 / 4	-0.84 / 2	0.00	3.92
AA	JPMorgan Multi-Cap Mrkt Netral C	OGNCX	C-	(800) 480-4111	E / 0.5	-1.89	-0.21	0.21 /16	-0.04 / 4	-0.85 / 2	0.00	3.84
AA	JPMorgan Multi-Cap Mrkt Netral Sel	OGNIX	C-	(800) 480-4111	E / 0.5	-1.75	0.10	0.90 /18	0.77 / 5	0.04 / 2	0.00	2.96
GR	JPMorgan Opportunistic Eqty L/S Sel	JOEQX	U	(800) 480-4111	U /	4.74	10.33	--	--	--	0.00	2.35
RE	JPMorgan Realty Income A	URTAX	C+	(800) 480-4111	B+ / 8.6	4.48	19.95	24.79 /98	13.05 /60	15.48 /90	1.14	1.40
RE	● JPMorgan Realty Income B	URTBX	C+	(800) 480-4111	A- / 9.0	4.39	19.63	24.27 /98	12.47 /56	14.90 /86	1.08	1.90
RE	JPMorgan Realty Income C	URTCX	C+	(800) 480-4111	A- / 9.0	4.36	19.71	24.29 /98	12.48 /56	14.88 /86	1.12	1.90
RE	JPMorgan Realty Income I	URTLX	B-	(800) 480-4111	A / 9.4	4.61	20.17	25.31 /98	13.48 /63	15.95 /93	1.30	1.00
RE	JPMorgan Realty Income R5	JRIRX	B-	(800) 480-4111	A / 9.4	4.62	20.18	25.43 /98	13.55 /64	16.00 /93	1.33	0.95
GR	JPMorgan Research Equity L/S A	JLSAX	C-	(800) 480-4111	D- / 1.0	-0.95	0.77	3.14 /27	5.34 /14	--	0.00	4.10
GR	JPMorgan Research Equity L/S C	JLSCX	C-	(800) 480-4111	D- / 1.3	-0.97	0.61	2.65 /25	4.84 /13	--	Incl.	4.59
GR	JPMorgan Research Equity L/S R5	JLSRX	C-	(800) 480-4111	D / 1.7	-0.75	1.05	3.62 /30	5.84 /16	--	0.00	3.58
GR	JPMorgan Research Equity L/S Sel	JLSSX	C-	(800) 480-4111	D / 1.6	-0.88	0.94	3.42 /29	5.62 /15	--	0.00	3.79
IN	JPMorgan Research Market Neut A	JMNAX	C-	(800) 480-4111	E / 0.5	-1.08	-0.36	1.32 /19	1.33 / 6	-0.41 / 2	0.00	4.35
IN	● JPMorgan Research Market Neut B	JMNBX	C-	(800) 480-4111	E+ / 0.6	-1.21	-0.65	0.81 /18	0.82 / 5	-0.90 / 2	0.00	4.94
IN	JPMorgan Research Market Neut C	JMNCX	C-	(800) 480-4111	E+ / 0.6	-1.28	-0.65	0.74 /18	0.82 / 5	-0.90 / 2	0.00	4.84
IN	JPMorgan Research Market Neut Inst	JPMNX	C-	(800) 480-4111	E+ / 0.7	-1.03	-0.21	1.72 /21	1.81 / 6	0.08 / 3	0.00	3.88
IN	JPMorgan Research Market Neut Sel	JMNSX	C-	(800) 480-4111	E+ / 0.7	-1.05	-0.28	1.55 /20	1.59 / 6	-0.16 / 2	0.00	3.99
RE	JPMorgan Secs Cap US Core RE A	CEEAX	C-	(800) 480-4111	C / 4.8	3.00	11.70	15.81 /93	9.62 /37	--	1.65	1.57
RE	JPMorgan Secs Cap US Core RE C	CEECX	C-	(800) 480-4111	C / 5.3	2.86	11.40	15.31 /92	9.07 /33	--	1.39	2.06
RE	JPMorgan Secs Cap US Core RE R5	CEEFX	C	(800) 480-4111	C+ / 6.0	3.11	11.96	16.37 /94	10.13 /40	--	2.08	1.12
RE	JPMorgan Secs Cap US Core RE R6	CEERX	C	(800) 480-4111	C+ / 6.0	3.18	12.04	16.49 /94	10.20 /40	--	2.12	1.05
RE	JPMorgan Secs Cap US Core RE Sel	CEESX	C	(800) 480-4111	C+ / 5.9	3.07	11.87	16.18 /94	9.91 /39	--	1.91	1.32
SC	JPMorgan Small Cap Core Sel	VSSCX	A	(800) 480-4111	A+ / 9.7	3.98	16.22	12.79 /86	19.68 /97	16.68 /95	0.16	1.15
SC	● JPMorgan Small Cap Equity A	VSEAX	B	(800) 480-4111	B+ / 8.3	5.51	14.54	10.49 /76	16.83 /89	16.63 /95	0.15	1.38
SC	● JPMorgan Small Cap Equity B	VSEBX	B	(800) 480-4111	B+ / 8.8	5.37	14.25	9.91 /74	16.25 /85	16.04 /93	0.00	1.88
SC	● JPMorgan Small Cap Equity C	JSECX	B	(800) 480-4111	B+ / 8.8	5.39	14.27	9.94 /74	16.26 /85	16.05 /93	0.00	1.86
SC	● JPMorgan Small Cap Equity R2	JSEZX	B+	(800) 480-4111	B+ / 8.9	5.44	14.40	10.22 /75	16.53 /87	16.33 /94	0.00	1.77
SC	● JPMorgan Small Cap Equity R5	JSERX	A-	(800) 480-4111	A / 9.3	5.65	14.85	11.04 /78	17.41 /92	17.21 /96	0.54	0.86

99 Pct = Best
0 Pct = Worst

● Denotes fund is closed to new investors
* Denotes fund is included in Section II

www.thestreetratings.com

RISK			NET ASSETS		ASSET				Portfolio	BULL / BEAR		FUND MANAGER		MINIMUMS		LOADS	
	3 Year		NAV							Last Bull	Last Bear	Manager	Manager	Initial	Additional	Front	Back
Risk	Standard		As of	Total	Cash	Stocks	Bonds	Other	Turnover	Market	Market	Quality	Tenure	Purch.	Purch.	End	End
Rating/Pts	Deviation	Beta	3/31/15	$(Mil)	%	%	%	%	Ratio	Return	Return	Pct	(Years)	$	$	Load	Load
C /5.4	11.3	1.02	13.00	10	3	96	0	1	25	104.1	-23.4	64	2	0	0	0.0	0.0
C /5.4	11.3	1.02	13.22	1,254	3	96	0	1	25	107.8	-23.2	70	2	1,000,000	0	0.0	0.0
B+ /9.7	3.2	0.10	14.58	23	97	2	0	1	781	-0.1	-4.3	34	1	1,000	50	5.3	0.0
B+ /9.6	3.2	0.10	14.06	17	97	2	0	1	781	-1.8	-4.5	28	1	1,000	50	0.0	0.0
B+ /9.7	3.1	0.10	14.87	60	97	2	0	1	781	0.7	-4.2	37	1	1,000,000	0	0.0	0.0
C+ /6.5	10.4	0.92	46.73	215	4	95	0	1	47	110.3	-20.6	86	13	1,000	50	5.3	0.0
C+ /6.5	10.4	0.92	45.84	25	4	95	0	1	47	106.7	-20.8	83	13	1,000	50	0.0	0.0
U /	N/A	N/A	47.07	1,138	4	95	0	1	47	N/A	N/A	N/A	13	15,000,000	0	0.0	0.0
C+ /6.5	10.4	0.92	47.06	1,840	4	95	0	1	47	112.8	-20.5	87	13	1,000,000	0	0.0	0.0
C /4.6	12.7	1.08	26.71	929	4	95	0	1	69	112.0	-23.8	59	11	1,000	50	5.3	0.0
C- /3.5	12.7	1.08	17.87	4	4	95	0	1	69	108.4	-24.0	51	11	1,000	50	0.0	0.0
C- /4.2	12.7	1.07	22.13	63	4	95	0	1	69	108.5	-24.0	52	11	1,000	50	0.0	0.0
C /4.8	12.7	1.08	28.89	6	4	95	0	1	69	110.8	-23.8	56	11	0	0	0.0	0.0
C+ /5.8	12.7	1.07	30.09	76	4	95	0	1	69	115.3	-23.7	66	11	0	0	0.0	0.0
C+ /5.8	12.7	1.07	30.16	187	4	95	0	1	69	115.7	-23.7	66	11	15,000,000	0	0.0	0.0
C /4.9	12.7	1.07	29.92	1,429	4	95	0	1	69	114.2	-23.7	64	11	1,000,000	0	0.0	0.0
B- /7.0	8.9	0.77	37.77	2,734	3	96	0	1	25	110.3	-17.7	94	18	1,000	50	5.3	0.0
B- /7.0	8.9	0.77	36.95	8	3	96	0	1	25	106.7	-17.9	93	18	1,000	50	0.0	0.0
B- /7.0	8.9	0.77	36.60	623	3	96	0	1	25	106.7	-17.9	93	18	1,000	50	0.0	0.0
C+ /6.9	8.9	0.77	38.52	10,694	3	96	0	1	25	113.9	-17.6	95	18	3,000,000	0	0.0	0.0
C+ /6.9	8.9	0.77	36.52	77	3	96	0	1	25	108.4	-17.8	93	18	0	0	0.0	0.0
B- /7.0	8.9	0.77	38.14	2,464	3	96	0	1	25	112.1	-17.6	94	18	1,000,000	0	0.0	0.0
B+ /9.9	2.9	0.18	9.89	7	98	1	0	1	227	3.8	-1.0	46	2	1,000	50	5.3	0.0
B+ /9.9	2.9	0.20	9.34	N/A	98	1	0	1	227	1.7	-1.4	36	2	1,000	50	0.0	0.0
B+ /9.9	2.9	0.19	9.35	7	98	1	0	1	227	1.7	-1.4	37	2	1,000	50	0.0	0.0
B+ /9.9	2.9	0.18	10.09	288	98	1	0	1	227	4.7	-0.9	50	2	1,000,000	0	0.0	0.0
U /	N/A	N/A	16.56	59	0	0	0	100	0	N/A	N/A	N/A	1	1,000,000	0	0.0	0.0
C- /3.7	13.3	1.06	14.47	178	0	99	0	1	105	81.8	-16.5	41	8	1,000	50	5.3	0.0
C- /3.6	13.3	1.06	14.28	N/A	0	99	0	1	105	78.8	-16.7	34	8	1,000	50	0.0	0.0
C- /3.6	13.3	1.06	14.13	11	0	99	0	1	105	78.6	-16.6	33	8	1,000	50	0.0	0.0
C- /3.7	13.3	1.06	14.59	235	0	99	0	1	105	84.2	-16.3	47	8	3,000,000	0	0.0	0.0
C- /3.7	13.3	1.06	14.60	1,686	0	99	0	1	105	84.5	-16.2	48	8	0	0	0.0	0.0
B+ /9.1	4.6	0.42	16.73	58	67	32	0	1	187	25.2	-7.9	51	1	1,000	50	5.3	0.0
B+ /9.1	4.5	0.42	16.31	1	67	32	0	1	187	23.0	-8.1	44	1	1,000	50	0.0	0.0
B+ /9.1	4.5	0.42	17.12	N/A	67	32	0	1	187	27.1	-7.7	59	1	0	0	0.0	0.0
B+ /9.1	4.5	0.42	16.94	82	67	32	0	1	187	26.2	-7.8	55	1	1,000,000	0	0.0	0.0
B+ /9.9	2.5	0.12	14.65	68	98	1	0	1	192	4.1	-3.3	60	1	1,000	50	5.3	0.0
B+ /9.8	2.5	0.11	13.93	N/A	98	1	0	1	192	2.4	-3.5	53	1	1,000	50	0.0	0.0
B+ /9.8	2.5	0.12	13.93	10	98	1	0	1	192	2.4	-3.5	52	1	1,000	50	0.0	0.0
B+ /9.9	2.5	0.12	15.36	269	98	1	0	1	192	6.0	-3.1	N/A	1	3,000,000	0	0.0	0.0
B+ /9.9	2.5	0.12	15.15	344	98	1	0	1	192	5.1	-3.1	64	1	1,000,000	0	0.0	0.0
C /5.4	8.0	0.64	18.81	9	6	80	12	2	106	53.8	N/A	75	4	1,000	50	5.3	0.0
C /5.4	8.0	0.64	18.81	N/A	6	80	12	2	106	51.2	N/A	70	4	1,000	50	0.0	0.0
C /5.4	8.0	0.64	18.88	N/A	6	80	12	2	106	56.2	N/A	79	4	0	0	0.0	0.0
C /5.4	8.0	0.64	18.89	28	6	80	12	2	106	56.5	N/A	79	4	15,000,000	0	0.0	0.0
C /5.4	8.0	0.64	18.86	67	6	80	12	2	106	55.2	N/A	77	4	1,000,000	0	0.0	0.0
C+ /5.9	13.9	1.02	56.48	808	2	97	0	1	51	122.7	-27.2	87	11	1,000,000	0	0.0	0.0
C /5.5	11.0	0.80	44.98	688	5	94	0	1	30	106.4	-20.5	90	8	1,000	50	5.3	0.0
C /4.9	11.0	0.80	35.74	2	5	94	0	1	30	103.0	-20.7	89	8	1,000	50	0.0	0.0
C /4.9	11.0	0.80	35.61	38	5	94	0	1	30	103.0	-20.7	89	8	1,000	50	0.0	0.0
C /5.5	11.0	0.80	44.36	4	5	94	0	1	30	104.6	-20.6	90	8	0	0	0.0	0.0
C+ /5.7	11.0	0.80	50.71	1,220	5	94	0	1	30	110.0	-20.4	92	8	0	0	0.0	0.0

Fund Type	Fund Name	Ticker Symbol	Overall Investment Rating	Phone	Performance Rating/Pts	3 Mo	6 Mo	1Yr / Pct	Annualized 3Yr / Pct	Annualized 5Yr / Pct	Dividend Yield	Expense Ratio
	99 Pct = Best *0 Pct = Worst*											
SC	● JPMorgan Small Cap Equity Sel	VSEIX	A-	(800) 480-4111	A- / 9.2	5.59	14.72	10.83 /78	17.18 /91	16.97 /96	0.38	1.13
SC	● JPMorgan Small Cap Growth A	PGSGX	C-	(800) 480-4111	B- / 7.1	5.97	15.95	5.23 /40	15.51 /79	15.75 /92	0.00	1.59
SC	● JPMorgan Small Cap Growth B	OGFBX	C-	(800) 480-4111	B / 7.7	5.86	15.68	4.81 /37	14.95 /74	15.17 /88	0.00	2.08
SC	● JPMorgan Small Cap Growth C	OSGCX	C-	(800) 480-4111	B / 7.7	5.89	15.67	4.79 /37	14.96 /75	15.18 /88	0.00	2.06
SC	● JPMorgan Small Cap Growth Inst	JISGX	C+	(800) 480-4111	B+ / 8.5	6.06	16.21	5.72 /44	15.98 /83	16.22 /94	0.00	1.12
SC	● JPMorgan Small Cap Growth R2	JSGZX	C	(800) 480-4111	B / 7.9	5.94	15.83	5.03 /39	15.22 /77	15.46 /90	0.00	1.96
SC	● JPMorgan Small Cap Growth R6	JGSMX	C+	(800) 480-4111	B+ / 8.6	6.10	16.29	5.83 /45	16.12 /84	16.25 /94	0.00	0.96
SC	● JPMorgan Small Cap Growth Sel	OGGFX	C+	(800) 480-4111	B+ / 8.4	6.04	16.14	5.55 /43	15.83 /82	16.05 /93	0.00	1.31
SC	JPMorgan Small Cap Value A	PSOAX	C+	(800) 480-4111	C+ / 6.9	2.59	12.98	5.84 /45	15.75 /81	13.75 /75	0.66	1.51
SC	● JPMorgan Small Cap Value B	PSOBX	B	(800) 480-4111	B- / 7.4	2.42	12.65	5.19 /40	15.07 /75	13.05 /69	0.40	2.01
SC	JPMorgan Small Cap Value C	OSVCX	B	(800) 480-4111	B- / 7.4	2.43	12.59	5.20 /40	15.04 /75	13.05 /69	0.44	1.98
SC	JPMorgan Small Cap Value R2	JSVZX	B	(800) 480-4111	B / 7.7	2.53	12.84	5.56 /43	15.45 /79	13.46 /72	0.49	1.90
SC	JPMorgan Small Cap Value R5	JSVRX	B+	(800) 480-4111	B / 8.2	2.65	13.15	6.21 /48	16.14 /84	14.13 /79	1.02	1.02
SC	JPMorgan Small Cap Value R6	JSVUX	B+	(800) 480-4111	B+ / 8.3	2.69	13.20	6.27 /49	16.21 /85	14.19 /79	1.10	0.88
SC	JPMorgan Small Cap Value Sel	PSOPX	B+	(800) 480-4111	B / 8.2	2.63	13.11	6.10 /47	16.05 /84	14.02 /78	0.92	1.23
AA	JPMorgan Smart Ret 2015 A	JSFAX	C	(800) 480-4111	D / 2.2	2.26	4.31	6.31 /49	7.52 /24	7.92 /29	2.39	1.09
AA	JPMorgan Smart Ret 2015 C	JSFCX	C	(800) 480-4111	D+ / 2.5	2.00	3.95	5.58 /43	6.80 /20	7.20 /24	1.90	1.62
AA	JPMorgan Smart Ret 2015 Inst	JSFIX	C+	(800) 480-4111	C- / 3.1	2.25	4.42	6.54 /51	7.77 /26	8.18 /31	2.72	0.68
AA	JPMorgan Smart Ret 2015 R2	JSFZX	C	(800) 480-4111	D+ / 2.7	2.15	4.14	6.03 /47	7.23 /23	7.64 /27	2.28	1.37
AA	JPMorgan Smart Ret 2015 Sel	JSFSX	C	(800) 480-4111	C- / 3.0	2.22	4.30	6.40 /50	7.61 /25	8.02 /30	2.59	0.85
AA	JPMorgan Smart Ret 2020 A	JTTAX	C	(800) 480-4111	C- / 3.3	2.60	5.34	7.78 /61	9.19 /34	9.14 /38	2.43	1.13
AA	JPMorgan Smart Ret 2020 C	JTTCX	C+	(800) 480-4111	C- / 3.5	2.46	5.04	7.09 /56	8.50 /30	8.43 /33	1.95	1.67
AA	JPMorgan Smart Ret 2020 Inst	JTTIX	C+	(800) 480-4111	C- / 4.1	2.65	5.43	7.99 /63	9.46 /36	9.40 /40	2.76	0.71
AA	JPMorgan Smart Ret 2020 R2	JTTZX	C+	(800) 480-4111	C- / 3.8	2.55	5.23	7.50 /59	8.91 /32	8.87 /36	2.33	1.40
AA	JPMorgan Smart Ret 2020 Sel	JTTSX	C+	(800) 480-4111	C- / 4.1	2.67	5.43	7.91 /62	9.31 /35	9.25 /39	2.63	0.88
AA	JPMorgan Smart Ret 2025 A	JNSAX	C+	(800) 480-4111	C- / 4.0	2.80	5.98	8.57 /67	10.48 /42	9.95 /44	2.42	1.16
AA	JPMorgan Smart Ret 2025 C	JNSCX	C+	(800) 480-4111	C / 4.3	2.67	5.70	7.90 /62	9.77 /38	9.25 /39	1.96	1.70
AA	JPMorgan Smart Ret 2025 Inst	JNSIX	B-	(800) 480-4111	C / 4.9	2.85	6.09	8.86 /68	10.75 /44	10.22 /46	2.75	0.75
AA	JPMorgan Smart Ret 2025 R2	JNSZX	C+	(800) 480-4111	C / 4.5	2.75	5.82	8.30 /65	10.19 /40	9.67 /42	2.32	1.44
AA	JPMorgan Smart Ret 2025 Sel	JNSSX	B-	(800) 480-4111	C / 4.8	2.87	6.08	8.72 /68	10.60 /43	10.06 /45	2.62	0.91
AA	JPMorgan Smart Ret 2030 A	JSMAX	C+	(800) 480-4111	C / 4.6	2.93	6.36	9.06 /70	11.49 /49	10.52 /49	2.36	1.18
AA	JPMorgan Smart Ret 2030 C	JSMCX	C+	(800) 480-4111	C / 4.9	2.80	6.03	8.35 /65	10.77 /44	9.80 /43	1.93	1.73
AA	JPMorgan Smart Ret 2030 Inst	JSMIX	B	(800) 480-4111	C+ / 5.6	3.03	6.51	9.39 /71	11.76 /51	10.78 /51	2.68	0.76
AA	JPMorgan Smart Ret 2030 R2	JSMZX	B-	(800) 480-4111	C / 5.2	2.93	6.31	8.85 /68	11.21 /47	10.24 /46	2.26	1.45
AA	JPMorgan Smart Ret 2030 Sel	JSMSX	B-	(800) 480-4111	C / 5.5	3.00	6.45	9.20 /70	11.61 /50	10.62 /50	2.55	0.94
AA	JPMorgan Smart Ret 2035 A	SRJAX	C+	(800) 480-4111	C / 5.1	3.03	6.70	9.36 /71	12.24 /54	11.01 /53	2.35	1.20
AA	JPMorgan Smart Ret 2035 C	SRJCX	C+	(800) 480-4111	C / 5.3	2.86	6.27	8.61 /67	11.49 /49	10.28 /47	1.96	1.70
AA	JPMorgan Smart Ret 2035 Inst	SRJIX	B-	(800) 480-4111	C+ / 6.0	3.13	6.79	9.63 /73	12.50 /56	11.28 /55	2.67	0.80
AA	JPMorgan Smart Ret 2035 R2	SRJZX	B-	(800) 480-4111	C+ / 5.6	2.98	6.54	9.08 /70	11.95 /52	10.73 /50	2.24	1.50
AA	JPMorgan Smart Ret 2035 Sel	SRJSX	B-	(800) 480-4111	C+ / 5.9	3.10	6.73	9.48 /72	12.36 /55	11.12 /54	2.53	0.97
AA	JPMorgan Smart Ret 2040 A	SMTAX	C+	(800) 480-4111	C / 5.3	3.11	6.79	9.55 /72	12.54 /56	11.21 /55	2.33	1.24
AA	JPMorgan Smart Ret 2040 C	SMTCX	C+	(800) 480-4111	C / 5.5	2.94	6.43	8.80 /68	11.80 /51	10.50 /49	1.95	1.82
AA	JPMorgan Smart Ret 2040 Inst	SMTIX	B-	(800) 480-4111	C+ / 6.2	3.21	6.94	9.81 /74	12.82 /58	11.50 /57	2.65	0.81
AA	JPMorgan Smart Ret 2040 R2	SMTZX	B-	(800) 480-4111	C+ / 5.8	3.03	6.65	9.25 /71	12.25 /54	10.94 /52	2.24	1.53
AA	JPMorgan Smart Ret 2040 Sel	SMTSX	B-	(800) 480-4111	C+ / 6.1	3.13	6.82	9.63 /73	12.65 /57	11.33 /55	2.52	1.00
AA	JPMorgan Smart Ret 2045 A	JSAAX	C+	(800) 480-4111	C / 5.3	3.19	6.86	9.55 /72	12.58 /57	11.19 /54	2.31	1.27
AA	JPMorgan Smart Ret 2045 C	JSACX	C+	(800) 480-4111	C+ / 5.6	2.98	6.50	8.86 /69	11.84 /51	10.48 /48	1.93	1.86
AA	JPMorgan Smart Ret 2045 Inst	JSAIX	B-	(800) 480-4111	C+ / 6.2	3.23	6.96	9.82 /74	12.86 /59	11.46 /57	2.63	0.84
AA	JPMorgan Smart Ret 2045 R2	JSAZX	B-	(800) 480-4111	C+ / 5.9	3.09	6.65	9.22 /70	12.27 /54	10.90 /52	2.21	1.59
AA	JPMorgan Smart Ret 2045 Sel	JSASX	B-	(800) 480-4111	C+ / 6.1	3.15	6.89	9.62 /73	12.67 /57	11.30 /55	2.50	1.05
AA	JPMorgan Smart Ret 2050 A	JTSAX	C+	(800) 480-4111	C / 5.2	3.08	6.78	9.49 /72	12.51 /56	11.24 /55	2.30	1.34
AA	JPMorgan Smart Ret 2050 C	JTSCX	C+	(800) 480-4111	C / 5.5	2.94	6.43	8.81 /68	11.78 /51	10.53 /49	1.92	1.92

● Denotes fund is closed to new investors
* Denotes fund is included in Section II

www.thestreetratings.com

RISK			NET ASSETS		ASSET					BULL / BEAR		FUND MANAGER		MINIMUMS		LOADS	
	3 Year		NAV						Portfolio	Last Bull	Last Bear	Manager	Manager	Initial	Additional	Front	Back
Risk Rating/Pts	Standard Deviation	Beta	As of 3/31/15	Total $(Mil)	Cash %	Stocks %	Bonds %	Other %	Turnover Ratio	Market Return	Market Return	Quality Pct	Tenure (Years)	Purch. $	Purch. $	End Load	End Load
C+ /5.8	11.0	0.80	50.61	1,444	5	94	0	1	30	108.6	-20.4	91	8	1,000,000	0	0.0	0.0
C- /3.6	15.4	1.07	14.02	265	1	98	0	1	58	101.3	-27.9	41	11	1,000	50	5.3	0.0
D+ /2.8	15.4	1.07	10.47	2	1	98	0	1	58	98.1	-28.1	34	11	1,000	50	0.0	0.0
C- /3.0	15.4	1.07	11.14	26	1	98	0	1	58	98.1	-28.1	34	11	1,000	50	0.0	0.0
C- /3.7	15.4	1.07	15.39	285	1	98	0	1	58	104.1	-27.8	47	11	3,000,000	0	0.0	0.0
C- /3.5	15.5	1.07	13.74	29	1	98	0	1	58	99.7	-28.0	37	11	0	0	0.0	0.0
C- /3.7	15.4	1.07	15.47	454	1	98	0	1	58	104.8	-27.8	49	11	15,000,000	0	0.0	0.0
C- /3.7	15.5	1.07	15.09	152	1	98	0	1	58	103.1	-27.9	44	11	1,000,000	0	0.0	0.0
C+ /6.2	13.3	0.97	27.21	574	4	95	0	1	40	101.4	-25.4	67	10	1,000	50	5.3	0.0
C+ /6.1	13.3	0.97	23.53	2	4	95	0	1	40	97.4	-25.6	59	10	1,000	50	0.0	0.0
C+ /6.1	13.3	0.97	23.27	51	4	95	0	1	40	97.2	-25.6	59	10	1,000	50	0.0	0.0
C+ /6.2	13.3	0.97	27.05	50	4	95	0	1	40	99.8	-25.5	64	10	0	0	0.0	0.0
C+ /6.2	13.3	0.97	28.59	93	4	95	0	1	40	103.8	-25.3	71	10	0	0	0.0	0.0
C+ /6.2	13.3	0.97	28.61	530	4	95	0	1	40	104.2	-25.3	72	10	15,000,000	0	0.0	0.0
C+ /6.2	13.3	0.97	28.59	481	4	95	0	1	40	103.2	-25.4	70	10	1,000,000	0	0.0	0.0
B /8.9	5.2	0.86	18.01	626	11	37	50	2	10	42.5	-10.8	43	9	1,000	50	4.5	0.0
B /8.9	5.3	0.87	17.88	25	11	37	50	2	10	39.4	-11.1	32	9	1,000	50	0.0	0.0
B /8.9	5.2	0.86	18.05	1,337	11	37	50	2	10	43.6	-10.7	46	9	3,000,000	0	0.0	0.0
B /8.9	5.3	0.86	17.95	127	11	37	50	2	10	41.2	-10.9	38	9	0	0	0.0	0.0
B /8.9	5.3	0.86	18.03	385	11	37	50	2	10	42.9	-10.7	43	9	1,000,000	0	0.0	0.0
B /8.5	6.3	1.04	18.75	1,321	6	52	40	2	9	52.5	-12.9	37	9	1,000	50	4.5	0.0
B /8.5	6.3	1.05	18.68	51	6	52	40	2	9	49.2	-13.1	29	9	1,000	50	0.0	0.0
B /8.5	6.3	1.05	18.82	2,945	6	52	40	2	9	53.8	-12.8	40	9	3,000,000	0	0.0	0.0
B /8.5	6.3	1.05	18.70	290	6	52	40	2	9	51.2	-12.9	33	9	0	0	0.0	0.0
B /8.5	6.3	1.05	18.81	955	6	52	40	2	9	53.1	-12.8	39	9	1,000,000	0	0.0	0.0
B /8.1	7.4	1.23	18.21	1,182	6	61	31	2	7	61.7	-15.6	28	8	1,000	50	4.5	0.0
B /8.1	7.3	1.22	18.15	51	6	61	31	2	7	58.1	-15.8	22	8	1,000	50	0.0	0.0
B /8.1	7.3	1.22	18.26	2,457	6	61	31	2	7	62.9	-15.5	32	8	3,000,000	0	0.0	0.0
B /8.1	7.3	1.22	18.15	251	6	61	31	2	7	60.2	-15.7	26	8	0	0	0.0	0.0
B /8.1	7.4	1.23	18.25	747	6	61	31	2	7	62.1	-15.5	30	8	1,000,000	0	0.0	0.0
B- /7.8	8.2	1.38	19.61	1,358	6	68	24	2	10	68.9	-17.8	22	N/A	1,000	50	4.5	0.0
B- /7.8	8.2	1.38	19.46	48	6	68	24	2	10	65.2	-18.0	16	N/A	1,000	50	0.0	0.0
B- /7.8	8.2	1.38	19.70	2,823	6	68	24	2	10	70.2	-17.6	24	N/A	3,000,000	0	0.0	0.0
B- /7.8	8.3	1.38	19.56	338	6	68	24	2	10	67.5	-17.9	19	N/A	0	0	0.0	0.0
B- /7.8	8.3	1.38	19.66	934	6	68	24	2	10	69.4	-17.7	22	N/A	1,000,000	0	0.0	0.0
B- /7.4	9.0	1.50	18.80	903	5	75	18	2	8	75.0	-19.3	17	8	1,000	50	4.5	0.0
B- /7.4	8.9	1.49	18.67	32	5	75	18	2	8	71.2	-19.5	13	8	1,000	50	0.0	0.0
B- /7.4	8.9	1.49	18.89	1,868	5	75	18	2	8	76.6	-19.2	19	8	3,000,000	0	0.0	0.0
B- /7.4	9.0	1.50	18.75	211	5	75	18	2	8	73.5	-19.4	15	8	0	0	0.0	0.0
B- /7.4	8.9	1.49	18.88	563	5	75	18	2	8	75.6	-19.2	18	8	1,000,000	0	0.0	0.0
B- /7.3	9.2	1.55	20.16	945	6	80	13	1	9	76.9	-19.4	15	9	1,000	50	4.5	0.0
B- /7.3	9.2	1.55	19.95	33	6	80	13	1	9	73.0	-19.6	11	9	1,000	50	0.0	0.0
B- /7.3	9.2	1.54	20.26	2,041	6	80	13	1	9	78.3	-19.3	17	9	3,000,000	0	0.0	0.0
B- /7.3	9.2	1.54	20.08	219	6	80	13	1	9	75.3	-19.5	14	9	0	0	0.0	0.0
B- /7.3	9.2	1.54	20.21	668	6	80	13	1	9	77.4	-19.3	16	9	1,000,000	0	0.0	0.0
B- /7.3	9.2	1.55	19.09	499	5	80	14	1	8	76.9	-19.3	15	N/A	1,000	50	4.5	0.0
B- /7.3	9.2	1.55	18.99	17	5	80	14	1	8	73.0	-19.5	12	N/A	1,000	50	0.0	0.0
B- /7.3	9.2	1.54	19.16	1,128	5	80	14	1	8	78.3	-19.2	18	N/A	3,000,000	0	0.0	0.0
B- /7.3	9.2	1.54	19.03	129	5	80	14	1	8	75.3	-19.4	14	N/A	0	0	0.0	0.0
B- /7.3	9.3	1.55	19.14	319	5	80	14	1	8	77.5	-19.3	16	N/A	1,000,000	0	0.0	0.0
B- /7.3	9.3	1.55	19.04	400	5	80	14	1	8	76.8	-19.4	15	N/A	1,000	50	4.5	0.0
B- /7.3	9.2	1.54	18.92	17	5	80	14	1	8	72.8	-19.6	11	N/A	1,000	50	0.0	0.0

Fund Type	Fund Name	Ticker Symbol	Overall Investment Rating	Phone	Performance Rating/Pts	3 Mo	6 Mo	1Yr / Pct	3Yr / Pct (Annualized)	5Yr / Pct (Annualized)	Dividend Yield	Expense Ratio
AA	JPMorgan Smart Ret 2050 Inst	JTSIX	B-	(800) 480-4111	C+ / 6.2	3.18	6.93	9.81 /74	12.80 /58	11.53 /57	2.61	0.85
AA	JPMorgan Smart Ret 2050 R2	JTSZX	B-	(800) 480-4111	C+ / 5.8	3.04	6.68	9.22 /70	12.22 /54	10.97 /52	2.20	1.65
AA	JPMorgan Smart Ret 2050 Sel	JTSSX	B-	(800) 480-4111	C+ / 6.1	3.15	6.87	9.62 /73	12.61 /57	11.37 /56	2.48	1.11
IX	JPMorgan Smart Ret 2055 A	JFFAX	B-	(800) 480-4111	C / 5.3	3.09	6.78	9.46 /72	12.69 /57	--	2.10	1.41
GI	JPMorgan Smart Ret 2055 C	JFFCX	B-	(800) 480-4111	C+ / 5.6	2.94	6.42	8.72 /68	11.97 /52	--	1.73	2.12
GI	JPMorgan Smart Ret 2055 Inst	JFFIX	B-	(800) 480-4111	C+ / 6.2	3.09	6.84	9.68 /73	12.96 /59	--	2.41	0.93
GI	JPMorgan Smart Ret 2055 R2	JFFRX	B-	(800) 480-4111	C+ / 5.9	3.00	6.63	9.19 /70	12.41 /55	--	2.00	1.73
GI	JPMorgan Smart Ret 2055 Select	JFFSX	B-	(800) 480-4111	C+ / 6.1	3.06	6.78	9.49 /72	12.80 /58	--	2.29	1.18
GI	JPMorgan Smart Ret Blend 2015 R5	JSBWX	U	(800) 480-4111	U /	1.74	3.42	5.49 /42	--	--	2.11	1.24
GI	JPMorgan Smart Ret Blend 2015 R6	JSBYX	U	(800) 480-4111	U /	1.75	3.50	5.54 /43	--	--	2.15	1.33
GI	JPMorgan Smart Ret Blend 2020 R5	JBSRX	U	(800) 480-4111	U /	2.06	4.40	6.84 /54	--	--	2.12	1.03
GI	JPMorgan Smart Ret Blend 2020 R6	JSYRX	U	(800) 480-4111	U /	2.08	4.42	6.89 /54	--	--	2.17	1.06
GI	JPMorgan Smart Ret Blend 2025 R5	JBBSX	U	(800) 480-4111	U /	2.15	4.68	7.37 /58	--	--	2.09	1.10
GI	JPMorgan Smart Ret Blend 2025 R6	JBYSX	U	(800) 480-4111	U /	2.22	4.76	7.42 /59	--	--	2.14	1.18
GI	JPMorgan Smart Ret Blend 2030 R5	JRBBX	U	(800) 480-4111	U /	2.25	4.90	7.72 /61	--	--	2.08	1.06
GI	JPMorgan Smart Ret Blend 2030 R6	JRBYX	U	(800) 480-4111	U /	2.32	4.97	7.76 /61	--	--	2.12	1.17
GI	JPMorgan Smart Ret Blend 2035 R5	JPBRX	U	(800) 480-4111	U /	2.35	5.08	7.91 /62	--	--	2.02	1.26
GI	JPMorgan Smart Ret Blend 2035 R6	JPYRX	U	(800) 480-4111	U /	2.36	5.11	7.96 /63	--	--	2.07	1.36
GI	JPMorgan Smart Ret Blend 2040 R5	JOBBX	U	(800) 480-4111	U /	2.37	5.20	8.07 /63	--	--	2.02	1.22
GI	JPMorgan Smart Ret Blend 2040 R6	JOBYX	U	(800) 480-4111	U /	2.43	5.23	8.12 /64	--	--	2.06	1.32
BA	JPMorgan Smart Ret Inc A	JSRAX	C-	(800) 480-4111	D / 1.6	2.05	3.79	5.53 /43	6.20 /18	6.68 /21	2.29	1.09
BA	JPMorgan Smart Ret Inc C	JSRCX	C	(800) 480-4111	D / 1.8	1.85	3.42	4.77 /37	5.49 /15	5.98 /17	1.79	1.62
BA	JPMorgan Smart Ret Inc Inst	JSIIX	C	(800) 480-4111	D+ / 2.3	2.10	3.85	5.76 /44	6.45 /19	6.94 /23	2.62	0.65
BA	JPMorgan Smart Ret Inc R2	JSIZX	C	(800) 480-4111	D / 2.0	2.00	3.62	5.25 /40	5.93 /16	6.42 /20	2.19	1.38
BA	JPMorgan Smart Ret Inc Sel	JSRSX	C	(800) 480-4111	D / 2.2	2.07	3.79	5.57 /43	6.29 /18	6.78 /22	2.50	0.85
GR	JPMorgan SmartAllocation Equity R6	JSARX	U	(800) 480-4111	U /	2.88	5.88	8.80 /68	--	--	2.00	1.65
GI	JPMorgan Systematic Alpha Select	SSALX	U	(800) 480-4111	U /	0.20	1.25	2.13 /22	--	--	1.04	3.06
GI	JPMorgan Tax Aware Equity A	JPEAX	B+	(800) 480-4111	B / 8.0	2.13	7.58	13.85 /89	16.80 /89	14.10 /79	0.74	0.98
GI	JPMorgan Tax Aware Equity C	JPECX	A-	(800) 480-4111	B+ / 8.5	1.95	7.28	13.25 /87	16.21 /85	13.53 /73	0.40	1.49
GI	JPMorgan Tax Aware Equity I	JPDEX	A+	(800) 480-4111	A- / 9.1	2.20	7.79	14.28 /90	17.28 /91	14.54 /83	1.11	0.56
GI	JPMorgan Tax Aware Equity Sel	JPESX	A	(800) 480-4111	A- / 9.0	2.16	7.69	14.13 /90	17.09 /90	14.38 /81	0.97	0.72
GL	JPMorgan Total Emerging Markets A	TMGGX	D-	(800) 480-4111	E / 0.5	1.23	0.07	1.09 /19	1.25 / 5	--	1.97	2.94
GL	JPMorgan Total Emerging Markets C	TMGHX	D-	(800) 480-4111	E+ / 0.6	1.10	-0.24	0.59 /17	0.72 / 5	--	1.82	3.36
GL	JPMorgan Total Emerging Markets	TMGTX	D-	(800) 480-4111	E+ / 0.6	1.16	-0.08	0.85 /18	1.00 / 5	--	1.87	3.08
GL	JPMorgan Total Emerging Markets	TMGRX	D-	(800) 480-4111	E+ / 0.7	1.35	0.24	1.53 /20	1.69 / 6	--	2.30	2.38
GL	JPMorgan Total Emerging Markets	TMGVX	D-	(800) 480-4111	E+ / 0.7	1.35	0.31	1.63 /20	1.76 / 6	--	2.33	2.33
GL	JPMorgan Total Emerging Markets	TMGSX	D-	(800) 480-4111	E+ / 0.7	1.29	0.16	1.34 /20	1.56 / 6	--	2.18	2.58
GR	JPMorgan US Dynamic Plus A	JPSAX	C+	(800) 480-4111	C+ / 6.6	-0.88	4.73	12.54 /85	15.36 /78	12.86 /67	0.37	2.48
GR	JPMorgan US Dynamic Plus C	JPSCX	B	(800) 480-4111	B- / 7.1	-1.08	4.47	11.90 /82	14.76 /73	12.29 /62	0.01	2.92
GR	JPMorgan US Dynamic Plus Sel	JILSX	B+	(800) 480-4111	B / 7.8	-0.87	4.83	12.76 /86	15.64 /80	13.13 /69	0.58	2.07
GI	JPMorgan US Equity A	JUEAX	B+	(800) 480-4111	B / 8.0	1.72	7.14	13.59 /88	16.94 /89	14.31 /80	0.81	1.09
GI	● JPMorgan US Equity B	JUEBX	B+	(800) 480-4111	B+ / 8.5	1.61	6.87	13.05 /87	16.37 /86	13.72 /75	0.41	1.58
GI	JPMorgan US Equity C	JUECX	B+	(800) 480-4111	B+ / 8.5	1.57	6.80	12.96 /86	16.33 /86	13.73 /75	0.47	1.57
GI	JPMorgan US Equity I	JMUEX	A	(800) 480-4111	A- / 9.1	1.80	7.29	13.98 /89	17.32 /91	14.68 /84	1.13	0.65
GI	JPMorgan US Equity R2	JUEZX	A-	(800) 480-4111	B+ / 8.7	1.66	7.01	13.28 /88	16.65 /88	14.02 /78	0.65	1.45
GI	JPMorgan US Equity R5	JUSRX	A	(800) 480-4111	A- / 9.1	1.82	7.38	14.02 /89	17.39 /92	14.75 /85	1.17	0.59
GI	JPMorgan US Equity R6	JUEMX	A	(800) 480-4111	A- / 9.1	1.76	7.33	14.06 /90	17.43 /92	14.81 /85	1.22	0.50
GI	JPMorgan US Equity Sel	JUESX	A-	(800) 480-4111	A- / 9.0	1.74	7.20	13.73 /89	17.15 /91	14.50 /82	0.98	0.78
GR	● JPMorgan US LgCap Core Plus A	JLCAX	B+	(800) 480-4111	B+ / 8.6	1.71	7.37	14.39 /90	17.77 /93	14.12 /79	0.34	2.52
GR	● JPMorgan US LgCap Core Plus C	JLPCX	A	(800) 480-4111	A- / 9.0	1.61	7.10	13.82 /89	17.18 /91	13.55 /73	0.00	3.01
GR	● JPMorgan US LgCap Core Plus R2	JLPZX	A	(800) 480-4111	A- / 9.1	1.67	7.24	14.09 /90	17.48 /92	13.83 /76	0.19	2.83
GR	● JPMorgan US LgCap Core Plus R5	JCPRX	A	(800) 480-4111	A / 9.4	1.86	7.66	14.92 /91	18.30 /95	14.64 /84	0.77	2.02

● Denotes fund is closed to new investors
* Denotes fund is included in Section II

99 Pct = Best
0 Pct = Worst

RISK			NET ASSETS		ASSET				Portfolio	BULL / BEAR		FUND MANAGER		MINIMUMS		LOADS	
	3 Year		NAV							Last Bull	Last Bear	Manager	Manager	Initial	Additional	Front	Back
Risk Rating/Pts	Standard Deviation	Beta	As of 3/31/15	Total $(Mil)	Cash %	Stocks %	Bonds %	Other %	Turnover Ratio	Market Return	Market Return	Quality Pct	Tenure (Years)	Purch. $	Purch. $	End Load	End Load
B- / 7.3	9.2	1.54	19.13	815	5	80	14	1	8	78.2	-19.3	17	N/A	3,000,000	0	0.0	0.0
B- / 7.3	9.2	1.54	18.99	105	5	80	14	1	8	75.2	-19.4	14	N/A	0	0	0.0	0.0
B- / 7.3	9.2	1.55	19.10	305	5	80	14	1	8	77.4	-19.3	16	N/A	1,000,000	0	0.0	0.0
B- / 7.8	9.2	0.90	21.04	60	4	86	8	2	49	N/A	N/A	45	N/A	1,000	50	4.5	0.0
B- / 7.7	9.2	0.90	20.98	2	4	86	8	2	49	N/A	N/A	35	N/A	1,000	50	0.0	0.0
B- / 7.8	9.2	0.90	21.07	151	4	86	8	2	49	N/A	N/A	48	N/A	3,000,000	0	0.0	0.0
B- / 7.7	9.2	0.90	21.01	22	4	86	8	2	49	N/A	N/A	41	N/A	0	0	0.0	0.0
B- / 7.8	9.2	0.90	21.06	37	4	86	8	2	49	N/A	N/A	46	N/A	1,000,000	0	0.0	0.0
U /	N/A	N/A	17.29	26	0	0	0	100	75	N/A	N/A	N/A	3	0	0	0.0	0.0
U /	N/A	N/A	17.30	25	0	0	0	100	75	N/A	N/A	N/A	3	15,000,000	0	0.0	0.0
U /	N/A	N/A	18.23	56	0	0	0	100	49	N/A	N/A	N/A	3	0	0	0.0	0.0
U /	N/A	N/A	18.23	74	0	0	0	100	49	N/A	N/A	N/A	3	15,000,000	0	0.0	0.0
U /	N/A	N/A	18.84	53	0	0	0	100	40	N/A	N/A	N/A	3	0	0	0.0	0.0
U /	N/A	N/A	18.84	54	0	0	0	100	40	N/A	N/A	N/A	3	15,000,000	0	0.0	0.0
U /	N/A	N/A	19.40	68	0	0	0	100	36	N/A	N/A	N/A	3	0	0	0.0	0.0
U /	N/A	N/A	19.41	49	0	0	0	100	36	N/A	N/A	N/A	3	15,000,000	0	0.0	0.0
U /	N/A	N/A	19.87	35	0	0	0	100	37	N/A	N/A	N/A	3	0	0	0.0	0.0
U /	N/A	N/A	19.87	41	0	0	0	100	37	N/A	N/A	N/A	3	15,000,000	0	0.0	0.0
U /	N/A	N/A	20.11	33	0	0	0	100	22	N/A	N/A	N/A	3	0	0	0.0	0.0
U /	N/A	N/A	20.11	35	0	0	0	100	22	N/A	N/A	N/A	3	15,000,000	0	0.0	0.0
B+ / 9.1	4.4	0.72	17.85	590	14	34	50	2	11	33.1	-7.5	46	9	1,000	50	4.5	0.0
B+ / 9.1	4.4	0.72	17.77	22	14	34	50	2	11	30.1	-7.7	35	9	1,000	50	0.0	0.0
B+ / 9.1	4.4	0.72	17.90	932	14	34	50	2	11	34.1	-7.4	49	9	3,000,000	0	0.0	0.0
B+ / 9.1	4.4	0.72	17.81	99	14	34	50	2	11	31.9	-7.6	42	9	0	0	0.0	0.0
B+ / 9.1	4.4	0.72	17.87	310	14	34	50	2	11	33.5	-7.5	47	9	1,000,000	0	0.0	0.0
U /	N/A	N/A	21.08	99	2	97	0	1	18	N/A	N/A	N/A	3	15,000,000	0	0.0	0.0
U /	N/A	N/A	15.07	264	0	0	0	100	113	N/A	N/A	N/A	2	1,000,000	0	0.0	0.0
C+ / 6.6	10.5	1.07	29.52	13	0	99	0	1	59	105.3	-18.6	60	7	1,000	50	5.3	0.0
C+ / 6.6	10.5	1.08	29.36	3	0	99	0	1	59	101.9	-18.8	52	7	1,000	50	0.0	0.0
C+ / 6.7	10.5	1.08	29.61	1,285	0	99	0	1	59	108.3	-18.5	66	7	3,000,000	0	0.0	0.0
C+ / 6.7	10.5	1.08	29.59	84	0	99	0	1	59	107.1	-18.6	63	7	1,000,000	0	0.0	0.0
B- / 7.0	11.4	1.47	15.66	1	2	59	37	2	113	N/A	N/A	1	3	1,000	50	4.5	0.0
C+ / 6.9	11.4	1.48	15.60	N/A	2	59	37	2	113	N/A	N/A	1	3	1,000	50	0.0	0.0
B- / 7.0	11.4	1.47	15.67	N/A	2	59	37	2	113	N/A	N/A	1	3	0	0	0.0	0.0
B- / 7.0	11.4	1.48	15.74	N/A	2	59	37	2	113	N/A	N/A	1	3	0	0	0.0	0.0
B- / 7.0	11.4	1.47	15.75	N/A	2	59	37	2	113	N/A	N/A	1	3	15,000,000	0	0.0	0.0
B- / 7.0	11.4	1.48	15.72	29	2	59	37	2	113	N/A	N/A	1	3	1,000,000	0	0.0	0.0
C+ / 6.8	10.8	1.10	17.98	122	2	97	0	1	109	98.8	-16.2	36	3	1,000	50	5.3	0.0
C+ / 6.9	10.9	1.10	17.43	1	2	97	0	1	109	95.5	-16.4	29	3	1,000	50	0.0	0.0
C+ / 6.8	10.8	1.09	18.16	179	2	97	0	1	109	100.6	-16.2	40	3	1,000,000	0	0.0	0.0
C+ / 6.3	10.3	1.06	14.74	1,341	2	97	0	1	73	105.8	-17.8	65	9	1,000	50	5.3	0.0
C+ / 6.3	10.3	1.06	14.50	4	2	97	0	1	73	102.3	-18.0	58	9	1,000	50	0.0	0.0
C+ / 6.2	10.3	1.06	14.39	237	2	97	0	1	73	102.5	-18.0	56	9	1,000	50	0.0	0.0
C+ / 6.3	10.3	1.06	14.78	4,977	2	97	0	1	73	108.2	-17.7	69	9	3,000,000	0	0.0	0.0
C+ / 6.3	10.3	1.06	14.65	167	2	97	0	1	73	104.1	-17.9	61	9	0	0	0.0	0.0
C+ / 6.3	10.3	1.06	14.79	489	2	97	0	1	73	108.5	-17.7	69	9	0	0	0.0	0.0
C+ / 6.3	10.3	1.06	14.80	2,799	2	97	0	1	73	108.7	-17.7	70	9	15,000,000	0	0.0	0.0
C+ / 6.3	10.3	1.06	14.76	2,394	2	97	0	1	73	107.0	-17.7	67	9	1,000,000	0	0.0	0.0
C+ / 6.3	10.6	1.09	29.69	931	1	98	0	1	122	108.4	-18.5	69	10	1,000	50	5.3	0.0
C+ / 6.3	10.6	1.08	28.99	270	1	98	0	1	122	105.0	-18.7	62	10	1,000	50	0.0	0.0
C+ / 6.3	10.6	1.08	29.30	6	1	98	0	1	122	106.6	-18.6	66	10	0	0	0.0	0.0
C+ / 6.2	10.6	1.09	30.06	302	1	98	0	1	122	111.7	-18.4	73	10	0	0	0.0	0.0

99 Pct = Best
0 Pct = Worst

Fund Type	Fund Name	Ticker Symbol	Overall Investment Rating	Phone	Performance Rating/Pts	Total Return % through 3/31/15			Annualized		Incl. in Returns	
						3 Mo	6 Mo	1Yr / Pct	3Yr / Pct	5Yr / Pct	Dividend Yield	Expense Ratio
GR	● JPMorgan US LgCap Core Plus Sel	JLPSX	A	(800) 480-4111	A / 9.3	1.80	7.54	14.67 /91	18.06 /94	14.41 /81	0.60	2.23
GR	JPMorgan US Research Eqty Plus A	JEPAX	B+	(800) 480-4111	B / 7.8	-0.09	6.42	13.52 /88	16.86 /89	--	0.11	3.86
GR	JPMorgan US Research Eqty Plus C	JEPCX	A-	(800) 480-4111	B+/ 8.3	-0.22	6.14	12.89 /86	16.26 /85	--	0.04	4.33
GR	JPMorgan US Research Eqty Plus R2	JEPZX	A-	(800) 480-4111	B+/ 8.5	-0.13	6.31	13.22 /87	16.56 /87	--	0.00	4.07
GR	JPMorgan US Research Eqty Plus R5	JEPRX	A	(800) 480-4111	A- / 9.0	0.00	6.63	13.97 /89	17.37 /92	--	0.41	3.37
GR	JPMorgan US Research Eqty Plus R6	JEPMX	A+	(800) 480-4111	A- / 9.0	0.04	6.71	14.10 /90	17.44 /92	--	0.45	3.32
GR	JPMorgan US Research Eqty Plus	JEPSX	A	(800) 480-4111	B+/ 8.9	0.00	6.56	13.82 /89	17.15 /91	--	0.25	3.57
SC	JPMorgan US Small Company A	JTUAX	A	(800) 480-4111	A- / 9.2	4.19	16.00	11.00 /78	18.56 /96	15.98 /93	0.00	1.41
SC	JPMorgan US Small Company C	JTUCX	A	(800) 480-4111	A / 9.4	4.05	15.73	10.47 /76	17.95 /94	15.42 /90	0.00	1.91
SC	JPMorgan US Small Company I	JUSSX	A+	(800) 480-4111	A+/ 9.7	4.24	16.22	11.49 /80	19.05 /97	16.45 /95	0.24	0.94
SC	JPMorgan US Small Company R2	JSCZX	A+	(800) 480-4111	A / 9.5	4.10	15.80	10.70 /77	18.25 /95	15.71 /91	0.00	1.64
SC	JPMorgan US Small Company R6	JUSMX	A+	(800) 480-4111	A+/ 9.7	4.30	16.26	11.54 /81	19.17 /97	--	0.28	0.78
SC	JPMorgan US Small Company Sel	JSCSX	A+	(800) 480-4111	A+/ 9.6	4.17	16.09	11.24 /79	18.84 /96	16.26 /94	0.09	1.12
GI	JPMorgan Value Advtg A	JVAAX	A	(800) 480-4111	B / 7.9	1.45	7.33	10.93 /78	17.18 /91	14.99 /87	0.80	1.48
GI	JPMorgan Value Advtg C	JVACX	A+	(800) 480-4111	B+/ 8.4	1.32	7.02	10.35 /76	16.58 /87	14.41 /81	0.52	1.84
GI	JPMorgan Value Advtg Inst	JVAIX	A+	(800) 480-4111	A- / 9.1	1.54	7.59	11.48 /80	17.75 /93	15.56 /90	1.22	0.90
GI	JPMorgan Value Advtg Sel	JVASX	A+	(800) 480-4111	A- / 9.0	1.51	7.45	11.19 /79	17.46 /92	15.28 /89	1.02	1.06
SC	Kalmar Growth With Value Sm Cap	KGSAX	U	(800) 282-2319	U /	5.52	13.56	1.48 /20	--	--	0.00	1.32
SC	Kalmar Growth With Value Sm Cap	KGSIX	U	(800) 282-2319	U /	5.51	13.59	1.53 /20	--	--	0.00	1.22
SC	Kalmar Growth With Value Sm Cap	KGSCX	D+	(800) 282-2319	C / 5.1	5.42	13.52	1.35 /20	11.77 /51	14.96 /86	0.00	1.29
GR	KCM Macro Trends R1	KCMTX	C-	(877) 275-5599	C / 5.1	2.09	3.98	9.51 /72	11.32 /48	5.40 /14	0.34	1.77
GL	KCM Macro Trends R2	KCMBX	C-	(877) 275-5599	C / 4.6	1.92	3.57	8.67 /67	10.47 /42	4.61 /11	0.00	2.52
MC	KEELEY All Cap Value A	KACVX	C+	(800) 533-5344	C+/ 5.9	1.79	2.75	2.08 /22	15.38 /78	13.67 /75	0.11	2.63
MC	KEELEY All Cap Value I	KACIX	C+	(800) 533-5344	C+/ 6.9	1.88	2.92	2.37 /23	15.68 /81	13.94 /77	0.37	2.38
GR	KEELEY Alternative Value A	KALVX	D-	(800) 533-5344	D- / 1.0	0.10	-2.61	-5.59 / 5	6.51 /19	--	0.00	1.44
GR	KEELEY Alternative Value I	KALIX	D-	(800) 533-5344	D- / 1.4	0.21	-2.57	-5.33 / 5	6.77 /20	--	0.00	1.19
IN	KEELEY Mid Cap Dividend Value A	KMDVX	A+	(800) 533-5344	A- / 9.0	4.38	10.30	13.73 /89	18.04 /94	--	0.97	1.60
IN	KEELEY Mid Cap Dividend Value I	KMDIX	A+	(800) 533-5344	A / 9.5	4.50	10.49	14.07 /90	18.35 /95	--	1.24	1.35
MC	KEELEY Mid Cap Value A	KMCVX	C	(800) 533-5344	C / 5.4	2.74	3.60	0.77 /18	14.42 /70	13.16 /70	0.61	1.46
MC	KEELEY Mid Cap Value I	KMCIX	C+	(800) 533-5344	C+/ 6.3	2.84	3.78	1.04 /19	14.72 /73	13.45 /72	1.08	1.21
MC	KEELEY Sm/Md Cap Val A	KSMVX	C+	(800) 533-5344	B / 8.1	4.56	8.12	4.49 /35	17.80 /94	15.34 /89	0.20	1.42
MC	KEELEY Sm/Md Cap Val I	KSMIX	C+	(800) 533-5344	A- / 9.0	4.55	8.26	4.74 /37	18.11 /95	15.62 /91	0.39	1.17
SC	KEELEY Small Cap Div Value A	KSDVX	C+	(800) 533-5344	C+/ 5.7	1.55	10.68	4.65 /36	13.86 /66	14.73 /85	1.41	1.45
SC	KEELEY Small Cap Div Value I	KSDIX	C+	(800) 533-5344	C+/ 6.6	1.56	10.80	4.86 /38	14.11 /68	15.01 /87	1.72	1.20
SC	KEELEY Small Cap Value A	KSCVX	C	(800) 533-5344	C+/ 6.1	2.35	8.43	2.66 /25	15.07 /75	13.24 /70	0.00	1.35
SC	KEELEY Small Cap Value I	KSCIX	C+	(800) 533-5344	B- / 7.1	2.43	8.59	2.94 /26	15.36 /78	13.53 /73	0.22	1.10
GL	Kellner Merger Fund Inst	GAKIX	U	(855) 535-5637	U /	2.09	3.42	5.22 /40	--	--	0.00	8.04
GI	Kinetics Alter Inc Inst	KWIIX	C-	(800) 930-3828	E+/ 0.9	1.49	0.64	2.14 /22	3.77 /10	1.93 / 4	0.00	2.22
GI	Kinetics Alter Inc NL	KWINX	C-	(800) 930-3828	E+/ 0.9	1.44	0.53	1.93 /22	3.56 / 9	1.65 / 4	0.00	2.27
GI	Kinetics Alternative Inc Advisor A	KWIAX	D+	(800) 930-3828	E+/ 0.6	1.39	0.41	1.67 /21	3.31 / 8	1.39 / 4	0.00	2.52
GI	Kinetics Alternative Inc Advisor C	KWICX	C-	(800) 930-3828	E+/ 0.7	1.25	0.16	1.17 /19	2.75 / 7	0.89 / 3	0.00	3.02
GL	Kinetics Global Advisor A	KGLAX	E+	(800) 930-3828	D- / 1.2	4.14	-4.15	-7.05 / 4	8.30 /29	6.81 /22	0.00	3.09
GL	Kinetics Global Advisor C	KGLCX	E+	(800) 930-3828	D- / 1.5	3.88	-4.45	-7.58 / 4	7.63 /25	6.21 /18	0.00	3.59
GL	Kinetics Global No Load	WWWEX	E+	(800) 930-3828	D / 1.8	4.13	-4.13	-7.03 / 4	8.41 /29	6.96 /23	0.00	2.84
TC	Kinetics Internet Advisor A	KINAX	C+	(800) 930-3828	C+/ 6.5	1.69	5.29	5.54 /43	16.64 /88	14.88 /86	0.00	2.09
TC	Kinetics Internet Advisor C	KINCX	C+	(800) 930-3828	B- / 7.1	1.54	5.03	5.05 /39	16.07 /84	14.32 /81	0.00	2.59
TC	Kinetics Internet NL	WWWFX	B	(800) 930-3828	B / 7.8	1.75	5.42	5.81 /45	16.93 /89	15.17 /88	0.00	1.84
GL	Kinetics Market Opps Advisor A	KMKAX	D+	(800) 930-3828	C- / 3.1	2.11	-2.36	-2.70 / 9	12.22 /54	10.42 /48	0.00	2.13
GL	Kinetics Market Opps Advisor C	KMKCX	C-	(800) 930-3828	C- / 3.7	1.97	-2.59	-3.16 / 8	11.67 /50	9.85 /43	0.00	2.63
GL	Kinetics Market Opps Inst	KMKYX	C-	(800) 930-3828	C / 4.4	2.26	-2.17	-2.28 /10	12.77 /58	10.93 /52	0.00	1.83
GL	Kinetics Market Opps NL	KMKNX	C-	(800) 930-3828	C- / 4.2	2.16	-2.29	-2.46 / 9	12.47 /56	10.68 /50	0.00	1.88
HL	Kinetics Medical Advisor A	KRXAX	B+	(800) 930-3828	A+/ 9.9	9.32	15.85	21.21 /97	24.59 /99	16.56 /95	0.00	2.34

● Denotes fund is closed to new investors
* Denotes fund is included in Section II

www.thestreetratings.com

RISK			NET ASSETS		ASSET				Portfolio	BULL / BEAR		FUND MANAGER		MINIMUMS		LOADS	
	3 Year		NAV							Last Bull	Last Bear	Manager	Manager	Initial	Additional	Front	Back
Risk Rating/Pts	Standard Deviation	Beta	As of 3/31/15	Total $(Mil)	Cash %	Stocks %	Bonds %	Other %	Portfolio Turnover Ratio	Market Return	Market Return	Quality Pct	Tenure (Years)	Purch. $	Purch. $	End Load	End Load
C+ / 6.2	10.6	1.09	29.93	10,336	1	98	0	1	122	110.3	-18.5	71	10	1,000,000	0	0.0	0.0
C+ / 6.7	10.3	1.07	23.48	3	1	98	0	1	101	105.3	-18.1	62	1	1,000	50	5.3	0.0
C+ / 6.7	10.4	1.07	23.16	1	1	98	0	1	101	101.7	-18.2	54	1	1,000	50	0.0	0.0
C+ / 6.7	10.4	1.07	23.42	N/A	1	98	0	1	101	103.5	-18.2	58	1	0	0	0.0	0.0
C+ / 6.7	10.4	1.07	23.72	N/A	1	98	0	1	101	108.5	-18.0	68	1	0	0	0.0	0.0
C+ / 6.7	10.4	1.07	23.75	N/A	1	98	0	1	101	108.7	-17.9	68	1	15,000,000	0	0.0	0.0
C+ / 6.7	10.3	1.07	23.66	21	1	98	0	1	101	107.0	-18.0	66	1	1,000,000	0	0.0	0.0
C+ / 6.1	13.8	1.01	16.92	204	5	94	0	1	51	118.5	-26.7	83	11	1,000	50	5.3	0.0
C+ / 6.1	13.9	1.02	16.44	38	5	94	0	1	51	114.7	-26.7	79	11	1,000	50	0.0	0.0
C+ / 6.2	13.7	1.01	17.21	314	5	94	0	1	51	121.5	-26.5	86	11	3,000,000	0	0.0	0.0
C+ / 6.2	13.8	1.01	16.74	13	5	94	0	1	51	116.9	-26.7	81	11		0	0.0	0.0
C+ / 6.2	13.8	1.01	17.22	67	5	94	0	1	51	N/A	N/A	86	11	15,000,000	0	0.0	0.0
C+ / 6.1	13.8	1.01	17.23	228	5	94	0	1	51	120.3	-26.5	84	11	1,000,000	0	0.0	0.0
B- / 7.6	9.4	0.95	30.10	2,333	9	90	0	1	36	103.7	-17.4	82	10	1,000	50	5.3	0.0
B- / 7.6	9.4	0.95	30.01	654	9	90	0	1	36	100.3	-17.5	78	10	1,000	50	0.0	0.0
B- / 7.6	9.5	0.95	30.27	4,908	9	90	0	1	36	107.3	-17.2	85	10	3,000,000	0	0.0	0.0
B- / 7.6	9.5	0.95	30.23	2,940	9	90	0	1	36	105.5	-17.3	84	10	1,000,000	0	0.0	0.0
U /	N/A	N/A	20.83	67	3	96	0	1	43	N/A	N/A	N/A	18	100,000	500	0.0	2.0
U /	N/A	N/A	20.86	442	3	96	0	1	43	N/A	N/A	N/A	18	250,000	500	0.0	2.0
C- / 4.1	14.2	0.99	20.80	217	3	96	0	1	43	77.6	-21.4	17	18	2,500	500	0.0	2.0
C+ / 5.6	10.2	0.95	12.68	95	13	86	0	1	272	57.2	-21.7	21	7	5,000	1,000	0.0	0.0
C / 5.5	10.3	0.53	12.19	N/A	13	86	0	1	272	53.2	-21.9	94	7	5,000	1,000	0.0	0.0
C+ / 6.6	11.0	0.94	18.75	65	1	98	0	1	35	93.7	-22.0	61	9	2,500	50	4.5	0.0
C+ / 6.7	10.9	0.93	18.92	55	1	98	0	1	35	95.5	-22.0	66	9	1,000,000	10,000	0.0	0.0
C+ / 6.3	8.8	0.68	9.58	14	41	58	0	1	66	35.8	-17.6	17	5	2,500	50	4.5	0.0
C+ / 6.4	8.8	0.68	9.73	11	41	58	0	1	66	37.2	-17.5	19	5	1,000,000	10,000	0.0	0.0
B- / 7.1	9.7	0.94	18.91	11	4	95	0	1	13	N/A	N/A	87	4	2,500	50	4.5	0.0
B- / 7.1	9.7	0.95	18.92	24	4	95	0	1	13	N/A	N/A	87	4	1,000,000	10,000	0.0	0.0
C+ / 6.2	11.9	1.01	16.11	50	0	99	0	1	29	90.1	-23.4	32	10	2,500	50	4.5	0.0
C+ / 6.2	11.9	1.01	16.27	32	0	99	0	1	29	91.9	-23.4	34	10	1,000,000	10,000	0.0	0.0
C- / 3.8	12.7	1.09	14.68	111	1	98	0	1	43	117.3	-28.1	55	8	2,500	50	4.5	0.0
C- / 3.8	12.7	1.09	14.93	195	1	98	0	1	43	119.1	-28.0	60	8	1,000,000	10,000	0.0	0.0
C+ / 6.7	11.7	0.81	17.46	51	4	95	0	1	39	83.0	-19.5	74	6	2,500	50	4.5	0.0
C+ / 6.7	11.8	0.82	17.48	103	4	95	0	1	39	84.5	-19.4	76	6	1,000,000	10,000	0.0	0.0
C+ / 5.6	13.7	0.98	39.22	1,439	0	99	0	1	43	92.0	-26.9	57	22	2,500	50	4.5	0.0
C+ / 5.6	13.7	0.98	39.58	1,044	0	99	0	1	43	93.6	-26.9	61	22	1,000,000	10,000	0.0	0.0
U /	N/A	N/A	10.77	61	56	43	0	1	144	N/A	N/A	N/A	3	100,000	100	0.0	0.0
B+ / 9.2	2.9	0.24	91.49	26	3	0	96	1	19	29.4	-16.3	68	5	1,000,000	0	0.0	2.0
B+ / 9.2	2.9	0.24	90.35	8	3	0	96	1	19	28.6	-16.4	66	5	2,500	0	0.0	2.0
B+ / 9.2	2.8	0.24	89.92	1	3	0	96	1	19	27.5	-16.5	63	5	2,500	0	5.8	2.0
B+ / 9.2	2.8	0.24	87.69	1	3	0	96	1	19	25.3	-16.6	54	5	2,500	0	0.0	2.0
C / 5.0	13.8	0.92	5.53	1	14	85	0	1	15	52.8	-20.4	62	16	2,500	0	5.8	2.0
C / 5.0	13.7	0.92	5.36	2	14	85	0	1	15	50.0	-20.8	53	16	2,500	0	0.0	2.0
C / 5.0	13.8	0.92	5.55	7	14	85	0	1	15	53.6	-20.4	63	16	2,500	0	0.0	2.0
C / 5.5	12.6	1.15	55.43	5	4	95	0	1	8	95.4	-22.2	39	16	2,500	0	5.8	2.0
C / 5.5	12.7	1.16	52.61	1	4	95	0	1	8	92.3	-22.4	32	16	2,500	0	0.0	2.0
C+ / 5.6	12.6	1.15	57.06	147	4	95	0	1	8	97.2	-22.1	43	16	2,500	0	0.0	2.0
C+ / 6.3	13.7	0.86	16.94	7	25	74	0	1	21	73.5	-18.7	91	9	2,500	0	5.8	2.0
C+ / 6.3	13.7	0.86	16.56	5	25	74	0	1	21	70.6	-18.9	89	9	2,500	0	0.0	2.0
C+ / 6.3	13.7	0.86	17.17	3	25	74	0	1	21	76.4	-18.6	92	9	1,000,000	0	0.0	2.0
C+ / 6.3	13.7	0.86	17.04	37	25	74	0	1	21	74.9	-18.6	91	9	2,500	0	0.0	2.0
C / 4.8	13.0	0.88	32.48	5	2	97	0	1	12	118.7	-15.5	97	14	2,500	0	5.8	2.0

Fund Type	Fund Name	Ticker Symbol	Overall Investment Rating	Phone	Performance Rating/Pts	3 Mo	6 Mo	1Yr / Pct	3Yr / Pct	5Yr / Pct	Dividend Yield	Expense Ratio
HL	Kinetics Medical Advisor C	KRXCX	B+	(800) 930-3828	A+ / 9.9	9.19	15.55	20.58 /97	23.94 /99	15.97 /93	0.00	2.84
HL	Kinetics Medical NL	MEDRX	B+	(800) 930-3828	A+ / 9.9	9.39	15.99	21.52 /97	24.89 /99	16.84 /96	0.00	2.09
GI	Kinetics Multi-Disciplinary Inc A	KMDAX	D-	(800) 930-3828	E+ / 0.7	1.62	1.99	2.27 /23	4.07 /10	6.29 /19	2.87	2.13
GI	Kinetics Multi-Disciplinary Inc C	KMDCX	D-	(800) 930-3828	E+ / 0.9	1.52	1.65	1.75 /21	3.52 / 9	5.74 /15	2.63	2.63
GI	Kinetics Multi-Disciplinary Inc I	KMDYX	D-	(800) 930-3828	D- / 1.1	1.72	2.22	2.71 /25	4.50 /11	6.74 /21	3.56	1.83
GI	Kinetics Multi-Disciplinary Inc NL	KMDNX	D-	(800) 930-3828	D- / 1.1	1.68	2.07	2.46 /24	4.28 /11	6.55 /20	3.32	1.88
GR	Kinetics Paradigm Fund A	KNPAX	C+	(800) 930-3828	C+ / 6.2	5.57	2.29	3.25 /28	16.34 /86	12.08 /61	0.00	1.97
GR	Kinetics Paradigm Fund C	KNPCX	C+	(800) 930-3828	C+ / 6.8	5.46	2.03	2.75 /25	15.74 /81	11.52 /57	0.00	2.47
GR	Kinetics Paradigm Fund I	KNPYX	B	(800) 930-3828	B / 7.6	5.69	2.50	3.71 /30	16.85 /89	12.57 /65	0.00	1.67
GR	Kinetics Paradigm Fund NL	WWNPX	B	(800) 930-3828	B- / 7.4	5.63	2.42	3.51 /29	16.63 /88	12.36 /63	0.00	1.72
GL	Kinetics Small Cap Opps Advisor A	KSOAX	C+	(800) 930-3828	C+ / 6.9	5.11	-2.50	-3.16 / 8	19.01 /97	12.98 /68	0.00	1.98
GL	Kinetics Small Cap Opps Advisor C	KSOCX	B-	(800) 930-3828	B- / 7.5	4.96	-2.74	-3.65 / 8	18.43 /95	12.42 /63	0.00	2.48
GL	Kinetics Small Cap Opps Inst	KSCYX	B	(800) 930-3828	B+ / 8.4	5.22	-2.27	-2.71 / 9	19.55 /97	13.48 /73	0.00	1.68
GL	Kinetics Small Cap Opps NL	KSCOX	B	(800) 930-3828	B / 8.2	5.16	-2.37	-2.90 / 9	19.32 /97	13.27 /71	0.00	1.73
MC	Kirr Marbach Parners Value	KMVAX	C+	(800) 870-8039	C+ / 6.4	3.35	6.45	2.77 /25	14.63 /72	16.33 /94	0.00	1.45
GL	Kopernik Global All-Cap A	KGGAX	U	(866) 777-7818	U /	-1.27	-17.08	-22.65 / 1	--	--	0.57	1.39
GL	Kopernik Global All-Cap Inst	KGGIX	U	(866) 777-7818	U /	-1.14	-16.94	-22.43 / 1	--	--	1.12	1.14
FO	KP International Equity Instl	KPIEX	U	(855) 457-3637	U /	4.73	0.82	0.22 /16	--	--	2.42	0.57
GR	KP Large Cap Equity Instl	KPLCX	U	(855) 457-3637	U /	2.22	7.45	12.44 /85	--	--	1.38	0.37
GI	KP Retirement Path 2015 Instl	KPRAX	U	(855) 457-3637	U /	1.99	3.40	5.15 /40	--	--	2.35	0.38
GI	KP Retirement Path 2020 Instl	KPRBX	U	(855) 457-3637	U /	2.27	3.83	5.38 /41	--	--	2.38	0.42
GI	KP Retirement Path 2025 Instl	KPRCX	U	(855) 457-3637	U /	2.57	4.20	5.54 /43	--	--	2.46	0.46
GI	KP Retirement Path 2030 Instl	KPRDX	U	(855) 457-3637	U /	2.97	4.67	5.70 /44	--	--	2.54	0.50
GI	KP Retirement Path 2035 Instl	KPREX	U	(855) 457-3637	U /	3.07	4.95	5.88 /45	--	--	2.55	0.53
GI	KP Retirement Path 2040 Instl	KPRFX	U	(855) 457-3637	U /	3.17	5.00	6.04 /47	--	--	2.56	0.54
GI	KP Retirement Path 2045 Instl	KPRGX	U	(855) 457-3637	U /	3.27	5.06	6.10 /47	--	--	2.56	0.54
GI	KP Retirement Path 2050 Instl	KPRHX	U	(855) 457-3637	U /	3.27	5.05	6.09 /47	--	--	2.56	0.54
SC	KP Small Cap Equity Instl	KPSCX	U	(855) 457-3637	U /	3.68	11.12	5.57 /43	--	--	0.82	0.54
GL	KS 529 LearningQuest ESP 100% Eq		C+	(800) 345-6488	C+ / 6.2	2.50	6.04	8.97 /69	13.17 /61	11.95 /60	0.00	0.99
GL	KS 529 LearningQuest ESP 100% Eq		C+	(800) 345-6488	C / 5.4	2.61	6.21	9.16 /70	13.33 /62	11.96 /60	0.00	1.52
GL	KS 529 LearningQuest ESP 100% Eq		C+	(800) 345-6488	C+ / 5.9	2.50	5.92	8.49 /66	12.51 /56	11.15 /54	0.00	2.27
IX	KS 529 LearningQuest ESP 500 Idx		A	(800) 345-6488	B / 8.1	0.87	5.76	12.47 /85	15.83 /82	14.14 /79	0.00	0.25
GL	KS 529 LearningQuest ESP Aggr A		C	(800) 345-6488	C- / 3.1	1.99	4.53	7.03 /55	9.59 /37	9.44 /40	0.00	1.37
GL	KS 529 LearningQuest ESP Aggr C		C+	(800) 345-6488	C- / 3.5	1.81	4.16	6.29 /49	8.72 /31	8.62 /34	0.00	2.12
GL	KS 529 LearningQuest ESP Aggr Idx		B	(800) 345-6488	C / 5.3	2.01	4.97	8.42 /66	11.72 /51	10.81 /51	0.00	0.50
GL	KS 529 LearningQuest ESP Aggr		C+	(800) 345-6488	C- / 4.1	1.90	4.46	7.00 /55	9.66 /37	9.68 /42	0.00	0.82
GL	KS 529 LearningQuest ESP Bal Idx		B	(800) 345-6488	C / 4.9	1.72	5.67	9.59 /72	10.83 /44	10.60 /49	0.00	0.28
GL	KS 529 LearningQuest ESP Csv A		C	(800) 345-6488	D / 1.7	1.33	3.30	5.20 /40	7.04 /22	7.38 /26	0.00	1.24
GL	KS 529 LearningQuest ESP Csv C		C	(800) 345-6488	D / 2.1	1.25	3.01	4.67 /36	6.31 /18	6.61 /21	0.00	1.99
GL	KS 529 LearningQuest ESP Csv Idx		C+	(800) 345-6488	D+ / 2.5	1.69	3.75	6.19 /48	6.80 /20	6.89 /22	0.00	0.50
GL	KS 529 LearningQuest ESP Csv Port		C+	(800) 345-6488	D+ / 2.6	1.26	3.43	5.39 /42	7.30 /23	7.68 /28	0.00	0.75
GL	KS 529 LearningQuest ESP Dsp Gr A		B-	(800) 345-6488	C+ / 6.3	1.46	5.85	12.28 /84	14.75 /73	15.67 /91	0.00	1.49
GL	KS 529 LearningQuest ESP Dsp Gr C		B-	(800) 345-6488	C+ / 6.8	1.31	5.44	11.50 /80	13.92 /67	14.79 /85	0.00	2.24
GL	KS 529 LearningQuest ESP Fndl Eq		B-	(800) 345-6488	C+ / 6.6	0.72	6.61	12.77 /86	15.19 /76	14.04 /78	0.00	1.46
GL	KS 529 LearningQuest ESP Fndl Eq		B+	(800) 345-6488	B- / 7.1	0.51	6.32	12.04 /83	14.35 /70	13.18 /70	0.00	2.21
GL	KS 529 LearningQuest ESP Heritage		C+	(800) 345-6488	C+ / 6.9	7.89	13.60	13.46 /88	14.19 /69	14.44 /82	0.00	1.46
GL	KS 529 LearningQuest ESP Heritage		B-	(800) 345-6488	B- / 7.4	7.73	13.20	12.63 /85	13.38 /62	13.62 /74	0.00	2.21
FO	KS 529 LearningQuest ESP Itl Gr A		D-	(800) 345-6488	D / 2.2	4.20	1.60	-1.55 /11	9.01 /33	7.34 /25	0.00	1.83
FO	KS 529 LearningQuest ESP Itl Gr C		D	(800) 345-6488	D+ / 2.6	4.25	1.31	-2.17 /10	8.31 /29	6.62 /21	0.00	2.58
GL	KS 529 LearningQuest ESP LvStr		C+	(800) 345-6488	D+ / 2.6	1.11	3.25	5.34 /41	7.23 /23	7.78 /29	0.00	1.00
GL	KS 529 LearningQuest ESP LvStr		C+	(800) 345-6488	C- / 3.4	1.66	4.26	6.38 /50	8.48 /30	8.82 /35	0.00	1.06
GL	KS 529 LearningQuest ESP MC Val		A	(800) 345-6488	B / 7.9	1.42	8.00	13.12 /87	17.02 /90	14.31 /80	0.00	1.45

• Denotes fund is closed to new investors
* Denotes fund is included in Section II

www.thestreetratings.com

I. Index of Stock Mutual Funds

RISK	3 Year		NET ASSETS		ASSET				Portfolio	BULL / BEAR		FUND MANAGER		MINIMUMS		LOADS	
Risk Rating/Pts	Standard Deviation	Beta	NAV As of 3/31/15	Total $(Mil)	Cash %	Stocks %	Bonds %	Other %	Portfolio Turnover Ratio	Last Bull Market Return	Last Bear Market Return	Manager Quality Pct	Manager Tenure (Years)	Initial Purch. $	Additional Purch. $	Front End Load	Back End Load
C / 4.9	13.0	0.87	31.83	1	2	97	0	1	12	114.8	-15.6	97	14	2,500	0	0.0	2.0
C / 4.8	13.0	0.88	33.55	24	2	97	0	1	12	120.4	-15.3	98	14	2,500	0	0.0	2.0
C+ / 6.2	6.3	0.47	10.83	12	7	0	79	14	54	34.5	-12.5	24	7	2,500	0	5.8	2.0
C+ / 6.1	6.4	0.48	10.73	11	7	0	79	14	54	32.2	-12.6	18	7	2,500	0	0.0	2.0
C+ / 6.1	6.4	0.48	10.90	109	7	0	79	14	54	36.5	-12.3	27	7	1,000,000	0	0.0	2.0
C+ / 6.2	6.3	0.47	10.87	10	7	0	79	14	54	35.6	-12.4	26	7	2,500	0	0.0	2.0
C+ / 6.2	12.4	1.07	35.25	175	13	86	0	1	4	92.2	-25.0	55	14	2,500	0	5.8	2.0
C+ / 6.2	12.4	1.07	33.62	140	13	86	0	1	4	88.9	-25.2	46	14	2,500	0	0.0	2.0
C+ / 6.2	12.4	1.07	36.02	355	13	86	0	1	4	95.2	-24.8	61	14	1,000,000	0	0.0	2.0
C+ / 6.2	12.4	1.07	36.00	461	13	86	0	1	4	93.8	-24.9	58	14	2,500	0	0.0	2.0
C+ / 5.6	14.2	0.84	38.28	23	9	90	0	1	6	108.5	-22.1	98	13	2,500	0	5.8	2.0
C / 5.5	14.3	0.85	37.22	13	9	90	0	1	6	105.1	-22.3	98	13	2,500	0	0.0	2.0
C+ / 5.6	14.2	0.84	39.52	72	9	90	0	1	6	111.7	-22.0	98	13	1,000,000	0	0.0	2.0
C+ / 5.6	14.2	0.84	39.12	231	9	90	0	1	6	110.4	-22.1	98	13	2,500	0	0.0	2.0
C+ / 6.6	12.8	1.03	23.77	78	5	94	0	1	11	100.2	-25.8	31	28	1,000	100	0.0	1.0
U /	N/A	N/A	7.79	73	12	87	0	1	42	N/A	N/A	N/A	2	3,000	250	5.8	0.0
U /	N/A	N/A	7.78	610	12	87	0	1	42	N/A	N/A	N/A	2	1,000,000	0	0.0	0.0
U /	N/A	N/A	9.74	1,002	4	95	0	1	0	N/A	N/A	N/A	1	0	0	0.0	0.0
U /	N/A	N/A	11.06	1,211	3	96	0	1	0	N/A	N/A	N/A	1	0	0	0.0	0.0
U /	N/A	N/A	10.27	527	1	34	64	1	0	N/A	N/A	N/A	1	0	0	0.0	0.0
U /	N/A	N/A	10.34	705	1	46	52	1	0	N/A	N/A	N/A	1	0	0	0.0	0.0
U /	N/A	N/A	10.37	692	0	60	38	2	0	N/A	N/A	N/A	1	0	0	0.0	0.0
U /	N/A	N/A	10.39	620	0	73	25	2	0	N/A	N/A	N/A	1	0	0	0.0	0.0
U /	N/A	N/A	10.41	668	0	81	17	2	0	N/A	N/A	N/A	1	0	0	0.0	0.0
U /	N/A	N/A	10.42	584	0	86	12	2	0	N/A	N/A	N/A	1	0	0	0.0	0.0
U /	N/A	N/A	10.42	387	0	89	10	1	0	N/A	N/A	N/A	1	0	0	0.0	0.0
U /	N/A	N/A	10.42	143	0	89	10	1	0	N/A	N/A	N/A	1	0	0	0.0	0.0
U /	N/A	N/A	10.70	847	5	94	0	1	0	N/A	N/A	N/A	1	0	0	0.0	0.0
C+ / 6.9	9.8	0.66	11.06	62	1	98	0	1	0	82.4	-19.1	96	N/A	500	50	0.0	0.0
C+ / 6.9	9.9	0.66	10.61	11	2	98	0	0	0	82.5	-19.6	96	N/A	500	50	5.8	0.0
C+ / 6.9	9.8	0.65	9.84	3	2	98	0	0	0	77.8	-19.8	95	N/A	500	50	0.0	0.0
B- / 7.3	9.5	0.99	10.46	40	0	99	0	1	0	98.3	-16.4	66	N/A	500	50	0.0	0.0
B / 8.4	7.0	0.47	7.16	31	0	68	31	1	0	55.1	-13.1	93	N/A	500	50	5.8	0.0
B / 8.4	7.1	0.48	6.76	10	0	68	31	1	0	51.0	-13.3	91	N/A	500	50	0.0	0.0
B / 8.1	7.9	0.52	7.60	19	0	79	19	2	0	68.2	-14.6	95	N/A	500	50	0.0	0.0
B / 8.5	6.9	0.47	7.49	176	1	68	29	2	0	55.7	-12.1	93	N/A	500	50	0.0	0.0
B / 8.7	5.7	0.86	10.06	36	0	60	39	1	0	58.3	-9.0	88	N/A	500	50	0.0	0.0
B+ / 9.3	5.0	0.34	6.88	34	10	49	40	1	0	38.7	-8.8	91	N/A	500	50	5.8	0.0
B+ / 9.3	5.0	0.34	6.50	14	10	49	40	1	0	35.4	-9.0	89	N/A	500	50	0.0	0.0
B+ / 9.8	3.9	0.26	7.20	8	15	39	44	2	0	34.2	-5.9	92	N/A	500	50	0.0	0.0
B+ / 9.5	4.9	0.33	7.24	381	11	49	38	2	0	39.2	-7.8	92	N/A	500	50	0.0	0.0
B- / 7.0	10.1	0.61	9.05	1	0	99	0	1	0	98.1	-16.6	97	N/A	100	50	5.8	0.0
B- / 7.0	10.2	0.61	8.53	1	0	99	0	1	0	93.1	-16.9	96	N/A	100	50	0.0	0.0
B- / 7.4	9.4	0.54	8.39	1	0	99	0	1	0	97.7	-16.6	98	N/A	100	50	5.8	0.0
B- / 7.3	9.5	0.55	7.91	1	0	99	0	1	0	92.6	-16.9	97	N/A	100	50	0.0	0.0
C+ / 5.8	11.6	0.65	9.44	1	2	97	0	1	0	86.8	-21.5	96	N/A	100	50	5.8	0.0
C+ / 5.8	11.7	0.65	8.92	1	2	97	0	1	0	82.5	-21.8	96	N/A	100	50	0.0	0.0
C+ / 5.8	12.6	0.94	5.70	1	0	99	0	1	0	55.5	-24.3	69	N/A	100	50	5.8	0.0
C+ / 5.7	12.7	0.94	5.40	1	0	99	0	1	0	51.9	-24.6	59	N/A	100	50	0.0	0.0
B+ / 9.4	4.8	0.74	7.30	2	10	42	46	2	0	40.1	-8.1	73	N/A	500	50	0.0	0.0
B+ / 9.1	5.8	0.90	7.34	3	6	52	40	2	0	48.2	-10.6	71	N/A	500	50	0.0	0.0
B- / 7.5	8.9	0.51	9.31	1	3	96	0	1	0	97.5	-17.3	98	N/A	100	50	5.8	0.0

Fund Type	Fund Name	Ticker Symbol	Overall Investment Rating	Phone	Perfor-mance Rating/Pts	3 Mo	6 Mo	1Yr / Pct	3Yr / Pct	5Yr / Pct	Dividend Yield	Expense Ratio
	99 Pct = Best							Total Return % through 3/31/15			Incl. in Returns	
	0 Pct = Worst								Annualized			
GL	KS 529 LearningQuest ESP MC Val		A+	(800) 345-6488	B+ / 8.3	1.27	7.48	12.29 /84	16.13 /84	13.43 /72	0.00	2.20
GL	KS 529 LearningQuest ESP Mdt A		C	(800) 345-6488	D+ / 2.4	1.73	3.98	6.33 /49	8.35 /29	8.48 /33	0.00	1.31
GL	KS 529 LearningQuest ESP Mdt C		C	(800) 345-6488	D+ / 2.8	1.37	3.58	5.38 /41	7.51 /24	7.64 /27	0.00	2.06
GL	KS 529 LearningQuest ESP Mdt Idx		C+	(800) 345-6488	C- / 3.8	1.78	4.36	7.23 /57	9.19 /34	8.79 /35	0.00	0.50
GL	KS 529 LearningQuest ESP Mdt Port		C+	(800) 345-6488	C- / 3.3	1.65	3.93	6.31 /49	8.45 /30	8.71 /35	0.00	0.79
GL	KS 529 LearningQuest ESP Nw Op II		C+	(800) 345-6488	B / 7.9	6.49	17.43	11.48 /80	15.83 /82	15.26 /89	0.00	1.81
GL	KS 529 LearningQuest ESP Nw Op II		B-	(800) 345-6488	B+ / 8.4	6.37	17.03	10.79 /78	15.01 /75	14.44 /82	0.00	2.56
RE	KS 529 LearningQuest ESP Rl Est A		C+	(800) 345-6488	B+ / 8.6	5.20	20.04	24.42 /98	13.29 /62	15.85 /92	0.00	1.61
RE	KS 529 LearningQuest ESP Rl Est C		B-	(800) 345-6488	B+ / 8.9	5.00	19.65	23.53 /98	12.39 /55	14.98 /87	0.00	2.36
GL	KS 529 LearningQuest ESP Tot Gr		B+	(800) 345-6488	B- / 7.2	2.12	5.89	10.06 /75	14.71 /73	13.03 /68	0.00	0.30
GL	KS 529 LearningQuest ESP Very Agg		C+	(800) 345-6488	C / 5.5	2.19	5.37	8.13 /64	11.95 /52	11.11 /54	0.00	0.93
GL	KS 529 LearningQuest ESP Very Agg		C	(800) 345-6488	C / 4.5	2.30	5.48	8.37 /65	11.98 /52	11.08 /53	0.00	1.47
GL	KS 529 LearningQuest ESP Very Agg		C+	(800) 345-6488	C / 5.0	2.13	5.16	7.52 /59	11.18 /47	10.28 /47	0.00	2.22
GL	KS 529 LearningQuest ESP Very Csv		C	(800) 345-6488	D- / 1.3	0.76	2.15	3.42 /29	4.54 /12	5.08 /12	0.00	0.70
GL	KS 529 LearningQuest ESP Very Csv		C-	(800) 345-6488	E+ / 0.9	0.80	2.12	3.29 /28	4.34 /11	4.76 /11	0.00	1.11
GL	KS 529 LearningQuest ESP Very Csv		C-	(800) 345-6488	D- / 1.0	0.51	1.55	2.43 /24	3.50 / 9	3.95 / 8	0.00	1.86
GL	KS 529 Schwab CSP Aggressive Port		B	(800) 345-6488	C+ / 5.8	2.51	6.15	6.28 /49	12.64 /57	11.13 /54	0.00	1.41
GL	KS 529 Schwab CSP Conservative		C	(800) 345-6488	D- / 1.0	0.59	1.48	2.51 /24	3.54 / 9	4.29 / 9	0.00	0.92
GL	KS 529 Schwab CSP Mdt Aggr Port		B-	(800) 345-6488	C / 4.7	2.10	5.31	5.92 /46	10.98 /45	10.04 /45	0.00	1.33
GL	KS 529 Schwab CSP Mdt Csv Port		C	(800) 345-6488	D / 2.0	1.21	2.91	3.92 /31	6.29 /18	6.76 /22	0.00	1.13
GL	KS 529 Schwab CSP Moderate Port		C+	(800) 345-6488	C- / 3.4	1.65	4.08	4.97 /38	8.79 /32	8.62 /34	0.00	1.24
GR	Lateef A	LIMAX	C	(866) 499-2151	C / 4.9	2.29	7.98	7.98 /63	12.94 /59	13.36 /72	0.09	1.41
GR	Lateef C	LIMCX	C	(866) 499-2151	C / 5.3	2.14	7.66	7.18 /57	12.11 /53	12.55 /64	0.00	2.16
GR	Lateef I	LIMIX	C+	(866) 499-2151	C+ / 6.0	2.33	8.14	8.22 /64	13.22 /61	13.67 /75	0.34	1.16
FO	Laudus Internatl MarketMasters Inv	SWOIX	D+	(800) 407-0256	C- / 3.1	5.23	3.22	-2.27 /10	9.51 /36	8.52 /33	1.36	1.60
FO	Laudus Internatl MarketMasters Sel	SWMIX	D+	(800) 407-0256	C- / 3.2	5.23	3.26	-2.15 /10	9.66 /37	8.67 /34	1.52	1.44
EM	Laudus Mondrian Emg Mkts Inst	LEMNX	E	(800) 407-0256	E / 0.3	-0.97	-5.21	-3.03 / 9	-2.72 / 2	0.71 / 3	2.91	1.52
EM	Laudus Mondrian Emg Mkts Inv	LEMIX	E	(800) 407-0256	E / 0.3	-1.09	-5.42	-3.46 / 8	-3.09 / 2	0.33 / 3	2.47	1.86
EM	Laudus Mondrian Emg Mkts Sel	LEMSX	E	(800) 407-0256	E / 0.3	-1.09	-5.33	-3.26 / 8	-2.84 / 2	0.62 / 3	2.79	1.59
FO	Laudus Mondrian Intl Eq Inst	LIEIX	E	(800) 407-0256	C- / 3.0	5.52	1.49	0.11 /16	9.16 /34	6.34 /19	11.41	1.07
FO	Laudus Mondrian Intl Eq Inv	LIEQX	E	(800) 407-0256	D+ / 2.8	5.39	1.37	-0.02 /15	8.87 /32	6.02 /17	11.38	1.29
FO	Laudus Mondrian Intl Eq Sel	LIEFX	E	(800) 407-0256	C- / 3.0	5.54	1.43	0.04 /16	9.12 /34	6.26 /18	11.36	1.08
SC	Laudus Small-Cap MarketMasters Inv	SWOSX	C+	(800) 407-0256	C+ / 6.6	5.95	15.10	6.59 /52	13.56 /64	11.99 /60	0.15	1.60
SC	Laudus Small-Cap MarketMasters Sel	SWMSX	C+	(800) 407-0256	C+ / 6.7	6.02	15.22	6.72 /53	13.73 /65	12.17 /62	0.30	1.54
GR	Laudus US Large Cap Growth	LGILX	C	(800) 407-0256	B / 8.0	3.61	9.29	14.99 /92	15.40 /78	15.76 /92	0.00	0.77
GL	Lazard Cap Alloc Srs Opp Stra Open	LCAOX	D	(800) 821-6474	D / 1.6	0.80	2.72	4.42 /35	5.67 /15	6.87 /22	2.39	2.29
GL	Lazard Capital Allocator Stra Inst	LCAIX	D+	(800) 821-6474	D / 1.8	0.90	2.82	4.72 /37	6.01 /17	7.22 /24	2.68	1.58
FO	Lazard Developing Markets Eq Inst	LDMIX	E	(800) 821-6474	E- / 0.2	-3.64	-9.64	-10.27 / 3	-6.35 / 1	-2.37 / 2	1.65	1.17
FO	Lazard Developing Markets Eq Open	LDMOX	E	(800) 821-6474	E- / 0.2	-3.74	-9.79	-10.58 / 3	-6.68 / 1	-2.68 / 1	1.31	1.45
CV	Lazard Emerging Markets Debt Inst	LEDIX	E-	(800) 821-6474	E / 0.4	-1.01	-6.41	-5.71 / 5	-0.21 / 4	--	5.65	0.97
CV	Lazard Emerging Markets Debt Open	LEDOX	E	(800) 821-6474	E / 0.4	-0.97	-6.61	-6.02 / 4	-0.40 / 4	--	4.94	1.39
EM	● Lazard Emerging Markets Inst	LZEMX	E	(800) 821-6474	E / 0.3	-1.92	-8.49	-5.60 / 5	-0.92 / 3	1.68 / 4	2.18	1.09
EM	● Lazard Emerging Markets Open	LZOEX	E	(800) 821-6474	E / 0.3	-1.98	-8.62	-5.90 / 5	-1.20 / 3	1.38 / 4	1.82	1.37
EM	Lazard Emerging Mkts Core Eq Inst	ECEIX	U	(800) 821-6474	U /	2.91	-0.89	2.46 /24	--	--	0.88	1.34
EM	Lazard Emerging Mkts Eq Blend Inst	EMBIX	E	(800) 821-6474	E- / 0.2	-1.80	-8.59	-7.49 / 4	-3.77 / 2	--	2.17	1.33
EM	Lazard Emerging Mkts Eq Blend	EMBOX	E	(800) 821-6474	E- / 0.2	-1.90	-8.72	-7.79 / 3	-4.05 / 2	--	1.85	1.69
GR	Lazard Fundamental Long/Short Inst	LLSIX	U	(800) 821-6474	U /	3.37	15.23	--	--	--	0.00	N/A
OT	Lazard Global Listed Infr Inst	GLIFX	A+	(800) 821-6474	A+ / 9.8	8.23	12.65	18.44 /96	21.93 /98	14.82 /85	6.30	1.01
OT	Lazard Global Listed Infr Open	GLFOX	A+	(800) 821-6474	A+ / 9.8	8.22	12.55	18.18 /96	21.60 /98	14.45 /82	6.04	1.32
RE	Lazard Global Realty Equity Inst	LITIX	C-	(800) 821-6474	C+ / 6.2	4.68	7.54	12.47 /85	12.55 /56	--	3.54	5.46
RE	Lazard Global Realty Equity Open	LITOX	C-	(800) 821-6474	C+ / 6.0	4.55	7.36	12.09 /83	12.21 /54	8.31 /32	3.26	5.81
FO	Lazard Intl Equity Inst	LZIEX	D+	(800) 821-6474	C- / 3.7	5.67	2.70	0.68 /18	9.93 /39	8.13 /31	0.90	0.95

● Denotes fund is closed to new investors
* Denotes fund is included in Section II

www.thestreetratings.com

RISK			NET ASSETS		ASSET					BULL / BEAR		FUND MANAGER		MINIMUMS		LOADS	
	3 Year		NAV						Portfolio	Last Bull	Last Bear	Manager	Manager	Initial	Additional	Front	Back
Risk Rating/Pts	Standard Deviation	Beta	As of 3/31/15	Total $(Mil)	Cash %	Stocks %	Bonds %	Other %	Turnover Ratio	Market Return	Market Return	Quality Pct	Tenure (Years)	Purch. $	Purch. $	End Load	End Load
B- /7.5	8.8	0.50	8.77	1	3	96	0	1	0	92.6	-17.7	98	N/A	100	50	0.0	0.0
B /8.9	6.0	0.41	7.06	47	5	58	35	2	0	46.7	-10.7	92	N/A	500	50	5.8	0.0
B /8.9	6.1	0.41	6.66	19	5	58	35	2	0	43.1	-11.0	90	N/A	500	50	0.0	0.0
B+ /9.1	5.9	0.40	7.42	13	10	59	29	2	0	50.1	-10.6	94	N/A	500	50	0.0	0.0
B+ /9.0	5.9	0.40	7.41	382	6	59	34	1	0	47.4	-10.0	92	N/A	500	50	0.0	0.0
C /4.9	14.0	0.67	9.03	N/A	2	97	0	1	0	103.9	-29.1	97	N/A	500	50	5.8	0.0
C /4.8	14.0	0.67	8.52	N/A	2	97	0	1	0	98.8	-29.2	97	N/A	500	50	0.0	0.0
C- /4.0	13.0	1.04	6.47	N/A	1	98	0	1	0	83.1	-14.9	49	N/A	100	50	5.8	0.0
C- /4.0	13.0	1.04	6.09	N/A	1	98	0	1	0	78.0	-15.1	36	N/A	100	50	0.0	0.0
B- /7.0	9.9	0.64	10.61	91	0	99	0	1	0	90.4	-18.8	97	N/A	500	50	0.0	0.0
B- /7.3	8.9	0.60	7.45	84	1	88	9	2	0	72.9	-16.8	95	N/A	500	50	0.0	0.0
B- /7.3	8.9	0.60	7.12	18	1	87	10	2	0	72.8	-17.3	95	N/A	500	50	5.8	0.0
B- /7.3	8.9	0.60	6.72	6	1	87	10	2	0	68.5	-17.6	94	N/A	500	50	0.0	0.0
B+ /9.9	3.1	0.20	6.65	161	35	29	34	2	0	23.5	-4.3	87	N/A	500	50	0.0	0.0
B+ /9.8	3.2	0.20	6.27	15	34	29	36	1	0	22.6	-4.8	86	N/A	500	50	4.5	0.0
B+ /9.8	3.1	0.20	5.91	8	34	29	36	1	0	19.5	-5.3	81	N/A	500	50	0.0	0.0
B- /7.6	9.6	0.64	24.87	554	0	0	0	100	0	77.2	-19.4	95	N/A	1,000	50	0.0	0.0
B+ /9.9	2.6	0.16	17.14	207	0	0	0	100	0	18.2	-3.3	84	N/A	1,000	50	0.0	0.0
B /8.2	8.1	0.54	23.80	778	0	0	0	100	0	64.5	-16.1	94	N/A	1,000	50	0.0	0.0
B+ /9.8	4.4	0.30	20.14	215	0	0	0	100	0	33.6	-7.5	90	N/A	1,000	50	0.0	0.0
B+ /9.1	6.3	0.43	22.17	443	0	0	0	100	0	49.3	-11.9	93	N/A	1,000	50	0.0	0.0
C+ /6.2	11.7	1.10	14.27	106	0	100	0	0	41	89.4	-15.7	15	8	5,000	250	5.0	2.0
C+ /6.2	11.7	1.10	13.38	49	0	100	0	0	41	84.6	-16.0	10	8	5,000	250	0.0	2.0
C+ /6.2	11.7	1.10	14.49	613	0	100	0	0	41	90.9	-15.6	15	8	1,000,000	0	0.0	2.0
C+ /6.3	12.1	0.90	23.35	624	25	74	0	1	74	56.8	-23.7	77	N/A	100	0	0.0	2.0
C+ /6.3	12.1	0.90	23.32	1,565	25	74	0	1	74	57.5	-23.7	78	N/A	50,000	0	0.0	2.0
C /4.4	14.7	1.02	8.18	575	2	97	0	1	69	17.5	-20.9	21	8	500,000	0	0.0	2.0
C /4.4	14.8	1.03	8.18	6	2	97	0	1	69	16.0	-21.0	17	8	100	0	0.0	2.0
C /4.4	14.8	1.03	8.18	11	2	97	0	1	69	17.2	-20.9	20	8	50,000	0	0.0	2.0
D- /1.5	13.0	0.95	6.50	91	1	98	0	1	25	45.7	-16.8	69	7	500,000	0	0.0	2.0
D- /1.5	13.0	0.95	6.45	3	1	98	0	1	25	44.2	-17.0	66	7	100	0	0.0	2.0
D- /1.5	13.0	0.94	6.48	3	1	98	0	1	25	45.3	-16.8	69	7	50,000	0	0.0	2.0
C+ /6.5	13.5	0.99	19.04	72	87	12	0	1	79	82.3	-25.9	34	5	100	0	0.0	2.0
C+ /6.5	13.5	0.99	19.36	134	87	12	0	1	79	83.5	-25.9	36	5	50,000	0	0.0	2.0
C- /3.2	12.0	1.07	17.22	2,254	1	98	0	1	124	101.1	-15.4	42	2	100	0	0.0	2.0
B- /7.4	7.9	0.55	10.10	4	33	52	12	3	193	36.0	-13.0	73	7	2,500	50	0.0	1.0
B- /7.4	7.9	0.55	10.11	181	33	52	12	3	193	37.4	-12.7	76	7	100,000	50	0.0	1.0
C- /3.9	15.5	0.93	10.05	404	2	97	0	1	48	3.6	-32.3	1	28	100,000	50	0.0	1.0
C- /3.9	15.6	0.93	10.04	13	2	97	0	1	48	2.5	-32.4	0	28	2,500	50	0.0	1.0
C- /3.4	9.2	0.62	8.66	375	5	0	94	1	108	11.6	-5.8	3	4	100,000	50	0.0	1.0
C- /3.5	9.3	0.62	8.74	1	5	0	94	1	108	10.9	-6.0	3	4	2,500	50	0.0	1.0
C- /4.2	16.0	1.13	16.86	12,248	3	96	0	1	16	22.9	-23.1	42	21	100,000	50	0.0	1.0
C /4.3	16.0	1.13	17.30	1,476	3	96	0	1	16	21.7	-23.2	38	21	2,500	50	0.0	1.0
U /	N/A	N/A	9.90	42	3	96	0	1	0	N/A	N/A	N/A	2	100,000	50	0.0	1.0
C /4.5	15.2	1.08	9.82	452	4	95	0	1	48	11.1	-27.0	13	5	100,000	50	0.0	1.0
C /4.5	15.2	1.08	9.80	124	4	95	0	1	48	10.0	-27.2	11	5	2,500	50	0.0	1.0
U /	N/A	N/A	11.64	55	70	29	0	1	0	N/A	N/A	N/A	1	100,000	50	0.0	1.0
B- /7.0	8.1	0.58	14.79	1,534	21	78	0	1	35	94.4	-9.8	98	10	100,000	50	0.0	1.0
B- /7.0	8.1	0.58	14.82	220	21	78	0	1	35	92.3	-10.1	98	10	2,500	50	0.0	1.0
C- /3.9	12.9	0.78	15.88	4	11	88	0	1	81	72.2	N/A	81	7	100,000	50	0.0	1.0
C- /4.0	12.9	0.78	15.85	2	11	88	0	1	81	70.6	-24.5	78	7	2,500	50	0.0	1.0
C+ /6.2	12.9	0.96	17.89	409	4	95	0	1	43	60.4	-19.6	75	24	100,000	50	0.0	1.0

Fund Type	Fund Name	Ticker Symbol	Overall Investment Rating	Phone	Perfor-mance Rating/Pts	3 Mo	6 Mo	1Yr / Pct	3Yr / Pct	5Yr / Pct	Dividend Yield	Expense Ratio
FO	Lazard Intl Equity Open	LZIOX	D+	(800) 821-6474	C- / 3.5	5.62	2.62	0.41 /17	9.63 /37	7.82 /29	0.62	1.23
FO	Lazard Intl Equity Select Inst	LZSIX	D-	(800) 821-6474	D / 1.9	3.68	-0.31	-1.57 /11	7.17 /22	6.53 /20	1.13	2.45
FO	Lazard Intl Equity Select Open	LZESX	D-	(800) 821-6474	D / 1.7	3.68	-0.42	-1.86 /11	6.81 /20	6.20 /18	0.82	3.03
FO	Lazard Intl Small Cap Eq Inst	LZISX	C	(800) 821-6474	C / 5.0	5.39	4.56	-1.00 /13	12.49 /56	10.50 /49	2.38	1.19
FO	Lazard Intl Small Cap Eq Open	LZSMX	C	(800) 821-6474	C / 4.8	5.38	4.45	-1.28 /12	12.18 /54	10.18 /46	2.08	1.48
FO	Lazard Intl Strategic Equity Inst	LISIX	C	(800) 821-6474	C / 5.2	4.88	3.17	1.99 /22	12.64 /57	10.02 /45	1.05	0.86
FO	Lazard Intl Strategic EquityOpen	LISOX	C	(800) 821-6474	C / 5.0	4.85	3.04	1.72 /21	12.34 /55	9.71 /42	0.81	1.10
GI	Lazard US Eqty Concentrated Inst	LEVIX	A+	(800) 821-6474	A+ / 9.6	3.21	12.14	20.31 /97	18.22 /95	14.19 /79	0.60	0.85
GI	Lazard US Eqty Concentrated Open	LEVOX	A+	(800) 821-6474	A / 9.5	3.04	11.79	19.71 /97	17.76 /93	13.77 /76	0.22	1.87
MC	Lazard US Mid Cap Eq Inst	LZMIX	A+	(800) 821-6474	A / 9.5	6.94	16.11	21.48 /97	15.57 /80	13.21 /70	0.44	1.19
MC	Lazard US Mid Cap Eq Open	LZMOX	A+	(800) 821-6474	A / 9.4	6.85	15.91	21.07 /97	15.22 /77	12.87 /67	0.20	1.43
RE	Lazard US Realty Equity Inst	LREIX	C	(800) 821-6474	B / 8.0	3.96	13.74	20.33 /97	12.85 /58	--	0.99	1.27
RE	Lazard US Realty Equity Open	LREOX	C	(800) 821-6474	B / 7.8	3.84	13.51	19.94 /97	12.57 /56	15.90 /92	0.72	1.41
RE	Lazard US Realty Income Inst	LRIIX	C-	(800) 821-6474	C+ / 6.9	3.19	10.66	14.62 /91	12.86 /59	--	3.37	0.98
RE	Lazard US Realty Income Open	LRIOX	C-	(800) 821-6474	C+ / 6.7	3.14	10.62	14.29 /90	12.57 /56	12.31 /63	3.19	1.24
SC	Lazard US Sm-Mid Cap Eq Inst	LZSCX	B-	(800) 821-6474	A / 9.5	6.12	15.35	14.48 /91	18.04 /94	14.50 /82	0.06	0.86
SC	Lazard US Sm-Mid Cap Eq Open	LZCOX	C+	(800) 821-6474	A / 9.4	6.05	15.15	14.18 /90	17.66 /93	14.15 /79	0.00	1.20
GR	Lazard US Strategic Equity Inst	LZUSX	B-	(800) 821-6474	B- / 7.5	-0.24	6.69	12.86 /86	15.16 /76	13.13 /69	0.94	0.93
GR	Lazard US Strategic Equity Open	LZUOX	C+	(800) 821-6474	B- / 7.2	-0.40	6.53	12.51 /85	14.80 /73	12.77 /66	0.67	1.33
SC	Lebenthal Lisanti Small Cap Growth	ASCGX	C+	(800) 754-8757	B+ / 8.9	5.61	16.33	7.52 /59	16.98 /90	16.52 /95	0.00	2.71
GR	Legg Mason CO Sc Cho Equity 80%		B	(877) 534-4627	C / 5.2	2.26	4.88	8.22 /64	12.59 /57	11.17 /54	0.00	1.16
GR	Legg Mason CO Sc Cho Equity 80%		B	(877) 534-4627	C / 5.3	2.12	4.56	7.52 /59	11.82 /51	10.39 /48	0.00	1.86
GR	Legg Mason CO Sc Cho Equity 80%		B	(877) 534-4627	C / 5.5	2.16	4.68	7.78 /61	12.06 /53	10.62 /50	0.00	1.66
GR	Legg Mason CO Sc Cho Equity 80%		B+	(877) 534-4627	C+ / 5.8	2.29	4.94	8.32 /65	12.64 /57	11.23 /55	0.00	1.09
GR	Legg Mason CO Sch Ch All Equity A		B-	(877) 534-4627	C+ / 6.3	2.30	5.42	9.01 /69	14.49 /71	12.20 /62	0.00	1.23
GR	Legg Mason CO Sch Ch All Equity B		B-	(877) 534-4627	C+ / 6.4	2.19	5.05	8.30 /65	13.70 /65	11.40 /56	0.00	1.93
GR	Legg Mason CO Sch Ch All Equity C		B-	(877) 534-4627	C+ / 6.6	2.19	5.11	8.49 /66	13.92 /67	11.64 /58	0.00	1.73
GR	Legg Mason CO Sch Ch All Equity O		B+	(877) 534-4627	B- / 7.0	2.34	5.44	9.14 /70	14.64 /72	12.32 /63	0.00	1.09
GI	Legg Mason WY Sch Ch Age-Bsd		C-	(877) 534-4627	E / 0.5	0.43	0.29	0.72 /18	0.36 / 5	0.86 / 3	0.00	0.86
GI	Legg Mason WY Sch Ch Age-Bsd		C-	(877) 534-4627	E / 0.5	0.24	-0.16	-0.08 /15	-0.34 / 4	0.13 / 3	0.00	1.56
GI	Legg Mason WY Sch Ch Age-Bsd		C-	(877) 534-4627	E / 0.5	0.31	0.08	0.23 /16	-0.13 / 4	0.34 / 3	0.00	1.36
GI	Legg Mason WY Sch Ch Age-Bsd		C-	(877) 534-4627	E / 0.5	0.30	0.07	0.23 /16	-0.07 / 4	0.42 / 3	0.00	1.09
GR	Legg Mason WY Sch Ch All Equity A		B-	(877) 534-4627	C+ / 6.3	2.30	5.42	9.01 /69	14.49 /71	12.20 /62	0.00	1.14
GR	Legg Mason WY Sch Ch All Equity B		B-	(877) 534-4627	C+ / 6.4	2.19	5.05	8.30 /65	13.70 /65	11.40 /56	0.00	1.84
GR	Legg Mason WY Sch Ch All Equity C		B-	(877) 534-4627	C+ / 6.6	2.19	5.11	8.49 /66	13.92 /67	11.64 /58	0.00	1.64
GR	Legg Mason WY Sch Ch All Equity O		B+	(877) 534-4627	B- / 7.0	2.34	5.44	9.14 /70	14.64 /72	12.32 /63	0.00	1.09
BA	Legg Mason WY Sch Ch Balanc		C+	(877) 534-4627	C- / 3.2	2.02	3.78	6.58 /52	9.08 /33	8.83 /36	0.00	0.99
BA	Legg Mason WY Sch Ch Balanc		C+	(877) 534-4627	C- / 3.2	1.81	3.35	5.84 /45	8.30 /29	8.06 /30	0.00	1.69
BA	Legg Mason WY Sch Ch Balanc		B-	(877) 534-4627	C- / 3.4	1.85	3.51	6.05 /47	8.54 /30	8.28 /32	0.00	1.49
BA	Legg Mason WY Sch Ch Balanc		B-	(877) 534-4627	C- / 3.7	1.99	3.70	6.52 /51	9.00 /33	8.74 /35	0.00	1.09
GR	Legg Mason WY Sch Ch Equity 80%		B	(877) 534-4627	C / 5.2	2.26	4.88	8.22 /64	12.59 /57	11.17 /54	0.00	1.10
GR	Legg Mason WY Sch Ch Equity 80%		B	(877) 534-4627	C / 5.3	2.12	4.56	7.52 /59	11.82 /51	10.39 /48	0.00	1.80
GR	Legg Mason WY Sch Ch Equity 80%		B	(877) 534-4627	C / 5.5	2.16	4.68	7.78 /61	12.06 /53	10.62 /50	0.00	1.60
GR	Legg Mason WY Sch Ch Equity 80%		B+	(877) 534-4627	C+ / 5.8	2.29	4.94	8.32 /65	12.64 /57	11.23 /55	0.00	1.09
GI	Legg Mason WY Schr Ch Age-Bsd		B	(877) 534-4627	C / 4.6	2.26	4.67	7.92 /62	11.63 /50	10.61 /50	0.00	1.06
GI	Legg Mason WY Schr Ch Age-Bsd		B	(877) 534-4627	C / 4.7	2.08	4.29	7.18 /57	10.85 /45	9.82 /43	0.00	1.76
GI	Legg Mason WY Schr Ch Age-Bsd		B	(877) 534-4627	C / 4.9	2.12	4.38	7.40 /58	11.08 /46	10.04 /45	0.00	N/A
GI	Legg Mason WY Schr Ch Age-Bsd		B+	(877) 534-4627	C / 5.2	2.25	4.66	7.92 /62	11.64 /50	10.61 /50	0.00	1.09
GI	Legg Mason WY Schr Ch Age-Bsd		B-	(877) 534-4627	C- / 4.1	2.22	4.40	7.65 /60	10.62 /43	10.02 /45	0.00	1.03
GI	Legg Mason WY Schr Ch Age-Bsd		B-	(877) 534-4627	C- / 4.2	2.03	4.05	6.87 /54	9.86 /39	9.25 /39	0.00	1.73
GI	Legg Mason WY Schr Ch Age-Bsd		B	(877) 534-4627	C / 4.3	2.08	4.13	7.10 /56	10.08 /40	9.46 /40	0.00	1.53
GI	Legg Mason WY Schr Ch Age-Bsd		B	(877) 534-4627	C / 4.6	2.23	4.41	7.62 /60	10.58 /43	9.98 /44	0.00	1.09

• Denotes fund is closed to new investors
* Denotes fund is included in Section II

www.thestreetratings.com

RISK			NET ASSETS		ASSET				Portfolio	BULL / BEAR		FUND MANAGER		MINIMUMS		LOADS	
	3 Year		NAV							Last Bull	Last Bear	Manager	Manager	Initial	Additional	Front	Back
Risk Rating/Pts	Standard Deviation	Beta	As of 3/31/15	Total $(Mil)	Cash %	Stocks %	Bonds %	Other %	Turnover Ratio	Market Return	Market Return	Quality Pct	Tenure (Years)	Purch. $	Purch. $	End Load	End Load
C+ / 6.1	12.9	0.96	18.03	63	4	95	0	1	43	58.8	-19.7	72	24	2,500	50	0.0	1.0
C+ / 6.1	12.8	0.93	9.58	15	6	93	0	1	36	48.8	-19.8	43	14	100,000	50	0.0	1.0
C+ / 6.1	12.8	0.94	9.59	3	6	93	0	1	36	47.3	-20.1	38	14	2,500	50	0.0	1.0
C+ / 6.2	11.7	0.81	10.55	49	5	94	0	1	58	65.9	-20.0	92	24	100,000	50	0.0	1.0
C+ / 6.3	11.7	0.80	10.57	26	5	94	0	1	58	64.3	-20.1	92	24	2,500	50	0.0	1.0
C+ / 6.0	12.7	0.93	14.39	4,176	5	94	0	1	42	71.4	-21.8	90	10	100,000	50	0.0	1.0
C+ / 6.0	12.8	0.94	14.49	1,750	5	94	0	1	42	70.0	-21.9	89	10	2,500	50	0.0	1.0
C+ / 6.6	10.1	0.99	13.84	391	17	82	0	1	108	111.8	-20.2	84	10	100,000	50	0.0	1.0
C+ / 6.7	10.1	0.99	13.91	33	17	82	0	1	108	109.0	-20.3	81	10	2,500	50	0.0	1.0
C+ / 6.6	11.5	0.97	20.18	8	9	90	0	1	133	88.4	-21.7	56	14	100,000	50	0.0	1.0
C+ / 6.6	11.5	0.97	19.82	30	9	90	0	1	133	86.5	-21.7	51	14	2,500	50	0.0	1.0
C- / 3.8	10.3	0.82	20.49	23	2	97	0	1	98	94.9	N/A	79	7	100,000	50	0.0	1.0
C- / 3.9	10.3	0.82	20.54	95	2	97	0	1	98	93.2	-19.3	77	7	2,500	50	0.0	1.0
C- / 3.6	9.5	0.69	8.61	71	3	96	0	1	104	72.8	N/A	88	7	100,000	50	0.0	1.0
C- / 3.6	9.5	0.70	8.59	93	3	96	0	1	104	71.1	-13.6	87	7	2,500	50	0.0	1.0
C- / 3.7	12.2	0.88	14.91	173	3	96	0	1	101	109.6	-29.1	90	12	100,000	50	0.0	1.0
C- / 3.4	12.1	0.87	14.19	19	3	96	0	1	101	107.2	-29.2	89	12	2,500	50	0.0	1.0
C+ / 5.6	10.5	1.07	12.40	121	3	96	0	1	71	92.1	-17.0	39	11	100,000	50	0.0	1.0
C+ / 5.6	10.6	1.08	12.43	7	3	96	0	1	71	90.2	-17.2	33	11	2,500	50	0.0	1.0
C- / 3.8	14.5	0.97	19.78	25	2	97	0	1	295	103.6	-26.4	77	11	2,000	250	0.0	1.0
B / 8.5	8.1	0.83	21.72	210	0	0	0	100	0	73.7	-15.7	59	16	250	50	3.5	0.0
B / 8.4	8.1	0.83	19.74	9	0	0	0	100	0	69.6	-16.0	48	16	250	50	0.0	0.0
B / 8.5	8.1	0.83	20.36	126	0	0	0	100	0	70.8	-15.9	52	16	250	50	0.0	0.0
B / 8.5	8.1	0.83	21.88	9	0	0	0	100	0	74.0	-15.7	60	16	250	50	0.0	0.0
B- / 7.1	10.0	1.02	16.93	324	4	95	0	1	0	89.3	-19.4	41	15	250	50	3.5	0.0
B- / 7.0	10.0	1.02	15.39	26	4	95	0	1	0	84.8	-19.7	32	15	250	50	0.0	0.0
B- / 7.0	10.0	1.02	15.85	234	4	95	0	1	0	86.2	-19.7	34	15	250	50	0.0	0.0
B- / 7.1	10.0	1.02	17.07	17	4	95	0	1	0	90.1	-19.4	43	15	250	50	0.0	0.0
B+ / 9.9	1.2	-0.01	13.91	102	0	0	0	100	0	1.8	-0.4	72	16	250	50	3.5	0.0
B+ / 9.9	1.2	-0.01	12.66	11	0	0	0	100	0	-0.6	-0.7	65	16	250	50	0.0	0.0
B+ / 9.9	1.2	-0.01	13.02	119	0	0	0	100	0	0.2	-0.6	67	16	250	50	0.0	0.0
B+ / 9.9	1.2	-0.01	13.35	16	0	0	0	100	0	0.3	-0.6	68	16	250	50	0.0	0.0
B- / 7.8	10.0	1.02	16.93	324	0	0	0	100	0	89.3	-19.4	41	15	250	50	3.5	0.0
B- / 7.7	10.0	1.02	15.39	26	0	0	0	100	0	84.8	-19.7	32	15	250	50	0.0	0.0
B- / 7.7	10.0	1.02	15.85	234	0	0	0	100	0	86.2	-19.7	34	15	250	50	0.0	0.0
B- / 7.8	10.0	1.02	17.07	17	0	0	0	100	0	90.1	-19.4	43	15	250	50	0.0	0.0
B+ / 9.6	5.3	0.91	21.69	403	0	0	0	100	0	49.0	-9.8	56	16	250	50	3.5	0.0
B+ / 9.5	5.3	0.92	19.74	35	0	0	0	100	0	45.4	-10.0	44	16	250	50	0.0	0.0
B+ / 9.5	5.3	0.92	20.33	295	0	0	0	100	0	46.5	-10.0	47	16	250	50	0.0	0.0
B+ / 9.6	5.3	0.92	21.56	28	0	0	0	100	0	48.6	-9.8	53	16	250	50	0.0	0.0
B / 8.5	8.1	0.83	21.72	210	0	0	0	100	0	73.7	-15.7	59	16	250	50	3.5	0.0
B / 8.4	8.1	0.83	19.74	9	0	0	0	100	0	69.6	-16.0	48	16	250	50	0.0	0.0
B / 8.5	8.1	0.83	20.36	126	0	0	0	100	0	70.8	-15.9	52	16	250	50	0.0	0.0
B / 8.5	8.1	0.83	21.88	9	0	0	0	100	0	74.0	-15.7	60	16	250	50	0.0	0.0
B / 8.9	7.2	0.73	22.20	112	0	0	0	100	0	66.3	-13.7	68	16	250	50	3.5	0.0
B / 8.8	7.2	0.73	20.16	3	0	0	0	100	0	62.4	-13.9	57	16	250	50	0.0	0.0
B / 8.8	7.2	0.73	20.75	56	0	0	0	100	0	63.4	-13.8	60	16	250	50	0.0	0.0
B / 8.9	7.2	0.73	22.22	3	0	0	0	100	0	66.3	-13.7	68	16	250	50	0.0	0.0
B+ / 9.2	6.3	0.63	22.08	187	0	0	0	100	0	58.8	-11.6	74	16	250	50	3.5	0.0
B+ / 9.2	6.2	0.63	20.06	12	0	0	0	100	0	55.0	-11.9	67	16	250	50	0.0	0.0
B+ / 9.2	6.2	0.63	20.66	114	0	0	0	100	0	56.0	-11.7	69	16	250	50	0.0	0.0
B+ / 9.2	6.3	0.63	22.04	6	0	0	0	100	0	58.6	-11.6	74	16	250	50	0.0	0.0

Fund Type	Fund Name	Ticker Symbol	Overall Investment Rating	Phone	PERFORMANCE Performance Rating/Pts	Total Return % through 3/31/15 3 Mo	6 Mo	1Yr / Pct	Annualized 3Yr / Pct	5Yr / Pct	Incl. in Returns Dividend Yield	Expense Ratio
	99 Pct = Best											
	0 Pct = Worst											
BA	LeggMason CO Sc Ch Balanced		C+	(877) 534-4627	C- / 3.2	2.02	3.78	6.58 /52	9.08 /33	8.83 /36	0.00	1.04
BA	LeggMason CO Sc Ch Balanced		C+	(877) 534-4627	C- / 3.2	1.81	3.35	5.84 /45	8.30 /29	8.06 /30	0.00	1.74
BA	LeggMason CO Sc Ch Balanced		B-	(877) 534-4627	C- / 3.4	1.85	3.51	6.05 /47	8.54 /30	8.28 /32	0.00	1.54
BA	LeggMason CO Sc Ch Balanced		B-	(877) 534-4627	C- / 3.7	1.99	3.70	6.52 /51	9.00 /33	8.74 /35	0.00	1.09
GI	LeggMason CO SC Yr to Enr 10-12 A		B-	(877) 534-4627	C- / 4.1	2.22	4.40	7.65 /60	10.62 /43	10.02 /45	0.00	1.07
GI	LeggMason CO SC Yr to Enr 10-12 B		B-	(877) 534-4627	C- / 4.2	2.03	4.05	6.87 /54	9.86 /39	9.25 /39	0.00	1.77
GI	LeggMason CO SC Yr to Enr 10-12 C		B	(877) 534-4627	C / 4.3	2.08	4.13	7.10 /56	10.08 /40	9.46 /40	0.00	1.57
GI	LeggMason CO SC Yr to Enr 10-12 O		B	(877) 534-4627	C / 4.6	2.23	4.41	7.62 /60	10.58 /43	9.98 /44	0.00	1.09
GI	LeggMason CO SC Yr to Enr 1-3 A		C	(877) 534-4627	D- / 1.0	0.88	1.78	3.75 /30	4.40 /11	4.76 /11	0.00	0.81
GI	LeggMason CO SC Yr to Enr 1-3 B		C	(877) 534-4627	D- / 1.1	0.71	1.43	2.97 /26	3.65 / 9	4.02 / 8	0.00	1.51
GI	LeggMason CO SC Yr to Enr 1-3 C		C	(877) 534-4627	D- / 1.1	0.75	1.52	3.21 /27	3.87 /10	4.23 / 9	0.00	1.31
GI	LeggMason CO SC Yr to Enr 1-3 O		C	(877) 534-4627	D- / 1.2	0.78	1.64	3.40 /28	4.05 /10	4.44 /10	0.00	1.09
GI	LeggMason CO SC Yr to Enr 4-6 A		C+	(877) 534-4627	D+ / 2.3	1.44	2.81	5.49 /42	7.69 /25	7.65 /27	0.00	1.12
GI	LeggMason CO SC Yr to Enr 4-6 B		C+	(877) 534-4627	D+ / 2.4	1.18	2.45	4.72 /37	6.93 /21	6.89 /22	0.00	1.65
GI	LeggMason CO SC Yr to Enr 4-6 C		C+	(877) 534-4627	D+ / 2.5	1.26	2.55	4.99 /38	7.14 /22	7.11 /24	0.00	1.45
GI	LeggMason CO SC Yr to Enr 4-6 O		C+	(877) 534-4627	D+ / 2.7	1.35	2.74	5.30 /41	7.50 /24	7.48 /26	0.00	1.09
GI	LeggMason CO SC Yr to Enr 7-9 A		C+	(877) 534-4627	C- / 3.2	2.02	3.78	6.58 /52	9.08 /33	8.83 /36	0.00	1.07
GI	LeggMason CO SC Yr to Enr 7-9 B		C+	(877) 534-4627	C- / 3.2	1.81	3.35	5.84 /45	8.30 /29	8.06 /30	0.00	1.74
GI	LeggMason CO SC Yr to Enr 7-9 C		B-	(877) 534-4627	C- / 3.4	1.85	3.51	6.05 /47	8.54 /30	8.28 /32	0.00	1.54
GI	LeggMason CO SC Yr to Enr 7-9 O		B-	(877) 534-4627	C- / 3.7	1.99	3.70	6.52 /51	9.00 /33	8.74 /35	0.00	1.09
GI	LeggMason CO Sch Ch Age-Bsd		C+	(877) 534-4627	C- / 3.2	2.02	3.78	6.58 /52	9.08 /33	8.83 /36	0.00	1.04
GI	LeggMason CO Sch Ch Age-Bsd		C+	(877) 534-4627	C- / 3.2	1.81	3.35	5.84 /45	8.30 /29	8.06 /30	0.00	1.74
GI	LeggMason CO Sch Ch Age-Bsd		C+	(877) 534-4627	C- / 3.4	1.85	3.51	6.05 /47	8.54 /30	8.28 /32	0.00	1.54
GI	LeggMason CO Sch Ch Age-Bsd		C+	(877) 534-4627	C- / 3.7	1.99	3.70	6.52 /51	9.00 /33	8.74 /35	0.00	1.09
GI	LeggMason CO Sch Ch Age-Bsd		C	(877) 534-4627	D+ / 2.3	1.44	2.81	5.49 /42	7.69 /25	7.65 /27	0.00	0.95
GI	LeggMason CO Sch Ch Age-Bsd		C	(877) 534-4627	D+ / 2.4	1.18	2.45	4.72 /37	6.93 /21	6.89 /22	0.00	1.65
GI	LeggMason CO Sch Ch Age-Bsd		C	(877) 534-4627	D+ / 2.5	1.26	2.55	4.99 /38	7.14 /22	7.11 /24	0.00	1.45
GI	LeggMason CO Sch Ch Age-Bsd		C+	(877) 534-4627	D+ / 2.7	1.35	2.74	5.30 /41	7.50 /24	7.48 /26	0.00	1.09
GI	LeggMason CO Sch Ch Age-Bsd		C-	(877) 534-4627	D- / 1.0	0.88	1.78	3.75 /30	4.40 /11	4.76 /11	0.00	0.81
GI	LeggMason CO Sch Ch Age-Bsd		C-	(877) 534-4627	D- / 1.1	0.71	1.43	2.97 /26	3.65 / 9	4.02 / 8	0.00	1.51
GI	LeggMason CO Sch Ch Age-Bsd		C-	(877) 534-4627	D- / 1.1	0.75	1.52	3.21 /28	3.87 /10	4.23 / 9	0.00	1.31
GI	LeggMason CO Sch Ch Age-Bsd		C-	(877) 534-4627	D- / 1.2	0.78	1.64	3.40 /28	4.05 /10	4.44 /10	0.00	1.09
GI	LeggMason CO Sch Ch Age-Bsd 19+		C-	(877) 534-4627	E / 0.5	0.43	0.29	0.72 /18	0.36 / 5	0.86 / 3	0.00	0.71
GI	LeggMason CO Sch Ch Age-Bsd 19+		C-	(877) 534-4627	E / 0.5	0.24	-0.16	-0.08 /15	-0.34 / 4	0.13 / 3	0.00	1.41
GI	LeggMason CO Sch Ch Age-Bsd 19+		C-	(877) 534-4627	E / 0.5	0.31	0.08	0.23 /16	-0.13 / 4	0.34 / 3	0.00	1.21
GI	LeggMason CO Sch Ch Age-Bsd 19+		C-	(877) 534-4627	E / 0.5	0.30	0.07	0.23 /16	-0.07 / 4	0.42 / 3	0.00	1.09
GR	LeggMason CO Schr Ch Age-Bsd 0-3		B-	(877) 534-4627	C / 5.2	2.26	4.88	8.22 /64	12.59 /57	11.17 /54	0.00	1.16
GR	LeggMason CO Schr Ch Age-Bsd 0-3		B-	(877) 534-4627	C / 5.3	2.12	4.56	7.52 /59	11.82 /51	10.39 /48	0.00	1.86
GR	LeggMason CO Schr Ch Age-Bsd 0-3		B	(877) 534-4627	C / 5.5	2.16	4.68	7.78 /61	12.06 /53	10.62 /50	0.00	1.66
GR	LeggMason CO Schr Ch Age-Bsd 0-3		B	(877) 534-4627	C+ / 5.8	2.29	4.94	8.32 /65	12.64 /57	11.23 /55	0.00	1.09
GI	LeggMason CO Schr Ch Age-Bsd 4-6		B-	(877) 534-4627	C / 4.6	2.26	4.67	7.92 /62	11.63 /50	10.61 /50	0.00	1.12
GI	LeggMason CO Schr Ch Age-Bsd 4-6		B-	(877) 534-4627	C / 4.7	2.08	4.29	7.18 /57	10.85 /45	9.82 /43	0.00	1.82
GI	LeggMason CO Schr Ch Age-Bsd 4-6		B-	(877) 534-4627	C / 4.9	2.12	4.38	7.40 /58	11.08 /46	10.04 /45	0.00	1.62
GI	LeggMason CO Schr Ch Age-Bsd 4-6		B	(877) 534-4627	C / 5.2	2.25	4.66	7.92 /62	11.64 /50	10.61 /50	0.00	1.09
GI	LeggMason CO Schr Ch Age-Bsd 7-9		C+	(877) 534-4627	C- / 4.1	2.22	4.40	7.65 /60	10.62 /43	10.02 /45	0.00	1.07
GI	LeggMason CO Schr Ch Age-Bsd 7-9		C+	(877) 534-4627	C- / 4.2	2.03	4.05	6.87 /54	9.86 /39	9.25 /39	0.00	1.77
GI	LeggMason CO Schr Ch Age-Bsd 7-9		C+	(877) 534-4627	C / 4.3	2.08	4.13	7.10 /56	10.08 /40	9.46 /40	0.00	1.57
GI	LeggMason CO Schr Ch Age-Bsd 7-9		B-	(877) 534-4627	C / 4.6	2.23	4.41	7.62 /60	10.58 /43	9.98 /44	0.00	1.09
GI	LeggMason WY SC Yrs To Enr 10-12		B-	(877) 534-4627	C- / 4.1	2.22	4.40	7.65 /60	10.62 /43	10.02 /45	0.00	1.03
GI	LeggMason WY SC Yrs To Enr 10-12		B-	(877) 534-4627	C- / 4.2	2.03	4.05	6.87 /54	9.86 /39	9.25 /39	0.00	1.73
GI	LeggMason WY SC Yrs To Enr 10-12		B	(877) 534-4627	C / 4.3	2.08	4.13	7.10 /56	10.08 /40	9.46 /40	0.00	1.53
GI	LeggMason WY SC Yrs To Enr 10-12		B	(877) 534-4627	C / 4.6	2.23	4.41	7.62 /60	10.58 /43	9.98 /44	0.00	1.09

● Denotes fund is closed to new investors
★ Denotes fund is included in Section II

RISK			NET ASSETS		ASSET				Portfolio	BULL / BEAR		FUND MANAGER		MINIMUMS		LOADS	
	3 Year		NAV							Last Bull	Last Bear	Manager	Manager	Initial	Additional	Front	Back
Risk Rating/Pts	Standard Deviation	Beta	As of 3/31/15	Total $(Mil)	Cash %	Stocks %	Bonds %	Other %	Turnover Ratio	Market Return	Market Return	Quality Pct	Tenure (Years)	Purch. $	Purch. $	End Load	End Load
B+ / 9.6	5.3	0.91	21.69	403	0	0	0	100	0	49.0	-9.8	56	16	250	50	3.5	0.0
B+ / 9.5	5.3	0.92	19.74	35	0	0	0	100	0	45.4	-10.0	44	16	250	50	0.0	0.0
B+ / 9.5	5.3	0.92	20.33	295	0	0	0	100	0	46.5	-10.0	47	16	250	50	0.0	0.0
B+ / 9.6	5.3	0.92	21.56	28	0	0	0	100	0	48.6	-9.8	53	16	250	50	0.0	0.0
B+ / 9.2	6.3	0.63	22.08	187	0	0	0	100	0	58.8	-11.6	74	16	250	50	3.5	0.0
B+ / 9.2	6.2	0.63	20.06	12	0	0	0	100	0	55.0	-11.9	67	16	250	50	0.0	0.0
B+ / 9.2	6.2	0.63	20.66	114	0	0	0	100	0	56.0	-11.7	69	16	250	50	0.0	0.0
B+ / 9.2	6.3	0.63	22.04	6	0	0	0	100	0	58.6	-11.6	74	16	250	50	0.0	0.0
B+ / 9.9	2.3	0.20	17.17	234	0	0	0	100	0	21.3	-3.3	79	16	250	50	3.5	0.0
B+ / 9.9	2.4	0.20	15.60	25	0	0	0	100	0	18.5	-3.6	72	16	250	50	0.0	0.0
B+ / 9.9	2.3	0.20	16.08	232	0	0	0	100	0	19.2	-3.5	75	16	250	50	0.0	0.0
B+ / 9.9	2.3	0.20	16.75	31	0	0	0	100	0	20.0	-3.5	76	16	250	50	0.0	0.0
B+ / 9.9	4.3	0.43	19.78	298	0	0	0	100	0	40.2	-7.5	77	16	250	50	3.5	0.0
B+ / 9.9	4.3	0.43	17.96	30	0	0	0	100	0	36.9	-7.8	70	16	250	50	0.0	0.0
B+ / 9.9	4.3	0.43	18.51	219	0	0	0	100	0	37.9	-7.7	72	16	250	50	0.0	0.0
B+ / 9.9	4.3	0.43	19.48	32	0	0	0	100	0	39.4	-7.6	76	16	250	50	0.0	0.0
B+ / 9.6	5.3	0.53	21.69	403	0	0	0	100	0	49.0	-9.8	75	16	250	50	3.5	0.0
B+ / 9.5	5.3	0.53	19.74	35	0	0	0	100	0	45.4	-10.0	N/A	16	250	50	0.0	0.0
B+ / 9.5	5.3	0.53	20.33	295	0	0	0	100	0	46.5	-10.0	70	16	250	50	0.0	0.0
B+ / 9.6	5.3	0.53	21.56	28	0	0	0	100	0	48.6	-9.8	74	16	250	50	0.0	0.0
B / 8.9	5.3	0.53	21.69	403	0	49	49	2	0	49.0	-9.8	75	16	250	50	3.5	0.0
B / 8.8	5.3	0.53	19.74	35	0	49	49	2	0	45.4	-10.0	N/A	16	250	50	0.0	0.0
B / 8.9	5.3	0.53	20.33	295	0	49	49	2	0	46.5	-10.0	70	16	250	50	0.0	0.0
B / 8.9	5.3	0.53	21.56	28	0	49	49	2	0	48.6	-9.8	74	16	250	50	0.0	0.0
B+ / 9.3	4.3	0.43	19.78	298	10	39	49	2	0	40.2	-7.5	77	16	250	50	3.5	0.0
B+ / 9.3	4.3	0.43	17.96	30	10	39	49	2	0	36.9	-7.8	70	16	250	50	0.0	0.0
B+ / 9.3	4.3	0.43	18.51	219	10	39	49	2	0	37.9	-7.7	72	16	250	50	0.0	0.0
B+ / 9.3	4.3	0.43	19.48	32	10	39	49	2	0	39.4	-7.6	76	16	250	50	0.0	0.0
B+ / 9.5	2.3	0.20	17.17	234	25	20	54	1	0	21.3	-3.3	79	16	250	50	3.5	0.0
B+ / 9.5	2.4	0.20	15.60	25	25	20	54	1	0	18.5	-3.6	72	16	250	50	0.0	0.0
B+ / 9.5	2.3	0.20	16.08	232	25	20	54	1	0	19.2	-3.5	75	16	250	50	0.0	0.0
B+ / 9.5	2.3	0.20	16.75	31	25	20	54	1	0	20.0	-3.5	76	16	250	50	0.0	0.0
B+ / 9.9	1.2	-0.01	13.91	102	51	0	48	1	0	1.8	-0.4	72	16	250	50	3.5	0.0
B+ / 9.9	1.2	-0.01	12.66	11	51	0	48	1	0	-0.6	-0.7	65	16	250	50	0.0	0.0
B+ / 9.9	1.2	-0.01	13.02	119	51	0	48	1	0	0.2	-0.6	67	16	250	50	0.0	0.0
B+ / 9.9	1.2	-0.01	13.35	16	51	0	48	1	0	0.3	-0.6	68	16	250	50	0.0	0.0
B / 8.0	8.1	0.83	21.72	210	2	77	20	1	0	73.7	-15.7	59	16	250	50	3.5	0.0
B / 8.0	8.1	0.83	19.74	9	2	77	20	1	0	69.6	-16.0	48	16	250	50	0.0	0.0
B / 8.0	8.1	0.83	20.36	126	2	77	20	1	0	70.8	-15.9	52	16	250	50	0.0	0.0
B / 8.0	8.1	0.83	21.88	9	2	77	20	1	0	74.0	-15.7	60	16	250	50	0.0	0.0
B / 8.4	7.2	0.73	22.20	112	1	67	30	2	0	66.3	-13.7	68	16	250	50	3.5	0.0
B / 8.3	7.2	0.73	20.16	3	1	67	30	2	0	62.4	-13.9	57	16	250	50	0.0	0.0
B / 8.3	7.2	0.73	20.75	56	1	67	30	2	0	63.4	-13.8	60	16	250	50	0.0	0.0
B / 8.4	7.2	0.73	22.22	3	1	67	30	2	0	66.3	-13.7	68	16	250	50	0.0	0.0
B / 8.6	6.3	0.63	22.08	187	0	58	40	2	0	58.8	-11.6	74	16	250	50	3.5	0.0
B / 8.6	6.2	0.63	20.06	12	0	58	40	2	0	55.0	-11.9	67	16	250	50	0.0	0.0
B / 8.6	6.2	0.63	20.66	114	0	58	40	2	0	56.0	-11.7	69	16	250	50	0.0	0.0
B / 8.6	6.3	0.63	22.04	6	0	58	40	2	0	58.6	-11.6	74	16	250	50	0.0	0.0
B+ / 9.2	6.3	0.63	22.08	187	0	0	0	100	0	58.8	-11.6	74	16	250	50	3.5	0.0
B+ / 9.2	6.2	0.63	20.06	12	0	0	0	100	0	55.0	-11.9	67	16	250	50	0.0	0.0
B+ / 9.2	6.2	0.63	20.66	114	0	0	0	100	0	56.0	-11.7	69	16	250	50	0.0	0.0
B+ / 9.2	6.3	0.63	22.04	6	0	0	0	100	0	58.6	-11.6	74	16	250	50	0.0	0.0

Fund Type	Fund Name	Ticker Symbol	Overall Investment Rating	Phone	Performance Rating/Pts	3 Mo	6 Mo	1Yr / Pct	3Yr / Pct	5Yr / Pct	Dividend Yield	Expense Ratio
	99 Pct = Best 0 Pct = Worst							Total Return % through 3/31/15			Incl. in Returns	
									Annualized			
GI	LeggMason WY Sch Ch Age-Bsd		C+	(877) 534-4627	C- / 3.2	2.02	3.78	6.58 /52	9.08 /34	8.83 /36	0.00	0.99
GI	LeggMason WY Sch Ch Age-Bsd		C+	(877) 534-4627	C- / 3.2	1.81	3.35	5.84 /45	8.30 /29	8.06 /30	0.00	1.69
GI	LeggMason WY Sch Ch Age-Bsd		B-	(877) 534-4627	C- / 3.4	1.85	3.51	6.05 /47	8.54 /30	8.28 /32	0.00	1.49
GI	LeggMason WY Sch Ch Age-Bsd		B-	(877) 534-4627	C- / 3.7	1.99	3.70	6.52 /51	9.00 /33	8.74 /35	0.00	1.09
GI	LeggMason WY Sch Ch Age-Bsd		C+	(877) 534-4627	D+ / 2.3	1.44	2.81	5.49 /42	7.69 /25	7.65 /27	0.00	0.96
GI	LeggMason WY Sch Ch Age-Bsd		C+	(877) 534-4627	D+ / 2.4	1.18	2.45	4.72 /37	6.93 /21	6.89 /22	0.00	1.66
GI	LeggMason WY Sch Ch Age-Bsd		C+	(877) 534-4627	D+ / 2.5	1.26	2.55	4.99 /38	7.14 /22	7.11 /24	0.00	1.46
GI	LeggMason WY Sch Ch Age-Bsd		C+	(877) 534-4627	D+ / 2.7	1.35	2.74	5.30 /41	7.50 /24	7.48 /26	0.00	1.09
GI	LeggMason WY Sch Ch Age-Bsd		C	(877) 534-4627	D- / 1.0	0.88	1.78	3.75 /30	4.40 /11	4.76 /11	0.00	0.86
GI	LeggMason WY Sch Ch Age-Bsd		C	(877) 534-4627	D- / 1.1	0.71	1.43	2.97 /26	3.65 / 9	4.02 / 8	0.00	1.56
GI	LeggMason WY Sch Ch Age-Bsd		C	(877) 534-4627	D- / 1.1	0.75	1.52	3.21 /28	3.87 /10	4.23 / 9	0.00	1.36
GI	LeggMason WY Sch Ch Age-Bsd		C	(877) 534-4627	D- / 1.2	0.78	1.64	3.40 /28	4.05 /10	4.44 /10	0.00	1.09
GI	LeggMason WY Sch Ch Yr To Enr		C	(877) 534-4627	D- / 1.0	0.88	1.78	3.75 /30	4.40 /11	4.76 /11	0.00	0.86
GI	LeggMason WY Sch Ch Yr To Enr		C	(877) 534-4627	D- / 1.1	0.71	1.43	2.97 /26	3.65 / 9	4.02 / 8	0.00	1.56
GI	LeggMason WY Sch Ch Yr To Enr		C	(877) 534-4627	D- / 1.1	0.75	1.52	3.21 /28	3.87 /10	4.23 / 9	0.00	1.36
GI	LeggMason WY Sch Ch Yr To Enr		C	(877) 534-4627	D- / 1.2	0.78	1.64	3.40 /28	4.05 /10	4.44 /10	0.00	1.09
GI	LeggMason WY Sch Ch Yr To Enr		C+	(877) 534-4627	D+ / 2.3	1.44	2.81	5.49 /42	7.69 /25	7.65 /27	0.00	0.96
GI	LeggMason WY Sch Ch Yr To Enr		C+	(877) 534-4627	D+ / 2.4	1.18	2.45	4.72 /37	6.93 /21	6.89 /22	0.00	1.66
GI	LeggMason WY Sch Ch Yr To Enr		C+	(877) 534-4627	D+ / 2.5	1.26	2.55	4.99 /38	7.14 /22	7.11 /24	0.00	1.46
GI	LeggMason WY Sch Ch Yr To Enr		C+	(877) 534-4627	D+ / 2.7	1.35	2.74	5.30 /41	7.50 /24	7.48 /26	0.00	1.09
GI	LeggMason WY Sch Ch Yr To Enr		C+	(877) 534-4627	C- / 3.2	2.02	3.78	6.58 /52	9.08 /34	8.83 /36	0.00	0.99
GI	LeggMason WY Sch Ch Yr To Enr		C+	(877) 534-4627	C- / 3.2	1.81	3.35	5.84 /45	8.30 /29	8.06 /30	0.00	1.69
GI	LeggMason WY Sch Ch Yr To Enr		B-	(877) 534-4627	C- / 3.4	1.85	3.51	6.05 /47	8.54 /30	8.28 /32	0.00	1.49
GI	LeggMason WY Sch Ch Yr To Enr		B-	(877) 534-4627	C- / 3.7	1.99	3.70	6.52 /51	9.00 /33	8.74 /35	0.00	1.09
GR	LeggMason WY Schr Ch Age-Bsd 0-3		B	(877) 534-4627	C / 5.2	2.26	4.88	8.22 /64	12.59 /57	11.17 /54	0.00	1.10
GR	LeggMason WY Schr Ch Age-Bsd 0-3		B	(877) 534-4627	C / 5.3	2.12	4.56	7.52 /59	11.82 /51	10.39 /48	0.00	1.80
GR	LeggMason WY Schr Ch Age-Bsd 0-3		B	(877) 534-4627	C / 5.5	2.16	4.68	7.78 /61	12.06 /53	10.62 /50	0.00	1.60
GR	LeggMason WY Schr Ch Age-Bsd 0-3		B+	(877) 534-4627	C+ / 5.8	2.29	4.94	8.32 /65	12.64 /57	11.23 /55	0.00	1.09
GI	Leigh Baldwin Total Return	LEBOX	D-	(866) 706-9790	E / 0.4	1.28	-0.08	0.45 /17	-1.31 / 3	-1.07 / 2	2.90	4.29
GI	Leuthold Core Investment Inst	LCRIX	C+	(888) 200-0409	C- / 4.2	2.01	6.23	6.68 /52	9.86 /39	6.71 /21	0.30	1.22
GI	Leuthold Core Investment Retail	LCORX	C+	(888) 200-0409	C- / 4.2	1.96	6.23	6.58 /52	9.74 /38	6.60 /21	0.21	1.32
GL	Leuthold Global Industries Instl	LGIIX	B+	(888) 200-0409	B- / 7.5	3.51	6.72	5.89 /45	15.53 /79	--	0.68	1.81
GL	Leuthold Global Industries Retail	LGINX	B+	(888) 200-0409	B- / 7.3	3.47	6.67	5.69 /44	15.22 /77	--	0.52	2.06
GL	Leuthold Global Instl	GLBIX	D+	(888) 200-0409	D+ / 2.7	1.26	2.02	1.43 /20	8.04 /27	7.23 /25	0.75	1.47
GL	Leuthold Global Retail	GLBLX	D	(888) 200-0409	D+ / 2.5	1.17	1.93	1.23 /19	7.79 /26	7.01 /23	0.64	1.68
SC	Leuthold Grizzly Short	GRZZX	E-	(888) 200-0409	E- / 0.1	-3.24	-6.92	-10.56 / 3	-16.25 / 0	-16.00 / 0	0.00	3.36
GR	Leuthold Select Industries	LSLTX	A+	(888) 200-0409	A+ / 9.8	4.38	14.39	15.08 /92	20.01 /98	12.51 /64	0.00	1.68
AA	● Lifetime Achievement	LFTAX	E-	(888) 339-4230	C- / 3.3	1.65	3.14	2.56 /24	9.78 /38	9.06 /37	0.07	2.08
SC	Lincoln Baron Growth Opps Svc		A+	(800) 992-2766	A / 9.5	5.49	12.37	10.53 /76	18.70 /96	17.62 /97	0.17	1.31
EM	Lincoln SSgA Emerging Mkts 100 Std		E	(800) 992-2766	E / 0.4	1.24	-1.34	1.31 /19	-2.03 / 3	2.05 / 4	3.12	0.49
GR	Linde Hansen Contrarian Value A	LHVAX	C-	(855) 754-7933	C- / 3.7	1.30	3.93	4.26 /33	11.39 /48	--	0.00	1.99
GR	Linde Hansen Contrarian Value I	LHVIX	C	(855) 754-7933	C / 4.7	1.37	4.03	4.52 /35	11.61 /50	--	0.03	1.74
GL	Listed Pvt Eq Plus A	LPEAX	E-	(866) 900-4223	E- / 0.2	-6.15	-11.89	-22.64 / 1	-1.72 / 3	-3.85 / 1	27.70	4.43
GL	Listed Pvt Eq Plus C	LPECX	E-	(866) 900-4223	E- / 0.2	-6.53	-12.50	-23.41 / 1	-2.48 / 3	-4.60 / 1	28.15	5.18
AA	Litman Gregory Masters Alt Str Inst	MASFX	C-	(800) 960-0188	D / 1.8	1.98	2.36	4.20 /33	5.70 /16	--	2.80	1.82
AA	Litman Gregory Masters Alt Str Inv	MASNX	D+	(800) 960-0188	D- / 1.5	1.94	2.24	3.95 /31	5.45 /15	--	2.57	2.07
GR	Litman Gregory Masters Equity Inst	MSEFX	B	(800) 960-0188	B- / 7.5	1.30	5.78	9.09 /70	15.45 /79	13.27 /71	0.00	1.30
GR	Litman Gregory Masters Equity Inv	MSENX	C+	(800) 960-0188	B- / 7.0	1.28	5.69	8.83 /68	15.31 /77	13.08 /69	0.00	1.55
FO	Litman Gregory Masters Intl Inst	MSILX	D+	(800) 960-0188	C- / 4.0	5.47	5.40	2.94 /26	9.69 /37	7.27 /25	1.15	1.30
FO	Litman Gregory Masters Intl Inv	MNILX	D	(800) 960-0188	C- / 3.5	5.44	5.31	2.66 /25	9.39 /36	7.00 /23	0.92	1.55
SC	Litman Gregory Masters Sm Co Inst	MSSFX	D	(800) 960-0188	D+ / 2.7	-1.38	-3.38	-8.79 / 3	10.41 /42	11.88 /60	0.00	1.54
AA	LJM Preservation and Growth A	LJMAX	U	(855) 556-3863	U /	7.28	-1.57	4.59 /36	--	--	0.00	2.89

● Denotes fund is closed to new investors
* Denotes fund is included in Section II

www.thestreetratings.com

RISK			NET ASSETS		ASSET					Portfolio	BULL / BEAR		FUND MANAGER		MINIMUMS		LOADS	
	3 Year		NAV								Last Bull	Last Bear	Manager	Manager	Initial	Additional	Front	Back
Risk	Standard		As of	Total	Cash	Stocks	Bonds	Other		Turnover	Market	Market	Quality	Tenure	Purch.	Purch.	End	End
Rating/Pts	Deviation	Beta	3/31/15	$(Mil)	%	%	%	%		Ratio	Return	Return	Pct	(Years)	$	$	Load	Load
B+ / 9.6	5.3	0.53	21.69	403	0	0	0	100	0	49.0	-9.8	75	16	250	50	3.5	0.0
B+ / 9.5	5.3	0.53	19.74	35	0	0	0	100	0	45.4	-10.0	N/A	16	250	50	0.0	0.0
B+ / 9.5	5.3	0.53	20.33	295	0	0	0	100	0	46.5	-10.0	70	16	250	50	0.0	0.0
B+ / 9.6	5.3	0.53	21.56	28	0	0	0	100	0	48.6	-9.8	74	16	250	50	0.0	0.0
B+ / 9.9	4.3	0.43	19.78	298	0	0	0	100	0	40.2	-7.5	77	16	250	50	3.5	0.0
B+ / 9.9	4.3	0.43	17.96	30	0	0	0	100	0	36.9	-7.8	70	16	250	50	0.0	0.0
B+ / 9.9	4.3	0.43	18.51	219	0	0	0	100	0	37.9	-7.7	72	16	250	50	0.0	0.0
B+ / 9.9	4.3	0.43	19.48	32	0	0	0	100	0	39.4	-7.6	76	16	250	50	0.0	0.0
B+ / 9.9	2.3	0.20	17.17	234	0	0	0	100	0	21.3	-3.3	79	16	250	50	3.5	0.0
B+ / 9.9	2.4	0.20	15.60	25	0	0	0	100	0	18.5	-3.6	72	16	250	50	0.0	0.0
B+ / 9.9	2.3	0.20	16.08	232	0	0	0	100	0	19.2	-3.5	75	16	250	50	0.0	0.0
B+ / 9.9	2.3	0.20	16.75	31	0	0	0	100	0	20.0	-3.5	76	16	250	50	0.0	0.0
B+ / 9.9	2.3	0.20	17.17	234	0	0	0	100	0	21.3	-3.3	80	16	250	50	3.5	0.0
B+ / 9.9	2.4	0.20	15.60	25	0	0	0	100	0	18.5	-3.6	72	16	250	50	0.0	0.0
B+ / 9.9	2.3	0.20	16.08	232	0	0	0	100	0	19.2	-3.5	75	16	250	50	0.0	0.0
B+ / 9.9	2.3	0.20	16.75	31	0	0	0	100	0	20.0	-3.5	76	16	250	50	0.0	0.0
B+ / 9.9	4.3	0.43	19.78	298	0	0	0	100	0	40.2	-7.5	77	16	250	50	3.5	0.0
B+ / 9.9	4.3	0.43	17.96	30	0	0	0	100	0	36.9	-7.8	70	16	250	50	0.0	0.0
B+ / 9.9	4.3	0.43	18.51	219	0	0	0	100	0	37.9	-7.7	72	16	250	50	0.0	0.0
B+ / 9.9	4.3	0.43	19.48	32	0	0	0	100	0	39.4	-7.6	76	16	250	50	0.0	0.0
B+ / 9.6	5.3	0.53	21.69	403	0	0	0	100	0	49.0	-9.8	75	16	250	50	3.5	0.0
B+ / 9.5	5.3	0.53	19.74	35	0	0	0	100	0	45.4	-10.0	N/A	16	250	50	0.0	0.0
B+ / 9.5	5.3	0.53	20.33	295	0	0	0	100	0	46.5	-10.0	70	16	250	50	0.0	0.0
B+ / 9.6	5.3	0.53	21.56	28	0	0	0	100	0	48.6	-9.8	74	16	250	50	0.0	0.0
B / 8.5	8.1	0.83	21.72	210	0	0	0	100	0	73.7	-15.7	59	16	250	50	3.5	0.0
B / 8.4	8.1	0.83	19.74	9	0	0	0	100	0	69.6	-16.0	48	16	250	50	0.0	0.0
B / 8.5	8.1	0.83	20.36	126	0	0	0	100	0	70.8	-15.9	52	16	250	50	0.0	0.0
B / 8.5	8.1	0.83	21.88	9	0	0	0	100	0	74.0	-15.7	60	16	250	50	0.0	0.0
B- / 7.5	4.6	0.32	7.39	4	5	89	5	1	650	-0.8	-6.3	6	7	1,000	100	0.0	0.0
B / 8.1	7.7	0.73	18.82	292	29	51	19	1	81	46.0	-15.3	45	7	1,000,000	100	0.0	0.0
B / 8.1	7.7	0.73	18.83	579	29	51	19	1	81	45.6	-15.4	43	7	10,000	100	0.0	0.0
B- / 7.1	11.5	0.75	17.39	17	2	97	0	1	107	84.4	-24.7	97	5	1,000,000	100	0.0	0.0
B- / 7.0	11.6	0.76	17.29	8	2	97	0	1	107	82.6	-24.7	96	5	10,000	100	0.0	0.0
C+ / 6.4	7.7	1.15	10.44	230	28	52	19	1	72	39.8	-14.3	34	N/A	1,000,000	100	0.0	0.0
C+ / 6.4	7.8	1.16	10.38	112	28	52	19	1	72	38.8	-14.3	31	N/A	10,000	100	0.0	0.0
D / 2.1	12.7	-0.82	6.86	76	100	0	0	0	0	-58.1	30.2	8	9	10,000	100	0.0	0.0
B- / 7.1	11.9	1.15	22.90	14	1	98	0	1	67	110.6	-25.3	78	2	10,000	100	0.0	0.0
E- / 0.1	10.3	1.61	18.08	12	4	93	1	2	11	62.1	-22.1	4	15	10,000	500	2.5	0.0
C+ / 6.3	10.6	0.73	49.61	578	4	95	0	1	12	103.1	-18.5	95	17	0	0	0.0	0.0
C- / 3.5	14.6	1.03	9.40	528	2	97	0	1	84	15.6	-26.6	28	7	0	0	0.0	0.0
C+ / 6.5	10.7	0.96	13.21	21	20	79	0	1	19	N/A	N/A	20	3	2,500	250	5.3	1.0
C+ / 6.6	10.7	0.96	13.28	24	20	79	0	1	19	N/A	N/A	21	3	1,000,000	1,000	0.0	1.0
D / 2.1	13.6	0.85	2.29	2	19	80	0	1	689	8.1	-34.3	2	8	2,500	50	5.8	2.0
D / 2.2	13.7	0.86	2.29	N/A	19	80	0	1	689	5.0	-34.5	2	8	2,500	50	0.0	2.0
B / 8.1	2.7	0.39	11.58	900	25	25	46	4	179	27.1	N/A	81	N/A	100,000	250	0.0	0.0
B / 8.1	2.7	0.38	11.59	167	25	25	46	4	179	26.2	N/A	80	N/A	1,000	100	0.0	2.0
C+ / 5.8	11.1	1.07	18.24	394	5	94	0	1	113	88.5	-19.9	43	19	100,000	250	0.0	0.0
C+ / 5.8	11.2	1.07	18.06	N/A	5	94	0	1	113	87.4	-19.9	41	19	1,000	100	0.0	2.0
C+ / 5.6	13.4	0.97	18.31	1,238	5	94	0	1	112	58.1	-26.3	71	18	100,000	250	0.0	0.0
C+ / 5.6	13.4	0.97	18.16	333	5	94	0	1	112	56.7	-26.4	69	18	1,000	100	0.0	2.0
C+ / 5.8	13.3	0.85	19.81	68	14	85	0	1	154	82.1	-24.7	26	12	10,000	250	0.0	0.0
U /	N/A	N/A	10.02	25	100	0	0	0	0	N/A	N/A	N/A	3	2,500	500	5.8	1.0

I. Index of Stock Mutual Funds

					PERFORMANCE						Incl. in Returns	
						Total Return % through 3/31/15						
			Overall		Perfor-				Annualized			
Fund		Ticker	Investment		mance						Dividend	Expense
Type	Fund Name	Symbol	Rating	Phone	Rating/Pts	3 Mo	6 Mo	1Yr / Pct	3Yr / Pct	5Yr / Pct	Yield	Ratio
AA	LJM Preservation and Growth I	LJMIX	U	(855) 556-3863	U /	7.46	-1.47	5.00 /38	--	--	0.00	2.66
GI	LK Balanced Institutional	LKBLX	U	(855) 698-1378	U /	2.11	-1.87	-0.38 /15	--	--	1.92	1.44
GR	LKCM Aquinas Growth	AQEGX	E	(800) 688-5526	C- / 3.3	1.69	4.17	5.17 /40	8.72 /31	10.38 /48	0.00	1.59
SC	LKCM Aquinas Small-Cap	AQBLX	E+	(800) 688-5526	C- / 3.1	4.18	10.64	0.84 /18	8.13 /28	12.96 /68	0.00	2.25
IN	LKCM Aquinas Value	AQEIX	C-	(800) 688-5526	C / 5.0	1.13	3.37	2.80 /25	12.47 /56	11.96 /60	1.03	1.52
BA	LKCM Balanced Institutional	LKBAX	C+	(800) 688-5526	C / 4.4	1.40	3.66	6.46 /50	10.74 /44	10.22 /46	1.19	1.04
GR	LKCM Equity Institutional	LKEQX	C+	(800) 688-5526	C / 5.4	0.39	2.96	5.13 /40	12.99 /60	13.21 /70	0.69	0.94
SC	LKCM Small Cap Equity Adv	LKSAX	E+	(800) 688-5526	C- / 4.0	4.28	12.29	2.24 /23	9.42 /36	13.56 /73	0.00	1.20
SC	LKCM Small Cap Equity Inst	LKSCX	D-	(800) 688-5526	C- / 4.1	4.37	12.48	2.50 /24	9.70 /37	13.85 /76	0.00	0.95
IN	LKCM Small-Mid Cap Eq Inst	LKSMX	C-	(800) 688-5526	C- / 3.8	4.88	7.48	0.97 /18	9.71 /38	--	0.00	1.19
GL	LM BW Absolute Return Opptys A	LROAX	D	(877) 534-4627	D- / 1.2	0.86	1.47	4.61 /36	4.77 /12	--	2.86	1.22
GL	LM BW Absolute Return Opptys C	LAOCX	C-	(877) 534-4627	D- / 1.2	0.81	1.25	4.01 /32	4.10 /10	--	2.26	1.91
GL	LM BW Absolute Return Opptys C1	LROCX	D	(877) 534-4627	D- / 1.3	0.81	1.27	4.11 /33	4.26 /11	--	2.36	1.73
GL	LM BW Absolute Return Opptys I	LROIX	D+	(877) 534-4627	D / 1.6	1.02	1.71	5.00 /38	5.18 /14	--	3.21	0.87
GL	LM BW Absolute Return Opptys IS	LROSX	U	(877) 534-4627	U /	0.97	1.77	5.13 /40	--	--	3.33	0.75
GL	LM BW Absolute Return OpptysR	LBARX	D	(877) 534-4627	D- / 1.3	0.86	1.39	4.35 /34	4.51 /12	--	2.27	1.65
FS	LM BW Alternative Credit A	LMAPX	U	(877) 534-4627	U /	1.56	0.44	7.45 /59	--	--	1.75	1.56
FS	LM BW Alternative Credit C	LMAQX	U	(877) 534-4627	U /	1.40	0.10	6.74 /53	--	--	1.18	2.25
FS	LM BW Alternative Credit I	LMANX	U	(877) 534-4627	U /	1.65	0.58	7.74 /61	--	--	2.00	1.26
FS	LM BW Alternative Credit IS	LMAMX	C	(877) 534-4627	C- / 3.8	1.74	0.67	7.73 /61	9.41 /36	--	1.99	1.30
GR	LM BW Diversified Large Cap Val A	LBWAX	C+	(877) 534-4627	C+ / 5.8	-0.93	3.48	8.61 /67	14.76 /73	--	0.96	1.37
GR	LM BW Diversified Large Cap Val C	LBWCX	C+	(877) 534-4627	C+ / 6.2	-1.13	3.01	7.70 /60	13.87 /66	--	0.58	2.14
GR	LM BW Diversified Large Cap Val I	LBWIX	B	(877) 534-4627	B- / 7.0	-0.87	3.55	8.85 /68	15.04 /75	--	1.19	1.00
GR	LM BW Diversified Large Cap Val IS	LBISX	B	(877) 534-4627	B- / 7.0	-0.87	3.62	8.87 /69	15.07 /75	--	1.20	0.81
GR	LM BW Dyn Lg Cap Val IS	LMBGX	A+	(877) 534-4627	A+ / 9.7	2.14	7.21	12.45 /85	20.77 /98	17.46 /97	0.41	N/A
GR	LM CM Opportunity Trust A	LGOAX	A+	(877) 534-4627	A+ / 9.9	6.03	13.59	12.95 /86	30.29 /99	13.37 /72	0.00	1.56
GR	LM CM Opportunity Trust C	LMOPX	A+	(877) 534-4627	A+ / 9.9	5.86	13.17	12.05 /83	29.27 /99	12.48 /64	0.00	2.37
GR	LM CM Opportunity Trust FI	LMOFX	A+	(877) 534-4627	A+ / 9.9	5.99	13.54	12.86 /86	30.20 /99	13.27 /71	0.00	1.62
GR	LM CM Opportunity Trust I	LMNOX	A+	(877) 534-4627	A+ / 9.9	6.09	13.74	13.24 /87	30.62 /99	13.70 /75	0.02	1.28
GR	LM CM Opportunity Trust R	LMORX	A+	(877) 534-4627	A+ / 9.9	5.94	13.33	12.45 /85	29.72 /99	12.87 /67	0.00	2.04
GL	LMCG Global Market Neutral Inst	GMNIX	U	(877) 591-4667	U /	2.59	2.59	9.50 /72	--	--	0.00	8.73
OT	LoCorr Lng/Sht Commodities Strat A	LCSAX	D+	(855) 523-8637	E+ / 0.6	3.75	2.79	18.60 /96	-0.73 / 4	--	8.91	4.69
OT	LoCorr Lng/Sht Commodities Strat C	LCSCX	D+	(855) 523-8637	E+ / 0.6	3.47	2.29	17.57 /95	-1.50 / 3	--	9.01	5.44
OT	LoCorr Lng/Sht Commodities Strat I	LCSIX	D+	(855) 523-8637	E+ / 0.8	3.73	2.87	18.74 /96	-0.53 / 4	--	9.50	4.44
GI	LoCorr Managed Futures Strategy A	LFMAX	D	(855) 523-8637	D+ / 2.6	5.52	8.67	19.63 /96	4.75 /12	--	10.93	2.58
GI	LoCorr Managed Futures Strategy C	LFMCX	D+	(855) 523-8637	C- / 3.1	5.42	8.32	18.84 /96	4.01 /10	--	11.25	3.33
GI	LoCorr Managed Futures Strategy I	LFMIX	C-	(855) 523-8637	C- / 3.8	5.72	8.85	20.01 /97	5.03 /13	--	11.74	2.33
IN	LoCorr Market Trend A	LOTAX	U	(855) 523-8637	U /	10.40	26.17	--	--	--	0.00	N/A
IN	LoCorr Market Trend I	LOTIX	U	(855) 523-8637	U /	10.48	26.29	--	--	--	0.00	N/A
AA	LoCorr Spectrum Income A	LSPAX	U	(855) 523-8637	U /	6.63	-0.50	-1.61 /11	--	--	5.75	2.18
AA	LoCorr Spectrum Income C	LSPCX	U	(855) 523-8637	U /	6.54	-0.79	-2.25 /10	--	--	5.31	2.93
AA	LoCorr Spectrum Income I	LSPIX	U	(855) 523-8637	U /	6.81	-0.27	-1.26 /12	--	--	6.36	1.93
IN	Longboard Managed Futures Strat I	WAVIX	U	(855) 294-7540	U /	12.53	24.10	34.12 /99	--	--	0.00	3.00
*GR	Longleaf Partners	LLPFX	D	(800) 445-9469	C / 4.8	-1.09	0.36	3.50 /29	12.27 /54	11.35 /56	0.56	0.92
GL	Longleaf Partners Global	LLGLX	U	(800) 445-9469	U /	-1.38	-4.60	-9.73 / 3	--	--	0.66	1.73
FO	Longleaf Partners International	LLINX	E-	(800) 445-9469	E+ / 0.7	-0.43	-6.99	-17.61 / 1	5.74 /16	3.20 / 6	3.68	1.27
SC	● Longleaf Partners Small-Cap	LLSCX	B	(800) 445-9469	A+ / 9.8	5.98	10.03	13.35 /88	20.28 /98	16.50 /95	0.00	0.91
SC	● Loomis Sayles Sm Cp Gr Inst	LSSIX	C	(800) 633-3330	B+ / 8.5	6.29	15.07	5.74 /44	16.20 /85	17.50 /97	0.00	0.94
SC	Loomis Sayles Sm Cp Gr N	LSSNX	U	(800) 633-3330	U /	6.32	15.14	5.86 /45	--	--	0.00	0.83
SC	● Loomis Sayles Sm Cp Gr Ret	LCGRX	C	(800) 633-3330	B / 8.2	6.24	14.96	5.46 /42	15.65 /80	17.02 /96	0.00	1.21
SC	● Loomis Sayles SmCp Val Adm	LSVAX	C+	(800) 633-3330	B / 8.0	4.61	13.23	8.79 /68	15.24 /77	14.70 /84	0.00	1.65
SC	● Loomis Sayles SmCp Val Inst	LSSCX	B-	(800) 633-3330	B+ / 8.4	4.73	13.49	9.32 /71	15.81 /82	15.26 /89	0.53	1.05

99 Pct = Best
0 Pct = Worst

● Denotes fund is closed to new investors
* Denotes fund is included in Section II

www.thestreetratings.com

I. Index of Stock Mutual Funds

RISK			NET ASSETS		ASSET					Portfolio	BULL / BEAR		FUND MANAGER		MINIMUMS		LOADS	
	3 Year		NAV								Last Bull	Last Bear	Manager	Manager	Initial	Additional	Front	Back
Risk Rating/Pts	Standard Deviation	Beta	As of 3/31/15	Total $(Mil)	Cash %	Stocks %	Bonds %	Other %		Turnover Ratio	Market Return	Market Return	Quality Pct	Tenure (Years)	Purch. $	Purch. $	End Load	End Load
U /	N/A	N/A	10.08	82	100	0	0	0	0	N/A	N/A	N/A	3	100,000	1,000	0.0	1.0
U /	N/A	N/A	44.05	27	11	58	29	2	20	N/A	N/A	N/A	29	50,000	500	0.0	0.0
D /2.0	11.2	1.08	17.50	30	0	100	0	0	44	64.3	-17.9	3	5	2,000	500	0.0	1.0
D+ /2.9	13.9	1.00	7.98	8	0	99	0	1	60	59.8	-20.7	4	21	2,000	500	0.0	1.0
C /5.4	12.2	1.20	17.06	52	1	98	0	1	9	79.7	-19.7	6	21	2,000	500	0.0	1.0
B- /7.9	7.4	1.25	20.34	38	1	71	27	1	10	61.4	-10.6	29	18	2,000	1,000	0.0	1.0
C+ /6.7	10.2	1.04	22.90	324	1	98	0	1	17	84.4	-16.4	22	19	2,000	1,000	0.0	1.0
D+ /2.9	14.1	1.01	24.10	15	0	100	0	0	47	66.0	-20.5	6	21	2,000	1,000	0.0	1.0
C- /3.0	14.1	1.01	25.10	821	0	100	0	0	47	67.4	-20.4	6	21	2,000	1,000	0.0	1.0
C+ /6.3	12.5	1.10	12.69	344	0	0	0	100	49	61.0	N/A	4	4	2,000	1,000	0.0	1.0
B- /7.7	4.6	0.38	12.47	429	3	0	96	1	64	22.0	-0.9	80	4	1,000	50	2.3	0.0
B /8.9	4.6	0.19	12.48	16	3	0	96	1	64	19.2	-1.1	86	4	1,000	50	0.0	0.0
B- /7.7	4.6	0.39	12.48	4	3	0	96	1	64	20.0	-1.1	75	4	1,000	50	0.0	0.0
B- /7.7	4.6	0.38	12.49	565	3	0	96	1	64	23.6	-0.7	83	4	1,000,000	0	0.0	0.0
U /	N/A	N/A	12.49	618	3	0	96	1	64	N/A	N/A	N/A	4	0	0	0.0	0.0
B- /7.7	4.6	0.39	12.52	N/A	3	0	96	1	64	N/A	N/A	77	4	0	0	0.0	0.0
U /	N/A	N/A	10.64	147	6	0	93	1	131	N/A	N/A	N/A	2	1,000	50	4.3	0.0
U /	N/A	N/A	10.64	36	6	0	93	1	131	N/A	N/A	N/A	2	1,000	50	0.0	0.0
U /	N/A	N/A	10.64	695	6	0	93	1	131	N/A	N/A	N/A	2	1,000,000	0	0.0	0.0
B- /7.2	3.7	N/A	10.65	133	6	0	93	1	131	44.2	4.8	98	2	0	0	0.0	0.0
C+ /6.6	10.1	1.03	19.25	3	0	99	0	1	47	92.7	-15.6	42	5	1,000	50	5.8	0.0
C+ /6.7	10.1	1.03	19.18	N/A	0	99	0	1	47	87.8	-15.9	31	5	1,000	50	0.0	0.0
C+ /6.6	10.1	1.03	19.27	19	0	99	0	1	47	94.5	-15.5	46	5	1,000,000	0	0.0	0.0
C+ /6.6	10.1	1.03	19.28	811	0	99	0	1	47	94.8	-15.5	46	5	0	0	0.0	0.0
B /8.1	11.3	1.12	10.48	19	0	0	0	100	0	127.9	-17.1	85	1	0	0	0.0	0.0
C+ /5.9	16.7	1.36	20.06	188	0	99	0	1	32	201.1	-38.6	95	16	1,000	50	5.8	0.0
C+ /5.9	16.7	1.37	19.34	939	0	99	0	1	32	193.4	-38.8	94	16	1,000	50	0.0	0.0
C+ /5.9	16.7	1.36	20.71	77	0	99	0	1	32	200.8	-38.7	95	16	0	0	0.0	0.0
C+ /5.9	16.7	1.36	21.60	1,064	0	99	0	1	32	203.8	-38.4	96	16	1,000,000	0	0.0	0.0
C+ /5.9	16.7	1.37	20.32	7	0	99	0	1	32	196.2	-38.6	95	16	0	0	0.0	0.0
U /	N/A	N/A	11.07	58	98	1	0	1	62	N/A	N/A	N/A	2	100,000	0	0.0	0.0
B+ /9.0	7.4	-0.13	8.86	16	34	0	65	1	59	N/A	N/A	79	2	2,500	500	5.8	1.0
B+ /9.1	7.3	-0.13	8.65	3	34	0	65	1	59	N/A	N/A	71	2	2,500	500	0.0	1.0
B+ /9.0	7.3	-0.13	8.91	12	34	0	65	1	59	N/A	N/A	80	2	100,000	500	0.0	1.0
C+ /6.3	9.2	0.10	8.98	235	26	0	73	1	46	2.2	-7.2	89	4	2,500	500	5.8	1.0
C+ /6.3	9.2	0.11	8.75	103	26	0	73	1	46	-0.6	-7.5	86	4	2,500	500	0.0	1.0
C+ /6.3	9.2	0.11	9.06	212	26	0	73	1	46	3.0	-7.1	90	4	100,000	500	0.0	1.0
U /	N/A	N/A	12.63	56	0	0	0	100	0	N/A	N/A	N/A	1	2,500	500	5.8	1.0
U /	N/A	N/A	12.65	121	0	0	0	100	0	N/A	N/A	N/A	1	100,000	500	0.0	1.0
U /	N/A	N/A	9.42	44	0	0	0	100	0	N/A	N/A	N/A	2	2,500	500	5.8	2.0
U /	N/A	N/A	9.42	32	0	0	0	100	0	N/A	N/A	N/A	2	2,500	500	0.0	2.0
U /	N/A	N/A	9.43	37	0	0	0	100	0	N/A	N/A	N/A	2	100,000	500	0.0	2.0
U /	N/A	N/A	12.93	232	62	0	37	1	0	N/A	N/A	N/A	3	10,000	2,500	0.0	1.0
C- /4.0	12.4	1.13	30.90	6,949	4	85	9	2	23	82.5	-20.7	9	28	10,000	0	0.0	0.0
U /	N/A	N/A	11.44	167	17	82	0	1	4	N/A	N/A	N/A	3	10,000	0	0.0	0.0
D+ /2.9	16.6	1.13	13.74	1,446	2	92	5	1	36	39.3	-24.5	12	17	10,000	0	0.0	0.0
C- /3.9	9.0	0.50	32.24	4,686	3	76	19	2	20	107.8	-16.7	98	26	10,000	0	0.0	0.0
C- /3.2	14.6	0.99	24.17	879	1	98	0	1	63	96.6	-22.5	68	10	100,000	0	0.0	0.0
U /	N/A	N/A	24.21	27	1	98	0	1	63	N/A	N/A	N/A	10	0	0	0.0	0.0
C- /3.0	14.6	0.99	22.80	177	1	98	0	1	63	93.3	-22.5	61	10	2,500	50	0.0	0.0
C /4.7	12.3	0.89	34.72	63	1	98	0	1	23	96.6	-24.0	76	15	0	0	0.0	0.0
C /4.7	12.3	0.89	36.10	804	1	98	0	1	23	100.0	-23.9	80	15	100,000	0	0.0	0.0

Data as of March 31, 2015

99 Pct = Best
0 Pct = Worst

Fund Type	Fund Name	Ticker Symbol	Overall Investment Rating	Phone	Performance Rating/Pts	3 Mo	6 Mo	1Yr / Pct	3Yr / Pct	5Yr / Pct	Dividend Yield	Expense Ratio
SC	● Loomis Sayles SmCp Val Ret	LSCRX	B-	(800) 633-3330	B+ / 8.3	4.66	13.33	9.03 /69	15.52 /79	14.98 /87	0.27	1.34
★ GI	Lord Abbett Affiliated A	LAFFX	B-	(888) 522-2388	C+ / 6.3	0.35	5.85	9.95 /74	15.22 /77	11.20 /54	1.96	0.74
GI	● Lord Abbett Affiliated B	LAFBX	B-	(888) 522-2388	C+ / 6.8	0.21	5.47	9.15 /70	14.44 /70	10.45 /48	1.29	1.49
GI	Lord Abbett Affiliated C	LAFCX	B-	(888) 522-2388	C+ / 6.8	0.23	5.47	9.19 /70	14.44 /70	10.45 /48	1.35	1.49
GI	Lord Abbett Affiliated F	LAAFX	B+	(888) 522-2388	B / 7.6	0.39	5.93	10.11 /75	15.45 /79	11.43 /56	2.22	0.59
GI	Lord Abbett Affiliated I	LAFYX	B+	(888) 522-2388	B / 7.7	0.47	5.96	10.26 /75	15.57 /80	11.54 /57	2.31	0.49
GI	● Lord Abbett Affiliated P	LAFPX	B+	(888) 522-2388	B- / 7.4	0.41	5.85	9.94 /74	15.21 /77	11.17 /54	2.00	0.94
GI	Lord Abbett Affiliated R2	LAFQX	B+	(888) 522-2388	B- / 7.1	0.27	5.68	9.58 /72	14.88 /74	10.88 /52	1.74	1.09
GI	Lord Abbett Affiliated R3	LAFRX	B+	(888) 522-2388	B- / 7.3	0.36	5.74	9.70 /73	15.02 /75	11.01 /53	1.85	0.99
GL	Lord Abbett Alpha Strategy I	ALFYX	B	(888) 522-2388	B / 8.2	5.71	12.41	6.20 /48	15.78 /82	14.27 /80	1.63	1.38
IN	Lord Abbett Calibrated Div Gr A	LAMAX	C	(888) 522-2388	C / 5.3	-0.12	6.37	9.77 /73	13.28 /62	12.00 /60	1.44	1.10
IN	● Lord Abbett Calibrated Div Gr B	LAMBX	C	(888) 522-2388	C+ / 5.7	-0.32	5.95	8.93 /69	12.46 /56	11.20 /54	0.80	1.85
IN	Lord Abbett Calibrated Div Gr C	LAMCX	C	(888) 522-2388	C+ / 5.7	-0.30	5.99	8.93 /69	12.47 /56	11.22 /55	0.85	1.85
IN	Lord Abbett Calibrated Div Gr F	LAMFX	C+	(888) 522-2388	C+ / 6.3	-0.15	6.37	9.86 /74	13.45 /63	12.22 /62	1.66	0.95
IN	Lord Abbett Calibrated Div Gr I	LAMYX	C+	(888) 522-2388	C+ / 6.5	-0.06	6.52	10.04 /74	13.59 /64	12.32 /63	1.74	0.85
IN	● Lord Abbett Calibrated Div Gr P	LAMPX	C+	(888) 522-2388	C+ / 6.1	-0.24	6.23	9.50 /72	13.04 /60	11.82 /59	1.32	1.30
IN	Lord Abbett Calibrated Div Gr R2	LAMQX	C	(888) 522-2388	C+ / 6.0	-0.25	6.09	9.31 /71	12.89 /59	11.65 /58	1.05	1.45
IN	Lord Abbett Calibrated Div Gr R3	LAMRX	C+	(888) 522-2388	C+ / 6.1	-0.18	6.21	9.49 /72	13.01 /60	11.78 /59	1.32	1.35
CV	Lord Abbett Convertible A	LACFX	C-	(888) 522-2388	C / 4.8	2.45	3.70	6.32 /49	11.92 /52	9.16 /38	2.22	1.12
CV	● Lord Abbett Convertible B	LBCFX	C-	(888) 522-2388	C / 4.6	2.23	3.30	5.46 /42	11.06 /46	8.33 /32	1.48	1.92
CV	Lord Abbett Convertible C	LACCX	C-	(888) 522-2388	C / 4.8	2.29	3.40	5.67 /44	11.25 /47	8.47 /33	1.66	1.74
CV	Lord Abbett Convertible F	LBFFX	C-	(888) 522-2388	C / 5.3	2.47	3.76	6.43 /50	12.03 /53	9.29 /39	2.37	1.02
CV	Lord Abbett Convertible I	LCFYX	C-	(888) 522-2388	C / 5.4	2.48	3.79	6.50 /51	12.14 /53	9.40 /40	2.45	0.92
CV	● Lord Abbett Convertible P	LCFPX	C-	(888) 522-2388	C / 5.0	2.45	3.64	6.08 /47	11.66 /50	8.92 /36	2.02	1.37
CV	Lord Abbett Convertible R2	LBCQX	C-	(888) 522-2388	C / 4.9	2.37	3.53	5.93 /46	11.49 /49	8.76 /35	1.88	1.52
CV	Lord Abbett Convertible R3	LCFRX	C-	(888) 522-2388	C / 5.0	2.38	3.50	5.96 /46	11.59 /50	8.87 /36	2.01	1.42
SC	● Lord Abbett Developing Growth A	LAGWX	C-	(888) 522-2388	A / 9.4	7.12	15.25	8.78 /68	19.61 /97	18.95 /98	0.00	0.98
SC	● Lord Abbett Developing Growth B	LADBX	D+	(888) 522-2388	A+ / 9.6	6.88	14.79	8.00 /63	18.79 /96	18.17 /98	0.00	1.73
SC	● Lord Abbett Developing Growth C	LADCX	D+	(888) 522-2388	A+ / 9.6	6.93	14.81	8.02 /63	18.79 /96	18.18 /98	0.00	1.73
SC	● Lord Abbett Developing Growth F	LADFX	C-	(888) 522-2388	A+ / 9.7	7.19	15.36	9.02 /69	19.88 /98	19.24 /98	0.00	0.83
SC	● Lord Abbett Developing Growth I	LADYX	C	(888) 522-2388	A+ / 9.7	7.18	15.39	9.07 /70	19.99 /98	19.36 /98	0.00	0.73
SC	● Lord Abbett Developing Growth P	LADPX	C-	(888) 522-2388	A+ / 9.7	7.14	15.23	8.79 /68	19.63 /97	18.94 /98	0.00	1.18
SC	● Lord Abbett Developing Growth R2	LADQX	C-	(888) 522-2388	A+ / 9.6	7.00	15.05	8.45 /66	19.27 /97	18.64 /98	0.00	1.33
SC	● Lord Abbett Developing Growth R3	LADRX	C-	(888) 522-2388	A+ / 9.7	7.06	15.12	8.57 /67	19.40 /97	18.77 /98	0.00	1.23
GL	Lord Abbett Eq Tr Calib LCV A	LCAAX	B-	(888) 522-2388	C+ / 6.8	-0.05	6.02	9.42 /72	16.01 /83	--	1.42	1.08
GL	Lord Abbett Eq Tr Calib LCV C	LCACX	A-	(888) 522-2388	B- / 7.2	-0.24	5.64	8.63 /67	15.16 /76	--	0.88	1.83
GL	Lord Abbett Eq Tr Calib LCV F	LCAFX	A	(888) 522-2388	B / 8.0	-0.05	6.06	9.56 /72	16.18 /85	--	1.67	0.93
GL	Lord Abbett Eq Tr Calib LCV I	LVCIX	A+	(888) 522-2388	B / 8.1	0.00	6.10	9.69 /73	16.28 /85	--	1.75	0.83
GL	Lord Abbett Eq Tr Calib LCV R2	LCAQX	A	(888) 522-2388	B / 7.7	-0.14	5.81	9.05 /70	15.86 /82	--	1.16	1.43
GL	Lord Abbett Eq Tr Calib LCV R3	LCARX	A	(888) 522-2388	B / 7.7	-0.10	5.88	9.14 /70	15.80 /82	--	1.35	1.33
GR	Lord Abbett Eq Tr Calib MCV A	LVMAX	A+	(888) 522-2388	A- / 9.1	3.13	12.13	14.41 /90	18.47 /96	--	1.02	1.09
GR	Lord Abbett Eq Tr Calib MCV C	LVMCX	A+	(888) 522-2388	A / 9.3	2.98	11.74	13.58 /88	17.63 /93	--	0.45	1.84
GR	Lord Abbett Eq Tr Calib MCV F	LVMFX	A+	(888) 522-2388	A+ / 9.6	3.18	12.24	14.58 /91	18.67 /96	--	1.22	0.94
GR	Lord Abbett Eq Tr Calib MCV I	LVMIX	A+	(888) 522-2388	A+ / 9.6	3.22	12.28	14.72 /91	18.80 /96	--	1.31	0.84
GR	Lord Abbett Eq Tr Calib MCV R2	LVMQX	A+	(888) 522-2388	A / 9.5	3.06	11.94	14.00 /89	18.34 /95	--	0.89	1.44
GR	Lord Abbett Eq Tr Calib MCV R3	LVMRX	A+	(888) 522-2388	A / 9.5	3.07	12.00	14.12 /90	18.40 /95	--	0.98	1.34
GI	Lord Abbett Fundamental Equity A	LDFVX	D-	(888) 522-2388	C / 4.7	-0.45	3.28	6.24 /49	13.10 /60	11.63 /58	0.61	0.95
GI	● Lord Abbett Fundamental Equity B	GILBX	D-	(888) 522-2388	C / 5.2	-0.56	2.91	5.56 /43	12.38 /55	10.91 /52	0.00	1.70
GI	Lord Abbett Fundamental Equity C	GILAX	D-	(888) 522-2388	C / 5.2	-0.65	2.87	5.46 /42	12.34 /55	10.90 /52	0.03	1.70
GI	Lord Abbett Fundamental Equity F	LAVFX	D	(888) 522-2388	C+ / 5.9	-0.37	3.39	6.51 /51	13.37 /62	11.90 /60	0.91	0.80
GI	Lord Abbett Fundamental Equity I	LAVYX	D	(888) 522-2388	C+ / 5.9	-0.37	3.46	6.61 /52	13.47 /63	12.02 /61	1.00	0.70
GI	● Lord Abbett Fundamental Equity P	LAVPX	D	(888) 522-2388	C+ / 5.6	-0.53	3.16	6.09 /47	12.98 /60	11.51 /57	0.50	1.15

● Denotes fund is closed to new investors
★ Denotes fund is included in Section II

www.thestreetratings.com

I. Index of Stock Mutual Funds

RISK	3 Year		NET ASSETS		ASSET				Portfolio	BULL / BEAR		FUND MANAGER		MINIMUMS		LOADS	
Risk Rating/Pts	Standard Deviation	Beta	NAV As of 3/31/15	Total $(Mil)	Cash %	Stocks %	Bonds %	Other %	Turnover Ratio	Last Bull Market Return	Last Bear Market Return	Manager Quality Pct	Manager Tenure (Years)	Initial Purch. $	Additional Purch. $	Front End Load	Back End Load
C / 4.7	12.3	0.89	35.68	357	1	98	0	1	23	98.3	-23.9	78	15	2,500	50	0.0	0.0
B- / 7.1	10.2	1.04	16.24	6,046	0	100	0	0	81	97.8	-24.1	46	2	1,000	0	5.8	0.0
B- / 7.1	10.2	1.04	16.34	59	0	100	0	0	81	93.2	-24.4	36	2	250	0	0.0	0.0
B- / 7.1	10.2	1.04	16.25	459	0	100	0	0	81	93.2	-24.4	36	2	1,000	0	0.0	0.0
B- / 7.1	10.2	1.04	16.24	161	0	100	0	0	81	99.2	-24.1	49	2	0	0	0.0	0.0
B- / 7.1	10.2	1.04	16.29	136	0	100	0	0	81	99.9	-24.1	51	2	1,000,000	0	0.0	0.0
B- / 7.1	10.2	1.04	16.22	27	0	100	0	0	81	97.8	-24.2	46	2	0	0	0.0	0.0
B- / 7.1	10.3	1.05	16.21	1	0	100	0	0	81	95.8	-24.2	40	2	0	0	0.0	0.0
B- / 7.1	10.2	1.04	16.23	58	0	100	0	0	81	96.7	-24.2	43	2	0	0	0.0	0.0
C+ / 5.8	12.7	0.67	31.67	51	22	77	0	1	5	95.7	-25.3	97	11	1,000,000	0	0.0	0.0
C+ / 5.8	9.5	0.96	14.76	1,619	0	99	0	1	73	80.8	-16.0	38	3	1,000	0	5.8	0.0
C+ / 5.8	9.5	0.96	14.63	29	0	99	0	1	73	76.4	-16.2	29	3	1,000	0	0.0	0.0
C+ / 5.8	9.5	0.96	14.62	273	0	99	0	1	73	76.4	-16.2	30	3	1,000	0	0.0	0.0
C+ / 5.8	9.5	0.96	14.74	124	0	99	0	1	73	82.0	-15.9	40	3	0	0	0.0	0.0
C+ / 5.8	9.5	0.96	14.86	17	0	99	0	1	73	82.4	-15.9	43	3	1,000,000	0	0.0	0.0
C+ / 5.8	9.5	0.96	14.81	2	0	99	0	1	73	79.9	-16.0	35	3	0	0	0.0	0.0
C+ / 5.9	9.6	0.97	14.86	1	0	99	0	1	73	79.0	-16.1	33	3	0	0	0.0	0.0
C+ / 5.8	9.5	0.96	14.70	23	0	99	0	1	73	79.6	-16.1	35	3	0	0	0.0	0.0
C / 5.5	8.2	1.08	12.22	132	3	27	0	70	174	59.6	-17.3	29	12	1,500	0	2.3	0.0
C / 5.5	8.1	1.08	12.22	2	3	27	0	70	174	55.2	-17.6	22	12	1,000	0	0.0	0.0
C / 5.5	8.1	1.08	12.16	64	3	27	0	70	174	56.2	-17.5	23	12	1,500	0	0.0	0.0
C / 5.5	8.2	1.09	12.22	119	3	27	0	70	174	60.1	-17.3	30	12	0	0	0.0	0.0
C / 5.5	8.1	1.08	12.28	463	3	27	0	70	174	60.7	-17.3	32	12	1,000,000	0	0.0	0.0
C / 5.5	8.1	1.08	12.39	N/A	3	27	0	70	174	58.3	-17.5	27	12	0	0	0.0	0.0
C / 5.5	8.1	1.08	12.37	N/A	3	27	0	70	174	57.4	-17.5	25	12	0	0	0.0	0.0
C / 5.5	8.1	1.08	12.18	3	3	27	0	70	174	58.0	-17.4	26	12	0	0	0.0	0.0
E+ / 0.8	15.7	1.04	23.78	1,203	2	97	0	1	242	109.2	-23.6	86	14	1,000	0	5.8	0.0
E- / 0.2	15.6	1.03	18.49	9	2	97	0	1	242	104.5	-23.9	82	14	1,000	0	0.0	0.0
E- / 0.2	15.6	1.03	18.68	113	2	97	0	1	242	104.6	-23.9	82	14	1,000	0	0.0	0.0
D- / 1.0	15.6	1.03	24.45	273	2	97	0	1	242	110.9	-23.6	87	14	0	0	0.0	0.0
D- / 1.5	15.7	1.04	26.72	1,594	2	97	0	1	242	111.6	-23.5	87	14	1,000,000	0	0.0	0.0
E+ / 0.8	15.6	1.03	23.12	37	2	97	0	1	242	109.3	-23.6	86	14	0	0	0.0	0.0
E+ / 0.8	15.7	1.04	23.07	14	2	97	0	1	242	107.3	-23.7	84	14	0	0	0.0	0.0
E+ / 0.8	15.6	1.03	23.35	302	2	97	0	1	242	108.1	-23.7	85	14	0	0	0.0	0.0
B- / 7.7	10.0	0.58	20.95	68	0	99	0	1	104	N/A	N/A	98	4	1,500	0	5.8	0.0
B- / 7.7	10.0	0.58	20.65	17	0	99	0	1	104	N/A	N/A	97	4	1,500	0	0.0	0.0
B- / 7.7	10.0	0.58	20.95	26	0	99	0	1	104	N/A	N/A	98	4	0	0	0.0	0.0
B- / 7.7	10.0	0.58	20.98	368	0	99	0	1	104	N/A	N/A	98	4	1,000,000	0	0.0	0.0
B- / 7.7	10.0	0.58	21.06	N/A	0	99	0	1	104	N/A	N/A	98	4	0	0	0.0	0.0
B- / 7.7	10.0	0.58	20.85	N/A	0	99	0	1	104	N/A	N/A	98	4	0	0	0.0	0.0
B- / 7.2	10.3	0.99	22.08	91	0	99	0	1	98	N/A	N/A	85	4	1,500	0	5.8	0.0
B- / 7.2	10.3	0.99	21.76	26	0	99	0	1	98	N/A	N/A	81	4	1,500	0	0.0	0.0
B- / 7.2	10.3	0.99	22.09	94	0	99	0	1	98	N/A	N/A	86	4	0	0	0.0	0.0
B- / 7.2	10.3	0.99	22.14	675	0	99	0	1	98	N/A	N/A	87	4	1,000,000	0	0.0	0.0
B- / 7.2	10.3	0.99	22.20	N/A	0	99	0	1	98	N/A	N/A	85	4	0	0	0.0	0.0
B- / 7.2	10.3	0.99	22.18	N/A	0	99	0	1	98	N/A	N/A	85	4	0	0	0.0	0.0
C- / 3.1	10.6	1.05	13.41	2,366	0	99	0	1	113	84.3	-22.0	21	5	1,500	0	5.8	0.0
D+ / 2.8	10.6	1.06	12.38	39	0	99	0	1	113	80.1	-22.2	15	5	1,000	0	0.0	0.0
D+ / 2.7	10.6	1.06	12.28	857	0	99	0	1	113	80.2	-22.2	15	5	1,500	0	0.0	0.0
C- / 3.0	10.7	1.06	13.31	605	0	99	0	1	113	85.7	-21.9	22	5	0	0	0.0	0.0
C- / 3.1	10.6	1.06	13.48	349	0	99	0	1	113	86.4	-21.9	24	5	1,000,000	0	0.0	0.0
C- / 3.1	10.6	1.06	13.21	18	0	99	0	1	113	83.5	-22.0	19	5	0	0	0.0	0.0

99 Pct = Best
0 Pct = Worst

Fund Type	Fund Name	Ticker Symbol	Overall Investment Rating	Phone	Performance Rating/Pts	3 Mo	6 Mo	1Yr / Pct	3Yr / Pct	5Yr / Pct	Dividend Yield	Expense Ratio
GI	Lord Abbett Fundamental Equity R2	LAVQX	D	(888) 522-2388	C / 5.5	-0.53	3.12	5.92 / 46	12.81 / 58	11.35 / 56	0.21	1.30
GI	Lord Abbett Fundamental Equity R3	LAVRX	D	(888) 522-2388	C+ / 5.6	-0.45	3.19	6.05 / 47	12.92 / 59	11.46 / 57	0.47	1.20
GL	Lord Abbett Growth Leaders A	LGLAX	B+	(888) 522-2388	B+ / 8.3	4.71	9.06	12.97 / 86	17.26 / 91	--	0.00	1.02
GL	Lord Abbett Growth Leaders C	LGLCX	B+	(888) 522-2388	B+ / 8.8	4.55	8.70	12.15 / 83	16.49 / 87	--	0.00	1.77
GL	Lord Abbett Growth Leaders F	LGLFX	A-	(888) 522-2388	A- / 9.2	4.73	9.16	13.16 / 87	17.49 / 92	--	0.00	0.87
GL	Lord Abbett Growth Leaders I	LGLIX	A-	(888) 522-2388	A / 9.3	4.76	9.19	13.23 / 87	17.62 / 93	--	0.00	0.77
GL	Lord Abbett Growth Leaders R2	LGLQX	A-	(888) 522-2388	A- / 9.1	4.60	8.89	12.56 / 85	17.28 / 91	--	0.00	1.37
GL	Lord Abbett Growth Leaders R3	LGLRX	A-	(888) 522-2388	A- / 9.1	4.63	8.94	12.69 / 86	17.06 / 90	--	0.00	1.27
GR	Lord Abbett Growth Opportunities A	LMGAX	C-	(888) 522-2388	B- / 7.4	7.61	12.99	13.04 / 87	15.17 / 76	13.16 / 70	0.00	1.30
GR	● Lord Abbett Growth Opportunities B	LMGBX	C-	(888) 522-2388	B / 8.0	7.44	12.61	12.20 / 83	14.41 / 70	12.42 / 64	0.00	2.05
GR	Lord Abbett Growth Opportunities C	LMGCX	C-	(888) 522-2388	B / 8.0	7.44	12.61	12.20 / 83	14.40 / 70	12.43 / 64	0.00	2.05
GR	Lord Abbett Growth Opportunities F	LGOFX	C+	(888) 522-2388	B+ / 8.7	7.65	13.06	13.20 / 87	15.43 / 78	13.42 / 72	0.00	1.15
GR	Lord Abbett Growth Opportunities I	LMGYX	C+	(888) 522-2388	B+ / 8.7	7.69	13.15	13.33 / 88	15.54 / 79	13.54 / 73	0.00	1.05
GR	● Lord Abbett Growth Opportunities P	LGOPX	C	(888) 522-2388	B+ / 8.4	7.56	12.91	12.81 / 86	15.02 / 75	13.02 / 68	0.00	1.50
GR	Lord Abbett Growth Opportunities R2	LGOQX	C	(888) 522-2388	B+ / 8.3	7.52	12.83	12.62 / 85	14.86 / 74	12.86 / 67	0.00	1.65
GR	Lord Abbett Growth Opportunities R3	LGORX	C	(888) 522-2388	B+ / 8.4	7.52	12.88	12.72 / 86	14.96 / 75	12.98 / 68	0.00	1.55
FO	Lord Abbett Intl Core Equity A	LICAX	D-	(888) 522-2388	E+ / 0.9	3.72	-1.85	-4.26 / 7	5.81 / 16	4.24 / 9	1.05	1.26
FO	● Lord Abbett Intl Core Equity B	LICBX	D-	(888) 522-2388	D- / 1.1	3.59	-2.16	-4.88 / 6	5.13 / 14	3.56 / 7	0.24	2.01
FO	Lord Abbett Intl Core Equity C	LICCX	D-	(888) 522-2388	D- / 1.1	3.59	-2.15	-4.87 / 6	5.13 / 14	3.58 / 7	0.41	2.01
FO	Lord Abbett Intl Core Equity F	LICFX	D-	(888) 522-2388	D- / 1.4	3.83	-1.73	-4.02 / 7	6.06 / 17	4.50 / 10	1.40	1.11
FO	Lord Abbett Intl Core Equity I	LICYX	D-	(888) 522-2388	D- / 1.5	3.86	-1.68	-3.87 / 7	6.18 / 17	4.61 / 11	1.49	1.01
FO	● Lord Abbett Intl Core Equity P	LICPX	D-	(888) 522-2388	D- / 1.3	3.72	-1.92	-4.34 / 6	5.71 / 16	4.14 / 9	0.75	1.46
FO	Lord Abbett Intl Core Equity R2	LICQX	D-	(888) 522-2388	D- / 1.2	3.73	-2.02	-4.50 / 6	5.54 / 15	3.99 / 8	0.88	1.61
FO	Lord Abbett Intl Core Equity R3	LICRX	D-	(888) 522-2388	D- / 1.3	3.78	-1.93	-4.38 / 6	5.65 / 15	4.10 / 9	1.00	1.51
FO	Lord Abbett Intl Dividend Inc A	LIDAX	E	(888) 522-2388	E+ / 0.7	0.04	-3.85	-5.15 / 5	5.01 / 13	3.96 / 8	3.85	1.14
FO	Lord Abbett Intl Dividend Inc C	LIDCX	E	(888) 522-2388	E+ / 0.8	-0.13	-4.20	-5.80 / 5	4.32 / 11	3.29 / 7	3.44	1.89
FO	Lord Abbett Intl Dividend Inc F	LIDFX	E	(888) 522-2388	D- / 1.0	0.09	-3.74	-4.92 / 6	5.25 / 14	4.23 / 9	4.32	0.99
FO	Lord Abbett Intl Dividend Inc I	LAIDX	E+	(888) 522-2388	D- / 1.1	0.12	-3.68	-4.81 / 6	5.38 / 14	4.32 / 9	4.41	0.89
FO	Lord Abbett Intl Dividend Inc R2	LIDRX	E	(888) 522-2388	E+ / 0.9	-0.03	-4.02	-5.52 / 5	4.71 / 12	3.86 / 8	3.74	1.49
FO	Lord Abbett Intl Dividend Inc R3	LIRRX	E	(888) 522-2388	E+ / 0.9	0.00	-4.00	-5.36 / 5	4.84 / 13	3.80 / 8	3.89	1.39
GL	Lord Abbett Inv Tr-Div Eq Strat A	LDSAX	C-	(888) 522-2388	C+ / 5.7	3.61	7.05	7.56 / 60	13.98 / 67	11.41 / 56	1.93	1.34
GL	● Lord Abbett Inv Tr-Div Eq Strat B	LDSBX	C	(888) 522-2388	C+ / 6.1	3.41	6.66	6.76 / 53	13.13 / 61	10.61 / 50	1.27	2.09
GL	Lord Abbett Inv Tr-Div Eq Strat C	LDSCX	C	(888) 522-2388	C+ / 6.1	3.43	6.71	6.81 / 54	13.15 / 61	10.64 / 50	1.43	2.09
GL	Lord Abbett Inv Tr-Div Eq Strat F	LDSFX	C	(888) 522-2388	C+ / 6.8	3.61	7.10	7.71 / 61	14.13 / 68	11.59 / 58	2.17	1.19
GL	Lord Abbett Inv Tr-Div Eq Strat I	LDSYX	C+	(888) 522-2388	C+ / 6.9	3.68	7.20	7.86 / 62	14.26 / 69	11.71 / 58	2.24	1.09
GL	Lord Abbett Inv Tr-Div Eq Strat R2	LDSQX	C	(888) 522-2388	C+ / 6.4	3.50	6.90	7.20 / 57	13.58 / 64	11.09 / 53	1.69	1.69
GL	Lord Abbett Inv Tr-Div Eq Strat R3	LDSRX	C	(888) 522-2388	C+ / 6.5	3.53	6.92	7.27 / 57	13.71 / 65	11.16 / 54	1.88	1.59
MC	Lord Abbett Mid Cap Stock A	LAVLX	B	(888) 522-2388	B- / 7.2	3.52	10.23	12.02 / 83	15.64 / 80	14.14 / 79	0.43	1.23
MC	● Lord Abbett Mid Cap Stock B	LMCBX	B	(888) 522-2388	B / 7.7	3.30	9.79	11.20 / 79	14.87 / 74	13.38 / 72	0.00	1.88
MC	Lord Abbett Mid Cap Stock C	LMCCX	B+	(888) 522-2388	B / 7.7	3.32	9.83	11.25 / 79	14.87 / 74	13.38 / 72	0.00	1.88
MC	Lord Abbett Mid Cap Stock F	LMCFX	B+	(888) 522-2388	B+ / 8.5	3.54	10.32	12.26 / 84	15.91 / 83	14.41 / 82	0.71	0.98
MC	Lord Abbett Mid Cap Stock I	LMCYX	A-	(888) 522-2388	B+ / 8.6	3.62	10.39	12.38 / 84	16.03 / 84	14.53 / 83	0.78	0.88
MC	Lord Abbett Mid Cap Stock P	LMCPX	B+	(888) 522-2388	B+ / 8.4	3.55	10.23	12.02 / 83	15.68 / 81	14.12 / 79	0.50	1.33
MC	Lord Abbett Mid Cap Stock R2	LMCQX	B+	(888) 522-2388	B / 8.1	3.41	10.02	11.69 / 81	15.33 / 78	13.83 / 76	0.20	1.48
MC	Lord Abbett Mid Cap Stock R3	LMCRX	B+	(888) 522-2388	B / 8.2	3.48	10.12	11.83 / 82	15.47 / 79	13.96 / 77	0.34	1.38
BA	Lord Abbett Multi Asset Bal Opp A	LABFX	C	(888) 522-2388	C- / 3.8	2.09	3.87	5.17 / 40	10.18 / 40	8.75 / 35	4.78	1.17
BA	● Lord Abbett Multi Asset Bal Opp B	LABBX	C-	(888) 522-2388	C- / 3.6	1.81	3.49	4.37 / 34	9.32 / 35	7.95 / 30	4.13	1.92
BA	Lord Abbett Multi Asset Bal Opp C	BFLAX	C	(888) 522-2388	C- / 3.7	1.91	3.53	4.44 / 35	9.37 / 35	7.96 / 30	4.19	1.92
BA	Lord Abbett Multi Asset Bal Opp F	BLAFX	C	(888) 522-2388	C / 4.3	2.12	3.95	5.32 / 41	10.32 / 41	8.94 / 36	5.04	1.02
BA	Lord Abbett Multi Asset Bal Opp I	LABYX	C	(888) 522-2388	C / 4.3	2.06	3.99	5.42 / 42	10.42 / 42	9.02 / 37	5.14	0.92
BA	● Lord Abbett Multi Asset Bal Opp P	LABPX	C	(888) 522-2388	C- / 4.0	1.96	3.78	4.89 / 38	9.93 / 39	8.54 / 33	4.71	1.37
BA	Lord Abbett Multi Asset Bal Opp R2	BLAQX	C	(888) 522-2388	C- / 4.0	2.04	3.77	4.85 / 37	9.78 / 38	8.41 / 33	4.43	1.52

● Denotes fund is closed to new investors
* Denotes fund is included in Section II

www.thestreetratings.com

RISK			NET ASSETS		ASSET				Portfolio	BULL / BEAR		FUND MANAGER		MINIMUMS		LOADS	
	3 Year		NAV							Last Bull	Last Bear	Manager	Manager	Initial	Additional	Front	Back
Risk Rating/Pts	Standard Deviation	Beta	As of 3/31/15	Total $(Mil)	Cash %	Stocks %	Bonds %	Other %	Turnover Ratio	Market Return	Market Return	Quality Pct	Tenure (Years)	Purch. $	Purch. $	End Load	End Load
C- / 3.1	10.6	1.05	13.17	15	0	99	0	1	113	82.5	-22.0	19	5	0	0	0.0	0.0
C- / 3.1	10.6	1.06	13.23	259	0	99	0	1	113	83.2	-22.0	19	5	0	0	0.0	0.0
C+ / 5.9	11.2	0.57	23.14	609	1	98	0	1	507	101.8	N/A	98	4	1,500	0	5.8	0.0
C+ / 5.8	11.2	0.58	22.54	307	1	98	0	1	507	97.3	N/A	98	4	1,500	0	0.0	0.0
C+ / 5.9	11.2	0.58	23.26	571	1	98	0	1	507	103.4	N/A	98	4	0	0	0.0	0.0
C+ / 5.9	11.2	0.57	23.32	84	1	98	0	1	507	104.2	N/A	98	4	1,000,000	0	0.0	0.0
C+ / 5.9	11.2	0.58	23.20	1	1	98	0	1	507	102.3	N/A	98	4	0	0	0.0	0.0
C+ / 5.9	11.2	0.58	23.07	12	1	98	0	1	507	101.3	N/A	98	4	0	0	0.0	0.0
C- / 3.2	12.3	1.11	22.07	433	0	100	0	0	207	97.0	-27.6	32	7	1,000	0	5.8	0.0
D / 2.1	12.3	1.10	18.06	10	0	100	0	0	207	92.4	-27.8	25	7	1,000	0	0.0	0.0
D / 2.1	12.4	1.11	18.05	65	0	100	0	0	207	92.6	-27.8	24	7	1,000	0	0.0	0.0
C- / 3.4	12.4	1.11	22.66	21	0	100	0	0	207	98.4	-27.5	35	7	0	0	0.0	0.0
C- / 3.7	12.3	1.10	24.24	152	0	100	0	0	207	99.1	-27.5	36	7	1,000,000	0	0.0	0.0
C- / 3.1	12.4	1.11	21.76	5	0	100	0	0	207	96.1	-27.6	30	7	0	0	0.0	0.0
C- / 3.1	12.4	1.11	21.45	1	0	100	0	0	207	95.0	-27.6	29	7	0	0	0.0	0.0
C- / 3.1	12.3	1.10	21.72	32	0	100	0	0	207	95.8	-27.6	30	7	0	0	0.0	0.0
C+ / 6.0	12.4	0.93	13.10	362	3	96	0	1	64	39.0	-23.5	27	12	1,500	0	5.8	0.0
C+ / 6.1	12.4	0.93	13.00	9	3	96	0	1	64	36.0	-23.7	20	12	1,000	0	0.0	0.0
C+ / 6.1	12.4	0.93	12.97	47	3	96	0	1	64	36.0	-23.7	20	12	1,500	0	0.0	0.0
C+ / 6.0	12.4	0.93	13.00	81	3	96	0	1	64	40.2	-23.4	30	12	0	0	0.0	0.0
C+ / 6.0	12.5	0.93	13.18	64	3	96	0	1	64	40.6	-23.3	31	12	1,000,000	0	0.0	0.0
C+ / 6.0	12.5	0.93	13.12	N/A	3	96	0	1	64	38.5	-23.4	26	12	0	0	0.0	0.0
C+ / 6.0	12.5	0.93	13.07	1	3	96	0	1	64	37.8	-23.5	24	12	0	0	0.0	0.0
C+ / 6.0	12.5	0.93	12.92	20	3	96	0	1	64	38.3	-23.5	25	12	0	0	0.0	0.0
C / 4.6	14.4	1.07	7.86	950	9	89	1	1	72	37.7	-22.9	11	7	1,500	0	5.8	0.0
C / 4.6	14.5	1.07	7.79	179	9	89	1	1	72	34.7	-23.0	8	7	1,500	0	0.0	0.0
C / 4.6	14.4	1.07	7.87	300	9	89	1	1	72	38.9	-22.7	12	7	0	0	0.0	0.0
C / 4.6	14.3	1.06	7.89	1,166	9	89	1	1	72	39.4	-22.7	13	7	1,000,000	0	0.0	0.0
C / 4.6	14.3	1.06	8.01	1	9	89	1	1	72	36.6	-22.9	10	7	0	0	0.0	0.0
C / 4.6	14.4	1.06	7.93	13	9	89	1	1	72	37.0	-22.9	10	7	0	0	0.0	0.0
C / 5.0	10.7	0.70	19.83	172	2	97	0	1	12	86.4	-23.3	96	9	1,500	0	5.8	0.0
C / 5.1	10.7	0.70	19.42	6	2	97	0	1	12	81.8	-23.5	95	9	1,000	0	0.0	0.0
C / 5.0	10.7	0.70	19.32	69	2	97	0	1	12	81.8	-23.5	95	9	1,500	0	0.0	0.0
C / 5.0	10.7	0.70	19.82	4	2	97	0	1	12	87.4	-23.3	96	8	0	0	0.0	0.0
C / 5.0	10.7	0.69	19.98	19	2	97	0	1	12	88.1	-23.2	96	9	1,000,000	0	0.0	0.0
C / 5.3	10.7	0.69	20.11	N/A	2	97	0	1	12	84.1	-23.4	96	8	0	0	0.0	0.0
C / 5.0	10.7	0.70	19.64	13	2	97	0	1	12	84.9	-23.4	96	8	0	0	0.0	0.0
C+ / 6.4	11.0	0.96	26.78	1,317	1	98	0	1	64	95.5	-24.2	58	7	1,000	0	5.8	0.0
C+ / 6.3	11.0	0.96	25.01	19	1	98	0	1	64	91.2	-24.4	48	7	1,000	0	0.0	0.0
C+ / 6.3	11.0	0.96	24.91	234	1	98	0	1	64	91.1	-24.3	49	7	1,000	0	0.0	0.0
C+ / 6.4	11.0	0.96	26.58	130	1	98	0	1	64	97.1	-24.1	62	7	0	0	0.0	0.0
C+ / 6.4	11.0	0.96	26.61	613	1	98	0	1	64	97.7	-24.0	64	7	1,000,000	0	0.0	0.0
C+ / 6.4	11.0	0.96	25.99	103	1	98	0	1	64	95.5	-24.2	59	7	0	0	0.0	0.0
C+ / 6.4	11.0	0.96	26.36	2	1	98	0	1	64	93.8	-24.2	54	7	0	0	0.0	0.0
C+ / 6.4	11.0	0.96	26.50	34	1	98	0	1	64	94.5	-24.2	56	7	0	0	0.0	0.0
B- / 7.2	7.8	1.29	12.12	1,575	2	52	37	9	45	58.7	-16.6	19	10	1,500	0	2.3	0.0
B- / 7.2	7.8	1.29	12.11	30	2	52	37	9	45	54.8	-17.0	14	10	1,000	0	0.0	0.0
B- / 7.2	7.8	1.29	12.06	403	2	52	37	9	45	54.7	-16.8	14	10	1,500	0	0.0	0.0
B- / 7.2	7.8	1.29	12.11	80	2	52	37	9	45	59.5	-16.7	20	10	0	0	0.0	0.0
B- / 7.2	7.8	1.29	12.11	35	2	52	37	9	45	60.0	-16.5	21	10	1,000,000	0	0.0	0.0
B- / 7.2	7.8	1.30	12.07	1	2	52	37	9	45	57.7	-16.7	17	10	0	0	0.0	0.0
B- / 7.2	7.8	1.29	12.33	1	2	52	37	9	45	56.8	-16.8	16	10	0	0	0.0	0.0

Fund Type	Fund Name	Ticker Symbol	Overall Investment Rating	Phone	Performance Rating/Pts	3 Mo	6 Mo	1Yr / Pct	3Yr / Pct	5Yr / Pct	Dividend Yield	Expense Ratio
BA	Lord Abbett Multi Asset Bal Opp R3	BLARX	C	(888) 522-2388	C- / 4.0	1.94	3.76	4.84 /37	9.87 /39	8.49 /33	4.66	1.42
GL	Lord Abbett Multi Asset Glbl Opp A	LAGEX	D	(888) 522-2388	D / 2.0	1.31	1.06	0.94 /18	7.51 /24	6.52 /20	3.81	1.51
GL	● Lord Abbett Multi Asset Glbl Opp B	LAGBX	D	(888) 522-2388	D / 1.9	1.07	0.70	0.17 /16	6.73 /20	5.74 /15	3.49	2.26
GL	Lord Abbett Multi Asset Glbl Opp C	LAGCX	D	(888) 522-2388	D / 1.9	1.08	0.72	0.23 /16	6.73 /20	5.76 /15	3.55	2.26
GL	Lord Abbett Multi Asset Glbl Opp F	LAGFX	D+	(888) 522-2388	D+ / 2.4	1.27	1.13	1.09 /19	7.67 /25	6.68 /21	4.05	1.36
GL	Lord Abbett Multi Asset Glbl Opp I	LGEYX	D+	(888) 522-2388	D+ / 2.5	1.37	1.26	1.26 /19	7.79 /26	6.80 /22	4.12	1.26
GL	Lord Abbett Multi Asset Glbl Opp R2	LAGQX	D+	(888) 522-2388	D / 2.1	1.22	0.90	0.60 /17	7.17 /22	6.36 /19	3.50	1.86
GL	Lord Abbett Multi Asset Glbl Opp R3	LARRX	D+	(888) 522-2388	D / 2.2	1.26	0.95	0.80 /18	7.31 /23	6.31 /19	3.66	1.76
IN	Lord Abbett Multi Asset Income A	ISFAX	D	(888) 522-2388	D / 2.2	2.10	2.18	3.19 /27	7.35 /23	7.62 /27	4.79	1.12
IN	● Lord Abbett Multi Asset Income B	ISFBX	D	(888) 522-2388	D / 2.0	1.94	1.85	2.49 /24	6.54 /19	6.84 /22	4.06	1.87
IN	Lord Abbett Multi Asset Income C	ISFCX	D	(888) 522-2388	D / 2.0	1.89	1.79	2.40 /24	6.53 /19	6.84 /22	4.10	1.87
IN	Lord Abbett Multi Asset Income F	LIGFX	D+	(888) 522-2388	D+ / 2.6	2.14	2.32	3.34 /28	7.50 /24	7.80 /29	5.04	0.97
IN	Lord Abbett Multi Asset Income I	ISFYX	D+	(888) 522-2388	D+ / 2.6	2.17	2.32	3.46 /29	7.59 /24	7.90 /29	5.17	0.87
IN	Lord Abbett Multi Asset Income R2	LIGQX	D	(888) 522-2388	D+ / 2.3	2.03	2.09	2.89 /26	6.96 /21	7.35 /25	4.43	1.47
IN	Lord Abbett Multi Asset Income R3	LIXRX	D	(888) 522-2388	D+ / 2.3	2.04	2.13	3.01 /26	7.09 /22	7.38 /26	4.65	1.37
GL	Lord Abbett Multi-Asset Growth A	LWSAX	C	(888) 522-2388	C / 4.7	2.41	5.35	7.02 /55	11.50 /49	9.78 /43	4.29	1.18
GL	● Lord Abbett Multi-Asset Growth B	LWSBX	C	(888) 522-2388	C / 4.6	2.16	4.98	6.23 /48	10.66 /43	8.98 /37	3.64	1.93
GL	Lord Abbett Multi-Asset Growth C	LWSCX	C	(888) 522-2388	C / 4.6	2.19	4.98	6.27 /49	10.70 /44	9.01 /37	3.73	1.93
GL	Lord Abbett Multi-Asset Growth F	LGXFX	C+	(888) 522-2388	C / 5.2	2.45	5.48	7.19 /57	11.68 /50	9.97 /44	4.54	1.03
GL	Lord Abbett Multi-Asset Growth I	LWSYX	C+	(888) 522-2388	C / 5.3	2.46	5.51	7.31 /58	11.77 /51	10.08 /45	4.60	0.93
GL	● Lord Abbett Multi-Asset Growth P	LWSPX	C	(888) 522-2388	C / 5.0	2.41	5.34	6.93 /54	11.33 /48	9.63 /42	4.21	1.38
GL	Lord Abbett Multi-Asset Growth R2	LGIQX	C	(888) 522-2388	C / 4.9	2.26	5.18	6.64 /52	11.12 /46	9.42 /40	3.96	1.53
GL	Lord Abbett Multi-Asset Growth R3	LGIRX	C	(888) 522-2388	C / 5.0	2.36	5.31	6.80 /53	11.24 /47	9.54 /41	4.17	1.43
GL	Lord Abbett Sec Tr-Alpha Stratg A	ALFAX	C+	(888) 522-2388	C+ / 6.8	5.64	12.24	5.93 /46	15.49 /79	13.96 /77	1.33	1.63
GL	● Lord Abbett Sec Tr-Alpha Stratg B	ALFBX	B-	(888) 522-2388	B- / 7.3	5.49	11.85	5.15 /40	14.63 /72	13.13 /69	0.65	2.38
GL	Lord Abbett Sec Tr-Alpha Stratg C	ALFCX	C+	(888) 522-2388	B- / 7.3	5.44	11.80	5.12 /39	14.62 /72	13.13 /69	0.87	2.38
GL	Lord Abbett Sec Tr-Alpha Stratg F	ALFFX	B	(888) 522-2388	B / 8.1	5.67	12.33	6.10 /47	15.65 /80	14.15 /79	1.56	1.48
GL	Lord Abbett Sec Tr-Alpha Stratg R2	ALFQX	B	(888) 522-2388	B / 7.6	5.54	12.06	5.56 /43	15.09 /76	13.58 /74	1.18	1.98
GL	Lord Abbett Sec Tr-Alpha Stratg R3	ALFRX	B	(888) 522-2388	B / 7.7	5.59	12.12	5.66 /44	15.19 /76	13.70 /75	1.20	1.88
FO	Lord Abbett Sec Tr-Intl Opp A	LAIEX	D+	(888) 522-2388	C- / 3.6	6.70	5.10	-0.81 /14	11.10 /46	9.26 /39	1.02	1.32
FO	● Lord Abbett Sec Tr-Intl Opp B	LINBX	D+	(888) 522-2388	C- / 4.0	6.48	4.72	-1.53 /11	10.35 /41	8.53 /33	0.26	2.07
FO	Lord Abbett Sec Tr-Intl Opp C	LINCX	D+	(888) 522-2388	C- / 4.0	6.49	4.75	-1.56 /11	10.37 /42	8.55 /33	0.47	2.07
FO	Lord Abbett Sec Tr-Intl Opp F	LINFX	C-	(888) 522-2388	C / 4.6	6.76	5.17	-0.67 /14	11.35 /48	9.51 /41	1.28	1.17
FO	Lord Abbett Sec Tr-Intl Opp I	LINYX	C-	(888) 522-2388	C / 4.7	6.73	5.19	-0.60 /14	11.43 /48	9.61 /41	1.34	1.07
FO	● Lord Abbett Sec Tr-Intl Opp P	LINPX	C-	(888) 522-2388	C / 4.4	6.65	4.97	-1.08 /13	10.96 /45	9.12 /38	0.90	1.52
FO	Lord Abbett Sec Tr-Intl Opp R2	LINQX	C-	(888) 522-2388	C / 4.3	6.56	4.89	-1.18 /12	10.78 /44	8.95 /36	0.80	1.67
FO	Lord Abbett Sec Tr-Intl Opp R3	LINRX	C-	(888) 522-2388	C / 4.4	6.60	4.99	-1.06 /13	10.92 /45	9.09 /37	0.91	1.57
SC	Lord Abbett Small Cap Value A	LRSCX	E+	(888) 522-2388	C / 4.8	4.64	11.53	5.68 /44	11.98 /52	11.54 /57	0.00	1.23
SC	Lord Abbett Small Cap Value B	LRSBX	E+	(888) 522-2388	C / 5.2	4.44	11.12	4.95 /38	11.19 /47	10.75 /51	0.00	1.93
SC	Lord Abbett Small Cap Value C	LSRCX	E+	(888) 522-2388	C / 5.2	4.44	11.11	4.91 /38	11.20 /47	10.75 /51	0.00	1.93
SC	Lord Abbett Small Cap Value F	LRSFX	E+	(888) 522-2388	C+ / 5.9	4.68	11.60	5.87 /45	12.19 /54	11.75 /59	0.17	1.03
SC	Lord Abbett Small Cap Value I	LRSYX	D-	(888) 522-2388	C+ / 5.9	4.71	11.66	6.00 /46	12.31 /55	11.87 /60	0.25	0.93
SC	Lord Abbett Small Cap Value P	LRSPX	E+	(888) 522-2388	C+ / 5.6	4.57	11.39	5.50 /42	11.79 /51	11.36 /56	0.00	1.38
SC	Lord Abbett Small Cap Value R2	LRSQX	E+	(888) 522-2388	C / 5.5	4.58	11.34	5.34 /41	11.62 /50	11.19 /54	0.00	1.53
SC	Lord Abbett Small Cap Value R3	LRSRX	E+	(888) 522-2388	C+ / 5.6	4.59	11.40	5.49 /42	11.77 /51	11.33 /55	0.00	1.43
MC	Lord Abbett Value Opportunities A	LVOAX	C+	(888) 522-2388	B- / 7.2	4.09	12.21	8.72 /68	15.88 /82	13.17 /70	0.00	1.17
MC	● Lord Abbett Value Opportunities B	LVOBX	C+	(888) 522-2388	B / 7.7	3.89	11.80	7.96 /63	15.10 /76	12.43 /64	0.00	1.92
MC	Lord Abbett Value Opportunities C	LVOCX	C+	(888) 522-2388	B / 7.7	3.89	11.80	7.96 /63	15.10 /76	12.43 /64	0.00	1.92
MC	Lord Abbett Value Opportunities F	LVOFX	B	(888) 522-2388	B+ / 8.5	4.14	12.33	8.97 /69	16.15 /84	13.44 /72	0.00	1.02
MC	Lord Abbett Value Opportunities I	LVOYX	B	(888) 522-2388	B+ / 8.6	4.17	12.36	9.04 /70	16.27 /85	13.55 /73	0.00	0.92
MC	● Lord Abbett Value Opportunities P	LVOPX	B-	(888) 522-2388	B+ / 8.3	4.07	12.10	8.59 /67	15.77 /81	13.06 /69	0.00	1.37
MC	Lord Abbett Value Opportunities R2	LVOQX	B-	(888) 522-2388	B / 8.1	4.02	12.04	8.43 /66	15.59 /80	12.88 /67	0.00	1.52

● Denotes fund is closed to new investors
* Denotes fund is included in Section II

www.thestreetratings.com

RISK			NET ASSETS		ASSET					BULL / BEAR		FUND MANAGER		MINIMUMS		LOADS	
	3 Year		NAV						Portfolio	Last Bull	Last Bear	Manager	Manager	Initial	Additional	Front	Back
Risk Rating/Pts	Standard Deviation	Beta	As of 3/31/15	Total $(Mil)	Cash %	Stocks %	Bonds %	Other %	Turnover Ratio	Market Return	Market Return	Quality Pct	Tenure (Years)	Purch. $	Purch. $	End Load	End Load
B- / 7.2	7.8	1.29	12.09	39	2	52	37	9	45	57.4	-16.7	17	10	0	0	0.0	0.0
B- / 7.1	9.8	0.72	12.12	171	4	62	32	2	23	46.7	-19.8	75	7	1,000	0	2.3	0.0
B- / 7.0	9.8	0.71	11.06	4	4	62	32	2	23	43.2	-20.1	67	7	1,000	0	0.0	0.0
B- / 7.0	9.8	0.72	11.06	48	4	62	32	2	23	43.1	-20.0	67	7	1,000	0	0.0	0.0
B- / 7.1	9.8	0.72	12.12	14	4	62	32	2	23	47.5	-19.8	76	7	0	0	0.0	0.0
B- / 7.1	9.8	0.72	12.20	44	4	62	32	2	23	47.9	-19.7	77	7	1,000,000	0	0.0	0.0
B- / 7.1	9.8	0.71	12.35	N/A	4	62	32	2	23	45.3	-19.9	72	7	0	0	0.0	0.0
B- / 7.1	9.8	0.71	12.19	7	4	62	32	2	23	45.6	-19.8	73	7	0	0	0.0	0.0
C+ / 6.7	5.3	0.48	15.13	1,089	3	22	65	10	43	39.6	-9.8	66	N/A	1,500	0	2.3	0.0
C+ / 6.7	5.2	0.47	15.33	6	3	22	65	10	43	36.0	-10.0	56	N/A	1,000	0	0.0	0.0
C+ / 6.7	5.3	0.48	15.32	799	3	22	65	10	43	36.0	-10.1	55	N/A	1,500	0	0.0	0.0
C+ / 6.7	5.3	0.47	15.13	563	3	22	65	10	43	40.2	-9.7	69	8	0	0	0.0	0.0
C+ / 6.7	5.3	0.48	15.06	21	3	22	65	10	43	40.6	-9.7	69	N/A	1,000,000	0	0.0	0.0
C+ / 6.8	5.3	0.47	15.48	1	3	22	65	10	43	37.8	-9.9	62	8	0	0	0.0	0.0
C+ / 6.7	5.3	0.48	15.14	13	3	22	65	10	43	38.3	-9.8	63	8	0	0	0.0	0.0
C+ / 6.8	8.6	0.59	17.91	863	2	69	27	2	38	67.7	-18.7	94	N/A	1,500	0	2.3	0.0
C+ / 6.8	8.5	0.59	17.80	20	2	69	27	2	38	63.3	-19.0	93	N/A	1,000	0	0.0	0.0
C+ / 6.8	8.6	0.59	17.77	235	2	69	27	2	38	63.4	-18.9	93	N/A	1,500	0	0.0	0.0
C+ / 6.7	8.6	0.59	17.90	64	2	69	27	2	38	68.5	-18.6	95	8	0	0	0.0	0.0
C+ / 6.7	8.6	0.59	17.99	15	2	69	27	2	38	69.1	-18.6	95	N/A	1,000,000	0	0.0	0.0
C+ / 6.8	8.6	0.59	18.11	N/A	2	69	27	2	38	66.7	-18.7	94	N/A	0	0	0.0	0.0
C+ / 6.8	8.6	0.59	18.20	N/A	2	69	27	2	38	65.8	-18.8	94	8	0	0	0.0	0.0
C+ / 6.7	8.6	0.59	17.87	25	2	69	27	2	38	66.2	-18.8	94	8	0	0	0.0	0.0
C+ / 5.8	12.7	0.67	31.28	612	22	77	0	1	5	94.0	-25.4	97	17	1,500	0	5.8	0.0
C+ / 5.7	12.7	0.67	28.65	14	22	77	0	1	5	89.1	-25.6	97	17	1,000	0	0.0	0.0
C+ / 5.6	12.7	0.67	28.29	336	22	77	0	1	5	89.1	-25.6	97	17	1,500	0	0.0	0.0
C+ / 5.8	12.7	0.67	31.33	279	22	77	0	1	5	95.0	-25.3	97	8	0	0	0.0	0.0
C+ / 5.7	12.7	0.67	30.68	4	22	77	0	1	5	91.7	-25.5	97	8	0	0	0.0	0.0
C+ / 5.8	12.7	0.67	30.81	38	22	77	0	1	5	92.4	-25.4	97	8	0	0	0.0	0.0
C+ / 5.7	13.5	0.95	16.57	116	2	97	0	1	80	65.5	-24.3	83	12	1,500	0	5.8	0.0
C+ / 5.7	13.4	0.95	15.77	4	2	97	0	1	80	61.8	-24.5	79	12	1,000	0	0.0	0.0
C+ / 5.7	13.4	0.95	15.58	22	2	97	0	1	80	61.8	-24.5	79	12	1,500	0	0.0	0.0
C+ / 5.7	13.4	0.95	16.43	40	2	97	0	1	80	66.8	-24.2	85	12	0	0	0.0	0.0
C+ / 5.7	13.5	0.95	16.96	293	2	97	0	1	80	67.4	-24.2	85	12	1,000,000	0	0.0	0.0
C+ / 5.8	13.4	0.95	16.84	1	2	97	0	1	80	64.8	-24.3	83	12	0	0	0.0	0.0
C+ / 5.8	13.4	0.95	16.41	N/A	2	97	0	1	80	64.0	-24.4	82	12	0	0	0.0	0.0
C+ / 5.7	13.4	0.95	16.32	7	2	97	0	1	80	64.6	-24.3	82	12	0	0	0.0	0.0
D- / 1.0	12.9	0.91	27.49	557	9	90	0	1	31	85.0	-28.3	31	2	1,000	0	5.8	0.0
D- / 1.0	12.9	0.91	20.45	3	9	90	0	1	31	80.6	-28.5	24	2	1,000	0	0.0	0.0
D- / 1.0	12.9	0.91	20.47	39	9	90	0	1	31	80.6	-28.5	23	2	1,000	0	0.0	0.0
D- / 1.0	12.9	0.91	27.50	28	9	90	0	1	31	86.2	-28.2	34	2	0	0	0.0	0.0
D- / 1.1	12.8	0.91	30.44	947	9	90	0	1	31	86.8	-28.2	35	2	1,000,000	0	0.0	0.0
D- / 1.0	12.9	0.91	26.77	96	9	90	0	1	31	84.0	-28.4	29	2	0	0	0.0	0.0
D- / 1.0	12.8	0.91	26.71	N/A	9	90	0	1	31	82.9	-28.4	28	2	0	0	0.0	0.0
D- / 1.0	12.8	0.91	26.87	9	9	90	0	1	31	83.8	-28.3	29	2	0	0	0.0	0.0
C / 5.0	12.1	1.06	20.37	1,279	1	98	0	1	54	92.6	-23.0	37	10	1,500	0	5.8	0.0
C / 4.8	12.1	1.07	18.94	17	1	98	0	1	54	88.2	-23.2	28	10	1,000	0	0.0	0.0
C / 4.8	12.1	1.07	18.94	405	1	98	0	1	54	88.2	-23.2	28	10	1,500	0	0.0	0.0
C / 5.0	12.1	1.06	20.65	535	1	98	0	1	54	94.1	-22.9	40	10	0	0	0.0	0.0
C / 5.1	12.1	1.07	20.96	643	1	98	0	1	54	94.8	-22.9	42	10	1,000,000	0	0.0	0.0
C / 4.9	12.1	1.06	20.18	50	1	98	0	1	54	92.0	-23.1	36	10	0	0	0.0	0.0
C / 4.9	12.1	1.06	19.91	10	1	98	0	1	54	90.9	-23.1	34	10	0	0	0.0	0.0

Fund Type	Fund Name	Ticker Symbol	Overall Investment Rating	Phone	Performance Rating/Pts	3 Mo	6 Mo	1Yr / Pct	3Yr / Pct	5Yr / Pct	Dividend Yield	Expense Ratio
	99 Pct = Best											
	0 Pct = Worst					PERFORMANCE		Total Return % through 3/31/15		Annualized	Incl. in Returns	
MC	Lord Abbett Value Opportunities R3	LVORX	B-	(888) 522-2388	B / 8.2	4.05	12.08	8.50 /66	15.69 /81	13.00 /68	0.00	1.42
GL	LS Opportunity	LSOFX	C-	(866) 954-6682	C- / 3.0	1.24	2.17	4.67 /36	8.77 /31	--	0.00	2.71
GR	LSV Conservative Value Eq Inst	LSVVX	B+	(866) 777-7818	B+ / 8.4	-0.90	3.46	8.58 /67	17.37 /92	13.72 /75	1.87	0.56
SC	LSV Small Cap Value Inst	LSVQX	U	(866) 777-7818	U /	3.19	13.40	10.08 /75	--	--	0.84	1.09
GR	LSV Value Equity Inst	LSVEX	A+	(866) 777-7818	A / 9.4	0.76	5.15	9.20 /70	19.66 /97	15.06 /87	1.52	0.66
GR	Lyrical US Value Equity Inst	LYRIX	U	(888) 884-8099	U /	1.67	8.84	12.25 /84	--	--	0.03	1.93
GR	Lyrical US Value Equity Inv	LYRBX	U	(888) 884-8099	U /	1.67	8.68	12.02 /83	--	--	0.00	N/A
GR	M Fund M Large Cap Value	MBOVX	B+	(800) 237-7119	B+ / 8.4	2.62	6.09	9.92 /74	16.49 /87	12.17 /62	1.10	0.72
AA	MA 529 Fidelity UF CIP 100% Eq Ptf		C+	(800) 544-8544	C+ / 6.3	3.42	6.07	8.37 /65	13.30 /62	10.92 /52	0.00	1.00
AA	MA 529 Fidelity UF CIP 70% Eq Ptf		C+	(800) 544-8544	C / 4.6	2.94	5.03	7.20 /57	10.61 /43	9.42 /40	0.00	0.94
AA	MA 529 Fidelity UF CIP College Ptf		C	(800) 544-8544	D- / 1.2	1.47	2.47	3.66 /30	3.91 /10	4.24 / 9	0.00	0.77
AA	MA 529 Fidelity UF CIP Consv Ptf		C-	(800) 544-8544	E+ / 0.7	0.87	1.41	2.38 /24	1.62 / 6	2.41 / 5	0.00	0.59
AA	MA 529 Fidelity UF CIP Idx 100% Eq		B-	(800) 544-8544	C+ / 6.0	2.65	4.62	6.87 /54	13.18 /61	11.53 /57	0.00	0.27
AA	MA 529 Fidelity UF CIP Idx 70% Eq		C+	(800) 544-8544	C- / 4.2	2.36	4.05	6.13 /48	10.12 /40	9.97 /44	0.00	0.30
AA	MA 529 Fidelity UF CIP Idx College		C	(800) 544-8544	D- / 1.0	1.16	2.04	3.10 /27	3.39 / 9	4.38 /10	0.00	0.33
AA	MA 529 Fidelity UF CIP Idx Consv		C-	(800) 544-8544	E+ / 0.7	0.69	1.48	2.44 /24	1.26 / 5	2.44 / 5	0.00	0.34
AA	MA 529 Fidelity UF CIP Idx Ptf 2015		C	(800) 544-8544	D- / 1.3	1.15	2.10	3.30 /28	4.44 /11	5.84 /16	0.00	0.32
AA	MA 529 Fidelity UF CIP Idx Ptf 2018		C	(800) 544-8544	D / 2.1	1.53	2.74	4.29 /34	6.34 /18	7.35 /25	0.00	0.31
AA	MA 529 Fidelity UF CIP Idx Ptf 2021		C+	(800) 544-8544	C- / 3.1	1.84	3.32	5.14 /40	8.13 /28	8.61 /34	0.00	0.30
AA	MA 529 Fidelity UF CIP Idx Ptf 2024		C+	(800) 544-8544	C- / 4.0	2.14	3.81	5.83 /45	9.80 /38	9.65 /42	0.00	0.29
AA	MA 529 Fidelity UF CIP Idx Ptf 2027		C+	(800) 544-8544	C / 4.8	2.31	4.19	6.31 /49	11.08 /46	10.41 /48	0.00	0.28
AA	MA 529 Fidelity UF CIP Port 2015		C	(800) 544-8544	D- / 1.5	1.53	2.58	3.96 /32	5.04 /13	5.51 /14	0.00	0.80
AA	MA 529 Fidelity UF CIP Port 2018		C	(800) 544-8544	D+ / 2.5	2.05	3.53	5.31 /41	7.02 /21	6.99 /23	0.00	0.87
AA	MA 529 Fidelity UF CIP Port 2021		C+	(800) 544-8544	C- / 3.6	2.47	4.30	6.25 /49	8.77 /31	8.18 /31	0.00	0.93
AA	MA 529 Fidelity UF CIP Port 2024		C+	(800) 544-8544	C / 4.4	2.72	4.76	6.82 /54	10.30 /41	9.15 /38	0.00	0.97
AA	MA 529 Fidelity UF CIP Port 2027		C+	(800) 544-8544	C / 5.2	2.87	5.08	7.32 /58	11.61 /50	9.89 /44	0.00	0.99
AA	MA 529 Fidelity UF CIP Tot Mkt Idx		A	(800) 544-8544	B+ / 8.3	1.74	7.03	12.06 /83	16.13 /84	14.52 /82	0.00	0.25
AA	Madison Aggressive Alloc A	MAGSX	C	(800) 877-6089	C / 4.3	2.37	5.61	8.02 /63	11.46 /49	9.69 /42	1.45	1.22
AA	Madison Aggressive Alloc B	MAGBX	C+	(800) 877-6089	C / 4.6	2.23	5.17	7.25 /57	10.61 /43	8.88 /36	0.99	1.97
AA	Madison Aggressive Alloc C	MAACX	C+	(800) 877-6089	C / 4.6	2.14	5.17	7.15 /56	10.60 /43	8.86 /36	0.99	1.97
AA	Madison Conservative Alloc A	MCNAX	C-	(800) 877-6089	D / 1.6	1.95	3.97	6.09 /47	6.50 /19	6.34 /19	1.43	1.19
AA	Madison Conservative Alloc B	MCNBX	C	(800) 877-6089	D / 1.9	1.65	3.50	5.20 /40	5.69 /16	5.54 /14	0.63	1.94
AA	Madison Conservative Alloc C	MCOCX	C	(800) 877-6089	D / 1.9	1.65	3.59	5.29 /41	5.72 /16	5.54 /14	0.63	1.94
IN	Madison Covered Call and Eq Inc A	MENAX	D	(800) 877-6089	D- / 1.5	0.93	1.49	4.77 /37	6.82 /20	7.61 /27	5.78	1.28
IN	Madison Covered Call and Eq Inc Y	MENYX	C-	(800) 877-6089	D+ / 2.4	0.92	1.58	4.93 /38	7.08 /22	7.88 /29	6.05	1.03
BA	Madison Diversified Income A	MBLAX	C	(800) 877-6089	D+ / 2.4	0.31	2.84	5.61 /43	8.62 /31	9.15 /38	1.47	1.10
BA	Madison Diversified Income B	MBLNX	C+	(800) 877-6089	D+ / 2.7	0.08	2.46	4.81 /37	7.79 /26	8.30 /32	0.82	1.85
BA	Madison Dividend Income Y	BHBFX	B-	(800) 336-3063	C+ / 6.1	-0.48	3.18	6.79 /53	13.73 /65	10.77 /51	1.50	1.10
FO	● Madison Hansberger Intl Gro I	HITGX	E+	(800) 414-6927	D / 1.9	7.73	3.87	0.05 /16	5.76 /16	3.95 / 8	4.73	1.00
FO	● Madison Hansberger Intl Gro Y	HIGGX	E+	(800) 414-6927	D / 1.8	7.73	3.79	-0.08 /15	5.54 /15	3.72 / 7	4.59	1.15
FO	Madison International Stock A	MINAX	D	(800) 877-6089	D+ / 2.4	5.43	2.15	-0.04 /15	9.11 /34	6.96 /23	2.22	1.60
FO	Madison International Stock B	MINBX	D	(800) 877-6089	D+ / 2.8	5.28	1.80	-0.73 /14	8.32 /29	6.16 /18	1.64	2.35
FO	Madison International Stock Y	MINYX	D+	(800) 877-6089	C- / 3.5	5.51	2.26	0.22 /16	9.39 /36	7.21 /24	2.60	1.35
GR	Madison Investors Y	MINVX	C	(800) 336-3063	B- / 7.4	1.39	7.38	10.00 /74	14.88 /74	12.06 /61	0.45	1.10
GR	Madison Large Cap Growth A	MCAAX	C+	(800) 877-6089	C+ / 5.8	2.58	7.66	14.41 /90	13.13 /61	11.88 /60	0.22	1.20
GR	Madison Large Cap Growth B	MCPBX	C+	(800) 877-6089	C+ / 6.2	2.40	7.24	13.58 /88	12.29 /55	11.05 /53	0.00	1.95
GR	Madison Large Cap Growth Y	MYLGX	B	(800) 877-6089	B- / 7.0	2.65	7.77	14.74 /91	13.42 /63	12.16 /62	0.47	0.95
GR	Madison Large Cap Value A	MGWAX	C	(800) 877-6089	C+ / 5.6	-0.12	5.00	8.58 /67	14.18 /68	12.20 /62	0.70	1.16
GR	Madison Large Cap Value B	MGWBX	C	(800) 877-6089	C+ / 6.0	-0.24	4.58	7.79 /61	13.33 /62	11.36 /56	0.02	1.91
GR	Madison Large Cap Value Y	MYLVX	C+	(800) 877-6089	C+ / 6.8	-0.06	5.11	8.87 /69	14.47 /71	12.48 /64	0.99	0.91
MC	Madison Mid Cap A	MERAX	U	(800) 336-3063	U /	3.68	12.59	13.45 /88	--	--	0.00	1.40
MC	Madison Mid Cap Y	GTSGX	C-	(800) 336-3063	A- / 9.2	3.82	12.76	13.72 /89	17.13 /90	16.73 /95	0.00	1.15

● Denotes fund is closed to new investors
* Denotes fund is included in Section II

www.thestreetratings.com

RISK			NET ASSETS		ASSET					Portfolio	BULL / BEAR		FUND MANAGER		MINIMUMS		LOADS	
	3 Year		NAV								Last Bull	Last Bear	Manager	Manager	Initial	Additional	Front	Back
Risk Rating/Pts	Standard Deviation	Beta	As of 3/31/15	Total $(Mil)	Cash %	Stocks %	Bonds %	Other %		Turnover Ratio	Market Return	Market Return	Quality Pct	Tenure (Years)	Purch. $	Purch. $	End Load	End Load
C / 4.9	12.1	1.06	20.02	135	1	98	0	1		54	91.4	-23.0	35	10	0	0	0.0	0.0
B- / 7.5	8.5	0.92	13.03	177	33	66	0	1		312	33.2	-11.3	72	N/A	5,000	100	0.0	2.0
C+ / 6.0	10.9	1.10	10.97	84	0	98	0	2		26	109.5	-21.1	62	8	100,000	0	0.0	0.0
U /	N/A	N/A	13.59	85	2	97	0	1		27	N/A	N/A	N/A	2	100,000	0	0.0	0.0
B- / 7.1	11.8	1.17	24.02	1,450	0	99	0	1		12	125.2	-23.3	72	16	100,000	0	0.0	0.0
U /	N/A	N/A	16.47	599	1	98	0	1		20	N/A	N/A	N/A	2	100,000	100	0.0	0.0
U /	N/A	N/A	16.44	115	1	98	0	1		20	N/A	N/A	N/A	2	2,500	0	0.0	0.0
C+ / 6.0	10.3	1.03	13.71	87	1	98	0	1		154	97.7	-19.3	65	2	0	0	0.0	0.0
C+ / 6.7	10.3	1.72	19.04	277	4	94	0	2		18	82.9	-23.0	9	10	50	25	0.0	0.0
B / 8.1	7.6	1.29	20.69	125	4	67	27	2		21	61.4	-17.3	23	10	50	25	0.0	0.0
B+ / 9.9	2.6	0.41	18.68	368	22	21	55	2		19	18.7	-4.4	61	10	50	25	0.0	0.0
B+ / 9.9	1.5	0.06	15.06	40	40	0	59	1		20	6.4	0.6	77	10	50	25	0.0	0.0
B- / 7.0	10.1	1.71	15.86	87	5	94	0	1		26	80.1	-19.4	9	9	50	25	0.0	0.0
B / 8.6	7.3	1.24	16.45	49	4	66	28	2		40	56.0	-11.3	23	9	50	25	0.0	0.0
B+ / 9.9	2.2	0.34	13.99	39	35	18	45	2		49	15.7	-0.3	65	9	50	25	0.0	0.0
B+ / 9.9	1.4	0.01	13.04	23	55	0	44	1		38	3.8	4.4	78	9	50	25	0.0	0.0
B+ / 9.9	3.1	0.50	14.08	89	33	20	45	2		21	23.5	-4.0	55	9	50	25	0.0	0.0
B+ / 9.6	4.4	0.74	14.60	116	22	33	43	2		27	34.5	-7.3	45	9	50	25	0.0	0.0
B+ / 9.1	5.8	0.98	14.93	114	14	46	39	1		24	45.5	-10.5	34	9	50	25	0.0	0.0
B / 8.6	7.1	1.21	15.25	129	8	59	32	1		20	56.5	-13.7	24	9	50	25	0.0	0.0
B / 8.1	8.2	1.39	14.16	104	4	70	24	2		14	65.2	-15.8	17	8	50	25	0.0	0.0
B+ / 9.6	3.6	0.58	17.86	740	21	23	54	2		17	27.5	-9.0	51	10	50	25	0.0	0.0
B+ / 9.2	4.9	0.82	18.46	888	13	37	48	2		18	39.3	-12.5	42	10	50	25	0.0	0.0
B / 8.7	6.2	1.05	19.88	669	8	50	40	2		16	51.1	-16.1	31	10	50	25	0.0	0.0
B / 8.2	7.5	1.27	17.38	305	6	62	31	1		14	62.1	-19.1	22	10	50	25	0.0	0.0
B- / 7.7	8.6	1.45	13.64	145	5	74	19	2		11	71.0	-21.2	16	8	50	25	0.0	0.0
B- / 7.2	9.7	1.68	18.12	92	2	97	0	1		0	100.1	-17.8	32	9	50	25	0.0	0.5
B- / 7.2	7.8	1.35	12.11	48	4	77	17	2		78	60.1	-13.3	24	N/A	1,000	50	5.8	0.0
B- / 7.3	7.8	1.35	11.94	13	4	77	17	2		78	56.2	-13.6	18	N/A	1,000	50	0.0	0.0
B- / 7.3	7.8	1.34	11.94	3	4	77	17	2		78	56.0	-13.6	18	N/A	1,000	50	0.0	0.0
B / 8.9	3.8	0.60	10.87	48	5	33	60	2		96	30.4	-5.2	68	7	1,000	50	5.8	0.0
B+ / 9.0	3.7	0.60	10.93	11	5	33	60	2		96	27.0	-5.4	57	7	1,000	50	0.0	0.0
B+ / 9.0	3.7	0.60	10.94	20	5	33	60	2		96	27.1	-5.5	58	7	1,000	50	0.0	0.0
B- / 7.5	6.4	0.58	9.53	15	22	73	4	1		139	50.0	-11.2	35	6	1,000	50	5.8	0.0
B- / 7.5	6.5	0.59	9.65	40	22	73	4	1		139	51.4	-11.2	37	6	25,000	1,000	0.0	0.0
B+ / 9.2	5.0	0.85	14.91	123	3	54	41	2		23	43.0	-5.0	60	17	1,000	50	5.8	0.0
B+ / 9.2	5.0	0.86	14.99	15	3	54	41	2		23	39.4	-5.3	46	17	1,000	50	0.0	0.0
B- / 7.2	9.0	1.49	22.39	22	2	97	0	1		29	71.7	-9.7	30	25	25,000	1,000	0.0	0.0
C / 4.8	13.4	0.97	16.58	52	0	99	0	1		48	44.0	-28.9	23	12	1,000,000	100,000	0.0	0.0
C / 4.8	13.4	0.97	16.58	3	0	99	0	1		48	42.9	-29.0	21	12	25,000	1,000	0.0	0.0
C+ / 6.0	12.8	0.95	13.21	23	4	95	0	1		44	54.8	-20.4	68	18	1,000	50	5.8	0.0
C+ / 6.0	12.8	0.95	12.96	2	4	95	0	1		44	50.8	-20.6	57	18	1,000	50	0.0	0.0
C+ / 6.0	12.9	0.96	13.21	12	4	95	0	1		44	56.0	-20.2	70	18	25,000	1,000	0.0	0.0
C- / 4.2	9.0	0.90	21.22	124	7	92	0	1		52	85.0	-15.0	72	25	25,000	1,000	0.0	0.0
C+ / 6.8	9.6	0.97	22.69	66	7	92	0	1		40	80.3	-15.9	36	2	1,000	50	5.8	0.0
C+ / 6.6	9.6	0.97	20.05	5	7	92	0	1		40	75.6	-16.1	26	2	1,000	50	0.0	0.0
C+ / 6.8	9.6	0.97	22.88	121	7	92	0	1		40	81.8	-15.8	39	2	25,000	1,000	0.0	0.0
C / 5.3	9.3	0.94	16.96	72	2	97	0	1		85	82.8	-14.5	55	6	1,000	50	5.8	0.0
C / 5.4	9.3	0.94	16.70	5	2	97	0	1		85	78.2	-14.8	43	6	1,000	50	0.0	0.0
C / 5.3	9.3	0.94	16.95	125	2	97	0	1		85	84.4	-14.4	60	6	25,000	1,000	0.0	0.0
U /	N/A	N/A	8.73	60	7	92	0	1		33	N/A	N/A	N/A	5	1,000	50	5.8	0.0
D- / 1.2	10.2	0.85	8.98	208	7	92	0	1		33	100.1	-18.5	86	5	25,000	1,000	0.0	0.0

					PERFORMANCE							
	99 Pct = Best 0 Pct = Worst					Total Return % through 3/31/15					Incl. in Returns	
			Overall		Perfor-				Annualized			
Fund		Ticker	Investment		mance						Dividend	Expense
Type	Fund Name	Symbol	Rating	Phone	Rating/Pts	3 Mo	6 Mo	1Yr / Pct	3Yr / Pct	5Yr / Pct	Yield	Ratio
AA	Madison Moderate Alloc A	MMDAX	C	(800) 877-6089	C- / 3.0	2.16	4.89	7.11 /56	9.23 /34	8.32 /32	1.29	1.21
AA	Madison Moderate Alloc B	MMDRX	C	(800) 877-6089	C- / 3.4	1.99	4.54	6.40 /50	8.45 /30	7.53 /27	0.86	1.96
AA	Madison Moderate Alloc C	MMDCX	C	(800) 877-6089	C- / 3.4	1.90	4.44	6.30 /49	8.41 /29	7.51 /26	0.86	1.96
FO	Madison NorthRoad International R6	NRRIX	D+	(800) 336-3063	D / 2.2	4.64	-0.31	-3.19 / 8	7.73 /26	--	1.92	0.82
SC	Madison NorthRoad International Y	NRIEX	D-	(800) 336-3063	D / 2.1	4.67	-0.40	-3.44 / 8	7.43 /24	7.11 /24	1.93	1.15
SC	Madison Small Cap A	MASVX	B-	(800) 877-6089	B- / 7.0	3.89	15.48	8.87 /69	15.15 /76	13.83 /76	0.21	1.50
SC	Madison Small Cap B	MBSVX	B	(800) 877-6089	B- / 7.4	3.71	15.05	8.05 /63	14.28 /69	12.98 /68	0.00	2.25
SC	Madison Small Cap Y	MYSVX	B+	(800) 877-6089	B+ / 8.3	3.95	15.66	9.13 /70	15.42 /78	14.12 /79	0.46	1.25
AA	Madison Target Retirement 2020 R6	MTWRX	U	(800) 336-3063	U /	2.01	4.89	--	--	--	0.00	0.55
AA	Madison Target Retirement 2030 R6	MTIRX	U	(800) 336-3063	U /	2.33	5.69	--	--	--	0.00	0.55
AA	Madison Target Retirement 2040 R6	MFRRX	U	(800) 336-3063	U /	2.45	6.01	--	--	--	0.00	0.55
EN	MainGate MLP A	AMLPX	C	(855) 657-3863	C- / 4.2	-1.32	-6.93	4.78 /37	13.35 /62	--	4.61	11.48
EN	MainGate MLP C	MLCPX	U	(855) 657-3863	U /	-1.54	-7.25	4.03 /32	--	--	4.88	N/A
EN	MainGate MLP I	IMLPX	C+	(855) 657-3863	C / 5.3	-1.30	-6.79	5.05 /39	13.66 /65	--	4.83	11.23
BA	MainStay Balanced A	MBNAX	C+	(800) 624-6782	C / 4.9	1.24	5.65	8.71 /68	12.52 /56	10.93 /52	0.84	1.14
BA	MainStay Balanced B	MBNBX	C+	(800) 624-6782	C / 5.1	1.00	5.18	7.71 /61	11.49 /49	9.90 /44	0.08	2.05
BA	MainStay Balanced C	MBACX	C+	(800) 624-6782	C / 5.1	1.00	5.19	7.72 /61	11.48 /49	9.90 /44	0.08	2.05
BA	MainStay Balanced I	MBAIX	B-	(800) 624-6782	C+ / 6.0	1.27	5.77	8.96 /69	12.80 /58	11.20 /54	1.12	0.89
BA	MainStay Balanced Inv	MBINX	C+	(800) 624-6782	C / 4.7	1.21	5.57	8.54 /67	12.31 /55	10.72 /50	0.70	1.30
BA	MainStay Balanced R1	MBNRX	B-	(800) 624-6782	C+ / 5.9	1.25	5.72	8.86 /69	12.69 /57	11.09 /53	1.02	0.98
BA	MainStay Balanced R2	MBCRX	B	(800) 624-6782	C+ / 5.7	1.22	5.60	8.59 /67	12.40 /55	10.81 /51	0.78	1.24
BA	MainStay Balanced R3	MBDRX	B-	(800) 624-6782	C / 5.5	1.14	5.48	8.31 /65	12.13 /53	10.54 /49	0.53	1.48
GI	MainStay Common Stock A	MSOAX	A	(800) 624-6782	B+ / 8.3	1.57	5.48	13.05 /87	17.82 /94	14.41 /82	0.70	1.03
GI	MainStay Common Stock B	MOPBX	A	(800) 624-6782	B+ / 8.4	1.38	4.97	11.97 /82	16.52 /87	13.07 /69	0.19	2.06
GI	MainStay Common Stock C	MGOCX	A	(800) 624-6782	B+ / 8.4	1.38	5.03	11.98 /82	16.50 /87	13.06 /69	0.19	2.06
GI	MainStay Common Stock I	MSOIX	A+	(800) 624-6782	A / 9.3	1.67	5.64	13.38 /88	18.12 /95	14.69 /84	0.90	0.78
GI	MainStay Common Stock Inv	MCSSX	A-	(800) 624-6782	B / 8.0	1.52	5.35	12.79 /86	17.37 /92	13.91 /77	0.53	1.31
AA	MainStay Conservative Alloc A	MCKAX	C-	(800) 624-6782	D / 1.9	1.89	2.63	4.41 /34	7.66 /25	7.82 /29	2.22	1.21
AA	MainStay Conservative Alloc B	MCKBX	C-	(800) 624-6782	D / 2.2	1.68	2.19	3.51 /29	6.69 /20	6.88 /22	1.48	2.11
AA	MainStay Conservative Alloc C	MCKCX	C-	(800) 624-6782	D / 2.2	1.68	2.27	3.59 /29	6.69 /20	6.88 /22	1.48	2.11
AA	MainStay Conservative Alloc I	MCKIX	C	(800) 624-6782	D+ / 2.9	1.94	2.73	4.72 /37	7.93 /27	8.09 /30	2.57	0.96
AA	MainStay Conservative Alloc Inv	MCKNX	C-	(800) 624-6782	D / 1.8	1.86	2.56	4.26 /33	7.46 /24	7.65 /27	2.09	1.36
CV	MainStay Convertible A	MCOAX	C	(800) 624-6782	C / 4.5	3.01	5.19	8.06 /63	11.76 /51	10.11 /46	2.31	0.97
CV	MainStay Convertible B	MCSVX	C	(800) 624-6782	C / 4.6	2.72	4.64	7.08 /56	10.67 /43	9.05 /37	1.89	1.91
CV	MainStay Convertible C	MCCVX	C	(800) 624-6782	C / 4.7	2.78	4.71	7.09 /56	10.68 /44	9.06 /37	1.89	1.91
CV	MainStay Convertible I	MCNVX	C+	(800) 624-6782	C+ / 5.6	3.07	5.31	8.32 /65	12.02 /53	10.37 /48	2.67	0.72
CV	MainStay Convertible Inv	MCINX	C-	(800) 624-6782	C / 4.3	2.91	5.03	7.87 /62	11.50 /49	9.86 /43	2.15	1.16
GR	MainStay CornerStone Growth A	KLGAX	D+	(800) 624-6782	C / 4.3	2.23	7.40	13.21 /87	10.37 /42	11.88 /60	0.00	1.21
GR	● MainStay CornerStone Growth B	KLGBX	U	(800) 624-6782	U /	1.98	6.90	12.16 /83	--	--	0.00	2.05
GR	MainStay CornerStone Growth I	KLGIX	C-	(800) 624-6782	C / 5.4	2.29	7.57	13.50 /88	10.65 /43	12.18 /62	0.00	0.96
GR	MainStay CornerStone Growth Inv	KLGNX	U	(800) 624-6782	U /	2.17	7.32	13.04 /87	--	--	0.00	1.30
IN	MainStay Cushing MLP Premier A	CSHAX	D-	(800) 624-6782	D- / 1.0	-1.71	-11.17	-0.63 /14	6.89 /21	--	6.11	9.42
IN	MainStay Cushing MLP Premier C	CSHCX	D-	(800) 624-6782	D- / 1.1	-1.87	-11.48	-1.37 /12	6.10 /17	--	6.72	10.17
IN	MainStay Cushing MLP Premier I	CSHZX	D-	(800) 624-6782	D- / 1.5	-1.64	-11.04	-0.39 /15	7.20 /22	--	6.38	9.17
EN	MainStay Cushing Ren Adv A	CRZAX	U	(800) 624-6782	U /	1.28	-12.79	-5.71 / 5	--	--	2.34	3.90
EN	MainStay Cushing Ren Adv C	CRZCX	U	(800) 624-6782	U /	1.03	-13.19	-6.49 / 4	--	--	2.51	4.77
EN	MainStay Cushing Ren Adv I	CRZZX	U	(800) 624-6782	U /	1.32	-12.72	-5.49 / 5	--	--	2.47	3.65
EN	MainStay Cushing Royalty En Inc A	CURAX	U	(800) 624-6782	U /	-10.59	-48.87	-47.18 / 0	--	--	14.92	2.69
EN	MainStay Cushing Royalty En Inc C	CURCX	U	(800) 624-6782	U /	-10.81	-49.08	-47.61 / 0	--	--	16.15	3.49
EN	MainStay Cushing Royalty En Inc I	CURZX	U	(800) 624-6782	U /	-10.61	-48.79	-47.06 / 0	--	--	15.66	2.44
EM	Mainstay Emerging Markets Opps I	MEOIX	U	(800) 624-6782	U /	4.56	0.78	6.65 /52	--	--	3.34	1.72
GL	MainStay Epoch Global Choice A	EPAPX	C	(800) 624-6782	C / 4.8	3.57	5.89	6.11 /47	12.64 /57	10.13 /46	0.42	1.34

RISK			NET ASSETS		ASSET					BULL / BEAR		FUND MANAGER		MINIMUMS		LOADS	
	3 Year		NAV						Portfolio	Last Bull	Last Bear	Manager	Manager	Initial	Additional	Front	Back
Risk Rating/Pts	Standard Deviation	Beta	As of 3/31/15	Total $(Mil)	Cash %	Stocks %	Bonds %	Other %	Turnover Ratio	Market Return	Market Return	Quality Pct	Tenure (Years)	Purch. $	Purch. $	End Load	End Load
B / 8.2	5.7	0.99	11.83	111	4	58	37	1	89	46.8	-9.5	46	7	1,000	50	5.8	0.0
B / 8.4	5.7	0.99	11.79	33	4	58	37	1	89	42.9	-9.7	35	7	1,000	50	0.0	0.0
B / 8.3	5.7	0.99	11.79	9	4	58	37	1	89	42.9	-9.8	35	7	1,000	50	0.0	0.0
B- / 7.0	12.6	0.94	11.06	10	3	96	0	1	30	N/A	N/A	51	4	500,000	50	0.0	0.0
C / 5.0	12.6	0.63	10.99	34	3	96	0	1	30	43.8	-20.7	32	4	25,000	1,000	0.0	0.0
C+ / 6.4	12.6	0.91	15.49	4	4	95	0	1	29	94.1	-22.0	71	9	1,000	50	5.8	0.0
C+ / 6.3	12.6	0.91	14.80	1	4	95	0	1	29	89.2	-22.3	61	9	1,000	50	0.0	0.0
C+ / 6.4	12.6	0.91	15.52	79	4	95	0	1	29	95.8	-21.9	73	9	25,000	1,000	0.0	0.0
U /	N/A	N/A	10.15	63	0	0	0	100	0	N/A	N/A	N/A	1	500,000	50,000	0.0	0.0
U /	N/A	N/A	10.09	86	0	0	0	100	0	N/A	N/A	N/A	1	500,000	50,000	0.0	0.0
U /	N/A	N/A	10.03	59	0	0	0	100	0	N/A	N/A	N/A	1	500,000	50,000	0.0	0.0
B- / 7.1	9.9	0.49	12.88	187	83	16	0	1	58	68.9	-6.9	98	4	2,500	100	5.8	0.0
U /	N/A	N/A	12.91	34	83	16	0	1	58	N/A	N/A	N/A	4	2,500	100	0.0	0.0
B- / 7.1	9.9	0.49	13.04	1,021	83	16	0	1	58	70.3	-6.7	98	4	1,000,000	10,000	0.0	0.0
B- / 7.8	6.3	1.07	33.04	261	44	16	39	1	162	64.6	-11.2	75	7	25,000	0	5.5	0.0
B- / 7.8	6.3	1.07	32.94	35	44	16	39	1	162	59.5	-11.5	65	7	1,000	50	0.0	0.0
B- / 7.8	6.3	1.07	32.92	110	44	16	39	1	162	59.5	-11.6	65	7	1,000	50	0.0	0.0
B- / 7.7	6.3	1.07	33.10	328	44	16	39	1	162	66.0	-11.1	77	7	5,000,000	0	0.0	0.0
B- / 7.8	6.3	1.07	33.06	82	44	16	39	1	162	63.6	-11.3	73	7	1,000	50	5.5	0.0
B- / 7.8	6.3	1.07	33.06	7	44	16	39	1	162	65.5	-11.2	76	7	0	0	0.0	0.0
B- / 7.8	6.3	1.07	33.03	50	44	16	39	1	162	64.0	-11.2	74	7	0	0	0.0	0.0
B- / 7.8	6.3	1.07	33.03	2	44	16	39	1	162	62.7	-11.3	72	7	0	0	0.0	0.0
B- / 7.2	10.3	1.06	20.02	48	0	99	0	1	165	107.4	-17.3	73	8	25,000	0	5.5	0.0
B- / 7.1	10.3	1.07	18.43	8	0	99	0	1	165	99.4	-17.7	58	8	1,000	50	0.0	0.0
B- / 7.2	10.3	1.07	18.42	28	0	99	0	1	165	99.3	-17.7	57	8	1,000	50	0.0	0.0
B- / 7.2	10.3	1.06	20.08	91	0	99	0	1	165	109.1	-17.2	75	8	5,000,000	0	0.0	0.0
B- / 7.2	10.3	1.06	20.03	23	0	99	0	1	165	104.6	-17.5	69	8	1,000	50	5.5	0.0
B / 8.1	4.7	0.80	12.11	257	15	36	48	1	45	41.5	-8.5	54	N/A	25,000	0	5.5	0.0
B / 8.2	4.6	0.79	12.07	39	15	36	48	1	45	37.3	-8.9	41	N/A	1,000	50	0.0	0.0
B / 8.2	4.7	0.80	12.07	77	15	36	48	1	45	37.3	-8.8	40	N/A	1,000	50	0.0	0.0
B / 8.1	4.6	0.80	12.20	16	15	36	48	1	45	42.8	-8.4	58	N/A	5,000,000	0	0.0	0.0
B / 8.1	4.7	0.81	12.11	68	15	36	48	1	45	40.7	-8.5	49	N/A	1,000	50	5.5	0.0
C+ / 6.4	7.9	1.01	17.04	392	11	7	2	80	59	65.4	-19.6	39	14	25,000	0	5.5	0.0
C+ / 6.4	7.9	1.02	17.01	29	11	7	2	80	59	60.0	-19.9	26	14	1,000	50	0.0	0.0
C+ / 6.4	7.9	1.02	17.00	94	11	7	2	80	59	60.0	-19.9	26	14	1,000	50	0.0	0.0
C+ / 6.4	7.9	1.02	17.06	301	11	7	2	80	59	66.8	-19.5	42	14	5,000,000	0	0.0	0.0
C+ / 6.4	7.9	1.02	17.03	86	11	7	2	80	59	64.1	-19.6	35	14	1,000	50	5.5	0.0
C / 4.8	11.2	1.04	32.12	308	2	97	0	1	88	75.4	-18.6	7	9	25,000	0	5.5	0.0
U /	N/A	N/A	31.40	48	2	97	0	1	88	N/A	N/A	N/A	9	2,500	50	0.0	0.0
C / 4.8	11.2	1.04	32.57	564	2	97	0	1	88	77.0	-18.5	8	9	5,000,000	0	0.0	0.0
U /	N/A	N/A	31.99	236	2	97	0	1	88	N/A	N/A	N/A	9	2,500	50	5.5	0.0
C+ / 6.5	9.4	0.58	20.74	504	77	22	0	1	21	36.4	-8.2	37	5	25,000	0	5.5	0.0
C+ / 6.4	9.3	0.58	19.94	827	77	22	0	1	21	32.9	-8.4	28	5	2,500	50	0.0	0.0
C+ / 6.5	9.4	0.58	21.00	620	77	22	0	1	21	37.7	-8.1	41	5	5,000,000	0	0.0	0.0
U /	N/A	N/A	22.63	55	12	87	0	1	115	N/A	N/A	N/A	2	25,000	0	5.5	0.0
U /	N/A	N/A	22.30	46	12	87	0	1	115	N/A	N/A	N/A	2	2,500	50	0.0	0.0
U /	N/A	N/A	22.71	277	12	87	0	1	115	N/A	N/A	N/A	2	5,000,000	0	0.0	0.0
U /	N/A	N/A	8.87	108	80	19	0	1	27	N/A	N/A	N/A	3	25,000	0	5.5	0.0
U /	N/A	N/A	8.67	50	80	19	0	1	27	N/A	N/A	N/A	3	2,500	50	0.0	0.0
U /	N/A	N/A	8.94	63	80	19	0	1	27	N/A	N/A	N/A	3	5,000,000	0	0.0	0.0
U /	N/A	N/A	9.85	199	3	96	0	1	153	N/A	N/A	N/A	2	5,000,000	0	0.0	0.0
C+ / 6.4	10.1	0.68	19.45	6	5	94	0	1	101	72.4	-17.2	95	6	25,000	0	5.5	0.0

99 Pct = Best
0 Pct = Worst

Fund Type	Fund Name	Ticker Symbol	Overall Investment Rating	Phone	Perfor-mance Rating/Pts	Total Return % through 3/31/15			Annualized		Incl. in Returns	
						3 Mo	6 Mo	1Yr / Pct	3Yr / Pct	5Yr / Pct	Dividend Yield	Expense Ratio
GL	MainStay Epoch Global Choice C	EPAKX	C	(800) 624-6782	C / 5.0	3.27	5.35	5.02 /39	11.50 /49	9.03 /37	0.00	2.34
GL	MainStay Epoch Global Choice I	EPACX	C+	(800) 624-6782	C+ / 6.0	3.63	6.06	6.38 /50	12.91 /59	10.39 /48	0.67	1.09
GL	MainStay Epoch Global Choice Inv	EPAIX	C	(800) 624-6782	C / 4.7	3.53	5.78	5.83 /45	12.38 /55	9.87 /43	0.21	1.59
GL	MainStay Epoch Global Equity Yd A	EPSPX	C-	(800) 624-6782	C- / 3.3	-0.32	0.26	2.67 /25	11.17 /47	11.03 /53	3.54	1.07
GL	MainStay Epoch Global Equity Yd C	EPSKX	C-	(800) 624-6782	C- / 3.7	-0.51	-0.12	1.92 /22	10.33 /41	10.23 /46	3.00	1.84
GL	MainStay Epoch Global Equity Yd I	EPSYX	C	(800) 624-6782	C / 4.4	-0.26	0.39	2.93 /26	11.46 /49	11.31 /55	3.99	0.82
GL	MainStay Epoch Global Equity Yd Inv	EPSIX	C-	(800) 624-6782	C- / 3.3	-0.32	0.25	2.66 /25	11.14 /47	11.04 /53	3.53	1.09
FO	MainStay Epoch Intl Small Cap A	EPIPX	E+	(800) 624-6782	D- / 1.3	6.79	-0.50	-10.23 / 3	7.80 /26	6.76 /22	0.48	1.55
FO	MainStay Epoch Intl Small Cap C	EPIKX	E+	(800) 624-6782	D- / 1.4	6.54	-1.01	-11.16 / 2	6.76 /20	5.82 /16	0.00	2.53
FO	MainStay Epoch Intl Small Cap I	EPIEX	D-	(800) 624-6782	D / 2.0	6.84	-0.40	-10.05 / 3	8.05 /27	7.01 /23	0.79	1.30
FO	MainStay Epoch Intl Small Cap Inv	EPIIX	E+	(800) 624-6782	D- / 1.2	6.75	-0.66	-10.48 / 3	7.58 /25	6.61 /21	0.22	1.78
GR	MainStay Epoch US All Cap A	MAAAX	C+	(800) 624-6782	B- / 7.1	1.42	8.47	14.21 /90	15.46 /79	13.55 /73	0.67	1.13
GR	MainStay Epoch US All Cap B	MAWBX	C+	(800) 624-6782	B- / 7.2	1.22	7.92	13.03 /87	14.13 /68	12.23 /62	0.00	2.24
GR	MainStay Epoch US All Cap C	MAWCX	C+	(800) 624-6782	B- / 7.2	1.17	7.87	13.01 /87	14.12 /68	12.22 /62	0.00	2.24
GR	MainStay Epoch US All Cap I	MATIX	B+	(800) 624-6782	B+ / 8.4	1.52	8.62	14.53 /91	15.73 /81	13.83 /76	0.86	0.88
GR	MainStay Epoch US All Cap Investor	MAWNX	C+	(800) 624-6782	C+ / 6.8	1.40	8.31	13.87 /89	15.00 /75	13.08 /69	0.39	1.49
GR	MainStay Epoch US Equity Yield A	EPLPX	D+	(800) 624-6782	C+ / 5.7	-0.76	5.39	10.69 /77	13.92 /67	12.08 /61	1.97	1.63
GR	MainStay Epoch US Equity Yield C	EPLKX	D+	(800) 624-6782	C+ / 5.9	-0.99	4.94	9.65 /73	12.97 /59	11.14 /54	1.31	2.58
GR	MainStay Epoch US Equity Yield I	EPLCX	C-	(800) 624-6782	C+ / 6.7	-0.77	5.46	10.86 /78	14.16 /68	12.33 /63	2.29	1.38
GR	MainStay Epoch US Equity Yield Inv	EPLIX	D+	(800) 624-6782	C+ / 5.6	-0.78	5.26	10.50 /76	13.79 /66	11.94 /60	1.85	1.83
AA	MainStay Growth Allocation A	MGXAX	C	(800) 624-6782	C / 5.2	2.66	4.87	7.39 /58	13.36 /62	11.56 /57	1.50	1.61
AA	MainStay Growth Allocation B	MGXBX	C+	(800) 624-6782	C / 5.5	2.45	4.36	6.37 /50	12.34 /55	10.62 /50	0.72	2.53
AA	MainStay Growth Allocation C	MGXCX	C+	(800) 624-6782	C / 5.5	2.45	4.36	6.36 /50	12.35 /55	10.60 /50	0.72	2.53
AA	MainStay Growth Allocation I	MGXIX	C+	(800) 624-6782	C+ / 6.4	2.76	4.99	7.68 /60	13.70 /65	11.86 /60	1.80	1.36
AA	MainStay Growth Allocation Inv	MGXNX	C	(800) 624-6782	C / 5.1	2.66	4.84	7.22 /57	13.21 /61	11.44 /56	1.35	1.78
GR	MainStay ICAP Equity Fd A	ICAUX	C	(800) 624-6782	C / 5.5	0.81	5.52	8.74 /68	13.69 /65	12.40 /63	1.61	1.14
GR	MainStay ICAP Equity Fd C	ICAVX	C+	(800) 624-6782	C+ / 5.7	0.57	5.03	7.74 /61	12.60 /57	11.28 /55	0.90	2.08
GR	MainStay ICAP Equity Fd I	ICAEX	C+	(800) 624-6782	C+ / 6.6	0.87	5.66	9.02 /69	13.98 /67	12.69 /66	1.93	0.89
GR	MainStay ICAP Equity Fd Inv	ICANX	C	(800) 624-6782	C / 5.3	0.78	5.45	8.56 /67	13.44 /63	12.12 /61	1.45	1.33
GR	MainStay ICAP Equity Fd R1	ICAWX	C+	(800) 624-6782	C+ / 6.5	0.84	5.60	8.90 /69	13.87 /66	12.59 /65	1.83	0.99
GR	MainStay ICAP Equity Fd R2	ICAYX	C+	(800) 624-6782	C+ / 6.3	0.78	5.46	8.63 /67	13.57 /64	12.29 /62	1.60	1.24
GR	MainStay ICAP Equity Fd R3	ICAZX	C+	(800) 624-6782	C+ / 6.1	0.72	5.34	8.35 /65	13.29 /62	12.00 /60	1.35	1.49
GL	MainStay ICAP Global Fund A	ICGLX	D	(800) 624-6782	D+ / 2.9	2.37	1.44	1.79 /21	10.08 /40	8.54 /33	1.93	1.27
GL	MainStay ICAP Global Fund C	ICGCX	D+	(800) 624-6782	C- / 3.2	2.20	1.03	0.94 /18	9.20 /34	7.67 /28	1.33	2.25
GL	MainStay ICAP Global Fund I	ICGRX	C-	(800) 624-6782	C- / 3.9	2.46	1.54	1.97 /22	10.34 /41	8.80 /35	2.29	1.02
GL	MainStay ICAP Global Fund Inv	ICGNX	D	(800) 624-6782	D+ / 2.9	2.37	1.48	1.74 /21	10.01 /39	8.48 /33	1.89	1.50
FO	MainStay ICAP International Fd A	ICEVX	D-	(800) 624-6782	D / 1.6	5.34	-0.78	-0.78 /14	7.68 /25	5.92 /16	2.48	1.21
FO	MainStay ICAP International Fd C	ICEWX	D-	(800) 624-6782	D / 1.9	5.08	-1.24	-1.66 /11	6.73 /20	4.98 /12	1.72	2.10
FO	MainStay ICAP International Fd I	ICEUX	D	(800) 624-6782	D+ / 2.6	5.40	-0.65	-0.49 /14	8.02 /27	6.27 /19	3.14	0.96
FO	MainStay ICAP International Fd Inv	ICELX	D-	(800) 624-6782	D / 1.6	5.31	-0.85	-0.88 /13	7.55 /24	5.76 /15	2.33	1.35
FO	MainStay ICAP International Fd R1	ICETX	D	(800) 624-6782	D+ / 2.5	5.38	-0.71	-0.62 /14	7.90 /26	6.17 /18	3.04	1.06
FO	MainStay ICAP International Fd R2	ICEYX	D-	(800) 624-6782	D+ / 2.3	5.31	-0.82	-0.82 /14	7.58 /25	5.81 /16	2.53	1.31
FO	MainStay ICAP International Fd R3	ICEZX	D-	(800) 624-6782	D / 2.2	5.22	-0.96	-1.13 /13	7.30 /23	5.54 /14	2.25	1.56
GR	MainStay ICAP Select Equity Fd A	ICSRX	C-	(800) 624-6782	C / 5.1	0.71	5.78	7.93 /62	13.17 /61	11.85 /60	2.23	1.23
GR	MainStay ICAP Select Equity Fd B	ICSQX	C-	(800) 624-6782	C / 5.3	0.48	5.28	6.95 /55	12.10 /53	10.77 /51	1.51	2.10
GR	MainStay ICAP Select Equity Fd C	ICSVX	C-	(800) 624-6782	C / 5.3	0.48	5.28	6.95 /55	12.09 /53	10.77 /51	1.51	2.10
GR	MainStay ICAP Select Equity Fd I	ICSLX	C	(800) 624-6782	C+ / 6.2	0.78	5.92	8.25 /65	13.48 /63	12.16 /62	2.61	0.98
GR	MainStay ICAP Select Equity Fd Inv	ICSOX	C-	(800) 624-6782	C / 5.0	0.67	5.68	7.76 /61	12.93 /59	11.60 /58	2.08	1.35
GR	MainStay ICAP Select Equity Fd R1	ICSWX	C	(800) 624-6782	C+ / 6.2	0.75	5.86	8.13 /64	13.37 /62	12.02 /61	2.51	1.08
GR	MainStay ICAP Select Equity Fd R2	ICSYX	C	(800) 624-6782	C+ / 6.0	0.69	5.73	7.85 /62	13.09 /60	11.74 /59	2.28	1.33
GR	MainStay ICAP Select Equity Fd R3	ICSZX	C	(800) 624-6782	C+ / 5.8	0.61	5.56	7.50 /59	12.70 /57	11.40 /56	1.95	1.58
GR	MainStay ICAP Select Equity R6	ICSDX	U	(800) 624-6782	U /	0.80	5.96	8.34 /65	--	--	2.69	0.82

● Denotes fund is closed to new investors
* Denotes fund is included in Section II

www.thestreetratings.com

RISK			NET ASSETS		ASSET				Portfolio Turnover Ratio	BULL / BEAR		FUND MANAGER		MINIMUMS		LOADS	
	3 Year		NAV							Last Bull	Last Bear	Manager	Manager	Initial	Additional	Front	Back
Risk Rating/Pts	Standard Deviation	Beta	As of 3/31/15	Total $(Mil)	Cash %	Stocks %	Bonds %	Other %		Market Return	Market Return	Quality Pct	Tenure (Years)	Purch. $	Purch. $	End Load	End Load
C+ / 6.3	10.0	0.68	18.61	2	5	94	0	1	101	66.6	-17.6	93	6	2,500	50	0.0	0.0
C+ / 6.4	10.1	0.68	20.00	231	5	94	0	1	101	73.7	-17.1	95	6	5,000,000	0	0.0	0.0
C+ / 6.4	10.1	0.68	19.37	1	5	94	0	1	101	71.0	-17.3	94	6	2,500	50	5.5	0.0
C+ / 6.9	9.6	0.64	19.34	1,085	4	95	0	1	15	62.0	-12.2	93	6	25,000	0	5.5	0.0
C+ / 6.9	9.6	0.64	19.23	270	4	95	0	1	15	57.8	-12.5	91	6	2,500	50	0.0	0.0
C+ / 6.9	9.6	0.65	19.31	3,739	4	95	0	1	15	63.4	-12.2	93	6	5,000,000	0	0.0	0.0
C+ / 6.9	9.6	0.65	19.31	10	4	95	0	1	15	61.9	-12.2	93	6	2,500	50	5.5	0.0
C / 5.3	12.9	0.87	20.92	4	0	99	0	1	54	44.3	-28.2	62	9	25,000	0	5.5	0.0
C / 5.2	12.9	0.87	20.53	1	0	99	0	1	54	39.7	-28.4	47	9	2,500	50	0.0	0.0
C / 5.2	12.9	0.87	21.55	83	0	99	0	1	54	45.6	-28.1	65	9	5,000,000	0	0.0	0.0
C / 5.3	12.9	0.87	20.87	1	0	99	0	1	54	43.4	-28.2	59	9	2,500	50	5.5	0.0
C+ / 5.6	10.2	1.03	27.10	23	3	96	0	1	31	99.4	-20.9	51	6	25,000	0	5.5	0.0
C / 5.4	10.3	1.04	24.11	5	3	96	0	1	31	91.8	-21.3	33	6	1,000	50	0.0	0.0
C / 5.4	10.2	1.03	24.13	5	3	96	0	1	31	91.7	-21.3	34	6	1,000	50	0.0	0.0
C+ / 5.8	10.2	1.04	29.46	674	3	96	0	1	31	101.1	-20.8	54	6	5,000,000	0	0.0	0.0
C+ / 5.7	10.2	1.03	26.74	13	3	96	0	1	31	96.7	-21.0	45	6	1,000	50	5.5	0.0
C- / 3.7	9.6	0.93	14.19	13	5	94	0	1	16	89.0	-19.0	54	7	25,000	0	5.5	0.0
C- / 3.6	9.6	0.92	13.80	5	5	94	0	1	16	83.6	-19.3	43	7	2,500	50	0.0	0.0
C- / 3.7	9.6	0.93	14.30	7	5	94	0	1	16	90.4	-18.9	58	7	5,000,000	0	0.0	0.0
C- / 3.6	9.6	0.93	14.14	2	5	94	0	1	16	88.4	-19.1	53	7	2,500	50	5.5	0.0
C+ / 6.5	10.3	1.73	15.82	136	4	95	0	1	37	83.4	-20.2	9	11	25,000	0	5.5	0.0
C+ / 6.5	10.2	1.72	15.45	59	4	95	0	1	37	78.0	-20.5	6	11	1,000	50	0.0	0.0
C+ / 6.5	10.3	1.73	15.47	25	4	95	0	1	37	78.0	-20.5	6	11	1,000	50	0.0	0.0
C+ / 6.5	10.3	1.73	16.02	4	4	95	0	1	37	85.1	-20.1	10	11	5,000,000	0	0.0	0.0
C+ / 6.5	10.2	1.72	15.81	117	4	95	0	1	37	82.6	-20.3	9	N/A	1,000	50	5.5	0.0
C+ / 6.2	10.5	1.06	51.51	46	2	97	0	1	58	90.0	-19.0	26	21	25,000	0	5.5	0.0
C+ / 6.2	10.5	1.06	50.85	15	2	97	0	1	58	83.9	-19.3	17	21	1,000	50	0.0	0.0
C+ / 6.2	10.5	1.06	51.60	936	2	97	0	1	58	91.8	-18.9	28	21	5,000,000	0	0.0	0.0
C+ / 6.2	10.5	1.06	51.44	15	2	97	0	1	58	88.6	-19.1	23	21	1,000	50	5.5	0.0
C+ / 6.2	10.5	1.06	51.63	9	2	97	0	1	58	91.1	-18.9	27	21	0	0	0.0	0.0
C+ / 6.2	10.4	1.05	51.51	15	2	97	0	1	58	89.4	-19.0	25	21	0	0	0.0	0.0
C+ / 6.2	10.5	1.05	51.40	4	2	97	0	1	58	87.8	-19.1	22	21	0	0	0.0	0.0
C+ / 6.1	10.8	0.76	11.23	5	2	97	0	1	63	65.6	-22.0	87	7	25,000	0	5.5	0.0
C+ / 6.1	10.7	0.76	11.14	1	2	97	0	1	63	61.0	-22.3	84	7	1,000	50	0.0	0.0
C+ / 6.1	10.8	0.76	11.25	62	2	97	0	1	63	67.1	-22.0	89	7	5,000,000	0	0.0	0.0
C+ / 6.1	10.7	0.75	11.21	1	2	97	0	1	63	65.3	-22.0	87	7	1,000	50	5.5	0.0
C+ / 5.6	11.8	0.87	34.53	89	0	98	0	2	56	47.1	-22.9	60	18	25,000	0	5.5	0.0
C+ / 5.7	11.8	0.87	33.95	17	0	98	0	2	56	42.8	-23.2	47	18	1,000	50	0.0	0.0
C+ / 5.6	11.8	0.87	34.56	1,925	0	98	0	2	56	48.7	-22.8	65	18	5,000,000	0	0.0	0.0
C+ / 5.7	11.8	0.87	34.53	9	0	98	0	2	56	46.4	-23.0	58	18	1,000	50	5.5	0.0
C+ / 5.6	11.8	0.87	34.50	2	0	98	0	2	56	48.2	-22.9	63	18	0	0	0.0	0.0
C+ / 5.6	11.8	0.87	34.51	49	0	98	0	2	56	46.6	-23.0	59	18	0	0	0.0	0.0
C+ / 5.7	11.8	0.87	34.29	11	0	98	0	2	56	45.4	-23.0	55	18	0	0	0.0	0.0
C / 5.3	10.7	1.09	46.09	810	2	97	0	1	65	88.0	-20.2	17	18	25,000	0	5.5	0.0
C / 5.3	10.7	1.09	45.66	45	2	97	0	1	65	82.0	-20.5	11	18	1,000	50	0.0	0.0
C / 5.3	10.8	1.09	45.65	102	2	97	0	1	65	82.0	-20.5	11	18	1,000	50	0.0	0.0
C / 5.3	10.7	1.08	46.17	3,164	2	97	0	1	65	89.8	-20.1	19	18	5,000,000	0	0.0	0.0
C / 5.3	10.8	1.09	46.09	188	2	97	0	1	65	86.7	-20.3	16	18	1,000	50	5.5	0.0
C / 5.3	10.7	1.09	46.19	49	2	97	0	1	65	89.1	-20.2	19	18	0	0	0.0	0.0
C / 5.3	10.8	1.09	46.09	26	2	97	0	1	65	87.5	-20.2	16	18	0	0	0.0	0.0
C / 5.3	10.8	1.09	46.03	13	2	97	0	1	65	85.4	-20.3	14	18	0	0	0.0	0.0
U /	N/A	N/A	46.16	124	2	97	0	1	65	N/A	N/A	N/A	18	250,000	0	0.0	0.0

						PERFORMANCE							
	99 Pct = Best							Total Return % through 3/31/15				Incl. in Returns	
	0 Pct = Worst		**Overall**		**Perfor-**					Annualized		Dividend	Expense
Fund		Ticker	**Investment**		**mance**								
Type	Fund Name	Symbol	**Rating**	Phone	**Rating/Pts**	3 Mo	6 Mo	1Yr / Pct	3Yr / Pct	5Yr / Pct		Yield	Ratio
BA	MainStay Income Builder A	MTRAX	**C**	(800) 624-6782	**C- / 4.0**	1.47	2.62	6.18 /48	11.46 /49	11.08 /53		3.34	1.01
BA	MainStay Income Builder B	MKTRX	**C**	(800) 624-6782	**C- / 4.1**	1.25	2.11	5.16 /40	10.35 /41	9.94 /44		2.62	1.98
BA	MainStay Income Builder C	MCTRX	**C**	(800) 624-6782	**C- / 4.1**	1.25	2.11	5.16 /40	10.35 /41	9.94 /44		2.63	1.98
BA	MainStay Income Builder I	MTOIX	**C+**	(800) 624-6782	**C / 5.0**	1.51	2.72	6.44 /50	11.75 /51	11.37 /56		3.74	0.76
BA	MainStay Income Builder Inv	MTINX	**C-**	(800) 624-6782	**C- / 3.8**	1.43	2.48	5.98 /46	11.18 /47	10.78 /51		3.16	1.23
FO	MainStay Intl Equity A	MSEAX	**D-**	(800) 624-6782	**D- / 1.3**	4.15	2.60	-0.32 /15	6.29 /18	3.13 / 6		0.64	1.34
FO	MainStay Intl Equity B	MINEX	**D-**	(800) 624-6782	**D- / 1.4**	3.96	2.07	-1.36 /12	5.16 /14	2.04 / 4		0.00	2.42
FO	MainStay Intl Equity C	MIECX	**D-**	(800) 624-6782	**D- / 1.4**	3.87	2.07	-1.36 /12	5.13 /14	2.02 / 4		0.00	2.42
FO	MainStay Intl Equity I	MSIIX	**D-**	(800) 624-6782	**D / 2.0**	4.21	2.79	-0.05 /15	6.54 /19	3.38 / 7		0.94	1.09
FO	MainStay Intl Equity Inv	MINNX	**D-**	(800) 624-6782	**D- / 1.2**	4.15	2.48	-0.60 /14	5.93 /16	2.80 / 6		0.32	1.67
FO	MainStay Intl Equity R1	MIERX	**D-**	(800) 624-6782	**D / 2.0**	4.23	2.77	-0.16 /15	6.45 /19	3.29 / 7		0.84	1.19
FO	MainStay Intl Equity R2	MIRRX	**D-**	(800) 624-6782	**D / 1.8**	4.21	2.63	-0.36 /15	6.20 /18	3.03 / 6		0.57	1.44
FO	MainStay Intl Equity R3	MIFRX	**D-**	(800) 624-6782	**D / 1.7**	4.07	2.49	-0.66 /14	5.92 /16	2.75 / 5		0.28	1.69
FO	MainStay Intl Opportunities A	MYITX	**C-**	(800) 624-6782	**C / 4.7**	6.61	3.31	0.59 /17	13.20 /61	9.46 /40		1.73	3.12
FO	MainStay Intl Opportunities C	MYICX	**C**	(800) 624-6782	**C / 5.0**	6.42	2.86	-0.15 /15	12.25 /54	8.51 /33		1.27	4.03
FO	MainStay Intl Opportunities I	MYIIX	**C**	(800) 624-6782	**C+/ 5.9**	6.70	3.53	0.93 /18	13.51 /63	9.71 /42		2.03	2.86
FO	MainStay Intl Opportunities Inv	MYINX	**C-**	(800) 624-6782	**C / 4.6**	6.50	3.22	0.50 /17	13.05 /60	9.30 /39		1.65	3.25
GR	MainStay Large Cap Growth Fd A	MLAAX	**C**	(800) 624-6782	**C+/ 6.7**	3.09	8.54	15.22 /92	14.36 /70	14.24 /80		0.00	0.99
GR	MainStay Large Cap Growth Fd B	MLABX	**C+**	(800) 624-6782	**B- / 7.0**	2.84	8.23	14.37 /90	13.43 /63	13.32 /71		0.00	1.79
GR	MainStay Large Cap Growth Fd C	MLACX	**C+**	(800) 624-6782	**B- / 7.0**	2.84	8.12	14.38 /90	13.44 /63	13.34 /71		0.00	1.79
GR	MainStay Large Cap Growth Fd I	MLAIX	**B-**	(800) 624-6782	**B / 8.0**	3.15	8.71	15.59 /93	14.67 /72	14.54 /83		0.00	0.74
GR	MainStay Large Cap Growth Fd Inv	MLINX	**C**	(800) 624-6782	**C+/ 6.7**	3.01	8.60	15.21 /92	14.28 /69	14.18 /79		0.00	1.04
GR	MainStay Large Cap Growth Fd R1	MLRRX	**B-**	(800) 624-6782	**B / 7.8**	3.10	8.63	15.37 /92	14.50 /71	14.44 /82		0.00	0.84
GR	MainStay Large Cap Growth Fd R2	MLRTX	**C+**	(800) 624-6782	**B / 7.6**	2.99	8.54	15.10 /92	14.22 /69	14.13 /79		0.00	1.09
GR	MainStay Large Cap Growth Fd R3	MLGRX	**C+**	(800) 624-6782	**B- / 7.4**	2.96	8.33	14.79 /91	13.96 /67	13.83 /76		0.00	1.34
GR	MainStay Large Cap Growth R6	MLRSX	**U**	(800) 624-6782	**U /**	3.15	8.80	15.68 /93	--	--		0.00	0.62
GI	MainStay MAP Fund A	MAPAX	**C+**	(800) 624-6782	**C+/ 5.9**	1.66	5.35	9.62 /73	14.22 /69	12.30 /63		1.33	1.11
GI	MainStay MAP Fund B	MAPBX	**C+**	(800) 624-6782	**C+/ 6.1**	1.44	4.91	8.66 /67	13.17 /61	11.26 /55		0.62	2.01
GI	MainStay MAP Fund C	MMPCX	**C+**	(800) 624-6782	**C+/ 6.1**	1.44	4.91	8.66 /67	13.17 /61	11.26 /55		0.62	2.01
GI	MainStay MAP Fund I	MUBFX	**B-**	(800) 624-6782	**B- / 7.0**	1.71	5.49	9.90 /74	14.50 /71	12.58 /65		1.62	0.86
GI	MainStay MAP Fund Inv	MSMIX	**C+**	(800) 624-6782	**C+/ 5.8**	1.63	5.30	9.48 /72	14.02 /67	12.09 /61		1.21	1.26
GI	MainStay MAP Fund R1	MAPRX	**C+**	(800) 624-6782	**C+/ 6.9**	1.70	5.43	9.79 /74	14.37 /70	12.46 /64		1.52	0.96
GI	MainStay MAP Fund R2	MPRRX	**C+**	(800) 624-6782	**C+/ 6.7**	1.63	5.29	9.51 /72	14.09 /68	12.18 /62		1.28	1.21
GI	MainStay MAP Fund R3	MMAPX	**C+**	(800) 624-6782	**C+/ 6.5**	1.56	5.16	9.22 /70	13.81 /66	11.90 /60		1.02	1.46
GR	MainStay Marketfield A	MFADX	**U**	(800) 624-6782	**U /**	-0.25	-3.88	-11.09 / 2	--	--		0.00	2.93
GR	MainStay Marketfield C	MFCDX	**U**	(800) 624-6782	**U /**	-0.44	-4.30	-11.77 / 2	--	--		0.00	3.68
IN	MainStay Marketfield I	MFLDX	**D-**	(800) 624-6782	**E+/ 0.6**	-0.18	-3.80	-10.84 / 3	2.85 / 8	4.82 /11		0.00	2.66
GR	MainStay Marketfield P	MFPDX	**U**	(800) 624-6782	**U /**	-0.25	-3.86	-10.89 / 3	--	--		0.00	2.66
AA	MainStay Moderate Allocation A	MMRAX	**C**	(800) 624-6782	**C- / 3.2**	2.11	3.42	5.60 /43	9.90 /39	9.34 /39		2.03	1.33
AA	MainStay Moderate Allocation B	MMRBX	**C**	(800) 624-6782	**C- / 3.4**	1.90	2.89	4.63 /36	8.91 /32	8.35 /32		1.27	2.25
AA	MainStay Moderate Allocation C	MMRCX	**C**	(800) 624-6782	**C- / 3.4**	1.90	2.90	4.56 /35	8.85 /32	8.34 /32		1.27	2.25
AA	MainStay Moderate Allocation I	MMRIX	**C+**	(800) 624-6782	**C- / 4.2**	2.18	3.51	5.83 /45	10.16 /40	9.63 /42		2.37	1.08
AA	MainStay Moderate Allocation Inv	MMRDX	**C-**	(800) 624-6782	**C- / 3.1**	2.11	3.33	5.43 /42	9.68 /37	9.15 /38		1.88	1.50
AA	MainStay Moderate Gr Allocation A	MGDAX	**C**	(800) 624-6782	**C / 4.4**	2.46	4.43	6.52 /51	11.93 /52	10.69 /50		1.69	1.47
AA	MainStay Moderate Gr Allocation B	MGDBX	**C+**	(800) 624-6782	**C / 4.6**	2.28	3.93	5.62 /43	10.92 /45	9.71 /42		0.90	2.39
AA	MainStay Moderate Gr Allocation C	MGDCX	**C+**	(800) 624-6782	**C / 4.6**	2.28	3.93	5.62 /43	10.92 /45	9.71 /42		0.90	2.39
AA	MainStay Moderate Gr Allocation I	MGDIX	**C+**	(800) 624-6782	**C / 5.5**	2.51	4.50	6.79 /53	12.23 /54	10.97 /52		2.01	1.22
AA	MainStay Moderate Gr Allocation Inv	MGDNX	**C**	(800) 624-6782	**C- / 4.2**	2.40	4.32	6.35 /49	11.72 /51	10.52 /49		1.54	1.64
BA	MainStay Retirement 2010 A	MYRAX	**C-**	(800) 624-6782	**D / 2.0**	1.55	3.24	5.63 /43	7.52 /24	7.79 /29		1.71	1.28
BA	MainStay Retirement 2010 I	MYRIX	**C**	(800) 624-6782	**C- / 3.0**	1.64	3.39	5.97 /46	7.81 /26	8.07 /30		2.05	1.03
BA	MainStay Retirement 2010 Inv	MYRDX	**C-**	(800) 624-6782	**D / 1.9**	1.54	3.16	5.55 /43	7.44 /24	7.69 /28		1.46	1.37
BA	MainStay Retirement 2010 R2	MYRWX	**C**	(800) 624-6782	**D+/ 2.7**	1.55	3.14	5.53 /43	7.42 /24	7.69 /28		1.62	1.38

● Denotes fund is closed to new investors
* Denotes fund is included in Section II

www.thestreetratings.com

RISK			NET ASSETS		ASSET					BULL / BEAR		FUND MANAGER		MINIMUMS		LOADS	
	3 Year		NAV						Portfolio	Last Bull	Last Bear	Manager	Manager	Initial	Additional	Front	Back
Risk	Standard		As of	Total	Cash	Stocks	Bonds	Other	Turnover	Market	Market	Quality	Tenure	Purch.	Purch.	End	End
Rating/Pts	Deviation	Beta	3/31/15	$(Mil)	%	%	%	%	Ratio	Return	Return	Pct	(Years)	$	$	Load	Load
B- / 7.0	7.1	1.16	19.55	573	10	48	41	1	15	62.7	-11.0	50	6	25,000	0	5.5	0.0
B- / 7.0	7.1	1.16	19.66	49	10	48	41	1	15	57.2	-11.4	35	6	1,000	50	0.0	0.0
B- / 7.0	7.1	1.17	19.63	208	10	48	41	1	15	57.2	-11.3	34	6	1,000	50	0.0	0.0
B- / 7.0	7.1	1.17	19.70	516	10	48	41	1	15	64.1	-10.9	53	6	5,000,000	0	0.0	0.0
B- / 7.0	7.1	1.16	19.56	163	10	48	41	1	15	61.3	-11.0	46	6	1,000	50	5.5	0.0
C+ / 6.0	11.4	0.80	13.55	46	3	96	0	1	37	45.9	-25.6	50	4	25,000	0	5.5	0.0
C+ / 5.9	11.4	0.80	12.35	10	3	96	0	1	37	40.7	-25.9	34	4	1,000	50	0.0	0.0
C+ / 5.9	11.4	0.80	12.35	9	3	96	0	1	37	40.7	-25.9	33	4	1,000	50	0.0	0.0
C+ / 5.9	11.4	0.80	13.61	217	3	96	0	1	37	47.1	-25.5	53	4	5,000,000	0	0.0	0.0
C+ / 5.9	11.4	0.80	13.54	35	3	96	0	1	37	44.2	-25.6	44	4	1,000	50	5.5	0.0
C+ / 5.9	11.4	0.80	13.54	3	3	96	0	1	37	46.7	-25.6	52	4	0	0	0.0	0.0
C+ / 5.9	11.4	0.80	13.60	3	3	96	0	1	37	45.4	-25.6	48	4	0	0	0.0	0.0
C+ / 5.9	11.4	0.80	13.55	1	3	96	0	1	37	44.1	-25.7	44	4	0	0	0.0	0.0
C+ / 5.9	13.1	0.96	8.71	32	0	99	0	1	136	71.7	-24.3	91	8	25,000	0	5.5	0.0
C+ / 5.9	13.2	0.97	8.46	13	0	99	0	1	136	66.6	-24.5	88	8	1,000	50	0.0	0.0
C+ / 5.9	13.2	0.97	8.76	417	0	99	0	1	136	73.2	-24.3	91	8	5,000,000	0	0.0	0.0
C+ / 5.9	13.2	0.97	8.68	2	0	99	0	1	136	70.7	-24.2	90	8	1,000	50	5.5	0.0
C / 5.1	12.0	1.12	10.35	1,248	0	99	0	1	67	95.6	-17.7	22	10	25,000	0	5.5	0.0
C / 4.9	12.0	1.12	9.41	50	0	99	0	1	67	90.3	-18.1	15	10	1,000	50	0.0	0.0
C / 4.9	12.1	1.13	9.40	406	0	99	0	1	67	90.5	-18.1	14	10	1,000	50	0.0	0.0
C / 5.2	12.0	1.12	10.79	13,473	0	99	0	1	67	97.3	-17.7	24	10	5,000,000	0	0.0	0.0
C / 5.1	12.0	1.12	10.28	202	0	99	0	1	67	95.4	-17.8	21	10	1,000	50	5.5	0.0
C / 5.1	12.0	1.12	10.63	2,177	0	99	0	1	67	96.8	-17.8	23	10	0	0	0.0	0.0
C / 5.1	12.1	1.12	10.35	920	0	99	0	1	67	95.1	-17.8	20	10	0	0	0.0	0.0
C / 5.0	12.0	1.12	10.08	143	0	99	0	1	67	93.4	-17.9	19	10	0	0	0.0	0.0
U /	N/A	N/A	10.81	1,059	0	99	0	1	67	N/A	N/A	N/A	10	250,000	0	0.0	0.0
C+ / 6.3	10.2	1.05	44.17	371	2	97	0	1	32	90.1	-19.8	32	9	25,000	0	5.5	0.0
C+ / 6.3	10.2	1.05	40.73	64	2	97	0	1	32	84.2	-20.1	22	9	1,000	50	0.0	0.0
C+ / 6.3	10.2	1.05	40.73	141	2	97	0	1	32	84.2	-20.1	22	9	1,000	50	0.0	0.0
C+ / 6.3	10.2	1.05	45.15	1,379	2	97	0	1	32	91.7	-19.7	35	9	5,000,000	0	0.0	0.0
C+ / 6.3	10.2	1.05	44.17	155	2	97	0	1	32	89.0	-19.8	30	9	1,000	50	5.5	0.0
C+ / 6.3	10.2	1.05	44.39	4	2	97	0	1	32	91.0	-19.7	34	9	0	0	0.0	0.0
C+ / 6.3	10.2	1.05	44.32	15	2	97	0	1	32	89.5	-19.8	31	9	0	0	0.0	0.0
C+ / 6.3	10.2	1.05	44.16	1	2	97	0	1	32	87.8	-19.9	28	9	0	0	0.0	0.0
U /	N/A	N/A	16.12	607	48	51	0	1	32	N/A	N/A	N/A	8	25,000	0	5.5	0.0
U /	N/A	N/A	15.82	749	48	51	0	1	32	N/A	N/A	N/A	8	2,500	50	0.0	0.0
B- / 7.2	6.7	0.39	16.21	4,914	48	51	0	1	32	24.8	-7.0	24	8	5,000,000	0	0.0	0.0
U /	N/A	N/A	16.20	111	48	51	0	1	32	N/A	N/A	N/A	8	0	0	0.0	0.0
B- / 7.7	6.6	1.13	13.55	361	14	56	29	1	47	56.7	-12.7	34	10	25,000	0	5.5	0.0
B- / 7.9	6.6	1.13	13.41	86	14	56	29	1	47	51.9	-13.1	24	10	1,000	50	0.0	0.0
B- / 7.9	6.6	1.13	13.40	71	14	56	29	1	47	51.8	-13.0	23	10	1,000	50	0.0	0.0
B- / 7.6	6.6	1.13	13.62	14	14	56	29	1	47	58.1	-12.6	37	10	5,000,000	0	0.0	0.0
B- / 7.7	6.6	1.13	13.55	154	14	56	29	1	47	55.8	-12.8	31	7	1,000	50	5.5	0.0
B- / 7.3	8.6	1.46	14.97	302	13	75	10	2	45	71.6	-17.1	18	10	25,000	0	5.5	0.0
B- / 7.3	8.6	1.45	14.78	103	13	75	10	2	45	66.5	-17.5	12	10	1,000	50	0.0	0.0
B- / 7.4	8.5	1.45	14.78	52	13	75	10	2	45	66.5	-17.5	12	10	1,000	50	0.0	0.0
B- / 7.3	8.6	1.45	15.10	9	13	75	10	2	45	73.2	-17.1	21	10	5,000,000	0	0.0	0.0
B- / 7.3	8.6	1.46	14.96	203	13	75	10	2	45	70.7	-17.2	16	N/A	1,000	50	5.5	0.0
B / 8.2	4.8	0.82	10.47	6	9	38	51	2	69	43.1	-10.6	49	N/A	25,000	0	5.5	0.0
B / 8.1	4.8	0.82	10.55	44	9	38	51	2	69	44.2	-10.4	53	N/A	5,000,000	0	0.0	0.0
B / 8.3	4.8	0.81	10.52	1	9	38	51	2	69	42.5	-10.6	48	N/A	1,000	50	5.5	0.0
B / 8.2	4.8	0.81	10.49	3	9	38	51	2	69	42.6	-10.6	48	N/A	0	0	0.0	0.0

Fund Type	Fund Name	Ticker Symbol	Overall Investment Rating	Phone	Performance Rating/Pts	Total Return % through 3/31/15			Annualized		Incl. in Returns	
						3 Mo	6 Mo	1Yr / Pct	3Yr / Pct	5Yr / Pct	Dividend Yield	Expense Ratio
BA	MainStay Retirement 2010 R3	MYREX	C	(800) 624-6782	D+ / 2.6	1.52	3.12	5.37 /41	7.20 /22	7.43 /26	1.34	1.63
GI	MainStay Retirement 2020 A	MYROX	C	(800) 624-6782	D+ / 2.8	1.87	3.95	6.50 /51	9.10 /34	8.81 /35	1.43	1.20
GI	MainStay Retirement 2020 I	MYRTX	C+	(800) 624-6782	C- / 3.9	1.86	3.99	6.72 /53	9.36 /35	9.05 /37	1.83	0.94
GI	MainStay Retirement 2020 Inv	MYRYX	C	(800) 624-6782	D+ / 2.8	1.77	3.81	6.35 /49	8.99 /33	8.69 /34	1.31	1.37
GI	MainStay Retirement 2020 R2	MYRVX	C+	(800) 624-6782	C- / 3.7	1.87	3.88	6.42 /50	9.01 /33	8.69 /34	1.45	1.29
GL	MainStay Retirement 2020 R3	MYRZX	C+	(800) 624-6782	C- / 3.4	1.76	3.65	6.07 /47	8.69 /31	8.39 /32	1.16	1.54
GI	MainStay Retirement 2030 A	MRTTX	C	(800) 624-6782	C- / 3.8	2.13	4.50	7.16 /56	10.74 /44	9.83 /43	1.31	1.25
GI	MainStay Retirement 2030 I	MRTIX	C+	(800) 624-6782	C / 4.8	2.21	4.57	7.30 /57	10.95 /45	10.09 /45	1.65	0.99
GI	MainStay Retirement 2030 Inv	MRTFX	C	(800) 624-6782	C- / 3.7	2.04	4.37	6.92 /54	10.57 /43	9.70 /42	1.20	1.46
GI	MainStay Retirement 2030 R2	MRTUX	C+	(800) 624-6782	C / 4.5	2.04	4.44	7.00 /55	10.58 /43	9.68 /42	1.32	1.34
GI	MainStay Retirement 2030 R3	MRTVX	C+	(800) 624-6782	C / 4.4	2.02	4.26	6.69 /53	10.31 /41	9.43 /40	1.10	1.59
GI	MainStay Retirement 2040 A	MSRTX	C	(800) 624-6782	C / 4.4	2.28	5.10	7.63 /60	11.69 /50	10.42 /48	1.21	1.34
GI	MainStay Retirement 2040 I	MSRYX	C+	(800) 624-6782	C / 5.4	2.35	5.17	7.87 /62	11.96 /52	10.72 /50	1.46	1.08
GI	MainStay Retirement 2040 Inv	MSRUX	C	(800) 624-6782	C / 4.3	2.27	5.00	7.52 /59	11.57 /49	10.32 /47	1.05	1.55
GI	MainStay Retirement 2040 R2	MSRQX	C+	(800) 624-6782	C / 5.2	2.28	4.98	7.49 /59	11.55 /49	10.32 /47	1.17	1.44
GI	MainStay Retirement 2040 R3	MSRZX	C+	(800) 624-6782	C / 5.0	2.26	4.94	7.25 /57	11.29 /48	10.04 /45	0.81	1.69
GI	MainStay Retirement 2050 A	MSRLX	C	(800) 624-6782	C / 4.6	2.48	5.38	7.73 /61	12.05 /53	10.66 /50	1.19	1.50
GI	MainStay Retirement 2050 I	MSRMX	C+	(800) 624-6782	C+ / 5.7	2.56	5.55	8.09 /64	12.36 /55	10.95 /52	1.43	1.26
GI	MainStay Retirement 2050 Inv	MSRVX	C	(800) 624-6782	C / 4.5	2.48	5.34	7.69 /60	11.93 /52	10.53 /49	1.06	1.75
GI	MainStay Retirement 2050 R2	MSRPX	C+	(800) 624-6782	C / 5.4	2.47	5.33	7.68 /60	11.95 /52	10.57 /49	1.13	1.61
GI	MainStay Retirement 2050 R3	MSRWX	C+	(800) 624-6782	C / 5.2	2.37	5.17	7.40 /58	11.66 /50	10.27 /47	0.91	1.86
GR	MainStay S&P 500 Index A	MSXAX	B+	(800) 624-6782	B- / 7.2	0.85	5.67	12.09 /83	15.44 /79	13.80 /76	1.28	0.62
GR	MainStay S&P 500 Index I	MSPIX	A-	(800) 624-6782	B / 8.0	0.90	5.80	12.38 /84	15.72 /81	14.08 /78	1.54	0.37
GR	MainStay S&P 500 Index Inv	MYSPX	B+	(800) 624-6782	B- / 7.1	0.80	5.61	12.00 /82	15.32 /77	13.68 /75	1.19	0.80
GI	MainStay US Eqty Opportunities A	MYCTX	C+	(800) 624-6782	A / 9.5	3.13	9.13	16.58 /94	19.85 /98	16.36 /94	0.00	2.48
GI	MainStay US Eqty Opportunities C	MYCCX	C	(800) 624-6782	A / 9.5	2.79	8.55	15.47 /92	18.66 /96	15.19 /88	0.00	3.45
GI	MainStay US Eqty Opportunities I	MYCIX	C+	(800) 624-6782	A+ / 9.8	3.11	9.20	16.89 /94	20.12 /98	16.58 /95	0.00	2.27
GI	MainStay US Eqty Opportunities Inv	MYCNX	C+	(800) 624-6782	A / 9.4	3.05	9.00	16.37 /94	19.58 /97	16.08 /93	0.00	2.73
SC	MainStay US Small Cap A	MOPAX	C+	(800) 624-6782	C+ / 6.4	2.98	11.71	7.66 /60	14.70 /72	13.50 /73	0.00	1.25
SC	MainStay US Small Cap B	MOTBX	C+	(800) 624-6782	C+ / 6.5	2.72	11.15	6.54 /51	13.52 /64	12.35 /63	0.00	2.28
SC	MainStay US Small Cap C	MOPCX	C+	(800) 624-6782	C+ / 6.5	2.68	11.11	6.54 /51	13.51 /63	12.34 /63	0.00	2.28
SC	MainStay US Small Cap I	MOPIX	B	(800) 624-6782	B / 7.6	3.03	11.85	7.93 /62	15.00 /75	13.78 /76	0.23	1.00
SC	MainStay US Small Cap Inv	MOINX	C+	(800) 624-6782	C+ / 6.2	2.90	11.57	7.36 /58	14.38 /70	13.20 /70	0.00	1.53
BA	Mairs & Power Balanced Fund	MAPOX	B-	(800) 304-7404	C / 4.9	0.78	4.61	6.73 /53	11.32 /48	11.21 /55	2.35	0.73
GR	Mairs & Power Growth Fund	MPGFX	A	(800) 304-7404	B / 7.9	0.82	7.20	7.63 /60	16.16 /85	14.58 /83	1.28	0.68
SC	Mairs & Power Small Cap	MSCFX	A+	(800) 304-7404	A / 9.5	2.61	9.57	6.09 /47	19.89 /98	--	0.34	1.18
GR	Managed Account Series Glbl SC	MGCSX	D+	(800) 441-7762	C+ / 6.1	2.69	3.82	1.47 /20	14.29 /69	12.13 /62	0.18	1.08
GR	Managed Account Series MCV Opp	MMCVX	C	(800) 441-7762	B- / 7.1	2.44	5.59	6.23 /48	15.14 /76	14.75 /85	1.41	0.81
IN	Manning & Napier Disciplined Val I	MNDFX	C+	(800) 466-3863	C+ / 5.7	0.42	1.86	8.44 /66	12.90 /59	12.07 /61	2.25	0.75
IN	Manning & Napier Disciplined Val S	MDFSX	B-	(800) 466-3863	C / 5.5	0.34	1.68	8.15 /64	12.55 /56	--	2.73	1.00
GR	Manning & Napier Equity Series	EXEYX	D	(800) 466-3863	C+ / 6.1	0.65	1.63	5.52 /43	14.07 /68	10.85 /51	0.02	1.08
GL	Manning & Napier Inflation Focus Eq	MNIFX	E+	(800) 466-3863	E+ / 0.6	-3.38	-4.41	-5.75 / 5	3.04 / 8	--	0.32	1.19
FO	Manning & Napier International I	MNIIX	D	(800) 466-3863	D / 1.9	2.67	-0.21	-2.52 / 9	7.00 /21	--	1.31	0.89
FO	Manning & Napier Overseas Srs	EXOSX	E	(800) 466-3863	E+ / 0.8	1.99	-2.84	-9.38 / 3	4.31 /11	3.46 / 7	1.53	0.75
GI	Manning & Napier Pro-Blend Csv Tm	MNCCX	D	(800) 466-3863	D- / 1.3	0.60	0.44	1.96 /22	4.92 /13	5.31 /13	1.13	1.69
GI	Manning & Napier Pro-Blend Csv Tm	MNCIX	D+	(800) 466-3863	D / 1.7	0.96	0.98	3.03 /27	5.97 /17	6.39 /19	2.00	0.69
AA	Manning & Napier Pro-Blend Csv Tm	MNCRX	D	(800) 466-3863	D- / 1.5	0.80	0.74	2.57 /24	5.46 /15	--	1.62	1.19
GI	Manning & Napier Pro-Blend Csv Tm	EXDAX	D+	(800) 466-3863	D / 1.6	0.82	0.87	2.76 /25	5.74 /16	6.15 /18	1.38	0.89
GI	Manning & Napier Pro-Blend Ext Tm	MNECX	D	(800) 466-3863	D+ / 2.7	0.76	0.66	2.11 /22	8.18 /28	7.74 /28	0.55	1.81
GI	Manning & Napier Pro-Blend Ext Tm I	MNBIX	D	(800) 466-3863	C- / 3.4	1.02	1.16	3.22 /28	9.30 /35	8.80 /35	1.59	0.81
GI	Manning & Napier Pro-Blend Ext Tm	MNBRX	D	(800) 466-3863	C- / 3.0	0.81	0.88	2.60 /25	8.72 /31	--	0.93	1.31
GI	Manning & Napier Pro-Blend Ext Tm	MNBAX	D+	(800) 466-3863	C- / 3.2	0.89	1.00	2.90 /26	9.00 /33	8.52 /33	0.73	1.06

• Denotes fund is closed to new investors
* Denotes fund is included in Section II

www.thestreetratings.com

RISK			NET ASSETS		ASSET				Portfolio Turnover Ratio	BULL / BEAR		FUND MANAGER		MINIMUMS		LOADS	
	3 Year		NAV							Last Bull Market Return	Last Bear Market Return	Manager Quality Pct	Manager Tenure (Years)	Initial Purch. $	Additional Purch. $	Front End Load	Back End Load
Risk Rating/Pts	Standard Deviation	Beta	As of 3/31/15	Total $(Mil)	Cash %	Stocks %	Bonds %	Other %									
B /8.6	4.8	0.83	10.68	N/A	9	38	51	2	69	41.5	-10.7	43	N/A	0	0	0.0	0.0
B /8.4	6.3	0.64	10.89	14	9	57	32	2	64	53.7	-13.9	55	N/A	25,000	0	5.5	0.0
B /8.4	6.3	0.63	10.94	118	9	57	32	2	64	55.1	-13.8	59	N/A	5,000,000	0	0.0	0.0
B /8.4	6.3	0.63	10.91	7	9	57	32	2	64	53.2	-13.9	54	N/A	1,000	50	5.5	0.0
B /8.4	6.3	0.63	10.90	5	9	57	32	2	64	53.1	-14.0	56	N/A	0	0	0.0	0.0
B /8.5	6.3	0.63	11.00	N/A	9	57	32	2	64	51.7	-14.0	50	N/A	0	0	0.0	0.0
B- /7.8	8.0	0.81	11.01	13	9	75	15	1	68	65.4	-17.3	38	N/A	25,000	0	5.5	0.0
B- /7.8	8.0	0.81	11.09	182	9	75	15	1	68	66.8	-17.3	40	N/A	5,000,000	0	0.0	0.0
B- /7.8	8.0	0.81	11.02	10	9	75	15	1	68	64.9	-17.4	37	N/A	1,000	50	5.5	0.0
B- /7.8	8.0	0.81	10.99	8	9	75	15	1	68	64.8	-17.4	36	N/A	0	0	0.0	0.0
B- /7.8	8.0	0.81	11.13	N/A	9	75	15	1	68	63.4	-17.4	33	N/A	0	0	0.0	0.0
B- /7.2	9.0	0.91	11.20	8	7	87	5	1	83	72.2	-18.9	29	N/A	25,000	0	5.5	0.0
B- /7.2	9.0	0.91	11.31	141	7	87	5	1	83	73.7	-18.8	33	N/A	5,000,000	0	0.0	0.0
B- /7.3	9.0	0.92	11.25	10	7	87	5	1	83	71.7	-18.9	28	N/A	1,000	50	5.5	0.0
B- /7.2	9.0	0.91	11.23	8	7	87	5	1	83	71.7	-18.9	28	N/A	0	0	0.0	0.0
B- /7.3	9.0	0.92	11.33	N/A	7	87	5	1	83	70.3	-19.0	25	N/A	0	0	0.0	0.0
B- /7.0	9.4	0.95	11.16	3	6	91	2	1	51	75.1	-19.7	26	N/A	25,000	0	5.5	0.0
B- /7.0	9.4	0.96	11.23	65	6	91	2	1	51	76.6	-19.6	29	N/A	5,000,000	0	0.0	0.0
B- /7.0	9.4	0.95	11.15	6	6	91	2	1	51	74.5	-19.8	26	N/A	1,000	50	5.5	0.0
B- /7.0	9.4	0.95	11.18	7	6	91	2	1	51	74.4	-19.8	26	N/A	0	0	0.0	0.0
B- /7.0	9.4	0.95	11.23	N/A	6	91	2	1	51	73.0	-19.8	22	N/A	0	0	0.0	0.0
B- /7.3	9.5	1.00	47.62	581	0	98	1	1	4	96.3	-16.5	59	19	25,000	0	3.0	0.0
B- /7.3	9.5	1.00	48.07	1,427	0	98	1	1	4	98.0	-16.4	63	19	5,000,000	0	0.0	0.0
B- /7.3	9.5	1.00	47.60	36	0	98	1	1	4	95.7	-16.5	57	19	1,000	50	3.0	0.0
D+ /2.5	10.8	1.08	8.56	44	0	99	0	1	163	116.5	-16.5	84	8	25,000	0	5.5	0.0
D /1.9	10.7	1.08	7.74	24	0	99	0	1	163	109.5	-16.9	77	8	1,000	50	0.0	0.0
D+ /2.5	10.8	1.08	8.61	530	0	99	0	1	163	118.1	-16.5	85	8	5,000,000	0	0.0	0.0
D+ /2.4	10.7	1.07	8.46	2	0	99	0	1	163	114.7	-16.6	83	8	1,000	50	5.5	0.0
C+ /6.1	12.8	0.93	27.28	135	1	98	0	1	36	90.2	-21.8	64	6	25,000	0	5.5	0.0
C+ /6.1	12.8	0.93	24.92	25	1	98	0	1	36	83.6	-22.2	48	6	1,000	50	0.0	0.0
C+ /6.1	12.8	0.93	24.91	22	1	98	0	1	36	83.7	-22.2	48	6	1,000	50	0.0	0.0
C+ /6.2	12.8	0.93	27.92	277	1	98	0	1	36	91.9	-21.8	67	6	5,000,000	0	0.0	0.0
C+ /6.1	12.8	0.93	27.00	90	1	98	0	1	36	88.3	-21.9	60	6	1,000	50	5.5	0.0
B /8.5	6.7	1.14	86.97	755	3	61	34	2	3	66.1	-11.5	51	23	2,500	100	0.0	0.0
B- /7.5	10.4	1.02	117.15	4,299	1	98	0	1	4	105.9	-18.1	64	16	2,500	100	0.0	0.0
C+ /6.9	12.0	0.82	21.21	191	1	98	0	1	35	139.7	N/A	95	4	2,500	100	0.0	0.0
C- /3.5	12.4	1.15	14.15	172	3	96	0	1	81	83.0	-23.2	18	10	0	0	0.0	0.0
C /4.3	11.8	1.11	14.25	166	3	96	0	1	61	95.8	-21.4	30	6	0	0	0.0	0.0
B- /7.1	9.4	0.93	15.97	194	2	97	0	1	23	73.8	-10.6	39	7	1,000,000	0	0.0	0.0
B- /7.7	9.4	0.93	11.90	15	2	97	0	1	23	N/A	N/A	36	7	2,000	0	0.0	0.0
D /2.1	11.4	1.10	17.14	828	2	97	0	1	61	84.7	-19.9	22	13	2,000	0	0.0	0.0
C /5.0	12.2	0.79	10.57	95	2	97	0	1	55	41.7	N/A	15	4	2,000	0	0.0	0.0
C+ /6.6	12.8	0.92	10.37	139	6	93	0	1	22	N/A	N/A	43	23	1,000,000	0	0.0	0.0
C- /3.3	13.4	0.97	22.04	2,309	4	95	0	1	39	39.8	-27.0	12	13	1,000,000	0	0.0	0.0
B- /7.4	4.0	0.35	10.07	142	5	34	60	1	45	24.5	-4.5	60	20	2,000	0	0.0	0.0
B- /7.4	4.0	0.35	10.48	380	5	34	60	1	45	28.7	-4.0	73	20	1,000,000	0	0.0	0.0
B- /7.4	4.0	0.64	10.07	66	5	34	60	1	45	26.5	-4.2	47	20	2,000	0	0.0	0.0
B- /7.9	4.0	0.35	13.46	1,070	5	34	60	1	45	27.9	-4.1	71	20	2,000	0	0.0	0.0
C /5.4	7.3	0.70	10.59	172	2	62	34	2	65	47.3	-13.4	29	20	2,000	0	0.0	0.0
C /5.1	7.3	0.70	9.92	631	2	62	34	2	65	52.5	-13.2	43	20	1,000,000	0	0.0	0.0
C+ /5.6	7.4	0.70	11.25	64	2	62	34	2	65	49.9	-13.2	35	20	2,000	0	0.0	0.0
C+ /6.6	7.3	0.70	16.97	837	2	62	34	2	65	51.1	-13.2	39	20	2,000	0	0.0	0.0

	99 Pct = Best 0 Pct = Worst				**PERFORMANCE**							
			Overall		**Perfor-**		Total Return % through 3/31/15				Incl. in Returns	
			Investment		**mance**				Annualized		Dividend	Expense
Fund		Ticker	**Rating**	Phone	**Rating/Pts**	3 Mo	6 Mo	1Yr / Pct	3Yr / Pct	5Yr / Pct	Yield	Ratio
Type	Fund Name	Symbol										
GL	Manning & Napier Pro-Blend Max Tm	MNHCX	D-	(800) 466-3863	C- / 4.2	0.36	0.96	3.05 /27	11.07 /46	8.81 /35	0.02	1.82
GL	Manning & Napier Pro-Blend Max Tm	MNHIX	D-	(800) 466-3863	C / 4.9	0.67	1.47	4.05 /32	12.17 /54	9.91 /44	0.89	0.82
GL	Manning & Napier Pro-Blend Max Tm	MNHRX	D	(800) 466-3863	C / 4.6	0.55	1.20	3.53 /29	11.62 /50	--	0.27	1.32
GL	Manning & Napier Pro-Blend Max Tm	EXHAX	D+	(800) 466-3863	C / 4.8	0.53	1.29	3.73 /30	11.89 /52	9.65 /42	0.29	1.07
GI	Manning & Napier Pro-Blend Mdt Tm	MNMIX	D	(800) 466-3863	D+ / 2.3	0.97	0.90	2.28 /23	7.26 /23	7.34 /25	1.54	0.81
GI	Manning & Napier Pro-Blend Mdt Tm	MNMRX	D	(800) 466-3863	D / 2.0	0.93	0.73	1.84 /21	6.76 /20	--	0.98	1.31
GI	Manning & Napier Pro-Blend Mdt Tm	EXBAX	D+	(800) 466-3863	D / 2.2	0.97	0.90	2.09 /22	7.05 /22	7.08 /24	0.95	1.06
GI	Manning & Napier Pro-Blend Mod Tm	MNMCX	D	(800) 466-3863	D / 1.7	0.77	0.47	1.25 /19	6.23 /18	6.29 /19	0.57	1.81
RE	Manning & Napier Real Estate I	MNRIX	U	(800) 466-3863	U /	4.85	19.26	24.76 /98	--	--	4.59	0.88
RE	Manning & Napier Real Estate S	MNREX	C+	(800) 466-3863	A / 9.5	4.79	19.18	24.46 /98	14.33 /70	15.11 /88	2.55	1.13
GI	Manning & Napier Target 2010 I	MTHIX	D	(800) 466-3863	D / 1.9	0.84	0.86	2.68 /25	6.46 /19	6.73 /21	2.91	0.96
GI	Manning & Napier Target 2010 K	MTHKX	D	(800) 466-3863	D / 1.8	0.74	0.71	2.43 /24	6.19 /18	6.47 /20	2.68	1.21
GI	Manning & Napier Target 2010 R	MTHRX	D	(800) 466-3863	D / 1.6	0.64	0.49	2.18 /23	5.88 /16	6.20 /18	2.33	1.46
GI	Manning & Napier Target 2020 I	MTNIX	D	(800) 466-3863	D+ / 2.8	0.93	0.97	2.55 /24	8.24 /28	8.09 /30	3.04	0.90
GI	Manning & Napier Target 2020 K	MTNKX	D	(800) 466-3863	D+ / 2.6	0.83	0.73	2.21 /23	7.94 /27	7.81 /29	2.81	1.15
GI	Manning & Napier Target 2020 R	MTNRX	D	(800) 466-3863	D+ / 2.4	0.73	0.71	2.07 /22	7.69 /25	7.52 /27	2.49	1.40
GI	Manning & Napier Target 2030 I	MTPIX	D+	(800) 466-3863	C- / 4.2	0.89	1.27	3.45 /29	10.74 /44	9.43 /40	4.23	0.90
GI	Manning & Napier Target 2030 K	MTPKX	D+	(800) 466-3863	C- / 4.0	0.90	1.14	3.13 /27	10.49 /42	9.16 /38	4.02	1.15
GI	Manning & Napier Target 2030 R	MTPRX	D	(800) 466-3863	C- / 3.8	0.80	1.00	2.87 /26	10.19 /40	8.89 /36	3.69	1.40
GI	Manning & Napier Target 2040 I	MTTIX	D	(800) 466-3863	C / 4.6	0.76	1.32	3.75 /30	11.57 /49	9.52 /41	5.36	0.93
GI	Manning & Napier Target 2040 K	MTTKX	D	(800) 466-3863	C / 4.4	0.67	1.18	3.51 /29	11.30 /48	9.23 /38	5.14	1.18
GI	Manning & Napier Target 2040 R	MTTRX	D	(800) 466-3863	C / 4.3	0.58	1.01	3.22 /28	11.03 /46	8.96 /36	4.79	1.43
GI	Manning & Napier Target 2050 I	MTYIX	D	(800) 466-3863	C / 4.9	0.68	1.48	4.06 /32	12.14 /53	9.84 /43	5.76	1.06
GI	Manning & Napier Target 2050 K	MTYKX	D	(800) 466-3863	C / 4.7	0.60	1.34	3.74 /30	11.82 /51	9.54 /41	5.55	1.31
GI	Manning & Napier Target 2050 R	MTYRX	D	(800) 466-3863	C / 4.6	0.52	1.25	3.54 /29	11.56 /49	9.29 /39	5.28	1.56
AA	Manning & Napier Target Income I	MTDIX	D	(800) 466-3863	D / 1.7	1.01	1.02	3.00 /26	5.92 /16	6.34 /19	3.00	0.84
AA	Manning & Napier Target Income K	MTDKX	D	(800) 466-3863	D / 1.6	0.81	0.77	2.74 /25	5.63 /15	6.07 /17	2.76	1.09
AA	Manning & Napier Target Income R	MTDRX	D	(800) 466-3863	D- / 1.5	0.82	0.73	2.51 /24	5.38 /14	5.80 /16	2.53	1.34
GI	Manning & Napier Tax Managed Srs	EXTAX	D+	(800) 466-3863	C+ / 6.6	1.44	1.80	6.80 /53	14.66 /72	11.17 /54	0.11	1.33
FO	Manning & Napier World Oppty A	EXWAX	E	(800) 466-3863	E+ / 0.7	1.36	-3.62	-10.22 / 3	3.72 / 9	2.90 / 6	1.23	1.07
MC	Manning and Napier Dynamic Opp I	MDOIX	U	(800) 466-3863	U /	7.98	12.99	8.01 /63	--	--	0.00	0.88
MC	Manning and Napier Dynamic Opp S	MDOSX	U	(800) 466-3863	U /	7.89	12.79	7.82 /61	--	--	0.00	1.08
EM	Manning and Napier Emerging Mkts	MNEMX	E+	(800) 466-3863	E / 0.3	-3.79	-13.64	-13.04 / 2	-0.41 / 4	--	3.11	1.27
IN	Manning and Napier Equity Income I	MNEIX	U	(800) 466-3863	U /	0.09	3.13	8.53 /66	--	--	2.25	1.40
GL	Manning and Napier Focused Opp I	MNFIX	U	(800) 466-3863	U /	-3.19	4.13	-0.01 /16	--	--	0.92	0.77
GL	Manning and Napier Focused Opp S	MNFSX	U	(800) 466-3863	U /	-3.19	4.14	-0.20 /15	--	--	0.74	0.97
GR	Manor Fund	MNRMX	B+	(800) 787-3334	B / 7.7	3.32	6.03	9.72 /73	15.38 /78	13.14 /69	0.57	1.50
GR	Manor Growth Fund	MNRGX	A+	(800) 787-3334	B+ / 8.8	3.48	10.40	15.14 /92	16.09 /84	14.77 /85	0.00	1.50
GR	Marathon Value Portfolio	MVPFX	B-	(800) 788-6086	C / 5.4	0.87	6.18	7.13 /56	12.11 /53	11.80 /59	0.61	1.10
AA	Mariner Managed Futures Strategy A	MHBAX	D	(855) 542-4642	E / 0.3	5.74	2.50	6.49 /51	-3.34 / 2	--	0.00	9.35
AA	Mariner Managed Futures Strategy C	MHBCX	D	(855) 542-4642	E / 0.3	5.83	2.53	6.21 /48	-3.81 / 2	--	0.00	7.92
AA	Mariner Managed Futures Strategy I	MHBIX	D	(855) 542-4642	E / 0.4	5.82	2.60	6.69 /53	-3.13 / 2	--	0.00	4.48
SC	Marketocracy Masters 100	MOFQX	E+	(888) 884-8482	D- / 1.3	3.89	9.58	-1.23 /12	4.15 /11	5.58 /15	1.87	2.04
MC	Marsico 21ST Century Fund	MXXIX	B	(888) 860-8686	B / 7.9	3.90	7.13	12.29 /84	15.24 /77	11.73 /59	0.00	1.43
GI	Marsico Flexible Capital Fd	MFCFX	B-	(888) 860-8686	B- / 7.5	2.30	6.37	9.52 /72	15.23 /77	16.86 /96	0.00	1.39
GR	Marsico Focus Fund	MFOCX	C	(888) 860-8686	B- / 7.5	2.51	4.04	15.48 /92	14.88 /74	13.91 /77	0.00	1.34
GL	Marsico Global Fd	MGLBX	C-	(888) 860-8686	B- / 7.4	5.10	6.16	9.89 /74	14.64 /72	13.73 /75	0.00	1.66
GR	Marsico Growth Fd	MGRIX	D+	(888) 860-8686	C+ / 6.3	1.59	3.30	11.71 /81	13.18 /61	13.43 /72	0.00	1.37
FO	Marsico International Oppty	MIOFX	D	(888) 860-8686	C- / 3.3	5.61	8.76	6.17 /48	7.61 /25	6.35 /19	0.00	1.69
AA	MassMutual Barings Dynamic All	MBGLX	C-	(800) 542-6767	C- / 3.5	3.97	5.77	8.98 /69	7.44 /24	--	5.10	2.69
AA	MassMutual Barings Dynamic All I	MPBZX	C-	(800) 542-6767	C- / 3.7	4.08	6.04	9.35 /71	7.80 /26	--	5.43	2.39
AA	MassMutual Barings Dynamic All R5	MPBSX	C-	(800) 542-6767	C- / 3.7	4.08	6.01	9.33 /71	7.69 /25	--	5.40	2.49

● Denotes fund is closed to new investors
* Denotes fund is included in Section II

RISK			NET ASSETS		ASSET						BULL / BEAR		FUND MANAGER		MINIMUMS		LOADS	
	3 Year		NAV							Portfolio	Last Bull	Last Bear	Manager	Manager	Initial	Additional	Front	Back
Risk Rating/Pts	Standard Deviation	Beta	As of 3/31/15	Total $(Mil)	Cash %	Stocks %	Bonds %	Other %		Turnover Ratio	Market Return	Market Return	Quality Pct	Tenure (Years)	Purch. $	Purch. $	End Load	End Load
C- / 3.1	10.4	0.69	11.01	59	1	90	8	1		74	67.7	-20.4	92	20	2,000	0	0.0	0.0
D+ / 2.7	10.4	0.69	10.47	495	1	90	8	1		74	73.5	-20.0	94	20	1,000,000	0	0.0	0.0
C- / 3.8	10.4	0.69	12.74	40	1	90	8	1		74	70.5	-20.2	93	20	2,000	0	0.0	0.0
C / 5.0	10.5	0.69	18.94	571	1	90	8	1		74	72.1	-20.2	93	20	2,000	0	0.0	0.0
C+ / 6.5	5.8	0.55	10.38	754	3	48	47	2		53	40.4	-9.9	50	22	1,000,000	0	0.0	0.0
C+ / 6.6	5.8	0.54	10.87	51	3	48	47	2		53	38.1	-10.1	43	22	2,000	0	0.0	0.0
B- / 7.0	5.8	0.55	13.55	771	3	48	47	2		53	39.3	-10.0	46	22	2,000	0	0.0	0.0
C+ / 6.6	5.8	0.55	10.49	160	3	48	47	2		53	35.7	-10.3	35	22	2,000	0	0.0	0.0
U /	N/A	N/A	9.29	57	2	97	0	1		40	N/A	N/A	N/A	6	1,000,000	0	0.0	0.0
D+ / 2.9	12.5	1.00	16.20	244	2	97	0	1		40	91.2	-17.2	70	6	2,000	0	0.0	0.0
B- / 7.1	4.7	0.43	9.56	17	4	37	57	2		39	34.7	-8.9	65	10	1,000,000	0	0.0	0.0
B- / 7.1	4.7	0.43	9.51	31	4	37	57	2		39	33.6	-8.9	61	10	2,000	0	0.0	0.0
B- / 7.1	4.7	0.43	9.43	2	4	37	57	2		39	32.4	-9.0	56	10	2,000	0	0.0	0.0
C+ / 6.3	6.5	0.61	9.79	79	3	54	42	1		37	46.1	-12.0	48	7	1,000,000	0	0.0	0.0
C+ / 6.3	6.5	0.62	9.74	99	3	54	42	1		37	44.9	-12.1	43	7	2,000	0	0.0	0.0
C+ / 6.3	6.5	0.62	9.62	15	3	54	42	1		37	43.7	-12.2	39	7	2,000	0	0.0	0.0
C / 5.3	8.1	0.78	10.22	76	2	70	26	2		27	59.4	-14.7	46	7	1,000,000	0	0.0	0.0
C / 5.3	8.0	0.77	10.13	123	2	70	26	2		27	58.0	-14.8	43	7	2,000	0	0.0	0.0
C / 5.3	8.1	0.78	10.05	16	2	70	26	2		27	56.5	-14.8	38	7	2,000	0	0.0	0.0
C- / 3.8	10.0	0.98	10.57	45	1	84	13	2		22	70.5	-20.2	19	7	1,000,000	0	0.0	0.0
C- / 3.8	10.0	0.98	10.49	87	1	84	13	2		22	68.8	-20.2	17	7	2,000	0	0.0	0.0
C- / 3.8	10.0	0.98	10.42	8	1	84	13	2		22	67.4	-20.3	15	7	2,000	0	0.0	0.0
C- / 4.1	10.4	1.02	11.84	15	1	90	8	1		13	73.1	-20.1	18	7	1,000,000	0	0.0	0.0
C- / 4.1	10.4	1.02	11.74	51	1	90	8	1		13	71.6	-20.2	16	7	2,000	0	0.0	0.0
C- / 4.1	10.4	1.02	11.66	4	1	90	8	1		13	70.2	-20.3	14	7	2,000	0	0.0	0.0
B- / 7.0	4.0	0.64	9.98	14	5	32	61	2		15	28.4	-4.0	54	7	1,000,000	0	0.0	0.0
B- / 7.0	4.0	0.65	9.94	51	5	32	61	2		15	27.3	-4.2	49	7	2,000	0	0.0	0.0
B- / 7.0	4.0	0.65	9.82	2	5	32	61	2		15	26.3	-4.3	44	7	2,000	0	0.0	0.0
D+ / 2.8	11.0	1.06	27.40	27	5	94	0	1		47	86.0	-21.5	35	20	2,000	0	0.0	0.0
C- / 3.1	13.6	0.98	7.43	3,831	3	96	0	1		46	37.3	-27.1	9	19	2,000	0	0.0	0.0
U /	N/A	N/A	10.69	65	0	0	0	100		0	N/A	N/A	N/A	2	1,000,000	0	0.0	0.0
U /	N/A	N/A	10.66	264	0	0	0	100		0	N/A	N/A	N/A	2	2,000	0	0.0	0.0
C+ / 6.3	14.3	0.97	8.89	91	3	96	0	1		44	N/A	N/A	51	4	2,000	0	0.0	0.0
U /	N/A	N/A	10.79	40	0	0	0	100		0	N/A	N/A	N/A	2	1,000,000	0	0.0	0.0
U /	N/A	N/A	9.71	58	0	0	0	100		0	N/A	N/A	N/A	2	1,000,000	0	0.0	0.0
U /	N/A	N/A	9.71	239	0	0	0	100		0	N/A	N/A	N/A	2	2,000	0	0.0	0.0
C+ / 6.6	10.7	1.06	25.55	6	2	97	0	1		22	86.4	-15.4	44	22	1,000	25	0.0	0.0
B- / 7.1	10.3	1.01	20.82	21	5	94	0	1		20	94.5	-15.7	65	16	1,000	25	0.0	0.0
B- / 7.6	8.7	0.88	23.27	67	4	88	7	1		16	73.5	-14.3	41	15	2,500	100	0.0	0.0
B / 8.0	8.7	0.13	9.03	1	75	24	0	1		181	N/A	N/A	12	4	2,500	250	5.5	1.0
B- / 7.9	8.7	0.10	8.90	N/A	75	24	0	1		181	N/A	N/A	10	4	1,000	100		1.0
B / 8.0	8.7	0.13	9.09	16	75	24	0	1		181	N/A	N/A	13	4	100,000	10,000		1.0
C / 5.2	13.8	0.88	10.41	6	19	80	0	1		566	36.4	-21.0	2	14	10,000	50	0.0	0.0
C+ / 5.9	11.2	0.87	22.39	314	0	99	0	1		83	98.2	-25.5	72	4	2,500	100	0.0	0.0
C+ / 5.6	10.1	0.90	17.79	698	4	91	4	1		118	94.6	-18.0	75	3	2,500	100	0.0	0.0
C- / 3.8	10.9	0.96	20.44	913	2	97	0	1		71	97.7	-17.7	62	18	2,500	100	0.0	0.0
C- / 3.5	11.9	0.73	13.61	73	0	99	0	1		129	97.2	-24.3	96	8	2,500	100	0.0	0.0
C- / 3.0	10.9	0.97	21.66	510	3	96	0	1		80	88.5	-17.4	35	18	2,500	100	0.0	0.0
C / 4.8	13.0	0.86	16.01	103	0	99	0	1		178	52.1	-25.2	60	5	2,500	100	0.0	0.0
C+ / 6.7	6.4	1.02	9.68	1	4	72	23	1		83	N/A	N/A	22	4	0	0	0.0	0.0
C+ / 6.9	6.4	1.02	9.70	3	4	72	23	1		83	N/A	N/A	25	4	0	0	0.0	0.0
C+ / 6.7	6.4	1.01	9.69	5	4	72	23	1		83	N/A	N/A	25	4	0	0	0.0	0.0

Data as of March 31, 2015

						PERFORMANCE							
	99 Pct = Best			Overall		Perfor-mance	Total Return % through 3/31/15					Incl. in Returns	
	0 Pct = Worst			Investment						Annualized		Dividend	Expense
Fund Type	Fund Name	Ticker Symbol	Rating	Phone	Rating/Pts	3 Mo	6 Mo	1Yr / Pct	3Yr / Pct	5Yr / Pct	Yield	Ratio
AA	MassMutual Barings Dynamic All Svc	MPBYX	C-	(800) 542-6767	C- / 3.6	4.06	5.94	9.16 /70	7.57 /24	--	4.80	2.59
AA	MassMutual Barings Dynamic Alloc A	MLBAX	D	(800) 542-6767	D+ / 2.4	3.87	5.71	8.73 /68	7.19 /22	--	4.73	2.94
BA	MassMutual Premier Balanced A	MMBDX	C-	(800) 542-6767	C- / 3.1	0.93	3.50	7.30 /57	9.63 /37	9.23 /38	1.18	1.22
BA	MassMutual Premier Balanced Adm	MMBLX	C	(800) 542-6767	C- / 4.2	0.99	3.63	7.50 /59	9.91 /39	9.49 /40	1.56	0.97
BA	MassMutual Premier Balanced I	MBBIX	C+	(800) 542-6767	C / 5.0	1.08	3.76	10.45 /76	11.09 /46	10.35 /47	1.82	0.67
BA	MassMutual Premier Balanced R5	MBLDX	C	(800) 542-6767	C / 4.3	1.08	3.78	7.84 /62	10.20 /40	9.83 /43	1.68	0.77
BA	MassMutual Premier Balanced Svc	MBAYX	C	(800) 542-6767	C- / 4.2	0.96	3.63	7.62 /60	10.03 /39	9.66 /42	1.55	0.87
GR	MassMutual Premier Dsp Growth A	MPGAX	C	(800) 542-6767	B / 7.7	3.44	7.87	14.24 /90	16.36 /86	15.25 /88	0.54	1.09
GR	MassMutual Premier Dsp Growth	MPGLX	C+	(800) 542-6767	B+ / 8.9	3.54	8.03	14.56 /91	16.64 /88	15.55 /90	0.76	0.84
GR	MassMutual Premier Dsp Growth I	MPDIX	A-	(800) 542-6767	A / 9.3	3.58	8.16	16.08 /93	17.35 /92	16.04 /93	1.02	0.54
GR	MassMutual Premier Dsp Growth R5	MPGSX	B-	(800) 542-6767	A- / 9.1	3.58	8.15	14.83 /91	16.93 /89	15.79 /92	0.94	0.64
GR	MassMutual Premier Dsp Growth Svc	DEIGX	C+	(800) 542-6767	A- / 9.0	3.49	8.03	14.60 /91	16.75 /88	15.67 /91	0.86	0.74
GR	MassMutual Premier Dsp Value A	MEPAX	B-	(800) 542-6767	C+ / 6.1	-1.06	3.29	7.09 /56	15.55 /80	12.65 /65	1.18	1.09
GR	MassMutual Premier Dsp Value Adm	MPILX	B+	(800) 542-6767	B- / 7.3	-0.98	3.39	7.38 /58	15.84 /82	12.96 /68	1.52	0.84
GR	MassMutual Premier Dsp Value I	MPIVX	B	(800) 542-6767	B / 7.8	-0.93	3.57	8.31 /65	16.35 /86	13.33 /71	1.80	0.54
GR	MassMutual Premier Dsp Value R3	MPINX	B-	(800) 542-6767	C+ / 6.9	-1.12	3.19	6.96 /55	15.26 /77	12.34 /63	1.10	1.24
GR	MassMutual Premier Dsp Value R5	MEPSX	A-	(800) 542-6767	B- / 7.5	-0.93	3.52	7.68 /60	16.12 /84	13.20 /70	1.68	0.64
GR	MassMutual Premier Dsp Value Svc	DENVX	A-	(800) 542-6767	B- / 7.5	-0.93	3.47	7.52 /59	16.01 /83	13.09 /69	1.63	0.74
GL	MassMutual Premier Global A	MGFAX	C	(800) 542-6767	C+ / 5.6	7.18	6.84	8.44 /66	13.36 /62	10.41 /48	0.56	1.40
GL	MassMutual Premier Global Adm	MGFLX	C+	(800) 542-6767	C+ / 6.8	7.33	6.98	8.71 /68	13.70 /65	10.71 /50	0.88	1.15
GL	MassMutual Premier Global I	MGFZX	C+	(800) 542-6767	B- / 7.4	7.40	7.16	10.14 /75	14.37 /70	11.23 /55	1.17	0.85
GL	MassMutual Premier Global R3	MGFNX	C+	(800) 542-6767	C+ / 6.5	7.23	6.76	8.28 /65	13.28 /62	10.30 /47	0.60	1.55
GL	MassMutual Premier Global R5	MGFSX	C+	(800) 542-6767	B- / 7.0	7.33	7.07	8.94 /69	13.95 /67	10.98 /53	1.09	0.95
GL	MassMutual Premier Global Svc	MGFYX	C+	(800) 542-6767	C+ / 6.9	7.31	6.97	8.78 /68	13.82 /66	10.82 /51	1.03	1.05
FO	MassMutual Premier Intl Equity A	MMIAX	E	(800) 542-6767	D / 1.8	3.86	2.61	-4.83 / 6	8.55 /30	7.89 /29	0.70	1.50
FO	MassMutual Premier Intl Equity Adm	MIELX	E	(800) 542-6767	D+ / 2.8	3.93	2.80	-4.55 / 6	8.82 /32	8.17 /31	0.95	1.25
FO	MassMutual Premier Intl Equity I	MIZIX	D	(800) 542-6767	C- / 3.1	4.07	2.94	-3.81 / 7	9.25 /35	8.50 /33	1.27	0.95
FO	MassMutual Premier Intl Equity R5	MIEDX	E	(800) 542-6767	D+ / 2.9	3.99	2.87	-4.38 / 6	9.03 /33	8.37 /32	1.14	1.05
FO	MassMutual Premier Intl Equity Svc	MYIEX	E	(800) 542-6767	D+ / 2.9	4.00	2.86	-4.47 / 6	8.95 /33	8.32 /32	1.07	1.15
GR	MassMutual Premier Main Street A	MSSAX	C+	(800) 542-6767	C+ / 5.8	1.49	4.58	10.72 /77	14.00 /67	13.30 /71	0.38	1.21
GR	MassMutual Premier Main Street	MMSLX	B-	(800) 542-6767	C+ / 6.9	1.62	4.80	10.98 /78	14.31 /69	13.58 /74	0.63	0.96
GR	MassMutual Premier Main Street I	MSZIX	B-	(800) 542-6767	B- / 7.4	1.69	4.93	12.26 /84	14.90 /74	14.05 /78	0.89	0.66
GR	MassMutual Premier Main Street R3	MMSNX	B-	(800) 542-6767	C+ / 6.6	1.48	4.51	10.52 /76	13.75 /65	13.00 /68	0.29	1.36
GR	MassMutual Premier Main Street R5	MMSSX	B+	(800) 542-6767	B- / 7.1	1.62	4.87	11.20 /79	14.54 /71	13.83 /76	0.83	0.76
GR	MassMutual Premier Main Street Svc	MMSYX	B	(800) 542-6767	B- / 7.0	1.59	4.79	11.04 /78	14.44 /70	13.76 /75	0.75	0.86
SC	MassMutual Premier Sm Cap Opp A	DLBMX	B+	(800) 542-6767	A- / 9.0	3.10	15.58	10.50 /76	18.56 /96	16.09 /93	0.41	1.24
SC	MassMutual Premier Sm Cap Opp	MSCLX	B+	(800) 542-6767	A+ / 9.6	3.12	15.67	10.79 /78	18.85 /96	16.39 /94	0.75	0.99
SC	MassMutual Premier Sm Cap Opp I	MSOOX	B+	(800) 542-6767	A+ / 9.7	3.17	15.83	12.53 /85	19.63 /97	16.91 /96	0.95	0.69
SC	MassMutual Premier Sm Cap Opp R5	MSCDX	B+	(800) 542-6767	A+ / 9.6	3.17	15.78	10.99 /78	19.08 /97	16.59 /95	0.85	0.79
SC	MassMutual Premier Sm Cap Opp	MSVYX	B+	(800) 542-6767	A+ / 9.6	3.17	15.76	10.90 /78	18.96 /97	16.47 /95	0.83	0.89
EM	MassMutual Premier Str Em Mkts A	MPASX	E	(800) 542-6767	E- / 0.2	-1.26	-7.96	-4.80 / 6	-3.24 / 2	-1.97 / 2	0.85	1.93
EM	MassMutual Premier Str Em Mkts	MPLSX	E	(800) 542-6767	E / 0.3	-1.16	-7.87	-4.57 / 6	-3.00 / 2	-1.71 / 2	0.92	1.68
EM	MassMutual Premier Str Em Mkts I	MPZSX	E	(800) 542-6767	E / 0.3	-1.08	-7.73	-4.26 / 7	-2.63 / 3	--	1.27	1.38
EM	MassMutual Premier Str Em Mkts R5	MPSMX	E	(800) 542-6767	E / 0.3	-1.15	-7.84	-4.41 / 6	-2.79 / 2	-1.51 / 2	1.13	1.48
EM	MassMutual Premier Str Em Mkts Svc	MPEYX	E	(800) 542-6767	E / 0.3	-1.17	-7.85	-4.45 / 6	-2.88 / 2	-1.59 / 2	1.08	1.58
GR	MassMutual Premier Value A	MCEAX	C+	(800) 542-6767	C / 5.3	-0.09	3.77	8.05 /63	13.88 /66	11.09 /53	1.28	1.23
GR	MassMutual Premier Value Adm	DLBVX	B-	(800) 542-6767	C+ / 6.5	-0.05	3.82	8.31 /65	14.17 /68	11.38 /56	1.60	0.98
GR	MassMutual Premier Value I	MCZIX	C+	(800) 542-6767	C+ / 6.9	0.00	4.01	9.27 /71	14.70 /72	11.77 /59	1.91	0.68
GR	MassMutual Premier Value R3	MCENX	B-	(800) 542-6767	C+ / 6.1	-0.14	3.67	7.86 /62	13.57 /64	10.77 /51	1.21	1.38
GR	MassMutual Premier Value R5	MVEDX	B-	(800) 542-6767	C+ / 6.7	0.00	3.99	8.50 /66	14.43 /70	11.62 /58	1.80	0.78
GR	MassMutual Premier Value Svc	MCEYX	B-	(800) 542-6767	C+ / 6.6	0.00	3.89	8.43 /66	14.30 /69	11.50 /57	1.72	0.88
AA	MassMutual RetireSMART 2010 A	MRXAX	C-	(800) 542-6767	D- / 1.4	1.72	2.77	3.86 /31	6.30 /18	6.76 /22	2.31	1.30

RISK			NET ASSETS		ASSET					BULL / BEAR		FUND MANAGER		MINIMUMS		LOADS	
	3 Year		NAV						Portfolio	Last Bull	Last Bear	Manager	Manager	Initial	Additional	Front	Back
Risk	Standard		As of	Total	Cash	Stocks	Bonds	Other	Turnover	Market	Market	Quality	Tenure	Purch.	Purch.	End	End
Rating/Pts	Deviation	Beta	3/31/15	$(Mil)	%	%	%	%	Ratio	Return	Return	Pct	(Years)	$	$	Load	Load
C+ / 6.5	6.3	1.01	9.73	1	4	72	23	1	83	N/A	N/A	24	4	0	0	0.0	0.0
C+ / 6.5	6.4	1.02	9.67	1	4	72	23	1	83	N/A	N/A	19	4	0	0	5.8	0.0
B- / 7.0	6.1	1.08	11.91	35	0	61	38	1	192	53.8	-10.4	38	15	0	0	5.8	0.0
C+ / 6.9	6.1	1.08	12.20	9	0	61	38	1	192	55.1	-10.3	41	15	0	0	0.0	0.0
C+ / 6.9	6.2	1.07	12.15	38	0	61	38	1	192	60.5	-10.1	59	15	0	0	0.0	0.0
C+ / 6.9	6.1	1.08	12.16	73	0	61	38	1	192	56.7	-10.1	46	15	0	0	0.0	0.0
B- / 7.0	6.2	1.09	12.65	14	0	61	38	1	192	55.9	-10.2	42	15	0	0	0.0	0.0
C- / 3.9	10.0	1.02	12.02	42	0	99	0	1	142	102.9	-16.0	67	15	0	0	5.8	0.0
C- / 3.9	10.0	1.02	12.27	34	0	99	0	1	142	104.6	-15.8	70	15	0	0	0.0	0.0
C+ / 5.7	9.9	1.01	12.14	209	0	99	0	1	142	108.4	-15.8	76	15	0	0	0.0	0.0
C- / 3.8	9.9	1.01	12.15	121	0	99	0	1	142	106.2	-15.8	73	15	0	0	0.0	0.0
C- / 3.9	9.9	1.01	12.17	92	0	99	0	1	142	105.3	-15.8	71	15	0	0	0.0	0.0
B- / 7.4	10.1	1.03	15.82	10	0	99	0	1	92	93.8	-18.5	54	15	0	0	5.8	0.0
B- / 7.4	10.1	1.02	16.19	9	0	99	0	1	92	95.7	-18.4	59	15	0	0	0.0	0.0
C+ / 5.7	10.1	1.02	16.02	198	0	99	0	1	92	98.2	-18.3	66	15	0	0	0.0	0.0
B- / 7.4	10.1	1.03	15.93	N/A	0	99	0	1	92	92.1	-18.6	50	15	0	0	0.0	0.0
B- / 7.4	10.1	1.02	16.04	68	0	99	0	1	92	97.1	-18.3	62	15	0	0	0.0	0.0
B- / 7.4	10.1	1.02	15.94	72	0	99	0	1	92	96.3	-18.3	62	15	0	0	0.0	0.0
C+ / 5.6	12.1	0.87	15.08	46	1	98	0	1	27	75.5	-23.3	93	11	0	0	5.8	0.0
C+ / 5.6	12.1	0.87	15.22	134	1	98	0	1	27	77.2	-23.1	93	11	0	0	0.0	0.0
C / 5.2	12.1	0.87	15.23	N/A	1	98	0	1	27	80.6	-23.1	94	11	0	0	0.0	0.0
C+ / 5.6	12.1	0.87	15.12	2	1	98	0	1	27	75.0	-23.3	93	11	0	0	0.0	0.0
C+ / 5.6	12.1	0.87	15.23	212	1	98	0	1	27	78.7	-23.1	94	11	0	0	0.0	0.0
C+ / 5.6	12.1	0.87	15.12	29	1	98	0	1	27	78.0	-23.2	94	11	0	0	0.0	0.0
D / 2.1	12.6	0.91	11.84	54	1	98	0	1	76	55.1	-20.9	66	17	0	0	5.8	0.0
D / 2.2	12.6	0.91	12.17	21	1	98	0	1	76	56.4	-20.8	69	17	0	0	0.0	0.0
C / 5.1	12.7	0.92	12.26	95	1	98	0	1	76	58.3	-20.7	73	17	0	0	0.0	0.0
D / 2.2	12.7	0.91	12.26	340	1	98	0	1	76	57.4	-20.7	71	17	0	0	0.0	0.0
D / 2.2	12.7	0.91	12.23	23	1	98	0	1	76	57.2	-20.7	70	17	0	0	0.0	0.0
B- / 7.0	10.1	1.03	14.34	14	2	97	0	1	53	92.6	-15.5	33	6	0	0	5.8	0.0
B- / 7.0	10.1	1.03	14.46	34	2	97	0	1	53	94.1	-15.3	37	6	0	0	0.0	0.0
C+ / 5.7	10.1	1.03	14.48	51	2	97	0	1	53	97.4	-15.2	45	6	0	0	0.0	0.0
B- / 7.0	10.1	1.03	14.43	N/A	2	97	0	1	53	90.8	-15.5	31	6	0	0	0.0	0.0
B- / 7.0	10.1	1.03	14.47	102	2	97	0	1	53	95.7	-15.2	40	6	0	0	0.0	0.0
B- / 7.0	10.1	1.03	14.66	7	2	97	0	1	53	95.2	-15.3	39	6	0	0	0.0	0.0
C / 5.1	12.8	0.92	15.28	77	2	97	0	1	66	117.3	-23.5	89	6	0	0	5.8	0.0
C / 5.1	12.8	0.92	15.52	21	2	97	0	1	66	119.0	-23.4	90	6	0	0	0.0	0.0
C / 5.1	12.6	0.90	15.62	5	2	97	0	1	66	123.6	-23.4	92	6	0	0	0.0	0.0
C / 5.1	12.8	0.92	15.62	82	2	97	0	1	66	120.5	-23.4	91	6	0	0	0.0	0.0
C / 5.1	12.8	0.92	15.61	8	2	97	0	1	66	119.8	-23.4	90	6	0	0	0.0	0.0
C / 4.3	14.9	1.05	10.98	1	6	93	0	1	108	7.5	-27.8	16	2	0	0	5.8	0.0
C / 4.4	14.9	1.05	11.09	1	6	93	0	1	108	8.4	-27.7	18	2	0	0	0.0	0.0
C / 4.4	14.9	1.05	11.03	148	6	93	0	1	108	9.9	-27.6	21	2	0	0	0.0	0.0
C / 4.4	14.9	1.05	11.16	9	6	93	0	1	108	9.3	-27.6	20	2	0	0	0.0	0.0
C / 4.4	14.9	1.05	11.02	8	6	93	0	1	108	8.9	-27.7	19	2	0	0	0.0	0.0
B- / 7.1	10.3	1.04	21.43	8	0	99	0	1	43	80.8	-21.1	30	2	0	0	5.8	0.0
B- / 7.1	10.2	1.04	21.43	14	0	99	0	1	43	82.6	-21.0	34	2	0	0	0.0	0.0
C / 5.5	10.2	1.04	21.37	N/A	0	99	0	1	43	85.3	-21.0	40	2	0	0	0.0	0.0
B- / 7.1	10.3	1.04	21.32	N/A	0	99	0	1	43	79.2	-21.2	27	2	0	0	0.0	0.0
B- / 7.1	10.3	1.04	21.37	64	0	99	0	1	43	83.9	-21.0	37	2	0	0	0.0	0.0
B- / 7.1	10.2	1.04	21.45	N/A	0	99	0	1	43	83.2	-21.0	36	2	0	0	0.0	0.0
B / 8.6	5.4	0.88	11.86	27	0	37	61	2	47	35.6	-10.0	26	12	0	0	5.8	0.0

						PERFORMANCE							
	99 Pct = Best					Perfor-	Total Return % through 3/31/15					Incl. in Returns	
	0 Pct = Worst			Overall		mance				Annualized		Dividend	Expense
Fund		Ticker	Investment		Rating/Pts	3 Mo	6 Mo	1Yr / Pct	3Yr / Pct	5Yr / Pct	Yield	Ratio
Type	Fund Name	Symbol	Rating	Phone								
AA	MassMutual RetireSMART 2010 Adm	MRXYX	C-	(800) 542-6767	D / 2.2	1.79	2.84	4.04 /32	6.60 /19	7.11 /24	2.90	1.05
AA	MassMutual RetireSMART 2010 R3	MRXNX	C-	(800) 542-6767	D / 1.9	1.74	2.72	3.73 /30	6.05 /17	6.49 /20	2.93	1.45
AA	MassMutual RetireSMART 2010 Svc	MRXSX	C	(800) 542-6767	D+ / 2.3	1.87	2.92	4.26 /33	6.78 /20	7.24 /25	2.76	0.95
GL	MassMutual RetireSMART 2015 A	MMJAX	C-	(800) 542-6767	D / 1.8	1.84	2.96	4.01 /32	7.44 /24	--	2.11	2.20
GL	MassMutual RetireSMART 2015 Adm	MMJYX	C	(800) 542-6767	D+ / 2.8	1.91	3.16	4.28 /34	7.78 /26	--	2.51	1.95
GL	MassMutual RetireSMART 2015 Svc	MMJSX	C	(800) 542-6767	D+ / 2.9	1.91	3.17	4.38 /34	7.87 /26	--	2.43	1.85
AA	MassMutual RetireSMART 2020 A	MRTAX	C-	(800) 542-6767	D+ / 2.3	1.96	3.23	4.14 /33	8.57 /30	8.35 /32	1.85	1.23
AA	MassMutual RetireSMART 2020	MRTYX	C	(800) 542-6767	C- / 3.4	1.95	3.29	4.34 /34	8.91 /32	8.70 /35	2.42	0.98
AA	MassMutual RetireSMART 2020 I	MRTDX	U	(800) 542-6767	U /	2.11	3.53	--	--	--	0.00	N/A
AA	MassMutual RetireSMART 2020 R3	MRTNX	C	(800) 542-6767	C- / 3.1	1.83	3.12	3.94 /31	8.28 /29	8.06 /30	2.49	1.38
AA	MassMutual RetireSMART 2020 Svc	MRTSX	C	(800) 542-6767	C- / 3.5	2.03	3.37	4.48 /35	9.02 /33	8.79 /35	2.31	0.88
GL	MassMutual RetireSMART 2025 A	MMSDX	C-	(800) 542-6767	D+ / 2.7	2.07	3.34	4.11 /33	9.35 /35	--	2.13	2.20
GL	MassMutual RetireSMART 2025	MMIYX	C	(800) 542-6767	C- / 3.9	2.14	3.53	4.38 /34	9.69 /37	--	2.45	1.95
GL	MassMutual RetireSMART 2025 R3	MMNRX	U	(800) 542-6767	U /	2.07	3.33	--	--	--	0.00	2.35
GL	MassMutual RetireSMART 2025	MMISX	C	(800) 542-6767	C- / 3.9	2.13	3.48	4.49 /35	9.76 /38	--	2.40	1.85
AA	MassMutual RetireSMART 2030 A	MRYAX	C-	(800) 542-6767	D+ / 2.9	2.17	3.52	4.11 /33	9.72 /38	9.14 /38	3.60	1.26
AA	MassMutual RetireSMART 2030 Adm	MRYYX	C	(800) 542-6767	C- / 4.1	2.24	3.64	4.39 /34	10.09 /40	9.52 /41	4.17	1.01
AA	MassMutual RetireSMART 2030 I	MRYUX	U	(800) 542-6767	U /	2.32	3.72	--	--	--	0.00	N/A
AA	MassMutual RetireSMART 2030 R3	MRYNX	C	(800) 542-6767	C- / 3.7	2.12	3.47	3.99 /32	9.49 /36	8.88 /36	4.10	1.41
AA	MassMutual RetireSMART 2030 Svc	MRYSX	C	(800) 542-6767	C- / 4.1	2.24	3.66	4.50 /35	10.19 /40	9.59 /41	4.20	0.91
GL	MassMutual RetireSMART 2035 A	MMXAX	C-	(800) 542-6767	C- / 3.1	2.25	3.73	4.31 /34	10.04 /40	--	1.95	2.46
GL	MassMutual RetireSMART 2035	MMXYX	C	(800) 542-6767	C- / 4.2	2.31	3.81	4.55 /35	10.36 /42	--	2.31	2.21
GL	MassMutual RetireSMART 2035 Svc	MMXSX	C	(800) 542-6767	C / 4.3	2.31	3.79	4.61 /36	10.44 /42	--	2.22	2.11
AA	MassMutual RetireSMART 2040 A	MRFAX	C-	(800) 542-6767	C- / 3.1	2.19	3.66	4.34 /34	10.01 /39	9.38 /40	3.14	1.29
AA	MassMutual RetireSMART 2040 Adm	MRFYX	C	(800) 542-6767	C / 4.3	2.26	3.88	4.63 /36	10.38 /42	9.72 /42	3.70	1.04
AA	MassMutual RetireSMART 2040 I	MRFUX	U	(800) 542-6767	U /	2.34	4.04	--	--	--	0.00	N/A
AA	MassMutual RetireSMART 2040 R3	MFRNX	C	(800) 542-6767	C- / 3.9	2.22	3.72	4.24 /33	9.80 /38	9.10 /37	3.62	1.44
AA	MassMutual RetireSMART 2040 Svc	MFRSX	C	(800) 542-6767	C / 4.3	2.33	3.97	4.73 /37	10.52 /42	9.84 /43	3.71	0.94
GL	MassMutual RetireSMART 2045 A	MMKAX	C-	(800) 542-6767	C- / 3.5	2.25	3.93	4.54 /35	10.77 /44	--	1.87	3.50
GL	MassMutual RetireSMART 2045 adm	MMKYX	C	(800) 542-6767	C / 4.7	2.39	4.09	4.77 /37	11.12 /46	--	2.22	3.25
GL	MassMutual RetireSMART 2045 Svc	MMKSX	C	(800) 542-6767	C / 4.7	2.39	4.11	4.87 /38	11.19 /47	--	2.16	3.15
AA	MassMutual RetireSMART 2050 A	MMARX	D+	(800) 542-6767	C- / 3.5	2.35	3.91	4.54 /35	10.77 /44	9.85 /43	1.73	1.48
AA	MassMutual RetireSMART 2050	MMRYX	C-	(800) 542-6767	C / 4.7	2.34	4.11	4.84 /37	11.15 /47	10.27 /47	2.12	1.23
AA	MassMutual RetireSMART 2050 R3	MMRNX	C-	(800) 542-6767	C / 4.3	2.25	3.86	4.39 /34	10.49 /42	9.55 /41	1.98	1.63
AA	MassMutual RetireSMART 2050 Svc	MMTSX	C-	(800) 542-6767	C / 4.7	2.34	4.12	4.74 /37	11.16 /47	10.24 /46	2.13	1.13
GL	MassMutual RetireSMART Consv A	MCTAX	D	(800) 542-6767	D- / 1.0	1.44	2.36	3.73 /30	5.00 /13	--	2.17	1.16
GL	MassMutual RetireSMART Consv	MRCLX	D+	(800) 542-6767	D / 1.6	1.64	2.65	4.02 /32	5.29 /14	--	2.56	0.91
GI	MassMutual RetireSMART Consv I	MRCUX	C-	(800) 542-6767	D / 1.8	1.64	2.73	4.51 /35	5.55 /15	--	2.84	N/A
GL	MassMutual RetireSMART Consv R5	MRCSX	D+	(800) 542-6767	D / 1.7	1.64	2.73	4.21 /33	5.45 /15	--	2.74	0.71
GL	MassMutual RetireSMART Consv	MRCYX	D+	(800) 542-6767	D / 1.7	1.65	2.67	4.15 /33	5.38 /14	--	2.69	0.81
GL	MassMutual RetireSMART Growth A	MRRAX	D	(800) 542-6767	C- / 3.6	2.31	3.99	4.55 /35	10.93 /45	--	1.75	1.41
GL	MassMutual RetireSMART Growth	MRGLX	D+	(800) 542-6767	C / 4.7	2.31	4.08	4.72 /37	11.17 /47	--	2.09	1.16
GI	MassMutual RetireSMART Growth I	MRGUX	C-	(800) 542-6767	C / 5.1	2.50	4.30	5.97 /46	11.69 /50	--	2.35	N/A
GL	MassMutual RetireSMART Growth	MRRSX	D+	(800) 542-6767	C / 4.8	2.41	4.18	4.99 /38	11.34 /48	--	2.25	0.96
GL	MassMutual RetireSMART Growth	MRGYX	D+	(800) 542-6767	C / 4.8	2.41	4.20	4.93 /38	11.30 /48	--	2.19	1.06
AA	MassMutual RetireSMART In Ret A	MRDAX	C-	(800) 542-6767	D- / 1.0	1.46	2.30	3.41 /29	5.05 /13	5.90 /16	1.90	1.32
AA	MassMutual RetireSMART In Ret	MDRYX	C-	(800) 542-6767	D / 1.6	1.54	2.47	3.76 /30	5.41 /15	6.25 /18	2.45	1.07
AA	MassMutual RetireSMART In Ret R3	MDRNX	C-	(800) 542-6767	D- / 1.4	1.47	2.23	3.39 /28	4.85 /13	5.64 /15	2.54	1.47
AA	MassMutual RetireSMART In Ret Svc	MDRSX	C-	(800) 542-6767	D / 1.7	1.63	2.47	3.89 /31	5.49 /15	6.31 /19	2.39	0.97
GL	MassMutual RetireSMART Modt A	MRMAX	D	(800) 542-6767	D / 1.9	1.83	3.12	4.14 /33	7.69 /25	--	2.11	1.19
GL	MassMutual RetireSMART Modt Adm	MRMLX	D+	(800) 542-6767	D+ / 2.9	1.93	3.30	4.43 /35	7.96 /27	--	2.50	0.94
GL	MassMutual RetireSMART Modt Gro	MOGAX	D-	(800) 542-6767	C- / 3.0	2.19	3.54	4.22 /33	9.81 /38	--	1.99	1.26

RISK			NET ASSETS		ASSET				Portfolio Turnover Ratio	BULL / BEAR		FUND MANAGER		MINIMUMS		LOADS	
Risk Rating/Pts	3 Year		NAV As of 3/31/15	Total $(Mil)	Cash %	Stocks %	Bonds %	Other %		Last Bull Market Return	Last Bear Market Return	Manager Quality Pct	Manager Tenure (Years)	Initial Purch. $	Additional Purch. $	Front End Load	Back End Load
	Standard Deviation	Beta															
B / 8.5	5.3	0.86	11.94	24	0	37	61	2	47	37.0	-9.9	31	12	0	0	0.0	0.0
B / 8.5	5.3	0.86	11.70	8	0	37	61	2	47	34.3	-10.0	25	12	0	0	0.0	0.0
B / 8.6	5.2	0.86	11.97	34	0	37	61	2	47	37.4	-9.7	33	12	0	0	0.0	0.0
B / 8.1	6.2	0.44	11.62	22	0	47	52	1	67	44.3	-13.3	89	5	0	0	5.8	0.0
B / 8.1	6.2	0.44	11.71	10	0	47	52	1	67	45.9	-13.2	90	5	0	0	0.0	0.0
B / 8.1	6.2	0.44	11.74	11	0	47	52	1	67	46.2	-13.2	90	5	0	0	0.0	0.0
B / 8.1	7.4	1.23	12.46	108	0	59	40	1	45	51.9	-15.7	13	12	0	0	5.8	0.0
B / 8.1	7.4	1.23	12.56	144	0	59	40	1	45	53.5	-15.6	15	12	0	0	0.0	0.0
U /	N/A	N/A	12.60	49	0	59	40	1	45	N/A	N/A	N/A	9	0	0	0.0	0.0
B / 8.1	7.4	1.23	12.21	56	0	59	40	1	45	50.6	-15.8	11	12	0	0	0.0	0.0
B / 8.1	7.4	1.23	12.59	200	0	59	40	1	45	54.1	-15.6	15	12	0	0	0.0	0.0
B- / 7.4	8.4	0.58	12.33	37	0	70	29	1	55	58.1	-17.7	90	5	0	0	5.8	0.0
B- / 7.4	8.4	0.58	12.43	29	0	70	29	1	55	59.9	-17.6	91	5	0	0	0.0	0.0
U /	N/A	N/A	12.31	26	0	70	29	1	55	N/A	N/A	N/A	N/A	0	0	0.0	0.0
B- / 7.4	8.4	0.59	12.45	17	0	70	29	1	55	60.3	-17.6	91	5	0	0	0.0	0.0
B- / 7.4	8.8	1.47	12.72	93	0	76	22	2	43	61.1	-18.4	7	12	0	0	5.8	0.0
B- / 7.3	8.8	1.47	12.79	135	0	76	22	2	43	62.8	-18.2	8	12	0	0	0.0	0.0
U /	N/A	N/A	12.80	56	0	76	22	2	43	N/A	N/A	N/A	9	0	0	0.0	0.0
B- / 7.3	8.9	1.48	12.54	66	0	76	22	2	43	59.6	-18.4	6	12	0	0	0.0	0.0
B- / 7.3	8.8	1.48	12.80	205	0	76	22	2	43	63.4	-18.3	8	12	0	0	0.0	0.0
B- / 7.1	9.2	1.42	12.73	27	2	79	17	2	36	63.1	-18.9	29	5	0	0	5.8	0.0
B- / 7.1	9.2	1.42	12.82	20	2	79	17	2	36	65.0	-18.8	33	5	0	0	0.0	0.0
B- / 7.1	9.2	1.42	12.85	11	2	79	17	2	36	65.4	-18.8	34	5	0	0	0.0	0.0
B- / 7.0	9.3	1.55	12.60	55	1	81	16	2	45	63.7	-19.1	5	12	0	0	5.8	0.0
B- / 7.0	9.3	1.55	12.68	90	1	81	16	2	45	65.5	-19.0	6	12	0	0	0.0	0.0
U /	N/A	N/A	12.70	47	1	81	16	2	45	N/A	N/A	N/A	9	0	0	0.0	0.0
B- / 7.0	9.3	1.55	12.42	26	1	81	16	2	45	62.1	-19.2	5	12	0	0	0.0	0.0
B- / 7.0	9.3	1.56	12.71	125	1	81	16	2	45	66.0	-19.0	6	12	0	0	0.0	0.0
C+ / 6.7	9.9	1.51	12.74	15	4	86	8	2	39	69.1	-20.5	28	5	0	0	5.8	0.0
C+ / 6.7	9.9	1.51	12.84	8	4	86	8	2	39	70.9	-20.4	31	5	0	0	0.0	0.0
C+ / 6.7	9.9	1.51	12.86	7	4	86	8	2	39	71.2	-20.3	32	5	0	0	0.0	0.0
C+ / 5.6	9.9	1.65	9.13	16	3	89	7	1	45	68.8	-20.2	5	N/A	0	0	5.8	0.0
C+ / 5.6	9.9	1.65	9.18	42	3	89	7	1	45	71.1	-20.1	5	N/A	0	0	0.0	0.0
C+ / 5.6	9.9	1.66	9.07	14	3	89	7	1	45	67.3	-20.4	4	N/A	0	0	0.0	0.0
C+ / 5.6	9.9	1.66	9.18	26	3	89	7	1	45	70.7	-20.0	5	N/A	0	0	0.0	0.0
B / 8.0	3.9	0.58	9.88	127	0	25	73	2	37	26.1	N/A	66	4	0	0	5.8	0.0
B- / 7.9	3.9	0.58	9.89	68	0	25	73	2	37	27.1	N/A	69	4	0	0	0.0	0.0
B / 8.5	3.8	0.31	9.89	N/A	0	25	73	2	37	28.3	N/A	75	4	0	0	0.0	0.0
B- / 7.9	3.8	0.57	9.89	4	0	25	73	2	37	27.8	N/A	72	4	0	0	0.0	0.0
B- / 7.9	3.8	0.56	9.88	20	0	25	73	2	37	27.6	N/A	71	4	0	0	0.0	0.0
C / 5.0	10.1	0.70	11.05	60	5	90	4	1	36	70.2	N/A	92	4	0	0	5.8	0.0
C / 5.0	10.0	0.69	11.06	43	5	90	4	1	36	71.7	N/A	92	4	0	0	0.0	0.0
C+ / 5.6	10.1	1.00	11.06	N/A	5	90	4	1	36	73.9	N/A	18	4	0	0	0.0	0.0
C / 5.0	10.1	0.70	11.06	6	5	90	4	1	36	72.4	N/A	92	4	0	0	0.0	0.0
C / 5.0	10.1	0.70	11.06	5	5	90	4	1	36	72.3	N/A	92	4	0	0	0.0	0.0
B / 8.9	4.3	0.68	11.11	22	0	28	70	2	41	27.4	-6.5	36	12	0	0	5.8	0.0
B / 8.8	4.2	0.66	11.19	33	0	28	70	2	41	28.8	-6.4	44	12	0	0	0.0	0.0
B / 8.8	4.3	0.67	11.02	6	0	28	70	2	41	26.4	-6.6	34	12	0	0	0.0	0.0
B / 8.8	4.3	0.67	11.19	22	0	28	70	2	41	29.3	-6.3	43	12	0	0	0.0	0.0
C+ / 6.4	6.4	0.45	10.02	199	0	53	46	1	37	44.6	N/A	90	4	0	0	5.8	0.0
C+ / 6.4	6.4	0.45	10.01	141	0	53	46	1	37	45.7	N/A	90	4	0	0	0.0	0.0
C / 5.0	8.8	1.36	10.28	154	3	77	19	1	36	61.2	N/A	32	4	0	0	5.8	0.0

Fund Type	Fund Name	Ticker Symbol	Overall Investment Rating	Phone	Performance Rating/Pts	3 Mo	6 Mo	1Yr / Pct	3Yr / Pct	5Yr / Pct	Dividend Yield	Expense Ratio
	99 Pct = Best 0 Pct = Worst				PERFORMANCE			Total Return % through 3/31/15			Incl. in Returns	
									Annualized			
GL	MassMutual RetireSMART Modt Gro	MRSLX	D	(800) 542-6767	C- / 4.1	2.19	3.67	4.43 /35	10.05 /40	--	2.39	1.01
GI	MassMutual RetireSMART Modt Gro I	MROUX	C-	(800) 542-6767	C / 4.4	2.30	3.79	5.48 /42	10.51 /42	--	2.67	N/A
GL	MassMutual RetireSMART Modt Gro	MRSSX	D	(800) 542-6767	C- / 4.2	2.30	3.70	4.65 /36	10.23 /41	--	2.58	0.81
GL	MassMutual RetireSMART Modt Gro	MROYX	D	(800) 542-6767	C- / 4.2	2.30	3.71	4.57 /36	10.19 /40	--	2.51	0.91
GI	MassMutual RetireSMART Modt I	MRMUX	C-	(800) 542-6767	C- / 3.2	2.04	3.42	5.23 /40	8.28 /29	--	2.79	N/A
GL	MassMutual RetireSMART Modt R5	MROSX	D+	(800) 542-6767	C- / 3.0	2.04	3.33	4.65 /36	8.09 /27	--	2.70	0.74
GL	MassMutual RetireSMART Modt Svc	MRMYX	D+	(800) 542-6767	C- / 3.0	1.94	3.32	4.54 /35	8.05 /27	--	2.60	0.84
MC	MassMutual Sel S and P MC Idx A	MDKAX	U	(800) 542-6767	U /	5.14	11.57	11.37 /80	--	--	0.57	0.86
MC	MassMutual Sel S and P MC Idx Adm	MDKYX	U	(800) 542-6767	U /	5.21	11.80	11.69 /81	--	--	0.80	0.61
MC	MassMutual Sel S and P MC Idx I	MDKZX	U	(800) 542-6767	U /	5.26	11.92	11.99 /82	--	--	1.02	0.26
SC	MassMutual Sel Small Cap Val Eq A	MMQAX	B	(800) 542-6767	B / 8.0	4.39	14.71	9.37 /71	16.74 /88	15.04 /87	0.14	1.46
SC	MassMutual Sel Small Cap Val Eq	MMQLX	A-	(800) 542-6767	A- / 9.1	4.45	14.93	9.66 /73	17.03 /90	15.28 /89	0.36	1.21
SC	MassMutual Sel Small Cap Val Eq I	MMQIX	B+	(800) 542-6767	A / 9.4	4.51	15.12	11.39 /80	17.85 /94	15.92 /93	0.65	N/A
SC	MassMutual Sel Small Cap Val Eq R5	MMQSX	A-	(800) 542-6767	A- / 9.2	4.50	14.98	9.87 /74	17.31 /91	15.60 /91	0.55	1.01
SC	MassMutual Sel Small Cap Val Eq	MMQYX	A-	(800) 542-6767	A- / 9.2	4.49	14.98	9.73 /73	17.21 /91	15.51 /90	0.22	1.11
GL	MassMutual Select BlackRock GA A	MGJAX	D	(800) 542-6767	D- / 1.4	2.62	1.88	3.72 /30	6.46 /19	6.00 /17	1.71	1.47
GL	MassMutual Select BlackRock GA	MGSLX	D	(800) 542-6767	D / 2.2	2.63	1.99	4.03 /32	6.70 /20	6.34 /19	1.98	1.22
GL	MassMutual Select BlackRock GA I	MGJIX	D+	(800) 542-6767	D+ / 2.5	2.80	2.14	4.76 /37	7.15 /22	6.65 /21	2.37	N/A
GL	MassMutual Select BlackRock GA R5	MGSSX	D+	(800) 542-6767	D+ / 2.4	2.67	2.07	4.08 /32	6.92 /21	6.51 /20	0.98	1.02
GL	MassMutual Select BlackRock GA	MGSYX	D	(800) 542-6767	D+ / 2.3	2.71	2.02	4.11 /33	6.87 /21	6.42 /20	2.17	1.12
GR	MassMutual Select Blue Chip Gr A	MBCGX	B	(800) 542-6767	B+ / 8.4	4.93	9.23	15.48 /92	16.93 /89	16.36 /94	0.00	1.23
GR	MassMutual Select Blue Chip Gr Adm	MBCLX	B+	(800) 542-6767	A / 9.3	5.02	9.38	15.80 /93	17.17 /91	16.61 /95	0.00	0.98
GR	MassMutual Select Blue Chip Gr I	MBCZX	A-	(800) 542-6767	A+ / 9.6	5.05	9.52	18.06 /96	18.12 /95	17.26 /96	0.00	N/A
GR	MassMutual Select Blue Chip Gr R3	MBCNX	B+	(800) 542-6767	A- / 9.0	4.89	9.16	15.30 /92	16.60 /87	16.00 /93	0.00	1.38
GR	MassMutual Select Blue Chip Gr R5	MBCSX	B+	(800) 542-6767	A / 9.3	4.99	9.47	16.00 /93	17.43 /92	16.85 /96	0.00	0.78
GR	MassMutual Select Blue Chip Gr Svc	MBCYX	B+	(800) 542-6767	A / 9.3	4.96	9.40	15.91 /93	17.33 /92	16.77 /95	0.00	0.88
FO	MassMutual Select Dvsfd Intl A	MMZAX	E+	(800) 542-6767	E+ / 0.9	4.19	-0.81	-4.63 / 6	5.85 /16	2.52 / 5	2.81	1.50
FO	MassMutual Select Dvsfd Intl Adm	MMZLX	E+	(800) 542-6767	D- / 1.4	4.33	-0.74	-4.41 / 6	5.92 /16	2.63 / 5	3.42	1.25
FO	MassMutual Select Dvsfd Intl I	MMZIX	E+	(800) 542-6767	D / 1.7	4.35	-0.56	-3.23 / 8	6.68 /20	3.16 / 6	3.75	N/A
FO	MassMutual Select Dvsfd Intl R5	MMZSX	E+	(800) 542-6767	D- / 1.5	4.19	-0.67	-4.22 / 7	6.31 /18	2.95 / 6	3.65	1.05
FO	MassMutual Select Dvsfd Intl Svc	MMZYX	E+	(800) 542-6767	D- / 1.5	4.39	-0.58	-4.18 / 7	6.23 /18	2.77 / 6	3.49	1.15
GI	MassMutual Select Dvsfd Value A	MDDAX	B-	(800) 542-6767	C+ / 6.3	-0.74	3.41	7.97 /63	15.81 /82	13.01 /68	1.33	1.10
GI	MassMutual Select Dvsfd Value Adm	MDDLX	A-	(800) 542-6767	B / 7.6	-0.67	3.55	8.23 /64	16.11 /84	13.33 /71	1.76	0.85
GI	MassMutual Select Dvsfd Value I	MDDIX	B	(800) 542-6767	B / 8.0	-0.61	3.74	9.00 /69	16.56 /87	13.66 /75	2.00	N/A
GI	MassMutual Select Dvsfd Value R3	MDVNX	B+	(800) 542-6767	B- / 7.2	-0.74	3.36	7.83 /62	15.50 /79	12.71 /66	1.30	1.25
GI	MassMutual Select Dvsfd Value R5	MDVSX	A	(800) 542-6767	B / 7.8	-0.67	3.64	8.43 /66	16.36 /86	13.54 /73	1.91	0.65
GI	MassMutual Select Dvsfd Value Svc	MDVYX	A-	(800) 542-6767	B / 7.7	-0.67	3.62	8.33 /65	16.26 /85	13.46 /72	1.82	0.75
GR	MassMutual Select Focused Value A	MFVAX	C+	(800) 542-6767	B- / 7.0	-1.89	3.76	10.79 /78	16.62 /88	14.82 /85	1.30	1.29
GR	MassMutual Select Focused Value	MMFVX	B-	(800) 542-6767	B+ / 8.3	-1.88	3.86	11.00 /78	16.91 /89	15.11 /88	1.56	1.04
MC	MassMutual Select Focused Value I	MFVZX	B	(800) 542-6767	B+ / 8.6	-1.81	4.05	11.36 /80	17.30 /91	--	1.84	0.74
GR	MassMutual Select Focused Value	MFVNX	C+	(800) 542-6767	B / 7.9	-1.96	3.65	10.55 /77	16.32 /86	14.49 /82	1.25	1.44
GR	MassMutual Select Focused Value	MFVSX	B	(800) 542-6767	B+ / 8.5	-1.80	4.02	11.27 /79	17.19 /91	15.38 /89	1.74	0.84
GR	MassMutual Select Focused Value	MMFYX	B-	(800) 542-6767	B+ / 8.4	-1.87	3.92	11.14 /79	17.07 /90	15.26 /89	1.67	0.94
IN	MassMutual Select Fundamental G A	MOTAX	C-	(800) 542-6767	C / 5.1	1.95	6.87	12.17 /83	12.39 /55	14.38 /81	0.45	1.34
IN	MassMutual Select Fundamental G	MOTLX	C	(800) 542-6767	C+ / 6.3	2.14	7.06	12.48 /85	12.68 /57	14.68 /84	0.70	1.09
GR	MassMutual Select Fundamental G I	MOTZX	C+	(800) 542-6767	C+ / 6.8	2.08	7.18	14.18 /90	13.43 /63	15.26 /89	0.97	N/A
IN	MassMutual Sel Fundamental G	MOTNX	C	(800) 542-6767	C+ / 5.9	1.90	6.81	12.02 /83	12.06 /53	14.06 /78	0.45	1.49
IN	MassMutual Select Fundamental G	MOTCX	C+	(800) 542-6767	C+ / 6.5	2.07	7.22	12.75 /86	12.95 /59	14.97 /87	0.80	0.89
IN	MassMutual Select Fundamental G	MOTYX	C+	(800) 542-6767	C+ / 6.4	2.11	7.06	12.52 /85	12.81 /58	14.83 /85	0.80	0.99
IN	MassMutual Select Fundamental V A	MFUAX	C+	(800) 542-6767	C+ / 6.1	0.94	5.55	10.10 /75	14.71 /73	12.03 /61	0.93	1.18
IN	MassMutual Select Fundamental V	MFULX	B	(800) 542-6767	B- / 7.3	1.00	5.72	10.39 /76	15.00 /75	12.32 /63	1.24	0.93
GR	MassMutual Select Fundamental V I	MFUZX	B+	(800) 542-6767	B / 7.6	1.07	5.85	10.69 /77	15.43 /78	--	1.61	0.63

RISK	3 Year		NET ASSETS		ASSET				Portfolio Turnover Ratio	BULL / BEAR		FUND MANAGER		MINIMUMS		LOADS	
Risk Rating/Pts	Standard Deviation	Beta	NAV As of 3/31/15	Total $(Mil)	Cash %	Stocks %	Bonds %	Other %		Last Bull Market Return	Last Bear Market Return	Manager Quality Pct	Manager Tenure (Years)	Initial Purch. $	Additional Purch. $	Front End Load	Back End Load
C / 4.9	8.8	1.36	10.26	142	3	77	19	1	36	62.5	N/A	35	4	0	0	0.0	0.0
C+ / 5.9	8.8	0.86	10.25	N/A	3	77	19	1	36	64.3	N/A	26	4	0	0	0.0	0.0
C / 4.8	8.8	1.36	10.25	11	3	77	19	1	36	63.2	N/A	38	4	0	0	0.0	0.0
C / 4.8	8.8	1.36	10.25	26	3	77	19	1	36	62.9	N/A	37	4	0	0	0.0	0.0
C+ / 6.9	6.4	0.62	9.99	1	0	53	46	1	37	47.1	N/A	48	4	0	0	0.0	0.0
C+ / 6.3	6.4	0.45	9.99	25	0	53	46	1	37	46.3	N/A	91	4	0	0	0.0	0.0
C+ / 6.3	6.4	0.45	10.00	40	0	53	46	1	37	46.2	N/A	91	4	0	0	0.0	0.0
U /	N/A	N/A	13.71	33	3	96	0	1	54	N/A	N/A	N/A	3	0	0	5.8	0.0
U /	N/A	N/A	13.73	51	3	96	0	1	54	N/A	N/A	N/A	3	0	0	0.0	0.0
U /	N/A	N/A	13.80	164	3	96	0	1	54	N/A	N/A	N/A	3	0	0	0.0	0.0
C+ / 5.9	13.6	0.98	16.40	7	4	95	0	1	28	118.0	-27.4	74	6	0	0	5.8	0.0
C+ / 5.9	13.6	0.98	16.44	5	4	95	0	1	28	119.6	-27.4	76	6	0	0	0.0	0.0
C / 5.0	13.5	0.97	16.47	67	4	95	0	1	28	124.4	-27.2	83	6	0	0	0.0	0.0
C+ / 5.9	13.6	0.98	16.48	104	4	95	0	1	28	121.5	-27.2	78	6	0	0	0.0	0.0
C+ / 5.9	13.6	0.99	16.53	3	4	95	0	1	28	120.9	-27.2	77	6	0	0	0.0	0.0
C+ / 6.7	6.6	1.03	10.95	9	1	64	30	5	66	36.8	-14.1	29	6	0	0	5.8	0.0
C+ / 6.7	6.7	1.04	11.31	17	1	64	30	5	66	37.7	-13.6	31	6	0	0	0.0	0.0
C+ / 6.6	6.6	1.04	11.03	635	1	64	30	5	66	39.9	-14.0	37	6	0	0	0.0	0.0
C+ / 6.9	6.7	1.04	11.16	8	1	64	30	5	66	39.1	-14.0	34	6	0	0	0.0	0.0
C+ / 6.6	6.7	1.04	11.01	12	1	64	30	5	66	38.7	-14.0	33	6	0	0	0.0	0.0
C / 5.4	11.4	1.03	17.23	166	0	99	0	1	33	110.1	-14.9	71	9	0	0	5.8	0.0
C / 5.4	11.4	1.03	17.79	280	0	99	0	1	33	111.7	-14.8	73	9	0	0	0.0	0.0
C / 5.4	11.2	1.02	18.11	304	0	99	0	1	33	117.2	-14.8	80	9	0	0	0.0	0.0
C / 5.3	11.4	1.03	16.51	1	0	99	0	1	33	108.2	-15.0	67	9	0	0	0.0	0.0
C / 5.5	11.3	1.02	18.09	588	0	99	0	1	33	113.4	-14.8	75	9	0	0	0.0	0.0
C / 5.5	11.4	1.03	17.97	181	0	99	0	1	33	112.9	-14.8	74	9	0	0	0.0	0.0
C / 5.2	14.4	1.07	6.96	1	3	96	0	1	56	41.6	-26.1	16	4	0	0	5.8	0.0
C / 5.1	14.3	1.06	7.23	N/A	3	96	0	1	56	42.0	-26.2	17	4	0	0	0.0	0.0
C / 4.7	14.3	1.06	6.96	70	3	96	0	1	56	45.2	-26.0	23	4	0	0	0.0	0.0
C / 5.1	14.2	1.06	6.96	3	3	96	0	1	56	43.7	-26.0	20	4	0	0	0.0	0.0
C / 5.1	14.4	1.07	7.14	N/A	3	96	0	1	56	43.1	-26.3	18	4	0	0	0.0	0.0
B- / 7.5	10.2	1.05	14.75	24	2	97	0	1	44	98.8	-18.9	52	5	0	0	5.8	0.0
B- / 7.5	10.2	1.05	14.83	10	2	97	0	1	44	100.8	-18.9	56	5	0	0	0.0	0.0
C+ / 5.7	10.2	1.04	14.77	104	2	97	0	1	44	103.0	-18.8	63	5	0	0	0.0	0.0
B- / 7.5	10.2	1.05	14.80	N/A	2	97	0	1	44	97.1	-19.1	49	5	0	0	0.0	0.0
B- / 7.5	10.2	1.05	14.77	234	2	97	0	1	44	102.0	-18.8	60	5	0	0	0.0	0.0
B- / 7.5	10.2	1.05	14.78	16	2	97	0	1	44	101.4	-18.8	58	5	0	0	0.0	0.0
C / 4.9	11.8	1.11	21.28	221	8	91	0	1	27	113.7	-20.9	50	17	0	0	5.8	0.0
C / 4.9	11.7	1.11	21.89	112	8	91	0	1	27	115.6	-20.8	54	17	0	0	0.0	0.0
C / 4.9	11.8	0.91	22.28	231	8	91	0	1	27	118.1	-20.7	82	17	0	0	0.0	0.0
C / 4.8	11.8	1.11	20.54	1	8	91	0	1	27	111.9	-21.0	45	17	0	0	0.0	0.0
C / 4.9	11.7	1.11	22.33	312	8	91	0	1	27	117.3	-20.7	58	17	0	0	0.0	0.0
C / 4.9	11.8	1.11	22.07	93	8	91	0	1	27	116.6	-20.8	55	17	0	0	0.0	0.0
C / 5.5	10.7	1.05	7.83	24	0	99	0	1	62	81.3	-11.0	16	3	0	0	5.8	0.0
C / 5.5	10.7	1.05	8.10	11	0	99	0	1	62	82.6	-10.8	18	3	0	0	0.0	0.0
C / 5.4	10.6	1.04	8.35	94	0	99	0	1	62	86.8	-10.8	26	3	0	0	0.0	0.0
C / 5.5	10.7	1.05	7.52	N/A	0	99	0	1	62	79.5	-11.0	14	3	0	0	0.0	0.0
C+ / 5.6	10.7	1.04	8.37	21	0	99	0	1	62	84.2	-10.8	21	3	0	0	0.0	0.0
C+ / 5.6	10.7	1.04	8.24	7	0	99	0	1	62	83.5	-10.8	20	3	0	0	0.0	0.0
C+ / 6.6	10.3	1.05	14.03	198	1	98	0	1	18	94.1	-20.7	37	7	0	0	5.8	0.0
C+ / 6.6	10.3	1.05	14.18	119	1	98	0	1	18	95.7	-20.5	41	7	0	0	0.0	0.0
C+ / 6.5	10.3	1.05	14.12	455	1	98	0	1	18	98.3	-20.4	47	7	0	0	0.0	0.0

99 Pct = Best
0 Pct = Worst

Fund Type	Fund Name	Ticker Symbol	Overall Investment Rating	Phone	PERFORMANCE: Performance Rating/Pts	Total Return % through 3/31/15: 3 Mo	6 Mo	1Yr / Pct	Annualized: 3Yr / Pct	5Yr / Pct	Incl. in Returns: Dividend Yield	Expense Ratio
IN	MassMutual Select Fundamental V	MFUNX	**C+**	(800) 542-6767	**C+ / 6.9**	0.87	5.45	9.87 /74	14.40 /70	11.72 /59	0.87	1.33
IN	MassMutual Select Fundamental V	MVUSX	**B**	(800) 542-6767	**B- / 7.5**	1.07	5.76	10.59 /77	15.21 /77	12.53 /64	1.48	0.73
IN	MassMutual Select Fundamental V	MFUYX	**B**	(800) 542-6767	**B- / 7.4**	1.00	5.70	10.47 /76	15.13 /76	12.47 /64	1.41	0.83
AG	MassMutual Select Growth Opps A	MMAAX	**C+**	(800) 542-6767	**C+ / 6.6**	1.47	6.51	11.73 /81	15.22 /77	17.38 /97	0.00	1.29
AG	MassMutual Select Growth Opps	MAGLX	**B-**	(800) 542-6767	**B / 7.9**	1.50	6.59	11.91 /82	15.48 /79	17.68 /97	0.00	1.04
GR	MassMutual Select Growth Opps I	MMAZX	**B**	(800) 542-6767	**B / 8.2**	1.60	6.75	12.22 /84	15.94 /83	--	0.00	0.74
AG	MassMutual Select Growth Opps R3	MMANX	**C+**	(800) 542-6767	**B- / 7.5**	1.45	6.44	11.48 /80	14.93 /74	17.09 /96	0.00	1.44
AG	MassMutual Select Growth Opps R5	MGRSX	**B**	(800) 542-6767	**B / 8.1**	1.52	6.69	12.19 /83	15.74 /81	17.94 /97	0.00	0.84
AG	MassMutual Select Growth Opps Svc	MAGYX	**B-**	(800) 542-6767	**B / 8.0**	1.55	6.62	12.01 /83	15.63 /80	17.81 /97	0.00	0.94
GR	MassMutual Select Lg Cap Val A	MMLAX	**E-**	(800) 542-6767	**D / 2.1**	-2.66	-0.94	-0.14 /15	9.65 /37	8.59 /34	2.37	1.22
GR	MassMutual Select Lg Cap Val Adm	MLVLX	**E**	(800) 542-6767	**C- / 3.2**	-2.54	-0.72	0.07 /16	9.95 /39	8.89 /36	2.79	0.97
GI	MassMutual Select Lg Cap Val I	MLVZX	**D**	(800) 542-6767	**C- / 3.5**	-2.53	-0.57	0.96 /18	10.42 /42	9.26 /39	3.13	N/A
GR	MassMutual Select Lg Cap Val R3	MLVNX	**E**	(800) 542-6767	**D+ / 2.9**	-2.71	-0.93	-0.33 /15	9.40 /36	8.34 /32	2.34	1.37
GR	MassMutual Select Lg Cap Val R5	MLVSX	**E**	(800) 542-6767	**C- / 3.3**	-2.65	-0.63	0.27 /16	10.17 /40	9.11 /38	2.98	0.77
GR	MassMutual Select Lg Cap Val Svc	MMLYX	**E**	(800) 542-6767	**C- / 3.3**	-2.64	-0.76	0.13 /16	10.08 /40	9.02 /37	2.74	0.87
MC	MassMutual Select Mid Cap Val A	MLUAX	**C+**	(800) 542-6767	**C / 5.4**	2.03	5.63	6.02 /47	13.97 /67	12.79 /66	0.53	1.35
MC	MassMutual Select Mid Cap Val Adm	MLULX	**C+**	(800) 542-6767	**C+ / 6.6**	2.08	5.77	6.30 /49	14.26 /69	13.01 /68	0.73	1.10
MC	MassMutual Select Mid Cap Val I	MLUZX	**B-**	(800) 542-6767	**C+ / 6.9**	2.23	5.99	6.66 /52	14.68 /72	--	1.13	0.80
MC	MassMutual Select Mid Cap Val R3	MLUNX	**C+**	(800) 542-6767	**C+ / 6.2**	2.04	5.65	5.90 /46	13.72 /65	12.49 /64	0.43	1.50
MC	MassMutual Select Mid Cap Val R5	MLUSX	**C+**	(800) 542-6767	**C+ / 6.8**	2.16	5.83	6.43 /50	14.52 /71	13.32 /71	0.81	0.90
MC	MassMutual Select Mid Cap Val Svc	MLUYX	**C+**	(800) 542-6767	**C+ / 6.7**	2.16	5.89	6.42 /50	14.45 /71	13.23 /70	0.92	1.00
MC	MassMutual Select Mid Cp GE II A	MEFAX	**B+**	(800) 542-6767	**A- / 9.2**	6.62	15.31	16.17 /94	17.75 /93	16.29 /94	0.00	1.30
MC	MassMutual Select Mid Cp GE II Adm	MMELX	**A-**	(800) 542-6767	**A+ / 9.6**	6.67	15.43	16.45 /94	18.05 /94	16.58 /95	0.00	1.05
MC	MassMutual Select Mid Cp GE II I	MEFZX	**A-**	(800) 542-6767	**A+ / 9.7**	6.81	15.61	16.83 /94	18.46 /96	--	0.00	0.75
MC	MassMutual Select Mid Cp GE II R3	MEFNX	**B+**	(800) 542-6767	**A / 9.5**	6.63	15.23	16.00 /93	17.48 /92	15.98 /93	0.00	1.45
MC	MassMutual Select Mid Cp GE II R5	MGRFX	**A-**	(800) 542-6767	**A+ / 9.7**	6.73	15.58	16.67 /94	18.31 /95	16.85 /96	0.00	0.85
MC	MassMutual Select Mid Cp GE II Svc	MEFYX	**A-**	(800) 542-6767	**A+ / 9.7**	6.74	15.48	16.59 /94	18.20 /95	16.74 /95	0.00	0.95
GR	MassMutual Select MSCI EAFE Itl	MKRYX	**U**	(800) 542-6767	**U /**	5.34	0.97	-1.39 /12	--	--	2.87	0.69
GR	MassMutual Select MSCI EAFE Itl I	MKRZX	**U**	(800) 542-6767	**U /**	5.49	1.17	-1.04 /13	--	--	3.04	0.34
FO	MassMutual Select Overseas A	MOSAX	**D-**	(800) 542-6767	**D / 2.2**	5.53	2.75	-0.65 /14	8.64 /31	6.52 /20	1.69	1.46
FO	MassMutual Select Overseas Admin	MOSLX	**D**	(800) 542-6767	**C- / 3.2**	5.65	2.81	-0.44 /14	8.87 /32	6.79 /22	2.07	1.21
FO	MassMutual Select Overseas I	MOSZX	**D+**	(800) 542-6767	**C- / 3.4**	5.67	2.94	-0.17 /15	9.26 /35	--	2.35	0.91
FO	MassMutual Select Overseas R3	MOSNX	**D**	(800) 542-6767	**D+ / 2.9**	5.40	2.63	-0.92 /13	8.36 /29	6.21 /18	0.00	1.61
FO	MassMutual Select Overseas R5	MOSSX	**D**	(800) 542-6767	**C- / 3.3**	5.54	2.93	-0.23 /15	9.05 /33	6.92 /23	2.05	1.01
FO	MassMutual Select Overseas Svc	MOSYX	**D**	(800) 542-6767	**C- / 3.2**	5.57	2.83	-0.32 /15	8.94 /33	6.85 /22	1.98	1.11
SC	MassMutual Select Russ 2K SCI Adm	MCJYX	**U**	(800) 542-6767	**U /**	4.26	14.31	7.91 /62	--	--	0.89	0.80
SC	MassMutual Select Russ 2K SCI I	MCJZX	**U**	(800) 542-6767	**U /**	4.25	14.48	8.25 /65	--	--	1.13	0.45
SC	MassMutual Select Small Cap GE A	MMGEX	**C-**	(800) 542-6767	**B+ / 8.7**	6.10	14.54	11.00 /78	17.54 /92	14.71 /84	0.00	1.41
SC	MassMutual Select Small Cap GE	MSGLX	**C**	(800) 542-6767	**A / 9.4**	6.23	14.72	11.29 /80	17.84 /94	15.01 /87	0.00	1.16
SC	MassMutual Select Small Cap GE I	MSGZX	**C**	(800) 542-6767	**A / 9.5**	6.29	14.89	11.61 /81	18.25 /95	--	0.00	0.86
SC	MassMutual Select Small Cap GE R3	MSGNX	**C-**	(800) 542-6767	**A / 9.3**	6.19	14.52	10.84 /78	17.24 /91	14.40 /81	0.00	1.56
SC	MassMutual Select Small Cap GE R5	MSGSX	**C**	(800) 542-6767	**A / 9.5**	6.20	14.78	11.49 /80	18.15 /95	15.31 /89	0.00	0.96
SC	MassMutual Select Small Cap GE	MSCYX	**C**	(800) 542-6767	**A / 9.5**	6.24	14.77	11.38 /80	18.00 /94	15.16 /88	0.00	1.06
SC	MassMutual Select Small Co Val A	MMYAX	**D**	(800) 542-6767	**C / 4.5**	1.01	8.36	2.30 /23	12.58 /57	11.48 /57	0.23	1.48
SC	MassMutual Select Small Co Val Adm	MMYLX	**D+**	(800) 542-6767	**C+ / 5.6**	1.05	8.46	2.50 /24	12.85 /58	11.76 /59	0.52	1.23
SC	MassMutual Select Small Co Val I	MSVZX	**D+**	(800) 542-6767	**C+ / 5.9**	1.18	8.66	2.82 /26	13.26 /61	--	0.87	0.93
SC	MassMutual Select Small Co Val R3	MSVNX	**D**	(800) 542-6767	**C / 5.3**	0.97	8.30	2.09 /22	12.30 /55	11.18 /54	0.11	1.63
SC	MassMutual Select Small Co Val R5	MSVSX	**D+**	(800) 542-6767	**C+ / 5.8**	1.11	8.61	2.72 /25	13.07 /60	11.98 /60	0.73	1.03
SC	MassMutual Select Small Co Val Svc	MMVYX	**D+**	(800) 542-6767	**C+ / 5.7**	1.11	8.61	2.63 /25	13.02 /60	11.93 /60	0.64	1.13
SC	MassMutual Select Small Comp Gr A	MRWAX	**D**	(800) 542-6767	**C+ / 6.1**	5.46	13.67	9.11 /70	13.55 /64	14.97 /87	0.00	1.69
SC	MassMutual Select Small Comp Gr	MMCLX	**C-**	(800) 542-6767	**B- / 7.3**	5.56	13.81	9.42 /72	13.83 /66	15.23 /88	0.00	1.44
SC	MassMutual Select Small Comp Gr I	MRWIX	**C+**	(800) 542-6767	**B / 8.0**	5.62	14.07	11.35 /80	14.63 /72	15.82 /92	0.00	N/A

● Denotes fund is closed to new investors
* Denotes fund is included in Section II

RISK	3 Year		NET ASSETS		ASSET					BULL / BEAR		FUND MANAGER		MINIMUMS		LOADS	
Risk Rating/Pts	Standard Deviation	Beta	NAV As of 3/31/15	Total $(Mil)	Cash %	Stocks %	Bonds %	Other %	Portfolio Turnover Ratio	Last Bull Market Return	Last Bear Market Return	Manager Quality Pct	Manager Tenure (Years)	Initial Purch. $	Additional Purch. $	Front End Load	Back End Load
C+ / 6.6	10.3	1.05	13.93	1	1	98	0	1	18	92.3	-20.7	34	7	0	0	0.0	0.0
C+ / 6.6	10.3	1.05	14.16	501	1	98	0	1	18	96.9	-20.5	44	7	0	0	0.0	0.0
C+ / 6.6	10.2	1.05	14.11	195	1	98	0	1	18	96.6	-20.5	44	7	0	0	0.0	0.0
C / 5.3	11.9	1.07	11.04	188	1	98	0	1	29	104.6	-12.4	39	11	0	0	5.8	0.0
C / 5.3	12.0	1.08	11.54	122	1	98	0	1	29	106.2	-12.2	41	11	0	0	0.0	0.0
C+ / 5.7	12.0	1.08	12.09	357	1	98	0	1	29	N/A	N/A	47	11	0	0	0.0	0.0
C / 5.2	12.0	1.08	10.49	N/A	1	98	0	1	29	102.6	-12.4	34	11	0	0	0.0	0.0
C / 5.3	12.0	1.08	12.03	277	1	98	0	1	29	107.9	-12.1	44	11	0	0	0.0	0.0
C / 5.3	12.0	1.08	11.82	162	1	98	0	1	29	107.0	-12.2	43	11	0	0	0.0	0.0
D- / 1.1	9.8	0.99	8.04	44	1	98	0	1	34	66.2	-20.3	8	3	0	0	5.8	0.0
D- / 1.1	9.8	0.99	8.06	22	1	98	0	1	34	67.5	-20.1	9	3	0	0	0.0	0.0
C / 5.4	9.9	1.00	8.08	150	1	98	0	1	34	69.8	-20.0	10	3	0	0	0.0	0.0
D- / 1.1	9.9	0.99	7.90	N/A	1	98	0	1	34	64.7	-20.3	7	3	0	0	0.0	0.0
D- / 1.1	9.9	1.00	8.08	156	1	98	0	1	34	68.9	-20.0	9	3	0	0	0.0	0.0
D- / 1.1	9.9	0.99	8.10	10	1	98	0	1	34	68.5	-20.1	9	3	0	0	0.0	0.0
C+ / 6.8	10.6	0.93	15.58	4	1	98	0	1	109	88.1	-22.0	43	6	0	0	5.8	0.0
C+ / 6.8	10.6	0.93	15.72	1	1	98	0	1	109	89.8	-22.1	47	6	0	0	0.0	0.0
B- / 7.2	10.6	0.93	15.59	155	1	98	0	1	109	N/A	N/A	52	6	0	0	0.0	0.0
C+ / 6.8	10.6	0.93	15.52	N/A	1	98	0	1	109	86.6	-22.1	40	6	0	0	0.0	0.0
C+ / 6.9	10.6	0.93	15.64	18	1	98	0	1	109	91.3	-21.8	51	6	0	0	0.0	0.0
C+ / 6.8	10.6	0.93	15.62	5	1	98	0	1	109	90.5	-21.8	49	6	0	0	0.0	0.0
C / 5.1	10.8	0.94	17.87	337	3	96	0	1	32	101.9	-20.4	82	15	0	0	5.8	0.0
C / 5.3	10.8	0.94	18.86	386	3	96	0	1	32	103.5	-20.3	83	15	0	0	0.0	0.0
C / 5.4	10.8	0.94	19.92	531	3	96	0	1	32	106.0	-20.2	85	15	0	0	0.0	0.0
C / 5.0	10.8	0.93	16.89	3	3	96	0	1	32	100.0	-20.5	80	15	0	0	0.0	0.0
C / 5.4	10.8	0.94	19.81	715	3	96	0	1	32	105.1	-20.2	85	15	0	0	0.0	0.0
C / 5.3	10.8	0.94	19.48	263	3	96	0	1	32	104.4	-20.2	84	15	0	0	0.0	0.0
U /	N/A	N/A	12.82	28	2	97	0	1	42	N/A	N/A	N/A	3	0	0	0.0	0.0
U /	N/A	N/A	12.87	246	2	97	0	1	42	N/A	N/A	N/A	3	0	0	0.0	0.0
C+ / 5.8	13.4	1.00	8.59	67	2	97	0	1	35	55.6	-24.2	56	14	0	0	5.8	0.0
C+ / 5.8	13.4	0.99	8.79	36	2	97	0	1	35	56.9	-24.0	59	14	0	0	0.0	0.0
C+ / 5.8	13.4	0.99	8.76	351	2	97	0	1	35	58.9	-23.9	65	14	0	0	0.0	0.0
C+ / 5.8	13.4	1.00	8.59	1	2	97	0	1	35	54.3	-24.3	52	14	0	0	0.0	0.0
C+ / 5.8	13.4	1.00	8.77	181	2	97	0	1	35	57.5	-24.0	61	14	0	0	0.0	0.0
C+ / 5.8	13.4	1.00	8.72	81	2	97	0	1	35	57.2	-24.1	60	14	0	0	0.0	0.0
U /	N/A	N/A	12.72	33	3	96	0	1	59	N/A	N/A	N/A	3	0	0	0.0	0.0
U /	N/A	N/A	12.76	108	3	96	0	1	59	N/A	N/A	N/A	3	0	0	0.0	0.0
D- / 1.3	13.3	0.95	14.95	57	1	98	0	1	97	105.9	-27.4	83	14	0	0	5.8	0.0
D / 1.6	13.3	0.95	16.04	35	1	98	0	1	97	107.6	-27.2	85	14	0	0	0.0	0.0
D / 2.1	13.2	0.95	17.40	570	1	98	0	1	97	110.2	-27.1	86	14	0	0	0.0	0.0
D- / 1.1	13.3	0.95	13.89	N/A	1	98	0	1	97	104.0	-27.4	81	14	0	0	0.0	0.0
D / 2.1	13.3	0.95	17.29	209	1	98	0	1	97	109.5	-27.2	86	14	0	0	0.0	0.0
D / 1.9	13.3	0.95	16.69	42	1	98	0	1	97	108.6	-27.2	85	14	0	0	0.0	0.0
C- / 3.8	12.5	0.91	14.07	43	2	97	0	1	44	80.7	-24.3	38	14	0	0	5.8	0.0
C- / 3.8	12.5	0.91	14.37	25	2	97	0	1	44	82.4	-24.3	43	14	0	0	0.0	0.0
C- / 3.7	12.5	0.91	14.55	134	2	97	0	1	44	84.6	-24.1	48	14	0	0	0.0	0.0
C- / 3.6	12.5	0.91	13.49	N/A	2	97	0	1	44	79.2	-24.5	35	14	0	0	0.0	0.0
C- / 3.8	12.5	0.91	14.59	190	2	97	0	1	44	83.6	-24.2	45	14	0	0	0.0	0.0
C- / 3.8	12.5	0.91	14.54	35	2	97	0	1	44	83.2	-24.2	44	14	0	0	0.0	0.0
D+ / 2.9	13.7	0.96	11.79	9	0	99	0	1	161	84.0	-22.4	41	2	0	0	5.8	0.0
C- / 3.0	13.7	0.96	12.34	5	0	99	0	1	161	85.5	-22.3	44	2	0	0	0.0	0.0
C / 4.8	13.5	0.95	12.78	19	0	99	0	1	161	89.5	-22.2	58	2	0	0	0.0	0.0

			99 Pct = Best 0 Pct = Worst		**PERFORMANCE**							
								Total Return % through 3/31/15			Incl. in Returns	
			Overall		**Perfor-**				Annualized			
Fund		Ticker	**Investment**		**mance**						Dividend	Expense
Type	Fund Name	Symbol	**Rating**	Phone	**Rating/Pts**	3 Mo	6 Mo	1Yr / Pct	3Yr / Pct	5Yr / Pct	Yield	Ratio
SC	MassMutual Select Small Comp Gr	MSCSX	C-	(800) 542-6767	B- / 7.5	5.62	13.98	9.71 /73	14.06 /68	15.48 /90	0.00	1.24
SC	MassMutual Select Small Comp Gr	MMCYX	C-	(800) 542-6767	B- / 7.4	5.50	13.92	9.53 /72	13.97 /67	15.43 /90	0.00	1.34
IN	Matisse Discounted CE Strategy Inst	MDCEX	U	(800) 773-3863	U /	3.32	4.13	8.37 /65	--	--	4.93	2.46
GI	Matrix Advisor Value Fund	MAVFX	C+	(800) 366-6223	C+ / 5.6	-1.73	1.41	5.81 /45	13.65 /65	10.02 /45	1.27	1.15
GI	Matthew 25 Fund	MXXVX	A-	(888) 625-3863	B / 7.8	1.82	3.47	9.09 /70	16.69 /88	20.89 /99	0.51	1.06
FO	● Matthews Asia Dividend Fund Instl	MIPIX	C	(800) 789-2742	C / 4.8	8.68	5.10	10.61 /77	9.68 /37	--	1.87	0.93
FO	● Matthews Asia Dividend Fund Inv	MAPIX	C	(800) 789-2742	C / 4.7	8.64	5.00	10.50 /76	9.53 /36	8.15 /31	1.78	1.06
FO	Matthews Asia Growth Fund Inst	MIAPX	C	(800) 789-2742	C / 5.1	6.75	4.41	11.05 /79	10.91 /45	--	1.84	0.93
FO	Matthews Asia Growth Fund Inv	MPACX	C	(800) 789-2742	C / 5.0	6.68	4.32	10.83 /78	10.71 /44	9.38 /40	1.70	1.12
TC	Matthews Asia Science and Tech Inst	MITEX	U	(800) 789-2742	U /	4.85	5.00	15.40 /92	--	--	0.60	1.00
TC	Matthews Asia Science and Tech Inv	MATFX	B	(800) 789-2742	B / 8.1	4.85	4.87	15.17 /92	15.85 /82	11.56 /57	0.42	1.18
CV	Matthews Asian Growth & Income	MICSX	D	(800) 789-2742	D / 1.7	2.00	-1.47	1.03 /19	6.85 /21	--	2.02	0.93
CV	Matthews Asian Growth & Income Inv	MACSX	D	(800) 789-2742	D / 1.6	2.00	-1.56	0.86 /18	6.69 /20	6.64 /21	1.85	1.08
FO	Matthews Asian Small Companies	MISMX	U	(800) 789-2742	U /	2.38	0.48	9.54 /72	--	--	0.56	1.25
FO	Matthews Asian Small Companies Inv	MSMLX	D+	(800) 789-2742	C- / 3.8	2.33	0.34	9.29 /71	9.85 /38	9.33 /39	0.38	1.47
FO	Matthews China Dividend Fund Instl	MICDX	C+	(800) 789-2742	C+ / 5.8	7.03	6.05	13.34 /88	11.25 /47	--	2.64	1.24
FO	Matthews China Dividend Fund Inv	MCDFX	C+	(800) 789-2742	C+ / 5.6	7.03	5.97	13.14 /87	11.04 /46	9.83 /43	2.48	1.08
FO	Matthews China Fund Institutional	MICFX	E+	(800) 789-2742	D+ / 2.5	6.90	9.24	11.80 /82	4.08 /10	--	1.31	0.92
FO	Matthews China Investor	MCHFX	E+	(800) 789-2742	D+ / 2.4	6.90	9.15	11.65 /81	3.90 /10	2.20 / 5	1.15	1.09
FO	Matthews China Small Companies	MCSMX	D	(800) 789-2742	D+ / 2.5	1.95	0.29	0.29 /16	8.67 /31	--	3.80	2.04
EM	Matthews Emerging Asia Inst	MIASX	U	(800) 789-2742	U /	-0.60	-0.40	9.88 /74	--	--	0.64	2.21
EM	Matthews Emerging Asia Investor	MEASX	U	(800) 789-2742	U /	-0.69	-0.63	9.63 /73	--	--	0.49	2.39
FO	Matthews India Fund Institutional	MIDNX	C+	(800) 789-2742	A+ / 9.9	10.42	19.33	58.00 /99	21.97 /98	--	0.27	0.95
FO	Matthews India Fund Inv	MINDX	C+	(800) 789-2742	A+ / 9.9	10.36	19.22	57.70 /99	21.77 /98	11.48 /57	0.16	1.13
FO	Matthews Japan Fund Institutional	MIJFX	A	(800) 789-2742	A- / 9.1	17.38	12.47	17.08 /95	15.66 /81	--	0.49	0.96
FO	Matthews Japan Fund Inv	MJFOX	A	(800) 789-2742	A- / 9.1	17.39	12.47	16.94 /94	15.52 /79	12.04 /61	0.44	1.10
FO	Matthews Korea Fund Institutional	MIKOX	D+	(800) 789-2742	C / 4.5	8.63	1.09	9.12 /70	10.38 /42	--	0.00	0.97
FO	Matthews Korea Fund Inv	MAKOX	D+	(800) 789-2742	C / 4.4	8.67	0.93	8.98 /69	10.30 /41	10.62 /50	0.00	1.13
FO	● Matthews Pacific Tiger Fund Instl	MIPTX	C	(800) 789-2742	C+ / 6.1	7.53	6.33	17.64 /95	10.93 /45	--	0.60	0.92
FO	● Matthews Pacific Tiger Fund Inv	MAPTX	C	(800) 789-2742	C+ / 6.0	7.53	6.26	17.47 /95	10.76 /44	9.75 /43	0.44	1.09
FO	McKinley Non-US Core Growth Y	MCNUX	U	(888) 458-1963	U /	3.05	2.34	--	--	--	0.00	N/A
IN	MD Sass Equity Income Plus Inst	MDEIX	U	(855) 637-3863	U /	2.01	3.18	8.18 /64	--	--	1.93	1.29
AG	Meeder Aggressive Growth	FLAGX	B-	(800) 325-3539	B / 8.1	2.29	8.36	13.59 /88	15.28 /77	12.03 /61	0.63	1.74
GR	Meeder Balanced	FLDFX	C	(800) 325-3539	C / 4.3	1.00	3.67	7.33 /58	10.14 /40	7.90 /29	2.27	1.79
GR	Meeder Dynamic Growth	FLDGX	C+	(800) 325-3539	B / 7.6	1.10	6.38	11.66 /81	15.08 /75	12.17 /62	2.61	1.66
GR	Meeder Muirfield	FLMFX	C+	(800) 325-3539	C+ / 6.8	1.00	5.47	10.69 /77	14.16 /68	10.45 /48	2.38	1.62
IX	Meeder Quantex	FLCGX	B+	(800) 325-3539	B+ / 8.3	0.14	4.49	6.86 /54	17.30 /91	13.95 /77	1.09	1.94
GR	Meeder Strategic Growth	FLFGX	D	(800) 325-3539	C / 4.4	2.31	3.12	5.44 /42	10.67 /43	9.37 /40	1.36	1.75
UT	Meeder Utilities and Infrastructure	FLRUX	C-	(800) 325-3539	C / 4.7	0.22	-0.16	4.33 /34	11.93 /52	10.80 /51	2.54	1.99
GR	Meehan Focus Fund	MEFOX	B-	(866) 884-5968	C+ / 6.2	2.37	3.07	8.85 /68	13.38 /62	11.46 /57	0.78	1.01
EM	Mercer Emerging Markets Equity Y-3	MEMQX	U	(800) 428-0980	U /	1.33	-4.08	-1.10 /13	--	--	0.00	1.04
GR	Merger Fund Institutional	MERIX	U	(800) 343-8959	U /	1.41	0.98	2.55 /24	--	--	2.80	1.46
GR	Merger Fund Investor	MERFX	D+	(800) 343-8959	E+ / 0.9	1.41	0.84	2.34 /23	2.99 / 8	2.67 / 5	2.47	1.70
GR	Meridian Contrarian Legacy	MVALX	B-	(800) 446-6662	B+ / 8.8	5.59	13.37	10.92 /78	16.85 /89	14.05 /78	0.18	1.13
IN	Meridian Equity Income Legacy	MEIFX	C-	(800) 446-6662	C / 5.4	2.82	4.04	6.68 /52	12.73 /58	12.18 /62	1.67	1.37
MC	Meridian Growth Investor	MRIGX	U	(800) 446-6662	U /	2.40	12.74	13.54 /88	--	--	0.00	1.30
GR	Meridian Growth Legacy	MERDX	D-	(800) 446-6662	C+ / 6.7	2.47	12.91	13.86 /89	12.77 /58	15.13 /88	0.00	0.86
SC	Meridian Small Cap Growth Advisor	MSGAX	U	(800) 446-6662	U /	3.60	16.94	16.62 /94	--	--	0.00	3.05
SC	Meridian Small Cap Growth Investor	MISGX	U	(800) 446-6662	U /	3.67	17.18	16.97 /95	--	--	0.00	3.69
SC	Meridian Small Cap Growth Legacy	MSGGX	U	(800) 446-6662	U /	3.75	17.17	17.06 /95	--	--	0.00	2.41
IN	Meritage Yield Focus Equity Inst	MPYIX	U	(855) 261-0104	U /	0.07	0.03	3.12 /27	--	--	2.58	2.96
OT	Merk Abs Rtn Currency Inst	MAAIX	D	(866) 637-5386	E / 0.3	-6.48	-6.28	-6.18 / 4	-0.81 / 4	--	2.23	1.05

● Denotes fund is closed to new investors
* Denotes fund is included in Section II

www.thestreetratings.com

RISK			NET ASSETS		ASSET				Portfolio	BULL / BEAR		FUND MANAGER		MINIMUMS		LOADS	
	3 Year		NAV							Last Bull	Last Bear	Manager	Manager	Initial	Additional	Front	Back
Risk Rating/Pts	Standard Deviation	Beta	As of 3/31/15	Total $(Mil)	Cash %	Stocks %	Bonds %	Other %	Turnover Ratio	Market Return	Market Return	Quality Pct	Tenure (Years)	Purch. $	Purch. $	End Load	End Load
C- / 3.1	13.7	0.96	12.77	26	0	99	0	1	161	86.7	-22.2	48	2	0	0	0.0	0.0
C- / 3.1	13.7	0.96	12.66	4	0	99	0	1	161	86.4	-22.3	47	2	0	0	0.0	0.0
U /	N/A	N/A	10.28	119	0	52	45	3	151	N/A	N/A	N/A	3	25,000	100	0.0	2.0
C+ / 6.4	12.7	1.24	62.36	75	0	99	0	1	41	91.6	-26.0	7	19	1,000	100	0.0	1.0
B- / 7.2	10.8	1.05	31.82	836	7	92	0	1	7	133.1	-16.0	64	20	10,000	100	0.0	2.0
C+ / 6.8	10.5	0.67	16.56	2,354	4	95	0	1	14	46.3	-13.4	89	4	3,000,000	100	0.0	2.0
C+ / 6.9	10.4	0.67	16.56	3,018	4	95	0	1	14	45.8	-13.6	89	4	2,500	100	0.0	2.0
C+ / 6.5	11.6	0.72	22.62	321	1	98	0	1	11	51.9	-17.3	91	8	3,000,000	100	0.0	2.0
C+ / 6.5	11.6	0.72	22.51	594	1	98	0	1	11	50.9	-17.3	90	8	2,500	100	0.0	2.0
U /	N/A	N/A	14.27	62	4	95	0	1	62	N/A	N/A	N/A	9	3,000,000	100	0.0	2.0
C+ / 5.9	12.1	0.91	14.27	127	4	95	0	1	62	75.9	-23.5	79	9	2,500	100	0.0	2.0
C+ / 6.5	9.8	0.74	18.36	1,169	3	85	0	12	15	37.2	-14.6	26	6	3,000,000	100	0.0	2.0
C+ / 6.5	9.8	0.74	18.37	3,029	3	85	0	12	15	36.5	-14.6	24	6	2,500	100	0.0	2.0
U /	N/A	N/A	21.97	105	2	97	0	1	37	N/A	N/A	N/A	7	3,000,000	100	0.0	2.0
C+ / 5.9	11.1	0.56	21.96	613	2	97	0	1	37	50.7	-21.7	92	7	2,500	100	0.0	2.0
C+ / 6.8	10.3	0.60	14.31	29	6	94	0	0	21	59.3	-19.0	94	3	3,000,000	100	0.0	2.0
C+ / 6.8	10.3	0.60	14.31	124	6	94	0	0	21	58.4	-19.2	94	3	2,500	100	0.0	2.0
C / 4.4	13.3	0.65	22.92	51	6	93	0	1	6	26.7	-26.3	39	16	3,000,000	100	0.0	2.0
C / 4.4	13.3	0.65	22.94	951	6	93	0	1	6	26.0	-26.3	36	16	2,500	100	0.0	2.0
C+ / 5.8	12.1	0.56	9.39	21	1	98	0	1	10	43.2	N/A	90	4	2,500	100	0.0	2.0
U /	N/A	N/A	11.53	37	3	96	0	1	2	N/A	N/A	N/A	2	3,000,000	100	0.0	2.0
U /	N/A	N/A	11.52	124	3	96	0	1	2	N/A	N/A	N/A	2	2,500	100	0.0	2.0
D / 2.0	23.3	0.96	29.25	164	2	97	0	1	9	87.0	-19.2	98	10	3,000,000	100	0.0	2.0
D / 2.0	23.3	0.96	29.20	1,339	2	97	0	1	9	86.0	-19.3	98	10	2,500	100	0.0	2.0
C+ / 6.5	14.1	0.67	18.44	170	2	97	0	1	23	52.4	-5.5	97	9	3,000,000	100	0.0	2.0
C+ / 6.5	14.1	0.67	18.43	516	2	97	0	1	23	51.7	-5.5	97	9	2,500	100	0.0	2.0
C / 5.0	13.8	0.71	6.17	54	4	95	0	1	46	55.1	-21.8	90	8	3,000,000	100	0.0	2.0
C / 5.0	13.8	0.71	6.14	133	4	95	0	1	46	54.5	-21.9	90	8	2,500	100	0.0	2.0
C / 5.4	12.2	0.72	28.56	5,636	0	100	0	0	8	55.7	-17.4	91	9	3,000,000	100	0.0	2.0
C / 5.4	12.2	0.72	28.57	3,260	0	100	0	0	8	54.9	-17.5	91	9	2,500	100	0.0	2.0
U /	N/A	N/A	19.91	40	1	98	0	1	0	N/A	N/A	N/A	1	40,000,000	0	0.0	0.0
U /	N/A	N/A	11.42	150	0	0	0	100	54	N/A	N/A	N/A	2	1,000,000	25,000	0.0	0.0
C / 4.9	10.7	1.07	10.71	99	6	92	0	2	272	91.2	-21.7	41	10	2,500	100	0.0	0.0
B- / 7.2	7.5	0.76	11.08	210	15	60	23	2	217	54.2	-14.1	42	9	2,500	100	0.0	0.0
C / 5.2	10.5	1.06	10.13	159	4	94	0	2	276	91.8	-20.3	40	10	2,500	100	0.0	0.0
C+ / 6.2	10.4	1.05	7.10	334	10	88	0	2	260	80.6	-19.8	32	10	2,500	100	0.0	0.0
C+ / 6.1	12.6	1.19	35.22	72	16	83	0	1	25	106.8	-23.1	39	10	2,500	100	0.0	0.0
C / 4.4	10.8	1.05	10.62	124	11	87	0	2	231	68.6	-23.3	8	9	2,500	100	0.0	0.0
C / 5.5	9.9	0.38	30.47	54	14	85	0	1	19	64.4	-15.8	96	20	2,500	100	0.0	0.0
B- / 7.1	10.6	1.06	22.07	60	2	97	0	1	23	79.1	-15.1	23	16	5,000	100	0.0	0.0
U /	N/A	N/A	9.88	1,085	0	0	0	100	64	N/A	N/A	N/A	3	0	0	0.0	2.0
U /	N/A	N/A	15.80	1,292	37	60	1	2	194	N/A	N/A	N/A	8	1,000,000	500	0.0	0.0
B / 8.4	2.4	0.14	15.85	4,009	37	60	1	2	194	13.7	-4.1	76	8	2,000	0	0.0	0.0
C / 4.3	11.2	1.02	40.96	704	7	92	0	1	67	104.0	-20.6	71	14	1,000	50	0.0	2.0
C / 4.5	9.5	0.92	12.40	10	5	89	4	2	35	79.0	-15.0	40	10	1,000	50	0.0	2.0
U /	N/A	N/A	37.11	42	8	91	0	1	96	N/A	N/A	N/A	2	1,000,000	0	0.0	2.0
E+ / 0.8	11.1	0.96	37.27	1,926	8	91	0	1	96	84.6	-19.1	34	2	1,000	50	0.0	2.0
U /	N/A	N/A	12.66	40	0	0	0	100	78	N/A	N/A	N/A	2	2,500	50	0.0	2.0
U /	N/A	N/A	12.71	112	0	0	0	100	78	N/A	N/A	N/A	2	1,000,000	0	0.0	2.0
U /	N/A	N/A	12.72	58	0	0	0	100	78	N/A	N/A	N/A	2	1,000	50	0.0	2.0
U /	N/A	N/A	10.51	32	20	79	0	1	63	N/A	N/A	N/A	2	100,000	1,000	0.0	0.0
B / 8.2	6.6	0.25	8.80	18	11	0	88	1	0	1.1	-10.4	12	6	250,000	0	0.0	0.0

Fund Type	Fund Name	Ticker Symbol	Overall Investment Rating	Phone	Performance Rating/Pts	Total Return % through 3/31/15			Annualized		Incl. in Returns	
						3 Mo	6 Mo	1Yr / Pct	3Yr / Pct	5Yr / Pct	Dividend Yield	Expense Ratio
OT	Merk Abs Rtn Currency Investor	MABFX	D	(866) 637-5386	E / 0.3	-6.64	-6.44	-6.59 / 4	-1.11 / 3	-0.98 / 2	2.19	1.30
OT	Merk Asian Currency Inst	MASIX	C-	(866) 637-5386	E / 0.5	1.37	0.52	1.05 /19	0.17 / 4	--	0.00	1.05
OT	Merk Asian Currency Investor	MEAFX	C-	(866) 637-5386	E / 0.5	1.28	0.32	0.74 /18	-0.07 / 4	0.24 / 3	0.00	1.30
GR	Merk Currency Enhanced US Eq Inst	MUSIX	C	(866) 637-5386	C / 5.2	-5.54	-2.34	2.78 /25	13.76 /65	--	1.86	1.12
GR	Merk Currency Enhanced US Eq Inv	MUSFX	C-	(866) 637-5386	C / 4.9	-5.75	-2.60	2.29 /23	13.37 /62	--	1.82	1.37
FS	● Merk Hard Currency Inst	MHCIX	E+	(866) 637-5386	E- / 0.1	-8.96	-12.22	-17.18 / 1	-5.94 / 2	--	0.93	1.05
FS	● Merk Hard Currency Investor	MERKX	E+	(866) 637-5386	E- / 0.1	-9.01	-12.29	-17.47 / 1	-6.22 / 1	-2.37 / 2	0.85	1.30
GR	Meyers Capital Aggressive Growth	MAGFX	E-	(866) 232-3837	D / 2.1	5.70	-5.66	-10.80 / 3	9.37 /35	10.06 /45	0.00	1.91
GL	MFS Absolute Return Fund R5	MRNVX	U	(800) 225-2606	U /	0.93	-0.51	-0.46 /14	--	--	0.80	1.13
AG	MFS Aggressive Gr Alloc 529A	EAGTX	C	(800) 225-2606	C / 4.4	3.26	5.60	5.87 /45	12.01 /53	11.14 /54	1.14	1.26
AG	MFS Aggressive Gr Alloc 529B	EBAAX	C	(800) 225-2606	C / 4.8	3.06	5.19	5.08 /39	11.16 /47	10.30 /47	0.43	2.01
AG	MFS Aggressive Gr Alloc 529C	ECAAX	C	(800) 225-2606	C / 4.8	3.03	5.20	5.09 /39	11.17 /47	10.31 /47	0.55	2.01
AG	MFS Aggressive Gr Alloc A	MAAGX	C	(800) 225-2606	C / 4.4	3.24	5.60	5.87 /45	12.05 /53	11.19 /54	1.16	1.16
AG	MFS Aggressive Gr Alloc B	MBAGX	C	(800) 225-2606	C / 4.8	3.07	5.21	5.15 /40	11.22 /47	10.36 /47	0.44	1.91
AG	MFS Aggressive Gr Alloc C	MCAGX	C	(800) 225-2606	C / 4.9	3.10	5.22	5.16 /40	11.23 /47	10.38 /48	0.57	1.91
AG	MFS Aggressive Gr Alloc I	MIAGX	C+	(800) 225-2606	C+ / 5.6	3.29	5.72	6.14 /48	12.32 /55	11.46 /57	1.45	0.91
AG	MFS Aggressive Gr Alloc R1	MAAFX	C	(800) 225-2606	C / 4.8	3.03	5.16	5.11 /39	11.21 /47	10.35 /47	0.41	1.91
AG	MFS Aggressive Gr Alloc R2	MAWAX	C+	(800) 225-2606	C / 5.2	3.19	5.48	5.64 /43	11.77 /51	10.91 /52	0.93	1.41
AG	MFS Aggressive Gr Alloc R3	MAAHX	C+	(800) 225-2606	C / 5.4	3.26	5.59	5.92 /46	12.06 /53	11.19 /54	1.24	1.16
AG	MFS Aggressive Gr Alloc R4	MAALX	C+	(800) 225-2606	C+ / 5.6	3.33	5.73	6.16 /48	12.36 /55	11.49 /57	1.47	0.91
GR	MFS Blended Research Core Eq A	MUEAX	B+	(800) 225-2606	B- / 7.3	1.60	5.97	12.02 /83	16.30 /85	14.34 /81	0.81	1.11
GR	MFS Blended Research Core Eq B	MUSBX	B+	(800) 225-2606	B / 7.7	1.41	5.58	11.25 /79	15.44 /79	13.48 /73	0.37	1.86
GR	MFS Blended Research Core Eq C	MUECX	B+	(800) 225-2606	B / 7.7	1.43	5.57	11.20 /79	15.43 /78	13.49 /73	0.47	1.86
GR	MFS Blended Research Core Eq I	MUSEX	A	(800) 225-2606	B+ / 8.6	1.67	6.12	12.37 /84	16.61 /87	14.63 /83	1.04	0.86
GR	MFS Blended Research Core Eq R1	MUERX	B+	(800) 225-2606	B / 7.7	1.41	5.58	11.24 /79	15.44 /79	13.49 /73	0.13	1.86
GR	MFS Blended Research Core Eq R2	MUESX	A-	(800) 225-2606	B / 8.2	1.51	5.82	11.75 /81	16.02 /84	14.05 /78	0.73	1.36
GR	MFS Blended Research Core Eq R3	MUETX	A	(800) 225-2606	B+ / 8.4	1.60	5.95	12.08 /83	16.30 /85	14.33 /81	0.86	1.11
GR	MFS Blended Research Core Eq R4	MUEUX	A	(800) 225-2606	B+ / 8.6	1.68	6.13	12.38 /84	16.60 /87	14.62 /83	1.05	0.86
GI	MFS Blended Research Core Eq R5	MUEVX	U	(800) 225-2606	U /	1.67	6.17	12.47 /85	--	--	1.13	0.74
SC	MFS Blended Research SC Eq Initial		C+	(800) 225-2606	A / 9.5	4.74	12.98	9.67 /73	18.70 /96	15.40 /90	0.91	0.51
SC	MFS Blended Research SC Eq		C+	(800) 225-2606	A / 9.4	4.70	12.87	9.45 /72	18.40 /95	15.12 /88	0.66	0.76
OT	● MFS Commodity Strategy Fund A	MCSAX	E-	(800) 225-2606	E- / 0.1	-5.12	-16.73	-26.46 / 0	-11.17 / 1	--	0.00	1.11
OT	● MFS Commodity Strategy Fund I	MCSIX	E-	(800) 225-2606	E- / 0.1	-5.12	-16.63	-26.37 / 0	-10.98 / 1	--	0.26	0.86
OT	MFS Commodity Strategy Fund R5	MCSRX	U	(800) 225-2606	U /	-5.12	-16.63	-26.37 / 0	--	--	0.26	0.86
AA	MFS Conservative Alloc 529A	ECLAX	C-	(800) 225-2606	D- / 1.4	1.85	3.13	4.27 /34	6.36 /18	7.00 /23	1.72	1.05
AA	MFS Conservative Alloc 529B	EBCAX	C	(800) 225-2606	D / 1.7	1.70	2.78	3.52 /29	5.56 /15	6.19 /18	1.07	1.80
AA	MFS Conservative Alloc 529C	ECACX	C	(800) 225-2606	D / 1.7	1.64	2.73	3.50 /29	5.56 /15	6.20 /18	1.11	1.80
AA	MFS Conservative Alloc A	MACFX	C-	(800) 225-2606	D- / 1.4	1.86	3.14	4.37 /34	6.41 /19	7.05 /23	1.75	0.95
AA	MFS Conservative Alloc B	MACBX	C	(800) 225-2606	D / 1.7	1.69	2.84	3.61 /30	5.61 /15	6.26 /18	1.12	1.70
AA	MFS Conservative Alloc C	MACVX	C	(800) 225-2606	D / 1.7	1.65	2.74	3.60 /29	5.60 /15	6.26 /18	1.16	1.70
AA	MFS Conservative Alloc I	MACIX	C	(800) 225-2606	D+ / 2.3	1.97	3.24	4.59 /36	6.66 /20	7.32 /25	2.09	0.70
AA	MFS Conservative Alloc R1	MACKX	C	(800) 225-2606	D / 1.7	1.68	2.77	3.56 /29	5.60 /15	6.26 /18	1.15	1.70
AA	MFS Conservative Alloc R2	MCARX	C	(800) 225-2606	D / 2.0	1.85	3.03	4.15 /33	6.15 /17	6.81 /22	1.66	1.20
AA	MFS Conservative Alloc R3	MACNX	C	(800) 225-2606	D / 2.1	1.87	3.17	4.33 /34	6.40 /18	7.05 /23	1.87	0.95
AA	MFS Conservative Alloc R4	MACJX	C	(800) 225-2606	D+ / 2.3	1.98	3.27	4.62 /36	6.69 /20	7.35 /25	2.10	0.70
GR	MFS Core Equity A	MRGAX	B	(800) 225-2606	B / 7.7	2.86	7.61	12.65 /85	16.62 /88	14.44 /82	0.39	1.05
GR	MFS Core Equity B	MRGBX	B+	(800) 225-2606	B / 8.2	2.70	7.25	11.85 /82	15.75 /81	13.58 /74	0.00	1.80
GR	MFS Core Equity C	MRGCX	B+	(800) 225-2606	B / 8.2	2.72	7.23	11.83 /82	15.76 /81	13.58 /74	0.00	1.80
GR	MFS Core Equity I	MRGRX	A-	(800) 225-2606	B+ / 8.9	2.95	7.77	12.96 /86	16.92 /89	14.73 /85	0.63	0.80
GR	MFS Core Equity R1	MRGGX	B+	(800) 225-2606	B / 8.2	2.69	7.24	11.84 /82	15.76 /81	13.59 /74	0.00	1.80
GR	MFS Core Equity R2	MRERX	A-	(800) 225-2606	B+ / 8.6	2.84	7.51	12.41 /84	16.33 /86	14.15 /79	0.10	1.30
GR	MFS Core Equity R3	MRGHX	A-	(800) 225-2606	B+ / 8.7	2.87	7.64	12.66 /85	16.63 /88	14.43 /82	0.42	1.05

● Denotes fund is closed to new investors
* Denotes fund is included in Section II

Risk Rating/Pts	Standard Deviation	Beta	NAV As of 3/31/15	Total $(Mil)	Cash %	Stocks %	Bonds %	Other %	Portfolio Turnover Ratio	Last Bull Market Return	Last Bear Market Return	Manager Quality Pct	Manager Tenure (Years)	Initial Purch. $	Additional Purch. $	Front End Load	Back End Load
B /8.2	6.6	0.25	8.72	24	11	0	88	1	0	0.1	-10.5	11	6	2,500	100	0.0	0.0
B+/9.8	3.2	0.15	9.59	7	18	0	81	1	0	1.2	-4.5	36	7	250,000	0	0.0	0.0
B+/9.8	3.2	0.15	9.50	18	18	0	81	1	0	0.3	-4.5	33	7	2,500	100	0.0	0.0
C+/5.9	13.1	1.18	16.04	N/A	2	92	5	1	17	94.6	N/A	12	4	250,000	0	0.0	0.0
C+/5.8	13.2	1.19	15.90	3	2	92	5	1	17	92.2	N/A	9	4	2,500	100	0.0	0.0
C+/5.8	7.3	0.40	9.55	29	23	0	76	1	45	-12.1	-7.8	1	10	250,000	0	0.0	0.0
C+/5.8	7.2	0.40	9.49	127	23	0	76	1	45	-13.0	-8.0	1	10	2,500	100	0.0	0.0
D-/1.1	19.1	1.39	7.60	3	13	86	0	1	752	70.6	-29.1	1	7	2,000	1,000	0.0	1.0
U /	N/A	N/A	9.51	202	7	0	92	1	28	N/A	N/A	N/A	4	0	0	0.0	0.0
C+/6.9	9.8	0.97	20.30	125	3	92	4	1	4	71.8	-19.0	24	13	250	0	5.8	0.0
C+/6.9	9.8	0.97	19.90	8	3	92	4	1	4	67.5	-19.3	17	13	250	0	0.0	0.0
C+/6.9	9.8	0.97	19.71	38	3	92	4	1	4	67.6	-19.3	17	13	250	0	0.0	0.0
C+/6.9	9.8	0.96	20.41	762	3	92	4	1	4	72.0	-19.0	25	13	1,000	50	5.8	0.0
C+/6.9	9.8	0.97	20.12	87	3	92	4	1	4	67.7	-19.3	17	13	1,000	50	0.0	0.0
C+/6.9	9.8	0.97	19.97	287	3	92	4	1	4	67.7	-19.2	18	13	1,000	50	0.0	0.0
C+/6.9	9.8	0.97	20.70	63	3	92	4	1	4	73.5	-18.9	27	13	0	0	0.0	0.0
C+/6.9	9.8	0.96	19.70	21	3	92	4	1	4	67.7	-19.2	18	N/A	0	0	0.0	0.0
C+/6.9	9.8	0.97	20.03	93	3	92	4	1	4	70.6	-19.1	22	12	0	0	0.0	0.0
C+/6.9	9.8	0.97	20.26	172	3	92	4	1	4	72.0	-19.0	25	N/A	0	0	0.0	0.0
C+/6.9	9.8	0.97	20.47	78	3	92	4	1	4	73.7	-18.9	27	N/A	0	0	0.0	0.0
B-/7.0	10.1	1.04	22.93	164	0	99	0	1	42	100.1	-16.9	61	10	1,000	50	5.8	0.0
B-/7.0	10.1	1.04	22.31	12	0	99	0	1	42	95.0	-17.1	49	10	1,000	50	0.0	0.0
B-/7.0	10.1	1.04	22.02	38	0	99	0	1	42	94.9	-17.1	48	10	1,000	50	0.0	0.0
B-/7.0	10.1	1.04	23.18	213	0	99	0	1	42	101.8	-16.8	65	10	0	0	0.0	0.0
B-/7.0	10.1	1.04	22.22	1	0	99	0	1	42	95.0	-17.1	49	10	0	0	0.0	0.0
B-/7.0	10.1	1.04	22.17	15	0	99	0	1	42	98.4	-17.0	57	10	0	0	0.0	0.0
B-/7.0	10.1	1.04	22.84	91	0	99	0	1	42	100.1	-16.8	60	10	0	0	0.0	0.0
B-/7.0	10.1	1.04	22.98	36	0	99	0	1	42	101.7	-16.8	64	10	0	0	0.0	0.0
U /	N/A	N/A	23.19	50	0	99	0	1	42	N/A	N/A	N/A	10	0	0	0.0	0.0
D+/2.7	13.2	0.97	16.80	32	0	99	0	1	67	111.0	-25.3	87	3	0	0	0.0	0.0
D+/2.7	13.2	0.97	16.49	100	0	99	0	1	67	109.3	-25.5	86	3	0	0	0.0	0.0
C-/3.6	12.6	0.70	6.67	N/A	3	0	96	1	21	-25.6	-21.0	0	5	1,000	50	5.8	0.0
C-/3.6	12.7	0.71	6.67	N/A	3	0	96	1	21	-25.0	-20.9	0	5	0	0	0.0	0.0
U /	N/A	N/A	6.67	565	3	0	96	1	21	N/A	N/A	N/A	5	0	0	0.0	0.0
B+/9.3	4.4	0.73	14.88	80	22	35	41	2	5	33.0	-6.4	47	13	250	0	5.8	0.0
B+/9.3	4.5	0.73	14.67	7	22	35	41	2	5	29.6	-6.7	35	13	250	0	0.0	0.0
B+/9.3	4.5	0.74	14.63	40	22	35	41	2	5	29.6	-6.7	34	13	250	0	0.0	0.0
B+/9.3	4.5	0.73	14.95	1,408	22	35	41	2	5	33.2	-6.3	47	13	1,000	50	5.8	0.0
B+/9.3	4.5	0.74	14.88	168	22	35	41	2	5	29.8	-6.7	35	13	1,000	50	0.0	0.0
B+/9.3	4.5	0.74	14.75	739	22	35	41	2	5	29.8	-6.7	35	13	1,000	50	0.0	0.0
B+/9.3	4.5	0.73	15.07	161	22	35	41	2	5	34.3	-6.3	50	13	0	0	0.0	0.0
B+/9.3	4.5	0.74	14.49	21	22	35	41	2	5	29.8	-6.7	35	N/A	0	0	0.0	0.0
B+/9.3	4.4	0.73	14.58	111	22	35	41	2	5	32.2	-6.5	43	12	0	0	0.0	0.0
B+/9.3	4.5	0.73	14.84	180	22	35	41	2	5	33.3	-6.4	47	N/A	0	0	0.0	0.0
B+/9.3	4.5	0.73	14.96	122	22	35	41	2	5	34.4	-6.3	50	N/A	0	0	0.0	0.0
C+/6.3	9.7	1.00	28.40	1,038	2	97	0	1	48	99.8	-17.6	73	7	1,000	0	5.8	0.0
C+/6.3	9.7	0.99	25.88	38	2	97	0	1	48	94.8	-17.9	64	7	1,000	0	0.0	0.0
C+/6.2	9.7	1.00	25.64	93	2	97	0	1	48	94.7	-17.9	64	7	1,000	0	0.0	0.0
C+/6.4	9.7	1.00	29.68	53	2	97	0	1	48	101.5	-17.5	75	7	0	0	0.0	0.0
C+/6.2	9.7	0.99	25.62	4	2	97	0	1	48	94.8	-17.9	64	7	0	0	0.0	0.0
C+/6.4	9.7	1.00	27.84	18	2	97	0	1	48	98.0	-17.7	70	7	0	0	0.0	0.0
C+/6.3	9.8	1.00	28.31	71	2	97	0	1	48	99.8	-17.7	72	7	0	0	0.0	0.0

Fund Type	Fund Name	Ticker Symbol	Overall Investment Rating	Phone	Performance Rating/Pts	3 Mo	6 Mo	1Yr / Pct	3Yr / Pct	5Yr / Pct	Dividend Yield	Expense Ratio
	99 Pct = Best				**PERFORMANCE**			Total Return % through 3/31/15			Incl. in Returns	
	0 Pct = Worst								Annualized			
GR	MFS Core Equity R4	MRGJX	A-	(800) 225-2606	B+ / 8.9	2.92	7.75	12.96 /86	16.92 /89	14.69 /84	0.67	0.80
AA	MFS Diversified Income Fund A	DIFAX	C	(800) 225-2606	D+ / 2.9	1.92	5.28	8.05 /63	8.52 /30	9.23 /38	2.69	1.08
AA	MFS Diversified Income Fund C	DIFCX	C	(800) 225-2606	C- / 3.1	1.73	4.89	7.25 /57	7.72 /25	8.42 /33	2.07	1.83
AA	MFS Diversified Income Fund I	DIFIX	C+	(800) 225-2606	C- / 3.8	1.99	5.41	8.32 /65	8.79 /32	9.50 /41	3.05	0.83
AA	MFS Diversified Income Fund R1	DIFDX	C	(800) 225-2606	C- / 3.1	1.73	4.89	7.25 /57	7.72 /25	8.41 /33	2.07	1.83
AA	MFS Diversified Income Fund R2	DIFEX	C	(800) 225-2606	C- / 3.4	1.86	5.15	7.78 /61	8.25 /28	8.96 /36	2.56	1.33
AA	MFS Diversified Income Fund R3	DIFFX	C+	(800) 225-2606	C- / 3.6	1.92	5.28	8.05 /63	8.55 /30	9.25 /39	2.80	1.08
AA	MFS Diversified Income Fund R4	DIFGX	C+	(800) 225-2606	C- / 3.8	1.99	5.41	8.32 /65	8.82 /32	9.52 /41	3.05	0.83
EM	MFS Emerging Mkt Equity Fund A	MEMAX	E	(800) 225-2606	E- / 0.2	0.40	-5.47	-4.58 / 6	-2.96 / 2	0.21 / 3	0.67	1.69
EM	MFS Emerging Mkt Equity Fund B	MEMBX	E	(800) 225-2606	E- / 0.2	0.20	-5.86	-5.31 / 5	-3.70 / 2	-0.54 / 2	0.00	2.44
EM	MFS Emerging Mkt Equity Fund C	MEMCX	E	(800) 225-2606	E- / 0.2	0.20	-5.85	-5.33 / 5	-3.70 / 2	-0.55 / 2	0.00	2.44
EM	MFS Emerging Mkt Equity Fund I	MEMIX	E	(800) 225-2606	E / 0.3	0.45	-5.38	-4.35 / 6	-2.73 / 2	0.46 / 3	0.98	1.44
EM	MFS Emerging Mkt Equity Fund R1	MEMRX	E	(800) 225-2606	E- / 0.2	0.20	-5.87	-5.34 / 5	-3.71 / 2	-0.55 / 2	0.28	2.44
EM	MFS Emerging Mkt Equity Fund R2	MEMFX	E	(800) 225-2606	E / 0.3	0.32	-5.62	-4.82 / 6	-3.21 / 2	-0.05 / 2	0.69	1.94
EM	MFS Emerging Mkt Equity Fund R3	MEMGX	E	(800) 225-2606	E / 0.3	0.37	-5.49	-4.60 / 6	-2.98 / 2	0.21 / 3	0.79	1.69
EM	MFS Emerging Mkt Equity Fund R4	MEMHX	E	(800) 225-2606	E / 0.3	0.44	-5.38	-4.35 / 6	-2.73 / 2	0.46 / 3	1.02	1.44
EM	MFS Emerging Mkt Equity Fund R5	MEMJX	U	(800) 225-2606	U /	0.45	-5.35	-4.26 / 7	--	--	1.07	1.34
IN	MFS Equity Income A	EQNAX	U	(800) 225-2606	U /	0.87	2.61	6.55 /51	--	--	1.79	1.68
GR	MFS Equity Opportunities Class A	SRFAX	B	(800) 225-2606	B- / 7.0	3.21	5.56	5.94 /46	16.70 /88	15.77 /92	0.25	1.20
GR	MFS Equity Opportunities Class B	SRFBX	B+	(800) 225-2606	B- / 7.5	3.04	5.19	5.15 /40	15.82 /82	14.90 /86	0.00	1.95
GR	MFS Equity Opportunities Class C	SRFCX	B+	(800) 225-2606	B- / 7.5	3.03	5.15	5.15 /40	15.82 /82	14.91 /86	0.00	1.95
GR	MFS Equity Opportunities Class I	SRFIX	A-	(800) 225-2606	B+ / 8.3	3.28	5.66	6.20 /48	16.99 /90	16.00 /93	0.50	0.95
GR	MFS Equity Opportunities Class R1	SRFDX	B+	(800) 225-2606	B- / 7.5	3.04	5.17	5.17 /40	15.82 /82	14.91 /86	0.00	1.95
GR	MFS Equity Opportunities Class R2	SRFEX	B+	(800) 225-2606	B / 7.9	3.19	5.43	5.71 /44	16.41 /86	15.49 /90	0.37	1.45
GR	MFS Equity Opportunities Class R3	SRFFX	A-	(800) 225-2606	B / 8.2	3.22	5.57	5.95 /46	16.70 /88	15.77 /92	0.39	1.20
GR	MFS Equity Opportunities Class R4	SRFGX	A-	(800) 225-2606	B+ / 8.3	3.28	5.69	6.18 /48	16.98 /90	16.06 /93	0.49	0.95
GR	MFS Equity Opportunities R5	SRFHX	A-	(800) 225-2606	B+ / 8.4	3.30	5.74	6.26 /49	17.05 /90	16.06 /93	0.57	0.86
GI	MFS Global Alternative Strategy A	DVRAX	C-	(800) 225-2606	D / 1.8	3.63	3.96	6.27 /49	6.85 /21	5.11 /12	0.81	1.64
GI	MFS Global Alternative Strategy B	DVRBX	C-	(800) 225-2606	D / 2.1	3.39	3.58	5.53 /43	6.03 /17	4.32 / 9	0.17	2.39
GI	MFS Global Alternative Strategy C	DVRCX	C-	(800) 225-2606	D / 2.1	3.40	3.64	5.48 /42	6.02 /17	4.31 / 9	0.22	2.39
GI	MFS Global Alternative Strategy I	DVRIX	C	(800) 225-2606	D+ / 2.7	3.60	4.04	6.45 /50	7.08 /22	5.37 /14	1.06	1.39
GI	MFS Global Alternative Strategy R1	DVRFX	C-	(800) 225-2606	D / 2.1	3.41	3.51	5.46 /42	6.01 /17	4.31 / 9	0.19	2.39
GI	MFS Global Alternative Strategy R2	DVRHX	C	(800) 225-2606	D+ / 2.4	3.56	3.79	6.03 /47	6.56 /19	4.82 /11	0.68	1.89
GI	MFS Global Alternative Strategy R3	DVRJX	C	(800) 225-2606	D+ / 2.6	3.52	3.89	6.21 /48	6.82 /20	5.08 /12	0.71	1.64
GI	MFS Global Alternative Strategy R4	DVRKX	C	(800) 225-2606	D+ / 2.8	3.59	4.01	6.51 /51	7.09 /22	5.35 /13	1.03	1.39
GI	MFS Global Alternative Strategy R5	DVRLX	C	(800) 225-2606	D+ / 2.8	3.67	4.18	6.67 /52	7.15 /22	5.36 /14	1.10	1.32
GL	MFS Global Equity Fund A	MWEFX	C+	(800) 225-2606	C / 5.3	2.93	6.30	6.21 /48	13.61 /64	11.79 /59	0.66	1.23
GL	MFS Global Equity Fund B	MWEBX	C+	(800) 225-2606	C+ / 5.8	2.75	5.91	5.42 /42	12.76 /58	10.96 /52	0.05	1.98
GL	MFS Global Equity Fund C	MWECX	C+	(800) 225-2606	C+ / 5.8	2.74	5.88	5.41 /42	12.76 /58	10.95 /52	0.16	1.98
GL	MFS Global Equity Fund I	MWEIX	C+	(800) 225-2606	C+ / 6.5	3.00	6.45	6.48 /51	13.90 /66	12.08 /61	0.90	0.98
GL	MFS Global Equity Fund R1	MWEGX	C+	(800) 225-2606	C+ / 5.8	2.75	5.91	5.41 /42	12.76 /58	10.97 /52	0.08	1.98
GL	MFS Global Equity Fund R2	MEQRX	C+	(800) 225-2606	C+ / 6.1	2.86	6.18	5.93 /46	13.32 /62	11.52 /57	0.45	1.48
GL	MFS Global Equity Fund R3	MWEHX	C+	(800) 225-2606	C+ / 6.3	2.95	6.30	6.21 /48	13.62 /64	11.80 /59	0.72	1.23
GL	MFS Global Equity Fund R4	MWELX	C+	(800) 225-2606	C+ / 6.5	3.01	6.44	6.47 /50	13.89 /66	12.08 /61	0.93	0.98
GL	MFS Global Equity Fund R5	MWEMX	U	(800) 225-2606	U /	3.03	6.51	6.57 /52	--	--	0.98	0.90
GL	MFS Global Growth Fund A	MWOFX	D+	(800) 225-2606	C- / 3.4	2.02	5.79	5.88 /45	10.07 /40	9.30 /39	0.27	1.45
GL	MFS Global Growth Fund B	MWOBX	C-	(800) 225-2606	C- / 3.8	1.81	5.42	5.11 /39	9.25 /35	8.49 /33	0.00	2.20
GL	MFS Global Growth Fund C	MWOCX	C-	(800) 225-2606	C- / 3.8	1.80	5.37	5.10 /39	9.24 /34	8.48 /33	0.00	2.20
GL	MFS Global Growth Fund I	MWOIX	C-	(800) 225-2606	C / 4.4	2.07	5.91	6.15 /48	10.34 /41	9.57 /41	0.52	1.20
GL	MFS Global Growth Fund R1	MWOGX	C-	(800) 225-2606	C- / 3.8	1.83	5.38	5.11 /39	9.25 /35	8.49 /33	0.00	2.20
GL	MFS Global Growth Fund R2	MGWRX	C-	(800) 225-2606	C- / 4.1	1.95	5.66	5.62 /43	9.79 /38	9.03 /37	0.01	1.70
GL	MFS Global Growth Fund R3	MWOHX	C-	(800) 225-2606	C / 4.3	2.00	5.78	5.87 /45	10.06 /40	9.30 /39	0.28	1.45

● Denotes fund is closed to new investors
* Denotes fund is included in Section II

Risk Rating/Pts	Standard Deviation (3 Year)	Beta	NAV As of 3/31/15	Total $(Mil)	Cash %	Stocks %	Bonds %	Other %	Portfolio Turnover Ratio	Last Bull Market Return	Last Bear Market Return	Manager Quality Pct	Manager Tenure (Years)	Initial Purch. $	Additional Purch. $	Front End Load	Back End Load
C+ / 6.3	9.7	0.99	28.58	23	2	97	0	1	48	101.4	-17.6	75	7	0	0	0.0	0.0
B / 8.4	5.3	0.80	12.65	1,372	31	35	32	2	63	46.8	-8.2	67	9	1,000	0	4.3	0.0
B / 8.4	5.3	0.79	12.64	891	31	35	32	2	63	43.2	-8.6	57	9	1,000	0	0.0	0.0
B / 8.4	5.3	0.79	12.65	752	31	35	32	2	63	48.1	-8.1	70	9	0	0	0.0	0.0
B / 8.4	5.3	0.79	12.63	1	31	35	32	2	63	43.2	-8.6	56	9	0	0	0.0	0.0
B / 8.4	5.3	0.79	12.64	2	31	35	32	2	63	45.6	-8.3	64	9	0	0	0.0	0.0
B / 8.3	5.3	0.79	12.65	8	31	35	32	2	63	47.0	-8.3	67	9	0	0	0.0	0.0
B / 8.4	5.3	0.79	12.65	5	31	35	32	2	63	48.2	-8.2	70	9	0	0	0.0	0.0
C / 4.6	13.9	1.00	27.34	135	1	98	0	1	44	11.6	-25.6	19	7	1,000	50	5.8	0.0
C / 4.6	13.9	1.00	25.56	9	1	98	0	1	44	8.9	-25.9	13	7	1,000	50	0.0	0.0
C / 4.6	13.9	1.00	24.96	30	1	98	0	1	44	8.8	-25.9	13	7	1,000	50	0.0	0.0
C / 4.6	13.9	1.00	28.74	51	1	98	0	1	44	12.6	-25.5	21	7	0	0	0.0	0.0
C / 4.5	13.9	1.00	24.75	1	1	98	0	1	44	8.8	-25.8	13	7	0	0	0.0	0.0
C / 4.5	13.9	1.00	25.13	2	1	98	0	1	44	10.7	-25.7	17	7	0	0	0.0	0.0
C / 4.6	13.9	1.00	27.17	5	1	98	0	1	44	11.7	-25.6	19	7	0	0	0.0	0.0
C / 4.6	13.9	1.00	27.23	5	1	98	0	1	44	12.6	-25.5	21	7	0	0	0.0	0.0
U /	N/A	N/A	28.76	547	1	98	0	1	44	N/A	N/A	N/A	7	0	0	0.0	0.0
U /	N/A	N/A	13.39	70	1	98	0	1	34	N/A	N/A	N/A	3	1,000	0	5.8	0.0
C+ / 6.8	11.0	1.02	29.24	245	0	99	0	1	106	100.1	-18.7	70	5	1,000	0	5.8	0.0
C+ / 6.8	11.0	1.02	28.16	19	0	99	0	1	106	95.0	-19.0	59	5	1,000	0	0.0	0.0
C+ / 6.8	11.0	1.02	28.18	110	0	99	0	1	106	94.9	-19.0	60	5	1,000	0	0.0	0.0
C+ / 6.8	11.0	1.02	29.30	126	0	99	0	1	106	101.7	-18.7	72	5	0	0	0.0	0.0
C+ / 6.8	11.0	1.02	28.09	1	0	99	0	1	106	95.0	-19.0	59	5	0	0	0.0	0.0
C+ / 6.8	11.0	1.02	28.50	2	0	99	0	1	106	98.3	-18.8	67	5	0	0	0.0	0.0
C+ / 6.8	11.0	1.02	29.14	2	0	99	0	1	106	100.0	-18.7	70	5	0	0	0.0	0.0
C+ / 6.8	11.0	1.02	29.32	14	0	99	0	1	106	101.6	-18.6	72	5	0	0	0.0	0.0
C+ / 6.8	11.0	1.02	29.76	2	0	99	0	1	106	102.1	-18.6	73	5	0	0	0.0	0.0
B / 8.6	3.5	0.20	10.86	149	12	67	19	2	94	25.9	1.2	91	8	1,000	0	5.8	0.0
B / 8.7	3.5	0.20	10.66	9	12	67	19	2	94	22.5	1.0	88	8	1,000	0	0.0	0.0
B / 8.7	3.5	0.20	10.65	44	12	67	19	2	94	22.6	0.9	88	8	1,000	0	0.0	0.0
B / 8.6	3.5	0.20	10.95	315	12	67	19	2	94	26.9	1.4	91	8	0	0	0.0	0.0
B / 8.7	3.6	0.20	10.61	N/A	12	67	19	2	94	22.6	1.0	88	8	0	0	0.0	0.0
B / 8.6	3.5	0.20	10.75	1	12	67	19	2	94	24.8	1.1	90	8	0	0	0.0	0.0
B / 8.6	3.5	0.20	10.87	N/A	12	67	19	2	94	25.8	1.2	90	8	0	0	0.0	0.0
B / 8.6	3.5	0.20	10.96	2	12	67	19	2	94	26.9	1.4	91	8	0	0	0.0	0.0
B / 8.6	3.5	0.21	11.01	1	12	67	19	2	94	27.0	1.3	91	8	0	0	0.0	0.0
C+ / 6.8	11.0	0.77	36.55	643	0	99	0	1	11	83.7	-19.7	95	23	1,000	0	5.8	0.0
C+ / 6.7	11.0	0.76	33.97	27	0	99	0	1	11	79.1	-20.0	94	23	1,000	0	0.0	0.0
C+ / 6.7	11.0	0.77	32.62	123	0	99	0	1	11	79.1	-20.0	94	23	1,000	0	0.0	0.0
C+ / 6.8	11.0	0.76	37.43	734	0	99	0	1	11	85.3	-19.6	95	23	0	0	0.0	0.0
C+ / 6.7	11.0	0.76	33.25	4	0	99	0	1	11	79.2	-20.0	94	23	0	0	0.0	0.0
C+ / 6.7	11.0	0.77	35.56	56	0	99	0	1	11	82.1	-19.8	94	23	0	0	0.0	0.0
C+ / 6.7	11.0	0.77	36.31	101	0	99	0	1	11	83.7	-19.7	95	23	0	0	0.0	0.0
C+ / 6.8	11.0	0.76	36.65	116	0	99	0	1	11	85.2	-19.7	95	23	0	0	0.0	0.0
U /	N/A	N/A	37.44	360	0	99	0	1	11	N/A	N/A	N/A	23	0	0	0.0	0.0
C+ / 6.3	10.8	0.76	34.33	187	1	98	0	1	27	68.1	-19.3	88	5	1,000	0	5.8	0.0
C+ / 6.3	10.8	0.75	30.94	7	1	98	0	1	27	63.9	-19.6	84	5	1,000	0	0.0	0.0
C+ / 6.3	10.8	0.76	30.60	14	1	98	0	1	27	63.9	-19.6	84	5	1,000	0	0.0	0.0
C+ / 6.3	10.8	0.76	35.04	14	1	98	0	1	27	69.5	-19.2	89	5	0	0	0.0	0.0
C+ / 6.3	10.8	0.76	30.55	1	1	98	0	1	27	63.8	-19.6	84	5	0	0	0.0	0.0
C+ / 6.3	10.8	0.76	33.47	3	1	98	0	1	27	66.7	-19.4	87	5	0	0	0.0	0.0
C+ / 6.3	10.8	0.75	34.17	4	1	98	0	1	27	68.1	-19.3	88	5	0	0	0.0	0.0

Fund Type	Fund Name	Ticker Symbol	Overall Investment Rating	Phone	Performance Rating/Pts	3 Mo	6 Mo	1Yr / Pct	3Yr / Pct	5Yr / Pct	Dividend Yield	Expense Ratio
									Annualized		Incl. in Returns	
	99 Pct = Best *0 Pct = Worst*							Total Return % through 3/31/15				
GL	MFS Global Growth Fund R4	MWOJX	C-	(800) 225-2606	C / 4.4	2.05	5.90	6.12 /48	10.34 /41	9.57 /41	0.52	1.20
GL	MFS Global Leaders Fund A	GLOAX	D+	(800) 225-2606	C- / 3.1	2.66	5.44	4.30 /34	9.80 /38	--	0.36	2.48
GL	MFS Global Leaders Fund B	GLOBX	D+	(800) 225-2606	C- / 3.5	2.40	5.03	3.49 /29	8.96 /33	--	0.00	3.23
GL	MFS Global Leaders Fund C	GLOCX	D+	(800) 225-2606	C- / 3.5	2.48	5.11	3.49 /29	8.97 /33	--	0.00	3.23
GL	MFS Global Leaders Fund I	GLODX	C-	(800) 225-2606	C- / 4.2	2.65	5.63	4.48 /35	10.04 /40	--	0.64	2.23
GL	MFS Global New Discovery A	GLNAX	D+	(800) 225-2606	C- / 3.2	3.29	5.61	-1.10 /13	10.73 /44	--	0.00	2.28
GL	MFS Global New Discovery B	GLNBX	C-	(800) 225-2606	C- / 3.6	3.16	5.23	-1.78 /11	9.92 /39	--	0.00	3.03
GL	MFS Global New Discovery C	GLNCX	C-	(800) 225-2606	C- / 3.6	3.09	5.15	-1.85 /11	9.90 /39	--	0.00	3.03
GL	MFS Global New Discovery I	GLNIX	C-	(800) 225-2606	C / 4.3	3.41	5.77	-0.84 /13	11.00 /45	--	0.00	2.03
GL	MFS Global New Discovery R1	GLNJX	C-	(800) 225-2606	C- / 3.6	3.09	5.15	-1.85 /11	9.90 /39	--	0.00	3.03
GL	MFS Global New Discovery R2	GLNKX	C-	(800) 225-2606	C- / 4.0	3.25	5.51	-1.30 /12	10.45 /42	--	0.00	2.53
GL	MFS Global New Discovery R3	GLNLX	C-	(800) 225-2606	C- / 4.1	3.29	5.61	-1.10 /13	10.73 /44	--	0.00	2.28
GL	MFS Global New Discovery R4	GLNMX	C-	(800) 225-2606	C / 4.3	3.41	5.77	-0.84 /13	11.00 /45	--	0.00	2.03
RE	MFS Global Real Estate A	MGLAX	C-	(800) 225-2606	C+ / 5.8	2.90	10.38	14.48 /91	12.48 /56	10.84 /51	2.35	1.22
RE	MFS Global Real Estate I	MGLIX	C	(800) 225-2606	B- / 7.0	3.03	10.49	14.73 /91	12.77 /58	11.12 /54	2.72	0.97
RE	MFS Global Real Estate R5	MGLRX	U	(800) 225-2606	U /	3.03	10.49	14.73 /91	--	--	2.72	0.97
GL	MFS Global Total Return Fund A	MFWTX	C-	(800) 225-2606	D / 1.9	0.82	1.89	2.65 /25	8.06 /27	7.83 /29	1.70	1.27
GL	MFS Global Total Return Fund B	MFWBX	C-	(800) 225-2606	D / 2.2	0.65	1.48	1.88 /21	7.26 /23	7.03 /23	1.13	2.02
GL	MFS Global Total Return Fund C	MFWCX	C-	(800) 225-2606	D / 2.2	0.60	1.45	1.88 /21	7.27 /23	7.03 /23	1.18	2.02
GL	MFS Global Total Return Fund I	MFWIX	C	(800) 225-2606	D+ / 2.9	0.94	2.03	2.93 /26	8.36 /29	8.11 /31	2.07	1.02
GL	MFS Global Total Return Fund R1	MFWGX	C-	(800) 225-2606	D / 2.2	0.66	1.49	1.86 /21	7.26 /23	7.02 /23	1.16	2.02
GL	MFS Global Total Return Fund R2	MGBRX	C	(800) 225-2606	D+ / 2.6	0.80	1.74	2.41 /24	7.80 /26	7.57 /27	1.57	1.52
GL	MFS Global Total Return Fund R3	MFWHX	C	(800) 225-2606	D+ / 2.7	0.82	1.89	2.65 /25	8.06 /27	7.84 /29	1.80	1.27
GL	MFS Global Total Return Fund R4	MFWJX	C	(800) 225-2606	D+ / 2.9	0.93	2.01	2.95 /26	8.34 /29	8.11 /31	2.05	1.02
GL	MFS Global Total Return Fund R5	MFWLX	U	(800) 225-2606	U /	0.96	2.08	3.02 /27	--	--	2.16	0.93
AA	MFS Growth Allocation 529A	EAGWX	C	(800) 225-2606	C- / 3.4	2.75	4.57	5.15 /40	10.27 /41	10.05 /45	1.44	1.17
AA	MFS Growth Allocation 529B	EBGWX	C	(800) 225-2606	C- / 3.8	2.55	4.20	4.38 /34	9.43 /36	9.22 /38	0.70	1.92
AA	MFS Growth Allocation 529C	ECGWX	C	(800) 225-2606	C- / 3.8	2.58	4.20	4.38 /34	9.45 /36	9.22 /38	0.88	1.92
AA	MFS Growth Allocation A	MAGWX	C	(800) 225-2606	C- / 3.4	2.79	4.58	5.22 /40	10.32 /41	10.11 /46	1.47	1.07
AA	MFS Growth Allocation B	MBGWX	C	(800) 225-2606	C- / 3.8	2.59	4.19	4.42 /35	9.48 /36	9.30 /39	0.77	1.82
AA	MFS Growth Allocation C	MCGWX	C	(800) 225-2606	C- / 3.8	2.55	4.18	4.41 /34	9.49 /36	9.29 /39	0.90	1.82
AA	MFS Growth Allocation I	MGWIX	C+	(800) 225-2606	C / 4.5	2.82	4.68	5.43 /42	10.57 /43	10.38 /48	1.78	0.82
AA	MFS Growth Allocation R1	MAGMX	C	(800) 225-2606	C- / 3.8	2.60	4.19	4.43 /35	9.49 /36	9.28 /39	0.84	1.82
AA	MFS Growth Allocation R2	MGALX	C+	(800) 225-2606	C- / 4.1	2.67	4.47	4.94 /38	10.03 /39	9.84 /43	1.33	1.32
AA	MFS Growth Allocation R3	MAGEX	C+	(800) 225-2606	C / 4.3	2.75	4.61	5.19 /40	10.31 /41	10.11 /46	1.56	1.07
AA	MFS Growth Allocation R4	MAGJX	C+	(800) 225-2606	C / 4.5	2.79	4.67	5.41 /42	10.55 /43	10.37 /48	1.80	0.82
GR	MFS Growth Fund A	MFEGX	B	(800) 225-2606	B- / 7.3	3.42	8.53	12.49 /85	15.81 /82	14.48 /82	0.00	1.03
GR	MFS Growth Fund B	MEGBX	B	(800) 225-2606	B / 7.7	3.22	8.12	11.64 /81	14.95 /74	13.63 /74	0.00	1.78
GR	MFS Growth Fund C	MFECX	B	(800) 225-2606	B / 7.7	3.23	8.13	11.65 /81	14.94 /74	13.62 /74	0.00	1.78
GR	MFS Growth Fund I	MFEIX	B+	(800) 225-2606	B+ / 8.6	3.47	8.65	12.76 /86	16.08 /84	14.76 /85	0.00	0.78
GR	MFS Growth Fund R1	MFELX	B	(800) 225-2606	B / 7.7	3.22	8.12	11.63 /81	14.94 /74	13.62 /74	0.00	1.78
GR	MFS Growth Fund R2	MEGRX	B+	(800) 225-2606	B / 8.2	3.35	8.39	12.21 /84	15.52 /79	14.19 /79	0.00	1.28
GR	MFS Growth Fund R3	MFEHX	B+	(800) 225-2606	B+ / 8.4	3.40	8.52	12.47 /85	15.81 /82	14.48 /82	0.00	1.03
GR	MFS Growth Fund R4	MFEJX	B+	(800) 225-2606	B+ / 8.6	3.48	8.66	12.76 /86	16.10 /84	14.76 /85	0.00	0.78
GR	MFS Growth R5	MFEKX	A-	(800) 225-2606	B+ / 8.6	3.51	8.72	12.88 /86	16.18 /85	--	0.00	0.69
* FO	MFS Inst Intl Equity Fund	MIEIX	D+	(800) 225-2606	C- / 3.5	6.12	3.36	2.66 /25	8.91 /32	7.99 /30	2.04	0.72
GR	MFS Inst Large Cap Value Fund	ILVAX	A-	(800) 225-2606	B / 8.0	0.71	6.37	9.69 /73	16.07 /84	13.30 /71	2.33	0.64
FO	MFS International Diversifictn 529A	MDIEX	D	(800) 225-2606	D / 1.7	4.91	2.42	0.91 /18	7.42 /24	6.99 /23	1.11	1.34
FO	MFS International Diversifictn 529B	MDIMX	D	(800) 225-2606	D / 2.0	4.73	2.08	0.13 /16	6.58 /19	6.17 /18	0.37	2.09
FO	MFS International Diversifictn 529C	MDINX	D	(800) 225-2606	D / 2.0	4.73	2.09	0.17 /16	6.58 /19	6.17 /18	0.41	2.09
FO	MFS International Diversifictn A	MDIDX	D	(800) 225-2606	D / 1.7	4.94	2.52	0.96 /18	7.45 /24	7.04 /23	1.10	1.24
FO	MFS International Diversifictn B	MDIFX	D	(800) 225-2606	D / 2.1	4.78	2.09	0.21 /16	6.64 /20	6.25 /18	0.26	1.99

● Denotes fund is closed to new investors
* Denotes fund is included in Section II

www.thestreetratings.com

RISK			NET ASSETS		ASSET				Portfolio	BULL / BEAR		FUND MANAGER		MINIMUMS		LOADS	
Risk Rating/Pts	3 Year		NAV As of 3/31/15	Total $(Mil)	Cash %	Stocks %	Bonds %	Other %	Turnover Ratio	Last Bull Market Return	Last Bear Market Return	Manager Quality Pct	Manager Tenure (Years)	Initial Purch. $	Additional Purch. $	Front End Load	Back End Load
	Standard Deviation	Beta															
C+ / 6.3	10.8	0.75	34.35	1	1	98	0	1	27	69.5	-19.2	89	5	0	0	0.0	0.0
C+ / 6.2	10.1	0.67	13.88	8	3	96	0	1	17	66.4	N/A	89	4	1,000	0	5.8	0.0
C+ / 6.2	10.1	0.68	13.65	1	3	96	0	1	17	62.2	N/A	86	4	1,000	0	0.0	0.0
C+ / 6.2	10.1	0.68	13.65	2	3	96	0	1	17	62.3	N/A	86	4	1,000	0	0.0	0.0
C+ / 6.2	10.1	0.67	13.93	3	3	96	0	1	17	67.8	N/A	90	4	0	0	0.0	0.0
C+ / 6.4	12.0	0.67	14.74	14	1	98	0	1	53	N/A	N/A	92	4	1,000	0	5.8	0.0
C+ / 6.4	12.0	0.67	14.36	1	1	98	0	1	53	N/A	N/A	90	4	1,000	0	0.0	0.0
C+ / 6.4	12.0	0.67	14.35	5	1	98	0	1	53	N/A	N/A	90	4	1,000	0	0.0	0.0
C+ / 6.4	12.0	0.67	14.87	4	1	98	0	1	53	N/A	N/A	92	4	0	0	0.0	0.0
C+ / 6.4	12.0	0.67	14.35	N/A	1	98	0	1	53	N/A	N/A	90	4	0	0	0.0	0.0
C+ / 6.4	12.0	0.67	14.61	N/A	1	98	0	1	53	N/A	N/A	91	4	0	0	0.0	0.0
C+ / 6.4	12.0	0.67	14.74	N/A	1	98	0	1	53	N/A	N/A	92	4	0	0	0.0	0.0
C+ / 6.4	12.0	0.67	14.87	N/A	1	98	0	1	53	N/A	N/A	92	4	0	0	0.0	0.0
C / 4.8	12.2	0.89	16.30	1	8	91	0	1	30	72.3	-19.7	68	6	1,000	0	5.8	0.0
C / 4.8	12.2	0.89	16.32	1	8	91	0	1	30	73.7	-19.5	71	6	0	0	0.0	0.0
U /	N/A	N/A	16.32	456	8	91	0	1	30	N/A	N/A	N/A	6	0	0	0.0	0.0
B / 8.5	6.9	0.49	16.60	803	4	59	35	2	23	42.6	-9.3	90	15	1,000	0	5.8	0.0
B / 8.5	6.9	0.48	17.00	64	4	59	35	2	23	39.0	-9.5	87	15	1,000	0	0.0	0.0
B / 8.5	6.9	0.48	16.78	322	4	59	35	2	23	39.0	-9.5	87	15	1,000	0	0.0	0.0
B / 8.5	6.9	0.48	16.45	200	4	59	35	2	23	43.8	-9.2	90	15	0	0	0.0	0.0
B / 8.5	6.9	0.49	16.72	3	4	59	35	2	23	39.1	-9.6	87	15	0	0	0.0	0.0
B / 8.5	6.9	0.48	16.48	10	4	59	35	2	23	41.5	-9.4	89	15	0	0	0.0	0.0
B / 8.5	6.9	0.48	16.55	13	4	59	35	2	23	42.7	-9.3	90	15	0	0	0.0	0.0
B / 8.5	6.8	0.48	16.62	9	4	59	35	2	23	43.8	-9.2	91	15	0	0	0.0	0.0
U /	N/A	N/A	16.45	79	4	59	35	2	23	N/A	N/A	N/A	15	0	0	0.0	0.0
B- / 7.9	8.1	1.36	18.69	200	8	72	18	2	2	59.4	-15.3	14	13	250	0	5.8	0.0
B- / 7.9	8.1	1.36	18.47	18	8	72	18	2	2	55.3	-15.4	10	13	250	0	0.0	0.0
B- / 7.9	8.1	1.36	18.28	75	8	72	18	2	2	55.3	-15.6	10	13	250	0	0.0	0.0
B- / 7.9	8.2	1.37	18.82	2,834	8	72	18	2	2	59.6	-15.2	14	13	1,000	50	5.8	0.0
B- / 7.9	8.2	1.37	18.64	299	8	72	18	2	2	55.5	-15.4	10	13	1,000	50	0.0	0.0
B- / 7.9	8.2	1.37	18.48	997	8	72	18	2	2	55.5	-15.5	10	13	1,000	50	0.0	0.0
B- / 7.9	8.1	1.36	18.96	106	8	72	18	2	2	60.9	-15.1	16	13	0	0	0.0	0.0
B- / 7.9	8.2	1.37	18.13	47	8	72	18	2	2	55.5	-15.5	10	N/A	0	0	0.0	0.0
B- / 7.9	8.2	1.37	18.43	237	8	72	18	2	2	58.3	-15.3	12	12	0	0	0.0	0.0
B- / 7.9	8.1	1.37	18.67	270	8	72	18	2	2	59.5	-15.2	14	N/A	0	0	0.0	0.0
B- / 7.9	8.1	1.37	18.80	238	8	72	18	2	2	60.8	-15.1	16	N/A	0	0	0.0	0.0
C+ / 6.3	10.5	1.00	70.52	4,329	2	97	0	1	33	96.5	-14.4	64	13	1,000	50	5.8	0.0
C+ / 6.2	10.5	1.00	59.56	141	2	97	0	1	33	91.5	-14.7	53	13	1,000	50	0.0	0.0
C+ / 6.2	10.5	1.00	59.15	495	2	97	0	1	33	91.5	-14.7	53	13	1,000	50	0.0	0.0
C+ / 6.3	10.5	1.00	73.99	3,350	2	97	0	1	33	98.1	-14.3	67	13	0	0	0.0	0.0
C+ / 6.2	10.5	1.00	59.34	15	2	97	0	1	33	91.5	-14.7	53	13	0	0	0.0	0.0
C+ / 6.2	10.5	1.00	67.56	162	2	97	0	1	33	94.8	-14.5	61	13	0	0	0.0	0.0
C+ / 6.3	10.5	1.00	70.21	466	2	97	0	1	33	96.5	-14.4	64	13	0	0	0.0	0.0
C+ / 6.3	10.5	1.00	72.16	888	2	97	0	1	33	98.2	-14.3	68	13	0	0	0.0	0.0
C+ / 6.3	10.5	1.00	74.05	2,180	2	97	0	1	33	98.5	N/A	68	13	0	0	0.0	0.0
C+ / 5.9	12.5	0.92	22.19	7,392	0	99	0	1	14	58.4	-23.1	69	14	3,000,000	0	0.0	0.0
B- / 7.0	10.4	1.07	12.82	96	1	98	0	1	18	99.1	-18.0	51	13	3,000,000	0	0.0	0.0
C+ / 6.4	11.5	0.86	16.25	6	2	97	0	1	2	46.9	-20.0	58	N/A	250	0	5.8	0.0
C+ / 6.4	11.6	0.86	16.17	N/A	2	97	0	1	2	43.0	-20.3	45	N/A	250	0	0.0	0.0
C+ / 6.4	11.6	0.86	15.94	2	2	97	0	1	2	43.2	-20.3	45	N/A	250	0	0.0	0.0
C+ / 6.4	11.5	0.86	16.37	2,342	2	97	0	1	2	47.2	-20.0	58	N/A	1,000	50	5.8	0.0
C+ / 6.4	11.5	0.86	16.23	48	2	97	0	1	2	43.4	-20.3	46	N/A	1,000	50	0.0	0.0

					PERFORMANCE							
	99 Pct = Best 0 Pct = Worst			Overall		Perfor-	Total Return % through 3/31/15			Annualized		Incl. in Returns
Fund Type	Fund Name	Ticker Symbol	Investment Rating	Phone	mance Rating/Pts	3 Mo	6 Mo	1Yr / Pct	3Yr / Pct	5Yr / Pct	Dividend Yield	Expense Ratio
FO	MFS International Diversifictn C	MDIGX	D	(800) 225-2606	D / 2.0	4.69	2.03	0.20 /16	6.61 /19	6.24 /18	0.43	1.99
FO	MFS International Diversifictn I	MDIJX	D	(800) 225-2606	D+ / 2.7	4.97	2.58	1.22 /19	7.68 /25	7.31 /25	1.41	0.99
FO	MFS International Diversifictn R1	MDIOX	D	(800) 225-2606	D / 2.1	4.76	2.09	0.23 /16	6.62 /20	6.24 /18	0.59	1.99
FO	MFS International Diversifictn R2	MDIKX	D	(800) 225-2606	D+ / 2.3	4.88	2.32	0.67 /17	7.16 /22	6.77 /22	0.95	1.49
FO	MFS International Diversifictn R3	MDIHX	D	(800) 225-2606	D+ / 2.5	4.90	2.44	0.94 /18	7.42 /24	7.04 /23	1.20	1.24
FO	MFS International Diversifictn R4	MDITX	D	(800) 225-2606	D+ / 2.7	4.98	2.59	1.22 /19	7.71 /25	7.31 /25	1.41	0.99
FO	MFS International Growth Fund A	MGRAX	D-	(800) 225-2606	D- / 1.1	5.03	2.69	0.44 /17	5.59 /15	6.36 /19	1.17	1.20
FO	MFS International Growth Fund B	MGRBX	D-	(800) 225-2606	D- / 1.4	4.83	2.30	-0.31 /15	4.80 /12	5.57 /15	0.45	1.95
FO	MFS International Growth Fund C	MGRCX	D-	(800) 225-2606	D- / 1.4	4.87	2.33	-0.30 /15	4.80 /12	5.57 /15	0.58	1.95
FO	MFS International Growth Fund I	MQGIX	D-	(800) 225-2606	D / 1.8	5.11	2.82	0.68 /18	5.87 /16	6.63 /21	1.30	0.95
FO	MFS International Growth Fund R1	MGRRX	D-	(800) 225-2606	D- / 1.4	4.85	2.33	-0.29 /15	4.81 /13	5.56 /14	0.71	1.95
FO	MFS International Growth Fund R2	MGRQX	D-	(800) 225-2606	D / 1.6	4.95	2.58	0.19 /16	5.33 /14	6.09 /17	1.08	1.45
FO	MFS International Growth Fund R3	MGRTX	D-	(800) 225-2606	D / 1.7	5.03	2.68	0.42 /17	5.59 /15	6.36 /19	1.19	1.20
FO	MFS International Growth Fund R4	MGRVX	D-	(800) 225-2606	D / 1.8	5.07	2.81	0.67 /17	5.85 /16	6.62 /21	1.46	0.95
FO	MFS International Growth R5	MGRDX	D-	(800) 225-2606	D / 1.9	5.15	2.89	0.82 /18	5.96 /17	6.65 /21	1.56	0.85
FO	MFS International Value R5	MINJX	C+	(800) 225-2606	C+ / 6.8	6.69	7.05	7.33 /58	13.88 /66	11.21 /55	2.23	0.76
FO	MFS Intl New Discovery 529A	EAIDX	D	(800) 225-2606	D / 2.2	2.91	2.44	-0.73 /14	8.97 /33	9.37 /40	1.07	1.46
FO	MFS Intl New Discovery 529B	EBIDX	D	(800) 225-2606	D+ / 2.5	2.71	2.01	-1.52 /11	8.12 /28	8.54 /33	0.13	2.21
FO	MFS Intl New Discovery 529C	ECIDX	D	(800) 225-2606	D+ / 2.6	2.73	2.03	-1.51 /11	8.13 /28	8.54 /33	0.45	2.21
FO	MFS Intl New Discovery A	MIDAX	D	(800) 225-2606	D / 2.2	2.90	2.42	-0.74 /14	8.99 /33	9.42 /40	1.03	1.36
FO	MFS Intl New Discovery B	MIDBX	D	(800) 225-2606	D+ / 2.6	2.72	2.04	-1.50 /11	8.18 /28	8.60 /34	0.12	2.11
FO	MFS Intl New Discovery C	MIDCX	D	(800) 225-2606	D+ / 2.6	2.73	2.04	-1.48 /11	8.17 /28	8.60 /34	0.38	2.11
FO	MFS Intl New Discovery I	MWNIX	D+	(800) 225-2606	C- / 3.3	2.97	2.56	-0.48 /14	9.27 /35	9.69 /42	1.33	1.11
FO	MFS Intl New Discovery R1	MIDGX	D	(800) 225-2606	D+ / 2.6	2.71	2.03	-1.51 /11	8.17 /28	8.59 /34	0.00	2.11
FO	MFS Intl New Discovery R2	MIDRX	D+	(800) 225-2606	D+ / 2.9	2.86	2.31	-0.97 /13	8.73 /31	9.15 /38	0.85	1.61
FO	MFS Intl New Discovery R3	MIDHX	D+	(800) 225-2606	C- / 3.1	2.93	2.43	-0.72 /14	8.98 /33	9.41 /40	1.13	1.36
FO	MFS Intl New Discovery R4	MIDJX	D+	(800) 225-2606	C- / 3.3	2.98	2.55	-0.47 /14	9.26 /35	9.69 /42	1.36	1.11
FO	MFS Intl New Discovery R5	MIDLX	U	(800) 225-2606	U /	3.00	2.63	-0.37 /15	--	--	1.44	1.00
* FO	MFS Intl Value Fund A	MGIAX	C+	(800) 225-2606	C+ / 5.6	6.59	6.85	6.94 /55	13.49 /63	10.92 /52	1.82	1.09
FO	MFS Intl Value Fund B	MGIBX	C+	(800) 225-2606	C+ / 6.0	6.42	6.47	6.17 /48	12.64 /57	10.09 /45	1.30	1.84
FO	MFS Intl Value Fund C	MGICX	C+	(800) 225-2606	C+ / 6.0	6.40	6.46	6.15 /48	12.65 /57	10.09 /45	1.54	1.84
FO	MFS Intl Value Fund I	MINIX	C+	(800) 225-2606	C+ / 6.7	6.66	6.98	7.22 /57	13.77 /65	11.19 /54	2.07	0.84
FO	MFS Intl Value Fund R1	MINRX	C+	(800) 225-2606	C+ / 6.0	6.43	6.45	6.18 /48	12.65 /57	10.10 /45	1.58	1.84
FO	MFS Intl Value Fund R2	MINFX	C+	(800) 225-2606	C+ / 6.3	6.56	6.71	6.71 /53	13.22 /61	10.64 /50	1.85	1.34
FO	MFS Intl Value Fund R3	MINGX	C+	(800) 225-2606	C+ / 6.5	6.60	6.87	6.96 /55	13.49 /63	10.92 /52	2.00	1.09
FO	MFS Intl Value Fund R4	MINHX	C+	(800) 225-2606	C+ / 6.7	6.67	7.00	7.22 /57	13.78 /65	11.20 /54	2.15	0.84
GI	MFS Lifetime 2015 R4	LFTUX	U	(800) 225-2606	U /	1.68	2.89	4.24 /33	--	--	2.04	1.08
AA	MFS Lifetime 2020 A	MFLAX	C	(800) 225-2606	D / 1.8	1.89	3.27	4.45 /35	7.34 /23	8.02 /30	1.83	1.07
AA	MFS Lifetime 2020 B	MFLBX	C	(800) 225-2606	D / 2.2	1.83	2.94	3.73 /30	6.55 /19	7.23 /25	1.23	1.82
AA	MFS Lifetime 2020 C	MFLCX	C	(800) 225-2606	D / 2.1	1.77	2.94	3.74 /30	6.53 /19	7.22 /24	1.29	1.82
AA	MFS Lifetime 2020 I	MFLIX	C+	(800) 225-2606	D+ / 2.8	2.04	3.40	4.81 /37	7.61 /25	8.30 /32	2.22	0.82
AA	MFS Lifetime 2020 R1	MFLEX	C	(800) 225-2606	D / 2.2	1.75	2.90	3.77 /30	6.54 /19	7.22 /24	1.19	1.82
AA	MFS Lifetime 2020 R2	MFLGX	C	(800) 225-2606	D+ / 2.5	1.91	3.14	4.25 /33	7.08 /22	7.76 /28	1.73	1.32
AA	MFS Lifetime 2020 R3	MFLHX	C	(800) 225-2606	D+ / 2.6	1.97	3.31	4.49 /35	7.34 /23	8.01 /30	1.98	1.07
AA	MFS Lifetime 2020 R4	MFLJX	C	(800) 225-2606	D+ / 2.8	1.96	3.40	4.73 /37	7.62 /25	8.27 /32	2.22	0.82
GI	MFS Lifetime 2025 R4	LTTUX	U	(800) 225-2606	U /	2.45	4.14	5.28 /41	--	--	1.82	0.98
AA	MFS Lifetime 2030 A	MLTAX	C	(800) 225-2606	C- / 3.6	2.78	4.67	5.27 /41	10.65 /43	10.36 /47	1.50	1.18
AA	MFS Lifetime 2030 B	MLTBX	C	(800) 225-2606	C- / 4.0	2.59	4.33	4.55 /35	9.81 /38	9.55 /41	0.87	1.93
AA	MFS Lifetime 2030 C	MLTCX	C	(800) 225-2606	C- / 4.0	2.61	4.32	4.55 /35	9.83 /38	9.53 /41	0.92	1.93
AA	MFS Lifetime 2030 I	MLTIX	C+	(800) 225-2606	C / 4.7	2.84	4.80	5.55 /43	10.92 /45	10.64 /50	1.81	0.93
AA	MFS Lifetime 2030 R1	MLTEX	C	(800) 225-2606	C- / 4.0	2.66	4.30	4.53 /35	9.83 /38	9.55 /41	0.85	1.93
AA	MFS Lifetime 2030 R2	MLTGX	C+	(800) 225-2606	C / 4.4	2.80	4.58	5.11 /39	10.37 /42	10.10 /46	1.34	1.43

● Denotes fund is closed to new investors
* Denotes fund is included in Section II

www.thestreetratings.com

RISK			NET ASSETS		ASSET					BULL / BEAR		FUND MANAGER		MINIMUMS		LOADS	
	3 Year		NAV						Portfolio	Last Bull	Last Bear	Manager	Manager	Initial	Additional	Front	Back
Risk Rating/Pts	Standard Deviation	Beta	As of 3/31/15	Total $(Mil)	Cash %	Stocks %	Bonds %	Other %	Turnover Ratio	Market Return	Market Return	Quality Pct	Tenure (Years)	Purch. $	Purch. $	End Load	End Load
C+ / 6.4	11.5	0.86	16.08	478	2	97	0	1	2	43.3	-20.2	46	N/A	1,000	50	0.0	0.0
C+ / 6.4	11.5	0.86	16.49	774	2	97	0	1	2	48.3	-19.9	61	N/A	0	0	0.0	0.0
C+ / 6.4	11.6	0.86	15.85	10	2	97	0	1	2	43.4	-20.2	46	N/A	0	0	0.0	0.0
C+ / 6.4	11.5	0.86	16.13	61	2	97	0	1	2	45.8	-20.1	54	N/A	0	0	0.0	0.0
C+ / 6.4	11.5	0.86	16.26	241	2	97	0	1	2	47.1	-20.0	58	N/A	0	0	0.0	0.0
C+ / 6.4	11.5	0.86	16.44	434	2	97	0	1	2	48.3	-19.9	62	N/A	0	0	0.0	0.0
C+ / 5.9	11.8	0.87	27.36	538	1	98	0	1	21	44.4	-21.8	31	5	1,000	50	5.8	0.0
C+ / 5.9	11.8	0.87	25.81	10	1	98	0	1	21	40.8	-22.1	22	5	1,000	50	0.0	0.0
C+ / 5.9	11.8	0.87	25.21	40	1	98	0	1	21	40.8	-22.1	22	5	1,000	50	0.0	0.0
C+ / 5.9	11.8	0.87	30.26	1,188	1	98	0	1	21	45.7	-21.7	34	5	0	0	0.0	0.0
C+ / 5.9	11.8	0.87	24.85	1	1	98	0	1	21	40.8	-22.1	22	5	0	0	0.0	0.0
C+ / 5.8	11.8	0.87	25.21	25	1	98	0	1	21	43.2	-21.9	28	5	0	0	0.0	0.0
C+ / 5.9	11.8	0.87	27.15	67	1	98	0	1	21	44.4	-21.8	31	5	0	0	0.0	0.0
C+ / 5.8	11.8	0.87	27.36	256	1	98	0	1	21	45.7	-21.8	34	5	0	0	0.0	0.0
C+ / 5.8	11.8	0.87	27.36	1,894	1	98	0	1	21	46.0	-21.8	35	5	0	0	0.0	0.0
C+ / 6.8	10.8	0.77	35.38	2,780	5	94	0	1	18	68.7	-13.2	95	N/A	0	0	0.0	0.0
C+ / 6.5	10.8	0.77	27.59	6	3	96	0	1	14	56.9	-20.2	82	18	250	0	5.8	0.0
C+ / 6.5	10.8	0.77	26.16	N/A	3	96	0	1	14	52.8	-20.4	76	18	250	0	0.0	0.0
C+ / 6.5	10.8	0.77	25.97	2	3	96	0	1	14	52.8	-20.4	76	18	250	0	0.0	0.0
C+ / 6.5	10.8	0.77	28.00	1,531	3	96	0	1	14	57.0	-20.2	82	18	1,000	50	5.8	0.0
C+ / 6.5	10.8	0.77	27.19	21	3	96	0	1	14	53.0	-20.4	76	18	1,000	50	0.0	0.0
C+ / 6.5	10.8	0.77	26.76	178	3	96	0	1	14	53.0	-20.4	76	18	1,000	50	0.0	0.0
C+ / 6.5	10.8	0.77	28.78	1,848	3	96	0	1	14	58.3	-20.1	83	18	0	0	0.0	0.0
C+ / 6.5	10.8	0.77	26.13	4	3	96	0	1	14	53.0	-20.4	76	18	0	0	0.0	0.0
C+ / 6.5	10.8	0.77	27.29	65	3	96	0	1	14	55.7	-20.3	80	18	0	0	0.0	0.0
C+ / 6.5	10.8	0.77	27.79	159	3	96	0	1	14	57.0	-20.2	82	18	0	0	0.0	0.0
C+ / 6.5	10.8	0.77	27.99	363	3	96	0	1	14	58.3	-20.1	83	18	0	0	0.0	0.0
U /	N/A	N/A	28.80	886	3	96	0	1	14	N/A	N/A	N/A	18	0	0	0.0	0.0
C+ / 6.9	10.9	0.77	35.24	6,403	5	94	0	1	18	66.9	-13.3	95	N/A	1,000	50	5.8	0.0
C+ / 6.9	10.9	0.77	33.67	56	5	94	0	1	18	62.7	-13.5	93	N/A	1,000	50	0.0	0.0
C+ / 6.9	10.9	0.77	32.25	717	5	94	0	1	18	62.7	-13.5	93	N/A	1,000	50	0.0	0.0
C+ / 6.9	10.9	0.77	36.84	11,253	5	94	0	1	18	68.4	-13.2	95	N/A	0	0	0.0	0.0
C+ / 6.8	10.9	0.77	32.63	12	5	94	0	1	18	62.7	-13.5	93	N/A	0	0	0.0	0.0
C+ / 6.8	10.9	0.77	33.13	459	5	94	0	1	18	65.5	-13.3	94	N/A	0	0	0.0	0.0
C+ / 6.9	10.9	0.77	35.06	985	5	94	0	1	18	66.9	-13.3	95	N/A	0	0	0.0	0.0
C+ / 6.8	10.9	0.77	35.35	977	5	94	0	1	18	68.3	-13.1	95	N/A	0	0	0.0	0.0
U /	N/A	N/A	10.87	42	29	28	42	1	0	N/A	N/A	N/A	3	0	0	0.0	0.0
B+ / 9.1	5.3	0.87	13.45	50	20	38	40	2	12	40.4	-10.1	38	10	1,000	50	5.8	0.0
B+ / 9.1	5.3	0.88	13.36	7	20	38	40	2	12	36.9	-10.3	28	10	1,000	50	0.0	0.0
B+ / 9.1	5.2	0.87	13.20	19	20	38	40	2	12	36.9	-10.3	29	10	1,000	50	0.0	0.0
B+ / 9.1	5.2	0.87	13.53	3	20	38	40	2	12	41.7	-10.0	43	10	0	0	0.0	0.0
B+ / 9.1	5.3	0.88	13.36	6	20	38	40	2	12	37.0	-10.4	28	10	0	0	0.0	0.0
B+ / 9.1	5.3	0.88	13.37	67	20	38	40	2	12	39.2	-10.1	34	10	0	0	0.0	0.0
B+ / 9.1	5.3	0.88	13.46	51	20	38	40	2	12	40.4	-10.1	37	10	0	0	0.0	0.0
B+ / 9.1	5.3	0.88	13.51	159	20	38	40	2	12	41.7	-10.0	41	10	0	0	0.0	0.0
U /	N/A	N/A	12.13	97	7	59	32	2	10	N/A	N/A	N/A	3	0	0	0.0	0.0
B- / 7.8	8.4	1.41	14.41	46	8	73	17	2	6	62.3	-16.3	13	N/A	1,000	50	5.8	0.0
B- / 7.8	8.4	1.41	14.24	8	8	73	17	2	6	58.2	-16.5	9	N/A	1,000	50	0.0	0.0
B- / 7.8	8.5	1.42	14.17	15	8	73	17	2	6	58.3	-16.6	9	N/A	1,000	50	0.0	0.0
B- / 7.8	8.4	1.41	14.49	12	8	73	17	2	6	63.7	-16.2	15	N/A	0	0	0.0	0.0
B- / 7.7	8.5	1.41	14.26	8	8	73	17	2	6	58.2	-16.6	9	N/A	0	0	0.0	0.0
B- / 7.8	8.4	1.41	14.30	78	8	73	17	2	6	61.0	-16.5	12	N/A	0	0	0.0	0.0

Data as of March 31, 2015

	99 Pct = Best 0 Pct = Worst		Overall		PERFORMANCE								
						Total Return % through 3/31/15					Incl. in Returns		
									Annualized				
Fund Type	Fund Name	Ticker Symbol	Investment Rating	Phone	Perfor-mance Rating/Pts	3 Mo	6 Mo	1Yr / Pct	3Yr / Pct	5Yr / Pct	Dividend Yield	Expense Ratio
AA	MFS Lifetime 2030 R3	MLTHX	C+	(800) 225-2606	C / 4.5	2.79	4.67	5.27 /41	10.64 /43	10.36 /47	1.59	1.18
AA	MFS Lifetime 2030 R4	MLTJX	C+	(800) 225-2606	C / 4.7	2.92	4.81	5.56 /43	10.90 /45	10.64 /50	1.81	0.93
GI	MFS Lifetime 2035 R4	LFEUX	U	(800) 225-2606	U /	3.13	5.24	5.83 /45	--	--	1.59	1.15
AA	MFS Lifetime 2040 A	MLFAX	C	(800) 225-2606	C- / 4.2	3.23	5.44	5.81 /45	11.62 /50	10.99 /53	1.32	1.25
AA	MFS Lifetime 2040 B	MLFBX	C	(800) 225-2606	C / 4.6	2.97	5.00	5.00 /39	10.76 /44	10.15 /46	0.67	2.00
AA	MFS Lifetime 2040 C	MLFCX	C	(800) 225-2606	C / 4.6	3.00	5.03	4.96 /38	10.78 /44	10.14 /46	0.73	2.00
AA	MFS Lifetime 2040 I	MLFIX	C+	(800) 225-2606	C / 5.3	3.21	5.57	6.01 /47	11.87 /52	11.26 /55	1.62	1.00
AA	MFS Lifetime 2040 R1	MLFEX	C	(800) 225-2606	C / 4.6	2.99	5.01	5.01 /39	10.76 /44	10.14 /46	0.59	2.00
AA	MFS Lifetime 2040 R2	MLFGX	C+	(800) 225-2606	C / 4.9	3.11	5.29	5.52 /43	11.32 /48	10.72 /50	1.17	1.50
AA	MFS Lifetime 2040 R3	MLFHX	C+	(800) 225-2606	C / 5.1	3.16	5.44	5.82 /45	11.59 /50	10.97 /52	1.40	1.25
AA	MFS Lifetime 2040 R4	MLFJX	C+	(800) 225-2606	C / 5.3	3.21	5.50	6.02 /47	11.88 /52	11.25 /55	1.62	1.00
GI	MFS Lifetime 2045 R4	LTMUX	U	(800) 225-2606	U /	3.25	5.48	5.99 /46	--	--	1.55	1.50
AA	MFS Lifetime 2050 A	MFFSX	C	(800) 225-2606	C- / 4.2	3.22	5.42	5.77 /44	11.60 /50	--	1.31	1.53
AA	MFS Lifetime 2050 B	MFFRX	C	(800) 225-2606	C / 4.6	2.98	4.99	4.99 /38	10.75 /44	--	0.67	2.28
AA	MFS Lifetime 2050 C	MFFDX	C	(800) 225-2606	C / 4.6	2.99	5.04	4.97 /38	10.76 /44	--	0.84	2.28
AA	MFS Lifetime 2050 I	MFFIX	C+	(800) 225-2606	C / 5.3	3.29	5.59	6.08 /47	11.88 /52	--	1.60	1.28
AA	MFS Lifetime 2050 R1	MFFMX	C	(800) 225-2606	C / 4.6	2.99	4.98	4.98 /38	10.77 /44	--	0.92	2.28
AA	MFS Lifetime 2050 R2	MFFNX	C+	(800) 225-2606	C / 4.9	3.11	5.30	5.51 /42	11.33 /48	--	1.24	1.78
AA	MFS Lifetime 2050 R3	MFFOX	C+	(800) 225-2606	C / 5.1	3.17	5.37	5.72 /44	11.57 /49	--	1.39	1.53
AA	MFS Lifetime 2050 R4	MFFPX	C+	(800) 225-2606	C / 5.3	3.29	5.52	6.08 /47	11.86 /52	--	1.60	1.28
AA	MFS Lifetime Income A	MLLAX	C	(800) 225-2606	D- / 1.1	1.64	2.70	3.81 /31	5.06 /13	5.91 /16	1.77	1.00
AA	MFS Lifetime Income B	MLLBX	C	(800) 225-2606	D- / 1.3	1.45	2.32	3.03 /27	4.28 /11	5.13 /13	1.13	1.75
AA	MFS Lifetime Income C	MLLCX	C	(800) 225-2606	D- / 1.3	1.45	2.32	3.03 /27	4.28 /11	5.13 /13	1.13	1.75
AA	MFS Lifetime Income I	MLLIX	C	(800) 225-2606	D / 1.6	1.62	2.83	3.98 /32	5.29 /14	6.16 /18	2.12	0.75
AA	MFS Lifetime Income R1	MLLEX	C	(800) 225-2606	D- / 1.3	1.45	2.32	3.03 /27	4.27 /11	5.12 /12	1.13	1.75
AA	MFS Lifetime Income R2	MLLGX	C	(800) 225-2606	D- / 1.4	1.50	2.57	3.46 /29	4.77 /12	5.63 /15	1.63	1.25
AA	MFS Lifetime Income R3	MLLHX	C	(800) 225-2606	D- / 1.5	1.56	2.70	3.81 /31	5.06 /13	5.91 /16	1.88	1.00
AA	MFS Lifetime Income R4	MLLJX	C	(800) 225-2606	D / 1.6	1.62	2.83	3.98 /32	5.26 /14	6.16 /18	2.12	0.75
GL	MFS Low Volatility Global Equity R5	MVGNX	U	(800) 225-2606	U /	3.11	7.44	10.15 /75	--	--	1.05	5.83
GR	MFS Managed Wealth I	MNWIX	U	(800) 225-2606	U /	1.40	2.59	--	--	--	0.00	N/A
GR	MFS Mass Investors Gr Stk 529A	EISTX	C+	(800) 225-2606	C+ / 6.4	1.65	9.24	12.36 /84	14.57 /72	14.01 /78	0.57	0.85
GR	MFS Mass Investors Gr Stk 529B	EMIVX	C+	(800) 225-2606	C+ / 6.8	1.40	8.78	11.41 /80	13.70 /65	13.16 /70	0.00	1.60
GR	MFS Mass Investors Gr Stk 529C	EMICX	C+	(800) 225-2606	C+ / 6.8	1.41	8.81	11.46 /80	13.69 /65	13.16 /70	0.03	1.60
GR	MFS Mass Investors Gr Stk A	MIGFX	C+	(800) 225-2606	C+ / 6.5	1.63	9.28	12.36 /84	14.61 /72	14.06 /78	0.56	0.75
GR	MFS Mass Investors Gr Stk B	MIGBX	C+	(800) 225-2606	C+ / 6.9	1.46	8.86	11.50 /80	13.75 /65	13.23 /70	0.00	1.50
GR	MFS Mass Investors Gr Stk C	MIGDX	C+	(800) 225-2606	C+ / 6.9	1.47	8.85	11.51 /80	13.76 /65	13.23 /70	0.00	1.50
GR	MFS Mass Investors Gr Stk I	MGTIX	B+	(800) 225-2606	B / 7.7	1.68	9.38	12.64 /85	14.89 /74	14.35 /81	0.83	0.50
GR	MFS Mass Investors Gr Stk R1	MIGMX	C+	(800) 225-2606	C+ / 6.9	1.44	8.83	11.50 /80	13.75 /65	13.23 /70	0.00	1.50
GR	MFS Mass Investors Gr Stk R2	MIRGX	B+	(800) 225-2606	B- / 7.3	1.54	9.08	12.03 /83	14.32 /69	13.79 /76	0.39	1.00
GR	MFS Mass Investors Gr Stk R3	MIGHX	B+	(800) 225-2606	B- / 7.5	1.65	9.27	12.39 /84	14.61 /72	14.08 /78	0.60	0.75
GR	MFS Mass Investors Gr Stk R4	MIGKX	B+	(800) 225-2606	B / 7.8	1.70	9.38	12.64 /85	14.90 /74	14.37 /81	0.82	0.50
GR	MFS Mass Investors Gr Stk R5	MIGNX	U	(800) 225-2606	U /	1.71	9.44	12.74 /86	--	--	0.90	0.41
GI	MFS Mass Investors Trust 529A	EAMTX	C+	(800) 225-2606	C+ / 6.7	1.24	6.98	10.82 /78	15.58 /80	13.00 /68	0.76	0.83
GI	MFS Mass Investors Trust 529B	EBMTX	B	(800) 225-2606	B- / 7.2	1.04	6.57	9.93 /74	14.70 /72	12.17 /62	0.14	1.58
GI	MFS Mass Investors Trust 529C	ECITX	B	(800) 225-2606	B- / 7.2	1.01	6.60	9.95 /74	14.69 /72	12.17 /62	0.10	1.58
GI	MFS Mass Investors Trust A	MITTX	C+	(800) 225-2606	C+ / 6.8	1.25	7.00	10.82 /78	15.61 /80	13.07 /69	0.75	0.73
GI	MFS Mass Investors Trust B	MITBX	B	(800) 225-2606	B- / 7.2	1.07	6.61	10.00 /74	14.74 /73	12.23 /62	0.09	1.48
GI	MFS Mass Investors Trust C	MITCX	B	(800) 225-2606	B- / 7.2	1.05	6.62	10.03 /74	14.75 /73	12.23 /62	0.13	1.48
GI	MFS Mass Investors Trust I	MITIX	B+	(800) 225-2606	B / 8.1	1.28	7.12	11.10 /79	15.88 /82	13.36 /72	1.04	0.48
GI	MFS Mass Investors Trust R1	MITGX	B	(800) 225-2606	B- / 7.2	1.05	6.58	9.99 /74	14.73 /73	12.23 /62	0.12	1.48
GI	MFS Mass Investors Trust R2	MIRTX	B+	(800) 225-2606	B / 7.6	1.19	6.86	10.55 /77	15.31 /77	12.80 /66	0.56	0.98
GI	MFS Mass Investors Trust R3	MITHX	B+	(800) 225-2606	B / 7.9	1.26	7.03	10.84 /78	15.61 /80	13.07 /69	0.78	0.73

RISK			NET ASSETS		ASSET					BULL / BEAR		FUND MANAGER		MINIMUMS		LOADS	
	3 Year		NAV						Portfolio	Last Bull	Last Bear	Manager	Manager	Initial	Additional	Front	Back
Risk Rating/Pts	Standard Deviation	Beta	As of 3/31/15	Total $(Mil)	Cash %	Stocks %	Bonds %	Other %	Turnover Ratio	Market Return	Market Return	Quality Pct	Tenure (Years)	Purch. $	Purch. $	End Load	End Load
B- / 7.8	8.4	1.40	14.38	70	8	73	17	2	6	62.3	-16.4	14	N/A	0	0	0.0	0.0
B- / 7.8	8.5	1.41	14.47	162	8	73	17	2	6	63.7	-16.2	14	N/A	0	0	0.0	0.0
U /	N/A	N/A	12.87	76	6	82	11	1	8	N/A	N/A	N/A	3	0	0	0.0	0.0
B- / 7.2	9.3	1.55	14.69	31	5	87	6	2	8	68.6	-18.0	10	N/A	1,000	50	5.8	0.0
B- / 7.2	9.3	1.54	14.57	4	5	87	6	2	8	64.4	-18.2	7	N/A	1,000	50	0.0	0.0
B- / 7.2	9.3	1.55	14.41	12	5	87	6	2	8	64.3	-18.2	7	N/A	1,000	50	0.0	0.0
B- / 7.2	9.3	1.55	14.78	9	5	87	6	2	8	70.1	-17.9	12	N/A	0	0	0.0	0.0
B- / 7.2	9.3	1.55	14.48	6	5	87	6	2	8	64.3	-18.2	7	N/A	0	0	0.0	0.0
B- / 7.2	9.3	1.55	14.59	61	5	87	6	2	8	67.2	-18.1	9	N/A	0	0	0.0	0.0
B- / 7.2	9.3	1.55	14.68	38	5	87	6	2	8	68.6	-18.0	10	N/A	0	0	0.0	0.0
B- / 7.2	9.3	1.54	14.77	146	5	87	6	2	8	70.2	-17.9	12	N/A	0	0	0.0	0.0
U /	N/A	N/A	13.02	46	5	87	7	1	10	N/A	N/A	N/A	3	0	0	0.0	0.0
B- / 7.2	9.3	1.55	15.73	7	5	87	7	1	9	68.5	-17.6	10	5	1,000	50	5.8	0.0
B- / 7.2	9.3	1.54	15.57	1	5	87	7	1	9	64.1	-17.9	7	5	1,000	50	0.0	0.0
B- / 7.2	9.3	1.55	15.49	2	5	87	7	1	9	64.1	-17.9	7	5	1,000	50	0.0	0.0
B- / 7.2	9.3	1.55	15.70	1	5	87	7	1	9	70.0	-17.6	12	5	0	0	0.0	0.0
B- / 7.2	9.3	1.55	15.50	N/A	5	87	7	1	9	64.1	-17.9	7	5	0	0	0.0	0.0
B- / 7.2	9.3	1.55	15.58	12	5	87	7	1	9	67.2	-17.8	9	5	0	0	0.0	0.0
B- / 7.2	9.3	1.55	15.64	9	5	87	7	1	9	68.4	-17.6	10	5	0	0	0.0	0.0
B- / 7.2	9.3	1.55	15.69	56	5	87	7	1	9	69.9	-17.6	11	5	0	0	0.0	0.0
B+ / 9.8	3.5	0.54	12.27	135	0	0	0	100	10	25.1	-4.1	58	N/A	1,000	50	5.8	0.0
B+ / 9.8	3.5	0.54	12.27	21	0	0	0	100	10	22.0	-4.4	46	N/A	1,000	50	0.0	0.0
B+ / 9.8	3.5	0.54	12.27	162	0	0	0	100	10	21.9	-4.4	47	N/A	1,000	50	0.0	0.0
B+ / 9.8	3.5	0.54	12.27	22	0	0	0	100	10	26.1	-3.9	61	N/A	0	0	0.0	0.0
B+ / 9.8	3.5	0.54	12.28	6	0	0	0	100	10	22.0	-4.4	47	N/A	0	0	0.0	0.0
B+ / 9.8	3.4	0.53	12.27	29	0	0	0	100	10	24.0	-4.2	54	N/A	0	0	0.0	0.0
B+ / 9.8	3.5	0.54	12.27	26	0	0	0	100	10	25.1	-4.1	57	N/A	0	0	0.0	0.0
B+ / 9.8	3.5	0.54	12.27	75	0	0	0	100	10	26.1	-3.9	61	N/A	0	0	0.0	0.0
U /	N/A	N/A	11.38	29	1	98	0	1	28	N/A	N/A	N/A	2	0	0	0.0	0.0
U /	N/A	N/A	10.11	27	0	0	0	100	0	N/A	N/A	N/A	N/A	0	0	0.0	0.0
C+ / 6.9	10.2	1.01	24.66	12	1	98	0	1	26	89.4	-13.2	44	N/A	250	0	5.8	0.0
C+ / 6.9	10.2	1.02	21.75	1	1	98	0	1	26	84.6	-13.4	33	N/A	250	0	0.0	0.0
C+ / 6.9	10.2	1.01	21.63	4	1	98	0	1	26	84.5	-13.5	33	N/A	250	0	0.0	0.0
C+ / 6.9	10.2	1.02	24.93	3,849	1	98	0	1	26	89.7	-13.1	44	N/A	1,000	50	5.8	0.0
C+ / 6.9	10.2	1.02	22.19	87	1	98	0	1	26	84.9	-13.5	33	N/A	1,000	50	0.0	0.0
C+ / 6.9	10.2	1.02	22.07	268	1	98	0	1	26	84.8	-13.4	33	N/A	1,000	50	0.0	0.0
C+ / 6.9	10.2	1.01	25.48	762	1	98	0	1	26	91.2	-13.0	48	N/A	0	0	0.0	0.0
C+ / 6.9	10.1	1.01	21.89	35	1	98	0	1	26	84.8	-13.5	34	N/A	0	0	0.0	0.0
C+ / 6.9	10.2	1.01	24.34	226	1	98	0	1	26	88.0	-13.3	40	N/A	0	0	0.0	0.0
C+ / 6.9	10.2	1.02	24.71	530	1	98	0	1	26	89.7	-13.2	44	N/A	0	0	0.0	0.0
C+ / 6.9	10.1	1.01	25.07	994	1	98	0	1	26	91.3	-13.1	49	N/A	0	0	0.0	0.0
U /	N/A	N/A	25.52	399	1	98	0	1	26	N/A	N/A	N/A	N/A	0	0	0.0	0.0
C+ / 6.7	10.3	1.05	28.63	7	1	98	0	1	19	96.8	-18.0	50	11	250	0	5.8	0.0
C+ / 6.8	10.3	1.05	27.31	N/A	1	98	0	1	19	91.8	-18.2	38	11	250	0	0.0	0.0
C+ / 6.7	10.3	1.05	27.02	3	1	98	0	1	19	91.7	-18.2	37	11	250	0	0.0	0.0
C+ / 6.7	10.3	1.05	29.18	3,445	1	98	0	1	19	97.0	-17.9	49	11	1,000	50	5.8	0.0
C+ / 6.8	10.3	1.05	28.43	94	1	98	0	1	19	92.0	-18.1	38	11	1,000	50	0.0	0.0
C+ / 6.8	10.3	1.05	28.02	304	1	98	0	1	19	91.9	-18.2	39	11	1,000	50	0.0	0.0
C+ / 6.7	10.3	1.05	28.53	2,883	1	98	0	1	19	98.7	-17.8	53	11	0	0	0.0	0.0
C+ / 6.8	10.3	1.05	27.87	10	1	98	0	1	19	91.9	-18.2	38	11	0	0	0.0	0.0
C+ / 6.7	10.3	1.05	28.07	202	1	98	0	1	19	95.3	-18.0	46	11	0	0	0.0	0.0
C+ / 6.7	10.2	1.05	28.97	389	1	98	0	1	19	97.0	-17.9	50	11	0	0	0.0	0.0

Fund Type	Fund Name	Ticker Symbol	Overall Investment Rating	Phone	Performance Rating/Pts	3 Mo	6 Mo	1Yr / Pct	3Yr / Pct	5Yr / Pct	Dividend Yield	Expense Ratio
GI	MFS Mass Investors Trust R4	MITDX	B+	(800) 225-2606	B / 8.1	1.31	7.13	11.10 /79	15.90 /83	13.36 /72	1.00	0.48
GI	MFS Mass Investors Trust R5	MITJX	U	(800) 225-2606	U /	1.35	7.19	11.22 /79	--	--	1.11	0.40
MC	MFS Mid Cap Value 529A	EACVX	A-	(800) 225-2606	B+ / 8.4	3.46	9.27	9.88 /74	17.98 /94	15.80 /92	0.36	1.31
MC	MFS Mid Cap Value 529B	EBCVX	A	(800) 225-2606	B+ / 8.8	3.29	8.85	9.03 /69	17.11 /90	14.93 /86	0.00	2.06
MC	MFS Mid Cap Value 529C	ECCVX	A	(800) 225-2606	B+ / 8.8	3.27	8.87	9.04 /70	17.10 /90	14.94 /86	0.00	2.06
MC	MFS Mid Cap Value A	MVCAX	A-	(800) 225-2606	B+ / 8.5	3.46	9.25	9.90 /74	18.04 /94	15.86 /92	0.41	1.21
MC	MFS Mid Cap Value B	MCBVX	A	(800) 225-2606	B+ / 8.8	3.30	8.88	9.10 /70	17.16 /91	15.01 /87	0.00	1.96
MC	MFS Mid Cap Value C	MVCCX	A	(800) 225-2606	B+ / 8.8	3.25	8.84	9.07 /70	17.15 /91	15.01 /87	0.00	1.96
MC	MFS Mid Cap Value I	MCVIX	A+	(800) 225-2606	A / 9.3	3.53	9.39	10.19 /75	18.34 /95	16.16 /94	0.63	0.96
MC	MFS Mid Cap Value Initial		C+	(800) 225-2606	A- / 9.1	3.57	9.49	10.46 /76	17.47 /92	15.85 /92	0.94	0.81
MC	MFS Mid Cap Value R1	MVCGX	A	(800) 225-2606	B+ / 8.8	3.30	8.86	9.09 /70	17.14 /91	14.99 /87	0.00	1.96
MC	MFS Mid Cap Value R2	MCVRX	A+	(800) 225-2606	A- / 9.1	3.43	9.17	9.67 /73	17.75 /93	15.57 /91	0.34	1.46
MC	MFS Mid Cap Value R3	MVCHX	A+	(800) 225-2606	A- / 9.2	3.47	9.27	9.87 /74	18.03 /94	15.87 /92	0.52	1.21
MC	MFS Mid Cap Value R4	MVCJX	A+	(800) 225-2606	A / 9.3	3.55	9.47	10.23 /75	18.34 /95	16.18 /94	0.65	0.96
MC	MFS Mid Cap Value R5	MVCKX	U	(800) 225-2606	U /	3.58	9.52	10.33 /76	--	--	0.70	0.84
MC	MFS Mid-Cap Growth 529A	EAMCX	B+	(800) 225-2606	B+ / 8.4	5.64	11.62	14.11 /90	16.92 /89	15.10 /88	0.00	1.32
MC	MFS Mid-Cap Growth 529B	EBCGX	B+	(800) 225-2606	B+ / 8.7	5.47	11.10	13.23 /87	15.98 /83	14.21 /80	0.00	2.07
MC	MFS Mid-Cap Growth 529C	ECGRX	B+	(800) 225-2606	B+ / 8.7	5.43	11.11	13.19 /87	15.99 /83	14.21 /80	0.00	2.07
MC	MFS Mid-Cap Growth A	OTCAX	B+	(800) 225-2606	B+ / 8.4	5.65	11.64	14.16 /90	16.95 /90	15.16 /88	0.00	1.22
MC	MFS Mid-Cap Growth B	OTCBX	B+	(800) 225-2606	B+ / 8.8	5.45	11.15	13.24 /87	16.04 /84	14.28 /80	0.00	1.97
MC	MFS Mid-Cap Growth C	OTCCX	B+	(800) 225-2606	B+ / 8.8	5.41	11.16	13.30 /88	16.05 /84	14.29 /80	0.00	1.97
MC	MFS Mid-Cap Growth I	OTCIX	A-	(800) 225-2606	A / 9.3	5.78	11.78	14.45 /90	17.24 /91	15.44 /90	0.00	0.97
MC	MFS Mid-Cap Growth R1	OTCGX	B+	(800) 225-2606	B+ / 8.8	5.46	11.20	13.30 /88	16.07 /84	14.28 /80	0.00	1.97
MC	MFS Mid-Cap Growth R2	MCPRX	B+	(800) 225-2606	A- / 9.1	5.58	11.48	13.83 /89	16.62 /88	14.84 /86	0.00	1.47
MC	MFS Mid-Cap Growth R3	OTCHX	A-	(800) 225-2606	A- / 9.2	5.68	11.62	14.16 /90	16.91 /89	15.16 /88	0.00	1.22
MC	MFS Mid-Cap Growth R4	OTCJX	A-	(800) 225-2606	A / 9.3	5.68	11.71	14.43 /90	17.21 /91	15.42 /90	0.00	0.97
MC	MFS Mid-Cap Growth R5	OTCKX	U	(800) 225-2606	U /	5.77	11.76	14.51 /91	--	--	0.00	0.91
AA	MFS Moderate Allocation 529A	EAMDX	C	(800) 225-2606	D+ / 2.4	2.32	3.92	4.84 /37	8.46 /30	8.72 /35	1.70	1.11
AA	MFS Moderate Allocation 529B	EBMDX	C	(800) 225-2606	D+ / 2.8	2.14	3.54	4.06 /32	7.66 /25	7.90 /29	1.09	1.86
AA	MFS Moderate Allocation 529C	ECMAX	C	(800) 225-2606	D+ / 2.8	2.09	3.50	4.05 /32	7.65 /25	7.89 /29	1.13	1.86
AA	MFS Moderate Allocation A	MAMAX	C	(800) 225-2606	D+ / 2.4	2.32	3.92	4.85 /37	8.50 /30	8.78 /35	1.73	1.01
AA	MFS Moderate Allocation B	MMABX	C	(800) 225-2606	D+ / 2.8	2.06	3.46	4.06 /32	7.66 /25	7.95 /30	1.12	1.76
AA	MFS Moderate Allocation C	MMACX	C	(800) 225-2606	D+ / 2.8	2.07	3.48	4.05 /32	7.68 /25	7.95 /30	1.14	1.76
AA	MFS Moderate Allocation I	MMAIX	C+	(800) 225-2606	C- / 3.5	2.35	4.06	5.11 /39	8.77 /31	9.04 /37	2.05	0.76
AA	MFS Moderate Allocation R1	MAMFX	C	(800) 225-2606	D+ / 2.8	2.11	3.48	4.05 /32	7.69 /25	7.96 /30	1.16	1.76
AA	MFS Moderate Allocation R2	MARRX	C	(800) 225-2606	C- / 3.1	2.25	3.74	4.55 /35	8.22 /28	8.50 /33	1.62	1.26
AA	MFS Moderate Allocation R3	MAMHX	C+	(800) 225-2606	C- / 3.3	2.27	3.88	4.82 /37	8.48 /30	8.76 /35	1.84	1.01
AA	MFS Moderate Allocation R4	MAMJX	C+	(800) 225-2606	C- / 3.5	2.32	3.99	5.12 /39	8.77 /31	9.04 /37	2.08	0.76
SC	MFS New Discovery 529A	EANDX	D	(800) 225-2606	C / 4.8	5.77	9.92	0.80 /18	12.78 /58	13.31 /71	0.00	1.43
SC	MFS New Discovery 529B	EBNDX	D	(800) 225-2606	C / 5.2	5.57	9.53	0.04 /16	11.92 /52	12.46 /64	0.00	2.18
SC	MFS New Discovery 529C	ECNDX	D	(800) 225-2606	C / 5.2	5.52	9.47	-0.01 /16	11.89 /52	12.45 /64	0.00	2.18
SC	MFS New Discovery A	MNDAX	D	(800) 225-2606	C / 4.8	5.78	9.95	0.82 /18	12.81 /58	13.37 /72	0.00	1.33
SC	MFS New Discovery B	MNDBX	D	(800) 225-2606	C / 5.2	5.56	9.51	0.09 /16	11.97 /52	12.53 /64	0.00	2.08
SC	MFS New Discovery C	MNDCX	D	(800) 225-2606	C / 5.2	5.55	9.55	0.08 /16	11.96 /52	12.52 /64	0.00	2.08
SC	MFS New Discovery I	MNDIX	D+	(800) 225-2606	C+ / 5.9	5.81	10.06	1.05 /19	13.08 /60	13.65 /74	0.00	1.08
SC	MFS New Discovery R1	MNDGX	D	(800) 225-2606	C / 5.2	5.54	9.52	0.09 /16	11.96 /52	12.52 /64	0.00	2.08
SC	MFS New Discovery R2	MNDRX	D	(800) 225-2606	C+ / 5.6	5.68	9.80	0.56 /17	12.51 /56	13.08 /69	0.00	1.58
SC	MFS New Discovery R3	MNDHX	D+	(800) 225-2606	C+ / 5.8	5.74	9.92	0.82 /18	12.81 /58	13.36 /72	0.00	1.33
SC	MFS New Discovery R4	MNDJX	D+	(800) 225-2606	C+ / 6.0	5.82	10.08	1.06 /19	13.09 /60	13.65 /74	0.00	1.08
SC	MFS New Discovery R5	MNDKX	U	(800) 225-2606	U /	5.83	10.15	1.19 /19	--	--	0.00	0.97
GL	MFS New Discovery Value A	NDVAX	C+	(800) 225-2606	C+ / 6.7	3.45	10.87	4.64 /36	15.76 /81	--	0.04	1.58
GL	MFS New Discovery Value B	NDVBX	C+	(800) 225-2606	B- / 7.1	3.27	10.48	3.86 /31	14.89 /74	--	0.00	2.33

99 Pct = Best
0 Pct = Worst

PERFORMANCE
Total Return % through 3/31/15
Annualized
Incl. in Returns

● Denotes fund is closed to new investors
* Denotes fund is included in Section II

RISK			NET ASSETS		ASSET				Portfolio	BULL / BEAR		FUND MANAGER		MINIMUMS		LOADS	
	3 Year		NAV							Last Bull	Last Bear	Manager	Manager	Initial	Additional	Front	Back
Risk Rating/Pts	Standard Deviation	Beta	As of 3/31/15	Total $(Mil)	Cash %	Stocks %	Bonds %	Other %	Turnover Ratio	Market Return	Market Return	Quality Pct	Tenure (Years)	Purch. $	Purch. $	End Load	End Load
C+ / 6.7	10.3	1.05	29.40	85	1	98	0	1	19	98.7	-17.9	54	11	0	0	0.0	0.0
U /	N/A	N/A	28.56	78	1	98	0	1	19	N/A	N/A	N/A	11	0	0	0.0	0.0
C+ / 6.7	10.2	0.89	20.33	5	1	97	0	2	34	104.4	-21.0	87	7	250	0	5.8	0.0
C+ / 6.7	10.2	0.89	19.17	N/A	1	97	0	2	34	99.2	-21.2	83	7	250	0	0.0	0.0
C+ / 6.7	10.2	0.88	19.25	2	1	97	0	2	34	99.2	-21.1	83	7	250	0	0.0	0.0
C+ / 6.7	10.2	0.89	20.63	692	1	97	0	2	34	104.7	-20.9	87	7	1,000	50	5.8	0.0
C+ / 6.7	10.2	0.89	19.73	21	1	97	0	2	34	99.5	-21.2	84	7	1,000	50	0.0	0.0
C+ / 6.7	10.2	0.89	19.68	100	1	97	0	2	34	99.5	-21.2	83	7	1,000	50	0.0	0.0
C+ / 6.8	10.1	0.88	21.09	287	1	97	0	2	34	106.4	-20.8	89	7	0	0	0.0	0.0
C- / 3.6	10.3	0.89	10.15	321	0	99	0	1	55	104.8	-19.8	85	3	0	0	0.0	0.0
C+ / 6.7	10.2	0.89	19.39	8	1	97	0	2	34	99.5	-21.1	84	7	0	0	0.0	0.0
C+ / 6.7	10.2	0.89	20.21	55	1	97	0	2	34	103.1	-21.0	86	7	0	0	0.0	0.0
C+ / 6.7	10.2	0.89	20.57	178	1	97	0	2	34	104.7	-20.9	87	7	0	0	0.0	0.0
C+ / 6.8	10.2	0.89	20.72	215	1	97	0	2	34	106.5	-20.8	88	7	0	0	0.0	0.0
U /	N/A	N/A	21.10	1,658	1	97	0	2	34	N/A	N/A	N/A	7	0	0	0.0	0.0
C+ / 5.8	10.8	0.89	14.23	3	1	98	0	1	59	94.2	-19.7	81	7	250	0	5.8	0.0
C+ / 5.6	10.8	0.90	12.54	N/A	1	98	0	1	59	88.8	-19.8	75	7	250	0	0.0	0.0
C / 5.5	10.8	0.89	12.23	1	1	98	0	1	59	89.0	-20.0	75	7	250	0	0.0	0.0
C+ / 5.8	10.8	0.89	14.59	290	1	98	0	1	59	94.3	-19.7	82	7	1,000	0	5.8	0.0
C+ / 5.6	10.8	0.89	12.78	18	1	98	0	1	59	89.3	-20.0	76	7	1,000	0	0.0	0.0
C+ / 5.6	10.8	0.89	12.47	41	1	98	0	1	59	89.2	-19.9	76	7	1,000	0	0.0	0.0
C+ / 5.8	10.8	0.90	15.19	18	1	98	0	1	59	95.8	-19.6	83	7	0	0	0.0	0.0
C+ / 5.6	10.8	0.89	12.74	2	1	98	0	1	59	89.4	-20.0	76	7	0	0	0.0	0.0
C+ / 5.7	10.8	0.89	14.00	5	1	98	0	1	59	92.6	-19.8	80	7	0	0	0.0	0.0
C+ / 5.8	10.7	0.89	14.51	5	1	98	0	1	59	94.3	-19.7	82	7	0	0	0.0	0.0
C+ / 5.8	10.8	0.89	14.89	2	1	98	0	1	59	95.8	-19.6	83	7	0	0	0.0	0.0
U /	N/A	N/A	15.21	1,393	1	98	0	1	59	N/A	N/A	N/A	7	0	0	0.0	0.0
B / 8.7	6.2	1.05	16.93	185	10	54	35	1	2	46.2	-10.8	28	13	250	0	5.8	0.0
B / 8.7	6.3	1.06	16.70	17	10	54	35	1	2	42.6	-11.1	20	13	250	0	0.0	0.0
B / 8.7	6.3	1.06	16.61	78	10	54	35	1	2	42.5	-11.1	20	13	250	0	0.0	0.0
B / 8.7	6.3	1.06	17.00	3,330	10	54	35	1	2	46.4	-10.8	28	13	1,000	50	5.8	0.0
B / 8.7	6.3	1.06	16.84	359	10	54	35	1	2	42.7	-11.0	20	13	1,000	50	0.0	0.0
B / 8.7	6.2	1.05	16.74	1,379	10	54	35	1	2	42.6	-11.0	20	13	1,000	50	0.0	0.0
B / 8.7	6.3	1.05	17.20	137	10	54	35	1	2	47.7	-10.7	31	13	0	0	0.0	0.0
B / 8.7	6.3	1.05	16.44	45	10	54	35	1	2	42.8	-11.1	20	N/A	0	0	0.0	0.0
B / 8.7	6.2	1.05	16.68	256	10	54	35	1	2	45.1	-10.8	26	12	0	0	0.0	0.0
B / 8.7	6.3	1.05	16.88	414	10	54	35	1	2	46.4	-10.8	28	N/A	0	0	0.0	0.0
B / 8.7	6.2	1.05	16.98	284	10	54	35	1	2	47.7	-10.7	31	N/A	0	0	0.0	0.0
C- / 3.4	14.9	1.01	23.66	5	2	97	0	1	98	78.0	-27.4	23	2	250	0	5.8	0.0
C- / 3.0	14.9	1.01	20.08	N/A	2	97	0	1	98	73.5	-27.6	16	2	250	0	0.0	0.0
C- / 3.0	14.8	1.01	20.08	1	2	97	0	1	98	73.3	-27.6	16	2	250	0	0.0	0.0
C- / 3.5	14.9	1.01	24.36	499	2	97	0	1	98	78.2	-27.4	23	2	1,000	0	5.8	0.0
C- / 3.1	14.9	1.01	20.70	29	2	97	0	1	98	73.7	-27.6	17	2	1,000	0	0.0	0.0
C- / 3.1	14.9	1.01	20.74	116	2	97	0	1	98	73.8	-27.6	16	2	1,000	0	0.0	0.0
C- / 3.7	14.8	1.01	26.41	273	2	97	0	1	98	79.7	-27.3	26	2	0	0	0.0	0.0
C- / 3.0	14.9	1.01	20.57	8	2	97	0	1	98	73.7	-27.6	17	2	0	0	0.0	0.0
C- / 3.4	14.9	1.01	23.26	63	2	97	0	1	98	76.6	-27.4	21	2	0	0	0.0	0.0
C- / 3.5	14.9	1.01	24.33	133	2	97	0	1	98	78.2	-27.3	24	2	0	0	0.0	0.0
C- / 3.6	14.9	1.01	25.26	211	2	97	0	1	98	79.8	-27.3	26	2	0	0	0.0	0.0
U /	N/A	N/A	26.51	342	2	97	0	1	98	N/A	N/A	N/A	2	0	0	0.0	0.0
C+ / 5.6	11.9	0.58	13.20	19	2	97	0	1	55	109.0	N/A	98	4	1,000	0	5.8	0.0
C / 5.5	11.9	0.58	12.96	2	2	97	0	1	55	103.8	N/A	97	4	1,000	0	0.0	0.0

Fund Type	Fund Name	Ticker Symbol	Overall Investment Rating	Phone	Performance Rating/Pts	3 Mo	6 Mo	1Yr / Pct	3Yr / Pct	5Yr / Pct	Dividend Yield	Expense Ratio
GL	MFS New Discovery Value C	NDVCX	C+	(800) 225-2606	B- / 7.1	3.27	10.50	3.87 /31	14.91 /74	--	0.00	2.33
GL	MFS New Discovery Value I	NDVIX	B	(800) 225-2606	B / 8.0	3.52	11.10	4.96 /38	16.08 /84	--	0.32	1.33
GL	MFS New Discovery Value R1	NDVRX	C+	(800) 225-2606	B- / 7.1	3.35	10.56	3.94 /31	14.92 /74	--	0.00	2.33
GL	MFS New Discovery Value R2	NDVSX	B-	(800) 225-2606	B / 7.6	3.45	10.74	4.44 /35	15.51 /79	--	0.00	1.83
GL	MFS New Discovery Value R3	NDVTX	B	(800) 225-2606	B / 7.8	3.52	10.99	4.77 /37	15.79 /82	--	0.09	1.58
GL	MFS New Discovery Value R4	NDVUX	B	(800) 225-2606	B / 8.0	3.52	11.06	4.92 /38	16.08 /84	--	0.30	1.33
GR	MFS New Discovery Value R5	NDVVX	U	(800) 225-2606	U /	3.60	11.18	5.12 /39	--	--	0.39	1.26
GR	MFS Research A	MFRFX	C+	(800) 225-2606	C+ / 6.6	1.88	6.15	10.99 /78	15.38 /78	13.57 /74	0.60	0.81
GR	MFS Research B	MFRBX	B	(800) 225-2606	B- / 7.0	1.69	5.75	10.16 /75	14.50 /71	12.72 /66	0.00	1.56
GR	MFS Research C	MFRCX	B	(800) 225-2606	B- / 7.0	1.70	5.75	10.19 /75	14.51 /71	12.72 /66	0.03	1.56
GR	MFS Research I	MRFIX	B+	(800) 225-2606	B / 7.9	1.95	6.30	11.27 /79	15.67 /81	13.86 /76	0.85	0.56
FO	MFS Research International 529A	EARSX	D-	(800) 225-2606	D- / 1.4	5.74	1.44	-1.16 /12	6.99 /21	5.97 /17	2.06	1.23
FO	MFS Research International 529B	EBRIX	D-	(800) 225-2606	D / 1.7	5.46	0.99	-1.93 /10	6.17 /17	5.15 /13	1.50	1.98
FO	MFS Research International 529C	ECRIX	D-	(800) 225-2606	D / 1.7	5.46	0.98	-1.97 /10	6.16 /17	5.16 /13	1.55	1.98
FO	MFS Research International A	MRSAX	D-	(800) 225-2606	D- / 1.5	5.72	1.41	-1.15 /13	7.03 /21	6.02 /17	2.08	1.13
FO	MFS Research International B	MRIBX	D-	(800) 225-2606	D / 1.7	5.43	1.00	-1.91 /11	6.21 /18	5.22 /13	1.25	1.88
FO	MFS Research International C	MRICX	D-	(800) 225-2606	D / 1.7	5.48	1.05	-1.91 /11	6.23 /18	5.23 /13	1.49	1.88
FO	MFS Research International I	MRSIX	D	(800) 225-2606	D+ / 2.3	5.78	1.56	-0.87 /13	7.30 /23	6.29 /19	2.37	0.88
FO	MFS Research International R1	MRSGX	D-	(800) 225-2606	D / 1.7	5.50	1.06	-1.88 /11	6.24 /18	5.23 /13	1.57	1.88
FO	MFS Research International R2	MRSRX	D-	(800) 225-2606	D / 2.0	5.58	1.28	-1.42 /12	6.76 /20	5.75 /15	2.05	1.38
FO	MFS Research International R3	MRSHX	D	(800) 225-2606	D / 2.2	5.66	1.40	-1.13 /13	7.03 /21	6.01 /17	2.21	1.13
FO	MFS Research International R4	MRSJX	D	(800) 225-2606	D+ / 2.3	5.78	1.55	-0.90 /13	7.30 /23	6.29 /19	2.45	0.88
FO	MFS Research International R5	MRSKX	D	(800) 225-2606	D+ / 2.4	5.74	1.60	-0.81 /14	7.38 /23	6.29 /19	2.56	0.79
GR	MFS Research R1	MFRLX	B	(800) 225-2606	B- / 7.0	1.69	5.77	10.16 /75	14.50 /71	12.72 /66	0.06	1.56
GR	MFS Research R2	MSRRX	B+	(800) 225-2606	B- / 7.5	1.82	6.02	10.71 /77	15.08 /75	13.29 /71	0.37	1.06
GR	MFS Research R3	MFRHX	B+	(800) 225-2606	B / 7.7	1.89	6.14	11.01 /78	15.37 /78	13.57 /74	0.63	0.81
GR	MFS Research R4	MFRJX	B+	(800) 225-2606	B / 7.9	1.96	6.30	11.29 /80	15.66 /81	13.84 /76	0.87	0.56
GR	MFS Research R5	MFRKX	A-	(800) 225-2606	B / 8.0	1.99	6.34	11.36 /80	15.75 /81	13.86 /76	0.93	0.49
TC	MFS Technology A	MTCAX	C	(800) 225-2606	C / 5.5	1.48	6.56	10.56 /77	13.44 /63	15.18 /88	0.00	1.33
TC	MFS Technology B	MTCBX	C	(800) 225-2606	C+ / 5.9	1.27	6.17	9.75 /73	12.59 /57	14.32 /81	0.00	2.08
TC	MFS Technology C	MTCCX	C	(800) 225-2606	C+ / 5.9	1.32	6.18	9.76 /73	12.59 /57	14.32 /81	0.00	2.08
TC	MFS Technology I	MTCIX	C+	(800) 225-2606	C+ / 6.7	1.56	6.68	10.86 /78	13.72 /65	15.48 /90	0.00	1.08
TC	MFS Technology R1	MTCKX	C	(800) 225-2606	C+ / 5.9	1.32	6.14	9.73 /73	12.60 /57	14.31 /81	0.00	2.08
TC	MFS Technology R2	MTERX	C+	(800) 225-2606	C+ / 6.3	1.40	6.43	10.27 /75	13.16 /61	14.89 /86	0.00	1.58
TC	MFS Technology R3	MTCHX	C+	(800) 225-2606	C+ / 6.5	1.52	6.56	10.56 /77	13.44 /63	15.18 /88	0.00	1.33
TC	MFS Technology R4	MTCJX	C+	(800) 225-2606	C+ / 6.7	1.56	6.68	10.86 /78	13.74 /65	15.48 /90	0.00	1.08
AA	MFS Total Return 529A	EATRX	C+	(800) 225-2606	C- / 3.5	1.04	4.19	7.30 /57	10.41 /42	9.31 /39	1.98	0.83
AA	MFS Total Return 529B	EBTRX	C+	(800) 225-2606	C- / 3.9	0.85	3.84	6.50 /51	9.59 /37	8.52 /33	1.32	1.58
AA	MFS Total Return 529C	ECTRX	C+	(800) 225-2606	C- / 3.9	0.90	3.83	6.55 /51	9.59 /37	8.51 /33	1.34	1.58
AA	MFS Total Return A	MSFRX	C+	(800) 225-2606	C- / 3.5	1.05	4.20	7.32 /58	10.46 /42	9.38 /40	2.01	0.73
AA	MFS Total Return B	MTRBX	C+	(800) 225-2606	C- / 4.0	0.86	3.81	6.56 /51	9.63 /37	8.57 /34	1.38	1.48
AA	MFS Total Return C	MTRCX	C+	(800) 225-2606	C- / 4.0	0.86	3.85	6.54 /51	9.64 /37	8.57 /34	1.38	1.48
AA	MFS Total Return I	MTRIX	B-	(800) 225-2606	C / 4.6	1.11	4.39	7.65 /60	10.73 /44	9.67 /42	2.37	0.48
AA	MFS Total Return R1	MSFFX	C+	(800) 225-2606	C- / 4.0	0.86	3.82	6.52 /51	9.64 /37	8.57 /34	1.39	1.48
AA	MFS Total Return R2	MTRRX	C+	(800) 225-2606	C / 4.3	0.98	4.06	7.09 /56	10.17 /40	9.11 /38	1.87	0.98
AA	MFS Total Return R3	MSFHX	B-	(800) 225-2606	C / 4.5	1.05	4.20	7.32 /58	10.45 /42	9.39 /40	2.12	0.73
AA	MFS Total Return R4	MSFJX	B-	(800) 225-2606	C / 4.6	1.11	4.38	7.64 /60	10.74 /44	9.67 /42	2.37	0.48
BA	MFS Total Return R5	MSFKX	U	(800) 225-2606	U /	1.13	4.37	7.73 /61	--	--	2.44	0.41
UT	MFS Utilities A	MMUFX	C	(800) 225-2606	C / 5.1	0.86	1.61	6.82 /54	13.70 /65	13.43 /72	2.42	0.97
UT	MFS Utilities B	MMUBX	C	(800) 225-2606	C / 5.5	0.68	1.25	6.05 /47	12.86 /59	12.59 /65	1.83	1.72
UT	MFS Utilities C	MMUCX	C	(800) 225-2606	C / 5.5	0.64	1.21	6.01 /47	12.84 /58	12.57 /65	1.84	1.72
UT	MFS Utilities I	MMUIX	C+	(800) 225-2606	C+ / 6.2	0.92	1.73	7.06 /55	13.97 /67	13.70 /75	2.80	0.72

Performance header: **PERFORMANCE** — Total Return % through 3/31/15; Annualized (3Yr, 5Yr); Incl. in Returns (Dividend Yield, Expense Ratio).

99 Pct = Best
0 Pct = Worst

● Denotes fund is closed to new investors
* Denotes fund is included in Section II

www.thestreetratings.com

Risk Rating/Pts	3 Year Standard Deviation	Beta	NAV As of 3/31/15	Total $(Mil)	Cash %	Stocks %	Bonds %	Other %	Portfolio Turnover Ratio	Last Bull Market Return	Last Bear Market Return	Manager Quality Pct	Manager Tenure (Years)	Initial Purch. $	Additional Purch. $	Front End Load	Back End Load
C / 5.5	11.9	0.58	12.93	4	2	97	0	1	55	103.8	N/A	97	4	1,000	0	0.0	0.0
C+ / 5.6	11.9	0.58	13.24	15	2	97	0	1	55	110.9	N/A	98	4	0	0	0.0	0.0
C / 5.5	11.9	0.59	12.97	N/A	2	97	0	1	55	103.8	N/A	97	4	0	0	0.0	0.0
C+ / 5.6	11.9	0.58	13.18	1	2	97	0	1	55	107.4	N/A	98	4	0	0	0.0	0.0
C+ / 5.6	11.9	0.58	13.23	1	2	97	0	1	55	109.0	N/A	98	4	0	0	0.0	0.0
C+ / 5.6	11.9	0.58	13.25	N/A	2	97	0	1	55	110.8	N/A	98	4	0	0	0.0	0.0
U /	N/A	N/A	13.25	317	2	97	0	1	55	N/A	N/A	N/A	4	0	0	0.0	0.0
C+ / 6.9	9.7	1.00	38.97	2,245	1	98	0	1	39	95.0	-16.9	58	7	1,000	50	5.8	0.0
C+ / 6.9	9.7	1.00	36.09	29	1	98	0	1	39	90.1	-17.2	46	7	1,000	50	0.0	0.0
C+ / 6.9	9.7	1.00	35.91	139	1	98	0	1	39	90.0	-17.2	46	7	1,000	50	0.0	0.0
C+ / 6.9	9.7	1.00	39.79	755	1	98	0	1	39	96.7	-16.8	62	7	0	0	0.0	0.0
C+ / 5.9	12.8	0.95	16.96	2	1	98	0	1	27	43.3	-22.0	38	10	250	0	5.8	0.0
C+ / 6.0	12.7	0.95	16.03	N/A	1	98	0	1	27	39.7	-22.3	29	10	250	0	0.0	0.0
C+ / 6.0	12.8	0.96	15.84	1	1	98	0	1	27	39.6	-22.3	28	10	250	0	0.0	0.0
C+ / 5.9	12.7	0.95	17.19	1,251	1	98	0	1	27	43.4	-22.0	39	10	1,000	0	5.8	0.0
C+ / 6.0	12.7	0.95	16.51	14	1	98	0	1	27	39.8	-22.2	29	10	1,000	0	0.0	0.0
C+ / 6.0	12.7	0.95	16.16	83	1	98	0	1	27	39.9	-22.3	29	10	1,000	0	0.0	0.0
C+ / 5.9	12.8	0.95	17.76	2,127	1	98	0	1	27	44.7	-21.9	42	10	0	0	0.0	0.0
C+ / 6.0	12.8	0.95	15.92	4	1	98	0	1	27	39.8	-22.2	29	10	0	0	0.0	0.0
C+ / 5.9	12.7	0.95	16.64	187	1	98	0	1	27	42.2	-22.1	36	10	0	0	0.0	0.0
C+ / 5.9	12.7	0.95	17.00	191	1	98	0	1	27	43.6	-22.0	39	10	0	0	0.0	0.0
C+ / 5.9	12.8	0.95	17.20	425	1	98	0	1	27	44.7	-21.9	42	10	0	0	0.0	0.0
C+ / 5.9	12.7	0.95	17.12	3,075	1	98	0	1	27	45.0	-22.0	44	10	0	0	0.0	0.0
C+ / 6.9	9.7	1.00	35.44	5	1	98	0	1	39	90.1	-17.2	46	7	0	0	0.0	0.0
C+ / 6.9	9.7	1.00	37.95	35	1	98	0	1	39	93.4	-17.0	54	7	0	0	0.0	0.0
C+ / 6.9	9.7	1.00	38.76	62	1	98	0	1	39	95.0	-16.9	58	7	0	0	0.0	0.0
C+ / 6.9	9.7	1.00	38.96	55	1	98	0	1	39	96.7	-16.8	62	7	0	0	0.0	0.0
C+ / 6.9	9.7	1.00	38.96	1,433	1	98	0	1	39	97.0	-16.9	63	7	0	0	0.0	0.0
C+ / 5.6	12.9	1.12	24.73	190	4	95	0	1	38	88.9	-12.5	15	4	1,000	0	5.8	0.0
C+ / 5.6	13.0	1.12	22.26	18	4	95	0	1	38	84.1	-12.7	11	4	1,000	0	0.0	0.0
C+ / 5.6	12.9	1.12	22.22	41	4	95	0	1	38	84.1	-12.7	11	4	1,000	0	0.0	0.0
C+ / 5.6	12.9	1.12	26.05	51	4	95	0	1	38	90.5	-12.4	17	4	0	0	0.0	0.0
C+ / 5.6	12.9	1.12	22.18	2	4	95	0	1	38	84.2	-12.8	11	4	0	0	0.0	0.0
C+ / 5.6	13.0	1.12	23.89	18	4	95	0	1	38	87.2	-12.6	14	4	0	0	0.0	0.0
C+ / 5.6	12.9	1.12	24.73	10	4	95	0	1	38	88.9	-12.5	15	4	0	0	0.0	0.0
C+ / 5.6	12.9	1.12	25.43	3	4	95	0	1	38	90.5	-12.4	17	4	0	0	0.0	0.0
B / 8.5	6.1	1.06	18.25	19	1	58	39	2	35	56.1	-10.4	52	13	250	0	5.8	0.0
B / 8.6	6.0	1.05	18.31	2	1	58	39	2	35	52.1	-10.6	41	13	250	0	0.0	0.0
B / 8.5	6.0	1.05	18.39	9	1	58	39	2	35	52.0	-10.7	42	13	250	0	0.0	0.0
B / 8.5	6.0	1.05	18.29	4,779	1	58	39	2	35	56.4	-10.4	53	13	1,000	50	5.8	0.0
B / 8.6	6.1	1.06	18.31	238	1	58	39	2	35	52.4	-10.6	41	13	1,000	50	0.0	0.0
B / 8.5	6.0	1.06	18.39	996	1	58	39	2	35	52.3	-10.6	41	13	1,000	50	0.0	0.0
B / 8.6	6.0	1.05	18.29	252	1	58	39	2	35	57.7	-10.2	57	13	0	0	0.0	0.0
B / 8.5	6.0	1.06	18.27	16	1	58	39	2	35	52.4	-10.6	42	13	0	0	0.0	0.0
B / 8.5	6.0	1.06	18.34	172	1	58	39	2	35	54.9	-10.4	49	13	0	0	0.0	0.0
B / 8.6	6.0	1.05	18.30	267	1	58	39	2	35	56.3	-10.3	54	13	0	0	0.0	0.0
B / 8.5	6.1	1.06	18.31	266	1	58	39	2	35	57.7	-10.2	56	13	0	0	0.0	0.0
U /	N/A	N/A	18.29	38	1	58	39	2	35	N/A	N/A	N/A	13	0	0	0.0	0.0
C+ / 6.0	10.2	0.48	21.60	3,497	14	84	0	2	46	68.0	-12.3	96	23	1,000	0	5.8	0.0
C+ / 6.0	10.2	0.47	21.51	317	14	84	0	2	46	63.8	-12.6	96	23	1,000	0	0.0	0.0
C+ / 6.0	10.2	0.48	21.50	1,129	14	84	0	2	46	63.9	-12.6	95	23	1,000	0	0.0	0.0
C+ / 6.0	10.2	0.48	21.67	801	14	84	0	2	46	69.5	-12.2	96	23	0	0	0.0	0.0

						PERFORMANCE							
	99 Pct = Best							Total Return % through 3/31/15				Incl. in Returns	
	0 Pct = Worst		**Overall**			**Perfor-**					Annualized	Dividend	Expense
Fund		Ticker	**Investment**		Phone	**mance**	3 Mo	6 Mo	1Yr / Pct	3Yr / Pct	5Yr / Pct	Yield	Ratio
Type	Fund Name	Symbol	**Rating**			**Rating/Pts**							
UT	MFS Utilities R1	MMUGX	C		(800) 225-2606	C / 5.5	0.69	1.25	6.02 /47	12.86 /59	12.59 /65	1.84	1.72
UT	MFS Utilities R2	MURRX	C+		(800) 225-2606	C+ / 5.9	0.80	1.49	6.57 /52	13.43 /63	13.15 /70	2.32	1.22
UT	MFS Utilities R3	MMUHX	C+		(800) 225-2606	C+ / 6.0	0.86	1.61	6.82 /54	13.71 /65	13.44 /72	2.57	0.97
UT	MFS Utilities R4	MMUJX	C+		(800) 225-2606	C+ / 6.2	0.92	1.78	7.08 /56	13.99 /67	13.71 /75	2.81	0.72
UT	MFS Utilities R5	MMUKX	U		(800) 225-2606	U /	0.94	1.78	7.20 /57	--	--	2.88	0.64
GR	MFS Value 529A	EAVLX	B-		(800) 225-2606	C+ / 6.8	0.74	6.51	9.71 /73	15.84 /82	13.17 /70	1.80	1.00
GR	MFS Value 529B	EBVLX	B+		(800) 225-2606	B- / 7.3	0.70	6.37	9.12 /70	15.03 /75	12.36 /63	1.31	1.75
GR	MFS Value 529C	ECVLX	B+		(800) 225-2606	B- / 7.1	0.52	6.10	8.86 /69	14.94 /74	12.30 /63	1.18	1.75
* GR	MFS Value A	MEIAX	B-		(800) 225-2606	C+ / 6.7	0.70	6.49	9.69 /73	15.84 /82	13.21 /70	1.77	0.90
GR	MFS Value B	MFEBX	B+		(800) 225-2606	B- / 7.2	0.53	6.12	8.88 /69	14.98 /75	12.36 /63	1.15	1.65
GR	MFS Value C	MEICX	B+		(800) 225-2606	B- / 7.2	0.51	6.10	8.86 /69	14.97 /75	12.36 /63	1.18	1.65
GR	MFS Value I	MEIIX	A		(800) 225-2606	B / 8.1	0.78	6.65	9.98 /74	16.13 /84	13.50 /73	2.11	0.65
GR	MFS Value R1	MEIGX	B+		(800) 225-2606	B- / 7.2	0.52	6.08	8.85 /68	14.98 /75	12.36 /63	1.19	1.65
GR	MFS Value R2	MVRRX	B+		(800) 225-2606	B / 7.6	0.65	6.38	9.41 /71	15.56 /80	12.92 /67	1.65	1.15
GR	MFS Value R3	MEIHX	A-		(800) 225-2606	B / 7.8	0.71	6.51	9.69 /73	15.85 /82	13.21 /70	1.89	0.90
GR	MFS Value R4	MEIJX	A		(800) 225-2606	B / 8.1	0.76	6.62	9.96 /74	16.12 /84	13.49 /73	2.12	0.65
GR	MFS Value R5	MEIKX	A		(800) 225-2606	B / 8.2	0.78	6.68	10.08 /75	16.27 /85	13.52 /73	2.22	0.55
SC	MH Elite Small Cap Fund of Funds	MHELX	C-		(800) 318-7969	C+ / 6.0	3.63	9.29	3.63 /30	13.14 /61	11.21 /55	0.00	2.37
PM	Midas Fund	MIDSX	E-		(800) 400-6432	E- / 0.0	-3.03	-22.58	-34.25 / 0	-34.14 / 0	-24.17 / 0	0.00	3.02
AG	Midas Magic Fund	MISEX	C		(800) 400-6432	C / 5.4	-0.22	1.60	3.30 /28	13.42 /63	11.52 /57	0.00	3.37
OT	Midas Perpetual Portfolio	MPERX	E		(800) 400-6432	E- / 0.2	-1.01	-5.11	-9.42 / 3	-5.33 / 2	0.30 / 3	0.00	2.22
CV	Miller Convertible Bond A	MCFAX	C		(877) 441-4434	D+ / 2.5	3.25	3.13	3.39 /28	8.97 /33	8.37 /32	2.62	1.45
CV	Miller Convertible Bond C	MCFCX	C		(877) 441-4434	C- / 3.1	3.09	2.81	2.83 /26	8.41 /29	7.87 /29	2.32	1.95
CV	Miller Convertible Bond I	MCIFX	C+		(877) 441-4434	C- / 3.7	3.43	3.38	3.97 /32	9.24 /34	8.78 /35	3.27	0.95
AA	Miller Income Oppty I	LMCLX	U		(877) 534-4627	U /	5.32	3.11	4.98 /38	--	--	6.52	1.80
AA	Miller Income Oppty IS	LMCMX	U		(877) 534-4627	U /	5.22	3.02	4.89 /38	--	--	6.55	2.11
FO	Mirae Asia A	MALAX	C		(888) 335-3417	C+ / 6.6	7.84	7.47	16.89 /94	13.08 /60	--	0.00	4.60
FO	Mirae Asia C	MCLAX	C		(888) 335-3417	B- / 7.0	7.65	7.00	15.94 /93	12.22 /54	--	0.00	7.22
FO	Mirae Asia I	MILAX	C+		(888) 335-3417	B / 7.8	7.83	7.47	16.97 /95	13.29 /62	--	0.00	3.46
EM	Mirae Emerging Markets A	MALGX	E+		(888) 335-3417	D- / 1.0	5.94	2.73	7.05 /55	2.95 / 8	--	0.00	4.45
EM	Mirae Emerging Markets C	MCLGX	E+		(888) 335-3417	D- / 1.1	5.71	2.40	6.16 /48	2.16 / 7	--	0.00	6.53
EM	Mirae Emerging Markets I	MILGX	E+		(888) 335-3417	D- / 1.5	5.99	2.80	7.20 /57	3.17 / 8	--	0.00	3.09
EM	Mirae Emg Mkts Great Cnsmr A	MECGX	E+		(888) 335-3417	D- / 1.3	5.25	-0.77	6.58 /52	5.56 /15	--	0.00	2.53
EM	Mirae Emg Mkts Great Cnsmr C	MCCGX	E+		(888) 335-3417	D / 1.6	5.07	-1.21	5.80 /45	4.76 /12	--	0.00	3.43
EM	Mirae Emg Mkts Great Cnsmr I	MICGX	D-		(888) 335-3417	D / 2.1	5.36	-0.69	6.87 /54	5.79 /16	--	0.00	2.30
FO	Mirae Glbl Asia Great Consumer A	MGCEX	C+		(888) 335-3417	B+ / 8.4	10.52	6.92	23.30 /98	14.35 /70	--	0.00	3.85
FO	Mirae Glbl Asia Great Consumer C	MGCCX	B-		(888) 335-3417	B+ / 8.7	10.37	6.58	22.48 /97	13.48 /63	--	0.00	5.61
FO	Mirae Glbl Asia Great Consumer I	MGCIX	B		(888) 335-3417	A / 9.3	10.67	7.01	23.67 /98	14.61 /72	--	0.00	2.98
OT	Mirae Global Great Consumer A	MGUAX	C		(888) 335-3417	C / 4.6	5.21	6.62	5.43 /42	12.14 /53	--	0.00	4.97
OT	Mirae Global Great Consumer C	MGUCX	C		(888) 335-3417	C / 5.0	5.10	6.30	4.71 /36	11.31 /48	--	0.00	6.40
OT	Mirae Global Great Consumer I	MGUIX	C+		(888) 335-3417	C+ / 5.8	5.26	6.81	5.77 /44	12.44 /56	--	0.00	3.14
GR	MM S and P 500 Index Administrative	MIEYX	A-		(800) 542-6767	B / 7.9	0.82	5.70	12.17 /83	15.59 /80	13.95 /77	1.49	0.48
GR	MM S and P 500 Index I	MMIZX	A		(800) 542-6767	B / 8.2	0.92	5.86	12.60 /85	16.02 /84	--	1.78	0.13
GR	MM S and P 500 Index R3	MMINX	B+		(800) 542-6767	B- / 7.5	0.78	5.48	11.80 /82	15.05 /75	13.40 /72	1.16	0.88
GR	MM S and P 500 Index R4	MIEAX	A-		(800) 542-6767	B / 7.7	0.82	5.64	12.04 /83	15.38 /78	13.73 /75	1.30	0.63
GR	MM S and P 500 Index R5	MIEZX	A		(800) 542-6767	B / 8.1	0.91	5.86	12.52 /85	15.90 /83	14.23 /80	1.67	0.23
GR	MM S and P 500 Index Service	MMIEX	A-		(800) 542-6767	B / 7.9	0.86	5.69	12.28 /84	15.64 /80	13.98 /78	1.53	0.38
GL	MO 529 MOST CSP Direct Vngd		C+		(800) 662-7447	C+ / 6.1	2.40	4.72	7.92 /62	13.21 /61	11.45 /56	0.00	0.55
GI	MO 529 MOST CSP Direct Vngd Csv		C+		(800) 662-7447	D+ / 2.8	2.00	4.15	6.94 /55	7.19 /22	7.36 /25	0.00	0.55
GI	MO 529 MOST CSP Direct Vngd		B-		(800) 662-7447	C / 4.9	2.32	4.62	7.72 /61	11.17 /47	10.19 /46	0.00	0.55
GI	MO 529 MOST CSP Direct Vngd Mdt		C+		(800) 662-7447	C- / 3.9	2.15	4.39	7.35 /58	9.18 /34	8.84 /36	0.00	0.55
SC	Monetta	MONTX	C		(800) 241-9772	C+ / 6.1	3.39	6.29	12.06 /83	12.33 /55	10.07 /45	0.00	1.54

● Denotes fund is closed to new investors
* Denotes fund is included in Section II

RISK Risk Rating/Pts	3 Year Standard Deviation	Beta	NET ASSETS NAV As of 3/31/15	Total $(Mil)	ASSET Cash %	Stocks %	Bonds %	Other %	Portfolio Turnover Ratio	BULL / BEAR Last Bull Market Return	Last Bear Market Return	FUND MANAGER Manager Quality Pct	Manager Tenure (Years)	MINIMUMS Initial Purch. $	Additional Purch. $	LOADS Front End Load	Back End Load
C+ / 6.0	10.3	0.48	21.47	14	14	84	0	2	46	63.9	-12.6	96	23	0	0	0.0	0.0
C+ / 6.0	10.2	0.48	21.55	135	14	84	0	2	46	66.6	-12.4	96	23	0	0	0.0	0.0
C+ / 6.0	10.2	0.48	21.59	175	14	84	0	2	46	68.1	-12.3	96	23	0	0	0.0	0.0
C+ / 6.0	10.2	0.48	21.62	128	14	84	0	2	46	69.5	-12.2	96	23	0	0	0.0	0.0
U /	N/A	N/A	21.68	50	14	84	0	2	46	N/A	N/A	N/A	23	0	0	0.0	0.0
B- / 7.3	10.4	1.08	34.75	17	1	98	0	1	13	97.6	-18.0	47	13	250	0	5.8	0.0
B- / 7.2	10.4	1.08	34.41	1	1	98	0	1	13	92.7	-18.2	36	13	250	0	0.0	0.0
B- / 7.2	10.4	1.08	34.29	5	1	98	0	1	13	92.4	-18.3	35	13	250	0	0.0	0.0
B- / 7.3	10.4	1.08	34.98	9,277	1	98	0	1	13	97.7	-18.0	47	13	1,000	0	5.8	0.0
B- / 7.3	10.4	1.07	34.83	173	1	98	0	1	13	92.6	-18.2	36	13	1,000	0	0.0	0.0
B- / 7.2	10.4	1.08	34.63	1,408	1	98	0	1	13	92.7	-18.2	36	13	1,000	0	0.0	0.0
B- / 7.3	10.4	1.08	35.16	14,457	1	98	0	1	13	99.4	-17.9	51	13	0	0	0.0	0.0
B- / 7.3	10.4	1.08	34.40	32	1	98	0	1	13	92.7	-18.2	36	13	0	0	0.0	0.0
B- / 7.3	10.4	1.08	34.68	567	1	98	0	1	13	96.0	-18.1	43	13	0	0	0.0	0.0
B- / 7.3	10.4	1.08	34.88	1,651	1	98	0	1	13	97.7	-18.0	47	13	0	0	0.0	0.0
B- / 7.3	10.4	1.07	34.98	3,043	1	98	0	1	13	99.4	-17.9	51	13	0	0	0.0	0.0
B- / 7.3	10.4	1.07	34.98	4,594	1	98	0	1	13	100.0	-17.9	53	13	0	0	0.0	0.0
C- / 3.9	12.5	0.92	7.32	6	8	86	5	1	31	84.3	-25.7	44	N/A	10,000	1,000	0.0	0.0
D- / 1.3	36.7	1.69	0.96	14	9	90	0	1	17	-71.8	-26.1	0	13	1,000	100	0.0	1.0
C+ / 6.2	12.3	1.21	23.00	15	0	100	0	0	13	93.2	-12.3	8	N/A	1,000	100	0.0	1.0
C / 4.5	9.2	0.49	0.98	6	31	46	22	1	0	-4.2	-6.6	1	7	1,000	100	0.0	1.0
B / 8.4	6.3	0.78	12.54	285	11	0	3	86	78	45.9	-15.2	46	8	2,500	100	5.8	0.0
B / 8.4	6.3	0.78	12.47	67	11	0	3	86	78	43.4	-15.3	38	8	2,500	100	0.0	0.0
B / 8.4	6.5	0.80	12.55	338	11	0	3	86	78	47.2	-15.0	45	8	1,000,000	100	0.0	0.0
U /	N/A	N/A	9.80	26	14	78	5	3	0	N/A	N/A	N/A	1	1,000,000	0	0.0	0.0
U /	N/A	N/A	9.79	45	14	78	5	3	0	N/A	N/A	N/A	1	0	0	0.0	0.0
C / 4.3	11.8	0.70	11.69	N/A	1	98	0	1	88	73.7	-30.5	95	5	2,000	100	5.8	0.0
C- / 4.2	11.8	0.70	11.26	N/A	1	98	0	1	88	69.3	-30.7	94	5	2,000	100	0.0	0.0
C / 4.3	11.8	0.70	11.85	21	1	98	0	1	88	75.1	-30.4	95	5	250,000	25,000	0.0	0.0
C / 5.1	13.3	0.92	10.17	N/A	3	96	0	1	77	31.4	-28.7	86	5	2,000	100	5.8	0.0
C / 5.1	13.2	0.92	9.82	1	3	96	0	1	77	27.8	-28.8	81	5	2,000	100	0.0	0.0
C / 5.1	13.3	0.92	10.27	9	3	96	0	1	77	32.4	-28.6	87	5	250,000	25,000	0.0	0.0
C / 5.1	13.0	0.82	12.44	22	11	88	0	1	29	43.0	-24.6	93	5	2,000	100	5.8	0.0
C / 5.0	12.9	0.82	12.02	20	11	88	0	1	29	39.2	-24.9	92	5	2,000	100	0.0	0.0
C / 5.1	12.9	0.82	12.57	137	11	88	0	1	29	44.0	-24.5	94	5	250,000	25,000	0.0	0.0
C / 4.4	13.2	0.53	13.76	6	6	93	0	1	35	74.0	-25.1	97	4	2,000	100	5.8	0.0
C / 4.4	13.2	0.53	13.30	5	6	93	0	1	35	69.3	-25.3	97	4	2,000	100	0.0	0.0
C / 4.4	13.2	0.53	13.90	89	6	93	0	1	35	75.1	-25.0	97	4	250,000	25,000	0.0	0.0
C+ / 6.3	12.7	1.02	13.53	1	3	96	0	1	38	N/A	N/A	18	3	2,000	100	5.8	0.0
C+ / 6.3	12.7	1.02	13.19	1	3	96	0	1	38	N/A	N/A	13	3	2,000	100	0.0	0.0
C+ / 6.4	12.7	1.02	13.62	12	3	96	0	1	38	N/A	N/A	20	3	250,000	25,000	0.0	0.0
B- / 7.2	9.6	1.00	18.54	576	2	97	0	1	10	97.3	-16.5	61	8	0	0	0.0	0.0
B- / 7.4	9.6	1.01	18.71	703	2	97	0	1	10	N/A	N/A	65	8	0	0	0.0	0.0
B- / 7.2	9.5	1.00	18.20	11	2	97	0	1	10	94.1	-16.7	54	8	0	0	0.0	0.0
B- / 7.2	9.6	1.00	18.40	573	2	97	0	1	10	95.8	-16.5	57	8	0	0	0.0	0.0
B- / 7.2	9.5	1.00	18.75	1,009	2	97	0	1	10	98.9	-16.4	65	8	0	0	0.0	0.0
B- / 7.2	9.6	1.00	18.76	696	2	97	0	1	10	97.5	-16.4	61	8	0	0	0.0	0.0
C+ / 6.9	10.1	0.69	16.63	467	0	99	0	1	0	81.5	-19.9	95	9	25	25	0.0	0.0
B+ / 9.6	4.1	0.37	16.33	443	0	39	59	2	0	35.5	-5.7	80	9	25	25	0.0	0.0
B / 8.1	8.0	0.80	16.75	237	0	79	19	2	0	64.8	-15.2	46	9	25	25	0.0	0.0
B+ / 9.0	6.0	0.59	16.66	317	0	59	39	2	0	49.7	-10.6	67	9	25	25	0.0	0.0
C / 5.5	11.9	0.72	18.28	56	4	95	0	1	96	76.2	-24.1	75	29	1,000	0	0.0	0.0

					PERFORMANCE							
						Total Return % through 3/31/15					Incl. in Returns	
					Perfor-				Annualized		Dividend	Expense
Fund Type	Fund Name	Ticker Symbol	Overall Investment Rating	Phone	mance Rating/Pts	3 Mo	6 Mo	1Yr / Pct	3Yr / Pct	5Yr / Pct	Yield	Ratio
GR	Monetta Young Investor	MYIFX	B	(800) 241-9772	B- / 7.1	1.84	5.00	11.22 /79	14.55 /71	14.40 /81	0.40	1.29
GR	Monteagle Informed Investor Gr Inst	MIIFX	D+	(888) 263-5593	B / 7.7	13.04	11.39	15.44 /92	11.51 /49	9.57 /41	0.00	1.39
GR	Monteagle Quality Growth Inst	MFGIX	C+	(888) 263-5593	C+ / 6.0	2.31	7.78	14.82 /91	11.52 /49	12.20 /62	0.17	1.31
GR	Monteagle Select Val Inst	MVEIX	A+	(888) 263-5593	A+ / 9.8	2.72	7.80	12.94 /86	22.40 /98	16.31 /94	0.83	1.36
GR	Monteagle Value Inst	MVRGX	D	(888) 263-5593	C / 4.3	0.90	0.84	0.74 /18	11.44 /48	10.40 /48	1.31	1.35
SC	Montibus Small Cap Growth A	SGWAX	C-	(888) 739-1390	C+ / 6.0	5.45	13.75	9.48 /72	13.58 /64	--	0.00	2.45
SC	Montibus Small Cap Growth Advisor	SGWYX	C	(888) 739-1390	C+ / 6.9	5.54	13.85	9.49 /72	13.59 /64	--	0.00	2.45
SC	Montiibus Small Cap Growth Instl	SGRIX	C	(888) 739-1390	B- / 7.1	5.54	13.91	9.76 /73	13.86 /66	15.64 /91	0.00	2.20
AA	Morgan Creek Tactical Allocation I	MIGTX	U	(855) 489-9939	U /	1.80	0.23	-7.80 / 3	--	--	0.00	3.98
SC	Morgan Dempsey Small/Micro Cap	MITYX	D-	(877) 642-7227	D+ / 2.4	0.81	2.67	-6.71 / 4	9.30 /35	--	0.28	3.43
FO	Morgan Stanley European Eq A	EUGAX	E+	(800) 869-6397	D / 1.6	4.94	-0.37	-5.47 / 5	8.74 /31	6.87 /22	3.57	1.57
FO	● Morgan Stanley European Eq B	EUGBX	D-	(800) 869-6397	D / 2.2	4.96	-0.37	-5.51 / 5	8.71 /31	6.86 /22	4.10	1.54
FO	Morgan Stanley European Eq I	EUGDX	D-	(800) 869-6397	D+ / 2.4	4.98	-0.21	-5.18 / 5	9.04 /33	7.14 /24	4.02	1.38
FO	Morgan Stanley European Eq L	EUGCX	E+	(800) 869-6397	D / 1.9	4.80	-0.59	-6.00 / 4	8.10 /28	6.16 /18	3.47	2.16
GR	Morgan Stanley Multi Cap Gr Trust A	CPOAX	D+	(800) 869-6397	C+ / 6.6	4.34	7.02	9.44 /72	15.10 /76	16.02 /93	0.00	1.33
GR	● Morgan Stanley Multi Cap Gr Trust B	CPOBX	D+	(800) 869-6397	C+ / 6.9	4.15	6.65	8.63 /67	14.23 /69	15.16 /88	0.00	2.12
GR	Morgan Stanley Multi Cap Gr Trust I	CPODX	C	(800) 869-6397	B / 7.9	4.44	7.23	9.83 /74	15.44 /79	16.36 /94	0.00	1.04
GR	Morgan Stanley Multi Cap Gr Trust L	CPOCX	D+	(800) 869-6397	B- / 7.1	4.22	6.76	8.90 /69	14.45 /71	15.29 /89	0.00	1.87
MC	Mosaic Mid Cap R6	MMCRX	A+	(800) 336-3063	A / 9.4	3.90	13.03	14.22 /90	17.65 /93	--	0.00	0.77
FO	Motley Fool Epic Voyage Investor	TMFEX	D-	(888) 863-8803	E+ / 0.6	-2.31	-8.04	-7.01 / 4	3.54 / 9	--	1.65	1.84
GL	Motley Fool Great America Investor	TMFGX	A+	(888) 863-8803	A- / 9.2	4.81	13.13	13.32 /88	17.46 /92	--	0.20	1.20
GL	Motley Fool Independence Investor	FOOLX	C	(888) 863-8803	C / 4.9	2.28	3.17	8.98 /69	11.60 /50	11.28 /55	0.52	1.17
GR	Mount Lucas US Focused Eq I	BMLEX	C+	(844) 261-6483	A / 9.4	1.72	8.86	9.78 /73	18.91 /96	14.89 /86	1.78	1.18
GR	MP 63 Fund	DRIPX	B+	(877) 676-3386	B- / 7.1	-1.61	4.83	8.60 /67	15.50 /79	12.34 /63	1.53	0.77
FO	MSIF Active Internatl Allocation A	MSIBX	D-	(800) 354-8185	D / 1.8	5.94	1.45	-1.23 /12	8.38 /29	5.21 /13	2.08	1.25
FO	MSIF Active Internatl Allocation I	MSACX	D	(800) 354-8185	D+ / 2.7	5.99	1.60	-0.91 /13	8.69 /31	5.50 /14	2.64	0.99
GR	MSIF Advantage A	MAPPX	A-	(800) 354-8185	B+ / 8.9	7.78	11.65	17.18 /95	16.46 /87	--	0.00	2.58
GR	MSIF Advantage I	MPAIX	A	(800) 354-8185	A / 9.5	7.84	11.82	17.65 /95	16.81 /89	17.06 /96	0.03	2.23
GR	● MSIF Advantage L	MAPLX	A	(800) 354-8185	A / 9.5	7.85	11.76	17.49 /95	16.71 /88	16.99 /96	0.01	3.00
FO	MSIF Asian Equity A	MEQPX	D-	(800) 354-8185	C- / 3.0	5.24	2.82	8.51 /66	9.46 /36	--	0.49	4.68
FO	MSIF Asian Equity I	MEQIX	D	(800) 354-8185	C- / 4.1	5.42	3.07	8.94 /69	9.81 /38	--	0.81	4.28
FO	MSIF Asian Equity L	MEQLX	D	(800) 354-8185	C- / 3.5	5.19	2.61	7.97 /63	8.94 /32	--	0.01	5.59
EM	MSIF Emerging Markets A	MMKBX	E	(800) 354-8185	E / 0.4	3.06	-3.38	-1.23 /12	1.01 / 5	1.99 / 4	0.41	1.78
EM	MSIF Emerging Markets I	MGEMX	E	(800) 354-8185	E+ / 0.6	3.16	-3.26	-0.93 /13	1.32 / 6	2.27 / 5	0.83	1.51
EM	MSIF Emerging Markets IS	MMMPX	U	(800) 354-8185	U /	3.16	-3.22	-0.85 /13	--	--	0.90	6.65
EM	MSIF Frontier Emerging Markets A	MFMPX	U	(800) 354-8185	U /	-1.21	-11.12	-5.16 / 5	--	--	0.71	1.95
EM	MSIF Frontier Emerging Markets I	MFMIX	C+	(800) 354-8185	C / 4.3	-1.15	-10.95	-4.87 / 6	14.26 /69	8.25 /32	1.01	1.89
EM	MSIF Global Advantage A	MIGPX	C-	(800) 354-8185	C / 5.3	5.51	6.62	6.86 /54	12.97 /59	--	0.06	8.33
EM	MSIF Global Advantage I	MIGIX	C	(800) 354-8185	C+ / 6.4	5.65	6.76	7.24 /57	13.32 /62	--	0.06	7.97
EM	MSIF Global Advantage L	MIGLX	C	(800) 354-8185	C+ / 5.8	5.41	6.37	6.36 /50	12.39 /55	--	0.06	8.97
GL	MSIF Global Discovery A	MGDPX	D-	(800) 354-8185	C+ / 5.8	1.60	2.20	-2.95 / 9	16.08 /84	--	2.44	3.87
GL	MSIF Global Discovery I	MLDIX	D	(800) 354-8185	C+ / 6.9	1.69	2.35	-2.65 / 9	16.44 /87	--	2.89	3.65
GL	MSIF Global Discovery L	MGDLX	D	(800) 354-8185	C+ / 6.2	1.51	1.94	-3.46 / 8	15.49 /79	--	1.88	4.62
GL	● MSIF Global Franchise A	MSFBX	D	(800) 354-8185	D+ / 2.4	0.45	1.46	4.21 /33	8.77 /31	11.07 /53	1.34	1.20
GL	MSIF Global Franchise I	MSFAX	D+	(800) 354-8185	C- / 3.4	0.49	1.63	4.53 /35	9.07 /33	11.39 /56	1.71	0.95
GL	MSIF Global Insight A	MBPHX	C	(800) 354-8185	C / 4.6	2.33	1.28	-3.01 / 9	13.99 /67	--	0.47	13.62
GL	MSIF Global Insight I	MBPIX	C+	(800) 354-8185	C+ / 5.7	2.42	1.48	-2.75 / 9	14.31 /69	--	0.82	14.22
GL	MSIF Global Insight L	MBPLX	C	(800) 354-8185	C / 5.1	2.17	1.05	-3.57 / 8	13.38 /62	--	0.29	17.73
GL	MSIF Global Opportunity A	MGGPX	B-	(800) 354-8185	B / 8.0	7.71	8.51	15.80 /93	15.98 /83	--	0.00	3.83
GL	MSIF Global Opportunity I	MGGIX	B+	(800) 354-8185	A- / 9.1	7.80	8.81	16.26 /94	16.35 /86	15.92 /93	0.00	3.26
GL	MSIF Global Opportunity L	MGGLX	B	(800) 354-8185	B+ / 8.9	7.64	8.43	15.62 /93	15.90 /83	15.52 /90	0.00	4.13
RE	MSIF Global Real Estate A	MRLBX	C	(800) 354-8185	C+ / 5.8	4.16	11.39	15.12 /92	11.66 /50	10.41 /48	1.43	1.32

● Denotes fund is closed to new investors
* Denotes fund is included in Section II

RISK			NET ASSETS		ASSET					BULL / BEAR		FUND MANAGER		MINIMUMS		LOADS	
Risk Rating/Pts	3 Year		NAV As of 3/31/15	Total $(Mil)	Cash %	Stocks %	Bonds %	Other %	Portfolio Turnover Ratio	Last Bull Market Return	Last Bear Market Return	Manager Quality Pct	Manager Tenure (Years)	Initial Purch. $	Additional Purch. $	Front End Load	Back End Load
	Standard Deviation	Beta															
C+ / 6.2	9.5	0.98	21.03	137	2	97	0	1	37	89.1	-13.4	51	9	1,000	0	0.0	0.0
D / 2.0	12.4	0.83	11.62	13	2	97	0	1	290	71.0	-17.5	43	7	50,000	0	0.0	0.0
C+ / 6.8	10.4	1.04	13.73	26	3	96	0	1	27	77.1	-15.9	12	8	50,000	0	0.0	0.0
C+ / 6.3	12.2	1.19	17.42	14	13	86	0	1	29	125.5	-22.9	87	N/A	50,000	0	0.0	0.0
C- / 4.1	11.0	1.06	15.02	20	5	94	0	1	37	72.0	-18.9	10	16	50,000	0	0.0	0.0
C / 4.3	14.3	0.99	13.73	1	3	96	0	1	93	93.7	-26.7	35	8	1,000	100	5.8	1.0
C- / 4.2	14.4	0.99	13.72	N/A	3	96	0	1	93	94.0	-26.8	35	8	1,000	100	0.0	1.0
C / 4.3	14.3	0.99	13.91	24	3	96	0	1	93	95.5	-26.6	39	8	100,000	0	0.0	1.0
U /	N/A	N/A	10.20	39	5	90	3	2	346	N/A	N/A	N/A	2	1,000,000	0	0.0	0.0
C / 5.1	13.4	0.92	12.50	39	3	96	0	1	14	58.0	-21.7	10	5	2,500	50	0.0	2.0
C / 4.9	14.4	1.06	18.48	9	0	99	0	1	19	54.0	-25.1	49	9	1,000	100	5.3	2.0
C / 4.8	14.4	1.05	17.56	143	0	99	0	1	19	54.0	-25.1	49	9	1,000	100	0.0	2.0
C / 4.9	14.4	1.05	19.19	1	0	99	0	1	19	55.5	-25.0	54	9	5,000,000	0	0.0	2.0
C / 4.9	14.4	1.05	17.68	3	0	99	0	1	19	50.7	-25.3	40	9	1,000	100	0.0	2.0
D+ / 2.9	14.8	1.13	33.41	284	2	97	0	1	39	92.6	-16.8	26	13	1,000	100	5.3	0.0
D+ / 2.5	14.8	1.14	28.13	4	2	97	0	1	39	87.7	-17.1	19	13	1,000	100	0.0	0.0
C- / 3.0	14.8	1.13	35.28	64	2	97	0	1	39	94.6	-16.7	30	13	5,000,000	0	0.0	0.0
D+ / 2.5	14.8	1.13	28.16	29	2	97	0	1	39	88.8	-17.1	21	13	1,000	100	0.0	0.0
B- / 7.4	10.3	0.86	9.06	7	7	92	0	1	33	N/A	N/A	88	5	500,000	50,000	0.0	0.0
C+ / 6.8	12.2	0.82	11.43	37	3	96	0	1	25	N/A	N/A	16	4	500	50	0.0	2.0
C+ / 6.9	10.3	0.57	20.05	260	4	95	0	1	18	105.1	-17.4	98	5	500	50	0.0	2.0
C+ / 6.9	9.4	0.62	20.66	413	6	93	0	1	24	68.4	-16.1	94	6	500	50	0.0	2.0
D+ / 2.9	13.3	1.18	10.04	58	1	98	0	1	54	116.8	-23.9	63	N/A	10,000	0	0.0	0.0
B- / 7.5	9.2	0.91	18.33	55	1	98	0	1	4	90.4	-16.9	75	16	500	50	0.0	1.0
C+ / 6.0	12.9	0.97	13.55	75	13	86	0	1	36	44.7	-23.6	55	20	1,000	0	5.3	2.0
C+ / 5.9	12.9	0.97	13.27	228	13	86	0	1	36	46.3	-23.6	60	20	5,000,000	0	0.0	2.0
C+ / 6.1	11.0	0.94	18.00	7	8	91	0	1	36	98.2	-10.7	78	7	1,000	0	5.3	0.0
C+ / 6.1	10.9	0.94	18.15	19	8	91	0	1	36	100.2	-10.6	81	7	5,000,000	0	0.0	0.0
C+ / 6.1	10.9	0.94	18.14	9	8	91	0	1	36	99.7	-10.6	80	7	1,000	0	0.0	0.0
C / 4.6	14.0	0.80	10.85	2	3	96	0	1	114	55.7	-25.2	83	3	1,000	0	5.3	2.0
C / 4.6	13.9	0.80	10.89	7	3	96	0	1	114	57.2	-25.2	85	3	5,000,000	0	0.0	2.0
C / 4.7	14.0	0.80	10.75	N/A	3	96	0	1	114	53.0	-25.3	79	3	1,000	0	0.0	2.0
C- / 4.2	12.9	0.92	22.23	27	4	95	0	1	49	20.8	-22.8	72	21	1,000	0	5.3	2.0
C- / 4.2	12.9	0.92	22.83	665	4	95	0	1	49	22.0	-22.8	74	21	5,000,000	0	0.0	2.0
U /	N/A	N/A	22.84	345	4	95	0	1	49	N/A	N/A	N/A	21	10,000,000	0	0.0	2.0
U /	N/A	N/A	18.84	67	6	93	0	1	34	N/A	N/A	N/A	7	1,000	0	5.3	2.0
B- / 7.6	11.3	0.43	18.94	540	6	93	0	1	34	63.8	-21.5	99	7	5,000,000	0	0.0	2.0
C / 5.2	10.8	0.58	13.40	1	3	96	0	1	57	82.0	-15.9	99	5	1,000	0	5.3	0.0
C / 5.2	10.8	0.58	13.46	4	3	96	0	1	57	84.0	-15.7	99	5	5,000,000	0	0.0	0.0
C / 5.2	10.8	0.58	13.24	N/A	3	96	0	1	57	78.8	-16.0	99	5	1,000	0	0.0	0.0
D / 2.0	13.5	0.88	10.79	4	12	87	0	1	100	103.2	-27.7	96	5	1,000	0	5.3	0.0
D / 2.0	13.5	0.88	10.80	7	12	87	0	1	100	105.1	-27.6	96	5	5,000,000	0	0.0	0.0
D / 2.1	13.6	0.88	10.75	N/A	12	87	0	1	100	99.8	-27.9	96	5	1,000	0	0.0	0.0
C+ / 6.3	11.4	0.76	20.01	63	2	97	0	1	24	56.1	-6.5	81	6	1,000	0	5.3	0.0
C+ / 6.3	11.5	0.76	20.37	494	2	97	0	1	24	57.7	-6.5	83	6	5,000,000	0	0.0	0.0
C+ / 6.3	12.4	0.85	11.86	N/A	2	97	0	1	59	N/A	N/A	94	4	1,000	0	5.3	0.0
C+ / 6.3	12.4	0.84	11.84	2	2	97	0	1	59	N/A	N/A	95	4	5,000,000	0	0.0	0.0
C+ / 6.3	12.4	0.84	11.75	N/A	2	97	0	1	59	N/A	N/A	93	4	1,000	0	0.0	0.0
C / 5.1	13.1	0.71	14.80	22	9	88	2	1	38	89.8	-21.4	97	7	1,000	0	5.3	0.0
C / 5.1	13.1	0.71	15.07	23	9	88	2	1	38	91.8	-21.4	97	7	5,000,000	0	0.0	0.0
C / 5.1	13.1	0.71	14.66	3	9	88	2	1	38	89.5	-21.5	97	7	1,000	0	0.0	0.0
C / 5.3	12.0	0.86	11.51	107	9	90	0	1	33	71.2	-21.9	62	9	1,000	0	5.3	0.0

	99 Pct = Best 0 Pct = Worst				PERFORMANCE							
			Overall		Perfor-	Total Return % through 3/31/15					Incl. in Returns	
			Investment		mance				Annualized		Dividend	Expense
Fund Type	Fund Name	Ticker Symbol	Rating	Phone	Rating/Pts	3 Mo	6 Mo	1Yr / Pct	3Yr / Pct	5Yr / Pct	Yield	Ratio
RE	MSIF Global Real Estate I	MRLAX	C+	(800) 354-8185	C+ / 6.9	4.23	11.38	15.30 /92	11.98 /52	10.68 /50	1.73	1.02
RE	MSIF Global Real Estate IS	MGREX	U	(800) 354-8185	U /	4.23	11.46	15.49 /92	--	--	1.80	0.97
RE	MSIF Global Real Estate L	MGRLX	C	(800) 354-8185	C+ / 6.3	4.03	11.00	14.54 /91	11.15 /47	9.87 /43	1.05	1.77
GR	MSIF Growth A	MSEGX	C+	(800) 354-8185	B / 8.2	6.14	7.80	13.68 /89	16.70 /88	16.93 /96	0.00	0.96
GR	MSIF Growth I	MSEQX	B	(800) 354-8185	A- / 9.1	6.20	7.92	13.89 /89	16.96 /90	17.20 /96	0.01	0.71
GR	MSIF Growth IS	MGRPX	U	(800) 354-8185	U /	6.22	7.98	14.03 /89	--	--	0.02	5.60
GR	MSIF Growth L	MSHLX	U	(800) 354-8185	U /	6.02	7.57	13.18 /87	--	--	0.02	1.72
GL	MSIF Insight A	MFPHX	A+	(800) 354-8185	B+ / 8.8	0.51	6.09	8.64 /67	19.42 /97	--	0.06	13.79
GL	MSIF Insight I	MFPIX	A+	(800) 354-8185	A / 9.5	0.66	6.29	9.07 /70	19.75 /98	--	0.23	10.83
GL	MSIF Insight L	MFPLX	A+	(800) 354-8185	A- / 9.2	0.44	5.86	8.13 /64	18.82 /96	--	0.06	12.31
FO	MSIF International Advantage A	MFAPX	D+	(800) 354-8185	C- / 3.4	6.71	7.70	8.28 /65	9.55 /36	--	0.22	6.89
FO	MSIF International Advantage I	MFAIX	C-	(800) 354-8185	C / 4.4	6.80	7.92	8.67 /67	9.89 /39	--	0.49	6.30
FO	MSIF International Advantage L	MSALX	C-	(800) 354-8185	C- / 3.9	6.58	7.45	7.86 /62	9.01 /33	--	0.06	7.43
FO	MSIF International Equity A	MIQBX	D-	(800) 354-8185	R- / 1.5	4.91	-0.70	-1.96 /10	7.93 /27	6.15 /18	2.51	1.25
FO	MSIF International Equity I	MSIQX	D-	(800) 354-8185	D+ / 2.3	4.98	-0.57	-1.64 /11	8.25 /28	6.43 /20	2.96	0.99
FO	MSIF International Equity IS	MIQPX	U	(800) 354-8185	U /	5.04	-0.56	-1.57 /11	--	--	2.97	0.91
FO	MSIF International Opportunity A	MIOPX	D+	(800) 354-8185	C- / 3.7	7.14	6.01	8.70 /68	10.29 /41	10.41 /48	0.04	4.49
FO	MSIF International Opportunity I	MIOIX	C-	(800) 354-8185	C / 4.8	7.26	6.28	9.13 /70	10.68 /43	10.74 /51	0.04	3.84
FO	MSIF International Opportunity L	MIOLX	D+	(800) 354-8185	C- / 4.2	7.01	5.71	8.14 /64	9.75 /38	9.86 /43	0.00	4.91
RE	MSIF International Real Estate A	IERBX	D+	(800) 354-8185	C- / 3.9	4.39	5.12	7.98 /63	11.13 /46	7.09 /24	1.80	1.53
RE	MSIF International Real Estate I	MSUAX	C-	(800) 354-8185	C / 5.0	4.44	5.27	8.34 /65	11.47 /49	7.38 /26	2.27	1.23
GL	MSIF Multi-Asset A	MMPPX	U	(800) 354-8185	U /	-1.48	-4.79	-2.94 / 9	--	--	1.58	2.26
GL	MSIF Multi-Asset I	MMPIX	U	(800) 354-8185	U /	-1.39	-4.63	-2.71 / 9	--	--	1.90	1.99
GL	MSIF Multi-Asset L	MMPLX	U	(800) 354-8185	U /	-1.58	-5.02	-3.40 / 8	--	--	1.24	2.75
GR	MSIF Opportunity A	MEGPX	C	(800) 354-8185	C+ / 6.7	7.74	8.23	13.12 /87	14.17 /68	--	0.00	1.22
GR	MSIF Opportunity I	MGEIX	B-	(800) 354-8185	B / 7.9	7.89	8.48	13.63 /89	14.54 /71	14.85 /86	0.00	0.87
GR	MSIF Opportunity L	MGELX	C+	(800) 354-8185	B- / 7.2	7.65	8.04	12.60 /85	13.61 /64	13.92 /77	0.00	1.67
OT	MSIF Select Global Infr A	MTIPX	C+	(800) 354-8185	C+ / 5.9	0.20	1.66	9.99 /74	14.54 /71	--	1.10	2.43
OT	MSIF Select Global Infr I	MTIIX	B	(800) 354-8185	B- / 7.3	0.19	1.81	10.27 /75	15.49 /79	--	1.35	2.04
OT	MSIF Select Global Infr L	MTILX	C+	(800) 354-8185	C+ / 6.6	-0.07	1.30	9.28 /71	14.55 /71	--	0.65	2.86
SC	● MSIF Small Company Growth A	MSSMX	D-	(800) 354-8185	C+ / 6.3	3.96	10.94	-1.61 /11	16.42 /86	14.81 /85	0.00	1.35
SC	● MSIF Small Company Growth I	MSSGX	D+	(800) 354-8185	B- / 7.5	4.06	11.10	-1.25 /12	16.79 /89	15.13 /88	0.00	1.08
GL	MSIF Small Company Growth IS	MFLLX	U	(800) 354-8185	U /	4.12	11.16	-1.20 /12	--	--	0.00	0.99
SC	● MSIF Small Company Growth L	MSSLX	D+	(800) 354-8185	C+ / 6.9	3.90	10.71	-2.04 /10	15.88 /82	--	0.00	1.92
BA	MSIF Trust Global Strategist A	MBAAX	D	(800) 354-8185	D / 1.8	0.25	-0.83	0.96 /18	8.27 /29	8.93 /36	1.67	1.14
BA	MSIF Trust Global Strategist I	MPBAX	C-	(800) 354-8185	D+ / 2.7	0.38	-0.62	1.29 /19	8.60 /30	9.24 /38	2.12	0.83
BA	MSIF Trust Global Strategist L	MSDLX	U	(800) 354-8185	U /	0.13	-1.07	0.43 /17	--	--	1.23	1.70
MC	MSIF Trust Mid Cap Growth A	MACGX	E	(800) 354-8185	C- / 3.3	2.89	5.58	3.99 /32	10.07 /40	12.64 /65	0.00	1.00
MC	MSIF Trust Mid Cap Growth I	MPEGX	E+	(800) 354-8185	C / 4.3	2.97	5.69	4.25 /33	10.35 /41	12.92 /67	0.20	0.75
MC	MSIF Trust Mid Cap Growth IS	MMCGX	U	(800) 354-8185	U /	3.00	5.77	4.42 /35	--	--	0.33	0.61
RE	MSIF US Real Estate A	MUSDX	C+	(800) 354-8185	B+ / 8.4	4.09	18.70	23.99 /98	13.19 /61	14.77 /85	1.23	1.29
RE	MSIF US Real Estate I	MSUSX	B	(800) 354-8185	A / 9.3	4.15	19.00	24.44 /98	13.54 /64	15.09 /87	1.58	1.03
RE	MSIF US Real Estate IS	MURSX	U	(800) 354-8185	U /	4.20	19.01	24.50 /98	--	--	1.63	6.19
RE	MSIF US Real Estate L	MSULX	B+	(800) 354-8185	B+ / 8.8	3.94	18.47	23.44 /98	12.63 /57	--	0.88	1.79
GI	Muhlenkamp Fund	MUHLX	D	(800) 860-3863	C / 4.3	1.11	0.94	2.40 /24	11.20 /47	8.03 /30	0.00	1.21
GR	Mundoval	MUNDX	D+	(800) 595-2877	C- / 3.8	0.46	-4.23	-0.43 /14	11.26 /47	8.49 /33	0.42	1.50
GR	Mutual of America Inst All Amer	MALLX	C-	(800) 914-8716	B / 7.7	1.87	7.47	11.72 /81	15.08 /75	13.35 /72	1.16	1.27
IX	Mutual of America Inst Eqty Idx	MAEQX	D+	(800) 914-8716	B / 8.2	0.90	5.83	12.55 /85	16.01 /83	14.09 /79	1.76	0.59
MC	Mutual of America Inst MCE Idx	MAMQX	C	(800) 914-8716	A- / 9.1	5.29	11.93	12.08 /83	16.91 /89	16.67 /95	1.24	0.63
SC	Mutual of America Inst SC Gro	MASSX	C	(800) 914-8716	B+ / 8.4	6.38	18.04	11.87 /82	14.75 /73	14.47 /82	0.00	1.50
SC	Mutual of America Inst SC Val	MAVSX	C	(800) 914-8716	C+ / 6.8	3.40	11.74	7.97 /63	13.72 /65	12.89 /67	0.77	1.43
GR	Mutual Recovery A	FMRAX	D+	(800) 342-5236	D / 2.2	0.87	-1.74	-1.66 /11	9.70 /37	7.00 /23	3.89	2.84

● Denotes fund is closed to new investors
* Denotes fund is included in Section II

RISK			NET ASSETS		ASSET					BULL / BEAR		FUND MANAGER		MINIMUMS		LOADS	
	3 Year		NAV						Portfolio	Last Bull	Last Bear	Manager	Manager	Initial	Additional	Front	Back
Risk Rating/Pts	Standard Deviation	Beta	As of 3/31/15	Total $(Mil)	Cash %	Stocks %	Bonds %	Other %	Turnover Ratio	Market Return	Market Return	Quality Pct	Tenure (Years)	Purch. $	Purch. $	End Load	End Load
C / 5.3	12.0	0.86	11.57	1,856	9	90	0	1	33	72.6	-21.8	66	9	5,000,000	0	0.0	0.0
U /	N/A	N/A	11.58	545	9	90	0	1	33	N/A	N/A	N/A	9	10,000,000	0	0.0	0.0
C / 5.3	12.0	0.86	11.35	5	9	90	0	1	33	68.2	-22.1	55	9	1,000	0	0.0	0.0
C / 4.6	13.8	1.06	40.29	1,625	2	97	0	1	31	102.2	-16.0	61	11	1,000	0	5.3	0.0
C / 4.6	13.8	1.06	41.25	836	2	97	0	1	31	103.8	-15.9	65	11	5,000,000	0	0.0	0.0
U /	N/A	N/A	41.33	1,026	2	97	0	1	31	N/A	N/A	N/A	11	10,000,000	0	0.0	0.0
U /	N/A	N/A	39.63	94	2	97	0	1	31	N/A	N/A	N/A	11	1,000	0	0.0	0.0
C+ / 6.9	10.0	0.51	13.73	N/A	2	97	0	1	51	N/A	N/A	99	4	1,000	0	5.3	0.0
C+ / 6.9	10.0	0.51	13.74	2	2	97	0	1	51	N/A	N/A	99	4	5,000,000	0	0.0	0.0
C+ / 6.9	10.0	0.51	13.56	N/A	2	97	0	1	51	N/A	N/A	99	4	1,000	0	0.0	0.0
C+ / 6.4	9.9	0.66	13.20	1	9	88	2	1	49	62.8	-15.9	89	5	1,000	0	5.3	2.0
C+ / 6.4	9.9	0.66	13.20	5	9	88	2	1	49	64.4	-15.7	90	5	5,000,000	0	0.0	2.0
C+ / 6.4	9.9	0.67	13.12	N/A	9	88	2	1	49	60.2	-16.1	87	5	1,000	0	0.0	2.0
C+ / 5.7	12.5	0.92	16.03	1,547	2	97	0	1	29	51.6	-20.1	56	16	1,000	0	5.3	2.0
C+ / 5.7	12.5	0.92	16.24	2,575	2	97	0	1	29	53.0	-20.0	61	16	5,000,000	0	0.0	2.0
U /	N/A	N/A	16.25	864	2	97	0	1	29	N/A	N/A	N/A	16	10,000,000	0	0.0	2.0
C+ / 5.7	11.3	0.66	14.85	1	10	87	2	1	40	62.3	-26.2	91	5	1,000	0	5.3	2.0
C+ / 5.7	11.3	0.66	14.92	12	10	87	2	1	40	63.9	-26.1	92	5	5,000,000	0	0.0	2.0
C+ / 5.6	11.2	0.66	14.66	N/A	10	87	2	1	40	59.6	-26.3	90	5	1,000	0	0.0	2.0
C / 5.5	14.5	0.77	20.71	3	16	83	0	1	40	66.6	-25.0	71	16	1,000	0	5.3	2.0
C / 5.5	14.5	0.77	20.72	91	16	83	0	1	40	68.2	-24.9	74	16	5,000,000	0	0.0	2.0
U /	N/A	N/A	11.33	51	76	20	2	2	223	N/A	N/A	N/A	3	1,000	0	5.3	0.0
U /	N/A	N/A	11.39	512	76	20	2	2	223	N/A	N/A	N/A	3	5,000,000	0	0.0	0.0
U /	N/A	N/A	11.21	39	76	20	2	2	223	N/A	N/A	N/A	3	1,000	0	0.0	0.0
C / 5.1	13.2	0.98	22.98	191	2	97	0	1	21	83.9	-14.9	47	9	1,000	0	5.3	0.0
C / 5.2	13.2	0.98	23.37	10	2	97	0	1	21	85.8	-14.8	52	9	5,000,000	0	0.0	0.0
C / 5.0	13.2	0.98	19.99	31	2	97	0	1	21	80.6	-15.0	39	9	1,000	0	0.0	0.0
C+ / 6.3	8.7	0.60	15.40	357	11	88	0	1	30	74.2	-6.8	93	5	1,000	0	5.3	0.0
C+ / 6.3	8.7	0.60	15.44	53	11	88	0	1	30	78.9	-6.7	94	5	5,000,000	0	0.0	0.0
C+ / 6.4	8.7	0.60	15.33	8	11	88	0	1	30	73.9	-7.0	93	5	1,000	0	0.0	0.0
D- / 1.5	17.1	1.12	15.49	184	5	94	0	1	43	91.7	-24.7	43	16	1,000	0	5.3	2.0
D / 1.8	17.0	1.11	17.18	1,089	5	94	0	1	43	93.7	-24.6	49	16	5,000,000	0	0.0	2.0
U /	N/A	N/A	17.20	755	5	94	0	1	43	N/A	N/A	N/A	16	10,000,000	0	0.0	2.0
D+ / 2.7	17.0	1.11	15.18	2	5	94	0	1	43	N/A	N/A	37	16	1,000	0	0.0	2.0
B- / 7.2	6.0	0.93	15.83	335	10	63	26	1	62	51.3	-9.4	42	4	1,000	0	5.3	0.0
B- / 7.1	6.0	0.93	15.90	78	10	63	26	1	62	52.8	-9.4	47	4	5,000,000	0	0.0	0.0
U /	N/A	N/A	15.78	28	10	63	26	1	62	N/A	N/A	N/A	4	1,000	0	0.0	0.0
D / 2.1	14.5	1.04	38.42	1,550	0	99	0	1	45	65.3	-21.2	5	13	1,000	0	5.3	0.0
D / 2.2	14.5	1.04	40.51	4,285	0	99	0	1	45	66.8	-21.1	5	13	5,000,000	0	0.0	0.0
U /	N/A	N/A	40.55	722	0	99	0	1	45	N/A	N/A	N/A	13	10,000,000	0	0.0	0.0
C / 4.4	12.0	0.96	20.86	110	2	97	0	1	24	81.0	-17.5	64	20	1,000	0	5.3	0.0
C / 4.4	12.0	0.96	21.33	777	2	97	0	1	24	82.9	-17.4	68	20	5,000,000	0	0.0	0.0
U /	N/A	N/A	21.34	167	2	97	0	1	24	N/A	N/A	N/A	20	10,000,000	0	0.0	0.0
C / 5.2	12.0	0.96	20.82	5	2	97	0	1	24	N/A	N/A	57	20	1,000	0	0.0	0.0
C / 4.4	11.4	1.11	60.16	416	7	92	0	1	26	66.8	-19.0	6	27	1,500	50	0.0	0.0
C / 5.5	13.8	1.21	15.35	22	0	99	0	1	33	69.2	-17.3	4	11	10,000	100	0.0	0.0
D+ / 2.6	9.6	1.00	10.60	10	2	96	0	2	20	92.9	-18.3	55	12	25,000	5,000	0.0	0.0
D- / 1.1	9.5	1.00	9.79	34	0	97	2	1	4	99.6	-16.3	67	1	25,000	5,000	0.0	0.0
D / 2.2	11.0	1.00	12.32	23	1	96	1	2	17	102.2	-22.6	66	1	25,000	5,000	0.0	0.0
D+ / 2.5	13.8	0.99	12.89	7	3	96	0	1	54	85.8	-23.9	50	8	25,000	5,000	0.0	0.0
C / 4.5	10.9	0.78	12.37	9	6	93	0	1	53	78.4	-21.7	77	8	25,000	5,000	0.0	0.0
B- / 7.4	7.0	0.55	11.56	21	13	50	32	5	58	54.0	-18.1	77	11	10,000	1,000	5.8	0.0

Fund Type	Fund Name	Ticker Symbol	Overall Investment Rating	Phone	PERFORMANCE Performance Rating/Pts	Total Return % through 3/31/15 3 Mo	6 Mo	1Yr / Pct	Annualized 3Yr / Pct	5Yr / Pct	Incl. in Returns Dividend Yield	Expense Ratio
GR	Mutual Recovery Adv	FMRVX	C-	(800) 321-8563	C- / 3.3	0.87	-1.63	-1.39 /12	10.01 /39	7.31 /25	4.45	2.54
GR	Mutual Recovery C	FCMRX	C-	(800) 342-5236	D+ / 2.6	0.62	-2.12	-2.36 /10	8.92 /32	6.25 /18	3.31	3.54
GR	NASDAQ-100 Index Direct	NASDX	A+	(800) 955-9988	A / 9.5	2.58	7.93	21.69 /97	17.85 /94	18.46 /98	0.68	0.73
GR	NASDAQ-100 Index K	NDXKX	A+	(800) 955-9988	A / 9.4	2.46	7.61	21.07 /97	17.29 /91	17.85 /97	0.18	1.23
GI	Nationwide A	NWFAX	B-	(800) 848-0920	C+ / 6.6	2.01	5.24	12.24 /84	15.12 /76	12.66 /65	0.91	1.00
SC	Nationwide Bailard Cognitive Val A	NWHDX	D	(800) 848-0920	C+ / 5.6	2.88	9.10	8.09 /64	13.46 /63	14.26 /80	0.50	1.35
SC	Nationwide Bailard Cognitive Val C	NWHEX	D	(800) 848-0920	C+ / 6.0	2.68	8.61	7.22 /57	12.71 /58	13.55 /73	0.00	2.11
SC	Nationwide Bailard Cognitive Val IS	NWHHX	D+	(800) 848-0920	C+ / 6.8	2.88	9.28	8.48 /66	13.79 /66	14.63 /83	0.72	1.09
SC	Nationwide Bailard Cognitive Val M	NWHFX	D+	(800) 848-0920	C+ / 6.8	2.89	9.18	8.35 /65	13.84 /66	14.71 /84	0.67	1.02
EM	Nationwide Bailard Em Mkts Eq M	NWWEX	U	(800) 848-0920	U /	0.60	-2.06	--	--	--	0.00	1.81
FO	Nationwide Bailard Intl Eq A	NWHJX	D	(800) 848-0920	D+ / 2.9	4.61	3.39	0.94 /18	9.97 /39	6.92 /23	3.66	1.26
FO	Nationwide Bailard Intl Eq C	NWHKX	D+	(800) 848-0920	C- / 3.3	4.36	2.89	-0.05 /15	9.18 /34	6.18 /18	3.18	1.98
FO	Nationwide Bailard Intl Eq IS	NWHNX	C-	(800) 848-0920	C- / 4.0	4.49	3.34	1.01 /18	10.15 /40	7.08 /24	4.19	0.98
FO	Nationwide Bailard Intl Eq M	NWHLX	C-	(800) 848-0920	C- / 4.1	4.62	3.50	1.17 /19	10.31 /41	7.26 /25	4.23	0.89
GR	Nationwide Bailard Tech and Scie A	NWHOX	C	(800) 848-0920	C+ / 6.1	2.45	8.16	15.48 /92	13.49 /63	14.08 /78	0.09	1.32
GR	Nationwide Bailard Tech and Scie C	NWHPX	C+	(800) 848-0920	C+ / 6.6	2.27	7.82	14.68 /91	12.76 /58	13.35 /72	0.00	2.04
GR	Nationwide Bailard Tech and Scie IS	NWHUX	B-	(800) 848-0920	B- / 7.4	2.49	8.32	15.71 /93	13.80 /66	14.44 /82	0.23	1.10
GR	Nationwide Bailard Tech and Scie M	NWHQX	B-	(800) 848-0920	B- / 7.5	2.55	8.39	15.91 /93	13.94 /67	14.52 /83	0.40	0.98
GI	Nationwide C	GTRCX	B-	(800) 848-0920	C+ / 6.9	1.79	4.81	11.38 /80	14.26 /69	11.84 /60	0.44	1.78
AA	Nationwide Destination 2010 A	NWDAX	D+	(800) 848-0920	D- / 1.4	2.15	3.60	4.57 /36	6.18 /17	5.86 /16	1.62	0.86
AA	Nationwide Destination 2010 C	NWDCX	C-	(800) 848-0920	D / 1.8	2.01	3.22	3.92 /31	5.60 /15	5.29 /13	1.08	1.52
AA	Nationwide Destination 2010 Inst	NWDIX	C-	(800) 848-0920	D+ / 2.4	2.24	3.75	5.00 /39	6.68 /20	6.37 /19	2.12	0.40
AA	Nationwide Destination 2010 IS	NWDSX	C-	(800) 848-0920	D+ / 2.4	2.36	3.87	5.12 /39	6.77 /20	6.40 /19	2.12	0.40
AA	Nationwide Destination 2010 R	NWDBX	C-	(800) 848-0920	D / 1.9	2.05	3.37	4.34 /34	5.90 /16	5.58 /15	1.37	1.15
AA	Nationwide Destination 2015 A	NWEAX	D+	(800) 848-0920	D / 1.8	2.25	3.87	4.80 /37	7.20 /22	6.74 /21	1.58	0.87
AA	Nationwide Destination 2015 C	NWECX	C-	(800) 848-0920	D+ / 2.3	2.22	3.53	4.11 /33	6.63 /20	6.17 /18	1.21	1.44
AA	Nationwide Destination 2015 Inst	NWEIX	C-	(800) 848-0920	D+ / 2.9	2.44	4.13	5.24 /40	7.68 /25	7.25 /25	2.18	0.40
AA	Nationwide Destination 2015 IS	NWESX	C-	(800) 848-0920	D+ / 2.7	2.38	3.90	4.98 /38	7.43 /24	6.98 /23	1.93	0.65
AA	Nationwide Destination 2015 R	NWEBX	C-	(800) 848-0920	D+ / 2.4	2.15	3.64	4.35 /34	6.85 /21	6.44 /20	1.43	1.15
AA	Nationwide Destination 2020 A	NWAFX	C-	(800) 848-0920	D+ / 2.3	2.28	3.91	4.77 /37	8.29 /29	7.60 /27	1.67	0.85
AA	Nationwide Destination 2020 C	NWFCX	C	(800) 848-0920	D+ / 2.8	2.17	3.47	4.06 /32	7.71 /25	7.04 /23	1.16	1.47
AA	Nationwide Destination 2020 Inst	NWFIX	C	(800) 848-0920	C- / 3.5	2.46	4.04	5.15 /40	8.79 /32	8.11 /31	2.14	0.40
AA	Nationwide Destination 2020 IS	NWFSX	C	(800) 848-0920	C- / 3.3	2.41	3.93	4.91 /38	8.55 /30	7.86 /29	1.90	0.65
AA	Nationwide Destination 2020 R	NWFTX	C	(800) 848-0920	C- / 3.0	2.18	3.68	4.29 /34	7.98 /27	7.30 /25	1.40	1.15
AA	Nationwide Destination 2025 A	NWHAX	C-	(800) 848-0920	C- / 3.0	2.51	4.29	4.93 /38	9.55 /36	8.58 /34	1.62	0.86
AA	Nationwide Destination 2025 C	NWHCX	C	(800) 848-0920	C- / 3.4	2.32	3.77	4.19 /33	8.90 /32	7.98 /30	1.19	1.47
AA	Nationwide Destination 2025 Inst	NWHIX	C	(800) 848-0920	C- / 4.2	2.58	4.41	5.33 /41	10.03 /39	9.08 /37	2.11	0.41
AA	Nationwide Destination 2025 IS	NWHSX	C	(800) 848-0920	C- / 4.0	2.43	4.20	4.99 /38	9.75 /38	8.79 /35	1.87	0.66
AA	Nationwide Destination 2025 R	NWHBX	C	(800) 848-0920	C- / 3.7	2.41	4.06	4.59 /36	9.24 /35	8.26 /32	1.38	1.16
AA	Nationwide Destination 2030 A	NWIAX	C-	(800) 848-0920	C- / 3.5	2.63	4.61	5.20 /40	10.45 /42	9.34 /39	1.40	0.89
AA	Nationwide Destination 2030 C	NWICX	C-	(800) 848-0920	C- / 4.0	2.51	4.24	4.60 /36	9.89 /39	8.77 /35	1.19	1.44
AA	Nationwide Destination 2030 Inst	NWIIX	C	(800) 848-0920	C / 4.7	2.74	4.83	5.70 /44	10.98 /45	9.87 /44	2.05	0.41
AA	Nationwide Destination 2030 IS	NWISX	C	(800) 848-0920	C / 4.6	2.79	4.72	5.47 /42	10.74 /44	9.60 /41	1.82	0.66
AA	Nationwide Destination 2030 R	NWBIX	C-	(800) 848-0920	C- / 4.2	2.60	4.41	4.89 /38	10.18 /40	9.06 /37	1.37	1.16
AA	Nationwide Destination 2035 A	NWLAX	C-	(800) 848-0920	C- / 3.9	2.68	4.84	5.24 /40	11.17 /47	9.97 /44	1.56	0.86
AA	Nationwide Destination 2035 C	NWLCX	C	(800) 848-0920	C / 4.4	2.57	4.47	4.58 /36	10.54 /43	9.38 /40	1.17	1.49
AA	Nationwide Destination 2035 Inst	NWLIX	C+	(800) 848-0920	C / 5.2	2.89	5.14	5.79 /45	11.74 /51	10.53 /49	2.08	0.41
AA	Nationwide Destination 2035 IS	NWLSX	C+	(800) 848-0920	C / 5.0	2.74	4.94	5.56 /43	11.42 /48	10.24 /46	1.85	0.66
AA	Nationwide Destination 2035 R	NWLBX	C	(800) 848-0920	C / 4.6	2.65	4.72	4.99 /38	10.86 /45	9.68 /42	1.39	1.16
AA	Nationwide Destination 2040 A	NWMAX	C	(800) 848-0920	C- / 4.2	2.88	5.27	5.60 /43	11.60 /50	10.21 /46	1.59	0.85
AA	Nationwide Destination 2040 C	NWMCX	C	(800) 848-0920	C / 4.7	2.82	5.03	5.08 /39	11.01 /45	9.65 /42	1.10	1.43
AA	Nationwide Destination 2040 Inst	NWMHX	C+	(800) 848-0920	C / 5.4	2.97	5.42	6.09 /47	12.10 /53	10.74 /51	2.07	0.40

RISK			NET ASSETS		ASSET				Portfolio Turnover Ratio	BULL / BEAR		FUND MANAGER		MINIMUMS		LOADS	
	3 Year		NAV							Last Bull	Last Bear	Manager	Manager	Initial	Additional	Front	Back
Risk Rating/Pts	Standard Deviation	Beta	As of 3/31/15	Total $(Mil)	Cash %	Stocks %	Bonds %	Other %		Market Return	Market Return	Quality Pct	Tenure (Years)	Purch. $	Purch. $	End Load	End Load
B- /7.4	7.0	0.55	11.64	22	13	50	32	5	58	55.4	-18.0	79	11	250,000	1,000	0.0	0.0
B- /7.6	6.9	0.55	11.42	8	13	50	32	5	58	50.4	-18.4	70	11	10,000	1,000	0.0	0.0
C+ /6.6	11.4	1.06	11.14	198	4	95	0	1	3	117.2	-10.8	74	12	1,000	250	0.0	0.0
C+ /6.6	11.4	1.06	10.84	20	4	95	0	1	3	113.4	-11.0	69	12	1,000	250	0.0	0.0
B- /7.0	10.1	1.04	22.40	82	1	98	0	1	48	93.6	-18.4	46	2	2,000	100	5.8	0.0
D+ /2.9	12.9	0.91	12.50	5	1	98	0	1	286	85.6	-23.3	51	2	2,000	100	5.8	0.0
D+ /2.6	12.9	0.91	11.88	1	1	98	0	1	286	81.4	-23.5	41	2	2,000	100	0.0	0.0
D+ /2.9	12.9	0.91	12.49	N/A	1	98	0	1	286	87.7	-23.2	56	2	50,000	0	0.0	0.0
D+ /2.8	12.9	0.91	12.47	90	1	98	0	1	286	87.9	-23.1	56	2	5,000	100	0.0	0.0
U /	N/A	N/A	10.00	33	2	97	0	1	64	N/A	N/A	N/A	1	5,000	100	0.0	0.0
C+ /6.0	12.9	0.96	8.17	4	1	98	0	1	84	57.5	-26.1	75	2	2,000	100	5.8	0.0
C+ /6.0	13.0	0.97	8.13	3	1	98	0	1	84	54.0	-26.4	67	2	2,000	100	0.0	0.0
C+ /6.0	13.0	0.96	8.14	98	1	98	0	1	84	58.7	-26.1	76	2	50,000	0	0.0	0.0
C+ /6.0	13.0	0.96	8.15	176	1	98	0	1	84	59.5	-26.1	77	2	5,000	100	0.0	0.0
C /5.5	13.0	1.19	16.73	3	0	99	0	1	37	96.9	-17.6	9	3	2,000	100	5.8	0.0
C /5.5	13.0	1.20	15.80	1	0	99	0	1	37	92.7	-17.9	7	3	2,000	100	0.0	0.0
C+ /5.6	13.0	1.20	17.26	1	0	99	0	1	37	98.8	-17.5	10	3	50,000	0	0.0	0.0
C+ /5.6	13.0	1.20	17.28	103	0	99	0	1	37	99.7	-17.5	11	3	5,000	100	0.0	0.0
B- /7.0	10.1	1.04	21.04	2	1	98	0	1	48	88.8	-18.7	35	2	2,000	100	0.0	0.0
B /8.2	5.2	0.83	8.70	4	12	41	46	1	30	30.3	-10.1	30	N/A	2,000	100	5.8	0.0
B /8.2	5.2	0.84	8.64	2	12	41	46	1	30	27.8	-10.4	23	N/A	2,000	100	0.0	0.0
B /8.2	5.2	0.83	8.71	8	12	41	46	1	30	32.4	-10.0	35	N/A	1,000,000	0	0.0	0.0
B /8.2	5.1	0.83	8.71	N/A	12	41	46	1	30	32.6	-10.0	37	N/A	50,000	0	0.0	0.0
B /8.2	5.1	0.83	8.68	15	12	41	46	1	30	28.9	-10.2	27	N/A	0	0	0.0	0.0
B- /7.7	5.8	0.96	9.25	12	13	49	37	1	27	36.1	-11.4	26	N/A	2,000	100	5.8	0.0
B- /7.8	5.8	0.95	9.21	1	13	49	37	1	27	33.7	-11.6	21	N/A	2,000	100	0.0	0.0
B- /7.8	5.8	0.96	9.28	30	13	49	37	1	27	38.3	-11.2	31	N/A	1,000,000	0	0.0	0.0
B- /7.8	5.8	0.95	9.26	48	13	49	37	1	27	37.1	-11.3	29	N/A	50,000	0	0.0	0.0
B- /7.8	5.8	0.95	9.21	49	13	49	37	1	27	34.8	-11.4	23	N/A	0	0	0.0	0.0
B /8.1	6.5	1.09	9.98	15	15	57	27	1	20	42.7	-12.8	22	N/A	2,000	100	5.8	0.0
B /8.1	6.6	1.10	9.87	3	15	57	27	1	20	40.1	-13.0	17	N/A	2,000	100	0.0	0.0
B /8.0	6.5	1.09	10.03	59	15	57	27	1	20	45.2	-12.7	27	N/A	1,000,000	0	0.0	0.0
B /8.1	6.5	1.09	10.00	102	15	57	27	1	20	43.9	-12.7	24	N/A	50,000	0	0.0	0.0
B /8.0	6.6	1.10	9.95	92	15	57	27	1	20	41.3	-12.9	19	N/A	0	0	0.0	0.0
B- /7.6	7.6	1.26	10.22	22	18	66	15	1	15	50.8	-14.8	17	N/A	2,000	100	5.8	0.0
B- /7.6	7.6	1.27	10.14	2	18	66	15	1	15	48.0	-15.0	13	N/A	2,000	100	0.0	0.0
B- /7.6	7.6	1.27	10.27	61	18	66	15	1	15	53.3	-14.6	20	N/A	1,000,000	0	0.0	0.0
B- /7.6	7.6	1.26	10.22	99	18	66	15	1	15	52.0	-14.8	18	N/A	50,000	0	0.0	0.0
B- /7.6	7.6	1.27	10.19	105	18	66	15	1	15	49.3	-14.8	14	N/A	0	0	0.0	0.0
C+ /6.6	8.4	1.41	9.90	22	18	74	7	1	24	58.3	-16.8	12	N/A	2,000	100	5.8	0.0
C+ /6.6	8.4	1.42	9.82	2	18	74	7	1	24	55.6	-17.0	9	N/A	2,000	100	0.0	0.0
C+ /6.6	8.4	1.40	9.95	56	18	74	7	1	24	61.0	-16.6	16	N/A	1,000,000	0	0.0	0.0
C+ /6.6	8.4	1.41	9.91	86	18	74	7	1	24	59.7	-16.7	14	N/A	50,000	0	0.0	0.0
C+ /6.6	8.4	1.41	9.85	114	18	74	7	1	24	56.8	-16.8	11	N/A	0	0	0.0	0.0
C+ /6.9	9.1	1.52	10.50	16	18	78	3	1	8	64.3	-17.8	10	N/A	2,000	100	5.8	0.0
C+ /6.9	9.1	1.52	10.37	2	18	78	3	1	8	61.4	-18.1	8	N/A	2,000	100	0.0	0.0
C+ /6.9	9.1	1.53	10.56	43	18	78	3	1	8	67.1	-17.7	12	N/A	1,000,000	0	0.0	0.0
C+ /6.9	9.1	1.52	10.51	64	18	78	3	1	8	65.6	-17.7	11	N/A	50,000	0	0.0	0.0
C+ /6.9	9.1	1.52	10.45	86	18	78	3	1	8	62.7	-17.9	8	N/A	0	0	0.0	0.0
C+ /6.7	9.4	1.57	10.24	15	14	82	2	2	10	67.2	-18.9	9	N/A	2,000	100	5.8	0.0
C+ /6.8	9.4	1.57	10.22	1	14	82	2	2	10	64.1	-19.0	7	N/A	2,000	100	0.0	0.0
C+ /6.7	9.5	1.58	10.30	36	14	82	2	2	10	69.8	-18.7	11	N/A	1,000,000	0	0.0	0.0

I. Index of Stock Mutual Funds

					PERFORMANCE							
						Total Return % through 3/31/15					Incl. in Returns	
									Annualized		Dividend	Expense
Fund Type	Fund Name	Ticker Symbol	Overall Investment Rating	Phone	Performance Rating/Pts	3 Mo	6 Mo	1Yr / Pct	3Yr / Pct	5Yr / Pct	Yield	Ratio
AA	Nationwide Destination 2040 IS	NWMSX	C+	(800) 848-0920	C / 5.3	3.02	5.41	5.85 /45	11.84 /51	10.48 /48	1.84	0.65
AA	Nationwide Destination 2040 R	NWMDX	C	(800) 848-0920	C / 4.9	2.82	5.10	5.38 /41	11.31 /48	9.92 /44	1.37	1.15
AA	Nationwide Destination 2045 A	NWNAX	C	(800) 848-0920	C / 4.4	3.14	5.63	5.97 /46	11.92 /52	10.43 /48	1.56	0.86
AA	Nationwide Destination 2045 C	NWNCX	C	(800) 848-0920	C / 4.9	2.89	5.26	5.21 /40	11.32 /48	9.85 /43	1.11	1.51
AA	Nationwide Destination 2045 Inst	NWNIX	C+	(800) 848-0920	C+ / 5.7	3.24	5.91	6.40 /50	12.44 /56	10.98 /53	2.06	0.40
AA	Nationwide Destination 2045 IS	NWNSX	C+	(800) 848-0920	C / 5.5	3.20	5.72	6.19 /48	12.21 /54	10.72 /50	1.84	0.64
AA	Nationwide Destination 2045 R	NWNBX	C	(800) 848-0920	C / 5.1	2.99	5.48	5.58 /43	11.64 /50	10.16 /46	1.36	1.15
AA	Nationwide Destination 2050 A	NWOAX	D+	(800) 848-0920	C / 4.4	3.08	5.60	5.86 /45	11.90 /52	10.35 /47	1.37	0.88
AA	Nationwide Destination 2050 C	NWOCX	C-	(800) 848-0920	C / 4.9	2.93	5.22	5.34 /41	11.31 /48	9.80 /43	1.13	1.44
AA	Nationwide Destination 2050 Inst	NWOIX	C	(800) 848-0920	C+ / 5.7	3.19	5.84	6.40 /50	12.44 /56	10.90 /52	2.05	0.40
AA	Nationwide Destination 2050 IS	NWOSX	C-	(800) 848-0920	C / 5.5	3.14	5.62	6.06 /47	12.13 /53	10.61 /50	1.82	0.65
AA	Nationwide Destination 2050 R	NWOBX	C-	(800) 848-0920	C / 5.1	3.05	5.40	5.58 /43	11.60 /50	10.06 /45	1.36	1.15
AA	Nationwide Destination 2055 A	NTDAX	C	(800) 848-0920	C / 4.4	3.07	5.59	5.88 /45	11.81 /51	--	1.58	0.85
AA	Nationwide Destination 2055 C	NTDCX	C	(800) 848-0920	C / 4.8	2.90	5.33	5.24 /40	11.21 /47	--	1.14	1.42
AA	Nationwide Destination 2055 Inst	NTDIX	C+	(800) 848-0920	C+ / 5.6	3.24	5.87	6.48 /51	12.35 /55	--	2.08	0.39
AA	Nationwide Destination 2055 IS	NTDSX	C+	(800) 848-0920	C / 5.4	3.11	5.75	6.15 /48	12.09 /53	--	1.85	0.64
AA	Nationwide Destination 2055 R	NTDTX	C	(800) 848-0920	C / 5.1	3.00	5.44	5.59 /43	11.53 /49	--	1.39	1.14
MC	Nationwide Geneva Mid Cap Growth	NWHVX	D+	(800) 848-0920	C / 5.1	5.12	12.67	11.28 /80	11.57 /49	14.68 /84	0.00	1.23
MC	Nationwide Geneva Mid Cap Growth	NWHWX	D+	(800) 848-0920	C+ / 5.6	4.97	12.27	10.52 /76	10.89 /45	13.98 /78	0.00	1.88
MC	Nationwide Geneva Mid Cap Growth	NWHYX	C-	(800) 848-0920	C+ / 6.2	5.21	12.83	11.60 /81	11.87 /52	14.99 /87	0.00	0.94
SC	Nationwide Geneva Small Cap Gro A	NWHZX	C+	(800) 848-0920	B- / 7.5	8.22	15.26	8.39 /65	15.69 /81	17.01 /96	0.00	1.57
SC	Nationwide Geneva Small Cap Gro C	NWKBX	B-	(800) 848-0920	B / 8.1	8.03	14.85	7.68 /60	14.97 /75	16.30 /94	0.00	2.28
SC	Nationwide Geneva Small Cap Gro IS	NWKDX	B	(800) 848-0920	B+ / 8.8	8.28	15.38	8.70 /68	16.00 /83	17.32 /97	0.00	1.29
GL	Nationwide Global Equity A	GGEAX	D	(800) 848-0920	D / 2.1	0.84	-0.92	-0.11 /15	9.28 /35	7.26 /25	1.23	1.48
GL	Nationwide Global Equity C	GGECX	D	(800) 848-0920	D+ / 2.5	0.61	-1.36	-0.96 /13	8.56 /30	6.51 /20	0.68	2.25
GL	Nationwide Global Equity Instl	GGEIX	D+	(800) 848-0920	C- / 3.2	0.94	-0.74	0.23 /16	9.61 /37	7.61 /27	1.72	1.18
GR	Nationwide Growth A	NMFAX	C-	(800) 848-0920	B- / 7.3	5.27	9.16	15.63 /93	14.79 /73	15.00 /87	0.15	1.22
GR	Nationwide Growth C	GCGRX	C-	(800) 848-0920	B / 7.7	5.12	8.73	14.82 /91	13.96 /67	14.16 /79	0.00	2.01
GR	Nationwide Growth Inst	MUIGX	C+	(800) 848-0920	B+ / 8.6	5.39	9.33	16.04 /93	15.13 /76	15.34 /89	0.48	0.91
GR	Nationwide Growth Institutional Svc	NGISX	A	(800) 848-0920	B+ / 8.4	5.31	9.24	15.84 /93	14.90 /74	--	0.23	1.11
GR	Nationwide Growth R	GGFRX	C	(800) 848-0920	B / 8.1	5.24	8.89	15.22 /92	14.46 /71	14.63 /83	0.00	1.66
BA	Nationwide HighMark Balanced A	NWGDX	D-	(800) 848-0920	D+ / 2.4	1.86	4.92	7.75 /61	8.03 /27	8.73 /35	0.85	1.77
BA	Nationwide HighMark Balanced IS	NWGGX	D-	(800) 848-0920	C- / 3.4	1.86	5.01	7.97 /63	8.27 /29	8.99 /37	1.33	1.70
BA	Nationwide HighMark BalancedC	NWGEX	D-	(800) 848-0920	D+ / 2.9	1.65	4.57	7.07 /56	7.38 /23	8.08 /30	0.38	2.52
GR	Nationwide HighMark Large Cp Gr A	NWGLX	E+	(800) 848-0920	C / 4.8	2.62	7.44	12.47 /85	11.40 /48	11.73 /59	0.27	1.41
GR	Nationwide HighMark Large Cp Gr C	NWGMX	E+	(800) 848-0920	C / 5.3	2.47	7.14	11.88 /82	10.76 /44	11.07 /53	0.04	2.10
GR	Nationwide HighMark Large Cp Gr IS	NWGOX	E+	(800) 848-0920	C+ / 5.9	2.64	7.52	12.77 /86	11.69 /50	12.03 /61	0.46	1.26
IN	Nationwide HighMark LC Core Eq A	NWGHX	B-	(800) 848-0920	C+ / 6.4	2.05	5.14	11.99 /82	14.93 /74	13.47 /73	0.92	1.30
IN	Nationwide HighMark LC Core Eq C	NWGIX	B-	(800) 848-0920	C+ / 6.9	1.86	4.87	11.33 /80	14.21 /69	12.80 /66	0.54	1.98
IN	Nationwide HighMark LC Core Eq IS	NWGKX	B+	(800) 848-0920	B / 7.8	2.13	5.39	12.39 /84	15.28 /77	13.80 /76	1.27	0.92
SC	Nationwide HighMark Sm Cp Core A	NWGPX	A	(800) 848-0920	A- / 9.2	4.49	15.92	14.17 /90	18.34 /95	17.07 /96	0.00	1.55
SC	Nationwide HighMark Sm Cp Core C	NWGQX	A	(800) 848-0920	A / 9.4	4.30	15.50	13.39 /88	17.59 /93	16.35 /94	0.00	2.29
SC	Nationwide HighMark Sm Cp Core IS	NWGSX	A+	(800) 848-0920	A+ / 9.7	4.54	16.12	14.51 /91	18.68 /96	17.42 /97	0.00	1.23
GI	Nationwide HighMark Value A	NWGTX	E+	(800) 848-0920	C- / 3.6	-0.39	1.08	2.05 /22	11.79 /51	11.10 /53	0.60	1.15
GI	Nationwide HighMark Value C	NWGUX	E+	(800) 848-0920	C- / 4.0	-0.59	0.66	1.24 /19	11.05 /46	10.40 /48	0.27	1.86
GI	Nationwide HighMark Value IS	NWKFX	E+	(800) 848-0920	C / 4.7	-0.41	1.13	2.26 /23	12.05 /53	11.37 /56	0.78	0.90
GI	Nationwide Inst Service	MUIFX	B+	(800) 848-0920	B / 7.8	2.10	5.34	12.52 /85	15.39 /78	12.91 /67	1.20	0.77
FO	Nationwide Internatl Index A	GIIAX	D-	(800) 848-0920	D / 1.9	5.27	0.78	-1.65 /11	8.36 /29	5.58 /15	2.65	0.70
FO	Nationwide Internatl Index C	GIICX	D-	(800) 848-0920	D+ / 2.3	5.06	0.50	-2.30 /10	7.69 /25	4.95 /12	2.51	1.38
FO	Nationwide Internatl Index Inst	GIXIX	D	(800) 848-0920	C- / 3.0	5.35	0.98	-1.25 /12	8.79 /32	6.01 /17	3.21	0.30
FO	Nationwide Internatl Index R	GIIRX	D	(800) 848-0920	D+ / 2.7	5.25	0.73	-1.85 /11	8.26 /29	5.50 /14	2.73	0.80
GL	Nationwide Inv Dest Aggressive A	NDAAX	C	(800) 848-0920	C / 4.5	2.88	5.45	5.96 /46	12.19 /54	10.67 /50	1.61	0.81

● Denotes fund is closed to new investors
* Denotes fund is included in Section II

446

RISK			NET ASSETS		ASSET					BULL / BEAR		FUND MANAGER		MINIMUMS		LOADS	
Risk Rating/Pts	3 Year Standard Deviation	Beta	NAV As of 3/31/15	Total $(Mil)	Cash %	Stocks %	Bonds %	Other %	Portfolio Turnover Ratio	Last Bull Market Return	Last Bear Market Return	Manager Quality Pct	Manager Tenure (Years)	Initial Purch. $	Additional Purch. $	Front End Load	Back End Load
C+ / 6.7	9.4	1.57	10.28	43	14	82	2	2	10	68.3	-18.7	10	N/A	50,000	0	0.0	0.0
C+ / 6.7	9.4	1.56	10.20	81	14	82	2	2	10	65.6	-19.0	8	N/A	0	0	0.0	0.0
C+ / 6.7	9.7	1.62	10.42	11	11	87	0	2	10	68.8	-19.1	8	N/A	2,000	100	5.8	0.0
C+ / 6.7	9.7	1.62	10.34	2	11	87	0	2	10	65.8	-19.2	6	N/A	2,000	100	0.0	0.0
C+ / 6.7	9.7	1.62	10.46	27	11	87	0	2	10	71.7	-18.9	10	N/A	1,000,000	0	0.0	0.0
C+ / 6.7	9.7	1.62	10.40	21	11	87	0	2	10	70.2	-19.0	9	N/A	50,000	0	0.0	0.0
C+ / 6.7	9.6	1.61	10.35	50	11	87	0	2	10	67.3	-19.1	8	N/A	0	0	0.0	0.0
C / 5.3	9.8	1.63	8.90	10	11	87	0	2	27	68.5	-19.2	8	N/A	2,000	100	5.8	0.0
C / 5.3	9.8	1.63	8.78	N/A	11	87	0	2	27	65.8	-19.5	6	N/A	2,000	100	0.0	0.0
C / 5.3	9.7	1.62	8.91	16	11	87	0	2	27	71.3	-19.2	10	N/A	1,000,000	0	0.0	0.0
C / 5.3	9.8	1.63	8.88	18	11	87	0	2	27	70.0	-19.2	9	N/A	50,000	0	0.0	0.0
C / 5.3	9.8	1.63	8.80	41	11	87	0	2	27	67.2	-19.4	7	N/A	0	0	0.0	0.0
C+ / 6.8	9.8	1.64	13.13	3	6	87	5	2	10	68.7	-19.3	7	5	2,000	100	5.0	0.0
C+ / 6.8	9.8	1.64	13.13	N/A	6	87	5	2	10	65.5	-19.4	6	5	2,000	100	0.0	0.0
C+ / 6.8	9.8	1.63	13.18	8	6	87	5	2	10	71.4	-19.2	9	5	1,000,000	0	0.0	0.0
C+ / 6.8	9.8	1.64	13.17	7	6	87	5	2	10	70.2	-19.2	8	5	50,000	0	0.0	0.0
C+ / 6.8	9.8	1.64	13.11	12	6	87	5	2	10	67.1	-19.4	6	5	0	0	0.0	0.0
C / 4.5	10.8	0.89	27.93	480	1	98	0	1	32	75.4	-17.1	24	6	2,000	100	5.8	0.0
C- / 4.1	10.8	0.89	24.50	89	1	98	0	1	32	71.7	-17.3	18	6	2,000	100	0.0	0.0
C / 4.6	10.8	0.89	28.48	659	1	98	0	1	32	76.9	-17.0	27	6	50,000	0	0.0	0.0
C / 5.2	11.9	0.80	43.69	33	2	97	0	1	27	88.0	-18.3	87	6	2,000	100	5.8	0.0
C / 5.0	11.9	0.80	41.99	16	2	97	0	1	27	84.0	-18.5	84	6	2,000	100	0.0	0.0
C / 5.2	11.9	0.80	44.45	107	2	97	0	1	27	89.6	-18.2	88	6	50,000	0	0.0	0.0
C+ / 6.2	11.9	0.86	15.63	44	0	100	0	0	50	70.2	-25.5	78	3	2,000	100	5.8	0.0
C+ / 6.2	12.0	0.86	14.85	17	0	100	0	0	50	66.4	-25.8	72	3	2,000	100	0.0	0.0
C+ / 6.2	11.9	0.86	16.07	13	0	100	0	0	50	71.9	-25.4	80	3	1,000,000	0	0.0	0.0
C- / 3.3	10.5	0.98	10.98	34	1	98	0	1	160	94.0	-17.0	55	1	2,000	100	5.8	0.0
D+ / 2.5	10.5	0.98	9.04	6	1	98	0	1	160	89.6	-17.4	44	1	2,000	100	0.0	0.0
C- / 3.5	10.5	0.98	11.45	166	1	98	0	1	160	96.3	-17.1	60	1	1,000,000	0	0.0	0.0
C+ / 6.9	10.5	0.98	11.50	21	1	98	0	1	160	N/A	N/A	56	1	50,000	0	0.0	0.0
C- / 3.3	10.5	0.98	10.84	1	1	98	0	1	160	92.2	-17.2	50	1	0	0	0.0	0.0
C / 4.6	5.4	0.93	13.55	11	1	59	39	1	51	48.9	-11.4	38	2	2,000	100	5.8	0.0
C / 4.5	5.3	0.93	13.55	4	1	59	39	1	51	50.2	-11.3	42	2	50,000	0	0.0	0.0
C / 4.6	5.3	0.92	13.43	5	1	59	39	1	51	46.0	-11.6	31	2	2,000	100	0.0	0.0
E+ / 0.9	8.9	0.88	8.79	16	2	97	0	1	41	75.6	-16.4	33	2	2,000	100	5.8	0.0
E+ / 0.9	8.9	0.88	7.47	2	2	97	0	1	41	72.1	-16.6	25	2	2,000	100	0.0	0.0
E+ / 0.9	8.9	0.88	9.08	21	2	97	0	1	41	77.0	-16.2	36	2	50,000	0	0.0	0.0
B- / 7.0	9.8	1.01	13.56	11	2	97	0	1	48	95.3	-15.1	49	2	2,000	100	5.8	0.0
B- / 7.0	9.8	1.01	13.11	1	2	97	0	1	48	91.3	-15.4	39	2	2,000	100	0.0	0.0
B- / 7.0	9.8	1.02	13.60	50	2	97	0	1	48	97.4	-15.1	53	2	50,000	0	0.0	0.0
C+ / 6.2	12.6	0.91	32.55	28	7	92	0	1	49	112.7	-26.0	89	2	2,000	100	5.8	0.0
C+ / 6.2	12.6	0.91	31.07	7	7	92	0	1	49	108.1	-26.1	86	2	2,000	100	0.0	0.0
C+ / 6.2	12.6	0.92	33.14	116	7	92	0	1	49	114.8	-25.9	90	2	50,000	0	0.0	0.0
D / 2.2	11.3	1.13	14.19	77	2	97	0	1	58	79.7	-20.0	7	17	2,000	100	5.8	0.0
D / 2.0	11.3	1.13	13.49	3	2	97	0	1	58	75.9	-20.2	6	17	2,000	100	0.0	0.0
D / 2.2	11.3	1.13	14.27	63	2	97	0	1	58	81.3	-20.0	8	17	50,000	0	0.0	0.0
B- / 7.0	10.1	1.04	22.08	822	1	98	0	1	48	95.2	-18.4	49	2	50,000	0	0.0	0.0
C+ / 5.7	13.3	1.00	8.12	195	1	98	0	1	6	49.1	-23.6	51	4	2,000	100	5.8	0.0
C+ / 5.7	13.3	1.01	7.70	5	1	98	0	1	6	45.9	-23.7	41	4	2,000	100	0.0	0.0
C+ / 5.7	13.3	1.00	8.16	1,646	1	98	0	1	6	51.1	-23.3	57	4	1,000,000	0	0.0	0.0
C+ / 5.7	13.3	1.00	8.13	3	1	98	0	1	6	48.6	-23.5	49	4	0	0	0.0	0.0
C+ / 6.8	9.7	1.48	11.21	62	10	85	4	1	8	73.4	-19.6	48	N/A	2,000	100	5.8	0.0

				Overall Investment Rating		PERFORMANCE							
						Perfor-mance Rating/Pts	Total Return % through 3/31/15			Annualized		Incl. in Returns	
Fund Type	Fund Name	Ticker Symbol	Phone				3 Mo	6 Mo	1Yr / Pct	3Yr / Pct	5Yr / Pct	Dividend Yield	Expense Ratio
GL	Nationwide Inv Dest Aggressive C	NDACX	C	(800) 848-0920		C / 4.9	2.73	5.07	5.22 /40	11.43 /48	9.89 /44	1.10	1.55
GL	Nationwide Inv Dest Aggressive Inst	GAIDX	C+	(800) 848-0920		C+ / 5.8	3.03	5.68	6.39 /50	12.60 /57	11.03 /53	2.05	0.45
GL	Nationwide Inv Dest Aggressive R	GAFRX	C+	(800) 848-0920		C / 5.2	2.86	5.30	5.68 /44	11.83 /51	10.28 /47	1.46	1.10
GL	Nationwide Inv Dest Aggressive Svc	NDASX	C+	(800) 848-0920		C / 5.4	2.96	5.43	5.93 /46	12.11 /53	10.57 /49	1.67	0.85
GL	Nationwide Inv Dest Cons A	NDCAX	C-	(800) 848-0920		E+ / 0.8	1.27	2.41	3.52 /29	3.78 /10	4.23 / 9	1.62	0.83
GL	Nationwide Inv Dest Cons C	NDCCX	C-	(800) 848-0920		D- / 1.0	1.11	2.09	2.85 /26	3.06 / 8	3.48 / 7	1.06	1.55
GL	Nationwide Inv Dest Cons Inst	GIMCX	C-	(800) 848-0920		D- / 1.3	1.35	2.57	3.98 /32	4.13 /11	4.54 /10	2.06	0.48
GL	Nationwide Inv Dest Cons R	GCFRX	C-	(800) 848-0920		D- / 1.1	1.19	2.26	3.32 /28	3.44 / 9	3.87 / 8	1.42	1.13
GL	Nationwide Inv Dest Cons Svc	NDCSX	C-	(800) 848-0920		D- / 1.1	1.25	2.38	3.57 /29	3.71 / 9	4.13 / 9	1.67	0.88
GL	Nationwide Inv Dest Mdt Aggr A	NDMAX	C	(800) 848-0920		C- / 3.6	2.63	4.75	5.48 /42	10.60 /43	9.56 /41	1.64	0.84
GL	Nationwide Inv Dest Mdt Aggr C	NDMCX	C	(800) 848-0920		C- / 4.0	2.47	4.43	4.71 /36	9.86 /39	8.79 /35	1.12	1.56
GL	Nationwide Inv Dest Mdt Aggr Inst	GMIAX	C+	(800) 848-0920		C / 4.7	2.73	4.94	5.87 /45	10.99 /45	9.90 /44	2.10	0.47
GL	Nationwide Inv Dest Mdt Aggr R	GMARX	C	(800) 848-0920		C / 4.3	2.62	4.70	5.21 /40	10.28 /41	9.20 /38	1.50	1.12
GL	Nationwide Inv Dest Mdt Aggr Svc	NDMSX	C+	(800) 848-0920		C / 4.5	2.63	4.83	5.45 /42	10.56 /43	9.47 /40	1.71	0.87
GL	Nationwide Inv Dest Mdt Consv A	NADCX	D+	(800) 848-0920		D- / 1.3	1.68	3.20	4.27 /34	5.79 /16	6.06 /17	1.67	0.85
GL	Nationwide Inv Dest Mdt Consv C	NCDCX	C-	(800) 848-0920		D / 1.6	1.52	2.77	3.57 /29	5.32 /14	5.48 /14	1.10	1.55
GL	Nationwide Inv Dest Mdt Consv I	GMIMX	C-	(800) 848-0920		D / 2.2	1.76	3.36	4.71 /36	6.41 /19	6.57 /20	2.12	0.47
GL	Nationwide Inv Dest Mdt Consv R	GMMRX	C-	(800) 848-0920		D / 1.8	1.70	3.05	4.06 /32	5.73 /16	5.89 /16	1.49	1.12
GL	Nationwide Inv Dest Mdt Consv Svc	NSDCX	C-	(800) 848-0920		D / 2.0	1.76	3.17	4.31 /34	6.01 /17	6.15 /18	1.73	0.87
GL	Nationwide Inv Dest Moderate A	NADMX	C-	(800) 848-0920		D+ / 2.3	2.20	3.89	4.74 /37	8.31 /29	7.91 /29	1.63	0.84
GL	Nationwide Inv Dest Moderate C	NCDMX	C	(800) 848-0920		D+ / 2.7	1.97	3.50	4.01 /32	7.55 /24	7.15 /24	1.08	1.55
GL	Nationwide Inv Dest Moderate Inst	GMDIX	C	(800) 848-0920		C- / 3.4	2.21	4.01	5.08 /39	8.62 /31	8.22 /31	2.12	0.46
GL	Nationwide Inv Dest Moderate R	GMDRX	C	(800) 848-0920		C- / 3.0	2.09	3.74	4.48 /35	7.96 /27	7.56 /27	1.51	1.11
GL	Nationwide Inv Dest Moderate Svc	NSDMX	C	(800) 848-0920		C- / 3.1	2.11	3.80	4.66 /36	8.22 /28	7.81 /29	1.73	0.86
MC	Nationwide Mid Cap Market Index A	GMXAX	B	(800) 848-0920		B / 7.8	5.13	11.65	11.46 /80	16.32 /86	14.91 /86	0.73	0.68
MC	Nationwide Mid Cap Market Index C	GMCCX	B+	(800) 848-0920		B+ / 8.3	4.96	11.24	10.75 /77	15.59 /80	14.19 /79	0.44	1.35
MC	Nationwide Mid Cap Market Index I	GMXIX	A-	(800) 848-0920		A- / 9.0	5.23	11.90	11.94 /82	16.79 /89	15.36 /89	1.13	0.27
MC	Nationwide Mid Cap Market Index R	GMXRX	A-	(800) 848-0920		B+ / 8.7	5.05	11.52	11.24 /79	16.15 /84	14.76 /85	0.48	0.96
AA	Nationwide Portfolio Comp A	NWAAX	D	(800) 848-0920		E / 0.5	0.11	-0.85	-0.76 /14	0.87 / 5	--	1.57	0.88
AA	Nationwide Portfolio Comp C	NWACX	D	(800) 848-0920		E / 0.5	0.00	-1.15	-1.45 /12	0.15 / 4	--	1.35	1.58
AA	Nationwide Portfolio Comp Instl	NAAIX	D	(800) 848-0920		E+ / 0.6	0.21	-0.66	-0.43 /14	1.19 / 5	--	1.84	0.51
AA	Nationwide Portfolio Comp IS	NAASX	D	(800) 848-0920		E+ / 0.6	0.21	-0.78	-0.50 /14	1.18 / 5	--	1.77	0.59
GI	Nationwide R	GNWRX	B+	(800) 848-0920		B- / 7.3	1.88	5.01	11.72 /81	14.72 /73	12.24 /62	0.65	1.46
AA	Nationwide Retirement Inc A	NWRAX	D+	(800) 848-0920		E+ / 0.8	1.74	2.89	3.84 /31	3.57 / 9	3.67 / 7	1.42	0.84
AA	Nationwide Retirement Inc C	NWRCX	C-	(800) 848-0920		D- / 1.0	1.48	2.54	3.20 /27	3.00 / 8	3.13 / 6	0.98	1.46
AA	Nationwide Retirement Inc Inst	NWRIX	C-	(800) 848-0920		D- / 1.3	1.80	3.02	4.24 /33	4.04 /10	4.18 / 9	1.89	0.40
AA	Nationwide Retirement Inc IS	NWRSX	C-	(800) 848-0920		D- / 1.2	1.74	2.89	4.09 /32	3.81 /10	3.93 / 8	1.65	0.65
AA	Nationwide Retirement Inc R	NWRBX	C-	(800) 848-0920		D- / 1.1	1.62	2.64	3.57 /29	3.29 / 8	3.42 / 7	1.14	1.15
IX	Nationwide S&P 500 Index A	GRMAX	C+	(800) 848-0920		C+ / 6.7	0.74	5.61	12.08 /83	15.46 /79	13.80 /76	1.32	0.58
IX	Nationwide S&P 500 Index C	GRMCX	B	(800) 848-0920		B- / 7.2	0.68	5.31	11.37 /80	14.76 /73	13.11 /69	0.85	1.24
IX	Nationwide S&P 500 Index Inst	GRMIX	A-	(800) 848-0920		B / 8.1	0.90	5.86	12.52 /85	15.92 /83	14.27 /80	1.77	0.17
IX	Nationwide S&P 500 Index IS	GRISX	B+	(800) 848-0920		B / 7.9	0.90	5.74	12.27 /84	15.65 /80	13.99 /78	1.54	0.42
IX	Nationwide S&P 500 Index R	GRMRX	B+	(800) 848-0920		B- / 7.5	0.74	5.52	11.74 /81	15.10 /76	13.43 /72	0.90	0.92
IX	Nationwide S&P 500 Index Svc	GRMSX	B+	(800) 848-0920		B / 7.8	0.80	5.62	12.08 /83	15.43 /78	13.80 /76	1.40	0.57
SC	Nationwide Small Cap Index A	GMRAX	C+	(800) 848-0920		B- / 7.2	4.20	14.30	7.84 /62	15.83 /82	14.08 /78	0.70	0.73
SC	Nationwide Small Cap Index C	GMRCX	B	(800) 848-0920		B / 7.8	4.01	13.79	7.06 /55	15.09 /76	13.39 /72	0.37	1.42
SC	Nationwide Small Cap Index Inst	GMRIX	B+	(800) 848-0920		B+ / 8.6	4.31	14.48	8.24 /64	16.28 /85	14.55 /83	1.10	0.33
SC	Nationwide Small Cap Index R	GMSRX	B	(800) 848-0920		B+ / 8.3	4.14	14.17	7.62 /60	15.71 /81	13.96 /77	0.69	0.83
SC	Nationwide Small Company Growth A	NWSAX	B-	(800) 848-0920		B / 8.0	3.93	11.86	7.57 /60	17.34 /92	--	0.00	1.95
SC	Nationwide Small Company Growth	NWSIX	B+	(800) 848-0920		A- / 9.1	4.07	12.05	7.90 /62	17.59 /93	--	0.00	1.80
SC	Nationwide US Sm Cp Val A	NWUAX	C-	(800) 848-0920		C+ / 6.3	2.89	7.81	2.37 /23	15.77 /81	13.53 /73	0.05	1.53
SC	Nationwide US Sm Cp Val C	NWUCX	C	(800) 848-0920		C+ / 6.7	2.72	7.43	1.63 /20	14.98 /75	12.74 /66	0.00	2.24

• Denotes fund is closed to new investors
* Denotes fund is included in Section II

www.thestreetratings.com

RISK			NET ASSETS		ASSET				Portfolio Turnover Ratio	BULL / BEAR		FUND MANAGER		MINIMUMS		LOADS	
	3 Year		NAV							Last Bull	Last Bear	Manager	Manager	Initial	Additional	Front	Back
Risk Rating/Pts	Standard Deviation	Beta	As of 3/31/15	Total $(Mil)	Cash %	Stocks %	Bonds %	Other %		Market Return	Market Return	Quality Pct	Tenure (Years)	Purch. $	Purch. $	End Load	End Load
C+ / 6.8	9.8	1.49	10.93	77	10	85	4	1	8	69.1	-19.8	37	N/A	2,000	100	0.0	0.0
C+ / 6.8	9.8	1.49	11.33	168	10	85	4	1	8	75.3	-19.4	53	N/A	1,000,000	0	0.0	0.0
C+ / 6.8	9.7	1.49	11.02	100	10	85	4	1	8	71.3	-19.6	43	N/A	0	0	0.0	0.0
C+ / 6.8	9.8	1.49	11.23	836	10	85	4	1	8	72.9	-19.6	46	N/A	50,000	0	0.0	0.0
B+ / 9.1	2.4	0.34	10.27	77	14	17	67	2	25	17.7	-2.3	75	N/A	2,000	100	5.8	0.0
B+ / 9.2	2.4	0.33	10.23	91	14	17	67	2	25	14.8	-2.6	68	N/A	2,000	100	0.0	0.0
B+ / 9.2	2.3	0.33	10.32	76	14	17	67	2	25	18.9	-2.2	78	N/A	1,000,000	0	0.0	0.0
B+ / 9.2	2.4	0.34	10.25	51	14	17	67	2	25	16.3	-2.4	72	N/A	0	0	0.0	0.0
B+ / 9.2	2.4	0.34	10.30	188	14	17	67	2	25	17.3	-2.4	74	N/A	50,000	0	0.0	0.0
B- / 7.5	8.4	1.29	11.47	125	12	75	12	1	10	61.3	-16.2	52	N/A	2,000	100	5.8	0.0
B- / 7.5	8.3	1.28	11.22	128	12	75	12	1	10	57.5	-16.4	43	N/A	2,000	100	0.0	0.0
B- / 7.5	8.3	1.28	11.46	349	12	75	12	1	10	63.1	-16.1	58	N/A	1,000,000	0	0.0	0.0
B- / 7.5	8.3	1.28	11.23	230	12	75	12	1	10	59.5	-16.3	48	N/A	0	0	0.0	0.0
B- / 7.5	8.4	1.29	11.45	1,216	12	75	12	1	10	61.0	-16.3	51	N/A	50,000	0	0.0	0.0
B / 8.4	4.1	0.64	10.53	59	13	36	49	2	18	30.3	-6.7	69	N/A	2,000	100	5.8	0.0
B / 8.4	4.1	0.64	10.48	58	13	36	49	2	18	28.3	-7.0	62	N/A	2,000	100	0.0	0.0
B / 8.4	4.2	0.65	10.63	122	13	36	49	2	18	32.8	-6.6	74	N/A	1,000,000	0	0.0	0.0
B / 8.4	4.1	0.64	10.55	76	13	36	49	2	18	30.0	-7.0	67	N/A	0	0	0.0	0.0
B / 8.4	4.1	0.64	10.59	270	13	36	49	2	18	31.1	-6.9	70	N/A	50,000	0	0.0	0.0
B / 8.3	6.1	0.95	11.05	140	14	56	29	1	17	45.6	-11.6	64	N/A	2,000	100	5.8	0.0
B / 8.3	6.2	0.96	10.87	139	14	56	29	1	17	42.2	-11.8	53	N/A	2,000	100	0.0	0.0
B / 8.3	6.2	0.96	11.00	364	14	56	29	1	17	47.4	-11.5	67	N/A	1,000,000	0	0.0	0.0
B / 8.3	6.2	0.96	10.81	181	14	56	29	1	17	44.1	-11.7	59	N/A	0	0	0.0	0.0
B / 8.3	6.2	0.96	11.00	949	14	56	29	1	17	45.3	-11.7	62	N/A	50,000	0	0.0	0.0
C+ / 6.2	11.0	1.00	19.58	341	1	98	0	1	14	98.5	-23.0	59	4	2,000	100	5.8	0.0
C+ / 6.1	11.0	1.00	18.61	9	1	98	0	1	14	94.3	-23.2	48	4	2,000	100	0.0	0.0
C+ / 6.2	11.0	1.00	19.81	943	1	98	0	1	14	101.2	-22.9	64	4	1,000,000	0	0.0	0.0
C+ / 6.2	11.0	1.00	19.43	11	1	98	0	1	14	97.6	-23.1	56	4	0	0	0.0	0.0
B / 8.3	6.4	0.82	9.46	3	48	9	41	2	40	11.2	N/A	3	4	2,000	100	2.3	0.0
B / 8.2	6.4	0.82	9.35	1	48	9	41	2	40	8.5	N/A	3	4	2,000	100	0.0	0.0
B / 8.3	6.4	0.82	9.49	997	48	9	41	2	40	12.4	N/A	4	4	1,000,000	0	0.0	0.0
B / 8.3	6.4	0.82	9.49	N/A	48	9	41	2	40	12.4	N/A	4	4	50,000	0	0.0	0.0
B- / 7.0	10.1	1.04	21.96	N/A	1	98	0	1	48	91.4	-18.6	41	2	0	0	0.0	0.0
B+ / 9.0	4.1	0.58	9.69	2	17	26	56	1	46	17.0	-7.1	30	N/A	2,000	100	5.8	0.0
B+ / 9.0	4.1	0.60	9.58	N/A	17	26	56	1	46	14.7	-7.2	23	N/A	2,000	100	0.0	0.0
B+ / 9.0	4.1	0.59	9.69	5	17	26	56	1	46	18.8	-6.9	35	N/A	1,000,000	0	0.0	0.0
B+ / 9.0	4.1	0.58	9.69	11	17	26	56	1	46	17.8	-7.0	33	N/A	50,000	0	0.0	0.0
B+ / 9.0	4.1	0.58	9.63	8	17	26	56	1	46	15.7	-7.2	27	N/A	0	0	0.0	0.0
C+ / 6.8	9.6	1.01	15.15	132	2	97	0	1	4	96.6	-16.5	58	4	2,000	100	5.8	0.0
C+ / 6.8	9.6	1.00	14.92	19	2	97	0	1	4	92.2	-16.7	49	4	2,000	100	0.0	0.0
C+ / 6.8	9.6	1.00	15.25	1,984	2	97	0	1	4	99.2	-16.4	64	4	1,000,000	0	0.0	0.0
C+ / 6.8	9.6	1.00	15.23	245	2	97	0	1	4	97.4	-16.5	61	4	50,000	0	0.0	0.0
C+ / 6.8	9.6	1.00	15.15	2	2	97	0	1	4	94.1	-16.6	54	4	0	0	0.0	0.0
C+ / 6.8	9.6	1.01	15.16	434	2	97	0	1	4	96.4	-16.5	57	4	25,000	0	0.0	0.0
C+ / 5.6	13.4	1.00	15.52	146	2	97	0	1	19	97.5	-25.2	62	4	2,000	100	5.8	0.0
C+ / 5.6	13.5	1.00	15.04	4	2	97	0	1	19	93.4	-25.4	52	4	2,000	100	0.0	0.0
C+ / 5.6	13.4	1.00	15.73	619	2	97	0	1	19	100.2	-25.0	67	4	1,000,000	0	0.0	0.0
C+ / 5.6	13.4	1.00	15.41	1	2	97	0	1	19	96.9	-25.2	60	4	0	0	0.0	0.0
C / 5.2	13.8	0.91	12.96	2	2	97	0	1	11	N/A	N/A	86	3	2,000	100	5.8	0.0
C / 5.2	13.7	0.91	13.03	23	2	97	0	1	11	N/A	N/A	87	3	50,000	0	0.0	0.0
C / 4.5	14.0	1.00	13.78	23	0	99	0	1	24	102.2	-26.6	61	3	2,000	100	5.8	0.0
C / 4.3	14.0	1.00	13.21	4	0	99	0	1	24	97.4	-26.9	50	3	2,000	100	0.0	0.0

					PERFORMANCE						Incl. in Returns	
						Total Return % through 3/31/15						
			Overall		**Perfor-**				Annualized		Dividend	Expense
Fund		Ticker	**Investment**		**mance**						Yield	Ratio
Type	Fund Name	Symbol	**Rating**	Phone	**Rating/Pts**	3 Mo	6 Mo	1Yr / Pct	3Yr / Pct	5Yr / Pct		
SC	Nationwide US Sm Cp Val Inst	NWUIX	C+	(800) 848-0920	B / 7.6	2.96	8.02	2.78 /25	16.18 /85	13.90 /77	0.15	1.15
SC	Nationwide US Sm Cp Val IS	NWUSX	C+	(800) 848-0920	B- / 7.4	2.97	7.93	2.58 /24	15.89 /82	13.61 /74	0.07	1.40
IN	Nationwide Ziegler Equity Income A	NWGYX	B-	(800) 848-0920	C+ / 5.8	0.36	5.57	8.71 /68	14.35 /70	13.76 /75	1.90	0.95
IN	Nationwide Ziegler Equity Income C	NWGZX	B-	(800) 848-0920	C+ / 6.2	0.19	5.25	7.89 /62	13.63 /64	13.04 /69	1.46	1.68
IN	Nationwide Ziegler Equity Income I	NWJAX	U	(800) 848-0920	U /	0.44	5.81	9.09 /70	--	--	2.31	0.61
IN	Nationwide Ziegler Equity Income IS	NWJBX	B-	(800) 848-0920	C+ / 6.9	0.42	5.75	8.95 /69	14.61 /72	14.08 /78	2.18	0.73
TC	Nationwide Ziegler NYSE Arc T100 A	NWJCX	B	(800) 848-0920	B- / 7.5	3.02	8.10	12.50 /85	16.29 /85	17.06 /96	0.64	0.83
TC	Nationwide Ziegler NYSE Arc T100 C	NWJDX	B+	(800) 848-0920	B / 8.0	2.81	7.69	11.67 /81	15.53 /79	16.32 /94	0.45	1.55
TC	Nationwide Ziegler NYSE Arc T100 IS	NWJFX	A-	(800) 848-0920	B+ / 8.8	3.07	8.22	12.75 /86	16.58 /87	17.36 /97	0.87	0.58
RE	Natixis AEW Real Estate A	NRFAX	D+	(800) 225-5478	B+ / 8.5	5.00	20.02	24.13 /98	13.20 /61	15.37 /89	1.07	1.36
RE	● Natixis AEW Real Estate B	NRFBX	C-	(800) 225-5478	B+ / 8.9	4.87	19.68	23.26 /98	12.37 /55	14.54 /83	0.32	2.10
RE	Natixis AEW Real Estate C	NRCFX	C-	(800) 225-5478	B+ / 8.9	4.85	19.65	23.19 /98	12.37 /55	14.53 /83	0.46	2.11
RE	Natixis AEW Real Estate Y	NRFYX	C-	(800) 225-5478	A / 9.4	5.10	20.26	24.45 /98	13.51 /63	15.68 /91	1.44	1.10
GL	Natixis ASG Glb Alternatives A	GAFAX	C	(800) 225-5478	C- / 3.8	5.94	8.59	11.15 /79	8.57 /30	6.11 /17	0.00	1.58
GL	Natixis ASG Glb Alternatives C	GAFCX	C	(800) 225-5478	C- / 4.1	5.75	8.12	10.25 /75	7.76 /26	5.33 /13	0.00	2.33
GL	Natixis ASG Glb Alternatives Y	GAFYX	C+	(800) 225-5478	C / 4.8	5.96	8.68	11.31 /80	8.80 /32	6.36 /19	0.00	1.33
IN	Natixis ASG Managed Futures Strat A	AMFAX	A+	(800) 225-5478	A+/ 9.7	11.75	21.82	39.33 /99	12.29 /55	--	2.03	1.78
IN	Natixis ASG Managed Futures Strat	ASFCX	A+	(800) 225-5478	A+/ 9.7	11.41	21.40	38.26 /99	11.45 /49	--	1.79	2.53
IN	Natixis ASG Managed Futures Strat Y	ASFYX	A+	(800) 225-5478	A+/ 9.8	11.72	21.93	39.66 /99	12.58 /57	--	2.34	1.53
GR	Natixis ASG Tactical US Market Y	USMYX	U	(800) 225-5478	U /	0.59	5.93	13.85 /89	--	--	0.05	1.53
GR	Natixis CGM Advisor Tgt Eqty A	NEFGX	D	(800) 225-5478	C / 4.9	1.68	6.74	10.09 /75	12.32 /55	8.80 /35	0.00	1.17
GR	● Natixis CGM Advisor Tgt Eqty B	NEBGX	D	(800) 225-5478	C / 5.3	1.44	6.27	9.24 /71	11.47 /49	7.98 /30	0.00	1.91
GR	Natixis CGM Advisor Tgt Eqty C	NEGCX	D	(800) 225-5478	C / 5.3	1.45	6.33	9.20 /70	11.46 /49	7.99 /30	0.00	1.91
GR	Natixis CGM Advisor Tgt Eqty Y	NEGYX	C-	(800) 225-5478	C+ / 6.0	1.79	6.85	10.37 /76	12.61 /57	9.09 /37	0.00	0.91
GI	Natixis Diversified Income A	IIDPX	C-	(800) 225-5478	C- / 3.6	1.94	7.64	10.12 /75	9.08 /34	10.39 /48	2.18	1.09
GI	Natixis Diversified Income C	CIDPX	C	(800) 225-5478	C- / 3.8	1.74	7.23	9.29 /71	8.25 /28	9.56 /41	1.61	1.84
GI	Natixis Loomis Sayles Div Inc A	LSCAX	B-	(800) 225-5478	C+ / 5.8	1.05	2.42	7.04 /55	14.84 /74	--	2.46	1.55
GI	Natixis Loomis Sayles Div Inc C	LSCCX	B-	(800) 225-5478	C+ / 6.1	0.80	1.99	6.19 /48	13.97 /67	--	1.88	2.21
GI	Natixis Loomis Sayles Div Inc Y	LSCYX	B-	(800) 225-5478	C+ / 6.9	1.03	2.46	7.21 /57	15.10 /76	--	2.84	1.34
GL	Natixis Loomis Sayles Gl Eq & Inc A	LGMAX	D+	(800) 225-5478	D+ / 2.7	3.64	4.09	6.90 /54	8.64 /31	10.55 /49	0.93	1.16
GL	Natixis Loomis Sayles Gl Eq & Inc C	LGMCX	D+	(800) 225-5478	C- / 3.1	3.40	3.69	6.09 /47	7.81 /26	9.72 /42	0.30	1.91
GL	Natixis Loomis Sayles Gl Eq & Inc Y	LSWWX	C-	(800) 225-5478	C- / 3.8	3.67	4.20	7.17 /56	8.90 /32	10.83 /51	1.25	0.91
GR	Natixis Loomis Sayles Growth Fund A	LGRRX	A-	(800) 225-5478	B+ / 8.6	2.93	8.39	14.06 /90	17.78 /94	15.09 /87	0.47	0.94
GR	● Natixis Loomis Sayles Growth Fund B	LGRBX	A	(800) 225-5478	B+ / 8.9	2.71	7.96	13.25 /87	16.90 /89	14.23 /80	0.00	1.69
GR	Natixis Loomis Sayles Growth Fund C	LGRCX	A	(800) 225-5478	B+ / 8.9	2.71	7.85	13.13 /87	16.87 /89	14.20 /79	0.00	1.69
GR	Natixis Loomis Sayles Growth Fund Y	LSGRX	A+	(800) 225-5478	A / 9.4	3.05	8.50	14.42 /90	18.05 /94	15.38 /89	0.66	0.69
GI	Natixis Loomis Sayles Value A	LSVRX	C+	(800) 225-5478	C+ / 6.7	-0.46	3.30	7.46 /59	16.58 /87	12.70 /66	1.73	0.96
GI	Natixis Loomis Sayles Value Adm	LSAVX	B	(800) 225-5478	B / 7.6	-0.50	3.19	7.20 /57	16.33 /86	12.43 /64	1.79	1.21
GI	● Natixis Loomis Sayles Value B	LSVBX	B	(800) 225-5478	B- / 7.2	-0.63	2.92	6.63 /52	15.73 /81	11.85 /60	0.00	1.71
GI	Natixis Loomis Sayles Value C	LSCVX	B-	(800) 225-5478	B- / 7.2	-0.65	2.92	6.63 /52	15.71 /81	11.85 /60	1.06	1.71
GI	Natixis Loomis Sayles Value N	LSVNX	U	(800) 225-5478	U /	-0.34	3.50	7.84 /62	--	--	2.16	0.57
GI	Natixis Loomis Sayles Value Y	LSGIX	B	(800) 225-5478	B / 8.1	-0.38	3.43	7.68 /60	16.88 /89	12.98 /68	1.99	0.71
GR	Natixis Oakmark A	NEFOX	C	(800) 225-5478	C+ / 6.0	-0.64	2.89	8.21 /64	15.21 /77	12.90 /67	0.28	1.30
GR	● Natixis Oakmark B	NEGBX	C	(800) 225-5478	C+ / 6.4	-0.76	2.49	7.41 /58	14.37 /70	12.07 /61	0.00	2.05
GR	Natixis Oakmark C	NECOX	C	(800) 225-5478	C+ / 6.4	-0.77	2.50	7.39 /58	14.38 /70	12.07 /61	0.10	2.05
FO	Natixis Oakmark International A	NOIAX	D+	(800) 225-5478	C- / 4.1	6.27	6.01	-0.81 /14	12.03 /53	--	1.77	1.44
FO	Natixis Oakmark International C	NOICX	C-	(800) 225-5478	C / 4.5	5.96	5.52	-1.62 /11	11.17 /47	--	1.22	2.19
GR	Natixis Oakmark Y	NEOYX	C+	(800) 225-5478	B- / 7.2	-0.56	3.00	8.47 /66	15.50 /79	13.20 /70	0.49	1.05
GI	Natixis US Equity Opportunities A	NEFSX	D+	(800) 225-5478	B / 7.9	2.34	6.51	12.05 /83	17.24 /91	15.54 /90	0.00	1.37
GI	● Natixis US Equity Opportunities B	NESBX	D+	(800) 225-5478	B+ / 8.4	2.13	6.12	11.22 /79	16.37 /86	14.69 /84	0.00	2.12
GI	Natixis US Equity Opportunities C	NECCX	D+	(800) 225-5478	B+ / 8.4	2.12	6.10	11.20 /79	16.36 /86	14.68 /84	0.00	2.12
GI	Natixis US Equity Opportunties Y	NESYX	C	(800) 225-5478	A- / 9.1	2.37	6.65	12.35 /84	17.54 /93	15.85 /92	0.00	1.12

● Denotes fund is closed to new investors
* Denotes fund is included in Section II

www.thestreetratings.com

Risk Rating/Pts	Standard Deviation	Beta	NAV As of 3/31/15	Total $(Mil)	Cash %	Stocks %	Bonds %	Other %	Portfolio Turnover Ratio	Last Bull Market Return	Last Bear Market Return	Manager Quality Pct	Manager Tenure (Years)	Initial Purch. $	Additional Purch. $	Front End Load	Back End Load
C / 4.6	14.0	1.00	14.05	3	0	99	0	1	24	104.3	-26.5	66	3	1,000,000	0	0.0	0.0
C / 4.5	14.0	1.00	13.87	133	0	99	0	1	24	102.5	-26.6	62	3	50,000	0	0.0	0.0
B- / 7.7	9.4	0.92	13.82	24	0	99	0	1	46	84.0	-14.1	63	6	2,000	100	5.8	0.0
B- / 7.7	9.4	0.91	13.72	7	0	99	0	1	46	80.1	-14.4	54	6	2,000	100	0.0	0.0
U /	N/A	N/A	13.87	359	0	99	0	1	46	N/A	N/A	N/A	6	1,000,000	0	0.0	0.0
B- / 7.7	9.3	0.92	13.87	11	0	99	0	1	46	85.6	-14.1	67	6	50,000	0	0.0	0.0
C+ / 6.1	11.8	1.09	57.37	280	0	99	0	1	22	108.9	-16.5	48	2	2,000	100	5.8	0.0
C+ / 6.1	11.8	1.09	52.01	29	0	99	0	1	22	104.4	-16.7	39	2	2,000	100	0.0	0.0
C+ / 6.2	11.9	1.10	57.86	62	0	99	0	1	22	110.7	-16.4	52	2	50,000	0	0.0	0.0
D- / 1.0	13.1	1.04	18.19	75	2	97	0	1	17	79.8	-15.0	47	15	2,500	100	5.8	0.0
D- / 1.0	13.1	1.05	18.29	N/A	2	97	0	1	17	75.2	-15.2	35	15	2,500	100	0.0	0.0
D- / 1.0	13.1	1.05	18.25	10	2	97	0	1	17	75.3	-15.2	35	15	2,500	100	0.0	0.0
E+ / 0.9	13.1	1.05	17.24	171	2	97	0	1	17	81.3	-14.8	50	15	100,000	0	0.0	0.0
B- / 7.6	6.7	0.39	11.78	184	25	1	73	1	0	32.0	-9.8	93	7	2,500	100	5.8	0.0
B- / 7.4	6.8	0.40	11.22	96	25	1	73	1	0	28.6	-10.0	91	7	2,500	100	0.0	0.0
B- / 7.7	6.7	0.39	11.92	3,199	25	1	73	1	0	33.0	-9.6	93	7	100,000	100	0.0	0.0
B- / 7.7	10.1	0.31	12.27	260	0	0	100	0	0	30.7	-6.3	96	5	2,500	100	5.8	0.0
B- / 7.7	10.1	0.31	11.91	59	0	0	100	0	0	27.4	-6.6	95	5	2,500	100	0.0	0.0
B- / 7.7	10.1	0.31	12.30	1,919	0	0	100	0	0	31.8	-6.2	96	5	100,000	100	0.0	0.0
U /	N/A	N/A	11.95	78	7	56	35	2	0	N/A	N/A	N/A	2	100,000	100	0.0	0.0
C- / 4.0	14.0	1.27	10.91	451	1	98	0	1	205	91.2	-28.9	4	39	2,500	100	5.8	0.0
C- / 3.1	14.1	1.27	9.18	1	1	98	0	1	205	86.3	-29.1	3	39	2,500	100	0.0	0.0
C- / 3.1	14.1	1.27	9.10	30	1	98	0	1	205	86.4	-29.2	3	39	2,500	100	0.0	0.0
C- / 4.2	14.0	1.27	11.36	33	1	98	0	1	205	92.8	-28.8	4	39	100,000	100	0.0	0.0
B- / 7.2	6.6	0.34	13.67	122	4	51	42	3	41	47.9	-7.5	90	10	2,500	100	4.5	0.0
B- / 7.2	6.6	0.34	13.62	56	4	51	42	3	41	44.3	-7.8	88	10	2,500	100	0.0	0.0
B- / 7.6	9.1	0.91	11.78	9	5	79	14	2	65	N/A	N/A	69	3	2,500	100	5.8	0.0
B- / 7.6	9.1	0.92	11.75	2	5	79	14	2	65	N/A	N/A	58	3	2,500	100	0.0	0.0
B- / 7.6	9.1	0.91	11.78	21	5	79	14	2	65	N/A	N/A	72	3	100,000	100	0.0	0.0
C+ / 6.7	8.4	0.58	19.38	242	1	70	26	3	49	54.0	-16.6	89	19	2,500	100	5.8	0.0
C+ / 6.7	8.4	0.57	19.18	379	1	70	26	3	49	50.0	-16.8	86	19	2,500	100	0.0	0.0
C+ / 6.6	8.4	0.58	19.47	621	1	70	26	3	49	55.2	-16.5	90	19	100,000	100	0.0	0.0
C+ / 6.6	10.9	1.06	10.19	84	1	98	0	1	14	101.4	-13.0	73	5	2,500	100	5.8	0.0
C+ / 6.6	11.0	1.06	9.49	N/A	1	98	0	1	14	96.0	-13.2	63	5	2,500	100	0.0	0.0
C+ / 6.6	10.9	1.05	9.48	39	1	98	0	1	14	96.1	-13.2	65	5	2,500	100	0.0	0.0
C+ / 6.6	10.9	1.06	10.82	982	1	98	0	1	14	103.0	-12.9	75	5	100,000	100	0.0	0.0
C+ / 5.9	10.4	1.06	26.24	242	2	97	0	1	28	103.0	-21.5	60	10	2,500	100	5.8	0.0
C+ / 5.9	10.4	1.06	26.09	N/A	2	97	0	1	28	101.4	-21.5	56	10	0	0	0.0	0.0
C+ / 6.4	10.4	1.06	26.96	N/A	2	97	0	1	28	98.0	-21.7	48	10	2,500	100	0.0	0.0
C+ / 6.1	10.4	1.06	26.02	18	2	97	0	1	28	97.9	-21.7	48	10	2,500	100	0.0	0.0
U /	N/A	N/A	26.31	609	2	97	0	1	28	N/A	N/A	N/A	10	0	0	0.0	0.0
C+ / 5.9	10.4	1.06	26.34	935	2	97	0	1	28	104.8	-21.4	63	10	100,000	100	0.0	0.0
C+ / 5.6	11.1	1.09	20.30	200	6	93	0	1	29	103.6	-19.1	35	13	2,500	100	5.8	0.0
C / 5.4	11.1	1.09	18.17	N/A	6	93	0	1	29	98.4	-19.4	26	13	2,500	100	0.0	0.0
C / 5.3	11.0	1.09	18.05	71	6	93	0	1	29	98.5	-19.4	26	13	2,500	100	0.0	0.0
C / 5.4	14.6	1.04	13.22	793	4	95	0	1	20	71.4	-22.8	83	5	2,500	100	5.8	0.0
C / 5.4	14.6	1.05	12.98	366	4	95	0	1	20	67.1	-23.1	78	5	2,500	100	0.0	0.0
C+ / 5.7	11.0	1.09	21.16	19	6	93	0	1	29	105.3	-19.0	38	13	100,000	100	0.0	0.0
D / 1.8	10.4	1.03	28.04	426	2	97	0	1	50	107.2	-20.1	73	4	2,500	100	5.8	0.0
E+ / 0.9	10.4	1.03	20.66	2	2	97	0	1	50	101.9	-20.4	65	4	2,500	100	0.0	0.0
E+ / 0.9	10.4	1.03	20.67	59	2	97	0	1	50	101.9	-20.3	65	4	2,500	100	0.0	0.0
D+ / 2.5	10.4	1.03	31.92	54	2	97	0	1	50	109.0	-20.0	75	4	100,000	100	0.0	0.0

99 Pct = Best
0 Pct = Worst

Fund Type	Fund Name	Ticker Symbol	Overall Investment Rating	Phone	PERFORMANCE Perfor- mance Rating/Pts	Total Return % through 3/31/15 3 Mo	6 Mo	1Yr / Pct	Annualized 3Yr / Pct	Annualized 5Yr / Pct	Incl. in Returns Dividend Yield	Expense Ratio
SC	● Natixis Vaug Nel Sm Cp Val A	NEFJX	B-	(800) 225-5478	A- / 9.1	6.15	13.60	13.25 /87	18.16 /95	15.23 /88	0.00	1.66
SC	● Natixis Vaug Nel Sm Cp Val B	NEJBX	C	(800) 225-5478	A / 9.3	6.05	13.19	12.48 /85	17.30 /91	14.39 /81	0.00	2.41
SC	● Natixis Vaug Nel Sm Cp Val C	NEJCX	C	(800) 225-5478	A / 9.3	5.99	13.21	12.43 /84	17.28 /91	14.38 /81	0.00	2.41
SC	● Natixis Vaug Nel Sm Cp Val Y	NEJYX	B	(800) 225-5478	A+ / 9.6	6.25	13.74	13.55 /88	18.47 /96	15.53 /90	0.00	1.41
GR	Natixis Vaughan Nelson Select Y	VNSYX	U	(800) 225-5478	U /	2.29	7.45	10.74 /77	--	--	0.06	1.80
GR	Natixis Vaughan Nelson Val Opp A	VNVAX	A+	(800) 225-5478	A / 9.5	7.00	13.25	12.73 /86	19.64 /97	16.48 /95	0.00	1.42
GR	Natixis Vaughan Nelson Val Opp C	VNVCX	A+	(800) 225-5478	A+/ 9.6	6.78	12.82	11.90 /82	18.76 /96	15.63 /91	0.00	2.17
GR	Natixis Vaughan Nelson Val Opp N	VNVNX	U	(800) 225-5478	U /	7.07	13.43	13.11 /87	--	--	0.00	2.22
GR	Natixis Vaughan Nelson Val Opp Y	VNVYX	A+	(800) 225-5478	A+/ 9.8	7.06	13.41	13.05 /87	19.95 /98	16.77 /95	0.00	1.17
GL	Navigator Equity Hedged A	NAVAX	D	(877) 766-2264	E+ / 0.8	2.67	4.29	3.01 /26	3.39 / 9	--	0.09	1.78
GL	Navigator Equity Hedged C	NAVCX	D	(877) 766-2264	E+ / 0.9	2.42	3.88	2.13 /22	2.57 / 7	--	0.00	2.53
GL	Navigator Equity Hedged I	NAVIX	D	(877) 766-2264	D- / 1.2	2.77	4.43	3.25 /28	3.65 / 9	--	0.33	1.53
GR	Navigator Sentry Managed Vol I	NVXIX	U	(877) 766-2264	U /	-6.74	-9.83	-28.25 / 0	--	--	0.00	1.73
FS	Navigator Tactical Fixed Income I	NTBIX	U	(877) 766-2264	U /	1.79	-0.16	-0.40 /14	--	--	2.36	1.80
GI	NE 529 State Farm CSP Opp 4-6		C+	(888) 470-0862	D+ / 2.9	2.02	3.95	6.99 /55	9.04 /33	8.68 /34	0.00	1.14
GI	NE 529 State Farm CSP Opp 4-6		C+	(888) 470-0862	C- / 3.2	1.81	3.60	6.17 /48	8.20 /28	7.85 /29	0.00	1.89
GL	NE 529 State Farm CSP Opp		C+	(888) 470-0862	C- / 4.0	2.21	4.22	6.86 /54	11.13 /46	9.95 /44	0.00	1.22
GL	NE 529 State Farm CSP Opp		C+	(888) 470-0862	C / 4.3	2.04	3.85	6.13 /48	10.34 /41	9.13 /38	0.00	1.97
BA	NE 529 State Farm CSP Opp Bal A		C+	(888) 470-0862	D+ / 2.8	2.02	3.96	6.93 /54	9.00 /33	8.64 /34	0.00	1.14
BA	NE 529 State Farm CSP Opp Bal B		C+	(888) 470-0862	C- / 3.2	1.81	3.61	6.10 /47	8.20 /28	7.83 /29	0.00	1.89
GI	NE 529 State Farm CSP Opp Col		C-	(888) 470-0862	E+ / 0.6	0.78	1.38	2.38 /24	1.84 / 6	2.64 / 5	0.00	0.92
GI	NE 529 State Farm CSP Opp Col		C-	(888) 470-0862	E+ / 0.7	0.72	1.04	1.78 /21	1.12 / 5	1.89 / 4	0.00	1.67
GL	NE 529 State Farm CSP Opp Gro A		C+	(888) 470-0862	C / 5.0	2.26	5.00	7.89 /62	12.92 /59	10.96 /52	0.00	1.23
GL	NE 529 State Farm CSP Opp Gro B		C+	(888) 470-0862	C / 5.4	2.02	4.60	7.06 /55	12.06 /53	10.12 /46	0.00	1.98
GL	NE 529 State Farm CSP Opp Mdt G		C+	(888) 470-0862	C- / 4.0	2.27	4.28	6.91 /54	11.18 /47	10.01 /45	0.00	1.22
GL	NE 529 State Farm CSP Opp Mdt G		C+	(888) 470-0862	C / 4.3	2.03	3.83	6.11 /47	10.33 /41	9.19 /38	0.00	1.97
GL	NE 529 State Farm CSP		C+	(888) 470-0862	C / 5.0	2.27	4.95	7.87 /62	12.92 /59	10.23 /46	0.00	1.23
GL	NE 529 State Farm CSP		C+	(888) 470-0862	C / 5.3	2.10	4.53	6.83 /54	12.01 /53	9.39 /40	0.00	1.98
GI	NE 529 State Farm CSP		C	(888) 470-0862	D- / 1.3	1.33	2.79	4.73 /37	5.75 /16	5.85 /16	0.00	1.01
GI	NE 529 State Farm CSP		C	(888) 470-0862	D- / 1.5	1.15	2.41	3.89 /31	4.96 /13	5.04 /12	0.00	1.76
AG	Needham Aggressive Growth	NEAGX	B-	(800) 625-7071	B / 7.6	3.78	14.09	14.25 /90	13.87 /66	13.56 /74	0.00	2.07
GR	Needham Growth Fund	NEEGX	C+	(800) 625-7071	B- / 7.1	3.59	12.32	11.95 /82	14.07 /68	12.73 /66	0.00	1.89
SC	Needham Small Cap Growth	NESGX	D	(800) 625-7071	C- / 3.8	6.64	13.37	9.45 /72	8.05 /27	9.20 /38	0.00	2.10
GL	Neiman Balanced Allocation A	NBAFX	C-		D / 2.0	1.29	3.71	4.57 /36	7.71 /25	--	1.28	3.01
GL	Neiman Balanced Allocation C	NBCFX	C-		D+ / 2.4	1.14	3.30	3.81 /31	6.98 /21	--	0.52	3.76
IN	Neiman Large Cap Value NL	NEIMX	B-		C+ / 5.9	1.91	6.62	10.84 /78	12.22 /54	11.14 /54	0.57	1.57
GL	Neuberger Berman Abs Ret Mlt-Mgr	NABCX	U	(800) 877-9700	U /	1.33	1.19	0.17 /16	--	--	0.00	3.80
GL	Neuberger Berman AbsRet MltMgr A	NABAX	U	(800) 877-9700	U /	1.58	1.56	1.01 /18	--	--	0.19	3.05
GL	Neuberger Berman AbsRet MltMgr	NABIX	U	(800) 877-9700	U /	1.67	1.74	1.29 /19	--	--	0.65	2.68
GR	Neuberger Berman All Cap Core A	NBEAX	E+	(800) 877-9700	C- / 3.5	1.80	-0.19	2.07 /22	11.46 /49	10.68 /50	0.00	1.49
GR	Neuberger Berman All Cap Core C	NBECX	E+	(800) 877-9700	C- / 3.9	1.57	-0.54	1.24 /19	10.64 /43	9.85 /43	0.00	2.24
GR	Neuberger Berman All Cap Core Inst	NBEIX	D-	(800) 877-9700	C / 4.7	1.76	-0.01	2.42 /24	11.93 /52	11.18 /54	0.00	1.11
BA	Neuberger Berman AMT Balanced I	NBABX	C-	(800) 877-9700	C / 4.3	5.34	10.48	9.99 /74	8.74 /31	9.82 /43	0.00	2.04
GR	Neuberger Berman AMT Guardian I		C	(800) 877-9700	B- / 7.5	0.29	4.23	9.63 /73	15.58 /80	13.58 /74	0.44	1.11
GR	Neuberger Berman AMT Social Resp		A-	(800) 877-9700	B / 8.0	1.63	6.96	11.57 /81	15.73 /81	13.73 /75	0.35	1.00
GR	Neuberger Berman AMT Social Resp		B+	(800) 877-9700	B / 7.9	1.63	6.89	11.34 /80	15.53 /79	13.57 /74	0.11	1.25
EM	Neuberger Berman Emg Mkt Eq A	NEMAX	E+	(800) 877-9700	E / 0.4	0.94	-3.01	-1.18 /12	1.29 / 6	0.90 / 3	0.77	2.01
EM	Neuberger Berman Emg Mkt Eq C	NEMCX	E+	(800) 877-9700	E / 0.5	0.77	-3.36	-1.91 /11	0.53 / 5	0.15 / 3	0.28	2.74
EM	Neuberger Berman Emg Mkt Eq I	NEMIX	E+	(800) 877-9700	E+ / 0.6	0.94	-2.92	-0.98 /13	1.51 / 6	1.16 / 3	1.06	1.60
EM	Neuberger Berman Emg Mkt Eq R3	NEMRX	E+	(800) 877-9700	E / 0.5	0.83	-3.21	-1.59 /11	0.85 / 5	0.49 / 3	0.57	2.32
EM	Neuberger Berman Emg Mkt Eq R6	NREMX	U	(800) 877-9700	U /	0.94	-2.85	-0.91 /13	--	--	1.14	1.57
IN	Neuberger Berman Eq Income A	NBHAX	C-	(800) 877-9700	C- / 3.0	0.93	4.10	7.39 /58	9.39 /36	10.29 /47	2.16	1.06

● Denotes fund is closed to new investors
* Denotes fund is included in Section II

www.thestreetratings.com

| RISK | | | NET ASSETS | | ASSET | | | | Portfolio | BULL / BEAR | | FUND MANAGER | | MINIMUMS | | LOADS | |
| Risk Rating/Pts | 3 Year | | NAV As of 3/31/15 | Total $(Mil) | Cash % | Stocks % | Bonds % | Other % | Turnover Ratio | Last Bull Market Return | Last Bear Market Return | Manager Quality Pct | Manager Tenure (Years) | Initial Purch. $ | Additional Purch. $ | Front End Load | Back End Load |
	Standard Deviation	Beta															
C- / 3.9	11.8	0.83	21.92	128	3	96	0	1	58	104.3	-23.3	92	11	2,500	100	5.8	0.0
D+ / 2.4	11.8	0.83	16.30	1	3	96	0	1	58	99.1	-23.5	90	11	2,500	100	0.0	0.0
D+ / 2.4	11.8	0.83	16.28	27	3	96	0	1	58	99.1	-23.6	90	11	2,500	100	0.0	0.0
C- / 4.0	11.8	0.83	22.45	187	3	96	0	1	58	105.9	-23.2	92	11	100,000	100	0.0	0.0
U /	N/A	N/A	14.74	61	3	96	0	1	64	N/A	N/A	N/A	3	100,000	100	0.0	0.0
C+ / 6.3	11.5	1.07	22.78	76	3	96	0	1	39	112.1	-23.9	84	7	2,500	100	5.8	0.0
C+ / 6.3	11.5	1.07	21.90	42	3	96	0	1	39	106.7	-24.2	79	7	2,500	100	0.0	0.0
U /	N/A	N/A	23.02	53	3	96	0	1	39	N/A	N/A	N/A	7	0	0	0.0	0.0
C+ / 6.3	11.5	1.07	23.04	740	3	96	0	1	39	114.0	-23.9	86	7	100,000	100	0.0	0.0
B- / 7.9	7.0	0.46	9.61	4	11	88	0	1	353	20.1	-15.4	55	5	5,000	500	5.5	0.0
B- / 7.8	7.0	0.46	9.31	2	11	88	0	1	353	17.0	-15.8	42	5	5,000	500	0.0	0.0
B- / 7.9	7.0	0.46	9.64	58	11	88	0	1	353	21.1	-15.4	59	5	25,000	0	0.0	0.0
U /	N/A	N/A	7.06	45	85	14	0	1	148	N/A	N/A	N/A	1	25,000	0	0.0	0.0
U /	N/A	N/A	9.74	269	0	0	0	100	7	N/A	N/A	N/A	N/A	25,000	0	0.0	0.0
B+ / 9.1	6.4	0.63	13.16	66	0	0	0	100	0	50.1	-11.7	55	7	250	50	5.5	0.0
B+ / 9.0	6.4	0.63	12.39	4	0	0	0	100	0	46.2	-12.0	43	7	250	50	0.0	0.0
B / 8.0	8.7	0.59	14.33	98	0	0	0	100	0	66.5	-17.7	94	7	250	50	5.5	0.0
B / 8.0	8.7	0.59	13.50	5	0	0	0	100	0	62.3	-18.1	92	7	250	50	0.0	0.0
B+ / 9.1	6.4	1.09	13.12	14	0	0	0	100	0	49.8	-11.6	29	6	250	50	5.5	0.0
B+ / 9.0	6.4	1.10	12.35	1	0	0	0	100	0	46.1	-12.0	21	6	250	50	0.0	0.0
B+ / 9.9	1.6	0.08	10.32	29	0	0	0	100	0	8.3	0.6	74	6	250	50	5.5	0.0
B+ / 9.9	1.7	0.08	9.73	2	0	0	0	100	0	5.7	0.3	66	6	250	50	0.0	0.0
B- / 7.4	10.3	0.68	14.50	54	0	0	0	100	0	80.0	-20.3	95	6	250	50	5.5	0.0
B- / 7.4	10.3	0.68	13.65	3	0	0	0	100	0	75.4	-20.4	94	6	250	50	0.0	0.0
B / 8.0	8.7	0.59	14.39	29	0	0	0	100	0	66.3	-17.4	94	6	250	50	5.5	0.0
B / 8.0	8.7	0.59	13.55	2	0	0	0	100	0	62.1	-17.7	92	6	250	50	0.0	0.0
B- / 7.4	10.2	0.68	13.98	40	0	0	0	100	0	79.7	-22.5	95	6	250	50	5.5	0.0
B- / 7.3	10.3	0.68	13.14	N/A	0	0	0	100	0	75.0	-22.8	94	6	250	50	0.0	0.0
B+ / 9.9	4.0	0.39	12.17	54	0	0	0	100	0	29.8	-6.0	64	N/A	250	50	5.5	0.0
B+ / 9.9	4.1	0.40	11.47	3	0	0	0	100	0	26.5	-6.2	51	N/A	250	50	0.0	0.0
C / 5.4	14.3	1.09	24.45	63	0	99	0	1	20	103.1	-30.3	22	5	2,000	100	0.0	2.0
C+ / 5.7	12.1	1.02	47.65	152	4	95	0	1	12	100.5	-28.5	36	6	2,000	100	0.0	2.0
C / 4.5	13.5	0.82	14.94	32	7	92	0	1	58	63.4	-29.1	12	7	2,000	100	0.0	2.0
B- / 7.9	6.4	0.96	12.52	15	8	61	29	2	72	43.0	-13.2	54	4	2,500	100	5.8	0.0
B / 8.1	6.2	0.95	12.39	6	8	61	29	2	72	39.5	-13.5	46	4	2,500	100	0.0	0.0
B- / 7.1	8.2	0.82	27.16	35	9	90	0	1	26	67.8	-14.6	56	12	1,000	100	0.0	0.0
U /	N/A	N/A	10.69	92	54	31	14	1	329	N/A	N/A	N/A	3	1,000	100	0.0	0.0
U /	N/A	N/A	10.91	215	54	31	14	1	329	N/A	N/A	N/A	3	1,000	100	5.8	0.0
U /	N/A	N/A	10.95	1,217	54	31	14	1	329	N/A	N/A	N/A	3	1,000,000	0	0.0	0.0
C- / 3.3	8.7	0.79	9.06	12	9	90	0	1	62	64.2	-15.1	52	8	1,000	100	5.8	0.0
C- / 3.0	8.8	0.79	8.43	11	9	90	0	1	62	60.2	-15.5	40	8	1,000	100	0.0	0.0
C- / 3.4	8.7	0.79	9.24	50	9	90	0	1	62	66.8	-15.0	59	8	1,000,000	0	0.0	0.0
C+ / 6.4	7.4	1.06	13.61	14	1	69	29	1	51	48.7	-12.0	30	12	0	0	0.0	0.0
C- / 4.0	10.7	1.05	24.16	14	2	97	0	1	31	90.9	-20.1	48	13	0	0	0.0	0.0
C+ / 6.9	10.3	1.01	24.27	310	4	95	0	1	29	90.9	-20.8	60	14	0	0	0.0	0.0
C+ / 6.9	10.3	1.01	24.32	80	4	95	0	1	29	89.8	-20.8	57	14	0	0	0.0	0.0
C+ / 5.9	12.1	0.86	16.10	15	4	95	0	1	36	24.1	-28.0	74	7	1,000	100	5.8	0.0
C+ / 6.0	12.1	0.86	15.63	7	4	95	0	1	36	21.0	-28.2	67	7	1,000	100	0.0	0.0
C+ / 5.9	12.1	0.86	16.16	410	4	95	0	1	36	25.3	-27.9	76	7	1,000,000	0	0.0	0.0
C+ / 6.0	12.1	0.86	15.81	1	4	95	0	1	36	22.4	-28.1	70	7	0	0	0.0	0.0
U /	N/A	N/A	16.17	92	4	95	0	1	36	N/A	N/A	N/A	7	0	0	0.0	0.0
B- / 7.2	7.7	0.64	12.59	339	6	90	0	4	41	47.8	-9.8	60	9	1,000	100	5.8	0.0

	99 Pct = Best 0 Pct = Worst					**PERFORMANCE**								
								Total Return % through 3/31/15					Incl. in Returns	
				Overall		Perfor-				Annualized			Dividend	Expense
Fund Type	Fund Name	Ticker Symbol	Investment Rating		Phone	mance Rating/Pts	3 Mo	6 Mo	1Yr / Pct	3Yr / Pct	5Yr / Pct		Yield	Ratio
IN	Neuberger Berman Eq Income C	NBHCX	C-		(800) 877-9700	C- / 3.4	0.83	3.83	6.67 / 52	8.62 / 31	9.50 / 41		1.60	1.81
IN	Neuberger Berman Eq Income I	NBHIX	C		(800) 877-9700	C- / 4.2	1.02	4.30	7.81 / 61	9.83 / 38	10.72 / 50		2.68	0.69
IN	Neuberger Berman Eq Income R3	NBHRX	C		(800) 877-9700	C- / 3.7	0.87	3.99	7.17 / 56	9.07 / 33	--		2.08	1.42
AA	Neuberger Berman Flexible Sel Inst	NFLIX	U		(800) 877-9700	U /	1.52	4.90	8.68 / 67	--	--		0.98	1.22
GR	Neuberger Berman Focus A	NFAAX	C-		(800) 877-9700	B- / 7.4	1.16	5.53	8.33 / 65	17.09 / 90	13.18 / 70		0.69	1.20
GR ●	Neuberger Berman Focus Adv	NBFAX	D+		(800) 877-9700	B+ / 8.3	1.14	5.52	8.14 / 64	16.91 / 89	12.99 / 68		1.19	1.29
GR	Neuberger Berman Focus C	NFACX	D		(800) 877-9700	B / 7.8	1.07	5.16	7.58 / 60	16.25 / 85	12.36 / 63		0.96	1.94
GR	Neuberger Berman Focus Inst	NFALX	B		(800) 877-9700	B+ / 8.7	1.27	5.74	8.71 / 68	17.52 / 92	13.59 / 74		0.69	0.78
GR ●	Neuberger Berman Focus Inv	NBSSX	B-		(800) 877-9700	B+ / 8.6	1.24	5.67	8.53 / 67	17.31 / 91	13.38 / 72		0.53	0.94
GR ●	Neuberger Berman Focus Tr	NBFCX	C		(800) 877-9700	B+ / 8.4	1.15	5.50	8.29 / 65	17.06 / 90	13.15 / 70		0.74	1.14
SC	Neuberger Berman Genesis Adv	NBGAX	D		(800) 877-9700	C+ / 6.2	4.20	9.97	4.99 / 38	13.22 / 61	13.24 / 70		0.12	1.38
SC	Neuberger Berman Genesis Inst	NBGIX	C+		(800) 877-9700	C+ / 6.7	4.35	10.28	5.58 / 43	13.83 / 66	13.84 / 76		0.29	0.86
SC	Neuberger Berman Genesis Inv	NBGNX	C-		(800) 877-9700	C+ / 6.6	4.31	10.21	5.42 / 42	13.65 / 65	13.64 / 74		0.32	1.02
SC	Neuberger Berman Genesis R6	NRGSX	U		(800) 877-9700	U /	4.36	10.32	5.65 / 44	--	--		0.37	0.80
SC	Neuberger Berman Genesis Tr	NBGEX	C+		(800) 877-9700	C+ / 6.5	4.27	10.15	5.31 / 41	13.55 / 64	13.55 / 73		0.05	1.11
GL	Neuberger Berman Gl Them Opp A	NGHAX	D-		(800) 877-9700	E+ / 0.7	0.70	-1.19	-3.90 / 7	3.99 / 10	--		0.43	2.02
GL	Neuberger Berman Gl Them Opp C	NGHCX	D-		(800) 877-9700	E+ / 0.7	0.51	-1.56	-4.58 / 6	3.22 / 8	--		0.22	2.87
GL	Neuberger Berman Gl Them Opp Inst	NGHIX	D-		(800) 877-9700	D- / 1.0	0.79	-1.10	-3.52 / 8	4.34 / 11	--		0.72	1.62
GL	Neuberger Berman Global Alloc A	NGLAX	D-		(800) 877-9700	D- / 1.3	1.40	3.91	0.51 / 17	6.37 / 18	--		2.12	3.51
GL	Neuberger Berman Global Alloc C	NGLCX	D		(800) 877-9700	D- / 1.5	1.23	3.49	-0.31 / 15	5.57 / 15	--		1.73	4.26
GL	Neuberger Berman Global Alloc Inst	NGLIX	D		(800) 877-9700	D / 2.1	1.49	4.11	0.91 / 18	6.76 / 20	--		2.54	3.13
GL	Neuberger Berman Global Equity A	NGQAX	E		(800) 877-9700	C- / 3.4	2.96	5.25	5.94 / 46	10.16 / 40	--		6.47	5.67
GL	Neuberger Berman Global Equity C	NGQCX	E		(800) 877-9700	C- / 3.8	2.73	4.83	5.13 / 40	9.30 / 35	--		6.09	6.51
GL	Neuberger Berman Global Equity Inst	NGQIX	E		(800) 877-9700	C / 4.6	2.93	5.44	6.31 / 49	10.54 / 43	--		6.94	5.16
FO	Neuberger Berman Grtr China Eq Inst	NCEIX	U		(800) 877-9700	U /	4.65	19.39	32.82 / 99	--	--		0.68	1.91
GI	Neuberger Berman Guardian A	NGDAX	C-		(800) 877-9700	C+ / 6.4	0.31	4.26	9.66 / 73	15.52 / 79	13.55 / 73		0.87	1.11
GI ●	Neuberger Berman Guardian Adv	NBGUX	C		(800) 877-9700	B- / 7.2	0.26	4.16	9.35 / 71	15.15 / 76	13.16 / 70		0.30	1.50
GI	Neuberger Berman Guardian C	NGDCX	C		(800) 877-9700	C+ / 6.8	0.13	3.91	8.80 / 68	14.65 / 72	12.70 / 66		0.00	1.87
GI	Neuberger Berman Guardian Inst	NGDLX	C+		(800) 877-9700	B / 7.8	0.38	4.48	10.03 / 74	15.93 / 83	13.98 / 78		0.86	0.73
GI ●	Neuberger Berman Guardian Inv	NGUAX	C+		(800) 877-9700	B / 7.6	0.33	4.40	9.85 / 74	15.73 / 81	13.78 / 76		0.70	0.91
GI	Neuberger Berman Guardian R3	NGDRX	C		(800) 877-9700	B- / 7.2	0.20	4.10	9.29 / 71	15.20 / 76	13.27 / 71		0.47	1.41
GI ●	Neuberger Berman Guardian Tr	NBGTX	C		(800) 877-9700	B- / 7.5	0.23	4.27	9.62 / 73	15.52 / 79	13.58 / 74		0.83	1.08
FO	Neuberger Berman Intl Equity A	NIQAX	D+		(800) 877-9700	D+ / 2.5	5.43	6.16	2.03 / 22	8.64 / 31	8.06 / 30		0.45	1.56
FO	Neuberger Berman Intl Equity C	NIQCX	C-		(800) 877-9700	D+ / 2.9	5.22	5.76	1.24 / 19	7.81 / 26	7.25 / 25		0.10	2.52
FO	Neuberger Berman Intl Equity Inst	NBIIX	D+		(800) 877-9700	C- / 3.4	5.55	6.37	2.34 / 23	9.16 / 34	8.48 / 33		1.75	1.15
FO ●	Neuberger Berman Intl Equity Inv	NIQVX	C-		(800) 877-9700	C- / 3.6	5.50	6.31	2.22 / 23	8.85 / 32	8.30 / 32		0.71	1.33
FO ●	Neuberger Berman Intl Equity Trust	NIQTX	C-		(800) 877-9700	C- / 3.5	5.47	6.24	2.11 / 22	8.77 / 31	8.25 / 32		0.34	1.43
FO	Neuberger Berman Intl Sel A	NBNAX	D		(800) 877-9700	D / 2.2	5.51	5.59	1.28 / 19	8.02 / 27	6.80 / 22		0.96	1.38
FO	Neuberger Berman Intl Sel C	NBNCX	D		(800) 877-9700	D+ / 2.5	5.19	5.16	0.44 / 17	7.17 / 22	5.97 / 17		0.32	2.10
FO	Neuberger Berman Intl Sel Inst	NILIX	D+		(800) 877-9700	C- / 3.2	5.59	5.73	1.62 / 20	8.36 / 29	7.15 / 24		1.42	0.98
FO	Neuberger Berman Intl Sel R3	NBNRX	D		(800) 877-9700	D+ / 2.8	5.36	5.38	0.95 / 18	7.70 / 25	6.50 / 20		0.89	1.61
FO ●	Neuberger Berman Intl Sel Trust	NILTX	D+		(800) 877-9700	C- / 3.0	5.47	5.58	1.30 / 19	8.01 / 27	6.80 / 22		1.04	1.38
GR	Neuberger Berman Intrinsic Val A	NINAX	B-		(800) 877-9700	B- / 7.5	5.26	12.36	6.42 / 50	16.53 / 87	12.93 / 68		0.00	1.58
GR	Neuberger Berman Intrinsic Val C	NINCX	B		(800) 877-9700	B / 8.0	5.09	11.95	5.62 / 43	15.68 / 81	12.13 / 62		0.00	2.32
GR	Neuberger Berman Intrinsic Val Inst	NINLX	B+		(800) 877-9700	B+ / 8.8	5.38	12.61	6.81 / 54	16.94 / 90	13.33 / 71		0.00	1.19
GR	Neuberger Berman Large Cap Val A	NPNAX	D		(800) 877-9700	C+ / 5.9	-0.53	4.38	6.88 / 54	15.08 / 75	--		0.99	1.12
GR ●	Neuberger Berman Large Cap Val	NBPBX	D		(800) 877-9700	C+ / 6.8	-0.56	4.32	6.72 / 53	14.95 / 74	9.53 / 41		1.24	1.22
GR	Neuberger Berman Large Cap Val C	NPNCX	D-		(800) 877-9700	C+ / 6.3	-0.71	4.05	6.08 / 47	14.23 / 69	8.83 / 36		0.90	1.87
GR	Neuberger Berman Large Cap Val	NBPIX	C		(800) 877-9700	B- / 7.2	-0.43	4.63	7.31 / 58	15.55 / 80	10.10 / 46		0.99	0.72
GR ●	Neuberger Berman Large Cap Val Inv	NPRTX	C		(800) 877-9700	B- / 7.1	-0.46	4.52	7.11 / 56	15.36 / 78	9.92 / 44		0.84	0.87
GR	Neuberger Berman Large Cap Val R3	NPNRX	D		(800) 877-9700	C+ / 6.7	-0.61	4.25	6.56 / 51	14.78 / 73	--		1.10	1.44
GR ●	Neuberger Berman Large Cap Val Tr	NBPTX	D+		(800) 877-9700	C+ / 6.9	-0.53	4.43	6.93 / 54	15.13 / 76	9.71 / 42		1.04	1.07

RISK			NET ASSETS		ASSET					BULL / BEAR		FUND MANAGER		MINIMUMS		LOADS	
	3 Year		NAV							Last Bull	Last Bear	Manager	Manager	Initial	Additional	Front	Back
Risk	Standard		As of	Total	Cash	Stocks	Bonds	Other	Portfolio	Market	Market	Quality	Tenure	Purch.	Purch.	End	End
Rating/Pts	Deviation	Beta	3/31/15	$(Mil)	%	%	%	%	Turnover Ratio	Return	Return	Pct	(Years)	$	$	Load	Load
B- / 7.2	7.7	0.63	12.53	442	6	90	0	4	41	44.2	-10.1	49	9	1,000	100	0.0	0.0
B- / 7.1	7.8	0.64	12.63	1,627	6	90	0	4	41	49.7	-9.7	65	9	1,000,000	0	0.0	0.0
B- / 7.2	7.8	0.64	12.57	4	6	90	0	4	41	46.3	-10.0	54	9	0	0	0.0	0.0
U /	N/A	N/A	12.00	100	6	87	6	1	50	N/A	N/A	N/A	2	1,000,000	0	0.0	0.0
D+ / 2.5	9.7	0.96	16.61	6	3	96	0	1	84	102.9	-20.5	80	7	1,000	100	5.8	0.0
D- / 1.0	9.8	0.96	8.88	6	3	96	0	1	84	101.7	-20.5	79	7	0	0	0.0	0.0
D- / 1.0	9.8	0.96	8.53	3	3	96	0	1	84	97.7	-20.6	75	7	1,000	0	0.0	0.0
C / 4.7	9.7	0.96	26.26	28	3	96	0	1	84	105.4	-20.4	83	7	1,000,000	0	0.0	0.0
C / 4.7	9.8	0.96	26.23	680	3	96	0	1	84	104.1	-20.4	82	7	1,000	100	0.0	0.0
D+ / 2.6	9.8	0.96	16.75	116	3	96	0	1	84	102.7	-20.4	80	7	0	0	0.0	0.0
D+ / 2.7	11.1	0.78	28.77	528	4	95	0	1	14	72.4	-17.7	74	21	0	0	0.0	0.0
C / 5.3	11.1	0.78	59.06	4,241	4	95	0	1	14	75.5	-17.5	79	21	1,000,000	0	0.0	0.0
C- / 3.9	11.1	0.78	37.99	2,260	4	95	0	1	14	74.5	-17.6	77	21	1,000	100	0.0	0.0
U /	N/A	N/A	59.06	3,074	4	95	0	1	14	N/A	N/A	N/A	21	0	0	0.0	0.0
C / 5.5	11.1	0.78	61.77	2,507	4	95	0	1	14	74.0	-17.6	77	21	0	0	0.0	0.0
C+ / 6.5	10.6	0.69	10.12	N/A	11	88	0	1	80	29.6	N/A	32	4	1,000	100	5.8	0.0
C+ / 6.5	10.6	0.69	9.92	N/A	11	88	0	1	80	26.2	N/A	24	4	1,000	100	0.0	0.0
C+ / 6.5	10.6	0.69	10.18	62	11	88	0	1	80	31.2	N/A	36	4	1,000,000	0	0.0	0.0
C+ / 6.7	9.3	1.28	10.83	9	100	0	0	0	228	33.7	-5.9	11	5	1,000	100	5.8	0.0
C+ / 6.7	9.2	1.27	10.69	7	100	0	0	0	228	30.4	-6.2	8	5	1,000	100	0.0	0.0
C+ / 6.6	9.3	1.28	10.87	11	100	0	0	0	228	35.2	-5.7	13	5	1,000,000	0	0.0	0.0
D- / 1.0	10.7	0.73	6.61	N/A	2	97	0	1	39	58.4	N/A	89	4	1,000	100	5.8	0.0
D- / 1.0	10.8	0.74	6.39	N/A	2	97	0	1	39	54.4	N/A	85	4	1,000	100	0.0	0.0
D- / 1.0	10.8	0.73	6.67	3	2	97	0	1	39	60.3	N/A	90	4	1,000,000	0	0.0	0.0
U /	N/A	N/A	13.27	131	7	92	0	1	171	N/A	N/A	N/A	2	1,000,000	0	0.0	0.0
C- / 3.5	10.6	1.05	12.80	84	1	98	0	1	37	90.1	-20.1	49	13	1,000	100	5.8	0.0
C / 4.5	10.6	1.04	15.44	N/A	1	98	0	1	37	88.0	-20.2	45	13	0	0	0.0	0.0
C / 4.5	10.7	1.05	15.06	3	1	98	0	1	37	85.2	-20.3	37	13	1,000	100	0.0	0.0
C / 5.0	10.7	1.05	18.41	128	1	98	0	1	37	92.6	-20.0	55	13	1,000,000	0	0.0	0.0
C / 5.0	10.7	1.05	18.38	1,156	1	98	0	1	37	91.4	-20.0	52	13	1,000	0	0.0	0.0
C / 4.5	10.7	1.05	15.39	1	1	98	0	1	37	88.5	-20.2	44	13	0	0	0.0	0.0
C- / 3.6	10.6	1.04	12.94	126	1	98	0	1	37	90.2	-20.1	50	13	0	0	0.0	0.0
B- / 7.0	11.2	0.80	23.48	65	2	97	0	1	34	46.9	-23.0	77	10	1,000	100	5.8	0.0
B- / 7.0	11.2	0.80	23.18	8	2	97	0	1	34	43.1	-23.3	70	10	1,000	100	0.0	0.0
C+ / 6.3	11.3	0.81	11.42	882	2	97	0	1	34	49.1	-23.0	80	10	1,000,000	0	0.0	2.0
B- / 7.0	11.2	0.80	21.10	124	2	97	0	1	34	47.9	-23.0	78	10	1,000	100	0.0	0.0
B- / 7.0	11.2	0.80	23.54	62	2	97	0	1	34	47.6	-23.0	78	10	0	0	0.0	0.0
C+ / 6.3	11.4	0.82	11.29	9	2	97	0	1	27	44.7	-24.6	70	9	1,000	100	5.8	0.0
C+ / 6.3	11.4	0.83	11.15	4	2	97	0	1	27	41.0	-24.7	58	9	1,000	100	0.0	0.0
C+ / 6.3	11.4	0.83	11.34	219	2	97	0	1	27	46.4	-24.4	73	9	1,000,000	0	0.0	0.0
C+ / 6.3	11.4	0.83	11.20	3	2	97	0	1	27	43.4	-24.6	66	9	0	0	0.0	0.0
C+ / 6.3	11.4	0.82	11.37	11	2	97	0	1	27	44.6	-24.5	70	9	1,000	100	0.0	0.0
C / 5.5	13.3	1.17	14.80	27	4	95	0	1	24	100.6	-29.4	34	18	1,000	100	5.8	0.0
C / 5.4	13.3	1.17	14.24	18	4	95	0	1	24	95.4	-29.6	25	18	1,000	100	0.0	0.0
C / 5.5	13.3	1.18	15.07	336	4	95	0	1	24	103.1	-29.3	38	18	1,000,000	0	0.0	0.0
D+ / 2.4	10.5	0.99	20.60	3	7	92	0	1	104	86.2	-26.4	56	4	1,000	100	5.8	0.0
D- / 1.4	10.4	0.99	16.09	199	7	92	0	1	104	85.6	-26.5	55	4	0	0	0.0	0.0
D- / 1.3	10.5	0.99	15.37	3	7	92	0	1	104	81.4	-26.7	44	4	1,000	100	0.0	0.0
C / 4.5	10.5	0.99	30.33	99	7	92	0	1	104	88.7	-26.3	63	4	1,000,000	0	0.0	0.0
C / 4.5	10.5	0.99	30.15	1,189	7	92	0	1	104	87.7	-26.4	60	4	1,000	100	0.0	0.0
D- / 1.4	10.5	0.99	16.30	N/A	7	92	0	1	104	84.6	-26.5	52	4	0	0	0.0	0.0
D+ / 2.4	10.5	0.99	20.60	132	7	92	0	1	104	86.5	-26.4	57	4	0	0	0.0	0.0

Fund Type	Fund Name	Ticker Symbol	Overall Investment Rating	Phone	Perfor-mance Rating/Pts	3 Mo	6 Mo	1Yr / Pct	3Yr / Pct	5Yr / Pct	Dividend Yield	Expense Ratio
GR	Neuberger Berman Lg Cap Disp Gr A	NLDAX	E	(800) 877-9700	C- / 3.3	1.27	4.04	8.29 /65	9.75 /38	9.67 /42	0.00	1.16
GR	Neuberger Berman Lg Cap Disp Gr C	NLDCX	E	(800) 877-9700	C- / 3.7	1.10	3.71	7.53 /59	8.97 /33	8.86 /36	0.00	1.92
GR	Neuberger Berman Lg Cap Disp Gr I	NLDLX	E	(800) 877-9700	C / 4.3	1.25	4.00	8.48 /66	10.06 /40	10.04 /45	0.13	0.80
GR ●	Neuberger Berman Lg Cap Disp Gr In	NBCIX	E	(800) 877-9700	C- / 4.2	1.26	4.03	8.27 /65	9.80 /38	9.72 /42	0.00	1.11
GR	Neuberger Berman Lg Cap Disp Gr	NLDRX	E	(800) 877-9700	C- / 4.0	1.03	3.85	7.83 /62	9.45 /36	9.38 /40	0.00	1.46
GR	Neuberger Berman Lng Sh MltMgr	NLMIX	U	(800) 877-9700	U /	2.32	3.08	2.88 /26	--	--	0.14	5.12
GR	Neuberger Berman Long Short A	NLSAX	C-	(800) 877-9700	D / 2.0	1.63	2.72	4.35 /34	7.95 /27	--	0.00	2.11
GR	Neuberger Berman Long Short C	NLSCX	C	(800) 877-9700	D+ / 2.4	1.43	2.29	3.53 /29	7.13 /22	--	0.00	2.85
GR	Neuberger Berman Long Short Inst	NLSIX	C+	(800) 877-9700	C- / 3.1	1.77	2.90	4.69 /36	8.33 /29	--	0.20	1.73
MC	Neuberger Berman MC Intrinsc V A	NBRAX	A-	(800) 877-9700	A- / 9.1	4.61	10.90	14.94 /92	18.49 /96	--	0.91	1.66
MC	Neuberger Berman MC Intrinsc V C	NBRCX	A	(800) 877-9700	A / 9.3	4.38	10.50	14.10 /90	17.60 /93	--	0.37	2.35
MC	Neuberger Berman MC Intrinsc V Inst	NBRTX	A+	(800) 877-9700	A+ / 9.6	4.72	11.12	15.35 /92	18.92 /97	15.27 /89	1.08	1.24
MC ●	Neuberger Berman MC Intrinsc V Inv	NBRVX	A+	(800) 877-9700	A+ / 9.6	4.63	10.98	15.11 /92	18.63 /96	14.95 /86	0.92	1.41
MC	Neuberger Berman MC Intrinsc V R3	NBRRX	A	(800) 877-9700	A / 9.5	4.55	10.75	14.67 /91	18.19 /95	14.57 /83	0.70	1.86
MC ●	Neuberger Berman MC Intrinsc V Tr	NBREX	A	(800) 877-9700	A+ / 9.6	4.61	10.89	14.87 /91	18.42 /95	14.78 /85	0.86	1.66
MC	Neuberger Berman MidCap Gr A	NMGAX	B-	(800) 877-9700	B- / 7.3	7.58	15.62	15.46 /92	14.26 /69	15.69 /91	0.00	1.18
MC ●	Neuberger Berman MidCap Gr Adv	NBMBX	B+	(800) 877-9700	B / 8.2	7.60	15.54	15.34 /92	14.06 /68	15.38 /89	0.00	1.30
MC	Neuberger Berman MidCap Gr C	NMGCX	B	(800) 877-9700	B / 7.7	7.41	15.19	14.63 /91	13.41 /63	14.82 /85	0.00	1.96
MC	Neuberger Berman MidCap Gr Inst	NBMLX	B	(800) 877-9700	A- / 9.1	7.67	15.78	15.94 /93	14.66 /72	16.09 /93	0.00	0.79
MC ●	Neuberger Berman MidCap Gr Inv	NMANX	B-	(800) 877-9700	B+ / 8.5	7.68	15.69	15.69 /93	14.43 /70	15.81 /92	0.00	0.98
MC	Neuberger Berman MidCap Gr R3	NMGRX	B	(800) 877-9700	B / 8.2	7.55	15.48	15.22 /92	13.98 /67	15.39 /89	0.00	1.43
GR	Neuberger Berman MidCap Gr R6	NRMGX	U	(800) 877-9700	U /	7.73	15.91	15.99 /93	--	--	0.00	7.22
MC ●	Neuberger Berman MidCap Gr Tr	NBMTX	B+	(800) 877-9700	B+ / 8.4	7.61	15.70	15.65 /93	14.36 /70	15.76 /92	0.00	1.04
GR	Neuberger Berman Mlt-Cp Opps Fd A	NMUAX	B	(800) 877-9700	B- / 7.1	0.77	4.09	5.91 /46	17.18 /91	14.43 /82	0.49	1.18
GR	Neuberger Berman Mlt-Cp Opps Fd C	NMUCX	B+	(800) 877-9700	B- / 7.5	0.59	3.69	5.13 /40	16.28 /85	13.56 /74	0.12	2.06
GR	Neuberger Berman Mlt-Cp Opps Fd	NMULX	A	(800) 877-9700	B+ / 8.5	0.89	4.29	6.37 /50	17.60 /93	14.86 /86	0.90	0.86
OT	Neuberger Berman RB Comm Strat A	NRBAX	U	(800) 877-9700	U /	-5.76	-19.45	-25.96 / 0	--	--	0.00	1.99
OT	Neuberger Berman RB Comm Strat	NRBIX	U	(800) 877-9700	U /	-5.71	-19.20	-25.61 / 0	--	--	0.00	1.63
RE	Neuberger Berman Real Est A	NREAX	C-	(800) 877-9700	C+ / 6.2	3.60	15.44	19.57 /96	11.12 /46	--	1.80	1.47
RE	Neuberger Berman Real Est C	NRECX	C-	(800) 877-9700	C+ / 6.6	3.41	15.00	18.65 /96	10.26 /41	--	1.20	2.24
RE	Neuberger Berman Real Est Inst	NBRIX	C	(800) 877-9700	B / 7.6	3.68	15.68	20.03 /97	11.51 /49	14.19 /79	2.23	1.07
RE	Neuberger Berman Real Est R3	NRERX	C-	(800) 877-9700	B- / 7.0	3.48	15.25	19.23 /96	10.82 /44	13.49 /73	1.69	1.70
RE	Neuberger Berman Real Est R6	NRREX	U	(800) 877-9700	U /	3.64	15.65	20.04 /97	--	--	2.30	1.11
RE ●	Neuberger Berman Real Est Trust	NBRFX	C	(800) 877-9700	B- / 7.4	3.65	15.54	19.77 /97	11.30 /48	13.99 /78	2.06	1.43
SC	Neuberger Berman SmallCap Gr A	NSNAX	C	(800) 877-9700	B / 7.7	5.00	16.25	9.44 /72	16.08 /84	14.50 /82	0.00	1.83
SC ●	Neuberger Berman SmallCap Gr Adv	NBMVX	C+	(800) 877-9700	B+ / 8.6	4.95	16.13	9.17 /70	15.79 /82	14.16 /79	0.00	1.93
SC	Neuberger Berman SmallCap Gr C	NSNCX	C+	(800) 877-9700	B / 8.2	4.84	15.82	8.66 /67	15.23 /77	13.66 /75	0.00	2.56
SC	Neuberger Berman SmallCap Gr Inst	NBSMX	B-	(800) 877-9700	A- / 9.0	5.08	16.44	9.81 /74	16.50 /87	14.91 /86	0.00	1.41
SC ●	Neuberger Berman SmallCap Gr Inv	NBMIX	C+	(800) 877-9700	B+ / 8.8	5.00	16.28	9.51 /72	16.13 /84	14.57 /83	0.00	1.64
SC	Neuberger Berman SmallCap Gr R3	NSNRX	C+	(800) 877-9700	B+ / 8.6	4.94	16.09	9.14 /70	15.80 /82	14.22 /80	0.00	2.15
SC ●	Neuberger Berman SmallCap Gr Tr	NBMOX	C+	(800) 877-9700	B+ / 8.6	4.97	16.19	9.26 /71	15.92 /83	14.35 /81	0.00	1.84
GR	Neuberger Berman Socially Resp A	NRAAX	C	(800) 877-9700	C+ / 6.9	1.56	6.91	11.40 /80	15.69 /81	13.67 /75	0.95	1.10
GR	Neuberger Berman Socially Resp C	NRACX	C+	(800) 877-9700	B- / 7.3	1.35	6.51	10.53 /76	14.83 /74	12.81 /66	0.55	1.86
GR	Neuberger Berman Socially Resp Inst	NBSLX	B+	(800) 877-9700	B+ / 8.3	1.65	7.09	11.82 /82	16.14 /84	14.10 /79	0.84	0.69
GR ●	Neuberger Berman Socially Resp Inv	NBSRX	B+	(800) 877-9700	B / 8.2	1.62	7.01	11.61 /81	15.92 /83	13.89 /77	0.66	0.87
GR	Neuberger Berman Socially Resp R3	NRARX	C+	(800) 877-9700	B / 7.8	1.48	6.78	11.10 /79	15.42 /78	13.41 /72	0.80	1.30
GR	Neuberger Berman Socially Resp R6	NRSRX	U	(800) 877-9700	U /	1.68	7.13	11.89 /82	--	--	0.90	0.62
GR ●	Neuberger Berman Socially Resp Tr	NBSTX	C+	(800) 877-9700	B / 8.0	1.59	6.91	11.46 /80	15.73 /81	13.70 /75	0.96	1.05
GL	Neuberger Berman Value A	NVAAX	C+	(800) 877-9700	C+ / 5.6	-0.64	3.63	5.74 /44	14.74 /73	12.74 /66	0.55	6.83
GL	Neuberger Berman Value C	NVACX	B-	(800) 877-9700	C+ / 6.0	-0.84	3.19	4.92 /38	13.85 /66	11.89 /60	0.02	7.33
GL	Neuberger Berman Value Inst	NLRLX	B-	(800) 877-9700	C+ / 6.9	-0.51	3.81	6.11 /47	15.21 /77	13.15 /70	0.88	5.95
GR	New Alternatives A	NALFX	C+	(800) 423-8383	B- / 7.2	13.16	4.66	6.45 /50	15.78 /82	7.76 /28	1.11	1.16

● Denotes fund is closed to new investors
★ Denotes fund is included in Section II

RISK			NET ASSETS		ASSET				BULL / BEAR		FUND MANAGER		MINIMUMS		LOADS	
	3 Year		NAV													
Risk Rating/Pts	Standard Deviation	Beta	As of 3/31/15	Total $(Mil)	Cash %	Stocks %	Bonds %	Other %	Portfolio Turnover Ratio	Last Bull Market Return	Last Bear Market Return	Manager Quality Pct	Manager Tenure (Years)	Initial Purch. $	Additional Purch. $	Front End Load	Back End Load
E+ / 0.8	10.1	1.01	4.00	4	2	97	0	1	61	66.1	-18.0	7	16	1,000	100	5.8	0.0
E+ / 0.8	10.0	1.00	3.67	13	2	97	0	1	61	61.7	-18.3	6	16	1,000	100	0.0	0.0
E+ / 0.8	10.0	0.99	4.05	68	2	97	0	1	61	68.2	-17.9	9	16	1,000,000	0	0.0	0.0
E+ / 0.8	10.1	1.00	4.01	11	2	97	0	1	61	66.2	-18.0	8	16	1,000	100	0.0	0.0
E+ / 0.8	10.0	1.00	3.93	N/A	2	97	0	1	61	64.5	-18.0	6	16	0	0	0.0	0.0
U /	N/A	N/A	10.58	30	0	0	0	100	168	N/A	N/A	N/A	N/A	1,000,000	0	0.0	0.0
B / 8.8	4.1	0.37	13.09	385	34	50	15	1	61	N/A	N/A	84	4	1,000	100	5.8	0.0
B / 8.8	4.2	0.38	12.79	208	34	50	15	1	61	N/A	N/A	79	4	1,000	100	0.0	0.0
B / 8.8	4.2	0.38	13.20	2,818	34	50	15	1	61	N/A	N/A	86	4	1,000,000	0	0.0	0.0
C+ / 5.9	10.1	0.86	19.28	9	5	94	0	1	34	110.2	-25.7	90	4	1,000	100	5.8	0.0
C+ / 6.0	10.1	0.86	19.07	3	5	94	0	1	34	105.1	-26.0	88	4	1,000	100	0.0	0.0
C+ / 6.2	10.1	0.85	22.87	28	5	94	0	1	34	113.0	-25.6	91	4	1,000,000	0	0.0	0.0
C+ / 6.2	10.1	0.85	22.84	48	5	94	0	1	34	111.5	-25.8	91	4	1,000	100	0.0	0.0
C+ / 5.9	10.0	0.85	19.30	N/A	5	94	0	1	34	108.6	-25.9	90	4	0	0	0.0	0.0
C+ / 5.9	10.1	0.86	19.30	15	5	94	0	1	34	109.9	-25.7	90	4	0	0	0.0	0.0
C+ / 5.8	11.1	0.93	24.13	99	4	95	0	1	63	83.0	-15.1	47	12	1,000	100	5.8	0.0
C+ / 5.8	11.1	0.93	24.62	12	4	95	0	1	63	81.8	-15.2	45	12	0	0	0.0	0.0
C+ / 5.8	11.1	0.93	24.06	7	4	95	0	1	63	78.4	-15.3	37	12	1,000	100	0.0	0.0
C / 4.9	11.1	0.93	14.74	427	4	95	0	1	63	85.5	-15.0	54	12	1,000,000	0	0.0	0.0
C / 4.8	11.1	0.93	14.45	449	4	95	0	1	63	83.9	-15.0	50	12	1,000	100	0.0	0.0
C+ / 5.8	11.1	0.93	24.63	10	4	95	0	1	63	81.6	-15.2	43	12	0	0	0.0	0.0
U /	N/A	N/A	14.77	49	4	95	0	1	63	N/A	N/A	N/A	12	0	0	0.0	0.0
C+ / 5.8	11.1	0.93	24.17	78	4	95	0	1	63	83.6	-15.0	49	12	0	0	0.0	0.0
C+ / 6.8	11.2	1.10	15.73	124	1	98	0	1	17	103.6	-17.7	58	6	1,000	100	5.8	0.0
C+ / 6.8	11.2	1.10	15.30	49	1	98	0	1	17	98.4	-18.0	46	6	1,000	100	0.0	0.0
C+ / 6.8	11.1	1.10	15.84	2,388	1	98	0	1	17	106.1	-17.6	65	6	1,000,000	0	0.0	0.0
U /	N/A	N/A	6.87	71	14	0	85	1	21	N/A	N/A	N/A	3	1,000	100	5.8	0.0
U /	N/A	N/A	6.94	26	14	0	85	1	21	N/A	N/A	N/A	3	1,000,000	0	0.0	0.0
C- / 3.6	11.7	0.94	15.17	188	0	99	0	1	36	73.0	-16.8	39	10	1,000	100	5.8	0.0
C- / 3.7	11.8	0.94	15.18	43	0	99	0	1	36	68.7	-17.1	29	10	1,000	100	0.0	0.0
C- / 3.6	11.8	0.94	15.21	467	0	99	0	1	36	75.2	-16.7	44	10	1,000,000	0	0.0	0.0
C- / 3.6	11.7	0.94	15.15	28	0	99	0	1	36	71.7	-16.9	36	10	0	0	0.0	0.0
U /	N/A	N/A	15.20	36	0	99	0	1	36	N/A	N/A	N/A	10	0	0	0.0	0.0
C- / 3.6	11.8	0.94	15.17	311	0	99	0	1	36	74.1	-16.7	42	10	1,000	100	0.0	0.0
C- / 3.9	15.2	1.04	33.63	5	1	98	0	1	284	90.9	-21.1	57	12	1,000	100	5.8	0.0
C- / 3.9	15.3	1.04	22.03	3	1	98	0	1	284	89.1	-21.2	52	12	0	0	0.0	0.0
C- / 3.8	15.2	1.04	21.45	2	1	98	0	1	284	86.1	-21.3	46	12	1,000	100	0.0	0.0
C+ / 3.9	15.2	1.04	31.45	21	1	98	0	1	284	93.3	-21.0	63	12	1,000,000	0	0.0	0.0
C- / 3.9	15.3	1.04	30.85	53	1	98	0	1	284	91.2	-21.1	57	12	1,000	100	0.0	0.0
C- / 3.9	15.2	1.04	22.08	1	1	98	0	1	284	89.3	-21.1	53	12	0	0	0.0	0.0
C- / 3.9	15.2	1.04	33.38	6	1	98	0	1	284	90.1	-21.1	55	12	0	0	0.0	0.0
C / 4.6	10.4	1.02	21.46	149	2	97	0	1	36	90.5	-20.7	57	18	1,000	100	5.8	0.0
C / 4.6	10.5	1.02	20.95	53	2	97	0	1	36	85.7	-20.9	45	18	1,000	100	0.0	0.0
C+ / 6.0	10.4	1.02	35.16	755	2	97	0	1	36	93.0	-20.5	63	18	1,000,000	0	0.0	0.0
C+ / 6.0	10.4	1.02	35.13	826	2	97	0	1	36	91.8	-20.6	60	18	1,000	100	0.0	0.0
C / 4.6	10.5	1.03	21.25	33	2	97	0	1	36	89.0	-20.7	52	18	0	0	0.0	0.0
U /	N/A	N/A	35.17	274	2	97	0	1	36	N/A	N/A	N/A	18	0	0	0.0	0.0
C / 4.6	10.5	1.02	21.66	377	2	97	0	1	36	90.7	-20.7	57	18	0	0	0.0	0.0
B- / 7.0	10.0	0.56	15.62	10	8	91	0	1	129	84.4	-15.8	97	4	1,000	100	5.8	0.0
B- / 7.1	10.0	0.56	15.41	1	8	91	0	1	129	79.8	-16.1	97	4	1,000	100	0.0	0.0
B- / 7.0	10.0	0.55	15.71	17	8	91	0	1	129	87.1	-15.8	98	4	1,000,000	0	0.0	0.0
C / 4.9	14.5	1.00	53.04	200	13	86	0	1	24	63.4	-24.7	64	33	2,500	250	4.8	0.0

Fund Type	Fund Name	Ticker Symbol	Overall Investment Rating	Phone	Performance Rating/Pts	3 Mo	6 Mo	1Yr / Pct	3Yr / Pct	5Yr / Pct	Dividend Yield	Expense Ratio
GI	New Century Alternative Strategies	NCHPX	D+	(888) 639-0102	E+ / 0.8	1.16	0.75	0.44 /17	3.31 / 8	3.56 / 7	1.04	2.25
GI	New Century Balanced	NCIPX	C-	(888) 639-0102	C- / 3.2	1.87	3.26	5.10 /39	8.99 /33	8.21 /31	1.14	2.04
GI	New Century Capital	NCCPX	C	(888) 639-0102	C+ / 5.9	2.97	6.76	9.51 /72	12.98 /60	11.32 /55	0.00	2.00
FO	New Century International	NCFPX	E+	(888) 639-0102	D+ / 2.3	6.99	5.09	2.82 /26	6.96 /21	4.98 /12	1.14	2.33
GL	New Covenant Balanced Growth	NCBGX	C+	(877) 835-4531	C- / 3.8	1.66	4.34	8.44 /66	8.96 /33	8.73 /35	2.78	1.20
BA	New Covenant Balanced Income	NCBIX	C	(877) 835-4531	D / 2.1	1.51	3.44	6.38 /50	5.93 /16	6.39 /19	2.15	1.13
GL	New Covenant Growth	NCGFX	C	(877) 835-4531	C+ / 6.8	1.88	5.48	11.43 /80	13.92 /67	12.31 /63	0.57	1.15
GL	Newfound Risk Managed Glbl Sector	NFGIX	U	(855) 394-9777	U /	0.80	0.89	--	--	--	0.00	N/A
GR	Newmark Risk-Managed	NEWRX	E-	(877) 772-7231	E / 0.5	1.65	11.31	13.36 /88	-2.58 / 3	-9.65 / 0	0.00	2.09
AA	NH 529 Fidelity UNIQUE CIP 100%		C+	(800) 544-8544	C+ / 6.3	3.44	6.05	8.42 /66	13.32 /62	10.91 /52	0.00	1.00
AA	NH 529 Fidelity UNIQUE CIP 70%E		C+	(800) 544-8544	C / 4.6	2.92	5.03	7.18 /57	10.61 /43	9.41 /40	0.00	0.93
AA	NH 529 Fidelity UNIQUE CIP Clg Ptf		C-	(800) 544-8544	D- / 1.2	1.43	2.42	3.65 /30	3.91 /10	4.23 / 9	0.00	0.67
AA	NH 529 Fidelity UNIQUE CIP Csv Ptf		C-	(800) 544-8544	E+ / 0.7	0.80	1.42	2.31 /23	1.62 / 6	2.41 / 5	0.00	0.59
AA	NH 529 Fidelity UNIQUE CIP Idx		B-	(800) 544-8544	C+ / 6.0	2.67	4.64	6.84 /54	13.14 /61	11.53 /57	0.00	0.27
AA	NH 529 Fidelity UNIQUE CIP Idx		C	(800) 544-8544	D- / 1.3	1.23	2.11	3.31 /28	4.46 /11	5.85 /16	0.00	0.32
AA	NH 529 Fidelity UNIQUE CIP Idx		C	(800) 544-8544	D / 2.1	1.54	2.76	4.31 /34	6.35 /18	7.35 /25	0.00	0.31
AA	NH 529 Fidelity UNIQUE CIP Idx		C+	(800) 544-8544	C- / 3.1	1.85	3.34	5.17 /40	8.12 /28	8.61 /34	0.00	0.30
AA	NH 529 Fidelity UNIQUE CIP Idx		C+	(800) 544-8544	C- / 4.0	2.08	3.81	5.83 /45	9.78 /38	9.66 /42	0.00	0.29
AA	NH 529 Fidelity UNIQUE CIP Idx		C+	(800) 544-8544	C / 4.8	2.31	4.19	6.31 /49	11.08 /46	10.41 /48	0.00	0.28
AA	NH 529 Fidelity UNIQUE CIP Idx		C+	(800) 544-8544	C- / 4.2	2.37	4.05	6.07 /47	10.10 /40	9.96 /44	0.00	0.30
AA	NH 529 Fidelity UNIQUE CIP Idx Clg		C	(800) 544-8544	D- / 1.0	1.16	2.05	3.10 /27	3.42 / 9	4.40 /10	0.00	0.33
AA	NH 529 Fidelity UNIQUE CIP Idx Csv		C-	(800) 544-8544	E+ / 0.7	0.70	1.48	2.44 /24	1.26 / 6	2.42 / 5	0.00	0.34
AA	NH 529 Fidelity UNIQUE CIP Ptf		C	(800) 544-8544	D- / 1.5	1.53	2.62	3.96 /32	5.03 /13	5.50 /14	0.00	0.80
AA	NH 529 Fidelity UNIQUE CIP Ptf		C	(800) 544-8544	D+ / 2.5	2.04	3.52	5.27 /41	7.00 /21	6.97 /23	0.00	0.86
AA	NH 529 Fidelity UNIQUE CIP Ptf		C+	(800) 544-8544	C- / 3.5	2.41	4.29	6.23 /48	8.73 /31	8.16 /31	0.00	0.92
AA	NH 529 Fidelity UNIQUE CIP Ptf		C+	(800) 544-8544	C / 4.4	2.70	4.80	6.85 /54	10.27 /41	9.09 /37	0.00	0.97
AA	NH 529 Fidelity UNIQUE CIP Ptf		C+	(800) 544-8544	C / 5.2	2.88	5.19	7.35 /58	11.59 /50	9.84 /43	0.00	0.99
GR	Nicholas	NICSX	A+	(800) 544-6547	A+ / 9.8	4.70	14.01	19.51 /96	21.92 /98	18.41 /98	0.27	0.73
IN	Nicholas Equity Income	NSEIX	A+	(800) 544-6547	A- / 9.0	3.91	9.50	13.13 /87	16.94 /90	14.83 /85	1.98	0.72
GR	Nicholas High Income I	NCINX	D	(800) 544-6547	D / 1.7	2.10	1.73	1.39 /20	5.95 /17	7.46 /26	5.21	0.66
GR	Nicholas High Income N	NNHIX	D	(800) 544-6547	D- / 1.5	1.97	1.43	1.10 /19	5.57 /15	7.07 /23	4.77	1.04
GR	Nicholas II I	NCTWX	B	(800) 544-6547	A- / 9.1	5.54	13.02	15.85 /93	16.15 /84	15.39 /89	0.32	0.62
GR	Nicholas II N	NNTWX	B	(800) 544-6547	B+ / 8.9	5.42	12.81	15.41 /92	15.73 /81	14.98 /87	0.00	0.97
GR	Nicholas Limited Edition I	NCLEX	C+	(800) 544-6547	B- / 7.2	4.76	14.56	9.71 /73	13.66 /65	14.98 /87	0.00	0.86
GR	Nicholas Limited Edition N	NNLEX	C+	(800) 544-6547	C+ / 6.9	4.66	14.33	9.33 /71	13.27 /62	14.59 /83	0.00	1.22
EM	Nile Pan Africa A	NAFAX	D-	(877) 682-3742	E+ / 0.8	-0.68	-6.88	-6.76 / 4	7.07 /22	--	0.00	2.50
EM	Nile Pan Africa C	NAFCX	D-	(877) 682-3742	D- / 1.0	-0.84	-7.27	-7.47 / 4	6.29 /18	--	0.00	3.25
EM	Nile Pan Africa Inst	NAFIX	D-	(877) 682-3742	D- / 1.2	-0.60	-6.79	-6.53 / 4	7.33 /23	--	0.00	2.25
GL	NJ 529 NJBest CSP Age-Based 0-8		B-	(800) 342-5236	C+ / 6.4	4.71	6.67	8.05 /63	13.39 /62	11.51 /57	0.00	1.23
GL	NJ 529 NJBest CSP Age-Based		C+	(800) 342-5236	C- / 3.0	2.68	3.62	5.18 /40	7.93 /27	7.63 /27	0.00	1.05
GL	NJ 529 NJBest CSP Age-Based 17 &		C	(800) 342-5236	D- / 1.5	1.71	2.13	3.92 /31	5.08 /13	5.60 /15	0.00	1.02
GL	NJ 529 NJBest CSP Age-Based 9-12		C+	(800) 342-5236	C / 4.6	3.60	5.09	6.54 /51	10.57 /43	9.55 /41	0.00	1.13
GL	NJ 529 NJBest CSP Corefolio Port		B-	(800) 342-5236	C+ / 6.6	3.23	5.56	7.95 /62	13.84 /66	11.78 /59	0.00	1.10
GL	NJ 529 NJBest CSP Gro & Inc Port		C+	(800) 342-5236	C- / 3.1	2.67	3.62	5.20 /40	7.96 /27	7.65 /27	0.00	1.09
GL	NJ 529 NJBest CSP Growth Port		B-	(800) 342-5236	C+ / 6.4	4.57	6.52	7.90 /62	13.35 /62	11.50 /57	0.00	1.23
IX	NJ 529 NJBest CSP S&P 500 Idx		A+	(800) 342-5236	B / 8.1	0.92	5.81	12.46 /85	15.81 /82	14.21 /80	0.00	0.85
GR	North Country Equity Growth	NCEGX	B	(888) 350-2990	B- / 7.4	2.94	6.39	12.01 /83	14.60 /72	12.43 /64	0.34	1.02
IN	North Star Dividend I	NSDVX	U	(800) 595-7827	U /	0.08	8.70	5.10 /39	--	--	3.22	1.69
SC	North Star Micro Cap I	NSMVX	U	(800) 595-7827	U /	-2.95	5.53	3.01 /26	--	--	0.46	1.52
AA	North Star Opportunity A	NSOPX	C	(800) 595-7827	C- / 3.8	0.52	2.80	7.26 /57	11.66 /50	--	1.26	1.74
AA	North Star Opportunity I	NSOIX	C+	(800) 595-7827	C / 5.5	0.52	2.79	7.18 /57	13.18 /61	--	1.33	1.49
GR	Northeast Investors Growth	NTHFX	D	(800) 225-6704	C+ / 5.8	3.44	7.05	13.50 /88	11.11 /46	9.48 /40	0.00	1.23

99 Pct = Best
0 Pct = Worst

● Denotes fund is closed to new investors
* Denotes fund is included in Section II

Risk Rating/Pts	3 Year Standard Deviation	Beta	NAV As of 3/31/15	Total $(Mil)	Cash %	Stocks %	Bonds %	Other %	Portfolio Turnover Ratio	Last Bull Market Return	Last Bear Market Return	Manager Quality Pct	Manager Tenure (Years)	Initial Purch. $	Additional Purch. $	Front End Load	Back End Load
B /8.8	4.8	0.44	13.10	117	27	46	23	4	29	23.1	-12.7	22	15	1,000	0	0.0	2.0
B- /7.2	7.0	0.69	15.76	73	11	53	30	6	16	49.3	-13.2	40	4	1,000	0	0.0	2.0
C /5.4	9.6	0.98	19.41	117	4	93	2	1	26	77.4	-18.9	32	4	1,000	0	0.0	2.0
C- /3.8	12.0	0.90	13.78	56	6	92	0	2	22	43.2	-25.0	46	15	1,000	0	0.0	2.0
B /8.8	6.2	0.94	102.27	304	9	58	32	1	6	51.1	-11.4	72	N/A	500	100	0.0	0.0
B+ /9.4	3.8	0.65	21.36	81	14	33	52	1	9	31.5	-6.2	53	N/A	500	100	0.0	0.0
C- /4.1	10.3	0.65	38.36	419	3	96	0	1	86	87.0	-19.0	96	4	500	100	0.0	0.0
U /	N/A	N/A	10.07	69	0	0	0	100	0	N/A	N/A	N/A	1	1,000,000	10,000	0.0	1.0
C- /3.3	15.3	1.01	2.46	6	5	94	0	1	233	9.0	-5.0	0	2	1,000	100	0.0	2.0
C+ /6.7	10.2	1.72	18.93	593	4	94	0	2	21	82.8	-23.0	9	10	50	25	0.0	0.0
B /8.1	7.6	1.29	20.46	284	4	67	27	2	24	61.4	-17.3	22	10	50	25	0.0	0.0
B+ /9.6	2.6	0.41	19.88	841	22	21	55	2	20	18.6	-4.4	62	10	50	25	0.0	0.0
B+ /9.9	1.4	0.05	15.05	95	40	0	59	1	15	6.4	0.7	77	10	50	25	0.0	0.0
B- /7.0	10.2	1.71	15.77	162	4	95	0	1	22	80.1	-19.4	9	9	50	25	0.0	0.0
B+ /9.9	3.1	0.49	14.03	163	33	20	45	2	30	23.6	-4.1	57	9	50	25	0.0	0.0
B+ /9.6	4.4	0.74	14.53	199	22	33	43	2	28	34.4	-7.2	44	9	50	25	0.0	0.0
B+ /9.1	5.8	0.98	14.84	207	14	46	39	1	25	45.5	-10.6	33	9	50	25	0.0	0.0
B /8.6	7.1	1.21	15.24	217	9	58	32	1	21	56.4	-13.7	24	9	50	25	0.0	0.0
B /8.1	8.2	1.39	14.16	196	3	70	25	2	16	65.2	-15.8	17	8	50	25	0.0	0.0
B /8.6	7.3	1.24	16.43	117	3	67	28	2	29	56.0	-11.3	23	9	50	25	0.0	0.0
B+ /9.9	2.2	0.34	13.95	90	35	18	45	2	37	15.8	-0.3	65	9	50	25	0.0	0.0
B+ /9.9	1.4	0.01	13.02	50	56	0	43	1	22	3.9	4.4	78	9	50	25	0.0	0.0
B+ /9.6	3.6	0.57	19.94	1,437	22	23	53	2	20	27.5	-9.1	52	10	50	25	0.0	0.0
B+ /9.2	5.0	0.83	19.99	1,686	13	37	48	2	21	39.1	-12.4	40	10	50	25	0.0	0.0
B /8.7	6.3	1.06	19.95	1,297	8	50	40	2	20	50.8	-16.2	30	10	50	25	0.0	0.0
B /8.2	7.5	1.27	17.47	669	5	62	31	2	18	61.3	-19.1	21	10	50	25	0.0	0.0
B- /7.6	8.7	1.47	13.59	294	5	74	19	2	16	70.2	-21.2	15	8	50	25	0.0	0.0
C+ /6.7	10.2	0.98	71.57	3,651	7	92	0	1	25	125.4	-15.7	94	46	500	100	0.0	0.0
B- /7.0	9.4	0.91	20.99	595	11	88	0	1	30	90.4	-15.1	84	22	500	100	0.0	0.0
C+ /6.5	3.9	0.27	9.72	104	10	3	86	1	51	33.5	-6.0	82	12	100,000	100	0.0	0.0
C+ /6.5	3.9	0.27	9.85	6	10	3	86	1	51	31.9	-6.2	80	12	500	100	0.0	0.0
C /5.0	10.3	0.96	27.24	639	4	95	0	1	26	99.0	-19.6	74	22	100,000	100	0.0	0.0
C /5.0	10.3	0.96	26.86	111	4	95	0	1	26	96.6	-19.7	70	22	500	100	0.0	0.0
C /5.3	12.4	1.07	26.85	294	10	89	0	1	32	81.3	-19.0	23	22	100,000	100	0.0	0.0
C /5.2	12.4	1.07	25.81	45	10	89	0	1	32	79.2	-19.1	19	22	500	100	0.0	0.0
C+ /6.1	11.4	0.58	13.24	25	0	99	0	1	113	56.0	-23.8	96	5	1,000	100	5.8	2.0
C+ /6.0	11.4	0.58	12.98	2	0	99	0	1	113	52.2	-24.0	95	5	1,000	100	0.0	2.0
C+ /6.2	11.4	0.58	13.31	7	0	99	0	1	113	57.4	-23.7	96	5	250,000	25,000	0.0	2.0
B- /7.2	10.2	0.68	30.88	133	0	0	0	100	0	79.5	-21.2	96	12	25	25	0.0	0.0
B+ /9.2	5.7	0.87	23.76	148	0	0	0	100	0	41.5	-10.7	69	12	25	25	0.0	0.0
B+ /9.9	3.6	0.56	19.63	101	0	0	0	100	0	25.4	-5.0	69	12	25	25	0.0	0.0
B /8.2	7.9	0.54	27.05	220	0	0	0	100	0	59.1	-15.9	94	12	25	25	0.0	0.0
B- /7.5	10.0	0.67	29.05	57	0	0	0	100	0	83.9	-18.9	96	12	25	25	0.0	0.0
B+ /9.2	5.7	0.39	23.48	45	0	0	0	100	0	41.7	-10.6	92	12	25	25	0.0	0.0
B- /7.2	10.2	0.68	30.86	91	0	0	0	100	0	79.2	-21.0	95	12	25	25	0.0	0.0
B /8.0	9.5	1.00	28.61	83	0	0	0	100	0	98.4	-16.4	64	12	25	25	0.0	0.0
C+ /6.4	9.9	1.00	15.43	119	1	98	0	1	29	88.6	-16.3	47	3	1,000	100	0.0	0.0
U /	N/A	N/A	18.35	51	0	0	0	100	22	N/A	N/A	N/A	2	5,000	500	0.0	2.0
U /	N/A	N/A	27.26	71	0	0	0	100	31	N/A	N/A	N/A	2	5,000	500	0.0	2.0
B- /7.2	10.5	1.70	12.51	N/A	3	89	5	3	53	N/A	N/A	5	4	2,500	500	5.8	2.0
B- /7.3	10.4	1.68	12.49	78	3	89	5	3	53	N/A	N/A	10	4	5,000	500	0.0	2.0
C- /3.3	10.5	0.98	17.15	64	0	100	0	0	82	71.2	-20.1	15	35	1,000	0	0.0	0.0

Fund Type	Fund Name	Ticker Symbol	Overall Investment Rating	Phone	Performance Rating/Pts	3 Mo	6 Mo	1Yr / Pct	3Yr / Pct	5Yr / Pct	Dividend Yield	Expense Ratio
								Total Return % through 3/31/15	Annualized		Incl. in Returns	
EM	Northern Emerg Mkts Eq Idx	NOEMX	U	(800) 595-9111	U /	2.36	-2.70	--	--	1.22 / 4	2.67	0.34
GR	Northern Funds Large Cap Equity	NOGEX	B+	(800) 595-9111	B- / 7.3	1.94	6.81	12.02 /83	14.46 /71	13.08 /69	0.88	0.95
EM	Northern Glbl Sustainability Index	NSRIX	C	(800) 595-9111	C / 5.0	2.67	3.38	5.82 /45	12.32 /55	9.76 /43	2.16	0.40
RE	Northern Global Real Estate Index	NGREX	C	(800) 595-9111	C+ / 5.8	4.01	10.82	13.82 /89	11.00 /45	10.26 /47	2.51	0.53
BA	Northern Global Tactical Asset Allo	BBALX	C-	(800) 637-1380	D / 2.2	1.69	2.02	2.51 /24	6.97 /21	7.39 /26	1.74	0.87
CV	Northern Income Equity	NOIEX	D	(800) 595-9111	C+ / 6.0	1.84	6.18	9.40 /71	12.69 /57	11.78 /59	3.39	1.10
FO	Northern Intl Eqty Index	NOINX	D	(800) 595-9111	D+ / 2.7	5.37	0.98	-1.29 /12	8.74 /31	5.93 /16	3.83	0.31
FO	Northern Intl Equity	NOIGX	D-	(800) 595-9111	D+ / 2.3	4.80	0.28	-2.91 / 9	8.31 /29	5.69 /15	3.77	1.17
GR	Northern Large Cap Core	NOLCX	A+	(800) 595-9111	B+ / 8.4	0.38	4.54	10.81 /78	16.81 /89	14.82 /85	1.29	1.24
GR	Northern Large Cap Value	NOLVX	B+	(800) 595-9111	B- / 7.4	0.50	5.68	10.39 /76	15.06 /75	10.71 /50	2.56	1.05
MC	Northern Midcap Index	NOMIX	A	(800) 595-9111	A- / 9.1	5.25	11.91	11.98 /82	16.82 /89	15.45 /90	1.10	0.18
OT	Northern Mlt-Mgr Glb Listed Infra	NMFIX	U	(800) 595-9111	U /	-0.57	-3.00	0.64 /17	--	--	1.82	1.04
EM	Northern Multi Mgr Emg Mkts Eqty	NMMEX	E+	(800) 595-9111	E / 0.4	1.11	-4.61	-2.80 / 9	0.38 / 5	2.85 / 6	1.07	1.41
RE	Northern Multi Mgr Glbl Rl Estate	NMMGX	D	(800) 595-9111	C / 5.4	3.96	11.63	12.76 /86	10.22 /41	9.89 /44	1.68	1.19
FO	Northern Multi Mgr Intl Equity Fd	NMIEX	D-	(800) 595-9111	D- / 1.3	3.57	-0.63	-2.27 /10	5.94 /17	4.22 / 9	2.17	1.25
GI	Northern Multi Mgr Large Cap	NMMLX	C-	(800) 595-9111	C+ / 6.4	1.40	4.88	10.08 /75	13.59 /64	12.97 /68	0.78	0.94
MC	Northern Multi Mgr Mid Cap	NMMCX	C	(800) 595-9111	B- / 7.5	3.85	9.44	9.20 /70	14.85 /74	13.92 /77	0.38	1.05
SC	Northern Multi Mgr Small Cap	NMMSX	D+	(800) 595-9111	B / 7.7	3.29	12.28	7.11 /56	15.19 /76	13.62 /74	0.09	1.17
SC	Northern Small Cap Core	NSGRX	A-	(800) 595-9111	A / 9.3	4.75	15.00	10.33 /76	17.46 /92	15.83 /92	0.49	0.86
SC	Northern Small Cap Index	NSIDX	B+	(800) 595-9111	B+ / 8.6	4.28	14.40	8.02 /63	16.14 /84	14.32 /81	1.02	0.19
SC	Northern Small Cap Value	NOSGX	B+	(800) 595-9111	B / 7.9	2.32	13.37	7.79 /61	15.45 /77	14.20 /80	0.86	1.26
* IX	Northern Stock Index	NOSIX	A	(800) 595-9111	B / 8.2	0.93	5.86	12.59 /85	15.98 /83	14.29 /80	1.78	0.12
TC	Northern Technology	NTCHX	C	(800) 595-9111	C+ / 6.5	3.18	11.26	15.54 /93	11.50 /49	14.33 /81	0.00	1.35
GR	NorthQuest Capital	NQCFX	C	(800) 698-5261	C / 4.3	-0.89	7.79	6.55 /51	10.15 /40	8.01 /30	0.00	1.79
GR	Nuance Concentrated Value Inst	NCVLX	C+	(855) 682-6233	C+ / 6.7	0.81	1.99	2.65 /25	15.46 /79	--	1.02	1.17
GR	Nuance Concentrated Value Inv	NCAVX	U	(855) 682-6233	U /	0.74	1.86	2.34 /23	--	--	0.75	1.47
MC	Nuance Mid Cap Value Institutional	NMVLX	U	(855) 682-6233	U /	1.51	4.34	4.57 /36	--	--	1.06	1.50
GR	Nuveen Concentrated Core A	NCADX	U	(800) 257-8787	U /	0.82	8.41	17.20 /95	--	--	0.06	1.85
GR	Nuveen Concentrated Core I	NCAFX	U	(800) 257-8787	U /	0.89	8.56	17.49 /95	--	--	0.29	1.71
IN	Nuveen Dividend Value A	FFEIX	C-	(800) 257-8787	C / 4.7	-0.62	2.69	6.14 /48	13.24 /61	12.66 /65	2.01	1.15
IN	Nuveen Dividend Value C	FFECX	C	(800) 257-8787	C / 5.1	-0.88	2.28	5.35 /41	12.40 /55	11.82 /59	1.40	1.90
IN	Nuveen Dividend Value I	FAQIX	C+	(800) 257-8787	C+ / 5.9	-0.61	2.81	6.43 /50	13.52 /64	12.95 /68	2.36	0.90
IN	Nuveen Dividend Value R3	FEISX	C	(800) 257-8787	C / 5.5	-0.68	2.57	5.95 /46	12.96 /59	12.40 /63	1.88	1.40
IN	Nuveen Dividend Value R6	FFEFX	U	(800) 257-8787	U /	-0.55	2.93	6.55 /51	--	--	2.36	0.81
IX	Nuveen Equity Index A	FAEIX	B+	(800) 257-8787	B / 7.7	0.81	5.64	12.09 /83	15.41 /78	13.77 /76	1.32	0.73
IX	Nuveen Equity Index C	FCEIX	B	(800) 257-8787	B- / 7.1	0.62	5.23	11.23 /79	14.55 /71	12.92 /67	0.61	1.48
IX	Nuveen Equity Index I	FEIIX	B+	(800) 257-8787	B / 7.9	0.87	5.74	12.33 /84	15.68 /81	14.05 /78	1.56	0.48
IX	Nuveen Equity Index R3	FADSX	B	(800) 257-8787	B- / 7.5	0.74	5.47	11.77 /82	15.11 /76	13.49 /73	1.09	0.98
GR	Nuveen Equity Long/Short A	NELAX	C	(800) 257-8787	C- / 3.6	-1.61	5.81	8.41 /66	10.47 /42	9.71 /42	0.00	4.24
GR	Nuveen Equity Long/Short C	NELCX	C	(800) 257-8787	C- / 4.0	-1.79	5.41	7.61 /60	9.63 /37	8.88 /36	0.00	5.04
GR	Nuveen Equity Long/Short I	NELIX	C+	(800) 257-8787	C / 4.7	-1.55	5.95	8.68 /67	10.75 /44	9.99 /44	0.00	4.20
GR	Nuveen Equity Market Neutral I	NIMEX	U	(800) 257-8787	U /	-2.55	0.05	1.09 /19	--	--	0.00	3.37
GL	Nuveen Global Growth A	NGGAX	C-	(800) 257-8787	C / 5.3	5.74	7.53	2.22 /23	13.73 /65	12.52 /64	0.00	2.47
GL	Nuveen Global Growth C	NGGCX	C-	(800) 257-8787	C+ / 5.7	5.55	7.15	1.49 /20	12.90 /59	11.68 /58	0.00	3.26
GL	Nuveen Global Growth I	NGWIX	C	(800) 257-8787	C+ / 6.5	5.83	7.69	2.48 /24	14.03 /67	12.80 /66	0.00	2.54
GL	Nuveen Global Growth R3	NGGRX	C-	(800) 257-8787	C+ / 6.1	5.68	7.40	1.99 /22	13.46 /63	12.27 /62	0.00	3.11
GL	Nuveen Global Infrastructure A	FGIAX	C-	(800) 257-8787	C / 4.7	0.56	2.64	8.36 /65	12.68 /57	11.40 /56	1.28	1.43
GL	Nuveen Global Infrastructure C	FGNCX	C	(800) 257-8787	C / 5.1	0.37	2.17	7.62 /60	11.83 /51	10.57 /49	0.53	2.18
GL	Nuveen Global Infrastructure I	FGIYX	C	(800) 257-8787	C+ / 5.8	0.56	2.72	8.60 /67	12.95 /59	11.67 /58	1.84	1.18
GL	Nuveen Global Infrastructure R3	FGNRX	C	(800) 257-8787	C / 5.4	0.46	2.46	8.09 /64	12.39 /55	11.02 /53	1.01	1.67
AA	Nuveen Gresham Divsfd Comm Str I	NGVIX	U	(800) 257-8787	U /	-5.93	-18.15	-25.73 / 0	--	--	0.00	1.83
MC	Nuveen Growth A	NSAGX	C+	(800) 257-8787	C+ / 6.9	1.87	8.88	16.18 /94	14.76 /73	13.34 /71	0.00	1.45

● Denotes fund is closed to new investors
* Denotes fund is included in Section II

www.thestreetratings.com

RISK			NET ASSETS		ASSET					BULL / BEAR		FUND MANAGER		MINIMUMS		LOADS	
	3 Year		NAV						Portfolio	Last Bull	Last Bear	Manager	Manager	Initial	Additional	Front	Back
Risk Rating/Pts	Standard Deviation	Beta	As of 3/31/15	Total $(Mil)	Cash %	Stocks %	Bonds %	Other %	Turnover Ratio	Market Return	Market Return	Quality Pct	Tenure (Years)	Purch. $	Purch. $	End Load	End Load
U /	13.9	1.01	10.86	1,711	4	95	0	1	32	22.5	-27.2	N/A	8	2,500	50	0.0	2.0
B- / 7.0	10.5	1.07	22.28	146	1	98	0	1	33	97.0	-19.4	31	4	2,500	50	0.0	0.0
C+ / 6.6	10.6	0.62	12.29	220	2	97	0	1	12	71.4	-19.3	99	7	2,500	50	0.0	2.0
C / 5.2	12.4	0.90	10.41	1,783	13	86	0	1	9	67.1	-20.7	45	7	2,500	50	0.0	2.0
B / 8.3	6.8	1.09	12.20	79	3	54	42	1	24	41.4	-11.2	13	4	2,500	50	0.0	0.0
D+ / 2.8	8.6	0.99	12.74	332	1	98	0	1	14	72.4	-15.3	57	8	2,500	50	0.0	0.0
C / 5.5	13.4	1.01	11.78	4,239	2	97	0	1	41	51.4	-23.6	56	8	2,500	50	0.0	2.0
C / 5.2	14.2	1.06	9.39	212	1	98	0	1	16	53.4	-26.1	43	4	2,500	50	0.0	2.0
B- / 7.5	10.2	1.06	15.42	170	2	97	0	1	95	104.2	-15.5	64	4	2,500	50	0.0	0.0
B- / 7.2	11.0	1.12	13.99	105	2	97	0	1	24	98.9	-25.5	29	11	2,500	50	0.0	0.0
C+ / 6.5	11.0	1.00	18.43	1,670	3	96	0	1	13	101.7	-22.7	65	9	2,500	50	0.0	0.0
U /	N/A	N/A	12.22	1,409	19	80	0	1	53	N/A	N/A	N/A	3	2,500	50	0.0	2.0
C / 5.3	13.7	0.99	18.25	1,326	3	96	0	1	55	25.8	-25.5	63	7	2,500	50	0.0	2.0
C- / 3.4	12.0	0.87	16.66	773	11	88	0	1	49	62.6	-20.0	40	6	2,500	50	0.0	2.0
C+ / 6.0	12.3	0.92	10.44	1,921	5	93	0	2	39	39.8	-23.3	30	9	2,500	50	0.0	2.0
C- / 3.9	9.7	0.98	9.26	520	5	94	0	1	43	86.4	-17.5	38	8	2,500	50	0.0	0.0
C- / 3.5	11.0	0.97	12.96	813	3	96	0	1	73	92.1	-22.5	45	9	2,500	50	0.0	0.0
D / 1.8	12.7	0.92	10.06	304	3	96	0	1	42	91.4	-24.0	70	5	2,500	50	0.0	0.0
C+ / 5.9	12.7	0.94	22.26	279	4	95	0	1	6	105.0	-23.8	84	5	2,500	50	0.0	0.0
C+ / 5.8	13.5	1.00	12.67	1,054	3	96	0	1	16	99.5	-25.1	65	9	2,500	50	0.0	0.0
C+ / 6.3	13.2	0.96	21.61	3,005	4	95	0	1	21	95.5	-21.4	66	14	2,500	50	0.0	0.0
B- / 7.3	9.6	1.00	25.41	6,969	3	96	0	1	8	99.4	-16.3	65	9	2,500	50	0.0	0.0
C / 4.9	14.5	1.20	23.72	84	3	96	0	1	35	81.0	-18.9	4	11	2,500	50	0.0	0.0
B- / 7.4	9.8	0.94	15.67	3	3	96	0	1	0	66.3	-16.9	14	13	1,000	100	0.0	0.0
C+ / 6.3	10.6	1.00	13.06	397	9	90	0	1	103	88.2	N/A	60	4	1,000,000	100	0.0	0.0
U /	N/A	N/A	13.04	173	9	90	0	1	103	N/A	N/A	N/A	4	2,500	100	5.8	0.0
U /	N/A	N/A	10.26	26	4	95	0	1	0	N/A	N/A	N/A	4	1,000,000	100	0.0	0.0
U /	N/A	N/A	28.27	48	0	99	0	1	88	N/A	N/A	N/A	2	3,000	100	5.8	0.0
U /	N/A	N/A	28.30	60	0	99	0	1	88	N/A	N/A	N/A	2	100,000	0	0.0	0.0
C+ / 6.1	10.1	1.02	16.33	351	1	98	0	1	27	84.5	-17.0	27	21	3,000	100	5.8	0.0
C+ / 6.1	10.1	1.02	16.12	62	1	98	0	1	27	79.7	-17.2	19	21	3,000	100	0.0	0.0
C+ / 6.1	10.1	1.02	16.48	1,101	1	98	0	1	27	86.0	-16.9	30	21	100,000	0	0.0	0.0
C+ / 6.1	10.1	1.02	16.30	48	1	98	0	1	27	83.0	-17.1	24	21	0	0	0.0	0.0
U /	N/A	N/A	16.51	60	1	98	0	1	27	N/A	N/A	N/A	21	5,000,000	0	0.0	0.0
C+ / 6.8	9.5	1.00	28.18	205	4	94	0	2	2	96.1	-16.5	59	16	3,000	100	0.0	0.0
C+ / 6.8	9.5	1.00	27.86	16	4	94	0	2	2	91.1	-16.7	47	16	3,000	100	0.0	0.0
C+ / 6.8	9.5	1.00	28.16	520	4	94	0	2	2	97.8	-16.4	63	16	100,000	0	0.0	0.0
C+ / 6.3	9.5	1.00	28.19	100	4	94	0	2	2	94.5	-16.6	55	16	0	0	0.0	0.0
B- / 7.5	10.5	0.99	33.06	21	34	65	0	1	232	74.9	-17.5	11	2	3,000	100	5.8	0.0
B- / 7.5	10.5	0.98	31.32	6	34	65	0	1	232	70.4	-17.8	8	2	3,000	100	0.0	0.0
B- / 7.5	10.5	0.99	33.61	47	34	65	0	1	232	76.4	-17.5	13	2	100,000	0	0.0	0.0
U /	N/A	N/A	21.39	35	99	0	0	1	187	N/A	N/A	N/A	2	100,000	0	0.0	0.0
C / 4.8	12.8	0.77	33.87	4	1	98	0	1	217	77.4	-21.5	95	6	3,000	100	5.8	0.0
C / 4.7	12.8	0.77	32.12	1	1	98	0	1	217	73.0	-21.7	94	6	3,000	100	0.0	0.0
C / 4.8	12.8	0.77	34.48	6	1	98	0	1	217	78.9	-21.4	95	6	100,000	0	0.0	0.0
C / 4.8	12.8	0.77	33.28	1	1	98	0	1	217	75.9	-21.6	95	6	0	0	0.0	0.0
C+ / 5.9	9.5	0.58	10.85	288	11	88	0	1	162	66.0	-15.5	96	8	3,000	100	5.8	0.0
C+ / 6.0	9.5	0.58	10.75	25	11	88	0	1	162	61.7	-15.7	95	8	3,000	100	0.0	0.0
C+ / 5.9	9.5	0.58	10.83	382	11	88	0	1	162	67.6	-15.5	96	8	100,000	0	0.0	0.0
C+ / 6.0	9.5	0.58	11.00	1	11	88	0	1	162	64.7	-16.0	96	8	0	0	0.0	0.0
U /	N/A	N/A	13.80	112	21	0	78	1	0	N/A	N/A	N/A	3	100,000	0	0.0	0.0
C+ / 6.4	10.7	0.85	29.92	9	1	98	0	1	41	92.4	-16.5	71	5	3,000	100	5.8	0.0

					PERFORMANCE							
	99 Pct = Best					Total Return % through 3/31/15					Incl. in Returns	
	0 Pct = Worst			Overall	Perfor-				Annualized			
Fund		Ticker	Investment		mance						Dividend	Expense
Type	Fund Name	Symbol	Rating	Phone	Rating/Pts	3 Mo	6 Mo	1Yr / Pct	3Yr / Pct	5Yr / Pct	Yield	Ratio
MC	Nuveen Growth C	NSRCX	B-	(800) 257-8787	B- / 7.3	1.68	8.47	15.27 /92	13.92 /67	12.49 /64	0.00	2.21
MC	Nuveen Growth I	NSRGX	B+	(800) 257-8787	B / 8.2	1.95	9.01	16.46 /94	15.05 /75	13.63 /74	0.00	1.20
MC	Nuveen Growth R3	NBGRX	B+	(800) 257-8787	B / 7.8	1.82	8.75	15.88 /93	14.49 /71	13.03 /68	0.00	1.70
FO	Nuveen International Growth A	NBQAX	D+	(800) 257-8787	C / 4.3	4.99	3.21	-3.26 / 8	13.15 /61	10.31 /47	0.00	1.52
FO	Nuveen International Growth C	NBQCX	D+	(800) 257-8787	C / 4.7	4.80	2.83	-3.95 / 7	12.34 /55	9.50 /41	0.00	2.28
FO	Nuveen International Growth I	NBQIX	C-	(800) 257-8787	C / 5.4	5.04	3.33	-3.01 / 9	13.42 /63	10.57 /49	0.20	1.27
FO	Nuveen International Growth R3	NBQBX	C-	(800) 257-8787	C / 5.0	4.92	3.07	-3.47 / 8	12.85 /58	10.01 /45	0.00	1.79
GR	Nuveen Large Cap Core A	NLACX	U	(800) 257-8787	U /	1.48	7.38	15.69 /93	--	--	0.08	1.26
GR	Nuveen Large Cap Core C	NLCDX	U	(800) 257-8787	U /	1.31	6.98	14.84 /91	--	--	0.00	1.99
GR	Nuveen Large Cap Core I	NLCIX	U	(800) 257-8787	U /	1.56	7.53	15.99 /93	--	--	0.31	1.01
GR	Nuveen Large Cap Core Plus I	NLPIX	U	(800) 257-8787	U /	0.30	7.35	14.46 /90	--	--	0.11	2.33
GR	Nuveen Large Cap Growth A	NLAGX	U	(800) 257-8787	U /	3.84	9.56	18.44 /96	--	--	0.10	1.35
GR	Nuveen Large Cap Growth I	NLIGX	U	(800) 257-8787	U /	3.92	9.72	18.75 /96	--	--	0.33	1.10
GR	Nuveen Large Cap Growth Opps A	FRGWX	D	(800) 257-8787	C+ / 6.2	4.79	9.74	14.36 /90	13.00 /60	14.37 /81	0.00	1.25
GR	Nuveen Large Cap Growth Opps C	FAWCX	D	(800) 257-8787	C+ / 6.6	4.60	9.31	13.47 /88	12.16 /54	13.52 /73	0.00	2.00
GR	Nuveen Large Cap Growth Opps I	FIGWX	C-	(800) 257-8787	B- / 7.4	4.86	9.85	14.61 /91	13.27 /62	14.65 /84	0.00	1.00
GR	Nuveen Large Cap Growth Opps R3	FLCYX	D+	(800) 257-8787	B- / 7.0	4.75	9.59	14.06 /90	12.73 /58	14.08 /78	0.00	1.50
GR	Nuveen Large Cap Select A	FLRAX	B+	(800) 257-8787	B- / 7.4	2.23	7.84	13.15 /87	16.14 /84	13.03 /68	0.34	1.31
GR	Nuveen Large Cap Select C	FLYCX	B+	(800) 257-8787	B / 7.8	2.06	7.41	12.27 /84	15.27 /77	12.19 /62	0.00	2.07
GR	Nuveen Large Cap Select I	FLRYX	A+	(800) 257-8787	B+ / 8.7	2.31	7.98	13.43 /88	16.43 /86	13.32 /71	0.59	1.06
GR	Nuveen Large Cap Value A	NNGAX	C+	(800) 257-8787	B- / 7.4	-0.04	5.19	10.95 /78	16.86 /89	13.34 /71	0.71	1.11
GR	Nuveen Large Cap Value C	NNGCX	B-	(800) 257-8787	B / 7.8	-0.20	4.80	10.12 /75	15.98 /83	12.50 /64	0.05	1.86
GR	Nuveen Large Cap Value I	NNGRX	B	(800) 257-8787	B+ / 8.6	0.04	5.34	11.21 /79	17.15 /91	13.64 /74	0.98	0.86
GR	Nuveen Large Cap Value R3	NMMTX	B	(800) 257-8787	B / 8.2	-0.12	4.93	10.52 /76	16.51 /87	13.03 /68	0.51	1.36
MC	Nuveen Mid Cap Growth Opps A	FRSLX	D+	(800) 257-8787	B- / 7.2	5.68	11.47	12.56 /85	15.26 /77	16.05 /93	0.00	1.30
MC	Nuveen Mid Cap Growth Opps C	FMECX	D	(800) 257-8787	B / 7.7	5.52	11.08	11.72 /81	14.40 /70	15.18 /88	0.00	2.05
MC	Nuveen Mid Cap Growth Opps I	FISGX	C	(800) 257-8787	B+ / 8.5	5.77	11.61	12.85 /86	15.55 /80	16.34 /94	0.00	1.05
MC	Nuveen Mid Cap Growth Opps R3	FMEYX	C-	(800) 257-8787	B / 8.2	5.64	11.34	12.29 /84	14.98 /75	15.76 /92	0.00	1.55
MC	Nuveen Mid Cap Growth Opps R6	FMEFX	U	(800) 257-8787	U /	5.80	11.69	13.01 /87	--	--	0.00	0.92
MC	Nuveen Mid Cap Index A	FDXAX	A-	(800) 257-8787	B+ / 8.7	5.06	11.55	11.36 /80	16.22 /85	14.99 /87	0.80	0.81
MC	Nuveen Mid Cap Index C	FDXCX	B+	(800) 257-8787	B / 8.2	4.89	11.11	10.54 /76	15.35 /78	14.12 /79	0.12	1.56
MC	Nuveen Mid Cap Index I	FIMEX	A	(800) 257-8787	B+ / 8.9	5.16	11.66	11.66 /81	16.53 /87	15.28 /89	1.03	0.56
MC	Nuveen Mid Cap Index R3	FMCYX	A-	(800) 257-8787	B+ / 8.6	5.01	11.43	11.11 /79	15.93 /83	14.70 /84	0.57	1.06
MC	Nuveen Mid Cap Value A	FASEX	C+	(800) 257-8787	C+ / 6.8	2.53	7.26	9.66 /73	15.66 /81	12.09 /61	0.77	1.42
MC	Nuveen Mid Cap Value C	FACSX	B	(800) 257-8787	B- / 7.2	2.33	6.88	8.83 /68	14.79 /73	11.25 /55	0.12	2.17
MC	Nuveen Mid Cap Value I	FSEIX	B+	(800) 257-8787	B / 8.1	2.58	7.40	9.93 /74	15.94 /83	12.35 /63	1.05	1.17
MC	Nuveen Mid Cap Value R3	FMVSX	B+	(800) 257-8787	B / 7.6	2.45	7.14	9.38 /71	15.36 /78	11.81 /59	0.58	1.67
IN	Nuveen NWQ Global Equity Income	NQGAX	D+	(800) 257-8787	C- / 4.1	3.02	4.26	4.03 /32	11.88 /52	10.31 /47	1.93	4.95
IN	Nuveen NWQ Global Equity Income	NQGCX	D+	(800) 257-8787	C / 4.5	2.83	3.88	3.26 /28	11.05 /46	9.48 /40	1.31	5.70
IN	Nuveen NWQ Global Equity Income I	NQGIX	C-	(800) 257-8787	C / 5.3	3.08	4.39	4.29 /34	12.17 /54	10.59 /49	2.28	4.88
GR	Nuveen NWQ Large Cap Value A	NQCAX	E	(800) 257-8787	C- / 3.1	0.24	2.05	5.06 /39	10.29 /41	8.82 /35	1.62	1.08
GR	Nuveen NWQ Large Cap Value C	NQCCX	E	(800) 257-8787	C- / 3.6	0.09	1.71	4.34 /34	9.49 /36	8.02 /30	0.93	1.83
GR	Nuveen NWQ Large Cap Value I	NQCRX	E	(800) 257-8787	C / 4.3	0.32	2.25	5.40 /42	10.61 /43	9.11 /38	1.92	0.83
GR	Nuveen NWQ Large Cap Value R3	NQCQX	E	(800) 257-8787	C- / 3.9	0.16	1.94	4.82 /37	10.03 /39	8.55 /33	1.42	1.33
GI	Nuveen NWQ Multi-Cap Value A	NQVAX	D	(800) 257-8787	D+ / 2.7	1.85	1.58	0.61 /17	10.00 /39	10.11 /46	0.64	1.28
GI	Nuveen NWQ Multi-Cap Value C	NQVCX	D+	(800) 257-8787	C- / 3.1	1.66	1.20	-0.16 /15	9.18 /34	9.29 /39	0.00	2.03
GI	Nuveen NWQ Multi-Cap Value I	NQVRX	C-	(800) 257-8787	C- / 3.8	1.92	1.68	0.86 /18	10.28 /41	10.39 /48	0.93	1.03
GI	Nuveen NWQ Multi-Cap Value R3	NMCTX	D+	(800) 257-8787	C- / 3.4	1.78	1.46	0.35 /17	9.72 /38	9.84 /43	0.43	1.53
SC	Nuveen NWQ Sm and MidCap VL A	NSMAX	D+	(800) 257-8787	C- / 4.0	1.91	4.81	-0.24 /15	12.35 /55	13.93 /77	0.00	1.31
SC	Nuveen NWQ Sm and MidCap VL C	NSMCX	C-	(800) 257-8787	C / 4.4	1.73	4.43	-0.97 /13	11.51 /49	13.08 /69	0.00	2.05
SC	Nuveen NWQ Sm and MidCap VL I	NSMRX	C-	(800) 257-8787	C / 5.1	1.96	4.96	--	12.64 /57	14.21 /80	0.00	1.05
MC	Nuveen NWQ Sm and MidCap VL R3	NWQRX	C-	(800) 257-8787	C / 4.8	1.87	4.73	-0.45 /14	12.07 /53	13.65 /74	0.00	1.56

● Denotes fund is closed to new investors
* Denotes fund is included in Section II

www.thestreetratings.com

RISK			NET ASSETS		ASSET					BULL / BEAR		FUND MANAGER		MINIMUMS		LOADS	
	3 Year		NAV						Portfolio	Last Bull	Last Bear	Manager	Manager	Initial	Additional	Front	Back
Risk	Standard		As of	Total	Cash	Stocks	Bonds	Other	Turnover	Market	Market	Quality	Tenure	Purch.	Purch.	End	End
Rating/Pts	Deviation	Beta	3/31/15	$(Mil)	%	%	%	%	Ratio	Return	Return	Pct	(Years)	$	$	Load	Load
C+ / 6.2	10.7	0.85	27.85	10	1	98	0	1	41	87.8	-16.7	62	5	3,000	100	0.0	0.0
C+ / 6.4	10.7	0.85	30.36	36	1	98	0	1	41	94.2	-16.4	74	5	100,000	0	0.0	0.0
C+ / 6.3	10.7	0.85	29.71	N/A	1	98	0	1	41	91.0	-16.6	68	5	0	0	0.0	0.0
C / 5.1	12.3	0.82	39.38	75	1	98	0	1	326	66.0	-25.4	93	6	3,000	100	5.8	0.0
C / 5.0	12.3	0.82	37.99	15	1	98	0	1	326	61.9	-25.6	92	6	3,000	100	0.0	0.0
C / 5.1	12.3	0.82	39.60	249	1	98	0	1	326	67.4	-25.3	94	6	100,000	0	0.0	0.0
C / 5.1	12.3	0.82	39.04	N/A	1	98	0	1	326	64.5	-25.5	93	6	0	0	0.0	0.0
U /	N/A	N/A	27.35	29	0	99	0	1	122	N/A	N/A	N/A	2	3,000	100	5.8	0.0
U /	N/A	N/A	27.09	31	0	99	0	1	122	N/A	N/A	N/A	2	3,000	100	0.0	0.0
U /	N/A	N/A	27.37	157	0	99	0	1	122	N/A	N/A	N/A	2	100,000	0	0.0	0.0
U /	N/A	N/A	26.75	93	0	99	0	1	152	N/A	N/A	N/A	2	100,000	0	0.0	0.0
U /	N/A	N/A	27.05	28	0	99	0	1	145	N/A	N/A	N/A	2	3,000	100	5.8	0.0
U /	N/A	N/A	27.07	50	0	99	0	1	145	N/A	N/A	N/A	2	100,000	0	0.0	0.0
D+ / 2.5	11.9	1.07	36.08	133	0	100	0	0	66	80.0	-15.3	18	13	3,000	100	5.8	0.0
D / 1.6	11.9	1.07	31.14	14	0	100	0	0	66	75.5	-15.6	13	13	3,000	100	0.0	0.0
D+ / 2.9	11.9	1.07	38.59	321	0	100	0	0	66	81.6	-15.2	20	13	100,000	0	0.0	0.0
D+ / 2.3	11.9	1.06	34.82	9	0	100	0	0	66	78.5	-15.4	17	13	0	0	0.0	0.0
B- / 7.0	10.6	1.07	21.07	7	2	97	0	1	154	105.8	-23.3	53	12	3,000	100	5.8	0.0
B- / 7.0	10.6	1.06	19.85	1	2	97	0	1	154	100.6	-23.5	42	12	3,000	100	0.0	0.0
B- / 7.0	10.6	1.06	21.22	38	2	97	0	1	154	107.8	-23.2	57	12	100,000	0	0.0	0.0
C / 5.4	11.3	1.16	25.53	295	0	99	0	1	153	104.3	-19.6	41	2	3,000	100	5.8	0.0
C / 5.4	11.4	1.16	24.55	34	0	99	0	1	153	99.1	-19.8	30	2	3,000	100	0.0	0.0
C / 5.3	11.4	1.16	25.67	132	0	99	0	1	153	106.1	-19.5	44	2	100,000	0	0.0	0.0
C / 5.4	11.4	1.16	25.69	N/A	0	99	0	1	153	102.3	-19.7	36	2	0	0	0.0	0.0
D / 2.0	12.6	1.02	42.98	393	0	99	0	1	106	89.2	-20.5	39	10	3,000	100	5.8	0.0
E+ / 0.9	12.6	1.02	35.36	25	0	99	0	1	106	84.3	-20.7	29	10	3,000	100	0.0	0.0
D+ / 2.7	12.6	1.02	49.11	808	0	99	0	1	106	90.8	-20.4	42	10	100,000	0	0.0	0.0
D / 1.7	12.6	1.02	41.02	71	0	99	0	1	106	87.5	-20.6	35	10	0	0	0.0	0.0
U /	N/A	N/A	49.27	35	0	99	0	1	106	N/A	N/A	N/A	10	5,000,000	0	0.0	0.0
C+ / 6.4	11.0	1.00	18.91	227	1	97	0	2	10	98.3	-22.7	57	14	3,000	100	0.0	0.0
C+ / 6.4	11.0	1.00	18.22	17	1	97	0	2	10	93.3	-22.9	46	14	3,000	100	0.0	0.0
C+ / 6.4	11.0	1.00	18.96	221	1	97	0	2	10	99.9	-22.6	61	14	100,000	0	0.0	0.0
C+ / 6.4	11.0	1.00	18.67	241	1	97	0	2	10	96.5	-22.7	53	14	0	0	0.0	0.0
C+ / 6.4	12.0	1.04	36.52	40	1	98	0	1	127	93.4	-24.2	39	3	3,000	100	5.8	0.0
C+ / 6.4	12.0	1.04	35.10	8	1	98	0	1	127	88.6	-24.4	30	3	3,000	100	0.0	0.0
C+ / 6.4	12.0	1.04	36.60	76	1	98	0	1	127	95.0	-24.1	43	3	100,000	0	0.0	0.0
C+ / 6.4	12.0	1.04	36.34	8	1	98	0	1	127	91.7	-24.3	36	3	0	0	0.0	0.0
C / 5.1	11.7	1.13	26.65	1	0	97	0	3	49	74.5	-20.3	7	2	3,000	100	5.8	0.0
C / 5.1	11.6	1.13	26.63	N/A	0	97	0	3	49	70.1	-20.6	5	2	3,000	100	0.0	0.0
C / 5.1	11.7	1.14	26.66	1	0	97	0	3	49	76.1	-20.3	8	2	100,000	0	0.0	0.0
D- / 1.3	12.0	1.14	12.35	16	0	100	0	0	45	68.3	-22.8	4	9	3,000	100	5.8	0.0
D- / 1.3	11.9	1.13	11.71	9	0	100	0	0	45	64.2	-23.0	3	9	3,000	100	0.0	0.0
D- / 1.3	11.9	1.13	12.38	201	0	100	0	0	45	69.9	-22.7	5	9	100,000	0	0.0	0.0
D- / 1.3	12.0	1.14	12.29	N/A	0	100	0	0	45	67.0	-22.8	4	9	0	0	0.0	0.0
C+ / 6.3	12.0	1.09	25.93	35	0	99	0	1	37	70.1	-23.8	5	18	3,000	100	5.8	0.0
C+ / 6.3	12.0	1.09	24.48	39	0	99	0	1	37	65.8	-24.0	4	18	3,000	100	0.0	0.0
C+ / 6.3	12.0	1.09	26.06	57	0	99	0	1	37	71.5	-23.7	5	18	100,000	0	0.0	0.0
C+ / 6.3	12.0	1.09	25.67	N/A	0	99	0	1	37	68.7	-23.9	4	18	0	0	0.0	0.0
C / 5.5	13.4	0.90	29.41	11	1	98	0	1	48	77.7	-23.0	37	9	3,000	100	5.8	0.0
C / 5.4	13.4	0.91	27.61	3	1	98	0	1	48	73.1	-23.3	28	9	3,000	100	0.0	0.0
C / 5.5	13.4	0.90	29.60	46	1	98	0	1	48	79.3	-23.0	41	9	100,000	0	0.0	0.0
C / 5.5	13.4	1.10	28.80	1	1	98	0	1	48	76.1	-23.1	7	9	0	0	0.0	0.0

	99 Pct = Best 0 Pct = Worst				**PERFORMANCE**							
			Overall		**Perfor-**		Total Return % through 3/31/15				Incl. in Returns	
			Investment		**mance**				Annualized		Dividend	Expense
Fund		Ticker	**Rating**	Phone	**Rating/Pts**	3 Mo	6 Mo	1Yr / Pct	3Yr / Pct	5Yr / Pct	Yield	Ratio
Type	Fund Name	Symbol										
SC	Nuveen NWQ Small Cap Value A	NSCAX	A-	(800) 257-8787	A- / 9.1	3.54	12.38	8.51 /66	19.20 /97	17.51 /97	0.00	1.36
SC	Nuveen NWQ Small Cap Value C	NSCCX	A-	(800) 257-8787	A / 9.3	3.34	11.93	7.69 /60	18.30 /95	16.63 /95	0.00	2.11
SC	Nuveen NWQ Small Cap Value I	NSCRX	A	(800) 257-8787	A+ / 9.6	3.59	12.50	8.77 /68	19.49 /97	17.81 /97	0.00	1.11
SC	Nuveen NWQ Small Cap Value R3	NSCQX	A	(800) 257-8787	A / 9.5	3.47	12.23	8.24 /64	18.91 /96	17.23 /96	0.00	1.61
AA	Nuveen Real Asset Income A	NRIAX	C	(800) 257-8787	C / 4.5	2.17	4.69	11.09 /79	11.54 /49	--	4.57	1.34
AA	Nuveen Real Asset Income C	NRICX	C+	(800) 257-8787	C / 4.9	1.98	4.33	10.26 /75	10.72 /44	--	4.06	2.09
AA	Nuveen Real Asset Income I	NRIIX	C+	(800) 257-8787	C+ / 5.6	2.24	4.84	11.37 /80	11.81 /51	--	5.10	1.10
RE	● Nuveen Real Estate Securities A	FREAX	C	(800) 257-8787	B+ / 8.4	4.11	18.49	23.47 /98	13.68 /65	15.53 /90	2.11	1.25
RE	● Nuveen Real Estate Securities C	FRLCX	C+	(800) 257-8787	B+ / 8.8	3.91	18.08	22.49 /97	12.83 /58	14.68 /84	1.55	2.00
RE	● Nuveen Real Estate Securities I	FARCX	C+	(800) 257-8787	A / 9.3	4.17	18.66	23.75 /98	13.97 /67	15.83 /92	2.46	1.00
RE	● Nuveen Real Estate Securities R3	FRSSX	C+	(800) 257-8787	A- / 9.1	4.03	18.40	23.11 /98	13.39 /62	15.26 /89	2.01	1.50
RE	Nuveen Real Estate Securities R6	FREGX	U	(800) 257-8787	U /	4.20	18.81	24.01 /98	--	--	2.46	0.88
GI	Nuveen Santa Barbara Div Gro A	NSBAX	B-	(800) 257-8787	C+ / 5.9	1.17	7.57	11.79 /82	13.76 /65	14.03 /78	1.29	1.01
GI	Nuveen Santa Barbara Div Gro C	NSBCX	B-	(800) 257-8787	C+ / 6.2	0.98	7.16	10.96 /78	12.91 /59	13.17 /70	0.66	1.76
GI	Nuveen Santa Barbara Div Gro I	NSBRX	B+	(800) 257-8787	B- / 7.0	1.23	7.70	12.06 /83	14.03 /67	14.31 /81	1.60	0.76
GI	Nuveen Santa Barbara Div Gro R3	NBDRX	B-	(800) 257-8787	C+ / 6.6	1.12	7.45	11.50 /80	13.48 /63	13.75 /75	1.13	1.26
IN	Nuveen Santa Barbara Div Gro R6	NSBFX	U	(800) 257-8787	U /	1.28	7.75	12.16 /83	--	--	1.60	0.68
SC	Nuveen Small Cap Growth Opps A	FRMPX	D+	(800) 257-8787	C+ / 6.8	4.47	14.61	9.30 /71	14.80 /73	14.53 /83	0.00	1.57
SC	Nuveen Small Cap Growth Opps C	FMPCX	D	(800) 257-8787	B- / 7.2	4.29	14.21	8.48 /66	13.94 /67	13.68 /75	0.00	2.32
SC	Nuveen Small Cap Growth Opps I	FIMPX	C	(800) 257-8787	B / 8.1	4.54	14.75	9.60 /73	15.09 /76	14.82 /85	0.00	1.32
SC	Nuveen Small Cap Growth Opps R3	FMPYX	C-	(800) 257-8787	B / 7.6	4.37	14.43	8.99 /69	14.50 /71	14.24 /80	0.00	1.82
SC	Nuveen Small Cap Index A	FMDAX	B	(800) 257-8787	B / 8.2	4.17	14.14	7.64 /60	15.62 /80	13.93 /77	0.80	1.09
SC	Nuveen Small Cap Index C	FPXCX	B-	(800) 257-8787	B- / 7.5	3.94	13.61	6.76 /53	14.73 /73	13.06 /69	0.10	1.84
SC	Nuveen Small Cap Index I	ASETX	B+	(800) 257-8787	B+ / 8.4	4.23	14.22	7.88 /62	15.89 /82	14.21 /80	1.03	0.84
SC	Nuveen Small Cap Index R3	ARSCX	B	(800) 257-8787	B / 8.0	4.07	13.93	7.35 /58	15.31 /77	13.62 /74	0.57	1.34
SC	Nuveen Small Cap Select A	EMGRX	D-	(800) 257-8787	C+ / 6.3	5.18	16.88	10.83 /78	13.37 /62	13.56 /74	0.00	1.55
SC	Nuveen Small Cap Select C	FHMCX	D-	(800) 257-8787	C+ / 6.7	4.95	16.41	9.91 /74	12.51 /56	12.69 /66	0.00	2.31
SC	Nuveen Small Cap Select I	ARSTX	D+	(800) 257-8787	B- / 7.5	5.28	17.06	11.02 /78	13.64 /64	13.81 /76	0.00	1.30
SC	Nuveen Small Cap Select R3	ASEIX	D-	(800) 257-8787	B- / 7.0	5.10	16.70	10.50 /76	13.06 /60	13.25 /71	0.00	1.80
SC	Nuveen Small Cap Value A	FSCAX	B	(800) 257-8787	B- / 7.1	4.75	13.15	6.78 /53	15.83 /82	15.27 /89	0.34	1.56
SC	Nuveen Small Cap Value C	FSCVX	B	(800) 257-8787	B / 7.6	4.50	12.66	5.99 /46	14.96 /75	14.41 /82	0.00	2.30
SC	Nuveen Small Cap Value I	FSCCX	B+	(800) 257-8787	B+ / 8.4	4.81	13.28	7.10 /56	16.14 /84	15.53 /90	0.59	1.31
SC	Nuveen Small Cap Value R3	FSVSX	B+	(800) 257-8787	B / 8.0	4.68	13.02	6.54 /51	15.55 /80	14.97 /87	0.13	1.81
AA	Nuveen Strategy Aggr Gro Alloc A	FAAGX	D+	(800) 257-8787	C- / 3.4	2.62	3.48	5.51 /43	10.46 /42	9.40 /40	2.83	1.59
AA	Nuveen Strategy Aggr Gro Alloc C	FSACX	C-	(800) 257-8787	C- / 3.8	2.44	3.11	4.66 /36	9.63 /37	8.58 /34	2.24	2.34
AA	Nuveen Strategy Aggr Gro Alloc I	FSAYX	C-	(800) 257-8787	C / 4.5	2.69	3.62	5.77 /44	10.76 /44	9.67 /42	3.24	1.34
AA	Nuveen Strategy Aggr Gro Alloc R3	FSASX	C-	(800) 257-8787	C- / 4.2	2.59	3.36	5.20 /40	10.21 /41	9.13 /38	2.74	1.84
AA	Nuveen Strategy Balanced Alloc A	FSGNX	D	(800) 257-8787	D+ / 2.3	2.17	3.09	5.46 /42	8.36 /29	8.08 /30	3.67	1.37
AA	Nuveen Strategy Balanced Alloc C	FSKCX	D+	(800) 257-8787	D+ / 2.8	2.01	2.71	4.70 /36	7.64 /25	7.32 /25	3.14	2.12
AA	Nuveen Strategy Balanced Alloc I	FSKYX	D+	(800) 257-8787	C- / 3.4	2.33	3.31	5.82 /45	8.63 /31	8.35 /32	4.12	1.12
AA	Nuveen Strategy Balanced Alloc R3	FSKSX	D+	(800) 257-8787	C- / 3.1	2.13	2.97	5.31 /41	8.11 /28	7.82 /29	3.63	1.62
AA	Nuveen Strategy Consv Alloc A	FSFIX	D+	(800) 257-8787	D- / 1.2	1.60	1.97	4.20 /33	5.71 /16	6.22 /18	2.35	1.29
AA	Nuveen Strategy Consv Alloc C	FSJCX	C-	(800) 257-8787	D- / 1.4	1.33	1.53	3.38 /28	4.82 /13	5.39 /14	1.70	2.04
AA	Nuveen Strategy Consv Alloc I	FSFYX	C-	(800) 257-8787	D / 1.9	1.67	2.12	4.48 /35	5.88 /16	6.44 /20	2.76	1.04
AA	Nuveen Strategy Consv Alloc R3	FSJSX	C-	(800) 257-8787	D / 1.6	1.54	1.82	3.93 /31	5.37 /14	5.92 /16	2.23	1.53
AA	Nuveen Strategy Growth Alloc A	FAGSX	D+	(800) 257-8787	C- / 3.1	2.40	3.69	6.04 /47	9.67 /37	8.90 /36	2.97	1.49
AA	Nuveen Strategy Growth Alloc C	FSNCX	C-	(800) 257-8787	C- / 3.5	2.29	3.33	5.32 /41	8.85 /32	8.09 /30	2.39	2.24
AA	Nuveen Strategy Growth Alloc I	FSGYX	C	(800) 257-8787	C- / 4.2	2.48	3.79	6.30 /49	9.97 /39	9.18 /34	3.38	1.24
AA	Nuveen Strategy Growth Alloc R3	FSNSX	C-	(800) 257-8787	C- / 3.8	2.35	3.52	5.81 /45	9.40 /36	8.64 /34	2.89	1.74
FO	Nuveen Symphony International Eq A	NSIAX	D	(800) 257-8787	D / 2.2	6.61	2.59	1.34 /20	8.26 /29	7.06 /23	0.77	2.22
FO	Nuveen Symphony International Eq C	NSECX	D	(800) 257-8787	D+ / 2.5	6.44	2.19	0.56 /17	7.43 /24	6.25 /18	0.08	3.12
FO	Nuveen Symphony International Eq I	NSIEX	D+	(800) 257-8787	C- / 3.2	6.67	2.69	1.61 /20	8.53 /30	7.32 /25	1.06	2.01

● Denotes fund is closed to new investors
* Denotes fund is included in Section II

www.thestreetratings.com

RISK			NET ASSETS		ASSET				Portfolio	BULL / BEAR		FUND MANAGER		MINIMUMS		LOADS	
	3 Year		NAV						Turnover	Last Bull	Last Bear	Manager	Manager	Initial	Additional	Front	Back
Risk	Standard		As of	Total	Cash	Stocks	Bonds	Other		Market	Market	Quality	Tenure	Purch.	Purch.	End	End
Rating/Pts	Deviation	Beta	3/31/15	$(Mil)	%	%	%	%	Ratio	Return	Return	Pct	(Years)	$	$	Load	Load
C+ / 5.9	13.9	0.98	44.75	120	6	93	0	1	49	110.8	-21.3	88	11	3,000	100	5.8	0.0
C+ / 5.9	13.9	0.97	41.74	29	6	93	0	1	49	105.5	-21.6	85	11	3,000	100	0.0	0.0
C+ / 6.0	13.9	0.97	45.53	415	6	93	0	1	49	112.6	-21.2	89	11	100,000	0	0.0	0.0
C+ / 5.9	13.9	0.97	44.42	6	6	93	0	1	49	109.1	-21.4	87	11	0	0	0.0	0.0
B- / 7.1	6.5	0.76	24.00	144	0	58	39	3	86	55.8	N/A	89	4	3,000	100	5.8	0.0
B- / 7.1	6.5	0.76	24.01	96	0	58	39	3	86	51.9	N/A	86	4	3,000	100	0.0	0.0
B- / 7.1	6.5	0.76	24.00	478	0	58	39	3	86	57.1	N/A	90	4	100,000	0	0.0	0.0
C- / 3.3	12.8	1.03	24.65	766	2	97	0	1	89	84.1	-16.5	56	16	3,000	100	5.8	0.0
C- / 3.3	12.9	1.03	24.08	99	2	97	0	1	89	79.5	-16.7	44	16	3,000	100	0.0	0.0
C- / 3.3	12.9	1.03	24.97	4,261	2	97	0	1	89	85.7	-16.4	60	16	100,000	0	0.0	0.0
C- / 3.3	12.9	1.03	25.00	71	2	97	0	1	89	82.6	-16.6	52	16	0	0	0.0	0.0
U /	N/A	N/A	25.05	259	2	97	0	1	89	N/A	N/A	N/A	16	5,000,000	0	0.0	0.0
B- / 7.4	9.4	0.95	36.01	737	3	96	0	1	29	84.9	-13.9	46	11	3,000	100	5.8	0.0
B- / 7.3	9.4	0.95	35.97	512	3	96	0	1	29	80.3	-14.3	36	11	3,000	100	0.0	0.0
B- / 7.4	9.4	0.95	36.02	1,433	3	96	0	1	29	86.5	-13.9	51	11	100,000	0	0.0	0.0
B- / 7.4	9.4	0.95	36.28	16	3	96	0	1	29	83.4	-14.1	43	11	0	0	0.0	0.0
U /	N/A	N/A	36.25	33	3	96	0	1	29	N/A	N/A	N/A	11	5,000,000	0	0.0	0.0
D+ / 2.7	14.4	1.00	23.35	38	3	96	0	1	125	97.8	-25.3	49	11	3,000	100	5.8	0.0
D / 1.7	14.4	1.00	19.45	3	3	96	0	1	125	92.9	-25.5	38	11	3,000	100	0.0	0.0
C- / 3.4	14.4	1.00	26.49	65	3	96	0	1	125	99.5	-25.2	53	11	100,000	0	0.0	0.0
D+ / 2.5	14.4	1.00	22.44	2	3	96	0	1	125	96.2	-25.4	45	11	0	0	0.0	0.0
C+ / 5.7	13.4	1.00	15.23	43	2	96	0	2	12	96.9	-25.3	59	14	3,000	100	0.0	0.0
C+ / 5.7	13.4	1.00	14.50	3	2	96	0	2	12	91.8	-25.5	47	14	3,000	100	0.0	0.0
C+ / 5.7	13.4	1.00	15.26	48	2	96	0	2	12	98.4	-25.2	63	14	100,000	0	0.0	0.0
C+ / 5.7	13.4	1.00	14.82	51	2	96	0	2	12	95.0	-25.3	55	14	0	0	0.0	0.0
D- / 1.0	13.6	0.99	11.57	98	1	98	0	1	90	94.8	-27.1	32	7	3,000	100	5.8	0.0
E+ / 0.9	13.7	0.99	9.12	9	1	98	0	1	90	89.9	-27.3	23	7	3,000	100	0.0	0.0
D / 1.7	13.7	0.99	13.57	124	1	98	0	1	90	96.5	-27.0	35	7	100,000	0	0.0	0.0
E+ / 0.9	13.7	0.99	10.92	8	1	98	0	1	90	93.3	-27.2	28	7	0	0	0.0	0.0
C+ / 6.3	12.9	0.91	19.83	47	0	99	0	1	55	101.0	-24.2	76	10	3,000	100	5.8	0.0
C+ / 6.2	12.9	0.91	17.17	3	0	99	0	1	55	96.1	-24.5	69	10	3,000	100	0.0	0.0
C+ / 6.3	12.9	0.91	20.48	72	0	99	0	1	55	102.8	-24.2	78	10	100,000	0	0.0	0.0
C+ / 6.3	12.9	0.92	19.47	13	0	99	0	1	55	99.3	-24.2	74	10	0	0	0.0	0.0
C+ / 6.0	9.4	1.59	14.86	55	5	78	15	2	42	64.2	-19.4	5	14	3,000	100	5.8	0.0
C+ / 6.0	9.4	1.59	14.29	13	5	78	15	2	42	60.1	-19.6	4	14	3,000	100	0.0	0.0
C+ / 6.0	9.4	1.59	14.90	25	5	78	15	2	42	65.8	-19.3	6	14	100,000	0	0.0	0.0
C+ / 6.0	9.4	1.58	14.68	4	5	78	15	2	42	62.9	-19.5	5	14	0	0	0.0	0.0
C+ / 6.4	6.7	1.14	10.69	169	6	53	39	2	28	47.8	-13.3	18	2	3,000	100	5.8	0.0
C+ / 6.4	6.7	1.13	10.53	40	6	53	39	2	28	44.4	-13.6	14	2	3,000	100	0.0	0.0
C+ / 6.4	6.7	1.13	10.66	130	6	53	39	2	28	49.0	-13.3	21	2	100,000	0	0.0	0.0
C+ / 6.4	6.7	1.13	10.57	6	6	53	39	2	28	46.8	-13.5	17	2	0	0	0.0	0.0
B / 8.5	4.2	0.66	11.80	66	7	33	59	1	20	30.2	-6.4	48	19	3,000	100	5.8	0.0
B / 8.5	4.2	0.66	11.72	24	7	33	59	1	20	26.6	-6.7	36	19	3,000	100	0.0	0.0
B / 8.5	4.2	0.65	11.79	28	7	33	59	1	20	30.8	-6.3	51	19	100,000	0	0.0	0.0
B / 8.5	4.1	0.65	11.77	1	7	33	59	1	20	28.7	-6.5	45	19	0	0	0.0	0.0
C+ / 6.7	8.1	1.38	12.35	96	6	70	23	1	31	56.9	-16.1	10	19	3,000	100	5.8	0.0
C+ / 6.8	8.2	1.38	12.04	25	6	70	23	1	31	52.9	-16.4	7	19	3,000	100	0.0	0.0
C+ / 6.7	8.1	1.38	12.41	43	6	70	23	1	31	58.3	-16.0	12	19	100,000	0	0.0	0.0
C+ / 6.7	8.1	1.38	12.19	8	6	70	23	1	31	55.6	-16.2	9	19	0	0	0.0	0.0
C+ / 6.2	12.2	0.92	19.03	1	0	99	0	1	42	52.5	-22.3	62	5	3,000	100	5.8	0.0
C+ / 6.2	12.2	0.92	18.84	N/A	0	99	0	1	42	48.7	-22.5	50	5	3,000	100	0.0	0.0
C+ / 6.2	12.2	0.91	19.02	18	0	99	0	1	42	53.8	-22.2	66	5	100,000	0	0.0	0.0

					PERFORMANCE							
						Total Return % through 3/31/15					Incl. in Returns	
									Annualized		Dividend	Expense
Fund Type	Fund Name	Ticker Symbol	Overall Investment Rating	Phone	Performance Rating/Pts	3 Mo	6 Mo	1Yr / Pct	3Yr / Pct	5Yr / Pct	Yield	Ratio
FO	Nuveen Symphony International Eq	NSREX	D+	(800) 257-8787	D+ / 2.9	6.59	2.48	1.13 /19	8.00 /27	--	0.57	2.62
GR	Nuveen Symphony Large-Cap	NCGAX	C+	(800) 257-8787	C+ / 5.8	3.08	6.87	14.12 /90	13.21 /61	15.39 /89	0.02	1.16
GR	Nuveen Symphony Large-Cap	NCGCX	C+	(800) 257-8787	C+ / 6.2	2.91	6.47	13.27 /87	12.36 /55	14.54 /83	0.00	1.91
GR	Nuveen Symphony Large-Cap	NSGIX	B	(800) 257-8787	B- / 7.0	3.14	7.01	14.38 /90	13.49 /63	15.66 /91	0.25	0.91
GR	Nuveen Symphony Large-Cap	NSGQX	C+	(800) 257-8787	C+ / 6.6	3.03	6.73	13.83 /89	12.92 /59	15.10 /88	0.00	1.41
GR	Nuveen Symphony Low Volatility Eq	NOPAX	C+	(800) 257-8787	B- / 7.5	2.91	8.18	14.86 /91	16.00 /83	14.68 /84	1.02	1.26
GR	Nuveen Symphony Low Volatility Eq	NOPCX	C+	(800) 257-8787	B / 8.0	2.72	7.73	13.96 /89	15.10 /76	13.81 /76	0.39	2.00
GR	Nuveen Symphony Low Volatility Eq I	NOPRX	B	(800) 257-8787	B+ / 8.8	2.98	8.29	15.12 /92	16.27 /85	14.96 /86	1.30	0.95
MC	Nuveen Symphony Mid-Cap Core A	NCCAX	C+	(800) 257-8787	C+ / 6.6	3.58	9.97	13.01 /87	14.52 /71	14.18 /79	0.00	1.60
MC	Nuveen Symphony Mid-Cap Core C	NCCCX	B-	(800) 257-8787	B- / 7.0	3.38	9.54	12.17 /83	13.66 /65	13.32 /71	0.00	2.35
MC	Nuveen Symphony Mid-Cap Core I	NCCIX	B+	(800) 257-8787	B / 7.9	3.63	10.09	13.29 /88	14.80 /73	14.47 /82	0.02	1.35
MC	Nuveen Symphony Mid-Cap Core R3	NMCRX	B	(800) 257-8787	B- / 7.5	3.51	9.83	12.74 /86	14.23 /69	13.90 /77	0.00	1.86
AA	Nuveen Tactical Market Opps A	NTMAX	D+	(800) 257-8787	E / 0.4	0.19	-0.90	0.57 /17	-0.39 / 4	--	2.77	1.38
AA	Nuveen Tactical Market Opps C	NTMCX	D+	(800) 257-8787	E / 0.4	0.10	-1.25	-0.14 /15	-1.15 / 3	--	2.16	2.13
AA	Nuveen Tactical Market Opps I	FGTYX	D+	(800) 257-8787	E / 0.5	0.28	-0.72	0.83 /18	-0.15 / 4	2.38 / 5	3.20	1.13
GL	Nuveen Tradewinds Global All-Cap A	NWGAX	E+	(800) 257-8787	E+ / 0.6	0.99	-2.78	-2.25 /10	3.37 / 9	3.47 / 7	1.30	1.37
GL	Nuveen Tradewinds Global All-Cap C	NWGCX	E+	(800) 257-8787	E+ / 0.7	0.76	-3.18	-3.01 / 9	2.59 / 7	2.69 / 5	0.60	2.12
GL	Nuveen Tradewinds Global All-Cap I	NWGRX	E+	(800) 257-8787	E+ / 0.8	1.06	-2.67	-2.00 /10	3.63 / 9	3.73 / 7	1.64	1.12
GL	Nuveen Tradewinds Global All-Cap	NGARX	E+	(800) 257-8787	E+ / 0.8	0.87	-2.94	-2.51 / 9	3.10 / 8	3.21 / 6	1.12	1.61
FO	Nuveen Tradewinds Intl Value A	NAIGX	E+	(800) 257-8787	E+ / 0.8	6.20	-0.85	-3.47 / 8	4.87 /13	1.96 / 4	3.74	1.42
FO	Nuveen Tradewinds Intl Value C	NCIGX	E+	(800) 257-8787	D- / 1.0	5.97	-1.27	-4.25 / 7	4.08 /10	1.19 / 4	3.16	2.16
FO	Nuveen Tradewinds Intl Value I	NGRRX	E+	(800) 257-8787	D- / 1.3	6.27	-0.75	-3.25 / 8	5.13 /14	2.21 / 5	4.24	1.16
FO	Nuveen Tradewinds Intl Value R3	NTITX	E+	(800) 257-8787	D- / 1.1	6.11	-1.00	-3.80 / 7	4.58 /12	1.69 / 4	3.70	1.67
IN	Nuveen Tradewinds Value Opp A	NVOAX	D-	(800) 257-8787	C- / 3.0	-0.83	3.93	5.51 /43	9.87 /39	8.99 /37	0.88	1.25
IN	Nuveen Tradewinds Value Opp C	NVOCX	D-	(800) 257-8787	C- / 3.4	-1.05	3.55	4.73 /37	9.04 /33	8.18 /31	0.20	2.00
IN	Nuveen Tradewinds Value Opp I	NVORX	D	(800) 257-8787	C- / 4.1	-0.80	4.07	5.78 /45	10.13 /40	9.26 /39	1.17	0.99
IN	Nuveen Tradewinds Value Opp R3	NTVTX	D-	(800) 257-8787	C- / 3.7	-0.93	3.81	5.24 /40	9.59 /37	8.73 /35	0.68	1.50
EM	Nuveen TW Emerging Markets A	NTEAX	E	(800) 257-8787	E- / 0.1	1.08	-11.17	-5.97 / 4	-7.22 / 1	-6.32 / 1	0.00	2.20
EM	Nuveen TW Emerging Markets C	NTECX	E-	(800) 257-8787	E- / 0.1	0.92	-11.48	-6.67 / 4	-7.91 / 1	-7.02 / 1	0.00	2.95
EM	Nuveen TW Emerging Markets I	NTEIX	E	(800) 257-8787	E- / 0.2	1.12	-11.08	-5.74 / 5	-7.00 / 1	-6.09 / 1	0.28	1.92
EM	Nuveen TW Emerging Markets R3	NTERX	E	(800) 257-8787	E- / 0.2	1.00	-11.30	-6.21 / 4	-7.44 / 1	-6.56 / 1	0.00	2.46
FO	Nuveen TW Japan A	NTJAX	D	(800) 257-8787	C- / 3.5	12.51	5.78	10.39 /76	8.61 /30	4.78 /11	4.36	3.46
FO	Nuveen TW Japan C	NTJCX	D+	(800) 257-8787	C- / 3.9	12.30	5.33	9.57 /72	7.76 /26	3.98 / 8	3.88	4.15
FO	Nuveen TW Japan I	NTJIX	C-	(800) 257-8787	C / 4.5	12.52	5.84	10.62 /77	8.85 /32	5.04 /12	4.87	3.19
GR	Nuveen Winslow Large-Cap Growth	NWCAX	C	(800) 257-8787	C+ / 6.6	3.04	8.61	15.22 /92	14.16 /68	14.08 /78	0.00	1.15
GL	Nuveen Winslow Large-Cap Growth	NWCCX	C	(800) 257-8787	B- / 7.0	2.83	8.19	14.35 /90	13.31 /62	13.23 /70	0.00	1.90
GR	Nuveen Winslow Large-Cap Growth I	NVLIX	C+	(800) 257-8787	B / 7.8	3.09	8.75	15.53 /93	14.45 /71	14.37 /81	0.00	0.90
GR	Nuveen Winslow Large-Cap Growth	NWCRX	C+	(800) 257-8787	B- / 7.4	2.97	8.47	14.95 /92	13.88 /66	13.80 /76	0.00	1.39
GR	Nuveen Winslow Large-Cap Growth	NWCFX	U	(800) 257-8787	U /	3.13	8.83	15.68 /93	--	--	0.00	0.74
AA	NWM Momentum	MOMOX	U	(888) 331-9609	U /	0.50	2.45	--	--	--	0.00	N/A
GL	NY 529 CSP Direct Aggr Gro Port		A+	(800) 662-7447	B+ / 8.4	1.80	7.07	12.22 /84	16.29 /85	14.59 /83	0.00	0.25
GI	NY 529 CSP Direct Csv Gro Port		C+	(800) 662-7447	D+ / 2.4	1.63	4.38	7.28 /57	6.24 /18	6.91 /22	0.00	0.25
FO	NY 529 CSP Direct Dev Mkts Idx Port		D+	(800) 662-7447	C- / 3.1	5.50	1.13	-1.01 /13	8.91 /32	6.15 /18	0.00	0.25
GL	NY 529 CSP Direct Gro Stk Idx Port		A+	(800) 662-7447	B+ / 8.9	3.42	8.67	16.56 /94	16.37 /86	15.53 /90	0.00	0.25
GI	NY 529 CSP Direct Growth Port		B	(800) 662-7447	C+ / 6.2	1.76	6.22	10.62 /77	12.94 /59	12.17 /62	0.00	0.25
AA	NY 529 CSP Direct Income Port		C-	(800) 662-7447	E+ / 0.8	1.14	2.04	3.58 /29	1.65 / 6	3.21 / 6	0.00	0.25
MC	NY 529 CSP Direct MC Stk Idx Port		A+	(800) 662-7447	A / 9.4	4.25	11.14	14.76 /91	17.82 /94	15.92 /93	0.00	0.25
BA	NY 529 CSP Direct Mdt Gro Port		B	(800) 662-7447	C- / 4.2	1.73	5.38	9.02 /69	9.61 /37	9.59 /41	0.00	0.25
SC	NY 529 CSP Direct SC Stk Idx Port		A	(800) 662-7447	A- / 9.2	4.78	11.91	9.73 /73	17.47 /92	15.67 /91	0.00	0.25
GI	NY 529 CSP Direct Val Stk Idx Port		A-	(800) 662-7447	B / 7.6	-0.58	4.09	9.36 /71	15.88 /82	13.30 /71	0.00	0.25
GR	NYSA Fund	NYSAX	E-	(800) 535-9169	E- / 0.1	9.09	-20.00	-36.52 / 0	-10.66 / 1	-9.01 / 1	0.00	6.16
TC	Oak Assoc-Black Oak Emerging Tech	BOGSX	C-	(888) 462-5386	C+ / 6.0	2.73	10.24	13.00 /87	11.39 /48	11.95 /60	0.00	1.31

● Denotes fund is closed to new investors
* Denotes fund is included in Section II

www.thestreetratings.com

RISK			NET ASSETS		ASSET					BULL / BEAR		FUND MANAGER		MINIMUMS		LOADS	
	3 Year		NAV						Portfolio	Last Bull	Last Bear	Manager	Manager	Initial	Additional	Front	Back
Risk Rating/Pts	Standard Deviation	Beta	As of 3/31/15	Total $(Mil)	Cash %	Stocks %	Bonds %	Other %	Turnover Ratio	Market Return	Market Return	Quality Pct	Tenure (Years)	Purch. $	Purch. $	End Load	End Load
C+ / 6.2	12.3	0.92	19.08	N/A	0	99	0	1	42	51.3	-22.4	58	5	0	0	0.0	0.0
C+ / 6.7	9.8	0.98	33.77	85	0	99	0	1	71	94.1	-16.5	35	5	3,000	100	5.8	0.0
C+ / 6.6	9.8	0.98	31.85	29	0	99	0	1	71	89.3	-16.8	26	5	3,000	100	0.0	0.0
C+ / 6.7	9.8	0.98	34.18	64	0	99	0	1	71	95.8	-16.5	38	5	100,000	0	0.0	0.0
C+ / 6.7	9.8	0.98	33.70	4	0	99	0	1	71	92.5	-16.6	31	5	0	0	0.0	0.0
C / 4.9	8.8	0.91	27.63	16	1	98	0	1	125	91.7	-13.3	79	5	3,000	100	5.8	0.0
C / 4.9	8.8	0.91	26.86	4	1	98	0	1	125	86.8	-13.6	73	5	3,000	100	0.0	0.0
C / 4.9	8.9	0.91	27.66	46	1	98	0	1	125	93.4	-13.3	81	5	100,000	0	0.0	0.0
C+ / 6.3	10.7	0.95	37.62	15	1	98	0	1	141	90.2	-22.8	48	5	3,000	100	5.8	0.0
C+ / 6.3	10.7	0.95	35.48	3	1	98	0	1	141	85.5	-23.0	36	5	3,000	100	0.0	0.0
C+ / 6.3	10.7	0.95	38.24	28	1	98	0	1	141	92.0	-22.7	51	5	100,000	0	0.0	0.0
C+ / 6.3	10.7	0.95	37.44	N/A	1	98	0	1	141	88.6	-22.8	43	5	0	0	0.0	0.0
B+ / 9.1	2.7	0.13	10.55	6	38	34	26	2	36	0.5	1.2	40	6	3,000	100	5.8	0.0
B+ / 9.0	2.7	0.14	10.40	5	38	34	26	2	36	-2.2	0.9	29	6	3,000	100	0.0	0.0
B+ / 9.1	2.7	0.14	10.59	79	38	34	26	2	36	1.3	1.4	43	6	100,000	0	0.0	0.0
C / 5.5	13.7	0.90	26.63	38	2	97	0	1	49	15.1	-14.6	11	3	3,000	100	5.8	0.0
C / 5.5	13.8	0.90	26.39	35	2	97	0	1	49	12.2	-14.9	8	3	3,000	100	0.0	0.0
C / 5.5	13.7	0.89	26.62	52	2	97	0	1	49	16.1	-14.5	13	3	100,000	0	0.0	0.0
C / 5.5	13.8	0.90	26.57	N/A	2	97	0	1	49	14.1	-14.7	10	3	0	0	0.0	0.0
C / 5.3	12.8	0.91	23.45	37	1	98	0	1	24	18.8	-18.4	20	6	3,000	100	5.8	0.0
C / 5.4	12.8	0.91	22.35	22	1	98	0	1	24	15.9	-18.7	14	6	3,000	100	0.0	0.0
C / 5.3	12.8	0.91	23.55	230	1	98	0	1	24	19.8	-18.4	22	6	100,000	0	0.0	0.0
C / 5.3	12.8	0.91	23.62	1	1	98	0	1	24	17.8	-18.5	17	6	0	0	0.0	0.0
C- / 4.0	12.2	1.14	32.09	116	1	98	0	1	107	48.3	-14.5	3	3	3,000	100	5.8	0.0
C- / 4.1	12.2	1.14	31.10	98	1	98	0	1	107	44.6	-14.8	3	3	3,000	100	0.0	0.0
C- / 4.0	12.2	1.14	32.23	165	1	98	0	1	107	49.6	-14.4	4	3	100,000	0	0.0	0.0
C- / 4.1	12.2	1.14	32.11	4	1	98	0	1	107	47.1	-14.6	3	3	0	0	0.0	0.0
C- / 3.7	17.1	1.14	24.42	2	2	97	0	1	101	-16.3	-28.6	3	7	3,000	100	5.8	0.0
C- / 3.6	17.1	1.14	24.05	1	2	97	0	1	101	-18.4	-28.8	2	7	3,000	100	0.0	0.0
C- / 3.7	17.1	1.14	24.43	26	2	97	0	1	101	-15.5	-28.5	3	7	100,000	0	0.0	0.0
C- / 3.7	17.1	1.14	24.33	N/A	2	97	0	1	101	-16.9	-28.7	3	7	0	0	0.0	0.0
C / 5.5	13.9	0.71	25.01	2	0	99	0	1	33	23.4	-2.5	83	7	3,000	100	5.8	0.0
C / 5.5	13.9	0.71	24.75	1	0	99	0	1	33	20.2	-2.7	77	7	3,000	100	0.0	0.0
C / 5.4	13.9	0.71	25.08	6	0	99	0	1	33	24.4	-2.3	84	7	100,000	0	0.0	0.0
C / 5.0	12.0	1.12	44.69	30	1	98	0	1	69	93.8	-17.7	20	6	3,000	100	5.8	0.0
C / 4.9	12.0	0.69	42.52	2	1	98	0	1	69	89.0	-18.0	95	6	3,000	100	0.0	0.0
C / 5.0	12.0	1.12	45.33	1,039	1	98	0	1	69	95.5	-17.6	23	6	100,000	0	0.0	0.0
C / 5.0	12.0	1.12	44.00	3	1	98	0	1	69	92.2	-17.8	18	6	0	0	0.0	0.0
U /	N/A	N/A	45.46	50	1	98	0	1	69	N/A	N/A	N/A	6	5,000,000	0	0.0	0.0
U /	N/A	N/A	9.96	33	0	0	0	100	0	N/A	N/A	N/A	1	5,000	100	0.0	2.0
B- / 7.2	9.7	0.59	25.43	2,531	0	99	0	1	0	101.1	-17.8	98	6	25	25	0.0	0.0
B+ / 9.7	3.0	0.21	18.13	2,337	0	25	74	1	0	28.4	-1.1	88	6	25	25	0.0	0.0
C+ / 6.0	13.2	1.00	20.54	266	1	98	0	1	0	51.8	-23.4	60	6	25	25	0.0	0.0
C+ / 6.8	10.1	0.61	25.69	685	0	99	0	1	0	103.8	-15.2	98	6	25	25	0.0	0.0
B / 8.6	7.2	0.75	24.26	2,137	0	74	24	2	0	73.9	-12.4	77	6	25	25	0.0	0.0
B+ / 9.6	2.8	0.01	15.04	1,896	25	0	74	1	0	6.3	3.9	80	6	25	25	0.0	0.0
C+ / 6.6	10.4	0.92	31.42	872	0	99	0	1	0	107.1	-21.4	84	6	25	25	0.0	0.0
B+ / 9.6	4.8	0.84	21.15	2,750	0	50	49	1	0	49.7	-7.0	73	6	25	25	0.0	0.0
C+ / 6.3	12.0	0.88	30.91	684	0	99	0	1	0	108.1	-24.6	88	6	25	25	0.0	0.0
B- / 7.7	9.7	0.99	24.18	775	0	99	0	1	0	96.4	-18.5	66	6	25	25	0.0	0.0
D / 1.6	19.3	0.89	4.92	2	3	96	0	1	128	-24.2	-21.4	0	2	1,000	250	2.5	0.0
C / 4.3	15.5	1.30	4.52	36	2	97	0	1	41	86.6	-28.7	2	9	2,000	25	0.0	0.0

					PERFORMANCE							
						Total Return % through 3/31/15					Incl. in Returns	
									Annualized		Dividend	Expense
Fund Type	Fund Name	Ticker Symbol	Overall Investment Rating	Phone	Perfor-mance Rating/Pts	3 Mo	6 Mo	1Yr / Pct	3Yr / Pct	5Yr / Pct	Yield	Ratio
HL	Oak Assoc-Live Oak Health Sciences	LOGSX	A+	(888) 462-5386	A+ / 9.9	7.46	16.46	21.12 /97	23.05 /99	18.64 /98	0.54	1.12
SC	Oak Assoc-Pin Oak Equity	POGSX	B+	(888) 462-5386	B- / 7.2	0.69	3.23	6.82 /54	15.51 /79	13.84 /76	1.06	1.13
TC	Oak Assoc-Red Oak Technology	ROGSX	B	(888) 462-5386	B / 7.6	-0.89	5.68	8.26 /65	15.91 /83	15.95 /93	0.97	1.15
GR	Oak Assoc-Rock Oak Core Gr Fund	RCKSX	D	(888) 462-5386	C / 4.7	-0.52	3.17	4.52 /35	11.57 /50	11.89 /60	0.31	1.58
GR	Oak Ridge Lrg Cap Growth A	ORILX	C+	(855) 551-5521	C+ / 5.8	3.25	8.62	13.48 /88	13.00 /60	11.64 /58	0.00	1.54
GR	Oak Ridge Lrg Cap Growth C	ORLCX	C+	(855) 551-5521	C+ / 6.1	3.04	8.17	12.49 /85	12.00 /52	10.65 /50	0.00	2.24
GR	Oak Ridge Lrg Cap Growth Y	PORYX	C+	(855) 551-5521	C+ / 6.9	3.29	8.68	13.65 /89	13.08 /60	11.80 /59	0.00	1.17
SC	Oak Ridge Sm Cap Growth A	ORIGX	B+	(855) 551-5521	B+ / 8.7	7.11	14.27	13.09 /87	17.23 /91	15.61 /91	0.00	1.40
SC	Oak Ridge Sm Cap Growth C	ORICX	B+	(855) 551-5521	A- / 9.0	6.91	13.84	12.26 /84	16.36 /86	14.73 /85	0.00	2.12
GR	Oak Ridge Sm Cap Growth K	ORIKX	A	(855) 551-5521	A / 9.5	7.22	14.53	13.65 /89	17.67 /93	15.87 /92	0.00	0.89
SC	Oak Ridge Sm Cap Growth Y	ORIYX	A-	(855) 551-5521	A / 9.5	7.18	14.43	13.47 /88	17.65 /93	16.01 /93	0.00	1.02
BA	Oakmark Equity and Income I	OAKBX	C	(800) 625-6275	C / 4.5	0.91	4.69	6.02 /47	10.65 /43	9.00 /37	0.77	0.74
BA	Oakmark Equity and Income II	OARBX	C	(800) 625-6275	C / 4.3	0.82	4.50	5.67 /44	10.30 /41	8.65 /34	0.46	1.05
GR	Oakmark Fund I	OAKMX	A-	(800) 625-6275	B+ / 8.3	-0.57	3.05	8.37 /65	17.18 /91	14.64 /84	0.61	0.87
GR	Oakmark Fund II	OARMX	B+	(800) 625-6275	B / 8.0	-0.65	2.88	8.03 /63	16.83 /89	14.28 /80	0.40	1.18
GL	Oakmark Global I	OAKGX	C	(800) 625-6275	C+ / 6.1	2.13	5.24	4.14 /33	13.81 /66	10.35 /47	1.12	1.11
GL	Oakmark Global II	OARGX	C	(800) 625-6275	C+ / 5.9	2.04	5.01	3.74 /30	13.43 /63	9.94 /44	0.78	1.45
GL	Oakmark Global Select I	OAKWX	C	(800) 625-6275	C+ / 6.0	2.43	4.31	3.50 /29	13.68 /65	11.35 /56	0.83	1.13
FO	● Oakmark International I	OAKIX	C	(800) 625-6275	C+ / 5.6	6.51	6.03	-0.05 /15	12.97 /59	9.73 /42	1.95	0.95
FO	● Oakmark International II	OARIX	C-	(800) 625-6275	C / 5.4	6.43	5.87	-0.41 /14	12.58 /57	9.34 /39	1.59	1.33
FO	Oakmark International Small Cap I	OAKEX	D-	(800) 625-6275	D+ / 2.9	9.20	6.31	-1.46 /12	8.34 /29	7.98 /30	1.51	1.31
FO	Oakmark International Small Cap II	OAREX	D-	(800) 625-6275	D+ / 2.7	9.04	6.05	-1.80 /11	8.00 /27	7.63 /27	1.15	1.62
MC	Oakmark Select I	OAKLX	B	(800) 625-6275	B+ / 8.7	-0.98	2.38	8.98 /69	18.00 /94	15.62 /91	0.00	0.95
MC	Oakmark Select II	OARLX	B	(800) 625-6275	B+ / 8.5	-1.09	2.23	8.68 /67	17.67 /93	15.28 /89	0.00	1.23
GR	Oakseed Opportunity Institutional	SEDEX	U	(888) 446-4460	U /	0.91	6.05	11.34 /80	--	--	0.05	1.55
FO	Oberweis Asia Opportunities	OBAOX	E+	(800) 245-7311	D / 1.7	4.05	1.93	2.77 /25	6.05 /17	4.42 /10	0.00	5.35
FO	Oberweis China Opportunities	OBCHX	C-	(800) 245-7311	B / 8.1	4.79	-0.01	-2.19 /10	18.81 /96	7.51 /27	0.62	2.07
SC	Oberweis Emerging Growth Portfolio	OBEGX	D	(800) 245-7311	C+ / 6.4	8.24	11.37	-1.39 /12	14.13 /68	11.88 /60	0.00	1.53
FO	Oberweis International Opptys Inst	OBIIX	U	(800) 245-7311	U /	7.13	4.12	0.22 /16	--	--	0.21	N/A
FO	Oberweis Internatl Opportunities	OBIOX	A-	(800) 245-7311	A / 9.5	7.06	4.36	0.20 /16	21.16 /98	17.80 /97	0.00	2.20
SC	Oberweis Micro Cap Portfolio	OBMCX	D	(800) 245-7311	C / 5.0	0.82	3.01	-9.79 / 3	14.40 /70	12.18 /62	0.00	1.87
MC	Oberweis Small Cap Opportunity	OBSOX	C+	(800) 245-7311	B / 8.2	12.50	16.88	7.03 /55	14.96 /75	15.16 /88	0.00	2.39
PM	OCM Gold Fund Advisor	OCMAX	E-	(800) 628-9403	E- / 0.0	-2.54	-12.10	-19.29 / 1	-22.96 / 0	--	0.00	1.69
PM	OCM Gold Fund Investor	OCMGX	E-	(800) 628-9403	E- / 0.0	-2.72	-12.37	-19.86 / 1	-23.46 / 0	-12.23 / 0	0.00	2.22
FO	OH 529 CollAdv Vngd Dev Mkt Itl Stk		D	(800) 662-7447	C- / 3.0	5.47	1.11	-1.09 /13	8.84 /32	6.12 /17	0.00	0.32
GR	OH CollegeAdv 529 BR Cap App Opt		C+	(800) 441-7762	C+ / 6.7	3.96	9.64	15.29 /92	13.95 /67	12.28 /62	0.00	1.26
GR	OH CollegeAdv 529 BR Cap App Opt		C+	(800) 441-7762	B- / 7.1	3.79	9.20	14.42 /90	13.10 /60	11.43 /56	0.00	2.01
AA	OH CollegeAdv 529 BR Csv 0-5 Opt		C	(800) 441-7762	C- / 3.5	2.28	3.84	6.18 /48	10.43 /42	9.38 /40	0.00	1.40
AA	OH CollegeAdv 529 BR Csv 0-5 Opt		C	(800) 441-7762	C- / 3.8	2.06	3.35	5.28 /41	9.57 /37	8.57 /34	0.00	2.15
AA	OH CollegeAdv 529 BR Csv 10-12		C-	(800) 441-7762	E+ / 0.7	1.01	1.10	2.13 /22	3.61 / 9	3.21 / 6	0.00	1.18
AA	OH CollegeAdv 529 BR Csv 10-12		C-	(800) 441-7762	E+ / 0.8	0.79	0.70	1.32 /19	2.85 / 8	2.45 / 5	0.00	1.93
AA	OH CollegeAdv 529 BR Csv 13-16		C-	(800) 441-7762	E+ / 0.6	0.81	0.45	0.81 /18	2.35 / 7	2.18 / 5	0.00	1.13
AA	OH CollegeAdv 529 BR Csv 13-16		C-	(800) 441-7762	E+ / 0.7	0.56	0.00	--	1.53 / 6	1.41 / 4	0.00	1.88
AA	OH CollegeAdv 529 BR Csv 17Pl Opt		C-	(800) 441-7762	E+ / 0.6	0.73	0.73	1.28 /19	2.16 / 7	1.91 / 4	0.00	1.10
AA	OH CollegeAdv 529 BR Csv 17Pl Opt		C-	(800) 441-7762	E+ / 0.7	0.57	0.28	0.47 /17	1.42 / 6	1.15 / 3	0.00	1.85
AA	OH CollegeAdv 529 BR Csv 6-9 Opt		C	(800) 441-7762	D / 1.8	1.91	2.93	5.19 /40	7.29 /23	6.54 /20	0.00	1.37
AA	OH CollegeAdv 529 BR Csv 6-9 Opt		C	(800) 441-7762	D / 2.2	1.76	2.52	4.45 /35	6.49 /19	5.78 /16	0.00	2.12
IN	OH CollegeAdv 529 BR Eq Div Opt A		C	(800) 441-7762	C- / 3.8	-1.13	2.95	6.37 /50	11.31 /48	11.31 /55	0.00	1.26
IN	OH CollegeAdv 529 BR Eq Div Opt C		C	(800) 441-7762	C- / 4.2	-1.29	2.56	5.62 /43	10.50 /42	10.47 /48	0.00	2.01
GL	OH CollegeAdv 529 BR Glbl All Opt A		D+	(800) 441-7762	D- / 1.4	2.62	1.95	3.83 /31	6.53 /19	6.23 /18	0.00	1.35
GL	OH CollegeAdv 529 BR Glbl All Opt C		C-	(800) 441-7762	D / 1.7	2.50	1.58	3.04 /27	5.75 /16	5.44 /14	0.00	2.10
SC	OH CollegeAdv 529 BR ING SmCo		C+	(800) 441-7762	C+ / 6.6	3.95	13.66	8.51 /66	14.78 /73	13.31 /71	0.00	1.75

● Denotes fund is closed to new investors
* Denotes fund is included in Section II

Risk Rating/Pts	3 Year Standard Deviation	Beta	NAV As of 3/31/15	Total $(Mil)	Cash %	Stocks %	Bonds %	Other %	Portfolio Turnover Ratio	Last Bull Market Return	Last Bear Market Return	Manager Quality Pct	Manager Tenure (Years)	Initial Purch. $	Additional Purch. $	Front End Load	Back End Load
C+ / 6.1	9.1	0.78	22.05	55	3	96	0	1	15	113.9	-10.4	98	14	2,000	25	0.0	0.0
B- / 7.0	11.7	0.74	49.79	92	0	99	0	1	5	103.2	-20.8	89	10	2,000	25	0.0	0.0
C+ / 6.5	12.7	1.19	16.69	146	2	97	0	1	7	105.9	-15.6	24	9	2,000	25	0.0	0.0
C / 4.3	13.0	1.19	13.38	8	0	99	0	1	29	81.2	-21.6	5	11	2,000	25	0.0	0.0
C+ / 6.6	10.5	1.01	20.03	45	2	97	0	1	29	88.1	-16.4	26	16	1,000	100	5.8	0.0
C+ / 6.6	10.5	1.01	18.28	18	2	97	0	1	29	82.4	-16.7	18	16	1,000	500	0.0	0.0
C+ / 6.6	10.4	1.01	20.40	16	2	97	0	1	29	88.6	-16.4	27	16	5,000,000	0	0.0	0.0
C+ / 5.7	12.7	0.86	40.95	462	2	98	0	0	23	92.3	-21.5	89	21	1,000	100	5.8	0.0
C / 5.4	12.7	0.86	33.44	96	2	98	0	0	23	87.6	-21.8	85	21	1,000	500	0.0	0.0
C+ / 5.9	12.7	1.00	41.45	127	2	98	0	0	23	94.4	-21.5	80	21	5,000,000	0	0.0	0.0
C+ / 5.7	12.7	0.86	41.80	1,693	2	98	0	0	23	94.8	-21.4	90	21	5,000,000	0	0.0	0.0
B- / 7.0	7.8	1.25	32.20	19,638	6	64	29	1	18	60.9	-13.7	27	20	1,000	100	0.0	0.0
B- / 7.1	7.8	1.26	32.00	1,106	6	64	29	1	18	59.2	-13.8	23	20	0	0	0.0	0.0
C+ / 6.7	10.8	1.10	66.00	17,844	2	94	2	2	25	109.8	-16.3	60	15	1,000	100	0.0	0.0
C+ / 6.7	10.8	1.09	65.75	224	2	94	2	2	25	107.7	-16.5	55	15	0	0	0.0	0.0
C+ / 5.6	13.2	0.90	29.79	3,520	1	98	0	1	31	81.3	-21.1	93	12	1,000	100	0.0	0.0
C+ / 5.6	13.2	0.90	29.03	39	1	98	0	1	31	79.2	-21.3	92	12	0	0	0.0	0.0
C+ / 5.6	12.4	0.83	16.41	2,037	5	94	0	1	24	85.3	-18.4	94	9	1,000	100	0.0	0.0
C / 5.4	14.4	1.03	24.86	29,018	2	96	1	1	39	74.8	-22.8	88	23	1,000	100	0.0	0.0
C / 5.4	14.4	1.03	24.98	623	2	96	1	1	39	72.7	-22.9	86	23	0	0	0.0	0.0
C / 4.6	13.8	0.97	16.15	3,129	3	96	0	1	38	57.0	-23.8	56	20	1,000	100	0.0	2.0
C / 4.6	13.8	0.96	16.05	3	3	96	0	1	38	55.5	-23.9	51	20	0	0	0.0	2.0
C / 4.9	11.6	0.88	40.39	6,433	4	95	0	1	37	112.8	-16.9	87	19	1,000	100	0.0	0.0
C / 4.9	11.6	0.89	39.93	39	4	95	0	1	37	110.8	-17.0	86	19	0	0	0.0	0.0
U /	N/A	N/A	13.30	113	20	77	1	2	71	N/A	N/A	N/A	3	10,000	250	0.0	0.0
C- / 4.2	15.9	0.72	10.03	5	6	93	0	1	241	36.6	-21.9	57	7	1,000	100	0.0	2.0
D / 1.9	17.7	0.58	14.45	153	1	98	0	1	140	98.6	-41.7	99	10	1,000	100	0.0	2.0
D / 2.2	17.4	1.14	27.84	50	0	99	0	1	70	79.7	-32.9	17	14	1,000	100	0.0	1.0
U /	N/A	N/A	9.61	222	1	94	3	2	0	N/A	N/A	N/A	1	1,000,000	0	0.0	2.0
C+ / 5.6	14.6	0.94	19.87	463	0	97	1	2	176	120.4	-25.4	98	8	1,000	100	0.0	2.0
C- / 3.2	16.2	1.06	17.26	27	0	100	0	0	71	91.1	-29.0	30	14	1,000	100	0.0	1.0
C- / 3.6	15.4	1.14	16.11	9	0	99	0	1	134	83.4	-23.4	17	14	1,000	100	0.0	1.0
E+ / 0.6	37.2	1.77	9.60	21	9	90	0	1	5	-52.1	-11.6	6	19	5,000	50	0.0	1.5
E+ / 0.6	37.2	1.77	9.29	36	9	90	0	1	5	-53.1	-11.8	5	19	1,000	50	4.5	1.5
C+ / 6.0	13.3	1.00	19.08	133	1	98	0	1	0	51.4	-23.4	58	6	25	0	0.0	0.0
C+ / 5.6	12.0	1.07	19.68	70	0	99	0	1	0	84.7	-20.6	25	N/A	25	25	5.8	0.0
C+ / 5.6	12.0	1.08	18.88	20	0	99	0	1	0	79.9	-20.8	18	N/A	25	25	0.0	0.0
B- / 7.7	8.3	1.41	17.02	7	2	79	17	2	0	61.5	-16.1	12	N/A	25	25	5.8	0.0
B- / 7.7	8.4	1.41	16.34	2	2	79	17	2	0	57.4	-16.4	8	N/A	25	25	0.0	0.0
B+ / 9.8	2.6	0.43	11.98	8	48	23	28	1	0	17.3	-4.1	53	N/A	25	25	5.8	0.0
B+ / 9.8	2.5	0.42	11.50	3	48	23	28	1	0	14.5	-4.6	43	N/A	25	25	0.0	0.0
B+ / 9.9	1.9	0.32	11.27	18	61	18	20	1	0	11.6	-3.3	52	N/A	25	25	5.8	0.0
B+ / 9.9	2.0	0.32	10.81	11	61	18	20	1	0	8.7	-3.6	39	N/A	25	25	0.0	0.0
B+ / 9.9	1.7	0.28	11.09	28	67	15	17	1	0	10.3	-3.0	56	N/A	25	25	5.8	0.0
B+ / 9.9	1.7	0.29	10.64	16	67	15	17	1	0	7.5	-3.2	43	N/A	25	25	0.0	0.0
B+ / 9.1	4.4	0.75	14.40	10	0	39	59	2	0	37.1	-7.9	56	N/A	25	25	5.8	0.0
B+ / 9.1	4.4	0.75	13.84	3	0	39	59	2	0	33.8	-8.2	45	N/A	25	25	0.0	0.0
B- / 7.7	9.1	0.93	19.21	128	3	96	0	1	0	69.4	-13.9	24	N/A	25	25	5.8	0.0
B- / 7.7	9.1	0.92	18.43	42	3	96	0	1	0	65.1	-14.3	17	N/A	25	25	0.0	0.0
B / 8.2	6.6	1.03	14.11	182	18	58	20	4	0	37.3	-13.8	30	N/A	25	25	5.8	0.0
B / 8.2	6.7	1.04	13.54	145	18	58	20	4	0	33.8	-14.1	21	N/A	25	25	0.0	0.0
C+ / 6.4	12.1	0.90	21.05	28	1	98	0	1	0	96.0	-24.1	70	N/A	25	25	5.8	0.0

			99 Pct = Best / 0 Pct = Worst		PERFORMANCE								
					Perfor-mance Rating/Pts	Total Return % through 3/31/15			Annualized		Incl. in Returns		
Fund Type	Fund Name	Ticker Symbol	Overall Investment Rating	Phone		3 Mo	6 Mo	1Yr / Pct	3Yr / Pct	5Yr / Pct	Dividend Yield	Expense Ratio
SC	OH CollegeAdv 529 BR ING SmCo		B	(800) 441-7762	B- / 7.1	3.80	13.33	7.78 /61	13.96 /67	12.49 /64	0.00	2.50
FO	OH CollegeAdv 529 BR Intl Opp Opt		E+	(800) 441-7762	D- / 1.1	5.18	1.25	-5.80 / 5	6.51 /19	4.73 /11	0.00	1.83
FO	OH CollegeAdv 529 BR Intl Opp Opt		E+	(800) 441-7762	D- / 1.3	4.97	0.89	-6.52 / 4	5.70 /16	3.94 / 8	0.00	2.58
GR	OH CollegeAdv 529 BR LC Core Opt		B-	(800) 441-7762	C+ / 5.9	0.10	5.16	9.15 /70	14.58 /72	11.99 /60	0.00	1.45
GR	OH CollegeAdv 529 BR LC Core Opt		B-	(800) 441-7762	C+ / 6.3	-0.11	4.74	8.30 /65	13.69 /65	11.15 /54	0.00	2.20
AA	OH CollegeAdv 529 BR Mdt 0-5 Opt		C	(800) 441-7762	C- / 3.5	2.30	3.81	6.16 /48	10.52 /42	9.57 /41	0.00	1.40
AA	OH CollegeAdv 529 BR Mdt 0-5 Opt		C	(800) 441-7762	C- / 3.9	2.08	3.44	5.39 /42	9.69 /37	8.76 /35	0.00	2.15
AA	OH CollegeAdv 529 BR Mdt 10-12		C	(800) 441-7762	D / 2.2	2.25	3.37	5.85 /45	8.05 /27	7.27 /25	0.00	1.39
AA	OH CollegeAdv 529 BR Mdt 10-12		C	(800) 441-7762	D+ / 2.6	1.98	3.01	5.04 /39	7.23 /23	6.45 /20	0.00	2.14
AA	OH CollegeAdv 529 BR Mdt 13-16		C-	(800) 441-7762	D- / 1.1	1.63	2.10	3.79 /30	5.32 /14	4.77 /11	0.00	1.27
AA	OH CollegeAdv 529 BR Mdt 13-16		C	(800) 441-7762	D- / 1.3	1.45	1.69	3.03 /27	4.54 /12	3.99 / 8	0.00	2.02
AA	OH CollegeAdv 529 BR Mdt 17Pl Op		C-	(800) 441-7762	E+ / 0.8	1.33	1.41	2.60 /25	4.10 /10	3.66 / 7	0.00	1.21
AA	OH CollegeAdv 529 BR Mdt 17Pl Op		C-	(800) 441-7762	D- / 1.0	1.12	1.03	1.82 /21	3.36 / 9	2.89 / 6	0.00	1.96
AA	OH CollegeAdv 529 BR Mdt 6-9 Opt		C	(800) 441-7762	C- / 3.5	2.30	4.02	6.39 /50	10.38 /42	9.48 /40	0.00	1.40
AA	OH CollegeAdv 529 BR Mdt 6-9 Opt		C	(800) 441-7762	C- / 3.9	2.09	3.61	5.58 /43	9.54 /36	8.69 /35	0.00	2.15
MC	OH CollegeAdv 529 BR Rain MCE		C	(800) 441-7762	C+ / 6.0	5.76	9.03	12.45 /85	13.44 /63	14.10 /79	0.00	1.56
MC	OH CollegeAdv 529 BR Rain MCE		C+	(800) 441-7762	C+ / 6.4	5.55	8.56	11.51 /80	12.57 /56	13.25 /71	0.00	2.31
EN	Oil Equip Distr & Serv UltSec ProFd	OEPIX	E-	(888) 776-3637	E- / 0.2	-3.28	-29.87	-26.05 / 0	0.35 / 5	3.61 / 7	0.00	1.73
GR	Old Westbury Large Cap Core	OWLCX	C+	(800) 607-2200	C / 5.5	2.67	4.21	7.92 /62	12.10 /53	6.56 /20	1.26	1.04
* FO	Old Westbury Large Cap Strategies	OWLSX	C+	(800) 607-2200	C+ / 5.7	3.10	6.46	8.64 /67	12.10 /53	8.62 /34	0.71	1.14
* GL	Old Westbury Small & Mid Cap	OWSMX	C	(800) 607-2200	C / 4.9	4.07	7.21	4.72 /37	11.03 /46	11.08 /53	0.72	1.18
GR	Olstein All Cap Value Adv	OFAFX	A+	(800) 799-2113	A / 9.5	2.04	11.92	16.74 /94	17.81 /94	14.80 /85	0.00	1.28
GR	Olstein All Cap Value C	OFALX	A+	(800) 799-2113	A- / 9.1	1.81	11.35	15.59 /93	16.79 /89	13.86 /76	0.00	2.28
GI	Olstein Strategic Opps Fd A	OFSAX	A	(800) 799-2113	A+ / 9.7	4.82	15.57	16.55 /94	20.23 /98	16.72 /95	0.00	1.61
GI	Olstein Strategic Opps Fd C	OFSCX	A	(800) 799-2113	A+ / 9.7	4.61	15.10	15.65 /93	19.33 /97	15.87 /92	0.00	2.36
AA	OnTrack Core Fund	OTRFX	U	(855) 747-9555	U /	1.91	2.76	1.39 /20	--	--	1.78	3.11
AA	Oppenheimer 529 BS AgeBsd 0-6yr 4		B	(888) 470-0862	C+ / 6.0	1.93	5.05	8.11 /64	12.96 /59	12.08 /61	0.00	0.60
AA	Oppenheimer 529 BS AgeBsd 0-6yr		C+	(888) 470-0862	C / 4.6	1.53	4.81	7.88 /62	11.73 /51	10.89 /52	0.00	0.96
AA	Oppenheimer 529 BS AgeBsd 0-6yr		C+	(888) 470-0862	C / 5.0	1.47	4.64	7.65 /60	11.43 /48	10.63 /50	0.00	1.21
AA	Oppenheimer 529 BS AgeBsd 0-6yr		B-	(888) 470-0862	C / 5.3	1.62	4.84	7.93 /62	11.74 /51	10.90 /52	0.00	0.96
AA	Oppenheimer 529 BS AgeBsd 0-6yr		B-	(888) 470-0862	C / 5.4	1.65	4.93	8.23 /64	12.01 /53	11.18 /54	0.00	0.71
AA	Oppenheimer 529 BS AgeBsd		B-	(888) 470-0862	C- / 3.7	1.68	3.97	6.37 /50	9.07 /33	9.12 /38	0.00	0.59
AA	Oppenheimer 529 BS AgeBsd		C	(888) 470-0862	D+ / 2.5	1.25	3.50	5.76 /44	8.12 /28	8.13 /31	0.00	0.93
AA	Oppenheimer 529 BS AgeBsd		C+	(888) 470-0862	D+ / 2.9	1.19	3.40	5.51 /43	7.82 /26	7.86 /29	0.00	1.18
AA	Oppenheimer 529 BS AgeBsd		C+	(888) 470-0862	C- / 3.1	1.28	3.56	5.81 /45	8.11 /29	8.14 /31	0.00	0.93
AA	Oppenheimer 529 BS AgeBsd		C+	(888) 470-0862	C- / 3.3	1.32	3.68	6.09 /47	8.37 /29	8.40 /32	0.00	0.68
AA	Oppenheimer 529 BS AgeBsd		C+	(888) 470-0862	D+ / 2.8	1.52	3.40	5.42 /42	7.63 /25	7.92 /29	0.00	0.59
AA	Oppenheimer 529 BS AgeBsd		C	(888) 470-0862	D / 1.9	1.21	3.09	5.04 /39	6.91 /21	7.13 /24	0.00	0.92
AA	Oppenheimer 529 BS AgeBsd		C	(888) 470-0862	D / 2.2	1.11	2.88	4.71 /36	6.61 /19	6.84 /22	0.00	1.17
AA	Oppenheimer 529 BS AgeBsd		C	(888) 470-0862	D+ / 2.4	1.20	3.03	5.00 /39	6.89 /21	7.11 /24	0.00	0.92
AA	Oppenheimer 529 BS AgeBsd		C+	(888) 470-0862	D+ / 2.5	1.24	3.17	5.31 /41	7.16 /22	7.37 /26	0.00	0.67
AA	Oppenheimer 529 BS AgeBsd		C	(888) 470-0862	D- / 1.4	1.16	2.35	3.71 /30	4.82 /13	5.21 /13	0.00	0.55
AA	Oppenheimer 529 BS AgeBsd		C	(888) 470-0862	D- / 1.0	1.02	2.26	3.53 /29	4.46 /11	4.90 /11	0.00	0.86
AA	Oppenheimer 529 BS AgeBsd		C	(888) 470-0862	D- / 1.2	0.93	2.07	3.33 /28	4.20 /11	4.66 /11	0.00	1.11
AA	Oppenheimer 529 BS AgeBsd		C	(888) 470-0862	D- / 1.3	0.97	2.17	3.55 /29	4.44 /11	4.90 /12	0.00	0.86
AA	Oppenheimer 529 BS AgeBsd		C	(888) 470-0862	D- / 1.4	1.09	2.34	3.84 /31	4.72 /12	5.19 /13	0.00	0.61
AA	Oppenheimer 529 BS AgeBsd 18yr 4		C-	(888) 470-0862	E+ / 0.8	0.75	1.36	2.05 /22	1.98 / 6	2.36 / 5	0.00	0.48
AA	Oppenheimer 529 BS AgeBsd 18yr A		C-	(888) 470-0862	E+ / 0.6	0.59	1.09	1.69 /21	1.69 / 6	2.15 / 5	0.00	0.73
AA	Oppenheimer 529 BS AgeBsd 18yr C		C-	(888) 470-0862	E+ / 0.7	0.60	1.00	1.41 /20	1.43 / 6	1.89 / 4	0.00	0.98
AA	Oppenheimer 529 BS AgeBsd 18yr G		C-	(888) 470-0862	E+ / 0.7	0.61	1.07	1.68 /21	1.66 / 6	2.15 / 5	0.00	0.73
AA	Oppenheimer 529 BS AgeBsd 18yr H		C-	(888) 470-0862	E+ / 0.7	0.67	1.20	1.88 /21	1.92 / 6	2.41 / 5	0.00	0.48
AA	Oppenheimer 529 BS AgeBsd 7-9yr 4		B-	(888) 470-0862	C / 4.4	1.70	4.29	6.90 /54	10.41 /42	10.25 /47	0.00	0.59

● Denotes fund is closed to new investors
* Denotes fund is included in Section II

www.thestreetratings.com

RISK			NET ASSETS		ASSET				Portfolio	BULL / BEAR		FUND MANAGER		MINIMUMS		LOADS	
	3 Year		NAV							Last Bull	Last Bear	Manager	Manager	Initial	Additional	Front	Back
Risk Rating/Pts	Standard Deviation	Beta	As of 3/31/15	Total $(Mil)	Cash %	Stocks %	Bonds %	Other %	Turnover Ratio	Market Return	Market Return	Quality Pct	Tenure (Years)	Purch. $	Purch. $	End Load	End Load
C+ / 6.3	12.2	0.90	20.23	9	1	98	0	1	0	91.2	-24.3	60	N/A	25	25	0.0	0.0
C / 5.5	12.4	0.90	13.00	41	1	98	0	1	0	41.2	-25.3	39	N/A	25	25	5.8	0.0
C / 5.4	12.4	0.90	12.47	14	1	98	0	1	0	37.7	-25.5	29	N/A	25	25	0.0	0.0
B- / 7.0	10.9	1.10	19.57	20	1	98	0	1	0	94.4	-22.6	27	N/A	25	25	5.8	0.0
B- / 7.0	10.9	1.10	18.78	9	1	98	0	1	0	89.6	-22.8	19	N/A	25	25	0.0	0.0
B- / 7.8	8.4	1.41	16.90	84	3	80	16	1	0	61.8	-15.9	12	N/A	25	25	5.8	0.0
B- / 7.8	8.4	1.41	16.22	34	3	80	16	1	0	57.8	-16.2	9	6	25	25	0.0	0.0
B+ / 9.0	5.0	0.85	15.01	322	0	45	54	1	0	41.8	-9.3	51	N/A	25	25	5.8	0.0
B+ / 9.0	5.0	0.86	14.39	64	0	45	54	1	0	38.3	-9.6	39	N/A	25	25	0.0	0.0
B+ / 9.6	3.4	0.57	13.13	607	26	31	41	2	0	26.1	-6.0	56	N/A	25	25	5.8	0.0
B+ / 9.6	3.3	0.57	12.60	103	26	31	41	2	0	23.0	-6.3	46	6	25	25	0.0	0.0
B+ / 9.7	2.7	0.46	12.23	391	43	25	30	2	0	19.9	-5.0	56	N/A	25	25	5.8	0.0
B+ / 9.7	2.8	0.47	11.75	84	43	25	30	2	0	16.9	-5.3	44	N/A	25	25	0.0	0.0
B- / 7.9	7.9	1.34	17.32	145	2	76	20	2	0	60.0	-15.0	17	N/A	25	25	5.8	0.0
B- / 7.9	8.0	1.35	16.64	49	2	76	20	2	0	55.9	-15.3	11	N/A	25	25	0.0	0.0
C+ / 5.8	11.5	1.00	22.22	13	0	99	0	1	0	89.0	-24.5	24	N/A	25	25	5.8	0.0
C+ / 5.8	11.6	1.00	21.31	7	0	99	0	1	0	84.1	-24.7	16	N/A	25	25	0.0	0.0
D- / 1.5	28.7	1.65	20.07	12	39	60	0	1	68	39.3	-47.1	7	2	15,000	100	0.0	0.0
C+ / 6.9	10.5	1.02	14.60	1,075	4	95	0	1	43	53.1	-18.3	18	4	1,000	100	0.0	0.0
C+ / 6.3	10.3	0.72	13.31	13,251	0	97	2	1	51	65.8	-25.5	93	4	1,000	100	0.0	0.0
C+ / 6.3	10.1	0.67	16.88	5,543	3	95	0	2	38	66.1	-22.0	92	10	1,000	100	0.0	0.0
B- / 7.2	10.8	1.06	25.46	154	10	89	0	1	51	114.4	-19.1	73	20	1,000	100	0.0	0.0
B- / 7.1	10.8	1.06	21.90	639	10	89	0	1	51	108.3	-19.4	62	20	1,000	100	0.0	0.0
C+ / 5.8	13.1	1.16	18.49	161	3	96	0	1	60	133.2	-24.0	77	9	1,000	100	5.5	0.0
C+ / 5.7	13.1	1.16	17.26	40	3	96	0	1	60	127.2	-24.2	71	9	1,000	100	0.0	0.0
U /	N/A	N/A	51.76	121	56	5	38	1	412	N/A	N/A	N/A	2	1,000	500	0.0	0.0
B / 8.0	8.9	1.53	18.52	132	0	0	0	100	0	78.6	-14.9	19	8	25	15	0.0	0.0
B- / 7.8	9.1	1.55	13.28	94	0	0	0	100	0	71.5	-16.9	11	8	25	15	3.5	0.0
B- / 7.8	9.2	1.56	13.09	55	0	0	0	100	0	70.0	-16.9	9	8	25	15	0.0	0.0
B- / 7.8	9.1	1.55	17.55	5	0	0	0	100	0	71.3	-16.8	11	8	25	15	0.0	0.0
B- / 7.8	9.1	1.55	17.89	2	0	0	0	100	0	72.9	-16.8	12	8	25	15	0.0	0.0
B+ / 9.3	5.9	1.02	17.53	183	0	0	0	100	0	50.5	-8.9	39	8	25	15	0.0	0.0
B+ / 9.0	6.1	1.05	12.12	28	0	0	0	100	0	45.9	-10.9	24	8	25	15	3.5	0.0
B+ / 9.0	6.2	1.07	11.87	30	0	0	0	100	0	44.8	-11.0	20	8	25	15	0.0	0.0
B+ / 9.0	6.2	1.06	16.58	67	0	0	0	100	0	46.0	-10.9	23	8	25	15	0.0	0.0
B+ / 9.0	6.2	1.07	16.90	40	0	0	0	100	0	47.3	-10.8	25	8	25	15	0.0	0.0
B+ / 9.6	4.9	0.86	16.72	307	0	0	0	100	0	41.4	-7.0	43	8	25	15	0.0	0.0
B+ / 9.4	5.2	0.90	11.67	41	0	0	0	100	0	38.2	-9.0	29	8	25	15	3.5	0.0
B+ / 9.4	5.3	0.91	11.79	51	0	0	0	100	0	37.0	-9.0	25	8	25	15	0.0	0.0
B+ / 9.4	5.2	0.90	15.96	149	0	0	0	100	0	38.1	-8.9	29	8	25	15	0.0	0.0
B+ / 9.4	5.3	0.91	16.27	75	0	0	0	100	0	39.4	-8.9	31	8	25	15	0.0	0.0
B+ / 9.9	3.0	0.53	14.80	235	0	0	0	100	0	24.3	-3.8	56	8	25	15	0.0	0.0
B+ / 9.9	3.4	0.58	10.85	30	0	0	0	100	0	23.4	-5.3	43	8	25	15	3.5	0.0
B+ / 9.9	3.3	0.57	10.85	54	0	0	0	100	0	22.3	-5.3	40	8	25	15	0.0	0.0
B+ / 9.9	3.4	0.58	14.57	131	0	0	0	100	0	23.4	-5.2	42	8	25	15	0.0	0.0
B+ / 9.9	3.4	0.58	14.86	73	0	0	0	100	0	24.4	-5.1	46	8	25	15	0.0	0.0
B+ / 9.9	1.2	0.18	13.45	149	0	0	0	100	0	8.8	-0.6	67	8	25	15	0.0	0.0
B+ / 9.9	1.4	0.22	10.22	14	0	0	0	100	0	8.1	-1.3	58	8	25	15	3.5	0.0
B+ / 9.9	1.4	0.22	10.09	38	0	0	0	100	0	7.2	-1.4	54	8	25	15	0.0	0.0
B+ / 9.9	1.4	0.22	13.28	103	0	0	0	100	0	8.1	-1.4	57	8	25	15	0.0	0.0
B+ / 9.9	1.4	0.22	13.54	55	0	0	0	100	0	9.1	-1.2	62	8	25	15	0.0	0.0
B / 8.9	6.8	1.19	17.98	172	0	0	0	100	0	59.7	-10.8	32	8	25	15	0.0	0.0

99 Pct = Best
0 Pct = Worst

Fund Type	Fund Name	Ticker Symbol	Overall Investment Rating	Phone	Performance Rating/Pts	3 Mo	6 Mo	1Yr / Pct	3Yr / Pct	5Yr / Pct	Dividend Yield	Expense Ratio
AA	Oppenheimer 529 BS AgeBsd 7-9yr		C	(888) 470-0862	C- / 3.2	1.34	3.88	6.37 /50	9.27 /35	9.00 /37	0.00	0.94
AA	Oppenheimer 529 BS AgeBsd 7-9yr		C+	(888) 470-0862	C- / 3.6	1.27	3.73	6.14 /48	8.99 /33	8.75 /35	0.00	1.19
AA	Oppenheimer 529 BS AgeBsd 7-9yr		C+	(888) 470-0862	C- / 3.8	1.32	3.87	6.35 /49	9.24 /35	9.02 /37	0.00	0.94
AA	Oppenheimer 529 BS AgeBsd 7-9yr		C+	(888) 470-0862	C- / 3.9	1.41	3.98	6.68 /52	9.53 /36	9.28 /39	0.00	0.69
BA	Oppenheimer 529 BS Bal Port 4		C+	(888) 470-0862	D+ / 2.9	1.50	3.37	5.48 /42	7.76 /26	8.16 /31	0.00	0.65
BA	Oppenheimer 529 BS Bal Port A		C	(888) 470-0862	D / 1.8	1.20	2.96	5.00 /39	6.78 /20	6.93 /23	0.00	0.88
BA	Oppenheimer 529 BS Bal Port C		C	(888) 470-0862	D / 2.2	1.11	2.87	4.69 /36	6.51 /19	6.64 /21	0.00	1.13
BA	Oppenheimer 529 BS Bal Port G		C	(888) 470-0862	D+ / 2.3	1.10	2.94	4.93 /38	6.79 /20	6.90 /22	0.00	0.88
BA	Oppenheimer 529 BS Bal Port H		C+	(888) 470-0862	D+ / 2.5	1.25	3.14	5.29 /41	7.06 /22	7.18 /24	0.00	0.63
GR	Oppenheimer 529 BS Eq Port 4		B-	(888) 470-0862	C+ / 6.6	2.08	5.25	8.44 /66	14.04 /67	12.91 /67	0.00	0.63
GR	Oppenheimer 529 BS Eq Port A		C+	(888) 470-0862	C / 5.3	1.59	5.10	8.51 /66	12.87 /59	11.57 /57	0.00	0.94
GR	Oppenheimer 529 BS Eq Port C		B-	(888) 470-0862	C+ / 5.8	1.58	4.91	8.28 /65	12.58 /57	11.29 /55	0.00	1.19
GR	Oppenheimer 529 BS Eq Port G		B-	(888) 470-0862	C+ / 6.0	1.61	5.11	8.61 /67	12.89 /59	11.58 /58	0.00	0.94
GR	Oppenheimer 529 BS Eq Port H		B-	(888) 470-0862	C+ / 6.1	1.63	5.19	8.81 /68	13.16 /61	11.84 /60	0.00	0.69
AA	Oppenheimer 529 BS Idx AB 0-6yr 4		B	(888) 470-0862	C+ / 6.4	2.20	5.30	9.13 /70	13.48 /63	12.08 /61	0.00	0.20
AA	Oppenheimer 529 BS Idx AB 10-11yr		B-	(888) 470-0862	C- / 4.0	1.83	4.23	7.12 /56	9.52 /36	9.19 /38	0.00	0.21
AA	Oppenheimer 529 BS Idx AB 12-14yr		B-	(888) 470-0862	C- / 3.2	1.63	3.67	6.24 /49	8.19 /28	8.27 /32	0.00	0.21
AA	Oppenheimer 529 BS Idx AB 15-17yr		C	(888) 470-0862	D / 1.7	1.36	2.83	4.73 /37	5.46 /15	6.02 /17	0.00	0.22
AA	Oppenheimer 529 BS Idx AB 18 yr 4		C	(888) 470-0862	E+ / 0.9	1.11	2.01	3.16 /27	2.88 / 8	3.98 / 8	0.00	0.22
AA	Oppenheimer 529 BS Idx AB 7-9 yr 4		B	(888) 470-0862	C / 4.7	1.91	4.48	7.72 /61	10.79 /44	10.10 /46	0.00	0.21
BA	Oppenheimer 529 BS Idx Bal Port 4		B-	(888) 470-0862	C- / 3.2	1.65	3.71	6.24 /49	8.17 /28	8.27 /32	0.00	0.21
AG	Oppenheimer 529 SE Aggressive 3		B-	(888) 470-0862	C / 5.5	2.52	5.15	7.54 /59	12.16 /54	10.10 /46	0.00	2.03
AG	Oppenheimer 529 SE Aggressive A		C+	(888) 470-0862	C / 5.3	2.72	5.55	8.36 /65	13.01 /60	10.94 /52	0.00	1.19
GR	Oppenheimer 529 SE Cap Apprec A		C+	(888) 470-0862	C / 5.1	2.65	5.92	9.05 /70	12.49 /56	10.93 /52	0.00	1.11
GR	Oppenheimer 529 SE Cap Apprec B		B-	(888) 470-0862	C / 5.3	2.46	5.51	8.22 /64	11.64 /50	10.08 /45	0.00	2.06
GR	Oppenheimer 529 SE Cap Apprec C		B-	(888) 470-0862	C / 5.3	2.47	5.51	8.23 /64	11.64 /50	10.08 /45	0.00	2.06
AA	Oppenheimer 529 SE Conserative 3		C	(888) 470-0862	D / 1.9	1.59	2.72	3.98 /32	5.88 /16	6.08 /17	0.00	2.04
AA	Oppenheimer 529 SE Conserative A		C	(888) 470-0862	D / 1.7	1.72	3.08	4.71 /37	6.66 /20	6.87 /22	0.00	1.06
GL	Oppenheimer 529 SE Global 2		D	(888) 470-0862	D+ / 2.3	5.45	3.68	-0.13 /15	6.90 /21	5.82 /16	0.00	2.12
GL	Oppenheimer 529 SE Global 3		D	(888) 470-0862	D+ / 2.3	5.44	3.68	-0.12 /15	6.89 /21	5.82 /16	0.00	2.12
GL	Oppenheimer 529 SE Global A		D	(888) 470-0862	D / 2.0	5.62	4.07	0.64 /17	7.71 /25	6.64 /21	0.00	1.37
SC	Oppenheimer 529 SE Main St		A-	(888) 470-0862	B / 7.8	3.39	8.92	11.90 /82	16.38 /86	14.70 /84	0.00	1.11
SC	Oppenheimer 529 SE Main St		A	(888) 470-0862	B / 8.0	3.19	8.52	11.06 /79	15.50 /79	13.84 /76	0.00	2.19
SC	Oppenheimer 529 SE Main St		A	(888) 470-0862	B / 8.0	3.19	8.52	11.05 /79	15.49 /79	13.84 /76	0.00	2.19
GI	Oppenheimer 529 SE MainStay MAP		B-	(888) 470-0862	C+ / 5.8	1.62	5.24	9.38 /71	13.87 /66	11.99 /60	0.00	1.37
GI	Oppenheimer 529 SE MainStay MAP		B-	(888) 470-0862	C+ / 6.0	1.41	4.84	8.51 /66	12.99 /60	11.14 /54	0.00	1.92
GI	Oppenheimer 529 SE MainStay MAP		B-	(888) 470-0862	C+ / 6.0	1.42	4.86	8.54 /67	13.01 /60	11.14 /54	0.00	1.92
AA	Oppenheimer 529 SE Moderate 3		C+	(888) 470-0862	C- / 3.2	1.97	3.57	5.22 /40	8.23 /28	7.81 /29	0.00	1.97
AA	Oppenheimer 529 SE Moderate A		C+	(888) 470-0862	D+ / 2.9	2.16	3.96	6.03 /47	9.04 /33	8.63 /34	0.00	1.13
AA	Oppenheimer 529 SE Moderately		C+	(888) 470-0862	C / 4.4	2.26	4.36	6.38 /50	10.35 /41	9.19 /38	0.00	2.03
AA	Oppenheimer 529 SE Moderately		C+	(888) 470-0862	C- / 4.2	2.45	4.76	7.20 /57	11.19 /47	10.01 /45	0.00	1.15
GR	Oppenheimer 529 SE Value A		B-	(888) 470-0862	C / 5.5	-0.16	3.66	8.04 /63	13.84 /66	11.09 /53	0.00	0.98
GR	Oppenheimer 529 SE Value B		B-	(888) 470-0862	C+ / 5.7	-0.34	3.27	7.21 /57	12.98 /60	10.24 /46	0.00	1.99
GR	Oppenheimer 529 SE Value C		B-	(888) 470-0862	C+ / 5.7	-0.33	3.27	7.22 /57	12.99 /60	10.25 /47	0.00	1.99
AG	Oppenheimer 529 TEP Aggressive		B-	(888) 470-0862	C+ / 6.6	2.89	5.90	8.60 /67	13.90 /66	11.90 /60	0.00	0.77
AA	Oppenheimer 529 TEP Cons Portfolio		C+	(888) 470-0862	D+ / 2.4	1.87	3.53	5.46 /42	6.83 /20	7.01 /23	0.00	0.67
AA	Oppenheimer 529 TEP Mod Agg Port		B	(888) 470-0862	C / 5.3	2.60	5.22	7.73 /61	11.66 /50	10.57 /49	0.00	0.75
AA	Oppenheimer 529 TEP Moderate Port		B-	(888) 470-0862	C- / 4.0	2.39	4.65	6.88 /54	9.38 /35	9.07 /37	0.00	0.72
AA	Oppenheimer 529 TEP Ultra Cons		C	(888) 470-0862	D- / 1.2	1.37	2.50	3.94 /31	4.10 /10	4.64 /11	0.00	0.61
AA	Oppenheimer Active Alloc A	OAAAX	C	(888) 470-0862	C- / 3.4	2.20	4.15	5.89 /45	10.37 /42	8.93 /36	0.92	1.23
AA	● Oppenheimer Active Alloc B	OAABX	C	(888) 470-0862	C- / 3.8	1.98	3.78	5.11 /39	9.51 /36	8.04 /30	0.01	1.98
AA	Oppenheimer Active Alloc C	OAACX	C	(888) 470-0862	C- / 3.8	2.00	3.75	4.99 /38	9.56 /37	8.11 /31	0.28	1.98

● Denotes fund is closed to new investors
* Denotes fund is included in Section II

www.thestreetratings.com

RISK			NET ASSETS		ASSET					BULL / BEAR		FUND MANAGER		MINIMUMS		LOADS	
	3 Year		NAV						Portfolio	Last Bull	Last Bear	Manager	Manager	Initial	Additional	Front	Back
Risk	Standard		As of	Total	Cash	Stocks	Bonds	Other	Turnover	Market	Market	Quality	Tenure	Purch.	Purch.	End	End
Rating/Pts	Deviation	Beta	3/31/15	$(Mil)	%	%	%	%	Ratio	Return	Return	Pct	(Years)	$	$	Load	Load
B /8.6	7.2	1.23	12.85	50	0	0	0	100	0	53.9	-12.9	17	8	25	15	3.5	0.0
B /8.6	7.2	1.23	12.79	48	0	0	0	100	0	52.5	-13.0	15	8	25	15	0.0	0.0
B /8.6	7.1	1.22	16.91	50	0	0	0	100	0	53.9	-13.0	18	8	25	15	0.0	0.0
B /8.6	7.1	1.22	17.24	25	0	0	0	100	0	55.2	-12.8	20	8	25	15	0.0	0.0
B+ /9.6	4.9	0.86	12.89	63	0	0	0	100	0	42.4	-6.9	46	8	25	15	0.0	0.0
B+ /9.5	5.1	0.87	10.08	23	0	0	0	100	0	37.6	-8.7	31	8	25	15	3.5	0.0
B+ /9.4	5.1	0.88	10.04	29	0	0	0	100	0	36.3	-8.7	28	8	25	15	0.0	0.0
B+ /9.5	5.1	0.88	11.91	23	0	0	0	100	0	37.5	-8.7	31	8	25	15	0.0	0.0
B+ /9.5	5.1	0.87	12.15	16	0	0	0	100	0	38.6	-8.5	34	8	25	15	0.0	0.0
B- /7.6	10.0	1.03	19.65	385	0	0	0	100	0	88.1	-16.8	34	8	25	15	0.0	0.0
B- /7.4	10.2	1.03	14.02	55	0	0	0	100	0	80.1	-19.1	22	8	25	15	3.5	0.0
B- /7.4	10.2	1.03	13.47	54	0	0	0	100	0	78.5	-19.2	19	8	25	15	0.0	0.0
B- /7.4	10.2	1.03	18.30	253	0	0	0	100	0	80.0	-19.0	22	8	25	15	0.0	0.0
B- /7.4	10.2	1.03	18.65	110	0	0	0	100	0	81.4	-19.0	24	8	25	15	0.0	0.0
B /8.1	8.8	1.52	15.30	302	0	0	0	100	0	79.8	-16.2	25	8	25	15	0.0	0.0
B+ /9.3	5.8	1.01	15.04	119	0	0	0	100	0	51.5	-9.7	46	8	25	15	0.0	0.0
B+ /9.7	4.8	0.84	14.98	173	0	0	0	100	0	43.1	-7.4	55	8	25	15	0.0	0.0
B+ /9.9	3.1	0.51	14.17	160	0	0	0	100	0	26.7	-3.2	67	8	25	15	0.0	0.0
B+ /9.9	2.0	0.18	13.72	106	0	0	0	100	0	12.2	1.6	77	8	25	15	0.0	0.0
B /8.9	6.8	1.19	14.93	206	0	0	0	100	0	60.5	-12.0	37	8	25	15	0.0	0.0
B+ /9.7	4.8	0.85	14.82	151	0	0	0	100	0	43.0	-7.4	54	8	25	15	0.0	0.0
B- /7.4	10.1	1.02	37.39	40	0	0	0	100	0	74.5	-20.1	18	10	250	25	0.0	0.0
B- /7.5	10.1	1.02	41.86	133	0	0	0	100	0	79.1	-19.8	25	10	250	25	4.8	0.0
B- /7.8	10.1	0.96	49.88	13	0	0	0	100	0	79.3	-16.5	29	10	250	25	4.8	0.0
B- /7.7	10.2	0.96	44.23	1	0	0	0	100	0	74.7	-16.8	21	10	250	25	0.0	0.0
B- /7.7	10.2	0.96	41.55	3	0	0	0	100	0	74.7	-16.8	21	10	250	25	0.0	0.0
B+ /9.7	4.5	0.77	28.74	13	0	0	0	100	0	31.9	-8.0	34	10	250	25	0.0	0.0
B+ /9.8	4.5	0.77	32.46	29	0	0	0	100	0	35.4	-7.7	45	10	250	25	4.8	0.0
C+ /6.3	11.8	0.86	46.44	1	0	0	0	100	0	44.1	-20.1	49	10	250	25	0.0	0.0
C+ /6.3	11.8	0.86	48.68	3	0	0	0	100	0	44.1	-20.1	49	10	250	25	0.0	0.0
C+ /6.4	11.8	0.86	50.15	12	0	0	0	100	0	47.9	-19.8	61	10	250	25	4.8	0.0
B- /7.3	10.9	0.76	83.04	16	0	0	0	100	0	107.8	-23.6	91	10	250	25	4.8	0.0
B- /7.3	10.9	0.76	75.30	1	0	0	0	100	0	102.5	-23.8	88	10	250	25	0.0	0.0
B- /7.3	10.9	0.76	77.06	4	0	0	0	100	0	102.5	-23.8	88	10	250	25	0.0	0.0
B- /7.5	10.1	1.04	52.61	9	0	0	0	100	0	88.0	-19.8	30	10	250	25	4.8	0.0
B- /7.4	10.1	1.04	48.07	N/A	0	0	0	100	0	83.2	-20.0	21	10	250	25	0.0	0.0
B- /7.4	10.1	1.04	50.08	2	0	0	0	100	0	83.2	-20.0	21	10	250	25	0.0	0.0
B+ /9.0	6.4	1.10	33.67	26	0	0	0	100	0	46.6	-12.1	21	10	250	25	0.0	0.0
B+ /9.0	6.4	1.10	37.30	73	0	0	0	100	0	50.3	-11.8	29	10	250	25	4.8	0.0
B /8.1	8.3	1.42	38.50	31	0	0	0	100	0	61.5	-17.5	11	10	250	25	0.0	0.0
B /8.1	8.3	1.41	42.72	99	0	0	0	100	0	65.7	-17.2	16	10	250	25	4.8	0.0
B- /7.5	10.2	1.03	57.54	9	0	0	0	100	0	80.3	-20.8	31	10	250	25	4.8	0.0
B- /7.5	10.2	1.03	52.06	N/A	0	0	0	100	0	75.7	-21.1	23	10	250	25	0.0	0.0
B- /7.5	10.2	1.03	50.78	3	0	0	0	100	0	75.7	-21.1	23	10	250	25	0.0	0.0
B- /7.5	10.2	1.03	19.58	79	0	0	0	100	0	84.2	-19.7	32	10	250	25	0.0	0.0
B+ /9.9	4.0	0.69	14.68	11	0	0	0	100	0	34.4	-5.8	59	10	250	25	0.0	0.0
B /8.4	8.0	1.37	18.96	30	0	0	0	100	0	66.9	-15.0	24	10	250	25	0.0	0.0
B+ /9.3	6.0	1.03	17.55	18	0	0	0	100	0	50.6	-10.2	42	10	250	25	0.0	0.0
B+ /9.9	2.3	0.36	11.88	5	0	0	0	100	0	18.3	-1.1	71	10	250	25	0.0	0.0
B /8.0	8.1	1.37	12.55	1,662	15	74	9	2	9	55.1	-15.7	15	10	1,000	50	5.8	0.0
B /8.0	8.1	1.37	12.37	128	15	74	9	2	9	50.8	-16.0	10	10	1,000	50	0.0	0.0
B /8.0	8.2	1.37	12.27	573	15	74	9	2	9	51.3	-16.1	10	10	1,000	50	0.0	0.0

99 Pct = Best
0 Pct = Worst

Fund Type	Fund Name	Ticker Symbol	Overall Investment Rating	Phone	Perfor-mance Rating/Pts	3 Mo	6 Mo	1Yr / Pct	3Yr / Pct	5Yr / Pct	Dividend Yield	Expense Ratio
								Total Return % through 3/31/15	Annualized		Incl. in Returns	
AA	Oppenheimer Active Alloc R	OAANX	C+	(888) 470-0862	C- / 4.2	2.13	4.05	5.62 /43	10.13 /40	8.69 /35	0.70	1.48
AA	Oppenheimer Active Alloc Y	OAAYX	C+	(888) 470-0862	C / 4.5	2.26	4.26	6.06 /47	10.69 /44	9.25 /39	1.28	0.98
GR	Oppenheimer Capital Appr A	OPTFX	C+	(888) 470-0862	B / 7.7	3.44	8.73	19.14 /96	15.34 /78	12.65 /65	0.00	1.07
GR	● Oppenheimer Capital Appr B	OTGBX	C+	(888) 470-0862	B / 8.2	3.26	8.32	18.24 /96	14.42 /70	11.73 /59	0.00	1.82
GR	Oppenheimer Capital Appr C	OTFCX	C+	(888) 470-0862	B / 8.2	3.26	8.31	18.25 /96	14.46 /71	11.78 /59	0.00	1.82
GR	Oppenheimer Capital Appr Fd/VA Svc		A-	(888) 470-0862	B+ / 8.8	3.47	8.76	19.24 /96	15.43 /78	12.77 /66	0.16	1.06
GR	Oppenheimer Capital Appr I	OPTIX	A	(888) 470-0862	A- / 9.0	3.56	8.96	19.67 /97	15.86 /82	--	0.00	0.63
GR	Oppenheimer Capital Appr R	OTCNX	B-	(888) 470-0862	B+ / 8.6	3.38	8.59	18.83 /96	15.04 /75	12.36 /63	0.00	1.32
GR	Oppenheimer Capital Appr Y	OTCYX	B	(888) 470-0862	A- / 9.0	3.52	8.86	19.44 /96	15.71 /81	13.06 /69	0.00	0.82
GI	Oppenheimer Capital Income A	OPPEX	C-	(888) 470-0862	D / 1.8	1.86	2.49	4.50 /35	7.32 /23	7.77 /28	2.92	1.06
GI	● Oppenheimer Capital Income B	OPEBX	C	(888) 470-0862	D / 2.0	1.61	2.03	3.67 /30	6.34 /18	6.77 /22	2.36	1.81
GI	Oppenheimer Capital Income C	OPECX	C	(888) 470-0862	D / 2.1	1.65	2.01	3.61 /30	6.44 /19	6.86 /22	2.51	1.81
GI	Oppenheimer Capital Income R	OCINX	C	(888) 470-0862	D+ / 2.4	1.72	2.29	4.10 /32	6.98 /21	7.40 /26	2.90	1.31
GI	Oppenheimer Capital Income Y	OCIYX	C	(888) 470-0862	D+ / 2.7	1.91	2.62	4.67 /36	7.58 /25	8.03 /30	3.36	0.81
EN	Oppenheimer Comm Str Tot Retn A	QRAAX	E-	(888) 470-0862	E- / 0.0	-6.93	-22.66	-31.75 / 0	-15.07 / 0	-7.30 / 1	0.00	1.73
EN	● Oppenheimer Comm Str Tot Retn B	QRABX	E-	(888) 470-0862	E- / 0.0	-7.14	-22.96	-32.47 / 0	-15.76 / 0	-8.06 / 1	0.00	2.49
EN	Oppenheimer Comm Str Tot Retn C	QRACX	E-	(888) 470-0862	E- / 0.0	-7.24	-22.93	-32.34 / 0	-15.68 / 0	-8.02 / 1	0.00	2.49
OT	Oppenheimer Comm Str Tot Retn I	QRAIX	U	(888) 470-0862	U /	-6.81	-22.34	-31.56 / 0	--	--	0.00	1.30
EN	Oppenheimer Comm Str Tot Retn R	QRANX	E-	(888) 470-0862	E- / 0.0	-7.08	-22.51	-32.04 / 0	-15.25 / 0	-7.55 / 1	0.00	1.99
EN	Oppenheimer Comm Str Tot Retn Y	QRAYX	E-	(888) 470-0862	E- / 0.0	-6.84	-22.42	-31.66 / 0	-14.76 / 0	-6.96 / 1	0.00	1.49
AA	Oppenheimer Conservative Inv A	OACIX	C-	(888) 470-0862	D- / 1.1	1.55	2.82	4.32 /34	5.28 /14	5.90 /16	1.58	1.08
AA	● Oppenheimer Conservative Inv B	OBCIX	C-	(888) 470-0862	D- / 1.3	1.33	2.41	3.56 /29	4.45 /11	5.05 /12	0.72	1.83
AA	Oppenheimer Conservative Inv C	OCCIX	C-	(888) 470-0862	D- / 1.3	1.34	2.44	3.60 /29	4.48 /11	5.11 /12	0.95	1.83
AA	Oppenheimer Conservative Inv R	ONCIX	C	(888) 470-0862	D- / 1.5	1.44	2.67	4.06 /32	4.97 /13	5.59 /15	1.42	1.33
AA	Oppenheimer Conservative Inv Y	OYCIX	C	(888) 470-0862	D / 1.8	1.66	2.91	4.63 /36	5.54 /15	6.21 /18	1.98	0.83
* EM	● Oppenheimer Developing Mkts A	ODMAX	E	(888) 470-0862	E / 0.4	-1.35	-8.00	-4.38 / 6	2.31 / 7	4.45 /10	0.27	1.33
EM	● Oppenheimer Developing Mkts B	ODVBX	E	(888) 470-0862	E / 0.5	-1.51	-8.32	-5.10 / 5	1.49 / 6	3.59 / 7	0.00	2.08
EM	● Oppenheimer Developing Mkts C	ODVCX	E	(888) 470-0862	E / 0.5	-1.54	-8.36	-5.11 / 5	1.58 / 6	3.70 / 7	0.00	2.08
EM	● Oppenheimer Developing Mkts I	ODVIX	D-	(888) 470-0862	E+ / 0.6	-1.23	-7.79	-3.95 / 7	2.79 / 7	--	0.85	0.87
EM	● Oppenheimer Developing Mkts R	ODVNX	E	(888) 470-0862	E / 0.5	-1.40	-8.11	-4.61 / 6	2.00 / 6	4.10 / 9	0.11	1.58
EM	● Oppenheimer Developing Mkts Y	ODVYX	E	(888) 470-0862	E+ / 0.6	-1.28	-7.89	-4.12 / 7	2.62 / 7	4.77 /11	0.64	1.08
SC	● Oppenheimer Discovery A	OPOCX	C	(888) 470-0862	B / 7.7	7.42	15.82	7.64 /60	16.17 /85	16.93 /96	0.00	1.11
SC	● Oppenheimer Discovery B	ODIBX	C	(888) 470-0862	B / 8.2	7.21	15.38	6.82 /54	15.24 /77	15.99 /93	0.00	1.86
SC	● Oppenheimer Discovery C	ODICX	C	(888) 470-0862	B / 8.2	7.21	15.40	6.84 /54	15.28 /77	16.03 /93	0.00	1.86
SC	● Oppenheimer Discovery I	ODIIX	B+	(888) 470-0862	A- / 9.1	7.52	16.06	8.11 /64	16.74 /88	17.29 /97	0.00	0.67
SC	Oppenheimer Discovery Mid Cap Gro	OEGAX	C+	(888) 470-0862	B- / 7.5	8.01	13.52	13.26 /87	15.21 /77	16.37 /94	0.00	1.36
SC	● Oppenheimer Discovery Mid Cap Gro	OEGBX	C+	(888) 470-0862	B / 7.9	7.76	13.12	12.38 /84	14.26 /69	15.44 /90	0.00	2.11
SC	Oppenheimer Discovery Mid Cap Gro	OEGCX	C+	(888) 470-0862	B / 8.0	7.85	13.10	12.44 /85	14.34 /70	15.50 /90	0.00	2.11
SC	Oppenheimer Discovery Mid Cap Gro	OEGNX	B-	(888) 470-0862	B+ / 8.4	7.91	13.40	13.00 /87	14.86 /74	16.06 /93	0.00	1.61
SC	Oppenheimer Discovery Mid Cap Gro	OEGYX	B	(888) 470-0862	B+ / 8.8	8.04	13.69	13.57 /88	15.62 /80	16.86 /96	0.00	1.11
SC	● Oppenheimer Discovery R	ODINX	C+	(888) 470-0862	B+ / 8.6	7.34	15.66	7.34 /58	15.84 /82	16.61 /95	0.00	1.36
SC	● Oppenheimer Discovery Y	ODIYX	C+	(888) 470-0862	B+ / 8.9	7.48	15.97	7.89 /62	16.50 /87	17.33 /97	0.00	0.86
GR	Oppenheimer Dividend Opportunity A	OSVAX	C-	(888) 470-0862	C- / 3.5	2.25	2.54	7.20 /57	10.35 /41	8.16 /31	2.54	1.13
GR	● Oppenheimer Dividend Opportunity B	OSVBX	C-	(888) 470-0862	C- / 3.8	2.05	2.15	6.40 /50	9.44 /36	7.27 /25	1.96	1.89
GR	Oppenheimer Dividend Opportunity C	OSCVX	C-	(888) 470-0862	C- / 3.8	2.06	2.14	6.39 /50	9.47 /36	7.31 /25	2.05	1.89
GR	Oppenheimer Dividend Opportunity R	OSVNX	C	(888) 470-0862	C- / 4.2	2.16	2.38	6.95 /55	10.06 /40	7.89 /29	2.47	1.38
GR	Oppenheimer Dividend Opportunity Y	OSVYX	C	(888) 470-0862	C / 4.6	2.31	2.68	7.49 /59	10.71 /44	8.57 /34	2.95	0.89
EM	Oppenheimer Em Mkts Innovators A	EMIAX	U	(888) 470-0862	U /	2.14	-5.48	--	--	--	0.00	1.79
EM	Oppenheimer Em Mkts Innovators Y	EMIYX	U	(888) 470-0862	U /	2.14	-5.42	--	--	--	0.00	1.54
GI	Oppenheimer Equity A	OEQAX	C+	(888) 470-0862	C+ / 6.5	1.74	6.32	13.66 /89	14.74 /73	12.05 /61	0.53	0.99
GI	● Oppenheimer Equity B	OEQBX	C+	(888) 470-0862	C+ / 6.8	1.49	5.81	12.72 /86	13.71 /65	11.00 /53	0.00	1.79
GI	Oppenheimer Equity C	OEQCX	C+	(888) 470-0862	C+ / 6.8	1.49	5.89	12.71 /86	13.77 /65	11.06 /53	0.00	1.78

● Denotes fund is closed to new investors
* Denotes fund is included in Section II

www.thestreetratings.com

Risk Rating/Pts	3 Year Standard Deviation	Beta	NAV As of 3/31/15	Total $(Mil)	Cash %	Stocks %	Bonds %	Other %	Portfolio Turnover Ratio	Last Bull Market Return	Last Bear Market Return	Manager Quality Pct	Manager Tenure (Years)	Initial Purch. $	Additional Purch. $	Front End Load	Back End Load
B / 8.0	8.1	1.37	12.48	124	15	74	9	2	9	53.9	-15.8	13	10	1,000	50	0.0	0.0
B / 8.0	8.1	1.37	12.69	32	15	74	9	2	9	56.7	-15.7	16	10	1,000	50	0.0	0.0
C / 4.5	10.3	0.98	61.37	3,558	0	99	0	1	67	94.1	-16.6	62	3	1,000	0	5.8	0.0
C- / 4.0	10.3	0.98	51.04	103	0	99	0	1	67	88.9	-16.9	49	3	1,000	0	0.0	0.0
C- / 3.9	10.3	0.98	50.69	459	0	99	0	1	67	89.1	-16.9	50	3	1,000	0	0.0	0.0
C+ / 6.4	10.3	0.99	66.53	348	0	99	0	1	77	95.2	-16.6	62	3	0	0	0.0	0.0
C+ / 6.5	10.3	0.98	65.14	1,060	0	99	0	1	67	N/A	N/A	68	3	5,000,000	0	0.0	0.0
C / 4.4	10.3	0.98	59.03	96	0	99	0	1	67	92.4	-16.7	58	3	1,000	0	0.0	0.0
C / 4.7	10.3	0.98	65.04	149	0	99	0	1	67	96.3	-16.4	66	3	1,000	0	0.0	0.0
B+ / 9.0	3.1	0.25	9.90	1,792	20	27	51	2	93	33.3	-4.9	90	6	1,000	0	5.8	0.0
B+ / 9.0	3.1	0.25	9.69	25	20	27	51	2	93	29.2	-5.3	86	6	1,000	0	0.0	0.0
B+ / 9.0	3.1	0.25	9.60	392	20	27	51	2	93	29.6	-5.2	87	6	1,000	0	0.0	0.0
B+ / 9.0	3.1	0.25	9.77	27	20	27	51	2	93	32.0	-5.1	89	6	1,000	0	0.0	0.0
B+ / 9.0	3.1	0.25	9.89	428	20	27	51	2	93	34.5	-4.7	90	6	1,000	0	0.0	0.0
D / 1.7	14.9	0.68	2.15	96	50	0	49	1	80	-26.7	-22.6	0	2	1,000	0	5.8	0.0
D / 1.6	14.9	0.69	2.08	3	50	0	49	1	80	-28.5	-23.1	0	2	1,000	0	0.0	0.0
D / 1.7	14.9	0.69	2.05	28	50	0	49	1	80	-28.4	-23.0	0	2	1,000	0	0.0	0.0
U /	N/A	N/A	2.19	132	50	0	49	1	80	N/A	N/A	N/A	2	5,000,000	0	0.0	0.0
D / 1.7	15.0	0.69	2.10	7	50	0	49	1	80	-27.2	-22.7	0	2	1,000	0	0.0	0.0
D / 1.7	14.8	0.68	2.18	47	50	0	49	1	80	-25.7	-22.6	0	2	1,000	0	0.0	0.0
B+ / 9.4	4.3	0.68	9.17	385	36	28	34	2	12	27.2	-7.3	39	10	1,000	50	5.8	0.0
B+ / 9.4	4.3	0.68	9.14	17	36	28	34	2	12	23.7	-7.5	28	10	1,000	50	0.0	0.0
B+ / 9.4	4.4	0.69	9.05	165	36	28	34	2	12	23.9	-7.5	27	10	1,000	50	0.0	0.0
B+ / 9.4	4.4	0.69	9.14	43	36	28	34	2	12	26.0	-7.3	34	10	1,000	50	0.0	0.0
B+ / 9.3	4.3	0.68	9.20	8	36	28	34	2	12	28.2	-7.2	43	10	1,000	50	0.0	0.0
C / 4.6	14.0	0.96	35.04	9,952	7	92	0	1	26	30.7	-23.2	82	8	1,000	0	5.8	0.0
C / 4.6	14.0	0.96	33.96	115	7	92	0	1	26	27.0	-23.5	76	8	1,000	0	0.0	0.0
C / 4.6	14.0	0.96	33.14	1,699	7	92	0	1	26	27.5	-23.4	76	8	1,000	0	0.0	0.0
C+ / 6.3	14.0	0.96	34.63	6,783	7	92	0	1	26	N/A	N/A	85	8	5,000,000	0	0.0	0.0
C / 4.6	14.0	0.96	33.70	801	7	92	0	1	26	29.3	-23.3	80	8	1,000	0	0.0	0.0
C / 4.6	14.0	0.96	34.61	19,209	7	92	0	1	26	32.0	-23.1	84	8	1,000	0	0.0	0.0
C- / 3.5	14.5	0.94	76.16	1,368	2	97	0	1	87	91.7	-22.3	75	9	1,000	0	5.8	0.0
D+ / 2.8	14.5	0.94	58.40	40	2	97	0	1	87	86.4	-22.6	67	9	1,000	0	0.0	0.0
D+ / 2.9	14.5	0.94	60.34	174	2	97	0	1	87	86.7	-22.6	67	9	1,000	0	0.0	0.0
C / 5.1	14.5	0.94	83.91	76	2	97	0	1	87	94.6	-22.3	79	9	5,000,000	0	0.0	0.0
C / 4.8	12.5	0.76	17.93	330	3	96	0	1	116	89.2	-19.7	87	8	1,000	0	5.8	0.0
C / 4.4	12.5	0.77	15.42	14	3	96	0	1	116	83.9	-20.0	83	8	1,000	0	0.0	0.0
C / 4.4	12.5	0.77	15.53	92	3	96	0	1	116	84.3	-20.0	83	8	1,000	0	0.0	0.0
C / 4.7	12.5	0.76	17.05	29	3	96	0	1	116	87.4	-19.8	86	8	1,000	0	0.0	0.0
C / 4.9	12.5	0.77	19.63	46	3	96	0	1	116	91.5	-19.5	89	8	1,000	0	0.0	0.0
C- / 3.5	14.5	0.94	72.21	57	2	97	0	1	87	89.8	-22.4	72	9	1,000	0	0.0	0.0
C- / 3.6	14.5	0.94	83.30	438	2	97	0	1	87	93.7	-22.2	78	9	1,000	0	0.0	0.0
C+ / 6.7	9.8	0.96	20.34	138	0	99	0	1	73	61.6	-24.7	13	2	1,000	0	5.8	0.0
C+ / 6.7	9.8	0.96	19.73	4	0	99	0	1	73	57.2	-24.9	8	2	1,000	0	0.0	0.0
C+ / 6.7	9.8	0.96	19.69	42	0	99	0	1	73	57.4	-25.0	9	2	1,000	0	0.0	0.0
C+ / 6.7	9.8	0.96	20.15	9	0	99	0	1	73	60.4	-24.8	11	2	0	0	0.0	0.0
C+ / 6.7	9.8	0.96	20.31	12	0	99	0	1	73	63.6	-24.5	15	2	0	0	0.0	0.0
U /	N/A	N/A	9.06	67	0	0	0	100	0	N/A	N/A	N/A	1	1,000	0	5.8	0.0
U /	N/A	N/A	9.06	35	0	0	0	100	0	N/A	N/A	N/A	1	1,000	0	0.0	0.0
C+ / 6.8	9.9	1.01	14.07	1,537	0	99	0	1	114	88.4	-18.8	47	3	1,000	50	5.8	0.0
C+ / 6.8	9.8	1.00	12.94	21	0	99	0	1	114	82.8	-19.2	35	3	1,000	50	0.0	0.0
C+ / 6.8	9.9	1.01	12.95	79	0	99	0	1	114	83.1	-19.2	35	3	1,000	50	0.0	0.0

99 Pct = Best
0 Pct = Worst

Fund Type	Fund Name	Ticker Symbol	Overall Investment Rating	Phone	Perfor-mance Rating/Pts	3 Mo	6 Mo	1Yr / Pct	3Yr / Pct	5Yr / Pct	Dividend Yield	Expense Ratio
GR	Oppenheimer Equity Income A	OAEIX	C+	(888) 470-0862	C+ / 6.2	1.05	4.32	9.16 /70	15.23 /77	12.94 /68	1.97	1.02
GR ●	Oppenheimer Equity Income B	OBEIX	C+	(888) 470-0862	C+ / 6.6	0.86	3.96	8.35 /65	14.23 /69	11.93 /60	1.84	1.77
GR	Oppenheimer Equity Income C	OCEIX	C+	(888) 470-0862	C+ / 6.7	0.86	3.93	8.34 /65	14.36 /70	12.07 /61	1.87	1.77
IN	Oppenheimer Equity Income I	OEIIX	A-	(888) 470-0862	B / 7.6	1.14	4.55	9.65 /73	15.69 /81	--	2.51	0.58
GR	Oppenheimer Equity Income R	ONEIX	B	(888) 470-0862	B- / 7.0	0.97	4.20	8.88 /69	14.85 /74	12.52 /64	1.93	1.27
GL	Oppenheimer Equity Income Y	OYEIX	B+	(888) 470-0862	B- / 7.5	1.10	4.45	9.42 /72	15.56 /80	13.20 /70	2.34	0.77
AG	Oppenheimer Equity Inv A	OAAIX	C-	(888) 470-0862	C- / 4.2	2.78	4.32	4.67 /36	11.90 /52	9.96 /44	0.70	1.19
AG ●	Oppenheimer Equity Inv B	OBAIX	C	(888) 470-0862	C / 4.5	2.57	3.91	3.91 /31	11.03 /46	9.09 /37	0.00	1.94
AG	Oppenheimer Equity Inv C	OCAIX	C	(888) 470-0862	C / 4.6	2.57	3.97	3.90 /31	11.07 /46	9.15 /38	0.06	1.94
AG	Oppenheimer Equity Inv R	ONAIX	C	(888) 470-0862	C / 5.0	2.72	4.23	4.44 /35	11.66 /50	9.74 /42	0.46	1.44
AG	Oppenheimer Equity Inv Y	OYAIX	C+	(888) 470-0862	C / 5.3	2.83	4.49	4.98 /38	12.25 /54	10.36 /47	0.99	0.94
GI	Oppenheimer Equity R	OEQNX	B	(888) 470-0862	B- / 7.2	1.62	6.08	13.28 /88	14.32 /69	11.61 /58	0.31	1.29
GI	Oppenheimer Equity Y	OEQYX	B+	(888) 470-0862	B / 7.7	1.74	6.37	13.80 /89	14.97 /75	12.22 /62	0.76	0.79
GR	Oppenheimer Flexible Strategies A	QVOPX	C-	(888) 470-0862	D- / 1.2	2.25	1.95	4.57 /36	5.72 /16	3.48 / 7	1.66	2.18
GR ●	Oppenheimer Flexible Strategies B	QOPBX	C-	(888) 470-0862	D- / 1.5	2.12	1.59	3.79 /30	4.87 /13	2.60 / 5	1.06	2.93
GR	Oppenheimer Flexible Strategies C	QOPCX	C-	(888) 470-0862	D- / 1.5	2.07	1.54	3.74 /30	4.92 /13	2.69 / 5	1.26	2.93
GR	Oppenheimer Flexible Strategies R	QOPNX	C	(888) 470-0862	D / 1.7	2.22	1.85	4.32 /34	5.43 /15	3.17 / 6	1.54	2.43
GR	Oppenheimer Flexible Strategies Y	QOPYX	C	(888) 470-0862	D / 2.0	2.34	2.08	4.83 /37	5.99 /17	3.76 / 8	2.00	1.93
* GL	Oppenheimer Global A	OPPAX	C	(888) 470-0862	C+ / 5.9	7.33	7.06	8.82 /68	13.78 /65	10.84 /51	0.74	1.13
BA	Oppenheimer Global Allocation A	QVGIX	D+	(888) 470-0862	D / 2.0	3.54	4.40	3.20 /27	7.66 /25	6.04 /17	1.11	1.35
BA ●	Oppenheimer Global Allocation B	QGRBX	D+	(888) 470-0862	D+ / 2.3	3.30	3.98	2.45 /24	6.78 /20	5.17 /13	0.64	2.10
BA	Oppenheimer Global Allocation C	QGRCX	D+	(888) 470-0862	D+ / 2.4	3.35	4.01	2.48 /24	6.89 /21	5.28 /13	0.67	2.10
AA	Oppenheimer Global Allocation I	QGRIX	C-	(888) 470-0862	C- / 3.1	3.64	4.62	3.70 /30	8.18 /28	--	1.60	0.91
BA	Oppenheimer Global Allocation R	QGRNX	C-	(888) 470-0862	D+ / 2.7	3.49	4.28	3.02 /27	7.40 /24	5.77 /15	0.98	1.60
BA	Oppenheimer Global Allocation Y	QGRYX	C-	(888) 470-0862	C- / 3.1	3.60	4.54	3.48 /29	8.03 /27	6.39 /19	1.44	1.10
GL ●	Oppenheimer Global B	OGLBX	C	(888) 470-0862	C+ / 6.3	7.12	6.65	7.99 /63	12.84 /58	9.89 /44	0.00	1.88
GL	Oppenheimer Global C	OGLCX	C	(888) 470-0862	C+ / 6.3	7.12	6.64	7.99 /63	12.95 /59	10.02 /45	0.14	1.88
GL	Oppenheimer Global I	OGLIX	B	(888) 470-0862	B- / 7.3	7.45	7.29	9.30 /71	14.30 /69	11.16 /54	1.19	0.69
AA	Oppenheimer Global Multi-Alt A	ODAAX	U	(888) 470-0862	U /	1.65	0.67	0.18 /16	--	--	2.62	1.37
GI	Oppenheimer Global MultiStrat A	OARAX	D	(888) 470-0862	D- / 1.5	2.40	5.05	5.82 /45	5.79 /16	3.22 / 6	4.62	1.57
IN	Oppenheimer Global MultiStrat C	OARCX	D	(888) 470-0862	D / 1.7	2.24	4.67	4.97 /38	4.95 /13	--	4.25	2.32
IN	Oppenheimer Global MultiStrat I	OAIIX	D+	(888) 470-0862	D+ / 2.4	2.54	5.27	6.18 /48	6.09 /17	--	5.17	1.13
IN	Oppenheimer Global MultiStrat Y	OARYX	D+	(888) 470-0862	D / 2.2	2.46	5.15	5.98 /46	5.80 /16	--	5.13	1.32
GL	Oppenheimer Global Opportunities A	OPGIX	E+	(888) 470-0862	D / 2.0	1.69	4.47	-3.21 / 8	8.80 /32	8.12 /31	Incl.	1.18
GL ●	Oppenheimer Global Opportunities B	OGGIX	E+	(888) 470-0862	D+ / 2.3	1.50	4.06	-3.93 / 7	7.87 /26	7.18 /24	0.00	1.93
GL	Oppenheimer Global Opportunities C	OGICX	E+	(888) 470-0862	D+ / 2.3	1.49	4.09	-3.93 / 7	7.98 /27	7.31 /25	0.00	1.93
GL	Oppenheimer Global Opportunities I	OGIIX	D	(888) 470-0862	C- / 3.1	1.80	4.70	-2.79 / 9	9.29 /35	8.43 /33	0.71	0.74
GL	Oppenheimer Global Opportunities R	OGINX	D-	(888) 470-0862	D+ / 2.6	1.64	4.35	-3.46 / 8	8.46 /30	7.77 /28	0.00	1.43
GL	Oppenheimer Global Opportunities Y	OGIYX	D-	(888) 470-0862	C- / 3.0	1.75	4.59	-2.98 / 9	9.08 /34	8.41 /33	0.52	0.93
GL	Oppenheimer Global R	OGLNX	C+	(888) 470-0862	C+ / 6.7	7.25	6.91	8.53 /67	13.46 /63	10.50 /49	0.54	1.38
RE	Oppenheimer Global Real Estate I	OIRGX	U	(888) 470-0862	U /	5.15	14.25	18.12 /96	--	--	4.18	1.06
GL	Oppenheimer Global Value A	GLVAX	D+	(888) 470-0862	C- / 4.2	1.42	5.46	-1.24 /12	12.74 /58	11.38 /56	0.00	1.29
GL	Oppenheimer Global Value C	GLVCX	D+	(888) 470-0862	C / 4.5	1.22	5.04	-1.99 /10	11.86 /52	10.52 /49	0.00	2.04
GL	Oppenheimer Global Value I	GLVIX	C	(888) 470-0862	C / 5.4	1.52	5.66	-0.81 /14	13.16 /61	11.63 /58	0.00	0.86
GL	Oppenheimer Global Value R	GLVNX	D+	(888) 470-0862	C / 4.9	1.36	5.30	-1.48 /11	12.43 /56	11.10 /53	0.00	1.53
GL	Oppenheimer Global Value Y	GLVYX	C-	(888) 470-0862	C / 5.3	1.48	5.55	-1.00 /13	13.05 /60	11.72 /59	0.00	1.05
GL	Oppenheimer Global Y	OGLYX	C+	(888) 470-0862	B- / 7.1	7.39	7.18	9.08 /70	14.08 /68	11.13 /54	0.98	0.88
PM	Oppenheimer Gold/Spec Min A	OPGSX	E-	(888) 470-0862	E / 0.0	-5.53	-16.72	-25.08 / 0	-27.27 / 0	-15.68 / 0	2.26	1.17
PM ●	Oppenheimer Gold/Spec Min B	OGMBX	E-	(888) 470-0862	E / 0.0	-5.70	-17.04	-25.63 / 0	-27.86 / 0	-16.37 / 0	1.12	1.92
PM	Oppenheimer Gold/Spec Min C	OGMCX	E-	(888) 470-0862	E / 0.0	-5.69	-17.00	-25.61 / 0	-27.81 / 0	-16.30 / 0	1.57	1.92
PM	Oppenheimer Gold/Spec Min I	OGMIX	U	(888) 470-0862	U /	-5.38	-16.50	-24.71 / 0	--	--	3.07	0.73
PM	Oppenheimer Gold/Spec Min R	OGMNX	E-	(888) 470-0862	E / 0.0	-5.60	-16.86	-25.29 / 0	-27.46 / 0	-15.93 / 0	2.28	1.42

● Denotes fund is closed to new investors
* Denotes fund is included in Section II

RISK			NET ASSETS		ASSET					BULL / BEAR		FUND MANAGER		MINIMUMS		LOADS	
	3 Year		NAV						Portfolio	Last Bull	Last Bear	Manager	Manager	Initial	Additional	Front	Back
Risk	Standard		As of	Total	Cash	Stocks	Bonds	Other	Turnover	Market	Market	Quality	Tenure	Purch.	Purch.	End	End
Rating/Pts	Deviation	Beta	3/31/15	$(Mil)	%	%	%	%	Ratio	Return	Return	Pct	(Years)	$	$	Load	Load
C+ / 6.9	10.9	1.08	32.29	4,129	7	83	1	9	40	94.0	-22.2	37	8	1,000	0	5.8	0.0
C+ / 6.6	10.9	1.08	26.55	149	7	83	1	9	40	88.3	-22.5	27	8	1,000	0	0.0	0.0
C+ / 6.6	10.9	1.08	26.58	1,040	7	83	1	9	40	88.9	-22.4	28	8	0.0	0.0	0.0	0.0
B- / 7.5	10.9	1.08	32.25	142	7	83	1	9	40	N/A	N/A	43	8	5,000,000	0	0.0	0.0
C+ / 6.8	10.9	1.08	31.07	200	7	83	1	9	40	91.7	-22.3	33	8	1,000	0	0.0	0.0
C+ / 6.9	10.9	0.63	32.26	717	7	83	1	9	40	95.8	-22.1	97	8	1,000	0	0.0	0.0
C+ / 6.6	10.6	1.03	15.53	535	7	92	0	1	6	70.4	-21.0	15	10	1,000	50	5.8	0.0
C+ / 6.6	10.6	1.03	15.14	43	7	92	0	1	6	65.8	-21.2	11	10	1,000	50	0.0	0.0
C+ / 6.6	10.6	1.03	15.14	192	7	92	0	1	6	66.0	-21.2	11	10	1,000	50	0.0	0.0
C+ / 6.6	10.6	1.03	15.51	51	7	92	0	1	6	69.1	-21.0	14	10	1,000	50	0.0	0.0
C+ / 6.6	10.6	1.03	15.61	22	7	92	0	1	6	72.3	-20.8	17	10	1,000	50	0.0	0.0
C+ / 6.8	9.9	1.01	13.80	20	0	99	0	1	114	86.2	-18.9	42	3	1,000	50	0.0	0.0
C+ / 6.8	9.9	1.01	14.07	20	0	99	0	1	114	89.6	-18.8	50	3	0	0	0.0	0.0
B+ / 9.3	2.6	0.18	26.85	641	48	29	21	2	44	19.4	-10.2	88	4	1,000	0	5.8	0.0
B+ / 9.3	2.7	0.18	24.13	21	48	29	21	2	44	16.0	-10.5	84	4	1,000	0	0.0	0.0
B+ / 9.3	2.6	0.18	24.12	111	48	29	21	2	44	16.3	-10.5	85	4	1,000	0	0.0	0.0
B+ / 9.3	2.7	0.18	25.79	17	48	29	21	2	44	18.2	-10.3	87	4	1,000	0	0.0	0.0
B+ / 9.3	2.6	0.18	27.50	29	48	29	21	2	44	20.4	-10.1	89	4	1,000	0	0.0	0.0
C / 5.5	12.2	0.88	81.59	7,679	0	99	0	1	11	77.9	-23.2	93	11	1,000	0	5.8	0.0
B- / 7.4	7.7	1.21	17.82	1,259	13	75	11	1	43	37.2	-15.0	9	3	1,000	0	5.8	0.0
B- / 7.4	7.8	1.22	17.24	46	13	75	11	1	43	33.5	-15.3	6	3	1,000	0	0.0	0.0
B- / 7.4	7.7	1.21	17.26	259	13	75	11	1	43	33.9	-15.2	7	3	1,000	0	0.0	0.0
B- / 7.2	7.7	1.21	17.80	1	13	75	11	1	43	N/A	N/A	12	3	5,000,000	0	0.0	0.0
B- / 7.4	7.7	1.21	17.54	39	13	75	11	1	43	36.0	-15.0	8	3	1,000	0	0.0	0.0
B- / 7.4	7.7	1.22	17.80	42	13	75	11	1	43	38.8	-14.8	11	3	1,000	0	0.0	0.0
C / 5.5	12.1	0.87	74.95	92	0	99	0	1	11	72.9	-23.5	92	11	1,000	0	0.0	0.0
C / 5.5	12.1	0.87	75.97	722	0	99	0	1	11	73.5	-23.4	92	11	1,000	0	0.0	0.0
C+ / 6.5	12.1	0.87	81.73	437	0	99	0	1	11	80.4	-23.2	94	11	5,000,000	0	0.0	0.0
U /	N/A	N/A	9.86	28	56	10	32	2	107	N/A	N/A	N/A	3	1,000	0	5.8	0.0
C+ / 6.8	3.9	0.22	26.84	15	10	5	83	2	59	14.1	-7.2	86	8	1,000	0	5.8	0.0
B- / 7.3	3.9	0.22	26.45	3	10	5	83	2	59	N/A	N/A	81	8	1,000	0	0.0	0.0
B- / 7.3	3.9	0.22	27.04	106	10	5	83	2	59	N/A	N/A	87	8	5,000,000	0	0.0	0.0
B- / 7.3	3.9	0.22	26.70	6	10	5	83	2	59	N/A	N/A	86	8	0	0	0.0	0.0
C / 4.4	14.6	0.77	40.29	2,293	3	96	0	1	16	61.1	-19.5	80	20	1,000	0	5.8	0.0
C / 4.3	14.6	0.77	36.64	46	3	96	0	1	16	56.4	-19.9	73	20	1,000	0	0.0	0.0
C / 4.3	14.6	0.77	36.68	414	3	96	0	1	16	57.0	-19.8	74	20	1,000	0	0.0	0.0
C / 5.3	14.6	1.68	40.73	66	3	96	0	1	16	63.3	-19.5	8	20	5,000,000	0	0.0	0.0
C / 4.4	14.6	0.77	39.09	91	3	96	0	1	16	59.3	-19.7	78	20	1,000	0	0.0	0.0
C / 4.4	14.6	0.77	40.65	401	3	96	0	1	16	62.6	-19.5	82	20	1,000	0	0.0	0.0
C / 5.5	12.1	0.87	81.22	242	0	99	0	1	11	76.1	-23.3	93	11	1,000	0	0.0	0.0
U /	N/A	N/A	11.57	164	7	92	0	1	100	N/A	N/A	N/A	2	5,000,000	0	0.0	0.0
C / 4.9	15.6	1.02	42.21	229	1	98	0	1	59	77.6	-22.1	88	8	1,000	0	5.8	0.0
C / 4.9	15.6	1.02	40.53	90	1	98	0	1	59	73.0	-22.3	84	8	1,000	0	0.0	0.0
C+ / 5.9	15.6	1.02	42.80	16	1	98	0	1	59	79.6	-22.1	89	8	5,000,000	0	0.0	0.0
C / 4.9	15.6	1.02	41.59	8	1	98	0	1	59	76.0	-22.1	86	8	0	0	0.0	0.0
C / 4.9	15.6	1.02	42.65	140	1	98	0	1	59	79.4	-22.0	89	8	0	0	0.0	0.0
C / 5.5	12.1	0.87	81.72	1,264	0	99	0	1	11	79.5	-23.1	94	11	1,000	0	0.0	0.0
E+ / 0.7	36.5	1.70	12.82	520	8	91	0	1	95	-59.8	-21.1	1	18	1,000	0	5.8	0.0
E+ / 0.7	36.5	1.70	12.07	13	8	91	0	1	95	-60.9	-21.3	1	18	1,000	0	0.0	0.0
E+ / 0.7	36.5	1.70	11.93	129	8	91	0	1	95	-60.8	-21.3	1	18	1,000	0	0.0	0.0
U /	N/A	N/A	12.83	40	8	91	0	1	95	N/A	N/A	N/A	18	5,000,000	0	0.0	0.0
E+ / 0.7	36.5	1.70	12.31	106	8	91	0	1	95	-60.1	-21.2	1	18	1,000	0	0.0	0.0

Fund Type	Fund Name	Ticker Symbol	Overall Investment Rating	Phone	Performance Rating/Pts	3 Mo	6 Mo	1Yr / Pct	3Yr / Pct	5Yr / Pct	Dividend Yield	Expense Ratio
								Total Return % through 3/31/15			Incl. in Returns	
									Annualized			
PM	Oppenheimer Gold/Spec Min Y	OGMYX	E-	(888) 470-0862	E- / 0.0	-5.40	-16.57	-24.86 / 0	-27.11 / 0	-15.49 / 0	2.75	0.92
FO	Oppenheimer International Value A	QIVAX	D+	(888) 470-0862	C- / 3.1	4.67	3.83	-1.52 /11	10.65 /43	4.89 /11	1.77	1.29
FO ●	Oppenheimer International Value B	QIVBX	D+	(888) 470-0862	C- / 3.5	4.47	3.41	-2.30 /10	9.82 /38	4.04 / 8	1.04	2.04
FO	Oppenheimer International Value C	QIVCX	D+	(888) 470-0862	C- / 3.5	4.48	3.48	-2.25 /10	9.81 /38	4.06 / 9	1.37	2.04
FO	Oppenheimer International Value I	QIVIX	U	(888) 470-0862	U /	4.76	4.08	-1.09 /13	--	--	2.37	0.86
FO	Oppenheimer International Value R	QIVNX	D+	(888) 470-0862	C- / 3.9	4.60	3.72	-1.80 /11	10.34 /41	4.58 /10	1.65	1.55
FO	Oppenheimer International Value Y	QIVYX	C-	(888) 470-0862	C- / 4.2	4.69	3.95	-1.31 /12	10.94 /45	5.27 /13	2.11	1.05
FO	Oppenheimer Intl Diversified A	OIDAX	D	(888) 470-0862	D / 2.2	3.60	1.63	-2.09 /10	9.29 /35	7.12 /24	0.59	1.29
FO ●	Oppenheimer Intl Diversified B	OIDBX	D+	(888) 470-0862	D+ / 2.6	3.38	1.22	-2.83 / 9	8.38 /29	6.20 /18	0.00	2.04
FO	Oppenheimer Intl Diversified C	OIDCX	D+	(888) 470-0862	D+ / 2.6	3.38	1.22	-2.84 / 9	8.46 /30	6.31 /19	0.00	2.04
FO	Oppenheimer Intl Diversified I	OIDIX	C	(888) 470-0862	C- / 3.5	3.70	1.89	-1.65 /11	9.90 /39	7.47 /26	1.09	0.85
FO	Oppenheimer Intl Diversified R	OIDNX	D+	(888) 470-0862	D+ / 2.9	3.57	1.51	-2.31 /10	8.97 /33	6.78 /22	0.43	1.54
FO	Oppenheimer Intl Diversified Y	OIDYX	C-	(888) 470-0862	C- / 3.3	3.64	1.78	-1.84 /11	9.55 /36	7.37 /26	0.91	1.04
FO	Oppenheimer Intl Growth A	OIGAX	D-	(888) 470-0862	D / 2.0	4.02	2.90	-4.38 / 6	8.98 /33	8.40 /32	0.76	1.14
FO ●	Oppenheimer Intl Growth B	IGRWX	D	(888) 470-0862	D+ / 2.4	3.85	2.51	-5.11 / 5	8.16 /28	7.56 /27	0.00	1.89
FO	Oppenheimer Intl Growth C	OIGCX	D	(888) 470-0862	D+ / 2.4	3.84	2.51	-5.09 / 5	8.17 /28	7.60 /27	0.20	1.89
FO	Oppenheimer Intl Growth I	OIGIX	C-	(888) 470-0862	C- / 3.2	4.16	3.13	-3.95 / 7	9.52 /36	--	1.29	0.70
FO	Oppenheimer Intl Growth R	OIGNX	D	(888) 470-0862	D+ / 2.7	3.98	2.75	-4.64 / 6	8.70 /31	8.13 /31	0.66	1.39
FO	Oppenheimer Intl Growth Svc		D	(888) 470-0862	C- / 3.0	4.17	2.88	-4.36 / 6	9.24 /35	8.54 /33	0.96	1.34
FO	Oppenheimer Intl Growth Y	OIGYX	D	(888) 470-0862	C- / 3.1	4.10	3.01	-4.15 / 7	9.31 /35	8.81 /35	1.12	0.89
FO	Oppenheimer Intl Small Comp A	OSMAX	B+	(888) 470-0862	B+ / 8.3	6.47	7.15	3.23 /28	18.61 /96	14.64 /84	0.42	1.22
FO ●	Oppenheimer Intl Small Comp B	OSMBX	B+	(888) 470-0862	B+ / 8.6	6.27	6.79	2.47 /24	17.66 /93	13.66 /75	0.00	1.97
FO	Oppenheimer Intl Small Comp C	OSMCX	B+	(888) 470-0862	B+ / 8.6	6.25	6.74	2.47 /24	17.71 /93	13.77 /76	0.00	1.97
FO	Oppenheimer Intl Small Comp I	OSCIX	A+	(888) 470-0862	A / 9.3	6.58	7.39	3.70 /30	19.13 /97	--	0.83	0.78
FO	Oppenheimer Intl Small Comp R	OSMNX	A-	(888) 470-0862	A- / 9.0	6.41	7.07	3.02 /27	18.27 /95	14.29 /80	0.21	1.47
FO	Oppenheimer Intl Small Comp Y	OSMYX	A-	(888) 470-0862	A / 9.3	6.52	7.30	3.50 /29	18.97 /97	15.05 /87	0.68	0.97
GI	Oppenheimer Main St Select A	OMSOX	C	(888) 470-0862	C / 4.5	1.37	3.43	7.78 /61	12.20 /54	11.82 /59	0.34	1.13
GI ●	Oppenheimer Main St Select B	OMOBX	C	(888) 470-0862	C / 4.8	1.20	3.02	6.95 /55	11.27 /47	10.88 /52	0.01	1.88
GI	Oppenheimer Main St Select C	OMSCX	C	(888) 470-0862	C / 4.8	1.19	3.04	6.99 /55	11.35 /48	10.98 /53	0.01	1.88
GI	Oppenheimer Main St Select R	OMSNX	C+	(888) 470-0862	C / 5.2	1.30	3.28	7.49 /59	11.87 /52	11.50 /57	0.09	1.38
GI	Oppenheimer Main St Select Y	OMSYX	C+	(888) 470-0862	C+ / 5.6	1.45	3.54	8.05 /63	12.49 /56	12.15 /62	0.62	0.88
* GI	Oppenheimer Main Street A	MSIGX	C+	(888) 470-0862	C+ / 6.0	1.61	4.86	11.07 /79	14.35 /70	13.59 /74	0.62	0.94
GI ●	Oppenheimer Main Street B	OMSBX	C+	(888) 470-0862	C+ / 6.3	1.41	4.48	10.24 /75	13.37 /62	12.61 /65	0.00	1.69
GI	Oppenheimer Main Street C	MIGCX	C+	(888) 470-0862	C+ / 6.4	1.44	4.49	10.25 /75	13.49 /63	12.74 /66	0.00	1.69
GI	Oppenheimer Main Street I	OMSIX	B+	(888) 470-0862	B- / 7.4	1.73	5.10	11.59 /81	14.84 /74	--	1.07	0.50
SC	Oppenheimer Main Street Mid Cap A	OPMSX	C+	(888) 470-0862	B / 7.7	3.39	8.97	11.95 /82	16.50 /87	14.83 /85	0.51	1.11
SC ●	Oppenheimer Main Street Mid Cap B	OPMBX	C+	(888) 470-0862	B / 8.1	3.16	8.54	11.09 /79	15.56 /80	13.91 /77	0.00	1.86
SC	Oppenheimer Main Street Mid Cap C	OPMCX	C+	(888) 470-0862	B / 8.1	3.18	8.56	11.09 /79	15.62 /80	13.97 /77	0.00	1.86
SC	Oppenheimer Main Street Mid Cap I	OPMIX	U	(888) 470-0862	U /	3.49	9.21	12.45 /85	--	--	0.92	0.67
SC	Oppenheimer Main Street Mid Cap R	OPMNX	B-	(888) 470-0862	B+ / 8.5	3.31	8.87	11.71 /81	16.18 /85	14.53 /83	0.34	1.36
SC	Oppenheimer Main Street Mid Cap Y	OPMYX	B	(888) 470-0862	B+ / 8.9	3.45	9.14	12.24 /84	16.88 /89	15.22 /88	0.77	0.86
GI	Oppenheimer Main Street R	OMGNX	C+	(888) 470-0862	C+ / 6.8	1.57	4.75	10.84 /78	14.06 /68	13.31 /71	0.43	1.19
SC	Oppenheimer Main Street Small Cap	OSCAX	U	(888) 470-0862	U /	2.97	15.42	10.31 /76	--	--	0.01	1.37
SC	Oppenheimer Main Street Small Cap	OSSIX	U	(888) 470-0862	U /	3.12	15.63	10.81 /78	--	--	0.16	0.93
SC	Oppenheimer Main Street Small Cap	OSCYX	U	(888) 470-0862	U /	3.04	15.51	10.60 /77	--	--	0.13	1.12
GI	Oppenheimer Main Street Y	MIGYX	B-	(888) 470-0862	B- / 7.2	1.68	5.00	11.36 /80	14.69 /72	13.99 /78	0.90	0.69
AA	Oppenheimer Moderate Inv A	OAMIX	C	(888) 470-0862	D+ / 2.5	1.86	3.79	5.85 /45	8.68 /31	8.09 /30	2.20	1.11
AA ●	Oppenheimer Moderate Inv B	OBMIX	C	(888) 470-0862	D+ / 2.9	1.60	3.43	5.02 /39	7.83 /26	7.22 /24	1.40	1.86
AA	Oppenheimer Moderate Inv C	OCMIX	C	(888) 470-0862	D+ / 2.9	1.61	3.41	5.01 /39	7.86 /26	7.28 /25	1.65	1.86
AA	Oppenheimer Moderate Inv R	ONMIX	C+	(888) 470-0862	C- / 3.3	1.87	3.71	5.68 /44	8.44 /30	7.82 /29	2.06	1.36
AA	Oppenheimer Moderate Inv Y	OYMIX	C+	(888) 470-0862	C- / 3.6	1.95	3.98	6.13 /48	8.93 /32	8.37 /32	2.52	0.86
RE	Oppenheimer Real Estate A	OREAX	B-	(888) 470-0862	A- / 9.2	5.01	21.82	25.98 /98	14.21 /69	15.52 /90	1.44	1.46

● Denotes fund is closed to new investors
* Denotes fund is included in Section II

www.thestreetratings.com

RISK			NET ASSETS		ASSET					BULL / BEAR		FUND MANAGER		MINIMUMS		LOADS	
	3 Year		NAV						Portfolio	Last Bull	Last Bear	Manager	Manager	Initial	Additional	Front	Back
Risk	Standard		As of	Total	Cash	Stocks	Bonds	Other	Turnover	Market	Market	Quality	Tenure	Purch.	Purch.	End	End
Rating/Pts	Deviation	Beta	3/31/15	$(Mil)	%	%	%	%	Ratio	Return	Return	Pct	(Years)	$	$	Load	Load
E+ / 0.7	36.5	1.70	12.78	109	8	91	0	1	95	-59.5	-20.9	1	18	1,000	0	0.0	0.0
C+ / 6.0	12.9	0.93	18.15	181	4	95	0	1	68	47.0	-26.8	82	2	1,000	0	5.8	0.0
C+ / 5.9	12.9	0.93	16.61	4	4	95	0	1	68	43.2	-27.1	77	2	1,000	0	0.0	0.0
C+ / 5.9	12.9	0.93	16.34	38	4	95	0	1	68	43.2	-27.1	76	2	1,000	0	0.0	0.0
U /	N/A	N/A	18.06	748	4	95	0	1	68	N/A	N/A	N/A	2	5,000,000	0	0.0	0.0
C+ / 6.0	13.0	0.93	17.98	8	4	95	0	1	68	45.7	-26.9	80	2	1,000	0	0.0	0.0
C+ / 6.0	13.0	0.93	18.31	11	4	95	0	1	68	48.6	-26.6	84	2	1,000	0	0.0	0.0
C+ / 6.7	11.7	0.86	14.37	1,476	25	74	0	1	18	49.8	-21.3	78	10	1,000	0	5.8	0.0
C+ / 6.7	11.8	0.87	14.06	42	25	74	0	1	18	45.6	-21.6	69	10	1,000	0	0.0	0.0
C+ / 6.7	11.8	0.87	14.05	480	25	74	0	1	18	46.0	-21.5	70	10	1,000	0	0.0	0.0
B- / 7.4	11.9	0.87	14.57	86	25	74	0	1	18	52.2	-21.3	81	10	5,000,000	0	0.0	0.0
C+ / 6.7	11.8	0.87	14.20	179	25	74	0	1	18	48.4	-21.3	74	10	0	0	0.0	0.0
C+ / 6.7	11.8	0.87	14.52	518	25	74	0	1	18	51.2	-21.2	79	10	0	0	0.0	0.0
C+ / 5.8	12.5	0.91	36.70	4,715	2	97	0	1	12	56.9	-20.4	71	19	1,000	0	5.8	0.0
C+ / 5.8	12.5	0.91	35.11	20	2	97	0	1	12	52.8	-20.6	62	19	1,000	0	0.0	0.0
C+ / 5.8	12.5	0.90	34.86	512	2	97	0	1	12	52.9	-20.6	62	19	1,000	0	0.0	0.0
C+ / 6.6	12.5	0.90	36.55	3,972	2	97	0	1	12	N/A	N/A	76	19	5,000,000	0	0.0	0.0
C+ / 5.8	12.5	0.91	36.07	379	2	97	0	1	12	55.5	-20.4	68	19	1,000	0	0.0	0.0
C / 5.5	12.7	0.91	2.50	158	2	97	0	1	32	58.0	-20.6	73	16	0	0	0.0	0.0
C+ / 5.9	12.5	0.91	36.52	9,982	2	97	0	1	12	58.6	-20.2	74	19	1,000	0	0.0	0.0
C+ / 5.9	12.2	0.84	34.54	1,321	9	90	0	1	18	89.8	-18.9	98	3	1,000	0	5.8	0.0
C+ / 5.9	12.2	0.84	32.72	9	9	90	0	1	18	84.5	-19.2	97	3	1,000	0	0.0	0.0
C+ / 5.9	12.2	0.84	32.30	205	9	90	0	1	18	85.1	-19.2	97	3	1,000	0	0.0	0.0
C+ / 6.5	12.2	0.84	34.33	883	9	90	0	1	18	N/A	N/A	98	3	5,000,000	0	0.0	0.0
C+ / 5.9	12.2	0.84	33.19	46	9	90	0	1	18	87.9	-19.0	98	3	1,000	0	0.0	0.0
C+ / 5.9	12.1	0.84	34.29	823	9	90	0	1	18	92.0	-18.8	98	3	1,000	0	0.0	0.0
C+ / 6.8	10.3	1.03	19.91	1,080	2	97	0	1	49	82.5	-14.5	16	1	1,000	50	5.8	0.0
C+ / 6.7	10.3	1.03	18.50	43	2	97	0	1	49	77.4	-14.8	12	1	1,000	50	0.0	0.0
C+ / 6.7	10.3	1.04	18.69	266	2	97	0	1	49	78.0	-14.8	12	1	1,000	50	0.0	0.0
C+ / 6.8	10.3	1.04	19.47	79	2	97	0	1	49	80.8	-14.6	14	1	1,000	50	0.0	0.0
C+ / 6.8	10.3	1.04	20.24	55	2	97	0	1	49	84.3	-14.4	18	1	1,000	50	0.0	0.0
C+ / 5.9	10.1	1.03	48.66	5,418	2	97	0	1	52	94.2	-15.1	37	6	1,000	0	5.8	0.0
C+ / 6.0	10.1	1.03	46.78	144	2	97	0	1	52	88.6	-15.5	26	6	1,000	0	0.0	0.0
C+ / 6.0	10.1	1.03	46.64	673	2	97	0	1	52	89.3	-15.4	28	6	1,000	0	0.0	0.0
B- / 7.3	10.1	1.03	48.30	278	2	97	0	1	52	N/A	N/A	44	6	5,000,000	0	0.0	0.0
C / 4.7	11.0	0.77	30.50	1,883	3	96	0	1	63	108.6	-23.6	91	6	1,000	0	5.8	0.0
C / 4.4	11.0	0.77	26.44	38	3	96	0	1	63	102.8	-23.8	88	6	1,000	0	0.0	0.0
C / 4.4	11.0	0.77	26.64	400	3	96	0	1	63	103.3	-23.8	89	6	1,000	0	0.0	0.0
U /	N/A	N/A	32.28	504	3	96	0	1	63	N/A	N/A	N/A	6	5,000,000	0	0.0	0.0
C / 4.7	11.0	0.77	29.32	232	3	96	0	1	63	106.6	-23.7	90	6	1,000	0	0.0	0.0
C / 4.8	11.0	0.77	32.34	695	3	96	0	1	63	110.9	-23.5	92	6	1,000	0	0.0	0.0
C+ / 6.0	10.1	1.03	48.02	120	2	97	0	1	52	92.5	-15.2	34	6	1,000	0	0.0	0.0
U /	N/A	N/A	13.17	39	2	97	0	1	52	N/A	N/A	N/A	2	1,000	0	5.8	0.0
U /	N/A	N/A	13.22	194	2	97	0	1	52	N/A	N/A	N/A	2	5,000,000	0	0.0	0.0
U /	N/A	N/A	13.21	44	2	97	0	1	52	N/A	N/A	N/A	2	0	0	0.0	0.0
C+ / 5.9	10.1	1.03	48.34	704	2	97	0	1	52	96.3	-15.0	42	6	1,000	0	0.0	0.0
B / 8.8	6.5	1.10	10.93	1,023	23	55	20	2	6	45.5	-11.9	25	10	1,000	50	5.8	0.0
B / 8.8	6.5	1.11	10.80	67	23	55	20	2	6	41.6	-12.3	17	10	1,000	50	0.0	0.0
B / 8.8	6.6	1.11	10.71	400	23	55	20	2	6	41.8	-12.2	16	10	1,000	50	0.0	0.0
B / 8.8	6.5	1.10	10.87	108	23	55	20	2	6	44.3	-12.0	22	10	1,000	50	0.0	0.0
B / 8.8	6.6	1.11	11.00	9	23	55	20	2	6	46.5	-11.7	26	10	1,000	50	0.0	0.0
C- / 3.8	13.3	1.06	30.02	683	0	100	0	0	123	85.7	-17.1	57	13	1,000	0	5.8	0.0

Fund Type	Fund Name	Ticker Symbol	Overall Investment Rating	Phone	Perfor-mance Rating/Pts	3 Mo	6 Mo	1Yr / Pct	3Yr / Pct	5Yr / Pct	Dividend Yield	Expense Ratio
RE	● Oppenheimer Real Estate B	OREBX	B-	(888) 470-0862	A / 9.4	4.81	21.35	25.03 /98	13.34 /62	14.67 /84	0.84	2.22
RE	Oppenheimer Real Estate C	ORECX	B-	(888) 470-0862	A / 9.4	4.82	21.32	25.04 /98	13.34 /62	14.65 /84	0.88	2.22
RE	Oppenheimer Real Estate I	OREIX	B+	(888) 470-0862	A+/ 9.7	5.10	22.04	26.55 /99	14.65 /72	15.79 /92	1.92	1.03
RE	Oppenheimer Real Estate R	ORENX	B	(888) 470-0862	A+/ 9.6	4.94	21.67	25.69 /98	13.92 /67	15.23 /88	1.31	1.72
RE	Oppenheimer Real Estate Y	OREYX	B	(888) 470-0862	A+/ 9.7	5.06	21.95	26.27 /99	14.49 /71	15.88 /92	1.74	1.22
GR	Oppenheimer Rising Dividends A	OARDX	C-	(888) 470-0862	C / 4.8	-0.15	5.44	9.64 /73	12.43 /56	12.09 /61	0.76	1.06
GR	● Oppenheimer Rising Dividends B	OBRDX	C-	(888) 470-0862	C / 5.1	-0.38	4.99	8.79 /68	11.45 /49	11.11 /54	0.20	1.81
GR	Oppenheimer Rising Dividends C	OCRDX	C	(888) 470-0862	C / 5.2	-0.32	5.05	8.85 /68	11.61 /50	11.25 /55	0.25	1.81
GR	Oppenheimer Rising Dividends I	OIRDX	B-	(888) 470-0862	C+/ 6.0	-0.06	5.62	10.12 /75	12.89 /59	--	1.20	0.62
GR	Oppenheimer Rising Dividends R	ONRDX	C	(888) 470-0862	C / 5.5	-0.21	5.33	9.41 /71	12.10 /53	11.73 /59	0.57	1.31
GR	Oppenheimer Rising Dividends Y	OYRDX	C+	(888) 470-0862	C+/ 5.9	-0.10	5.56	9.89 /74	12.66 /57	12.34 /63	1.00	0.81
SC	Oppenheimer Small & Mid Cap Value	QVSCX	B	(888) 470-0862	B- / 7.5	2.84	10.85	10.01 /74	16.40 /86	12.41 /63	0.52	1.17
SC	● Oppenheimer Small & Mid Cap Value	QSCBX	B+	(888) 470-0862	B / 7.9	2.63	10.45	9.18 /70	15.45 /79	11.50 /57	0.02	1.92
SC	Oppenheimer Small & Mid Cap Value	QSCCX	B+	(888) 470-0862	B / 7.9	2.63	10.43	9.20 /70	15.51 /79	11.55 /57	0.04	1.92
MC	Oppenheimer Small & Mid Cap Value	QSCIX	A	(888) 470-0862	B+/ 8.7	2.93	11.09	10.46 /76	16.51 /87	12.48 /64	0.94	0.73
SC	Oppenheimer Small & Mid Cap Value	QSCNX	B+	(888) 470-0862	B+/ 8.4	2.76	10.70	9.72 /73	16.08 /84	12.11 /61	0.35	1.42
SC	Oppenheimer Small & Mid Cap Value	QSCYX	A-	(888) 470-0862	B+/ 8.8	2.88	10.98	10.29 /75	16.75 /88	12.75 /66	0.78	0.92
EN	Oppenheimer SteelPath MLP Alp Pls	MLPLX	D+	(888) 614-6614	D / 1.6	-3.10	-14.22	-1.26 /12	9.97 /39	--	5.26	20.44
EN	Oppenheimer SteelPath MLP Alp Pls	MLPMX	C-	(888) 614-6614	D+/ 2.3	-3.32	-14.48	-2.02 /10	9.81 /38	--	5.71	21.25
EN	Oppenheimer SteelPath MLP Alp Pls	MLPNX	C-	(888) 614-6614	D+/ 2.6	-2.99	-14.03	-1.01 /13	10.28 /41	--	5.53	20.20
GI	Oppenheimer SteelPath MLP Alpha A	MLPAX	D	(888) 614-6614	D- / 1.2	-2.36	-10.67	-0.36 /15	7.82 /26	7.19 /24	5.46	15.40
EN	Oppenheimer SteelPath MLP Alpha C	MLPGX	D	(888) 614-6614	D- / 1.4	-2.50	-11.04	-1.11 /13	7.00 /21	--	5.94	16.13
GI	Oppenheimer SteelPath MLP Alpha Y	MLPOX	D	(888) 614-6614	D / 1.8	-2.25	-10.60	-0.11 /15	8.11 /28	7.48 /26	5.71	15.19
GI	Oppenheimer SteelPath MLP Income	MLPDX	D	(888) 614-6614	E+/ 0.7	-2.10	-9.43	1.08 /19	4.93 /13	4.89 /11	6.51	9.22
EN	Oppenheimer SteelPath MLP Income	MLPRX	D	(888) 614-6614	E+/ 0.8	-2.25	-9.84	0.33 /17	4.13 /11	--	7.11	9.94
GI	Oppenheimer SteelPath MLP Income	MLPZX	D	(888) 614-6614	D- / 1.1	-1.98	-9.31	1.45 /20	5.21 /14	5.18 /13	6.81	8.95
GI	Oppenheimer SteelPath MLP Sel 40	MLPFX	D	(888) 614-6614	D- / 1.1	-1.95	-9.83	0.44 /17	7.24 /23	6.06 /17	5.65	13.84
EN	Oppenheimer SteelPath MLP Sel 40	MLPEX	D	(888) 614-6614	D- / 1.3	-2.16	-10.24	-0.31 /15	6.44 /19	--	6.13	14.55
EN	Oppenheimer SteelPath MLP Sel 40 I	OSPSX	U	(888) 614-6614	U /	-1.92	-9.75	0.76 /18	--	--	5.89	13.38
GI	Oppenheimer SteelPath MLP Sel 40	MLPYX	D	(888) 614-6614	D / 1.7	-1.84	-9.75	0.76 /18	7.52 /24	7.39 /26	5.89	13.61
GI	Oppenheimer SteelPath MLP Sel 40	MLPTX	D	(888) 614-6614	D / 1.7	-1.84	-9.75	0.68 /18	7.52 /24	7.04 /23	5.89	13.69
GR	Oppenheimer Value A	CGRWX	C+	(888) 470-0862	C / 5.4	-0.19	3.72	8.10 /64	13.96 /67	11.18 /54	1.03	0.96
GR	● Oppenheimer Value B	CGRBX	C+	(888) 470-0862	C+/ 5.8	-0.36	3.33	7.27 /57	13.07 /60	10.27 /47	0.33	1.71
GR	Oppenheimer Value C	CGRCX	C+	(888) 470-0862	C+/ 5.8	-0.35	3.33	7.28 /57	13.11 /60	10.34 /47	0.42	1.71
GR	Oppenheimer Value I	OGRIX	B-	(888) 470-0862	C+/ 6.7	-0.07	3.94	8.57 /67	14.48 /71	11.49 /57	1.49	0.52
GR	Oppenheimer Value R	CGRNX	B-	(888) 470-0862	C+/ 6.1	-0.25	3.60	7.82 /61	13.67 /65	10.88 /52	0.87	1.21
GR	Oppenheimer Value Y	CGRYX	B-	(888) 470-0862	C+/ 6.6	-0.14	3.83	8.35 /65	14.32 /69	11.58 /58	1.26	0.71
FO	Optimum Intl Equity A	OAIEX	E+	(800) 523-1918	E+/ 0.8	2.10	-2.50	-6.25 / 4	5.33 /14	4.05 / 8	1.02	1.61
FO	Optimum Intl Equity C	OCIEX	D-	(800) 523-1918	E+/ 0.9	1.88	-2.89	-6.99 / 4	4.59 /12	3.35 / 7	0.18	2.36
FO	Optimum Intl Equity I	OIIEX	D-	(800) 523-1918	D- / 1.2	2.18	-2.37	-6.04 / 4	5.66 /15	4.39 /10	1.34	1.36
GR	Optimum Large Cap Growth A	OALGX	B+	(800) 523-1918	B+/ 8.5	5.52	9.97	17.27 /95	16.52 /87	14.92 /86	0.00	1.48
GR	Optimum Large Cap Growth C	OCLGX	B+	(800) 523-1918	B+/ 8.9	5.32	9.53	16.44 /94	15.74 /81	14.14 /79	0.00	2.23
GR	Optimum Large Cap Growth I	OILGX	A-	(800) 523-1918	A / 9.4	5.53	10.04	17.55 /95	16.89 /89	15.28 /89	0.00	1.23
GR	Optimum Large Cap Value A	OALVX	C	(800) 523-1918	C / 4.4	1.07	2.73	5.34 /41	12.44 /56	11.64 /58	0.98	1.44
GR	Optimum Large Cap Value C	OCLVX	C+	(800) 523-1918	C / 4.8	0.89	2.32	4.48 /35	11.67 /50	10.89 /52	0.32	2.19
GR	Optimum Large Cap Value I	OILVX	C+	(800) 523-1918	C / 5.5	1.13	2.86	5.60 /43	12.78 /58	11.99 /60	1.28	1.19
SC	Optimum Small Mid Cap Growth A	OASGX	C	(800) 523-1918	C+/ 6.2	4.34	10.86	8.93 /69	14.23 /69	13.27 /71	0.00	1.90
SC	Optimum Small Mid Cap Growth C	OCSGX	C	(800) 523-1918	C+/ 6.6	4.13	10.50	8.08 /63	13.42 /63	12.50 /64	0.00	2.65
SC	Optimum Small Mid Cap Growth I	OISGX	C+	(800) 523-1918	B- / 7.5	4.39	11.02	9.18 /70	14.59 /72	13.63 /74	0.00	1.65
SC	Optimum Small Mid Cap Value A	OASVX	D	(800) 523-1918	C- / 3.3	1.64	4.13	-0.69 /14	11.07 /46	11.63 /58	0.00	1.81
SC	Optimum Small Mid Cap Value C	OCSVX	D	(800) 523-1918	C- / 3.7	1.49	3.73	-1.45 /12	10.30 /41	10.88 /52	0.00	2.56
SC	Optimum Small Mid Cap Value I	OISVX	C-	(800) 523-1918	C / 4.4	1.71	4.23	-0.53 /14	11.37 /48	11.97 /60	0.00	1.56

RISK Risk Rating/Pts	3 Year Standard Deviation	Beta	NET ASSETS NAV As of 3/31/15	Total $(Mil)	ASSET Cash %	Stocks %	Bonds %	Other %	Portfolio Turnover Ratio	BULL / BEAR Last Bull Market Return	Last Bear Market Return	FUND MANAGER Manager Quality Pct	Manager Tenure (Years)	MINIMUMS Initial Purch. $	Additional Purch. $	LOADS Front End Load	Back End Load
C- /3.8	13.3	1.06	29.44	19	0	100	0	0	123	81.0	-17.3	46	13	1,000	0	0.0	0.0
C- /3.8	13.3	1.06	29.38	137	0	100	0	0	123	81.0	-17.3	46	13	1,000	0	0.0	0.0
C /4.9	13.3	1.06	30.26	161	0	100	0	0	123	87.9	-17.1	64	13	5,000,000	0	0.0	0.0
C- /3.8	13.3	1.06	29.90	120	0	100	0	0	123	84.2	-17.2	53	13	0	0	0.0	0.0
C- /3.8	13.3	1.06	30.28	444	0	100	0	0	123	87.4	-16.9	61	13	0	0	0.0	0.0
C+ /6.0	10.3	1.05	19.91	2,773	2	97	0	1	90	80.3	-15.9	16	8	1,000	0	5.8	0.0
C+ /5.7	10.3	1.05	17.60	118	2	97	0	1	90	74.9	-16.2	11	8	1,000	0	0.0	0.0
C+ /5.7	10.2	1.05	17.48	768	2	97	0	1	90	75.6	-16.1	12	8	1,000	0	0.0	0.0
B- /7.1	10.3	1.05	20.45	48	2	97	0	1	90	N/A	N/A	19	8	5,000,000	0	0.0	0.0
C+ /6.0	10.3	1.05	19.81	150	2	97	0	1	90	78.2	-16.0	14	8	1,000	0	0.0	0.0
C+ /6.0	10.3	1.05	20.47	2,025	2	97	0	1	90	81.5	-15.8	18	8	1,000	0	0.0	0.0
C+ /6.5	11.6	0.78	50.05	1,142	1	98	0	1	51	90.5	-24.3	90	2	1,000	0	5.8	0.0
C+ /6.4	11.7	0.79	42.07	33	1	98	0	1	51	85.3	-24.6	87	2	1,000	0	0.0	0.0
C+ /6.4	11.6	0.78	42.13	290	1	98	0	1	51	85.5	-24.5	87	2	1,000	0	0.0	0.0
C+ /6.9	11.7	1.01	50.85	1	1	98	0	1	51	91.0	-24.3	59	2	5,000,000	0	0.0	0.0
C+ /6.5	11.6	0.78	48.07	121	1	98	0	1	51	88.7	-24.4	89	2	1,000	0	0.0	0.0
C+ /6.5	11.6	0.78	51.28	54	1	98	0	1	51	92.5	-24.2	91	2	1,000	0	0.0	0.0
B- /7.8	12.5	0.53	11.77	175	96	3	0	1	21	N/A	N/A	96	4	1,000	50	5.8	0.0
B- /7.9	12.1	0.50	11.52	57	96	3	0	1	21	N/A	N/A	96	4	1,000	50	0.0	0.0
B- /7.7	12.5	0.53	11.89	126	96	3	0	1	21	N/A	N/A	97	4	1,000	50	0.0	0.0
B- /7.1	9.7	0.58	11.90	1,730	97	2	0	1	17	37.2	-8.9	50	5	1,000	50	5.8	0.0
B- /7.1	9.7	0.42	11.61	1,011	97	2	0	1	17	33.6	N/A	94	5	1,000	50	0.0	0.0
B- /7.2	9.7	0.58	12.08	2,193	97	2	0	1	17	38.3	-8.7	55	5	1,000	50	0.0	0.0
B- /7.5	9.0	0.56	10.29	1,953	97	2	0	1	14	25.4	-12.3	20	5	1,000	50	5.8	0.0
B- /7.4	9.0	0.37	10.00	1,588	97	2	0	1	14	22.1	N/A	87	5	1,000	50	0.0	0.0
B- /7.6	9.0	0.55	10.44	925	97	2	0	1	14	26.5	-12.3	23	5	1,000	50	0.0	0.0
B- /7.2	9.8	0.61	11.78	825	98	1	0	1	12	34.8	-10.4	36	5	1,000	50	5.8	0.0
B- /7.1	9.8	0.45	11.52	492	98	1	0	1	12	31.6	N/A	93	5	1,000	50	0.0	0.0
U /	N/A	N/A	11.98	140	98	1	0	1	12	N/A	N/A	N/A	5	5,000,000	0	0.0	0.0
B- /7.2	9.8	0.61	11.98	53	98	1	0	1	12	36.0	-10.2	39	5	1,000	50	0.0	0.0
B- /7.2	9.8	0.61	11.98	1,604	98	1	0	1	12	36.0	-10.2	39	5	1,000	50	0.0	0.0
B- /7.0	10.3	1.04	32.16	616	0	100	0	0	46	80.9	-20.9	31	2	1,000	0	5.8	0.0
B- /7.0	10.2	1.04	31.71	13	0	100	0	0	46	76.0	-21.2	23	2	1,000	0	0.0	0.0
B- /7.0	10.3	1.04	30.84	137	0	100	0	0	46	76.3	-21.2	23	2	1,000	0	0.0	0.0
B- /7.3	10.2	1.04	32.76	1,260	0	100	0	0	46	83.4	-20.9	38	2	5,000,000	0	0.0	0.0
B- /7.0	10.3	1.04	31.58	60	0	100	0	0	46	79.3	-21.0	29	2	1,000	0	0.0	0.0
B- /7.0	10.2	1.04	32.81	110	0	100	0	0	46	83.0	-20.7	36	2	1,000	0	0.0	0.0
C+ /6.0	12.3	0.91	11.66	10	2	97	0	1	126	34.4	-21.0	24	3	1,000	100	5.8	0.0
C+ /6.0	12.2	0.91	11.41	36	2	97	0	1	126	31.3	-21.2	18	3	1,000	100	0.0	0.0
C+ /6.1	12.2	0.91	11.74	478	2	97	0	1	126	35.8	-20.9	28	3	0	0	0.0	0.0
C+ /5.8	10.5	0.99	17.00	41	3	96	0	1	98	103.7	-18.2	73	7	1,000	100	5.8	0.0
C /5.4	10.5	0.99	15.44	138	3	96	0	1	98	99.3	-18.5	66	7	1,000	100	0.0	0.0
C+ /5.9	10.5	0.99	17.76	1,413	3	96	0	1	98	106.1	-18.1	76	7	0	0	0.0	0.0
B- /7.2	10.3	1.06	16.01	36	2	97	0	1	37	81.8	-17.0	15	12	1,000	100	5.8	0.0
B- /7.2	10.3	1.06	15.85	123	2	97	0	1	37	77.5	-17.2	12	12	1,000	100	0.0	0.0
B- /7.2	10.3	1.06	16.04	1,146	2	97	0	1	37	83.9	-16.9	18	12	0	0	0.0	0.0
C /5.1	12.5	0.89	15.37	7	3	96	0	1	58	88.4	-24.5	65	7	1,000	100	5.8	0.0
C /4.9	12.5	0.90	13.86	23	3	96	0	1	58	84.2	-24.7	53	7	1,000	100	0.0	0.0
C /5.1	12.5	0.89	16.17	528	3	96	0	1	58	90.5	-24.4	69	7	0	0	0.0	0.0
C+ /5.6	12.6	0.89	13.64	5	11	88	0	1	33	83.5	-25.7	27	9	1,000	100	5.8	0.0
C /5.4	12.6	0.88	12.30	19	11	88	0	1	33	79.1	-25.9	20	9	1,000	100	0.0	0.0
C+ /5.7	12.6	0.88	14.31	500	11	88	0	1	33	85.3	-25.6	30	9	0	0	0.0	0.0

Fund Type	Fund Name	Ticker Symbol	Overall Investment Rating	Phone	Perfor-mance Rating/Pts	3 Mo	6 Mo	1Yr / Pct	3Yr / Pct	5Yr / Pct	Dividend Yield	Expense Ratio
GL	Orinda Income Opportunities Fund A	OIOAX	U	(855) 467-4632	U /	1.69	0.88	3.12 /27	--	--	5.46	4.25
GL	Orinda Income Opportunities Fund I	OIOIX	U	(855) 467-4632	U /	1.79	1.10	3.45 /29	--	--	5.94	3.95
GR	O'Shaughnessy All Cap Core A	OFAAX	C	(877) 291-7827	C+ / 6.5	1.47	5.62	9.39 /71	15.89 /82	--	0.37	1.48
GR	O'Shaughnessy All Cap Core C	OFACX	C+	(877) 291-7827	C+ / 6.8	1.32	5.23	8.56 /67	14.99 /75	--	0.16	2.23
GR	O'Shaughnessy All Cap Core I	OFAIX	C+	(877) 291-7827	B / 7.6	1.55	5.71	9.62 /73	16.16 /85	--	0.84	0.76
IN	O'Shaughnessy Enh Div I	OFDIX	E	(877) 291-7827	E / 0.5	-1.15	-12.10	-11.05 / 2	3.29 / 8	--	5.79	1.24
GR	O'Shaughnessy S/M Cap Growth I	OFMIX	C	(877) 291-7827	B- / 7.4	4.76	7.14	4.94 /38	15.97 /83	--	0.00	2.79
GI	Osterweis	OSTFX	B	(800) 700-3316	B / 7.8	4.27	6.25	8.70 /68	15.59 /80	11.66 /58	1.34	1.01
GI	Osterweis Institutional Equity Inv	OSTEX	U	(800) 700-3316	U /	4.29	6.29	8.84 /68	--	--	1.32	1.13
GL	Osterweis Strat Invest	OSTVX	C+	(800) 700-3316	C+ / 6.1	3.44	4.17	6.30 /49	13.34 /62	--	2.54	1.15
GR	Otter Creek Long/Short Oppty Inst	OTTRX	U		U /	0.82	1.35	5.21 /40	--	--	0.00	3.15
AA	Outfitter Fund	OTFTX	D	(888) 450-4517	D+ / 2.7	1.14	3.44	5.34 /41	8.11 /28	--	1.47	1.20
GL	PACE Alternatives Strat Invst A	PASIX	C-	(888) 793-8637	D- / 1.2	2.51	3.37	5.35 /41	5.65 /15	4.14 / 9	0.00	2.02
GL	PACE Alternatives Strat Invst C	PASOX	C	(888) 793-8637	D- / 1.5	2.41	3.02	4.64 /36	4.93 /13	3.41 / 7	0.20	2.76
GL	PACE Alternatives Strat Invst P	PASPX	C	(888) 793-8637	D / 1.7	2.70	3.65	5.81 /45	5.97 /17	4.44 /10	0.97	1.79
GL	PACE Alternatives Strat Invst Y	PASYX	C	(888) 793-8637	D / 1.9	2.70	3.58	5.74 /44	5.93 /16	4.40 /10	0.93	1.80
RE	PACE Glb Real Est Sec Inv Cl A	PREAX	C	(888) 793-8637	C+ / 6.4	4.39	12.46	16.30 /94	12.77 /58	11.39 /56	0.00	1.59
RE	PACE Glb Real Est Sec Inv Cl C	PREEX	C+	(888) 793-8637	C+ / 6.8	4.28	12.04	15.54 /93	12.01 /53	10.57 /49	2.58	2.30
RE	PACE Glb Real Est Sec Inv Cl P	PREQX	C+	(888) 793-8637	B- / 7.2	4.40	12.45	16.62 /94	13.08 /60	11.63 /58	3.34	1.63
RE	PACE Glb Real Est Sec Inv Cl Y	PREYX	C+	(888) 793-8637	B / 7.6	4.52	12.56	16.54 /94	13.08 /60	11.66 /58	3.39	1.38
EM	PACE Intertl Emg Mkts Eq Inve A	PWEAX	E+	(888) 793-8637	E / 0.4	0.63	-1.62	0.87 /18	0.01 / 4	1.67 / 4	0.44	1.83
EM	PACE Intertl Emg Mkts Eq Inve C	PWECX	E+	(888) 793-8637	E / 0.4	0.43	-1.99	0.17 /16	-0.72 / 4	0.91 / 3	0.25	2.58
EM	PACE Intertl Emg Mkts Eq Inve P	PCEMX	E+	(888) 793-8637	E / 0.4	0.63	-1.55	1.06 /19	0.14 / 4	1.74 / 4	1.17	1.67
EM	PACE Intertl Emg Mkts Eq Inve Y	PWEYX	E+	(888) 793-8637	E / 0.5	0.63	-1.57	1.10 /19	0.25 / 4	1.89 / 4	1.24	1.58
FO	PACE Intrntl Eq Inve A	PWGAX	D	(888) 793-8637	D / 1.9	4.57	0.93	-1.68 /11	8.69 /31	5.82 /16	2.09	1.70
FO	PACE Intrntl Eq Inve C	PWGCX	D	(888) 793-8637	D / 2.2	4.36	0.55	-2.43 /10	7.80 /26	4.97 /12	1.60	2.51
FO	PACE Intrntl Eq Inve P	PCIEX	D	(888) 793-8637	D+ / 2.6	4.67	1.15	-1.34 /12	8.99 /33	6.09 /17	2.64	1.45
FO	PACE Intrntl Eq Inve Y	PWIYX	D+	(888) 793-8637	D+ / 2.9	4.66	1.10	-1.39 /12	9.01 /33	6.12 /17	2.71	1.42
GR	PACE Large Co Gr Eq Inve A	PLAAX	C	(888) 793-8637	C+ / 6.8	3.06	8.54	14.68 /91	15.02 /75	14.17 /79	0.00	1.18
GR	PACE Large Co Gr Eq Inve C	PLACX	C	(888) 793-8637	B- / 7.1	2.85	8.12	13.75 /89	14.07 /68	13.22 /70	0.00	2.00
GR	PACE Large Co Gr Eq Inve P	PCLCX	C+	(888) 793-8637	B / 7.7	3.16	8.73	15.03 /92	15.33 /78	14.48 /82	0.20	0.93
GR	PACE Large Co Gr Eq Inve Y	PLAYX	B-	(888) 793-8637	B / 8.1	3.14	8.73	15.04 /92	15.33 /78	14.47 /82	0.21	0.93
GI	PACE Large Co Val Eq Inve A	PCPAX	C+	(888) 793-8637	C+ / 5.9	-0.80	4.79	8.10 /64	15.00 /75	12.30 /63	1.09	1.32
GI	PACE Large Co Val Eq Inve C	PLVCX	C+	(888) 793-8637	C+ / 6.2	-1.00	4.35	7.26 /57	14.10 /68	11.41 /56	0.43	2.10
GI	PACE Large Co Val Eq Inve P	PCLVX	C+	(888) 793-8637	C+ / 6.6	-0.76	4.91	8.35 /65	15.28 /77	12.55 /64	1.41	1.08
GI	PACE Large Co Val Eq Inve Y	PLVYX	B-	(888) 793-8637	B- / 7.0	-0.75	4.90	8.37 /65	15.27 /77	12.56 /65	1.45	1.07
MC	PACE Smal/Med Co Val Eq Inve A	PEVAX	C	(888) 793-8637	C+ / 6.7	4.39	10.56	9.05 /70	15.34 /78	12.90 /67	0.12	1.29
MC	PACE Smal/Med Co Val Eq Inve C	PEVCX	C	(888) 793-8637	B- / 7.1	4.15	10.12	8.16 /64	14.46 /71	12.04 /61	0.00	2.05
MC	PACE Smal/Med Co Val Eq Inve P	PCSVX	C+	(888) 793-8637	B- / 7.5	4.39	10.63	9.16 /70	15.48 /79	13.04 /69	0.42	1.16
MC	PACE Smal/Med Co Val Eq Inve Y	PVEYX	C+	(888) 793-8637	B / 7.8	4.40	10.63	9.17 /70	15.46 /79	13.07 /69	0.46	1.16
MC	PACE Smal/Med Comp Gr Eq Inve A	PQUAX	D+	(888) 793-8637	C+ / 6.5	5.71	14.97	8.53 /67	14.52 /71	14.86 /86	0.00	1.25
MC	PACE Smal/Med Comp Gr Eq Inve C	PUMCX	D+	(888) 793-8637	C+ / 6.9	5.50	14.53	7.70 /60	13.66 /65	13.98 /78	0.00	2.01
MC	PACE Smal/Med Comp Gr Eq Inve P	PCSGX	C-	(888) 793-8637	B- / 7.3	5.77	15.00	8.68 /67	14.67 /72	15.02 /87	0.00	1.13
MC	PACE Smal/Med Comp Gr Eq Inve Y	PUMYX	C	(888) 793-8637	B / 7.6	5.75	15.03	8.68 /67	14.66 /72	15.05 /87	0.00	1.14
BA	Pacific Advisors Balanced A	PAABX	E	(800) 282-6693	E+ / 0.7	-1.32	-4.09	-6.13 / 4	5.78 /16	5.77 /15	0.00	3.07
BA	Pacific Advisors Balanced C	PGBCX	E	(800) 282-6693	E+ / 0.8	-1.52	-4.48	-6.88 / 4	4.96 /13	4.95 /12	0.00	3.86
GR	Pacific Advisors Large Cap Value A	PAGTX	C+	(800) 282-6693	C- / 4.1	-1.04	4.32	9.40 /71	12.11 /53	10.49 /49	0.00	4.02
GR	Pacific Advisors Large Cap Value C	PGCCX	C+	(800) 282-6693	C / 4.5	-1.24	3.91	8.55 /67	11.26 /47	9.68 /42	0.00	4.77
GR	Pacific Advisors Mid Cap Value A	PAMVX	E	(800) 282-6693	E / 0.4	-1.73	-2.83	-8.97 / 3	3.18 / 8	7.37 /26	0.00	3.69
GR	Pacific Advisors Mid Cap Value C	PMVCX	E	(800) 282-6693	E / 0.5	-1.94	-3.23	-9.68 / 3	2.42 / 7	6.53 /20	0.00	4.42
SC	Pacific Advisors Small Cap Value A	PASMX	E-	(800) 282-6693	E / 0.3	-5.05	-14.09	-21.88 / 1	4.68 /12	10.37 /48	0.00	2.31
SC	Pacific Advisors Small Cap Value C	PGSCX	E-	(800) 282-6693	E / 0.4	-5.23	-14.42	-22.48 / 1	3.90 /10	9.55 /41	0.00	3.08

Risk Rating/Pts	Standard Deviation	Beta	NAV As of 3/31/15	Total $(Mil)	Cash %	Stocks %	Bonds %	Other %	Portfolio Turnover Ratio	Last Bull Market Return	Last Bear Market Return	Manager Quality Pct	Manager Tenure (Years)	Initial Purch. $	Additional Purch. $	Front End Load	Back End Load
U /	N/A	N/A	24.81	74	13	86	0	1	119	N/A	N/A	N/A	2	5,000	0	5.0	0.0
U /	N/A	N/A	24.86	153	13	86	0	1	119	N/A	N/A	N/A	2	500,000	0	0.0	0.0
C / 5.3	10.2	1.02	15.85	3	1	98	0	1	72	99.5	-19.7	60	5	2,500	100	5.3	2.0
C / 5.3	10.3	1.02	15.38	11	1	98	0	1	72	94.4	-20.0	48	5	2,500	100	0.0	2.0
C / 5.2	10.3	1.02	15.76	120	1	98	0	1	72	101.0	-19.7	64	5	1,000,000	0	0.0	2.0
C- / 3.4	14.1	1.10	10.44	73	1	98	0	1	45	33.8	-16.7	1	5	1,000,000	0	0.0	2.0
C- / 3.5	11.5	1.04	14.74	18	0	99	0	1	99	94.5	-28.4	56	5	1,000,000	0	0.0	2.0
C+ / 6.0	10.0	0.97	34.90	1,179	14	85	0	1	31	86.5	-20.6	68	22	5,000	100	0.0	0.0
U /	N/A	N/A	13.60	44	11	88	0	1	31	N/A	N/A	N/A	3	100,000	100	0.0	0.0
C+ / 6.8	7.2	0.43	15.34	339	8	58	31	3	61	69.7	-13.9	97	5	5,000	100	0.0	0.0
U /	N/A	N/A	11.06	97	10	88	0	2	37	N/A	N/A	N/A	2	100,000	0	0.0	1.0
C+ / 5.9	6.3	1.07	12.42	23	5	58	36	1	21	N/A	N/A	23	3	5,000	100	0.0	2.0
B+ / 9.6	3.9	0.26	11.03	8	71	10	17	2	114	27.3	-8.4	89	9	1,000	100	5.5	1.0
B+ / 9.6	3.9	0.26	10.62	8	71	10	17	2	114	24.4	-8.8	86	9	1,000	100	0.0	1.0
B+ / 9.6	3.9	0.25	11.02	742	71	10	17	2	114	28.6	-8.4	90	9	10,000	500	2.0	1.0
B+ / 9.6	3.9	0.26	11.05	3	71	10	17	2	114	28.4	-8.3	90	9	5,000,000	0	0.0	1.0
C / 5.2	12.1	0.90	7.85	1	10	89	0	1	53	75.7	-20.1	69	6	1,000	100	5.5	1.0
C / 5.2	12.1	0.89	7.56	N/A	10	89	0	1	53	71.2	-20.4	61	6	1,000	100	0.0	1.0
C / 5.2	12.1	0.90	7.60	156	10	89	0	1	53	77.1	-20.0	72	6	10,000	500	2.0	1.0
C / 5.2	12.0	0.89	7.63	N/A	10	89	0	1	53	77.4	-20.1	73	6	5,000,000	0	0.0	1.0
C+ / 5.7	13.3	0.96	12.71	7	45	54	0	1	74	23.3	-25.4	58	11	1,000	100	5.5	1.0
C+ / 5.7	13.3	0.95	11.79	2	45	54	0	1	74	20.3	-25.6	47	11	1,000	100	0.0	1.0
C+ / 5.7	13.3	0.95	12.81	443	45	54	0	1	74	23.7	-25.3	60	11	10,000	500	2.0	1.0
C+ / 5.7	13.3	0.96	12.87	10	45	54	0	1	74	24.3	-25.3	62	11	5,000,000	0	0.0	1.0
C+ / 6.3	12.5	0.94	14.88	35	40	59	0	1	86	50.3	-22.3	64	6	1,000	100	5.5	1.0
C+ / 6.3	12.5	0.94	14.60	3	40	59	0	1	86	46.2	-22.7	52	6	1,000	100	0.0	1.0
C+ / 6.3	12.5	0.94	14.80	1,010	40	59	0	1	86	51.6	-22.2	68	6	10,000	500	2.0	1.0
C+ / 6.3	12.5	0.94	14.83	19	40	59	0	1	86	51.7	-22.3	68	6	5,000,000	0	0.0	1.0
C / 5.0	10.2	1.02	25.24	47	2	97	0	1	40	96.6	-17.4	48	8	1,000	100	5.5	1.0
C / 4.6	10.3	1.02	21.98	4	2	97	0	1	40	91.1	-17.7	36	8	1,000	100	0.0	1.0
C / 5.0	10.3	1.02	25.79	1,350	2	97	0	1	40	98.3	-17.3	52	8	10,000	500	2.0	1.0
C / 5.0	10.3	1.02	25.94	16	2	97	0	1	40	98.3	-17.3	52	8	5,000,000	0	0.0	1.0
C+ / 6.0	10.8	1.09	23.63	129	22	77	0	1	71	97.0	-20.6	33	7	1,000	100	5.5	1.0
C+ / 6.2	10.8	1.09	23.66	15	22	77	0	1	71	91.8	-20.9	24	7	1,000	100	0.0	1.0
C+ / 6.0	10.8	1.09	23.58	1,279	22	77	0	1	71	98.4	-20.5	36	7	10,000	500	2.0	1.0
C+ / 6.0	10.8	1.09	23.67	20	22	77	0	1	71	98.6	-20.6	36	7	5,000,000	0	0.0	1.0
C / 4.8	12.1	1.07	21.15	19	26	73	0	1	86	99.4	-27.7	31	8	1,000	100	5.5	1.0
C- / 4.2	12.1	1.07	18.32	5	26	73	0	1	86	94.4	-28.0	22	8	1,000	100	0.0	1.0
C / 4.9	12.1	1.07	21.63	547	26	73	0	1	86	100.2	-27.7	32	8	10,000	500	2.0	1.0
C / 4.9	12.1	1.07	21.82	1	26	73	0	1	86	100.3	-27.7	32	8	5,000,000	0	0.0	1.0
C- / 3.3	13.5	1.09	19.45	28	33	66	0	1	94	89.4	-22.9	19	10	1,000	100	5.5	1.0
D+ / 2.4	13.5	1.09	16.31	4	33	66	0	1	94	84.4	-23.2	14	10	1,000	100	0.0	1.0
C- / 3.5	13.4	1.08	20.35	533	33	66	0	1	94	90.2	-22.9	21	10	10,000	500	2.0	1.0
C- / 3.5	13.5	1.09	20.61	1	33	66	0	1	94	90.3	-22.9	21	10	5,000,000	0	0.0	1.0
C / 4.8	10.1	1.50	14.21	5	1	70	28	1	23	40.7	-14.6	2	8	1,000	25	5.8	2.0
C / 4.4	10.1	1.50	12.79	4	1	70	28	1	23	37.0	-14.9	2	8	10,000	500	0.0	2.0
B- / 7.7	9.9	1.00	14.04	7	1	98	0	1	24	74.9	-10.9	20	5	1,000	25	5.8	2.0
B- / 7.7	9.9	1.00	12.23	1	1	98	0	1	24	70.4	-11.2	14	5	10,000	500	0.0	2.0
C / 4.3	17.0	1.53	13.22	6	0	100	0	0	15	49.5	-33.5	0	8	1,000	25	5.8	2.0
C- / 4.2	17.0	1.53	11.86	1	0	100	0	0	15	45.8	-33.8	0	8	10,000	500	0.0	2.0
D / 1.8	19.3	1.11	42.26	91	0	100	0	0	9	71.8	-30.0	1	22	1,000	25	5.8	2.0
D / 1.7	19.3	1.11	34.68	9	0	100	0	0	9	67.5	-30.2	1	22	10,000	500	0.0	2.0

Fund Type	Fund Name	Ticker Symbol	Overall Investment Rating	Phone	Performance Rating/Pts	3 Mo	6 Mo	1Yr / Pct	3Yr / Pct	5Yr / Pct	Dividend Yield	Expense Ratio
SC	Pacific Advisors Small Cap Value I	PGISX	E-	(800) 282-6693	E / 0.5	-4.74	-13.77	-21.46 / 1	5.99 /17	11.29 /55	0.00	2.06
IN	Pacific Financial Core Eqty Inst	PFGQX	C	(800) 637-1380	C+ / 5.6	1.56	5.13	6.74 /53	12.48 /56	9.78 /43	1.19	2.14
IN	Pacific Financial Core Eqty Inv	PFLQX	C	(800) 637-1380	C / 5.0	1.40	4.71	6.03 /47	11.62 /50	8.95 /36	0.77	2.88
OT	Pacific Financial Explorer Inst	PFGPX	B	(800) 637-1380	B- / 7.1	3.09	7.90	10.86 /78	14.07 /68	9.23 /38	0.00	2.07
GR	Pacific Financial Explorer Inv	PFLPX	C+	(800) 258-9232	C+ / 6.5	2.87	7.48	10.05 /75	13.26 /61	8.38 /32	0.00	2.83
EM	Pacific Financial Intl Inst	PFGIX	D	(800) 637-1380	D / 2.1	3.17	4.27	0.17 /16	6.58 /19	1.29 / 4	0.00	2.70
FO	Pacific Financial Intl Investor	PFLIX	D-	(800) 637-1380	D / 1.7	2.92	3.87	-0.53 /14	5.82 /16	0.59 / 3	0.00	3.45
AA	Pacific Financial Stg Csv Inst	PFGSX	C-	(800) 637-1380	E+ / 0.9	1.16	1.30	2.25 /23	2.76 / 7	3.59 / 7	1.91	2.10
AA	Pacific Financial Stg Csv Inv	PFLSX	C-	(800) 637-1380	E+ / 0.7	0.95	0.95	1.53 /20	2.00 / 6	2.89 / 6	1.09	2.85
GL	Palmer Square Absolute Return A	PSQAX	D+	(866) 933-9033	E / 0.5	0.93	0.01	0.38 /17	2.12 / 6	--	1.81	2.29
GL	Palmer Square Absolute Return I	PSQIX	D+	(866) 933-9033	E+ / 0.8	0.93	0.13	0.62 /17	2.37 / 7	--	2.25	2.04
CV	Palmer Square SSI Alternative Inc I	PSCIX	U	(866) 933-9033	U /	0.61	-1.27	-1.25 /12	--	--	1.22	2.10
FO	Papp Small and Mid Cap Growth	PAPPX	C+	(877) 370-7277	C+ / 5.8	5.18	10.45	10.77 /77	11.45 /49	13.15 /70	0.00	1.86
GR	Paradigm Micro-Cap	PVIVX	C	(877) 593-8637	B- / 7.3	4.93	19.46	7.47 /59	14.28 /69	13.25 /71	0.00	1.25
SC	Paradigm Opportunity	PFOPX	C	(877) 593-8637	C+ / 6.1	7.52	13.34	11.17 /79	11.97 /52	12.40 /63	0.00	2.01
SC	Paradigm Select	PFSLX	D	(877) 593-8637	C+ / 6.2	5.84	12.73	11.16 /79	12.46 /56	13.78 /76	0.00	1.50
SC	Paradigm Value	PVFAX	E-	(877) 593-8637	D / 2.0	1.88	6.46	-1.29 /12	7.24 /23	9.47 /40	0.00	1.91
IX	Parametric Absolute Return Inst	EOAIX	D-	(800) 262-1122	E+ / 0.6	2.85	-0.91	0.83 /18	1.25 / 5	--	0.00	1.49
IX	Parametric Absolute Return Inv	EOAAX	D-	(800) 262-1122	E+ / 0.6	2.77	-1.13	0.52 /17	0.98 / 5	--	0.00	1.74
OT	Parametric Commodity Strategy Inst	EIPCX	E	(800) 262-1122	E- / 0.1	-5.86	-17.01	-23.65 / 1	-10.88 / 1	--	0.00	1.14
OT	Parametric Commodity Strategy Inv	EAPCX	D-	(800) 262-1122	E- / 0.1	-5.90	-17.10	-23.77 / 1	-11.11 / 1	--	0.00	1.39
EM	● Parametric Emerging Markets C	ECEMX	E+	(800) 262-1122	E / 0.3	-0.86	-9.33	-6.34 / 4	-0.89 / 4	0.58 / 3	0.39	2.13
EM	Parametric Emerging Markets Inst	EIEMX	E+	(800) 262-1122	E / 0.4	-0.64	-8.86	-5.40 / 5	0.09 / 4	1.58 / 4	1.60	1.13
EM	Parametric Emerging Markets Inv	EAEMX	E+	(800) 262-1122	E / 0.4	-0.72	-8.98	-5.64 / 5	-0.16 / 4	1.32 / 4	1.29	1.38
EM	Parametric Emerging Markets R6	EREMX	E	(800) 262-1122	E / 0.4	-0.64	-8.89	-5.38 / 5	0.10 / 4	1.59 / 4	1.63	N/A
FO	Parametric International Eqty Inst	EIISX	D	(800) 262-1122	D+ / 2.9	4.95	1.81	-1.22 /12	8.50 /30	--	2.42	1.09
FO	Parametric International Eqty Inv	EAISX	D-	(800) 262-1122	D+ / 2.7	4.96	1.67	-1.36 /12	8.22 /28	--	2.04	1.34
FO	● Parametric Tax-Mgd Intl Equity C	ECIGX	D-	(800) 262-1122	D / 2.0	4.27	0.86	-2.78 / 9	7.00 /21	3.26 / 6	1.68	2.35
FO	Parametric Tax-Mgd Intl Equity Inst	EITIX	D	(800) 262-1122	D+ / 2.6	4.50	1.38	-1.81 /11	8.09 /27	4.32 / 9	2.65	1.35
FO	Parametric Tax-Mgd Intl Equity Inv	ETIGX	D	(800) 262-1122	D+ / 2.4	4.38	1.19	-2.08 /10	7.79 /26	4.03 / 8	2.36	1.60
EM	Parametric TxMg Em Mk Inst	EITEX	E+	(800) 262-1122	E / 0.4	-0.35	-8.63	-5.15 / 5	0.88 / 5	2.43 / 5	2.14	0.95
GR	Parnassus	PARNX	B+	(800) 999-3505	A+ / 9.6	2.79	10.97	14.28 /90	19.26 /97	15.59 /91	3.10	0.86
IN	Parnassus Core Equity Inst	PRILX	A+	(800) 999-3505	A- / 9.1	-0.73	5.57	12.90 /86	17.94 /94	13.91 /77	1.60	0.69
★ IN	Parnassus Core Equity Inv	PRBLX	A+	(800) 999-3505	A- / 9.0	-0.78	5.47	12.70 /86	17.75 /93	13.69 /75	1.41	0.87
GR	Parnassus Endeavor	PARWX	A+	(800) 999-3505	A+ / 9.7	2.94	10.53	18.69 /96	19.20 /97	15.87 /92	1.59	1.07
MC	Parnassus Mid Cap	PARMX	A	(800) 999-3505	B / 8.0	1.82	8.84	13.22 /87	15.30 /77	14.79 /85	0.70	1.14
SC	Parnassus Small Cap	PARSX	E+	(800) 999-3505	D+ / 2.9	-2.65	5.50	2.22 /23	8.49 /30	9.78 /43	0.01	1.20
GR	Pathway Advisors Aggressive Growth	PWAGX	U	(888) 288-1121	U /	1.35	2.79	4.34 /34	--	--	1.03	3.59
AA	Pathway Advisors Conservative	PWCNX	U	(888) 288-1121	U /	0.76	1.55	3.38 /28	--	--	1.28	5.19
GR	Patriot A	TRFAX	B-	(855) 527-2363	C+ / 6.7	3.23	8.31	14.27 /90	15.31 /77	--	0.00	2.90
GR	Patriot C	TRFCX	A-	(855) 527-2363	B- / 7.2	3.09	7.87	13.41 /88	14.51 /71	--	0.00	3.65
GR	Patriot I	TRFTX	A+	(855) 527-2363	B / 8.0	3.28	8.39	14.48 /91	15.61 /80	--	0.00	2.65
GR	Pax Ellevate Glbl Women's Idx Inst	PXWIX	C-	(800) 767-1729	C / 4.6	1.71	3.45	6.41 /50	10.88 /45	8.46 /33	2.20	0.74
GR	Pax Ellevate Glbl Women's Idx Inv	PXWEX	C-	(800) 767-1729	C / 4.4	1.62	3.29	6.10 /47	10.59 /43	8.18 /31	1.98	0.99
FO	Pax MSCI International ESG Ind Inv	PXINX	D	(800) 767-1729	C- / 3.5	6.11	2.47	-0.67 /14	9.54 /36	--	1.32	0.80
FO	Pax MSCI International ESG Inst	PXNIX	D-	(800) 767-1729	C- / 3.7	6.21	2.75	-0.40 /14	9.83 /38	--	3.45	N/A
FO	Pax MSCI International ESG R	PXIRX	D	(800) 767-1729	C- / 3.4	6.15	2.54	-0.85 /13	9.30 /35	--	1.40	1.05
BA	Pax World Balanced Ind Inv	PAXWX	C-	(800) 767-1729	C- / 3.6	0.72	3.55	7.54 /59	8.87 /32	8.43 /33	0.85	0.91
BA	Pax World Balanced Inst	PAXIX	C-	(800) 767-1729	C- / 3.8	0.79	3.65	7.81 /61	9.15 /34	8.70 /35	1.08	0.66
BA	Pax World Balanced R	PAXRX	D+	(800) 767-1729	C- / 3.4	0.67	3.41	7.27 /57	8.60 /30	8.15 /31	0.64	1.16
GL	Pax World Global Envi Mkts A	PXEAX	C-	(800) 767-1729	C- / 3.6	3.11	4.47	0.05 /16	11.31 /48	9.39 /40	0.96	1.54
GL	Pax World Global Envi Mkts Ind Inv	PGRNX	C-	(800) 767-1729	C / 4.5	3.10	4.53	--	11.30 /48	9.38 /40	0.97	1.54

● Denotes fund is closed to new investors
★ Denotes fund is included in Section II

99 Pct = Best
0 Pct = Worst

www.thestreetratings.com

RISK Rating/Pts	Standard Deviation (3 Year)	Beta	NAV As of 3/31/15	Total $(Mil)	Cash %	Stocks %	Bonds %	Other %	Portfolio Turnover Ratio	Last Bull Market Return	Last Bear Market Return	Manager Quality Pct	Manager Tenure (Years)	Initial Purch. $	Additional Purch. $	Front End Load	Back End Load
D / 1.9	19.4	1.09	50.54	N/A	0	100	0	0	9	78.5	-29.9	2	22	250,000	500	0.0	2.0
C+ / 6.0	10.0	1.02	9.77	53	4	94	1	1	267	76.1	-22.3	20	8	5,000	250	0.0	0.0
C+ / 6.0	10.0	1.02	9.43	260	4	94	1	1	267	71.9	-22.5	15	8	5,000	250	0.0	0.0
C+ / 6.8	9.8	0.95	10.35	37	0	99	0	1	300	81.4	-25.3	52	8	5,000	250	0.0	0.0
C+ / 6.8	9.8	0.95	10.04	161	0	99	0	1	300	76.7	-25.4	41	8	5,000	250	0.0	0.0
C+ / 6.2	10.3	0.57	5.86	8	4	93	2	1	136	33.2	-30.1	95	8	5,000	250	0.0	0.0
C+ / 6.2	10.2	0.69	5.64	35	4	93	2	1	136	29.8	-30.2	58	8	5,000	250	0.0	0.0
B+ / 9.6	2.5	0.09	9.59	27	6	5	86	3	218	9.8	1.3	83	8	5,000	250	0.0	0.0
B+ / 9.7	2.6	0.08	9.55	143	6	5	86	3	218	7.0	1.0	78	8	5,000	250	0.0	0.0
B / 8.7	2.2	0.11	9.78	6	32	1	61	6	230	8.8	N/A	78	4	2,500	100	5.8	0.0
B / 8.7	2.3	0.11	9.81	306	32	1	61	6	230	9.7	N/A	80	4	1,000,000	5,000	0.0	0.0
U /	N/A	N/A	9.94	439	48	0	0	52	60	N/A	N/A	N/A	3	1,000,000	5,000	0.0	0.0
C+ / 6.5	10.6	0.54	18.29	27	2	97	0	1	14	71.6	-19.2	95	N/A	5,000	1,000	0.0	0.0
C / 4.4	15.7	1.14	28.74	28	4	95	0	1	70	87.9	-21.2	18	4	2,500	100	0.0	2.0
C / 5.1	12.9	0.87	35.18	7	8	91	0	1	44	70.1	-19.1	40	2	2,500	100	0.0	2.0
D+ / 2.7	12.1	0.83	34.09	7	1	98	0	1	47	74.9	-18.8	55	2	2,500	100	0.0	2.0
D- / 1.5	12.8	0.88	49.26	83	2	97	0	1	48	51.3	-21.6	6	2	2,500	100	0.0	0.0
C+ / 6.9	4.5	-0.30	9.75	26	0	0	99	1	85	4.0	-0.1	95	5	50,000	0	0.0	0.0
C+ / 6.9	4.5	-0.31	9.66	8	0	0	99	1	85	3.1	-0.2	94	5	1,000	0	0.0	0.0
C- / 3.8	11.9	0.69	6.10	89	22	0	77	1	2,797	-23.8	N/A	0	4	50,000	0	0.0	0.0
B- / 7.0	11.9	0.69	6.06	2	22	0	77	1	2,797	-24.5	N/A	0	4	1,000	0	0.0	0.0
C / 5.3	12.8	0.91	13.77	15	1	98	0	1	7	17.7	-24.9	45	8	1,000	0	0.0	0.0
C / 5.3	12.8	0.91	13.92	3,171	1	98	0	1	7	21.8	-24.6	60	8	50,000	0	0.0	0.0
C / 5.3	12.8	0.90	13.88	694	1	98	0	1	7	20.7	-24.7	56	8	1,000	0	0.0	0.0
C / 5.0	12.8	0.91	13.92	655	1	98	0	1	7	21.9	-24.6	60	8	1,000,000	0	0.0	0.0
C / 5.3	12.3	0.92	11.88	105	1	98	0	1	35	47.3	-21.2	64	5	50,000	0	0.0	0.0
C / 5.3	12.3	0.92	11.86	9	1	98	0	1	35	46.0	-21.3	61	5	1,000	0	0.0	0.0
C+ / 6.0	12.3	0.92	9.27	10	2	98	0	0	53	48.7	-28.1	42	3	1,000	0	0.0	0.0
C+ / 5.9	12.3	0.92	9.75	5	2	98	0	0	53	54.0	-27.8	58	3	50,000	0	0.0	0.0
C+ / 5.9	12.3	0.92	9.77	25	2	98	0	0	53	52.5	-27.8	54	3	1,000	0	0.0	0.0
C / 5.3	12.7	0.90	45.89	3,679	1	97	0	2	6	24.8	-24.2	70	8	50,000	0	0.0	2.0
C / 5.1	12.5	1.17	49.43	730	1	98	0	1	65	136.9	-25.9	68	31	2,000	50	0.0	0.0
B- / 7.1	9.3	0.92	40.35	3,324	5	94	0	1	17	98.7	-14.7	88	14	100,000	0	0.0	0.0
B- / 7.1	9.3	0.92	40.29	8,745	5	94	0	1	17	97.6	-14.8	87	14	2,000	50	0.0	0.0
C+ / 6.8	9.8	0.96	30.83	991	11	88	0	1	41	122.6	-19.9	89	10	2,000	50	0.0	0.0
B- / 7.3	9.1	0.76	27.90	334	5	94	0	1	21	95.6	-20.4	86	7	2,000	50	0.0	0.0
C- / 3.1	14.8	1.00	23.14	437	0	99	0	1	49	68.6	-28.9	4	4	2,000	50	0.0	0.0
U /	N/A	N/A	11.98	38	3	80	15	2	18	N/A	N/A	N/A	3	2,500	0	0.0	0.0
U /	N/A	N/A	10.61	32	4	28	66	2	38	N/A	N/A	N/A	3	2,500	0	0.0	0.0
B- / 7.8	9.3	0.93	14.68	3	4	95	0	1	23	N/A	N/A	70	3	1,000	100	5.8	2.0
B- / 7.8	9.2	0.93	14.36	N/A	4	95	0	1	23	N/A	N/A	63	3	1,000	100	0.0	2.0
B- / 7.8	9.2	0.93	14.80	13	4	95	0	1	23	N/A	N/A	74	3	1,000,000	25,000	0.0	2.0
C+ / 5.9	10.8	1.04	20.87	16	0	100	0	0	28	68.3	-22.2	9	N/A	250,000	0	0.0	0.0
C+ / 5.9	10.8	1.04	20.76	60	0	100	0	0	28	66.8	-22.2	8	N/A	1,000	50	0.0	0.0
C / 5.0	13.2	0.99	8.69	54	2	97	0	1	12	51.8	-21.2	68	4	1,000	50	0.0	0.0
C- / 3.7	13.1	0.99	8.55	188	2	97	0	1	12	53.0	-21.1	71	4	0	0	0.0	0.0
C / 5.0	13.1	0.99	8.63	1	2	97	0	1	12	50.4	-21.3	66	4	0	0	0.0	0.0
C+ / 6.3	7.2	1.22	23.87	1,728	1	62	36	1	62	52.8	-15.9	16	17	1,000	50	0.0	0.0
C+ / 6.3	7.2	1.21	24.16	254	1	62	36	1	62	54.1	-15.8	18	17	250,000	0	0.0	0.0
C+ / 6.3	7.2	1.22	24.00	6	1	62	36	1	62	51.5	-15.9	14	17	0	0	0.0	0.0
C+ / 6.7	11.6	0.75	12.61	11	0	100	0	0	20	71.5	-23.7	91	7	1,000	50	5.5	0.0
C+ / 6.2	11.6	0.75	12.63	103	0	100	0	0	20	71.5	-23.7	91	7	1,000	50	0.0	0.0

Fund Type	Fund Name	Ticker Symbol	Overall Investment Rating	Phone	Performance Rating/Pts	3 Mo	6 Mo	1Yr / Pct	3Yr / Pct	5Yr / Pct	Dividend Yield	Expense Ratio
	99 Pct = Best 0 Pct = Worst							Total Return % through 3/31/15	Annualized		Incl. in Returns	
GL	Pax World Global Envi Mkts Inst	PGINX	C-	(800) 767-1729	C / 4.6	3.17	4.64	0.25 /16	11.60 /50	9.67 /42	1.21	1.29
GL	Pax World Global Envi Mkts R	PGRGX	C-	(800) 767-1729	C / 4.3	3.12	4.42	-0.17 /15	11.07 /46	9.12 /38	0.72	1.79
GR	Pax World Growth A	PXGAX	C+	(800) 767-1729	C+ / 5.9	2.14	7.67	12.68 /86	13.62 /64	13.53 /73	0.57	1.35
GR	Pax World Growth Ind Inv	PXWGX	C+	(800) 767-1729	C+ / 6.9	2.08	7.58	12.66 /85	13.60 /64	13.52 /73	0.55	1.35
GR	Pax World Growth Inst	PWGIX	B-	(800) 767-1729	B- / 7.1	2.20	7.77	12.94 /86	13.88 /66	13.79 /76	0.76	1.10
GR	Pax World Growth R	PXGRX	C+	(800) 767-1729	C+ / 6.6	2.04	7.43	12.38 /84	13.29 /62	13.21 /70	0.43	1.60
GR	Pax World Small Cap A	PXSAX	A-	(800) 767-1729	B+ / 8.6	4.17	10.47	9.31 /71	18.10 /95	15.39 /89	0.68	1.66
SC	Pax World Small Cap Ind Inv	PXSCX	A-	(800) 767-1729	A / 9.3	4.24	10.53	9.34 /71	18.11 /95	15.40 /90	0.69	1.66
SC	Pax World Small Cap Inst	PXSIX	A-	(800) 767-1729	A / 9.4	4.29	10.66	9.58 /72	18.42 /95	15.68 /91	0.88	1.41
SC	Pax World Small Cap R	PXSRX	B+	(800) 767-1729	A- / 9.2	4.20	10.43	9.09 /70	17.82 /94	15.11 /88	0.48	1.91
GI	Payden Equity Income Adviser	PYVAX	B-	(888) 409-8007	C+ / 6.5	1.63	3.73	11.27 /79	13.63 /64	--	2.09	1.08
GI	Payden Equity Income Investor	PYVLX	B-	(888) 409-8007	C+ / 6.8	1.70	3.84	11.48 /80	14.01 /67	13.94 /77	2.34	0.83
IN	Payden Equity Income SI	PYVSX	U	(888) 409-8007	U /	1.73	3.89	--	--	--	0.00	0.83
GL	Payden Strategic Income Investor	PYSGX	U	(888) 409-8007	U /	2.19	2.41	--	--	--	0.00	1.20
GL	Payden Strategic Income SI	PYSIX	U	(888) 409-8007	U /	2.32	2.47	--	--	--	0.00	1.17
GR	Payson Total Return	PBFDX	C-	(800) 805-8258	C- / 4.1	-0.11	2.46	6.32 /49	10.10 /40	10.99 /53	1.01	1.01
EM	Pear Tree PanAgora Dyn Emg Mkt	QEMAX	E+	(800) 326-2151	E / 0.5	1.00	-2.87	0.77 /18	0.56 / 5	2.46 / 5	1.64	1.44
EM	Pear Tree PanAgora Emg Markets	QFFOX	E+	(800) 326-2151	E / 0.5	0.97	-2.97	0.49 /17	0.31 / 5	2.21 / 5	1.44	1.69
EM	Pear Tree PanAgora RskPrity EM Inst	EMRPX	U	(800) 326-2151	U /	-0.31	-7.37	-4.41 / 6	--	--	0.91	1.59
FO	Pear Tree Polaris Foreign Val Inst	QFVIX	C	(800) 326-2151	C / 4.9	6.14	3.82	-2.29 /10	12.23 /54	9.61 /41	1.30	1.28
FO	Pear Tree Polaris Foreign Val Ord	QFVOX	C	(800) 326-2151	C / 4.7	6.02	3.67	-2.53 / 9	11.94 /52	9.33 /39	1.07	1.54
FO	Pear Tree Polaris Foreign VSC Inst	QUSIX	B+	(800) 326-2151	B- / 7.3	4.86	5.18	2.87 /26	15.76 /81	10.13 /46	1.36	1.33
FO	Pear Tree Polaris Foreign VSC Ord	QUSOX	B+	(800) 326-2151	B- / 7.1	4.79	4.93	2.54 /24	15.45 /79	9.83 /43	1.08	1.58
SC	Pear Tree Polaris Sm Cap Inst	QBNAX	D	(800) 326-2151	C / 4.5	3.73	10.06	-0.11 /15	10.84 /45	11.28 /55	0.85	1.19
SC	Pear Tree Polaris Sm Cap Ord	USBNX	D	(800) 326-2151	C / 4.4	3.66	9.96	-0.36 /15	10.57 /43	11.01 /53	0.73	1.44
GI	Pear Tree Quality Inst	QGIAX	C	(800) 326-2151	C+ / 5.7	0.49	5.02	9.34 /71	12.46 /56	12.98 /68	1.86	1.31
GI	Pear Tree Quality Ord	USBOX	C	(800) 326-2151	C / 5.5	0.46	4.94	9.12 /70	12.09 /53	12.58 /65	1.71	1.55
GR	Perkins Discovery Fund	PDFDX	C-	(800) 998-3190	C / 5.5	3.93	7.56	-3.69 / 7	13.61 /64	9.90 /44	0.00	2.83
GL	Perkins Global Value A	JPPAX	D+	(800) 295-2687	D+ / 2.9	0.65	0.91	2.88 /26	10.20 /40	9.19 /38	1.70	1.09
GL	Perkins Global Value C	JPPCX	C-	(800) 295-2687	C- / 3.3	0.44	0.52	2.09 /22	9.33 /35	8.55 /33	1.36	1.85
GL	● Perkins Global Value D	JNGOX	C-	(800) 295-2687	C- / 3.9	0.72	0.97	3.06 /27	10.35 /42	9.37 /40	1.91	0.95
GL	Perkins Global Value I	JPPIX	C	(800) 295-2687	C- / 4.0	0.73	1.02	3.14 /27	10.48 /42	9.42 /40	2.12	0.81
GL	Perkins Global Value N	JPPNX	C+	(800) 295-2687	C- / 4.0	0.73	1.12	3.25 /28	10.54 /43	9.46 /40	2.15	0.76
GL	Perkins Global Value S	JPPSX	C-	(800) 295-2687	C- / 3.7	0.64	0.86	2.74 /25	10.02 /39	9.04 /37	1.60	1.26
GL	Perkins Global Value T	JGVAX	C-	(800) 295-2687	C- / 3.9	0.72	1.01	2.96 /26	10.27 /41	9.30 /39	1.88	1.01
GL	Perkins Lg Cp Value A	JAPAX	C	(800) 295-2687	C / 4.6	-0.79	3.27	7.15 /56	12.78 /58	10.85 /51	1.31	0.90
GL	Perkins Lg Cp Value C	JAPCX	C	(800) 295-2687	C / 5.0	-0.99	2.87	6.26 /49	11.98 /52	10.02 /45	0.67	1.72
GL	● Perkins Lg Cp Value D	JNPLX	C+	(800) 295-2687	C+ / 5.7	-0.73	3.33	7.24 /57	12.96 /59	10.93 /52	1.38	0.83
GL	Perkins Lg Cp Value I	JAPIX	C+	(800) 295-2687	C+ / 5.8	-0.79	3.31	7.39 /58	13.10 /60	11.18 /54	1.54	0.64
GR	Perkins Lg Cp Value N	JPLNX	B-	(800) 295-2687	C+ / 5.8	-0.73	3.41	7.43 /59	13.15 /61	11.21 /55	1.57	0.64
GL	Perkins Lg Cp Value S	JAPSX	C+	(800) 295-2687	C / 5.5	-0.85	3.13	6.84 /54	12.66 /57	10.72 /50	1.26	1.15
GL	Perkins Lg Cp Value T	JPLTX	C+	(800) 295-2687	C+ / 5.6	-0.80	3.28	7.12 /56	12.87 /59	10.94 /52	1.32	0.89
GL	● Perkins Mid Cap Value A	JDPAX	E+	(800) 295-2687	C- / 3.8	0.05	4.30	6.62 /52	11.07 /46	9.74 /42	1.83	0.93
GL	● Perkins Mid Cap Value C	JMVCX	D-	(800) 295-2687	C- / 4.2	-0.15	3.89	5.83 /45	10.24 /41	8.93 /36	1.20	1.70
GL	● Perkins Mid Cap Value D	JNMCX	D-	(800) 295-2687	C / 4.9	0.10	4.44	6.90 /54	11.38 /48	10.04 /45	3.00	0.65
GL	● Perkins Mid Cap Value I	JMVAX	D-	(800) 295-2687	C / 4.9	0.10	4.47	6.92 /54	11.40 /48	10.07 /45	2.98	0.63
GL	● Perkins Mid Cap Value L	JMIVX	D-	(800) 295-2687	C / 4.9	0.10	4.41	6.79 /53	11.38 /48	10.08 /45	2.81	0.75
GR	● Perkins Mid Cap Value N	JDPNX	C+	(800) 295-2687	C / 5.0	0.15	4.53	7.03 /55	11.54 /49	10.09 /45	3.24	0.49
GL	● Perkins Mid Cap Value R	JDPRX	D-	(800) 295-2687	C / 4.5	-0.05	4.14	6.24 /49	10.72 /44	9.39 /40	1.80	1.25
GL	● Perkins Mid Cap Value S	JMVIX	D-	(800) 295-2687	C / 4.6	0.00	4.24	6.51 /51	11.00 /45	9.66 /42	1.86	0.99
GL	● Perkins Mid Cap Value T	JMCVX	D-	(800) 295-2687	C / 4.8	0.05	4.36	6.77 /53	11.27 /47	9.93 /44	2.72	0.74
GL	Perkins Select Value A	JVSAX	C	(800) 295-2687	C- / 3.6	1.96	6.44	5.93 /46	10.50 /42	--	1.23	1.34

Risk Rating/Pts	Standard Deviation	Beta	NAV As of 3/31/15	Total $(Mil)	Cash %	Stocks %	Bonds %	Other %	Portfolio Turnover Ratio	Last Bull Market Return	Last Bear Market Return	Manager Quality Pct	Manager Tenure (Years)	Initial Purch. $	Additional Purch. $	Front End Load	Back End Load
C+ / 6.2	11.7	0.75	12.70	110	0	100	0	0	20	73.1	-23.7	92	7	250,000	0	0.0	0.0
C+ / 6.2	11.7	0.75	12.54	2	0	100	0	0	20	70.1	-23.8	91	7	0	0	0.0	0.0
C+ / 6.8	10.8	1.07	18.62	2	0	100	0	0	27	87.4	-20.1	23	12	1,000	50	5.5	0.0
C+ / 6.3	10.8	1.07	18.64	163	0	100	0	0	27	87.3	-20.1	23	12	1,000	50	0.0	0.0
C+ / 6.3	10.8	1.07	19.07	36	0	100	0	0	27	88.9	-20.0	26	12	250,000	0	0.0	0.0
C+ / 6.3	10.8	1.07	18.55	2	0	100	0	0	27	85.7	-20.2	21	12	0	0	0.0	0.0
C+ / 6.6	10.3	0.86	14.48	25	0	100	0	0	162	105.2	-23.9	91	7	1,000	50	5.5	0.0
C+ / 5.7	10.2	0.71	14.51	175	0	100	0	0	162	105.2	-23.9	95	7	1,000	50	0.0	0.0
C+ / 5.7	10.3	0.71	14.60	141	0	100	0	0	162	107.2	-23.8	95	7	250,000	0	0.0	0.0
C+ / 5.7	10.3	0.71	14.39	2	0	100	0	0	162	103.5	-23.9	95	7	0	0	0.0	0.0
B- / 7.7	8.4	0.75	14.10	5	5	94	0	1	51	N/A	N/A	81	N/A	5,000	250	0.0	0.0
B- / 7.4	8.3	0.75	14.09	300	5	94	0	1	51	77.7	-5.6	83	N/A	100,000	250	0.0	0.0
U /	N/A	N/A	14.09	272	5	94	0	1	51	N/A	N/A	N/A	N/A	50,000,000	250	0.0	0.0
U /	N/A	N/A	10.07	83	0	0	0	100	0	N/A	N/A	N/A	1	100,000	250	0.0	0.0
U /	N/A	N/A	10.06	27	0	0	0	100	0	N/A	N/A	N/A	1	50,000,000	250	0.0	0.0
C+ / 6.7	10.6	1.04	15.21	77	1	98	0	1	47	72.2	-14.5	6	24	2,000	250	0.0	0.0
C / 5.2	13.8	1.00	22.25	12	1	98	0	1	61	23.1	-25.0	66	9	1,000,000	0	0.0	0.0
C / 5.3	13.8	1.00	21.94	127	1	98	0	1	61	22.1	-25.0	62	9	2,500	0	0.0	0.0
U /	N/A	N/A	9.78	39	4	95	0	1	42	N/A	N/A	N/A	2	1,000,000	0	0.0	0.0
C+ / 6.3	12.9	0.92	18.68	595	0	100	0	0	3	68.9	-23.6	89	17	1,000,000	0	0.0	0.0
C+ / 6.3	12.9	0.93	18.67	1,031	0	100	0	0	3	67.3	-23.7	88	17	2,500	0	0.0	0.0
B- / 7.1	10.0	0.67	13.37	200	0	100	0	0	4	75.7	-22.1	97	7	1,000,000	0	0.0	0.0
B- / 7.1	10.0	0.67	13.35	233	0	100	0	0	4	74.2	-22.2	97	7	2,500	0	0.0	0.0
C- / 4.2	12.9	0.89	28.39	4	0	100	0	0	67	72.7	-21.6	23	19	1,000,000	0	0.0	0.0
C- / 4.0	12.9	0.90	24.65	98	0	100	0	0	67	71.2	-21.7	20	19	2,500	0	0.0	0.0
C+ / 5.9	9.2	0.93	18.39	11	0	100	0	0	35	76.3	-7.8	35	4	1,000,000	0	0.0	0.0
C+ / 5.9	9.1	0.93	17.47	116	0	100	0	0	35	74.1	-7.9	31	4	2,500	0	0.0	0.0
C / 4.7	15.7	0.94	37.54	10	2	97	0	1	24	60.6	-26.7	47	17	2,500	100	0.0	1.0
C+ / 6.9	8.0	0.54	13.94	26	8	82	8	2	19	54.8	-10.5	93	10	2,500	0	5.8	0.0
B- / 7.0	8.0	0.54	13.64	13	8	82	8	2	19	51.6	-10.7	91	10	2,500	0	0.0	0.0
C+ / 6.9	7.9	0.54	14.07	101	8	82	8	2	19	55.4	-10.4	93	10	2,500	0	0.0	0.0
C+ / 6.9	8.0	0.54	13.85	65	8	82	8	2	19	56.3	-10.4	94	10	1,000,000	0	0.0	0.0
B / 8.0	8.0	0.54	13.80	3	8	82	8	2	19	56.3	-10.5	94	10	0	0	0.0	0.0
B- / 7.0	8.0	0.54	14.13	N/A	8	82	8	2	19	53.8	-10.6	93	10	2,500	0	0.0	0.0
C+ / 6.9	8.0	0.54	14.04	75	8	82	8	2	19	55.2	-10.5	93	10	2,500	0	0.0	0.0
C+ / 6.5	9.0	0.53	16.30	4	5	94	0	1	34	77.5	-17.5	96	7	2,500	0	5.8	0.0
C+ / 6.6	9.0	0.53	16.08	3	5	94	0	1	34	73.1	-17.7	96	7	2,500	0	0.0	0.0
C+ / 6.5	9.0	0.53	16.21	41	5	94	0	1	34	78.5	-17.3	96	7	2,500	100	0.0	0.0
C+ / 6.5	9.0	0.53	16.26	44	5	94	0	1	34	79.5	-17.3	96	7	1,000,000	0	0.0	0.0
B- / 7.7	9.0	0.92	16.25	82	5	94	0	1	34	79.6	-17.3	46	7	0	0	0.0	0.0
C+ / 6.7	9.0	0.53	16.40	N/A	5	94	0	1	34	76.9	-17.5	96	7	2,500	0	0.0	0.0
C+ / 6.5	9.0	0.53	16.18	4	5	94	0	1	34	78.0	-17.4	96	7	2,500	0	0.0	0.0
D+ / 2.9	9.3	0.54	20.18	277	2	94	3	1	51	66.7	-19.2	95	17	2,500	0	5.8	0.0
C- / 3.0	9.3	0.54	19.89	136	2	94	3	1	51	62.5	-19.4	93	17	2,500	0	0.0	0.0
D+ / 2.6	9.3	0.54	20.01	890	2	94	3	1	51	68.3	-19.1	95	17	2,500	100	0.0	0.0
D+ / 2.7	9.3	0.54	20.02	1,810	2	94	3	1	51	68.4	-19.1	95	17	1,000,000	0	0.0	0.0
D+ / 2.7	9.3	0.54	20.30	16	2	94	3	1	51	68.2	-19.1	95	17	250,000	0	0.0	0.0
B- / 7.3	9.3	0.92	19.98	326	2	94	3	1	51	69.0	-19.2	27	17	0	0	0.0	0.0
D+ / 2.9	9.3	0.54	20.01	99	2	94	3	1	51	64.9	-19.3	94	17	2,500	0	0.0	0.0
D+ / 2.9	9.3	0.54	20.16	245	2	94	3	1	51	66.4	-19.3	94	17	2,500	0	0.0	0.0
D+ / 2.7	9.3	0.54	20.06	2,962	2	94	3	1	51	67.7	-19.2	95	17	2,500	0	0.0	0.0
B- / 7.5	8.4	0.50	12.50	N/A	11	88	0	1	76	N/A	N/A	94	4	2,500	0	5.8	0.0

	99 Pct = Best 0 Pct = Worst				PERFORMANCE							
			Overall		Perfor-	Total Return % through 3/31/15					Incl. in Returns	
			Investment		mance				Annualized		Dividend	Expense
Fund Type	Fund Name	Ticker Symbol	Rating	Phone	Rating/Pts	3 Mo	6 Mo	1Yr / Pct	3Yr / Pct	5Yr / Pct	Yield	Ratio
GL	Perkins Select Value C	JVSCX	C	(800) 295-2687	C- / 4.0	1.72	6.01	5.07 /39	9.68 /37	--	0.40	2.10
GL	● Perkins Select Value D	JSVDX	C+	(800) 295-2687	C / 4.7	2.04	6.64	6.21 /48	10.76 /44	--	1.57	1.06
GL	Perkins Select Value I	JVSIX	C+	(800) 295-2687	C / 4.8	1.95	6.55	6.30 /49	10.91 /45	--	1.73	0.89
GL	Perkins Select Value S	JSVSX	C+	(800) 295-2687	C / 4.4	1.96	6.40	5.89 /45	10.33 /41	--	1.51	1.40
GL	Perkins Select Value T	JSVTX	C+	(800) 295-2687	C / 4.6	2.04	6.53	6.11 /47	10.68 /44	--	1.55	1.16
SC	Perkins Small Cap Value A	JDSAX	D	(800) 295-2687	C / 5.3	3.18	10.36	8.21 /64	12.87 /59	10.57 /49	0.05	1.05
SC	Perkins Small Cap Value C	JCSCX	D	(800) 295-2687	C+ / 5.8	2.95	9.99	7.50 /59	12.04 /53	9.74 /42	0.00	1.79
SC	Perkins Small Cap Value D	JNPSX	D+	(800) 295-2687	C+ / 6.5	3.24	10.55	8.57 /67	13.21 /61	10.89 /52	0.81	0.74
SC	Perkins Small Cap Value I	JSCOX	D+	(800) 295-2687	C+ / 6.5	3.23	10.59	8.61 /67	13.24 /61	10.95 /52	0.75	0.73
SC	● Perkins Small Cap Value L	JSIVX	C-	(800) 295-2687	C+ / 6.6	3.26	10.61	8.71 /68	13.35 /62	11.05 /53	0.92	0.80
SC	Perkins Small Cap Value N	JDSNX	B-	(800) 295-2687	C+ / 6.6	3.24	10.63	8.74 /68	13.39 /62	11.07 /53	0.96	0.58
SC	Perkins Small Cap Value R	JDSRX	D+	(800) 295-2687	C+ / 6.1	3.09	10.23	7.93 /62	12.54 /56	10.24 /46	0.00	1.33
SC	Perkins Small Cap Value S	JISCX	D+	(800) 295-2687	C+ / 6.2	3.16	10.37	8.22 /64	12.82 /58	10.51 /49	0.37	1.08
SC	Perkins Small Cap Value T	JSCVX	D+	(800) 295-2687	C+ / 6.4	3.19	10.51	8.49 /66	13.10 /60	10.79 /51	0.67	0.83
GI	Perkins Value Plus Income A	JPVAX	C-	(800) 295-2687	C- / 3.2	1.15	4.67	7.17 /56	9.77 /38	--	2.21	1.35
GI	Perkins Value Plus Income C	JPVCX	C	(800) 295-2687	C- / 3.6	0.88	4.28	6.31 /49	8.94 /33	--	1.65	2.04
GI	● Perkins Value Plus Income D	JPVDX	C	(800) 295-2687	C- / 4.2	1.09	4.74	7.25 /57	9.90 /39	--	2.48	1.15
GI	Perkins Value Plus Income I	JPVIX	C	(800) 295-2687	C / 4.3	1.19	4.77	7.34 /58	10.02 /39	--	2.57	1.02
GI	Perkins Value Plus Income S	JPVSX	C	(800) 295-2687	C- / 4.0	1.10	4.55	7.02 /55	9.62 /37	--	2.12	1.50
GI	Perkins Value Plus Income T	JPVTX	C	(800) 295-2687	C- / 4.2	1.15	4.68	7.21 /57	9.85 /38	--	2.37	1.25
AA	Permal Alternative Core A	LPTAX	D	(877) 534-4627	D / 2.1	3.01	4.33	6.45 /50	7.50 /24	6.44 /20	5.03	2.35
AA	Permal Alternative Core C	LPTCX	D+	(877) 534-4627	D+ / 2.5	2.85	4.01	5.68 /44	6.70 /20	5.65 /15	4.48	3.07
AA	Permal Alternative Core FI	LPTFX	C-	(877) 534-4627	C- / 3.0	3.02	4.32	6.43 /50	7.49 /24	6.42 /20	5.06	2.37
AA	Permal Alternative Core I	LPTIX	C-	(877) 534-4627	C- / 3.1	3.01	4.45	6.65 /52	7.75 /26	6.68 /21	5.58	2.07
AA	Permal Alternative Core IS	LPTSX	C-	(877) 534-4627	C- / 3.1	3.11	4.46	6.67 /52	7.76 /26	6.69 /21	5.33	2.10
* AA	Permanent Portfolio	PRPFX	E	(800) 531-5142	E / 0.5	1.06	-0.48	-1.93 /10	-0.24 / 4	4.49 /10	0.63	0.77
AG	Permanent Portfolio Aggress Gr	PAGRX	B+	(800) 531-5142	B+ / 8.3	0.20	1.56	7.58 /60	17.39 /92	13.50 /73	0.29	1.20
SC	Perritt MicroCap Opportunities	PRCGX	C-	(800) 332-3133	C / 5.2	-0.58	4.87	-1.06 /13	13.81 /66	11.64 /58	0.00	1.21
GR	Perritt Ultra MicroCap	PREOX	D	(800) 332-3133	C / 4.4	0.40	2.01	-5.18 / 5	13.13 /61	12.15 /62	0.00	1.58
GR	Persimmon Long/Short I	LSEIX	U	(855) 233-8300	U /	1.38	3.39	3.11 /27	--	--	0.00	4.14
GR	PF Comstock P		B-	(800) 722-2333	B- / 7.1	-0.23	1.84	7.22 /57	15.65 /80	13.05 /69	2.02	0.97
EM	PF Emerging Mkts P		E	(800) 722-2333	E+ / 0.6	-1.09	-7.89	-4.15 / 7	2.51 / 7	4.60 /11	1.39	1.27
GL	PF Global Absolute Ret P		U	(800) 722-2333	U /	3.19	4.19	9.13 /70	--	--	5.25	1.36
GR	PF Growth P		B+	(800) 722-2333	B / 7.9	3.49	8.69	12.96 /86	14.98 /75	12.34 /63	0.65	0.79
FO	PF International Val P		E+	(800) 722-2333	D / 1.6	4.62	-0.30	-4.07 / 7	6.45 /19	3.70 / 7	4.09	0.91
FO	PF Intl Large Cap P		D+	(800) 722-2333	C- / 3.2	5.84	2.87	1.70 /21	8.50 /30	7.43 /26	1.42	1.10
GI	PF Large-Cap Growth P		C	(800) 722-2333	B+ / 8.3	3.58	9.31	14.84 /91	15.18 /76	15.76 /92	0.00	0.97
GI	PF Large-Cap Value P		B	(800) 722-2333	B- / 7.3	-0.36	4.22	9.40 /71	15.34 /78	13.35 /72	2.11	0.86
GI	PF Main Street Core P		C+	(800) 722-2333	B- / 7.1	1.64	5.00	11.36 /80	14.57 /72	13.82 /76	0.88	0.67
MC	PF Mid-Cap Equity P		C+	(800) 722-2333	C+ / 6.7	6.11	7.61	7.44 /59	13.62 /64	12.02 /61	0.23	0.87
MC	PF Mid-Cap Growth P		D	(800) 722-2333	C+ / 6.1	4.06	10.76	11.57 /81	11.47 /49	13.11 /69	0.08	0.93
GR	PF Port Optz Aggr Gro A	POEAX	C-	(800) 722-2333	C- / 3.0	2.52	4.46	6.18 /48	9.35 /35	9.29 /39	1.88	1.56
GR	PF Port Optz Aggr Gro Adv	POEDX	C	(800) 722-2333	C- / 4.0	2.59	4.57	6.50 /51	9.53 /36	9.40 /40	2.22	1.31
GR	PF Port Optz Aggr Gro B	POEBX	C-	(800) 722-2333	C- / 3.5	2.37	4.16	5.55 /43	8.74 /31	8.70 /35	1.26	2.31
GR	PF Port Optz Aggr Gro C	POCEX	C-	(800) 722-2333	C- / 3.5	2.37	4.14	5.54 /43	8.74 /31	8.70 /35	1.31	2.31
GR	PF Port Optz Aggr Gro R	POERX	C	(800) 722-2333	C- / 3.8	2.47	4.36	5.94 /46	9.14 /34	9.09 /37	1.75	1.81
AA	PF Port Optz Consrv Class A	POAAX	D	(800) 722-2333	E+ / 0.9	1.72	2.09	3.71 /30	4.00 /10	4.87 /11	1.86	1.40
AA	PF Port Optz Consrv Class Adv	PLCDX	C-	(800) 722-2333	D- / 1.3	1.72	2.20	4.01 /32	4.13 /11	4.95 /12	2.16	1.15
AA	PF Port Optz Consrv Class B	POABX	D+	(800) 722-2333	D- / 1.0	1.56	1.72	3.00 /26	3.30 / 8	4.13 / 9	1.44	2.15
AA	PF Port Optz Consrv Class C	POACX	D+	(800) 722-2333	D- / 1.0	1.56	1.72	3.09 /27	3.30 / 8	4.15 / 9	1.43	2.15
AA	PF Port Optz Consrv Class R	POARX	D+	(800) 722-2333	D- / 1.1	1.64	1.94	3.48 /29	3.77 /10	4.62 /11	1.82	1.65
GR	PF Port Optz Growth A	PODAX	C-	(800) 722-2333	D+ / 2.8	2.54	4.24	6.36 /50	8.97 /33	9.03 /37	2.04	1.51

RISK	3 Year		NET ASSETS		ASSET				Portfolio	BULL / BEAR		FUND MANAGER		MINIMUMS		LOADS	
Risk Rating/Pts	Standard Deviation	Beta	NAV As of 3/31/15	Total $(Mil)	Cash %	Stocks %	Bonds %	Other %	Turnover Ratio	Last Bull Market Return	Last Bear Market Return	Manager Quality Pct	Manager Tenure (Years)	Initial Purch. $	Additional Purch. $	Front End Load	Back End Load
B- / 7.5	8.4	0.49	12.41	N/A	11	88	0	1	76	N/A	N/A	93	4	2,500	0	0.0	0.0
B- / 7.5	8.4	0.49	12.52	7	11	88	0	1	76	N/A	N/A	95	4	2,500	100	0.0	0.0
B- / 7.5	8.4	0.50	12.52	71	11	88	0	1	76	N/A	N/A	95	4	1,000,000	0	0.0	0.0
B- / 7.5	8.4	0.49	12.49	N/A	11	88	0	1	76	N/A	N/A	94	4	2,500	0	0.0	0.0
B- / 7.5	8.4	0.49	12.50	3	11	88	0	1	76	N/A	N/A	95	4	2,500	0	0.0	0.0
C- / 3.4	10.7	0.77	22.38	48	7	91	1	1	62	73.0	-20.8	73	28	2,500	0	5.8	0.0
C- / 3.2	10.8	0.77	21.62	14	7	91	1	1	62	68.9	-21.0	64	28	2,500	0	0.0	0.0
C- / 3.2	10.7	0.77	22.28	79	7	91	1	1	62	74.9	-20.6	76	28	2,500	100	0.0	0.0
C- / 3.2	10.8	0.77	22.36	546	7	91	1	1	62	75.1	-20.7	76	28	1,000,000	0	0.0	0.0
C- / 3.3	10.7	0.77	22.81	193	7	91	1	1	62	75.7	-20.6	77	28	250,000	0	0.0	0.0
B- / 7.1	10.7	0.77	22.32	208	7	91	1	1	62	75.9	-20.6	77	28	0	0	0.0	0.0
C- / 3.3	10.7	0.76	22.00	19	7	91	1	1	62	71.4	-20.9	70	28	2,500	0	0.0	0.0
C- / 3.3	10.7	0.77	22.17	68	7	91	1	1	62	72.8	-20.8	73	28	2,500	0	0.0	0.0
C- / 3.2	10.8	0.77	22.30	601	7	91	1	1	62	74.3	-20.7	75	28	2,500	0	0.0	0.0
B- / 7.3	5.4	0.53	11.46	7	3	56	39	2	95	50.6	-9.3	80	5	2,500	0	5.8	0.0
B- / 7.3	5.4	0.53	11.48	7	3	56	39	2	95	47.3	-9.6	74	5	2,500	0	0.0	0.0
B- / 7.3	5.4	0.53	11.46	30	3	56	39	2	95	51.2	-9.3	81	5	2,500	100	0.0	0.0
B- / 7.3	5.4	0.53	11.47	4	3	56	39	2	95	51.8	-9.2	82	5	1,000,000	0	0.0	0.0
B- / 7.3	5.3	0.52	11.47	2	3	56	39	2	95	49.8	-9.4	80	5	2,500	0	0.0	0.0
B- / 7.3	5.4	0.53	11.47	4	3	56	39	2	95	51.0	-9.3	81	5	2,500	0	0.0	0.0
C+ / 6.9	5.7	0.88	14.38	15	27	60	11	2	93	35.9	-12.4	40	N/A	1,000	50	5.8	0.0
B- / 7.1	5.7	0.88	14.43	27	27	60	11	2	93	32.6	-12.6	30	N/A	1,000	50	0.0	0.0
B- / 7.3	5.7	0.88	14.68	N/A	27	60	11	2	93	35.9	-12.4	39	N/A	0	0	0.0	0.0
C+ / 6.9	5.7	0.88	14.36	72	27	60	11	2	93	37.0	-12.2	42	N/A	1,000,000	0	0.0	0.0
B- / 7.1	5.7	0.88	14.57	N/A	27	60	11	2	93	37.0	-12.2	43	N/A	0	0	0.0	0.0
C / 5.1	7.3	0.73	39.99	5,133	20	39	39	2	4	9.2	-8.3	3	12	1,000	100	0.0	0.0
C+ / 6.0	12.8	1.22	70.22	47	0	99	0	1	0	113.7	-25.3	34	12	1,000	100	0.0	0.0
C / 5.3	14.0	0.97	34.06	445	6	93	0	1	29	92.3	-29.0	42	19	1,000	50	0.0	2.0
C- / 4.1	10.9	0.72	14.88	68	3	96	0	1	64	71.0	-22.7	81	11	1,000	50	0.0	2.0
U /	N/A	N/A	11.03	30	39	60	0	1	181	N/A	N/A	N/A	2	100,000	100	0.0	1.0
C+ / 6.2	10.5	1.05	17.07	270	3	96	0	1	14	97.7	-20.0	50	12	0	0	0.0	0.0
C / 4.4	14.0	0.96	13.58	138	6	93	0	1	31	31.4	-23.2	83	8	0	0	0.0	0.0
U /	N/A	N/A	10.03	178	14	1	84	1	115	N/A	N/A	N/A	N/A	0	0	0.0	0.0
C+ / 6.6	9.9	0.92	19.30	148	3	96	0	1	76	93.1	-18.4	70	2	0	0	0.0	0.0
C / 5.0	14.2	1.06	9.51	143	2	97	0	1	54	44.3	-24.8	21	4	0	0	0.0	0.0
C+ / 5.9	12.6	0.93	18.50	221	0	98	1	1	14	56.4	-23.5	63	11	0	0	0.0	0.0
C- / 3.1	12.0	1.07	10.71	199	0	99	0	1	163	100.2	-15.4	40	2	0	0	0.0	0.0
C+ / 6.3	10.0	1.02	16.46	344	1	98	0	1	13	96.8	-16.4	54	N/A	0	0	0.0	0.0
C / 5.1	10.0	1.03	14.26	271	2	97	0	1	66	95.4	-14.9	41	6	0	0	0.0	0.0
C / 5.2	11.1	0.96	12.15	218	3	96	0	1	114	79.6	-21.5	33	2	0	0	0.0	0.0
D+ / 2.8	11.1	0.88	8.71	86	2	97	0	1	135	65.9	-21.5	25	12	0	0	0.0	0.0
B- / 7.1	9.0	0.89	15.85	177	6	84	9	1	5	61.7	-19.4	14	9	1,000	50	5.5	0.0
B- / 7.4	9.0	0.89	15.86	7	6	84	9	1	5	62.4	-19.4	15	12	0	0	0.0	0.0
B- / 7.1	9.2	0.91	15.57	36	6	84	9	1	5	59.4	-20.0	9	9	1,000	50	0.0	0.0
B- / 7.0	9.2	0.91	15.55	110	6	84	9	1	5	59.4	-20.0	9	9	1,000	50	0.0	0.0
B- / 7.1	9.1	0.90	15.77	9	6	84	9	1	5	60.8	-19.6	12	9	0	0	0.0	0.0
B / 8.1	3.1	0.46	11.22	170	0	19	80	1	11	21.8	-4.6	55	12	1,000	50	5.5	0.0
B / 8.7	3.2	0.46	11.23	8	0	19	80	1	11	22.2	-4.6	56	12	0	0	0.0	0.0
B / 8.2	3.2	0.47	11.05	38	0	19	80	1	11	19.0	-4.9	43	12	1,000	50	0.0	0.0
B / 8.2	3.2	0.47	11.05	192	0	19	80	1	11	19.0	-4.9	43	12	1,000	50	0.0	0.0
B / 8.2	3.2	0.47	11.16	12	0	19	80	1	11	20.8	-4.6	50	10	0	0	0.0	0.0
B- / 7.4	7.9	0.78	15.34	607	3	75	20	2	1	56.2	-16.0	24	12	1,000	50	5.5	0.0

Fund Type	Fund Name	Ticker Symbol	Overall Investment Rating	Phone	Performance Rating/Pts	3 Mo	6 Mo	1Yr / Pct	3Yr / Pct	5Yr / Pct	Dividend Yield	Expense Ratio
								Total Return % through 3/31/15			Incl. in Returns	
									Annualized			
GR	PF Port Optz Growth Advisor	PMADX	C	(800) 722-2333	C- / 3.8	2.61	4.41	6.61 /52	9.18 /34	9.16 /38	2.39	1.26
GR	PF Port Optz Growth B	PODBX	C-	(800) 722-2333	C- / 3.2	2.35	3.90	5.61 /43	8.23 /28	8.31 /32	1.42	2.26
GR	PF Port Optz Growth C	PODCX	C-	(800) 722-2333	C- / 3.2	2.36	3.88	5.59 /43	8.27 /29	8.32 /32	1.46	2.26
GR	PF Port Optz Growth R	PODRX	C	(800) 722-2333	C- / 3.5	2.47	4.12	6.10 /47	8.69 /31	8.76 /35	1.91	1.76
GR	PF Port Optz Mod Class A	POCAX	C-	(800) 722-2333	D / 1.9	2.01	3.16	5.30 /41	7.38 /23	7.79 /29	2.13	1.47
BA	PF Port Optz Mod Class Adv	POMDX	E	(800) 722-2333	D+ / 2.8	2.01	3.26	5.55 /43	7.56 /24	7.90 /29	2.49	1.22
GR	PF Port Optz Mod Class B	POMBX	C-	(800) 722-2333	D / 2.2	1.81	2.71	4.49 /35	6.61 /19	7.03 /23	1.54	2.22
GR	PF Port Optz Mod Class C	POMCX	C-	(800) 722-2333	D / 2.2	1.81	2.73	4.51 /35	6.62 /20	7.04 /23	1.55	2.22
GR	PF Port Optz Mod Class R	POCRX	C	(800) 722-2333	D+ / 2.5	1.94	3.01	5.00 /39	7.11 /22	7.54 /27	1.97	1.72
GI	PF Port Optz Mod-Consrv A	POBAX	D+	(800) 722-2333	D- / 1.3	1.69	2.56	4.69 /36	5.66 /15	6.26 /18	1.86	1.43
AA	PF Port Optz Mod-Consrv Advisor	PMCDX	C	(800) 722-2333	D / 1.9	1.77	2.67	4.89 /38	5.77 /16	6.33 /19	2.15	1.18
GI	PF Port Optz Mod-Consrv B	POBBX	C-	(800) 722-2333	D- / 1.5	1.55	2.25	3.90 /31	4.94 /13	5.52 /14	1.43	2.18
GI	PF Port Optz Mod-Consrv C	POBCX	C-	(800) 722-2333	D- / 1.5	1.55	2.19	3.93 /31	4.91 /13	5.52 /14	1.45	2.18
GI	PF Port Optz Mod-Consrv R	POBRX	C-	(800) 722-2333	D / 1.7	1.70	2.45	4.42 /35	5.41 /15	6.00 /17	1.78	1.68
PM	PF Precious Metals P		U	(800) 722-2333	U /	-5.86	-16.36	-21.33 / 1	--	--	0.00	1.01
RE	PF Real Estate P		B	(800) 722-2333	A- / 9.0	4.26	18.91	23.69 /98	12.83 /58	14.74 /85	1.82	1.12
MC	PF Small-Cap Growth P		C-	(800) 722-2333	B- / 7.1	7.09	15.26	8.36 /65	13.34 /62	12.91 /67	0.00	0.83
SC	PF Small-Cap Val P		C-	(800) 722-2333	B+ / 8.6	4.50	17.17	11.55 /81	15.43 /78	14.26 /80	0.93	0.98
GL	Philadelphia Invest Part New Gnrtn	PIPGX	E	(800) 749-9933	E / 0.3	-2.06	-6.90	-8.93 / 3	-0.37 / 4	--	0.00	4.62
RE	Phocas Real Estate	PHREX	B	(866) 746-2271	A+ / 9.8	5.95	22.36	27.96 /99	16.45 /87	16.02 /93	0.07	3.85
GR	Piedmont Select Equity	PSVFX	C	(888) 859-5865	C / 4.8	3.64	5.28	4.70 /36	11.19 /47	11.32 /55	0.00	1.73
AA	PIMCO All Asset A	PASAX	E+	(800) 426-0107	E+ / 0.6	0.00	-2.97	-1.85 /11	2.90 / 8	5.35 /13	4.07	1.50
AA	PIMCO All Asset Admin	PAALX	D-	(800) 426-0107	E+ / 0.8	0.06	-2.91	-1.68 /11	3.14 / 8	5.62 /15	4.51	1.25
AA	PIMCO All Asset All Authority A	PAUAX	E	(800) 426-0107	E / 0.3	-0.43	-4.92	-5.26 / 5	-0.03 / 4	3.39 / 7	4.91	2.40
AA	PIMCO All Asset All Authority C	PAUCX	E	(800) 426-0107	E / 0.4	-0.60	-5.34	-5.98 / 4	-0.81 / 4	2.61 / 5	4.38	3.15
AA	PIMCO All Asset All Authority D	PAUDX	E	(800) 426-0107	E / 0.4	-0.31	-4.91	-5.11 / 5	0.03 / 4	3.50 / 7	5.29	2.35
AA	PIMCO All Asset All Authority Inst	PAUIX	E	(800) 426-0107	E / 0.4	-0.32	-4.77	-4.80 / 6	0.41 / 5	3.89 / 8	5.73	1.95
AA	PIMCO All Asset All Authority P	PAUPX	E	(800) 426-0107	E / 0.4	-0.35	-4.73	-4.89 / 6	0.32 / 5	3.79 / 8	5.61	2.05
AA	PIMCO All Asset C	PASCX	E+	(800) 426-0107	E+ / 0.6	-0.17	-3.37	-2.58 / 9	2.13 / 6	4.57 /10	3.47	2.25
AA	PIMCO All Asset D	PASDX	D-	(800) 426-0107	E+ / 0.7	0.02	-2.92	-1.75 /11	3.01 / 8	5.48 /14	4.35	1.40
AA	PIMCO All Asset Inst	PAAIX	D-	(800) 426-0107	E+ / 0.8	0.11	-2.79	-1.36 /12	3.40 / 9	5.90 /16	4.77	1.00
AA	PIMCO All Asset P	PALPX	E+	(800) 426-0107	E+ / 0.8	0.09	-2.84	-1.53 /11	3.30 / 8	5.78 /16	4.66	1.10
AA	PIMCO All Asset R	PATRX	E+	(800) 426-0107	E+ / 0.7	-0.06	-3.12	-2.10 /10	2.63 / 7	5.07 /12	4.00	1.75
OT	PIMCO CommoditiesPLUS Strategy	PCLAX	E-	(800) 426-0107	E- / 0.0	-6.04	-26.40	-32.54 / 0	-12.11 / 1	--	4.99	1.37
OT	PIMCO CommoditiesPLUS Strategy	PCPCX	E-	(800) 426-0107	E- / 0.0	-6.17	-26.65	-33.02 / 0	-12.76 / 1	--	4.74	2.12
OT	PIMCO CommoditiesPLUS Strategy	PCLDX	E-	(800) 426-0107	E- / 0.1	-6.03	-26.36	-32.53 / 0	-12.10 / 1	--	5.37	1.37
OT	PIMCO CommoditiesPLUS Strategy	PCLIX	E-	(800) 426-0107	E- / 0.1	-5.86	-26.21	-32.21 / 0	-11.68 / 1	--	5.84	0.87
OT	PIMCO CommoditiesPLUS Strategy	PCLPX	E-	(800) 426-0107	E- / 0.1	-6.01	-26.26	-32.32 / 0	-11.79 / 1	--	5.77	0.97
OT	PIMCO CommoditiesPLUS Strategy	PCPRX	E-	(800) 426-0107	E- / 0.1	-5.95	-26.40	-32.67 / 0	-12.31 / 1	--	5.23	1.62
IN	PIMCO Commodity Real Ret Str A	PCRAX	E-	(800) 426-0107	E- / 0.0	-5.23	-18.71	-28.12 / 0	-12.65 / 1	-4.19 / 1	0.18	1.35
IN	PIMCO Commodity Real Ret Str Adm	PCRRX	E-	(800) 426-0107	E- / 0.1	-5.22	-18.83	-27.97 / 0	-12.47 / 1	-4.01 / 1	0.37	1.15
IN	PIMCO Commodity Real Ret Str C	PCRCX	E-	(800) 426-0107	E- / 0.1	-5.42	-18.99	-28.52 / 0	-13.26 / 1	-4.88 / 1	0.00	2.10
IN	PIMCO Commodity Real Ret Str D	PCRDX	E-	(800) 426-0107	E- / 0.1	-5.22	-18.68	-28.03 / 0	-12.63 / 1	-4.18 / 1	0.25	1.35
IN	PIMCO Commodity Real Ret Str Inst	PCRIX	E-	(800) 426-0107	E- / 0.1	-5.13	-18.58	-27.79 / 0	-12.24 / 1	-3.73 / 1	0.52	0.90
IN	PIMCO Commodity Real Ret Str P	PCRPX	E-	(800) 426-0107	E- / 0.1	-5.15	-18.62	-27.75 / 0	-12.32 / 1	-3.84 / 1	0.47	1.00
OT	PIMCO Commodity Real Ret Str R	PCSRX	E-	(800) 426-0107	E- / 0.1	-5.31	-18.81	-28.25 / 0	-12.85 / 1	-4.41 / 1	0.13	1.60
CV	● PIMCO Convertible A	PACNX	D-	(800) 426-0107	C- / 3.6	1.12	3.35	8.81 /68	10.37 /42	9.43 /40	8.99	1.11
CV	● PIMCO Convertible Bond Admin	PFCAX	D	(800) 426-0107	C / 4.6	1.05	3.35	9.01 /69	10.56 /43	9.55 /41	8.97	0.96
CV	● PIMCO Convertible Bond P	PCVPX	D	(800) 426-0107	C / 4.6	1.11	3.44	9.05 /70	10.67 /43	9.70 /42	9.74	0.81
CV	● PIMCO Convertible C	PCCNX	D-	(800) 426-0107	C- / 4.0	0.94	2.94	8.05 /63	9.56 /37	8.60 /34	8.97	1.86
CV	● PIMCO Convertible D	PCVDX	C+	(800) 426-0107	C / 4.5	1.11	3.32	8.84 /68	10.37 /42	9.43 /40	9.45	1.11
CV	● PIMCO Convertible Institutional	PFCIX	D	(800) 426-0107	C / 4.8	1.19	3.50	9.26 /71	10.81 /44	9.82 /43	9.67	0.71

● Denotes fund is closed to new investors
* Denotes fund is included in Section II

Risk Rating/Pts	3 Year Standard Deviation	Beta	NAV As of 3/31/15	Total $(Mil)	Cash %	Stocks %	Bonds %	Other %	Portfolio Turnover Ratio	Last Bull Market Return	Last Bear Market Return	Manager Quality Pct	Manager Tenure (Years)	Initial Purch. $	Additional Purch. $	Front End Load	Back End Load
B- / 7.5	7.9	0.79	15.35	10	3	75	20	2	1	57.0	-16.0	25	12	0	0	0.0	0.0
B- / 7.3	8.0	0.80	15.22	119	3	75	20	2	1	53.1	-16.5	16	12	1,000	50	0.0	0.0
B- / 7.3	8.0	0.80	15.18	399	3	75	20	2	1	53.1	-16.4	16	12	1,000	50	0.0	0.0
B- / 7.4	7.9	0.79	15.32	21	3	75	20	2	1	55.0	-16.1	21	10	0	0	0.0	0.0
B / 8.3	6.1	0.60	14.20	844	0	55	44	1	1	44.6	-12.2	39	12	1,000	50	5.5	0.0
D- / 1.4	6.1	1.03	14.20	22	0	55	44	1	1	45.4	-12.2	21	12	0	0	0.0	0.0
B / 8.3	6.1	0.61	14.10	160	0	55	44	1	1	41.5	-12.5	29	12	1,000	50	0.0	0.0
B / 8.3	6.1	0.61	14.08	602	0	55	44	1	1	41.5	-12.6	29	12	1,000	50	0.0	0.0
B / 8.4	6.1	0.61	14.18	28	0	55	44	1	1	43.6	-12.3	34	10	0	0	0.0	0.0
B / 8.5	4.5	0.43	12.61	277	0	35	64	1	5	32.5	-8.3	54	12	1,000	50	5.5	0.0
B+ / 9.1	4.5	0.75	12.62	6	0	35	64	1	5	33.0	-8.3	36	12	0	0	0.0	0.0
B / 8.6	4.5	0.43	12.46	51	0	35	64	1	5	29.7	-8.8	43	12	1,000	50	0.0	0.0
B / 8.6	4.5	0.42	12.45	241	0	35	64	1	5	29.6	-8.8	44	12	1,000	50	0.0	0.0
B / 8.6	4.5	0.42	12.56	7	0	35	64	1	5	31.5	-8.5	51	10	0	0	0.0	0.0
U /	N/A	N/A	4.50	40	5	94	0	1	12	N/A	N/A	N/A	3	0	0	0.0	0.0
C / 4.4	12.2	0.97	16.87	49	3	96	0	1	18	80.8	-18.0	56	11	0	0	0.0	0.0
C- / 3.5	14.2	1.13	14.80	84	3	96	0	1	84	84.7	-26.1	9	8	0	0	0.0	0.0
D- / 1.3	12.3	0.86	10.45	146	1	98	0	1	41	81.8	-18.5	80	1	0	0	0.0	0.0
C / 4.6	10.5	0.64	12.82	10	22	76	1	1	335	16.8	N/A	6	4	2,500	100	0.0	2.0
C- / 4.2	13.0	1.04	34.37	12	0	99	0	1	29	99.1	-18.0	81	9	5,000	200	0.0	1.0
C+ / 6.7	9.8	0.92	16.80	27	0	100	0	0	24	75.1	-14.4	23	9	5,000	250	0.0	0.0
C+ / 6.2	6.7	0.87	11.60	1,437	16	1	81	2	54	22.6	-7.5	6	13	1,000	50	3.8	0.0
C+ / 6.1	6.7	0.86	11.60	442	16	1	81	2	54	23.7	-7.4	7	13	1,000,000	0	0.0	0.0
C- / 3.7	7.1	0.77	9.08	1,610	0	1	98	1	65	14.2	-7.4	3	12	1,000	50	5.5	0.0
C- / 3.8	7.2	0.78	9.08	2,049	0	1	98	1	65	11.4	-7.7	2	12	1,000	50	0.0	0.0
C- / 3.7	7.1	0.77	9.05	805	0	1	98	1	65	14.5	-7.4	3	12	1,000	50	0.0	0.0
C- / 3.6	7.1	0.77	9.07	11,807	0	1	98	1	65	16.0	-7.3	4	12	1,000,000	0	0.0	0.0
C- / 3.6	7.1	0.77	9.08	2,677	0	1	98	1	65	15.6	-7.2	3	12	1,000,000	0	0.0	0.0
C+ / 6.2	6.7	0.87	11.56	1,445	16	1	81	2	54	19.5	-7.8	5	13	1,000	50	0.0	0.0
C+ / 6.2	6.7	0.87	11.59	700	16	1	81	2	54	23.0	-7.4	6	13	1,000	50	0.0	0.0
C+ / 6.1	6.7	0.87	11.58	25,895	16	1	81	2	54	24.7	-7.4	8	13	1,000,000	0	0.0	0.0
C+ / 6.1	6.7	0.87	11.60	1,231	16	1	81	2	54	24.2	-7.3	7	13	1,000,000	0	0.0	0.0
C+ / 6.2	6.7	0.87	11.54	117	16	1	81	2	54	21.6	-7.6	6	13	0	0	0.0	0.0
D+ / 2.8	16.1	0.96	7.16	61	22	0	77	1	102	-18.8	-21.8	0	5	1,000	50	5.5	0.0
D+ / 2.8	16.0	0.95	6.99	16	22	0	77	1	102	-20.8	-22.1	0	5	1,000	50	0.0	0.0
D+ / 2.8	16.1	0.95	7.17	246	22	0	77	1	102	-18.8	-21.8	0	5	1,000	50	0.0	0.0
D+ / 2.8	16.1	0.95	7.23	2,868	22	0	77	1	102	-17.5	-21.6	0	5	1,000,000	0	0.0	0.0
D+ / 2.8	16.1	0.96	7.19	1,548	22	0	77	1	102	-17.8	-21.6	0	5	1,000,000	0	0.0	0.0
D+ / 2.8	16.0	0.95	7.11	2	22	0	77	1	102	-19.5	-21.9	0	5	0	0	0.0	0.0
D / 1.8	14.4	0.78	4.17	494	0	0	99	1	49	-25.4	-20.0	0	8	1,000	50	5.5	0.0
D / 1.8	14.5	0.79	4.18	235	0	0	99	1	49	-24.8	-20.1	0	8	1,000,000	0	0.0	0.0
D / 1.8	14.5	0.78	4.01	232	0	0	99	1	49	-27.2	-20.3	0	8	1,000	50	0.0	0.0
D / 1.8	14.5	0.79	4.18	447	0	0	99	1	49	-25.4	-20.1	0	8	1,000	50	0.0	0.0
D / 1.8	14.6	0.79	4.25	8,264	0	0	99	1	49	-24.2	-19.9	0	8	1,000,000	0	0.0	0.0
D / 1.8	14.5	0.79	4.24	1,025	0	0	99	1	49	-24.4	-19.9	0	8	1,000,000	0	0.0	0.0
D / 1.8	14.5	0.80	4.10	52	0	0	99	1	49	-26.0	-20.1	0	8	0	0	0.0	0.0
C- / 3.8	7.8	0.99	11.77	64	7	15	11	67	103	53.2	-12.6	27	5	1,000	50	5.5	0.0
C- / 4.2	7.8	0.99	12.48	2	7	15	11	67	103	54.2	-12.6	29	5	1,000,000	0	0.0	0.0
C- / 3.9	7.8	0.99	11.79	21	7	15	11	67	103	54.7	-12.4	30	5	1,000	50	0.0	0.0
C- / 3.8	7.8	0.99	11.77	49	7	15	11	67	103	49.3	-12.9	20	5	1,000	50	0.0	0.0
B- / 7.7	7.8	0.99	11.85	36	7	15	11	67	103	53.2	-12.5	27	5	1,000	50	0.0	0.0
C- / 3.9	7.8	0.99	11.92	68	7	15	11	67	103	55.2	-12.5	32	5	1,000,000	0	0.0	0.0

Fund Type	Fund Name	Ticker Symbol	Overall Investment Rating	Phone	Perfor-mance Rating/Pts	3 Mo	6 Mo	1Yr / Pct	3Yr / Pct	5Yr / Pct	Dividend Yield	Expense Ratio
							Total Return % through 3/31/15		Annualized		Incl. in Returns	
GL	PIMCO Div and Inc Builder A	PQIZX	C	(800) 426-0107	C- / 3.3	2.91	4.21	4.64 /36	10.06 /40	--	3.08	1.57
GL	PIMCO Div and Inc Builder C	PQICX	C+	(800) 426-0107	C- / 3.6	2.64	3.75	3.78 /30	9.23 /34	--	2.52	2.32
GL	PIMCO Div and Inc Builder D	PQIDX	C+	(800) 426-0107	C- / 4.1	2.91	4.21	4.64 /36	10.04 /40	--	3.26	1.57
GL	PIMCO Div and Inc Builder Inst	PQIIX	C+	(800) 426-0107	C / 4.4	2.91	4.39	4.96 /38	10.41 /42	--	3.56	1.22
GL	PIMCO Div and Inc Builder P	PQIPX	C+	(800) 426-0107	C / 4.3	2.97	4.34	4.90 /38	10.35 /42	--	3.50	1.32
GL	PIMCO Div and Inc Builder R	PQIBX	C+	(800) 426-0107	C- / 4.0	2.76	4.08	4.38 /34	9.80 /38	--	3.01	1.82
EM	PIMCO EM Fdmtl Index+AR Str	PEFAX	E+	(800) 426-0107	E / 0.4	-1.06	-6.49	-1.15 /13	-0.06 / 4	2.98 / 6	0.02	1.40
EM	PIMCO EM Fdmtl Index+AR Str Inst	PEFIX	E-	(800) 426-0107	E / 0.5	-0.94	-6.35	-0.94 /13	0.20 / 4	3.24 / 6	0.13	1.15
EM	PIMCO EM Fdmtl Index+AR Str P	PEFPX	E-	(800) 426-0107	E / 0.4	-1.05	-6.35	-1.00 /13	0.07 / 4	3.12 / 6	0.18	1.25
GL	PIMCO Emerging Multi-Asset A	PEAAX	E	(800) 426-0107	E / 0.3	0.75	-3.35	-1.08 /13	-1.31 / 3	--	4.16	2.78
GL	PIMCO Emerging Multi-Asset Admin	PEAMX	E	(800) 426-0107	E / 0.4	0.88	-3.33	-0.94 /13	-1.24 / 3	--	4.42	2.68
GL	PIMCO Emerging Multi-Asset C	PEACX	E	(800) 426-0107	E / 0.3	0.63	-3.71	-1.76 /11	-2.04 / 3	--	4.03	3.53
GL	PIMCO Emerging Multi-Asset D	PEAEX	E+	(800) 426-0107	E / 0.4	0.75	-3.46	-1.08 /13	-1.33 / 3	--	4.26	2.78
GL	PIMCO Emerging Multi-Asset Instl	PEAWX	E+	(800) 426-0107	E / 0.4	0.87	-3.30	-0.83 /14	-0.97 / 3	--	4.63	2.43
GL	PIMCO Emerging Multi-Asset P	PEAQX	E+	(800) 426-0107	E / 0.4	0.87	-3.27	-0.78 /14	-1.10 / 3	--	4.56	2.53
GL	PIMCO Emerging Multi-Asset R	PEARX	E	(800) 426-0107	E / 0.4	0.75	-3.53	-1.25 /12	-1.56 / 3	--	4.39	3.03
EM	PIMCO EMG Itl LV RAFI-PLUS AR I	PLVLX	U	(800) 426-0107	U /	0.00	-6.30	0.52 /17	--	--	2.69	1.15
GL	PIMCO EqS Dividend A	PQDAX	C	(800) 426-0107	C- / 3.3	2.50	3.69	3.87 /31	10.29 /41	--	2.55	1.60
GL	PIMCO EqS Dividend C	PQDCX	C	(800) 426-0107	C- / 3.6	2.32	3.35	3.06 /27	9.48 /36	--	1.97	2.35
GL	PIMCO EqS Dividend D	PQDDX	C+	(800) 426-0107	C- / 4.2	2.50	3.77	3.87 /31	10.29 /41	--	2.64	1.60
GL	PIMCO EqS Dividend Institutional	PQDIX	C+	(800) 426-0107	C / 4.4	2.59	3.98	4.29 /34	10.68 /44	--	2.91	1.25
GL	PIMCO EqS Dividend P	PQDPX	C+	(800) 426-0107	C / 4.3	2.56	3.84	4.14 /33	10.55 /43	--	2.86	1.35
GL	PIMCO EqS Dividend R	PQDRX	C	(800) 426-0107	C- / 4.0	2.57	3.69	3.74 /30	10.08 /40	--	2.42	1.85
EM	PIMCO EqS Emerging Markets A	PEQAX	E	(800) 426-0107	E / 0.3	1.78	-0.58	2.51 /24	-1.24 / 3	--	0.00	1.80
EM	PIMCO EqS Emerging Markets Admn	PEQTX	E+	(800) 426-0107	E / 0.5	1.77	-0.58	2.62 /25	-1.12 / 3	--	0.00	1.70
EM	PIMCO EqS Emerging Markets C	PEQEX	E	(800) 426-0107	E / 0.4	1.58	-0.95	1.70 /21	-1.98 / 3	--	0.00	2.55
EM	PIMCO EqS Emerging Markets D	PEQDX	E+	(800) 426-0107	E / 0.4	1.78	-0.58	2.51 /24	-1.26 / 3	--	0.00	1.80
EM	PIMCO EqS Emerging Markets Instl	PEQWX	E+	(800) 426-0107	E / 0.5	1.88	-0.34	2.84 /26	-0.91 / 3	--	0.00	1.45
EM	PIMCO EqS Emerging Markets P	PEQQX	E+	(800) 426-0107	E / 0.5	1.88	-0.46	2.73 /25	-1.01 / 3	--	0.00	1.55
EM	PIMCO EqS Emerging Markets R	PEQHX	E+	(800) 426-0107	E / 0.4	1.79	-0.70	2.28 /23	-1.50 / 3	--	0.00	2.05
GR	PIMCO Eqs Long Short A	PMHAX	U	(800) 426-0107	U /	4.49	6.73	1.99 /22	--	--	0.00	2.38
GR	PIMCO Eqs Long Short C	PMHCX	U	(800) 426-0107	U /	4.30	6.30	1.25 /19	--	--	0.00	3.13
GR	PIMCO Eqs Long Short D	PMHDX	U	(800) 426-0107	U /	4.48	6.73	1.99 /22	--	--	0.00	2.38
GR	PIMCO Eqs Long Short Inst	PMHIX	C+	(800) 426-0107	C- / 3.7	4.53	6.94	2.31 /23	9.14 /34	5.14 /13	0.00	2.03
GR	PIMCO Eqs Long Short P	PMHBX	U	(800) 426-0107	U /	4.55	6.87	2.32 /23	--	--	0.00	2.13
GR	PIMCO EqS Pathfinder A	PATHX	E	(800) 426-0107	D / 2.0	3.60	0.75	2.25 /23	8.06 /27	--	1.68	1.40
GR	PIMCO EqS Pathfinder C	PTHCX	E	(800) 426-0107	D+ / 2.3	3.37	0.32	1.49 /20	7.25 /23	--	1.49	2.15
GR	PIMCO EqS Pathfinder D	PTHDX	E	(800) 426-0107	D+ / 2.8	3.61	0.73	2.22 /23	8.07 /27	--	1.74	1.40
GR	PIMCO EqS Pathfinder Inst	PTHWX	E	(800) 426-0107	C- / 3.0	3.68	0.88	2.62 /25	8.43 /29	--	1.87	1.05
GR	PIMCO EqS Pathfinder P	PTHPX	E	(800) 426-0107	D+ / 2.9	3.58	0.78	2.44 /24	8.30 /29	--	1.86	1.15
GR	PIMCO EqS Pathfinder R	PTHRX	E	(800) 426-0107	D+ / 2.6	3.55	0.54	1.96 /22	7.79 /26	--	1.76	1.65
GI	PIMCO Fdmental Advtg Abs Rtn Stg	PTFAX	E+	(800) 426-0107	E+ / 0.6	-1.35	-1.57	-2.82 / 9	3.35 / 9	3.23 / 6	6.64	1.29
GI	PIMCO Fdmental Advtg Abs Rtn Stg	PTRCX	E+	(800) 426-0107	E+ / 0.7	-1.65	-2.08	-3.65 / 8	2.55 / 7	2.39 / 5	6.26	2.04
GI	PIMCO Fdmental Advtg Abs Rtn Stg	PFSDX	E+	(800) 426-0107	E+ / 0.8	-1.36	-1.79	-3.02 / 9	3.29 / 8	3.16 / 6	7.05	1.29
GI	PIMCO Fdmental Advtg Abs Rtn Stg I	PFATX	E+	(800) 426-0107	E+ / 0.8	-1.24	-1.57	-2.61 / 9	3.73 / 9	3.60 / 7	7.27	0.89
GR	PIMCO Fdmental Advtg Abs Rtn Stg	PFAPX	E+	(800) 426-0107	E+ / 0.8	-1.27	-1.36	-2.45 / 9	3.71 / 9	3.52 / 7	7.16	0.99
IN	PIMCO Fundamental IndexPLUS AR	PIXAX	B-	(800) 426-0107	B+ / 8.4	-0.41	3.86	8.24 /64	18.54 /96	18.11 /98	6.00	1.19
IN	PIMCO Fundamental IndexPLUS AR	PXTAX	B	(800) 426-0107	A- / 9.0	-0.38	3.73	8.40 /66	18.64 /96	18.25 /98	6.24	1.04
IN	PIMCO Fundamental IndexPLUS AR	PIXCX	B-	(800) 426-0107	B+ / 8.5	-0.58	3.44	7.54 /59	17.62 /93	17.20 /96	5.94	1.94
IN	PIMCO Fundamental IndexPLUS AR	PIXDX	B	(800) 426-0107	A- / 9.0	-0.26	3.88	8.43 /66	18.53 /96	18.13 /98	6.21	1.19
IN	PIMCO Fundamental IndexPLUS AR	PXTIX	B+	(800) 426-0107	A- / 9.2	-0.17	4.08	8.80 /68	19.05 /97	18.61 /98	6.34	0.79
IN	PIMCO Fundamental IndexPLUS AR	PIXPX	B	(800) 426-0107	A- / 9.2	-0.34	3.90	8.61 /67	18.87 /96	18.45 /98	6.31	0.89

Legend (top left): 99 Pct = Best   0 Pct = Worst

● Denotes fund is closed to new investors

* Denotes fund is included in Section II

RISK			NET ASSETS		ASSET				BULL / BEAR		FUND MANAGER		MINIMUMS		LOADS	
	3 Year		NAV						Last Bull	Last Bear	Manager	Manager	Initial	Additional	Front	Back
Risk	Standard		As of	Total	Cash	Stocks	Bonds	Other	Market	Market	Quality	Tenure	Purch.	Purch.	End	End
Rating/Pts	Deviation	Beta	3/31/15	$(Mil)	%	%	%	%	Return	Return	Pct	(Years)	$	$	Load	Load
B /8.3	8.2	0.54	12.57	275	3	85	11	1	N/A	N/A	93	4	1,000	50	5.5	0.0
B /8.3	8.2	0.54	12.54	336	3	85	11	1	N/A	N/A	91	4	1,000	50	0.0	0.0
B /8.3	8.2	0.54	12.57	30	3	85	11	1	N/A	N/A	93	4	1,000	50	0.0	0.0
B /8.3	8.2	0.54	12.57	66	3	85	11	1	N/A	N/A	94	4	1,000,000	0	0.0	0.0
B /8.3	8.3	0.54	12.58	143	3	85	11	1	N/A	N/A	93	4	1,000,000	0	0.0	0.0
B /8.3	8.3	0.54	12.57	N/A	3	85	11	1	N/A	N/A	92	4	0	0	0.0	0.0
C+ /5.9	16.7	1.18	9.37	N/A	21	0	78	1	31.2	-29.1	55	1	1,000,000	0	0.0	0.0
C- /3.1	16.6	1.18	9.44	3,407	21	0	78	1	32.3	-29.0	59	1	1,000,000	0	0.0	0.0
C- /3.0	16.7	1.19	9.44	8	21	0	78	1	31.8	-29.1	57	1	1,000,000	0	0.0	0.0
C /5.2	10.6	1.40	8.07	4	4	50	45	1	6.5	-17.7	1	4	1,000	50	5.5	0.0
C /5.2	10.6	1.40	8.07	N/A	4	50	45	1	6.7	-17.6	1	4	1,000,000	0	0.0	0.0
C /5.1	10.6	1.40	7.94	2	4	50	45	1	3.9	-18.0	1	4	1,000	50	0.0	0.0
C /5.2	10.6	1.40	8.10	1	4	50	45	1	6.5	-17.7	1	4	1,000	50	0.0	0.0
C /5.2	10.6	1.40	8.13	6	4	50	45	1	7.7	-17.6	1	4	1,000,000	0	0.0	0.0
C /5.2	10.5	1.40	8.11	1	4	50	45	1	7.4	-17.6	1	4	1,000,000	0	0.0	0.0
C /5.1	10.6	1.41	8.01	N/A	4	50	45	1	5.7	-17.8	1	4	0	0	0.0	0.0
U /	N/A	N/A	9.73	4,883	39	0	60	1	N/A	N/A	N/A	1	1,000,000	0	0.0	0.0
B- /7.8	9.3	1.35	7.39	40	2	94	2	2	N/A	N/A	40	4	1,000	50	5.5	0.0
B- /7.7	9.2	1.34	7.35	28	2	94	2	2	N/A	N/A	31	4	1,000	50	0.0	0.0
B- /7.8	9.2	1.34	7.39	3	2	94	2	2	N/A	N/A	41	4	1,000	50	0.0	0.0
B- /7.8	9.2	1.34	7.39	55	2	94	2	2	N/A	N/A	46	4	1,000,000	0	0.0	0.0
B- /7.8	9.2	1.34	7.39	3	2	94	2	2	N/A	N/A	45	4	1,000,000	0	0.0	0.0
B- /7.8	9.2	1.34	7.39	N/A	2	94	2	2	N/A	N/A	38	4	0	0	0.0	0.0
C /5.2	13.9	0.98	8.57	5	2	95	2	1	13.7	-28.6	39	4	1,000	50	5.5	0.0
C /5.3	13.8	0.98	8.62	N/A	2	95	2	1	14.3	-28.5	40	4	1,000,000	0	0.0	0.0
C /5.2	13.9	0.98	8.36	2	2	95	2	1	10.9	-28.7	29	4	1,000	50	0.0	0.0
C /5.2	13.9	0.98	8.57	1	2	95	2	1	13.7	-28.5	38	4	1,000	50	0.0	0.0
C /5.2	13.9	0.98	8.68	69	2	95	2	1	15.1	-28.4	44	4	1,000,000	0	0.0	0.0
C /5.2	13.9	0.98	8.65	N/A	2	95	2	1	14.6	-28.3	42	4	1,000,000	0	0.0	0.0
C /5.2	13.9	0.98	8.52	N/A	2	95	2	1	12.9	-28.5	35	4	0	0	0.0	0.0
U /	N/A	N/A	12.11	180	40	39	20	1	N/A	N/A	N/A	3	1,000	50	5.5	0.0
U /	N/A	N/A	11.88	150	40	39	20	1	N/A	N/A	N/A	3	1,000	50	0.0	0.0
U /	N/A	N/A	12.12	48	40	39	20	1	N/A	N/A	N/A	3	1,000	50	0.0	0.0
B /8.5	8.7	0.59	12.23	347	40	39	20	1	30.4	-7.6	66	3	1,000,000	0	0.0	0.0
U /	N/A	N/A	12.19	215	40	39	20	1	N/A	N/A	N/A	3	1,000,000	0	0.0	0.0
D /2.0	9.5	0.86	9.50	63	3	90	5	2	48.0	-16.4	10	5	1,000	50	5.5	0.0
D /1.9	9.5	0.87	9.21	48	3	90	5	2	44.2	-16.7	6	5	1,000	50	0.0	0.0
D /2.0	9.5	0.86	9.46	9	3	90	5	2	48.0	-16.4	10	5	1,000	50	0.0	0.0
D /2.0	9.5	0.86	9.59	804	3	90	5	2	49.7	-16.3	11	5	1,000,000	0	0.0	0.0
D /2.0	9.5	0.86	9.54	23	3	90	5	2	49.4	-16.4	10	5	1,000,000	0	0.0	0.0
D /1.9	9.5	0.87	9.33	N/A	3	90	5	2	46.5	-16.6	8	5	0	0	0.0	0.0
C+ /6.1	3.3	0.14	3.57	32	38	0	60	2	14.7	-5.3	79	1	1,000	50	3.8	0.0
C+ /6.1	3.3	0.12	3.58	24	38	0	60	2	11.8	-5.6	74	1	1,000	50	0.0	0.0
C+ /5.9	3.3	0.13	3.54	51	38	0	60	2	14.8	-5.3	79	1	1,000	50	0.0	0.0
C+ /6.0	3.2	0.13	3.62	2,487	38	0	60	2	16.3	-5.1	82	1	1,000,000	0	0.0	0.0
C+ /6.0	3.4	0.13	3.62	26	38	0	60	2	15.6	-5.1	81	1	1,000,000	0	0.0	0.0
C /4.8	10.8	1.09	6.32	839	33	0	66	1	122.2	-18.4	75	1	1,000	50	3.8	0.0
C /4.8	10.9	1.10	6.43	43	33	0	66	1	123.7	-18.6	74	1	1,000,000	0	0.0	0.0
C /4.6	10.9	1.10	5.96	575	33	0	66	1	117.0	-18.8	64	1	1,000	50	0.0	0.0
C /4.8	10.8	1.09	6.31	660	33	0	66	1	122.5	-18.5	74	1	1,000	50	0.0	0.0
C /4.9	10.8	1.09	6.56	1,085	33	0	66	1	125.6	-18.3	79	1	1,000,000	0	0.0	0.0
C /4.9	10.8	1.10	6.52	640	33	0	66	1	124.4	-18.4	76	1	1,000,000	0	0.0	0.0

I. Index of Stock Mutual Funds

Spring 2015

Fund Type	Fund Name	Ticker Symbol	Overall Investment Rating	Phone	Performance Rating/Pts	3 Mo	6 Mo	1Yr / Pct	3Yr / Pct	5Yr / Pct	Dividend Yield	Expense Ratio
GL	PIMCO Global Multi Asset A	PGMAX	E+	(800) 426-0107	E+ / 0.9	4.17	4.46	10.48 /76	1.60 / 6	3.59 / 7	0.26	2.10
GL	PIMCO Global Multi Asset Admin	PGAAX	D-	(800) 426-0107	D- / 1.4	4.27	4.64	10.84 /78	1.96 / 6	3.91 / 8	0.41	1.75
GL	PIMCO Global Multi Asset C	PGMCX	D-	(800) 426-0107	D- / 1.0	3.96	4.06	9.73 /73	0.86 / 5	2.81 / 6	0.00	2.85
GL	PIMCO Global Multi Asset D	PGMDX	D-	(800) 426-0107	D- / 1.2	4.17	4.46	10.48 /76	1.61 / 6	3.57 / 7	0.27	2.10
GL	PIMCO Global Multi Asset I	PGAIX	D-	(800) 426-0107	D- / 1.4	4.26	4.74	11.10 /79	2.21 / 7	4.18 / 9	0.55	1.50
GL	PIMCO Global Multi Asset P	PGAPX	D-	(800) 426-0107	D- / 1.4	4.36	4.74	11.05 /79	2.14 / 6	4.09 / 9	0.51	1.60
GL	PIMCO Global Multi Asset R	PGMRX	D-	(800) 426-0107	D- / 1.2	4.11	4.40	10.24 /75	1.37 / 6	3.32 / 7	0.18	2.35
AA	PIMCO Infl Response MultiAsset A	PZRMX	E+	(800) 426-0107	E / 0.3	1.63	-0.36	-1.23 /12	-0.63 / 4	--	7.83	1.61
AA	PIMCO Infl Response MultiAsset C	PCRMX	E+	(800) 426-0107	E / 0.4	1.42	-0.71	-1.97 /10	-1.34 / 3	--	7.85	2.36
AA	PIMCO Infl Response MultiAsset D	PDRMX	E+	(800) 426-0107	E / 0.5	1.74	-0.23	-1.21 /12	-0.60 / 4	--	8.27	1.61
AA	PIMCO Infl Response MultiAsset Inst	PIRMX	E+	(800) 426-0107	E / 0.5	1.85	0.00	-0.67 /14	-0.13 / 4	--	8.59	1.16
AA	PIMCO Infl Response MultiAsset P	PPRMX	E+	(800) 426-0107	E / 0.5	1.74	-0.15	-0.88 /13	-0.25 / 4	--	8.49	1.26
AA	PIMCO Infl Response Multi-Asset R	PQRMX	E+	(800) 426-0107	E / 0.4	1.63	-0.40	-1.53 /11	-0.84 / 4	--	8.17	1.86
FO	PIMCO Int StkPlus AR St Unhdg A	PPUAX	D-	(800) 426-0107	C- / 3.5	4.81	1.27	-0.68 /14	10.84 /45	8.71 /35	4.99	1.04
FO	PIMCO Int StkPlus AR St Unhdg	PSKAX	D	(800) 426-0107	C / 4.4	5.00	1.55	-0.48 /14	11.31 /48	9.07 /37	5.33	0.89
FO	PIMCO Int StkPlus AR St Unhdg C	PPUCX	D-	(800) 426-0107	C- / 3.6	4.63	0.92	-1.40 /12	10.02 /39	7.92 /29	4.61	1.79
FO	PIMCO Int StkPlus AR St Unhdg D	PPUDX	D	(800) 426-0107	C- / 4.1	4.97	1.29	-0.64 /14	10.85 /45	8.78 /35	5.19	1.04
FO	PIMCO Int StkPlus AR St Unhdg Inst	PSKIX	D	(800) 426-0107	C / 4.4	5.14	1.63	-0.27 /15	11.31 /48	9.18 /38	5.48	0.64
FO	PIMCO Int StkPlus AR St Unhdg P	PPLPX	D	(800) 426-0107	C / 4.3	4.92	1.55	-0.39 /15	11.21 /47	9.09 /37	5.35	0.74
GR	PIMCO Intl Fdl IdxPLUS AR Str Inst	PTSIX	E-	(800) 426-0107	C- / 3.4	2.40	-2.78	-6.53 / 4	11.06 /46	--	2.95	0.83
FO	PIMCO Intl StkPlus AR Strat (DH) P	PIUHX	A+	(800) 426-0107	A+ / 9.6	10.63	12.08	16.97 /95	17.83 /94	11.84 /60	12.62	0.88
FO	PIMCO Itl Low Vol RAFI-PLUS AR	PLVTX	U	(800) 426-0107	U /	4.12	0.22	3.62 /30	--	--	3.59	0.82
GI	PIMCO Low Vol RAFI-PLUS AR Inst	PILVX	U	(800) 426-0107	U /	-0.73	4.59	11.15 /79	--	--	6.23	0.79
RE	PIMCO RealEstate RlRetrn Str A	PETAX	D+	(800) 426-0107	A / 9.3	6.51	22.50	29.19 /99	13.54 /64	20.71 /99	33.66	1.18
RE	PIMCO RealEstate RlRetrn Str C	PETCX	D+	(800) 426-0107	A / 9.5	6.56	22.33	28.56 /99	12.77 /58	19.84 /99	39.28	1.93
RE	PIMCO RealEstate RlRetrn Str D	PETDX	D+	(800) 426-0107	A+ / 9.7	6.47	22.38	29.37 /99	13.58 /64	20.73 /99	35.44	1.18
RE	PIMCO RealEstate RlRetrn Str Inst	PRRSX	D+	(800) 426-0107	A+ / 9.7	6.82	22.89	29.93 /99	13.97 /67	21.20 /99	32.96	0.78
RE	PIMCO RealEstate RlRetrn Str P	PETPX	D+	(800) 426-0107	A+ / 9.7	6.65	22.59	29.71 /99	13.85 /66	21.08 /99	33.48	0.88
AA	PIMCO RealPath 2020 A	PTYAX	D	(800) 426-0107	D- / 1.1	2.14	2.88	5.06 /39	4.67 /12	5.10 /12	4.08	1.63
AA	PIMCO RealPath 2020 Admin	PFNAX	D+	(800) 426-0107	D / 1.7	2.26	2.92	5.30 /41	4.95 /13	5.39 /14	4.44	1.38
AA	PIMCO RealPath 2020 C	PTYCX	D	(800) 426-0107	D- / 1.3	2.08	2.43	4.26 /33	3.91 /10	4.33 / 9	3.55	2.38
AA	PIMCO RealPath 2020 D	PTYDX	D+	(800) 426-0107	D- / 1.5	2.13	2.86	5.04 /39	4.67 /12	5.10 /12	4.30	1.63
AA	PIMCO RealPath 2020 Inst	PRWIX	D+	(800) 426-0107	D / 1.8	2.36	3.12	5.54 /43	5.22 /14	5.63 /15	4.79	1.13
GL	PIMCO RealPath 2020 P	PTYPX	D+	(800) 426-0107	D / 1.8	2.33	3.14	5.53 /43	5.11 /13	5.58 /15	4.16	1.23
AA	PIMCO RealPath 2020 R	PTYRX	D	(800) 426-0107	D- / 1.4	2.17	2.69	4.73 /37	4.44 /11	4.85 /11	4.01	1.88
AA	PIMCO RealPath 2025 A	PENZX	D	(800) 426-0107	D- / 1.2	2.54	3.01	5.23 /40	5.32 /14	--	4.90	1.69
AA	PIMCO RealPath 2025 Admin	PENMX	D+	(800) 426-0107	D / 1.9	2.61	3.07	5.42 /42	5.54 /15	--	5.47	1.44
AA	PIMCO RealPath 2025 C	PENWX	D	(800) 426-0107	D- / 1.4	2.40	2.66	4.44 /35	4.53 /12	--	4.52	2.44
AA	PIMCO RealPath 2025 D	PENDX	D+	(800) 426-0107	D / 1.8	2.55	3.03	5.16 /40	5.31 /14	--	5.22	1.69
AA	PIMCO RealPath 2025 Inst	PENTX	D+	(800) 426-0107	D / 2.0	2.66	3.20	5.67 /44	5.78 /16	--	5.72	1.19
AA	PIMCO RealPath 2025 P	PENPX	C-	(800) 426-0107	D / 1.9	2.63	3.15	5.58 /43	5.69 /16	--	1.72	1.29
AA	PIMCO RealPath 2025 R	PENRX	D+	(800) 426-0107	D / 1.6	2.47	2.86	4.88 /38	5.01 /13	--	4.95	1.94
AA	PIMCO RealPath 2030 A	PEHAX	D	(800) 426-0107	D- / 1.5	2.71	3.11	5.31 /41	6.16 /17	5.84 /16	4.93	1.72
AA	PIMCO RealPath 2030 Admin	PNLAX	D+	(800) 426-0107	D+ / 2.3	2.75	3.23	5.55 /43	6.39 /18	6.14 /18	5.44	1.47
AA	PIMCO RealPath 2030 C	PEHCX	D	(800) 426-0107	D / 1.7	2.57	2.73	4.58 /36	5.35 /14	5.06 /12	4.51	2.47
AA	PIMCO RealPath 2030 D	PEHDX	D+	(800) 426-0107	D / 2.1	2.70	2.98	5.31 /41	6.15 /17	5.83 /16	5.22	1.72
AA	PIMCO RealPath 2030 Inst	PRLIX	D+	(800) 426-0107	D+ / 2.4	2.67	3.24	5.81 /45	6.67 /20	6.39 /19	5.70	1.22
AA	PIMCO RealPath 2030 P	PEHPX	C-	(800) 426-0107	D+ / 2.4	2.79	3.25	5.65 /44	6.59 /19	6.34 /19	1.36	1.32
AA	PIMCO RealPath 2030 R	PEHRX	D+	(800) 426-0107	D / 1.9	2.48	2.80	4.99 /38	5.84 /16	5.55 /14	4.90	1.97
AA	PIMCO RealPath 2035 A	PIVAX	D+	(800) 426-0107	D / 1.8	2.72	3.41	5.65 /44	6.87 /21	--	5.15	1.74
AA	PIMCO RealPath 2035 Admin	PIVNX	C-	(800) 426-0107	D+ / 2.7	2.87	3.65	6.03 /47	7.15 /22	--	5.71	1.49
AA	PIMCO RealPath 2035 C	PIVWX	D+	(800) 426-0107	D / 2.1	2.54	3.00	4.99 /38	6.08 /17	--	4.71	2.49

● Denotes fund is closed to new investors
* Denotes fund is included in Section II

www.thestreetratings.com

I. Index of Stock Mutual Funds

RISK			NET ASSETS		ASSET					BULL / BEAR		FUND MANAGER		MINIMUMS		LOADS	
	3 Year		NAV						Portfolio	Last Bull	Last Bear	Manager	Manager	Initial	Additional	Front	Back
Risk Rating/Pts	Standard Deviation	Beta	As of 3/31/15	Total $(Mil)	Cash %	Stocks %	Bonds %	Other %	Turnover Ratio	Market Return	Market Return	Quality Pct	Tenure (Years)	Purch. $	Purch. $	End Load	End Load
C+ / 6.0	7.9	1.01	11.48	176	0	22	77	1	94	13.3	-10.1	4	7	1,000	50	5.5	0.0
C+ / 6.0	7.9	1.02	11.49	N/A	0	22	77	1	94	14.7	-10.1	5	7	1,000,000	0	0.0	0.0
C+ / 6.0	7.8	1.01	11.28	172	0	22	77	1	94	10.4	-10.5	3	7	1,000	50	0.0	0.0
C+ / 6.0	7.9	1.02	11.48	33	0	22	77	1	94	13.3	-10.1	4	7	1,000	50	0.0	0.0
C+ / 6.0	7.8	1.00	11.50	597	0	22	77	1	94	15.7	-10.0	5	7	1,000,000	0	0.0	0.0
C+ / 6.0	7.9	1.02	11.50	91	0	22	77	1	94	15.2	-10.0	5	7	1,000,000	0	0.0	0.0
C+ / 6.0	7.9	1.01	11.40	11	0	22	77	1	94	12.4	-10.3	4	7	0	0	0.0	0.0
C+ / 5.8	6.8	0.54	8.73	12	0	4	95	1	80	5.5	N/A	6	4	1,000	50	5.5	0.0
C+ / 5.7	6.8	0.54	8.60	3	0	4	95	1	80	2.7	N/A	4	4	1,000	50	0.0	0.0
C+ / 5.8	6.9	0.54	8.75	16	0	4	95	1	80	5.3	N/A	6	4	1,000	50	0.0	0.0
C+ / 5.8	6.8	0.54	8.79	645	0	4	95	1	80	7.0	N/A	7	4	1,000,000	0	0.0	0.0
C+ / 5.8	6.9	0.55	8.79	2	0	4	95	1	80	6.6	N/A	7	4	1,000,000	0	0.0	0.0
C+ / 5.8	6.9	0.54	8.74	N/A	0	4	95	1	80	4.6	N/A	5	4	0	0	0.0	0.0
C- / 4.1	14.0	1.04	6.37	24	37	0	62	1	395	67.3	-24.7	76	1	1,000	50	3.8	0.0
C- / 4.1	14.1	1.04	6.42	3	37	0	62	1	395	69.1	-24.5	79	1	1,000,000	0	0.0	0.0
C- / 4.1	14.1	1.04	6.18	8	37	0	62	1	395	62.9	-24.7	68	1	1,000	50	0.0	0.0
C- / 4.1	14.1	1.05	6.40	36	37	0	62	1	395	67.3	-24.5	75	1	1,000	50	0.0	0.0
C- / 4.2	14.1	1.05	6.50	1,081	37	0	62	1	395	69.6	-24.5	79	1	1,000,000	0	0.0	0.0
C- / 4.2	14.2	1.05	6.52	13	37	0	62	1	395	69.2	-24.5	78	1	1,000,000	0	0.0	0.0
E- / 0.0	15.7	1.25	8.95	1,215	51	0	48	1	414	62.5	N/A	3	1	1,000,000	0	0.0	0.0
B / 8.0	10.3	0.73	8.19	157	65	0	34	1	733	94.1	-19.5	98	N/A	1,000,000	0	0.0	0.0
U /	N/A	N/A	10.12	2,663	23	0	76	1	0	N/A	N/A	N/A	1	1,000,000	0	0.0	0.0
U /	N/A	N/A	10.81	1,253	29	0	70	1	0	N/A	N/A	N/A	1	1,000,000	0	0.0	0.0
E- / 0.0	19.2	1.45	3.82	324	0	0	99	1	81	92.4	-10.3	5	8	1,000	50	5.5	0.0
E- / 0.0	19.2	1.46	3.40	184	0	0	99	1	81	87.1	-10.6	4	8	1,000	50	0.0	0.0
E- / 0.0	19.1	1.45	3.84	273	0	0	99	1	81	92.5	-10.3	6	8	1,000	50	0.0	0.0
E- / 0.0	19.2	1.45	4.17	1,725	0	0	99	1	81	95.1	-10.2	6	8	1,000,000	0	0.0	0.0
E- / 0.0	19.1	1.45	4.10	132	0	0	99	1	81	94.3	-10.1	6	8	1,000,000	0	0.0	0.0
B- / 7.6	4.9	0.63	8.27	8	0	11	88	1	38	22.3	-4.8	38	7	1,000	50	5.5	0.0
B- / 7.6	4.8	0.61	8.47	61	0	11	88	1	38	23.3	-4.7	44	7	1,000,000	0	0.0	0.0
B- / 7.6	4.8	0.62	8.33	4	0	11	88	1	38	19.2	-5.0	30	7	1,000	50	0.0	0.0
B- / 7.6	4.8	0.62	8.30	3	0	11	88	1	38	22.3	-4.8	39	7	1,000	50	0.0	0.0
B- / 7.6	4.9	0.62	8.29	32	0	11	88	1	38	24.4	-4.6	47	7	1,000,000	0	0.0	0.0
B- / 7.6	4.8	0.24	8.34	N/A	0	11	88	1	38	24.0	-4.6	88	7	1,000,000	0	0.0	0.0
B- / 7.6	4.9	0.62	8.33	2	0	11	88	1	38	21.3	-4.9	36	7	0	0	0.0	0.0
B- / 7.6	5.6	0.78	10.04	2	13	10	75	2	29	27.1	N/A	27	4	1,000	50	5.5	0.0
B- / 7.6	5.6	0.79	10.01	57	13	10	75	2	29	28.0	N/A	28	4	1,000,000	0	0.0	0.0
B- / 7.6	5.6	0.79	10.03	1	13	10	75	2	29	23.9	N/A	18	4	1,000	50	0.0	0.0
B- / 7.6	5.7	0.79	10.02	3	13	10	75	2	29	27.1	N/A	25	4	1,000	50	0.0	0.0
B- / 7.6	5.6	0.79	10.01	25	13	10	75	2	29	29.3	N/A	30	4	1,000,000	0	0.0	0.0
B / 8.0	5.6	0.79	10.41	N/A	13	10	75	2	29	28.9	N/A	29	4	1,000,000	0	0.0	0.0
B- / 7.6	5.7	0.80	10.02	1	13	10	75	2	29	26.0	N/A	22	4	0	0	0.0	0.0
B- / 7.1	6.3	0.91	7.92	7	6	19	74	1	29	29.2	-7.7	21	7	1,000	50	5.5	0.0
B- / 7.1	6.3	0.91	7.96	75	6	19	74	1	29	30.3	-7.7	23	7	1,000,000	0	0.0	0.0
B- / 7.2	6.3	0.91	7.98	3	6	19	74	1	29	25.8	-8.0	15	7	1,000	50	0.0	0.0
B- / 7.1	6.3	0.92	7.94	3	6	19	74	1	29	29.1	-7.7	20	7	1,000	50	0.0	0.0
B- / 7.1	6.3	0.92	7.95	41	6	19	74	1	29	31.5	-7.6	25	7	1,000,000	0	0.0	0.0
B- / 7.5	6.3	0.92	8.30	N/A	6	19	74	1	29	31.1	-7.6	24	7	1,000,000	0	0.0	0.0
B- / 7.2	6.3	0.92	7.97	2	6	19	74	1	29	28.0	-7.8	18	7	0	0	0.0	0.0
B- / 7.5	6.9	1.04	10.16	2	14	16	69	1	30	35.3	N/A	15	4	1,000	50	5.5	0.0
B- / 7.5	7.0	1.05	10.18	56	14	16	69	1	30	36.4	N/A	17	4	1,000,000	0	0.0	0.0
B- / 7.5	7.0	1.05	10.23	N/A	14	16	69	1	30	31.8	N/A	11	4	1,000	50	0.0	0.0

Fund Type	Fund Name	Ticker Symbol	Overall Investment Rating	Phone	Performance Rating/Pts	Total Return % through 3/31/15					Incl. in Returns	
						3 Mo	6 Mo	1Yr / Pct	3Yr / Pct (Annualized)	5Yr / Pct (Annualized)	Dividend Yield	Expense Ratio
AA	PIMCO RealPath 2035 D	PIVDX	C-	(800) 426-0107	D+ / 2.5	2.69	3.39	5.74 /44	6.89 /21	--	5.44	1.74
AA	PIMCO RealPath 2035 Inst	PIVIX	C-	(800) 426-0107	D+ / 2.9	2.82	3.67	6.27 /49	7.43 /24	--	5.95	1.24
AA	PIMCO RealPath 2035 P	PIVPX	C-	(800) 426-0107	D+ / 2.8	2.82	3.64	6.19 /48	7.33 /23	--	3.22	1.34
AA	PIMCO Realpath 2035 R	PIVSX	C-	(800) 426-0107	D+ / 2.4	2.74	3.34	5.51 /43	6.62 /20	--	5.21	1.99
AA	PIMCO RealPath 2040 A	POFAX	D+	(800) 426-0107	D / 1.9	2.88	3.68	5.66 /44	7.28 /23	6.86 /22	5.31	1.75
AA	PIMCO RealPath 2040 Admin	PEOAX	C-	(800) 426-0107	D+ / 2.9	3.05	3.80	6.03 /47	7.56 /24	7.12 /24	5.84	1.50
AA	PIMCO RealPath 2040 C	POFCX	D+	(800) 426-0107	D+ / 2.3	2.74	3.34	4.86 /38	6.50 /19	6.03 /17	4.96	2.50
AA	PIMCO RealPath 2040 D	POFDX	C-	(800) 426-0107	D+ / 2.7	2.87	3.68	5.66 /44	7.27 /23	6.85 /22	5.61	1.75
AA	PIMCO RealPath 2040 Inst	PROIX	C-	(800) 426-0107	C- / 3.1	2.97	3.93	6.15 /48	7.82 /26	7.39 /26	6.09	1.25
GL	PIMCO RealPath 2040 P	POFPX	C	(800) 426-0107	C- / 3.0	2.94	3.88	6.05 /47	7.71 /25	7.32 /25	1.40	1.35
AA	PIMCO RealPath 2040 R	POFRX	C-	(800) 426-0107	D+ / 2.5	2.72	3.49	5.34 /41	6.98 /21	6.53 /20	5.18	2.00
GI	PIMCO RealPath 2045 A	PFZAX	C-	(800) 426-0107	D / 2.1	2.89	3.50	5.41 /42	7.69 /25	--	5.68	1.75
GI	PIMCO RealPath 2045 Admin	PFZMX	C	(800) 426-0107	C- / 3.1	2.85	3.58	5.53 /43	7.92 /27	--	6.32	1.50
GI	PIMCO RealPath 2045 C	PFZCX	C-	(800) 426-0107	D+ / 2.4	2.64	3.06	4.51 /35	6.87 /21	--	5.32	2.50
GI	PIMCO RealPath 2045 D	PFZDX	C	(800) 426-0107	D+ / 2.9	2.90	3.46	5.39 /42	7.69 /25	--	6.09	1.75
GI	PIMCO RealPath 2045 Inst	PFZIX	C	(800) 426-0107	C- / 3.3	3.00	3.71	5.87 /45	8.22 /28	--	6.56	1.25
GI	PIMCO RealPath 2045 P	PFZPX	C	(800) 426-0107	C- / 3.2	2.87	3.66	5.68 /44	8.09 /27	--	2.64	1.35
GI	PIMCO RealPath 2045 R	PFZRX	C	(800) 426-0107	D+ / 2.7	2.81	3.31	5.03 /39	7.42 /24	--	5.63	2.00
AA	PIMCO RealPath 2050 A	PFYAX	D+	(800) 426-0107	D / 2.1	2.92	3.80	5.90 /46	7.60 /25	6.73 /21	5.17	1.76
AA	PIMCO RealPath 2050 Admin	POTAX	C-	(800) 426-0107	C- / 3.1	3.10	3.90	6.24 /49	7.88 /26	6.99 /23	5.67	1.51
AA	PIMCO RealPath 2050 C	PFYCX	C-	(800) 426-0107	D+ / 2.4	2.77	3.38	5.12 /39	6.79 /20	5.92 /16	4.71	2.51
AA	PIMCO RealPath 2050 D	PFYDX	C-	(800) 426-0107	D+ / 2.9	2.92	3.65	5.79 /45	7.55 /24	6.68 /21	5.37	1.76
AA	PIMCO RealPath 2050 Inst	PRMIX	C	(800) 426-0107	C- / 3.3	3.14	4.02	6.46 /50	8.13 /28	7.29 /25	5.88	1.26
GL	PIMCO RealPath 2050 P	PFYPX	C	(800) 426-0107	C- / 3.2	2.93	3.86	6.26 /49	8.00 /27	7.21 /24	3.50	1.36
AA	PIMCO RealPath 2050 R	PFYRX	C-	(800) 426-0107	D+ / 2.7	2.73	3.50	5.48 /42	7.26 /23	6.41 /20	5.20	2.01
AA	PIMCO RealPath Income A	PTNAX	D	(800) 426-0107	D- / 1.0	2.16	2.46	4.74 /37	4.51 /12	5.27 /13	4.32	1.56
AA	PIMCO RealPath Income Admn	PRNAX	D	(800) 426-0107	D- / 1.5	2.09	2.59	5.02 /39	4.77 /12	5.52 /14	4.84	1.31
AA	PIMCO RealPath Income C	PTNCX	D	(800) 426-0107	D- / 1.2	1.89	2.07	4.03 /32	3.71 / 9	4.47 /10	3.88	2.31
AA	PIMCO RealPath Income D	PTNDX	D	(800) 426-0107	D- / 1.4	2.15	2.47	4.80 /37	4.50 /11	5.26 /13	4.63	1.56
AA	PIMCO RealPath Income Inst	PRIEX	D	(800) 426-0107	D / 1.7	2.25	2.72	5.27 /41	5.04 /13	5.81 /16	5.08	1.06
GL	PIMCO RealPath Income P	PTNPX	D	(800) 426-0107	D / 1.6	2.22	2.71	5.21 /40	4.92 /13	5.74 /15	4.91	1.16
AA	PIMCO RealPath Income R	PTNRX	D	(800) 426-0107	D- / 1.4	2.06	2.30	4.49 /35	4.25 /11	4.98 /12	4.33	1.81
IN	PIMCO SmallCap StkPlus AR Strat A	PCKAX	B	(800) 426-0107	A / 9.3	4.65	14.89	9.50 /72	19.01 /97	18.09 /97	3.79	1.09
IN	PIMCO SmallCap StkPlus AR Strat C	PCKCX	B	(800) 426-0107	A / 9.4	4.47	14.55	8.62 /67	18.13 /95	17.20 /96	3.93	1.84
IN	PIMCO SmallCap StkPlus AR Strat D	PCKDX	B+	(800) 426-0107	A+ / 9.6	4.79	14.97	9.56 /72	19.00 /97	18.10 /97	3.95	1.09
IN	PIMCO SmallCap StkPlus AR Strat I	PSCSX	B+	(800) 426-0107	A+ / 9.7	4.80	15.14	9.93 /74	19.46 /97	18.55 /98	4.08	0.69
IN	PIMCO SmallCap StkPlus AR Strat P	PCKPX	B+	(800) 426-0107	A+ / 9.6	4.72	15.08	9.71 /73	19.32 /97	18.38 /98	4.06	0.79
GR	PIMCO SmCo Fdl IdxPLUS AR Str	PCFIX	C	(800) 426-0107	A / 9.4	2.06	12.70	6.82 /54	19.01 /97	--	6.21	0.84
GI	PIMCO StockPlus Long Duration Fd I	PSLDX	C-	(800) 426-0107	A+ / 9.9	4.21	14.73	29.07 /99	24.14 /99	24.94 /99	4.55	0.59
IX	PIMCO StocksPLUS A	PSPAX	C+	(800) 426-0107	B+ / 8.4	1.47	6.14	12.89 /86	17.38 /92	15.58 /91	0.03	0.91
IX	PIMCO StocksPLUS Absolute Return	PTOAX	C+	(800) 426-0107	B+ / 8.5	0.94	5.84	12.88 /86	17.68 /93	17.28 /96	2.87	1.04
IX	PIMCO StocksPLUS Absolute Return	PSOCX	C	(800) 426-0107	B+ / 8.6	0.78	5.46	12.12 /83	16.79 /89	16.41 /94	2.90	1.79
IX	PIMCO StocksPLUS Absolute Return	PSTDX	C+	(800) 426-0107	A- / 9.0	0.96	5.81	12.94 /86	17.61 /93	17.27 /96	3.00	1.04
IX	PIMCO StocksPLUS Absolute Return	PSPTX	C+	(800) 426-0107	A- / 9.2	1.04	6.01	13.29 /88	18.12 /95	17.76 /97	3.10	0.64
IX	PIMCO StocksPLUS Absolute Return	PTOPX	C+	(800) 426-0107	A- / 9.2	1.05	5.92	13.24 /87	18.00 /94	17.63 /97	3.09	0.74
IX	PIMCO StocksPLUS Admin	PPLAX	B-	(800) 426-0107	A- / 9.1	1.57	6.24	13.13 /87	17.71 /93	15.85 /92	0.10	0.76
IX	PIMCO StocksPLUS C	PSPCX	C+	(800) 426-0107	B+ / 8.7	1.41	5.91	12.36 /84	16.82 /89	15.04 /87	0.00	1.41
IX	PIMCO StocksPLUS D	PSPDX	C+	(800) 426-0107	A- / 9.0	1.48	6.18	12.98 /86	17.39 /92	15.60 /91	0.05	0.91
IX	PIMCO StocksPLUS Inst	PSTKX	B	(800) 426-0107	A- / 9.2	1.59	6.35	13.37 /88	17.83 /94	16.06 /93	0.19	0.51
IX	PIMCO StocksPLUS P	PSKPX	B-	(800) 426-0107	A- / 9.1	1.49	6.24	13.24 /87	17.69 /93	15.90 /92	0.17	0.61
IX	PIMCO StocksPLUS R	PSPRX	C+	(800) 426-0107	B+ / 8.8	1.43	6.10	12.77 /86	17.09 /90	15.34 /89	0.00	1.16
IN	PIMCO TRENDS Mgd Fut Str D	PQTDX	U	(800) 426-0107	U /	2.30	6.97	21.00 /97	--	--	6.84	1.83

www.thestreetratings.com

RISK			NET ASSETS		ASSET					Portfolio	BULL / BEAR		FUND MANAGER		MINIMUMS		LOADS	
	3 Year		NAV								Last Bull	Last Bear	Manager	Manager	Initial	Additional	Front	Back
Risk Rating/Pts	Standard Deviation	Beta	As of 3/31/15	Total $(Mil)	Cash %	Stocks %	Bonds %	Other %		Turnover Ratio	Market Return	Market Return	Quality Pct	Tenure (Years)	Purch. $	Purch. $	End Load	End Load
B- / 7.5	6.9	1.04	10.17	1	14	16	69	1		30	35.3	N/A	16	4	1,000	50	0.0	0.0
B- / 7.4	7.0	1.06	10.18	30	14	16	69	1		30	37.6	N/A	18	4	1,000,000	0	0.0	0.0
B- / 7.8	7.0	1.05	10.45	N/A	14	16	69	1		30	37.0	N/A	18	4	1,000,000	0	0.0	0.0
B- / 7.5	7.0	1.05	10.19	1	14	16	69	1		30	34.2	N/A	13	4	0	0	0.0	0.0
B- / 7.5	7.4	1.12	7.90	6	21	23	55	1		34	36.6	-10.6	13	7	1,000	50	5.5	0.0
B- / 7.5	7.3	1.11	7.94	52	21	23	55	1		34	37.8	-10.6	15	7	1,000,000	0	0.0	0.0
B- / 7.6	7.4	1.11	7.87	2	21	23	55	1		34	33.2	-11.0	9	7	1,000	50	0.0	0.0
B- / 7.5	7.3	1.10	7.92	2	21	23	55	1		34	36.6	-10.7	14	7	1,000	50	0.0	0.0
B- / 7.5	7.3	1.11	7.94	47	21	23	55	1		34	38.7	-10.4	17	7	1,000,000	0	0.0	0.0
B- / 7.9	7.5	0.45	8.31	N/A	21	23	55	1		34	38.4	-10.4	90	7	1,000,000	0	0.0	0.0
B- / 7.6	7.3	1.11	7.94	1	21	23	55	1		34	35.3	-10.7	12	7	0	0	0.0	0.0
B / 8.5	7.7	0.64	10.68	1	17	19	62	2		31	N/A	N/A	34	3	1,000	50	5.5	0.0
B / 8.5	7.8	0.65	10.66	18	17	19	62	2		31	N/A	N/A	36	3	1,000,000	0	0.0	0.0
B / 8.3	7.7	0.64	10.67	N/A	17	19	62	2		31	N/A	N/A	26	3	1,000	50	0.0	0.0
B / 8.5	7.7	0.64	10.65	1	17	19	62	2		31	N/A	N/A	34	3	1,000	50	0.0	0.0
B / 8.5	7.7	0.64	10.67	41	17	19	62	2		31	N/A	N/A	41	3	1,000,000	0	0.0	0.0
B / 8.5	7.8	0.65	11.07	N/A	17	19	62	2		31	N/A	N/A	38	3	1,000,000	0	0.0	0.0
B / 8.4	7.7	0.65	10.72	N/A	17	19	62	2		31	N/A	N/A	31	3	0	0	0.0	0.0
B- / 7.7	7.7	1.17	8.20	3	22	26	51	1		41	38.6	-12.0	12	7	1,000	50	5.5	0.0
B- / 7.7	7.6	1.16	8.23	40	22	26	51	1		41	39.5	-11.9	13	7	1,000,000	0	0.0	0.0
B- / 7.7	7.7	1.17	8.19	1	22	26	51	1		41	35.1	-12.3	8	7	1,000	50	0.0	0.0
B- / 7.7	7.7	1.17	8.21	2	22	26	51	1		41	38.3	-12.0	11	7	1,000	50	0.0	0.0
B- / 7.6	7.7	1.18	8.26	48	22	26	51	1		41	40.7	-11.8	14	7	1,000,000	0	0.0	0.0
B- / 7.9	7.7	0.47	8.44	N/A	22	26	51	1		41	40.4	-11.8	90	7	1,000,000	0	0.0	0.0
B- / 7.7	7.7	1.18	8.19	1	22	26	51	1		41	37.2	-12.1	9	7	0	0	0.0	0.0
B- / 7.2	4.4	0.47	8.61	9	1	5	93	1		26	19.8	-2.0	61	N/A	1,000	50	5.5	0.0
B- / 7.2	4.4	0.47	8.61	59	1	5	93	1		26	20.9	-1.8	64	N/A	1,000,000	0	0.0	0.0
B- / 7.2	4.4	0.47	8.61	3	1	5	93	1		26	16.7	-2.2	48	N/A	1,000	50	0.0	0.0
B- / 7.2	4.5	0.49	8.60	4	1	5	93	1		26	19.8	-1.9	58	N/A	1,000	50	0.0	0.0
B- / 7.1	4.4	0.47	8.62	31	1	5	93	1		26	21.8	-1.7	68	N/A	1,000,000	0	0.0	0.0
B- / 7.2	4.4	0.18	8.63	N/A	1	5	93	1		26	21.4	-1.7	89	N/A	1,000,000	0	0.0	0.0
B- / 7.2	4.5	0.48	8.63	N/A	1	5	93	1		26	18.8	-2.0	56	N/A	0	0	0.0	0.0
C / 4.7	13.5	1.18	9.45	367	35	0	64	1		428	125.1	-28.1	63	1	1,000	50	3.8	0.0
C / 4.4	13.5	1.18	8.89	165	35	0	64	1		428	119.2	-28.2	53	1	1,000	50	0.0	0.0
C / 4.7	13.5	1.18	9.40	347	35	0	64	1		428	124.8	-27.9	65	1	1,000	50	0.0	0.0
C / 4.8	13.5	1.18	9.60	279	35	0	64	1		428	128.0	-27.8	70	1	1,000,000	0	0.0	0.0
C / 4.8	13.5	1.18	9.54	199	35	0	64	1		428	127.4	-28.0	68	1	1,000,000	0	0.0	0.0
D / 1.7	14.2	1.26	12.39	395	24	0	74	2		378	121.8	N/A	46	1	1,000,000	0	0.0	0.0
E- / 0.1	10.8	0.72	7.56	692	4	0	95	1		73	146.0	-5.9	98	8	1,000,000	0	0.0	0.0
C- / 3.9	9.8	1.02	8.98	237	35	0	64	1		169	111.1	-18.8	75	1	1,000	50	3.8	0.0
C- / 3.4	10.3	1.05	9.62	353	37	0	61	2		392	119.3	-19.0	73	1	1,000	50	3.8	0.0
C- / 3.0	10.3	1.05	9.03	225	37	0	61	2		392	113.8	-19.3	65	1	1,000	50	0.0	0.0
C- / 3.3	10.3	1.05	9.49	314	37	0	61	2		392	119.2	-19.1	74	1	1,000	50	0.0	0.0
C- / 3.4	10.3	1.05	9.72	409	37	0	61	2		392	122.3	-18.9	77	1	1,000,000	0	0.0	0.0
C- / 3.3	10.3	1.05	9.64	146	37	0	61	2		392	121.4	-18.9	76	1	1,000,000	0	0.0	0.0
C- / 3.9	9.8	1.02	9.05	7	35	0	64	1		169	112.6	-18.7	78	1	1,000,000	0	0.0	0.0
C- / 3.7	9.8	1.02	8.61	149	35	0	64	1		169	107.3	-18.9	70	1	1,000	50	0.0	0.0
C- / 3.9	9.8	1.02	8.94	36	35	0	64	1		169	110.8	-18.7	75	1	1,000	50	0.0	0.0
C- / 4.2	9.8	1.02	9.56	620	35	0	64	1		169	113.7	-18.6	79	1	1,000,000	0	0.0	0.0
C- / 4.2	9.8	1.03	9.54	22	35	0	64	1		169	113.3	-18.9	77	1	1,000,000	0	0.0	0.0
C- / 4.0	9.9	1.03	9.22	15	35	0	64	1		169	109.5	-18.9	72	1	0	0	0.0	0.0
U /	N/A	N/A	11.14	41	21	0	78	1		0	N/A	N/A	N/A	2	1,000	50	0.0	0.0

Fund Type	Fund Name	Ticker Symbol	Overall Investment Rating	Phone	Performance Rating/Pts	3 Mo	6 Mo	1Yr / Pct	3Yr / Pct	5Yr / Pct	Dividend Yield	Expense Ratio
	99 Pct = Best							Total Return % through 3/31/15			Incl. in Returns	
	0 Pct = Worst								Annualized			
IN	PIMCO TRENDS Mgd Fut Str Inst	PQTIX	U	(800) 426-0107	U /	2.38	7.20	21.53 /97	--	--	6.91	1.43
GL	PIMCO Wrldwd Fndmntl Adv AR St	PWWIX	U	(800) 426-0107	U /	-2.09	-4.17	-5.77 / 5	--	--	2.08	0.99
GR	Pinnacle Value Fund	PVFIX	C+	(877) 369-3705	C- / 3.9	0.23	3.09	3.97 /32	10.38 /42	8.26 /32	0.00	1.76
BA	Pioneer Classic Balanced Fund A	AOBLX	D+	(800) 225-6292	C / 4.3	1.96	4.85	9.72 /73	11.03 /46	9.73 /42	1.73	1.25
BA	Pioneer Classic Balanced Fund C	PCBCX	D+	(800) 225-6292	C / 4.5	1.75	4.39	8.81 /68	10.14 /40	8.82 /35	1.18	1.95
BA	Pioneer Classic Balanced Fund Y	AYBLX	C-	(800) 225-6292	C / 5.2	2.06	4.88	9.94 /74	11.36 /48	10.05 /45	2.13	0.95
GR	Pioneer Core Equity A	PIOTX	C+	(800) 225-6292	C / 5.3	0.41	4.50	9.36 /71	13.58 /64	13.24 /70	0.89	0.99
GR	Pioneer Core Equity C	PCOTX	C+	(800) 225-6292	C+ / 5.6	0.13	4.02	8.36 /65	12.55 /56	12.20 /62	0.40	1.92
GR	Pioneer Core Equity Y	PVFYX	B-	(800) 225-6292	C+ / 6.5	0.46	4.65	9.67 /73	13.88 /66	13.55 /73	1.24	0.75
GR	Pioneer Disciplined Growth A	PINDX	B	(800) 225-6292	B- / 7.0	1.65	7.03	14.89 /91	15.44 /79	14.98 /87	0.81	1.18
GR	Pioneer Disciplined Growth C	INDCX	B+	(800) 225-6292	B- / 7.4	1.41	6.56	13.89 /89	14.44 /70	13.98 /78	0.30	2.04
GR	Pioneer Disciplined Growth Y	INYDX	A	(800) 225-6292	B+ / 8.4	1.74	7.19	15.26 /92	15.83 /82	15.37 /89	1.16	0.75
GR	Pioneer Disciplined Value A	CVFCX	D	(800) 225-6292	C / 4.6	-0.45	4.15	7.23 /57	12.68 /57	11.13 /54	0.51	1.19
GR	Pioneer Disciplined Value C	CVCFX	D	(800) 225-6292	C / 5.0	-0.63	3.76	6.50 /51	11.84 /51	10.18 /46	0.01	1.88
GR	Pioneer Disciplined Value R	CVRFX	C+	(800) 225-6292	C / 5.4	-0.46	4.07	7.00 /55	12.42 /55	10.87 /52	0.45	1.58
GR	Pioneer Disciplined Value Y	CVFYX	C-	(800) 225-6292	C+ / 5.9	-0.34	4.33	7.62 /60	13.11 /60	11.51 /57	0.90	0.82
GR	Pioneer Disciplined Value Z	CVFZX	B-	(800) 225-6292	C+ / 5.7	-0.40	4.26	7.47 /59	12.86 /59	11.23 /55	0.86	1.17
EM	Pioneer Emerging Markets A	PEMFX	E-	(800) 225-6292	E- / 0.1	-3.00	-14.56	-13.34 / 2	-6.31 / 1	-4.48 / 1	1.81	1.91
EM	Pioneer Emerging Markets C	PCEFX	E-	(800) 225-6292	E- / 0.1	-3.22	-14.94	-14.07 / 2	-7.09 / 1	-5.26 / 1	1.38	2.73
EM	Pioneer Emerging Markets R	PEMRX	E-	(800) 225-6292	E- / 0.1	-3.08	-14.67	-13.59 / 2	-6.48 / 1	-4.68 / 1	1.81	2.08
EM	Pioneer Emerging Markets Y	PYEFX	E-	(800) 225-6292	E- / 0.2	-2.87	-14.35	-12.93 / 2	-5.78 / 2	-3.96 / 1	2.35	1.33
IN	Pioneer Equity Income A	PEQIX	B-	(800) 225-6292	C+ / 6.4	1.08	8.61	10.94 /78	14.75 /73	14.26 /80	2.21	1.09
IN	Pioneer Equity Income C	PCEQX	B-	(800) 225-6292	C+ / 6.8	0.89	8.20	10.12 /75	13.92 /67	13.44 /72	1.67	1.80
IN	Pioneer Equity Income K	PEQKX	A	(800) 225-6292	B / 7.7	1.14	8.79	11.38 /80	15.10 /76	14.48 /82	2.69	0.69
IN	Pioneer Equity Income R	PQIRX	B+	(800) 225-6292	B- / 7.1	0.98	8.41	10.53 /76	14.38 /70	13.92 /77	1.94	1.43
IN	Pioneer Equity Income Y	PYEQX	B+	(800) 225-6292	B / 7.7	1.13	8.75	11.25 /79	15.12 /76	14.68 /84	2.59	0.79
IN	Pioneer Equity Income Z	PEZQX	B+	(800) 225-6292	B / 7.6	1.11	8.69	11.09 /79	14.96 /75	14.56 /83	2.42	0.88
GI	Pioneer Fund A	PIODX	D	(800) 225-6292	C+ / 5.8	0.74	5.93	9.26 /71	14.14 /68	11.36 /56	0.80	0.97
GI	Pioneer Fund C	PCODX	D	(800) 225-6292	C+ / 6.1	0.53	5.51	8.41 /66	13.26 /61	10.49 /49	0.23	1.74
GI	Pioneer Fund R	PIORX	D	(800) 225-6292	C+ / 6.5	0.65	5.73	8.94 /69	13.76 /65	11.00 /53	0.54	1.34
GI	Pioneer Fund Y	PYODX	D+	(800) 225-6292	B- / 7.0	0.81	6.10	9.63 /73	14.51 /71	11.75 /59	1.12	0.63
GI	Pioneer Fund Z	PIOZX	D+	(800) 225-6292	C+ / 6.8	0.76	6.04	9.45 /72	14.30 /69	11.58 /58	1.00	0.85
GR	Pioneer Fundamental Growth A	PIGFX	A-	(800) 225-6292	B / 7.8	2.58	8.91	17.60 /95	16.03 /84	14.82 /85	0.23	1.13
GR	Pioneer Fundamental Growth C	FUNCX	A	(800) 225-6292	B+ / 8.3	2.42	8.56	16.81 /94	15.19 /76	13.96 /77	0.00	1.83
GR	Pioneer Fundamental Growth K	PFGKX	A+	(800) 225-6292	A- / 9.0	2.70	9.19	18.11 /96	16.39 /86	15.03 /87	0.60	0.71
GR	Pioneer Fundamental Growth R	PFGRX	A+	(800) 225-6292	B+ / 8.6	2.44	8.73	17.23 /95	15.69 /81	14.50 /82	0.00	1.39
GR	Pimeer Fundamental Growth Y	FUNYX	A+	(800) 225-6292	A- / 9.0	2.67	9.13	17.98 /95	16.37 /86	15.23 /88	0.51	0.82
GR	Pioneer Fundamental Growth Z	PFGZX	A+	(800) 225-6292	A- / 9.0	2.59	9.00	17.78 /95	16.27 /85	14.96 /87	0.43	0.99
GL	Pioneer Global Equity A	GLOSX	C+	(800) 225-6292	C+ / 5.6	2.74	3.32	8.92 /69	13.93 /67	9.75 /43	2.60	1.61
GL	Pioneer Global Equity C	GCSLX	C+	(800) 225-6292	C+ / 5.9	2.48	2.87	7.97 /63	12.90 /59	8.78 /35	2.24	2.40
GL	Pioneer Global Equity K	PGEKX	C+	(800) 225-6292	C+ / 6.6	2.81	3.39	9.00 /69	13.96 /67	9.77 /43	2.76	N/A
GL	Pioneer Global Equity Y	PGSYX	B-	(800) 225-6292	C+ / 6.9	2.73	3.50	9.41 /71	14.46 /71	10.28 /47	3.23	1.00
FO	Pioneer International Value A	PIIFX	D-	(800) 225-6292	D / 1.6	4.50	0.80	1.16 /19	7.34 /23	4.91 /12	5.40	1.69
FO	Pioneer International Value C	PCITX	D-	(800) 225-6292	D / 1.9	4.33	0.36	0.26 /16	6.39 /18	3.99 / 8	5.65	2.41
FO	Pioneer International Value Y	INVYX	D	(800) 225-6292	D+ / 2.6	4.60	0.96	1.55 /20	7.77 /26	5.34 /13	6.12	1.04
MC	Pioneer Mid Cap Value A	PCGRX	C+	(800) 225-6292	C+ / 6.6	1.71	8.40	10.88 /78	15.13 /76	12.20 /62	0.36	1.04
MC	Pioneer Mid Cap Value C	PCCGX	C+	(800) 225-6292	C+ / 6.9	1.49	7.95	9.96 /74	14.15 /68	11.25 /55	0.00	1.86
MC	Pioneer Mid Cap Value R	PCMRX	B-	(800) 225-6292	B- / 7.4	1.66	8.24	10.50 /76	14.73 /73	11.83 /59	0.05	1.43
MC	Pioneer Mid Cap Value Y	PYCGX	B	(800) 225-6292	B / 8.0	1.80	8.57	11.28 /80	15.55 /80	12.63 /65	0.65	0.67
GL	Pioneer Multi-Asset Income Fund A	PMAIX	C-	(800) 225-6292	D+ / 2.5	2.93	-0.24	1.26 /19	9.10 /34	--	5.71	1.40
GL	Pioneer Multi-Asset Income Fund C	PMACX	C-	(800) 225-6292	D+ / 2.5	2.64	-0.72	0.35 /17	8.13 /28	--	5.16	2.12
GL	Pioneer Multi-Asset Income Fund K	PMFKX	C-	(800) 225-6292	C- / 3.2	3.00	-0.11	1.38 /20	9.15 /34	--	6.10	N/A

● Denotes fund is closed to new investors

* Denotes fund is included in Section II

www.thestreetratings.com

RISK	3 Year		NET ASSETS		ASSET				Portfolio	BULL / BEAR		FUND MANAGER		MINIMUMS		LOADS	
Risk Rating/Pts	Standard Deviation	Beta	NAV As of 3/31/15	Total $(Mil)	Cash %	Stocks %	Bonds %	Other %	Turnover Ratio	Last Bull Market Return	Last Bear Market Return	Manager Quality Pct	Manager Tenure (Years)	Initial Purch. $	Additional Purch. $	Front End Load	Back End Load
U /	N/A	N/A	11.18	412	21	0	78	1	0	N/A	N/A	N/A	2	1,000,000	0	0.0	0.0
U /	N/A	N/A	9.29	1,904	33	0	66	1	394	N/A	N/A	N/A	1	1,000,000	0	0.0	0.0
B / 8.5	5.4	0.43	17.26	66	45	54	0	1	4	50.1	-7.7	90	12	2,500	100	0.0	1.0
C / 4.9	6.5	1.13	9.34	174	0	64	34	2	49	61.0	-12.1	49	10	1,000	100	4.5	0.0
C / 4.9	6.4	1.13	9.28	36	0	64	34	2	49	56.7	-12.4	37	10	1,000	500	0.0	0.0
C / 4.9	6.4	1.12	9.38	74	0	64	34	2	49	62.7	-11.9	55	10	5,000,000	0	0.0	0.0
B- / 7.1	10.0	1.03	17.25	1,574	0	99	0	1	67	87.5	-16.3	29	10	1,000	100	5.8	0.0
B- / 7.1	10.0	1.04	15.50	14	0	99	0	1	67	82.0	-16.7	19	10	1,000	500	0.0	0.0
B- / 7.2	10.0	1.03	17.42	66	0	99	0	1	67	89.3	-16.3	31	10	5,000,000	0	0.0	0.0
B- / 7.0	10.3	1.04	17.84	1,028	1	98	0	1	47	101.2	-17.6	50	5	1,000	100	5.8	0.0
C+ / 6.9	10.3	1.04	16.59	24	1	98	0	1	47	95.5	-17.9	36	5	1,000	500	0.0	0.0
B- / 7.0	10.3	1.04	18.14	10	1	98	0	1	47	103.6	-17.5	54	5	5,000,000	0	0.0	0.0
C- / 4.0	11.0	1.12	17.61	470	0	99	0	1	66	81.2	-18.5	12	4	1,000	100	5.8	0.0
C- / 3.9	11.0	1.11	17.37	193	0	99	0	1	66	76.3	-18.9	8	4	1,000	500	0.0	0.0
B- / 7.2	11.0	1.12	17.21	19	0	99	0	1	66	79.8	-18.6	10	10	0	0	0.0	0.0
C- / 4.0	11.0	1.11	17.67	204	0	99	0	1	66	83.5	-18.5	14	4	5,000,000	0	0.0	0.0
B- / 7.2	11.0	1.11	17.47	2	0	99	0	1	66	82.1	-18.5	13	10	0	0	0.0	0.0
D+ / 2.9	15.2	1.06	18.44	89	0	97	2	1	141	-5.5	-27.6	4	2	1,000	100	5.8	0.0
D+ / 2.7	15.2	1.06	15.33	16	0	97	2	1	141	-8.2	-27.9	3	2	1,000	500	0.0	0.0
D+ / 2.9	15.2	1.06	17.65	29	0	97	2	1	141	-6.3	-27.7	4	2	0	0	0.0	0.0
C- / 3.0	15.2	1.06	20.27	7	0	97	2	1	141	-3.7	-27.5	5	2	5,000,000	0	0.0	0.0
B- / 7.0	9.7	0.95	34.59	759	2	97	0	1	29	81.6	-14.4	62	25	1,000	100	5.8	0.0
B- / 7.0	9.7	0.95	34.13	123	2	97	0	1	29	77.2	-14.7	50	25	1,000	500	0.0	0.0
B- / 7.6	9.7	0.95	34.62	16	2	97	0	1	29	83.3	-14.4	66	25	5,000,000	0	0.0	0.0
B- / 7.0	9.7	0.95	35.04	77	2	97	0	1	29	79.8	-14.6	57	25	0	0	0.0	0.0
B- / 7.0	9.7	0.95	34.89	529	2	97	0	1	29	83.8	-14.3	67	25	5,000,000	0	0.0	0.0
B- / 7.0	9.7	0.95	34.64	1	2	97	0	1	29	82.9	-14.2	64	25	0	0	0.0	0.0
D+ / 2.5	10.3	1.07	36.85	4,712	0	99	0	1	7	84.9	-20.2	28	29	1,000	100	5.8	0.0
D / 2.1	10.3	1.07	34.12	160	0	99	0	1	7	80.0	-20.4	20	29	1,000	500	0.0	0.0
D+ / 2.5	10.3	1.07	36.98	63	0	99	0	1	7	82.8	-20.3	25	29	0	0	0.0	0.0
D+ / 2.5	10.3	1.07	37.12	290	0	99	0	1	7	86.9	-20.1	32	29	5,000,000	0	0.0	0.0
D+ / 2.5	10.3	1.07	36.98	1	0	99	0	1	7	85.8	-20.1	30	29	0	0	0.0	0.0
B- / 7.3	9.9	1.00	19.06	797	3	96	0	1	21	99.4	-11.3	67	8	1,000	100	5.8	0.0
B- / 7.3	9.9	1.00	17.81	246	3	96	0	1	21	94.4	-11.6	55	8	1,000	500	0.0	0.0
B- / 7.3	9.9	1.00	19.05	97	3	96	0	1	21	101.3	-11.3	70	8	5,000,000	0	0.0	0.0
B- / 7.3	9.9	1.00	18.86	37	3	96	0	1	21	97.5	-11.4	62	8	0	0	0.0	0.0
B- / 7.3	9.9	1.00	19.20	1,262	3	96	0	1	21	101.5	-11.1	69	8	5,000,000	0	0.0	0.0
B- / 7.3	9.9	1.00	19.03	4	3	96	0	1	21	100.7	-11.3	68	8	0	0	0.0	0.0
B- / 7.0	10.3	0.72	13.88	80	2	97	0	1	121	80.4	-21.3	96	5	1,000	100	5.8	0.0
B- / 7.0	10.4	0.72	13.62	13	2	97	0	1	121	75.0	-21.6	95	5	1,000	500	0.0	0.0
C+ / 5.7	10.3	0.72	13.89	59	2	97	0	1	121	80.6	-21.3	96	5	5,000,000	250	0.0	0.0
B- / 7.0	10.3	0.72	13.92	14	2	97	0	1	121	83.2	-21.1	96	5	5,000,000	0	0.0	0.0
C+ / 5.6	12.4	0.92	21.38	82	4	95	0	1	100	43.5	-22.1	49	7	1,000	100	5.8	0.0
C+ / 5.6	12.4	0.92	18.81	11	4	95	0	1	100	39.3	-22.4	35	7	1,000	500	0.0	0.0
C+ / 5.6	12.4	0.92	21.39	96	4	95	0	1	100	45.4	-21.9	54	7	5,000,000	0	0.0	0.0
C+ / 5.8	11.1	0.97	26.73	970	0	99	0	1	61	91.3	-22.9	49	10	1,000	100	5.8	0.0
C / 5.0	11.1	0.97	20.48	70	0	99	0	1	61	85.8	-23.2	37	10	1,000	500	0.0	0.0
C+ / 5.7	11.2	0.97	26.32	25	0	99	0	1	61	89.0	-23.1	44	10	0	0	0.0	0.0
C+ / 5.9	11.1	0.97	28.31	37	0	99	0	1	61	93.8	-22.8	55	10	5,000,000	0	0.0	0.0
B / 8.0	6.2	0.91	11.32	233	3	53	42	2	99	N/A	N/A	76	4	1,000	100	4.5	0.0
B / 8.0	6.2	0.91	11.28	313	3	53	42	2	99	N/A	N/A	67	4	1,000	500	0.0	0.0
C+ / 6.8	6.3	0.91	11.32	N/A	3	53	42	2	99	N/A	N/A	76	4	5,000,000	0	0.0	0.0

Fund Type	Fund Name	Ticker Symbol	Overall Investment Rating	Phone	Perfor-mance Rating/Pts	3 Mo	6 Mo	1Yr / Pct	3Yr / Pct	5Yr / Pct	Dividend Yield	Expense Ratio
								Total Return % through 3/31/15	Annualized		Incl. in Returns	
GL	Pioneer Multi-Asset Income Fund R	PMFRX	D+	(800) 225-6292	C- / 3.0	2.87	-0.33	1.03 /19	8.84 /32	--	5.74	N/A
GL	Pioneer Multi-Asset Income Fund Y	PMFYX	C	(800) 225-6292	C- / 3.2	2.98	-0.21	1.39 /20	9.23 /34	--	6.22	1.11
GI	Pioneer Multi-Asset Real Return A	PMARX	C-	(800) 225-6292	C- / 3.0	7.28	9.35	5.65 /44	8.07 /27	--	1.83	1.27
GI	Pioneer Multi-Asset Real Return C	PRRCX	C-	(800) 225-6292	C- / 3.1	6.99	8.86	4.78 /37	7.24 /23	--	1.23	2.01
GL	Pioneer Multi-Asset Real Return R	MUARX	C	(800) 225-6292	C- / 3.4	6.90	8.84	5.03 /39	7.69 /25	--	1.35	1.59
GI	Pioneer Multi-Asset Real Return Y	PMYRX	C-	(800) 225-6292	C- / 3.9	7.42	9.54	5.97 /46	8.38 /29	--	2.21	1.04
GL	Pioneer Multi-Asset Real Return Z	PMZYX	C	(800) 225-6292	C- / 3.5	7.00	9.17	5.01 /39	7.94 /32	--	1.54	1.67
RE	Pioneer Real Estate Shares A	PWREX	C+	(800) 225-6292	B+ / 8.5	5.11	20.02	23.88 /98	13.16 /61	15.29 /89	1.72	1.48
RE	Pioneer Real Estate Shares C	PCREX	C+	(800) 225-6292	B+ / 8.8	4.91	19.52	22.83 /98	12.22 /54	14.32 /81	1.08	2.32
RE	Pioneer Real Estate Shares Y	PYREX	B	(800) 225-6292	A / 9.4	5.22	20.23	24.41 /98	13.69 /65	15.87 /92	2.19	1.01
MC	Pioneer Sel Mid Cap Growth A	PGOFX	C+	(800) 225-6292	B / 8.0	6.08	11.10	13.35 /88	16.38 /86	14.99 /87	0.00	1.08
MC	Pioneer Sel Mid Cap Growth C	GOFCX	C+	(800) 225-6292	B+ / 8.4	5.86	10.65	12.46 /85	15.36 /78	13.96 /77	0.00	1.90
MC	Pioneer Sel Mid Cap Growth I	GROYX	B+	(800) 225-6292	A- / 9.2	6.15	11.26	13.73 /89	16.79 /89	15.45 /90	0.00	0.75
MC	Pioneer Sel Mid Cap Growth K	PSMKX	B+	(800) 225-6292	A- / 9.0	6.16	11.18	13.44 /88	16.41 /86	15.01 /87	0.00	N/A
AA	Pioneer Solutions Balanced A	PIALX	C-	(800) 225-6292	D / 2.1	2.18	2.76	4.58 /36	8.01 /27	7.44 /26	2.71	1.43
AA	Pioneer Solutions Balanced C	PIDCX	C-	(800) 225-6292	D+ / 2.5	1.91	2.38	3.88 /31	7.24 /23	6.70 /21	2.43	2.12
AA	Pioneer Solutions Balanced Y	IMOYX	C	(800) 225-6292	C- / 3.2	2.23	2.91	4.86 /38	8.31 /29	7.79 /29	3.09	1.19
AA	Pioneer Solutions Conservative A	PIAVX	D+	(800) 225-6292	D- / 1.2	1.55	1.92	3.49 /29	5.65 /15	5.68 /15	2.51	1.46
AA	Pioneer Solutions Conservative C	PICVX	C-	(800) 225-6292	D- / 1.4	1.42	1.50	2.76 /25	4.86 /13	4.90 /12	2.02	2.19
AA	Pioneer Solutions Conservative Y	IBBCX	D+	(800) 225-6292	D- / 1.5	1.73	2.08	3.17 /27	4.97 /13	5.24 /13	3.04	1.68
AA	Pioneer Solutions Growth A	GRAAX	C-	(800) 225-6292	D+ / 2.8	2.71	3.79	6.05 /47	9.17 /34	8.32 /32	3.00	1.51
AA	Pioneer Solutions Growth C	GRACX	C	(800) 225-6292	C- / 3.3	2.54	3.41	5.30 /41	8.43 /29	7.58 /27	2.24	2.20
AA	Pioneer Solutions Growth Y	IBGYX	C+	(800) 225-6292	C- / 3.9	2.81	3.96	6.26 /49	9.44 /36	8.40 /32	3.50	1.23
BA	Plumb Balanced Fund	PLBBX	C	(866) 987-7888	C- / 4.0	1.29	4.90	9.65 /73	9.15 /34	8.60 /34	1.02	1.60
GR	Plumb Equity Fund	PLBEX	C+	(866) 987-7888	C+ / 5.8	1.42	7.38	13.76 /89	11.51 /49	9.89 /44	0.15	1.69
GL	PMC Diversified Equity	PMDEX	C+	(866) 762-7338	C+ / 5.9	2.30	5.32	7.10 /56	12.85 /59	11.57 /58	0.47	1.61
BA	PNC Balanced Allocation A	PBAAX	C	(800) 551-2145	C- / 3.0	2.45	4.79	6.52 /51	8.96 /33	8.96 /36	1.16	1.50
BA	PNC Balanced Allocation C	PBCCX	C	(800) 551-2145	C- / 3.2	2.26	4.45	5.81 /45	8.20 /28	8.15 /31	0.73	2.21
BA	PNC Balanced Allocation I	PBLIX	C+	(800) 551-2145	C- / 3.9	2.54	4.95	6.74 /53	9.24 /35	9.22 /38	1.48	1.21
FO	PNC International Equity A	PMIEX	C-	(800) 551-2145	C- / 4.0	6.55	4.46	-1.29 /12	11.84 /51	8.69 /35	1.03	1.33
FO	PNC International Equity C	PIUCX	C-	(800) 551-2145	C / 4.4	6.41	4.20	-1.87 /11	11.10 /46	7.92 /29	0.67	2.03
FO	PNC International Equity I	PIUIX	C	(800) 551-2145	C / 5.0	6.61	4.70	-0.97 /13	12.18 /54	8.99 /37	1.33	1.03
GR	PNC Large Cap Core A	PLEAX	A	(800) 551-2145	B / 8.0	4.42	10.90	19.35 /96	14.96 /75	14.29 /80	0.52	1.44
GR	PNC Large Cap Core C	PLECX	A	(800) 551-2145	B+ / 8.4	4.23	10.52	18.47 /96	14.11 /68	13.43 /72	0.05	2.16
GR	PNC Large Cap Core I	PLEIX	A+	(800) 551-2145	A- / 9.0	4.51	11.08	19.51 /96	15.23 /77	14.57 /83	0.76	1.16
GR	PNC Large Cap Growth A	PEWAX	A+	(800) 551-2145	A / 9.3	5.47	13.45	22.83 /98	16.61 /88	15.90 /92	0.14	1.41
GR	PNC Large Cap Growth C	PEWCX	A+	(800) 551-2145	A / 9.5	5.32	13.14	22.40 /97	15.92 /83	15.15 /88	0.00	2.11
GR	PNC Large Cap Growth I	PEWIX	A+	(800) 551-2145	A+ / 9.7	5.59	13.66	22.97 /98	16.87 /89	16.17 /94	0.37	1.11
GR	PNC Large Cap Value A	PLVAX	B-	(800) 551-2145	C+ / 6.5	1.31	6.41	10.22 /75	15.20 /76	12.49 /64	0.81	1.30
GR	PNC Large Cap Value C	PALVX	B+	(800) 551-2145	B- / 7.0	1.24	6.20	9.78 /73	14.52 /71	11.73 /59	0.33	2.00
GR	PNC Large Cap Value I	PLIVX	A-	(800) 551-2145	B / 7.7	1.35	6.60	10.40 /76	15.52 /79	12.77 /66	1.18	1.00
MC	PNC Mid Cap A	PMCAX	C+	(800) 551-2145	C+ / 6.4	2.87	9.94	7.22 /57	14.94 /74	11.32 /55	0.00	2.02
MC	PNC Mid Cap C	PMFCX	C+	(800) 551-2145	C+ / 6.8	2.66	9.61	6.39 /50	14.11 /68	10.47 /48	0.00	2.74
MC	PNC Mid Cap I	PMVIX	B+	(800) 551-2145	B / 7.6	2.95	10.10	7.27 /57	15.22 /77	11.55 /57	0.00	1.74
SC	PNC Multi-Factor Small Cap Core A	PLOAX	A+	(800) 551-2145	A+ / 9.8	3.95	14.65	13.56 /88	22.34 /98	19.63 /99	0.08	1.54
SC	PNC Multi-Factor Small Cap Core I	PLOIX	A+	(800) 551-2145	A+ / 9.8	4.02	14.81	13.84 /89	22.66 /98	19.94 /99	0.20	1.26
SC	PNC Multi-Factor Small Cap Growth	PLWAX	A	(800) 551-2145	A+ / 9.6	7.19	16.87	13.75 /89	19.74 /98	19.21 /98	0.00	1.94
SC	PNC Multi-Factor Small Cap Growth	PLWCX	A	(800) 551-2145	A+ / 9.7	6.92	16.47	12.90 /86	18.88 /96	18.34 /98	0.00	2.66
SC	PNC Multi-Factor Small Cap Growth I	PLTIX	A+	(800) 551-2145	A+ / 9.8	7.23	17.02	13.89 /89	20.05 /98	19.51 /99	0.00	1.66
SC	PNC Multi-Factor Small Cap Value A	PMRRX	A	(800) 551-2145	A- / 9.0	5.08	13.93	12.90 /86	18.04 /94	15.69 /91	0.66	1.86
SC	PNC Multi-Factor Small Cap Value C	PSVCX	A+	(800) 551-2145	A / 9.3	5.08	13.68	12.32 /84	17.28 /91	14.89 /86	0.19	2.58
SC	PNC Multi-Factor Small Cap Value I	PMUIX	A+	(800) 551-2145	A+ / 9.6	5.13	14.06	12.94 /86	18.29 /95	15.95 /93	0.87	1.58

99 Pct = Best
0 Pct = Worst

● Denotes fund is closed to new investors
* Denotes fund is included in Section II

www.thestreetratings.com

RISK			NET ASSETS		ASSET				BULL / BEAR		FUND MANAGER		MINIMUMS		LOADS	
	3 Year		NAV						Last Bull	Last Bear	Manager	Manager	Initial	Additional	Front	Back
Risk Rating/Pts	Standard Deviation	Beta	As of 3/31/15	Total $(Mil)	Cash %	Stocks %	Bonds %	Other %	Portfolio Turnover Ratio	Market Return	Market Return	Quality Pct	Tenure (Years)	Purch. $	Purch. $	End Load	End Load
C+ / 6.8	6.2	0.91	11.32	N/A	3	53	42	2	99	N/A	N/A	74	4	0	0	0.0	0.0
B / 8.0	6.2	0.91	11.30	302	3	53	42	2	99	N/A	N/A	77	4	5,000,000	0	0.0	0.0
C+ / 6.9	8.9	0.66	13.17	198	12	66	20	2	383	36.1	-5.7	35	5	1,000	100	4.5	0.0
C+ / 6.9	8.9	0.66	13.01	214	12	66	20	2	383	32.7	-6.0	26	5	1,000	500	0.0	0.0
B- / 7.7	8.9	1.21	13.16	N/A	12	66	20	2	383	34.9	-5.8	25	5	0	0	0.0	0.0
C+ / 6.9	9.0	0.66	13.21	333	12	66	20	2	383	37.5	-5.6	39	5	5,000,000	0	0.0	0.0
B- / 7.7	9.1	1.24	13.14	N/A	12	66	20	2	383	36.1	-5.7	25	5	0	0	0.0	0.0
C- / 4.0	13.1	1.04	30.97	112	2	97	0	1	17	79.3	-15.7	47	11	1,000	100	5.8	0.0
C- / 4.0	13.0	1.04	30.52	15	2	97	0	1	17	74.2	-16.0	35	11	1,000	500	0.0	0.0
C- / 4.0	13.0	1.04	30.93	52	2	97	0	1	17	82.2	-15.4	54	11	5,000,000	0	0.0	0.0
C / 4.8	12.2	1.01	39.25	1,078	1	98	0	1	105	101.1	-21.0	56	6	1,000	100	5.8	0.0
C- / 4.1	12.2	1.01	31.25	77	1	98	0	1	105	95.0	-21.3	42	6	1,000	500	0.0	0.0
C / 4.9	12.2	1.02	41.58	136	1	98	0	1	105	103.7	-20.9	61	6	5,000,000	0	0.0	0.0
C / 5.2	12.2	1.01	39.28	14	1	98	0	1	105	101.2	-21.0	57	6	5,000,000	0	0.0	0.0
B / 8.3	6.6	1.11	12.67	143	5	52	41	2	10	44.9	-13.4	18	11	1,000	100	5.8	0.0
B / 8.3	6.6	1.11	11.76	78	5	52	41	2	10	41.4	-13.5	13	11	1,000	500	0.0	0.0
B / 8.3	6.6	1.11	12.82	3	5	52	41	2	10	46.4	-13.3	20	11	5,000,000	0	0.0	0.0
B / 8.4	3.9	0.64	11.76	51	6	21	70	3	12	28.8	-7.5	50	N/A	1,000	100	5.8	0.0
B / 8.5	3.9	0.63	11.42	23	6	21	70	3	12	25.7	-7.8	40	N/A	1,000	500	0.0	0.0
B / 8.3	3.9	0.61	11.18	N/A	6	21	70	3	12	26.5	-8.0	44	N/A	5,000,000	0	0.0	0.0
B- / 7.9	7.9	1.34	13.64	276	9	74	16	1	8	53.9	-16.1	10	11	1,000	100	5.8	0.0
B- / 7.9	8.0	1.34	12.92	92	9	74	16	1	8	50.2	-16.3	7	11	1,000	500	0.0	0.0
B- / 7.9	7.9	1.34	13.90	1	9	74	16	1	8	55.1	-16.9	11	11	5,000,000	0	0.0	0.0
B- / 7.5	7.7	1.30	22.75	35	4	63	32	1	46	53.8	-13.1	12	8	2,500	100	0.0	0.0
C+ / 6.3	10.9	1.10	24.26	24	2	97	0	1	52	72.3	-18.8	8	8	2,500	100	0.0	0.0
C+ / 6.5	10.3	0.68	24.94	295	3	96	0	1	30	79.3	-20.8	95	6	1,000	50	0.0	0.0
B / 8.2	6.3	1.08	13.78	10	5	58	35	2	55	53.0	-12.4	30	1	1,000	50	4.8	0.0
B / 8.2	6.3	1.08	13.59	1	5	58	35	2	55	49.0	-12.6	23	1	1,000	50	0.0	0.0
B / 8.2	6.3	1.08	13.74	54	5	58	35	2	55	54.0	-12.3	34	1	0	0	0.0	0.0
C+ / 6.0	12.6	0.91	19.86	17	4	95	0	1	31	67.5	-25.4	88	18	1,000	50	5.5	0.0
C+ / 6.0	12.6	0.91	19.09	2	4	95	0	1	31	63.4	-25.6	86	18	1,000	50	0.0	0.0
C+ / 6.0	12.6	0.91	20.00	586	4	95	0	1	31	68.9	-25.3	89	18	0	0	0.0	0.0
B- / 7.3	10.1	1.03	17.02	3	1	98	0	1	69	89.9	-15.3	45	6	1,000	50	5.5	0.0
B- / 7.3	10.1	1.03	15.76	N/A	1	98	0	1	69	85.2	-15.6	34	6	1,000	50	0.0	0.0
B- / 7.3	10.1	1.03	17.38	22	1	98	0	1	69	91.2	-15.2	48	6	0	0	0.0	0.0
B- / 7.0	10.9	1.07	28.93	16	2	97	0	1	70	102.1	-15.4	57	6	1,000	50	5.5	0.0
B- / 7.0	10.9	1.07	26.34	1	2	97	0	1	70	97.7	-15.6	49	6	1,000	50	0.0	0.0
B- / 7.0	10.9	1.07	29.47	82	2	97	0	1	70	103.6	-15.3	62	6	0	0	0.0	0.0
B- / 7.5	10.1	1.02	21.68	25	0	99	0	1	57	91.8	-17.5	51	2	1,000	50	5.5	0.0
B- / 7.5	10.1	1.02	21.31	N/A	0	99	0	1	57	87.5	-17.8	41	2	1,000	50	0.0	0.0
B- / 7.5	10.1	1.02	21.73	90	0	99	0	1	57	93.3	-17.5	55	2	0	0	0.0	0.0
C+ / 6.8	12.4	1.02	19.02	9	3	96	0	1	25	83.2	-22.7	37	2	1,000	50	5.5	0.0
C+ / 6.8	12.4	1.01	18.14	1	3	96	0	1	25	78.2	-22.9	28	2	1,000	50	0.0	0.0
C+ / 6.8	12.4	1.01	19.18	2	3	96	0	1	25	84.0	-22.6	40	2	0	0	0.0	0.0
C+ / 6.4	13.5	0.97	21.34	53	2	97	0	1	102	124.6	-19.9	94	10	1,000	50	5.5	0.0
C+ / 6.4	13.5	0.97	21.47	55	2	97	0	1	102	126.6	-19.8	95	10	0	0	0.0	0.0
C+ / 6.0	13.4	0.97	20.58	23	1	98	0	1	85	105.8	-20.0	90	10	1,000	50	5.5	0.0
C+ / 5.9	13.4	0.97	20.23	1	1	98	0	1	85	100.6	-20.2	88	10	1,000	50	0.0	0.0
C+ / 6.0	13.4	0.97	20.90	16	1	98	0	1	85	107.3	-19.9	91	10	0	0	0.0	0.0
C+ / 6.6	13.0	0.93	19.87	14	6	93	0	1	109	96.0	-19.6	87	10	1,000	50	5.5	0.0
C+ / 6.6	13.0	0.93	17.80	1	6	93	0	1	109	91.5	-19.9	83	10	1,000	50	0.0	0.0
C+ / 6.6	13.1	0.94	21.53	13	6	93	0	1	109	97.2	-19.5	88	10	0	0	0.0	0.0

Fund Type	Fund Name	Ticker Symbol	Overall Investment Rating	Phone	PERFORMANCE Performance Rating/Pts	Total Return % through 3/31/15 3 Mo	6 Mo	1Yr / Pct	Annualized 3Yr / Pct	5Yr / Pct	Incl. in Returns Dividend Yield	Expense Ratio
IX	PNC S&P 500 Index A	PIIAX	B+	(800) 551-2145	B- / 7.4	0.87	5.70	12.31 /84	15.56 /80	13.90 /77	1.46	0.52
IX	PNC S&P 500 Index C	PPICX	B+	(800) 551-2145	B- / 7.2	0.68	5.29	11.38 /80	14.70 /73	13.04 /69	0.75	1.27
IX	PNC S&P 500 Index I	PSXIX	A	(800) 551-2145	B / 8.1	0.92	5.80	12.52 /85	15.83 /82	14.17 /79	1.72	0.27
GR	PNC S&P 500 Index R4	PSPEX	B	(800) 551-2145	B / 8.1	0.92	5.77	12.49 /85	15.82 /82	14.16 /79	1.69	0.42
GR	PNC S&P 500 Index R5	PSFFX	B	(800) 551-2145	B / 8.1	0.92	5.81	12.52 /85	15.83 /82	14.17 /79	1.72	0.32
SC	PNC Small Cap A	PPCAX	A+	(800) 551-2145	A / 9.3	6.34	17.32	9.74 /73	18.89 /96	17.68 /97	0.00	1.48
SC	PNC Small Cap C	PPCCX	A+	(800) 551-2145	A / 9.5	6.18	16.92	8.99 /69	18.06 /94	16.85 /96	0.00	2.18
SC	PNC Small Cap I	PPCIX	A+	(800) 551-2145	A+ / 9.7	6.40	17.52	10.06 /75	19.23 /97	18.01 /97	0.07	1.18
GL	Polaris Global Value	PGVFX	B+	(888) 263-5594	B / 7.8	5.17	7.68	4.43 /35	16.27 /85	13.53 /73	1.35	1.32
GR	Polen Growth Inst	POLIX	B	(888) 678-6024	B- / 7.4	3.41	13.62	19.90 /97	12.30 /55	--	0.09	1.27
GR	Polen Growth Retail	POLRX	B-	(888) 678-6024	B- / 7.1	3.38	13.49	19.59 /96	12.02 /53	--	0.00	1.52
GR	Poplar Forest Partners Fund A	PFPFX	B-	(888) 263-6443	B- / 7.0	-0.64	-0.23	4.78 /37	17.56 /93	13.02 /68	0.32	1.40
GR	Poplar Forest Partners Fund Inst	IPFPX	B+	(888) 263-6443	B / 8.2	-0.59	-0.10	5.06 /39	17.86 /94	13.31 /71	0.54	1.15
GL	Portfolio 21 Global Equity Retail	PORTX	D+	(877) 351-4115	C- / 4.0	3.93	4.81	2.82 /26	9.80 /38	7.59 /27	0.74	1.37
GL	Portfolio 21 Global Equity Inst	PORIX	D+	(877) 351-4115	C- / 4.1	4.00	4.96	3.11 /27	10.11 /40	7.91 /29	1.18	1.07
IN	Power Dividend Index A	PWDAX	U	(877) 779-7462	U /	-1.92	-0.32	7.15 /56	--	--	2.30	1.76
IN	Power Dividend Index I	PWDIX	U	(877) 779-7462	U /	-1.87	-0.22	7.36 /58	--	--	2.62	1.51
BA	Praxis Genesis Balanced A	MBAPX	C-	(800) 977-2947	D / 2.1	1.66	3.95	6.00 /46	8.18 /28	7.93 /29	1.21	1.21
GI	Praxis Genesis Conservative A	MCONX	C-	(800) 977-2947	D- / 1.1	1.37	3.13	5.63 /43	5.52 /15	5.89 /16	1.66	1.20
GR	Praxis Genesis Growth A	MGAFX	C-	(800) 977-2947	D+ / 2.9	1.81	4.44	6.13 /48	9.82 /38	9.17 /38	0.86	1.30
GR	Praxis Growth Index Fund A	MGNDX	B+	(800) 977-2947	B- / 7.0	1.86	6.82	15.54 /93	15.79 /82	14.57 /83	0.58	1.01
GR	Praxis Growth Index Fund I	MMDEX	A+	(800) 977-2947	B+ / 8.5	1.96	7.00	16.04 /93	16.36 /86	15.17 /88	1.06	0.47
FO	Praxis International Index Fd A	MPLAX	E+	(800) 977-2947	E+ / 0.9	3.86	-0.66	-1.60 /11	5.37 /14	--	1.71	1.43
FO	Praxis International Index Fd I	MPLIX	D-	(800) 977-2947	D- / 1.4	4.04	-0.42	-1.16 /12	6.02 /17	--	2.31	0.80
SC	Praxis Small Cap Fund A	MMSCX	E	(800) 977-2947	D+ / 2.8	4.18	12.17	1.22 /19	9.28 /35	13.65 /74	0.00	1.90
SC	Praxis Small Cap Fund I	MMSIX	E+	(800) 977-2947	C- / 4.1	4.33	12.54	1.83 /21	10.05 /40	14.37 /81	0.00	1.04
GR	Praxis Value Index A	MVIAX	B-	(800) 977-2947	C+ / 5.7	-0.96	3.29	8.59 /67	15.06 /75	11.73 /59	0.61	1.03
GR	Praxis Value Index I	MVIIX	B+	(800) 977-2947	B- / 7.0	-0.88	3.48	9.00 /69	15.70 /81	12.45 /64	1.07	0.48
AA	Presidential Managed Risk 2010 A	PZAAX	C-	(800) 234-3500	D- / 1.1	1.41	2.36	3.80 /31	5.21 /14	--	1.10	2.26
AA	Presidential Managed Risk 2010 C	PZACX	C	(800) 234-3500	D- / 1.5	1.32	2.21	3.46 /29	4.94 /13	--	0.93	2.51
AA	Presidential Managed Risk 2010 I	PZAIX	C	(800) 234-3500	D / 1.7	1.41	2.44	3.97 /32	5.44 /15	--	1.41	2.01
GI	Presidential Managed Risk 2020 A	PZBAX	C-	(800) 234-3500	D- / 1.3	1.61	2.71	4.21 /33	6.04 /17	--	1.18	2.09
GI	Presidential Managed Risk 2020 C	PZBCX	C	(800) 234-3500	D / 1.8	1.53	2.64	3.96 /32	5.76 /16	--	1.01	2.34
GI	Presidential Managed Risk 2020 I	PZBIX	C	(800) 234-3500	D / 2.1	1.70	2.88	4.47 /35	6.30 /18	--	1.50	1.84
GI	Presidential Managed Risk 2030 A	PZCAX	C-	(800) 234-3500	D- / 1.2	1.47	2.22	3.53 /29	5.89 /16	--	1.32	2.46
GI	Presidential Managed Risk 2030 C	PZCCX	C-	(800) 234-3500	D / 1.7	1.47	2.15	3.28 /28	5.61 /15	--	1.16	2.71
GI	Presidential Managed Risk 2030 I	PZCIX	C	(800) 234-3500	D / 1.9	1.56	2.39	3.79 /30	6.15 /17	--	1.65	2.21
GI	Presidential Managed Risk 2040 A	PZDAX	D	(800) 234-3500	D- / 1.4	1.65	2.26	3.62 /30	6.53 /19	--	1.18	2.83
GI	Presidential Managed Risk 2040 C	PZDCX	D+	(800) 234-3500	D / 2.0	1.65	2.17	3.36 /28	6.28 /18	--	1.00	3.08
GI	Presidential Managed Risk 2040 I	PZDIX	C-	(800) 234-3500	D+ / 2.3	1.73	2.42	3.87 /31	6.82 /20	--	1.49	2.58
GI	Presidential Managed Risk 2050 A	PZEAX	D+	(800) 234-3500	D / 1.6	2.30	2.36	3.88 /31	6.94 /21	--	1.20	3.72
GI	Presidential Managed Risk 2050 C	PZECX	C-	(800) 234-3500	D / 2.2	2.31	2.28	3.63 /30	6.67 /20	--	1.03	3.97
GI	Presidential Managed Risk 2050 I	PZEIX	C-	(800) 234-3500	D+ / 2.5	2.39	2.54	4.14 /33	7.21 /22	--	1.52	3.47
GI	Primary Trend Fund	PTFDX	E+	(800) 443-6544	D- / 1.1	-0.58	-5.34	-3.15 / 8	5.41 /15	5.54 /14	0.00	1.92
* AG ●	PRIMECAP Odyssey Agg Growth Fd	POAGX	A	(800) 729-2307	A+ / 9.9	5.92	14.71	17.96 /95	26.39 /99	20.62 /99	0.16	0.63
* MC	PRIMECAP Odyssey Growth Fd	POGRX	A+	(800) 729-2307	A+ / 9.7	3.53	9.41	13.10 /87	19.63 /97	15.20 /88	0.59	0.63
GR	PRIMECAP Odyssey Stock Fd	POSKX	A+	(800) 729-2307	A / 9.4	2.49	7.54	13.56 /88	18.33 /95	14.44 /82	1.26	0.63
IN	Princeton Futures Strategy A	PFFAX	D-	(888) 868-9501	E+ / 0.8	2.40	4.55	16.01 /93	0.29 / 4	--	0.00	2.53
AA	Princeton Futures Strategy C	PFFTX	D-	(888) 868-9501	E+ / 0.7	2.24	4.10	15.10 /92	-0.46 / 4	--	0.00	3.28
IN	Princeton Futures Strategy I	PFFNX	D-	(888) 868-9501	D- / 1.2	2.48	4.62	16.24 /94	0.54 / 5	--	0.00	2.28
GR	Principal Blue Chip Inst	PBCKX	U	(800) 222-5852	U /	2.83	8.61	12.63 /85	--	--	0.55	0.72
GR	Principal Cap Appreciation Fd A	CMNWX	B+	(800) 222-5852	B- / 7.1	2.03	7.52	12.35 /84	15.67 /81	13.46 /72	0.82	0.82

99 Pct = Best
0 Pct = Worst

RISK			NET ASSETS		ASSET					BULL / BEAR		FUND MANAGER		MINIMUMS		LOADS	
	3 Year		NAV						Portfolio	Last Bull	Last Bear	Manager	Manager	Initial	Additional	Front	Back
Risk Rating/Pts	Standard Deviation	Beta	As of 3/31/15	Total $(Mil)	Cash %	Stocks %	Bonds %	Other %	Turnover Ratio	Market Return	Market Return	Quality Pct	Tenure (Years)	Purch. $	Purch. $	End Load	End Load
B- /7.3	9.6	1.00	16.32	21	1	98	0	1	18	96.8	-16.5	60	N/A	1,000	50	2.5	0.0
B- /7.2	9.6	1.00	16.17	8	1	98	0	1	18	91.8	-16.6	48	N/A	1,000	50	0.0	0.0
B- /7.3	9.5	0.99	16.39	168	1	98	0	1	18	98.5	-16.4	65	N/A	0	0	0.0	0.0
C+ /5.8	9.5	0.99	16.39	3	1	98	0	1	18	98.4	-16.4	65	N/A	0	0	0.0	0.0
C+ /5.8	9.5	0.99	16.39	N/A	1	98	0	1	18	98.5	-16.4	65	N/A	0	0	0.0	0.0
C+ /6.8	12.6	0.88	21.81	65	4	95	0	1	24	119.2	-21.0	92	11	1,000	50	5.5	0.0
C+ /6.7	12.6	0.88	20.11	21	4	95	0	1	24	113.7	-21.2	90	11	1,000	50	0.0	0.0
C+ /6.8	12.6	0.88	22.43	508	4	95	0	1	24	121.1	-20.9	92	11	0	0	0.0	0.0
B- /7.0	11.6	0.78	22.19	313	0	99	0	1	14	95.7	-22.5	97	26	2,500	250	0.0	1.0
C+ /6.2	10.3	0.90	18.20	377	4	95	0	1	40	81.7	-8.8	39	5	100,000	0	0.0	2.0
C+ /6.1	10.3	0.90	18.05	30	4	95	0	1	40	80.1	-8.9	35	5	3,000	100	0.0	2.0
C+ /6.3	13.1	1.22	43.81	218	4	95	0	1	23	110.6	-21.7	37	6	25,000	1,000	5.0	0.0
C+ /6.2	13.1	1.22	43.98	370	4	95	0	1	23	112.5	-21.6	41	6	1,000,000	1,000	0.0	0.0
C /5.2	10.8	0.77	37.56	287	0	99	0	1	40	55.0	-19.5	86	16	5,000	100	0.0	0.0
C /5.1	10.8	0.77	37.47	167	0	99	0	1	40	56.7	-19.5	87	16	100,000	1,000	0.0	0.0
U /	N/A	N/A	10.89	97	1	98	0	1	22	N/A	N/A	N/A	N/A	1,000	100	5.0	1.0
U /	N/A	N/A	10.89	243	1	98	0	1	22	N/A	N/A	N/A	N/A	100,000	0	0.0	1.0
B /8.7	5.9	1.02	12.96	60	0	60	39	1	20	44.7	-10.9	28	N/A	1,000	50	5.3	2.0
B+ /9.4	3.3	0.28	11.47	20	0	30	69	1	26	26.3	-3.8	79	N/A	1,000	50	5.3	2.0
B- /7.7	8.0	0.81	14.04	51	0	79	20	1	21	57.7	-15.4	28	N/A	1,000	50	5.3	2.0
B- /7.2	9.4	0.97	17.57	57	0	99	0	1	15	100.1	-13.8	70	8	2,500	100	5.3	2.0
B- /7.2	9.4	0.96	17.68	122	0	99	0	1	15	103.5	-13.5	75	8	100,000	0	0.0	2.0
C+ /5.8	12.8	0.96	10.23	19	0	99	0	1	11	39.0	-25.3	20	4	2,500	100	5.3	2.0
C+ /5.8	12.8	0.96	10.29	161	0	99	0	1	11	42.2	-25.3	27	4	100,000	0	0.0	2.0
D+ /2.5	13.9	0.99	11.97	8	0	99	0	1	49	65.3	-19.6	6	8	2,500	100	5.3	2.0
D+ /2.7	13.9	1.00	12.53	55	0	99	0	1	49	69.2	-19.5	8	8	100,000	0	0.0	2.0
B- /7.3	10.0	1.01	12.42	17	0	99	0	1	30	91.2	-19.5	50	14	2,500	100	5.3	2.0
B- /7.3	10.1	1.02	12.35	111	0	99	0	1	30	95.1	-19.2	57	14	100,000	0	0.0	2.0
B+ /9.6	4.7	0.77	11.54	18	2	46	50	2	48	N/A	N/A	27	4	1,000	0	5.8	0.0
B+ /9.6	4.6	0.76	11.52	N/A	2	46	50	2	48	N/A	N/A	24	4	1,000	0	0.0	0.0
B+ /9.6	4.7	0.77	11.54	N/A	2	46	50	2	48	N/A	N/A	29	4	0	0	0.0	0.0
B+ /9.4	5.2	0.49	11.96	21	3	57	38	2	38	N/A	N/A	45	4	1,000	0	5.8	0.0
B+ /9.4	5.2	0.50	11.95	N/A	3	57	38	2	38	N/A	N/A	39	4	1,000	0	0.0	0.0
B+ /9.4	5.3	0.50	11.97	1	3	57	38	2	38	N/A	N/A	47	4	0	0	0.0	0.0
B+ /9.2	5.9	0.57	11.72	10	4	63	31	2	32	N/A	N/A	27	4	1,000	0	5.8	0.0
B+ /9.2	5.9	0.57	11.71	N/A	4	63	31	2	32	N/A	N/A	24	4	1,000	0	0.0	0.0
B+ /9.2	5.9	0.57	11.73	N/A	4	63	31	2	32	N/A	N/A	30	4	0	0	0.0	0.0
B- /7.6	6.7	0.65	12.33	6	5	73	20	2	22	N/A	N/A	21	4	1,000	0	5.8	0.0
B- /7.5	6.7	0.65	12.32	N/A	5	73	20	2	22	N/A	N/A	19	4	1,000	0	0.0	0.0
B- /7.7	6.6	0.65	12.34	3	5	73	20	2	22	N/A	N/A	24	4	0	0	0.0	0.0
B- /7.8	7.4	0.71	12.43	2	8	84	7	1	18	N/A	N/A	16	4	1,000	0	5.8	0.0
B- /7.8	7.4	0.71	12.42	N/A	8	84	7	1	18	N/A	N/A	15	4	1,000	0	0.0	0.0
B- /7.8	7.4	0.71	12.44	3	8	84	7	1	18	N/A	N/A	18	4	0	0	0.0	0.0
C+ /5.8	9.2	0.81	12.00	11	6	93	0	1	14	43.3	-13.4	5	26	500	100	0.0	0.0
C+ /5.6	14.3	1.15	34.88	6,831	3	96	0	1	13	154.7	-20.5	95	11	2,000	150	0.0	0.0
C+ /6.7	11.4	0.91	26.98	5,528	6	92	0	2	10	110.2	-20.1	91	11	2,000	150	0.0	0.0
B- /7.7	8.7	0.88	24.25	4,276	10	89	0	1	8	101.3	-16.0	91	11	2,000	150	0.0	0.0
C+ /6.4	7.7	N/A	9.39	16	60	0	39	1	24	-6.6	-7.4	70	N/A	2,500	100	5.8	0.0
C+ /6.2	7.6	0.05	9.12	7	60	0	39	1	24	-9.0	N/A	52	N/A	2,500	100	0.0	0.0
C+ /6.5	7.7	0.01	9.49	61	60	0	39	1	24	-5.9	-7.3	72	N/A	100,000	100	0.0	0.0
U /	N/A	N/A	15.65	910	0	99	0	1	34	N/A	N/A	N/A	3	0	0	0.0	0.0
B- /7.1	9.7	1.00	58.68	844	2	97	0	1	8	95.0	-17.6	61	13	1,000	100	5.5	0.0

99 Pct = Best
0 Pct = Worst

Fund Type	Fund Name	Ticker Symbol	Overall Investment Rating	Phone	Perfor-mance Rating/Pts	3 Mo	6 Mo	1Yr / Pct	3Yr / Pct	5Yr / Pct	Dividend Yield	Expense Ratio
GR	Principal Cap Appreciation Fd C	CMNCX	B+	(800) 222-5852	B- / 7.4	1.83	7.07	11.38 /80	14.68 /72	12.48 /64	0.39	1.67
GR	Principal Cap Appreciation Fd Inst	PWCIX	A	(800) 222-5852	B+ / 8.5	2.13	7.72	12.75 /86	16.14 /84	13.94 /77	1.18	0.46
GR	Principal Cap Appreciation Fd P	PCFPX	A	(800) 222-5852	B+ / 8.3	2.10	7.69	12.61 /85	15.95 /83	13.70 /75	1.07	0.60
GR	Principal Cap Appreciation Fd R1	PCAMX	B+	(800) 222-5852	B / 7.7	1.91	7.24	11.76 /82	15.12 /76	12.95 /68	0.39	1.34
GR	Principal Cap Appreciation Fd R2	PCANX	A-	(800) 222-5852	B / 7.8	1.94	7.32	11.91 /82	15.27 /77	13.09 /69	0.47	1.21
GR	Principal Cap Appreciation Fd R3	PCAOX	A-	(800) 222-5852	B / 8.0	1.98	7.40	12.10 /83	15.48 /79	13.30 /71	0.72	1.03
GR	Principal Cap Appreciation Fd R4	PCAPX	A	(800) 222-5852	B / 8.2	2.04	7.52	12.32 /84	15.70 /81	13.51 /73	0.86	0.84
GR	Principal Cap Appreciation Fd R5	PCAQX	A	(800) 222-5852	B+ / 8.3	2.07	7.59	12.46 /85	15.85 /82	13.65 /74	0.94	0.72
FO	Principal Divers Intl A	PRWLX	D	(800) 222-5852	D / 1.8	4.11	0.82	-0.02 /15	8.02 /27	6.56 /20	0.98	1.33
FO	Principal Divers Intl C	PDNCX	D	(800) 222-5852	D / 2.2	3.92	0.42	-0.75 /14	7.27 /23	5.85 /16	0.25	2.22
FO	Principal Divers Intl Inst	PIIIX	D+	(800) 222-5852	C- / 3.0	4.22	0.99	0.48 /17	8.60 /30	7.12 /24	1.54	0.85
FO	Principal Divers Intl J	PIIJX	D	(800) 222-5852	D+ / 2.5	4.07	0.81	0.05 /16	8.10 /28	6.60 /21	1.12	1.27
FO	Principal Divers Intl P	PDIPX	D	(800) 222-5852	D+ / 2.8	4.14	0.88	0.20 /16	8.38 /29	6.85 /22	1.43	1.57
FO	Principal Divers Intl R1	PDVIX	D	(800) 222-5852	D+ / 2.4	3.94	0.59	-0.42 /14	7.63 /25	6.18 /18	0.57	1.73
FO	Principal Divers Intl R2	PINNX	D	(800) 222-5852	D+ / 2.5	3.96	0.59	-0.33 /15	7.78 /26	6.32 /19	0.74	1.60
FO	Principal Divers Intl R3	PINRX	D	(800) 222-5852	D+ / 2.6	4.13	0.77	-0.07 /15	7.97 /27	6.52 /20	0.91	1.42
FO	Principal Divers Intl R4	PINLX	D	(800) 222-5852	D+ / 2.7	4.07	0.80	0.06 /16	8.17 /28	6.72 /21	1.11	1.23
FO	Principal Divers Intl R5	PINPX	D	(800) 222-5852	D+ / 2.8	4.08	0.86	0.20 /16	8.29 /29	6.85 /22	1.25	1.11
GI	Principal Diversified Real Ast A	PRDAX	D	(800) 222-5852	E+ / 0.6	-0.41	-3.57	-1.87 /11	3.37 / 9	5.98 /17	0.66	1.27
GI	Principal Diversified Real Ast C	PRDCX	D	(800) 222-5852	E+ / 0.7	-0.59	-3.91	-2.58 / 9	2.59 / 7	5.20 /13	0.00	2.04
GI	Principal Diversified Real Ast Inst	PDRDX	D	(800) 222-5852	E+ / 0.8	-0.33	-3.37	-1.51 /11	3.77 /10	6.38 /19	1.06	0.86
AA	Principal Diversified Real Ast P	PRDPX	D	(800) 222-5852	E+ / 0.8	-0.42	-3.51	-1.73 /11	3.61 / 9	6.21 /18	0.92	1.13
IN	Principal Equity Inc Fd A	PQIAX	B	(800) 222-5852	C+ / 5.8	0.52	5.28	9.27 /71	14.17 /68	13.15 /70	1.65	0.89
IN	Principal Equity Inc Fd C	PEUCX	B-	(800) 222-5852	C+ / 6.1	0.35	4.91	8.44 /66	13.33 /62	12.33 /63	1.08	1.63
IN	Principal Equity Inc Fd Inst	PEIIX	B+	(800) 222-5852	B- / 7.0	0.66	5.47	9.72 /73	14.64 /72	13.63 /74	2.12	0.52
IN	Principal Equity Inc Fd P	PEQPX	B-	(800) 222-5852	C+ / 6.9	0.60	5.43	9.58 /72	14.49 /71	13.44 /72	2.03	0.62
IN	Principal Equity Inc Fd R1	PIEMX	B-	(800) 222-5852	C+ / 6.3	0.42	5.01	8.73 /68	13.62 /64	12.52 /64	1.27	1.39
IN	Principal Equity Inc Fd R2	PEINX	B-	(800) 222-5852	C+ / 6.4	0.46	5.07	8.89 /69	13.78 /65	12.78 /66	1.36	1.26
IN	Principal Equity Inc Fd R3	PEIOX	B-	(800) 222-5852	C+ / 6.6	0.51	5.19	9.09 /70	13.98 /67	12.98 /68	1.56	1.08
IN	Principal Equity Inc Fd R4	PEIPX	B-	(800) 222-5852	C+ / 6.7	0.57	5.29	9.29 /71	14.19 /69	13.20 /70	1.75	0.89
IN	Principal Equity Inc Fd R5	PEIQX	B-	(800) 222-5852	C+ / 6.8	0.56	5.35	9.41 /71	14.32 /69	13.19 /70	1.87	0.77
RE	Principal Glb Real Est Sec A	POSAX	C+	(800) 222-5852	B- / 7.3	4.53	13.56	16.30 /94	13.91 /66	12.61 /65	2.67	1.32
RE	Principal Glb Real Est Sec C	POSCX	C+	(800) 222-5852	B / 7.6	4.33	13.10	15.45 /92	12.99 /60	11.77 /59	2.17	2.14
RE	Principal Glb Real Est Sec Inst	POSIX	B	(800) 222-5852	B+ / 8.7	4.68	13.90	16.85 /94	14.42 /70	14.12 /79	3.01	0.90
RE	Principal Glb Real Est Sec P	POSPX	B	(800) 222-5852	B+ / 8.6	4.66	13.71	16.71 /94	14.23 /69	6.17 /18	2.88	1.06
GL	Principal Global Multi-Strat A	PMSAX	C-	(800) 222-5852	D- / 1.3	2.20	3.81	5.25 /40	4.61 /12	--	0.48	2.58
GL	Principal Global Multi-Strat C	PMSCX	U	(800) 222-5852	U /	2.04	3.51	4.48 /35	--	--	0.00	3.39
GL	Principal Global Multi-Strat Inst	PSMIX	C-	(800) 222-5852	D / 1.7	2.28	4.02	5.64 /44	4.77 /12	--	0.90	2.18
GL	Principal Global Multi-Strat P	PMSPX	C-	(800) 222-5852	D / 1.7	2.29	4.03	5.56 /43	4.67 /12	--	0.81	2.31
GL	Principal Global Opportunities Inst	PGOIX	U	(800) 222-5852	U /	2.06	2.60	5.71 /44	--	--	0.90	0.84
EM	Principal Intl Emrg Mkts A	PRIAX	E	(800) 222-5852	E / 0.4	3.00	-1.42	1.50 /20	-0.51 / 4	1.37 / 4	1.07	1.76
EM	Principal Intl Emrg Mkts C	PMKCX	E	(800) 222-5852	E / 0.4	2.79	-1.86	0.60 /17	-1.46 / 3	0.42 / 3	0.25	2.70
EM	Principal Intl Emrg Mkts Inst	PIEIX	E+	(800) 222-5852	E+ / 0.6	3.16	-1.18	2.06 /22	0.05 / 4	1.93 / 4	1.71	1.23
EM	Principal Intl Emrg Mkts J	PIEJX	E	(800) 222-5852	E / 0.5	3.02	-1.37	1.61 /20	-0.40 / 4	1.47 / 4	1.32	1.66
EM	Principal Intl Emrg Mkts P	PIEPX	E	(800) 222-5852	E / 0.5	3.11	-1.22	1.90 /21	-0.09 / 4	1.74 / 4	1.52	2.05
EM	Principal Intl Emrg Mkts R1	PIXEX	E	(800) 222-5852	E / 0.5	2.94	-1.57	1.18 /19	-0.80 / 4	1.05 / 3	0.73	2.10
EM	Principal Intl Emrg Mkts R2	PEASX	E	(800) 222-5852	E / 0.5	2.96	-1.57	1.28 /19	-0.69 / 4	1.18 / 4	0.91	1.97
EM	Principal Intl Emrg Mkts R3	PEAPX	E	(800) 222-5852	E / 0.5	3.03	-1.42	1.49 /20	-0.50 / 4	1.36 / 4	1.04	1.79
EM	Principal Intl Emrg Mkts R4	PESSX	E	(800) 222-5852	E / 0.5	3.07	-1.33	1.66 /21	-0.31 / 4	1.56 / 4	1.28	1.60
EM	Principal Intl Emrg Mkts R5	PEPSX	E	(800) 222-5852	E / 0.5	3.06	-1.29	1.77 /21	-0.19 / 4	1.68 / 4	1.43	1.48
FO	Principal Intl Equity Index Inst	PIDIX	E+	(800) 222-5852	D+ / 2.9	5.33	0.96	-1.44 /12	8.60 /30	5.64 /15	2.56	0.34
FO	Principal Intl Equity Index R1	PILIX	E+	(800) 222-5852	D+ / 2.3	5.15	0.49	-2.34 /10	7.65 /25	4.73 /11	2.05	1.21

● Denotes fund is closed to new investors
* Denotes fund is included in Section II

www.thestreetratings.com

Risk Rating/Pts	Standard Deviation	Beta	NAV As of 3/31/15	Total $(Mil)	Cash %	Stocks %	Bonds %	Other %	Portfolio Turnover Ratio	Last Bull Market Return	Last Bear Market Return	Manager Quality Pct	Manager Tenure (Years)	Initial Purch. $	Additional Purch. $	Front End Load	Back End Load
B- / 7.1	9.7	1.01	48.46	47	2	97	0	1	8	89.5	-17.9	47	13	1,000	100	0.0	0.0
B- / 7.1	9.7	1.00	59.49	1,539	2	97	0	1	8	97.8	-17.5	67	13	1,000,000	0	0.0	0.0
B- / 7.1	9.7	1.00	59.33	28	2	97	0	1	8	96.6	-17.5	65	13	0	0	0.0	0.0
B- / 7.1	9.7	1.00	58.73	2	2	97	0	1	8	91.9	-17.8	54	13	0	0	0.0	0.0
B- / 7.1	9.7	1.00	58.82	2	2	97	0	1	8	92.8	-17.7	56	13	0	0	0.0	0.0
B- / 7.1	9.7	1.00	58.70	26	2	97	0	1	8	94.0	-17.7	59	13	0	0	0.0	0.0
B- / 7.1	9.7	1.00	59.07	16	2	97	0	1	8	95.2	-17.6	62	13	0	0	0.0	0.0
B- / 7.1	9.7	1.00	59.23	37	2	97	0	1	8	96.1	-17.6	63	13	0	0	0.0	0.0
C+ / 6.2	12.7	0.93	11.91	254	2	97	0	1	67	49.2	-22.4	56	12	1,000	100	5.5	0.0
C+ / 6.2	12.7	0.94	11.92	13	2	97	0	1	67	45.7	-22.5	45	12	1,000	100	0.0	0.0
C+ / 6.2	12.7	0.93	11.85	4,632	2	97	0	1	67	51.9	-22.2	64	12	1,000,000	0	0.0	0.0
C+ / 6.2	12.7	0.94	11.77	193	2	97	0	1	67	49.6	-22.4	57	12	1,000	100	0.0	1.0
C+ / 6.2	12.7	0.93	11.81	5	2	97	0	1	67	50.9	-22.3	61	12	0	0	0.0	0.0
C+ / 6.2	12.7	0.94	11.86	6	2	97	0	1	67	47.3	-22.5	50	12	0	0	0.0	0.0
C+ / 6.2	12.7	0.93	11.80	9	2	97	0	1	67	48.0	-22.4	52	12	0	0	0.0	0.0
C+ / 6.2	12.7	0.94	11.85	42	2	97	0	1	67	49.0	-22.4	55	12	0	0	0.0	0.0
C+ / 6.2	12.7	0.93	12.01	37	2	97	0	1	67	49.9	-22.3	58	12	0	0	0.0	0.0
C+ / 6.2	12.7	0.93	11.98	74	2	97	0	1	67	50.5	-22.2	60	12	0	0	0.0	0.0
B- / 7.6	6.5	0.48	12.02	120	20	39	39	2	67	24.6	-12.8	17	N/A	1,000	100	3.8	0.0
B- / 7.7	6.6	0.49	11.80	53	20	39	39	2	67	21.6	-13.1	12	N/A	1,000	100	0.0	0.0
B- / 7.6	6.6	0.48	12.03	3,324	20	39	39	2	67	26.3	-12.7	19	N/A	0	0	0.0	0.0
B- / 7.6	6.5	0.90	11.99	366	20	39	39	2	67	25.7	-12.8	7	N/A	0	0	0.0	0.0
B- / 7.7	9.3	0.94	26.69	1,019	5	94	0	1	15	82.7	-14.2	55	7	1,000	100	5.5	0.0
B- / 7.6	9.3	0.94	26.11	200	5	94	0	1	15	78.3	-14.5	43	7	1,000	100	0.0	0.0
B- / 7.7	9.3	0.94	26.72	4,291	5	94	0	1	15	85.4	-14.1	61	7	1,000,000	0	0.0	0.0
B- / 7.7	9.3	0.94	26.69	135	5	94	0	1	15	84.4	-14.1	59	7	0	0	0.0	0.0
B- / 7.6	9.3	0.94	26.60	3	5	94	0	1	15	79.9	-14.4	48	7	0	0	0.0	0.0
B- / 7.6	9.3	0.94	26.69	7	5	94	0	1	15	80.7	-14.3	50	7	0	0	0.0	0.0
B- / 7.6	9.3	0.94	26.62	74	5	94	0	1	15	81.8	-14.3	52	7	0	0	0.0	0.0
B- / 7.7	9.3	0.94	26.66	59	5	94	0	1	15	82.9	-14.2	55	7	0	0	0.0	0.0
B- / 7.7	9.3	0.94	26.69	170	5	94	0	1	15	83.7	-14.1	57	7	0	0	0.0	0.0
C / 5.2	12.0	0.89	8.97	129	11	88	0	1	29	80.7	-21.0	79	8	1,000	100	5.5	0.0
C / 5.2	12.0	0.90	8.74	57	11	88	0	1	29	76.1	-21.2	71	8	1,000	100	0.0	0.0
C / 5.2	12.0	0.90	9.55	2,573	11	88	0	1	29	83.4	-20.7	82	8	1,000,000	0	0.0	0.0
C / 5.2	12.0	0.89	9.54	142	11	88	0	1	29	82.5	-20.8	81	8	0	0	0.0	0.0
B+ / 9.1	2.5	0.14	11.15	156	34	33	28	5	166	N/A	N/A	89	4	1,000	100	3.8	0.0
U /	N/A	N/A	11.01	51	34	33	28	5	166	N/A	N/A	N/A	4	1,000	100	0.0	0.0
B+ / 9.1	2.5	0.14	11.22	2,530	34	33	28	5	166	N/A	N/A	90	4	0	0	0.0	0.0
B+ / 9.1	2.5	0.14	11.19	217	34	33	28	5	166	N/A	N/A	89	4	0	0	0.0	0.0
U /	N/A	N/A	11.89	1,295	1	98	0	1	128	N/A	N/A	N/A	3	0	0	0.0	0.0
C / 5.1	13.8	0.99	24.07	91	1	98	0	1	115	19.1	-26.2	49	8	1,000	100	5.5	0.0
C / 5.0	13.8	1.00	23.19	10	1	98	0	1	115	15.2	-26.5	35	8	1,000	100	0.0	0.0
C / 5.1	13.8	0.99	23.86	1,457	1	98	0	1	115	21.3	-26.0	58	8	1,000,000	0	0.0	0.0
C / 5.1	13.8	0.99	23.20	119	1	98	0	1	115	19.5	-26.2	51	8	1,000	100	0.0	0.0
C / 5.1	13.8	0.99	23.85	2	1	98	0	1	115	20.8	-26.1	56	8	0	0	0.0	0.0
C / 5.1	13.8	0.99	23.80	3	1	98	0	1	115	17.8	-26.3	45	8	0	0	0.0	0.0
C / 5.1	13.8	1.00	23.63	5	1	98	0	1	115	18.3	-26.3	47	8	0	0	0.0	0.0
C / 5.1	13.8	0.99	23.78	13	1	98	0	1	115	19.1	-26.2	50	8	0	0	0.0	0.0
C / 5.1	13.8	0.99	23.87	13	1	98	0	1	115	19.8	-26.2	53	8	0	0	0.0	0.0
C / 5.1	13.8	0.99	23.91	27	1	98	0	1	115	20.3	-26.1	55	8	0	0	0.0	0.0
C- / 3.7	13.3	1.00	10.08	716	2	97	0	1	46	50.0	-23.4	54	4	0	0	0.0	0.0
C- / 3.7	13.3	1.00	9.80	1	2	97	0	1	46	45.6	-23.5	41	4	0	0	0.0	0.0

	99 Pct = Best 0 Pct = Worst			**Overall**		**PERFORMANCE**					**Incl. in Returns**	
								Total Return % through 3/31/15				
										Annualized		Dividend	Expense
Fund Type	Fund Name	Ticker Symbol	**Investment Rating**	Phone	**Perfor- mance Rating/Pts**	3 Mo	6 Mo	1Yr / Pct	3Yr / Pct	5Yr / Pct	Yield	Ratio
FO	Principal Intl Equity Index R2	PINEX	E+	(800) 222-5852	D+ / 2.4	5.13	0.57	-2.21 /10	7.79 /26	4.84 /11	1.80	1.08
FO	Principal Intl Equity Index R3	PIIOX	E+	(800) 222-5852	D+ / 2.5	5.09	0.54	-2.08 /10	7.95 /27	5.03 /12	2.08	0.90
FO	Principal Intl Equity Index R4	PIIPX	E+	(800) 222-5852	D+ / 2.6	5.15	0.68	-1.92 /11	8.17 /28	5.23 /13	2.20	0.71
FO	Principal Intl Equity Index R5	PIIQX	E+	(800) 222-5852	D+ / 2.7	5.25	0.72	-1.78 /11	8.28 /29	5.38 /14	2.33	0.59
FO	Principal Intl I Inst	PINIX	C-	(800) 222-5852	C / 4.6	4.47	4.96	7.19 /57	10.45 /42	7.24 /25	2.29	0.99
FO	Principal Intl I R1	PPISX	C-	(800) 222-5852	C- / 4.1	4.25	4.50	6.33 /49	9.50 /36	6.32 /19	1.41	1.83
FO	Principal Intl I R2	PSPPX	C-	(800) 222-5852	C- / 4.1	4.31	4.57	6.40 /50	9.63 /37	6.46 /20	1.41	1.70
FO	Principal Intl I R3	PRPPX	C-	(800) 222-5852	C / 4.3	4.32	4.65	6.65 /52	9.83 /38	6.66 /21	1.63	1.52
FO	Principal Intl I R4	PUPPX	C-	(800) 222-5852	C / 4.4	4.40	4.82	6.82 /54	10.05 /40	6.87 /22	1.94	1.33
FO	Principal Intl I R5	PTPPX	C-	(800) 222-5852	C / 4.5	4.48	4.84	6.99 /55	10.21 /41	7.00 /23	2.10	1.21
GR	Principal LgCap Growth A	PRGWX	C	(800) 222-5852	C+ / 6.9	3.83	7.03	14.95 /92	14.92 /74	13.27 /71	0.00	1.07
GR	Principal LgCap Growth C	PLGCX	C+	(800) 222-5852	B- / 7.2	3.62	6.55	14.09 /90	13.94 /67	12.32 /63	0.00	1.91
GR	Principal LgCap Growth Inst	PGLIX	B	(800) 222-5852	B+ / 8.4	3.98	7.23	15.42 /92	15.48 /79	13.88 /77	0.14	0.65
GR	Principal LgCap Growth J	PGLJX	C+	(800) 222-5852	B / 8.0	3.95	7.12	15.01 /92	14.99 /75	13.34 /71	0.00	1.05
GR	Principal LgCap Growth P	PGLPX	B-	(800) 222-5852	B / 8.2	3.90	7.11	15.22 /92	15.27 /74	13.62 /74	0.00	0.84
GR	Principal LgCap Growth R1	PLSGX	C+	(800) 222-5852	B / 7.6	3.77	6.79	14.50 /91	14.51 /71	12.91 /67	0.00	1.50
GR	Principal LgCap Growth R2	PCPPX	C+	(800) 222-5852	B / 7.7	3.72	6.79	14.62 /91	14.65 /72	13.04 /69	0.00	1.37
GR	Principal LgCap Growth R3	PLGPX	B-	(800) 222-5852	B / 7.9	3.79	6.90	14.87 /91	14.86 /74	13.25 /71	0.00	1.19
GR	Principal LgCap Growth R4	PEPPX	B-	(800) 222-5852	B / 8.1	3.90	7.13	15.07 /92	15.08 /76	13.48 /73	0.00	1.00
GR	Principal LgCap Growth R5	PDPPX	B-	(800) 222-5852	B / 8.2	3.94	7.12	15.24 /92	15.21 /77	13.59 /74	0.00	0.88
IX	Principal LgCap S&P 500 A	PLSAX	B+	(800) 222-5852	B- / 7.5	0.83	5.69	12.18 /83	15.45 /79	13.79 /76	1.47	0.49
IX	Principal LgCap S&P 500 C	PLICX	B+	(800) 222-5852	B- / 7.1	0.63	5.30	11.29 /80	14.61 /72	12.98 /68	0.91	1.39
IX	Principal LgCap S&P 500 Inst	PLFIX	A	(800) 222-5852	B / 8.1	0.90	5.86	12.53 /85	15.91 /83	14.25 /80	1.79	0.16
IX	Principal LgCap S&P 500 J	PSPJX	A-	(800) 222-5852	B / 7.8	0.84	5.66	12.13 /83	15.48 /79	13.81 /76	1.49	0.51
IX	Principal LgCap S&P 500 R1	PLPIX	B+	(800) 222-5852	B- / 7.3	0.69	5.39	11.56 /81	14.88 /74	13.25 /71	0.97	1.03
IX	Principal LgCap S&P 500 R2	PLFNX	B+	(800) 222-5852	B- / 7.5	0.76	5.43	11.72 /81	15.06 /75	13.41 /72	1.03	0.90
IX	Principal LgCap S&P 500 R3	PLFMX	A-	(800) 222-5852	B / 7.6	0.83	5.62	11.94 /82	15.26 /77	13.63 /74	1.21	0.72
IX	Principal LgCap S&P 500 R4	PLFSX	A-	(800) 222-5852	B / 7.8	0.83	5.64	12.10 /83	15.48 /79	13.84 /76	1.45	0.53
IX	Principal LgCap S&P 500 R5	PLFPX	A-	(800) 222-5852	B / 7.9	0.82	5.70	12.20 /83	15.60 /80	13.95 /77	1.54	0.41
GR	Principal LgCap Val Fd A	PCACX	C+	(800) 222-5852	C+ / 5.8	-0.31	3.97	6.78 /53	14.80 /73	12.94 /68	1.03	0.85
GR	Principal LgCap Val Fd C	PLUCX	C+	(800) 222-5852	C+ / 6.1	-0.48	3.59	5.96 /46	13.84 /66	12.03 /61	0.37	1.87
GR	Principal LgCap Val Fd Inst	PVLIX	B-	(800) 222-5852	B- / 7.1	-0.16	4.25	7.22 /57	15.35 /78	13.50 /73	1.48	0.41
GR	Principal LgCap Val Fd J	PVLJX	C+	(800) 222-5852	C+ / 6.7	-0.24	4.08	6.86 /54	14.81 /73	12.93 /68	1.14	0.84
GR	Principal LgCap Val Fd R1	PLSVX	C+	(800) 222-5852	C+ / 6.4	-0.39	3.80	6.31 /49	14.36 /70	12.52 /64	0.68	1.29
GR	Principal LgCap Val Fd R2	PLVNX	C+	(800) 222-5852	C+ / 6.5	-0.39	3.82	6.48 /51	14.48 /71	12.65 /65	0.85	1.16
GR	Principal LgCap Val Fd R3	PLVMX	C+	(800) 222-5852	C+ / 6.6	-0.32	3.94	6.61 /52	14.67 /72	12.86 /67	1.04	0.98
GR	Principal LgCap Val Fd R4	PLVSX	C+	(800) 222-5852	C+ / 6.8	-0.32	4.04	6.87 /54	14.91 /74	13.07 /69	1.12	0.79
GR	Principal LgCap Val Fd R5	PLVPX	C+	(800) 222-5852	C+ / 6.9	-0.24	4.12	6.93 /54	15.03 /75	13.20 /70	1.22	0.67
GR	Principal LgCp Blend II Inst	PLBIX	D	(800) 222-5852	B- / 7.0	1.10	4.79	10.04 /74	14.55 /71	12.72 /66	0.87	0.79
GR	Principal LgCp Blend II J	PLBJX	D	(800) 222-5852	C+ / 6.7	0.94	4.69	9.72 /73	14.15 /68	12.27 /62	0.63	1.13
GR	Principal LgCp Blend II R1	PLBSX	D	(800) 222-5852	C+ / 6.3	0.81	4.38	9.14 /70	13.58 /64	11.77 /59	0.13	1.64
GR	Principal LgCp Blend II R2	PPZNX	D	(800) 222-5852	C+ / 6.4	0.81	4.39	9.26 /71	13.71 /65	11.90 /60	0.04	1.51
GR	Principal LgCp Blend II R3	PPZMX	D	(800) 222-5852	C+ / 6.6	0.91	4.53	9.52 /72	13.95 /67	12.11 /61	0.24	1.33
GR	Principal LgCp Blend II R4	PPZSX	D	(800) 222-5852	C+ / 6.7	1.01	4.59	9.64 /73	14.15 /68	12.30 /63	0.60	1.14
GR	Principal LgCp Blend II R5	PPZPX	D	(800) 222-5852	C+ / 6.8	0.91	4.60	9.77 /73	14.26 /69	12.45 /64	0.68	1.02
GR	Principal LgCp Gr I A	PLGAX	C+	(800) 222-5852	C+ / 6.8	4.46	9.34	12.72 /86	14.71 /73	15.09 /87	0.00	1.50
GR	Principal LgCp Gr I Inst	PLGIX	B	(800) 222-5852	B+ / 8.3	4.66	9.73	13.45 /88	15.31 /77	15.56 /90	0.26	0.63
GR	Principal LgCp Gr I J	PLGJX	B-	(800) 222-5852	B / 7.9	4.52	9.49	13.11 /87	14.81 /73	14.97 /87	0.00	1.02
GR	Principal LgCp Gr I R1	PCRSX	C+	(800) 222-5852	B- / 7.5	4.40	9.23	12.49 /85	14.30 /69	14.55 /83	0.00	1.49
GR	Principal LgCp Gr I R2	PPUNX	C+	(800) 222-5852	B / 7.6	4.41	9.25	12.57 /85	14.45 /71	14.68 /84	0.00	1.36
GR	Principal LgCp Gr I R3	PPUMX	B-	(800) 222-5852	B / 7.8	4.51	9.37	12.90 /86	14.67 /72	14.89 /86	0.00	1.18
GR	Principal LgCp Gr I R4	PPUSX	B	(800) 222-5852	B / 8.0	4.56	9.48	13.08 /87	14.88 /74	15.12 /88	0.00	0.99

● Denotes fund is closed to new investors
* Denotes fund is included in Section II

www.thestreetratings.com

I. Index of Stock Mutual Funds

RISK			NET ASSETS		ASSET					BULL / BEAR		FUND MANAGER		MINIMUMS		LOADS	
Risk Rating/Pts	3 Year		NAV As of 3/31/15	Total $(Mil)	Cash %	Stocks %	Bonds %	Other %	Portfolio Turnover Ratio	Last Bull Market Return	Last Bear Market Return	Manager Quality Pct	Manager Tenure (Years)	Initial Purch. $	Additional Purch. $	Front End Load	Back End Load
	Standard Deviation	Beta															
C- / 3.8	13.3	1.01	10.05	1	2	97	0	1	46	46.1	-23.6	42	4	0	0	0.0	0.0
C- / 3.7	13.3	1.01	9.91	14	2	97	0	1	46	47.1	-23.5	45	4	0	0	0.0	0.0
C- / 3.7	13.3	1.00	10.01	12	2	97	0	1	46	48.0	-23.4	48	4	0	0	0.0	0.0
C- / 3.7	13.3	1.00	10.02	36	2	97	0	1	46	48.6	-23.4	50	4	0	0	0.0	0.0
C+ / 6.1	12.9	0.94	13.78	320	2	97	0	1	128	59.9	-26.0	80	1	1,000,000	0	0.0	0.0
C+ / 6.1	12.8	0.93	13.74	4	2	97	0	1	128	55.3	-26.2	73	1	0	0	0.0	0.0
C+ / 6.1	12.8	0.93	13.78	3	2	97	0	1	128	56.0	-26.2	74	1	0	0	0.0	0.0
C+ / 6.1	12.8	0.93	13.76	5	2	97	0	1	128	56.8	-26.1	76	1	0	0	0.0	0.0
C+ / 6.0	12.9	0.94	13.76	5	2	97	0	1	128	57.9	-26.0	78	1	0	0	0.0	0.0
C+ / 6.0	12.9	0.94	13.76	10	2	97	0	1	128	58.7	-26.1	79	1	0	0	0.0	0.0
C / 4.9	10.8	0.97	10.84	389	1	98	0	1	58	93.0	-16.7	59	10	1,000	100	5.5	0.0
C / 4.7	10.8	0.96	10.01	18	1	98	0	1	58	87.7	-17.1	47	10	1,000	100	0.0	0.0
C / 5.0	10.8	0.97	11.24	2,836	1	98	0	1	58	96.7	-16.6	66	10	1,000,000	0	0.0	0.0
C / 4.8	10.8	0.97	10.27	68	1	98	0	1	58	93.5	-16.7	60	10	1,000	100	0.0	0.0
C / 5.0	10.8	0.96	11.18	12	1	98	0	1	58	95.4	-16.7	65	10	0	0	0.0	0.0
C / 4.8	10.8	0.97	10.45	6	1	98	0	1	58	90.9	-16.9	54	10	0	0	0.0	0.0
C / 4.9	10.8	0.96	10.60	5	1	98	0	1	58	91.7	-16.9	57	10	0	0	0.0	0.0
C / 5.1	10.8	0.96	11.51	19	1	98	0	1	58	92.7	-16.7	59	10	0	0	0.0	0.0
C / 5.0	10.8	0.97	11.45	17	1	98	0	1	58	94.3	-16.7	61	10	0	0	0.0	0.0
C / 5.0	10.8	0.97	11.33	75	1	98	0	1	58	95.0	-16.7	63	10	0	0	0.0	0.0
B- / 7.3	9.5	1.00	14.58	261	1	98	0	1	6	96.2	-16.4	59	4	1,000	100	1.5	0.0
B- / 7.3	9.5	1.00	14.35	32	1	98	0	1	6	91.4	-16.7	49	4	1,000	100	0.0	0.0
B- / 7.3	9.5	1.00	14.56	2,638	1	98	0	1	6	98.9	-16.3	66	4	1,000,000	0	0.0	0.0
B- / 7.3	9.5	1.00	14.44	528	1	98	0	1	6	96.5	-16.5	60	4	1,000	100	0.0	0.0
B- / 7.3	9.5	0.99	14.53	20	1	98	0	1	6	93.0	-16.5	53	4	0	0	0.0	0.0
B- / 7.3	9.5	1.00	14.62	36	1	98	0	1	6	94.1	-16.6	54	4	0	0	0.0	0.0
B- / 7.3	9.5	0.99	14.59	231	1	98	0	1	6	95.1	-16.5	58	4	0	0	0.0	0.0
B- / 7.3	9.5	1.00	14.62	226	1	98	0	1	6	96.5	-16.5	60	4	0	0	0.0	0.0
B- / 7.3	9.5	1.00	14.73	420	1	98	0	1	6	97.3	-16.4	61	4	0	0	0.0	0.0
C+ / 6.1	10.2	1.02	12.72	210	1	98	0	1	119	94.8	-19.9	45	8	1,000	100	5.5	0.0
C+ / 6.2	10.2	1.02	12.45	8	1	98	0	1	119	89.1	-20.0	33	8	1,000	100	0.0	0.0
C+ / 6.0	10.2	1.02	12.69	2,879	1	98	0	1	119	98.0	-19.7	52	8	1,000,000	0	0.0	0.0
C+ / 6.0	10.2	1.03	12.50	73	1	98	0	1	119	94.7	-19.8	44	8	1,000	100	0.0	0.0
C+ / 6.2	10.2	1.02	12.61	2	1	98	0	1	119	92.2	-20.0	40	8	0	0	0.0	0.0
C+ / 6.1	10.2	1.02	12.64	3	1	98	0	1	119	92.8	-19.9	41	8	0	0	0.0	0.0
C+ / 6.1	10.2	1.02	12.61	5	1	98	0	1	119	94.3	-19.9	43	8	0	0	0.0	0.0
C+ / 6.1	10.1	1.02	12.59	3	1	98	0	1	119	95.4	-19.8	48	8	0	0	0.0	0.0
C+ / 6.1	10.2	1.02	12.71	8	1	98	0	1	119	96.2	-19.8	49	8	0	0	0.0	0.0
D / 1.8	9.7	1.01	10.07	414	1	98	0	1	35	91.7	-17.7	45	8	1,000,000	0	0.0	0.0
D- / 1.5	9.7	1.01	9.64	113	1	98	0	1	35	89.3	-17.8	40	8	1,000	100	0.0	0.0
D / 1.9	9.7	1.01	10.00	3	1	98	0	1	35	86.3	-18.0	33	8	0	0	0.0	0.0
D / 1.9	9.7	1.01	9.99	3	1	98	0	1	35	87.1	-18.0	33	8	0	0	0.0	0.0
D / 1.8	9.7	1.01	9.97	14	1	98	0	1	35	88.2	-17.9	36	8	0	0	0.0	0.0
D / 1.8	9.7	1.01	10.05	12	1	98	0	1	35	89.6	-17.9	40	8	0	0	0.0	0.0
D / 1.8	9.7	1.01	10.01	21	1	98	0	1	35	90.3	-17.8	40	8	0	0	0.0	0.0
C+ / 6.5	11.1	1.05	12.89	9	2	97	0	1	38	98.2	-17.5	38	11	1,000	100	5.5	0.0
C / 5.5	11.1	1.05	13.02	6,803	2	97	0	1	38	101.5	-17.4	45	11	1,000,000	0	0.0	0.0
C / 5.2	11.1	1.05	11.32	111	2	97	0	1	38	98.4	-17.6	39	11	1,000	100	0.0	0.0
C / 5.3	11.1	1.06	11.86	8	2	97	0	1	38	95.4	-17.7	32	11	0	0	0.0	0.0
C / 5.3	11.1	1.06	11.60	22	2	97	0	1	38	96.4	-17.7	34	11	0	0	0.0	0.0
C / 5.4	11.1	1.05	12.28	155	2	97	0	1	38	97.6	-17.5	37	11	0	0	0.0	0.0
C / 5.4	11.1	1.05	12.38	98	2	97	0	1	38	98.8	-17.5	40	11	0	0	0.0	0.0

Fund Type	Fund Name	Ticker Symbol	Overall Investment Rating	Phone	PERFORMANCE Perfor-mance Rating/Pts	Total Return % through 3/31/15 3 Mo	6 Mo	1Yr / Pct	Annualized 3Yr / Pct	5Yr / Pct	Incl. in Returns Dividend Yield	Expense Ratio
GR	Principal LgCp Gr I R5	PPUPX	B	(800) 222-5852	B / 8.1	4.61	9.58	13.20 /87	15.01 /75	15.26 /89	0.07	0.87
GR	Principal LgCp Gr II Inst	PPIIX	C-	(800) 222-5852	B- / 7.5	2.77	8.83	14.08 /90	14.22 /69	13.43 /72	0.55	0.88
GR	Principal LgCp Gr II J	PPLJX	D+	(800) 222-5852	B- / 7.1	2.57	8.52	13.58 /88	13.68 /65	12.85 /67	0.32	1.32
GR	Principal LgCp Gr II R1	PDASX	D+	(800) 222-5852	C+ / 6.7	2.48	8.33	13.05 /87	13.20 /61	12.42 /64	0.00	1.76
GR	Principal LgCp Gr II R2	PPTNX	D+	(800) 222-5852	C+ / 6.8	2.59	8.32	13.21 /87	13.38 /62	12.57 /65	0.00	1.63
GR	Principal LgCp Gr II R3	PPTMX	D+	(800) 222-5852	B- / 7.0	2.63	8.51	13.40 /88	13.59 /64	12.79 /66	0.03	1.45
GR	Principal LgCp Gr II R4	PPTSX	D+	(800) 222-5852	B- / 7.1	2.54	8.53	13.52 /88	13.75 /65	12.98 /68	0.29	1.26
GR	Principal LgCp Gr II R5	PPTPX	C-	(800) 222-5852	B- / 7.3	2.63	8.59	13.75 /89	13.94 /67	13.15 /70	0.31	1.14
GR	Principal LgCp Val III Inst	PLVIX	B+	(800) 222-5852	B- / 7.5	0.38	5.22	9.63 /73	15.55 /80	12.09 /61	1.54	0.77
GR	Principal LgCp Val III J	PLVJX	B+	(800) 222-5852	B- / 7.2	0.32	5.02	9.25 /71	15.08 /76	11.58 /58	1.17	1.17
GR	Principal LgCp Val III R1	PESAX	B-	(800) 222-5852	C+ / 6.8	0.19	4.70	8.66 /67	14.55 /71	11.13 /54	0.90	1.64
GR	Principal LgCp Val III R2	PPSNX	B-	(800) 222-5852	C+ / 6.9	0.19	4.77	8.74 /68	14.71 /73	11.26 /55	0.90	1.51
GR	Principal LgCp Val III R3	PPSFX	B+	(800) 222-5852	B- / 7.1	0.31	4.91	9.02 /69	14.92 /74	11.48 /57	0.98	1.33
GR	Principal LgCp Val III R4	PPSSX	B+	(800) 222-5852	B- / 7.2	0.32	4.99	9.17 /70	15.15 /76	11.70 /58	1.25	1.14
GR	Principal LgCp Val III R5	PPSRX	B+	(800) 222-5852	B- / 7.4	0.38	5.08	9.38 /71	15.28 /77	11.82 /59	1.29	1.02
AA	Principal LifeTime 2010 A	PENAX	C	(800) 222-5852	D / 2.0	2.00	3.24	5.01 /39	7.19 /22	7.60 /27	1.71	1.11
AA	Principal LifeTime 2010 Inst	PTTIX	C	(800) 222-5852	D+ / 2.8	2.08	3.42	5.36 /41	7.59 /25	7.99 /30	2.17	0.69
AA	Principal LifeTime 2010 J	PTAJX	C	(800) 222-5852	D+ / 2.7	2.09	3.37	5.16 /40	7.30 /23	7.65 /27	1.89	0.99
AA	Principal LifeTime 2010 R1	PVASX	C	(800) 222-5852	D+ / 2.3	1.94	2.99	4.47 /35	6.66 /20	7.06 /23	1.23	1.56
AA	Principal LifeTime 2010 R2	PTANX	C	(800) 222-5852	D+ / 2.3	1.94	3.04	4.60 /36	6.79 /20	7.19 /24	1.28	1.43
AA	Principal LifeTime 2010 R3	PTAMX	C	(800) 222-5852	D+ / 2.5	2.02	3.21	4.85 /37	7.00 /21	7.39 /26	1.58	1.25
AA	Principal LifeTime 2010 R4	PTASX	C	(800) 222-5852	D+ / 2.6	2.02	3.27	5.06 /39	7.22 /23	7.60 /27	1.72	1.06
AA	Principal LifeTime 2010 R5	PTAPX	C	(800) 222-5852	D+ / 2.7	2.09	3.39	5.19 /40	7.35 /23	7.73 /28	1.92	0.94
AA	Principal LifeTime 2015 Inst	LTINX	C	(800) 222-5852	C- / 3.3	2.15	3.68	5.67 /44	8.35 /29	8.59 /34	2.35	0.70
AA	Principal LifeTime 2015 R1	LTSGX	C	(800) 222-5852	D+ / 2.7	1.90	3.18	4.72 /37	7.37 /23	7.63 /27	1.48	1.57
AA	Principal LifeTime 2015 R2	LTASX	C	(800) 222-5852	D+ / 2.7	1.90	3.22	4.85 /37	7.52 /24	7.76 /28	1.62	1.44
AA	Principal LifeTime 2015 R3	LTAPX	C	(800) 222-5852	D+ / 2.9	1.99	3.37	5.00 /39	7.71 /25	7.96 /30	1.85	1.26
AA	Principal LifeTime 2015 R4	LTSLX	C	(800) 222-5852	C- / 3.0	2.08	3.42	5.23 /40	7.92 /27	8.18 /31	1.99	1.07
AA	Principal LifeTime 2015 R5	LTPFX	C	(800) 222-5852	C- / 3.1	2.08	3.47	5.38 /41	8.05 /27	8.29 /32	2.13	0.95
AA	Principal LifeTime 2020 A	PTBAX	C	(800) 222-5852	D+ / 2.7	2.18	4.01	5.80 /45	8.96 /33	8.86 /36	1.95	1.12
AA	Principal LifeTime 2020 Inst	PLWIX	C+	(800) 222-5852	C- / 3.9	2.27	4.26	6.21 /48	9.40 /36	9.27 /39	2.43	0.73
AA	Principal LifeTime 2020 J	PLFJX	C+	(800) 222-5852	C- / 3.7	2.20	4.13	5.94 /46	9.06 /33	8.91 /36	2.16	1.03
AA	Principal LifeTime 2020 R1	PWASX	C	(800) 222-5852	C- / 3.3	2.06	3.81	5.33 /41	8.43 /29	8.32 /32	1.58	1.60
AA	Principal LifeTime 2020 R2	PTBNX	C	(800) 222-5852	C- / 3.4	2.14	3.91	5.43 /42	8.59 /30	8.45 /33	1.67	1.47
AA	Principal LifeTime 2020 R3	PTBMX	C	(800) 222-5852	C- / 3.5	2.14	3.92	5.59 /43	8.76 /31	8.64 /34	1.89	1.29
AA	Principal LifeTime 2020 R4	PTBSX	C	(800) 222-5852	C- / 3.6	2.21	4.08	5.89 /45	8.98 /33	8.86 /36	2.04	1.10
AA	Principal LifeTime 2020 R5	PTBPX	C+	(800) 222-5852	C- / 3.7	2.28	4.17	5.98 /46	9.12 /34	9.00 /37	2.20	0.98
AA	Principal LifeTime 2025 Inst	LTSTX	C+	(800) 222-5852	C / 4.3	2.52	4.60	6.81 /54	9.99 /39	9.68 /42	2.61	0.75
AA	Principal LifeTime 2025 R1	LTSNX	C	(800) 222-5852	C- / 3.7	2.29	4.11	5.89 /45	9.06 /33	8.74 /35	1.87	1.62
AA	Principal LifeTime 2025 R2	LTADX	C	(800) 222-5852	C- / 3.8	2.38	4.24	6.02 /47	9.17 /34	8.87 /36	1.90	1.49
AA	Principal LifeTime 2025 R3	LTVPX	C+	(800) 222-5852	C- / 3.9	2.37	4.31	6.18 /48	9.38 /35	9.06 /37	2.14	1.31
AA	Principal LifeTime 2025 R4	LTEEX	C+	(800) 222-5852	C- / 4.0	2.45	4.44	6.39 /50	9.59 /37	9.28 /39	2.28	1.12
AA	Principal LifeTime 2025 R5	LTPDX	C+	(800) 222-5852	C- / 4.1	2.44	4.45	6.49 /51	9.73 /38	9.40 /40	2.38	1.00
AA	Principal LifeTime 2030 A	PTCAX	C	(800) 222-5852	C- / 3.5	2.51	4.63	6.62 /52	10.16 /40	9.65 /42	2.08	1.17
AA	Principal LifeTime 2030 Inst	PMTIX	C+	(800) 222-5852	C / 4.6	2.66	4.87	7.01 /55	10.60 /43	10.06 /45	2.55	0.77
AA	Principal LifeTime 2030 J	PLTJX	C+	(800) 222-5852	C / 4.4	2.59	4.72	6.72 /53	10.23 /41	9.69 /42	2.27	1.08
AA	Principal LifeTime 2030 R1	PXASX	C+	(800) 222-5852	C- / 4.0	2.39	4.37	6.09 /47	9.61 /37	9.11 /38	1.74	1.64
AA	Principal LifeTime 2030 R2	PTCNX	C+	(800) 222-5852	C- / 4.1	2.45	4.50	6.22 /48	9.76 /38	9.25 /39	1.80	1.51
AA	Principal LifeTime 2030 R3	PTCMX	C+	(800) 222-5852	C- / 4.2	2.52	4.58	6.44 /50	9.95 /39	9.44 /40	2.01	1.33
AA	Principal LifeTime 2030 R4	PTCSX	C+	(800) 222-5852	C / 4.4	2.52	4.61	6.63 /52	10.17 /40	9.64 /42	2.10	1.14
AA	Principal LifeTime 2030 R5	PTCPX	C+	(800) 222-5852	C / 4.4	2.59	4.76	6.76 /53	10.31 /41	9.80 /43	2.31	1.02
AA	Principal LifeTime 2035 Inst	LTIUX	C+	(800) 222-5852	C / 5.0	2.63	5.01	7.26 /57	11.21 /47	10.43 /48	2.59	0.78

• Denotes fund is closed to new investors
* Denotes fund is included in Section II

www.thestreetratings.com

RISK	3 Year		NET ASSETS		ASSET				Portfolio	BULL / BEAR		FUND MANAGER		MINIMUMS		LOADS	
Risk Rating/Pts	Standard Deviation	Beta	NAV As of 3/31/15	Total $(Mil)	Cash %	Stocks %	Bonds %	Other %	Turnover Ratio	Last Bull Market Return	Last Bear Market Return	Manager Quality Pct	Manager Tenure (Years)	Initial Purch. $	Additional Purch. $	Front End Load	Back End Load
C / 5.5	11.1	1.05	12.70	334	2	97	0	1	38	99.8	-17.5	41	11	0	0	0.0	0.0
D+ / 2.8	9.7	0.98	8.89	642	2	97	0	1	84	90.8	-15.7	47	15	1,000,000	0	0.0	0.0
D / 2.1	9.8	0.99	7.59	36	2	97	0	1	84	87.8	-15.9	38	15	1,000	100	0.0	0.0
D+ / 2.6	9.8	0.99	8.28	1	2	97	0	1	84	85.3	-16.0	32	15	0	0	0.0	0.0
D+ / 2.4	9.7	0.98	7.92	2	2	97	0	1	84	86.0	-15.9	35	15	0	0	0.0	0.0
D+ / 2.5	9.8	0.99	8.18	8	2	97	0	1	84	87.2	-15.9	36	15	0	0	0.0	0.0
D+ / 2.7	9.8	0.99	8.47	2	2	97	0	1	84	88.5	-15.9	38	15	0	0	0.0	0.0
D+ / 2.7	9.8	0.98	8.59	7	2	97	0	1	84	89.3	-15.9	42	15	0	0	0.0	0.0
B- / 7.3	9.9	1.02	15.82	2,192	3	96	0	1	41	95.8	-21.2	55	6	1,000,000	0	0.0	0.0
B- / 7.3	9.9	1.02	15.65	77	3	96	0	1	41	92.8	-21.3	50	6	1,000	100	0.0	0.0
B- / 7.3	9.9	1.02	15.79	5	3	96	0	1	41	90.1	-21.5	43	6	0	0	0.0	0.0
B- / 7.3	9.9	1.02	15.76	6	3	96	0	1	41	91.0	-21.4	44	6	0	0	0.0	0.0
B- / 7.3	9.9	1.01	16.38	14	3	96	0	1	41	92.0	-21.3	48	6	0	0	0.0	0.0
B- / 7.3	9.9	1.02	15.81	7	3	96	0	1	41	93.4	-21.3	50	6	0	0	0.0	0.0
B- / 7.3	9.9	1.02	15.92	12	3	96	0	1	41	94.1	-21.3	53	6	0	0	0.0	0.0
B+ / 9.0	5.0	0.83	13.80	43	8	35	56	1	24	38.9	-10.1	42	10	1,000	100	3.8	0.0
B / 8.9	5.0	0.83	13.72	975	8	35	56	1	24	40.7	-10.0	48	14	1,000,000	0	0.0	0.0
B+ / 9.0	5.0	0.84	13.68	258	8	35	56	1	24	39.1	-10.2	43	14	1,000	100	0.0	0.0
B+ / 9.0	5.0	0.84	13.67	14	8	35	56	1	24	36.5	-10.3	34	11	0	0	0.0	0.0
B+ / 9.0	5.0	0.83	13.66	14	8	35	56	1	24	37.2	-10.3	37	14	0	0	0.0	0.0
B+ / 9.0	5.0	0.84	13.62	70	8	35	56	1	24	37.9	-10.2	39	14	0	0	0.0	0.0
B+ / 9.0	5.0	0.84	13.65	49	8	35	56	1	24	38.9	-10.1	42	14	0	0	0.0	0.0
B / 8.9	5.0	0.84	13.67	108	8	35	56	1	24	39.3	-10.0	43	14	0	0	0.0	0.0
B / 8.2	5.8	0.98	10.94	625	9	44	46	1	25	47.3	-12.6	36	8	1,000,000	0	0.0	0.0
B / 8.4	5.9	1.00	10.70	13	9	44	46	1	25	43.0	-12.8	23	8	0	0	0.0	0.0
B / 8.4	5.8	0.99	10.74	13	9	44	46	1	25	43.7	-12.8	26	8	0	0	0.0	0.0
B / 8.3	5.8	0.99	10.74	91	9	44	46	1	25	44.5	-12.8	27	8	0	0	0.0	0.0
B / 8.3	5.8	0.98	10.80	64	9	44	46	1	25	45.4	-12.6	31	8	0	0	0.0	0.0
B / 8.3	5.8	0.98	10.82	88	9	44	46	1	25	46.1	-12.6	32	8	0	0	0.0	0.0
B / 8.2	6.8	1.14	14.51	138	10	55	34	1	19	53.1	-14.7	23	10	1,000	100	5.5	0.0
B / 8.2	6.8	1.14	14.43	4,392	10	55	34	1	19	55.1	-14.6	27	14	1,000,000	0	0.0	0.0
B / 8.2	6.7	1.14	14.37	904	10	55	34	1	19	53.4	-14.6	24	14	1,000	100	0.0	0.0
B / 8.3	6.8	1.15	14.35	52	10	55	34	1	19	50.5	-14.8	18	11	0	0	0.0	0.0
B / 8.3	6.8	1.14	14.32	68	10	55	34	1	19	51.1	-14.8	19	14	0	0	0.0	0.0
B / 8.2	6.7	1.14	14.31	303	10	55	34	1	19	52.1	-14.8	21	14	0	0	0.0	0.0
B / 8.2	6.8	1.14	14.34	222	10	55	34	1	19	53.0	-14.7	23	14	0	0	0.0	0.0
B / 8.2	6.7	1.14	14.37	487	10	55	34	1	19	53.7	-14.6	25	14	0	0	0.0	0.0
B- / 7.9	7.2	1.22	11.38	1,095	9	61	29	1	16	59.4	-15.7	24	7	1,000,000	0	0.0	0.0
B / 8.0	7.2	1.21	11.18	19	9	61	29	1	16	54.6	-16.1	17	7	0	0	0.0	0.0
B / 8.0	7.2	1.21	11.20	20	9	61	29	1	16	55.2	-15.9	18	7	0	0	0.0	0.0
B / 8.0	7.2	1.21	11.21	171	9	61	29	1	16	56.3	-15.9	20	7	0	0	0.0	0.0
B / 8.0	7.2	1.22	11.29	92	9	61	29	1	16	57.3	-15.8	21	7	0	0	0.0	0.0
B- / 7.9	7.2	1.22	11.32	146	9	61	29	1	16	58.0	-15.8	22	7	0	0	0.0	0.0
B- / 7.8	7.8	1.31	14.72	127	8	68	22	2	15	61.0	-16.6	17	10	1,000	100	5.5	0.0
B- / 7.7	7.8	1.31	14.68	4,610	8	68	22	2	15	63.1	-16.5	21	14	1,000,000	0	0.0	0.0
B- / 7.8	7.8	1.31	14.65	1,049	8	68	22	2	15	61.2	-16.6	18	14	1,000	100	0.0	0.0
B- / 7.8	7.8	1.32	14.59	47	8	68	22	2	15	58.3	-16.9	14	11	0	0	0.0	0.0
B- / 7.8	7.8	1.31	14.61	67	8	68	22	2	15	59.0	-16.8	14	14	0	0	0.0	0.0
B- / 7.8	7.7	1.31	14.63	271	8	68	22	2	15	60.0	-16.7	16	14	0	0	0.0	0.0
B- / 7.8	7.7	1.31	15.04	207	8	68	22	2	15	61.0	-16.7	17	14	0	0	0.0	0.0
B- / 7.8	7.8	1.31	14.67	471	8	68	22	2	15	61.7	-16.6	18	14	0	0	0.0	0.0
B- / 7.5	8.3	1.40	11.70	834	9	72	17	2	13	67.5	-17.5	17	7	1,000,000	0	0.0	0.0

Data as of March 31, 2015

Fund Type	Fund Name	Ticker Symbol	Overall Investment Rating	Phone	Performance Rating/Pts	3 Mo	6 Mo	1Yr / Pct	3Yr / Pct	5Yr / Pct	Dividend Yield	Expense Ratio
AA	Principal LifeTime 2035 R1	LTANX	C+	(800) 222-5852	C / 4.4	2.40	4.55	6.37 /50	10.25 /41	9.49 /40	1.78	1.65
AA	Principal LifeTime 2035 R2	LTVIX	C+	(800) 222-5852	C / 4.4	2.40	4.60	6.42 /50	10.36 /42	9.61 /41	1.91	1.52
AA	Principal LifeTime 2035 R3	LTAOX	C+	(800) 222-5852	C / 4.6	2.48	4.70	6.70 /53	10.58 /43	9.82 /43	2.10	1.34
AA	Principal LifeTime 2035 R4	LTSEX	C+	(800) 222-5852	C / 4.7	2.56	4.79	6.87 /54	10.79 /44	10.03 /45	2.28	1.15
AA	Principal LifeTime 2035 R5	LTPEX	C+	(800) 222-5852	C / 4.8	2.55	4.88	6.96 /55	10.91 /45	10.17 /46	2.37	1.03
AA	Principal LifeTime 2040 A	PTDAX	C	(800) 222-5852	C- / 4.0	2.61	4.89	7.00 /55	11.16 /47	10.26 /47	2.18	1.23
AA	Principal LifeTime 2040 Inst	PTDIX	C+	(800) 222-5852	C / 5.2	2.71	5.11	7.40 /58	11.59 /50	10.68 /50	2.61	0.79
AA	Principal LifeTime 2040 J	PTDJX	C+	(800) 222-5852	C / 4.9	2.66	4.95	7.05 /55	11.19 /47	10.23 /46	2.32	1.14
AA	Principal LifeTime 2040 R1	PYASX	C+	(800) 222-5852	C / 4.6	2.52	4.68	6.49 /51	10.63 /43	9.72 /42	1.80	1.66
AA	Principal LifeTime 2040 R2	PTDNX	C+	(800) 222-5852	C / 4.6	2.52	4.74	6.63 /52	10.75 /44	9.84 /43	1.86	1.53
AA	Principal LifeTime 2040 R3	PTDMX	C+	(800) 222-5852	C / 4.8	2.60	4.87	6.83 /54	10.97 /45	10.05 /45	2.10	1.35
AA	Principal LifeTime 2040 R4	PTDSX	C+	(800) 222-5852	C / 4.9	2.60	4.94	6.97 /55	11.18 /47	10.25 /47	2.24	1.16
AA	Principal LifeTime 2040 R5	PTDPX	C+	(800) 222-5852	C / 5.0	2.65	5.02	7.11 /56	11.32 /48	10.38 /48	2.39	1.04
AA	Principal LifeTime 2045 Inst	LTRIX	C+	(800) 222-5852	C / 5.4	2.75	5.23	7.53 /59	11.92 /52	10.88 /52	2.66	0.80
AA	Principal LifeTime 2045 R1	LTRGX	C+	(800) 222-5852	C / 4.8	2.55	4.79	6.59 /52	10.94 /45	9.93 /44	1.94	1.68
AA	Principal LifeTime 2045 R2	LTRSX	C+	(800) 222-5852	C / 4.8	2.55	4.80	6.69 /53	11.08 /46	10.06 /45	2.04	1.55
AA	Principal LifeTime 2045 R3	LTRVX	C+	(800) 222-5852	C / 4.9	2.53	4.87	6.85 /54	11.25 /47	10.24 /46	2.21	1.37
AA	Principal LifeTime 2045 R4	LTRLX	C+	(800) 222-5852	C / 5.1	2.61	4.96	7.10 /56	11.49 /49	10.48 /48	2.38	1.18
AA	Principal LifeTime 2045 R5	LTRDX	C+	(800) 222-5852	C / 5.2	2.69	5.06	7.30 /57	11.62 /50	10.60 /50	2.48	1.06
AA	Principal LifeTime 2050 A	PPEAX	C	(800) 222-5852	C / 4.4	2.71	5.08	7.14 /56	11.72 /51	10.61 /50	2.21	1.28
AA	Principal LifeTime 2050 Inst	PPLIX	C+	(800) 222-5852	C+ / 5.6	2.80	5.25	7.55 /60	12.15 /53	11.00 /53	2.68	0.80
AA	Principal LifeTime 2050 J	PFLJX	C+	(800) 222-5852	C / 5.2	2.72	5.03	7.08 /56	11.62 /50	10.45 /48	2.35	1.26
AA	Principal LifeTime 2050 R1	PZASX	C+	(800) 222-5852	C / 4.9	2.53	4.81	6.61 /52	11.18 /47	10.05 /45	1.92	1.67
AA	Principal LifeTime 2050 R2	PTENX	C+	(800) 222-5852	C / 5.0	2.68	4.89	6.84 /54	11.33 /48	10.18 /46	1.98	1.54
AA	Principal LifeTime 2050 R3	PTERX	C+	(800) 222-5852	C / 5.1	2.68	4.95	6.97 /55	11.52 /49	10.37 /48	2.18	1.36
AA	Principal LifeTime 2050 R4	PTESX	C+	(800) 222-5852	C / 5.3	2.74	5.07	7.16 /56	11.75 /51	10.60 /50	2.29	1.17
AA	Principal LifeTime 2050 R5	PTEFX	C+	(800) 222-5852	C / 5.4	2.73	5.18	7.34 /58	11.86 /52	10.73 /50	2.47	1.05
AA	Principal LifeTime 2055 Inst	LTFIX	C+	(800) 222-5852	C / 5.5	2.77	5.24	7.60 /60	12.06 /53	10.88 /52	2.64	0.83
AA	Principal LifeTime 2055 R1	LTFGX	C+	(800) 222-5852	C / 4.9	2.50	4.71	6.58 /52	11.13 /46	9.92 /44	2.00	1.69
AA	Principal LifeTime 2055 R2	LTFSX	C+	(800) 222-5852	C / 4.9	2.58	4.82	6.77 /53	11.26 /47	10.06 /45	2.10	1.56
AA	Principal LifeTime 2055 R3	LTFDX	C+	(800) 222-5852	C / 5.1	2.65	4.94	6.98 /55	11.46 /49	10.27 /47	2.24	1.38
AA	Principal LifeTime 2055 R4	LTFLX	C+	(800) 222-5852	C / 5.2	2.72	5.09	7.21 /57	11.67 /50	10.47 /48	2.39	1.19
AA	Principal LifeTime 2055 R5	LTFPX	C+	(800) 222-5852	C / 5.3	2.72	5.10	7.30 /57	11.83 /51	10.61 /50	2.49	1.07
GI	Principal LifeTime 2060 Inst	PLTZX	U	(800) 222-5852	U /	2.81	5.18	7.48 /59	--	--	2.60	1.03
AA	Principal LifeTime Strg Inc A	PALTX	C-	(800) 222-5852	D- / 1.3	1.82	2.75	4.37 /34	5.28 /14	6.09 /17	1.65	1.09
AA	Principal LifeTime Strg Inc Inst	PLSIX	C-	(800) 222-5852	D / 1.8	1.92	2.90	4.72 /37	5.67 /15	6.50 /20	2.11	0.64
AA	Principal LifeTime Strg Inc J	PLSJX	C-	(800) 222-5852	D / 1.7	1.84	2.68	4.41 /34	5.31 /14	6.10 /17	1.80	0.98
AA	Principal LifeTime Strg Inc R1	PLAIX	C-	(800) 222-5852	D- / 1.4	1.67	2.41	3.79 /30	4.75 /12	5.55 /14	1.13	1.52
AA	Principal LifeTime Strg Inc R2	PLSNX	C-	(800) 222-5852	D- / 1.5	1.67	2.44	3.90 /31	4.88 /13	5.69 /15	1.24	1.39
AA	Principal LifeTime Strg Inc R3	PLSMX	C-	(800) 222-5852	D / 1.6	1.76	2.64	4.12 /33	5.07 /13	5.89 /16	1.51	1.21
AA	Principal LifeTime Strg Inc R4	PLSSX	C-	(800) 222-5852	D / 1.6	1.85	2.68	4.32 /34	5.28 /14	6.09 /17	1.71	1.02
AA	Principal LifeTime Strg Inc R5	PLSPX	C-	(800) 222-5852	D / 1.7	1.84	2.74	4.38 /34	5.38 /14	6.20 /18	1.86	0.90
MC	Principal MdCp Gr III Inst	PPIMX	D	(800) 222-5852	B- / 7.2	5.19	11.49	11.76 /82	13.58 /64	13.55 /73	0.00	0.97
MC	Principal MdCp Gr III J	PPQJX	D-	(800) 222-5852	C+ / 6.8	5.06	11.20	11.31 /80	13.02 /60	13.00 /68	0.00	1.44
MC	Principal MdCp Gr III R1	PHASX	D-	(800) 222-5852	C+ / 6.5	5.07	11.09	10.89 /78	12.59 /57	12.60 /65	0.00	1.85
MC	Principal MdCp Gr III R2	PPQNX	D-	(800) 222-5852	C+ / 6.6	5.01	11.08	10.98 /78	12.73 /58	12.71 /66	0.00	1.72
MC	Principal MdCp Gr III R3	PPQMX	D-	(800) 222-5852	C+ / 6.7	4.99	11.12	11.12 /79	12.94 /59	12.92 /67	0.00	1.54
MC	Principal MdCp Gr III R4	PPQSX	D	(800) 222-5852	C+ / 6.9	5.09	11.31	11.40 /80	13.14 /61	13.14 /69	0.00	1.35
MC	Principal MdCp Gr III R5	PPQPX	D	(800) 222-5852	B- / 7.0	5.22	11.44	11.53 /81	13.28 /62	13.26 /71	0.00	1.23
MC	Principal MdCp Value I Inst	PVMIX	C+	(800) 222-5852	A- / 9.1	2.22	8.52	11.50 /80	17.68 /93	14.90 /86	0.48	1.01
MC	Principal MdCp Value I J	PVEJX	C+	(800) 222-5852	B+ / 8.9	2.10	8.28	11.07 /79	17.15 /91	14.33 /81	0.16	1.44
MC	Principal MdCp Value I R1	PLASX	C	(800) 222-5852	B+ / 8.6	2.01	8.07	10.55 /77	16.66 /88	13.92 /77	0.00	1.87

RISK			NET ASSETS		ASSET					BULL / BEAR		FUND MANAGER		MINIMUMS		LOADS	
	3 Year		NAV						Portfolio	Last Bull	Last Bear	Manager	Manager	Initial	Additional	Front	Back
Risk Rating/Pts	Standard Deviation	Beta	As of 3/31/15	Total $(Mil)	Cash %	Stocks %	Bonds %	Other %	Turnover Ratio	Market Return	Market Return	Quality Pct	Tenure (Years)	Purch. $	Purch. $	End Load	End Load
B- / 7.6	8.2	1.39	11.53	14	9	72	17	2	13	62.4	-17.8	12	7	0	0	0.0	0.0
B- / 7.5	8.3	1.40	11.51	15	9	72	17	2	13	63.2	-17.8	12	7	0	0	0.0	0.0
B- / 7.5	8.3	1.40	11.56	112	9	72	17	2	13	64.3	-17.7	13	7	0	0	0.0	0.0
B- / 7.5	8.3	1.39	11.62	71	9	72	17	2	13	65.3	-17.6	15	7	0	0	0.0	0.0
B- / 7.5	8.3	1.40	11.65	113	9	72	17	2	13	66.0	-17.6	16	7	0	0	0.0	0.0
B- / 7.3	8.7	1.47	14.94	90	9	77	12	2	12	68.0	-18.3	12	10	1,000	100	5.5	0.0
B- / 7.3	8.7	1.48	15.16	3,063	9	77	12	2	12	70.1	-18.1	14	14	1,000,000	0	0.0	0.0
B- / 7.4	8.8	1.47	15.06	603	9	77	12	2	12	68.1	-18.4	12	14	1,000	100	0.0	0.0
B- / 7.4	8.8	1.48	15.04	34	9	77	12	2	12	65.2	-18.5	9	11	0	0	0.0	0.0
B- / 7.4	8.8	1.49	15.03	45	9	77	12	2	12	65.8	-18.4	10	14	0	0	0.0	0.0
B- / 7.4	8.8	1.48	15.01	167	9	77	12	2	12	67.0	-18.4	11	14	0	0	0.0	0.0
B- / 7.3	8.8	1.48	15.02	138	9	77	12	2	12	68.0	-18.3	12	14	0	0	0.0	0.0
B- / 7.3	8.8	1.48	15.10	318	9	77	12	2	12	68.8	-18.3	13	14	0	0	0.0	0.0
B- / 7.2	9.0	1.52	11.96	495	10	79	9	2	9	72.2	-18.5	14	7	1,000,000	0	0.0	0.0
B- / 7.2	9.0	1.52	11.67	9	10	79	9	2	9	67.2	-18.9	9	7	0	0	0.0	0.0
B- / 7.2	9.0	1.51	11.66	12	10	79	9	2	9	67.9	-18.8	10	7	0	0	0.0	0.0
B- / 7.2	9.0	1.52	11.73	61	10	79	9	2	9	69.2	-18.8	10	7	0	0	0.0	0.0
B- / 7.2	9.0	1.52	11.80	35	10	79	9	2	9	70.2	-18.7	11	7	0	0	0.0	0.0
B- / 7.2	9.0	1.52	11.82	93	10	79	9	2	9	70.8	-18.7	12	7	0	0	0.0	0.0
B- / 7.1	9.3	1.57	14.78	66	10	82	6	2	10	72.2	-19.3	10	10	1,000	100	5.5	0.0
B- / 7.1	9.3	1.57	14.71	1,629	10	82	6	2	10	74.5	-19.3	12	14	1,000,000	0	0.0	0.0
B- / 7.1	9.3	1.56	14.37	175	10	82	6	2	10	71.5	-19.4	10	14	1,000	100	0.0	0.0
B- / 7.1	9.4	1.58	14.58	19	10	82	6	2	10	69.2	-19.5	7	11	0	0	0.0	0.0
B- / 7.1	9.3	1.57	14.57	25	10	82	6	2	10	70.0	-19.5	8	14	0	0	0.0	0.0
B- / 7.1	9.3	1.56	14.58	79	10	82	6	2	10	71.1	-19.5	9	14	0	0	0.0	0.0
B- / 7.1	9.3	1.57	14.64	63	10	82	6	2	10	72.1	-19.3	10	14	0	0	0.0	0.0
B- / 7.1	9.3	1.57	14.66	187	10	82	6	2	10	72.9	-19.3	10	14	0	0	0.0	0.0
B- / 7.1	9.3	1.57	12.23	138	11	82	6	1	9	74.2	-19.4	11	7	1,000,000	0	0.0	0.0
B- / 7.1	9.4	1.58	11.90	2	11	82	6	1	9	69.2	-19.8	7	7	0	0	0.0	0.0
B- / 7.1	9.4	1.57	11.93	2	11	82	6	1	9	69.9	-19.7	8	7	0	0	0.0	0.0
B- / 7.1	9.4	1.58	12.00	14	11	82	6	1	9	71.1	-19.7	8	7	0	0	0.0	0.0
B- / 7.1	9.3	1.57	12.07	10	11	82	6	1	9	71.9	-19.6	10	7	0	0	0.0	0.0
B- / 7.1	9.3	1.57	12.10	23	11	82	6	1	9	72.7	-19.5	10	7	0	0	0.0	0.0
U /	N/A	N/A	12.46	60	10	82	6	2	16	N/A	N/A	N/A	2	1,000,000	0	0.0	0.0
B / 8.9	3.5	0.52	12.30	32	5	20	73	2	27	25.9	-4.7	63	8	1,000	100	3.8	0.0
B / 8.9	3.5	0.53	12.22	549	5	20	73	2	27	27.6	-4.6	68	8	1,000,000	0	0.0	0.0
B / 8.9	3.5	0.53	12.16	83	5	20	73	2	27	26.1	-4.7	63	8	1,000	100	0.0	0.0
B+ / 9.0	3.5	0.53	12.21	7	5	20	73	2	27	23.7	-4.9	55	8	0	0	0.0	0.0
B+ / 9.0	3.5	0.52	12.21	8	5	20	73	2	27	24.3	-4.8	58	8	0	0	0.0	0.0
B / 8.9	3.5	0.53	12.12	32	5	20	73	2	27	25.2	-4.8	59	8	0	0	0.0	0.0
B / 8.9	3.5	0.52	12.14	19	5	20	73	2	27	26.0	-4.7	63	8	0	0	0.0	0.0
B / 8.9	3.5	0.53	12.20	50	5	20	73	2	27	26.4	-4.7	64	8	0	0	0.0	0.0
D / 1.6	11.6	1.00	10.94	1,422	5	94	0	1	131	81.6	-22.4	25	N/A	1,000,000	0	0.0	0.0
E+ / 0.9	11.6	1.00	9.34	39	5	94	0	1	131	78.6	-22.4	20	N/A	1,000	100	0.0	0.0
D- / 1.0	11.7	1.01	9.54	3	5	94	0	1	131	76.2	-22.6	16	N/A	0	0	0.0	0.0
D- / 1.1	11.6	1.00	9.85	5	5	94	0	1	131	76.7	-22.5	18	N/A	0	0	0.0	0.0
D- / 1.3	11.6	1.00	10.52	11	5	94	0	1	131	78.0	-22.5	19	N/A	0	0	0.0	0.0
D- / 1.4	11.6	1.00	10.73	15	5	94	0	1	131	79.1	-22.4	21	N/A	0	0	0.0	0.0
D / 1.6	11.6	1.01	11.09	14	5	94	0	1	131	80.0	-22.4	22	N/A	0	0	0.0	0.0
C- / 3.1	9.8	0.87	15.18	1,781	3	96	0	1	85	105.3	-22.0	87	12	1,000,000	0	0.0	0.0
C- / 3.1	9.8	0.87	15.05	81	3	96	0	1	85	102.0	-22.2	85	12	1,000	100	0.0	0.0
C- / 3.1	9.8	0.87	14.69	7	3	96	0	1	85	99.3	-22.3	83	12	0	0	0.0	0.0

Fund Type	Fund Name	Ticker Symbol	Overall Investment Rating	Phone	Perfor-mance Rating/Pts	3 Mo	6 Mo	1Yr / Pct	3Yr / Pct	5Yr / Pct	Dividend Yield	Expense Ratio
MC	Principal MdCp Value I R2	PABUX	C	(800) 222-5852	B+ / 8.7	2.00	8.17	10.71 /77	16.81 /89	14.08 /78	0.00	1.74
MC	Principal MdCp Value I R3	PMPRX	C+	(800) 222-5852	B+ / 8.8	2.04	8.21	10.86 /78	17.03 /90	14.26 /80	0.00	1.56
MC	Principal MdCp Value I R4	PABWX	C+	(800) 222-5852	B+ / 8.9	2.11	8.35	11.14 /79	17.25 /91	14.48 /82	0.19	1.37
MC	Principal MdCp Value I R5	PABVX	C+	(800) 222-5852	A- / 9.0	2.17	8.40	11.26 /79	17.40 /92	14.63 /83	0.28	1.25
MC	● Principal MidCap A	PEMGX	A+	(800) 222-5852	A+ / 9.6	6.38	13.60	18.04 /96	19.27 /97	18.56 /98	0.00	1.00
MC	● Principal MidCap C	PMBCX	A+	(800) 222-5852	A+ / 9.7	6.21	13.15	17.17 /95	18.39 /95	17.65 /97	0.00	1.74
MC	● Principal MidCap Inst	PCBIX	A+	(800) 222-5852	A+ / 9.8	6.48	13.78	18.44 /96	19.70 /97	19.02 /98	0.32	0.68
MC	● Principal MidCap J	PMBJX	A+	(800) 222-5852	A+ / 9.8	6.38	13.62	18.16 /96	19.34 /97	18.57 /98	0.12	0.93
MC	● Principal MidCap P	PMCPX	A+	(800) 222-5852	A+ / 9.8	6.45	13.78	18.40 /96	19.62 /97	18.84 /98	0.29	0.71
MC	● Principal MidCap R1	PMSBX	A+	(800) 222-5852	A+ / 9.7	6.21	13.28	17.43 /95	18.71 /96	18.02 /97	0.00	1.47
MC	● Principal MidCap R2	PMBNX	A+	(800) 222-5852	A+ / 9.7	6.30	13.41	17.66 /95	18.88 /96	18.18 /98	0.00	1.34
MC	● Principal MidCap R3	PMBMX	A+	(800) 222-5852	A+ / 9.7	6.33	13.49	17.86 /95	19.10 /97	18.39 /98	0.00	1.16
MC	● Principal MidCap R4	PMBSX	A+	(800) 222-5852	A+ / 9.8	6.34	13.57	18.06 /96	19.33 /97	18.62 /98	0.05	0.97
MC	● Principal MidCap R5	PMBPX	A+	(800) 222-5852	A+ / 9.8	6.45	13.68	18.21 /96	19.48 /97	18.77 /98	0.17	0.85
MC	Principal MidCp Grw Inst	PGWIX	C	(800) 222-5852	A+ / 9.7	9.01	13.70	17.30 /95	18.02 /94	16.60 /95	0.00	0.78
MC	Principal MidCp Grw J	PMGJX	C-	(800) 222-5852	A+ / 9.6	8.99	13.40	16.79 /94	17.44 /92	16.00 /93	0.00	1.21
MC	Principal MidCp Grw R1	PMSGX	C-	(800) 222-5852	A / 9.4	8.72	13.12	16.36 /94	17.04 /90	15.59 /91	0.00	1.56
MC	Principal MidCp Grw R2	PGPPX	C-	(800) 222-5852	A / 9.5	8.80	13.28	16.52 /94	17.21 /91	15.78 /92	0.00	1.43
MC	Principal MidCp Grw R3	PFPPX	C-	(800) 222-5852	A+ / 9.6	8.97	13.53	16.80 /94	17.46 /92	15.99 /93	0.00	1.25
MC	Principal MidCp Grw R4	PIPPX	C-	(800) 222-5852	A+ / 9.6	9.01	13.53	16.97 /95	17.65 /93	16.18 /94	0.00	1.06
MC	Principal MidCp Grw R5	PHPPX	C	(800) 222-5852	A+ / 9.6	9.00	13.55	17.04 /95	17.80 /94	16.34 /94	0.00	0.94
MC	Principal MidCp S&P 400 Idx Inst	MPSIX	A	(800) 222-5852	A- / 9.0	5.26	11.87	11.93 /82	16.75 /88	15.46 /90	1.08	0.20
MC	Principal MidCp S&P 400 Idx J	PMFJX	A-	(800) 222-5852	B+ / 8.8	5.16	11.63	11.51 /80	16.26 /85	14.92 /86	0.77	0.61
MC	Principal MidCp S&P 400 Idx R1	PMSSX	B+	(800) 222-5852	B+ / 8.5	5.04	11.40	10.99 /78	15.76 /81	14.49 /82	0.35	1.04
MC	Principal MidCp S&P 400 Idx R2	PMFNX	A-	(800) 222-5852	B+ / 8.6	5.11	11.51	11.17 /79	15.95 /83	14.64 /84	0.41	0.91
MC	Principal MidCp S&P 400 Idx R3	PMFMX	A-	(800) 222-5852	B+ / 8.7	5.13	11.54	11.37 /80	16.13 /84	14.84 /86	0.60	0.73
MC	Principal MidCp S&P 400 Idx R4	PMFSX	A-	(800) 222-5852	B+ / 8.8	5.17	11.71	11.59 /81	16.36 /86	15.07 /87	0.76	0.54
MC	Principal MidCp S&P 400 Idx R5	PMFPX	A	(800) 222-5852	B+ / 8.9	5.19	11.75	11.70 /81	16.50 /87	15.21 /88	0.87	0.42
MC	Principal MidCp Value III Inst	PVUIX	A+	(800) 222-5852	A- / 9.1	2.52	8.38	9.97 /74	17.92 /94	15.74 /91	1.12	0.66
MC	Principal MidCp Value III J	PMCJX	A+	(800) 222-5852	B+ / 8.9	2.39	8.15	9.59 /72	17.44 /92	15.17 /88	0.85	1.05
MC	Principal MidCp Value III R1	PMSVX	A	(800) 222-5852	B+ / 8.6	2.32	7.89	9.03 /69	16.89 /89	14.66 /84	0.67	1.53
MC	Principal MidCp Value III R2	PKPPX	A	(800) 222-5852	B+ / 8.7	2.36	7.98	9.17 /70	17.05 /90	14.82 /85	0.64	1.40
MC	Principal MidCp Value III R3	PJPPX	A	(800) 222-5852	B+ / 8.8	2.38	8.07	9.39 /71	17.26 /91	15.03 /87	0.82	1.22
MC	Principal MidCp Value III R4	PMPPX	A+	(800) 222-5852	B+ / 8.9	2.46	8.17	9.56 /72	17.48 /92	15.23 /88	0.95	1.03
MC	Principal MidCp Value III R5	PLPPX	A+	(800) 222-5852	A- / 9.0	2.44	8.22	9.71 /73	17.64 /93	15.37 /89	1.04	0.91
FO	Principal Overseas Institutional	PINZX	D-	(800) 222-5852	D / 2.2	3.11	-2.06	-3.54 / 8	8.14 /28	6.07 /17	2.52	1.09
FO	Principal Overseas R-1	PINQX	D	(800) 222-5852	D / 1.7	2.82	-2.51	-4.41 / 6	7.21 /22	5.36 /14	1.65	1.96
FO	Principal Overseas R-2	PINSX	D	(800) 222-5852	D / 1.8	2.92	-2.38	-4.28 / 7	7.33 /23	5.47 /14	1.78	1.83
FO	Principal Overseas R-3	PINTX	D	(800) 222-5852	D / 1.9	2.93	-2.40	-4.14 / 7	7.50 /24	5.59 /15	2.02	1.65
FO	Principal Overseas R-4	PINUX	D	(800) 222-5852	D / 2.0	2.92	-2.28	-3.93 / 7	7.72 /25	5.78 /16	2.13	1.46
FO	Principal Overseas R-5	PINGX	D+	(800) 222-5852	D / 2.2	2.92	-2.24	-3.89 / 7	8.12 /28	6.06 /17	2.26	1.34
RE	Principal Real Est Securities A	PRRAX	C	(800) 222-5852	A / 9.4	5.11	21.45	26.07 /98	14.90 /74	15.67 /91	0.94	1.30
RE	Principal Real Est Securities C	PRCEX	C	(800) 222-5852	A / 9.5	4.92	20.98	25.07 /98	13.97 /67	14.75 /85	0.31	2.09
RE	Principal Real Est Securities Inst	PIREX	C+	(800) 222-5852	A+ / 9.7	5.19	21.63	26.56 /99	15.40 /78	16.22 /94	1.32	0.90
RE	Principal Real Est Securities J	PREJX	C+	(800) 222-5852	A+ / 9.7	5.15	21.42	26.11 /98	14.93 /74	15.70 /91	1.04	1.28
RE	Principal Real Est Securities P	PIRPX	C+	(800) 222-5852	A+ / 9.7	5.19	21.61	26.44 /99	15.27 /77	--	1.26	1.00
RE	Principal Real Est Securities R1	PRAEX	C+	(800) 222-5852	A+ / 9.6	5.02	21.20	25.52 /98	14.46 /71	15.25 /88	0.61	1.71
RE	Principal Real Est Securities R2	PRENX	C	(800) 222-5852	A+ / 9.6	5.01	21.23	25.72 /98	14.61 /72	15.39 /89	0.76	1.58
RE	Principal Real Est Securities R3	PRERX	C+	(800) 222-5852	A+ / 9.7	5.08	21.36	25.86 /98	14.80 /73	15.60 /91	0.89	1.40
RE	Principal Real Est Securities R4	PRETX	C+	(800) 222-5852	A+ / 9.7	5.13	21.46	26.14 /99	15.04 /75	15.84 /92	1.08	1.21
RE	Principal Real Est Securities R5	PREPX	C+	(800) 222-5852	A+ / 9.7	5.16	21.54	26.29 /99	15.16 /76	15.96 /93	1.18	1.09
BA	Principal SAM Bal Port A	SABPX	C	(800) 222-5852	C- / 3.2	2.03	4.42	6.74 /53	9.74 /38	9.25 /39	1.81	1.33

99 Pct = Best
0 Pct = Worst

PERFORMANCE — Total Return % through 3/31/15 — Annualized — Incl. in Returns

● Denotes fund is closed to new investors
* Denotes fund is included in Section II

www.thestreetratings.com

Risk Rating/Pts	3 Year Standard Deviation	Beta	NAV As of 3/31/15	Total $(Mil)	Cash %	Stocks %	Bonds %	Other %	Portfolio Turnover Ratio	Last Bull Market Return	Last Bear Market Return	Manager Quality Pct	Manager Tenure (Years)	Initial Purch. $	Additional Purch. $	Front End Load	Back End Load
C- / 3.1	9.8	0.87	14.78	11	3	96	0	1	85	100.3	-22.3	84	12	0	0	0.0	0.0
C- / 3.1	9.8	0.87	14.98	36	3	96	0	1	85	101.5	-22.2	85	12	0	0	0.0	0.0
C- / 3.1	9.8	0.87	15.02	34	3	96	0	1	85	102.8	-22.2	86	12	0	0	0.0	0.0
C- / 3.1	9.7	0.86	15.09	83	3	96	0	1	85	103.5	-22.1	87	12	0	0	0.0	0.0
C+ / 6.8	10.4	0.89	23.00	2,037	1	98	0	1	18	113.3	-15.9	91	15	1,000	100	5.5	0.0
C+ / 6.8	10.4	0.89	21.56	373	1	98	0	1	18	107.8	-16.1	89	15	1,000	100	0.0	0.0
C+ / 6.8	10.4	0.89	23.33	4,884	1	98	0	1	18	116.0	-15.7	92	15	1,000,000	0	0.0	0.0
C+ / 6.8	10.4	0.89	22.18	304	1	98	0	1	18	113.5	-15.8	91	15	1,000	100	0.0	0.0
C+ / 6.8	10.4	0.88	23.27	2,186	1	98	0	1	18	115.5	-15.7	92	15	0	0	0.0	0.0
C+ / 6.8	10.4	0.89	21.88	45	1	98	0	1	18	110.0	-16.0	89	15	0	0	0.0	0.0
C+ / 6.8	10.4	0.89	22.10	44	1	98	0	1	18	111.0	-16.0	90	15	0	0	0.0	0.0
C+ / 6.8	10.4	0.89	22.67	167	1	98	0	1	18	112.2	-15.9	90	15	0	0	0.0	0.0
C+ / 6.8	10.4	0.89	23.31	164	1	98	0	1	18	113.6	-15.8	91	15	0	0	0.0	0.0
C+ / 6.8	10.4	0.89	23.12	291	1	98	0	1	18	114.6	-15.8	91	15	0	0	0.0	0.0
D- / 1.2	12.8	0.98	7.50	26	0	99	0	1	185	99.8	-22.3	78	N/A	1,000,000	0	0.0	0.0
E / 0.4	12.8	0.99	6.06	52	0	99	0	1	185	96.7	-22.4	73	N/A	1,000	100	0.0	0.0
E / 0.4	12.8	0.99	6.36	2	0	99	0	1	185	94.4	-22.5	70	N/A	0	0	0.0	0.0
E+ / 0.6	12.8	0.98	6.80	3	0	99	0	1	185	94.9	-22.5	71	N/A	0	0	0.0	0.0
E+ / 0.9	12.8	0.99	7.17	6	0	99	0	1	185	96.2	-22.4	73	N/A	0	0	0.0	0.0
D- / 1.2	12.8	0.98	7.50	6	0	99	0	1	185	97.5	-22.4	76	N/A	0	0	0.0	0.0
D- / 1.5	12.7	0.98	7.75	17	0	99	0	1	185	98.5	-22.4	76	N/A	0	0	0.0	0.0
C+ / 6.4	11.0	1.00	20.41	592	1	98	0	1	14	101.1	-22.6	65	4	1,000,000	0	0.0	0.0
C+ / 6.4	11.0	1.00	19.97	98	1	98	0	1	14	98.2	-22.7	58	4	1,000	100	0.0	0.0
C+ / 6.4	11.0	1.00	20.23	22	1	98	0	1	14	95.5	-22.8	51	4	0	0	0.0	0.0
C+ / 6.4	11.0	1.00	20.77	20	1	98	0	1	14	96.4	-22.8	54	4	0	0	0.0	0.0
C+ / 6.4	11.0	1.00	20.70	122	1	98	0	1	14	97.7	-22.8	57	4	0	0	0.0	0.0
C+ / 6.4	11.0	1.00	20.74	127	1	98	0	1	14	98.8	-22.7	59	4	0	0	0.0	0.0
C+ / 6.4	11.0	1.00	20.89	222	1	98	0	1	14	99.7	-22.7	62	4	0	0	0.0	0.0
C+ / 6.9	10.2	0.89	19.92	840	4	95	0	1	70	110.0	-19.9	86	10	1,000,000	0	0.0	0.0
C+ / 6.8	10.2	0.89	18.82	115	4	95	0	1	70	106.9	-20.2	84	10	1,000	100	0.0	0.0
C+ / 6.8	10.2	0.90	18.95	1	4	95	0	1	70	103.9	-20.3	81	10	0	0	0.0	0.0
C+ / 6.9	10.1	0.89	19.08	2	4	95	0	1	70	104.7	-20.3	82	10	0	0	0.0	0.0
C+ / 6.8	10.1	0.89	18.94	13	4	95	0	1	70	105.9	-20.2	84	10	0	0	0.0	0.0
C+ / 6.8	10.2	0.89	18.76	17	4	95	0	1	70	107.3	-20.2	84	10	0	0	0.0	0.0
C+ / 6.8	10.1	0.89	18.92	28	4	95	0	1	70	108.1	-20.1	86	10	0	0	0.0	0.0
C / 4.9	13.2	0.98	10.62	2,731	4	95	0	1	35	52.6	-24.9	51	7	1,000,000	0	0.0	0.0
C+ / 6.9	13.2	0.98	10.57	N/A	4	95	0	1	35	48.4	-25.0	37	7	0	0	0.0	0.0
C+ / 6.9	13.2	0.98	10.58	N/A	4	95	0	1	35	49.0	-25.0	39	7	0	0	0.0	0.0
C+ / 6.9	13.2	0.98	10.55	N/A	4	95	0	1	35	49.8	-25.0	42	7	0	0	0.0	0.0
C+ / 6.9	13.2	0.98	10.58	1	4	95	0	1	35	50.8	-24.9	45	7	0	0	0.0	0.0
C+ / 6.9	13.1	0.98	10.58	1	4	95	0	1	35	52.5	-24.9	51	7	0	0	0.0	0.0
D+ / 2.3	13.1	1.05	24.00	317	0	99	0	1	11	90.7	-16.3	68	15	1,000	100	5.5	0.0
D+ / 2.3	13.2	1.05	23.68	41	0	99	0	1	11	85.5	-16.6	56	15	1,000	100	0.0	0.0
D+ / 2.3	13.2	1.05	24.01	1,508	0	99	0	1	11	93.7	-16.2	72	15	1,000,000	0	0.0	0.0
D / 2.2	13.2	1.05	23.40	209	0	99	0	1	11	90.8	-16.3	68	15	0	100	0.0	0.0
D+ / 2.3	13.1	1.05	23.99	70	0	99	0	1	11	92.8	-16.2	72	15	0	0	0.0	0.0
D+ / 2.3	13.2	1.05	23.75	9	0	99	0	1	11	88.1	-16.4	63	15	0	0	0.0	0.0
D / 2.2	13.1	1.05	23.01	20	0	99	0	1	11	89.0	-16.4	65	15	0	0	0.0	0.0
D+ / 2.3	13.2	1.05	23.49	67	0	99	0	1	11	90.2	-16.3	67	15	0	0	0.0	0.0
D / 2.2	13.2	1.05	23.27	77	0	99	0	1	11	91.5	-16.3	69	15	0	0	0.0	0.0
D / 2.2	13.2	1.05	23.31	195	0	99	0	1	11	92.2	-16.3	70	15	0	0	0.0	0.0
B / 8.6	6.5	1.12	16.19	2,183	12	55	31	2	3	53.9	-12.2	34	15	1,000	100	5.5	0.0

Fund Type	Fund Name	Ticker Symbol	Overall Investment Rating	Phone	Performance Rating/Pts	Total Return % through 3/31/15			Annualized		Incl. in Returns	
						3 Mo	6 Mo	1Yr / Pct	3Yr / Pct	5Yr / Pct	Dividend Yield	Expense Ratio
BA	Principal SAM Bal Port C	SCBPX	C+	(800) 222-5852	C- / 3.6	1.81	4.03	5.90 /46	8.91 /32	8.44 /33	1.22	2.08
BA	Principal SAM Bal Port Inst	PSBIX	B-	(800) 222-5852	C / 4.3	2.07	4.59	7.04 /55	10.10 /40	9.62 /41	2.27	0.99
BA	Principal SAM Bal Port J	PSAJX	C+	(800) 222-5852	C- / 4.1	2.10	4.51	6.78 /53	9.79 /38	9.26 /39	2.02	1.30
BA	Principal SAM Bal Port R1	PSBGX	C+	(800) 222-5852	C- / 3.7	1.92	4.14	6.15 /48	9.15 /34	8.67 /34	1.43	1.87
BA	Principal SAM Bal Port R2	PSBVX	C+	(800) 222-5852	C- / 3.8	1.90	4.21	6.20 /48	9.29 /35	8.81 /35	1.54	1.74
BA	Principal SAM Bal Port R3	PBAPX	C+	(800) 222-5852	C- / 4.0	2.00	4.31	6.46 /50	9.50 /36	9.01 /37	1.72	1.56
BA	Principal SAM Bal Port R4	PSBLX	C+	(800) 222-5852	C- / 4.1	2.04	4.39	6.65 /52	9.71 /38	9.22 /38	1.90	1.37
BA	Principal SAM Bal Port R5	PSBFX	C+	(800) 222-5852	C- / 4.2	2.08	4.46	6.78 /53	9.83 /38	9.36 /39	2.02	1.25
BA	Principal SAM Consv Bal A	SAIPX	C	(800) 222-5852	D / 2.1	1.82	3.70	5.78 /45	7.62 /25	7.67 /28	2.13	1.29
BA	Principal SAM Consv Bal C	SCIPX	C	(800) 222-5852	D+ / 2.4	1.65	3.27	4.97 /38	6.80 /20	6.86 /22	1.54	2.04
BA	Principal SAM Consv Bal Inst	PCCIX	C+	(800) 222-5852	C- / 3.1	2.00	3.89	6.16 /48	7.95 /27	8.01 /30	2.58	0.96
BA	Principal SAM Consv Bal J	PCBJX	C	(800) 222-5852	D+ / 2.9	1.85	3.68	5.79 /45	7.63 /25	7.65 /28	2.31	1.26
BA	Principal SAM Consv Bal R1	PCSSX	C	(800) 222-5852	D+ / 2.5	1.78	3.46	5.25 /40	7.04 /22	7.11 /24	1.72	1.83
BA	Principal SAM Consv Bal R2	PCNSX	C	(800) 222-5852	D+ / 2.6	1.74	3.42	5.36 /41	7.16 /22	7.22 /24	1.83	1.70
BA	Principal SAM Consv Bal R3	PCBPX	C	(800) 222-5852	D+ / 2.7	1.77	3.52	5.56 /43	7.37 /23	7.43 /26	2.01	1.52
BA	Principal SAM Consv Bal R4	PCBLX	C	(800) 222-5852	D+ / 2.8	1.81	3.61	5.77 /44	7.57 /24	7.64 /27	2.21	1.33
BA	Principal SAM Consv Bal R5	PCBFX	C	(800) 222-5852	D+ / 2.9	1.85	3.68	5.89 /45	7.70 /25	7.75 /28	2.33	1.21
AA	Principal SAM Consv Growth A	SAGPX	C+	(800) 222-5852	C / 4.3	2.15	5.12	7.50 /59	11.57 /50	10.56 /49	1.51	1.37
AA	Principal SAM Consv Growth C	SCGPX	C+	(800) 222-5852	C / 4.6	1.98	4.74	6.76 /53	10.74 /44	9.74 /42	1.00	2.12
AA	Principal SAM Consv Growth Inst	PCWIX	B-	(800) 222-5852	C / 5.4	2.25	5.27	7.94 /62	11.96 /52	10.95 /52	1.95	1.04
AA	Principal SAM Consv Growth J	PCGJX	B-	(800) 222-5852	C / 5.2	2.21	5.15	7.60 /60	11.60 /50	10.56 /49	1.69	1.35
AA	Principal SAM Consv Growth R1	PCGGX	C+	(800) 222-5852	C / 4.8	2.04	4.80	6.95 /55	10.99 /45	9.98 /44	1.14	1.91
AA	Principal SAM Consv Growth R2	PCGVX	C+	(800) 222-5852	C / 4.9	2.10	4.90	7.11 /56	11.13 /46	10.13 /46	1.29	1.78
AA	Principal SAM Consv Growth R3	PCGPX	C+	(800) 222-5852	C / 5.0	2.10	5.02	7.29 /57	11.33 /48	10.33 /47	1.40	1.60
AA	Principal SAM Consv Growth R4	PCWSX	B-	(800) 222-5852	C / 5.2	2.20	5.10	7.54 /59	11.55 /49	10.55 /49	1.62	1.41
AA	Principal SAM Consv Growth R5	PCWPX	B-	(800) 222-5852	C / 5.2	2.20	5.17	7.61 /60	11.66 /50	10.68 /50	1.73	1.29
AA	Principal SAM Flex Inc A	SAUPX	C-	(800) 222-5852	D / 1.7	1.52	2.91	4.97 /38	6.39 /18	6.77 /22	2.62	1.21
AA	Principal SAM Flex Inc C	SCUPX	C-	(800) 222-5852	D / 1.7	1.35	2.55	4.22 /33	5.60 /15	5.97 /17	1.99	1.97
AA	Principal SAM Flex Inc Inst	PIFIX	C	(800) 222-5852	D+ / 2.3	1.52	3.00	5.22 /40	6.72 /20	7.10 /24	3.04	0.89
AA	Principal SAM Flex Inc J	PFIJX	C-	(800) 222-5852	D / 2.2	1.54	2.95	5.03 /39	6.41 /19	6.74 /21	2.77	1.19
AA	Principal SAM Flex Inc R1	PFIGX	C-	(800) 222-5852	D / 1.8	1.39	2.64	4.41 /34	5.80 /16	6.20 /18	2.18	1.76
AA	Principal SAM Flex Inc R2	PFIVX	C-	(800) 222-5852	D / 1.9	1.34	2.62	4.44 /35	5.95 /17	6.33 /19	2.30	1.63
AA	Principal SAM Flex Inc R3	PFIPX	C-	(800) 222-5852	D / 2.0	1.46	2.80	4.73 /37	6.15 /17	6.52 /20	2.49	1.45
AA	Principal SAM Flex Inc R4	PFILX	C-	(800) 222-5852	D / 2.1	1.51	2.89	4.92 /38	6.34 /18	6.74 /21	2.67	1.26
AA	Principal SAM Flex Inc R5	PFIFX	C	(800) 222-5852	D / 2.2	1.46	2.87	4.97 /38	6.44 /19	6.84 /22	2.80	1.14
AA	Principal SAM Strat Growth A	SACAX	C+	(800) 222-5852	C / 5.1	1.94	5.50	8.51 /66	12.99 /60	11.58 /58	1.61	1.33
AA	Principal SAM Strat Growth C	SWHCX	C+	(800) 222-5852	C / 5.5	1.71	5.06	7.71 /61	12.14 /53	10.74 /51	1.13	2.08
AA	Principal SAM Strat Growth Inst	PSWIX	C+	(800) 222-5852	C+ / 6.3	2.02	5.66	8.88 /69	13.43 /63	12.00 /61	2.06	0.98
AA	Principal SAM Strat Growth J	PSWJX	C+	(800) 222-5852	C+ / 6.1	1.94	5.50	8.53 /67	13.05 /60	11.60 /58	1.79	1.30
AA	Principal SAM Strat Growth R1	PSGGX	C+	(800) 222-5852	C+ / 5.7	1.84	5.23	7.95 /62	12.44 /56	11.04 /53	1.19	1.85
AA	Principal SAM Strat Growth R2	PSGVX	C+	(800) 222-5852	C+ / 5.8	1.84	5.31	8.13 /64	12.57 /56	11.18 /54	1.36	1.72
AA	Principal SAM Strat Growth R3	PSGPX	C+	(800) 222-5852	C+ / 5.9	1.84	5.33	8.25 /65	12.77 /58	11.37 /56	1.53	1.54
AA	Principal SAM Strat Growth R4	PSGLX	C+	(800) 222-5852	C+ / 6.0	1.93	5.47	8.48 /66	12.98 /60	11.59 /58	1.72	1.35
AA	Principal SAM Strat Growth R5	PSGFX	C+	(800) 222-5852	C+ / 6.1	1.99	5.56	8.64 /67	13.13 /61	11.73 /59	1.85	1.23
IN	Principal Small-MidCap Div Inc A	PMDAX	B-	(800) 222-5852	C+ / 5.9	2.19	7.02	6.68 /52	14.55 /71	--	1.86	1.47
IN	Principal Small-MidCap Div Inc C	PMDDX	U	(800) 222-5852	U /	2.02	6.63	5.94 /46	--	--	1.32	2.28
IN	Principal Small-MidCap Div Inc Inst	PMDIX	B+	(800) 222-5852	B- / 7.3	2.32	7.23	7.15 /56	15.06 /75	--	2.34	1.07
IN	Principal Small-MidCap Div Inc P	PMDPX	B+	(800) 222-5852	B- / 7.1	2.30	7.16	7.02 /55	14.86 /74	--	2.26	1.21
SC	Principal SmCap Blend Fd A	PLLAX	B+	(800) 222-5852	A- / 9.2	7.20	16.26	9.22 /70	18.82 /96	16.05 /93	0.00	1.25
SC	Principal SmCap Blend Fd C	PSMCX	B+	(800) 222-5852	A / 9.4	6.95	15.75	8.26 /65	17.85 /94	15.16 /88	0.00	2.10
SC	Principal SmCap Blend Fd Inst	PSLIX	B+	(800) 222-5852	A+ / 9.7	7.30	16.46	9.65 /73	19.38 /97	16.68 /95	0.00	0.81
SC	Principal SmCap Blend Fd J	PSBJX	B+	(800) 222-5852	A+ / 9.6	7.24	16.31	9.33 /71	18.95 /97	16.20 /94	0.00	1.16

99 Pct = Best
0 Pct = Worst

• Denotes fund is closed to new investors
* Denotes fund is included in Section II

www.thestreetratings.com

Risk Rating/Pts	3 Year Standard Deviation	Beta	NAV As of 3/31/15	Total $(Mil)	Cash %	Stocks %	Bonds %	Other %	Portfolio Turnover Ratio	Last Bull Market Return	Last Bear Market Return	Manager Quality Pct	Manager Tenure (Years)	Initial Purch. $	Additional Purch. $	Front End Load	Back End Load
B /8.6	6.5	1.12	16.00	765	12	55	31	2	3	49.9	-12.4	25	13	1,000	100	0.0	0.0
B /8.6	6.5	1.13	15.97	797	12	55	31	2	3	55.7	-12.1	37	8	1,000,000	0	0.0	0.0
B /8.6	6.5	1.11	15.75	1,015	12	55	31	2	3	54.1	-12.3	35	8	1,000	100	0.0	0.0
B /8.6	6.5	1.12	15.95	5	12	55	31	2	3	51.1	-12.4	27	8	0	0	0.0	0.0
B /8.6	6.5	1.12	15.90	9	12	55	31	2	3	51.8	-12.4	29	8	0	0	0.0	0.0
B /8.6	6.5	1.12	15.93	64	12	55	31	2	3	52.7	-12.3	31	8	0	0	0.0	0.0
B /8.6	6.4	1.11	15.96	53	12	55	31	2	3	53.7	-12.3	34	8	0	0	0.0	0.0
B /8.6	6.5	1.12	15.96	116	12	55	31	2	3	54.4	-12.2	35	8	0	0	0.0	0.0
B /8.9	4.7	0.80	12.29	515	9	38	51	2	3	39.8	-8.4	52	15	1,000	100	5.5	0.0
B /8.9	4.8	0.81	12.18	255	9	38	51	2	3	36.3	-8.7	40	13	1,000	100	0.0	0.0
B /8.9	4.7	0.80	12.19	295	9	38	51	2	3	41.3	-8.3	58	8	1,000,000	0	0.0	0.0
B /8.9	4.7	0.80	12.15	544	9	38	51	2	3	39.9	-8.4	53	8	1,000	100	0.0	0.0
B /8.9	4.7	0.80	12.16	3	9	38	51	2	3	37.2	-8.7	44	8	0	0	0.0	0.0
B /8.9	4.7	0.80	12.21	3	9	38	51	2	3	37.8	-8.6	48	8	0	0	0.0	0.0
B /8.9	4.7	0.80	12.17	18	9	38	51	2	3	38.7	-8.6	50	8	0	0	0.0	0.0
B /8.9	4.7	0.80	12.18	20	9	38	51	2	3	39.5	-8.4	53	8	0	0	0.0	0.0
B /8.9	4.7	0.80	12.18	40	9	38	51	2	3	40.1	-8.3	54	8	0	0	0.0	0.0
B- /7.9	8.2	1.42	18.53	1,568	16	71	12	1	4	67.9	-16.2	19	15	1,000	100	5.5	0.0
B- /7.8	8.2	1.42	17.52	566	16	71	12	1	4	63.5	-16.4	13	13	1,000	100	0.0	0.0
B- /7.9	8.2	1.41	18.20	529	16	71	12	1	4	69.8	-16.0	22	8	1,000,000	0	0.0	0.0
B- /7.8	8.3	1.42	18.01	511	16	71	12	1	4	68.0	-16.1	19	8	1,000	100	0.0	0.0
B- /7.8	8.2	1.42	17.97	4	16	71	12	1	4	65.0	-16.4	15	8	0	0	0.0	0.0
B- /7.8	8.3	1.42	17.97	9	16	71	12	1	4	65.6	-16.3	15	8	0	0	0.0	0.0
B- /7.9	8.2	1.42	18.00	27	16	71	12	1	4	66.6	-16.2	17	8	0	0	0.0	0.0
B- /7.8	8.3	1.42	18.14	23	16	71	12	1	4	67.6	-16.1	18	8	0	0	0.0	0.0
B- /7.8	8.3	1.43	18.09	88	16	71	12	1	4	68.4	-16.1	19	8	0	0	0.0	0.0
B /8.7	3.7	0.59	12.53	839	4	28	67	1	4	32.0	-5.6	68	15	1,000	100	3.8	0.0
B /8.7	3.8	0.59	12.42	332	4	28	67	1	4	28.6	-5.8	57	13	1,000	100	0.0	0.0
B /8.7	3.7	0.59	12.49	180	4	28	67	1	4	33.5	-5.4	71	8	1,000,000	0	0.0	0.0
B /8.7	3.8	0.60	12.44	789	4	28	67	1	4	32.1	-5.5	67	8	1,000	100	0.0	0.0
B /8.7	3.8	0.60	12.45	1	4	28	67	1	4	29.5	-5.7	60	8	0	0	0.0	0.0
B /8.7	3.7	0.59	12.47	1	4	28	67	1	4	30.1	-5.7	63	8	0	0	0.0	0.0
B /8.7	3.7	0.59	12.47	11	4	28	67	1	4	31.0	-5.7	65	8	0	0	0.0	0.0
B /8.7	3.8	0.60	12.48	10	4	28	67	1	4	31.8	-5.5	66	8	0	0	0.0	0.0
B /8.7	3.7	0.59	12.47	21	4	28	67	1	4	32.4	-5.5	69	8	0	0	0.0	0.0
C+ /6.8	9.6	1.64	21.07	1,050	6	91	1	2	66	79.1	-18.9	12	15	1,000	100	5.5	0.0
C+ /6.8	9.6	1.64	19.63	338	6	91	1	2	66	74.7	-19.2	8	13	1,000	100	0.0	0.0
C+ /6.8	9.6	1.64	20.68	282	6	91	1	2	66	81.5	-18.8	14	8	1,000,000	0	0.0	0.0
C+ /6.8	9.6	1.64	20.51	290	6	91	1	2	66	79.4	-18.9	12	8	1,000	100	0.0	0.0
C+ /6.8	9.6	1.65	20.43	3	6	91	1	2	66	76.2	-19.1	9	8	0	0	0.0	0.0
C+ /6.8	9.6	1.64	20.46	6	6	91	1	2	66	76.9	-19.0	10	8	0	0	0.0	0.0
C+ /6.8	9.6	1.64	20.47	17	6	91	1	2	66	78.1	-19.0	10	8	0	0	0.0	0.0
C+ /6.8	9.6	1.64	20.58	19	6	91	1	2	66	79.3	-18.9	12	8	0	0	0.0	0.0
C+ /6.8	9.6	1.64	20.53	36	6	91	1	2	66	80.0	-18.9	13	8	0	0	0.0	0.0
B- /7.3	9.9	0.91	13.96	194	15	84	0	1	18	90.6	N/A	N/A	4	1,000	100	5.5	0.0
U /	N/A	N/A	13.89	136	15	84	0	1	18	N/A	N/A	N/A	4	1,000	100	0.0	0.0
B- /7.3	9.8	0.90	14.02	792	15	84	0	1	18	93.4	N/A	73	4	0	0	0.0	0.0
B- /7.3	9.8	0.90	14.14	627	15	84	0	1	18	92.6	N/A	71	4	0	0	0.0	0.0
C /5.0	13.5	0.97	21.60	212	2	97	0	1	68	115.4	-24.8	87	9	1,000	100	5.5	0.0
C /4.8	13.5	0.97	20.17	18	2	97	0	1	68	109.8	-25.1	83	9	1,000	100	0.0	0.0
C /5.1	13.5	0.97	22.78	87	2	97	0	1	68	119.3	-24.7	89	9	1,000,000	0	0.0	0.0
C /5.0	13.5	0.97	20.75	215	2	97	0	1	68	116.4	-24.8	88	9	1,000	100	0.0	0.0

Fund Type	Fund Name	Ticker Symbol	Overall Investment Rating	Phone	Perfor-mance Rating/Pts	3 Mo	6 Mo	1Yr / Pct	3Yr / Pct	5Yr / Pct	Dividend Yield	Expense Ratio
	99 Pct = Best							Total Return % through 3/31/15	Annualized		Incl. in Returns	
SC	Principal SmCap Blend Fd R1	PSABX	B+	(800) 222-5852	A / 9.5	7.08	15.97	8.75 /68	18.38 /95	15.70 /91	0.00	1.66
SC	Principal SmCap Blend Fd R2	PSBNX	B+	(800) 222-5852	A+ / 9.6	7.07	16.06	8.89 /69	18.52 /96	15.84 /92	0.00	1.53
SC	Principal SmCap Blend Fd R3	PSBMX	B+	(800) 222-5852	A+ / 9.6	7.14	16.12	9.10 /70	18.77 /96	16.06 /93	0.00	1.35
SC	Principal SmCap Blend Fd R4	PSBSX	B+	(800) 222-5852	A+ / 9.6	7.22	16.24	9.28 /71	18.99 /97	16.28 /94	0.00	1.16
SC	Principal SmCap Blend Fd R5	PSBPX	B+	(800) 222-5852	A+ / 9.7	7.20	16.29	9.42 /72	19.11 /97	16.42 /94	0.00	1.04
SC	Principal SmCap S&P 600 Indx Inst	PSSIX	A-	(800) 222-5852	A- / 9.0	3.95	14.13	8.54 /67	17.02 /90	15.99 /93	0.99	0.22
SC	Principal SmCap S&P 600 Indx J	PSSJX	B+	(800) 222-5852	B+ / 8.7	3.86	13.93	8.18 /64	16.56 /87	15.46 /90	0.72	0.59
SC	Principal SmCap S&P 600 Indx R1	PSAPX	B+	(800) 222-5852	B+ / 8.4	3.73	13.68	7.64 /60	16.07 /84	15.01 /87	0.21	1.06
SC	Principal SmCap S&P 600 Indx R2	PSSNX	B+	(800) 222-5852	B+ / 8.5	3.74	13.70	7.78 /61	16.20 /85	15.16 /88	0.31	0.93
SC	Principal SmCap S&P 600 Indx R3	PSSMX	B+	(800) 222-5852	B+ / 8.6	3.80	13.81	7.96 /63	16.42 /86	15.37 /89	0.52	0.75
SC	Principal SmCap S&P 600 Indx R4	PSSSX	B+	(800) 222-5852	B+ / 8.8	3.81	13.95	8.17 /64	16.63 /88	15.58 /91	0.67	0.56
SC	Principal SmCap S&P 600 Indx R5	PSSPX	A-	(800) 222-5852	B+ / 8.8	3.88	14.02	8.31 /65	16.78 /89	15.73 /91	0.75	0.44
SC	Principal SmCp Gr I Inst	PGRTX	C	(800) 222-5852	B+ / 8.4	6.73	14.51	7.84 /62	15.66 /81	17.18 /96	0.00	1.09
SC	Principal SmCp Gr I J	PSIJX	D+	(800) 222-5852	B / 8.0	6.66	14.38	7.37 /58	15.09 /76	16.51 /95	0.00	1.64
SC	Principal SmCp Gr I R1	PNASX	D+	(800) 222-5852	B / 7.7	6.66	14.15	6.96 /55	14.66 /72	16.18 /94	0.00	1.95
SC	Principal SmCp Gr I R2	PPNNX	D+	(800) 222-5852	B / 7.8	6.54	14.11	7.03 /55	14.81 /73	16.29 /94	0.00	1.82
SC	Principal SmCp Gr I R3	PPNMX	C-	(800) 222-5852	B / 7.9	6.65	14.23	7.28 /57	15.00 /75	16.53 /95	0.00	1.64
SC	Principal SmCp Gr I R4	PPNSX	C-	(800) 222-5852	B / 8.1	6.73	14.41	7.50 /59	15.22 /77	16.75 /95	0.00	1.45
SC	Principal SmCp Gr I R5	PPNPX	C-	(800) 222-5852	B / 8.2	6.69	14.43	7.61 /60	15.35 /78	16.90 /96	0.00	1.33
SC	Principal SmCp Value II Inst	PPVIX	B+	(800) 222-5852	A- / 9.1	4.25	12.73	8.76 /68	17.42 /92	14.46 /82	0.30	1.08
SC	Principal SmCp Value II J	PSMJX	B+	(800) 222-5852	B+ / 8.8	4.17	12.51	8.24 /64	16.76 /89	13.69 /75	0.00	1.60
SC	Principal SmCp Value II R1	PCPTX	B	(800) 222-5852	B+ / 8.6	4.13	12.29	7.87 /62	16.45 /87	13.46 /72	0.00	1.95
SC	Principal SmCp Value II R2	PKARX	B	(800) 222-5852	B+ / 8.7	4.17	12.37	8.05 /63	16.61 /88	13.59 /74	0.00	1.82
SC	Principal SmCp Value II R3	PJARX	B+	(800) 222-5852	B+ / 8.8	4.14	12.38	8.16 /64	16.79 /89	13.79 /76	0.00	1.64
SC	Principal SmCp Value II R4	PSTWX	B+	(800) 222-5852	B+ / 8.9	4.18	12.53	8.42 /66	17.01 /90	14.02 /78	0.00	1.45
SC	Principal SmCp Value II R5	PLARX	B+	(800) 222-5852	A- / 9.0	4.23	12.62	8.53 /67	17.16 /91	14.13 /79	0.09	1.33
GL	Private Capital Management Value A	VFPAX	B	(888) 739-1390	B- / 7.4	2.67	12.36	16.53 /94	15.26 /77	--	0.00	1.74
GL	Private Capital Management Value I	VFPIX	B+	(888) 739-1390	B+ / 8.6	2.77	12.47	16.84 /94	15.54 /79	14.17 /79	0.00	1.49
GR	Probabilities I	PROTX	U	(855) 224-7204	U /	-2.49	2.19	2.97 /26	--	--	0.00	2.08
GI	Profit	PVALX	D	(888) 744-2337	C+ / 6.5	-2.22	2.44	10.51 /76	14.27 /69	12.84 /67	0.00	2.21
EN	ProFunds Oil Eqpt Svcs & Dist Svc	OEPSX	E-	(888) 776-3637	E- / 0.2	-3.51	-30.20	-26.79 / 0	-0.66 / 4	2.56 / 5	0.00	2.73
EN	ProFunds Short Oil & Gas Inv	SNPIX	E-	(888) 776-3637	E- / 0.2	0.16	11.90	7.69 /60	-8.26 / 1	-13.29 / 0	0.00	2.60
EN	ProFunds Short Oil & Gas Svc	SNPSX	E-	(888) 776-3637	E- / 0.2	-0.16	11.27	6.51 /51	-9.06 / 1	-14.06 / 0	0.00	3.60
PM	ProFunds Short Precious Metals Inv	SPPIX	D+	(888) 776-3637	B+ / 8.8	-1.79	14.45	18.85 /96	15.53 /79	3.07 / 6	0.00	1.87
PM	ProFunds Short Precious Metals Svc	SPPSX	D	(888) 776-3637	B / 8.1	-2.02	13.85	17.80 /95	14.49 /71	2.15 / 5	0.00	2.87
RE	ProFunds Short Real Estate Inv	SRPIX	E-	(888) 776-3637	E- / 0.1	-5.20	-16.22	-20.74 / 1	-15.02 / 0	-18.07 / 0	0.00	2.28
RE	ProFunds Short Real Estate Svc	SRPSX	E-	(888) 776-3637	E- / 0.0	-5.40	-16.59	-21.44 / 1	-15.85 / 0	-18.82 / 0	0.00	3.28
GR	ProFunds Ultra Short NASDAQ-100	USPIX	E-	(888) 776-3637	E- / 0.0	-6.85	-17.43	-37.80 / 0	-33.34 / 0	-36.21 / 0	0.00	1.96
GR	ProFunds Ultra Short NASDAQ-100	USPSX	E-	(888) 776-3637	E- / 0.0	-7.07	-17.83	-38.26 / 0	-33.95 / 0	-36.81 / 0	0.00	2.96
FS	ProFunds-Banks UltraSector Inv	BKPIX	C	(888) 776-3637	B+ / 8.7	-5.57	1.57	1.30 /19	19.68 /97	6.25 /18	0.00	1.75
FS	ProFunds-Banks UltraSector Svc	BKPSX	C-	(888) 776-3637	B / 8.0	-5.79	1.04	0.31 /16	18.58 /96	5.20 /13	0.00	2.75
GR	ProFunds-Basic Mat UltraSector Inv	BMPIX	E+	(888) 776-3637	D / 1.8	-1.18	-7.13	-2.31 /10	7.93 /27	6.91 /22	0.00	1.73
GR	ProFunds-Basic Mat UltraSector Svc	BMPSX	E	(888) 776-3637	D- / 1.4	-1.42	-7.60	-3.29 / 8	6.87 /21	5.85 /16	0.00	2.73
GR	ProFunds-Bear Fund Inv	BRPIX	E-	(888) 776-3637	E- / 0.1	-1.66	-7.16	-13.69 / 2	-16.40 / 0	-16.21 / 0	0.00	1.72
GR	ProFunds-Bear Fund Svc	BRPSX	E-	(888) 776-3637	E- / 0.1	-2.04	-7.68	-14.67 / 2	-17.28 / 0	-17.06 / 0	0.00	2.72
GR	ProFunds-Biotech Ultra Sector Inv	BIPIX	C	(888) 776-3637	A+ / 9.9	8.35	18.73	56.98 /99	64.49 /99	42.17 /99	0.00	1.57
GR	ProFunds-Biotech Ultra Sector Svc	BIPSX	C	(888) 776-3637	A+ / 9.9	8.10	18.14	55.44 /99	62.85 /99	40.79 /99	0.00	2.57
AG	ProFunds-Bull Inv	BLPIX	B	(888) 776-3637	C+ / 6.6	0.44	4.88	10.55 /77	13.84 /66	12.18 /62	0.00	1.58
AG	ProFunds-Bull Svc	BLPSX	B-	(888) 776-3637	C+ / 5.8	0.20	4.36	9.44 /72	12.70 /57	11.06 /53	0.00	2.58
GR	ProFunds-Consumer Goods Ultra Inv	CNPIX	A+	(888) 776-3637	A+ / 9.8	0.93	10.56	17.15 /95	20.41 /98	19.79 /99	0.00	1.97
GR	ProFunds-Consumer Goods Ultra Svc	CNPSX	A+	(888) 776-3637	A+ / 9.6	0.67	10.01	15.99 /93	19.22 /97	18.59 /98	0.00	2.97
GR	ProFunds-Consumer Srvs Ultra Inv	CYPIX	A+	(888) 776-3637	A+ / 9.9	6.99	24.10	30.03 /99	32.78 /99	28.29 /99	0.00	1.73

● Denotes fund is closed to new investors
* Denotes fund is included in Section II

www.thestreetratings.com

RISK			NET ASSETS		ASSET					BULL / BEAR		FUND MANAGER		MINIMUMS		LOADS	
	3 Year		NAV						Portfolio	Last Bull	Last Bear	Manager	Manager	Initial	Additional	Front	Back
Risk	Standard		As of	Total	Cash	Stocks	Bonds	Other	Turnover	Market	Market	Quality	Tenure	Purch.	Purch.	End	End
Rating/Pts	Deviation	Beta	3/31/15	$(Mil)	%	%	%	%	Ratio	Return	Return	Pct	(Years)	$	$	Load	Load
C /4.9	13.5	0.97	20.87	3	2	97	0	1	68	113.0	-24.9	85	9	0	0	0.0	0.0
C /5.0	13.5	0.97	21.04	4	2	97	0	1	68	113.9	-24.8	86	9	0	0	0.0	0.0
C /5.0	13.5	0.97	21.62	7	2	97	0	1	68	115.3	-24.8	87	9	0	0	0.0	0.0
C /5.1	13.6	0.97	22.27	6	2	97	0	1	68	116.7	-24.8	88	9	0	0	0.0	0.0
C /5.1	13.5	0.97	22.64	19	2	97	0	1	68	117.7	-24.7	88	9	0	0	0.0	0.0
C+ /6.1	12.8	0.94	24.99	542	3	96	0	1	19	106.7	-22.1	81	4	1,000,000	0	0.0	0.0
C+ /6.1	12.7	0.94	23.96	151	3	96	0	1	19	103.7	-22.2	78	4	1,000	100	0.0	0.0
C+ /6.1	12.8	0.94	24.72	13	3	96	0	1	19	100.9	-22.4	75	4	0	0	0.0	0.0
C+ /6.1	12.8	0.94	25.24	18	3	96	0	1	19	101.6	-22.3	76	4	0	0	0.0	0.0
C+ /6.1	12.8	0.94	25.39	139	3	96	0	1	19	103.0	-22.3	77	4	0	0	0.0	0.0
C+ /6.1	12.8	0.94	25.58	94	3	96	0	1	19	104.3	-22.2	79	4	0	0	0.0	0.0
C+ /6.1	12.8	0.94	25.69	195	3	96	0	1	19	105.0	-22.1	80	4	0	0	0.0	0.0
D+ /2.6	14.2	0.99	12.68	1,571	6	93	0	1	66	102.7	-25.1	62	N/A	1,000,000	0	0.0	0.0
D- /1.4	14.2	0.99	10.09	54	6	93	0	1	66	99.3	-25.3	54	N/A	1,000	100	0.0	0.0
D /1.8	14.2	0.99	11.05	3	6	93	0	1	66	96.9	-25.4	48	N/A	0	0	0.0	0.0
D /1.7	14.2	0.99	10.75	7	6	93	0	1	66	97.7	-25.3	50	N/A	0	0	0.0	0.0
D /1.9	14.2	0.99	11.23	20	6	93	0	1	66	99.0	-25.3	53	N/A	0	0	0.0	0.0
D /2.2	14.2	0.99	11.73	17	6	93	0	1	66	100.2	-25.2	56	N/A	0	0	0.0	0.0
D+ /2.4	14.2	0.99	12.12	38	6	93	0	1	66	100.9	-25.2	57	N/A	0	0	0.0	0.0
C /5.5	12.9	0.95	13.48	1,303	3	96	0	1	42	105.7	-25.9	83	10	1,000,000	0	0.0	0.0
C /5.5	13.0	0.95	13.23	20	3	96	0	1	42	101.4	-26.1	79	10	1,000	100	0.0	0.0
C /5.3	13.0	0.95	12.62	2	3	96	0	1	42	99.6	-26.1	77	10	0	0	0.0	0.0
C /5.4	12.9	0.94	12.74	5	3	96	0	1	42	100.7	-26.1	78	10	0	0	0.0	0.0
C /5.4	13.0	0.95	13.09	12	3	96	0	1	42	101.6	-26.0	79	10	0	0	0.0	0.0
C /5.5	13.0	0.95	13.21	14	3	96	0	1	42	103.0	-26.0	80	10	0	0	0.0	0.0
C /5.5	13.0	0.95	13.32	24	3	96	0	1	42	103.9	-25.9	81	10	0	0	0.0	0.0
C+ /6.1	12.7	0.63	16.91	8	5	94	0	1	20	94.7	-20.3	97	5	5,000	50	5.0	2.0
C+ /6.1	12.7	0.63	17.05	62	5	94	0	1	20	96.4	-20.2	97	5	750,000	0	0.0	2.0
U /	N/A	N/A	10.57	50	0	0	0	100	2,750	N/A	N/A	N/A	2	100,000	100	0.0	0.0
D /2.2	11.1	1.11	21.61	15	2	97	0	1	46	101.0	-16.9	23	18	2,500	0	0.0	0.0
D- /1.5	28.7	1.65	18.42	1	39	60	0	1	68	34.6	-47.3	5	2	5,000	100	0.0	0.0
D+ /2.4	15.3	-0.98	6.30	2	100	0	0	0	0	-41.4	26.8	10	2	15,000	100	0.0	0.0
D+ /2.3	15.3	-0.98	6.22	N/A	100	0	0	0	0	-43.0	26.2	7	2	5,000	100	0.0	0.0
E+ /0.8	29.9	-1.26	9.90	6	100	0	0	0	0	30.4	15.3	70	2	15,000	100	0.0	0.0
E+ /0.7	29.9	-1.26	10.19	N/A	100	0	0	0	0	26.4	14.9	57	2	5,000	100	0.0	0.0
C- /3.1	12.3	-1.00	18.96	1	100	0	0	0	0	-52.6	13.9	23	2	15,000	100	0.0	0.0
D+ /2.9	12.3	-0.99	17.70	N/A	100	0	0	0	0	-54.2	13.4	14	2	5,000	100	0.0	0.0
E- /0.0	23.2	-2.10	12.51	8	100	0	0	0	0	-84.2	13.0	2	2	15,000	100	0.0	0.0
E- /0.0	23.3	-2.10	12.53	N/A	100	0	0	0	0	-84.7	12.5	2	2	5,000	100	0.0	0.0
D+ /2.7	24.6	1.93	30.34	14	33	66	0	1	173	192.4	-46.1	1	2	15,000	100	0.0	0.0
D+ /2.6	24.6	1.93	29.11	1	33	66	0	1	173	182.5	-46.2	1	2	5,000	100	0.0	0.0
C- /4.1	20.6	1.81	54.46	8	23	76	0	1	110	86.6	-45.7	0	2	15,000	100	0.0	0.0
C- /4.1	20.6	1.81	50.59	2	23	76	0	1	110	80.4	-46.0	0	2	5,000	100	0.0	0.0
D+ /2.8	9.5	-1.00	9.46	15	100	0	0	0	0	-55.5	14.8	24	2	15,000	100	0.0	0.0
D+ /2.7	9.5	-0.99	9.13	6	100	0	0	0	0	-57.1	14.4	15	2	5,000	100	0.0	0.0
D- /1.0	24.9	1.37	68.48	730	35	64	0	1	47	533.0	-16.7	99	2	15,000	100	0.0	0.0
D- /1.0	24.9	1.37	57.28	38	35	64	0	1	47	511.8	-17.0	99	2	5,000	100	0.0	0.0
B /8.0	9.6	1.00	94.09	107	57	42	0	1	78	87.2	-17.1	37	2	15,000	100	0.0	0.0
B- /7.9	9.6	1.00	81.35	12	57	42	0	1	78	80.8	-17.4	25	2	5,000	100	0.0	0.0
C+ /6.9	14.9	1.35	83.99	11	37	62	0	1	327	131.1	-13.6	43	2	15,000	100	0.0	0.0
C+ /6.8	14.9	1.35	78.41	2	37	62	0	1	327	123.5	-14.0	30	2	5,000	100	0.0	0.0
C+ /6.8	16.3	1.54	84.39	99	29	70	0	1	57	232.8	-19.7	94	2	15,000	100	0.0	0.0

99 Pct = Best
0 Pct = Worst

Fund Type	Fund Name	Ticker Symbol	Overall Investment Rating	Phone	PERFORMANCE Performance Rating/Pts	3 Mo	6 Mo	1Yr / Pct	3Yr / Pct	5Yr / Pct	Dividend Yield	Expense Ratio
GR	ProFunds-Consumer Srvs Ultra Svc	CYPSX	A+	(888) 776-3637	A+ / 9.9	6.72	23.50	28.75 /99	31.46 /99	27.02 /99	0.00	2.73
FO	ProFunds-Europe 30 Inv	UEPIX	E	(888) 776-3637	E+ / 0.8	-1.80	-9.12	-10.79 / 3	5.32 /14	2.88 / 6	1.15	1.79
FO	ProFunds-Europe 30 Svc	UEPSX	E	(888) 776-3637	E+ / 0.6	-2.02	-9.48	-11.56 / 2	4.33 /11	1.89 / 4	0.23	2.79
FS	ProFunds-Financial UltraSector Inv	FNPIX	B+	(888) 776-3637	A+ / 9.8	-1.93	9.76	14.01 /89	23.60 /99	13.18 /70	0.00	1.87
FS	ProFunds-Financial UltraSector Svc	FNPSX	B+	(888) 776-3637	A+ / 9.8	-2.10	9.27	12.86 /86	22.36 /98	12.04 /61	0.00	2.87
GR	ProFunds-HlthCare UltraSector Inv	HCPIX	A+	(888) 776-3637	A+ / 9.9	10.39	22.59	39.64 /99	40.16 /99	28.68 /99	0.00	1.74
GR	ProFunds-HlthCare UltraSector Svc	HCPSX	A+	(888) 776-3637	A+ / 9.9	10.12	21.97	38.24 /99	38.76 /99	27.38 /99	0.00	2.74
GR	ProFunds-Industrial UltraSector Inv	IDPIX	A	(888) 776-3637	A+ / 9.8	1.59	10.14	10.59 /77	22.81 /98	19.45 /98	0.00	1.86
GR	ProFunds-Industrial UltraSector Svc	IDPSX	A	(888) 776-3637	A+ / 9.8	1.35	9.60	9.50 /72	21.61 /98	18.28 /98	0.00	2.86
SC	ProFunds-Internet UltraSector Inv	INPIX	C-	(888) 776-3637	A+ / 9.9	8.29	8.56	11.77 /82	28.90 /99	26.56 /99	0.00	1.59
SC	ProFunds-Internet UltraSector Svc	INPSX	C-	(888) 776-3637	A+ / 9.9	8.05	8.07	10.72 /77	27.61 /99	25.30 /99	0.00	2.59
GR	ProFunds-Large Cap Growth Inv	LGPIX	B+	(888) 776-3637	B- / 7.5	2.01	6.64	13.83 /89	14.55 /71	13.43 /72	0.00	1.99
GR	ProFunds-Large Cap Growth Svc	LGPSX	B-	(888) 776-3637	C+ / 6.6	1.77	6.16	12.73 /86	13.40 /63	12.30 /63	0.00	2.99
GR	ProFunds-Large Cap Value Inv	LVPIX	C+	(888) 776-3637	C+ / 5.8	-1.11	3.20	7.19 /57	13.20 /61	11.05 /53	0.59	1.89
GR	ProFunds-Large Cap Value Svc	LVPSX	C+	(888) 776-3637	C / 5.0	-1.38	2.69	6.08 /47	12.07 /53	9.94 /44	0.00	2.89
GR	ProFunds-Mble Telcm UltraSector Inv	WCPIX	C+	(888) 776-3637	A+ / 9.9	13.17	0.16	-8.03 / 3	27.37 /99	18.72 /98	0.00	1.99
GR	ProFunds-Mble Telcm UltraSector	WCPSX	C+	(888) 776-3637	A+ / 9.8	12.93	-0.34	-8.98 / 3	26.05 /99	17.50 /97	0.00	2.99
GR	ProFunds-Mid Cap Growth Inv	MGPIX	B+	(888) 776-3637	B / 7.7	6.95	12.61	11.05 /79	14.20 /69	14.07 /78	0.00	1.97
GR	ProFunds-Mid Cap Growth Svc	MGPSX	C+	(888) 776-3637	C+ / 6.8	6.68	12.06	9.91 /74	13.07 /60	12.94 /68	0.00	2.97
MC	ProFunds-Mid Cap Inv	MDPIX	A	(888) 776-3637	B / 7.8	4.91	10.98	10.21 /75	14.88 /74	13.49 /73	0.00	1.43
MC	ProFunds-Mid Cap Svc	MDPSX	B-	(888) 776-3637	C+ / 6.9	4.65	10.44	9.12 /70	13.76 /65	12.37 /63	0.00	2.43
MC	ProFunds-Mid Cap Value Inv	MLPIX	B	(888) 776-3637	B- / 7.5	2.29	8.76	8.51 /66	15.16 /76	12.85 /67	0.00	1.95
MC	ProFunds-Mid Cap Value Svc	MLPSX	C+	(888) 776-3637	C+ / 6.7	2.03	8.20	7.44 /59	14.02 /67	11.73 /59	0.00	2.95
AG	ProFunds-Nasdaq-100 Inv	OTPIX	A+	(888) 776-3637	B+ / 8.4	2.04	6.47	19.35 /96	15.30 /77	16.05 /93	0.00	1.65
AG	ProFunds-Nasdaq-100 Svc	OTPSX	B+	(888) 776-3637	B- / 7.5	1.78	5.93	18.16 /96	14.13 /68	14.90 /86	0.00	2.65
EN	ProFunds-Oil & Gas UltraSector Inv	ENPIX	E-	(888) 776-3637	E / 0.3	-4.07	-22.66	-21.02 / 1	2.43 / 7	7.56 /27	0.00	1.64
EN	ProFunds-Oil & Gas UltraSector Svc	ENPSX	E-	(888) 776-3637	E / 0.3	-4.30	-23.03	-21.79 / 1	1.43 / 6	6.50 /20	0.00	2.64
GR	ProFunds-Pharm UltraSector Inv	PHPIX	A+	(888) 776-3637	A+ / 9.9	8.98	15.21	25.70 /98	33.55 /99	25.59 /99	0.00	1.74
GR	ProFunds-Pharm UltraSector Svc	PHPSX	A+	(888) 776-3637	A+ / 9.9	8.67	14.60	24.39 /98	32.15 /99	24.32 /99	0.00	2.74
PM	ProFunds-Precious Metals Ultra Inv	PMPIX	E-	(888) 776-3637	E- / 0.0	-5.14	-33.45	-41.61 / 0	-38.19 / 0	-24.97 / 0	0.00	1.75
PM	ProFunds-Precious Metals Ultra Svc	PMPSX	E-	(888) 776-3637	E- / 0.0	-5.38	-33.80	-42.21 / 0	-38.81 / 0	-25.71 / 0	0.00	2.75
RE	ProFunds-Real Est UltraSector Inv	REPIX	B-	(888) 776-3637	A+ / 9.8	5.62	24.76	30.97 /99	16.93 /89	18.17 /98	0.31	1.78
RE	ProFunds-Real Est UltraSector Svc	REPSX	C+	(888) 776-3637	A+ / 9.8	5.31	24.12	29.63 /99	15.77 /81	17.02 /96	0.00	2.78
FS	ProFunds-Rising Rates Opp 10 Inv	RTPIX	E+	(888) 776-3637	E- / 0.2	-3.21	-7.06	-11.17 / 2	-5.79 / 2	-8.38 / 1	0.00	1.65
FS	ProFunds-Rising Rates Opp 10 Svc	RTPSX	E+	(888) 776-3637	E- / 0.2	-3.48	-7.51	-12.04 / 2	-6.73 / 1	-9.31 / 1	0.00	2.65
OT	ProFunds-Rising Rates Opport Inv	RRPIX	E-	(888) 776-3637	E- / 0.0	-7.44	-18.60	-28.12 / 0	-13.80 / 1	-17.94 / 0	0.00	1.57
OT	ProFunds-Rising Rates Opport Svc	RRPSX	E-	(888) 776-3637	E- / 0.0	-7.66	-19.04	-28.83 / 0	-14.69 / 0	-18.76 / 0	0.00	2.57
GR	ProFunds-Rising US Dollar Inv	RDPIX	B-	(888) 776-3637	C / 4.5	8.07	12.98	19.79 /97	5.04 /13	1.14 / 3	0.00	1.80
GR	ProFunds-Rising US Dollar Svc	RDPSX	C+	(888) 776-3637	C- / 3.8	7.76	12.38	18.53 /96	3.98 /10	0.12 / 3	0.00	2.80
GR	ProFunds-Semicond UltraSector Inv	SMPIX	C+	(888) 776-3637	A+ / 9.8	-3.59	7.04	34.76 /99	19.54 /97	16.84 /96	0.00	1.76
GR	ProFunds-Semicond UltraSector Svc	SMPSX	C+	(888) 776-3637	A+ / 9.7	-3.81	6.50	33.49 /99	18.32 /95	15.68 /91	0.00	2.76
GR	ProFunds-Short OTC Inv	SOPIX	E-	(888) 776-3637	E- / 0.0	-4.01	-9.71	-21.99 / 1	-19.26 / 0	-20.37 / 0	0.00	2.05
GR	ProFunds-Short OTC Svc	SOPSX	E-	(888) 776-3637	E- / 0.0	-4.26	-10.14	-22.68 / 1	-20.13 / 0	-21.19 / 0	0.00	3.05
SC	ProFunds-Short Small Cap Inv	SHPIX	E-	(888) 776-3637	E- / 0.0	-5.30	-14.95	-12.15 / 2	-18.37 / 0	-19.27 / 0	0.00	2.10
SC	ProFunds-Short Small Cap Svc	SHPSX	E-	(888) 776-3637	E- / 0.0	-5.54	-15.36	-13.05 / 2	-19.10 / 0	-20.00 / 0	0.00	3.10
SC	ProFunds-Small Cap Growth Inv	SGPIX	B+	(888) 776-3637	B+ / 8.4	6.08	15.32	8.59 /67	15.48 /79	15.31 /89	0.00	2.04
SC	ProFunds-Small Cap Growth Svc	SGPSX	B-	(888) 776-3637	B- / 7.5	5.83	14.77	7.50 /59	14.32 /69	14.16 /79	0.00	3.04
SC	ProFunds-Small Cap Inv	SLPIX	B	(888) 776-3637	B- / 7.1	3.86	13.20	6.00 /46	14.30 /69	12.88 /67	0.00	1.80
SC	ProFunds-Small Cap Svc	SLPSX	C+	(888) 776-3637	C+ / 6.3	3.61	12.64	4.96 /38	13.17 /61	11.75 /59	0.00	2.80
SC	ProFunds-Small Cap Value Inv	SVPIX	C+	(888) 776-3637	C+ / 6.7	0.77	10.64	3.97 /32	14.41 /70	12.62 /65	0.00	1.80
SC	ProFunds-Small Cap Value Svc	SVPSX	C	(888) 776-3637	C+ / 5.9	0.52	10.09	2.92 /26	13.24 /61	11.49 /57	0.00	2.80
TC	ProFunds-Tech UltraSector Inv	TEPIX	B-	(888) 776-3637	B+ / 8.5	0.45	5.88	23.10 /98	15.13 /76	17.26 /96	0.00	1.80

● Denotes fund is closed to new investors
★ Denotes fund is included in Section II

RISK			NET ASSETS		ASSET					Portfolio	BULL / BEAR		FUND MANAGER		MINIMUMS		LOADS	
	3 Year		NAV								Last Bull	Last Bear	Manager	Manager	Initial	Additional	Front	Back
Risk	Standard		As of	Total	Cash	Stocks	Bonds	Other		Turnover	Market	Market	Quality	Tenure	Purch.	Purch.	End	End
Rating/Pts	Deviation	Beta	3/31/15	$(Mil)	%	%	%	%		Ratio	Return	Return	Pct	(Years)	$	$	Load	Load
C+ / 6.7	16.3	1.54	76.52	12	29	70	0	1		57	221.6	-20.0	92	2	5,000	100	0.0	0.0
C / 4.8	15.2	1.09	14.15	15	0	100	0	0		485	44.6	-27.7	11	6	15,000	100	0.0	0.0
C / 4.9	15.1	1.09	14.52	2	0	100	0	0		485	40.0	-28.0	7	6	5,000	100	0.0	0.0
C / 5.0	17.2	1.50	14.73	11	46	53	0	1		124	187.6	-37.4	27	2	15,000	100	0.0	0.0
C / 4.9	17.3	1.51	13.08	2	46	53	0	1		124	178.1	-37.8	16	2	5,000	100	0.0	0.0
B- / 7.3	15.0	1.27	50.13	103	43	56	0	1		156	256.7	-16.7	99	2	15,000	100	0.0	0.0
B- / 7.2	15.0	1.27	44.30	13	43	56	0	1		156	244.8	-17.0	99	2	5,000	100	0.0	0.0
C+ / 5.8	16.9	1.64	71.04	50	32	67	0	1		365	181.3	-35.6	16	2	15,000	100	0.0	0.0
C+ / 5.7	16.9	1.64	65.11	3	32	67	0	1		365	171.9	-35.9	10	2	5,000	100	0.0	0.0
E / 0.5	23.5	1.29	39.34	56	21	78	0	1		133	207.5	-32.9	95	2	15,000	100	0.0	0.0
E / 0.5	23.5	1.29	33.00	3	21	78	0	1		133	197.1	-33.2	93	2	5,000	100	0.0	0.0
B- / 7.2	9.4	0.96	63.87	7	0	99	0	1		749	88.5	-13.7	55	2	15,000	100	0.0	0.0
B- / 7.1	9.4	0.96	56.38	8	0	99	0	1		749	82.2	-14.1	40	2	5,000	100	0.0	0.0
B- / 7.0	10.2	1.04	53.40	12	0	99	0	1		593	86.3	-20.1	24	2	15,000	100	0.0	0.0
B- / 7.0	10.2	1.04	49.49	1	0	99	0	1		593	80.0	-20.4	15	2	5,000	100	0.0	0.0
D / 2.2	29.1	1.12	50.25	6	49	50	0	1		298	183.5	-29.8	96	2	15,000	100	0.0	0.0
D / 2.1	29.1	1.12	43.23	1	49	50	0	1		298	173.9	-30.1	96	2	5,000	100	0.0	0.0
C+ / 6.4	11.0	0.96	71.88	27	0	99	0	1		924	81.5	-21.6	51	2	15,000	100	0.0	0.0
C+ / 6.4	11.0	0.96	62.46	10	0	99	0	1		924	75.5	-21.9	36	2	5,000	100	0.0	0.0
B- / 7.5	11.1	1.00	75.92	109	60	39	0	1		211	90.1	-23.3	38	2	15,000	100	0.0	0.0
B- / 7.4	11.1	1.00	66.84	5	60	39	0	1		211	83.8	-23.6	26	2	5,000	100	0.0	0.0
C+ / 6.4	11.5	1.03	68.35	8	0	100	0	0		689	97.8	-24.7	37	2	15,000	100	0.0	0.0
C+ / 6.3	11.5	1.03	59.83	3	0	100	0	0		689	91.2	-25.0	25	2	5,000	100	0.0	0.0
B- / 7.3	11.6	1.06	132.88	53	62	37	0	1		147	101.5	-11.4	42	2	15,000	100	0.0	0.0
B- / 7.2	11.6	1.06	113.70	10	62	37	0	1		147	94.6	-11.8	29	2	5,000	100	0.0	0.0
D / 2.1	23.8	1.51	44.29	29	30	69	0	1		68	48.5	-37.7	22	2	15,000	100	0.0	0.0
D / 2.0	23.8	1.51	38.30	6	30	69	0	1		68	43.6	-38.0	14	2	5,000	100	0.0	0.0
C+ / 6.5	15.1	1.18	24.63	29	31	68	0	1		92	195.4	-8.4	99	2	15,000	100	0.0	0.0
C+ / 6.4	15.1	1.18	22.56	4	31	68	0	1		92	185.1	-8.9	98	2	5,000	100	0.0	0.0
D / 1.6	46.7	1.90	7.38	18	32	67	0	1		177	-72.5	-26.6	0	2	15,000	100	0.0	0.0
D / 1.6	46.6	1.90	6.68	1	32	67	0	1		177	-73.4	-26.9	0	2	5,000	100	0.0	0.0
C- / 3.1	18.8	1.51	40.78	36	38	61	0	1		162	118.7	-26.4	15	2	15,000	100	0.0	0.0
C- / 3.1	18.7	1.50	30.68	2	38	61	0	1		162	111.6	-26.7	9	2	5,000	100	0.0	0.0
C+ / 6.4	6.4	0.27	15.67	20	100	0	0	0		0	-15.6	-13.8	2	6	15,000	100	0.0	0.0
C+ / 5.9	6.4	0.27	15.27	1	100	0	0	0		0	-18.4	-14.2	1	6	5,000	100	0.0	0.0
D- / 1.4	17.4	0.92	5.47	55	100	0	0	0		0	-31.7	-33.2	0	6	15,000	100	0.0	0.0
D- / 1.4	17.3	0.92	5.06	5	100	0	0	0		0	-33.9	-33.5	0	6	5,000	100	0.0	0.0
B / 8.6	6.5	-0.40	29.60	60	100	0	0	0		0	11.4	6.2	98	6	15,000	100	0.0	0.0
B / 8.3	6.5	-0.40	27.51	14	100	0	0	0		0	7.7	5.7	98	6	5,000	100	0.0	0.0
D+ / 2.7	23.5	1.83	28.73	104	31	68	0	1		193	158.5	-29.9	2	2	15,000	100	0.0	0.0
D+ / 2.6	23.5	1.83	25.23	1	31	68	0	1		193	150.1	-30.2	2	2	5,000	100	0.0	0.0
D+ / 2.3	11.5	-1.05	17.95	9	100	0	0	0		0	-61.5	7.2	7	6	15,000	100	0.0	0.0
D / 2.2	11.5	-1.05	16.84	N/A	100	0	0	0		0	-62.8	6.6	5	6	5,000	100	0.0	0.0
D / 2.0	13.4	-1.00	20.02	2	100	0	0	0		0	-59.8	24.2	9	6	15,000	100	0.0	0.0
D / 1.9	13.5	-1.00	20.12	5	100	0	0	0		0	-61.0	23.9	6	6	5,000	100	0.0	0.0
C+ / 5.7	12.6	0.92	69.43	40	0	99	0	1		654	92.7	-22.0	72	2	15,000	100	0.0	0.0
C+ / 5.6	12.7	0.92	59.94	20	0	99	0	1		654	86.1	-22.3	59	2	5,000	100	0.0	0.0
C+ / 6.7	13.5	1.00	69.39	44	61	38	0	1		252	89.6	-25.2	40	2	15,000	100	0.0	0.0
C+ / 6.6	13.5	1.00	60.50	5	61	38	0	1		252	83.4	-25.6	28	2	5,000	100	0.0	0.0
C+ / 5.9	13.2	0.96	71.02	10	0	99	0	1		413	97.2	-23.2	51	2	15,000	100	0.0	0.0
C+ / 5.8	13.3	0.97	62.43	3	0	99	0	1		413	90.4	-23.5	36	2	5,000	100	0.0	0.0
C / 4.6	18.8	1.65	60.65	47	43	56	0	1		322	139.7	-20.7	2	2	15,000	100	0.0	0.0

Fund Type	Fund Name	Ticker Symbol	Overall Investment Rating	Phone	Performance Rating/Pts	3 Mo	6 Mo	1Yr / Pct	3Yr / Pct	5Yr / Pct	Dividend Yield	Expense Ratio
	99 Pct = Best 0 Pct = Worst				PERFORMANCE Total Return % through 3/31/15 Annualized						Incl. in Returns	
TC	ProFunds-Tech UltraSector Svc	TEPSX	C+	(888) 776-3637	B / 7.6	0.21	5.35	21.78 /97	13.97 /67	16.06 /93	0.00	2.80
GR	ProFunds-Telecom UltraSector Inv	TCPIX	C	(888) 776-3637	C / 5.3	2.31	-4.96	3.04 /27	13.46 /63	15.42 /90	0.31	2.41
GR	ProFunds-Telecom UltraSector Svc	TCPSX	C-	(888) 776-3637	C / 4.6	2.04	-5.48	1.99 /22	12.32 /55	14.27 /80	0.00	3.41
GR	ProFunds-Ultra Bear Inv	URPIX	E-	(888) 776-3637	E- / 0.0	-3.28	-13.71	-25.33 / 0	-30.50 / 0	-30.91 / 0	0.00	1.67
GR	ProFunds-Ultra Bear Svc	URPSX	E-	(888) 776-3637	E- / 0.0	-3.63	-14.21	-26.14 / 0	-31.22 / 0	-31.57 / 0	0.00	2.67
AG	ProFunds-Ultra Bull Inv	ULPIX	A-	(888) 776-3637	A+ / 9.9	0.73	9.68	22.07 /97	29.19 /99	23.90 /99	0.00	1.57
AG	ProFunds-Ultra Bull Svc	ULPSX	A-	(888) 776-3637	A+ / 9.9	0.48	9.16	20.88 /97	27.92 /99	22.68 /99	0.00	2.57
FO	Profunds-Ultra China Inv	UGPIX	E+	(888) 776-3637	C+ / 6.6	7.35	-2.64	14.70 /91	13.54 /64	3.18 / 6	0.00	1.79
FO	Profunds-Ultra China Svc	UGPSX	E+	(888) 776-3637	C+ / 5.8	7.04	-3.14	13.47 /88	12.38 /55	2.13 / 5	0.00	2.79
GR	Profunds-Ultra Dow 30 Inv	UDPIX	A-	(888) 776-3637	A+ / 9.8	-0.53	8.77	17.20 /95	22.94 /98	21.85 /99	0.00	2.49
GR	Profunds-Ultra Dow 30 Svc	UDPSX	A-	(888) 776-3637	A+ / 9.8	-0.77	8.22	16.05 /93	21.72 /98	20.64 /99	0.00	3.49
EM	Profunds-Ultra Emerging Mkt Inv	UUPIX	E-	(888) 776-3637	E- / 0.1	-5.42	-21.40	-8.89 / 3	-11.95 / 1	-10.22 / 0	0.40	1.79
EM	Profunds-Ultra Emerging Mkt Svc	UUPSX	E-	(888) 776-3637	E- / 0.1	-5.54	-21.73	-9.68 / 3	-12.84 / 1	-11.13 / 0	0.00	2.79
EM	ProFunds-Ultra Intl Inv	UNPIX	E	(888) 776-3637	C- / 4.1	9.15	-1.05	-7.58 / 4	11.59 /50	3.62 / 7	0.00	1.52
EM	ProFunds-Ultra Intl Svc	UNPSX	E-	(888) 776-3637	C- / 3.4	8.91	-1.58	-8.47 / 3	10.50 /42	2.59 / 5	0.00	2.52
FO	ProFunds-Ultra Japan Inv	UJPIX	C-	(888) 776-3637	A+ / 9.9	21.85	34.54	56.95 /99	39.03 /99	13.83 /76	0.00	1.76
FO	ProFunds-Ultra Japan Svc	UJPSX	C-	(888) 776-3637	A+ / 9.9	21.57	33.94	55.50 /99	37.64 /99	12.68 /66	0.00	2.76
FO	ProFunds-Ultra Latin America Inv	UBPIX	E-	(888) 776-3637	E- / 0.0	-21.19	-44.54	-47.50 / 0	-33.71 / 0	-22.76 / 0	1.53	1.87
FO	ProFunds-Ultra Latin America Svc	UBPSX	E-	(888) 776-3637	E- / 0.0	-21.31	-44.73	-47.92 / 0	-34.32 / 0	-23.49 / 0	0.00	2.87
AG	ProFunds-Ultra Mid Cap Inv	UMPIX	B+	(888) 776-3637	A+ / 9.9	9.77	22.76	20.96 /97	31.11 /99	26.08 /99	0.00	1.60
AG	ProFunds-Ultra Mid Cap Svc	UMPSX	B	(888) 776-3637	A+ / 9.9	9.49	22.15	19.75 /97	29.78 /99	24.82 /99	0.00	2.60
GR	ProFunds-Ultra Nasdaq-100 Inv	UOPIX	B	(888) 776-3637	A+ / 9.9	4.02	12.99	42.21 /99	32.78 /99	33.24 /99	0.00	1.57
GR	ProFunds-Ultra Nasdaq-100 Svc	UOPSX	B	(888) 776-3637	A+ / 9.9	3.76	12.44	40.79 /99	31.48 /99	31.95 /99	0.00	2.57
EM	Profunds-Ultra Sh Emer Mkt Inv	UVPIX	E-	(888) 776-3637	E / 0.3	0.76	14.09	-7.70 / 3	-4.51 / 2	-12.11 / 0	0.00	1.86
EM	Profunds-Ultra Sh Emer Mkt Svc	UVPSX	E-	(888) 776-3637	E- / 0.2	0.69	13.66	-8.60 / 3	-5.44 / 2	-12.91 / 0	0.00	2.86
EM	Profunds-Ultra Sh Intl Inv	UXPIX	E-	(888) 776-3637	E- / 0.0	-12.28	-7.14	-5.26 / 5	-22.87 / 0	-24.18 / 0	0.00	2.62
EM	Profunds-Ultra Sh Intl Svc	UXPSX	E-	(888) 776-3637	E- / 0.0	-12.48	-7.55	-6.18 / 4	-23.68 / 0	-24.93 / 0	0.00	3.62
FO	ProFunds-Ultra Sh Latin America Inv	UFPIX	D+	(888) 776-3637	A+ / 9.9	16.44	47.75	42.32 /99	19.90 /98	-2.50 / 1	0.00	2.42
FO	ProFunds-Ultra Sh Latin America Svc	UFPSX	D+	(888) 776-3637	A+ / 9.9	16.23	47.07	41.00 /99	18.71 /96	-3.41 / 1	0.00	3.42
FO	Profunds-Ultra Short China Inv	UHPIX	E-	(888) 776-3637	E- / 0.0	-10.25	-7.42	-28.61 / 0	-29.14 / 0	-27.22 / 0	0.00	3.05
FO	Profunds-Ultra Short China Svc	UHPSX	E-	(888) 776-3637	E- / 0.0	-10.51	-7.92	-29.33 / 0	-29.92 / 0	-27.95 / 0	0.00	4.05
GR	ProFunds-Ultra Short Dow 30 Inv	UWPIX	E-	(888) 776-3637	E- / 0.0	-2.64	-13.64	-22.78 / 1	-26.53 / 0	-28.49 / 0	0.00	1.82
GR	ProFunds-Ultra Short Dow 30 Svc	UWPSX	E-	(888) 776-3637	E- / 0.0	-2.84	-14.03	-23.62 / 1	-27.30 / 0	-29.26 / 0	0.00	2.82
FO	Profunds-Ultra Short Japan Inv	UKPIX	E-	(888) 776-3637	E- / 0.0	-21.49	-34.26	-47.54 / 0	-44.33 / 0	-32.86 / 0	0.00	2.49
FO	Profunds-Ultra Short Japan Svc	UKPSX	E-	(888) 776-3637	E- / 0.0	-21.66	-34.56	-48.02 / 0	-44.85 / 0	-33.50 / 0	0.00	3.49
MC	ProFunds-Ultra Short Mid-Cap Inv	UIPIX	E-	(888) 776-3637	E- / 0.0	-11.68	-23.59	-25.97 / 0	-32.69 / 0	-34.59 / 0	0.00	2.76
MC	ProFunds-Ultra Short Mid-Cap Svc	UIPSX	E-	(888) 776-3637	E- / 0.0	-12.05	-24.06	-26.81 / 0	-33.27 / 0	-35.19 / 0	0.00	3.76
SC	ProFunds-Ultra Short Small-Cap Inv	UCPIX	E-	(888) 776-3637	E- / 0.0	-10.38	-28.06	-23.29 / 1	-33.64 / 0	-36.85 / 0	0.00	1.93
SC	ProFunds-Ultra Short Small-Cap Svc	UCPSX	E-	(888) 776-3637	E- / 0.0	-10.66	-28.44	-24.05 / 1	-34.34 / 0	-37.51 / 0	0.00	2.93
SC	ProFunds-Ultra Small Cap Inv	UAPIX	C+	(888) 776-3637	A+ / 9.9	7.58	27.59	11.57 /81	29.42 /99	22.79 /99	0.00	1.73
SC	ProFunds-Ultra Small Cap Svc	UAPSX	C+	(888) 776-3637	A+ / 9.9	7.35	27.03	10.53 /76	28.11 /99	21.54 /99	0.00	2.73
UT	ProFunds-Utilities UltraSector Inv	UTPIX	B-	(888) 776-3637	B+ / 8.5	-7.88	10.49	13.84 /89	16.82 /89	17.11 /96	0.60	1.77
UT	ProFunds-Utilities UltraSector Svc	UTPSX	C+	(888) 776-3637	B / 7.7	-8.13	9.96	12.74 /86	15.69 /81	15.97 /93	0.19	2.77
IN	Prospector Capital Appreciation Fd	PCAFX	D	(877) 734-7862	C- / 3.1	2.43	3.10	3.10 /27	9.04 /33	7.89 /29	1.51	1.77
MC	Prospector Opportunity	POPFX	C+	(877) 734-7862	C+ / 6.3	2.80	8.59	8.64 /67	13.72 /65	12.47 /64	0.67	1.58
GI	Provident Trust Strategy Fd	PROVX	C+	(855) 739-9950	C / 5.1	4.08	7.66	6.92 /54	11.07 /46	9.34 /39	0.11	0.93
BA	Prudential Asset Allocation A	PIBAX	C	(800) 225-1852	C- / 4.1	1.78	4.83	9.07 /70	11.07 /46	10.49 /49	1.12	1.24
BA	● Prudential Asset Allocation B	PBFBX	C	(800) 225-1852	C / 4.5	1.57	4.48	8.30 /65	10.30 /41	9.71 /42	0.51	1.94
BA	Prudential Asset Allocation C	PABCX	C	(800) 225-1852	C / 4.5	1.64	4.48	8.30 /65	10.30 /41	9.71 /42	0.51	1.94
BA	Prudential Asset Allocation R	PALRX	C+	(800) 225-1852	C / 4.8	1.71	4.69	8.86 /69	10.86 /45	10.25 /47	0.99	1.69
BA	Prudential Asset Allocation Z	PABFX	C+	(800) 225-1852	C / 5.2	1.90	4.98	9.41 /71	11.43 /48	10.83 /51	1.46	0.94
AA	Prudential Conservative Alloc A	JDUAX	C-	(800) 225-1852	D- / 1.4	1.93	3.45	4.62 /36	6.25 /18	6.41 /20	1.73	1.61

● Denotes fund is closed to new investors
* Denotes fund is included in Section II

RISK			NET ASSETS		ASSET					BULL / BEAR		FUND MANAGER		MINIMUMS		LOADS	
	3 Year		NAV						Portfolio	Last Bull	Last Bear	Manager	Manager	Initial	Additional	Front	Back
Risk	Standard		As of	Total	Cash	Stocks	Bonds	Other	Turnover	Market	Market	Quality	Tenure	Purch.	Purch.	End	End
Rating/Pts	Deviation	Beta	3/31/15	$(Mil)	%	%	%	%	Ratio	Return	Return	Pct	(Years)	$	$	Load	Load
C / 4.5	18.8	1.65	53.39	3	43	56	0	1	322	131.5	-21.0	1	2	5,000	100	0.0	0.0
C+ / 5.7	19.4	0.70	20.39	7	45	54	0	1	664	79.1	-15.3	85	2	15,000	100	0.0	0.0
C+ / 5.6	19.5	0.70	19.50	1	45	54	0	1	664	73.1	-15.7	78	2	5,000	100	0.0	0.0
E- / 0.0	19.3	-1.99	5.60	12	100	0	0	0	0	-80.8	28.1	5	6	15,000	100	0.0	0.0
E- / 0.0	19.2	-1.98	5.31	1	100	0	0	0	0	-81.5	27.7	3	6	5,000	100	0.0	0.0
C / 5.2	19.4	2.01	103.64	76	37	62	0	1	509	242.3	-33.2	14	2	15,000	100	0.0	0.0
C / 5.2	19.4	2.01	89.74	4	37	62	0	1	509	231.0	-33.4	9	2	5,000	100	0.0	0.0
E- / 0.0	34.3	1.80	12.56	18	0	0	0	100	266	80.0	-54.1	19	6	15,000	100	0.0	0.0
E- / 0.0	34.3	1.81	11.71	N/A	0	0	0	100	266	74.0	-54.2	12	6	5,000	100	0.0	0.0
C / 5.4	20.3	2.03	65.47	27	47	52	0	1	82	183.2	-28.5	2	2	15,000	100	0.0	0.0
C / 5.4	20.3	2.03	59.35	1	47	52	0	1	82	173.5	-28.8	2	2	5,000	100	0.0	0.0
D- / 1.3	35.0	2.36	9.24	13	17	77	5	1	264	1.6	-45.8	1	6	15,000	100	0.0	0.0
D- / 1.3	34.9	2.36	8.86	1	17	77	5	1	264	-2.0	-46.0	1	6	5,000	100	0.0	0.0
E / 0.5	27.6	1.63	15.98	54	100	0	0	0	0	85.5	-46.5	98	6	15,000	100	0.0	0.0
E / 0.4	27.6	1.63	14.91	N/A	100	0	0	0	0	79.3	-46.8	98	6	5,000	100	0.0	0.0
E- / 0.0	38.6	1.75	21.58	61	100	0	0	0	0	253.3	-27.4	99	6	15,000	100	0.0	0.0
E- / 0.0	38.6	1.74	19.22	4	100	0	0	0	0	241.2	-27.7	99	6	5,000	100	0.0	0.0
D- / 1.1	42.9	2.34	3.31	13	18	81	0	1	490	-47.1	-47.5	0	6	15,000	100	0.0	0.0
D- / 1.1	42.8	2.33	3.25	N/A	18	81	0	1	490	-48.9	-47.7	0	6	5,000	100	0.0	0.0
C- / 4.2	22.5	2.04	94.50	83	35	64	0	1	40	246.1	-43.3	21	2	15,000	100	0.0	0.0
C- / 4.1	22.5	2.04	81.90	2	35	64	0	1	40	234.3	-43.6	14	2	5,000	100	0.0	0.0
C- / 4.0	23.7	2.13	90.90	245	36	63	0	1	5	300.8	-23.3	20	2	15,000	100	0.0	0.0
C- / 4.0	23.7	2.13	77.73	10	36	63	0	1	5	287.7	-23.6	13	2	5,000	100	0.0	0.0
E- / 0.0	34.4	-2.32	9.23	7	100	0	0	0	0	-50.4	51.8	23	6	15,000	100	0.0	0.0
E- / 0.0	34.5	-2.33	8.82	2	100	0	0	0	0	-52.0	51.4	15	6	5,000	100	0.0	0.0
E- / 0.0	27.5	-1.62	23.42	2	100	0	0	0	0	-70.9	47.2	0	6	15,000	100	0.0	0.0
E- / 0.0	27.4	-1.61	22.16	1	100	0	0	0	0	-71.9	46.5	0	6	5,000	100	0.0	0.0
E- / 0.0	42.0	-2.30	21.32	7	100	0	0	0	0	-19.2	55.6	99	6	15,000	100	0.0	0.0
E- / 0.0	42.0	-2.29	19.84	2	100	0	0	0	0	-22.0	55.4	99	6	5,000	100	0.0	0.0
E- / 0.0	33.3	-1.76	16.72	1	0	0	0	100	0	-76.6	72.5	0	6	15,000	100	0.0	0.0
E- / 0.0	33.4	-1.75	15.59	N/A	0	0	0	100	0	-77.4	72.0	0	6	5,000	100	0.0	0.0
E / 0.3	20.2	-2.02	6.27	4	100	0	0	0	0	-75.9	23.5	56	2	15,000	100	0.0	0.0
E- / 0.2	20.1	-2.01	5.82	N/A	100	0	0	0	0	-76.7	23.1	38	2	5,000	100	0.0	0.0
E- / 0.0	38.5	-1.69	14.83	2	100	0	0	0	0	-88.0	21.7	0	6	15,000	100	0.0	0.0
E- / 0.0	38.6	-1.69	14.07	N/A	100	0	0	0	0	-88.4	21.2	0	6	5,000	100	0.0	0.0
E- / 0.0	22.2	-1.98	4.76	2	100	0	0	0	0	-82.8	43.7	3	2	15,000	100	0.0	0.0
E- / 0.0	22.2	-1.98	4.45	N/A	100	0	0	0	0	-83.4	43.6	2	2	5,000	100	0.0	0.0
E- / 0.0	27.2	-1.99	19.33	9	100	0	0	0	0	-84.8	47.6	1	2	15,000	100	0.0	0.0
E- / 0.0	27.2	-1.99	18.95	4	100	0	0	0	0	-85.3	46.5	1	2	5,000	100	0.0	0.0
D+ / 2.8	27.5	2.01	42.73	47	29	70	0	1	45	234.7	-47.5	13	2	15,000	100	0.0	0.0
D+ / 2.7	27.6	2.01	36.94	1	29	70	0	1	45	223.3	-47.7	8	2	5,000	100	0.0	0.0
C / 4.6	20.4	1.44	33.20	15	30	69	0	1	294	77.9	0.1	40	2	15,000	100	0.0	0.0
C / 4.6	20.4	1.44	31.66	2	30	69	0	1	294	72.1	-0.3	28	2	5,000	100	0.0	0.0
C+ / 5.6	9.1	0.82	15.99	38	5	76	0	19	31	45.0	-16.1	19	8	10,000	1,000	0.0	2.0
C+ / 6.4	9.4	0.79	21.33	93	7	91	0	2	25	77.0	-15.6	71	8	10,000	1,000	0.0	2.0
C+ / 6.9	9.7	0.89	11.49	131	10	89	0	1	14	65.1	-15.6	27	13	1,000	100	0.0	0.0
B- / 7.0	6.2	1.10	15.48	313	0	62	37	1	215	60.5	-10.5	54	10	2,500	100	5.5	0.0
B- / 7.1	6.3	1.11	15.54	14	0	62	37	1	215	56.9	-10.8	42	10	2,500	100	0.0	0.0
B- / 7.1	6.2	1.10	15.54	27	0	62	37	1	215	56.8	-10.8	44	10	2,500	100	0.0	0.0
B- / 7.0	6.2	1.10	15.48	1	0	62	37	1	215	59.5	-10.6	51	10	0	0	0.0	0.0
B- / 7.0	6.2	1.10	15.58	58	0	62	37	1	215	62.3	-10.5	59	10	0	0	0.0	0.0
B / 8.6	4.6	0.77	13.21	78	5	39	55	1	46	32.8	-8.1	39	11	2,500	100	5.5	0.0

99 Pct = Best
0 Pct = Worst

Fund Type	Fund Name	Ticker Symbol	Overall Investment Rating	Phone	Perfor-mance Rating/Pts	3 Mo	6 Mo	1Yr / Pct	3Yr / Pct	5Yr / Pct	Dividend Yield	Expense Ratio
AA	● Prudential Conservative Alloc B	JDABX	C-	(800) 225-1852	D / 1.7	1.78	3.06	3.85 /31	5.48 /15	5.63 /15	1.10	2.31
AA	Prudential Conservative Alloc C	JDACX	C-	(800) 225-1852	D / 1.7	1.70	3.06	3.85 /31	5.45 /15	5.61 /15	1.10	2.31
AA	Prudential Conservative Alloc R	JDARX	C-	(800) 225-1852	D / 2.0	1.84	3.30	4.34 /34	5.99 /17	6.14 /18	1.57	2.06
AA	Prudential Conservative Alloc Z	JDAZX	C	(800) 225-1852	D+ / 2.3	2.00	3.56	4.94 /38	6.51 /19	6.68 /21	2.06	1.31
AA	Prudential Defensive Equity A	PAMGX	C-	(800) 225-1852	C- / 3.8	-0.07	3.24	8.69 /67	10.92 /45	9.50 /41	0.81	1.45
AA	● Prudential Defensive Equity B	DMGBX	C	(800) 225-1852	C- / 4.2	-0.30	2.89	7.87 /62	10.11 /40	8.68 /34	0.14	2.15
AA	Prudential Defensive Equity C	PIMGX	C	(800) 225-1852	C- / 4.2	-0.22	2.89	7.87 /62	10.11 /40	8.68 /34	0.14	2.15
AA	Prudential Defensive Equity R	SPMRX	C	(800) 225-1852	C / 4.5	-0.15	3.15	8.44 /66	10.67 /43	9.22 /38	0.61	1.90
AA	Prudential Defensive Equity Z	PDMZX	C	(800) 225-1852	C / 4.9	-0.07	3.41	8.94 /69	11.20 /47	9.77 /43	1.09	1.15
FS	Prudential Financial Services A	PFSAX	E	(800) 225-1852	D- / 1.4	-0.97	-6.64	-7.79 / 3	9.26 /35	7.66 /28	1.41	1.31
FS	● Prudential Financial Services B	PUFBX	E	(800) 225-1852	D / 1.7	-1.16	-6.94	-8.45 / 3	8.50 /30	6.92 /23	0.89	2.01
FS	Prudential Financial Services C	PUFCX	E	(800) 225-1852	D / 1.7	-1.16	-6.94	-8.39 / 3	8.50 /30	6.92 /23	0.89	2.01
FS	Prudential Financial Services R	PSSRX	D-	(800) 225-1852	D / 2.0	-0.97	-6.72	-7.93 / 3	9.08 /34	7.36 /25	1.27	1.76
FS	Prudential Financial Services Z	PFSZX	E	(800) 225-1852	D+ / 2.3	-0.87	-6.47	-7.49 / 4	9.59 /37	7.99 /30	1.76	1.01
RE	Prudential Global Real Estate A	PURAX	C-	(800) 225-1852	C+ / 5.7	4.03	11.31	15.26 /92	11.47 /49	11.25 /55	2.41	1.26
RE	● Prudential Global Real Estate B	PURBX	C	(800) 225-1852	C+ / 6.0	3.88	10.95	14.44 /90	10.71 /44	10.48 /48	2.00	1.96
RE	Prudential Global Real Estate C	PURCX	C	(800) 225-1852	C+ / 6.1	3.88	10.95	14.49 /91	10.71 /44	10.48 /48	2.00	1.96
RE	Prudential Global Real Estate Q	PGRQX	C+	(800) 225-1852	C+ / 6.9	4.19	11.61	15.82 /93	11.81 /51	11.58 /58	3.06	0.83
RE	Prudential Global Real Estate R	PURRX	C	(800) 225-1852	C+ / 6.4	3.99	11.22	15.03 /92	11.26 /47	11.03 /53	2.37	1.71
RE	Prudential Global Real Estate Z	PURZX	C	(800) 225-1852	C+ / 6.8	4.11	11.52	15.60 /93	11.82 /51	11.58 /58	2.87	0.96
GR	Prudential Growth Allocation A	JDAAX	C	(800) 225-1852	C- / 3.9	2.60	4.81	6.03 /47	11.05 /46	9.72 /42	1.87	2.00
GR	● Prudential Growth Allocation B	JDGBX	C	(800) 225-1852	C / 4.3	2.39	4.42	5.24 /40	10.22 /41	8.90 /36	1.33	2.70
GR	Prudential Growth Allocation C	JDGCX	C	(800) 225-1852	C / 4.3	2.39	4.42	5.23 /40	10.23 /41	8.91 /36	1.33	2.70
GR	Prudential Growth Allocation R	JGARX	C	(800) 225-1852	C / 4.6	2.50	4.66	5.70 /44	10.75 /44	9.47 /40	1.76	2.45
GR	Prudential Growth Allocation Z	JDGZX	C+	(800) 225-1852	C / 5.0	2.63	4.95	6.28 /49	11.33 /48	10.01 /45	2.20	1.70
AA	Prudential Income Builder A	PCGAX	E	(800) 225-1852	D / 1.6	1.63	1.83	4.21 /33	6.93 /21	7.08 /24	2.28	1.75
AA	● Prudential Income Builder B	PBCFX	E+	(800) 225-1852	D / 1.9	1.47	1.46	3.50 /29	6.16 /17	6.31 /19	1.71	2.45
AA	Prudential Income Builder C	PCCFX	E+	(800) 225-1852	D / 1.9	1.47	1.46	3.50 /29	6.16 /17	6.31 /19	1.71	2.45
AA	Prudential Income Builder R	PCLRX	E+	(800) 225-1852	D / 2.2	1.67	1.69	3.98 /32	6.70 /20	6.83 /22	2.09	2.20
AA	Prudential Income Builder Z	PDCZX	E+	(800) 225-1852	D+ / 2.5	1.68	1.95	4.50 /35	7.21 /22	7.37 /26	2.67	1.45
FO	Prudential International Equity A	PJRAX	D-	(800) 225-1852	D- / 1.5	2.32	-2.45	-3.11 / 8	8.21 /28	5.69 /15	2.30	1.59
FO	● Prudential International Equity B	PJRBX	D-	(800) 225-1852	D / 1.8	2.11	-2.86	-3.80 / 7	7.47 /24	4.95 /12	1.81	2.29
FO	Prudential International Equity C	PJRCX	D-	(800) 225-1852	D / 1.8	2.11	-2.72	-3.80 / 7	7.47 /24	4.99 /12	1.81	2.29
FO	Prudential International Equity Z	PJIZX	D	(800) 225-1852	D+ / 2.4	2.31	-2.39	-2.91 / 9	8.48 /30	5.93 /16	2.74	1.29
RE	Prudential International Real Est A	PUEAX	D	(800) 225-1852	D+ / 2.7	2.53	3.68	7.12 /56	8.67 /31	--	3.69	2.48
RE	● Prudential International Real Est B	PUEBX	D	(800) 225-1852	C- / 3.1	2.44	3.30	6.34 /49	7.88 /26	--	3.16	3.18
RE	Prudential International Real Est C	PUECX	D	(800) 225-1852	C- / 3.6	2.54	3.71	7.17 /56	8.74 /31	--	3.93	3.18
RE	Prudential International Real Est Z	PUEZX	D+	(800) 225-1852	C- / 3.7	2.64	3.77	7.33 /58	8.95 /33	--	4.18	2.18
GI	Prudential Jennison 20/20 Focus A	PTWAX	D	(800) 225-1852	C / 4.5	3.11	3.56	8.96 /69	11.76 /51	10.29 /47	0.00	1.18
GI	● Prudential Jennison 20/20 Focus B	PTWBX	D-	(800) 225-1852	C / 4.8	2.89	3.22	8.18 /64	10.98 /45	9.52 /41	0.00	1.88
GI	Prudential Jennison 20/20 Focus C	PTWCX	D-	(800) 225-1852	C / 4.8	2.88	3.23	8.18 /64	10.97 /45	9.52 /41	0.00	1.88
GR	Prudential Jennison 20/20 Focus Q	PJTQX	D+	(800) 225-1852	C+ / 5.7	3.19	3.78	9.41 /72	12.23 /54	10.73 /51	0.00	0.76
GI	Prudential Jennison 20/20 Focus R	JTWRX	D	(800) 225-1852	C / 5.2	3.01	3.47	8.69 /67	11.52 /49	10.05 /45	0.00	1.63
GI	Prudential Jennison 20/20 Focus Z	PTWZX	D+	(800) 225-1852	C+ / 5.6	3.15	3.69	9.27 /71	12.08 /53	10.62 /50	0.00	0.88
GI	Prudential Jennison Blend A	PBQAX	C-	(800) 225-1852	C / 5.4	2.85	6.02	9.06 /70	13.34 /62	11.56 /57	0.16	0.95
GI	● Prudential Jennison Blend B	PBQFX	C-	(800) 225-1852	C+ / 5.9	2.65	5.64	8.32 /65	12.55 /56	10.78 /51	0.00	1.65
GI	Prudential Jennison Blend C	PRECX	C-	(800) 225-1852	C+ / 5.9	2.65	5.64	8.31 /65	12.55 /56	10.78 /51	0.00	1.65
GI	Prudential Jennison Blend Z	PEQZX	C	(800) 225-1852	C+ / 6.6	2.94	6.23	9.43 /72	13.68 /65	11.90 /60	0.45	0.65
GR	Prudential Jennison Conserv Gro A	TBDAX	B	(800) 225-1852	B- / 7.2	2.56	6.23	11.81 /82	16.12 /84	12.87 /67	0.27	1.31
GR	● Prudential Jennison Conserv Gro B	TBDBX	B	(800) 225-1852	B / 7.7	2.42	5.91	11.01 /78	15.27 /77	12.07 /61	0.00	2.01
GR	Prudential Jennison Conserv Gro C	TBDCX	B	(800) 225-1852	B / 7.7	2.42	5.91	11.01 /78	15.32 /77	12.07 /61	0.00	2.01
IN	Prudential Jennison Equity Income A	SPQAX	C+	(800) 225-1852	C+ / 6.2	2.47	4.62	10.19 /75	14.66 /72	13.31 /71	1.93	1.21

● Denotes fund is closed to new investors
* Denotes fund is included in Section II

www.thestreetratings.com

RISK Rating/Pts	Standard Deviation	Beta	NAV As of 3/31/15	Total $(Mil)	Cash %	Stocks %	Bonds %	Other %	Portfolio Turnover Ratio	Last Bull Market Return	Last Bear Market Return	Manager Quality Pct	Manager Tenure (Years)	Initial Purch. $	Additional Purch. $	Front End Load	Back End Load
B /8.7	4.6	0.76	13.15	38	5	39	55	1	46	29.5	-8.5	30	11	2,500	100	0.0	0.0
B /8.6	4.6	0.76	13.15	31	5	39	55	1	46	29.5	-8.5	30	11	2,500	100	0.0	0.0
B /8.6	4.6	0.76	13.25	N/A	5	39	55	1	46	31.7	-8.3	36	8	0	0	0.0	0.0
B /8.6	4.6	0.76	13.27	6	5	39	55	1	46	34.1	-8.1	43	11	0	0	0.0	0.0
B- /7.0	8.2	1.39	13.51	182	4	95	0	1	87	60.2	-12.3	16	2	2,500	100	5.5	0.0
B- /7.1	8.2	1.39	13.46	15	4	95	0	1	87	56.2	-12.6	12	2	2,500	100	0.0	0.0
B- /7.1	8.2	1.40	13.46	48	4	95	0	1	87	56.1	-12.6	11	2	2,500	100	0.0	0.0
B- /7.0	8.2	1.39	13.50	N/A	4	95	0	1	87	58.9	-12.4	15	2			0.0	0.0
C+ /6.9	8.2	1.39	13.53	4	4	95	0	1	87	61.7	-12.2	18	2	0	0	0.0	0.0
D+ /2.6	15.9	1.17	13.24	143	3	96	0	1	66	71.1	-30.1	2	6	2,500	100	5.5	0.0
D+ /2.4	15.9	1.17	11.95	11	3	96	0	1	66	67.0	-30.2	2	6	2,500	100	0.0	0.0
D+ /2.4	15.9	1.17	11.95	52	3	96	0	1	66	67.0	-30.2	2	6	2,500	100	0.0	0.0
C+ /5.9	15.9	1.17	13.24	5	3	96	0	1	66	69.8	-30.2	2	6	0	0	0.0	0.0
D+ /2.6	15.9	1.17	13.63	88	3	96	0	1	66	72.8	-30.0	2	6	0	0	0.0	0.0
C /5.0	12.3	0.90	25.36	992	11	88	0	1	32	69.0	-19.0	53	8	2,500	100	5.5	0.0
C /5.0	12.3	0.90	24.93	17	11	88	0	1	32	65.0	-19.2	42	8	2,500	100	0.0	0.0
C /5.0	12.3	0.90	24.93	192	11	88	0	1	32	65.0	-19.2	42	8	2,500	100	0.0	0.0
C+ /6.0	12.3	0.90	25.46	238	11	88	0	1	32	70.7	-18.9	56	8	0	0	0.0	0.0
C /5.0	12.3	0.90	25.31	24	11	88	0	1	32	67.8	-19.1	50	8	0	0	0.0	0.0
C /5.0	12.3	0.90	25.46	2,573	11	88	0	1	32	70.8	-18.9	58	8	0	0	0.0	0.0
B- /7.1	9.3	0.91	17.74	62	6	87	5	2	24	65.6	-18.8	24	11	2,500	100	5.5	0.0
B- /7.1	9.3	0.91	17.12	24	6	87	5	2	24	61.6	-19.1	17	11	2,500	100	0.0	0.0
B- /7.1	9.3	0.91	17.14	13	6	87	5	2	24	61.6	-19.1	17	11	2,500	100	0.0	0.0
B- /7.1	9.2	0.91	17.61	N/A	6	87	5	2	24	64.3	-18.9	21	8			0.0	0.0
B- /7.1	9.2	0.91	17.93	1	6	87	5	2	24	67.0	-18.7	27	11	0	0	0.0	0.0
C- /3.8	4.4	0.72	9.95	105	18	33	46	3	478	36.4	-6.6	56	1	2,500	100	5.5	0.0
C- /3.8	4.4	0.72	9.79	4	18	33	46	3	478	33.0	-7.0	45	1	2,500	100	0.0	0.0
C- /3.9	4.4	0.73	9.79	36	18	33	46	3	478	33.0	-7.0	44	1	2,500	100	0.0	0.0
C- /3.9	4.4	0.71	9.94	N/A	18	33	46	3	478	35.1	-6.7	54	1	0	0	0.0	0.0
C- /3.8	4.4	0.72	10.01	41	18	33	46	3	478	37.6	-6.5	60	1	0	0	0.0	0.0
C+ /6.0	13.3	0.99	7.06	236	2	97	0	1	134	51.6	-24.1	50	12	2,500	100	5.5	0.0
C+ /6.0	13.3	0.99	6.79	5	2	97	0	1	134	48.1	-24.3	40	12	2,500	100	0.0	0.0
C+ /6.0	13.3	1.00	6.79	21	2	97	0	1	134	48.1	-24.3	39	12	2,500	100	0.0	0.0
C+ /5.9	13.2	0.99	7.10	58	2	97	0	1	134	53.2	-24.0	54	12	0	0	0.0	0.0
C /5.4	14.2	0.79	10.55	3	30	69	0	1	48	50.6	-20.6	36	5	2,500	100	5.5	0.0
C /5.4	14.2	0.79	10.49	N/A	30	69	0	1	48	46.9	-21.4	27	5	2,500	100	0.0	0.0
C /5.4	14.2	0.79	10.48	1	30	69	0	1	48	50.7	-21.3	36	5	2,500	100	0.0	0.0
C /5.4	14.2	0.79	10.49	29	30	69	0	1	48	52.2	-21.1	39	5	0	0	0.0	0.0
C- /3.8	11.4	1.03	16.93	847	0	99	0	1	88	74.3	-18.6	14	17	2,500	100	5.5	0.0
D+ /2.9	11.4	1.03	13.90	102	0	99	0	1	88	70.1	-18.8	10	17	2,500	100	0.0	0.0
D+ /2.9	11.4	1.03	13.91	306	0	99	0	1	88	70.1	-18.8	10	17	2,500	100	0.0	0.0
C- /4.1	11.4	1.03	18.11	14	0	99	0	1	88	76.8	-18.4	17	17	0	0	0.0	0.0
C- /3.7	11.4	1.03	16.45	97	0	99	0	1	88	73.1	-18.6	13	17	0	0	0.0	0.0
C- /4.1	11.4	1.03	18.02	544	0	99	0	1	88	76.0	-18.4	16	17	0	0	0.0	0.0
C /5.0	11.2	1.08	21.68	1,039	0	99	0	1	54	83.4	-21.0	20	10	2,500	100	5.5	0.0
C /4.8	11.2	1.08	20.11	18	0	99	0	1	54	79.1	-21.2	14	10	2,500	100	0.0	0.0
C /4.8	11.2	1.08	20.12	25	0	99	0	1	54	79.1	-21.2	14	10	2,500	100	0.0	0.0
C /5.0	11.1	1.07	21.70	40	0	99	0	1	54	85.2	-20.8	23	10	0	0	0.0	0.0
C+ /6.2	10.1	1.03	11.61	183	1	98	0	1	234	95.2	-15.5	61	10	2,500	100	5.5	0.0
C+ /6.0	10.1	1.03	10.17	5	1	98	0	1	234	90.4	-15.8	50	10	2,500	100	0.0	0.0
C+ /6.0	10.0	1.02	10.17	57	1	98	0	1	234	90.4	-15.8	52	10	2,500	100	0.0	0.0
C+ /6.7	9.6	0.96	17.64	1,822	3	88	8	1	57	82.3	-17.2	57	15	2,500	100	5.5	0.0

99 Pct = Best
0 Pct = Worst

Fund Type	Fund Name	Ticker Symbol	Overall Investment Rating	Phone	Performance Rating/Pts	3 Mo	6 Mo	1Yr / Pct	3Yr / Pct	5Yr / Pct	Dividend Yield	Expense Ratio
IN	● Prudential Jennison Equity Income B	JEIBX	C+	(800) 225-1852	C+ / 6.5	2.25	4.25	9.31 /71	13.79 /66	12.45 /64	1.48	1.91
IN	Prudential Jennison Equity Income C	AGOCX	C+	(800) 225-1852	C+ / 6.5	2.25	4.26	9.33 /71	13.80 /66	12.46 /64	1.49	1.91
IN	Prudential Jennison Equity Income Q	PJIQX	B+	(800) 225-1852	B- / 7.5	2.60	4.86	10.56 /77	15.08 /76	13.65 /74	2.38	0.81
IN	Prudential Jennison Equity Income R	PJERX	C+	(800) 225-1852	C+ / 6.9	2.42	4.49	9.92 /74	14.39 /70	12.99 /68	1.80	1.66
IN	Prudential Jennison Equity Income Z	JDEZX	B	(800) 225-1852	B- / 7.4	2.53	4.75	10.47 /76	14.96 /75	13.60 /74	2.28	0.91
GR	Prudential Jennison Equity Oppty A	PJIAX	C+	(800) 225-1852	C+ / 6.7	3.90	6.46	7.36 /58	15.66 /81	13.71 /75	0.15	1.07
GR	● Prudential Jennison Equity Oppty B	PJIBX	C+	(800) 225-1852	B- / 7.1	3.70	6.07	6.64 /52	14.86 /74	12.94 /68	0.00	1.77
GR	Prudential Jennison Equity Oppty C	PJGCX	C+	(800) 225-1852	B- / 7.1	3.76	6.07	6.58 /52	14.86 /74	12.94 /68	0.00	1.77
GR	Prudential Jennison Equity Oppty R	PJORX	B-	(800) 225-1852	B- / 7.5	3.85	6.35	7.17 /56	15.43 /78	13.49 /73	0.01	1.52
GR	Prudential Jennison Equity Oppty Z	PJGZX	B	(800) 225-1852	B / 8.0	3.93	6.60	7.67 /60	16.02 /84	14.06 /78	0.43	0.77
OT	Prudential Jennison Global Infra Z	PGJZX	U	(800) 225-1852	U /	2.31	-0.96	8.35 /65	--	--	0.75	1.99
IN	Prudential Jennison Global Oppty A	PRJAX	C+	(800) 225-1852	C+ / 6.9	9.84	11.29	10.24 /75	14.55 /71	--	0.00	2.19
IN	Prudential Jennison Global Oppty C	PRJCX	C+	(800) 225-1852	B- / 7.3	9.69	10.92	9.45 /72	13.70 /65	--	0.00	2.89
IN	Prudential Jennison Global Oppty Z	PRJZX	B-	(800) 225-1852	B / 8.2	9.91	11.52	10.55 /77	14.85 /74	--	0.00	1.89
GR	Prudential Jennison Growth A	PJFAX	B-	(800) 225-1852	B / 7.7	5.55	8.99	15.82 /93	15.41 /78	14.68 /84	0.00	1.05
GR	● Prudential Jennison Growth B	PJFBX	B	(800) 225-1852	B / 8.2	5.33	8.61	15.04 /92	14.62 /72	13.89 /77	0.00	1.75
GR	Prudential Jennison Growth C	PJFCX	B	(800) 225-1852	B / 8.2	5.33	8.59	15.02 /92	14.61 /72	13.88 /77	0.00	1.75
GR	Prudential Jennison Growth R	PJGRX	B	(800) 225-1852	B+ / 8.6	5.49	8.88	15.61 /93	15.20 /76	14.48 /82	0.00	1.50
GR	Prudential Jennison Growth Z	PJFZX	B+	(800) 225-1852	B+ / 8.9	5.59	9.14	16.15 /93	15.75 /81	15.03 /87	0.00	0.75
HL	● Prudential Jennison Health Sci A	PHLAX	B-	(800) 225-1852	A+ / 9.9	13.24	31.76	43.17 /99	36.97 /99	29.20 /99	0.00	1.15
HL	● Prudential Jennison Health Sci B	PHLBX	C+	(800) 225-1852	A+ / 9.9	13.03	31.29	42.15 /99	36.01 /99	28.30 /99	0.00	1.85
HL	● Prudential Jennison Health Sci C	PHLCX	C+	(800) 225-1852	A+ / 9.9	13.06	31.30	42.17 /99	36.02 /99	28.30 /99	0.00	1.85
HL	● Prudential Jennison Health Sci R	PJHRX	B+	(800) 225-1852	A+ / 9.9	13.19	31.64	42.88 /99	36.69 /99	28.82 /99	0.00	1.60
HL	● Prudential Jennison Health Sci Z	PHSZX	B-	(800) 225-1852	A+ / 9.9	13.32	31.95	43.58 /99	37.38 /99	29.58 /99	0.00	0.85
FO	Prudential Jennison Intl Opptys Z	PWJZX	U	(800) 225-1852	U /	8.35	6.51	2.15 /22	--	--	0.00	1.54
MC	● Prudential Jennison Mid-Cap Gro A	PEEAX	B-	(800) 225-1852	B- / 7.5	6.11	13.01	14.53 /91	14.46 /71	14.57 /83	0.00	1.05
MC	● Prudential Jennison Mid-Cap Gro B	PEEBX	B	(800) 225-1852	B / 8.0	5.96	12.64	13.76 /89	13.66 /65	13.77 /76	0.00	1.76
MC	● Prudential Jennison Mid-Cap Gro C	PEGCX	B-	(800) 225-1852	B / 8.0	5.93	12.60	13.76 /89	13.66 /65	13.77 /76	0.00	1.76
MC	● Prudential Jennison Mid-Cap Gro Q	PJGQX	B+	(800) 225-1852	B+ / 8.9	6.22	13.27	15.09 /92	14.99 /75	15.07 /87	0.00	0.58
MC	● Prudential Jennison Mid-Cap Gro R	JDERX	B	(800) 225-1852	B+ / 8.4	6.05	12.90	14.30 /90	14.23 /69	14.34 /81	0.00	1.51
MC	● Prudential Jennison Mid-Cap Gro Z	PEGZX	B+	(800) 225-1852	B+ / 8.7	6.20	13.16	14.90 /91	14.79 /73	14.91 /86	0.00	0.77
EN	Prudential Jennison MLP A	PRPAX	U	(800) 225-1852	U /	-1.40	-6.85	5.52 /43	--	--	3.81	3.71
EN	Prudential Jennison MLP Z	PRPZX	U	(800) 225-1852	U /	-1.39	-6.76	5.71 /44	--	--	4.02	3.72
EN	Prudential Jennison Natural Res A	PGNAX	E-	(800) 225-1852	E- / 0.1	-2.35	-24.40	-25.81 / 0	-7.47 / 1	-3.04 / 1	0.00	1.17
EN	● Prudential Jennison Natural Res B	PRGNX	E-	(800) 225-1852	E- / 0.1	-2.55	-24.69	-26.33 / 0	-8.11 / 1	-3.72 / 1	0.00	1.87
EN	Prudential Jennison Natural Res C	PNRCX	E-	(800) 225-1852	E- / 0.1	-2.55	-24.68	-26.32 / 0	-8.11 / 1	-3.72 / 1	0.00	1.87
EN	Prudential Jennison Natural Res Q	PJNQX	E+	(800) 225-1852	E- / 0.1	-2.25	-24.23	-25.48 / 0	-7.06 / 1	-2.78 / 1	0.00	0.74
EN	Prudential Jennison Natural Res R	JNRRX	E-	(800) 225-1852	E- / 0.1	-2.43	-24.50	-25.96 / 0	-7.65 / 1	-3.23 / 1	0.00	1.62
EN	Prudential Jennison Natural Res Z	PNRZX	E-	(800) 225-1852	E- / 0.1	-2.29	-24.29	-25.58 / 0	-7.19 / 1	-2.75 / 1	0.00	0.87
GR	Prudential Jennison Select Growth A	SPFAX	C	(800) 225-1852	C+ / 6.4	4.74	7.44	14.04 /89	14.04 /67	14.05 /78	0.00	1.49
GR	● Prudential Jennison Select Growth B	SPFBX	C+	(800) 225-1852	C+ / 6.8	4.48	7.05	13.15 /87	13.19 /61	13.18 /70	0.00	2.19
GR	Prudential Jennison Select Growth C	SPFCX	C+	(800) 225-1852	C+ / 6.8	4.48	6.97	13.16 /87	13.16 /61	13.20 /70	0.00	2.19
GR	Prudential Jennison Select Growth Q	PSGQX	B-	(800) 225-1852	B / 7.6	4.84	7.60	14.22 /90	14.28 /69	14.33 /81	0.00	0.99
GR	Prudential Jennison Select Growth Z	SPFZX	B-	(800) 225-1852	B / 7.7	4.84	7.59	14.37 /90	14.33 /70	14.36 /81	0.00	1.19
SC	Prudential Jennison Small Company	PGOAX	C+	(800) 225-1852	B / 7.6	5.62	10.94	11.42 /80	15.99 /83	14.59 /83	0.19	1.14
SC	● Prudential Jennison Small Company	CHNDX	C-	(800) 225-1852	B / 8.1	5.57	10.57	10.69 /77	15.21 /77	13.80 /76	0.00	1.84
SC	Prudential Jennison Small Company	PSCCX	C-	(800) 225-1852	B / 8.0	5.44	10.52	10.63 /77	15.17 /76	13.79 /76	0.00	1.84
SC	Prudential Jennison Small Company	PJSQX	B	(800) 225-1852	A- / 9.0	5.81	11.21	12.01 /83	16.56 /87	14.69 /84	0.59	0.69
SC	Prudential Jennison Small Company	JSCRX	C+	(800) 225-1852	B+ / 8.5	5.57	10.76	11.12 /79	15.75 /81	14.35 /81	0.03	1.59
SC	Prudential Jennison Small Company	PSCZX	B-	(800) 225-1852	B+ / 8.8	5.69	11.01	11.69 /81	16.29 /85	14.88 /86	0.45	0.84
UT	Prudential Jennison Utility A	PRUAX	B	(800) 225-1852	B / 7.9	-0.43	1.37	11.02 /78	18.01 /94	16.06 /93	1.38	0.82
UT	● Prudential Jennison Utility B	PRUTX	B+	(800) 225-1852	B+ / 8.3	-0.60	1.08	10.21 /75	17.21 /91	15.27 /89	0.78	1.52

● Denotes fund is closed to new investors
* Denotes fund is included in Section II

www.thestreetratings.com

RISK Risk Rating/Pts	3 Year Standard Deviation	Beta	NET ASSETS NAV As of 3/31/15	Total $(Mil)	ASSET Cash %	Stocks %	Bonds %	Other %	Portfolio Turnover Ratio	BULL/BEAR Last Bull Market Return	Last Bear Market Return	FUND MANAGER Manager Quality Pct	Manager Tenure (Years)	MINIMUMS Initial Purch. $	Additional Purch. $	LOADS Front End Load	Back End Load
C+ / 6.6	9.6	0.96	16.51	170	3	88	8	1	57	77.7	-17.4	46	15	2,500	100	0.0	0.0
C+ / 6.6	9.6	0.96	16.47	1,402	3	88	8	1	57	77.8	-17.5	46	15	2,500	100	0.0	0.0
C+ / 6.6	9.6	0.96	17.65	7	3	88	8	1	57	84.5	-17.0	63	15	0	0	0.0	0.0
C+ / 6.7	9.6	0.96	17.64	46	3	88	8	1	57	80.8	-17.3	55	15	0	0	0.0	0.0
C+ / 6.6	9.6	0.96	17.63	1,838	3	88	8	1	57	83.9	-17.1	61	15	0	0	0.0	0.0
C / 5.5	10.4	0.99	20.77	297	2	97	0	1	47	95.0	-20.0	63	15	2,500	100	5.5	0.0
C / 5.3	10.4	1.00	17.95	12	2	97	0	1	47	90.5	-20.2	52	15	2,500	100	0.0	0.0
C / 5.2	10.4	1.00	17.95	51	2	97	0	1	47	90.5	-20.2	52	15	2,500	100	0.0	0.0
C / 5.4	10.4	0.99	18.88	8	2	97	0	1	47	93.7	-20.0	60	15	0	0	0.0	0.0
C / 5.5	10.4	1.00	21.41	178	2	97	0	1	47	97.1	-19.8	67	15	0	0	0.0	0.0
U /	N/A	N/A	12.40	40	16	83	0	1	49	N/A	N/A	N/A	2	0	0	0.0	0.0
C / 5.1	13.9	1.04	15.18	25	0	99	0	1	68	N/A	N/A	37	3	2,500	100	5.5	0.0
C / 5.1	13.8	1.04	14.83	8	0	99	0	1	68	N/A	N/A	29	3	2,500	100	0.0	0.0
C / 5.1	13.9	1.04	15.30	36	0	99	0	1	68	N/A	N/A	41	3	0	0	0.0	0.0
C / 5.4	11.7	1.03	30.23	1,085	0	99	0	1	38	98.5	-14.0	52	16	2,500	100	5.5	0.0
C / 5.3	11.7	1.03	25.67	24	0	99	0	1	38	93.9	-14.3	41	16	2,500	100	0.0	0.0
C / 5.3	11.7	1.03	25.71	84	0	99	0	1	38	93.8	-14.2	42	16	2,500	100	0.0	0.0
C / 5.3	11.7	1.02	27.27	53	0	99	0	1	38	97.4	-14.1	50	16	0	0	0.0	0.0
C / 5.4	11.7	1.02	31.91	1,669	0	99	0	1	38	100.7	-13.9	57	16	0	0	0.0	0.0
C- / 3.2	16.6	0.74	53.98	1,680	7	92	0	1	57	226.8	-14.4	99	16	2,500	100	5.5	0.0
D+ / 2.9	16.6	0.74	44.60	63	7	92	0	1	57	219.1	-14.6	99	16	2,500	100	0.0	0.0
D+ / 2.9	16.6	0.74	44.59	342	7	92	0	1	57	219.2	-14.6	99	16	2,500	100	0.0	0.0
C / 4.6	16.6	0.74	53.56	22	7	92	0	1	57	224.2	-14.5	99	16	0	0	0.0	0.0
C- / 3.3	16.6	0.74	57.84	1,475	7	92	0	1	57	230.1	-14.3	99	16	0	0	0.0	0.0
U /	N/A	N/A	13.75	49	4	95	0	1	61	N/A	N/A	N/A	3	0	0	0.0	0.0
C / 5.5	10.5	0.90	40.44	3,475	1	98	0	1	42	87.6	-17.3	57	10	2,500	100	5.5	0.0
C / 5.1	10.5	0.90	34.32	37	1	98	0	1	42	83.2	-17.5	46	10	2,500	100	0.0	0.0
C / 5.1	10.5	0.90	34.32	215	1	98	0	1	42	83.2	-17.5	47	10	2,500	100	0.0	0.0
C+ / 5.6	10.5	0.90	42.69	796	1	98	0	1	42	90.6	-17.1	64	10	0	0	0.0	0.0
C / 5.5	10.5	0.90	39.61	371	1	98	0	1	42	86.3	-17.3	55	10	0	0	0.0	0.0
C+ / 5.6	10.5	0.90	42.51	5,388	1	98	0	1	42	89.5	-17.2	62	10	0	0	0.0	0.0
U /	N/A	N/A	10.83	25	93	6	0	1	67	N/A	N/A	N/A	2	2,500	100	5.5	0.0
U /	N/A	N/A	10.86	80	93	6	0	1	67	N/A	N/A	N/A	2	0	0	0.0	0.0
D / 2.2	19.4	1.13	38.69	1,064	4	95	0	1	24	-2.5	-33.0	1	10	2,500	100	5.5	0.0
D / 2.1	19.4	1.13	31.70	56	4	95	0	1	24	-4.9	-33.2	1	10	2,500	100	0.0	0.0
D / 2.1	19.4	1.13	31.71	359	4	95	0	1	24	-4.9	-33.2	1	10	2,500	100	0.0	0.0
D / 2.2	19.4	1.13	40.41	211	4	95	0	1	24	-1.1	-32.8	1	10	0	0	0.0	0.0
D / 2.2	19.4	1.13	38.19	69	4	95	0	1	24	-3.2	-33.0	1	10	0	0	0.0	0.0
D / 2.2	19.4	1.13	40.18	1,391	4	95	0	1	24	-1.5	-32.9	1	10	0	0	0.0	0.0
C / 5.4	12.5	1.05	13.93	198	2	97	0	1	49	92.2	-13.0	31	15	2,500	100	5.5	0.0
C / 5.3	12.5	1.05	12.37	11	2	97	0	1	49	87.3	-13.2	22	15	2,500	100	0.0	0.0
C / 5.3	12.5	1.05	12.36	51	2	97	0	1	49	87.2	-13.1	22	15	2,500	100	0.0	0.0
C+ / 5.7	12.5	1.05	14.50	N/A	2	97	0	1	49	93.6	-12.8	33	15	0	0	0.0	0.0
C / 5.4	12.5	1.05	14.52	108	2	97	0	1	49	93.8	-12.8	33	15	0	0	0.0	0.0
C / 4.4	11.7	0.83	26.67	979	4	95	0	1	41	95.2	-23.9	86	15	2,500	100	5.5	0.0
D+ / 2.6	11.6	0.83	17.64	14	4	95	0	1	41	90.3	-24.0	82	15	2,500	100	0.0	0.0
D+ / 2.6	11.6	0.83	17.82	141	4	95	0	1	41	90.4	-24.1	82	15	2,500	100	0.0	0.0
C / 4.5	11.6	0.83	27.87	538	4	95	0	1	41	98.7	-25.4	88	15	0	0	0.0	0.0
C / 4.4	11.6	0.83	26.17	53	4	95	0	1	41	93.6	-23.9	85	15	0	0	0.0	0.0
C / 4.5	11.6	0.83	28.23	1,807	4	95	0	1	41	96.7	-23.6	87	15	0	0	0.0	0.0
C+ / 5.9	10.6	0.61	15.34	3,268	14	85	0	1	42	90.1	-12.2	98	15	2,500	100	5.5	0.0
C+ / 5.9	10.6	0.61	15.31	72	14	85	0	1	42	85.7	-12.5	97	15	2,500	100	0.0	0.0

						PERFORMANCE						
	99 Pct = Best 0 Pct = Worst			Overall		Perfor-	Total Return % through 3/31/15				Incl. in Returns	
				Investment		mance				Annualized		Dividend	Expense
Fund Type	Fund Name	Ticker Symbol	Rating	Phone		Rating/Pts	3 Mo	6 Mo	1Yr / Pct	3Yr / Pct	5Yr / Pct	Yield	Ratio
UT	Prudential Jennison Utility C	PCUFX	B+	(800) 225-1852		B+ / 8.3	-0.60	1.02	10.15 /75	17.17 /91	15.24 /88	0.78	1.52
UT	Prudential Jennison Utility R	JDURX	B+	(800) 225-1852		B+ / 8.7	-0.48	1.27	10.74 /77	17.76 /93	15.84 /92	1.26	1.27
UT	Prudential Jennison Utility Z	PRUZX	A-	(800) 225-1852		A- / 9.0	-0.35	1.52	11.34 /80	18.38 /95	16.41 /94	1.74	0.52
GR	Prudential Jennison Value A	PBEAX	C	(800) 225-1852		C / 4.8	-1.06	1.20	5.81 /45	13.42 /63	10.25 /47	0.46	1.06
GR ●	Prudential Jennison Value B	PBQIX	C	(800) 225-1852		C / 5.2	-1.23	0.84	5.06 /39	12.65 /57	9.48 /40	0.00	1.76
GR	Prudential Jennison Value C	PEICX	C	(800) 225-1852		C / 5.2	-1.23	0.84	5.11 /39	12.64 /57	9.47 /40	0.00	1.76
GR	Prudential Jennison Value Q	PJVQX	C+	(800) 225-1852		C+ / 6.0	-0.91	1.46	6.33 /49	13.95 /67	10.35 /47	0.90	0.63
GR	Prudential Jennison Value R	JDVRX	C+	(800) 225-1852		C+ / 5.6	-1.06	1.13	5.66 /44	13.21 /61	10.03 /45	0.29	1.51
GR	Prudential Jennison Value Z	PEIZX	C+	(800) 225-1852		C+ / 5.9	-1.01	1.33	6.14 /48	13.77 /65	10.59 /49	0.78	0.76
GR	Prudential Large-Cap Core Equity A	PTMAX	B	(800) 225-1852		B- / 7.5	1.33	7.11	13.14 /87	16.33 /86	14.27 /80	0.60	1.21
GR ●	Prudential Large-Cap Core Equity B	PTMBX	B+	(800) 225-1852		B / 7.9	1.09	6.68	12.27 /84	15.46 /79	13.43 /72	0.01	1.91
GR	Prudential Large-Cap Core Equity C	PTMCX	B+	(800) 225-1852		B / 7.9	1.16	6.68	12.26 /84	15.47 /79	13.43 /72	0.01	1.91
GR	Prudential Large-Cap Core Equity Z	PTEZX	A-	(800) 225-1852		B+ / 8.7	1.37	7.21	13.35 /88	16.62 /88	14.55 /83	0.83	0.91
GR	Prudential Long-Short Equity Z	PLHZX	U	(800) 225-1852		U /	4.06	7.90	--	--	--	0.00	N/A
MC	Prudential Mid-Cap Value A	SPRAX	A+	(800) 225-1852		A- / 9.1	2.69	8.70	12.41 /84	19.13 /97	15.41 /90	0.52	1.39
MC ●	Prudential Mid-Cap Value B	SVUBX	A+	(800) 225-1852		A / 9.3	2.55	8.31	11.61 /81	18.26 /95	14.56 /83	0.00	2.09
MC	Prudential Mid-Cap Value C	NCBVX	A+	(800) 225-1852		A / 9.3	2.56	8.34	11.65 /81	18.25 /95	14.55 /83	0.00	2.09
MC	Prudential Mid-Cap Value Q	PMVQX	A+	(800) 225-1852		A+ / 9.6	2.82	8.91	12.77 /86	19.61 /97	15.82 /92	0.90	0.95
MC	Prudential Mid-Cap Value Z	SPVZX	A+	(800) 225-1852		A+ / 9.6	2.77	8.85	12.75 /86	19.44 /97	15.72 /91	0.77	1.09
AA	Prudential Moderate Allocation A	JDTAX	C-	(800) 225-1852		D+ / 2.7	2.32	4.38	5.77 /44	8.90 /32	8.23 /31	1.88	1.71
AA ●	Prudential Moderate Allocation B	JDMBX	C	(800) 225-1852		C- / 3.1	2.12	3.91	4.96 /38	8.09 /27	7.43 /26	1.26	2.41
AA	Prudential Moderate Allocation C	JDMCX	C	(800) 225-1852		C- / 3.1	2.12	3.99	4.96 /38	8.09 /27	7.43 /26	1.26	2.41
AA	Prudential Moderate Allocation R	JMARX	C	(800) 225-1852		C- / 3.4	2.26	4.21	5.53 /43	8.58 /30	7.96 /30	1.74	2.16
AA	Prudential Moderate Allocation Z	JDMZX	C	(800) 225-1852		C- / 3.8	2.39	4.50	6.03 /47	9.18 /34	8.50 /33	2.22	1.41
AA	Prudential Real Assets Fund A	PUDAX	D	(800) 225-1852		E+ / 0.6	0.50	-0.87	0.67 /17	2.45 / 7	--	1.19	1.92
AA ●	Prudential Real Assets Fund B	PUDBX	D	(800) 225-1852		E+ / 0.7	0.40	-1.25	-0.10 /15	1.69 / 6	--	0.52	2.62
AA	Prudential Real Assets Fund C	PUDCX	D	(800) 225-1852		E+ / 0.6	0.30	-1.26	-0.10 /15	1.66 / 6	--	0.52	2.62
AA	Prudential Real Assets Fund Z	PUDZX	D	(800) 225-1852		E+ / 0.8	0.50	-0.81	0.83 /18	2.70 / 7	--	1.51	1.62
SC	Prudential Small-Cap Value A	PZVAX	C+	(800) 225-1852		C+ / 6.8	2.20	13.00	8.54 /67	15.25 /77	13.90 /77	0.89	1.35
SC ●	Prudential Small-Cap Value B	PZVBX	B-	(800) 225-1852		B- / 7.3	2.06	12.68	7.83 /62	14.45 /71	13.12 /69	0.45	2.05
SC	Prudential Small-Cap Value C	PZVCX	B-	(800) 225-1852		B- / 7.2	2.06	12.62	7.76 /61	14.44 /70	13.10 /69	0.45	2.05
SC	Prudential Small-Cap Value R	PSVRX	B	(800) 225-1852		B / 7.7	2.20	12.93	8.36 /65	15.04 /75	13.74 /75	0.73	1.80
SC	Prudential Small-Cap Value Z	PSVZX	B+	(800) 225-1852		B / 8.1	2.31	13.18	8.89 /69	15.60 /80	14.17 /79	1.23	1.05
IX	Prudential Stock Index A	PSIAX	B+	(800) 225-1852		B- / 7.2	0.83	5.64	12.14 /83	15.50 /79	13.90 /77	1.32	0.60
IX	Prudential Stock Index C	PSICX	B+	(800) 225-1852		B- / 7.3	0.67	5.33	11.46 /80	14.79 /73	13.22 /70	0.80	1.22
IX	Prudential Stock Index I	PDSIX	A-	(800) 225-1852		B / 8.1	0.92	5.83	12.56 /85	15.91 /83	14.30 /80	1.66	0.26
IX	Prudential Stock Index Z	PSIFX	A-	(800) 225-1852		B / 8.1	0.90	5.82	12.47 /85	15.83 /82	14.24 /80	1.61	0.32
GR	Prudential Strategic Value A	SUVAX	C+	(800) 225-1852		C+ / 5.8	-1.61	2.58	7.54 /59	15.03 /75	12.24 /62	0.68	1.49
GR ●	Prudential Strategic Value B	SUVBX	B-	(800) 225-1852		C+ / 6.2	-1.70	2.29	6.79 /53	14.20 /69	11.43 /56	0.05	2.19
GR	Prudential Strategic Value C	SUVCX	B-	(800) 225-1852		C+ / 6.2	-1.70	2.23	6.79 /53	14.21 /69	11.41 /56	0.05	2.19
GR	Prudential Strategic Value Z	SUVZX	B	(800) 225-1852		B- / 7.0	-1.52	2.76	7.82 /61	15.33 /78	12.54 /64	0.93	1.19
GI	Prudential US Real Estate Fund A	PJEAX	C+	(800) 225-1852		B / 8.2	4.14	18.67	23.06 /98	13.06 /60	--	0.77	2.04
GI ●	Prudential US Real Estate Fund B	PJEBX	C+	(800) 225-1852		B+ / 8.5	3.98	18.22	22.05 /97	12.20 /54	--	0.34	2.74
GI	Prudential US Real Estate Fund C	PJECX	C+	(800) 225-1852		B+ / 8.5	3.99	18.25	22.09 /97	12.23 /54	--	0.34	2.74
GI	Prudential US Real Estate Fund Z	PJEZX	B-	(800) 225-1852		A- / 9.2	4.26	18.89	23.35 /98	13.36 /62	--	1.04	1.74
AA	PSI Calendar Effects A	FXCAX	U	(888) 928-9774		U /	-2.87	-0.86	0.55 /17	--	--	0.00	2.37
IN	PSI Market Neutral A	FXMAX	D	(888) 928-9774		E- / 0.2	-0.72	-0.48	-4.26 / 7	-3.05 / 2	--	0.00	2.96
GI	PSI Strategic Growth A	FXSAX	D	(888) 928-9774		E+ / 0.6	0.30	-2.68	0.74 /18	3.14 / 8	--	0.00	2.77
GR	PSI Tactical Growth A	FXTAX	D	(888) 928-9774		D- / 1.0	3.86	4.38	2.96 /26	5.32 /14	--	0.15	2.54
GL	PSI Total Return A	FXBAX	D-	(888) 928-9774		E- / 0.2	-1.01	-3.52	-5.04 / 5	-1.52 / 3	--	2.28	2.25
AA	PSP Multi-Manager Investor	CEFFX	D+	(855) 318-2804		D / 1.6	5.04	4.73	8.04 /63	3.50 / 9	3.14 / 6	0.00	4.47
GR	Purisima All-Purpose	PURLX	C-	(800) 550-1071		E / 0.4	-0.32	-0.74	-1.48 /11	-1.39 / 3	-1.34 / 2	0.00	N/A

● Denotes fund is closed to new investors
* Denotes fund is included in Section II

www.thestreetratings.com

RISK			NET ASSETS		ASSET					BULL / BEAR		FUND MANAGER		MINIMUMS		LOADS	
	3 Year		NAV						Portfolio	Last Bull	Last Bear	Manager	Manager	Initial	Additional	Front	Back
Risk Rating/Pts	Standard Deviation	Beta	As of 3/31/15	Total $(Mil)	Cash %	Stocks %	Bonds %	Other %	Turnover Ratio	Market Return	Market Return	Quality Pct	Tenure (Years)	Purch. $	Purch. $	End Load	End Load
C+ / 5.9	10.6	0.61	15.29	159	14	85	0	1	42	85.8	-12.5	97	15	2,500	100	0.0	0.0
C+ / 5.9	10.6	0.61	15.33	59	14	85	0	1	42	88.9	-12.3	98	15	0	0	0.0	0.0
C+ / 5.9	10.6	0.60	15.35	224	14	85	0	1	42	92.1	-12.1	98	15	0	0	0.0	0.0
C+ / 6.4	10.9	1.06	20.59	522	0	99	0	1	39	83.2	-23.2	23	11	2,500	100	5.5	0.0
C+ / 6.4	10.9	1.06	20.02	9	0	99	0	1	39	78.9	-23.5	17	11	2,500	100	0.0	0.0
C+ / 6.4	10.9	1.06	20.01	27	0	99	0	1	39	78.8	-23.4	17	11	2,500	100	0.0	0.0
C+ / 6.4	10.9	1.06	20.60	14	0	99	0	1	39	85.9	-23.5	27	11	0	0	0.0	0.0
C+ / 6.4	10.8	1.06	20.55	13	0	99	0	1	39	81.9	-23.2	21	11	0	0	0.0	0.0
C+ / 6.4	10.9	1.06	20.61	78	0	99	0	1	39	84.9	-23.1	26	11	0	0	0.0	0.0
C+ / 6.6	10.0	1.04	15.96	92	1	98	0	1	91	104.8	-17.7	62	10	2,500	100	5.5	0.0
C+ / 6.6	10.0	1.04	14.85	3	1	98	0	1	91	99.7	-18.0	50	10	2,500	100	0.0	0.0
C+ / 6.6	10.0	1.03	14.87	40	1	98	0	1	91	99.5	-17.9	51	10	2,500	100	0.0	0.0
C+ / 6.6	10.0	1.04	16.26	49	1	98	0	1	91	106.7	-17.7	65	10	0	0	0.0	0.0
U /	N/A	N/A	11.03	39	58	40	0	2	0	N/A	N/A	N/A	1	0	0	0.0	0.0
C+ / 6.8	10.4	0.91	21.35	277	2	97	0	1	87	109.0	-21.2	89	8	2,500	100	5.5	0.0
C+ / 6.6	10.4	0.91	18.90	8	2	97	0	1	87	103.7	-21.4	87	8	2,500	100	0.0	0.0
C+ / 6.6	10.3	0.90	18.83	61	2	97	0	1	87	103.6	-21.4	87	8	2,500	100	0.0	0.0
C+ / 6.7	10.3	0.90	21.49	38	2	97	0	1	87	111.9	-21.0	91	8	0	0	0.0	0.0
C+ / 6.7	10.4	0.91	21.53	261	2	97	0	1	87	110.7	-21.1	90	8	0	0	0.0	0.0
B / 8.1	6.9	1.16	14.99	101	6	64	29	1	35	49.5	-13.6	20	11	2,500	100	5.5	0.0
B / 8.1	6.9	1.16	14.90	49	6	64	29	1	35	45.7	-13.9	15	11	2,500	100	0.0	0.0
B / 8.1	6.9	1.16	14.90	33	6	64	29	1	35	45.8	-13.9	15	11	2,500	100	0.0	0.0
B / 8.1	6.9	1.16	14.94	N/A	6	64	29	1	35	48.1	-13.7	18	8	0	0	0.0	0.0
B / 8.0	6.9	1.15	15.00	4	6	64	29	1	35	50.8	-13.6	24	11	0	0	0.0	0.0
B- / 7.8	7.4	0.85	10.04	12	36	38	24	2	114	16.0	-8.0	6	5	2,500	100	5.5	0.0
B- / 7.8	7.3	0.85	10.02	1	36	38	24	2	114	13.1	-8.2	4	5	2,500	100	0.0	0.0
B- / 7.8	7.4	0.85	10.01	5	36	38	24	2	114	13.1	-8.2	4	5	2,500	100	0.0	0.0
B- / 7.8	7.4	0.85	10.05	99	36	38	24	2	114	17.1	-7.8	6	5	0	0	0.0	0.0
C+ / 6.2	13.6	0.97	18.62	145	0	99	0	1	89	91.6	-21.4	62	8	2,500	100	5.5	0.0
C+ / 6.0	13.6	0.97	16.35	4	0	99	0	1	89	87.0	-21.6	51	8	2,500	100	0.0	0.0
C+ / 6.0	13.6	0.97	16.33	38	0	99	0	1	89	86.9	-21.5	51	8	2,500	100	0.0	0.0
C+ / 6.2	13.6	0.96	18.62	2	0	99	0	1	89	91.2	-21.4	60	8	0	0	0.0	0.0
C+ / 6.2	13.6	0.97	18.61	17	0	99	0	1	89	93.6	-21.3	66	8	0	0	0.0	0.0
B- / 7.1	9.5	1.00	43.69	215	3	96	0	1	4	96.8	-16.5	60	23	2,500	100	3.3	0.0
B- / 7.1	9.5	1.00	43.46	47	3	96	0	1	4	92.6	-16.6	50	23	2,500	100	0.0	0.0
B- / 7.1	9.5	1.00	43.80	303	3	96	0	1	4	99.1	-16.3	65	23	0	0	0.0	0.0
B- / 7.1	9.5	1.00	43.80	460	3	96	0	1	4	98.7	-16.3	64	23	0	0	0.0	0.0
B- / 7.0	10.5	1.05	14.63	24	0	99	0	1	77	89.7	-18.3	41	10	2,500	100	5.5	0.0
B- / 7.0	10.5	1.05	13.87	1	0	99	0	1	77	85.0	-18.6	32	10	2,500	100	0.0	0.0
B- / 7.0	10.5	1.05	13.86	14	0	99	0	1	77	84.9	-18.6	32	10	2,500	100	0.0	0.0
B- / 7.0	10.5	1.05	14.89	36	0	99	0	1	77	91.3	-18.2	46	10	0	0	0.0	0.0
C- / 3.8	13.0	0.43	14.80	7	0	99	0	1	66	80.2	-18.2	95	5	2,500	100	5.5	0.0
C- / 3.8	12.9	0.43	14.62	2	0	99	0	1	66	75.5	-18.5	94	5	2,500	100	0.0	0.0
C- / 3.8	13.0	0.43	14.60	2	0	99	0	1	66	75.7	-18.6	94	5	2,500	100	0.0	0.0
C- / 3.8	13.0	0.43	14.81	35	0	99	0	1	66	81.7	-18.2	95	5	0	0	0.0	0.0
U /	N/A	N/A	9.83	27	20	65	14	1	1,038	N/A	N/A	N/A	2	2,500	500	5.8	2.0
B / 8.4	3.1	0.11	8.31	14	37	21	31	11	3,987	-12.7	-7.6	12	5	2,500	500	5.8	2.0
B / 8.3	6.2	0.48	10.20	29	21	62	15	2	4,725	23.6	-18.6	16	5	2,500	500	5.8	2.0
B- / 7.5	5.2	0.47	10.22	16	14	51	34	1	1,927	24.7	-13.7	40	5	2,500	500	5.8	2.0
B- / 7.5	3.5	0.12	8.81	20	9	4	83	4	2,108	-3.9	-0.3	29	5	2,500	500	5.8	2.0
B- / 7.7	6.5	0.72	10.62	3	11	77	10	2	0	14.2	-10.5	16	1	1,000	250	0.0	1.0
B+ / 9.9	0.1	N/A	9.34	N/A	100	0	0	0	0	-4.7	-0.6	45	10	25,000	1,000	0.0	0.0

						PERFORMANCE							
							Total Return % through 3/31/15					Incl. in Returns	
					Perfor-					Annualized		Dividend	Expense
Fund		Ticker	Overall Investment		mance								
Type	Fund Name	Symbol	Rating	Phone	Rating/Pts	3 Mo	6 Mo	1Yr / Pct	3Yr / Pct	5Yr / Pct		Yield	Ratio
AA	Purisima Total Return	PURIX	D	(800) 550-1071	C- / 3.0	1.12	2.63	4.64 /36	8.15 /28	7.01 /23		0.59	1.35
FO	Putnam Asia Pacific Equity Fd A	PAPAX	D-	(800) 225-1581	D- / 1.2	3.15	2.07	5.45 /42	5.03 /13	2.47 / 5		0.25	2.58
FO	Putnam Asia Pacific Equity Fd B	PAPBX	D-	(800) 225-1581	D- / 1.4	2.93	1.64	4.56 /35	4.26 /11	1.71 / 4		0.00	3.33
FO	Putnam Asia Pacific Equity Fd C	PAPCX	D-	(800) 225-1581	D- / 1.4	2.94	1.74	4.58 /36	4.24 /11	1.70 / 4		0.00	3.33
FO	Putnam Asia Pacific Equity Fd M	PAPMX	D-	(800) 225-1581	D- / 1.2	2.99	1.81	4.91 /38	4.53 /12	1.96 / 4		0.00	3.08
FO	Putnam Asia Pacific Equity Fd R	PAPLX	D-	(800) 225-1581	D / 1.6	3.07	1.92	5.10 /39	4.78 /12	2.21 / 5		0.02	2.83
FO	Putnam Asia Pacific Equity Fd Y	PAPYX	D	(800) 225-1581	D / 1.8	3.24	2.24	5.72 /44	5.31 /14	2.73 / 5		0.52	2.33
SC	Putnam Capital Opportunities A	PCOAX	D+	(800) 225-1581	C / 5.0	2.28	9.14	5.02 /39	13.04 /60	13.22 /70		0.43	1.18
SC	Putnam Capital Opportunities B	POPBX	D+	(800) 225-1581	C / 5.4	2.02	8.69	4.15 /33	12.19 /54	12.38 /63		0.00	1.93
SC	Putnam Capital Opportunities C	PCOCX	C-	(800) 225-1581	C / 5.5	2.07	8.72	4.16 /33	12.21 /54	12.37 /63		0.00	1.93
SC	Putnam Capital Opportunities M	POPMX	D+	(800) 225-1581	C / 5.0	2.13	8.82	4.41 /34	12.48 /56	12.65 /65		0.00	1.68
SC	Putnam Capital Opportunities R	PCORX	C-	(800) 225-1581	C+ / 5.8	2.21	9.00	4.72 /37	12.76 /58	12.92 /67		0.26	1.43
SC	Putnam Capital Opportunities Y	PYCOX	C	(800) 225-1581	C+ / 6.2	2.29	9.23	5.26 /41	13.33 /62	13.52 /73		0.67	0.93
GI	Putnam Capital Spectrum Fund A	PVSAX	B+	(800) 225-1581	B- / 7.3	-1.01	5.02	6.68 /52	17.51 /92	18.16 /98		0.00	1.27
GI	Putnam Capital Spectrum Fund B	PVSBX	B+	(800) 225-1581	B / 7.8	-1.19	4.65	5.90 /46	16.64 /88	17.28 /96		0.00	2.02
GI	Putnam Capital Spectrum Fund C	PVSCX	B+	(800) 225-1581	B / 7.8	-1.22	4.63	5.89 /46	16.64 /88	17.28 /96		0.00	2.02
GI	Putnam Capital Spectrum Fund M	PVSMX	B+	(800) 225-1581	B- / 7.3	-1.13	4.75	6.14 /48	16.93 /89	17.57 /97		0.00	1.77
GI	Putnam Capital Spectrum Fund R	PVSRX	A-	(800) 225-1581	B / 8.2	-1.07	4.88	6.44 /50	17.23 /91	17.87 /97		0.00	1.52
GI	Putnam Capital Spectrum Fund Y	PVSYX	A	(800) 225-1581	B+ / 8.6	-0.95	5.15	6.96 /55	17.80 /94	18.44 /98		0.00	1.02
CV	Putnam Convertible Securities A	PCONX	C	(800) 225-1581	C / 4.3	2.23	3.89	6.65 /52	11.90 /52	10.23 /46		2.01	1.06
CV	Putnam Convertible Securities B	PCNBX	C+	(800) 225-1581	C / 4.7	2.04	3.50	5.86 /45	11.08 /46	9.42 /40		1.44	1.81
CV	Putnam Convertible Securities C	PRCCX	C+	(800) 225-1581	C / 4.7	2.03	3.52	5.83 /45	11.07 /46	9.40 /40		1.44	1.81
CV	Putnam Convertible Securities M	PCNMX	C	(800) 225-1581	C / 4.3	2.13	3.64	6.11 /47	11.35 /48	9.69 /42		1.62	1.56
CV	Putnam Convertible Securities R	PCVRX	C+	(800) 225-1581	C / 5.0	2.18	3.78	6.38 /50	11.63 /50	9.96 /44		1.90	1.31
CV	Putnam Convertible Securities Y	PCGYX	B-	(800) 225-1581	C / 5.4	2.29	4.02	6.92 /54	12.18 /54	10.52 /49		2.37	0.81
AA	Putnam Dynamic Asset Alloc Bal A	PABAX	B-	(800) 225-1581	C / 4.8	2.99	6.68	10.14 /75	11.93 /52	10.63 /50		1.29	1.00
AA	Putnam Dynamic Asset Alloc Bal B	PABBX	B	(800) 225-1581	C / 5.1	2.81	6.31	9.28 /71	11.07 /46	9.81 /43		0.65	1.75
AA	Putnam Dynamic Asset Alloc Bal C	AABCX	B	(800) 225-1581	C / 5.2	2.89	6.32	9.30 /71	11.08 /46	9.81 /43		0.72	1.75
AA	Putnam Dynamic Asset Alloc Bal M	PABMX	B-	(800) 225-1581	C / 4.7	2.87	6.43	9.55 /72	11.35 /48	10.09 /45		0.86	1.50
AA	Putnam Dynamic Asset Alloc Bal R	PAARX	B	(800) 225-1581	C / 5.5	2.96	6.53	9.80 /74	11.63 /50	10.35 /47		1.14	1.25
AA	Putnam Dynamic Asset Alloc Bal R6	PAAEX	U	(800) 225-1581	U /	3.15	6.92	10.50 /76	--	--		1.69	0.65
AA	Putnam Dynamic Asset Alloc Bal Y	PABYX	B	(800) 225-1581	C+ / 5.9	3.05	6.80	10.33 /76	12.18 /54	10.91 /52		1.60	0.75
AA	Putnam Dynamic Asset Alloc Consv	PACAX	C	(800) 225-1581	D+ / 2.7	2.69	5.50	8.43 /66	8.45 /30	7.78 /29		1.54	1.04
AA	Putnam Dynamic Asset Alloc Consv	PACBX	C	(800) 225-1581	C- / 3.2	2.43	5.15	7.66 /60	7.62 /25	7.00 /23		0.90	1.79
AA	Putnam Dynamic Asset Alloc Consv	PACCX	C	(800) 225-1581	C- / 3.2	2.35	5.09	7.64 /60	7.60 /25	6.96 /23		0.95	1.79
AA	Putnam Dynamic Asset Alloc Consv	PACMX	C	(800) 225-1581	D+ / 2.8	2.40	5.20	7.90 /62	7.86 /26	7.23 /25		1.14	1.54
AA	Purisima Dynamic Asset Alloc Consv	PACRX	C	(800) 225-1581	C- / 3.5	2.57	5.35	8.17 /64	8.16 /28	7.55 /27		1.37	1.29
AA	Putnam Dynamic Asset Alloc Consv	PACYX	C+	(800) 225-1581	C- / 3.8	2.65	5.62	8.68 /67	8.69 /31	8.05 /30		1.86	0.79
GR	Putnam Dynamic Asset Alloc Equity A		C	(800) 225-1581	B- / 7.0	3.82	8.00	11.71 /81	15.60 /80	12.92 /67		1.38	1.91
GR	Putnam Dynamic Asset Alloc Equity Y		C+	(800) 225-1581	B / 8.1	3.82	7.91	11.69 /81	15.56 /80	12.90 /67		1.45	1.66
AA	Putnam Dynamic Asst Alloc Growth A	PAEAX	C	(800) 225-1581	C+ / 5.7	3.36	6.94	10.20 /75	13.63 /64	11.46 /57		1.77	1.07
AA	Putnam Dynamic Asst Alloc Growth B	PAEBX	C+	(800) 225-1581	C+ / 6.1	3.16	6.50	9.36 /71	12.77 /58	10.63 /50		1.07	1.82
AA	Putnam Dynamic Asst Alloc Growth C	PAECX	C+	(800) 225-1581	C+ / 6.1	3.12	6.44	9.30 /71	12.76 /58	10.61 /50		1.29	1.82
AA	Putnam Dynamic Asst Alloc Growth	PAGMX	C	(800) 225-1581	C+ / 5.7	3.23	6.64	9.63 /73	13.07 /60	10.89 /52		1.36	1.57
AA	Putnam Dynamic Asst Alloc Growth R	PASRX	C+	(800) 225-1581	C+ / 6.5	3.23	6.72	9.90 /74	13.34 /62	11.17 /54		1.76	1.32
AA	Putnam Dynamic Asst Alloc Growth	PAEEX	U	(800) 225-1581	U /	3.39	7.06	10.54 /76	--	--		2.18	0.72
AA	Putnam Dynamic Asst Alloc Growth Y	PAGYX	C+	(800) 225-1581	C+ / 6.9	3.40	7.05	10.47 /76	13.91 /66	11.73 /59		2.11	0.82
GL	Putnam Dynamic Risk Allocation A	PDREX	D	(800) 225-1581	D- / 1.0	2.41	2.19	2.74 /25	4.75 /12	--		1.33	1.52
GL	Putnam Dynamic Risk Allocation B	PDRBX	D	(800) 225-1581	D- / 1.3	2.16	1.77	1.95 /22	4.70 /12	--		0.83	2.27
GL	Putnam Dynamic Risk Allocation C	PDRFX	D	(800) 225-1581	D- / 1.3	2.16	1.85	1.94 /22	4.70 /12	--		0.73	2.27
GL	Putnam Dynamic Risk Allocation M	PDRTX	D	(800) 225-1581	D- / 1.1	2.31	2.03	2.21 /23	4.97 /13	--		0.97	2.02
GL	Putnam Dynamic Risk Allocation R	PDRRX	D	(800) 225-1581	D- / 1.5	2.34	2.10	2.46 /24	5.21 /14	--		1.33	1.77

www.thestreetratings.com

RISK			NET ASSETS		ASSET					BULL / BEAR		FUND MANAGER		MINIMUMS		LOADS	
	3 Year		NAV						Portfolio	Last Bull	Last Bear	Manager	Manager	Initial	Additional	Front	Back
Risk	Standard		As of	Total	Cash	Stocks	Bonds	Other	Turnover	Market	Market	Quality	Tenure	Purch.	Purch.	End	End
Rating/Pts	Deviation	Beta	3/31/15	$(Mil)	%	%	%	%	Ratio	Return	Return	Pct	(Years)	$	$	Load	Load
C+ / 5.9	11.5	1.92	22.55	305	0	99	0	1	20	56.3	-23.0	1	19	25,000	1,000	0.0	0.0
C+ / 6.4	11.5	0.70	10.81	7	2	97	0	1	108	45.3	-32.8	45	4	500	0	5.8	0.0
C+ / 6.4	11.5	0.70	10.54	N/A	2	97	0	1	108	41.9	-33.0	34	4	500	0	0.0	0.0
C+ / 6.4	11.5	0.69	10.51	1	2	97	0	1	108	41.8	-33.0	35	4	500	0	0.0	0.0
C+ / 6.4	11.5	0.70	10.69	N/A	2	97	0	1	108	43.0	-33.0	38	4	500	0	3.5	0.0
C+ / 6.4	11.5	0.70	10.75	N/A	2	97	0	1	108	44.2	-32.9	42	4	500	0	0.0	0.0
C+ / 6.4	11.5	0.70	10.82	1	2	97	0	1	108	46.7	-32.7	50	4	500	0	0.0	0.0
C / 4.8	12.3	0.87	15.68	300	2	97	0	1	90	94.0	-28.4	55	16	500	0	5.8	0.0
C / 4.4	12.4	0.87	13.61	12	2	97	0	1	90	89.1	-28.6	42	16	500	0	0.0	0.0
C / 4.5	12.3	0.87	13.80	28	2	97	0	1	90	89.1	-28.6	42	16	500	0	0.0	0.0
C / 4.6	12.3	0.87	14.40	5	2	97	0	1	90	90.8	-28.5	46	16	500	0	3.5	0.0
C / 4.7	12.3	0.87	15.26	23	2	97	0	1	90	92.2	-28.4	50	16	500	0	0.0	0.0
C / 4.9	12.3	0.87	16.11	53	2	97	0	1	90	95.8	-28.3	58	16	500	0	0.0	0.0
B- / 7.0	9.0	0.68	38.19	3,088	19	77	2	2	53	110.2	-14.2	95	6	500	0	5.8	0.0
B- / 7.0	9.1	0.69	37.31	106	19	77	2	2	53	104.9	-14.4	94	6	500	0	0.0	0.0
B- / 7.0	9.0	0.68	37.22	2,018	19	77	2	2	53	104.9	-14.4	94	6	500	0	0.0	0.0
B- / 7.0	9.0	0.68	37.62	16	19	77	2	2	53	106.6	-14.4	94	6	500	0	3.5	0.0
B- / 7.0	9.0	0.68	37.91	18	19	77	2	2	53	108.4	-14.2	95	6	500	0	0.0	0.0
B- / 7.0	9.0	0.68	38.44	5,549	19	77	2	2	53	112.0	-14.1	95	6	500	0	0.0	0.0
B- / 7.5	7.2	0.94	24.99	583	9	15	0	76	63	60.7	-16.0	55	9	500	0	5.8	0.0
B- / 7.5	7.2	0.94	24.53	13	9	15	0	76	63	56.6	-16.3	44	9	500	0	0.0	0.0
B- / 7.5	7.2	0.94	24.72	76	9	15	0	76	63	56.7	-16.3	43	9	500	0	0.0	0.0
B- / 7.5	7.2	0.94	24.75	5	9	15	0	76	63	57.9	-16.2	48	9	500	0	3.5	0.0
B- / 7.5	7.2	0.95	24.89	7	9	15	0	76	63	59.4	-16.1	50	9	0	0	0.0	0.0
B- / 7.5	7.2	0.94	24.98	291	9	15	0	76	63	62.1	-15.9	59	9	0	0	0.0	0.0
B / 8.2	6.5	1.13	14.84	1,224	13	54	32	1	351	64.9	-13.8	62	13	500	0	5.8	0.0
B / 8.2	6.5	1.12	14.78	81	13	54	32	1	351	60.7	-14.0	51	13	500	0	0.0	0.0
B / 8.2	6.5	1.12	14.51	168	13	54	32	1	351	60.7	-14.0	51	13	500	0	0.0	0.0
B / 8.2	6.4	1.12	14.81	31	13	54	32	1	351	62.1	-13.9	56	13	500	0	3.5	0.0
B / 8.2	6.4	1.12	14.73	16	13	54	32	1	351	63.5	-13.8	59	13	500	0	0.0	0.0
U /	N/A	N/A	14.87	33	13	54	32	1	351	N/A	N/A	N/A	13	0	0	0.0	0.0
B / 8.2	6.4	1.12	14.86	170	13	54	32	1	351	66.3	-13.7	66	13	500	0	0.0	0.0
B / 8.2	4.0	0.63	10.96	471	5	40	54	1	583	39.8	-7.0	82	13	500	0	5.8	0.0
B / 8.2	4.0	0.64	10.88	23	5	40	54	1	583	36.2	-7.3	75	13	500	0	0.0	0.0
B / 8.2	4.0	0.63	10.83	69	5	40	54	1	583	36.2	-7.3	75	13	500	0	0.0	0.0
B / 8.2	4.0	0.63	10.84	11	5	40	54	1	583	37.3	-7.2	77	13	500	0	3.5	0.0
B / 8.3	4.0	0.63	11.23	8	5	40	54	1	583	38.7	-7.1	80	13	500	0	0.0	0.0
B / 8.2	4.0	0.63	10.99	100	5	40	54	1	583	40.8	-6.8	83	13	500	0	0.0	0.0
C / 4.4	9.9	1.01	11.95	N/A	6	93	0	1	69	96.8	-21.6	59	6	500	0	5.8	0.0
C / 4.4	9.9	1.01	11.95	40	6	93	0	1	69	96.7	-21.6	59	6	500	0	0.0	0.0
C+ / 5.9	8.5	1.46	16.30	1,476	17	62	20	1	351	80.5	-19.2	33	13	500	0	5.8	0.0
C+ / 6.1	8.4	1.46	16.00	106	17	62	20	1	351	76.0	-19.6	25	13	500	0	0.0	0.0
C+ / 5.9	8.4	1.46	15.53	189	17	62	20	1	351	76.0	-19.5	25	13	500	0	0.0	0.0
C+ / 6.0	8.4	1.46	15.97	32	17	62	20	1	351	77.6	-19.5	28	13	500	0	3.5	0.0
C+ / 5.9	8.4	1.45	15.97	23	17	62	20	1	351	79.1	-19.4	31	13	500	0	0.0	0.0
U /	N/A	N/A	16.47	49	17	62	20	1	351	N/A	N/A	N/A	13	0	0	0.0	0.0
C+ / 5.9	8.4	1.46	16.44	194	17	62	20	1	351	82.1	-19.2	37	13	500	0	0.0	0.0
B- / 7.6	6.7	0.93	11.03	28	0	0	0	100	117	28.9	N/A	21	4	500	0	5.8	0.0
B- / 7.5	6.8	0.93	10.88	4	0	0	0	100	117	28.3	N/A	20	4	500	0	0.0	0.0
B- / 7.5	6.8	0.93	10.89	16	0	0	0	100	117	28.3	N/A	21	4	500	0	0.0	0.0
B- / 7.7	6.8	0.94	11.05	N/A	0	0	0	100	117	29.4	N/A	22	4	500	0	3.5	0.0
B- / 7.5	6.8	0.94	10.95	1	0	0	0	100	117	30.5	N/A	25	4	500	0	0.0	0.0

					PERFORMANCE							
99 Pct = Best						Total Return % through 3/31/15					Incl. in Returns	
0 Pct = Worst			**Overall**		**Perfor-**				Annualized		Dividend	Expense
Fund Type	Fund Name	Ticker Symbol	**Investment Rating**	Phone	**mance Rating/Pts**	3 Mo	6 Mo	1Yr / Pct	3Yr / Pct	5Yr / Pct	Yield	Ratio
GL	Putnam Dynamic Risk Allocation R6	PDRGX	U	(800) 225-1581	U /	2.42	2.36	2.99 /26	--	--	1.92	1.13
GL	Putnam Dynamic Risk Allocation Y	PDRYX	D+	(800) 225-1581	D / 1.8	2.42	2.27	2.90 /26	5.74 /16	--	1.75	1.27
FO	Putnam Emerging Markets Eq A	PEMMX	E+	(800) 225-1581	E / 0.5	1.23	-2.86	-0.24 /15	1.30 / 6	0.48 / 3	0.72	1.83
FO	Putnam Emerging Markets Eq B	PEMBX	E+	(800) 225-1581	E / 0.5	1.05	-3.23	-0.93 /13	0.56 / 5	-0.26 / 2	0.00	2.58
FO	Putnam Emerging Markets Eq C	PEMZX	E+	(800) 225-1581	E / 0.5	1.16	-3.13	-0.82 /14	0.60 / 5	-0.24 / 2	0.12	2.58
FO	Putnam Emerging Markets Eq M	PEMAX	E+	(800) 225-1581	E / 0.5	1.25	-3.08	-0.61 /14	0.85 / 5	--	0.20	2.33
FO	Putnam Emerging Markets Eq R	PEMLX	E+	(800) 225-1581	E+ / 0.6	1.24	-2.99	-0.45 /14	1.08 / 5	0.24 / 3	0.56	2.08
FO	Putnam Emerging Markets Eq Y	PEMYX	E+	(800) 225-1581	E+ / 0.6	1.42	-2.76	0.14 /16	1.58 / 6	0.74 / 3	1.02	1.58
IN	Putnam Equity Income A	PEYAX	B	(800) 225-1581	B- / 7.4	1.24	5.95	10.80 /78	16.76 /89	14.31 /81	1.29	1.02
IN	Putnam Equity Income B	PEQNX	B+	(800) 225-1581	B / 7.9	1.06	5.57	9.99 /74	15.90 /83	13.47 /73	0.66	1.77
IN	Putnam Equity Income C	PEQCX	B+	(800) 225-1581	B / 7.9	1.13	5.60	10.04 /74	15.91 /83	13.47 /73	0.70	1.77
IN	Putnam Equity Income M	PEIMX	B	(800) 225-1581	B- / 7.4	1.14	5.72	10.29 /75	16.19 /85	13.75 /75	0.88	1.52
IN	Putnam Equity Income R	PEQRX	B+	(800) 225-1581	B+ / 8.3	1.20	5.88	10.58 /77	16.47 /87	14.03 /78	1.15	1.27
IN	Putnam Equity Income R5	PEQLX	U	(800) 225-1581	U /	1.38	6.18	11.22 /79	--	--	1.68	0.66
IN	Putnam Equity Income R6	PEQSX	U	(800) 225-1581	U /	1.40	6.22	11.31 /80	--	--	1.76	0.56
IN	Putnam Equity Income Y	PEIYX	A-	(800) 225-1581	B+ / 8.7	1.31	6.13	11.13 /79	17.05 /90	14.60 /83	1.60	0.77
GR	Putnam Equity Spectrum A	PYSAX	C+	(800) 225-1581	C+ / 6.1	-1.85	1.66	0.29 /16	16.83 /89	18.04 /97	0.00	1.36
GR	Putnam Equity Spectrum B	PYSOX	C+	(800) 225-1581	C+ / 6.5	-2.01	1.29	-0.44 /14	15.96 /83	17.16 /96	0.00	2.11
GR	Putnam Equity Spectrum C	PYSCX	C+	(800) 225-1581	C+ / 6.5	-2.04	1.27	-0.44 /14	15.96 /83	17.17 /96	0.00	2.11
GR	Putnam Equity Spectrum M	PYSMX	C+	(800) 225-1581	C+ / 6.1	-1.96	1.40	-0.20 /15	16.25 /85	17.45 /97	0.00	1.86
GR	Putnam Equity Spectrum R	PYSRX	C+	(800) 225-1581	C+ / 6.9	-1.92	1.53	0.03 /16	16.53 /87	17.75 /97	0.00	1.61
GR	Putnam Equity Spectrum Y	PYSYX	B	(800) 225-1581	B- / 7.4	-1.79	1.78	0.56 /17	17.12 /90	18.35 /98	0.00	1.11
FO	Putnam Europe Equity A	PEUGX	D+	(800) 225-1581	C- / 3.8	5.60	3.08	-3.31 / 8	12.26 /54	8.93 /36	1.30	1.41
FO	Putnam Europe Equity B	PEUBX	D+	(800) 225-1581	C- / 4.2	5.41	2.68	-4.04 / 7	11.43 /48	8.11 /31	0.74	2.16
FO	Putnam Europe Equity C	PEECX	D+	(800) 225-1581	C- / 4.2	5.40	2.71	-4.05 / 7	11.42 /48	8.12 /31	0.72	2.16
FO	Putnam Europe Equity M	PEUMX	D+	(800) 225-1581	C- / 3.9	5.44	2.80	-3.82 / 7	11.70 /50	8.38 /32	0.81	1.91
FO	Putnam Europe Equity R	PEERX	C-	(800) 225-1581	C / 4.5	5.50	2.91	-3.59 / 8	11.95 /52	8.64 /34	1.16	1.66
FO	Putnam Europe Equity Y	PEUYX	C-	(800) 225-1581	C / 4.9	5.62	3.16	-3.09 / 8	12.53 /56	9.19 /38	1.61	1.16
* GI	Putnam Fund for Gr & Inc A	PGRWX	C+	(800) 225-1581	C+ / 6.4	0.02	3.10	7.66 /60	16.00 /83	12.79 /66	1.37	0.97
GI	Putnam Fund for Gr & Inc B	PGIBX	C+	(800) 225-1581	C+ / 6.9	-0.12	2.72	6.89 /54	15.14 /76	11.95 /60	0.73	1.72
GI	Putnam Fund for Gr & Inc C	PGRIX	C+	(800) 225-1581	C+ / 6.9	-0.11	2.75	6.86 /54	15.17 /76	11.96 /60	0.74	1.72
GI	Putnam Fund for Gr & Inc M	PGRMX	C+	(800) 225-1581	C+ / 6.4	-0.10	2.83	7.08 /56	15.44 /79	12.23 /62	0.94	1.47
GI	Putnam Fund for Gr & Inc R	PGCRX	B+	(800) 225-1581	B- / 7.3	-0.03	2.96	7.35 /58	15.72 /81	12.51 /64	1.19	1.22
GI	Putnam Fund for Gr & Inc Y	PGIYX	B+	(800) 225-1581	B / 7.7	0.13	3.23	7.97 /63	16.30 /85	13.09 /69	1.70	0.72
GL	Putnam Glob Telecommunications A	PGBZX	D-	(800) 225-1581	C+ / 6.0	3.54	6.61	2.60 /25	15.23 /77	15.74 /91	11.80	1.67
GL	Putnam Glob Telecommunications B	PGBBX	D	(800) 225-1581	C+ / 6.4	3.41	6.24	1.86 /21	14.39 /70	14.89 /86	11.70	2.42
GL	Putnam Glob Telecommunications C	PGBNX	D	(800) 225-1581	C+ / 6.4	3.42	6.27	1.89 /21	14.39 /70	14.90 /86	12.14	2.42
GL	Putnam Glob Telecommunications M	PGBMX	D-	(800) 225-1581	C+ / 6.0	3.50	6.42	2.14 /22	14.68 /72	15.19 /88	11.62	2.17
GL	Putnam Glob Telecommunications R	PGBTX	D	(800) 225-1581	C+ / 6.8	3.57	6.50	2.41 /24	14.95 /74	15.47 /90	12.12	1.92
GL	Putnam Glob Telecommunications Y	PGBYX	D	(800) 225-1581	B- / 7.2	3.67	6.75	2.87 /26	15.53 /79	16.05 /93	12.74	1.42
OT	Putnam Global Consumer Fund A	PGCOX	C-	(800) 225-1581	C+ / 6.0	5.00	10.32	7.05 /55	14.15 /68	13.45 /72	0.32	1.70
OT	Putnam Global Consumer Fund B	PGCKX	C	(800) 225-1581	C+ / 6.4	4.77	9.93	6.20 /48	13.30 /62	12.58 /65	0.00	2.45
OT	Putnam Global Consumer Fund C	PGCNX	C	(800) 225-1581	C+ / 6.4	4.79	9.92	6.23 /48	13.30 /62	12.59 /65	0.00	2.45
OT	Putnam Global Consumer Fund M	PGCMX	C-	(800) 225-1581	C+ / 6.0	4.86	10.01	6.44 /50	13.58 /64	12.87 /67	0.00	2.20
OT	Putnam Global Consumer Fund R	PGCIX	C	(800) 225-1581	C+ / 6.8	4.93	10.19	6.73 /53	13.86 /66	13.17 /70	0.30	1.95
OT	Putnam Global Consumer Fund Y	PGCYX	C+	(800) 225-1581	B- / 7.2	5.05	10.51	7.30 /57	14.43 /70	13.73 /75	0.61	1.45
EN	Putnam Global Energy Fund A	PGEAX	E-	(800) 225-1581	E- / 0.1	-4.98	-26.30	-25.56 / 0	-4.77 / 2	-0.28 / 2	0.00	1.59
EN	Putnam Global Energy Fund B	PGEDX	E-	(800) 225-1581	E- / 0.1	-5.18	-26.61	-26.16 / 0	-5.51 / 2	-1.03 / 2	0.00	2.34
EN	Putnam Global Energy Fund C	PGECX	E-	(800) 225-1581	E- / 0.1	-5.08	-26.53	-26.09 / 0	-5.48 / 2	-1.02 / 2	0.00	2.34
EN	Putnam Global Energy Fund M	PGENX	E-	(800) 225-1581	E- / 0.1	-5.12	-26.47	-25.93 / 0	-5.26 / 2	-0.78 / 2	0.00	2.09
EN	Putnam Global Energy Fund R	PGETX	E-	(800) 225-1581	E- / 0.1	-5.03	-26.41	-25.82 / 0	-5.02 / 2	-0.54 / 2	0.00	1.84
EN	Putnam Global Energy Fund Y	PGEIX	E-	(800) 225-1581	E- / 0.1	-4.86	-26.19	-25.36 / 0	-4.52 / 2	-0.02 / 2	0.00	1.34

● Denotes fund is closed to new investors
* Denotes fund is included in Section II

www.thestreetratings.com

RISK			NET ASSETS		ASSET					BULL / BEAR		FUND MANAGER		MINIMUMS		LOADS	
	3 Year		NAV						Portfolio	Last Bull	Last Bear	Manager	Manager	Initial	Additional	Front	Back
Risk Rating/Pts	Standard Deviation	Beta	As of 3/31/15	Total $(Mil)	Cash %	Stocks %	Bonds %	Other %	Turnover Ratio	Market Return	Market Return	Quality Pct	Tenure (Years)	Purch. $	Purch. $	End Load	End Load
U /	N/A	N/A	11.02	30	0	0	0	100	117	N/A	N/A	N/A	4	0	0	0.0	0.0
B- / 7.5	6.8	0.93	11.02	137	0	0	0	100	117	32.8	N/A	31	4	500	0	0.0	0.0
C+ / 5.7	13.2	0.85	9.89	24	2	97	0	1	125	31.1	-34.3	5	7	500	0	5.8	0.0
C+ / 5.6	13.2	0.85	9.58	2	2	97	0	1	125	27.8	-34.6	4	7	500	0	0.0	0.0
C+ / 5.7	13.2	0.85	9.56	3	2	97	0	1	125	27.7	-34.6	4	7	500	0	0.0	0.0
C+ / 5.6	13.2	0.85	9.72	N/A	2	97	0	1	125	28.8	-34.5	5	7	500	0	3.5	0.0
C+ / 5.7	13.2	0.85	9.80	1	2	97	0	1	125	29.8	-34.4	5	7	500	0	0.0	0.0
C+ / 5.7	13.2	0.85	9.99	7	2	97	0	1	125	32.0	-34.2	6	7	500	0	0.0	0.0
C+ / 6.5	10.4	1.05	21.23	3,615	4	94	0	2	29	105.1	-19.7	65	3	500	0	5.8	0.0
C+ / 6.5	10.4	1.05	21.01	113	4	94	0	2	29	100.0	-19.9	54	3	500	0	0.0	0.0
C+ / 6.5	10.4	1.05	21.02	333	4	94	0	2	29	100.0	-19.9	54	3	500	0	0.0	0.0
C+ / 6.5	10.4	1.05	20.99	52	4	94	0	2	29	101.6	-19.8	58	3	500	0	3.5	0.0
C+ / 6.5	10.4	1.05	21.08	128	4	94	0	2	29	103.4	-19.7	61	3	500	0	0.0	0.0
U /	N/A	N/A	21.24	101	4	94	0	2	29	N/A	N/A	N/A	3	0	0	0.0	0.0
U /	N/A	N/A	21.24	402	4	94	0	2	29	N/A	N/A	N/A	3	0	0	0.0	0.0
C+ / 6.5	10.4	1.05	21.23	1,461	4	94	0	2	29	106.9	-19.6	68	3	0	0	0.0	0.0
C+ / 6.2	10.6	0.83	42.39	2,247	16	83	0	1	55	112.6	-14.4	89	6	500	0	5.8	0.0
C+ / 6.2	10.6	0.83	40.91	62	16	83	0	1	55	107.3	-14.7	86	6	500	0	0.0	0.0
C+ / 6.2	10.6	0.83	40.83	572	16	83	0	1	55	107.2	-14.7	86	6	500	0	0.0	0.0
C+ / 6.2	10.6	0.84	41.45	5	16	83	0	1	55	109.0	-14.6	87	6	500	0	3.5	0.0
C+ / 6.2	10.6	0.84	41.95	13	16	83	0	1	55	110.8	-14.5	88	6	500	0	0.0	0.0
C+ / 6.2	10.6	0.83	42.80	1,833	16	83	0	1	55	114.4	-14.3	90	6	500	0	0.0	0.0
C / 5.3	14.6	1.04	25.84	211	1	98	0	1	64	78.1	-27.8	85	9	500	0	5.8	0.0
C / 5.3	14.6	1.04	24.74	4	1	98	0	1	64	73.6	-28.0	80	9	500	0	0.0	0.0
C / 5.3	14.6	1.04	25.18	19	1	98	0	1	64	73.6	-28.0	80	9	500	0	0.0	0.0
C / 5.3	14.6	1.04	25.60	3	1	98	0	1	64	75.0	-27.9	82	9	500	0	3.5	0.0
C / 5.3	14.6	1.04	25.49	1	1	98	0	1	64	76.6	-27.9	83	9	500	0	0.0	0.0
C / 5.3	14.6	1.04	25.94	53	1	98	0	1	64	79.6	-27.7	86	9	0	0	0.0	0.0
C+ / 6.9	10.7	1.08	21.60	5,350	5	94	0	1	41	102.9	-22.2	48	7	500	0	5.8	0.0
C+ / 6.9	10.7	1.07	21.22	89	5	94	0	1	41	97.7	-22.4	38	7	500	0	0.0	0.0
C+ / 6.9	10.7	1.08	21.51	62	5	94	0	1	41	97.6	-22.4	38	7	500	0	0.0	0.0
C+ / 6.9	10.7	1.08	21.42	38	5	94	0	1	41	99.3	-22.3	41	7	500	0	3.5	0.0
C+ / 6.9	10.7	1.07	21.49	3	5	94	0	1	41	101.1	-22.2	46	7	500	0	0.0	0.0
C+ / 6.9	10.7	1.08	21.65	67	5	94	0	1	41	104.6	-22.1	52	7	500	0	0.0	0.0
D / 1.7	11.9	0.65	14.62	15	0	99	0	1	75	79.1	-13.6	97	7	500	0	5.8	0.0
D / 1.8	11.9	0.65	14.27	1	0	99	0	1	75	74.6	-13.8	97	7	500	0	0.0	0.0
D / 1.7	11.9	0.65	14.22	2	0	99	0	1	75	74.5	-13.8	97	7	500	0	0.0	0.0
D / 1.8	11.9	0.65	14.48	N/A	0	99	0	1	75	76.1	-13.8	97	7	500	0	3.5	0.0
D / 1.7	11.9	0.65	14.52	1	0	99	0	1	75	77.5	-13.6	97	7	500	0	0.0	0.0
D / 1.7	11.9	0.65	14.68	3	0	99	0	1	75	80.6	-13.5	97	7	500	0	0.0	0.0
C / 4.7	11.3	1.06	18.07	13	2	97	0	1	102	88.3	-17.7	30	7	500	0	5.8	0.0
C / 4.6	11.4	1.06	17.58	1	2	97	0	1	102	83.5	-18.0	22	7	500	0	0.0	0.0
C / 4.6	11.3	1.06	17.50	4	2	97	0	1	102	83.5	-18.0	22	7	500	0	0.0	0.0
C / 4.7	11.3	1.05	17.90	N/A	2	97	0	1	102	85.1	-17.9	25	7	500	0	3.5	0.0
C / 4.6	11.3	1.06	17.89	1	2	97	0	1	102	86.7	-17.9	27	7	500	0	0.0	0.0
C / 4.6	11.4	1.06	18.11	4	2	97	0	1	102	89.9	-17.7	33	7	500	0	0.0	0.0
D / 2.0	18.1	1.09	9.92	17	8	91	0	1	118	8.5	-27.8	2	3	500	0	5.8	0.0
D / 2.0	18.1	1.09	9.70	3	8	91	0	1	118	5.6	-28.0	2	3	500	0	0.0	0.0
D / 2.0	18.0	1.09	9.71	5	8	91	0	1	118	5.7	-28.1	2	3	500	0	0.0	0.0
D / 2.0	18.0	1.09	9.83	N/A	8	91	0	1	118	6.6	-28.0	2	3	500	0	3.5	0.0
D / 2.0	18.1	1.09	9.81	2	8	91	0	1	118	7.5	-27.9	2	3	500	0	0.0	0.0
D / 2.0	18.1	1.09	9.98	3	8	91	0	1	118	9.3	-27.8	2	3	500	0	0.0	0.0

Fund Type	Fund Name	Ticker Symbol	Overall Investment Rating	Phone	Perfor- mance Rating/Pts	3 Mo	6 Mo	1Yr / Pct	3Yr / Pct	5Yr / Pct	Dividend Yield	Expense Ratio
GL	Putnam Global Equity Fd A	PEQUX	C	(800) 225-1581	C / 5.2	4.95	4.66	4.58 /36	13.52 /64	11.18 /54	0.53	1.27
GL	Putnam Global Equity Fd B	PEQBX	C	(800) 225-1581	C+ / 5.6	4.72	4.26	3.81 /31	12.67 /57	10.34 /47	0.00	2.02
GL	Putnam Global Equity Fd C	PUGCX	C	(800) 225-1581	C+ / 5.6	4.64	4.21	3.78 /30	12.67 /57	10.34 /47	0.00	2.02
GL	Putnam Global Equity Fd M	PEQMX	C	(800) 225-1581	C / 5.2	4.84	4.43	4.09 /32	12.96 /59	10.63 /50	0.10	1.77
GL	Putnam Global Equity Fd R	PGLRX	C+	(800) 225-1581	C+ / 6.0	4.85	4.49	4.33 /34	13.25 /61	10.91 /52	0.36	1.52
GL	Putnam Global Equity Fd Y	PEQYX	C+	(800) 225-1581	C+ / 6.3	4.95	4.69	4.77 /37	13.79 /66	11.45 /56	0.78	1.02
FS	Putnam Global Financials Fund A	PGFFX	E+	(800) 225-1581	C- / 4.0	1.88	2.99	-0.54 /14	12.58 /57	5.97 /17	0.16	1.72
FS	Putnam Global Financials Fund B	PGFOX	E+	(800) 225-1581	C / 4.4	1.66	2.60	-1.29 /12	11.73 /51	5.17 /13	0.00	2.47
FS	Putnam Global Financials Fund C	PGFDX	E+	(800) 225-1581	C / 4.4	1.67	2.55	-1.30 /12	11.73 /51	5.17 /13	0.00	2.47
FS	Putnam Global Financials Fund M	PGFMX	E+	(800) 225-1581	C- / 4.1	1.81	2.74	-0.99 /13	12.06 /53	5.45 /14	0.00	2.22
FS	Putnam Global Financials Fund R	PGFRX	E+	(800) 225-1581	C / 4.8	1.81	2.82	-0.80 /14	12.29 /55	5.71 /15	0.00	1.97
FS	Putnam Global Financials Fund Y	PGFYX	D-	(800) 225-1581	C / 5.2	1.96	3.10	-0.29 /15	12.89 /59	6.23 /18	0.46	1.47
HL	Putnam Global Health Care Fund A	PHSTX	A-	(800) 225-1581	A+ / 9.9	8.80	16.05	31.06 /99	29.35 /99	18.07 /97	0.37	1.21
HL	Putnam Global Health Care Fund B	PHSBX	B+	(800) 225-1581	A+ / 9.9	8.59	15.61	30.06 /99	28.38 /99	17.19 /96	0.00	1.96
HL	Putnam Global Health Care Fund C	PCHSX	A-	(800) 225-1581	A+ / 9.9	8.60	15.62	30.08 /99	28.39 /99	17.18 /96	0.00	1.96
HL	Putnam Global Health Care Fund M	PHLMX	A-	(800) 225-1581	A+ / 9.9	8.65	15.76	30.39 /99	28.71 /99	17.48 /97	0.08	1.71
HL	Putnam Global Health Care Fund R	PHSRX	A-	(800) 225-1581	A+ / 9.9	8.73	15.91	30.71 /99	29.02 /99	17.77 /97	0.25	1.46
HL	Putnam Global Health Care Fund Y	PHSYX	A	(800) 225-1581	A+ / 9.9	8.86	16.20	31.37 /99	29.68 /99	18.36 /98	0.58	0.96
GL	Putnam Global Industrials Fund A	PGIAX	C+	(800) 225-1581	B / 7.6	5.13	6.19	3.81 /31	17.60 /93	14.06 /78	0.50	1.85
GL	Putnam Global Industrials Fund B	PGIVX	C+	(800) 225-1581	B / 8.0	4.87	5.81	3.00 /26	16.72 /88	13.23 /70	0.06	2.60
GL	Putnam Global Industrials Fund C	PGIEX	C+	(800) 225-1581	B / 8.0	4.92	5.86	3.05 /27	16.72 /88	13.22 /70	0.00	2.60
GL	Putnam Global Industrials Fund M	PGIHX	C+	(800) 225-1581	B / 7.6	5.01	5.98	3.32 /28	17.03 /90	13.53 /73	0.00	2.35
GL	Putnam Global Industrials Fund R	PGIOX	C+	(800) 225-1581	B+ / 8.4	5.09	6.11	3.57 /29	17.33 /92	13.82 /76	0.40	2.10
GL	Putnam Global Industrials Fund Y	PGILX	B-	(800) 225-1581	B+ / 8.8	5.17	6.31	4.05 /32	17.91 /94	14.35 /81	0.85	1.60
EN	Putnam Global Natural Resources A	EBERX	E-	(800) 225-1581	E- / 0.2	-1.47	-14.33	-16.58 / 2	-2.40 / 3	0.35 / 3	0.06	1.23
EN	Putnam Global Natural Resources B	PNRBX	E-	(800) 225-1581	E- / 0.2	-1.66	-14.67	-17.18 / 1	-3.12 / 2	-0.39 / 2	0.00	1.98
EN	Putnam Global Natural Resources C	PGLCX	E-	(800) 225-1581	E- / 0.2	-1.63	-14.66	-17.20 / 1	-3.11 / 2	-0.39 / 2	0.00	1.98
EN	Putnam Global Natural Resources M	PGLMX	E-	(800) 225-1581	E- / 0.2	-1.61	-14.60	-16.99 / 2	-2.89 / 2	-0.14 / 2	0.00	1.73
EN	Putnam Global Natural Resources R	PGNRX	E-	(800) 225-1581	E- / 0.2	-1.50	-14.47	-16.79 / 2	-2.63 / 3	0.11 / 3	0.00	1.48
EN	Putnam Global Natural Resources Y	PGRYX	E-	(800) 225-1581	E- / 0.2	-1.40	-14.26	-16.37 / 2	-2.16 / 3	0.60 / 3	0.37	0.98
GL	Putnam Global Sector A	PPGAX	D+	(800) 225-1581	C / 4.3	3.03	4.01	4.51 /35	12.49 /56	9.85 /43	3.53	2.53
GL	Putnam Global Sector B	PPGBX	D+	(800) 225-1581	C / 4.7	2.79	3.64	3.64 /30	11.59 /50	9.00 /37	3.15	3.28
GL	Putnam Global Sector C	PPGCX	D+	(800) 225-1581	C / 4.7	2.79	3.60	3.69 /30	11.63 /50	9.01 /37	3.28	3.28
GL	Putnam Global Sector M	PPGMX	D+	(800) 225-1581	C / 4.3	2.85	3.74	3.99 /32	11.91 /52	9.29 /39	3.14	3.03
GL	Putnam Global Sector R	PPGSX	C-	(800) 225-1581	C / 5.1	2.94	3.92	4.26 /33	12.18 /54	9.57 /41	3.50	2.78
GL	Putnam Global Sector Y	PPGYX	C-	(800) 225-1581	C / 5.4	3.02	4.16	4.74 /37	12.74 /58	10.11 /46	3.96	2.28
TC	Putnam Global Technology Fund A	PGTAX	D	(800) 225-1581	C- / 3.5	0.00	3.53	12.99 /86	9.93 /39	10.11 /46	0.00	1.84
TC	Putnam Global Technology Fund B	PGTPX	D+	(800) 225-1581	C- / 3.9	-0.20	3.14	12.13 /83	9.10 /34	9.28 /39	0.00	2.59
TC	Putnam Global Technology Fund C	PGTDX	D+	(800) 225-1581	C- / 3.9	-0.15	3.14	12.13 /83	9.10 /34	9.28 /39	0.00	2.59
TC	Putnam Global Technology Fund M	PGTMX	D	(800) 225-1581	C- / 3.5	-0.15	3.24	12.38 /84	9.36 /35	9.55 /41	0.00	2.34
TC	Putnam Global Technology Fund R	PGTRX	D+	(800) 225-1581	C / 4.3	-0.05	3.43	12.73 /86	9.65 /37	9.83 /43	0.00	2.09
TC	Putnam Global Technology Fund Y	PGTYX	C-	(800) 225-1581	C / 4.6	0.05	3.62	13.24 /87	10.19 /40	10.37 /48	0.00	1.59
UT	Putnam Global Utilities Fund A	PUGIX	D	(800) 225-1581	D / 1.9	-3.32	1.58	2.60 /25	8.41 /29	5.41 /14	1.62	1.25
UT	Putnam Global Utilities Fund B	PUTBX	D+	(800) 225-1581	D / 2.2	-3.53	1.20	1.83 /21	7.59 /25	4.63 /11	0.94	2.00
UT	Putnam Global Utilities Fund C	PUTCX	D+	(800) 225-1581	D / 2.2	-3.46	1.21	1.87 /21	7.58 /25	4.63 /11	0.97	2.00
UT	Putnam Global Utilities Fund M	PUTMX	D	(800) 225-1581	D / 1.9	-3.45	1.32	2.09 /22	7.87 /26	4.88 /11	1.16	1.75
UT	Putnam Global Utilities Fund R	PULRX	D+	(800) 225-1581	D+ / 2.5	-3.39	1.46	2.37 /23	8.13 /28	5.15 /13	1.48	1.50
UT	Putnam Global Utilities Fund Y	PUTYX	C-	(800) 225-1581	D+ / 2.8	-3.26	1.63	2.86 /26	8.65 /31	5.66 /15	1.98	1.00
GR	Putnam Growth Opportunities A	POGAX	C+	(800) 225-1581	B / 7.9	2.63	7.34	15.15 /92	16.65 /88	15.01 /87	0.43	1.10
GR	Putnam Growth Opportunities B	POGBX	C+	(800) 225-1581	B+ / 8.4	2.48	6.98	14.32 /90	15.81 /82	14.15 /79	0.00	1.85
GR	Putnam Growth Opportunities C	POGCX	C+	(800) 225-1581	B+ / 8.4	2.44	6.96	14.29 /90	15.79 /82	14.15 /79	0.00	1.85
GR	Putnam Growth Opportunities M	PGOMX	C+	(800) 225-1581	B / 7.9	2.50	7.09	14.57 /91	16.07 /84	14.43 /82	0.09	1.60

Legend (top-left):
- 99 Pct = Best
- 0 Pct = Worst

PERFORMANCE — Total Return % through 3/31/15 — Annualized — Incl. in Returns

RISK			NET ASSETS		ASSET					BULL / BEAR		FUND MANAGER		MINIMUMS		LOADS	
	3 Year		NAV						Portfolio	Last Bull	Last Bear	Manager	Manager	Initial	Additional	Front	Back
Risk	Standard		As of	Total	Cash	Stocks	Bonds	Other	Turnover	Market	Market	Quality	Tenure	Purch.	Purch.	End	End
Rating/Pts	Deviation	Beta	3/31/15	$(Mil)	%	%	%	%	Ratio	Return	Return	Pct	(Years)	$	$	Load	Load
C+ / 6.0	11.7	0.80	13.35	835	2	97	0	1	80	84.2	-23.4	94	4	500	0	5.8	0.0
C+ / 6.0	11.8	0.81	11.99	17	2	97	0	1	80	79.5	-23.6	93	4	500	0	0.0	0.0
C+ / 6.0	11.8	0.81	12.62	18	2	97	0	1	80	79.6	-23.6	93	4	500	0	0.0	0.0
C+ / 6.0	11.8	0.81	12.79	13	2	97	0	1	80	80.9	-23.5	93	4	500	0	3.5	0.0
C+ / 6.0	11.8	0.81	13.20	2	2	97	0	1	80	82.5	-23.5	94	4	0	0	0.0	0.0
C+ / 6.0	11.8	0.81	13.77	34	2	97	0	1	80	85.6	-23.2	94	4	0	0	0.0	0.0
D / 2.0	14.9	1.18	11.91	6	5	94	0	1	55	84.6	-32.1	4	7	500	0	5.8	0.0
D / 1.9	14.9	1.19	11.66	1	5	94	0	1	55	80.1	-32.4	3	7	500	0	0.0	0.0
D / 1.9	14.9	1.18	11.55	1	5	94	0	1	55	80.1	-32.3	3	7	500	0	0.0	0.0
D / 2.0	14.9	1.18	11.84	N/A	5	94	0	1	55	81.6	-32.3	4	7	500	0	3.5	0.0
D / 2.0	14.9	1.18	11.80	1	5	94	0	1	55	83.2	-32.2	4	7	500	0	0.0	0.0
D / 2.0	14.8	1.18	11.94	3	5	94	0	1	55	86.3	-32.1	5	7	500	0	0.0	0.0
C / 5.3	10.9	0.89	71.94	1,568	0	99	0	1	22	152.2	-19.4	99	10	500	0	5.8	1.0
C / 4.6	10.9	0.89	52.36	38	0	99	0	1	22	145.8	-19.6	99	10	500	0	0.0	1.0
C / 5.0	10.9	0.89	60.11	52	0	99	0	1	22	145.8	-19.6	99	10	500	0	0.0	1.0
C / 5.0	10.9	0.89	61.40	17	0	99	0	1	22	147.8	-19.5	99	10	500	0	3.5	1.0
C / 5.3	10.9	0.89	68.78	8	0	99	0	1	22	150.0	-19.4	99	10	500	0	0.0	1.0
C / 5.4	10.9	0.89	75.32	60	0	99	0	1	22	154.3	-19.3	99	10	500	0	0.0	1.0
C / 4.4	11.6	0.71	17.61	10	7	92	0	1	227	109.6	-30.7	98	6	500	0	5.8	0.0
C / 4.4	11.6	0.71	17.02	1	7	92	0	1	227	104.4	-30.9	98	6	500	0	0.0	0.0
C / 4.4	11.6	0.71	17.06	1	7	92	0	1	227	104.5	-30.9	98	6	500	0	0.0	0.0
C / 4.5	11.6	0.71	17.40	N/A	7	92	0	1	227	106.4	-30.9	98	6	500	0	3.5	0.0
C / 4.4	11.6	0.71	17.55	N/A	7	92	0	1	227	108.0	-30.8	98	6	500	0	0.0	0.0
C / 4.4	11.6	0.71	17.69	5	7	92	0	1	227	111.5	-30.6	98	6	500	0	0.0	0.0
C- / 3.2	15.8	0.92	18.81	188	7	92	0	1	101	21.4	-32.6	7	3	500	0	5.8	0.0
C- / 3.1	15.8	0.92	16.58	8	7	92	0	1	101	18.3	-32.9	5	3	500	0	0.0	0.0
C- / 3.1	15.9	0.92	16.94	10	7	92	0	1	101	18.3	-32.8	5	3	500	0	0.0	0.0
C- / 3.1	15.8	0.92	17.73	3	7	92	0	1	101	19.3	-32.8	6	3	500	0	3.5	0.0
C- / 3.1	15.9	0.92	18.38	12	7	92	0	1	101	20.3	-32.7	6	3	500	0	0.0	0.0
C- / 3.2	15.9	0.92	18.95	13	7	92	0	1	101	22.4	-32.6	7	3	500	0	0.0	0.0
C / 5.1	11.0	0.77	11.57	4	3	96	0	1	39	78.3	-24.3	93	4	500	0	5.8	1.0
C / 5.1	11.0	0.77	11.41	N/A	3	96	0	1	39	73.8	-24.6	91	4	500	0	0.0	1.0
C / 5.1	11.0	0.77	11.41	1	3	96	0	1	39	74.0	-24.6	92	4	500	0	0.0	1.0
C / 5.1	11.0	0.77	11.54	N/A	3	96	0	1	39	75.3	-24.4	92	4	500	0	3.5	1.0
C / 5.1	11.1	0.77	11.56	N/A	3	96	0	1	39	77.1	-24.5	92	4	0	0	0.0	1.0
C / 5.0	11.0	0.77	11.59	4	3	96	0	1	39	80.0	-24.2	93	4	0	0	0.0	1.0
C / 5.5	12.4	1.05	21.28	16	1	98	0	1	50	72.7	-15.5	6	3	500	0	5.8	0.0
C / 5.5	12.4	1.05	20.26	2	1	98	0	1	50	68.3	-15.7	4	3	500	0	0.0	0.0
C / 5.5	12.4	1.05	20.26	2	1	98	0	1	50	68.3	-15.7	4	3	500	0	0.0	0.0
C / 5.5	12.4	1.05	20.61	N/A	1	98	0	1	50	69.6	-15.6	5	3	500	0	3.5	0.0
C / 5.5	12.4	1.05	20.98	N/A	1	98	0	1	50	71.2	-15.5	5	3	500	0	0.0	0.0
C / 5.5	12.4	1.04	21.60	4	1	98	0	1	50	74.1	-15.4	7	3	500	0	0.0	0.0
B- / 7.1	10.9	0.65	12.35	198	0	99	0	1	27	37.5	-10.6	70	3	500	0	5.8	0.0
B- / 7.1	11.0	0.65	12.31	6	0	99	0	1	27	34.0	-10.9	60	3	500	0	0.0	0.0
B- / 7.1	11.0	0.65	12.26	6	0	99	0	1	27	34.0	-10.8	60	3	500	0	0.0	0.0
B- / 7.1	10.9	0.65	12.34	1	0	99	0	1	27	35.2	-10.8	64	3	500	0	3.5	0.0
B- / 7.1	10.9	0.65	12.31	1	0	99	0	1	27	36.3	-10.7	67	3	500	0	0.0	0.0
B- / 7.1	11.0	0.65	12.34	4	0	99	0	1	27	38.8	-10.6	72	3	500	0	0.0	0.0
C / 4.7	11.0	1.06	24.57	455	3	96	0	1	83	110.9	-20.3	60	7	500	0	5.8	0.0
C / 4.5	11.0	1.06	21.52	21	3	96	0	1	83	105.6	-20.6	49	7	500	0	0.0	0.0
C / 4.5	11.0	1.07	21.87	28	3	96	0	1	83	105.5	-20.6	48	7	500	0	0.0	0.0
C / 4.6	11.0	1.07	22.58	7	3	96	0	1	83	107.3	-20.5	52	7	500	0	3.5	0.0

99 Pct = Best
0 Pct = Worst

Fund Type	Fund Name	Ticker Symbol	Overall Investment Rating	Phone	Perfor-mance Rating/Pts	3 Mo	6 Mo	1Yr / Pct	3Yr / Pct	5Yr / Pct	Dividend Yield	Expense Ratio
GR	Putnam Growth Opportunities R	PGORX	B	(800) 225-1581	B+ / 8.7	2.58	7.25	14.87 /91	16.38 /86	14.72 /84	0.44	1.35
GR	Putnam Growth Opportunities Y	PGOYX	B	(800) 225-1581	A- / 9.0	2.70	7.46	15.45 /92	16.94 /90	15.30 /89	0.70	0.85
FO	Putnam International Capital Opp A	PNVAX	E+	(800) 225-1581	E+ / 0.8	5.93	1.03	-9.25 / 3	5.55 /15	4.28 / 9	1.92	1.43
FO	Putnam International Capital Opp B	PVNBX	E+	(800) 225-1581	D- / 1.0	5.75	0.65	-9.93 / 3	4.77 /12	3.51 / 7	1.06	2.18
FO	Putnam International Capital Opp C	PUVCX	E+	(800) 225-1581	D- / 1.0	5.77	0.65	-9.92 / 3	4.77 /12	3.50 / 7	1.17	2.18
FO	Putnam International Capital Opp M	PIVMX	E+	(800) 225-1581	E+ / 0.8	5.83	0.78	-9.69 / 3	5.03 /13	3.77 / 8	1.41	1.93
FO	Putnam International Capital Opp R	PICRX	E+	(800) 225-1581	D- / 1.0	5.86	0.89	-9.49 / 3	5.28 /14	4.02 / 8	1.78	1.68
FO	Putnam International Capital Opp Y	PIVYX	E+	(800) 225-1581	D- / 1.3	6.03	1.15	-9.01 / 3	5.82 /16	4.55 /10	2.33	1.18
FO	Putnam International Equity A	POVSX	D	(800) 225-1581	C- / 3.1	6.30	2.22	-0.35 /15	10.32 /41	7.17 /24	0.85	1.30
FO	Putnam International Equity B	POVBX	D+	(800) 225-1581	C- / 3.4	6.03	1.79	-1.12 /13	9.49 /36	6.37 /19	0.05	2.05
FO	Putnam International Equity C	PIGCX	D+	(800) 225-1581	C- / 3.4	6.04	1.81	-1.09 /13	9.48 /36	6.37 /19	0.18	2.05
FO	Putnam International Equity M	POVMX	D	(800) 225-1581	C- / 3.1	6.14	1.91	-0.85 /13	9.76 /38	6.63 /21	0.39	1.80
FO	Putnam International Equity R	PIERX	D+	(800) 225-1581	C- / 3.8	6.18	2.05	-0.64 /14	10.03 /39	6.90 /22	0.76	1.55
FO	Putnam International Equity Y	POVYX	C-	(800) 225-1581	C / 4.1	6.31	2.29	-0.13 /15	10.58 /43	7.44 /26	1.18	1.05
FO	Putnam International Growth A	PINOX	D-	(800) 225-1581	D / 1.6	4.16	-0.11	-3.16 / 8	8.00 /27	5.76 /15	0.00	1.50
FO	Putnam International Growth B	PINWX	D-	(800) 225-1581	D / 1.9	3.97	-0.46	-3.89 / 7	7.18 /22	4.97 /12	0.00	2.25
FO	Putnam International Growth C	PIOCX	D-	(800) 225-1581	D / 1.9	3.93	-0.51	-3.91 / 7	7.19 /22	4.95 /12	0.00	2.25
FO	Putnam International Growth M	PINMX	D-	(800) 225-1581	D / 1.6	4.01	-0.33	-3.66 / 8	7.45 /24	5.23 /13	0.00	2.00
FO	Putnam International Growth R	PNPRX	D-	(800) 225-1581	D / 2.2	4.06	-0.21	-3.46 / 8	7.71 /25	5.50 /14	0.00	1.75
FO	Putnam International Growth Y	PINYX	D	(800) 225-1581	D+ / 2.5	4.19	0.00	-2.94 / 9	8.25 /28	6.02 /17	0.00	1.25
FO	Putnam International Value A	PNGAX	E+	(800) 225-1581	D- / 1.3	4.62	-1.90	-5.01 / 5	7.59 /25	5.10 /12	1.81	1.34
FO	Putnam International Value B	PGNBX	D-	(800) 225-1581	D / 1.6	4.44	-2.26	-5.72 / 5	6.80 /20	4.33 / 9	0.97	2.09
FO	Putnam International Value C	PIGRX	D-	(800) 225-1581	D / 1.6	4.45	-2.14	-5.69 / 5	6.83 /20	4.34 /10	1.18	2.09
FO	Putnam International Value M	PIGMX	D-	(800) 225-1581	D- / 1.4	4.51	-2.13	-5.48 / 5	7.08 /22	4.59 /11	1.29	1.84
FO	Putnam International Value R	PIIRX	D-	(800) 225-1581	D / 1.8	4.59	-1.98	-5.22 / 5	7.36 /23	4.86 /11	1.73	1.59
FO	Putnam International Value Y	PNGYX	D-	(800) 225-1581	D / 2.1	4.72	-1.69	-4.72 / 6	7.90 /26	5.38 /14	2.22	1.09
GR	Putnam Investors Fund A	PINVX	B+	(800) 225-1581	B- / 7.3	0.87	4.98	11.94 /82	16.52 /87	14.36 /81	0.84	1.08
GR	Putnam Investors Fund B	PNVBX	B+	(800) 225-1581	B / 7.7	0.66	4.59	11.13 /79	15.64 /80	13.50 /73	0.26	1.83
GR	Putnam Investors Fund C	PCINX	B+	(800) 225-1581	B / 7.7	0.67	4.63	11.11 /79	15.62 /80	13.52 /73	0.37	1.83
GR	Putnam Investors Fund M	PNVMX	B+	(800) 225-1581	B- / 7.3	0.77	4.72	11.41 /80	15.92 /83	13.80 /76	0.48	1.58
GR	Putnam Investors Fund R	PIVRX	A	(800) 225-1581	B / 8.2	0.79	4.83	11.62 /81	16.21 /85	14.08 /78	0.73	1.33
GR	Putnam Investors Fund Y	PNVYX	A+	(800) 225-1581	B+ / 8.6	0.90	5.10	12.23 /84	16.79 /89	14.64 /84	1.16	0.83
GI	Putnam Low Volatility Equity Y	PLVKX	U	(800) 225-1581	U /	0.88	5.01	8.82 /68	--	--	0.61	1.26
GR	Putnam Multi-Cap Core Fund A	PMYAX	A	(800) 225-1581	B+ / 8.7	1.65	5.26	12.01 /83	18.71 /96	--	0.33	1.52
GR	Putnam Multi-Cap Core Fund B	PMYBX	A+	(800) 225-1581	A- / 9.0	1.45	4.86	11.17 /79	17.83 /94	--	0.00	2.27
GR	Putnam Multi-Cap Core Fund C	PMYCX	A+	(800) 225-1581	A- / 9.0	1.45	4.83	11.21 /79	17.83 /94	--	0.08	2.27
GR	Putnam Multi-Cap Core Fund M	PMYMX	A	(800) 225-1581	B+ / 8.7	1.49	4.98	11.44 /80	18.14 /95	--	0.25	2.02
GR	Putnam Multi-Cap Core Fund R	PMYZX	A+	(800) 225-1581	A / 9.3	1.59	5.13	11.75 /81	18.43 /95	--	0.28	1.77
GR	Putnam Multi-Cap Core Fund Y	PMYYX	A+	(800) 225-1581	A / 9.4	1.70	5.40	12.34 /84	19.01 /97	--	0.44	1.27
GR	Putnam Multi-Cap Growth Fund A	PNOPX	B-	(800) 225-1581	B / 7.8	3.30	8.52	14.67 /91	16.44 /87	14.98 /87	0.25	1.04
GR	Putnam Multi-Cap Growth Fund B	PNOBX	B-	(800) 225-1581	B+ / 8.3	3.10	8.11	13.82 /89	15.57 /80	14.12 /79	0.00	1.79
GR	Putnam Multi-Cap Growth Fund C	PNOCX	B-	(800) 225-1581	B+ / 8.3	3.10	8.10	13.81 /89	15.57 /80	14.12 /79	0.00	1.79
GR	Putnam Multi-Cap Growth Fund M	PNOMX	C+	(800) 225-1581	B / 7.8	3.16	8.24	14.10 /90	15.86 /82	14.41 /82	0.00	1.54
GR	Putnam Multi-Cap Growth Fund R	PNORX	B	(800) 225-1581	B+ / 8.7	3.23	8.39	14.38 /90	16.15 /84	14.69 /84	0.01	1.29
GR	Putnam Multi-Cap Growth Fund Y	PNOYX	B+	(800) 225-1581	A- / 9.0	3.35	8.64	14.94 /92	16.74 /88	15.27 /89	0.48	0.79
MC	Putnam Multi-Cap Value Fund A	PMVAX	A-	(800) 225-1581	B+ / 8.9	4.42	11.56	12.24 /84	18.33 /95	15.29 /89	0.56	1.11
MC	Putnam Multi-Cap Value Fund B	PMVBX	A	(800) 225-1581	A- / 9.2	4.22	11.17	11.35 /80	17.43 /92	14.42 /82	0.00	1.86
MC	Putnam Multi-Cap Value Fund C	PMPCX	A	(800) 225-1581	A- / 9.2	4.24	11.15	11.39 /80	17.43 /92	14.43 /82	0.00	1.86
MC	Putnam Multi-Cap Value Fund M	PMCVX	A-	(800) 225-1581	B+ / 8.9	4.27	11.26	11.61 /81	17.72 /93	14.71 /84	0.14	1.61
MC	Putnam Multi-Cap Value Fund R	PMVRX	A	(800) 225-1581	A / 9.4	4.35	11.42	11.94 /82	18.02 /94	15.00 /87	0.42	1.36
MC	Putnam Multi-Cap Value Fund Y	PMVYX	A+	(800) 225-1581	A / 9.5	4.47	11.70	12.50 /85	18.63 /96	15.56 /90	0.81	0.86
GR	Putnam Research Fund A	PNRAX	A-	(800) 225-1581	B / 8.0	1.90	6.49	13.77 /89	17.07 /90	14.68 /84	0.91	1.14

● Denotes fund is closed to new investors
* Denotes fund is included in Section II

RISK			NET ASSETS		ASSET					BULL / BEAR		FUND MANAGER		MINIMUMS		LOADS	
	3 Year		NAV						Portfolio	Last Bull	Last Bear	Manager	Manager	Initial	Additional	Front	Back
Risk	Standard		As of	Total	Cash	Stocks	Bonds	Other	Turnover	Market	Market	Quality	Tenure	Purch.	Purch.	End	End
Rating/Pts	Deviation	Beta	3/31/15	$(Mil)	%	%	%	%	Ratio	Return	Return	Pct	(Years)	$	$	Load	Load
C /4.7	11.0	1.07	23.88	5	3	96	0	1	83	109.2	-20.4	56	7	500	0	0.0	0.0
C /4.8	11.0	1.07	25.49	61	3	96	0	1	83	112.7	-20.2	63	7	0	0	0.0	0.0
C /5.1	13.6	0.98	35.90	464	0	99	0	1	84	40.8	-27.8	20	16	500	0	5.8	0.0
C /5.2	13.6	0.98	35.86	12	0	99	0	1	84	37.3	-28.0	14	16	500	0	0.0	0.0
C /5.2	13.6	0.98	35.75	33	0	99	0	1	84	37.3	-28.0	15	16	500	0	0.0	0.0
C /5.2	13.6	0.98	35.77	7	0	99	0	1	84	38.4	-27.9	16	16	500	0	3.5	0.0
C /5.2	13.6	0.97	35.43	33	0	99	0	1	84	39.6	-27.9	18	16	500	0	0.0	1.0
C /5.1	13.6	0.98	35.89	81	0	99	0	1	84	42.1	-27.7	23	16	500	0	0.0	0.0
C+ /5.8	13.2	0.98	23.97	823	0	99	0	1	67	64.8	-26.2	77	4	500	0	5.8	0.0
C+ /5.8	13.2	0.97	22.85	16	0	99	0	1	67	60.7	-26.4	70	4	500	0	0.0	0.0
C+ /5.8	13.1	0.97	23.18	58	0	99	0	1	67	60.6	-26.4	70	4	500	0	0.0	0.0
C+ /5.7	13.2	0.98	23.34	16	0	99	0	1	67	62.0	-26.3	72	4	500	0	3.5	0.0
C+ /5.7	13.2	0.97	23.54	4	0	99	0	1	67	63.3	-26.2	74	4	0	0	0.0	0.0
C+ /5.8	13.1	0.97	24.25	70	0	99	0	1	67	66.1	-26.1	79	4	0	0	0.0	0.0
C+ /5.6	12.7	0.94	19.03	295	2	97	0	1	110	54.6	-27.8	55	7	500	0	5.8	0.0
C+ /5.6	12.7	0.94	17.30	6	2	97	0	1	110	50.8	-28.1	43	7	500	0	0.0	0.0
C+ /5.6	12.7	0.94	17.71	9	2	97	0	1	110	50.6	-28.1	43	7	500	0	0.0	0.0
C+ /5.6	12.7	0.94	17.90	6	2	97	0	1	110	52.0	-28.0	47	7	500	0	3.5	0.0
C+ /5.6	12.7	0.94	18.70	2	2	97	0	1	110	53.3	-27.9	51	7	500	0	0.0	0.0
C+ /5.6	12.7	0.94	19.15	22	2	97	0	1	110	55.9	-27.8	59	7	500	0	0.0	0.0
C /5.5	13.5	1.00	10.86	167	3	96	0	1	50	49.2	-24.8	40	10	500	0	5.8	0.0
C+ /5.6	13.5	1.01	10.81	5	3	96	0	1	50	45.5	-25.1	30	10	500	0	0.0	0.0
C+ /5.6	13.5	1.01	10.79	9	3	96	0	1	50	45.5	-25.1	30	10	500	0	0.0	0.0
C+ /5.6	13.6	1.01	10.89	3	3	96	0	1	50	46.8	-25.0	33	10	500	0	3.5	0.0
C+ /5.6	13.5	1.01	10.70	3	3	96	0	1	50	48.0	-24.9	37	10	500	0	0.0	0.0
C /5.5	13.5	1.01	10.88	5	3	96	0	1	50	50.4	-24.7	44	10	500	0	0.0	0.0
B- /7.1	10.3	1.07	22.10	1,629	0	98	0	2	63	106.6	-18.9	58	7	500	0	5.8	0.0
B- /7.1	10.3	1.07	19.83	48	0	98	0	2	63	101.2	-19.0	46	7	500	0	0.0	0.0
B- /7.1	10.3	1.07	20.89	51	0	98	0	2	63	101.3	-19.1	45	7	500	0	0.0	0.0
B- /7.1	10.3	1.06	20.82	24	0	98	0	2	63	103.1	-19.0	50	7	500	0	3.5	0.0
B- /7.1	10.3	1.07	21.73	5	0	98	0	2	63	104.9	-19.0	54	7	500	0	0.0	0.0
B- /7.2	10.3	1.07	22.42	97	0	98	0	2	63	108.3	-18.7	61	7	0	0	0.0	0.0
U /	N/A	N/A	11.49	45	2	97	0	1	91	N/A	N/A	N/A	2	500	0	0.0	0.0
C+ /6.7	10.5	1.07	17.88	163	4	95	0	1	100	120.1	-20.1	79	5	500	0	5.8	0.0
C+ /6.7	10.5	1.07	17.53	7	4	95	0	1	100	114.5	-20.3	72	5	500	0	0.0	0.0
C+ /6.7	10.5	1.07	17.49	64	4	95	0	1	100	114.5	-20.3	72	5	500	0	0.0	0.0
C+ /6.7	10.5	1.07	17.66	4	4	95	0	1	100	116.4	-20.3	74	5	500	0	3.5	0.0
C+ /6.7	10.4	1.06	17.84	2	4	95	0	1	100	118.3	-20.2	77	5	500	0	0.0	0.0
C+ /6.7	10.5	1.07	17.94	149	4	95	0	1	100	122.0	-20.1	80	5	500	0	0.0	0.0
C /5.1	11.1	1.06	78.84	3,780	2	97	0	1	88	109.8	-22.2	57	5	500	0	5.8	0.0
C /4.7	11.1	1.06	65.15	91	2	97	0	1	88	104.5	-22.4	46	5	500	0	0.0	0.0
C /4.9	11.1	1.06	69.74	68	2	97	0	1	88	104.5	-22.4	46	5	500	0	0.0	0.0
C /4.9	11.1	1.06	70.44	60	2	97	0	1	88	106.3	-22.3	49	5	500	0	3.5	0.0
C /5.1	11.1	1.06	76.95	9	2	97	0	1	88	108.0	-22.2	53	5	500	0	0.0	0.0
C /5.2	11.1	1.06	83.21	153	2	97	0	1	88	111.6	-22.1	61	5	0	0	0.0	0.0
C+ /6.2	11.4	0.97	20.10	361	3	96	0	1	77	114.4	-22.2	82	11	500	0	5.8	0.0
C+ /6.1	11.4	0.97	18.75	9	3	96	0	1	77	108.8	-22.5	76	11	500	0	0.0	0.0
C+ /6.1	11.4	0.97	18.68	24	3	96	0	1	77	108.9	-22.5	76	11	500	0	0.0	0.0
C+ /6.2	11.4	0.97	19.28	5	3	96	0	1	77	110.8	-22.5	78	11	500	0	3.5	0.0
C+ /6.2	11.4	0.97	19.67	17	3	96	0	1	77	112.6	-22.4	80	11	500	0	0.0	0.0
C+ /6.2	11.4	0.97	20.12	31	3	96	0	1	77	116.2	-22.2	83	11	500	0	0.0	0.0
B- /7.1	9.7	1.01	26.23	246	5	94	0	1	96	107.0	-19.0	75	5	500	0	5.8	0.0

Fund Type	Fund Name	Ticker Symbol	Overall Investment Rating	Phone	Performance Rating/Pts	3 Mo	6 Mo	1Yr / Pct	3Yr / Pct	5Yr / Pct	Dividend Yield	Expense Ratio
	99 Pct = Best						**PERFORMANCE** Total Return % through 3/31/15			Annualized	Incl. in Returns	
GR	Putnam Research Fund B	PRFBX	A	(800) 225-1581	B+ / 8.4	1.73	6.13	12.97 /86	16.21 /85	13.82 /76	0.27	1.89
GR	Putnam Research Fund C	PRACX	A	(800) 225-1581	B+ / 8.4	1.73	6.12	12.95 /86	16.21 /85	13.83 /76	0.35	1.89
GR	Putnam Research Fund M	PRFMX	A-	(800) 225-1581	B / 7.9	1.77	6.25	13.21 /87	16.49 /87	14.11 /79	0.54	1.64
GR	Putnam Research Fund R	PRSRX	A+	(800) 225-1581	B+ / 8.8	1.84	6.35	13.51 /88	16.78 /89	14.38 /81	1.02	1.39
GR	Putnam Research Fund Y	PURYX	A+	(800) 225-1581	A- / 9.1	1.97	6.65	14.07 /90	17.38 /92	14.97 /87	1.18	0.89
AA	Putnam Ret Income Fd Lifestyle 1 A	PRMAX	C-	(800) 225-1581	D- / 1.1	1.37	2.66	4.28 /34	4.68 /12	4.26 / 9	2.21	1.29
AA	Putnam Ret Income Fd Lifestyle 1 B	PRMLX	C-	(800) 225-1581	D- / 1.2	1.16	2.27	3.46 /29	3.89 /10	3.49 / 7	1.90	2.04
AA	Putnam Ret Income Fd Lifestyle 1 C	PRMCX	C-	(800) 225-1581	D- / 1.2	1.15	2.21	3.45 /29	3.88 /10	3.48 / 7	1.90	2.04
AA	Putnam Ret Income Fd Lifestyle 1 M	PRMMX	C-	(800) 225-1581	D- / 1.1	1.30	2.46	4.00 /32	4.41 /11	3.93 / 8	1.97	1.54
AA	Putnam Ret Income Fd Lifestyle 1 R	PRMKX	C-	(800) 225-1581	D- / 1.3	1.31	2.53	4.01 /32	4.40 /11	4.00 / 8	2.05	1.54
AA	Putnam Ret Income Fd Lifestyle 1 Y	PRMYX	C-	(800) 225-1581	D- / 1.5	1.37	2.72	4.47 /35	4.92 /13	4.51 /10	2.55	1.04
AA	Putnam Retirement Ready 2015 A	PRRHX	C-	(800) 225-1581	D- / 1.2	1.43	2.88	4.67 /36	5.45 /15	5.17 /13	1.23	1.25
AA	Putnam Retirement Ready 2015 B		C-	(800) 225-1581	D- / 1.4	1.30	2.54	3.90 /31	4.66 /12	4.39 /10	0.58	2.00
AA	Putnam Retirement Ready 2015 C		C-	(800) 225-1581	D- / 1.4	1.25	2.48	3.84 /31	4.66 /12	4.38 /10	0.58	2.00
AA	Putnam Retirement Ready 2015 M		C-	(800) 225-1581	D- / 1.2	1.33	2.64	4.15 /33	4.93 /13	4.65 /11	0.74	1.75
AA	Putnam Retirement Ready 2015 R		C-	(800) 225-1581	D / 1.6	1.42	2.75	4.41 /34	5.20 /14	4.92 /12	1.06	1.50
AA	Putnam Retirement Ready 2015 Y	PRRLX	C	(800) 225-1581	D / 1.8	1.48	2.96	4.92 /38	5.70 /16	5.42 /14	1.49	1.00
AA	Putnam Retirement Ready 2020 A	PRRMX	C	(800) 225-1581	D / 1.9	1.87	3.98	6.21 /48	7.21 /22	6.68 /21	1.07	1.21
AA	Putnam Retirement Ready 2020 B		C	(800) 225-1581	D / 2.2	1.71	3.60	5.44 /42	6.41 /19	5.89 /16	0.28	1.96
AA	Putnam Retirement Ready 2020 C		C	(800) 225-1581	D / 2.2	1.71	3.58	5.40 /42	6.40 /18	5.88 /16	0.54	1.96
AA	Putnam Retirement Ready 2020 M		C	(800) 225-1581	D / 1.9	1.79	3.73	5.70 /44	6.68 /20	6.16 /18	0.60	1.71
AA	Putnam Retirement Ready 2020 R		C	(800) 225-1581	D+ / 2.5	1.83	3.83	5.90 /46	6.93 /21	6.42 /20	0.88	1.46
AA	Putnam Retirement Ready 2020 Y	PRRNX	C+	(800) 225-1581	D+ / 2.9	1.96	4.11	6.47 /50	7.48 /24	6.95 /23	1.15	0.96
AA	Putnam Retirement Ready 2025 A	PRROX	C	(800) 225-1581	D+ / 2.9	2.27	4.91	7.49 /59	8.98 /33	8.04 /30	1.17	1.21
AA	Putnam Retirement Ready 2025 B		C+	(800) 225-1581	C- / 3.3	2.07	4.46	6.65 /52	8.15 /28	7.22 /24	0.62	1.96
AA	Putnam Retirement Ready 2025 C		C+	(800) 225-1581	C- / 3.3	2.12	4.50	6.69 /53	8.16 /28	7.23 /25	0.66	1.96
AA	Putnam Retirement Ready 2025 M		C	(800) 225-1581	D+ / 2.9	2.14	4.58	6.90 /54	8.42 /29	7.48 /26	0.81	1.71
AA	Putnam Retirement Ready 2025 R		C+	(800) 225-1581	C- / 3.6	2.18	4.75	7.17 /56	8.71 /31	7.76 /28	1.10	1.46
AA	Putnam Retirement Ready 2025 Y	PRRPX	C+	(800) 225-1581	C- / 4.0	2.36	5.01	7.79 /61	9.25 /35	8.30 /32	1.45	0.96
AA	Putnam Retirement Ready 2030 A	PRRQX	C+	(800) 225-1581	C- / 3.8	2.61	5.59	8.38 /65	10.49 /42	9.12 /38	2.16	1.25
AA	Putnam Retirement Ready 2030 B		C+	(800) 225-1581	C- / 4.2	2.43	5.15	7.51 /59	9.67 /37	8.31 /32	1.58	2.00
AA	Putnam Retirement Ready 2030 C		C+	(800) 225-1581	C- / 4.2	2.48	5.17	7.59 /60	9.69 /37	8.31 /32	1.75	2.00
AA	Putnam Retirement Ready 2030 M		C+	(800) 225-1581	C- / 3.8	2.48	5.30	7.79 /61	9.95 /39	8.58 /34	1.73	1.75
AA	Putnam Retirement Ready 2030 R		B-	(800) 225-1581	C / 4.5	2.55	5.43	8.10 /64	10.23 /41	8.85 /36	2.13	1.50
AA	Putnam Retirement Ready 2030 Y	PRRTX	B-	(800) 225-1581	C / 4.9	2.72	5.72	8.65 /67	10.78 /44	9.40 /40	2.17	1.00
AA	Putnam Retirement Ready 2035 A	PRRWX	C+	(800) 225-1581	C / 4.6	2.94	6.13	9.06 /70	11.81 /51	10.08 /45	3.39	1.33
AA	Putnam Retirement Ready 2035 B		B-	(800) 225-1581	C / 5.0	2.76	5.74	8.27 /65	10.96 /45	9.27 /39	3.19	2.08
AA	Putnam Retirement Ready 2035 C		B-	(800) 225-1581	C / 5.0	2.77	5.76	8.29 /65	10.98 /45	9.26 /39	3.40	2.08
AA	Putnam Retirement Ready 2035 M		C+	(800) 225-1581	C / 4.6	2.84	5.85	8.55 /67	11.25 /47	9.54 /41	3.08	1.83
AA	Putnam Retirement Ready 2035 R		B	(800) 225-1581	C / 5.4	2.91	6.01	8.83 /68	11.54 /49	9.82 /43	3.48	1.58
AA	Putnam Retirement Ready 2035 Y	PRRYX	B	(800) 225-1581	C+ / 5.7	3.04	6.28	9.37 /71	12.09 /53	10.36 /47	3.27	1.08
AA	Putnam Retirement Ready 2040 A	PRRZX	B-	(800) 225-1581	C / 5.2	3.18	6.59	9.71 /73	12.81 /58	10.85 /51	4.40	1.48
AA	Putnam Retirement Ready 2040 B		B-	(800) 225-1581	C+ / 5.6	3.00	6.20	8.92 /69	11.97 /52	10.01 /45	4.07	2.23
AA	Putnam Retirement Ready 2040 C		B-	(800) 225-1581	C+ / 5.6	2.99	6.17	8.92 /69	11.98 /52	10.02 /45	4.39	2.23
AA	Putnam Retirement Ready 2040 M		B-	(800) 225-1581	C / 5.2	3.06	6.30	9.20 /70	12.25 /54	10.29 /47	4.35	1.98
AA	Putnam Retirement Ready 2040 R		B-	(800) 225-1581	C+ / 6.0	3.15	6.43	9.48 /72	12.53 /56	10.56 /49	4.24	1.73
AA	Putnam Retirement Ready 2040 Y	PRZZX	B-	(800) 225-1581	C+ / 6.4	3.28	6.74	10.04 /74	13.10 /60	11.12 /54	4.13	1.23
AA	Putnam Retirement Ready 2045 A	PRVLX	B-	(800) 225-1581	C+ / 5.6	3.36	6.89	10.13 /75	13.32 /62	11.22 /55	4.68	1.64
AA	Putnam Retirement Ready 2045 B		B-	(800) 225-1581	C+ / 5.9	3.13	6.48	9.29 /71	12.45 /56	10.37 /48	4.65	2.39
AA	Putnam Retirement Ready 2045 C		B-	(800) 225-1581	C+ / 5.9	3.13	6.50	9.30 /71	12.46 /56	10.38 /48	4.86	2.39
AA	Putnam Retirement Ready 2045 M		B-	(800) 225-1581	C+ / 5.6	3.23	6.66	9.61 /73	12.76 /58	10.66 /50	4.59	2.14
AA	Putnam Retirement Ready 2045 R		B-	(800) 225-1581	C+ / 6.3	3.28	6.79	9.90 /74	13.04 /60	10.93 /52	4.60	1.89

● Denotes fund is closed to new investors
* Denotes fund is included in Section II

www.thestreetratings.com

RISK	3 Year		NET ASSETS		ASSET				Portfolio	BULL / BEAR		FUND MANAGER		MINIMUMS		LOADS	
Risk Rating/Pts	Standard Deviation	Beta	NAV As of 3/31/15	Total $(Mil)	Cash %	Stocks %	Bonds %	Other %	Turnover Ratio	Last Bull Market Return	Last Bear Market Return	Manager Quality Pct	Manager Tenure (Years)	Initial Purch. $	Additional Purch. $	Front End Load	Back End Load
B- / 7.0	9.7	1.01	24.65	10	5	94	0	1	96	101.7	-19.3	67	5	500	0	0.0	0.0
B- / 7.0	9.7	1.01	24.66	16	5	94	0	1	96	101.8	-19.3	67	5	500	0	0.0	0.0
B- / 7.0	9.7	1.00	25.25	5	5	94	0	1	96	103.6	-19.2	70	5	500	0	3.5	0.0
B- / 7.1	9.7	1.00	26.02	1	5	94	0	1	96	105.3	-19.1	73	5	500	0	0.0	0.0
B- / 7.1	9.7	1.01	26.40	19	5	94	0	1	96	108.9	-19.0	77	5	500	0	0.0	0.0
B+ / 9.0	2.2	0.34	17.70	19	22	21	56	1	98	21.8	-5.8	78	N/A	500	0	4.0	0.0
B+ / 9.0	2.2	0.33	17.48	N/A	22	21	56	1	98	18.7	-6.1	71	N/A	500	0	0.0	0.0
B+ / 9.0	2.2	0.34	17.52	1	22	21	56	1	98	18.7	-6.1	71	N/A	500	0	0.0	0.0
B+ / 9.0	2.2	0.34	17.74	N/A	22	21	56	1	98	20.8	-5.9	75	N/A	500	0	3.3	0.0
B+ / 9.0	2.2	0.34	17.69	1	22	21	56	1	98	20.7	-5.8	75	N/A	500	0	0.0	0.0
B+ / 9.0	2.2	0.34	17.75	1	22	21	56	1	98	22.8	-5.7	79	N/A	500	0	0.0	0.0
B+ / 9.1	2.7	0.44	18.43	29	22	24	53	1	87	27.2	-7.9	75	N/A	500	0	5.8	0.0
B+ / 9.1	2.7	0.44	17.86	1	22	24	53	1	87	24.0	-8.2	67	N/A	500	0	0.0	0.0
B+ / 9.1	2.7	0.44	17.87	1	22	24	53	1	87	23.9	-8.2	67	N/A	500	0	0.0	0.0
B+ / 9.1	2.8	0.44	18.22	N/A	22	24	53	1	87	25.1	-8.0	70	N/A	500	0	3.5	0.0
B+ / 9.1	2.8	0.44	17.80	3	22	24	53	1	87	26.1	-7.9	72	N/A	500	0	0.0	0.0
B+ / 9.1	2.8	0.45	18.47	6	22	24	53	1	87	28.4	-7.8	76	N/A	500	0	0.0	0.0
B+ / 9.1	3.8	0.64	19.11	52	21	33	45	1	75	37.4	-10.1	71	N/A	500	0	5.8	0.0
B+ / 9.1	3.8	0.64	18.43	1	21	33	45	1	75	33.8	-10.4	61	N/A	500	0	0.0	0.0
B+ / 9.1	3.8	0.64	18.44	2	21	33	45	1	75	33.8	-10.4	61	N/A	500	0	0.0	0.0
B+ / 9.1	3.8	0.65	18.79	N/A	21	33	45	1	75	35.0	-10.3	64	N/A	500	0	3.5	0.0
B+ / 9.1	3.8	0.64	18.39	6	21	33	45	1	75	36.2	-10.2	68	N/A	500	0	0.0	0.0
B+ / 9.1	3.8	0.64	21.32	5	21	33	45	1	75	38.5	-10.0	73	N/A	500	0	0.0	0.0
B / 8.8	5.0	0.87	21.61	35	17	41	40	2	74	48.6	-13.1	62	N/A	500	0	5.8	0.0
B / 8.8	5.0	0.86	20.22	1	17	41	40	2	74	44.9	-13.3	51	N/A	500	0	0.0	0.0
B / 8.8	5.0	0.86	20.21	1	17	41	40	2	74	44.9	-13.3	51	N/A	500	0	0.0	0.0
B / 8.8	5.0	0.87	20.52	N/A	17	41	40	2	74	46.1	-13.2	54	N/A	500	0	3.5	0.0
B / 8.8	5.1	0.87	20.19	7	17	41	40	2	74	47.4	-13.2	58	N/A	500	0	0.0	0.0
B / 8.8	5.0	0.86	21.70	12	17	41	40	2	74	49.8	-12.9	67	N/A	500	0	0.0	0.0
B / 8.4	6.2	1.08	21.23	47	19	48	31	2	77	59.5	-16.0	49	11	500	0	5.8	0.0
B / 8.4	6.2	1.08	20.23	1	19	48	31	2	77	55.4	-16.2	39	11	500	0	0.0	0.0
B / 8.4	6.2	1.08	20.21	1	19	48	31	2	77	55.4	-16.2	39	11	500	0	0.0	0.0
B / 8.4	6.2	1.08	20.64	N/A	19	48	31	2	77	56.7	-16.1	42	11	500	0	3.5	0.0
B / 8.4	6.2	1.08	20.11	8	19	48	31	2	77	58.1	-16.0	47	11	500	0	0.0	0.0
B / 8.4	6.2	1.08	24.16	13	19	48	31	2	77	60.7	-15.8	54	11	500	0	0.0	0.0
B / 8.1	7.3	1.26	21.37	27	20	55	24	1	79	68.9	-17.8	40	11	500	0	5.8	0.0
B / 8.0	7.3	1.26	19.71	1	20	55	24	1	79	64.5	-18.0	30	11	500	0	0.0	0.0
B / 8.0	7.2	1.25	19.68	1	20	55	24	1	79	64.6	-18.1	31	11	500	0	0.0	0.0
B / 8.1	7.3	1.26	20.62	1	20	55	24	1	79	66.0	-18.0	33	11	500	0	3.5	0.0
B / 8.1	7.3	1.25	20.53	5	20	55	24	1	79	67.4	-17.9	37	11	500	0	0.0	0.0
B / 8.1	7.3	1.26	24.78	13	20	55	24	1	79	70.3	-17.7	43	11	500	0	0.0	0.0
B- / 7.7	8.0	1.39	21.08	34	15	65	19	1	90	76.1	-18.8	33	11	500	0	5.8	0.0
B- / 7.7	8.0	1.38	19.57	1	15	65	19	1	90	71.7	-19.1	26	11	500	0	0.0	0.0
B- / 7.7	8.0	1.39	19.32	1	15	65	19	1	90	71.7	-19.1	25	11	500	0	0.0	0.0
B- / 7.7	8.0	1.38	19.88	N/A	15	65	19	1	90	73.1	-19.0	28	11	500	0	3.5	0.0
B- / 7.7	8.0	1.39	21.63	5	15	65	19	1	90	74.6	-18.9	31	11	500	0	0.0	0.0
B- / 7.7	8.0	1.38	24.59	9	15	65	19	1	90	77.6	-18.8	38	11	500	0	0.0	0.0
B- / 7.5	8.4	1.44	19.40	15	12	73	14	1	92	79.9	-19.4	32	N/A	500	0	5.8	0.0
B- / 7.5	8.4	1.45	17.77	N/A	12	73	14	1	92	75.4	-19.6	23	11	500	0	0.0	0.0
B- / 7.5	8.4	1.45	17.81	1	12	73	14	1	92	75.5	-19.7	23	11	500	0	0.0	0.0
B- / 7.5	8.4	1.45	18.86	N/A	12	73	14	1	92	76.9	-19.6	26	11	500	0	3.5	0.0
B- / 7.5	8.4	1.45	19.84	3	12	73	14	1	92	78.5	-19.5	29	11	500	0	0.0	0.0

Data as of March 31, 2015

					PERFORMANCE							
	99 Pct = Best *0 Pct = Worst*					Total Return % through 3/31/15					Incl. in Returns	
			Overall		Perfor-				Annualized		Dividend	Expense
Fund Type	Fund Name	Ticker Symbol	Investment Rating	Phone	mance Rating/Pts	3 Mo	6 Mo	1Yr / Pct	3Yr / Pct	5Yr / Pct	Yield	Ratio
AA	Putnam Retirement Ready 2045 Y	PRVYX	B-	(800) 225-1581	C+ / 6.7	3.41	7.03	10.42 /76	13.61 /64	11.49 /57	4.34	1.39
AA	Putnam Retirement Ready 2050 A		B-	(800) 225-1581	C+ / 5.8	3.42	7.12	10.46 /76	13.69 /65	11.48 /57	4.65	1.69
AA	Putnam Retirement Ready 2050 B		B-	(800) 225-1581	C+ / 6.2	3.22	6.70	9.61 /73	12.84 /58	10.65 /50	4.22	2.44
AA	Putnam Retirement Ready 2050 C		B-	(800) 225-1581	C+ / 6.2	3.25	6.74	9.60 /73	12.84 /58	10.65 /50	4.36	2.44
AA	Putnam Retirement Ready 2050 M		B-	(800) 225-1581	C+ / 5.8	3.33	6.86	9.91 /74	13.12 /61	10.94 /52	4.32	2.19
AA	Putnam Retirement Ready 2050 R		B-	(800) 225-1581	C+ / 6.6	3.36	6.94	10.13 /75	13.41 /63	11.20 /54	4.74	1.94
AA	Putnam Retirement Ready 2050 Y		B-	(800) 225-1581	C+ / 6.9	3.47	7.20	10.66 /77	13.96 /67	11.75 /59	5.07	1.44
GL	Putnam Retirement Ready 2055 A		C	(800) 225-1581	C+ / 5.9	3.51	7.27	10.63 /77	13.85 /66	--	4.90	4.41
GL	Putnam Retirement Ready 2055 B		C+	(800) 225-1581	C+ / 6.3	3.35	6.89	9.80 /74	13.00 /60	--	4.58	5.16
GL	Putnam Retirement Ready 2055 C		C+	(800) 225-1581	C+ / 6.3	3.29	6.77	9.80 /74	13.00 /60	--	4.71	5.16
GL	Putnam Retirement Ready 2055 M		C	(800) 225-1581	C+ / 5.9	3.42	6.95	10.04 /74	13.28 /62	--	4.41	4.91
GL	Putnam Retirement Ready 2055 R		C+	(800) 225-1581	C+ / 6.7	3.44	7.05	10.32 /76	13.56 /64	--	5.06	4.66
GL	Putnam Retirement Ready 2055 Y		C+	(800) 225-1581	B- / 7.1	3.59	7.43	10.88 /78	14.12 /68	--	5.33	4.16
SC	Putnam Small Cap Growth A	PNSAX	B	(800) 225-1581	B / 8.2	6.28	15.60	8.39 /66	16.82 /89	15.69 /91	0.00	1.24
SC	Putnam Small Cap Growth B	PNSBX	B	(800) 225-1581	B+ / 8.6	6.09	15.14	7.60 /60	15.95 /83	14.89 /86	0.00	1.99
SC	Putnam Small Cap Growth C	PNSCX	B	(800) 225-1581	B+ / 8.5	6.11	15.16	7.59 /60	15.94 /83	14.83 /85	0.00	1.99
SC	Putnam Small Cap Growth M	PSGMX	B	(800) 225-1581	B / 8.1	6.13	15.27	7.84 /62	16.22 /85	15.10 /88	0.00	1.74
SC	Putnam Small Cap Growth R	PSGRX	B+	(800) 225-1581	B+ / 8.9	6.24	15.44	8.15 /64	16.52 /87	15.40 /90	0.00	1.49
SC	Putnam Small Cap Growth Y	PSYGX	B+	(800) 225-1581	A- / 9.2	6.34	15.71	8.68 /67	17.09 /90	15.97 /93	0.00	0.99
SC	Putnam Small Cap Value Fund A	PSLAX	C+	(800) 225-1581	C+ / 5.8	1.97	8.83	2.68 /25	14.78 /73	13.35 /72	0.68	1.41
SC	Putnam Small Cap Value Fund B	PSLBX	C+	(800) 225-1581	C+ / 6.2	1.77	8.43	1.93 /22	13.90 /66	12.50 /64	0.08	2.16
SC	Putnam Small Cap Value Fund C	PSLCX	C+	(800) 225-1581	C+ / 6.2	1.77	8.43	1.87 /21	13.91 /66	12.50 /64	0.30	2.16
SC	Putnam Small Cap Value Fund M	PSLMX	C+	(800) 225-1581	C+ / 5.8	1.79	8.53	2.16 /23	14.16 /68	12.79 /66	0.33	1.91
SC	Putnam Small Cap Value Fund R	PSCRX	C+	(800) 225-1581	C+ / 6.5	1.87	8.64	2.35 /23	14.47 /71	13.05 /69	0.58	1.66
SC	Putnam Small Cap Value Fund Y	PYSVX	C+	(800) 225-1581	C+ / 6.9	2.03	8.96	2.93 /26	15.02 /75	13.64 /74	0.96	1.16
GR	Putnam Voyager A	PVOYX	C	(800) 225-1581	C+ / 6.8	2.90	7.11	12.02 /83	15.35 /78	11.27 /55	0.37	0.98
GR	Putnam Voyager B	PVOBX	C	(800) 225-1581	B- / 7.3	2.71	6.71	11.18 /79	14.49 /71	10.43 /48	0.00	1.73
GR	Putnam Voyager C	PVFCX	C+	(800) 225-1581	B- / 7.2	2.68	6.69	11.18 /79	14.48 /71	10.43 /48	0.00	1.73
GR	Putnam Voyager M	PVOMX	C	(800) 225-1581	C+ / 6.8	2.77	6.83	11.47 /80	14.78 /73	10.71 /50	0.00	1.48
GR	Putnam Voyager R	PVYRX	C+	(800) 225-1581	B / 7.7	2.83	6.99	11.74 /81	15.07 /75	10.99 /53	0.12	1.23
GR	Putnam Voyager R6	PVOEX	U	(800) 225-1581	U /	2.97	7.30	12.47 /85	--	--	0.74	0.56
GR	Putnam Voyager Y	PVYYX	B-	(800) 225-1581	B / 8.2	2.95	7.23	12.29 /84	15.65 /80	11.55 /57	0.61	0.73
AA	QCI Balanced Institutional	QCIBX	U	(800) 773-3863	U /	0.59	2.85	5.25 /40	--	--	0.66	1.69
EM	QS Batterymarch Emerging Markets	LMRAX	E	(877) 534-4627	E- / 0.2	1.69	-4.30	-1.18 /12	-3.12 / 2	-2.04 / 2	0.84	1.72
EM	QS Batterymarch Emerging Markets	LMEMX	E	(877) 534-4627	E / 0.3	1.46	-4.69	-1.95 /10	-3.85 / 2	-2.79 / 1	0.23	2.48
EM	QS Batterymarch Emerging Markets	LGFMX	E	(877) 534-4627	E / 0.3	1.71	-4.27	-1.17 /12	-3.11 / 2	-2.04 / 2	1.07	1.63
EM	QS Batterymarch Emerging Markets I	LGEMX	E	(877) 534-4627	E / 0.3	1.71	-4.21	-1.16 /13	-3.07 / 2	-1.92 / 2	0.76	1.51
EM	QS Batterymarch Emerging Markets	LGMSX	E	(877) 534-4627	E / 0.3	2.04	-4.02	-0.76 /14	-2.75 / 2	-1.72 / 2	1.11	1.47
EM	QS Batterymarch Emerging Markets	LBERX	E	(877) 534-4627	E / 0.3	1.62	-4.40	-1.03 /13	-3.24 / 2	--	0.00	2.28
GL	● QS Batterymarch Global Equity 1	LMPEX	B+	(877) 534-4627	B / 7.8	4.93	7.95	12.63 /85	14.83 /74	11.13 /54	0.92	1.67
GL	QS Batterymarch Global Equity A	CFIPX	B-	(877) 534-4627	C+ / 6.7	4.99	7.98	12.65 /85	14.77 /73	11.03 /53	0.92	1.75
GL	QS Batterymarch Global Equity C	SILLX	B+	(877) 534-4627	B- / 7.1	4.78	7.58	11.76 /82	13.91 /66	10.18 /46	0.02	2.42
GL	QS Batterymarch Global Equity I	SMYIX	A-	(877) 534-4627	B / 8.1	5.08	8.20	13.06 /87	15.14 /76	11.37 /56	1.30	1.14
FO	QS Batterymarch International Eq A	LMEAX	D	(877) 534-4627	D+ / 2.9	6.27	3.59	3.17 /27	9.32 /35	5.76 /15	1.71	1.37
FO	QS Batterymarch International Eq C	LMGEX	D+	(877) 534-4627	C- / 3.3	6.06	3.22	2.37 /23	8.51 /30	5.00 /12	1.19	2.18
FO	QS Batterymarch International Eq FI	LGFEX	D+	(877) 534-4627	C- / 3.8	6.20	3.56	3.08 /27	9.31 /35	5.76 /15	1.77	1.44
FO	QS Batterymarch International Eq I	LGIEX	C-	(877) 534-4627	C- / 4.0	6.35	3.74	3.46 /29	9.70 /37	6.14 /18	2.13	1.04
FO	QS Batterymarch International Eq IS	LIESX	C-	(877) 534-4627	C- / 4.1	6.36	3.79	3.56 /29	9.79 /38	6.22 /18	2.29	0.91
FO	QS Batterymarch International Eq R	LMIRX	D+	(877) 534-4627	C- / 3.6	6.18	3.49	2.87 /26	9.06 /33	5.48 /14	1.26	1.87
GR	QS Batterymarch S&P 500 Index A	SBSPX	A-	(877) 534-4627	B / 7.8	0.87	5.65	12.08 /83	15.48 /79	13.86 /76	1.23	0.62
GR	QS Batterymarch S&P 500 Index D	SBSDX	A-	(877) 534-4627	B / 8.0	0.91	5.77	12.28 /84	15.71 /81	14.08 /78	1.42	0.53
GR	QS Batterymarch US Large Cap Eq	LMUSX	A+	(877) 534-4627	B+ / 8.8	1.78	7.32	13.48 /88	16.73 /88	14.50 /82	0.64	1.43

● Denotes fund is closed to new investors
* Denotes fund is included in Section II

RISK			NET ASSETS		ASSET					BULL / BEAR		FUND MANAGER		MINIMUMS		LOADS	
	3 Year		NAV						Portfolio	Last Bull	Last Bear	Manager	Manager	Initial	Additional	Front	Back
Risk	Standard		As of	Total	Cash	Stocks	Bonds	Other	Turnover	Market	Market	Quality	Tenure	Purch.	Purch.	End	End
Rating/Pts	Deviation	Beta	3/31/15	$(Mil)	%	%	%	%	Ratio	Return	Return	Pct	(Years)	$	$	Load	Load
B- / 7.6	8.4	1.44	23.07	6	12	73	14	1	92	81.5	-19.3	35	11	500	0	0.0	0.0
B- / 7.5	8.7	1.50	17.52	10	19	74	6	1	100	83.0	-19.8	30	10	500	0	5.8	0.0
B- / 7.5	8.7	1.50	17.32	N/A	19	74	6	1	100	78.2	-20.0	21	10	500	0	0.0	0.0
B- / 7.5	8.7	1.50	17.17	1	19	74	6	1	100	78.4	-20.1	21	10	500	0	0.0	0.0
B- / 7.5	8.7	1.50	17.70	N/A	19	74	6	1	100	79.8	-20.0	23	10	500	0	3.5	0.0
B- / 7.5	8.7	1.50	17.25	3	19	74	6	1	100	81.3	-20.0	27	10	500	0	0.0	0.0
B- / 7.5	8.7	1.50	17.58	5	19	74	6	1	100	84.6	-19.8	32	10	500	0	0.0	0.0
C+ / 5.8	8.8	1.34	11.49	1	10	81	8	1	202	83.2	-20.6	80	5	500	0	5.8	0.0
C+ / 5.9	8.8	1.34	11.42	N/A	10	81	8	1	202	78.7	-20.8	74	5	500	0	0.0	0.0
C+ / 5.8	8.7	1.33	11.29	1	10	81	8	1	202	78.6	-20.8	76	5	500	0	0.0	0.0
C+ / 5.9	8.8	1.33	11.49	N/A	10	81	8	1	202	80.4	-20.8	77	5	500	0	3.5	0.0
C+ / 5.8	8.7	1.33	11.44	N/A	10	81	8	1	202	81.8	-20.7	79	5	500	0	0.0	0.0
C+ / 5.8	8.8	1.34	11.54	2	10	81	8	1	202	85.0	-20.6	82	5	500	0	0.0	0.0
C / 5.4	14.0	1.00	31.65	123	0	100	0	0	57	107.4	-27.5	72	5	500	0	5.8	0.0
C / 5.3	14.0	1.00	28.59	2	0	100	0	0	57	102.8	-27.8	63	5	500	0	0.0	0.0
C / 5.3	14.0	1.00	28.49	8	0	100	0	0	57	102.2	-27.8	62	5	500	0	0.0	0.0
C / 5.3	14.0	1.00	29.59	1	0	100	0	0	57	104.0	-27.7	66	5	500	0	3.5	0.0
C / 5.4	14.0	1.00	30.80	11	0	100	0	0	57	105.7	-27.6	69	5	500	0	0.0	0.0
C / 5.4	13.9	1.00	32.56	14	0	100	0	0	57	109.1	-27.5	74	5	0	0	0.0	0.0
C+ / 6.6	11.9	0.87	15.52	173	9	90	0	1	68	94.0	-24.8	74	7	500	0	5.8	0.0
C+ / 6.6	11.9	0.87	13.25	3	9	90	0	1	68	89.0	-25.0	67	7	500	0	0.0	0.0
C+ / 6.6	11.9	0.86	13.23	18	9	90	0	1	68	89.3	-25.2	67	7	500	0	0.0	0.0
C+ / 6.6	11.9	0.87	14.22	2	9	90	0	1	68	90.9	-25.1	69	7	500	0	3.5	0.0
C+ / 6.6	11.9	0.86	15.29	1	9	90	0	1	68	92.4	-24.9	72	7	500	0	0.0	0.0
C+ / 6.7	11.9	0.86	16.05	148	9	90	0	1	68	95.7	-24.8	77	7	0	0	0.0	0.0
C / 4.8	13.3	1.24	31.19	3,608	5	94	0	1	146	104.7	-28.6	15	7	500	0	5.8	0.0
C / 4.3	13.2	1.23	25.37	104	5	94	0	1	146	99.6	-28.8	11	7	500	0	0.0	0.0
C / 4.6	13.3	1.23	28.35	169	5	94	0	1	146	99.5	-28.8	11	7	500	0	0.0	0.0
C / 4.6	13.2	1.23	28.24	29	5	94	0	1	146	101.2	-28.7	12	7	500	0	3.5	0.0
C / 4.8	13.2	1.23	30.53	17	5	94	0	1	146	102.9	-28.6	14	7	500	0	0.0	0.0
U /	N/A	N/A	32.92	39	5	94	0	1	146	N/A	N/A	N/A	7	0	0	0.0	0.0
C / 4.8	13.2	1.23	32.81	408	5	94	0	1	146	106.5	-28.5	17	7	0	0	0.0	0.0
U /	N/A	N/A	10.72	40	0	0	0	100	29	N/A	N/A	N/A	1	25,000	250	0.0	0.0
C / 4.7	13.9	1.01	18.02	5	1	98	0	1	140	7.5	-28.4	17	N/A	1,000	50	5.8	0.0
C / 4.7	13.9	1.01	18.02	58	1	98	0	1	140	4.9	-28.7	12	N/A	1,000	50	0.0	0.0
C / 4.7	13.9	1.01	18.42	4	1	98	0	1	140	7.6	-28.4	17	N/A	0	0	0.0	0.0
C / 4.8	13.9	1.01	18.46	21	1	98	0	1	140	7.9	-28.4	18	N/A	1,000,000	0	0.0	0.0
C / 4.7	13.9	1.01	18.47	N/A	1	98	0	1	140	8.9	-28.3	20	N/A	0	0	0.0	0.0
C / 4.8	13.9	1.01	18.24	N/A	1	98	0	1	140	7.1	N/A	16	N/A	0	0	0.0	0.0
B- / 7.0	10.5	0.74	13.62	2	1	98	0	1	35	84.4	-20.4	96	4	0	0	0.0	0.0
B- / 7.1	10.4	0.74	13.68	126	1	98	0	1	35	83.9	-20.4	96	4	1,000	50	5.8	0.0
B- / 7.0	10.5	0.74	13.80	14	1	98	0	1	35	79.1	-20.6	95	4	1,000	50	0.0	0.0
B- / 7.1	10.5	0.74	13.65	1	1	98	0	1	35	85.5	-20.1	96	4	1,000,000	0	0.0	0.0
C+ / 6.1	13.0	0.98	14.74	6	2	97	0	1	55	49.9	-23.7	67	4	1,000	50	5.8	0.0
C+ / 6.0	13.0	0.97	14.71	56	2	97	0	1	55	46.2	-24.0	57	4	1,000	50	0.0	0.0
C+ / 6.1	13.0	0.97	15.25	9	2	97	0	1	55	49.9	-23.7	68	4	0	0	0.0	0.0
C+ / 6.1	13.0	0.98	15.24	19	2	97	0	1	55	51.7	-23.6	71	4	1,000,000	0	0.0	0.0
C+ / 6.1	12.9	0.97	15.21	291	2	97	0	1	55	52.2	-23.6	73	4	0	0	0.0	0.0
C+ / 6.1	13.0	0.97	15.28	N/A	2	97	0	1	55	48.8	-23.9	65	4	0	0	0.0	0.0
B- / 7.3	9.5	1.00	20.93	242	0	99	0	1	12	96.5	-16.5	59	N/A	0	0	0.0	0.0
B- / 7.3	9.6	1.00	21.06	9	0	99	0	1	12	97.8	-16.4	62	N/A	0	0	0.0	0.0
B- / 7.6	10.2	1.06	17.19	1	0	0	0	100	86	103.9	-17.6	63	7	0	0	0.0	0.0

Fund Type	Fund Name	Ticker Symbol	Overall Investment Rating	Phone	Performance Rating/Pts	3 Mo	6 Mo	1Yr / Pct	3Yr / Pct	5Yr / Pct	Dividend Yield	Expense Ratio
GR	QS Batterymarch US Large Cap Eq	LMISX	A+	(877) 534-4627	B+ / 8.9	1.84	7.43	13.81 /89	17.03 /90	14.81 /85	0.85	0.79
SC	QS Batterymarch US Small Cap Eq A	LMBAX	B+	(877) 534-4627	B+ / 8.9	4.98	17.79	12.96 /86	17.45 /92	16.08 /93	0.00	1.26
SC	QS Batterymarch US Small Cap Eq C	LMBCX	B+	(877) 534-4627	A- / 9.2	4.89	17.43	12.19 /83	16.59 /87	15.21 /88	0.00	2.06
SC	QS Batterymarch US Small Cap Eq	LGSCX	A-	(877) 534-4627	A / 9.4	5.07	17.76	13.05 /87	17.46 /92	15.96 /93	0.00	1.34
SC	QS Batterymarch US Small Cap Eq I	LMSIX	A-	(877) 534-4627	A+ / 9.6	5.15	18.08	13.53 /88	18.03 /94	16.47 /95	0.19	0.80
SC	QS Batterymarch US Small Cap Eq	LMBMX	A+	(877) 534-4627	A+ / 9.6	5.22	18.08	13.56 /88	18.01 /94	--	0.20	0.77
AA	QS LM Lifestyle Allocation 30% A	SBCPX	D+	(877) 534-4627	D- / 1.5	1.65	1.95	3.75 /30	6.40 /19	6.94 /23	2.45	1.20
AA	● QS LM Lifestyle Allocation 30% B	SBCBX	D+	(877) 534-4627	D / 1.7	1.46	1.62	3.02 /27	5.67 /15	6.24 /18	1.72	1.90
AA	QS LM Lifestyle Allocation 30% C	LWLAX	C-	(877) 534-4627	D / 1.6	1.43	1.59	2.95 /26	5.58 /15	6.13 /18	1.77	2.13
AA	● QS LM Lifestyle Allocation 30% C1	SBCLX	D+	(877) 534-4627	D / 1.8	1.58	1.75	3.26 /28	5.81 /16	6.44 /20	1.96	1.75
AA	QS LM Lifestyle Allocation 30% I	LMGIX	C-	(877) 534-4627	D / 2.1	1.66	2.03	3.94 /31	6.58 /19	--	2.83	1.11
BA	QS LM Lifestyle Allocation 50% A	SBBAX	C-	(877) 534-4627	D / 2.2	1.57	2.27	3.80 /31	8.37 /29	8.47 /33	1.87	1.24
BA	● QS LM Lifestyle Allocation 50% B	SCBBX	C-	(877) 534-4627	D+ / 2.4	1.35	1.84	2.81 /26	7.34 /23	7.52 /27	0.88	2.17
BA	QS LM Lifestyle Allocation 50% C	SCBCX	C-	(877) 534-4627	D+ / 2.5	1.34	1.90	3.00 /26	7.58 /25	7.78 /29	1.20	1.97
GR	QS LM Lifestyle Allocation 70% A	SCGRX	C	(877) 534-4627	C- / 3.2	1.58	2.70	4.02 /32	10.28 /41	9.68 /42	1.46	1.32
GR	● QS LM Lifestyle Allocation 70% B	SGRBX	C	(877) 534-4627	C- / 3.4	1.37	2.21	2.98 /26	9.25 /35	8.77 /35	0.25	2.24
GR	QS LM Lifestyle Allocation 70% C	SCGCX	C	(877) 534-4627	C- / 3.6	1.44	2.32	3.31 /28	9.53 /36	9.04 /37	0.95	2.01
GR	QS LM Lifestyle Allocation 70% I	LLAIX	C+	(877) 534-4627	C- / 4.2	1.77	2.92	4.38 /34	10.53 /42	9.96 /44	1.89	1.21
GR	QS LM Lifestyle Allocation 85% A	SCHAX	C	(877) 534-4627	C- / 3.8	1.81	3.12	3.94 /31	11.47 /49	10.36 /47	0.98	1.42
GR	● QS LM Lifestyle Allocation 85% B	SCHBX	C	(877) 534-4627	C- / 4.1	1.56	2.63	2.95 /26	10.44 /42	9.45 /40	0.05	2.30
GR	QS LM Lifestyle Allocation 85% C	SCHCX	C	(877) 534-4627	C / 4.3	1.61	2.79	3.22 /28	10.76 /44	9.81 /43	0.68	2.08
GR	QS LM Lifestyle Allocation 85% I	LANIX	C+	(877) 534-4627	C / 4.9	1.93	3.26	4.20 /33	11.80 /51	10.75 /51	1.34	1.18
GI	QS LM Strategic Real Return A	LRRAX	E+	(877) 534-4627	E- / 0.2	-2.52	-8.86	-12.05 / 2	-1.92 / 3	2.42 / 5	0.00	1.61
GI	QS LM Strategic Real Return C	LRRCX	E+	(877) 534-4627	E- / 0.2	-2.71	-9.25	-12.71 / 2	-2.66 / 2	1.66 / 4	0.00	2.45
GI	QS LM Strategic Real Return I	LRRIX	E+	(877) 534-4627	E / 0.3	-2.40	-8.67	-11.76 / 2	-1.66 / 3	2.68 / 5	0.28	1.47
GI	QS LM Strategic Real Return IS	LRRSX	D-	(877) 534-4627	E / 0.3	-2.44	-8.70	-11.70 / 2	-1.57 / 3	--	0.37	1.11
GR	Quaker Event Arbitrage A	QEAAX	D	(800) 220-8888	D- / 1.0	1.23	3.07	2.02 /22	5.18 /14	3.25 / 6	0.77	2.15
GR	Quaker Event Arbitrage C	QEACX	D	(800) 220-8888	D- / 1.2	1.03	2.71	1.33 /19	4.40 /11	--	0.19	2.90
GR	Quaker Event Arbitrage Inst	QEAIX	D	(800) 220-8888	D / 1.6	1.38	3.23	2.40 /24	5.47 /15	--	1.11	1.90
GL	Quaker Global Tactical Alloc A	QTRAX	C+	(800) 220-8888	C+ / 6.6	3.96	7.63	13.82 /89	14.42 /70	10.88 /52	0.00	2.19
GL	Quaker Global Tactical Alloc C	QTRCX	C+	(800) 220-8888	C+ / 6.9	3.78	7.21	12.97 /86	13.58 /64	10.07 /45	0.00	2.94
GL	Quaker Global Tactical Alloc I	QTRIX	B+	(800) 220-8888	B / 7.8	4.02	7.74	14.10 /90	14.71 /73	11.13 /54	0.00	1.94
MC	Quaker Mid-Cap Value A	QMCVX	C+	(800) 220-8888	C+ / 6.7	3.27	6.63	11.27 /79	15.18 /76	14.20 /80	0.00	2.03
MC	Quaker Mid-Cap Value C	QMCCX	B	(800) 220-8888	B- / 7.1	3.07	6.19	10.42 /76	14.32 /69	13.35 /72	0.00	2.78
MC	Quaker Mid-Cap Value Inst	QMVIX	B+	(800) 220-8888	B / 8.0	3.35	6.76	11.51 /80	15.48 /79	14.49 /82	0.00	1.78
SC	Quaker Small-Cap Value A	QUSVX	C+	(800) 220-8888	C+ / 6.3	3.94	9.87	6.90 /54	14.81 /73	14.85 /86	0.00	1.84
SC	Quaker Small-Cap Value C	QSVCX	C+	(800) 220-8888	C+ / 6.7	3.71	9.41	6.12 /48	13.95 /67	13.97 /77	0.00	2.59
SC	Quaker Small-Cap Value Inst	QSVIX	B	(800) 220-8888	B / 7.6	3.98	9.97	7.16 /56	15.10 /76	15.12 /88	0.00	1.59
GL	Quaker Strategic Growth A	QUAGX	C+	(800) 220-8888	C+ / 6.5	1.65	5.45	12.51 /85	14.86 /74	11.27 /55	0.00	2.24
GL	Quaker Strategic Growth C	QAGCX	C+	(800) 220-8888	C+ / 6.8	1.52	5.08	11.67 /81	14.00 /67	10.44 /48	0.00	2.99
GL	Quaker Strategic Growth Inst	QAGIX	B+	(800) 220-8888	B / 7.7	1.74	5.61	12.81 /86	15.14 /76	11.52 /57	0.00	1.99
GR	Quality Dividend A	QDVAX	U	(888) 739-1390	U /	-1.24	2.71	9.62 /73	--	--	2.27	2.97
GL	Quantified Market Leaders Fund Inv	QMLFX	U	(855) 747-9555	U /	4.86	8.62	6.77 /53	--	--	0.00	1.80
SC	Queens Road Small Cap Value Fund	QRSVX	C+	(800) 595-3088	C / 5.0	1.21	8.12	5.64 /44	11.41 /48	10.00 /45	0.00	1.27
GI	Queens Road Value Fund	QRVLX	B-	(800) 595-3088	C+ / 6.0	-0.90	4.12	7.69 /60	13.35 /62	11.31 /55	1.09	0.96
FO	Rainier International Discv Instl	RAIIX	A+	(800) 248-6314	A / 9.3	9.93	10.11	4.81 /37	18.52 /96	--	0.06	1.61
MC	Rainier Invt Mang Mid Cap Eq Inst	RAIMX	C+	(800) 248-6314	B- / 7.5	5.87	9.23	12.90 /86	14.04 /67	14.75 /85	0.00	1.10
MC	Rainier Invt Mang Mid Cap Eq Orig	RIMMX	C+	(800) 248-6314	B- / 7.3	5.80	9.09	12.57 /85	13.73 /65	14.45 /82	0.00	1.34
IN	Rainier Large Cap Equity Inst	RAIEX	D	(800) 248-6314	B- / 7.5	3.23	7.43	14.45 /90	14.22 /69	12.68 /66	0.01	0.90
IN	Rainier Large Cap Equity Original	RIMEX	D	(800) 248-6314	B- / 7.2	3.16	7.29	14.12 /90	13.90 /66	12.37 /63	0.00	1.19
SC	● Rainier Small-Mid Cap Equity Inst	RAISX	C-	(800) 248-6314	B- / 7.0	6.57	8.80	9.64 /73	13.75 /65	14.62 /83	0.00	1.01
SC	● Rainier Small-Mid Cap Equity Orig	RIMSX	C-	(800) 248-6314	C+ / 6.8	6.50	8.62	9.29 /71	13.42 /63	14.30 /80	0.00	1.32

● Denotes fund is closed to new investors
* Denotes fund is included in Section II

www.thestreetratings.com

Risk Rating/Pts	Standard Deviation	Beta	NAV As of 3/31/15	Total $(Mil)	Cash %	Stocks %	Bonds %	Other %	Portfolio Turnover Ratio	Last Bull Market Return	Last Bear Market Return	Manager Quality Pct	Manager Tenure (Years)	Initial Purch. $	Additional Purch. $	Front End Load	Back End Load
B- / 7.6	10.2	1.06	17.17	759	0	0	0	100	86	105.8	-17.5	67	7	0	0	0.0	0.0
C+ / 5.6	13.3	0.98	14.13	18	0	99	0	1	85	107.6	-25.4	80	15	1,000	50	5.8	0.0
C / 5.5	13.3	0.98	13.51	7	0	99	0	1	85	102.0	-25.6	74	15	1,000	50	0.0	0.0
C / 5.5	13.3	0.98	13.69	1	0	99	0	1	85	107.5	-25.5	79	15	0	0	0.0	0.0
C+ / 5.6	13.3	0.98	14.30	16	0	99	0	1	85	110.7	-25.3	83	15	1,000,000	0	0.0	0.0
C+ / 6.3	13.3	0.98	14.11	797	0	99	0	1	85	N/A	N/A	83	15	0	0	0.0	0.0
B / 8.0	4.2	0.69	13.42	131	0	25	74	1	12	33.8	-7.3	53	19	1,000	50	4.3	0.0
B / 8.0	4.2	0.69	13.71	6	0	25	74	1	12	30.7	-7.6	42	19	1,000	50	0.0	0.0
B / 8.2	4.2	0.69	13.36	3	0	25	74	1	12	30.3	-7.6	41	12	1,000	50	0.0	0.0
B / 8.0	4.2	0.69	13.68	5	0	25	74	1	12	31.3	-7.6	45	19	1,000	50	0.0	0.0
B / 8.2	4.2	0.69	13.39	3	0	25	74	1	12	N/A	N/A	56	14	1,000,000	0	0.0	0.0
B / 8.2	5.8	0.99	15.03	282	0	43	55	2	13	47.5	-11.4	34	19	1,000	50	5.8	0.0
B / 8.2	5.9	1.00	15.51	14	0	43	55	2	13	42.8	-11.8	22	19	1,000	50	0.0	0.0
B / 8.2	5.8	0.99	15.53	21	0	43	55	2	13	43.8	-11.7	26	19	1,000	50	0.0	0.0
B- / 7.9	7.8	0.78	17.36	447	1	62	35	2	12	61.1	-15.4	38	19	1,000	50	5.8	0.0
B- / 7.9	7.7	0.78	17.71	25	1	62	35	2	12	56.2	-15.8	27	19	1,000	50	0.0	0.0
B- / 7.9	7.7	0.78	17.59	27	1	62	35	2	12	57.4	-15.7	30	19	1,000	50	0.0	0.0
B- / 7.9	7.7	0.78	17.26	6	1	62	35	2	12	62.3	-15.4	43	19	1,000,000	0	0.0	0.0
B- / 7.3	9.3	0.93	17.98	688	2	76	20	2	11	70.3	-18.6	24	19	1,000	50	5.8	0.0
B- / 7.3	9.3	0.93	16.95	49	2	76	20	2	11	65.3	-18.9	16	19	1,000	50	0.0	0.0
B- / 7.3	9.3	0.93	17.07	25	2	76	20	2	11	66.8	-18.8	18	19	1,000	50	0.0	0.0
B- / 7.3	9.3	0.93	17.93	2	2	76	20	2	11	72.1	-18.6	27	19	1,000,000	0	0.0	0.0
C+ / 6.0	9.4	0.72	12.38	2	21	40	38	1	55	9.5	-13.1	1	5	1,000	50	5.8	0.0
C+ / 5.8	9.4	0.71	12.19	1	21	40	38	1	55	6.8	-13.4	1	5	1,000	50	0.0	0.0
C+ / 6.0	9.4	0.71	12.59	1	21	40	38	1	55	10.5	-13.0	1	5	1,000,000	0	0.0	0.0
B- / 7.3	9.4	0.71	12.42	138	21	40	38	1	55	N/A	N/A	1	5	0	0	0.0	0.0
B- / 7.4	5.5	0.46	13.13	32	18	71	8	3	280	31.4	-11.8	38	12	2,000	100	5.5	0.0
B- / 7.4	5.5	0.46	12.79	6	18	71	8	3	280	28.1	-12.1	30	12	2,000	100	0.0	0.0
B- / 7.4	5.5	0.46	13.20	70	18	71	8	3	280	32.6	-11.8	44	12	1,000,000	0	0.0	0.0
C+ / 6.5	10.5	0.63	11.28	5	2	94	2	2	130	77.0	-18.1	97	7	2,000	100	5.5	0.0
C+ / 6.5	10.5	0.63	10.71	2	2	94	2	2	130	72.7	-18.4	96	7	2,000	100	0.0	0.0
C+ / 6.5	10.5	0.63	12.95	2	2	94	2	2	130	78.7	-18.0	97	7	1,000,000	0	0.0	0.0
C+ / 6.6	11.7	1.00	25.58	6	0	99	0	1	62	98.6	-23.0	42	7	2,000	100	5.5	0.0
C+ / 6.5	11.6	1.00	22.47	2	0	99	0	1	62	93.5	-23.2	33	7	2,000	100	0.0	0.0
C+ / 6.6	11.7	1.00	26.83	2	0	99	0	1	62	100.3	-22.9	46	7	1,000,000	0	0.0	0.0
C+ / 6.3	13.0	0.92	23.98	8	1	98	0	1	176	94.1	-24.2	67	19	2,000	100	5.5	0.0
C+ / 6.2	13.0	0.92	19.85	2	1	98	0	1	176	89.1	-24.4	56	19	2,000	100	0.0	0.0
C+ / 6.3	13.0	0.92	25.09	28	1	98	0	1	176	95.8	-24.1	70	19	1,000,000	0	0.0	0.0
C+ / 6.5	10.8	0.63	25.91	78	4	95	0	1	170	86.6	-19.3	97	19	2,000	100	5.5	0.0
C+ / 6.4	10.9	0.64	22.77	21	4	95	0	1	170	81.8	-19.6	96	19	2,000	100	0.0	0.0
C+ / 6.5	10.8	0.63	26.94	64	4	95	0	1	170	88.1	-19.3	97	19	1,000,000	0	0.0	0.0
U /	N/A	N/A	11.33	34	13	86	0	1	11	N/A	N/A	N/A	2	1,000	100	5.8	1.0
U /	N/A	N/A	10.57	104	3	96	0	1	887	N/A	N/A	N/A	2	10,000	1,000	0.0	0.0
B- / 7.5	10.1	0.73	24.20	78	23	76	0	1	10	55.7	-14.6	65	13	2,500	1,000	0.0	0.0
B- / 7.6	8.8	0.89	19.79	38	16	83	0	1	4	71.3	-10.3	57	11	2,500	1,000	0.0	0.0
B- / 7.0	11.3	0.74	15.50	40	7	92	0	1	80	N/A	N/A	98	3	100,000	1,000	0.0	0.0
C / 5.0	11.5	1.00	55.34	868	4	95	0	1	150	92.3	-24.3	29	10	100,000	1,000	0.0	0.0
C / 5.0	11.5	1.00	53.78	104	4	95	0	1	150	90.5	-24.3	26	10	2,500	250	0.0	0.0
D- / 1.4	11.2	1.08	25.87	226	1	98	0	1	82	87.2	-18.7	26	19	100,000	1,000	0.0	0.0
D- / 1.3	11.2	1.08	25.43	126	1	98	0	1	82	85.5	-18.7	23	19	2,500	250	0.0	0.0
C- / 3.8	12.1	0.83	47.20	673	0	99	0	1	140	93.6	-25.1	71	21	100,000	1,000	0.0	0.0
C- / 3.7	12.1	0.83	45.23	609	0	99	0	1	140	91.7	-25.2	68	21	2,500	250	0.0	0.0

99 Pct = Best
0 Pct = Worst

Fund Type	Fund Name	Ticker Symbol	Overall Investment Rating	Phone	PERFORMANCE Perfor-mance Rating/Pts	Total Return % through 3/31/15 3 Mo	6 Mo	1Yr / Pct	Annualized 3Yr / Pct	5Yr / Pct	Incl. in Returns Dividend Yield	Expense Ratio
GL	Ramius Hedged Alpha A	RDRAX	D	(877) 672-6487	E / 0.3	0.55	-2.13	-5.45 / 5	-1.38 / 3	--	0.00	1.92
GL	Ramius Hedged Alpha I	RDRIX	D	(877) 672-6487	E / 0.3	0.65	-2.01	-5.31 / 5	-1.13 / 3	--	0.00	1.67
AA	Ranger Quest for Inc and Gro Inst	RFIDX	C-	(866) 458-4744	C- / 3.0	0.20	0.12	1.82 / 21	8.92 / 32	--	5.69	1.82
SC	Ranger Small Cap Inst	RFISX	C-	(866) 458-4744	C+ / 6.1	8.08	15.58	11.81 / 82	10.99 / 45	--	0.00	1.49
AA	RBB Free Market Fixed Income Inst	FMFIX	C-	(888) 261-4073	E+ / 0.6	0.78	1.08	1.45 / 20	0.66 / 5	1.46 / 4	0.67	0.78
EM	RBB Free Market Intl Eq Inst	FMNEX	D-	(888) 261-4073	D / 1.9	3.72	-1.24	-5.02 / 5	7.56 / 24	5.50 / 14	2.18	1.07
IN	RBB Free Market US Equity Inst	FMUEX	A-	(888) 261-4073	B+ / 8.3	1.61	7.20	6.69 / 53	16.82 / 89	14.43 / 82	0.63	0.83
IN	RBC BlueBay Absolute Return I	RBARX	U	(800) 422-2766	U /	1.50	1.14	0.25 / 16	--	--	0.93	1.02
CV	RBC BlueBay Global Convertible Bd I	RGCBX	B	(800) 422-2766	C- / 3.9	4.62	6.99	7.40 / 58	9.27 / 35	--	1.78	1.55
SC	RBC Enterprise A	TETAX	D	(800) 422-2766	C / 4.8	1.67	7.79	-2.09 / 10	14.42 / 70	14.37 / 81	0.00	1.75
SC	RBC Enterprise I	TETIX	C	(800) 422-2766	C+ / 6.6	1.70	7.93	-1.86 / 11	15.85 / 82	14.64 / 84	0.00	1.20
SC	RBC Micro Cap Value A	TMVAX	A	(800) 422-2766	B+ / 8.8	4.42	13.89	9.15 / 70	18.86 / 96	15.86 / 92	0.31	1.70
SC	RBC Micro Cap Value I	RMVIX	A+	(800) 422-2766	A / 9.5	4.49	14.01	9.38 / 71	19.16 / 97	16.15 / 94	0.57	1.24
SC	RBC Mid Cap Value I	RBMVX	B	(800) 422-2766	A / 9.4	3.32	11.69	15.19 / 92	18.14 / 95	16.34 / 94	0.30	3.71
SC	RBC Small Cap Core A	TEEAX	C+	(800) 422-2766	C+ / 6.6	3.90	12.63	7.07 / 56	15.59 / 80	15.67 / 91	0.00	1.58
SC	RBC Small Cap Core I	RCSIX	B	(800) 422-2766	B / 7.8	3.95	12.76	7.34 / 58	15.87 / 82	15.95 / 93	0.00	1.14
MC	RBC SMID Cap Growth A	TMCAX	D+	(800) 422-2766	C / 5.1	3.09	10.63	7.60 / 60	13.23 / 61	15.63 / 91	0.00	1.47
MC	RBC SMID Cap Growth I	TMCIX	C-	(800) 422-2766	C+ / 6.3	3.12	10.74	7.83 / 62	13.51 / 63	15.91 / 92	0.00	1.04
IN	Redmont Resolute I A	RMRFX	C-	(855) 268-2242	E+ / 0.9	3.99	4.85	5.14 / 40	3.60 / 9	--	0.00	6.15
IN	Redmont Resolute I I	RMREX	C-	(855) 268-2242	E+ / 0.9	1.69	2.59	3.16 / 27	3.18 / 8	--	0.07	7.52
IN	Redmont Resolute II I	RMRGX	C-	(877) 665-1287	D- / 1.3	1.62	3.24	4.16 / 33	4.94 / 13	--	2.14	3.84
MC	Reinhart Mid Cap Priv Mrkt Val Adv	RPMVX	U	(855) 774-3863	U /	4.73	6.67	8.87 / 69	--	--	0.45	1.76
GL	REMS Real Estate Income 50/50 Inst	RREIX	C	(800) 527-9525	C+ / 6.7	2.81	11.15	18.65 / 96	11.96 / 52	--	4.68	0.86
RE	REMS Real Estate Value Opp Fd Inst	HLRRX	B+	(800) 527-9525	A- / 9.2	3.55	13.86	17.50 / 95	16.06 / 84	16.20 / 94	1.66	1.45
RE	REMS Real Estate Value Opp Fd Plat	HLPPX	B+	(800) 527-9525	A- / 9.1	3.52	13.76	17.26 / 95	15.77 / 81	15.90 / 92	1.41	1.45
GR	Renaissance Global IPO	IPOSX	D+	(888) 476-3863	C+ / 5.9	6.54	6.40	9.44 / 72	12.74 / 58	7.73 / 28	0.00	2.84
IN	RESQ Dynamic Allocation A	RQEAX	U	(877) 940-2526	U /	2.69	4.91	7.49 / 59	--	--	0.00	3.16
GL	RESQ Strategic Income A	RQIAX	U	(877) 940-2526	U /	-0.12	2.51	5.07 / 39	--	--	1.98	3.56
GR	Reynolds Blue Chip Growth	RBCGX	D-	(800) 773-9665	C+ / 5.7	3.39	5.28	7.31 / 58	12.33 / 55	12.32 / 63	0.00	1.59
SC	Rice Hall James Micro Cap Port	RHJSX	B-	(866) 777-7818	B / 7.6	6.61	14.67	6.68 / 53	15.11 / 76	15.88 / 92	0.00	1.54
SC	Rice Hall James Small Cap Port	RHJMX	D	(866) 777-7818	B / 8.1	6.47	15.94	10.56 / 77	14.61 / 72	17.10 / 96	0.00	1.51
MC	Rice Hall James SMID Cap Investor	RHJVX	C	(866) 777-7818	C / 5.3	4.89	8.52	7.04 / 55	11.18 / 47	10.69 / 50	0.00	2.71
AG	RidgeWorth Aggr Gr Alloc Str A	SLAAX	E+	(888) 784-3863	C- / 3.7	1.94	5.55	7.56 / 60	10.53 / 42	9.57 / 41	1.73	1.76
AG	RidgeWorth Aggr Gr Alloc Str C	CLVLX	D-	(888) 784-3863	C- / 4.2	1.87	5.19	6.89 / 54	9.82 / 38	8.87 / 36	1.41	2.37
AG	RidgeWorth Aggr Gr Alloc Str I	CVMGX	D-	(888) 784-3863	C / 4.8	2.05	5.67	7.79 / 61	10.76 / 44	9.86 / 43	1.95	1.75
AG	RidgeWorth Aggressive Gr Stock A	SAGAX	D	(888) 784-3863	C+ / 5.6	2.57	-0.48	4.47 / 35	15.07 / 75	13.41 / 72	0.00	1.41
AG	RidgeWorth Aggressive Gr Stock I	SCATX	C-	(888) 784-3863	C+ / 6.7	2.58	-0.37	4.61 / 36	15.27 / 77	13.68 / 75	0.00	1.35
AA	RidgeWorth Cons Alloc Str A	SVCAX	C-	(888) 784-3863	D- / 1.5	1.76	3.88	5.86 / 45	6.09 / 17	6.46 / 20	2.07	1.24
AA	RidgeWorth Cons Alloc Str C	SCCLX	C-	(888) 784-3863	D / 1.8	1.61	3.54	5.20 / 40	5.36 / 14	5.73 / 15	1.51	1.90
AA	RidgeWorth Cons Alloc Str I	SCCTX	C-	(888) 784-3863	D+ / 2.3	1.84	4.10	6.25 / 49	6.39 / 18	6.78 / 22	2.46	0.96
AA	RidgeWorth Grow Alloc Str A	SGIAX	D+	(888) 784-3863	C- / 3.4	2.06	5.34	7.38 / 58	10.06 / 40	9.20 / 38	1.72	1.43
AA	RidgeWorth Grow Alloc Str C	SGILX	C-	(888) 784-3863	C- / 3.9	1.91	4.91	6.70 / 53	9.36 / 35	8.47 / 33	1.36	2.04
AA	RidgeWorth Grow Alloc Str I	CLVGX	C-	(888) 784-3863	C / 4.5	2.05	5.32	7.54 / 59	10.27 / 41	9.43 / 40	1.99	1.43
FO	RidgeWorth Intl Equity A	SCIIX	E	(888) 784-3863	D- / 1.5	4.76	1.36	-4.87 / 6	7.79 / 26	5.61 / 15	1.78	1.58
FO	RidgeWorth Intl Equity I	STITX	E	(888) 784-3863	D+ / 2.3	4.92	1.43	-4.59 / 6	7.97 / 27	5.83 / 16	2.02	1.35
GI	RidgeWorth Large Cap Val Equity A	SVIIX	C	(888) 784-3863	C+ / 5.7	-1.96	2.60	6.98 / 55	14.99 / 75	12.88 / 67	0.95	1.37
GI	RidgeWorth Large Cap Val Equity C	SVIFX	C+	(888) 784-3863	C+ / 6.3	-2.06	2.42	6.50 / 51	14.40 / 70	12.21 / 62	0.57	1.71
GI	RidgeWorth Large Cap Val Equity I	STVTX	C+	(888) 784-3863	C+ / 6.9	-1.89	2.78	7.25 / 57	15.30 / 77	13.20 / 70	1.29	1.06
GI	RidgeWorth Large Cap Val Equity IS	STVZX	C+	(888) 784-3863	C+ / 6.9	-1.83	2.91	7.45 / 59	15.37 / 78	13.24 / 71	1.13	N/A
GR	RidgeWorth Lrg-Cap Growth Stock A	STCIX	D-	(888) 784-3863	B- / 7.3	5.93	10.08	14.83 / 91	14.68 / 72	15.15 / 88	0.00	1.19
GR	RidgeWorth Lrg-Cap Growth Stock C	STCFX	D	(888) 784-3863	B / 7.9	5.98	9.85	14.20 / 90	13.93 / 67	14.40 / 81	0.00	1.87
GR	RidgeWorth Lrg-Cap Growth Stock I	STCAX	D+	(888) 784-3863	B+ / 8.6	6.06	10.15	15.03 / 92	14.93 / 74	15.45 / 90	0.00	1.09

● Denotes fund is closed to new investors
★ Denotes fund is included in Section II

www.thestreetratings.com

RISK Rating/Pts	3 Year Standard Deviation	3 Year Beta	NAV As of 3/31/15	Total $(Mil)	Cash %	Stocks %	Bonds %	Other %	Portfolio Turnover Ratio	Last Bull Market Return	Last Bear Market Return	Manager Quality Pct	Manager Tenure (Years)	Initial Purch. $	Additional Purch. $	Front End Load	Back End Load
B /8.3	4.2	0.21	9.20	N/A	100	0	0	0	49	1.0	-7.7	22	5	1,000	50	5.5	2.0
B /8.3	4.3	0.21	9.28	79	100	0	0	0	49	2.0	-7.6	24	5	1,000,000	100,000	0.0	2.0
B- /7.6	9.1	1.20	12.73	16	16	83	0	1	39	50.9	N/A	18	4	250,000	0	0.0	0.0
C /4.7	15.0	1.00	16.98	23	3	96	0	1	79	88.9	N/A	12	4	250,000	0	0.0	0.0
B+ /9.7	1.4	0.02	10.29	1,956	3	0	96	1	0	2.3	2.0	72	8	0	0	0.0	0.0
C /5.3	13.9	0.86	9.75	1,473	1	98	0	1	2	48.4	-26.3	96	8	0	0	0.0	0.0
C+ /6.6	12.0	1.17	17.09	2,079	0	99	0	1	3	105.2	-24.1	39	8	0	0	0.0	0.0
U /	N/A	N/A	10.18	610	40	0	57	3	218	N/A	N/A	N/A	3	1,000,000	10,000	0.0	2.0
B+ /9.7	5.3	0.63	10.66	22	0	0	0	100	139	N/A	N/A	76	4	1,000,000	10,000	0.0	2.0
C- /4.2	14.3	0.99	23.81	2	0	99	0	1	19	89.6	-22.0	46	16	1,000	100	5.8	2.0
C /4.3	14.2	0.97	24.50	128	0	99	0	1	19	91.2	-22.0	68	16	250,000	0	0.0	2.0
C+ /6.7	13.0	0.94	29.53	10	2	97	0	1	11	109.6	-20.4	89	6	1,000	100	5.8	2.0
C+ /6.8	13.0	0.94	29.54	149	2	97	0	1	11	111.4	-20.3	90	6	250,000	0	0.0	2.0
C- /4.2	12.0	0.79	12.44	5	0	99	0	1	162	122.4	-26.4	93	6	250,000	0	0.0	2.0
C+ /5.9	13.6	0.96	33.31	9	1	98	0	1	29	97.2	-24.0	67	24	1,000	100	5.8	2.0
C+ /6.0	13.6	0.96	34.50	271	1	98	0	1	29	99.0	-23.9	70	24	250,000	0	0.0	2.0
C- /4.0	11.0	0.92	14.69	13	2	97	0	1	17	83.1	-17.8	37	6	1,000	100	5.8	2.0
C /4.4	11.0	0.92	15.87	61	2	97	0	1	17	84.6	-17.7	40	6	250,000	0	0.0	2.0
B+ /9.3	4.7	0.39	10.94	N/A	41	32	24	3	91	N/A	N/A	33	4	2,500	0	5.5	2.0
B+ /9.3	4.5	0.41	10.82	3	41	32	24	3	91	N/A	N/A	25	4	1,000,000	0	0.0	2.0
B+ /9.2	4.6	0.42	11.32	685	41	31	23	5	114	N/A	N/A	44	4	1,000,000	0	0.0	2.0
U /	N/A	N/A	14.60	83	11	88	0	1	41	N/A	N/A	N/A	3	5,000	100	0.0	0.0
C /4.7	8.2	0.24	14.91	101	5	94	0	1	40	62.7	-9.3	98	5	50,000	5,000	0.0	2.0
C /5.5	9.7	0.70	18.37	393	14	85	0	1	41	110.6	-24.1	95	13	50,000	5,000	0.0	0.0
C /5.5	9.7	0.70	18.22	42	14	85	0	1	41	108.7	-24.2	94	13	2,500	100	0.0	0.0
C- /3.8	15.6	1.09	17.28	10	10	89	0	1	198	71.3	-27.6	14	18	5,000	100	0.0	2.0
U /	N/A	N/A	10.30	50	0	54	38	8	376	N/A	N/A	N/A	2	1,000	0	5.8	2.0
U /	N/A	N/A	10.15	53	17	38	39	6	325	N/A	N/A	N/A	2	1,000	0	4.8	2.0
D /2.0	11.2	1.05	60.43	134	1	98	0	1	102	82.2	-22.9	16	27	1,000	100	0.0	0.0
C /5.5	14.0	0.98	30.17	44	5	94	0	1	57	106.1	-23.8	56	21	2,500	100	0.0	2.0
E+ /0.9	14.1	0.98	13.98	50	1	98	0	1	46	81.0	-19.0	49	19	2,500	100	0.0	0.0
C+ /5.7	13.5	1.15	20.38	6	5	94	0	1	50	75.0	-25.5	4	11	2,500	100	0.0	0.0
C- /3.1	9.2	0.92	7.87	5	4	84	11	1	12	69.8	-21.4	18	23	2,000	1,000	5.8	0.0
C- /3.0	9.2	0.92	7.61	1	4	84	11	1	12	66.5	-21.7	13	23	5,000	1,000	0.0	0.0
C- /3.1	9.3	0.93	7.97	5	4	84	11	1	12	71.3	-21.4	18	23	0	0	0.0	0.0
C- /3.2	17.3	1.20	20.76	11	1	98	0	1	49	96.1	-26.2	16	11	2,000	1,000	5.8	0.0
C- /3.2	17.3	1.20	21.49	24	1	98	0	1	49	97.5	-26.1	18	11	0	0	0.0	0.0
B /8.5	3.9	0.64	12.75	16	3	35	61	1	24	31.1	-5.3	57	12	2,000	1,000	4.8	0.0
B /8.6	3.9	0.64	12.61	18	3	35	61	1	24	28.0	-5.6	46	12	5,000	1,000	0.0	0.0
B /8.4	4.0	0.65	12.76	33	3	35	61	1	24	32.4	-5.2	60	12	0	0	0.0	0.0
C+ /6.3	7.8	1.33	11.41	9	3	74	22	1	14	59.8	-15.4	15	23	2,000	1,000	5.8	0.0
C+ /6.3	7.8	1.33	11.18	3	3	74	22	1	14	56.4	-15.7	11	23	5,000	1,000	0.0	0.0
C+ /6.2	7.8	1.32	11.46	53	3	74	22	1	14	60.9	-15.3	17	23	0	0	0.0	0.0
C- /3.2	13.7	1.02	10.34	4	2	97	0	1	43	51.8	-25.6	40	15	2,000	1,000	5.8	0.0
C- /3.2	13.8	1.02	10.45	19	2	97	0	1	43	52.7	-25.5	43	15	0	0	0.0	0.0
C+ /5.8	10.3	1.05	16.48	461	4	95	0	1	81	95.3	-19.5	42	20	2,000	1,000	5.8	0.0
C+ /5.8	10.3	1.04	16.15	21	4	95	0	1	81	91.6	-19.7	36	20	5,000	1,000	0.0	0.0
C+ /5.8	10.3	1.04	16.60	1,927	4	95	0	1	81	97.1	-19.3	47	20	0	0	0.0	0.0
C+ /5.7	10.3	1.04	16.66	38	4	95	0	1	81	97.4	-19.3	48	20	2,500,000	0	0.0	0.0
E+ /0.7	11.7	1.06	8.75	66	0	99	0	1	21	98.7	-16.9	36	8	2,000	1,000	5.8	0.0
E+ /0.7	11.7	1.05	6.38	47	0	99	0	1	21	94.3	-17.1	28	8	5,000	1,000	0.0	0.0
E+ /0.7	11.7	1.05	10.32	127	0	99	0	1	21	100.3	-16.7	41	8	0	0	0.0	0.0

		99 Pct = Best				**PERFORMANCE**					
		0 Pct = Worst		**Overall**		**Perfor-**	Total Return % through 3/31/15			Incl. in Returns	
Fund			Ticker	**Investment**		**mance**			Annualized	Dividend	Expense
Type	Fund Name		Symbol	**Rating**	Phone	**Rating/Pts**	3 Mo	6 Mo	1Yr / Pct	3Yr / Pct	5Yr / Pct	Yield	Ratio

Fund Type	Fund Name	Ticker Symbol	Overall Investment Rating	Phone	Performance Rating/Pts	3 Mo	6 Mo	1Yr / Pct	3Yr / Pct	5Yr / Pct	Dividend Yield	Expense Ratio
GR	RidgeWorth Lrg-Cap Growth Stock IS	STCZX	B	(888) 784-3863	B+ / 8.6	6.06	10.25	15.14 /92	14.97 /75	15.47 /90	0.00	0.87
MC	RidgeWorth Mid Cap Value Eq A	SAMVX	C+	(888) 784-3863	C+ / 6.6	0.29	5.11	7.45 /59	16.01 /83	13.07 /69	0.51	1.40
MC	RidgeWorth Mid Cap Value Eq C	SMVFX	B-	(888) 784-3863	B- / 7.3	0.23	4.92	7.06 /55	15.52 /79	12.46 /64	0.22	1.76
MC	RidgeWorth Mid Cap Value Eq I	SMVTX	B	(888) 784-3863	B / 7.9	0.37	5.23	7.76 /61	16.34 /86	13.39 /72	0.82	1.10
MC	RidgeWorth Mid Cap Value Eq IS	SMVZX	B	(888) 784-3863	B / 8.0	0.51	5.43	8.05 /63	16.44 /87	13.45 /72	0.87	N/A
AA	RidgeWorth Mod Alloc Str A	SVMAX	D+	(888) 784-3863	D+ / 2.4	1.94	4.59	6.65 /52	8.14 /28	7.95 /30	2.00	1.29
AA	RidgeWorth Mod Alloc Str C	SVGLX	C-	(888) 784-3863	D+ / 2.9	1.77	4.28	6.07 /47	7.50 /24	7.26 /25	1.55	1.88
AA	RidgeWorth Mod Alloc Str I	CLVBX	C-	(888) 784-3863	C- / 3.4	1.93	4.71	6.77 /53	8.29 /29	8.17 /31	2.24	1.21
SC	RidgeWorth Sm Cap Gr Stock A	SCGIX	D-	(888) 784-3863	C+ / 6.2	5.50	14.29	4.21 /33	14.39 /70	13.98 /78	0.00	1.29
SC	RidgeWorth Sm Cap Gr Stock C	SSCFX	D-	(888) 784-3863	C+ / 6.6	5.30	13.96	3.55 /29	13.64 /64	13.20 /70	0.00	1.94
SC	RidgeWorth Sm Cap Gr Stock I	SSCTX	D	(888) 784-3863	B- / 7.2	5.48	14.30	4.24 /33	14.46 /71	14.15 /79	0.00	1.31
SC	RidgeWorth Sm Cap Gr Stock IS	SCGZX	C+	(888) 784-3863	B- / 7.4	5.62	14.51	4.50 /35	14.56 /71	14.20 /80	0.00	N/A
SC ●	RidgeWorth Small Cap Val Eq A	SASVX	D+	(888) 784-3863	C / 5.4	2.28	12.34	3.79 /30	13.60 /64	12.95 /68	0.51	1.50
SC ●	RidgeWorth Small Cap Val Eq C	STCEX	C-	(888) 784-3863	C+ / 6.1	2.21	12.14	3.42 /29	13.14 /61	12.36 /63	0.27	1.87
SC ●	RidgeWorth Small Cap Val Eq I	SCETX	C-	(888) 784-3863	C+ / 6.6	2.36	12.47	4.07 /32	13.92 /67	13.27 /71	0.84	1.22
SC	River Oak Discovery Fund	RIVSX	D-	(888) 462-5386	C / 4.9	2.99	9.29	4.06 /32	11.07 /46	11.43 /56	0.00	1.48
GR	Riverbridge Growth Institutional	RIVBX	U	(888) 447-4470	U /	2.46	9.33	5.12 /39	--	--	0.00	2.02
GI	RiverFront Dynamic Equity Income A	RLGAX	D+	(866) 759-5679	C- / 3.6	5.43	6.72	7.83 /62	9.82 /38	--	1.56	1.78
GI	RiverFront Dynamic Equity Income C	RLGCX	D+	(866) 759-5679	C- / 4.0	5.25	6.26	6.98 /55	8.99 /33	--	1.19	2.54
GI	RiverFront Dynamic Equity Income I	RLIIX	C-	(866) 759-5679	C / 4.6	5.47	6.81	8.06 /63	10.06 /40	--	1.81	1.54
GI	RiverFront Global Allocation A	RMGAX	D	(866) 759-5679	C- / 3.7	5.72	6.85	7.10 /56	10.00 /39	--	1.43	1.89
GI	RiverFront Global Allocation C	RMGCX	D	(866) 759-5679	C- / 4.0	5.45	6.39	6.23 /48	9.16 /34	--	1.05	2.64
GI	RiverFront Global Allocation I	RMGIX	D+	(866) 759-5679	C / 4.7	5.75	6.89	7.31 /58	10.25 /41	--	1.68	1.65
GL	RiverFront Global Growth A	RLTAX	D-	(866) 759-5679	C / 4.4	6.39	7.33	7.75 /61	11.13 /46	--	1.48	1.78
GL	RiverFront Global Growth C	RLTCX	D	(866) 759-5679	C / 4.8	6.26	6.96	7.03 /55	10.31 /41	--	1.10	2.53
GL	RiverFront Global Growth I	RLFIX	D	(866) 759-5679	C / 5.5	6.43	7.41	8.04 /63	11.39 /48	--	1.71	1.76
GL ●	RiverFront Global Growth Inv	RLTSX	D	(866) 759-5679	C / 5.3	6.42	7.30	7.79 /61	11.11 /46	8.33 /32	1.56	1.78
GL ●	RiverFront Global Growth L	RLTIX	D	(866) 759-5679	C / 5.5	6.44	7.43	8.06 /63	11.41 /48	8.61 /34	1.72	1.42
GI	RiverFront Moderate Growth & Inc A	RMIAX	D	(866) 759-5679	D+ / 2.3	3.32	4.64	6.51 /51	7.78 /26	--	1.66	1.66
GI	RiverFront Moderate Growth & Inc C	RMICX	D	(866) 759-5679	D+ / 2.6	3.17	4.28	5.76 /44	6.97 /21	--	1.12	2.42
GI	RiverFront Moderate Growth & Inc I	RMIIX	D+	(866) 759-5679	C- / 3.3	3.38	4.74	6.76 /53	8.04 /27	--	1.97	1.42
AA	RiverNorth Core Oppty I	RNCIX	U	(888) 848-7549	U /	1.74	3.23	--	--	--	0.00	2.16
IN	RiverNorth Core Oppty R	RNCOX	C-	(888) 848-7549	C- / 3.3	1.74	3.16	5.34 /41	9.12 /34	9.20 /38	3.34	2.41
GR	RiverPark Large Growth Instl	RPXIX	C+	(888) 564-4517	C+ / 6.0	0.98	3.84	4.68 /36	13.67 /65	--	0.25	1.00
GR	RiverPark Large Growth Retail	RPXFX	C+	(888) 564-4517	C+ / 5.7	0.93	3.75	4.15 /33	13.31 /62	--	0.00	1.26
GL	RiverPark Long/Short Oppty Instl	RLSIX	D	(888) 564-4517	E+ / 0.7	0.96	0.57	-1.49 /11	2.19 / 7	8.31 /32	0.00	3.22
GL	RiverPark Long/Short Oppty Retail	RLSFX	D	(888) 564-4517	E+ / 0.7	0.86	0.48	-1.68 /11	1.99 / 6	--	0.00	3.37
AA	RiverPark Strategic Income Inst	RSIIX	U	(888) 564-4517	U /	1.44	1.07	3.00 /26	--	--	5.70	0.91
AA	RiverPark Strategic Income Rtl	RSIVX	U	(888) 564-4517	U /	1.38	0.95	2.65 /25	--	--	5.45	1.24
GR	RiverPark/Gargoyle Hedged Val nstl	RGHIX	U	(888) 564-4517	U /	3.30	1.60	5.20 /40	--	--	1.49	1.25
GR	RiverPark/Wedgewood Instl	RWGIX	B-	(888) 564-4517	C+ / 6.3	0.70	5.99	7.99 /63	13.70 /65	--	0.04	0.88
GR	RiverPark/Wedgewood Retail	RWGFX	B-	(888) 564-4517	C+ / 6.2	0.66	5.83	7.72 /61	13.43 /63	--	0.00	1.05
GI	RNC Genter Dividend Income Fund	GDIIX	C-	(800) 545-4322	C- / 3.2	-1.51	-1.69	2.23 /23	10.27 /41	11.05 /53	1.96	2.25
GR	Robeco Boston Ptrs All Cap Val I	BPAIX	A+	(888) 261-4073	A- / 9.1	2.14	7.00	10.89 /78	17.81 /94	14.16 /79	0.92	0.94
GR	Robeco Boston Ptrs All Cap Val Inv	BPAVX	A+	(888) 261-4073	A- / 9.0	2.06	6.83	10.58 /77	17.56 /93	13.92 /77	0.71	1.19
GL	Robeco Boston Ptrs Glbl Lg/Sh Instl	BGLSX	U	(888) 261-4073	U /	0.99	0.79	2.20 /23	--	--	0.00	4.89
GL	Robeco Boston Ptrs Glo Eqty Inst	BPGIX	B-	(888) 261-4073	C+ / 6.3	3.63	5.59	6.30 /49	13.99 /67	--	0.87	1.39
AA ●	Robeco Boston Ptrs Lg/Sh Equit I	BPLSX	D-	(888) 261-4073	E+ / 0.8	-4.11	-5.61	-2.06 /10	4.90 /13	8.24 /31	0.00	4.33
AA ●	Robeco Boston Ptrs Lg/Sh Equit Inv	BPLEX	E+	(888) 261-4073	E+ / 0.8	-4.23	-5.77	-2.35 /10	4.63 /12	7.97 /30	0.00	4.58
IN ●	Robeco Boston Ptrs Lng/Shrt Rs Inst	BPIRX	C+	(888) 261-4073	C- / 4.1	0.52	4.03	6.23 /48	10.20 /40	--	0.00	2.52
IN ●	Robeco Boston Ptrs Lng/Shrt Rs Inv	BPRRX	C+	(888) 261-4073	C- / 3.9	0.46	3.94	6.01 /47	9.93 /39	--	0.00	2.77
SC	Robeco Boston Ptrs Sm/Cp Val II I	BPSIX	B+	(888) 261-4073	B / 8.1	3.31	10.08	6.25 /49	16.39 /86	13.27 /71	0.65	1.23

● Denotes fund is closed to new investors
* Denotes fund is included in Section II

www.thestreetratings.com

RISK			NET ASSETS		ASSET				Portfolio Turnover Ratio	BULL / BEAR		FUND MANAGER		MINIMUMS		LOADS	
	3 Year		NAV							Last Bull Market Return	Last Bear Market Return	Manager Quality Pct	Manager Tenure (Years)	Initial Purch. $	Additional Purch. $	Front End Load	Back End Load
Risk Rating/Pts	Standard Deviation	Beta	As of 3/31/15	Total $(Mil)	Cash %	Stocks %	Bonds %	Other %									
C / 5.2	11.7	1.05	10.33	53	0	99	0	1	21	100.5	-16.7	41	8	2,500,000	0	0.0	0.0
C+ / 5.6	11.0	0.95	13.60	593	4	95	0	1	108	105.1	-27.8	67	14	2,000	1,000	5.8	0.0
C+ / 5.6	11.1	0.95	13.34	87	4	95	0	1	108	101.9	-28.1	60	14	5,000	1,000	0.0	0.0
C+ / 5.6	11.1	0.95	13.74	3,559	4	95	0	1	108	107.1	-27.8	70	14	0	0	0.0	0.0
C+ / 5.6	11.1	0.95	13.76	23	4	95	0	1	108	107.5	-27.8	70	14	2,500,000	0	0.0	0.0
B- / 7.3	5.8	0.99	11.04	17	3	54	41	2	18	45.3	-10.4	32	23	2,000	1,000	5.8	0.0
B- / 7.4	5.8	0.99	10.95	14	3	54	41	2	18	42.3	-10.8	26	23	5,000	1,000	0.0	0.0
B- / 7.3	5.8	1.00	11.07	95	3	54	41	2	18	46.2	-10.3	33	23	0	0	0.0	0.0
E+ / 0.8	14.6	1.02	13.23	10	1	98	0	1	90	90.1	-25.6	37	8	2,000	1,000	5.8	0.0
E / 0.4	14.6	1.02	9.53	6	1	98	0	1	90	85.9	-25.9	29	8	5,000	1,000	0.0	0.0
D- / 1.0	14.6	1.02	14.82	126	1	98	0	1	90	90.8	-25.5	39	8	0	0	0.0	0.0
C / 4.6	14.6	1.02	14.85	6	1	98	0	1	90	91.1	-25.5	40	8	2,500,000	0	0.0	0.0
C- / 4.0	14.0	0.99	15.25	163	0	99	0	1	37	79.7	-20.9	36	21	2,000	1,000	5.8	0.0
C- / 3.9	14.0	0.98	14.31	34	0	99	0	1	37	77.0	-21.1	31	21	5,000	1,000	0.0	0.0
C- / 4.1	14.0	0.99	15.59	1,121	0	99	0	1	37	81.6	-20.8	40	21	0	0	0.0	0.0
C- / 3.0	13.5	0.93	14.82	15	6	93	0	1	96	78.3	-26.0	20	10	2,000	25	0.0	0.0
U /	N/A	N/A	14.14	41	1	98	0	1	9	N/A	N/A	N/A	3	1,000,000	0	0.0	1.0
C+ / 5.8	8.0	0.76	13.20	18	5	78	15	2	99	53.3	-16.0	37	5	2,500	0	5.5	0.0
C+ / 5.8	8.0	0.76	13.03	33	5	78	15	2	99	49.4	-16.3	27	5	2,500	0	0.0	0.0
C+ / 5.7	8.1	0.77	13.11	22	5	78	15	2	99	54.7	-16.0	39	5	1,000,000	0	0.0	0.0
C / 4.9	9.0	0.84	12.75	9	3	89	6	2	113	55.3	-19.0	25	5	2,500	0	5.5	0.0
C / 4.9	9.0	0.84	12.57	16	3	89	6	2	113	51.4	-19.3	17	5	2,500	0	0.0	0.0
C / 4.8	8.9	0.84	12.51	15	3	89	6	2	113	56.5	-18.9	27	5	1,000,000	0	0.0	0.0
C- / 3.4	10.0	0.71	14.66	18	2	97	0	1	85	64.1	-22.1	92	7	2,500	0	5.5	0.0
C- / 3.4	10.0	0.71	14.43	13	2	97	0	1	85	59.9	-22.4	90	7	2,500	0	0.0	0.0
C- / 3.4	10.0	0.71	14.73	15	2	97	0	1	85	65.4	-22.0	92	7	1,000,000	0	0.0	0.0
C- / 3.4	10.0	0.71	14.58	8	2	97	0	1	85	64.2	-22.1	92	7	2,500	0	0.0	0.0
C- / 3.4	9.9	0.71	14.70	27	2	97	0	1	85	65.6	-22.0	92	7	1,000,000	0	0.0	0.0
C+ / 6.1	6.2	0.60	11.79	27	7	60	32	1	98	41.3	-10.6	45	5	2,500	0	5.5	0.0
C+ / 6.1	6.2	0.60	11.74	69	7	60	32	1	98	37.6	-11.0	34	5	2,500	0	0.0	0.0
C+ / 6.1	6.1	0.59	11.78	46	7	60	32	1	98	42.5	-10.6	49	5	1,000,000	0	0.0	0.0
U /	N/A	N/A	12.26	168	0	0	0	100	46	N/A	N/A	N/A	9	5,000,000	100	0.0	2.0
C+ / 6.8	6.5	0.63	12.25	642	0	0	0	100	46	53.7	-13.9	57	9	5,000	100	0.0	2.0
C+ / 6.6	10.9	1.04	18.51	20	11	88	0	1	33	94.1	-13.4	29	5	100,000	100	0.0	0.0
C+ / 6.6	10.9	1.04	18.36	52	11	88	0	1	33	91.9	-13.5	25	5	1,000	100	0.0	0.0
B / 8.4	6.9	0.36	10.57	98	54	45	0	1	59	39.2	-6.2	51	3	100,000	100	0.0	0.0
B / 8.3	6.9	0.36	10.51	14	54	45	0	1	59	N/A	N/A	47	3	1,000	100	0.0	0.0
U /	N/A	N/A	10.04	280	16	0	83	1	61	N/A	N/A	N/A	2	100,000	100	0.0	0.0
U /	N/A	N/A	10.04	385	16	0	83	1	61	N/A	N/A	N/A	2	1,000	100	0.0	0.0
U /	N/A	N/A	13.79	58	0	100	0	0	42	N/A	N/A	N/A	N/A	100,000	100	0.0	0.0
B- / 7.1	10.2	0.97	18.60	1,862	9	90	0	1	24	95.3	-10.4	41	5	100,000	100	0.0	0.0
B- / 7.1	10.2	0.97	18.41	183	9	90	0	1	24	93.8	-10.5	38	5	1,000	100	0.0	0.0
B- / 7.4	10.2	0.99	15.63	18	4	95	0	1	14	68.5	-12.2	10	11	2,500	500	0.0	2.0
B- / 7.2	10.8	1.08	22.92	790	1	98	0	1	26	111.0	-19.9	71	8	100,000	5,000	0.0	0.0
B- / 7.2	10.8	1.08	22.83	224	1	98	0	1	26	109.7	-20.1	68	8	2,500	100	0.0	0.0
U /	N/A	N/A	10.24	211	0	0	0	100	72	N/A	N/A	N/A	1	100,000	5,000	0.0	1.0
B- / 7.5	11.0	0.75	15.14	79	4	95	0	1	136	N/A	N/A	95	4	100,000	5,000	0.0	1.0
C+ / 6.2	7.1	0.43	18.90	556	73	26	0	1	65	31.7	-4.2	71	18	100,000	5,000	0.0	2.0
C+ / 6.0	7.1	0.43	17.67	132	73	26	0	1	65	30.6	-4.2	68	18	2,500	100	0.0	2.0
B / 8.8	6.1	0.57	15.37	6,139	54	45	0	1	57	57.2	-10.5	79	5	100,000	5,000	0.0	1.0
B / 8.8	6.1	0.56	15.20	251	54	45	0	1	57	55.9	-10.5	77	5	2,500	100	0.0	1.0
C+ / 6.7	12.2	0.88	23.09	151	2	97	0	1	16	101.6	-23.5	84	17	100,000	5,000	0.0	1.0

99 Pct = Best
0 Pct = Worst

Fund Type	Fund Name	Ticker Symbol	Overall Investment Rating	Phone	Performance Rating/Pts	3 Mo	6 Mo	1Yr / Pct	3Yr / Pct	5Yr / Pct	Dividend Yield	Expense Ratio
								Total Return % through 3/31/15	Annualized		Incl. in Returns	
SC	Robeco Boston Ptrs Sm/Cp Val II Inv	BPSCX	B+	(888) 261-4073	B / 7.8	3.30	9.99	6.02 /47	16.12 /84	13.00 /68	0.46	1.48
GR	Robeco WPG Small/Micro Cap Val	WPGTX	D	(888) 261-4073	C / 5.2	1.82	4.04	-2.54 / 9	13.91 /66	11.73 /59	0.65	1.35
GL	Roge Partners	ROGEX	C-	(888) 800-7643	C- / 4.1	1.06	3.92	4.45 /35	10.30 /41	8.45 /33	0.90	2.18
GR	Roosevelt Multi-Cap Inst	BULRX	U	(877) 322-0576	U /	2.73	4.37	8.80 /68	--	--	0.51	1.00
GR	Roosevelt Multi-Cap Investor	BULLX	D+	(877) 322-0576	C / 4.7	2.70	4.22	8.51 /66	10.62 /43	9.58 /41	0.25	1.25
GL	Rothschild Larch Lane Alt Inst	RLLIX	U	(866) 777-7818	U /	7.82	13.57	--	--	--	0.00	4.34
GI	Roumell Opportunistic Value A	RAMVX	E	(800) 773-3863	E / 0.5	-3.50	-4.60	-8.93 / 3	3.36 / 9	--	2.31	1.84
GI	Roumell Opportunistic Value Inst	RAMSX	E	(800) 773-3863	E+ / 0.6	-3.36	-4.59	-8.81 / 3	3.52 / 9	--	2.36	1.59
SC	Roxbury/Hood River Sm-Cap Gr Inst	RSCIX	A	(800) 336-9970	A+ / 9.8	8.02	17.59	16.85 /94	21.31 /98	17.68 /97	0.00	1.49
GR	Roxbury/Mar Vista Strategic Growth	RMSIX	A+	(800) 227-6681	B+ / 8.6	2.40	8.09	15.14 /92	16.19 /85	--	0.37	2.80
GR	Royce 100 Inv	ROHHX	E	(800) 221-4268	D+ / 2.3	0.57	3.98	-2.78 / 9	8.12 /28	9.40 /40	0.00	1.21
GR	Royce 100 K	ROHKX	E+	(800) 221-4268	D / 2.2	0.44	3.90	-3.13 / 8	7.69 /25	8.94 /36	0.00	1.79
GR	Royce 100 R	ROHRX	E+	(800) 221-4268	D / 2.1	0.45	3.78	-3.33 / 8	7.43 /24	8.66 /34	0.00	2.29
GR	Royce 100 Svc	RYOHX	E	(800) 221-4268	D / 2.1	0.46	3.90	-3.01 / 9	7.82 /26	9.09 /37	0.00	1.51
IN	Royce Dividend Value Instl	RDIIX	U	(800) 221-4268	U /	1.11	3.57	-0.84 /13	--	--	1.62	1.15
GR	Royce Dividend Value Inv	RDVIX	D+	(800) 221-4268	C- / 3.8	1.05	3.46	-0.99 /13	10.82 /44	11.82 /59	1.35	1.25
GR	Royce Dividend Value Svc	RYDVX	D+	(800) 221-4268	C- / 3.7	1.10	3.39	-1.23 /12	10.56 /43	11.56 /57	0.85	1.52
GR	● Royce Enterprise Select Inv	RMISX	C-	(800) 221-4268	C / 5.5	1.84	7.07	5.33 /41	12.63 /57	12.16 /62	0.00	3.08
FO	Royce Euro Smaller Company Fd Ser	RISCX	E	(800) 221-4268	E+ / 0.7	4.74	-3.94	-14.21 / 2	4.78 /12	6.74 /21	1.16	2.27
GR	Royce Financial Services Svc	RYFSX	B	(800) 221-4268	B / 7.7	2.69	7.01	4.62 /36	16.42 /86	12.94 /68	0.66	1.97
GL	● Royce Global Dividend Value Fd Ser	RGVDX	E+	(800) 221-4268	E+ / 0.8	0.40	-4.62	-7.78 / 3	4.79 /12	--	1.77	2.99
FO	Royce Global Value Fd Consultant	RGVHX	E	(800) 221-4268	E / 0.4	2.16	-3.97	-8.19 / 3	-0.54 / 4	--	1.17	2.54
GL	Royce Global Value Fd Investment	RGVIX	E	(800) 221-4268	E / 0.4	2.38	-3.45	-7.26 / 4	0.49 / 5	--	2.09	1.50
GL	Royce Global Value Fd K	RGVKX	D-	(800) 221-4268	E / 0.4	2.37	-3.70	-7.53 / 4	0.14 / 4	--	2.67	19.22
GL	Royce Global Value Fd R	RGVRX	D-	(800) 221-4268	E / 0.4	2.26	-3.79	-7.79 / 3	-0.09 / 4	--	2.49	9.51
GL	Royce Global Value Fd Ser	RIVFX	E	(800) 221-4268	E / 0.4	2.37	-3.67	-7.52 / 4	0.22 / 4	3.96 / 8	1.84	1.84
GR	Royce Heritage Cons	RYGCX	E+	(800) 221-4268	D+ / 2.3	1.05	4.58	-1.31 /12	7.45 /24	8.62 /34	0.00	2.41
GR	Royce Heritage Inv	RHFHX	D-	(800) 221-4268	D+ / 2.9	1.25	5.09	-0.19 /15	8.78 /32	9.93 /44	0.31	1.17
GR	Royce Heritage K	RHFKX	E+	(800) 221-4268	D+ / 2.8	1.21	4.90	-0.63 /14	8.30 /29	9.44 /40	0.00	1.74
GR	Royce Heritage R	RHFRX	E+	(800) 221-4268	D+ / 2.6	1.13	4.75	-0.90 /13	8.02 /27	9.18 /38	0.00	1.94
GR	Royce Heritage Svc	RGFAX	D-	(800) 221-4268	D+ / 2.7	1.19	4.96	-0.45 /14	8.46 /30	9.64 /42	0.00	1.49
FO	Royce International Premier Fd Svc	RYIPX	D-	(800) 221-4268	D / 1.7	5.35	-0.58	-4.13 / 7	7.14 /22	--	1.05	2.82
FO	Royce Intl Micro-Cap Svc	ROIMX	D-	(800) 221-4268	E+ / 0.9	1.76	-5.01	-3.54 / 8	5.08 /13	--	1.41	3.88
FO	Royce Intl Smaller-Companies Svc	RYGSX	E	(800) 221-4268	E / 0.5	-0.51	-6.90	-9.79 / 3	2.95 / 8	4.22 / 9	1.96	2.08
SC	Royce Low Priced Stock I	RLPIX	E-	(800) 221-4268	E+ / 0.6	0.63	-0.93	-4.43 / 6	1.23 / 5	4.59 /11	0.29	1.08
SC	Royce Low Priced Stock Inv	RLPHX	E-	(800) 221-4268	E / 0.5	0.53	-1.19	-4.67 / 6	1.12 / 5	4.50 /10	0.07	1.23
SC	Royce Low Priced Stock K	RLPKX	E-	(800) 221-4268	E / 0.5	0.68	-1.18	-4.83 / 6	0.81 / 5	4.16 / 9	0.00	1.78
SC	Royce Low Priced Stock R	RLPRX	E-	(800) 221-4268	E / 0.5	0.44	-1.43	-5.22 / 5	0.52 / 5	3.88 / 8	0.00	2.07
SC	Royce Low Priced Stock Svc	RYLPX	E-	(800) 221-4268	E / 0.5	0.53	-1.19	-4.81 / 6	0.91 / 5	4.26 / 9	0.00	1.51
SC	Royce Micro-Cap Cons	RYMCX	E	(800) 221-4268	E+ / 0.7	-0.57	4.61	-4.65 / 6	2.66 / 7	5.40 /14	0.00	2.55
SC	Royce Micro-Cap Discovery Svc	RYDFX	D	(800) 221-4268	C- / 3.9	2.83	12.68	3.37 /28	9.29 /35	9.98 /44	0.00	2.50
SC	Royce Micro-Cap Inv	RYOTX	E	(800) 221-4268	E+ / 0.9	-0.28	5.20	-3.64 / 8	3.72 / 9	6.45 /20	0.00	1.56
SC	Royce Micro-Cap Port Inv	RCMCX	E+	(800) 221-4268	D- / 1.0	-0.18	5.10	-2.99 / 9	3.84 /10	6.39 /19	0.00	1.34
SC	Royce Micro-Cap Port Svc	RCMSX	E+	(800) 221-4268	E+ / 0.9	-0.27	4.89	-3.26 / 8	3.58 / 9	6.17 /18	0.00	1.62
SC	Royce Micro-Cap Svc	RMCFX	E	(800) 221-4268	E+ / 0.9	-0.28	5.12	-3.81 / 7	3.61 / 9	6.31 /19	0.00	1.77
SC	Royce Opportunity Fd Cons	ROFCX	D	(800) 221-4268	C / 5.3	0.85	6.77	-3.86 / 7	13.33 /62	11.51 /57	0.00	2.32
SC	Royce Opportunity Fd Inst	ROFIX	C-	(800) 221-4268	C+ / 6.2	1.17	7.47	-2.65 / 9	14.80 /73	12.93 /68	0.00	1.04
SC	Royce Opportunity Fd Inv	RYPNX	D+	(800) 221-4268	C+ / 5.9	1.11	7.33	-2.81 / 9	14.66 /72	12.81 /66	0.00	1.17
SC	Royce Opportunity Fd K	ROFKX	D	(800) 221-4268	C+ / 5.8	0.95	7.07	-3.28 / 8	14.22 /69	12.36 /63	0.00	1.47
SC	Royce Opportunity Fd R	ROFRX	D+	(800) 221-4268	C+ / 5.6	0.96	6.94	-3.45 / 8	13.91 /66	12.05 /61	0.00	1.83
SC	Royce Opportunity Fd Svc	RYOFX	D+	(800) 221-4268	C+ / 5.7	1.02	7.31	-3.05 / 9	14.30 /69	12.46 /64	0.00	1.48
GR	Royce Opportunity Select Fd Inv	ROSFX	C+	(800) 221-4268	B / 8.1	5.08	8.26	-5.71 / 5	18.23 /95	--	0.00	1.78

● Denotes fund is closed to new investors
* Denotes fund is included in Section II

www.thestreetratings.com

RISK			NET ASSETS		ASSET					BULL / BEAR		FUND MANAGER		MINIMUMS		LOADS	
	3 Year		NAV						Portfolio	Last Bull	Last Bear	Manager	Manager	Initial	Additional	Front	Back
Risk Rating/Pts	Standard Deviation	Beta	As of 3/31/15	Total $(Mil)	Cash %	Stocks %	Bonds %	Other %	Turnover Ratio	Market Return	Market Return	Quality Pct	Tenure (Years)	Purch. $	Purch. $	End Load	End Load
C+ / 6.7	12.2	0.88	22.22	131	2	97	0	1	16	99.9	-23.7	82	17	2,500	100	0.0	1.0
C- / 3.6	13.7	1.18	17.30	42	4	95	0	1	75	92.9	-29.0	12	16	100,000	5,000	0.0	2.0
C+ / 6.4	8.6	0.56	13.40	21	1	80	18	1	103	53.8	-15.6	93	11	5,000	100	0.0	0.0
U /	N/A	N/A	17.30	75	5	94	0	1	87	N/A	N/A	N/A	14	100,000	0	0.0	0.0
C / 4.4	10.1	0.90	17.14	66	5	94	0	1	87	67.0	-17.0	21	14	1,000	500	0.0	0.0
U /	N/A	N/A	11.30	58	0	0	0	100	0	N/A	N/A	N/A	1	10,000	0	0.0	0.0
C- / 3.7	10.7	0.53	8.27	2	24	58	15	3	93	18.7	-13.2	12	5	2,500	100	4.5	1.0
C- / 3.7	10.6	0.53	8.33	40	24	58	15	3	93	19.3	-13.1	13	5	25,000	1,000	0.0	1.0
C+ / 5.7	12.8	0.88	33.42	83	1	98	0	1	115	131.6	-25.3	95	8	25,000	0	0.0	1.0
B- / 7.2	9.3	0.94	15.39	20	7	92	0	1	31	N/A	N/A	77	4	25,000	0	0.0	0.8
D+ / 2.9	13.5	1.15	8.79	65	9	90	0	1	31	65.2	-27.0	2	12	100,000	50	0.0	1.0
C- / 3.9	13.6	1.16	11.39	1	9	90	0	1	31	62.9	-27.2	2	12	0	0	0.0	1.0
C- / 3.8	13.6	1.16	11.19	2	9	90	0	1	31	61.4	-27.2	2	12	0	0	0.0	1.0
D+ / 2.9	13.6	1.15	8.69	138	9	90	0	1	31	63.5	-27.0	2	12	2,000	50	0.0	1.0
U /	N/A	N/A	8.14	41	8	91	0	1	36	N/A	N/A	N/A	11	1,000,000	0	0.0	0.0
C+ / 5.8	11.8	1.12	8.17	164	8	91	0	1	36	73.4	-21.9	6	11	100,000	50	0.0	1.0
C+ / 5.9	11.8	1.11	8.28	271	8	91	0	1	36	71.9	-22.1	5	11	2,000	50	0.0	1.0
C / 4.5	9.4	0.84	10.59	3	28	69	1	2	154	82.8	-19.3	56	8	2,000	50	0.0	1.0
C / 4.5	14.8	0.97	10.82	19	7	92	0	1	53	34.6	-27.8	15	9	2,000	50	0.0	2.0
C+ / 6.2	11.9	1.12	9.53	51	2	97	0	1	23	96.0	-23.5	45	12	2,000	50	0.0	1.0
C / 5.5	12.0	0.83	9.96	7	3	96	0	1	82	38.7	-21.6	27	4	2,000	50	0.0	2.0
C / 5.2	13.5	0.88	12.79	18	3	96	0	1	41	12.3	N/A	3	6	2,000	50	0.0	0.0
C / 5.2	13.4	0.87	12.88	36	3	96	0	1	41	16.3	-24.7	4	6	100,000	50	0.0	2.0
C+ / 6.7	13.5	0.88	9.52	N/A	3	96	0	1	41	N/A	N/A	3	6	0	0	0.0	0.0
C+ / 6.7	13.4	0.87	9.51	N/A	3	96	0	1	41	N/A	N/A	3	6	0	0	0.0	0.0
C / 5.2	13.4	0.88	12.95	27	3	96	0	1	41	15.3	-24.7	3	6	2,000	50	0.0	2.0
C- / 4.0	12.3	1.10	11.59	13	10	89	0	1	79	55.9	-27.1	2	20	2,000	50	0.0	0.0
C / 4.9	12.3	1.10	15.40	167	10	89	0	1	79	62.5	-26.7	3	20	100,000	50	0.0	1.0
C- / 3.9	12.3	1.10	10.83	6	10	89	0	1	79	59.9	-26.8	3	20	0	0	0.0	0.0
C- / 3.8	12.3	1.10	10.72	3	10	89	0	1	79	58.6	-27.0	2	20	0	0	0.0	0.0
C / 5.0	12.3	1.10	15.35	165	10	89	0	1	79	60.9	-26.8	3	20	2,000	50	0.0	1.0
C+ / 5.9	10.8	0.74	10.83	4	2	97	0	1	51	44.0	-21.8	69	4	2,000	50	0.0	2.0
C+ / 6.5	11.3	0.69	9.83	7	6	92	0	2	103	33.7	-26.5	47	4	2,000	50	0.0	2.0
C- / 3.8	12.0	0.84	9.75	30	4	95	0	1	64	27.7	-24.9	12	6	2,000	50	0.0	2.0
D- / 1.0	14.7	0.92	9.52	74	10	89	0	1	16	25.6	-27.3	1	2	1,000,000	0	0.0	0.0
D- / 1.0	14.7	0.92	9.51	47	10	89	0	1	16	25.4	-27.3	1	2	100,000	50	0.0	1.0
D- / 1.0	14.7	0.92	2.97	2	10	89	0	1	16	24.0	-27.4	1	2	0	0	0.0	0.0
D- / 1.0	14.6	0.92	9.12	2	10	89	0	1	16	22.8	-27.5	1	2	0	0	0.0	0.0
D- / 1.0	14.7	0.92	9.51	488	10	89	0	1	16	24.4	-27.4	1	2	2,000	50	0.0	1.0
C- / 3.3	14.3	1.00	12.16	68	8	91	0	1	22	32.3	-27.3	1	11	2,000	50	0.0	0.0
C / 5.0	15.2	1.05	6.18	6	11	88	0	1	81	60.6	-19.4	4	12	2,000	50	0.0	1.0
C- / 3.9	14.3	1.00	14.43	388	8	91	0	1	22	36.8	-27.1	1	11	2,000	50	0.0	1.0
C / 4.9	13.7	0.96	11.35	467	11	88	0	1	30	37.0	-27.0	2	5	0	0	0.0	0.0
C / 4.9	13.7	0.96	11.20	27	11	88	0	1	30	35.9	-27.1	1	5	0	0	0.0	0.0
C- / 3.8	14.3	1.00	14.22	37	8	91	0	1	22	36.3	-27.1	1	11	2,000	50	0.0	1.0
C- / 3.2	14.7	1.05	11.89	23	19	80	0	1	39	99.8	-31.8	22	17	2,000	50	0.0	0.0
C- / 3.9	14.7	1.05	13.80	801	19	80	0	1	39	108.6	-31.4	38	17	1,000,000	0	0.0	0.0
C- / 3.9	14.7	1.05	13.61	1,234	19	80	0	1	39	108.1	-31.5	36	17	2,000	50	0.0	0.0
C- / 3.2	14.7	1.05	11.68	21	19	80	0	1	39	105.2	-31.6	30	17	0	0	0.0	0.0
C- / 3.5	14.7	1.05	12.68	34	19	80	0	1	39	103.1	-31.7	27	17	0	0	0.0	0.0
C- / 3.6	14.7	1.05	12.93	149	19	80	0	1	39	105.6	-31.6	31	17	2,000	50	0.0	1.0
C / 4.7	15.6	1.19	17.36	18	7	92	0	1	129	118.6	-32.5	52	5	2,000	50	0.0	1.0

99 Pct = Best
0 Pct = Worst

Fund Type	Fund Name	Ticker Symbol	Overall Investment Rating	Phone	Performance Rating/Pts	3 Mo	6 Mo	1Yr / Pct	3Yr / Pct	5Yr / Pct	Dividend Yield	Expense Ratio
SC	Royce PA Mutual Fd Cons	RYPCX	D	(800) 221-4268	C- / 3.9	0.90	5.95	-0.84 /13	10.41 /42	10.52 /49	0.00	1.95
SC	Royce PA Mutual Fd Inst	RPMIX	D+	(800) 221-4268	C / 4.7	1.15	6.56	0.23 /16	11.67 /50	--	0.45	0.80
SC	Royce PA Mutual Fd Inv	PENNX	D+	(800) 221-4268	C / 4.5	1.15	6.52	0.11 /16	11.57 /50	11.64 /58	0.32	0.93
SC	Royce PA Mutual Fd K	RPMKX	D	(800) 221-4268	C / 4.3	0.97	6.15	-0.43 /14	11.05 /46	11.04 /53	0.00	1.38
SC	Royce PA Mutual Fd R	RPMRX	D	(800) 221-4268	C- / 4.2	1.04	6.23	-0.39 /15	10.92 /45	10.97 /52	0.00	1.57
SC	Royce PA Mutual Fd Svc	RYPFX	D	(800) 221-4268	C- / 4.2	1.08	6.33	-0.24 /15	11.20 /47	11.33 /55	0.00	1.26
GR	● Royce Partners Fund Ser	RPTRX	E+	(800) 221-4268	C- / 4.1	0.91	2.76	-0.22 /15	11.34 /48	10.40 /48	0.39	3.97
SC	Royce Premier Cons	RPRCX	E+	(800) 221-4268	D+ / 2.5	2.46	3.24	-0.97 /13	7.93 /27	10.12 /46	0.00	2.13
SC	Royce Premier Fd	RYPRX	D-	(800) 221-4268	C- / 3.1	2.64	3.67	-0.01 /16	9.06 /33	11.23 /55	0.37	1.09
SC	Royce Premier Inst	RPFIX	D-	(800) 221-4268	C- / 3.3	2.66	3.76	0.10 /16	9.16 /34	11.34 /56	0.47	0.98
SC	Royce Premier K	RPRKX	E	(800) 221-4268	D+ / 2.9	2.60	3.38	-0.67 /14	8.51 /30	10.68 /50	0.57	1.59
SC	Royce Premier R	RPRRX	E+	(800) 221-4268	D+ / 2.8	2.50	3.41	-0.61 /14	8.37 /29	10.53 /49	0.00	1.74
SC	Royce Premier Svc	RPFFX	D-	(800) 221-4268	D+ / 2.9	2.59	3.64	-0.26 /15	8.75 /31	10.93 /52	0.00	1.38
SC	Royce Premier W	RPRWX	D-	(800) 221-4268	C- / 3.2	2.68	3.73	0.01 /16	9.06 /33	11.26 /55	0.38	1.09
GR	● Royce Select Fund II Investment	RSFDX	E	(800) 221-4268	D- / 1.3	-1.51	-3.62	-6.04 / 4	7.32 /23	6.75 /22	2.04	3.30
GR	Royce Select I Investment	RYSFX	E+	(800) 221-4268	D+ / 2.5	0.23	2.55	-3.65 / 8	8.87 /32	9.06 /37	0.00	1.20
SC	Royce Small-Cap Port Inv	RCPFX	C	(800) 221-4268	C+ / 6.1	3.00	11.47	5.58 /43	12.90 /59	12.13 /62	0.12	1.05
SC	Royce Small-Cap Port Svc	RCSSX	C	(800) 221-4268	C+ / 6.0	2.97	11.33	5.30 /41	12.62 /57	11.86 /60	0.00	1.31
MC	● Royce SMid Cap Value Fd Svc	RMVSX	D-	(800) 221-4268	D / 1.6	2.40	-2.32	-6.02 / 4	7.42 /24	8.25 /32	0.39	2.20
SC	Royce Special Equity Cons	RSQCX	D+	(800) 221-4268	C / 4.6	2.21	10.65	3.26 /28	10.54 /43	10.31 /47	0.00	2.17
SC	Royce Special Equity Inst	RSEIX	C-	(800) 221-4268	C / 5.4	2.47	11.27	4.42 /35	11.81 /51	11.57 /58	0.58	1.01
SC	Royce Special Equity Inv	RYSEX	C-	(800) 221-4268	C / 5.2	2.41	11.21	4.32 /34	11.68 /50	11.45 /56	0.47	1.13
GR	Royce Special Equity Multi-Cap Inst	RMUIX	U	(800) 221-4268	U /	-0.45	3.86	8.42 /66	--	--	0.73	0.95
GR	Royce Special Equity Multi-Cap Inv	RSMCX	B-	(800) 221-4268	C+ / 6.2	-0.45	3.82	8.32 /65	14.10 /68	--	0.69	1.01
GR	Royce Special Equity Multi-Cap Svc	RSEMX	B-	(800) 221-4268	C+ / 6.0	-0.58	3.60	8.00 /63	13.80 /66	--	0.43	1.46
SC	Royce Special Equity Svc	RSEFX	C-	(800) 221-4268	C / 4.9	2.37	11.05	4.01 /32	11.39 /48	11.17 /54	0.18	1.45
GI	Royce Total Return Cons	RYTCX	C-	(800) 221-4268	C / 4.8	1.53	6.84	1.54 /20	11.72 /51	11.12 /54	0.27	2.20
GI	Royce Total Return Fd	RYTRX	C-	(800) 221-4268	C / 5.4	1.77	7.33	2.57 /24	12.90 /59	12.12 /61	1.86	1.18
GI	Royce Total Return Inst	RTRIX	C-	(800) 221-4268	C+ / 5.7	1.78	7.40	2.73 /25	13.01 /60	12.25 /62	2.06	1.05
GI	Royce Total Return K	RTRKX	D+	(800) 221-4268	C / 5.4	1.73	7.27	2.26 /23	12.52 /56	11.77 /59	1.34	1.55
GI	Royce Total Return R	RTRRX	C-	(800) 221-4268	C / 5.2	1.66	7.09	2.01 /22	12.20 /54	11.46 /57	0.88	1.80
GI	Royce Total Return Svc	RYTFX	C-	(800) 221-4268	C / 5.2	1.71	7.37	2.34 /23	12.57 /56	11.81 /59	0.99	1.53
GI	Royce Total Return W	RTRWX	C-	(800) 221-4268	C+ / 5.6	1.77	7.35	2.59 /24	12.88 /59	12.15 /62	1.87	1.20
SC	Royce Value Fd Cons	RVFCX	D-	(800) 221-4268	C- / 3.1	3.22	5.45	1.49 /20	8.45 /30	8.94 /36	0.00	2.29
SC	Royce Value Fd Inst	RVFIX	D	(800) 221-4268	C- / 4.0	3.47	5.95	2.62 /25	9.75 /38	10.24 /46	0.37	1.05
SC	Royce Value Fd Inv	RVVHX	D-	(800) 221-4268	C- / 3.7	3.39	5.94	2.45 /24	9.58 /37	10.09 /45	0.22	1.21
SC	Royce Value Fd K	RVFKX	E+	(800) 221-4268	C- / 3.5	3.26	5.61	1.88 /21	9.09 /34	9.64 /42	0.00	1.62
SC	Royce Value Fd R	RVVRX	D-	(800) 221-4268	C- / 3.4	3.24	5.61	1.81 /21	8.90 /32	9.43 /40	0.00	1.83
SC	Royce Value Fd Svc	RYVFX	D-	(800) 221-4268	C- / 3.5	3.32	5.81	2.23 /23	9.31 /35	9.80 /43	0.00	1.48
SC	Royce Value Plus Fd Cons	RVPCX	D	(800) 221-4268	C+ / 5.7	4.57	11.46	4.37 /34	12.04 /53	10.31 /47	0.00	2.37
SC	Royce Value Plus Fd Inst	RVPIX	D+	(800) 221-4268	C+ / 6.6	4.91	12.07	5.61 /43	13.49 /63	11.67 /58	0.00	1.08
SC	Royce Value Plus Fd Inv	RVPHX	D+	(800) 221-4268	C+ / 6.2	4.81	11.93	5.33 /41	13.18 /61	11.45 /56	0.00	1.38
SC	Royce Value Plus Fd K	RVPKX	D-	(800) 221-4268	C+ / 6.2	4.75	11.77	5.08 /39	12.87 /59	11.08 /53	0.00	2.63
SC	Royce Value Plus Fd R	RVPRX	D	(800) 221-4268	C+ / 6.0	4.69	11.64	4.80 /37	12.58 /57	10.78 /51	0.00	2.42
SC	Royce Value Plus Fd Svc	RYVPX	D	(800) 221-4268	C+ / 6.1	4.78	11.90	5.25 /40	13.05 /60	11.24 /55	0.00	1.49
FO	RS China A	RSCHX	C+	(800) 766-3863	C+ / 6.8	7.25	12.98	20.96 /97	11.34 /48	--	0.94	2.05
FO	RS China C	RCHCX	B-	(800) 766-3863	B- / 7.2	7.18	12.62	20.13 /97	10.62 /43	--	0.47	2.82
FO	RS China K	RCHKX	B	(800) 766-3863	B- / 7.4	7.17	12.67	20.40 /97	10.97 /45	--	0.80	2.46
FO	RS China Y	RCHYX	B+	(800) 766-3863	B / 8.0	7.35	13.09	21.42 /97	11.70 /50	--	1.42	1.73
EM	RS Emerging Markets Fund A	GBEMX	E-	(800) 766-3863	E / 0.3	1.92	-2.35	0.81 /18	-3.32 / 2	-0.42 / 2	0.84	1.67
EM	RS Emerging Markets Fund C	REMGX	E-	(800) 766-3863	E / 0.3	1.64	-2.74	-0.02 /15	-4.09 / 2	-1.19 / 2	0.51	2.45
EM	RS Emerging Markets Fund K	REMKX	E-	(800) 766-3863	E / 0.3	1.84	-2.47	0.52 /17	-3.59 / 2	-0.74 / 2	0.88	1.92

● Denotes fund is closed to new investors
* Denotes fund is included in Section II

www.thestreetratings.com

RISK			NET ASSETS		ASSET					BULL / BEAR		FUND MANAGER		MINIMUMS		LOADS	
Risk Rating/Pts	3 Year		NAV As of 3/31/15	Total $(Mil)	Cash %	Stocks %	Bonds %	Other %	Portfolio Turnover Ratio	Last Bull Market Return	Last Bear Market Return	Manager Quality Pct	Manager Tenure (Years)	Initial Purch. $	Additional Purch. $	Front End Load	Back End Load
	Standard Deviation	Beta															
C- / 4.2	13.1	0.94	11.26	653	2	97	0	1	26	68.3	-24.5	15	43	2,000	50	0.0	0.0
C / 4.7	13.1	0.94	13.17	797	2	97	0	1	26	75.0	N/A	24	43	1,000,000	0	0.0	0.0
C / 4.7	13.1	0.94	13.15	3,579	2	97	0	1	26	74.4	-24.2	23	43	2,000	50	0.0	1.0
C / 4.3	13.1	0.94	11.41	11	2	97	0	1	26	71.6	-24.4	19	43	0	0	0.0	0.0
C / 4.6	13.1	0.93	12.63	35	2	97	0	1	26	70.7	-24.4	18	43	0	0	0.0	0.0
C / 4.7	13.1	0.94	13.10	307	2	97	0	1	26	72.5	-24.3	20	43	2,000	50	0.0	1.0
D+ / 2.3	11.2	1.03	10.86	3	18	81	0	1	53	76.0	-25.2	12	8	2,000	50	0.0	1.0
C- / 3.7	13.0	0.86	17.51	55	5	94	0	1	11	54.9	-21.9	9	23	2,000	50	0.0	0.0
C- / 4.1	13.0	0.86	20.24	3,803	5	94	0	1	11	60.4	-21.6	14	23	2,000	50	0.0	1.0
C- / 4.1	13.0	0.86	20.45	568	5	94	0	1	11	61.0	-21.5	15	23	1,000,000	0	0.0	0.0
D- / 1.1	13.0	0.86	5.91	6	5	94	0	1	11	57.7	-21.7	11	23	0	0	0.0	0.0
C- / 4.0	13.0	0.86	19.29	26	5	94	0	1	11	57.0	-21.7	11	23	0	0	0.0	0.0
C- / 4.1	13.0	0.86	19.83	150	5	94	0	1	11	58.9	-21.7	13	23	2,000	50	0.0	1.0
C- / 4.1	13.0	0.86	20.29	421	5	94	0	1	11	60.4	-21.5	14	23	1,000,000	0	0.0	0.0
C- / 3.3	11.3	0.96	9.81	5	5	94	0	1	159	59.7	-29.2	4	10	2,000	50	0.0	2.0
C- / 3.8	12.9	1.10	17.31	27	9	90	0	1	56	64.7	-24.0	3	17	2,000	50	0.0	1.0
C / 5.2	13.8	0.97	13.03	565	3	96	0	1	43	73.6	-19.3	31	12	0	0	0.0	0.0
C / 5.1	13.8	0.97	12.81	220	3	96	0	1	43	72.1	-19.4	29	12	0	0	0.0	0.0
C / 5.5	13.2	1.01	14.35	14	3	96	0	1	31	55.8	-26.6	2	12	2,000	50	0.0	1.0
C / 4.9	12.4	0.87	21.74	62	5	94	0	1	28	66.7	-18.4	24	17	2,000	50	0.0	0.0
C / 5.1	12.4	0.87	23.27	640	5	94	0	1	28	73.4	-18.0	38	17	1,000,000	0	0.0	0.0
C / 5.2	12.4	0.87	23.41	1,811	5	94	0	1	28	72.7	-18.0	37	17	2,000	50	0.0	0.0
U /	N/A	N/A	15.49	78	8	91	0	1	44	N/A	N/A	N/A	4	1,000,000	0	0.0	0.0
B- / 7.5	11.2	1.08	15.48	125	8	91	0	1	44	N/A	N/A	26	4	100,000	50	0.0	1.0
B- / 7.0	11.2	1.08	15.51	92	8	91	0	1	44	84.8	-12.1	24	4	2,000	50	0.0	1.0
C / 5.2	12.4	0.87	23.35	207	5	94	0	1	28	71.3	-18.1	33	17	2,000	50	0.0	1.0
C / 5.1	11.3	1.04	15.27	350	8	91	0	1	21	69.1	-19.4	13	22	2,000	50	0.0	0.0
C / 4.9	11.3	1.04	14.95	2,965	8	91	0	1	21	75.2	-19.5	20	22	2,000	50	0.0	1.0
C / 4.8	11.3	1.04	14.82	565	8	91	0	1	21	75.7	-19.4	22	22	1,000,000	0	0.0	0.0
C- / 3.8	11.3	1.04	10.87	96	8	91	0	1	21	73.1	-19.6	18	22	0	0	0.0	0.0
C / 5.1	11.3	1.04	15.29	66	8	91	0	1	21	71.6	-19.7	15	22	0	0	0.0	0.0
C / 5.1	11.4	1.04	15.20	222	8	91	0	1	21	73.4	-19.6	18	22	2,000	50	0.0	1.0
C / 4.9	11.3	1.04	14.93	260	8	91	0	1	21	75.0	-19.4	21	22	1,000,000	0	0.0	0.0
C- / 3.9	14.0	0.92	11.21	26	3	96	0	1	51	54.2	-26.2	7	13	2,000	50	0.0	0.0
C- / 4.2	14.0	0.92	12.22	192	3	96	0	1	51	60.6	-25.8	13	13	1,000,000	0	0.0	0.0
C / 4.3	14.0	0.92	12.21	133	3	96	0	1	51	60.0	-25.8	11	13	100,000	50	0.0	1.0
C- / 3.2	14.0	0.93	9.19	9	3	96	0	1	51	57.7	-26.0	9	13	0	0	0.0	0.0
C- / 4.1	14.0	0.92	11.80	28	3	96	0	1	51	56.5	-26.1	8	13	0	0	0.0	0.0
C / 4.3	14.0	0.93	12.15	443	3	96	0	1	51	58.4	-25.9	10	13	2,000	50	0.0	1.0
D+ / 2.5	14.5	1.03	13.72	17	6	93	0	1	45	78.8	-26.6	15	13	2,000	50	0.0	0.0
C- / 3.0	14.4	1.03	15.17	39	6	93	0	1	45	86.8	-26.3	26	13	1,000,000	0	0.0	0.0
C- / 3.0	14.5	1.03	15.05	302	6	93	0	1	45	85.2	-26.3	23	13	100,000	50	0.0	1.0
E+ / 0.9	14.5	1.03	9.48	1	6	93	0	1	45	83.5	-26.4	20	13	0	0	0.0	0.0
D+ / 2.7	14.5	1.04	14.28	1	6	93	0	1	45	82.0	-26.5	18	13	0	0	0.0	0.0
D+ / 2.9	14.5	1.03	14.91	567	6	93	0	1	45	84.4	-26.4	22	13	2,000	50	0.0	1.0
C+ / 6.1	13.1	0.67	11.69	12	1	98	0	1	200	67.7	N/A	93	2	2,500	100	4.8	0.0
C+ / 6.1	13.2	0.68	11.64	5	1	98	0	1	200	63.3	N/A	91	2	2,500	100	0.0	0.0
C+ / 6.1	13.2	0.68	11.66	5	1	98	0	1	200	65.3	N/A	92	2	1,000	0	0.0	0.0
C+ / 6.1	13.1	0.67	11.69	6	1	98	0	1	200	69.8	N/A	93	2	0	100	0.0	0.0
D / 2.0	14.3	1.01	17.55	113	1	98	0	1	224	16.4	-27.9	16	2	2,500	100	4.8	0.0
D / 1.6	14.2	1.01	13.65	20	1	98	0	1	224	13.3	-28.1	11	2	2,500	100	0.0	0.0
D / 1.9	14.2	1.01	16.61	25	1	98	0	1	224	15.3	-28.0	14	2	1,000	0	0.0	0.0

					PERFORMANCE						Incl. in Returns	
99 Pct = Best 0 Pct = Worst			Overall		Perfor-	Total Return % through 3/31/15						
			Investment		mance				Annualized		Dividend	Expense
Fund Type	Fund Name	Ticker Symbol	Rating	Phone	Rating/Pts	3 Mo	6 Mo	1Yr / Pct	3Yr / Pct	5Yr / Pct	Yield	Ratio
EM	RS Emerging Markets Fund Y	RSENX	E-	(800) 766-3863	E / 0.3	1.97	-2.18	1.13 / 19	-2.98 / 2	-0.11 / 2	1.45	1.33
GL	RS Global A	RSGGX	C	(800) 766-3863	C+ / 5.8	4.58	5.00	8.57 / 67	13.75 / 65	--	0.62	1.68
GL	RS Global C	RGGCX	C+	(800) 766-3863	C+ / 6.0	4.37	4.60	7.76 / 61	12.97 / 59	--	0.00	2.43
GL	RS Global K	RGGKX	C+	(800) 766-3863	C+ / 6.3	4.52	4.89	8.12 / 64	13.39 / 63	--	0.21	2.07
EN	RS Global Natural Resources Fund A	RSNRX	E-	(800) 766-3863	E- / 0.1	-3.14	-23.45	-27.54 / 0	-8.70 / 1	-2.13 / 2	0.05	1.46
EN	RS Global Natural Resources Fund C	RGNCX	E-	(800) 766-3863	E- / 0.1	-3.37	-23.76	-28.11 / 0	-9.40 / 1	-2.87 / 1	0.05	2.24
EN	RS Global Natural Resources Fund K	RSNKX	E-	(800) 766-3863	E- / 0.1	-3.23	-23.60	-27.82 / 0	-9.03 / 1	-2.51 / 1	0.05	1.82
EN	RS Global Natural Resources Fund Y	RSNYX	E-	(800) 766-3863	E- / 0.1	-3.10	-23.33	-27.32 / 0	-8.39 / 1	-1.80 / 2	0.05	1.15
GL	RS Global Y	RGGYX	C+	(800) 766-3863	C+ / 6.8	4.57	5.16	8.82 / 68	14.14 / 68	--	0.89	1.33
GR	RS Growth Fund A	RSGRX	B-	(800) 766-3863	B+ / 8.5	3.22	7.94	13.64 / 89	17.40 / 92	15.40 / 90	0.00	1.21
GR	RS Growth Fund C	RGWCX	B-	(800) 766-3863	B+ / 8.6	3.04	7.51	12.70 / 86	16.37 / 86	14.22 / 80	0.00	2.11
GR	RS Growth Fund K	RSGKX	B-	(800) 766-3863	B+ / 8.8	3.12	7.68	13.01 / 87	16.67 / 88	14.74 / 85	0.00	1.79
GR	RS Growth Fund Y	RGRYX	B	(800) 766-3863	A / 9.3	3.33	8.15	14.01 / 89	17.69 / 93	15.71 / 91	0.00	0.93
FO	RS International Fund A	GUBGX	E-	(800) 766-3863	D- / 1.1	4.46	1.86	-2.49 / 9	5.86 / 16	5.35 / 14	1.59	1.61
FO	RS International Fund C	RIGCX	E-	(800) 766-3863	D- / 1.2	4.21	1.32	-3.61 / 8	4.74 / 12	4.38 / 10	1.33	2.55
FO	RS International Fund K	RIGKX	E-	(800) 766-3863	D- / 1.4	4.42	1.63	-3.00 / 9	5.33 / 14	4.84 / 11	1.36	1.99
FO	RS International Fund Y	RSIGX	E-	(800) 766-3863	D / 1.8	4.64	2.05	-2.05 / 10	6.30 / 18	5.72 / 15	2.04	1.01
GL	RS Investors Fund A	RSINX	B	(800) 766-3863	B / 7.8	0.08	3.51	0.75 / 18	18.88 / 96	15.17 / 88	0.87	1.89
GL	RS Investors Fund C	RIVCX	B	(800) 766-3863	B / 8.1	-0.16	3.13	-0.01 / 16	18.00 / 94	14.43 / 82	0.57	2.66
GL	RS Investors Fund K	RSIKX	B+	(800) 766-3863	B+ / 8.3	-0.08	3.24	0.19 / 16	18.32 / 95	14.78 / 85	0.76	2.56
GL	RS Investors Fund Y	RSIYX	B+	(800) 766-3863	B+ / 8.9	0.15	3.70	1.11 / 19	19.21 / 97	15.43 / 90	1.25	1.44
IN	RS Large Cap Alpha Fd A	GPAFX	B	(800) 766-3863	B+ / 8.3	0.00	5.25	10.17 / 75	18.11 / 95	12.55 / 65	0.79	0.92
IN	RS Large Cap Alpha Fd C	RCOCX	B	(800) 766-3863	B+ / 8.5	-0.20	4.82	9.26 / 71	17.16 / 91	11.66 / 58	0.17	1.74
IN	RS Large Cap Alpha Fd K	RCEKX	B+	(800) 766-3863	B+ / 8.8	-0.10	5.04	9.71 / 73	17.67 / 93	12.12 / 61	0.42	1.31
IN	RS Large Cap Alpha Fd Y	RCEYX	B+	(800) 766-3863	A- / 9.1	0.05	5.37	10.42 / 76	18.41 / 95	12.87 / 67	1.08	0.65
MC	RS Mid Cap Growth Fund A	RSMOX	B+	(800) 766-3863	B+ / 8.6	6.50	13.31	13.85 / 89	16.72 / 88	17.91 / 97	0.00	1.45
MC	RS Mid Cap Growth Fund C	RMOCX	B+	(800) 766-3863	B+ / 8.7	6.33	12.93	13.00 / 87	15.72 / 81	16.87 / 96	0.00	2.31
MC	RS Mid Cap Growth Fund K	RSMKX	A-	(800) 766-3863	B+ / 8.9	6.36	13.08	13.27 / 87	16.12 / 84	17.32 / 97	0.00	1.94
MC	RS Mid Cap Growth Fund Y	RMOYX	A	(800) 766-3863	A / 9.3	6.61	13.50	14.15 / 90	17.02 / 90	18.25 / 98	0.00	1.23
SC	● RS Partners Fund A	RSPFX	E+	(800) 766-3863	C- / 4.0	-1.38	0.51	-6.33 / 4	13.55 / 64	11.31 / 55	0.00	1.51
SC	RS Partners Fund K	RSPKX	E+	(800) 766-3863	C / 4.5	-1.48	0.31	-6.69 / 4	13.12 / 61	10.84 / 51	0.00	1.85
SC	RS Partners Fund Y	RSPYX	E+	(800) 766-3863	C / 4.9	-1.31	0.67	-6.02 / 4	13.92 / 67	11.67 / 58	0.00	1.17
SC	RS Select Growth Fund A	RSDGX	C+	(800) 766-3863	B- / 7.3	6.17	15.28	7.66 / 60	15.35 / 78	17.80 / 97	0.00	1.45
SC	RS Select Growth Fund C	RSGFX	C+	(800) 766-3863	B- / 7.5	5.95	14.81	6.79 / 53	14.44 / 70	16.74 / 95	0.00	2.26
SC	RS Select Growth Fund K	RSDKX	C+	(800) 766-3863	B / 7.7	6.04	14.97	7.09 / 56	14.60 / 72	17.05 / 96	0.00	2.02
SC	RS Select Growth Fund Y	RSSYX	B	(800) 766-3863	B+ / 8.4	6.23	15.41	7.93 / 62	15.65 / 80	18.15 / 98	0.00	1.19
SC	● RS Small Cap Equity Fund A	GPSCX	C+	(800) 766-3863	A+ / 9.8	9.19	24.88	18.29 / 96	21.26 / 98	18.94 / 98	0.00	1.29
SC	● RS Small Cap Equity Fund C	RSCCX	C-	(800) 766-3863	A+ / 9.8	9.02	24.37	17.37 / 95	20.25 / 98	17.94 / 97	0.00	2.08
SC	● RS Small Cap Equity Fund K	RSCKX	C+	(800) 766-3863	A+ / 9.8	9.06	24.59	17.79 / 95	20.85 / 98	18.55 / 98	0.00	1.69
SC	● RS Small Cap Equity Fund Y	RSCYX	C+	(800) 766-3863	A+ / 9.8	8.68	24.37	18.02 / 95	21.37 / 98	19.12 / 98	0.00	1.00
SC	RS Small Cap Growth Fund A	RSEGX	B+	(800) 766-3863	A+ / 9.8	8.55	23.76	17.00 / 95	21.19 / 98	18.83 / 98	0.73	1.41
SC	RS Small Cap Growth Fund C	REGWX	B+	(800) 766-3863	A+ / 9.8	8.35	23.30	16.10 / 93	19.86 / 98	17.36 / 97	0.24	2.32
SC	RS Small Cap Growth Fund K	RSEKX	B+	(800) 766-3863	A+ / 9.8	8.45	23.52	16.48 / 94	20.63 / 98	18.23 / 98	0.47	1.92
SC	RS Small Cap Growth Fund Y	RSYEX	B+	(800) 766-3863	A+ / 9.8	8.62	23.93	17.32 / 95	21.07 / 98	18.93 / 98	0.99	1.17
TC	RS Technology Fund A	RSIFX	E+	(800) 766-3863	C / 4.9	2.15	10.23	9.13 / 70	11.85 / 51	13.31 / 71	0.00	1.49
TC	RS Technology Fund C	RINCX	E+	(800) 766-3863	C / 5.1	1.91	9.70	8.15 / 64	10.92 / 45	12.38 / 63	0.00	2.34
TC	RS Technology Fund K	RIFKX	E+	(800) 766-3863	C / 5.4	2.02	9.94	8.54 / 67	11.30 / 48	12.70 / 66	0.00	2.02
TC	RS Technology Fund Y	RIFYX	D-	(800) 766-3863	C+ / 6.0	2.18	10.39	9.43 / 72	12.19 / 54	13.64 / 74	0.00	1.22
MC	RS Value Fund A	RSVAX	B	(800) 766-3863	A / 9.3	4.78	10.88	14.08 / 90	18.98 / 97	12.92 / 67	0.85	1.35
MC	RS Value Fund C	RVACX	B+	(800) 766-3863	A / 9.4	4.57	10.46	13.20 / 87	18.09 / 95	12.08 / 61	0.35	2.11
MC	RS Value Fund K	RSVKX	B+	(800) 766-3863	A / 9.5	4.68	10.64	13.62 / 88	18.51 / 96	12.48 / 64	0.69	1.70
MC	RS Value Fund Y	RSVYX	B+	(800) 766-3863	A+ / 9.7	4.85	11.02	14.36 / 90	19.27 / 97	13.23 / 70	1.26	1.14

● Denotes fund is closed to new investors
* Denotes fund is included in Section II

RISK			NET ASSETS		ASSET					BULL / BEAR		FUND MANAGER		MINIMUMS		LOADS	
	3 Year		NAV						Portfolio	Last Bull	Last Bear	Manager	Manager	Initial	Additional	Front	Back
Risk	Standard		As of	Total	Cash	Stocks	Bonds	Other	Turnover	Market	Market	Quality	Tenure	Purch.	Purch.	End	End
Rating/Pts	Deviation	Beta	3/31/15	$(Mil)	%	%	%	%	Ratio	Return	Return	Pct	(Years)	$	$	Load	Load
D /1.9	14.3	1.01	17.56	113	1	98	0	1	224	17.6	-27.8	18	2	0	100	0.0	0.0
C+/5.7	11.3	0.79	12.09	12	1	98	0	1	137	80.8	N/A	95	2	2,500	100	4.8	0.0
C+/5.8	11.3	0.79	11.93	7	1	98	0	1	137	76.6	N/A	93	2	2,500	100	0.0	0.0
C+/5.8	11.3	0.80	12.02	6	1	98	0	1	137	79.0	N/A	94	2	1,000	0	0.0	0.0
D /2.0	17.9	0.92	24.03	623	5	94	0	1	39	-7.4	-25.2	1	10	2,500	100	4.8	0.0
D /1.9	17.9	0.92	22.39	58	5	94	0	1	39	-9.8	-25.4	1	10	2,500	100	0.0	0.0
D /2.0	17.9	0.92	23.05	6	5	94	0	1	39	-8.6	-25.3	1	10	1,000	0	0.0	0.0
D /2.0	17.9	0.92	24.69	2,336	5	94	0	1	39	-6.3	-25.1	1	10	0	100	0.0	0.0
C+/5.7	11.3	0.79	12.12	16	1	98	0	1	137	83.3	N/A	95	2	0	100	0.0	0.0
C /4.6	11.3	1.04	18.60	213	1	98	0	1	101	104.5	-16.0	73	6	2,500	100	4.8	0.0
C /4.3	11.3	1.04	16.95	14	1	98	0	1	101	97.6	-16.3	63	6	2,500	100	0.0	0.0
C /4.5	11.4	1.04	17.85	1	1	98	0	1	101	100.3	-16.1	66	6	1,000	0	0.0	0.0
C /4.7	11.3	1.04	18.94	36	1	98	0	1	101	106.2	-15.9	76	6	0	100	0.0	0.0
D-/1.3	13.3	0.96	10.31	22	2	97	0	1	41	43.9	-25.1	24	6	2,500	100	4.8	0.0
D-/1.3	13.3	0.96	7.67	2	2	97	0	1	41	39.0	-25.3	15	6	2,500	100	0.0	0.0
D-/1.3	13.3	0.96	9.68	4	2	97	0	1	41	41.3	-25.3	19	6	1,000	0	0.0	0.0
D-/1.3	13.5	0.97	10.15	4	2	97	0	1	41	45.7	-25.0	28	12	0	100	0.0	0.0
C+/6.0	12.9	0.68	12.96	61	1	98	0	1	128	114.4	-24.0	98	10	2,500	100	4.8	0.0
C+/5.9	12.9	0.68	12.24	32	1	98	0	1	128	108.9	-24.2	98	10	2,500	100	0.0	0.0
C+/6.0	12.9	0.68	12.29	2	1	98	0	1	128	110.9	-24.0	98	10	1,000	0	0.0	0.0
C+/6.0	12.9	0.68	13.07	116	1	98	0	1	128	116.2	-23.9	99	10	0	100	0.0	0.0
C+/5.7	11.1	1.12	59.25	617	6	93	0	1	48	107.0	-24.8	67	3	2,500	100	4.8	0.0
C+/5.6	11.1	1.11	53.85	36	6	93	0	1	48	101.3	-25.0	55	3	2,500	100	0.0	0.0
C+/5.8	11.1	1.12	59.09	15	6	93	0	1	48	104.3	-24.9	62	3	1,000	0	0.0	0.0
C+/5.7	11.1	1.12	59.11	37	6	93	0	1	48	108.8	-24.7	70	3	0	100	0.0	0.0
C+/6.0	12.0	0.99	21.45	112	2	97	0	1	119	102.2	-19.0	67	7	2,500	100	4.8	0.0
C+/6.0	12.0	0.99	19.82	15	2	97	0	1	119	96.4	-19.3	53	7	2,500	100	0.0	0.0
C+/6.0	12.0	0.99	20.40	2	2	97	0	1	119	98.7	-19.1	58	7	1,000	0	0.0	0.0
C+/6.0	12.0	0.98	21.94	87	2	97	0	1	119	103.9	-18.9	70	7	0	100	0.0	0.0
D /1.9	12.4	0.83	30.65	742	2	97	0	1	49	81.2	-24.4	69	3	2,500	100	4.8	0.0
D /1.8	12.4	0.83	29.28	4	2	97	0	1	49	78.7	-24.6	64	3	1,000	0	0.0	0.0
D /1.9	12.4	0.83	31.53	819	2	97	0	1	49	83.1	-24.4	72	3	0	100	0.0	0.0
C /5.2	12.7	0.84	50.75	273	1	98	0	1	105	91.4	-19.4	81	8	2,500	100	4.8	0.0
C /5.1	12.7	0.84	47.22	90	1	98	0	1	105	86.4	-19.9	75	8	2,500	100	0.0	0.0
C /5.1	12.6	0.84	47.08	1	1	98	0	1	105	87.3	-19.7	77	8	1,000	0	0.0	0.0
C /5.2	12.7	0.84	51.64	478	1	98	0	1	105	93.2	-19.3	83	8	0	100	0.0	0.0
C-/3.0	14.1	0.94	21.63	75	1	98	0	1	107	121.9	-25.7	94	6	2,500	100	4.8	0.0
E+/0.8	14.1	0.94	14.63	1	1	98	0	1	107	115.4	-26.0	92	6	2,500	100	0.0	0.0
D+/2.4	14.1	0.94	19.62	5	1	98	0	1	107	119.3	-25.8	93	6	1,000	0	0.0	0.0
C-/3.0	14.2	0.95	21.78	9	1	98	0	1	107	122.5	-25.6	94	6	0	100	0.0	0.0
C /4.9	14.2	0.95	71.13	724	0	99	0	1	115	120.5	-25.1	93	8	2,500	100	4.8	0.0
C /4.7	14.2	0.94	65.17	19	0	99	0	1	115	111.0	-25.5	91	8	2,500	100	0.0	0.0
C /4.9	14.2	0.95	67.54	4	0	99	0	1	115	116.9	-25.3	92	8	1,000	0	0.0	0.0
C /5.0	14.2	0.94	72.82	782	0	99	0	1	115	120.1	-25.0	93	8	0	100	0.0	0.0
D /1.8	16.6	1.15	18.52	128	1	98	0	1	141	83.0	-26.8	7	14	2,500	100	4.8	0.0
D-/1.2	16.5	1.15	16.58	12	1	98	0	1	141	77.8	-27.0	5	14	2,500	100	0.0	0.0
D-/1.3	16.6	1.15	17.19	2	1	98	0	1	141	79.7	-27.0	6	14	1,000	0	0.0	0.0
D /1.9	16.6	1.15	19.19	42	1	98	0	1	141	84.6	-26.7	7	14	0	100	0.0	0.0
C /4.7	11.4	0.98	34.62	439	3	96	0	1	48	103.7	-26.0	84	2	2,500	100	4.8	0.0
C /4.7	11.4	0.98	32.98	31	3	96	0	1	48	98.5	-26.3	79	2	2,500	100	0.0	0.0
C /4.7	11.4	0.98	33.80	4	3	96	0	1	48	101.0	-26.1	81	2	1,000	0	0.0	0.0
C /4.6	11.4	0.98	34.84	861	3	96	0	1	48	105.4	-25.9	85	2	0	100	0.0	0.0

	99 Pct = Best						**PERFORMANCE**							
	0 Pct = Worst			**Overall**		**Perfor-**			Total Return % through 3/31/15				Incl. in Returns	
				Investment		**mance**					Annualized		Dividend	Expense
Fund		Ticker		**Rating**	Phone	**Rating/Pts**	3 Mo	6 Mo	1Yr / Pct	3Yr / Pct	5Yr / Pct		Yield	Ratio
Type	Fund Name	Symbol												
FO	RSQ International Equity Instl	RSQIX	U	(855) 355-4777		U /	6.32	3.23	-3.32 / 8	--	--		3.16	1.71
AA	● Russell 2020 Strategy A	RLLAX	E-	(800) 832-6688		D- / 1.5	1.75	3.17	4.50 /35	6.44 /19	6.85 /22		2.12	0.86
AA	Russell 2020 Strategy E	RLLEX	E	(800) 832-6688		D / 2.2	1.75	3.19	4.58 /36	6.48 /19	6.93 /23		2.25	0.86
AA	Russell 2020 Strategy R1	RLLRX	E	(800) 832-6688		D+ / 2.3	1.75	3.25	4.76 /37	6.74 /20	7.13 /24		2.51	0.61
AA	Russell 2020 Strategy R4	RLLUX	C-	(800) 832-6688		D / 2.1	1.75	3.28	4.45 /35	6.28 /18	6.64 /21		2.12	0.86
AA	Russell 2020 Strategy R5	RLLVX	C-	(800) 832-6688		D / 1.9	1.76	3.09	4.20 /33	5.98 /17	6.39 /19		1.83	1.11
AA	Russell 2020 Strategy S	RLLSX	E	(800) 832-6688		D+ / 2.3	1.75	3.33	4.76 /37	6.74 /20	7.15 /24		2.51	0.61
AA	Russell 2025 Strategy R1	RPLRX	D-	(800) 832-6688		D+ / 2.9	2.13	3.64	4.91 /38	7.75 /26	7.80 /29		2.36	0.63
GI	Russell 2025 Strategy R4	RPLUX	D	(800) 832-6688		D+ / 2.6	2.01	3.48	4.49 /35	7.26 /23	7.29 /25		2.00	0.88
GI	Russell 2025 Strategy R5	RPLVX	D-	(800) 832-6688		D+ / 2.4	1.90	3.32	4.19 /33	6.98 /21	6.99 /23		1.72	1.13
AA	● Russell 2030 Strategy A	RRLAX	E	(800) 832-6688		D+ / 2.3	2.07	3.62	4.41 /34	8.43 /30	8.01 /30		1.91	0.92
AA	Russell 2030 Strategy E	RRLEX	E	(800) 832-6688		C- / 3.2	2.10	3.66	4.46 /35	8.43 /30	7.93 /29		1.97	0.92
AA	Russell 2030 Strategy R1	RRLRX	E	(800) 832-6688		C- / 3.4	2.21	3.77	4.70 /36	8.70 /31	8.25 /32		2.25	0.67
AA	Russell 2030 Strategy R4	RRLUX	D+	(800) 832-6688		C- / 3.1	2.10	3.53	4.19 /33	8.18 /28	7.70 /28		1.87	0.92
AA	Russell 2030 Strategy R5	RRLVX	D+	(800) 832-6688		D+ / 2.9	1.98	3.45	3.98 /32	7.94 /27	7.46 /26		1.58	1.17
AA	Russell 2030 Strategy S	RRLSX	E	(800) 832-6688		C- / 3.4	2.21	3.69	4.62 /36	8.71 /31	8.23 /31		2.25	0.67
AA	Russell 2035 Strategy R1	RVLRX	D-	(800) 832-6688		C- / 4.0	2.27	3.89	4.38 /34	9.82 /38	9.00 /37		2.01	0.70
GI	Russell 2035 Strategy R4	RVLUX	C-	(800) 832-6688		C- / 3.6	2.15	3.65	3.97 /32	9.32 /35	8.45 /33		1.65	0.95
GI	Russell 2035 Strategy R5	RVLVX	D+	(800) 832-6688		C- / 3.5	2.15	3.59	3.79 /30	9.05 /33	8.21 /31		1.40	1.20
AA	● Russell 2040 Strategy A	RXLAX	E	(800) 832-6688		D+ / 2.9	2.36	3.85	4.21 /33	9.54 /36	8.72 /35		1.70	0.96
AA	Russell 2040 Strategy E	RXLEX	E	(800) 832-6688		C- / 3.8	2.36	3.79	4.15 /33	9.56 /37	8.69 /35		1.71	0.96
AA	Russell 2040 Strategy R1	RXLRX	E	(800) 832-6688		C- / 4.0	2.36	3.94	4.42 /35	9.84 /38	9.00 /37		2.01	0.71
AA	Russell 2040 Strategy R4	RXLUX	D+	(800) 832-6688		C- / 3.7	2.36	3.84	4.06 /32	9.32 /35	8.47 /33		1.64	0.96
AA	Russell 2040 Strategy R5	RXLVX	D+	(800) 832-6688		C- / 3.5	2.37	3.73	3.82 /31	9.06 /33	8.22 /31		1.41	1.21
AA	Russell 2040 Strategy S	RXLSX	E	(800) 832-6688		C- / 3.9	2.36	3.90	4.38 /34	9.79 /38	9.00 /37		2.01	0.71
AA	Russell 2045 Strategy R1	RWLRX	E+	(800) 832-6688		C- / 4.0	2.32	3.94	4.44 /35	9.89 /39	9.00 /37		1.97	0.71
GI	Russell 2045 Strategy R4	RWLUX	D+	(800) 832-6688		C- / 3.7	2.32	3.89	4.04 /32	9.39 /36	8.54 /33		1.59	0.96
GI	Russell 2045 Strategy R5	RWLVX	D+	(800) 832-6688		C- / 3.5	2.33	3.78	3.80 /31	9.11 /34	8.24 /31		1.40	1.21
AA	Russell 2050 Strategy R1	RYLRX	E	(800) 832-6688		C- / 4.0	2.35	3.92	4.43 /35	9.86 /39	9.00 /37		1.98	0.71
GI	Russell 2050 Strategy R4	RYLUX	D+	(800) 832-6688		C- / 3.7	2.34	3.87	4.01 /32	9.37 /35	8.53 /33		1.58	0.96
GI	Russell 2050 Strategy R5	RYLWX	D+	(800) 832-6688		C- / 3.5	2.19	3.63	3.75 /30	9.09 /34	8.22 /31		1.39	1.21
AA	Russell 2055 Strategy R1	RQLRX	C-	(800) 832-6688		C- / 4.0	2.42	3.91	4.44 /35	9.83 /38	--		1.95	0.71
GI	Russell 2055 Strategy R4	RQLUX	D+	(800) 832-6688		C- / 3.7	2.33	3.77	3.96 /32	9.35 /35	--		1.58	0.96
GI	Russell 2055 Strategy R5	RQLVX	D+	(800) 832-6688		C- / 3.5	2.24	3.76	3.76 /30	9.04 /33	--		1.39	1.21
GL	Russell Bal Strat A	RBLAX	C-	(800) 832-6688		D / 1.8	1.89	3.46	4.70 /36	7.31 /23	7.13 /24		2.26	1.47
GL	Russell Bal Strat C	RBLCX	C-	(800) 832-6688		D / 2.2	1.66	3.06	3.92 /31	6.50 /19	6.33 /19		1.94	2.22
GL	Russell Bal Strat E	RBLEX	C	(800) 832-6688		D+ / 2.6	1.88	3.44	4.68 /36	7.28 /23	7.13 /24		2.38	1.47
GL	Russell Bal Strat R1	RBLRX	C	(800) 832-6688		D+ / 2.9	1.95	3.60	5.12 /39	7.71 /25	7.54 /27		2.65	1.22
BA	Russell Bal Strat R4	RBLUX	D	(800) 832-6688		D+ / 2.6	1.88	3.48	4.74 /37	7.21 /22	7.03 /23		2.35	1.47
BA	Russell Bal Strat R5	RBLVX	D	(800) 832-6688		D+ / 2.4	1.80	3.33	4.37 /34	6.96 /21	6.76 /22		2.16	1.72
GL	Russell Bal Strat S	RBLSX	C	(800) 832-6688		D+ / 2.8	1.87	3.49	4.94 /38	7.54 /24	7.39 /26		2.55	1.22
OT	Russell Commodity Strategies A	RCSAX	E	(800) 832-6688		E- / 0.0	-6.21	-18.72	-27.38 / 0	-12.94 / 1	--		0.00	2.11
OT	Russell Commodity Strategies C	RCSCX	E	(800) 832-6688		E- / 0.1	-6.38	-18.95	-27.87 / 0	-13.60 / 1	--		0.00	2.86
OT	Russell Commodity Strategies E	RCSEX	E	(800) 832-6688		E- / 0.1	-6.21	-18.72	-27.29 / 0	-12.94 / 1	--		0.00	2.11
OT	Russell Commodity Strategies S	RCCSX	E	(800) 832-6688		E- / 0.1	-6.02	-18.57	-27.11 / 0	-12.70 / 1	--		0.00	1.86
OT	Russell Commodity Strategies Y	RCSYX	E	(800) 832-6688		E- / 0.1	-5.99	-18.48	-26.98 / 0	-12.55 / 1	--		0.00	1.66
GL	Russell Cons Strat A	RCLAX	C-	(800) 832-6688		E+ / 0.8	1.30	2.32	3.53 /29	4.04 /10	4.86 /11		2.04	1.41
GL	Russell Cons Strat C	RCLCX	C-	(800) 832-6688		D- / 1.0	1.13	1.99	2.83 /26	3.29 / 8	4.05 / 8		1.47	2.16
GL	Russell Cons Strat E	RCLEX	C-	(800) 832-6688		D- / 1.2	1.30	2.23	3.53 /29	4.03 /10	4.83 /11		2.16	1.41
GL	Russell Cons Strat R1	RCLRX	C-	(800) 832-6688		D- / 1.3	1.39	2.42	3.91 /31	4.44 /11	5.24 /13		2.53	1.16
AA	Russell Cons Strat R4	RCLUX	C-	(800) 832-6688		D- / 1.2	1.39	2.38	3.62 /30	3.96 /10	4.76 /11		2.15	1.41
AA	Russell Cons Strat R5	RCLVX	C-	(800) 832-6688		D- / 1.1	1.29	2.22	3.32 /28	3.69 / 9	4.48 /10		1.87	1.66

RISK			NET ASSETS		ASSET				Portfolio Turnover Ratio	BULL / BEAR		FUND MANAGER		MINIMUMS		LOADS	
Risk Rating/Pts	3 Year Standard Deviation	Beta	NAV As of 3/31/15	Total $(Mil)	Cash %	Stocks %	Bonds %	Other %		Last Bull Market Return	Last Bear Market Return	Manager Quality Pct	Manager Tenure (Years)	Initial Purch. $	Additional Purch. $	Front End Load	Back End Load
U /	N/A	N/A	9.59	50	6	93	0	1	107	N/A	N/A	N/A	N/A	1,000,000	0	0.0	0.0
D /2.0	5.0	0.82	8.70	N/A	3	36	59	2	42	35.3	-10.2	35	N/A	0	0	5.8	0.0
D /2.0	5.0	0.81	8.72	2	3	36	59	2	42	35.4	-10.2	35	N/A	0	0	0.0	0.0
D /1.9	5.0	0.81	8.70	51	3	36	59	2	42	36.5	-10.2	39	N/A	0	0	0.0	0.0
B /8.4	5.0	0.81	8.70	13	3	36	59	2	42	34.3	-10.3	33	1	0	0	0.0	0.0
B /8.4	5.0	0.82	8.68	24	3	36	59	2	42	33.2	-10.4	29	1	0	0	0.0	0.0
D /1.9	5.0	0.82	8.70	9	3	36	59	2	42	36.5	-10.1	38	N/A	0	0	0.0	0.0
C- /4.0	6.1	1.01	8.62	19	4	46	48	2	67	43.9	-13.4	25	7	0	0	0.0	0.0
C+ /5.8	6.2	0.58	8.62	8	4	46	48	2	67	41.7	-13.6	42	1	0	0	0.0	0.0
C /5.2	6.2	0.58	8.58	10	4	46	48	2	67	40.4	-13.7	39	1	0	0	0.0	0.0
D /1.6	7.7	1.28	8.86	1	7	58	34	1	60	51.0	-17.6	10	N/A	0	0	5.8	0.0
D /1.6	7.7	1.28	8.77	N/A	7	58	34	1	60	50.9	-17.6	10	N/A	0	0	0.0	0.0
D /1.6	7.7	1.27	8.79	55	7	58	34	1	60	52.1	-17.5	11	N/A	0	0	0.0	0.0
C+ /6.6	7.7	1.27	8.76	15	7	58	34	1	60	49.6	-17.7	9	1	0	0	0.0	0.0
C+ /6.6	7.7	1.28	8.77	26	7	58	34	1	60	48.5	-17.7	8	1	0	0	0.0	0.0
D /1.6	7.7	1.27	8.78	13	7	58	34	1	60	52.2	-17.5	11	N/A	0	0	0.0	0.0
C- /3.1	9.3	1.53	9.03	12	9	71	18	2	80	60.1	-19.0	5	7	0	0	0.0	0.0
C+ /6.3	9.2	0.90	9.01	9	9	71	18	2	80	57.6	-19.2	13	1	0	0	0.0	0.0
C+ /6.3	9.3	0.90	9.01	8	9	71	18	2	80	56.2	-19.4	11	1	0	0	0.0	0.0
D- /1.4	9.4	1.56	8.67	1	11	81	7	1	64	59.0	-19.1	5	N/A	0	0	5.8	0.0
D- /1.4	9.4	1.57	8.67	N/A	11	81	7	1	64	59.1	-19.1	4	N/A	0	0	0.0	0.0
D- /1.4	9.3	1.55	8.68	46	11	81	7	1	64	60.3	-19.0	5	N/A	0	0	0.0	0.0
C+ /5.9	9.4	1.56	8.68	9	11	81	7	1	64	57.8	-19.2	4	1	0	0	0.0	0.0
C+ /5.9	9.4	1.56	8.65	18	11	81	7	1	64	56.4	-19.3	4	1	0	0	0.0	0.0
D- /1.4	9.3	1.55	8.68	13	11	81	7	1	64	60.4	-19.0	5	N/A	0	0	0.0	0.0
D+ /2.8	9.4	1.56	8.81	7	11	81	7	1	84	60.5	-19.0	5	7	0	0	0.0	0.0
C+ /6.0	9.4	0.92	8.83	4	11	81	7	1	84	58.1	-19.2	12	1	0	0	0.0	0.0
C+ /6.0	9.4	0.92	8.78	4	11	81	7	1	84	56.6	-19.3	10	1	0	0	0.0	0.0
D- /1.4	9.4	1.56	6.54	8	11	81	7	1	84	60.4	-19.0	5	7	0	0	0.0	0.0
C+ /6.0	9.4	0.92	6.56	2	11	81	7	1	84	58.0	-19.2	11	1	0	0	0.0	0.0
C+ /6.0	9.5	0.93	6.53	4	11	81	7	1	84	56.7	-19.2	9	1	0	0	0.0	0.0
C+ /5.9	9.4	1.56	11.42	1	2	87	9	2	132	60.1	-19.0	5	5	0	0	0.0	0.0
C+ /5.9	9.4	0.92	11.42	2	2	87	9	2	132	57.7	-19.2	11	1	0	0	0.0	0.0
C+ /5.8	9.4	0.92	11.41	1	2	87	9	2	132	56.0	-19.3	9	1	0	0	0.0	0.0
B /8.4	6.7	1.06	12.41	1,027	12	53	33	2	19	41.6	-13.6	37	N/A	0	0	5.8	0.0
B /8.4	6.6	1.04	12.22	1,210	12	53	33	2	19	38.0	-13.8	29	N/A	0	0	0.0	0.0
B /8.4	6.7	1.05	12.46	57	12	53	33	2	19	41.6	-13.6	37	N/A	0	0	0.0	0.0
B /8.4	6.7	1.06	12.54	250	12	53	33	2	19	43.5	-13.4	42	N/A	0	0	0.0	0.0
C+ /6.2	6.7	1.12	12.44	185	12	53	33	2	19	41.2	-13.6	12	1	0	0	0.0	0.0
C+ /6.1	6.7	1.12	12.45	126	12	53	33	2	19	40.0	-13.6	11	1	0	0	0.0	0.0
B /8.4	6.7	1.05	12.53	558	12	53	33	2	19	42.6	-13.4	40	N/A	0	0	0.0	0.0
C- /3.9	12.1	0.72	6.34	8	18	0	81	1	302	-30.2	-19.5	0	N/A	0	0	5.8	0.0
C- /3.8	12.1	0.72	6.16	6	18	0	81	1	302	-32.0	-19.8	0	N/A	0	0	0.0	0.0
C- /3.9	12.0	0.72	6.34	15	18	0	81	1	302	-30.3	-19.6	0	N/A	0	0	0.0	0.0
C- /3.9	12.1	0.72	6.40	690	18	0	81	1	302	-29.6	-19.5	0	N/A	0	0	0.0	0.0
C- /3.9	12.1	0.72	6.44	278	18	0	81	1	302	-29.2	-19.4	0	N/A	10,000,000	0	0.0	0.0
B+ /9.0	3.1	0.44	10.89	115	4	20	74	2	26	20.0	-4.2	69	N/A	0	0	5.8	0.0
B+ /9.0	3.2	0.44	10.78	206	4	20	74	2	26	16.9	-4.5	59	N/A	0	0	0.0	0.0
B+ /9.0	3.1	0.43	10.93	22	4	20	74	2	26	19.9	-4.3	69	N/A	0	0	0.0	0.0
B+ /9.0	3.1	0.43	10.96	30	4	20	74	2	26	21.6	-4.1	73	N/A	0	0	0.0	0.0
B /8.8	3.1	0.45	10.91	22	4	20	74	2	26	19.6	-4.3	56	1	0	0	0.0	0.0
B /8.8	3.1	0.44	10.98	25	4	20	74	2	26	18.6	-4.4	53	1	0	0	0.0	0.0

					PERFORMANCE							
					Perfor-mance Rating/Pts	Total Return % through 3/31/15					Incl. in Returns	
									Annualized		Dividend	Expense
Fund Type	Fund Name	Ticker Symbol	Overall Investment Rating	Phone		3 Mo	6 Mo	1Yr / Pct	3Yr / Pct	5Yr / Pct	Yield	Ratio
GL	Russell Cons Strat S	RCLSX	C-	(800) 832-6688	D- / 1.3	1.39	2.44	3.87 /31	4.31 /11	5.11 /12	2.40	1.16
EM	Russell Emerging Markets A	REMAX	E	(800) 832-6688	E / 0.4	0.83	-4.65	-1.43 /12	0.04 / 4	1.54 / 4	1.19	1.76
EM	Russell Emerging Markets C	REMCX	E	(800) 832-6688	E / 0.4	0.69	-4.98	-2.13 /10	-0.71 / 4	0.78 / 3	0.55	2.51
EM	Russell Emerging Markets E	REMEX	E	(800) 832-6688	E / 0.5	0.89	-4.65	-1.39 /12	0.04 / 4	1.55 / 4	1.24	1.76
EM	Russell Emerging Markets S	REMSX	E	(800) 832-6688	E / 0.5	0.88	-4.57	-1.15 /13	0.29 / 5	1.80 / 4	1.54	1.51
EM	Russell Emerging Markets Y	REMYX	E	(800) 832-6688	E / 0.5	0.94	-4.42	-0.94 /13	0.48 / 5	1.99 / 4	1.74	1.31
GL	Russell Eq Gr Strat A	REAAX	D+	(800) 832-6688	D+ / 2.5	2.09	3.28	3.92 /31	8.96 /33	7.82 /29	2.16	1.56
GL	Russell Eq Gr Strat C	RELCX	C-	(800) 832-6688	D+ / 2.9	1.83	2.94	3.15 /27	8.15 /28	7.01 /23	2.06	2.31
GL	Russell Eq Gr Strat E	RELEX	C-	(800) 832-6688	C- / 3.4	2.05	3.35	3.92 /31	8.95 /33	7.82 /29	2.34	1.56
GL	Russell Eq Gr Strat R1	RELRX	C-	(800) 832-6688	C- / 3.7	2.16	3.55	4.29 /34	9.37 /35	8.25 /32	2.66	1.31
GL	Russell Eq Gr Strat R4	RELUX	C-	(800) 832-6688	C- / 3.4	2.04	3.40	3.89 /31	8.86 /32	7.75 /28	2.34	1.56
GL	Russell Eq Gr Strat R5	RELVX	D+	(800) 832-6688	C- / 3.2	1.97	3.23	3.62 /30	8.60 /30	7.46 /26	2.19	1.81
GL	Russell Eq Gr Strat S	RELSX	C-	(800) 832-6688	C- / 3.6	2.08	3.40	4.08 /32	9.23 /34	8.10 /31	2.53	1.31
GL	Russell Global Equity A	RGEAX	C-	(800) 832-6688	C / 4.7	3.67	7.30	7.96 /63	12.06 /53	9.71 /42	1.14	1.49
GL	Russell Global Equity C	RGECX	C	(800) 832-6688	C / 5.1	3.52	6.92	7.20 /57	11.21 /47	8.89 /36	0.46	2.24
GL	Russell Global Equity E	RGEEX	C	(800) 832-6688	C+ / 5.7	3.66	7.43	7.99 /63	12.07 /53	9.72 /42	1.15	1.49
GL	Russell Global Equity S	RGESX	C+	(800) 832-6688	C+ / 5.9	3.75	7.53	8.28 /65	12.33 /55	9.99 /44	1.43	1.24
GL	Russell Global Equity Y	RLGYX	C+	(800) 832-6688	C+ / 6.0	3.74	7.55	8.39 /66	12.56 /56	10.19 /46	1.62	1.04
GL	Russell Global Infrastructure A	RGIAX	D	(800) 832-6688	C- / 3.2	-0.17	0.91	3.53 /29	10.76 /44	--	1.82	1.81
GL	Russell Global Infrastructure C	RGCIX	D+	(800) 832-6688	C- / 3.6	-0.25	0.61	2.80 /25	9.93 /39	--	1.22	2.56
GL	Russell Global Infrastructure E	RGIEX	C-	(800) 832-6688	C- / 4.1	-0.08	0.97	3.51 /29	10.74 /44	--	1.90	1.81
GL	Russell Global Infrastructure S	RGISX	C-	(800) 832-6688	C / 4.3	0.00	1.04	3.86 /31	11.06 /46	--	2.16	1.56
GL	Russell Global Infrastructure Y	RGIYX	C-	(800) 832-6688	C / 4.4	0.00	1.13	3.96 /32	11.22 /47	--	2.33	1.36
RE	Russell Global Real Estate Sec A	RREAX	C-	(800) 832-6688	C+ / 5.7	4.28	11.67	14.88 /91	11.68 /50	10.37 /48	2.42	1.36
RE	Russell Global Real Estate Sec C	RRSCX	C-	(800) 832-6688	C+ / 6.1	4.07	11.22	13.99 /89	10.85 /45	9.54 /41	1.93	2.11
RE	Russell Global Real Estate Sec E	RREEX	C	(800) 832-6688	C+ / 6.7	4.27	11.66	14.87 /91	11.68 /50	10.37 /48	2.54	1.36
RE	Russell Global Real Estate Sec S	RRESX	C	(800) 832-6688	C+ / 6.9	4.33	11.77	15.15 /92	11.96 /52	10.64 /50	2.73	1.11
RE	Russell Global Real Estate Sec Y	RREYX	C	(800) 832-6688	B- / 7.0	4.38	11.89	15.35 /92	12.18 /54	10.84 /51	2.91	0.91
GL	Russell Gr Strat A	RALAX	D+	(800) 832-6688	D / 2.1	1.85	3.11	3.79 /30	8.05 /27	7.46 /26	2.17	1.51
GL	Russell Gr Strat C	RALCX	C-	(800) 832-6688	D+ / 2.5	1.73	2.79	3.10 /27	7.28 /23	6.65 /21	1.94	2.26
GL	Russell Gr Strat E	RALEX	C-	(800) 832-6688	D+ / 2.9	1.85	3.09	3.76 /30	8.07 /27	7.45 /26	2.28	1.51
GL	Russell Gr Strat R1	RALRX	C-	(800) 832-6688	C- / 3.2	2.00	3.36	4.23 /33	8.50 /30	7.86 /29	2.66	1.26
GL	Russell Gr Strat R4	RALUX	D+	(800) 832-6688	D+ / 2.9	1.85	3.16	3.86 /31	7.98 /27	7.34 /25	2.29	1.51
GL	Russell Gr Strat R5	RALVX	D+	(800) 832-6688	D+ / 2.7	1.85	3.04	3.61 /30	7.72 /25	7.08 /24	2.12	1.76
GL	Russell Gr Strat S	RALSX	C-	(800) 832-6688	C- / 3.1	1.92	3.21	4.10 /32	8.32 /29	7.72 /28	2.53	1.26
GI	● Russell In Ret A	RZLAX	E-	(800) 832-6688	D- / 1.2	1.54	2.92	4.35 /34	5.37 /14	--	2.18	0.84
AA	Russell In Ret R1	RZLRX	E-	(800) 832-6688	D / 1.8	1.71	3.01	4.59 /36	5.61 /15	6.30 /19	2.56	0.59
GI	Russell In Ret R4	RZLUX	C-	(800) 832-6688	D / 1.6	1.70	2.96	4.38 /34	5.15 /14	5.81 /16	2.17	0.84
GI	Russell In Ret R5	RZLVX	C-	(800) 832-6688	D- / 1.5	1.58	2.78	3.94 /31	4.88 /13	5.52 /14	1.88	1.09
FO	Russell Internatl Developed Mkts A	RLNAX	D-	(800) 832-6688	D / 1.7	4.55	0.44	-1.84 /11	8.10 /28	5.30 /13	1.45	1.26
FO	Russell Internatl Developed Mkts C	RLNCX	D	(800) 832-6688	D / 2.1	4.36	0.05	-2.59 / 9	7.30 /23	4.54 /10	0.67	2.01
FO	Russell Internatl Developed Mkts E	RIFEX	D	(800) 832-6688	D+ / 2.5	4.55	0.43	-1.84 /11	8.12 /28	5.35 /14	1.47	1.26
FO	Russell Internatl Developed Mkts I	RINSX	D	(800) 832-6688	D+ / 2.7	4.63	0.60	-1.51 /11	8.46 /30	5.66 /15	1.86	0.93
FO	Russell Internatl Developed Mkts S	RINTX	D	(800) 832-6688	D+ / 2.7	4.61	0.53	-1.61 /11	8.37 /29	5.58 /15	1.79	1.01
FO	Russell Internatl Developed Mkts Y	RINYX	D	(800) 832-6688	D+ / 2.8	4.64	0.65	-1.41 /12	8.58 /30	5.74 /15	1.98	0.81
GL	Russell Mod Strategy A	RMLAX	C-	(800) 832-6688	D- / 1.2	1.63	2.98	4.41 /34	5.55 /15	6.04 /17	2.26	1.39
GL	Russell Mod Strategy C	RMLCX	C-	(800) 832-6688	D- / 1.4	1.47	2.56	3.70 /30	4.76 /12	5.25 /13	1.78	2.14
GL	Russell Mod Strategy E	RMLEX	C-	(800) 832-6688	D / 1.8	1.62	2.97	4.39 /34	5.55 /15	6.04 /17	2.37	1.39
GL	Russell Mod Strategy R1	RMLRX	C	(800) 832-6688	D / 2.0	1.71	3.18	4.89 /38	5.96 /17	6.47 /20	2.76	1.14
AA	Russell Mod Strategy R4	RMLUX	C-	(800) 832-6688	D / 1.7	1.71	3.04	4.49 /35	5.48 /15	5.96 /17	2.38	1.39
AA	Russell Mod Strategy R5	RMLVX	C-	(800) 832-6688	D / 1.6	1.53	2.89	4.19 /33	5.17 /14	5.67 /15	2.10	1.64
GL	Russell Mod Strategy S	RMLSX	C	(800) 832-6688	D / 1.9	1.71	3.11	4.66 /36	5.80 /16	6.30 /19	2.63	1.14

● Denotes fund is closed to new investors
★ Denotes fund is included in Section II

www.thestreetratings.com

RISK	3 Year		NET ASSETS		ASSET					BULL / BEAR		FUND MANAGER		MINIMUMS		LOADS	
Risk Rating/Pts	Standard Deviation	Beta	NAV As of 3/31/15	Total $(Mil)	Cash %	Stocks %	Bonds %	Other %	Portfolio Turnover Ratio	Last Bull Market Return	Last Bear Market Return	Manager Quality Pct	Manager Tenure (Years)	Initial Purch. $	Additional Purch. $	Front End Load	Back End Load
B+ / 9.0	3.1	0.44	10.97	82	4	20	74	2	26	20.9	-4.2	72	N/A	0	0	0.0	0.0
C / 5.0	14.2	1.03	17.03	20	14	84	1	1	67	23.2	-26.5	58	N/A	0	0	5.8	0.0
C / 5.1	14.2	1.03	15.97	25	14	84	1	1	67	20.1	-26.7	46	N/A	0	0	0.0	0.0
C / 5.0	14.2	1.03	17.09	48	14	84	1	1	67	23.2	-26.5	58	N/A	0	0	0.0	0.0
C / 5.0	14.2	1.03	17.12	2,138	14	84	1	1	67	24.2	-26.4	62	N/A	0	0	0.0	0.0
C / 5.0	14.2	1.03	17.15	614	14	84	1	1	67	25.1	-26.4	64	N/A	10,000,000	0	0.0	0.0
B- / 7.0	9.8	1.52	11.73	226	19	72	8	1	23	57.2	-20.8	13	N/A	0	0	5.8	0.0
B- / 7.0	9.8	1.52	10.59	313	19	72	8	1	23	53.1	-21.0	9	N/A	0	0	0.0	0.0
B- / 7.0	9.8	1.51	11.47	21	19	72	8	1	23	57.1	-20.9	13	N/A	0	0	0.0	0.0
B- / 7.0	9.8	1.52	11.80	40	19	72	8	1	23	59.2	-20.6	15	N/A	0	0	0.0	0.0
C+ / 6.5	9.8	0.70	11.51	51	19	72	8	1	23	56.7	-20.8	85	1	0	0	0.0	0.0
C+ / 6.5	9.8	0.70	11.37	44	19	72	8	1	23	55.4	-20.9	83	1	0	0	0.0	0.0
B- / 7.0	9.8	1.52	11.77	206	19	72	8	1	23	58.5	-20.7	14	N/A	0	0	0.0	0.0
C+ / 6.0	11.5	0.80	11.59	14	7	92	0	1	39	72.0	-22.0	92	N/A	0	0	5.8	0.0
C+ / 6.0	11.5	0.80	11.48	15	7	92	0	1	39	67.7	-22.3	90	N/A	0	0	0.0	0.0
C+ / 6.0	11.5	0.80	11.61	52	7	92	0	1	39	71.9	-22.0	92	N/A	0	0	0.0	0.0
C+ / 6.0	11.5	0.80	11.63	2,183	7	92	0	1	39	73.5	-21.9	92	N/A	0	0	0.0	0.0
C+ / 6.0	11.5	0.80	11.64	928	7	92	0	1	39	74.6	-21.9	93	N/A	10,000,000	0	0.0	0.0
C+ / 5.8	10.0	0.63	11.88	9	13	86	0	1	119	58.8	-16.1	92	N/A	0	0	5.8	0.0
C+ / 5.9	10.0	0.63	11.84	9	13	86	0	1	119	54.9	-16.4	91	N/A	0	0	0.0	0.0
C+ / 5.9	10.0	0.64	11.89	23	13	86	0	1	119	58.9	-16.1	92	N/A	0	0	0.0	0.0
C+ / 5.9	9.9	0.63	11.91	1,063	13	86	0	1	119	60.3	-16.0	93	N/A	0	0	0.0	0.0
C+ / 5.8	10.0	0.63	11.91	405	13	86	0	1	119	61.2	-15.9	93	N/A	10,000,000	0	0.0	0.0
C / 4.4	12.1	0.89	39.25	31	19	80	0	1	69	69.3	-20.7	57	N/A	0	0	5.8	0.0
C / 4.4	12.1	0.89	38.12	42	19	80	0	1	69	65.0	-21.0	45	N/A	0	0	0.0	0.0
C / 4.4	12.1	0.89	39.29	31	19	80	0	1	69	69.3	-20.7	56	N/A	0	0	0.0	0.0
C / 4.5	12.1	0.89	40.04	1,443	19	80	0	1	69	70.7	-20.6	61	N/A	0	0	0.0	0.0
C / 4.5	12.1	0.89	40.03	160	19	80	0	1	69	71.8	-20.6	63	N/A	10,000,000	0	0.0	0.0
B- / 7.6	8.5	1.32	12.08	738	17	65	17	1	22	49.6	-18.0	19	N/A	0	0	5.8	0.0
B- / 7.6	8.5	1.32	11.77	725	17	65	17	1	22	45.7	-18.2	14	N/A	0	0	0.0	0.0
B- / 7.6	8.4	1.32	12.12	45	17	65	17	1	22	49.4	-17.9	19	N/A	0	0	0.0	0.0
B- / 7.6	8.5	1.33	12.22	120	17	65	17	1	22	51.5	-17.8	22	N/A	0	0	0.0	0.0
C+ / 6.6	8.5	1.32	12.12	137	17	65	17	1	22	49.1	-17.9	18	1	0	0	0.0	0.0
C+ / 6.6	8.5	1.32	12.13	83	17	65	17	1	22	47.9	-18.1	16	1	0	0	0.0	0.0
B- / 7.6	8.5	1.33	12.21	308	17	65	17	1	22	50.9	-17.9	20	N/A	0	0	0.0	0.0
D / 2.1	3.8	0.31	7.91	1	2	27	70	1	34	27.2	-6.1	74	5	0	0	5.8	0.0
D / 2.0	3.8	0.59	7.75	27	2	27	70	1	34	28.1	-6.0	58	7	0	0	0.0	0.0
B / 8.6	3.8	0.31	7.76	11	2	27	70	1	34	26.2	-6.2	71	1	0	0	0.0	0.0
B / 8.6	3.9	0.31	7.73	12	2	27	70	1	34	25.2	-6.2	68	1	0	0	0.0	0.0
C+ / 6.0	12.8	0.96	35.82	31	24	75	0	1	74	48.9	-24.6	53	N/A	0	0	5.8	0.0
C+ / 6.0	12.8	0.96	35.88	36	24	75	0	1	74	45.4	-24.9	42	N/A	0	0	0.0	0.0
C+ / 6.0	12.7	0.96	35.88	84	24	75	0	1	74	49.1	-24.6	54	N/A	0	0	0.0	0.0
C+ / 6.0	12.8	0.96	35.90	687	24	75	0	1	74	50.7	-24.5	59	N/A	100,000	0	0.0	0.0
C+ / 6.0	12.8	0.96	35.85	2,505	24	75	0	1	74	50.4	-24.5	57	N/A	0	0	0.0	0.0
C+ / 6.0	12.8	0.96	35.85	32	24	75	0	1	74	51.1	-24.5	60	N/A	10,000,000	0	0.0	0.0
B+ / 9.0	4.7	0.72	11.87	224	7	33	58	2	14	29.6	-8.6	56	N/A	0	0	5.8	0.0
B+ / 9.0	4.7	0.72	11.74	294	7	33	58	2	14	26.3	-8.9	43	N/A	0	0	0.0	0.0
B+ / 9.0	4.7	0.71	11.89	33	7	33	58	2	14	29.7	-8.7	56	N/A	0	0	0.0	0.0
B+ / 9.0	4.7	0.71	11.93	41	7	33	58	2	14	31.4	-8.4	62	N/A	0	0	0.0	0.0
B / 8.6	4.7	0.74	11.89	42	7	33	58	2	14	29.3	-8.7	33	1	0	0	0.0	0.0
B / 8.6	4.7	0.74	11.93	31	7	33	58	2	14	28.2	-8.8	30	1	0	0	0.0	0.0
B+ / 9.0	4.6	0.71	11.92	141	7	33	58	2	14	30.7	-8.5	60	N/A	0	0	0.0	0.0

Fund Type	Fund Name	Ticker Symbol	Overall Investment Rating	Phone	Performance Rating/Pts	3 Mo	6 Mo	1Yr / Pct	3Yr / Pct	5Yr / Pct	Dividend Yield	Expense Ratio
IN	Russell Multi Strat Alternative S	RMSSX	U	(800) 832-6688	U /	0.31	-0.39	-0.29 /15	--	--	2.84	2.19
FO	Russell Select International Eq Y	RTIYX	U	(800) 832-6688	U /	4.62	0.15	--	--	--	0.00	0.80
GR	Russell Select US Equity Y	RTDYX	U	(800) 832-6688	U /	1.41	5.99	--	--	--	0.00	0.52
GR	Russell Strat Call Overwriting S	ROWSX	U	(800) 832-6688	U /	1.12	1.17	0.95 /18	--	--	0.85	1.19
SC	Russell Tax-Magd US Mid-Sm Cap A	RTSAX	C+	(800) 832-6688	C+ / 6.4	3.66	11.26	6.49 /51	14.98 /75	--	0.00	1.58
SC	Russell Tax-Magd US Mid-Sm Cap C	RTSCX	C+	(800) 832-6688	C+ / 6.8	3.46	10.87	5.70 /44	14.15 /68	13.87 /77	0.00	2.33
SC	Russell Tax-Magd US Mid-Sm Cap E	RTSEX	B-	(800) 832-6688	B- / 7.5	3.70	11.29	6.52 /51	15.01 /75	14.72 /84	0.00	1.58
SC	Russell Tax-Magd US Mid-Sm Cap S	RTSSX	B	(800) 832-6688	B / 7.7	3.72	11.42	6.79 /53	15.30 /77	15.01 /87	0.00	1.33
GR	Russell Tax-Managed US Large Cap	RTLAX	C+	(800) 832-6688	C+ / 6.0	1.12	5.71	10.97 /78	14.32 /69	--	0.40	1.24
GR	Russell Tax-Managed US Large Cap	RTLCX	C+	(800) 832-6688	C+ / 6.4	0.94	5.30	10.13 /75	13.46 /63	12.75 /66	0.00	1.99
GR	Russell Tax-Managed US Large Cap	RTLEX	B-	(800) 832-6688	B- / 7.0	1.12	5.72	10.99 /78	14.32 /69	13.60 /74	0.39	1.24
GR	Russell Tax-Managed US Large Cap	RETSX	B	(800) 832-6688	B- / 7.2	1.18	5.85	11.25 /79	14.60 /72	13.89 /77	0.62	0.99
IX	Russell US Core Equity A	RSQAX	C	(800) 832-6688	C+ / 6.1	1.12	5.79	10.55 /77	14.58 /72	12.56 /65	0.86	1.09
IX	Russell US Core Equity C	REQSX	C+	(800) 832-6688	C+ / 6.5	0.90	5.40	9.72 /73	13.72 /65	11.72 /59	0.35	1.84
IX	Russell US Core Equity E	REAEX	C+	(800) 832-6688	B- / 7.1	1.12	5.79	10.57 /77	14.59 /72	12.59 /65	0.85	1.09
IX	Russell US Core Equity I	REASX	B-	(800) 832-6688	B- / 7.4	1.20	5.96	10.94 /78	14.97 /75	12.93 /68	1.21	0.76
IX	Russell US Core Equity S	RLISX	C+	(800) 832-6688	B- / 7.3	1.18	5.94	10.84 /78	14.87 /74	12.84 /67	1.13	0.84
IX	Russell US Core Equity Y	REAYX	B-	(800) 832-6688	B- / 7.5	1.23	6.03	11.05 /79	15.10 /76	13.04 /69	1.32	0.64
GR	Russell US Defensive Equity A	REQAX	C+	(800) 832-6688	C / 5.5	0.79	6.17	11.30 /80	13.33 /62	12.87 /67	0.97	1.09
GR	Russell US Defensive Equity C	REQCX	B-	(800) 832-6688	C+ / 5.9	0.60	5.77	10.48 /76	12.48 /56	12.02 /61	0.33	1.84
GR	Russell US Defensive Equity E	REQEX	B-	(800) 832-6688	C+ / 6.4	0.79	6.16	11.30 /80	13.33 /62	12.91 /67	0.97	1.09
GR	Russell US Defensive Equity I	REDSX	B-	(800) 832-6688	C+ / 6.7	0.88	6.35	11.66 /81	13.69 /65	13.24 /71	1.34	0.76
GR	Russell US Defensive Equity S	REQTX	B-	(800) 832-6688	C+ / 6.6	0.85	6.30	11.58 /81	13.60 /64	13.15 /70	1.26	0.84
GR	Russell US Defensive Equity Y	REUYX	B-	(800) 832-6688	C+ / 6.8	0.90	6.41	11.79 /82	13.82 /66	13.36 /72	1.45	0.64
GR	Russell US Dynamic Equity C	RSGCX	C	(800) 832-6688	B- / 7.3	2.30	7.16	11.63 /81	14.55 /71	13.82 /76	0.00	2.27
GR	Russell US Dynamic Equity E	RSGEX	C+	(800) 832-6688	B / 8.0	2.54	7.61	12.43 /84	15.38 /78	14.68 /84	0.00	1.52
GR	Russell US Dynamic Equity I	RSGIX	B-	(800) 832-6688	B+ / 8.3	2.59	7.70	12.73 /86	15.78 /82	15.09 /87	0.15	1.19
GR	Russell US Dynamic Equity S	RSGSX	C+	(800) 832-6688	B / 8.2	2.63	7.69	12.66 /85	15.65 /80	14.94 /86	0.09	1.27
GR	Russell US Dynamic Equity Y	RSGTX	U	(800) 832-6688	U /	2.60	7.72	12.88 /86	--	--	0.23	1.07
GR	Russell US Large Cap Equity A	RLCZX	B-	(800) 832-6688	C+ / 6.1	0.76	5.57	10.49 /76	14.70 /73	--	0.86	1.26
GR	Russell US Large Cap Equity C	RLCCX	B-	(800) 832-6688	C+ / 6.5	0.54	5.22	9.68 /73	13.85 /66	--	0.26	2.01
GR	Russell US Large Cap Equity S	RLCSX	B+	(800) 832-6688	B- / 7.4	0.84	5.76	10.80 /78	15.02 /75	--	1.12	1.01
MC	Russell US Mid Cap Equity A	RMCAX	C+	(800) 832-6688	C+ / 6.9	3.02	9.43	11.46 /80	15.36 /78	--	0.15	1.42
MC	Russell US Mid Cap Equity C	RMCCX	B+	(800) 832-6688	B- / 7.4	2.83	9.01	10.58 /77	14.51 /71	--	0.00	2.17
MC	Russell US Mid Cap Equity S	RMCSX	A-	(800) 832-6688	B+ / 8.3	3.10	9.54	11.77 /82	15.64 /80	--	0.37	1.17
GR	Russell US Small Cap Equity A	RLACX	C	(800) 832-6688	C+ / 6.8	3.67	13.74	6.13 /48	15.45 /79	14.31 /81	0.06	1.25
GR	Russell US Small Cap Equity C	RLECX	C	(800) 832-6688	B- / 7.3	3.50	13.37	5.34 /41	14.60 /72	13.45 /72	0.00	2.00
GR	Russell US Small Cap Equity E	REBEX	C+	(800) 832-6688	B / 7.9	3.69	13.76	6.14 /48	15.47 /79	14.35 /81	0.03	1.25
GR	Russell US Small Cap Equity I	REBSX	C+	(800) 832-6688	B / 8.2	3.77	13.95	6.49 /51	15.84 /82	14.68 /84	0.35	0.92
GR	Russell US Small Cap Equity S	RLESX	C+	(800) 832-6688	B / 8.1	3.75	13.90	6.41 /50	15.74 /81	14.60 /83	0.29	1.00
GR	Russell US Small Cap Equity Y	REBYX	C+	(800) 832-6688	B+ / 8.3	3.78	13.99	6.61 /52	15.96 /83	14.80 /85	0.47	0.80
GR	Russell US Strategic Equity E	RSEEX	U	(800) 832-6688	U /	0.96	5.53	10.52 /76	--	--	0.85	1.32
GR	Russell US Strategic Equity S	RSESX	U	(800) 832-6688	U /	1.04	5.67	10.89 /78	--	--	1.09	1.07
AA	Rx Dynamic Growth Fund Advisor	FMGCX	C+	(877) 773-3863	B- / 7.0	8.56	11.16	12.53 /85	11.97 /52	--	0.80	2.06
AA	Rx Dynamic Growth Fund Inst	FMGRX	B	(877) 773-3863	B / 7.9	8.79	11.70	13.61 /88	13.09 /60	10.08 /45	0.78	1.06
GL	Rx Fundamental Growth Inst	FMFGX	U	(877) 773-3863	U /	7.49	7.76	13.89 /89	--	--	0.00	1.63
GL	Rx Tactical Rotation Institutional	FMARX	U	(877) 773-3863	U /	1.60	6.86	11.37 /80	--	--	0.47	1.61
GL	Rx Traditional Equity Institutional	FMSQX	U	(877) 773-3863	U /	2.45	4.23	5.87 /45	--	--	0.43	1.93
FS	Rydex Banking A	RYBKX	D	(800) 820-0888	D+ / 2.9	-2.09	0.56	-0.98 /13	10.75 /44	4.57 /10	0.70	1.62
FS	Rydex Banking Adv	RYKAX	D+	(800) 820-0888	C- / 3.5	-2.10	0.47	-1.19 /12	10.52 /42	4.32 / 9	0.75	1.87
FS	Rydex Banking C	RYKCX	D+	(800) 820-0888	C- / 3.1	-2.25	0.21	-1.71 /11	9.93 /39	3.80 / 8	0.79	2.37
FS	Rydex Banking Inv	RYKIX	D+	(800) 820-0888	C- / 3.8	-2.02	0.71	-0.73 /14	11.02 /46	4.84 /11	0.67	1.37

● Denotes fund is closed to new investors
* Denotes fund is included in Section II

www.thestreetratings.com

RISK			NET ASSETS		ASSET					BULL / BEAR		FUND MANAGER		MINIMUMS		LOADS	
	3 Year		NAV						Portfolio	Last Bull	Last Bear	Manager	Manager	Initial	Additional	Front	Back
Risk Rating/Pts	Standard Deviation	Beta	As of 3/31/15	Total $(Mil)	Cash %	Stocks %	Bonds %	Other %	Turnover Ratio	Market Return	Market Return	Quality Pct	Tenure (Years)	Purch. $	Purch. $	End Load	End Load
U /	N/A	N/A	9.81	587	31	15	53	1	478	N/A	N/A	N/A	N/A	0	0	0.0	0.0
U /	N/A	N/A	9.52	938	0	0	0	100	0	N/A	N/A	N/A	N/A	10,000,000	0	0.0	0.0
U /	N/A	N/A	10.76	896	0	0	0	100	0	N/A	N/A	N/A	1	10,000,000	0	0.0	0.0
U /	N/A	N/A	10.87	88	0	0	0	100	5	N/A	N/A	N/A	3	0	0	0.0	0.0
C+ / 5.8	12.4	0.91	21.52	9	9	90	0	1	80	94.4	-23.0	69	11	0	0	5.8	0.0
C / 5.5	12.5	0.92	18.86	12	9	90	0	1	80	89.6	-23.2	59	11	0	0	0.0	0.0
C+ / 5.8	12.5	0.92	21.56	7	9	90	0	1	80	94.6	-23.0	69	11	0	0	0.0	0.0
C+ / 5.9	12.4	0.91	22.31	330	9	90	0	1	80	96.3	-22.9	72	11	0	0	0.0	0.0
C+ / 6.8	9.9	1.02	31.48	22	0	91	7	2	63	94.2	-18.3	38	19	0	0	5.8	0.0
C+ / 6.8	9.9	1.03	30.03	22	0	91	7	2	63	89.4	-18.6	28	19	0	0	0.0	0.0
C+ / 6.8	9.9	1.03	31.61	48	0	91	7	2	63	94.3	-18.4	38	19	0	0	0.0	0.0
C+ / 6.8	9.9	1.02	31.75	1,316	0	91	7	2	63	95.9	-18.2	42	19	0	0	0.0	0.0
C / 5.5	10.4	1.07	38.74	36	36	63	0	1	73	93.5	-19.6	32	N/A	0	0	5.8	0.0
C / 5.5	10.4	1.07	38.09	55	36	63	0	1	73	88.6	-19.9	23	N/A	0	0	0.0	0.0
C+ / 5.6	10.4	1.07	38.77	10	36	63	0	1	73	93.5	-19.6	32	N/A	0	0	0.0	0.0
C / 5.5	10.4	1.07	38.69	532	36	63	0	1	73	95.7	-19.5	36	N/A	100,000	0	0.0	0.0
C / 5.5	10.4	1.07	38.71	408	36	63	0	1	73	95.1	-19.5	35	N/A	0	0	0.0	0.0
C / 5.5	10.4	1.07	38.65	73	36	63	0	1	73	96.4	-19.5	38	N/A	10,000,000	0	0.0	0.0
B- / 7.3	9.3	0.96	47.17	26	5	94	0	1	105	86.7	-16.7	40	16	0	0	5.8	0.0
B- / 7.3	9.4	0.96	46.87	51	5	94	0	1	105	82.0	-17.0	30	16	0	0	0.0	0.0
B- / 7.3	9.4	0.96	47.22	9	5	94	0	1	105	86.8	-16.7	40	16	0	0	0.0	0.0
B- / 7.3	9.4	0.96	47.19	231	5	94	0	1	105	88.8	-16.6	45	16	100,000	0	0.0	0.0
B- / 7.3	9.4	0.96	47.25	241	5	94	0	1	105	88.2	-16.6	44	16	0	0	0.0	0.0
B- / 7.3	9.4	0.96	47.20	602	5	94	0	1	105	89.5	-16.6	47	16	10,000,000	0	0.0	0.0
C- / 3.7	10.8	1.08	9.33	12	2	97	0	1	146	94.5	-17.4	31	8	0	0	0.0	0.0
C / 4.5	10.8	1.08	10.88	2	2	97	0	1	146	99.6	-17.2	40	8	0	0	0.0	0.0
C / 4.7	10.7	1.07	11.50	21	2	97	0	1	146	102.2	-17.1	46	8	100,000	0	0.0	0.0
C / 4.7	10.7	1.07	11.32	42	2	97	0	1	146	101.2	-17.1	45	8	0	0	0.0	0.0
U /	N/A	N/A	11.46	588	2	97	0	1	146	N/A	N/A	N/A	8	10,000,000	0	0.0	0.0
B- / 7.3	10.0	1.03	13.19	8	6	93	0	1	81	N/A	N/A	41	3	0	0	5.8	0.0
B- / 7.3	10.0	1.04	13.14	2	6	93	0	1	81	N/A	N/A	31	3	0	0	0.0	0.0
B- / 7.3	10.0	1.04	13.23	439	6	93	0	1	81	N/A	N/A	44	3	0	0	0.0	0.0
C+ / 6.8	10.9	0.96	12.95	5	6	93	0	1	96	N/A	N/A	54	3	0	0	5.8	0.0
C+ / 6.8	11.0	0.97	12.71	2	6	93	0	1	96	N/A	N/A	42	3	0	0	0.0	0.0
C+ / 6.8	10.9	0.96	12.99	213	6	93	0	1	96	N/A	N/A	58	3	0	0	0.0	0.0
C / 4.4	13.7	1.19	30.76	26	10	89	0	1	86	98.8	-24.6	21	20	0	0	5.8	0.0
C / 4.3	13.7	1.19	29.59	33	10	89	0	1	86	93.8	-24.9	15	20	0	0	0.0	0.0
C / 4.5	13.7	1.19	30.89	40	10	89	0	1	86	98.9	-24.6	21	20	0	0	0.0	0.0
C / 4.5	13.7	1.19	31.14	200	10	89	0	1	86	101.0	-24.6	24	20	100,000	0	0.0	0.0
C / 4.5	13.7	1.19	31.00	1,528	10	89	0	1	86	100.5	-24.6	24	20	0	0	0.0	0.0
C / 4.4	13.7	1.19	31.01	568	10	89	0	1	86	101.8	-24.5	25	20	10,000,000	0	0.0	0.0
U /	N/A	N/A	12.66	111	4	95	0	1	85	N/A	N/A	N/A	N/A	0	0	0.0	0.0
U /	N/A	N/A	12.67	4,027	4	95	0	1	85	N/A	N/A	N/A	N/A	0	0	0.0	0.0
C / 5.5	10.9	1.57	12.43	1	7	92	0	1	425	57.9	-17.4	11	1	250	50	0.0	0.0
C+ / 5.6	10.8	1.55	12.75	21	7	92	0	1	425	63.0	-17.0	18	1	250	50	0.0	0.0
U /	N/A	N/A	12.63	48	1	98	0	1	71	N/A	N/A	N/A	2	250	50	0.0	0.0
U /	N/A	N/A	12.07	65	0	0	0	100	394	N/A	N/A	N/A	3	250	50	0.0	0.0
U /	N/A	N/A	12.96	31	0	0	0	100	4	N/A	N/A	N/A	N/A	250	50	0.0	0.0
C+ / 6.0	13.7	1.13	57.76	1	0	99	0	1	481	84.1	-30.1	3	17	2,500	0	4.8	0.0
C+ / 6.0	13.7	1.14	56.30	1	0	99	0	1	481	82.8	-30.2	3	17	2,500	0	0.0	0.0
C+ / 6.0	13.7	1.14	53.34	3	0	99	0	1	481	79.5	-30.3	2	17	2,500	0	0.0	0.0
C+ / 6.0	13.7	1.14	62.72	44	0	99	0	1	481	85.7	-30.0	3	17	2,500	0	0.0	0.0

					PERFORMANCE							
	99 Pct = Best 0 Pct = Worst					Total Return % through 3/31/15					Incl. in Returns	
Fund Type	Fund Name	Ticker Symbol	Overall Investment Rating	Phone	Perfor- mance Rating/Pts	3 Mo	6 Mo	1Yr / Pct	Annualized		Dividend Yield	Expense Ratio
									3Yr / Pct	5Yr / Pct		
GR	Rydex Basic Materials A	RYBMX	E	(800) 820-0888	E / 0.4	0.76	-3.18	-4.05 / 7	0.57 / 5	2.50 / 5	0.76	1.63
GR	Rydex Basic Materials Adv	RYBAX	E+	(800) 820-0888	E / 0.5	0.68	-3.33	-4.30 / 6	0.31 / 5	2.24 / 5	0.82	1.88
GR	Rydex Basic Materials C	RYBCX	E	(800) 820-0888	E / 0.4	0.58	-3.54	-4.76 / 6	-0.18 / 4	1.73 / 4	0.87	2.38
GR	Rydex Basic Materials Inv	RYBIX	E+	(800) 820-0888	E / 0.5	0.84	-3.04	-3.77 / 7	0.83 / 5	2.76 / 6	0.75	1.38
HL	Rydex Biotechnology A	RYBOX	B-	(800) 820-0888	A+ / 9.9	13.85	27.02	41.83 /99	37.84 /99	28.59 /99	0.00	1.61
HL	Rydex Biotechnology Adv	RYOAX	B-	(800) 820-0888	A+ / 9.9	13.79	26.86	41.49 /99	37.51 /99	28.27 /99	0.00	1.86
HL	Rydex Biotechnology C	RYCFX	B-	(800) 820-0888	A+ / 9.9	13.63	26.52	40.75 /99	36.80 /99	27.64 /99	0.00	2.36
HL	Rydex Biotechnology Inv	RYOIX	B-	(800) 820-0888	A+ / 9.9	13.92	27.18	42.19 /99	38.18 /99	28.92 /99	0.00	1.36
OT	Rydex Commodities Strgy A	RYMEX	E-	(800) 820-0888	E- / 0.0	-8.71	-34.04	-41.00 / 0	-18.52 / 0	-9.92 / 0	0.00	1.64
OT	Rydex Commodities Strgy C	RYMJX	E-	(800) 820-0888	E- / 0.0	-8.85	-34.18	-41.35 / 0	-19.06 / 0	-10.55 / 0	0.00	2.39
OT	Rydex Commodities Strgy H	RYMBX	E-	(800) 820-0888	E- / 0.0	-8.70	-33.94	-40.94 / 0	-18.46 / 0	-9.88 / 0	0.00	1.64
GR	Rydex Consumer Products A	RYPDX	B	(800) 820-0888	B- / 7.0	2.05	8.04	13.47 /88	15.10 /76	14.94 /86	0.43	1.62
GR	Rydex Consumer Products Adv	RYCAX	B+	(800) 820-0888	B / 7.7	2.00	7.93	13.19 /87	14.81 /73	14.65 /84	0.46	1.87
GR	Rydex Consumer Products C	RYCPX	B	(800) 820-0888	B- / 7.2	1.86	7.64	12.62 /85	14.23 /69	14.08 /78	0.50	2.37
GR	Rydex Consumer Products Inv	RYCIX	A-	(800) 820-0888	B / 8.1	2.13	8.20	13.77 /89	15.39 /78	15.21 /88	0.42	1.37
AG	Rydex Dow 2x Strategy A	RYLDX	A	(800) 820-0888	A+ / 9.8	-0.59	8.66	17.18 /95	22.98 /99	21.60 /99	0.00	1.76
AG	Rydex Dow 2x Strategy C	RYCYX	A	(800) 820-0888	A+ / 9.8	-0.77	8.24	16.32 /94	22.10 /98	20.69 /99	0.00	2.50
AG	Rydex Dow 2x Strategy H	RYCVX	A	(800) 820-0888	A+ / 9.8	-0.61	8.62	17.10 /95	22.95 /98	21.54 /99	0.00	1.77
AG	Rydex Dyn-NASDAQ 100 2x Strgy A	RYVLX	B	(800) 820-0888	A+ / 9.9	4.08	13.06	42.33 /99	33.02 /99	33.41 /99	0.00	1.76
AG	Rydex Dyn-NASDAQ 100 2x Strgy C	RYCCX	B	(800) 820-0888	A+ / 9.9	3.90	12.62	41.24 /99	31.99 /99	32.39 /99	0.00	2.52
AG	Rydex Dyn-NASDAQ 100 2x Strgy H	RYVYX	B	(800) 820-0888	A+ / 9.9	4.08	13.06	42.33 /99	32.99 /99	33.39 /99	0.00	1.77
TC	Rydex Electronics A	RYELX	C+	(800) 820-0888	B / 8.2	6.49	11.27	19.36 /96	14.63 /72	9.54 /41	0.00	1.62
TC	Rydex Electronics Adv	RYSAX	B-	(800) 820-0888	B+ / 8.8	6.41	11.09	19.04 /96	14.28 /69	9.26 /39	0.00	1.87
TC	Rydex Electronics C	RYSCX	C+	(800) 820-0888	B+ / 8.4	6.31	10.86	18.50 /96	13.72 /65	8.74 /35	0.00	2.37
TC	Rydex Electronics Inv	RYSIX	B	(800) 820-0888	A- / 9.1	6.54	11.39	19.65 /96	14.91 /74	9.82 /43	0.00	1.37
EM	Rydex Emerging Mkts 2x Strat A	RYWTX	E-	(800) 820-0888	E- / 0.1	-5.02	-20.70	-8.72 / 3	-11.54 / 1	--	0.00	1.81
EM	Rydex Emerging Mkts 2x Strat C	RYWUX	E-	(800) 820-0888	E- / 0.1	-5.16	-20.96	-9.32 / 3	-12.07 / 1	--	0.00	2.66
EM	Rydex Emerging Mkts 2x Strat H	RYWVX	E-	(800) 820-0888	E- / 0.1	-5.05	-20.72	-8.71 / 3	-11.61 / 1	--	0.00	1.80
EN	Rydex Energy A	RYENX	E-	(800) 820-0888	E- / 0.2	-1.44	-21.46	-21.49 / 1	-1.24 / 3	2.42 / 5	0.49	1.62
EN	Rydex Energy Advisor	RYEAX	E-	(800) 820-0888	E- / 0.2	-1.61	-21.61	-21.76 / 1	-1.53 / 3	2.16 / 5	0.53	1.87
EN	Rydex Energy C	RYECX	E-	(800) 820-0888	E- / 0.2	-1.77	-21.87	-22.18 / 1	-2.03 / 3	1.64 / 4	0.57	2.37
EN	Rydex Energy Inv	RYEIX	E-	(800) 820-0888	E- / 0.2	-1.53	-21.47	-21.42 / 1	-1.03 / 3	2.67 / 5	0.49	1.37
EN	Rydex Energy Srsvices A	RYESX	E-	(800) 820-0888	E- / 0.1	-7.49	-32.76	-37.11 / 0	-8.42 / 1	-1.92 / 2	0.00	1.62
EN	Rydex Energy Srsvices Advisor	RYVAX	E-	(800) 820-0888	E- / 0.1	-7.59	-32.89	-37.33 / 0	-8.68 / 1	-2.18 / 2	0.00	1.87
EN	Rydex Energy Srsvices C	RYVCX	E-	(800) 820-0888	E- / 0.1	-7.65	-33.01	-37.58 / 0	-9.11 / 1	-2.66 / 1	0.00	2.37
EN	Rydex Energy Srsvices Inv	RYVIX	E-	(800) 820-0888	E- / 0.1	-7.41	-32.66	-36.95 / 0	-8.20 / 1	-1.68 / 2	0.00	1.37
FO	Rydex Eurp 1.25x Strgy A	RYAEX	E	(800) 820-0888	D- / 1.1	3.53	-6.58	-10.33 / 3	7.55 /24	1.98 / 4	0.33	1.72
FO	Rydex Eurp 1.25x Strgy C	RYCEX	E	(800) 820-0888	D- / 1.1	3.38	-6.86	-10.94 / 3	6.32 /18	1.02 / 3	0.40	2.47
FO	Rydex Eurp 1.25x Strgy H	RYEUX	E+	(800) 820-0888	D- / 1.3	3.56	-6.57	-10.36 / 3	7.20 /22	1.78 / 4	0.35	1.71
FS	Rydex Financial Srsvice A	RYFNX	C+	(800) 820-0888	C+ / 5.9	-0.11	6.83	8.89 /69	14.06 /68	9.31 /39	0.22	1.65
FS	Rydex Financial Srsvice Advisor	RYFAX	C+	(800) 820-0888	C+ / 6.4	-0.17	6.70	8.63 /67	13.78 /65	9.04 /37	0.24	1.90
FS	Rydex Financial Srsvice C	RYFCX	C+	(800) 820-0888	C+ / 6.1	-0.29	6.44	8.08 /63	13.23 /61	8.51 /33	0.26	2.40
FS	Rydex Financial Srsvice Inv	RYFIX	C+	(800) 820-0888	C+ / 6.8	-0.05	6.96	9.17 /70	14.34 /70	9.58 /41	0.22	1.40
HL	Rydex Health Care A	RYHEX	A+	(800) 820-0888	A+ / 9.9	10.34	19.88	30.21 /99	26.61 /99	19.23 /98	0.00	1.62
HL	Rydex Health Care Advisor	RYHAX	A+	(800) 820-0888	A+ / 9.9	10.25	19.74	29.89 /99	26.31 /99	18.96 /98	0.00	1.87
HL	Rydex Health Care C	RYHCX	A+	(800) 820-0888	A+ / 9.9	10.15	19.47	29.21 /99	25.67 /99	18.39 /98	0.00	2.37
HL	Rydex Health Care Inv	RYHIX	A+	(800) 820-0888	A+ / 9.9	10.38	20.04	30.51 /99	26.93 /99	19.50 /99	0.00	1.37
TC	Rydex Internet A	RYINX	C-	(800) 820-0888	C+ / 6.8	2.49	2.46	6.12 /48	16.33 /86	14.26 /80	0.00	1.62
TC	Rydex Internet Advisor	RYIAX	C	(800) 820-0888	B- / 7.4	2.43	2.32	5.80 /45	16.01 /83	13.96 /77	0.00	1.87
TC	Rydex Internet C	RYICX	C	(800) 820-0888	B- / 7.0	2.30	2.07	5.34 /41	15.44 /79	13.39 /72	0.00	2.37
TC	Rydex Internet Inv	RYIIX	C+	(800) 820-0888	B / 7.9	2.55	2.59	6.40 /50	16.61 /88	14.54 /83	0.00	1.37
AG	Rydex Inv Dow 2x Strategy A	RYIDX	E-	(800) 820-0888	E- / 0.0	-2.44	-13.41	-22.85 / 1	-26.18 / 0	-28.42 / 0	0.00	1.75

RISK	3 Year		NET ASSETS		ASSET				Portfolio	BULL / BEAR		FUND MANAGER		MINIMUMS		LOADS	
Risk Rating/Pts	Standard Deviation	Beta	NAV As of 3/31/15	Total $(Mil)	Cash %	Stocks %	Bonds %	Other %	Turnover Ratio	Last Bull Market Return	Last Bear Market Return	Manager Quality Pct	Manager Tenure (Years)	Initial Purch. $	Additional Purch. $	Front End Load	Back End Load
C / 5.2	14.0	1.07	47.54	6	0	99	0	1	349	27.6	-27.3	0	17	2,500	0	4.8	0.0
C / 5.2	14.0	1.07	46.18	3	0	99	0	1	349	26.5	-27.3	0	17	2,500	0	0.0	0.0
C / 5.1	14.0	1.07	43.36	3	0	99	0	1	349	24.4	-27.5	0	17	2,500	0	0.0	0.0
C / 5.2	14.0	1.07	50.18	47	0	99	0	1	349	28.7	-27.2	1	17	2,500	0	0.0	0.0
C- / 3.2	19.6	0.85	87.63	91	0	99	0	1	119	246.1	-14.5	99	17	2,500	0	4.8	0.0
C- / 3.2	19.6	0.85	85.39	73	0	99	0	1	119	243.3	-14.6	99	17	2,500	0	0.0	0.0
C- / 3.2	19.6	0.85	80.88	41	0	99	0	1	119	237.2	-14.8	99	17	2,500	0	0.0	0.0
C- / 3.2	19.6	0.85	93.63	496	0	99	0	1	119	249.1	-14.5	99	17	2,500	0	0.0	0.0
E+ / 0.6	18.5	1.01	9.01	1	100	0	0	0	0	-33.3	-24.0	0	10	2,500	0	4.8	0.0
E+ / 0.6	18.4	1.00	8.34	1	100	0	0	0	0	-34.9	-24.2	0	10	2,500	0	0.0	0.0
E+ / 0.7	18.5	1.00	9.03	3	100	0	0	0	0	-33.1	-24.0	0	10	2,500	0	0.0	0.0
C+ / 6.9	10.1	0.89	54.66	33	0	99	0	1	112	77.1	-4.7	75	17	2,500	0	4.8	0.0
C+ / 6.9	10.1	0.89	52.94	47	0	99	0	1	112	75.6	-4.8	72	17	2,500	0	0.0	0.0
C+ / 6.8	10.1	0.89	49.18	18	0	99	0	1	112	72.7	-5.0	67	17	2,500	0	0.0	0.0
C+ / 6.9	10.1	0.89	58.55	224	0	99	0	1	112	78.7	-4.6	77	17	2,500	0	0.0	0.0
C+ / 5.6	20.3	2.04	50.69	14	79	20	0	1	3,338	182.5	-28.7	2	11	2,500	0	4.8	0.0
C / 5.5	20.3	2.04	46.62	4	79	20	0	1	3,338	175.3	-28.9	2	11	2,500	0	0.0	0.0
C+ / 5.6	20.3	2.04	50.54	25	79	20	0	1	3,338	182.1	-28.8	2	11	2,500	0	0.0	0.0
C- / 3.8	23.6	2.13	369.52	21	19	80	0	1	346	303.1	-23.4	23	15	2,500	0	4.8	0.0
C- / 3.7	23.6	2.13	316.07	23	19	80	0	1	346	292.7	-23.7	16	15	2,500	0	0.0	0.0
C- / 3.8	23.6	2.13	369.50	293	19	80	0	1	346	302.9	-23.4	23	15	2,500	0	0.0	0.0
C / 4.3	16.5	1.31	78.62	2	0	99	0	1	1,436	86.4	-28.4	7	17	2,500	0	4.8	0.0
C- / 4.2	16.5	1.30	76.66	6	0	99	0	1	1,436	84.6	-28.4	6	17	2,500	0	0.0	0.0
C- / 4.2	16.5	1.31	72.76	1	0	99	0	1	1,436	81.5	-28.6	5	17	2,500	0	0.0	0.0
C / 4.3	16.5	1.31	83.54	18	0	99	0	1	1,436	88.0	-28.3	8	17	2,500	0	0.0	0.0
D- / 1.3	34.6	2.35	60.49	3	24	75	0	1	1,412	3.8	-47.9	1	5	2,500	0	4.8	0.0
D- / 1.3	34.6	2.35	59.36	1	24	75	0	1	1,412	1.9	-47.5	1	5	2,500	0	0.0	0.0
D- / 1.3	34.6	2.35	60.59	8	24	75	0	1	1,412	3.8	-47.7	1	5	2,500	0	0.0	0.0
D+ / 2.5	18.3	1.14	21.94	5	0	99	0	1	231	22.8	-31.2	8	17	2,500	0	4.8	0.0
D+ / 2.5	18.3	1.14	21.34	3	0	99	0	1	231	21.7	-31.3	7	17	2,500	0	0.0	0.0
D+ / 2.5	18.3	1.14	19.98	7	0	99	0	1	231	19.5	-31.5	6	17	2,500	0	0.0	0.0
D+ / 2.5	18.3	1.14	23.24	26	0	99	0	1	231	23.8	-31.2	9	17	2,500	0	0.0	0.0
D / 1.9	22.3	1.32	37.32	4	0	99	0	1	350	1.0	-34.8	1	17	2,500	0	4.8	0.0
D / 1.9	22.3	1.32	36.28	3	0	99	0	1	350	0.1	-34.9	1	17	2,500	0	0.0	0.0
D / 1.9	22.3	1.32	34.28	4	0	99	0	1	350	-1.6	-35.1	1	17	2,500	0	0.0	0.0
D / 2.0	22.3	1.32	39.36	14	0	99	0	1	350	1.8	-34.8	1	17	2,500	0	0.0	0.0
C / 4.4	18.6	1.34	15.55	1	53	46	0	1	654	55.0	-31.9	11	15	2,500	0	4.8	0.0
C / 4.3	18.4	1.33	13.77	1	53	46	0	1	654	49.8	-32.3	6	15	2,500	0	0.0	0.0
C / 4.4	18.5	1.34	15.42	10	53	46	0	1	654	53.5	-31.9	9	15	2,500	0	0.0	0.0
C+ / 6.1	11.0	0.94	109.65	3	0	99	0	1	414	92.6	-26.6	38	17	2,500	0	4.8	0.0
C+ / 6.1	11.0	0.94	106.60	5	0	99	0	1	414	91.0	-26.6	34	17	2,500	0	0.0	0.0
C+ / 6.1	11.0	0.94	100.28	1	0	99	0	1	414	87.9	-26.8	29	17	2,500	0	0.0	0.0
C+ / 6.1	11.0	0.94	115.57	50	0	99	0	1	414	94.3	-26.5	41	17	2,500	0	0.0	0.0
C+ / 6.6	10.5	0.83	33.60	29	1	98	0	1	277	141.6	-14.6	99	17	2,500	0	4.8	0.0
C+ / 6.6	10.5	0.83	32.71	49	1	98	0	1	277	139.8	-14.7	98	17	2,500	0	0.0	0.0
C+ / 6.5	10.5	0.83	30.82	12	1	98	0	1	277	135.6	-14.9	98	17	2,500	0	0.0	0.0
C+ / 6.6	10.5	0.83	35.83	175	1	98	0	1	277	143.6	-14.5	99	17	2,500	0	0.0	0.0
C- / 4.0	15.6	1.18	73.71	2	0	99	0	1	472	102.9	-25.0	32	15	2,500	0	4.8	0.0
C- / 4.0	15.6	1.18	71.64	2	0	99	0	1	472	101.1	-25.2	28	15	2,500	0	0.0	0.0
C- / 4.0	15.6	1.18	67.17	2	0	99	0	1	472	97.8	-25.3	23	15	2,500	0	0.0	0.0
C- / 4.0	15.6	1.17	77.87	8	0	99	0	1	472	104.7	-25.0	35	15	2,500	0	0.0	0.0
E / 0.5	20.0	-2.00	30.36	1	100	0	0	0	15,091	-75.8	23.4	59	7	2,500	0	4.8	0.0

99 Pct = Best
0 Pct = Worst

Fund Type	Fund Name	Ticker Symbol	Overall Investment Rating	Phone	Perfor-mance Rating/Pts	3 Mo	6 Mo	1Yr / Pct	3Yr / Pct	5Yr / Pct	Dividend Yield	Expense Ratio
AG	Rydex Inv Dow 2x Strategy C	RYCZX	E-	(800) 820-0888	E- / 0.0	-2.63	-13.72	-23.46 / 1	-26.79 / 0	-29.01 / 0	0.00	2.47
AG	Rydex Inv Dow 2x Strategy H	RYCWX	E-	(800) 820-0888	E- / 0.0	-2.47	-13.37	-22.86 / 1	-26.09 / 0	-28.39 / 0	0.00	1.77
MC	Rydex Inv Mid-Cap Stgy A	RYAGX	E-	(800) 820-0888	E- / 0.0	-5.64	-12.14	-13.47 / 2	-17.42 / 0	-17.83 / 0	0.00	1.67
MC	Rydex Inv Mid-Cap Stgy C	RYCLX	E-	(800) 820-0888	E- / 0.0	-5.79	-12.44	-14.09 / 2	-18.06 / 0	-18.45 / 0	0.00	2.42
MC	Rydex Inv Mid-Cap Stgy H	RYMHX	E-	(800) 820-0888	E- / 0.0	-5.62	-12.11	-13.47 / 2	-17.44 / 0	-17.84 / 0	0.00	1.67
AG	Rydex Inv NASDAQ 100 2x Stgy A	RYVTX	E-	(800) 820-0888	E- / 0.0	-6.38	-16.59	-37.04 / 0	-32.89 / 0	-36.00 / 0	0.00	1.76
AG	Rydex Inv NASDAQ 100 2x Stgy C	RYCDX	E-	(800) 820-0888	E- / 0.0	-6.59	-17.03	-37.53 / 0	-33.62 / 0	-36.53 / 0	0.00	2.54
AG	Rydex Inv NASDAQ 100 2x Stgy H	RYVNX	E-	(800) 820-0888	E- / 0.0	-6.34	-16.71	-37.02 / 0	-32.98 / 0	-35.97 / 0	0.00	1.78
AG	Rydex Inv NASDAQ 100 Strgy A	RYAPX	E-	(800) 820-0888	E- / 0.0	-3.09	-8.56	-20.50 / 1	-17.77 / 0	-19.21 / 0	0.00	1.71
AG	Rydex Inv NASDAQ 100 Strgy Adv	RYAAX	E-	(800) 820-0888	E- / 0.0	-3.21	-8.74	-20.86 / 1	-18.08 / 0	-19.39 / 0	0.00	1.96
AG	Rydex Inv NASDAQ 100 Strgy C	RYACX	E-	(800) 820-0888	E- / 0.0	-3.30	-8.92	-21.13 / 1	-18.39 / 0	-19.81 / 0	0.00	2.46
AG	Rydex Inv NASDAQ 100 Strgy Inv	RYAIX	E-	(800) 820-0888	E- / 0.0	-3.05	-8.44	-20.31 / 1	-17.49 / 0	-18.94 / 0	0.00	1.46
SC	Rydex Inv Rusl 2000 2x Strtgy A	RYIUX	E-	(800) 820-0888	E- / 0.0	-10.31	-27.89	-23.39 / 1	-33.63 / 0	-36.31 / 0	0.00	1.77
SC	Rydex Inv Rusl 2000 2x Strtgy C	RYIZX	E-	(800) 820-0888	E- / 0.0	-10.51	-28.22	-24.08 / 1	-34.04 / 0	-36.70 / 0	0.00	2.49
SC	Rydex Inv Rusl 2000 2x Strtgy H	RYIRX	E-	(800) 820-0888	E- / 0.0	-10.38	-27.94	-23.48 / 1	-33.57 / 0	-36.30 / 0	0.00	1.79
SC	Rydex Inv Russell 2000 Stgy A	RYAFX	E-	(800) 820-0888	E- / 0.0	-4.98	-14.59	-11.48 / 2	-17.68 / 0	-18.45 / 0	0.00	1.72
SC	Rydex Inv Russell 2000 Stgy C	RYCQX	E-	(800) 820-0888	E- / 0.0	-5.19	-14.95	-12.19 / 2	-18.29 / 0	-19.05 / 0	0.00	2.47
SC	Rydex Inv Russell 2000 Stgy H	RYSHX	E-	(800) 820-0888	E- / 0.0	-4.99	-14.60	-11.51 / 2	-17.62 / 0	-18.41 / 0	0.00	1.72
AG	Rydex Inv S&P 500 2x Strategy A	RYTMX	E-	(800) 820-0888	E- / 0.0	-3.32	-13.86	-25.38 / 0	-29.97 / 0	-30.46 / 0	0.00	1.74
AG	Rydex Inv S&P 500 2x Strategy C	RYCBX	E-	(800) 820-0888	E- / 0.0	-3.47	-14.17	-25.96 / 0	-30.45 / 0	-30.93 / 0	0.00	2.49
AG	Rydex Inv S&P 500 2x Strategy H	RYTPX	E-	(800) 820-0888	E- / 0.0	-3.31	-13.85	-25.42 / 0	-30.00 / 0	-30.45 / 0	0.00	1.74
AG	Rydex Inv S&P 500 Stgry A	RYARX	E-	(800) 820-0888	E- / 0.0	-1.52	-6.98	-13.49 / 2	-16.21 / 0	-15.97 / 0	0.00	1.68
AG	Rydex Inv S&P 500 Stgry Adv	RYUAX	E-	(800) 820-0888	E- / 0.1	-1.48	-6.94	-13.54 / 2	-16.38 / 0	-16.16 / 0	0.00	1.93
AG	Rydex Inv S&P 500 Stgry C	RYUCX	E-	(800) 820-0888	E- / 0.1	-1.64	-7.31	-14.09 / 2	-16.83 / 0	-16.60 / 0	0.00	2.42
AG	Rydex Inv S&P 500 Stgry Inv	RYURX	E-	(800) 820-0888	E- / 0.1	-1.49	-6.83	-13.26 / 2	-15.99 / 0	-15.75 / 0	0.00	1.42
EM	Rydex Inverse Emg Mkts 2x Str A	RYWWX	E-	(800) 820-0888	E- / 0.2	0.42	13.67	-7.96 / 3	-4.33 / 2	--	0.00	1.78
EM	Rydex Inverse Emg Mkts 2x Str C	RYWZX	E-	(800) 820-0888	E- / 0.2	0.23	13.02	-8.78 / 3	-5.00 / 2	--	0.00	2.48
EM	Rydex Inverse Emg Mkts 2x Str H	RYWYX	E-	(800) 820-0888	E / 0.3	0.42	13.13	-8.35 / 3	-4.50 / 2	--	0.00	1.78
FO	Rydex Japan 2x Strategy Fd A	RYJSX	C-	(800) 820-0888	A- / 9.0	22.45	15.99	20.61 / 97	14.66 / 72	7.15 / 24	0.00	1.52
FO	Rydex Japan 2x Strategy Fd C	RYJTX	C-	(800) 820-0888	A- / 9.2	22.34	15.66	20.23 / 97	14.04 / 67	6.49 / 20	0.00	2.27
FO	Rydex Japan 2x Strategy Fd H	RYJHX	C-	(800) 820-0888	A / 9.4	22.47	16.03	20.64 / 97	14.71 / 73	7.24 / 25	0.00	1.52
GR	Rydex Leisure A	RYLSX	A+	(800) 820-0888	A- / 9.0	2.71	8.73	10.86 / 78	18.79 / 96	17.50 / 97	0.19	1.62
GR	Rydex Leisure Adv	RYLAX	A+	(800) 820-0888	A / 9.3	2.66	8.65	10.66 / 77	18.51 / 96	17.23 / 96	0.21	1.87
GR	Rydex Leisure C	RYLCX	A+	(800) 820-0888	A- / 9.1	2.55	8.34	10.04 / 74	17.92 / 94	16.63 / 95	0.22	2.37
GR	Rydex Leisure Inv	RYLIX	A+	(800) 820-0888	A / 9.5	2.79	8.86	11.15 / 79	19.09 / 97	17.82 / 97	0.19	1.37
MC	Rydex Mid Cap 1.5x Strgy A	RYAHX	A+	(800) 820-0888	A+ / 9.8	7.35	16.77	15.50 / 92	23.07 / 99	20.23 / 99	0.00	1.67
MC	Rydex Mid Cap 1.5x Strgy C	RYDCX	A+	(800) 820-0888	A+ / 9.8	7.15	16.35	14.63 / 91	22.16 / 98	19.35 / 98	0.00	2.42
MC	Rydex Mid Cap 1.5x Strgy H	RYMDX	A+	(800) 820-0888	A+ / 9.9	7.42	16.86	15.56 / 93	23.11 / 99	20.27 / 99	0.00	1.68
MC	Rydex MidCap 400 Pure Growth A	RYMGX	C-	(800) 820-0888	C+ / 6.1	8.81	8.38	7.18 / 57	13.81 / 66	15.08 / 87	0.00	1.52
MC	Rydex MidCap 400 Pure Growth C	RYCKX	D+	(800) 820-0888	C+ / 6.3	8.60	7.99	6.39 / 50	12.97 / 60	14.22 / 80	0.00	2.27
MC	Rydex MidCap 400 Pure Growth H	RYBHX	C-	(800) 820-0888	C+ / 6.9	8.80	8.38	7.18 / 57	13.81 / 66	15.07 / 87	0.00	1.52
MC	Rydex MidCap 400 Pure Value A	RYMVX	C+	(800) 820-0888	C+ / 5.7	0.79	6.97	6.25 / 49	14.15 / 68	10.52 / 49	0.10	1.56
MC	Rydex MidCap 400 Pure Value C	RYMMX	C+	(800) 820-0888	C+ / 6.0	0.60	6.58	5.47 / 42	13.29 / 62	9.68 / 42	0.12	2.32
MC	Rydex MidCap 400 Pure Value H	RYAVX	C+	(800) 820-0888	C+ / 6.5	0.80	6.98	6.26 / 49	14.13 / 68	10.50 / 49	0.11	1.56
AG	Rydex NASDAQ 100 A	RYATX	A-	(800) 820-0888	B / 8.2	2.37	6.89	20.24 / 97	16.16 / 85	16.82 / 96	0.00	1.54
AG	Rydex NASDAQ 100 Advisor	RYAOX	A	(800) 820-0888	B+ / 8.8	2.31	6.78	19.94 / 97	15.84 / 82	16.51 / 95	0.00	1.79
AG	Rydex NASDAQ 100 C	RYCOX	A-	(800) 820-0888	B+ / 8.4	2.18	6.48	19.37 / 96	15.31 / 77	15.97 / 93	0.00	2.29
AG	Rydex NASDAQ 100 Investor	RYOCX	A+	(800) 820-0888	A- / 9.1	2.42	7.01	20.53 / 97	16.45 / 87	17.14 / 96	0.00	1.29
AG	Rydex Nova A	RYANX	A+	(800) 820-0888	A+ / 9.8	0.91	7.79	17.09 / 95	22.38 / 98	19.28 / 98	0.10	1.53
AG	Rydex Nova Advisor	RYNAX	A+	(800) 820-0888	A+ / 9.8	0.85	7.65	16.79 / 94	22.06 / 98	18.98 / 98	0.11	1.78
AG	Rydex Nova C	RYNCX	A+	(800) 820-0888	A+ / 9.8	0.73	7.39	16.19 / 94	21.46 / 98	18.40 / 98	0.11	2.28
AG	Rydex Nova Investor	RYNVX	A+	(800) 820-0888	A+ / 9.8	0.98	7.92	17.36 / 95	22.68 / 98	19.57 / 99	0.10	1.28

● Denotes fund is closed to new investors
* Denotes fund is included in Section II

RISK Rating/Pts	3 Year Standard Deviation	Beta	NAV As of 3/31/15	Total $(Mil)	Cash %	Stocks %	Bonds %	Other %	Portfolio Turnover Ratio	Last Bull Market Return	Last Bear Market Return	Manager Quality Pct	Manager Tenure (Years)	Initial Purch. $	Additional Purch. $	Front End Load	Back End Load
E / 0.4	20.3	-2.03	27.74	1	100	0	0	0	15,091	-76.5	22.9	51	7	2,500	0	0.0	0.0
E / 0.5	20.0	-2.01	30.44	8	100	0	0	0	15,091	-75.8	23.3	61	7	2,500	0	0.0	0.0
D+ / 2.5	11.0	-1.00	30.76	N/A	100	0	0	0	0	-57.1	22.5	20	11	2,500	0	4.8	0.0
D+ / 2.5	11.1	-1.00	28.16	N/A	100	0	0	0	0	-58.2	22.0	15	11	2,500	0	0.0	0.0
D+ / 2.5	11.0	-1.00	30.71	4	100	0	0	0	0	-57.1	22.5	20	11	2,500	0	0.0	0.0
E- / 0.0	23.2	-2.10	19.36	N/A	60	0	39	1	0	-83.9	12.5	2	15	2,500	0	4.8	0.0
E- / 0.0	23.2	-2.10	17.30	1	60	0	39	1	0	-84.5	12.6	2	15	2,500	0	0.0	0.0
E- / 0.0	23.2	-2.10	19.34	22	60	0	39	1	0	-84.0	12.8	2	15	2,500	0	0.0	0.0
D+ / 2.4	11.5	-1.06	25.44	1	100	0	0	0	94	-59.2	7.8	17	17	2,500	0	4.8	0.0
D+ / 2.4	11.5	-1.06	24.74	N/A	100	0	0	0	94	-59.5	7.8	14	17	2,500	0	0.0	0.0
D+ / 2.4	11.5	-1.06	22.58	1	100	0	0	0	94	-60.2	7.4	13	17	2,500	0	0.0	0.0
D+ / 2.5	11.5	-1.05	26.37	7	100	0	0	0	94	-58.7	8.0	19	17	2,500	0	0.0	0.0
E- / 0.0	27.3	-1.99	25.05	1	100	0	0	0	0	-84.7	49.4	1	9	2,500	0	4.8	0.0
E- / 0.0	27.2	-1.99	23.33	1	100	0	0	0	0	-85.1	49.5	1	9	2,500	0	0.0	0.0
E- / 0.0	27.2	-1.99	24.96	11	100	0	0	0	0	-84.7	49.6	1	9	2,500	0	0.0	0.0
D / 2.1	13.4	-1.00	29.22	1	100	0	0	0	0	-58.6	25.1	13	11	2,500	0	4.8	0.0
D / 2.0	13.4	-1.00	26.86	2	100	0	0	0	0	-59.6	24.7	9	11	2,500	0	0.0	0.0
D / 2.1	13.4	-1.00	29.30	7	100	0	0	0	0	-58.5	25.0	13	11	2,500	0	0.0	0.0
E / 0.3	19.4	-2.00	23.87	3	74	0	25	1	0	-80.3	28.4	7	15	2,500	0	4.8	0.0
E- / 0.2	19.4	-2.00	21.45	2	74	0	25	1	0	-80.8	28.1	5	15	2,500	0	0.0	0.0
E- / 0.2	19.4	-2.00	23.94	27	74	0	25	1	0	-80.3	28.6	7	15	2,500	0	0.0	0.0
D+ / 2.8	9.5	-1.00	13.59	5	64	0	35	1	0	-55.2	14.9	27	21	2,500	0	4.8	0.0
D+ / 2.8	9.6	-1.00	13.28	2	64	0	35	1	0	-55.5	14.8	25	21	2,500	0	0.0	0.0
D+ / 2.7	9.5	-1.00	12.56	5	64	0	35	1	0	-56.3	14.6	19	21	2,500	0	0.0	0.0
D+ / 2.8	9.5	-1.00	14.59	61	64	0	35	1	0	-54.8	15.0	30	21	2,500	0	0.0	0.0
E- / 0.0	34.5	-2.34	16.88	N/A	100	0	0	0	0	-50.0	51.9	25	5	2,500	0	4.8	0.0
E- / 0.0	34.5	-2.34	17.36	N/A	100	0	0	0	0	-49.9	54.9	18	5	2,500	0	0.0	0.0
E- / 0.0	34.5	-2.33	16.80	23	100	0	0	0	0	-50.3	52.0	23	5	2,500	0	0.0	0.0
D- / 1.2	29.5	1.44	23.29	N/A	100	0	0	0	0	73.4	-20.5	73	7	2,500	0	4.8	0.0
D- / 1.1	29.5	1.44	22.23	N/A	100	0	0	0	0	70.1	-20.8	68	7	2,500	0	0.0	0.0
D- / 1.2	29.5	1.45	23.38	18	100	0	0	0	0	73.7	-20.5	74	7	2,500	0	0.0	0.0
B- / 7.1	10.8	1.04	56.88	10	0	99	0	1	265	122.1	-18.7	82	17	2,500	0	4.8	0.0
B- / 7.1	10.8	1.04	55.50	8	0	99	0	1	265	120.3	-18.7	81	17	2,500	0	0.0	0.0
B- / 7.1	10.8	1.04	52.72	2	0	99	0	1	265	116.6	-18.9	77	17	2,500	0	0.0	0.0
B- / 7.2	10.8	1.04	60.75	48	0	99	0	1	265	124.0	-18.6	84	17	2,500	0	0.0	0.0
C+ / 5.9	16.8	1.51	67.32	5	56	43	0	1	563	159.7	-33.8	26	14	2,500	0	4.8	0.0
C+ / 5.9	16.8	1.51	60.27	5	56	43	0	1	563	153.3	-33.9	18	14	2,500	0	0.0	0.0
C+ / 5.9	16.8	1.51	67.45	15	56	43	0	1	563	160.3	-33.7	26	14	2,500	0	0.0	0.0
C- / 3.8	12.3	1.05	53.86	41	0	99	0	1	131	75.4	-18.5	19	11	2,500	0	4.8	0.0
C- / 3.5	12.3	1.05	48.60	27	0	99	0	1	131	71.0	-18.7	14	11	2,500	0	0.0	0.0
C- / 3.8	12.3	1.05	53.91	125	0	99	0	1	131	75.4	-18.5	19	11	2,500	0	0.0	0.0
C+ / 6.4	13.7	1.16	45.68	2	0	99	0	1	506	94.2	-24.9	10	11	2,500	0	4.8	0.0
C+ / 6.4	13.7	1.16	41.59	3	0	99	0	1	506	89.2	-25.1	7	11	2,500	0	0.0	0.0
C+ / 6.4	13.7	1.16	45.62	9	0	99	0	1	506	94.0	-24.9	10	11	2,500	0	0.0	0.0
C+ / 6.9	11.5	1.06	23.78	71	37	62	0	1	141	106.4	-11.1	55	21	2,500	0	4.8	0.0
C+ / 6.8	11.5	1.06	23.06	67	37	62	0	1	141	104.6	-11.2	51	21	2,500	0	0.0	0.0
C+ / 6.8	11.5	1.06	21.60	32	37	62	0	1	141	101.3	-11.4	43	21	2,500	0	0.0	0.0
C+ / 6.9	11.5	1.06	25.38	770	37	62	0	1	141	108.3	-11.0	60	21	2,500	0	0.0	0.0
C+ / 6.6	14.5	1.51	46.40	4	47	52	0	1	259	161.8	-25.1	33	19	2,500	0	4.8	0.0
C+ / 6.6	14.5	1.51	45.08	4	47	52	0	1	259	159.6	-25.2	30	19	2,500	0	0.0	0.0
C+ / 6.6	14.5	1.51	42.50	12	47	52	0	1	259	155.3	-25.3	25	19	2,500	0	0.0	0.0
C+ / 6.6	14.5	1.51	49.42	148	47	52	0	1	259	164.0	-25.0	37	19	2,500	0	0.0	0.0

						PERFORMANCE							
99 Pct = Best							Total Return % through 3/31/15					Incl. in Returns	
0 Pct = Worst						Perfor-				Annualized		Dividend	Expense
Fund Type	Fund Name	Ticker Symbol	Overall Investment Rating	Phone		mance Rating/Pts	3 Mo	6 Mo	1Yr / Pct	3Yr / Pct	5Yr / Pct	Yield	Ratio
PM	Rydex Precious Metal A	RYMNX	E-	(800) 820-0888		E- / 0.0	-5.05	-19.85	-28.13 / 0	-25.99 / 0	-15.48 / 0	3.15	1.52
PM	Rydex Precious Metal Advisor	RYMPX	E-	(800) 820-0888		E- / 0.0	-5.02	-19.90	-28.24 / 0	-26.15 / 0	-15.67 / 0	3.40	1.77
PM	Rydex Precious Metal C	RYZCX	E-	(800) 820-0888		E- / 0.0	-5.21	-20.13	-28.64 / 0	-26.53 / 0	-16.10 / 0	3.71	2.27
PM	Rydex Precious Metal Investor	RYPMX	E-	(800) 820-0888		E- / 0.0	-4.89	-19.68	-27.88 / 0	-25.78 / 0	-15.25 / 0	3.20	1.27
RE	Rydex Real Estate A	RYREX	D+	(800) 820-0888		C+ / 5.7	3.18	13.81	15.58 /93	10.96 /45	12.06 /61	0.81	1.65
RE	Rydex Real Estate C	RYCRX	D+	(800) 820-0888		C+ / 5.9	2.99	13.39	14.73 /91	10.12 /40	11.16 /54	0.93	2.38
RE	Rydex Real Estate H	RYHRX	C-	(800) 820-0888		C+ / 6.5	3.18	13.81	15.55 /93	10.91 /45	12.03 /61	0.85	1.64
GR	Rydex Retailing A	RYRTX	A+	(800) 820-0888		A / 9.5	6.29	18.28	19.44 /96	16.99 /90	16.95 /96	0.00	1.62
GR	Rydex Retailing Advisor	RYRAX	A+	(800) 820-0888		A+ / 9.7	6.24	18.16	19.18 /96	16.81 /89	16.72 /95	0.00	1.87
GR	Rydex Retailing C	RYRCX	A+	(800) 820-0888		A+ / 9.6	6.07	17.77	18.51 /96	16.12 /84	16.06 /93	0.00	2.37
GR	Rydex Retailing Investor	RYRIX	A+	(800) 820-0888		A+ / 9.7	6.35	18.39	19.50 /96	17.25 /91	17.21 /96	0.00	1.37
AG	Rydex Russell 2000 1.5x Strgy A	RYAKX	B+	(800) 820-0888		A+ / 9.8	5.95	20.80	9.48 /72	21.86 /98	18.22 /98	0.000	1.78
AG	Rydex Russell 2000 1.5x Strgy C	RYCMX	B+	(800) 820-0888		A+ / 9.8	5.73	20.33	8.64 /67	20.95 /98	17.32 /97	0.000	2.53
AG	Rydex Russell 2000 1.5x Strgy H	RYMKX	B+	(800) 820-0888		A+ / 9.8	5.92	20.80	9.48 /72	21.88 /98	18.20 /98	0.000	1.78
SC	Rydex Russell 2000 2x Strtgy A	RYRUX	C+	(800) 820-0888		A+ / 9.9	7.60	27.85	11.52 /81	28.83 /99	22.08 /99	0.00	1.81
SC	Rydex Russell 2000 2x Strtgy C	RYRLX	C+	(800) 820-0888		A+ / 9.9	7.42	27.40	10.71 /77	27.93 /99	21.23 /99	0.00	2.55
SC	Rydex Russell 2000 2x Strtgy H	RYRSX	C+	(800) 820-0888		A+ / 9.9	7.60	27.86	11.52 /81	28.80 /99	22.05 /99	0.00	1.83
SC	Rydex Russell 2000 A	RYRRX	C+	(800) 820-0888		C+ / 6.4	3.90	13.41	6.42 /50	14.36 /70	12.93 /68	0.00	1.65
SC	Rydex Russell 2000 C	RYROX	C+	(800) 820-0888		C+ / 6.6	3.75	12.95	5.61 /43	13.45 /63	12.01 /61	0.00	2.42
SC	Rydex Russell 2000 H	RYRHX	B	(800) 820-0888		B- / 7.2	3.88	13.38	6.37 /50	14.33 /70	12.90 /67	0.00	1.64
AG	Rydex S&P 500 2x Strategy A	RYTTX	A-	(800) 820-0888		A+ / 9.9	0.88	9.93	22.51 /97	29.80 /99	24.33 /99	0.00	1.73
AG	Rydex S&P 500 2x Strategy C	RYCTX	A-	(800) 820-0888		A+ / 9.9	0.69	9.53	21.59 /97	28.84 /99	23.44 /99	0.00	2.50
AG	Rydex S&P 500 2x Strategy H	RYTNX	A-	(800) 820-0888		A+ / 9.9	0.88	9.93	22.51 /97	29.75 /99	24.30 /99	0.00	1.74
IX	Rydex S&P 500 A	RYSOX	B-	(800) 820-0888		C+ / 6.0	0.66	5.06	10.90 /78	14.23 /69	12.64 /65	0.04	1.57
IX	Rydex S&P 500 C	RYSYX	B-	(800) 820-0888		C+ / 6.3	0.47	4.65	10.04 /74	13.37 /62	11.75 /59	0.04	2.32
IX	Rydex S&P 500 H	RYSPX	B-	(800) 820-0888		C+ / 6.8	0.66	5.03	10.90 /78	14.23 /69	12.65 /65	0.04	1.56
GR	Rydex S&P500 Pure Growth A	RYLGX	A-	(800) 820-0888		A- / 9.0	4.35	7.20	12.98 /86	18.45 /96	16.88 /96	0.00	1.52
GR	Rydex S&P500 Pure Growth C	RYGRX	A	(800) 820-0888		A- / 9.1	4.17	6.80	12.13 /83	17.58 /93	16.00 /93	0.00	2.27
GR	Rydex S&P500 Pure Growth H	RYAWX	A+	(800) 820-0888		A / 9.4	4.35	7.20	12.98 /86	18.47 /96	16.88 /96	0.00	1.52
GR	Rydex S&P500 Pure Value A	RYLVX	B+	(800) 820-0888		B / 7.9	-1.50	2.32	5.60 /43	18.65 /96	14.79 /85	0.09	1.52
GR	Rydex S&P500 Pure Value C	RYVVX	B+	(800) 820-0888		B / 8.2	-1.68	1.93	4.81 /37	17.76 /93	13.94 /77	0.10	2.27
GR	Rydex S&P500 Pure Value H	RYZAX	A-	(800) 820-0888		B+ / 8.8	-1.49	2.33	5.60 /43	18.65 /96	14.79 /85	0.09	1.52
SC	Rydex SmCp 600 Pure Growth A	RYSGX	B	(800) 820-0888		B / 8.2	9.36	16.22	11.15 /79	15.76 /81	15.63 /91	0.00	1.53
SC	Rydex SmCp 600 Pure Growth C	RYWCX	B	(800) 820-0888		B+ / 8.4	9.17	15.78	10.30 /76	14.89 /74	14.78 /85	0.00	2.28
SC	Rydex SmCp 600 Pure Growth H	RYWAX	B+	(800) 820-0888		B+ / 8.9	9.36	16.22	11.13 /79	15.75 /81	15.64 /91	0.00	1.52
SC	Rydex SmCp 600 Pure Value A	RYSVX	C	(800) 820-0888		C+ / 5.7	0.90	8.81	0.58 /17	14.78 /73	9.65 /42	0.00	1.52
SC	Rydex SmCp 600 Pure Value C	RYYCX	C	(800) 820-0888		C+ / 6.0	0.71	8.42	-0.13 /15	13.94 /67	8.81 /35	0.00	2.27
SC	Rydex SmCp 600 Pure Value H	RYAZX	C	(800) 820-0888		C+ / 6.5	0.90	8.85	0.63 /17	14.78 /73	9.61 /41	0.00	1.53
TC	Rydex Technology A	RYTHX	C-	(800) 820-0888		C / 4.9	1.60	5.33	9.28 /71	12.27 /54	10.85 /51	0.00	1.61
TC	Rydex Technology Advisor	RYTAX	C	(800) 820-0888		C / 5.5	1.53	5.17	9.00 /69	12.01 /53	10.60 /50	0.00	1.86
TC	Rydex Technology C	RYCHX	C-	(800) 820-0888		C / 5.1	1.42	4.92	8.52 /66	11.46 /49	10.05 /45	0.00	2.36
TC	Rydex Technology Investor	RYTIX	C	(800) 820-0888		C+ / 5.9	1.66	5.44	9.53 /72	12.56 /56	11.15 /54	0.00	1.36
TC	Rydex Telecomm A	RYTLX	E+	(800) 820-0888		D- / 1.0	0.47	-0.04	2.75 /25	5.15 /14	3.97 / 8	2.91	1.63
TC	Rydex Telecomm Advisor	RYMAX	D-	(800) 820-0888		D- / 1.3	0.39	-0.16	2.42 /24	4.84 /13	3.71 / 7	3.13	1.88
TC	Rydex Telecomm C	RYCSX	E+	(800) 820-0888		D- / 1.2	0.28	-0.44	1.86 /21	4.56 /12	3.39 / 7	3.31	2.38
TC	Rydex Telecomm Investor	RYMIX	D-	(800) 820-0888		D- / 1.5	0.51	0.07	2.93 /26	5.38 /14	4.20 / 9	2.86	1.38
GR	Rydex Transportation A	RYTSX	A+	(800) 820-0888		A+ / 9.8	-0.94	11.24	16.34 /94	24.25 /99	16.70 /95	0.00	1.62
GR	Rydex Transportation Advisor	RYPAX	A+	(800) 820-0888		A+ / 9.8	-1.01	11.08	16.03 /93	23.92 /99	16.40 /94	0.00	1.87
GR	Rydex Transportation C	RYCNX	A+	(800) 820-0888		A+ / 9.8	-1.11	10.81	15.46 /92	23.30 /99	15.85 /92	0.00	2.37
GR	Rydex Transportation Investor	RYPIX	A+	(800) 820-0888		A+ / 9.9	-0.86	11.38	16.65 /94	24.53 /99	16.96 /96	0.00	1.37
UT	Rydex Utilities A	RYUTX	C-	(800) 820-0888		C- / 4.1	-4.09	7.34	8.78 /68	11.23 /47	11.69 /58	0.36	1.63
UT	Rydex Utilities Advisor	RYAUX	C-	(800) 820-0888		C / 4.7	-4.14	7.25	8.53 /67	10.95 /45	11.42 /56	0.39	1.88

● Denotes fund is closed to new investors
* Denotes fund is included in Section II

www.thestreetratings.com

RISK Risk Rating/Pts	3 Year Standard Deviation	Beta	NAV As of 3/31/15	Total $(Mil)	Cash %	Stocks %	Bonds %	Other %	Portfolio Turnover Ratio	Last Bull Market Return	Last Bear Market Return	Manager Quality Pct	Manager Tenure (Years)	Initial Purch. $	Additional Purch. $	Front End Load	Back End Load
E- / 0.2	35.3	1.58	24.28	3	0	99	0	1	348	-54.2	-22.6	1	22	2,500	0	4.8	0.0
E- / 0.2	35.3	1.58	23.64	4	0	99	0	1	348	-54.5	-22.7	1	22	2,500	0	0.0	0.0
E- / 0.2	35.3	1.58	21.67	6	0	99	0	1	348	-55.3	-22.8	1	22	2,500	0	0.0	0.0
E- / 0.2	35.4	1.58	25.11	31	0	99	0	1	348	-53.8	-22.5	1	22	2,500	0	0.0	0.0
C- / 3.8	11.9	0.96	38.34	7	0	100	0	0	788	70.0	-19.7	33	11	2,500	0	4.8	0.0
C- / 3.7	11.9	0.96	34.81	3	0	100	0	0	788	65.5	-20.0	25	11	2,500	0	0.0	0.0
C- / 3.8	11.9	0.96	38.25	38	0	100	0	0	788	69.8	-19.7	33	11	2,500	0	0.0	0.0
C+ / 6.5	12.7	1.12	26.85	20	0	99	0	1	671	99.4	-11.1	52	17	2,500	0	4.8	0.0
C+ / 6.5	12.7	1.12	26.22	9	0	99	0	1	671	98.1	-11.1	50	17	2,500	0	0.0	0.0
C+ / 6.5	12.7	1.12	24.46	4	0	99	0	1	671	94.3	-11.3	41	17	2,500	0	0.0	0.0
C+ / 6.5	12.7	1.11	28.13	46	0	99	0	1	671	101.0	-11.0	57	17	2,500	0	0.0	0.0
C / 4.9	20.4	1.74	58.05	1	54	45	0	1	472	154.1	-37.3	6	15	2,500	0	4.8	0.0
C / 4.8	20.4	1.74	52.01	2	54	45	0	1	472	147.6	-37.5	5	15	2,500	0	0.0	0.0
C / 4.9	20.4	1.74	57.94	18	54	45	0	1	472	154.2	-37.3	6	15	2,500	0	0.0	0.0
D+ / 2.8	27.5	2.01	349.40	5	35	64	0	1	515	227.1	-47.8	10	9	2,500	0	4.8	0.0
D+ / 2.7	27.5	2.01	326.49	1	35	64	0	1	515	219.3	-47.9	8	9	2,500	0	0.0	0.0
D+ / 2.8	27.5	2.01	348.85	105	35	64	0	1	515	226.7	-47.8	10	9	2,500	0	0.0	0.0
C+ / 6.5	13.4	1.00	38.88	14	45	54	0	1	267	90.7	-25.6	43	9	2,500	0	4.8	0.0
C+ / 6.5	13.4	1.00	36.00	4	45	54	0	1	267	85.5	-25.8	32	9	2,500	0	0.0	0.0
C+ / 6.5	13.4	1.00	38.79	28	45	54	0	1	267	90.5	-25.6	42	9	2,500	0	0.0	0.0
C / 5.1	19.4	2.01	70.18	13	23	76	0	1	396	247.1	-33.0	17	15	2,500	0	4.8	0.0
C / 5.0	19.4	2.01	62.57	12	23	76	0	1	396	238.6	-33.2	12	15	2,500	0	0.0	0.0
C / 5.1	19.4	2.01	70.12	122	23	76	0	1	396	246.8	-33.1	17	15	2,500	0	0.0	0.0
B- / 7.5	9.5	1.00	41.40	28	18	81	0	1	157	89.3	-16.8	43	17	2,500	0	4.8	0.0
B- / 7.5	9.5	1.00	38.58	21	18	81	0	1	157	84.5	-17.2	33	17	2,500	0	0.0	0.0
B- / 7.5	9.5	1.00	41.40	245	18	81	0	1	157	89.4	-16.8	43	17	2,500	0	0.0	0.0
C+ / 6.2	11.4	1.08	55.85	26	0	99	0	1	594	105.8	-18.0	76	11	2,500	0	4.8	0.0
C+ / 6.2	11.4	1.08	51.23	23	0	99	0	1	594	100.7	-18.2	69	11	2,500	0	0.0	0.0
C+ / 6.3	11.4	1.07	55.84	104	0	99	0	1	594	105.9	-17.9	76	11	2,500	0	0.0	0.0
C+ / 6.2	13.7	1.29	145.09	16	0	99	0	1	410	118.3	-22.2	35	11	2,500	0	4.8	0.0
C+ / 6.1	13.7	1.29	130.15	6	0	99	0	1	410	112.8	-22.4	26	11	2,500	0	0.0	0.0
C+ / 6.2	13.7	1.29	145.62	53	0	99	0	1	410	118.3	-22.2	35	11	2,500	0	0.0	0.0
C / 5.4	13.7	0.97	58.90	3	0	99	0	1	677	90.5	-20.4	67	11	2,500	0	4.8	0.0
C / 5.4	13.7	0.97	54.28	5	0	99	0	1	677	85.7	-20.7	56	11	2,500	0	0.0	0.0
C / 5.4	13.7	0.97	58.89	50	0	99	0	1	677	90.5	-20.5	67	11	2,500	0	0.0	0.0
C / 5.2	17.1	1.17	25.81	2	0	99	0	1	658	98.8	-26.2	17	11	2,500	0	4.8	0.0
C / 5.2	17.1	1.17	22.78	3	0	99	0	1	658	93.7	-26.5	12	11	2,500	0	0.0	0.0
C / 5.2	17.1	1.18	25.71	12	0	99	0	1	658	98.6	-26.3	16	11	2,500	0	0.0	0.0
C / 5.4	13.8	1.23	57.69	10	0	99	0	1	321	83.4	-22.0	5	17	2,500	0	4.8	0.0
C / 5.4	13.7	1.23	56.54	3	0	99	0	1	321	81.9	-22.1	4	17	2,500	0	0.0	0.0
C / 5.3	13.8	1.23	53.50	3	0	99	0	1	321	78.8	-22.3	4	17	2,500	0	0.0	0.0
C / 5.4	13.8	1.23	61.23	21	0	99	0	1	321	85.1	-21.9	5	17	2,500	0	0.0	0.0
C+ / 5.6	11.5	1.02	42.63	1	1	98	0	1	1,271	41.4	-23.1	2	17	2,500	0	4.8	0.0
C+ / 5.6	11.5	1.02	41.59	N/A	1	98	0	1	1,271	40.1	-23.2	2	17	2,500	0	0.0	0.0
C+ / 5.6	11.5	1.02	39.35	1	1	98	0	1	1,271	38.8	-23.4	2	17	2,500	0	0.0	0.0
C+ / 5.6	11.5	1.01	45.56	1	1	98	0	1	1,271	42.3	-23.1	2	17	2,500	0	0.0	0.0
C+ / 6.9	12.1	0.96	48.41	16	0	99	0	1	593	147.7	-26.0	96	17	2,500	0	4.8	0.0
C+ / 6.9	12.1	0.96	47.12	6	0	99	0	1	593	145.5	-26.0	96	17	2,500	0	0.0	0.0
C+ / 6.8	12.0	0.96	45.63	7	0	99	0	1	593	141.3	-26.1	96	17	2,500	0	0.0	0.0
C+ / 6.9	12.1	0.96	52.06	43	0	99	0	1	593	149.7	-25.9	97	17	2,500	0	0.0	0.0
C+ / 6.2	13.2	0.93	34.70	10	0	99	0	1	508	48.9	-2.1	60	15	2,500	0	4.8	0.0
C+ / 6.1	13.2	0.93	33.61	11	0	99	0	1	508	47.6	-2.2	55	15	2,500	0	0.0	0.0

Fund Type	Fund Name	Ticker Symbol	Overall Investment Rating	Phone	Perfor- mance Rating/Pts	Total Return % through 3/31/15			Annualized		Incl. in Returns	
						3 Mo	6 Mo	1Yr / Pct	3Yr / Pct	5Yr / Pct	Dividend Yield	Expense Ratio
UT	Rydex Utilities C	RYCUX	C-	(800) 820-0888	C / 4.4	-4.27	6.98	7.99 /63	10.41 /42	10.85 /51	0.43	2.38
UT	Rydex Utilities Investor	RYUIX	C	(800) 820-0888	C / 5.1	-4.02	7.51	9.12 /70	11.52 /49	11.97 /60	0.36	1.40
IX	S&P 500 Index Direct	SPFIX	A	(800) 955-9988	B / 8.0	0.87	5.85	12.46 /85	15.76 /81	14.21 /80	1.63	0.50
IX	S&P 500 Index K	SPXKX	A-	(800) 955-9988	B / 7.6	0.77	5.59	11.90 /82	15.20 /76	13.64 /74	1.16	1.00
MC	S&P MidCap Index Direct	SPMIX	A-	(800) 955-9988	B+ / 8.9	5.20	11.75	11.89 /82	16.54 /87	15.21 /88	0.88	0.63
MC	S&P MidCap Index K	MIDKX	B+	(800) 955-9988	B+ / 8.6	5.06	11.49	11.33 /80	15.96 /83	13.75 /75	0.47	1.13
SC	S&P SmallCap Index Direct	SMCIX	A-	(800) 955-9988	A- / 9.2	4.70	15.37	9.87 /74	17.18 /91	15.78 /92	0.60	0.82
SC	S&P SmallCap Index K	SMLKX	B+	(800) 955-9988	B+ / 8.9	4.58	15.06	9.34 /71	16.60 /87	14.49 /82	0.11	1.32
EM	SA Emerging Markets Value	SAEMX	E	(800) 366-7266	E- / 0.2	-1.43	-8.62	-7.51 / 4	-3.65 / 2	-2.04 / 2	1.45	1.93
FO	SA International Sm Comp Fund	SAISX	D-	(800) 366-7266	D / 1.7	3.62	-1.60	-8.13 / 3	7.42 /24	6.68 /21	1.61	1.64
EM	SA International Value Fund	SAHMX	E+	(800) 366-7266	D / 1.6	3.54	-1.72	-4.89 / 6	6.73 /20	3.88 / 8	3.53	1.26
RE	SA Real Estate Securities Fund	SAREX	B-	(800) 366-7266	A- / 9.0	4.48	19.22	23.07 /98	12.94 /59	14.84 /86	2.10	1.31
GR	SA US Core Market Fund	SAMKX	A-	(800) 366-7266	B / 7.8	1.51	6.33	11.14 /79	15.54 /80	13.92 /77	0.81	1.02
SC	SA US Small Company	SAUMX	B+	(800) 366-7266	B+ / 8.6	3.81	12.55	6.84 /54	16.69 /88	15.35 /89	0.10	1.35
GR	SA US Value Fund	SABTX	A-	(800) 366-7266	B+ / 8.4	0.12	2.16	6.99 /55	17.59 /93	13.90 /77	0.94	1.06
GL	Salient Broadmark Tactical Plus F	BTPIX	U	(866) 667-9228	U /	-4.13	1.31	2.75 /25	--	--	0.00	4.40
GL	Salient Global Equity I	SGEIX	U	(866) 667-9228	U /	1.29	2.13	2.39 /24	--	--	0.60	2.13
EN	Salient MLP and Energy Infr A	SMAPX	U	(866) 667-9228	U /	0.91	-12.05	5.56 /43	--	--	3.92	2.65
EN	Salient MLP and Energy Infr C	SMFPX	U	(866) 667-9228	U /	0.65	-12.44	4.72 /37	--	--	3.56	3.40
EN	Salient MLP and Energy Infr I	SMLPX	U	(866) 667-9228	U /	0.98	-11.95	5.78 /45	--	--	4.46	2.40
GL	Salient Risk Parity I	SRPFX	U	(866) 667-9228	U /	4.48	13.01	12.54 /85	--	--	0.00	1.59
GR	Salient Trend I	SPTIX	U	(866) 667-9228	U /	6.97	30.20	46.66 /99	--	--	0.00	1.73
AA	Sandalwood Opportunity A	SANAX	U	(888) 868-9501	U /	0.24	-3.22	-0.77 /14	--	--	5.84	3.19
AA	Sandalwood Opportunity I	SANIX	U	(888) 868-9501	U /	0.20	-3.19	-0.61 /14	--	--	6.47	2.97
GL	Sands Global Capital Growth Inst	SCMGX	C-	(866) 777-7818	C / 5.0	3.00	4.36	6.70 /53	11.91 /52	14.00 /78	0.48	1.13
GL	Sands Global Capital Growth Inv	SCGVX	C-	(866) 777-7818	C / 4.8	2.96	4.28	6.39 /50	11.65 /50	13.74 /75	0.21	1.38
FO	Sanford Bernstein T/M Intl	SNIVX	D-	(212) 486-5800	D / 1.6	4.19	0.65	-3.41 / 8	6.14 /17	2.48 / 5	2.22	1.16
EM	Sanford C Bernstein Emerg Mkts Val	SNEMX	E+	(212) 486-5800	E+ / 0.7	3.23	-0.10	4.68 /36	1.08 / 5	0.80 / 3	1.30	1.49
FO	Sanford C Bernstein Internatl II	SIMTX	E+	(212) 486-5800	D- / 1.5	4.14	0.47	-3.49 / 8	5.96 /17	2.39 / 5	2.11	1.20
EN	Saratoga Adv Tr Energy&Basic Mat A	SBMBX	E-	(800) 807-3863	E- / 0.2	2.79	-15.84	-19.52 / 1	-2.28 / 3	0.29 / 3	0.00	3.04
EN	Saratoga Adv Tr Energy&Basic Mat C	SEPCX	E-	(800) 807-3863	E- / 0.2	2.58	-16.11	-20.03 / 1	-2.85 / 2	-0.32 / 2	0.00	3.62
EN	Saratoga Adv Tr Energy&Basic Mat I	SEPIX	E-	(800) 807-3863	E- / 0.2	2.87	-15.67	-19.23 / 1	-1.88 / 3	0.68 / 3	0.00	2.64
FS	Saratoga Adv Tr Financial Service A	SFPAX	D	(800) 807-3863	D+ / 2.9	-3.41	1.19	3.66 /30	11.05 /46	5.39 /14	0.00	4.30
FS	Saratoga Adv Tr Financial Service C	SFPCX	D+	(800) 807-3863	C- / 3.4	-3.54	0.92	3.10 /27	10.39 /42	4.78 /11	0.00	4.89
FS	Saratoga Adv Tr Financial Service I	SFPIX	C-	(800) 807-3863	C- / 4.1	-3.34	1.36	4.07 /32	11.46 /49	5.80 /16	0.00	3.89
FO	Saratoga Adv Tr Intl Equity A	SIEYX	E+	(800) 807-3863	E / 0.4	2.79	-4.97	-8.59 / 3	2.39 / 7	0.14 / 3	0.00	2.78
FO	Saratoga Adv Tr Intl Equity C	SIECX	E+	(800) 807-3863	E / 0.5	2.61	-5.42	-9.24 / 3	1.67 / 6	-0.55 / 2	0.00	3.29
FO	Saratoga Adv Tr Intl Equity I	SIEPX	E+	(800) 807-3863	E+ / 0.6	2.90	-4.80	-8.18 / 3	2.71 / 7	0.47 / 3	0.47	2.31
GR	Saratoga Adv Tr Large Cap Value A	SLVYX	B+	(800) 807-3863	B+ / 8.8	3.64	8.01	10.36 /76	19.34 /97	13.80 /76	0.00	1.61
GR	Saratoga Adv Tr Large Cap Value C	SLVCX	A-	(800) 807-3863	A- / 9.2	3.50	7.82	9.82 /74	18.59 /96	13.09 /69	0.00	2.21
GR	Saratoga Adv Tr Large Cap Value I	SLCVX	A	(800) 807-3863	A / 9.5	3.69	8.21	10.83 /78	19.73 /98	14.20 /80	0.00	1.21
MC	Saratoga Adv Tr Mid Cap A	SPMAX	B	(800) 807-3863	A- / 9.2	6.96	13.03	12.31 /84	19.15 /97	15.68 /91	0.00	2.03
MC	Saratoga Adv Tr Mid Cap C	SPMCX	B	(800) 807-3863	A / 9.4	6.79	12.92	11.86 /82	18.54 /96	15.02 /87	0.00	2.63
MC	Saratoga Adv Tr Mid Cap I	SMIPX	B+	(800) 807-3863	A+ / 9.7	7.11	13.31	12.78 /86	19.65 /97	16.14 /94	0.00	1.63
SC	Saratoga Adv Tr Small Cap A	SSCYX	D	(800) 807-3863	C- / 3.8	2.33	6.98	1.02 /18	12.08 /53	10.02 /45	0.00	1.76
SC	Saratoga Adv Tr Small Cap C	SSCCX	D-	(800) 807-3863	C- / 4.2	2.23	6.68	0.43 /17	11.23 /47	9.23 /38	0.00	2.35
SC	Saratoga Adv Tr Small Cap I	SSCPX	C-	(800) 807-3863	C / 4.9	2.55	7.36	1.58 /20	12.39 /55	10.35 /47	0.00	1.35
TC	Saratoga Adv Tr Technology &	STPAX	D	(800) 807-3863	C- / 3.8	0.80	5.68	8.10 /64	11.36 /48	16.58 /95	0.00	2.27
TC	Saratoga Adv Tr Technology &	STPCX	D	(800) 807-3863	C / 4.3	0.70	5.40	7.48 /59	10.70 /44	15.89 /92	0.00	2.87
TC	Saratoga Adv Tr Technology &	STPIX	C-	(800) 807-3863	C / 5.0	0.87	5.89	8.54 /67	11.80 /51	17.03 /96	0.00	1.87
HL	Saratoga Adv Tr-Health & Biotech A	SHPAX	A+	(800) 807-3863	A+ / 9.8	7.31	15.48	19.51 /96	21.87 /98	17.78 /97	0.00	2.38
HL	Saratoga Adv Tr-Health & Biotech C	SHPCX	A+	(800) 807-3863	A+ / 9.8	7.16	15.10	18.77 /96	21.14 /98	17.08 /96	0.00	2.98

RISK			NET ASSETS		ASSET					BULL / BEAR		FUND MANAGER		MINIMUMS		LOADS	
	3 Year		NAV						Portfolio	Last Bull	Last Bear	Manager	Manager	Initial	Additional	Front	Back
Risk Rating/Pts	Standard Deviation	Beta	As of 3/31/15	Total $(Mil)	Cash %	Stocks %	Bonds %	Other %	Turnover Ratio	Market Return	Market Return	Quality Pct	Tenure (Years)	Purch. $	Purch. $	End Load	End Load
C+ / 5.9	13.2	0.93	30.70	8	0	99	0	1	508	45.2	-2.5	48	15	2,500	0	0.0	0.0
C+ / 6.2	13.2	0.93	36.98	55	0	99	0	1	508	50.2	-2.0	63	15	2,500	0	0.0	0.0
B- / 7.3	9.6	1.00	41.66	130	1	98	0	1	1	98.1	-16.1	62	12	1,000	250	0.0	0.0
B- / 7.3	9.5	1.00	41.65	9	1	98	0	1	1	94.8	-16.3	55	12	1,000	250	0.0	0.0
C+ / 6.3	11.0	1.00	30.50	156	0	99	0	1	10	99.1	-22.4	61	12	1,000	250	0.0	0.0
C+ / 6.3	11.0	1.00	30.27	6	0	99	0	1	10	88.3	-22.5	54	12	1,000	250	0.0	0.0
C+ / 5.8	12.5	0.92	21.78	45	0	99	0	1	13	102.4	-21.7	84	12	1,000	250	0.0	0.0
C+ / 5.8	12.5	0.92	21.42	11	0	99	0	1	13	92.7	-21.8	81	12	1,000	250	0.0	0.0
C / 4.6	15.0	1.07	8.95	158	1	98	0	1	10	8.5	-30.2	13	8	100,000	0	0.0	0.0
C+ / 5.7	13.3	0.95	19.47	308	14	85	0	1	7	45.2	-23.7	44	16	100,000	0	0.0	0.0
C / 5.2	14.2	0.83	11.12	669	0	99	0	1	15	41.3	-26.3	95	16	100,000	0	0.0	0.0
C- / 3.9	13.3	1.07	11.20	184	0	99	0	1	2	80.1	-16.6	38	3	100,000	0	0.0	0.0
B- / 7.1	9.8	1.02	19.49	682	0	99	0	1	11	96.4	-17.7	54	9	100,000	0	0.0	0.0
C+ / 6.0	13.2	0.97	25.62	382	0	99	0	1	13	102.5	-24.6	75	3	100,000	0	0.0	0.0
C+ / 6.9	11.5	1.13	17.25	518	0	99	0	1	20	112.1	-24.3	58	3	100,000	0	0.0	0.0
U /	N/A	N/A	11.37	29	0	0	0	100	153	N/A	N/A	N/A	3	100,000	0	0.0	0.0
U /	N/A	N/A	11.75	55	2	97	0	1	104	N/A	N/A	N/A	2	1,000,000	0	0.0	0.0
U /	N/A	N/A	13.28	181	39	60	0	1	64	N/A	N/A	N/A	3	2,500	0	5.5	0.0
U /	N/A	N/A	13.19	156	39	60	0	1	64	N/A	N/A	N/A	3	2,500	0	0.0	0.0
U /	N/A	N/A	13.26	1,309	39	60	0	1	64	N/A	N/A	N/A	3	1,000,000	0	0.0	0.0
U /	N/A	N/A	9.56	96	100	0	0	0	0	N/A	N/A	N/A	N/A	1,000,000	0	0.0	0.0
U /	N/A	N/A	12.74	45	100	0	0	0	0	N/A	N/A	N/A	N/A	1,000,000	0	0.0	0.0
U /	N/A	N/A	10.11	41	11	0	88	1	197	N/A	N/A	N/A	3	2,500	100	5.8	0.0
U /	N/A	N/A	10.11	181	11	0	88	1	197	N/A	N/A	N/A	3	100,000	100	0.0	0.0
C / 5.1	13.0	0.83	18.22	695	2	97	0	1	24	79.3	-17.4	91	7	1,000,000	0	0.0	2.0
C / 5.1	13.0	0.83	18.10	7	2	97	0	1	24	77.8	-17.5	90	7	100,000	0	0.0	2.0
C / 5.4	13.7	1.02	15.68	3,764	1	98	0	1	64	39.8	-25.5	22	3	25,000	0	0.0	0.0
C / 5.1	14.7	1.05	27.48	1,308	2	97	0	1	53	25.6	-30.4	71	4	25,000	0	0.0	1.0
C / 5.3	13.7	1.02	15.60	1,556	0	99	0	1	67	39.0	-25.5	20	16	25,000	0	0.0	0.0
D+ / 2.5	16.9	1.03	13.28	1	2	97	0	1	114	19.5	-34.9	6	4	250	0	5.8	2.0
D+ / 2.5	16.9	1.03	11.14	N/A	2	97	0	1	114	17.1	-35.1	5	4	250	0	0.0	2.0
D+ / 2.5	16.9	1.03	14.32	3	2	97	0	1	114	21.1	-34.8	7	4	250	0	0.0	2.0
C+ / 6.1	13.0	1.11	8.49	N/A	3	96	0	1	18	76.9	-26.7	4	9	250	0	5.8	2.0
C+ / 6.1	12.9	1.11	7.64	N/A	3	96	0	1	18	73.5	-26.9	3	9	250	0	0.0	2.0
C+ / 6.1	12.9	1.11	8.96	2	3	96	0	1	18	79.2	-26.6	5	9	250	0	0.0	2.0
C+ / 5.7	13.0	0.93	10.32	N/A	8	91	0	1	125	24.3	-28.0	6	3	250	0	5.8	2.0
C+ / 5.6	13.1	0.93	9.43	N/A	8	91	0	1	125	21.3	-28.2	5	3	250	0	0.0	2.0
C+ / 5.6	13.1	0.93	10.28	7	8	91	0	1	125	25.7	-27.9	7	3	250	0	0.0	2.0
C+ / 5.9	12.8	1.18	22.79	N/A	4	95	0	1	104	113.5	-25.3	67	7	250	0	5.8	2.0
C+ / 5.8	12.8	1.19	20.13	1	4	95	0	1	104	108.9	-25.4	57	7	250	0	0.0	2.0
C+ / 5.9	12.8	1.19	23.34	29	4	95	0	1	104	116.0	-25.2	71	7	250	0	0.0	2.0
C / 4.7	11.6	1.00	13.52	4	1	98	0	1	57	109.1	-25.3	83	9	250	0	5.8	2.0
C- / 4.2	11.6	1.00	11.95	1	1	98	0	1	57	105.2	-25.4	79	9	250	0	0.0	2.0
C / 5.0	11.6	1.00	14.62	15	1	98	0	1	57	111.9	-25.2	85	9	250	0	0.0	2.0
C / 5.0	11.1	0.79	9.67	N/A	6	93	0	1	32	74.1	-23.0	60	9	250	0	5.8	2.0
C- / 3.8	11.1	0.79	6.89	1	6	93	0	1	32	69.6	-23.2	49	9	250	0	0.0	2.0
C / 5.1	11.1	0.79	10.07	13	6	93	0	1	32	75.9	-22.9	63	9	250	0	0.0	2.0
C / 4.7	12.4	1.12	16.35	17	4	95	0	1	25	85.2	-24.2	7	4	250	0	5.8	2.0
C / 4.3	12.4	1.12	14.30	7	4	95	0	1	25	81.4	-24.4	5	4	250	0	0.0	2.0
C / 4.9	12.4	1.12	17.39	22	4	95	0	1	25	87.8	-24.1	8	4	250	0	0.0	2.0
C+ / 6.4	9.0	0.77	31.71	9	2	97	0	1	14	107.7	-10.2	97	10	250	0	5.8	2.0
C+ / 6.2	9.0	0.77	28.45	3	2	97	0	1	14	103.5	-10.4	97	10	250	0	0.0	2.0

					PERFORMANCE							
99 Pct = Best						Total Return % through 3/31/15					Incl. in Returns	
0 Pct = Worst				Overall	Perfor-				Annualized		Dividend	Expense
Fund		Ticker		Investment	mance						Yield	Ratio
Type	Fund Name	Symbol		Rating	Phone	Rating/Pts	3 Mo	6 Mo	1Yr / Pct	3Yr / Pct	5Yr / Pct	
HL	Saratoga Adv Tr-Health & Biotech I	SBHIX	A+	(800) 807-3863	A+ / 9.8	7.39	15.70	19.95 /97	22.37 /98	18.26 /98	0.00	1.98
GR	Saratoga Adv Tr-Large Cap Growth A	SLGYX	B+	(800) 807-3863	B+ / 8.3	2.80	9.03	14.59 /91	17.67 /93	18.20 /98	0.00	1.59
GR	Saratoga Adv Tr-Large Cap Growth C	SLGCX	B+	(800) 807-3863	B+ / 8.7	2.67	8.67	13.92 /89	16.95 /90	17.48 /97	0.00	2.20
GR	Saratoga Adv Tr-Large Cap Growth I	SLCGX	A	(800) 807-3863	A / 9.3	2.92	9.25	15.08 /92	18.14 /95	18.65 /98	0.04	1.21
GL	Saratoga JamesAlpha Gl Enh Rl Rtn	GRRAX	D+	(800) 807-3863	E+ / 0.7	2.95	5.86	6.08 /47	1.51 / 6	--	0.00	2.30
GL	Saratoga JamesAlpha Gl Enh Rl Rtn	GRRCX	C-	(800) 807-3863	E+ / 0.7	2.70	5.44	5.23 /40	0.71 / 5	--	0.00	3.03
GL	Saratoga JamesAlpha Gl Enh Rl Rtn I	GRRIX	D+	(800) 807-3863	D- / 1.0	3.04	6.05	6.37 /50	1.75 / 6	--	0.00	2.01
RE	Saratoga JamesAlpha Gl RE Invest A	JAREX	C	(800) 807-3863	C+ / 6.4	8.38	12.92	13.76 /89	12.85 /59	11.77 /59	1.56	2.04
RE	Saratoga JamesAlpha Gl RE Invest C	JACRX	B+	(800) 807-3863	B- / 7.0	8.16	12.56	13.07 /87	12.34 /55	--	2.61	2.79
RE	Saratoga JamesAlpha Gl RE Invest I	JARIX	B-	(800) 807-3863	B / 8.0	8.50	13.23	14.39 /90	13.55 /64	--	1.88	1.78
GL	Sarofim Equity	SRFMX	U	(866) 777-7818	U /	-0.65	1.31	7.79 /61	--	--	2.20	0.87
SC	Satuit Capital US Emerging Co NL	SATMX	D-	(800) 527-9525	C- / 4.0	3.64	9.15	-0.70 /14	10.62 /43	11.40 /56	0.00	1.84
GL	Saturna Sextant Global High Income	SGHIX	D	(800) 728-8762	E+ / 0.9	-1.25	-2.98	-1.74 /11	4.29 /11	--	4.80	1.25
MC	SC 529 CO FS Acorn A	CACAX	C-	(800) 345-6611	C- / 4.1	3.85	7.78	4.39 /34	11.42 /48	12.08 /61	0.00	1.29
MC	SC 529 CO FS Acorn B		C-	(800) 345-6611	C / 4.5	3.69	7.39	3.64 /30	10.59 /43	11.26 /55	0.00	2.04
MC	SC 529 CO FS Acorn C	CACBX	C-	(800) 345-6611	C / 4.5	3.68	7.39	3.62 /30	10.59 /43	11.25 /55	0.00	2.04
MC	SC 529 CO FS Acorn E	CACEX	C	(800) 345-6611	C / 4.9	3.82	7.65	4.15 /33	11.14 /47	11.80 /59	0.00	1.54
MC	SC 529 CO FS Acorn Z		C	(800) 345-6611	C / 5.3	3.90	7.88	4.66 /36	11.68 /50	12.36 /63	0.00	1.04
AG	SC 529 CO FS Aggressive Growth A	CAGGX	C-	(800) 345-6611	C / 5.0	3.00	6.66	8.48 /66	12.63 /57	11.47 /57	0.00	1.43
AG	SC 529 CO FS Aggressive Growth B		C-	(800) 345-6611	C / 5.4	2.78	6.23	7.65 /60	11.80 /51	10.68 /50	0.00	2.18
AG	● SC 529 CO FS Aggressive Growth		C	(800) 345-6611	C+ / 5.7	2.89	6.43	7.97 /63	12.16 /54	11.70 /58	0.00	1.88
AG	SC 529 CO FS Aggressive Growth C	CCGGX	C	(800) 345-6611	C / 5.4	2.80	6.28	7.68 /60	11.83 /51	10.67 /50	0.00	2.18
AG	SC 529 CO FS Aggressive Growth		C	(800) 345-6611	C+ / 5.8	2.94	6.55	8.22 /64	12.39 /57	11.23 /55	0.00	1.68
AG	SC 529 CO FS Aggressive Growth		C+	(800) 345-6611	C+ / 6.2	2.70	6.17	8.96 /69	13.02 /60	12.07 /61	0.00	0.50
AG	SC 529 CO FS Aggressive Growth E	CEGGX	C	(800) 345-6611	C+ / 5.8	2.91	6.52	8.17 /64	12.37 /55	11.23 /55	0.00	1.68
AG	SC 529 CO FS Aggressive Growth Z		C	(800) 345-6611	C+ / 6.2	3.03	6.76	8.73 /68	12.94 /59	11.78 /59	0.00	1.18
GR	SC 529 CO FS Growth A	CGAGX	C	(800) 345-6611	C / 4.5	2.72	6.17	8.30 /65	11.73 /51	10.69 /50	0.00	1.41
GR	SC 529 CO FS Growth B		C	(800) 345-6611	C / 4.8	2.54	5.79	7.54 /59	10.87 /45	9.94 /44	0.00	2.16
GR	● SC 529 CO FS Growth BX		C+	(800) 345-6611	C / 5.1	2.57	5.93	7.83 /62	11.21 /47	10.80 /51	0.00	1.86
GR	SC 529 CO FS Growth C	CGCGX	C	(800) 345-6611	C / 4.9	2.53	5.77	7.52 /59	10.87 /45	9.91 /44	0.00	2.16
GR	SC 529 CO FS Growth CX		C+	(800) 345-6611	C / 5.2	2.65	6.03	8.05 /63	11.42 /48	10.51 /49	0.00	1.66
GR	SC 529 CO FS Growth Dir		C+	(800) 345-6611	C / 5.5	2.38	5.81	8.74 /68	11.86 /52	11.23 /55	0.00	0.51
GR	SC 529 CO FS Growth E	CGAAX	C+	(800) 345-6611	C / 5.2	2.68	6.08	8.05 /63	11.42 /48	10.45 /48	0.00	1.66
GR	SC 529 CO FS Growth Z		C+	(800) 345-6611	C+ / 5.6	2.81	6.32	8.62 /67	12.00 /52	11.04 /53	0.00	1.16
GR	SC 529 CO FS Marsico Growth A	CMRAX	C+	(800) 345-6611	C / 5.4	1.83	3.56	12.06 /83	13.22 /61	13.16 /70	0.00	1.50
GR	SC 529 CO FS Marsico Growth B		C+	(800) 345-6611	C+ / 5.8	1.62	3.21	11.26 /79	12.37 /55	12.37 /63	0.00	2.25
GR	SC 529 CO FS Marsico Growth C	CMRCX	C+	(800) 345-6611	C+ / 5.8	1.61	3.19	11.24 /79	12.37 /55	12.33 /63	0.00	2.25
GR	SC 529 CO FS Marsico Growth E	CMREX	C+	(800) 345-6611	C+ / 6.2	1.77	3.46	11.80 /82	12.94 /59	11.48 /57	0.00	1.75
GR	SC 529 CO FS Marsico Growth Z		C+	(800) 345-6611	C+ / 6.5	1.87	3.72	12.35 /84	13.50 /63	13.44 /72	0.00	1.25
GI	SC 529 CO FS Mod Conservative A	MDOCX	C-	(800) 345-6611	D- / 1.1	1.27	2.99	4.40 /34	5.30 /14	5.30 /13	0.00	1.14
GI	SC 529 CO FS Mod Conservative B		C	(800) 345-6611	D- / 1.3	1.15	2.70	3.65 /30	4.52 /12	4.59 /11	0.00	1.89
GI	● SC 529 CO FS Mod Conservative BX		C	(800) 345-6611	D- / 1.5	1.19	2.79	3.93 /31	4.84 /13	5.24 /13	0.00	1.59
GI	SC 529 CO FS Mod Conservative C	CMCNX	C	(800) 345-6611	D- / 1.4	1.14	2.69	3.64 /30	4.53 /12	4.58 /10	0.00	1.89
GI	SC 529 CO FS Mod Conservative CX		C	(800) 345-6611	D- / 1.5	1.31	2.97	4.17 /33	5.04 /13	5.11 /12	0.00	1.39
GI	SC 529 CO FS Mod Conservative Dir		C	(800) 345-6611	D / 1.9	1.47	3.52	5.40 /42	5.67 /15	5.70 /15	0.00	0.57
GI	SC 529 CO FS Mod Conservative E	CEGMX	C	(800) 345-6611	D- / 1.5	1.24	2.92	4.18 /33	5.04 /13	5.11 /12	0.00	1.39
GI	SC 529 CO FS Mod Conservative Z		C	(800) 345-6611	D / 1.8	1.38	3.19	4.66 /36	5.56 /15	5.63 /15	0.00	0.89
BA	SC 529 CO FS Moderate A	CMAGX	C	(800) 345-6611	D+ / 2.3	2.01	4.65	6.57 /52	8.07 /27	7.81 /29	0.00	1.29
BA	SC 529 CO FS Moderate B		C	(800) 345-6611	D+ / 2.7	1.86	4.28	5.75 /44	7.27 /23	7.07 /24	0.00	2.04
BA	● SC 529 CO FS Moderate BX		C+	(800) 345-6611	D+ / 2.9	1.91	4.39	6.07 /47	7.59 /25	7.75 /28	0.00	1.74
BA	SC 529 CO FS Moderate C	CMCGX	C	(800) 345-6611	D+ / 2.7	1.84	4.27	5.78 /45	7.27 /23	7.05 /23	0.00	2.04
BA	SC 529 CO FS Moderate CX		C+	(800) 345-6611	C- / 3.1	1.98	4.53	6.29 /49	7.81 /26	7.58 /27	0.00	1.54

● Denotes fund is closed to new investors
★ Denotes fund is included in Section II

RISK			NET ASSETS		ASSET				Portfolio	BULL / BEAR		FUND MANAGER		MINIMUMS		LOADS	
Risk Rating/Pts	3 Year		NAV As of 3/31/15	Total $(Mil)	Cash %	Stocks %	Bonds %	Other %	Portfolio Turnover Ratio	Last Bull Market Return	Last Bear Market Return	Manager Quality Pct	Manager Tenure (Years)	Initial Purch. $	Additional Purch. $	Front End Load	Back End Load
	Standard Deviation	Beta															
C+ / 6.6	9.0	0.77	33.43	14	2	97	0	1	14	110.5	-10.0	97	10	250	0	0.0	2.0
C+ / 6.2	11.1	1.07	26.46	2	1	98	0	1	14	101.3	-13.4	71	N/A	250	0	5.8	2.0
C+ / 6.1	11.1	1.07	22.70	3	1	98	0	1	14	97.1	-13.5	63	N/A	250	0	0.0	2.0
C+ / 6.2	11.1	1.07	27.51	32	1	98	0	1	14	104.0	-13.2	74	N/A	250	0	0.0	2.0
B / 8.7	3.4	-0.08	10.47	3	14	20	65	1	260	3.6	-0.5	85	4	2,500	0	5.8	2.0
B+ / 9.2	3.4	-0.07	10.27	2	14	20	65	1	260	N/A	N/A	79	4	2,500	0	0.0	2.0
B / 8.7	3.4	-0.08	10.52	8	14	20	65	1	260	4.4	-0.5	86	4	1,000,000	0	0.0	2.0
C / 5.0	11.7	0.77	20.98	95	5	94	0	1	219	76.1	-21.3	84	4	2,500	0	5.8	2.0
B- / 7.2	11.6	0.77	21.10	75	5	94	0	1	219	N/A	N/A	81	4	2,500	0	0.0	2.0
C / 5.2	11.6	0.77	21.28	212	5	94	0	1	219	79.6	N/A	87	4	2,000,000	0	0.0	2.0
U /	N/A	N/A	10.55	108	3	95	0	2	0	N/A	N/A	N/A	1	2,500	100	0.0	2.0
C- / 3.3	13.8	0.95	34.19	136	0	0	0	100	110	71.9	-26.1	14	15	1,000	250	0.0	2.0
B- / 7.2	7.4	1.05	10.27	8	9	52	38	1	11	N/A	N/A	11	N/A	1,000	25	0.0	0.0
C+ / 6.2	11.7	1.02	20.22	13	2	97	0	1	20	75.4	-22.3	9	N/A	250	50	5.8	0.0
C+ / 6.2	11.7	1.03	21.06	1	2	97	0	1	20	71.0	-22.5	6	N/A	250	50	0.0	0.0
C+ / 6.2	11.7	1.03	18.88	6	2	97	0	1	20	70.9	-22.6	6	N/A	250	50	0.0	0.0
C+ / 6.2	11.7	1.03	16.05	1	2	97	0	1	20	73.9	-22.4	8	N/A	250	50	0.0	0.0
C+ / 6.2	11.7	1.03	19.99	2	2	97	0	1	20	76.9	-22.3	10	N/A	250	50	0.0	0.0
C / 5.5	9.9	1.00	21.62	119	0	92	6	2	0	81.1	-20.7	25	N/A	250	50	5.8	0.0
C / 5.4	9.9	1.00	26.61	7	0	92	6	2	0	76.6	-20.9	18	N/A	250	50	0.0	0.0
C / 5.4	9.9	1.00	21.01	1	0	92	6	2	0	78.4	-20.9	21	N/A	250	50	0.0	0.0
C / 5.4	9.9	1.00	26.07	37	0	92	6	2	0	76.6	-21.0	18	N/A	250	50	0.0	0.0
C / 5.5	9.9	1.00	20.67	1	0	92	6	2	0	79.6	-20.8	23	N/A	250	50	0.0	0.0
C+ / 5.7	9.2	0.94	23.23	149	0	92	6	2	0	82.7	-19.4	40	N/A	250	50	0.0	0.0
C / 5.4	9.9	1.00	27.94	6	0	92	6	2	0	79.6	-20.8	23	N/A	250	50	0.0	0.0
C / 5.5	9.9	1.00	28.90	6	0	92	6	2	0	82.7	-20.7	28	N/A	250	50	0.0	0.0
C+ / 6.9	9.0	0.91	21.52	156	0	82	15	3	0	73.0	-19.2	31	N/A	250	50	5.8	0.0
C+ / 6.9	9.0	0.90	25.39	14	0	82	15	3	0	68.6	-19.4	23	N/A	250	50	0.0	0.0
C+ / 6.9	8.9	0.90	20.37	1	0	82	15	3	0	70.3	-19.4	27	N/A	250	50	0.0	0.0
C+ / 6.9	9.0	0.91	24.75	58	0	82	15	3	0	68.6	-19.5	23	N/A	250	50	0.0	0.0
C+ / 6.9	9.0	0.90	20.93	2	0	82	15	3	0	71.5	-19.3	29	N/A	250	50	0.0	0.0
B- / 7.2	8.1	0.83	22.76	116	0	82	15	3	0	73.7	-17.7	49	N/A	250	50	0.0	0.0
C+ / 6.9	9.2	0.92	26.86	8	0	82	15	3	0	72.8	-19.3	25	N/A	250	50	0.0	0.0
C+ / 6.9	9.0	0.90	27.09	8	0	82	15	3	0	74.5	-19.1	35	N/A	250	50	0.0	0.0
C+ / 6.6	10.9	0.97	26.20	14	4	95	0	1	62	89.0	-18.3	35	N/A	250	50	5.8	0.0
C+ / 6.6	10.9	0.97	23.81	1	4	95	0	1	62	84.2	-18.5	26	N/A	250	50	0.0	0.0
C+ / 6.6	10.9	0.97	22.66	7	4	95	0	1	62	84.3	-18.5	26	N/A	250	50	0.0	0.0
C+ / 6.6	10.9	0.97	23.02	1	4	95	0	1	62	87.4	-18.4	32	N/A	250	50	0.0	0.0
C+ / 6.6	10.9	0.97	21.74	1	4	95	0	1	62	90.6	-18.2	39	N/A	250	50	0.0	0.0
B+ / 9.6	3.3	0.33	17.57	91	5	31	62	2	0	27.6	-7.5	70	N/A	250	50	5.8	0.0
B+ / 9.6	3.3	0.33	16.76	6	5	31	62	2	0	24.4	-7.8	60	N/A	250	50	0.0	0.0
B+ / 9.6	3.3	0.33	16.94	1	5	31	62	2	0	25.6	-7.6	65	N/A	250	50	0.0	0.0
B+ / 9.6	3.3	0.33	16.79	44	5	31	62	2	0	24.4	-7.7	61	N/A	250	50	0.0	0.0
B+ / 9.6	3.3	0.32	17.00	4	5	31	62	2	0	26.5	-7.6	67	N/A	250	50	0.0	0.0
B+ / 9.6	3.1	0.29	17.96	62	5	31	62	2	0	28.5	-6.1	78	N/A	250	50	0.0	0.0
B+ / 9.6	3.4	0.33	17.95	3	5	31	62	2	0	26.6	-7.6	67	N/A	250	50	0.0	0.0
B+ / 9.6	3.3	0.32	19.08	3	5	31	62	2	0	28.7	-7.4	73	N/A	250	50	0.0	0.0
B+ / 9.0	5.5	0.96	20.27	193	0	51	47	2	0	45.0	-11.8	35	N/A	250	50	5.8	0.0
B+ / 9.0	5.5	0.96	20.22	16	0	51	47	2	0	41.4	-12.1	27	N/A	250	50	0.0	0.0
B+ / 9.0	5.5	0.96	19.74	3	0	51	47	2	0	42.8	-12.0	30	N/A	250	50	0.0	0.0
B+ / 9.0	5.5	0.96	20.50	73	0	51	47	2	0	41.4	-12.1	26	N/A	250	50	0.0	0.0
B+ / 9.0	5.6	0.96	19.60	5	0	51	47	2	0	43.8	-11.9	31	N/A	250	50	0.0	0.0

Fund Type	Fund Name	Ticker Symbol	Overall Investment Rating	Phone	Performance Rating/Pts	3 Mo	6 Mo	1Yr / Pct	Annualized 3Yr / Pct	Annualized 5Yr / Pct	Dividend Yield	Expense Ratio
BA	SC 529 CO FS Moderate Dir		C+	(800) 345-6611	C- / 3.6	2.01	4.88	7.42 /59	8.60 /30	8.25 /32	0.00	0.60
BA	SC 529 CO FS Moderate E	CMEGX	C+	(800) 345-6611	C- / 3.1	1.96	4.49	6.28 /49	7.81 /26	7.60 /27	0.00	1.54
BA	SC 529 CO FS Moderate Growth A	CGAMX	C	(800) 345-6611	C- / 3.3	2.41	5.41	7.44 /59	9.74 /38	9.34 /39	0.00	1.36
BA	SC 529 CO FS Moderate Growth B		C	(800) 345-6611	C- / 3.7	2.25	5.02	6.61 /52	8.94 /33	8.62 /34	0.00	2.11
BA	● SC 529 CO FS Moderate Growth BX		C+	(800) 345-6611	C- / 3.9	2.36	5.21	6.97 /55	9.26 /35	9.35 /39	0.00	1.81
BA	SC 529 CO FS Moderate Growth C	CMCTX	C	(800) 345-6611	C- / 3.7	2.26	5.05	6.65 /52	8.93 /32	8.57 /34	0.00	2.11
BA	SC 529 CO FS Moderate Growth CX		C+	(800) 345-6611	C- / 4.1	2.35	5.29	7.16 /56	9.46 /36	9.12 /38	0.00	1.61
BA	SC 529 CO FS Moderate Growth Dir		C+	(800) 345-6611	C- / 4.2	2.25	5.42	8.03 /63	9.71 /38	9.47 /40	0.00	0.56
BA	SC 529 CO FS Moderate Growth E	CMGEX	C+	(800) 345-6611	C- / 4.1	2.34	5.28	7.13 /56	9.47 /36	9.13 /38	0.00	1.61
BA	SC 529 CO FS Moderate Growth Z		C+	(800) 345-6611	C / 4.4	2.53	5.56	7.72 /61	10.02 /39	9.64 /42	0.00	1.11
BA	SC 529 CO FS Moderate Z		C+	(800) 345-6611	C- / 3.4	2.09	4.79	6.84 /54	8.35 /29	8.14 /31	0.00	1.04
GI	Scharf Balanced Opportunity Inv	LOGOX	U	(866) 572-4273	U /	2.71	6.24	11.66 /81	--	--	0.30	1.71
GL	Scharf Institutional	LOGIX	A+	(866) 572-4273	B+ / 8.7	3.36	8.03	16.45 /94	16.49 /87	--	0.07	1.31
SC	Schneider Small Cap Value	SCMVX	E-	(888) 520-3277	E+ / 0.9	-5.90	-6.32	-16.23 / 2	7.75 /26	5.34 /13	0.00	1.50
GR	Schneider Value	SCMLX	C-	(888) 520-3277	C / 4.6	-1.87	0.03	-0.55 /14	12.83 /58	7.47 /26	0.45	1.55
GI	Schooner Fund Adv	SCNAX	D-	(866) 724-5997	E+ / 0.6	-2.31	-1.58	-2.58 / 9	2.90 / 8	5.11 /12	0.50	1.74
GR	Schooner Fund I	SCNIX	U	(866) 724-5997	U /	-2.26	-1.44	-2.32 /10	--	--	0.66	1.49
EM	Schroder Emerging Market Equity	SEMVX	E+	(800) 464-3108	E / 0.5	2.85	-1.89	0.62 /17	0.64 / 5	1.58 / 4	0.30	1.65
EM	Schroder Emerging Market Equity Inv	SEMNX	E+	(800) 464-3108	E / 0.5	2.94	-1.74	0.84 /18	0.88 / 5	1.81 / 4	0.96	1.40
GL	Schroder Global Multi-Cp Eq Inv	SQQJX	C	(800) 464-3108	C- / 3.6	1.86	0.68	2.47 /24	10.48 /42	--	3.20	0.96
GL	Schroder Global Multi-Cp Eq R6	SQQIX	E-	(800) 464-3108	C- / 3.7	1.86	0.70	2.48 /24	10.55 /43	--	3.29	0.81
FO	Schroder International Alpha Adv	SCVEX	D-	(800) 464-3108	D / 2.2	5.11	0.55	0.63 /17	7.66 /25	6.23 /18	0.00	1.43
FO	Schroder International Alpha Inv	SCIEX	D-	(800) 464-3108	D+ / 2.4	5.18	0.65	0.90 /18	7.92 /27	6.52 /20	2.45	1.18
FO	Schroder Intl Multi-Cap Value Adv	SIDVX	D-	(800) 464-3108	D / 1.7	3.11	-2.54	-3.41 / 8	7.58 /25	6.49 /20	2.82	1.54
FO	Schroder Intl Multi-Cap Value Inv	SIDNX	D-	(800) 464-3108	D / 1.9	3.17	-2.41	-3.06 / 9	7.96 /27	6.78 /22	3.19	1.29
GL	Schroder North American Equity Adv	SNAVX	B+	(800) 464-3108	B- / 7.0	0.54	5.08	10.62 /77	14.62 /72	13.13 /69	1.55	0.66
GL	Schroder North American Equity Inv	SNAEX	B+	(800) 464-3108	B- / 7.4	0.60	5.20	10.94 /78	15.01 /75	13.52 /73	1.86	0.31
SC	● Schroder US Opportunities Adv	SCUVX	C+	(800) 464-3108	B+ / 8.3	4.68	13.38	11.02 /78	15.91 /83	13.27 /71	0.00	1.63
SC	● Schroder US Opportunities Inv	SCUIX	C+	(800) 464-3108	B+ / 8.5	4.74	13.51	11.37 /80	16.26 /85	13.58 /74	0.00	1.38
MC	Schroder US Smll & Mid Cap Opp	SMDVX	C	(800) 464-3108	B+ / 8.5	5.04	12.10	13.40 /88	16.08 /84	13.93 /77	0.00	1.77
MC	Schroder US Smll & Mid Cap Opp Inv	SMDIX	C	(800) 464-3108	B+ / 8.7	5.14	12.29	13.81 /89	16.39 /86	14.23 /80	0.00	1.52
* GI	Schwab 1000 Index Fund	SNXFX	B+	(800) 407-0256	B / 7.8	1.54	6.50	12.39 /84	15.98 /83	14.33 /81	1.57	0.34
BA	Schwab Balanced Fund	SWOBX	B-	(800) 407-0256	C / 4.5	2.45	6.68	10.16 /75	10.43 /42	10.04 /45	2.13	0.71
GR	Schwab Core Equity Fd	SWANX	B	(800) 407-0256	B+ / 8.4	2.08	7.45	14.89 /91	16.29 /85	13.78 /76	1.26	0.73
IN	Schwab Dividend Equity Fund	SWDSX	C+	(800) 407-0256	B- / 7.1	0.91	5.23	10.09 /75	15.28 /77	13.44 /72	1.47	0.89
FS	Schwab Financial Services Focus	SWFFX	B	(800) 407-0256	B / 7.7	0.12	8.24	10.20 /75	16.09 /84	10.50 /49	0.78	1.03
FO	Schwab Fundm Intl Lg Co Index	SFNNX	D-	(800) 407-0256	D / 2.1	3.65	-1.87	-4.42 / 6	8.44 /30	5.03 /12	3.48	0.52
FO	Schwab Fundm Intl Sm Co Index	SFILX	D	(800) 407-0256	D+ / 2.9	5.63	2.09	-1.16 /13	9.13 /34	7.70 /28	1.64	0.94
GR	Schwab Fundm US Large Co Index	SFLNX	B+	(800) 407-0256	B / 7.6	-0.07	4.46	9.94 /74	16.30 /86	13.97 /77	1.68	0.41
MC	Schwab Fundm US Small Co Index	SFSNX	B+	(800) 407-0256	B+ / 8.8	4.13	12.83	9.50 /72	17.18 /91	14.89 /86	1.12	0.48
EM	Schwab Fundmntl EM Large Co	SFENX	E	(800) 407-0256	E- / 0.2	0.53	-9.21	-8.36 / 3	-4.27 / 2	-1.77 / 2	2.81	0.89
RE	Schwab Global Real Estate Fund	SWASX	C	(800) 407-0256	C / 5.5	4.55	10.98	14.04 /89	10.14 /40	9.77 /43	5.12	1.17
HL	Schwab Health Care	SWHFX	B+	(800) 407-0256	A+ / 9.9	9.61	15.14	26.92 /99	26.82 /99	21.25 /99	0.70	0.83
IN	Schwab Hedged Equity	SWHEX	C-	(800) 407-0256	C- / 3.7	1.05	4.64	8.37 /65	9.42 /36	7.59 /27	0.00	2.52
FO	Schwab International Core Equity Fd	SICNX	C-	(800) 407-0256	C- / 4.1	6.53	1.23	-1.18 /12	11.44 /49	8.56 /34	1.53	1.10
FO	Schwab International Index	SWISX	D	(800) 407-0256	D+ / 2.7	5.30	0.98	-1.29 /12	8.82 /32	6.10 /17	3.20	0.23
GR	Schwab Large-Cap Growth Fund	SWLSX	A-	(800) 407-0256	B+ / 8.9	4.87	9.99	17.92 /95	16.15 /84	14.48 /82	0.46	1.05
GR	Schwab MarketTrack All Eq Port Inv	SWEGX	C+	(800) 407-0256	C+ / 5.7	2.52	5.78	6.35 /49	13.22 /61	11.40 /56	1.34	0.64
BA	Schwab MarketTrack Bal Port Inv	SWBGX	C+	(800) 407-0256	C- / 3.4	1.95	4.84	6.12 /48	9.04 /33	8.64 /34	1.54	0.65
AA	Schwab MarketTrack Consv Port Inv	SWCGX	C	(800) 407-0256	D / 2.2	1.78	4.19	5.69 /44	6.73 /20	6.95 /23	1.56	0.70
AA	Schwab MarketTrack Growth Port Inv	SWHGX	C+	(800) 407-0256	C / 4.6	2.12	5.40	6.48 /51	11.29 /48	10.19 /46	1.50	0.64
GL	Schwab Monthly Income Fund	SWKRX	C	(800) 407-0256	D / 1.9	1.76	3.80	5.67 /44	5.43 /15	6.06 /17	2.44	0.71

● Denotes fund is closed to new investors
* Denotes fund is included in Section II

www.thestreetratings.com

RISK			NET ASSETS		ASSET					BULL / BEAR		FUND MANAGER		MINIMUMS		LOADS	
	3 Year		NAV						Portfolio	Last Bull	Last Bear	Manager	Manager	Initial	Additional	Front	Back
Risk	Standard		As of	Total	Cash	Stocks	Bonds	Other	Turnover	Market	Market	Quality	Tenure	Purch.	Purch.	End	End
Rating/Pts	Deviation	Beta	3/31/15	$(Mil)	%	%	%	%	Ratio	Return	Return	Pct	(Years)	$	$	Load	Load
B+ / 9.2	5.1	0.88	20.85	128	0	51	47	2	0	45.8	-9.9	54	N/A	250	50	0.0	0.0
B+ / 9.0	5.5	0.96	22.34	9	0	51	47	2	0	43.8	-11.9	32	N/A	250	50	0.0	0.0
B / 8.0	7.1	1.22	21.24	197	0	61	37	2	0	58.7	-16.0	22	N/A	250	50	5.8	0.0
B / 8.0	7.1	1.22	23.22	17	0	61	37	2	0	54.7	-16.2	16	N/A	250	50	0.0	0.0
B / 8.0	7.1	1.21	20.40	1	0	61	37	2	0	56.2	-16.2	19	N/A	250	50	0.0	0.0
B / 8.0	7.1	1.22	23.11	69	0	61	37	2	0	54.6	-16.2	16	N/A	250	50	0.0	0.0
B / 8.0	7.1	1.22	20.50	2	0	61	37	2	0	57.3	-16.0	20	N/A	250	50	0.0	0.0
B / 8.3	6.2	1.07	21.79	130	0	61	37	2	0	57.0	-14.1	40	N/A	250	50	0.0	0.0
B / 8.0	7.1	1.22	24.94	8	0	61	37	2	0	57.4	-16.0	20	N/A	250	50	0.0	0.0
B / 8.0	7.1	1.21	26.78	7	0	61	37	2	0	59.9	-15.9	25	N/A	250	50	0.0	0.0
B+ / 9.0	5.5	0.96	23.42	6	0	51	47	2	0	46.3	-11.6	39	N/A	250	50	0.0	0.0
U /	N/A	N/A	31.03	48	23	69	6	2	36	N/A	N/A	N/A	3	10,000	500	0.0	0.0
B / 8.5	8.8	0.55	40.65	289	0	0	0	100	31	N/A	N/A	98	4	5,000,000	0	0.0	2.0
D- / 1.0	17.0	1.06	12.77	39	5	92	0	3	72	85.5	-37.3	3	17	20,000	2,500	0.0	1.8
C / 5.5	15.7	1.43	18.92	28	6	93	0	1	44	82.8	-30.7	2	13	20,000	2,500	0.0	1.0
B- / 7.3	6.0	0.56	24.92	106	5	93	0	2	114	29.0	-8.1	8	7	5,000	500	4.8	0.0
U /	N/A	N/A	25.03	181	5	93	0	2	114	N/A	N/A	N/A	7	1,000,000	0	0.0	0.0
C / 5.4	13.8	0.99	12.97	50	0	99	0	1	58	25.1	-27.3	67	9	2,500	1,000	0.0	2.0
C / 5.4	13.8	0.99	12.96	763	0	99	0	1	58	25.9	-27.2	70	9	250,000	1,000	0.0	2.0
B- / 7.9	10.7	0.77	12.02	64	0	0	0	100	93	64.9	-19.3	89	5	250,000	1,000	0.0	2.0
E- / 0.0	10.7	0.77	12.03	146	0	0	0	100	93	65.3	-19.3	89	5	5,000,000	0	0.0	2.0
C+ / 5.7	12.4	0.93	11.73	4	0	100	0	0	54	49.9	-27.2	51	5	2,500	1,000	0.0	2.0
C / 5.2	12.5	0.93	11.37	116	0	100	0	0	54	51.2	-27.1	55	5	250,000	1,000	0.0	2.0
C+ / 5.8	12.6	0.94	9.00	24	8	91	0	1	66	45.3	-22.3	49	9	2,500	1,000	0.0	2.0
C+ / 5.8	12.5	0.93	9.00	281	8	91	0	1	66	46.7	-22.2	55	9	250,000	1,000	0.0	2.0
B- / 7.2	9.9	0.58	14.95	N/A	0	99	0	1	48	91.8	-16.6	97	12	2,500	1,000	0.0	2.0
B- / 7.2	9.8	0.58	14.99	809	0	99	0	1	48	94.1	-16.5	97	12	250,000	1,000	0.0	0.0
C- / 3.7	10.9	0.80	25.52	1	3	93	3	1	66	90.2	-23.0	88	12	2,500	1,000	0.0	2.0
C- / 3.8	10.9	0.80	26.30	139	3	93	3	1	66	92.1	-22.9	89	12	250,000	1,000	0.0	2.0
D+ / 2.7	10.5	0.93	12.51	6	3	93	3	1	62	93.0	-21.0	70	9	2,500	1,000	0.0	2.0
D+ / 2.8	10.5	0.93	12.88	58	3	93	3	1	62	94.8	-21.0	73	9	250,000	1,000	0.0	2.0
B- / 7.0	9.6	1.01	53.29	6,824	0	99	0	1	4	99.1	-17.2	65	7	100	0	0.0	2.0
B / 8.7	6.2	1.07	15.46	233	8	53	37	2	27	57.1	-10.3	51	N/A	100	0	0.0	2.0
C / 5.3	9.8	1.02	23.06	2,400	1	98	0	1	63	100.7	-19.1	66	3	100	0	0.0	2.0
C / 5.5	9.9	1.01	17.08	2,065	1	98	0	1	72	90.4	-15.1	55	3	100	0	0.0	2.0
C+ / 6.3	12.3	1.07	16.27	81	0	99	0	1	75	107.1	-25.9	35	3	100	0	0.0	2.0
C / 5.3	14.6	1.09	8.52	1,047	0	99	0	1	8	50.1	-26.3	40	6	100	0	0.0	2.0
C+ / 6.1	12.5	0.90	11.25	363	2	97	0	1	41	47.6	-19.4	73	6	100	0	0.0	2.0
B- / 7.3	10.0	1.03	15.28	5,077	0	99	0	1	14	99.7	-18.5	64	6	100	0	0.0	2.0
C+ / 5.7	12.8	1.12	13.62	1,455	0	99	0	1	29	107.3	-25.5	41	6	100	0	0.0	2.0
C- / 4.1	15.6	1.11	7.64	383	0	99	0	1	19	8.4	-27.2	10	3	100	0	0.0	2.0
C / 5.5	11.9	0.88	7.28	263	10	89	0	1	98	62.2	-21.4	38	3	100	0	0.0	2.0
C / 4.7	10.2	0.89	27.37	1,152	2	97	0	1	57	134.8	-9.6	98	3	100	0	0.0	2.0
C+ / 6.2	6.5	0.63	17.27	208	37	62	0	1	142	52.6	-14.0	61	3	100	0	0.0	2.0
C+ / 5.9	12.8	0.95	9.63	487	0	98	0	2	90	61.3	-21.3	85	3	100	0	0.0	2.0
C+ / 5.7	13.3	1.00	19.08	2,616	5	94	0	1	2	52.5	-23.9	58	4	100	0	0.0	2.0
C+ / 6.1	10.0	1.01	17.66	265	0	99	0	1	82	102.9	-18.8	66	3	100	0	0.0	2.0
C+ / 6.8	10.5	1.05	17.48	623	3	96	0	1	9	80.7	-20.5	22	7	100	0	0.0	2.0
B / 8.8	6.2	1.07	19.39	526	4	58	36	2	16	49.1	-10.9	32	7	100	0	0.0	2.0
B+ / 9.6	4.3	0.72	16.22	229	2	39	57	2	9	34.0	-6.0	53	7	100	0	0.0	2.0
B- / 7.9	8.3	1.41	23.15	757	6	78	15	1	7	65.5	-15.8	17	7	100	0	0.0	2.0
B+ / 9.6	3.5	0.49	11.33	101	1	30	67	2	14	24.6	-1.8	77	N/A	100	0	0.0	0.0

					PERFORMANCE						
	99 Pct = Best					Total Return % through 3/31/15				Incl. in Returns	
	0 Pct = Worst		Overall		Perfor-				Annualized	Dividend	Expense
Fund		Ticker	Investment		mance						
Type	Fund Name	Symbol	Rating	Phone	Rating/Pts	3 Mo	6 Mo	1Yr / Pct	3Yr / Pct	5Yr / Pct	Yield	Ratio
GL	Schwab Monthly Income Fund	SWLRX	C	(800) 407-0256	D- / 1.3	1.69	3.38	5.29 /41	3.85 /10	4.50 /10	2.24	0.66
GL	Schwab Monthly Income Fund	SWJRX	C	(800) 407-0256	D+ / 2.6	2.01	4.25	6.14 /48	6.96 /21	7.25 /25	2.61	0.96
* IX	Schwab S&P 500 Index Fund	SWPPX	A-	(800) 407-0256	B / 7.8	0.90	5.86	12.60 /85	16.01 /83	14.36 /81	1.78	0.09
SC	Schwab Small-Cap Equity Fund	SWSCX	B-	(800) 407-0256	A+ / 9.6	5.12	14.14	10.32 /76	19.81 /98	17.61 /97	0.07	1.11
SC	Schwab Small-Cap Index	SWSSX	B	(800) 407-0256	B+ / 8.3	4.30	14.46	8.30 /65	16.30 /86	14.84 /86	1.16	0.20
GR	Schwab Target 2010	SWBRX	C	(800) 407-0256	D / 2.2	1.88	3.94	5.76 /44	6.85 /21	7.21 /24	2.00	0.67
GI	Schwab Target 2015	SWGRX	C	(800) 407-0256	D+ / 2.6	1.82	4.03	5.88 /45	7.68 /25	8.01 /30	2.11	0.64
GR	Schwab Target 2020	SWCRX	C+	(800) 407-0256	C- / 3.5	2.05	4.65	6.54 /51	9.29 /35	9.25 /39	2.14	0.65
GI	Schwab Target 2025	SWHRX	C+	(800) 407-0256	C- / 4.2	2.23	5.11	7.06 /55	10.40 /42	10.11 /46	2.19	0.73
GR	Schwab Target 2030 Fund	SWDRX	C+	(800) 407-0256	C / 4.7	2.47	5.57	7.44 /59	11.31 /48	10.70 /50	2.26	0.75
GI	Schwab Target 2035	SWIRX	C+	(800) 407-0256	C / 5.2	2.55	5.83	7.71 /61	12.13 /53	11.28 /55	2.26	0.82
GR	Schwab Target 2040	SWERX	B-	(800) 407-0256	C+ / 5.7	2.78	6.20	8.05 /63	12.78 /58	11.73 /59	2.31	0.82
GI	Schwab Target 2045	SWMRX	U	(800) 407-0256	U /	2.92	6.36	8.20 /64	--	--	2.29	1.12
GI	Schwab Target 2050	SWNRX	U	(800) 407-0256	U /	2.90	6.40	8.23 /64	--	--	2.29	1.20
GR	Schwab Total Stock Market Index Fd	SWTSX	A	(800) 407-0256	B / 8.1	1.76	7.09	12.20 /83	16.31 /86	14.72 /84	1.62	0.10
GR	Schwartz Value Fund	RCMFX	E	(888) 449-9240	E+ / 0.6	-4.23	-7.80	-11.43 / 2	3.87 /10	6.07 /17	0.00	1.47
GR	Scotia Dynamic US Growth I	DWUGX	D+	(888) 261-4073	B / 7.8	8.87	11.48	17.57 /95	12.77 /58	20.42 /99	0.00	1.20
GL	Scout Global Equity	SCGLX	C	(800) 996-2862	C / 5.5	5.29	5.55	7.59 /60	11.77 /51	--	0.42	3.87
FO	Scout Internl Fund	UMBWX	D-	(800) 996-2862	D / 1.9	4.08	2.64	0.38 /17	6.34 /18	5.77 /15	1.42	1.01
MC	Scout Mid Cap Fund	UMBMX	C-	(800) 996-2862	C+ / 6.4	5.96	7.34	6.93 /54	13.34 /62	15.13 /88	0.08	1.02
SC	Scout Small Cap Fund	UMBHX	B+	(800) 996-2862	B+ / 8.6	4.55	10.10	9.05 /70	16.58 /87	14.90 /86	0.00	1.27
AA	SCS Tactical Allocation Fund	SCSGX	D-	(800) 773-3863	E / 0.4	-1.04	-12.48	-15.08 / 2	3.73 / 9	--	0.00	3.81
FO	Seafarer Overseas Gr and Inc Inst	SIGIX	C-	(855) 732-9220	C- / 3.4	8.58	5.23	7.47 /59	8.18 /28	--	1.73	1.51
FO	Seafarer Overseas Gr and Inc Inv	SFGIX	C-	(855) 732-9220	C- / 3.3	8.58	5.22	7.35 /58	8.08 /27	--	1.62	1.66
GR	Sector Rotation No Load	NAVFX	D+	(800) 527-9525	C / 4.9	2.81	7.33	10.20 /75	10.13 /40	9.65 /42	0.86	2.11
GL	Seeyond Multi-Asset Allocation Y	SAFYX	U	(800) 225-5478	U /	2.48	1.85	--	--	--	0.00	N/A
SC	Segall Bryant & Hamill Sm Cap Val	SBHVX	U	(866) 490-4999	U /	2.16	10.72	6.35 /50	--	--	0.13	2.21
AA	● SEI Asset Alloc Core Mkt Str Al A	SKTAX	B-	(800) 342-5734	C+ / 5.8	2.56	4.90	6.84 /54	12.68 /57	11.39 /56	0.97	1.38
AA	SEI Asset Alloc- Moderate Strgy A	SMOAX	C	(800) 342-5734	D / 2.1	2.10	3.19	5.74 /44	6.05 /17	6.51 /20	2.97	1.27
AA	SEI Asset Alloc- Moderate Strgy D	SMSDX	C-	(800) 342-5734	D / 1.6	1.92	2.87	4.88 /38	5.15 /14	--	2.33	2.23
AA	SEI Asset Alloc- Moderate Strgy I	SMSIX	C-	(800) 342-5734	D / 2.0	2.04	3.13	5.55 /43	5.81 /16	6.26 /18	2.77	1.52
GI	● SEI Asset Alloc Tr Tax Mgd Strgy A	SXMAX	A-	(800) 342-5734	B- / 7.0	2.82	7.62	10.87 /78	14.05 /67	13.30 /71	2.73	1.35
AA	SEI Asset Alloc Trust Cons Strat I	SICIX	C-	(800) 342-5734	D- / 1.1	1.24	1.75	3.20 /27	3.85 /10	4.18 / 9	1.63	1.40
AA	SEI Asset Alloc-Agg Strgy A	SSGAX	C+	(800) 342-5734	C- / 4.2	3.16	4.29	6.55 /51	9.82 /38	9.55 /41	2.82	1.49
AA	SEI Asset Alloc-Agg Strgy D	SASDX	C	(800) 342-5734	C- / 3.7	3.01	3.94	5.74 /44	9.01 /33	--	2.28	2.49
AA	SEI Asset Alloc-Agg Strgy I	SEAIX	C+	(800) 342-5734	C- / 4.1	3.16	4.25	6.41 /50	9.62 /37	9.30 /39	2.76	1.74
GI	● SEI Asset Alloc-Cons Str All A	SMGAX	B-	(800) 342-5734	C+ / 6.6	3.01	8.94	12.20 /83	13.08 /60	13.32 /71	3.29	1.35
AA	SEI Asset Alloc-Cons Strat A	SVSAX	C-	(800) 342-5734	D- / 1.2	1.26	1.85	3.39 /28	4.07 /10	4.44 /10	1.89	1.15
AA	SEI Asset Alloc-Cons Strat D	SSTDX	C-	(800) 342-5734	D- / 1.0	1.16	1.51	2.60 /25	3.15 / 8	--	1.22	2.06
GL	SEI Asset Alloc-Core Mrkt Strat A	SOKAX	C-	(800) 342-5734	D+ / 2.3	2.73	3.23	5.33 /41	6.52 /19	7.44 /26	2.56	1.36
GL	SEI Asset Alloc-Core Mrkt Strat I	SCMSX	C-	(800) 342-5734	D / 2.2	2.70	3.20	5.15 /40	6.28 /18	7.29 /25	2.33	1.61
AA	SEI Asset Alloc-Defensive Strat A	SNSAX	C-	(800) 342-5734	E+ / 0.8	0.82	1.01	2.18 /23	2.05 / 6	2.45 / 5	1.34	1.06
AA	SEI Asset Alloc-Defensive Strat I	SEDIX	C-	(800) 342-5734	E+ / 0.7	0.73	0.86	1.87 /21	1.78 / 6	2.04 / 4	1.13	1.31
AA	● SEI Asset Alloc-Mkt Gr Str Alloc A	SGOAX	B-	(800) 342-5734	C+ / 5.8	2.54	4.95	6.83 /54	12.71 /58	11.45 /56	0.98	1.38
AA	SEI Asset Alloc-Mkt Gr Strgy A	SRWAX	C	(800) 342-5734	D+ / 2.7	2.86	3.36	5.48 /42	7.36 /23	8.03 /30	2.82	1.42
AA	SEI Asset Alloc-Mkt Gr Strgy D	SMKDX	C-	(800) 342-5734	D+ / 2.3	2.70	3.06	4.78 /37	6.52 /19	--	2.23	2.42
AA	SEI Asset Alloc-Mkt Gr Strgy I	SMGSX	C	(800) 342-5734	D+ / 2.6	2.82	3.25	5.24 /40	7.10 /22	7.76 /28	2.64	1.67
AA	● SEI Asset Alloc-Tax Mgd Agg Strgy A	SISAX	B-	(800) 342-5734	C+ / 5.8	2.55	4.92	6.83 /54	12.73 /58	11.43 /56	0.97	1.38
EM	SEI Inst Intl Emerging Mkts Eqty A	SIEMX	E	(800) 342-5734	E / 0.3	-0.40	-5.65	-3.86 / 7	-1.15 / 3	-0.47 / 2	1.12	1.84
FO	SEI Inst Intl International Eqty A	SEITX	D	(800) 342-5734	D+ / 2.6	5.54	1.72	-1.07 /13	8.08 /27	5.75 /15	1.95	1.25
FO	SEI Inst Intl International Eqty I	SEEIX	D	(800) 342-5734	D+ / 2.4	5.43	1.61	-1.37 /12	7.80 /26	5.49 /14	1.65	1.50
GL	SEI Inst Inv Dynamic Asset All A	SDLAX	A+	(800) 342-5734	A+ / 9.8	5.06	11.93	23.80 /98	19.13 /97	--	4.54	0.66

● Denotes fund is closed to new investors
* Denotes fund is included in Section II

www.thestreetratings.com

RISK			NET ASSETS		ASSET					BULL / BEAR		FUND MANAGER		MINIMUMS		LOADS	
	3 Year		NAV						Portfolio	Last Bull	Last Bear	Manager	Manager	Initial	Additional	Front	Back
Risk	Standard		As of	Total	Cash	Stocks	Bonds	Other	Turnover	Market	Market	Quality	Tenure	Purch.	Purch.	End	End
Rating/Pts	Deviation	Beta	3/31/15	$(Mil)	%	%	%	%	Ratio	Return	Return	Pct	(Years)	$	$	Load	Load
B+ / 9.6	2.6	0.27	10.50	53	0	16	83	1	16	15.3	0.6	80	N/A	100	0	0.0	0.0
B+ / 9.2	4.6	0.69	11.39	52	3	44	51	2	16	34.3	-5.9	75	N/A	100	0	0.0	0.0
B- / 7.3	9.5	1.00	32.45	21,704	1	98	0	1	2	99.5	-16.2	66	7	100	0	0.0	2.0
C- / 3.4	13.4	0.98	22.17	705	0	99	0	1	103	121.7	-24.3	90	3	100	0	0.0	2.0
C+ / 5.7	13.4	1.00	28.13	2,635	0	99	0	1	12	99.8	-23.7	68	7	100	0	0.0	2.0
B+ / 9.5	4.4	0.41	12.48	66	8	36	54	2	29	35.1	-6.7	73	10	100	0	0.0	2.0
B / 8.6	5.0	0.48	12.29	115	7	41	50	2	32	41.5	-9.5	70	N/A	100	0	0.0	2.0
B / 8.9	6.2	0.62	14.42	524	7	53	38	2	26	51.5	-11.8	62	10	100	0	0.0	2.0
B / 8.3	7.2	0.72	14.22	381	8	62	29	1	27	59.3	-13.6	55	N/A	100	0	0.0	2.0
B / 8.1	7.9	0.79	15.74	770	8	69	21	2	26	65.6	-15.3	50	10	100	0	0.0	2.0
B- / 7.6	8.6	0.86	14.86	310	9	75	15	1	24	71.4	-16.5	45	N/A	100	0	0.0	2.0
B- / 7.5	9.1	0.92	16.63	821	9	80	9	2	23	76.1	-17.5	42	10	100	0	0.0	2.0
U /	N/A	N/A	12.69	51	8	84	6	2	23	N/A	N/A	N/A	2	100	0	0.0	2.0
U /	N/A	N/A	12.78	42	8	86	4	2	23	N/A	N/A	N/A	2	100	0	0.0	2.0
B- / 7.2	9.7	1.01	37.63	4,458	1	98	0	1	1	100.9	-17.5	N/A	3	100	0	0.0	2.0
C / 4.8	11.5	1.01	24.00	27	12	87	0	1	57	38.8	-11.2	1	31	2,500	0	0.0	0.0
D / 1.9	18.5	0.98	27.62	59	2	97	0	1	277	81.2	-14.3	29	6	25,000	0	0.0	0.0
C+ / 6.3	10.5	0.71	13.33	10	3	96	0	1	81	65.9	N/A	93	7	1,000	100	0.0	0.0
C / 5.3	11.5	0.84	33.92	5,112	1	98	0	1	12	45.3	-24.2	45	22	1,000	100	0.0	0.0
C- / 4.1	12.4	1.05	16.36	1,778	0	99	0	1	134	77.3	-15.7	16	9	1,000	100	0.0	0.0
C+ / 5.7	13.1	0.92	26.17	250	2	97	0	1	17	101.9	-26.6	81	5	1,000	100	0.0	0.0
C+ / 6.9	11.7	1.18	10.43	5	20	76	3	1	156	N/A	N/A	3	N/A	2,000	100	4.8	0.0
B- / 7.0	11.8	0.71	11.90	110	3	91	3	3	51	N/A	N/A	80	3	100,000	500	0.0	2.0
B- / 7.0	11.8	0.71	11.89	37	3	91	3	3	51	N/A	N/A	79	3	2,500	500	0.0	2.0
C / 4.3	7.6	0.72	11.72	23	0	0	0	100	218	54.5	-14.8	51	6	2,500	100	0.0	0.0
U /	N/A	N/A	9.93	50	79	11	9	1	0	N/A	N/A	N/A	1	100,000	100	0.0	0.0
U /	N/A	N/A	11.33	29	4	95	0	1	55	N/A	N/A	N/A	2	2,500	100	0.0	2.0
B- / 7.3	9.5	1.60	16.43	27	7	81	11	1	49	77.9	-18.7	13	12	100,000	1,000	0.0	0.0
B / 8.8	3.9	0.58	11.69	263	16	29	54	1	47	29.3	-3.8	65	12	100,000	1,000	0.0	0.0
B / 8.8	3.9	0.59	11.66	3	16	29	54	1	47	25.6	-4.2	52	12	150,000	1,000	0.0	0.0
B / 8.9	3.8	0.58	11.98	7	16	29	54	1	47	28.3	-4.0	63	12	100,000	1,000	0.0	0.0
B / 8.3	7.3	0.70	19.71	95	6	75	17	2	41	76.0	-12.5	87	12	100,000	1,000	0.0	0.0
B+ / 9.3	2.4	0.34	10.63	5	24	19	56	1	47	17.5	-2.1	70	12	100,000	1,000	0.0	0.0
B- / 7.8	8.2	1.37	13.39	261	16	61	22	1	50	63.4	-17.5	11	12	100,000	1,000	0.0	0.0
B- / 7.8	8.2	1.38	13.33	14	16	61	22	1	50	59.1	-17.8	8	12	150,000	1,000	0.0	0.0
B- / 7.8	8.2	1.37	13.06	31	16	61	22	1	50	62.0	-17.5	10	12	100,000	1,000	0.0	0.0
B- / 7.8	6.5	0.49	14.73	44	5	62	31	2	64	68.7	-10.2	93	12	100,000	1,000	0.0	0.0
B+ / 9.3	2.3	0.33	10.46	107	24	19	56	1	47	18.6	-1.9	73	12	100,000	1,000	0.0	0.0
B+ / 9.3	2.4	0.34	10.45	5	24	19	56	1	47	15.0	-2.4	61	12	150,000	1,000	0.0	0.0
B / 8.5	5.3	0.80	11.66	117	14	33	51	2	52	37.7	-9.0	58	12	100,000	1,000	0.0	0.0
B / 8.5	5.4	0.81	12.16	1	14	33	51	2	52	36.8	-9.1	54	12	100,000	1,000	0.0	0.0
B+ / 9.6	1.5	0.18	9.82	35	39	8	52	1	60	8.5	N/A	69	N/A	100,000	1,000	0.0	0.0
B+ / 9.6	1.5	0.18	9.66	4	39	8	52	1	60	7.6	-0.2	66	12	100,000	1,000	0.0	0.0
B- / 7.3	9.5	1.61	19.79	135	7	80	11	2	34	78.2	-18.5	12	12	100,000	1,000	0.0	0.0
B / 8.3	6.4	1.05	12.21	361	13	45	40	2	50	46.8	-13.6	18	12	100,000	1,000	0.0	0.0
B / 8.3	6.5	1.06	12.17	6	13	45	40	2	50	42.8	-14.0	12	12	150,000	1,000	0.0	0.0
B / 8.3	6.4	1.06	12.04	13	13	45	40	2	50	45.5	-13.6	15	12	100,000	1,000	0.0	0.0
B- / 7.3	9.5	1.60	18.12	64	7	81	11	1	37	78.3	-18.9	13	N/A	100,000	1,000	0.0	0.0
C / 5.2	13.9	1.01	10.04	1,644	2	96	0	2	59	16.7	-28.6	40	5	100,000	1,000	0.0	1.3
C+ / 6.1	12.2	0.92	9.91	2,683	8	90	0	2	60	47.0	-24.3	59	6	100,000	1,000	0.0	0.8
C+ / 6.1	12.2	0.92	9.91	5	8	90	0	2	60	45.5	-24.3	54	6	100,000	1,000	0.0	0.8
B- / 7.2	7.5	0.82	16.62	1,932	1	98	0	1	11	95.0	-9.2	98	3	100,000	1,000	0.0	0.0

	99 Pct = Best 0 Pct = Worst				PERFORMANCE							
						Total Return % through 3/31/15					Incl. in Returns	
			Overall		Perfor-				Annualized		Dividend	Expense
Fund Type	Fund Name	Ticker Symbol	Investment Rating	Phone	mance Rating/Pts	3 Mo	6 Mo	1Yr / Pct	3Yr / Pct	5Yr / Pct	Yield	Ratio
GL	SEI Inst Inv Extended Mkt Index A	SMXAX	U	(800) 342-5734	U /	5.21	12.00	10.44 /76	--	--	1.06	0.18
GI	SEI Inst Inv Large Cap A	SLCAX	B+	(800) 342-5734	B+ / 8.5	2.22	6.78	12.11 /83	16.45 /87	14.54 /83	0.90	0.46
GR	SEI Inst Inv Large Cap Index A	LCIAX	B+	(800) 342-5734	B+ / 8.5	1.61	6.56	12.73 /86	16.42 /86	14.71 /84	1.38	0.23
GR	SEI Inst Inv LC Disciplined Eq A	SCPAX	B+	(800) 342-5734	B+ / 8.7	2.10	7.13	13.14 /87	16.57 /87	14.54 /83	1.42	0.46
IN	SEI Inst Inv Managed Vol Fund A	SVYAX	A+	(800) 342-5734	A / 9.5	2.74	10.35	15.66 /93	18.42 /95	16.60 /95	1.58	0.71
AA	SEI Inst Inv Multi-Asset RI Rtn A	SEIAX	D-	(800) 342-5734	E / 0.3	0.82	-3.75	-4.07 / 7	-2.78 / 2	--	2.08	0.64
SC	SEI Inst Inv Small Cap A	SLPAX	B-	(800) 342-5734	B / 7.9	4.66	12.49	7.35 /58	15.30 /77	13.63 /74	0.50	0.72
SC	SEI Inst Inv Small Cap II A	SECAX	U	(800) 342-5734	U /	5.03	12.77	8.39 /66	--	--	0.44	0.72
MC	SEI Inst Inv Small/Mid Cap Equity A	SSMAX	B+	(800) 342-5734	B+ / 8.9	4.69	11.94	10.12 /75	16.69 /88	14.76 /85	0.43	0.71
GR	SEI Inst Inv Tr-Tax Mgd Volty A	TMMAX	A+	(800) 342-5734	B+ / 8.8	2.20	9.35	14.10 /90	16.63 /88	15.33 /89	0.99	1.23
EM	SEI Inst Screened World Eq Ex-US A	SSEAX	D-	(800) 342-5734	D / 1.9	2.45	0.54	-1.16 /13	6.87 /21	5.04 /12	1.71	0.85
* EM	SEI Inst World Equity Ex US A	WEUSX	D-	(800) 342-5734	D+ / 2.7	3.73	0.90	0.98 /18	7.96 /27	6.29 /19	2.00	0.62
GI	SEI Insti Inv Tr LrgCap Diver Alp A	SCDAX	A-	(800) 342-5734	B+ / 8.7	2.25	7.06	13.28 /88	16.56 /87	14.89 /86	1.48	0.47
GR	SEI Instl Managed Tr-Lg Cap Gro A	SELCX	B+	(800) 342-5734	B / 8.2	4.11	10.69	14.67 /91	14.99 /75	14.53 /83	0.07	0.97
GR	SEI Instl Managed Tr-Lg Cap Gro I	SPGIX	B+	(800) 342-5734	B / 7.9	4.08	10.57	14.42 /90	14.75 /73	14.28 /80	0.01	1.22
GI	SEI Instl Managed Tr-Lg Cap Val A	TRMVX	A-	(800) 342-5734	B / 7.8	1.12	5.07	9.22 /70	16.18 /85	13.58 /74	0.61	0.92
GI	SEI Instl Managed Tr-Lg Cap Val I	SEUIX	B+	(800) 342-5734	B / 7.7	1.08	5.00	8.99 /69	15.94 /83	13.33 /71	0.48	1.17
MC	SEI Instl Managed Tr-Mid Cap I	SIPIX	A	(800) 342-5734	A / 9.3	5.09	10.77	12.82 /86	17.59 /93	15.03 /87	0.00	1.23
MC	SEI Instl Managed Tr-MidCap Portf A	SEMCX	A	(800) 342-5734	A / 9.3	5.20	10.92	13.11 /87	17.88 /94	15.31 /89	0.05	0.98
RE	SEI Instl Managed Tr-Real Est A	SETAX	B	(800) 342-5734	A- / 9.2	4.68	20.37	24.46 /98	13.16 /61	15.09 /87	1.35	1.23
RE	SEI Instl Managed Tr-Real Est I	SEIRX	B-	(800) 342-5734	A- / 9.1	4.63	20.30	24.24 /98	12.91 /59	14.86 /86	1.18	1.48
IX	SEI Instl Managed Tr-S&P 500 Idx A	SSPIX	B+	(800) 342-5734	B / 7.9	0.87	5.73	12.29 /84	15.64 /80	14.06 /78	1.20	0.54
IX	SEI Instl Managed Tr-S&P 500 Idx E	TRQIX	B+	(800) 342-5734	B / 8.1	0.91	5.84	12.49 /85	15.85 /82	14.27 /80	1.31	0.29
IX	SEI Instl Managed Tr-S&P 500 Idx I	SPIIX	B+	(800) 342-5734	B / 7.7	0.81	5.61	12.03 /83	15.38 /78	13.81 /76	1.03	0.79
SC	SEI Instl Managed Tr-Sm Cap Gr A	SSCGX	B+	(800) 342-5734	A- / 9.0	6.08	14.95	10.44 /76	16.72 /88	15.45 /90	0.00	1.23
SC	SEI Instl Managed Tr-Sm Cap Gr I	SPWIX	B	(800) 342-5734	B+ / 8.8	6.02	14.83	10.19 /75	16.44 /87	15.16 /88	0.00	1.48
GI	SEI Instl Managed Tr-Sm Cap Val A	SESVX	C+	(800) 342-5734	C+ / 6.3	3.31	10.51	4.43 /35	13.81 /66	12.32 /63	0.55	1.22
GI	SEI Instl Managed Tr-Sm Cap Val I	SMVIX	C+	(800) 342-5734	C+ / 6.2	3.25	10.35	4.17 /33	13.55 /64	12.07 /61	0.37	1.47
GR	SEI Instl Managed Tr-T/M Lg Cap A	TMLCX	A-	(800) 342-5734	B / 7.9	1.71	6.23	11.07 /79	15.78 /82	13.99 /78	0.43	0.97
EM	SEI Instl Mgd Tr-Glb Mngd Volty A	SVTAX	B+	(800) 342-5734	B / 7.7	3.91	9.00	14.41 /90	14.57 /72	11.21 /55	4.80	1.23
EM	SEI Instl Mgd Tr-Glb Mngd Volty I	SGMIX	B	(800) 342-5734	B- / 7.5	3.89	8.80	14.19 /90	14.31 /69	10.93 /52	4.65	1.48
GL	SEI Instl Mgd Tr-Mlt-Asst Infl A	SIFAX	U	(800) 342-5734	U /	0.56	-4.05	-4.76 / 6	--	--	0.00	1.25
GL	SEI Instl Mgd Tr-Multi-Asset Inc A	SIOAX	U	(800) 342-5734	U /	2.44	4.03	4.98 /38	--	--	3.96	1.24
AA	SEI Instl Mgd Tr-Multi-Asst Accum A	SAAAX	U	(800) 342-5734	U /	4.55	6.50	10.66 /77	--	--	0.99	1.37
AG	SEI Instl Mgd Tr-Multi-Strat Alt A	SMSAX	C-	(800) 342-5734	E+ / 0.8	1.01	0.97	0.66 /17	2.42 / 7	1.26 / 4	1.56	3.43
GL	SEI Instl Mgd Tr-T Mlt-Asst Captl A	SCLAX	U	(800) 342-5734	U /	0.80	0.87	3.18 /27	--	--	0.05	0.99
IN	SEI Instl Mgd Tr-US Mgd Volty A	SVOAX	A+	(800) 342-5734	A- / 9.2	2.46	9.60	14.61 /91	17.60 /93	15.86 /92	1.04	1.22
IN	SEI Instl Mgd Tr-US Mgd Volty I	SEVIX	A	(800) 342-5734	A- / 9.1	2.34	9.42	14.29 /90	17.28 /91	15.56 /90	0.87	1.47
GI	SEI Large Cap Fund A	SLGAX	B+	(800) 342-5734	B / 7.7	1.98	6.46	11.09 /79	15.50 /79	13.62 /74	0.37	0.96
SC	SEI Small Cap A	SLLAX	B-	(800) 342-5734	B- / 7.5	4.42	11.99	6.27 /49	15.25 /77	13.33 /71	0.00	1.23
GI	Selected American Shares D	SLADX	C-	(800) 279-0279	C+ / 6.3	2.18	5.13	6.36 /50	13.74 /65	11.20 /54	0.74	0.61
GI	Selected American Shares S	SLASX	C-	(800) 279-0279	C+ / 6.0	2.11	4.97	6.00 /46	13.36 /62	10.83 /51	0.43	0.94
FO	Selected International Fund D	SLSDX	D+	(800) 279-0279	C- / 3.3	2.51	-0.41	-1.01 /13	9.70 /37	5.17 /13	0.62	0.83
FO	Selected International Fund S	SLSSX	D	(800) 279-0279	D+ / 2.9	2.34	-0.73	-1.51 /11	9.09 /34	4.60 /11	0.14	1.44
BA	Sentinel Balanced A	SEBLX	C	(800) 282-3863	C- / 3.2	0.99	3.26	6.93 /54	9.72 /38	9.89 /44	1.36	1.06
BA	Sentinel Balanced C	SBACX	C	(800) 282-3863	C- / 3.5	0.84	2.89	6.13 /48	8.86 /32	9.02 /37	0.67	1.86
BA	Sentinel Balanced I	SIBLX	C+	(800) 282-3863	C- / 4.1	1.06	3.36	7.13 /56	9.94 /39	10.05 /45	1.69	0.77
GI	Sentinel Common Stock A	SENCX	C+	(800) 282-3863	C+ / 6.1	1.30	5.38	10.38 /76	14.36 /70	13.08 /69	1.13	1.03
GI	Sentinel Common Stock C	SCSCX	C+	(800) 282-3863	C+ / 6.3	1.09	4.94	9.52 /72	13.43 /63	12.14 /62	0.50	1.84
GI	Sentinel Common Stock I	SICWX	B	(800) 282-3863	B- / 7.2	1.37	5.51	10.68 /77	14.69 /72	13.43 /72	1.46	0.72
FO	Sentinel International Equity A	SWRLX	E+	(800) 282-3863	D+ / 2.5	6.55	6.28	0.15 /16	9.14 /34	6.05 /17	1.63	1.44
FO	Sentinel International Equity C	SWFCX	E	(800) 282-3863	D+ / 2.3	6.23	5.62	-1.19 /12	7.47 /24	4.50 /10	0.37	3.04

● Denotes fund is closed to new investors
* Denotes fund is included in Section II

www.thestreetratings.com

RISK			NET ASSETS		ASSET				Portfolio Turnover Ratio	BULL / BEAR		FUND MANAGER		MINIMUMS		LOADS	
Risk Rating/Pts	3 Year		NAV As of 3/31/15	Total $(Mil)	Cash %	Stocks %	Bonds %	Other %		Last Bull Market Return	Last Bear Market Return	Manager Quality Pct	Manager Tenure (Years)	Initial Purch. $	Additional Purch. $	Front End Load	Back End Load
	Standard Deviation	Beta															
U /	N/A	N/A	13.72	622	6	93	0	1	17	N/A	N/A	N/A	2	100,000	1,000	0.0	0.0
C+ / 5.8	10.1	1.05	22.55	2,419	5	94	0	1	59	103.6	-17.7	62	19	100,000	1,000	0.0	0.0
C+ / 5.9	9.6	1.00	166.79	1,905	3	96	0	1	10	101.7	-17.0	70	10	100,000	1,000	0.0	0.0
C+ / 5.8	9.8	1.02	14.11	4,505	3	96	0	1	110	102.9	-17.3	68	12	100,000	1,000	0.0	0.0
C+ / 6.3	8.3	0.75	14.64	1,406	3	96	0	1	72	93.9	-9.7	95	11	100,000	1,000	0.0	0.0
B- / 7.7	4.5	0.40	8.58	743	0	0	99	1	122	-4.1	N/A	4	4	100,000	1,000	0.0	0.0
C / 5.1	13.0	0.96	19.31	689	5	93	0	2	63	97.6	-26.1	63	18	100,000	1,000	0.0	0.0
U /	N/A	N/A	12.95	314	7	92	0	1	108	N/A	N/A	N/A	3	100,000	1,000	0.0	0.0
C / 5.3	12.1	1.05	14.97	1,922	5	94	0	1	54	103.3	-24.2	51	12	100,000	1,000	0.0	0.0
B- / 7.4	8.1	0.74	14.43	882	7	92	0	1	58	85.0	-9.4	92	8	100,000	1,000	0.0	0.5
C+ / 6.1	12.2	0.79	9.21	87	8	91	0	1	45	45.9	-24.9	95	7	100,000	1,000	0.0	0.0
C / 5.3	12.4	0.79	12.23	7,174	6	93	0	1	46	50.8	-24.2	96	10	100,000	1,000	0.0	0.0
C+ / 6.2	9.8	1.01	14.98	105	17	82	0	1	121	101.6	-16.2	70	10	100,000	1,000	0.0	0.0
C+ / 6.3	10.2	1.01	34.72	1,610	5	94	0	1	61	96.2	-16.6	51	12	100,000	1,000	0.0	0.5
C+ / 6.2	10.2	1.01	34.22	6	5	94	0	1	61	94.8	-16.7	48	12	100,000	1,000	0.0	0.5
B- / 7.1	10.7	1.09	25.20	1,517	6	93	0	1	58	101.1	-19.8	48	21	100,000	1,000	0.0	0.5
B- / 7.1	10.7	1.09	25.20	8	6	93	0	1	58	99.6	-19.9	45	21	100,000	1,000	0.0	0.5
C+ / 6.0	11.0	0.98	27.65	1	7	92	0	1	66	109.6	-23.8	75	22	100,000	1,000	0.0	0.8
C+ / 6.0	11.0	0.98	27.70	88	7	92	0	1	66	111.3	-23.7	78	22	100,000	1,000	0.0	0.8
C- / 4.2	13.0	1.03	19.89	242	3	96	0	1	57	79.7	-16.4	48	12	100,000	1,000	0.0	1.0
C- / 4.2	13.0	1.03	19.88	1	3	96	0	1	57	78.4	-16.5	45	12	100,000	1,000	0.0	1.0
C+ / 6.5	9.6	1.00	50.85	412	1	97	0	2	10	97.6	-16.4	61	4	100,000	1,000	0.0	0.2
C+ / 6.5	9.6	1.00	51.18	280	1	97	0	2	10	98.8	-16.4	64	4	5,000,000	1,000	0.0	0.2
C+ / 6.5	9.6	1.00	51.09	8	1	97	0	2	10	96.1	-16.5	58	4	100,000	1,000	0.0	0.2
C / 5.3	14.0	1.01	29.83	366	4	94	0	2	70	107.7	-26.9	71	4	100,000	1,000	0.0	1.0
C / 5.2	13.9	1.00	28.88	3	4	94	0	2	70	106.0	-27.0	68	4	100,000	1,000	0.0	1.0
C+ / 5.7	12.6	1.12	24.32	391	7	91	0	2	52	88.0	-24.6	17	21	100,000	1,000	0.0	1.0
C+ / 5.7	12.6	1.12	24.14	4	7	91	0	2	52	86.7	-24.7	16	21	100,000	1,000	0.0	1.0
B- / 7.0	10.2	1.05	20.81	3,210	7	92	0	1	39	100.4	-18.0	52	14	100,000	1,000	0.0	0.5
C+ / 6.4	7.0	0.30	11.15	1,929	11	88	0	1	68	65.3	-4.1	99	9	100,000	1,000	0.0	0.8
C+ / 6.4	7.0	0.30	10.96	1	11	88	0	1	68	63.9	-4.2	99	9	100,000	1,000	0.0	0.8
U /	N/A	N/A	9.01	884	0	23	76	1	119	N/A	N/A	N/A	3	100,000	1,000	0.0	0.8
U /	N/A	N/A	10.76	566	0	4	95	1	124	N/A	N/A	N/A	3	100,000	1,000	0.0	0.5
U /	N/A	N/A	10.57	1,924	57	6	35	2	55	N/A	N/A	N/A	3	100,000	1,000	0.0	0.8
B+ / 9.2	2.7	0.20	9.99	532	38	32	27	3	72	9.6	-5.2	57	2	100,000	1,000	0.0	0.3
U /	N/A	N/A	10.14	520	82	0	16	2	246	N/A	N/A	N/A	3	100,000	1,000	0.0	0.3
C+ / 6.5	8.2	0.75	17.11	1,013	5	94	0	1	71	90.2	-10.1	93	N/A	100,000	1,000	0.0	0.5
C+ / 6.5	8.2	0.75	17.08	2	5	94	0	1	71	88.6	-10.2	93	N/A	100,000	1,000	0.0	0.5
C+ / 6.4	10.1	1.04	14.91	2,587	8	90	0	2	57	98.1	-18.0	51	6	100,000	1,000	0.0	0.5
C / 5.5	13.3	0.98	13.46	533	4	94	0	2	72	98.6	-26.7	58	4	100,000	1,000	0.0	1.0
C- / 4.2	10.4	1.05	44.07	3,296	2	97	0	1	26	84.7	-19.7	27	21	10,000	25	0.0	0.0
C / 4.3	10.4	1.05	44.07	1,452	2	97	0	1	26	82.6	-19.8	23	21	1,000	25	0.0	0.0
C+ / 5.8	13.0	0.89	11.45	80	8	91	0	1	49	60.4	-32.6	79	14	10,000	25	0.0	0.0
C+ / 5.8	13.0	0.88	11.38	10	8	91	0	1	49	57.3	-32.7	74	14	1,000	25	0.0	0.0
B- / 7.9	6.7	1.16	19.98	277	6	64	28	2	94	57.6	-11.4	28	11	1,000	50	5.0	0.0
B- / 7.9	6.7	1.16	20.07	33	6	64	28	2	94	53.4	-11.7	20	11	1,000	50	0.0	0.0
B- / 7.9	6.7	1.16	19.88	13	6	64	28	2	94	58.5	-11.3	31	11	1,000,000	0	0.0	0.0
C+ / 6.7	10.1	1.04	42.89	1,528	0	99	0	1	19	88.9	-17.0	36	21	1,000	50	5.0	0.0
C+ / 6.6	10.0	1.03	41.24	91	0	99	0	1	19	83.7	-17.3	27	21	1,000	50	0.0	0.0
C+ / 6.6	10.0	1.03	42.85	836	0	99	0	1	19	90.8	-16.8	41	21	1,000,000	0	0.0	0.0
C- / 3.1	12.9	0.94	16.92	113	4	95	0	1	50	55.4	-24.1	69	3	1,000	50	5.0	2.0
C- / 3.2	13.0	0.94	16.20	4	4	95	0	1	50	47.6	-24.5	46	3	1,000	50	0.0	2.0

					PERFORMANCE						Incl. in Returns	
						Total Return % through 3/31/15						
			Overall		Perfor-				Annualized		Dividend	Expense
Fund Type	Fund Name	Ticker Symbol	Investment Rating	Phone	mance Rating/Pts	3 Mo	6 Mo	1Yr / Pct	3Yr / Pct	5Yr / Pct	Yield	Ratio
FO	Sentinel International Equity I	SIIEX	E+	(800) 282-3863	C- / 3.7	6.75	6.51	0.64 /17	9.71 /38	6.56 /20	2.24	0.89
MC	Sentinel Mid Cap A	SNTNX	D-	(800) 282-3863	C / 5.2	4.64	8.08	6.00 /46	12.91 /59	13.81 /76	0.00	1.35
MC	Sentinel Mid Cap C	SMGCX	E+	(800) 282-3863	C / 5.4	4.41	7.61	5.07 /39	11.79 /51	12.49 /64	0.00	2.29
MC	Sentinel Mid Cap I	SIMGX	D+	(800) 282-3863	C+ / 6.3	4.68	8.21	6.27 /49	13.24 /61	14.16 /79	0.00	0.96
GL	Sentinel Multi-Asset Income A	SECMX	D-	(800) 282-3863	D- / 1.5	2.48	2.20	4.70 /36	6.46 /19	6.97 /23	2.15	1.03
GL	Sentinel Multi-Asset Income C	SMKCX	D-	(800) 282-3863	D / 1.8	2.30	1.76	3.91 /31	5.68 /15	6.20 /18	1.58	1.77
GL	Sentinel Multi-Asset Income I	SCSIX	D	(800) 282-3863	D+ / 2.3	2.63	2.36	5.04 /39	6.70 /20	7.12 /24	2.56	0.80
SC	Sentinel Small Company Fd A	SAGWX	D-	(800) 282-3863	B- / 7.3	6.81	16.27	11.40 /80	15.29 /77	15.31 /89	0.01	1.21
SC	Sentinel Small Company Fd C	SSCOX	D	(800) 282-3863	B- / 7.5	6.36	15.63	10.40 /76	14.39 /70	14.47 /82	0.00	1.93
SC	Sentinel Small Company Fd I	SIGWX	D+	(800) 282-3863	B+ / 8.5	6.82	16.35	11.66 /81	15.67 /81	15.75 /92	0.23	0.81
GR	Sentinel Sustainable Core Oppor A	MYPVX	B-	(800) 282-3863	C+ / 5.8	0.34	4.64	9.83 /74	14.16 /68	12.70 /66	0.76	1.26
GR	Sentinel Sustainable Core Oppor I	CVALX	B-	(800) 282-3863	C+ / 6.9	0.39	4.79	10.19 /75	14.46 /71	13.04 /69	1.04	1.00
GR	Sentinel Sustainable Mid Cap Opps A	WAEGX	C-	(800) 282-3863	C+ / 6.0	5.36	10.76	9.37 /71	13.49 /63	13.75 /75	0.00	1.35
GR	Sentinel Sustainable Mid Cap Opps I	CEGIX	C	(800) 282-3863	C+ / 6.9	5.35	10.76	9.42 /72	13.59 /64	13.77 /76	0.00	1.15
* GR ●	Sequoia Fund	SEQUX	A+	(800) 686-6884	A / 9.5	7.67	15.51	13.77 /89	17.63 /93	17.69 /97	0.00	1.02
GI	Sextant Core Fund	SCORX	C-	(800) 728-8762	D / 1.9	0.90	1.43	4.69 /36	6.16 /17	6.36 /19	1.70	1.01
GR	Sextant Growth Fund	SSGFX	B+	(800) 728-8762	B / 7.8	1.91	6.49	12.40 /84	15.20 /76	12.33 /63	0.05	0.94
FO	Sextant International Fund	SSIFX	E+	(800) 728-8762	D- / 1.0	4.89	1.03	1.72 /21	3.24 / 8	3.27 / 7	4.01	0.66
GL	SFG Futures Strategy A	EFSAX	C	(855) 256-0149	D / 2.0	4.36	8.91	15.82 /93	3.83 /10	--	0.00	3.10
GL	SFG Futures Strategy C	EFSCX	C	(855) 256-0149	D / 2.2	4.14	8.42	14.91 /91	3.09 / 8	--	0.00	3.85
GL	SFG Futures Strategy I	EFSIX	C+	(855) 256-0149	D+ / 2.8	4.45	9.03	16.03 /93	4.06 /10	--	0.42	2.85
GL	SFG Futures Strategy N	EFSNX	C+	(855) 256-0149	D+ / 2.4	4.36	8.91	15.82 /93	3.30 / 8	--	0.00	3.10
IN	Shelton Core Value Direct	EQTIX	B+	(800) 955-9988	B- / 7.3	-0.11	5.00	11.63 /81	14.96 /75	13.73 /75	1.56	0.83
IN	Shelton Core Value K	EQTKX	B-	(800) 955-9988	C+ / 6.9	-0.19	4.77	11.11 /79	14.40 /70	13.19 /70	0.96	1.33
FO	Shelton Greater China Fund	SGCFX	C-	(800) 955-9988	C- / 4.2	4.90	10.00	14.09 /90	7.56 /24	3.79 / 8	1.30	3.00
OT	Shelton Green Alpha	NEXTX	U	(800) 955-9988	U /	5.47	3.01	-1.40 /12	--	--	0.00	1.36
AA	Sierra Core Retirement A	SIRAX	D	(800) 595-9111	E+ / 0.8	1.88	2.22	4.29 /34	3.57 / 9	3.82 / 8	2.14	2.28
AA	Sierra Core Retirement C	SIRCX	D	(800) 595-9111	D- / 1.0	1.69	1.84	3.54 /29	2.80 / 7	3.06 / 6	1.52	3.03
AA	Sierra Core Retirement I	SIRIX	D+	(800) 595-9111	D- / 1.2	1.92	2.22	4.34 /34	3.58 / 9	3.79 / 8	2.27	2.28
GL	Sierra Core Retirement I1	SIRJX	U	(800) 595-9111	U /	1.88	2.13	4.17 /33	--	--	2.11	2.43
AA	Sierra Core Retirement R	SIRRX	D+	(800) 595-9111	D- / 1.2	1.94	2.31	4.55 /35	3.80 /10	4.07 / 9	2.51	2.03
GL	SilverPepper Cmdty Str Gl Mac Adv	SPCAX	U	(855) 554-5540	U /	-3.54	-8.73	-10.28 / 3	--	--	0.00	3.07
GL	SilverPepper Cmdty Str Gl Mac Inst	SPCIX	U	(855) 554-5540	U /	-3.53	-8.70	-10.07 / 3	--	--	0.00	2.82
GI	SiM Dynamic Alloc Equity Inc A	SDEAX	C	(855) 746-3863	C- / 4.1	2.29	6.06	8.50 /66	10.95 /45	--	1.07	1.93
GL	Sirios Focus Institutional	SFDIX	U	(888) 739-1390	U /	4.46	10.10	11.39 /80	--	--	2.81	1.64
BA	Sit Balanced Fund	SIBAX	C+	(800) 332-5580	C / 4.6	2.13	6.05	10.60 /77	9.96 /39	9.45 /40	1.23	1.01
EM	Sit Developing Mkts Growth Fund	SDMGX	E-	(800) 332-5580	E / 0.3	1.45	-4.73	-4.79 / 6	-1.99 / 3	-0.77 / 2	0.00	2.00
GI	Sit Dividend Growth I	SDVGX	C+	(800) 332-5580	C+ / 6.9	1.39	6.45	12.21 /84	14.49 /71	13.83 /76	1.33	1.34
GI	Sit Dividend Growth S	SDVSX	C+	(800) 332-5580	C+ / 6.7	1.33	6.33	11.94 /82	14.20 /69	13.54 /73	1.08	1.59
GL	Sit Global Dividend Growth Class I	GDGIX	C-	(800) 332-5580	C- / 3.7	1.44	3.79	5.25 /40	9.88 /39	8.94 /36	1.29	1.43
GL	Sit Global Dividend Growth Class S	GDGSX	C-	(800) 332-5580	C- / 3.5	1.38	3.66	4.98 /38	9.62 /37	8.67 /34	1.04	1.68
FO	Sit International Growth Fund	SNGRX	D-	(800) 332-5580	D / 2.0	6.12	2.55	-1.60 /11	7.15 /22	5.34 /13	1.61	1.50
GR	Sit Large Cap Growth	SNIGX	C-	(800) 332-5580	C+ / 6.7	2.86	8.16	14.05 /89	13.45 /63	12.29 /62	0.42	1.00
MC	Sit Mid Cap Growth Fund	NBNGX	C	(800) 332-5580	C+ / 6.9	5.45	11.03	10.77 /77	13.83 /66	14.09 /79	0.00	1.25
SC	Sit Small Cap Growth Fund	SSMGX	C	(800) 332-5580	C+ / 6.1	6.27	12.54	7.86 /62	12.63 /57	14.48 /82	0.00	1.50
IN	SkyBridge Dividend Value A	SKYAX	U	(888) 739-1390	U /	4.14	6.71	--	--	--	0.00	N/A
IN	SkyBridge Dividend Value I	SKYIX	U	(888) 739-1390	U /	4.28	6.62	--	--	--	0.00	2.07
GR	Small Cap Value Fund Inc	SCAPX	E	(800) 704-6072	D / 2.2	-6.53	-5.40	-14.75 / 2	11.67 /50	12.24 /62	0.00	0.95
GR	Smead Value Fund A	SVFAX	U	(877) 807-4122	U /	1.77	9.16	12.61 /85	--	--	0.49	1.46
GR	Smead Value Fund I1	SVFFX	A+	(877) 807-4122	A+ / 9.8	1.85	9.35	13.03 /87	21.86 /98	17.90 /97	0.62	1.19
GR ●	Smead Value Fund Investor	SMVLX	A+	(877) 807-4122	A+ / 9.8	1.80	9.19	12.72 /86	21.57 /98	17.61 /97	0.39	1.46
BA	SMI Conservative Allocation	SMILX	D	(877) 764-3863	C- / 3.3	2.14	4.45	3.36 /28	9.24 /35	--	0.77	1.93

● Denotes fund is closed to new investors
* Denotes fund is included in Section II

www.thestreetratings.com

Risk Rating/Pts	3 Year Standard Deviation	Beta	NAV As of 3/31/15	Total $(Mil)	Cash %	Stocks %	Bonds %	Other %	Portfolio Turnover Ratio	Last Bull Market Return	Last Bear Market Return	Manager Quality Pct	Manager Tenure (Years)	Initial Purch. $	Additional Purch. $	Front End Load	Back End Load
C- / 3.0	13.0	0.94	16.76	11	4	95	0	1	50	58.2	-24.0	74	3	1,000,000	0	0.0	2.0
D+ / 2.6	10.8	0.94	20.30	113	3	96	0	1	56	77.9	-17.4	28	3	1,000	50	5.0	0.0
D- / 1.4	10.8	0.95	15.40	10	3	96	0	1	56	72.0	-17.9	18	3	1,000	50	0.0	0.0
D+ / 2.9	10.7	0.94	21.02	7	3	96	0	1	56	79.9	-17.4	32	3	1,000,000	0	0.0	0.0
C+ / 6.0	4.8	0.74	13.24	136	10	16	72	2	166	35.8	-8.1	66	9	1,000	50	5.0	0.0
C+ / 6.0	4.8	0.74	13.18	115	10	16	72	2	166	32.7	-8.4	55	9	1,000	50	0.0	0.0
C+ / 6.0	4.8	0.74	13.22	57	10	16	72	2	166	36.8	-8.1	68	9	1,000,000	0	0.0	0.0
E+ / 0.6	10.9	0.76	5.80	686	1	98	0	1	59	88.6	-20.3	88	3	1,000	50	5.0	2.0
E+ / 0.6	10.9	0.76	4.18	117	1	98	0	1	59	84.2	-20.6	84	3	1,000	50	0.0	2.0
E+ / 0.6	10.8	0.75	6.11	244	1	98	0	1	59	90.6	-20.1	89	3	1,000,000	0	0.0	2.0
B- / 7.2	9.9	1.01	20.64	234	2	97	0	1	20	89.1	-17.2	39	N/A	1,000	50	5.0	0.0
B- / 7.2	9.9	1.01	20.70	15	2	97	0	1	20	90.9	-17.1	42	N/A	1,000,000	0	0.0	0.0
C / 4.7	11.0	1.03	18.49	132	2	97	0	1	62	76.8	-15.2	27	3	1,000	50	5.0	0.0
C / 4.9	11.0	1.04	19.31	7	2	97	0	1	62	77.4	-15.2	28	3	1,000,000	0	0.0	0.0
B- / 7.2	9.2	0.77	253.02	8,616	0	81	18	1	2	103.8	-11.5	93	35	5,000	0	0.0	0.0
B / 8.6	5.1	0.49	12.38	9	13	48	37	2	14	34.4	-9.8	47	7	1,000	25	0.0	0.0
C+ / 6.6	9.3	0.91	26.67	47	10	89	0	1	23	88.8	-16.9	72	2	1,000	25	0.0	0.0
C+ / 5.8	11.2	0.79	15.67	95	0	99	0	1	3	25.0	-15.6	16	20	1,000	25	0.0	0.0
B+ / 9.4	6.2	-0.01	10.76	N/A	87	5	2	6	4	N/A	N/A	91	4	2,500	250	4.5	1.0
B+ / 9.4	6.2	-0.01	10.56	N/A	87	5	2	6	4	N/A	N/A	89	4	1,000	100	0.0	1.0
B+ / 9.4	6.2	N/A	10.79	29	87	5	2	6	4	N/A	N/A	91	4	500,000	10,000	0.0	1.0
B+ / 9.4	6.2	-0.02	10.76	N/A	87	5	2	6	4	N/A	N/A	90	4	2,500	100	0.0	1.0
B- / 7.4	9.7	0.99	26.59	196	1	98	0	1	3	90.4	-16.7	54	12	1,000	250	0.0	0.0
B- / 7.4	9.7	0.99	26.43	6	1	98	0	1	3	87.1	-16.8	47	12	1,000	250	0.0	0.0
C+ / 6.1	11.0	0.58	7.92	10	0	0	0	100	10	32.7	-26.3	84	3	1,000	100	0.0	2.0
U /	N/A	N/A	15.42	27	6	93	0	1	5	N/A	N/A	N/A	2	1,000	250	0.0	0.0
B / 8.1	2.9	0.13	23.51	83	8	8	82	2	78	13.1	-1.4	85	8	10,000	1,000	5.8	0.0
B / 8.1	2.9	0.14	23.68	97	8	8	82	2	78	10.2	-1.7	79	8	10,000	1,000	0.0	0.0
B / 8.1	3.0	0.14	23.48	81	8	8	82	2	78	13.1	-1.5	85	8	10,000	1,000	0.0	0.0
U /	N/A	N/A	23.62	39	8	8	82	2	78	N/A	N/A	N/A	8	10,000	1,000	0.0	0.0
B / 8.0	2.9	0.14	23.34	274	8	8	82	2	78	13.9	-1.3	86	8	100,000	1,000	0.0	0.0
U /	N/A	N/A	8.99	154	100	0	0	0	0	N/A	N/A	N/A	2	5,000	100	0.0	2.0
U /	N/A	N/A	9.02	26	100	0	0	0	0	N/A	N/A	N/A	2	500,000	100	0.0	2.0
B- / 7.4	8.2	0.81	12.94	40	3	86	7	4	10	66.1	N/A	40	4	2,500	100	5.5	0.0
U /	N/A	N/A	11.01	33	0	0	0	100	0	N/A	N/A	N/A	2	100,000	0	0.0	2.0
B / 8.2	6.6	1.15	21.62	21	1	64	33	2	55	55.8	-9.4	32	20	5,000	100	0.0	0.0
D+ / 2.7	14.4	1.03	14.66	9	1	98	0	1	21	12.2	-24.4	28	18	5,000	100	0.0	2.0
C+ / 6.0	9.3	0.96	17.55	977	1	98	0	1	44	88.4	-16.0	55	12	100,000	100	0.0	2.0
C+ / 6.0	9.3	0.96	17.49	88	1	98	0	1	44	86.7	-16.0	51	12	5,000	100	0.0	2.0
C+ / 6.6	10.0	0.68	14.75	21	2	97	0	1	49	64.3	-19.2	90	7	100,000	100	0.0	2.0
C+ / 6.6	10.0	0.68	14.73	6	2	97	0	1	49	62.8	-19.3	89	7	5,000	100	0.0	2.0
C+ / 5.8	12.1	0.90	16.47	22	2	98	0	0	47	48.2	-24.4	48	24	5,000	100	0.0	2.0
C- / 3.4	10.5	1.06	46.81	156	1	98	0	1	27	87.4	-15.5	22	31	5,000	100	0.0	2.0
C / 4.9	11.9	1.00	20.13	173	1	98	0	1	28	95.8	-22.8	27	18	5,000	100	0.0	2.0
C / 5.0	12.1	0.84	58.95	103	0	99	0	1	33	88.3	-22.0	56	14	5,000	100	0.0	2.0
U /	N/A	N/A	10.89	34	0	0	0	100	0	N/A	N/A	N/A	1	1,000	50	5.8	0.0
U /	N/A	N/A	10.89	48	0	0	0	100	0	N/A	N/A	N/A	1	50,000	0	0.0	0.0
C- / 3.3	19.7	1.29	33.64	17	3	96	0	1	469	83.8	-22.0	3	10	100,000	100	0.0	0.0
U /	N/A	N/A	40.16	63	2	97	0	1	16	N/A	N/A	N/A	7	3,000	100	5.8	0.0
B- / 7.5	10.9	1.06	40.27	606	2	97	0	1	16	137.0	-15.3	91	7	1,000,000	100	0.0	0.0
B- / 7.5	10.9	1.06	40.25	384	2	97	0	1	16	135.0	-15.4	91	7	3,000	100	0.0	0.0
C+ / 5.7	6.5	1.01	10.48	30	6	57	35	2	349	47.7	-13.2	44	5	2,500	100	0.0	2.0

					PERFORMANCE						Incl. in Returns	
99 Pct = Best, 0 Pct = Worst			Overall Investment Rating		Perfor-mance Rating/Pts	Total Return % through 3/31/15			Annualized		Dividend Yield	Expense Ratio
Fund Type	Fund Name	Ticker Symbol		Phone		3 Mo	6 Mo	1Yr / Pct	3Yr / Pct	5Yr / Pct		
AA	SMI Dynamic Allocation	SMIDX	U	(877) 764-3863	U /	2.78	11.36	13.88 /89	--	--	1.84	1.44
GR	Smith Group Lg Cap Core Grow Inst	BSLGX	B	(877) 764-8465	B+ / 8.4	3.35	9.62	13.30 /88	15.71 /81	15.72 /91	0.60	1.05
GR	Snow Capital Opportunity A	SNOAX	D+	(877) 766-9363	C / 5.3	-3.10	-3.21	0.57 /17	15.83 /82	10.04 /45	0.12	1.53
GR	Snow Capital Opportunity C	SNOCX	C-	(877) 766-9363	C+ / 5.6	-3.27	-3.57	-0.13 /15	15.03 /75	9.28 /39	0.00	2.24
GR	Snow Capital Opportunity Inst	SNOIX	C-	(877) 766-9363	C+ / 6.3	-3.04	-3.10	0.84 /18	16.12 /84	10.31 /47	0.40	1.28
GL	Snow Capital Small Cap Value A	SNWAX	D+	(877) 766-9363	C / 4.8	-1.74	1.03	0.34 /17	14.46 /71	--	0.00	2.00
GL	Snow Capital Small Cap Value C	SNWCX	D+	(877) 766-9363	C / 5.1	-1.93	0.64	-0.42 /14	13.60 /64	--	0.00	2.72
GL	Snow Capital Small Cap Value Inst	SNWIX	C-	(877) 766-9363	C+ / 5.9	-1.69	1.14	0.58 /17	14.75 /73	--	0.00	1.74
GR	Sound Mind Investing	SMIFX	D+	(877) 764-3863	C+ / 5.6	2.59	5.96	4.90 /38	13.16 /61	10.50 /49	0.47	2.03
GR	Sound Shore Inst	SSHVX	U	(800) 754-8758	U /	0.94	3.96	9.06 /70	--	--	1.90	0.87
GR	Sound Shore Investor	SSHFX	A-	(800) 754-8758	A- / 9.0	0.90	3.89	8.88 /69	18.33 /95	13.96 /77	1.86	0.93
GR	Sparrow Growth Fd A	SGFFX	C	(888) 727-3301	C+ / 5.9	8.37	12.52	11.92 /82	12.67 /57	13.31 /71	0.00	2.38
GR	Sparrow Growth Fd C	SGFCX	B	(888) 727-3301	B / 7.8	8.22	12.26	11.32 /80	14.17 /68	--	0.00	2.85
GR	Sparrow Growth Fd NL	SGNFX	C+	(888) 727-3301	B- / 7.1	8.42	12.67	12.16 /83	12.94 /59	13.59 /74	0.00	2.16
EN	Spirit of America Energy A	SOAEX	U	(800) 452-4892	U /	-2.43	-17.58	--	--	--	0.00	1.86
AA	Spirit Of America Inc and Opp A	SOAOX	U	(800) 452-4892	U /	1.98	1.13	8.00 /63	--	--	4.66	2.74
GR	Spirit Of America Large Cap Value	SOAVX	C+	(800) 452-4892	C / 4.9	0.52	4.84	10.82 /78	12.44 /56	11.35 /56	0.69	1.68
RE	Spirit Of America Real Estate A	SOAAX	C+	(800) 452-4892	B / 8.0	3.63	15.85	24.09 /98	13.11 /60	13.72 /75	1.22	1.68
RE	● SSgA Clarion Real Estate N	SSREX	B-	(800) 843-2639	A / 9.3	4.50	20.44	24.97 /98	13.33 /62	15.39 /89	1.53	1.39
SC	● SSgA Dynamic Small Cap N	SVSCX	A-	(800) 843-2639	A- / 9.1	4.30	13.53	7.84 /62	17.41 /92	18.20 /98	0.73	2.16
EM	SSgA Emerging Markets N	SSEMX	E-	(800) 843-2639	E / 0.4	1.61	-3.56	-1.54 /11	-1.63 / 3	0.26 / 3	2.67	1.17
EM	SSgA Emerging Markets Sel	SEMSX	E-	(800) 843-2639	E / 0.4	1.71	-3.36	-1.30 /12	-1.38 / 3	0.51 / 3	2.97	0.95
SC	● SSgA Enhanced Small Cap N	SESPX	B+	(800) 843-2639	A / 9.5	5.56	16.95	11.34 /80	18.12 /95	17.08 /96	0.87	1.41
FO	● SSgA Intl Stock Selection N	SSAIX	D+	(800) 843-2639	C- / 3.7	5.56	2.29	1.05 /19	9.61 /37	5.65 /15	2.15	1.17
IX	SSgA S&P 500 Index N	SVSPX	A+	(800) 843-2639	B / 8.2	0.90	5.82	12.53 /85	15.98 /83	14.31 /81	1.77	0.17
GL	STAAR Inv Trust International Fund	SITIX	E	(800) 332-7738	E- / 0.2	-5.78	-11.00	-13.57 / 2	-1.78 / 3	-0.74 / 2	0.00	2.84
AA	STAAR Inv Trust Lg Comp Stock	SITLX	D-	(800) 332-7738	C- / 3.6	-9.95	2.49	4.22 /33	10.42 /42	9.10 /37	0.00	2.53
SC	STAAR Inv Trust Sm Comp Stock	SITSX	E+	(800) 332-7738	D / 1.8	-3.35	0.14	-4.50 / 6	7.83 /26	7.79 /29	0.00	2.79
AA	Stadion Managed Risk 100 A	ETFFX	D-	(866) 383-7636	E / 0.3	-5.75	-5.19	-4.14 / 7	-0.49 / 4	0.45 / 3	0.00	1.70
AA	Stadion Managed Risk 100 C	ETFYX	D-	(866) 383-7636	E / 0.3	-6.00	-5.61	-4.92 / 6	-1.25 / 3	-0.34 / 2	0.00	2.46
AA	Stadion Managed Risk 100 I	ETFVX	D-	(866) 383-7636	E / 0.4	-5.79	-5.14	-4.00 / 7	-0.31 / 4	0.66 / 3	0.00	1.48
AA	Stadion Tactical Defensive A	ETFRX	D	(866) 383-7636	D- / 1.2	-1.71	1.71	3.80 /31	5.88 /16	5.33 /13	0.00	2.17
AA	Stadion Tactical Defensive C	ETFZX	D	(866) 383-7636	D- / 1.3	-1.87	1.25	2.97 /26	5.01 /13	4.50 /10	0.00	2.95
AA	Stadion Tactical Defensive I	ETFWX	D+	(866) 383-7636	D / 1.8	-1.69	1.69	3.94 /31	6.04 /17	5.53 /14	0.00	2.01
GR	Stadion Tactical Growth A	ETFAX	U	(866) 383-7636	U /	2.54	7.23	11.45 /80	--	--	0.29	2.10
GR	Stadion Tactical Growth I	ETFOX	D+	(866) 383-7636	C / 5.1	2.53	7.22	11.63 /81	10.30 /41	11.26 /55	0.40	1.84
AA	Stadion Trilogy Alternative Ret A	STTGX	U	(866) 383-7636	U /	0.48	1.38	0.88 /18	--	--	0.29	1.91
AA	Stadion Trilogy Alternative Ret I	STTIX	U	(866) 383-7636	U /	0.57	1.52	1.11 /19	--	--	0.44	1.72
BA	State Farm Balanced Fund	STFBX	C+	(800) 447-4930	C- / 3.7	0.70	3.15	8.53 /67	8.98 /33	8.15 /31	2.55	0.13
IX	State Farm Equity & Bond A	NBSAX	B	(800) 447-4930	C / 4.8	2.54	7.50	11.58 /81	11.37 /48	10.07 /45	1.15	1.07
IX	State Farm Equity & Bond B	NBSBX	B+	(800) 447-4930	C / 5.2	2.44	7.12	10.92 /78	10.73 /44	9.37 /40	0.63	1.77
IX	State Farm Equity & Bond Inst	SEBIX	A-	(800) 447-4930	C+ / 5.9	2.71	7.70	12.02 /83	11.67 /50	10.35 /47	1.42	0.82
IX	State Farm Equity & Bond Legacy A	SLBAX	B+	(800) 447-4930	C / 5.1	2.60	7.51	11.67 /81	11.39 /48	10.04 /45	1.15	1.07
IX	State Farm Equity & Bond Legacy B	SLBBX	B+	(800) 447-4930	C / 5.3	2.51	7.28	11.20 /79	10.96 /45	9.62 /41	0.80	1.47
IX	State Farm Equity & Bond R1	REBOX	B+	(800) 447-4930	C / 5.4	2.57	7.32	11.40 /80	11.04 /46	9.71 /42	0.92	1.39
IX	State Farm Equity & Bond R2	REBTX	B+	(800) 447-4930	C+ / 5.6	2.56	7.42	11.60 /81	11.24 /47	9.91 /44	1.12	1.19
IX	State Farm Equity & Bond R3	REBHX	A-	(800) 447-4930	C+ / 5.8	2.65	7.65	11.88 /82	11.62 /50	10.26 /47	1.38	0.89
IN	State Farm Equity A	SNEAX	A+	(800) 447-4930	B+ / 8.6	2.98	10.32	15.83 /93	17.22 /91	13.97 /77	0.52	1.17
IN	State Farm Equity B	SNEBX	A+	(800) 447-4930	B+ / 8.9	2.79	9.78	14.91 /91	16.35 /86	13.17 /70	0.00	1.86
IN	State Farm Equity Inst	SLEIX	A+	(800) 447-4930	A / 9.3	3.07	10.35	16.09 /93	17.46 /92	14.26 /80	0.73	0.92
IN	State Farm Equity LegA	SLEAX	A+	(800) 447-4930	B+ / 8.9	2.96	10.17	15.70 /93	17.15 /91	13.97 /77	0.46	1.17
IN	State Farm Equity LegB	SLEBX	A+	(800) 447-4930	A- / 9.1	2.87	10.05	15.23 /92	16.74 /88	13.51 /73	0.03	1.57

● Denotes fund is closed to new investors
* Denotes fund is included in Section II

www.thestreetratings.com

| RISK | 3 Year | | NET ASSETS | | ASSET | | | | Portfolio | BULL / BEAR | | FUND MANAGER | | MINIMUMS | | LOADS | |
Risk Rating/Pts	Standard Deviation	Beta	NAV As of 3/31/15	Total $(Mil)	Cash %	Stocks %	Bonds %	Other %	Turnover Ratio	Last Bull Market Return	Last Bear Market Return	Manager Quality Pct	Manager Tenure (Years)	Initial Purch. $	Additional Purch. $	Front End Load	Back End Load
U /	N/A	N/A	12.22	204	1	98	0	1	135	N/A	N/A	N/A	2	2,500	100	0.0	2.0
C /5.4	11.0	1.09	11.11	59	0	0	0	100	47	98.4	-19.1	41	8	25,000	100	0.0	0.0
C /4.4	13.9	1.31	27.51	114	4	95	0	1	91	102.4	-26.9	11	9	2,500	0	5.3	0.5
C- /4.2	13.9	1.31	26.05	54	4	95	0	1	91	97.7	-27.0	8	9	2,500	0	0.0	0.5
C /4.4	13.9	1.31	27.75	168	4	95	0	1	91	104.1	-26.8	12	9	1,000,000	0	0.0	0.5
C /4.6	15.5	0.78	30.55	31	0	99	0	1	66	105.2	-28.4	96	5	2,500	0	5.3	0.5
C /4.5	15.5	0.78	29.40	19	0	99	0	1	66	100.0	-28.7	95	5	2,500	0	0.0	0.5
C /4.7	15.5	0.78	30.92	53	0	99	0	1	66	106.9	-28.4	96	5	1,000,000	0	0.0	0.5
C- /3.6	10.9	1.05	12.29	260	4	95	0	1	136	74.1	-21.3	22	10	2,500	100	0.0	2.0
U /	N/A	N/A	49.33	689	2	97	0	1	44	N/A	N/A	N/A	30	1,000,000	0	0.0	0.0
C+ /6.2	11.2	1.10	49.23	1,727	2	97	0	1	44	117.4	-22.7	72	30	10,000	0	0.0	0.0
C /5.2	11.5	0.99	20.06	9	0	100	0	0	254	86.2	-16.0	27	17	1,000	50	5.8	0.0
C+ /5.8	12.2	1.01	19.35	N/A	0	100	0	0	254	N/A	N/A	39	17	1,000	50	0.0	0.0
C /5.2	11.6	0.99	19.32	2	0	100	0	0	254	87.9	-15.9	29	17	2,500	100	0.0	0.0
U /	N/A	N/A	7.85	199	0	0	0	100	0	N/A	N/A	N/A	N/A	500	50	5.8	0.0
U /	N/A	N/A	10.35	44	23	28	48	1	0	N/A	N/A	N/A	2	500	50	4.8	0.0
B- /7.6	9.1	0.94	19.85	78	5	94	0	1	22	81.5	-17.3	33	N/A	500	50	5.3	0.0
C /4.7	11.7	0.93	13.56	141	9	90	0	1	31	79.5	-20.4	68	N/A	500	50	5.3	0.0
C- /3.9	13.3	1.06	17.41	55	0	99	0	1	32	85.1	-16.4	45	2	1,000	100	0.0	0.0
C+ /6.2	13.0	0.95	39.54	25	1	98	0	1	147	114.7	-23.3	83	5	1,000	100	0.0	0.0
D- /1.5	14.3	1.03	10.70	263	1	98	0	1	89	16.1	-27.8	33	8	1,000	100	0.0	0.0
D- /1.5	14.3	1.04	10.72	14	1	98	0	1	89	17.0	-27.7	36	8	20,000,000	1,000	0.0	0.0
C /5.1	13.4	0.98	15.95	39	1	98	0	1	71	110.2	-22.8	83	10	1,000	100	0.0	0.0
C+ /5.8	13.3	0.99	11.02	348	2	97	0	1	74	54.0	-26.0	69	5	1,000	100	0.0	0.0
B- /7.8	9.5	1.00	32.80	1,605	0	0	0	100	4	99.6	-16.4	66	11	10,000	100	0.0	0.0
C- /3.6	12.6	1.78	10.76	2	3	89	6	2	14	10.3	-24.0	0	18	1,000	50	0.0	0.0
C /4.4	12.9	1.63	15.20	4	3	96	0	1	16	64.5	-17.9	5	18	1,000	50	0.0	0.0
C /4.6	12.4	0.86	14.42	4	4	95	0	1	11	52.1	-23.2	8	18	1,000	50	0.0	0.0
C+ /6.9	7.3	0.74	9.50	132	2	97	0	1	1,079	4.4	-8.2	3	9	1,000	250	5.8	0.0
C+ /6.7	7.3	0.75	9.09	56	2	97	0	1	1,079	1.8	-8.6	2	9	1,000	250	0.0	0.0
C+ /6.9	7.3	0.75	9.60	63	2	97	0	1	1,079	5.2	-8.2	3	9	500,000	5,000	0.0	0.0
B- /7.8	7.8	1.25	12.07	35	49	50	0	1	529	30.1	-12.2	4	9	1,000	250	5.8	0.0
B- /7.7	7.8	1.26	11.54	11	49	50	0	1	529	26.7	-12.5	3	N/A	1,000	250	0.0	0.0
B- /7.8	7.8	1.27	12.19	22	49	50	0	1	529	31.1	-12.2	4	N/A	500,000	5,000	0.0	0.0
U /	N/A	N/A	10.48	48	3	86	9	2	324	N/A	N/A	N/A	2	1,000	250	5.8	0.0
C- /4.1	8.6	0.82	10.52	78	3	86	9	2	324	64.7	-15.5	32	2	500,000	5,000	0.0	0.0
U /	N/A	N/A	10.53	42	3	47	49	1	15	N/A	N/A	N/A	3	1,000	250	5.8	0.0
U /	N/A	N/A	10.56	56	3	47	49	1	15	N/A	N/A	N/A	3	500,000	5,000	0.0	0.0
B /8.8	5.5	0.92	67.53	1,715	1	62	35	2	4	46.2	-9.1	53	24	250	50	0.0	0.0
B+ /9.1	6.0	0.60	11.32	128	1	60	38	1	0	59.6	-10.2	83	N/A	250	50	5.0	0.0
B+ /9.1	6.0	0.59	11.32	15	1	60	38	1	0	56.2	-10.4	80	N/A	250	50	0.0	0.0
B+ /9.1	6.0	0.60	11.35	31	1	60	38	1	0	61.0	-10.1	85	N/A	250	50	0.0	0.0
B+ /9.1	6.0	0.59	11.43	114	1	60	38	1	0	59.5	-10.1	84	N/A	250	50	3.0	0.0
B+ /9.1	6.0	0.60	11.45	25	1	60	38	1	0	57.5	-10.3	80	N/A	250	50	0.0	0.0
B+ /9.1	6.0	0.59	11.18	3	1	60	38	1	0	57.9	-10.3	81	N/A	0	0	0.0	0.0
B+ /9.1	6.0	0.59	11.20	7	1	60	38	1	0	58.9	-10.1	83	N/A	0	0	0.0	0.0
B+ /9.1	6.0	0.60	11.23	2	1	60	38	1	0	60.5	-10.1	84	N/A	0	0	0.0	0.0
B- /7.2	9.9	1.01	10.02	125	2	97	0	1	69	104.5	-19.4	75	N/A	250	50	5.0	0.0
B- /7.1	10.0	1.03	9.95	3	2	97	0	1	69	99.5	-19.6	65	N/A	250	50	0.0	0.0
B- /7.2	9.9	1.01	10.07	251	2	97	0	1	69	106.3	-19.3	77	N/A	250	50	0.0	0.0
B- /7.2	10.0	1.02	10.42	117	2	97	0	1	69	104.4	-19.3	73	N/A	250	50	3.0	0.0
B- /7.2	9.9	1.01	10.39	9	2	97	0	1	69	101.7	-19.5	71	N/A	250	50	0.0	0.0

99 Pct = Best
0 Pct = Worst

Fund Type	Fund Name	Ticker Symbol	Overall Investment Rating	Phone	Performance Rating/Pts	3 Mo	6 Mo	1Yr / Pct	3Yr / Pct	5Yr / Pct	Dividend Yield	Expense Ratio
IN	State Farm Equity R1	SREOX	A+	(800) 447-4930	A- / 9.1	2.98	10.08	15.32 /92	16.80 /89	13.59 /74	0.23	1.48
IN	State Farm Equity R2	SRETX	A+	(800) 447-4930	A- / 9.2	2.88	10.10	15.61 /93	17.02 /90	13.80 /76	0.43	1.29
IN	State Farm Equity R3	SREHX	A+	(800) 447-4930	A / 9.3	3.07	10.27	15.87 /93	17.41 /92	14.16 /79	0.65	0.98
GR	State Farm Growth Fund	STFGX	B-	(800) 447-4930	C+ / 5.6	-0.66	2.14	9.04 /70	12.69 /57	10.82 /51	2.16	0.12
FO	State Farm Intl Equity A	SNIAX	D-	(800) 447-4930	D- / 1.5	5.46	4.11	0.67 /17	6.47 /19	5.66 /15	0.61	1.53
FO	State Farm Intl Equity B	SNIBX	D-	(800) 447-4930	D / 1.8	5.34	3.80	-0.05 /15	5.89 /16	5.02 /12	0.04	2.23
FO	State Farm Intl Equity Inst	SFIIX	D-	(800) 447-4930	D+ / 2.3	5.60	4.22	0.90 /18	6.74 /20	5.90 /16	0.87	1.28
FO	State Farm Intl Equity LegA	SFFAX	D-	(800) 447-4930	D / 1.8	5.60	4.13	0.73 /18	6.49 /19	5.66 /15	0.59	1.53
FO	State Farm Intl Equity LegB	SFFBX	D-	(800) 447-4930	D / 1.9	5.38	3.95	0.23 /16	6.05 /17	5.23 /13	0.22	1.93
FO	State Farm Intl Equity R1	RIEOX	D-	(800) 447-4930	D / 2.0	5.49	3.99	0.35 /17	6.14 /17	5.33 /13	0.25	1.85
FO	State Farm Intl Equity R2	RIETX	D-	(800) 447-4930	D / 2.1	5.56	4.10	0.57 /17	6.36 /18	5.53 /14	0.55	1.65
FO	State Farm Intl Equity R3	RIEHX	D-	(800) 447-4930	D / 2.2	5.60	4.25	0.84 /18	6.66 /20	5.84 /16	0.80	1.35
FO	State Farm Intl Index A	NFSAX	D-	(800) 447-4930	D / 1.7	5.08	0.52	-2.04 /10	7.87 /26	5.11 /12	2.33	1.22
FO	State Farm Intl Index B	NFSBX	D-	(800) 447-4930	D / 2.1	4.99	0.20	-2.67 / 9	7.26 /23	4.45 /10	1.81	1.92
FO	State Farm Intl Index Inst	SFFFX	D	(800) 447-4930	D+ / 2.6	5.16	0.67	-1.81 /11	8.15 /28	5.37 /14	2.67	0.97
FO	State Farm Intl Index LegA	SIIAX	D-	(800) 447-4930	D / 2.0	5.18	0.64	-2.01 /10	7.92 /27	5.10 /12	2.33	1.22
FO	State Farm Intl Index LegB	SIIBX	D-	(800) 447-4930	D / 2.2	4.97	0.33	-2.46 / 9	7.44 /24	4.69 /11	1.94	1.62
FO	State Farm Intl Index R1	RIIOX	D-	(800) 447-4930	D / 2.2	4.99	0.42	-2.38 /10	7.53 /24	4.77 /11	2.02	1.54
FO	State Farm Intl Index R2	RIITX	D	(800) 447-4930	D+ / 2.4	5.10	0.46	-2.19 /10	7.75 /26	4.97 /12	2.31	1.34
FO	State Farm Intl Index R3	RIIHX	D	(800) 447-4930	D+ / 2.6	5.16	0.67	-1.89 /11	8.08 /27	5.30 /13	2.59	1.04
AA	State Farm LifePath 2020 A	NLWAX	D+	(800) 447-4930	D / 1.6	1.85	3.31	5.00 /39	6.47 /19	6.88 /22	1.07	1.57
AA	State Farm LifePath 2020 B	NLWBX	C-	(800) 447-4930	D / 1.8	1.65	2.96	4.23 /33	5.71 /16	6.13 /18	0.38	2.26
AA	State Farm LifePath 2020 Inst	SAWIX	C-	(800) 447-4930	D+ / 2.4	1.91	3.46	5.22 /40	6.72 /20	7.15 /24	1.33	1.31
AA	State Farm LifePath 2020 LegA	SAWAX	C-	(800) 447-4930	D / 1.8	1.86	3.28	4.98 /38	6.45 /19	6.88 /22	1.06	1.56
AA	State Farm LifePath 2020 LegB	SAWBX	C-	(800) 447-4930	D / 2.0	1.77	3.09	4.56 /36	6.04 /17	6.46 /20	0.52	1.96
AA	State Farm LifePath 2020 R1	RAWOX	C-	(800) 447-4930	D / 2.0	1.71	3.08	4.63 /36	6.11 /17	6.55 /20	0.76	1.88
AA	State Farm LifePath 2020 R2	RAWTX	C-	(800) 447-4930	D / 2.1	1.79	3.23	4.78 /37	6.33 /18	6.76 /22	1.03	1.68
AA	State Farm LifePath 2020 R3	RAWHX	C-	(800) 447-4930	D+ / 2.3	1.85	3.39	5.15 /40	6.65 /20	7.07 /24	1.26	1.38
AA	State Farm LifePath 2030 A	NLHAX	D+	(800) 447-4930	D+ / 2.3	2.17	3.72	5.59 /43	7.92 /27	7.83 /29	1.02	1.60
AA	State Farm LifePath 2030 B	NLHBX	C-	(800) 447-4930	D+ / 2.6	1.98	3.35	4.82 /37	7.17 /22	7.08 /24	0.34	2.30
AA	State Farm LifePath 2030 Inst	SAYIX	C-	(800) 447-4930	C- / 3.2	2.16	3.78	5.78 /45	8.17 /28	8.09 /30	1.28	1.35
AA	State Farm LifePath 2030 LegA	SAYAX	C-	(800) 447-4930	D+ / 2.6	2.10	3.66	5.53 /43	7.92 /27	7.82 /29	1.00	1.60
AA	State Farm LifePath 2030 LegB	SAYBX	C-	(800) 447-4930	D+ / 2.8	2.03	3.48	5.15 /40	7.49 /24	7.40 /26	0.49	2.00
AA	State Farm LifePath 2030 R1	RAYOX	C-	(800) 447-4930	D+ / 2.8	2.05	3.53	5.21 /40	7.58 /25	7.49 /26	0.70	1.93
AA	State Farm LifePath 2030 R2	RAYTX	C-	(800) 447-4930	D+ / 2.9	2.11	3.60	5.41 /42	7.78 /26	7.69 /28	0.96	1.73
AA	State Farm LifePath 2030 R3	RAYHX	C-	(800) 447-4930	C- / 3.2	2.16	3.78	5.70 /44	8.11 /28	8.02 /30	1.21	1.43
AA	State Farm LifePath 2040 A	NLOAX	D+	(800) 447-4930	D+ / 2.9	2.35	3.95	6.00 /46	9.08 /34	8.55 /33	1.03	1.64
AA	State Farm LifePath 2040 B	NLBOX	C-	(800) 447-4930	C- / 3.2	2.23	3.65	5.26 /41	8.33 /29	7.82 /29	0.37	2.34
AA	State Farm LifePath 2040 Inst	SAUIX	C-	(800) 447-4930	C- / 3.9	2.40	4.08	6.25 /49	9.35 /35	8.82 /35	1.29	1.39
AA	State Farm LifePath 2040 LegA	SAUAX	C-	(800) 447-4930	C- / 3.2	2.41	3.96	6.01 /47	9.08 /34	8.56 /34	1.01	1.64
AA	State Farm LifePath 2040 LegB	SAUBX	C-	(800) 447-4930	C- / 3.4	2.27	3.77	5.56 /43	8.66 /31	8.12 /31	0.52	2.04
AA	State Farm LifePath 2040 R1	RAUOX	C-	(800) 447-4930	C- / 3.5	2.30	3.81	5.67 /44	8.75 /31	8.22 /31	0.70	1.96
AA	State Farm LifePath 2040 R2	RAUTX	C-	(800) 447-4930	C- / 3.6	2.35	3.85	5.84 /45	8.95 /33	8.42 /33	0.99	1.76
AA	State Farm LifePath 2040 R3	RAUHX	C-	(800) 447-4930	C- / 3.8	2.44	4.05	6.19 /48	9.27 /35	8.75 /35	1.21	1.46
AA	State Farm LifePath 2050 A	NLPAX	C-	(800) 447-4930	C- / 3.4	2.39	4.16	6.25 /49	9.98 /39	9.12 /38	0.96	1.71
AA	State Farm LifePath 2050 R1	RAVRX	C	(800) 447-4930	C- / 4.0	2.38	3.99	5.98 /46	9.65 /37	8.80 /35	0.68	2.03
AA	State Farm LifePath 2050 R2	RAVSX	C	(800) 447-4930	C- / 4.1	2.38	4.15	6.14 /48	9.83 /38	9.01 /37	0.92	1.83
GI	State Farm LifePath Retirement A	NILAX	C-	(800) 447-4930	D- / 1.1	1.72	2.80	4.32 /34	5.09 /13	5.94 /17	0.85	1.56
GI	State Farm LifePath Retirement B	NILBX	C-	(800) 447-4930	D- / 1.4	1.54	2.71	3.86 /31	4.67 /12	5.39 /14	0.76	2.26
GI	State Farm LifePath Retirement Inst	SLRIX	C-	(800) 447-4930	D / 1.8	1.74	3.15	4.77 /37	5.43 /15	6.24 /18	1.39	1.31
GI	State Farm LifePath Retirement LegA	SLRAX	C-	(800) 447-4930	D- / 1.3	1.67	3.02	4.57 /36	5.17 /14	5.99 /17	1.09	1.56
GI	State Farm LifePath Retirement LegB	SLRBX	C-	(800) 447-4930	D- / 1.5	1.64	2.86	4.17 /33	4.75 /12	5.57 /15	0.69	1.95

● Denotes fund is closed to new investors
* Denotes fund is included in Section II

www.thestreetratings.com

RISK			NET ASSETS		ASSET					BULL / BEAR		FUND MANAGER		MINIMUMS		LOADS	
Risk Rating/Pts	3 Year		NAV As of 3/31/15	Total $(Mil)	Cash %	Stocks %	Bonds %	Other %	Portfolio Turnover Ratio	Last Bull Market Return	Last Bear Market Return	Manager Quality Pct	Manager Tenure (Years)	Initial Purch. $	Additional Purch. $	Front End Load	Back End Load
	Standard Deviation	Beta															
B- / 7.2	9.9	1.02	10.02	2	2	97	0	1	69	102.5	-19.6	71	N/A	0	0	0.0	0.0
B- / 7.2	9.9	1.02	9.99	15	2	97	0	1	69	103.8	-19.5	73	N/A	0	0	0.0	0.0
B- / 7.2	9.8	1.01	10.07	2	2	97	0	1	69	105.5	-19.3	77	N/A	0	0	0.0	0.0
B- / 7.5	9.5	0.95	74.96	4,210	0	99	0	1	1	76.0	-17.3	34	24	250	50	0.0	0.0
C / 5.5	12.2	0.89	11.21	44	3	96	0	1	77	48.2	-25.6	40	9	250	50	5.0	0.0
C / 5.5	12.1	0.89	11.04	10	3	96	0	1	77	45.3	-25.9	33	9	250	50	0.0	0.0
C / 5.5	12.2	0.89	11.32	20	3	96	0	1	77	49.3	-25.5	43	9	250	50	0.0	0.0
C / 5.5	12.2	0.89	11.32	49	3	96	0	1	77	48.0	-25.5	40	9	250	50	3.0	0.0
C / 5.5	12.3	0.89	11.16	11	3	96	0	1	77	46.1	-25.7	34	9	250	50	0.0	0.0
C / 5.5	12.2	0.89	11.15	3	3	96	0	1	77	46.5	-25.6	35	9	0	0	0.0	0.0
C / 5.5	12.2	0.89	11.20	6	3	96	0	1	77	47.5	-25.6	38	9	0	0	0.0	0.0
C / 5.5	12.2	0.89	11.31	2	3	96	0	1	77	48.9	-25.5	42	9	0	0	0.0	0.0
C+ / 5.7	13.2	1.00	11.99	85	2	97	0	1	1	47.1	-23.5	45	22	250	50	5.0	0.0
C+ / 5.7	13.2	1.00	11.99	12	2	97	0	1	1	44.1	-23.8	36	22	250	50	0.0	0.0
C+ / 5.7	13.2	1.00	12.02	46	2	97	0	1	1	48.3	-23.5	48	22	250	50	0.0	0.0
C+ / 5.7	13.2	1.00	11.98	94	2	97	0	1	1	47.0	-23.5	45	22	250	50	3.0	0.0
C+ / 5.7	13.3	1.00	12.03	15	2	97	0	1	1	45.0	-23.6	38	22	250	50	0.0	0.0
C+ / 5.7	13.2	1.00	12.00	3	2	97	0	1	1	45.5	-23.6	39	22	0	0	0.0	0.0
C+ / 5.7	13.2	1.00	11.96	8	2	97	0	1	1	46.4	-23.6	43	22	0	0	0.0	0.0
C+ / 5.7	13.3	1.00	12.03	2	2	97	0	1	1	48.0	-23.5	47	22	0	0	0.0	0.0
B / 8.1	5.6	0.92	14.32	1,280	6	40	52	2	19	37.5	-10.0	22	N/A	250	50	5.0	0.0
B / 8.2	5.6	0.92	14.20	33	6	40	52	2	19	34.2	-10.3	16	N/A	250	50	0.0	0.0
B / 8.0	5.6	0.92	14.37	203	6	40	52	2	19	38.6	-10.0	25	N/A	250	50	0.0	0.0
B / 8.1	5.6	0.91	14.27	459	6	40	52	2	19	37.4	-9.9	23	N/A	250	50	3.0	0.0
B / 8.2	5.5	0.91	14.34	21	6	40	52	2	19	35.6	-10.1	20	N/A	250	50	0.0	0.0
B / 8.2	5.6	0.92	14.24	20	6	40	52	2	19	36.0	-10.1	20	N/A	0	0	0.0	0.0
B / 8.1	5.5	0.91	14.25	61	6	40	52	2	19	36.8	-10.0	22	N/A	0	0	0.0	0.0
B / 8.0	5.6	0.92	14.33	4	6	40	52	2	19	38.3	-9.9	24	N/A	0	0	0.0	0.0
B- / 7.5	7.1	1.18	15.05	1,224	13	57	28	2	22	47.6	-13.7	13	N/A	250	50	5.0	0.0
B- / 7.6	7.1	1.18	14.95	43	13	57	28	2	22	44.2	-13.9	9	N/A	250	50	0.0	0.0
B- / 7.4	7.1	1.18	15.15	232	13	57	28	2	22	49.0	-13.6	14	N/A	250	50	0.0	0.0
B- / 7.5	7.1	1.19	15.07	370	13	57	28	2	22	47.7	-13.7	12	N/A	250	50	3.0	0.0
B- / 7.6	7.1	1.18	15.09	20	13	57	28	2	22	45.7	-13.9	10	N/A	250	50	0.0	0.0
B- / 7.5	7.1	1.18	14.96	30	13	57	28	2	22	46.2	-13.9	11	N/A	0	0	0.0	0.0
B- / 7.5	7.1	1.19	15.02	54	13	57	28	2	22	47.1	-13.7	11	N/A	0	0	0.0	0.0
B- / 7.5	7.1	1.18	15.16	5	13	57	28	2	22	48.7	-13.7	14	N/A	0	0	0.0	0.0
C+ / 6.9	8.3	1.39	15.67	762	19	71	8	2	26	56.5	-16.7	7	N/A	250	50	5.0	0.0
B- / 7.0	8.4	1.39	15.56	44	19	71	8	2	26	52.9	-17.0	6	N/A	250	50	0.0	0.0
C+ / 6.8	8.3	1.39	15.81	280	19	71	8	2	26	57.9	-16.7	8	N/A	250	50	0.0	0.0
C+ / 6.9	8.3	1.38	15.73	272	19	71	8	2	26	56.5	-16.7	8	N/A	250	50	3.0	0.0
B- / 7.0	8.3	1.39	15.76	20	19	71	8	2	26	54.5	-16.9	6	N/A	250	50	0.0	0.0
C+ / 6.9	8.4	1.40	15.60	21	19	71	8	2	26	54.9	-16.8	6	N/A	0	0	0.0	0.0
C+ / 6.9	8.3	1.39	15.66	45	19	71	8	2	26	55.9	-16.7	7	N/A	0	0	0.0	0.0
C+ / 6.9	8.3	1.39	15.98	5	19	71	8	2	26	57.5	-16.7	8	N/A	0	0	0.0	0.0
B- / 7.3	9.3	1.54	10.71	261	77	20	1	2	28	63.8	-19.2	6	7	250	50	5.0	0.0
B- / 7.4	9.4	1.55	10.74	7	77	20	1	2	28	62.2	-19.3	5	7	0	0	0.0	0.0
B- / 7.3	9.3	1.55	10.75	12	77	20	1	2	28	63.1	-19.2	5	7	0	0	0.0	0.0
B / 8.7	4.3	0.37	12.33	812	2	29	67	2	17	27.7	-5.5	60	N/A	250	50	5.0	0.0
B / 8.8	4.3	0.37	12.41	13	2	29	67	2	17	25.9	-5.7	53	N/A	250	50	0.0	0.0
B / 8.7	4.3	0.36	12.61	99	2	29	67	2	17	29.1	-5.4	65	N/A	250	50	0.0	0.0
B / 8.8	4.3	0.36	12.61	279	2	29	67	2	17	28.0	-5.4	63	N/A	250	50	3.0	0.0
B / 8.8	4.3	0.36	12.68	8	2	29	67	2	17	26.3	-5.6	56	N/A	250	50	0.0	0.0

Fund Type	Fund Name	Ticker Symbol	Overall Investment Rating	Phone	Performance Rating/Pts	3 Mo	6 Mo	1Yr / Pct	3Yr / Pct	5Yr / Pct	Dividend Yield	Expense Ratio
GI	State Farm LifePath Retirement R1	RLROX	C-	(800) 447-4930	D- / 1.5	1.64	2.92	4.26 /33	4.88 /13	5.67 /15	0.85	1.88
GI	State Farm LifePath Retirement R2	RLRTX	C-	(800) 447-4930	D / 1.6	1.64	3.03	4.45 /35	5.05 /13	5.87 /16	1.02	1.67
GI	State Farm LifePath Retirement R3	RLRHX	C-	(800) 447-4930	D / 1.7	1.73	3.21	4.78 /37	5.38 /14	6.18 /18	1.31	1.38
GI	State Farm S&P 500 Index A	SNPAX	B-	(800) 447-4930	C+ / 6.7	0.77	5.52	11.94 /82	15.23 /77	13.61 /74	1.08	0.75
GI	State Farm S&P 500 Index B	SNPBX	B+	(800) 447-4930	B- / 7.0	0.58	5.17	11.10 /79	14.41 /70	12.79 /66	0.41	1.44
GI	State Farm S&P 500 Index Inst	SFXIX	A-	(800) 447-4930	B / 7.8	0.83	5.67	12.20 /83	15.53 /79	13.90 /77	1.32	0.50
GI	State Farm S&P 500 Index LegA	SLIAX	B+	(800) 447-4930	B- / 7.0	0.77	5.50	11.81 /82	15.21 /77	13.59 /74	1.05	0.75
GI	State Farm S&P 500 Index LegB	SLIBX	B+	(800) 447-4930	B- / 7.2	0.64	5.29	11.40 /80	14.77 /73	13.15 /70	0.57	1.14
GI	State Farm S&P 500 Index R1	RSPOX	B+	(800) 447-4930	B- / 7.3	0.64	5.33	11.50 /80	14.84 /74	13.23 /70	0.77	1.07
GI	State Farm S&P 500 Index R2	RSPTX	B+	(800) 447-4930	B- / 7.5	0.77	5.51	11.80 /82	15.12 /76	13.46 /72	0.99	0.86
GI	State Farm S&P 500 Index R3	RSPHX	A-	(800) 447-4930	B / 7.7	0.83	5.59	12.05 /83	15.42 /78	13.80 /76	1.24	0.57
SC	State Farm Small Cap Index A	SNRAX	C+	(800) 447-4930	C+ / 6.9	4.07	13.93	7.24 /57	15.21 /77	13.53 /73	0.28	1.05
SC	State Farm Small Cap Index B	SNRBX	B-	(800) 447-4930	B- / 7.3	3.90	13.55	6.48 /51	14.50 /71	12.79 /66	0.00	1.75
SC	State Farm Small Cap Index Inst	SMIIX	B	(800) 447-4930	B / 8.1	4.10	14.06	7.48 /59	15.51 /79	13.82 /76	0.50	0.80
SC	State Farm Small Cap Index LegA	SMIAX	B-	(800) 447-4930	B- / 7.3	4.10	13.95	7.27 /57	15.25 /77	13.54 /73	0.26	1.05
SC	State Farm Small Cap Index LegB	SMIBX	B-	(800) 447-4930	B / 7.6	4.01	13.75	6.87 /54	14.77 /73	13.10 /69	0.00	1.45
SC	State Farm Small Cap Index R1	RSIOX	B	(800) 447-4930	B / 7.6	4.01	13.77	6.93 /54	14.87 /74	13.18 /70	0.00	1.37
SC	State Farm Small Cap Index R2	RSITX	B	(800) 447-4930	B / 7.8	4.00	13.83	7.07 /56	15.07 /75	13.39 /72	0.15	1.17
SC	State Farm Small Cap Index R3	RSIHX	B	(800) 447-4930	B / 8.1	4.16	14.04	7.46 /59	15.45 /79	13.75 /75	0.42	0.87
SC	State Farm Small Mid Cap Eq A	SSNAX	C-	(800) 447-4930	C+ / 5.9	3.39	8.77	5.83 /45	14.14 /68	13.66 /75	0.00	1.46
SC	State Farm Small Mid Cap Eq B	SSNBX	C-	(800) 447-4930	C+ / 6.2	3.17	8.35	5.08 /39	13.46 /63	12.96 /68	0.00	2.16
SC	State Farm Small Mid Cap Eq Inst	SFEIX	C	(800) 447-4930	C+ / 6.9	3.39	8.82	6.01 /47	14.40 /70	13.92 /77	0.00	1.21
SC	State Farm Small Mid Cap Eq LegA	SFSAX	C-	(800) 447-4930	C+ / 6.2	3.38	8.70	5.87 /45	14.12 /68	13.65 /74	0.00	1.46
SC	State Farm Small Mid Cap Eq LegB	SFSBX	C-	(800) 447-4930	C+ / 6.4	3.27	8.42	5.41 /42	13.66 /65	13.19 /70	0.00	1.86
SC	State Farm Small Mid Cap Eq R1	RSEOX	C	(800) 447-4930	C+ / 6.5	3.30	8.50	5.52 /43	13.78 /65	13.29 /71	0.00	1.78
SC	State Farm Small Mid Cap Eq R2	RSETX	C	(800) 447-4930	C+ / 6.6	3.39	8.65	5.72 /44	14.00 /67	13.52 /73	0.00	1.58
SC	State Farm Small Mid Cap Eq R3	RSEHX	C	(800) 447-4930	C+ / 6.9	3.43	8.75	6.00 /46	14.33 /70	13.84 /76	0.00	1.28
GR	State Street Equity 500 Index Adm	STFAX	A+	(800) 882-0052	B / 8.0	0.87	5.73	12.43 /84	15.82 /82	14.19 /79	1.79	0.31
GR	State Street Equity 500 Index B	STBIX	A+	(800) 882-0052	B / 7.9	0.87	5.69	12.34 /84	15.69 /81	14.07 /78	1.69	0.41
IX	State Street Equity 500 Index II	SSEYX	U	(800) 882-0052	U /	0.95	5.91	--	--	--	0.00	N/A
IX	State Street Equity 500 Index R	SSFRX	A	(800) 882-0052	B / 7.6	0.75	5.52	11.95 /82	15.30 /77	13.66 /75	1.33	0.76
FO	State Street Global Eq ex-US Id K	SSGLX	U	(800) 882-0052	U /	3.82	-0.87	--	--	--	0.00	N/A
FO	State Street Global Eq ex-US Indx	SSGVX	U	(800) 882-0052	U /	3.82	-0.82	--	--	--	0.00	N/A
GL	State Street/Ramius Mgd Fut Strat A	RTSRX	B-	(877) 672-6487	C / 5.3	6.56	16.19	25.24 /98	7.49 /24	--	8.17	4.61
GL	State Street/Ramius Mgd Fut Strat I	RTSIX	B-	(877) 672-6487	C+ / 6.4	6.64	16.30	25.54 /98	7.76 /26	--	9.25	4.36
GL	Steben Managed Futures I	SKLIX	U	(855) 775-5571	U /	4.17	11.16	--	--	--	0.00	N/A
GL	Steinberg Select Institutional	STMIX	U		U /	2.60	1.45	6.65 /52	--	--	0.42	1.55
GI	Sterling Capital Beh LC Val Eq A	BBTGX	B-	(800) 228-1872	C+ / 6.0	0.70	5.53	11.07 /79	14.46 /71	11.40 /56	1.03	1.18
GI	● Sterling Capital Beh LC Val Eq B	BGISX	B-	(800) 228-1872	C+ / 6.4	0.46	5.11	10.23 /75	13.61 /64	10.55 /49	0.36	1.93
GI	Sterling Capital Beh LC Val Eq C	BCVCX	B-	(800) 228-1872	C+ / 6.4	0.47	5.13	10.22 /75	13.62 /64	10.56 /49	0.50	1.93
GI	Sterling Capital Beh LC Val Eq Inst	BBISX	B+	(800) 228-1872	B- / 7.3	0.81	5.68	11.34 /80	14.76 /73	11.67 /58	1.33	0.93
SC	Sterling Capital Beh SC Val Eq A	SPSAX	C	(800) 228-1872	C / 5.5	3.49	11.43	6.46 /50	13.35 /62	11.93 /60	0.55	1.61
SC	● Sterling Capital Beh SC Val Eq B	SPSBX	C	(800) 228-1872	C+ / 5.9	3.32	10.97	5.65 /44	12.51 /56	11.11 /54	0.00	2.36
SC	Sterling Capital Beh SC Val Eq C	SPSDX	C	(800) 228-1872	C+ / 5.9	3.25	10.91	5.58 /43	12.48 /56	11.08 /53	0.00	2.36
SC	Sterling Capital Beh SC Val Eq Inst	SPSCX	C+	(800) 228-1872	C+ / 6.7	3.53	11.53	6.66 /52	13.62 /64	12.22 /62	0.82	1.36
SC	Sterling Capital Beh SC Val Eq R	SPSRX	C	(866) 777-7818	C+ / 6.4	3.29	11.28	6.22 /48	13.20 /61	11.83 /59	0.30	1.86
IN	Sterling Capital Equity Income Fd A	BAEIX	C-	(800) 228-1872	C- / 3.2	1.15	2.61	5.39 /42	10.31 /41	11.20 /54	1.53	1.20
IN	● Sterling Capital Equity Income Fd B	BEIBX	C	(800) 228-1872	C- / 3.6	0.91	2.17	4.56 /36	9.48 /36	10.35 /47	0.82	1.95
IN	Sterling Capital Equity Income Fd C	BCEGX	C	(800) 228-1872	C- / 3.6	0.99	2.22	4.61 /36	9.49 /36	10.35 /47	0.90	1.95
IN	Sterling Capital Equity Income Fd I	BEGIX	C	(800) 228-1872	C / 4.3	1.21	2.73	5.59 /43	10.57 /43	11.47 /57	1.87	0.95
IN	Sterling Capital Equity Income Fd R	BAERX	C	(800) 228-1872	C- / 4.0	1.06	2.46	5.10 /39	10.04 /40	10.97 /52	1.37	1.45
GR	Sterling Capital Long Short Eq Inst	SLSIX	U	(800) 228-1872	U /	2.03	-5.18	-4.12 / 7	--	--	0.00	2.81

www.thestreetratings.com

RISK			NET ASSETS		ASSET					Portfolio	BULL / BEAR		FUND MANAGER		MINIMUMS		LOADS	
	3 Year		NAV								Last Bull	Last Bear	Manager	Manager	Initial	Additional	Front	Back
Risk	Standard		As of	Total	Cash	Stocks	Bonds	Other		Turnover	Market	Market	Quality	Tenure	Purch.	Purch.	End	End
Rating/Pts	Deviation	Beta	3/31/15	$(Mil)	%	%	%	%		Ratio	Return	Return	Pct	(Years)	$	$	Load	Load
B / 8.7	4.3	0.36	12.38	7	2	29	67	2		17	26.7	-5.6	57	N/A	0	0	0.0	0.0
B / 8.8	4.3	0.37	12.65	23	2	29	67	2		17	27.5	-5.5	59	N/A	0	0	0.0	0.0
B / 8.8	4.3	0.37	12.60	2	2	29	67	2		17	28.8	-5.4	64	N/A	0	0	0.0	0.0
B- / 7.3	9.5	1.00	15.64	414	1	98	0	1		3	95.2	-16.5	56	7	250	50	5.0	0.0
B- / 7.3	9.6	1.00	15.69	13	1	98	0	1		3	90.4	-16.8	45	7	250	50	0.0	0.0
B- / 7.3	9.6	1.00	15.78	156	1	98	0	1		3	96.8	-16.5	59	7	250	50	0.0	0.0
B- / 7.3	9.5	0.99	15.72	449	1	98	0	1		3	95.2	-16.6	57	7	250	50	3.0	0.0
B- / 7.3	9.5	1.00	15.83	28	1	98	0	1		3	92.6	-16.8	50	7	250	50	0.0	0.0
B- / 7.3	9.6	1.00	15.69	7	1	98	0	1		3	93.1	-16.7	50	7	0	0	0.0	0.0
B- / 7.3	9.5	1.00	15.62	20	1	98	0	1		3	94.4	-16.7	55	7	0	0	0.0	0.0
B- / 7.3	9.6	1.00	15.75	2	1	98	0	1		3	96.3	-16.5	58	7	0	0	0.0	0.0
C+ / 5.7	13.5	1.00	16.89	114	2	96	0	2		14	94.4	-25.4	53	N/A	250	50	5.0	0.0
C+ / 5.7	13.4	1.00	16.50	15	2	96	0	2		14	90.5	-25.7	44	N/A	250	50	0.0	0.0
C+ / 5.7	13.4	1.00	17.01	86	2	96	0	2		14	96.3	-25.3	58	N/A	250	50	0.0	0.0
C+ / 5.7	13.4	1.00	16.74	207	2	96	0	2		14	94.4	-25.4	54	N/A	250	50	3.0	0.0
C+ / 5.7	13.4	1.00	16.36	29	2	96	0	2		14	92.0	-25.6	48	N/A	250	50	0.0	0.0
C+ / 5.7	13.4	1.00	16.84	4	2	96	0	2		14	92.5	-25.5	49	N/A	0	0	0.0	0.0
C+ / 5.7	13.5	1.00	16.88	9	2	96	0	2		14	93.7	-25.4	51	N/A	0	0	0.0	0.0
C+ / 5.7	13.4	1.00	17.02	3	2	96	0	2		14	95.9	-25.4	57	N/A	0	0	0.0	0.0
C / 4.7	12.6	0.90	12.21	95	1	98	0	1		116	88.3	-24.1	63	N/A	250	50	5.0	0.0
C / 4.4	12.6	0.90	11.39	13	1	98	0	1		116	84.5	-24.4	52	N/A	250	50	0.0	0.0
C / 4.8	12.5	0.90	12.52	49	1	98	0	1		116	90.0	-24.1	66	N/A	250	50	0.0	0.0
C / 4.6	12.5	0.90	11.94	101	1	98	0	1		116	88.3	-24.2	63	N/A	250	50	3.0	0.0
C / 4.3	12.5	0.90	11.05	12	1	98	0	1		116	85.8	-24.3	57	N/A	250	50	0.0	0.0
C / 4.5	12.5	0.90	11.59	3	1	98	0	1		116	86.3	-24.3	58	N/A	0	0	0.0	0.0
C / 4.6	12.5	0.90	11.89	12	1	98	0	1		116	87.6	-24.2	61	N/A	0	0	0.0	0.0
C / 4.7	12.5	0.90	12.38	3	1	98	0	1		116	89.5	-24.1	66	N/A	0	0	0.0	0.0
B / 8.0	9.5	1.00	17.42	251	0	0	0	100		4	98.6	-16.4	64	11	25,000,000	0	0.0	0.0
B / 8.0	9.5	1.00	17.40	131	0	0	0	100		4	98.0	-16.5	63	11	25,000,000	0	0.0	0.0
U /	N/A	N/A	10.65	484	0	0	0	100		0	N/A	N/A	N/A	1	0	0	0.0	0.0
B / 8.0	9.5	1.00	17.39	43	0	0	0	100		4	95.7	-16.6	57	11	25,000,000	0	0.0	0.0
U /	N/A	N/A	9.52	45	0	0	0	100		0	N/A	N/A	N/A	1	10,000,000	0	0.0	0.0
U /	N/A	N/A	9.52	92	0	0	0	100		0	N/A	N/A	N/A	1	0	0	0.0	0.0
B- / 7.6	9.5	N/A	10.89	4	20	0	79	1		98	15.4	N/A	96	4	1,000	50	5.5	1.0
B- / 7.6	9.6	0.01	10.92	164	20	0	79	1		98	16.3	N/A	96	4	1,000,000	100,000	0.0	1.0
U /	N/A	N/A	11.75	78	34	0	65	1		0	N/A	N/A	N/A	1	1,000,000	25,000	0.0	1.0
U /	N/A	N/A	10.25	59	10	89	0	1		44	N/A	N/A	N/A	N/A	100,000	0	0.0	0.0
B- / 7.5	9.4	0.94	18.07	36	0	99	0	1		114	90.4	-19.9	60	2	1,000	0	5.8	0.0
B- / 7.5	9.4	0.94	17.75	1	0	99	0	1		114	85.6	-20.2	49	2	1,000	0	0.0	0.0
B- / 7.5	9.4	0.94	17.58	1	0	99	0	1		114	85.6	-20.2	48	2	1,000	0	0.0	0.0
B- / 7.5	9.4	0.94	18.17	250	0	99	0	1		114	92.0	-19.9	64	2	1,000,000	0	0.0	0.0
C / 5.3	13.9	0.99	15.42	14	2	97	0	1		69	81.8	-25.6	32	2	1,000	0	5.8	0.0
C / 5.3	13.9	0.99	14.94	N/A	2	97	0	1		69	77.2	-25.9	24	2	1,000	0	0.0	0.0
C / 5.3	13.9	0.99	14.92	N/A	2	97	0	1		69	77.1	-25.9	23	2	1,000	0	0.0	0.0
C / 5.4	13.9	0.99	15.54	122	2	97	0	1		69	83.4	-25.5	35	2	1,000,000	0	0.0	0.0
C / 5.3	13.8	0.98	15.38	N/A	2	97	0	1		69	81.8	-25.5	32	2	1,000	0	0.0	0.0
B- / 7.4	8.9	0.85	18.74	553	2	97	0	1		16	62.1	-10.3	26	11	1,000	0	5.8	0.0
B- / 7.4	8.9	0.85	18.70	6	2	97	0	1		16	58.0	-10.6	19	11	1,000	0	0.0	0.0
B- / 7.4	8.9	0.85	18.59	307	2	97	0	1		16	58.1	-10.5	19	11	1,000	0	0.0	0.0
B- / 7.4	8.9	0.85	18.78	927	2	97	0	1		16	63.5	-10.2	29	11	1,000,000	0	0.0	0.0
B- / 7.4	8.9	0.85	18.63	2	2	97	0	1		16	60.8	-10.3	23	11	1,000	0	0.0	0.0
U /	N/A	N/A	10.06	102	49	50	0	1		194	N/A	N/A	N/A	2	1,000,000	0	0.0	0.0

Fund Type	Fund Name	Ticker Symbol	Overall Investment Rating	Phone	PERFORMANCE Perfor- mance Rating/Pts	Total Return % through 3/31/15 3 Mo	6 Mo	1Yr / Pct	Annualized 3Yr / Pct	5Yr / Pct	Incl. in Returns Dividend Yield	Expense Ratio
	99 Pct = Best 0 Pct = Worst											
MC	Sterling Capital Mid Value A	OVEAX	B+	(800) 228-1872	B / 8.0	5.13	10.97	10.91 /78	16.86 /89	14.10 /79	0.49	1.18
MC	● Sterling Capital Mid Value B	OVEBX	A-	(800) 228-1872	B+ / 8.5	4.97	10.56	10.13 /75	16.01 /83	13.26 /71	0.00	1.93
MC	Sterling Capital Mid Value C	OVECX	A-	(800) 228-1872	B+ / 8.5	5.00	10.57	10.14 /75	16.02 /84	13.24 /71	0.08	1.93
MC	Sterling Capital Mid Value I	OVEIX	A+	(800) 228-1872	A- / 9.1	5.20	11.09	11.21 /79	17.16 /91	14.38 /81	0.74	0.93
MC	Sterling Capital Mid Value R	OVERX	A	(800) 228-1872	B+ / 8.6	4.90	10.88	10.77 /77	16.21 /85	13.57 /74	0.26	1.43
GR	Sterling Capital Special Opptys A	BOPAX	B-	(800) 228-1872	B- / 7.2	4.05	5.69	13.42 /88	15.74 /81	12.61 /65	0.00	1.21
GR	● Sterling Capital Special Opptys B	BOPBX	B	(800) 228-1872	B / 7.6	3.90	5.33	12.59 /85	14.88 /74	11.76 /59	0.00	1.96
GR	Sterling Capital Special Opptys C	BOPCX	B	(800) 228-1872	B / 7.6	3.85	5.27	12.58 /85	14.87 /74	11.75 /59	0.00	1.96
GR	Sterling Capital Special Opptys Ins	BOPIX	B+	(800) 228-1872	B+ / 8.5	4.13	5.81	13.76 /89	16.03 /84	12.89 /67	0.00	0.96
GR	Sterling Capital Special Opptys R	BOPRX	B+	(800) 228-1872	B / 8.1	3.99	5.56	13.15 /87	15.45 /79	12.38 /63	0.00	1.46
GI	Sterling Capital Strat Alloc Bal A	BAMGX	C	(800) 228-1872	D+ / 2.5	2.59	3.29	7.11 /56	8.39 /29	7.68 /28	1.49	1.43
GI	● Sterling Capital Strat Alloc Bal B	BBMGX	C+	(800) 228-1872	D+ / 2.9	2.44	2.84	6.29 /49	7.58 /25	6.88 /22	0.81	2.18
GI	Sterling Capital Strat Alloc Bal C	BCMCX	C+	(800) 228-1872	D+ / 2.9	2.45	2.88	6.28 /49	7.57 /24	6.89 /22	0.90	2.18
GI	Sterling Capital Strat Alloc Bal I	BCGTX	C+	(800) 228-1872	C- / 3.6	2.64	3.40	7.33 /58	8.68 /31	7.96 /30	1.81	1.18
GI	Sterling Capital Strat Alloc Csv A	BCGAX	C	(800) 228-1872	D / 1.6	2.26	3.20	6.30 /49	6.64 /20	6.71 /21	2.20	1.41
GI	● Sterling Capital Strat Alloc Csv B	BCGBX	C	(800) 228-1872	D / 2.0	1.97	2.74	5.50 /42	5.84 /16	5.90 /16	1.68	2.16
GI	Sterling Capital Strat Alloc Csv C	BCCCX	C	(800) 228-1872	D / 1.9	2.00	2.77	5.45 /42	5.80 /16	5.90 /16	1.70	2.16
GI	Sterling Capital Strat Alloc Csv I	BMGTX	C+	(800) 228-1872	D+ / 2.6	2.30	3.29	6.59 /52	6.90 /21	6.96 /23	2.55	1.16
GI	Sterling Capital Strat Alloc Gro A	BCMAX	C	(800) 228-1872	C- / 3.2	2.83	3.28	7.61 /60	9.68 /37	8.41 /33	1.14	1.51
GI	● Sterling Capital Strat Alloc Gro B	BCMBX	C+	(800) 228-1872	C- / 3.6	2.77	2.91	6.80 /53	8.88 /32	7.61 /27	0.52	2.26
GI	Sterling Capital Strat Alloc Gro C	BCGCX	C+	(800) 228-1872	C- / 3.6	2.68	2.95	6.79 /53	8.84 /32	7.61 /27	0.58	2.26
GI	Sterling Capital Strat Alloc Gro I	BCMTX	C+	(800) 228-1872	C / 4.3	2.98	3.49	7.85 /62	9.96 /39	8.71 /35	1.45	1.26
GL	Steward Global Equity Income Indv	SGIDX	C	(800) 262-6631	C- / 3.8	-0.46	3.87	6.19 /48	9.58 /37	10.07 /45	2.00	1.06
GL	Steward Global Equity Income Inst	SGISX	C	(800) 262-6631	C- / 4.1	-0.39	4.08	6.59 /52	9.96 /39	10.45 /48	2.35	0.71
FO	Steward Intl Enhanced Index Indv	SNTKX	E+	(800) 262-6631	E / 0.5	-0.18	-7.22	-4.79 / 6	1.91 / 6	1.16 / 3	2.56	1.08
FO	Steward Intl Enhanced Index Inst	SNTCX	E+	(800) 262-6631	E+ / 0.6	-0.11	-7.04	-4.44 / 6	2.27 / 7	1.51 / 4	2.94	0.73
GR	Steward Large Cap Enhan Index Indv	SEEKX	A-	(800) 262-6631	B+ / 8.4	1.07	5.33	11.14 /79	16.65 /88	14.75 /85	0.83	0.90
GR	Steward Large Cap Enhan Index Inst	SEECX	A	(800) 262-6631	B+ / 8.7	1.14	5.54	11.54 /81	17.05 /90	15.15 /88	1.16	0.54
SC	Steward SMCap Enh Idx Indv	TRDFX	B	(800) 262-6631	B+ / 8.5	4.95	11.93	8.91 /69	16.04 /84	14.95 /86	0.42	0.92
SC	Steward SMCap Enh Idx Inst	SCECX	B	(800) 262-6631	B+ / 8.7	4.95	12.10	9.18 /70	16.35 /86	15.26 /89	0.68	0.64
MC	Stewart Capital Mid Cap Fund	SCMFX	C+	(800) 262-6631	C+ / 6.8	2.87	3.43	8.84 /68	14.38 /70	15.12 /88	0.06	1.56
GI	Stock Dividend Fund	SDIVX	D	(800) 704-6072	D / 2.2	-1.54	-3.40	-3.95 / 7	9.36 /35	11.13 /54	2.39	0.85
GL	Stone Harbor Local Markets Inst	SHLMX	E-	(866) 699-8125	E- / 0.2	-3.15	-10.77	-13.26 / 2	-6.50 / 1	--	1.45	0.89
AG	Stonebridge Small Cap Growth	SBSGX	E-	(800) 639-3935	E / 0.5	0.73	3.99	-10.13 / 3	1.41 / 6	4.20 / 9	0.00	2.25
GR	Stralem Equity Fund Adv	STRAX	E		C- / 4.0	-0.26	1.79	4.54 /35	10.61 /43	10.85 /51	1.13	1.72
GR	Stralem Equity Fund Inst	STEFX	E		C / 4.3	-0.20	2.49	5.43 /42	11.10 /46	11.26 /55	1.43	1.12
GL	Strategic Latin America A	SLATX	E	(888) 716-7116	E- / 0.2	-4.08	-9.27	-5.45 / 5	-4.59 / 2	--	0.28	2.09
GR	Stratton Mid Cap Value Fund	STRGX	B+	(800) 634-5726	B+ / 8.4	5.10	8.22	8.00 /63	16.86 /89	11.28 /55	0.04	1.16
RE	Stratton Real Estate Fund	STMDX	B	(800) 634-5726	A / 9.4	4.28	18.61	25.52 /98	14.34 /70	14.74 /85	1.55	0.97
SC	Stratton Small Cap Value	STSCX	B	(800) 634-5726	B- / 7.2	4.05	6.39	2.25 /23	16.10 /84	14.27 /80	0.03	1.15
GR	Stratus Growth A	STWAX	C+	(888) 769-2362	C+ / 5.6	0.30	5.68	10.19 /75	13.41 /63	10.81 /51	2.04	1.19
GR	Stratus Growth Inst	STPGX	B-	(888) 769-2362	C+ / 6.4	0.34	5.75	10.20 /75	13.44 /63	10.80 /51	2.10	1.19
GR	Summit Glbl Inv US Low Vol Eq I	SILVX	A+	(888) 261-4073	B- / 7.2	1.07	8.65	13.93 /89	14.42 /70	--	1.13	2.74
GI	SunAmerica Alternative Strat A	SUNAX	E+	(800) 858-8850	E- / 0.2	0.27	-3.84	-6.47 / 4	-5.92 / 2	-4.86 / 1	0.00	2.22
GI	SunAmerica Alternative Strat C	SUNCX	E+	(800) 858-8850	E- / 0.2	0.14	-3.92	-6.96 / 4	-6.46 / 1	-5.43 / 1	0.00	2.97
GI	SunAmerica Alternative Strat W	SUNWX	E+	(800) 858-8850	E- / 0.2	0.40	-3.56	-6.18 / 4	-5.66 / 2	-4.62 / 1	0.00	2.18
BA	SunAmerica Foc Balanced Strategy A	FBAAX	C	(800) 858-8850	D+ / 2.4	1.78	4.27	6.47 /50	8.26 /29	7.66 /28	1.56	1.64
BA	SunAmerica Foc Balanced Strategy B	FBABX	C	(800) 858-8850	D+ / 2.8	1.61	3.89	5.73 /44	7.54 /24	6.96 /23	0.99	2.34
BA	SunAmerica Foc Balanced Strategy C	FBACX	C	(800) 858-8850	D+ / 2.9	1.67	3.95	5.82 /45	7.58 /25	6.98 /23	1.03	2.28
BA	SunAmerica Foc Balanced Strategy I		C	(800) 858-8850	C- / 3.3	1.76	4.24	6.42 /50	8.23 /28	7.64 /27	1.62	3.41
GI	SunAmerica Foc Dividend Strategy A	FDSAX	A	(800) 858-8850	B / 8.2	2.13	6.37	12.37 /84	17.64 /93	16.10 /93	2.14	1.07
GI	SunAmerica Foc Dividend Strategy B	FDSBX	A+	(800) 858-8850	B+ / 8.7	1.97	6.07	11.70 /81	16.86 /89	15.35 /89	1.69	1.72

● Denotes fund is closed to new investors
* Denotes fund is included in Section II

RISK			NET ASSETS		ASSET				Portfolio	BULL / BEAR		FUND MANAGER		MINIMUMS		LOADS	
	3 Year		NAV							Last Bull	Last Bear	Manager	Manager	Initial	Additional	Front	Back
Risk Rating/Pts	Standard Deviation	Beta	As of 3/31/15	Total $(Mil)	Cash %	Stocks %	Bonds %	Other %	Turnover Ratio	Market Return	Market Return	Quality Pct	Tenure (Years)	Purch. $	Purch. $	End Load	End Load
C+ / 6.7	12.6	1.04	20.08	45	2	97	0	1	27	104.3	-23.7	56	10	1,000	0	5.8	0.0
C+ / 6.6	12.6	1.04	18.79	1	2	97	0	1	27	99.2	-23.9	45	10	1,000	0	0.0	0.0
C+ / 6.6	12.6	1.04	18.70	5	2	97	0	1	27	99.3	-24.0	45	10	1,000	0	0.0	0.0
C+ / 6.6	12.7	1.04	20.24	721	2	97	0	1	27	106.2	-23.7	59	10	1,000,000	0	0.0	0.0
C+ / 6.7	12.5	1.03	19.68	N/A	2	97	0	1	27	101.0	-23.8	50	10	1,000	0	0.0	0.0
C+ / 6.2	10.0	0.92	23.39	259	2	97	0	1	32	93.4	-18.1	76	12	1,000	0	5.8	0.0
C+ / 5.9	10.0	0.92	20.78	6	2	97	0	1	32	88.5	-18.3	69	12	1,000	0	0.0	0.0
C+ / 5.9	10.0	0.92	20.79	137	2	97	0	1	32	88.5	-18.3	68	12	1,000	0	0.0	0.0
C+ / 6.2	10.0	0.92	24.19	506	2	97	0	1	32	95.0	-17.9	78	12	1,000,000	0	0.0	0.0
C+ / 6.2	9.9	0.92	23.74	N/A	2	97	0	1	32	91.7	-18.1	74	12	1,000	0	0.0	0.0
B+ / 9.1	5.7	0.55	10.91	36	4	57	37	2	6	46.6	-15.1	65	N/A	1,000	0	5.8	0.0
B+ / 9.0	5.7	0.55	10.69	2	4	57	37	2	6	42.9	-15.3	53	N/A	1,000	0	0.0	0.0
B+ / 9.0	5.7	0.55	10.71	1	4	57	37	2	6	42.9	-15.3	53	N/A	1,000	0	0.0	0.0
B+ / 9.0	5.7	0.55	10.98	N/A	4	57	37	2	6	47.9	-14.9	68	N/A	1,000,000	0	0.0	0.0
B+ / 9.4	4.0	0.37	10.81	15	3	38	57	2	9	34.0	-8.6	77	N/A	1,000	0	5.8	0.0
B+ / 9.4	3.9	0.36	10.82	1	3	38	57	2	9	30.6	-8.8	70	N/A	1,000	0	0.0	0.0
B+ / 9.4	4.0	0.36	10.73	N/A	3	38	57	2	9	30.6	-8.9	69	N/A	1,000	0	0.0	0.0
B+ / 9.4	4.0	0.36	10.93	2	3	38	57	2	9	35.1	-8.5	79	N/A	1,000,000	0	0.0	0.0
B / 8.6	7.1	0.70	10.65	24	4	72	23	1	9	56.2	-18.7	49	N/A	1,000	0	5.8	0.0
B / 8.5	7.2	0.70	10.39	2	4	72	23	1	9	52.2	-18.9	37	N/A	1,000	0	0.0	0.0
B / 8.6	7.1	0.70	10.34	1	4	72	23	1	9	52.3	-19.0	37	N/A	1,000	0	0.0	0.0
B / 8.6	7.1	0.69	10.68	1	4	72	23	1	9	57.7	-18.6	54	N/A	1,000,000	0	0.0	0.0
B- / 7.1	9.8	0.62	29.80	25	1	98	0	1	40	59.6	-13.1	90	7	200	0	0.0	0.0
B- / 7.1	9.8	0.62	29.84	138	1	98	0	1	40	61.5	-13.0	91	7	25,000	1,000	0.0	0.0
C / 5.4	13.7	0.98	21.02	15	0	99	0	1	11	26.5	-24.3	4	9	200	0	0.0	0.0
C / 5.4	13.7	0.98	21.06	271	0	99	0	1	11	28.0	-24.2	5	9	25,000	1,000	0.0	0.0
C+ / 6.6	10.3	1.07	38.70	50	0	99	0	1	30	102.1	-17.8	60	11	200	0	0.0	0.0
C+ / 6.6	10.3	1.06	38.51	289	0	99	0	1	30	104.4	-17.7	65	11	25,000	1,000	0.0	0.0
C / 4.9	12.2	0.89	15.54	61	0	99	0	1	29	98.4	-22.4	81	17	200	0	0.0	0.0
C / 5.0	12.2	0.89	15.71	95	0	99	0	1	29	100.3	-22.3	83	17	25,000	1,000	0.0	0.0
C+ / 6.4	10.8	0.87	16.51	98	7	92	0	1	35	86.2	-17.7	65	9	1,000	100	0.0	0.0
C+ / 6.2	12.0	0.99	24.87	39	4	95	0	1	71	65.9	-13.5	7	11	100,000	100	0.0	2.0
D+ / 2.7	11.2	0.66	8.29	1,552	0	0	0	100	181	-7.5	-8.9	1	5	1,000,000	250,000	0.0	0.0
C- / 3.3	18.3	1.33	8.31	16	0	99	0	1	152	41.8	-27.6	0	36	2,500	100	0.0	2.0
D- / 1.2	9.2	0.93	15.11	6	5	94	0	1	19	67.6	-11.5	17	15	1,000	100	0.0	1.0
D- / 1.2	9.2	0.93	15.15	254	5	94	0	1	19	70.1	-11.4	22	15	250,000	100	0.0	1.0
C- / 4.0	9.7	0.95	7.76	25	7	61	31	1	176	16.5	-21.7	1	5	1,000	100	5.0	2.0
C+ / 6.4	11.6	1.11	58.33	75	3	96	0	1	24	97.7	-25.5	51	36	2,000	100	0.0	1.5
C- / 4.1	12.4	0.99	38.00	107	4	95	0	1	18	85.7	-16.6	70	35	2,000	100	0.0	1.5
C+ / 6.5	11.7	0.81	77.05	1,459	6	93	0	1	9	91.4	-21.2	87	15	2,000	100	0.0	1.5
B- / 7.0	10.7	1.09	20.10	N/A	1	98	0	1	8	85.2	-19.4	18	8	1,000	0	4.5	0.0
B- / 7.0	10.7	1.09	20.41	42	1	98	0	1	8	85.3	-19.4	19	8	250,000	0	0.0	0.0
B / 8.7	8.3	0.77	14.16	72	0	0	0	100	110	N/A	N/A	84	3	1,000,000	0	0.0	1.5
C+ / 6.4	6.2	-0.04	7.52	39	4	0	95	1	16	-32.5	5.7	8	7	500	100	5.8	0.0
C+ / 6.2	6.2	-0.04	7.35	7	4	0	95	1	16	-33.9	5.3	6	7	500	100	0.0	0.0
C+ / 6.5	6.3	-0.03	7.59	6	4	0	95	1	16	-31.9	5.8	8	7	50,000	0	0.0	0.0
B / 8.5	6.6	1.14	15.86	92	5	68	26	1	38	43.1	-10.0	17	13	500	100	5.8	0.0
B / 8.5	6.6	1.14	15.73	18	5	68	26	1	38	39.9	-10.3	13	13	500	100	0.0	0.0
B / 8.5	6.6	1.14	15.79	65	5	68	26	1	38	40.0	-10.2	13	13	500	100	0.0	0.0
B / 8.5	6.7	1.15	15.89	1	5	68	26	1	38	43.0	-10.0	17	13	0	0	0.0	0.0
B- / 7.2	10.0	0.92	17.40	3,880	0	98	0	2	47	100.8	-8.9	87	2	500	100	5.8	0.0
B- / 7.2	10.0	0.92	17.30	311	0	98	0	2	47	96.4	-9.2	83	2	500	100	0.0	0.0

Fund Type	Fund Name	Ticker Symbol	Overall Investment Rating	Phone	Perfor-mance Rating/Pts	3 Mo	6 Mo	1Yr / Pct	3Yr / Pct	5Yr / Pct	Dividend Yield	Expense Ratio
			99 Pct = Best 0 Pct = Worst		**PERFORMANCE** Total Return % through 3/31/15				Annualized		Incl. in Returns	
GI	SunAmerica Foc Dividend Strategy C	FDSTX	A+	(800) 858-8850	B+ / 8.7	1.98	6.02	11.71 /81	16.88 /89	15.37 /89	1.70	1.72
GI	SunAmerica Foc Dividend Strategy W	FDSWX	A+	(800) 858-8850	A- / 9.2	2.19	6.48	12.64 /85	17.80 /94	16.20 /94	2.48	0.87
GR	SunAmerica Foc Multi-Asset Strat A	FASAX	C-	(800) 858-8850	D+ / 2.4	1.87	4.39	6.60 /52	8.16 /28	6.91 /22	1.43	1.61
GR	SunAmerica Foc Multi-Asset Strat B	FMABX	C	(800) 858-8850	D+ / 2.8	1.75	4.03	5.91 /46	7.44 /24	6.19 /18	0.80	2.29
GR	SunAmerica Foc Multi-Asset Strat C	FMATX	C	(800) 858-8850	D+ / 2.8	1.75	4.05	5.93 /46	7.47 /24	6.22 /18	0.89	2.25
GR	SunAmerica Foc Multi-Asset Strat I		C	(800) 858-8850	C- / 3.2	1.87	4.33	6.54 /51	8.09 /27	--	1.46	1.94
GR	SunAmerica Focused Alpha Gr C	FOCCX	C+	(800) 858-8850	C+ / 6.4	2.13	4.13	11.65 /81	13.33 /62	--	0.00	2.37
GR	SunAmerica Focused Alpha Growth A	FOCAX	C+	(800) 858-8850	C+ / 6.0	2.28	4.47	12.41 /84	14.07 /68	16.40 /94	0.00	1.65
GR	SunAmerica Focused Alpha Growth	FOCWX	B	(800) 858-8850	B- / 7.1	2.34	4.60	12.60 /85	14.27 /69	16.58 /95	0.00	1.50
GR	SunAmerica Focused Alpha LCF A	SFLAX	B+	(800) 858-8850	B- / 7.4	0.75	6.79	14.57 /91	16.19 /85	16.49 /95	0.00	1.66
GR	SunAmerica Focused Alpha LCF C	SFLCX	A-	(800) 858-8850	B / 8.0	0.62	6.44	13.78 /89	15.46 /79	--	0.00	2.32
GR	SunAmerica Focused Alpha LCF W	SFLWX	A+	(800) 858-8850	B+ / 8.6	0.79	6.86	14.69 /91	16.40 /86	16.63 /95	0.00	1.65
GL	SunAmerica Global Trends A	GTFAX	D-	(800) 858-8850	E / 0.5	3.15	4.30	2.17 /23	0.31 / 5	--	0.00	2.33
GL	SunAmerica Global Trends C	GTFCX	D-	(800) 858-8850	E+ / 0.6	2.98	4.00	1.61 /20	-0.32 / 4	--	0.00	2.94
GL	SunAmerica Global Trends W	GTFWX	D-	(800) 858-8850	E+ / 0.7	3.20	4.42	2.45 /24	0.54 / 5	--	0.00	2.13
FO	SunAmerica Intl Dividend Strat A	SIEAX	E	(800) 858-8850	E- / 0.2	-1.02	-13.73	-15.16 / 2	-3.08 / 2	-2.51 / 1	2.75	1.91
FO	SunAmerica Intl Dividend Strat C	SIETX	E	(800) 858-8850	E- / 0.2	-1.22	-14.02	-15.70 / 2	-3.71 / 2	-3.16 / 1	2.39	2.56
FO	● SunAmerica Intl Dividend Strat I	NAOIX	E	(800) 858-8850	E- / 0.2	-1.01	-13.72	-15.01 / 2	-2.94 / 2	-2.40 / 1	3.03	1.78
FO	SunAmerica Japan A	SAESX	C-	(800) 858-8850	C- / 3.7	10.28	4.87	9.40 /71	9.40 /36	--	0.60	2.19
FO	SunAmerica Japan C	SAJCX	C	(800) 858-8850	C- / 4.1	10.06	4.64	8.73 /68	8.64 /31	--	0.18	3.39
IN	SunAmerica Select Dividend Growth	SDVAX	U	(800) 858-8850	U /	0.69	7.99	--	--	--	0.00	1.63
SC	SunAmerica Small Cap A	SASAX	U	(800) 858-8850	U /	5.47	16.79	7.88 /62	--	--	0.00	1.98
GR	SunAmerica Strat Value Portfolio A	SFVAX	B-	(800) 858-8850	C+ / 6.7	0.04	6.57	11.29 /80	15.53 /79	12.37 /63	0.96	1.42
GR	SunAmerica Strat Value Portfolio C	SFVTX	B+	(800) 858-8850	B- / 7.2	-0.16	6.22	10.57 /77	14.76 /73	11.62 /58	0.51	2.08
AA	SunAmerica VAL Co I Asset Alloc	VCAAX	C	(800) 858-8850	C- / 3.9	3.00	5.03	7.15 /56	9.17 /34	9.73 /42	2.06	0.71
GR	SunAmerica VAL Co I Bluechip Gro	VCBCX	A	(800) 858-8850	A / 9.4	5.84	10.32	16.86 /94	17.57 /93	16.84 /96	0.00	0.84
GI	SunAmerica VAL Co I Brcap Val inc	VBCVX	B+	(800) 858-8850	B- / 7.1	1.42	5.44	7.33 /58	15.13 /76	13.07 /69	1.65	0.95
GR	SunAmerica VAL Co I Core Eq Fd	VCCEX	B+	(800) 858-8850	B- / 7.4	0.98	5.57	9.83 /74	15.17 /76	12.87 /67	0.92	0.93
GI	SunAmerica VAL Co I Dividend Val	VCIGX	B-	(800) 858-8850	C+ / 6.5	0.19	4.35	8.94 /69	14.05 /67	13.51 /73	2.02	0.83
GL	SunAmerica VAL Co I Emg	VCGEX	E+	(800) 858-8850	E / 0.4	2.44	-2.73	-1.36 /12	-1.10 / 3	1.18 / 4	2.15	0.95
FO	SunAmerica VAL Co I Fr Val Fd	VCFVX	E+	(800) 858-8850	D / 1.6	4.95	-5.63	-7.75 / 3	7.49 /24	5.43 /14	2.64	0.80
RE	SunAmerica VAL Co I Glb Real Est	VGREX	C	(800) 858-8850	C+ / 6.7	4.18	10.41	13.81 /89	12.12 /53	10.84 /51	2.59	0.86
GR	SunAmerica VAL Co I Glb Soc Awr	VCSOX	B	(800) 858-8850	B- / 7.0	3.01	5.57	8.48 /66	14.52 /71	11.38 /56	2.02	0.64
GL	SunAmerica VAL Co I Glb Str Fd	VGLSX	C	(800) 858-8850	C- / 3.9	1.88	0.42	1.29 /19	10.51 /42	9.21 /38	2.72	0.64
GI	SunAmerica VAL Co I Growth & Inc	VCGAX	B+	(800) 858-8850	B- / 7.4	0.85	6.41	12.75 /86	14.62 /72	12.19 /62	0.95	0.93
GR	SunAmerica VAL Co I Growth Fd	VCULX	B	(800) 858-8850	B- / 7.1	3.02	8.05	12.63 /85	13.93 /67	14.06 /78	0.59	0.81
HL	SunAmerica VAL Co I Health Sci Fd	VCHSX	A-	(800) 858-8850	A+ / 9.9	13.98	26.66	41.62 /99	36.21 /99	28.54 /99	0.00	1.11
FO	SunAmerica VAL Co I Intl Growth	VCINX	D+	(800) 858-8850	C- / 3.4	4.57	2.42	0.94 /18	9.27 /35	7.97 /30	1.47	1.06
GR	SunAmerica VAL Co I Lg Cptl Gro Fd	VLCGX	C	(800) 858-8850	C+ / 6.3	1.69	9.27	12.40 /84	12.58 /57	11.69 /58	0.54	0.76
GI	SunAmerica VAL Co I Lgcap Core Fd	VLCCX	B+	(800) 858-8850	A- / 9.0	1.30	6.07	13.47 /88	17.32 /91	15.16 /88	1.05	0.84
MC	SunAmerica VAL Co I MdCp Strt Gr	VMSGX	C-	(800) 858-8850	C / 5.4	4.12	7.26	6.49 /51	11.75 /51	12.58 /65	0.00	0.82
MC	SunAmerica VAL Co I Midcap Idx Fd	VMIDX	A	(800) 858-8850	A- / 9.0	5.23	11.80	11.80 /82	16.68 /88	15.36 /89	0.98	0.36
GR	SunAmerica VAL Co I Nsdq 100 IdX	VCNIX	A+	(800) 858-8850	A / 9.4	2.49	7.37	21.35 /97	17.26 /91	17.99 /97	0.93	0.57
GR	SunAmerica VAL Co I Sc&Tech Fd	VCSTX	B+	(800) 858-8850	B+ / 8.7	3.15	7.24	14.93 /91	16.34 /86	15.97 /93	0.00	0.99
AG	SunAmerica VAL Co I SmCp Agg Gro	VSAGX	B-	(800) 858-8850	A+ / 9.8	8.88	24.39	17.67 /95	21.28 /98	16.23 /94	0.00	1.02
SC	SunAmerica VAL Co I Smcp Fd	VCSMX	B	(800) 858-8850	B+ / 8.5	4.32	13.07	7.61 /60	16.21 /85	15.82 /92	0.00	1.01
SC	SunAmerica VAL Co I Smcp Idx Fd	VCSLX	B+	(800) 858-8850	B+ / 8.6	4.29	14.46	8.10 /64	16.12 /84	14.36 /81	1.02	0.40
SC	SunAmerica VAL Co I Smcp Spl Val	VSSVX	A	(800) 858-8850	B+ / 8.5	4.24	12.16	7.64 /60	16.38 /86	13.73 /75	0.92	0.88
SC	SunAmerica VAL Co I Sm-Mid Gro Fd	VSSGX	C	(800) 858-8850	B / 8.2	4.57	13.27	12.08 /83	15.06 /75	14.70 /84	0.00	1.03
GR	SunAmerica VAL Co I Stk Idx Fd	VSTIX	A-	(800) 858-8850	B / 8.0	0.86	5.74	12.34 /84	15.70 /81	14.07 /78	1.62	0.35
GR	SunAmerica VAL Co I Val Fd	VAVAX	B+	(800) 858-8850	B / 7.6	1.15	5.88	10.75 /77	15.27 /77	13.05 /69	1.47	0.93
AA	SunAmerica VAL Co II Agg Gr Life Fd	VAGLX	C+	(800) 858-8850	C / 4.7	3.21	4.99	6.27 /49	10.85 /45	10.86 /52	0.89	0.89

● Denotes fund is closed to new investors
* Denotes fund is included in Section II

RISK			NET ASSETS		ASSET				BULL / BEAR		FUND MANAGER		MINIMUMS		LOADS	
	3 Year		NAV						Portfolio	Last Bull	Last Bear	Manager	Manager	Initial	Additional	Front	Back
Risk	Standard		As of	Total	Cash	Stocks	Bonds	Other	Turnover	Market	Market	Quality	Tenure	Purch.	Purch.	End	End
Rating/Pts	Deviation	Beta	3/31/15	$(Mil)	%	%	%	%	Ratio	Return	Return	Pct	(Years)	$	$	Load	Load
B- / 7.2	10.0	0.92	17.29	2,707	0	98	0	2	47	96.4	-9.1	83	2	500	100	0.0	0.0
B- / 7.9	10.0	0.92	17.39	1,955	0	98	0	2	47	101.6	-8.9	87	2	50,000	0	0.0	0.0
B / 8.3	7.3	0.73	16.32	180	5	73	20	2	32	34.6	-9.6	24	13	500	100	5.8	0.0
B / 8.3	7.3	0.73	16.27	30	5	73	20	2	32	31.5	-9.8	18	13	500	100	0.0	0.0
B / 8.3	7.3	0.73	16.26	118	5	73	20	2	32	31.6	-9.8	18	13	500	100	0.0	0.0
B / 8.3	7.3	0.73	16.31	N/A	5	73	20	2	32	34.3	N/A	24	13	0	0	0.0	0.0
C+ / 6.6	10.1	0.86	26.35	106	2	97	0	1	74	N/A	N/A	62	4	500	100	0.0	0.0
C+ / 6.7	10.1	0.86	26.95	463	2	97	0	1	74	85.2	-20.0	70	4	500	100	5.8	0.0
C+ / 6.7	10.1	0.86	27.12	60	2	97	0	1	74	86.6	-20.0	72	4	50,000	0	0.0	0.0
B- / 7.1	11.0	1.03	26.75	533	0	99	0	1	57	105.4	-21.7	61	3	500	100	5.8	0.0
B- / 7.0	11.0	1.03	26.17	130	0	99	0	1	57	N/A	N/A	51	3	500	100	0.0	0.0
B- / 7.1	11.0	1.03	26.93	19	0	99	0	1	57	106.7	-21.7	64	3	50,000	0	0.0	0.0
C+ / 6.7	4.9	0.61	13.77	34	100	0	0	0	0	5.4	N/A	10	4	500	100	5.8	0.0
C+ / 6.4	4.9	0.61	13.47	10	100	0	0	0	0	3.1	N/A	8	4	500	100	0.0	0.0
C+ / 6.9	4.9	0.61	13.88	4	100	0	0	0	0	6.2	N/A	11	4	50,000	0	0.0	0.0
C- / 3.8	15.5	1.02	9.73	105	2	97	0	1	80	7.8	-25.3	1	3	500	100	5.8	0.0
C- / 3.7	15.5	1.02	8.87	33	2	97	0	1	80	5.5	-25.7	1	3	500	100	0.0	0.0
C- / 3.8	15.5	1.02	9.83	N/A	2	97	0	1	80	8.4	-25.4	1	3	0	0	0.0	0.0
C+ / 6.8	14.0	0.79	7.40	33	2	97	0	1	77	N/A	N/A	83	3	500	100	5.8	0.0
C+ / 6.9	13.9	0.79	7.11	4	2	97	0	1	77	N/A	N/A	78	3	500	100	0.0	0.0
U /	N/A	N/A	16.47	58	0	99	0	1	0	N/A	N/A	N/A	1	500	100	5.8	0.0
U /	N/A	N/A	16.97	53	1	98	0	1	61	N/A	N/A	N/A	1	500	100	5.8	0.0
B- / 7.4	10.2	1.03	26.35	202	0	99	0	1	64	95.9	-19.3	53	2	500	100	5.8	0.0
B- / 7.3	10.2	1.03	24.47	61	0	99	0	1	64	91.5	-19.6	43	2	500	100	0.0	0.0
B- / 7.6	6.3	1.07	12.23	178	8	60	31	1	99	53.3	-11.0	33	13	0	0	0.0	0.0
C+ / 5.9	11.3	1.01	17.73	653	0	99	0	1	34	113.2	-14.7	78	15	0	0	0.0	0.0
B- / 7.3	10.1	1.02	15.47	62	1	98	0	1	27	93.5	-18.7	50	3	0	0	0.0	0.0
C+ / 6.8	11.3	1.14	20.00	265	1	98	0	1	39	97.1	-20.5	26	3	0	0	0.0	0.0
B- / 7.5	9.1	0.91	12.97	655	1	98	0	1	37	82.5	-11.8	60	2	0	0	0.0	0.0
C / 5.5	14.4	0.91	7.54	653	0	99	0	1	55	20.9	-23.6	2	4	0	0	0.0	0.0
C / 5.2	15.4	1.10	10.02	966	3	96	0	1	27	43.7	-24.7	28	7	0	0	0.0	0.0
C / 4.5	11.9	0.85	8.76	521	10	89	0	1	41	72.2	-21.0	70	7	0	0	0.0	0.0
C+ / 6.7	10.6	1.05	21.62	424	1	98	0	1	99	82.5	-19.9	36	13	0	0	0.0	0.0
B- / 7.3	9.6	0.71	13.20	504	4	69	25	2	25	57.1	-15.2	90	10	0	0	0.0	0.0
C+ / 6.9	9.8	1.01	19.30	120	1	98	0	1	169	94.3	-19.7	46	N/A	0	0	0.0	0.0
C+ / 6.4	10.0	1.00	16.20	1,032	0	99	0	1	90	91.1	-17.3	39	8	0	0	0.0	0.0
C / 5.2	13.1	0.86	25.70	881	3	96	0	1	59	217.9	-14.7	99	2	0	0	0.0	0.0
C+ / 6.1	12.2	0.91	13.66	606	2	97	0	1	53	57.6	-23.1	74	10	0	0	0.0	0.0
C / 4.7	10.9	1.07	12.55	421	0	99	0	1	137	82.9	-18.9	15	N/A	0	0	0.0	0.0
C / 5.2	10.4	1.07	13.30	179	0	99	0	1	76	109.4	-20.0	67	4	0	0	0.0	0.0
C / 4.6	13.3	1.03	15.28	292	2	97	0	1	65	74.9	-21.7	9	10	0	0	0.0	0.0
C+ / 6.5	11.0	1.00	28.46	3,339	1	97	0	2	11	100.8	-22.7	63	3	0	0	0.0	0.0
C+ / 6.4	11.5	1.06	9.95	321	3	96	0	1	8	113.2	-10.9	69	3	0	0	0.0	0.0
C / 5.3	13.5	1.13	25.52	989	2	96	0	2	102	102.1	-19.4	40	6	0	0	0.0	0.0
C- / 3.2	14.2	0.98	14.31	113	1	98	0	1	111	120.2	-25.7	93	4	0	0	0.0	0.0
C / 5.0	12.4	0.91	14.22	362	1	98	0	1	32	102.8	-24.9	80	15	0	0	0.0	0.0
C+ / 5.7	13.4	1.00	21.30	1,133	0	98	1	1	13	99.6	-25.2	65	3	0	0	0.0	0.0
C+ / 6.8	12.4	0.90	13.92	246	5	94	0	1	65	101.7	-24.0	82	10	0	0	0.0	0.0
C- / 3.5	12.8	0.90	13.26	131	0	99	0	1	148	92.7	-23.2	72	2	0	0	0.0	0.0
B- / 7.3	9.5	1.00	35.81	4,487	0	98	0	2	4	97.8	-16.4	62	3	0	0	0.0	0.0
B- / 7.1	10.2	1.05	15.18	117	0	99	0	1	16	98.1	-20.6	46	4	0	0	0.0	0.0
B- / 7.9	8.2	1.38	12.21	541	4	77	18	1	32	63.2	-14.0	16	N/A	0	0	0.0	0.0

	99 Pct = Best
	0 Pct = Worst

Fund Type	Fund Name	Ticker Symbol	Overall Investment Rating	Phone	Performance Rating/Pts	3 Mo	6 Mo	1Yr / Pct	Annualized 3Yr / Pct	Annualized 5Yr / Pct	Dividend Yield	Expense Ratio
GR	SunAmerica VAL Co II Capital App	VCCAX	B+	(800) 858-8850	B / 7.9	2.95	6.55	10.19 /75	15.61 /80	13.61 /74	0.40	1.01
AA	SunAmerica VAL Co II Con Gr Life Fd	VCGLX	C-	(800) 858-8850	D+ / 2.4	2.57	3.05	4.47 /35	6.91 /21	8.04 /30	1.92	0.92
GR	SunAmerica VAL Co II Lrg Cp Val	VACVX	A-	(800) 858-8850	B / 8.2	0.94	5.14	9.00 /69	16.61 /88	13.02 /68	1.04	0.91
MC	SunAmerica VAL Co II MdCp Value	VMCVX	B	(800) 858-8850	B / 7.8	3.37	8.45	6.85 /54	15.80 /82	13.09 /69	0.28	1.08
MC	SunAmerica VAL Co II Mid Cap	VAMGX	D+	(800) 858-8850	C / 5.4	5.87	10.85	8.90 /69	10.89 /45	11.08 /53	0.06	1.18
AA	SunAmerica VAL Co II Mod Gro LfSt	VMGLX	C+	(800) 858-8850	C- / 3.8	2.93	4.36	5.74 /44	9.24 /35	9.70 /42	1.24	0.88
SC	SunAmerica VAL Co II SmCp Growth	VASMX	C	(800) 858-8850	B+ / 8.3	6.23	16.36	5.68 /44	15.68 /81	15.70 /91	0.00	1.31
SC	SunAmerica VAL Co II SmCp Value	VCSVX	C+	(800) 858-8850	B / 7.6	2.76	12.13	7.28 /57	15.10 /76	12.92 /67	0.88	1.05
GR	SunAmerica VAL Co II Soc Resp	VCSRX	A+	(800) 858-8850	B+ / 8.8	0.57	6.33	13.51 /88	17.01 /90	14.88 /86	1.24	0.62
IX	Swan Defined Risk A	SDRAX	U	(877) 896-2590	U /	0.42	1.57	5.33 /41	--	--	0.35	1.63
IX	Swan Defined Risk C	SDRCX	U	(877) 896-2590	U /	0.26	1.20	4.62 /36	--	--	0.00	2.38
IX	Swan Defined Risk I	SDRIX	U	(877) 896-2590	U /	0.51	1.74	5.59 /43	--	--	0.55	1.38
GR	Symons Alpha Value Inst	SAVIX	D	(800) 408-4682	D+ / 2.7	-1.19	2.02	1.89 /21	8.93 /32	8.66 /34	1.61	1.36
FO	T Rowe Price Africa and Middle East	TRAMX	C	(800) 638-5660	C / 4.9	1.03	-5.65	3.25 /28	13.41 /63	7.47 /26	1.32	1.42
FO	T Rowe Price Asia Opportunities	TRAOX	U	(800) 638-5660	U /	7.55	7.67	--	--	--	0.00	2.92
BA	T Rowe Price Balanced	RPBAX	C+	(800) 638-5660	C / 4.7	2.93	4.72	7.63 /60	10.65 /43	10.15 /46	1.91	0.68
★ GR	T Rowe Price Blue Chip Growth	TRBCX	A	(800) 638-5660	A / 9.5	5.96	10.49	17.08 /95	17.80 /94	17.07 /96	0.00	0.74
GR	T Rowe Price Blue Chip Growth Adv	PABGX	A-	(800) 638-5660	A / 9.4	5.89	10.33	16.75 /94	17.50 /92	16.78 /95	0.00	1.00
GR	T Rowe Price Blue Chip Growth R	RRBGX	A-	(800) 638-5660	A / 9.3	5.83	10.19	16.46 /94	17.20 /91	16.49 /95	0.00	1.25
★ AA	T Rowe Price Cap Appreciation	PRWCX	B	(800) 638-5660	B- / 7.3	3.21	8.19	12.66 /85	14.11 /68	12.59 /65	1.27	0.71
AA	T Rowe Price Cap Appreciation Adv	PACLX	B	(800) 638-5660	B- / 7.0	3.13	8.03	12.28 /84	13.76 /65	12.26 /62	1.04	1.02
GR	T Rowe Price Cap Opportunity	PRCOX	B+	(800) 638-5660	B / 7.9	1.34	6.18	12.36 /84	15.56 /80	13.81 /76	1.07	0.71
GR	T Rowe Price Cap Opportunity Adv	PACOX	B+	(800) 638-5660	B / 7.6	1.21	6.02	12.02 /83	15.20 /76	13.46 /73	0.82	1.02
GR	T Rowe Price Cap Opportunity R	RRCOX	B+	(800) 638-5660	B- / 7.4	1.17	5.89	11.74 /81	14.85 /74	13.14 /69	0.49	1.35
MC	T Rowe Price Diversified MidCap Gr	PRDMX	A	(800) 638-5660	A / 9.4	6.32	13.60	16.13 /93	17.12 /90	16.23 /94	0.00	0.91
SC	T Rowe Price Diversified Sm-Cap Gr	PRDSX	A	(800) 638-5660	A+ / 9.7	8.21	15.53	15.57 /93	18.97 /97	19.03 /98	0.00	0.82
IN	T Rowe Price Dividend Growth	PRDGX	A+	(800) 638-5660	B+ / 8.3	1.77	8.30	12.65 /85	15.82 /82	13.90 /77	1.59	0.66
IN	T Rowe Price Dividend Growth Adv	TADGX	A	(800) 638-5660	B / 8.0	1.69	8.16	12.35 /84	15.51 /79	13.61 /74	1.33	0.93
EM	T Rowe Price Emer Europe	TREMX	E-	(800) 638-5660	E- / 0.1	-0.80	-22.22	-25.78 / 0	-11.73 / 1	-7.90 / 1	1.53	1.51
★ EM	T Rowe Price Emerging Mkts Stk	PRMSX	E+	(800) 638-5660	E+ / 0.9	3.61	0.67	5.73 /44	2.17 / 7	2.36 / 5	0.57	1.24
★ IN	T Rowe Price Equity Income	PRFDX	C+	(800) 638-5660	C+ / 5.6	-1.03	1.95	4.71 /37	13.31 /62	11.67 /58	1.67	0.67
IN	T Rowe Price Equity Income Adv	PAFDX	C+	(800) 638-5660	C / 5.4	-1.10	1.83	4.44 /35	13.01 /60	11.39 /56	1.38	0.94
IN	T Rowe Price Equity Income R	RRFDX	C+	(800) 638-5660	C / 5.2	-1.19	1.68	4.13 /33	12.71 /58	11.08 /53	1.15	1.20
★ IX	T Rowe Price Equity Index 500	PREIX	A-	(800) 638-5660	B / 8.0	0.90	5.83	12.46 /85	15.82 /82	14.17 /79	1.81	0.28
FO	T Rowe Price European Stk	PRESX	C-	(800) 638-5660	C / 4.5	3.98	4.20	-4.82 / 6	12.67 /57	10.01 /45	1.60	0.96
MC	T Rowe Price Extended Eq Mkt Indx	PEXMX	A	(800) 638-5660	A- / 9.2	5.24	12.17	10.38 /76	17.68 /93	16.08 /93	0.99	0.45
FS	T Rowe Price Financial Services	PRISX	A	(800) 638-5660	A- / 9.0	1.26	8.51	9.50 /72	17.76 /93	10.89 /52	1.07	0.88
RE	T Rowe Price Glbl Real Estate	TRGRX	C+	(800) 638-5660	C+ / 6.6	5.45	12.65	15.59 /93	11.65 /50	11.94 /60	1.86	1.09
RE	T Rowe Price Glbl Real Estate Adv	PAGEX	C+	(800) 638-5660	C+ / 6.6	5.43	12.61	15.44 /92	11.55 /49	11.82 /59	1.82	1.33
GL	T Rowe Price Global Allocation	RPGAX	U	(800) 638-5660	U /	3.27	4.00	5.94 /46	--	--	0.98	1.88
GL	T Rowe Price Global Stock	PRGSX	C+	(800) 638-5660	C+ / 6.6	5.33	6.90	10.11 /75	13.81 /66	10.66 /50	0.26	0.89
GL	T Rowe Price Global Stock Adv	PAGSX	C	(800) 638-5660	C+ / 6.4	5.27	6.80	9.80 /74	13.52 /64	10.36 /47	0.26	1.39
TC	T Rowe Price Global Technology	PRGTX	C	(800) 638-5660	A+ / 9.8	4.14	7.79	21.40 /97	19.92 /98	20.12 /99	0.00	0.95
GI	T Rowe Price Growth and Inc	PRGIX	A	(800) 638-5660	B+ / 8.3	1.21	7.97	12.72 /86	15.88 /82	13.60 /74	0.96	0.68
★ GR	T Rowe Price Growth Stock	PRGFX	B+	(800) 638-5660	A / 9.3	6.04	10.61	16.85 /94	17.05 /90	16.23 /94	0.00	0.69
GR	T Rowe Price Growth Stock Adv	TRSAX	B+	(800) 638-5660	A / 9.3	5.97	10.48	16.56 /94	16.77 /89	15.96 /93	0.00	0.93
GR	T Rowe Price Growth Stock R	RRGSX	B+	(800) 638-5660	A- / 9.1	5.90	10.33	16.26 /94	16.47 /87	15.66 /91	0.00	1.19
★ HL	T Rowe Price Health Sciences	PRHSX	A-	(800) 638-5660	A+ / 9.9	14.00	26.77	41.92 /99	36.57 /99	28.92 /99	0.00	0.79
FO	T Rowe Price Ins Intl Core Eqty	TRCEX	D	(800) 638-5660	C- / 3.2	5.69	2.24	0.69 /18	9.33 /35	--	3.18	0.93
GL	T Rowe Price Inst Glbl Gr Eq	RPIGX	C+	(800) 638-5660	C+ / 6.2	5.17	7.16	12.06 /83	12.82 /58	10.43 /48	0.42	0.81
EM	T Rowe Price Inst Global Foc Gr Eq	TRGSX	D	(800) 638-5660	C+ / 6.5	5.39	7.07	10.17 /75	13.72 /65	10.62 /50	0.42	0.95
FO	T Rowe Price Inst Intl Gro Eqty	PRFEX	D	(800) 638-5660	D+ / 2.9	6.41	4.85	4.71 /37	7.91 /26	6.73 /21	1.42	1.02

● Denotes fund is closed to new investors
★ Denotes fund is included in Section II

RISK			NET ASSETS		ASSET					BULL / BEAR		FUND MANAGER		MINIMUMS		LOADS	
	3 Year		NAV						Portfolio	Last Bull	Last Bear	Manager	Manager	Initial	Additional	Front	Back
Risk	Standard		As of	Total	Cash	Stocks	Bonds	Other	Turnover	Market	Market	Quality	Tenure	Purch.	Purch.	End	End
Rating/Pts	Deviation	Beta	3/31/15	$(Mil)	%	%	%	%	Ratio	Return	Return	Pct	(Years)	$	$	Load	Load
C+ / 6.7	10.7	1.01	16.75	86	1	98	0	1	44	100.8	-19.4	59	4	0	0	0.0	0.0
B / 8.4	5.0	0.78	13.18	336	5	40	53	2	31	37.7	-7.5	47	N/A	0	0	0.0	0.0
B- / 7.0	10.5	1.06	18.19	208	1	98	0	1	54	103.1	-22.4	60	5	0	0	0.0	0.0
C+ / 6.1	11.5	1.01	25.80	957	5	94	0	1	29	104.1	-25.6	50	13	0	0	0.0	0.0
C- / 4.2	12.2	1.03	10.83	159	0	99	0	1	175	69.9	-23.6	7	2	0	0	0.0	0.0
B / 8.4	6.7	1.11	15.81	835	4	61	33	2	27	52.4	-11.4	29	N/A	0	0	0.0	0.0
D+ / 2.6	15.4	1.07	18.07	118	1	98	0	1	63	102.0	-28.2	43	8	0	0	0.0	0.0
C / 4.8	13.4	0.97	17.47	562	2	97	0	1	47	92.2	-28.1	59	10	0	0	0.0	0.0
B- / 7.1	9.7	1.01	19.49	744	0	91	8	1	26	104.2	-16.5	73	3	0	0	0.0	0.0
U /	N/A	N/A	11.90	154	10	89	0	1	3	N/A	N/A	N/A	3	2,500	500	5.5	0.0
U /	N/A	N/A	11.78	79	10	89	0	1	3	N/A	N/A	N/A	3	2,500	500	0.0	0.0
U /	N/A	N/A	11.93	854	10	89	0	1	3	N/A	N/A	N/A	3	100,000	500	0.0	0.0
C+ / 5.6	7.7	0.60	11.05	84	12	87	0	1	58	48.5	-7.4	61	35	5,000	250	0.0	2.0
C+ / 6.0	10.4	0.51	9.82	212	16	83	0	1	59	76.7	-17.1	97	4	2,500	100	0.0	2.0
U /	N/A	N/A	11.11	25	7	92	0	1	0	N/A	N/A	N/A	1	2,500	100	0.0	2.0
B- / 7.4	6.8	1.16	23.43	4,221	1	64	33	2	54	59.6	-11.8	40	4	2,500	100	0.0	0.0
C+ / 5.8	11.3	1.01	71.28	25,005	0	99	0	1	35	115.0	-14.8	79	22	2,500	100	0.0	0.0
C+ / 5.8	11.3	1.01	70.68	2,800	0	99	0	1	35	113.1	-14.9	77	22	2,500	100	0.0	0.0
C+ / 5.7	11.3	1.01	68.66	472	0	99	0	1	35	111.4	-15.0	75	22	2,500	100	0.0	0.0
C+ / 6.6	5.9	1.01	26.97	22,644	8	63	27	2	57	78.8	-12.5	88	9	2,500	100	0.0	0.0
C+ / 6.6	5.9	1.01	26.71	1,220	8	63	27	2	57	76.9	-12.6	86	9	2,500	100	0.0	0.0
C+ / 6.9	9.8	1.02	23.48	691	0	99	0	1	31	98.5	-16.5	56	N/A	2,500	100	0.0	0.0
C+ / 6.9	9.8	1.02	23.38	11	0	99	0	1	31	96.5	-16.7	51	N/A	2,500	100	0.0	0.0
C+ / 6.9	9.8	1.02	23.37	8	0	99	0	1	31	94.5	-16.7	47	N/A	2,500	100	0.0	0.0
C+ / 6.0	11.4	0.97	24.91	420	0	99	0	1	18	105.1	-22.9	72	12	2,500	100	0.0	0.0
C+ / 5.9	12.3	0.88	27.68	1,182	1	98	0	1	13	117.4	-23.8	92	9	2,500	100	0.0	1.0
B- / 7.4	9.1	0.94	36.54	4,503	4	95	0	1	13	94.0	-15.3	74	15	2,500	100	0.0	0.0
B- / 7.4	9.1	0.94	36.50	251	4	95	0	1	13	92.3	-15.4	72	15	2,500	100	0.0	0.0
D / 1.6	23.8	1.36	12.44	184	1	98	0	1	32	-15.0	-34.2	1	2	2,500	100	0.0	2.0
C / 5.3	14.2	1.02	33.55	8,168	3	96	0	1	23	27.4	-26.0	81	7	2,500	100	0.0	2.0
B- / 7.3	9.4	0.96	32.35	27,934	6	92	0	2	10	85.1	-18.1	40	30	2,500	100	0.0	0.0
B- / 7.3	9.4	0.96	32.29	1,266	6	92	0	2	10	83.5	-18.2	36	30	2,500	100	0.0	0.0
B- / 7.3	9.4	0.96	32.22	347	6	92	0	2	10	81.9	-18.3	32	30	2,500	100	0.0	0.0
B- / 7.3	9.5	1.00	55.70	25,248	0	99	0	1	10	98.5	-16.4	64	13	2,500	100	0.0	0.5
C / 5.5	13.8	1.00	20.64	1,549	1	98	0	1	59	80.3	-27.3	88	10	2,500	100	0.0	2.0
C+ / 6.2	11.9	1.07	26.32	759	3	96	0	1	22	109.4	-23.9	61	13	2,500	100	0.0	0.5
C+ / 6.3	12.6	1.07	22.50	519	4	95	0	1	49	118.8	-27.6	55	5	2,500	100	0.0	0.0
C / 5.5	12.1	0.89	21.00	213	16	83	0	1	23	68.6	-17.9	57	7	2,500	100	0.0	2.0
C / 5.5	12.1	0.89	20.88	24	16	83	0	1	23	68.1	-17.9	55	7	2,500	100	0.0	2.0
U /	N/A	N/A	11.06	88	17	57	25	1	33	N/A	N/A	N/A	2	2,500	100	0.0	0.0
C / 5.5	12.2	0.82	26.89	511	1	98	0	1	138	87.5	-22.7	94	4	2,500	100	0.0	2.0
C / 5.4	12.2	0.82	26.79	2	1	98	0	1	138	85.8	-22.8	94	4	2,500	100	0.0	2.0
D- / 1.2	14.0	1.16	12.83	1,883	7	92	0	1	93	139.4	-20.4	76	3	2,500	100	0.0	0.0
B- / 7.1	9.5	0.98	32.58	1,619	2	97	0	1	14	94.8	-16.6	68	8	2,500	100	0.0	0.0
C / 5.0	11.0	0.97	55.09	40,960	1	98	0	1	35	111.0	-16.5	79	1	2,500	100	0.0	0.0
C / 5.0	11.0	0.97	54.29	3,633	1	98	0	1	35	109.2	-16.6	77	1	2,500	100	0.0	0.0
C / 5.0	11.0	0.97	53.12	1,007	1	98	0	1	35	107.5	-16.7	75	1	2,500	100	0.0	0.0
C / 5.0	13.1	0.85	77.51	13,647	2	97	0	1	46	219.8	-14.4	99	2	2,500	100	0.0	0.0
C+ / 5.9	12.5	0.94	12.25	131	0	99	0	1	19	57.0	-23.4	71	5	1,000,000	0	0.0	2.0
C+ / 5.7	11.2	0.77	22.80	291	0	99	0	1	101	80.8	-22.5	94	7	1,000,000	0	0.0	2.0
D+ / 2.3	12.1	0.68	11.35	93	3	96	0	1	160	86.6	-22.4	99	3	1,000,000	0	0.0	2.0
C+ / 5.7	12.1	0.88	22.40	71	3	96	0	1	50	53.5	-23.7	61	8	1,000,000	0	0.0	2.0

						PERFORMANCE							
	99 Pct = Best					Perfor-mance Rating/Pts	Total Return % through 3/31/15					Incl. in Returns	
	0 Pct = Worst			Overall						Annualized		Dividend	Expense
Fund Type	Fund Name	Ticker Symbol	Investment Rating	Phone			3 Mo	6 Mo	1Yr / Pct	3Yr / Pct	5Yr / Pct	Yield	Ratio
FO	T Rowe Price Instl Africa & ME	TRIAX	D+	(800) 638-5660		C / 5.3	1.01	-5.12	4.25 /33	13.94 /67	7.74 /28	1.59	1.17
EM	T Rowe Price Instl Emer Mkt Eqty	IEMFX	E+	(800) 638-5660		E+ / 0.9	3.65	0.73	5.96 /46	2.31 / 7	2.60 / 5	0.78	1.10
EM	T Rowe Price Instl Fron Mkt Eq	PRFFX	U	(800) 638-5660		U /	-3.69	-12.39	--	--	--	0.00	1.44
FO	T Rowe Price Instl Intl Conc Eqty	RPICX	D	(800) 638-5660		C- / 3.4	3.75	-0.36	-2.63 / 9	10.62 /43	--	1.53	0.94
GR	T Rowe Price Instl Lg Cap Core Gr	TPLGX	A	(800) 638-5660		A / 9.5	6.03	10.58	17.17 /95	17.86 /94	17.06 /96	0.08	0.59
★ GR	T Rowe Price Instl Lg Cap Gr	TRLGX	B+	(800) 638-5660		A / 9.4	5.49	10.32	14.61 /91	17.69 /93	16.55 /95	0.06	0.56
GI	T Rowe Price Instl Lg Cap Val	TILCX	A	(800) 638-5660		B+ / 8.5	-0.29	4.10	9.99 /74	17.27 /91	13.61 /74	1.54	0.58
MC	● T Rowe Price Instl Mid-Cap Eq Gr	PMEGX	A+	(800) 638-5660		A+ / 9.8	6.70	16.24	18.05 /96	19.09 /97	17.60 /97	0.00	0.61
SC	● T Rowe Price Instl Small Cap Stk	TRSSX	A	(800) 638-5660		A / 9.3	4.10	13.96	9.50 /72	17.63 /93	17.58 /97	0.31	0.68
GR	T Rowe Price Instl US Stru Res	TRISX	B+	(800) 638-5660		B / 8.0	1.34	6.23	12.50 /85	15.66 /81	13.98 /78	1.30	0.55
FO	T Rowe Price Intl Discovery	PRIDX	C-	(800) 638-5660		C / 4.3	4.15	3.39	1.11 /19	11.50 /49	10.27 /47	0.79	1.21
FO	T Rowe Price Intl Equity Index	PIEQX	D-	(800) 638-5660		D+ / 2.4	5.52	0.89	-1.34 /12	8.32 /29	5.88 /16	3.16	0.50
GL	T Rowe Price Intl Glbl Grow Stk	RPGEX	C-	(800) 638-5660		C+ / 6.1	5.14	7.11	11.94 /82	12.68 /57	10.26 /47	0.48	1.16
GL	T Rowe Price Intl Glbl Grow Stk Adv	PAGLX	C-	(800) 638-5660		C+ / 6.0	5.11	7.05	11.84 /82	12.57 /56	10.15 /46	0.44	1.58
★ FO	T Rowe Price Intl Gr and Inc	TRIGX	D-	(800) 638-5660		D / 1.9	3.92	-0.97	-3.17 / 8	7.65 /25	6.18 /18	3.11	0.85
FO	T Rowe Price Intl Gr and Inc Adv	PAIGX	D-	(800) 638-5660		D / 1.7	3.79	-1.12	-3.40 / 8	7.41 /24	5.95 /17	2.73	1.07
FO	T Rowe Price Intl Gr and Inc R	RRIGX	E+	(800) 638-5660		D / 1.6	3.76	-1.22	-3.66 / 8	7.12 /22	5.65 /15	2.36	1.35
★ FO	T Rowe Price Intl Stock	PRITX	D	(800) 638-5660		D+ / 2.9	6.34	4.82	4.69 /36	7.92 /27	6.75 /22	1.12	0.83
FO	T Rowe Price Intl Stock Adv	PAITX	D	(800) 638-5660		D+ / 2.8	6.31	4.80	4.60 /36	7.70 /25	6.55 /20	1.31	1.09
FO	T Rowe Price Intl Stock R	RRITX	D	(800) 638-5660		D+ / 2.5	6.19	4.50	4.06 /32	7.33 /23	6.17 /18	0.59	1.47
FO	T Rowe Price Japan	PRJPX	C	(800) 638-5660		C / 5.0	13.04	6.33	8.97 /69	10.55 /43	7.89 /29	0.67	1.05
FO	T Rowe Price Latin America	PRLAX	E-	(800) 638-5660		E- / 0.1	-6.75	-19.19	-18.26 / 1	-12.68 / 1	-8.13 / 1	1.72	1.31
TC	T Rowe Price Media and Telecomm	PRMTX	C+	(800) 638-5660		B / 8.2	3.00	3.84	9.32 /71	16.42 /86	17.28 /96	2.21	0.80
★ MC	● T Rowe Price Mid-Cap Growth	RPMGX	A	(800) 638-5660		A+ / 9.7	6.52	15.69	17.20 /95	18.41 /95	17.02 /96	0.00	0.78
MC	● T Rowe Price Mid-Cap Growth Adv	PAMCX	A	(800) 638-5660		A+ / 9.7	6.45	15.54	16.91 /94	18.12 /95	16.73 /95	0.00	1.03
MC	● T Rowe Price Mid-Cap Growth R	RRMGX	A	(800) 638-5660		A+ / 9.6	6.39	15.40	16.63 /94	17.81 /94	16.42 /95	0.00	1.29
MC	● T Rowe Price Mid-Cap Value Adv	TAMVX	B	(800) 638-5660		B+ / 8.5	2.79	6.40	9.39 /71	16.82 /89	13.05 /69	0.69	1.06
★ MC	● T Rowe Price Mid-Cap Value Fd	TRMCX	B+	(800) 638-5660		B+ / 8.7	2.88	6.59	9.70 /73	17.12 /90	13.34 /71	0.92	0.80
MC	● T Rowe Price Mid-Cap Value R	RRMVX	B	(800) 638-5660		B+ / 8.3	2.72	6.30	9.11 /70	16.51 /87	12.76 /66	0.42	1.31
GR	T Rowe Price New Amer Growth	PRWAX	B	(800) 638-5660		A / 9.4	5.78	10.40	16.88 /94	17.15 /91	15.24 /88	0.00	0.81
GR	T Rowe Price New Amer Growth Adv	PAWAX	B	(800) 638-5660		A / 9.3	5.70	10.23	16.55 /94	16.85 /89	14.94 /86	0.00	1.07
FO	T Rowe Price New Asia	PRASX	D	(800) 638-5660		C- / 3.0	5.22	4.38	11.21 /79	6.70 /20	7.33 /25	0.90	0.94
EN	T Rowe Price New Era	PRNEX	E-	(800) 638-5660		E / 0.4	-0.64	-13.48	-11.14 / 2	1.31 / 6	2.20 / 5	1.05	0.66
★ SC	● T Rowe Price New Horizons	PRNHX	B	(800) 638-5660		A+ / 9.6	6.40	13.82	10.99 /78	19.03 /97	20.72 /99	0.00	0.80
★ FO	T Rowe Price Overseas Stock Fund	TROSX	D+	(800) 638-5660		C- / 3.2	5.63	2.40	1.09 /19	9.24 /35	7.26 /25	2.71	0.84
BA	T Rowe Price Personal Strategy Bal	TRPBX	C	(800) 638-5660		C / 4.4	2.87	4.39	6.98 /55	10.28 /41	10.06 /45	1.77	0.85
GR	T Rowe Price Personal Strategy Gr	TRSGX	C+	(800) 638-5660		C+ / 5.9	3.44	5.32	8.26 /65	12.60 /57	11.75 /59	1.40	0.90
AA	T Rowe Price Personal Strategy Inc	PRSIX	C-	(800) 638-5660		D+ / 2.9	2.21	3.21	5.26 /41	7.71 /25	7.99 /30	1.94	0.73
OT	T Rowe Price Real Assets	PRAFX	E	(800) 638-5660		E / 0.5	1.02	-2.63	-2.03 /10	1.29 / 6	--	1.56	0.85
RE	T Rowe Price Real Estate	TRREX	B	(800) 638-5660		A / 9.4	5.55	20.57	24.49 /98	13.73 /65	15.86 /92	2.13	0.79
RE	T Rowe Price Real Estate Adv	PAREX	B	(800) 638-5660		A / 9.3	5.53	20.43	24.21 /98	13.45 /63	15.58 /91	1.89	1.03
AA	T Rowe Price Retire Balanced	TRRIX	C	(800) 638-5660		D / 1.9	1.47	2.04	3.96 /32	6.06 /17	6.51 /20	1.60	0.57
AA	T Rowe Price Retire Balanced Adv	PARIX	C-	(800) 638-5660		D / 1.8	1.48	1.98	3.77 /30	5.80 /16	6.26 /18	1.35	0.82
AA	T Rowe Price Retire Balanced R	RRTIX	C-	(800) 638-5660		D / 1.6	1.35	1.79	3.51 /29	5.53 /15	6.00 /17	1.10	1.07
GI	T Rowe Price Retirement 2005	TRRFX	C	(800) 638-5660		D+ / 2.3	1.62	2.45	4.63 /36	6.78 /20	7.25 /25	1.93	0.59
GI	T Rowe Price Retirement 2005 Adv	PARGX	C-	(800) 638-5660		D / 2.2	1.54	2.30	4.41 /34	6.52 /19	6.99 /23	1.71	0.84
GI	T Rowe Price Retirement 2005 R	RRTLX	C-	(800) 638-5660		D / 2.0	1.54	2.22	4.09 /32	6.27 /18	6.72 /21	1.41	1.09
★ AA	T Rowe Price Retirement 2010	TRRAX	C	(800) 638-5660		D+ / 2.8	1.75	2.73	5.05 /39	7.60 /25	7.94 /30	1.98	0.59
AA	T Rowe Price Retirement 2010 Adv	PARAX	C	(800) 638-5660		D+ / 2.6	1.70	2.63	4.80 /37	7.33 /23	7.69 /28	1.67	0.84
AA	T Rowe Price Retirement 2010 R	RRTAX	C-	(800) 638-5660		D+ / 2.4	1.65	2.48	4.54 /35	7.07 /22	7.41 /26	1.46	1.09
★ GI	T Rowe Price Retirement 2015	TRRGX	C	(800) 638-5660		C- / 3.5	2.07	3.37	5.86 /45	8.88 /32	8.94 /36	1.79	0.63
GI	T Rowe Price Retirement 2015 Adv	PARHX	C	(800) 638-5660		C- / 3.4	2.08	3.24	5.59 /43	8.62 /31	8.67 /34	1.53	0.88

● Denotes fund is closed to new investors
★ Denotes fund is included in Section II

www.thestreetratings.com

RISK			NET ASSETS		ASSET				Portfolio Turnover Ratio	BULL / BEAR		FUND MANAGER		MINIMUMS		LOADS	
Risk Rating/Pts	3 Year		NAV As of 3/31/15	Total $(Mil)	Cash %	Stocks %	Bonds %	Other %		Last Bull Market Return	Last Bear Market Return	Manager Quality Pct	Manager Tenure (Years)	Initial Purch. $	Additional Purch. $	Front End Load	Back End Load
	Standard Deviation	Beta															
C /4.5	10.3	0.50	6.99	226	5	85	8	2	58	79.3	-17.0	97	4	1,000,000	0	0.0	2.0
C /5.2	14.2	1.02	30.64	997	2	97	0	1	24	28.4	-26.0	82	7	1,000,000	0	0.0	2.0
U /	N/A	N/A	8.62	41	0	0	0	100	0	N/A	N/A	N/A	1	1,000,000	0	0.0	2.0
C /5.0	11.4	0.84	11.62	227	15	84	0	1	122	63.5	-18.7	87	5	1,000,000	0	0.0	2.0
C+ /6.0	11.3	1.01	26.36	1,671	0	99	0	1	47	115.0	-14.8	80	12	1,000,000	0	0.0	0.0
C /5.3	12.2	1.07	28.99	12,332	0	99	0	1	42	114.7	-16.7	70	13	1,000,000	0	0.0	0.0
B- /7.1	10.1	1.03	20.54	2,234	2	97	0	1	11	104.2	-20.5	74	11	1,000,000	0	0.0	0.0
C+ /6.2	11.1	0.96	46.00	4,990	2	97	0	1	34	110.7	-20.6	86	19	1,000,000	0	0.0	0.0
C+ /6.2	12.1	0.89	21.32	2,085	2	97	0	1	20	113.1	-24.1	88	15	1,000,000	0	0.0	0.0
C+ /6.2	9.8	1.02	12.81	775	0	99	0	1	37	99.2	-16.4	57	N/A	1,000,000	0	0.0	0.0
C+ /5.8	10.5	0.74	53.72	3,681	4	95	0	1	42	64.4	-21.8	92	17	2,500	100	0.0	2.0
C+ /5.6	13.1	0.99	12.99	532	1	98	0	1	7	50.0	-24.2	53	10	2,500	100	0.0	2.0
C /4.5	11.2	0.77	20.47	96	0	99	0	1	104	79.5	-22.4	93	7	2,500	100	0.0	2.0
C /4.5	11.2	0.77	20.35	1	0	99	0	1	104	78.8	-22.5	93	7	2,500	100	0.0	2.0
C /5.1	12.5	0.94	14.31	11,173	5	94	0	1	45	50.2	-24.5	50	5	2,500	100	0.0	2.0
C /5.2	12.4	0.93	14.52	168	5	94	0	1	45	49.2	-24.6	47	5	2,500	100	0.0	2.0
C /5.2	12.4	0.93	14.36	45	5	94	0	1	45	47.6	-24.7	43	5	2,500	100	0.0	2.0
C+ /5.6	12.1	0.88	16.60	13,671	3	96	0	1	39	53.5	-23.5	62	8	2,500	100	0.0	2.0
C+ /5.6	12.1	0.88	16.50	620	3	96	0	1	39	52.4	-23.6	59	8	2,500	100	0.0	2.0
C+ /5.6	12.1	0.88	16.48	8	3	96	0	1	39	50.6	-23.7	53	8	2,500	100	0.0	2.0
C+ /6.4	14.0	0.74	10.40	279	0	99	0	1	38	42.4	-6.9	90	2	2,500	100	0.0	2.0
D- /1.2	21.1	1.14	20.46	720	1	98	0	1	21	-14.1	-29.3	0	1	2,500	100	0.0	2.0
C- /3.8	11.5	0.97	67.02	3,272	0	99	0	1	54	101.7	-16.9	75	2	2,500	100	0.0	0.0
C+ /5.8	10.8	0.93	80.36	23,932	3	96	0	1	26	106.2	-20.2	86	23	2,500	100	0.0	0.0
C+ /5.8	10.8	0.93	78.38	1,223	3	96	0	1	26	104.4	-20.2	84	23	2,500	100	0.0	0.0
C+ /5.9	10.8	0.93	76.72	264	3	96	0	1	26	102.6	-20.3	82	23	2,500	100	0.0	0.0
C /5.4	10.3	0.88	29.49	737	10	89	0	1	32	94.3	-19.5	82	15	2,500	100	0.0	0.0
C /5.4	10.2	0.88	29.65	11,520	10	89	0	1	32	95.9	-19.5	84	15	2,500	100	0.0	0.0
C /5.4	10.3	0.88	29.12	302	10	89	0	1	32	92.6	-19.6	80	15	2,500	100	0.0	0.0
C /4.3	10.8	0.97	44.44	3,966	0	99	0	1	92	100.2	-16.7	80	2	2,500	100	0.0	0.0
C /4.3	10.8	0.97	43.75	488	0	99	0	1	92	98.4	-16.7	78	2	2,500	100	0.0	0.0
C+ /5.9	11.0	0.64	17.14	4,405	2	97	0	1	59	43.4	-19.4	74	1	2,500	100	0.0	2.0
D /1.9	15.0	0.90	34.23	3,648	2	97	0	1	55	26.2	-31.0	35	5	2,500	100	0.0	0.0
C- /4.2	12.6	0.87	46.58	15,974	1	97	0	2	35	119.6	-18.1	92	5	2,500	100	0.0	0.0
C+ /6.1	12.1	0.91	9.95	10,272	4	95	0	1	8	56.1	-23.2	73	9	2,500	100	0.0	2.0
C+ /6.9	7.0	1.17	22.86	2,070	4	59	35	2	53	59.4	-13.1	33	4	2,500	100	0.0	0.0
C+ /6.3	8.9	0.87	30.67	1,626	2	79	18	1	46	76.3	-17.0	51	4	2,500	100	0.0	0.0
B- /7.9	5.3	0.87	18.44	1,471	14	39	46	1	59	42.6	-9.5	44	4	2,500	100	0.0	0.0
C /4.8	12.3	0.81	10.92	4,602	5	94	0	1	52	25.0	-25.2	1	4	2,500	100	0.0	2.0
C /4.5	12.4	0.98	28.23	5,053	5	93	0	2	4	85.7	-16.4	66	18	2,500	100	0.0	1.0
C /4.5	12.4	0.99	28.54	350	5	93	0	2	4	84.2	-16.5	62	18	2,500	100	0.0	1.0
B+ /9.0	4.7	0.79	15.01	2,955	3	39	56	2	13	34.0	-8.4	34	13	2,500	100	0.0	0.0
B+ /9.0	4.8	0.80	15.02	397	3	39	56	2	13	32.8	-8.5	29	12	2,500	100	0.0	0.0
B+ /9.0	4.8	0.80	15.01	332	3	39	56	2	13	31.7	-8.6	26	12	2,500	100	0.0	0.0
B /8.6	5.1	0.48	13.21	1,466	4	39	55	2	18	38.3	-9.3	59	11	2,500	100	0.0	0.0
B /8.7	5.1	0.48	13.17	90	4	39	55	2	18	37.1	-9.4	55	8	2,500	100	0.0	0.0
B /8.7	5.1	0.47	13.19	90	4	39	55	2	18	35.9	-9.5	52	8	2,500	100	0.0	0.0
B /8.3	5.7	0.96	18.04	5,233	4	45	49	2	19	44.0	-11.1	30	13	2,500	100	0.0	0.0
B /8.4	5.7	0.96	17.96	741	4	45	49	2	19	42.7	-11.2	27	12	2,500	100	0.0	0.0
B /8.4	5.7	0.96	17.84	473	4	45	49	2	19	41.5	-11.3	25	12	2,500	100	0.0	0.0
B /8.3	6.6	0.64	14.77	9,003	4	55	40	1	15	52.0	-13.0	52	11	2,500	100	0.0	0.0
B /8.3	6.6	0.64	14.72	831	4	55	40	1	15	50.8	-13.1	48	8	2,500	100	0.0	0.0

					PERFORMANCE								
	99 Pct = Best 0 Pct = Worst			Overall		Perfor-	Total Return % through 3/31/15					Incl. in Returns	
				Investment		mance				Annualized		Dividend	Expense
Fund Type	Fund Name	Ticker Symbol	Rating	Phone		Rating/Pts	3 Mo	6 Mo	1Yr / Pct	3Yr / Pct	5Yr / Pct	Yield	Ratio
GI	T Rowe Price Retirement 2015 R	RRTMX	C	(800) 638-5660		C- / 3.2	2.03	3.13	5.35 /41	8.35 /29	8.42 /33	1.34	1.13
★ AA	T Rowe Price Retirement 2020	TRRBX	C+	(800) 638-5660		C- / 4.2	2.51	4.00	6.56 /51	10.03 /39	9.80 /43	1.66	0.67
AA	T Rowe Price Retirement 2020 Adv	PARBX	C+	(800) 638-5660		C- / 4.1	2.43	3.88	6.30 /49	9.74 /38	9.52 /41	1.39	0.92
AA	T Rowe Price Retirement 2020 R	RRTBX	C+	(800) 638-5660		C- / 3.9	2.35	3.72	6.00 /46	9.48 /36	9.24 /39	1.22	1.17
★ GI	T Rowe Price Retirement 2025	TRRHX	C+	(800) 638-5660		C / 4.9	2.86	4.52	7.20 /57	11.05 /46	10.50 /49	1.52	0.70
GI	T Rowe Price Retirement 2025 Adv	PARJX	C+	(800) 638-5660		C / 4.7	2.75	4.42	6.97 /55	10.78 /44	10.21 /46	1.28	0.95
GI	T Rowe Price Retirement 2025 R	RRTNX	C+	(800) 638-5660		C / 4.5	2.71	4.26	6.69 /53	10.48 /42	9.94 /44	1.11	1.20
★ AA	T Rowe Price Retirement 2030	TRRCX	B-	(800) 638-5660		C / 5.4	3.08	4.91	7.70 /60	11.88 /52	11.10 /53	1.44	0.73
AA	T Rowe Price Retirement 2030 Adv	PARCX	C+	(800) 638-5660		C / 5.2	3.02	4.82	7.44 /59	11.60 /50	10.82 /51	1.20	1.00
AA	T Rowe Price Retirement 2030 R	RRTCX	C+	(800) 638-5660		C / 5.0	3.00	4.72	7.22 /57	11.34 /48	10.56 /49	1.00	1.23
★ GI	T Rowe Price Retirement 2035	TRRJX	B-	(800) 638-5660		C+ / 5.8	3.36	5.30	8.11 /64	12.49 /56	11.51 /57	1.36	0.75
GI	T Rowe Price Retirement 2035 Adv	PARKX	C+	(800) 638-5660		C+ / 5.6	3.25	5.14	7.83 /62	12.19 /54	11.21 /55	1.14	1.00
GI	T Rowe Price Retirement 2035 R	RRTPX	C+	(800) 638-5660		C / 5.4	3.22	5.00	7.58 /60	11.94 /52	10.96 /52	0.98	1.25
★ AA	T Rowe Price Retirement 2040	TRRDX	B-	(800) 638-5660		C+ / 6.0	3.47	5.49	8.34 /65	12.87 /59	11.75 /59	1.26	0.76
AA	T Rowe Price Retirement 2040 Adv	PARDX	B-	(800) 638-5660		C+ / 5.9	3.41	5.37	8.05 /63	12.58 /57	11.47 /57	0.99	1.01
AA	T Rowe Price Retirement 2040 R	RRTDX	C+	(800) 638-5660		C+ / 5.7	3.34	5.27	7.83 /62	12.31 /55	11.20 /54	0.76	1.26
★ GI	T Rowe Price Retirement 2045	TRRKX	B-	(800) 638-5660		C+ / 6.1	3.50	5.53	8.40 /66	12.87 /59	11.75 /59	1.30	0.76
GI	T Rowe Price Retirement 2045 Adv	PARLX	B-	(800) 638-5660		C+ / 5.9	3.39	5.37	8.04 /63	12.59 /57	11.47 /57	1.07	1.01
GI	T Rowe Price Retirement 2045 R	RRTRX	C+	(800) 638-5660		C+ / 5.7	3.36	5.29	7.85 /62	12.31 /55	11.19 /54	0.84	1.26
GI	T Rowe Price Retirement 2050	TRRMX	B-	(800) 638-5660		C+ / 6.0	3.43	5.47	8.34 /65	12.86 /59	11.74 /59	1.20	0.76
GI	T Rowe Price Retirement 2050 Adv	PARFX	B-	(800) 638-5660		C+ / 5.9	3.46	5.44	8.09 /64	12.58 /57	11.46 /57	1.00	1.01
GI	T Rowe Price Retirement 2050 R	RRTFX	C+	(800) 638-5660		C+ / 5.7	3.40	5.25	7.83 /62	12.34 /55	11.20 /54	0.79	1.26
GI	T Rowe Price Retirement 2055	TRRNX	B-	(800) 638-5660		C+ / 6.0	3.46	5.52	8.34 /65	12.85 /59	11.77 /59	1.21	0.76
GI	T Rowe Price Retirement 2055 Adv	PAROX	B-	(800) 638-5660		C+ / 5.9	3.47	5.39	8.14 /64	12.60 /57	11.49 /57	1.00	1.01
GI	T Rowe Price Retirement 2055 R	RRTVX	C+	(800) 638-5660		C+ / 5.7	3.41	5.26	7.85 /62	12.31 /55	11.20 /54	0.79	1.26
TC	T Rowe Price Science and Tech	PRSCX	D+	(800) 638-5660		C+ / 6.8	3.24	6.26	13.53 /88	13.41 /63	14.10 /79	0.00	0.86
TC	T Rowe Price Science and Tech Adv	PASTX	D+	(800) 638-5660		C+ / 6.6	3.19	6.13	13.28 /88	13.16 /61	13.88 /77	0.00	1.05
★ SC	● T Rowe Price Small Cap Stock	OTCFX	A-	(800) 638-5660		B+ / 8.8	3.90	13.44	8.82 /68	16.72 /88	16.86 /96	0.10	0.91
SC	● T Rowe Price Small Cap Stock Adv	PASSX	B+	(800) 638-5660		B+ / 8.6	3.82	13.24	8.49 /66	16.40 /86	16.55 /95	0.00	1.19
★ SC	T Rowe Price Small Cap Value	PRSVX	C	(800) 638-5660		C / 5.1	1.13	8.07	0.32 /17	12.66 /57	12.83 /67	0.67	0.96
SC	T Rowe Price Small Cap Value Adv	PASVX	C-	(800) 638-5660		C / 4.9	1.05	7.91	0.02 /16	12.35 /55	12.53 /64	0.34	1.24
GI	T Rowe Price Spectrum Growth	PRSGX	C+	(800) 638-5660		C+ / 6.3	3.58	5.51	8.21 /64	13.28 /62	12.22 /62	1.08	0.80
FO	T Rowe Price Spectrum Internatl	PSILX	D	(800) 638-5660		D+ / 2.6	4.95	2.22	0.71 /18	8.17 /28	7.00 /23	1.65	0.94
GI	T Rowe Price Target Retire 2010	TRROX	U	(800) 638-5660		U /	1.58	2.33	4.35 /34	--	--	1.37	0.59
GI	T Rowe Price Target Retire 2015	TRRTX	U	(800) 638-5660		U /	1.85	2.68	4.79 /37	--	--	1.26	0.62
GI	T Rowe Price Target Retire 2020	TRRUX	U	(800) 638-5660		U /	2.10	3.12	5.31 /41	--	--	1.16	0.65
GI	T Rowe Price Target Retire 2025	TRRVX	U	(800) 638-5660		U /	2.44	3.63	6.00 /46	--	--	1.23	0.68
GI	T Rowe Price Target Retire 2030	TRRWX	U	(800) 638-5660		U /	2.77	4.22	6.68 /53	--	--	1.29	0.71
GI	T Rowe Price Target Retire 2035	RPGRX	U	(800) 638-5660		U /	3.01	4.73	7.37 /58	--	--	1.28	0.74
GI	T Rowe Price Target Retire 2040	TRHRX	U	(800) 638-5660		U /	3.25	5.05	7.78 /61	--	--	1.18	0.75
MC	T Rowe Price Tax-Efficient Equity	PREFX	A-	(800) 638-5660		A- / 9.2	6.00	12.66	16.50 /94	16.21 /85	.15.73 /91	0.04	0.89
GR	T Rowe Price Total Eq Mkt Index	POMIX	A	(800) 638-5660		B+ / 8.4	1.75	7.04	12.09 /83	16.37 /86	14.54 /83	1.38	0.35
GR	T Rowe Price US Large-Cap Core	PAULX	B+	(800) 638-5660		B+ / 8.8	3.01	7.96	13.50 /88	16.61 /88	14.40 /81	0.43	1.44
GR	T Rowe Price US Large-Cap Core Inc	TRULX	B+	(800) 638-5660		B+ / 8.9	3.06	8.06	13.60 /88	16.68 /88	14.47 /82	0.48	1.15
★ GI	T Rowe Price Value	TRVLX	A	(800) 638-5660		A / 9.3	0.89	5.60	10.36 /76	18.65 /96	14.96 /87	1.13	0.84
GI	T Rowe Price Value Adv	PAVLX	A	(800) 638-5660		A- / 9.2	0.85	5.49	10.13 /75	18.38 /95	14.73 /85	1.01	1.04
AA	Tactical Asset Allocation A	GVTAX	U	(877) 940-3435		U /	3.06	4.96	5.36 /41	--	--	0.98	2.19
GR	Tanaka Growth R	TGFRX	B+	(877) 482-6252		A / 9.5	9.33	11.08	16.83 /94	17.18 /91	10.60 /50	0.00	2.49
FO	Target International Equity Q	TIEQX	D	(800) 225-1852		D+ / 2.6	5.67	1.36	-0.78 /14	7.82 /26	5.79 /16	2.64	0.81
FO	Target International Equity R	TEQRX	D	(800) 225-1852		D / 2.2	5.44	1.02	-1.48 /11	7.18 /22	5.16 /13	2.02	1.67
FO	Target International Equity T	TAIEX	D	(800) 225-1852		D+ / 2.5	5.59	1.32	-0.96 /13	7.72 /25	5.68 /15	2.53	0.92
GR	Target Large Capitalization Gr R	TLCRX	C+	(800) 225-1852		C+ / 6.9	3.71	8.71	11.33 /80	13.64 /64	12.98 /68	0.00	1.56

● Denotes fund is closed to new investors
★ Denotes fund is included in Section II

www.thestreetratings.com

RISK			NET ASSETS		ASSET					BULL / BEAR		FUND MANAGER		MINIMUMS		LOADS	
	3 Year		NAV						Portfolio	Last Bull	Last Bear	Manager	Manager	Initial	Additional	Front	Back
Risk Rating/Pts	Standard Deviation	Beta	As of 3/31/15	Total $(Mil)	Cash %	Stocks %	Bonds %	Other %	Turnover Ratio	Market Return	Market Return	Quality Pct	Tenure (Years)	Purch. $	Purch. $	End Load	End Load
B /8.3	6.5	0.63	14.60	561	4	55	40	1	15	49.5	-13.2	46	8	2,500	100	0.0	0.0
B /8.1	7.3	1.23	21.23	19,731	4	63	31	2	14	59.5	-14.7	24	13	2,500	100	0.0	0.0
B /8.1	7.3	1.23	21.09	3,388	4	63	31	2	14	58.1	-14.8	21	12	2,500	100	0.0	0.0
B /8.1	7.3	1.23	20.90	2,124	4	63	31	2	14	56.8	-14.9	19	12	2,500	100	0.0	0.0
B- /7.8	8.0	0.79	16.16	14,858	4	71	24	1	12	66.1	-16.1	48	11	2,500	100	0.0	0.0
B- /7.8	8.0	0.78	16.08	1,641	4	71	24	1	12	64.8	-16.2	45	8	2,500	100	0.0	0.0
B- /7.8	8.0	0.78	15.94	1,115	4	71	24	1	12	63.3	-16.3	41	8	2,500	100	0.0	0.0
B- /7.5	8.5	1.44	23.73	18,380	4	77	18	1	12	72.1	-17.4	19	13	2,500	100	0.0	0.0
B- /7.5	8.6	1.44	23.55	3,389	4	77	18	1	12	70.7	-17.5	17	12	2,500	100	0.0	0.0
B- /7.5	8.6	1.44	23.38	2,272	4	77	18	1	12	69.3	-17.6	15	12	2,500	100	0.0	0.0
B- /7.2	9.0	0.89	17.22	10,716	3	82	13	2	12	76.3	-18.3	44	11	2,500	100	0.0	0.0
B- /7.2	9.0	0.89	17.14	1,276	3	82	13	2	12	74.8	-18.4	40	8	2,500	100	0.0	0.0
B- /7.2	9.0	0.89	16.98	892	3	82	13	2	12	73.4	-18.5	37	8	2,500	100	0.0	0.0
B- /7.0	9.3	1.56	24.75	12,343	3	87	9	1	13	78.9	-18.7	16	13	2,500	100	0.0	0.0
B- /7.0	9.3	1.56	24.56	2,594	3	87	9	1	13	77.3	-18.7	15	12	2,500	100	0.0	0.0
B+ /7.0	9.3	1.56	24.42	1,614	3	87	9	1	13	75.9	-18.8	13	12	2,500	100	0.0	0.0
B- /7.1	9.3	0.92	16.56	6,023	3	87	9	1	15	78.7	-18.5	43	10	2,500	100	0.0	0.0
B- /7.1	9.3	0.92	16.46	748	3	87	9	1	15	77.1	-18.6	39	8	2,500	100	0.0	0.0
B- /7.1	9.3	0.92	16.32	561	3	87	9	1	15	75.7	-18.7	36	8	2,500	100	0.0	0.0
B- /7.1	9.3	0.91	13.87	3,836	3	87	9	1	16	78.7	-18.5	44	9	2,500	100	0.0	0.0
B- /7.1	9.3	0.91	13.77	950	3	87	9	1	16	77.2	-18.6	40	9	2,500	100	0.0	0.0
B- /7.1	9.2	0.91	13.67	641	3	87	9	1	16	75.5	-18.6	37	9	2,500	100	0.0	0.0
B- /7.1	9.3	0.92	13.77	1,331	3	87	9	1	20	78.6	-18.5	43	9	2,500	100	0.0	0.0
B- /7.1	9.3	0.92	13.71	183	3	87	9	1	20	77.2	-18.6	40	8	2,500	100	0.0	0.0
B- /7.1	9.3	0.91	13.65	150	3	87	9	1	20	75.7	-18.6	36	8	2,500	100	0.0	0.0
C- /3.0	14.8	1.25	38.61	3,426	6	93	0	1	72	92.3	-19.0	6	6	2,500	100	0.0	0.0
C- /3.0	14.8	1.25	38.21	494	6	93	0	1	72	91.0	-19.1	6	6	2,500	100	0.0	0.0
C+ /6.1	11.8	0.87	46.05	9,111	6	93	0	1	22	107.6	-23.8	86	23	2,500	100	0.0	0.0
C+ /6.1	11.8	0.87	45.61	373	6	93	0	1	22	105.7	-23.9	84	23	2,500	100	0.0	0.0
C+ /5.9	12.0	0.87	47.33	7,888	3	95	0	2	6	81.6	-21.9	49	24	2,500	100	0.0	1.0
C+ /5.9	12.0	0.87	46.98	1,093	3	95	0	2	6	80.0	-21.9	45	24	2,500	100	0.0	1.0
C+ /6.2	10.1	0.99	24.28	4,023	3	96	0	1	10	84.1	-19.4	32	N/A	2,500	100	0.0	0.0
C+ /6.1	11.9	0.88	12.71	1,213	3	96	0	1	5	53.0	-23.5	65	N/A	2,500	100	0.0	2.0
U /	N/A	N/A	10.90	29	5	36	57	2	21	N/A	N/A	N/A	2	2,500	100	0.0	0.0
U /	N/A	N/A	11.04	84	4	44	51	1	15	N/A	N/A	N/A	2	2,500	100	0.0	0.0
U /	N/A	N/A	11.18	86	4	51	44	1	25	N/A	N/A	N/A	2	2,500	100	0.0	0.0
U /	N/A	N/A	11.35	74	4	58	37	1	26	N/A	N/A	N/A	2	2,500	100	0.0	0.0
U /	N/A	N/A	11.52	70	3	65	30	2	11	N/A	N/A	N/A	2	2,500	100	0.0	0.0
U /	N/A	N/A	11.65	45	4	71	23	2	25	N/A	N/A	N/A	2	2,500	100	0.0	0.0
U /	N/A	N/A	11.77	35	4	76	19	1	15	N/A	N/A	N/A	2	2,500	100	0.0	0.0
C+ /6.0	11.1	0.90	22.61	173	0	99	0	1	18	100.0	-17.7	75	15	2,500	100	0.0	1.0
B- /7.2	9.8	1.02	23.85	1,200	2	97	0	1	6	101.4	-17.9	66	13	2,500	100	0.0	0.5
C+ /6.0	9.3	0.96	19.14	2	3	96	0	1	69	100.4	-17.8	78	6	2,500	100	0.0	0.0
C+ /6.0	9.2	0.95	19.17	107	3	96	0	1	69	100.6	-17.8	79	6	2,500	100	0.0	0.0
C+ /6.3	10.3	1.05	34.96	22,100	1	98	0	1	44	112.1	-20.6	80	6	2,500	100	0.0	0.0
C+ /6.3	10.3	1.04	34.47	684	1	98	0	1	44	110.5	-20.7	79	6	2,500	100	0.0	0.0
U /	N/A	N/A	10.75	60	4	71	23	2	397	N/A	N/A	N/A	2	1,000	100	5.8	1.0
C /4.9	19.4	1.29	21.45	16	4	95	0	1	26	116.3	-24.9	21	17	2,000	500	0.0	0.0
C+ /6.1	12.3	0.92	13.23	188	5	94	0	1	23	46.5	-24.1	54	10	0	0	0.0	0.0
C+ /6.2	12.3	0.93	13.19	279	5	94	0	1	23	43.6	-24.3	45	10	0	0	0.0	0.0
C+ /6.1	12.3	0.93	13.22	58	5	94	0	1	23	46.1	-24.2	52	10	0	0	0.0	0.0
C+ /6.4	10.0	0.96	20.42	213	3	96	0	1	21	87.2	-17.1	44	4	0	0	0.0	0.0

						PERFORMANCE						
							Total Return % through 3/31/15				Incl. in Returns	
	99 Pct = Best 0 Pct = Worst			**Overall Investment Rating**		**Perfor-mance Rating/Pts**				Annualized		Dividend	Expense
Fund Type	Fund Name	Ticker Symbol			Phone		3 Mo	6 Mo	1Yr / Pct	3Yr / Pct	5Yr / Pct	Yield	Ratio
GR	Target Large Capitalization Gro T	TALGX	B		(800) 225-1852	B- / 7.4	3.84	8.97	11.89 /82	14.20 /69	13.53 /73	0.00	0.81
IN	Target Large Capitalization Val R	TLVRX	A-		(800) 225-1852	B / 7.8	-0.30	4.73	9.49 /72	16.08 /84	12.26 /62	1.52	1.54
IN	Target Large Capitalization Val T	TALVX	A+		(800) 225-1852	B+ / 8.3	-0.18	4.94	10.04 /74	16.65 /88	12.82 /67	1.99	0.79
SC	Target Sm Capitalization Growth R	TSCRX	C		(800) 225-1852	B- / 7.1	6.47	16.16	8.38 /65	13.37 /62	14.27 /80	0.00	1.64
SC	Target Sm Capitalization Growth T	TASGX	C+		(800) 225-1852	B / 7.6	6.62	16.42	8.97 /69	13.96 /67	14.84 /86	0.00	0.89
SC	Target Sm Capitalization Value Q	TSVQX	U		(800) 225-1852	U /	2.70	10.20	--	--	--	0.00	0.64
SC	Target Sm Capitalization Value R	TSVRX	B-		(800) 225-1852	B- / 7.1	2.56	9.88	6.79 /53	14.63 /72	13.23 /70	0.49	1.43
SC	Target Sm Capitalization Value T	TASVX	B		(800) 225-1852	B / 7.6	2.70	10.14	7.35 /58	15.20 /76	13.81 /76	0.96	0.68
GR	Tax Mgd US MktWide Val II Inst	DFMVX	A+		(800) 984-9472	A / 9.3	0.88	5.01	9.89 /74	19.07 /97	15.54 /90	1.60	0.22
SC	Tax-Managed Small/Mid Cap A	STMSX	B		(800) 342-5734	B / 7.8	4.05	10.54	7.78 /61	15.61 /80	13.78 /76	0.10	1.23
GR	TCM Small Cap Growth	TCMSX	C		(800) 536-3230	A+ / 9.6	7.36	15.35	9.35 /71	18.89 /96	15.43 /90	0.00	0.92
MC	TCM Small Mid Cap Growth	TCMMX	D+		(800) 536-3230	A / 9.3	6.69	14.92	14.24 /90	17.06 /90	14.73 /85	0.00	1.23
GR	TCW Concentrated Value I	TGFFX	A+		(800) 386-3829	A / 9.4	0.25	7.34	15.46 /92	18.57 /96	13.26 /71	0.38	1.95
GR	TCW Concentrated Value N	TGFVX	A+		(800) 386-3829	A / 9.5	0.25	7.30	15.51 /92	18.66 /96	13.02 /68	0.38	4.15
AA	TCW Conservative Alloc I	TGPCX	C+		(800) 386-3829	C- / 3.2	2.21	5.69	7.75 /61	7.52 /24	7.39 /26	1.08	0.91
AA	TCW Conservative Alloc N	TGPNX	C		(800) 386-3829	D+ / 2.9	2.04	5.37	7.16 /56	7.03 /21	7.09 /24	0.45	3.82
GL	TCW Emerg Mkts Multi Asset Opps I	TGMAX	U		(800) 386-3829	U /	1.36	-1.67	-0.19 /15	--	--	1.89	1.72
OT	TCW Enhanced Commodity Strategy	TGGWX	E-		(800) 386-3829	E- / 0.1	-6.02	-16.83	-25.99 / 0	-8.94 / 1	--	1.46	5.67
OT	TCW Enhanced Commodity Strategy	TGABX	E-		(800) 386-3829	E- / 0.1	-6.03	-16.72	-25.91 / 0	-8.91 / 1	--	1.39	6.14
MC	TCW Growth Equities I	TGGEX	E+		(800) 386-3829	C+ / 5.9	5.63	10.34	6.40 /50	12.08 /53	11.43 /56	0.00	1.32
MC	TCW Growth Equities N	TGDNX	E+		(800) 386-3829	C+ / 5.9	5.67	10.42	6.53 /51	12.11 /53	11.43 /56	0.00	1.93
FO	TCW International Small Cap I	TGICX	E		(800) 386-3829	E+ / 0.6	3.82	-8.06	-7.56 / 4	2.77 / 7	--	0.64	1.36
FO	TCW International Small Cap N	TGNIX	E		(800) 386-3829	E+ / 0.6	3.69	-8.13	-7.73 / 3	2.66 / 7	--	0.56	1.67
IN	TCW Relative Value Dividend App I	TGDFX	B+		(800) 386-3829	B / 7.6	-0.73	3.80	8.08 /63	16.07 /84	14.44 /82	1.57	0.82
IN	TCW Relative Value Dividend App N	TGIGX	B+		(800) 386-3829	B- / 7.4	-0.72	3.68	7.84 /62	15.78 /82	14.10 /79	1.32	1.11
GR	TCW Relative Value Large Cap I	TGDIX	A-		(800) 386-3829	B / 8.2	0.18	5.39	9.01 /69	16.61 /88	13.98 /78	0.97	0.87
GR	TCW Relative Value Large Cap N	TGDVX	B+		(800) 386-3829	B / 7.9	0.09	5.22	8.69 /67	16.32 /86	13.71 /75	0.80	1.13
MC	TCW Relative Value Mid Cap I	TGVOX	C+		(800) 386-3829	B- / 7.4	2.80	6.33	4.49 /35	15.76 /81	13.88 /77	0.43	0.94
MC	TCW Relative Value Mid Cap N	TGVNX	C+		(800) 386-3829	B- / 7.2	2.73	6.23	4.24 /33	15.45 /79	13.55 /73	0.31	1.32
GR	TCW Select Equities I	TGCEX	C		(800) 386-3829	C+ / 6.4	3.19	8.70	11.91 /82	12.73 /58	14.25 /80	0.00	0.83
GR	TCW Select Equities N	TGCNX	C		(800) 386-3829	C+ / 6.2	3.10	8.59	11.61 /81	12.43 /56	13.92 /77	0.00	1.10
SC	TCW Small Cap Growth I	TGSCX	D-		(800) 386-3829	C+ / 6.7	6.92	17.49	9.31 /71	12.39 /55	10.38 /48	0.00	1.18
SC	TCW Small Cap Growth N	TGSNX	D-		(800) 386-3829	C+ / 6.5	6.85	17.33	9.10 /70	12.09 /53	10.08 /45	0.00	1.47
GR	TCW SMID Cap Growth I	TGSDX	C-		(800) 386-3829	C+ / 6.3	6.16	12.02	5.32 /41	12.94 /59	--	0.00	1.34
GR	TCW SMID Cap Growth N	TGMDX	C-		(800) 386-3829	C+ / 6.3	6.16	12.02	5.32 /41	12.94 /59	--	0.00	1.61
MC	TDAM US Sm Md Cp Equity Inst	TDUSX	U			U /	2.22	9.39	7.39 /58	--	--	0.49	3.95
AA	Teberg Fund	TEBRX	C-		(866) 209-1964	D+ / 2.6	-1.62	7.51	11.75 /81	5.85 /16	6.13 /18	0.21	2.77
EM	Templeton BRIC A	TABRX	E		(800) 342-5236	E- / 0.2	-1.11	-8.25	-3.89 / 7	-5.59 / 2	-5.39 / 1	1.35	2.10
EM	Templeton BRIC Adv	TZBRX	E		(800) 321-8563	E- / 0.2	-1.12	-8.11	-3.55 / 8	-5.31 / 2	-5.13 / 1	1.82	1.82
EM	Templeton BRIC C	TPBRX	E		(800) 342-5236	E- / 0.2	-1.33	-8.53	-4.57 / 6	-6.26 / 1	-6.07 / 1	0.59	2.82
FO	Templeton China World A	TCWAX	E		(800) 342-5236	E+ / 0.7	3.08	2.55	6.27 /49	1.86 / 6	3.57 / 7	1.19	1.85
FO	Templeton China World Adv	TACWX	E		(800) 342-5236	D- / 1.0	3.12	2.65	6.53 /51	2.15 / 6	3.88 / 8	1.45	1.55
FO	Templeton China World C	TCWCX	E		(800) 342-5236	E+ / 0.8	2.88	2.18	5.53 /43	1.15 / 5	2.85 / 6	0.74	2.55
FO	Templeton China World R6	FCWRX	D		(800) 342-5236	D- / 1.1	3.19	2.77	6.78 /53	2.28 / 7	3.95 / 8	1.61	1.39
EM	Templeton Developing Markets A	TEDMX	E-		(800) 342-5236	E / 0.3	1.58	-3.92	-3.36 / 8	-2.10 / 3	0.08 / 3	1.49	1.71
EM	Templeton Developing Markets Adv	TDADX	E-		(800) 321-8563	E / 0.3	1.59	-3.83	-3.09 / 9	-1.84 / 3	0.36 / 3	1.89	1.44
EM	Templeton Developing Markets C	TDMTX	E-		(800) 342-5236	E / 0.3	1.32	-4.33	-4.07 / 7	-2.83 / 2	-0.64 / 2	0.82	2.44
EM	Templeton Developing Markets R	TDMRX	E-		(800) 342-5236	E / 0.3	1.55	-4.01	-3.57 / 8	-2.32 / 3	-0.09 / 2	1.38	1.94
EM	Templeton Developing Markets R6	FDEVX	E+		(800) 342-5236	E / 0.3	1.65	-3.72	-2.94 / 9	-1.83 / 3	0.25 / 3	2.08	1.30
EM	Templeton Emerg Mkts Small Cap A	TEMMX	D-		(800) 342-5236	D- / 1.1	0.25	-4.52	5.40 /42	6.02 /17	3.05 / 6	0.15	2.12
EM	Templeton Emerg Mkts Small Cap	TEMZX	D		(800) 321-8563	D / 1.8	0.24	-4.42	5.66 /44	6.34 /18	3.35 / 7	0.46	1.82
EM	Templeton Emerg Mkts Small Cap C	TCEMX	D-		(800) 342-5236	D- / 1.4	0.00	-4.91	4.60 /36	5.26 /14	2.32 / 5	0.00	2.82

RISK			NET ASSETS		ASSET				Portfolio Turnover Ratio	BULL / BEAR		FUND MANAGER		MINIMUMS		LOADS	
	3 Year		NAV							Last Bull	Last Bear	Manager	Manager	Initial	Additional	Front	Back
Risk Rating/Pts	Standard Deviation	Beta	As of 3/31/15	Total $(Mil)	Cash %	Stocks %	Bonds %	Other %		Market Return	Market Return	Quality Pct	Tenure (Years)	Purch. $	Purch. $	End Load	End Load
C+ / 6.4	10.0	0.96	20.84	89	3	96	0	1	21	90.4	-16.9	51	4	0	0	0.0	0.0
B- / 7.4	10.4	1.07	16.35	217	1	98	0	1	23	97.3	-18.6	52	10	0	0	0.0	0.0
B- / 7.5	10.4	1.06	16.41	86	1	98	0	1	23	100.8	-18.4	61	10	0	0	0.0	0.0
C / 4.7	14.8	1.03	17.78	112	1	98	0	1	74	81.9	-21.7	26	7	0	0	0.0	0.0
C / 4.7	14.8	1.03	18.53	42	1	98	0	1	74	85.0	-21.6	31	7	0	0	0.0	0.0
U /	N/A	N/A	26.29	41	3	96	0	1	42	N/A	N/A	N/A	N/A	0	0	0.0	0.0
C+ / 6.1	12.1	0.87	26.09	161	3	96	0	1	42	86.2	-22.0	72	N/A	0	0	0.0	0.0
C+ / 6.0	12.1	0.87	26.28	1,878	3	96	0	1	42	89.4	-21.8	77	N/A	0	0	0.0	0.0
B- / 7.0	11.3	1.12	24.91	1,520	0	99	0	1	2	120.1	-23.7	74	N/A	0	0	0.0	0.0
C+ / 6.2	12.1	0.88	19.27	631	8	91	0	1	61	96.8	-23.6	79	10	100,000	1,000	0.0	1.0
D / 1.6	14.1	1.14	34.00	304	1	98	0	1	149	118.0	-28.1	70	11	100,000	2,500	0.0	1.0
E / 0.4	13.2	1.11	16.90	51	1	98	0	1	149	103.9	-25.5	42	8	100,000	2,500	0.0	1.0
C+ / 6.7	11.0	1.09	20.21	13	7	92	0	1	40	118.1	-24.9	75	11	2,000	250	0.0	0.0
C+ / 6.7	11.0	1.09	20.00	3	7	92	0	1	40	117.7	-25.3	76	11	2,000	250	0.0	0.0
B / 8.9	4.7	0.76	12.51	32	4	49	46	1	41	38.2	-8.2	59	9	2,000	250	0.0	0.0
B / 8.9	4.7	0.76	12.49	1	4	49	46	1	41	36.4	-8.2	52	9	2,000	250	0.0	0.0
U /	N/A	N/A	10.41	49	9	58	32	1	152	N/A	N/A	N/A	2	2,000	250	0.0	0.0
D+ / 2.3	13.2	0.75	5.98	2	57	0	42	1	4	-17.1	-20.7	0	4	2,000	250	0.0	0.0
D+ / 2.3	13.2	0.75	5.99	1	57	0	42	1	4	-17.0	-20.8	0	4	2,000	250	0.0	0.0
E / 0.5	15.2	1.18	12.56	21	2	97	0	1	49	76.6	-22.7	4	3	2,000	250	0.0	0.0
E / 0.5	15.1	1.18	12.48	5	2	97	0	1	49	76.7	-22.7	4	3	2,000	250	0.0	0.0
C- / 3.8	15.4	0.94	8.43	19	0	100	0	0	260	33.9	-29.8	7	4	2,000	250	0.0	0.0
C- / 3.8	15.4	0.94	8.43	9	0	100	0	0	260	33.4	-29.9	7	4	2,000	250	0.0	0.0
B- / 7.0	11.5	1.16	16.97	203	1	98	0	1	17	106.8	-21.4	31	14	2,000	250	0.0	0.0
B- / 7.0	11.4	1.16	17.26	983	1	98	0	1	17	104.8	-21.5	29	14	2,000	250	0.0	0.0
C+ / 6.9	12.1	1.22	22.62	696	0	99	0	1	19	110.0	-23.5	27	16	2,000	250	0.0	0.0
C+ / 6.9	12.1	1.22	22.57	27	0	99	0	1	19	108.2	-23.6	24	16	2,000	250	0.0	0.0
C / 4.7	13.2	1.14	24.60	115	0	100	0	0	22	109.4	-26.0	22	4	2,000	250	0.0	0.0
C / 4.7	13.2	1.14	24.05	28	0	100	0	0	22	107.6	-26.1	20	4	2,000	250	0.0	0.0
C / 5.0	11.9	1.08	27.17	1,620	0	99	0	1	26	82.0	-12.3	15	11	2,000	250	0.0	0.0
C / 5.0	11.9	1.08	25.62	214	0	99	0	1	26	80.3	-12.5	13	11	2,000	250	0.0	0.0
D- / 1.2	18.5	1.21	30.74	129	3	96	0	1	76	71.7	-27.7	5	3	2,000	250	0.0	0.0
E+ / 0.9	18.5	1.21	28.70	31	3	96	0	1	76	70.1	-27.8	5	3	2,000	250	0.0	0.0
C- / 4.1	17.0	1.30	15.52	24	1	98	0	1	67	76.5	-27.7	4	3	2,000	250	0.0	0.0
C- / 4.1	16.9	1.30	15.52	25	1	98	0	1	67	76.5	-27.7	4	3	2,000	250	0.0	0.0
U /	N/A	N/A	11.83	109	0	0	0	100	16	N/A	N/A	N/A	N/A	0	0	0.0	0.0
B- / 7.9	7.9	0.97	11.55	36	63	36	0	1	304	33.7	-6.5	14	13	2,000	100	0.0	0.0
C- / 3.8	16.7	1.15	9.78	145	2	97	0	1	20	-1.1	-29.9	5	9	1,000	0	5.8	0.0
C- / 3.8	16.6	1.14	9.74	7	2	97	0	1	20	N/A	-29.8	6	9	1,000,000	0	0.0	0.0
C- / 3.9	16.6	1.14	9.64	44	2	97	0	1	20	-3.4	-30.1	4	9	1,000	0	0.0	0.0
C- / 3.5	12.8	0.66	31.50	318	0	100	0	0	4	24.6	-23.1	15	22	1,000	0	5.8	0.0
C- / 3.5	12.8	0.65	31.70	179	0	100	0	0	4	25.8	-23.0	17	22	1,000	0	0.0	0.0
C- / 3.6	12.8	0.65	31.08	86	0	100	0	0	4	21.7	-23.3	11	22	1,000	0	0.0	0.0
B- / 7.2	12.8	0.65	31.70	71	0	100	0	0	4	26.2	-23.0	18	22	1,000,000	0	0.0	0.0
D / 1.7	14.6	1.01	17.36	1,213	5	94	0	1	48	14.0	-24.8	27	24	1,000	0	5.8	0.0
D / 1.7	14.6	1.01	17.28	173	5	94	0	1	48	15.1	-24.7	30	24	1,000,000	0	0.0	0.0
D / 1.7	14.6	1.01	16.84	187	5	94	0	1	48	11.2	-25.0	20	24	1,000	0	0.0	0.0
D / 1.7	14.6	1.01	17.06	27	5	94	0	1	48	13.2	-24.9	25	24	1,000	0	0.0	0.0
C+ / 6.5	14.6	1.01	17.27	54	5	94	0	1	48	14.9	-24.8	31	24	1,000,000	0	0.0	0.0
C+ / 6.6	11.7	0.75	12.25	280	17	82	0	1	22	39.8	-28.9	94	9	1,000	0	5.8	0.0
C+ / 6.6	11.7	0.75	12.37	371	17	82	0	1	22	41.2	-28.8	95	9	1,000,000	0	0.0	0.0
C+ / 6.6	11.6	0.75	11.82	75	17	82	0	1	22	36.5	-29.1	93	9	1,000	0	0.0	0.0

Fund Type	Fund Name	Ticker Symbol	Overall Investment Rating	Phone	Perfor-mance Rating/Pts	3 Mo	6 Mo	1Yr / Pct	3Yr / Pct	5Yr / Pct	Dividend Yield	Expense Ratio
	99 Pct = Best				PERFORMANCE			Total Return % through 3/31/15			Incl. in Returns	
	0 Pct = Worst								Annualized			
EM	Templeton Emerg Mkts Small Cap R		D	(800) 342-5236	D / 1.6	0.08	-4.63	5.10 /39	5.82 /16	2.83 / 6	0.00	2.32
EM	Templeton Emg Markets Balanced A	TAEMX	E	(800) 342-5236	E- / 0.2	-0.30	-5.09	-3.66 / 8	-3.33 / 2	--	3.77	2.04
EM	Templeton Emg Markets Balanced	TZEMX	E	(800) 342-5236	E / 0.3	-0.25	-4.83	-3.28 / 8	-3.07 / 2	--	4.28	1.74
EM	Templeton Emg Markets Balanced C		E	(800) 342-5236	E- / 0.2	-0.53	-5.39	-4.27 / 7	-4.04 / 2	--	3.26	2.74
EM	Templeton Emg Markets Balanced R		E	(800) 342-5236	E / 0.3	-0.33	-5.09	-3.85 / 7	-3.55 / 2	--	3.79	2.24
FO	Templeton Foreign A	TEMFX	E	(800) 342-5236	D- / 1.2	4.59	-5.45	-7.15 / 4	7.78 /26	5.94 /17	2.65	1.19
FO	Templeton Foreign Adv	TFFAX	E+	(800) 321-8563	D / 1.9	4.66	-5.34	-7.06 / 4	8.00 /27	6.17 /18	3.15	0.94
FO	Templeton Foreign C	TEFTX	E+	(800) 342-5236	D- / 1.4	4.25	-5.79	-7.99 / 3	6.96 /21	5.12 /12	2.05	1.94
FO	Templeton Foreign R	TEFRX	E+	(800) 342-5236	D / 1.6	4.38	-5.55	-7.51 / 4	7.46 /24	5.64 /15	2.62	1.44
FO	Templeton Foreign R6	FTFGX	D	(800) 342-5236	D / 1.9	4.66	-5.15	-6.76 / 4	8.10 /28	6.13 /18	3.35	0.74
FO ●	Templeton Foreign Smaller Co A	FINEX	E+	(800) 342-5236	D- / 1.0	4.68	0.57	-4.13 / 7	5.72 /16	5.33 /13	1.25	1.67
FO ●	Templeton Foreign Smaller Co Adv	FTFAX	E+	(800) 321-8563	D- / 1.5	4.76	0.68	-3.92 / 7	5.98 /17	5.60 /15	1.65	1.42
FO ●	Templeton Foreign Smaller Co C	FCFSX	E+	(800) 342-5236	D- / 1.1	4.46	0.12	-4.92 / 6	4.91 /13	4.55 /10	0.58	2.42
FO ●	Templeton Foreign Smaller Co R6		D-	(800) 342-5236	D / 1.6	4.83	0.83	-3.61 / 8	6.09 /17	5.55 /14	2.02	1.11
EM ●	Templeton Frontier Markets A	TFMAX	E-	(800) 342-5236	E- / 0.2	-6.20	-23.75	-19.91 / 1	0.62 / 5	0.51 / 3	3.68	1.99
EM ●	Templeton Frontier Markets Adv	FFRZX	E-	(800) 342-5236	E / 0.3	-6.18	-23.68	-19.78 / 1	0.88 / 5	0.78 / 3	4.25	1.74
EM ●	Templeton Frontier Markets C	FFRMX	E-	(800) 342-5236	E- / 0.2	-6.35	-24.06	-20.53 / 1	-0.12 / 4	-0.21 / 2	2.93	2.74
EM ●	Templeton Frontier Markets R		E-	(800) 342-5236	E- / 0.2	-6.29	-23.89	-20.17 / 1	0.38 / 5	0.28 / 3	3.68	2.24
EM ●	Templeton Frontier Markets R6	FFMRX	D-	(800) 342-5236	E / 0.3	-6.12	-23.62	-19.63 / 1	0.97 / 5	0.84 / 3	4.45	1.61
GL	Templeton Global Balanced A	TAGBX	D	(800) 342-5236	D / 2.1	3.32	1.18	0.38 /17	8.73 /31	7.84 /29	5.31	1.14
GL ●	Templeton Global Balanced A1	TINCX	D	(800) 342-5236	D+ / 2.4	3.32	1.18	0.36 /17	8.82 /32	7.81 /29	5.38	1.14
GL	Templeton Global Balanced Adv	TZINX	D+	(800) 342-5236	C- / 3.2	3.35	1.30	0.62 /17	9.07 /33	8.06 /30	5.87	0.89
GL	Templeton Global Balanced C	FCGBX	D+	(800) 342-5236	D+ / 2.6	3.20	1.12	-0.04 /15	8.07 /27	7.02 /23	4.91	1.89
GL ●	Templeton Global Balanced C1	TCINX	D+	(800) 342-5236	D+ / 2.8	3.26	0.97	0.26 /16	8.39 /29	7.37 /26	5.20	1.54
GL	Templeton Global Balanced R		D+	(800) 342-5236	D+ / 2.9	3.27	1.06	0.43 /17	8.54 /30	7.52 /27	5.36	1.39
GL	Templeton Global Balanced R6		C-	(800) 342-5236	C- / 3.3	3.37	1.35	1.02 /18	9.14 /34	8.10 /31	5.97	2.32
EM	Templeton Global Equity Series	TGESX	D	(800) 342-5236	C / 5.0	2.70	0.49	-2.25 /10	13.11 /60	10.35 /47	2.27	0.94
GL	Templeton Global Opportunities A	TEGOX	D-	(800) 342-5236	D+ / 2.4	2.09	-1.88	-3.38 / 8	10.20 /40	7.14 /24	2.04	1.32
GL	Templeton Global Opportunities Adv	FGOZX	D	(800) 321-8563	C- / 3.4	2.14	-1.76	-3.13 / 8	10.50 /42	7.42 /26	2.45	1.07
GL	Templeton Global Opportunities C	TEGPX	D	(800) 342-5236	D+ / 2.7	1.89	-2.26	-4.12 / 7	9.37 /35	6.34 /19	1.39	2.07
GL	Templeton Global Smaller Co A	TEMGX	D	(800) 342-5236	D+ / 2.6	2.20	2.52	-1.66 /11	9.94 /39	7.67 /28	0.47	1.39
GL	Templeton Global Smaller Co Adv	TGSAX	C-	(800) 321-8563	C- / 3.6	2.20	2.61	-1.34 /12	10.20 /40	7.93 /29	0.70	1.14
GL	Templeton Global Smaller Co C	TESGX	D+	(800) 342-5236	C- / 3.0	1.93	2.08	-2.36 /10	9.13 /34	6.85 /22	0.00	2.14
GL	Templeton Global Smaller Co R6	FBOGX	C-	(800) 342-5236	C- / 3.7	2.31	2.73	-1.22 /12	10.26 /41	7.85 /29	0.93	3.26
* GL	Templeton Growth A	TEPLX	D+	(800) 342-5236	C- / 3.3	1.47	-1.22	-3.26 / 8	11.97 /52	9.39 /40	2.61	1.07
GL	Templeton Growth Adv	TGADX	C-	(800) 321-8563	C / 4.4	1.47	-1.13	-3.06 / 9	12.24 /54	9.66 /42	3.05	0.82
GL	Templeton Growth C	TEGTX	D+	(800) 342-5236	C- / 3.7	1.25	-1.65	-4.00 / 7	11.12 /46	8.58 /34	2.05	1.82
GL	Templeton Growth R	TEGRX	C-	(800) 342-5236	C- / 4.0	1.36	-1.39	-3.52 / 8	11.67 /50	9.11 /38	2.52	1.32
GL	Templeton Growth R6	FTGFX	C	(800) 342-5236	C / 4.4	1.51	-1.09	-2.94 / 9	12.22 /54	9.53 /41	3.14	0.71
EM	Templeton Inst-Emerg Markets Mkts	TEEMX	E-	(800) 321-8563	E / 0.4	1.96	-3.50	-2.61 / 9	-0.82 / 4	2.03 / 4	2.87	1.33
* FO	Templeton Inst-Foreign Eq Prm	TFEQX	D-	(800) 321-8563	D+ / 2.5	5.29	0.52	-3.34 / 8	8.21 /28	5.87 /16	3.69	0.79
FO	Templeton Inst-Foreign Eq Svc	TFESX	D-	(800) 321-8563	D+ / 2.4	5.22	0.39	-3.49 / 8	8.03 /27	5.71 /15	3.52	0.94
FO ●	Templeton Inst-Foreign Small Comp	TFSCX	C-	(800) 321-8563	C- / 3.6	5.14	3.02	0.02 /16	9.57 /37	9.36 /39	0.73	0.99
* GL	Templeton World A	TEMWX	D-	(800) 342-5236	D+ / 2.7	1.69	-1.78	-2.82 / 9	10.84 /45	9.03 /37	2.64	1.05
GL	Templeton World Adv	TWDAX	D	(800) 321-8563	C- / 3.8	1.69	-1.66	-2.61 / 9	11.11 /46	9.30 /39	3.08	0.81
GL	Templeton World C	TEWTX	D	(800) 342-5236	C- / 3.1	1.51	-2.15	-3.54 / 8	10.00 /39	8.23 /31	2.10	1.81
GL	Templeton World R6	FTWRX	C-	(800) 342-5236	C- / 3.8	1.75	-1.63	-2.53 / 9	11.06 /46	9.16 /38	3.16	0.72
BA	TETON Westwood Balanced A	WEBCX	C-	(800) 422-3554	C- / 3.3	1.37	4.94	7.20 /57	9.46 /36	8.27 /32	0.74	1.52
BA	TETON Westwood Balanced AAA	WEBAX	C	(800) 422-3554	C- / 4.2	1.44	5.10	7.51 /59	9.72 /38	8.56 /34	1.01	1.27
BA	TETON Westwood Balanced C	WBCCX	C	(800) 422-3554	C- / 3.6	1.23	4.63	6.68 /53	8.89 /32	7.74 /28	0.29	2.02
BA	TETON Westwood Balanced I	WBBIX	C	(800) 422-3554	C / 4.3	1.42	5.15	7.71 /61	9.98 /39	8.80 /35	1.26	1.02
IN	TETON Westwood Equity A	WEECX	C+	(800) 422-3554	C+ / 6.3	1.23	6.56	10.03 /74	14.36 /70	11.60 /58	0.16	1.84

● Denotes fund is closed to new investors
* Denotes fund is included in Section II

www.thestreetratings.com

RISK			NET ASSETS		ASSET				BULL / BEAR		FUND MANAGER		MINIMUMS		LOADS	
	3 Year		NAV						Last Bull	Last Bear	Manager	Manager	Initial	Additional	Front	Back
Risk Rating/Pts	Standard Deviation	Beta	As of 3/31/15	Total $(Mil)	Cash %	Stocks %	Bonds %	Other %	Portfolio Turnover Ratio	Market Return	Market Return	Quality Pct	Tenure (Years)	Purch. $	Purch. $	End Load	End Load
C+ / 6.6	11.7	0.75	12.16	1	17	82	0	1	22	38.8	-28.9	94	9	1,000	0	0.0	0.0
C- / 3.8	11.6	0.82	9.36	32	10	57	32	1	69	N/A	N/A	16	4	1,000	0	5.8	0.0
C- / 3.8	11.6	0.82	9.38	8	10	57	32	1	69	N/A	N/A	19	4	1,000,000	0	0.0	0.0
C- / 3.8	11.6	0.82	9.30	4	10	57	32	1	69	N/A	N/A	12	4	1,000	0	0.0	0.0
C- / 3.8	11.6	0.82	9.35	N/A	10	57	32	1	69	N/A	N/A	15	4	1,000	0	0.0	0.0
C / 4.3	15.0	1.05	7.29	4,588	3	96	0	1	31	45.3	-25.0	36	8	1,000	0	5.8	0.0
C- / 4.2	15.0	1.05	7.19	1,438	3	96	0	1	31	46.3	-24.9	40	8	1,000	0	0.0	0.0
C / 4.4	15.0	1.05	7.11	526	3	96	0	1	31	41.5	-25.2	27	8	1,000	0	0.0	0.0
C / 4.3	15.0	1.05	7.15	189	3	96	0	1	31	43.7	-25.0	32	8	1,000	0	0.0	0.0
C+ / 6.5	15.0	1.05	7.19	665	3	96	0	1	31	46.4	-25.0	41	8	1,000,000	0	0.0	0.0
C / 5.2	13.8	0.95	16.77	92	5	94	0	1	37	38.4	-26.0	25	8	1,000	0	5.8	0.0
C / 5.2	13.8	0.95	16.72	39	5	94	0	1	37	39.5	-25.9	27	8	1,000,000	0	0.0	0.0
C / 5.2	13.8	0.95	16.16	12	5	94	0	1	37	34.8	-26.2	18	8	1,000	0	0.0	0.0
C+ / 6.5	13.8	0.95	16.72	1	5	94	0	1	37	39.8	-26.0	28	8	1,000,000	0	0.0	0.0
C- / 3.4	12.4	0.57	13.47	146	10	88	0	2	13	20.3	-19.6	70	7	1,000	0	5.8	0.0
C- / 3.4	12.3	0.56	13.51	578	10	88	0	2	13	21.4	-19.5	72	7	1,000,000	0	0.0	0.0
C- / 3.5	12.4	0.57	13.27	40	10	88	0	2	13	17.3	-19.8	60	7	1,000	0	0.0	0.0
C- / 3.4	12.4	0.57	13.40	N/A	10	88	0	2	13	19.4	-19.6	67	7	1,000	0	0.0	0.0
B- / 7.6	12.3	0.56	13.51	143	10	88	0	2	13	21.7	-19.5	73	7	1,000,000	0	0.0	0.0
C+ / 6.6	9.6	1.46	3.13	1,116	1	67	28	4	13	51.3	-17.2	15	10	1,000	0	5.8	0.0
C+ / 6.6	9.6	1.45	3.13	475	1	67	28	4	13	51.6	-17.6	16	10	1,000	0	4.3	0.0
C+ / 6.6	9.6	1.45	3.14	409	1	67	28	4	13	52.7	-17.4	18	10	1,000,000	0	0.0	0.0
C+ / 6.7	9.6	1.45	3.12	511	1	67	28	4	13	47.8	-17.7	12	10	1,000	0	0.0	0.0
C+ / 6.6	9.7	1.47	3.13	301	1	67	28	4	13	49.6	-17.5	13	10	1,000	0	0.0	0.0
C+ / 6.6	9.8	1.48	3.14	6	1	67	28	4	13	49.8	-17.3	13	10	1,000	0	0.0	0.0
B- / 7.4	9.8	1.48	3.14	N/A	1	67	28	4	13	53.0	-17.4	16	10	1,000,000	0	0.0	0.0
C- / 3.5	11.7	0.65	9.90	495	5	94	0	1	43	75.3	-19.0	99	7	1,000,000	0	0.0	0.0
C / 5.3	12.6	0.91	21.01	471	2	97	0	1	28	59.0	-23.4	81	5	1,000	0	5.8	0.0
C / 5.3	12.6	0.91	20.99	13	2	97	0	1	28	60.5	-23.4	82	5	1,000,000	0	0.0	0.0
C / 5.3	12.6	0.91	20.52	34	2	97	0	1	28	55.1	-23.7	74	5	1,000	0	0.0	0.0
C+ / 6.2	12.5	0.79	8.81	1,018	6	93	0	1	26	58.6	-27.3	86	8	1,000	0	5.8	0.0
C+ / 6.2	12.4	0.79	8.84	50	6	93	0	1	26	60.0	-27.2	87	8	1,000	0	0.0	0.0
C+ / 6.2	12.4	0.79	8.46	41	6	93	0	1	26	54.7	-27.6	81	8	1,000	0	0.0	0.0
C+ / 6.9	12.5	0.79	8.84	25	6	93	0	1	26	60.0	-27.3	87	8	1,000,000	0	0.0	0.0
C+ / 6.2	13.1	0.94	24.16	13,002	1	98	0	1	17	72.1	-22.8	88	8	1,000	0	5.8	0.0
C+ / 6.2	13.1	0.94	24.19	424	1	98	0	1	17	73.6	-22.8	89	8	1,000	0	0.0	0.0
C+ / 6.2	13.1	0.94	23.55	828	1	98	0	1	17	67.9	-23.1	84	8	1,000	0	0.0	0.0
C+ / 6.2	13.1	0.94	23.93	141	1	98	0	1	17	70.7	-22.9	87	8	1,000	0	0.0	0.0
C+ / 6.9	13.0	0.94	24.15	2,249	1	98	0	1	17	73.2	-22.8	89	8	1,000	0	0.0	0.0
D- / 1.3	14.8	1.02	4.68	112	3	96	0	1	52	19.9	-21.1	45	22	1,000,000	0	0.0	0.0
C / 5.3	13.0	0.96	21.11	6,305	4	95	0	1	16	47.9	-24.5	55	16	1,000,000	0	0.0	0.0
C / 5.3	13.0	0.96	21.16	8	4	95	0	1	16	47.0	-24.5	53	16	1,000,000	0	0.0	0.0
C+ / 6.7	10.6	0.73	21.87	1,340	5	94	0	1	24	54.5	-19.8	87	8	1,000,000	0	0.0	0.0
C / 5.0	12.7	0.90	17.49	5,372	1	98	0	1	19	66.1	-20.4	85	8	1,000	0	5.8	0.0
C / 5.0	12.8	0.90	17.46	236	1	98	0	1	19	67.7	-20.3	86	8	1,000	0	0.0	0.0
C / 5.1	12.8	0.91	16.86	217	1	98	0	1	19	61.9	-20.7	79	8	1,000	0	0.0	0.0
B- / 7.0	12.8	0.90	17.45	52	1	98	0	1	19	67.1	-20.4	86	8	1,000,000	0	0.0	0.0
B- / 7.5	6.3	1.07	12.44	7	3	63	33	1	39	52.2	-12.1	37	3	1,000	0	4.0	0.0
B- / 7.4	6.2	1.06	12.38	61	3	63	33	1	39	53.4	-12.0	41	3	1,000	0	0.0	0.0
B- / 7.5	6.2	1.06	12.59	6	3	63	33	1	39	49.7	-12.3	32	3	1,000	0	0.0	0.0
B- / 7.4	6.2	1.07	12.36	2	3	63	33	1	39	54.7	-11.9	45	3	500,000	0	0.0	0.0
C+ / 6.7	10.1	1.02	13.13	3	1	98	0	1	52	89.6	-20.4	39	3	1,000	0	4.0	0.0

Fund Type	Fund Name	Ticker Symbol	Overall Investment Rating	Phone	Perfor-mance Rating/Pts	3 Mo	6 Mo	1Yr / Pct	3Yr / Pct	5Yr / Pct	Dividend Yield	Expense Ratio
	99 Pct = Best 0 Pct = Worst				PERFORMANCE Total Return % through 3/31/15 / Annualized / Incl. in Returns							
IN	TETON Westwood Equity AAA	WESWX	B	(800) 422-3554	B- / 7.2	1.31	6.64	10.36 /76	14.65 /72	11.86 /60	0.38	1.59
IN	TETON Westwood Equity C	WEQCX	C+	(800) 422-3554	C+ / 6.6	1.20	6.27	9.51 /72	13.82 /66	11.03 /53	0.00	2.34
IN	TETON Westwood Equity I	WEEIX	B	(800) 422-3554	B- / 7.4	1.39	6.78	10.59 /77	14.88 /74	12.09 /61	0.64	1.34
IN	TETON Westwood Income A	WEIAX	C	(800) 422-3554	C- / 4.0	0.72	0.48	6.79 /53	11.17 /47	10.36 /47	0.14	2.67
IN	TETON Westwood Income AAA	WESRX	C+	(800) 422-3554	C / 4.8	0.81	0.56	7.08 /56	11.44 /49	10.63 /50	0.30	2.42
IN	TETON Westwood Income C	WEICX	C	(800) 422-3554	C / 4.3	0.62	0.24	6.35 /50	10.63 /43	9.81 /43	0.01	3.17
IN	TETON Westwood Income I	WESIX	C+	(800) 422-3554	C / 4.9	0.79	0.70	7.36 /58	11.73 /51	10.91 /52	0.48	2.17
SC	TETON Westwood Mighty Mites A	WMMAX	C+	(800) 422-3554	C+ / 6.2	1.31	8.48	1.56 /20	15.31 /77	13.42 /72	0.00	1.68
SC	TETON Westwood Mighty Mites AAA	WEMMX	B	(800) 422-3554	B- / 7.1	1.36	8.58	1.81 /21	15.61 /80	13.69 /75	0.00	1.43
SC	TETON Westwood Mighty Mites C	WMMCX	C+	(800) 422-3554	C+ / 6.5	1.12	8.19	1.02 /18	14.72 /73	12.83 /67	0.00	2.18
SC	TETON Westwood Mighty Mites I	WEIMX	B	(800) 422-3554	B- / 7.4	1.39	8.75	2.08 /22	15.89 /82	13.97 /77	0.00	1.18
SC	TETON Westwood Sm Cap Equity A	WWSAX	D	(800) 422-3554	C- / 3.4	1.96	6.83	0.85 /18	10.30 /41	10.62 /50	0.00	1.82
SC	TETON Westwood Sm Cap Equity	WESCX	D	(800) 422-3554	C- / 4.2	2.01	6.97	1.06 /19	10.57 /43	10.87 /52	0.00	1.57
SC	TETON Westwood Sm Cap Equity C	WWSCX	D	(800) 422-3554	C- / 3.7	1.79	6.55	0.28 /16	9.75 /38	10.05 /45	0.00	2.32
SC	TETON Westwood Sm Cap Equity I	WWSIX	D+	(800) 422-3554	C / 4.4	2.07	7.11	1.33 /19	10.87 /45	11.16 /54	0.00	1.32
IN	TFS Hedged Futures	TFSHX	C-	(800) 534-2001	E / 0.3	0.51	-0.50	-2.18 /10	-2.43 / 3	--	0.00	2.24
IN	TFS Market Neutral	TFSMX	C-	(800) 534-2001	D / 1.8	2.50	5.31	8.82 /68	4.08 /10	4.08 / 9	0.00	8.40
SC	TFS Small Cap	TFSSX	C+	(800) 534-2001	A+ / 9.7	5.08	15.89	9.97 /74	19.74 /98	16.70 /95	0.00	1.58
FO	Third Avenue International Val Inst	TAVIX	E	(800) 443-1021	E / 0.4	-3.16	-5.38	-14.35 / 2	2.57 / 7	3.10 / 6	7.54	1.44
FO	Third Avenue International Val Inv	TVIVX	E	(800) 443-1021	E / 0.4	-3.21	-5.49	-14.55 / 2	2.32 / 7	2.86 / 6	6.96	1.69
RE	Third Avenue Real Estate Value Inst	TAREX	A	(800) 443-1021	B / 8.1	3.05	7.99	10.30 /76	16.11 /84	13.09 /69	1.54	1.08
RE	Third Avenue Real Estate Value Inv	TVRVX	A-	(800) 443-1021	B / 7.9	2.97	7.88	10.02 /74	15.83 /82	12.83 /67	1.34	1.33
GL	Third Avenue Small-Cap Value Inst	TASCX	C-	(800) 443-1021	B- / 7.0	3.83	10.82	6.61 /52	14.60 /72	12.12 /61	0.00	1.12
GL	Third Avenue Small-Cap Value Inv	TVSVX	C-	(800) 443-1021	C+ / 6.8	3.76	10.69	6.35 /50	14.32 /69	11.87 /60	0.00	1.37
GR	Third Avenue Value Inst	TAVFX	C	(800) 443-1021	C / 4.7	0.44	0.57	4.45 /35	12.06 /53	7.20 /24	3.88	1.10
GR	Third Avenue Value Inv	TVFVX	C	(800) 443-1021	C / 4.5	0.39	0.46	4.20 /33	11.78 /51	6.96 /23	3.60	1.35
GR	Third Avenue Value Portfolio		C	(800) 443-1021	C / 4.7	0.48	0.48	4.06 /32	11.84 /51	6.98 /23	3.01	1.20
MC	Thomas White American Opps	TWAOX	B	(800) 811-0535	B / 7.7	2.80	9.87	13.15 /87	15.20 /76	14.05 /78	0.36	1.24
EM	Thomas White Emerging Markets A	TWIAX	D-	(800) 811-0535	E / 0.3	2.08	-4.16	-0.58 /14	-1.08 / 3	--	0.69	1.72
EM	Thomas White Emerging Markets C	TWICX	D-	(800) 811-0535	E / 0.3	1.89	-4.40	-0.83 /14	-1.49 / 3	--	1.04	2.26
EM	Thomas White Emerging Markets I	TWIIX	D-	(800) 811-0535	E / 0.4	2.16	-3.94	-0.10 /15	-0.62 / 4	--	1.12	1.26
EM	Thomas White Emerging Markets Inv	TWEMX	E	(800) 811-0535	E / 0.4	2.17	-3.98	-0.32 /15	-0.81 / 4	--	1.09	1.35
FO	Thomas White International A	TWWAX	D-	(800) 811-0535	E+ / 0.6	3.75	-1.71	-5.24 / 5	4.39 /11	3.80 / 8	1.25	1.41
FO	Thomas White International C	TWWCX	D-	(800) 811-0535	E+ / 0.7	3.50	-1.96	-5.76 / 5	3.76 /10	3.11 / 6	0.66	2.05
FO	Thomas White International I	TWWIX	D-	(800) 811-0535	E+ / 0.9	3.79	-1.53	-4.85 / 6	4.77 /12	4.13 / 9	1.69	1.05
FO	Thomas White International Investor	TWWDX	E	(800) 811-0535	E+ / 0.9	3.74	-1.69	-5.11 / 5	4.52 /12	3.98 / 8	1.44	1.27
GR	Thompson LargeCap	THPGX	B	(800) 999-0887	B / 7.6	-1.08	4.56	9.37 /71	15.92 /83	12.97 /68	0.53	1.22
MC	Thompson MidCap Fund	THPMX	B	(800) 999-0887	B+ / 8.3	3.19	8.18	9.07 /70	16.20 /85	14.54 /83	0.00	1.63
SC	Thomson Hrstmnn and Brynt MicCp	THBIX	C-	(855) 842-3863	C / 5.1	-0.87	4.15	-5.67 / 5	14.43 /70	--	0.00	1.80
SC	Thomson Hrstmnn and Brynt MicCp	THBVX	C-	(855) 842-3863	C / 4.8	-0.95	3.89	-6.10 / 4	13.96 /67	--	0.00	2.31
GR	Thornburg Core Growth A	THCGX	C	(800) 847-0200	C+ / 6.3	3.58	7.11	6.23 /48	14.84 /74	14.48 /82	0.00	1.40
GR	Thornburg Core Growth C	TCGCX	C	(800) 847-0200	C+ / 6.5	3.39	6.71	5.42 /42	13.99 /67	13.64 /74	0.00	2.14
GR	Thornburg Core Growth I	THIGX	C+	(800) 847-0200	B- / 7.5	3.67	7.31	6.66 /52	15.34 /78	15.01 /87	0.00	1.03
GR	Thornburg Core Growth R3	THCRX	C+	(800) 847-0200	B- / 7.0	3.56	7.05	6.12 /48	14.74 /73	14.43 /82	0.00	1.80
GR	Thornburg Core Growth R4	TCGRX	C+	(800) 847-0200	B- / 7.1	3.57	7.12	6.20 /48	14.86 /74	14.54 /83	0.00	1.77
GR	Thornburg Core Growth R5	THGRX	C+	(800) 847-0200	B- / 7.5	3.67	7.32	6.67 /52	15.35 /78	15.02 /87	0.00	1.28
EM	Thornburg Developing World A	THDAX	E+	(800) 847-0200	E+ / 0.7	-2.15	-4.46	-4.77 / 6	4.64 /12	7.10 /24	0.00	1.45
EM	Thornburg Developing World C	THDCX	E+	(800) 847-0200	E+ / 0.7	-2.28	-4.83	-5.45 / 5	3.85 /10	6.34 /19	0.00	2.23
EM	Thornburg Developing World I	THDIX	E+	(800) 847-0200	D- / 1.0	-2.06	-4.30	-4.39 / 6	5.13 /14	7.65 /28	0.38	1.09
EM	Thornburg Developing World R6	TDWRX	U	(800) 847-0200	U /	-2.00	-4.23	-4.26 / 7	--	--	0.47	1.10
GL	Thornburg Globl Opportunities A	THOAX	A	(800) 847-0200	A+ / 9.8	6.66	13.31	21.60 /97	20.32 /98	13.93 /77	0.11	1.41
GL	Thornburg Globl Opportunities C	THOCX	A	(800) 847-0200	A+ / 9.8	6.41	12.83	20.62 /97	19.37 /97	13.06 /69	0.00	2.17

● Denotes fund is closed to new investors
* Denotes fund is included in Section II

Risk Rating/Pts	Standard Deviation	Beta	NAV As of 3/31/15	Total $(Mil)	Cash %	Stocks %	Bonds %	Other %	Portfolio Turnover Ratio	Last Bull Market Return	Last Bear Market Return	Manager Quality Pct	Manager Tenure (Years)	Initial Purch. $	Additional Purch. $	Front End Load	Back End Load
C+ / 6.7	10.1	1.02	13.15	60	1	98	0	1	52	91.0	-20.3	43	3	1,000	0	0.0	0.0
C+ / 6.7	10.0	1.02	12.66	1	1	98	0	1	52	86.3	-20.5	34	3	1,000	0	0.0	0.0
C+ / 6.6	10.0	1.02	13.12	4	1	98	0	1	52	92.2	-20.2	47	3	500,000	0	0.0	0.0
B- / 7.4	9.6	0.94	12.22	1	2	93	3	2	31	62.9	-12.6	20	N/A	1,000	0	4.0	0.0
B- / 7.4	9.6	0.94	11.83	6	2	93	3	2	31	64.1	-12.6	22	N/A	1,000	0	0.0	0.0
B- / 7.4	9.6	0.94	13.07	1	2	93	3	2	31	60.1	-12.8	16	N/A	1,000	0	0.0	0.0
B- / 7.4	9.6	0.94	11.85	N/A	2	93	3	2	31	65.6	-12.5	25	N/A	500,000	0	0.0	0.0
C+ / 6.2	11.9	0.84	23.91	184	0	75	23	2	14	81.6	-19.3	81	17	10,000	0	4.0	0.0
C+ / 6.3	11.8	0.84	24.54	344	0	75	23	2	14	83.1	-19.3	83	17	10,000	0	0.0	0.0
C+ / 6.1	11.9	0.84	21.67	223	0	75	23	2	14	78.5	-19.5	78	17	10,000	0	0.0	0.0
C+ / 6.3	11.8	0.84	24.86	595	0	75	23	2	14	84.6	-19.2	85	17	500,000	0	0.0	0.0
C / 4.7	14.7	1.04	19.79	4	0	98	1	1	52	73.7	-28.9	7	7	1,000	0	4.0	0.0
C / 4.8	14.7	1.04	20.32	13	0	98	1	1	52	75.1	-28.8	7	7	1,000	0	0.0	0.0
C / 4.6	14.7	1.04	18.15	4	0	98	1	1	52	70.7	-29.0	6	7	1,000	0	0.0	0.0
C / 4.8	14.7	1.04	20.70	18	0	98	1	1	52	76.8	-28.8	8	7	500,000	0	0.0	0.0
B+ / 9.5	5.7	0.22	9.85	17	77	0	22	1	0	N/A	N/A	7	4	5,000	100	0.0	0.0
B / 8.4	4.4	0.16	15.60	743	71	22	5	2	669	22.0	-10.4	81	11	5,000	100	0.0	0.0
D+ / 2.5	13.1	0.96	14.28	111	2	97	0	1	579	119.8	-26.4	90	9	5,000	100	0.0	0.0
C- / 3.9	13.0	0.89	15.93	255	6	93	0	1	22	28.1	-22.8	8	14	100,000	0	0.0	2.0
C- / 4.0	13.0	0.89	15.96	8	6	93	0	1	22	27.1	-22.8	7	14	2,500	1,000	0.0	2.0
B- / 7.3	9.2	0.52	32.43	3,073	21	75	2	2	14	98.0	-22.5	97	17	100,000	0	0.0	1.0
B- / 7.3	9.2	0.52	32.25	424	21	75	2	2	14	96.4	-22.5	97	17	2,500	1,000	0.0	1.0
C- / 3.4	12.0	0.61	23.85	466	1	98	0	1	40	76.3	-19.6	97	2	100,000	0	0.0	1.0
C- / 3.3	12.0	0.61	23.73	11	1	98	0	1	40	75.0	-19.7	97	2	2,500	1,000	0.0	1.0
C+ / 6.7	10.6	0.93	57.01	1,942	4	95	0	1	31	67.4	-26.9	31	2	100,000	0	0.0	1.0
C+ / 6.7	10.6	0.93	56.96	34	4	95	0	1	31	66.1	-27.0	28	2	2,500	1,000	0.0	1.0
C+ / 6.8	10.7	0.93	16.88	135	8	91	0	1	23	67.0	-27.6	29	2	0	0	0.0	0.0
C+ / 5.9	10.5	0.92	16.86	36	1	98	0	1	32	90.6	-19.7	63	16	2,500	100	0.0	2.0
C+ / 6.8	14.3	0.99	10.81	N/A	2	97	0	1	64	20.1	-27.2	41	5	2,500	100	5.8	2.0
C+ / 6.8	14.2	0.99	10.77	N/A	2	97	0	1	64	18.2	-27.4	35	5	2,500	100	0.0	2.0
C+ / 6.8	14.3	0.99	10.90	76	2	97	0	1	64	21.9	-27.1	48	5	1,000,000	100	0.0	2.0
C / 5.1	14.3	0.99	10.85	5	2	97	0	1	64	21.2	-27.1	45	5	2,500	100	0.0	2.0
B- / 7.0	12.5	0.92	16.62	1	2	97	0	1	62	37.8	-23.9	16	21	2,500	100	5.8	2.0
B- / 7.0	12.5	0.92	16.56	N/A	2	97	0	1	62	34.9	-24.2	12	21	2,500	100	0.0	2.0
B- / 7.0	12.5	0.92	16.70	386	2	97	0	1	62	39.5	-23.9	18	21	1,000,000	100	0.0	2.0
C / 4.6	12.5	0.92	16.66	336	2	97	0	1	62	38.5	-23.9	16	21	2,500	100	0.0	2.0
C+ / 6.4	11.8	1.16	53.08	125	0	99	0	1	27	106.3	-21.6	31	23	1,000	100	0.0	0.0
C / 5.3	12.0	1.02	13.25	42	0	99	0	1	34	103.2	-23.0	51	7	1,000	100	0.0	0.0
C+ / 5.7	14.3	0.98	13.73	71	2	97	0	1	57	N/A	N/A	48	3	100,000	2,500	0.0	2.0
C+ / 5.7	14.3	0.97	13.58	4	2	97	0	1	57	N/A	N/A	43	3	100	0	0.0	2.0
C / 5.2	12.3	1.01	28.32	272	2	91	5	2	101	112.5	-21.0	48	3	5,000	100	4.5	0.0
C / 5.2	12.3	1.01	25.28	203	2	91	5	2	101	107.0	-21.2	37	3	5,000	100	0.0	0.0
C / 5.3	12.3	1.01	29.94	264	2	91	5	2	101	115.6	-20.8	55	3	2,500,000	100	0.0	0.0
C / 5.2	12.3	1.01	28.25	86	2	91	5	2	101	112.0	-21.0	47	3	0	0	0.0	0.0
C / 5.3	12.3	1.01	28.43	11	2	91	5	2	101	112.6	-20.9	48	3	0	0	0.0	0.0
C / 5.3	12.3	1.01	29.91	58	2	91	5	2	101	115.7	-20.9	55	3	0	0	0.0	0.0
C / 5.5	13.2	0.84	17.78	365	1	91	6	2	61	45.0	-25.3	91	N/A	5,000	100	4.5	0.0
C / 5.5	13.2	0.84	17.16	216	1	91	6	2	61	41.3	-25.6	89	N/A	5,000	100	0.0	0.0
C / 5.5	13.2	0.84	18.10	2,177	1	91	6	2	61	47.5	-25.2	92	N/A	2,500,000	100	0.0	0.0
U /	N/A	N/A	18.10	31	1	91	6	2	61	N/A	N/A	N/A	N/A	0	0	0.0	0.0
C+ / 5.8	10.9	0.67	26.90	381	3	87	9	1	60	110.8	-23.6	99	9	5,000	100	4.5	0.0
C+ / 5.8	10.8	0.66	26.21	218	3	87	9	1	60	105.2	-23.8	99	9	5,000	100	0.0	0.0

					PERFORMANCE						Incl. in Returns	
99 Pct = Best						Total Return % through 3/31/15						
0 Pct = Worst			Overall		Perfor-				Annualized		Dividend	Expense
Fund Type	Fund Name	Ticker Symbol	Investment Rating	Phone	mance Rating/Pts	3 Mo	6 Mo	1Yr / Pct	3Yr / Pct	5Yr / Pct	Yield	Ratio
GL	Thornburg Globl Opportunities Inst	THOIX	A	(800) 847-0200	A+ / 9.8	6.72	13.47	22.04 /97	20.84 /98	14.46 /82	0.38	1.08
GL	Thornburg Globl Opportunities R3	THORX	A	(800) 847-0200	A+ / 9.8	6.60	13.21	21.40 /97	20.21 /98	13.87 /77	0.00	2.59
GL	Thornburg Globl Opportunities R4	THOVX	A	(800) 847-0200	A+ / 9.8	6.59	13.24	21.50 /97	20.34 /98	13.98 /78	0.13	2.23
GL	Thornburg Globl Opportunities R5	THOFX	A	(800) 847-0200	A+ / 9.8	6.72	13.46	22.01 /97	20.82 /98	14.44 /82	0.37	1.10
BA	Thornburg Income Builder A	TIBAX	C	(800) 847-0200	C- / 3.4	3.44	2.10	4.85 /37	10.09 /40	8.96 /36	4.15	1.33
BA	Thornburg Income Builder C	TIBCX	C	(800) 847-0200	C- / 3.6	3.25	1.74	4.11 /33	9.31 /35	8.21 /31	3.64	2.08
BA	Thornburg Income Builder I	TIBIX	C+	(800) 847-0200	C / 4.3	3.50	2.25	5.17 /40	10.44 /42	9.32 /39	4.67	1.01
BA	Thornburg Income Builder R3	TIBRX	C	(800) 847-0200	C- / 3.9	3.35	1.98	4.57 /36	9.76 /38	8.64 /34	4.03	1.70
BA	Thornburg Income Builder R4	TIBGX	C	(800) 847-0200	C- / 4.0	3.38	2.00	4.66 /36	9.90 /39	8.77 /35	4.17	1.55
BA	Thornburg Income Builder R5	TIBMX	C+	(800) 847-0200	C- / 4.2	3.47	2.19	5.05 /39	10.31 /41	9.19 /38	4.55	1.25
FO	Thornburg International Growth A	TIGAX	D-	(800) 847-0200	D+ / 2.7	4.77	4.11	-3.19 / 8	9.55 /36	12.12 /61	0.00	1.33
FO	Thornburg International Growth C	TIGCX	D-	(800) 847-0200	D+ / 2.9	4.61	3.75	-3.86 / 7	8.73 /31	11.27 /55	0.00	2.09
FO	Thornburg International Growth I	TINGX	D	(800) 847-0200	C- / 3.7	4.94	4.31	-2.76 / 9	10.01 /39	12.65 /65	0.36	0.98
FO	Thornburg International Growth R3	TIGVX	D-	(800) 847-0200	C- / 3.3	4.75	4.08	-3.26 / 8	9.45 /36	12.07 /61	0.00	1.86
FO	Thornburg International Growth R4	TINVX	D-	(800) 847-0200	C- / 3.4	4.86	4.13	-3.16 / 8	9.58 /37	12.20 /62	0.00	1.63
FO	Thornburg International Growth R5	TINFX	D	(800) 847-0200	C- / 3.7	4.92	4.35	-2.78 / 9	9.99 /39	12.64 /65	0.33	1.18
FO	Thornburg International Value A	TGVAX	D-	(800) 847-0200	D / 2.1	7.45	5.53	6.15 /48	6.59 /19	5.44 /14	0.79	1.26
FO	● Thornburg International Value B	THGBX	D-	(800) 847-0200	D / 2.2	7.22	5.02	5.17 /40	5.67 /15	4.55 /10	0.24	2.13
FO	Thornburg International Value C	THGCX	D-	(800) 847-0200	D+ / 2.3	7.24	5.11	5.35 /41	5.80 /16	4.66 /11	0.26	1.99
FO	Thornburg International Value Inst	TGVIX	D	(800) 847-0200	C- / 3.0	7.55	5.72	6.49 /51	7.00 /21	5.85 /16	1.35	0.88
FO	Thornburg International Value R3	TGVRX	D	(800) 847-0200	D+ / 2.6	7.37	5.41	5.93 /46	6.38 /18	5.24 /13	0.66	1.61
FO	Thornburg International Value R4	THVRX	D	(800) 847-0200	D+ / 2.8	7.46	5.52	6.13 /48	6.60 /19	5.46 /14	0.91	1.49
FO	Thornburg International Value R5	TIVRX	D	(800) 847-0200	D+ / 2.9	7.52	5.66	6.42 /50	6.89 /21	5.74 /15	1.22	1.12
FO	Thornburg International Value R6	TGIRX	U	(800) 847-0200	U /	7.57	5.78	6.70 /53	--	--	1.59	0.73
GI	Thornburg Value A	TVAFX	C+	(800) 847-0200	B- / 7.2	3.47	7.90	12.53 /85	15.32 /77	9.93 /44	0.40	1.37
GI	● Thornburg Value B	TVBFX	C+	(800) 847-0200	B- / 7.2	3.21	7.33	11.43 /80	14.21 /69	8.88 /36	0.00	2.55
GI	Thornburg Value C	TVCFX	C+	(800) 847-0200	B- / 7.4	3.29	7.50	11.70 /81	14.44 /70	9.09 /37	0.00	2.14
GI	Thornburg Value Fund R4	TVIRX	B-	(800) 847-0200	B / 8.2	3.50	7.95	12.67 /85	15.47 /79	10.04 /45	0.53	1.69
GI	Thornburg Value Inst	TVIFX	B-	(800) 847-0200	B+ / 8.4	3.56	8.09	12.95 /86	15.78 /82	10.36 /47	0.78	1.06
GI	Thornburg Value R3	TVRFX	B-	(800) 847-0200	B / 8.1	3.47	7.89	12.55 /85	15.35 /78	9.92 /44	0.45	1.77
GI	Thornburg Value R5	TVRRX	B-	(800) 847-0200	B+ / 8.4	3.57	8.09	12.97 /86	15.77 /81	10.32 /47	0.78	1.42
AA	Thrivent Aggressive Allocation A	TAAAX	C-	(800) 847-4836	C / 4.6	3.13	5.22	7.59 /60	12.06 /53	10.56 /49	0.46	1.31
AA	Thrivent Aggressive Allocation Inst	TAAIX	C	(800) 847-4836	C+ / 5.8	3.18	5.36	7.93 /62	12.48 /56	10.98 /53	0.83	0.91
BA	Thrivent Balanced Income Plus A	AABFX	D+	(800) 847-4836	C- / 3.4	2.84	4.75	6.87 /54	10.03 /39	9.49 /40	1.81	1.11
BA	Thrivent Balanced Income Plus Inst	IBBFX	C-	(800) 847-4836	C / 4.6	2.95	4.95	7.20 /57	10.46 /42	9.97 /44	2.28	1.12
IN	Thrivent Growth and Inc Plus A	TEIAX	U	(800) 847-4836	U /	2.65	4.08	4.55 /35	--	--	1.67	1.53
GR	Thrivent Large Cap Growth A	AAAGX	B+	(800) 847-4836	B- / 7.5	4.16	5.67	13.88 /89	16.11 /84	12.46 /64	0.00	1.41
GR	Thrivent Large Cap Growth Inst	THLCX	A	(800) 847-4836	B+ / 8.8	4.19	5.83	14.24 /90	16.57 /87	12.89 /67	0.00	0.82
GR	Thrivent Large Cap Stock A	AALGX	C-	(800) 847-4836	C / 4.9	4.19	4.23	6.99 /55	12.68 /57	10.09 /45	0.80	1.05
GR	Thrivent Large Cap Stock Inst	IILGX	C+	(800) 847-4836	C+ / 6.1	4.33	4.44	7.45 /59	13.17 /61	10.61 /50	1.21	0.61
GR	Thrivent Large Cap Value A	AAUTX	C+	(800) 847-4836	C / 5.5	0.20	3.76	6.06 /47	14.40 /70	11.54 /57	0.86	0.98
GR	Thrivent Large Cap Value Inst	TLVIX	B-	(800) 847-4836	C+ / 6.8	0.30	4.00	6.56 /51	14.93 /74	12.09 /61	1.30	0.52
MC	Thrivent Mid Cap Growth A	LBMGX	C+	(800) 847-4836	B- / 7.4	5.82	13.97	15.58 /93	13.94 /67	13.34 /71	0.00	1.00
MC	Thrivent Mid Cap Growth Inst	LBMIX	B	(800) 847-4836	B+ / 8.8	5.98	14.27	16.16 /93	14.47 /71	13.91 /77	0.00	0.52
MC	Thrivent Mid Cap Stock A	AASCX	C+	(800) 847-4836	B- / 7.4	2.77	7.92	9.26 /71	16.57 /87	13.93 /77	0.18	1.15
MC	Thrivent Mid Cap Stock Inst	TMSIX	B+	(800) 847-4836	B+ / 8.7	2.83	8.11	9.65 /73	17.05 /90	14.46 /82	0.50	0.71
AA	Thrivent Moderate Aggr Alloc A	TMAAX	C-	(800) 847-4836	C- / 3.8	2.81	4.79	6.69 /53	10.80 /44	9.59 /41	0.98	1.21
AA	Thrivent Moderate Aggr Alloc Inst	TMAFX	C	(800) 847-4836	C / 5.0	2.87	4.96	7.01 /55	11.20 /47	9.99 /44	1.36	0.84
AA	Thrivent Moderate Allocation A	THMAX	C-	(800) 847-4836	D+ / 2.8	2.46	4.29	6.06 /47	9.02 /33	8.34 /32	1.25	1.11
AA	Thrivent Moderate Allocation Inst	TMAIX	C	(800) 847-4836	C- / 3.9	2.54	4.45	6.40 /50	9.39 /36	8.71 /35	1.65	0.77
AA	Thrivent Moderate Consv Alloc A	TCAAX	C-	(800) 847-4836	D / 1.7	2.06	3.42	5.12 /40	6.90 /21	6.56 /20	1.57	1.05
AA	Thrivent Moderate Consv Alloc Inst	TCAIX	C	(800) 847-4836	D+ / 2.7	2.14	3.58	5.45 /42	7.22 /23	6.89 /22	1.98	0.72

RISK			NET ASSETS		ASSET					BULL / BEAR		FUND MANAGER		MINIMUMS		LOADS	
	3 Year		NAV						Portfolio	Last Bull	Last Bear	Manager	Manager	Initial	Additional	Front	Back
Risk	Standard		As of	Total	Cash	Stocks	Bonds	Other	Turnover	Market	Market	Quality	Tenure	Purch.	Purch.	End	End
Rating/Pts	Deviation	Beta	3/31/15	$(Mil)	%	%	%	%	Ratio	Return	Return	Pct	(Years)	$	$	Load	Load
C+ / 5.8	10.8	0.66	26.98	958	3	87	9	1	60	114.0	-23.4	99	9	2,500,000	100	0.0	0.0
C+ / 5.8	10.8	0.66	26.66	4	3	87	9	1	60	110.3	-23.6	99	9	0	0	0.0	0.0
C+ / 5.8	10.8	0.66	26.69	10	3	87	9	1	60	111.0	-23.6	99	9	0	0	0.0	0.0
C+ / 5.8	10.8	0.66	27.00	100	3	87	9	1	60	114.0	-23.4	99	9	0	0	0.0	0.0
B- / 7.8	8.3	1.26	21.40	4,718	4	87	8	1	39	49.9	-12.2	21	13	5,000	100	4.5	0.0
B- / 7.8	8.3	1.26	21.39	6,471	4	87	8	1	39	46.4	-12.5	16	13	5,000	100	0.0	0.0
B- / 7.8	8.3	1.26	21.55	7,955	4	87	8	1	39	51.7	-12.1	25	13	2,500,000	100	0.0	0.0
B- / 7.8	8.3	1.26	21.40	86	4	87	8	1	39	48.5	-12.4	19	13	0	0	0.0	0.0
B- / 7.8	8.3	1.26	21.44	44	4	87	8	1	39	49.1	-12.4	20	13	0	0	0.0	0.0
B- / 7.8	8.3	1.25	21.54	79	4	87	8	1	39	50.9	-12.2	24	13	0	0	0.0	0.0
C / 4.5	12.8	0.79	18.88	258	2	95	2	1	106	55.5	-12.4	84	3	5,000	100	4.5	0.0
C / 4.4	12.8	0.79	18.14	120	2	95	2	1	106	51.5	-12.7	79	3	5,000	100	0.0	0.0
C / 4.5	12.8	0.79	19.34	1,072	2	95	2	1	106	57.6	-12.2	86	3	2,500,000	100	0.0	0.0
C / 4.5	12.8	0.79	18.76	23	2	95	2	1	106	54.9	-12.4	83	3	0	0	0.0	0.0
C / 4.5	12.8	0.79	18.78	40	2	95	2	1	106	55.6	-12.3	84	3	0	0	0.0	0.0
C / 4.5	12.8	0.79	19.39	67	2	95	2	1	106	57.6	-12.2	86	3	0	0	0.0	0.0
C+ / 5.6	11.8	0.83	28.84	1,544	4	92	2	2	37	40.3	-24.3	49	17	5,000	100	4.5	0.0
C / 5.4	11.8	0.83	26.45	11	4	92	2	2	37	36.3	-24.5	37	17	5,000	100	0.0	0.0
C / 5.4	11.8	0.83	26.66	772	4	92	2	2	37	36.8	-24.5	38	17	5,000	100	0.0	0.0
C+ / 5.6	11.8	0.83	29.48	6,370	4	92	2	2	37	42.1	-24.2	56	17	2,500,000	100	0.0	0.0
C+ / 5.6	11.8	0.83	28.83	597	4	92	2	2	37	39.4	-24.3	47	17	0	0	0.0	0.0
C / 5.5	11.8	0.83	28.67	448	4	92	2	2	37	40.4	-24.2	50	17	0	0	0.0	0.0
C+ / 5.6	11.8	0.83	29.45	916	4	92	2	2	37	41.7	-24.2	54	17	0	0	0.0	0.0
U /	N/A	N/A	29.41	494	4	92	2	2	37	N/A	N/A	N/A	17	0	0	0.0	0.0
C / 4.9	13.2	1.23	51.87	409	5	89	4	2	72	89.3	-25.1	15	9	5,000	100	4.5	0.0
C / 4.9	13.2	1.23	47.28	3	5	89	4	2	72	83.1	-25.4	10	9	5,000	100	0.0	0.0
C / 4.9	13.2	1.23	48.32	184	5	89	4	2	72	84.4	-25.4	10	9	5,000	100	0.0	0.0
C / 4.9	13.2	1.23	52.04	11	5	89	4	2	72	90.1	-25.1	16	9	0	0	0.0	0.0
C / 5.0	13.2	1.23	53.20	301	5	89	4	2	72	91.9	-25.0	18	9	2,500,000	100	0.0	0.0
C / 4.9	13.2	1.23	51.54	71	5	89	4	2	72	89.5	-25.1	15	9	0	0	0.0	0.0
C / 5.0	13.2	1.23	53.12	28	5	89	4	2	72	91.8	-25.0	18	9	0	0	0.0	0.0
C+ / 5.6	9.5	1.60	14.19	727	2	81	16	1	51	72.1	-19.9	9	N/A	2,000	50	5.5	0.0
C / 5.5	9.5	1.61	14.29	116	2	81	16	1	51	74.4	-19.8	11	N/A	50,000	0	0.0	0.0
C+ / 6.1	6.8	1.11	13.13	233	4	48	46	2	124	58.0	-15.4	38	10	2,000	50	5.5	0.0
C+ / 6.0	6.8	1.12	13.10	56	4	48	46	2	124	60.3	-15.2	42	10	50,000	0	0.0	0.0
U /	N/A	N/A	10.25	77	3	68	28	1	162	N/A	N/A	N/A	7	2,000	50	5.5	0.0
C+ / 6.7	10.9	1.04	8.51	198	6	92	0	2	45	102.8	-20.1	59	4	2,000	50	5.5	0.0
C+ / 6.7	10.9	1.04	9.20	452	6	92	0	2	45	105.5	-20.0	64	4	50,000	0	0.0	0.0
C+ / 5.8	10.0	1.00	26.08	1,607	10	87	2	1	65	82.1	-20.8	26	4	2,000	50	5.5	0.0
C+ / 5.7	10.0	0.99	26.27	180	10	87	2	1	65	84.9	-20.7	31	4	50,000	0	0.0	0.0
B- / 7.0	10.5	1.05	20.16	242	4	95	0	1	24	92.3	-21.6	34	2	2,000	50	5.5	0.0
B- / 7.0	10.5	1.05	20.27	583	4	95	0	1	24	95.3	-21.4	40	2	50,000	0	0.0	0.0
C / 4.6	11.8	0.99	20.55	293	4	95	0	1	45	80.4	-20.2	30	12	2,000	50	5.5	0.0
C / 5.1	11.8	0.99	24.47	161	4	95	0	1	45	83.2	-20.0	36	12	50,000	0	0.0	0.0
C / 5.4	11.6	1.02	21.90	694	5	94	0	1	27	99.8	-25.9	58	11	2,000	50	5.5	0.0
C / 5.5	11.6	1.02	23.95	277	5	94	0	1	27	102.7	-25.8	64	11	50,000	0	0.0	0.0
C+ / 6.7	7.9	1.34	13.88	1,830	1	66	32	1	61	62.1	-17.1	20	10	2,000	50	5.5	0.0
C+ / 6.6	7.8	1.33	13.97	125	1	66	32	1	61	64.2	-17.0	24	10	50,000	0	0.0	0.0
B- / 7.6	5.9	1.01	13.09	1,737	0	50	49	1	73	48.9	-13.2	40	10	2,000	50	5.5	0.0
B- / 7.6	5.9	1.01	13.12	100	0	50	49	1	73	50.6	-13.0	45	10	50,000	0	0.0	0.0
B / 8.2	4.1	0.68	12.08	742	0	32	67	1	140	34.9	-9.2	62	10	2,000	50	5.5	0.0
B / 8.2	4.1	0.67	12.11	34	0	32	67	1	140	36.3	-9.0	68	10	50,000	0	0.0	0.0

					PERFORMANCE							
99 Pct = Best *0 Pct = Worst*					Perfor- mance Rating/Pts	Total Return % through 3/31/15					Incl. in Returns	
			Ticker	Overall Investment					Annualized		Dividend	Expense
Fund Type	Fund Name		Symbol	Rating	Phone	3 Mo	6 Mo	1Yr / Pct	3Yr / Pct	5Yr / Pct	Yield	Ratio
RE	Thrivent Natural Resources A		TREFX	E-	(800) 847-4836	E- / 0.1	-1.86	-21.25	-22.02 / 1	-6.38 / 1	-0.31 / 2	0.39	1.82
RE	Thrivent Natural Resources Inst		TREIX	E-	(800) 847-4836	E- / 0.1	-1.73	-21.10	-21.71 / 1	-6.05 / 2	0.04 / 2	0.78	0.98
MC	Thrivent Partner Mid Cap Value A		TPMAX	C	(800) 847-4836	B / 7.6	1.89	7.47	11.05 /79	16.77 /89	13.86 /76	0.13	1.43
MC	Thrivent Partner Mid Cap Value I		TPMIX	B-	(800) 847-4836	B+ / 8.9	2.02	7.71	11.58 /81	17.20 /91	14.29 /80	0.44	0.90
SC	Thrivent Partner Small Cap Gr A		TPSAX	C-	(800) 847-4836	B / 7.7	7.63	16.15	11.13 /79	15.42 /78	14.20 /80	0.00	1.55
SC	Thrivent Partner Small Cap Gr I		TPGIX	C+	(800) 847-4836	B+ / 8.9	7.64	16.13	11.36 /80	15.77 /81	14.59 /83	0.00	1.04
SC	Thrivent Partner Small Cap Value A		AALVX	C-	(800) 847-4836	C / 5.3	1.14	10.99	2.50 /24	13.68 /65	12.14 /62	0.42	1.52
SC	Thrivent Partner Small Cap Value I		TPSIX	C	(800) 847-4836	C+ / 6.5	1.23	11.26	2.96 /26	14.20 /69	12.71 /66	0.76	1.04
GL	Thrivent Partner Worldwide Alloc A		TWAAX	D-	(800) 847-4836	D- / 1.2	4.39	0.92	-2.46 / 9	6.48 /19	5.77 /16	1.85	1.60
GL	Thrivent Partner Worldwide Alloc I		TWAIX	D-	(800) 847-4836	D / 1.9	4.37	1.08	-2.10 /10	6.86 /21	6.12 /17	2.40	0.98
SC	Thrivent Small Cap Stock A		AASMX	C-	(800) 847-4836	C / 5.4	3.46	11.55	7.19 /57	12.92 /59	12.12 /61	0.00	1.30
SC	Thrivent Small Cap Stock I		TSCSX	C+	(800) 847-4836	C+ / 6.7	3.60	11.87	7.72 /61	13.49 /63	12.75 /66	0.00	0.77
EM	TIAA-CREF EM Equity Idx Fund Inst		TEQLX	E	(800) 842-2252	E / 0.5	2.54	-2.26	0.12 /16	-0.05 / 4	--	2.10	0.23
EM	TIAA-CREF EM Equity Idx Fund		TEQPX	E	(800) 842-2252	E / 0.4	2.44	-2.29	-0.11 /15	-0.22 / 4	--	1.98	0.39
EM	TIAA-CREF EM Equity Idx Fund Ret		TEQSX	E	(800) 842-2252	E / 0.4	2.45	-2.38	-0.19 /15	-0.33 / 4	--	1.90	0.48
EM	TIAA-CREF EM Equity Idx Fund Rtl		TEQKX	E	(800) 842-2252	E / 0.4	2.44	-2.36	-0.27 /15	-0.46 / 4	--	1.73	0.64
EM	TIAA-CREF Emg Mkt Equity Fund		TEMLX	E	(800) 842-2252	E / 0.4	2.51	-4.21	-3.68 / 7	-0.14 / 4	--	1.28	0.95
EM	TIAA-CREF Emg Mkt Equity Fund		TEMPX	E	(800) 842-2252	E / 0.4	2.40	-4.25	-3.81 / 7	-0.30 / 4	--	1.14	1.10
EM	TIAA-CREF Emg Mkt Equity Fund		TEMSX	E	(800) 842-2252	E / 0.4	2.41	-4.28	-4.01 / 7	-0.40 / 4	--	1.04	1.20
EM	TIAA-CREF Emg Mkt Equity Fund Rtl		TEMRX	E	(800) 842-2252	E / 0.4	2.41	-4.35	-4.08 / 7	-0.52 / 4	--	0.88	1.33
GI	TIAA-CREF Enhanced LCG Idx Inst		TLIIX	B	(800) 842-2252	B / 8.0	4.18	9.14	15.76 /93	14.33 /70	14.69 /84	1.10	0.35
FO	TIAA-CREF Enhncd Intl Eq Idx Inst		TFIIX	D	(800) 842-2252	C- / 3.6	5.01	1.99	-0.62 /14	10.33 /41	7.32 /25	3.62	0.44
GR	TIAA-CREF Enhncd LgCp Val Idx Inst		TEVIX	B-	(800) 842-2252	B- / 7.4	0.49	4.81	8.67 /67	15.40 /78	12.99 /68	1.59	0.35
GR	TIAA-CREF Equity Index Inst		TIEIX	A	(800) 842-2252	B+ / 8.5	1.81	7.12	12.33 /84	16.38 /86	14.67 /84	1.78	0.05
GR	TIAA-CREF Equity Index Premier		TCEPX	A	(800) 842-2252	B+ / 8.4	1.74	7.06	12.21 /84	16.20 /85	14.49 /82	1.66	0.20
GR	TIAA-CREF Equity Index Retail		TINRX	A	(800) 842-2252	B+ / 8.3	1.71	6.97	12.01 /83	16.04 /84	14.32 /81	1.48	0.36
GR	TIAA-CREF Equity Index Retire		TIQRX	A	(800) 842-2252	B+ / 8.3	1.72	6.97	12.02 /83	16.09 /84	14.37 /81	1.53	0.30
EN	TIAA-CREF Gl Nat Res Instl		TNRIX	E+	(800) 842-2252	E- / 0.2	-2.56	-9.90	-14.50 / 2	-5.76 / 2	--	1.78	0.74
EN	TIAA-CREF Gl Nat Res Prm		TNRPX	E+	(800) 842-2252	E- / 0.2	-2.56	-9.94	-14.63 / 2	-5.92 / 2	--	1.64	0.89
EN	TIAA-CREF Gl Nat Res Ret		TNRRX	E+	(800) 842-2252	E- / 0.1	-2.67	-9.98	-14.67 / 2	-6.00 / 2	--	1.48	0.99
EN	TIAA-CREF Gl Nat Res Rtl		TNRLX	E+	(800) 842-2252	E- / 0.1	-2.56	-9.93	-14.72 / 2	-6.14 / 1	--	1.33	1.13
GI	TIAA-CREF Growth and Inc Inst		TIGRX	B+	(800) 842-2252	B+ / 8.5	2.97	7.29	13.04 /87	16.15 /84	14.75 /85	1.08	0.42
GI	TIAA-CREF Growth and Inc Premier		TRPGX	B	(800) 842-2252	B+ / 8.4	2.84	7.12	12.77 /86	15.97 /83	14.58 /83	0.94	0.57
GI	TIAA-CREF Growth and Inc Retail		TIIRX	B+	(800) 842-2252	B / 8.2	2.82	7.06	12.65 /85	15.75 /81	14.40 /81	0.57	0.74
GI	TIAA-CREF Growth and Inc Retire		TRGIX	B	(800) 842-2252	B+ / 8.3	2.86	7.05	12.67 /85	15.84 /82	14.45 /82	0.83	0.67
FO	TIAA-CREF International Opptys Inst		TIOIX	U	(800) 842-2252	U /	6.10	3.83	-1.96 /10	--	--	0.97	0.64
FO	TIAA-CREF Intl Equity Index Inst		TCIEX	D	(800) 842-2252	D+ / 2.8	5.45	1.16	-1.03 /13	9.07 /33	6.30 /19	3.74	0.06
FO	TIAA-CREF Intl Equity Index Premier		TRIPX	D	(800) 842-2252	D+ / 2.7	5.40	1.12	-1.13 /13	8.91 /32	6.15 /18	3.60	0.21
FO	TIAA-CREF Intl Equity Index Retire		TRIEX	D	(800) 842-2252	D+ / 2.7	5.33	1.02	-1.29 /12	8.79 /32	6.03 /17	3.39	0.31
FO	TIAA-CREF Intl Equity Inst		TIIEX	D	(800) 842-2252	C- / 3.7	7.26	5.45	-4.10 / 7	10.59 /43	7.54 /27	1.36	0.49
FO	TIAA-CREF Intl Equity Premier		TREPX	D	(800) 842-2252	C- / 3.6	7.27	5.40	-4.25 / 7	10.46 /42	7.39 /26	1.22	0.64
FO	TIAA-CREF Intl Equity Retail		TIERX	D	(800) 842-2252	C- / 3.5	7.22	5.33	-4.41 / 6	10.21 /41	7.20 /24	1.65	0.83
FO	TIAA-CREF Intl Equity Retire		TRERX	D	(800) 842-2252	C- / 3.6	7.29	5.42	-4.33 / 6	10.34 /41	7.29 /25	1.04	0.74
GR	TIAA-CREF Large Cap Gr Idx Inst		TILIX	A+	(800) 842-2252	B+ / 8.9	3.84	8.79	16.04 /93	16.27 /85	15.54 /90	1.32	0.06
GR	TIAA-CREF Large Cap Gr Idx Retire		TRIRX	A	(800) 842-2252	B+ / 8.7	3.72	8.64	15.71 /93	15.98 /83	15.26 /89	1.10	0.31
GR	TIAA-CREF Large Cap Gr Inst		TILGX	B+	(800) 842-2252	A / 9.5	4.32	10.03	18.36 /96	17.83 /94	15.96 /93	0.28	0.44
GR	TIAA-CREF Large Cap Gr Premier		TILPX	B+	(800) 842-2252	A / 9.5	4.33	9.95	18.12 /96	17.65 /93	15.79 /92	0.16	0.59
GR	TIAA-CREF Large Cap Gr Ret		TILRX	B+	(800) 842-2252	A / 9.5	4.27	9.93	18.06 /96	17.55 /93	15.67 /91	0.00	0.69
GR	TIAA-CREF Large Cap Gr Retail		TIRTX	B+	(800) 842-2252	A / 9.4	4.26	9.91	17.94 /95	17.41 /92	15.56 /90	0.00	0.79
GR	TIAA-CREF Large Cap Val Idx Inst		TILVX	A-	(800) 842-2252	B / 7.8	-0.74	4.15	9.24 /71	16.30 /86	13.65 /74	1.82	0.06
GR	TIAA-CREF Large Cap Val Idx Ret		TRCVX	B+	(800) 842-2252	B / 7.7	-0.78	4.09	8.98 /69	16.04 /84	13.37 /72	1.57	0.31
GR	TIAA-CREF Large Cap Val Inst		TRLIX	B+	(800) 842-2252	B / 8.0	1.34	5.28	9.00 /69	16.29 /85	12.94 /68	1.73	0.42

● Denotes fund is closed to new investors
★ Denotes fund is included in Section II

www.thestreetratings.com

Risk Rating/Pts	Standard Deviation (3 Year)	Beta	NAV As of 3/31/15	Total $(Mil)	Cash %	Stocks %	Bonds %	Other %	Portfolio Turnover Ratio	Last Bull Market Return	Last Bear Market Return	Manager Quality Pct	Manager Tenure (Years)	Initial Purch. $	Additional Purch. $	Front End Load	Back End Load
D+ / 2.6	17.3	0.41	7.93	18	1	98	0	1	36	-6.3	-16.5	1	4	2,000	50	5.5	0.0
D+ / 2.7	17.3	0.40	7.94	70	1	98	0	1	36	-5.1	-16.4	1	4	50,000	0	0.0	0.0
C- / 4.0	9.7	0.85	14.04	30	3	96	0	1	92	98.3	-22.3	85	N/A	2,000	50	5.5	0.0
C- / 4.0	9.7	0.85	14.12	158	3	96	0	1	92	100.7	-22.2	87	N/A	50,000	0	0.0	0.0
D+ / 2.9	13.7	0.96	14.96	17	3	96	0	1	438	94.2	-28.2	65	N/A	2,000	50	5.5	0.0
C- / 3.1	13.7	0.96	15.63	N/A	3	96	0	1	438	96.4	-28.1	69	N/A	50,000	0	0.0	0.0
C / 4.6	12.9	0.93	18.57	97	2	97	0	1	20	88.3	-24.4	49	11	2,000	50	5.5	0.0
C / 4.8	12.8	0.93	19.73	122	2	97	0	1	20	91.2	-24.3	56	11	50,000	0	0.0	0.0
C+ / 6.1	12.1	1.81	9.99	175	2	87	10	1	77	41.4	-20.4	2	7	2,000	50	5.5	0.0
C+ / 6.1	12.1	1.81	10.03	662	2	87	10	1	77	43.4	-20.4	2	7	50,000	0	0.0	0.0
C / 5.2	12.6	0.90	18.85	260	3	96	0	1	56	82.6	-27.6	45	2	2,000	50	5.5	0.0
C / 5.3	12.6	0.90	21.85	97	3	96	0	1	56	85.8	-27.4	53	2	50,000	0	0.0	0.0
C / 5.1	13.8	1.01	10.08	990	0	97	1	2	13	22.3	-27.3	57	5	10,000,000	1,000	0.0	2.0
C / 5.1	13.9	1.01	10.06	6	0	97	1	2	13	21.6	-27.3	54	5	5,000,000	0	0.0	2.0
C / 5.1	13.8	1.01	10.05	65	0	97	1	2	13	21.2	-27.4	52	5	0	0	0.0	2.0
C / 5.1	13.9	1.01	10.06	9	0	97	1	2	13	20.5	-27.4	50	5	2,500	100	0.0	2.0
C / 5.0	13.9	0.99	10.22	919	0	99	0	1	104	18.6	-27.3	55	5	2,000,000	1,000	0.0	2.0
C / 5.0	13.9	0.99	10.22	8	0	99	0	1	104	18.0	-27.3	53	5	1,000,000	0	0.0	2.0
C / 5.0	13.9	0.99	10.19	27	0	99	0	1	104	17.6	-27.4	51	5	0	0	0.0	2.0
C / 5.0	13.9	0.99	10.20	6	0	99	0	1	104	17.0	-27.4	49	5	2,500	100	0.0	2.0
C+ / 5.6	10.3	1.02	11.71	1,898	0	98	0	2	105	92.6	-15.0	38	8	2,000,000	1,000	0.0	0.0
C / 5.1	13.1	0.98	7.54	1,204	1	98	0	1	71	57.4	-23.5	76	8	2,000,000	1,000	0.0	0.0
C+ / 5.9	10.3	1.05	10.27	1,757	0	99	0	1	91	95.2	-18.8	46	8	2,000,000	1,000	0.0	0.0
B- / 7.1	9.7	1.01	15.79	8,501	0	100	0	0	6	101.5	-17.8	68	10	10,000,000	1,000	0.0	0.0
B- / 7.1	9.7	1.01	15.75	81	0	100	0	0	6	100.3	-17.7	66	10	5,000,000	0	0.0	0.0
B- / 7.1	9.7	1.01	16.06	694	0	100	0	0	6	99.2	-17.8	63	10	2,500	100	0.0	0.0
B- / 7.1	9.7	1.01	16.01	355	0	100	0	0	6	99.8	-17.9	65	10	0	0	0.0	0.0
C+ / 6.2	14.4	0.75	8.39	238	2	97	0	1	169	N/A	N/A	2	4	2,000,000	1,000	0.0	2.0
C+ / 6.2	14.4	0.75	8.38	4	2	97	0	1	169	N/A	N/A	2	4	1,000,000	0	0.0	2.0
C+ / 6.2	14.4	0.75	8.39	13	2	97	0	1	169	N/A	N/A	2	4	0	0	0.0	2.0
C+ / 6.2	14.4	0.75	8.39	7	2	97	0	1	169	N/A	N/A	2	4	2,500	100	0.0	2.0
C+ / 5.6	10.2	1.04	12.37	3,130	0	99	0	1	98	100.7	-16.1	59	10	2,000,000	1,000	0.0	0.0
C+ / 5.6	10.2	1.04	12.37	153	0	99	0	1	98	99.7	-16.3	57	10	1,000,000	0	0.0	0.0
C+ / 6.1	10.2	1.04	15.89	996	0	99	0	1	98	98.4	-16.2	53	10	2,500	100	0.0	0.0
C+ / 5.6	10.2	1.04	12.54	672	0	99	0	1	98	99.0	-16.2	54	10	0	0	0.0	0.0
U /	N/A	N/A	10.79	1,122	0	96	3	1	46	N/A	N/A	N/A	2	2,000,000	1,000	0.0	2.0
C / 5.5	13.3	1.00	18.39	5,326	1	98	0	1	5	52.7	-23.3	61	10	10,000,000	1,000	0.0	2.0
C / 5.5	13.3	1.01	18.36	211	1	98	0	1	5	52.0	-23.3	58	10	5,000,000	0	0.0	2.0
C / 5.5	13.3	1.01	18.76	713	1	98	0	1	5	51.4	-23.3	57	10	0	0	0.0	2.0
C / 5.2	14.4	1.03	11.38	2,775	0	99	0	1	85	66.2	-31.2	75	16	2,000,000	1,000	0.0	2.0
C / 5.2	14.4	1.02	11.36	225	0	99	0	1	85	65.5	-31.3	74	16	1,000,000	0	0.0	2.0
C / 5.2	14.4	1.02	7.72	325	0	99	0	1	85	64.1	-31.3	72	16	2,500	100	0.0	2.0
C / 5.2	14.4	1.03	11.77	736	0	99	0	1	85	64.7	-31.2	73	16	0	0	0.0	2.0
C+ / 6.9	9.8	0.99	21.62	1,997	0	99	0	1	21	101.5	-15.3	71	10	10,000,000	1,000	0.0	0.0
C+ / 6.9	9.8	0.99	21.77	338	0	99	0	1	21	99.9	-15.4	68	10	0	0	0.0	0.0
C / 4.6	11.3	1.06	15.68	2,335	1	98	0	1	96	110.3	-15.4	73	9	2,000,000	1,000	0.0	0.0
C / 4.6	11.3	1.06	15.67	10	1	98	0	1	96	109.3	-15.5	72	9	1,000,000	0	0.0	0.0
C / 4.7	11.3	1.06	15.62	114	1	98	0	1	96	108.7	-15.5	71	9	0	0	0.0	0.0
C / 4.7	11.3	1.06	15.65	618	1	98	0	1	96	107.5	-15.5	69	9	2,500	100	0.0	0.0
B- / 7.2	9.9	1.01	17.50	2,647	0	99	0	1	21	100.3	-18.7	68	10	10,000,000	1,000	0.0	0.0
B- / 7.2	9.9	1.01	17.77	416	0	99	0	1	21	98.6	-18.8	64	10	0	0	0.0	0.0
C+ / 6.4	10.4	1.06	18.19	4,039	0	99	0	1	49	101.1	-22.9	57	13	2,000,000	1,000	0.0	0.0

99 Pct = Best
0 Pct = Worst

Fund Type	Fund Name	Ticker Symbol	Overall Investment Rating	Phone	PERFORMANCE Perfor-mance Rating/Pts	Total Return % through 3/31/15 3 Mo	6 Mo	1Yr / Pct	Annualized 3Yr / Pct	5Yr / Pct	Incl. in Returns Dividend Yield	Expense Ratio
GR	TIAA-CREF Large Cap Val Premier	TRCPX	B+	(800) 842-2252	B / 7.9	1.28	5.20	8.80 /68	16.11 /84	12.78 /66	1.59	0.57
GR	TIAA-CREF Large Cap Val Ret	TRLCX	B+	(800) 842-2252	B / 7.8	1.28	5.17	8.72 /68	16.00 /83	12.67 /65	1.47	0.67
GR	TIAA-CREF Large Cap Val Retail	TCLCX	B+	(800) 842-2252	B / 7.7	1.27	5.12	8.65 /67	15.88 /82	12.58 /65	1.48	0.74
AA	TIAA-CREF Lifecycle 2010 Inst	TCTIX	C	(800) 842-2252	C- / 3.2	2.60	4.16	5.90 /46	8.00 /27	8.28 /32	2.90	0.52
AA	TIAA-CREF Lifecycle 2010 Premier	TCTPX	C	(800) 842-2252	C- / 3.1	2.60	4.10	5.74 /44	7.85 /26	8.14 /31	2.75	0.67
AA	TIAA-CREF Lifecycle 2010 Ret	TCLEX	C	(800) 842-2252	C- / 3.0	2.49	3.98	5.66 /44	7.74 /26	8.03 /30	2.27	0.82
AA	TIAA-CREF Lifecycle 2015 Inst	TCNIX	C	(800) 842-2252	C- / 3.6	2.76	4.47	6.25 /49	8.71 /31	8.79 /35	2.96	0.53
AA	TIAA-CREF Lifecycle 2015 Premier	TCFPX	C	(800) 842-2252	C- / 3.4	2.67	4.32	6.10 /47	8.51 /30	8.62 /34	2.82	0.68
AA	TIAA-CREF Lifecycle 2015 Ret	TCLIX	C	(800) 842-2252	C- / 3.4	2.66	4.26	5.93 /46	8.40 /29	8.49 /33	2.27	0.83
AA	TIAA-CREF Lifecycle 2020 Inst	TCWIX	C	(800) 842-2252	C- / 4.1	2.92	4.75	6.51 /51	9.58 /37	9.41 /40	2.97	0.54
AA	TIAA-CREF Lifecycle 2020 Premier	TCWPX	C	(800) 842-2252	C- / 4.0	2.83	4.61	6.28 /49	9.41 /36	9.24 /39	2.84	0.69
AA	TIAA-CREF Lifecycle 2020 Ret	TCLTX	C	(800) 842-2252	C- / 3.9	2.82	4.56	6.20 /48	9.31 /35	9.12 /38	2.23	0.84
AA	TIAA-CREF Lifecycle 2025 Inst	TCYIX	C+	(800) 842-2252	C / 4.6	3.11	5.05	6.81 /54	10.48 /42	10.00 /45	3.04	0.56
AA	TIAA-CREF Lifecycle 2025 Premier	TCQPX	C	(800) 842-2252	C / 4.5	3.02	4.91	6.68 /53	10.32 /41	9.81 /43	2.91	0.71
AA	TIAA-CREF Lifecycle 2025 Ret	TCLFX	C+	(800) 842-2252	C / 4.4	3.02	4.92	6.54 /51	10.22 /41	9.72 /42	2.27	0.86
AA	TIAA-CREF Lifecycle 2030 Inst	TCRIX	C+	(800) 842-2252	C / 5.1	3.31	5.30	7.07 /56	11.33 /48	10.54 /49	3.08	0.57
AA	TIAA-CREF Lifecycle 2030 Premier	TCHPX	C+	(800) 842-2252	C / 5.0	3.23	5.26	6.94 /55	11.14 /47	10.38 /48	2.95	0.72
AA	TIAA-CREF Lifecycle 2030 Ret	TCLNX	C+	(800) 842-2252	C / 4.9	3.14	5.13	6.74 /53	11.03 /46	10.25 /47	2.27	0.87
AA	TIAA-CREF Lifecycle 2035 Inst	TCIIX	C+	(800) 842-2252	C / 5.5	3.29	5.46	7.12 /56	11.99 /52	10.99 /53	3.07	0.58
AA	TIAA-CREF Lifecycle 2035 Premier	TCYPX	C+	(800) 842-2252	C / 5.4	3.29	5.41	7.07 /56	11.82 /51	10.83 /51	2.93	0.73
AA	TIAA-CREF Lifecycle 2035 Ret	TCLRX	C+	(800) 842-2252	C / 5.3	3.31	5.40	6.98 /55	11.73 /51	10.73 /51	2.22	0.88
AA	TIAA-CREF Lifecycle 2040 Inst	TCOIX	C+	(800) 842-2252	C+ / 5.8	3.45	5.70	7.35 /58	12.47 /56	11.33 /55	3.10	0.58
AA	TIAA-CREF Lifecycle 2040 Premier	TCZPX	C+	(800) 842-2252	C+ / 5.6	3.37	5.56	7.11 /56	12.30 /55	11.15 /54	2.97	0.73
AA	TIAA-CREF Lifecycle 2040 Ret	TCLOX	C+	(800) 842-2252	C+ / 5.6	3.46	5.57	7.12 /56	12.22 /54	11.04 /53	2.20	0.88
GI	TIAA-CREF Lifecycle 2045 Inst	TTFIX	C+	(800) 842-2252	C+ / 5.8	3.52	5.76	7.40 /58	12.50 /56	11.28 /55	2.83	0.60
GI	TIAA-CREF Lifecycle 2045 Premier	TTFPX	C+	(800) 842-2252	C+ / 5.7	3.44	5.63	7.18 /57	12.33 /55	11.13 /54	2.71	0.75
GI	TIAA-CREF Lifecycle 2045 Ret	TTFRX	C+	(800) 842-2252	C+ / 5.6	3.45	5.53	7.08 /56	12.20 /54	11.00 /53	2.60	0.90
GI	TIAA-CREF Lifecycle 2050 Inst	TFTIX	C+	(800) 842-2252	C+ / 5.8	3.53	5.73	7.38 /58	12.47 /56	11.30 /55	2.81	0.61
GI	TIAA-CREF Lifecycle 2050 Premier	TCLPX	C+	(800) 842-2252	C+ / 5.7	3.45	5.53	7.18 /57	12.30 /55	11.12 /54	2.70	0.76
GI	TIAA-CREF Lifecycle 2050 Ret	TLFRX	C+	(800) 842-2252	C+ / 5.6	3.45	5.51	7.07 /56	12.18 /54	11.03 /53	2.59	0.91
AA	TIAA-CREF Lifecycle 2055 Inst	TTRIX	C+	(800) 842-2252	C+ / 5.8	3.49	5.68	7.34 /58	12.48 /56	--	2.78	0.78
AA	TIAA-CREF Lifecycle 2055 Prm	TTRPX	C+	(800) 842-2252	C+ / 5.7	3.50	5.58	7.15 /56	12.30 /55	--	2.67	0.93
AA	TIAA-CREF Lifecycle 2055 Ret	TTRLX	C+	(800) 842-2252	C+ / 5.6	3.41	5.56	7.04 /55	12.21 /54	--	2.58	1.08
GI	TIAA-CREF Lifecycle Idx Ret Inc Ins	TRILX	C+	(800) 842-2252	D+ / 2.6	2.10	3.95	6.56 /51	6.94 /21	7.55 /27	2.11	0.55
GI	TIAA-CREF Lifecycle Idx Ret Inc Prm	TLIPX	C+	(800) 842-2252	D+ / 2.5	2.06	3.87	6.40 /50	6.82 /20	7.39 /26	1.96	0.70
GI	TIAA-CREF Lifecycle Idx Ret Inc Ret	TRCIX	C+	(800) 842-2252	D+ / 2.4	2.04	3.75	6.25 /49	6.67 /20	7.28 /25	1.89	0.87
AA	TIAA-CREF Lifecycle Index 2010 Inst	TLTIX	C+	(800) 842-2252	C- / 3.1	2.12	4.06	6.70 /53	7.76 /26	8.09 /30	2.05	0.30
AA	TIAA-CREF Lifecycle Index 2010	TLTPX	C+	(800) 842-2252	C- / 3.0	2.12	3.99	6.56 /51	7.60 /25	7.94 /30	1.91	0.45
AA	TIAA-CREF Lifecycle Index 2010 Ret	TLTRX	C+	(800) 842-2252	D+ / 2.9	2.13	3.95	6.53 /51	7.50 /24	7.82 /29	1.86	0.60
AA	TIAA-CREF Lifecycle Index 2015 Inst	TLFIX	C+	(800) 842-2252	C- / 3.4	2.19	4.21	6.92 /54	8.43 /30	8.55 /33	2.04	0.26
AA	TIAA-CREF Lifecycle Index 2015	TLFPX	C+	(800) 842-2252	C- / 3.3	2.20	4.14	6.79 /53	8.29 /29	8.40 /32	1.90	0.41
AA	TIAA-CREF Lifecycle Index 2015 Ret	TLGRX	C+	(800) 842-2252	C- / 3.3	2.21	4.10	6.67 /52	8.18 /28	8.29 /32	1.86	0.56
AA	TIAA-CREF Lifecycle Index 2020 Inst	TLWIX	C+	(800) 842-2252	C- / 4.0	2.32	4.42	7.20 /57	9.37 /35	9.18 /38	2.03	0.24
AA	TIAA-CREF Lifecycle Index 2020	TLWPX	C+	(800) 842-2252	C- / 3.8	2.26	4.29	7.01 /55	9.20 /34	9.00 /37	1.90	0.39
AA	TIAA-CREF Lifecycle Index 2020 Ret	TLWRX	C+	(800) 842-2252	C- / 3.8	2.20	4.21	6.92 /54	9.11 /34	8.91 /36	1.88	0.54
AA	TIAA-CREF Lifecycle Index 2025 Inst	TLQIX	B-	(800) 842-2252	C / 4.4	2.38	4.54	7.38 /58	10.26 /41	9.79 /43	2.07	0.23
AA	TIAA-CREF Lifecycle Index 2025	TLVPX	B-	(800) 842-2252	C / 4.4	2.39	4.48	7.32 /58	10.10 /40	9.63 /42	1.93	0.38
AA	TIAA-CREF Lifecycle Index 2025 Ret	TLQRX	C+	(800) 842-2252	C / 4.3	2.33	4.45	7.16 /56	9.99 /39	9.51 /41	1.90	0.53
AA	TIAA-CREF Lifecycle Index 2030 Inst	TLHIX	B-	(800) 842-2252	C / 4.9	2.50	4.72	7.69 /60	11.15 /47	10.39 /48	2.08	0.23
AA	TIAA-CREF Lifecycle Index 2030	TLHPX	B-	(800) 842-2252	C / 4.8	2.44	4.60	7.50 /59	10.98 /45	10.20 /46	1.96	0.38
AA	TIAA-CREF Lifecycle Index 2030 Ret	TLHRX	B-	(800) 842-2252	C / 4.8	2.39	4.52	7.36 /58	10.86 /45	10.09 /45	1.94	0.53
AA	TIAA-CREF Lifecycle Index 2035 Inst	TLYIX	B-	(800) 842-2252	C / 5.4	2.55	4.83	7.85 /62	11.99 /52	10.95 /52	2.12	0.22

RISK			NET ASSETS		ASSET				Portfolio	BULL / BEAR		FUND MANAGER		MINIMUMS		LOADS	
	3 Year		NAV							Last Bull	Last Bear	Manager	Manager	Initial	Additional	Front	Back
Risk Rating/Pts	Standard Deviation	Beta	As of 3/31/15	Total $(Mil)	Cash %	Stocks %	Bonds %	Other %	Turnover Ratio	Market Return	Market Return	Quality Pct	Tenure (Years)	Purch. $	Purch. $	End Load	End Load
C+ / 6.4	10.5	1.06	18.15	314	0	99	0	1	49	100.1	-22.9	54	13	1,000,000	0	0.0	0.0
C+ / 6.4	10.4	1.06	18.13	1,060	0	99	0	1	49	99.5	-23.0	53	13	0	0	0.0	0.0
C+ / 6.4	10.4	1.06	17.57	142	0	99	0	1	49	98.8	-23.0	52	13	2,500	100	0.0	0.0
B / 8.3	5.4	0.90	11.45	523	0	44	55	1	28	43.4	-9.1	42	8	2,000,000	1,000	0.0	0.0
B / 8.4	5.4	0.91	11.43	121	0	44	55	1	28	42.5	-9.1	40	8	1,000,000	0	0.0	0.0
B / 8.6	5.4	0.90	13.18	456	0	44	55	1	28	42.1	-9.2	39	8	0	0	0.0	0.0
B- / 7.4	6.0	1.00	10.43	844	0	49	50	1	20	48.2	-10.9	37	8	2,000,000	1,000	0.0	0.0
B- / 7.5	6.0	1.00	10.39	210	0	49	50	1	20	47.6	-11.0	35	8	1,000,000	0	0.0	0.0
B- / 7.9	6.0	1.01	12.37	718	0	49	50	1	20	47.0	-11.1	32	8	0	0	0.0	0.0
B- / 7.5	6.8	1.14	10.56	1,359	0	57	42	1	15	54.5	-12.9	30	8	2,000,000	1,000	0.0	0.0
B- / 7.5	6.8	1.15	10.53	364	0	57	42	1	15	53.8	-13.0	27	8	1,000,000	0	0.0	0.0
B- / 7.9	6.8	1.14	12.77	1,026	0	57	42	1	15	53.3	-13.0	26	8	0	0	0.0	0.0
B- / 7.3	7.6	1.28	10.62	1,414	0	65	34	1	12	61.1	-14.9	22	8	2,000,000	1,000	0.0	0.0
B- / 7.3	7.6	1.29	10.58	364	0	65	34	1	12	60.3	-15.0	20	8	1,000,000	0	0.0	0.0
B- / 7.7	7.6	1.28	12.97	992	0	65	34	1	12	59.7	-15.0	20	8	0	0	0.0	0.0
B- / 7.0	8.5	1.42	10.60	1,431	0	73	26	1	11	67.4	-16.8	16	8	2,000,000	1,000	0.0	0.0
B- / 7.1	8.4	1.42	10.56	364	0	73	26	1	11	66.5	-16.8	15	N/A	1,000,000	0	0.0	0.0
B- / 7.4	8.4	1.42	13.13	885	0	73	26	1	11	66.0	-16.8	15	N/A	0	0	0.0	0.0
C+ / 6.7	9.3	1.56	10.68	1,497	0	82	17	1	10	73.2	-18.5	11	8	2,000,000	1,000	0.0	0.0
C+ / 6.8	9.2	1.56	10.66	363	0	82	17	1	10	72.5	-18.6	11	8	1,000,000	0	0.0	0.0
B- / 7.0	9.2	1.55	13.44	840	0	82	17	1	10	71.8	-18.6	11	8	0	0	0.0	0.0
C+ / 6.4	9.8	1.64	10.78	1,919	0	89	10	1	9	76.3	-18.8	9	8	2,000,000	1,000	0.0	0.0
C+ / 6.4	9.7	1.63	10.75	490	0	89	10	1	9	75.4	-19.0	9	8	1,000,000	0	0.0	0.0
C+ / 6.7	9.7	1.63	13.77	1,077	0	89	10	1	9	75.0	-19.0	9	8	0	0	0.0	0.0
C+ / 6.9	9.7	0.97	11.17	699	0	89	10	1	6	76.4	-18.9	29	8	2,000,000	1,000	0.0	0.0
C+ / 6.9	9.7	0.97	11.13	193	0	89	10	1	6	75.3	-18.9	27	8	1,000,000	0	0.0	0.0
C+ / 6.9	9.7	0.96	11.10	372	0	89	10	1	6	74.8	-18.9	26	8	0	0	0.0	0.0
C+ / 6.9	9.7	0.97	11.15	392	0	89	10	1	6	76.3	-18.8	28	8	2,000,000	1,000	0.0	0.0
C+ / 6.9	9.7	0.96	11.11	122	0	89	10	1	6	75.3	-18.9	27	8	1,000,000	0	0.0	0.0
C+ / 6.9	9.7	0.96	11.08	220	0	89	10	1	6	74.7	-18.9	26	8	0	0	0.0	0.0
C+ / 6.9	9.7	1.63	12.46	53	0	89	10	1	10	76.7	-18.9	10	4	2,000,000	1,000	0.0	0.0
C+ / 6.9	9.7	1.63	12.43	23	0	89	10	1	10	75.6	-18.9	9	4	1,000,000	0	0.0	0.0
C+ / 6.9	9.7	1.63	12.43	50	0	89	10	1	10	75.2	-19.0	9	4	0	0	0.0	0.0
B+ / 9.4	4.2	0.36	13.27	27	0	40	59	1	26	35.4	-5.3	79	6	2,000,000	1,000	0.0	0.0
B+ / 9.4	4.3	0.37	13.27	10	0	40	59	1	26	34.7	-5.3	78	6	5,000,000	0	0.0	0.0
B+ / 9.5	4.3	0.37	13.26	6	0	40	59	1	26	34.3	-5.3	77	6	0	0	0.0	0.0
B+ / 9.3	4.8	0.80	13.97	123	0	46	53	1	17	40.9	-7.6	55	6	2,000,000	1,000	0.0	0.0
B+ / 9.3	4.8	0.80	13.94	23	0	46	53	1	17	40.3	-7.7	52	6	5,000,000	0	0.0	0.0
B+ / 9.3	4.8	0.81	13.88	40	0	46	53	1	17	39.8	-7.7	50	6	0	0	0.0	0.0
B+ / 9.2	5.3	0.91	14.44	219	0	51	48	1	16	45.8	-9.4	48	6	2,000,000	1,000	0.0	0.0
B+ / 9.2	5.3	0.91	14.40	55	0	51	48	1	16	45.0	-9.3	46	6	5,000,000	0	0.0	0.0
B+ / 9.2	5.4	0.91	14.36	63	0	51	48	1	16	44.6	-9.4	44	6	0	0	0.0	0.0
B / 8.9	6.1	1.04	14.98	319	0	59	40	1	10	52.0	-11.2	40	6	2,000,000	1,000	0.0	0.0
B / 8.9	6.1	1.04	14.92	116	0	59	40	1	10	51.3	-11.3	37	6	5,000,000	0	0.0	0.0
B / 8.9	6.0	1.04	14.88	103	0	59	40	1	10	50.6	-11.3	37	6	0	0	0.0	0.0
B / 8.6	6.8	1.17	15.47	329	0	67	32	1	11	58.4	-13.1	33	6	2,000,000	1,000	0.0	0.0
B / 8.6	6.8	1.17	15.43	115	0	67	32	1	11	57.6	-13.1	31	6	5,000,000	0	0.0	0.0
B / 8.6	6.9	1.18	15.38	91	0	67	32	1	11	57.1	-13.2	29	6	0	0	0.0	0.0
B / 8.2	7.6	1.31	15.99	352	0	75	24	1	10	65.0	-15.0	26	6	2,000,000	1,000	0.0	0.0
B / 8.2	7.6	1.31	15.93	126	0	75	24	1	10	64.2	-15.0	24	6	5,000,000	0	0.0	0.0
B / 8.2	7.6	1.31	15.88	87	0	75	24	1	10	63.6	-15.0	23	6	0	0	0.0	0.0
B- / 7.8	8.5	1.45	16.47	362	0	83	16	1	9	71.6	-16.8	19	6	2,000,000	1,000	0.0	0.0

99 Pct = Best 0 Pct = Worst					**PERFORMANCE**								
							Total Return % through 3/31/15					Incl. in Returns	
				Overall Investment Rating	Perfor-mance Rating/Pts					Annualized		Dividend Yield	Expense Ratio
Fund Type	Fund Name	Ticker Symbol	Phone			3 Mo	6 Mo	1Yr / Pct	3Yr / Pct	5Yr / Pct			
AA	TIAA-CREF Lifecycle Index 2035	TLYPX	B-	(800) 842-2252	C / 5.3	2.44	4.70	7.66 /60	11.81 /51	10.76 /51	1.99	0.37
AA	TIAA-CREF Lifecycle Index 2035 Ret	TLYRX	B-	(800) 842-2252	C / 5.3	2.51	4.67	7.57 /60	11.70 /50	10.65 /50	1.95	0.52
AA	TIAA-CREF Lifecycle Index 2040 Inst	TLZIX	B-	(800) 842-2252	C+ / 5.8	2.58	4.89	7.94 /62	12.53 /56	11.30 /55	2.16	0.22
AA	TIAA-CREF Lifecycle Index 2040	TLPRX	B-	(800) 842-2252	C+ / 5.7	2.59	4.83	7.82 /61	12.37 /55	11.12 /54	2.03	0.37
AA	TIAA-CREF Lifecycle Index 2040 Ret	TLZRX	B-	(800) 842-2252	C+ / 5.6	2.53	4.81	7.73 /61	12.27 /54	11.01 /53	2.00	0.52
AA	TIAA-CREF Lifecycle Index 2045 Inst	TLXIX	B-	(800) 842-2252	C+ / 5.8	2.59	4.95	8.01 /63	12.55 /56	11.28 /55	2.15	0.25
AA	TIAA-CREF Lifecycle Index 2045	TLMPX	B-	(800) 842-2252	C+ / 5.7	2.53	4.83	7.83 /62	12.37 /55	11.11 /54	2.02	0.40
AA	TIAA-CREF Lifecycle Index 2045 Ret	TLMRX	B-	(800) 842-2252	C+ / 5.6	2.54	4.80	7.74 /61	12.25 /54	11.01 /53	1.99	0.55
AA	TIAA-CREF Lifecycle Index 2050 Inst	TLLIX	B-	(800) 842-2252	C+ / 5.8	2.59	4.91	7.97 /63	12.52 /56	11.29 /55	2.14	0.28
AA	TIAA-CREF Lifecycle Index 2050	TLLPX	B-	(800) 842-2252	C+ / 5.7	2.54	4.85	7.79 /61	12.37 /55	11.12 /54	2.02	0.43
AA	TIAA-CREF Lifecycle Index 2050 Ret	TLLRX	B-	(800) 842-2252	C+ / 5.6	2.54	4.76	7.70 /60	12.25 /54	11.02 /53	1.99	0.58
AA	TIAA-CREF Lifecycle Index 2055 Inst	TTIIX	B-	(800) 842-2252	C+ / 5.8	2.56	4.84	7.93 /62	12.54 /56	--	2.14	0.61
AA	TIAA-CREF Lifecycle Index 2055 Prm	TTIPX	B-	(800) 842-2252	C+ / 5.6	2.48	4.79	7.72 /61	12.36 /55	--	2.02	0.76
AA	TIAA-CREF Lifecycle Index 2055 Ret	TTIRX	B-	(800) 842-2252	C+ / 5.6	2.48	4.77	7.70 /60	12.24 /54	--	2.00	0.92
GL	TIAA-CREF Lifecycle Ret Inc Inst	TLRIX	C	(800) 842-2252	D+ / 2.7	2.50	3.91	5.60 /43	7.28 /23	7.70 /28	2.64	0.55
GL	TIAA-CREF Lifecycle Ret Inc Premier	TPILX	C	(800) 842-2252	D+ / 2.6	2.37	3.74	5.35 /41	7.09 /22	7.53 /27	2.49	0.70
GL	TIAA-CREF Lifecycle Ret Inc Ret	TLIRX	C	(800) 842-2252	D+ / 2.6	2.44	3.78	5.35 /41	6.99 /21	7.45 /26	2.40	0.85
GL	TIAA-CREF Lifecycle Ret Inc Retail	TLRRX	C	(800) 842-2252	D+ / 2.6	2.44	3.78	5.35 /41	6.99 /21	7.47 /26	2.40	0.84
GR	TIAA-CREF Lifestyle Aggrv Gro Inst	TSAIX	C+	(800) 842-2252	C+ / 6.5	3.73	6.18	7.80 /61	13.64 /64	--	2.62	0.98
GR	TIAA-CREF Lifestyle Aggrv Gro Prmr	TSAPX	C+	(800) 842-2252	C+ / 6.3	3.66	6.11	7.58 /60	13.45 /63	--	2.49	1.13
GR	TIAA-CREF Lifestyle Aggrv Gro Ret	TSARX	C+	(800) 842-2252	C+ / 6.3	3.59	6.01	7.49 /59	13.31 /62	--	2.39	1.22
GR	TIAA-CREF Lifestyle Aggrv Gro Rtl	TSALX	C+	(800) 842-2252	C+ / 6.2	3.60	5.98	7.38 /58	13.26 /61	--	2.36	1.31
GL	TIAA-CREF Lifestyle Cons Inst	TCSIX	C+	(800) 842-2252	D+ / 2.8	2.45	3.89	5.50 /42	7.45 /24	--	2.54	0.75
GL	TIAA-CREF Lifestyle Cons Prmr	TLSPX	C+	(800) 842-2252	D+ / 2.7	2.41	3.81	5.34 /41	7.28 /23	--	2.38	0.90
GL	TIAA-CREF Lifestyle Cons Ret	TSCTX	C	(800) 842-2252	D+ / 2.6	2.38	3.76	5.25 /40	7.17 /22	--	2.30	0.99
GL	TIAA-CREF Lifestyle Cons Rtl	TSCLX	C	(800) 842-2252	D+ / 2.6	2.38	3.76	5.23 /40	7.15 /22	--	2.28	1.02
GR	TIAA-CREF Lifestyle Growth Fund Rtl	TSGLX	B-	(800) 842-2252	C / 5.1	3.28	5.41	6.89 /54	11.45 /49	--	2.47	1.22
GR	TIAA-CREF Lifestyle Growth Inst	TSGGX	B-	(800) 842-2252	C / 5.4	3.43	5.56	7.28 /57	11.79 /51	--	2.70	0.93
GR	TIAA-CREF Lifestyle Growth Premier	TSGPX	B-	(800) 842-2252	C / 5.3	3.35	5.49	7.13 /56	11.64 /50	--	2.56	1.08
GR	TIAA-CREF Lifestyle Growth Ret	TSGRX	B-	(800) 842-2252	C / 5.2	3.36	5.42	6.98 /55	11.52 /49	--	2.49	1.17
AA	TIAA-CREF Lifestyle Income Inst	TSITX	C-	(800) 842-2252	D- / 1.5	1.85	2.81	4.19 /33	4.97 /13	--	2.20	0.86
AA	TIAA-CREF Lifestyle Income Premier	TSIPX	C-	(800) 842-2252	D- / 1.5	1.72	2.72	3.95 /31	4.79 /12	--	2.06	1.01
AA	TIAA-CREF Lifestyle Income Retail	TSILX	C-	(800) 842-2252	D- / 1.4	1.78	2.67	3.92 /31	4.68 /12	--	1.94	1.13
AA	TIAA-CREF Lifestyle Income Retire	TLSRX	C-	(800) 842-2252	D- / 1.4	1.79	2.67	3.94 /31	4.71 /12	--	1.96	1.10
BA	TIAA-CREF Lifestyle Moderate Inst	TSIMX	C+	(800) 842-2252	C / 4.3	3.11	5.06	6.94 /55	10.01 /39	--	2.88	0.76
BA	TIAA-CREF Lifestyle Moderate Prmr	TSMPX	C+	(800) 842-2252	C- / 4.2	3.07	4.97	6.78 /53	9.85 /38	--	2.73	0.90
BA	TIAA-CREF Lifestyle Moderate Ret	TSMTX	C+	(800) 842-2252	C- / 4.2	3.05	4.93	6.60 /52	9.73 /38	--	2.64	1.00
BA	TIAA-CREF Lifestyle Moderate Rtl	TSMLX	C+	(800) 842-2252	C- / 4.1	3.05	4.84	6.58 /52	9.67 /37	--	2.62	1.04
BA	TIAA-CREF Mgd Alloc Inst	TIMIX	C+	(800) 842-2252	C / 4.3	3.04	4.96	6.98 /55	9.98 /39	9.70 /42	3.04	0.46
BA	TIAA-CREF Mgd Alloc Ret	TIMRX	C+	(800) 842-2252	C- / 4.1	2.97	4.82	6.69 /53	9.68 /37	9.43 /40	2.79	0.77
BA	TIAA-CREF Mgd Alloc Retire	TITRX	C+	(800) 842-2252	C- / 4.2	3.07	4.92	6.72 /53	9.70 /37	9.43 /40	2.80	0.71
MC	TIAA-CREF Mid Cap Value Inst	TIMVX	A	(800) 842-2252	B+ / 8.9	2.85	8.98	11.47 /80	16.95 /90	14.68 /84	1.34	0.41
MC	TIAA-CREF Mid Cap Value Prmr	TRVPX	A	(800) 842-2252	B+ / 8.8	2.82	8.91	11.30 /80	16.77 /89	14.50 /82	1.19	0.56
MC	TIAA-CREF Mid Cap Value Retail	TCMVX	A	(800) 842-2252	B+ / 8.7	2.78	8.86	11.15 /79	16.58 /87	14.35 /81	1.10	0.72
MC	TIAA-CREF Mid Cap Value Retire	TRVRX	A	(800) 842-2252	B+ / 8.7	2.78	8.84	11.19 /79	16.66 /88	14.39 /81	1.06	0.66
MC	TIAA-CREF Mid/Cp Growth Inst	TRPWX	C+	(800) 842-2252	B+ / 8.7	5.69	11.32	12.32 /84	16.08 /84	15.72 /91	0.43	0.47
MC	TIAA-CREF Mid/Cp Growth Prmr	TRGPX	C+	(800) 842-2252	B+ / 8.7	5.67	11.28	12.18 /83	15.92 /83	15.56 /90	0.27	0.62
MC	TIAA-CREF Mid/Cp Growth Retail	TCMGX	C+	(800) 842-2252	B+ / 8.5	5.63	11.15	11.97 /82	15.70 /81	15.36 /89	0.14	0.79
MC	TIAA-CREF Mid/Cp Growth Retire	TRGMX	C+	(800) 842-2252	B+ / 8.6	5.63	11.16	12.07 /83	15.80 /82	15.43 /90	0.18	0.72
RE	TIAA-CREF Real Est Secs Instl	TIREX	B	(800) 842-2252	A / 9.4	5.17	20.05	24.80 /98	13.56 /64	15.63 /91	1.55	0.52
RE	TIAA-CREF Real Est Secs Premier	TRRPX	B	(800) 842-2252	A / 9.3	5.12	19.94	24.59 /98	13.38 /62	15.44 /90	1.41	0.67
RE	TIAA-CREF Real Est Secs Retail	TCREX	B	(800) 842-2252	A / 9.3	5.05	19.93	24.41 /98	13.19 /61	15.28 /89	1.28	0.86

● Denotes fund is closed to new investors
* Denotes fund is included in Section II

www.thestreetratings.com

RISK	3 Year		NET ASSETS		ASSET				Portfolio	BULL / BEAR		FUND MANAGER		MINIMUMS		LOADS	
Risk Rating/Pts	Standard Deviation	Beta	NAV As of 3/31/15	Total $(Mil)	Cash %	Stocks %	Bonds %	Other %	Turnover Ratio	Last Bull Market Return	Last Bear Market Return	Manager Quality Pct	Manager Tenure (Years)	Initial Purch. $	Additional Purch. $	Front End Load	Back End Load
B- / 7.8	8.4	1.45	16.40	104	0	83	16	1	9	70.8	-16.8	18	6	5,000,000	0	0.0	0.0
B- / 7.8	8.4	1.44	16.36	65	0	83	16	1	9	70.1	-16.8	18	6	0	0	0.0	0.0
B- / 7.5	9.0	1.53	16.72	463	0	89	10	1	8	75.2	-17.2	16	6	2,000,000	1,000	0.0	0.0
B- / 7.5	9.0	1.53	16.66	99	0	89	10	1	8	74.4	-17.2	15	6	5,000,000	0	0.0	0.0
B- / 7.5	9.0	1.53	16.62	67	0	89	10	1	8	73.8	-17.3	14	6	0	0	0.0	0.0
B- / 7.5	9.0	1.54	16.65	184	0	89	10	1	13	75.0	-17.1	16	6	2,000,000	1,000	0.0	0.0
B- / 7.5	8.9	1.53	16.59	75	0	89	10	1	13	74.3	-17.3	15	6	5,000,000	0	0.0	0.0
B- / 7.5	9.0	1.54	16.54	41	0	89	10	1	13	73.6	-17.2	14	6	0	0	0.0	0.0
B- / 7.5	9.0	1.54	16.63	118	0	89	10	1	20	75.1	-17.2	16	6	2,000,000	1,000	0.0	0.0
B- / 7.5	8.9	1.53	16.57	51	0	89	10	1	20	74.4	-17.2	15	6	5,000,000	0	0.0	0.0
B- / 7.5	8.9	1.53	16.52	28	0	89	10	1	20	73.7	-17.3	15	6	0	0	0.0	0.0
B- / 7.5	8.9	1.52	13.23	32	0	89	9	2	25	75.2	-17.2	17	4	2,000,000	1,000	0.0	0.0
B- / 7.5	9.0	1.53	13.21	7	0	89	9	2	25	74.5	-17.3	15	4	5,000,000	0	0.0	0.0
B- / 7.5	8.9	1.53	13.20	7	0	89	9	2	25	73.8	-17.3	14	4	0	0	0.0	0.0
B / 8.8	4.7	0.72	11.27	125	0	39	60	1	31	37.9	-6.9	75	8	2,000,000	1,000	0.0	0.0
B / 8.8	4.7	0.73	11.26	26	0	39	60	1	31	37.1	-7.0	73	8	1,000,000	0	0.0	0.0
B / 8.8	4.7	0.73	11.25	127	0	39	60	1	31	36.7	-7.0	72	8	0	0	0.0	0.0
B / 8.8	4.7	0.73	11.26	79	0	39	60	1	31	36.6	-6.9	72	8	2,500	100	0.0	0.0
C+ / 6.8	10.7	1.06	14.74	3	1	98	0	1	24	N/A	N/A	25	4	2,000,000	1,000	0.0	0.0
C+ / 6.8	10.7	1.06	14.73	2	1	98	0	1	24	N/A	N/A	23	4	1,000,000	0	0.0	0.0
C+ / 6.8	10.7	1.06	14.70	21	1	98	0	1	24	N/A	N/A	22	4	0	0	0.0	0.0
C+ / 6.8	10.7	1.06	14.69	27	1	98	0	1	24	N/A	N/A	21	4	2,500	100	0.0	0.0
B+ / 9.2	4.7	0.33	12.00	4	0	38	61	1	9	N/A	N/A	92	4	2,000,000	1,000	0.0	0.0
B+ / 9.2	4.7	0.33	12.00	1	0	38	61	1	9	N/A	N/A	92	4	1,000,000	0	0.0	0.0
B+ / 9.2	4.8	0.33	11.99	22	0	38	61	1	9	N/A	N/A	91	4	0	0	0.0	0.0
B+ / 9.2	4.7	0.33	11.99	81	0	38	61	1	9	N/A	N/A	91	4	2,500	100	0.0	0.0
B- / 7.8	8.7	0.86	13.84	47	0	78	21	1	16	N/A	N/A	38	4	2,500	100	0.0	0.0
B- / 7.9	8.6	0.85	13.89	2	0	78	21	1	16	N/A	N/A	44	4	2,000,000	1,000	0.0	0.0
B- / 7.8	8.7	0.86	13.88	2	0	78	21	1	16	N/A	N/A	40	4	1,000,000	0	0.0	0.0
B- / 7.8	8.7	0.86	13.86	22	0	78	21	1	16	N/A	N/A	38	4	0	0	0.0	0.0
B+ / 9.1	2.9	0.44	10.99	2	0	19	80	1	16	N/A	N/A	70	4	2,000,000	1,000	0.0	0.0
B+ / 9.1	2.9	0.44	10.98	1	0	19	80	1	16	N/A	N/A	68	4	1,000,000	0	0.0	0.0
B+ / 9.1	3.0	0.44	10.99	36	0	19	80	1	16	N/A	N/A	67	4	2,500	100	0.0	0.0
B+ / 9.1	2.9	0.44	10.99	15	0	19	80	1	16	N/A	N/A	67	4	0	0	0.0	0.0
B / 8.0	6.7	1.13	13.05	3	0	57	42	1	17	N/A	N/A	36	4	2,000,000	1,000	0.0	0.0
B- / 7.9	6.7	1.12	13.05	1	0	57	42	1	17	N/A	N/A	34	4	1,000,000	0	0.0	0.0
B- / 7.9	6.8	1.13	13.04	39	0	57	42	1	17	N/A	N/A	32	4	0	0	0.0	0.0
B- / 7.9	6.7	1.12	13.03	98	0	57	42	1	17	N/A	N/A	32	4	2,500	100	0.0	0.0
B / 8.2	6.7	1.13	12.23	13	0	58	41	1	15	55.7	-12.1	35	N/A	2,000,000	1,000	0.0	0.0
B / 8.2	6.6	1.12	12.26	713	0	58	41	1	15	54.3	-12.2	33	N/A	2,500	100	0.0	0.0
B / 8.2	6.6	1.12	12.23	47	0	58	41	1	15	54.2	-12.1	33	N/A	0	0	0.0	0.0
C+ / 6.7	9.7	0.87	24.88	3,434	2	97	0	1	28	101.2	-21.2	84	13	2,000,000	1,000	0.0	0.0
C+ / 6.7	9.7	0.87	24.83	375	2	97	0	1	28	100.1	-21.2	83	13	1,000,000	0	0.0	0.0
C+ / 6.7	9.7	0.87	24.38	332	2	97	0	1	28	98.9	-21.2	82	13	2,500	100	0.0	0.0
C+ / 6.7	9.8	0.87	24.75	1,247	2	97	0	1	28	99.4	-21.2	82	13	0	0	0.0	0.0
C- / 3.4	11.8	0.99	22.46	1,021	0	99	0	1	104	100.8	-24.1	57	9	2,000,000	1,000	0.0	0.0
C- / 3.4	11.8	0.99	22.35	120	0	99	0	1	104	99.8	-24.2	55	9	1,000,000	0	0.0	0.0
C- / 3.4	11.8	0.99	21.94	191	0	99	0	1	104	98.4	-24.2	52	9	2,500	100	0.0	0.0
C- / 3.4	11.8	0.99	21.94	523	0	99	0	1	104	99.1	-24.2	53	9	0	0	0.0	0.0
C- / 4.2	12.1	0.97	15.92	1,379	0	95	3	2	65	86.3	-17.1	67	10	2,000,000	1,000	0.0	0.0
C- / 4.2	12.1	0.97	15.93	65	0	95	3	2	65	85.4	-17.3	64	10	1,000,000	0	0.0	0.0
C- / 4.2	12.2	0.97	15.82	239	0	95	3	2	65	84.1	-17.3	61	10	2,500	100	0.0	0.0

Fund Type	Fund Name	Ticker Symbol	Overall Investment Rating	Phone	Performance Rating/Pts	3 Mo	6 Mo	1Yr / Pct	3Yr / Pct	5Yr / Pct	Dividend Yield	Expense Ratio
									Annualized		Incl. in Returns	
RE	TIAA-CREF Real Est Secs Retire	TRRSX	B	(800) 842-2252	A / 9.3	5.12	19.97	24.50 /98	13.26 /61	15.33 /89	1.28	0.77
IX	TIAA-CREF S&P 500 Idx Inst	TISPX	A	(800) 842-2252	B / 8.2	0.91	5.88	12.62 /85	16.03 /84	14.36 /81	1.76	0.06
IX	TIAA-CREF S&P 500 Idx Retire	TRSPX	A-	(800) 842-2252	B / 8.0	0.87	5.72	12.34 /84	15.74 /81	14.09 /79	1.55	0.31
SC	TIAA-CREF Sm Cap Equity Inst	TISEX	B-	(800) 842-2252	B+ / 8.8	5.21	14.68	10.67 /77	16.70 /88	15.06 /87	0.69	0.49
SC	TIAA-CREF Sm Cap Equity Prmr	TSRPX	C+	(800) 842-2252	B+ / 8.7	5.17	14.59	10.51 /76	16.53 /87	14.89 /86	0.62	0.64
SC	TIAA-CREF Sm Cap Equity Retail	TCSEX	C+	(800) 842-2252	B+ / 8.5	5.06	14.44	10.29 /75	16.27 /85	14.68 /84	0.55	0.83
SC	TIAA-CREF Sm Cap Equity Retire	TRSEX	C+	(800) 842-2252	B+ / 8.6	5.14	14.50	10.43 /76	16.40 /86	14.78 /85	0.59	0.74
SC	TIAA-CREF Sm Cp Blend Idx Inst	TISBX	B+	(800) 842-2252	B+ / 8.5	4.39	14.64	8.50 /66	16.53 /87	14.72 /84	1.53	0.13
SC	TIAA-CREF Sm Cp Blend Idx Ret	TRBIX	B+	(800) 842-2252	B+ / 8.3	4.32	14.46	8.23 /64	16.25 /85	14.44 /82	1.27	0.38
GR	TIAA-CREF Social Ch Eq Inst	TISCX	B+	(800) 842-2252	B / 7.6	0.77	4.86	10.12 /75	15.50 /79	13.50 /73	1.39	0.18
GR	TIAA-CREF Social Ch Eq Premier	TRPSX	B+	(800) 842-2252	B- / 7.5	0.78	4.86	9.99 /74	15.35 /78	13.33 /71	1.26	0.33
GR	TIAA-CREF Social Ch Eq Retail	TICRX	B+	(800) 842-2252	B- / 7.4	0.72	4.82	9.91 /74	15.20 /76	13.19 /70	1.36	0.46
GR	TIAA-CREF Social Ch Eq Retire	TRSCX	B+	(800) 842-2252	B- / 7.4	0.71	4.77	9.90 /74	15.22 /77	13.22 /70	1.12	0.43
AG	Timothy Plan Aggressive Growth A	TAAGX	C	(800) 662-0201	C+ / 6.5	5.79	11.85	10.29 /76	14.27 /69	16.07 /93	0.00	1.75
AG	Timothy Plan Aggressive Growth C	TCAGX	C	(800) 662-0201	C+ / 6.9	5.45	11.37	9.35 /71	13.42 /63	15.19 /88	0.00	2.50
AA	Timothy Plan Conservative Growth A	TCGAX	D+	(800) 662-0201	E+ / 0.9	1.78	1.97	1.78 /21	4.78 /12	6.04 /17	0.47	2.49
AA	Timothy Plan Conservative Growth C	TCVCX	D+	(800) 662-0201	D- / 1.1	1.62	1.56	0.97 /18	3.99 /10	5.23 /13	0.00	3.23
IN	Timothy Plan Defensive Strat A	TPDAX	D-	(800) 662-0201	E / 0.4	1.16	0.81	0.63 /17	-0.84 / 4	4.28 / 9	0.99	1.36
IN	Timothy Plan Defensive Strat C	TPDCX	D-	(800) 662-0201	E / 0.4	0.91	0.39	-0.15 /15	-1.60 / 3	3.46 / 7	0.27	2.12
GI	Timothy Plan Growth and Income A	TGIAX	U	(800) 662-0201	U /	1.00	1.55	1.55 /20	--	--	0.00	1.69
FO	Timothy Plan International A	TPIAX	D	(800) 662-0201	D / 1.9	3.31	1.91	0.44 /17	7.98 /27	4.37 /10	0.00	1.70
FO	Timothy Plan International C	TPICX	D	(800) 662-0201	D / 2.2	3.04	1.61	-0.34 /15	7.14 /22	3.60 / 7	0.00	2.45
FO	Timothy Plan Israel Common Values	TPAIX	E+	(800) 662-0201	E+ / 0.8	7.03	-2.27	-10.09 / 3	5.22 /14	--	0.00	1.99
FO	Timothy Plan Israel Common Values	TPCIX	E+	(800) 662-0201	E+ / 0.9	6.83	-2.66	-10.87 / 3	4.41 /11	--	0.00	2.75
GR	Timothy Plan Large Mid Cap Growth	TLGAX	C+	(800) 662-0201	C+ / 6.4	3.69	8.27	11.35 /80	14.38 /70	14.17 /79	0.00	1.58
GR	Timothy Plan Large Mid Cap Growth	TLGCX	C+	(800) 662-0201	C+ / 6.7	3.57	7.94	10.56 /77	13.48 /63	13.33 /71	0.00	2.33
MC	Timothy Plan Large/Mid Cap Val A	TLVAX	B	(800) 662-0201	B- / 7.2	3.20	8.01	11.01 /78	15.96 /83	14.68 /84	0.00	1.51
MC	Timothy Plan Large/Mid Cap Val C	TLVCX	B	(800) 662-0201	B / 7.6	2.96	7.60	10.16 /75	15.08 /76	13.81 /76	0.00	2.26
SC	Timothy Plan Small Cap Value A	TPLNX	B-	(800) 662-0201	B+ / 8.7	2.50	11.16	6.89 /54	18.77 /96	16.14 /94	0.00	1.54
SC	Timothy Plan Small Cap Value C	TSVCX	C+	(800) 662-0201	A- / 9.0	2.30	10.71	6.06 /47	17.87 /94	15.26 /89	0.00	2.29
GR	Timothy Plan Strategic Growth A	TSGAX	D+	(800) 662-0201	D- / 1.5	2.16	2.10	1.64 /21	7.05 /22	7.44 /26	1.21	2.73
GR	Timothy Plan Strategic Growth C	TSGCX	D+	(800) 662-0201	D / 1.8	2.11	1.78	0.92 /18	6.28 /18	6.59 /21	0.66	3.48
GR	Tocqueville	TOCQX	C+	(800) 697-3863	C+ / 6.5	-0.97	4.91	8.93 /69	14.69 /72	12.18 /62	0.72	1.28
IN	Tocqueville Alternative Strategies	TALSX	U	(800) 697-3863	U /	1.18	3.11	5.77 /44	--	--	0.00	3.11
PM	Tocqueville Gold	TGLDX	E-	(800) 697-3863	E- / 0.0	-6.15	-16.46	-21.15 / 1	-24.24 / 0	-11.44 / 0	0.00	1.35
FO	Tocqueville International Value	TIVFX	D+	(800) 697-3863	C- / 3.8	8.67	4.35	0.64 /17	10.11 /40	7.68 /28	2.12	1.55
SC	Tocqueville Opportunity	TOPPX	B	(800) 697-3863	A+ / 9.7	11.30	21.78	20.77 /97	17.77 /93	17.96 /97	0.00	1.30
MC	Tocqueville Select	TSELX	D	(800) 697-3863	C / 4.5	-1.95	3.34	3.84 /31	11.98 /52	11.08 /53	0.00	1.35
EM	Toews Hedged Core Frontier	THEMX	E+	(877) 558-6397	E / 0.3	-5.19	-6.54	--	-3.76 / 2	-8.90 / 1	0.00	2.36
AA	Toews Hedged Core L	THLGX	C-	(877) 558-6397	C / 4.3	-1.07	0.96	4.64 /36	11.15 /47	--	0.00	1.41
AA	Toews Hedged Core S	THSMX	D+	(877) 558-6397	C- / 3.9	1.57	4.36	0.66 /17	10.20 /40	--	0.00	1.41
FO	Toews Hedged Core W	THIDX	D-	(877) 558-6397	E+ / 0.7	3.11	-2.38	-2.82 / 9	2.38 / 7	--	0.00	1.44
FO	Toews Hedged Growth Allocation	THGWX	C	(877) 558-6397	D / 2.2	1.47	0.76	0.57 /17	7.44 /24	--	0.02	1.56
GR	Toreador Core Fund Institutional	TORZX	B	(800) 408-4682	B+ / 8.4	0.76	4.43	12.99 /86	17.04 /90	14.38 /81	0.23	1.34
GR	Toreador Core Fund Retail	TORLX	B	(800) 408-4682	B / 8.2	0.76	4.37	12.78 /86	16.78 /89	14.13 /79	0.03	1.59
EM	Toreador International Inst	TMRIX	U	(800) 527-9525	U /	3.34	0.04	-4.21 / 7	--	--	0.82	2.05
GR	Torray	TORYX	B-	(800) 443-3036	C+ / 6.1	-1.12	2.82	8.68 /67	13.71 /65	12.12 /61	0.93	1.15
EN	Tortoise MLP & Pipeline C	TORCX	U	(855) 822-3863	U /	-1.23	-9.64	3.26 /28	--	--	0.19	2.08
EN	Tortoise MLP & Pipeline Institution	TORIX	C-	(855) 822-3863	C+ / 5.8	-0.97	-9.21	4.28 /34	14.80 /73	--	0.96	1.08
EN	Tortoise MLP & Pipeline Investor	TORTX	D	(855) 822-3863	C / 4.6	-1.10	-9.33	4.02 /32	14.52 /71	--	0.70	1.33
EN	Tortoise Select Opportunity Inst	TOPIX	U	(855) 822-3863	U /	7.53	-13.79	-4.66 / 6	--	--	0.17	1.42
FS	Touchstone Arbitrage Y	TMAYX	U	(800) 543-0407	U /	0.80	1.47	0.46 /17	--	--	0.00	2.21

99 Pct = Best
0 Pct = Worst

● Denotes fund is closed to new investors
* Denotes fund is included in Section II

www.thestreetratings.com

RISK	3 Year		NET ASSETS		ASSET				Portfolio	BULL / BEAR		FUND MANAGER		MINIMUMS		LOADS	
Risk Rating/Pts	Standard Deviation	Beta	NAV As of 3/31/15	Total $(Mil)	Cash %	Stocks %	Bonds %	Other %	Turnover Ratio	Last Bull Market Return	Last Bear Market Return	Manager Quality Pct	Manager Tenure (Years)	Initial Purch. $	Additional Purch. $	Front End Load	Back End Load
C- / 4.2	12.2	0.97	16.47	370	0	95	3	2	65	84.7	-17.3	62	10	0	0	0.0	0.0
B- / 7.3	9.6	1.00	23.26	2,087	0	99	0	1	9	99.6	-16.3	66	10	10,000,000	1,000	0.0	0.0
B- / 7.3	9.5	1.00	23.14	693	0	99	0	1	9	97.9	-16.3	64	10	0	0	0.0	0.0
C- / 4.2	12.8	0.94	18.17	2,118	0	99	0	1	94	104.2	-25.7	79	11	2,000,000	1,000	0.0	2.0
C- / 4.2	12.8	0.95	18.09	157	0	99	0	1	94	103.2	-25.8	78	11	1,000,000	0	0.0	2.0
C- / 4.1	12.8	0.94	17.66	109	0	99	0	1	94	101.7	-25.8	76	11	2,500	100	0.0	2.0
C- / 4.1	12.8	0.94	17.81	566	0	99	0	1	94	102.5	-25.8	77	11	0	0	0.0	2.0
C+ / 5.8	13.4	1.00	19.51	1,311	0	99	0	1	24	102.0	-25.1	70	10	10,000,000	1,000	0.0	2.0
C+ / 5.8	13.4	1.00	19.58	481	0	99	0	1	24	100.3	-25.2	68	10	0	0	0.0	2.0
B- / 7.1	10.0	1.03	16.91	1,380	0	97	2	1	7	94.4	-17.5	53	10	2,000,000	1,000	0.0	0.0
B- / 7.1	10.0	1.03	16.87	75	0	97	2	1	7	93.4	-17.6	51	10	1,000,000	0	0.0	0.0
B- / 7.0	10.0	1.02	15.42	940	0	97	2	1	7	92.4	-17.6	50	10	2,500	100	0.0	0.0
B- / 7.1	10.0	1.03	17.13	380	0	97	2	1	7	92.8	-17.7	49	10	0	0	0.0	0.0
C / 5.1	12.6	1.13	9.14	22	4	95	0	1	91	94.9	-22.1	19	7	1,000	0	5.5	0.0
C / 4.7	12.5	1.13	7.93	4	4	95	0	1	91	89.9	-22.4	14	7	1,000	0	5.5	0.0
B / 8.4	5.9	0.97	10.84	48	8	48	43	1	19	29.8	-10.8	9	N/A	1,000	0	5.5	0.0
B / 8.4	5.9	0.96	10.05	12	8	48	43	1	19	26.6	-11.0	6	N/A	1,000	0	0.0	0.0
B- / 7.1	7.8	0.45	11.34	55	9	56	33	2	24	11.6	-7.1	3	6	1,000	0	5.5	0.0
B- / 7.0	7.8	0.45	11.04	14	9	56	33	2	24	8.8	-7.4	3	6	1,000	0	0.0	0.0
U /	N/A	N/A	11.12	30	3	47	49	1	21	N/A	N/A	N/A	2	1,000	0	5.5	0.0
C+ / 6.5	11.4	0.83	9.06	59	6	93	0	1	31	49.3	-27.2	69	8	1,000	0	5.5	0.0
C+ / 6.5	11.4	0.82	8.81	4	6	93	0	1	31	45.4	-27.4	58	8	1,000	0	0.0	0.0
C / 5.5	11.8	0.65	12.03	15	3	96	0	1	11	N/A	N/A	55	4	1,000	0	5.5	0.0
C / 5.4	11.8	0.65	11.73	3	3	96	0	1	11	N/A	N/A	43	4	1,000	0	0.0	0.0
C+ / 5.8	10.7	1.04	8.42	61	4	95	0	1	61	91.0	-20.1	35	7	1,000	0	5.5	0.0
C / 5.3	10.8	1.05	7.25	7	4	95	0	1	61	85.8	-20.2	25	7	1,000	0	0.0	0.0
C+ / 6.8	10.2	0.88	19.35	155	14	85	0	1	37	93.6	-18.8	77	10	1,000	0	5.5	0.0
C+ / 6.4	10.2	0.88	16.67	19	14	85	0	1	37	88.7	-19.1	69	10	1,000	0	0.0	0.0
C / 4.5	13.7	0.98	18.46	84	16	83	0	1	71	120.9	-24.7	86	5	1,000	0	5.5	0.0
C- / 3.3	13.8	0.98	14.68	10	16	83	0	1	71	115.3	-24.8	82	5	1,000	0	0.0	0.0
B- / 7.8	8.6	0.82	8.97	38	8	70	21	1	14	46.9	-19.3	8	N/A	1,000	0	5.5	0.0
B- / 7.7	8.6	0.82	8.24	8	8	70	21	1	14	43.6	-20.4	6	N/A	1,000	0	0.0	0.0
C+ / 6.9	10.3	1.03	33.74	379	0	99	0	1	19	91.4	-18.2	42	23	1,000	100	0.0	2.0
U /	N/A	N/A	27.33	41	55	5	14	26	69	N/A	N/A	N/A	3	1,000	100	0.0	2.0
E / 0.3	34.2	1.63	30.05	1,147	1	95	3	1	10	-52.9	-17.4	2	18	1,000	100	0.0	2.0
C+ / 5.6	11.8	0.85	14.66	243	4	95	0	1	31	47.7	-21.7	84	14	1,000	100	0.0	2.0
C- / 4.2	14.7	0.94	22.75	96	1	98	0	1	922	109.4	-21.3	85	5	1,000	100	0.0	2.0
C- / 4.2	14.1	1.13	13.09	98	7	83	9	1	32	81.6	-27.5	6	17	1,000	100	0.0	2.0
C+ / 6.6	8.8	0.30	6.57	3	66	0	33	1	0	-14.9	-22.0	16	6	10,000	100	0.0	0.0
C+ / 5.8	8.6	1.36	11.14	85	88	0	11	1	18	51.5	-13.8	21	5	10,000	100	0.0	0.0
C+ / 5.7	10.9	1.51	11.03	119	85	0	14	1	0	42.8	-19.1	7	5	10,000	100	0.0	0.0
B- / 7.2	9.8	0.53	8.62	86	88	0	11	1	0	-4.6	-11.3	31	N/A	10,000	100	0.0	0.0
B / 8.6	7.2	0.44	10.50	30	64	0	34	2	193	27.2	-12.8	89	5	10,000	100	0.0	0.0
C / 5.2	13.0	1.19	14.60	74	2	97	0	1	95	103.2	-19.0	36	9	10,000	100	0.0	2.0
C / 5.2	13.0	1.19	14.59	77	2	97	0	1	95	101.6	-19.1	33	9	1,000	100	0.0	2.0
U /	N/A	N/A	17.65	46	2	97	0	1	163	N/A	N/A	N/A	3	100,000	10,000	0.0	1.0
B- / 7.7	9.9	0.99	47.46	415	13	86	0	1	14	78.9	-12.3	37	18	2,000	500	0.0	0.0
U /	N/A	N/A	16.07	82	26	73	0	1	34	N/A	N/A	N/A	4	2,500	100	0.0	0.0
C / 4.5	12.6	0.57	16.34	1,751	26	73	0	1	34	85.4	N/A	99	4	1,000,000	100	0.0	0.0
C / 4.5	12.6	0.57	16.24	264	26	73	0	1	34	83.8	N/A	99	4	2,500	100	5.8	0.0
U /	N/A	N/A	10.43	38	10	89	0	1	131	N/A	N/A	N/A	2	1,000,000	100	0.0	0.0
U /	N/A	N/A	10.04	108	46	49	4	1	293	N/A	N/A	N/A	2	2,500	50	0.0	0.0

Fund Type	Fund Name	Ticker Symbol	Overall Investment Rating	Phone	Perfor-mance Rating/Pts	3 Mo	6 Mo	1Yr / Pct	3Yr / Pct	5Yr / Pct	Dividend Yield	Expense Ratio
AA	Touchstone Balanced Allocation A	TBAAX	C-	(800) 543-0407	D / 1.7	1.25	2.10	3.61 /30	7.29 /23	7.42 /26	1.71	1.68
AA	Touchstone Balanced Allocation C	TBACX	C-	(800) 543-0407	D / 2.0	1.18	1.76	2.96 /26	6.53 /19	6.62 /21	0.87	2.40
AA	Touchstone Balanced Allocation Inst	TBAIX	C	(800) 543-0407	D+ / 2.7	1.40	2.32	3.98 /32	7.61 /25	7.69 /28	2.08	63.93
AA	Touchstone Balanced Allocation Y	TBAYX	C	(800) 543-0407	D+ / 2.6	1.31	2.23	3.87 /31	7.57 /24	7.68 /28	2.07	1.41
GR	Touchstone Capital Growth A	TSCGX	C	(800) 543-0407	C / 5.4	4.03	7.71	10.21 /75	12.92 /59	13.05 /69	0.00	2.66
GR	Touchstone Capital Growth Inst	TCGNX	C+	(800) 543-0407	C+ / 6.7	4.13	7.93	10.64 /77	13.31 /62	13.44 /72	0.00	24.91
GR	Touchstone Capital Growth Y	TCGYX	C+	(800) 543-0407	C+ / 6.6	4.12	7.84	10.53 /76	13.21 /61	13.34 /71	0.00	1.10
AA	Touchstone Conservative Alloc A	TSAAX	C-	(800) 543-0407	E+ / 0.9	0.81	1.12	2.50 /24	4.53 /12	5.13 /13	1.82	1.59
AA	Touchstone Conservative Alloc C	TSACX	C-	(800) 543-0407	D- / 1.0	0.62	0.84	1.74 /21	3.76 /10	4.34 /10	1.19	2.34
AA	Touchstone Conservative Alloc Inst	TVAIX	C-	(800) 543-0407	D- / 1.3	0.79	1.25	2.67 /25	4.76 /12	5.40 /14	2.20	5.55
AA	Touchstone Conservative Alloc Y	TSAYX	C-	(800) 543-0407	D- / 1.3	0.88	1.26	2.76 /25	4.76 /12	5.40 /14	2.20	1.32
IN	Touchstone Dynamic Equity A	TDEAX	C-	(800) 543-0407	D / 2.0	2.21	1.75	4.10 /32	7.86 /26	8.58 /34	0.26	2.42
IN	Touchstone Dynamic Equity C	TDECX	C-	(800) 543-0407	D+ / 2.3	2.05	1.33	3.35 /28	7.06 /22	7.76 /28	0.00	3.21
IN	Touchstone Dynamic Equity Inst	TDELX	C	(800) 543-0407	C- / 3.0	2.31	1.89	4.43 /35	8.20 /28	8.89 /36	0.66	1.96
IN	Touchstone Dynamic Equity Y	TDEYX	C	(800) 543-0407	C- / 3.0	2.32	1.94	4.49 /35	8.17 /28	8.86 /36	0.70	1.96
EM	Touchstone Emerging Mkts Eq A	TEMAX	E	(800) 543-0407	E- / 0.2	1.36	-3.60	0.71 /18	-3.10 / 2	0.03 / 2	0.50	2.18
EM	Touchstone Emerging Mkts Eq C	TEFCX	E	(800) 543-0407	E / 0.3	1.20	-4.02	-0.09 /15	-3.85 / 2	-0.71 / 2	0.00	3.01
EM	Touchstone Emerging Mkts Eq Inst	TMEIX	E	(800) 543-0407	E / 0.3	1.46	-3.50	1.01 /18	-2.73 / 2	0.43 / 3	1.09	1.29
EM	Touchstone Emerging Mkts Eq Y	TEMYX	E	(800) 543-0407	E / 0.3	1.46	-3.53	0.99 /18	-2.82 / 2	0.33 / 3	0.98	1.36
GR	Touchstone Focused A	TFOAX	B+	(800) 543-0407	B- / 7.2	2.54	6.01	6.99 /55	16.83 /89	13.72 /75	0.29	1.47
GR	Touchstone Focused Inst	TFFIX	A+	(800) 543-0407	B+ / 8.6	2.63	6.20	7.40 /58	17.30 /91	14.18 /79	0.51	1.01
GR	Touchstone Focused Y	TFFYX	A	(800) 543-0407	B+ / 8.5	2.58	6.15	7.29 /57	17.13 /90	14.02 /78	0.41	1.03
RE	Touchstone Global Real Est A	TGAAX	D	(800) 543-0407	C / 5.1	4.08	9.74	13.48 /88	11.22 /47	10.96 /52	4.90	3.56
RE	Touchstone Global Real Est C	TGACX	D	(800) 543-0407	C+ / 5.6	3.89	9.35	12.66 /85	10.38 /42	10.13 /46	4.51	4.89
RE	Touchstone Global Real Est Inst	TRFIX	D+	(800) 543-0407	C+ / 6.4	4.23	10.03	13.97 /89	11.67 /50	11.41 /56	5.35	1.68
RE	Touchstone Global Real Est Y	TRFYX	D+	(800) 543-0407	C+ / 6.3	4.18	9.90	13.81 /89	11.50 /49	11.25 /55	5.31	4.57
AA	Touchstone Growth Allocation A	TGQAX	C-	(800) 543-0407	C- / 3.3	2.46	3.64	5.12 /40	10.14 /40	9.64 /42	1.34	1.98
AA	Touchstone Growth Allocation C	TGQCX	C-	(800) 543-0407	C- / 3.7	2.26	3.26	4.26 /33	9.33 /35	8.83 /36	0.68	2.70
AA	Touchstone Growth Allocation Inst	TGQIX	C	(800) 543-0407	C / 4.3	2.53	3.73	5.34 /41	10.30 /41	9.83 /43	1.76	99.04
AA	Touchstone Growth Allocation Y	TGQYX	C	(800) 543-0407	C / 4.3	2.51	3.74	5.35 /41	10.42 /42	9.92 /44	1.60	1.65
GR	Touchstone Growth Opps A	TGVFX	B	(800) 543-0407	A- / 9.0	4.10	11.17	14.99 /92	18.18 /95	15.31 /89	0.00	1.43
GR	Touchstone Growth Opps C	TGVCX	B	(800) 543-0407	A / 9.3	3.87	10.75	14.11 /90	17.30 /91	14.47 /82	0.00	2.25
GR	Touchstone Growth Opps Inst	TGVVX	B+	(800) 543-0407	A+ / 9.6	4.16	11.33	15.39 /92	18.62 /96	15.75 /92	0.07	0.98
GR	Touchstone Growth Opps Y	TGVYX	B+	(800) 543-0407	A+ / 9.6	4.16	11.34	15.32 /92	18.52 /96	15.62 /91	0.03	1.03
SC	Touchstone International SC A	TNSAX	C	(800) 543-0407	C+ / 5.6	7.59	7.36	2.89 /26	13.91 /66	12.52 /64	0.42	2.14
SC	Touchstone International SC Inst	TNSIX	C+	(800) 543-0407	C+ / 6.9	7.71	7.52	3.31 /28	14.43 /70	13.03 /69	0.77	1.35
SC	Touchstone International SC Y	TNSYX	C+	(800) 543-0407	C+ / 6.7	7.61	7.41	3.11 /27	14.21 /69	12.81 /66	0.64	1.46
FO	Touchstone International Value Inst	FIVIX	U	(800) 543-0407	U /	1.08	-3.71	-4.66 / 6	--	--	3.51	1.29
FO	Touchstone Internatl Value A	FSIEX	E+	(800) 543-0407	E+ / 0.9	1.08	-3.79	-4.95 / 6	5.96 /17	3.88 / 8	2.91	1.79
FO	Touchstone Internatl Value C	FTECX	E+	(800) 543-0407	D- / 1.0	0.78	-4.25	-5.72 / 5	5.11 /13	3.08 / 6	2.67	6.04
FO	Touchstone Internatl Value Y	FIEIX	D-	(800) 543-0407	D- / 1.3	1.08	-3.66	-4.72 / 6	6.28 /18	4.16 / 9	3.45	1.33
GR	Touchstone Large Cap Growth A	TEQAX	C	(800) 543-0407	B / 7.6	7.31	12.40	17.17 /95	13.92 /67	14.61 /83	0.13	1.29
GR	● Touchstone Large Cap Growth B	TEQBX	C+	(800) 543-0407	B / 8.1	7.12	11.95	16.27 /94	13.24 /61	14.04 /78	0.00	1.79
GR	Touchstone Large Cap Growth C	TEQCX	C	(800) 543-0407	B / 8.0	7.15	11.97	16.30 /94	13.07 /60	13.75 /75	0.00	2.04
GR	Touchstone Large Cap Growth I	TIQIX	C+	(800) 543-0407	B+ / 8.8	7.40	12.55	17.48 /95	14.23 /69	14.91 /86	0.28	1.05
GR	Touchstone Large Cap Inst	TLCIX	U	(800) 543-0407	U /	0.09	6.75	--	--	--	0.00	N/A
GL	● Touchstone Merger Arbitrage A	TMGAX	D	(800) 543-0407	E / 0.5	0.76	1.78	-0.13 /15	2.00 / 6	--	0.00	2.54
GL	● Touchstone Merger Arbitrage C	TMGCX	D+	(800) 543-0407	E+ / 0.6	0.58	1.43	-0.89 /13	1.20 / 5	--	0.00	3.34
GL	● Touchstone Merger Arbitrage Inst	TMGLX	D+	(800) 543-0407	E+ / 0.8	0.85	1.95	0.25 /16	2.35 / 7	--	0.00	2.22
GL	● Touchstone Merger Arbitrage Y	TMGYX	D+	(800) 543-0407	E+ / 0.8	0.85	1.96	0.15 /16	2.30 / 7	--	0.00	2.26
MC	Touchstone Mid Cap A	TMAPX	A+	(800) 543-0407	B+ / 8.7	3.59	9.59	12.73 /86	17.98 /94	15.68 /91	0.00	1.38
MC	Touchstone Mid Cap C	TMCJX	A+	(800) 543-0407	A- / 9.0	3.42	9.14	11.87 /82	17.11 /90	14.82 /85	0.00	2.14

● Denotes fund is closed to new investors
* Denotes fund is included in Section II

| RISK | | | NET ASSETS | | ASSET | | | | BULL / BEAR | | FUND MANAGER | | MINIMUMS | | LOADS | |
| | 3 Year | | NAV | | | | | | Last Bull | Last Bear | Manager | Manager | Initial | Additional | Front | Back |
Risk Rating/Pts	Standard Deviation	Beta	As of 3/31/15	Total $(Mil)	Cash %	Stocks %	Bonds %	Other %	Portfolio Turnover Ratio	Market Return	Market Return	Quality Pct	Tenure (Years)	Purch. $	Purch. $	End Load	End Load
B /8.7	5.9	1.00	12.80	36	8	58	32	2	32	42.6	-11.2	22	N/A	2,500	50	5.8	0.0
B /8.7	6.0	1.01	12.82	32	8	58	32	2	32	39.1	-11.4	15	N/A	2,500	50	0.0	0.0
B /8.7	6.0	1.01	12.77	N/A	8	58	32	2	32	43.9	-11.1	24	N/A	500,000	50	0.0	0.0
B /8.7	6.0	1.01	12.82	24	8	58	32	2	32	43.8	-11.1	24	N/A	2,500	50	0.0	0.0
C+ /5.9	12.3	1.16	28.88	2	1	98	0	1	30	87.3	-17.9	9	8	2,500	50	5.8	0.0
C+ /5.9	12.3	1.16	29.76	1	1	98	0	1	30	89.6	-17.8	11	8	500,000	50	0.0	0.0
C+ /5.9	12.3	1.16	29.54	191	1	98	0	1	30	89.0	-17.9	10	8	2,500	50	0.0	0.0
B+ /9.1	3.3	0.54	11.14	17	14	32	51	3	30	23.1	-4.7	50	N/A	2,500	50	5.8	0.0
B+ /9.1	3.4	0.55	11.09	13	14	32	51	3	30	20.0	-5.1	37	N/A	2,500	50	0.0	0.0
B+ /9.1	3.4	0.55	11.15	N/A	14	32	51	3	30	24.1	-4.7	52	N/A	500,000	50	0.0	0.0
B+ /9.1	3.3	0.53	11.14	12	14	32	51	3	30	24.1	-4.7	55	N/A	2,500	50	0.0	0.0
B /8.3	6.3	0.50	13.89	11	2	97	0	1	382	49.2	-9.9	69	37	2,500	50	5.8	0.0
B /8.3	6.3	0.50	12.96	11	2	97	0	1	382	45.5	-10.1	58	37	2,500	50	0.0	0.0
B /8.3	6.3	0.50	14.15	12	2	97	0	1	382	50.7	-9.7	72	37	500,000	50	0.0	0.0
B /8.3	6.3	0.50	14.12	40	2	97	0	1	382	50.4	-9.7	72	37	2,500	50	0.0	0.0
C /4.4	14.1	0.99	11.19	5	1	98	0	1	38	10.3	-21.0	18	6	2,500	50	5.8	0.0
C /4.4	14.1	0.99	10.97	2	1	98	0	1	38	7.5	-21.2	12	6	2,500	50	0.0	0.0
C /4.4	14.0	0.99	11.11	237	1	98	0	1	38	11.9	-20.9	21	6	500,000	50	0.0	0.0
C /4.4	14.0	0.99	11.11	86	1	98	0	1	38	11.5	-21.0	20	6	2,500	50	0.0	0.0
B- /7.1	10.7	1.02	37.19	297	6	93	0	1	27	110.4	-18.6	70	3	2,500	50	5.8	0.0
B- /7.1	10.7	1.02	37.91	52	6	93	0	1	27	113.2	-18.4	75	3	500,000	50	0.0	0.0
B- /7.1	10.7	1.02	37.76	757	6	93	0	1	27	112.2	-18.5	73	3	2,500	50	0.0	0.0
C- /3.1	11.9	0.83	11.19	5	23	76	0	1	53	68.5	-19.1	62	2	2,500	50	5.8	0.0
C- /3.1	11.9	0.84	11.22	1	23	76	0	1	53	64.0	-19.4	50	2	2,500	50	0.0	0.0
C- /3.1	11.9	0.84	11.48	11	23	76	0	1	53	70.7	-19.1	67	2	500,000	50	0.0	0.0
C- /3.1	11.8	0.83	11.34	6	23	76	0	1	53	69.9	-19.1	66	2	2,500	50	0.0	0.0
B- /7.0	9.3	1.55	14.56	26	3	92	3	2	50	65.3	-19.1	6	N/A	2,500	50	5.8	0.0
C+ /6.9	9.3	1.56	14.02	21	3	92	3	2	50	61.0	-19.4	4	N/A	2,500	50	0.0	0.0
C+ /6.9	9.2	1.55	13.36	N/A	3	92	3	2	50	65.9	-19.1	6	N/A	500,000	50	0.0	0.0
B- /7.0	9.2	1.55	14.71	10	3	92	3	2	50	66.7	-19.0	6	N/A	2,500	50	0.0	0.0
C /5.0	12.3	1.18	33.29	49	1	98	0	1	79	112.9	-23.1	53	9	2,500	50	5.8	0.0
C /4.7	12.3	1.19	29.27	14	1	98	0	1	79	107.6	-23.4	41	9	2,500	50	0.0	0.0
C /5.1	12.3	1.18	34.05	135	1	98	0	1	79	115.5	-23.0	59	9	500,000	50	0.0	0.0
C /5.1	12.3	1.18	33.81	107	1	98	0	1	79	114.8	-23.0	57	9	2,500	50	0.0	0.0
C+ /6.2	12.0	0.65	15.74	14	1	98	0	1	60	72.3	-21.3	89	4	2,500	50	5.8	0.0
C+ /6.3	12.0	0.66	16.20	29	1	98	0	1	60	75.1	-21.1	90	4	500,000	50	0.0	0.0
C+ /6.3	12.0	0.65	16.12	127	1	98	0	1	60	74.0	-21.3	90	4	2,500	50	0.0	0.0
U /	N/A	N/A	8.42	73	4	95	0	1	31	N/A	N/A	N/A	3	500,000	50	0.0	0.0
C+ /5.7	13.3	0.98	8.41	5	4	95	0	1	31	40.1	-25.0	24	3	2,500	50	5.8	0.0
C+ /5.7	13.3	0.98	7.77	N/A	4	95	0	1	31	36.7	-25.4	16	3	2,500	50	0.0	0.0
C+ /5.7	13.3	0.98	8.41	35	4	95	0	1	31	41.5	-25.0	27	3	2,500	50	0.0	0.0
C- /4.0	9.6	0.76	30.96	258	1	98	0	1	92	75.4	-10.8	82	18	2,500	50	5.8	0.0
C- /3.7	9.6	0.76	28.73	2	1	98	0	1	92	72.1	-10.8	78	18	2,500	50	0.0	0.0
C- /3.6	9.7	0.76	28.32	104	1	98	0	1	92	70.9	-11.0	76	18	2,500	50	0.0	0.0
C- /4.0	9.6	0.76	31.49	417	1	98	0	1	92	76.9	-10.7	84	18	2,500	50	0.0	0.0
U /	N/A	N/A	10.77	81	0	0	0	100	0	N/A	N/A	N/A	1	500,000	50	0.0	0.0
B /8.5	2.0	0.06	10.63	41	47	46	5	2	271	10.9	N/A	80	4	2,500	50	5.8	0.0
B /8.5	2.0	0.06	10.36	26	47	46	5	2	271	7.9	N/A	74	4	2,500	50	0.0	0.0
B /8.5	2.0	0.06	10.73	112	47	46	5	2	271	12.1	N/A	82	4	500,000	0	0.0	0.0
B /8.5	2.0	0.06	10.71	122	47	46	5	2	271	12.0	N/A	82	4	2,500	50	0.0	0.0
B- /7.1	11.4	0.88	25.95	52	2	97	0	1	26	102.0	-19.0	88	4	2,500	50	5.8	0.0
B- /7.1	11.4	0.88	25.07	57	2	97	0	1	26	97.0	-19.3	84	4	2,500	50	0.0	0.0

				PERFORMANCE								
	99 Pct = Best						Total Return % through 3/31/15				Incl. in Returns	
	0 Pct = Worst			Perfor-					Annualized		Dividend	Expense
Fund		Ticker		Overall Investment		mance						
Type	Fund Name	Symbol	Phone	Rating	Rating/Pts	3 Mo	6 Mo	1Yr / Pct	3Yr / Pct	5Yr / Pct	Yield	Ratio
MC	Touchstone Mid Cap Growth A	TEGAX	(800) 543-0407	B	A- / 9.2	6.20	14.44	16.34 /94	17.86 /94	14.25 /80	0.00	1.38
MC	● Touchstone Mid Cap Growth B	TBEGX	(800) 543-0407	B	A / 9.5	6.00	14.02	15.72 /93	17.39 /92	13.83 /76	0.00	1.73
MC	Touchstone Mid Cap Growth C	TOECX	B-	(800) 543-0407	A / 9.4	5.95	14.00	15.51 /92	17.00 /90	13.38 /72	0.00	2.11
MC	Touchstone Mid Cap Growth Inst	TEGIX	B+	(800) 543-0407	A+ / 9.7	6.22	14.58	16.73 /94	18.32 /95	--	0.00	0.97
MC	Touchstone Mid Cap Growth Y	TEGYX	B+	(800) 543-0407	A+ / 9.6	6.21	14.57	16.69 /94	18.20 /95	14.55 /83	0.00	1.07
MC	Touchstone Mid Cap Inst	TMPIX	A+	(800) 543-0407	A / 9.4	3.69	9.77	13.09 /87	18.38 /95	--	0.26	0.99
MC	Touchstone Mid Cap Value A	TCVAX	C+	(800) 543-0407	C+ / 6.8	2.69	7.95	9.26 /71	15.70 /81	13.66 /75	0.38	1.57
MC	Touchstone Mid Cap Value C	TMFCX	B	(800) 543-0407	B- / 7.3	2.47	7.53	8.55 /67	14.90 /74	12.84 /67	0.08	3.04
MC	Touchstone Mid Cap Value Inst	TCVIX	B+	(800) 543-0407	B+ / 8.3	2.78	8.19	9.73 /73	16.17 /85	14.12 /79	0.81	1.03
MC	Touchstone Mid Cap Value Y	TCVYX	B+	(800) 543-0407	B / 8.2	2.76	8.10	9.57 /72	16.01 /83	13.95 /77	0.71	1.13
MC	Touchstone Mid Cap Y	TMCPX	A+	(800) 543-0407	A / 9.4	3.69	9.75	13.03 /87	18.30 /95	15.98 /93	0.20	1.04
MC	Touchstone Mid Cap Z	TMCTX	A+	(800) 543-0407	A / 9.3	3.62	9.56	12.72 /86	17.98 /94	15.67 /91	0.00	1.53
AA	Touchstone Moderate Gr Alloc A	TSMAX	C-	(800) 543-0407	D+ / 2.7	1.91	3.21	4.93 /38	9.09 /34	8.81 /35	1.46	1.82
AA	Touchstone Moderate Gr Alloc C	TSMCX	C-	(800) 543-0407	C- / 3.1	1.74	2.78	4.14 /33	8.27 /29	7.98 /30	0.97	2.54
AA	Touchstone Moderate Gr Alloc Inst	TSMIX	C	(800) 543-0407	C- / 3.7	1.96	3.25	5.18 /40	9.39 /36	9.09 /37	1.78	42.53
AA	Touchstone Moderate Gr Alloc Y	TSMYX	C	(800) 543-0407	C- / 3.7	2.03	3.31	5.16 /40	9.33 /35	9.06 /37	1.78	1.49
GI	Touchstone Premium Yield Eq A	TPYAX	C-	(800) 543-0407	C- / 4.0	0.82	1.45	9.00 /69	11.40 /48	12.67 /65	2.48	1.31
GI	Touchstone Premium Yield Eq C	TPYCX	C	(800) 543-0407	C / 4.4	0.64	1.09	8.12 /64	10.57 /43	11.84 /60	1.92	2.04
GI	Touchstone Premium Yield Eq Y	TPYYX	C	(800) 543-0407	C / 5.1	0.89	1.58	9.19 /70	11.70 /50	12.94 /68	2.89	0.98
EM	Touchstone Sands Cap Em Mkt Gr	TSEGX	U	(800) 543-0407	U /	1.37	0.88	--	--	--	0.00	1.65
EM	Touchstone Sands Cap Em Mkt Gr Y	TSEMX	U	(800) 543-0407	U /	1.37	0.88	--	--	--	0.00	1.81
GR	● Touchstone Sands Cap Sel Gr A	TSNAX	C-	(800) 543-0407	C+ / 5.8	0.17	4.03	7.65 /60	14.69 /72	--	0.00	1.31
GR	● Touchstone Sands Cap Sel Gr C	TSNCX	C-	(800) 543-0407	C+ / 6.2	0.00	3.69	6.85 /54	13.84 /66	--	0.00	2.07
GR	● Touchstone Sands Cap Sel Gr Y	CFSIX	C	(800) 543-0407	B- / 7.0	0.33	4.21	7.98 /63	15.02 /75	18.50 /98	0.00	1.01
GR	● Touchstone Sands Cap Sel Gr Z	PTSGX	C	(800) 543-0407	C+ / 6.8	0.22	4.09	7.71 /61	14.72 /73	18.20 /98	0.00	1.33
GR	● Touchstone Sands Capital Inst Gro	CISGX	C	(800) 543-0407	B- / 7.2	0.31	4.25	8.10 /64	15.26 /77	18.87 /98	0.00	0.80
SC	● Touchstone Small Cap Core A	TSFAX	C+	(800) 543-0407	B- / 7.1	10.05	10.49	8.22 /64	15.37 /78	16.07 /93	0.01	1.41
SC	● Touchstone Small Cap Core C	TSFCX	B-	(800) 543-0407	B / 7.6	9.84	10.11	7.38 /58	14.51 /71	15.21 /88	0.00	2.15
SC	● Touchstone Small Cap Core Inst	TSFIX	B+	(800) 543-0407	B+ / 8.5	10.13	10.67	8.52 /66	15.80 /82	16.50 /95	0.05	1.02
SC	● Touchstone Small Cap Core Y	TSFYX	B	(800) 543-0407	B+ / 8.5	10.11	10.64	8.50 /66	15.71 /81	16.40 /94	0.04	1.06
SC	Touchstone Small Cap Growth A	MXCAX	B-	(800) 543-0407	B / 8.1	8.57	13.03	11.52 /81	16.29 /85	13.94 /77	0.00	1.83
SC	Touchstone Small Cap Growth C	MXCSX	B	(800) 543-0407	B+ / 8.5	8.39	12.67	10.64 /77	15.43 /78	13.12 /69	0.00	2.67
SC	Touchstone Small Cap Growth Y	MXAIX	B+	(800) 543-0407	A- / 9.2	8.58	13.38	12.01 /83	16.60 /87	14.26 /80	0.00	1.52
GR	Touchstone Small Cap Val Opps A	TSOAX	C+	(800) 543-0407	B+ / 8.9	5.56	11.34	5.73 /44	19.18 /97	14.59 /83	1.35	1.94
GR	Touchstone Small Cap Val Opps Inst	TSOIX	B-	(800) 543-0407	A+ / 9.6	5.68	11.52	6.11 /47	19.64 /97	15.05 /87	1.55	1.38
GR	Touchstone Small Cap Val Opps Y	TSOYX	B-	(800) 543-0407	A+ / 9.6	5.59	11.43	6.02 /47	19.52 /97	14.91 /86	1.52	1.25
SC	Touchstone Small Cap Value A	TVOAX	D+	(800) 543-0407	C- / 3.9	-1.45	6.85	-0.88 /13	12.39 /55	12.39 /63	1.43	1.62
SC	Touchstone Small Cap Value C	TVOCX	C-	(800) 543-0407	C / 4.3	-1.62	6.43	-1.62 /11	11.58 /50	--	0.78	3.20
SC	Touchstone Small Cap Value Inst	TVOIX	C	(800) 543-0407	C / 5.1	-1.35	7.06	-0.47 /14	12.84 /58	--	1.91	1.25
SC	Touchstone Small Cap Value Y	TVOYX	C-	(800) 543-0407	C / 5.0	-1.39	6.98	-0.62 /14	12.66 /57	--	1.76	1.60
GR	Touchstone Value A	TVLAX	B	(800) 543-0407	C+ / 5.7	0.10	3.53	7.50 /59	14.66 /72	12.43 /64	1.72	1.30
GR	Touchstone Value Institutional	TVLIX	B+	(800) 543-0407	B- / 7.0	0.21	3.73	7.90 /62	15.10 /76	12.85 /67	2.20	0.86
GR	Touchstone Value Y	TVLYX	B-	(800) 543-0407	C+ / 6.9	0.21	3.77	7.76 /61	14.98 /75	12.73 /66	2.08	0.98
SC	Towle Deep Value	TDVFX	B	(888) 998-6953	B+ / 8.6	-0.80	11.00	1.13 /19	18.78 /96	--	0.00	1.32
GR	Transamerica Arbitrage Strategy I2		D+	(888) 233-4339	E+ / 0.6	0.92	1.21	1.51 /20	0.55 / 5	--	0.05	2.00
AA	Transamerica Asset Alloc Consv A	ICLAX	D+	(888) 233-4339	D- / 1.4	2.23	3.51	5.40 /42	6.07 /17	6.20 /18	1.97	1.29
AA	● Transamerica Asset Alloc Consv B	ICLBX	D+	(888) 233-4339	D / 1.7	1.94	3.02	4.48 /35	5.29 /14	5.45 /14	1.29	2.06
AA	Transamerica Asset Alloc Consv C	ICLLX	D+	(888) 233-4339	D / 1.7	1.98	3.09	4.61 /36	5.37 /14	5.53 /14	1.40	2.00
AA	Transamerica Asset Alloc Consv I	TACIX	C-	(888) 233-4339	D+ / 2.3	2.20	3.64	5.57 /43	6.39 /18	6.54 /20	2.32	1.04
AA	Transamerica Asset Alloc Consv R	ICVRX	D+	(888) 233-4339	D / 1.9	2.12	3.35	5.04 /39	5.82 /16	5.93 /16	1.69	1.60
AA	Transamerica Asset Alloc Growth A	IAAAX	C	(888) 233-4339	C / 4.7	3.45	6.32	8.62 /67	11.91 /52	10.41 /48	1.26	1.47
AA	● Transamerica Asset Alloc Growth B	IAABX	C	(888) 233-4339	C / 5.0	3.24	5.85	7.77 /61	11.06 /46	9.60 /41	0.38	2.27

● Denotes fund is closed to new investors
* Denotes fund is included in Section II

www.thestreetratings.com

Risk Rating/Pts	3 Year Standard Deviation	Beta	NAV As of 3/31/15	Total $(Mil)	Cash %	Stocks %	Bonds %	Other %	Portfolio Turnover Ratio	Last Bull Market Return	Last Bear Market Return	Manager Quality Pct	Manager Tenure (Years)	Initial Purch. $	Additional Purch. $	Front End Load	Back End Load
C /4.8	11.3	0.97	27.06	269	3	96	0	1	79	103.7	-26.0	79	16	2,500	50	5.8	0.0
C- /3.9	11.3	0.97	20.32	3	3	96	0	1	79	100.5	-26.0	76	16	2,500	50	0.0	0.0
C- /3.8	11.3	0.97	19.78	157	3	96	0	1	79	98.6	-26.2	72	16	2,500	50	0.0	0.0
C /4.9	11.3	0.97	27.85	102	3	96	0	1	79	106.5	-25.9	81	16	500,000	50	0.0	0.0
C /4.9	11.3	0.97	27.71	299	3	96	0	1	79	105.6	-25.9	81	16	2,500	50	0.0	0.0
B- /7.1	11.4	0.88	26.11	97	2	97	0	1	26	N/A	N/A	89	4	500,000	50	0.0	0.0
C+ /6.4	10.5	0.92	17.19	9	0	100	0	0	85	95.0	-23.3	69	N/A	2,500	50	5.8	0.0
C+ /6.4	10.5	0.92	16.98	2	0	100	0	0	85	90.4	-23.5	60	N/A	2,500	50	0.0	0.0
C+ /6.4	10.5	0.92	17.33	135	0	100	0	0	85	97.8	-23.2	73	N/A	500,000	50	0.0	0.0
C+ /6.4	10.4	0.91	17.26	204	0	100	0	0	85	96.7	-23.2	72	N/A	2,500	50	0.0	0.0
B- /7.1	11.4	0.88	26.10	340	2	97	0	1	26	103.8	-18.9	89	4	2,500	50	0.0	0.0
B- /7.1	11.4	0.88	25.79	24	2	97	0	1	26	101.9	-19.0	88	4	2,500	50	0.0	0.0
B- /7.7	7.6	1.28	13.13	57	4	75	19	2	38	55.3	-15.3	13	N/A	2,500	50	5.8	0.0
B- /7.7	7.7	1.30	12.89	43	4	75	19	2	38	51.5	-15.6	8	N/A	2,500	50	0.0	0.0
B- /7.7	7.6	1.29	13.17	N/A	4	75	19	2	38	56.8	-15.2	14	N/A	500,000	50	0.0	0.0
B- /7.7	7.6	1.29	13.23	16	4	75	19	2	38	56.7	-15.3	14	N/A	2,500	50	0.0	0.0
C+ /6.5	8.8	0.77	9.52	49	2	97	0	1	26	67.0	-9.3	57	7	2,500	50	5.8	0.0
C+ /6.5	8.8	0.77	9.51	37	2	97	0	1	26	62.6	-9.4	46	7	2,500	50	0.0	0.0
C+ /6.5	8.8	0.77	9.50	127	2	97	0	1	26	68.3	-9.2	60	7	2,500	50	0.0	0.0
U /	N/A	N/A	10.37	33	0	0	0	100	0	N/A	N/A	N/A	1	500,000	50	0.0	0.0
U /	N/A	N/A	10.37	39	0	0	0	100	0	N/A	N/A	N/A	1	2,500	50	0.0	0.0
C /4.7	13.9	1.12	17.99	298	3	96	0	1	30	106.1	-12.0	24	15	2,500	50	5.8	0.0
C /4.7	13.9	1.13	17.38	200	3	96	0	1	30	100.8	-12.2	17	15	2,500	50	0.0	0.0
C /4.7	13.9	1.12	18.50	3,887	3	96	0	1	30	107.7	-11.8	28	15	2,500	50	0.0	0.0
C /4.7	13.9	1.12	18.00	1,697	3	96	0	1	30	106.1	-12.0	25	15	2,500	50	0.0	0.0
C /4.3	13.9	1.13	22.32	3,841	1	98	0	1	37	109.7	-11.8	29	10	500,000	50	0.0	0.0
C /5.5	12.7	0.75	20.92	81	1	98	0	1	17	96.5	-17.9	89	6	2,500	50	5.8	0.0
C /5.4	12.7	0.75	20.32	27	1	98	0	1	17	91.4	-18.1	86	6	2,500	50	0.0	0.0
C /5.5	12.7	0.75	21.10	390	1	98	0	1	17	98.9	-17.7	90	6	500,000	50	0.0	0.0
C /5.5	12.7	0.75	21.13	327	1	98	0	1	17	98.5	-17.8	90	6	2,500	50	0.0	0.0
C /5.3	12.7	0.90	5.70	34	4	95	0	1	195	94.2	-21.6	81	5	2,500	50	5.8	0.0
C /4.9	12.7	0.90	4.78	13	4	95	0	1	195	89.6	-21.8	75	5	2,500	50	0.0	0.0
C /5.5	12.7	0.91	6.33	314	4	95	0	1	195	95.8	-21.4	82	5	2,500	50	0.0	0.0
C- /3.1	13.8	1.17	19.16	18	3	96	0	1	73	111.3	-22.9	68	14	2,500	50	5.8	0.0
C- /3.4	13.7	1.17	20.45	31	3	96	0	1	73	114.2	-22.8	73	14	500,000	50	0.0	0.0
C- /3.4	13.8	1.17	20.20	152	3	96	0	1	73	113.5	-22.8	72	14	2,500	50	0.0	0.0
C+ /5.8	14.2	1.00	23.67	31	4	95	0	1	100	89.5	-22.7	21	5	2,500	50	5.8	0.0
C+ /5.8	14.2	1.00	23.44	2	4	95	0	1	100	84.9	-22.9	16	5	2,500	50	0.0	0.0
C+ /5.8	14.3	1.00	23.69	31	4	95	0	1	100	92.2	-22.6	25	5	500,000	50	0.0	0.0
C+ /5.8	14.2	1.00	23.70	9	4	95	0	1	100	91.0	-22.4	24	5	2,500	50	0.0	0.0
B- /7.7	9.5	0.95	9.70	55	1	98	0	1	26	92.9	-16.5	59	9	2,500	50	5.8	0.0
B- /7.7	9.4	0.95	9.72	248	1	98	0	1	26	95.4	-16.4	65	9	500,000	50	0.0	0.0
B- /7.7	9.4	0.95	9.74	113	1	98	0	1	26	94.9	-16.5	65	9	2,500	50	0.0	0.0
C /4.7	18.8	1.18	16.11	73	5	94	0	1	23	N/A	N/A	59	4	50,000	5,000	0.0	2.0
B /8.5	2.5	0.08	9.89	145	41	45	13	1	683	3.4	N/A	56	4	0	0	0.0	0.0
B- /7.7	4.1	0.68	11.62	402	4	34	60	2	26	31.3	-8.3	50	N/A	1,000	50	5.5	0.0
B- /7.7	4.2	0.69	11.56	32	4	34	60	2	26	28.0	-8.5	37	N/A	1,000	50	0.0	0.0
B- /7.7	4.1	0.67	11.53	490	4	34	60	2	26	28.3	-8.5	41	N/A	1,000	50	0.0	0.0
B- /7.7	4.1	0.68	11.64	30	4	34	60	2	26	32.6	-8.2	54	6	1,000,000	0	0.0	0.0
B- /7.7	4.1	0.68	11.72	2	4	34	60	2	26	30.2	-8.5	46	N/A	0	0	0.0	0.0
C+ /6.6	9.6	1.60	15.88	749	7	88	4	1	31	73.0	-20.1	9	N/A	1,000	50	5.5	0.0
C+ /6.7	9.6	1.61	15.60	65	7	88	4	1	31	68.6	-20.3	6	N/A	1,000	50	0.0	0.0

					PERFORMANCE							
99 Pct = Best						Total Return % through 3/31/15					Incl. in Returns	
0 Pct = Worst				Perfor-					Annualized		Dividend	Expense
Fund Type	Fund Name	Ticker Symbol	Overall Investment Rating	Phone	mance Rating/Pts	3 Mo	6 Mo	1Yr / Pct	3Yr / Pct	5Yr / Pct	Yield	Ratio
AA	Transamerica Asset Alloc Growth C	IAALX	C	(888) 233-4339	C / 5.1	3.26	5.93	7.86 /62	11.16 /47	9.69 /42	0.67	2.19
AA	Transamerica Asset Alloc Growth I	TAGIX	C+	(888) 233-4339	C+/ 5.8	3.52	6.44	8.87 /69	12.29 /55	10.80 /51	1.61	1.19
AA	Transamerica Asset Alloc Growth R	IGWRX	C+	(888) 233-4339	C / 5.4	3.34	6.17	8.27 /65	11.65 /50	10.19 /46	1.04	1.78
AA	Transamerica Asset Alloc Mod A	IMOAX	D+	(888) 233-4339	D / 2.1	2.51	4.26	6.00 /46	7.66 /25	7.52 /27	1.91	1.33
AA	● Transamerica Asset Alloc Mod B	IMOBX	C-	(888) 233-4339	D+/ 2.4	2.23	3.77	5.10 /39	6.80 /20	6.72 /21	1.00	2.13
AA	Transamerica Asset Alloc Mod C	IMOLX	D+	(888) 233-4339	D+/ 2.5	2.27	3.83	5.17 /40	6.90 /21	6.80 /22	1.31	2.05
AA	Transamerica Asset Alloc Mod Gr A	IMLAX	C-	(888) 233-4339	C-/ 3.4	2.90	5.14	7.14 /56	9.83 /38	8.86 /36	1.66	1.37
AA	● Transamerica Asset Alloc Mod Gr B	IMLBX	C-	(888) 233-4339	C-/ 3.7	2.73	4.72	6.28 /49	8.98 /33	8.06 /30	0.73	2.17
AA	Transamerica Asset Alloc Mod Gr C	IMLLX	C-	(888) 233-4339	C-/ 3.8	2.77	4.74	6.38 /50	9.08 /34	8.13 /31	1.03	2.10
AA	Transamerica Asset Alloc Mod Gr I	TMGIX	C	(888) 233-4339	C / 4.4	2.91	5.22	7.36 /58	10.13 /40	9.19 /38	2.01	1.12
AA	Transamerica Asset Alloc Mod Gr R	IMGRX	C	(888) 233-4339	C-/ 4.1	2.84	5.01	6.87 /54	9.60 /37	8.65 /34	1.48	1.62
AA	Transamerica Asset Alloc Mod I	TMMIX	C-	(888) 233-4339	C-/ 3.2	2.59	4.31	6.21 /48	7.97 /27	7.84 /29	2.28	1.08
AA	Transamerica Asset Alloc Mod R	IMDRX	C-	(888) 233-4339	D+/ 2.8	2.44	4.13	5.79 /45	7.44 /24	7.31 /25	1.81	1.56
AA	Transamerica Asst All Interm Hrz	DVMSX	C+	(888) 233-4339	C-/ 3.1	2.91	4.58	5.72 /44	7.91 /26	8.17 /31	1.64	1.23
AA	Transamerica Asst All Int-Lng Hrzn	DVASX	C+	(888) 233-4339	C / 4.3	3.63	5.68	6.69 /53	9.77 /38	9.64 /42	1.43	1.29
AA	Transamerica Asst All Lg Horizon	DVLSX	C+	(888) 233-4339	C / 5.3	4.14	6.63	7.38 /58	11.48 /49	10.82 /51	1.21	1.34
AA	Transamerica Asst All Short Hrzn	DVCSX	C	(888) 233-4339	D-/ 1.2	1.60	2.32	3.43 /29	3.87 /10	4.97 /12	2.24	1.13
AA	Transamerica Asst All Shrt-Int Hrz	DVSIX	C	(888) 233-4339	D / 2.0	2.16	3.28	4.62 /36	5.94 /17	6.57 /20	1.96	1.18
GI	Transamerica Capital Growth A	IALAX	C+	(888) 233-4339	B / 8.0	6.36	7.51	13.17 /87	16.64 /88	16.72 /95	0.00	1.25
GI	● Transamerica Capital Growth B	IACBX	C+	(888) 233-4339	B+/ 8.3	6.11	7.05	12.12 /83	15.68 /81	15.83 /92	0.00	2.20
GI	Transamerica Capital Growth C	ILLLX	B-	(888) 233-4339	B+/ 8.5	6.18	7.16	12.38 /84	15.92 /83	15.99 /93	0.00	1.95
GI	Transamerica Capital Growth I	TFOIX	B	(888) 233-4339	A-/ 9.1	6.43	7.69	13.53 /88	17.11 /90	17.21 /96	0.00	0.95
GR	Transamerica Capital Growth I2		B	(888) 233-4339	A-/ 9.2	6.50	7.77	13.71 /89	17.30 /91	--	0.00	0.81
EN	Transamerica Commodity Str I2		E	(888) 233-4339	E-/ 0.1	-5.63	-15.51	-24.89 / 0	-11.91 / 1	-7.10 / 1	0.00	0.86
GR	Transamerica Concentrated Growth I	TOREX	B+	(888) 233-4339	B / 7.8	2.97	9.14	11.56 /81	14.97 /75	--	0.11	0.95
GR	Transamerica Concentrated Growth		U	(888) 233-4339	U /	3.00	9.18	11.80 /82	--	--	0.24	0.77
GL	Transamerica Developing Mkts Eq I2	TDMIX	E-	(888) 233-4339	E / 0.4	-1.66	-9.26	-6.62 / 4	1.18 / 5	3.61 / 7	0.11	1.32
IN	Transamerica Dividend Focused A	TDFAX	U	(888) 233-4339	U /	0.10	3.73	6.60 /52	--	--	1.47	0.96
IN	Transamerica Dividend Focused I2		U	(888) 233-4339	U /	0.17	3.87	6.88 /54	--	--	1.80	0.70
EM	Transamerica Emerging Mkts Eqty I2		U	(888) 233-4339	U /	0.51	-1.20	2.84 /26	--	--	1.38	1.17
RE	Transamerica Gl Real Est I2	TRSIX	C	(888) 233-4339	C+/ 6.6	4.41	11.64	15.03 /92	11.38 /48	10.66 /50	2.54	1.11
FO	Transamerica Global Equity A	IMNAX	D-	(888) 233-4339	D-/ 1.5	1.26	2.19	1.72 /21	7.05 /22	5.70 /15	0.00	1.35
FO	● Transamerica Global Equity B	IMNBX	D-	(888) 233-4339	D / 1.8	1.09	1.74	0.91 /18	6.20 /18	4.89 /11	0.00	2.25
FO	Transamerica Global Equity C	IMNCX	D-	(888) 233-4339	D / 1.8	1.00	1.74	0.91 /18	6.25 /18	4.96 /12	0.00	2.10
FO	Transamerica Global Equity I	TMUIX	D	(888) 233-4339	D+/ 2.4	1.35	2.28	2.00 /22	7.44 /24	6.08 /17	0.00	1.05
FO	Transamerica Global Equity I2		U	(888) 233-4339	U /	1.36	2.28	--	--	--	0.00	1.08
GR	Transamerica Growth I2	TJNIX	C	(888) 233-4339	B+/ 8.8	5.49	8.93	16.00 /93	15.73 /81	15.00 /87	0.00	0.84
MC	Transamerica Growth Opps A	ITSAX	E	(888) 233-4339	D+/ 2.6	2.85	4.38	1.94 /22	9.10 /34	11.51 /57	0.00	1.35
MC	● Transamerica Growth Opps B	ITCBX	E	(888) 233-4339	D+/ 2.9	2.76	4.07	1.17 /19	8.22 /28	10.70 /50	0.00	2.23
MC	Transamerica Growth Opps C	ITSLX	E	(888) 233-4339	D+/ 2.9	2.73	4.04	1.16 /19	8.28 /29	10.74 /51	0.00	2.14
MC	Transamerica Growth Opps I	TGPIX	E+	(888) 233-4339	C-/ 3.7	2.95	4.57	2.35 /23	9.58 /37	12.07 /61	0.00	0.99
MC	Transamerica Growth Opps I2		D-	(888) 233-4339	C-/ 3.9	3.01	4.72	2.52 /24	9.76 /38	12.30 /63	0.10	0.83
GR	Transamerica Income and Growth A	TAIGX	U	(888) 233-4339	U /	0.07	0.05	0.62 /17	--	--	4.53	1.28
GR	Transamerica Income and Growth C	TCIGX	U	(888) 233-4339	U /	-0.20	-0.47	-0.26 /15	--	--	4.09	2.03
GR	Transamerica Income and Growth I	TIIGX	U	(888) 233-4339	U /	0.03	0.09	0.79 /18	--	--	5.05	1.04
GR	Transamerica Income and Growth I2		U	(888) 233-4339	U /	0.06	0.14	0.97 /18	--	--	5.14	0.94
AA	Transamerica Inst Asst All InLg Hrz	DILHX	C+	(888) 233-4339	C / 4.5	3.69	5.83	6.99 /55	10.09 /40	9.90 /44	2.09	0.97
AA	Transamerica Inst Asst All Int Hrz	DIIHX	C+	(888) 233-4339	C-/ 3.3	3.04	4.82	6.10 /47	8.24 /28	8.48 /33	2.18	0.92
AA	Transamerica Inst Asst All Lg Hrz	DILSX	C+	(888) 233-4339	C+/ 5.6	4.24	6.78	7.73 /61	11.85 /51	11.18 /54	1.94	1.03
AA	Transamerica Inst Asst All ShIntHrz	DIHSX	C	(888) 233-4339	D / 2.2	2.32	3.39	4.83 /37	6.28 /18	6.96 /23	2.42	0.86
AA	Transamerica Inst Asst All Sht Hrz	DISHX	C-	(888) 233-4339	D-/ 1.3	1.71	2.50	3.92 /31	4.24 /11	5.34 /13	2.57	0.80
FO	Transamerica International Eqty A	TRWAX	D+	(888) 233-4339	C-/ 3.0	5.29	1.38	-0.19 /15	10.36 /42	--	1.53	1.28

● Denotes fund is closed to new investors
* Denotes fund is included in Section II

RISK			NET ASSETS		ASSET				Portfolio Turnover Ratio	BULL / BEAR		FUND MANAGER		MINIMUMS		LOADS	
Risk Rating/Pts	3 Year		NAV As of 3/31/15	Total $(Mil)	Cash %	Stocks %	Bonds %	Other %		Last Bull Market Return	Last Bear Market Return	Manager Quality Pct	Manager Tenure (Years)	Initial Purch. $	Additional Purch. $	Front End Load	Back End Load
	Standard Deviation	Beta															
C+ / 6.7	9.6	1.60	15.50	753	7	88	4	1	31	69.1	-20.3	7	N/A	1,000	50	0.0	0.0
C+ / 6.6	9.6	1.60	15.87	32	7	88	4	1	31	75.0	-19.9	10	6	1,000,000	0	0.0	0.0
C+ / 6.7	9.6	1.60	15.79	2	7	88	4	1	31	71.6	-20.2	8	N/A	0	0	0.0	0.0
B- / 7.2	5.5	0.93	12.68	887	4	46	48	2	27	42.1	-11.8	33	N/A	1,000	50	5.5	0.0
B- / 7.5	5.5	0.93	12.81	62	4	46	48	2	27	38.4	-12.1	25	N/A	1,000	50	0.0	0.0
B- / 7.3	5.5	0.93	12.62	1,121	4	46	48	2	27	38.9	-12.1	26	N/A	1,000	50	0.0	0.0
C+ / 6.8	7.4	1.25	14.17	1,325	4	67	27	2	33	56.5	-16.3	19	N/A	1,000	50	5.5	0.0
B- / 7.1	7.4	1.26	14.28	113	4	67	27	2	33	52.5	-16.5	13	N/A	1,000	50	0.0	0.0
B- / 7.0	7.4	1.26	14.12	1,520	4	67	27	2	33	52.9	-16.5	14	N/A	1,000	50	0.0	0.0
C+ / 6.8	7.4	1.26	14.14	54	4	67	27	2	33	58.2	-16.2	22	6	1,000,000	0	0.0	0.0
C+ / 6.9	7.4	1.26	14.11	5	4	67	27	2	33	55.5	-16.4	17	N/A	0	0	0.0	0.0
B- / 7.1	5.5	0.93	12.66	47	4	46	48	2	27	43.5	-11.6	38	6	1,000,000	0	0.0	0.0
B- / 7.2	5.4	0.93	12.62	5	4	46	48	2	27	41.1	-11.8	32	N/A	0	0	0.0	0.0
B / 8.9	5.8	0.97	13.39	359	4	48	47	1	61	43.2	-10.4	32	19	5,000	0	0.0	0.0
B / 8.2	7.6	1.28	14.14	204	1	69	29	1	61	56.7	-14.8	17	19	5,000	0	0.0	0.0
B- / 7.3	9.5	1.59	12.81	106	2	87	9	2	66	70.3	-19.3	8	17	5,000	0	0.0	0.0
B+ / 9.7	2.9	0.30	11.66	123	0	10	89	1	55	18.1	-1.1	74	19	5,000	0	0.0	0.0
B / 8.9	3.9	0.63	11.20	212	0	29	70	1	66	30.3	-6.0	56	17	5,000	0	0.0	0.0
C / 4.5	13.9	1.07	24.90	130	2	97	0	1	30	99.7	-16.3	58	4	1,000	50	5.5	0.0
C / 4.5	13.9	1.07	22.04	4	2	97	0	1	30	94.4	-16.5	45	4	1,000	50	0.0	0.0
C / 4.5	13.9	1.07	22.15	54	2	97	0	1	30	95.7	-16.5	48	4	1,000	50	0.0	0.0
C / 4.6	13.9	1.07	25.48	159	2	97	0	1	30	102.8	-16.1	64	4	1,000,000	0	0.0	0.0
C / 4.5	13.9	1.07	17.05	911	2	97	0	1	30	103.8	N/A	66	4	0	0	0.0	0.0
C- / 3.9	12.0	0.56	6.70	54	28	0	71	1	0	-27.6	-19.2	1	5	0	0	0.0	0.0
B- / 7.0	9.5	0.92	16.99	23	2	97	0	1	18	91.9	-12.8	70	5	1,000,000	0	0.0	0.0
U /	N/A	N/A	17.16	439	2	97	0	1	18	N/A	N/A	N/A	5	0	0	0.0	0.0
C- / 3.3	14.2	0.92	10.08	403	5	94	0	1	57	26.7	-23.2	4	8	0	0	0.0	0.0
U /	N/A	N/A	13.12	52	2	97	0	1	21	N/A	N/A	N/A	2	1,000	50	5.5	0.0
U /	N/A	N/A	13.12	869	2	97	0	1	21	N/A	N/A	N/A	2	0	0	0.0	0.0
U /	N/A	N/A	9.93	266	1	98	0	1	69	N/A	N/A	N/A	3	0	0	0.0	0.0
C / 5.0	12.5	0.91	14.85	54	9	90	0	1	60	65.7	-18.9	49	12	0	0	0.0	0.0
C+ / 6.2	11.5	0.83	11.22	55	3	96	0	1	150	44.7	-24.3	56	N/A	1,000	50	5.5	0.0
C+ / 6.1	11.4	0.83	11.11	5	3	96	0	1	150	41.0	-24.6	44	N/A	1,000	50	0.0	0.0
C+ / 6.1	11.6	0.84	11.09	71	3	96	0	1	150	41.2	-24.5	44	N/A	1,000	50	0.0	0.0
C+ / 6.2	11.5	0.83	11.22	39	3	96	0	1	150	46.5	-24.2	62	6	1,000,000	0	0.0	0.0
U /	N/A	N/A	11.22	144	3	96	0	1	150	N/A	N/A	N/A	9	0	0	0.0	0.0
D+ / 2.5	11.8	1.03	14.21	542	0	100	0	0	31	99.4	-13.8	55	11	0	0	0.0	0.0
D+ / 2.9	14.6	1.06	10.12	100	5	94	0	1	53	60.2	-22.2	3	4	1,000	50	5.5	0.0
D+ / 2.4	14.6	1.05	8.57	3	5	94	0	1	53	56.2	-22.5	2	4	1,000	50	0.0	0.0
D+ / 2.5	14.7	1.06	8.64	13	5	94	0	1	53	56.3	-22.4	2	4	1,000	50	0.0	0.0
C- / 3.0	14.7	1.06	10.83	61	5	94	0	1	53	62.9	-21.9	4	4	1,000,000	0	0.0	0.0
C- / 3.1	14.6	1.05	10.95	633	5	94	0	1	53	63.8	-22.0	4	4	0	0	0.0	0.0
U /	N/A	N/A	10.54	71	17	82	0	1	23	N/A	N/A	N/A	3	1,000	50	5.5	0.0
U /	N/A	N/A	10.49	107	17	82	0	1	23	N/A	N/A	N/A	3	1,000	50	0.0	0.0
U /	N/A	N/A	10.55	80	17	82	0	1	23	N/A	N/A	N/A	3	1,000,000	0	0.0	0.0
U /	N/A	N/A	10.56	599	17	82	0	1	23	N/A	N/A	N/A	3	0	0	0.0	0.0
B / 8.2	7.6	1.29	11.99	56	1	69	29	1	109	58.4	-14.7	19	19	5,000	0	0.0	0.0
B / 8.9	5.7	0.96	11.87	93	0	50	49	1	76	44.8	-10.4	37	19	5,000	0	0.0	0.0
B- / 7.3	9.6	1.59	11.35	37	2	87	9	2	69	72.1	-19.0	9	17	5,000	0	0.0	0.0
B / 8.9	4.0	0.64	11.15	23	0	30	69	1	106	31.8	-5.7	59	17	5,000	0	0.0	0.0
B+ / 9.5	2.9	0.29	11.19	17	0	10	89	1	133	19.6	-0.9	78	19	5,000	0	0.0	0.0
C+ / 6.1	12.1	0.91	17.52	182	3	96	0	1	19	61.9	-22.2	81	4	1,000	50	5.5	0.0

Fund Type	Fund Name	Ticker Symbol	Overall Investment Rating	Phone	Performance Rating/Pts	3 Mo	6 Mo	1Yr / Pct	3Yr / Pct	5Yr / Pct	Dividend Yield	Expense Ratio
	99 Pct = Best / 0 Pct = Worst											
FO	Transamerica International Eqty C	TRWCX	D+	(888) 233-4339	C- / 3.5	5.09	1.11	-0.86 /13	9.67 /37	--	0.87	1.98
FO	Transamerica International Eqty I	TSWIX	C-	(888) 233-4339	C- / 4.2	5.35	1.62	0.17 /16	10.77 /44	8.94 /36	1.74	0.95
FO	Transamerica International Eqty I2	TRWIX	D+	(888) 233-4339	C- / 3.6	5.41	1.67	0.28 /16	9.68 /37	--	1.79	0.85
FO	Transamerica International Sm Cp I2		D	(888) 233-4339	C- / 3.9	7.50	2.80	-2.18 /10	10.25 /41	8.74 /35	1.29	1.15
FO	Transamerica Internatl Eqty Opps I2		D-	(888) 233-4339	C- / 3.3	6.21	3.23	2.51 /24	8.58 /30	7.60 /27	1.77	1.00
FO	Transamerica Internatl Sm Cp Val I	TISVX	U	(888) 233-4339	U /	6.09	3.79	-1.37 /12	--	--	1.48	1.15
FO	● Transamerica Internatl Sm Cp Val I2		U	(888) 233-4339	U /	6.08	3.83	-1.33 /12	--	--	1.52	1.05
GR	Transamerica Large Cap Value A	TWQAX	C+	(888) 233-4339	B- / 7.5	2.34	6.91	10.47 /76	16.62 /88	--	1.05	1.06
GR	Transamerica Large Cap Value C	TWQCX	C+	(888) 233-4339	B / 7.9	2.10	6.47	9.60 /73	15.82 /82	--	0.41	1.79
GR	Transamerica Large Cap Value I	TWQIX	B	(888) 233-4339	B+ / 8.7	2.32	7.02	10.70 /77	17.03 /90	--	1.34	0.79
GR	Transamerica Large Cap Value I2	TWQZX	B	(888) 233-4339	B+ / 8.6	2.34	7.09	10.84 /78	17.13 /90	--	1.45	0.69
GR	Transamerica Long/Short Strategy I2		C	(888) 233-4339	D / 1.7	-0.73	1.21	3.84 /31	5.99 /17	2.85 / 6	0.00	3.19
GL	Transamerica Managed Future Str I2		A+	(888) 233-4339	B+ / 8.7	8.77	18.97	26.52 /99	10.45 /42	--	0.64	1.71
MC	Transamerica Mid Cap Growth I2		U	(888) 233-4339	U /	7.36	13.68	13.47 /88	--	--	0.60	0.99
MC	Transamerica Mid Cap Value I2		A	(888) 233-4339	A+ / 9.8	3.73	12.32	15.96 /93	19.87 /98	17.45 /97	0.90	0.89
MC	Transamerica Mid Cap Value Opps I2		U	(888) 233-4339	U /	3.85	11.43	--	--	--	0.00	0.86
EN	Transamerica MLP & Energy Income	TMLAX	U	(888) 233-4339	U /	0.30	-10.66	1.22 /19	--	--	2.32	1.53
EN	Transamerica MLP & Energy Income	TMCLX	U	(888) 233-4339	U /	0.13	-10.94	0.57 /17	--	--	1.78	2.26
EN	Transamerica MLP & Energy Income	TMLPX	U	(888) 233-4339	U /	0.37	-10.60	1.48 /20	--	--	2.72	1.27
EN	Transamerica MLP & Energy Income		U	(888) 233-4339	U /	0.30	-10.55	1.57 /20	--	--	2.82	1.17
BA	Transamerica Multi-Managed Bal A	IBALX	C+	(888) 233-4339	C- / 3.9	1.08	4.87	9.27 /71	10.65 /43	12.32 /63	0.94	1.21
BA	● Transamerica Multi-Managed Bal B	IBABX	C+	(888) 233-4339	C- / 4.1	0.85	4.43	8.26 /65	9.68 /37	11.37 /56	0.08	2.14
BA	Transamerica Multi-Managed Bal C	IBLLX	C+	(888) 233-4339	C / 4.3	0.91	4.51	8.52 /66	9.96 /39	11.65 /58	0.40	1.89
BA	Transamerica Multi-Managed Bal I	TBLIX	B-	(888) 233-4339	C / 5.0	1.18	5.04	9.59 /72	11.07 /46	12.72 /66	1.26	0.91
AA	Transamerica Multi-Mgr Alter Strg A	IMUAX	C-	(888) 233-4339	E+ / 0.9	1.63	1.47	4.86 /38	4.17 /11	3.65 / 7	0.66	2.28
AA	Transamerica Multi-Mgr Alter Strg C	IMUCX	C-	(888) 233-4339	D- / 1.1	1.45	1.10	4.10 /32	3.40 / 9	2.94 / 6	0.04	3.03
AA	Transamerica Multi-Mgr Alter Strg I	TASIX	C	(888) 233-4339	D- / 1.4	1.73	1.72	5.21 /40	4.53 /12	4.02 / 8	1.12	1.99
BA	Transamerica Prt Balanced	DVIBX	B	(888) 233-4339	C / 4.9	1.11	4.86	9.21 /70	10.91 /45	10.52 /49	1.12	1.29
BA	Transamerica Prt Inst Balanced	DIBFX	B	(888) 233-4339	C / 5.1	1.19	5.07	9.59 /72	11.29 /48	10.91 /52	1.48	1.56
FO	Transamerica Prt Inst Intl Eq	DIIEX	D-	(888) 233-4339	D- / 1.1	4.31	-1.48	-4.22 / 7	4.81 /13	4.50 /10	2.61	1.19
GI	Transamerica Prt Inst Large Core	DIGIX	A+	(888) 233-4339	A+ / 9.6	3.12	8.27	16.68 /94	18.61 /96	16.00 /93	0.65	1.46
GR	Transamerica Prt Inst Large Growth	DIEGX	B+	(888) 233-4339	B+ / 8.5	5.14	9.84	15.75 /93	14.90 /74	14.34 /81	0.17	1.00
IN	Transamerica Prt Inst Large Value	DIVIX	A+	(888) 233-4339	B+ / 8.7	2.53	6.17	9.76 /73	17.15 /91	15.01 /87	0.91	0.83
MC	Transamerica Prt Inst Mid Growth	DIMGX	C-	(888) 233-4339	B+ / 8.3	7.53	14.05	14.01 /89	14.46 /71	14.31 /81	0.38	1.18
MC	Transamerica Prt Inst Mid Value	DIMVX	B+	(888) 233-4339	A / 9.5	3.69	11.56	14.37 /90	18.13 /95	15.48 /90	1.12	1.03
IN	Transamerica Prt Inst Small Core	DISEX	C+	(888) 233-4339	C+ / 6.1	2.10	8.08	3.13 /27	13.53 /64	13.41 /72	0.78	1.27
GL	Transamerica Prt Inst Small Growth	DISGX	C	(888) 233-4339	C+ / 6.2	8.23	15.82	12.09 /83	11.13 /46	11.08 /53	0.29	1.50
SC	Transamerica Prt Inst Small Value	DIVSX	A	(888) 233-4339	B+ / 8.9	4.12	16.44	9.94 /74	16.40 /86	15.00 /87	0.81	1.42
IX	Transamerica Prt Inst Stock Index	DISFX	A	(888) 233-4339	B / 8.1	0.91	5.82	12.44 /85	15.81 /82	14.15 /79	1.80	0.38
FO	Transamerica Prt International Eq	DVIEX	D-	(888) 233-4339	D- / 1.0	4.28	-1.65	-4.50 / 6	4.53 /12	4.25 / 9	2.21	1.44
GI	Transamerica Prt Large Core	DVGIX	A+	(888) 233-4339	A / 9.5	3.11	8.22	16.36 /94	18.26 /95	15.70 /91	0.44	1.26
GR	Transamerica Prt Large Growth	DVEGX	B-	(888) 233-4339	B+ / 8.3	5.12	9.70	15.37 /92	14.54 /71	13.97 /77	0.00	1.25
IN	Transamerica Prt Large Value	DVEIX	A+	(888) 233-4339	B+ / 8.5	2.52	6.05	9.51 /72	16.87 /89	14.75 /85	0.67	1.07
MC	Transamerica Prt Mid Growth	DVMGX	C-	(888) 233-4339	B / 7.9	7.47	13.82	13.55 /88	14.03 /67	13.87 /77	0.07	1.41
MC	Transamerica Prt Mid Value	DVMVX	A+	(888) 233-4339	A / 9.4	3.60	11.36	13.99 /89	17.73 /93	15.09 /87	0.85	1.30
IN	Transamerica Prt Small Core	DVPEX	C+	(888) 233-4339	C+ / 5.8	2.02	7.91	2.80 /25	13.09 /60	12.99 /68	0.44	1.46
SC	Transamerica Prt Small Growth	DVSGX	C-	(888) 233-4339	C+ / 5.9	8.13	15.56	11.60 /81	10.67 /43	10.64 /50	0.18	1.67
SC	Transamerica Prt Small Value	DVSVX	A-	(888) 233-4339	B+ / 8.6	3.96	16.14	9.53 /72	15.93 /83	14.53 /83	0.58	1.58
IX	Transamerica Prt Stock Index	DSKIX	A-	(888) 233-4339	B / 7.7	0.82	5.67	12.03 /83	15.39 /78	13.76 /75	1.45	0.69
SC	Transamerica Sm Cap Value I2		U	(888) 233-4339	U /	0.00	8.64	2.22 /23	--	--	1.14	1.24
SC	Transamerica Sm/Mid Cap Value A	IIVAX	C	(888) 233-4339	C+ / 6.1	3.69	8.53	5.95 /46	14.64 /72	14.17 /79	0.10	1.28
SC	● Transamerica Sm/Mid Cap Value B	IIVBX	C	(888) 233-4339	C+ / 6.5	3.48	8.14	5.19 /40	13.82 /66	13.39 /72	0.00	2.01

RISK			NET ASSETS		ASSET					BULL / BEAR		FUND MANAGER		MINIMUMS		LOADS	
	3 Year		NAV						Portfolio	Last Bull	Last Bear	Manager	Manager	Initial	Additional	Front	Back
Risk Rating/Pts	Standard Deviation	Beta	As of 3/31/15	Total $(Mil)	Cash %	Stocks %	Bonds %	Other %	Turnover Ratio	Market Return	Market Return	Quality Pct	Tenure (Years)	Purch. $	Purch. $	End Load	End Load
C+ / 6.2	12.1	0.91	17.33	42	3	96	0	1	19	58.2	-22.4	77	4	1,000	50	0.0	0.0
C+ / 6.1	12.2	0.92	17.71	763	3	96	0	1	19	63.9	-22.1	84	4	1,000,000	0	0.0	0.0
C+ / 6.1	12.3	0.91	17.72	551	3	96	0	1	19	59.1	-22.1	77	4	0	0	0.0	0.0
C / 5.1	13.0	0.91	9.75	804	3	96	0	1	34	56.2	-25.4	81	7	0	0	0.0	0.0
C / 4.7	12.7	0.94	8.04	471	1	98	0	1	39	56.3	-23.4	63	9	0	0	0.0	0.0
U /	N/A	N/A	12.02	306	3	96	0	1	21	N/A	N/A	N/A	2	1,000,000	0	0.0	0.0
U /	N/A	N/A	12.03	510	3	96	0	1	21	N/A	N/A	N/A	2	0	0	0.0	0.0
C / 4.7	10.9	1.11	12.76	23	2	97	0	1	87	99.8	-19.2	50	3	1,000	50	5.5	0.0
C / 4.7	11.0	1.11	12.72	10	2	97	0	1	87	95.4	-19.4	40	3	1,000	50	0.0	0.0
C / 4.7	10.9	1.11	12.81	12	2	97	0	1	87	102.2	-19.0	56	3	1,000,000	0	0.0	0.0
C / 4.7	10.9	1.11	12.80	1,833	2	97	0	1	87	102.7	-19.0	57	3	0	0	0.0	1.0
B+ / 9.2	4.5	0.41	9.47	155	67	32	0	1	339	27.5	-7.5	63	4	0	0	0.0	0.0
B / 8.2	9.3	-0.15	11.78	480	75	0	24	1	0	24.4	-5.4	99	5	0	0	0.0	0.0
U /	N/A	N/A	12.11	262	0	99	0	1	67	N/A	N/A	N/A	1	0	0	0.0	0.0
C / 5.5	9.0	0.78	16.68	285	2	97	0	1	44	115.8	-17.6	95	10	0	0	0.0	0.0
U /	N/A	N/A	11.32	451	0	0	0	100	23	N/A	N/A	N/A	N/A	0	0	0.0	0.0
U /	N/A	N/A	10.58	64	39	54	6	1	46	N/A	N/A	N/A	2	1,000	50	5.5	0.0
U /	N/A	N/A	10.54	53	39	54	6	1	46	N/A	N/A	N/A	2	1,000	50	0.0	0.0
U /	N/A	N/A	10.58	103	39	54	6	1	46	N/A	N/A	N/A	2	1,000,000	0	0.0	0.0
U /	N/A	N/A	10.58	485	39	54	6	1	46	N/A	N/A	N/A	2	1,000,000	0	0.0	0.0
B / 8.1	6.0	1.06	25.04	196	0	58	41	1	102	58.6	-9.1	55	4	1,000	50	5.5	0.0
B / 8.1	6.0	1.06	24.90	6	0	58	41	1	102	53.8	-9.4	42	4	1,000	50	0.0	0.0
B / 8.1	5.9	1.05	24.64	169	0	58	41	1	102	55.2	-9.3	46	4	1,000	50	0.0	0.0
B / 8.1	5.9	1.05	25.14	206	0	58	41	1	102	60.6	-8.9	62	4	1,000,000	0	0.0	0.0
B+ / 9.5	3.4	0.46	10.61	122	50	25	23	2	79	19.1	-8.3	56	N/A	1,000	50	5.5	0.0
B+ / 9.5	3.5	0.48	10.52	119	50	25	23	2	79	16.3	-8.6	43	N/A	1,000	50	0.0	0.0
B+ / 9.5	3.4	0.46	10.60	233	50	25	23	2	79	20.6	-8.1	62	6	1,000,000	0	0.0	0.0
B / 8.6	5.9	1.04	19.92	88	0	56	43	1	92	60.2	-9.3	62	5	5,000	0	0.0	0.0
B / 8.5	5.9	1.04	12.79	6	0	56	43	1	92	62.3	-9.2	67	5	5,000	0	0.0	0.0
C+ / 6.0	12.0	0.87	7.01	54	7	92	0	1	28	36.6	-25.7	22	2	5,000	0	0.0	0.0
B- / 7.6	10.0	1.03	7.66	10	1	98	0	1	70	114.2	-16.2	82	6	5,000	0	0.0	0.0
C+ / 6.0	11.2	1.05	11.82	119	0	99	0	1	73	97.3	-16.9	40	8	5,000	0	0.0	0.0
B- / 7.4	10.5	1.06	14.93	106	2	97	0	1	69	104.8	-18.2	67	6	5,000	0	0.0	0.0
D+ / 2.4	12.9	1.09	13.99	23	1	98	0	1	60	82.7	-22.5	19	2	5,000	0	0.0	0.0
C / 5.0	9.3	0.82	19.82	405	3	96	0	1	92	105.5	-20.4	91	14	5,000	0	0.0	0.0
C+ / 6.4	12.7	1.15	15.56	28	1	98	0	1	148	84.5	-22.9	13	2	5,000	0	0.0	0.0
C / 4.7	15.1	0.69	19.76	12	2	97	0	1	78	75.1	-25.5	92	N/A	5,000	0	0.0	0.0
C+ / 6.5	12.8	0.93	22.94	9	4	95	0	1	18	100.4	-21.3	78	5	5,000	0	0.0	0.0
B- / 7.3	9.5	1.00	13.83	805	1	98	0	1	3	98.4	-16.4	64	7	5,000	0	0.0	0.0
C+ / 6.1	12.0	0.88	11.00	173	7	92	0	1	28	35.5	-25.8	20	2	5,000	0	0.0	0.0
B- / 7.6	10.0	1.03	33.88	97	1	98	0	1	70	112.3	-16.3	80	6	5,000	0	0.0	0.0
C / 4.8	11.2	1.04	29.38	282	0	99	0	1	73	94.9	-17.0	37	8	5,000	0	0.0	0.0
B- / 7.4	10.5	1.06	27.95	295	2	97	0	1	69	103.1	-18.3	64	6	5,000	0	0.0	0.0
D+ / 2.7	12.9	1.09	10.79	64	1	98	0	1	60	80.3	-22.6	16	2	5,000	0	0.0	0.0
B- / 7.6	9.4	0.82	21.95	168	3	96	0	1	92	103.1	-20.6	90	14	5,000	0	0.0	0.0
C+ / 6.4	12.7	1.15	29.40	81	1	98	0	1	148	82.1	-23.0	10	2	5,000	0	0.0	0.0
C / 4.5	15.1	1.03	17.87	44	2	97	0	1	78	72.8	-25.7	9	N/A	5,000	0	0.0	0.0
C+ / 6.4	12.8	0.93	17.71	44	4	95	0	1	18	97.8	-21.5	75	5	5,000	0	0.0	0.0
B- / 7.3	9.6	1.00	16.08	393	1	98	0	1	3	96.1	-16.6	58	7	5,000	0	0.0	0.0
U /	N/A	N/A	11.99	603	2	96	0	2	37	N/A	N/A	N/A	3	0	0	0.0	0.0
C+ / 5.6	11.2	0.79	27.52	464	1	98	0	1	96	93.1	-25.9	82	4	1,000	50	5.5	0.0
C / 5.4	11.2	0.79	25.31	25	1	98	0	1	96	88.5	-26.1	77	4	1,000	50	0.0	0.0

99 Pct = Best
0 Pct = Worst

Fund Type	Fund Name	Ticker Symbol	Overall Investment Rating	Phone	Performance Rating/Pts	3 Mo	6 Mo	1Yr / Pct	3Yr / Pct	5Yr / Pct	Dividend Yield	Expense Ratio
								Total Return % through 3/31/15	Annualized		Incl. in Returns	
SC	Transamerica Sm/Mid Cap Value C	IIVLX	C+	(888) 233-4339	C+ / 6.5	3.52	8.19	5.25 /41	13.89 /66	13.46 /73	0.00	1.97
SC	Transamerica Sm/Mid Cap Value I	TSVIX	B-	(888) 233-4339	B- / 7.4	3.79	8.75	6.30 /49	15.08 /76	14.64 /84	0.48	0.96
SC	Transamerica Sm/Mid Cap Value I2	TSMVX	B-	(888) 233-4339	B- / 7.5	3.78	8.79	6.43 /50	15.19 /76	14.76 /85	0.57	0.85
SC	Transamerica Small Cap Core I2		U	(888) 233-4339	U /	2.08	8.14	3.13 /27	--	--	0.66	1.06
SC	Transamerica Small Cap Growth I2		U	(888) 233-4339	U /	8.28	16.08	12.44 /85	--	--	0.00	0.89
GL	Transamerica Tactical Inc A	IGTAX	D	(888) 233-4339	D- / 1.3	1.55	2.53	4.53 /35	5.47 /15	--	3.02	1.19
GL	Transamerica Tactical Inc C	IGTCX	D	(888) 233-4339	D- / 1.4	1.37	2.15	3.66 /30	4.67 /12	--	2.42	1.95
GL	Transamerica Tactical Inc I	IGTIX	D+	(888) 233-4339	D / 1.8	1.61	2.64	4.78 /37	5.68 /15	--	3.40	0.96
GI	Transamerica US Growth A	TADAX	C-	(888) 233-4339	C+ / 6.7	4.79	10.70	14.93 /91	13.67 /65	12.49 /64	0.10	1.22
GI	● Transamerica US Growth B	TADBX	C-	(888) 233-4339	B- / 7.0	4.59	10.18	13.84 /89	12.73 /58	11.63 /58	0.00	2.08
GI	Transamerica US Growth C	TADCX	C-	(888) 233-4339	B- / 7.1	4.66	10.26	14.06 /90	12.81 /58	11.67 /58	0.00	2.02
GI	Transamerica US Growth I	TDEIX	C	(888) 233-4339	B / 8.2	4.90	10.89	15.39 /92	14.17 /68	12.95 /68	0.43	0.86
GI	Transamerica US Growth I2		C+	(888) 233-4339	B / 8.2	4.92	10.95	15.46 /92	14.30 /69	13.18 /70	0.57	0.73
GI	● Transamerica US Growth T	TWMTX	C+	(888) 233-4339	C+ / 6.6	4.92	10.91	15.39 /92	14.19 /69	--	0.16	0.83
AA	Transparent Value Dir Alloc A	TVRAX	U	(888) 727-6885	U /	1.82	1.12	1.55 /20	--	--	0.00	1.50
AA	Transparent Value Dir Alloc C	TVRCX	U	(888) 727-6885	U /	1.61	0.76	0.90 /18	--	--	0.00	2.10
AA	Transparent Value Dir Alloc F1	TVFRX	U	(888) 727-6885	U /	1.82	1.12	1.69 /21	--	--	0.00	1.35
AA	Transparent Value Dir Alloc I	TVRIX	U	(888) 727-6885	U /	1.88	1.26	1.90 /21	--	--	0.00	1.10
IN	Transparent Value Dividend A	TVEAX	B	(888) 727-6885	C+ / 5.7	1.01	6.71	7.49 /59	14.13 /68	--	1.66	1.86
IN	Transparent Value Dividend C	TVECX	B-	(888) 727-6885	C+ / 6.2	0.85	6.41	6.90 /54	13.45 /63	--	1.04	2.46
IN	Transparent Value Dividend F1	TVEFX	B-	(888) 727-6885	C+ / 6.8	1.11	6.85	7.75 /61	14.34 /70	--	1.84	1.71
IN	Transparent Value Dividend I	TVEIX	B+	(888) 727-6885	B- / 7.0	1.18	7.02	7.98 /63	14.62 /72	--	1.94	1.46
GR	Transparent Value LgCp Aggr A	TVAAX	E+	(888) 727-6885	C+ / 5.6	4.43	6.20	8.24 /65	13.57 /64	--	0.00	1.71
GR	Transparent Value LgCp Aggr C	TVCAX	D-	(888) 727-6885	C+ / 6.1	4.27	5.97	7.60 /60	12.92 /59	--	0.00	2.31
GR	Transparent Value LgCp Aggr F1	TVFAX	D-	(888) 727-6885	C+ / 6.6	4.50	6.36	8.39 /66	13.68 /65	--	0.00	1.56
GR	Transparent Value LgCp Aggr I	TVIAX	D-	(888) 727-6885	C+ / 6.8	4.56	6.45	8.55 /67	13.91 /66	--	0.00	1.31
GR	Transparent Value LgCp Cor C	TVBCX	C+	(888) 727-6885	C+ / 5.7	-0.19	4.50	5.51 /43	13.04 /60	--	0.03	2.99
GR	Transparent Value LgCp Core A	TVBAX	C+	(888) 727-6885	C / 5.1	0.00	4.84	6.19 /48	13.70 /65	--	0.19	2.39
GR	Transparent Value LgCp Core F1	TVFBX	B-	(888) 727-6885	C+ / 6.3	0.00	4.96	6.38 /50	13.92 /67	--	0.25	2.24
GR	Transparent Value LgCp Core I	TVBIX	B-	(888) 727-6885	C+ / 6.4	0.09	5.12	6.63 /52	14.19 /69	--	0.31	1.99
GR	Transparent Value LgCp Defensive A	TVDAX	D-	(888) 727-6885	C / 5.2	0.54	6.66	8.54 /67	13.24 /61	--	0.53	1.68
GR	Transparent Value LgCp Defensive C	TVDCX	D	(888) 727-6885	C+ / 5.8	0.45	6.33	7.96 /63	12.59 /57	--	0.26	2.28
GR	Transparent Value LgCp Defensive	TVFDX	D+	(888) 727-6885	C+ / 6.3	0.62	6.67	8.69 /68	13.42 /63	--	0.63	1.53
GR	Transparent Value LgCp Defensive I	TVIDX	D+	(888) 727-6885	C+ / 6.5	0.62	6.80	8.99 /69	13.69 /65	--	0.79	1.28
GR	Transparent Value LgCp Growth A	TVGAX	C+	(888) 727-6885	C+ / 6.6	1.80	8.39	9.71 /73	15.21 /77	--	0.00	3.29
GR	Transparent Value LgCp Growth C	TVGCX	B	(888) 727-6885	B- / 7.1	1.69	8.13	9.07 /70	14.58 /72	--	0.00	3.89
GR	Transparent Value LgCp Growth F1	TVGFX	B+	(888) 727-6885	B / 7.8	1.95	8.49	9.88 /74	15.40 /78	--	0.00	3.14
GR	Transparent Value LgCp Growth I	TVGIX	B+	(888) 727-6885	B / 8.0	1.92	8.56	10.10 /75	15.66 /81	--	0.00	2.89
GR	Transparent Value LgCp Market A	TVMAX	D-	(888) 727-6885	C+ / 6.2	3.91	7.91	8.84 /68	14.61 /72	--	0.00	1.62
GR	Transparent Value LgCp Market C	TVMCX	D-	(888) 727-6885	C+ / 6.7	3.76	7.51	8.10 /64	13.87 /66	--	0.00	2.22
GR	Transparent Value LgCp Market F1	TVFMX	D	(888) 727-6885	B- / 7.4	3.93	7.95	9.03 /69	14.77 /73	--	0.00	1.47
GR	Transparent Value LgCp Market I	TVIMX	D	(888) 727-6885	B / 7.6	4.07	8.12	9.28 /71	15.06 /75	--	0.00	1.22
GR	Transparent Value LgCp Value A	TVVAX	B-	(888) 727-6885	C+ / 6.0	-1.19	5.28	8.83 /68	14.90 /74	--	0.98	4.44
GR	Transparent Value LgCp Value C	TVVCX	B-	(888) 727-6885	C+ / 6.3	-1.70	4.62	7.79 /61	14.05 /67	--	0.63	5.04
GR	Transparent Value LgCp Value F1	TVVFX	B+	(888) 727-6885	B- / 7.0	-1.22	5.29	8.90 /69	15.01 /75	--	1.15	4.29
GR	Transparent Value LgCp Value I	TVVIX	B+	(888) 727-6885	B- / 7.3	-1.20	5.43	9.19 /70	15.33 /78	--	1.31	4.04
BA	Tributary Balanced Fund Inst	FOBAX	C+	(800) 662-4203	C / 5.2	5.19	7.84	9.40 /71	10.82 /44	11.55 /57	0.03	1.30
BA	Tributary Balanced Inst Plus	FOBPX	C+	(800) 662-4203	C / 5.4	5.26	7.92	9.67 /73	11.09 /46	--	0.23	1.09
GR	Tributary Growth Opps Inst	FOGRX	B	(800) 662-4203	B+ / 8.6	7.52	10.91	12.93 /86	15.53 /79	15.86 /92	0.00	1.20
GR	Tributary Growth Opps Inst Plus	FOGPX	B	(800) 662-4203	B+ / 8.8	7.57	11.04	13.18 /87	15.79 /82	--	0.00	1.01
SC	Tributary Small Company Inst	FOSCX	C+	(800) 662-4203	C+ / 6.7	3.13	11.98	6.97 /55	13.54 /64	13.75 /75	0.03	1.32
SC	Tributary Small Company Inst Plus	FOSBX	C+	(800) 662-4203	C+ / 6.8	3.17	12.08	7.17 /56	13.80 /66	--	0.14	1.09

● Denotes fund is closed to new investors
* Denotes fund is included in Section II

616

RISK			NET ASSETS		ASSET					BULL / BEAR		FUND MANAGER		MINIMUMS		LOADS	
	3 Year		NAV						Portfolio	Last Bull	Last Bear	Manager	Manager	Initial	Additional	Front	Back
Risk	Standard		As of	Total	Cash	Stocks	Bonds	Other	Turnover	Market	Market	Quality	Tenure	Purch.	Purch.	End	End
Rating/Pts	Deviation	Beta	3/31/15	$(Mil)	%	%	%	%	Ratio	Return	Return	Pct	(Years)	$	$	Load	Load
C /5.4	11.2	0.79	25.02	316	1	98	0	1	96	88.7	-26.0	77	4	1,000	50	0.0	0.0
C+/5.6	11.2	0.79	28.23	222	1	98	0	1	96	95.6	-25.7	85	4	1,000,000	0	0.0	0.0
C+/5.6	11.2	0.79	28.26	21	1	98	0	1	96	96.2	-25.7	85	4	0	0	0.0	0.0
U /	N/A	N/A	10.82	265	1	98	0	1	140	N/A	N/A	N/A	2	0	0	0.0	0.0
U /	N/A	N/A	13.21	563	3	96	0	1	73	N/A	N/A	N/A	3	0	0	0.0	0.0
B- /7.3	4.9	0.67	10.27	241	3	31	61	5	102	N/A	N/A	60	3	1,000	50	4.8	0.0
B- /7.3	4.9	0.67	10.23	380	3	31	61	5	102	N/A	N/A	49	3	1,000	50	0.0	0.0
B- /7.3	4.9	0.67	10.27	223	3	31	61	5	102	N/A	N/A	64	3	1,000,000	0	0.0	0.0
C- /3.7	11.0	1.06	16.86	475	0	99	0	1	111	91.8	-20.1	25	4	1,000	50	5.5	0.0
C- /3.6	10.9	1.06	16.41	13	0	99	0	1	111	86.5	-20.3	18	4	1,000	50	0.0	0.0
C- /3.6	11.0	1.06	16.40	52	0	99	0	1	111	86.8	-20.3	18	4	1,000	50	0.0	0.0
C- /3.7	10.9	1.06	17.11	197	0	99	0	1	111	94.8	-20.0	30	4	1,000,000	0	0.0	0.0
C- /3.6	10.9	1.06	17.07	387	0	99	0	1	111	95.7	-19.9	32	4	0	0	0.0	0.0
C+/6.6	10.9	1.06	40.95	106	0	99	0	1	111	N/A	N/A	30	4	1,000	50	8.5	0.0
U /	N/A	N/A	12.86	334	0	99	0	1	300	N/A	N/A	N/A	3	5,000	100	5.8	0.0
U /	N/A	N/A	12.63	524	0	99	0	1	300	N/A	N/A	N/A	3	5,000	100	0.0	0.0
U /	N/A	N/A	12.89	85	0	99	0	1	300	N/A	N/A	N/A	3	5,000	100	0.0	0.0
U /	N/A	N/A	12.99	845	0	99	0	1	300	N/A	N/A	N/A	3	2,000,000	100,000	0.0	0.0
B- /7.7	9.4	0.81	11.24	10	0	99	0	1	181	84.7	-16.3	78	4	5,000	100	5.8	0.0
B- /7.7	9.4	0.82	11.19	11	0	99	0	1	181	81.1	-16.5	72	4	5,000	100	0.0	0.0
B- /7.7	9.4	0.81	11.33	3	0	99	0	1	181	85.9	-16.3	79	4	5,000	100	0.0	0.0
B- /7.7	9.4	0.81	11.10	19	0	99	0	1	181	87.4	-16.1	81	4	2,000,000	100,000	0.0	0.0
D- /1.0	13.9	1.29	7.54	2	0	99	0	1	196	84.8	-26.8	5	5	5,000	100	5.8	0.0
D- /1.0	13.9	1.29	7.33	2	0	99	0	1	196	81.4	-27.1	4	5	5,000	100	0.0	0.0
D- /1.0	13.9	1.29	7.67	14	0	99	0	1	196	85.4	-26.9	5	5	5,000	100	0.0	0.0
D- /1.0	14.0	1.29	7.80	5	0	99	0	1	196	86.8	-26.8	6	5	2,000,000	100,000	0.0	0.0
B- /7.1	11.1	1.08	10.52	1	0	99	0	1	175	90.1	-17.6	17	4	5,000	100	0.0	0.0
B- /7.1	11.1	1.08	10.67	2	0	99	0	1	175	93.8	-17.4	22	4	5,000	100	5.8	0.0
B- /7.1	11.1	1.07	10.75	N/A	0	99	0	1	175	95.0	-17.3	26	4	5,000	100	0.0	0.0
B- /7.1	11.1	1.08	10.73	12	0	99	0	1	175	96.7	-17.2	27	4	2,000,000	100,000	0.0	0.0
D+/2.8	9.2	0.84	11.14	10	0	99	0	1	236	77.5	-11.6	66	5	5,000	100	5.8	0.0
D+/2.7	9.2	0.83	11.08	15	0	99	0	1	236	73.8	-11.7	59	5	5,000	100	0.0	0.0
D+/2.8	9.2	0.83	11.31	19	0	99	0	1	236	78.2	-11.5	69	5	5,000	100	0.0	0.0
D+/2.9	9.2	0.83	11.40	17	0	99	0	1	236	79.9	-11.4	72	5	2,000,000	100,000	0.0	0.0
C+/6.7	12.5	1.21	12.99	1	1	98	0	1	136	98.8	-17.8	16	4	5,000	100	5.8	0.0
C+/6.7	12.5	1.22	12.62	1	1	98	0	1	136	95.3	-18.2	13	4	5,000	100	0.0	0.0
C+/6.7	12.6	1.22	13.10	N/A	1	98	0	1	136	100.5	-18.0	17	4	5,000	100	0.0	0.0
C+/6.7	12.6	1.22	13.24	4	1	98	0	1	136	102.0	-17.9	19	4	2,000,000	100,000	0.0	0.0
D- /1.0	11.4	1.12	10.37	9	0	99	0	1	268	88.0	-16.9	24	5	5,000	100	5.8	0.0
D- /1.0	11.4	1.12	10.21	17	0	99	0	1	268	84.2	-17.1	18	5	5,000	100	0.0	0.0
D- /1.0	11.4	1.12	10.59	19	0	99	0	1	268	88.9	-17.0	25	5	5,000	100	0.0	0.0
D- /1.1	11.4	1.12	10.74	22	0	99	0	1	268	90.6	-16.9	29	5	2,000,000	100,000	0.0	0.0
B- /7.5	9.9	0.95	9.95	N/A	1	98	0	1	138	96.9	-18.9	62	4	5,000	100	5.8	0.0
B- /7.5	10.0	0.96	9.81	1	1	98	0	1	138	92.2	-19.2	49	4	5,000	100	0.0	0.0
B- /7.5	9.9	0.95	9.75	N/A	1	98	0	1	138	97.4	-18.9	64	4	5,000	100	0.0	0.0
B- /7.5	10.0	0.96	9.89	4	1	98	0	1	138	99.4	-18.9	67	4	2,000,000	100,000	0.0	0.0
C+/6.8	7.8	1.26	17.66	71	5	68	25	2	91	56.9	-9.9	28	N/A	1,000	50	0.0	0.0
C+/6.8	7.7	1.26	17.57	36	5	68	25	2	91	N/A	N/A	31	N/A	5,000,000	50	0.0	0.0
C /4.9	12.4	1.12	19.02	56	2	97	0	1	56	96.4	-24.4	32	9	1,000	50	0.0	0.0
C /4.9	12.4	1.13	19.19	119	2	97	0	1	56	N/A	N/A	35	9	5,000,000	50	0.0	0.0
C+/6.2	13.2	0.96	24.06	51	4	95	0	1	21	83.4	-21.4	40	16	1,000	50	0.0	0.0
C+/6.2	13.3	0.96	24.12	218	4	95	0	1	21	84.9	-21.3	43	16	5,000,000	50	0.0	0.0

Fund Type	Fund Name	Ticker Symbol	Overall Investment Rating	Phone	Performance Rating/Pts	3 Mo	6 Mo	1Yr / Pct	3Yr / Pct	5Yr / Pct	Dividend Yield	Expense Ratio
								Total Return % through 3/31/15	Annualized		Incl. in Returns	
SC	Turner Emerging Growth Inst	TMCOX	E+	(800) 224-6312	C+ / 6.7	5.24	11.54	2.84 /26	14.05 /67	14.51 /82	0.00	1.42
SC	Turner Emerging Growth Inv	TMCGX	E+	(800) 224-6312	C+ / 6.5	5.17	11.38	2.57 /24	13.75 /65	14.22 /80	0.00	1.67
HL	Turner Medical Sci Long/Short C	TMSCX	A+	(800) 224-6312	A+ / 9.6	24.57	15.85	21.22 /97	15.02 /75	--	0.00	4.54
HL	Turner Medical Sci Long/Short Inst	TMSEX	A+	(800) 224-6312	A+ / 9.7	24.89	16.45	22.42 /97	16.16 /85	--	0.00	3.54
HL	Turner Medical Sci Long/Short Inv	TMSFX	A+	(800) 224-6312	A+ / 9.7	24.76	16.27	22.18 /97	15.89 /82	--	0.00	3.79
MC	Turner Midcap Growth Inst	TMGEX	D-	(800) 224-6312	C+ / 6.5	5.26	9.26	8.89 /69	13.09 /60	12.58 /65	0.00	1.17
MC	Turner Midcap Growth Inv	TMGFX	E+	(800) 224-6312	C+ / 6.3	5.18	9.08	8.59 /67	12.77 /58	12.29 /62	0.00	1.42
MC	Turner Midcap Growth Retire	TMIIX	E+	(800) 224-6312	C+ / 6.4	5.14	8.95	8.38 /65	13.01 /60	12.04 /61	0.00	1.67
SC	Turner Small Cap Growth Fund	TSCEX	D-	(800) 224-6312	B- / 7.3	7.63	10.74	7.48 /59	14.20 /69	13.54 /73	0.00	1.66
GR	Turner Spectrum Fund C	TSCCX	E-	(800) 224-6312	E+ / 0.8	6.35	1.52	1.07 /19	1.93 / 6	1.81 / 4	0.00	3.84
GR	Turner Spectrum Fund Inst	TSPEX	E	(800) 224-6312	D- / 1.0	6.61	2.02	2.10 /22	2.96 / 8	2.84 / 6	0.00	2.84
GR	Turner Spectrum Fund Inv	TSPCX	E	(800) 224-6312	E+ / 0.9	6.50	1.86	1.77 /21	2.69 / 7	2.57 / 5	0.00	3.09
GR	● Turner Titan C	TTLCX	D	(800) 224-6312	D / 2.0	4.32	4.89	7.13 /56	4.57 /12	--	0.00	3.87
GR	● Turner Titan Institutional	TTLEX	D+	(800) 224-6312	D+ / 2.6	4.51	5.43	8.27 /65	5.70 /16	--	0.00	2.87
GR	● Turner Titan Investor	TTLFX	D+	(800) 224-6312	D+ / 2.4	4.47	5.30	7.88 /62	5.39 /14	--	0.00	3.12
EM	● Tweedy Browne Glbl Val II Cr Uhngd	TBCUX	D	(800) 432-4789	D / 1.6	0.72	-3.68	-4.71 / 6	7.71 /25	7.72 /28	1.33	1.39
* FO	Tweedy Browne Global Value	TBGVX	C	(800) 432-4789	C- / 4.1	3.57	1.58	3.69 /30	10.99 /45	9.25 /39	1.20	1.38
GR	Tweedy Browne Value Fund	TWEBX	C	(800) 432-4789	C / 4.4	1.37	-0.60	3.08 /27	11.40 /48	9.20 /38	1.12	1.38
GL	Tweedy Browne Wdwide Hi Div Yd	TBHDX	D-	(800) 432-4789	D / 1.7	0.18	-2.23	-2.22 /10	7.71 /25	8.07 /30	2.17	1.37
AA	Two Oaks Diversified Gro and Inc A	TWOAX	D+	(855) 896-6257	D / 2.1	2.98	2.37	4.46 /35	7.96 /27	9.09 /37	1.26	1.76
GL	UBS Asset Growth A	BGFAX	C-	(888) 793-8637	C- / 3.0	6.88	4.06	8.22 /64	9.02 /33	7.60 /27	0.00	2.36
GL	UBS Asset Growth C	BGFCX	C-	(888) 793-8637	C- / 3.4	6.60	3.65	7.33 /58	8.21 /28	6.79 /22	0.00	3.13
GL	UBS Asset Growth P	BGFYX	C	(888) 793-8637	C- / 4.1	6.87	4.17	8.46 /66	9.30 /35	7.83 /29	0.00	2.11
GL	UBS Dynamic Alpha A	BNAAX	C-	(888) 793-8637	D- / 1.5	2.67	3.18	5.63 /43	6.42 /19	4.36 /10	3.31	1.42
GL	UBS Dynamic Alpha C	BNACX	C-	(888) 793-8637	D / 1.7	2.39	2.73	4.87 /38	5.61 /15	3.58 / 7	3.10	2.18
GL	UBS Dynamic Alpha P	BNAYX	C-	(888) 793-8637	D+ / 2.3	2.62	3.28	5.97 /46	6.67 /20	4.64 /11	3.86	1.15
GL	UBS Equity Lg-Sht Multi-Strategy A	BMNAX	C	(888) 793-8637	D / 1.7	2.51	5.23	10.53 /76	5.56 /15	--	0.00	6.31
GL	UBS Equity Lg-Sht Multi-Strategy C	BMNCX	C	(888) 793-8637	D / 2.0	2.41	4.91	9.70 /73	4.75 /12	--	0.00	6.46
GL	UBS Equity Lg-Sht Multi-Strategy P	BMNYX	C+	(888) 793-8637	D+ / 2.6	2.58	5.36	10.82 /78	5.81 /16	--	0.00	5.48
GL	UBS Global Allocation A	BNGLX	C-	(888) 793-8637	D / 2.0	2.33	3.45	8.05 /63	7.38 /23	6.30 /19	0.00	1.36
GL	UBS Global Allocation C	BNPCX	C-	(888) 793-8637	D+ / 2.3	2.12	2.97	7.16 /56	6.55 /19	5.48 /14	0.00	2.14
GL	UBS Global Allocation P	BPGLX	C	(888) 793-8637	C- / 3.0	2.37	3.56	8.27 /65	7.68 /25	6.62 /21	0.00	1.06
FO	UBS Global Sustainable Equity A	BNIEX	D+	(888) 793-8637	C- / 3.8	5.83	6.80	9.67 /73	10.17 /40	6.60 /21	1.10	2.74
FO	UBS Global Sustainable Equity C	BNICX	D+	(888) 793-8637	C- / 4.2	5.59	6.35	8.75 /68	9.36 /35	5.78 /16	1.00	3.54
FO	UBS Global Sustainable Equity P	BNUEX	C-	(888) 793-8637	C / 4.9	5.82	6.85	9.84 /74	10.45 /42	6.85 /22	1.44	2.45
AA	UBS US Allocation A	PWTAX	C+	(888) 793-8637	C- / 4.2	2.22	6.16	9.73 /73	11.34 /48	10.77 /51	0.20	1.03
AA	UBS US Allocation C	KPAAX	B-	(888) 793-8637	C / 4.6	2.02	5.76	8.89 /69	10.50 /42	9.94 /44	0.00	1.79
AA	UBS US Allocation P	PWTYX	B	(888) 793-8637	C / 5.3	2.29	6.30	10.01 /74	11.65 /50	11.08 /53	0.39	0.75
GI	UBS US Defensive Equity A	BEAAX	C+	(888) 793-8637	C+ / 5.9	2.77	8.19	13.09 /87	13.68 /65	10.86 /52	0.00	3.80
GI	UBS US Defensive Equity C	BEACX	C+	(888) 793-8637	C+ / 6.2	2.49	7.70	12.20 /83	12.81 /58	10.04 /45	0.00	4.61
GI	UBS US Defensive Equity P	BEAYX	B	(888) 793-8637	B- / 7.0	2.76	8.24	13.31 /88	13.95 /67	11.11 /54	0.00	3.53
IN	UBS US Equity Opportunity A	BNVAX	C+	(888) 793-8637	C+ / 6.0	0.98	7.80	13.13 /87	14.17 /68	11.42 /56	0.03	1.72
IN	UBS US Equity Opportunity C	BNVCX	C+	(888) 793-8637	C+ / 6.4	0.81	7.43	12.26 /84	13.34 /62	10.61 /50	0.00	2.50
IN	UBS US Equity Opportunity P	BUSVX	B-	(888) 793-8637	B- / 7.2	1.08	8.02	13.45 /88	14.46 /71	11.73 /59	0.28	1.52
GI	UBS US Large Cap Eq A	BNEQX	B+	(888) 793-8637	B / 7.7	3.23	9.23	14.80 /91	16.38 /86	13.43 /72	0.44	1.29
GI	UBS US Large Cap Eq C	BNQCX	B+	(888) 793-8637	B / 8.1	3.00	8.79	13.94 /89	15.51 /79	12.58 /65	0.00	2.08
GI	UBS US Large Cap Eq P	BPEQX	A	(888) 793-8637	B+ / 8.9	3.29	9.35	15.09 /92	16.67 /88	13.72 /75	0.71	0.99
SC	UBS US Small Cap Growth A	BNSCX	C	(888) 793-8637	B+ / 8.5	5.16	15.52	10.63 /77	17.51 /92	19.51 /99	0.00	1.46
SC	UBS US Small Cap Growth C	BNMCX	C	(888) 793-8637	B+ / 8.8	4.98	15.07	9.78 /73	16.63 /88	18.62 /98	0.00	2.25
SC	UBS US Small Cap Growth P	BISCX	C+	(888) 793-8637	A / 9.4	5.21	15.71	10.95 /78	17.86 /94	19.84 /99	0.00	1.10
GR	Undiscovered Mgrs Behavior Val A	UBVAX	B	(800) 480-4111	B- / 7.1	3.74	8.09	6.93 /54	16.30 /86	16.24 /94	0.71	2.03
GR	● Undiscovered Mgrs Behavior Val B	UBVBX	B+	(800) 480-4111	B / 7.7	3.61	7.82	6.39 /50	15.73 /81	15.66 /91	0.00	2.56

● Denotes fund is closed to new investors
* Denotes fund is included in Section II

www.thestreetratings.com

RISK			NET ASSETS		ASSET					BULL / BEAR		FUND MANAGER		MINIMUMS		LOADS	
	3 Year		NAV						Portfolio	Last Bull	Last Bear	Manager	Manager	Initial	Additional	Front	Back
Risk	Standard		As of	Total	Cash	Stocks	Bonds	Other	Turnover	Market	Market	Quality	Tenure	Purch.	Purch.	End	End
Rating/Pts	Deviation	Beta	3/31/15	$(Mil)	%	%	%	%	Ratio	Return	Return	Pct	(Years)	$	$	Load	Load
E- / 0.1	14.0	0.97	32.51	19	1	98	0	1	78	82.9	-22.1	45	N/A	250,000	5,000	0.0	0.0
E- / 0.1	14.0	0.97	31.34	82	1	98	0	1	78	81.4	-22.2	41	N/A	2,500	50	0.0	0.0
C+ / 6.2	13.6	0.31	13.89	4	64	35	0	1	409	41.1	-1.9	98	2	2,500	50	0.0	0.0
C+ / 6.3	13.6	0.32	14.50	29	64	35	0	1	409	46.0	-1.5	98	2	100,000	5,000	0.0	0.0
C+ / 6.3	13.6	0.32	14.36	38	64	35	0	1	409	44.9	-1.6	98	2	2,500	50	0.0	0.0
E / 0.4	13.2	1.06	24.62	43	2	97	0	1	89	77.2	-23.9	14	7	250,000	5,000	0.0	0.0
E / 0.4	13.2	1.06	23.75	185	2	97	0	1	89	75.7	-24.0	12	7	2,500	50	0.0	0.0
E / 0.4	12.6	1.01	21.46	4	2	97	0	1	89	74.5	-24.1	19	7	2,500	50	0.0	0.0
E- / 0.0	14.8	1.01	18.77	56	1	98	0	1	127	91.4	-29.4	37	2	2,500	50	0.0	0.0
D+ / 2.6	5.4	0.29	8.71	2	71	28	0	1	443	6.1	-4.8	31	7	2,500	50	0.0	0.0
C- / 3.0	5.4	0.28	9.36	38	71	28	0	1	443	9.8	-4.4	47	7	100,000	5,000	0.0	0.0
D+ / 2.9	5.4	0.28	9.17	9	71	28	0	1	443	8.8	-4.5	42	7	2,500	50	0.0	0.0
C+ / 6.5	5.7	0.31	10.14	N/A	63	36	0	1	777	22.4	-5.7	66	4	2,500	50	0.0	0.0
C+ / 6.8	5.7	0.31	10.65	11	63	36	0	1	777	27.0	-5.4	77	4	100,000	5,000	0.0	0.0
C+ / 6.7	5.7	0.31	10.52	N/A	63	36	0	1	777	25.9	-5.4	74	4	2,500	50	0.0	0.0
C+ / 6.9	10.1	0.59	14.02	450	21	78	0	1	4	43.7	-14.0	96	6	2,500	200	0.0	2.0
B- / 7.3	7.7	0.54	26.97	9,596	16	74	8	2	4	56.8	-14.2	94	22	2,500	200	0.0	2.0
C+ / 6.6	8.6	0.81	22.14	622	12	84	2	2	7	63.6	-15.2	47	22	2,500	200	0.0	2.0
C+ / 6.0	10.4	0.76	10.84	569	8	90	0	2	10	43.9	-11.8	73	8	2,500	200	0.0	2.0
B- / 7.4	7.7	1.22	12.04	24	9	73	11	7	43	47.9	-10.5	10	10	2,500	1,000	5.8	0.0
B- / 7.0	10.5	0.73	9.48	14	28	1	67	4	112	55.1	-23.7	84	6	1,000	100	5.5	1.0
B- / 7.0	10.4	0.72	9.37	7	28	1	67	4	112	51.0	-23.9	80	6	1,000	100	0.0	1.0
B- / 7.1	10.5	0.73	9.49	6	28	1	67	4	112	56.4	-23.6	86	6	1,000	100	0.0	1.0
B / 8.5	4.4	0.49	7.31	88	15	0	84	1	45	27.1	-2.1	84	7	1,000	100	5.5	1.0
B / 8.5	4.4	0.50	6.86	48	15	0	84	1	45	23.9	-2.5	78	7	1,000	100	0.0	1.0
B / 8.5	4.3	0.49	7.44	183	15	0	84	1	45	28.1	-2.1	86	7	1,000	100	0.0	1.0
B+ / 9.6	4.0	0.03	11.01	N/A	71	18	10	1	148	16.1	-2.7	94	N/A	1,000	100	5.5	1.0
B+ / 9.6	4.0	0.03	10.63	1	71	18	10	1	148	13.0	-3.1	92	N/A	1,000	100	0.0	1.0
B+ / 9.6	4.0	0.03	11.15	16	71	18	10	1	148	16.9	-2.6	94	N/A	1,000	100	0.0	1.0
B / 8.2	7.2	1.11	11.41	240	41	43	15	1	49	40.8	-16.0	32	6	1,000	100	5.5	1.0
B / 8.2	7.2	1.10	11.08	153	41	43	15	1	49	37.2	-16.3	24	6	1,000	100	0.0	1.0
B / 8.2	7.2	1.10	11.65	127	41	43	15	1	49	42.2	-15.9	36	6	1,000	100	0.0	1.0
C+ / 5.6	12.5	0.91	9.26	6	0	100	0	0	137	62.9	-27.9	80	2	1,000	100	5.5	1.0
C+ / 5.6	12.5	0.91	9.07	2	0	100	0	0	137	58.8	-28.1	74	2	1,000	100	0.0	1.0
C+ / 5.6	12.4	0.90	9.28	16	0	100	0	0	137	64.1	-27.8	82	2	1,000	100	0.0	1.0
B / 8.4	7.1	1.22	41.44	174	33	44	21	2	240	65.0	-12.2	39	6	1,000	100	5.5	1.0
B / 8.4	7.2	1.23	40.41	73	33	44	21	2	240	60.8	-12.5	29	6	1,000	100	0.0	1.0
B / 8.4	7.1	1.22	42.03	26	33	44	21	2	240	66.7	-12.1	43	6	5,000,000	0	0.0	1.0
C+ / 6.6	10.0	0.97	13.74	9	3	96	0	1	60	86.8	-19.8	42	9	1,000	100	5.5	1.0
C+ / 6.6	10.0	0.96	13.15	2	3	96	0	1	60	82.1	-20.0	32	9	1,000	100	0.0	1.0
C+ / 6.7	10.0	0.97	13.79	5	3	96	0	1	60	88.3	-19.7	47	9	1,000	100	0.0	1.0
C+ / 6.0	12.2	1.19	10.28	39	3	96	0	1	62	98.4	-21.8	13	14	1,000	100	5.5	1.0
C+ / 6.0	12.2	1.18	9.98	4	3	96	0	1	62	93.5	-22.2	10	14	1,000	100	0.0	1.0
C+ / 6.0	12.2	1.18	10.34	2	3	96	0	1	62	100.1	-21.7	15	14	1,000	100	0.0	1.0
C+ / 6.4	11.3	1.13	26.88	10	1	98	0	1	55	103.0	-19.5	41	21	1,000	100	5.5	1.0
C+ / 6.4	11.3	1.13	25.74	3	1	98	0	1	55	97.8	-19.7	31	21	1,000	100	0.0	1.0
C+ / 6.4	11.3	1.13	26.98	28	1	98	0	1	55	104.6	-19.3	45	21	1,000	100	0.0	1.0
C- / 3.3	15.1	1.02	22.41	39	2	97	0	1	57	112.5	-21.6	75	18	1,000	100	5.5	1.0
D+ / 2.8	15.1	1.02	19.60	4	2	97	0	1	57	107.2	-21.9	67	18	1,000	100	0.0	1.0
C- / 3.5	15.1	1.02	23.83	154	2	97	0	1	57	114.6	-21.5	78	18	1,000	100	0.0	1.0
C+ / 6.5	11.8	1.10	56.33	545	6	93	0	1	44	123.2	-27.3	47	17	1,000	50	5.3	0.0
C+ / 6.5	11.8	1.10	53.91	N/A	6	93	0	1	44	119.4	-27.5	39	17	1,000	50	0.0	0.0

					PERFORMANCE							
	99 Pct = Best *0 Pct = Worst*			Overall Investment Rating	Perfor-mance	Total Return % through 3/31/15			Annualized		Incl. in Returns	
Fund Type	Fund Name	Ticker Symbol	Phone		Rating/Pts	3 Mo	6 Mo	1Yr / Pct	3Yr / Pct	5Yr / Pct	Dividend Yield	Expense Ratio
GR	Undiscovered Mgrs Behavior Val C	UBVCX	(800) 480-4111	B+	B / 7.7	3.62	7.84	6.41 /50	15.73 /81	15.66 /91	0.44	2.54
GR	Undiscovered Mgrs Behavior Val Inst	UBVLX	(800) 480-4111	A-	B+ / 8.5	3.85	8.30	7.35 /58	16.70 /88	16.57 /95	1.03	1.63
GR	Undiscovered Mgrs Behavior Val R2	UBVRX	(800) 480-4111	B+	B / 7.9	3.69	7.97	6.67 /52	16.01 /83	15.93 /93	0.53	2.26
GR	Undiscovered Mgrs Behavior Val R6	UBVFX	(800) 480-4111	A	B+ / 8.5	3.86	8.36	7.46 /59	16.78 /89	16.62 /95	1.09	1.51
GR	Undiscovered Mgrs Behavior Val Sel	UBVSX	(800) 480-4111	B+	B / 7.8	3.80	8.22	7.20 /57	15.73 /81	15.99 /93	0.95	1.81
GR	Unified Srs Tr Auer Growth Fd	AUERX	(800) 408-4682	E	E+ / 0.7	-3.39	-11.06	-14.84 / 2	5.18 /14	2.82 / 6	0.00	1.98
GR	Union Street Partners Value A	USPVX	(800) 527-9525	C-	C- / 3.9	0.14	-1.65	4.02 /32	12.19 /54	--	0.64	2.11
GR	Union Street Partners Value C	USPCX	(800) 527-9525	C	C / 4.6	-0.07	-0.96	4.36 /34	11.73 /51	--	0.05	2.86
EM	Universal Inst Emer Markets Eqty I	UEMEX	(800) 869-6397	E+	E+ / 0.6	3.00	-3.36	-1.22 /12	1.11 / 5	2.29 / 5	0.39	1.71
EM	Universal Inst Emer Markets Eqty II	UEMBX	(800) 869-6397	E+	E+ / 0.6	3.02	-3.37	-1.27 /12	1.07 / 5	2.24 / 5	0.34	2.06
FO	Universal Inst Glbl Tact Ast All I	UIMPX	(800) 869-6397	D	D / 2.1	0.19	-1.62	0.27 /16	7.62 /25	6.48 /20	0.84	1.33
GL	Universal Inst Global Franchise II	UGIIX	(800) 869-6397	E+	C- / 3.3	0.44	1.51	4.23 /33	8.96 /33	11.29 /55	2.06	1.63
RE	Universal Inst Global Real Est II	UGETX	(800) 869-6397	C	C+ / 6.5	4.07	11.22	14.92 /91	11.43 /48	10.66 /50	0.67	1.69
MC	● Universal Inst Mid Cap Growth I	UMGPX	(800) 869-6397	E+	C- / 4.2	2.91	5.65	4.50 /35	10.13 /40	12.56 /65	0.00	1.09
SC	● Universal Inst Small Co Growth II	USIIX	(800) 869-6397	D-	B- / 7.2	4.14	10.10	-5.22 / 5	16.36 /86	14.94 /86	0.00	2.25
RE	Universal Inst US Real Estate I	UUSRX	(800) 869-6397	B	A- / 9.0	4.32	18.44	23.70 /98	12.99 /60	14.84 /86	1.24	1.10
RE	Universal Inst US Real Estate II	USRBX	(800) 869-6397	B-	B+ / 8.9	4.25	18.31	23.34 /98	12.70 /57	14.56 /83	1.08	1.45
GR	Upright Growth Fund	UPUPX		C	C+ / 5.9	3.83	-2.81	5.50 /42	14.29 /69	15.07 /87	0.00	2.16
GR	US Global Inv All American Equity	GBTFX	(800) 873-8637	D	C / 4.5	0.47	0.54	1.47 /20	11.76 /51	11.68 /58	0.00	2.45
GL	US Global Inv China Region Opport	USCOX	(800) 873-8637	D-	D / 2.0	4.02	9.64	6.62 /52	4.83 /13	0.52 / 3	0.00	2.77
EN	US Global Inv Global Resources	PSPFX	(800) 873-8637	E-	E- / 0.0	-12.59	-35.29	-38.31 / 0	-14.89 / 0	-6.86 / 1	0.00	1.60
EN	US Global Inv Global Resources Inst	PIPFX	(800) 873-8637	E-	E- / 0.0	-12.29	-34.93	-37.83 / 0	-14.34 / 0	-6.27 / 1	0.00	1.25
PM	US Global Inv Gold & PMetals Fd	USERX	(800) 873-8637	E-	E- / 0.0	2.33	-14.01	-21.31 / 1	-24.65 / 0	-14.87 / 0	0.00	2.15
GR	US Global Inv Holmes Macro Trends	MEGAX	(800) 873-8637	E+	D / 2.2	2.91	-1.38	-2.45 / 9	7.92 /27	9.16 /38	0.00	2.00
PM	US Global Inv World Prec Min	UNWPX	(800) 873-8637	E-	E- / 0.0	-6.74	-23.22	-31.95 / 0	-30.61 / 0	-20.17 / 0	0.00	1.86
PM	US Global Inv World Prec Min Inst	UNWIX	(800) 873-8637	E-	E- / 0.0	-6.90	-23.14	-31.85 / 0	-30.40 / 0	-19.84 / 0	0.00	3.31
EM	US Global Investors Em Europe	EUROX	(800) 873-8637	E-	E- / 0.1	-5.79	-15.27	-21.23 / 1	-10.60 / 1	-7.43 / 1	3.46	1.84
GR	US Lg Cap Core Eqty Svc	GEVSX	(800) 242-0134	D+	B- / 7.0	0.21	3.32	8.63 /67	14.99 /75	12.61 /65	1.16	0.68
GR	US Lg-Cap Core Eqty Inv	GEIVX	(800) 242-0134	D+	B- / 7.2	0.31	3.46	8.83 /68	15.30 /77	12.90 /67	1.39	0.43
GR	USA Mutuals Barrier A	VICAX	(866) 264-8783	C	C- / 3.9	0.66	1.00	0.32 /17	12.87 /59	--	1.31	1.47
GR	USA Mutuals Barrier C	VICCX	(866) 264-8783	C	C / 4.3	0.49	0.63	-0.40 /14	12.04 /53	--	0.91	2.22
GR	USA Mutuals Barrier Inv	VICEX	(866) 264-8783	C	C / 4.9	0.69	1.03	0.34 /17	12.90 /59	14.86 /86	1.37	1.47
GR	USA Mutuals Gen Wave Growth Inv	GWGFX	(866) 264-8783	D-	E+ / 0.6	0.00	-7.75	-9.91 / 3	3.68 / 9	3.67 / 7	0.00	2.39
AG	USAA Aggressive Growth Fund	USAUX	(800) 382-8722	C	B- / 7.0	2.61	7.94	13.97 /89	13.61 /64	13.32 /71	1.78	0.93
AG	USAA Aggressive Growth Fund I	UIAGX	(800) 382-8722	C+	B- / 7.3	2.67	8.09	14.27 /90	13.95 /67	13.71 /75	1.96	0.68
GR	USAA Capital Growth	USCGX	(800) 382-8722	A-	B / 7.9	3.98	7.58	12.51 /85	15.17 /76	10.92 /52	1.48	1.28
GR	USAA Cornerstone Aggressive	UCAGX	(800) 382-8722	U	U /	1.94	2.29	3.64 /30	--	--	1.37	1.65
AA	USAA Cornerstone Conservative	USCCX	(800) 382-8722	U	U /	1.33	1.88	3.72 /30	--	--	2.97	0.77
GR	USAA Cornerstone Equity	UCEQX	(800) 382-8722	U	U /	2.48	3.09	4.12 /33	--	--	1.82	1.24
BA	USAA Cornerstone Moderate	USBSX	(800) 382-8722	C-	D+ / 2.4	1.64	2.09	4.19 /33	7.00 /21	6.92 /23	2.49	1.33
GL	USAA Cornerstone Moderately Aggr	USCRX	(800) 382-8722	C-	D+ / 2.5	1.41	1.78	4.02 /32	7.30 /23	6.66 /21	2.47	1.26
GI	USAA Cornerstone Moderately Consv	UCMCX	(800) 382-8722	U	U /	1.40	1.98	4.03 /32	--	--	2.39	1.17
EM	USAA Emerging Markets Adviser	UAEMX	(800) 382-8722	E	E- / 0.2	-1.57	-8.95	-7.47 / 4	-3.33 / 2	--	1.29	1.79
EM	USAA Emerging Markets Fund	USEMX	(800) 382-8722	E	E- / 0.2	-1.50	-8.86	-7.22 / 4	-3.00 / 2	-2.26 / 2	1.52	1.52
EM	USAA Emerging Markets Inst	UIEMX	(800) 382-8722	E	E / 0.3	-1.51	-8.77	-7.13 / 4	-2.78 / 2	-1.98 / 2	1.76	1.31
GR	USAA Extended Market Index	USMIX	(800) 382-8722	A-	B+ / 8.9	5.16	11.89	9.85 /74	16.74 /88	15.29 /89	0.84	0.51
GR	USAA First Start Growth Fund	UFSGX	(800) 382-8722	C	C / 4.5	2.15	3.88	7.15 /56	10.43 /42	9.65 /42	1.30	1.84
GI	USAA Growth & Income Fund	USGRX	(800) 382-8722	C+	B- / 7.1	0.74	4.54	10.66 /77	14.76 /73	12.81 /66	0.74	0.94
GL	USAA Growth & Income Fund	USGIX	(800) 382-8722	C+	C+ / 6.9	0.69	4.36	10.31 /76	14.39 /70	--	0.46	1.22
AA	USAA Growth & Tax Strategy Fund	USBLX	(800) 382-8722	B-	C- / 4.1	0.91	3.93	8.56 /67	9.60 /37	9.50 /41	2.34	0.92
GR	USAA Growth Fund	USAAX	(800) 382-8722	A+	A / 9.5	2.75	10.02	16.22 /94	18.29 /95	15.48 /90	1.07	1.12
GR	USAA Growth Fund Inst	UIGRX	(800) 382-8722	A+	A / 9.5	2.76	10.02	16.24 /94	18.31 /95	15.53 /90	1.09	1.00

● Denotes fund is closed to new investors
* Denotes fund is included in Section II

www.thestreetratings.com

RISK	3 Year		NET ASSETS		ASSET				Portfolio	BULL / BEAR		FUND MANAGER		MINIMUMS		LOADS	
Risk Rating/Pts	Standard Deviation	Beta	NAV As of 3/31/15	Total $(Mil)	Cash %	Stocks %	Bonds %	Other %	Turnover Ratio	Last Bull Market Return	Last Bear Market Return	Manager Quality Pct	Manager Tenure (Years)	Initial Purch. $	Additional Purch. $	Front End Load	Back End Load
C+ / 6.5	11.8	1.10	53.52	153	6	93	0	1	44	119.4	-27.5	39	17	1,000	50	0.0	0.0
C+ / 6.5	11.8	1.10	57.48	859	6	93	0	1	44	125.7	-27.3	52	17	3,000,000	0	0.0	0.0
C+ / 6.9	11.8	1.10	56.18	2	6	93	0	1	44	121.3	-27.5	42	17	0	0	0.0	0.0
B- / 7.0	11.8	1.10	57.53	61	6	93	0	1	44	126.1	-27.3	53	17	15,000,000	0	0.0	0.0
C+ / 6.9	11.8	1.09	57.36	447	6	93	0	1	44	120.2	-27.3	41	17	1,000,000	0	0.0	0.0
C- / 4.1	16.8	1.34	7.40	55	10	89	0	1	140	48.7	-33.7	1	28	2,000	100	0.0	0.0
C+ / 6.7	11.7	1.11	14.65	13	6	93	0	1	7	82.7	-18.4	10	5	2,500	50	5.8	0.0
C+ / 6.7	11.6	1.11	14.34	9	6	93	0	1	7	80.2	-18.6	8	5	2,500	50	0.0	0.0
C / 5.5	12.9	0.92	14.40	271	3	96	0	1	45	21.4	-22.6	72	19	0	0	0.0	0.0
C / 5.5	12.9	0.92	14.35	89	3	96	0	1	45	21.2	-22.7	72	19	0	0	0.0	0.0
C+ / 6.6	7.1	0.51	10.30	146	18	53	27	2	82	45.6	-15.3	87	5	0	0	0.0	0.0
C- / 3.5	11.5	0.76	16.11	51	1	98	0	1	20	57.4	-6.8	82	6	0	0	0.0	0.0
C / 5.1	12.3	0.88	11.00	106	9	90	0	1	31	70.8	-22.3	55	9	0	0	0.0	0.0
D- / 1.5	14.3	1.03	13.10	65	0	99	0	1	44	65.5	-21.6	5	12	0	0	0.0	0.0
E- / 0.1	18.3	1.15	17.11	16	5	93	0	2	50	90.9	-23.8	34	12	0	0	0.0	0.0
C / 4.4	12.0	0.95	21.00	211	5	93	1	1	25	80.6	-17.3	62	18	0	0	0.0	0.0
C / 4.5	12.0	0.95	20.87	311	5	93	1	1	25	78.9	-17.3	58	18	0	0	0.0	0.0
C / 5.0	15.2	1.05	12.73	10	14	84	0	2	47	115.7	-20.7	32	16	2,000	100	0.0	2.0
C / 4.3	10.3	1.00	27.97	22	1	98	0	1	150	78.5	-18.3	17	26	5,000	100	0.0	0.0
C / 5.5	13.3	0.70	8.53	21	2	97	0	1	201	22.3	-29.0	42	N/A	5,000	100	0.0	0.0
D / 2.1	17.5	0.95	5.83	143	6	90	3	1	138	-22.2	-31.8	0	26	5,000	100	0.0	0.0
D / 2.1	17.4	0.95	5.85	12	6	90	3	1	138	-20.7	-31.6	0	26	1,000,000	0	0.0	0.0
E+ / 0.7	34.8	1.64	5.28	63	7	89	3	1	64	-57.0	-18.0	2	26	5,000	100	0.0	0.0
C- / 3.7	12.1	0.99	20.84	47	5	93	0	2	109	54.0	-21.9	4	21	5,000	100	0.0	0.0
D- / 1.3	34.9	1.71	4.43	95	10	82	7	1	34	-64.2	-28.5	0	26	5,000	100	0.0	0.0
D- / 1.3	34.9	1.71	4.45	N/A	10	82	7	1	34	-63.8	-28.3	0	26	1,000,000	0	0.0	0.0
E+ / 0.9	18.8	1.20	6.18	62	0	0	0	100	74	-12.1	-32.7	1	18	5,000	100	0.0	0.0
D+ / 2.4	10.3	1.05	9.59	5	4	95	0	1	45	94.2	-19.2	40	13	5,000,000	0	0.0	0.0
D+ / 2.4	10.3	1.06	9.67	97	4	95	0	1	45	96.0	-19.1	44	13	5,000,000	0	0.0	0.0
B- / 7.2	10.6	0.88	29.00	23	0	99	0	1	167	N/A	N/A	51	4	2,000	100	5.8	1.0
B- / 7.2	10.6	0.88	28.60	20	0	99	0	1	167	N/A	N/A	40	4	2,000	100	0.0	1.0
C+ / 6.8	10.6	0.88	29.11	219	0	99	0	1	167	91.2	-13.9	52	4	2,000	100	0.0	1.0
B- / 7.1	7.4	0.57	8.09	10	25	54	20	1	392	28.8	-20.2	11	4	2,000	100	0.0	1.0
C / 4.7	11.4	1.09	40.47	1,198	0	99	0	1	68	91.5	-18.7	19	5	3,000	50	0.0	0.0
C / 4.7	11.4	1.09	40.80	156	0	99	0	1	68	93.5	-18.6	22	5	1,000,000	0	0.0	0.0
C+ / 6.9	10.7	1.03	9.93	746	1	98	0	1	36	86.0	-22.1	48	4	3,000	50	0.0	0.0
U /	N/A	N/A	12.07	187	6	79	14	1	46	N/A	N/A	N/A	3	1,000	50	0.0	0.0
U /	N/A	N/A	10.64	139	2	16	80	2	1	N/A	N/A	N/A	3	1,000	50	0.0	0.0
U /	N/A	N/A	13.20	83	4	95	0	1	2	N/A	N/A	N/A	3	1,000	50	0.0	0.0
B / 8.0	5.3	0.85	15.26	1,132	3	51	45	1	46	39.1	-13.4	36	11	1,000	50	0.0	0.0
B- / 7.9	6.1	0.95	25.83	2,492	4	59	35	2	57	38.6	-14.0	51	8	1,000	50	0.0	0.0
U /	N/A	N/A	11.33	196	8	43	47	2	36	N/A	N/A	N/A	3	1,000	50	0.0	0.0
C / 4.6	15.1	1.08	15.68	4	3	96	0	1	48	7.8	-29.0	15	3	3,000	50	0.0	1.0
C / 4.6	15.0	1.07	15.74	481	3	96	0	1	48	9.1	-28.9	18	3	3,000	50	0.0	0.0
C / 4.6	15.0	1.07	15.68	623	3	96	0	1	48	10.1	-28.8	20	3	1,000,000	0	0.0	0.0
C+ / 6.3	11.7	1.08	18.95	687	1	98	0	1	18	103.3	-23.6	58	5	3,000	50	0.0	0.0
B- / 7.0	7.3	0.73	13.32	374	3	73	22	2	64	57.6	-15.6	53	6	1,000	50	0.0	0.0
C+ / 5.7	10.7	1.10	21.37	1,552	2	97	0	1	61	94.1	-19.6	28	9	3,000	50	0.0	0.0
C+ / 5.7	10.7	0.64	21.31	9	2	97	0	1	61	92.0	-19.7	97	9	3,000	50	0.0	0.0
B / 8.8	4.6	0.78	17.44	277	0	45	54	1	5	51.2	-4.0	78	10	3,000	50	0.0	0.0
C+ / 6.6	10.6	1.06	25.02	1,215	1	98	0	1	31	110.3	-17.3	77	8	3,000	50	0.0	0.0
C+ / 6.6	10.6	1.05	24.96	858	1	98	0	1	31	110.3	-17.2	78	8	1,000,000	0	0.0	0.0

Data as of March 31, 2015

Fund Type	Fund Name	Ticker Symbol	Overall Investment Rating	Phone	Performance Rating/Pts	Total Return % through 3/31/15			Annualized		Incl. in Returns	
						3 Mo	6 Mo	1Yr / Pct	3Yr / Pct	5Yr / Pct	Dividend Yield	Expense Ratio
IN	USAA Income Stock Fund	USISX	B-	(800) 382-8722	C+ / 5.8	-1.90	2.49	7.13 /56	13.46 /63	12.48 /64	2.47	0.80
IN	USAA Income Stock Fund Inst	UIISX	B-	(800) 382-8722	C+ / 5.9	-1.89	2.52	7.20 /57	13.56 /64	12.63 /65	2.53	0.73
FO	USAA International Fund	USIFX	D	(800) 382-8722	C- / 3.1	5.98	2.75	1.79 /21	8.34 /29	7.34 /25	1.66	1.16
FO	USAA International Fund Adv	UAIFX	D	(800) 382-8722	D+ / 2.7	5.93	2.64	1.51 /20	8.00 /27	--	1.37	1.46
FO	USAA International Fund Inst	UIIFX	D	(800) 382-8722	C- / 3.2	6.04	2.82	1.93 /22	8.53 /30	7.57 /27	1.79	1.01
AA	USAA Managed Allocation Fund	UMAFX	D+	(800) 382-8722	D- / 1.3	2.52	2.24	2.32 /23	4.41 /11	6.56 /20	1.94	1.01
GR	USAA Nasdaq 100 Index	USNQX	A+	(800) 382-8722	A / 9.3	2.45	7.32	21.08 /97	17.13 /91	17.76 /97	0.21	0.64
PM	USAA Precious Mtls&Minerals Fund	USAGX	E-	(800) 382-8722	E- / 0.0	-4.07	-16.55	-22.99 / 1	-27.15 / 0	-15.55 / 0	1.42	1.24
PM	USAA Precious Mtls&Minerals Inst	UIPMX	E-	(800) 382-8722	E- / 0.0	-3.97	-16.37	-22.75 / 1	-26.98 / 0	-15.35 / 0	1.74	1.00
IX	USAA S&P 500 Index Members	USSPX	A	(800) 382-8722	B / 8.1	0.92	5.83	12.47 /85	15.83 /82	14.18 /79	1.68	0.30
IX	USAA S&P 500 Index Reward	USPRX	A	(800) 382-8722	B / 8.2	0.91	5.84	12.57 /85	15.93 /83	14.30 /80	1.77	0.20
TC	USAA Science & Tech Adv	USTCX	A-	(800) 382-8722	A+ / 9.8	5.53	13.05	20.65 /97	21.32 /98	--	1.41	1.41
TC	USAA Science & Technology Fund	USSCX	A-	(800) 382-8722	A+ / 9.8	5.56	13.10	20.82 /97	21.55 /98	18.24 /98	1.29	1.24
SC	USAA Small Cap Stock Fund	USCAX	C+	(800) 382-8722	B- / 7.5	4.03	12.70	6.19 /48	14.92 /74	14.01 /78	0.12	1.15
SC	USAA Small Cap Stock Fund Inst	UISCX	B-	(800) 382-8722	B / 7.7	4.06	12.75	6.33 /49	15.23 /77	14.38 /81	0.23	1.00
AA	USAA Target Retirement 2020 Fund	URTNX	C-	(800) 382-8722	D / 2.0	1.43	1.95	3.38 /28	6.27 /18	6.88 /22	2.84	0.74
AA	USAA Target Retirement 2030 Fund	URTRX	C-	(800) 382-8722	D+ / 2.7	1.69	2.52	3.83 /31	7.67 /25	8.11 /31	2.59	0.80
AA	USAA Target Retirement 2040 Fund	URFRX	C-	(800) 382-8722	C- / 3.1	1.78	2.78	3.88 /31	8.50 /30	8.60 /34	2.26	0.86
GI	USAA Target Retirement 2050 Fund	URFFX	C-	(800) 382-8722	C- / 3.3	1.87	3.10	4.06 /32	8.66 /31	8.72 /35	1.99	0.91
GI	USAA Target Retirement 2060	URSIX	U	(800) 382-8722	U /	1.92	3.27	4.02 /32	--	--	1.61	2.60
AA	USAA Target Retirement Income	URINX	C-	(800) 382-8722	D- / 1.4	1.30	1.64	3.11 /27	4.98 /13	5.85 /16	2.79	0.68
GI	USAA Total Return Strategy Fund	USTRX	D	(800) 382-8722	E+ / 0.7	-0.17	-1.79	-1.27 /12	2.27 / 7	2.61 / 5	0.72	1.45
AA	USAA Total Return Strategy Inst	UTRIX	U	(800) 382-8722	U /	-0.12	-1.66	-1.02 /13	--	--	0.97	1.23
GR	USAA Value Fund	UVALX	B+	(800) 382-8722	B- / 7.1	1.34	6.20	7.48 /59	15.01 /75	12.92 /67	1.19	1.11
GL	USAA Value Fund Adv	UAVAX	B-	(800) 382-8722	C+ / 6.9	1.29	6.05	7.23 /57	14.63 /72	--	0.99	1.35
GR	USAA Value Fund I	UIVAX	B+	(800) 382-8722	B- / 7.2	1.39	6.25	7.59 /60	15.14 /76	13.11 /69	1.33	1.00
GR	USAA World Growth Adv	USWGX	C+	(800) 382-8722	C+ / 6.1	2.94	6.13	6.05 /47	13.52 /64	--	0.86	1.35
GL	USAA World Growth Fund	USAWX	C+	(800) 382-8722	C+ / 6.4	3.04	6.27	6.27 /49	13.79 /66	11.91 /60	0.98	1.19
GL	UTC North American Fund	UTCNX	C+	(800) 368-3322	C / 4.9	3.31	8.98	12.65 /85	9.85 /39	6.48 /20	0.39	2.27
FO	VALIC Co II Intl Opportunities	VISEX	D	(800) 858-8850	D+ / 2.5	4.26	2.99	-2.24 /10	7.87 /26	6.25 /18	1.28	1.31
FO	VALIC Company International Eq Idx	VCIEX	D	(800) 858-8850	D+ / 2.5	5.44	0.82	-1.41 /12	7.83 /26	5.25 /13	3.64	0.46
GR	Valley Forge Fund	VAFGX	E-	(800) 548-1942	E / 0.3	-1.01	-15.88	-20.07 / 1	1.63 / 6	3.98 / 8	0.00	1.77
AA	Value Line Asset Allocation	VLAAX	B-	(800) 243-2729	C / 5.2	2.30	7.40	8.39 /66	11.20 /47	12.47 /64	0.35	1.19
GI	Value Line Income & Growth Fund	VALIX	C	(800) 243-2729	C+ / 5.7	2.14	5.99	10.48 /76	11.97 /52	9.57 /41	0.94	1.16
GR	Value Line Larger Companies	VALLX	B	(800) 243-2729	A- / 9.1	5.78	10.56	16.85 /94	15.99 /83	14.36 /81	0.35	1.25
GI	Value Line Mid Cap Focused	VLIFX	B+	(800) 243-2729	B- / 7.2	3.50	9.49	10.13 /75	14.22 /69	15.62 /91	0.04	1.26
GR	Value Line Premier Growth	VALSX	C+	(800) 243-2729	C+ / 6.2	2.69	7.60	8.54 /67	12.99 /60	14.64 /84	0.02	1.24
SC	Value Line Small Cap Opportunities	VLEOX	A	(800) 243-2729	A- / 9.2	4.90	13.82	10.96 /78	17.13 /91	16.96 /96	0.00	1.26
IN	Van Eck CM Commodity Index A	CMCAX	E-	(800) 826-1115	E- / 0.0	-6.57	-19.63	-27.33 / 0	-12.62 / 1	--	0.00	1.31
IN	Van Eck CM Commodity Index I	COMIX	E-	(800) 826-1115	E- / 0.1	-6.49	-19.55	-27.18 / 0	-12.40 / 1	--	0.00	0.95
IN	Van Eck CM Commodity Index Y	CMCYX	E-	(800) 826-1115	E- / 0.1	-6.50	-19.58	-27.21 / 0	-12.41 / 1	--	0.00	1.07
EM	Van Eck Emerging Mkts A	GBFAX	D-	(800) 826-1115	D- / 1.1	1.12	-1.71	0.56 /17	6.25 /18	5.89 /16	0.00	1.63
EM	Van Eck Emerging Mkts C	EMRCX	D-	(800) 826-1115	D- / 1.3	0.92	-2.15	-0.38 /15	5.33 /14	5.03 /12	0.00	2.63
EM	Van Eck Emerging Mkts I	EMRIX	D-	(800) 826-1115	D / 1.9	1.28	-1.51	1.07 /19	6.74 /20	6.41 /20	0.00	1.77
EM	Van Eck Emerging Mkts Y	EMRYX	D-	(800) 826-1115	D / 1.7	1.26	-1.56	0.90 /18	6.49 /19	6.05 /17	0.00	1.50
EN	Van Eck Global Hard Assets A	GHAAX	E-	(800) 826-1115	E- / 0.1	0.82	-19.80	-20.11 / 1	-4.69 / 2	-1.01 / 2	0.10	1.45
EN	Van Eck Global Hard Assets C	GHACX	E-	(800) 826-1115	E- / 0.1	0.64	-20.12	-20.74 / 1	-5.47 / 2	-1.79 / 2	0.12	2.23
EN	Van Eck Global Hard Assets I	GHAIX	E-	(800) 826-1115	E- / 0.2	0.94	-19.63	-19.79 / 1	-4.32 / 2	-0.63 / 2	0.10	1.03
EN	Van Eck Global Hard Assets Y	GHAYX	E-	(800) 826-1115	E- / 0.2	0.92	-19.68	-19.89 / 1	-4.45 / 2	-0.77 / 2	0.11	1.19
PM	Van Eck Intl Investors Gold A	INIVX	E-	(800) 826-1115	E- / 0.0	-5.37	-18.25	-22.28 / 1	-25.00 / 0	-13.24 / 0	0.00	1.46
PM	Van Eck Intl Investors Gold C	IIGCX	E-	(800) 826-1115	E- / 0.0	-5.52	-18.47	-22.71 / 1	-25.54 / 0	-13.87 / 0	0.00	2.30
PM	Van Eck Intl Investors Gold I	INIIX	E-	(800) 826-1115	E- / 0.0	-5.23	-18.00	-21.81 / 1	-24.66 / 0	-12.90 / 0	0.00	1.08

Notes at top left of table:
99 Pct = Best
0 Pct = Worst

- Denotes fund is closed to new investors
* Denotes fund is included in Section II

www.thestreetratings.com

RISK Risk Rating/Pts	3 Year Standard Deviation	Beta	NET ASSETS NAV As of 3/31/15	Total $(Mil)	ASSET Cash %	Stocks %	Bonds %	Other %	Portfolio Turnover Ratio	BULL/BEAR Last Bull Market Return	Last Bear Market Return	FUND MANAGER Manager Quality Pct	Manager Tenure (Years)	MINIMUMS Initial Purch. $	Additional Purch. $	LOADS Front End Load	Back End Load
B- / 7.5	9.4	0.96	17.73	1,672	3	96	0	1	57	85.9	-16.7	40	5	3,000	50	0.0	0.0
B- / 7.5	9.4	0.96	17.71	1,138	3	96	0	1	57	86.4	-16.5	42	5	1,000,000	0	0.0	0.0
C+ / 5.8	12.7	0.93	29.76	1,871	1	98	0	1	14	55.3	-23.2	61	13	3,000	50	0.0	0.0
C+ / 5.8	12.6	0.93	29.66	7	1	98	0	1	14	53.5	-23.3	56	13	3,000	50	0.0	1.0
C+ / 5.8	12.6	0.93	29.68	1,664	1	98	0	1	14	56.1	-23.1	63	13	1,000,000	0	0.0	0.0
B / 8.2	7.2	1.12	11.79	1,353	6	64	28	2	65	24.8	-1.6	4	5	0	0	0.0	0.0
C+ / 6.6	11.6	1.06	12.53	778	1	98	0	1	11	112.2	-11.0	67	9	3,000	50	0.0	0.0
E+ / 0.6	37.5	1.78	11.32	532	1	97	0	2	10	-60.8	-12.0	1	7	3,000	50	0.0	0.0
E+ / 0.6	37.5	1.78	11.36	145	1	97	0	2	10	-60.5	-11.9	1	7	1,000,000	0	0.0	0.0
B- / 7.3	9.6	1.00	29.54	2,788	4	95	0	1	3	98.6	-16.4	64	9	3,000	50	0.0	0.0
B- / 7.3	9.5	1.00	29.54	2,410	4	95	0	1	3	99.2	-16.3	65	9	100,000	50	0.0	0.0
C / 5.2	12.1	1.00	21.39	89	2	97	0	1	91	124.0	-16.4	92	13	3,000	50	0.0	0.0
C / 5.3	12.1	1.00	21.64	745	2	97	0	1	91	125.6	-16.3	93	13	3,000	50	0.0	0.0
C / 5.3	12.9	0.94	18.07	841	26	73	0	1	45	95.3	-24.1	63	12	3,000	50	0.0	0.0
C / 5.3	12.9	0.94	18.18	710	26	73	0	1	45	97.2	-23.9	66	12	1,000,000	0	0.0	0.0
B / 8.4	5.1	0.84	12.74	646	4	45	49	2	20	34.6	-9.2	29	7	1,000	50	0.0	0.0
B / 8.1	7.0	1.17	13.27	1,145	4	68	27	1	17	45.8	-13.3	12	7	1,000	50	0.0	0.0
B- / 7.5	8.5	1.41	13.12	1,194	5	80	14	1	17	54.0	-17.4	5	7	1,000	50	0.0	0.0
B- / 7.0	9.6	0.94	13.05	627	6	87	6	1	19	57.8	-19.5	7	7	1,000	50	0.0	0.0
U /	N/A	N/A	11.14	31	7	89	3	1	0	N/A	N/A	N/A	2	1,000	50	0.0	0.0
B / 8.9	3.9	0.63	11.93	364	4	33	61	2	31	25.8	-5.7	42	7	1,000	50	0.0	0.0
B- / 7.5	6.6	0.50	9.04	95	15	73	11	1	105	21.3	-11.1	9	9	3,000	50	0.0	0.0
U /	N/A	N/A	9.04	88	15	73	11	1	105	N/A	N/A	N/A	9	1,000,000	0	0.0	0.0
B- / 7.1	10.4	1.05	20.41	943	4	95	0	1	20	97.1	-20.9	41	11	3,000	50	0.0	0.0
B- / 7.1	10.4	0.60	20.35	9	4	95	0	1	20	94.7	-21.1	97	11	3,000	50	0.0	0.0
B- / 7.1	10.4	1.05	20.39	457	4	95	0	1	20	97.9	-20.9	42	11	1,000,000	0	0.0	0.0
C+ / 6.7	11.1	1.07	28.03	26	1	98	0	1	9	82.7	-19.9	23	13	3,000	50	0.0	1.0
C+ / 6.7	11.1	0.77	28.16	1,178	1	98	0	1	9	84.2	-19.7	95	13	3,000	50	0.0	0.0
B- / 7.8	6.8	0.38	12.16	42	0	79	20	1	93	51.9	-15.4	95	7	250	100	0.0	2.0
C+ / 5.8	12.3	0.88	15.16	597	4	95	0	1	72	46.2	-24.2	62	3	0	0	0.0	0.0
C+ / 6.0	13.0	0.98	6.87	1,035	3	96	0	1	60	46.8	-23.7	46	14	0	0	0.0	0.0
D / 1.8	15.8	0.88	7.86	10	31	61	0	8	52	28.1	-13.4	1	2	1,000	100	0.0	0.0
B / 8.1	6.8	1.12	28.88	271	7	68	24	1	29	64.0	-10.9	53	22	1,000	100	0.0	0.0
C+ / 5.9	6.5	0.67	9.58	390	5	73	20	2	27	60.8	-12.8	79	4	1,000	100	0.0	0.0
C / 4.9	9.7	0.96	26.74	231	0	99	0	1	8	96.0	-18.4	72	1	1,000	100	0.0	0.0
B- / 7.1	9.7	0.93	15.07	127	5	94	0	1	7	79.1	-13.6	59	6	1,000	100	0.0	0.0
C+ / 6.2	9.8	0.95	34.75	376	3	96	0	1	11	81.3	-16.1	36	19	1,000	100	0.0	0.0
C+ / 6.3	10.5	0.74	49.50	364	4	95	0	1	15	101.2	-16.6	93	17	1,000	100	0.0	0.0
C- / 3.6	12.5	0.81	5.69	29	5	0	94	1	0	-24.6	-17.7	0	5	1,000	100	5.8	0.0
C- / 3.6	12.5	0.81	5.76	178	5	0	94	1	0	-23.8	-17.5	0	5	1,000,000	0	0.0	0.0
C- / 3.6	12.5	0.81	5.75	31	5	0	94	1	0	-23.9	-17.5	0	5	1,000	100	0.0	0.0
C+ / 5.9	13.1	0.88	14.40	116	5	94	0	1	75	49.1	-29.7	94	17	1,000	100	5.8	0.0
C+ / 5.8	13.1	0.88	13.20	26	5	94	0	1	75	44.9	-29.9	93	17	1,000	100	0.0	0.0
C+ / 5.9	13.1	0.88	15.05	122	5	94	0	1	75	51.5	-29.5	95	17	1,000,000	0	0.0	0.0
C+ / 5.9	13.1	0.88	14.51	103	5	94	0	1	75	50.4	-29.7	95	17	1,000	100	0.0	0.0
D / 2.0	18.5	1.08	39.21	566	7	92	0	1	33	2.2	-29.5	2	20	1,000	100	5.8	0.0
D / 2.0	18.4	1.08	34.54	189	7	92	0	1	33	-0.6	-29.8	2	20	1,000	100	0.0	0.0
D / 2.0	18.5	1.08	40.69	2,229	7	92	0	1	33	3.5	-29.4	3	20	1,000,000	0	0.0	0.0
D / 2.0	18.4	1.07	39.69	390	7	92	0	1	33	3.0	-29.5	2	20	1,000	100	0.0	0.0
E- / 0.0	38.1	1.80	7.57	266	1	98	0	1	40	-56.4	-16.5	3	19	1,000	100	5.8	0.0
E- / 0.0	38.0	1.80	6.84	48	1	98	0	1	40	-57.5	-16.8	2	19	1,000	100	0.0	0.0
E- / 0.0	38.0	1.80	9.43	159	1	98	0	1	40	-55.8	-16.4	3	19	1,000,000	0	0.0	0.0

Fund Type	Fund Name	Ticker Symbol	Overall Investment Rating	Phone	Performance Rating/Pts	3 Mo	6 Mo	1Yr / Pct	3Yr / Pct	5Yr / Pct	Dividend Yield	Expense Ratio
PM	Van Eck Intl Investors Gold Y	INIYX	E-	(800) 826-1115	E- / 0.0	-5.20	-18.07	-21.92 / 1	-24.77 / 0	-13.04 / 0	0.00	1.34
AA	● Van Eck Multi-Manager Altern A	VMAAX	D	(800) 826-1115	E / 0.3	-1.45	-2.93	-3.98 / 7	-0.22 / 4	0.54 / 3	0.00	3.51
AA	● Van Eck Multi-Manager Altern I	VMAIX	D+	(800) 826-1115	E / 0.4	-1.31	-2.76	-3.59 / 8	0.22 / 4	0.92 / 3	0.00	3.41
AA	● Van Eck Multi-Manager Altern Y	VMAYX	D+	(800) 826-1115	E / 0.4	-1.32	-2.77	-3.49 / 8	0.22 / 4	--	0.00	3.55
IX	Vanguard 500 Index Adm	VFIAX	A	(800) 662-7447	B+ / 8.3	0.94	5.91	12.69 /86	16.07 /84	14.43 /82	1.95	0.05
* IX	Vanguard 500 Index Inv	VFINX	A	(800) 662-7447	B / 8.2	0.91	5.85	12.56 /85	15.93 /83	14.29 /80	1.84	0.17
GR	Vanguard 529 500 Index Portfolio		A	(800) 662-7447	B / 8.1	0.91	5.85	12.52 /85	15.86 /82	14.18 /79	0.00	0.25
GR	Vanguard 529 Aggressive Growth		C+	(800) 662-7447	C+ / 6.1	2.47	4.81	8.02 /63	13.27 /62	11.65 /58	0.00	0.25
BA	Vanguard 529 Conservative Gr Port		C	(800) 662-7447	D / 2.0	1.89	3.84	6.26 /49	5.53 /15	6.22 /18	0.00	0.25
GI	Vanguard 529 Growth Fund		B-	(800) 662-7447	C / 4.7	2.26	4.58	7.57 /60	10.74 /44	10.04 /45	0.00	0.25
GR	Vanguard 529 Growth Index Port		A+	(800) 662-7447	B+ / 8.9	3.38	8.57	16.36 /94	16.23 /85	15.41 /90	0.00	0.31
MC	Vanguard 529 Mid Cap Index Port		A+	(800) 662-7447	A / 9.4	4.27	11.11	14.69 /91	17.70 /93	15.84 /92	0.00	0.31
GI	Vanguard 529 Moderate Growth Port		C+	(800) 662-7447	C- / 3.3	2.07	4.27	6.97 /55	8.20 /28	8.24 /31	0.00	0.25
AG	Vanguard 529 ND Aggressive Gr Fd		C+	(800) 662-7447	C+ / 5.7	2.27	4.51	7.35 /58	12.59 /57	11.16 /54	0.00	0.85
AA	Vanguard 529 ND Conservative Gr		C	(800) 662-7447	D / 1.8	1.73	3.67	6.06 /47	5.05 /13	5.71 /15	0.00	0.85
GR	Vanguard 529 ND Growth Fd		C+	(800) 662-7447	C / 4.4	2.18	4.26	7.05 /55	10.18 /40	9.64 /42	0.00	0.85
AA	Vanguard 529 ND Moderate Growth		C+	(800) 662-7447	C- / 3.0	1.96	4.07	6.63 /52	7.60 /25	7.71 /28	0.00	0.85
AG	Vanguard 529 PA Agg Gr Port		C+	(800) 662-7447	C+ / 6.0	2.37	4.66	7.84 /62	13.05 /60	11.88 /60	0.00	0.53
AA	Vanguard 529 PA Consrv Gr Port		C+	(800) 662-7447	D+ / 2.4	1.92	3.98	6.42 /50	6.40 /19	7.24 /25	0.00	0.51
AA	Vanguard 529 PA Consrv Inc Port		C-	(800) 662-7447	E+ / 0.7	1.06	1.92	3.26 /28	1.29 / 6	2.81 / 6	0.00	0.55
GR	Vanguard 529 PA Growth Port		C+	(800) 662-7447	C / 4.8	2.30	4.44	7.38 /58	10.93 /45	10.50 /49	0.00	0.53
AA	Vanguard 529 PA Moderate Gr Port		B-	(800) 662-7447	C- / 3.9	2.10	4.55	7.41 /58	9.23 /34	9.25 /39	0.00	0.52
GR	Vanguard 529 PA Social Idx Port		A+	(800) 662-7447	A / 9.4	1.64	8.58	14.37 /90	18.35 /95	14.61 /83	0.00	0.64
FO	Vanguard 529 PA Ttl Stk Mkt Idx		A	(800) 662-7447	B / 8.2	1.72	6.92	11.97 /82	15.98 /83	14.32 /81	0.00	0.49
SC	Vanguard 529 Small Cap Index Port		A	(800) 662-7447	A- / 9.1	4.74	11.85	9.60 /73	17.33 /92	15.56 /90	0.00	0.31
FO	Vanguard 529 Ttl Intl St Index Port		D-	(800) 662-7447	D / 1.7	4.03	-0.41	-1.32 /12	6.27 /18	4.53 /10	0.00	0.55
OT	Vanguard 529 Ttl Stock Market Port		A	(800) 662-7447	B+ / 8.4	1.72	7.02	12.11 /83	16.22 /85	14.53 /83	0.00	0.25
GR	Vanguard 529 Value Index Port		A-	(800) 662-7447	B- / 7.5	-0.62	4.02	9.24 /71	15.71 /81	13.19 /70	0.00	0.31
GR	Vanguard AR Aggressive Gr Port		C+	(800) 662-7447	C+ / 5.8	2.30	4.54	7.43 /59	12.67 /57	11.14 /54	0.00	0.75
GI	Vanguard Balanced Index Adm	VBIAX	B	(800) 662-7447	C / 5.0	1.74	5.73	9.72 /73	11.01 /45	10.77 /51	1.93	0.09
GI	Vanguard Balanced Index Inst	VBAIX	B	(800) 662-7447	C / 5.1	1.78	5.77	9.77 /73	11.03 /46	10.80 /51	1.94	0.08
GI	Vanguard Balanced Index Inv	VBINX	B	(800) 662-7447	C / 4.9	1.71	5.65	9.57 /72	10.85 /45	10.62 /50	1.79	0.24
GR	● Vanguard Capital Opportunity Adm	VHCAX	A+	(800) 662-7447	A+ / 9.9	4.25	11.31	17.76 /95	23.49 /99	15.79 /92	0.62	0.40
GR	● Vanguard Capital Opportunity Inv	VHCOX	A+	(800) 662-7447	A+ / 9.9	4.23	11.28	17.69 /95	23.41 /99	15.71 /91	0.54	0.47
GR	Vanguard Capital Value Inv	VCVLX	C+	(800) 662-7447	B+ / 8.5	4.84	3.63	4.79 /37	17.50 /92	13.14 /69	1.12	0.47
GI	Vanguard Cons Discn Idx Adm	VCDAX	A+	(800) 662-7447	A+ / 9.8	4.80	14.26	17.09 /95	20.67 /98	19.95 /99	1.17	0.12
GI	Vanguard Cons Stap Idx Adm	VCSAX	A+	(800) 662-7447	B+ / 8.9	1.54	10.20	16.90 /94	16.43 /86	15.42 /90	1.90	0.12
CV	Vanguard Convertible Sec Inv	VCVSX	C-	(800) 662-7447	C / 4.3	5.09	4.64	3.52 /29	10.25 /41	9.11 /38	2.17	0.63
FO	Vanguard Developed Markets Idx	VTMGX	D	(800) 662-7447	C- / 3.1	5.56	1.23	-0.89 /13	8.93 /32	6.18 /18	2.89	0.09
FO	Vanguard Developed Markets Idx Inst	VTMNX	D	(800) 662-7447	C- / 3.1	5.55	1.16	-0.87 /13	8.95 /33	6.22 /18	2.90	0.07
FO	Vanguard Developed Markets Idx Inv	VDVIX	U	(800) 662-7447	U /	5.53	1.12	-0.99 /13	--	--	2.77	0.20
FO	Vanguard Developed Markets Idx IP	VDIPX	U	(800) 662-7447	U /	5.51	1.19	-0.91 /13	--	--	2.91	0.06
AA	Vanguard Diversified Equity Inv	VDEQX	A	(800) 662-7447	B+ / 8.7	3.09	8.04	12.31 /84	16.51 /87	14.62 /83	0.99	0.41
IN	Vanguard Dividend Apprec Idx Adm	VDADX	U	(800) 662-7447	U /	-0.08	5.98	9.53 /72	--	--	2.12	0.10
GR	Vanguard Dividend Apprec Idx Inv	VDAIX	B-	(800) 662-7447	C+ / 6.4	-0.08	5.98	9.43 /72	13.61 /64	12.89 /67	2.03	0.20
* GI	Vanguard Dividend Growth Inv	VDIGX	A-	(800) 662-7447	B- / 7.4	0.86	6.40	10.72 /77	15.01 /75	14.11 /79	1.83	0.31
EM	Vanguard Emg Mkts Sel Stk Idx Inv	VMMSX	E	(800) 662-7447	E / 0.4	1.58	-6.96	-4.51 / 6	0.43 / 5	--	1.37	0.94
EM	Vanguard Emg Mkts Stk Idx Admiral	VEMAX	E	(800) 662-7447	E+ / 0.6	2.10	-1.68	3.08 /27	0.57 / 5	1.82 / 4	2.72	0.15
EM	Vanguard Emg Mkts Stk Idx Inst	VEMIX	E	(800) 662-7447	E+ / 0.6	2.08	-1.67	3.08 /27	0.60 / 5	1.87 / 4	2.75	0.12
EM	Vanguard Emg Mkts Stk Idx Inst Plus	VEMRX	E	(800) 662-7447	E+ / 0.6	2.09	-1.66	3.10 /27	0.62 / 5	--	2.77	0.10
EM	Vanguard Emg Mkts Stk Idx Investor	VEIEX	E	(800) 662-7447	E+ / 0.6	2.06	-1.77	2.90 /26	0.39 / 5	1.67 / 4	2.53	0.33
EN	Vanguard Energy Adm	VGELX	E-	(800) 662-7447	E- / 0.2	-1.56	-17.70	-17.61 / 1	-0.60 / 4	2.84 / 6	2.26	0.32

● Denotes fund is closed to new investors
* Denotes fund is included in Section II

RISK			NET ASSETS		ASSET					BULL / BEAR		FUND MANAGER		MINIMUMS		LOADS	
	3 Year		NAV						Portfolio	Last Bull	Last Bear	Manager	Manager	Initial	Additional	Front	Back
Risk Rating/Pts	Standard Deviation	Beta	As of 3/31/15	Total $(Mil)	Cash %	Stocks %	Bonds %	Other %	Turnover Ratio	Market Return	Market Return	Quality Pct	Tenure (Years)	Purch. $	Purch. $	End Load	End Load
E- / 0.0	38.1	1.80	7.66	47	1	98	0	1	40	-56.0	-16.5	3	19	1,000	100	0.0	0.0
B / 8.7	3.8	0.52	8.82	6	57	31	9	3	249	3.0	-5.6	8	N/A	1,000	100	5.8	0.0
B / 8.8	3.8	0.51	9.01	3	57	31	9	3	249	4.4	-5.4	10	N/A	1,000,000	0	0.0	0.0
B / 8.8	3.8	0.51	9.00	1	57	31	9	3	249	4.4	-5.4	10	N/A	1,000	100	0.0	0.0
B- / 7.3	9.5	1.00	190.71	149,150	0	99	0	1	3	100.0	-16.3	67	24	10,000	100	0.0	0.0
B- / 7.3	9.5	1.00	190.71	28,828	0	99	0	1	3	99.2	-16.3	65	24	3,000	100	0.0	0.0
B- / 7.4	9.5	1.00	27.87	637	0	99	0	1	0	98.6	-16.3	65	13	3,000	50	0.0	0.0
C+ / 6.9	10.1	1.02	28.57	1,181	0	99	0	1	0	81.7	-19.8	27	13	3,000	50	0.0	0.0
B+ / 9.7	3.2	0.44	20.53	1,134	0	25	74	1	0	25.1	-1.7	76	13	3,000	50	0.0	0.0
B / 8.3	7.5	0.75	24.88	1,731	0	74	24	2	0	61.2	-13.9	52	13	3,000	50	0.0	0.0
C+ / 6.8	10.1	1.01	30.01	181	0	99	0	1	0	103.0	-15.2	67	13	3,000	50	0.0	0.0
C+ / 6.6	10.4	0.92	39.59	364	0	99	0	1	0	106.5	-21.4	83	N/A	3,000	50	0.0	0.0
B+ / 9.4	5.1	0.48	22.70	1,807	0	50	49	1	0	42.6	-8.0	74	N/A	3,000	50	0.0	0.0
C+ / 6.9	10.1	1.02	15.77	57	0	99	0	1	0	78.0	-19.3	21	9	25	25	0.0	0.0
B+ / 9.6	3.1	0.43	14.69	79	0	25	74	1	0	23.2	-1.7	72	9	25	25	0.0	0.0
B / 8.3	7.5	0.75	16.40	60	0	74	24	2	0	58.5	-13.7	44	9	25	25	0.0	0.0
B+ / 9.3	5.1	0.87	15.61	109	0	49	49	2	0	39.9	-7.9	43	9	25	25	0.0	0.0
C+ / 6.9	10.1	1.02	15.95	276	0	99	0	1	0	82.1	-18.9	26	9	25	25	0.0	0.0
B+ / 9.7	3.8	0.60	15.42	258	0	35	64	1	0	32.9	-4.7	67	9	25	25	0.0	0.0
B+ / 9.6	2.8	0.02	13.29	64	25	0	74	1	0	5.0	3.8	78	9	25	25	0.0	0.0
B / 8.0	8.0	0.80	16.00	361	0	79	19	2	0	64.9	-14.3	42	9	25	25	0.0	0.0
B+ / 9.0	6.0	1.03	16.08	413	0	60	39	1	0	50.6	-9.6	40	9	25	25	0.0	0.0
B- / 7.0	10.4	1.06	16.08	20	0	100	0	0	0	108.2	-15.8	77	9	25	25	0.0	0.0
B- / 7.2	9.7	0.59	17.77	94	0	99	0	1	0	99.3	-17.8	98	9	25	25	0.0	0.0
C+ / 6.3	12.0	0.88	40.86	373	0	99	0	1	0	107.2	-24.6	88	13	3,000	50	0.0	0.0
C+ / 6.0	12.8	0.95	26.87	497	1	98	0	1	0	42.0	-24.5	30	13	3,000	50	0.0	0.0
B- / 7.2	9.7	1.01	30.17	650	0	99	0	1	0	100.7	-17.8	66	13	3,000	50	0.0	0.0
B- / 7.6	9.8	0.99	28.74	211	0	99	0	1	0	95.7	-18.5	64	N/A	3,000	50	0.0	0.0
C+ / 6.9	10.1	1.02	18.65	55	0	99	0	1	0	78.3	-19.9	21	6	25	10	0.0	0.0
B / 8.7	5.7	0.58	30.05	14,788	0	59	39	2	53	59.3	-9.0	82	2	10,000	100	0.0	0.0
B / 8.7	5.7	0.58	30.06	7,645	0	59	39	2	53	59.5	-9.0	83	2	5,000,000	100	0.0	0.0
B / 8.7	5.7	0.58	30.05	3,257	0	59	39	2	53	58.6	-9.0	81	2	3,000	100	0.0	0.0
C+ / 6.8	10.9	0.97	126.92	11,406	5	94	0	1	7	132.0	-21.7	96	17	50,000	100	0.0	0.0
C+ / 6.8	10.9	0.97	54.97	2,964	5	94	0	1	7	131.5	-21.8	96	17	3,000	100	0.0	0.0
C / 4.3	13.5	1.24	14.07	1,420	0	100	0	0	90	113.2	-29.7	32	7	3,000	100	0.0	0.0
C+ / 6.8	11.8	1.11	63.35	101	0	100	0	0	7	131.1	-15.2	86	5	100,000	0	0.0	0.0
B- / 7.1	9.9	0.83	62.59	301	1	98	0	1	5	85.6	-4.3	88	5	100,000	0	0.0	0.0
C+ / 6.0	6.8	0.85	13.26	1,927	4	4	0	92	85	52.5	-16.7	49	19	3,000	100	0.0	0.0
C+ / 5.8	13.3	1.00	12.79	6,785	1	98	0	1	4	51.8	-23.3	59	2	10,000	100	0.0	0.0
C+ / 5.8	13.3	1.00	12.80	8,102	1	98	0	1	4	51.9	-23.3	59	2	5,000,000	100	0.0	0.0
U /	N/A	N/A	9.90	1,357	1	98	0	1	4	N/A	N/A	N/A	2	3,000	100	0.0	0.0
U /	N/A	N/A	20.01	6,924	1	98	0	1	4	N/A	N/A	N/A	2	0	0	0.0	0.0
C+ / 6.7	10.4	1.74	33.38	1,543	2	97	0	1	5	104.1	-19.2	29	N/A	3,000	100	0.0	0.0
U /	N/A	N/A	21.89	3,009	0	99	0	1	3	N/A	N/A	N/A	9	10,000	100	0.0	0.0
B- / 7.6	9.7	0.98	32.28	1,489	0	99	0	1	3	81.8	-14.3	40	9	3,000	100	0.0	0.0
B- / 7.7	8.8	0.90	22.92	24,440	1	97	0	2	18	85.6	-10.0	73	9	3,000	100	0.0	0.0
C / 4.7	14.8	1.06	18.59	287	6	92	0	2	54	26.4	N/A	64	4	3,000	1	0.0	0.0
C / 4.9	14.4	1.04	33.89	8,755	0	99	0	1	9	25.5	-27.2	66	7	10,000	100	0.0	0.0
C / 4.9	14.4	1.04	25.77	3,939	0	99	0	1	9	25.7	-27.2	66	7	5,000,000	100	0.0	0.0
C / 4.9	14.4	1.04	85.72	2,765	0	99	0	1	9	25.8	-27.2	66	7	100,000,000	100	0.0	0.0
C / 4.9	14.4	1.04	25.81	1,969	0	99	0	1	9	24.8	-27.2	63	7	3,000	100	0.0	0.0
D+ / 2.7	15.9	0.99	99.09	7,073	2	96	1	1	17	22.0	-27.6	14	23	50,000	100	0.0	0.0

						PERFORMANCE						
						Total Return % through 3/31/15					Incl. in Returns	
										Annualized	Dividend	Expense
Fund Type	Fund Name	Ticker Symbol	Overall Investment Rating	Phone	Performance Rating/Pts	3 Mo	6 Mo	1Yr / Pct	3Yr / Pct	5Yr / Pct	Yield	Ratio
EN	Vanguard Energy Index Adm	VENAX	E	(800) 662-7447	E / 0.5	-2.21	-14.97	-13.18 / 2	3.20 / 8	7.21 / 24	2.02	0.12
EN	Vanguard Energy Inv	VGENX	E-	(800) 662-7447	E- / 0.2	-1.58	-17.73	-17.67 / 1	-0.66 / 4	2.78 / 6	2.17	0.38
IN	Vanguard Equity Income Adm	VEIRX	B+	(800) 662-7447	B- / 7.0	-0.04	3.98	8.78 / 68	14.95 / 74	14.91 / 86	2.63	0.20
★ IN	Vanguard Equity Income Inv	VEIPX	B-	(800) 662-7447	C+ / 6.9	-0.07	3.93	8.67 / 67	14.85 / 74	14.81 / 85	2.54	0.29
FO	Vanguard European Stk Idx Inst	VESIX	D	(800) 662-7447	C- / 3.0	3.92	-0.79	-4.96 / 6	9.64 / 37	6.73 / 21	3.47	0.09
FO	Vanguard European Stk Idx Inst Adm	VEUSX	D	(800) 662-7447	C- / 3.0	3.91	-0.81	-4.99 / 5	9.61 / 37	6.69 / 21	3.43	0.12
FO	Vanguard European Stk Idx Investor	VEURX	D-	(800) 662-7447	D+ / 2.9	3.89	-0.85	-5.10 / 5	9.45 / 36	6.56 / 20	3.28	0.26
SC	Vanguard Explorer Fund Adm	VEXRX	B-	(800) 662-7447	A- / 9.2	6.34	13.33	9.75 / 73	17.27 / 91	16.30 / 94	0.31	0.35
SC	Vanguard Explorer Fund Inv	VEXPX	B-	(800) 662-7447	A- / 9.1	6.30	13.24	9.58 / 72	17.09 / 90	16.11 / 93	0.14	0.52
GR	Vanguard Explorer Value Inv	VEVFX	A-	(800) 662-7447	B+ / 8.7	4.57	11.53	7.50 / 59	16.81 / 89	15.58 / 91	0.80	0.66
IN	Vanguard Extended Market Index	VEXAX	A	(800) 662-7447	A- / 9.2	5.30	12.07	10.25 / 75	17.51 / 92	15.96 / 93	1.28	0.10
IN	Vanguard Extended Market Index Inst	VIEIX	A	(800) 662-7447	A- / 9.2	5.31	12.09	10.27 / 75	17.54 / 93	15.98 / 93	1.29	0.08
IN	Vanguard Extended Market Index Inv	VEXMX	A	(800) 662-7447	A- / 9.2	5.26	11.99	10.10 / 75	17.35 / 92	15.80 / 92	1.13	0.24
MC	Vanguard Extended Mkt Id Inst Plus	VEMPX	A	(800) 662-7447	A- / 9.2	5.31	12.09	10.29 / 76	17.56 / 93	--	1.31	0.06
FS	Vanguard Financial Index Fd Adm	VFAIX	B+	(800) 662-7447	B+ / 8.4	-0.65	7.07	10.21 / 75	16.67 / 88	10.83 / 51	1.80	0.12
FO	Vanguard FTSE All-Wld ex-US S/C	VFSVX	D-	(800) 662-7447	D- / 1.4	3.40	-1.72	-5.72 / 5	6.46 / 19	5.88 / 16	2.40	0.40
FO	Vanguard FTSE All-World ex-US	VFWAX	D-	(800) 662-7447	D / 1.9	4.12	-0.12	-0.48 / 14	6.61 / 19	--	2.93	0.15
FO	Vanguard FTSE All-World ex-US InsP	VFWPX	D-	(800) 662-7447	D / 1.9	4.12	-0.09	-0.45 / 14	6.65 / 20	--	2.96	0.10
FO	Vanguard FTSE All-World ex-US Inst	VFWSX	D-	(800) 662-7447	D / 1.9	4.11	-0.10	-0.48 / 14	6.63 / 20	5.06 / 12	2.94	0.12
FO	Vanguard FTSE All-World ex-US Inv	VFWIX	D-	(800) 662-7447	D / 1.8	4.10	-0.18	-0.65 / 14	6.46 / 19	4.86 / 11	2.77	0.30
FO	Vanguard FTSE All-World ex-US S/C	VFSNX	D-	(800) 662-7447	D- / 1.5	3.47	-1.62	-5.52 / 5	6.68 / 20	6.12 / 18	2.64	0.19
GR	Vanguard FTSE Social Index Inst	VFTNX	A+	(800) 662-7447	A / 9.5	1.73	8.77	14.79 / 91	18.83 / 96	15.08 / 87	1.30	0.16
GR	Vanguard FTSE Social Index Inv	VFTSX	A+	(800) 662-7447	A / 9.5	1.73	8.67	14.60 / 91	18.67 / 96	14.96 / 87	1.22	0.27
GL	Vanguard Global Equity Inv	VHGEX	C+	(800) 662-7447	C+ / 6.1	3.73	4.98	6.03 / 47	13.27 / 62	10.79 / 51	1.50	0.61
RE	Vanguard Global ex-US RE Admiral	VGRLX	C-	(800) 662-7447	C / 4.8	4.59	5.27	7.98 / 63	10.77 / 44	--	3.92	0.32
RE	Vanguard Global ex-US RE Inst	VGRNX	C-	(800) 662-7447	C / 4.9	4.60	5.29	7.99 / 63	10.80 / 44	--	3.98	0.24
RE	Vanguard Global ex-US RE Investor	VGXRX	C-	(800) 662-7447	C / 4.7	4.58	5.20	7.84 / 62	10.65 / 43	--	3.78	0.40
GL	Vanguard Global Minimum Vol Adm	VMNVX	U	(800) 662-7447	U /	5.26	11.76	16.79 / 94	--	--	2.44	0.27
GL	Vanguard Global Minimum Vol Inv	VMVFX	U	(800) 662-7447	U /	5.26	11.79	16.77 / 94	--	--	2.33	N/A
GI	Vanguard Growth & Income Adm	VGIAX	A+	(800) 662-7447	B+ / 8.8	1.53	6.46	13.95 / 89	16.73 / 88	14.90 / 86	1.64	0.26
GI	Vanguard Growth & Income Inv	VQNPX	A+	(800) 662-7447	B+ / 8.7	1.51	6.41	13.83 / 89	16.61 / 88	14.77 / 85	1.53	0.37
GR	Vanguard Growth Index Adm	VIGAX	A+	(800) 662-7447	A- / 9.0	3.46	8.72	16.63 / 94	16.47 / 87	15.68 / 91	1.22	0.09
GR	Vanguard Growth Index Inst	VIGIX	A+	(800) 662-7447	A- / 9.0	3.44	8.70	16.62 / 94	16.49 / 87	15.70 / 91	1.23	0.08
GR	Vanguard Growth Index Inv	VIGRX	A	(800) 662-7447	B+ / 8.9	3.40	8.62	16.44 / 94	16.30 / 86	15.51 / 90	1.09	0.24
HL	Vanguard Health Care Adm	VGHAX	A	(800) 662-7447	A+ / 9.9	9.66	18.51	29.53 / 99	29.17 / 99	21.76 / 99	1.16	0.30
★ HL	Vanguard Health Care Inv	VGHCX	A	(800) 662-7447	A+ / 9.9	9.64	18.48	29.47 / 99	29.10 / 99	21.70 / 99	1.11	0.35
HL	Vanguard HealthCare Index Adm	VHCIX	A+	(800) 662-7447	A+ / 9.9	7.81	16.86	27.85 / 99	27.67 / 99	20.76 / 99	0.95	0.12
IN	Vanguard High Div Yield Index Inv	VHDYX	A	(800) 662-7447	B- / 7.4	-0.27	4.10	10.93 / 78	15.36 / 78	14.78 / 85	2.81	0.19
OT	Vanguard Industrials Index Adm	VINAX	A+	(800) 662-7447	B+ / 8.7	0.46	7.53	8.41 / 66	17.40 / 92	15.11 / 88	1.56	0.12
TC	Vanguard Info Tech Ind Adm	VITAX	B	(800) 662-7447	B- / 7.5	1.61	7.31	17.37 / 95	14.01 / 67	14.68 / 84	1.11	0.12
★ IX	Vanguard Instl Index Inst	VINIX	A	(800) 662-7447	B+ / 8.3	0.94	5.92	12.71 / 86	16.08 / 84	14.44 / 82	2.30	0.04
IX	Vanguard Instl Index Inst Plus	VIIIX	A	(800) 662-7447	B+ / 8.3	0.95	5.93	12.73 / 86	16.11 / 84	14.46 / 82	2.32	0.02
GR	Vanguard Instl TtlStk Mkt Inst	VITNX	A+	(800) 662-7447	B+ / 8.6	1.81	7.14	12.37 / 84	16.45 / 87	14.80 / 85	2.11	0.04
GI	Vanguard Instl TtlStk Mkt Inst Plus	VITPX	A+	(800) 662-7447	B+ / 8.6	1.79	7.12	12.37 / 84	16.48 / 87	14.83 / 85	2.13	0.02
FO	Vanguard International Explorer Inv	VINEX	C-	(800) 662-7447	C / 4.7	7.29	3.53	-0.14 / 15	11.53 / 49	8.61 / 34	1.74	0.36
FO	Vanguard International Growth Adm	VWILX	D	(800) 662-7447	C- / 3.3	5.49	2.40	0.43 / 17	8.98 / 33	7.56 / 27	2.34	0.34
★ FO	Vanguard International Growth Inv	VWIGX	D	(800) 662-7447	C- / 3.2	5.48	2.35	0.32 / 17	8.83 / 32	7.42 / 26	2.17	0.47
★ FO	Vanguard International Value Inv	VTRIX	D	(800) 662-7447	D+ / 2.5	4.18	-1.73	-2.71 / 9	8.33 / 29	5.20 / 13	2.68	0.43
GR	Vanguard Large Cap Index Adm	VLCAX	A	(800) 662-7447	B+ / 8.3	1.31	6.24	12.73 / 86	16.15 / 85	14.54 / 83	1.82	0.09
GR	Vanguard Large Cap Index Inst	VLISX	A	(800) 662-7447	B+ / 8.3	1.29	6.23	12.73 / 86	16.16 / 85	14.56 / 83	1.82	0.08
GR	Vanguard Large Cap Index Inv	VLACX	A	(800) 662-7447	B / 8.2	1.25	6.16	12.56 / 85	15.98 / 83	14.37 / 81	1.68	0.24
★ AA	Vanguard LifeStrategy Consv Gr Inv	VSCGX	C+	(800) 662-7447	D+ / 2.9	2.07	4.25	7.11 / 56	7.36 / 23	7.31 / 25	2.00	0.15

● Denotes fund is closed to new investors
★ Denotes fund is included in Section II

www.thestreetratings.com

RISK			NET ASSETS		ASSET				Portfolio	BULL / BEAR		FUND MANAGER		MINIMUMS		LOADS	
	3 Year		NAV							Last Bull	Last Bear	Manager	Manager	Initial	Additional	Front	Back
Risk Rating/Pts	Standard Deviation	Beta	As of 3/31/15	Total $(Mil)	Cash %	Stocks %	Bonds %	Other %	Turnover Ratio	Market Return	Market Return	Quality Pct	Tenure (Years)	Purch. $	Purch. $	End Load	End Load
C- / 3.5	15.8	1.01	54.55	722	0	99	0	1	4	38.9	-26.9	57	5	100,000	0	0.0	0.0
D+ / 2.7	15.9	0.99	52.80	3,578	2	96	1	1	17	21.7	-27.6	14	23	3,000	100	0.0	0.0
B- / 7.6	9.2	0.94	64.95	13,608	1	97	0	2	33	90.2	-12.1	66	12	50,000	100	0.0	0.0
B- / 7.6	9.2	0.94	30.99	5,742	1	97	0	2	33	89.7	-12.1	65	12	3,000	100	0.0	0.0
C / 5.1	14.7	1.09	28.92	1,028	0	99	0	1	7	59.5	-27.2	57	7	5,000,000	100	0.0	0.0
C / 5.1	14.7	1.09	67.82	4,092	0	99	0	1	7	59.3	-27.2	57	7	10,000	100	0.0	0.0
C / 5.1	14.7	1.09	29.13	793	0	99	0	1	7	58.5	-27.2	55	7	3,000	100	0.0	0.0
C- / 3.9	12.9	0.92	91.93	8,192	2	97	0	1	66	105.9	-23.2	84	21	50,000	100	0.0	0.0
C- / 3.9	12.9	0.92	98.85	4,560	2	97	0	1	66	104.8	-23.3	83	21	3,000	100	0.0	0.0
C+ / 6.2	12.2	1.11	32.52	311	6	93	0	1	36	102.8	-22.9	51	5	3,000	1	0.0	0.0
C+ / 6.3	11.8	1.08	70.11	13,496	0	99	0	1	11	108.2	-23.9	67	18	10,000	100	0.0	0.0
C+ / 6.3	11.8	1.08	70.11	9,144	0	99	0	1	11	108.4	-23.9	67	18	5,000,000	100	0.0	0.0
C+ / 6.3	11.8	1.08	70.11	2,409	0	99	0	1	11	107.3	-23.9	66	18	3,000	100	0.0	0.0
C+ / 6.3	11.8	1.05	173.01	14,899	0	99	0	1	11	108.5	-23.9	62	18	100,000,000	100	0.0	0.0
C+ / 6.2	11.5	1.01	24.69	176	0	100	0	0	5	112.4	-26.3	57	5	100,000	0	0.0	0.0
C+ / 5.6	13.0	0.92	37.62	419	3	96	0	1	13	41.6	-25.9	35	2	3,000	100	0.8	0.0
C+ / 5.8	12.9	0.96	30.22	2,888	1	98	0	1	4	43.9	N/A	33	7	10,000	100	0.0	0.0
C+ / 5.8	12.9	0.96	101.44	2,461	1	98	0	1	4	44.2	-24.5	33	7	100,000,000	100	0.0	0.0
C+ / 5.8	12.9	0.96	95.79	4,808	1	98	0	1	4	44.1	-24.5	33	7	5,000,000	100	0.0	0.0
C+ / 5.8	12.9	0.96	19.18	569	1	98	0	1	4	43.2	-24.5	31	7	3,000	100	0.0	0.0
C+ / 5.6	12.9	0.92	188.45	59	3	96	0	1	13	42.6	-25.8	38	2	5,000,000	100	0.8	0.0
B- / 7.0	10.4	1.06	13.50	599	1	98	0	1	14	111.1	-15.6	80	4	5,000,000	100	0.0	0.0
B- / 7.0	10.3	1.06	13.49	1,077	1	98	0	1	14	110.3	-15.7	80	4	3,000	0	0.0	0.0
C+ / 6.8	10.8	0.76	25.01	4,654	3	96	0	1	45	76.8	-22.2	94	11	3,000	100	0.0	0.0
C+ / 5.6	13.7	0.77	33.95	326	19	80	0	1	8	62.4	-21.6	68	2	10,000	100	0.3	0.3
C+ / 5.6	13.7	0.77	113.08	209	19	80	0	1	8	62.5	-21.6	69	2	5,000,000	100	0.3	0.3
C+ / 5.6	13.7	0.77	22.42	58	19	80	0	1	8	61.7	-21.7	67	2	3,000	100	0.3	0.3
U /	N/A	N/A	23.22	275	4	95	0	1	49	N/A	N/A	N/A	2	50,000	100	0.0	0.0
U /	N/A	N/A	11.61	428	4	95	0	1	49	N/A	N/A	N/A	2	3,000	100	0.0	0.0
B- / 7.0	9.5	1.00	69.13	3,264	1	98	0	1	133	104.6	-16.4	73	4	50,000	100	0.0	0.0
B- / 7.1	9.5	1.00	42.34	3,132	1	98	0	1	133	103.9	-16.5	72	4	3,000	100	0.0	0.0
C+ / 6.8	10.1	1.01	55.39	15,879	0	99	0	1	32	104.5	-15.2	70	21	10,000	100	0.0	0.0
C+ / 6.8	10.1	1.01	55.38	10,140	0	99	0	1	32	104.6	-15.2	70	21	5,000,000	100	0.0	0.0
C+ / 6.8	10.1	1.01	55.39	3,395	0	99	0	1	32	103.5	-15.2	68	21	3,000	100	0.0	0.0
C+ / 5.6	9.5	0.76	95.21	36,252	1	95	3	1	21	142.2	-7.5	99	7	50,000	100	0.0	0.0
C+ / 5.6	9.5	0.76	225.70	12,287	1	95	3	1	21	141.8	-7.5	99	7	3,000	100	0.0	0.0
B / 8.2	10.0	0.85	67.68	642	0	99	0	1	10	149.0	-11.3	99	11	100,000	0	0.0	0.0
B / 8.0	9.3	0.93	26.97	4,477	0	96	0	1	13	91.2	-11.2	72	9	3,000	100	0.0	0.0
B- / 7.0	11.4	1.09	55.12	75	0	100	0	0	5	115.6	-25.1	64	5	100,000	0	0.0	0.0
C+ / 6.3	12.0	1.11	54.36	334	0	99	0	1	6	100.7	-14.1	21	5	100,000	0	0.0	0.0
B- / 7.3	9.5	1.00	188.84	106,126	0	99	0	1	5	100.1	-16.3	67	15	5,000,000	100	0.0	0.0
B- / 7.3	9.5	1.00	188.85	89,823	0	99	0	1	5	100.2	-16.3	N/A	15	200,000,000	100	0.0	0.0
B- / 7.1	9.7	1.01	47.27	2,691	0	99	0	1	9	102.1	-17.7	68	14	5,000,000	100	0.0	0.0
B- / 7.1	9.7	1.01	47.27	40,865	0	99	0	1	9	102.2	-17.7	69	14	200,000,000	100	0.0	0.0
C / 5.2	12.3	0.88	17.67	2,601	7	92	0	1	39	59.8	-25.7	88	15	3,000	100	0.0	0.0
C / 5.4	13.4	0.98	72.23	14,185	1	98	0	1	21	57.4	-25.6	62	12	50,000	0	0.0	0.0
C / 5.4	13.4	0.98	22.72	8,143	1	98	0	1	21	56.7	-25.6	60	12	3,000	0	0.0	0.0
C+ / 5.6	13.5	1.00	35.37	8,319	5	94	0	1	37	51.7	-24.2	50	7	3,000	100	0.0	0.0
B- / 7.3	9.5	1.00	48.06	3,288	0	99	0	1	9	100.4	-16.7	68	11	10,000	100	0.0	0.0
B- / 7.3	9.5	1.00	197.79	866	0	99	0	1	9	100.6	-16.8	68	11	5,000,000	100	0.0	0.0
B- / 7.3	9.5	1.00	38.44	416	0	99	0	1	9	99.5	-16.8	66	11	3,000	100	0.0	0.0
B+ / 9.3	4.2	0.69	18.74	7,693	0	39	60	1	15	36.3	-7.4	67	N/A	3,000	100	0.0	0.0

I. Index of Stock Mutual Funds

Spring 2015

99 Pct = Best
0 Pct = Worst

Fund Type	Fund Name	Ticker Symbol	Overall Investment Rating	Phone	Performance Rating/Pts	3 Mo	6 Mo	1Yr / Pct	3Yr / Pct	5Yr / Pct	Dividend Yield	Expense Ratio
* AA	Vanguard LifeStrategy Growth Inv	VASGX	B-	(800) 662-7447	C / 5.1	2.33	4.70	7.79 /61	11.35 /48	10.34 /47	2.03	0.17
AA	Vanguard LifeStrategy Income Inv	VASIX	C	(800) 662-7447	D / 2.0	1.93	4.01	6.66 /52	5.32 /14	5.77 /16	2.03	0.14
* AA	Vanguard LifeStrategy Mod Gro Inv	VSMGX	C+	(800) 662-7447	C- / 4.0	2.20	4.53	7.48 /59	9.38 /35	9.01 /37	2.04	0.16
GI	Vanguard Managed Payout Investor	VPGDX	C	(800) 662-7447	C- / 3.5	2.27	3.51	5.89 /46	8.84 /32	9.16 /38	3.74	0.34
IN	Vanguard Market Neutral Fund Inst	VMNIX	D+	(800) 662-7447	D- / 1.0	0.17	0.70	1.68 /21	3.66 / 9	3.38 / 7	0.00	1.50
IN	Vanguard Market Neutral Fund Inv	VMNFX	D+	(800) 662-7447	D- / 1.0	0.17	0.61	1.59 /20	3.56 / 9	3.28 / 7	0.00	1.60
PM	Vanguard Materials Index Fd Adm	VMIAX	C	(800) 662-7447	C / 4.7	1.06	0.32	3.99 /32	11.76 /51	11.10 /53	1.74	0.12
GR	Vanguard Mega Cap Gr Index I	VMGAX	A+	(800) 662-7447	B+ / 8.8	2.81	7.87	16.62 /94	16.38 /86	15.51 /90	1.28	0.10
MC	Vanguard Mega Cap Index Inst	VMCTX	A	(800) 662-7447	B / 8.0	0.68	5.23	12.27 /84	15.79 /82	14.22 /80	1.89	0.08
GR	Vanguard Mega Cap Value Index I	VMVLX	B+	(800) 662-7447	B- / 7.2	-1.02	3.15	8.94 /69	15.47 /79	13.07 /69	2.40	0.08
MC	Vanguard Mid Cap Growth Admiral	VMGMX	A	(800) 662-7447	A / 9.5	6.05	12.70	17.23 /95	16.84 /89	--	0.75	0.09
MC	Vanguard Mid Cap Value Index Adm	VMVAX	A+	(800) 662-7447	A / 9.5	2.58	9.72	12.56 /85	18.86 /96	--	1.64	0.09
MC	Vanguard Mid-Cap Growth Fd	VMGRX	B+	(800) 662-7447	A / 9.4	6.90	15.24	16.71 /94	16.72 /88	16.76 /95	0.13	0.51
MC	Vanguard Mid-Cap Growth Index Inv	VMGIX	A	(800) 662-7447	A / 9.4	6.02	12.67	17.09 /95	16.68 /88	16.19 /94	0.61	0.24
MC	Vanguard Mid-Cap Index Adm	VIMAX	A+	(800) 662-7447	A / 9.5	4.28	11.21	14.87 /91	17.93 /94	16.08 /93	1.24	0.09
MC	Vanguard Mid-Cap Index Inst	VMCIX	A+	(800) 662-7447	A / 9.5	4.28	11.21	14.89 /91	17.94 /94	16.10 /93	1.24	0.08
MC	Vanguard Mid-Cap Index Inst Plus	VMCPX	A+	(800) 662-7447	A / 9.5	4.30	11.22	14.91 /91	17.96 /94	--	1.26	0.06
MC	Vanguard Mid-Cap Index Inv	VIMSX	A+	(800) 662-7447	A / 9.4	4.23	11.13	14.72 /91	17.76 /93	15.91 /92	1.09	0.24
MC	Vanguard Mid-Cap Value Index Inv	VMVIX	A+	(800) 662-7447	A / 9.5	2.55	9.68	12.44 /85	18.69 /96	15.48 /90	1.49	0.24
MC	Vanguard Morgan Growth Adm	VMRAX	B	(800) 662-7447	B+ / 8.5	4.55	9.78	15.11 /92	15.51 /79	14.79 /85	0.80	0.26
MC	Vanguard Morgan Growth Inv	VMRGX	B	(800) 662-7447	B+ / 8.4	4.54	9.73	14.95 /92	15.36 /78	14.64 /84	0.65	0.40
BA	Vanguard OH Col Ad Welli Opti Port		B	(800) 662-7447	C / 5.0	0.81	3.98	8.08 /63	11.39 /48	10.51 /49	0.00	0.42
GR	Vanguard OH Col Adv Agg Gr Idx		B+	(800) 662-7447	B- / 7.2	2.49	5.84	9.42 /72	14.80 /73	12.94 /68	0.00	0.24
AA	Vanguard OH Col Adv Con Gr Idx		C	(800) 662-7447	D / 2.2	1.88	4.06	6.52 /51	5.88 /16	6.56 /20	0.00	0.25
MC	Vanguard OH Col Adv Ext Mkt Idx		A	(800) 662-7447	A- / 9.2	5.25	11.99	10.08 /75	17.32 /91	15.78 /92	0.00	0.28
GR	Vanguard OH Col Adv Grow Index		B+	(800) 662-7447	C / 5.5	2.31	5.35	8.57 /67	11.87 /52	10.99 /53	0.00	0.24
AA	Vanguard OH Col Adv Mod Gr Idx		B-	(800) 662-7447	C- / 3.7	2.08	4.73	7.63 /60	8.88 /32	8.86 /36	0.00	0.25
IX	Vanguard OH Coll Adv 500 Idx		A	(800) 662-7447	B / 8.1	0.88	5.83	12.50 /85	15.91 /83	14.30 /80	0.00	0.19
GR	Vanguard OH Coll Adv Morgan Gr		A-	(800) 662-7447	B+ / 8.4	4.48	9.63	14.83 /91	15.28 /77	14.69 /84	0.00	0.48
GI	Vanguard OH Coll Adv Windsor II Opt		B-	(800) 662-7447	C+ / 6.6	-0.11	3.40	7.80 /61	14.55 /71	12.61 /65	0.00	0.48
FO	Vanguard Pacific Stock Index Adm	VPADX	D+	(800) 662-7447	C- / 3.4	8.09	4.20	5.87 /45	7.88 /26	5.63 /15	2.49	0.12
FO	Vanguard Pacific Stock Index Inst	VPKIX	D+	(800) 662-7447	C- / 3.4	8.13	4.18	5.91 /46	7.91 /26	5.66 /15	2.52	0.09
FO	Vanguard Pacific Stock Index Inv	VPACX	D+	(800) 662-7447	C- / 3.3	8.02	4.07	5.70 /44	7.70 /25	5.48 /14	2.35	0.26
PM	Vanguard Prec Metals & Mining Inv	VGPMX	E-	(800) 662-7447	E- / 0.0	-3.68	-12.64	-20.37 / 1	-22.27 / 0	-13.00 / 0	1.70	0.25
MC	● Vanguard PRIMECAP Adm	VPMAX	A+	(800) 662-7447	A+ / 9.8	2.27	7.64	15.68 /93	21.11 /98	16.01 /93	1.22	0.35
* GR	● Vanguard PRIMECAP Core Inv	VPCCX	A+	(800) 662-7447	A+ / 9.7	1.85	7.99	15.49 /92	20.14 /98	15.55 /90	1.16	0.50
* MC	● Vanguard PRIMECAP Inv	VPMCX	A+	(800) 662-7447	A+ / 9.8	2.25	7.60	15.58 /93	21.00 /98	15.91 /93	1.05	0.44
RE	Vanguard REIT Index Adm	VGSLX	B-	(800) 662-7447	A / 9.4	4.72	19.70	24.09 /98	14.11 /68	15.84 /92	3.53	0.10
RE	Vanguard REIT Index Inst	VGSNX	B-	(800) 662-7447	A / 9.4	4.74	19.71	24.09 /98	14.12 /68	15.86 /92	3.55	0.08
RE	Vanguard REIT Index Inv	VGSIX	B-	(800) 662-7447	A / 9.4	4.67	19.61	23.95 /98	13.94 /67	15.68 /91	3.40	0.24
GR	Vanguard Russell 1000 Gro Idx Inst	VRGWX	A+	(800) 662-7447	B+ / 8.9	3.81	8.77	16.01 /93	16.26 /85	--	1.46	0.08
GR	Vanguard Russell 1000 Index Inst	VRNIX	A+	(800) 662-7447	B+ / 8.5	1.57	6.51	12.65 /85	16.35 /86	--	1.71	0.08
GR	Vanguard Russell 1000 Val Index Ins	VRVIX	A+	(800) 662-7447	B / 7.9	-0.73	4.19	9.26 /71	16.34 /86	--	2.19	0.08
SC	Vanguard Russell 2000 Gro Idx Inst	VRTGX	A-	(800) 662-7447	A / 9.5	6.66	17.43	12.27 /84	17.86 /94	--	0.69	0.08
GR	Vanguard Russell 2000 Index Inst	VRTIX	B+	(800) 662-7447	B+ / 8.7	4.33	14.50	8.32 /65	16.35 /86	--	1.12	0.08
SC	Vanguard Russell 2000 Val Index Ins	VRTVX	U	(800) 662-7447	U /	1.98	11.57	4.43 /35	--	--	1.77	0.08
IN	Vanguard Russell 3000 Index Inst	VRTTX	A	(800) 662-7447	B+ / 8.5	1.79	7.10	12.32 /84	16.35 /86	--	1.73	0.08
MC	Vanguard S&P Mid-Cap 400 Gro Inst	VMFGX	A	(800) 662-7447	A- / 9.1	7.54	13.80	13.21 /87	16.39 /86	--	0.84	0.08
MC	Vanguard S&P Mid-Cap 400 Index	VSPMX	A	(800) 662-7447	A- / 9.1	5.30	11.96	12.15 /83	16.97 /90	--	1.26	0.08
MC	Vanguard S&P Mid-Cap 400 Value	VMFVX	A+	(800) 662-7447	A- / 9.1	2.81	9.85	10.75 /77	17.48 /92	--	1.53	0.10
SC	Vanguard S&P SC 600 Indx Inst	VSMSX	A	(800) 662-7447	A- / 9.1	3.96	14.18	8.67 /67	17.22 /91	--	1.07	0.11
* MC	Vanguard Selected Value Inv	VASVX	A	(800) 662-7447	B / 8.1	1.30	4.27	5.50 /42	16.95 /90	14.55 /83	1.35	0.44

● Denotes fund is closed to new investors
* Denotes fund is included in Section II

www.thestreetratings.com

Risk Rating/Pts	3 Year Standard Deviation	Beta	NAV As of 3/31/15	Total $(Mil)	Cash %	Stocks %	Bonds %	Other %	Portfolio Turnover Ratio	Last Bull Market Return	Last Bear Market Return	Manager Quality Pct	Manager Tenure (Years)	Initial Purch. $	Additional Purch. $	Front End Load	Back End Load
B /8.0	8.0	1.37	29.48	11,267	0	79	20	1	10	65.4	-16.2	21	N/A	3,000	100	0.0	0.0
B+ /9.2	2.8	0.34	15.13	3,313	0	19	80	1	12	23.1	-2.5	82	N/A	3,000	100	0.0	0.0
B /8.9	6.0	1.03	24.61	12,479	0	59	40	1	12	50.2	-11.4	42	N/A	3,000	100	0.0	0.0
B /8.1	6.7	0.65	19.15	1,622	7	73	19	1	48	49.4	-12.6	48	7	25,000	100	0.0	0.0
B /8.8	3.8	0.08	11.47	58	4	95	0	1	73	11.2	2.6	86	8	5,000,000	100	0.0	0.0
B /8.8	3.8	0.09	11.52	304	4	95	0	1	73	10.8	2.6	85	8	250,000	100	0.0	0.0
C+ /6.3	12.3	0.25	55.29	199	0	100	0	0	4	88.9	-28.1	99	5	100,000	0	0.0	0.0
B- /7.0	10.1	1.01	165.40	25	1	98	0	1	11	105.5	-13.7	69	5	5,000,000	0	0.0	0.0
B- /7.3	9.5	0.75	138.66	374	0	99	0	1	6	99.1	-15.8	88	8	5,000,000	0	0.0	0.0
B- /7.7	9.8	0.98	118.39	223	1	98	0	1	8	94.0	-17.8	63	5	5,000,000	0	0.0	0.0
C+ /6.1	11.1	0.96	46.36	2,596	0	99	0	1	17	101.6	N/A	72	2	10,000	100	0.0	0.0
B- /7.0	10.2	0.89	47.48	3,324	0	99	0	1	46	113.3	N/A	90	9	10,000	100	0.0	0.0
C /5.1	11.4	0.97	25.89	3,805	4	94	0	2	82	99.5	-18.5	69	9	3,000	100	0.0	0.0
C+ /6.1	11.1	0.96	42.34	593	0	99	0	1	17	100.6	-21.8	70	2	3,000	100	0.0	0.0
C+ /6.9	10.4	0.92	159.49	23,777	0	99	0	1	16	107.8	-21.4	84	17	10,000	100	0.0	0.0
C+ /6.9	10.4	0.92	35.23	12,028	0	99	0	1	16	107.9	-21.4	84	17	5,000,000	100	0.0	0.0
C+ /6.9	10.4	0.92	173.77	11,624	0	99	0	1	16	108.1	-21.4	84	17	100,000,000	100	0.0	0.0
C+ /6.9	10.5	0.92	35.14	4,844	0	99	0	1	16	106.8	-21.4	83	17	3,000	100	0.0	0.0
B- /7.0	10.3	0.89	36.08	671	0	99	0	1	46	112.3	-21.0	89	9	3,000	100	0.0	0.0
C /5.4	10.7	0.88	82.08	6,885	1	98	0	1	52	98.9	-18.6	74	10	50,000	100	0.0	0.0
C /5.5	10.7	0.87	26.49	4,736	1	98	0	1	52	98.0	-18.6	73	10	3,000	100	0.0	0.0
B /8.8	6.1	1.07	22.46	143	0	65	34	1	0	62.5	-10.5	63	6	25	0	0.0	0.0
B- /7.1	10.0	1.02	23.01	449	0	99	0	1	0	90.3	-18.9	45	6	25	0	0.0	0.0
B+ /9.7	3.1	0.43	18.47	335	0	25	74	1	0	26.6	-1.5	79	6	25	0	0.0	0.0
C+ /6.2	11.8	1.05	29.05	194	0	99	0	1	0	107.0	-23.9	59	6	25	0	0.0	0.0
B /8.7	7.4	0.75	21.66	571	0	74	24	2	0	67.0	-13.3	67	6	25	0	0.0	0.0
B+ /9.5	5.0	0.86	20.16	545	0	49	49	2	0	45.7	-7.5	61	6	25	0	0.0	0.0
B- /7.4	9.5	1.00	22.86	345	0	99	0	1	0	99.1	-16.3	65	6	25	0	0.0	0.0
C+ /6.6	10.7	1.04	18.89	40	1	98	0	1	0	97.6	-18.3	48	6	25	0	0.0	0.0
B- /7.7	9.7	1.00	17.96	71	2	97	0	1	0	93.5	-17.1	47	6	25	0	0.0	0.0
C+ /6.2	13.2	0.85	75.62	2,038	3	96	0	1	5	40.6	-15.3	65	18	10,000	100	0.0	0.0
C+ /6.2	13.2	0.85	11.57	335	3	96	0	1	5	40.9	-15.2	65	18	5,000,000	100	0.0	0.0
C+ /6.2	13.2	0.85	11.65	352	3	96	0	1	5	40.0	-15.3	62	18	3,000	100	0.0	0.0
E+ /0.8	24.2	1.00	8.68	2,120	3	96	0	1	34	-47.0	-25.3	1	2	3,000	100	0.0	0.0
C+ /6.9	9.5	0.75	108.97	38,092	4	95	0	1	11	119.5	-18.4	96	30	50,000	100	0.0	0.0
B- /7.0	9.1	0.90	22.04	7,687	7	92	0	1	13	111.1	-17.6	93	11	3,000	100	0.0	0.0
C+ /7.0	9.5	0.75	105.16	9,938	4	95	0	1	11	118.8	-18.4	96	30	3,000	100	0.0	0.0
C- /3.8	13.4	1.07	119.54	15,301	0	99	0	1	11	86.3	-16.3	53	19	10,000	100	0.0	0.0
C- /3.8	13.4	1.07	18.50	6,629	0	99	0	1	11	86.3	-16.3	53	19	5,000,000	100	0.0	0.0
C- /3.8	13.4	1.07	28.02	3,110	0	99	0	1	11	85.5	-16.3	51	19	3,000	100	0.0	0.0
B- /7.1	9.8	0.99	195.05	1,475	2	97	0	1	18	101.6	-15.4	70	5	5,000,000	0	0.0	0.0
B- /7.3	9.6	1.00	185.47	1,192	0	99	0	1	11	101.3	-17.1	69	5	5,000,000	0	0.0	0.0
B- /7.8	9.9	1.01	175.98	1,227	0	0	0	100	16	100.6	-18.8	68	5	5,000,000	0	0.0	0.0
C /5.4	14.1	1.04	209.99	187	0	99	0	1	50	109.4	N/A	76	2	5,000,000	0	0.0	0.0
C+ /5.9	13.4	1.15	190.66	330	0	99	0	1	16	100.9	-25.1	36	2	5,000,000	0	0.0	0.0
U /	N/A	N/A	176.91	84	0	99	0	1	36	N/A	N/A	N/A	2	5,000,000	0	0.0	0.0
B- /7.2	9.7	1.01	185.88	653	0	99	0	1	8	101.3	-17.8	67	5	5,000,000	0	0.0	0.0
C+ /6.5	11.0	0.98	209.97	97	0	99	0	1	38	93.7	-21.0	64	2	5,000,000	0	0.0	0.0
C+ /6.5	11.0	1.00	204.78	567	0	99	0	1	14	102.5	-22.6	67	2	5,000,000	100	0.0	0.0
C+ /6.6	11.5	1.02	198.20	160	0	99	0	1	35	111.7	-24.2	67	2	5,000,000	100	0.0	0.0
C+ /6.2	12.8	0.94	214.28	205	0	99	0	1	16	107.9	-22.1	82	2	5,000,000	100	0.0	0.0
B- /7.2	10.2	0.86	28.75	10,454	7	92	0	1	18	102.4	-19.1	85	16	3,000	100	0.0	0.0

Fund Type	Fund Name	Ticker Symbol	Overall Investment Rating	Phone	PERFORMANCE Performance Rating/Pts	3 Mo	6 Mo	1Yr / Pct	3Yr / Pct	5Yr / Pct	Dividend Yield	Expense Ratio
SC	Vanguard Small Cap Growth Adm	VSGAX	B+	(800) 662-7447	B+ / 8.8	6.30	12.34	8.84 /68	16.47 /87	--	0.96	0.09
SC	Vanguard Small Cap Value Index	VSIAX	A+	(800) 662-7447	A / 9.4	3.51	11.65	10.62 /77	18.29 /95	--	1.76	0.09
SC	Vanguard Small-Cap Grwth Index Inst	VSGIX	B+	(800) 662-7447	B+ / 8.8	6.28	12.33	8.86 /69	16.49 /87	16.30 /94	0.96	0.08
SC	Vanguard Small-Cap Grwth Index Inv	VISGX	B+	(800) 662-7447	B+ / 8.7	6.29	12.26	8.69 /68	16.31 /86	16.12 /94	0.81	0.24
SC	Vanguard Small-Cap Index Adm	VSMAX	A	(800) 662-7447	A- / 9.2	4.81	11.98	9.83 /74	17.57 /93	15.81 /92	1.40	0.09
SC	Vanguard Small-Cap Index Inst	VSCIX	A	(800) 662-7447	A- / 9.2	4.81	11.97	9.84 /74	17.59 /93	15.84 /92	1.41	0.08
SC	Vanguard Small-Cap Index InstP	VSCPX	A	(800) 662-7447	A- / 9.2	4.81	11.99	9.85 /74	17.61 /93	--	1.43	0.06
SC	Vanguard Small-Cap Index Inv	NAESX	A	(800) 662-7447	A- / 9.1	4.75	11.89	9.66 /73	17.40 /92	15.65 /91	1.25	0.24
SC	Vanguard Small-Cap Value Index Inst	VSIIX	A+	(800) 662-7447	A / 9.4	3.50	11.66	10.64 /77	18.30 /95	15.12 /88	1.76	0.08
SC	Vanguard Small-Cap Value Index Inv	VISVX	A+	(800) 662-7447	A / 9.3	3.46	11.56	10.45 /76	18.12 /95	14.94 /86	1.62	0.24
* GI	Vanguard STAR Fund	VGSTX	B-	(800) 662-7447	C / 4.7	2.60	4.96	7.78 /61	10.69 /44	9.89 /44	2.09	0.34
GR	Vanguard Str Brd Mrkt Inst Inst	VSBMX	A-	(800) 662-7447	A / 9.4	2.58	8.30	13.96 /89	18.29 /95	16.65 /95	1.60	0.24
GR	Vanguard Str Brd Mrkt Inst plus	VSBPX	A-	(800) 662-7447	A / 9.4	2.58	8.32	14.04 /89	18.37 /95	16.73 /95	1.65	0.17
* SC	Vanguard Strategic Equity Inv	VSEQX	A+	(800) 662-7447	A+ / 9.8	5.16	12.00	14.29 /90	20.78 /98	18.19 /98	1.00	0.27
SC	Vanguard Strategic Sm-Cp Equity Inv	VSTCX	A+	(800) 662-7447	A+ / 9.7	4.80	13.10	11.51 /80	19.59 /97	17.65 /97	0.71	0.38
GR	Vanguard Structured Lg-Cp Eq Inst	VSLIX	A+	(800) 662-7447	A- / 9.0	1.40	6.70	14.13 /90	17.32 /91	15.86 /92	2.49	0.24
GR	Vanguard Structured Lg-Cp Eq	VSLPX	A+	(800) 662-7447	A- / 9.1	1.41	6.72	14.20 /90	17.40 /92	15.94 /93	2.48	0.17
* AA	Vanguard Target Retirement 2010 Inv	VTENX	C+	(800) 662-7447	D+ / 2.6	1.86	3.57	6.12 /48	7.02 /21	7.63 /27	1.69	0.16
* AA	Vanguard Target Retirement 2015 Inv	VTXVX	C+	(800) 662-7447	C- / 3.4	2.03	4.01	6.84 /54	8.49 /30	8.56 /34	1.80	0.16
* AA	Vanguard Target Retirement 2025 Inv	VTTVX	B-	(800) 662-7447	C / 4.5	2.24	4.59	7.65 /60	10.35 /42	9.78 /43	1.90	0.17
* AA	Vanguard Target Retirement 2030	VTHRX	B-	(800) 662-7447	C / 4.9	2.31	4.68	7.77 /61	11.10 /46	10.28 /47	1.88	0.17
* AA	Vanguard Target Retirement 2035 Inv	VTTHX	B-	(800) 662-7447	C / 5.4	2.35	4.77	7.92 /62	11.85 /51	10.76 /51	2.02	0.18
* AA	Vanguard Target Retirement 2040 Inv	VFORX	B-	(800) 662-7447	C+ / 5.6	2.39	4.75	7.91 /62	12.30 /55	11.06 /53	1.87	0.18
* AA	Vanguard Target Retirement 2045 Inv	VTIVX	B-	(800) 662-7447	C+ / 5.6	2.41	4.73	7.92 /62	12.31 /55	11.06 /53	2.01	0.18
* AA	Vanguard Target Retirement 2050 Inv	VFIFX	B-	(800) 662-7447	C+ / 5.6	2.36	4.73	7.91 /62	12.30 /55	11.06 /53	1.97	0.18
AA	Vanguard Target Retirement 2055 Inv	VFFVX	B-	(800) 662-7447	C+ / 5.6	2.38	4.74	7.90 /62	12.32 /55	--	1.68	0.18
GI	Vanguard Target Retirement 2060 Inv	VTTSX	B	(800) 662-7447	C+ / 5.7	2.38	4.70	7.89 /62	12.41 /55	--	1.59	0.18
* AA	Vanguard Target Retirement Income	VTINX	C	(800) 662-7447	D / 2.0	1.75	3.29	5.71 /44	5.79 /16	6.70 /21	1.79	0.16
BA	Vanguard Tax-Managed Bal Admiral	VTMFX	B-	(800) 662-7447	C- / 4.2	1.47	4.29	8.76 /68	9.76 /38	9.56 /41	2.00	0.12
* GR	Vanguard Tax-Managed Cap Appr	VTCLX	A+	(800) 662-7447	B+ / 8.5	1.92	6.55	12.29 /84	16.45 /87	14.69 /84	1.54	0.12
GR	Vanguard Tax-Managed Cap Appr	VTCIX	A+	(800) 662-7447	B+ / 8.5	1.94	6.58	12.34 /84	16.49 /87	14.74 /85	1.57	0.08
SC	Vanguard Tax-Managed Small-Cap	VTSIX	A	(800) 662-7447	A- / 9.2	4.05	14.58	9.31 /71	17.38 /92	16.31 /94	1.01	0.10
SC	Vanguard Tax-Managed Small-Cap	VTMSX	A	(800) 662-7447	A- / 9.2	4.04	14.57	9.27 /71	17.33 /92	16.25 /94	0.97	0.14
GR	Vanguard Telecom Services Index	VTCAX	C+	(800) 662-7447	C+ / 5.9	1.97	1.93	4.47 /35	13.68 /65	12.58 /65	2.59	0.12
* AA	Vanguard Tgt Retirement 2020 Inv	VTWNX	B-	(800) 662-7447	C- / 4.1	2.18	4.48	7.51 /59	9.62 /37	9.27 /39	1.85	0.16
FO	Vanguard Total Intl Stk Id Ins +	VTPSX	D-	(800) 662-7447	D / 1.9	4.07	-0.28	-1.03 /13	6.66 /20	--	2.90	0.10
FO	Vanguard Total Intl Stock Index Adm	VTIAX	D-	(800) 662-7447	D / 1.8	4.09	-0.27	-1.05 /13	6.62 /20	--	2.86	0.14
FO	Vanguard Total Intl Stock Index Ins	VTSNX	D-	(800) 662-7447	D / 1.8	4.07	-0.29	-1.05 /13	6.64 /20	--	2.88	0.12
* FO	Vanguard Total Intl Stock Index Inv	VGTSX	D-	(800) 662-7447	D / 1.8	4.03	-0.32	-1.14 /13	6.55 /19	4.83 /11	2.78	0.22
GR	Vanguard Total Stock Market Admiral	VTSAX	A	(800) 662-7447	B+ / 8.5	1.79	7.12	12.30 /84	16.39 /86	14.76 /85	1.82	0.05
GI	Vanguard Total Stock Mkt Index Inst	VITSX	A	(800) 662-7447	B+ / 8.5	1.81	7.13	12.32 /84	16.40 /86	14.76 /85	1.82	0.04
* GR	Vanguard Total Stock Mkt Index Inv	VTSMX	A	(800) 662-7447	B+ / 8.4	1.76	7.07	12.17 /83	16.24 /85	14.62 /83	1.71	0.17
EM	Vanguard Total Wld Stk Index Inst	VTWIX	C	(800) 662-7447	C / 4.7	2.85	3.27	5.47 /42	11.19 /47	9.30 /39	2.37	0.16
EM	Vanguard Total Wld Stk Index Inv	VTWSX	C	(800) 662-7447	C / 4.6	2.78	3.19	5.35 /41	11.04 /46	9.13 /38	2.26	0.30
GR	Vanguard US Growth Adm	VWUAX	A-	(800) 662-7447	A / 9.4	4.51	10.94	17.49 /95	17.19 /91	15.45 /90	0.72	0.30
GR	Vanguard US Growth Inv	VWUSX	A-	(800) 662-7447	A / 9.4	4.48	10.89	17.34 /95	17.04 /90	15.30 /89	0.58	0.44
GR	Vanguard US Value Inv	VUVLX	A+	(800) 662-7447	A- / 9.0	0.40	5.90	10.12 /75	18.03 /94	15.13 /88	1.60	0.29
UT	Vanguard Utilities Index Adm	VUIAX	C+	(800) 662-7447	C+ / 6.0	-4.66	7.83	10.57 /77	12.99 /60	13.14 /69	3.29	0.12
GR	Vanguard Value Index Adm	VVIAX	A-	(800) 662-7447	B / 7.7	-0.57	4.11	9.45 /72	15.97 /83	13.45 /72	2.33	0.09
GR	Vanguard Value Index Inst	VIVIX	A-	(800) 662-7447	B / 7.7	-0.56	4.12	9.46 /72	15.98 /83	13.48 /73	2.34	0.08
GR	Vanguard Value Index Inv	VIVAX	A-	(800) 662-7447	B- / 7.5	-0.60	4.04	9.33 /71	15.80 /82	13.29 /71	2.19	0.24
AA	Vanguard Wellesley Income Adm	VWIAX	C+	(800) 662-7447	C- / 3.3	1.26	3.63	6.68 /53	8.32 /29	9.26 /39	2.97	0.18

● Denotes fund is closed to new investors
* Denotes fund is included in Section II

RISK			NET ASSETS		ASSET					BULL / BEAR		FUND MANAGER		MINIMUMS		LOADS	
	3 Year		NAV						Portfolio	Last Bull	Last Bear	Manager	Manager	Initial	Additional	Front	Back
Risk	Standard		As of	Total	Cash	Stocks	Bonds	Other	Turnover	Market	Market	Quality	Tenure	Purch.	Purch.	End	End
Rating/Pts	Deviation	Beta	3/31/15	$(Mil)	%	%	%	%	Ratio	Return	Return	Pct	(Years)	$	$	Load	Load
C /5.5	12.4	0.89	47.04	5,806	0	99	0	1	50	104.2	N/A	83	11	10,000	100	0.0	0.0
C+ /6.8	12.0	0.87	46.98	6,123	0	99	0	1	47	111.3	N/A	91	17	10,000	100	0.0	0.0
C /5.5	12.4	0.89	37.67	3,814	0	99	0	1	50	104.3	-25.1	83	11	5,000,000	100	0.0	0.0
C /5.5	12.4	0.89	37.62	2,394	0	99	0	1	50	103.2	-25.1	82	11	3,000	100	0.0	0.0
C+ /6.3	12.0	0.88	58.53	21,343	0	99	0	1	29	108.7	-24.5	88	24	10,000	100	0.0	0.0
C+ /6.3	12.0	0.88	58.53	10,213	0	99	0	1	29	108.8	-24.5	88	24	5,000,000	100	0.0	0.0
C+ /6.3	12.0	0.88	168.95	6,586	0	99	0	1	29	109.0	-24.5	89	24	100,000,000	100	0.0	0.0
C+ /6.3	12.0	0.88	58.49	4,792	0	99	0	1	29	107.7	-24.6	88	24	3,000	100	0.0	0.0
C+ /6.8	12.0	0.87	26.26	2,124	0	99	0	1	47	111.4	-24.0	91	17	5,000,000	100	0.0	0.0
C+ /6.8	12.0	0.87	26.20	2,363	0	99	0	1	47	110.2	-24.0	90	17	3,000	100	0.0	0.0
B /8.6	6.5	0.64	25.26	19,282	0	60	39	1	6	58.2	-11.4	73	N/A	1,000	100	0.0	0.0
C+ /5.8	10.1	1.03	35.02	26	0	99	0	1	60	112.7	-17.5	80	11	5,000,000	100	0.0	0.0
C+ /5.7	10.1	1.04	69.98	553	0	99	0	1	60	113.3	-17.5	80	11	200,000,000	100	0.0	0.0
C+ /6.7	11.1	0.76	33.84	6,151	0	99	0	1	60	126.3	-22.2	96	9	3,000	100	0.0	0.0
C+ /6.2	12.4	0.90	32.07	757	0	99	0	1	64	117.8	-24.1	92	9	3,000	100	0.0	0.0
B- /7.3	9.8	1.02	40.44	82	0	99	0	1	68	107.6	-15.1	75	9	5,000,000	100	0.0	0.0
B- /7.3	9.8	1.02	80.05	488	0	99	0	1	68	108.1	-15.0	75	9	200,000,000	100	0.0	0.0
B+ /9.3	4.2	0.70	26.81	7,140	0	35	64	1	13	36.7	-6.9	61	9	1,000	100	0.0	0.0
B+ /9.1	5.4	0.92	15.60	22,508	0	50	49	1	10	45.7	-9.6	47	12	1,000	100	0.0	0.0
B /8.5	7.0	1.21	16.90	34,238	0	67	32	1	7	58.5	-13.5	30	12	1,000	100	0.0	0.0
B /8.1	7.8	1.33	29.71	25,532	0	74	25	1	7	64.3	-15.2	23	9	1,000	100	0.0	0.0
B- /7.7	8.5	1.46	18.26	26,044	0	82	17	1	6	70.3	-17.0	17	12	1,000	100	0.0	0.0
B- /7.5	9.1	1.55	30.47	17,706	0	89	10	1	6	73.3	-17.4	14	9	1,000	100	0.0	0.0
B- /7.5	9.1	1.55	19.10	16,047	0	89	10	1	7	73.3	-17.4	14	12	1,000	100	0.0	0.0
B- /7.4	9.1	1.55	30.32	8,341	0	89	10	1	7	73.4	-17.4	14	9	1,000	100	0.0	0.0
B- /7.5	9.0	1.54	32.74	2,133	1	88	9	2	7	73.5	-17.3	14	5	1,000	100	0.0	0.0
B- /7.7	9.0	0.91	28.87	643	0	89	9	2	11	N/A	N/A	39	3	1,000	100	0.0	0.0
B+ /9.6	3.4	0.51	13.09	11,678	0	29	70	1	6	28.1	-3.0	71	12	1,000	100	0.0	0.0
B /8.9	4.8	0.83	27.05	2,060	0	48	51	1	9	51.3	-6.5	75	16	10,000	100	0.0	0.0
B- /7.2	9.7	1.02	105.80	5,972	0	99	0	1	4	102.2	-17.4	68	21	10,000	100	0.0	0.0
B- /7.2	9.7	1.02	52.58	557	0	99	0	1	4	102.5	-17.4	68	21	5,000,000	100	0.0	0.0
C+ /6.2	12.6	0.93	47.73	248	0	99	0	1	31	109.0	-21.9	84	16	5,000,000	100	0.0	0.0
C+ /6.2	12.6	0.93	47.62	3,469	0	99	0	1	31	108.6	-21.9	84	16	10,000	100	0.0	0.0
C+ /6.7	11.5	0.71	44.03	26	0	99	0	1	19	66.9	-13.5	85	11	100,000	0	0.0	0.0
B /8.8	6.3	1.07	29.08	30,226	0	59	40	1	7	52.8	-11.6	38	9	1,000	100	0.0	0.0
C+ /5.9	12.8	0.96	107.89	39,875	1	98	0	1	5	43.9	-24.3	34	7	100,000,000	100	0.0	0.0
C+ /5.9	12.8	0.96	26.98	33,703	1	98	0	1	5	43.6	-24.3	33	7	10,000	100	0.0	0.0
C+ /5.9	12.8	0.96	107.88	15,032	1	98	0	1	5	43.7	-24.3	34	7	5,000,000	100	0.0	0.0
C+ /5.9	12.8	0.96	16.13	54,433	1	98	0	1	5	43.3	-24.4	32	7	3,000	100	0.0	0.0
B- /7.1	9.7	1.01	52.28	122,631	0	99	0	1	4	101.7	-17.7	68	21	10,000	100	0.0	0.0
B- /7.1	9.7	1.01	52.29	103,733	0	99	0	1	4	101.7	-17.7	68	21	5,000,000	100	0.0	0.0
B- /7.1	9.7	1.01	52.26	124,041	0	99	0	1	4	100.9	-17.7	66	21	3,000	100	0.0	0.0
C+ /6.5	10.7	0.66	125.48	1,526	1	98	0	1	7	68.3	-21.1	98	2	5,000,000	100	0.0	0.0
C+ /6.5	10.7	0.66	25.04	914	1	98	0	1	7	67.4	-21.2	98	2	3,000	100	0.0	0.0
C+ /5.7	11.2	1.07	80.88	2,154	3	96	0	1	36	110.8	-17.3	65	5	50,000	0	0.0	0.0
C+ /5.7	11.2	1.08	31.25	4,247	3	96	0	1	36	109.8	-17.4	62	5	3,000	0	0.0	0.0
B- /7.4	10.1	1.01	17.66	1,265	0	99	0	1	57	109.7	-18.4	80	7	3,000	100	0.0	0.0
C+ /6.4	13.4	0.95	48.56	487	0	99	0	1	7	55.3	1.4	75	5	100,000	100	0.0	0.0
B- /7.6	9.8	0.99	32.56	10,043	0	99	0	1	25	97.1	-18.4	67	21	10,000	100	0.0	0.0
B- /7.6	9.8	0.99	32.56	8,032	0	99	0	1	25	97.2	-18.4	67	21	5,000,000	100	0.0	0.0
B- /7.6	9.8	0.99	32.57	1,607	0	99	0	1	25	96.2	-18.5	65	21	3,000	100	0.0	0.0
B /8.9	3.9	0.60	62.29	28,914	0	37	62	1	109	40.0	-1.9	83	8	50,000	100	0.0	0.0

Fund Type	Fund Name	Ticker Symbol	Overall Investment Rating	Phone	Perfor-mance Rating/Pts	3 Mo	6 Mo	1Yr / Pct	3Yr / Pct	5Yr / Pct	Dividend Yield	Expense Ratio
								Total Return % through 3/31/15	Annualized		Incl. in Returns	

99 Pct = Best
0 Pct = Worst

Fund Type	Fund Name	Ticker Symbol	Overall Investment Rating	Phone	Perfor-mance Rating/Pts	3 Mo	6 Mo	1Yr / Pct	3Yr / Pct	5Yr / Pct	Dividend Yield	Expense Ratio
★ AA	Vanguard Wellesley Income Inv	VWINX	C+	(800) 662-7447	C- / 3.2	1.27	3.63	6.63 /52	8.25 /28	9.19 /38	2.90	0.25
BA	Vanguard Wellington Adm	VWENX	B	(800) 662-7447	C / 5.1	0.86	4.05	8.27 /65	11.61 /50	10.72 /50	2.50	0.18
★ BA	Vanguard Wellington Inv	VWELX	B	(800) 662-7447	C / 5.1	0.85	4.02	8.20 /64	11.53 /49	10.64 /50	2.42	0.26
MC	Vanguard Windsor-I Adm	VWNEX	A+	(800) 662-7447	A- / 9.0	1.59	6.10	9.84 /74	17.81 /94	14.15 /79	1.38	0.27
★ MC	Vanguard Windsor-I Inv	VWNDX	A+	(800) 662-7447	B+/ 8.9	1.54	6.02	9.71 /73	17.69 /93	14.04 /78	1.27	0.37
GR	Vanguard Windsor-II Adm	VWNAX	C+	(800) 662-7447	C+/ 6.8	-0.08	3.49	8.03 /63	14.75 /73	12.77 /66	2.26	0.28
★ GR	Vanguard Windsor-II Inv	VWNFX	C+	(800) 662-7447	C+/ 6.7	-0.08	3.45	7.96 /63	14.67 /72	12.69 /66	2.18	0.36
GR	Vanguard WY College Inv Agg Gr		B-	(800) 662-7447	C+/ 6.7	2.15	5.43	9.21 /70	14.04 /67	12.39 /63	0.00	0.52
GI	Vanguard WY College Inv Con Gr		C+	(800) 662-7447	D / 2.1	1.80	4.09	6.81 /54	5.68 /15	6.35 /19	0.00	0.52
GI	Vanguard WY College Inv Gr Port		B	(800) 662-7447	C / 5.1	2.06	5.07	8.49 /66	11.29 /48	10.54 /49	0.00	0.52
GI	Vanguard WY College Inv Mod Gr		B-	(800) 662-7447	C- / 3.6	1.98	4.66	7.79 /61	8.53 /30	8.52 /33	0.00	0.52
GR	Vanguard WY College Inv St Ind Port		A+	(800) 662-7447	B / 8.2	1.73	6.96	11.95 /82	15.98 /83	14.34 /81	0.00	0.52
IX	Vantagepoint 500 Stock Index I	VPFIX	A-	(800) 669-7400	B / 7.9	0.81	5.68	12.27 /84	15.66 /81	14.02 /78	1.36	0.41
IX	Vantagepoint 500 Stock Index II	VPSKX	A	(800) 669-7400	B / 8.1	0.93	5.88	12.52 /85	15.89 /82	14.26 /80	1.69	0.21
GR	Vantagepoint 500 Stock Index T	VQFIX	U	(800) 669-7400	U /	0.93	5.88	12.55 /85	--	--	1.56	0.21
MC	Vantagepoint Aggressive Opport Inv	VPAOX	C+	(800) 669-7400	B / 8.1	5.21	9.08	9.59 /72	15.54 /80	11.88 /60	0.00	0.84
MC	Vantagepoint Aggressive Opport T	VQAOX	U	(800) 669-7400	U /	5.21	9.15	9.82 /74	--	--	0.20	0.59
GR	Vantagepoint Broad Market Index I	VPMIX	A	(800) 669-7400	B / 8.2	1.73	6.95	12.06 /83	15.95 /83	14.30 /80	1.41	0.41
GR	Vantagepoint Broad Market Index II	VPBMX	A	(800) 669-7400	B+/ 8.4	1.79	7.09	12.27 /84	16.18 /85	14.55 /83	1.67	0.21
GR	Vantagepoint Broad Market Index T	VQMIX	U	(800) 669-7400	U /	1.79	7.12	12.36 /84	--	--	1.63	0.21
GR	Vantagepoint Discovery Inv	VPDSX	C	(800) 669-7400	B+/ 8.6	3.98	13.43	6.86 /54	16.43 /87	14.63 /84	0.49	0.96
GR	Vantagepoint Discovery T	VQDSX	U	(800) 669-7400	U /	4.08	13.64	7.16 /56	--	--	0.68	0.71
GL	Vantagepoint Diversifying Strat T	VPDAX	D+	(800) 669-7400	D / 1.8	3.46	7.13	6.52 /51	4.82 /13	4.18 / 9	2.13	0.49
IN	Vantagepoint Equity Income Inv	VPEIX	C-	(800) 669-7400	C+/ 5.9	0.10	3.22	6.70 /53	13.40 /63	11.68 /58	1.51	0.78
IN	Vantagepoint Equity Income T	VQEIX	U	(800) 669-7400	U /	0.20	3.43	7.00 /55	--	--	1.78	0.53
GI	Vantagepoint Growth and Income Inv	VPGIX	B-	(800) 669-7400	B / 8.0	2.12	6.19	11.75 /82	15.68 /81	13.73 /75	1.27	0.79
GI	Vantagepoint Growth and Income T	VQGIX	U	(800) 669-7400	U /	2.20	6.34	12.06 /83	--	--	1.55	0.54
GR	Vantagepoint Growth Inv	VPGRX	B	(800) 669-7400	B- / 7.5	2.80	7.07	13.23 /87	14.58 /72	12.84 /67	0.22	0.78
GR	Vantagepoint Growth T	VQGRX	U	(800) 669-7400	U /	2.88	7.17	13.41 /88	--	--	0.54	0.53
FO	Vantagepoint International Inv	VPINX	D	(800) 669-7400	D+/ 2.8	4.15	1.36	0.28 /16	8.21 /28	6.65 /21	3.40	1.00
FO	Vantagepoint International T	VQINX	U	(800) 669-7400	U /	4.25	1.45	0.46 /17	--	--	3.58	0.75
MC	Vantagepoint Mid-Small Comp Indx I	VPSIX	A-	(800) 669-7400	B+/ 8.9	5.07	12.10	9.82 /74	16.70 /88	15.28 /89	1.20	0.42
MC	Vantagepoint Mid-Small Comp Indx II	VPMSX	A-	(800) 669-7400	A- / 9.0	5.16	12.27	10.08 /75	16.94 /90	15.51 /90	1.54	0.22
MC	Vantagepoint Mid-Small Comp Indx T	VQSIX	U	(800) 669-7400	U /	5.12	12.25	10.08 /75	--	--	1.42	0.22
AA	Vantagepoint Milestone 2010 Inv M	VPRQX	D+	(800) 669-7400	D+/ 2.3	1.96	3.42	4.96 /38	6.65 /20	6.73 /21	1.75	0.82
AA	Vantagepoint Milestone 2010 TM	VQRQX	U	(800) 669-7400	U /	1.96	3.50	5.13 /40	--	--	2.00	0.57
AA	Vantagepoint Milestone 2015 Inv M	VPRPX	D+	(800) 669-7400	D+/ 2.8	1.97	3.68	5.23 /40	7.53 /24	7.47 /26	1.83	0.82
AA	Vantagepoint Milestone 2015 TM	VQRPX	U	(800) 669-7400	U /	2.06	3.85	5.49 /42	--	--	2.07	0.57
AA	Vantagepoint Milestone 2020 Inv M	VPROX	C-	(800) 669-7400	C- / 3.4	2.22	4.18	5.69 /44	8.65 /31	8.23 /31	1.92	0.83
AA	Vantagepoint Milestone 2020 TM	VQROX	U	(800) 669-7400	U /	2.30	4.26	5.94 /46	--	--	2.15	0.58
AA	Vantagepoint Milestone 2025 Inv M	VPRNX	C	(800) 669-7400	C- / 4.0	2.34	4.48	6.03 /47	9.69 /37	9.01 /37	2.00	0.85
AA	Vantagepoint Milestone 2025 TM	VQRNX	U	(800) 669-7400	U /	2.42	4.63	6.27 /49	--	--	2.22	0.60
AA	Vantagepoint Milestone 2030 Inv M	VPRMX	C	(800) 669-7400	C / 4.6	2.52	4.79	6.46 /50	10.63 /43	9.76 /43	2.04	0.87
AA	Vantagepoint Milestone 2030 TM	VQRMX	U	(800) 669-7400	U /	2.52	4.87	6.70 /53	--	--	2.27	0.62
AA	Vantagepoint Milestone 2035 Inv M	VPRLX	C	(800) 669-7400	C / 5.1	2.57	5.08	6.73 /53	11.56 /49	10.49 /49	2.09	0.88
AA	Vantagepoint Milestone 2035 TM	VQRLX	U	(800) 669-7400	U /	2.65	5.17	6.98 /55	--	--	2.31	0.63
AA	Vantagepoint Milestone 2040 Inv M	VPRKX	C	(800) 669-7400	C+/ 5.6	2.61	5.14	6.83 /54	12.28 /54	11.06 /53	2.10	0.90
AA	Vantagepoint Milestone 2040 TM	VQRKX	U	(800) 669-7400	U /	2.61	5.22	7.07 /56	--	--	2.32	0.65
AA	Vantagepoint Milestone 2045 Inv M	VPRJX	C+	(800) 669-7400	C+/ 5.7	2.63	5.23	6.87 /54	12.47 /56	11.06 /53	2.09	0.98
AA	Vantagepoint Milestone 2045 TM	VQRJX	U	(800) 669-7400	U /	2.70	5.31	7.17 /56	--	--	2.30	0.73
GI	Vantagepoint Milestone 2050 TM	VQRHX	U	(800) 669-7400	U /	2.71	5.35	7.06 /55	--	--	2.23	1.30
IN	Vantagepoint Milestone Ret Inc Inv	VPRRX	D+	(800) 669-7400	D- / 1.5	1.69	2.99	4.20 /33	4.77 /12	5.12 /12	1.74	0.81

● Denotes fund is closed to new investors
★ Denotes fund is included in Section II

www.thestreetratings.com

RISK			NET ASSETS		ASSET				BULL / BEAR		FUND MANAGER		MINIMUMS		LOADS	
	3 Year		NAV						Last Bull	Last Bear	Manager	Manager	Initial	Additional	Front	Back
Risk Rating/Pts	Standard Deviation	Beta	As of 3/31/15	Total $(Mil)	Cash %	Stocks %	Bonds %	Other %	Portfolio Turnover Ratio	Market Return	Market Return	Quality Pct	Tenure (Years)	Purch. $	Purch. $	End Load	End Load
B /9.0	3.9	0.59	25.72	12,774	0	37	62	1	109	39.7	-1.9	83	8	3,000	100	0.0	0.0
B /8.3	6.1	1.07	67.78	67,194	0	64	35	1	71	63.5	-10.4	66	15	50,000	100	0.0	0.0
B /8.3	6.2	1.07	39.25	23,519	0	64	35	1	71	63.0	-10.4	65	15	3,000	100	0.0	0.0
C+ /6.8	10.9	0.90	73.52	12,791	1	97	0	2	38	111.1	-21.1	85	7	50,000	100	0.0	0.0
C+ /6.8	10.9	0.90	21.79	5,917	1	97	0	2	38	110.3	-21.1	85	7	3,000	100	0.0	0.0
C+ /6.8	9.7	1.00	66.15	33,517	3	96	0	1	27	94.9	-17.1	50	30	50,000	100	0.0	0.0
C+ /6.8	9.7	1.00	37.28	17,346	3	96	0	1	27	94.5	-17.2	49	30	3,000	100	0.0	0.0
B- /7.6	9.9	1.02	21.34	419	0	0	0	100	0	86.6	-19.2	36	6	25	15	0.0	0.0
B+ /9.9	3.0	0.21	17.56	365	0	0	0	100	0	25.7	-1.6	86	6	25	15	0.0	0.0
B /8.7	7.3	0.75	20.32	454	0	0	0	100	0	64.5	-13.5	60	6	25	15	0.0	0.0
B+ /9.6	5.0	0.48	19.10	431	0	0	0	100	0	44.3	-7.8	77	6	25	15	0.0	0.0
B- /7.9	9.7	1.01	23.51	218	0	0	0	100	0	99.3	-17.8	63	6	25	15	0.0	0.0
B- /7.3	9.5	1.00	16.21	51	2	97	0	1	8	97.6	-16.4	62	11	0	0	0.0	0.0
B- /7.2	9.6	1.00	15.23	21	2	97	0	1	8	98.8	-16.3	65	11	0	0	0.0	0.0
U /	N/A	N/A	16.24	814	2	97	0	1	8	N/A	N/A	N/A	11	0	0	0.0	0.0
C /4.3	11.2	0.98	12.11	35	3	96	0	1	51	94.1	-25.2	54	13	0	0	0.0	0.0
U /	N/A	N/A	12.12	1,101	3	96	0	1	51	N/A	N/A	N/A	13	0	0	0.0	0.0
B- /7.1	9.7	1.01	17.61	49	2	97	0	1	9	98.8	-17.5	62	11	0	0	0.0	0.0
B- /7.1	9.8	1.02	16.46	13	2	97	0	1	9	100.1	-17.4	65	11	0	0	0.0	0.0
U /	N/A	N/A	17.63	851	2	97	0	1	9	N/A	N/A	N/A	11	0	0	0.0	0.0
D+ /2.7	13.4	1.16	10.44	6	2	48	48	2	77	100.3	-24.8	37	8	0	0	0.0	0.0
U /	N/A	N/A	10.46	300	2	48	48	2	77	N/A	N/A	N/A	8	0	0	0.0	0.0
B- /7.5	4.6	0.19	10.48	1,124	2	6	55	37	70	18.1	-3.4	88	8	0	0	0.0	0.0
C /4.3	10.1	1.02	9.96	54	6	93	0	1	18	84.5	-18.8	28	16	0	0	0.0	0.0
U /	N/A	N/A	9.97	2,304	6	93	0	1	18	N/A	N/A	N/A	16	0	0	0.0	0.0
C /5.3	9.8	1.01	13.00	39	3	96	0	1	35	99.2	-18.3	60	14	0	0	0.0	0.0
U /	N/A	N/A	13.01	1,695	3	96	0	1	35	N/A	N/A	N/A	14	0	0	0.0	0.0
C+ /6.4	10.8	1.04	13.94	25	3	96	0	1	53	91.6	-17.8	39	10	0	0	0.0	0.0
U /	N/A	N/A	13.94	2,316	3	96	0	1	53	N/A	N/A	N/A	10	0	0	0.0	0.0
C+ /6.0	12.0	0.89	10.79	26	3	96	0	1	51	49.6	-20.9	64	13	0	0	0.0	0.0
U /	N/A	N/A	10.80	1,561	3	96	0	1	51	N/A	N/A	N/A	13	0	0	0.0	0.0
C+ /6.0	11.8	1.05	20.92	33	0	99	0	1	37	102.1	-23.2	50	11	0	0	0.0	0.0
C+ /6.0	11.8	1.06	19.55	16	0	99	0	1	37	103.5	-23.1	53	11	0	0	0.0	0.0
U /	N/A	N/A	20.94	713	0	99	0	1	37	N/A	N/A	N/A	11	0	0	0.0	0.0
B- /7.5	4.8	0.81	10.94	73	3	33	59	5	15	36.0	-8.6	37	10	0	0	0.0	0.0
U /	N/A	N/A	10.94	219	3	33	59	5	15	N/A	N/A	N/A	10	0	0	0.0	0.0
B- /7.0	5.5	0.94	11.36	115	3	40	52	5	11	41.7	-10.5	32	10	0	0	0.0	0.0
U /	N/A	N/A	11.37	466	3	40	52	5	11	N/A	N/A	N/A	10	0	0	0.0	0.0
B- /7.3	6.3	1.07	11.99	126	3	47	44	6	9	48.4	-12.3	28	10	0	0	0.0	0.0
U /	N/A	N/A	12.00	655	3	47	44	6	9	N/A	N/A	N/A	10	0	0	0.0	0.0
B- /7.0	7.2	1.21	12.25	113	3	54	36	7	8	55.3	-14.1	22	10	0	0	0.0	0.0
U /	N/A	N/A	12.27	566	3	54	36	7	8	N/A	N/A	N/A	10	0	0	0.0	0.0
C+ /6.6	7.9	1.34	12.59	102	3	62	28	7	8	62.2	-15.8	19	10	0	0	0.0	0.0
U /	N/A	N/A	12.60	461	3	62	28	7	8	N/A	N/A	N/A	10	0	0	0.0	0.0
C+ /6.3	8.8	1.48	12.78	75	3	70	20	7	8	69.4	-17.6	14	10	0	0	0.0	0.0
U /	N/A	N/A	12.79	316	3	70	20	7	8	N/A	N/A	N/A	10	0	0	0.0	0.0
C+ /5.8	9.4	1.58	12.95	69	3	77	13	7	8	74.8	-18.7	12	10	0	0	0.0	0.0
U /	N/A	N/A	12.96	306	3	77	13	7	8	N/A	N/A	N/A	10	0	0	0.0	0.0
C+ /6.2	9.6	1.61	14.43	36	3	91	4	2	9	76.2	-18.9	11	5	0	0	0.0	0.0
U /	N/A	N/A	14.45	115	3	91	4	2	9	N/A	N/A	N/A	5	0	0	0.0	0.0
U /	N/A	N/A	12.88	38	3	91	4	2	24	N/A	N/A	N/A	3	0	0	0.0	0.0
B /8.4	3.4	0.31	10.80	89	3	29	65	3	10	24.1	-4.7	68	10	0	0	0.0	0.0

Fund Type	Fund Name	Ticker Symbol	Overall Investment Rating	Phone	PERFORMANCE						Incl. in Returns	
	99 Pct = Best 0 Pct = Worst				Perfor-mance Rating/Pts	Total Return % through 3/31/15			Annualized		Dividend Yield	Expense Ratio
						3 Mo	6 Mo	1Yr / Pct	3Yr / Pct	5Yr / Pct		
AA	Vantagepoint Milestone Ret Inc TM	VQRRX	U	(800) 669-7400	U /	1.79	3.06	4.46 /35	--	--	1.99	0.56
GR	Vantagepoint Mod Port All-E G Inv M	VPAGX	C+	(800) 669-7400	C+ / 6.1	2.54	5.41	7.35 /58	13.31 /62	11.55 /57	2.42	0.94
GR	Vantagepoint Mod Port All-E G TM	VQAGX	U	(800) 669-7400	U /	2.58	5.51	7.60 /60	--	--	2.66	0.69
GR	Vantagepoint Mod Port Cons Gr Inv	VPCGX	D+	(800) 669-7400	D / 2.0	1.76	2.93	3.92 /31	6.22 /18	6.32 /19	1.87	0.87
BA	Vantagepoint Mod Port Cons Gr TM	VQCGX	U	(800) 669-7400	U /	1.84	3.11	4.21 /33	--	--	2.11	0.62
GR	Vantagepoint Mod Port Lg-Tm G Inv	VPLGX	C	(800) 669-7400	C / 4.7	2.53	5.12	6.79 /53	10.82 /44	9.70 /42	2.34	0.91
GR	Vantagepoint Mod Port Lg-Tm G TM	VQLGX	U	(800) 669-7400	U /	2.57	5.21	7.04 /55	--	--	2.58	0.66
GR	Vantagepoint Mod Port Trad Gr Inv M	VPTGX	C	(800) 669-7400	C- / 3.6	2.24	4.28	5.69 /44	8.94 /33	8.36 /32	2.14	0.88
BA	Vantagepoint Mod Port Trad Gr TM	VQTGX	U	(800) 669-7400	U /	2.28	4.41	5.94 /46	--	--	2.37	0.63
FO	Vantagepoint Overseas Eqty Index I	VPOIX	D	(800) 669-7400	D+ / 2.9	5.31	0.96	-1.51 /11	8.59 /30	5.85 /16	3.01	0.55
FO	Vantagepoint Overseas Eqty Index II	VPOEX	D	(800) 669-7400	C- / 3.0	5.33	1.00	-1.31 /12	8.79 /32	6.04 /17	3.46	0.35
FO	Vantagepoint Overseas Eqty Index T	VQOIX	U	(800) 669-7400	U /	5.31	1.05	-1.34 /12	--	--	3.26	0.35
GI	Vantagepoint Select Value Inv	VPSVX	C+	(800) 669-7400	B / 7.8	2.53	7.42	8.07 /63	15.77 /81	14.56 /83	1.00	0.98
GI	Vantagepoint Select Value T	VQSVX	U	(800) 669-7400	U /	2.61	7.56	8.29 /65	--	--	1.28	0.73
SC	Vericimetry US Small Cap Value	VYSVX	B+	(855) 755-7550	B / 7.9	2.60	9.83	3.67 /30	16.39 /86	--	0.67	0.72
BA	Victory Balanced A	SBALX	C	(800) 539-3863	C- / 3.5	0.27	2.92	7.41 /58	10.62 /43	8.91 /36	1.98	1.34
BA	Victory Balanced C	VBFCX	C	(800) 539-3863	C- / 4.0	0.06	2.55	6.61 /52	9.83 /38	8.11 /31	1.45	2.14
BA	Victory Balanced I	VBFIX	C+	(800) 539-3863	C / 4.6	0.33	3.10	7.64 /60	10.89 /45	9.34 /39	2.32	4.80
BA	Victory Balanced R	VBFGX	C+	(800) 539-3863	C- / 4.2	0.21	2.78	7.10 /56	10.30 /41	8.57 /34	1.75	1.72
GR	Victory Diversified Stk A	SRVEX	C-	(800) 539-3863	C+ / 5.7	-0.90	2.77	8.69 /68	14.67 /72	11.59 /58	0.83	1.10
GR	Victory Diversified Stk C	VDSCX	C	(800) 539-3863	C+ / 6.1	-1.09	2.35	7.79 /61	13.74 /65	10.69 /50	0.18	1.89
GR	Victory Diversified Stk I	VDSIX	C+	(800) 539-3863	C+ / 6.9	-0.84	2.91	8.94 /69	14.95 /75	11.90 /60	1.14	0.82
GR	Victory Diversified Stk R	GRINX	C	(800) 539-3863	C+ / 6.5	-0.92	2.67	8.40 /66	14.34 /70	11.28 /55	0.63	1.38
GR	Victory Inst Diversified Stock Fund	VIDSX	C-	(800) 539-3863	B- / 7.0	-0.82	2.92	9.03 /69	15.12 /76	11.97 /60	1.33	0.61
SC	Victory Integrity Micro-Cap Eq A	MMEAX	C+	(800) 539-3863	A- / 9.1	4.80	15.35	8.25 /65	18.87 /96	18.10 /97	0.00	1.86
SC	Victory Integrity Micro-Cap Eq C	MMECX	C+	(800) 539-3863	A / 9.3	4.58	14.89	7.40 /58	17.97 /94	17.21 /96	0.00	2.61
SC	Victory Integrity Micro-Cap Eq R	MMERX	B-	(800) 539-3863	A / 9.4	4.64	15.05	7.81 /61	18.52 /96	17.77 /97	0.00	2.11
SC	Victory Integrity Micro-Cap Eq Y	MMEYX	B	(800) 539-3863	A+ / 9.6	4.87	15.50	8.52 /66	19.17 /97	18.39 /98	0.00	1.61
MC	Victory Integrity Mid-Cap Value A	MAIMX	B	(800) 539-3863	B- / 7.4	2.06	7.47	6.98 /55	17.09 /90	--	0.00	4.76
MC	Victory Integrity Mid-Cap Value Y	MYIMX	A-	(800) 539-3863	B+ / 8.7	2.25	7.71	7.35 /58	17.42 /92	--	0.00	4.81
GR	Victory Integrity Sm/Mid-Cap Val A	MAISX	C+	(800) 539-3863	C+ / 6.2	2.99	8.40	5.72 /44	15.01 /75	--	0.00	6.55
GR	Victory Integrity Sm/Mid-Cap Val Y	MYISX	B	(800) 539-3863	B- / 7.5	3.11	8.59	6.05 /47	15.33 /78	--	0.00	1.54
SC	Victory Integrity Small Cap Val C	MCVSX	B+	(800) 539-3863	B+ / 8.8	3.64	12.35	8.45 /66	16.75 /88	--	0.00	2.32
SC	Victory Integrity Small Cap Val R	MRVSX	A-	(800) 539-3863	A- / 9.1	3.78	12.60	9.00 /69	17.33 /92	--	0.00	1.79
SC	Victory Integrity Small Cap Val R6	MVSSX	U	(800) 539-3863	U /	3.96	13.01	9.77 /73	--	--	0.00	1.11
SC	Victory Integrity Small Cap Val Y	VSVIX	A	(800) 539-3863	A / 9.3	3.92	12.94	9.58 /72	17.93 /94	15.16 /88	0.00	1.31
SC	Victory Integrity Small Cap Value A	VSCVX	B+	(800) 539-3863	B+ / 8.4	3.84	12.77	9.29 /71	17.62 /93	14.87 /86	0.00	1.56
FO	● Victory International A	VIAFX	E	(800) 539-3863	D- / 1.4	2.92	0.29	-2.08 /10	7.25 /23	6.31 /19	0.65	2.46
FO	● Victory International C	VICFX	E	(800) 539-3863	D / 1.6	2.71	-0.03	-2.90 / 9	6.44 /19	5.49 /14	0.69	2.55
FO	● Victory International I	VIIFX	E	(800) 539-3863	D / 2.2	3.08	0.47	-1.88 /11	7.58 /25	6.61 /21	1.66	1.10
FO	● Victory International Select A	VISFX	D-	(800) 539-3863	D+ / 2.5	3.50	2.78	2.63 /25	8.97 /33	7.02 /23	0.86	2.34
FO	● Victory International Select C	VISKX	D-	(800) 539-3863	D+ / 2.9	3.32	2.38	1.86 /21	8.16 /28	6.21 /18	0.45	2.80
FO	● Victory International Select I	VISIX	D	(800) 539-3863	C- / 3.6	3.54	2.87	2.87 /26	9.29 /35	7.34 /25	1.28	1.08
FO	● Victory International Select Y	VISYX	C-	(800) 539-3863	C- / 3.5	3.58	2.89	2.89 /26	9.24 /35	--	1.21	1.52
FO	● Victory International Y	VIYFX	D+	(800) 539-3863	D / 2.2	3.02	0.45	-1.93 /10	7.52 /24	--	1.67	1.54
CV	Victory Invt Grade Conv A	SBFCX	C+	(800) 539-3863	C / 4.5	0.72	3.98	8.69 /68	10.95 /45	8.71 /35	1.70	1.52
CV	Victory Invt Grade Conv I	VICIX	B-	(800) 539-3863	C / 5.1	0.81	4.15	9.19 /70	11.48 /49	9.17 /38	2.18	1.08
TC	Victory Munder Growth Opps A	MNNAX	B+	(800) 539-3863	B- / 7.5	4.48	9.43	17.74 /95	14.89 /74	13.99 /78	0.00	1.63
TC	Victory Munder Growth Opps C	MNNCX	B+	(800) 539-3863	B / 7.9	4.24	8.99	16.82 /94	14.02 /67	13.13 /69	0.00	2.38
TC	Victory Munder Growth Opps R	MNNRX	A-	(800) 539-3863	B+ / 8.3	4.34	9.19	17.30 /95	14.56 /71	13.68 /75	0.00	1.88
TC	Victory Munder Growth Opps Y	MNNYX	A	(800) 539-3863	B+ / 8.8	4.57	9.63	18.06 /96	15.20 /76	14.29 /80	0.00	1.38
IX	Victory Munder Index 500 A	MUXAX	C+	(800) 539-3863	B- / 7.2	0.82	5.64	12.02 /83	15.32 /77	13.68 /75	1.26	0.83

● Denotes fund is closed to new investors
* Denotes fund is included in Section II

RISK	3 Year		NET ASSETS		ASSET					BULL / BEAR		FUND MANAGER		MINIMUMS		LOADS	
Risk Rating/Pts	Standard Deviation	Beta	NAV As of 3/31/15	Total $(Mil)	Cash %	Stocks %	Bonds %	Other %	Portfolio Turnover Ratio	Last Bull Market Return	Last Bear Market Return	Manager Quality Pct	Manager Tenure (Years)	Initial Purch. $	Additional Purch. $	Front End Load	Back End Load
U /	N/A	N/A	10.81	245	3	29	65	3	10	N/A	N/A	N/A	10	0	0	0.0	0.0
C+ / 6.2	10.2	1.03	26.64	55	4	92	3	1	8	82.6	-20.4	27	11	0	0	0.0	0.0
U /	N/A	N/A	26.66	917	4	92	3	1	8	N/A	N/A	N/A	11	0	0	0.0	0.0
B- / 7.2	4.5	0.43	25.43	104	3	28	64	5	11	33.2	-7.9	61	11	0	0	0.0	0.0
U /	N/A	N/A	25.46	563	3	28	64	5	11	N/A	N/A	N/A	11	0	0	0.0	0.0
C+ / 6.9	8.0	0.80	25.92	115	3	68	23	6	10	62.1	-15.4	42	11	0	0	0.0	0.0
U /	N/A	N/A	25.94	2,171	3	68	23	6	10	N/A	N/A	N/A	11	0	0	0.0	0.0
B- / 7.5	6.4	0.64	26.02	144	3	51	40	6	9	49.6	-12.2	52	11	0	0	0.0	0.0
U /	N/A	N/A	26.04	1,606	3	51	40	6	9	N/A	N/A	N/A	11	0	0	0.0	0.0
C+ / 5.6	13.3	1.00	12.10	12	1	98	0	1	11	50.5	-23.4	54	11	0	0	0.0	0.0
C+ / 5.6	13.3	1.01	11.26	4	1	98	0	1	11	51.4	-23.4	57	11	0	0	0.0	0.0
U /	N/A	N/A	12.10	276	1	98	0	1	11	N/A	N/A	N/A	11	0	0	0.0	0.0
C / 4.4	10.3	0.99	12.16	8	5	94	0	1	77	98.0	-21.2	65	8	0	0	0.0	0.0
U /	N/A	N/A	12.17	442	5	94	0	1	77	N/A	N/A	N/A	8	0	0	0.0	0.0
C+ / 6.6	13.9	1.00	16.72	196	0	99	0	1	16	N/A	N/A	68	4	0	0	0.0	0.0
B- / 7.6	7.0	1.18	14.97	10	1	64	34	1	66	61.7	-14.0	36	12	2,500	250	5.8	0.0
B- / 7.6	7.0	1.18	14.84	3	1	64	34	1	66	57.7	-14.3	27	12	2,500	250	0.0	0.0
B- / 7.6	7.1	1.18	15.03	N/A	1	64	34	1	66	63.1	-13.9	40	12	2,000,000	0	0.0	0.0
B- / 7.6	7.0	1.17	14.96	2	1	64	34	1	66	60.0	-14.1	33	12	0	0	0.0	0.0
C / 5.0	11.1	1.11	20.41	666	1	98	0	1	70	98.9	-22.6	26	26	2,500	250	5.8	0.0
C / 5.0	11.1	1.11	19.74	74	1	98	0	1	70	93.6	-22.9	18	26	2,500	250	0.0	0.0
C / 5.0	11.1	1.11	20.38	342	1	98	0	1	70	100.8	-22.5	28	26	2,000,000	0	0.0	0.0
C / 5.0	11.1	1.12	20.16	98	1	98	0	1	70	97.0	-22.7	22	26	0	0	0.0	0.0
C- / 3.4	11.0	1.10	12.14	481	1	98	0	1	79	100.6	-22.1	32	10	10,000,000	0	0.0	0.0
C- / 3.7	13.6	0.98	36.93	69	1	98	0	1	62	121.7	-24.9	87	N/A	2,500	250	5.8	0.0
D+ / 2.9	13.6	0.98	29.94	17	1	98	0	1	62	116.2	-25.1	82	N/A	2,500	250	0.0	0.0
C- / 3.6	13.6	0.98	36.06	1	1	98	0	1	62	119.6	-24.9	85	N/A	0	0	0.0	0.0
C- / 3.8	13.6	0.98	39.21	27	1	98	0	1	62	123.6	-24.8	88	N/A	1,000,000	0	0.0	0.0
C+ / 6.4	11.7	1.03	15.83	9	2	97	0	1	51	108.5	N/A	61	N/A	2,500	250	5.8	0.0
C+ / 6.4	11.7	1.03	15.94	5	2	97	0	1	51	111.0	N/A	66	N/A	1,000,000	0	0.0	0.0
C+ / 6.0	12.6	1.16	14.48	1	7	92	0	1	50	98.3	N/A	21	4	2,500	250	5.8	0.0
C+ / 6.1	12.6	1.16	14.57	20	7	92	0	1	50	100.3	N/A	24	4	1,000,000	0	0.0	0.0
C+ / 6.1	13.1	0.95	31.30	28	1	98	0	1	92	101.5	N/A	78	4	2,500	250	0.0	0.0
C+ / 6.1	13.1	0.95	33.79	11	1	98	0	1	92	105.0	N/A	82	4	0	0	0.0	0.0
U /	N/A	N/A	35.17	393	1	98	0	1	92	N/A	N/A	N/A	4	0	0	0.0	0.0
C+ / 6.2	13.1	0.95	35.01	714	1	98	0	1	92	108.5	-25.0	85	4	1,000,000	0	0.0	0.0
C+ / 6.2	13.1	0.95	34.36	238	1	98	0	1	92	106.7	-25.0	84	4	2,500	250	5.8	0.0
D+ / 2.8	12.2	0.90	11.16	N/A	4	95	0	1	50	48.8	-24.9	49	1	2,500	250	5.8	0.0
D+ / 2.7	12.1	0.90	10.93	1	4	95	0	1	50	45.1	-25.2	38	1	2,500	250	0.0	0.0
D+ / 2.7	12.2	0.90	11.20	N/A	4	95	0	1	50	50.3	-24.8	54	1	2,000,000	0	0.0	0.0
C / 5.1	12.4	0.91	13.62	1	5	94	0	1	63	57.6	-26.5	71	1	2,500	250	5.8	0.0
C / 5.1	12.4	0.90	13.40	1	5	94	0	1	63	53.6	-26.8	62	1	2,500	250	0.0	0.0
C / 5.1	12.4	0.90	13.74	1	5	94	0	1	63	59.2	-26.5	74	1	2,000,000	0	0.0	0.0
B- / 7.0	12.4	0.90	13.61	1	5	94	0	1	63	N/A	N/A	74	1	0	0	0.0	0.0
B- / 7.2	12.2	0.90	11.05	1	4	95	0	1	50	N/A	N/A	53	1	0	0	0.0	0.0
B / 8.1	6.4	0.80	14.08	8	19	12	2	67	28	53.3	-12.2	68	19	2,500	250	2.0	0.0
B / 8.1	6.4	0.80	14.06	39	19	12	2	67	28	55.8	-12.1	73	19	2,000,000	0	0.0	0.0
C+ / 6.7	10.9	1.07	44.55	386	0	99	0	1	124	93.6	-20.7	36	16	2,500	250	5.8	0.0
C+ / 6.7	10.9	1.07	39.06	82	0	99	0	1	124	88.6	-20.9	27	16	2,500	250	0.0	0.0
C+ / 6.7	10.9	1.07	43.26	1	0	99	0	1	124	91.7	-20.8	33	16	0	0	0.0	0.0
C+ / 6.7	10.9	1.07	46.68	26	0	99	0	1	124	95.3	-20.6	40	16	1,000,000	0	0.0	0.0
C / 5.5	9.6	1.00	22.29	217	3	96	0	1	3	95.6	-16.5	57	7	2,500	250	2.5	0.0

						PERFORMANCE							
							Total Return % through 3/31/15					Incl. in Returns	
										Annualized			
Fund Type	Fund Name	Ticker Symbol	Overall Investment Rating	Phone		Performance Rating/Pts	3 Mo	6 Mo	1Yr / Pct	3Yr / Pct	5Yr / Pct	Dividend Yield	Expense Ratio
IX	Victory Munder Index 500 R	MUXRX	B-	(800) 539-3863		B- / 7.4	0.70	5.44	11.63 /81	14.91 /74	13.28 /71	0.98	1.08
IX	Victory Munder Index 500 Y	MUXYX	B	(800) 539-3863		B / 7.8	0.86	5.74	12.19 /83	15.51 /79	13.87 /77	1.43	0.58
MC	Victory Munder MidCap Core Gro A	MGOAX	B	(800) 539-3863		B+ / 8.3	6.00	12.06	14.61 /91	16.52 /87	15.83 /92	0.00	1.38
MC	Victory Munder MidCap Core Gro C	MGOTX	B+	(800) 539-3863		B+ / 8.7	5.82	11.67	13.78 /89	15.65 /80	14.97 /87	0.00	2.13
MC	Victory Munder MidCap Core Gro R	MMSRX	B+	(800) 539-3863		A- / 9.0	5.92	11.84	14.25 /90	16.20 /85	15.52 /90	0.00	1.63
MC	Victory Munder MidCap Core Gro R6	MGOSX	U	(800) 539-3863		U /	6.10	12.21	15.02 /92	--	--	0.05	0.95
MC	Victory Munder MidCap Core Gro Y	MGOYX	A-	(800) 539-3863		A- / 9.2	6.06	12.16	14.88 /91	16.80 /89	16.12 /94	0.03	1.13
GL	Victory Newbridge Global Equity A	VPGEX	C-	(800) 539-3863		C / 5.1	4.74	7.24	9.25 /71	12.43 /56	11.73 /59	0.19	1.95
GL	Victory Newbridge Global Equity C	VPGCX	C	(800) 539-3863		C / 5.5	4.48	6.78	8.40 /66	11.60 /50	10.88 /52	0.00	2.72
GL	Victory Newbridge Global Equity I	VPGYX	C	(800) 539-3863		C+ / 6.2	4.74	7.32	9.41 /72	12.69 /57	12.00 /61	0.42	1.67
GR	Victory Newbridge Large Cap Grow A	VFGAX	C-	(800) 539-3863		C / 5.1	3.65	6.61	12.32 /84	12.13 /53	12.50 /64	0.00	1.26
GR	Victory Newbridge Large Cap Grow C	VFGCX	C-	(800) 539-3863		C / 5.5	3.45	6.25	11.46 /80	11.26 /47	11.61 /58	0.00	2.10
GR	Victory Newbridge Large Cap Grow I	VFGIX	C	(800) 539-3863		C+ / 6.3	3.77	6.81	12.65 /85	12.50 /56	--	0.00	1.00
GR	Victory Newbridge Large Cap Grow R	VFGRX	C-	(800) 539-3863		C+ / 5.9	3.58	6.51	12.00 /82	11.75 /51	12.10 /61	0.00	2.72
MC	Victory Special Value A	SSVSX	C-	(800) 539-3863		C- / 3.1	-1.21	2.80	2.51 /24	10.68 /44	8.96 /36	0.00	1.31
MC	Victory Special Value C	VSVCX	C-	(800) 539-3863		C- / 3.4	-1.38	2.40	1.62 /20	9.70 /37	7.98 /30	0.00	2.20
MC	Victory Special Value I	VSPIX	C	(800) 539-3863		C- / 4.2	-1.15	2.95	2.76 /25	10.97 /45	9.29 /39	0.00	1.01
MC	Victory Special Value R	VSVGX	C-	(800) 539-3863		C- / 3.8	-1.26	2.66	2.22 /23	10.33 /41	8.63 /34	0.00	1.61
GR	Victory Sycamore Established Val A	VETAX	B+	(800) 539-3863		B+ / 8.6	4.73	12.78	13.80 /89	17.24 /91	15.07 /87	0.90	1.04
GR	Victory Sycamore Established Val I	VEVIX	A	(800) 539-3863		A / 9.4	4.81	12.98	14.25 /90	17.70 /93	15.47 /90	1.28	0.66
GR	Victory Sycamore Established Val R	GETGX	A-	(800) 539-3863		A- / 9.2	4.68	12.70	13.62 /88	17.06 /90	14.88 /86	0.82	1.20
GR	Victory Sycamore Established Val R6	VEVRX	U	(800) 539-3863		U /	4.81	12.98	14.24 /90	--	--	1.29	0.91
SC	Victory Sycamore Small Co Oppty A	SSGSX	C	(800) 539-3863		C+ / 5.8	2.42	11.52	5.77 /44	14.10 /68	13.26 /71	0.00	1.31
SC	Victory Sycamore Small Co Oppty I	VSOIX	B-	(800) 539-3863		B- / 7.1	2.53	11.74	6.14 /48	14.50 /71	13.66 /75	0.21	0.98
SC	Victory Sycamore Small Co Oppty R	GOGFX	C+	(800) 539-3863		C+ / 6.6	2.38	11.39	5.48 /42	13.82 /66	13.00 /68	0.00	1.58
SC	Victory Sycamore Small Co Oppty Y	VSOYX	U	(800) 539-3863		U /	2.47	11.63	5.92 /46	--	--	0.06	1.18
FO	Victory Trivalent Intl Core Eq A	MAICX	D+	(800) 539-3863		C- / 3.2	5.02	1.52	1.97 /22	10.35 /42	6.54 /20	0.98	2.01
FO	Victory Trivalent Intl Core Eq C	MICCX	D+	(800) 539-3863		C- / 3.5	4.73	1.04	1.19 /19	9.50 /36	5.73 /15	0.29	3.48
FO	Victory Trivalent Intl Core Eq I	MICIX	C-	(800) 539-3863		C / 4.5	5.16	1.87	2.61 /25	11.03 /46	7.16 /24	1.37	8.54
FO	Victory Trivalent Intl Core Eq Y	MICYX	C-	(800) 539-3863		C- / 4.2	5.02	1.64	2.23 /23	10.58 /43	6.82 /22	1.29	1.37
FO	Victory Trivalent Intl Sm Cap A	MISAX	C	(800) 539-3863		C+ / 5.6	6.65	4.81	1.09 /19	14.52 /71	12.77 /66	1.13	1.67
FO	Victory Trivalent Intl Sm Cap C	MCISX	C+	(800) 539-3863		C+ / 6.0	6.38	4.35	0.30 /16	13.71 /65	11.91 /60	0.71	2.42
FO	Victory Trivalent Intl Sm Cap I	MISIX	C+	(800) 539-3863		C+ / 6.9	6.72	4.94	1.50 /20	15.03 /75	13.28 /71	1.50	1.27
FO	Victory Trivalent Intl Sm Cap Y	MYSIX	C+	(800) 539-3863		C+ / 6.7	6.64	4.81	1.27 /19	14.81 /73	13.02 /68	1.37	1.45
BA	Villere Balanced	VILLX	C-	(866) 209-1129		C / 4.4	4.40	1.86	2.67 /25	10.97 /45	14.22 /80	1.17	0.87
GR	Villere Equity	VLEQX	U	(866) 209-1129		U /	5.18	2.40	2.40 /24	--	--	0.00	1.26
GL	Virtus Allocator Prem AlphaSector A	VAAAX	D-	(800) 243-1574		E+ / 0.7	-1.14	-3.98	-2.76 / 9	4.23 /11	--	0.61	1.88
GL	Virtus Allocator Prem AlphaSector C	VAACX	D-	(800) 243-1574		E+ / 0.7	-1.34	-4.32	-3.50 / 8	3.48 / 9	--	0.00	2.63
GL	Virtus Allocator Prem AlphaSector I	VAISX	D	(800) 243-1574		E+ / 0.9	-1.04	-3.86	-2.52 / 9	4.48 /11	--	0.89	1.63
GR	Virtus AlphaSector Rotation A	PWBAX	D-	(800) 243-1574		C- / 3.9	-3.20	-1.93	2.89 /26	12.81 /58	11.28 /55	0.63	0.99
GR	Virtus AlphaSector Rotation C	PWBCX	D-	(800) 243-1574		C / 4.3	-3.34	-2.27	2.17 /23	12.00 /52	10.49 /49	0.18	1.74
GR	Virtus AlphaSector Rotation I	VARIX	D-	(800) 243-1574		C / 5.0	-3.12	-1.80	3.14 /27	13.08 /60	11.55 /57	0.82	0.74
FS	Virtus Alternative Income Sol I	VAIIX	U	(804) 333-7384		U /	1.48	-1.61	--	--	--	0.00	3.73
GR	Virtus Alternative Inflation Sol I	VIASX	U	(804) 333-7384		U /	0.30	-0.92	--	--	--	0.00	3.99
GI	Virtus Alternative Total Sol I	VATIX	U	(804) 333-7384		U /	2.02	0.67	--	--	--	0.00	3.89
AA	Virtus Alternatives Diversifier A	PDPAX	D	(800) 243-1574		E / 0.5	-0.18	-1.16	-1.54 /11	2.19 / 7	3.91 / 8	1.79	1.70
AA	Virtus Alternatives Diversifier C	PDPCX	D	(800) 243-1574		E+ / 0.6	-0.36	-1.48	-2.30 /10	1.41 / 6	3.13 / 6	1.12	2.45
AA	Virtus Alternatives Diversifier I	VADIX	D	(800) 243-1574		E+ / 0.7	-0.18	-1.02	-1.37 /12	2.43 / 7	4.16 / 9	2.17	1.45
BA	Virtus Balanced A	PHBLX	D	(800) 243-1574		D / 2.1	2.09	2.92	4.08 /32	8.13 /28	8.73 /35	1.78	1.10
BA	● Virtus Balanced B	PBCBX	D+	(800) 243-1574		D+ / 2.5	1.83	2.48	3.29 /28	7.31 /23	7.92 /29	1.13	1.85
BA	Virtus Balanced C	PSBCX	D+	(800) 243-1574		D+ / 2.5	1.86	2.45	3.29 /28	7.30 /23	7.92 /29	1.19	1.85
MC	Virtus Contrarian Value A	FMIVX	D+	(800) 243-1574		C- / 3.2	-0.99	-0.98	-1.73 /11	11.85 /51	12.54 /64	0.81	1.40

99 Pct = Best
0 Pct = Worst

● Denotes fund is closed to new investors
* Denotes fund is included in Section II

www.thestreetratings.com

RISK			NET ASSETS		ASSET					BULL / BEAR		FUND MANAGER		MINIMUMS		LOADS	
	3 Year		NAV						Portfolio	Last Bull	Last Bear	Manager	Manager	Initial	Additional	Front	Back
Risk Rating/Pts	Standard Deviation	Beta	As of 3/31/15	Total $(Mil)	Cash %	Stocks %	Bonds %	Other %	Turnover Ratio	Market Return	Market Return	Quality Pct	Tenure (Years)	Purch. $	Purch. $	End Load	End Load
C+ / 5.6	9.6	1.00	22.26	16	3	96	0	1	3	93.3	-16.6	51	7	0	0	0.0	0.0
C / 5.5	9.6	1.00	22.39	44	3	96	0	1	3	96.6	-16.5	59	7	1,000,000	0	0.0	0.0
C+ / 5.7	11.0	0.96	43.66	1,306	0	99	0	1	37	96.2	-19.0	70	14	2,500	250	5.8	0.0
C / 5.4	11.0	0.96	38.88	260	0	99	0	1	37	91.3	-19.3	60	14	2,500	250	0.0	0.0
C+ / 5.6	11.0	0.96	42.58	59	0	99	0	1	37	94.4	-19.1	66	14	0	0	0.0	0.0
U /	N/A	N/A	45.42	692	0	99	0	1	37	N/A	N/A	N/A	14	0	0	0.0	0.0
C+ / 5.7	11.0	0.96	45.18	4,240	0	99	0	1	37	97.9	-18.9	72	14	1,000,000	0	0.0	0.0
C+ / 5.6	10.8	0.75	13.69	4	5	94	0	1	83	77.6	-21.4	93	1	2,500	250	5.8	0.0
C+ / 5.6	10.8	0.75	13.53	3	5	94	0	1	83	73.0	-21.7	92	1	2,500	250	0.0	0.0
C+ / 5.6	10.8	0.75	13.71	5	5	94	0	1	83	79.0	-21.3	94	1	2,000,000	0	0.0	0.0
C / 4.7	12.0	1.06	18.46	22	3	96	0	1	47	79.1	-18.2	13	12	2,500	250	5.8	0.0
C / 4.4	12.0	1.07	16.51	10	3	96	0	1	47	74.4	-18.5	9	12	2,500	250	0.0	0.0
C / 4.8	12.0	1.06	18.72	132	3	96	0	1	47	81.1	-18.1	15	12	2,000,000	0	0.0	0.0
C / 4.6	12.0	1.06	17.65	1	3	96	0	1	47	77.1	-18.3	11	12	0	0	0.0	0.0
C+ / 6.9	10.9	0.89	22.06	60	0	99	0	1	174	74.9	-27.0	17	N/A	2,500	250	5.8	0.0
C+ / 6.9	10.9	0.89	20.08	14	0	99	0	1	174	69.7	-27.2	11	N/A	2,500	250	0.0	0.0
C+ / 6.9	10.9	0.89	22.34	8	0	99	0	1	174	76.7	-26.9	19	N/A	2,000,000	0	0.0	0.0
C+ / 6.9	10.9	0.89	21.22	53	0	99	0	1	174	73.1	-27.1	15	N/A	0	0	0.0	0.0
C+ / 5.9	10.0	0.95	35.20	1,038	2	97	0	1	51	102.0	-20.8	82	17	2,500	250	5.8	0.0
C+ / 5.9	10.0	0.95	35.20	580	2	97	0	1	51	104.7	-20.7	85	17	2,000,000	0	0.0	0.0
C+ / 5.9	10.0	0.95	34.84	718	2	97	0	1	51	100.8	-20.8	81	17	0	0	0.0	0.0
U /	N/A	N/A	35.20	34	2	97	0	1	51	N/A	N/A	N/A	17	0	0	0.0	0.0
C+ / 5.9	12.9	0.93	40.18	454	5	94	0	1	47	85.6	-20.8	54	17	2,500	250	5.8	0.0
C+ / 5.8	12.9	0.93	40.47	1,773	5	94	0	1	47	87.9	-20.7	60	17	2,000,000	0	0.0	0.0
C+ / 5.8	12.9	0.93	38.27	297	5	94	0	1	47	84.1	-20.9	51	17	0	0	0.0	0.0
U /	N/A	N/A	40.24	84	5	94	0	1	47	N/A	N/A	N/A	17	0	0	0.0	0.0
C+ / 6.0	13.0	0.96	6.91	6	1	98	0	1	61	60.0	-27.1	78	8	2,500	250	5.8	0.0
C+ / 6.0	13.0	0.97	6.87	1	1	98	0	1	61	55.9	-27.4	70	8	2,500	250	0.0	0.0
C+ / 5.9	13.1	0.97	6.93	N/A	1	98	0	1	61	63.1	-27.0	82	8	2,000,000	0	0.0	0.0
C+ / 5.9	13.1	0.97	6.90	19	1	98	0	1	61	61.5	-27.1	79	8	1,000,000	0	0.0	0.0
C+ / 6.2	12.9	0.92	11.23	46	2	97	0	1	54	80.0	-23.1	94	8	2,500	250	5.8	0.0
C+ / 6.2	12.9	0.91	11.01	3	2	97	0	1	54	75.6	-23.4	93	8	2,500	250	0.0	0.0
C+ / 6.2	12.9	0.91	11.28	245	2	97	0	1	54	83.0	-23.0	95	8	2,000,000	0	0.0	0.0
C+ / 6.2	13.0	0.92	11.24	145	2	97	0	1	54	81.8	-23.1	94	8	1,000,000	0	0.0	0.0
C+ / 6.0	8.0	1.08	24.42	808	3	71	25	1	25	63.7	-12.8	56	16	2,000	500	0.0	0.0
U /	N/A	N/A	11.16	46	9	90	0	1	13	N/A	N/A	N/A	2	2,000	500	0.0	2.0
B- / 7.2	6.4	0.92	10.44	100	0	70	28	2	337	22.5	-8.6	18	N/A	2,500	100	5.8	0.0
B- / 7.1	6.4	0.93	10.33	235	0	70	28	2	337	19.5	-8.8	13	N/A	2,500	100	0.0	0.0
B- / 7.2	6.4	0.92	10.47	156	0	70	28	2	337	23.5	-8.4	19	N/A	100,000	0	0.0	0.0
C- / 3.0	8.8	0.83	11.49	300	0	100	0	0	129	63.4	-11.1	62	6	2,500	100	5.8	0.0
D+ / 2.9	8.7	0.83	11.29	293	0	100	0	0	129	59.4	-11.3	51	6	2,500	100	0.0	0.0
C- / 3.0	8.8	0.83	11.50	270	0	100	0	0	129	64.7	-10.9	65	6	100,000	0	0.0	0.0
U /	N/A	N/A	9.69	41	0	0	0	100	49	N/A	N/A	N/A	1	100,000	0	0.0	0.0
U /	N/A	N/A	9.95	32	0	0	0	100	31	N/A	N/A	N/A	1	100,000	0	0.0	0.0
U /	N/A	N/A	10.09	71	0	0	0	100	195	N/A	N/A	N/A	1	100,000	0	0.0	0.0
B- / 7.7	8.0	1.09	11.02	34	6	56	36	2	27	21.8	-14.9	2	7	2,500	100	5.8	0.0
B- / 7.6	8.1	1.10	10.92	33	6	56	36	2	27	18.8	-15.0	2	7	2,500	100	0.0	0.0
B- / 7.7	8.1	1.09	11.01	46	6	56	36	2	27	22.9	-14.8	2	7	100,000	0	0.0	0.0
C+ / 6.8	6.9	1.16	15.18	542	3	57	38	2	57	50.9	-12.3	15	3	2,500	100	5.8	0.0
C+ / 6.8	7.0	1.17	15.10	1	3	57	38	2	57	47.1	-12.6	10	3	2,500	100	0.0	0.0
C+ / 6.8	6.9	1.16	15.06	47	3	57	38	2	57	47.0	-12.6	10	3	2,500	100	0.0	0.0
C+ / 6.1	11.5	0.91	36.18	192	2	97	0	1	15	90.8	-22.8	23	18	2,500	100	5.8	0.0

```
99 Pct = Best
0 Pct = Worst
```

Fund Type	Fund Name	Ticker Symbol	Overall Investment Rating	Phone	Performance Rating/Pts	3 Mo	6 Mo	1Yr / Pct	3Yr / Pct	5Yr / Pct	Dividend Yield	Expense Ratio
MC	Virtus Contrarian Value C	FMICX	D+	(800) 243-1574	C- / 3.6	-1.17	-1.36	-2.44 /10	11.02 /46	11.71 /59	0.16	2.15
MC	Virtus Contrarian Value I	PIMVX	C-	(800) 243-1574	C / 4.3	-0.93	-0.87	-1.48 /12	12.12 /53	12.83 /67	1.13	1.15
GR	Virtus Dynamic AlphaSector A	EMNAX	E+	(800) 243-1574	D / 1.6	-2.49	-7.06	-5.35 / 5	9.59 /37	3.86 / 8	0.00	2.88
GR	● Virtus Dynamic AlphaSector B	EMNBX	E+	(800) 243-1574	D / 1.9	-2.74	-7.42	-6.05 / 4	8.77 /31	3.05 / 6	0.00	3.63
GR	Virtus Dynamic AlphaSector C	EMNCX	E+	(800) 243-1574	D / 1.9	-2.75	-7.46	-6.08 / 4	8.76 /31	3.08 / 6	0.00	3.63
GR	Virtus Dynamic AlphaSector I	VIMNX	D-	(800) 243-1574	D+ / 2.5	-2.46	-6.96	-5.05 / 5	9.86 /39	4.17 / 9	0.00	2.63
EM	Virtus Emerging Markets Eqty Inc I	VEIIX	U	(800) 243-1574	U /	-0.10	-3.87	-1.37 /12	--	--	2.30	1.76
EM	Virtus Emerging Mkt Opp A	HEMZX	E	(800) 243-1574	E+ / 0.6	1.77	-1.15	5.06 /39	2.14 / 6	7.52 /27	0.59	1.57
EM	Virtus Emerging Mkt Opp C	PICEX	E	(800) 243-1574	E+ / 0.7	1.60	-1.53	4.24 /33	1.40 / 6	6.71 /21	0.07	2.32
EM	Virtus Emerging Mkt Opp I	HIEMX	E	(800) 243-1574	E+ / 0.9	1.82	-1.07	5.37 /41	2.40 / 7	7.79 /29	0.86	1.37
FO	Virtus Foreign Opportunities A	JVIAX	D-	(800) 243-1574	D- / 1.1	2.05	1.33	0.39 /17	6.00 /17	7.59 /27	0.77	1.43
FO	Virtus Foreign Opportunities C	JVICX	D-	(800) 243-1574	D- / 1.4	1.89	0.96	-0.36 /15	5.22 /14	6.79 /22	0.21	2.18
FO	Virtus Foreign Opportunities I	JVXIX	D	(800) 243-1574	D / 1.8	2.13	1.47	0.65 /17	6.27 /18	7.86 /29	1.08	1.18
GL	Virtus Global Commodities Stock A	VGCAX	E-	(800) 243-1574	E- / 0.1	-5.05	-16.45	-22.49 / 1	-9.37 / 1	--	0.00	1.82
GL	Virtus Global Commodities Stock C	VGCCX	E-	(800) 243-1574	E- / 0.1	-5.29	-16.85	-23.14 / 1	-9.98 / 1	--	0.00	2.57
GL	Virtus Global Commodities Stock I	VGCIX	E-	(800) 243-1574	E- / 0.1	-4.88	-16.23	-22.26 / 1	-9.06 / 1	--	0.00	1.57
UT	Virtus Global Dividend A	PGUAX	D+	(800) 243-1574	C- / 3.1	-0.86	-0.30	3.73 /30	10.81 /44	11.29 /55	3.64	1.29
UT	Virtus Global Dividend C	PGUCX	C-	(800) 243-1574	C- / 3.5	-1.09	-0.67	2.92 /26	10.00 /39	10.46 /48	3.18	2.04
UT	Virtus Global Dividend I	PGIUX	C-	(800) 243-1574	C- / 4.2	-0.80	-0.11	3.98 /32	11.10 /46	11.58 /58	4.11	1.04
GL	Virtus Global Opportunities A	NWWOX	C-	(800) 243-1574	C- / 3.6	2.43	4.89	7.01 /55	10.47 /42	11.77 /59	0.54	1.48
GL	● Virtus Global Opportunities B	WWOBX	C-	(800) 243-1574	C- / 4.0	2.19	4.50	6.19 /48	9.67 /37	10.95 /52	0.21	2.23
GL	Virtus Global Opportunities C	WWOCX	C-	(800) 243-1574	C- / 4.0	2.21	4.52	6.22 /48	9.65 /37	10.96 /52	0.20	2.23
GL	Virtus Global Opportunities I	WWOIX	C	(800) 243-1574	C / 4.7	2.43	4.95	7.19 /57	10.69 /44	11.91 /60	0.82	1.23
GL	Virtus Global Premium AlphaSector A	VGPAX	E+	(800) 243-1574	E+ / 0.7	-1.59	-6.63	-5.18 / 5	5.42 /15	--	0.56	1.91
GL	Virtus Global Premium AlphaSector C	VGPCX	E+	(800) 243-1574	E+ / 0.8	-1.80	-7.06	-5.90 / 5	4.64 /12	--	0.00	2.66
GL	Virtus Global Premium AlphaSector I	VGPIX	E+	(800) 243-1574	D- / 1.0	-1.59	-6.58	-5.05 / 5	5.64 /15	--	0.89	1.66
RE	Virtus Global Real Estate Sec A	VGSAX	C	(800) 243-1574	C+ / 6.5	4.15	13.72	17.65 /95	12.33 /55	13.41 /72	2.17	1.57
RE	Virtus Global Real Estate Sec C	VGSCX	C+	(800) 243-1574	B- / 7.0	4.01	13.37	16.81 /94	11.50 /49	12.58 /65	1.79	2.32
RE	Virtus Global Real Estate Sec I	VGISX	B-	(800) 243-1574	B / 7.8	4.24	13.90	17.95 /95	12.62 /57	13.71 /75	2.47	1.32
FO	Virtus Greater European Opport Fd A	VGEAX	D-	(800) 243-1574	D- / 1.4	2.96	1.79	-4.10 / 7	7.55 /24	8.02 /30	0.63	1.92
FO	Virtus Greater European Opport Fd C	VGECX	D-	(800) 243-1574	D / 1.7	2.72	1.44	-4.81 / 6	6.74 /20	7.24 /25	0.00	2.67
FO	Virtus Greater European Opport Fd I	VGEIX	D	(800) 243-1574	D / 2.2	3.02	1.94	-3.82 / 7	7.79 /26	8.28 /32	0.95	1.67
GI	Virtus Growth & Income A	PDIAX	C	(800) 243-1574	C / 5.3	0.38	5.67	9.75 /73	13.42 /63	12.21 /62	0.32	1.39
GI	Virtus Growth & Income C	PGICX	C+	(800) 243-1574	C+ / 5.8	0.21	5.24	8.91 /69	12.56 /56	11.37 /56	0.02	2.14
GI	Virtus Growth & Income I	PXIIX	C+	(800) 243-1574	C+ / 6.5	0.48	5.78	10.06 /75	13.67 /65	12.49 /64	0.45	1.14
FO	Virtus International Equity Fund A	VIEAX	D-	(800) 243-1574	D / 1.6	5.56	0.09	-1.98 /10	7.79 /26	--	0.67	2.43
FO	Virtus International Equity Fund C	VIECX	D-	(800) 243-1574	D / 1.9	5.45	-0.16	-2.63 / 9	6.95 /21	--	0.11	3.18
FO	Virtus International Equity Fund I	VIIEX	D-	(800) 243-1574	D+ / 2.6	5.68	0.24	-1.66 /11	8.04 /27	--	0.95	2.18
FO	Virtus International Small-Cap I	VIISX	U	(804) 333-7384	U /	5.24	-1.41	-3.31 / 8	--	--	3.21	1.50
FO	Virtus Intl Real Estate Sec A	PXRAX	C-	(800) 243-1574	C- / 4.2	4.21	5.50	9.56 /72	10.93 /45	10.69 /50	6.39	1.73
FO	Virtus Intl Real Estate Sec C	PXRCX	C-	(800) 243-1574	C / 4.6	4.06	5.31	8.90 /69	10.10 /40	9.89 /44	5.87	2.48
FO	Virtus Intl Real Estate Sec I	PXRIX	C	(800) 243-1574	C / 5.3	4.21	5.74	9.96 /74	11.21 /47	10.97 /52	7.01	1.48
MC	Virtus Mid Cap Growth A	PHSKX	C-	(800) 243-1574	C / 4.4	5.07	11.25	10.50 /76	10.51 /42	10.90 /52	0.00	1.45
MC	● Virtus Mid Cap Growth B	PSKBX	C-	(800) 243-1574	C / 4.8	4.91	10.87	9.68 /73	9.68 /37	10.08 /45	0.00	2.20
MC	Virtus Mid Cap Growth C	PSKCX	C-	(800) 243-1574	C / 4.8	4.85	10.81	9.68 /73	9.68 /37	10.08 /45	0.00	2.20
MC	Virtus Mid Cap Growth I	PICMX	C	(800) 243-1574	C / 5.5	5.15	11.42	10.79 /78	10.78 /44	11.19 /54	0.00	1.20
MC	Virtus Mid-Cap Core Fund A	VMACX	A+	(800) 243-1574	A / 9.5	6.04	16.62	22.75 /98	16.97 /90	15.46 /90	0.00	3.09
MC	Virtus Mid-Cap Core Fund C	VMCCX	A+	(800) 243-1574	A+ / 9.6	5.83	16.16	21.84 /97	16.12 /84	14.59 /83	0.00	3.84
MC	Virtus Mid-Cap Core Fund I	VIMCX	A+	(800) 243-1574	A+ / 9.8	6.09	16.76	23.05 /98	17.27 /91	15.73 /91	0.00	2.84
GI	Virtus Premium AlphaSector A	VAPAX	E	(800) 243-1574	D- / 1.4	-3.86	-6.90	-3.54 / 8	8.88 /32	--	0.26	1.61
GI	Virtus Premium AlphaSector C	VAPCX	E	(800) 243-1574	D / 1.6	-4.00	-7.25	-4.30 / 6	8.07 /27	--	0.00	2.36
GI	Virtus Premium AlphaSector I	VAPIX	E	(800) 243-1574	D / 2.2	-3.77	-6.76	-3.28 / 8	9.18 /34	--	0.46	1.36

● Denotes fund is closed to new investors
* Denotes fund is included in Section II

RISK			NET ASSETS		ASSET				BULL / BEAR			FUND MANAGER		MINIMUMS		LOADS	
	3 Year		NAV														
Risk Rating/Pts	Standard Deviation	Beta	As of 3/31/15	Total $(Mil)	Cash %	Stocks %	Bonds %	Other %	Portfolio Turnover Ratio	Last Bull Market Return	Last Bear Market Return	Manager Quality Pct	Manager Tenure (Years)	Initial Purch. $	Additional Purch. $	Front End Load	Back End Load
C+ / 6.1	11.4	0.91	34.62	61	2	97	0	1	15	86.1	-23.0	17	18	2,500	100	0.0	0.0
C+ / 6.1	11.5	0.91	36.18	176	2	97	0	1	15	92.5	-22.7	26	18	100,000	0	0.0	0.0
C / 4.7	10.2	0.86	10.56	285	55	44	0	1	233	37.7	-7.5	19	1	2,500	100	5.8	0.0
C / 4.4	10.2	0.86	9.60	N/A	55	44	0	1	233	34.3	-8.0	14	1	2,500	100	0.0	0.0
C / 4.3	10.2	0.86	9.54	348	55	44	0	1	233	34.3	-7.8	13	1	2,500	100	0.0	0.0
C / 4.8	10.2	0.86	10.72	545	55	44	0	1	233	39.2	-7.5	21	1	100,000	0	0.0	0.0
U /	N/A	N/A	9.93	69	3	96	0	1	72	N/A	N/A	N/A	3	100,000	0	0.0	0.0
C / 4.6	13.9	0.89	9.75	813	5	94	0	1	31	31.8	-12.7	81	9	2,500	100	5.8	0.0
C / 4.6	13.9	0.89	9.52	251	5	94	0	1	31	28.5	-13.0	75	9	2,500	100	0.0	0.0
C / 4.6	13.8	0.89	10.07	8,683	5	94	0	1	31	33.0	-12.7	83	9	100,000	0	0.0	0.0
C+ / 6.3	11.3	0.77	28.33	492	2	97	0	1	31	45.7	-14.0	49	13	2,500	100	5.8	0.0
C+ / 6.4	11.3	0.77	28.09	122	2	97	0	1	31	42.0	-14.3	38	13	2,500	100	0.0	0.0
C+ / 6.3	11.3	0.77	28.35	1,331	2	97	0	1	31	47.0	-13.9	53	13	100,000	0	0.0	0.0
D+ / 2.5	15.1	0.83	6.96	N/A	2	97	0	1	164	-7.2	-26.0	0	4	2,500	100	5.8	0.0
D+ / 2.5	15.1	0.83	6.81	N/A	2	97	0	1	164	-9.4	-26.2	0	4	2,500	100	0.0	0.0
D+ / 2.5	15.1	0.83	7.02	10	2	97	0	1	164	-6.2	-25.9	0	4	100,000	0	0.0	0.0
C+ / 6.5	9.5	0.47	15.01	74	9	90	0	1	24	55.6	-9.6	93	11	2,500	100	5.8	0.0
C+ / 6.5	9.5	0.47	14.95	46	9	90	0	1	24	51.9	-10.0	91	11	2,500	100	0.0	0.0
C+ / 6.5	9.5	0.47	15.02	65	9	90	0	1	24	57.1	-9.6	93	11	100,000	0	0.0	0.0
C+ / 6.4	11.0	0.74	12.65	89	1	98	0	1	41	67.9	-9.1	89	6	2,500	100	5.8	0.0
C+ / 6.4	11.0	0.74	11.19	1	1	98	0	1	41	63.8	-9.4	87	6	2,500	100	0.0	0.0
C+ / 6.4	11.0	0.74	11.12	9	1	98	0	1	41	63.9	-9.4	86	6	2,500	100	0.0	0.0
C+ / 6.8	11.0	0.74	12.63	40	1	98	0	1	41	69.0	-9.1	90	6	100,000	0	0.0	0.0
C / 5.5	9.0	1.30	10.50	36	0	99	0	1	205	29.6	-13.0	7	4	2,500	100	5.8	0.0
C / 5.5	9.0	1.30	10.35	38	0	99	0	1	205	26.5	-13.4	5	4	2,500	100	0.0	0.0
C / 5.5	9.0	1.30	10.52	37	0	99	0	1	205	30.7	-13.0	7	4	100,000	0	0.0	0.0
C / 5.3	12.0	0.93	27.88	37	11	88	0	1	29	74.7	-18.1	57	6	2,500	100	5.8	0.0
C / 5.3	12.0	0.94	27.48	8	11	88	0	1	29	70.2	-18.3	45	6	2,500	100	0.0	0.0
C / 5.3	12.0	0.93	28.04	40	11	88	0	1	29	76.1	-17.9	61	6	100,000	0	0.0	0.0
C+ / 6.2	11.2	0.78	15.29	13	4	95	0	1	65	51.0	-15.4	69	6	2,500	100	5.8	0.0
C+ / 6.3	11.2	0.78	15.10	1	4	95	0	1	65	47.3	-15.7	58	6	2,500	100	0.0	0.0
C+ / 6.2	11.2	0.78	15.33	6	4	95	0	1	65	52.3	-15.3	71	6	100,000	0	0.0	0.0
C+ / 6.3	10.2	1.01	20.97	117	2	97	0	1	283	89.8	-20.1	30	1	2,500	100	5.8	0.0
C+ / 6.1	10.2	1.01	19.42	37	2	97	0	1	283	84.9	-20.4	22	1	2,500	100	0.0	0.0
C+ / 6.2	10.1	1.01	20.96	9	2	97	0	1	283	91.4	-20.0	33	1	100,000	0	0.0	0.0
C / 5.3	10.6	0.76	10.83	2	6	93	0	1	115	43.2	-14.9	74	2	2,500	100	5.8	0.0
C / 5.3	10.6	0.76	10.65	1	6	93	0	1	115	39.0	-15.3	65	2	2,500	100	0.0	0.0
C / 5.2	10.6	0.75	10.79	4	6	93	0	1	115	43.8	-14.9	76	2	100,000	0	0.0	0.0
U /	N/A	N/A	12.26	46	10	89	0	1	44	N/A	N/A	N/A	3	100,000	0	0.0	0.0
C+ / 6.1	12.5	0.74	6.93	13	24	75	0	1	32	64.5	-21.0	91	8	2,500	100	5.8	0.0
C+ / 6.2	12.6	0.74	6.92	2	24	75	0	1	32	60.4	-21.3	88	8	2,500	100	0.0	0.0
C+ / 6.1	12.5	0.73	6.93	29	24	75	0	1	32	66.1	-21.0	91	8	100,000	0	0.0	0.0
C+ / 5.6	11.7	0.94	22.80	83	0	99	0	1	32	78.3	-26.8	11	3	2,500	100	5.8	0.0
C+ / 5.6	11.6	0.94	19.02	1	0	99	0	1	32	73.8	-27.1	8	3	2,500	100	0.0	0.0
C+ / 5.6	11.7	0.94	19.02	6	0	99	0	1	32	73.9	-27.1	8	3	2,500	100	0.0	0.0
C+ / 5.7	11.7	0.94	23.26	3	0	99	0	1	32	79.8	-26.7	13	3	100,000	0	0.0	0.0
B- / 7.0	10.5	0.88	23.00	13	2	97	0	1	30	98.4	-16.3	83	6	2,500	100	5.8	0.0
B- / 7.0	10.5	0.87	22.13	4	2	97	0	1	30	93.3	-16.6	79	6	2,500	100	0.0	0.0
B- / 7.0	10.5	0.88	23.17	5	2	97	0	1	30	100.0	-16.3	85	6	100,000	0	0.0	0.0
C- / 3.3	8.8	0.81	12.96	1,161	0	99	0	1	227	46.8	-11.6	19	1	2,500	100	5.8	0.0
C- / 3.2	8.9	0.82	12.72	1,358	0	99	0	1	227	43.1	-11.8	13	1	2,500	100	0.0	0.0
C- / 3.3	8.9	0.82	13.00	1,556	0	99	0	1	227	48.0	-11.5	20	1	100,000	0	0.0	0.0

99 Pct = Best
0 Pct = Worst

Fund Type	Fund Name	Ticker Symbol	Overall Investment Rating	Phone	Perfor- mance Rating/Pts	3 Mo	6 Mo	1Yr / Pct	3Yr / Pct	5Yr / Pct	Dividend Yield	Expense Ratio
GR	Virtus Quality Large-Cap Value A	PPTAX	B-	(800) 243-1574	C+ / 5.7	0.06	6.05	11.45 /80	13.74 /65	12.03 /61	0.74	1.43
GR	Virtus Quality Large-Cap Value C	PPTCX	B-	(800) 243-1574	C+ / 6.1	-0.13	5.62	10.64 /77	12.89 /59	11.20 /54	0.53	2.18
GR	Virtus Quality Large-Cap Value I	PIPTX	B-	(800) 243-1574	C+ / 6.8	0.06	6.10	11.72 /81	14.02 /67	12.31 /63	1.02	1.18
SC	Virtus Quality SmCap A	PQSAX	C	(800) 243-1574	C / 5.3	3.04	14.62	9.33 /71	12.34 /55	13.94 /77	0.15	1.32
SC	Virtus Quality SmCap C	PQSCX	C	(800) 243-1574	C+ / 5.8	2.82	14.19	8.49 /66	11.49 /49	13.08 /69	0.00	2.07
SC	Virtus Quality SmCap I	PXQSX	C+	(800) 243-1574	C+ / 6.5	3.10	14.74	9.59 /72	12.61 /57	14.21 /80	0.39	1.07
RE	Virtus Real Estate Securities A	PHRAX	C	(800) 243-1574	B / 8.2	4.16	19.98	23.31 /98	12.98 /60	15.40 /90	1.02	1.38
RE	● Virtus Real Estate Securities B	PHRBX	C+	(800) 243-1574	B+ / 8.6	3.96	19.51	22.35 /97	12.12 /53	14.54 /83	0.36	2.13
RE	Virtus Real Estate Securities C	PHRCX	C+	(800) 243-1574	B+ / 8.6	3.96	19.50	22.39 /97	12.14 /53	14.54 /83	0.41	2.13
RE	Virtus Real Estate Securities I	PHRIX	C+	(800) 243-1574	A- / 9.2	4.20	20.11	23.60 /98	13.25 /61	15.69 /91	1.30	1.13
SC	Virtus Small Cap Sustainable Gr A	PSGAX	B-	(800) 243-1574	B / 8.0	4.04	17.84	14.56 /91	15.63 /80	16.14 /94	0.00	1.57
SC	Virtus Small Cap Sustainable Gr C	PSGCX	B	(800) 243-1574	B+ / 8.4	3.82	17.45	13.68 /89	14.76 /73	15.26 /89	0.00	2.32
SC	Virtus Small Cap Sustainable Gr I	PXSGX	B+	(800) 243-1574	A- / 9.1	4.06	18.02	14.83 /91	15.94 /83	16.42 /95	0.00	1.32
SC	Virtus Small-Cap Core A	PKSAX	C+	(800) 243-1574	C / 5.5	3.64	13.42	13.28 /88	12.02 /53	14.50 /82	0.00	1.40
SC	Virtus Small-Cap Core C	PKSCX	C+	(800) 243-1574	C+ / 5.9	3.47	13.02	12.44 /85	11.20 /47	13.66 /75	0.00	2.15
SC	Virtus Small-Cap Core I	PKSFX	B	(800) 243-1574	B- / 7.0	3.67	13.52	13.57 /88	12.30 /55	14.79 /85	0.00	1.15
GR	Virtus Strategic Growth A	PSTAX	B	(800) 243-1574	B- / 7.5	5.49	11.65	19.29 /96	13.89 /66	12.89 /67	0.00	1.28
GR	● Virtus Strategic Growth B	PBTHX	B	(800) 243-1574	B / 7.9	5.30	11.24	18.40 /96	13.02 /60	12.06 /61	0.00	2.03
GR	Virtus Strategic Growth C	SSTFX	B	(800) 243-1574	B / 7.9	5.30	11.23	18.28 /96	13.02 /60	12.06 /61	0.00	2.03
GR	Virtus Strategic Growth I	PLXGX	A-	(800) 243-1574	B+ / 8.7	5.60	11.80	19.50 /96	14.15 /68	13.18 /70	0.00	1.03
AA	Virtus Tactical Allocation CL A	NAINX	D	(800) 243-1574	D+ / 2.3	1.91	2.62	3.60 /29	8.71 /31	8.94 /36	1.88	1.29
AA	● Virtus Tactical Allocation CL B	NBINX	D+	(800) 243-1574	D+ / 2.7	1.69	2.19	2.83 /26	7.91 /26	8.11 /31	1.18	2.04
AA	Virtus Tactical Allocation CL C	POICX	D+	(800) 243-1574	D+ / 2.7	1.69	2.13	2.81 /26	7.87 /26	8.10 /31	1.28	2.04
SC	Virtus Wealth Masters A	VWMAX	U	(804) 333-7384	U /	2.92	6.77	7.37 /58	--	--	0.28	1.46
SC	Virtus Wealth Masters C	VWMCX	U	(804) 333-7384	U /	2.68	6.39	6.61 /52	--	--	0.00	2.21
SC	Virtus Wealth Masters I	VWMIX	U	(804) 333-7384	U /	2.91	6.90	7.63 /60	--	--	0.49	1.21
GL	Vivaldi Orinda Hedged Equity A	OHEAX	E	(855) 467-4632	E+ / 0.6	0.36	3.11	-0.25 /15	2.20 / 7	--	0.00	3.75
GL	Vivaldi Orinda Hedged Equity I	OHEIX	E	(855) 467-4632	E+ / 0.8	0.44	3.24	0.07 /16	2.51 / 7	--	0.00	3.46
GR	Volumetric Fund	VOLMX	D-	(800) 541-3863	D / 1.6	-6.88	-3.56	-2.82 / 9	7.70 /25	8.33 /32	0.00	1.94
EM	● Vontobel Global Em Mkts Eq Inst I	VTGIX	U	(866) 252-5393	U /	1.82	-0.97	4.93 /38	--	--	1.92	1.00
GI	Voya Aggregate Bond Adv	IPRAX	D+	(800) 992-0180	D- / 1.3	1.89	3.94	5.52 /43	3.34 / 9	3.99 / 8	1.56	1.09
GI	Voya Aggregate Bond Inl	IPTIX	D+	(800) 992-0180	D- / 1.4	2.01	4.18	6.04 /47	3.83 /10	4.51 /10	2.06	0.59
GI	Voya Aggregate Bond Svc	IPTSX	D+	(800) 992-0180	D- / 1.3	1.94	4.14	5.85 /45	3.60 / 9	4.26 / 9	1.76	0.84
BA	Voya Balanced Inc I	IBPIX	C	(800) 992-0180	C- / 4.2	2.53	4.39	7.22 /57	9.87 /39	9.15 /38	1.54	0.69
BA	Voya Balanced Inc S	IBPSX	C	(800) 992-0180	C- / 4.1	2.41	4.20	6.93 /54	9.59 /37	8.87 /36	1.32	0.94
AA	Voya Capital Allocation A	ATLAX	D+	(800) 992-0180	D / 1.8	2.50	2.76	3.54 /29	7.51 /24	7.81 /29	2.54	1.52
AA	● Voya Capital Allocation B	ALYBX	C-	(800) 992-0180	D / 2.2	2.27	2.31	2.70 /25	6.70 /20	6.99 /23	1.71	2.27
AA	Voya Capital Allocation C	ACLGX	C-	(800) 992-0180	D / 2.2	2.39	2.38	2.86 /26	6.73 /20	7.00 /23	1.95	2.27
AA	Voya Capital Allocation I	ALEGX	C-	(800) 992-0180	D+ / 2.8	2.56	2.81	3.77 /30	7.79 /26	8.10 /31	2.92	1.17
AA	Voya Capital Allocation O	IDSIX	C-	(800) 992-0180	D+ / 2.7	2.51	2.79	3.57 /29	7.53 /24	7.79 /29	2.72	1.52
AA	Voya Capital Allocation W	IAFWX	C-	(800) 992-0180	D+ / 2.8	2.56	2.86	3.82 /31	7.82 /26	--	2.98	1.27
GI	Voya Corp Leaders Trust	LEXCX	B-	(800) 992-0180	C+ / 5.7	-3.07	0.49	4.73 /37	13.78 /66	15.10 /88	5.82	0.49
GR	Voya Corporate Leaders 100 A	IACLX	B-	(800) 992-0180	C+ / 6.7	-0.62	3.59	10.85 /78	16.00 /83	14.06 /78	0.88	0.97
GR	● Voya Corporate Leaders 100 B	IBCLX	B+	(800) 992-0180	B- / 7.1	-0.78	3.21	10.00 /74	15.14 /76	13.23 /70	0.00	1.72
GR	Voya Corporate Leaders 100 C	ICCLX	B+	(800) 992-0180	B- / 7.3	-0.73	3.33	10.27 /75	15.42 /78	13.40 /72	0.68	1.72
GR	Voya Corporate Leaders 100 I	IICLX	A	(800) 992-0180	B / 8.1	-0.51	3.84	11.19 /79	16.35 /86	14.38 /81	1.23	0.58
GR	Voya Corporate Leaders 100 O	IOCLX	A	(800) 992-0180	B / 7.8	-0.56	3.67	10.81 /78	15.99 /83	--	0.89	0.97
GR	Voya Corporate Leaders 100 R	IRCLX	A-	(800) 992-0180	B / 7.6	-0.62	3.52	10.61 /77	15.76 /81	--	0.75	1.22
GR	Voya Corporate Leaders 100 W	IWCLX	A	(800) 992-0180	B / 8.0	-0.51	3.80	11.14 /79	16.27 /85	14.34 /81	1.20	0.72
FO	Voya Diversified International A	IFFAX	E+	(800) 992-0180	D- / 1.1	4.55	0.76	-1.40 /12	5.92 /16	4.54 /10	4.01	1.66
FO	● Voya Diversified International B	IFFBX	D-	(800) 992-0180	D- / 1.3	4.24	0.28	-2.17 /10	5.11 /13	3.75 / 8	3.04	2.41
FO	Voya Diversified International C	IFFCX	D-	(800) 992-0180	D- / 1.3	4.37	0.37	-2.09 /10	5.13 /14	3.74 / 8	3.42	2.41

● Denotes fund is closed to new investors
* Denotes fund is included in Section II

RISK			NET ASSETS		ASSET					BULL / BEAR		FUND MANAGER		MINIMUMS		LOADS	
	3 Year		NAV						Portfolio	Last Bull	Last Bear	Manager	Manager	Initial	Additional	Front	Back
Risk Rating/Pts	Standard Deviation	Beta	As of 3/31/15	Total $(Mil)	Cash %	Stocks %	Bonds %	Other %	Turnover Ratio	Market Return	Market Return	Quality Pct	Tenure (Years)	Purch. $	Purch. $	End Load	End Load
B- / 7.6	9.6	0.96	15.40	55	3	96	0	1	23	83.3	-17.0	44	6	2,500	100	5.8	0.0
B- / 7.6	9.5	0.96	15.03	20	3	96	0	1	23	78.8	-17.3	34	6	2,500	100	0.0	0.0
B- / 7.6	9.6	0.96	15.40	10	3	96	0	1	23	84.9	-16.9	48	6	100,000	0	0.0	0.0
C+ / 5.9	13.6	0.90	16.61	75	3	96	0	1	24	70.6	-16.2	37	7	2,500	100	5.8	0.0
C+ / 5.8	13.6	0.90	16.41	26	3	96	0	1	24	66.3	-16.5	28	7	2,500	100	0.0	0.0
C+ / 5.9	13.6	0.90	16.64	163	3	96	0	1	24	72.1	-16.2	41	7	100,000	0	0.0	0.0
C- / 3.6	13.4	1.07	41.73	857	3	96	0	1	28	82.7	-16.5	39	17	2,500	100	5.8	0.0
C- / 3.6	13.4	1.07	41.11	2	3	96	0	1	28	78.1	-16.7	29	17	2,500	100	0.0	0.0
C- / 3.6	13.4	1.07	41.64	76	3	96	0	1	28	78.1	-16.7	29	17	2,500	100	0.0	0.0
C- / 3.6	13.4	1.07	41.69	759	3	96	0	1	28	84.3	-16.4	43	17	100,000	0	0.0	0.0
C / 5.4	12.5	0.85	17.53	84	3	96	0	1	23	81.5	-8.3	82	7	2,500	100	5.8	0.0
C / 5.3	12.5	0.85	16.32	16	3	96	0	1	23	76.8	-8.6	77	7	2,500	100	0.0	0.0
C / 5.4	12.5	0.85	17.70	33	3	96	0	1	23	83.1	-8.2	84	7	100,000	0	0.0	0.0
C+ / 6.7	9.9	0.65	25.65	68	4	95	0	1	31	69.7	-14.0	81	7	2,500	100	5.8	0.0
C+ / 6.7	9.9	0.65	22.98	34	4	95	0	1	31	65.4	-14.3	75	7	2,500	100	0.0	0.0
C+ / 6.7	9.9	0.65	26.58	249	4	95	0	1	31	71.1	-13.9	82	7	100,000	0	0.0	0.0
C+ / 6.2	10.4	0.97	14.23	434	0	99	0	1	26	95.1	-23.3	44	4	2,500	100	5.8	0.0
C+ / 6.1	10.4	0.97	11.93	2	0	99	0	1	26	90.1	-23.6	33	4	2,500	100	0.0	0.0
C+ / 6.1	10.4	0.98	11.93	12	0	99	0	1	26	90.3	-23.6	33	4	2,500	100	0.0	0.0
C+ / 6.2	10.5	0.98	14.53	9	0	99	0	1	26	96.9	-23.3	47	4	100,000	0	0.0	0.0
C+ / 6.5	7.8	1.31	9.75	181	2	61	35	2	61	53.1	-12.0	9	6	2,500	100	5.8	0.0
C+ / 6.6	7.8	1.31	9.88	N/A	2	61	35	2	61	49.3	-12.3	7	6	2,500	100	0.0	0.0
C+ / 6.6	7.8	1.31	9.96	6	2	61	35	2	61	49.3	-12.4	7	6	2,500	100	0.0	0.0
U /	N/A	N/A	15.17	62	0	99	0	1	62	N/A	N/A	N/A	3	2,500	100	5.8	0.0
U /	N/A	N/A	14.96	38	0	99	0	1	62	N/A	N/A	N/A	3	2,500	100	0.0	0.0
U /	N/A	N/A	15.21	47	0	99	0	1	62	N/A	N/A	N/A	3	100,000	0	0.0	0.0
C / 4.3	6.3	0.28	22.44	15	58	41	0	1	157	20.8	-9.4	61	4	5,000	0	5.0	1.0
C / 4.4	6.3	0.28	22.77	43	58	41	0	1	157	22.1	-9.3	66	4	500,000	0	0.0	1.0
C+ / 6.2	10.4	0.94	20.31	28	0	99	0	1	57	45.6	-16.7	5	37	500	200	0.0	0.0
U /	N/A	N/A	9.51	1,039	10	89	0	1	43	N/A	N/A	N/A	2	1,000,000	0	0.0	0.0
B / 8.4	3.4	0.02	11.86	160	4	0	95	1	874	14.0	-0.8	89	1	0	0	0.0	0.0
B / 8.3	3.4	0.02	12.20	177	4	0	95	1	874	15.9	-0.7	90	1	0	0	0.0	0.0
B / 8.4	3.4	0.02	12.08	286	4	0	95	1	874	15.0	-0.7	90	1	0	0	0.0	0.0
B- / 7.1	7.2	1.23	15.01	507	8	60	31	1	192	54.5	-13.0	22	8	0	0	0.0	0.0
B- / 7.2	7.2	1.23	14.90	5	8	60	31	1	192	53.1	-13.0	20	8	0	0	0.0	0.0
B- / 7.9	7.6	1.26	10.68	78	2	64	33	1	46	43.8	-13.1	7	8	1,000	0	5.8	0.0
B / 8.0	7.6	1.26	10.80	2	2	64	33	1	46	40.1	-13.4	5	8	1,000	0	0.0	0.0
B / 8.0	7.6	1.26	10.73	26	2	64	33	1	46	40.2	-13.4	5	8	1,000	0	0.0	0.0
B- / 7.9	7.5	1.25	10.83	15	2	64	33	1	46	45.3	-13.1	8	8	250,000	0	0.0	0.0
B- / 7.9	7.6	1.26	10.62	62	2	64	33	1	46	43.9	-13.2	7	8	1,000	0	0.0	0.0
B- / 7.9	7.6	1.26	10.82	N/A	2	64	33	1	46	45.2	N/A	8	8	1,000	0	0.0	0.0
B- / 7.5	9.3	0.89	32.16	1,639	1	98	0	1	277	90.7	-16.4	61	N/A	1,000	50	0.0	0.0
B- / 7.4	9.7	1.00	17.69	298	0	99	0	1	14	100.2	-16.5	65	7	1,000	0	5.8	0.0
B- / 7.3	9.7	1.01	17.71	2	0	99	0	1	14	95.4	-16.9	53	7	1,000	0	0.0	0.0
B- / 7.3	9.7	1.01	17.61	101	0	99	0	1	14	96.6	-16.8	57	7	1,000	0	0.0	0.0
B- / 7.4	9.7	1.00	17.69	285	0	99	0	1	14	101.8	-16.4	69	7	250,000	0	0.0	0.0
B- / 7.5	9.7	1.01	17.68	86	0	99	0	1	14	N/A	N/A	64	7	1,000	0	0.0	0.0
B- / 7.5	9.7	1.01	17.62	44	0	99	0	1	14	N/A	N/A	61	7	0	0	0.0	0.0
B- / 7.4	9.6	1.00	17.71	63	0	99	0	1	14	101.6	-16.4	69	7	1,000	0	0.0	0.0
C / 5.5	12.3	0.92	10.10	31	3	96	0	1	25	40.5	-24.0	30	10	1,000	0	5.8	0.0
C+ / 5.7	12.3	0.92	10.08	3	3	96	0	1	25	37.1	-24.3	21	10	1,000	0	0.0	0.0
C+ / 5.6	12.3	0.92	10.03	18	3	96	0	1	25	37.0	-24.2	22	10	1,000	0	0.0	0.0

99 Pct = Best
0 Pct = Worst

Fund Type	Fund Name	Ticker Symbol	Overall Investment Rating	Phone	PERFORMANCE Perfor- mance Rating/Pts	Total Return % through 3/31/15 3 Mo	6 Mo	1Yr / Pct	Annualized 3Yr / Pct	5Yr / Pct	Incl. in Returns Dividend Yield	Expense Ratio
FO	Voya Diversified International I	IFFIX	D-	(800) 992-0180	D / 1.7	4.56	0.86	-1.12 /13	6.17 /17	4.79 /11	4.56	1.36
FO	Voya Diversified International O	IFFOX	D-	(800) 992-0180	D / 1.6	4.60	0.78	-1.41 /12	5.95 /17	4.54 /10	4.31	1.66
FO	Voya Diversified International R	IFFRX	D-	(800) 992-0180	D- / 1.5	4.41	0.54	-1.65 /11	5.67 /15	4.28 / 9	4.00	1.91
FO	Voya Diversified International W	IDFWX	D-	(800) 992-0180	D / 1.7	4.58	0.81	-1.18 /12	6.15 /17	4.78 /11	4.61	1.41
FO	Voya Emerging Markets Equity Div A	IFCAX	E	(800) 992-0180	E / 0.3	-1.31	-7.58	-5.63 / 5	-0.30 / 4	0.39 / 3	2.26	2.50
FO	● Voya Emerging Markets Equity Div B	IFCBX	E	(800) 992-0180	E / 0.3	-1.56	-7.98	-6.36 / 4	-1.05 / 3	-0.38 / 2	1.16	3.25
FO	Voya Emerging Markets Equity Div C	IFCCX	E	(800) 992-0180	E / 0.3	-1.49	-7.90	-6.35 / 4	-1.05 / 3	-0.37 / 2	1.54	3.25
FO	Voya Emerging Markets Equity Div I	IFCIX	E	(800) 992-0180	E / 0.4	-1.30	-7.48	-5.41 / 5	-0.04 / 4	0.71 / 3	2.76	2.15
FO	Voya Emerging Markets Equity Div O	IFCOX	E	(800) 992-0180	E / 0.4	-1.32	-7.61	-5.64 / 5	-0.32 / 4	0.39 / 3	2.48	2.50
FO	Voya Emerging Markets Equity Div W	IFCWX	E	(800) 992-0180	E / 0.4	-1.23	-7.43	-5.34 / 5	-0.04 / 4	--	2.71	2.25
IN	Voya Fidelity VIP Equity-Inc Adv	VPEAX	C+	(800) 992-0180	C+ / 5.6	-0.08	1.75	5.59 /43	13.21 /61	11.53 /57	4.11	1.48
IN	Voya Fidelity VIP Equity-Inc S2	VPESX	B-	(800) 992-0180	C+ / 5.8	-0.08	1.83	5.81 /45	13.47 /63	11.80 /59	4.24	1.23
MC	Voya Fidelity VIP Mid Cap Adv	VPFAX	C+	(800) 992-0180	B- / 7.5	5.05	9.39	9.43 /72	14.59 /72	12.70 /66	4.55	1.56
MC	Voya Fidelity VIP Mid Cap S	VPFSX	C+	(800) 992-0180	B / 7.7	5.15	9.57	9.69 /73	14.85 /74	12.99 /68	4.83	1.56
GL	Voya Global Equity Dividend A	IAGEX	D	(800) 992-0180	D / 1.8	-0.23	-2.81	-1.28 /12	8.90 /32	7.52 /27	2.73	1.46
GL	● Voya Global Equity Dividend B	IBGEX	D	(800) 992-0180	D / 2.1	-0.38	-3.19	-1.97 /10	8.09 /27	6.73 /21	2.03	2.21
GL	Voya Global Equity Dividend C	ICGEX	D	(800) 992-0180	D / 2.1	-0.46	-3.17	-2.00 /10	8.05 /27	6.71 /21	2.09	2.21
GL	Voya Global Equity Dividend I	IGEIX	D+	(800) 992-0180	D+ / 2.8	-0.15	-2.72	-1.00 /13	9.25 /35	7.90 /29	3.19	1.11
GL	Voya Global Equity Dividend O	IDGEX	D+	(800) 992-0180	D+ / 2.6	-0.23	-2.83	-1.30 /13	8.88 /32	7.52 /27	2.89	1.46
GL	Voya Global Equity Dividend W	IGEWX	D+	(800) 992-0180	D+ / 2.7	-0.21	-2.76	-1.05 /13	9.15 /34	7.77 /28	2.88	1.21
EN	Voya Global Natural Resources A	LEXMX	E-	(800) 992-0180	E- / 0.2	-2.31	-18.33	-18.01 / 1	-2.95 / 2	0.17 / 3	0.37	1.57
EN	Voya Global Natural Resources I	IRGNX	E-	(800) 992-0180	E- / 0.2	-2.19	-18.19	-17.80 / 1	-2.57 / 3	0.54 / 3	0.79	1.21
EN	Voya Global Natural Resources W	IGNWX	E-	(800) 992-0180	E- / 0.2	-2.18	-18.22	-17.79 / 1	-2.71 / 2	0.43 / 3	0.49	1.32
RE	Voya Global Real Estate A	IGLAX	C-	(800) 992-0180	C / 5.3	3.84	11.39	14.59 /91	11.01 /45	10.26 /47	2.13	1.26
RE	● Voya Global Real Estate B	IGBAX	C-	(800) 992-0180	C+ / 5.7	3.58	10.97	13.71 /89	10.19 /40	9.44 /40	2.17	2.01
RE	Voya Global Real Estate C	IGCAX	C-	(800) 992-0180	C+ / 5.7	3.64	10.98	13.79 /89	10.21 /41	9.45 /40	1.98	2.01
RE	Voya Global Real Estate I	IGLIX	C	(800) 992-0180	C+ / 6.5	3.89	11.60	14.94 /92	11.32 /48	10.61 /50	2.55	0.98
RE	Voya Global Real Estate O	IDGTX	C	(800) 992-0180	C+ / 6.3	3.84	11.41	14.61 /91	11.01 /45	10.28 /47	2.28	1.26
RE	Voya Global Real Estate R	IGARX	C	(800) 992-0180	C+ / 6.1	3.75	11.25	14.34 /90	10.76 /44	--	2.08	1.51
FO	Voya Global Real Estate R6	VGRQX	U	(800) 992-0180	U /	3.94	11.65	--	--	--	0.00	0.87
RE	Voya Global Real Estate W	IRGWX	C	(800) 992-0180	C+ / 6.5	3.88	11.52	14.86 /91	11.31 /48	10.54 /49	2.51	1.01
GL	Voya Global Target Payment A	IGPAX	D+	(800) 992-0180	D / 1.7	2.58	3.33	4.69 /36	7.09 /22	6.89 /22	5.76	1.32
GL	Voya Global Target Payment C	IGPCX	C-	(800) 992-0180	D / 2.1	2.36	2.95	3.88 /31	6.29 /18	6.09 /17	5.38	2.07
GL	Voya Global Target Payment I	IGPIX	C-	(800) 992-0180	D+ / 2.7	2.57	3.51	4.89 /38	7.37 /23	7.15 /24	6.43	1.06
GL	Voya Global Target Payment R	IGPRX	C-	(800) 992-0180	D+ / 2.4	2.43	3.23	4.45 /35	6.87 /21	--	5.88	1.57
GL	Voya Global Target Payment W	IGPWX	C-	(800) 992-0180	D+ / 2.7	2.66	3.48	4.98 /38	7.37 /23	7.15 /24	6.40	1.07
GL	Voya Global Val Advantage A	NAWGX	D-	(800) 992-0180	D- / 1.3	3.95	1.79	-0.13 /15	6.33 /18	5.08 /12	3.05	1.49
GL	● Voya Global Val Advantage B	NAWBX	D-	(800) 992-0180	D- / 1.5	3.77	1.40	-0.90 /13	5.53 /15	4.29 / 9	2.01	2.24
GL	Voya Global Val Advantage C	NAWCX	D-	(800) 992-0180	D- / 1.5	3.74	1.39	-0.90 /13	5.54 /15	4.29 / 9	2.67	2.24
GL	Voya Global Val Advantage I	NAWIX	D-	(800) 992-0180	D / 2.0	4.02	1.91	0.10 /16	6.56 /19	5.36 /14	3.52	1.21
GL	Voya Global Val Advantage W	IGVWX	D-	(800) 992-0180	D / 2.0	3.99	1.92	0.11 /16	6.61 /20	5.35 /14	3.44	1.24
GL	Voya Global Value Advantage Adv	IGHAX	C-	(800) 992-0180	C- / 4.2	4.06	4.29	7.11 /56	9.73 /38	7.39 /26	2.54	1.27
GL	Voya Global Value Advantage S	IGHSX	C-	(800) 992-0180	C / 4.4	4.13	4.36	7.30 /57	9.98 /39	7.66 /28	2.76	1.02
GI	Voya Growth and Income Adv	IAVGX	C+	(800) 992-0180	C+ / 6.8	1.88	4.78	10.60 /77	14.13 /68	12.60 /65	1.51	1.09
GI	Voya Growth and Income I	IIVGX	C+	(800) 992-0180	B- / 7.2	1.99	5.03	11.13 /79	14.67 /72	13.12 /69	1.95	0.59
GI	Voya Growth and Income S	ISVGX	C+	(800) 992-0180	B- / 7.0	1.91	4.89	10.85 /78	14.37 /70	12.83 /67	1.71	0.84
GR	Voya Growth Opportunities A	NLCAX	C+	(800) 992-0180	B- / 7.5	4.06	9.33	17.93 /95	14.95 /75	16.07 /93	0.00	1.48
GR	● Voya Growth Opportunities B	NLCBX	B-	(800) 992-0180	B / 8.1	3.90	9.01	17.20 /95	14.20 /69	15.32 /89	0.00	2.13
GR	Voya Growth Opportunities C	NLCCX	B-	(800) 992-0180	B / 8.1	3.92	9.00	17.19 /95	14.20 /69	15.33 /89	0.00	2.13
GR	Voya Growth Opportunities I	PLCIX	B+	(800) 992-0180	B+ / 8.8	4.19	9.56	18.39 /96	15.38 /78	16.47 /95	0.00	0.91
GR	Voya Growth Opportunities W	IGOWX	B+	(800) 992-0180	B+ / 8.8	4.19	9.54	18.37 /96	15.34 /78	16.48 /95	0.00	1.13
AA	Voya Index Solution 2015 Adv	ISAAX	C-	(800) 992-0180	D+ / 2.6	2.07	3.73	5.78 /45	6.95 /21	6.56 /20	1.93	1.18

● Denotes fund is closed to new investors
* Denotes fund is included in Section II

www.thestreetratings.com

RISK			NET ASSETS		ASSET					BULL / BEAR		FUND MANAGER		MINIMUMS		LOADS	
	3 Year		NAV						Portfolio	Last Bull	Last Bear	Manager	Manager	Initial	Additional	Front	Back
Risk	Standard		As of	Total	Cash	Stocks	Bonds	Other	Turnover	Market	Market	Quality	Tenure	Purch.	Purch.	End	End
Rating/Pts	Deviation	Beta	3/31/15	$(Mil)	%	%	%	%	Ratio	Return	Return	Pct	(Years)	$	$	Load	Load
C / 5.5	12.4	0.92	10.08	4	3	96	0	1	25	41.8	-24.0	32	10	250,000	0	0.0	0.0
C / 5.5	12.4	0.92	10.00	5	3	96	0	1	25	40.5	-24.0	30	10	1,000	0	0.0	0.0
C / 5.5	12.4	0.92	9.95	N/A	3	96	0	1	25	39.5	-24.1	26	10	0	0	0.0	0.0
C / 5.5	12.4	0.92	10.04	1	3	96	0	1	25	41.8	-23.9	32	10	1,000	0	0.0	0.0
C- / 3.6	13.4	0.79	12.09	10	3	96	0	1	46	20.3	-26.8	4	3	1,000	0	5.8	0.0
C- / 3.8	13.5	0.79	11.96	N/A	3	96	0	1	46	17.2	-27.0	3	3	1,000	0	0.0	0.0
C- / 3.7	13.4	0.79	11.88	2	3	96	0	1	46	17.3	-27.0	3	3	1,000	0	0.0	0.0
C- / 3.6	13.4	0.79	12.13	1	3	96	0	1	46	21.6	-26.7	4	3	250,000	0	0.0	0.0
C- / 3.6	13.4	0.79	11.95	3	3	96	0	1	46	20.3	-26.8	4	3	1,000	0	0.0	0.0
C- / 3.6	13.4	0.79	12.09	N/A	3	96	0	1	46	21.4	N/A	4	3	1,000	0	0.0	0.0
B- / 7.1	9.2	0.93	12.23	N/A	8	87	0	5	32	80.6	-17.9	45	4	0	0	0.0	0.0
B- / 7.1	9.2	0.93	12.23	12	8	87	0	5	32	82.0	-17.8	48	4	0	0	0.0	0.0
C / 4.8	11.5	1.01	17.47	1	0	99	0	1	132	77.6	-21.3	34	14	0	0	0.0	0.0
C / 4.8	11.5	1.00	17.75	39	0	99	0	1	132	79.1	-21.3	38	14	0	0	0.0	0.0
C+ / 6.7	11.2	0.80	13.04	43	4	96	0	0	40	55.3	-16.9	79	9	1,000	0	5.8	0.0
C+ / 6.7	11.2	0.80	13.01	2	4	96	0	0	40	51.4	-17.1	72	9	1,000	0	0.0	0.0
C+ / 6.7	11.3	0.81	12.94	29	4	96	0	0	40	51.3	-17.1	72	9	1,000	0	0.0	0.0
C+ / 6.7	11.2	0.80	13.06	8	4	96	0	0	40	56.9	-16.7	81	9	250,000	0	0.0	0.0
C+ / 6.7	11.2	0.80	13.01	14	4	96	0	0	40	55.3	-16.9	79	9	1,000	0	0.0	0.0
C+ / 6.7	11.2	0.80	14.40	1	4	96	0	0	40	56.4	-16.7	80	9	1,000	0	0.0	0.0
D+ / 2.9	17.0	1.05	8.46	62	2	97	0	1	58	11.7	-30.1	4	5	1,000	0	5.8	0.0
D+ / 2.9	16.9	1.04	8.49	5	2	97	0	1	58	12.9	-30.0	5	5	250,000	0	0.0	0.0
D+ / 2.9	17.0	1.05	10.75	1	2	97	0	1	58	12.6	-30.0	5	5	1,000	0	0.0	0.0
C / 5.0	12.6	0.92	21.10	1,174	11	88	0	1	40	64.5	-18.5	41	14	1,000	0	5.8	0.0
C / 5.0	12.6	0.92	17.05	6	11	88	0	1	40	60.4	-18.8	31	14	1,000	0	0.0	0.0
C / 5.0	12.6	0.93	18.21	215	11	88	0	1	40	60.3	-18.8	31	14	1,000	0	0.0	0.0
C / 5.0	12.6	0.92	21.11	3,312	11	88	0	1	40	66.1	-18.4	45	14	250,000	0	0.0	0.0
C / 5.0	12.6	0.92	21.10	14	11	88	0	1	40	64.5	-18.5	41	14	1,000	0	0.0	0.0
C / 5.0	12.6	0.92	21.04	2	11	88	0	1	40	63.1	N/A	38	14	0	0	0.0	0.0
U /	N/A	N/A	21.12	104	11	88	0	1	40	N/A	N/A	N/A	14	1,000,000	0	0.0	0.0
C / 5.0	12.6	0.92	21.15	405	11	88	0	1	40	65.9	-18.5	45	14	1,000	0	0.0	0.0
B- / 7.8	6.5	1.01	8.84	130	6	55	37	2	22	40.9	-14.0	40	7	1,000	0	5.8	0.0
B- / 7.8	6.5	1.01	9.14	137	6	55	37	2	22	37.4	-14.2	29	7	1,000	0	0.0	0.0
B- / 7.8	6.5	1.01	8.82	87	6	55	37	2	22	42.1	-13.9	44	7	250,000	0	0.0	0.0
B- / 7.8	6.5	1.01	8.83	N/A	6	55	37	2	22	39.7	N/A	36	7	0	0	0.0	0.0
B- / 7.8	6.5	1.01	8.81	31	6	55	37	2	22	42.2	-13.9	43	7	1,000	0	0.0	0.0
C+ / 5.7	13.9	1.01	31.29	178	2	97	0	1	57	25.1	-15.1	25	3	1,000	0	5.8	0.0
C+ / 5.7	13.9	1.01	33.89	2	2	97	0	1	57	21.9	-15.3	17	3	1,000	0	0.0	0.0
C+ / 5.7	13.9	1.01	29.13	106	2	97	0	1	57	21.9	-15.3	18	3	1,000	0	0.0	0.0
C+ / 5.7	13.9	1.01	31.58	39	2	97	0	1	57	26.1	-14.9	27	3	250,000	0	0.0	0.0
C+ / 5.7	13.9	1.01	31.55	3	2	97	0	1	57	26.2	-14.9	27	3	1,000	0	0.0	0.0
C+ / 5.9	11.5	0.83	9.48	26	2	97	0	1	122	51.3	-19.9	83	2	0	0	0.0	0.0
C+ / 5.9	11.5	0.83	9.58	509	2	97	0	1	122	52.8	-19.8	84	2	0	0	0.0	0.0
C+ / 5.7	9.7	1.00	30.85	1,322	3	96	0	1	87	93.3	-18.2	41	11	0	0	0.0	0.0
C+ / 5.7	9.7	1.00	31.24	2,127	3	96	0	1	87	96.3	-18.0	49	11	0	0	0.0	0.0
C+ / 5.7	9.7	1.00	30.89	777	3	96	0	1	87	94.6	-18.1	45	11	0	0	0.0	0.0
C / 5.3	10.3	1.00	32.77	66	0	99	0	1	133	98.8	-14.6	52	6	1,000	0	5.8	0.0
C / 5.1	10.3	1.00	29.28	1	0	99	0	1	133	94.4	-14.8	42	6	1,000	0	0.0	0.0
C / 5.0	10.3	1.00	29.18	28	0	99	0	1	133	94.5	-14.8	42	6	1,000	0	0.0	0.0
C / 5.5	10.3	1.00	35.56	29	0	99	0	1	133	101.3	-14.5	58	6	250,000	0	0.0	0.0
C / 5.5	10.3	1.00	34.83	5	0	99	0	1	133	101.1	-14.5	57	6	1,000	0	0.0	0.0
B- / 7.8	4.9	0.81	10.85	115	0	38	61	1	43	36.2	-8.3	42	7	0	0	0.0	0.0

						PERFORMANCE							
	99 Pct = Best							Total Return % through 3/31/15				Incl. in Returns	
	0 Pct = Worst					Perfor-					Annualized	Dividend	Expense
Fund			Ticker	Overall Investment		mance							
Type	Fund Name		Symbol	Rating	Phone	Rating/Pts	3 Mo	6 Mo	1Yr / Pct	3Yr / Pct	5Yr / Pct	Yield	Ratio
AA	Voya Index Solution 2015 I		ISSIX	C-	(800) 992-0180	D+ / 2.9	2.12	3.94	6.29 /49	7.46 /24	7.08 /24	2.37	0.68
AA	Voya Index Solution 2015 S		ISASX	C-	(800) 992-0180	D+ / 2.7	2.05	3.78	5.96 /46	7.18 /22	6.81 /22	2.12	0.93
AA	Voya Index Solution 2015 T		ISATX	C-	(800) 992-0180	D+ / 2.4	1.96	3.51	5.56 /43	6.72 /20	6.36 /19	1.76	1.43
AA	Voya Index Solution 2025 Adv		ISDAX	C	(800) 992-0180	C- / 3.9	2.44	4.25	6.25 /49	9.43 /36	8.50 /33	1.56	1.17
AA	Voya Index Solution 2025 I		ISDIX	C	(800) 992-0180	C / 4.3	2.56	4.52	6.77 /53	9.96 /39	9.04 /37	1.94	0.67
AA	Voya Index Solution 2025 S		ISDSX	C	(800) 992-0180	C- / 4.1	2.50	4.29	6.50 /51	9.69 /37	8.76 /35	1.75	0.92
AA	Voya Index Solution 2025 T		ISDTX	C	(800) 992-0180	C- / 3.8	2.43	4.24	6.15 /48	9.24 /35	8.28 /32	1.32	1.42
AA	Voya Index Solution 2035 Adv		ISEAX	C	(800) 992-0180	C / 4.8	2.53	4.47	6.72 /53	11.02 /46	9.64 /42	1.36	1.17
AA	Voya Index Solution 2035 I		ISEIX	C+	(800) 992-0180	C / 5.2	2.64	4.81	7.30 /57	11.57 /50	10.16 /46	1.73	0.67
AA	Voya Index Solution 2035 S		ISESX	C+	(800) 992-0180	C / 5.0	2.59	4.59	6.97 /55	11.30 /48	9.90 /44	1.55	0.92
AA	Voya Index Solution 2035 T		ISETX	C	(800) 992-0180	C / 4.7	2.52	4.46	6.64 /52	10.83 /44	9.42 /40	1.14	1.42
AA	Voya Index Solution 2045 Adv		ISJAX	C+	(800) 992-0180	C / 5.2	2.63	4.61	7.10 /56	11.68 /50	10.16 /46	1.10	1.17
AA	Voya Index Solution 2045 I		ISJIX	C+	(800) 992-0180	C+ / 5.6	2.81	5.00	7.67 /60	12.25 /54	10.72 /50	1.43	0.67
AA	Voya Index Solution 2045 S		ISJSX	C+	(800) 992-0180	C / 5.4	2.76	4.89	7.46 /59	11.98 /52	10.44 /48	1.26	0.92
AA	Voya Index Solution 2045 T		ISJTX	C+	(800) 992-0180	C / 5.1	2.54	4.59	6.96 /56	11.46 /49	9.93 /44	0.84	1.42
GI	Voya Index Solution 2050 Adv		IDXPX	C+	(800) 992-0180	C / 5.0	2.56	4.47	6.89 /54	11.45 /49	--	1.24	83.70
GI	Voya Index Solution 2050 I		IDXQX	C+	(800) 992-0180	C / 5.4	2.68	4.73	7.45 /59	12.02 /53	--	1.69	83.20
GI	Voya Index Solution 2050 S		IDXRX	C+	(800) 992-0180	C / 5.3	2.68	4.73	7.18 /57	11.74 /51	--	1.46	83.45
GI	Voya Index Solution 2050 S2		IDXSX	C+	(800) 992-0180	C / 5.1	2.63	4.54	7.04 /55	11.56 /49	--	1.31	83.70
GI	Voya Index Solution 2050 T		IDXTX	C+	(800) 992-0180	C / 4.9	2.57	4.41	6.71 /53	11.26 /47	--	1.13	83.95
GL	Voya Index Solution 2055 Adv		IISAX	C+	(800) 992-0180	C / 5.3	2.59	4.80	7.35 /58	11.78 /51	10.26 /47	0.90	1.22
GL	Voya Index Solution 2055 I		IISNX	C+	(800) 992-0180	C+ / 5.6	2.68	5.00	7.85 /62	12.30 /55	10.78 /51	1.18	0.72
GL	Voya Index Solution 2055 S		IISSX	C+	(800) 992-0180	C / 5.5	2.63	4.90	7.61 /60	12.06 /53	10.52 /49	1.05	0.97
GL	Voya Index Solution 2055 S2		IISTX	C+	(800) 992-0180	C / 5.4	2.65	4.86	7.41 /58	11.88 /52	10.37 /48	0.90	1.22
GL	Voya Index Solution 2055 T		ITISX	C+	(800) 992-0180	C / 5.1	2.59	4.73	7.16 /56	11.57 /50	10.04 /45	0.66	1.47
AA	Voya Index Solution Income Adv		ISKAX	C-	(800) 992-0180	D / 2.2	1.90	3.57	5.81 /45	6.31 /18	6.16 /18	2.01	1.17
AA	Voya Index Solution Income I		ISKIX	C-	(800) 992-0180	D+ / 2.6	2.04	3.88	6.36 /50	6.86 /21	6.71 /21	2.40	0.67
AA	Voya Index Solution Income S		ISKSX	C-	(800) 992-0180	D+ / 2.4	2.06	3.72	6.13 /48	6.60 /19	6.43 /20	2.16	1.17
AA	Voya Index Solution Income T		ISKTX	C-	(800) 992-0180	D / 2.1	1.98	3.54	5.70 /44	6.14 /17	5.98 /17	1.76	1.42
FO	Voya International Core I		IICFX	E+	(800) 992-0180	D+ / 2.8	4.89	2.85	1.92 /22	7.89 /26	--	0.86	1.05
FO	Voya International Core W		IICWX	U	(800) 992-0180	U /	5.00	2.85	1.92 /22	--	--	0.86	1.05
FO	Voya International Index Adv		IIIAX	D-	(800) 992-0180	D+ / 2.6	5.11	0.62	-1.94 /10	8.14 /28	5.53 /14	0.83	1.05
FO	Voya International Index I		IIIIX	D	(800) 992-0180	D+ / 2.9	5.34	0.92	-1.41 /12	8.67 /31	6.05 /17	0.82	0.55
FO	Voya International Index S		INTIX	D	(800) 992-0180	D+ / 2.7	5.27	0.82	-1.73 /11	8.40 /29	5.78 /16	0.60	0.80
RE	Voya International Real Estate A		IIRAX	D+	(800) 992-0180	C- / 4.2	4.92	5.63	9.18 /70	11.02 /46	8.19 /31	4.19	1.42
RE	● Voya International Real Estate B		IIRBX	C-	(800) 992-0180	C / 4.7	4.82	5.32	8.45 /66	10.24 /41	7.40 /26	3.66	2.17
RE	Voya International Real Estate C		IIRCX	C-	(800) 992-0180	C / 4.6	4.71	5.23	8.39 /66	10.19 /40	7.39 /26	3.71	2.17
RE	Voya International Real Estate I		IIRIX	C-	(800) 992-0180	C / 5.4	5.03	5.79	9.50 /72	11.36 /48	8.53 /33	4.74	1.12
RE	Voya International Real Estate W		IIRWX	C-	(800) 992-0180	C / 5.4	5.02	5.74	9.41 /72	11.31 /48	8.47 /33	4.67	1.17
GR	Voya Large Cap Growth A		ILCAX	B+	(800) 992-0180	B / 7.8	4.16	9.32	17.96 /95	15.44 /79	--	0.02	1.23
GR	Voya Large Cap Growth Adv		IEOPX	B+	(800) 992-0180	B+ / 8.9	4.10	9.32	17.99 /95	15.60 /80	15.15 /88	0.07	1.43
GR	Voya Large Cap Growth C		ILCCX	A-	(800) 992-0180	B+ / 8.3	3.88	8.94	17.07 /95	14.58 /72	--	0.00	1.98
GR	Voya Large Cap Growth I		ILCIX	A+	(800) 992-0180	A- / 9.0	4.14	9.48	18.26 /96	15.79 /82	--	0.21	0.94
GR	Voya Large Cap Growth Inst		IEOHX	A-	(800) 992-0180	A- / 9.2	4.24	9.65	18.68 /96	16.20 /85	15.79 /92	0.45	0.68
GR	Voya Large Cap Growth R		ILCRX	A	(800) 992-0180	B+ / 8.6	4.03	9.24	17.62 /95	15.16 /76	--	0.00	1.48
GR	Voya Large Cap Growth R6		ILCZX	U	(800) 992-0180	U /	4.13	9.50	18.36 /96	--	--	0.23	0.94
GR	Voya Large Cap Growth Svc		IEOSX	A-	(800) 992-0180	A- / 9.0	4.16	9.49	18.32 /96	15.90 /83	15.49 /90	0.30	0.93
GR	Voya Large Cap Growth Svc 2		IEOTX	A-	(800) 992-0180	A- / 9.0	4.13	9.43	18.17 /96	15.75 /81	15.33 /89	0.17	1.18
GR	Voya Large Cap Growth W		ILCWX	A+	(800) 992-0180	A- / 9.0	4.14	9.53	18.24 /96	15.73 /81	--	0.18	0.98
GI	Voya Large Cap Value A		IEDAX	C+	(800) 992-0180	C / 5.5	0.43	3.62	7.82 /61	14.10 /68	13.32 /71	1.50	1.17
IN	Voya Large Cap Value Adv		IPEAX	B-	(800) 992-0180	C+ / 6.3	0.41	3.52	7.74 /61	13.99 /67	13.53 /73	1.76	1.52
GI	● Voya Large Cap Value B		IBEDX	C+	(800) 992-0180	C+ / 5.9	0.26	3.23	7.04 /55	13.23 /61	12.47 /64	0.77	1.92

● Denotes fund is closed to new investors

* Denotes fund is included in Section II

644

Risk Rating/Pts	3 Year Standard Deviation	Beta	NAV As of 3/31/15	Total $(Mil)	Cash %	Stocks %	Bonds %	Other %	Portfolio Turnover Ratio	Last Bull Market Return	Last Bear Market Return	Manager Quality Pct	Manager Tenure (Years)	Initial Purch. $	Additional Purch. $	Front End Load	Back End Load
B- /7.7	4.9	0.81	11.07	27	0	38	61	1	43	38.5	-8.1	49	7	0	0	0.0	0.0
B- /7.8	4.9	0.81	10.97	113	0	38	61	1	43	37.2	-8.2	46	7	0	0	0.0	0.0
B- /7.9	4.9	0.81	10.91	N/A	0	38	61	1	43	35.2	-8.4	39	7	0	0	0.0	0.0
B- /7.5	7.1	1.21	11.77	248	2	61	35	2	40	52.7	-14.0	20	7	0	0	0.0	0.0
B- /7.5	7.1	1.22	12.02	50	2	61	35	2	40	55.4	-13.9	25	7	0	0	0.0	0.0
B- /7.5	7.1	1.20	11.90	201	2	61	35	2	40	54.1	-14.0	23	7	0	0	0.0	0.0
B- /7.6	7.1	1.21	11.81	N/A	2	61	35	2	40	51.8	-14.1	18	7	0	0	0.0	0.0
B- /7.0	8.7	1.49	12.16	220	4	80	14	2	45	65.3	-17.4	11	7	0	0	0.0	0.0
B- /7.0	8.7	1.48	12.43	36	4	80	14	2	45	68.2	-17.2	14	7	0	0	0.0	0.0
B- /7.0	8.7	1.49	12.30	157	4	80	14	2	45	66.9	-17.4	12	7	0	0	0.0	0.0
B- /7.1	8.7	1.49	12.19	N/A	4	80	14	2	45	64.4	-17.5	10	7	0	0	0.0	0.0
C+ /6.7	9.6	1.62	12.48	142	4	90	5	1	48	70.7	-19.3	7	7	0	0	0.0	0.0
C+ /6.7	9.6	1.62	12.81	22	4	90	5	1	48	73.5	-19.1	9	7	0	0	0.0	0.0
C+ /6.7	9.6	1.63	12.66	98	4	90	5	1	48	72.2	-19.2	8	7	0	0	0.0	0.0
C+ /6.8	9.6	1.63	12.53	N/A	4	90	5	1	48	69.5	-19.3	7	7	0	0	0.0	0.0
B- /7.4	9.5	0.95	14.03	N/A	2	93	4	1	39	N/A	N/A	22	4	0	0	0.0	0.0
B- /7.4	9.5	0.95	14.16	N/A	2	93	4	1	39	N/A	N/A	26	4	0	0	0.0	0.0
B- /7.4	9.4	0.94	14.17	N/A	2	93	4	1	39	N/A	N/A	25	4	0	0	0.0	0.0
B- /7.4	9.5	0.95	14.06	N/A	2	93	4	1	39	N/A	N/A	23	4	0	0	0.0	0.0
B- /7.4	9.5	0.95	13.98	N/A	2	93	4	1	39	N/A	N/A	20	4	0	0	0.0	0.0
C+ /6.8	9.6	1.49	15.07	34	1	93	4	2	50	71.0	-19.2	42	5	0	0	0.0	0.0
C+ /6.8	9.6	1.49	15.34	5	1	93	4	2	50	73.9	-19.1	49	5	0	0	0.0	0.0
C+ /6.8	9.7	1.49	15.21	23	1	93	4	2	50	72.4	-19.2	45	5	0	0	0.0	0.0
C+ /6.8	9.6	1.49	15.11	5	1	93	4	2	50	71.5	-19.2	44	5	0	0	0.0	0.0
C+ /6.9	9.6	1.48	15.05	N/A	1	93	4	2	50	69.7	-19.3	40	5	0	0	0.0	0.0
B- /7.6	4.0	0.65	10.73	36	0	31	68	1	39	30.4	-4.6	58	7	0	0	0.0	0.0
B- /7.6	4.1	0.66	10.98	5	0	31	68	1	39	32.8	-4.5	64	7	0	0	0.0	0.0
B- /7.6	4.1	0.66	10.88	125	0	31	68	1	39	31.5	-4.5	61	7	0	0	0.0	0.0
B- /7.7	4.1	0.66	10.81	N/A	0	31	68	1	39	29.5	-4.7	55	7	0	0	0.0	0.0
C- /3.4	11.2	0.82	9.66	269	3	96	0	1	93	49.3	-24.3	68	4	250,000	0	0.0	0.0
U /	N/A	N/A	9.66	36	3	96	0	1	93	N/A	N/A	N/A	4	1,000	0	0.0	0.0
C /5.3	13.3	1.01	9.66	932	2	97	0	1	3	48.3	-23.4	47	3	0	0	0.0	0.0
C /5.3	13.3	1.00	9.87	562	2	97	0	1	3	51.0	-23.3	55	3	0	0	0.0	0.0
C /5.3	13.3	1.00	9.79	95	2	97	0	1	3	49.7	-23.4	52	3	0	0	0.0	0.0
C /5.4	14.6	0.81	9.38	178	20	79	0	1	67	59.5	-20.7	65	9	1,000	0	5.8	0.0
C /5.4	14.6	0.81	9.35	1	20	79	0	1	67	55.5	-21.0	53	9	1,000	0	0.0	0.0
C /5.4	14.7	0.81	9.33	15	20	79	0	1	67	55.5	-20.9	52	9	1,000	0	0.0	0.0
C /5.4	14.6	0.80	9.39	444	20	79	0	1	67	61.2	-20.6	69	9	250,000	0	0.0	0.0
C /5.4	14.7	0.81	9.42	39	20	79	0	1	67	61.0	-20.6	67	9	1,000	0	0.0	0.0
C+ /6.8	10.1	0.99	15.28	7	2	97	0	1	75	N/A	N/A	60	3	1,000	0	5.8	0.0
C+ /6.0	10.1	1.00	19.82	2,478	1	98	0	1	77	99.3	-14.5	62	5	0	0	0.0	0.0
C+ /6.8	10.2	1.00	14.98	3	2	97	0	1	75	N/A	N/A	47	3	1,000	0	0.0	0.0
C+ /6.8	10.2	1.00	15.36	223	2	97	0	1	75	N/A	N/A	64	3	250,000	0	0.0	0.0
C+ /6.0	10.1	0.99	20.90	1,901	1	98	0	1	77	103.1	-14.4	70	5	0	0	0.0	0.0
C+ /6.8	10.2	1.00	15.24	1	2	97	0	1	75	N/A	N/A	55	3	0	0	0.0	0.0
U /	N/A	N/A	15.37	61	2	97	0	1	75	N/A	N/A	N/A	3	1,000,000	0	0.0	0.0
C+ /6.0	10.2	1.00	20.54	2,342	1	98	0	1	77	101.3	-14.4	65	5	0	0	0.0	0.0
C+ /6.0	10.1	0.99	20.43	86	1	98	0	1	77	100.3	-14.5	65	5	0	0	0.0	0.0
C+ /6.8	10.2	1.00	15.35	2	2	97	0	1	75	N/A	N/A	63	3	1,000	0	0.0	0.0
C+ /6.4	9.8	1.00	11.98	525	3	96	0	1	149	86.3	-15.7	41	4	1,000	0	5.8	0.0
B- /7.7	9.8	1.00	12.37	65	0	0	0	100	104	86.4	-15.8	39	4	0	0	0.0	0.0
C+ /6.4	9.8	1.00	11.92	6	3	96	0	1	149	81.5	-16.0	31	4	1,000	0	0.0	0.0

Fund Type	Fund Name	Ticker Symbol	Overall Investment Rating	Phone	Performance Rating/Pts	3 Mo	6 Mo	1Yr / Pct	3Yr / Pct	5Yr / Pct	Dividend Yield	Expense Ratio
GI	Voya Large Cap Value C	IEDCX	C+	(800) 992-0180	C+ / 5.9	0.26	3.16	7.05 /55	13.25 /61	12.46 /64	0.80	1.92
GI	Voya Large Cap Value I	IEDIX	C+	(800) 992-0180	C+ / 6.7	0.56	3.74	8.21 /64	14.47 /71	13.65 /74	1.90	0.81
IN	Voya Large Cap Value Inst	IPEIX	B-	(800) 992-0180	C+ / 6.8	0.56	3.80	8.41 /66	14.64 /72	14.22 /80	2.05	0.77
IN	Voya Large Cap Value O	ILVOX	U	(800) 992-0180	U /	0.43	3.63	7.85 /62	--	--	1.60	1.17
GI	Voya Large Cap Value R	IEDRX	C+	(800) 992-0180	C+ / 6.3	0.40	3.53	7.62 /60	13.89 /66	--	1.39	1.42
IN	Voya Large Cap Value R6	IEDZX	U	(800) 992-0180	U /	0.56	3.77	8.24 /65	--	--	1.92	0.81
IN	Voya Large Cap Value Svc	IPESX	B-	(800) 992-0180	C+ / 6.6	0.49	3.65	8.03 /63	14.36 /70	13.93 /77	1.89	1.02
GI	Voya Large Cap Value W	IWEDX	C+	(800) 992-0180	C+ / 6.6	0.44	3.66	8.07 /63	14.37 /70	13.61 /74	1.76	0.92
MC	Voya Mid Cap Opportunities A	NMCAX	C+	(800) 992-0180	B- / 7.0	5.13	12.34	14.51 /91	14.00 /67	15.35 /89	0.00	1.34
MC	● Voya Mid Cap Opportunities B	NMCBX	C+	(800) 992-0180	B- / 7.5	4.90	11.91	13.70 /89	13.17 /61	14.48 /82	0.00	2.09
MC	Voya Mid Cap Opportunities C	NMCCX	C	(800) 992-0180	B- / 7.5	4.94	11.94	13.69 /89	13.16 /61	14.49 /82	0.00	2.09
MC	Voya Mid Cap Opportunities I	NMCIX	B	(800) 992-0180	B+ / 8.4	5.23	12.49	14.88 /91	14.44 /70	15.81 /92	0.11	0.96
MC	Voya Mid Cap Opportunities O	NMCOX	B-	(800) 992-0180	B / 8.1	5.10	12.29	14.51 /91	13.99 /67	15.33 /89	0.00	1.34
MC	Voya Mid Cap Opportunities R6	IMOZX	U	(800) 992-0180	U /	5.26	12.58	15.02 /92	--	--	0.13	0.90
MC	Voya Mid Cap Opportunities W	IMOWX	B	(800) 992-0180	B+ / 8.3	5.20	12.45	14.82 /91	14.29 /69	15.64 /91	0.06	1.09
MC	Voya Mid Cap Opps Port Adv	IAMOX	C+	(800) 992-0180	B / 8.1	5.10	12.26	14.39 /90	14.03 /67	15.37 /89	0.24	1.30
MC	Voya Mid Cap Opps Port I	IIMOX	C+	(800) 992-0180	B+ / 8.5	5.27	12.60	15.00 /92	14.61 /72	15.95 /93	0.35	0.80
MC	Voya Mid Cap Opps Port S	ISMOX	C+	(800) 992-0180	B+ / 8.3	5.18	12.43	14.68 /91	14.33 /70	15.65 /91	0.29	1.05
MC	Voya Mid Cap Value Advantage A	AIMAX	D+	(800) 992-0180	C+ / 6.2	1.57	8.54	9.09 /70	14.60 /72	13.25 /71	1.45	1.02
MC	● Voya Mid Cap Value Advantage B	APMBX	D+	(800) 992-0180	C+ / 6.6	1.40	8.15	8.27 /65	13.73 /65	12.40 /63	0.00	1.77
MC	Voya Mid Cap Value Advantage C	APMCX	C-	(800) 992-0180	C+ / 6.8	1.48	8.27	8.56 /67	14.02 /67	12.70 /66	1.11	1.52
MC	Voya Mid Cap Value Advantage I	AIMIX	C-	(800) 992-0180	B- / 7.4	1.65	8.66	9.42 /72	14.93 /74	13.58 /74	1.79	0.68
MC	Voya Mid Cap Value Advantage O	IDMOX	C-	(800) 992-0180	B- / 7.2	1.56	8.51	9.11 /70	14.59 /72	13.25 /71	1.51	1.02
MC	Voya Mid Cap Value Advantage R	AIMRX	C-	(800) 992-0180	C+ / 6.9	1.53	8.41	8.85 /68	14.30 /69	12.98 /68	1.34	1.27
MC	Voya Mid Cap Value Advantage W	AIMWX	C-	(800) 992-0180	B- / 7.4	1.65	8.72	9.43 /72	14.85 /74	--	1.73	0.77
MC	Voya MidCap Opportunities R	IMORX	B-	(800) 992-0180	B / 7.9	5.05	12.15	14.23 /90	13.73 /65	--	0.01	1.59
FO	Voya Multi Manager Internatl SC A	NTKLX	D-	(800) 992-0180	D / 2.0	4.83	0.44	-4.52 / 6	9.06 /33	8.12 /31	0.63	1.78
FO	● Voya Multi Manager Internatl SC B	NAPBX	D	(800) 992-0180	D+ / 2.4	4.67	0.12	-5.15 / 5	8.35 /29	7.42 /26	0.00	2.43
FO	Voya Multi Manager Internatl SC C	NARCX	D	(800) 992-0180	D+ / 2.4	4.66	0.13	-5.15 / 5	8.34 /29	7.42 /26	0.10	2.43
FO	Voya Multi Manager Internatl SC I	NAPIX	D+	(800) 992-0180	C- / 3.2	4.98	0.70	-4.06 / 7	9.59 /37	8.65 /34	1.28	1.32
FO	Voya Multi Manager Internatl SC O	NAPOX	D	(800) 992-0180	D+ / 2.9	4.86	0.51	-4.41 / 6	9.17 /34	8.23 /31	0.88	1.68
FO	Voya Multi Manager Internatl SC W	ISCWX	D+	(800) 992-0180	C- / 3.1	4.92	0.62	-4.20 / 7	9.44 /36	8.50 /33	0.93	1.43
EM	Voya Multi Mgr Emg Mrkts Eqty A	IEMHX	E	(800) 992-0180	E- / 0.2	-0.95	-8.13	-5.24 / 5	-2.00 / 3	--	1.06	1.83
EM	Voya Multi Mgr Emg Mrkts Eqty C	IEMJX	E	(800) 992-0180	E / 0.3	-1.14	-8.52	-6.04 / 4	-2.75 / 2	--	0.12	2.58
EM	Voya Multi Mgr Emg Mrkts Eqty I	IEMGX	E	(800) 992-0180	E / 0.3	-0.76	-7.90	-4.92 / 6	-1.67 / 3	--	1.62	1.30
EM	Voya Multi Mgr Emg Mrkts Eqty R	IEMKX	E	(800) 992-0180	E / 0.3	-0.96	-8.20	-5.46 / 5	-2.22 / 3	--	0.82	2.08
EM	Voya Multi Mgr Emg Mrkts Eqty W	IEMLX	E	(800) 992-0180	E / 0.3	-0.86	-7.99	-5.02 / 5	-1.74 / 3	--	1.53	1.58
FO	Voya Multi-Manager Intl Eqty I	IIGIX	D-	(800) 992-0180	D+ / 2.6	5.69	2.46	-0.95 /13	7.88 /26	--	2.28	0.99
GI	Voya Multi-Manager Lg Cap Core	IPFAX	B	(800) 992-0180	B- / 7.3	0.45	6.68	13.03 /87	14.44 /70	11.39 /56	0.64	1.50
GI	Voya Multi-Manager Lg Cap Core Inst	IPPIX	B+	(800) 992-0180	B / 7.8	0.64	6.97	13.67 /89	15.12 /76	12.05 /61	1.14	0.75
GI	Voya Multi-Manager Lg Cap Core Svc	IPPSX	B	(800) 992-0180	B- / 7.5	0.58	6.82	13.36 /88	14.82 /73	11.75 /59	0.94	1.00
MC	Voya Multi-Manager Mid Cap Val I	IMCVX	C+	(800) 992-0180	A- / 9.0	3.91	10.25	10.79 /78	17.10 /90	--	1.10	0.87
RE	Voya Real Estate A	CLARX	C+	(800) 992-0180	B+ / 8.4	4.64	20.40	23.92 /98	13.08 /60	15.31 /89	2.04	1.29
RE	● Voya Real Estate B	CRBCX	C+	(800) 992-0180	B+ / 8.7	4.41	19.77	22.74 /98	12.17 /54	14.41 /82	1.44	2.04
RE	Voya Real Estate C	CRCRX	C+	(800) 992-0180	B+ / 8.5	4.24	18.86	22.17 /97	11.97 /52	14.29 /80	1.42	2.04
RE	Voya Real Estate I	CRARX	B-	(800) 992-0180	A- / 9.1	4.38	18.98	23.04 /98	13.09 /60	15.46 /90	2.37	0.91
RE	Voya Real Estate O	IDROX	B-	(800) 992-0180	A- / 9.2	4.60	20.37	23.95 /98	13.07 /60	15.31 /89	2.16	1.29
RE	Voya Real Estate R	CRWRX	B-	(800) 992-0180	A- / 9.1	4.55	20.27	23.63 /98	12.83 /58	--	2.00	1.54
RE	Voya Real Estate W	IREWX	C+	(800) 992-0180	B+ / 8.3	3.87	16.65	20.96 /97	12.37 /55	14.99 /87	1.95	1.04
GI	Voya Retirement Conservative Adv	IRCAX	C-	(800) 992-0180	D / 1.8	1.60	3.37	5.90 /46	5.29 /14	6.14 /18	3.01	1.18
GI	Voya Retirement Conservative I	IRCPX	C-	(800) 992-0180	D / 1.9	1.58	3.42	6.00 /46	5.43 /15	6.40 /19	3.25	0.68
AA	Voya Retirement Growth Adv	IRGPX	C+	(800) 992-0180	C- / 4.2	2.42	4.41	6.50 /51	9.99 /39	9.02 /37	1.58	1.14

● Denotes fund is closed to new investors
* Denotes fund is included in Section II

www.thestreetratings.com

RISK			NET ASSETS		ASSET					BULL / BEAR		FUND MANAGER		MINIMUMS		LOADS	
	3 Year		NAV						Portfolio	Last Bull	Last Bear	Manager	Manager	Initial	Additional	Front	Back
Risk Rating/Pts	Standard Deviation	Beta	As of 3/31/15	Total $(Mil)	Cash %	Stocks %	Bonds %	Other %	Turnover Ratio	Market Return	Market Return	Quality Pct	Tenure (Years)	Purch. $	Purch. $	End Load	End Load
C+ / 6.4	9.8	1.00	11.93	101	3	96	0	1	149	81.7	-16.0	31	4	1,000	0	0.0	0.0
C+ / 6.5	9.7	0.99	12.79	286	3	96	0	1	149	88.5	-15.6	47	4	250,000	0	0.0	0.0
B- / 7.7	9.8	1.01	12.57	640	0	0	0	100	104	90.2	-15.6	47	4	0	0	0.0	0.0
U /	N/A	N/A	11.97	30	3	96	0	1	149	N/A	N/A	N/A	4	1,000	0	0.0	0.0
C+ / 6.4	9.7	1.00	11.96	6	3	96	0	1	149	85.2	N/A	39	4	0	0	0.0	0.0
U /	N/A	N/A	12.78	264	3	96	0	1	149	N/A	N/A	N/A	4	1,000,000	0	0.0	0.0
B- / 7.7	9.8	1.00	12.43	1,021	0	0	0	100	104	88.6	-15.7	43	4	0	0	0.0	0.0
C+ / 6.5	9.7	1.00	12.75	51	3	96	0	1	149	87.9	-15.6	46	4	1,000	0	0.0	0.0
C / 5.1	11.1	0.95	23.99	375	1	98	0	1	92	87.7	-20.0	40	10	1,000	0	5.8	0.0
C / 4.4	11.0	0.94	20.11	4	1	98	0	1	92	83.0	-20.2	31	10	1,000	0	0.0	0.0
C / 4.4	11.1	0.95	19.96	131	1	98	0	1	92	83.0	-20.2	31	10	1,000	0	0.0	0.0
C / 5.3	11.1	0.95	26.35	712	1	98	0	1	92	90.3	-19.8	46	10	250,000	0	0.0	0.0
C / 5.1	11.0	0.94	23.91	56	1	98	0	1	92	87.6	-20.0	41	10	1,000	0	0.0	0.0
U /	N/A	N/A	26.40	130	1	98	0	1	92	N/A	N/A	N/A	10	1,000,000	0	0.0	0.0
C / 5.3	11.0	0.94	26.11	96	1	98	0	1	92	89.2	-19.9	45	10	1,000	0	0.0	0.0
C- / 3.8	11.1	0.95	15.24	146	0	99	0	1	81	87.9	-20.1	41	10	0	0	0.0	0.0
C- / 4.0	11.1	0.95	15.97	751	0	99	0	1	81	91.1	-19.9	48	10	0	0	0.0	0.0
C- / 3.8	11.1	0.95	15.42	614	0	99	0	1	81	89.4	-20.0	44	10	0	0	0.0	0.0
C- / 3.4	10.2	0.91	16.86	61	2	97	0	1	122	94.1	-22.6	58	3	1,000	0	5.8	0.0
C- / 3.2	10.2	0.90	15.22	N/A	2	97	0	1	122	89.1	-22.8	47	3	1,000	0	0.0	0.0
C- / 3.1	10.2	0.90	15.80	9	2	97	0	1	122	90.8	-22.7	51	3	1,000	0	0.0	0.0
C- / 3.4	10.2	0.91	17.26	11	2	97	0	1	122	96.1	-22.5	63	3	250,000	0	0.0	0.0
C- / 3.4	10.2	0.90	16.91	96	2	97	0	1	122	94.2	-22.6	59	3	1,000	0	0.0	0.0
C- / 3.3	10.1	0.90	16.62	21	2	97	0	1	122	92.4	-22.6	55	3	0	0	0.0	0.0
C- / 3.4	10.1	0.90	17.24	N/A	2	97	0	1	122	95.7	N/A	62	3	1,000	0	0.0	0.0
C / 5.0	11.0	0.94	23.73	2	1	98	0	1	92	86.2	N/A	38	10	0	0	0.0	0.0
C+ / 6.1	12.8	0.91	47.56	67	1	98	0	1	46	54.3	-24.7	71	10	1,000	0	5.8	0.0
C+ / 6.0	12.8	0.91	50.61	1	1	98	0	1	46	50.9	-24.9	64	10	1,000	0	0.0	0.0
C+ / 6.0	12.8	0.91	44.22	19	1	98	0	1	46	50.9	-25.0	63	10	1,000	0	0.0	0.0
C+ / 6.0	12.9	0.91	47.47	110	1	98	0	1	46	56.8	-24.6	76	10	250,000	0	0.0	0.0
C+ / 6.1	12.9	0.91	46.99	3	1	98	0	1	46	54.8	-24.7	72	10	1,000	0	0.0	0.0
C+ / 6.1	12.8	0.91	56.89	48	1	98	0	1	46	56.2	-24.6	75	10	1,000	0	0.0	0.0
C / 4.9	14.6	1.05	10.41	30	1	98	0	1	68	N/A	N/A	28	4	1,000	0	5.8	0.0
C / 5.0	14.6	1.05	10.38	6	1	98	0	1	68	N/A	N/A	20	4	1,000	0	0.0	0.0
C / 4.8	14.7	1.05	10.43	186	1	98	0	1	68	N/A	N/A	32	4	250,000	0	0.0	0.0
C / 4.9	14.6	1.05	10.37	N/A	1	98	0	1	68	N/A	N/A	26	4	0	0	0.0	0.0
C / 4.9	14.7	1.05	10.41	36	1	98	0	1	68	N/A	N/A	31	4	1,000	0	0.0	0.0
C / 4.8	12.6	0.93	11.15	502	0	0	0	100	45	50.7	-22.9	54	4	250,000	0	0.0	0.0
C+ / 6.4	10.1	1.04	15.61	2	2	97	0	1	105	86.9	-20.4	36	2	0	0	0.0	0.0
C+ / 6.4	10.1	1.05	15.73	254	2	97	0	1	105	90.6	-20.2	44	2	0	0	0.0	0.0
C+ / 6.4	10.1	1.04	15.73	77	2	97	0	1	105	89.0	-20.3	41	2	0	0	0.0	0.0
C- / 3.1	11.3	0.98	13.02	305	1	98	0	1	141	N/A	N/A	71	4	250,000	0	0.0	0.0
C- / 3.9	13.5	1.07	20.74	251	1	98	0	1	45	82.1	-16.0	39	19	1,000	0	5.8	0.0
C- / 3.9	13.4	1.07	20.82	1	1	98	0	1	45	77.4	-16.2	29	19	1,000	0	0.0	0.0
C- / 3.9	13.2	1.06	21.62	34	1	98	0	1	45	76.4	-16.2	29	19	1,000	0	0.0	0.0
C- / 3.9	13.1	1.05	22.16	1,140	1	98	0	1	45	82.5	-15.8	45	19	250,000	0	0.0	0.0
C- / 3.9	13.4	1.07	20.71	41	1	98	0	1	45	82.2	-15.9	39	19	1,000	0	0.0	0.0
C- / 3.9	13.5	1.08	20.67	3	1	98	0	1	45	80.7	N/A	35	19	0	0	0.0	0.0
C- / 4.0	12.6	1.01	24.72	99	1	98	0	1	45	79.4	-15.9	42	19	1,000	0	0.0	0.0
B / 8.4	3.7	0.27	9.51	520	0	29	70	1	26	26.1	-2.8	78	8	0	0	0.0	0.0
B / 8.4	3.7	0.27	9.67	N/A	0	29	70	1	26	26.8	-2.6	79	8	0	0	0.0	0.0
B / 8.3	7.7	1.31	13.96	4,221	0	72	27	1	21	56.5	-14.6	16	9	0	0	0.0	0.0

Data as of March 31, 2015

Fund Type	Fund Name	Ticker Symbol	Overall Investment Rating	Phone	PERFORMANCE Performance Rating/Pts	3 Mo	6 Mo	1Yr / Pct	3Yr / Pct	5Yr / Pct	Dividend Yield	Expense Ratio
AA	Voya Retirement Growth I	IIRGX	C+	(800) 992-0180	C / 4.5	2.48	4.54	6.90 /54	10.41 /42	9.49 /40	1.98	0.64
AA	Voya Retirement Moderate Adv	IRMPX	C	(800) 992-0180	D+ / 2.6	1.97	3.52	5.78 /45	7.09 /22	7.25 /25	2.86	1.16
AA	Voya Retirement Moderate Gro Adv	IRMGX	C+	(800) 992-0180	C- / 3.7	2.22	4.21	6.55 /51	9.05 /33	8.45 /33	1.57	1.14
AA	Voya Retirement Moderate Gro I	IRGMX	C+	(800) 992-0180	C- / 4.0	2.30	4.38	6.98 /55	9.48 /36	8.88 /36	1.96	0.64
AA	Voya Retirement Moderate I	IRMIX	C	(800) 992-0180	D+ / 2.8	2.03	3.73	6.17 /48	7.45 /24	7.62 /27	3.18	0.66
GI	Voya Russell Large Cap Index Adv	IRLIX	B+	(800) 992-0180	B- / 7.2	0.32	4.59	11.42 /80	14.78 /73	13.19 /70	1.16	0.89
GI	Voya Russell Large Cap Index I	IIRLX	B+	(800) 992-0180	B / 7.6	0.44	4.78	11.93 /82	15.38 /78	13.77 /76	1.48	0.39
GI	Voya Russell Large Cap Index S	IRLCX	B+	(800) 992-0180	B- / 7.4	0.38	4.68	11.69 /81	15.08 /76	13.47 /73	1.28	0.64
GI	Voya Russell Mid Cap Index Adv	IRMAX	A-	(800) 992-0180	A- / 9.1	3.72	9.69	12.67 /85	17.08 /90	15.20 /88	0.67	0.93
GI	Voya Russell Mid Cap Index I	IIRMX	A-	(800) 992-0180	A / 9.3	3.88	9.92	13.18 /87	17.68 /93	15.78 /92	0.96	0.43
GI	Voya Russell Mid Cap Index S	IRMCX	A-	(800) 992-0180	A- / 9.2	3.85	9.81	13.00 /87	17.40 /92	15.50 /90	0.79	0.68
GI	Voya Russell Small Cap Index Adv	IRSIX	C+	(800) 992-0180	B / 8.2	4.09	14.07	7.55 /60	15.59 /80	13.92 /77	0.63	0.97
GI	Voya Russell Small Cap Index I	IIRSX	B-	(800) 992-0180	B+ / 8.6	4.24	14.36	8.11 /64	16.20 /85	14.51 /82	0.95	0.47
GI	Voya Russell Small Cap Index S	IRSSX	B-	(800) 992-0180	B+ / 8.4	4.15	14.20	7.79 /61	15.90 /83	14.21 /80	0.75	0.72
EM	Voya Russia A	LETRX	E-	(800) 992-0180	E- / 0.1	18.87	-11.75	-14.41 / 2	-10.51 / 1	-7.24 / 1	3.02	2.07
EM	Voya Russia I	IIRFX	E-	(800) 992-0180	E- / 0.1	18.97	-11.56	-14.21 / 2	-10.40 / 1	-7.01 / 1	3.61	1.88
EM	Voya Russia W	IWRFX	E-	(800) 992-0180	E- / 0.1	18.92	-11.58	-14.24 / 2	-10.31 / 1	--	3.73	1.82
RE	Voya Short Term Bond R6	IGZAX	U	(800) 992-0180	U /	0.80	1.01	1.53 /20	--	--	1.92	0.55
SC	Voya Small Cap Opps Port I	IVSOX	B-	(800) 992-0180	B+ / 8.9	5.26	14.11	10.57 /77	16.43 /87	16.73 /95	0.00	0.89
SC	Voya Small Cap Opps Port S	IVPOX	B-	(800) 992-0180	B+ / 8.7	5.19	13.98	10.27 /75	16.15 /85	16.44 /95	0.00	1.14
SC	Voya Small Company A	AESAX	C+	(800) 992-0180	C+ / 6.8	4.05	13.79	8.73 /68	15.02 /75	13.50 /73	0.00	1.36
SC	● Voya Small Company B	ASMLX	C+	(800) 992-0180	B- / 7.2	3.85	13.36	7.91 /62	14.16 /68	12.65 /65	0.00	2.11
SC	Voya Small Company C	ASCCX	C+	(800) 992-0180	B- / 7.2	3.83	13.37	7.93 /62	14.15 /68	12.65 /65	0.00	2.11
SC	Voya Small Company I	AESGX	B	(800) 992-0180	B / 8.2	4.10	13.97	9.06 /70	15.39 /78	13.91 /77	0.38	1.15
SC	Voya Small Company O	ISCOX	B-	(800) 992-0180	B / 7.9	4.05	13.75	8.75 /68	15.01 /75	13.50 /73	0.01	1.36
SC	Voya Small Company Port I	IVCSX	B-	(800) 992-0180	B+ / 8.5	4.22	14.24	9.52 /72	15.84 /82	14.33 /81	0.32	0.85
SC	Voya Small Company Port S	IVPSX	C+	(800) 992-0180	B+ / 8.3	4.16	14.10	9.24 /71	15.56 /80	14.03 /78	0.09	1.10
SC	Voya Small Company R6	ISMZX	U	(800) 992-0180	U /	4.16	14.01	9.16 /70	--	--	0.47	1.00
SC	Voya Small Company W	ISMWX	B	(800) 992-0180	B / 8.1	4.05	13.87	8.96 /69	15.28 /77	13.77 /76	0.33	1.11
SC	Voya SmallCap Opportunities A	NSPAX	C+	(800) 992-0180	B- / 7.3	5.05	13.59	9.78 /73	15.58 /80	15.94 /93	0.00	1.42
SC	● Voya SmallCap Opportunities B	NSPBX	B-	(800) 992-0180	B / 7.7	4.86	13.15	8.96 /69	14.71 /73	15.07 /87	0.00	2.17
SC	Voya SmallCap Opportunities C	NSPCX	B-	(800) 992-0180	B / 7.7	4.87	13.18	8.97 /69	14.71 /73	15.08 /87	0.00	2.17
SC	Voya SmallCap Opportunities I	NSPIX	B+	(800) 992-0180	B+ / 8.6	5.15	13.75	10.09 /75	15.97 /83	16.37 /94	0.00	1.18
SC	Voya SmallCap Opportunities R	ISORX	B	(800) 992-0180	B / 8.2	4.99	13.45	9.50 /72	15.31 /77	--	0.00	1.67
SC	Voya SmallCap Opportunities R6	ISOZX	U	(800) 992-0180	U /	5.17	13.83	10.21 /75	--	--	0.00	1.03
SC	Voya SmallCap Opportunities W	ISOWX	B+	(800) 992-0180	B+ / 8.6	5.11	13.72	10.05 /75	15.87 /82	16.24 /94	0.00	1.17
AA	Voya Solution 2015 Adv	ISOAX	C	(800) 992-0180	D+ / 2.5	2.23	4.03	5.99 /46	6.72 /20	6.77 /22	2.24	1.37
AA	Voya Solution 2015 I	ISOIX	C	(800) 992-0180	D+ / 2.8	2.34	4.37	6.58 /52	7.26 /23	7.29 /25	2.78	0.87
AA	Voya Solution 2015 S	ISOSX	C	(800) 992-0180	D+ / 2.6	2.28	4.24	6.32 /49	6.98 /21	7.03 /23	2.51	1.12
AA	Voya Solution 2015 T	ISOTX	C	(800) 992-0180	D+ / 2.4	2.19	4.05	5.87 /45	6.51 /19	6.57 /20	1.79	1.62
AA	Voya Solution 2025 Adv	ISZAX	C	(800) 992-0180	C- / 3.8	2.88	5.10	6.82 /54	8.96 /33	8.53 /33	1.69	1.45
AA	Voya Solution 2025 I	ISZIX	C	(800) 992-0180	C- / 4.1	2.97	5.30	7.35 /58	9.50 /36	9.06 /37	2.19	0.95
AA	Voya Solution 2025 S	ISZSX	C	(800) 992-0180	C- / 4.0	2.92	5.27	7.13 /56	9.25 /35	8.80 /35	1.95	1.20
AA	Voya Solution 2025 T	ISZTX	C	(800) 992-0180	C- / 3.6	2.75	4.92	6.59 /52	8.75 /31	8.31 /32	1.57	1.70
AA	Voya Solution 2035 Adv	ISQAX	C-	(800) 992-0180	C / 4.5	3.18	5.49	7.65 /60	10.25 /41	9.44 /40	1.72	1.50
AA	Voya Solution 2035 I	ISQIX	C	(800) 992-0180	C / 4.9	3.26	5.68	8.17 /64	10.81 /44	9.98 /44	2.20	1.00
AA	Voya Solution 2035 S	ISQSX	C	(800) 992-0180	C / 4.7	3.21	5.58	7.93 /62	10.53 /42	9.71 /42	1.95	1.25
AA	Voya Solution 2035 T	ISQTX	C-	(800) 992-0180	C / 4.4	3.04	5.30	7.39 /58	10.02 /39	9.21 /38	1.47	1.75
AA	Voya Solution 2045 Adv	ISRAX	C-	(800) 992-0180	C / 5.2	3.24	5.80	8.22 /64	11.27 /47	10.16 /46	1.42	1.52
AA	Voya Solution 2045 I	ISRIX	C	(800) 992-0180	C / 5.5	3.31	5.98	8.69 /68	11.81 /51	10.69 /50	1.87	1.02
AA	Voya Solution 2045 S	ISRSX	C	(800) 992-0180	C / 5.3	3.27	5.97	8.46 /66	11.54 /49	10.42 /48	1.62	1.27
AA	Voya Solution 2045 T	ISRTX	C-	(800) 992-0180	C / 5.0	3.20	5.65	7.95 /63	11.01 /46	9.92 /44	1.27	1.77

● Denotes fund is closed to new investors
* Denotes fund is included in Section II

www.thestreetratings.com

RISK			NET ASSETS		ASSET					Portfolio Turnover Ratio	BULL / BEAR		FUND MANAGER		MINIMUMS		LOADS	
Risk Rating/Pts	3 Year		NAV As of 3/31/15	Total $(Mil)	Cash %	Stocks %	Bonds %	Other %		Last Bull Market Return	Last Bear Market Return	Manager Quality Pct	Manager Tenure (Years)	Initial Purch. $	Additional Purch. $	Front End Load	Back End Load
	Standard Deviation	Beta															
B /8.3	7.7	1.30	14.06	52	0	72	27	1	21	58.9	-14.4	20	9	0	0	0.0	0.0
B+ /9.0	5.4	0.89	12.93	1,594	0	48	51	1	20	37.7	-8.2	33	9	0	0	0.0	0.0
B /8.7	6.7	1.13	13.84	2,933	0	62	37	1	21	49.8	-12.0	25	9	0	0	0.0	0.0
B /8.7	6.7	1.13	13.81	26	0	62	37	1	21	51.6	-11.9	29	9	0	0	0.0	0.0
B /8.9	5.3	0.88	13.08	20	0	48	51	1	20	39.5	-8.2	38	9	0	0	0.0	0.0
B- /7.0	9.6	1.00	15.71	37	2	97	0	1	6	93.4	-15.8	49	3	0	0	0.0	0.0
B- /7.0	9.6	1.00	16.00	188	2	97	0	1	6	96.8	-15.5	58	3	0	0	0.0	0.0
B- /7.0	9.6	1.00	15.88	625	2	97	0	1	6	95.1	-15.6	53	3	0	0	0.0	0.0
C+ /5.8	10.2	1.00	17.55	145	0	99	0	1	14	102.9	-21.3	75	3	0	0	0.0	0.0
C+ /5.8	10.2	1.00	17.95	1,829	0	99	0	1	14	106.3	-21.1	80	3	0	0	0.0	0.0
C+ /5.8	10.2	1.00	17.79	390	0	99	0	1	14	104.5	-21.1	78	3	0	0	0.0	0.0
C /4.5	13.4	1.16	16.78	83	0	99	0	1	13	96.4	-25.1	28	3	0	0	0.0	0.0
C /4.5	13.4	1.15	17.20	603	0	99	0	1	13	99.8	-25.0	34	3	0	0	0.0	0.0
C /4.5	13.4	1.16	17.05	308	0	99	0	1	13	98.2	-25.0	30	3	0	0	0.0	0.0
D- /1.5	27.6	1.49	23.43	87	1	98	0	1	76	-13.9	-34.9	1	3	1,000	0	5.8	0.0
D- /1.5	27.5	1.49	23.58	3	1	98	0	1	76	-13.4	-34.7	1	3	250,000	0	0.0	0.0
D- /1.5	27.5	1.49	23.44	N/A	1	98	0	1	76	-13.2	N/A	1	3	1,000	0	0.0	0.0
U /	N/A	N/A	9.98	133	1	0	98	1	116	N/A	N/A	N/A	3	1,000,000	0	0.0	0.0
C /4.3	12.8	0.93	29.42	211	1	98	0	1	40	107.1	-22.2	78	10	0	0	0.0	0.0
C- /4.2	12.8	0.94	28.19	80	1	98	0	1	40	105.4	-22.3	76	10	0	0	0.0	0.0
C /5.3	12.1	0.89	16.19	49	3	96	0	1	34	97.3	-24.0	73	10	1,000	0	5.8	0.0
C /4.8	12.1	0.89	14.29	1	3	96	0	1	34	92.2	-24.2	64	10	1,000	0	0.0	0.0
C /4.8	12.1	0.89	14.11	7	3	96	0	1	34	92.3	-24.2	64	10	1,000	0	0.0	0.0
C+ /5.6	12.1	0.90	18.28	513	3	96	0	1	34	99.6	-23.8	75	10	250,000	0	0.0	0.0
C /5.3	12.1	0.89	16.17	2	3	96	0	1	34	97.2	-23.9	73	10	1,000	0	0.0	0.0
C /4.4	12.2	0.90	24.23	527	2	97	0	1	36	102.2	-23.7	78	10	0	0	0.0	0.0
C /4.4	12.1	0.90	23.79	116	2	97	0	1	36	100.5	-23.8	76	10	0	0	0.0	0.0
U /	N/A	N/A	18.29	28	3	96	0	1	34	N/A	N/A	N/A	10	1,000,000	0	0.0	0.0
C+ /5.6	12.1	0.90	18.24	1	3	96	0	1	34	98.8	-23.9	74	10	1,000	0	0.0	0.0
C+ /5.6	12.6	0.92	57.83	167	2	97	0	1	31	102.2	-22.5	73	10	1,000	0	5.8	0.0
C /5.3	12.6	0.92	47.88	1	2	97	0	1	31	97.0	-22.7	64	10	1,000	0	0.0	0.0
C /5.3	12.6	0.92	47.78	51	2	97	0	1	31	97.1	-22.7	64	10	1,000	0	0.0	0.0
C+ /5.7	12.6	0.92	61.70	369	2	97	0	1	31	104.6	-22.4	76	10	250,000	0	0.0	0.0
C /5.6	12.6	0.92	57.21	2	2	97	0	1	31	100.4	N/A	71	10	0	0	0.0	0.0
U /	N/A	N/A	61.80	113	2	97	0	1	31	N/A	N/A	N/A	10	1,000,000	0	0.0	0.0
C+ /5.7	12.6	0.92	61.06	48	2	97	0	1	31	103.9	-22.4	75	10	1,000	0	0.0	0.0
B /8.5	4.9	0.82	12.39	213	2	39	57	2	68	38.0	-11.2	38	8	0	0	0.0	0.0
B /8.5	4.9	0.82	12.66	84	2	39	57	2	68	40.4	-11.0	45	8	0	0	0.0	0.0
B /8.5	4.9	0.82	12.55	230	2	39	57	2	68	39.2	-11.1	41	8	0	0	0.0	0.0
B /8.6	4.9	0.82	12.59	1	2	39	57	2	68	37.1	-11.2	35	8	0	0	0.0	0.0
B- /7.5	7.0	1.19	13.20	417	3	62	33	2	72	53.2	-16.1	18	8	0	0	0.0	0.0
B- /7.4	7.0	1.19	13.51	209	3	62	33	2	72	56.0	-15.9	23	8	0	0	0.0	0.0
B- /7.5	7.0	1.20	13.38	484	3	62	33	2	72	54.6	-16.0	20	8	0	0	0.0	0.0
B- /7.6	7.0	1.19	13.43	1	3	62	33	2	72	52.2	-16.1	16	8	0	0	0.0	0.0
C+ /6.3	8.5	1.44	13.64	350	4	81	13	2	74	63.9	-18.9	9	8	0	0	0.0	0.0
C+ /6.2	8.5	1.44	13.95	227	4	81	13	2	74	66.7	-18.8	12	8	0	0	0.0	0.0
C+ /6.2	8.5	1.45	13.82	442	4	81	13	2	74	65.4	-18.8	10	8	0	0	0.0	0.0
C+ /6.4	8.5	1.45	13.91	1	4	81	13	2	74	62.8	-18.9	8	8	0	0	0.0	0.0
C+ /5.7	9.4	1.60	14.04	228	4	91	4	1	72	70.2	-19.8	7	8	0	0	0.0	0.0
C+ /5.6	9.4	1.60	14.36	174	4	91	4	1	72	73.0	-19.6	9	8	0	0	0.0	0.0
C+ /5.6	9.4	1.60	14.21	310	4	91	4	1	72	71.5	-19.7	8	8	0	0	0.0	0.0
C+ /5.7	9.4	1.60	14.21	N/A	4	91	4	1	72	68.8	-19.8	6	8	0	0	0.0	0.0

Fund Type	Fund Name	Ticker Symbol	Overall Investment Rating	Phone	Perfor-mance Rating/Pts	Total Return % through 3/31/15 3 Mo	6 Mo	1Yr / Pct	Annualized 3Yr / Pct	5Yr / Pct	Incl. in Returns Dividend Yield	Expense Ratio
AA	Voya Solution 2050 Adv	ISNPX	C+	(800) 992-0180	C / 5.3	3.28	5.68	8.98 /69	11.40 /48	--	0.10	85.14
AA	Voya Solution 2050 I	ISNQX	C+	(800) 992-0180	C+ / 5.7	3.50	6.09	9.63 /73	12.02 /53	--	0.00	84.64
AA	Voya Solution 2050 S	ISNRX	C+	(800) 992-0180	C / 5.5	3.45	5.90	9.22 /70	11.64 /50	--	0.00	84.89
AA	Voya Solution 2050 S2	ISNSX	C+	(800) 992-0180	C / 5.4	3.41	5.88	9.22 /70	11.47 /49	--	0.00	85.14
AA	Voya Solution 2050 T	ISNTX	C+	(800) 992-0180	C / 5.3	3.34	5.75	8.94 /69	11.35 /48	--	0.00	85.39
GL	Voya Solution 2055 Adv	IASPX	C	(800) 992-0180	C / 5.2	3.15	5.82	8.32 /65	11.33 /48	10.21 /46	1.12	1.54
GL	Voya Solution 2055 I	IISPX	C+	(800) 992-0180	C+ / 5.6	3.24	6.10	8.90 /69	11.89 /52	10.75 /51	1.45	1.04
GL	Voya Solution 2055 S	ISSPX	C	(800) 992-0180	C / 5.4	3.27	6.00	8.68 /67	11.64 /50	10.49 /49	1.28	1.29
GL	Voya Solution 2055 S2	ITSPX	C	(800) 992-0180	C / 5.3	3.21	5.95	8.48 /66	11.48 /49	10.33 /47	1.21	1.54
GL	Voya Solution 2055 T	ISTPX	C	(800) 992-0180	C / 5.1	3.09	5.84	8.30 /65	11.19 /47	10.01 /45	1.08	1.79
GL	Voya Solution Balanced Adv	ISGAX	C	(800) 992-0180	C- / 3.9	2.65	5.03	7.37 /58	9.06 /33	8.49 /33	1.74	1.48
GL	Voya Solution Balanced I	ISGJX	C	(800) 992-0180	C- / 4.2	2.84	5.26	7.86 /62	9.54 /36	9.09 /37	2.15	0.98
GL	Voya Solution Balanced S	ISGKX	C	(800) 992-0180	C- / 4.0	2.71	5.07	7.56 /60	9.31 /35	8.79 /35	1.97	1.23
AA	Voya Solution Income Adv	ISWAX	C-	(800) 992-0180	D / 2.1	2.07	3.86	5.83 /45	5.98 /17	6.04 /17	2.26	1.33
AA	Voya Solution Income I	ISWIX	C-	(800) 992-0180	D+ / 2.4	2.19	4.12	6.31 /49	6.51 /19	6.57 /20	2.78	0.83
AA	Voya Solution Income S	ISWSX	C-	(800) 992-0180	D / 2.2	2.21	3.98	6.06 /47	6.23 /18	6.31 /19	2.52	1.08
AA	Voya Solution Income T	ISWTX	C-	(800) 992-0180	D / 2.0	2.07	3.79	5.59 /43	5.77 /16	5.85 /16	1.68	1.58
BA	Voya Solution Moderately Consv Adv	ISPGX	C-	(800) 992-0180	D+ / 2.6	2.58	4.48	6.14 /48	6.95 /21	6.95 /23	2.05	1.43
BA	Voya Solution Moderately Consv Inl	ISPRX	C-	(800) 992-0180	D+ / 2.9	2.67	4.79	6.66 /52	7.43 /24	7.58 /27	2.47	0.93
BA	Voya Solution Moderately Consv S2	ISPTX	C-	(800) 992-0180	D+ / 2.7	2.55	4.52	6.24 /49	7.06 /22	--	2.18	1.43
BA	Voya Solution Moderately Consv Svc	ISPSX	C-	(800) 992-0180	D+ / 2.8	2.53	4.59	6.41 /50	7.22 /23	7.28 /25	2.27	1.18
AA	Voya Strategic Alloc Consv I	ISAIX	C	(800) 992-0180	C- / 3.8	2.61	4.43	7.29 /57	8.93 /32	8.56 /34	2.49	0.74
AA	Voya Strategic Alloc Consv S	ISCVX	C	(800) 992-0180	C- / 3.6	2.55	4.30	7.05 /55	8.67 /31	8.29 /32	2.32	0.99
AA	Voya Strategic Alloc Gr Cl I	ISAGX	C+	(800) 992-0180	C / 5.5	3.19	5.64	8.41 /66	11.85 /51	10.37 /48	1.93	0.80
AA	Voya Strategic Alloc Gr Cl S	ISGRX	C+	(800) 992-0180	C / 5.3	3.21	5.53	8.24 /65	11.56 /49	10.11 /46	1.74	1.05
AA	Voya Strategic Alloc Mod Cl I	IIMDX	C+	(800) 992-0180	C / 4.5	2.89	5.21	8.06 /63	10.26 /41	9.38 /40	2.22	0.77
AA	Voya Strategic Alloc Mod Cl S	ISMDX	C+	(800) 992-0180	C / 4.4	2.83	5.16	7.88 /62	9.99 /39	9.12 /38	2.03	1.02
GI	Voya US Stock Index Inst	INGIX	B	(800) 992-0180	B / 8.1	0.89	5.82	12.44 /85	15.84 /82	14.17 /79	1.66	0.27
GI	Voya US Stock Index Svc 2	ISIPX	B	(800) 992-0180	B / 7.7	0.83	5.60	12.01 /83	15.37 /78	13.71 /75	1.35	0.77
GR	Voya VP Index Plus Large Cap I	IPLIX	A	(800) 992-0180	B+ / 8.3	1.38	5.51	13.45 /88	16.01 /83	13.68 /75	1.38	0.44
GR	Voya VP Index Plus Large Cap S	IPLSX	A-	(800) 992-0180	B / 8.1	1.35	5.41	13.19 /87	15.74 /81	13.40 /72	1.16	0.69
MC	Voya VP Index Plus MidCap I	IPMIX	A	(800) 992-0180	A- / 9.1	5.13	10.90	12.37 /84	16.94 /90	14.91 /86	0.70	0.49
MC	Voya VP Index Plus MidCap S	IPMSX	A	(800) 992-0180	B+ / 8.9	5.02	10.77	12.06 /83	16.65 /88	14.62 /83	0.48	0.74
SC	Voya VP Index Plus SmallCap I	IPSIX	A-	(800) 992-0180	B+ / 8.7	3.58	13.66	8.42 /66	16.61 /88	14.60 /83	0.59	0.49
SC	Voya VP Index Plus SmallCap S	IPSSX	B+	(800) 992-0180	B+ / 8.6	3.49	13.50	8.16 /64	16.31 /86	14.31 /81	0.37	0.74
GR	Vulcan Value Partners	VVPLX	A+	(877) 421-5078	A / 9.3	-0.41	6.83	14.59 /91	18.68 /96	15.96 /93	0.85	1.09
GR	● Vulcan Value Partners Small Cap	VVPSX	A-	(877) 421-5078	B+ / 8.7	3.20	11.15	7.71 /61	17.50 /92	16.49 /95	0.52	1.31
SC	VY American Century Sm-MC Val	IASAX	C+	(800) 992-0180	B+ / 8.6	2.03	9.64	11.05 /79	16.42 /86	13.59 /74	1.07	1.65
SC	VY American Century Sm-MC Val I	IACIX	B-	(800) 992-0180	B+ / 8.9	2.08	9.87	11.61 /81	16.96 /90	14.16 /79	1.46	1.15
SC	VY American Century Sm-MC Val S	IASSX	B-	(800) 992-0180	B+ / 8.7	2.04	9.74	11.31 /80	16.67 /88	13.87 /77	1.21	1.40
SC	VY Baron Growth Adv	IBSAX	A-	(800) 992-0180	A / 9.4	5.04	11.94	9.71 /73	18.13 /95	16.89 /96	0.00	1.50
SC	VY Baron Growth I	IBGIX	A	(800) 992-0180	A / 9.5	5.17	12.22	10.20 /75	18.71 /96	17.47 /97	0.27	1.00
SC	VY Baron Growth S	IBSSX	A	(800) 992-0180	A / 9.4	5.10	12.10	9.95 /74	18.41 /95	17.19 /96	0.07	1.25
RE	VY Clarion Global Real Estate Adv	ICRNX	C-	(800) 992-0180	C+ / 6.1	3.82	11.41	14.42 /90	10.82 /44	10.28 /47	0.83	1.73
RE	VY Clarion Global Real Estate Inst	IRGIX	C	(800) 992-0180	C+ / 6.6	3.97	11.76	15.13 /92	11.51 /49	10.94 /52	1.24	0.98
RE	VY Clarion Global Real Estate Svc	IRGTX	C-	(800) 992-0180	C+ / 6.4	3.83	11.55	14.85 /91	11.20 /47	10.64 /50	1.01	1.23
RE	VY Clarion Global Real Estate Svc 2	IRGSX	C-	(800) 992-0180	C+ / 6.3	3.81	11.49	14.69 /91	11.06 /46	10.48 /48	0.86	1.48
RE	VY Clarion Real Estate Adv	ICRPX	C+	(800) 992-0180	B+ / 8.9	4.40	19.00	22.84 /98	12.75 /58	15.06 /87	1.02	1.61
RE	VY Clarion Real Estate Inst	IVRIX	B-	(800) 992-0180	A- / 9.2	4.55	19.38	23.61 /98	13.43 /63	15.74 /91	1.37	0.86
RE	VY Clarion Real Estate Svc	IVRSX	B-	(800) 992-0180	A- / 9.1	4.51	19.23	23.29 /98	13.14 /61	15.46 /90	1.16	1.11
RE	VY Clarion Real Estate Svc 2	IVRTX	C+	(800) 992-0180	A- / 9.0	4.45	19.15	23.10 /98	12.97 /60	15.28 /89	1.04	1.36
GI	VY Columbia Contrarian Core Adv	ISBAX	B-	(800) 992-0180	B / 7.9	1.17	5.61	12.66 /85	15.52 /79	11.85 /60	0.63	1.46

● Denotes fund is closed to new investors
* Denotes fund is included in Section II

650

Risk Rating/Pts	Standard Deviation	Beta	NAV As of 3/31/15	Total $(Mil)	Cash %	Stocks %	Bonds %	Other %	Portfolio Turnover Ratio	Last Bull Market Return	Last Bear Market Return	Manager Quality Pct	Manager Tenure (Years)	Initial Purch. $	Additional Purch. $	Front End Load	Back End Load
B- / 7.1	9.5	1.60	15.44	N/A	2	93	4	1	65	N/A	N/A	7	4	0	0	0.0	0.0
B- / 7.1	9.4	1.60	15.68	N/A	2	93	4	1	65	N/A	N/A	10	4	0	0	0.0	0.0
B- / 7.1	9.5	1.60	15.61	N/A	2	93	4	1	65	N/A	N/A	8	4	0	0	0.0	0.0
B- / 7.1	9.4	1.60	15.48	N/A	2	93	4	1	65	N/A	N/A	8	4	0	0	0.0	0.0
B- / 7.1	9.5	1.60	15.45	N/A	2	93	4	1	65	N/A	N/A	7	4	0	0	0.0	0.0
C+ / 6.4	9.5	0.64	14.72	40	5	90	3	2	73	70.6	-19.8	93	5	0	0	0.0	0.0
C+ / 6.4	9.5	0.64	14.96	28	5	90	3	2	73	73.5	-19.6	94	5	0	0	0.0	0.0
C+ / 6.4	9.5	0.64	14.84	47	5	90	3	2	73	72.0	-19.7	94	5	0	0	0.0	0.0
C+ / 6.4	9.5	0.64	14.77	3	5	90	3	2	73	71.1	-19.7	94	5	0	0	0.0	0.0
C+ / 6.4	9.5	0.64	14.69	N/A	5	90	3	2	73	69.7	-19.8	93	5	0	0	0.0	0.0
B- / 7.1	6.9	1.06	10.85	29	4	64	31	1	78	53.8	-15.2	60	8	0	0	0.0	0.0
B- / 7.0	6.9	1.07	11.21	N/A	4	64	31	1	78	56.2	-15.0	66	8	0	0	0.0	0.0
B- / 7.0	6.9	1.06	10.99	24	4	64	31	1	78	55.1	-15.2	64	8	0	0	0.0	0.0
B / 8.5	4.2	0.68	11.85	82	2	32	64	2	70	31.6	-8.2	49	8	0	0	0.0	0.0
B / 8.4	4.2	0.67	12.12	24	2	32	64	2	70	33.9	-8.1	58	8	0	0	0.0	0.0
B / 8.4	4.2	0.68	12.02	56	2	32	64	2	70	32.7	-8.1	53	8	0	0	0.0	0.0
B / 8.5	4.2	0.68	12.32	N/A	2	32	64	2	70	30.8	-8.3	46	8	0	0	0.0	0.0
B- / 7.4	5.1	0.85	10.72	22	2	42	54	2	85	39.4	-11.4	37	8	0	0	0.0	0.0
B- / 7.4	5.1	0.85	11.16	N/A	2	42	54	2	85	41.7	-11.2	43	8	0	0	0.0	0.0
B- / 7.4	5.1	0.85	10.86	1	2	42	54	2	85	40.0	-11.4	38	8	0	0	0.0	0.0
B- / 7.4	5.0	0.84	10.94	22	2	42	54	2	85	40.6	-11.3	41	8	0	0	0.0	0.0
B / 8.0	5.2	0.87	12.97	87	2	41	55	2	55	44.3	-7.9	61	8	0	0	0.0	0.0
B / 8.0	5.2	0.87	12.85	3	2	41	55	2	55	43.1	-8.0	57	8	0	0	0.0	0.0
B- / 7.3	8.9	1.51	14.24	157	3	83	12	2	54	68.1	-16.7	14	8	0	0	0.0	0.0
B- / 7.4	8.8	1.50	14.13	3	3	83	12	2	54	66.6	-16.7	13	8	0	0	0.0	0.0
B- / 7.9	6.9	1.19	13.52	153	3	63	33	1	54	54.9	-12.4	31	8	0	0	0.0	0.0
B / 8.0	6.9	1.19	13.44	2	3	63	33	1	54	53.6	-12.4	28	8	0	0	0.0	0.0
C+ / 6.0	9.5	1.00	14.81	4,168	0	99	0	1	9	98.5	-16.4	64	3	0	0	0.0	0.0
C+ / 5.9	9.5	1.00	14.58	181	0	99	0	1	9	95.8	-16.5	58	3	0	0	0.0	0.0
B- / 7.0	9.8	1.02	22.79	631	0	100	0	0	80	99.5	-17.6	62	9	0	0	0.0	0.0
B- / 7.1	9.8	1.02	22.59	125	0	100	0	0	80	97.7	-17.7	57	9	0	0	0.0	0.0
C+ / 6.5	11.2	1.00	25.84	592	1	98	0	1	66	102.2	-22.3	66	9	0	0	0.0	0.0
C+ / 6.5	11.2	1.00	25.51	124	1	98	0	1	66	100.4	-22.4	62	9	0	0	0.0	0.0
C+ / 6.2	12.3	0.91	23.72	229	1	98	0	1	55	101.8	-23.0	82	9	0	0	0.0	0.0
C+ / 6.2	12.3	0.91	23.45	92	1	98	0	1	55	100.1	-23.0	80	9	0	0	0.0	0.0
B- / 7.1	10.7	1.04	19.44	1,681	0	99	0	1	56	120.5	-13.6	81	6	5,000	500	0.0	2.0
C+ / 6.2	11.6	0.99	18.41	1,101	4	95	0	1	70	114.6	-21.3	80	6	5,000	500	0.0	2.0
C- / 4.1	9.8	0.70	14.10	87	3	96	0	1	84	96.5	-19.9	93	13	0	0	0.0	0.0
C- / 4.2	9.8	0.69	14.70	138	3	96	0	1	84	99.9	-19.7	94	13	0	0	0.0	0.0
C- / 4.2	9.8	0.69	14.54	93	3	96	0	1	84	98.0	-19.7	93	13	0	0	0.0	0.0
C+ / 5.9	10.6	0.72	31.88	113	2	97	0	1	8	100.0	-19.5	95	13	0	0	0.0	0.0
C+ / 5.9	10.6	0.72	33.98	247	2	97	0	1	8	103.4	-19.3	95	13	0	0	0.0	0.0
C+ / 5.9	10.6	0.72	32.99	704	2	97	0	1	8	101.8	-19.4	95	13	0	0	0.0	0.0
C / 4.4	12.6	0.92	12.50	30	9	90	0	1	40	63.2	-18.5	38	9	0	0	0.0	0.0
C / 4.4	12.6	0.92	12.83	168	9	90	0	1	40	66.7	-18.3	48	9	0	0	0.0	0.0
C / 4.4	12.6	0.92	12.75	166	9	90	0	1	40	65.3	-18.4	44	9	0	0	0.0	0.0
C / 4.5	12.6	0.92	12.81	2	9	90	0	1	40	64.5	-18.5	41	9	0	0	0.0	0.0
C- / 3.8	13.2	1.05	35.13	99	1	98	0	1	52	80.5	-16.2	39	13	0	0	0.0	0.0
C- / 3.8	13.2	1.05	36.77	150	1	98	0	1	52	84.1	-16.0	47	13	0	0	0.0	0.0
C- / 3.8	13.2	1.05	36.64	508	1	98	0	1	52	82.6	-16.1	44	13	0	0	0.0	0.0
C- / 3.8	13.2	1.05	36.40	29	1	98	0	1	52	81.7	-16.1	41	13	0	0	0.0	0.0
C / 5.5	10.2	1.04	24.28	19	0	99	0	1	128	93.5	-20.1	50	2	0	0	0.0	0.0

99 Pct = Best
0 Pct = Worst

					PERFORMANCE						Incl. in Returns	
			Overall		Perfor-	Total Return % through 3/31/15						
			Investment		mance				Annualized		Dividend	Expense
Fund Type	Fund Name	Ticker Symbol	Rating	Phone	Rating/Pts	3 Mo	6 Mo	1Yr / Pct	3Yr / Pct	5Yr / Pct	Yield	Ratio
GI	VY Columbia Contrarian Core Init	ISFIX	B	(800) 992-0180	B+ / 8.3	1.29	5.85	13.24 /87	16.13 /84	12.44 /64	0.89	0.96
GI	VY Columbia Contrarian Core S	ISCSX	B	(800) 992-0180	B / 8.1	1.23	5.77	12.97 /86	15.83 /82	12.14 /62	0.75	1.21
SC	VY Columbia Small Cap Val II Adv	ICSAX	B+	(800) 992-0180	B / 7.8	3.94	11.06	5.92 /46	15.63 /80	14.15 /79	0.25	1.38
SC	VY Columbia Small Cap Val II Init	ICISX	B+	(800) 992-0180	B+ / 8.3	4.08	11.36	6.48 /51	16.20 /85	14.73 /85	0.37	0.88
SC	VY Columbia Small Cap Val II Svc	ICSSX	B+	(800) 992-0180	B / 8.1	4.04	11.22	6.15 /48	15.91 /83	14.42 /82	0.17	1.13
GI	VY DFA World Equity Port Adv	IFPAX	C-	(800) 992-0180	C- / 4.1	2.65	2.27	2.12 /22	10.55 /43	9.81 /43	1.39	1.46
GI	VY DFA World Equity Port Inst	IFPIX	C	(800) 992-0180	C / 4.5	2.87	2.58	2.76 /25	11.20 /47	10.52 /49	1.77	0.71
GI	VY DFA World Equity Port Svc	IFFSX	C	(800) 992-0180	C / 4.4	2.78	2.49	2.53 /24	10.94 /45	10.23 /46	1.54	0.96
GR	VY Fidelity VIP Contrafund Adv	VPCAX	B+	(800) 992-0180	B- / 7.2	2.21	5.98	11.57 /81	14.47 /71	12.82 /67	0.35	1.54
GR	VY Fidelity VIP Contrafund S	VPCSX	B+	(800) 992-0180	B- / 7.5	2.33	6.14	11.89 /82	14.79 /73	13.11 /69	0.51	1.29
MC	VY FMR Div Mid Cap Adv	IFDMX	C-	(800) 992-0180	B / 7.6	5.04	9.46	9.52 /72	14.84 /74	12.89 /67	0.17	1.39
MC	VY FMR Div Mid Cap Inst	IFDIX	C	(800) 992-0180	B / 8.2	5.27	9.84	10.23 /75	15.53 /79	13.59 /74	0.37	0.64
MC	VY FMR Div Mid Cap Svc	IFDSX	C	(800) 992-0180	B / 8.0	5.15	9.66	9.94 /74	15.25 /77	13.30 /71	0.21	0.89
MC	VY FMR Div Mid Cap Svc 2	IFDTX	C	(800) 992-0180	B / 7.8	5.19	9.62	9.79 /74	15.08 /76	13.13 /69	0.16	1.14
IN	VY Franklin Income Adv	IIFAX	D+	(800) 992-0180	D+ / 2.6	0.18	-1.60	0.47 /17	8.59 /30	8.46 /33	3.97	1.51
IN	VY Franklin Income Inst	IIFIX	D+	(800) 992-0180	C- / 3.1	0.44	-1.29	1.11 /19	9.24 /35	9.11 /38	4.13	0.76
IN	VY Franklin Income Svc	IIFSX	D+	(800) 992-0180	D+ / 2.9	0.35	-1.47	0.88 /18	8.98 /33	8.84 /36	3.93	1.01
IN	VY Franklin Income Svc 2	IIFTX	D+	(800) 992-0180	D+ / 2.8	0.27	-1.56	0.66 /17	8.82 /32	8.66 /34	3.80	1.26
GI	VY Franklin Mutual Shs Port Adv	IFMAX	B-	(800) 992-0180	C+ / 6.0	2.38	3.94	7.15 /56	13.29 /62	10.55 /49	0.77	1.53
GI	VY Franklin Mutual Shs Port Inst	IFMIX	B-	(800) 992-0180	C+ / 6.5	2.41	4.20	7.74 /61	13.95 /67	11.20 /54	1.20	0.78
GI	VY Franklin Mutual Shs Port Svc	IFMSX	B-	(800) 992-0180	C+ / 6.3	2.33	4.13	7.42 /59	13.64 /64	10.92 /52	0.97	1.03
GI	VY Franklin Temp Found Stratg Adv	ITFAX	C	(800) 992-0180	C- / 4.1	1.30	0.18	0.94 /18	11.08 /46	9.38 /40	2.20	1.65
GI	VY Franklin Temp Found Stratg Inst	ITFIX	C	(800) 992-0180	C / 4.5	1.45	0.54	1.62 /20	11.74 /51	10.03 /45	2.48	0.90
GI	VY Franklin Temp Found Stratg Svc	ITFSX	C	(800) 992-0180	C / 4.4	1.37	0.36	1.31 /19	11.47 /49	9.76 /43	2.27	1.15
GI	VY Invesco ComStock Adv	IVKAX	B-	(800) 992-0180	C+ / 6.9	-0.24	1.72	6.67 /52	15.45 /79	12.85 /67	1.69	1.25
GI	VY Invesco ComStock I	IVKIX	B+	(800) 992-0180	B- / 7.4	-0.12	1.99	7.24 /57	16.02 /84	13.42 /72	2.15	0.75
GI	VY Invesco ComStock Svc	IVKSX	B+	(800) 992-0180	B- / 7.1	-0.18	1.81	6.93 /54	15.71 /81	13.13 /69	1.90	1.00
GI	VY Invesco Eq and Inc Adv	IUAAX	B-	(800) 992-0180	C / 5.0	-0.04	1.88	6.04 /47	12.00 /52	9.50 /41	1.15	1.18
GI	VY Invesco Eq and Inc I	IUAIX	B	(800) 992-0180	C / 5.4	0.09	2.13	6.58 /52	12.56 /56	10.05 /45	1.51	0.68
GI	VY Invesco Eq and Inc Svc	IUASX	B-	(800) 992-0180	C / 5.2	0.02	1.99	6.31 /49	12.28 /54	9.78 /43	1.37	0.93
GI	VY Invesco Gr & Inc Adv	IVGAX	C+	(800) 992-0180	C+ / 6.5	-0.70	1.33	6.41 /50	14.76 /73	11.13 /54	0.92	1.40
GI	VY Invesco Gr & Inc Inst	IVGIX	B-	(800) 992-0180	B- / 7.0	-0.54	1.64	7.08 /56	15.44 /79	11.80 /59	1.37	0.65
GI	VY Invesco Gr & Inc Svc	IVGSX	C+	(800) 992-0180	C+ / 6.8	-0.60	1.51	6.82 /54	15.16 /76	11.52 /57	1.13	0.90
GI	VY Invesco Gr & Inc Svc 2	IVITX	C+	(800) 992-0180	C+ / 6.7	-0.63	1.45	6.64 /52	14.98 /75	11.35 /56	0.97	1.15
EM	VY JPMorgan Emer Mkt Eqty Adv	IJEAX	E	(800) 992-0180	E / 0.5	1.92	-1.22	0.01 /16	-0.05 / 4	1.33 / 4	0.70	2.01
EM	VY JPMorgan Emer Mkt Eqty Inst	IJEMX	E	(800) 992-0180	E+ / 0.6	2.07	-0.95	0.58 /17	0.54 / 5	1.93 / 4	1.19	1.26
EM	VY JPMorgan Emer Mkt Eqty Svc	IJPIX	E	(800) 992-0180	E / 0.5	2.03	-1.07	0.36 /17	0.29 / 5	1.68 / 4	0.92	1.51
EM	VY JPMorgan Emer Mkt Eqty Svc 2	IJPTX	E	(800) 992-0180	E / 0.5	1.93	-1.14	0.17 /16	0.14 / 4	1.53 / 4	0.79	1.76
MC	● VY JPMorgan Mid Cap Val Adv	IJMAX	A+	(800) 992-0180	A+ / 9.7	3.60	12.13	15.28 /92	18.94 /97	16.57 /95	0.56	1.37
MC	● VY JPMorgan Mid Cap Val I	IJMIX	A+	(800) 992-0180	A+ / 9.7	3.72	12.38	15.80 /93	19.51 /97	17.16 /96	0.96	0.87
MC	● VY JPMorgan Mid Cap Val Svc	IJMSX	A+	(800) 992-0180	A+ / 9.7	3.66	12.25	15.53 /93	19.21 /97	16.86 /96	0.73	1.12
SC	VY JPMorgan Sm Cap Eqty Adv	IJSAX	B+	(800) 992-0180	A / 9.4	4.69	15.27	11.34 /80	17.75 /93	16.15 /94	0.17	1.62
SC	VY JPMorgan Sm Cap Eqty Inst	IJSIX	B+	(800) 992-0180	A+ / 9.6	4.83	15.61	11.97 /82	18.45 /96	16.84 /96	0.51	0.87
SC	VY JPMorgan Sm Cap Eqty Svc	IJSSX	B+	(800) 992-0180	A / 9.5	4.78	15.49	11.69 /81	18.17 /95	16.55 /95	0.32	1.12
SC	VY JPMorgan Sm Cap Eqty Svc 2	IJSTX	B+	(800) 992-0180	A / 9.5	4.72	15.46	11.55 /81	18.00 /94	16.37 /94	0.17	1.37
GL	VY Morgan Stanley Glbl Franch Adv	IGFAX	D	(800) 992-0180	C- / 3.0	0.48	1.46	3.90 /31	8.55 /30	10.89 /52	1.57	1.71
GL	VY Morgan Stanley Glbl Franch Svc	IVGTX	D	(800) 992-0180	C- / 3.3	0.58	1.64	4.28 /34	8.93 /32	11.27 /55	1.67	1.21
GL	VY Morgan Stanley Glbl Franch Svc 2	IGFSX	D	(800) 992-0180	C- / 3.2	0.53	1.53	4.09 /32	8.76 /31	11.11 /54	1.53	1.46
GL	VY Oppenheimer Global Adv	IGMAX	C+	(800) 992-0180	C+ / 6.9	7.36	6.89	8.64 /67	13.73 /65	10.84 /51	0.74	1.26
GL	VY Oppenheimer Global I	IGMIX	B-	(800) 992-0180	B- / 7.3	7.54	7.20	9.17 /70	14.31 /69	11.39 /56	1.10	0.76
GL	VY Oppenheimer Global S	IGMSX	B-	(800) 992-0180	B- / 7.1	7.44	7.03	8.92 /69	14.03 /67	11.11 /54	0.91	1.01
AA	VY T Rowe Price Cap App Adv	ITRAX	C+	(800) 992-0180	C+ / 6.9	3.10	7.91	12.17 /83	13.53 /64	12.02 /61	0.95	1.39

● Denotes fund is closed to new investors
* Denotes fund is included in Section II

RISK			NET ASSETS		ASSET				Portfolio	BULL / BEAR		FUND MANAGER		MINIMUMS		LOADS	
	3 Year		NAV							Last Bull	Last Bear	Manager	Manager	Initial	Additional	Front	Back
Risk Rating/Pts	Standard Deviation	Beta	As of 3/31/15	Total $(Mil)	Cash %	Stocks %	Bonds %	Other %	Turnover Ratio	Market Return	Market Return	Quality Pct	Tenure (Years)	Purch. $	Purch. $	End Load	End Load
C / 5.5	10.2	1.04	25.14	12	0	99	0	1	128	96.9	-20.0	59	2	0	0	0.0	0.0
C / 5.5	10.2	1.04	24.75	326	0	99	0	1	128	95.0	-20.0	54	2	0	0	0.0	0.0
C+ / 6.3	12.5	0.91	16.87	30	2	97	0	1	39	98.1	-27.2	75	9	0	0	0.0	0.0
C+ / 6.3	12.5	0.91	17.35	49	2	97	0	1	39	101.2	-27.0	79	9	0	0	0.0	0.0
C+ / 6.4	12.4	0.91	17.25	159	2	97	0	1	39	99.6	-27.0	78	9	0	0	0.0	0.0
C+ / 6.5	11.3	1.07	10.83	6	2	97	0	1	4	65.5	-23.1	7	N/A	0	0	0.0	0.0
C+ / 6.5	11.2	1.06	11.13	4	2	97	0	1	4	68.9	-22.8	9	N/A	0	0	0.0	0.0
C+ / 6.5	11.2	1.06	11.10	171	2	97	0	1	4	67.6	-22.9	8	N/A	0	0	0.0	0.0
C+ / 6.9	9.6	0.99	15.25	7	2	97	0	1	86	88.1	-18.9	49	8	0	0	0.0	0.0
C+ / 6.9	9.6	0.98	15.39	290	2	97	0	1	86	89.7	-18.8	54	8	0	0	0.0	0.0
C- / 3.1	11.6	1.01	18.97	69	0	99	0	1	132	79.2	-21.6	36	11	0	0	0.0	0.0
C- / 3.2	11.5	1.01	19.59	111	0	99	0	1	132	83.0	-21.4	46	11	0	0	0.0	0.0
C- / 3.2	11.5	1.01	19.41	867	0	99	0	1	132	81.4	-21.5	42	11	0	0	0.0	0.0
C- / 3.1	11.6	1.01	19.26	75	0	99	0	1	132	80.5	-21.5	39	11	0	0	0.0	0.0
C+ / 6.7	6.8	0.60	11.05	79	3	56	36	5	23	46.7	-11.2	57	9	0	0	0.0	0.0
C+ / 6.7	6.8	0.60	11.48	302	3	56	36	5	23	49.7	-11.0	66	9	0	0	0.0	0.0
C+ / 6.8	6.8	0.60	11.39	528	3	56	36	5	23	48.5	-11.1	62	9	0	0	0.0	0.0
C+ / 6.8	6.8	0.60	11.35	11	3	56	36	5	23	47.7	-11.2	60	9	0	0	0.0	0.0
B- / 7.3	9.0	0.91	11.61	10	3	83	12	2	25	77.2	-17.3	50	8	0	0	0.0	0.0
B- / 7.3	9.0	0.91	11.90	290	3	83	12	2	25	80.6	-17.0	60	8	0	0	0.0	0.0
B- / 7.4	9.0	0.91	11.86	203	3	83	12	2	25	79.2	-17.2	55	8	0	0	0.0	0.0
B- / 7.1	9.2	0.89	10.90	13	3	80	15	2	11	64.2	-17.1	27	8	0	0	0.0	0.0
B- / 7.1	9.2	0.89	11.20	4	3	80	15	2	11	67.7	-16.9	34	8	0	0	0.0	0.0
B- / 7.1	9.2	0.89	11.13	855	3	80	15	2	11	66.2	-17.0	31	8	0	0	0.0	0.0
B- / 7.2	10.5	1.05	16.38	40	3	96	0	1	15	96.4	-20.4	48	13	0	0	0.0	0.0
B- / 7.2	10.5	1.05	16.53	141	3	96	0	1	15	99.6	-20.2	55	13	0	0	0.0	0.0
B- / 7.2	10.5	1.05	16.50	370	3	96	0	1	15	98.1	-20.3	52	13	0	0	0.0	0.0
B / 8.1	7.1	0.72	46.23	53	5	65	22	8	37	65.8	-15.4	73	14	0	0	0.0	0.0
B / 8.1	7.1	0.72	46.97	679	5	65	22	8	37	68.6	-15.2	78	14	0	0	0.0	0.0
B / 8.1	7.1	0.72	46.60	850	5	65	22	8	37	67.2	-15.3	76	14	0	0	0.0	0.0
C+ / 6.3	9.9	1.00	31.27	16	3	96	0	1	28	89.1	-20.2	51	16	0	0	0.0	0.0
C+ / 6.2	9.9	1.00	31.54	25	3	96	0	1	28	93.1	-20.0	60	16	0	0	0.0	0.0
C+ / 6.3	9.9	1.00	31.64	511	3	96	0	1	28	91.4	-20.1	56	16	0	0	0.0	0.0
C+ / 6.3	9.9	1.00	31.43	44	3	96	0	1	28	90.4	-20.1	54	16	0	0	0.0	0.0
C- / 3.8	15.3	1.06	16.95	42	0	99	0	1	45	25.0	-25.6	56	10	0	0	0.0	0.0
C- / 3.9	15.3	1.06	17.72	72	0	99	0	1	45	27.6	-25.5	65	10	0	0	0.0	0.0
C- / 3.9	15.3	1.06	17.61	488	0	99	0	1	45	26.5	-25.5	61	10	0	0	0.0	0.0
C- / 3.9	15.3	1.06	17.41	22	0	99	0	1	45	25.8	-25.6	59	10	0	0	0.0	0.0
C+ / 6.6	9.0	0.78	23.28	97	2	97	0	1	25	110.1	-17.9	94	11	0	0	0.0	0.0
C+ / 6.6	9.0	0.78	23.70	275	2	97	0	1	25	113.6	-17.7	95	11	0	0	0.0	0.0
C+ / 6.6	9.0	0.78	23.53	357	2	97	0	1	25	111.8	-17.8	94	11	0	0	0.0	0.0
C / 4.7	12.4	0.91	20.76	109	3	96	0	1	41	111.2	-24.1	87	11	0	0	0.0	0.0
C / 4.7	12.3	0.91	21.70	174	3	96	0	1	41	115.7	-24.0	89	11	0	0	0.0	0.0
C / 4.7	12.3	0.91	21.47	471	3	96	0	1	41	113.9	-24.1	89	11	0	0	0.0	0.0
C / 4.7	12.3	0.91	21.28	49	3	96	0	1	41	112.7	-24.1	88	11	0	0	0.0	0.0
C / 5.4	11.4	0.76	16.64	56	1	98	0	1	21	55.1	-6.9	79	6	0	0	0.0	0.0
C / 5.4	11.4	0.76	17.33	330	1	98	0	1	21	57.0	-6.8	82	6	0	0	0.0	0.0
C / 5.4	11.4	0.76	17.21	52	1	98	0	1	21	56.2	-6.8	81	6	0	0	0.0	0.0
C+ / 5.9	12.1	0.87	19.55	107	1	98	0	1	11	77.6	-23.0	93	11	0	0	0.0	0.0
C+ / 5.9	12.1	0.88	20.26	1,383	1	98	0	1	11	80.7	-22.9	94	11	0	0	0.0	0.0
C+ / 5.9	12.1	0.87	19.64	229	1	98	0	1	11	79.2	-23.0	94	11	0	0	0.0	0.0
C+ / 6.6	5.9	1.01	28.89	498	7	63	28	2	69	75.6	-12.9	86	9	0	0	0.0	0.0

Fund Type	Fund Name	Ticker Symbol	Overall Investment Rating	Phone	Performance Rating/Pts	3 Mo	6 Mo	1Yr / Pct	3Yr / Pct	5Yr / Pct	Dividend Yield	Expense Ratio
								Total Return % through 3/31/15		Annualized	Incl. in Returns	
AA	VY T Rowe Price Cap App Inst	ITRIX	B+	(800) 992-0180	B- / 7.4	3.30	8.25	12.83 /86	14.22 /69	12.70 /66	1.38	0.64
AA	VY T Rowe Price Cap App Svc	ITCSX	B	(800) 992-0180	B- / 7.2	3.23	8.11	12.57 /85	13.93 /67	12.42 /64	1.16	0.89
AA	VY T Rowe Price Cap App Svc 2	ITCTX	B	(800) 992-0180	B- / 7.0	3.18	8.03	12.35 /84	13.75 /65	12.24 /62	1.03	1.14
GR	VY T Rowe Price Dvs Mid Cap G Adv	IAXAX	B+	(800) 992-0180	A / 9.3	6.21	13.56	15.80 /93	16.82 /89	16.01 /93	0.03	1.27
GR	VY T Rowe Price Dvs Mid Cap G I	IAXIX	A-	(800) 992-0180	A / 9.5	6.43	13.91	16.42 /94	17.42 /92	16.59 /95	0.23	0.77
GR	VY T Rowe Price Dvs Mid Cap G S	IAXSX	A-	(800) 992-0180	A / 9.4	6.32	13.81	16.17 /94	17.10 /90	16.30 /94	0.03	1.02
IN	VY T Rowe Price Eqty Income Adv	ITEAX	C	(800) 992-0180	C / 5.3	-1.23	1.71	4.24 /33	12.85 /59	11.18 /54	1.49	1.39
IN	VY T Rowe Price Eqty Income Inst	ITEIX	C+	(800) 992-0180	C+ / 5.7	-1.09	1.98	4.86 /38	13.52 /64	11.84 /60	2.05	0.64
IN	VY T Rowe Price Eqty Income Svc	IRPSX	C+	(800) 992-0180	C / 5.5	-1.09	1.90	4.66 /36	13.25 /61	11.56 /57	1.80	0.89
IN	VY T Rowe Price Eqty Income Svc 2	ITETX	C	(800) 992-0180	C / 5.4	-1.16	1.85	4.50 /35	13.07 /60	11.40 /56	1.68	1.14
GR	VY T Rowe Price Growth Eq Adv	IGEAX	B+	(800) 992-0180	A- / 9.1	5.85	10.28	16.08 /93	16.41 /86	15.58 /91	0.00	1.24
GR	VY T Rowe Price Growth Eq I	ITGIX	A-	(800) 992-0180	A / 9.3	5.98	10.55	16.65 /94	16.99 /90	16.16 /94	0.00	0.74
GR	VY T Rowe Price Growth Eq S	ITGSX	B+	(800) 992-0180	A- / 9.2	5.92	10.42	16.37 /94	16.71 /88	15.87 /92	0.00	0.99
FO	VY T Rowe Price Intl Stk Adv	IMIOX	D	(800) 992-0180	D+ / 2.8	6.01	4.48	3.94 / 31	7.30 /23	6.69 /21	0.85	1.52
FO	VY T Rowe Price Intl Stk Inst	IMASX	D	(800) 992-0180	C- / 3.3	6.24	4.86	4.66 /36	7.95 /27	7.33 /25	1.32	0.77
FO	VY T Rowe Price Intl Stk Svc	IMISX	D	(800) 992-0180	C- / 3.1	6.18	4.73	4.37 /34	7.69 /25	7.07 /24	1.11	1.02
FO	VY Templeton Foreign Equity Adv	IFTAX	D	(800) 992-0180	D+ / 2.5	5.71	0.80	-3.11 / 8	8.15 /28	5.70 /15	2.09	1.44
FO	VY Templeton Foreign Equity I	IFTIX	D	(800) 992-0180	D+ / 2.9	5.90	1.03	-2.56 / 9	8.68 /31	6.23 /18	2.54	0.94
FO	VY Templeton Foreign Equity S	IFTSX	D	(800) 992-0180	D+ / 2.7	5.86	0.96	-2.82 / 9	8.40 /29	5.96 /17	2.30	1.19
GL	VY Templeton Glb Growth Adv	IGGAX	C-	(800) 992-0180	C- / 3.8	1.53	-1.54	-4.26 / 7	11.45 /49	9.00 /37	0.92	1.64
GL	VY Templeton Glb Growth Inst	IIGGX	C-	(800) 992-0180	C- / 4.2	1.69	-1.26	-3.68 / 7	12.12 /53	9.75 /43	1.44	0.89
GL	VY Templeton Glb Growth Svc	ISGGX	C-	(800) 992-0180	C- / 4.1	1.55	-1.38	-3.95 / 7	11.82 /51	9.47 /40	1.19	1.14
GL	VY Templeton Glb Growth Svc 2	ICGGX	C-	(800) 992-0180	C- / 4.0	1.56	-1.45	-4.10 / 7	11.67 /50	9.30 /39	1.06	1.39
GR	Waddell & Reed Adv Accumulative A	UNACX	C+	(888) 923-3355	B / 7.9	4.37	10.09	16.54 /94	15.76 /81	14.03 /78	0.16	1.15
GR	Waddell & Reed Adv Accumulative B	WAABX	C+	(888) 923-3355	B / 8.0	4.12	9.49	15.26 /92	14.33 /70	12.61 /65	0.00	2.38
GR	Waddell & Reed Adv Accumulative C	WAACX	C+	(888) 923-3355	B / 8.2	4.16	9.59	15.38 /92	14.62 /72	12.87 /67	0.00	2.12
GR	Waddell & Reed Adv Accumulative Y	WAAYX	B	(888) 923-3355	A- / 9.1	4.54	10.29	16.82 /94	16.08 /84	14.34 /81	0.37	0.89
GL	Waddell & Reed Adv Asset Strat A	UNASX	E	(888) 923-3355	D- / 1.5	1.46	1.19	-2.56 / 9	7.90 /26	7.32 /25	0.68	1.10
GL	Waddell & Reed Adv Asset Strat B	WBASX	E	(888) 923-3355	D / 1.7	1.29	0.72	-3.48 / 8	6.87 /21	6.30 /19	0.02	2.08
GL	Waddell & Reed Adv Asset Strat C	WCASX	E	(888) 923-3355	D / 1.8	1.28	0.80	-3.29 / 8	7.01 /21	6.46 /20	0.17	1.92
GL	Waddell & Reed Adv Asset Strat Y	WYASX	E	(888) 923-3355	D+ / 2.5	1.68	1.39	-2.18 /10	8.23 /28	7.65 /28	0.87	0.82
BA	Waddell & Reed Adv Continentl Inc A	UNCIX	C	(888) 923-3355	C / 4.4	2.53	5.91	9.01 /69	11.46 /49	11.47 /57	0.63	1.18
BA	Waddell & Reed Adv Continentl Inc B	WACBX	C+	(888) 923-3355	C / 4.5	2.26	5.30	7.92 /62	10.23 /41	10.26 /47	0.00	2.29
BA	Waddell & Reed Adv Continentl Inc C	WACCX	C+	(888) 923-3355	C / 4.7	2.44	5.56	8.29 /65	10.55 /43	10.51 /49	0.00	2.02
BA	Waddell & Reed Adv Continentl Inc Y	WACYX	B-	(888) 923-3355	C+ / 5.6	2.69	6.11	9.42 /72	11.81 /51	11.82 /59	0.94	0.90
GR	Waddell & Reed Adv Core Invest A	UNCMX	C	(888) 923-3355	C+ / 6.5	1.70	4.75	10.33 /76	15.37 /78	14.90 /86	0.25	1.06
GR	Waddell & Reed Adv Core Invest B	UNIBX	C-	(888) 923-3355	C+ / 6.6	1.32	4.12	9.02 /69	14.05 /67	13.53 /73	0.00	2.22
GR	Waddell & Reed Adv Core Invest C	WCCIX	C-	(888) 923-3355	C+ / 6.7	1.29	4.07	9.20 /70	14.25 /69	13.75 /75	0.00	2.00
GR	Waddell & Reed Adv Core Invest Y	UNIYX	C+	(888) 923-3355	B / 7.8	1.69	4.84	10.54 /77	15.67 /81	15.20 /88	0.48	0.80
GI	Waddell & Reed Adv Dividend Oppty	WDVAX	D+	(888) 923-3355	C / 5.1	0.64	4.49	8.13 /64	13.30 /62	11.41 /56	0.98	1.26
GI	Waddell & Reed Adv Dividend Oppty	WDVBX	D+	(888) 923-3355	C / 5.2	0.42	3.98	6.99 /55	12.03 /53	10.17 /46	0.09	2.39
GI	Waddell & Reed Adv Dividend Oppty	WDVCX	C-	(888) 923-3355	C / 5.5	0.47	4.14	7.28 /57	12.35 /55	10.44 /48	0.24	2.11
GI	Waddell & Reed Adv Dividend Oppty	WDVYX	C-	(888) 923-3355	C+ / 6.3	0.71	4.68	8.48 /66	13.69 /65	11.82 /59	1.34	0.95
EN	Waddell & Reed Adv Energy Fund A	WEGAX	E-	(888) 923-3355	E / 0.4	2.07	-16.47	-13.75 / 2	3.79 /10	4.95 /12	0.00	1.57
EN	Waddell & Reed Adv Energy Fund B	WEGBX	E-	(888) 923-3355	E / 0.4	1.74	-16.99	-14.80 / 2	2.50 / 7	3.69 / 7	0.00	2.78
EN	Waddell & Reed Adv Energy Fund C	WEGCX	E-	(888) 923-3355	E / 0.5	1.84	-16.81	-14.46 / 2	2.92 / 8	4.10 / 9	0.00	2.42
EN	Waddell & Reed Adv Energy Fund Y	WEGYX	E-	(888) 923-3355	E+ / 0.6	2.19	-16.23	-13.31 / 2	4.33 /11	5.51 /14	0.00	1.09
FO	Waddell & Reed Adv Glbl Growth A	UNCGX	D+	(888) 923-3355	C- / 3.6	5.96	5.69	5.43 /42	10.22 /41	9.53 /41	0.37	1.45
FO	Waddell & Reed Adv Glbl Growth B	WAIBX	D+	(888) 923-3355	C- / 3.5	5.52	4.85	4.01 /32	8.68 /31	8.00 /30	0.00	2.79
FO	Waddell & Reed Adv Glbl Growth C	WAICX	D+	(888) 923-3355	C- / 3.8	5.67	5.10	4.29 /34	9.09 /34	8.38 /32	0.00	2.52
FO	Waddell & Reed Adv Glbl Growth Y	WAIYX	C-	(888) 923-3355	C / 4.8	5.95	5.82	5.73 /44	10.64 /43	9.95 /44	0.59	1.08
MC	Waddell & Reed Adv New Concepts	UNECX	C-	(888) 923-3355	C+ / 5.8	4.04	10.65	10.84 /78	13.25 /61	15.06 /87	0.00	1.37

• Denotes fund is closed to new investors
* Denotes fund is included in Section II

www.thestreetratings.com

RISK			NET ASSETS		ASSET					BULL / BEAR		FUND MANAGER		MINIMUMS		LOADS	
	3 Year		NAV						Portfolio	Last Bull	Last Bear	Manager	Manager	Initial	Additional	Front	Back
Risk Rating/Pts	Standard Deviation	Beta	As of 3/31/15	Total $(Mil)	Cash %	Stocks %	Bonds %	Other %	Turnover Ratio	Market Return	Market Return	Quality Pct	Tenure (Years)	Purch. $	Purch. $	End Load	End Load
C+ / 6.7	5.9	1.01	29.74	1,076	7	63	28	2	69	79.3	-12.7	88	9	0	0	0.0	0.0
C+ / 6.7	5.9	1.01	29.74	4,180	7	63	28	2	69	77.7	-12.8	87	9	0	0	0.0	0.0
C+ / 6.7	5.9	1.01	29.57	93	7	63	28	2	69	76.8	-12.9	86	9	0	0	0.0	0.0
C / 5.5	11.4	1.05	12.14	30	0	99	0	1	20	103.1	-22.9	65	13	0	0	0.0	0.0
C+ / 5.7	11.3	1.05	12.91	839	0	99	0	1	20	106.4	-22.7	72	13	0	0	0.0	0.0
C+ / 5.6	11.3	1.04	12.62	29	0	99	0	1	20	104.8	-22.8	69	13	0	0	0.0	0.0
C+ / 6.3	9.5	0.96	16.09	60	7	92	0	1	12	82.8	-18.4	33	16	0	0	0.0	0.0
C+ / 6.4	9.5	0.97	16.29	193	7	92	0	1	12	86.6	-18.2	41	16	0	0	0.0	0.0
C+ / 6.4	9.5	0.97	16.31	960	7	92	0	1	12	85.0	-18.3	37	16	0	0	0.0	0.0
C+ / 6.3	9.5	0.97	16.16	125	7	92	0	1	12	84.1	-18.3	35	16	0	0	0.0	0.0
C+ / 5.6	11.0	0.97	91.60	180	1	98	0	1	41	107.0	-16.7	74	1	0	0	0.0	0.0
C+ / 5.7	11.0	0.97	95.54	1,032	1	98	0	1	41	110.6	-16.5	78	1	0	0	0.0	0.0
C+ / 5.7	11.0	0.97	93.56	392	1	98	0	1	41	108.8	-16.6	76	1	0	0	0.0	0.0
C+ / 5.7	12.3	0.89	13.76	14	3	96	0	1	48	51.4	-24.1	51	4	0	0	0.0	0.0
C+ / 5.7	12.2	0.89	13.80	52	3	96	0	1	48	54.5	-23.8	61	4	0	0	0.0	0.0
C+ / 5.7	12.2	0.89	13.74	193	3	96	0	1	48	53.2	-23.9	57	4	0	0	0.0	0.0
C+ / 5.7	13.6	1.01	12.59	41	2	97	0	1	12	48.0	-25.1	47	9	0	0	0.0	0.0
C+ / 5.7	13.7	1.01	12.75	224	2	97	0	1	12	50.5	-24.9	54	9	0	0	0.0	0.0
C+ / 5.7	13.7	1.01	12.65	597	2	97	0	1	12	49.3	-25.0	51	9	0	0	0.0	0.0
C+ / 6.3	12.8	0.93	15.31	N/A	2	97	0	1	12	70.4	-22.6	86	10	0	0	0.0	0.0
C+ / 6.3	12.9	0.93	15.66	294	2	97	0	1	12	74.1	-22.3	89	10	0	0	0.0	0.0
C+ / 6.3	12.9	0.93	15.70	250	2	97	0	1	12	72.6	-22.4	88	10	0	0	0.0	0.0
C+ / 6.3	12.9	0.93	15.58	5	2	97	0	1	12	71.7	-22.5	87	10	0	0	0.0	0.0
C / 4.7	9.9	0.96	10.99	1,423	1	95	2	2	104	96.1	-17.6	70	11	750	0	5.8	0.0
C / 4.5	10.0	0.97	9.60	5	1	95	2	2	104	88.1	-18.1	51	11	750	0	0.0	0.0
C / 4.5	10.0	0.97	9.77	6	1	95	2	2	104	89.6	-18.1	56	11	750	0	0.0	0.0
C / 4.6	10.0	0.97	11.05	5	1	95	2	2	104	98.3	-17.7	72	11	0	0	0.0	0.0
D+ / 2.7	10.5	1.41	9.01	3,194	5	74	19	2	83	54.4	-22.2	13	18	750	0	5.8	0.0
D+ / 2.6	10.5	1.42	8.67	35	5	74	19	2	83	49.5	-22.5	8	18	750	0	0.0	0.0
D+ / 2.6	10.6	1.42	8.72	57	5	74	19	2	83	50.3	-22.5	8	18	750	0	0.0	0.0
D+ / 2.7	10.5	1.41	9.07	67	5	74	19	2	83	56.0	-22.0	15	18	0	0	0.0	0.0
B- / 7.4	7.9	1.32	10.53	1,500	1	67	31	1	34	67.0	-12.3	28	1	750	0	5.8	0.0
B- / 7.5	7.9	1.32	10.40	5	1	67	31	1	34	60.7	-12.6	17	1	750	0	0.0	0.0
B- / 7.5	7.9	1.33	10.49	16	1	67	31	1	34	62.3	-12.7	19	1	750	0	0.0	0.0
B- / 7.4	7.8	1.31	10.54	6	1	67	31	1	34	68.7	-12.3	32	1	0	0	0.0	0.0
C / 4.5	10.7	1.08	7.18	4,479	2	95	1	2	52	98.5	-17.2	39	9	750	0	5.8	0.0
C- / 4.0	10.7	1.08	6.14	13	2	95	1	2	52	90.6	-17.6	25	9	750	0	0.0	0.0
C- / 4.1	10.7	1.08	6.26	23	2	95	1	2	52	92.4	-17.6	27	9	750	0	0.0	0.0
C / 4.5	10.7	1.08	7.21	103	2	95	1	2	52	100.5	-17.2	44	9	0	0	0.0	0.0
C / 4.4	10.5	1.07	17.33	676	4	90	5	1	47	87.9	-23.9	20	1	750	0	5.8	0.0
C / 4.4	10.5	1.07	16.92	5	4	90	5	1	47	80.8	-24.2	12	1	750	0	0.0	0.0
C / 4.4	10.5	1.07	17.05	9	4	90	5	1	47	82.3	-24.1	14	1	750	0	0.0	0.0
C / 4.4	10.5	1.07	17.34	5	4	90	5	1	47	90.2	-23.7	24	1	750	0	0.0	0.0
D+ / 2.6	17.3	1.03	14.30	260	10	85	3	2	43	39.4	-32.2	65	9	750	0	5.8	0.0
D+ / 2.6	17.3	1.03	12.90	1	10	85	3	2	43	33.5	-32.4	46	9	750	0	0.0	0.0
D+ / 2.6	17.3	1.03	13.31	3	10	85	3	2	43	35.5	-32.4	52	9	750	0	0.0	0.0
D+ / 2.7	17.3	1.03	14.92	3	10	85	3	2	43	41.9	-32.0	71	9	0	0	0.0	0.0
C+ / 6.0	11.1	0.81	12.45	566	1	89	8	2	49	63.4	-22.2	86	1	750	0	5.8	0.0
C+ / 5.9	11.0	0.81	11.27	1	1	89	8	2	49	55.6	-22.6	77	1	750	0	0.0	0.0
C+ / 6.0	11.1	0.81	11.75	2	1	89	8	2	49	57.7	-22.6	79	1	750	0	0.0	0.0
C+ / 6.0	11.1	0.81	12.46	63	1	89	8	2	49	65.6	-22.1	88	1	0	0	0.0	0.0
C / 4.5	10.7	0.91	11.32	1,840	0	97	2	1	51	86.3	-21.2	39	14	750	0	5.8	0.0

99 Pct = Best
0 Pct = Worst

Fund Type	Fund Name	Ticker Symbol	Overall Investment Rating	Phone	Performance Rating/Pts	3 Mo	6 Mo	1Yr / Pct	3Yr / Pct	5Yr / Pct	Dividend Yield	Expense Ratio
MC	Waddell & Reed Adv New Concepts	UNEBX	D	(888) 923-3355	C+ / 5.9	3.66	9.93	9.57 /72	11.97 /52	13.76 /75	0.00	2.51
MC	Waddell & Reed Adv New Concepts	WNCCX	D+	(888) 923-3355	C+ / 6.1	3.77	10.04	9.92 /74	12.22 /54	13.98 /78	0.00	2.28
MC	Waddell & Reed Adv New Concepts	UNEYX	C+	(888) 923-3355	B- / 7.1	4.07	10.73	11.25 /79	13.65 /65	15.51 /90	0.00	1.03
TC	Waddell & Reed Adv Science & Tech	UNSCX	B+	(888) 923-3355	A+ / 9.6	5.27	6.86	7.52 /59	21.68 /98	17.54 /97	0.00	1.26
TC	Waddell & Reed Adv Science & Tech	USTBX	B	(888) 923-3355	A+ / 9.6	5.02	6.25	6.34 /49	20.36 /98	16.24 /94	0.00	2.32
TC	Waddell & Reed Adv Science & Tech	WCSTX	B	(888) 923-3355	A+ / 9.6	5.04	6.33	6.50 /51	20.52 /98	16.39 /94	0.00	2.19
TC	Waddell & Reed Adv Science & Tech	USTFX	A-	(888) 923-3355	A+ / 9.8	5.34	7.02	7.81 /61	22.04 /98	17.92 /97	0.00	0.99
SC	Waddell & Reed Adv Small Cap A	UNSAX	C	(888) 923-3355	B / 7.6	5.58	16.30	7.87 /62	16.04 /84	15.66 /91	0.00	1.45
SC	Waddell & Reed Adv Small Cap B	WRSBX	C-	(888) 923-3355	B / 7.7	5.30	15.66	6.71 /53	14.72 /73	14.37 /81	0.00	2.55
SC	Waddell & Reed Adv Small Cap C	WSCCX	C	(888) 923-3355	B / 8.0	5.37	15.86	7.07 /56	15.09 /76	14.71 /84	0.00	2.27
SC	Waddell & Reed Adv Small Cap Y	WRSYX	B-	(888) 923-3355	B+ / 8.9	5.68	16.54	8.32 /65	16.52 /87	16.17 /94	0.00	1.06
GR	Waddell & Reed Adv Tax Managed	WTEAX	B+	(888) 923-3355	B / 8.2	4.66	8.49	17.49 /95	16.31 /86	14.19 /79	0.02	1.09
GR	Waddell & Reed Adv Tax Managed	WBTMX	B+	(888) 923-3355	B+ / 8.4	4.37	7.91	16.29 /94	15.13 /76	13.08 /69	0.00	2.06
GR	Waddell & Reed Adv Tax Managed	WCTMX	B+	(888) 923-3355	B+ / 8.5	4.44	8.05	16.45 /94	15.28 /77	13.18 /70	0.00	1.95
GR	Waddell & Reed Adv Value A	WVAAX	C	(888) 923-3355	C / 5.3	-2.32	-1.55	5.65 /44	14.82 /73	11.74 /59	0.28	1.26
GR	Waddell & Reed Adv Value B	WVABX	C	(888) 923-3355	C / 5.4	-2.52	-2.05	4.48 /35	13.52 /64	10.45 /48	0.00	2.41
GR	Waddell & Reed Adv Value C	WVACX	C	(888) 923-3355	C+ / 5.6	-2.48	-1.95	4.73 /37	13.80 /66	10.73 /51	0.00	2.14
GR	Waddell & Reed Adv Value Y	WVAYX	C+	(888) 923-3355	C+ / 6.5	-2.19	-1.39	5.97 /46	15.26 /77	12.20 /62	0.61	0.91
GR	Waddell & Reed Adv Vanguard A	UNVGX	C+	(888) 923-3355	B / 7.9	5.23	10.40	17.63 /95	15.22 /77	14.32 /81	0.00	1.19
GR	Waddell & Reed Adv Vanguard B	WRVBX	C	(888) 923-3355	B / 8.0	5.04	9.93	16.41 /94	13.83 /66	12.94 /68	0.00	2.39
GR	Waddell & Reed Adv Vanguard C	WAVCX	C	(888) 923-3355	B / 8.1	5.06	9.95	16.58 /94	14.04 /67	13.15 /70	0.00	2.18
GR	Waddell & Reed Adv Vanguard Y	WAVYX	B	(888) 923-3355	A- / 9.1	5.33	10.64	18.06 /96	15.56 /80	14.70 /84	0.14	0.88
BA	Walden Asset Management	WSBFX	C	(800) 282-8782	C- / 3.7	-0.25	3.86	7.00 /55	9.14 /34	9.21 /38	1.01	1.05
GI	Walden Equity	WSEFX	C+	(800) 282-8782	C / 5.2	-0.64	4.45	8.13 /64	11.89 /52	12.08 /61	0.90	1.08
GL	Walden Mid Cap Fund	WAMFX	B-	(800) 282-8782	C+ / 6.6	2.71	9.22	12.25 /84	12.95 /59	--	0.33	1.04
SC	● Walden Small Cap Innovations	WASOX	C-	(800) 282-8782	C / 5.1	3.09	11.56	3.86 /31	11.33 /48	12.05 /61	0.08	1.05
GL	Walden SMID Cap Innovations	WASMX	U	(800) 282-8782	U /	4.70	12.26	7.60 /60	--	--	0.04	1.12
GR	Wall Street Fund	WALLX	A-	(800) 443-4693	B / 8.2	1.32	8.49	14.50 /91	15.35 /78	14.65 /84	0.16	1.25
GR	Walthausen Select Value Inst	WSVIX	B+	(888) 925-8428	B / 8.2	3.20	4.30	1.68 /21	18.10 /95	--	0.92	1.46
GR	Walthausen Select Value Retail	WSVRX	B+	(888) 925-8428	B / 8.0	3.23	4.27	1.50 /20	17.83 /94	--	0.75	1.46
SC	● Walthausen Small Cap Value Fund	WSCVX	C+	(888) 925-8428	B / 8.0	0.36	7.59	3.81 /31	17.49 /92	16.67 /95	0.00	1.25
FO	Wanger International	WSCAX	D-	(800) 492-6437	C- / 3.0	4.33	1.42	-1.46 /12	8.81 /32	8.90 /36	1.40	1.07
FO	Wanger International Select Fund	WAFFX	E+	(800) 492-6437	D- / 1.0	1.56	-6.83	-8.20 / 3	5.84 /16	7.22 /24	1.51	1.52
MC	Wanger Select Fund	WATWX	C-	(800) 492-6437	C+ / 5.7	2.52	5.79	6.06 /47	12.64 /57	10.17 /46	0.00	0.93
SC	Wanger USA	WUSAX	C	(800) 492-6437	B / 7.8	5.25	12.95	9.33 /71	14.72 /73	14.56 /83	0.00	0.96
GR	Wasatch Core Growth Fund Inst	WIGRX	A+	(800) 551-1700	A / 9.3	7.31	17.91	15.20 /92	16.84 /89	--	0.00	1.18
GR	Wasatch Core Growth Investor	WGROX	A	(800) 551-1700	A / 9.3	7.30	17.85	15.11 /92	16.75 /88	17.15 /96	0.00	1.18
FO	Wasatch Emerging India Investor	WAINX	C+	(800) 551-1700	A+ / 9.9	5.76	14.35	43.20 /99	18.63 /96	--	0.05	2.57
EM	● Wasatch Emerging Markets SC	WAEMX	E	(800) 551-1700	E+ / 0.6	0.37	-2.06	4.42 /35	1.57 / 6	7.06 /23	0.14	2.02
EM	Wasatch Emerging Markets Sel Inst	WIESX	U	(800) 766-8938	U /	-0.49	-1.26	3.52 /29	--	--	0.48	1.71
EM	Wasatch Emerging Markets Sel Inv	WAESX	U	(800) 766-8938	U /	-0.59	-1.41	3.30 /28	--	--	0.34	1.88
EM	● Wasatch Frntr Em Sml Countries Inv	WAFMX	C	(800) 551-1700	C- / 4.1	-4.52	-9.04	-4.74 / 6	13.89 /66	--	0.53	2.24
GL	Wasatch Global Opportunities Inv	WAGOX	D	(800) 551-1700	C / 5.5	4.04	5.71	5.71 /44	12.77 /58	12.01 /61	0.25	1.78
GR	● Wasatch Heritage Growth Investor	WAHGX	D-	(800) 551-1700	C+ / 6.4	5.98	13.81	9.33 /71	13.00 /60	13.53 /73	0.00	0.95
FO	● Wasatch International Growth Inv	WAIGX	C-	(800) 551-1700	C / 4.3	6.21	4.75	-1.70 /11	11.51 /49	12.97 /68	0.02	1.46
FO	Wasatch International Opps Inv	WAIOX	C	(800) 551-1700	C+ / 5.7	5.22	1.43	5.53 /43	13.41 /63	11.24 /55	0.00	2.41
GI	Wasatch Large Cap Value Fund Inst	WILCX	C	(800) 766-8938	C- / 3.7	-0.28	1.07	4.39 /34	10.43 /42	--	1.55	1.25
IN	Wasatch Large Cap Value Investor	FMIEX	E	(800) 766-8938	C- / 3.6	-0.31	1.01	4.18 /33	10.29 /41	8.47 /33	1.44	1.12
GR	Wasatch Long-Short Institutional	WILSX	U	(800) 766-8938	U /	-1.68	-4.31	-4.37 / 6	--	--	1.11	1.42
AA	Wasatch Long-Short Investor	FMLSX	D-	(800) 766-8938	E+ / 0.9	-1.68	-4.38	-4.56 / 6	5.21 /14	6.05 /17	0.91	1.53
SC	Wasatch Micro Cap Investor	WMICX	C+	(800) 551-1700	B / 7.7	6.87	17.23	6.79 /53	15.02 /75	14.42 /82	0.02	1.90
SC	Wasatch Micro Cap Value Investor	WAMVX	C	(800) 551-1700	B+ / 8.5	5.78	12.29	4.34 /34	17.18 /91	13.40 /72	0.00	2.02

● Denotes fund is closed to new investors
* Denotes fund is included in Section II

Risk Rating/Pts	3 Year Standard Deviation	Beta	NAV As of 3/31/15	Total $(Mil)	Cash %	Stocks %	Bonds %	Other %	Portfolio Turnover Ratio	Last Bull Market Return	Last Bear Market Return	Manager Quality Pct	Manager Tenure (Years)	Initial Purch. $	Additional Purch. $	Front End Load	Back End Load
C- /3.2	10.7	0.91	8.22	8	0	97	2	1	51	79.2	-21.6	26	14	750	0	0.0	0.0
C- /3.3	10.7	0.91	8.54	12	0	97	2	1	51	80.3	-21.4	28	14	750	0	0.0	0.0
C /4.8	10.7	0.91	12.52	93	0	97	2	1	51	88.6	-21.0	45	14	0	0	0.0	0.0
C /5.0	12.7	1.03	15.78	3,706	0	98	1	1	41	128.2	-20.9	92	14	750	0	5.8	0.0
C- /4.1	12.7	1.03	11.50	20	0	98	1	1	41	119.7	-21.3	89	14	750	0	0.0	0.0
C- /4.2	12.6	1.03	11.68	21	0	98	1	1	41	120.8	-21.2	90	14	750	0	0.0	0.0
C /5.2	12.6	1.03	17.56	138	0	98	1	1	41	130.6	-20.8	93	14	0	0	0.0	0.0
C- /3.8	13.7	0.96	17.60	857	0	96	3	1	47	92.3	-25.3	71	5	750	0	5.8	0.0
D+ /2.9	13.7	0.97	13.72	7	0	96	3	1	47	84.9	-25.6	55	5	750	0	0.0	0.0
C- /3.1	13.7	0.97	14.52	9	0	96	3	1	47	87.0	-25.5	60	5	750	0	0.0	0.0
C- /4.0	13.7	0.96	19.55	24	0	96	3	1	47	95.2	-25.2	75	5	0	0	0.0	0.0
C+ /5.9	11.1	1.03	18.21	349	0	97	2	1	30	99.3	-16.0	64	1	750	0	5.8	0.0
C+ /5.7	11.1	1.03	15.75	1	0	97	2	1	30	92.4	-16.3	48	1	750	0	0.0	0.0
C+ /5.7	11.1	1.03	15.75	5	0	97	2	1	30	93.2	-16.2	49	1	750	0	0.0	0.0
C+ /5.7	10.9	1.04	16.01	924	8	83	8	1	72	95.2	-22.3	42	12	750	0	5.8	0.0
C+ /5.8	10.9	1.04	15.07	4	8	83	8	1	72	87.6	-22.7	27	12	750	0	0.0	0.0
C+ /5.8	10.9	1.03	15.31	7	8	83	8	1	72	89.5	-22.6	31	12	750	0	0.0	0.0
C+ /5.7	10.8	1.03	16.08	16	8	83	8	1	72	98.0	-22.2	49	12	0	0	0.0	0.0
C- /4.2	11.5	1.01	10.46	1,428	1	97	1	1	43	97.7	-14.8	53	18	750	0	5.8	0.0
C- /3.1	11.5	1.01	7.92	5	1	97	1	1	43	89.8	-15.4	34	18	750	0	0.0	0.0
C- /3.3	11.5	1.02	8.10	6	1	97	1	1	43	90.9	-15.2	36	18	750	0	0.0	0.0
C /4.4	11.5	1.01	11.07	97	1	97	1	1	43	100.0	-14.8	57	18	0	0	0.0	0.0
B /8.2	7.2	1.22	15.96	85	1	74	23	2	7	55.7	-11.5	17	3	100,000	1,000	0.0	0.0
B- /7.0	9.9	1.01	18.55	157	0	99	0	1	12	79.7	-16.4	18	5	100,000	1,000	0.0	0.0
B- /7.3	9.7	0.50	15.18	35	1	98	0	1	15	82.3	N/A	97	4	100,000	1,000	0.0	0.0
C /5.2	12.8	0.92	19.66	88	1	98	0	1	37	73.6	-21.6	24	7	100,000	1,000	0.0	0.0
U /	N/A	N/A	14.70	28	1	98	0	1	52	N/A	N/A	N/A	3	100,000	1,000	0.0	0.0
C+ /6.7	11.0	1.07	14.58	102	6	93	0	1	37	98.4	-16.8	41	5	1,000	100	0.0	0.0
C+ /6.1	13.8	1.27	15.81	51	2	97	0	1	78	112.2	-22.8	34	5	100,000	1,000	0.0	2.0
C+ /6.1	13.9	1.27	15.66	33	2	97	0	1	78	110.5	-22.9	30	5	2,500	100	0.0	2.0
C /4.7	14.7	1.03	22.28	903	4	95	0	1	70	113.6	-24.9	74	7	2,500	100	0.0	2.0
C- /4.2	11.3	0.82	30.33	675	8	91	0	1	44	52.1	-21.8	77	14	0	0	0.0	0.0
C /5.1	10.7	0.61	18.21	20	19	80	0	1	74	35.1	-18.7	68	14	0	0	0.0	0.0
C /5.1	11.0	0.93	33.82	171	4	95	0	1	24	82.5	-27.8	28	11	0	0	0.0	0.0
C- /4.0	13.1	0.94	39.69	812	2	97	0	1	15	96.0	-24.3	61	20	0	0	0.0	0.0
C+ /6.4	11.5	1.00	61.63	64	4	95	0	1	26	N/A	N/A	74	15	500,000	5,000	0.0	2.0
C+ /6.4	11.5	1.00	61.47	1,035	4	95	0	1	26	91.9	-14.5	73	15	2,000	100	0.0	2.0
D+ /2.4	18.9	0.73	3.12	77	4	95	0	1	13	73.8	-8.5	98	4	2,000	100	0.0	2.0
C /4.4	12.3	0.79	2.68	1,246	0	99	0	1	55	29.0	-17.9	77	8	2,000	100	0.0	2.0
U /	N/A	N/A	10.21	31	11	88	0	1	59	N/A	N/A	N/A	3	500,000	5,000	0.0	2.0
U /	N/A	N/A	10.14	27	11	88	0	1	59	N/A	N/A	N/A	3	2,000	100	0.0	2.0
B- /7.2	10.7	0.50	2.96	1,224	7	85	6	2	22	N/A	N/A	99	3	2,000	100	0.0	2.0
C- /3.0	10.6	0.66	3.86	183	0	98	1	1	42	75.2	-22.0	95	4	2,000	100	0.0	2.0
E+ /0.8	11.6	1.07	6.40	77	3	96	0	1	15	77.9	-16.6	17	11	2,000	100	0.0	2.0
C+ /5.7	12.1	0.80	27.86	1,322	0	100	0	0	42	67.7	-21.4	91	9	2,000	100	0.0	2.0
C /5.4	10.2	0.64	2.82	425	3	96	0	1	38	68.2	-20.0	96	10	2,000	100	0.0	2.0
B- /7.6	10.2	1.01	9.64	3	0	99	0	1	53	N/A	N/A	10	2	500,000	5,000	0.0	2.0
D- /1.5	10.2	1.01	9.64	312	0	99	0	1	53	66.7	-21.1	9	2	2,000	100	0.0	2.0
U /	N/A	N/A	14.66	929	26	73	0	1	47	N/A	N/A	N/A	7	25,000,000	10,000	0.0	2.0
C+ /6.7	8.6	1.23	14.65	1,216	26	73	0	1	47	37.6	-13.9	3	7	2,000	100	0.0	2.0
C /4.7	14.7	1.00	8.25	325	3	96	0	1	26	90.2	-24.3	51	11	2,000	100	0.0	2.0
D+ /2.8	13.1	0.91	2.93	160	0	99	0	1	71	93.5	-22.2	85	12	2,000	100	0.0	2.0

99 Pct = Best
0 Pct = Worst

Fund Type	Fund Name	Ticker Symbol	Overall Investment Rating	Phone	Performance Rating/Pts	Total Return % through 3/31/15 3 Mo	6 Mo	1Yr / Pct	Annualized 3Yr / Pct	5Yr / Pct	Incl. in Returns Dividend Yield	Expense Ratio
SC	Wasatch Small Cap Growth Investor	WAAEX	C+	(800) 551-1700	B- / 7.3	7.58	15.26	9.43 /72	14.03 /67	15.69 /91	0.00	1.21
SC	Wasatch Small Cap Value Inst	WICVX	A+	(800) 551-1700	A / 9.5	8.38	13.11	10.79 /78	18.89 /96	--	0.00	1.44
SC	Wasatch Small Cap Value Investor	WMCVX	A+	(800) 551-1700	A / 9.5	8.24	13.18	10.84 /78	18.81 /96	15.97 /93	0.00	1.20
GI	Wasatch Strategic Income Investor	WASIX	A-	(800) 551-1700	B / 7.7	1.72	4.88	11.03 /78	16.05 /84	15.81 /92	2.79	1.02
MC	Wasatch Ultra Growth Investor	WAMCX	D-	(800) 551-1700	B- / 7.2	7.19	17.67	7.05 /55	14.06 /68	15.17 /88	0.04	1.49
TC	Wasatch World Innovators Investor	WAGTX	D	(800) 551-1700	C- / 3.7	2.93	3.26	-1.49 /11	10.75 /44	13.84 /76	0.00	1.74
IN	WBI Absolute Return Bal Plus Inst	WBBPX	U	(888) 263-6443	U /	-1.36	-0.10	4.53 /35	--	--	0.84	9.27
GL	WBI Absolute Return Balanced Instl	WBBAX	D	(855) 924-3863	E+ / 0.7	-2.17	-1.68	0.16 /16	2.76 / 7	--	0.46	1.96
GL	WBI Absolute Return Balanced No Ld	WBADX	D	(855) 924-3863	E+ / 0.6	-2.34	-1.97	-0.28 /15	2.43 / 7	--	0.30	2.22
GL	WBI Absolute Return Dividend Gro In	WBDGX	D-	(855) 924-3863	D- / 1.2	-3.10	-3.74	-3.08 / 9	6.59 /19	--	0.37	1.94
GL	WBI Absolute Return Dividend Gro	WBIDX	D-	(855) 924-3863	D- / 1.1	-3.11	-3.78	-3.32 / 8	6.24 /18	--	0.20	2.20
FO	WCM Focused International Gro Inst	WCMIX	D+	(888) 988-9801	C- / 3.5	5.13	5.08	3.76 /30	8.91 /32	--	0.22	1.09
FO	WCM Focused International Gro Inv	WCMRX	D+	(888) 988-9801	C- / 3.3	5.06	4.97	3.47 /29	8.64 /31	--	0.02	1.34
BA	Weitz Balanced Fund	WBALX	C	(800) 232-4161	D+ / 2.8	1.37	3.69	3.73 /30	7.83 /26	8.30 /32	0.00	1.10
GR	Weitz Funds Part III Oppty	WPOPX	A+	(800) 232-4161	B- / 7.4	4.34	7.72	7.76 /61	14.90 /74	14.64 /84	0.00	1.45
GR	Weitz Partners III Oppty Inv	WPOIX	A	(800) 232-4161	B- / 7.1	4.26	7.54	7.38 /58	14.59 /72	--	0.00	1.86
GI	Weitz Partners-Partners Value Ins	WPVIX	U	(800) 232-4161	U /	3.33	8.41	--	--	--	0.00	N/A
GR	Weitz Partners-Partners Value Inv	WPVLX	A	(800) 232-4161	B / 8.1	3.27	8.35	8.99 /69	15.89 /82	14.68 /84	0.00	1.22
GR	Weitz Research Fund	WRESX	C+	(800) 232-4161	B- / 7.0	3.30	11.46	12.22 /84	13.39 /63	--	0.00	1.59
GR	Weitz Series-Hickory Fund	WEHIX	B	(800) 232-4161	B- / 7.0	4.50	11.90	8.31 /65	13.80 /66	14.56 /83	0.00	1.22
GI	Weitz Series-Value Institutional	WVAIX	U	(800) 232-4161	U /	3.64	7.86	--	--	--	0.00	N/A
MC	Weitz Series-Value Investor	WVALX	B+	(800) 232-4161	B / 8.0	3.60	7.75	10.19 /75	15.61 /80	14.34 /81	0.00	1.21
GL	Wells Fargo Adv Absolute Return A	WARAX	C-	(800) 222-8222	E+ / 0.9	1.29	0.30	0.66 /17	4.78 /12	--	2.24	1.57
GL	Wells Fargo Adv Absolute Return	WARDX	C-	(800) 222-8222	D- / 1.3	1.29	0.38	0.82 /18	4.94 /13	--	2.54	1.41
GL	Wells Fargo Adv Absolute Return C	WARCX	C-	(800) 222-8222	D- / 1.0	1.12	-0.02	-0.02 /16	4.00 /10	--	1.81	2.32
IN	Wells Fargo Adv Absolute Return Ins	WABIX	U	(800) 222-8222	U /	1.29	0.45	1.07 /19	--	--	2.88	1.14
FO	Wells Fargo Adv Asia Pac A	WFAAX	C	(800) 222-8222	C / 4.6	5.96	5.47	12.03 /83	10.89 /45	8.17 /31	1.08	1.72
FO	Wells Fargo Adv Asia Pac Adm	WFADX	C+	(800) 222-8222	C+ / 5.7	5.98	5.54	12.12 /83	11.08 /46	--	1.37	1.56
FO	Wells Fargo Adv Asia Pac C	WFCAX	C	(800) 222-8222	C / 5.0	5.72	5.01	11.09 /79	10.05 /40	7.37 /26	0.69	2.47
FO	Wells Fargo Adv Asia Pac Inst	WFPIX	C+	(800) 222-8222	C+ / 5.8	5.98	5.56	12.33 /84	11.24 /47	--	1.55	1.29
FO	Wells Fargo Adv Asia Pac Inv	SASPX	C+	(800) 222-8222	C+ / 5.6	5.96	5.47	11.95 /82	10.82 /44	8.11 /31	1.09	1.78
GL	Wells Fargo Adv Asset Alloc A	EAAFX	D+	(800) 222-8222	E+ / 0.9	0.95	-0.50	-0.15 /15	5.47 /15	5.82 /16	2.70	1.36
GL	Wells Fargo Adv Asset Alloc Adm	EAIFX	D+	(800) 222-8222	D- / 1.5	1.09	-0.32	0.10 /16	5.73 /16	6.05 /17	2.94	1.20
GL	● Wells Fargo Adv Asset Alloc B	EABFX	D+	(800) 222-8222	D- / 1.1	0.81	-0.87	-0.95 /13	4.68 /12	5.02 /12	1.64	2.11
GL	Wells Fargo Adv Asset Alloc C	EACFX	D+	(800) 222-8222	D- / 1.1	0.83	-0.86	-0.93 /13	4.70 /12	5.02 /12	2.03	2.11
GL	Wells Fargo Adv Asset Alloc Inst	EAAIX	U	(800) 222-8222	U /	1.17	-0.25	0.31 /17	--	--	3.39	0.93
GL	Wells Fargo Adv Asset Alloc R	EAXFX	D+	(800) 222-8222	D- / 1.3	0.96	-0.56	-0.35 /15	5.22 /14	5.55 /14	2.62	1.61
GR	Wells Fargo Adv C&B Lg Cp Val Adm	CBLLX	A-	(800) 222-8222	B / 7.7	1.33	8.01	10.94 /78	15.21 /77	12.66 /65	0.92	1.15
GR	● Wells Fargo Adv C&B Lg Cp Val B	CBEBX	B-	(800) 222-8222	C+ / 6.9	1.08	7.45	9.97 /74	14.14 /68	11.60 /58	0.00	2.06
GR	Wells Fargo Adv C&B Lg Cp Val C	CBECX	B-	(800) 222-8222	C+ / 6.9	1.10	7.46	9.93 /74	14.15 /68	11.59 /58	0.06	2.06
GR	Wells Fargo Adv C&B Lg Cp Val D	CBEQX	A-	(800) 222-8222	B- / 7.5	1.25	7.81	10.73 /77	14.91 /74	12.39 /63	0.65	1.37
GR	Wells Fargo Adv C&B Lg Cp Val I	CBLSX	A	(800) 222-8222	B / 7.9	1.40	8.15	11.26 /79	15.53 /79	12.94 /68	1.14	0.88
MC	Wells Fargo Adv C&B MdCp Val A	CBMAX	B+	(800) 222-8222	B- / 7.1	3.75	9.72	7.38 /58	16.14 /84	14.52 /83	0.17	1.36
MC	Wells Fargo Adv C&B MdCp Val Adm	CBMIX	A	(800) 222-8222	B+ / 8.3	3.74	9.75	7.43 /59	16.20 /85	14.56 /83	0.16	1.20
MC	● Wells Fargo Adv C&B MdCp Val B	CBMBX	B+	(800) 222-8222	B- / 7.5	3.54	9.27	6.56 /51	15.26 /77	13.66 /75	0.00	2.11
MC	Wells Fargo Adv C&B MdCp Val C	CBMCX	B+	(800) 222-8222	B- / 7.5	3.55	9.30	6.58 /52	15.27 /77	13.67 /75	0.00	2.11
MC	Wells Fargo Adv C&B MdCp Val D	CBMDX	A	(800) 222-8222	B / 8.2	3.73	9.67	7.30 /57	16.09 /84	14.46 /82	0.11	1.42
MC	Wells Fargo Adv C&B MdCp Val I	CBMSX	A	(800) 222-8222	B+ / 8.5	3.84	9.89	7.73 /61	16.51 /87	14.86 /86	0.47	0.93
GR	Wells Fargo Adv Cap Gr A	WFCGX	D-	(800) 222-8222	C+ / 6.3	3.13	7.15	12.80 /86	14.30 /69	13.65 /75	0.00	1.26
GR	Wells Fargo Adv Cap Gr Adm	WFCDX	D	(800) 222-8222	B- / 7.5	3.18	7.23	13.00 /87	14.55 /71	13.90 /77	0.00	1.10
GR	Wells Fargo Adv Cap Gr C	WFCCX	D-	(800) 222-8222	C+ / 6.7	2.94	6.73	11.91 /82	13.45 /63	12.80 /66	0.00	2.01
GR	Wells Fargo Adv Cap Gr I	WWCIX	D+	(800) 222-8222	B / 7.8	3.23	7.41	13.36 /88	14.86 /74	14.21 /80	0.00	0.83

● Denotes fund is closed to new investors
* Denotes fund is included in Section II

www.thestreetratings.com

RISK			NET ASSETS		ASSET				Portfolio Turnover Ratio	BULL / BEAR		FUND MANAGER		MINIMUMS		LOADS	
	3 Year		NAV							Last Bull	Last Bear	Manager	Manager	Initial	Additional	Front	Back
Risk Rating/Pts	Standard Deviation	Beta	As of 3/31/15	Total $(Mil)	Cash %	Stocks %	Bonds %	Other %		Market Return	Market Return	Quality Pct	Tenure (Years)	Purch. $	Purch. $	End Load	End Load
C / 5.4	11.1	0.77	52.78	2,397	4	95	0	1	23	86.5	-17.8	80	29	2,000	100	0.0	2.0
B- / 7.0	12.0	0.83	6.47	19	7	92	0	1	50	N/A	N/A	93	16	500,000	5,000	0.0	2.0
C+ / 6.6	12.1	0.83	6.44	283	7	92	0	1	50	102.6	-21.8	93	16	2,000	100	0.0	2.0
B- / 7.5	10.1	0.94	12.43	119	13	86	0	1	69	93.8	-14.8	75	9	2,000	100	0.0	2.0
E+ / 0.6	15.2	1.12	20.43	113	5	94	0	1	38	78.2	-19.6	13	3	2,000	100	0.0	2.0
C / 4.7	11.0	1.05	20.76	207	11	88	0	1	111	66.8	-13.2	8	7	2,000	100	0.0	2.0
U /	N/A	N/A	10.46	29	30	42	27	1	200	N/A	N/A	N/A	2	250,000	250	0.0	2.0
B / 8.2	4.2	0.51	10.54	49	15	49	34	2	176	22.6	-8.7	42	5	250,000	250	0.0	2.0
B / 8.2	4.3	0.51	10.49	33	15	49	34	2	176	21.5	-8.7	37	5	2,500	250	0.0	2.0
C+ / 6.4	9.9	0.61	11.39	43	11	88	0	1	266	57.5	-20.9	76	5	250,000	250	0.0	2.0
C+ / 6.4	9.9	0.61	11.35	28	11	88	0	1	266	55.7	-20.9	73	5	2,500	250	0.0	2.0
C+ / 6.2	11.1	0.78	12.29	1,008	6	93	0	1	36	56.5	N/A	80	4	100,000	5,000	0.0	1.0
C+ / 6.2	11.1	0.78	12.25	67	6	93	0	1	36	55.2	N/A	79	4	1,000	100	0.0	1.0
B / 8.5	4.8	0.76	14.07	126	2	51	45	2	36	46.4	-10.2	64	12	2,500	25	0.0	0.0
B / 8.6	8.8	0.80	17.31	1,012	39	60	0	1	20	83.7	-14.4	83	32	1,000,000	25	0.0	0.0
B / 8.5	8.8	0.80	17.12	68	39	60	0	1	20	81.9	N/A	82	32	2,500	25	0.0	0.0
U /	N/A	N/A	35.09	314	2	80	17	1	19	N/A	N/A	N/A	32	1,000,000	25	0.0	0.0
B- / 7.4	8.2	0.79	35.05	791	2	80	17	1	19	92.7	-16.1	89	32	2,500	25	0.0	0.0
C / 5.5	12.1	1.04	12.21	26	21	78	0	1	58	82.1	-11.4	26	10	1,000,000	25	0.0	0.0
C+ / 6.5	9.2	0.81	59.51	448	1	82	15	2	30	82.1	-18.3	75	12	2,500	25	0.0	0.0
U /	N/A	N/A	46.99	199	2	82	15	1	19	N/A	N/A	N/A	29	1,000,000	25	0.0	0.0
C+ / 6.7	8.4	0.62	46.93	948	2	82	15	1	19	88.8	-12.1	93	29	2,500	25	0.0	0.0
B+ / 9.2	5.5	0.81	10.96	1,936	12	53	34	1	0	N/A	N/A	33	3	1,000	100	5.8	0.0
B+ / 9.2	5.5	0.81	10.98	3,729	12	53	34	1	0	N/A	N/A	34	3	1,000,000	0	0.0	0.0
B+ / 9.2	5.4	0.80	10.83	1,797	12	53	34	1	0	N/A	N/A	25	3	1,000	100	0.0	0.0
U /	N/A	N/A	10.99	4,674	12	53	34	1	0	N/A	N/A	N/A	3	5,000,000	0	0.0	0.0
C+ / 6.7	10.8	0.69	12.63	7	5	94	0	1	113	57.0	-19.4	92	22	1,000	100	5.8	0.0
C+ / 6.7	10.9	0.69	12.40	15	5	94	0	1	113	58.2	-19.4	92	22	1,000,000	0	0.0	0.0
C+ / 6.7	10.9	0.69	12.01	3	5	94	0	1	113	53.1	-19.6	90	22	1,000	100	0.0	0.0
C+ / 6.7	10.8	0.69	12.40	2	5	94	0	1	113	58.9	-19.3	92	22	5,000,000	0	0.0	0.0
C+ / 6.7	10.9	0.70	12.44	153	5	94	0	1	113	56.7	-19.4	91	22	2,500	100	0.0	0.0
B / 8.3	6.9	1.04	13.82	2,039	7	58	34	1	1	33.2	-8.2	19	19	1,000	100	5.8	0.0
B / 8.3	6.9	1.04	13.95	427	7	58	34	1	1	34.2	-8.1	21	19	1,000,000	0	0.0	0.0
B / 8.5	6.9	1.04	13.75	176	7	58	34	1	1	29.8	-8.5	13	19	1,000	100	0.0	0.0
B / 8.4	6.9	1.05	13.35	2,051	7	58	34	1	1	29.8	-8.5	13	19	1,000	100	0.0	0.0
U /	N/A	N/A	13.87	1,021	7	58	34	1	1	N/A	N/A	N/A	19	5,000,000	0	0.0	0.0
B / 8.3	6.9	1.04	13.68	30	7	58	34	1	1	32.1	-8.3	17	19	0	0	0.0	0.0
B- / 7.4	10.1	1.03	12.96	56	9	90	0	1	22	87.8	-15.5	50	25	1,000,000	0	0.0	0.0
B- / 7.4	10.1	1.02	13.13	N/A	9	90	0	1	22	81.6	-15.7	37	25	1,000	100	0.0	0.0
B- / 7.4	10.1	1.02	12.92	8	9	90	0	1	22	81.7	-15.8	37	25	1,000	100	0.0	0.0
B- / 7.4	10.1	1.02	12.97	71	9	90	0	1	22	86.0	-15.6	47	25	2,500	100	0.0	0.0
B- / 7.4	10.1	1.02	13.00	137	9	90	0	1	22	89.2	-15.3	55	25	5,000,000	0	0.0	0.0
B- / 7.1	11.4	1.00	27.66	23	3	96	0	1	55	101.2	-19.8	56	17	1,000	100	5.8	0.0
B- / 7.1	11.5	1.00	27.98	13	3	96	0	1	55	101.5	-19.8	57	17	1,000,000	0	0.0	0.0
B- / 7.1	11.5	1.00	26.63	N/A	3	96	0	1	55	96.1	-20.1	44	17	1,000	100	0.0	0.0
B- / 7.1	11.5	1.00	26.55	8	3	96	0	1	55	96.2	-20.1	45	17	1,000	100	0.0	0.0
B- / 7.1	11.4	1.00	27.80	122	3	96	0	1	55	100.9	-19.8	55	17	2,500	100	0.0	0.0
B- / 7.1	11.5	1.00	27.87	32	3	96	0	1	55	103.2	-19.7	61	17	5,000,000	0	0.0	0.0
D- / 1.0	11.0	1.01	17.14	18	3	96	0	1	94	96.1	-21.2	41	11	1,000	100	5.8	0.0
D- / 1.3	11.0	1.01	18.16	35	3	96	0	1	94	97.6	-21.1	45	11	1,000,000	0	0.0	0.0
E+ / 0.7	11.0	1.01	15.74	5	3	96	0	1	94	91.2	-21.4	31	11	1,000	100	0.0	0.0
D- / 1.4	11.0	1.01	18.55	48	3	96	0	1	94	99.4	-21.0	49	11	5,000,000	0	0.0	0.0

| | | | | | | Total Return % through 3/31/15 | | | | | Incl. in Returns | |
Fund Type	Fund Name	Ticker Symbol	Overall Investment Rating	Phone	Performance Rating/Pts	3 Mo	6 Mo	1Yr / Pct	3Yr / Pct	5Yr / Pct	Dividend Yield	Expense Ratio
GR	Wells Fargo Adv Cap Gr Inv	SLGIX	D	(800) 222-8222	B- / 7.3	3.10	7.10	12.74 /86	14.24 /69	13.57 /74	0.00	1.32
GI	Wells Fargo Adv Cap Gr R6	WFCRX	U	(800) 222-8222	U /	3.22	7.39	13.34 /88	--	--	0.00	0.78
GR	Wells Fargo Adv CB Lg Cp VI A	CBEAX	B-	(800) 222-8222	C+ / 6.5	1.25	7.86	10.79 /78	14.99 /75	12.42 /64	0.66	1.31
MC	Wells Fargo Adv Comm Stk A	SCSAX	C	(800) 222-8222	C+ / 6.0	4.20	8.14	6.85 /54	14.43 /70	13.42 /72	0.00	1.30
MC	Wells Fargo Adv Comm Stk Adm	SCSDX	C+	(800) 222-8222	B- / 7.1	4.21	8.25	7.05 /55	14.62 /72	--	0.00	1.14
MC	● Wells Fargo Adv Comm Stk B	SCSKX	C-	(800) 222-8222	C+ / 6.4	3.97	7.72	6.00 /46	13.56 /64	12.55 /65	0.00	2.05
MC	Wells Fargo Adv Comm Stk C	STSAX	C-	(800) 222-8222	C+ / 6.4	3.97	7.72	6.05 /47	13.56 /64	12.56 /65	0.00	2.05
MC	Wells Fargo Adv Comm Stk Inst	SCNSX	C+	(800) 222-8222	B- / 7.3	4.28	8.37	7.31 /58	14.87 /74	--	0.00	0.87
GR	Wells Fargo Adv Comm Stk R6	SCSRX	U	(800) 222-8222	U /	4.28	8.40	7.34 /58	--	--	0.00	0.82
MC	Wells Fargo Adv Comm Stk Z	STCSX	C+	(800) 222-8222	C+ / 6.9	4.13	8.11	6.80 /53	14.37 /70	13.36 /72	0.00	1.36
SC	● Wells Fargo Adv Discovery A	WFDAX	C	(800) 222-8222	C+ / 6.6	6.49	12.10	8.58 /67	14.63 /72	17.18 /96	0.00	1.25
SC	● Wells Fargo Adv Discovery Adm	WFDDX	C+	(800) 222-8222	B / 7.8	6.51	12.18	8.69 /68	14.76 /73	17.32 /97	0.00	1.09
SC	● Wells Fargo Adv Discovery C	WDSCX	C	(800) 222-8222	B- / 7.0	6.28	11.69	7.75 /61	13.77 /65	16.29 /94	0.00	2.00
SC	● Wells Fargo Adv Discovery Inst	WFDSX	C+	(800) 222-8222	B / 8.0	6.59	12.32	9.00 /69	15.05 /75	17.63 /97	0.00	0.82
SC	● Wells Fargo Adv Discovery Inv	STDIX	C+	(800) 222-8222	B / 7.6	6.48	12.10	8.52 /66	14.55 /71	17.10 /96	0.00	1.31
GR	● Wells Fargo Adv Discovery R6	WFDRX	U	(800) 222-8222	U /	6.61	12.34	9.05 /70	--	--	0.00	0.77
AA	Wells Fargo Adv DJ Tgt 2010 A	STNRX	D+	(800) 222-8222	E+ / 0.7	0.77	1.46	2.23 /23	3.02 / 8	4.36 /10	0.83	1.01
AA	Wells Fargo Adv DJ Tgt 2010 Adm	WFLGX	C-	(800) 222-8222	E+ / 0.9	0.76	1.50	2.41 /24	3.16 / 8	4.52 /10	1.00	0.85
AA	● Wells Fargo Adv DJ Tgt 2010 B	SPTBX	C-	(800) 222-8222	E+ / 0.8	0.68	1.15	1.60 /20	2.27 / 7	3.59 / 7	0.00	1.76
AA	Wells Fargo Adv DJ Tgt 2010 C	WFOCX	C-	(800) 222-8222	E+ / 0.8	0.53	1.05	1.42 /20	2.24 / 7	3.58 / 7	0.27	1.76
AA	Wells Fargo Adv DJ Tgt 2010 Inv	WFCTX	C-	(800) 222-8222	E+ / 0.9	0.76	1.43	2.19 /23	3.03 / 8	4.41 /10	0.86	1.07
AA	Wells Fargo Adv DJ Tgt 2010 R4	WFORX	U	(800) 222-8222	U /	0.84	1.67	2.59 /24	--	--	1.17	0.68
AA	Wells Fargo Adv DJ Tgt 2010 R6	WFOAX	C-	(800) 222-8222	D- / 1.0	0.91	1.72	2.71 /25	3.52 / 9	4.90 /12	1.29	0.53
AA	Wells Fargo Adv DJ Tgt 2015 Adm	WFFFX	C-	(800) 222-8222	D- / 1.2	1.04	1.91	2.85 /26	4.18 /11	5.28 /13	1.35	0.85
AA	Wells Fargo Adv DJ Tgt 2015 Inv	WFQEX	C-	(800) 222-8222	D- / 1.1	0.90	1.81	2.63 /25	4.01 /10	5.15 /13	1.14	1.07
AA	Wells Fargo Adv DJ Tgt 2015 R4	WFSRX	U	(800) 222-8222	U /	1.09	2.04	3.10 /27	--	--	1.57	0.68
AA	Wells Fargo Adv DJ Tgt 2015 R6	WFSCX	C-	(800) 222-8222	D- / 1.3	1.03	2.02	3.26 /28	4.53 /12	5.65 /15	1.73	0.53
AA	Wells Fargo Adv DJ Tgt 2020 A	STTRX	C-	(800) 222-8222	D- / 1.1	1.33	2.42	3.43 /29	5.42 /15	6.13 /18	1.37	0.98
AA	Wells Fargo Adv DJ Tgt 2020 Adm	WFLPX	C-	(800) 222-8222	D / 1.7	1.41	2.46	3.59 /29	5.57 /15	6.31 /19	1.63	0.82
AA	● Wells Fargo Adv DJ Tgt 2020 B	STPBX	C-	(800) 222-8222	D- / 1.3	1.17	1.96	2.64 /25	4.61 /12	5.34 /13	0.37	1.73
AA	Wells Fargo Adv DJ Tgt 2020 C	WFLAX	C-	(800) 222-8222	D- / 1.3	1.12	1.99	2.63 /25	4.62 /12	5.34 /13	0.60	1.73
AA	Wells Fargo Adv DJ Tgt 2020 Inv	WFDTX	C-	(800) 222-8222	D / 1.6	1.30	2.36	3.35 /28	5.40 /15	6.19 /18	1.40	1.04
AA	Wells Fargo Adv DJ Tgt 2020 R4	WFLRX	U	(800) 222-8222	U /	1.45	2.55	3.83 /31	--	--	1.87	0.65
AA	Wells Fargo Adv DJ Tgt 2020 R6	WFOBX	C-	(800) 222-8222	D / 1.9	1.48	2.63	3.95 /31	5.93 /16	6.68 /21	2.05	0.50
AA	Wells Fargo Adv DJ Tgt 2025 Adm	WFTRX	C-	(800) 222-8222	D+ / 2.5	1.87	3.15	4.43 /35	7.04 /22	7.41 /26	1.28	0.82
AA	Wells Fargo Adv DJ Tgt 2025 Inv	WFGYX	C-	(800) 222-8222	D+ / 2.4	1.74	3.05	4.22 /33	6.90 /21	7.28 /25	1.08	1.04
BA	Wells Fargo Adv DJ Tgt 2025 R4	WFGRX	U	(800) 222-8222	U /	1.92	3.26	4.65 /36	--	--	1.48	0.65
AA	Wells Fargo Adv DJ Tgt 2025 R6	WFTYX	C	(800) 222-8222	D+ / 2.7	1.95	3.34	4.80 /37	7.42 /24	7.78 /29	1.63	0.50
AA	Wells Fargo Adv DJ Tgt 2030 A	STHRX	C-	(800) 222-8222	D+ / 2.3	2.30	3.87	5.20 /40	8.34 /29	8.23 /31	1.21	0.98
AA	Wells Fargo Adv DJ Tgt 2030 Adm	WFLIX	C	(800) 222-8222	C- / 3.3	2.30	3.96	5.34 /41	8.52 /30	8.39 /32	1.46	0.82
AA	● Wells Fargo Adv DJ Tgt 2030 B	SGPBX	C-	(800) 222-8222	D+ / 2.7	2.11	3.44	4.35 /34	7.53 /24	7.40 /26	0.14	1.73
AA	Wells Fargo Adv DJ Tgt 2030 C	WFDMX	C-	(800) 222-8222	D+ / 2.7	2.07	3.46	4.32 /34	7.53 /24	7.41 /26	0.50	1.73
AA	Wells Fargo Adv DJ Tgt 2030 Inv	WFETX	C	(800) 222-8222	C- / 3.3	2.32	3.87	5.10 /39	8.36 /29	8.27 /32	1.22	1.04
AA	Wells Fargo Adv DJ Tgt 2030 R4	WTHRX	U	(800) 222-8222	U /	2.40	4.06	5.53 /43	--	--	1.69	0.65
AA	Wells Fargo Adv DJ Tgt 2030 R6	WFOOX	C	(800) 222-8222	C- / 3.6	2.44	4.14	5.72 /44	8.88 /32	8.77 /35	1.87	0.50
AA	Wells Fargo Adv DJ Tgt 2035 Adm	WFQWX	C	(800) 222-8222	C- / 4.1	2.81	4.70	6.10 /47	9.78 /38	9.22 /38	1.20	0.85
AA	Wells Fargo Adv DJ Tgt 2035 Inv	WFQTX	C	(800) 222-8222	C- / 4.0	2.66	4.49	5.86 /45	9.59 /37	9.10 /37	0.99	1.07
AA	Wells Fargo Adv DJ Tgt 2035 R4	WTTRX	U	(800) 222-8222	U /	2.77	4.73	6.33 /49	--	--	1.40	0.68
AA	Wells Fargo Adv DJ Tgt 2035 R6	WFQRX	C+	(800) 222-8222	C / 4.4	2.89	4.81	6.49 /51	10.15 /40	9.61 /41	1.54	0.53
AA	Wells Fargo Adv DJ Tgt 2040 A	STFRX	C	(800) 222-8222	C- / 3.7	3.02	5.05	6.51 /51	10.55 /43	9.67 /42	0.99	0.99
AA	Wells Fargo Adv DJ Tgt 2040 Adm	WFLWX	C+	(800) 222-8222	C / 4.7	3.07	5.16	6.67 /52	10.74 /44	9.84 /43	1.19	0.83
AA	● Wells Fargo Adv DJ Tgt 2040 B	SLPBX	C	(800) 222-8222	C- / 4.1	2.82	4.65	5.69 /44	9.70 /37	8.83 /36	0.12	1.74

● Denotes fund is closed to new investors
* Denotes fund is included in Section II

RISK			NET ASSETS		ASSET				Portfolio	BULL / BEAR		FUND MANAGER		MINIMUMS		LOADS	
	3 Year		NAV							Last Bull	Last Bear	Manager	Manager	Initial	Additional	Front	Back
Risk Rating/Pts	Standard Deviation	Beta	As of 3/31/15	Total $(Mil)	Cash %	Stocks %	Bonds %	Other %	Turnover Ratio	Market Return	Market Return	Quality Pct	Tenure (Years)	Purch. $	Purch. $	End Load	End Load
D- / 1.0	11.0	1.01	16.97	88	3	96	0	1	94	95.7	-21.2	41	11	2,500	100	0.0	0.0
U /	N/A	N/A	18.58	152	3	96	0	1	94	N/A	N/A	N/A	11	0	0	0.0	0.0
B- / 7.4	10.1	1.02	12.96	27	9	90	0	1	22	86.3	-15.6	47	25	1,000	100	5.8	0.0
C / 5.0	12.0	1.02	23.80	189	5	94	0	1	38	93.3	-22.4	30	14	1,000	100	5.8	0.0
C / 5.0	12.0	1.02	24.03	39	5	94	0	1	38	94.3	-22.3	32	14	1,000,000	0	0.0	0.0
C / 4.4	12.0	1.02	19.64	N/A	5	94	0	1	38	88.2	-22.6	22	14	1,000	100	0.0	0.0
C / 4.3	12.0	1.02	19.64	30	5	94	0	1	38	88.4	-22.6	22	14	1,000	100	0.0	0.0
C / 5.0	12.0	1.02	24.35	225	5	94	0	1	38	95.9	-22.3	35	14	5,000,000	0	0.0	0.0
U /	N/A	N/A	24.38	102	5	94	0	1	38	N/A	N/A	N/A	14	0	0	0.0	0.0
C / 5.0	12.0	1.02	24.44	985	5	94	0	1	38	93.0	-22.4	30	14	2,500	100	0.0	0.0
C / 4.6	12.8	0.88	33.47	340	1	98	0	1	84	98.5	-22.9	72	14	1,000	100	5.8	0.0
C / 4.6	12.8	0.88	34.20	678	1	98	0	1	84	99.2	-22.8	72	14	1,000,000	0	0.0	0.0
C / 4.4	12.8	0.88	31.12	81	1	98	0	1	84	93.5	-23.1	63	14	1,000	100	0.0	0.0
C / 4.6	12.8	0.88	35.11	1,504	1	98	0	1	84	101.0	-22.7	75	14	5,000,000	0	0.0	0.0
C / 4.6	12.8	0.88	33.21	610	1	98	0	1	84	98.0	-22.8	71	14	2,500	100	0.0	0.0
U /	N/A	N/A	35.15	265	1	98	0	1	84	N/A	N/A	N/A	14	0	0	0.0	0.0
B+ / 9.1	3.3	0.40	13.14	27	7	17	75	1	40	15.0	-2.5	49	9	1,000	100	5.8	0.0
B+ / 9.1	3.3	0.40	13.27	168	7	17	75	1	40	15.6	-2.4	51	9	1,000,000	0	0.0	0.0
B+ / 9.2	3.2	0.40	13.36	N/A	7	17	75	1	40	12.1	-2.8	39	9	1,000	100	0.0	0.0
B+ / 9.2	3.3	0.40	13.33	3	7	17	75	1	40	12.1	-2.8	38	9	1,000	100	0.0	0.0
B+ / 9.1	3.3	0.40	13.24	60	7	17	75	1	40	15.1	-2.5	49	9	2,500	100	0.0	0.0
U /	N/A	N/A	13.28	148	7	17	75	1	40	N/A	N/A	N/A	9	0	0	0.0	0.0
B+ / 9.1	3.3	0.41	13.27	186	7	17	75	1	40	17.1	-2.4	56	9	0	0	0.0	0.0
B+ / 9.0	3.8	0.55	10.48	189	1	25	73	1	38	21.4	-4.7	44	N/A	1,000,000	0	0.0	0.0
B+ / 9.0	3.8	0.55	10.49	107	1	25	73	1	38	20.8	-4.8	40	N/A	2,500	100	0.0	0.0
U /	N/A	N/A	10.36	177	1	25	73	1	38	N/A	N/A	N/A	N/A	0	0	0.0	0.0
B+ / 9.0	3.8	0.54	10.34	407	1	25	73	1	38	22.9	-4.5	50	N/A	0	0	0.0	0.0
B / 8.8	4.7	0.74	15.16	65	3	32	63	2	35	28.7	-7.5	32	9	1,000	100	5.8	0.0
B / 8.8	4.7	0.75	15.38	680	3	32	63	2	35	29.4	-7.5	33	9	1,000,000	0	0.0	0.0
B / 8.9	4.7	0.74	15.19	N/A	3	32	63	2	35	25.4	-7.8	23	9	1,000	100	0.0	0.0
B / 8.8	4.7	0.74	15.10	6	3	32	63	2	35	25.4	-7.8	24	9	1,000	100	0.0	0.0
B / 8.8	4.8	0.75	15.36	202	3	32	63	2	35	28.8	-7.5	31	9	2,500	100	0.0	0.0
U /	N/A	N/A	15.42	770	3	32	63	2	35	N/A	N/A	N/A	9	0	0	0.0	0.0
B / 8.8	4.7	0.74	15.41	1,133	3	32	63	2	35	31.0	-7.4	39	9	0	0	0.0	0.0
B / 8.3	5.8	0.96	10.68	359	2	50	47	1	32	38.8	-10.7	24	8	1,000,000	0	0.0	0.0
B / 8.3	5.8	0.95	10.67	242	2	50	47	1	32	38.0	-10.6	23	8	2,500	100	0.0	0.0
U /	N/A	N/A	10.66	380	2	50	47	1	32	N/A	N/A	N/A	8	0	0	0.0	0.0
B / 8.3	5.8	0.95	10.65	1,474	2	50	47	1	32	40.3	-10.4	29	8	0	0	0.0	0.0
B- / 7.9	7.0	1.15	16.89	62	3	58	37	2	29	47.4	-13.8	17	9	1,000	100	5.8	0.0
B- / 7.9	7.0	1.16	17.10	653	3	58	37	2	29	48.2	-13.7	18	9	1,000,000	0	0.0	0.0
B- / 7.9	7.0	1.16	16.68	N/A	3	58	37	2	29	43.6	-14.0	12	9	1,000	100	0.0	0.0
B- / 7.9	7.0	1.16	16.51	5	3	58	37	2	29	43.6	-14.0	12	9	1,000	100	0.0	0.0
B- / 7.9	7.0	1.15	17.06	215	3	58	37	2	29	47.6	-13.7	17	9	2,500	100	0.0	0.0
U /	N/A	N/A	17.11	897	3	58	37	2	29	N/A	N/A	N/A	9	0	0	0.0	0.0
B- / 7.9	7.0	1.15	17.09	1,211	3	58	37	2	29	50.1	-13.6	21	9	0	0	0.0	0.0
B- / 7.5	8.0	1.33	11.31	233	3	72	23	2	26	56.8	-16.2	14	8	1,000,000	0	0.0	0.0
B- / 7.5	8.0	1.33	11.35	203	3	72	23	2	26	55.9	-16.1	13	8	2,500	100	0.0	0.0
U /	N/A	N/A	11.27	330	3	72	23	2	26	N/A	N/A	N/A	8	0	0	0.0	0.0
B- / 7.5	8.0	1.33	11.27	681	3	72	23	2	26	58.5	-16.0	16	8	0	0	0.0	0.0
B- / 7.2	8.8	1.46	19.45	112	3	80	16	1	25	62.3	-17.8	10	9	1,000	100	5.8	0.0
B- / 7.2	8.8	1.46	19.82	437	3	80	16	1	25	63.2	-17.8	11	9	1,000,000	0	0.0	0.0
B- / 7.2	8.8	1.46	18.59	N/A	3	80	16	1	25	58.2	-18.2	7	9	1,000	100	0.0	0.0

					PERFORMANCE						Incl. in Returns	
							Total Return % through 3/31/15					
			Overall		Perfor-				Annualized		Dividend	Expense
Fund Type	Fund Name	Ticker Symbol	Investment Rating	Phone	mance Rating/Pts	3 Mo	6 Mo	1Yr / Pct	3Yr / Pct	5Yr / Pct	Yield	Ratio
AA	Wells Fargo Adv DJ Tgt 2040 C	WFOFX	C	(800) 222-8222	C- / 4.1	2.87	4.68	5.75 /44	9.66 /37	8.82 /35	0.48	1.74
AA	Wells Fargo Adv DJ Tgt 2040 Inv	WFFTX	C	(800) 222-8222	C / 4.6	2.97	5.00	6.42 /50	10.55 /43	9.71 /42	1.01	1.05
AA	Wells Fargo Adv DJ Tgt 2040 R4	WTFRX	U	(800) 222-8222	U /	3.12	5.27	6.92 /54	--	--	1.38	0.66
AA	Wells Fargo Adv DJ Tgt 2040 R6	WFOSX	C+	(800) 222-8222	C / 4.9	3.12	5.31	7.02 /55	11.11 /46	10.22 /46	1.52	0.51
AA	Wells Fargo Adv DJ Tgt 2045 Adm	WFQYX	C+	(800) 222-8222	C / 5.0	3.26	5.49	7.07 /56	11.24 /47	10.18 /46	1.16	0.88
AA	Wells Fargo Adv DJ Tgt 2045 Inv	WFQSX	C+	(800) 222-8222	C / 4.9	3.20	5.37	6.82 /54	11.04 /46	10.03 /45	0.95	1.10
AA	Wells Fargo Adv DJ Tgt 2045 R4	WFFRX	U	(800) 222-8222	U /	3.32	5.54	7.23 /57	--	--	1.36	0.71
AA	Wells Fargo Adv DJ Tgt 2045 R6	WFQPX	C+	(800) 222-8222	C / 5.3	3.35	5.62	7.40 /58	11.64 /50	10.55 /49	1.50	0.56
AA	Wells Fargo Adv DJ Tgt 2050 Adm	WFQDX	C+	(800) 222-8222	C / 5.1	3.29	5.58	7.16 /56	11.34 /48	10.24 /46	1.18	0.85
AA	Wells Fargo Adv DJ Tgt 2050 Inv	WFQGX	C+	(800) 222-8222	C / 5.0	3.28	5.41	6.92 /54	11.16 /47	10.10 /46	0.98	1.07
AA	Wells Fargo Adv DJ Tgt 2050 R4	WQFRX	U	(800) 222-8222	U /	3.28	5.63	7.35 /58	--	--	1.36	0.68
AA	Wells Fargo Adv DJ Tgt 2050 R6	WFQFX	C+	(800) 222-8222	C / 5.4	3.38	5.67	7.50 /59	11.74 /51	10.63 /50	1.50	0.53
AA	Wells Fargo Adv DJ Tgt 2055 Adm	WFLHX	C+	(800) 222-8222	C / 5.1	3.26	5.52	7.08 /56	11.31 /48	--	1.14	1.05
AA	Wells Fargo Adv DJ Tgt 2055 Inv	WFQHX	C+	(800) 222-8222	C / 5.0	3.25	5.47	6.94 /55	11.15 /47	--	0.96	1.07
AA	Wells Fargo Adv DJ Tgt 2055 R4	WFVRX	U	(800) 222-8222	U /	3.37	5.60	7.34 /58	--	--	1.31	0.88
AA	Wells Fargo Adv DJ Tgt 2055 R6	WFQUX	C+	(800) 222-8222	C / 5.3	3.41	5.77	7.51 /59	11.69 /50	--	1.45	0.73
AA	Wells Fargo Adv DJ Tgt Today A	STWRX	D+	(800) 222-8222	E+ / 0.6	0.65	1.26	1.91 /22	2.31 / 7	3.82 / 8	0.77	1.01
AA	Wells Fargo Adv DJ Tgt Today Adm	WFLOX	C-	(800) 222-8222	E+ / 0.8	0.73	1.36	2.10 /22	2.46 / 7	3.99 / 8	0.92	0.85
AA	● Wells Fargo Adv DJ Tgt Today B	WFOKX	C-	(800) 222-8222	E+ / 0.7	0.45	0.86	1.13 /19	1.53 / 6	3.04 / 6	0.00	1.76
AA	Wells Fargo Adv DJ Tgt Today C	WFODX	C-	(800) 222-8222	E+ / 0.7	0.45	0.88	1.16 /19	1.57 / 6	3.05 / 6	0.19	1.76
AA	Wells Fargo Adv DJ Tgt Today Inv	WFBTX	C-	(800) 222-8222	E+ / 0.8	0.64	1.20	1.84 /21	2.32 / 7	3.86 / 8	0.76	1.07
AA	Wells Fargo Adv DJ Tgt Today R4	WOTRX	U	(800) 222-8222	U /	0.73	1.43	2.26 /23	--	--	1.09	0.68
AA	Wells Fargo Adv DJ Tgt Today R6	WOTDX	C-	(800) 222-8222	E+ / 0.9	0.82	1.55	2.48 /24	2.85 / 8	4.37 /10	1.20	0.53
GR	Wells Fargo Adv Dscpld US Core A	EVSAX	C	(800) 222-8222	B / 7.7	1.34	6.33	14.46 /90	16.65 /88	14.55 /83	0.89	0.93
GR	Wells Fargo Adv Dscpld US Core	EVSYX	B-	(800) 222-8222	B+ / 8.9	1.38	6.43	14.61 /91	16.87 /89	14.75 /85	1.05	0.77
GR	Wells Fargo Adv Dscpld US Core C	EVSTX	C+	(800) 222-8222	B / 8.2	1.14	5.94	13.58 /88	15.78 /82	13.70 /75	0.52	1.68
GR	Wells Fargo Adv Dscpld US Core I	EVSIX	B-	(800) 222-8222	A- / 9.0	1.39	6.58	14.91 /91	17.15 /91	--	1.30	0.50
BA	Wells Fargo Adv Dvsfd Cap Bldr A	EKBAX	B-	(800) 222-8222	C+ / 6.8	2.05	8.14	12.02 /83	15.27 /77	12.59 /65	0.95	1.21
BA	Wells Fargo Adv Dvsfd Cap Bldr Adm	EKBDX	A	(800) 222-8222	B / 8.1	2.11	8.28	12.30 /84	15.56 /80	--	1.25	1.05
BA	● Wells Fargo Adv Dvsfd Cap Bldr B	EKBBX	B+	(800) 222-8222	B- / 7.2	1.87	7.75	11.27 /80	14.43 /70	11.74 /59	0.24	1.96
BA	Wells Fargo Adv Dvsfd Cap Bldr C	EKBCX	B+	(800) 222-8222	B- / 7.3	1.90	7.74	11.20 /79	14.45 /71	11.73 /59	0.31	1.96
BA	Wells Fargo Adv Dvsfd Cap Bldr I	EKBYX	A	(800) 222-8222	B+ / 8.3	2.15	8.30	12.56 /85	15.79 /82	13.06 /69	1.41	0.78
GR	Wells Fargo Adv Dvsfd Eqty A	NVDAX	C	(800) 222-8222	C+ / 5.7	2.67	6.59	9.30 /71	13.81 /66	12.39 /63	0.41	1.43
GR	Wells Fargo Adv Dvsfd Eqty Adm	NVDEX	C+	(800) 222-8222	C+ / 6.9	2.70	6.72	9.53 /72	14.08 /68	12.66 /65	0.64	1.27
GR	● Wells Fargo Adv Dvsfd Eqty B	NVDBX	C	(800) 222-8222	C+ / 6.1	2.47	6.15	8.43 /66	12.94 /59	11.53 /57	0.00	2.18
GR	Wells Fargo Adv Dvsfd Eqty C	WFDEX	C	(800) 222-8222	C+ / 6.1	2.44	6.17	8.44 /66	12.95 /59	11.55 /57	0.00	2.18
FO	Wells Fargo Adv Dvsfd Intl A	SILAX	D	(800) 222-8222	D+ / 2.8	5.80	3.26	2.08 /22	9.35 /35	7.24 /25	2.16	1.76
FO	Wells Fargo Adv Dvsfd Intl Adm	WFIEX	C-	(800) 222-8222	C- / 3.8	5.87	3.31	2.23 /23	9.51 /36	7.44 /26	2.43	1.60
FO	● Wells Fargo Adv Dvsfd Intl B	SILBX	D+	(800) 222-8222	C- / 3.1	5.57	2.84	1.19 /19	8.49 /30	6.44 /20	0.00	2.51
FO	Wells Fargo Adv Dvsfd Intl C	WFECX	D+	(800) 222-8222	C- / 3.2	5.70	2.86	1.32 /19	8.54 /30	6.44 /20	1.60	2.51
FO	Wells Fargo Adv Dvsfd Intl Inst	WFISX	C-	(800) 222-8222	C- / 3.9	5.90	3.44	2.47 /24	9.67 /37	7.62 /27	2.84	1.33
FO	Wells Fargo Adv Dvsfd Intl Inv	WIEVX	D+	(800) 222-8222	C- / 3.6	5.83	3.24	2.05 /22	9.28 /35	7.18 /24	2.27	1.82
EM	Wells Fargo Adv Em Mkts Eq Inc	EQIDX	U	(800) 222-8222	U /	0.74	-2.24	3.35 /28	--	--	2.60	1.92
EM	Wells Fargo Adv Em Mkts Eq Inc Inst	EQIIX	U	(800) 222-8222	U /	0.74	-2.16	3.46 /29	--	--	2.80	1.65
EM	● Wells Fargo Adv Emerg Mkts Eq A	EMGAX	E	(800) 222-8222	E / 0.3	0.10	-5.66	-3.79 / 7	-1.76 / 3	1.25 / 4	0.68	1.65
EM	● Wells Fargo Adv Emerg Mkts Eq Adm	EMGYX	E	(800) 222-8222	E / 0.3	0.14	-5.62	-3.67 / 7	-1.62 / 3	1.43 / 4	0.55	1.49
EM	● Wells Fargo Adv Emerg Mkts Eq B	EMGBX	E	(800) 222-8222	E / 0.3	-0.12	-6.05	-4.51 / 6	-2.51 / 3	0.50 / 3	0.00	2.40
EM	● Wells Fargo Adv Emerg Mkts Eq C	EMGCX	E	(800) 222-8222	E / 0.3	-0.12	-6.04	-4.54 / 6	-2.51 / 3	0.49 / 3	0.00	2.40
EM	● Wells Fargo Adv Emerg Mkts Eq Inst	EMGNX	E	(800) 222-8222	E / 0.3	0.19	-5.49	-3.41 / 8	-1.34 / 3	--	1.20	1.22
EM	● Wells Fargo Adv Emerg Mkts Eq R6	EMGDX	U	(800) 222-8222	U /	0.19	-5.44	-3.36 / 8	--	--	1.25	1.17
EM	● Wells Fargo Adv Emerging Gr A	WEMAX	C-	(800) 222-8222	B- / 7.3	9.07	20.19	10.74 /77	14.35 /70	17.64 /97	0.00	1.39
EM	● Wells Fargo Adv Emerging Gr Adm	WFGDX	C	(800) 222-8222	B+ / 8.5	9.11	20.28	10.89 /78	14.54 /71	17.85 /97	0.00	1.23

● Denotes fund is closed to new investors
* Denotes fund is included in Section II

www.thestreetratings.com

Risk Rating/Pts	3 Year Standard Deviation	Beta	NAV As of 3/31/15	Total $(Mil)	Cash %	Stocks %	Bonds %	Other %	Portfolio Turnover Ratio	Last Bull Market Return	Last Bear Market Return	Manager Quality Pct	Manager Tenure (Years)	Initial Purch. $	Additional Purch. $	Front End Load	Back End Load
B- / 7.2	8.8	1.46	18.30	6	3	80	16	1	25	57.9	-18.1	7	9	1,000	100	0.0	0.0
B- / 7.2	8.8	1.46	19.77	138	3	80	16	1	25	62.5	-17.8	10	9	2,500	100	0.0	0.0
U /	N/A	N/A	19.86	678	3	80	16	1	25	N/A	N/A	N/A	9	0	0	0.0	0.0
B- / 7.2	8.8	1.46	19.85	886	3	80	16	1	25	65.1	-17.6	13	9	0	0	0.0	0.0
B- / 7.0	9.2	1.53	11.88	136	4	85	9	2	24	66.5	-18.5	9	8	1,000,000	0	0.0	0.0
B- / 7.0	9.2	1.54	11.92	114	4	85	9	2	24	65.6	-18.5	8	8	2,500	100	0.0	0.0
U /	N/A	N/A	11.82	201	4	85	9	2	24	N/A	N/A	N/A	8	0	0	0.0	0.0
B- / 7.0	9.2	1.54	11.80	373	4	85	9	2	24	68.4	-18.3	11	8	0	0	0.0	0.0
B- / 7.0	9.3	1.54	11.30	237	4	86	8	2	23	66.9	-18.4	10	N/A	1,000,000	0	0.0	0.0
B- / 7.0	9.3	1.55	11.33	67	4	86	8	2	23	66.3	-18.5	8	N/A	2,500	100	0.0	0.0
U /	N/A	N/A	11.33	365	4	86	8	2	23	N/A	N/A	N/A	N/A	0	0	0.0	0.0
B- / 7.0	9.2	1.54	11.33	874	4	86	8	2	23	69.0	-18.3	11	N/A	0	0	0.0	0.0
B- / 7.1	9.2	1.54	13.21	13	4	86	8	2	23	66.4	N/A	10	4	1,000,000	0	0.0	0.0
B- / 7.1	9.3	1.55	13.10	9	4	86	8	2	23	65.8	N/A	8	4	2,500	100	0.0	0.0
U /	N/A	N/A	13.24	36	4	86	8	2	23	N/A	N/A	N/A	N/A	0	0	0.0	0.0
B- / 7.1	9.3	1.54	13.22	130	4	86	8	2	23	68.4	N/A	11	4	0	0	0.0	0.0
B+ / 9.1	2.9	0.31	10.80	15	8	14	76	2	40	11.1	-0.7	53	9	1,000	100	5.8	0.0
B+ / 9.1	3.0	0.32	11.02	99	8	14	76	2	40	11.7	-0.6	54	9	1,000,000	0	0.0	0.0
B+ / 9.3	3.0	0.32	11.27	N/A	8	14	76	2	40	8.3	-0.9	39	9	1,000	100	0.0	0.0
B+ / 9.2	3.0	0.32	11.06	4	8	14	76	2	40	8.3	-1.0	40	9	1,000	100	0.0	0.0
B+ / 9.1	2.9	0.32	11.00	65	8	14	76	2	40	11.3	-0.7	52	9	2,500	100	0.0	0.0
U /	N/A	N/A	11.05	336	8	14	76	2	40	N/A	N/A	N/A	9	0	0	0.0	0.0
B+ / 9.0	3.0	0.32	11.04	237	8	14	76	2	40	13.1	-0.5	60	9	0	0	0.0	0.0
C- / 4.0	9.9	1.02	15.09	329	1	98	0	1	71	104.4	-16.8	68	4	1,000	100	5.8	0.0
C- / 4.1	9.8	1.02	15.43	56	1	98	0	1	71	105.7	-16.8	71	4	1,000,000	0	0.0	0.0
C- / 3.9	9.8	1.02	14.20	19	1	98	0	1	71	99.3	-17.1	58	4	1,000	100	0.0	0.0
C- / 4.0	9.8	1.02	15.27	103	1	98	0	1	71	107.4	-16.6	73	4	5,000,000	0	0.0	0.0
B- / 7.2	9.3	1.53	10.01	453	4	78	16	2	82	87.9	-23.2	44	8	1,000	100	5.8	0.0
B- / 7.2	9.3	1.53	10.02	11	4	78	16	2	82	89.4	-23.1	47	8	1,000,000	0	0.0	0.0
B- / 7.2	9.2	1.53	10.09	5	4	78	16	2	82	83.1	-23.4	34	8	1,000	100	0.0	0.0
B- / 7.2	9.2	1.52	10.02	54	4	78	16	2	82	83.1	-23.4	34	8	1,000	100	0.0	0.0
B- / 7.2	9.2	1.52	9.96	107	4	78	16	2	82	90.6	-23.1	51	8	5,000,000	0	0.0	0.0
C+ / 5.6	10.4	1.05	31.87	82	3	96	0	1	37	86.6	-19.6	27	10	1,000	100	5.8	0.0
C+ / 5.6	10.4	1.05	31.93	212	3	96	0	1	37	88.2	-19.5	30	10	1,000,000	0	0.0	0.0
C / 5.3	10.4	1.05	29.04	N/A	3	96	0	1	37	81.8	-19.8	20	10	1,000	100	0.0	0.0
C / 5.4	10.4	1.06	29.78	4	3	96	0	1	37	81.9	-19.8	19	10	1,000	100	0.0	0.0
C+ / 6.2	12.2	0.91	12.22	25	3	96	0	1	33	57.1	-24.3	74	11	1,000	100	5.8	0.0
C+ / 6.2	12.2	0.91	12.44	8	3	96	0	1	33	57.9	-24.2	75	11	1,000,000	0	0.0	0.0
C+ / 6.3	12.2	0.91	11.94	N/A	3	96	0	1	33	53.3	-24.5	65	11	1,000	100	0.0	0.0
C+ / 6.2	12.2	0.91	11.32	2	3	96	0	1	33	53.2	-24.5	66	11	1,000	100	0.0	0.0
C+ / 6.0	12.2	0.91	11.66	3	3	96	0	1	33	58.9	-24.2	76	11	5,000,000	0	0.0	0.0
C+ / 6.2	12.2	0.92	12.17	50	3	96	0	1	33	56.8	-24.3	73	11	2,500	100	0.0	0.0
U /	N/A	N/A	10.96	40	10	89	0	1	91	N/A	N/A	N/A	3	1,000,000	0	0.0	0.0
U /	N/A	N/A	10.95	45	10	89	0	1	91	N/A	N/A	N/A	3	5,000,000	0	0.0	0.0
C / 5.0	13.5	0.97	19.82	1,462	4	95	0	1	7	10.3	-20.4	32	9	1,000	100	5.8	0.0
C / 5.1	13.5	0.97	20.79	373	4	95	0	1	7	11.0	-20.4	33	9	1,000,000	0	0.0	0.0
C / 5.0	13.5	0.97	16.94	3	4	95	0	1	7	7.5	-20.7	23	9	1,000	100	0.0	0.0
C / 5.0	13.5	0.97	16.81	113	4	95	0	1	7	7.5	-20.7	23	9	1,000	100	0.0	0.0
C / 5.0	13.5	0.97	20.76	2,712	4	95	0	1	7	11.9	-20.3	37	9	5,000,000	0	0.0	0.0
U /	N/A	N/A	20.76	39	4	95	0	1	7	N/A	N/A	N/A	9	0	0	0.0	0.0
D+ / 2.8	17.0	0.44	16.71	134	2	97	0	1	63	95.6	-23.5	99	8	1,000	100	5.8	0.0
D+ / 2.8	17.0	0.44	17.00	173	2	97	0	1	63	96.6	-23.4	99	8	1,000,000	0	0.0	0.0

Fund Type	Fund Name	Ticker Symbol	Overall Investment Rating	Phone	Performance Rating/Pts	3 Mo	6 Mo	1Yr / Pct	3Yr / Pct	5Yr / Pct	Dividend Yield	Expense Ratio
								Total Return % through 3/31/15	Annualized		Incl. in Returns	
EM	● Wells Fargo Adv Emerging Gr C	WEMCX	C-	(800) 222-8222	B / 7.7	8.80	19.65	9.91 /74	13.48 /63	16.78 /95	0.00	2.14
EM	● Wells Fargo Adv Emerging Gr I	WEMIX	C	(800) 222-8222	B+ / 8.7	9.17	20.39	11.23 /79	14.89 /74	18.20 /98	0.00	0.96
EM	● Wells Fargo Adv Emerging Gr Inv	WFGTX	C	(800) 222-8222	B+ / 8.3	9.07	20.17	10.67 /77	14.28 /69	17.59 /97	0.00	1.45
OT	Wells Fargo Adv Endeavor Sel A	STAEX	C-	(800) 222-8222	C+ / 5.8	2.79	7.17	11.30 /80	13.56 /64	13.29 /71	0.00	1.25
OT	Wells Fargo Adv Endeavor Sel Adm	WECDX	C	(800) 222-8222	C+ / 6.9	2.86	7.37	11.65 /81	13.84 /66	13.56 /74	0.00	1.09
OT	● Wells Fargo Adv Endeavor Sel B	WECBX	C-	(800) 222-8222	C+ / 6.2	2.57	6.76	10.49 /76	12.71 /58	12.43 /64	0.00	2.00
OT	Wells Fargo Adv Endeavor Sel C	WECCX	C-	(800) 222-8222	C+ / 6.2	2.66	6.83	10.57 /77	12.74 /58	12.44 /64	0.00	2.00
OT	Wells Fargo Adv Endeavor Sel I	WFCIX	C	(800) 222-8222	B- / 7.1	2.89	7.47	11.85 /82	14.09 /68	13.80 /76	0.00	0.82
MC	Wells Fargo Adv Enterprise Adm	SEPKX	C	(800) 222-8222	B- / 7.4	5.87	10.82	8.86 /69	14.38 /70	14.86 /86	0.00	1.13
MC	Wells Fargo Adv Enterprise Adv	SENAX	C-	(800) 222-8222	C+ / 6.3	5.85	10.73	8.74 /68	14.29 /69	14.75 /85	0.00	1.29
MC	● Wells Fargo Adv Enterprise B	WENBX	C-	(800) 222-8222	C+ / 6.7	5.63	10.32	7.93 /62	13.44 /63	--	0.00	2.04
MC	Wells Fargo Adv Enterprise C	WENCX	C-	(800) 222-8222	C+ / 6.7	5.63	10.32	7.93 /62	13.44 /63	13.90 /77	0.00	2.04
MC	Wells Fargo Adv Enterprise I	WFEIX	C	(800) 222-8222	B / 7.6	5.94	10.94	9.11 /70	14.67 /72	15.16 /88	0.00	0.86
MC	Wells Fargo Adv Enterprise Inv	SENTX	C	(800) 222-8222	B- / 7.3	5.83	10.71	8.68 /67	14.22 /69	14.67 /84	0.00	1.35
GL	Wells Fargo Adv Global Opps A	EKGAX	D	(800) 222-8222	C / 4.4	4.71	7.66	2.60 /25	12.16 /54	10.05 /45	0.05	1.58
GL	Wells Fargo Adv Global Opps Adm	EKGYX	D+	(800) 222-8222	C / 5.5	4.75	7.75	2.75 /25	12.33 /55	10.24 /46	0.07	1.42
GL	● Wells Fargo Adv Global Opps B	EKGBX	D-	(800) 222-8222	C / 4.8	4.55	7.27	1.81 /21	11.32 /48	9.23 /38	0.00	2.33
GL	Wells Fargo Adv Global Opps C	EKGCX	D-	(800) 222-8222	C / 4.8	4.52	7.26	1.80 /21	11.32 /48	9.22 /38	0.00	2.33
GL	Wells Fargo Adv Global Opps Inst	EKGIX	D+	(800) 222-8222	C+ / 5.7	4.82	7.89	3.01 /26	12.62 /57	--	0.48	1.15
BA	Wells Fargo Adv Gro Bal A	WFGBX	C+	(800) 222-8222	C / 4.5	2.72	6.14	8.78 /68	11.73 /51	10.75 /51	0.39	1.39
BA	Wells Fargo Adv Gro Bal Adm	NVGBX	B	(800) 222-8222	C+ / 5.6	2.75	6.24	9.04 /70	12.00 /53	11.02 /53	0.57	1.23
BA	● Wells Fargo Adv Gro Bal B	NVGRX	C+	(800) 222-8222	C / 4.9	2.53	5.74	7.95 /63	10.88 /45	9.91 /44	0.00	2.14
BA	Wells Fargo Adv Gro Bal C	WFGWX	C+	(800) 222-8222	C / 4.9	2.55	5.75	7.97 /63	10.89 /45	9.93 /44	0.21	2.14
GR	● Wells Fargo Adv Growth Adm	SGRKX	C-	(800) 222-8222	C+ / 6.3	4.80	9.78	11.23 /79	12.44 /56	16.90 /96	0.00	1.02
GR	● Wells Fargo Adv Growth Adv	SGRAX	D	(800) 222-8222	C / 5.2	4.77	9.67	11.01 /78	12.20 /54	16.61 /95	0.00	1.18
GR	● Wells Fargo Adv Growth C	WGFCX	D	(800) 222-8222	C+ / 5.6	4.55	9.25	10.15 /75	11.35 /48	15.75 /92	0.00	1.93
GR	● Wells Fargo Adv Growth Instl	SGRNX	C-	(800) 222-8222	C+ / 6.5	4.86	9.90	11.47 /80	12.69 /57	17.13 /96	0.00	0.75
GR	● Wells Fargo Adv Growth Inv	SGROX	C-	(800) 222-8222	C+ / 6.1	4.75	9.62	10.94 /78	12.13 /53	16.54 /95	0.00	1.24
IX	● Wells Fargo Adv Index A	WFILX	B-	(800) 222-8222	C+ / 6.7	0.86	5.67	12.15 /83	15.50 /79	13.86 /76	1.36	0.67
IX	Wells Fargo Adv Index Adm	WFIOX	A	(800) 222-8222	B / 8.1	0.93	5.84	12.48 /85	15.85 /82	14.22 /80	1.73	0.36
AA	Wells Fargo Adv Index Asst All A	SFAAX	B	(800) 222-8222	C+ / 6.1	1.29	7.76	14.58 /91	13.89 /66	13.25 /71	1.11	1.20
AA	Wells Fargo Adv Index Asst All Adm	WFAIX	A+	(800) 222-8222	B- / 7.3	1.35	7.90	14.83 /91	14.16 /68	13.53 /73	1.43	1.04
AA	● Wells Fargo Adv Index Asst All B	SASBX	B	(800) 222-8222	C+ / 6.5	1.16	7.40	13.69 /89	13.06 /60	12.41 /63	0.33	1.95
AA	Wells Fargo Adv Index Asst All C	WFALX	B	(800) 222-8222	C+ / 6.5	1.14	7.39	13.75 /89	13.04 /60	12.41 /63	0.57	1.95
IX	● Wells Fargo Adv Index B	WFIMX	B+	(800) 222-8222	B- / 7.1	0.66	5.27	11.31 /80	14.63 /72	13.01 /68	0.43	1.42
IX	● Wells Fargo Adv Index C	WFINX	B+	(800) 222-8222	B- / 7.2	0.67	5.29	11.30 /80	14.64 /72	13.01 /68	0.73	1.42
IX	Wells Fargo Adv Index Inv	WFIRX	A-	(800) 222-8222	B / 7.9	0.89	5.74	12.26 /84	15.62 /80	--	1.57	0.73
FO	Wells Fargo Adv Intl Equity A	WFEAX	D	(800) 222-8222	C- / 3.0	8.74	7.26	5.61 /43	8.53 /30	6.20 /18	3.96	1.53
FO	Wells Fargo Adv Intl Equity Adm	WFEDX	D+	(800) 222-8222	C- / 3.9	8.80	7.31	5.63 /43	8.52 /30	--	4.28	1.37
FO	● Wells Fargo Adv Intl Equity B	WFEBX	D+	(800) 222-8222	C- / 3.3	8.55	6.87	4.81 /37	7.70 /25	5.42 /14	3.28	2.28
FO	Wells Fargo Adv Intl Equity C	WFEFX	D+	(800) 222-8222	C- / 3.4	8.58	6.80	4.86 /38	7.71 /25	5.41 /14	3.50	2.28
FO	Wells Fargo Adv Intl Equity Inst	WFENX	D+	(800) 222-8222	C- / 4.1	8.88	7.39	5.92 /46	8.79 /32	6.47 /20	4.47	1.10
FO	Wells Fargo Adv Intl Equity R	WFERX	D+	(800) 222-8222	C- / 3.7	8.81	7.11	5.39 /42	8.25 /28	5.95 /17	3.84	1.78
FO	Wells Fargo Adv Intl Val A	WFFAX	D-	(800) 222-8222	D- / 1.3	4.66	-1.47	-3.82 / 7	7.28 /23	4.76 /11	2.20	1.51
FO	Wells Fargo Adv Intl Val Adm	WFVDX	D-	(800) 222-8222	D / 2.1	4.70	-1.34	-3.58 / 8	7.53 /24	4.99 /12	2.69	1.35
FO	● Wells Fargo Adv Intl Val B	WFVBX	D-	(800) 222-8222	D- / 1.5	4.40	-1.96	-4.61 / 6	6.47 /19	3.95 / 8	0.00	2.26
FO	Wells Fargo Adv Intl Val C	WFVCX	D-	(800) 222-8222	D- / 1.5	4.44	-1.88	-4.60 / 6	6.47 /19	3.96 / 8	1.73	2.26
FO	Wells Fargo Adv Intl Val Inst	WFVIX	D-	(800) 222-8222	D / 2.2	4.77	-1.26	-3.43 / 8	7.75 /26	5.22 /13	2.91	1.08
SC	Wells Fargo Adv Intr Sm Cp VI A	WFSMX	B-	(800) 222-8222	B- / 7.3	2.82	10.58	8.37 /65	16.25 /85	13.03 /69	0.00	1.59
SC	Wells Fargo Adv Intr Sm Cp VI Adm	WFSDX	B+	(800) 222-8222	B+ / 8.5	2.85	10.66	8.58 /67	16.51 /87	13.30 /71	0.00	1.43
SC	Wells Fargo Adv Intr Sm Cp VI C	WSCDX	B	(800) 222-8222	B / 7.7	2.60	10.12	7.56 /60	15.38 /78	12.18 /62	0.00	2.34
SC	Wells Fargo Adv Intr Sm Cp VI Inst	WFSSX	B+	(800) 222-8222	B+ / 8.7	2.90	10.75	8.83 /68	16.79 /89	13.53 /73	0.37	1.16

● Denotes fund is closed to new investors
* Denotes fund is included in Section II

RISK			NET ASSETS		ASSET					BULL / BEAR		FUND MANAGER		MINIMUMS		LOADS	
	3 Year		NAV						Portfolio	Last Bull	Last Bear	Manager	Manager	Initial	Additional	Front	Back
Risk	Standard		As of	Total	Cash	Stocks	Bonds	Other	Turnover	Market	Market	Quality	Tenure	Purch.	Purch.	End	End
Rating/Pts	Deviation	Beta	3/31/15	$(Mil)	%	%	%	%	Ratio	Return	Return	Pct	(Years)	$	$	Load	Load
D+ / 2.6	17.0	0.44	15.70	5	2	97	0	1	63	90.4	-23.7	99	8	1,000	100	0.0	0.0
D+ / 2.8	17.1	0.44	17.39	717	2	97	0	1	63	98.6	-23.3	99	8	5,000,000	0	0.0	0.0
D+ / 2.7	17.0	0.44	16.60	45	2	97	0	1	63	95.0	-23.4	99	8	2,500	100	0.0	0.0
C / 4.5	11.1	0.99	13.28	28	6	93	0	1	100	90.8	-19.9	37	15	1,000	100	5.8	0.0
C / 4.6	11.2	0.99	13.65	46	6	93	0	1	100	92.6	-19.8	40	15	1,000,000	0	0.0	0.0
C- / 4.1	11.2	0.99	11.56	N/A	6	93	0	1	100	85.9	-20.1	27	15	1,000	100	0.0	0.0
C- / 4.1	11.2	0.99	11.57	7	6	93	0	1	100	86.1	-20.2	28	15	1,000	100	0.0	0.0
C / 4.6	11.2	0.99	13.89	509	6	93	0	1	100	93.7	-19.7	44	15	5,000,000	0	0.0	0.0
C- / 4.0	12.4	1.03	48.52	42	0	99	0	1	98	96.9	-24.8	28	15	1,000,000	0	0.0	0.0
C- / 3.9	12.4	1.02	46.71	434	0	99	0	1	98	96.4	-24.9	28	15	1,000	100	5.8	0.0
C- / 3.6	12.4	1.03	43.35	1	0	99	0	1	98	91.5	N/A	20	15	1,000	100	0.0	0.0
C- / 3.6	12.4	1.03	43.36	10	0	99	0	1	98	91.5	-25.1	20	15	1,000	100	0.0	0.0
C- / 4.1	12.4	1.03	49.94	77	0	99	0	1	98	98.6	-24.8	31	15	5,000,000	0	0.0	0.0
C- / 3.8	12.4	1.02	45.90	209	0	99	0	1	98	96.0	-24.9	27	15	2,500	100	0.0	0.0
C- / 3.9	11.8	0.76	38.66	165	6	93	0	1	66	71.9	-29.1	93	10	1,000	100	5.8	0.0
C- / 4.0	11.8	0.76	40.10	38	6	93	0	1	66	72.8	-29.0	93	10	1,000,000	0	0.0	0.0
D+ / 2.9	11.8	0.76	29.43	9	6	93	0	1	66	67.5	-29.3	91	10	1,000	100	0.0	0.0
D+ / 2.9	11.8	0.76	29.61	41	6	93	0	1	66	67.6	-29.3	91	10	1,000	100	0.0	0.0
C- / 4.0	11.8	0.76	40.02	8	6	93	0	1	66	74.3	-28.9	93	10	5,000,000	0	0.0	0.0
B- / 7.8	8.0	1.35	40.46	64	1	62	35	2	77	69.4	-16.4	27	10	1,000	100	5.8	0.0
B- / 7.8	8.0	1.35	36.22	182	1	62	35	2	77	70.9	-16.3	29	10	1,000,000	0	0.0	0.0
B- / 7.7	8.0	1.35	36.13	N/A	1	62	35	2	77	65.1	-16.7	19	10	1,000	100	0.0	0.0
B- / 7.7	8.0	1.35	35.38	14	1	62	35	2	77	65.2	-16.7	20	10	1,000	100	0.0	0.0
C- / 3.9	12.7	1.08	51.09	2,529	0	99	0	1	42	87.6	-16.2	14	13	1,000,000	0	0.0	0.0
C- / 3.8	12.7	1.08	47.89	1,558	0	99	0	1	42	86.1	-16.3	12	13	1,000	100	5.8	0.0
C- / 3.4	12.7	1.08	43.16	478	0	99	0	1	42	81.4	-16.5	9	13	1,000	100	0.0	0.0
C- / 4.0	12.7	1.08	53.12	3,789	0	99	0	1	42	88.9	-16.1	15	13	5,000,000	0	0.0	0.0
C- / 3.7	12.7	1.08	47.68	2,123	0	99	0	1	42	85.7	-16.3	12	13	2,500	100	0.0	0.0
B- / 7.2	9.5	1.00	65.90	445	1	98	0	1	5	96.6	-16.4	60	2	1,000	100	5.8	0.0
B- / 7.2	9.6	1.00	66.34	1,911	1	98	0	1	5	98.6	-16.3	64	2	1,000,000	0	0.0	0.0
B / 8.6	6.7	1.14	29.92	784	7	57	35	1	9	76.5	-8.9	79	9	1,000	100	5.8	0.0
B / 8.6	6.6	1.14	29.93	109	7	57	35	1	9	78.0	-8.8	81	9	1,000,000	0	0.0	0.0
B / 8.6	6.7	1.14	18.40	N/A	7	57	35	1	9	72.0	-9.1	73	9	1,000	100	0.0	0.0
B / 8.6	6.6	1.14	18.24	51	7	57	35	1	9	72.0	-9.2	73	9	1,000	100	0.0	0.0
B- / 7.2	9.6	1.00	67.08	2	1	98	0	1	5	91.5	-16.7	48	2	1,000	100	0.0	0.0
B- / 7.2	9.5	1.00	66.21	83	1	98	0	1	5	91.6	-16.7	48	2	1,000	100	0.0	0.0
B- / 7.2	9.6	1.00	66.08	232	1	98	0	1	5	97.3	-16.4	61	2	2,500	100	0.0	0.0
C+ / 5.8	12.7	0.91	11.82	100	5	94	0	1	32	48.7	-26.0	66	3	1,000	100	5.8	0.0
C+ / 5.8	12.7	0.91	11.62	12	5	94	0	1	32	48.5	-26.0	66	3	1,000,000	0	0.0	0.0
C+ / 5.8	12.7	0.91	11.55	4	5	94	0	1	32	44.9	-26.3	55	3	1,000	100	0.0	0.0
C+ / 5.8	12.7	0.91	11.64	17	5	94	0	1	32	44.8	-26.3	54	3	1,000	100	0.0	0.0
C+ / 5.8	12.7	0.91	11.77	65	5	94	0	1	32	49.9	-25.9	69	3	5,000,000	0	0.0	0.0
C+ / 5.8	12.7	0.91	11.98	2	5	94	0	1	32	47.4	-26.1	62	3	0	0	0.0	0.0
C+ / 5.8	13.2	0.99	14.16	6	4	95	0	1	11	43.0	-23.0	38	12	1,000	100	5.8	0.0
C+ / 5.8	13.3	0.99	14.04	467	4	95	0	1	11	44.2	-22.9	41	12	1,000,000	0	0.0	0.0
C+ / 6.2	13.2	0.99	14.47	N/A	4	95	0	1	11	39.3	-23.2	28	12	1,000	100	0.0	0.0
C+ / 5.9	13.2	0.99	13.88	1	4	95	0	1	11	39.4	-23.2	28	12	1,000	100	0.0	0.0
C+ / 5.8	13.2	0.99	14.06	4	4	95	0	1	11	45.2	-22.8	44	12	5,000,000	0	0.0	0.0
C+ / 6.1	13.7	0.96	25.50	1	5	94	0	1	75	108.6	-28.0	74	5	1,000	100	5.8	0.0
C+ / 6.1	13.6	0.95	25.95	5	5	94	0	1	75	110.3	-27.9	76	5	1,000,000	0	0.0	0.0
C+ / 6.0	13.6	0.95	24.04	N/A	5	94	0	1	75	103.2	-28.2	66	5	1,000	100	0.0	0.0
C+ / 6.1	13.6	0.95	26.22	85	5	94	0	1	75	111.7	-27.9	78	5	5,000,000	0	0.0	0.0

Fund Type	Fund Name	Ticker Symbol	Overall Investment Rating	Phone	Performance Rating/Pts	3 Mo	6 Mo	1Yr / Pct	3Yr / Pct	5Yr / Pct	Dividend Yield	Expense Ratio
SC	Wells Fargo Adv Intr Sm Cp VI Inv	SCOVX	B+	(800) 222-8222	B+ / 8.3	2.77	10.51	8.28 /65	16.20 /85	12.97 /68	0.00	1.65
GR	Wells Fargo Adv Intr Value A	EIVAX	C+	(800) 222-8222	C+ / 6.1	1.06	5.63	8.72 /68	14.91 /74	13.34 /71	0.49	1.22
GR	Wells Fargo Adv Intr Value Adm	EIVDX	B+	(800) 222-8222	B- / 7.3	1.09	5.75	8.97 /69	15.12 /76	--	0.72	1.06
GR	● Wells Fargo Adv Intr Value B	EIVBX	C+	(800) 222-8222	C+ / 6.5	0.84	5.25	7.88 /62	14.03 /67	12.47 /64	0.00	1.97
GR	Wells Fargo Adv Intr Value C	EIVCX	C+	(800) 222-8222	C+ / 6.5	0.84	5.21	7.94 /62	14.02 /67	12.47 /64	0.00	1.97
GR	Wells Fargo Adv Intr Value Inst	EIVIX	B+	(800) 222-8222	B- / 7.5	1.13	5.87	9.19 /70	15.40 /78	13.76 /76	0.95	0.79
GL	Wells Fargo Adv Intr World Eq A	EWEAX	C-	(800) 222-8222	C- / 3.2	3.08	3.58	2.76 /25	10.37 /42	11.07 /53	0.50	1.47
GL	Wells Fargo Adv Intr World Eq Adm	EWEIX	C	(800) 222-8222	C / 4.3	3.18	3.77	3.08 /27	10.66 /43	11.35 /56	0.78	1.31
GL	Wells Fargo Adv Intr World Eq C	EWECX	C-	(800) 222-8222	C- / 3.6	2.94	3.22	2.05 /22	9.57 /37	10.24 /46	0.00	2.22
GL	Wells Fargo Adv Intr World Eq Inst	EWENX	C	(800) 222-8222	C / 4.5	3.27	3.89	3.29 /28	10.89 /45	--	0.99	1.04
GR	Wells Fargo Adv Large Cap Core A	EGOAX	A+	(800) 222-8222	A- / 9.0	3.47	8.19	15.51 /92	18.55 /96	15.38 /89	0.28	1.29
GR	Wells Fargo Adv Large Cap Core	WFLLX	A+	(800) 222-8222	A+ / 9.6	3.52	8.33	15.81 /93	18.86 /96	--	0.44	1.13
GR	Wells Fargo Adv Large Cap Core C	EGOCX	A+	(800) 222-8222	A / 9.3	3.30	7.78	14.64 /91	17.69 /93	14.52 /83	0.00	2.04
GR	Wells Fargo Adv Large Cap Core I	EGOIX	A+	(800) 222-8222	A+ / 9.6	3.59	8.42	16.06 /93	19.14 /97	15.93 /93	0.53	0.86
GR	Wells Fargo Adv Large Cap Core Inv	WFLNX	A+	(800) 222-8222	A / 9.5	3.46	8.17	15.41 /92	18.47 /96	--	0.12	1.35
GR	Wells Fargo Adv Large Cap Gr A	STAFX	C+	(800) 222-8222	C+ / 6.0	3.54	8.76	13.46 /88	13.29 /62	--	0.00	1.22
GR	Wells Fargo Adv Large Cap Gr Adm	STDFX	B-	(800) 222-8222	B- / 7.1	3.59	8.80	13.59 /88	13.42 /63	--	0.00	1.06
GR	Wells Fargo Adv Large Cap Gr C	STOFX	C+	(800) 222-8222	C+ / 6.4	3.35	8.35	12.60 /85	12.44 /56	--	0.00	1.97
GR	Wells Fargo Adv Large Cap Gr Inst	STNFX	B-	(800) 222-8222	B- / 7.4	3.65	8.96	13.92 /89	13.73 /65	--	0.06	0.79
GR	Wells Fargo Adv Large Cap Gr Inv	STRFX	C+	(800) 222-8222	C+ / 6.9	3.53	8.70	13.39 /88	13.21 /61	14.57 /83	0.00	1.28
GI	Wells Fargo Adv Lg Co Val A	WLCAX	C+	(800) 222-8222	C+ / 5.7	1.22	4.11	7.23 /57	14.53 /71	11.34 /56	0.51	1.28
GI	Wells Fargo Adv Lg Co Val Adm	WWIDX	C+	(800) 222-8222	C+ / 6.9	1.33	4.25	7.52 /59	14.81 /73	11.63 /58	0.78	1.12
GI	Wells Fargo Adv Lg Co Val C	WFLVX	C+	(800) 222-8222	C+ / 6.1	1.03	3.71	6.41 /50	13.67 /65	10.51 /49	0.05	2.03
GI	Wells Fargo Adv Lg Co Val Inst	WLCIX	B-	(800) 222-8222	B- / 7.1	1.37	4.31	7.72 /61	15.08 /76	11.87 /60	0.95	0.85
GI	Wells Fargo Adv Lg Co Val Inv	SDVIX	C+	(800) 222-8222	C+ / 6.7	1.24	4.08	7.22 /57	14.46 /71	11.26 /55	0.47	1.34
BA	Wells Fargo Adv Modt Bal A	WFMAX	C	(800) 222-8222	D+ / 2.6	2.31	4.88	7.08 /56	8.51 /30	8.21 /31	1.74	1.36
BA	Wells Fargo Adv Modt Bal Adm	NVMBX	C+	(800) 222-8222	C- / 3.7	2.34	5.01	7.34 /58	8.76 /31	8.47 /33	2.16	1.20
BA	● Wells Fargo Adv Modt Bal B	WMOBX	C	(800) 222-8222	C- / 3.0	2.11	4.45	6.23 /48	7.68 /25	7.38 /26	0.00	2.11
BA	Wells Fargo Adv Modt Bal C	WFBCX	C	(800) 222-8222	C- / 3.0	2.12	4.47	6.28 /49	7.69 /25	7.39 /26	0.99	2.11
GR	Wells Fargo Adv Omega Growth A	EKOAX	D+	(800) 222-8222	C+ / 5.8	2.90	6.07	8.15 /64	14.21 /69	14.09 /79	0.00	1.32
GR	Wells Fargo Adv Omega Growth	EOMYX	C	(800) 222-8222	B- / 7.0	2.95	6.20	8.41 /66	14.49 /71	14.37 /81	0.00	1.16
GR	● Wells Fargo Adv Omega Growth B	EKOBX	D	(800) 222-8222	C+ / 6.2	2.68	5.66	7.31 /58	13.35 /62	13.24 /71	0.00	2.07
GR	Wells Fargo Adv Omega Growth C	EKOCX	D	(800) 222-8222	C+ / 6.2	2.70	5.67	7.35 /58	13.37 /62	13.24 /71	0.00	2.07
GR	Wells Fargo Adv Omega Growth Inst	EKONX	C	(800) 222-8222	B- / 7.2	3.01	6.32	8.67 /67	14.78 /73	--	0.00	0.89
GR	Wells Fargo Adv Omega Growth R	EKORX	C-	(800) 222-8222	C+ / 6.6	2.84	5.95	7.86 /62	13.92 /67	13.81 /76	0.00	1.57
GR	Wells Fargo Adv Oppty Adm	WOFDX	B-	(800) 222-8222	B- / 7.4	3.39	8.78	10.92 /78	14.42 /70	12.47 /64	0.00	1.11
SC	Wells Fargo Adv Oppty Adv	SOPVX	C+	(800) 222-8222	C+ / 6.1	3.34	8.66	10.70 /77	14.16 /68	12.21 /62	0.00	1.27
GR	● Wells Fargo Adv Oppty B	SOPBX	C+	(800) 222-8222	C+ / 6.5	3.13	8.26	9.86 /74	13.30 /62	--	0.00	2.02
GR	Wells Fargo Adv Oppty C	WFOPX	C+	(800) 222-8222	C+ / 6.6	3.15	8.26	9.88 /74	13.31 /62	11.37 /56	0.00	2.02
GR	Wells Fargo Adv Oppty Inst	WOFNX	B	(800) 222-8222	B / 7.6	3.47	8.92	11.22 /79	14.71 /73	--	0.00	0.84
GR	Wells Fargo Adv Oppty Inv	SOPFX	C+	(800) 222-8222	B- / 7.1	3.33	8.64	10.63 /77	14.09 /68	12.14 /62	0.00	1.33
PM	Wells Fargo Adv Precious Mtls A	EKWAX	E-	(800) 222-8222	E- / 0.0	-5.39	-15.46	-20.90 / 1	-24.56 / 0	-13.26 / 0	0.00	1.23
PM	Wells Fargo Adv Precious Mtls Adm	EKWDX	E-	(800) 222-8222	E- / 0.0	-5.35	-15.38	-20.78 / 1	-24.45 / 0	--	0.00	1.07
PM	● Wells Fargo Adv Precious Mtls B	EKWBX	E-	(800) 222-8222	E- / 0.0	-5.56	-15.80	-21.50 / 1	-25.13 / 0	-13.91 / 0	0.00	1.98
PM	Wells Fargo Adv Precious Mtls C	EKWCX	E-	(800) 222-8222	E- / 0.0	-5.56	-15.76	-21.49 / 1	-25.12 / 0	-13.91 / 0	0.00	1.98
PM	Wells Fargo Adv Precious Mtls Inst	EKWYX	E-	(800) 222-8222	E- / 0.0	-5.30	-15.33	-20.64 / 1	-24.32 / 0	-12.97 / 0	0.00	0.80
GR	Wells Fargo Adv Prmr Lg Co Gr A	EKJAX	C+	(800) 222-8222	C+ / 6.0	3.46	8.45	12.70 /86	13.64 /64	14.82 /85	0.00	1.17
GR	Wells Fargo Adv Prmr Lg Co Gr	WFPDX	B-	(800) 222-8222	B- / 7.2	3.50	8.53	12.84 /86	13.83 /66	--	0.00	1.01
GR	● Wells Fargo Adv Prmr Lg Co Gr B	EKJBX	C+	(800) 222-8222	C+ / 6.4	3.25	8.01	11.84 /82	12.79 /58	13.96 /77	0.00	1.92
GR	Wells Fargo Adv Prmr Lg Co Gr C	EKJCX	C+	(800) 222-8222	C+ / 6.4	3.26	8.03	11.87 /82	12.79 /58	13.98 /78	0.00	1.92
GR	Wells Fargo Adv Prmr Lg Co Gr Inst	EKJYX	B	(800) 222-8222	B- / 7.4	3.59	8.71	13.22 /87	14.13 /68	15.31 /89	0.00	0.74
GR	Wells Fargo Adv Prmr Lg Co Gr Inv	WFPNX	C+	(800) 222-8222	C+ / 6.9	3.40	8.41	12.68 /86	13.56 /64	--	0.00	1.23

● Denotes fund is closed to new investors
* Denotes fund is included in Section II

www.thestreetratings.com

RISK			NET ASSETS		ASSET					BULL / BEAR		FUND MANAGER		MINIMUMS		LOADS	
	3 Year		NAV						Portfolio	Last Bull	Last Bear	Manager	Manager	Initial	Additional	Front	Back
Risk	Standard		As of	Total	Cash	Stocks	Bonds	Other	Turnover	Market	Market	Quality	Tenure	Purch.	Purch.	End	End
Rating/Pts	Deviation	Beta	3/31/15	$(Mil)	%	%	%	%	Ratio	Return	Return	Pct	(Years)	$	$	Load	Load
C+ / 6.1	13.6	0.96	25.23	59	5	94	0	1	75	108.1	-28.0	74	5	2,500	100	0.0	0.0
C+ / 6.8	9.8	1.01	13.39	383	1	98	0	1	23	90.5	-19.5	49	9	1,000	100	5.8	0.0
C+ / 6.8	9.8	1.01	13.89	530	1	98	0	1	23	91.7	-19.4	53	9	1,000,000	0	0.0	0.0
C+ / 6.9	9.8	1.01	13.24	3	1	98	0	1	23	85.6	-19.8	38	9	1,000	100	0.0	0.0
C+ / 6.9	9.8	1.01	13.15	37	1	98	0	1	23	85.6	-19.7	37	9	1,000	100	0.0	0.0
C+ / 6.7	9.8	1.01	13.44	247	1	98	0	1	23	93.2	-19.3	56	9	5,000,000	0	0.0	0.0
C+ / 6.8	11.3	0.79	22.79	158	0	99	0	1	23	71.3	-17.3	88	8	1,000	100	5.8	0.0
C+ / 6.8	11.2	0.78	22.70	6	0	99	0	1	23	72.8	-17.2	89	8	1,000,000	0	0.0	0.0
C+ / 6.8	11.3	0.79	22.07	10	0	99	0	1	23	67.0	-17.5	84	8	1,000	100	0.0	0.0
C+ / 6.8	11.3	0.79	22.75	5	0	99	0	1	23	74.0	-17.1	89	8	5,000,000	0	0.0	0.0
B- / 7.4	10.2	1.02	15.82	69	2	97	0	1	61	116.2	-19.7	83	8	1,000	100	5.8	0.0
B- / 7.4	10.2	1.02	15.87	44	2	97	0	1	61	118.0	-19.5	84	8	1,000,000	0	0.0	0.0
B- / 7.4	10.2	1.02	15.66	40	2	97	0	1	61	110.8	-19.9	78	8	1,000	100	0.0	0.0
B- / 7.4	10.3	1.02	15.89	37	2	97	0	1	61	119.9	-19.5	85	8	5,000,000	0	0.0	0.0
B- / 7.4	10.2	1.02	15.86	273	2	97	0	1	61	115.7	-19.7	82	8	2,500	100	0.0	0.0
C+ / 5.9	11.6	1.06	47.95	197	1	98	0	1	35	89.3	-14.1	22	13	1,000	100	5.8	0.0
C+ / 5.9	11.6	1.06	48.21	256	1	98	0	1	35	90.1	-14.1	23	13	1,000,000	0	0.0	0.0
C+ / 5.9	11.6	1.06	46.26	23	1	98	0	1	35	84.6	-14.4	15	13	1,000	100	0.0	0.0
C+ / 5.9	11.6	1.06	48.61	638	1	98	0	1	35	92.0	-14.0	26	13	5,000,000	0	0.0	0.0
C+ / 5.9	11.6	1.06	47.84	483	1	98	0	1	35	88.9	-14.2	21	13	2,500	100	0.0	0.0
C+ / 6.2	10.5	1.06	16.13	110	1	98	0	1	59	87.1	-19.2	34	7	1,000	100	5.8	0.0
C+ / 6.2	10.5	1.06	16.23	33	1	98	0	1	59	88.9	-19.1	37	7	1,000,000	0	0.0	0.0
C+ / 6.2	10.5	1.06	16.45	5	1	98	0	1	59	82.6	-19.5	25	7	1,000	100	0.0	0.0
C+ / 6.1	10.5	1.06	16.20	2	1	98	0	1	59	90.2	-19.0	40	7	5,000,000	0	0.0	0.0
C+ / 6.2	10.5	1.06	16.60	145	1	98	0	1	59	86.9	-19.3	33	7	2,500	100	0.0	0.0
B / 8.6	5.1	0.87	23.48	22	2	38	58	2	89	45.1	-9.7	56	10	1,000	100	5.8	0.0
B / 8.6	5.0	0.87	23.65	154	2	38	58	2	89	46.3	-9.6	59	10	1,000,000	0	0.0	0.0
B / 8.7	5.0	0.86	23.74	N/A	2	38	58	2	89	41.3	-10.0	45	10	1,000	100	0.0	0.0
B / 8.7	5.0	0.86	23.12	6	2	38	58	2	89	41.4	-10.0	44	10	1,000	100	0.0	0.0
C- / 3.7	11.9	1.08	46.78	691	2	97	0	1	101	96.6	-23.0	27	5	1,000	100	5.8	0.0
C- / 4.0	11.9	1.08	49.55	91	2	97	0	1	101	98.2	-22.9	30	5	1,000,000	0	0.0	0.0
D+ / 2.6	11.9	1.08	36.35	10	2	97	0	1	101	91.6	-23.2	19	5	1,000	100	0.0	0.0
D+ / 2.7	11.9	1.08	36.47	102	2	97	0	1	101	91.7	-23.2	19	5	1,000	100	0.0	0.0
C- / 4.1	11.9	1.08	50.29	67	2	97	0	1	101	99.9	-22.8	32	5	5,000,000	0	0.0	0.0
C- / 3.6	11.9	1.08	45.23	17	2	97	0	1	101	94.9	-23.0	24	5	0	0	0.0	0.0
C+ / 5.8	11.1	1.08	51.20	261	4	95	0	1	32	88.7	-22.9	29	14	1,000,000	0	0.0	0.0
C+ / 5.7	11.1	1.08	48.20	456	4	95	0	1	32	87.2	-23.0	27	14	1,000	100	5.8	0.0
C+ / 5.6	11.1	1.08	46.42	5	4	95	0	1	32	82.5	N/A	19	14	1,000	100	0.0	0.0
C+ / 5.6	11.1	1.08	46.43	44	4	95	0	1	32	82.5	-23.2	19	14	1,000	100	0.0	0.0
C+ / 5.9	11.1	1.08	51.87	23	4	95	0	1	32	90.3	-22.9	32	14	5,000,000	0	0.0	0.0
C+ / 5.8	11.1	1.08	49.34	1,195	4	95	0	1	32	86.8	-23.0	26	14	2,500	100	0.0	0.0
E+ / 0.7	35.3	1.73	28.99	212	10	89	0	1	16	-55.4	-11.7	2	8	1,000	100	5.8	0.0
E+ / 0.7	35.3	1.73	29.17	22	10	89	0	1	16	-55.2	-11.6	3	8	1,000,000	0	0.0	0.0
E+ / 0.7	35.3	1.73	26.33	3	10	89	0	1	16	-56.5	-11.9	2	8	1,000	100	0.0	0.0
E+ / 0.7	35.3	1.73	25.97	59	10	89	0	1	16	-56.5	-11.9	2	8	1,000	100	0.0	0.0
E+ / 0.7	35.3	1.73	29.33	43	10	89	0	1	16	-54.9	-11.5	3	8	5,000,000	0	0.0	0.0
C+ / 6.0	11.8	1.07	15.86	2,253	0	99	0	1	37	93.2	-15.0	23	5	1,000	100	5.8	0.0
C+ / 6.0	11.8	1.07	15.97	1,278	0	99	0	1	37	94.4	-15.0	25	5	1,000,000	0	0.0	0.0
C+ / 5.9	11.8	1.07	13.97	3	0	99	0	1	37	88.3	-15.2	17	5	1,000	100	0.0	0.0
C+ / 5.9	11.8	1.07	13.94	400	0	99	0	1	37	88.4	-15.3	17	5	1,000	100	0.0	0.0
C+ / 6.0	11.8	1.07	16.16	1,189	0	99	0	1	37	96.1	-14.9	28	5	5,000,000	0	0.0	0.0
C+ / 6.0	11.8	1.07	15.80	198	0	99	0	1	37	93.1	-15.1	23	5	2,500	100	0.0	0.0

99 Pct = Best
0 Pct = Worst

Fund Type	Fund Name	Ticker Symbol	Overall Investment Rating	Phone	PERFORMANCE Perfor-mance Rating/Pts	3 Mo	6 Mo	1Yr / Pct	3Yr / Pct	5Yr / Pct	Dividend Yield	Expense Ratio
GR	Wells Fargo Adv Prmr Lg Co Gr R6	EKJFX	U	(800) 222-8222	U /	3.59	8.71	13.22 /87	--	--	0.00	0.69
SC	Wells Fargo Adv Sm Co Gro A	WFSAX	B+	(800) 222-8222	A / 9.3	6.69	15.04	13.19 /87	18.75 /96	18.80 /98	0.00	1.45
SC	Wells Fargo Adv Sm Co Gro Adm	NVSCX	A-	(800) 222-8222	A+ / 9.7	6.73	15.14	13.41 /88	19.01 /97	19.07 /98	0.00	1.29
SC	● Wells Fargo Adv Sm Co Gro B	WFSBX	A-	(800) 222-8222	A / 9.5	6.48	14.59	12.36 /84	17.86 /94	17.91 /97	0.00	2.20
SC	Wells Fargo Adv Sm Co Gro C	WSMCX	A-	(800) 222-8222	A / 9.5	6.50	14.61	12.38 /84	17.88 /94	17.91 /97	0.00	2.20
SC	Wells Fargo Adv Sm Co Gro Inst	WSCGX	A	(800) 222-8222	A+ / 9.7	6.80	15.28	13.70 /89	19.31 /97	19.37 /98	0.00	1.02
SC	Wells Fargo Adv Sm Co Val A	SCVAX	C+	(800) 222-8222	C+ / 5.9	3.28	11.57	5.84 /45	14.09 /68	13.71 /75	0.00	1.56
SC	Wells Fargo Adv Sm Co Val Adm	SCVIX	B-	(800) 222-8222	B- / 7.0	3.31	11.64	6.06 /47	14.32 /69	13.96 /77	0.00	1.40
SC	● Wells Fargo Adv Sm Co Val B	SCVBX	C+	(800) 222-8222	C+ / 6.3	3.07	11.19	5.07 /39	13.32 /62	12.91 /67	0.00	2.31
SC	Wells Fargo Adv Sm Co Val C	SCVFX	C+	(800) 222-8222	C+ / 6.3	3.09	11.14	5.05 /39	13.23 /61	12.86 /67	0.00	2.31
SC	Wells Fargo Adv Sm Co Val Inst	SCVNX	B-	(800) 222-8222	B- / 7.2	3.34	11.74	6.23 /48	14.57 /72	--	0.00	1.13
SC	Wells Fargo Adv Sm Cp Opp Adm	NVSOX	D+	(800) 222-8222	A- / 9.0	4.87	14.37	11.75 /82	16.49 /87	13.70 /75	0.00	1.24
SC	Wells Fargo Adv Sm Cp Val A	SMVAX	E-	(800) 222-8222	D- / 1.0	-2.83	-0.44	-7.29 / 4	7.22 /23	6.60 /21	0.37	1.35
SC	Wells Fargo Adv Sm Cp Val Adm	SMVDX	E	(800) 222-8222	D- / 1.5	-2.82	-0.40	-7.16 / 4	7.43 /24	--	0.00	1.19
SC	● Wells Fargo Adv Sm Cp Val B	SMVBX	E-	(800) 222-8222	D- / 1.2	-3.01	-0.82	-8.01 / 3	6.43 /19	5.80 /16	0.00	2.10
SC	Wells Fargo Adv Sm Cp Val C	SMVCX	E-	(800) 222-8222	D- / 1.2	-3.02	-0.84	-8.00 / 3	6.42 /19	5.80 /16	0.21	2.10
SC	Wells Fargo Adv Sm Cp Val Inst	WFSVX	E	(800) 222-8222	D / 1.6	-2.75	-0.27	-6.95 / 4	7.64 /25	7.03 /23	0.58	0.92
SC	Wells Fargo Adv Sm Cp Val R6	SMVRX	U	(800) 222-8222	U /	-2.75	-0.24	-6.90 / 4	--	--	0.61	0.87
SC	Wells Fargo Adv Sm Cp Val Z	SSMVX	E	(800) 222-8222	D- / 1.5	-2.86	-0.45	-7.30 / 4	7.20 /22	6.57 /20	0.33	1.41
SC	Wells Fargo Adv Sm/Mid Cp Val A	WFVAX	E-	(800) 222-8222	E / 0.3	-2.74	-6.41	-16.66 / 2	2.53 / 7	3.86 / 8	0.00	1.58
SC	Wells Fargo Adv Sm/Mid Cp Val Adm	WWMDX	E-	(800) 222-8222	E / 0.5	-2.74	-6.32	-16.48 / 2	2.76 / 7	4.11 / 9	0.00	1.42
SC	Wells Fargo Adv Sm/Mid Cp Val C	WFCVX	E-	(800) 222-8222	E / 0.4	-2.97	-6.74	-17.26 / 1	1.78 / 6	3.10 / 6	0.00	2.33
SC	Wells Fargo Adv Sm/Mid Cp Val Inst	WWMSX	E-	(800) 222-8222	E / 0.5	-2.72	-6.27	-16.34 / 2	2.97 / 8	4.32 / 9	0.00	1.15
SC	Wells Fargo Adv Sm/Mid Cp Val Inv	SMMVX	E-	(800) 222-8222	E / 0.4	-2.81	-6.51	-16.71 / 2	2.46 / 7	3.79 / 8	0.00	1.64
MC	Wells Fargo Adv Spec Mid Cp Vl A	WFPAX	A+	(800) 222-8222	A / 9.4	3.61	10.02	11.83 /82	19.88 /98	15.96 /93	0.47	1.29
MC	Wells Fargo Adv Spec Mid Cp Vl Adm	WFMDX	A+	(800) 222-8222	A+ / 9.7	3.68	10.11	12.04 /83	20.05 /98	16.11 /93	0.40	1.13
MC	Wells Fargo Adv Spec Mid Cp Vl C	WFPCX	A+	(800) 222-8222	A / 9.5	3.45	9.64	11.03 /78	19.00 /97	15.10 /88	0.00	2.04
MC	Wells Fargo Adv Spec Mid Cp Vl I	WFMIX	A+	(800) 222-8222	A+ / 9.7	3.75	10.25	12.31 /84	20.41 /98	16.43 /95	0.60	0.86
MC	Wells Fargo Adv Spec Mid Cp Vl Inv	SMCDX	A+	(800) 222-8222	A+ / 9.7	3.61	10.00	11.79 /82	19.82 /98	15.89 /92	0.15	1.35
SC	Wells Fargo Adv Spec Sm Cp Val A	ESPAX	C	(800) 222-8222	B- / 7.2	4.05	12.75	7.56 /60	15.96 /83	14.03 /78	0.59	1.41
SC	Wells Fargo Adv Spec Sm Cp Val	ESPIX	B-	(800) 222-8222	B+ / 8.5	4.14	12.89	7.82 /61	16.26 /85	14.32 /81	0.78	1.25
SC	● Wells Fargo Adv Spec Sm Cp Val B	ESPBX	C+	(800) 222-8222	B / 7.6	3.85	12.34	6.76 /53	15.09 /76	13.17 /70	0.00	2.16
SC	Wells Fargo Adv Spec Sm Cp Val C	ESPCX	C+	(800) 222-8222	B / 7.6	3.87	12.35	6.75 /53	15.10 /76	13.18 /70	0.02	2.16
SC	Wells Fargo Adv Spec Sm Cp Val I	ESPNX	B-	(800) 222-8222	B+ / 8.6	4.14	12.96	7.96 /63	16.42 /86	--	0.95	0.98
TC	Wells Fargo Adv Spec Tech A	WFSTX	C	(800) 222-8222	B- / 7.1	2.29	5.88	13.24 /87	15.78 /82	15.67 /91	0.00	1.51
TC	Wells Fargo Adv Spec Tech Adm	WFTDX	B-	(800) 222-8222	B+ / 8.4	2.36	6.01	13.42 /88	16.01 /83	--	0.00	1.35
TC	● Wells Fargo Adv Spec Tech B	WFTBX	C+	(800) 222-8222	B- / 7.5	2.07	5.51	12.39 /84	14.92 /74	14.82 /85	0.00	2.26
TC	Wells Fargo Adv Spec Tech C	WFTCX	C+	(800) 222-8222	B- / 7.5	2.08	5.53	12.44 /85	14.92 /74	14.80 /85	0.00	2.26
TC	Wells Fargo Adv Spec Tech Z	WFTZX	C+	(800) 222-8222	B / 8.1	2.31	5.85	13.17 /87	15.69 /81	15.60 /91	0.00	1.57
SC	Wells Fargo Adv Trad Sm Cap Gr A	EGWAX	D-	(800) 222-8222	C+ / 6.0	2.62	12.87	6.77 /53	14.15 /68	14.05 /78	0.00	1.55
SC	Wells Fargo Adv Trad Sm Cap Gr	EGWDX	D	(800) 222-8222	B- / 7.1	2.59	12.93	6.93 /54	14.31 /69	--	0.00	1.39
SC	Wells Fargo Adv Trad Sm Cap Gr C	EGWCX	D-	(800) 222-8222	C+ / 6.4	2.38	12.48	5.98 /46	13.30 /62	--	0.00	2.30
SC	Wells Fargo Adv Trad Sm Cap Gr I	EGRYX	D	(800) 222-8222	B- / 7.3	2.66	13.06	7.16 /56	14.53 /71	14.45 /82	0.00	1.12
UT	Wells Fargo Adv Util and Tel A	EVUAX	C	(800) 222-8222	C- / 4.1	-3.28	5.64	4.82 /37	12.15 /53	12.01 /61	1.74	1.23
UT	Wells Fargo Adv Util and Tel Adm	EVUDX	C+	(800) 222-8222	C / 5.2	-3.18	5.73	5.01 /39	12.39 /55	--	2.03	1.07
UT	● Wells Fargo Adv Util and Tel B	EVUBX	C	(800) 222-8222	C / 4.5	-3.46	5.22	3.98 /32	11.32 /48	11.18 /54	0.98	1.98
UT	Wells Fargo Adv Util and Tel C	EVUCX	C	(800) 222-8222	C / 4.5	-3.43	5.24	4.04 /32	11.32 /48	11.19 /54	1.09	1.98
UT	Wells Fargo Adv Util and Tel Inst	EVUYX	C+	(800) 222-8222	C / 5.3	-3.15	5.83	5.02 /39	12.51 /56	12.38 /63	2.21	0.80
AA	Wells Fargo Adv Wlth Bldr Consv All	WBCAX	D+	(800) 222-8222	E+ / 0.9	1.53	2.50	2.76 /25	3.33 / 9	4.19 / 9	0.40	2.08
GR	Wells Fargo Adv Wlth Bldr Eqty	WBGIX	C	(800) 222-8222	C / 4.7	2.55	4.82	6.31 /49	11.29 /48	9.78 /43	0.00	2.39
AA	Wells Fargo Adv Wlth Bldr Gro All	WBGGX	C	(800) 222-8222	C- / 3.8	2.88	4.93	5.51 /43	9.68 /37	9.36 /39	0.80	2.29
GI	Wells Fargo Adv Wlth Bldr Gro Bal	WBGBX	C-	(800) 222-8222	C- / 3.0	2.57	4.32	4.90 /38	8.37 /29	8.36 /32	0.69	2.21

● Denotes fund is closed to new investors
* Denotes fund is included in Section II

www.thestreetratings.com

RISK			NET ASSETS		ASSET				BULL / BEAR		FUND MANAGER		MINIMUMS		LOADS	
	3 Year		NAV						Last Bull	Last Bear	Manager	Manager	Initial	Additional	Front	Back
Risk Rating/Pts	Standard Deviation	Beta	As of 3/31/15	Total $(Mil)	Cash %	Stocks %	Bonds %	Other %	Portfolio Turnover Ratio	Market Return	Market Return	Quality Pct	Tenure (Years)	Purch. $	Purch. $	End Load	End Load
U /	N/A	N/A	16.16	163	0	99	0	1	37	N/A	N/A	N/A	5	0	0	0.0	0.0
C / 5.5	14.1	1.00	43.86	66	3	96	0	1	77	120.0	-26.8	85	31	1,000	100	5.8	0.0
C / 5.5	14.1	1.00	45.33	166	3	96	0	1	77	121.7	-26.7	86	31	1,000,000	0	0.0	0.0
C / 5.5	14.1	1.00	39.46	N/A	3	96	0	1	77	114.4	-27.0	80	31	1,000	100	0.0	0.0
C / 5.5	14.1	1.00	39.97	13	3	96	0	1	77	114.4	-27.0	80	31	1,000	100	0.0	0.0
C / 5.5	14.1	1.00	46.02	423	3	96	0	1	77	123.6	-26.7	87	31	0	0	0.0	0.0
C+ / 6.0	13.3	0.95	21.40	27	2	97	0	1	47	96.1	-26.2	49	13	1,000	100	5.8	0.0
C+ / 6.0	13.3	0.95	21.87	69	2	97	0	1	47	97.7	-26.2	53	13	1,000,000	0	0.0	0.0
C+ / 5.9	13.3	0.95	19.47	N/A	2	97	0	1	47	91.7	-26.5	39	13	1,000	100	0.0	0.0
C+ / 5.9	13.3	0.95	19.35	3	2	97	0	1	47	91.1	-26.4	38	13	1,000	100	0.0	0.0
C+ / 6.0	13.3	0.95	21.99	17	2	97	0	1	47	98.9	-26.1	56	13	5,000,000	0	0.0	0.0
E+ / 0.8	11.1	0.81	25.19	334	8	91	0	1	26	92.6	-22.8	89	12	1,000,000	0	0.0	0.0
D+ / 2.3	12.9	0.78	27.51	290	12	87	0	1	18	49.9	-22.3	11	18	1,000	100	5.8	0.0
D+ / 2.5	12.9	0.78	28.30	75	12	87	0	1	18	51.0	-22.3	13	18	1,000,000	0	0.0	0.0
D / 2.0	12.9	0.78	23.84	N/A	12	87	0	1	18	46.2	-22.6	8	18	1,000	100	0.0	0.0
D / 1.9	12.9	0.78	23.80	81	12	87	0	1	18	46.2	-22.6	8	18	1,000	100	0.0	0.0
D+ / 2.4	12.9	0.78	28.29	1,017	12	87	0	1	18	52.0	-22.2	14	18	5,000,000	0	0.0	0.0
U /	N/A	N/A	28.29	52	12	87	0	1	18	N/A	N/A	N/A	18	0	0	0.0	0.0
D+ / 2.5	12.9	0.78	28.21	480	12	87	0	1	18	49.9	-22.3	11	18	2,500	100	0.0	0.0
D- / 1.1	14.8	0.85	11.36	11	1	98	0	1	29	30.8	-22.2	2	18	1,000	100	5.8	0.0
D- / 1.1	14.9	0.86	11.70	4	1	98	0	1	29	31.9	-22.1	2	18	1,000,000	0	0.0	0.0
D- / 1.1	14.9	0.85	10.79	5	1	98	0	1	29	27.5	-22.4	1	18	1,000	100	0.0	0.0
D- / 1.2	14.9	0.85	11.79	5	1	98	0	1	29	32.9	-22.1	2	18	5,000,000	0	0.0	0.0
D- / 1.1	14.8	0.85	11.40	41	1	98	0	1	29	30.5	-22.2	2	18	2,500	100	0.0	0.0
C+ / 6.4	10.7	0.93	32.68	472	8	91	0	1	58	118.4	-22.3	90	6	1,000	100	5.8	0.0
C+ / 6.5	10.7	0.93	33.25	256	8	91	0	1	58	119.4	-22.2	91	6	1,000,000	0	0.0	0.0
C+ / 6.5	10.7	0.93	31.81	45	8	91	0	1	58	112.8	-22.5	88	6	1,000	100	0.0	0.0
C+ / 6.4	10.7	0.93	33.48	313	8	91	0	1	58	121.6	-22.1	91	6	5,000,000	0	0.0	0.0
C+ / 6.5	10.7	0.93	33.29	569	8	91	0	1	58	117.9	-22.2	90	6	2,500	100	0.0	0.0
C / 4.6	12.4	0.89	29.27	449	8	91	0	1	65	100.8	-22.4	80	13	1,000	100	5.8	0.0
C / 4.6	12.4	0.89	29.95	69	8	91	0	1	65	102.5	-22.3	82	13	1,000,000	0	0.0	0.0
C / 4.3	12.4	0.89	26.69	3	8	91	0	1	65	95.7	-22.6	74	13	1,000	100	0.0	0.0
C / 4.4	12.4	0.89	26.81	44	8	91	0	1	65	95.8	-22.6	74	13	1,000	100	0.0	0.0
C / 4.6	12.4	0.89	29.93	190	8	91	0	1	65	103.6	-22.2	83	13	5,000,000	0	0.0	0.0
C / 4.7	13.6	1.07	10.74	168	2	97	0	1	132	94.6	-21.5	46	N/A	1,000	100	5.8	0.0
C / 4.8	13.6	1.07	10.86	32	2	97	0	1	132	95.6	-21.3	49	N/A	1,000,000	0	0.0	0.0
C / 4.4	13.6	1.08	9.36	N/A	2	97	0	1	132	89.7	-21.7	35	N/A	1,000	100	0.0	0.0
C / 4.4	13.6	1.07	9.33	14	2	97	0	1	132	89.5	-21.6	36	N/A	1,000	100	0.0	0.0
C / 4.7	13.5	1.07	10.62	119	2	97	0	1	132	94.1	-21.4	47	N/A	2,500	100	0.0	0.0
D- / 1.1	15.1	1.00	18.04	124	2	97	0	1	77	95.7	-27.7	40	24	1,000	100	5.8	0.0
D- / 1.5	15.1	0.99	19.44	3	2	97	0	1	77	96.7	-27.6	43	24	1,000,000	0	0.0	0.0
D- / 1.0	15.1	1.00	17.21	N/A	2	97	0	1	77	90.8	-27.9	30	24	1,000	100	0.0	0.0
D / 1.6	15.1	1.00	19.69	12	2	97	0	1	77	98.0	-27.5	46	24	5,000,000	0	0.0	0.0
B- / 7.1	10.3	0.67	18.23	341	4	95	0	1	20	62.8	-5.2	90	13	1,000	100	5.8	0.0
B- / 7.1	10.3	0.67	18.25	8	4	95	0	1	20	63.9	-5.1	90	13	1,000,000	0	0.0	0.0
B- / 7.1	10.3	0.67	18.28	8	4	95	0	1	20	58.6	-5.5	87	13	1,000	100	0.0	0.0
B- / 7.1	10.3	0.67	18.25	64	4	95	0	1	20	58.6	-5.5	87	13	1,000	100	0.0	0.0
B- / 7.1	10.3	0.67	18.23	14	4	95	0	1	20	64.5	-5.1	91	13	5,000,000	0	0.0	0.0
B / 8.7	3.3	0.54	10.82	546	0	18	81	1	139	18.9	-5.7	33	2	1,000	100	1.5	0.0
C+ / 6.8	10.4	1.04	15.66	147	9	90	0	1	26	73.2	-22.0	11	2	1,000	100	1.5	0.0
B- / 7.2	9.6	1.59	14.67	440	5	72	21	2	60	65.4	-20.9	4	N/A	1,000	100	1.5	0.0
B- / 7.8	8.1	0.81	14.35	995	1	55	42	2	94	55.0	-18.2	16	N/A	1,000	100	1.5	0.0

Fund Type	Fund Name	Ticker Symbol	Overall Investment Rating	Phone	Performance Rating/Pts	3 Mo	6 Mo	1Yr / Pct	3Yr / Pct	5Yr / Pct	Dividend Yield	Expense Ratio
GI	Wells Fargo Adv Wlth Bldr Modt Bal	WBBBX	C-	(800) 222-8222	D / 1.7	2.02	3.44	3.78 /30	5.76 /16	6.15 /18	0.52	2.14
AA	Wells Fargo Adv Wlth Bldr Tact Eqty	WBGAX	C	(800) 222-8222	C / 4.3	3.09	5.44	6.26 /49	10.35 /42	10.29 /47	0.00	2.32
GL	Wells Fargo Advtg Alt Strat Inst	WAITX	U	(800) 222-8222	U /	4.18	6.00	--	--	--	0.00	3.41
GR	● Wells Fargo Avtg VT Dscvry 2		C-	(800) 222-8222	B / 8.2	6.61	12.28	8.59 /67	15.40 /78	17.71 /97	0.00	1.16
AA	Wells Fargo Avtg VT Idx Asset All 2		A+	(800) 222-8222	B- / 7.3	1.37	8.07	15.08 /92	14.07 /68	13.42 /72	1.40	1.11
IN	Wells Fargo Avtg VT Intrinsic Val 2		B+	(800) 222-8222	B- / 7.3	1.16	5.82	8.94 /69	15.15 /76	12.96 /68	0.72	1.13
GR	Wells Fargo Avtg VT Opp 2		B+	(800) 222-8222	B / 7.6	3.50	8.66	10.94 /78	14.82 /73	13.27 /71	0.05	1.10
SC	● Wells Fargo Avtg VT Sm Cap Growth		C-	(800) 222-8222	B+ / 8.6	9.14	20.38	11.36 /80	14.71 /73	13.45 /72	0.00	1.18
GR	Wells Fargo Avtg VT Sm Cap Val 2		D-	(800) 222-8222	D / 1.7	-2.96	0.65	-6.73 / 4	7.62 /25	6.73 /21	0.37	1.36
BA	WesMark Balanced Fund	WMBLX	C	(800) 341-7400	D+ / 2.8	0.75	2.93	6.19 /48	7.51 /24	8.64 /34	1.50	1.30
GR	WesMark Growth Fund	WMKGX	B+	(800) 341-7400	B- / 7.3	1.60	5.75	9.71 /73	14.89 /74	12.24 /62	0.45	1.15
SC	WesMark Small Company Growth	WMKSX	B	(800) 341-7400	B- / 7.5	6.09	10.42	6.72 /53	14.86 /74	13.31 /71	0.00	1.25
RE	West Loop Realty Institutional	REIIX	U	(877) 672-6487	U /	4.74	18.35	26.25 /99	--	--	0.81	2.59
AA	West Shore Real Return Income I	IWSFX	U		U /	-1.78	-3.44	-3.40 / 8	--	--	0.03	2.33
GI	Westcore Blue Chip Dividend Inst	WIMVX	E	(800) 392-2673	C- / 3.4	-1.64	0.74	0.54 /17	9.95 /39	9.07 /37	2.16	0.98
GI	Westcore Blue Chip Dividend Rtl	WTMVX	E	(800) 392-2673	C- / 3.2	-1.67	0.66	0.28 /16	9.73 /38	8.89 /36	1.89	1.14
GR	Westcore Growth Inst	WILGX	D-	(800) 392-2673	B- / 7.0	4.66	8.86	13.02 /87	13.45 /63	13.60 /74	0.00	1.14
GR	Westcore Growth Rtl	WTEIX	D-	(800) 392-2673	C+ / 6.9	4.56	8.73	12.79 /86	13.22 /61	13.41 /72	0.00	1.09
FO	● Westcore International SC Rtl	WTIFX	E	(800) 392-2673	E+ / 0.6	3.53	-6.35	-13.97 / 2	3.33 / 9	9.59 /41	0.04	1.63
SC	Westcore Micro-Cap Oppty Retail	WTMIX	B	(800) 392-2673	B- / 7.5	1.50	12.97	3.91 /31	16.03 /84	15.54 /90	0.00	1.99
MC	Westcore Mid-Cap Value Div Rtl	WTMCX	A	(800) 392-2673	B+ / 8.8	2.64	10.57	14.09 /90	16.22 /85	13.63 /74	1.01	1.24
MC	Westcore MIDCO Growth Inst	WIMGX	D-	(800) 392-2673	B- / 7.1	6.75	7.40	8.01 /63	14.23 /69	13.71 /75	0.00	0.95
MC	Westcore MIDCO Growth Rtl	WTMGX	D-	(800) 392-2673	C+ / 6.9	6.70	7.37	7.68 /60	13.98 /67	13.51 /73	0.00	1.05
MC	Westcore Select Rtl	WTSLX	E+	(800) 392-2673	C- / 3.3	3.71	5.93	4.87 /38	8.14 /28	8.54 /33	0.00	1.08
SC	● Westcore Small-Cap Value Div Inst	WISVX	D+	(800) 392-2673	C+ / 6.3	-0.89	9.95	6.56 /51	13.56 /64	12.48 /64	1.16	1.22
SC	● Westcore Small-Cap Value Div Rtl	WTSVX	D+	(800) 392-2673	C+ / 6.2	-0.97	9.86	6.39 /50	13.35 /62	12.30 /63	1.00	1.39
IN	Westfield Capital Dividend Gro Inst	WDIVX	U	(866) 777-7818	U /	2.64	9.14	11.48 /80	--	--	1.84	1.10
GR	Westfield Capital Lg Cap Gro Inst	WCLGX	A-	(866) 454-0738	B+ / 8.8	2.71	7.91	13.72 /89	16.54 /87	--	0.32	0.89
GR	Westfield Capital Lg Cap Gro Inv	WCLCX	B+	(866) 454-0738	B+ / 8.6	2.62	7.83	13.52 /88	16.27 /85	--	0.11	1.14
MC	Westport Fund I	WPFIX	C+	(888) 593-7878	C+ / 5.9	1.76	8.19	8.90 /69	12.47 /56	13.22 /70	0.00	1.05
MC	Westport Fund R	WPFRX	C+	(888) 593-7878	C+ / 5.8	1.74	8.11	8.74 /68	12.26 /54	13.00 /68	0.00	1.23
SC	Westport Select Cap I	WPSCX	E+	(888) 593-7878	C+ / 5.6	-0.31	6.03	5.35 /41	12.72 /58	10.56 /49	0.00	1.21
SC	Westport Select Cap R	WPSRX	E+	(888) 593-7878	C / 5.4	-0.38	5.84	5.03 /39	12.49 /56	10.34 /47	0.00	1.37
GR	Westwood Dividend Growth Inst	WHGDX	B	(877) 386-3944	B / 8.0	2.94	9.54	12.86 /86	15.10 /76	--	0.83	0.91
EM	Westwood Emerging Markets Inst	WWEMX	U	(866) 777-7818	U /	1.46	-3.31	3.91 /31	--	--	1.37	1.86
GI	Westwood Income Opportunity A	WWIAX	C	(877) 386-3944	D+ / 2.6	0.37	2.12	6.53 /51	8.86 /32	9.56 /41	1.27	1.11
GI	Westwood Income Opportunity Inst	WHGIX	C+	(877) 386-3944	C- / 3.6	0.43	2.24	6.79 /53	9.11 /34	9.83 /43	1.57	0.86
GR	Westwood Large Cap Value A	WWLAX	C+	(877) 386-3944	C+ / 6.5	1.35	6.68	10.51 /76	14.99 /75	12.09 /61	0.34	1.14
GR	Westwood Large Cap Value Inst	WHGLX	B-	(877) 386-3944	B / 7.6	1.44	6.78	10.87 /78	15.28 /77	12.37 /63	1.04	0.89
SC	Westwood SmallCap Value Inst	WHGSX	A+	(877) 386-3944	A+ / 9.6	2.94	12.39	8.63 /67	19.62 /97	16.82 /96	0.27	1.12
MC	Westwood SMidCap Institutional	WHGMX	C+	(877) 386-3944	B- / 7.1	4.85	9.30	6.40 /50	14.55 /71	13.87 /77	0.11	0.95
MC	Westwood SMidCap Plus Inst	WHGPX	A	(877) 386-3944	B+ / 8.5	5.75	10.07	8.70 /68	16.21 /85	--	0.23	1.00
GR	White Oak Select Growth	WOGSX	C	(888) 462-5386	C / 5.3	0.30	4.85	6.22 /48	12.20 /54	11.65 /58	1.59	1.10
GR	Whitebox Market Neutral Equity Inst	WBLFX	U	(855) 296-2866	U /	2.19	1.74	-0.27 /15	--	--	0.00	3.03
AA	Whitebox Tact Opportunities Inst	WBMIX	D+	(855) 296-2866	E+ / 0.7	-2.99	-4.32	-6.41 / 4	3.68 / 9	--	0.00	2.32
AA	Whitebox Tact Opportunities Inv	WBMAX	D+	(855) 296-2866	E+ / 0.7	-3.02	-4.44	-6.77 / 4	3.40 / 9	--	0.00	2.57
FO	WHV International Equity A	WHVAX	E	(888) 739-1390	E / 0.3	-1.50	-13.08	-13.34 / 2	1.25 / 5	1.83 / 4	0.74	1.49
FO	WHV International Equity I	WHVIX	E	(888) 739-1390	E / 0.4	-1.45	-12.96	-13.11 / 2	1.51 / 6	2.10 / 5	1.08	1.24
EM	William Blair EM Leaders I	WBELX	E+	(800) 742-7272	D- / 1.0	2.09	0.89	4.77 /37	2.64 / 7	4.16 / 9	0.24	1.58
EM	William Blair EM Leaders Inst	WELIX	E+	(800) 742-7272	D- / 1.0	2.21	0.95	4.94 /38	2.79 / 7	4.29 / 9	0.39	1.42
EM	William Blair EM Leaders N	WELNX	E+	(800) 742-7272	E+ / 0.9	2.10	0.77	4.54 /35	2.38 / 7	--	0.02	1.83
EM	William Blair EM Sm Cap Gro I	BESIX	B-	(800) 742-7272	B / 8.1	3.45	4.41	14.75 /91	15.48 /79	--	0.49	1.72

● Denotes fund is closed to new investors
* Denotes fund is included in Section II

RISK	NET ASSETS				ASSET				Portfolio	BULL / BEAR		FUND MANAGER		MINIMUMS		LOADS	
	3 Year		NAV							Last Bull	Last Bear	Manager	Manager	Initial	Additional	Front	Back
Risk Rating/Pts	Standard Deviation	Beta	As of 3/31/15	Total $(Mil)	Cash %	Stocks %	Bonds %	Other %	Turnover Ratio	Market Return	Market Return	Quality Pct	Tenure (Years)	Purch. $	Purch. $	End Load	End Load
B /8.3	5.6	0.55	12.11	886	0	36	63	1	110	34.9	-11.7	30	N/A	1,000	100	1.5	0.0
B- /7.1	10.0	1.66	19.01	438	9	89	0	2	23	69.7	-20.2	4	2	1,000	100	1.5	0.0
U /	N/A	N/A	10.71	126	0	0	0	100	0	N/A	N/A	N/A	1	5,000,000	0	0.0	0.0
D+ /2.6	13.0	1.07	32.74	144	1	98	0	1	88	104.1	-23.5	41	14	0	0	0.0	0.0
B /8.6	6.6	1.13	18.61	92	6	57	36	1	11	77.9	-8.9	81	2	0	0	0.0	0.0
B- /7.4	9.9	1.02	20.90	45	1	98	0	1	22	92.8	-19.7	50	5	0	0	0.0	0.0
C+ /6.5	11.1	1.08	29.87	202	4	95	0	1	26	92.1	-22.6	33	14	0	0	0.0	0.0
D /1.6	17.1	1.11	10.87	242	3	96	0	1	67	97.1	-23.4	26	4	0	0	0.0	0.0
C+ /5.7	13.4	1.00	10.82	13	2	97	0	1	18	51.9	-22.4	3	14	0	0	0.0	0.0
B /8.5	5.8	1.02	12.60	103	5	59	35	1	26	46.2	-7.8	22	17	1,000	100	0.0	0.0
B- /7.0	10.4	1.07	19.31	362	0	100	0	0	19	95.1	-22.7	37	18	1,000	100	0.0	0.0
C+ /5.9	13.4	0.94	14.63	103	9	90	0	1	15	85.8	-24.1	63	15	1,000	100	0.0	0.0
U /	N/A	N/A	13.34	37	0	99	0	1	0	N/A	N/A	N/A	2	1,000,000	100,000	0.0	0.0
U /	N/A	N/A	9.92	38	64	33	1	2	0	N/A	N/A	N/A	2	100,000	1,000	0.0	1.0
D /1.7	9.8	0.94	10.24	5	0	99	0	1	91	68.8	-13.1	12	13	500,000	0	0.0	0.0
D /1.7	9.8	0.95	10.30	44	0	99	0	1	91	67.7	-13.1	11	13	2,500	25	0.0	0.0
D- /1.0	10.7	0.99	13.48	5	2	98	0	0	182	88.2	-15.8	34	11	500,000	0	0.0	0.0
D- /1.0	10.7	0.99	13.30	30	2	98	0	0	182	87.1	-15.9	31	11	2,500	25	0.0	0.0
C /4.6	13.7	0.83	17.30	281	0	100	0	0	57	36.6	-19.2	14	12	2,500	25	0.0	0.0
C+ /6.1	14.8	1.06	18.23	38	0	99	0	1	52	100.6	-24.2	50	7	2,500	25	0.0	2.0
C+ /6.8	9.5	0.80	27.58	58	2	97	0	1	51	87.8	-17.8	87	13	2,500	25	0.0	0.0
E+ /0.7	14.6	1.10	5.85	21	3	96	0	1	117	92.5	-26.8	16	10	500,000	0	0.0	0.0
E+ /0.7	14.7	1.11	5.73	79	3	96	0	1	117	91.2	-26.9	14	10	2,500	25	0.0	0.0
C- /3.3	15.8	1.12	26.25	87	2	97	0	1	106	59.9	-29.3	2	5	2,500	25	0.0	0.0
C- /3.3	12.4	0.86	13.35	182	3	96	0	1	53	79.8	-20.0	64	11	500,000	0	0.0	0.0
C- /3.3	12.5	0.86	13.32	129	3	96	0	1	53	78.9	-20.1	60	11	2,500	25	0.0	0.0
U /	N/A	N/A	10.89	100	7	92	0	1	101	N/A	N/A	N/A	2	50,000	0	0.0	0.0
C+ /6.2	11.1	1.08	14.00	209	2	97	0	1	49	101.4	N/A	55	4	50,000	0	0.0	0.0
C+ /6.2	11.1	1.08	14.12	N/A	2	97	0	1	49	100.1	N/A	52	4	2,500	0	0.0	0.0
C+ /6.8	10.4	0.89	34.74	143	2	97	0	1	12	87.0	-19.5	33	18	250,000	0	0.0	0.0
C+ /6.8	10.4	0.89	34.50	481	2	97	0	1	12	85.8	-19.5	31	18	2,500	0	0.0	0.0
D- /1.0	14.1	0.96	19.56	174	0	99	0	1	2	74.1	-22.3	30	18	250,000	0	0.0	0.0
D- /1.0	14.1	0.96	18.24	169	0	99	0	1	2	73.0	-22.4	28	18	5,000	0	0.0	0.0
C /5.4	9.6	0.97	11.90	85	1	98	0	1	67	86.1	-14.1	60	11	5,000	0	0.0	0.0
U /	N/A	N/A	9.05	244	0	92	6	2	28	N/A	N/A	N/A	3	100,000	0	0.0	0.0
B+ /9.0	5.4	0.49	14.70	232	31	57	11	1	19	46.4	-6.6	78	10	5,000	0	5.0	0.0
B+ /9.0	5.4	0.49	14.71	2,555	31	57	11	1	19	47.6	-6.5	80	10	100,000	0	0.0	0.0
C /5.4	10.1	1.03	12.00	2	0	100	0	0	47	92.5	-20.0	47	9	5,000	0	5.0	0.0
C /5.3	10.1	1.02	11.95	140	0	100	0	0	47	94.1	-19.9	52	9	100,000	0	0.0	0.0
C+ /6.4	13.5	0.96	14.34	134	2	97	0	1	68	126.6	-23.8	90	2	5,000	0	0.0	0.0
C /5.0	12.0	1.04	16.87	548	1	98	0	1	51	92.3	-24.2	27	2	5,000	0	0.0	0.0
C+ /6.8	10.9	0.95	14.34	127	5	94	0	1	51	97.4	-22.5	68	2	5,000	0	0.0	0.0
C+ /6.3	12.2	1.15	60.73	251	0	99	0	1	1	77.8	-16.2	7	23	2,000	25	0.0	0.0
U /	N/A	N/A	10.28	45	0	0	0	100	298	N/A	N/A	N/A	3	5,000,000	0	0.0	0.0
B /8.6	7.0	0.55	11.69	717	86	13	0	1	154	N/A	N/A	36	4	5,000,000	0	0.0	0.0
B /8.5	7.0	0.55	11.57	120	86	13	0	1	154	N/A	N/A	32	4	5,000	1,000	0.0	0.0
C- /4.2	13.9	0.89	19.70	31	3	96	0	1	6	30.8	-29.0	5	7	5,000	100	5.8	0.0
C- /4.2	13.9	0.89	19.73	350	3	96	0	1	6	31.9	-29.0	5	7	500,000	0	0.0	0.0
C /5.4	13.4	0.93	9.27	34	2	97	0	1	131	30.5	-23.0	84	7	500,000	0	0.0	0.0
C /5.4	13.4	0.93	9.27	69	2	97	0	1	131	31.2	-23.0	85	7	5,000,000	0	0.0	0.0
C /5.4	13.5	0.93	9.25	2	2	97	0	1	131	29.3	-23.2	82	7	2,500	1,000	0.0	0.0
C /4.8	13.1	0.80	17.09	157	1	98	0	1	124	N/A	N/A	99	4	500,000	0	0.0	0.0

					PERFORMANCE								
	99 Pct = Best				Perfor-	Total Return % through 3/31/15					Incl. in Returns		
	0 Pct = Worst			Overall	mance				Annualized			Dividend	Expense
Fund		Ticker		Investment	Rating/Pts	3 Mo	6 Mo	1Yr / Pct	3Yr / Pct	5Yr / Pct	Yield	Ratio
Type	Fund Name	Symbol	Rating		Phone								
EM	William Blair EM Sm Cap Gro Inst	WESJX	U	(800) 742-7272	U /	3.45	4.46	14.87 /91	--	--	0.59	1.56
EM	William Blair EM Sm Cap Gro N	WESNX	C+	(800) 742-7272	B / 7.9	3.33	4.22	14.43 /90	15.16 /76	--	0.15	2.19
EM	● William Blair Emrg Mkts Gr I	WBEIX	E+	(800) 742-7272	D- / 1.2	2.77	0.58	5.65 /44	3.70 / 9	5.66 /15	0.81	1.41
EM	● William Blair Emrg Mkts Gr Inst	BIEMX	E+	(800) 742-7272	D- / 1.3	2.83	0.65	5.84 /45	3.92 /10	5.86 /16	1.01	1.19
EM	● William Blair Emrg Mkts Gr N	WBENX	E+	(800) 742-7272	D- / 1.2	2.71	0.45	5.41 /42	3.44 / 9	5.38 /14	0.55	1.68
GL	William Blair Global Leaders I	WGFIX	C	(800) 742-7272	C / 5.2	5.49	8.56	9.22 /70	10.64 /43	11.97 /60	0.14	1.35
GL	William Blair Global Leaders Inst	BGGIX	U	(800) 742-7272	U /	5.49	8.63	9.38 /71	--	--	0.28	1.14
GL	William Blair Global Leaders N	WGGNX	C	(800) 742-7272	C / 5.0	5.41	8.42	8.89 /69	10.36 /42	11.69 /58	0.00	1.63
GL	William Blair Global Sm Cp Gro I	WGLIX	U	(800) 742-7272	U /	6.93	10.82	7.34 /58	--	--	0.00	2.20
GR	William Blair Growth I	BGFIX	C+	(800) 742-7272	B / 7.8	3.67	9.07	11.32 /80	14.97 /75	13.18 /70	0.00	0.85
GR	William Blair Growth N	WBGSX	C	(800) 742-7272	B- / 7.5	3.54	8.89	10.96 /78	14.59 /72	12.80 /66	0.00	1.19
FO	William Blair Instl Int Eqty Fd	WIIEX	C-	(800) 742-7272	C- / 3.9	6.33	4.16	4.75 /37	9.20 /34	6.92 /23	1.93	1.02
FO	William Blair Instl Intl Gr	WBIIX	D	(800) 742-7272	C- / 4.1	5.64	3.96	3.48 /29	9.91 /39	8.73 /35	1.84	0.97
FO	William Blair Internatl Leaders Ins	WILJX	U	(800) 742-7272	U /	7.11	6.54	6.03 /47	--	--	0.88	1.25
FO	William Blair Intl Equity I	WIEIX	C-	(800) 742-7272	C- / 4.0	6.33	4.15	4.58 /36	9.37 /35	6.87 /22	0.79	1.31
FO	William Blair Intl Equity N	WIENX	C-	(800) 742-7272	C- / 3.8	6.25	3.99	4.36 /34	9.10 /34	6.60 /21	0.54	1.55
FO	William Blair Intl Grwth I	BIGIX	C-	(800) 742-7272	C- / 4.1	5.65	3.94	3.40 /28	9.83 /38	8.59 /34	1.18	1.11
FO	William Blair Intl Grwth N	WBIGX	C-	(800) 742-7272	C- / 3.8	5.59	3.76	3.08 /27	9.49 /36	8.27 /32	0.84	1.44
FO	● William Blair Intl Sm Cap Gr I	WISIX	E+	(800) 742-7272	D+ / 2.7	4.17	1.82	-5.66 / 5	8.97 /33	9.31 /39	1.52	1.30
FO	● William Blair Intl Sm Cap Gr Inst	WIISX	E+	(800) 742-7272	D+ / 2.9	4.15	1.90	-5.48 / 5	9.21 /34	9.55 /41	1.78	1.06
FO	● William Blair Intl Sm Cap Gr N	WISNX	E+	(800) 742-7272	D+ / 2.5	4.06	1.61	-6.00 / 4	8.62 /31	8.97 /36	1.19	1.59
GR	William Blair Large Cap Growth I	LCGFX	A	(800) 742-7272	A+ / 9.6	5.72	12.19	19.81 /97	17.51 /92	15.75 /92	0.00	1.11
GR	William Blair Large Cap Growth N	LCGNX	A-	(800) 742-7272	A+ / 9.6	5.64	12.02	19.42 /96	17.20 /91	15.46 /90	0.00	1.36
GR	William Blair Large Cap Value I	BLVIX	C	(800) 742-7272	C+ / 5.8	-1.04	2.86	4.84 /37	13.61 /64	--	1.02	2.96
GR	William Blair Large Cap Value N	WLVNX	C	(800) 742-7272	C+ / 5.6	-1.04	2.72	4.62 /36	13.35 /62	--	0.74	3.34
GL	William Blair Macro Alloc I	WMCIX	C+	(800) 742-7272	C- / 3.6	5.73	3.76	7.27 /57	8.40 /29	--	5.17	1.41
GL	William Blair Macro Alloc Inst	WMCJX	U	(800) 742-7272	U /	5.72	3.71	7.38 /58	--	--	5.20	1.19
GL	William Blair Macro Alloc N	WMCNX	C	(800) 742-7272	C- / 3.4	5.60	3.57	6.93 /55	8.12 /28	--	5.16	1.74
MC	William Blair Mid Cap Gr Fd I	WCGIX	B-	(800) 742-7272	B / 8.2	6.42	14.57	14.64 /91	13.34 /62	14.31 /81	0.00	1.15
MC	William Blair Mid Cap Gr Fd N	WCGNX	C+	(800) 742-7272	B- / 7.4	6.41	14.50	14.35 /90	13.04 /60	14.03 /78	0.00	1.42
GR	William Blair Mid Cap Value Fund I	WMVIX	B	(800) 742-7272	B+ / 8.6	3.42	11.83	11.35 /80	16.01 /83	--	0.55	3.04
GR	William Blair Mid Cap Value Fund N	WMVNX	B	(800) 742-7272	B+ / 8.4	3.26	11.69	11.05 /79	15.70 /81	--	0.28	3.37
SC	William Blair Small Cap Gr I	WBSIX	C	(800) 742-7272	A / 9.4	3.81	12.14	5.25 /41	19.06 /97	12.46 /64	0.00	1.27
SC	William Blair Small Cap Gr N	WBSNX	C	(800) 742-7272	A / 9.3	3.75	12.03	5.00 /39	18.76 /96	12.17 /62	0.00	1.57
SC	William Blair Small Cap Value I	BVDIX	B-	(800) 742-7272	B- / 7.5	2.04	12.36	5.58 /43	15.17 /76	13.49 /73	0.11	1.25
SC	William Blair Small Cap Value N	WBVDX	C+	(800) 742-7272	B- / 7.2	1.91	12.15	5.23 /40	14.87 /74	13.20 /70	0.00	1.55
MC	William Blair Small-Mid Cap Gr I	WSMDX	A	(800) 742-7272	A+ / 9.7	7.54	17.23	15.49 /92	18.41 /95	16.61 /95	0.00	1.10
MC	William Blair Small-Mid Cap Gr N	WSMNX	A-	(800) 742-7272	A+ / 9.7	7.48	17.06	15.21 /92	18.09 /95	16.33 /94	0.00	1.46
MC	William Blair Small-Mid Cap Val I	WSMIX	B	(800) 742-7272	B- / 7.5	3.30	12.90	6.98 /55	14.89 /74	--	0.34	4.24
MC	William Blair Small-Mid Cap Val N	BSMNX	B	(800) 742-7272	B- / 7.3	3.23	12.76	6.68 /53	14.55 /71	--	0.00	4.50
SC	Williston Basin/Mid-Nrth Amer Stk A	ICPAX	E-	(800) 601-5593	E / 0.5	3.28	-16.80	-13.23 / 2	5.14 /14	12.67 /65	0.00	1.42
EN	Williston Basin/Mid-Nrth Amer Stk C	ICPUX	U	(800) 601-5593	U /	3.28	-16.94	--	--	--	0.00	N/A
GR	Wilmington Large-Cap Strategy Inst	WMLIX	A	(800) 336-9970	B+ / 8.8	2.65	7.69	14.04 /89	16.55 /87	14.39 /81	1.41	0.88
MC	Wilmington Mid-Cap Growth A	AMCRX	D	(800) 336-9970	C- / 3.8	2.26	6.76	5.36 /41	10.79 /44	12.96 /68	0.00	1.53
MC	Wilmington Mid-Cap Growth Inst	ARMEX	C-	(800) 336-9970	C / 4.8	2.30	6.83	5.52 /43	10.96 /45	13.17 /70	0.00	1.28
RE	Wilmington Mul Mgr Real Asset A	WMMRX	D-	(800) 336-9970	E+ / 0.7	1.87	2.37	2.46 /24	2.71 / 7	5.00 /12	1.33	1.62
RE	Wilmington Mul Mgr Real Asset I	WMRIX	D	(800) 336-9970	D- / 1.0	1.93	2.50	2.72 /25	2.99 / 8	5.27 /13	1.52	1.37
FO	Wilmington Multi Manager Intl A	GVIEX	D-	(800) 336-9970	D- / 1.3	5.53	1.65	0.58 /17	6.11 /17	4.24 / 9	1.47	1.75
FO	Wilmington Multi Manager Intl Inst	MVIEX	D-	(800) 336-9970	D / 2.0	5.66	1.80	0.77 /18	6.26 /18	4.40 /10	1.61	1.50
BA	Wilmington Multi-Manager Altern A	WRAAX	D+	(800) 336-9970	D- / 1.0	3.32	4.29	3.61 /30	4.22 /11	--	0.05	3.39
AA	Wilmington Multi-Manager Altern I	WRAIX	D+	(800) 336-9970	D- / 1.5	3.44	4.50	3.82 /31	4.49 /11	--	0.07	3.14
SC	Wilmington Sm Cap Strat Inst	WMSIX	B+	(800) 336-9970	B+ / 8.9	5.01	15.42	9.62 /73	16.39 /86	14.61 /83	1.18	1.18

● Denotes fund is closed to new investors
* Denotes fund is included in Section II

www.thestreetratings.com

RISK			NET ASSETS		ASSET				Portfolio Turnover Ratio	BULL / BEAR		FUND MANAGER		MINIMUMS		LOADS	
Risk Rating/Pts	3 Year Standard Deviation	Beta	NAV As of 3/31/15	Total $(Mil)	Cash %	Stocks %	Bonds %	Other %		Last Bull Market Return	Last Bear Market Return	Manager Quality Pct	Manager Tenure (Years)	Initial Purch. $	Additional Purch. $	Front End Load	Back End Load
U /	N/A	N/A	17.10	133	1	98	0	1	124	N/A	N/A	N/A	4	5,000,000	0	0.0	0.0
C /4.8	13.1	0.80	17.07	12	1	98	0	1	124	N/A	N/A	99	4	2,500	1,000	0.0	0.0
C /5.4	12.7	0.88	13.37	181	5	94	0	1	101	36.7	-22.9	89	10	500,000	0	0.0	0.0
C /5.4	12.7	0.89	13.46	857	5	94	0	1	101	37.7	-22.8	90	10	5,000,000	0	0.0	0.0
C /5.4	12.7	0.88	13.26	14	5	94	0	1	101	35.5	-22.9	88	10	2,500	1,000	0.0	0.0
C+/6.6	10.5	0.70	12.50	60	1	98	0	1	60	69.4	-18.8	91	7	500,000	0	0.0	0.0
U /	N/A	N/A	12.50	127	1	98	0	1	60	N/A	N/A	N/A	7	5,000,000	0	0.0	0.0
C+/6.6	10.4	0.70	12.48	5	1	98	0	1	60	68.1	-18.9	90	7	2,500	1,000	0.0	0.0
U /	N/A	N/A	13.11	52	2	97	0	1	117	N/A	N/A	N/A	2	500,000	0	0.0	0.0
C /4.5	11.3	1.07	14.96	661	3	96	0	1	100	91.9	-17.0	37	14	500,000	0	0.0	0.0
C /4.3	11.4	1.07	14.03	243	3	96	0	1	100	89.9	-17.2	32	14	2,500	1,000	0.0	0.0
C+/6.2	11.6	0.85	12.77	15	1	98	0	1	61	54.4	-23.0	78	7	5,000,000	0	0.0	0.0
C /5.0	11.4	0.83	16.12	2,419	1	98	0	1	83	59.1	-21.8	84	2	5,000,000	0	0.0	0.0
U /	N/A	N/A	13.11	85	2	97	0	1	79	N/A	N/A	N/A	3	5,000,000	0	0.0	0.0
C+/6.2	11.4	0.84	14.79	71	1	98	0	1	73	54.5	-23.3	79	7	500,000	0	0.0	0.0
C+/6.2	11.5	0.85	14.62	4	1	98	0	1	73	53.2	-23.4	77	7	2,500	1,000	0.0	0.0
C+/6.2	11.5	0.84	27.28	2,812	1	98	0	1	79	58.4	-22.2	83	2	500,000	0	0.0	0.0
C+/6.2	11.5	0.83	26.65	1,018	1	98	0	1	79	56.9	-22.3	81	2	2,500	1,000	0.0	0.0
C-/3.3	11.1	0.75	13.23	371	1	98	0	1	127	49.6	-20.9	83	10	500,000	0	0.0	0.0
C-/3.2	11.1	0.75	13.30	248	1	98	0	1	127	50.7	-20.8	84	10	5,000,000	0	0.0	0.0
C-/3.3	11.1	0.75	13.07	12	1	98	0	1	127	48.2	-21.1	80	10	2,500	1,000	0.0	0.0
C+/5.7	11.5	1.09	11.46	53	2	97	0	1	50	113.3	-17.6	66	10	500,000	0	0.0	0.0
C+/5.6	11.5	1.09	11.05	9	2	97	0	1	50	111.8	-17.8	61	10	2,500	1,000	0.0	0.0
C+/5.7	10.6	1.07	13.28	3	1	98	0	1	37	N/A	N/A	23	4	500,000	0	0.0	0.0
C+/5.8	10.6	1.07	13.27	1	1	98	0	1	37	N/A	N/A	21	4	2,500	1,000	0.0	0.0
B /8.4	7.8	0.92	12.92	836	25	33	40	2	59	N/A	N/A	69	4	500,000	0	0.0	0.0
U /	N/A	N/A	12.93	188	25	33	40	2	59	N/A	N/A	N/A	4	5,000,000	0	0.0	0.0
B /8.4	7.8	0.92	12.82	195	25	33	40	2	59	N/A	N/A	66	4	2,500	1,000	0.0	0.0
C /4.8	11.5	0.97	15.59	318	1	98	0	1	81	79.7	-17.7	29	9	500,000	0	0.0	0.0
C /4.7	11.5	0.97	15.11	37	1	98	0	1	81	78.1	-17.8	25	9	2,500	1,000	0.0	0.0
C /5.3	10.0	0.92	13.32	3	0	99	0	1	33	95.5	-19.7	78	5	500,000	0	0.0	0.0
C /5.4	10.0	0.93	13.30	N/A	0	99	0	1	33	93.9	-19.8	75	5	2,500	1,000	0.0	0.0
D /2.0	13.9	0.97	28.36	371	1	98	0	1	82	114.1	-25.8	88	16	500,000	0	0.0	0.0
D /1.6	13.9	0.97	26.57	149	1	98	0	1	82	112.3	-25.8	87	16	2,500	1,000	0.0	0.0
C+/5.6	13.5	0.97	18.54	555	1	98	0	1	39	90.6	-24.2	60	19	500,000	0	0.0	0.0
C+/5.6	13.5	0.97	18.10	39	1	98	0	1	39	88.9	-24.3	55	19	2,500	1,000	0.0	0.0
C+/5.6	12.3	1.04	20.82	877	3	96	0	1	49	103.1	-20.8	74	12	500,000	0	0.0	0.0
C /5.5	12.3	1.04	20.12	118	3	96	0	1	49	101.4	-20.9	71	12	2,500	1,000	0.0	0.0
C+/6.3	12.8	1.11	14.08	4	1	98	0	1	69	N/A	N/A	19	4	500,000	0	0.0	0.0
C+/6.3	12.8	1.11	14.07	1	1	98	0	1	69	N/A	N/A	17	4	2,500	1,000	0.0	0.0
D+/2.5	18.3	0.76	5.99	786	0	100	0	0	86	54.7	-32.6	5	5	1,000	50	5.0	0.0
U /	N/A	N/A	5.98	43	0	100	0	0	86	N/A	N/A	N/A	5	1,000	50	5.0	0.0
C+/6.9	9.6	1.00	18.36	468	0	99	0	1	29	102.5	-17.1	71	4	1,000,000	25	0.0	0.0
C /5.2	12.9	1.08	17.62	57	0	99	0	1	32	73.3	-22.4	5	12	1,000	25	5.5	0.0
C /5.2	12.9	1.08	18.24	288	0	99	0	1	32	74.3	-22.3	5	12	1,000,000	25	0.0	0.0
B-/7.2	7.1	0.50	14.71	2	0	35	64	1	149	19.9	-10.5	16	7	1,000	25	5.5	0.0
B-/7.2	7.1	0.50	14.80	463	0	35	64	1	149	21.0	-10.4	19	7	1,000,000	25	0.0	0.0
C+/5.9	12.3	0.92	7.74	6	3	96	0	1	49	37.4	-25.1	31	3	1,000	25	5.5	0.0
C+/5.9	12.4	0.92	7.79	519	3	96	0	1	49	37.9	-24.9	33	3	1,000,000	25	0.0	0.0
B /8.2	2.7	0.23	11.05	4	38	32	28	2	403	N/A	N/A	82	3	1,000	25	5.5	0.0
B /8.2	2.7	0.25	11.07	205	38	32	28	2	403	N/A	N/A	83	3	1,000,000	25	0.0	0.0
C+/5.6	13.4	1.00	15.43	94	0	99	0	1	47	101.2	-25.0	68	N/A	1,000,000	25	0.0	0.0

| | | | | | PERFORMANCE | | | | | | | |
| | | | | | Perfor-mance Rating/Pts | Total Return % through 3/31/15 | | | | | Incl. in Returns | |

Fund Type	Fund Name	Ticker Symbol	Overall Investment Rating	Phone	Perfor-mance Rating/Pts	3 Mo	6 Mo	1Yr / Pct	3Yr / Pct	5Yr / Pct	Dividend Yield	Expense Ratio
SC	Wilmington Small-Cap Growth A	ARPAX	C-	(800) 336-9970	C+ / 6.5	6.61	15.51	9.07 /70	14.05 /68	12.53 /64	0.00	1.75
SC	Wilmington Small-Cap Growth Inst	ARPEX	C	(800) 336-9970	B / 7.7	6.67	15.59	9.32 /71	14.28 /69	12.76 /66	0.00	1.50
AA	Wilmington Strat Alloc Aggr A	WAAAX	C-	(800) 336-9970	C- / 3.3	3.64	5.08	4.82 /37	9.83 /38	8.62 /34	0.64	2.23
AA	Wilmington Strat Alloc Aggr Inst	WAAIX	C	(800) 336-9970	C / 4.3	3.62	5.13	5.11 /39	10.10 /40	8.90 /36	0.80	1.98
AA	Wilmington Strat Alloc Conserv A	WCAAX	C-	(800) 336-9970	E+ / 0.8	1.80	2.60	3.19 /27	3.67 / 9	4.58 /10	1.00	1.99
AA	Wilmington Strat Alloc Conserv Inst	WCAIX	C-	(800) 336-9970	D- / 1.2	1.86	2.73	3.44 /29	3.92 /10	4.83 /11	1.30	1.74
AA	Wilmington Strategic Alloc Mdt A	ARBAX	C-	(800) 336-9970	D / 1.7	2.77	4.03	4.43 /35	6.74 /20	6.35 /19	1.07	2.05
AA	Wilmington Strategic Alloc Mdt Inst	ARGIX	C	(800) 336-9970	D+ / 2.6	2.83	4.15	4.69 /36	7.03 /21	--	1.38	1.80
GR	Wilshire 5000 Index Inst	WINDX	A-	(888) 200-6796	B / 8.0	1.33	6.48	11.55 /81	15.75 /81	14.08 /78	1.40	0.46
GR	Wilshire 5000 Index Inv	WFIVX	A-	(888) 200-6796	B / 7.8	1.28	6.35	11.35 /80	15.51 /79	13.82 /76	1.21	0.68
GR	Wilshire International Equity Inst	WLTTX	D-	(888) 200-6796	D- / 1.4	4.00	1.06	-1.79 /11	5.73 /16	6.55 /20	0.60	1.50
GR	Wilshire International Equity Inv	WLCTX	D-	(888) 200-6796	D- / 1.3	3.97	0.98	-2.05 /10	5.53 /15	6.34 /19	0.23	1.58
GR	Wilshire Large Co Growth Inst	WLCGX	C	(888) 200-6796	C+ / 6.7	3.32	7.79	13.95 /89	12.91 /59	13.47 /73	0.01	1.06
GR	Wilshire Large Co Growth Inv	DTLGX	C-	(888) 200-6796	C+ / 6.5	3.23	7.61	13.59 /88	12.58 /57	13.10 /69	0.00	1.36
GR	Wilshire Large Co Val Inst	WLCVX	B-	(888) 200-6796	B- / 7.2	-0.66	3.66	7.56 /60	15.56 /80	12.63 /65	1.20	0.97
GR	Wilshire Large Co Val Inv	DTLVX	B-	(888) 200-6796	B- / 7.0	-0.71	3.56	7.28 /57	15.27 /77	12.33 /63	0.97	1.25
SC	Wilshire Small Co Growth Inst	WSMGX	A-	(888) 200-6796	A / 9.5	7.96	16.97	12.31 /84	17.77 /93	16.07 /93	0.00	1.20
SC	Wilshire Small Co Growth Inv	DTSGX	A-	(888) 200-6796	A / 9.5	7.94	16.80	12.01 /83	17.51 /92	15.78 /92	0.00	1.62
SC	Wilshire Small Co Val Inst	WSMVX	A-	(888) 200-6796	A / 9.5	3.49	13.99	9.03 /69	18.63 /96	14.10 /79	0.00	1.20
SC	Wilshire Small Co Val Inv	DTSVX	A-	(888) 200-6796	A / 9.4	3.37	13.77	8.68 /67	18.31 /95	13.72 /75	0.00	1.58
GL	Wintergreen Fund Inc Inst	WGRIX	D-	(888) 468-6473	E+ / 0.8	-3.34	-4.54	-6.51 / 4	4.96 /13	--	1.59	1.63
GR	Wintergreen Fund Inc Investor	WGRNX	D-	(888) 468-6473	E+ / 0.7	-3.39	-4.64	-6.71 / 4	4.71 /12	6.41 /20	1.30	1.85
GR	Wireless Fund	WIREX	B-	(800) 590-0898	B- / 7.3	5.67	5.11	20.10 /97	13.31 /62	9.66 /42	2.80	1.95
AA	WOA All Asset I I	WOAIX	U	(855) 754-7935	U /	3.36	1.66	-0.87 /13	--	--	1.70	1.69
FO	Wright Intl Blue Chip Equities	WIBCX	D-	(800) 232-0013	D- / 1.5	4.27	-0.20	-2.77 / 9	6.66 /20	3.84 / 8	2.11	2.01
GI	Wright Major Blue Chip Equities	WQCEX	C	(800) 232-0013	C / 5.2	-1.56	2.30	8.27 /65	12.13 /53	10.97 /52	0.80	1.87
GI	Wright Selected Blue Chip Equities	WSBEX	A-	(800) 232-0013	A+ / 9.6	7.37	15.75	13.79 /89	18.25 /95	16.07 /93	0.24	1.43
FS	WST Asset Manager US Bond Inv	WAMBX	U	(866) 515-4626	U /	0.17	-0.98	--	--	--	0.00	N/A
GR	YCG Enhanced R	YCGEX	U	(855) 444-9243	U /	2.12	6.39	11.99 /82	--	--	0.42	1.70
IN	Zacks All-Cap Core A	CZOAX	B-	(800) 245-2934	C+ / 6.1	2.58	8.32	12.48 /85	14.47 /71	13.17 /70	0.00	1.86
IN	Zacks All-Cap Core C	CZOCX	B-	(800) 245-2934	C+ / 6.4	2.40	7.86	11.61 /81	13.59 /64	12.30 /63	0.00	2.61
GI	Zacks Market Neutral A	ZMNAX	D	(800) 245-2934	E / 0.4	-0.53	2.63	2.40 /24	-0.20 / 4	0.47 / 3	0.00	4.93
GI	Zacks Market Neutral C	ZMNCX	D	(800) 245-2934	E / 0.4	-0.71	2.27	1.61 /20	-0.96 / 3	-0.28 / 2	0.00	5.68
GR	Zacks Small-Cap Core Investor	ZSCCX	A+	(800) 245-2934	A+ / 9.7	6.44	17.40	11.83 /82	19.62 /97	--	0.00	2.27

● Denotes fund is closed to new investors
* Denotes fund is included in Section II

RISK	3 Year		NET ASSETS		ASSET					BULL / BEAR		FUND MANAGER		MINIMUMS		LOADS	
Risk Rating/Pts	Standard Deviation	Beta	NAV As of 3/31/15	Total $(Mil)	Cash %	Stocks %	Bonds %	Other %	Portfolio Turnover Ratio	Last Bull Market Return	Last Bear Market Return	Manager Quality Pct	Manager Tenure (Years)	Initial Purch. $	Additional Purch. $	Front End Load	Back End Load
C- / 3.8	13.8	0.99	20.65	40	1	98	0	1	37	89.4	-29.8	41	N/A	1,000	25	5.5	0.0
C- / 3.9	13.8	0.99	21.59	20	1	98	0	1	37	90.9	-29.7	44	N/A	1,000,000	25	0.0	0.0
B- / 7.1	9.4	1.56	11.97	3	5	90	3	2	72	60.2	-19.6	5	N/A	1,000	25	5.5	0.0
B- / 7.1	9.4	1.56	12.02	30	5	90	3	2	72	61.4	-19.4	5	N/A	1,000,000	25	0.0	0.0
B+ / 9.3	3.1	0.45	10.96	4	10	25	64	1	33	22.4	-8.4	51	N/A	1,000	25	5.5	0.0
B+ / 9.2	3.1	0.46	10.98	35	10	25	64	1	33	23.3	-8.3	53	N/A	1,000,000	25	0.0	0.0
B / 8.5	6.3	1.05	10.87	53	8	59	32	1	54	39.9	-15.1	14	5	1,000	25	5.5	0.0
B / 8.5	6.3	1.05	10.87	1	8	59	32	1	54	41.2	-15.1	16	5	1,000,000	25	0.0	0.0
B- / 7.2	9.6	1.00	18.24	68	0	99	0	1	2	97.5	-17.6	62	16	250,000	100,000	0.0	0.0
B- / 7.2	9.6	1.00	18.24	159	0	99	0	1	2	96.1	-17.7	59	16	1,000	100	0.0	0.0
C+ / 6.3	11.1	1.00	9.35	167	2	97	0	1	368	50.0	-19.5	2	2	250,000	100,000	0.0	1.0
C+ / 6.3	11.1	1.00	9.42	12	2	97	0	1	368	48.9	-19.6	2	2	2,500	100	0.0	1.0
C / 4.4	10.6	1.02	41.97	135	2	97	0	1	136	85.9	-17.9	25	8	250,000	100,000	0.0	0.0
C / 4.3	10.7	1.02	39.91	106	2	97	0	1	136	84.0	-17.9	22	8	2,500	100	0.0	0.0
C+ / 6.1	11.0	1.11	21.10	62	2	97	0	1	101	99.7	-21.5	36	11	250,000	100,000	0.0	0.0
C+ / 6.1	11.1	1.11	21.04	63	2	97	0	1	101	97.9	-21.7	32	11	2,500	100	0.0	0.0
C / 5.5	13.7	0.99	26.72	16	1	98	0	1	88	106.4	-25.1	80	13	250,000	100,000	0.0	0.0
C / 5.5	13.7	0.99	25.30	13	1	98	0	1	88	104.8	-25.2	79	13	2,500	100	0.0	0.0
C+ / 5.7	13.8	1.00	24.02	16	3	96	0	1	60	109.4	-25.2	84	8	250,000	100,000	0.0	0.0
C+ / 5.6	13.7	1.00	23.63	16	3	96	0	1	60	107.3	-25.4	83	8	2,500	100	0.0	0.0
B- / 7.2	11.2	0.68	16.50	382	0	94	5	1	12	N/A	N/A	47	10	100,000	1,000	0.0	2.0
C+ / 6.3	11.2	0.97	16.51	785	0	94	5	1	12	37.5	-13.4	2	10	10,000	1,000	0.0	2.0
C+ / 5.9	11.0	0.84	8.01	4	0	100	0	0	29	74.2	-20.9	67	15	5,000	100	0.0	2.0
U /	N/A	N/A	10.76	119	2	68	28	2	230	N/A	N/A	N/A	4	1,000,000	25,000	0.0	0.0
C+ / 5.6	14.1	1.05	15.52	30	1	98	0	1	45	42.3	-25.4	24	19	1,000	0	0.0	2.0
C+ / 6.4	11.8	1.20	18.80	15	1	98	0	1	64	80.5	-19.0	5	6	1,000	0	0.0	0.0
C / 5.4	12.1	1.13	13.07	40	0	99	0	1	76	108.4	-22.8	67	7	1,000	0	0.0	0.0
U /	N/A	N/A	9.83	40	0	0	0	100	0	N/A	N/A	N/A	1	1,000	250	0.0	0.0
U /	N/A	N/A	13.48	90	16	83	0	1	25	N/A	N/A	N/A	3	2,500	100	0.0	2.0
B- / 7.0	9.9	1.00	24.26	35	1	98	0	1	46	84.8	-17.1	45	10	2,500	100	5.8	2.0
B- / 7.0	9.9	1.00	22.59	15	1	98	0	1	46	80.1	-17.4	35	10	2,500	100	0.0	2.0
B / 8.3	4.6	-0.08	13.25	9	97	2	0	1	144	2.4	3.0	76	7	2,500	100	5.8	2.0
B / 8.1	4.6	-0.08	12.60	1	97	2	0	1	144	-0.2	2.7	69	7	2,500	100	0.0	2.0
C+ / 6.5	14.3	1.16	24.78	60	1	98	0	1	154	114.6	N/A	74	4	2,500	100	0.0	2.0

Section II

Analysis of Largest Stock Mutual Funds

A summary analysis of the 183 largest retail

Equity Mutual Funds

receiving a TheStreet Investment Rating.

Funds are listed in alphabetical order.

Section II Contents

1. Fund Name
The name of the mutual fund as stated in its prospectus, which can sometimes differ slightly from the name that the company uses for advertising. If you cannot find the paritcular mutual fund you are interested in, or if you have any doubts regarding the precise name, verify the information with your broker or on your account statement. Also, use the fund's ticker symbol for confirmation.

2. Ticker Symbol
The unique alphabetic symbol used for identifying and trading a specific mutual fund. No two funds can have the same ticker symbol, and the ticker symbol for mutual funds always ends with an "X".

A handful of funds currently show no associated ticker symbol. This means that the fund is either small or new since the NASD only assigns a ticker symbol to funds with at least $25 million in assets or 1,000 shareholders.

3. Investment Rating
Our overall rating is measured on a scale from A to E based on each fund's risk-adjusted performance. Please see page 10 for specific descriptions of each letter grade. Also refer to page 7 for information on how our ratings are derived. Most important, when using this rating, please be sure to consider the warnings beginning on page 11 regarding the ratings' limitations and the underlying assumptions.

4. Major Rating Factors
A synopsis of the key ratios and sub-factors that have most influenced the rating of a particular mutual fund, including an examination of the fund's performance, risk, and managerial performance. There may be additional factors which have influenced the rating but do not appear due to space limitations.

5. Services Offered
Services and/or benefits offered by the fund.

6. Address
The address of the company managing the fund.

7. Phone
The telephone number of the company managing the fund. Call this number to receive a prospectus or other information about the fund.

8. Fund Family
The umbrella group of mutual funds to which the fund belongs. In many cases, investors may move their assets from one fund to another within the same family at little or no cost.

9. Fund Type   The mutual fund's peer category based on an analysis of its investment portfolio.

AG	Aggressive Growth	HL	Health
AA	Asset Allocation	IN	Income
BA	Balanced	IX	Index
CV	Convertible	MC	Mid Cap
EM	Emerging Market	OT	Other
EN	Energy/Natural Resources	PM	Precious Metals
FS	Financial Services	RE	Real Estate
FO	Foreign	SC	Small Cap
GL	Global	TC	Technology
GR	Growth	UT	Utilities
GI	Growth and Income		

A blank fund type means that the mutual fund has not yet been categorized.

How to Read the Historical Data Table

Data Date:
The quarter-end or year-end as of date used for evaluating the mutual fund.

NAV:
The fund's share price as of the date indicated. A fund's NAV is computed by dividing the value of the fund's asset holdings, less accrued fees and expenses, by the number of its shares outstanding.

Risk Rating/Pts:
A letter grade rating based solely on the mutual fund's risk as determined by its monthly performance volatility over the trailing three years. Pts are rating points where 0=worst and 10=best.

Data Date	Investment Rating	Net Assets ($Mil)	NAV	Performance Rating/Pts	Total Return Y-T-D	Risk Rating/Pts
3-15	D	55	36.50	C- / 3.7	25.01%	C- / 4.1
2014	D+	66	35.69	C+ / 5.9	19.98%	D+ / 2.0
2013	C	823	14.46	C+ / 6.1	4.18%	C / 4.8
2012	B+	760	20.11	B / 7.8	-3.28%	B / 8.5
2011	B-	155	41.31	C+ / 6.4	-1.41%	C+ / 5.2
2010	C+	105	38.99	C+ / 6.3	20.69%	D+ / 2.9

Investment Rating:
Our overall opinion of the fund's risk-adjusted performance at the specified time period.

Net Assets $(Mil):
The total value of all of the fund's asset holdings (in millions) including stocks, bonds, cash, and other financial instruments, less accrued expenses and fees.

Performance Rating/Pts:
A letter grade rating based solely on the mutual fund's return to shareholders over the trailing three years, without any consideration for the amount of risk the fund poses. Pts are rating points where 0=worst and 10=best

Total Return Y-T-D:
The fund's total return to shareholders since the beginning of the calendar year specified.

American Funds AMCAP A (AMCPX) B+ Good

Fund Family: American Funds **Phone:** (800) 421-0180
Address: 333 South Hope Street, Los Angeles, CA 90071
Fund Type: GR - Growth
Major Rating Factors: Strong performance is the major factor driving the B+ (Good) TheStreet.com Investment Rating for American Funds AMCAP A. The fund currently has a performance rating of B (Good) based on an average return of 17.23% over the last three years and 2.39% over the last three months. Factored into the performance evaluation is an expense ratio of 0.70% (very low) and a 5.8% front-end load that is levied at the time of purchase.

The fund's risk rating is currently C+ (Fair). It carries a beta of 0.94, meaning that its performance tracks fairly well with that of the overall stock market. Volatility, as measured by both the semi-deviation and a drawdown factor, is considered low.

Claudia P. Huntington has been running the fund for 19 years and currently receives a manager quality ranking of 84 (0=worst, 99=best). If you desire only a moderate level of risk and strong performance, then this fund is an excellent option.

Services Offered: Automated phone transactions, payroll deductions, an IRA investment plan, a 401K investment plan, a Keogh investment plan, wire transfers and a systematic withdrawal plan.

Data Date	Investment Rating	Net Assets ($Mil)	NAV	Performance Rating/Pts	Total Return Y-T-D	Risk Rating/Pts
3-15	B+	25,520	28.67	B / 7.8	2.39%	C+ / 6.5
2014	B+	24,627	28.00	B / 8.0	12.10%	C+ / 6.5
2013	A-	21,061	27.33	B+ / 8.3	36.86%	C / 5.5
2012	C	15,410	21.69	C / 4.9	15.67%	C / 5.4
2011	B+	13,708	18.83	B- / 7.4	0.38%	C / 5.4
2010	C	14,061	18.83	C / 5.0	13.98%	C- / 3.9

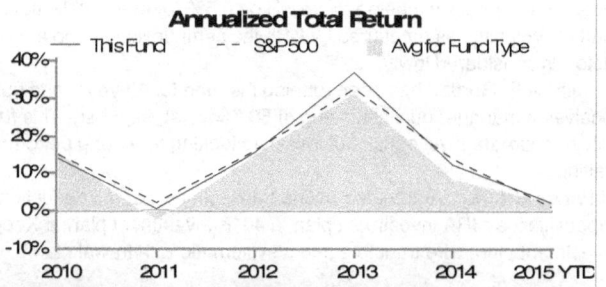

American Funds Amer Balncd Fd A (ABALX) C+ Fair

Fund Family: American Funds **Phone:** (800) 421-0180
Address: 333 South Hope Street, Los Angeles, CA 90071
Fund Type: BA - Balanced
Major Rating Factors: Middle of the road best describes American Funds Amer Balncd Fd A whose TheStreet.com Investment Rating is currently a C+ (Fair). The fund currently has a performance rating of C (Fair) based on an average return of 11.94% over the last three years and 0.77% over the last three months. Factored into the performance evaluation is an expense ratio of 0.59% (very low) and a 5.8% front-end load that is levied at the time of purchase.

The fund's risk rating is currently B (Good). It carries a beta of 1.20, meaning it is expected to move 12.0% for every 10% move in the market. Volatility, as measured by both the semi-deviation and a drawdown factor, is considered low.

Gregory D. Johnson has been running the fund for 12 years and currently receives a manager quality ranking of 50 (0=worst, 99=best). If you desire an average level of risk, then this fund may be an option.

Services Offered: Automated phone transactions, payroll deductions, bank draft capabilities, an IRA investment plan, a 401K investment plan, a Keogh investment plan, wire transfers and a systematic withdrawal plan.

Data Date	Investment Rating	Net Assets ($Mil)	NAV	Performance Rating/Pts	Total Return Y-T-D	Risk Rating/Pts
3-15	C+	47,852	24.75	C / 4.3	0.77%	B / 8.0
2014	B-	46,928	24.75	C / 4.8	8.85%	B / 8.1
2013	B-	42,030	24.42	C / 4.6	21.73%	B- / 7.7
2012	B-	34,272	20.40	C / 4.9	14.19%	B- / 7.6
2011	C+	30,569	18.21	C / 4.5	3.82%	B- / 7.0
2010	C+	31,409	17.93	C / 4.7	13.02%	C+ / 6.8

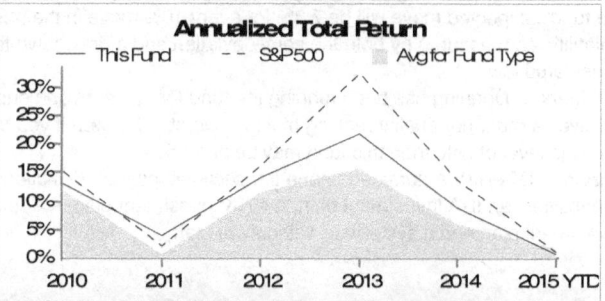

American Funds Amer Mutual Fd A (AMRMX) B- Good

Fund Family: American Funds **Phone:** (800) 421-0180
Address: 333 South Hope Street, Los Angeles, CA 90071
Fund Type: GI - Growth and Income
Major Rating Factors: American Funds Amer Mutual Fd A receives a TheStreet.com Investment Rating of B- (Good). The fund currently has a performance rating of C+ (Fair) based on an average return of 14.67% over the last three years and 0.10% over the last three months. Factored into the performance evaluation is an expense ratio of 0.59% (very low) and a 5.8% front-end load that is levied at the time of purchase.

The fund's risk rating is currently B- (Good). It carries a beta of 0.81, meaning the fund's expected move will be 8.1% for every 10% move in the market. Volatility, as measured by both the semi-deviation and a drawdown factor, is considered low.

Joyce E. Gordon has been running the fund for 9 years and currently receives a manager quality ranking of 81 (0=worst, 99=best). If you desire an average level of risk, then this fund may be an option.

Services Offered: Automated phone transactions, payroll deductions, an IRA investment plan, a 401K investment plan, a Keogh investment plan, wire transfers and a systematic withdrawal plan.

Data Date	Investment Rating	Net Assets ($Mil)	NAV	Performance Rating/Pts	Total Return Y-T-D	Risk Rating/Pts
3-15	B-	22,822	36.99	C+ / 6.1	0.10%	B- / 7.7
2014	B-	22,698	37.14	C+ / 6.4	12.61%	B- / 7.8
2013	C+	20,139	34.81	C+ / 5.7	27.91%	C+ / 6.7
2012	C	15,651	28.36	C- / 3.5	12.33%	C+ / 6.5
2011	C+	13,620	25.86	C+ / 6.2	4.77%	C+ / 5.9
2010	C	13,636	25.32	C- / 3.9	12.23%	C+ / 5.8

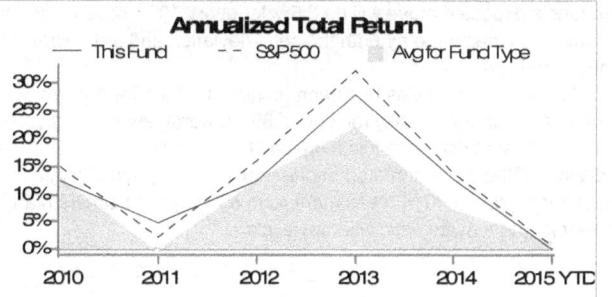

American Funds Cap Inc Builder A (CAIBX)   C-   Fair

Fund Family: American Funds   **Phone:** (800) 421-0180
Address: 333 South Hope Street, Los Angeles, CA 90071
Fund Type: IN - Income
Major Rating Factors: Disappointing performance is the major factor driving the
C- (Fair) TheStreet.com Investment Rating for American Funds Cap Inc Builder
A. The fund currently has a performance rating of D+ (Weak) based on an
average return of 9.40% over the last three years and 0.63% over the last three
months. Factored into the performance evaluation is an expense ratio of 0.59%
(very low) and a 5.8% front-end load that is levied at the time of purchase.

The fund's risk rating is currently B- (Good). It carries a beta of 0.65,
meaning the fund's expected move will be 6.5% for every 10% move in the
market. Volatility, as measured by both the semi-deviation and a drawdown
factor, is considered low.

Joyce E. Gordon has been running the fund for 15 years and currently
receives a manager quality ranking of 56 (0=worst, 99=best). This fund offers
only a moderate level of risk but investors looking for strong performance are still
waiting.

Services Offered: Automated phone transactions, payroll deductions, bank draft
capabilities, an IRA investment plan, a 401K investment plan, a Keogh
investment plan, wire transfers and a systematic withdrawal plan.

Data Date	Investment Rating	Net Assets ($Mil)	NAV	Performance Rating/Pts	Total Return Y-T-D	Risk Rating/Pts
3-15	C-	70,612	59.45	D+ / 2.7	0.63%	B- / 7.8
2014	C	69,896	59.58	C- / 3.0	6.61%	B- / 7.9
2013	C	65,416	58.55	D+ / 2.7	14.90%	B- / 7.4
2012	C-	58,079	52.77	D / 1.9	11.81%	B- / 7.3
2011	C	54,764	49.22	D+ / 2.5	2.86%	B- / 7.5
2010	C-	58,576	49.91	D- / 1.4	8.66%	C+ / 6.2

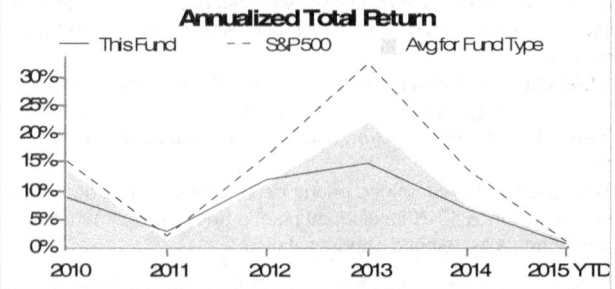

American Funds Cap Wld Gr&Inc A (CWGIX)   C   Fair

Fund Family: American Funds   **Phone:** (800) 421-0180
Address: 333 South Hope Street, Los Angeles, CA 90071
Fund Type: GL - Global
Major Rating Factors: Middle of the road best describes American Funds Cap
Wld Gr&Inc A whose TheStreet.com Investment Rating is currently a C (Fair).
The fund currently has a performance rating of C (Fair) based on an average
return of 12.61% over the last three years and 2.65% over the last three months.
Factored into the performance evaluation is an expense ratio of 0.77% (very low)
and a 5.8% front-end load that is levied at the time of purchase.

The fund's risk rating is currently C+ (Fair). It carries a beta of 0.73, meaning
the fund's expected move will be 7.3% for every 10% move in the market.
Volatility, as measured by both the semi-deviation and a drawdown factor, is
considered low.

Mark E. Denning has been running the fund for 22 years and currently
receives a manager quality ranking of 94 (0=worst, 99=best). If you desire an
average level of risk, then this fund may be an option.

Services Offered: Automated phone transactions, payroll deductions, bank draft
capabilities, an IRA investment plan, a 401K investment plan, a Keogh
investment plan and a systematic withdrawal plan.

Data Date	Investment Rating	Net Assets ($Mil)	NAV	Performance Rating/Pts	Total Return Y-T-D	Risk Rating/Pts
3-15	C	56,439	47.14	C / 4.5	2.65%	C+ / 6.9
2014	C	55,529	46.09	C / 4.5	4.02%	C+ / 6.9
2013	C-	54,676	45.32	C / 4.5	24.84%	C / 4.9
2012	D	46,651	37.20	C- / 3.0	19.12%	C / 4.6
2011	D	45,595	32.12	D- / 1.2	-7.53%	C / 5.3
2010	D	55,061	35.72	D- / 1.2	7.71%	C- / 4.1

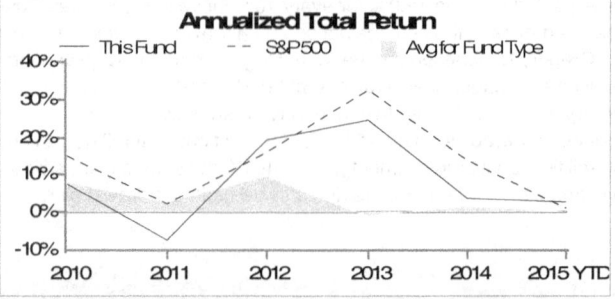

American Funds EuroPacific Gr A (AEPGX)   D   Weak

Fund Family: American Funds   **Phone:** (800) 421-0180
Address: 333 South Hope Street, Los Angeles, CA 90071
Fund Type: FO - Foreign
Major Rating Factors: American Funds EuroPacific Gr A receives a
TheStreet.com Investment Rating of D (Weak). The fund currently has a
performance rating of C- (Fair) based on an average return of 9.57% over the
last three years and 5.90% over the last three months. Factored into the
performance evaluation is an expense ratio of 0.84% (very low) and a 5.8%
front-end load that is levied at the time of purchase.

The fund's risk rating is currently C+ (Fair). It carries a beta of 0.85, meaning
the fund's expected move will be 8.5% for every 10% move in the market.
Volatility, as measured by both the semi-deviation and a drawdown factor, is
considered low.

Jonathan O. Knowles has been running the fund for 9 years and currently
receives a manager quality ranking of 80 (0=worst, 99=best). If you desire an
average level of risk, then this fund may be an option.

Services Offered: Automated phone transactions, payroll deductions, an IRA
investment plan, a 401K investment plan, a Keogh investment plan, wire
transfers and a systematic withdrawal plan.

Data Date	Investment Rating	Net Assets ($Mil)	NAV	Performance Rating/Pts	Total Return Y-T-D	Risk Rating/Pts
3-15	D	30,814	49.91	C- / 3.0	5.90%	C+ / 5.9
2014	D	29,419	47.13	D+ / 2.4	-2.64%	C+ / 5.9
2013	D-	32,428	49.07	C- / 3.0	20.15%	C- / 4.0
2012	D-	29,498	41.22	D / 2.2	19.21%	C- / 3.9
2011	D-	30,358	35.16	E+ / 0.8	-13.58%	C / 4.7
2010	D	39,210	41.37	D / 1.7	9.40%	C- / 4.0

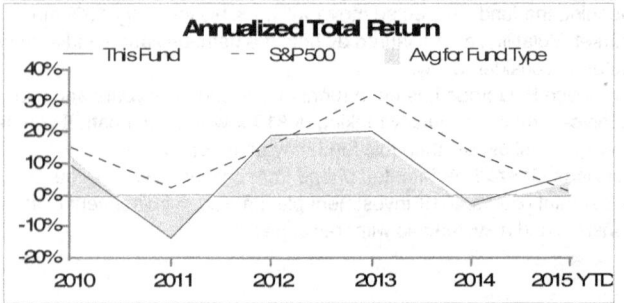

American Funds Fundamntl Invs A (ANCFX)   C+   Fair

Fund Family: American Funds   **Phone:** (800) 421-0180
Address: 333 South Hope Street, Los Angeles, CA 90071
Fund Type: GI - Growth and Income
Major Rating Factors: Middle of the road best describes American Funds Fundamntl Invs A whose TheStreet.com Investment Rating is currently a C+ (Fair). The fund currently has a performance rating of C+ (Fair) based on an average return of 15.19% over the last three years and 1.60% over the last three months. Factored into the performance evaluation is an expense ratio of 0.61% (very low) and a 5.8% front-end load that is levied at the time of purchase.

The fund's risk rating is currently C+ (Fair). It carries a beta of 1.00, meaning that its performance tracks fairly well with that of the overall stock market. Volatility, as measured by both the semi-deviation and a drawdown factor, is considered low.

Dina N. Perry has been running the fund for 22 years and currently receives a manager quality ranking of 56 (0=worst, 99=best). If you desire an average level of risk, then this fund may be an option.

Services Offered: Automated phone transactions, payroll deductions, bank draft capabilities, an IRA investment plan, a 401K investment plan, a Keogh investment plan and a systematic withdrawal plan.

Data Date	Investment Rating	Net Assets ($Mil)	NAV	Perfor-mance Rating/Pts	Total Return Y-T-D	Risk Rating/Pts
3-15	C+	44,458	52.13	C+ / 6.4	1.60%	C+ / 6.7
2014	C+	43,940	52.06	C+ / 6.6	8.96%	C+ / 6.7
2013	C+	40,703	51.97	C+ / 6.4	31.50%	C / 5.3
2012	C	32,568	40.78	C+ / 5.6	17.14%	C / 4.9
2011	C	30,354	35.39	C / 5.2	-1.89%	C / 5.5
2010	C-	33,089	36.70	D+ / 2.7	14.05%	C / 4.5

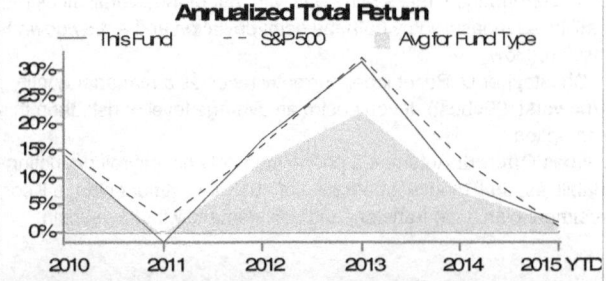

American Funds Gr Fnd of Amer A (AGTHX)   B   Good

Fund Family: American Funds   **Phone:** (800) 421-0180
Address: 333 South Hope Street, Los Angeles, CA 90071
Fund Type: GR - Growth
Major Rating Factors: Strong performance is the major factor driving the B (Good) TheStreet.com Investment Rating for American Funds Gr Fnd of Amer A. The fund currently has a performance rating of B (Good) based on an average return of 16.72% over the last three years and 3.37% over the last three months. Factored into the performance evaluation is an expense ratio of 0.66% (very low) and a 5.8% front-end load that is levied at the time of purchase.

The fund's risk rating is currently C+ (Fair). It carries a beta of 0.95, meaning that its performance tracks fairly well with that of the overall stock market. Volatility, as measured by both the semi-deviation and a drawdown factor, is considered low.

James F. Rothenberg has been running the fund for 27 years and currently receives a manager quality ranking of 79 (0=worst, 99=best). If you desire only a moderate level of risk and strong performance, then this fund is an excellent option.

Services Offered: Automated phone transactions, payroll deductions, bank draft capabilities, an IRA investment plan, a 401K investment plan, a Keogh investment plan, wire transfers and a systematic withdrawal plan.

Data Date	Investment Rating	Net Assets ($Mil)	NAV	Perfor-mance Rating/Pts	Total Return Y-T-D	Risk Rating/Pts
3-15	B	74,756	44.12	B / 7.6	3.37%	C+ / 5.7
2014	B-	72,970	42.68	B / 7.6	9.30%	C+ / 5.7
2013	B-	69,385	43.00	B- / 7.1	33.79%	C / 5.1
2012	C	55,970	34.35	C+ / 5.9	20.54%	C / 4.9
2011	C-	54,830	28.73	C- / 3.1	-4.89%	C+ / 5.6
2010	D+	66,101	30.44	D+ / 2.5	12.28%	C / 4.4

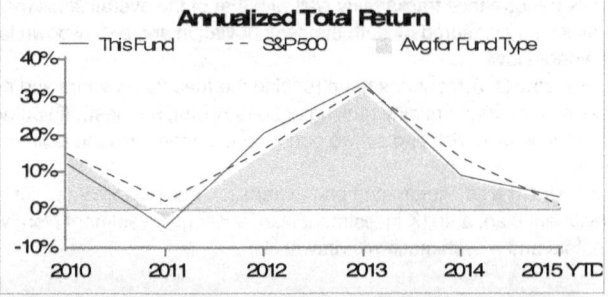

American Funds Inc Fnd of Amr A (AMECX)   C+   Fair

Fund Family: American Funds   **Phone:** (800) 421-0180
Address: 333 South Hope Street, Los Angeles, CA 90071
Fund Type: IN - Income
Major Rating Factors: Middle of the road best describes American Funds Inc Fnd of Amr A whose TheStreet.com Investment Rating is currently a C+ (Fair). The fund currently has a performance rating of C- (Fair) based on an average return of 11.21% over the last three years and 0.96% over the last three months. Factored into the performance evaluation is an expense ratio of 0.57% (very low) and a 5.8% front-end load that is levied at the time of purchase.

The fund's risk rating is currently B (Good). It carries a beta of 0.65, meaning the fund's expected move will be 6.5% for every 10% move in the market. Volatility, as measured by both the semi-deviation and a drawdown factor, is considered low.

Dina N. Perry has been running the fund for 23 years and currently receives a manager quality ranking of 76 (0=worst, 99=best). If you desire an average level of risk, then this fund may be an option.

Services Offered: Automated phone transactions, payroll deductions, bank draft capabilities, an IRA investment plan, a 401K investment plan, a Keogh investment plan, wire transfers and a systematic withdrawal plan.

Data Date	Investment Rating	Net Assets ($Mil)	NAV	Perfor-mance Rating/Pts	Total Return Y-T-D	Risk Rating/Pts
3-15	C+	73,697	21.62	C- / 3.8	0.96%	B / 8.1
2014	C+	72,851	21.58	C- / 3.8	8.39%	B / 8.1
2013	C	67,055	20.65	C- / 3.7	18.26%	B- / 7.2
2012	C+	57,662	18.06	C- / 3.9	11.95%	B- / 7.1
2011	C+	51,410	16.76	C+ / 6.1	5.58%	C+ / 6.7
2010	C	52,075	16.55	C- / 3.5	11.97%	C+ / 6.2

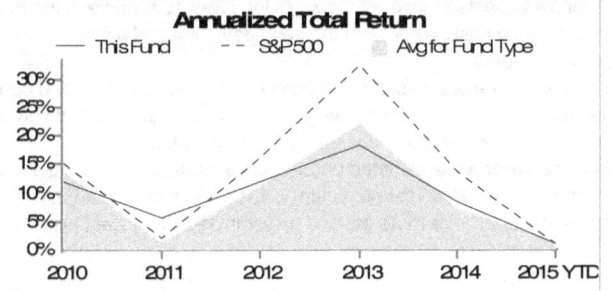

American Funds Inv Co of Amer A (AIVSX)   C+   Fair

Fund Family: American Funds   **Phone:** (800) 421-0180
Address: 333 South Hope Street, Los Angeles, CA 90071
Fund Type: GI - Growth and Income

Major Rating Factors: Middle of the road best describes American Funds Inv
Co of Amer A whose TheStreet.com Investment Rating is currently a C+ (Fair).
The fund currently has a performance rating of C+ (Fair) based on an average
return of 15.82% over the last three years and 0.57% over the last three months.
Factored into the performance evaluation is an expense ratio of 0.59% (very low)
and a 5.8% front-end load that is levied at the time of purchase.

The fund's risk rating is currently C+ (Fair). It carries a beta of 0.93, meaning
that its performance tracks fairly well with that of the overall stock market.
Volatility, as measured by both the semi-deviation and a drawdown factor, is
considered low.

Christopher D. Buchbinder currently receives a manager quality ranking of
76 (0=worst, 99=best). If you desire an average level of risk, then this fund may
be an option.

Services Offered: Automated phone transactions, payroll deductions, bank draft
capabilities, an IRA investment plan, a 401K investment plan, a Keogh
investment plan, wire transfers and a systematic withdrawal plan.

Data Date	Investment Rating	Net Assets ($Mil)	NAV	Perfor- mance Rating/Pts	Total Return Y-T-D	Risk Rating/Pts
3-15	C+	58,368	36.88	C+ / 6.6	0.57%	C+ / 6.1
2014	B	58,436	37.08	B- / 7.2	12.09%	C+ / 6.5
2013	C+	54,123	36.70	C+ / 6.6	32.43%	C+ / 5.7
2012	D+	44,501	30.16	D+ / 2.9	15.60%	C / 5.5
2011	C-	42,794	27.09	D+ / 2.8	-1.76%	C+ / 5.7
2010	C-	48,789	28.16	D / 2.2	10.86%	C / 5.1

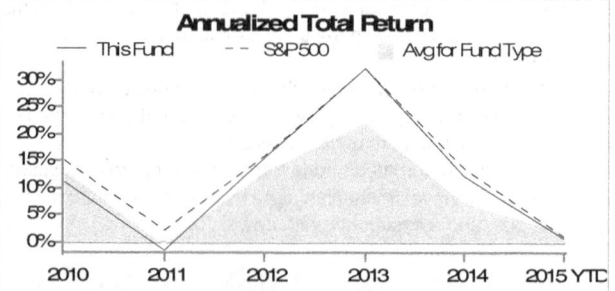

American Funds New Economy A (ANEFX)   B   Good

Fund Family: American Funds   **Phone:** (800) 421-0180
Address: 333 South Hope Street, Los Angeles, CA 90071
Fund Type: GR - Growth

Major Rating Factors: Strong performance is the major factor driving the B
(Good) TheStreet.com Investment Rating for American Funds New Economy A.
The fund currently has a performance rating of B (Good) based on an average
return of 18.19% over the last three years and 3.56% over the last three months.
Factored into the performance evaluation is an expense ratio of 0.79% (very low)
and a 5.8% front-end load that is levied at the time of purchase.

The fund's risk rating is currently C+ (Fair). It carries a beta of 0.93, meaning
that its performance tracks fairly well with that of the overall stock market.
Volatility, as measured by both the semi-deviation and a drawdown factor, is
considered low.

Timothy D. Armour has been running the fund for 24 years and currently
receives a manager quality ranking of 88 (0=worst, 99=best). If you desire only a
moderate level of risk and strong performance, then this fund is an excellent
option.

Services Offered: Automated phone transactions, payroll deductions, an IRA
investment plan, a 401K investment plan, a Keogh investment plan, wire
transfers and a systematic withdrawal plan.

Data Date	Investment Rating	Net Assets ($Mil)	NAV	Perfor- mance Rating/Pts	Total Return Y-T-D	Risk Rating/Pts
3-15	B	10,130	38.09	B / 8.1	3.56%	C+ / 5.9
2014	B+	9,776	36.78	B+ / 8.3	4.59%	C+ / 6.1
2013	A	8,920	38.22	A+ / 9.6	43.36%	C / 4.8
2012	B	5,978	28.43	B / 7.7	24.02%	C / 4.7
2011	C	5,298	23.78	C / 5.4	-5.65%	C / 5.3
2010	C-	6,036	25.33	C- / 3.7	13.40%	C / 4.5

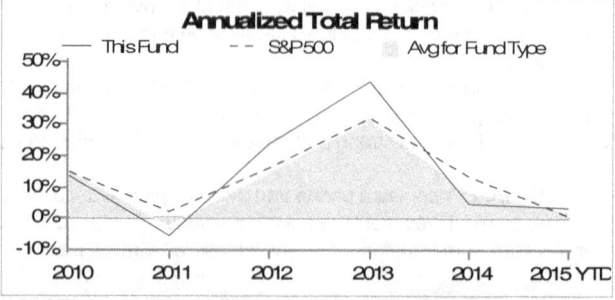

American Funds New Perspectve A (ANWPX)   C   Fair

Fund Family: American Funds   **Phone:** (800) 421-0180
Address: 333 South Hope Street, Los Angeles, CA 90071
Fund Type: GL - Global

Major Rating Factors: Middle of the road best describes American Funds New
Perspectve A whose TheStreet.com Investment Rating is currently a C (Fair).
The fund currently has a performance rating of C (Fair) based on an average
return of 13.31% over the last three years and 4.69% over the last three months.
Factored into the performance evaluation is an expense ratio of 0.76% (very low)
and a 5.8% front-end load that is levied at the time of purchase.

The fund's risk rating is currently C+ (Fair). It carries a beta of 0.74, meaning
the fund's expected move will be 7.4% for every 10% move in the market.
Volatility, as measured by both the semi-deviation and a drawdown factor, is
considered low.

Gregg E. Ireland has been running the fund for 23 years and currently
receives a manager quality ranking of 95 (0=worst, 99=best). If you desire an
average level of risk, then this fund may be an option.

Services Offered: Automated phone transactions, payroll deductions, bank draft
capabilities, an IRA investment plan, a 401K investment plan, a Keogh
investment plan, wire transfers and a systematic withdrawal plan.

Data Date	Investment Rating	Net Assets ($Mil)	NAV	Perfor- mance Rating/Pts	Total Return Y-T-D	Risk Rating/Pts
3-15	C	37,580	37.98	C / 5.4	4.69%	C+ / 6.2
2014	C	36,228	36.28	C / 4.9	3.23%	C+ / 6.2
2013	C	36,449	37.56	C / 5.1	26.77%	C / 5.1
2012	C	30,245	31.26	C+ / 5.7	20.77%	C / 4.9
2011	D+	28,548	26.16	D+ / 2.4	-7.60%	C+ / 5.6
2010	C	33,224	28.62	C- / 3.9	12.76%	C / 5.4

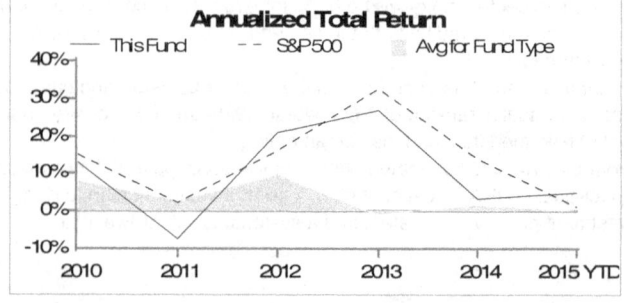

American Funds New World A (NEWFX)   E+   Very Weak

Fund Family: American Funds   **Phone:** (800) 421-0180
Address: 333 South Hope Street, Los Angeles, CA 90071
Fund Type: GL - Global
Major Rating Factors: Very poor performance is the major factor driving the E+ (Very Weak) TheStreet.com Investment Rating for American Funds New World A. The fund currently has a performance rating of E+ (Very Weak) based on an average return of 5.12% over the last three years and 2.86% over the last three months. Factored into the performance evaluation is an expense ratio of 1.03% (low) and a 5.8% front-end load that is levied at the time of purchase.

The fund's risk rating is currently C (Fair). It carries a beta of 0.79, meaning the fund's expected move will be 7.9% for every 10% move in the market. Volatility, as measured by both the semi-deviation and a drawdown factor, is considered average.

Carl M. Kawaja has been running the fund for 16 years and currently receives a manager quality ranking of 34 (0=worst, 99=best). This fund offers an average level of risk but investors looking for strong performance will be frustrated.
Services Offered: Automated phone transactions, payroll deductions, bank draft capabilities, an IRA investment plan, a 401K investment plan, a Keogh investment plan, wire transfers and a systematic withdrawal plan.

Data Date	Investment Rating	Net Assets ($Mil)	NAV	Performance Rating/Pts	Total Return Y-T-D	Risk Rating/Pts
3-15	E+	12,667	55.03	E+ / 0.9	2.86%	C / 5.2
2014	E+	12,449	53.50	D- / 1.0	-3.66%	C / 5.4
2013	E+	13,284	58.75	E+ / 0.9	10.01%	C- / 4.2
2012	D+	12,180	54.49	C / 4.5	19.71%	C / 4.3
2011	D+	11,444	46.12	C- / 3.1	-14.13%	C / 5.1
2010	C-	13,861	54.59	C- / 3.9	17.32%	C- / 3.5

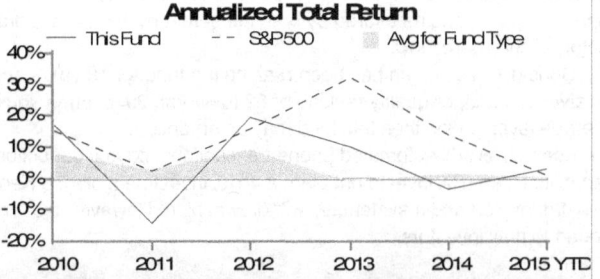

Annualized Total Return

American Funds SMALLCAP World A (SMCWX)   C-   Fair

Fund Family: American Funds   **Phone:** (800) 421-0180
Address: 333 South Hope Street, Los Angeles, CA 90071
Fund Type: SC - Small Cap
Major Rating Factors: Middle of the road best describes American Funds SMALLCAP World A whose TheStreet.com Investment Rating is currently a C- (Fair). The fund currently has a performance rating of C (Fair) based on an average return of 13.11% over the last three years and 5.39% over the last three months. Factored into the performance evaluation is an expense ratio of 1.07% (low) and a 5.8% front-end load that is levied at the time of purchase.

The fund's risk rating is currently C (Fair). It carries a beta of 0.73, meaning the fund's expected move will be 7.3% for every 10% move in the market. Volatility, as measured by both the semi-deviation and a drawdown factor, is considered average.

Mark E. Denning has been running the fund for 24 years and currently receives a manager quality ranking of 79 (0=worst, 99=best). If you desire an average level of risk, then this fund may be an option.
Services Offered: Automated phone transactions, payroll deductions, bank draft capabilities, an IRA investment plan, a 401K investment plan, a Keogh investment plan and a systematic withdrawal plan.

Data Date	Investment Rating	Net Assets ($Mil)	NAV	Performance Rating/Pts	Total Return Y-T-D	Risk Rating/Pts
3-15	C-	17,744	47.75	C / 5.3	5.39%	C / 5.3
2014	C-	16,972	45.31	C / 5.1	1.82%	C / 5.5
2013	D	17,118	49.15	C / 4.5	29.29%	C- / 3.5
2012	C	13,566	39.91	C+ / 6.9	21.94%	C- / 3.6
2011	C	12,578	33.18	C+ / 5.7	-14.34%	C / 4.3
2010	C	15,874	38.86	C+ / 6.2	24.92%	C- / 3.2

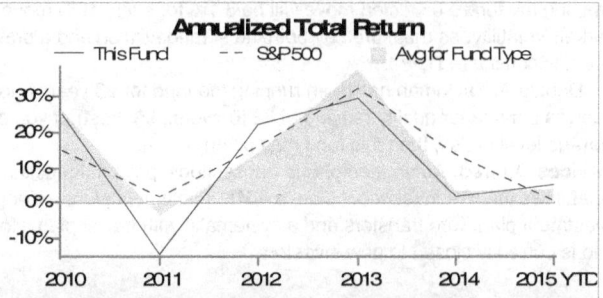

Annualized Total Return

American Funds Wash Mutl Invs A (AWSHX)   B-   Good

Fund Family: American Funds   **Phone:** (800) 421-0180
Address: 333 South Hope Street, Los Angeles, CA 90071
Fund Type: GI - Growth and Income
Major Rating Factors: American Funds Wash Mutl Invs A receives a TheStreet.com Investment Rating of B- (Good). The fund currently has a performance rating of C+ (Fair) based on an average return of 15.38% over the last three years and 0.22% over the last three months. Factored into the performance evaluation is an expense ratio of 0.60% (very low) and a 5.8% front-end load that is levied at the time of purchase.

The fund's risk rating is currently B- (Good). It carries a beta of 0.91, meaning that its performance tracks fairly well with that of the overall stock market. Volatility, as measured by both the semi-deviation and a drawdown factor, is considered low.

Alan N. Berro has been running the fund for 18 years and currently receives a manager quality ranking of 75 (0=worst, 99=best). If you desire an average level of risk, then this fund may be an option.
Services Offered: Automated phone transactions, payroll deductions, bank draft capabilities, an IRA investment plan, a 401K investment plan, a Keogh investment plan and a systematic withdrawal plan.

Data Date	Investment Rating	Net Assets ($Mil)	NAV	Performance Rating/Pts	Total Return Y-T-D	Risk Rating/Pts
3-15	B-	52,290	40.86	C+ / 6.3	0.22%	B- / 7.3
2014	B-	52,722	40.95	C+ / 6.5	11.22%	B- / 7.5
2013	A-	49,202	39.43	B- / 7.2	31.92%	C+ / 6.6
2012	C+	39,823	31.21	C / 4.8	12.50%	C+ / 6.4
2011	C+	37,594	28.40	C+ / 5.9	7.05%	C / 5.2
2010	D+	38,822	27.21	D / 2.0	13.34%	C / 5.0

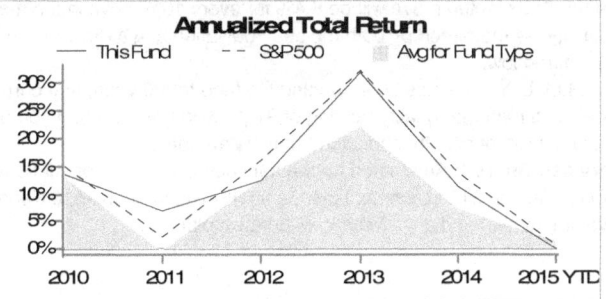

Annualized Total Return

AMG Yacktman Focused Svc (YAFFX)   C+   Fair

Fund Family: Managers Funds LLC   **Phone:** (800) 835-3879
Address: 800 Connecticut Ave., Norwalk, CT 06854
Fund Type: GI - Growth and Income
Major Rating Factors: Middle of the road best describes AMG Yacktman
Focused Svc whose TheStreet.com Investment Rating is currently a C+ (Fair).
The fund currently has a performance rating of C (Fair) based on an average
return of 12.23% over the last three years and -2.90% over the last three
months. Factored into the performance evaluation is an expense ratio of 1.26%
(average) and a 2.0% back-end load levied at the time of sale.

The fund's risk rating is currently B- (Good). It carries a beta of 0.79,
meaning the fund's expected move will be 7.9% for every 10% move in the
market. Volatility, as measured by both the semi-deviation and a drawdown
factor, is considered low.

Donald A. Yacktman has been running the fund for 18 years and currently
receives a manager quality ranking of 62 (0=worst, 99=best). If you desire an
average level of risk, then this fund may be an option.

Services Offered: Automated phone transactions, payroll deductions, bank draft
capabilities, an IRA investment plan, a 401K investment plan, a Keogh
investment plan and a systematic withdrawal plan. However, the fund is currently
closed to new investors.

Data Date	Investment Rating	Net Assets ($Mil)	NAV	Perfor-mance Rating/Pts	Total Return Y-T-D	Risk Rating/Pts
3-15	C+	7,072	25.13	C / 4.7	-2.90%	B- / 7.2
2014	B	7,850	25.88	C+ / 6.0	10.67%	B / 8.3
2013	B	8,627	25.15	C+ / 5.7	27.01%	B / 8.0
2012	B-	6,599	20.52	C / 4.3	10.57%	B- / 7.6
2011	A+	4,424	18.78	A+ / 9.8	7.41%	C / 5.4
2010	A+	1,984	17.68	A+ / 9.7	11.84%	C+ / 5.8

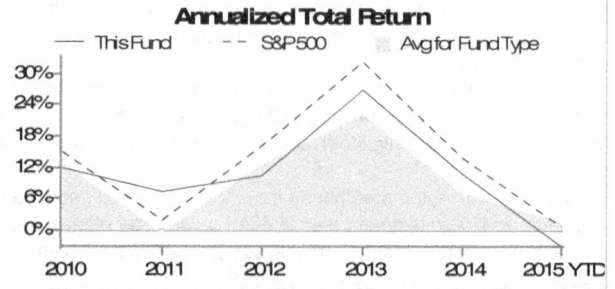

AMG Yacktman Svc (YACKX)   C+   Fair

Fund Family: Managers Funds LLC   **Phone:** (800) 835-3879
Address: 800 Connecticut Ave., Norwalk, CT 06854
Fund Type: GI - Growth and Income
Major Rating Factors: Middle of the road best describes AMG Yacktman Svc
whose TheStreet.com Investment Rating is currently a C+ (Fair). The fund
currently has a performance rating of C (Fair) based on an average return of
12.56% over the last three years and -3.30% over the last three months.
Factored into the performance evaluation is an expense ratio of 0.76% (very low)
and a 2.0% back-end load levied at the time of sale.

The fund's risk rating is currently B- (Good). It carries a beta of 0.81,
meaning the fund's expected move will be 8.1% for every 10% move in the
market. Volatility, as measured by both the semi-deviation and a drawdown
factor, is considered low.

Donald A. Yacktman has been running the fund for 23 years and currently
receives a manager quality ranking of 63 (0=worst, 99=best). If you desire an
average level of risk, then this fund may be an option.

Services Offered: Automated phone transactions, payroll deductions, bank draft
capabilities, an IRA investment plan, a 401K investment plan, a Keogh
investment plan, wire transfers and a systematic withdrawal plan. However, the
fund is currently closed to new investors.

Data Date	Investment Rating	Net Assets ($Mil)	NAV	Perfor-mance Rating/Pts	Total Return Y-T-D	Risk Rating/Pts
3-15	C+	13,053	24.29	C / 4.9	-3.30%	B- / 7.6
2014	B	14,219	25.12	C+ / 6.5	11.33%	B / 8.2
2013	B-	13,918	23.54	C+ / 6.0	27.74%	B- / 7.6
2012	C+	8,670	19.12	C / 5.2	11.47%	C+ / 6.9
2011	A+	6,280	17.51	A+ / 9.8	7.30%	C / 5.1
2010	A+	3,403	16.54	A / 9.5	12.64%	C+ / 6.0

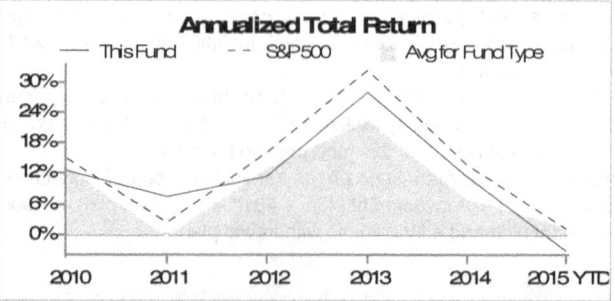

Artisan International Fund Inv (ARTIX)   C   Fair

Fund Family: Artisan Funds   **Phone:** (800) 344-1770
Address: P.O. Box 8412, Boston, MA 02266
Fund Type: FO - Foreign
Major Rating Factors: Middle of the road best describes Artisan International
Fund Inv whose TheStreet.com Investment Rating is currently a C (Fair). The
fund currently has a performance rating of C (Fair) based on an average return
of 11.95% over the last three years and 4.24% over the last three months.
Factored into the performance evaluation is an expense ratio of 1.17% (low) and
a 2.0% back-end load levied at the time of sale.

The fund's risk rating is currently C+ (Fair). It carries a beta of 0.84, meaning
the fund's expected move will be 8.4% for every 10% move in the market.
Volatility, as measured by both the semi-deviation and a drawdown factor, is
considered low.

Mark L. Yockey has been running the fund for 20 years and currently
receives a manager quality ranking of 91 (0=worst, 99=best). If you desire an
average level of risk, then this fund may be an option.

Services Offered: Automated phone transactions, payroll deductions, bank draft
capabilities, an IRA investment plan, a 401K investment plan, a Keogh
investment plan and a systematic withdrawal plan.

Data Date	Investment Rating	Net Assets ($Mil)	NAV	Perfor-mance Rating/Pts	Total Return Y-T-D	Risk Rating/Pts
3-15	C	15,064	31.23	C / 4.9	4.24%	C+ / 6.9
2014	C	14,389	29.96	C / 4.7	-0.97%	C+ / 6.8
2013	C-	10,764	30.48	C+ / 5.7	25.18%	C- / 3.7
2012	C+	7,498	24.59	B / 7.8	25.39%	C- / 3.3
2011	D	6,151	19.83	D+ / 2.3	-7.26%	C- / 4.0
2010	E+	7,489	21.70	E / 0.5	5.91%	D+ / 2.7

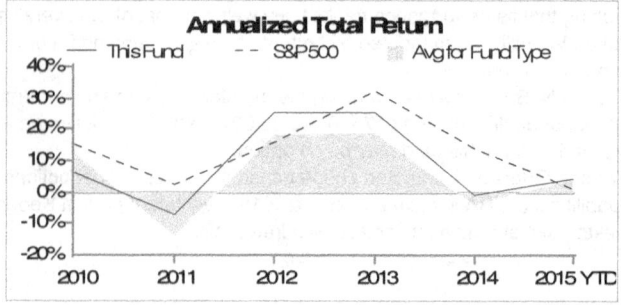

Artisan International Value Inv (ARTKX)   C+   Fair

Fund Family: Artisan Funds   **Phone:** (800) 344-1770
Address: P.O. Box 8412, Boston, MA 02266
Fund Type: FO - Foreign

Major Rating Factors: Middle of the road best describes Artisan International Value Inv whose TheStreet.com Investment Rating is currently a C+ (Fair). The fund currently has a performance rating of C+ (Fair) based on an average return of 14.06% over the last three years and 3.65% over the last three months. Factored into the performance evaluation is an expense ratio of 1.20% (average) and a 2.0% back-end load levied at the time of sale.

  The fund's risk rating is currently C+ (Fair). It carries a beta of 0.78, meaning the fund's expected move will be 7.8% for every 10% move in the market. Volatility, as measured by both the semi-deviation and a drawdown factor, is considered low.

  David Samra has been running the fund for 13 years and currently receives a manager quality ranking of 95 (0=worst, 99=best). If you desire an average level of risk, then this fund may be an option.

Services Offered: Automated phone transactions, payroll deductions, bank draft capabilities, an IRA investment plan, a 401K investment plan, a Keogh investment plan, wire transfers and a systematic withdrawal plan. However, the fund is currently closed to new investors.

Data Date	Investment Rating	Net Assets ($Mil)	NAV	Perfor- mance Rating/Pts	Total Return Y-T-D	Risk Rating/Pts
3-15	C+	8,894	35.46	C+ / 5.8	3.65%	C+ / 6.0
2014	C	8,865	34.21	C / 5.0	-0.59%	C+ / 6.2
2013	C+	8,565	36.77	C+ / 6.6	30.49%	C / 5.1
2012	A+	5,650	30.38	A / 9.3	22.82%	C / 4.9
2011	C-	3,451	25.09	C / 4.4	-7.14%	C / 4.7
2010	B+	3,081	27.11	B+ / 8.7	18.90%	C / 5.2

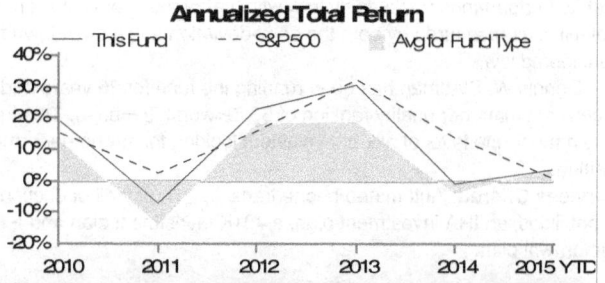

Artisan Mid Cap Value Inv (ARTQX)   C   Fair

Fund Family: Artisan Funds   **Phone:** (800) 344-1770
Address: P.O. Box 8412, Boston, MA 02266
Fund Type: MC - Mid Cap

Major Rating Factors: Middle of the road best describes Artisan Mid Cap Value Inv whose TheStreet.com Investment Rating is currently a C (Fair). The fund currently has a performance rating of C (Fair) based on an average return of 12.72% over the last three years and 2.03% over the last three months. Factored into the performance evaluation is an expense ratio of 1.19% (average).

  The fund's risk rating is currently C+ (Fair). It carries a beta of 0.95, meaning that its performance tracks fairly well with that of the overall stock market. Volatility, as measured by both the semi-deviation and a drawdown factor, is considered low.

  James C. Kieffer has been running the fund for 14 years and currently receives a manager quality ranking of 26 (0=worst, 99=best). If you desire an average level of risk, then this fund may be an option.

Services Offered: Automated phone transactions, payroll deductions, bank draft capabilities, an IRA investment plan, a 401K investment plan, a Keogh investment plan and a systematic withdrawal plan. However, the fund is currently closed to new investors.

Data Date	Investment Rating	Net Assets ($Mil)	NAV	Perfor- mance Rating/Pts	Total Return Y-T-D	Risk Rating/Pts
3-15	C	8,048	25.14	C / 5.3	2.03%	C+ / 5.7
2014	C-	8,817	24.64	C / 5.0	1.52%	C+ / 5.7
2013	A	10,039	27.00	B+ / 8.6	35.80%	C+ / 5.9
2012	A-	7,595	20.79	B- / 7.5	11.39%	C+ / 5.8
2011	A+	7,162	19.70	A / 9.4	6.42%	C / 5.2
2010	A-	6,327	20.08	B+ / 8.8	14.37%	C / 5.1

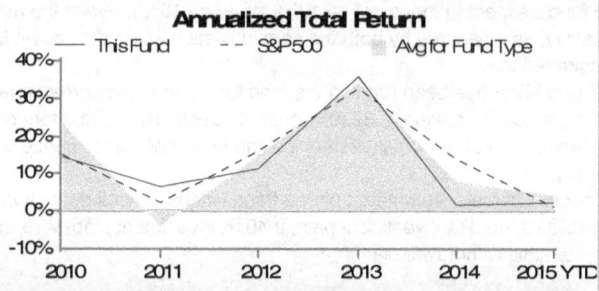

BlackRock Eq Dividend Inv A (MDDVX)   C   Fair

Fund Family: BlackRock Funds   **Phone:** (800) 441-7762
Address: c/o PFPC, Inc., Providence, RI 02940
Fund Type: IN - Income

Major Rating Factors: Middle of the road best describes BlackRock Eq Dividend Inv A whose TheStreet.com Investment Rating is currently a C (Fair). The fund currently has a performance rating of C- (Fair) based on an average return of 11.61% over the last three years and -1.08% over the last three months. Factored into the performance evaluation is an expense ratio of 0.95% (low) and a 5.3% front-end load that is levied at the time of purchase.

  The fund's risk rating is currently B- (Good). It carries a beta of 0.92, meaning that its performance tracks fairly well with that of the overall stock market. Volatility, as measured by both the semi-deviation and a drawdown factor, is considered low.

  Robert M. Shearer has been running the fund for 14 years and currently receives a manager quality ranking of 27 (0=worst, 99=best). If you desire an average level of risk, then this fund may be an option.

Services Offered: Automated phone transactions, payroll deductions, bank draft capabilities, an IRA investment plan, a 401K investment plan and a systematic withdrawal plan.

Data Date	Investment Rating	Net Assets ($Mil)	NAV	Perfor- mance Rating/Pts	Total Return Y-T-D	Risk Rating/Pts
3-15	C	7,825	24.63	C- / 4.0	-1.08%	B- / 7.5
2014	C+	8,484	24.90	C / 5.0	9.06%	B- / 7.6
2013	C+	10,965	24.28	C / 5.3	24.35%	C+ / 6.8
2012	C	9,157	19.89	C- / 3.9	11.92%	C+ / 6.7
2011	C+	6,765	18.15	C+ / 6.0	5.60%	C / 5.3
2010	C	4,724	17.52	D+ / 2.7	12.92%	C+ / 6.0

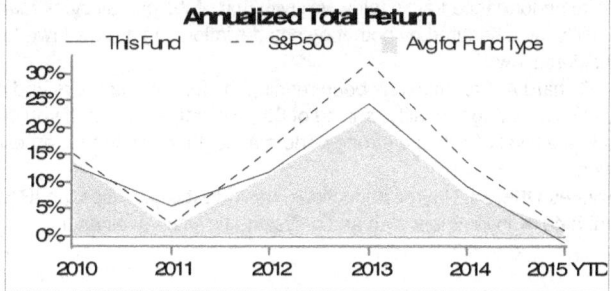

BlackRock Global Allocation Inv A (MDLOX) — D — Weak

Fund Family: BlackRock Funds **Phone:** (800) 441-7762
Address: c/o PFPC, Inc., Providence, RI 02940
Fund Type: GL - Global

Major Rating Factors: Disappointing performance is the major factor driving the D (Weak) TheStreet.com Investment Rating for BlackRock Global Allocation Inv A. The fund currently has a performance rating of D (Weak) based on an average return of 6.80% over the last three years and 2.68% over the last three months. Factored into the performance evaluation is an expense ratio of 1.13% (low) and a 5.3% front-end load that is levied at the time of purchase.

The fund's risk rating is currently C+ (Fair). It carries a beta of 1.03, meaning that its performance tracks fairly well with that of the overall stock market. Volatility, as measured by both the semi-deviation and a drawdown factor, is considered low.

Dennis W. Stattman has been running the fund for 26 years and currently receives a manager quality ranking of 33 (0=worst, 99=best). This fund offers only a moderate level of risk but investors looking for strong performance are still waiting.

Services Offered: Automated phone transactions, payroll deductions, bank draft capabilities, an IRA investment plan, a 401K investment plan and a systematic withdrawal plan.

Data Date	Investment Rating	Net Assets ($Mil)	NAV	Performance Rating/Pts	Total Return Y-T-D	Risk Rating/Pts
3-15	D	17,135	20.30	D / 1.6	2.68%	C+ / 6.9
2014	D	17,221	19.77	D / 1.7	1.87%	C+ / 6.9
2013	D+	19,299	21.33	D / 1.9	14.43%	C+ / 6.9
2012	D	17,292	19.74	E+ / 0.9	10.01%	B- / 7.0
2011	C-	17,029	18.16	D- / 1.2	-3.71%	B- / 7.2
2010	B-	16,633	19.42	C / 5.1	9.85%	B- / 7.6

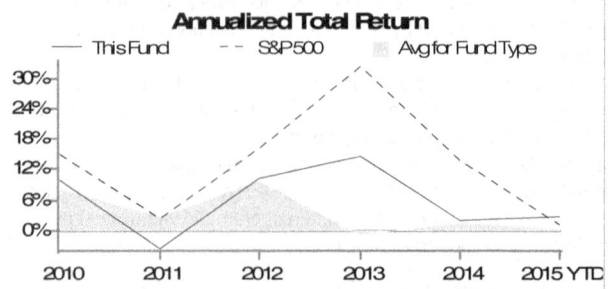
Annualized Total Return

BlackRock Strategic Inc Opps Inv A (BASIX) — D+ — Weak

Fund Family: BlackRock Funds **Phone:** (800) 441-7762
Address: c/o PFPC, Inc., Providence, RI 02940
Fund Type: AA - Asset Allocation

Major Rating Factors: Disappointing performance is the major factor driving the D+ (Weak) TheStreet.com Investment Rating for BlackRock Strategic Inc Opps Inv A. The fund currently has a performance rating of D- (Weak) based on an average return of 4.62% over the last three years and 1.49% over the last three months. Factored into the performance evaluation is an expense ratio of 1.18% (low) and a 4.0% front-end load that is levied at the time of purchase.

The fund's risk rating is currently B (Good). It carries a beta of 0.19, meaning the fund's expected move will be 1.9% for every 10% move in the market. Volatility, as measured by both the semi-deviation and a drawdown factor, is considered low.

Bob Miller has been running the fund for 4 years and currently receives a manager quality ranking of 87 (0=worst, 99=best). This fund offers only a moderate level of risk but investors looking for strong performance are still waiting.

Services Offered: Automated phone transactions, payroll deductions, bank draft capabilities, an IRA investment plan, a 401K investment plan, wire transfers and a systematic withdrawal plan.

Data Date	Investment Rating	Net Assets ($Mil)	NAV	Performance Rating/Pts	Total Return Y-T-D	Risk Rating/Pts
3-15	D+	5,995	10.22	D- / 1.0	1.49%	B / 8.6
2014	D+	4,042	10.11	D- / 1.0	3.59%	B / 8.3
2013	D	3,173	10.16	E+ / 0.7	3.01%	B- / 7.7
2012	C-	1,074	10.10	D / 1.7	9.64%	B- / 7.5
2011	B+	903	9.51	C- / 3.0	-0.98%	B+ / 9.9
2010	U	467	9.96	U / --	13.10%	U / --

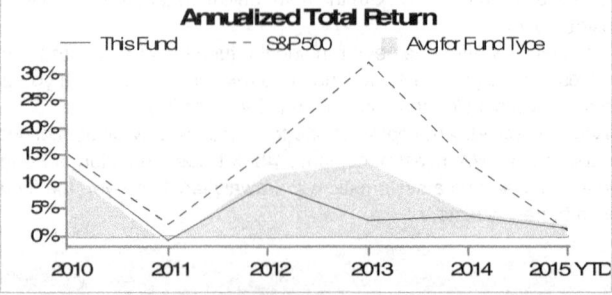
Annualized Total Return

CB Aggressive Growth A (SHRAX) — A+ — Excellent

Fund Family: Legg Mason Partners Funds **Phone:** (877) 534-4627
Address: 100 Light Street, Baltimore, MD 21202
Fund Type: AG - Aggressive Growth

Major Rating Factors: Exceptional performance is the major factor driving the A+ (Excellent) TheStreet.com Investment Rating for CB Aggressive Growth A. The fund currently has a performance rating of A (Excellent) based on an average return of 20.93% over the last three years and 3.01% over the last three months. Factored into the performance evaluation is an expense ratio of 1.15% (low) and a 5.8% front-end load that is levied at the time of purchase.

The fund's risk rating is currently C+ (Fair). It carries a beta of 1.06, meaning that its performance tracks fairly well with that of the overall stock market. Volatility, as measured by both the semi-deviation and a drawdown factor, is considered low.

Richard A. Freeman has been running the fund for 32 years and currently receives a manager quality ranking of 89 (0=worst, 99=best). If you desire only a moderate level of risk and strong performance, then this fund is an excellent option.

Services Offered: Payroll deductions, bank draft capabilities, an IRA investment plan, a 401K investment plan and a systematic withdrawal plan.

Data Date	Investment Rating	Net Assets ($Mil)	NAV	Performance Rating/Pts	Total Return Y-T-D	Risk Rating/Pts
3-15	A+	6,034	209.82	A / 9.4	3.01%	C+ / 6.6
2014	A+	5,666	203.68	A+ / 9.7	14.55%	C+ / 6.7
2013	A	4,405	181.37	A / 9.5	44.62%	C / 4.6
2012	B+	2,994	126.44	B+ / 8.6	18.53%	C- / 4.2
2011	B+	2,715	109.85	B+ / 8.3	1.41%	C / 4.4
2010	C+	2,996	110.87	C+ / 6.4	23.92%	C / 4.3

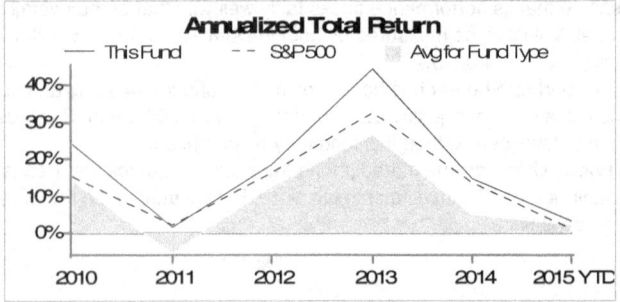
Annualized Total Return

Cohen & Steers Realty Shares (CSRSX)   B-   Good

Fund Family: Cohen & Steers Funds   **Phone:** (800) 330-7348
Address: 280 Park Avenue, New York, NY 10017
Fund Type: RE - Real Estate
Major Rating Factors: Exceptional performance is the major factor driving the B- (Good) TheStreet.com Investment Rating for Cohen & Steers Realty Shares. The fund currently has a performance rating of A (Excellent) based on an average return of 13.93% over the last three years and 5.14% over the last three months. Factored into the performance evaluation is an expense ratio of 0.97% (low).

The fund's risk rating is currently C- (Fair). It carries a beta of 1.05, meaning that its performance tracks fairly well with that of the overall stock market. Volatility, as measured by both the semi-deviation and a drawdown factor, is considered average.

Joseph M. Harvey has been running the fund for 10 years and currently receives a manager quality ranking of 56 (0=worst, 99=best). If you desire an average level of risk and strong performance, then this fund is a good option.
Services Offered: Automated phone transactions, bank draft capabilities and wire transfers.

Data Date	Investment Rating	Net Assets ($Mil)	NAV	Perfor- mance Rating/Pts	Total Return Y-T-D	Risk Rating/Pts
3-15	B-	6,506	80.43	A / 9.5	5.14%	C- / 3.7
2014	B-	6,339	76.86	A / 9.4	30.18%	C- / 3.6
2013	E+	5,158	62.82	D / 1.6	3.09%	D+ / 2.9
2012	B	4,879	64.57	A / 9.5	15.72%	C- / 3.1
2011	C	3,671	60.83	A+ / 9.6	6.18%	D- / 1.0
2010	C+	2,833	58.46	A / 9.5	27.14%	D- / 1.5

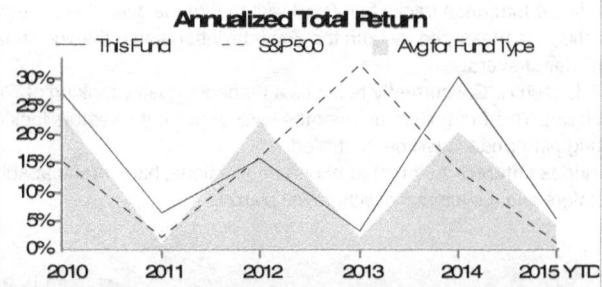

Annualized Total Return

Davis New York Venture Fund A (NYVTX)   C-   Fair

Fund Family: Davis Funds   **Phone:** (800) 279-0279
Address: 2949 East Elvira Road, Tuscon, AZ 85756
Fund Type: GR - Growth
Major Rating Factors: Middle of the road best describes Davis New York Venture Fund A whose TheStreet.com Investment Rating is currently a C- (Fair). The fund currently has a performance rating of C+ (Fair) based on an average return of 13.89% over the last three years and 1.98% over the last three months. Factored into the performance evaluation is an expense ratio of 0.86% (very low) and a 4.8% front-end load that is levied at the time of purchase.

The fund's risk rating is currently C (Fair). It carries a beta of 1.07, meaning that its performance tracks fairly well with that of the overall stock market. Volatility, as measured by both the semi-deviation and a drawdown factor, is considered average.

Christopher C. Davis has been running the fund for 20 years and currently receives a manager quality ranking of 25 (0=worst, 99=best). If you desire an average level of risk, then this fund may be an option.
Services Offered: Automated phone transactions, payroll deductions, bank draft capabilities, an IRA investment plan, a 401K investment plan and a systematic withdrawal plan.

Data Date	Investment Rating	Net Assets ($Mil)	NAV	Perfor- mance Rating/Pts	Total Return Y-T-D	Risk Rating/Pts
3-15	C-	9,588	37.57	C+ / 5.6	1.98%	C / 5.0
2014	C-	9,963	36.84	C+ / 5.8	6.55%	C / 5.0
2013	C+	11,711	41.41	C+ / 6.2	34.56%	C / 5.4
2012	D-	10,814	34.78	D- / 1.5	12.73%	C / 5.2
2011	D+	14,056	32.50	C- / 3.1	-4.78%	C- / 4.2
2010	D+	20,100	34.34	D / 1.9	12.11%	C / 4.5

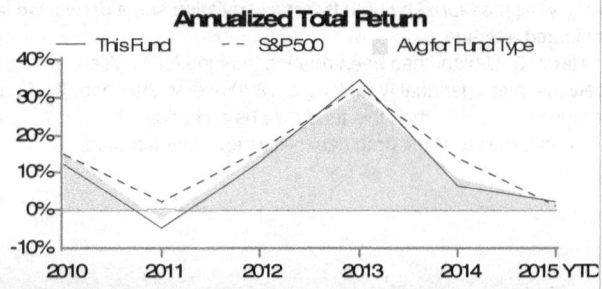

Annualized Total Return

DFA Emerging Markets Sm Cap Inst (DEMSX)   E+   Very Weak

Fund Family: Dimensional Investment Group   **Phone:** (800) 984-9472
Address: 1299 Ocean Avenue, Santa Monica, CA 90401
Fund Type: FO - Foreign
Major Rating Factors: Disappointing performance is the major factor driving the E+ (Very Weak) TheStreet.com Investment Rating for DFA Emerging Markets Sm Cap Inst. The fund currently has a performance rating of D- (Weak) based on an average return of 3.70% over the last three years and 3.42% over the last three months. Factored into the performance evaluation is an expense ratio of 0.72% (very low).

The fund's risk rating is currently C (Fair). It carries a beta of 0.80, meaning the fund's expected move will be 8.0% for every 10% move in the market. Volatility, as measured by both the semi-deviation and a drawdown factor, is considered average.

Karen E. Umland has been running the fund for 17 years and currently receives a manager quality ranking of 19 (0=worst, 99=best). This fund offers an average level of risk but investors looking for strong performance will be frustrated.
Services Offered: Automated phone transactions, bank draft capabilities and a systematic withdrawal plan.

Data Date	Investment Rating	Net Assets ($Mil)	NAV	Perfor- mance Rating/Pts	Total Return Y-T-D	Risk Rating/Pts
3-15	E+	5,189	20.57	D- / 1.1	3.42%	C / 5.4
2014	D-	4,772	19.89	D / 1.8	3.00%	C / 5.2
2013	E	3,992	20.11	E / 0.4	-1.38%	D+ / 2.5
2012	C+	3,461	21.17	B+ / 8.7	24.44%	D+ / 2.5
2011	B	1,716	17.83	A / 9.3	-22.62%	C- / 3.3
2010	B	1,918	24.06	A+ / 9.6	30.18%	D+ / 2.7

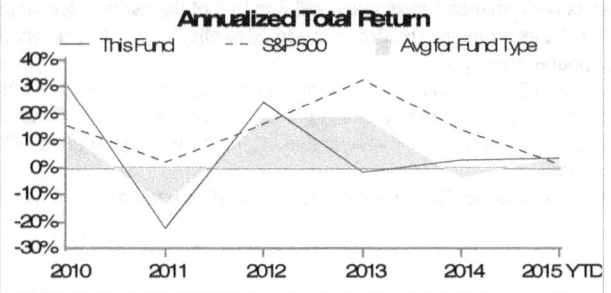

Annualized Total Return

DFA Emerging Markts Core Eqty Inst (DFCEX)   E+   Very Weak

Fund Family: Dimensional Investment Group   **Phone:** (800) 984-9472
Address: 1299 Ocean Avenue, Santa Monica, CA 90401
Fund Type: EM - Emerging Market
Major Rating Factors: Very poor performance is the major factor driving the E+
(Very Weak) TheStreet.com Investment Rating for DFA Emerging Markts Core
Eqty Inst. The fund currently has a performance rating of E+ (Very Weak) based
on an average return of 0.98% over the last three years and 1.96% over the last
three months. Factored into the performance evaluation is an expense ratio of
0.61% (very low).

The fund's risk rating is currently C (Fair). It carries a beta of 0.99, meaning
that its performance tracks fairly well with that of the overall stock market.
Volatility, as measured by both the semi-deviation and a drawdown factor, is
considered average.

Joseph H. Chi currently receives a manager quality ranking of 71 (0=worst,
99=best). This fund offers an average level of risk but investors looking for
strong performance will be frustrated.
Services Offered: Automated phone transactions, bank draft capabilities, wire
transfers and a systematic withdrawal plan.

Data Date	Investment Rating	Net Assets ($Mil)	NAV	Performance Rating/Pts	Total Return Y-T-D	Risk Rating/Pts
3-15	E+	16,162	19.29	E+ / 0.6	1.96%	C / 5.4
2014	E+	15,122	18.92	E+ / 0.8	-0.91%	C / 5.1
2013	E	13,152	19.46	E / 0.3	-2.64%	D+ / 2.8
2012	C-	9,739	20.40	C+ / 6.7	20.49%	D+ / 2.9
2011	B-	5,472	17.24	B / 8.2	-20.65%	C- / 3.6
2010	B	4,585	22.16	A- / 9.1	23.62%	C- / 3.2

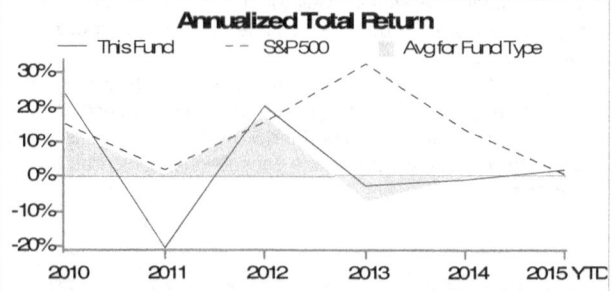

DFA International Sm Cap Val Inst (DISVX)   D+   Weak

Fund Family: Dimensional Investment Group   **Phone:** (800) 984-9472
Address: 1299 Ocean Avenue, Santa Monica, CA 90401
Fund Type: FO - Foreign
Major Rating Factors: DFA International Sm Cap Val Inst receives a
TheStreet.com Investment Rating of D+ (Weak). The fund currently has a
performance rating of C- (Fair) based on an average return of 11.31% over the
last three years and 4.68% over the last three months. Factored into the
performance evaluation is an expense ratio of 0.68% (very low).

The fund's risk rating is currently C (Fair). It carries a beta of 1.06, meaning
that its performance tracks fairly well with that of the overall stock market.
Volatility, as measured by both the semi-deviation and a drawdown factor, is
considered average.

Karen E. Umland has been running the fund for 17 years and currently
receives a manager quality ranking of 78 (0=worst, 99=best). If you desire an
average level of risk, then this fund may be an option.
Services Offered: Bank draft capabilities and wire transfers.

Data Date	Investment Rating	Net Assets ($Mil)	NAV	Performance Rating/Pts	Total Return Y-T-D	Risk Rating/Pts
3-15	D+	12,311	19.47	C- / 3.9	4.68%	C / 5.3
2014	D+	11,499	18.60	C- / 4.0	-4.99%	C / 5.1
2013	D+	11,533	20.35	C+ / 5.9	32.39%	C- / 3.1
2012	C	8,920	15.98	B / 8.0	22.26%	D+ / 2.7
2011	E+	6,915	13.58	D- / 1.2	-17.46%	C- / 3.4
2010	C+	8,359	17.20	B- / 7.0	18.10%	C- / 4.0

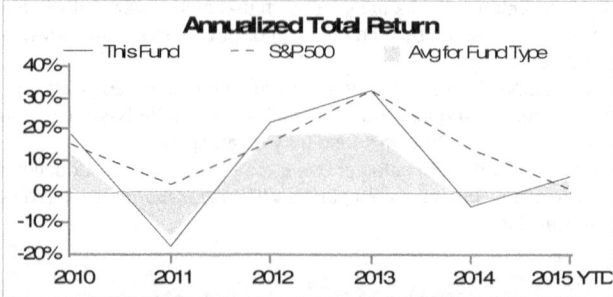

DFA International Small Co Inst (DFISX)   D-   Weak

Fund Family: Dimensional Investment Group   **Phone:** (800) 984-9472
Address: 1299 Ocean Avenue, Santa Monica, CA 90401
Fund Type: FO - Foreign
Major Rating Factors: Disappointing performance is the major factor driving the
D- (Weak) TheStreet.com Investment Rating for DFA International Small Co Inst.
The fund currently has a performance rating of D+ (Weak) based on an average
return of 8.81% over the last three years and 3.89% over the last three months.
Factored into the performance evaluation is an expense ratio of 0.53% (very
low).

The fund's risk rating is currently C (Fair). It carries a beta of 0.95, meaning
that its performance tracks fairly well with that of the overall stock market.
Volatility, as measured by both the semi-deviation and a drawdown factor, is
considered average.

Karen E. Umland has been running the fund for 17 years and currently
receives a manager quality ranking of 65 (0=worst, 99=best). This fund offers an
average level of risk but investors looking for strong performance will be
frustrated.
Services Offered: Bank draft capabilities and wire transfers.

Data Date	Investment Rating	Net Assets ($Mil)	NAV	Performance Rating/Pts	Total Return Y-T-D	Risk Rating/Pts
3-15	D-	8,805	17.64	D+ / 2.5	3.89%	C / 5.3
2014	D-	8,640	16.98	D+ / 2.8	-6.30%	C / 5.2
2013	D+	8,792	19.21	C / 4.9	27.44%	C- / 3.7
2012	C+	6,730	15.93	B / 7.8	18.86%	C- / 3.3
2011	D	5,463	13.84	C- / 3.0	-15.35%	C- / 3.9
2010	B-	5,974	17.18	B / 8.0	23.91%	C- / 3.9

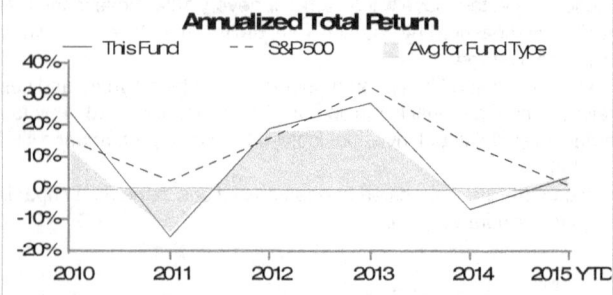

DFA Intl Core Equity Port Inst (DFIEX)   D   Weak

Fund Family: Dimensional Investment Group   **Phone:** (800) 984-9472
Address: 1299 Ocean Avenue, Santa Monica, CA 90401
Fund Type: FO - Foreign
Major Rating Factors: Disappointing performance is the major factor driving the D (Weak) TheStreet.com Investment Rating for DFA Intl Core Equity Port Inst. The fund currently has a performance rating of D+ (Weak) based on an average return of 8.34% over the last three years and 4.13% over the last three months. Factored into the performance evaluation is an expense ratio of 0.38% (very low).

The fund's risk rating is currently C+ (Fair). It carries a beta of 1.01, meaning that its performance tracks fairly well with that of the overall stock market. Volatility, as measured by both the semi-deviation and a drawdown factor, is considered low.

Joseph H. Chi currently receives a manager quality ranking of 49 (0=worst, 99=best). This fund offers only a moderate level of risk but investors looking for strong performance are still waiting.
Services Offered: Automated phone transactions, bank draft capabilities, wire transfers and a systematic withdrawal plan.

Data Date	Investment Rating	Net Assets ($Mil)	NAV	Perfor- mance Rating/Pts	Total Return Y-T-D	Risk Rating/Pts
3-15	D	13,369	12.17	D+ / 2.4	4.13%	C+ / 5.8
2014	D-	11,998	11.70	D+ / 2.4	-5.98%	C / 5.5
2013	D	10,220	12.81	C- / 4.0	23.43%	C- / 3.5
2012	D+	6,936	10.66	C / 5.5	18.74%	C- / 3.3
2011	D-	5,089	9.26	D- / 1.3	-15.11%	C- / 3.9
2010	C-	5,222	11.26	C- / 3.5	13.91%	C- / 3.7

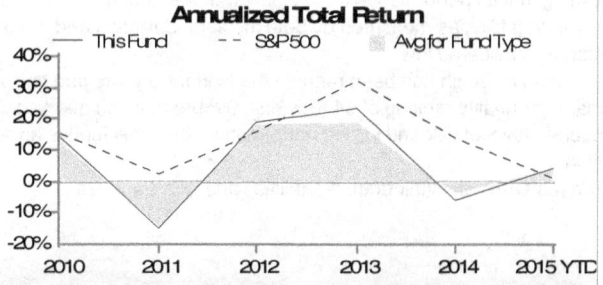

DFA Real Estate Securities Ptf Inst (DFREX)   B-   Good

Fund Family: Dimensional Investment Group   **Phone:** (800) 984-9472
Address: 1299 Ocean Avenue, Santa Monica, CA 90401
Fund Type: RE - Real Estate
Major Rating Factors: Exceptional performance is the major factor driving the B- (Good) TheStreet.com Investment Rating for DFA Real Estate Securities Ptf Inst. The fund currently has a performance rating of A (Excellent) based on an average return of 13.94% over the last three years and 4.76% over the last three months. Factored into the performance evaluation is an expense ratio of 0.19% (very low).

The fund's risk rating is currently C- (Fair). It carries a beta of 1.08, meaning that its performance tracks fairly well with that of the overall stock market. Volatility, as measured by both the semi-deviation and a drawdown factor, is considered average.

Bhanu P. Singh has been running the fund for 3 years and currently receives a manager quality ranking of 49 (0=worst, 99=best). If you desire an average level of risk and strong performance, then this fund is a good option.
Services Offered: Bank draft capabilities and wire transfers.

Data Date	Investment Rating	Net Assets ($Mil)	NAV	Perfor- mance Rating/Pts	Total Return Y-T-D	Risk Rating/Pts
3-15	B-	7,216	34.34	A / 9.4	4.76%	C- / 3.7
2014	B-	6,874	33.07	A / 9.5	31.11%	C- / 3.8
2013	E+	4,581	25.93	D / 1.7	1.39%	C- / 3.2
2012	A	3,835	26.34	A+ / 9.8	17.48%	C- / 3.9
2011	C+	3,100	23.09	A+ / 9.7	8.95%	D- / 1.5
2010	C	2,727	21.56	A- / 9.2	28.67%	E+ / 0.8

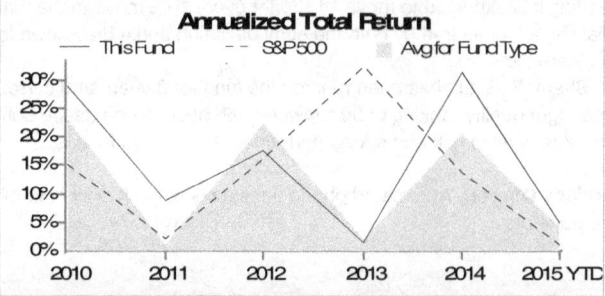

DFA TA US Core Equity 2 Inst (DFTCX)   A+   Excellent

Fund Family: Dimensional Investment Group   **Phone:** (800) 984-9472
Address: 1299 Ocean Avenue, Santa Monica, CA 90401
Fund Type: GR - Growth
Major Rating Factors: Strong performance is the major factor driving the A+ (Excellent) TheStreet.com Investment Rating for DFA TA US Core Equity 2 Inst. The fund currently has a performance rating of B+ (Good) based on an average return of 17.24% over the last three years and 2.21% over the last three months. Factored into the performance evaluation is an expense ratio of 0.24% (very low).

The fund's risk rating is currently C+ (Fair). It carries a beta of 1.10, meaning it is expected to move 11.0% for every 10% move in the market. Volatility, as measured by both the semi-deviation and a drawdown factor, is considered low.

Bhanu P. Singh has been running the fund for 3 years and currently receives a manager quality ranking of 59 (0=worst, 99=best). If you desire only a moderate level of risk and strong performance, then this fund is an excellent option.
Services Offered: N/A

Data Date	Investment Rating	Net Assets ($Mil)	NAV	Perfor- mance Rating/Pts	Total Return Y-T-D	Risk Rating/Pts
3-15	A+	5,462	14.53	B+ / 8.8	2.21%	C+ / 6.9
2014	A	5,191	14.26	B+ / 8.9	9.56%	C+ / 6.9
2013	A-	4,372	13.39	A- / 9.0	37.55%	C / 4.8
2012	B	2,962	9.97	B+ / 8.9	17.93%	C- / 3.6
2011	C-	2,458	8.62	B- / 7.5	-1.96%	D- / 1.5
2010	C-	2,277	8.92	B / 8.0	21.67%	E- / 0.2

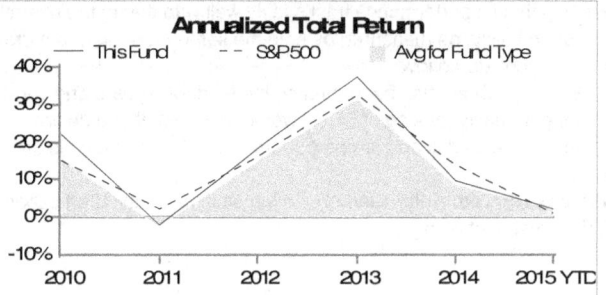

DFA US Core Equity 1 Ptf Inst (DFEOX)   A+   Excellent

Fund Family: Dimensional Investment Group   **Phone:** (800) 984-9472
Address: 1299 Ocean Avenue, Santa Monica, CA 90401
Fund Type: IN - Income

Major Rating Factors: Strong performance is the major factor driving the A+ (Excellent) TheStreet.com Investment Rating for DFA US Core Equity 1 Ptf Inst. The fund currently has a performance rating of B+ (Good) based on an average return of 16.93% over the last three years and 2.23% over the last three months. Factored into the performance evaluation is an expense ratio of 0.19% (very low).

The fund's risk rating is currently B- (Good). It carries a beta of 1.06, meaning that its performance tracks fairly well with that of the overall stock market. Volatility, as measured by both the semi-deviation and a drawdown factor, is considered low.

Bhanu P. Singh has been running the fund for 3 years and currently receives a manager quality ranking of 64 (0=worst, 99=best). If you desire only a moderate level of risk and strong performance, then this fund is an excellent option.

Services Offered: Bank draft capabilities and wire transfers.

Data Date	Investment Rating	Net Assets ($Mil)	NAV	Performance Rating/Pts	Total Return Y-T-D	Risk Rating/Pts
3-15	A+	12,357	18.26	B+ / 8.7	2.23%	B- / 7.0
2014	A	11,383	17.92	B+ / 8.8	10.52%	B- / 7.0
2013	A-	8,261	16.54	B+ / 8.9	36.60%	C / 5.2
2012	A-	5,140	12.35	B+ / 8.5	16.91%	C / 4.9
2011	B-	3,843	10.76	B / 7.8	-0.64%	C / 4.3
2010	B	3,222	11.00	B- / 7.5	20.11%	C / 4.8

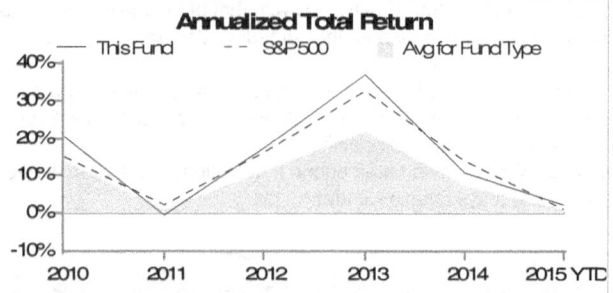

DFA US Core Equity 2 Ptf Inst (DFQTX)   A+   Excellent

Fund Family: Dimensional Investment Group   **Phone:** (800) 984-9472
Address: 1299 Ocean Avenue, Santa Monica, CA 90401
Fund Type: IN - Income

Major Rating Factors: Strong performance is the major factor driving the A+ (Excellent) TheStreet.com Investment Rating for DFA US Core Equity 2 Ptf Inst. The fund currently has a performance rating of B+ (Good) based on an average return of 17.22% over the last three years and 2.14% over the last three months. Factored into the performance evaluation is an expense ratio of 0.22% (very low).

The fund's risk rating is currently B- (Good). It carries a beta of 1.10, meaning it is expected to move 11.0% for every 10% move in the market. Volatility, as measured by both the semi-deviation and a drawdown factor, is considered low.

Bhanu P. Singh has been running the fund for 3 years and currently receives a manager quality ranking of 59 (0=worst, 99=best). If you desire only a moderate level of risk and strong performance, then this fund is an excellent option.

Services Offered: Automated phone transactions, bank draft capabilities and wire transfers.

Data Date	Investment Rating	Net Assets ($Mil)	NAV	Performance Rating/Pts	Total Return Y-T-D	Risk Rating/Pts
3-15	A+	14,374	17.82	B+ / 8.7	2.14%	B- / 7.0
2014	A	13,377	17.50	B+ / 8.9	9.32%	C+ / 6.9
2013	A-	10,717	16.37	A- / 9.1	37.76%	C / 4.8
2012	A-	7,195	12.18	B+ / 8.9	18.08%	C / 4.4
2011	C+	5,871	10.59	B / 7.6	-2.09%	C- / 3.8
2010	B	5,489	10.97	B / 7.8	21.81%	C / 4.5

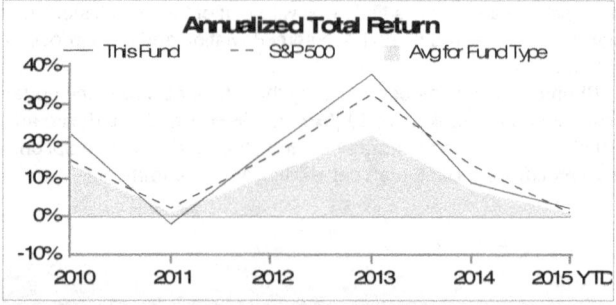

DFA US Large Company Portfolio Inst (DFUSX)   A   Excellent

Fund Family: Dimensional Investment Group   **Phone:** (800) 984-9472
Address: 1299 Ocean Avenue, Santa Monica, CA 90401
Fund Type: GR - Growth

Major Rating Factors: Strong performance is the major factor driving the A (Excellent) TheStreet.com Investment Rating for DFA US Large Company Portfolio Inst. The fund currently has a performance rating of B (Good) based on an average return of 16.00% over the last three years and 0.96% over the last three months. Factored into the performance evaluation is an expense ratio of 0.08% (very low).

The fund's risk rating is currently B- (Good). It carries a beta of 1.00, meaning that its performance tracks fairly well with that of the overall stock market. Volatility, as measured by both the semi-deviation and a drawdown factor, is considered low.

Bhanu P. Singh has been running the fund for 3 years and currently receives a manager quality ranking of 65 (0=worst, 99=best). If you desire only a moderate level of risk and strong performance, then this fund is an excellent option.

Services Offered: Automated phone transactions, bank draft capabilities and a 401K investment plan.

Data Date	Investment Rating	Net Assets ($Mil)	NAV	Performance Rating/Pts	Total Return Y-T-D	Risk Rating/Pts
3-15	A	5,775	16.31	B / 8.2	0.96%	B- / 7.3
2014	A+	5,764	16.22	B+ / 8.9	13.53%	B- / 7.4
2013	A	5,166	14.56	B / 8.2	32.33%	C+ / 6.1
2012	A	4,051	11.22	B- / 7.4	15.82%	C+ / 6.2
2011	C	3,761	9.90	B- / 7.3	2.10%	C- / 3.2
2010	D	3,860	9.90	C / 4.6	15.00%	E+ / 0.8

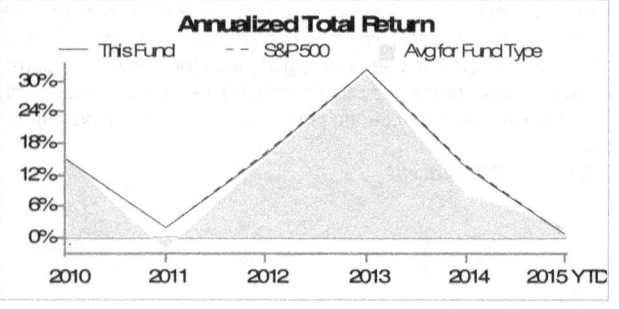

DFA US Micro Cap Portfolio Inst (DFSCX)   B+   Good

Fund Family: Dimensional Investment Group   **Phone:** (800) 984-9472
Address: 1299 Ocean Avenue, Santa Monica, CA 90401
Fund Type: SC - Small Cap

Major Rating Factors: Strong performance is the major factor driving the B+ (Good) TheStreet.com Investment Rating for DFA US Micro Cap Portfolio Inst. The fund currently has a performance rating of B+ (Good) based on an average return of 17.49% over the last three years and 3.13% over the last three months. Factored into the performance evaluation is an expense ratio of 0.53% (very low).

The fund's risk rating is currently C+ (Fair). It carries a beta of 1.03, meaning that its performance tracks fairly well with that of the overall stock market. Volatility, as measured by both the semi-deviation and a drawdown factor, is considered low.

Bhanu P. Singh has been running the fund for 3 years and currently receives a manager quality ranking of 74 (0=worst, 99=best). If you desire only a moderate level of risk and strong performance, then this fund is an excellent option.

Services Offered: Bank draft capabilities and wire transfers.

Data Date	Investment Rating	Net Assets ($Mil)	NAV	Performance Rating/Pts	Total Return Y-T-D	Risk Rating/Pts
3-15	B+	5,263	19.96	B+ / 8.9	3.13%	C+ / 5.8
2014	B+	5,092	19.37	B+ / 8.4	2.92%	C+ / 5.8
2013	B+	4,911	20.11	A+ / 9.7	45.06%	C- / 3.9
2012	B+	3,537	14.60	A / 9.5	18.24%	C- / 3.6
2011	C+	3,225	13.22	B+ / 8.5	-3.25%	D+ / 2.5
2010	B+	3,488	13.77	A+ / 9.7	31.29%	C- / 3.7

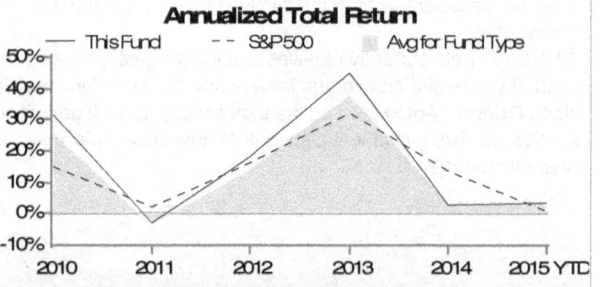

DFA US Small Cap Port Inst (DFSTX)   A-   Excellent

Fund Family: Dimensional Investment Group   **Phone:** (800) 984-9472
Address: 1299 Ocean Avenue, Santa Monica, CA 90401
Fund Type: SC - Small Cap

Major Rating Factors: Exceptional performance is the major factor driving the A- (Excellent) TheStreet.com Investment Rating for DFA US Small Cap Port Inst. The fund currently has a performance rating of A- (Excellent) based on an average return of 17.52% over the last three years and 3.99% over the last three months. Factored into the performance evaluation is an expense ratio of 0.37% (very low).

The fund's risk rating is currently C+ (Fair). It carries a beta of 0.98, meaning that its performance tracks fairly well with that of the overall stock market. Volatility, as measured by both the semi-deviation and a drawdown factor, is considered low.

Bhanu P. Singh has been running the fund for 3 years and currently receives a manager quality ranking of 80 (0=worst, 99=best). If you desire only a moderate level of risk and strong performance, then this fund is an excellent option.

Services Offered: Bank draft capabilities and wire transfers.

Data Date	Investment Rating	Net Assets ($Mil)	NAV	Performance Rating/Pts	Total Return Y-T-D	Risk Rating/Pts
3-15	A-	10,590	32.33	A- / 9.1	3.99%	C+ / 5.9
2014	B+	9,666	31.15	B+ / 8.4	4.44%	C+ / 6.0
2013	B+	8,139	31.00	A / 9.5	42.21%	C- / 3.8
2012	B+	4,719	22.67	A / 9.5	18.39%	C- / 3.5
2011	B-	3,817	20.52	A- / 9.2	-3.15%	D+ / 2.9
2010	B+	3,825	21.36	A / 9.5	30.70%	C- / 4.0

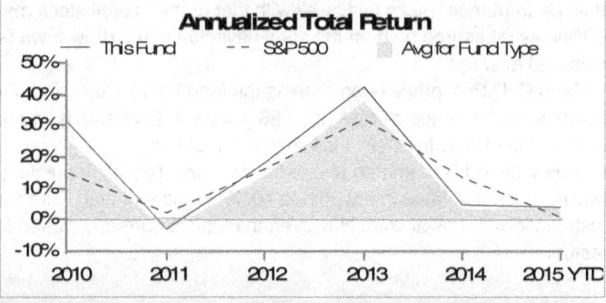

DFA US Small Cap Value I Inst (DFSVX)   B+   Good

Fund Family: Dimensional Investment Group   **Phone:** (800) 984-9472
Address: 1299 Ocean Avenue, Santa Monica, CA 90401
Fund Type: SC - Small Cap

Major Rating Factors: Strong performance is the major factor driving the B+ (Good) TheStreet.com Investment Rating for DFA US Small Cap Value I Inst. The fund currently has a performance rating of B+ (Good) based on an average return of 17.46% over the last three years and 2.44% over the last three months. Factored into the performance evaluation is an expense ratio of 0.53% (very low).

The fund's risk rating is currently C+ (Fair). It carries a beta of 1.02, meaning that its performance tracks fairly well with that of the overall stock market. Volatility, as measured by both the semi-deviation and a drawdown factor, is considered low.

Henry F. Gray has been running the fund for 3 years and currently receives a manager quality ranking of 75 (0=worst, 99=best). If you desire only a moderate level of risk and strong performance, then this fund is an excellent option.

Services Offered: Bank draft capabilities and wire transfers.

Data Date	Investment Rating	Net Assets ($Mil)	NAV	Performance Rating/Pts	Total Return Y-T-D	Risk Rating/Pts
3-15	B+	12,330	35.82	B+ / 8.6	2.44%	C+ / 5.8
2014	B+	11,681	34.97	B+ / 8.5	3.48%	C+ / 5.9
2013	B	10,249	35.41	A / 9.4	42.38%	C- / 3.1
2012	B-	7,044	26.21	A+ / 9.6	21.72%	D+ / 2.6
2011	C	6,451	23.16	B / 8.0	-7.55%	D / 2.2
2010	B	7,335	25.57	A / 9.5	30.90%	C- / 3.4

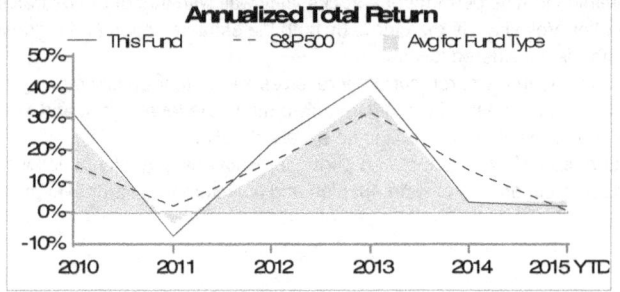

Dodge & Cox Global Stock (DODWX)   C+   Fair

Fund Family: Dodge & Cox   **Phone:** (800) 621-3979
Address: 555 California Street, San Francisco, CA 94104
Fund Type: GL - Global

Major Rating Factors: Middle of the road best describes Dodge & Cox Global Stock whose TheStreet.com Investment Rating is currently a C+ (Fair). The fund currently has a performance rating of C+ (Fair) based on an average return of 15.42% over the last three years and 1.44% over the last three months. Factored into the performance evaluation is an expense ratio of 0.65% (very low).

The fund's risk rating is currently C+ (Fair). It carries a beta of 0.83, meaning the fund's expected move will be 8.3% for every 10% move in the market. Volatility, as measured by both the semi-deviation and a drawdown factor, is considered low.

Charles F. Pohl currently receives a manager quality ranking of 96 (0=worst, 99=best). If you desire an average level of risk, then this fund may be an option.
Services Offered: Automated phone transactions, payroll deductions, bank draft capabilities, an IRA investment plan, a 401K investment plan, wire transfers and a systematic withdrawal plan.

Data Date	Investment Rating	Net Assets ($Mil)	NAV	Performance Rating/Pts	Total Return Y-T-D	Risk Rating/Pts
3-15	C+	6,260	12.00	C+ / 6.8	1.44%	C+ / 6.1
2014	B	5,895	11.83	B- / 7.4	6.95%	C+ / 6.0
2013	C+	3,712	11.48	C+ / 6.8	33.17%	C- / 4.1
2012	C	2,695	8.99	B- / 7.2	21.11%	C- / 3.1
2011	D	1,873	7.68	C / 4.8	-11.39%	D- / 1.3
2010	U	1,518	8.90	U / --	13.51%	U / --

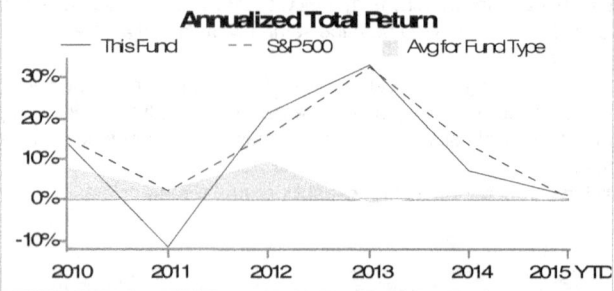

Dodge & Cox International Stock (DODFX)   C-   Fair

Fund Family: Dodge & Cox   **Phone:** (800) 621-3979
Address: 555 California Street, San Francisco, CA 94104
Fund Type: FO - Foreign

Major Rating Factors: Middle of the road best describes Dodge & Cox International Stock whose TheStreet.com Investment Rating is currently a C- (Fair). The fund currently has a performance rating of C (Fair) based on an average return of 12.25% over the last three years and 4.20% over the last three months. Factored into the performance evaluation is an expense ratio of 0.64% (very low).

The fund's risk rating is currently C (Fair). It carries a beta of 1.01, meaning that its performance tracks fairly well with that of the overall stock market. Volatility, as measured by both the semi-deviation and a drawdown factor, is considered average.

Mario C. DiPrisco has been running the fund for 11 years and currently receives a manager quality ranking of 86 (0=worst, 99=best). If you desire an average level of risk, then this fund may be an option.
Services Offered: Automated phone transactions, payroll deductions, bank draft capabilities, an IRA investment plan, a 401K investment plan, wire transfers and a systematic withdrawal plan. However, the fund is currently closed to new investors.

Data Date	Investment Rating	Net Assets ($Mil)	NAV	Performance Rating/Pts	Total Return Y-T-D	Risk Rating/Pts
3-15	C-	68,696	43.88	C / 4.9	4.20%	C / 5.4
2014	D+	64,040	42.11	C / 4.4	0.08%	C / 5.3
2013	D	52,538	43.04	C / 4.7	26.31%	C- / 3.3
2012	C	40,556	34.64	B- / 7.0	21.03%	C- / 3.2
2011	D-	37,795	29.24	D / 1.9	-15.97%	C- / 3.9
2010	D+	41,949	35.71	C- / 3.6	13.69%	C- / 3.4

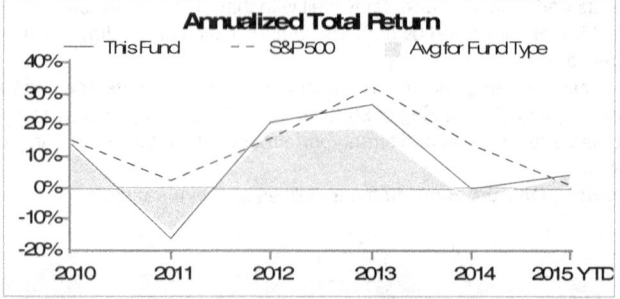

Dodge & Cox Stk Fund (DODGX)   A   Excellent

Fund Family: Dodge & Cox   **Phone:** (800) 621-3979
Address: 555 California Street, San Francisco, CA 94104
Fund Type: GI - Growth and Income

Major Rating Factors: Strong performance is the major factor driving the A (Excellent) TheStreet.com Investment Rating for Dodge & Cox Stk Fund. The fund currently has a performance rating of B+ (Good) based on an average return of 18.20% over the last three years and -1.19% over the last three months. Factored into the performance evaluation is an expense ratio of 0.52% (very low).

The fund's risk rating is currently B- (Good). It carries a beta of 1.08, meaning that its performance tracks fairly well with that of the overall stock market. Volatility, as measured by both the semi-deviation and a drawdown factor, is considered low.

C. Bryan Cameron currently receives a manager quality ranking of 73 (0=worst, 99=best). If you desire only a moderate level of risk and strong performance, then this fund is an excellent option.
Services Offered: Automated phone transactions, payroll deductions, bank draft capabilities, an IRA investment plan and a systematic withdrawal plan.

Data Date	Investment Rating	Net Assets ($Mil)	NAV	Performance Rating/Pts	Total Return Y-T-D	Risk Rating/Pts
3-15	A	60,672	176.55	B+ / 8.5	-1.19%	B- / 7.0
2014	A+	60,260	180.94	A+ / 9.6	10.40%	B- / 7.1
2013	A	53,874	168.87	A / 9.5	40.55%	C / 5.0
2012	B+	39,841	121.90	B+ / 8.6	22.01%	C / 4.5
2011	C-	36,876	101.64	C / 4.8	-4.08%	C- / 4.0
2010	D	41,481	107.76	D / 2.1	13.49%	C- / 4.0

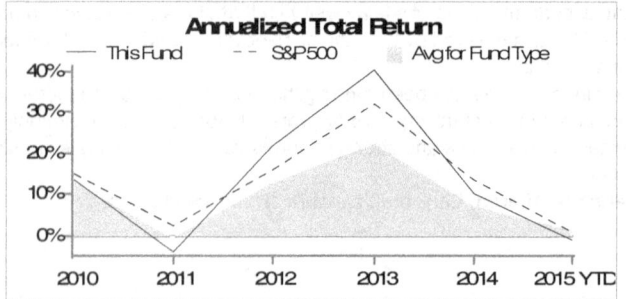

Emerging Markets Growth (EMRGX)   E   Very Weak

Fund Family: American Funds   **Phone:** (800) 421-0180
Address: 333 South Hope Street, Los Angeles, CA 90071
Fund Type: EM - Emerging Market
Major Rating Factors: Very poor performance is the major factor driving the E (Very Weak) TheStreet.com Investment Rating for Emerging Markets Growth. The fund currently has a performance rating of E (Very Weak) based on an average return of -1.58% over the last three years and 1.77% over the last three months. Factored into the performance evaluation is an expense ratio of 0.77% (very low).

The fund's risk rating is currently C (Fair). It carries a beta of 0.94, meaning that its performance tracks fairly well with that of the overall stock market. Volatility, as measured by both the semi-deviation and a drawdown factor, is considered average.

Christopher K. Choe currently receives a manager quality ranking of 34 (0=worst, 99=best). This fund offers an average level of risk but investors looking for strong performance will be frustrated.
Services Offered: Bank draft capabilities.

Data Date	Investment Rating	Net Assets ($Mil)	NAV	Performance Rating/Pts	Total Return Y-T-D	Risk Rating/Pts
3-15	E	7,195	6.90	E / 0.4	1.77%	C / 4.4
2014	E	7,195	6.78	E / 0.3	-7.52%	C- / 4.1
2013	E	1	7.77	E / 0.3	0.43%	C- / 3.1
2012	E	11,624	8.15	D- / 1.4	14.18%	D- / 1.4
2011	E+	14,151	7.36	D+ / 2.4	-25.43%	D / 1.9

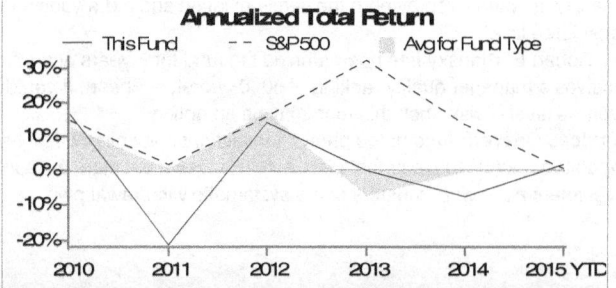

Fairholme (FAIRX)   E   Very Weak

Fund Family: Fairholme Capital Management LLC   **Phone:** (866) 202-2263
Address: 4400 Biscayne Boulevard, Miami, FL 33137
Fund Type: GR - Growth
Major Rating Factors: Disappointing performance is the major factor driving the E (Very Weak) TheStreet.com Investment Rating for Fairholme. The fund currently has a performance rating of D (Weak) based on an average return of 10.21% over the last three years and -1.97% over the last three months. Factored into the performance evaluation is an expense ratio of 1.02% (low) and a 2.0% back-end load levied at the time of sale.

The fund's risk rating is currently C- (Fair). It carries a beta of 1.33, meaning it is expected to move 13.3% for every 10% move in the market. Volatility, as measured by both the semi-deviation and a drawdown factor, is considered average.

Bruce R. Berkowitz has been running the fund for 16 years and currently receives a manager quality ranking of 2 (0=worst, 99=best). This fund offers an average level of risk but investors looking for strong performance will be frustrated.
Services Offered: Automated phone transactions, payroll deductions, bank draft capabilities, an IRA investment plan and wire transfers.

Data Date	Investment Rating	Net Assets ($Mil)	NAV	Performance Rating/Pts	Total Return Y-T-D	Risk Rating/Pts
3-15	E	5,750	34.39	D / 2.2	-1.97%	C- / 3.2
2014	C	6,558	35.08	C+ / 6.5	-2.72%	C / 5.0
2013	D-	8,534	39.20	C / 4.6	35.54%	D / 1.9
2012	C-	7,253	31.44	C+ / 6.9	35.81%	D / 2.2
2011	E-	6,962	23.15	E- / 0.1	-32.42%	D / 2.2
2010	B+	18,838	35.58	A+ / 9.8	25.47%	C- / 4.0

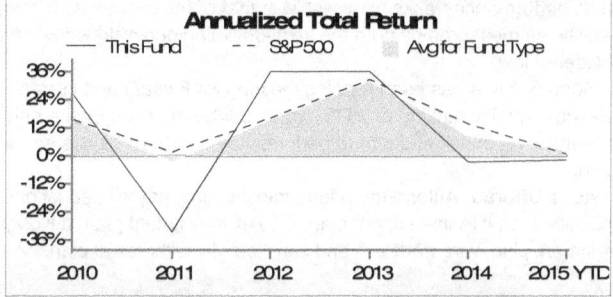

Fidelity Adv New Insights A (FNIAX)   C   Fair

Fund Family: Fidelity Advisor   **Phone:** (800) 522-7297
Address: 245 Summer Street, Boston, MA 02210
Fund Type: GR - Growth
Major Rating Factors: Middle of the road best describes Fidelity Adv New Insights A whose TheStreet.com Investment Rating is currently a C (Fair). The fund currently has a performance rating of C+ (Fair) based on an average return of 14.49% over the last three years and 2.76% over the last three months. Factored into the performance evaluation is an expense ratio of 0.92% (low) and a 5.8% front-end load that is levied at the time of purchase.

The fund's risk rating is currently C+ (Fair). It carries a beta of 0.92, meaning that its performance tracks fairly well with that of the overall stock market. Volatility, as measured by both the semi-deviation and a drawdown factor, is considered low.

William A. Danoff has been running the fund for 12 years and currently receives a manager quality ranking of 65 (0=worst, 99=best). If you desire an average level of risk, then this fund may be an option.
Services Offered: Automated phone transactions, payroll deductions, bank draft capabilities, an IRA investment plan, a 401K investment plan, a Keogh investment plan and a systematic withdrawal plan.

Data Date	Investment Rating	Net Assets ($Mil)	NAV	Performance Rating/Pts	Total Return Y-T-D	Risk Rating/Pts
3-15	C	8,519	27.25	C+ / 6.0	2.76%	C+ / 5.6
2014	C+	8,482	26.67	C+ / 6.5	9.20%	C+ / 5.6
2013	C+	8,646	26.32	C+ / 6.6	32.36%	C / 5.1
2012	C-	6,465	22.75	C- / 4.0	15.84%	C+ / 5.8
2011	C+	5,923	19.72	C / 5.1	-1.04%	C+ / 5.8
2010	C	5,582	19.96	C- / 3.1	16.07%	C+ / 5.9

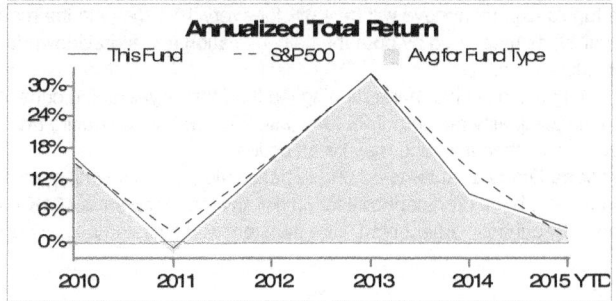

Fidelity Balanced Fd (FBALX)

B-   **Good**

Fund Family: Fidelity Investments   **Phone:** (800) 544-8544
Address: 245 Summer Street, Boston, MA 02210
Fund Type: BA - Balanced
Major Rating Factors: Fidelity Balanced Fd receives a TheStreet.com Investment Rating of B- (Good). The fund currently has a performance rating of C+ (Fair) based on an average return of 12.05% over the last three years and 2.24% over the last three months. Factored into the performance evaluation is an expense ratio of 0.56% (very low).

The fund's risk rating is currently B- (Good). It carries a beta of 1.15, meaning it is expected to move 11.5% for every 10% move in the market. Volatility, as measured by both the semi-deviation and a drawdown factor, is considered low.

Robert E. Stansky has been running the fund for 7 years and currently receives a manager quality ranking of 60 (0=worst, 99=best). If you desire an average level of risk, then this fund may be an option.

Services Offered: Automated phone transactions, payroll deductions, bank draft capabilities, an IRA investment plan, a 401K investment plan, a Keogh investment plan, wire transfers and a systematic withdrawal plan.

Data Date	Investment Rating	Net Assets ($Mil)	NAV	Performance Rating/Pts	Total Return Y-T-D	Risk Rating/Pts
3-15	B-	20,775	23.28	C+ / 5.7	2.24%	B- / 7.5
2014	C+	20,044	22.77	C / 5.5	10.37%	B- / 7.3
2013	B-	17,916	22.75	C / 4.7	20.50%	B- / 7.6
2012	B-	14,827	20.18	C / 5.3	12.90%	B- / 7.7
2011	B-	15,004	18.19	C+ / 6.8	1.68%	B- / 7.3
2010	C+	17,288	18.23	C+ / 6.0	13.76%	C+ / 6.4

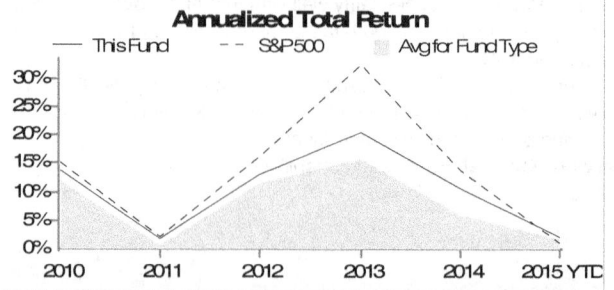
Annualized Total Return

Fidelity Blue Chip Growth Fd (FBGRX)

A   **Excellent**

Fund Family: Fidelity Investments   **Phone:** (800) 544-8544
Address: 245 Summer Street, Boston, MA 02210
Fund Type: GR - Growth
Major Rating Factors: Exceptional performance is the major factor driving the A (Excellent) TheStreet.com Investment Rating for Fidelity Blue Chip Growth Fd. The fund currently has a performance rating of A+ (Excellent) based on an average return of 18.79% over the last three years and 5.47% over the last three months. Factored into the performance evaluation is an expense ratio of 0.80% (very low).

The fund's risk rating is currently C+ (Fair). It carries a beta of 1.08, meaning that its performance tracks fairly well with that of the overall stock market. Volatility, as measured by both the semi-deviation and a drawdown factor, is considered low.

Sonu B. Kalra has been running the fund for 6 years and currently receives a manager quality ranking of 78 (0=worst, 99=best). If you desire only a moderate level of risk and strong performance, then this fund is an excellent option.

Services Offered: Automated phone transactions, payroll deductions, bank draft capabilities, an IRA investment plan, a 401K investment plan, a Keogh investment plan, wire transfers and a systematic withdrawal plan.

Data Date	Investment Rating	Net Assets ($Mil)	NAV	Performance Rating/Pts	Total Return Y-T-D	Risk Rating/Pts
3-15	A	14,299	72.16	A+ / 9.7	5.47%	C+ / 5.9
2014	A-	13,368	68.42	A+ / 9.8	14.60%	C+ / 5.7
2013	B+	11,347	63.37	A / 9.4	39.84%	C / 4.3
2012	B-	11,305	49.05	B / 7.8	17.77%	C- / 4.2
2011	A-	10,597	42.43	B+ / 8.7	-2.72%	C / 4.6
2010	B+	12,068	45.35	B+ / 8.6	19.61%	C / 4.6

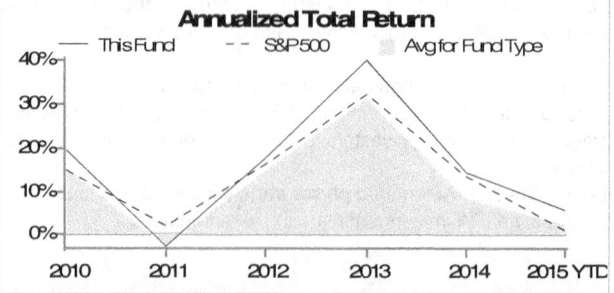
Annualized Total Return

Fidelity Capital and Income (FAGIX)

C-   **Fair**

Fund Family: Fidelity Investments   **Phone:** (800) 544-8544
Address: 245 Summer Street, Boston, MA 02210
Fund Type: GI - Growth and Income
Major Rating Factors: Middle of the road best describes Fidelity Capital and Income whose TheStreet.com Investment Rating is currently a C- (Fair). The fund currently has a performance rating of C- (Fair) based on an average return of 9.37% over the last three years and 4.01% over the last three months. Factored into the performance evaluation is an expense ratio of 0.71% (very low) and a 1.0% back-end load levied at the time of sale.

The fund's risk rating is currently C+ (Fair). It carries a beta of 0.40, meaning the fund's expected move will be 4.0% for every 10% move in the market. Volatility, as measured by both the semi-deviation and a drawdown factor, is considered low.

Mark J. Notkin has been running the fund for 12 years and currently receives a manager quality ranking of 89 (0=worst, 99=best). If you desire an average level of risk, then this fund may be an option.

Services Offered: Automated phone transactions, check writing, payroll deductions, bank draft capabilities, an IRA investment plan, a 401K investment plan, a Keogh investment plan, wire transfers and a systematic withdrawal plan.

Data Date	Investment Rating	Net Assets ($Mil)	NAV	Performance Rating/Pts	Total Return Y-T-D	Risk Rating/Pts
3-15	C-	10,985	9.97	C- / 3.9	4.01%	C+ / 6.5
2014	D+	10,388	9.68	C- / 3.3	6.14%	C+ / 6.5
2013	D	9,851	9.86	D / 2.2	9.71%	C / 5.2
2012	B+	9,657	9.50	B / 7.7	16.41%	C / 5.1
2011	A+	8,939	8.67	A+ / 9.8	-1.91%	C+ / 5.7
2010	A+	12,278	9.43	A+ / 9.8	17.13%	C+ / 6.4

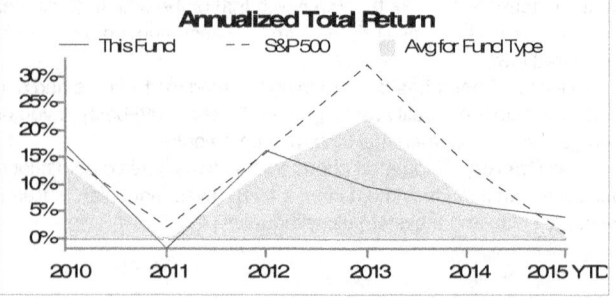
Annualized Total Return

Fidelity Capital Appreciation Fd (FDCAX)   A-   Excellent

Fund Family: Fidelity Investments   **Phone:** (800) 544-8544
Address: 245 Summer Street, Boston, MA 02210
Fund Type: GR - Growth
Major Rating Factors: Exceptional performance is the major factor driving the A- (Excellent) TheStreet.com Investment Rating for Fidelity Capital Appreciation Fd. The fund currently has a performance rating of A (Excellent) based on an average return of 17.88% over the last three years and 4.16% over the last three months. Factored into the performance evaluation is an expense ratio of 0.82% (very low).

The fund's risk rating is currently C+ (Fair). It carries a beta of 0.87, meaning the fund's expected move will be 8.7% for every 10% move in the market. Volatility, as measured by both the semi-deviation and a drawdown factor, is considered low.

J. Fergus Shiel has been running the fund for 10 years and currently receives a manager quality ranking of 90 (0=worst, 99=best). If you desire only a moderate level of risk and strong performance, then this fund is an excellent option.

Services Offered: Automated phone transactions, payroll deductions, bank draft capabilities, an IRA investment plan, a 401K investment plan, a Keogh investment plan and a systematic withdrawal plan.

Data Date	Investment Rating	Net Assets ($Mil)	NAV	Performance Rating/Pts	Total Return Y-T-D	Risk Rating/Pts
3-15	A-	6,285	37.53	A / 9.3	4.16%	C+ / 5.7
2014	B+	6,097	36.03	A / 9.5	10.84%	C / 5.4
2013	A	6,261	36.18	A- / 9.2	35.96%	C / 5.3
2012	A+	4,759	29.38	A- / 9.0	22.45%	C+ / 5.7
2011	B-	4,136	24.62	B / 7.7	-2.67%	C / 4.4
2010	C+	4,880	25.34	C+ / 6.3	18.34%	C / 4.4

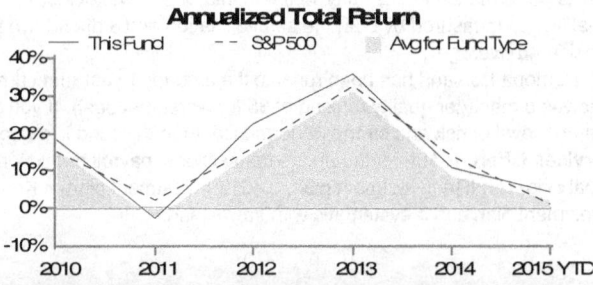

Fidelity Contrafund Fd (FCNTX)   B+   Good

Fund Family: Fidelity Investments   **Phone:** (800) 544-8544
Address: 245 Summer Street, Boston, MA 02210
Fund Type: GR - Growth
Major Rating Factors: Strong performance is the major factor driving the B+ (Good) TheStreet.com Investment Rating for Fidelity Contrafund Fd. The fund currently has a performance rating of B+ (Good) based on an average return of 15.64% over the last three years and 4.05% over the last three months. Factored into the performance evaluation is an expense ratio of 0.64% (very low).

The fund's risk rating is currently C+ (Fair). It carries a beta of 0.93, meaning that its performance tracks fairly well with that of the overall stock market. Volatility, as measured by both the semi-deviation and a drawdown factor, is considered low.

William A. Danoff has been running the fund for 25 years and currently receives a manager quality ranking of 74 (0=worst, 99=best). If you desire only a moderate level of risk and strong performance, then this fund is an excellent option.
Services Offered: Automated phone transactions, payroll deductions, bank draft capabilities, an IRA investment plan, a 401K investment plan, a Keogh investment plan and a systematic withdrawal plan.

Data Date	Investment Rating	Net Assets ($Mil)	NAV	Performance Rating/Pts	Total Return Y-T-D	Risk Rating/Pts
3-15	B+	77,111	100.96	B+ / 8.3	4.05%	C+ / 6.5
2014	B+	76,030	97.97	B / 8.0	9.56%	C+ / 6.4
2013	A	75,076	96.14	B+ / 8.6	34.15%	C+ / 5.8
2012	B+	58,819	77.57	B- / 7.0	16.24%	C+ / 5.8
2011	B+	56,074	67.46	B- / 7.2	-0.12%	C+ / 5.7
2010	C+	61,431	67.73	C+ / 5.7	16.93%	C / 5.5

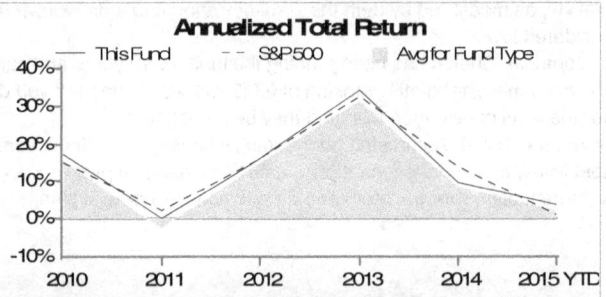

Fidelity Diversified Intl Fd (FDIVX)   C-   Fair

Fund Family: Fidelity Investments   **Phone:** (800) 544-8544
Address: 245 Summer Street, Boston, MA 02210
Fund Type: FO - Foreign
Major Rating Factors: Middle of the road best describes Fidelity Diversified Intl Fd whose TheStreet.com Investment Rating is currently a C- (Fair). The fund currently has a performance rating of C (Fair) based on an average return of 10.97% over the last three years and 6.36% over the last three months. Factored into the performance evaluation is an expense ratio of 0.91% (low) and a 1.0% back-end load levied at the time of sale.

The fund's risk rating is currently C+ (Fair). It carries a beta of 0.89, meaning the fund's expected move will be 8.9% for every 10% move in the market. Volatility, as measured by both the semi-deviation and a drawdown factor, is considered low.

William J. Bower has been running the fund for 14 years and currently receives a manager quality ranking of 86 (0=worst, 99=best). If you desire an average level of risk, then this fund may be an option.
Services Offered: Automated phone transactions, payroll deductions, bank draft capabilities, an IRA investment plan, a 401K investment plan, a Keogh investment plan and a systematic withdrawal plan.

Data Date	Investment Rating	Net Assets ($Mil)	NAV	Performance Rating/Pts	Total Return Y-T-D	Risk Rating/Pts
3-15	C-	14,143	36.64	C / 4.6	6.36%	C+ / 6.0
2014	D+	13,425	34.45	C- / 3.4	-3.20%	C+ / 6.0
2013	D	14,907	36.91	C / 4.5	25.19%	C- / 3.9
2012	D	13,545	29.94	C- / 3.5	19.41%	C- / 3.7
2011	D-	16,185	25.52	E+ / 0.7	-13.78%	C / 4.3
2010	E+	26,013	30.15	E+ / 0.9	9.65%	C- / 3.1

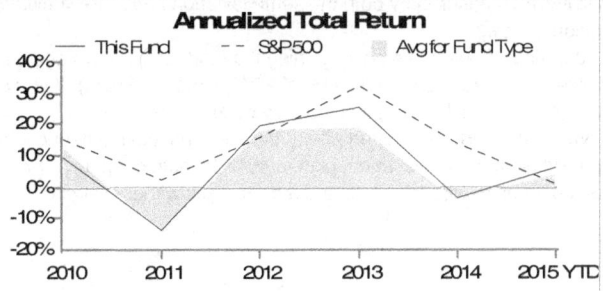

Fidelity Dividend Growth Fd (FDGFX)

C+   **Fair**

Fund Family: Fidelity Investments   **Phone:** (800) 544-8544
Address: 245 Summer Street, Boston, MA 02210
Fund Type: GR - Growth
Major Rating Factors: Strong performance is the major factor driving the C+ (Fair) TheStreet.com Investment Rating for Fidelity Dividend Growth Fd. The fund currently has a performance rating of B- (Good) based on an average return of 14.97% over the last three years and 1.17% over the last three months. Factored into the performance evaluation is an expense ratio of 0.56% (very low).

The fund's risk rating is currently C (Fair). It carries a beta of 1.08, meaning that its performance tracks fairly well with that of the overall stock market. Volatility, as measured by both the semi-deviation and a drawdown factor, is considered average.

Ramona Persaud has been running the fund for 1 year and currently receives a manager quality ranking of 35 (0=worst, 99=best). If you desire an average level of risk and strong performance, then this fund is a good option.
Services Offered: Automated phone transactions, payroll deductions, bank draft capabilities, an IRA investment plan, a 401K investment plan, a Keogh investment plan and a systematic withdrawal plan.

Data Date	Investment Rating	Net Assets ($Mil)	NAV	Perfor-mance Rating/Pts	Total Return Y-T-D	Risk Rating/Pts
3-15	C+	6,529	33.81	B- / 7.4	1.17%	C / 5.0
2014	B	6,614	33.42	B+ / 8.8	11.87%	C / 5.0
2013	C	6,864	35.39	C+ / 6.5	31.61%	C- / 4.0
2012	C+	5,964	29.90	B / 7.7	18.70%	C- / 3.5
2011	B	7,813	25.87	B+ / 8.3	-8.51%	C- / 3.8
2010	B	9,429	28.43	B+ / 8.6	21.19%	C- / 3.7

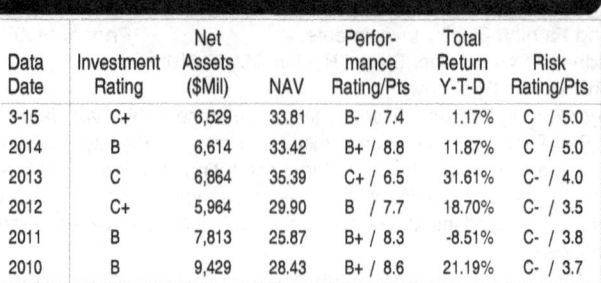

Annualized Total Return

Fidelity Freedom 2015 (FFVFX)

C   **Fair**

Fund Family: Fidelity Investments   **Phone:** (800) 544-8544
Address: 245 Summer Street, Boston, MA 02210
Fund Type: AA - Asset Allocation
Major Rating Factors: Middle of the road best describes Fidelity Freedom 2015 whose TheStreet.com Investment Rating is currently a C (Fair). The fund currently has a performance rating of C- (Fair) based on an average return of 7.65% over the last three years and 2.46% over the last three months. Factored into the performance evaluation is an expense ratio of 0.64% (very low).

The fund's risk rating is currently B (Good). It carries a beta of 0.94, meaning that its performance tracks fairly well with that of the overall stock market. Volatility, as measured by both the semi-deviation and a drawdown factor, is considered low.

Jonathan Shelon has been running the fund for 10 years and currently receives a manager quality ranking of 33 (0=worst, 99=best). If you desire an average level of risk, then this fund may be an option.
Services Offered: Automated phone transactions, payroll deductions, bank draft capabilities, an IRA investment plan, a 401K investment plan, a Keogh investment plan, wire transfers and a systematic withdrawal plan.

Data Date	Investment Rating	Net Assets ($Mil)	NAV	Perfor-mance Rating/Pts	Total Return Y-T-D	Risk Rating/Pts
3-15	C	6,063	12.92	C- / 3.0	2.46%	B / 8.8
2014	C	6,076	12.61	D+ / 2.9	5.17%	B / 8.8
2013	C	6,578	12.75	D+ / 2.3	11.88%	B / 8.1
2012	C	6,533	11.81	D+ / 2.7	10.68%	B / 8.1
2011	B-	7,518	10.93	C / 4.5	-0.34%	B- / 7.9
2010	C+	8,851	11.34	C+ / 6.2	11.75%	C+ / 6.9

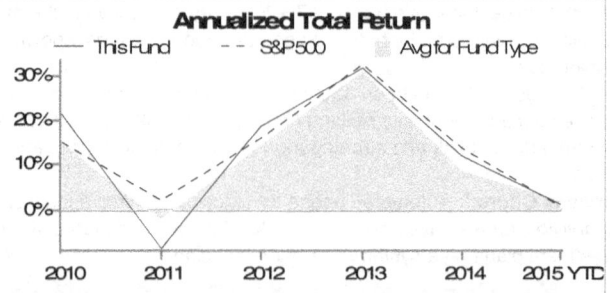

Annualized Total Return

Fidelity Freedom 2020 (FFFDX)

C   **Fair**

Fund Family: Fidelity Investments   **Phone:** (800) 544-8544
Address: 245 Summer Street, Boston, MA 02210
Fund Type: AA - Asset Allocation
Major Rating Factors: Middle of the road best describes Fidelity Freedom 2020 whose TheStreet.com Investment Rating is currently a C (Fair). The fund currently has a performance rating of C- (Fair) based on an average return of 8.21% over the last three years and 2.60% over the last three months. Factored into the performance evaluation is an expense ratio of 0.67% (very low).

The fund's risk rating is currently B (Good). It carries a beta of 1.04, meaning that its performance tracks fairly well with that of the overall stock market. Volatility, as measured by both the semi-deviation and a drawdown factor, is considered low.

Jonathan Shelon has been running the fund for 10 years and currently receives a manager quality ranking of 26 (0=worst, 99=best). If you desire an average level of risk, then this fund may be an option.
Services Offered: Automated phone transactions, payroll deductions, bank draft capabilities, an IRA investment plan, a 401K investment plan, a Keogh investment plan, wire transfers and a systematic withdrawal plan.

Data Date	Investment Rating	Net Assets ($Mil)	NAV	Perfor-mance Rating/Pts	Total Return Y-T-D	Risk Rating/Pts
3-15	C	12,880	15.76	C- / 3.3	2.60%	B / 8.5
2014	C	12,905	15.36	C- / 3.2	5.34%	B / 8.5
2013	C	13,702	15.61	D+ / 2.5	13.22%	B- / 7.6
2012	C	13,721	14.31	C- / 3.3	11.77%	B- / 7.5
2011	B-	15,910	13.12	C / 5.3	-1.36%	B- / 7.2
2010	C+	19,974	13.79	C+ / 5.6	12.93%	C+ / 5.8

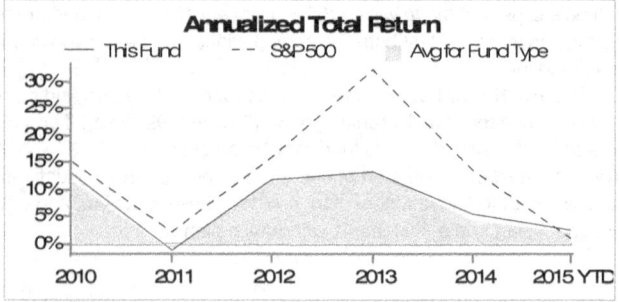

Annualized Total Return

Fidelity Freedom 2025 (FFTWX)   C+   Fair

Fund Family: Fidelity Investments   **Phone:** (800) 544-8544
Address: 245 Summer Street, Boston, MA 02210
Fund Type: AA - Asset Allocation
Major Rating Factors: Middle of the road best describes Fidelity Freedom 2025 whose TheStreet.com Investment Rating is currently a C+ (Fair). The fund currently has a performance rating of C- (Fair) based on an average return of 9.43% over the last three years and 2.82% over the last three months. Factored into the performance evaluation is an expense ratio of 0.72% (very low).

The fund's risk rating is currently B (Good). It carries a beta of 1.22, meaning it is expected to move 12.2% for every 10% move in the market. Volatility, as measured by both the semi-deviation and a drawdown factor, is considered low.

Jonathan Shelon has been running the fund for 10 years and currently receives a manager quality ranking of 19 (0=worst, 99=best). If you desire an average level of risk, then this fund may be an option.

Services Offered: Automated phone transactions, payroll deductions, bank draft capabilities, an IRA investment plan, a 401K investment plan, a Keogh investment plan, wire transfers and a systematic withdrawal plan.

Data Date	Investment Rating	Net Assets ($Mil)	NAV	Perfor- mance Rating/Pts	Total Return Y-T-D	Risk Rating/Pts
3-15	C+	9,056	13.51	C- / 4.0	2.82%	B / 8.1
2014	C+	8,887	13.14	C- / 3.9	5.63%	B / 8.0
2013	C	8,988	13.32	C- / 3.2	16.50%	C+ / 6.9
2012	C+	8,013	11.95	C- / 4.1	13.15%	C+ / 6.8
2011	C+	8,595	10.81	C / 5.2	-2.65%	C+ / 6.7
2010	C+	9,831	11.52	C+ / 5.8	13.82%	C / 5.5

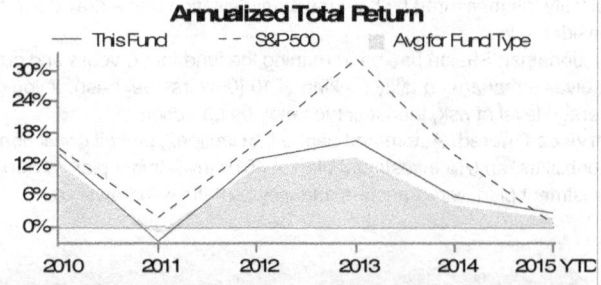

Annualized Total Return

Fidelity Freedom 2030 (FFFEX)   C+   Fair

Fund Family: Fidelity Investments   **Phone:** (800) 544-8544
Address: 245 Summer Street, Boston, MA 02210
Fund Type: AA - Asset Allocation
Major Rating Factors: Middle of the road best describes Fidelity Freedom 2030 whose TheStreet.com Investment Rating is currently a C+ (Fair). The fund currently has a performance rating of C (Fair) based on an average return of 10.02% over the last three years and 3.04% over the last three months. Factored into the performance evaluation is an expense ratio of 0.77% (very low).

The fund's risk rating is currently B- (Good). It carries a beta of 1.34, meaning it is expected to move 13.4% for every 10% move in the market. Volatility, as measured by both the semi-deviation and a drawdown factor, is considered low.

Jonathan Shelon has been running the fund for 10 years and currently receives a manager quality ranking of 14 (0=worst, 99=best). If you desire an average level of risk, then this fund may be an option.

Services Offered: Automated phone transactions, payroll deductions, bank draft capabilities, an IRA investment plan, a 401K investment plan, a Keogh investment plan, wire transfers and a systematic withdrawal plan.

Data Date	Investment Rating	Net Assets ($Mil)	NAV	Perfor- mance Rating/Pts	Total Return Y-T-D	Risk Rating/Pts
3-15	C+	10,889	16.62	C / 4.4	3.04%	B- / 7.7
2014	C+	10,752	16.13	C- / 4.1	5.67%	B- / 7.7
2013	C	11,328	16.30	C- / 3.5	18.13%	C+ / 6.7
2012	C	10,568	14.23	C- / 4.2	13.47%	C+ / 6.5
2011	C+	11,719	12.84	C / 5.1	-3.15%	C+ / 6.2
2010	C	14,727	13.77	C / 4.6	14.04%	C / 4.8

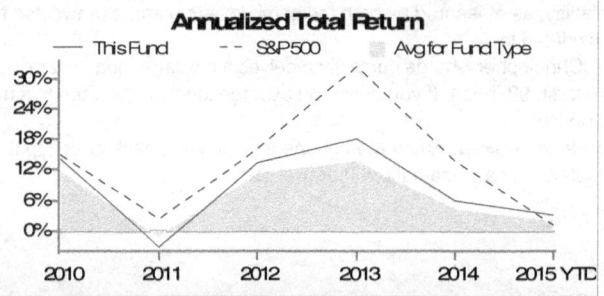

Annualized Total Return

Fidelity Freedom 2035 (FFTHX)   C+   Fair

Fund Family: Fidelity Investments   **Phone:** (800) 544-8544
Address: 245 Summer Street, Boston, MA 02210
Fund Type: AA - Asset Allocation
Major Rating Factors: Middle of the road best describes Fidelity Freedom 2035 whose TheStreet.com Investment Rating is currently a C+ (Fair). The fund currently has a performance rating of C (Fair) based on an average return of 10.80% over the last three years and 3.09% over the last three months. Factored into the performance evaluation is an expense ratio of 0.78% (very low).

The fund's risk rating is currently B- (Good). It carries a beta of 1.48, meaning it is expected to move 14.8% for every 10% move in the market. Volatility, as measured by both the semi-deviation and a drawdown factor, is considered low.

Jonathan Shelon has been running the fund for 10 years and currently receives a manager quality ranking of 10 (0=worst, 99=best). If you desire an average level of risk, then this fund may be an option.

Services Offered: Automated phone transactions, payroll deductions, bank draft capabilities, an IRA investment plan, a 401K investment plan, a Keogh investment plan, wire transfers and a systematic withdrawal plan.

Data Date	Investment Rating	Net Assets ($Mil)	NAV	Perfor- mance Rating/Pts	Total Return Y-T-D	Risk Rating/Pts
3-15	C+	6,295	13.67	C / 4.8	3.09%	B- / 7.3
2014	C	6,136	13.26	C / 4.6	5.75%	B- / 7.2
2013	C	6,319	13.48	C- / 4.1	20.68%	C+ / 6.1
2012	C	5,469	11.83	C / 4.4	14.45%	C+ / 5.9
2011	C	5,743	10.55	C / 4.6	-4.59%	C+ / 5.9
2010	C	6,591	11.47	C / 4.8	14.46%	C / 4.6

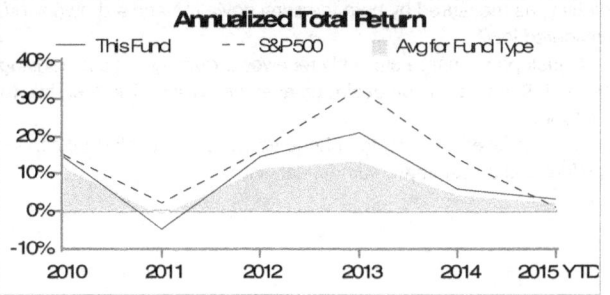

Annualized Total Return

Fidelity Freedom 2040 (FFFFX)   C+   Fair

Fund Family: Fidelity Investments   **Phone:** (800) 544-8544
Address: 245 Summer Street, Boston, MA 02210
Fund Type: AA - Asset Allocation
Major Rating Factors: Middle of the road best describes Fidelity Freedom 2040 whose TheStreet.com Investment Rating is currently a C+ (Fair). The fund currently has a performance rating of C (Fair) based on an average return of 10.92% over the last three years and 3.10% over the last three months. Factored into the performance evaluation is an expense ratio of 0.78% (very low).

The fund's risk rating is currently B- (Good). It carries a beta of 1.49, meaning it is expected to move 14.9% for every 10% move in the market. Volatility, as measured by both the semi-deviation and a drawdown factor, is considered low.

Jonathan Shelon has been running the fund for 10 years and currently receives a manager quality ranking of 10 (0=worst, 99=best). If you desire an average level of risk, then this fund may be an option.
Services Offered: Automated phone transactions, payroll deductions, bank draft capabilities, an IRA investment plan, a 401K investment plan, a Keogh investment plan, wire transfers and a systematic withdrawal plan.

Data Date	Investment Rating	Net Assets ($Mil)	NAV	Performance Rating/Pts	Total Return Y-T-D	Risk Rating/Pts
3-15	C+	6,903	9.63	C / 4.9	3.10%	B- / 7.3
2014	C+	6,863	9.34	C / 4.6	5.71%	B- / 7.2
2013	C	7,352	9.52	C- / 4.2	21.05%	C+ / 6.0
2012	C	6,675	8.26	C / 4.5	14.53%	C+ / 5.7
2011	C	7,163	7.36	C / 4.8	-4.63%	C+ / 5.7
2010	C	9,017	8.01	C / 4.4	14.62%	C / 4.4

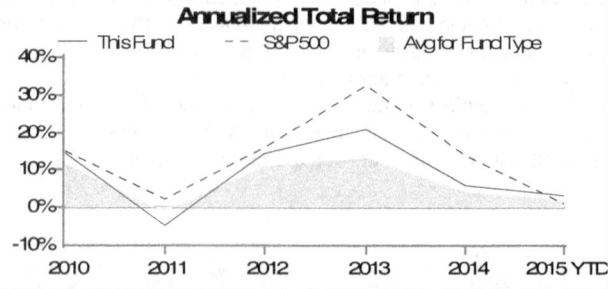

Fidelity Freedom K 2015 (FKVFX)   C   Fair

Fund Family: Fidelity Investments   **Phone:** (800) 544-8544
Address: 245 Summer Street, Boston, MA 02210
Fund Type: GI - Growth and Income
Major Rating Factors: Middle of the road best describes Fidelity Freedom K 2015 whose TheStreet.com Investment Rating is currently a C (Fair). The fund currently has a performance rating of C- (Fair) based on an average return of 7.74% over the last three years and 2.50% over the last three months. Factored into the performance evaluation is an expense ratio of 0.55% (very low).

The fund's risk rating is currently B (Good). It carries a beta of 0.54, meaning the fund's expected move will be 5.4% for every 10% move in the market. Volatility, as measured by both the semi-deviation and a drawdown factor, is considered low.

Christopher Sharpe currently receives a manager quality ranking of 59 (0=worst, 99=best). If you desire an average level of risk, then this fund may be an option.
Services Offered: Automated phone transactions, bank draft capabilities, wire transfers and a systematic withdrawal plan.

Data Date	Investment Rating	Net Assets ($Mil)	NAV	Performance Rating/Pts	Total Return Y-T-D	Risk Rating/Pts
3-15	C	6,739	13.94	C- / 3.1	2.50%	B / 8.3
2014	C	6,859	13.60	D+ / 2.9	5.25%	B / 8.2
2013	C	7,454	14.24	D+ / 2.4	11.96%	B / 8.0
2012	C+	6,602	12.96	D+ / 2.8	10.81%	B / 8.5
2011	U	4,171	12.13	U / --	-0.34%	U / --
2010	U	2,466	12.72	U / --	11.93%	U / --

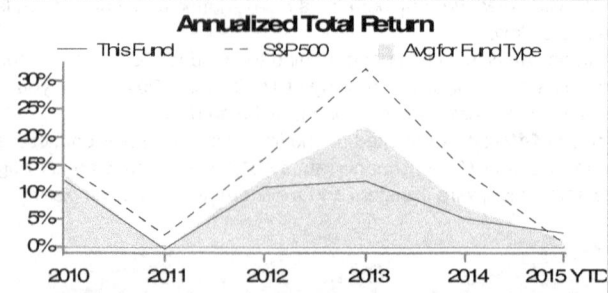

Fidelity Freedom K 2020 (FFKDX)   C   Fair

Fund Family: Fidelity Investments   **Phone:** (800) 544-8544
Address: 245 Summer Street, Boston, MA 02210
Fund Type: GI - Growth and Income
Major Rating Factors: Middle of the road best describes Fidelity Freedom K 2020 whose TheStreet.com Investment Rating is currently a C (Fair). The fund currently has a performance rating of C- (Fair) based on an average return of 8.31% over the last three years and 2.67% over the last three months. Factored into the performance evaluation is an expense ratio of 0.57% (very low).

The fund's risk rating is currently B (Good). It carries a beta of 0.60, meaning the fund's expected move will be 6.0% for every 10% move in the market. Volatility, as measured by both the semi-deviation and a drawdown factor, is considered low.

Christopher Sharpe currently receives a manager quality ranking of 53 (0=worst, 99=best). If you desire an average level of risk, then this fund may be an option.
Services Offered: Automated phone transactions, bank draft capabilities, wire transfers and a systematic withdrawal plan.

Data Date	Investment Rating	Net Assets ($Mil)	NAV	Performance Rating/Pts	Total Return Y-T-D	Risk Rating/Pts
3-15	C	17,529	14.62	C- / 3.4	2.67%	B / 8.1
2014	C	17,398	14.24	C- / 3.3	5.40%	B / 8.1
2013	C-	17,539	14.88	D+ / 2.6	13.35%	B- / 7.5
2012	C+	14,625	13.39	C- / 3.5	11.86%	B / 8.0
2011	U	9,146	12.43	U / --	-1.24%	U / --
2010	U	5,171	13.19	U / --	13.07%	U / --

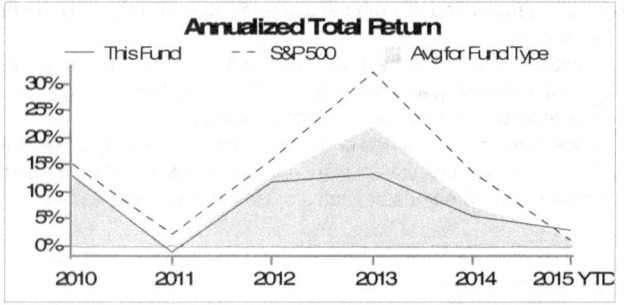

Fidelity Freedom K 2025 (FKTWX)   C   Fair

Fund Family: Fidelity Investments   **Phone:** (800) 544-8544
Address: 245 Summer Street, Boston, MA 02210
Fund Type: GI - Growth and Income
Major Rating Factors: Middle of the road best describes Fidelity Freedom K 2025 whose TheStreet.com Investment Rating is currently a C (Fair). The fund currently has a performance rating of C- (Fair) based on an average return of 9.53% over the last three years and 2.76% over the last three months. Factored into the performance evaluation is an expense ratio of 0.61% (very low).

The fund's risk rating is currently B- (Good). It carries a beta of 0.71, meaning the fund's expected move will be 7.1% for every 10% move in the market. Volatility, as measured by both the semi-deviation and a drawdown factor, is considered low.

Christopher Sharpe currently receives a manager quality ranking of 44 (0=worst, 99=best). If you desire an average level of risk, then this fund may be an option.
Services Offered: Automated phone transactions, bank draft capabilities, wire transfers and a systematic withdrawal plan.

Data Date	Investment Rating	Net Assets ($Mil)	NAV	Performance Rating/Pts	Total Return Y-T-D	Risk Rating/Pts
3-15	C	12,953	15.27	C- / 4.1	2.76%	B- / 7.7
2014	C	12,592	14.86	C- / 3.9	5.75%	B- / 7.7
2013	C-	11,681	15.51	C- / 3.2	16.65%	C+ / 6.8
2012	C+	8,751	13.58	C- / 4.2	13.26%	B- / 7.5
2011	U	4,781	12.44	U / --	-2.50%	U / --
2010	U	2,705	13.40	U / --	13.89%	U / --

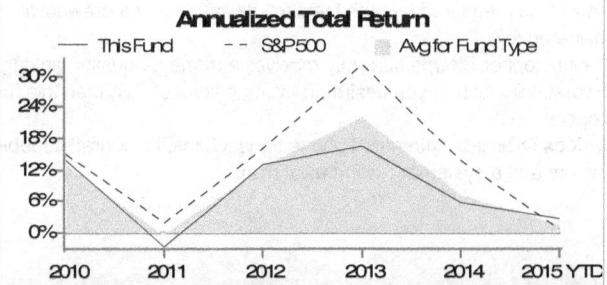

Fidelity Freedom K 2030 (FFKEX)   C   Fair

Fund Family: Fidelity Investments   **Phone:** (800) 544-8544
Address: 245 Summer Street, Boston, MA 02210
Fund Type: GL - Global
Major Rating Factors: Middle of the road best describes Fidelity Freedom K 2030 whose TheStreet.com Investment Rating is currently a C (Fair). The fund currently has a performance rating of C (Fair) based on an average return of 10.12% over the last three years and 2.97% over the last three months. Factored into the performance evaluation is an expense ratio of 0.65% (very low).

The fund's risk rating is currently B- (Good). It carries a beta of 1.22, meaning it is expected to move 12.2% for every 10% move in the market. Volatility, as measured by both the semi-deviation and a drawdown factor, is considered low.

Christopher Sharpe has been running the fund for 6 years and currently receives a manager quality ranking of 55 (0=worst, 99=best). If you desire an average level of risk, then this fund may be an option.
Services Offered: Automated phone transactions, bank draft capabilities, wire transfers and a systematic withdrawal plan.

Data Date	Investment Rating	Net Assets ($Mil)	NAV	Performance Rating/Pts	Total Return Y-T-D	Risk Rating/Pts
3-15	C	16,027	15.62	C / 4.5	2.97%	B- / 7.3
2014	C	15,582	15.17	C- / 4.2	5.86%	B- / 7.2
2013	C-	14,913	15.86	C- / 3.6	18.21%	C+ / 6.5
2012	C+	11,521	13.72	C / 4.4	13.65%	B- / 7.2
2011	U	6,774	12.54	U / --	-3.09%	U / --
2010	U	3,836	13.60	U / --	14.18%	U / --

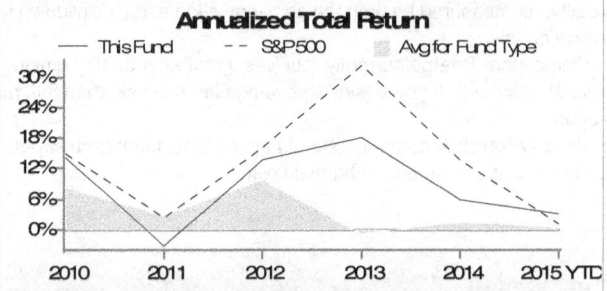

Fidelity Freedom K 2035 (FKTHX)   C   Fair

Fund Family: Fidelity Investments   **Phone:** (800) 544-8544
Address: 245 Summer Street, Boston, MA 02210
Fund Type: GI - Growth and Income
Major Rating Factors: Middle of the road best describes Fidelity Freedom K 2035 whose TheStreet.com Investment Rating is currently a C (Fair). The fund currently has a performance rating of C (Fair) based on an average return of 10.94% over the last three years and 3.14% over the last three months. Factored into the performance evaluation is an expense ratio of 0.66% (very low).

The fund's risk rating is currently C+ (Fair). It carries a beta of 0.87, meaning the fund's expected move will be 8.7% for every 10% move in the market. Volatility, as measured by both the semi-deviation and a drawdown factor, is considered low.

Christopher Sharpe currently receives a manager quality ranking of 28 (0=worst, 99=best). If you desire an average level of risk, then this fund may be an option.
Services Offered: Automated phone transactions, bank draft capabilities, wire transfers and a systematic withdrawal plan.

Data Date	Investment Rating	Net Assets ($Mil)	NAV	Performance Rating/Pts	Total Return Y-T-D	Risk Rating/Pts
3-15	C	10,139	16.10	C / 4.9	3.14%	C+ / 6.9
2014	C	9,815	15.61	C / 4.7	5.88%	C+ / 6.9
2013	C-	8,930	16.38	C- / 4.2	20.86%	C+ / 5.9
2012	C+	6,375	13.87	C / 4.7	14.60%	C+ / 6.7
2011	U	3,361	12.53	U / --	-4.53%	U / --
2010	U	1,816	13.78	U / --	14.72%	U / --

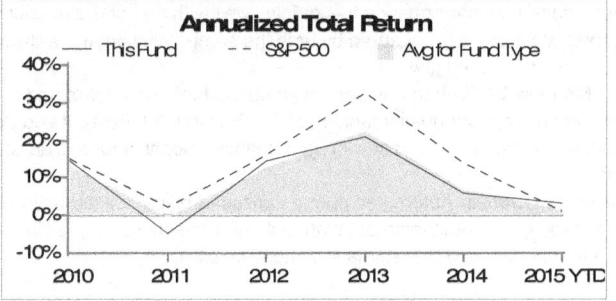

Fidelity Freedom K 2040 (FFKFX)   C+   Fair

Fund Family: Fidelity Investments   **Phone:** (800) 544-8544
Address: 245 Summer Street, Boston, MA 02210
Fund Type: GI - Growth and Income

Major Rating Factors: Middle of the road best describes Fidelity Freedom K 2040 whose TheStreet.com Investment Rating is currently a C+ (Fair). The fund currently has a performance rating of C (Fair) based on an average return of 11.04% over the last three years and 3.13% over the last three months. Factored into the performance evaluation is an expense ratio of 0.66% (very low).

The fund's risk rating is currently C+ (Fair). It carries a beta of 0.88, meaning the fund's expected move will be 8.8% for every 10% move in the market. Volatility, as measured by both the semi-deviation and a drawdown factor, is considered low.

Christopher Sharpe currently receives a manager quality ranking of 28 (0=worst, 99=best). If you desire an average level of risk, then this fund may be an option.

Services Offered: Automated phone transactions, bank draft capabilities, wire transfers and a systematic withdrawal plan.

Data Date	Investment Rating	Net Assets ($Mil)	NAV	Performance Rating/Pts	Total Return Y-T-D	Risk Rating/Pts
3-15	C+	10,934	16.14	C / 5.0	3.13%	C+ / 6.9
2014	C	10,527	15.65	C / 4.7	5.88%	C+ / 6.8
2013	C-	9,793	16.47	C- / 4.2	21.25%	C+ / 5.7
2012	C+	7,184	13.91	C / 4.6	14.61%	C+ / 6.6
2011	U	4,035	12.57	U / --	-4.64%	U / --
2010	U	2,284	13.86	U / --	14.79%	U / --

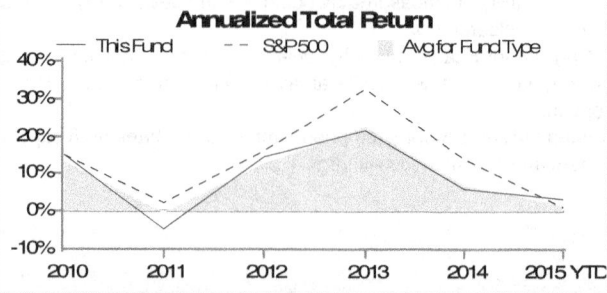

Fidelity Freedom K 2045 (FFKGX)   C+   Fair

Fund Family: Fidelity Investments   **Phone:** (800) 544-8544
Address: 245 Summer Street, Boston, MA 02210
Fund Type: GI - Growth and Income

Major Rating Factors: Middle of the road best describes Fidelity Freedom K 2045 whose TheStreet.com Investment Rating is currently a C+ (Fair). The fund currently has a performance rating of C (Fair) based on an average return of 11.26% over the last three years and 3.18% over the last three months. Factored into the performance evaluation is an expense ratio of 0.66% (very low).

The fund's risk rating is currently C+ (Fair). It carries a beta of 0.90, meaning the fund's expected move will be 9.0% for every 10% move in the market. Volatility, as measured by both the semi-deviation and a drawdown factor, is considered low.

Christopher Sharpe currently receives a manager quality ranking of 28 (0=worst, 99=best). If you desire an average level of risk, then this fund may be an option.

Services Offered: Automated phone transactions, bank draft capabilities, wire transfers and a systematic withdrawal plan.

Data Date	Investment Rating	Net Assets ($Mil)	NAV	Performance Rating/Pts	Total Return Y-T-D	Risk Rating/Pts
3-15	C+	5,971	16.57	C / 5.1	3.18%	C+ / 6.9
2014	C	5,658	16.06	C / 4.9	5.90%	C+ / 6.8
2013	C-	4,838	16.80	C / 4.4	21.84%	C+ / 5.6
2012	C+	3,219	14.09	C / 4.8	14.97%	C+ / 6.5
2011	U	1,519	12.66	U / --	-4.95%	U / --
2010	U	682	13.96	U / --	14.97%	U / --

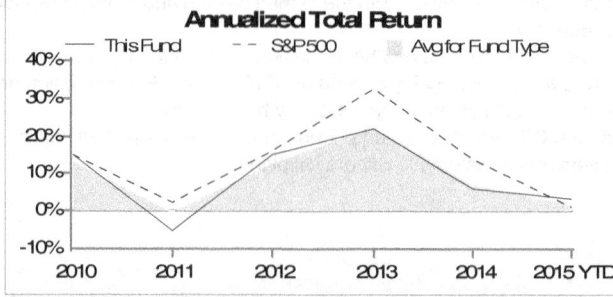

Fidelity Growth and Income (FGRIX)   B+   Good

Fund Family: Fidelity Investments   **Phone:** (800) 544-8544
Address: 245 Summer Street, Boston, MA 02210
Fund Type: GI - Growth and Income

Major Rating Factors: Strong performance is the major factor driving the B+ (Good) TheStreet.com Investment Rating for Fidelity Growth and Income. The fund currently has a performance rating of B (Good) based on an average return of 15.77% over the last three years and 0.36% over the last three months. Factored into the performance evaluation is an expense ratio of 0.66% (very low).

The fund's risk rating is currently B- (Good). It carries a beta of 1.05, meaning that its performance tracks fairly well with that of the overall stock market. Volatility, as measured by both the semi-deviation and a drawdown factor, is considered low.

Matthew W. Fruhan has been running the fund for 4 years and currently receives a manager quality ranking of 51 (0=worst, 99=best). If you desire only a moderate level of risk and strong performance, then this fund is an excellent option.

Services Offered: Automated phone transactions, payroll deductions, bank draft capabilities, an IRA investment plan, a 401K investment plan, a Keogh investment plan and a systematic withdrawal plan.

Data Date	Investment Rating	Net Assets ($Mil)	NAV	Performance Rating/Pts	Total Return Y-T-D	Risk Rating/Pts
3-15	B+	6,587	30.32	B / 7.6	0.36%	B- / 7.2
2014	A	6,699	30.21	B+ / 8.6	10.38%	B- / 7.2
2013	A+	6,471	27.86	B+ / 8.6	33.40%	C+ / 6.1
2012	A+	4,949	21.26	B+ / 8.6	19.10%	C+ / 5.6
2011	C+	4,627	18.24	C+ / 6.3	1.39%	C / 4.5
2010	E+	5,612	18.30	E / 0.3	14.57%	C- / 3.2

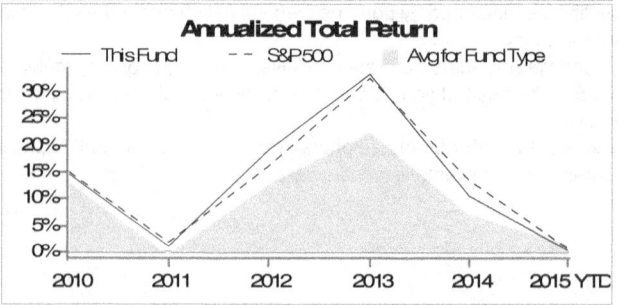

Fidelity Growth Company Fd (FDGRX)   A-   Excellent

Fund Family: Fidelity Investments   **Phone:** (800) 544-8544
Address: 245 Summer Street, Boston, MA 02210
Fund Type: GR - Growth

Major Rating Factors: Exceptional performance is the major factor driving the A- (Excellent) TheStreet.com Investment Rating for Fidelity Growth Company Fd. The fund currently has a performance rating of A (Excellent) based on an average return of 17.33% over the last three years and 4.86% over the last three months. Factored into the performance evaluation is an expense ratio of 0.82% (very low).

The fund's risk rating is currently C+ (Fair). It carries a beta of 1.09, meaning that its performance tracks fairly well with that of the overall stock market. Volatility, as measured by both the semi-deviation and a drawdown factor, is considered low.

Steven S. Wymer has been running the fund for 18 years and currently receives a manager quality ranking of 64 (0=worst, 99=best). If you desire only a moderate level of risk and strong performance, then this fund is an excellent option.

Services Offered: Automated phone transactions, payroll deductions, bank draft capabilities, an IRA investment plan, a 401K investment plan, a Keogh investment plan and a systematic withdrawal plan. However, the fund is currently closed to new investors.

Data Date	Investment Rating	Net Assets ($Mil)	NAV	Performance Rating/Pts	Total Return Y-T-D	Risk Rating/Pts
3-15	A-	23,244	138.08	A / 9.4	4.86%	C+ / 5.8
2014	A-	24,026	131.89	A+ / 9.7	14.44%	C+ / 5.6
2013	A-	23,381	119.88	A / 9.3	37.61%	C / 4.6
2012	B+	22,700	93.38	B+ / 8.5	18.52%	C / 4.4
2011	A	24,680	80.89	A- / 9.1	0.67%	C / 4.7
2010	B	28,622	83.15	B / 7.9	20.55%	C / 4.6

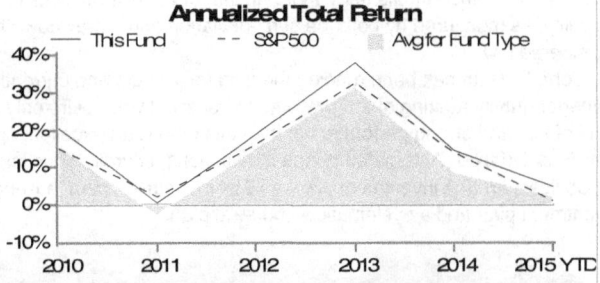

Fidelity Low-Priced Stock Fd (FLPSX)   B   Good

Fund Family: Fidelity Investments   **Phone:** (800) 544-8544
Address: 245 Summer Street, Boston, MA 02210
Fund Type: MC - Mid Cap

Major Rating Factors: Strong performance is the major factor driving the B (Good) TheStreet.com Investment Rating for Fidelity Low-Priced Stock Fd. The fund currently has a performance rating of B- (Good) based on an average return of 15.23% over the last three years and 1.77% over the last three months. Factored into the performance evaluation is an expense ratio of 0.82% (very low) and a 1.5% back-end load levied at the time of sale.

The fund's risk rating is currently B- (Good). It carries a beta of 0.86, meaning the fund's expected move will be 8.6% for every 10% move in the market. Volatility, as measured by both the semi-deviation and a drawdown factor, is considered low.

Joel C. Tillinghast has been running the fund for 26 years and currently receives a manager quality ranking of 74 (0=worst, 99=best). If you desire only a moderate level of risk and strong performance, then this fund is an excellent option.

Services Offered: Automated phone transactions, payroll deductions, bank draft capabilities, an IRA investment plan, a 401K investment plan, a Keogh investment plan and a systematic withdrawal plan.

Data Date	Investment Rating	Net Assets ($Mil)	NAV	Performance Rating/Pts	Total Return Y-T-D	Risk Rating/Pts
3-15	B	30,086	51.14	B- / 7.0	1.77%	B- / 7.0
2014	B+	30,318	50.25	B / 7.6	7.65%	B- / 7.0
2013	B	31,079	49.46	B / 8.2	34.31%	C / 4.8
2012	A-	23,433	39.50	A- / 9.0	18.50%	C / 4.5
2011	A-	23,926	35.73	B+ / 8.7	-0.06%	C / 5.0
2010	B	27,094	38.38	B+ / 8.3	20.70%	C- / 4.0

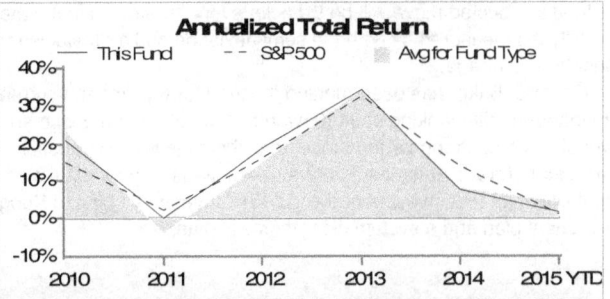

Fidelity Magellan Fund (FMAGX)   A   Excellent

Fund Family: Fidelity Investments   **Phone:** (800) 544-8544
Address: 245 Summer Street, Boston, MA 02210
Fund Type: GR - Growth

Major Rating Factors: Exceptional performance is the major factor driving the A (Excellent) TheStreet.com Investment Rating for Fidelity Magellan Fund. The fund currently has a performance rating of A- (Excellent) based on an average return of 17.18% over the last three years and 2.83% over the last three months. Factored into the performance evaluation is an expense ratio of 0.53% (very low).

The fund's risk rating is currently C+ (Fair). It carries a beta of 1.05, meaning that its performance tracks fairly well with that of the overall stock market. Volatility, as measured by both the semi-deviation and a drawdown factor, is considered low.

Jeffrey S. Feingold has been running the fund for 4 years and currently receives a manager quality ranking of 69 (0=worst, 99=best). If you desire only a moderate level of risk and strong performance, then this fund is an excellent option.

Services Offered: Automated phone transactions, payroll deductions, bank draft capabilities, an IRA investment plan, a 401K investment plan, a Keogh investment plan and a systematic withdrawal plan.

Data Date	Investment Rating	Net Assets ($Mil)	NAV	Performance Rating/Pts	Total Return Y-T-D	Risk Rating/Pts
3-15	A	14,225	95.14	A- / 9.1	2.83%	C+ / 6.3
2014	A	14,107	92.52	A+ / 9.6	14.08%	C+ / 6.2
2013	C+	13,542	92.37	B- / 7.0	35.30%	C- / 4.1
2012	D-	11,869	73.27	D+ / 2.6	17.99%	C- / 3.9
2011	D	13,313	62.98	D+ / 2.7	-11.55%	C- / 4.1
2010	E+	19,913	71.67	D- / 1.3	12.41%	D+ / 2.7

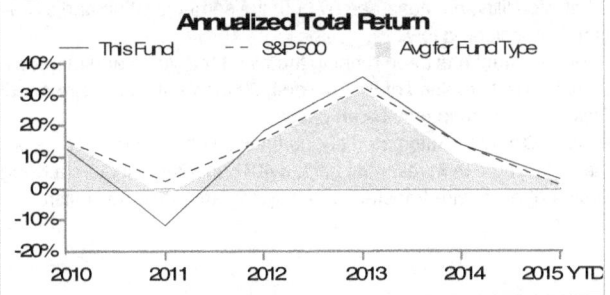

Fidelity Mid-Cap Stock Fund (FMCSX)   B+   Good

Fund Family: Fidelity Investments   **Phone:** (800) 544-8544
Address: 245 Summer Street, Boston, MA 02210
Fund Type: MC - Mid Cap
Major Rating Factors: Strong performance is the major factor driving the B+ (Good) TheStreet.com Investment Rating for Fidelity Mid-Cap Stock Fund. The fund currently has a performance rating of B (Good) based on an average return of 16.35% over the last three years and 4.40% over the last three months. Factored into the performance evaluation is an expense ratio of 0.81% (very low) and a 0.8% back-end load levied at the time of sale.

The fund's risk rating is currently C+ (Fair). It carries a beta of 0.95, meaning that its performance tracks fairly well with that of the overall stock market. Volatility, as measured by both the semi-deviation and a drawdown factor, is considered low.

John D. Roth has been running the fund for 4 years and currently receives a manager quality ranking of 70 (0=worst, 99=best). If you desire only a moderate level of risk and strong performance, then this fund is an excellent option.

Services Offered: Automated phone transactions, payroll deductions, bank draft capabilities, an IRA investment plan, a 401K investment plan, a Keogh investment plan and a systematic withdrawal plan.

Data Date	Investment Rating	Net Assets ($Mil)	NAV	Performance Rating/Pts	Total Return Y-T-D	Risk Rating/Pts
3-15	B+	5,904	40.08	B / 8.2	4.40%	C+ / 6.1
2014	B	5,860	38.39	B- / 7.5	7.11%	C+ / 6.0
2013	B	5,608	39.51	B+ / 8.7	38.97%	C- / 4.2
2012	C	4,282	29.38	B- / 7.5	14.93%	C- / 3.3
2011	B+	5,327	26.66	A / 9.4	-2.41%	C- / 3.4
2010	C+	6,724	28.85	B / 8.1	23.57%	D+ / 2.6

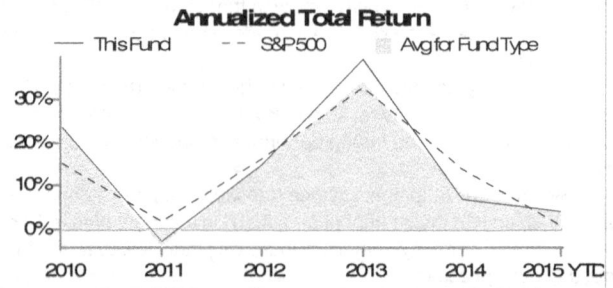

Fidelity OTC Portfolio Fd (FOCPX)   B+   Good

Fund Family: Fidelity Investments   **Phone:** (800) 544-8544
Address: 245 Summer Street, Boston, MA 02210
Fund Type: SC - Small Cap
Major Rating Factors: Exceptional performance is the major factor driving the B+ (Good) TheStreet.com Investment Rating for Fidelity OTC Portfolio Fd. The fund currently has a performance rating of A+ (Excellent) based on an average return of 19.32% over the last three years and 4.83% over the last three months. Factored into the performance evaluation is an expense ratio of 0.77% (very low).

The fund's risk rating is currently C (Fair). It carries a beta of 0.81, meaning the fund's expected move will be 8.1% for every 10% move in the market. Volatility, as measured by both the semi-deviation and a drawdown factor, is considered average.

Gavin S. Baker has been running the fund for 6 years and currently receives a manager quality ranking of 94 (0=worst, 99=best). If you desire an average level of risk and strong performance, then this fund is a good option.

Services Offered: Automated phone transactions, payroll deductions, bank draft capabilities, an IRA investment plan, a 401K investment plan, a Keogh investment plan and a systematic withdrawal plan.

Data Date	Investment Rating	Net Assets ($Mil)	NAV	Performance Rating/Pts	Total Return Y-T-D	Risk Rating/Pts
3-15	B+	9,198	83.40	A+ / 9.7	4.83%	C / 4.8
2014	B	8,596	79.56	A+ / 9.8	16.49%	C / 4.3
2013	A-	7,544	77.39	A+ / 9.6	46.50%	C / 4.3
2012	C-	5,288	60.59	C / 5.1	11.29%	C / 4.4
2011	A	5,967	54.70	A+ / 9.7	-0.42%	C- / 4.1
2010	C+	5,640	54.93	B+ / 8.6	20.14%	D+ / 2.8

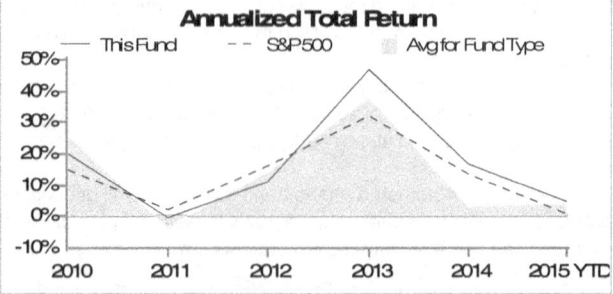

Fidelity Puritan Fd (FPURX)   B-   Good

Fund Family: Fidelity Investments   **Phone:** (800) 544-8544
Address: 245 Summer Street, Boston, MA 02210
Fund Type: GI - Growth and Income
Major Rating Factors: Fidelity Puritan Fd receives a TheStreet.com Investment Rating of B- (Good). The fund currently has a performance rating of C+ (Fair) based on an average return of 12.15% over the last three years and 2.65% over the last three months. Factored into the performance evaluation is an expense ratio of 0.56% (very low).

The fund's risk rating is currently B- (Good). It carries a beta of 0.67, meaning the fund's expected move will be 6.7% for every 10% move in the market. Volatility, as measured by both the semi-deviation and a drawdown factor, is considered low.

Ramin Arani has been running the fund for 8 years and currently receives a manager quality ranking of 81 (0=worst, 99=best). If you desire an average level of risk, then this fund may be an option.

Services Offered: Automated phone transactions, payroll deductions, bank draft capabilities, an IRA investment plan, a 401K investment plan, a Keogh investment plan, wire transfers and a systematic withdrawal plan.

Data Date	Investment Rating	Net Assets ($Mil)	NAV	Performance Rating/Pts	Total Return Y-T-D	Risk Rating/Pts
3-15	B-	19,514	22.06	C+ / 5.9	2.65%	B- / 7.2
2014	C+	18,754	21.49	C+ / 5.7	10.75%	B- / 7.1
2013	C+	17,308	21.23	C / 4.6	20.34%	B- / 7.2
2012	B-	15,209	19.41	C / 5.5	13.79%	B- / 7.2
2011	B-	15,013	17.69	C+ / 6.1	0.67%	B- / 7.5
2010	C+	16,688	17.91	C+ / 6.8	14.04%	C+ / 6.8

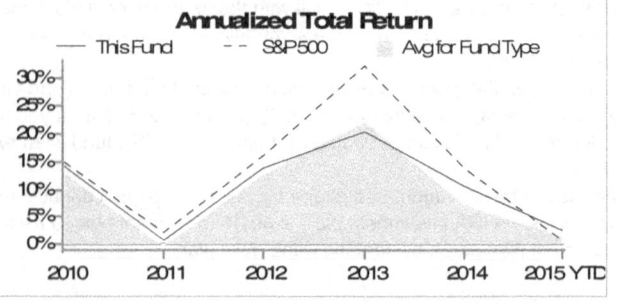

Fidelity Select Biotech Port (FBIOX)   C+   Fair

Fund Family: Fidelity Select Funds   **Phone:** (800) 544-8888
Address: 245 Summer Street, Boston, MA 02210
Fund Type: HL - Health
Major Rating Factors: Fidelity Select Biotech Port has adopted a risky asset allocation strategy and currently receives an overall TheStreet.com Investment Rating of C+ (Fair). The fund has shown an above average level of volatility, as measured by both semi-deviation and drawdown factors. It carries a beta of 0.85, meaning the fund's expected move will be 8.5% for every 10% move in the market. The high level of risk (D+, Weak) did however, reward investors with excellent performance.

  The fund's performance rating is currently A+ (Excellent). It has registered an average return of 43.52% over the last three years and is up 16.02% over the last three months. Factored into the performance evaluation is an expense ratio of 0.76% (very low) and a 0.8% back-end load levied at the time of sale.

  Rajiv Kaul has been running the fund for 10 years and currently receives a manager quality ranking of 99 (0=worst, 99=best). If you are comfortable owning a high risk investment, this fund may be an option.
Services Offered: Automated phone transactions, payroll deductions, bank draft capabilities, an IRA investment plan, a 401K investment plan, a Keogh investment plan and a systematic withdrawal plan.

Data Date	Investment Rating	Net Assets ($Mil)	NAV	Perfor-mance Rating/Pts	Total Return Y-T-D	Risk Rating/Pts
3-15	C+	14,209	256.71	A+ / 9.9	16.02%	D+ / 2.6
2014	C+	10,924	221.27	A+ / 9.9	35.05%	D+ / 2.4
2013	A-	7,959	181.73	A+ / 9.9	65.66%	C- / 4.0
2012	A	2,731	109.99	A+ / 9.9	36.59%	C- / 4.0
2011	B+	1,232	86.10	B+ / 8.5	18.18%	C / 4.3
2010	B	1,039	72.96	B / 7.9	11.41%	C / 5.0

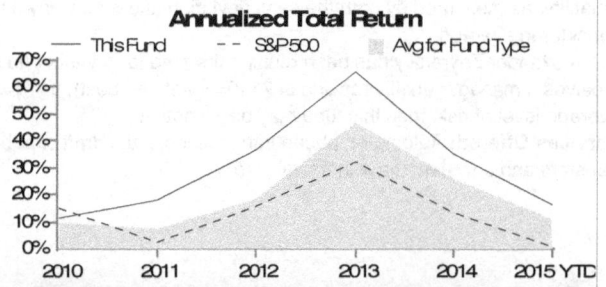

Fidelity Select Health Care (FSPHX)   B   Good

Fund Family: Fidelity Select Funds   **Phone:** (800) 544-8888
Address: 245 Summer Street, Boston, MA 02210
Fund Type: HL - Health
Major Rating Factors: Exceptional performance is the major factor driving the B (Good) TheStreet.com Investment Rating for Fidelity Select Health Care. The fund currently has a performance rating of A+ (Excellent) based on an average return of 36.11% over the last three years and 11.77% over the last three months. Factored into the performance evaluation is an expense ratio of 0.77% (very low) and a 0.8% back-end load levied at the time of sale.

  The fund's risk rating is currently C- (Fair). It carries a beta of 0.85, meaning the fund's expected move will be 8.5% for every 10% move in the market. Volatility, as measured by both the semi-deviation and a drawdown factor, is considered average.

  Edward L. Yoon has been running the fund for 7 years and currently receives a manager quality ranking of 99 (0=worst, 99=best). If you desire an average level of risk and strong performance, then this fund is a good option.
Services Offered: Automated phone transactions, payroll deductions, bank draft capabilities, an IRA investment plan, a 401K investment plan, a Keogh investment plan and a systematic withdrawal plan.

Data Date	Investment Rating	Net Assets ($Mil)	NAV	Perfor-mance Rating/Pts	Total Return Y-T-D	Risk Rating/Pts
3-15	B	10,328	243.32	A+ / 9.9	11.77%	C- / 4.1
2014	B	8,618	217.70	A+ / 9.9	32.88%	C- / 4.0
2013	A-	4,883	188.51	A+ / 9.9	56.27%	C- / 4.1
2012	A+	2,483	134.05	A / 9.5	21.39%	C / 4.8
2011	A+	1,988	122.36	A- / 9.1	7.82%	C / 5.4
2010	B	1,807	124.61	B / 7.8	16.96%	C / 5.0

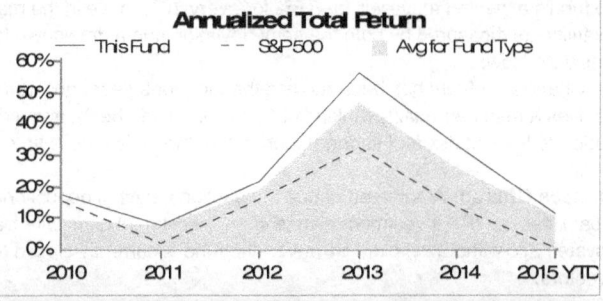

Fidelity Series International Gr F (FFIGX)   C-   Fair

Fund Family: Fidelity Investments   **Phone:** (800) 544-8544
Address: 245 Summer Street, Boston, MA 02210
Fund Type: FO - Foreign
Major Rating Factors: Middle of the road best describes Fidelity Series International Gr F whose TheStreet.com Investment Rating is currently a C- (Fair). The fund currently has a performance rating of C (Fair) based on an average return of 10.19% over the last three years and 6.65% over the last three months. Factored into the performance evaluation is an expense ratio of 0.80% (very low).

  The fund's risk rating is currently C+ (Fair). It carries a beta of 0.83, meaning the fund's expected move will be 8.3% for every 10% move in the market. Volatility, as measured by both the semi-deviation and a drawdown factor, is considered low.

  Jed Weiss has been running the fund for 6 years and currently receives a manager quality ranking of 85 (0=worst, 99=best). If you desire an average level of risk, then this fund may be an option.
Services Offered: Automated phone transactions, bank draft capabilities, wire transfers and a systematic withdrawal plan.

Data Date	Investment Rating	Net Assets ($Mil)	NAV	Perfor-mance Rating/Pts	Total Return Y-T-D	Risk Rating/Pts
3-15	C-	6,784	14.43	C / 4.5	6.65%	C+ / 6.2
2014	D+	6,451	13.53	C- / 3.4	-3.19%	C+ / 6.1
2013	D+	6,829	14.40	C / 4.6	22.36%	C / 4.6
2012	C	4,349	11.91	B / 7.7	19.80%	C- / 3.1
2011	U	2,336	10.12	U / --	-9.24%	U / --
2010	U	993	11.31	U / --	16.74%	U / --

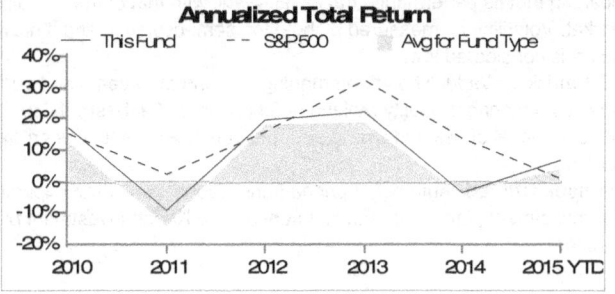

Fidelity Series International Val F (FFVNX)   D   Weak

Fund Family: Fidelity Investments   **Phone:** (800) 544-8544
Address: 245 Summer Street, Boston, MA 02210
Fund Type: FO - Foreign
Major Rating Factors: Fidelity Series International Val F receives a TheStreet.com Investment Rating of D (Weak). The fund currently has a performance rating of C- (Fair) based on an average return of 9.80% over the last three years and 4.96% over the last three months. Factored into the performance evaluation is an expense ratio of 0.65% (very low).

The fund's risk rating is currently C (Fair). It carries a beta of 0.99, meaning that its performance tracks fairly well with that of the overall stock market. Volatility, as measured by both the semi-deviation and a drawdown factor, is considered average.

Alexander Zavratsky has been running the fund for 4 years and currently receives a manager quality ranking of 71 (0=worst, 99=best). If you desire an average level of risk, then this fund may be an option.
Services Offered: Automated phone transactions, bank draft capabilities, wire transfers and a systematic withdrawal plan.

Data Date	Investment Rating	Net Assets ($Mil)	NAV	Performance Rating/Pts	Total Return Y-T-D	Risk Rating/Pts
3-15	D	6,690	10.15	C- / 3.4	4.96%	C / 4.8
2014	D-	6,296	9.67	D+ / 2.3	-7.30%	C / 5.0
2013	D-	6,754	11.24	C- / 3.7	22.78%	C- / 3.4
2012	E+	4,464	9.40	D+ / 2.7	20.40%	D+ / 2.4
2011	U	2,108	8.09	U / --	-16.37%	U / --
2010	U	976	9.96	U / --	4.44%	U / --

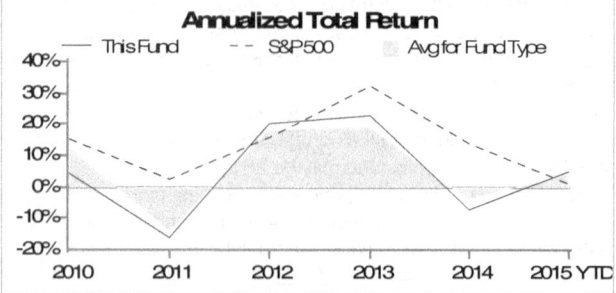

Fidelity Small Cap Discovery Fund (FSCRX)   A-   Excellent

Fund Family: Fidelity Investments   **Phone:** (800) 544-8544
Address: 245 Summer Street, Boston, MA 02210
Fund Type: SC - Small Cap
Major Rating Factors: Exceptional performance is the major factor driving the A- (Excellent) TheStreet.com Investment Rating for Fidelity Small Cap Discovery Fund. The fund currently has a performance rating of A- (Excellent) based on an average return of 18.23% over the last three years and 1.93% over the last three months. Factored into the performance evaluation is an expense ratio of 1.01% (low) and a 1.5% back-end load levied at the time of sale.

The fund's risk rating is currently C+ (Fair). It carries a beta of 0.88, meaning the fund's expected move will be 8.8% for every 10% move in the market. Volatility, as measured by both the semi-deviation and a drawdown factor, is considered low.

Charles L. Myers has been running the fund for 9 years and currently receives a manager quality ranking of 90 (0=worst, 99=best). If you desire only a moderate level of risk and strong performance, then this fund is an excellent option.
Services Offered: Automated phone transactions, payroll deductions, bank draft capabilities, an IRA investment plan, a 401K investment plan, wire transfers and a systematic withdrawal plan. However, the fund is currently closed to new investors.

Data Date	Investment Rating	Net Assets ($Mil)	NAV	Performance Rating/Pts	Total Return Y-T-D	Risk Rating/Pts
3-15	A-	6,115	30.67	A- / 9.1	1.93%	C+ / 6.1
2014	A-	6,119	30.09	A / 9.3	7.00%	C+ / 6.2
2013	B+	6,985	31.26	A / 9.5	38.22%	C- / 3.9
2012	A-	3,880	24.07	A+ / 9.9	24.03%	C- / 3.6
2011	B	1,960	20.03	A+ / 9.8	0.36%	D+ / 2.7
2010	A	885	20.47	A+ / 9.9	32.38%	C / 4.7

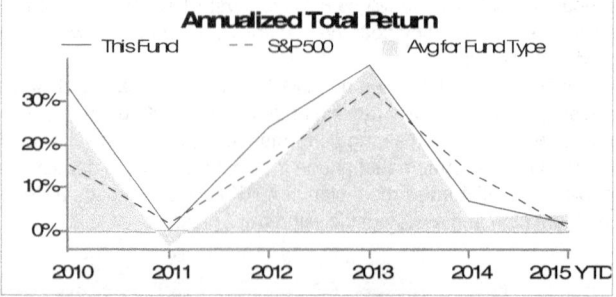

Fidelity Spartan 500 Index Inv (FUSEX)   A   Excellent

Fund Family: Fidelity Investments   **Phone:** (800) 544-8544
Address: 245 Summer Street, Boston, MA 02210
Fund Type: IX - Index
Major Rating Factors: Strong performance is the major factor driving the A (Excellent) TheStreet.com Investment Rating for Fidelity Spartan 500 Index Inv. The fund currently has a performance rating of B (Good) based on an average return of 16.01% over the last three years and 0.92% over the last three months. Factored into the performance evaluation is an expense ratio of 0.10% (very low).

The fund's risk rating is currently B- (Good). It carries a beta of 1.00, meaning that its performance tracks fairly well with that of the overall stock market. Volatility, as measured by both the semi-deviation and a drawdown factor, is considered low.

Patrick J. Waddell has been running the fund for 9 years and currently receives a manager quality ranking of 66 (0=worst, 99=best). If you desire only a moderate level of risk and strong performance, then this fund is an excellent option.
Services Offered: Automated phone transactions, bank draft capabilities, an IRA investment plan, a 401K investment plan, a Keogh investment plan and wire transfers.

Data Date	Investment Rating	Net Assets ($Mil)	NAV	Performance Rating/Pts	Total Return Y-T-D	Risk Rating/Pts
3-15	A	7,112	73.52	B / 8.2	0.92%	B- / 7.3
2014	A+	7,122	72.85	B+ / 8.9	13.59%	B- / 7.3
2013	A	5,695	65.48	B / 8.2	32.25%	C+ / 6.1
2012	B+	10,370	50.49	B- / 7.4	15.93%	C+ / 5.8
2011	B	16,455	44.49	B- / 7.2	2.03%	C / 5.0
2010	C	26,412	44.48	C / 4.4	14.98%	C / 4.9

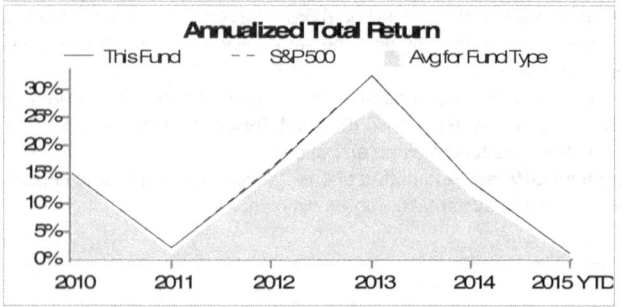

Fidelity Srs Emerging Markets Fd (FEMSX)   E+   Very Weak

Fund Family: Fidelity Investments   **Phone:** (800) 544-8544
Address: 245 Summer Street, Boston, MA 02210
Fund Type: EM - Emerging Market
Major Rating Factors: Very poor performance is the major factor driving the E+ (Very Weak) TheStreet.com Investment Rating for Fidelity Srs Emerging Markets Fd. The fund currently has a performance rating of E+ (Very Weak) based on an average return of 2.10% over the last three years and 2.04% over the last three months. Factored into the performance evaluation is an expense ratio of 1.06% (low).

The fund's risk rating is currently C (Fair). It carries a beta of 1.00, meaning that its performance tracks fairly well with that of the overall stock market. Volatility, as measured by both the semi-deviation and a drawdown factor, is considered average.

James J. Hayes has been running the fund for 6 years and currently receives a manager quality ranking of 80 (0=worst, 99=best). This fund offers an average level of risk but investors looking for strong performance will be frustrated.
Services Offered: Automated phone transactions, bank draft capabilities, wire transfers and a systematic withdrawal plan.

Data Date	Investment Rating	Net Assets ($Mil)	NAV	Performance Rating/Pts	Total Return Y-T-D	Risk Rating/Pts
3-15	E+	5,418	17.00	E+ / 0.7	2.04%	C / 5.3
2014	E+	4,792	16.66	E+ / 0.9	-4.30%	C / 5.2
2013	E	4,221	17.55	E / 0.5	3.35%	D+ / 2.7
2012	D+	3,325	17.15	C+ / 6.1	21.79%	D+ / 2.6
2011	D	3,204	14.28	C / 5.3	-22.33%	D- / 1.2
2010	U	2,670	19.15	U / --	21.85%	U / --

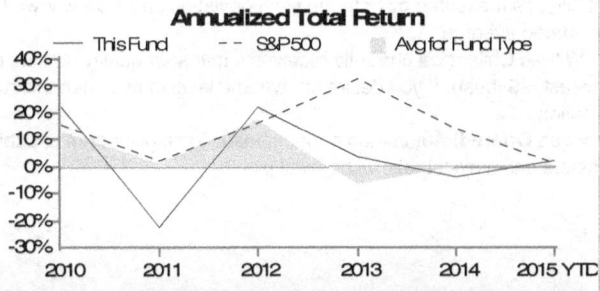

Fidelity Strategic Advisers Core (FCSAX)   B   Good

Fund Family: Fidelity Investments   **Phone:** (800) 544-8544
Address: 245 Summer Street, Boston, MA 02210
Fund Type: IN - Income
Major Rating Factors: Strong performance is the major factor driving the B (Good) TheStreet.com Investment Rating for Fidelity Strategic Advisers Core. The fund currently has a performance rating of B (Good) based on an average return of 15.71% over the last three years and 1.41% over the last three months. Factored into the performance evaluation is an expense ratio of 0.97% (low).

The fund's risk rating is currently C+ (Fair). It carries a beta of 1.01, meaning that its performance tracks fairly well with that of the overall stock market. Volatility, as measured by both the semi-deviation and a drawdown factor, is considered low.

Ronald S. Temple has been running the fund for 6 years and currently receives a manager quality ranking of 60 (0=worst, 99=best). If you desire only a moderate level of risk and strong performance, then this fund is an excellent option.
Services Offered: Automated phone transactions, bank draft capabilities, wire transfers and a systematic withdrawal plan.

Data Date	Investment Rating	Net Assets ($Mil)	NAV	Performance Rating/Pts	Total Return Y-T-D	Risk Rating/Pts
3-15	B	23,744	15.79	B / 8.0	1.41%	C+ / 6.0
2014	B+	22,831	15.57	B+ / 8.6	12.11%	C+ / 6.0
2013	B-	12,505	14.93	B- / 7.5	32.84%	C / 4.8
2012	C+	9,094	12.15	C+ / 6.6	16.11%	C / 5.3
2011	U	8,069	10.77	U / --	-2.34%	U / --
2010	U	7,424	11.36	U / --	0.00%	U / --

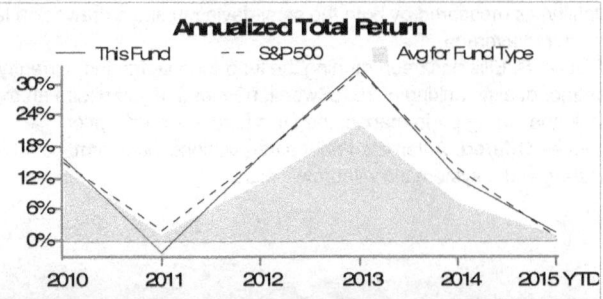

Fidelity Strategic Advisers Growth (FSGFX)   B+   Good

Fund Family: Fidelity Investments   **Phone:** (800) 544-8544
Address: 245 Summer Street, Boston, MA 02210
Fund Type: GR - Growth
Major Rating Factors: Strong performance is the major factor driving the B+ (Good) TheStreet.com Investment Rating for Fidelity Strategic Advisers Growth. The fund currently has a performance rating of B+ (Good) based on an average return of 15.57% over the last three years and 3.84% over the last three months. Factored into the performance evaluation is an expense ratio of 0.78% (very low).

The fund's risk rating is currently C+ (Fair). It carries a beta of 1.03, meaning that its performance tracks fairly well with that of the overall stock market. Volatility, as measured by both the semi-deviation and a drawdown factor, is considered low.

John Stone has been running the fund for 5 years and currently receives a manager quality ranking of 54 (0=worst, 99=best). If you desire only a moderate level of risk and strong performance, then this fund is an excellent option.
Services Offered: N/A

Data Date	Investment Rating	Net Assets ($Mil)	NAV	Performance Rating/Pts	Total Return Y-T-D	Risk Rating/Pts
3-15	B+	12,814	17.32	B+ / 8.4	3.84%	C+ / 6.1
2014	B+	12,366	16.68	B+ / 8.4	11.26%	C+ / 6.1
2013	B+	11,303	16.03	B+ / 8.6	35.78%	C / 4.6
2012	U	7,719	12.90	U / --	13.51%	U / --
2011	U	7,426	11.44	U / --	-0.42%	U / --
2010	U	5,609	11.66	U / --	0.00%	U / --

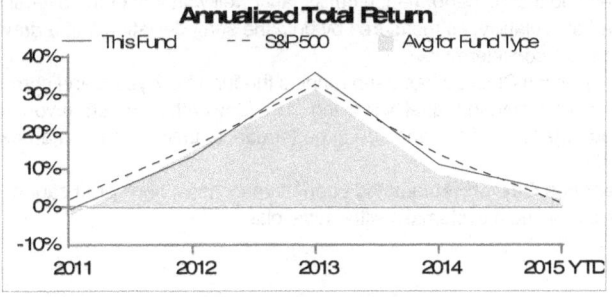

Fidelity Strategic Advisers Intl (FILFX)   D   Weak

Fund Family: Fidelity Investments   **Phone:** (800) 544-8544
Address: 245 Summer Street, Boston, MA 02210
Fund Type: FO - Foreign

Major Rating Factors: Fidelity Strategic Advisers Intl receives a TheStreet.com Investment Rating of D (Weak). The fund currently has a performance rating of C- (Fair) based on an average return of 9.24% over the last three years and 5.72% over the last three months. Factored into the performance evaluation is an expense ratio of 1.14% (low).

The fund's risk rating is currently C (Fair). It carries a beta of 0.90, meaning the fund's expected move will be 9.0% for every 10% move in the market. Volatility, as measured by both the semi-deviation and a drawdown factor, is considered average.

Wilfred Chilangwa currently receives a manager quality ranking of 74 (0=worst, 99=best). If you desire an average level of risk, then this fund may be an option.

Services Offered: Automated phone transactions, bank draft capabilities, wire transfers and a systematic withdrawal plan.

Data Date	Investment Rating	Net Assets ($Mil)	NAV	Performance Rating/Pts	Total Return Y-T-D	Risk Rating/Pts
3-15	D	21,571	10.35	C- / 3.5	5.72%	C / 5.2
2014	D	22,865	9.79	D+ / 2.8	-5.08%	C / 5.3
2013	D	20,404	10.72	C- / 4.0	22.20%	C- / 3.4
2012	D+	12,308	8.93	C+ / 6.2	20.01%	D+ / 2.6
2011	E-	11,211	7.60	D- / 1.1	-12.43%	D- / 1.2
2010	E	10,470	9.00	D / 2.1	11.78%	E- / 0.0

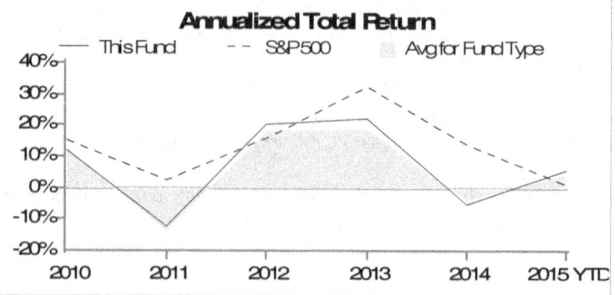

Fidelity Strategic Advisers Sm-Mid (FSCFX)   C   Fair

Fund Family: Fidelity Investments   **Phone:** (800) 544-8544
Address: 245 Summer Street, Boston, MA 02210
Fund Type: GR - Growth

Major Rating Factors: Strong performance is the major factor driving the C (Fair) TheStreet.com Investment Rating for Fidelity Strategic Advisers Sm-Mid. The fund currently has a performance rating of B- (Good) based on an average return of 14.73% over the last three years and 4.22% over the last three months. Factored into the performance evaluation is an expense ratio of 1.17% (low).

The fund's risk rating is currently C- (Fair). It carries a beta of 1.06, meaning that its performance tracks fairly well with that of the overall stock market. Volatility, as measured by both the semi-deviation and a drawdown factor, is considered average.

Juliet S. Ellis has been running the fund for 5 years and currently receives a manager quality ranking of 36 (0=worst, 99=best). If you desire an average level of risk and strong performance, then this fund is a good option.

Services Offered: Automated phone transactions, bank draft capabilities, wire transfers and a systematic withdrawal plan.

Data Date	Investment Rating	Net Assets ($Mil)	NAV	Performance Rating/Pts	Total Return Y-T-D	Risk Rating/Pts
3-15	C	7,210	13.84	B- / 7.4	4.22%	C- / 4.0
2014	C-	6,969	13.28	C+ / 6.6	3.99%	C- / 3.8
2013	C+	5,071	13.92	B / 7.9	36.26%	C- / 3.2
2012	C	2,705	11.41	B / 8.1	15.32%	D / 2.1
2011	C-	2,469	10.35	B / 8.1	-4.31%	E / 0.5
2010	C	2,013	11.33	B+ / 8.8	24.48%	E- / 0.0

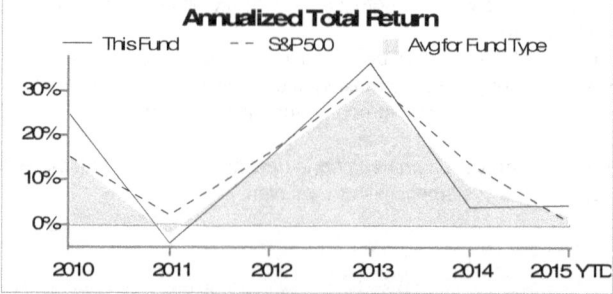

Fidelity Strategic Advisers Val Fd (FVSAX)   A-   Excellent

Fund Family: Fidelity Investments   **Phone:** (800) 544-8544
Address: 245 Summer Street, Boston, MA 02210
Fund Type: GR - Growth

Major Rating Factors: Strong performance is the major factor driving the A- (Excellent) TheStreet.com Investment Rating for Fidelity Strategic Advisers Val Fd. The fund currently has a performance rating of B (Good) based on an average return of 16.10% over the last three years and 0.48% over the last three months. Factored into the performance evaluation is an expense ratio of 0.79% (very low).

The fund's risk rating is currently B- (Good). It carries a beta of 1.04, meaning that its performance tracks fairly well with that of the overall stock market. Volatility, as measured by both the semi-deviation and a drawdown factor, is considered low.

Kristina Stookey has been running the fund for 7 years and currently receives a manager quality ranking of 57 (0=worst, 99=best). If you desire only a moderate level of risk and strong performance, then this fund is an excellent option.

Services Offered: Automated phone transactions, bank draft capabilities, wire transfers and a systematic withdrawal plan.

Data Date	Investment Rating	Net Assets ($Mil)	NAV	Performance Rating/Pts	Total Return Y-T-D	Risk Rating/Pts
3-15	A-	12,858	18.82	B / 7.9	0.48%	B- / 7.0
2014	A	12,982	18.73	B+ / 8.9	12.43%	B- / 7.1
2013	B+	11,516	18.25	B / 7.9	33.32%	C / 5.5
2012	C+	7,894	14.53	C+ / 6.5	16.59%	C / 5.1
2011	D	6,572	13.03	C- / 3.5	-0.77%	C- / 3.4
2010	U	6,639	13.55	U / --	12.23%	U / --

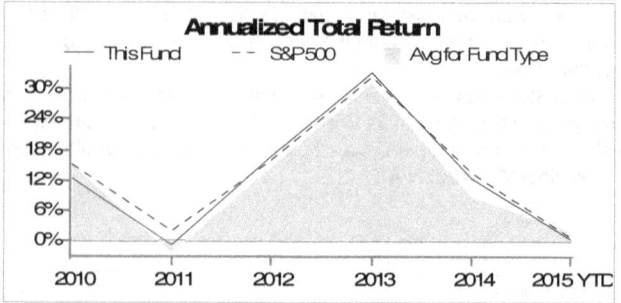

Fidelity Value Fd (FDVLX)   A+   Excellent

Fund Family: Fidelity Investments   **Phone:** (800) 544-8544
Address: 245 Summer Street, Boston, MA 02210
Fund Type: GI - Growth and Income
Major Rating Factors: Exceptional performance is the major factor driving the A+ (Excellent) TheStreet.com Investment Rating for Fidelity Value Fd. The fund currently has a performance rating of A (Excellent) based on an average return of 18.97% over the last three years and 3.05% over the last three months. Factored into the performance evaluation is an expense ratio of 0.76% (very low).

The fund's risk rating is currently C+ (Fair). It carries a beta of 1.05, meaning that its performance tracks fairly well with that of the overall stock market. Volatility, as measured by both the semi-deviation and a drawdown factor, is considered low.

Matthew H. Friedman has been running the fund for 5 years and currently receives a manager quality ranking of 82 (0=worst, 99=best). If you desire only a moderate level of risk and strong performance, then this fund is an excellent option.

Services Offered: Automated phone transactions, payroll deductions, bank draft capabilities, an IRA investment plan, a 401K investment plan, a Keogh investment plan and a systematic withdrawal plan.

Data Date	Investment Rating	Net Assets ($Mil)	NAV	Performance Rating/Pts	Total Return Y-T-D	Risk Rating/Pts
3-15	A+	8,133	116.72	A / 9.5	3.05%	C+ / 6.9
2014	A+	8,106	113.26	A+ / 9.6	11.72%	C+ / 6.7
2013	B	7,360	103.58	B+ / 8.5	37.07%	C / 4.3
2012	B+	5,613	76.34	A / 9.3	21.90%	C- / 3.7
2011	C+	5,825	63.47	B / 8.2	-6.71%	C- / 3.0
2010	C	7,668	68.69	C+ / 6.9	22.27%	D+ / 2.7

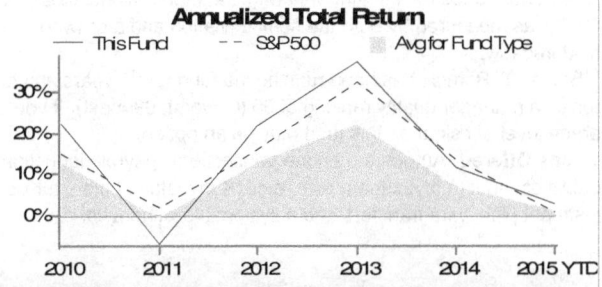

First Eagle Global A (SGENX)   D+   Weak

Fund Family: First Eagle   **Phone:** (800) 334-2143
Address: 1345 Avenue of the Americas, New York, NY 10105
Fund Type: GL - Global
Major Rating Factors: Disappointing performance is the major factor driving the D+ (Weak) TheStreet.com Investment Rating for First Eagle Global A. The fund currently has a performance rating of D (Weak) based on an average return of 7.97% over the last three years and 2.25% over the last three months. Factored into the performance evaluation is an expense ratio of 1.11% (low) and a 5.0% front-end load that is levied at the time of purchase.

The fund's risk rating is currently B- (Good). It carries a beta of 0.55, meaning the fund's expected move will be 5.5% for every 10% move in the market. Volatility, as measured by both the semi-deviation and a drawdown factor, is considered low.

Matthew B. McLennan has been running the fund for 7 years and currently receives a manager quality ranking of 87 (0=worst, 99=best). This fund offers only a moderate level of risk but investors looking for strong performance are still waiting.

Services Offered: Automated phone transactions, payroll deductions, bank draft capabilities, an IRA investment plan, a 401K investment plan, wire transfers and a systematic withdrawal plan.

Data Date	Investment Rating	Net Assets ($Mil)	NAV	Performance Rating/Pts	Total Return Y-T-D	Risk Rating/Pts
3-15	D+	17,476	53.62	D / 2.0	2.25%	B- / 7.4
2014	D+	17,506	52.44	D+ / 2.4	2.94%	B- / 7.3
2013	C-	19,398	53.61	D+ / 2.7	15.49%	B- / 7.3
2012	C+	16,115	48.59	C- / 3.9	12.46%	B- / 7.3
2011	C	14,220	45.12	C- / 3.5	-0.19%	C+ / 6.9
2010	A	13,251	46.36	B / 8.1	17.58%	B- / 7.0

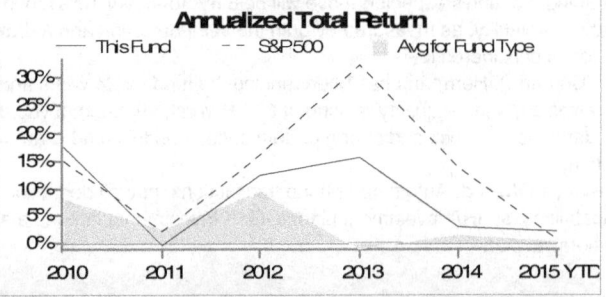

FMI Large Cap (FMIHX)   B+   Good

Fund Family: Fiduciary Management Funds   **Phone:** (800) 811-5311
Address: 225 E. Mason St., Milwaukee, WI 53202
Fund Type: GR - Growth
Major Rating Factors: Strong performance is the major factor driving the B+ (Good) TheStreet.com Investment Rating for FMI Large Cap. The fund currently has a performance rating of B (Good) based on an average return of 15.56% over the last three years and 1.79% over the last three months. Factored into the performance evaluation is an expense ratio of 0.94% (low).

The fund's risk rating is currently C+ (Fair). It carries a beta of 0.91, meaning that its performance tracks fairly well with that of the overall stock market. Volatility, as measured by both the semi-deviation and a drawdown factor, is considered low.

Patrick J. English has been running the fund for 14 years and currently receives a manager quality ranking of 76 (0=worst, 99=best). If you desire only a moderate level of risk and strong performance, then this fund is an excellent option.

Services Offered: Automated phone transactions, payroll deductions, bank draft capabilities, an IRA investment plan, a 401K investment plan, a Keogh investment plan and a systematic withdrawal plan. However, the fund is currently closed to new investors.

Data Date	Investment Rating	Net Assets ($Mil)	NAV	Performance Rating/Pts	Total Return Y-T-D	Risk Rating/Pts
3-15	B+	9,559	21.60	B / 8.0	1.79%	C+ / 6.5
2014	B+	9,631	21.22	B / 8.0	12.36%	C+ / 6.9
2013	B+	8,690	20.86	B- / 7.0	30.48%	C+ / 6.5
2012	C+	6,233	17.10	C+ / 5.8	14.86%	C+ / 6.2
2011	C+	4,477	15.25	C+ / 6.7	1.49%	C / 5.3
2010	B+	3,676	15.61	B- / 7.4	11.41%	C+ / 6.2

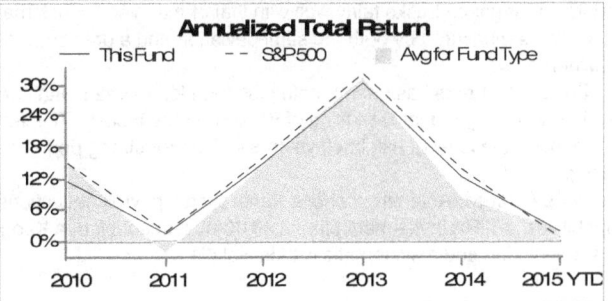

FPA Crescent (FPACX)

C+   **Fair**

Fund Family: FPA Funds   **Phone:** (800) 982-4372
Address: 11400 West Olympic Blvd, Los Angeles, CA 90064
Fund Type: BA - Balanced
Major Rating Factors: Middle of the road best describes FPA Crescent whose TheStreet.com Investment Rating is currently a C+ (Fair). The fund currently has a performance rating of C- (Fair) based on an average return of 10.45% over the last three years and 0.15% over the last three months. Factored into the performance evaluation is an expense ratio of 1.23% (average) and a 2.0% back-end load levied at the time of sale.

The fund's risk rating is currently B (Good). It carries a beta of 1.04, meaning that its performance tracks fairly well with that of the overall stock market. Volatility, as measured by both the semi-deviation and a drawdown factor, is considered low.

Steven T. Romick has been running the fund for 22 years and currently receives a manager quality ranking of 56 (0=worst, 99=best). If you desire an average level of risk, then this fund may be an option.

Services Offered: Automated phone transactions, payroll deductions, bank draft capabilities, an IRA investment plan, a 401K investment plan, a Keogh investment plan, wire transfers and a systematic withdrawal plan.

Data Date	Investment Rating	Net Assets ($Mil)	NAV	Perfor- mance Rating/Pts	Total Return Y-T-D	Risk Rating/Pts
3-15	C+	19,966	33.79	C- / 3.8	0.15%	B / 8.5
2014	C+	19,970	33.74	C- / 4.2	6.64%	B / 8.5
2013	B-	15,882	32.96	C / 4.4	21.95%	B- / 7.8
2012	C+	9,917	29.29	C- / 3.6	10.33%	B- / 7.8
2011	B	7,465	26.78	C+ / 6.7	3.02%	B / 8.2
2010	A+	4,813	26.79	B / 8.1	12.04%	B- / 7.9

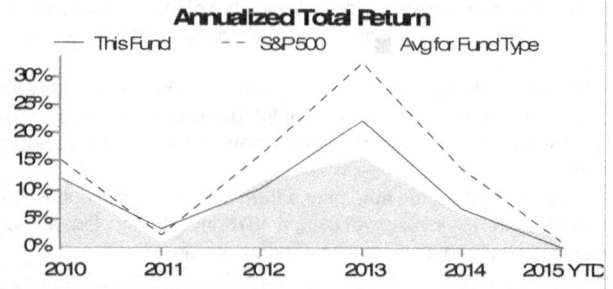

Franklin Growth A (FKGRX)

A-   **Excellent**

Fund Family: Franklin Templeton Investments   **Phone:** (800) 342-5236
Address: One Franklin Parkway, San Mateo, CA 94403
Fund Type: GR - Growth
Major Rating Factors: Strong performance is the major factor driving the A- (Excellent) TheStreet.com Investment Rating for Franklin Growth A. The fund currently has a performance rating of B (Good) based on an average return of 15.61% over the last three years and 3.31% over the last three months. Factored into the performance evaluation is an expense ratio of 0.90% (low) and a 5.8% front-end load that is levied at the time of purchase.

The fund's risk rating is currently B- (Good). It carries a beta of 0.88, meaning the fund's expected move will be 8.8% for every 10% move in the market. Volatility, as measured by both the semi-deviation and a drawdown factor, is considered low.

Conrad B. Herrmann has been running the fund for 24 years and currently receives a manager quality ranking of 80 (0=worst, 99=best). If you desire only a moderate level of risk and strong performance, then this fund is an excellent option.

Services Offered: Automated phone transactions, payroll deductions, bank draft capabilities, an IRA investment plan, a 401K investment plan and a systematic withdrawal plan.

Data Date	Investment Rating	Net Assets ($Mil)	NAV	Perfor- mance Rating/Pts	Total Return Y-T-D	Risk Rating/Pts
3-15	A-	7,603	77.16	B / 7.6	3.31%	B- / 7.3
2014	B+	7,193	74.69	B- / 7.5	14.88%	B- / 7.3
2013	C+	5,992	65.18	C+ / 6.0	29.39%	C+ / 6.2
2012	C-	4,226	50.61	C- / 3.9	13.69%	C+ / 5.8
2011	C+	3,397	44.64	C+ / 6.9	0.62%	C / 5.2
2010	C+	3,047	44.64	C+ / 6.0	14.86%	C / 5.3

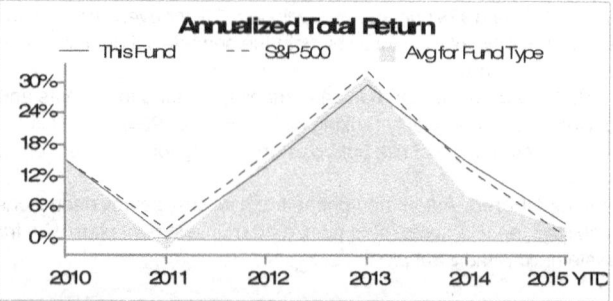

Franklin Income A (FKINX)

D   **Weak**

Fund Family: Franklin Templeton Investments   **Phone:** (800) 342-5236
Address: One Franklin Parkway, San Mateo, CA 94403
Fund Type: GL - Global
Major Rating Factors: Disappointing performance is the major factor driving the D (Weak) TheStreet.com Investment Rating for Franklin Income A. The fund currently has a performance rating of D (Weak) based on an average return of 8.92% over the last three years and 0.84% over the last three months. Factored into the performance evaluation is an expense ratio of 0.61% (very low) and a 4.3% front-end load that is levied at the time of purchase.

The fund's risk rating is currently C+ (Fair). It carries a beta of 1.04, meaning that its performance tracks fairly well with that of the overall stock market. Volatility, as measured by both the semi-deviation and a drawdown factor, is considered low.

Edward D. Perks has been running the fund for 13 years and currently receives a manager quality ranking of 61 (0=worst, 99=best). This fund offers only a moderate level of risk but investors looking for strong performance are still waiting.

Services Offered: Automated phone transactions, payroll deductions, bank draft capabilities, an IRA investment plan, a 401K investment plan, a Keogh investment plan and a systematic withdrawal plan.

Data Date	Investment Rating	Net Assets ($Mil)	NAV	Perfor- mance Rating/Pts	Total Return Y-T-D	Risk Rating/Pts
3-15	D	53,635	2.39	D / 2.2	0.84%	C+ / 6.8
2014	D+	52,523	2.40	D+ / 2.5	4.12%	B- / 7.1
2013	D+	50,515	2.42	D+ / 2.9	14.23%	C+ / 6.3
2012	C+	42,511	2.24	C / 5.1	13.68%	C+ / 5.9
2011	B+	34,617	2.10	B / 7.6	2.83%	C+ / 5.7
2010	C+	34,274	2.18	C+ / 6.1	12.91%	C / 4.8

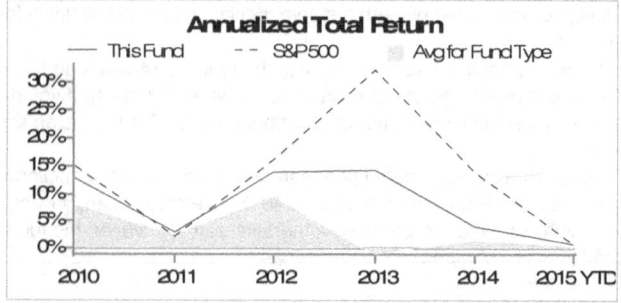

Franklin Mutual Global Discovery A (TEDIX)   C   Fair

Fund Family: Franklin Templeton Investments   **Phone:** (800) 342-5236
Address: One Franklin Parkway, San Mateo, CA 94403
Fund Type: GL - Global
Major Rating Factors: Middle of the road best describes Franklin Mutual Global Discovery A whose TheStreet.com Investment Rating is currently a C (Fair). The fund currently has a performance rating of C (Fair) based on an average return of 12.72% over the last three years and 3.14% over the last three months. Factored into the performance evaluation is an expense ratio of 1.28% (average) and a 5.8% front-end load that is levied at the time of purchase.

The fund's risk rating is currently C+ (Fair). It carries a beta of 0.58, meaning the fund's expected move will be 5.8% for every 10% move in the market. Volatility, as measured by both the semi-deviation and a drawdown factor, is considered low.

Peter A. Langerman has been running the fund for 10 years and currently receives a manager quality ranking of 96 (0=worst, 99=best). If you desire an average level of risk, then this fund may be an option.

Services Offered: Automated phone transactions, payroll deductions, bank draft capabilities, an IRA investment plan, a 401K investment plan, a Keogh investment plan, wire transfers and a systematic withdrawal plan.

Data Date	Investment Rating	Net Assets ($Mil)	NAV	Perfor- mance Rating/Pts	Total Return Y-T-D	Risk Rating/Pts
3-15	C	12,100	33.84	C / 4.7	3.14%	C+ / 6.9
2014	C	11,577	32.81	C- / 4.1	5.01%	C+ / 6.8
2013	C-	10,609	33.24	C / 4.4	25.26%	C / 5.4
2012	D	8,007	28.27	D / 2.1	13.34%	C+ / 5.7
2011	D+	7,648	27.14	D- / 1.4	-2.99%	C+ / 6.5
2010	C+	8,119	29.19	C- / 3.2	11.08%	B- / 7.7

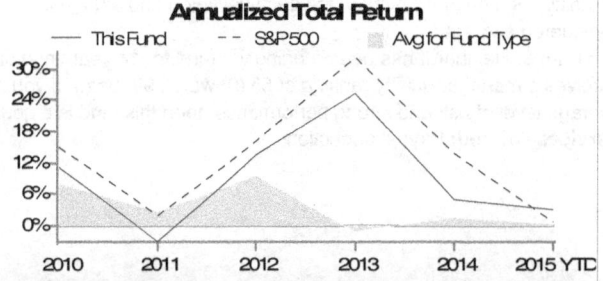

Annualized Total Return

Franklin Mutual Shares A (TESIX)   C+   Fair

Fund Family: Franklin Templeton Investments   **Phone:** (800) 342-5236
Address: One Franklin Parkway, San Mateo, CA 94403
Fund Type: GI - Growth and Income
Major Rating Factors: Middle of the road best describes Franklin Mutual Shares A whose TheStreet.com Investment Rating is currently a C+ (Fair). The fund currently has a performance rating of C (Fair) based on an average return of 13.81% over the last three years and 2.39% over the last three months. Factored into the performance evaluation is an expense ratio of 1.09% (low) and a 5.8% front-end load that is levied at the time of purchase.

The fund's risk rating is currently B- (Good). It carries a beta of 0.90, meaning the fund's expected move will be 9.0% for every 10% move in the market. Volatility, as measured by both the semi-deviation and a drawdown factor, is considered low.

Deborah A. Turner has been running the fund for 14 years and currently receives a manager quality ranking of 60 (0=worst, 99=best). If you desire an average level of risk, then this fund may be an option.

Services Offered: Automated phone transactions, payroll deductions, bank draft capabilities, an IRA investment plan, a 401K investment plan, a Keogh investment plan, wire transfers and a systematic withdrawal plan.

Data Date	Investment Rating	Net Assets ($Mil)	NAV	Perfor- mance Rating/Pts	Total Return Y-T-D	Risk Rating/Pts
3-15	C+	5,539	29.99	C / 5.4	2.39%	B- / 7.5
2014	C+	5,396	29.29	C / 5.1	7.30%	B- / 7.4
2013	C+	5,425	28.12	C / 5.1	27.74%	C+ / 5.8
2012	D+	4,643	22.31	D+ / 2.9	14.75%	C+ / 5.8
2011	C-	4,688	19.81	C- / 3.0	-1.79%	C+ / 5.9
2010	D+	5,367	20.64	D- / 1.3	11.41%	C / 5.3

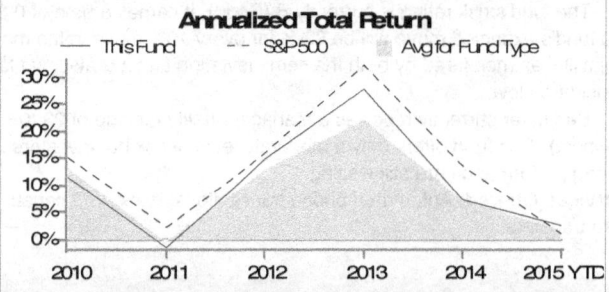

Annualized Total Return

Franklin Rising Dividends A (FRDPX)   B-   Good

Fund Family: Franklin Templeton Investments   **Phone:** (800) 342-5236
Address: One Franklin Parkway, San Mateo, CA 94403
Fund Type: GI - Growth and Income
Major Rating Factors: Franklin Rising Dividends A receives a TheStreet.com Investment Rating of B- (Good). The fund currently has a performance rating of C (Fair) based on an average return of 13.43% over the last three years and 0.10% over the last three months. Factored into the performance evaluation is an expense ratio of 0.91% (low) and a 5.8% front-end load that is levied at the time of purchase.

The fund's risk rating is currently B- (Good). It carries a beta of 0.92, meaning that its performance tracks fairly well with that of the overall stock market. Volatility, as measured by both the semi-deviation and a drawdown factor, is considered low.

Bruce C. Baughman has been running the fund for 28 years and currently receives a manager quality ranking of 51 (0=worst, 99=best). If you desire an average level of risk, then this fund may be an option.

Services Offered: Automated phone transactions, payroll deductions, bank draft capabilities, an IRA investment plan, a 401K investment plan, a Keogh investment plan and a systematic withdrawal plan.

Data Date	Investment Rating	Net Assets ($Mil)	NAV	Perfor- mance Rating/Pts	Total Return Y-T-D	Risk Rating/Pts
3-15	B-	11,609	52.04	C / 5.3	0.10%	B- / 7.7
2014	B-	11,389	52.06	C+ / 5.6	9.72%	B- / 7.8
2013	B-	9,764	48.47	C+ / 6.0	29.30%	B- / 7.1
2012	C+	5,935	37.82	C+ / 6.3	10.29%	C+ / 6.9
2011	B	3,928	34.80	B- / 7.0	7.21%	C / 5.5
2010	C+	2,614	32.85	C+ / 6.0	19.08%	C+ / 5.7

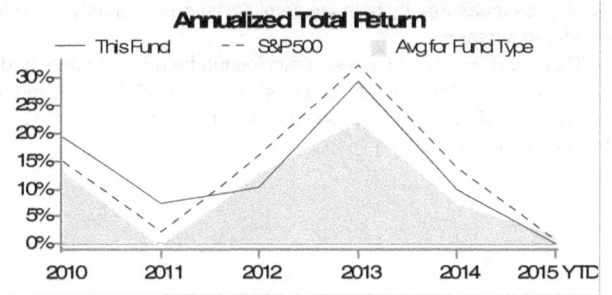

Annualized Total Return

GE RSP US Equity (GESSX)   B   Good

Fund Family: GE Investment Funds   **Phone:** (800) 242-0134
Address: PO Box 9838, Providence, RI 02940
Fund Type: GI - Growth and Income

Major Rating Factors: Strong performance is the major factor driving the B (Good) TheStreet.com Investment Rating for GE RSP US Equity. The fund currently has a performance rating of B (Good) based on an average return of 16.30% over the last three years and 0.79% over the last three months. Factored into the performance evaluation is an expense ratio of 0.17% (very low).

The fund's risk rating is currently C (Fair). It carries a beta of 1.06, meaning that its performance tracks fairly well with that of the overall stock market. Volatility, as measured by both the semi-deviation and a drawdown factor, is considered average.

Paul C. Reinhardt has been running the fund for 14 years and currently receives a manager quality ranking of 56 (0=worst, 99=best). If you desire an average level of risk and strong performance, then this fund is a good option.

Services Offered: Payroll deductions.

Data Date	Investment Rating	Net Assets ($Mil)	NAV	Performance Rating/Pts	Total Return Y-T-D	Risk Rating/Pts
3-15	B	5,412	54.74	B / 8.2	0.79%	C / 5.3
2014	A-	5,446	54.31	A / 9.3	13.27%	C+ / 5.8
2013	B+	5,057	54.73	B / 8.2	35.15%	C / 5.5
2012	C	3,960	44.41	C / 5.3	16.78%	C / 5.3
2011	C+	3,596	38.75	C+ / 5.6	-2.16%	C / 5.2
2010	C	3,930	40.23	C / 4.7	10.71%	C / 5.3

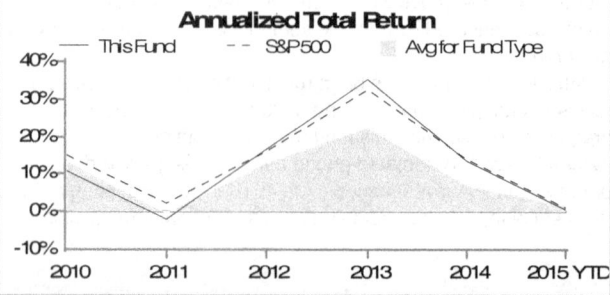

GMO Benchmark-Free Allocation III (GBMFX)   D+   Weak

Fund Family: GMO Funds   **Phone:** N/A
Address: 40 Rowes Wharf, Boston, MA 02110
Fund Type: AA - Asset Allocation

Major Rating Factors: Disappointing performance is the major factor driving the D+ (Weak) TheStreet.com Investment Rating for GMO Benchmark-Free Allocation III. The fund currently has a performance rating of D- (Weak) based on an average return of 5.70% over the last three years and 1.42% over the last three months. Factored into the performance evaluation is an expense ratio of 1.08% (low), a 0.1% front-end load that is levied at the time of purchase and a 0.1% back-end load levied at the time of sale.

The fund's risk rating is currently B (Good). It carries a beta of 0.84, meaning the fund's expected move will be 8.4% for every 10% move in the market. Volatility, as measured by both the semi-deviation and a drawdown factor, is considered low.

Ben Inker currently receives a manager quality ranking of 23 (0=worst, 99=best). This fund offers only a moderate level of risk but investors looking for strong performance are still waiting.

Services Offered: Automated phone transactions, bank draft capabilities and wire transfers.

Data Date	Investment Rating	Net Assets ($Mil)	NAV	Performance Rating/Pts	Total Return Y-T-D	Risk Rating/Pts
3-15	D+	6,036	26.39	D- / 1.5	1.42%	B / 8.0
2014	C-	5,108	26.02	D / 1.6	1.21%	B / 8.3
2013	C+	2,767	26.95	D+ / 2.3	10.73%	B+ / 9.3
2012	C+	853	25.03	D / 2.1	10.01%	B+ / 9.4
2011	B	162	22.92	C- / 3.2	3.86%	B+ / 9.2
2010	A	2,351	22.40	B- / 7.2	4.91%	B- / 7.7

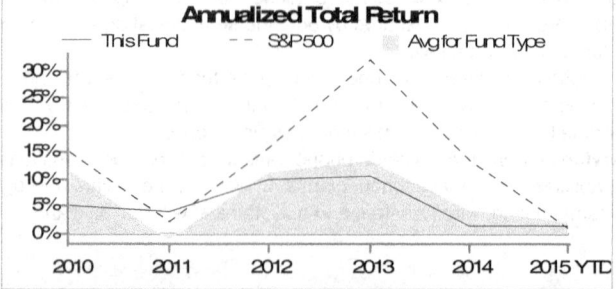

GMO Quality Equity III (GQETX)   C-   Fair

Fund Family: GMO Funds   **Phone:** N/A
Address: 40 Rowes Wharf, Boston, MA 02110
Fund Type: IN - Income

Major Rating Factors: Middle of the road best describes GMO Quality Equity III whose TheStreet.com Investment Rating is currently a C- (Fair). The fund currently has a performance rating of C+ (Fair) based on an average return of 13.15% over the last three years and 0.49% over the last three months. Factored into the performance evaluation is an expense ratio of 0.49% (very low).

The fund's risk rating is currently C (Fair). It carries a beta of 0.92, meaning that its performance tracks fairly well with that of the overall stock market. Volatility, as measured by both the semi-deviation and a drawdown factor, is considered average.

Thomas R. Hancock has been running the fund for 11 years and currently receives a manager quality ranking of 47 (0=worst, 99=best). If you desire an average level of risk, then this fund may be an option.

Services Offered: Wire transfers.

Data Date	Investment Rating	Net Assets ($Mil)	NAV	Performance Rating/Pts	Total Return Y-T-D	Risk Rating/Pts
3-15	C-	5,144	22.50	C+ / 6.2	0.49%	C / 4.3
2014	C	5,157	22.39	C+ / 6.8	12.50%	C / 4.3
2013	B-	5,871	24.92	C+ / 6.8	25.36%	B- / 7.0
2012	A+	6,069	22.34	B / 7.7	15.71%	C+ / 6.8
2011	A	6,018	22.04	B- / 7.4	11.75%	C+ / 6.4
2010	C+	5,099	20.11	C- / 3.6	5.47%	C+ / 6.8

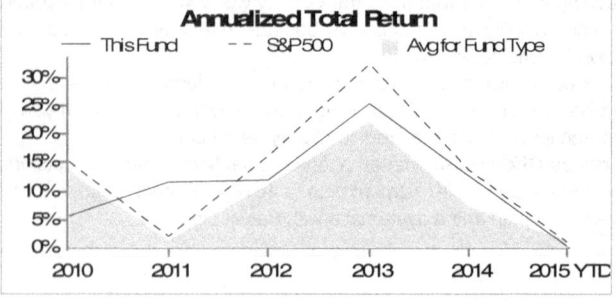

Hartford Capital Apprec A (ITHAX)   D+   Weak

Fund Family: Hartford Mutual Funds **Phone:** (888) 843-7824
Address: P.O. Box 64387, St. Paul, MN 55164
Fund Type: GR - Growth
Major Rating Factors: Hartford Capital Apprec A has adopted a very risky asset allocation strategy and currently receives an overall TheStreet.com Investment Rating of D+ (Weak). The fund has shown a high level of volatility, as measured by both semi-deviation and drawdown factors. It carries a beta of 1.10, meaning it is expected to move 11.0% for every 10% move in the market. The high level of risk (D, Weak) did however, reward investors with excellent performance.

The fund's performance rating is currently B (Good). It has registered an average return of 17.46% over the last three years and is up 3.34% over the last three months. Factored into the performance evaluation is an expense ratio of 1.10% (low) and a 5.5% front-end load that is levied at the time of purchase.

Saul J. Pannell has been running the fund for 19 years and currently receives a manager quality ranking of 63 (0=worst, 99=best). If you are comfortable owning a very high risk investment, this fund may be an option.
Services Offered: Automated phone transactions, payroll deductions, bank draft capabilities, an IRA investment plan, a 401K investment plan, wire transfers and a systematic withdrawal plan.

Data Date	Investment Rating	Net Assets ($Mil)	NAV	Performance Rating/Pts	Total Return Y-T-D	Risk Rating/Pts
3-15	D+	5,744	38.33	B / 8.0	3.34%	D / 1.6
2014	C-	5,684	37.09	B / 8.2	7.33%	D / 1.6
2013	C+	6,064	46.67	B- / 7.1	41.67%	C- / 4.0
2012	D	4,898	34.40	C- / 3.0	20.16%	C- / 4.0
2011	D-	5,243	28.82	D- / 1.2	-15.24%	C / 4.5
2010	D	8,648	34.63	D / 1.8	12.87%	C / 4.3

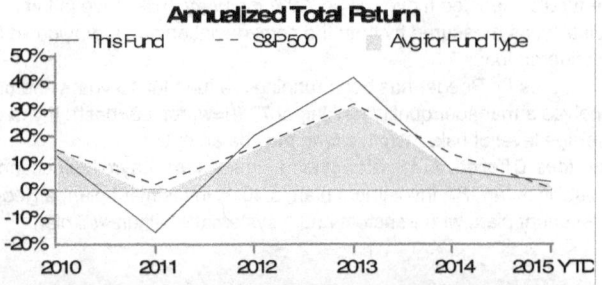

Invesco American Franchise A (VAFAX)   C+   Fair

Fund Family: Invesco Investments Funds **Phone:** (800) 959-4246
Address: P.O. Box 4739, Houston, TX 77210
Fund Type: IN - Income
Major Rating Factors: Middle of the road best describes Invesco American Franchise A whose TheStreet.com Investment Rating is currently a C+ (Fair). The fund currently has a performance rating of C+ (Fair) based on an average return of 14.64% over the last three years and 3.54% over the last three months. Factored into the performance evaluation is an expense ratio of 1.08% (low) and a 5.5% front-end load that is levied at the time of purchase.

The fund's risk rating is currently C (Fair). It carries a beta of 1.11, meaning it is expected to move 11.1% for every 10% move in the market. Volatility, as measured by both the semi-deviation and a drawdown factor, is considered average.

Erik J. Voss has been running the fund for 5 years and currently receives a manager quality ranking of 26 (0=worst, 99=best). If you desire an average level of risk, then this fund may be an option.
Services Offered: Automated phone transactions, payroll deductions, bank draft capabilities, an IRA investment plan, a 401K investment plan, wire transfers and a systematic withdrawal plan.

Data Date	Investment Rating	Net Assets ($Mil)	NAV	Performance Rating/Pts	Total Return Y-T-D	Risk Rating/Pts
3-15	C+	9,012	17.26	C+ / 6.5	3.54%	C / 5.4
2014	C+	8,871	16.67	B- / 7.0	8.32%	C / 5.1
2013	B	8,995	16.91	B+ / 8.3	39.72%	C / 4.3
2012	D	4,594	12.63	D+ / 2.3	13.20%	C / 4.8
2011	D+	4,553	11.16	C- / 3.5	-6.85%	C / 4.8
2010	A	215	12.11	B+ / 8.8	21.46%	C+ / 6.4

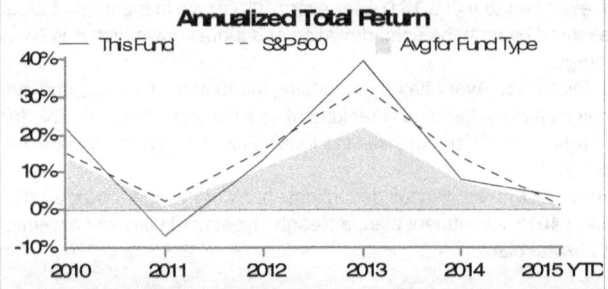

Invesco Comstock A (ACSTX)   B-   Good

Fund Family: Invesco Investments Funds **Phone:** (800) 959-4246
Address: P.O. Box 4739, Houston, TX 77210
Fund Type: GI - Growth and Income
Major Rating Factors: Invesco Comstock A receives a TheStreet.com Investment Rating of B- (Good). The fund currently has a performance rating of C+ (Fair) based on an average return of 15.81% over the last three years and -0.12% over the last three months. Factored into the performance evaluation is an expense ratio of 0.83% (very low) and a 5.5% front-end load that is levied at the time of purchase.

The fund's risk rating is currently B- (Good). It carries a beta of 1.04, meaning that its performance tracks fairly well with that of the overall stock market. Volatility, as measured by both the semi-deviation and a drawdown factor, is considered low.

Jason S. Leder has been running the fund for 20 years and currently receives a manager quality ranking of 55 (0=worst, 99=best). If you desire an average level of risk, then this fund may be an option.
Services Offered: Automated phone transactions, payroll deductions, bank draft capabilities, an IRA investment plan, a 401K investment plan, a Keogh investment plan, wire transfers and a systematic withdrawal plan.

Data Date	Investment Rating	Net Assets ($Mil)	NAV	Performance Rating/Pts	Total Return Y-T-D	Risk Rating/Pts
3-15	B-	7,541	25.41	C+ / 6.2	-0.12%	B- / 7.1
2014	B+	7,609	25.52	B- / 7.4	9.12%	B- / 7.3
2013	B	7,185	23.77	B / 7.6	35.24%	C / 5.4
2012	B	5,371	17.81	B- / 7.2	18.90%	C / 5.2
2011	C-	5,079	15.21	C / 4.8	-1.97%	C / 4.5
2010	C	133	15.73	C / 4.4	15.60%	C / 4.8

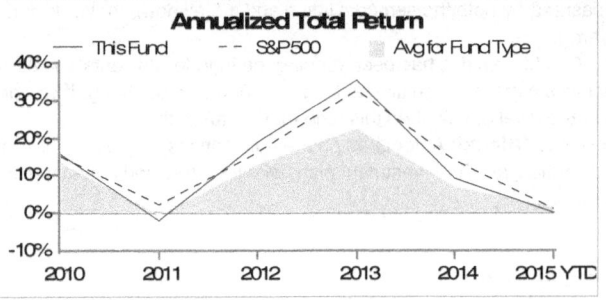

Invesco Equity and Income A (ACEIX)   C   Fair

Fund Family: Invesco Investments Funds   **Phone:** (800) 959-4246
Address: P.O. Box 4739, Houston, TX 77210
Fund Type: GI - Growth and Income
Major Rating Factors: Middle of the road best describes Invesco Equity and Income A whose TheStreet.com Investment Rating is currently a C (Fair). The fund currently has a performance rating of C (Fair) based on an average return of 12.51% over the last three years and 0.01% over the last three months. Factored into the performance evaluation is an expense ratio of 0.81% (very low) and a 5.5% front-end load that is levied at the time of purchase.

The fund's risk rating is currently C+ (Fair). It carries a beta of 0.72, meaning the fund's expected move will be 7.2% for every 10% move in the market. Volatility, as measured by both the semi-deviation and a drawdown factor, is considered low.

James O. Roeder has been running the fund for 16 years and currently receives a manager quality ranking of 77 (0=worst, 99=best). If you desire an average level of risk, then this fund may be an option.

Services Offered: Automated phone transactions, payroll deductions, bank draft capabilities, an IRA investment plan, a 401K investment plan, a Keogh investment plan, wire transfers and a systematic withdrawal plan.

Data Date	Investment Rating	Net Assets ($Mil)	NAV	Performance Rating/Pts	Total Return Y-T-D	Risk Rating/Pts
3-15	C	10,226	10.32	C / 4.4	0.01%	C+ / 6.8
2014	C+	10,172	10.36	C / 5.0	9.07%	C+ / 6.8
2013	C	9,543	10.66	C / 4.3	24.96%	C+ / 6.5
2012	D+	7,805	9.19	D / 2.2	12.88%	C+ / 6.5
2011	C-	7,802	8.32	D+ / 2.6	-1.23%	C+ / 6.9
2010	B-	8,297	8.59	C+ / 5.9	12.39%	B- / 7.0

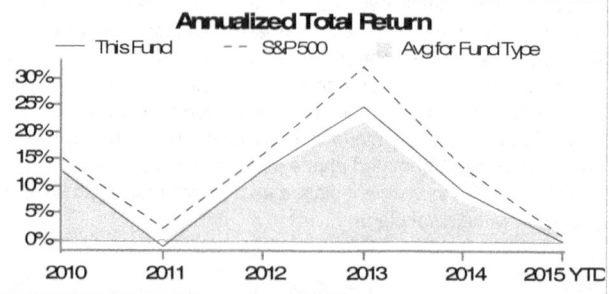

Annualized Total Return

Ivy Asset Strategy A (WASAX)   E   Very Weak

Fund Family: Ivy Funds   **Phone:** (800) 777-6472
Address: PO Box 29217, Shawnee Mission, KS 66201
Fund Type: GL - Global
Major Rating Factors: Disappointing performance is the major factor driving the E (Very Weak) TheStreet.com Investment Rating for Ivy Asset Strategy A. The fund currently has a performance rating of D- (Weak) based on an average return of 7.79% over the last three years and 1.57% over the last three months. Factored into the performance evaluation is an expense ratio of 0.96% (low) and a 5.8% front-end load that is levied at the time of purchase.

The fund's risk rating is currently C- (Fair). It carries a beta of 1.40, meaning it is expected to move 14.0% for every 10% move in the market. Volatility, as measured by both the semi-deviation and a drawdown factor, is considered average.

Michael L. Avery has been running the fund for 18 years and currently receives a manager quality ranking of 13 (0=worst, 99=best). This fund offers an average level of risk but investors looking for strong performance will be frustrated.

Services Offered: Payroll deductions, bank draft capabilities, an IRA investment plan, a 401K investment plan, a Keogh investment plan and a systematic withdrawal plan.

Data Date	Investment Rating	Net Assets ($Mil)	NAV	Performance Rating/Pts	Total Return Y-T-D	Risk Rating/Pts
3-15	E	6,593	25.89	D- / 1.5	1.57%	C- / 3.7
2014	E+	7,447	25.49	D+ / 2.5	-5.02%	C- / 3.8
2013	C-	9,049	32.02	C / 4.8	24.32%	C / 4.6
2012	D+	7,445	25.88	C- / 4.2	19.33%	C / 4.5
2011	D-	7,215	22.26	E+ / 0.8	-7.68%	C / 5.2
2010	C+	8,535	24.41	C- / 4.2	9.77%	B- / 7.0

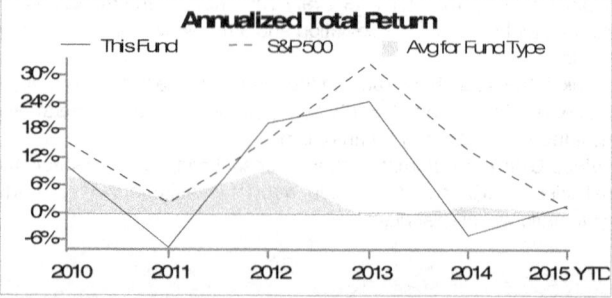

Annualized Total Return

Longleaf Partners (LLPFX)   D   Weak

Fund Family: Longleaf Partners   **Phone:** (800) 445-9469
Address: 6075 Poplar Avenue, Memphis, TN 38119
Fund Type: GR - Growth
Major Rating Factors: Longleaf Partners receives a TheStreet.com Investment Rating of D (Weak). The fund currently has a performance rating of C (Fair) based on an average return of 12.27% over the last three years and -1.09% over the last three months. Factored into the performance evaluation is an expense ratio of 0.92% (low).

The fund's risk rating is currently C- (Fair). It carries a beta of 1.13, meaning it is expected to move 11.3% for every 10% move in the market. Volatility, as measured by both the semi-deviation and a drawdown factor, is considered average.

Otis M Hawkins has been running the fund for 28 years and currently receives a manager quality ranking of 9 (0=worst, 99=best). If you desire an average level of risk, then this fund may be an option.

Services Offered: Automated phone transactions, payroll deductions, bank draft capabilities, an IRA investment plan, wire transfers and a systematic withdrawal plan.

Data Date	Investment Rating	Net Assets ($Mil)	NAV	Performance Rating/Pts	Total Return Y-T-D	Risk Rating/Pts
3-15	D	6,949	30.90	C / 4.8	-1.09%	C- / 4.0
2014	C-	7,550	31.24	C+ / 6.1	4.92%	C- / 3.8
2013	C+	8,599	33.75	B / 7.6	32.12%	C- / 3.3
2012	C+	7,731	26.39	B / 7.9	16.53%	C- / 3.8
2011	A	7,959	26.65	A- / 9.2	-2.85%	C / 4.9
2010	D+	8,119	28.26	C- / 3.7	17.89%	C- / 3.0

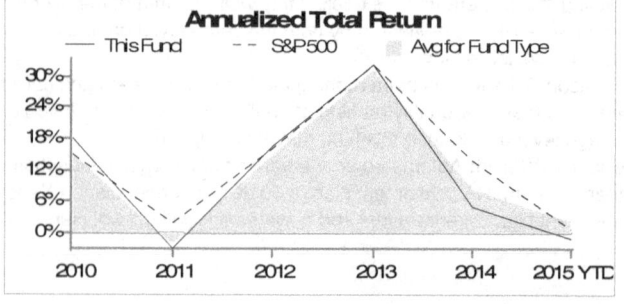

Annualized Total Return

Lord Abbett Affiliated A (LAFFX)   B-   Good

Fund Family: Lord Abbett Funds   **Phone:** (888) 522-2388
Address: 90 Hudson Street, Jersey City, NJ 07302
Fund Type: GI - Growth and Income
Major Rating Factors: Lord Abbett Affiliated A receives a TheStreet.com
Investment Rating of B- (Good). The fund currently has a performance rating of
C+ (Fair) based on an average return of 15.22% over the last three years and
0.35% over the last three months. Factored into the performance evaluation is
an expense ratio of 0.74% (very low) and a 5.8% front-end load that is levied at
the time of purchase.

The fund's risk rating is currently B- (Good). It carries a beta of 1.04,
meaning that its performance tracks fairly well with that of the overall stock
market. Volatility, as measured by both the semi-deviation and a drawdown
factor, is considered low.

Frederick J. Ruvkun has been running the fund for 2 years and currently
receives a manager quality ranking of 46 (0=worst, 99=best). If you desire an
average level of risk, then this fund may be an option.

Services Offered: Automated phone transactions, payroll deductions, an IRA
investment plan, a 401K investment plan and a systematic withdrawal plan.

Data Date	Investment Rating	Net Assets ($Mil)	NAV	Performance Rating/Pts	Total Return Y-T-D	Risk Rating/Pts
3-15	B-	6,046	16.24	C+ / 6.3	0.35%	B- / 7.1
2014	B+	6,128	16.27	B- / 7.5	12.07%	B- / 7.1
2013	C-	6,129	15.57	C / 5.4	32.15%	C / 4.4
2012	D-	5,354	12.02	D+ / 2.3	15.90%	C- / 3.9
2011	E+	5,518	10.54	D- / 1.0	-7.84%	C- / 3.5
2010	D+	7,349	11.58	D / 1.7	14.30%	C / 4.5

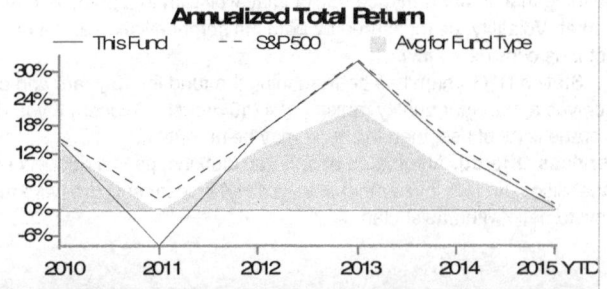

MFS Inst Intl Equity Fund (MIEIX)   D+   Weak

Fund Family: MFS Funds   **Phone:** (800) 225-2606
Address: P.O. Box 55824, Boston, MA 02205
Fund Type: FO - Foreign
Major Rating Factors: MFS Inst Intl Equity Fund receives a TheStreet.com
Investment Rating of D+ (Weak). The fund currently has a performance rating of
C- (Fair) based on an average return of 8.91% over the last three years and
6.12% over the last three months. Factored into the performance evaluation is
an expense ratio of 0.72% (very low).

The fund's risk rating is currently C+ (Fair). It carries a beta of 0.92, meaning
that its performance tracks fairly well with that of the overall stock market.
Volatility, as measured by both the semi-deviation and a drawdown factor, is
considered low.

Marcus L. Smith has been running the fund for 14 years and currently
receives a manager quality ranking of 69 (0=worst, 99=best). If you desire an
average level of risk, then this fund may be an option.

Services Offered: Automated phone transactions, bank draft capabilities and a
systematic withdrawal plan.

Data Date	Investment Rating	Net Assets ($Mil)	NAV	Performance Rating/Pts	Total Return Y-T-D	Risk Rating/Pts
3-15	D+	7,392	22.19	C- / 3.5	6.12%	C+ / 5.9
2014	D	6,892	20.91	D+ / 2.8	-4.21%	C+ / 5.8
2013	D	6,691	22.43	C- / 4.0	18.56%	C- / 4.2
2012	B-	4,643	19.25	B+ / 8.3	22.55%	C- / 3.9
2011	D	2,904	15.92	D / 1.6	-9.55%	C / 4.5
2010	C	2,957	17.94	C / 5.3	10.97%	C / 4.9

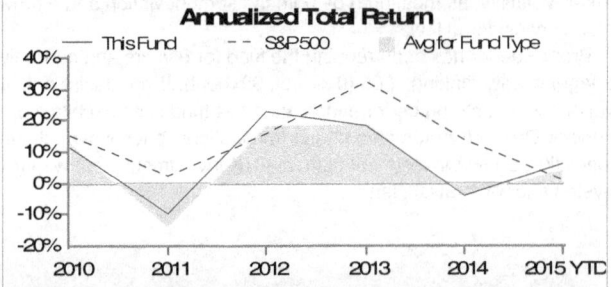

MFS Intl Value Fund A (MGIAX)   C+   Fair

Fund Family: MFS Funds   **Phone:** (800) 225-2606
Address: P.O. Box 55824, Boston, MA 02205
Fund Type: FO - Foreign
Major Rating Factors: Middle of the road best describes MFS Intl Value Fund A
whose TheStreet.com Investment Rating is currently a C+ (Fair). The fund
currently has a performance rating of C+ (Fair) based on an average return of
13.49% over the last three years and 6.59% over the last three months. Factored
into the performance evaluation is an expense ratio of 1.09% (low) and a 5.8%
front-end load that is levied at the time of purchase.

The fund's risk rating is currently C+ (Fair). It carries a beta of 0.77, meaning
the fund's expected move will be 7.7% for every 10% move in the market.
Volatility, as measured by both the semi-deviation and a drawdown factor, is
considered low.

Michael W. Roberge currently receives a manager quality ranking of 95
(0=worst, 99=best). If you desire an average level of risk, then this fund may be
an option.

Services Offered: Automated phone transactions, payroll deductions, bank draft
capabilities, an IRA investment plan, a 401K investment plan and a systematic
withdrawal plan.

Data Date	Investment Rating	Net Assets ($Mil)	NAV	Performance Rating/Pts	Total Return Y-T-D	Risk Rating/Pts
3-15	C+	6,403	35.24	C+ / 5.6	6.59%	C+ / 6.9
2014	C-	5,628	33.06	C- / 3.7	1.28%	C+ / 6.8
2013	C+	4,489	33.72	C / 4.9	27.35%	C+ / 6.5
2012	C-	2,451	27.04	C- / 3.2	15.81%	C+ / 6.4
2011	D	1,499	23.75	D / 1.6	-1.96%	C / 4.8
2010	C-	1,710	24.59	D / 2.0	9.13%	C / 5.1

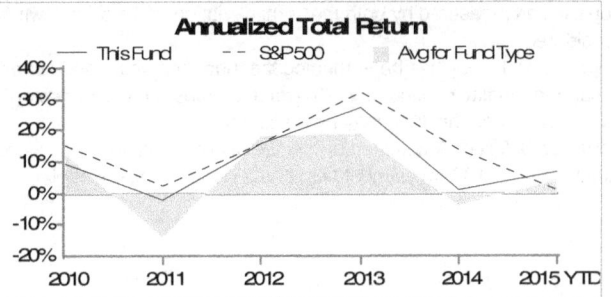

MFS Value A (MEIAX)

B- Good

Fund Family: MFS Funds   **Phone:** (800) 225-2606
Address: P.O. Box 55824, Boston, MA 02205
Fund Type: GR - Growth
Major Rating Factors: MFS Value A receives a TheStreet.com Investment Rating of B- (Good). The fund currently has a performance rating of C+ (Fair) based on an average return of 15.84% over the last three years and 0.70% over the last three months. Factored into the performance evaluation is an expense ratio of 0.90% (low) and a 5.8% front-end load that is levied at the time of purchase.

The fund's risk rating is currently B- (Good). It carries a beta of 1.08, meaning that its performance tracks fairly well with that of the overall stock market. Volatility, as measured by both the semi-deviation and a drawdown factor, is considered low.

Steven R. Gorham has been running the fund for 13 years and currently receives a manager quality ranking of 47 (0=worst, 99=best). If you desire an average level of risk, then this fund may be an option.

Services Offered: Automated phone transactions, payroll deductions, bank draft capabilities, an IRA investment plan, a 401K investment plan, wire transfers and a systematic withdrawal plan.

Data Date	Investment Rating	Net Assets ($Mil)	NAV	Performance Rating/Pts	Total Return Y-T-D	Risk Rating/Pts
3-15	B-	9,277	34.98	C+ / 6.7	0.70%	B- / 7.3
2014	B+	9,340	34.94	B / 7.6	10.29%	B- / 7.4
2013	B+	9,229	33.20	B / 7.6	35.48%	C+ / 5.8
2012	C-	6,662	25.35	C- / 4.0	16.13%	C+ / 5.6
2011	D	5,100	22.38	D+ / 2.3	-0.21%	C / 4.9
2010	C-	5,758	22.81	D / 1.8	11.41%	C+ / 5.6

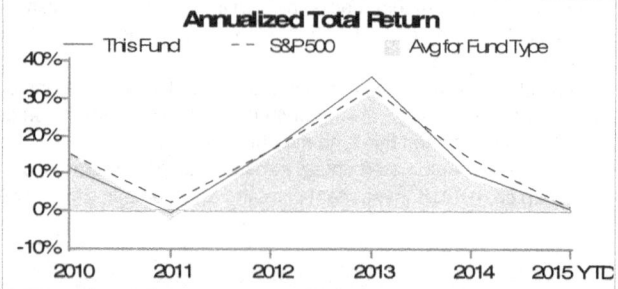

Northern Stock Index (NOSIX)

A Excellent

Fund Family: Northern Funds   **Phone:** (800) 595-9111
Address: PO Box 75986, Chicago, IL 60675
Fund Type: IX - Index
Major Rating Factors: Strong performance is the major factor driving the A (Excellent) TheStreet.com Investment Rating for Northern Stock Index. The fund currently has a performance rating of B (Good) based on an average return of 15.98% over the last three years and 0.93% over the last three months. Factored into the performance evaluation is an expense ratio of 0.12% (very low).

The fund's risk rating is currently B- (Good). It carries a beta of 1.00, meaning that its performance tracks fairly well with that of the overall stock market. Volatility, as measured by both the semi-deviation and a drawdown factor, is considered low.

Brent Reeder has been running the fund for 9 years and currently receives a manager quality ranking of 65 (0=worst, 99=best). If you desire only a moderate level of risk and strong performance, then this fund is an excellent option.

Services Offered: Automated phone transactions, payroll deductions, bank draft capabilities, an IRA investment plan, a 401K investment plan, wire transfers and a systematic withdrawal plan.

Data Date	Investment Rating	Net Assets ($Mil)	NAV	Performance Rating/Pts	Total Return Y-T-D	Risk Rating/Pts
3-15	A	6,969	25.41	B / 8.2	0.93%	B- / 7.3
2014	A+	6,657	25.28	B+ / 8.9	13.55%	B- / 7.4
2013	A	5,495	22.86	B / 8.1	32.23%	C+ / 6.1
2012	B+	4,216	17.68	B- / 7.3	15.86%	C+ / 5.6
2011	B-	2,718	15.58	B- / 7.1	1.89%	C / 5.0
2010	C	1,866	15.57	C- / 4.2	14.82%	C / 5.0

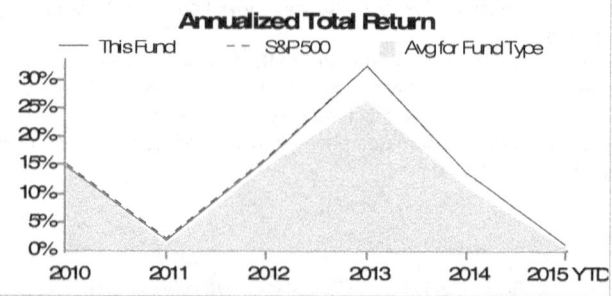

Old Westbury Large Cap Strategies (OWLSX)

C+ Fair

Fund Family: Old Westbury Funds   **Phone:** (800) 607-2200
Address: 630 5th Ave., New York, NY 10111
Fund Type: FO - Foreign
Major Rating Factors: Middle of the road best describes Old Westbury Large Cap Strategies whose TheStreet.com Investment Rating is currently a C+ (Fair). The fund currently has a performance rating of C+ (Fair) based on an average return of 12.10% over the last three years and 3.10% over the last three months. Factored into the performance evaluation is an expense ratio of 1.14% (low).

The fund's risk rating is currently C+ (Fair). It carries a beta of 0.72, meaning the fund's expected move will be 7.2% for every 10% move in the market. Volatility, as measured by both the semi-deviation and a drawdown factor, is considered low.

Hank R. Hagey has been running the fund for 4 years and currently receives a manager quality ranking of 93 (0=worst, 99=best). If you desire an average level of risk, then this fund may be an option.

Services Offered: Automated phone transactions, payroll deductions, bank draft capabilities, an IRA investment plan and a Keogh investment plan.

Data Date	Investment Rating	Net Assets ($Mil)	NAV	Performance Rating/Pts	Total Return Y-T-D	Risk Rating/Pts
3-15	C+	13,251	13.31	C+ / 5.7	3.10%	C+ / 6.3
2014	C+	12,970	12.91	C+ / 5.7	7.15%	C+ / 6.5
2013	D	10,106	12.47	C- / 3.7	25.31%	C- / 3.9
2012	E+	4,315	10.02	D / 1.8	15.09%	C- / 3.7
2011	E+	2,850	8.77	E / 0.3	-16.06%	C- / 4.0
2010	C	2,747	10.62	C / 4.6	15.11%	C / 4.9

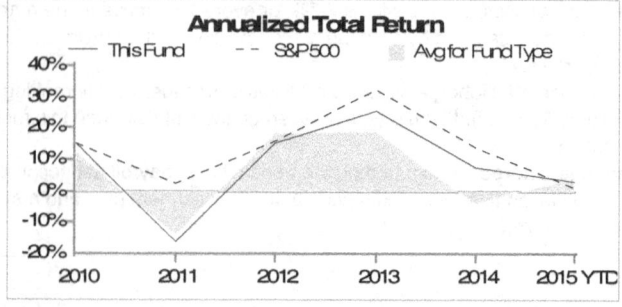

Old Westbury Small & Mid Cap (OWSMX)   C   Fair

Fund Family: Old Westbury Funds   **Phone:** (800) 607-2200
Address: 630 5th Ave., New York, NY 10111
Fund Type: GL - Global

Major Rating Factors: Middle of the road best describes Old Westbury Small & Mid Cap whose TheStreet.com Investment Rating is currently a C (Fair). The fund currently has a performance rating of C (Fair) based on an average return of 11.03% over the last three years and 4.07% over the last three months. Factored into the performance evaluation is an expense ratio of 1.18% (low).

The fund's risk rating is currently C+ (Fair). It carries a beta of 0.67, meaning the fund's expected move will be 6.7% for every 10% move in the market. Volatility, as measured by both the semi-deviation and a drawdown factor, is considered low.

Karen E. Umland has been running the fund for 10 years and currently receives a manager quality ranking of 92 (0=worst, 99=best). If you desire an average level of risk, then this fund may be an option.

Services Offered: Automated phone transactions, bank draft capabilities, an IRA investment plan, a 401K investment plan and wire transfers.

Data Date	Investment Rating	Net Assets ($Mil)	NAV	Performance Rating/Pts	Total Return Y-T-D	Risk Rating/Pts
3-15	C	5,543	16.88	C / 4.9	4.07%	C+ / 6.3
2014	C-	6,437	16.22	C / 4.6	2.09%	C+ / 6.2
2013	D+	6,803	17.18	C / 4.8	24.16%	C / 4.3
2012	B	4,930	14.69	B+ / 8.6	17.32%	C- / 3.8
2011	C-	4,655	13.47	C+ / 5.7	-7.84%	C- / 3.4
2010	B-	4,541	15.47	A+ / 9.7	24.13%	D / 2.1

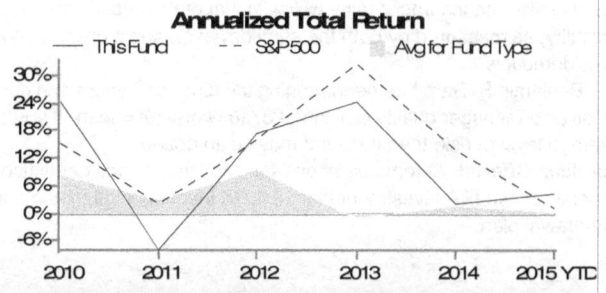

Annualized Total Return

Oppenheimer Developing Mkts A (ODMAX)   E   Very Weak

Fund Family: OppenheimerFunds   **Phone:** (888) 470-0862
Address: P.O. Box 219534, Denver, CO 80217
Fund Type: EM - Emerging Market

Major Rating Factors: Very poor performance is the major factor driving the E (Very Weak) TheStreet.com Investment Rating for Oppenheimer Developing Mkts A. The fund currently has a performance rating of E (Very Weak) based on an average return of 2.31% over the last three years and -1.35% over the last three months. Factored into the performance evaluation is an expense ratio of 1.33% (average) and a 5.8% front-end load that is levied at the time of purchase.

The fund's risk rating is currently C (Fair). It carries a beta of 0.96, meaning that its performance tracks fairly well with that of the overall stock market. Volatility, as measured by both the semi-deviation and a drawdown factor, is considered average.

Justin M. Leverenz has been running the fund for 8 years and currently receives a manager quality ranking of 82 (0=worst, 99=best). This fund offers an average level of risk but investors looking for strong performance will be frustrated.

Services Offered: Automated phone transactions, payroll deductions, an IRA investment plan, a 401K investment plan, wire transfers and a systematic withdrawal plan. However, the fund is currently closed to new investors.

Data Date	Investment Rating	Net Assets ($Mil)	NAV	Performance Rating/Pts	Total Return Y-T-D	Risk Rating/Pts
3-15	E	9,952	35.04	E / 0.4	-1.35%	C / 4.6
2014	E	10,523	35.52	E+ / 0.8	-4.81%	C / 4.5
2013	E+	13,930	38.02	E+ / 0.7	8.65%	C- / 3.9
2012	C-	12,172	35.29	C+ / 6.0	20.85%	C- / 3.8
2011	B+	9,505	29.32	B+ / 8.5	-18.10%	C / 4.3
2010	C+	11,469	36.47	A / 9.4	26.98%	D / 2.1

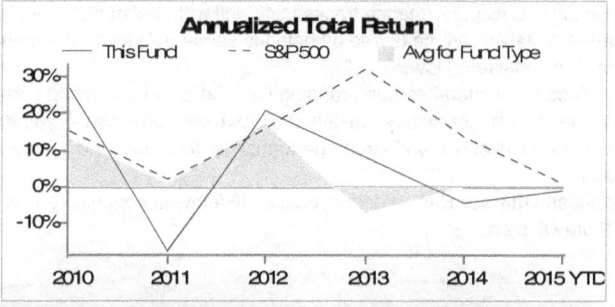

Annualized Total Return

Oppenheimer Global A (OPPAX)   C   Fair

Fund Family: OppenheimerFunds   **Phone:** (888) 470-0862
Address: P.O. Box 219534, Denver, CO 80217
Fund Type: GL - Global

Major Rating Factors: Middle of the road best describes Oppenheimer Global A whose TheStreet.com Investment Rating is currently a C (Fair). The fund currently has a performance rating of C+ (Fair) based on an average return of 13.78% over the last three years and 7.33% over the last three months. Factored into the performance evaluation is an expense ratio of 1.13% (low) and a 5.8% front-end load that is levied at the time of purchase.

The fund's risk rating is currently C (Fair). It carries a beta of 0.88, meaning the fund's expected move will be 8.8% for every 10% move in the market. Volatility, as measured by both the semi-deviation and a drawdown factor, is considered average.

Rajeev Bhaman has been running the fund for 11 years and currently receives a manager quality ranking of 93 (0=worst, 99=best). If you desire an average level of risk, then this fund may be an option.

Services Offered: Automated phone transactions, payroll deductions, bank draft capabilities, an IRA investment plan, a 401K investment plan, a Keogh investment plan, wire transfers and a systematic withdrawal plan.

Data Date	Investment Rating	Net Assets ($Mil)	NAV	Performance Rating/Pts	Total Return Y-T-D	Risk Rating/Pts
3-15	C	7,679	81.59	C+ / 5.9	7.33%	C / 5.5
2014	C-	7,316	76.02	C / 4.5	2.06%	C+ / 5.6
2013	D+	7,885	78.78	C / 5.0	26.77%	C- / 4.1
2012	C+	6,713	64.50	B / 7.6	20.75%	C- / 4.1
2011	D+	6,347	54.04	D+ / 2.7	-8.69%	C / 4.9
2010	C-	7,744	60.37	C- / 4.0	15.68%	C- / 4.0

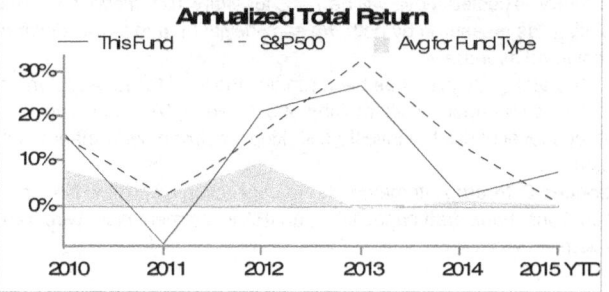

Annualized Total Return

Oppenheimer Main Street A (MSIGX)   C+   Fair

Fund Family: OppenheimerFunds   **Phone:** (888) 470-0862
Address: P.O. Box 219534, Denver, CO 80217
Fund Type: GI - Growth and Income
Major Rating Factors: Middle of the road best describes Oppenheimer Main Street A whose TheStreet.com Investment Rating is currently a C+ (Fair). The fund currently has a performance rating of C+ (Fair) based on an average return of 14.35% over the last three years and 1.61% over the last three months. Factored into the performance evaluation is an expense ratio of 0.94% (low) and a 5.8% front-end load that is levied at the time of purchase.

The fund's risk rating is currently C+ (Fair). It carries a beta of 1.03, meaning that its performance tracks fairly well with that of the overall stock market. Volatility, as measured by both the semi-deviation and a drawdown factor, is considered low.

Benjamin E. Ram has been running the fund for 6 years and currently receives a manager quality ranking of 37 (0=worst, 99=best). If you desire an average level of risk, then this fund may be an option.
Services Offered: Automated phone transactions, payroll deductions, bank draft capabilities, an IRA investment plan, a 401K investment plan and a systematic withdrawal plan.

Data Date	Investment Rating	Net Assets ($Mil)	NAV	Performance Rating/Pts	Total Return Y-T-D	Risk Rating/Pts
3-15	C+	5,418	48.66	C+ / 6.0	1.61%	C+ / 5.9
2014	C+	5,407	47.89	C+ / 6.9	10.46%	C+ / 5.9
2013	C+	5,157	48.46	C+ / 6.9	31.55%	C+ / 6.5
2012	C+	4,280	37.08	C / 5.5	16.55%	C+ / 6.0
2011	C	4,029	32.16	C+ / 5.8	-0.22%	C / 4.7
2010	C-	4,583	32.39	D+ / 2.9	15.78%	C / 4.8

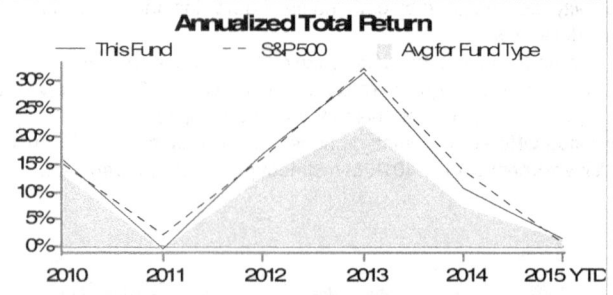

Parnassus Core Equity Inv (PRBLX)   A+   Excellent

Fund Family: Parnassus Investments   **Phone:** (800) 999-3505
Address: 1 Market Street, San Francisco, CA 94105
Fund Type: IN - Income
Major Rating Factors: Exceptional performance is the major factor driving the A+ (Excellent) TheStreet.com Investment Rating for Parnassus Core Equity Inv. The fund currently has a performance rating of A- (Excellent) based on an average return of 17.75% over the last three years and -0.78% over the last three months. Factored into the performance evaluation is an expense ratio of 0.87% (low).

The fund's risk rating is currently B- (Good). It carries a beta of 0.92, meaning that its performance tracks fairly well with that of the overall stock market. Volatility, as measured by both the semi-deviation and a drawdown factor, is considered low.

Todd C. Ahlsten has been running the fund for 14 years and currently receives a manager quality ranking of 87 (0=worst, 99=best). If you desire only a moderate level of risk and strong performance, then this fund is an excellent option.
Services Offered: Payroll deductions, an IRA investment plan and a systematic withdrawal plan.

Data Date	Investment Rating	Net Assets ($Mil)	NAV	Performance Rating/Pts	Total Return Y-T-D	Risk Rating/Pts
3-15	A+	8,745	40.29	A- / 9.0	-0.78%	B- / 7.1
2014	A+	8,543	40.69	A / 9.3	14.48%	B- / 7.1
2013	A+	6,282	36.68	B+ / 8.7	34.01%	C+ / 6.2
2012	C+	4,022	29.20	C+ / 6.4	15.43%	C+ / 6.0
2011	C+	3,399	26.35	C+ / 6.7	3.13%	C / 5.2
2010	B+	3,150	26.31	B / 7.6	8.89%	C+ / 6.3

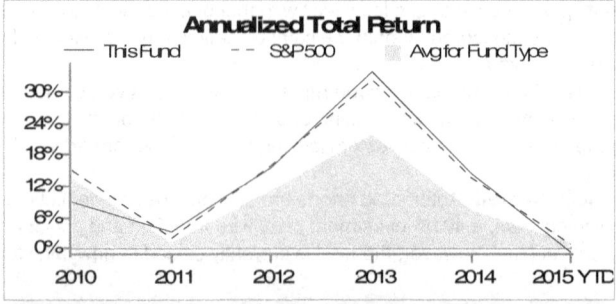

Permanent Portfolio (PRPFX)   E   Very Weak

Fund Family: Permanent Portfolios Family of Fund   **Phone:** (800) 531-5142
Address: 600 Montgomery Street, San Francisco, CA 94111
Fund Type: AA - Asset Allocation
Major Rating Factors: Very poor performance is the major factor driving the E (Very Weak) TheStreet.com Investment Rating for Permanent Portfolio. The fund currently has a performance rating of E (Very Weak) based on an average return of -0.24% over the last three years and 1.06% over the last three months. Factored into the performance evaluation is an expense ratio of 0.77% (very low).

The fund's risk rating is currently C (Fair). It carries a beta of 0.73, meaning the fund's expected move will be 7.3% for every 10% move in the market. Volatility, as measured by both the semi-deviation and a drawdown factor, is considered average.

Michael J. Cuggino has been running the fund for 12 years and currently receives a manager quality ranking of 3 (0=worst, 99=best). This fund offers an average level of risk but investors looking for strong performance will be frustrated.
Services Offered: Automated phone transactions, check writing, payroll deductions, bank draft capabilities, an IRA investment plan, wire transfers and a systematic withdrawal plan.

Data Date	Investment Rating	Net Assets ($Mil)	NAV	Performance Rating/Pts	Total Return Y-T-D	Risk Rating/Pts
3-15	E	5,133	39.99	E / 0.5	1.06%	C / 5.1
2014	E	5,669	39.57	E / 0.4	-0.82%	C / 5.0
2013	D-	9,616	43.06	E+ / 0.6	-2.02%	C+ / 6.7
2012	B-	16,842	48.64	C- / 3.9	6.91%	B / 8.1
2011	B	15,405	46.09	C+ / 6.0	2.13%	B / 8.4
2010	A+	10,152	45.81	A+ / 9.7	19.31%	B / 8.9

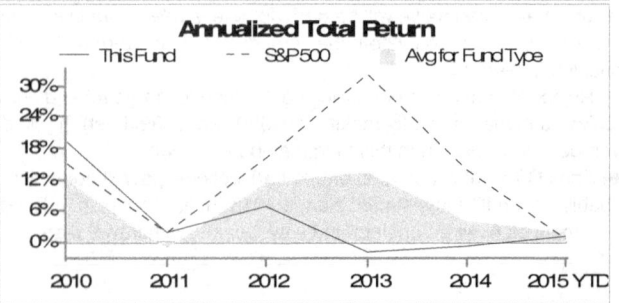

PRIMECAP Odyssey Agg Growth Fd (POAGX)   A   Excellent

Fund Family: PRIMECAP Odyssey Funds   **Phone:** (800) 729-2307
Address: c/o US Bancorp Fund Services L, Milwaukee, WI 53201
Fund Type: AG - Aggressive Growth
Major Rating Factors: Exceptional performance is the major factor driving the A (Excellent) TheStreet.com Investment Rating for PRIMECAP Odyssey Agg Growth Fd. The fund currently has a performance rating of A+ (Excellent) based on an average return of 26.39% over the last three years and 5.92% over the last three months. Factored into the performance evaluation is an expense ratio of 0.63% (very low).

The fund's risk rating is currently C+ (Fair). It carries a beta of 1.15, meaning it is expected to move 11.5% for every 10% move in the market. Volatility, as measured by both the semi-deviation and a drawdown factor, is considered low.

Theofanis A. Kolokotrones has been running the fund for 11 years and currently receives a manager quality ranking of 95 (0=worst, 99=best). If you desire only a moderate level of risk and strong performance, then this fund is an excellent option.

Services Offered: Automated phone transactions, payroll deductions, bank draft capabilities, an IRA investment plan, wire transfers and a systematic withdrawal plan. However, the fund is currently closed to new investors.

Data Date	Investment Rating	Net Assets ($Mil)	NAV	Performance Rating/Pts	Total Return Y-T-D	Risk Rating/Pts
3-15	A	6,831	34.88	A+ / 9.9	5.92%	C+ / 5.6
2014	A-	6,376	32.93	A+ / 9.9	16.55%	C+ / 5.6
2013	A-	5,030	29.65	A+ / 9.9	54.88%	C- / 3.9
2012	B	1,688	19.48	A- / 9.0	21.22%	C- / 3.4
2011	A-	1,086	16.07	A / 9.4	-0.45%	C- / 4.2
2010	A-	914	16.47	A / 9.3	21.57%	C / 4.9

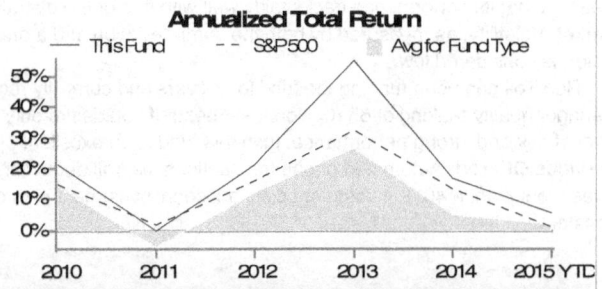

PRIMECAP Odyssey Growth Fd (POGRX)   A+   Excellent

Fund Family: PRIMECAP Odyssey Funds   **Phone:** (800) 729-2307
Address: c/o US Bancorp Fund Services L, Milwaukee, WI 53201
Fund Type: MC - Mid Cap
Major Rating Factors: Exceptional performance is the major factor driving the A+ (Excellent) TheStreet.com Investment Rating for PRIMECAP Odyssey Growth Fd. The fund currently has a performance rating of A+ (Excellent) based on an average return of 19.63% over the last three years and 3.53% over the last three months. Factored into the performance evaluation is an expense ratio of 0.63% (very low).

The fund's risk rating is currently C+ (Fair). It carries a beta of 0.91, meaning that its performance tracks fairly well with that of the overall stock market. Volatility, as measured by both the semi-deviation and a drawdown factor, is considered low.

Theofanis A. Kolokotrones has been running the fund for 11 years and currently receives a manager quality ranking of 91 (0=worst, 99=best). If you desire only a moderate level of risk and strong performance, then this fund is an excellent option.

Services Offered: Automated phone transactions, payroll deductions, bank draft capabilities, an IRA investment plan, wire transfers and a systematic withdrawal plan.

Data Date	Investment Rating	Net Assets ($Mil)	NAV	Performance Rating/Pts	Total Return Y-T-D	Risk Rating/Pts
3-15	A+	5,528	26.98	A+ / 9.7	3.53%	C+ / 6.7
2014	A+	5,003	26.06	A+ / 9.7	13.92%	C+ / 6.7
2013	B+	3,884	23.61	B+ / 8.7	39.30%	C / 4.8
2012	C+	2,221	17.34	C+ / 6.9	16.76%	C / 4.4
2011	B+	1,798	14.94	B / 7.6	-2.22%	C / 5.2
2010	B+	1,623	15.40	B / 7.8	15.37%	C / 5.2

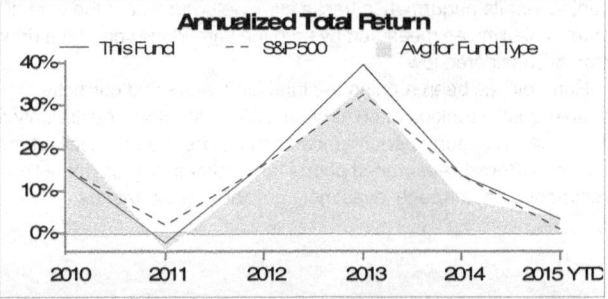

Putnam Fund for Gr & Inc A (PGRWX)   C+   Fair

Fund Family: Putnam Funds   **Phone:** (800) 225-1581
Address: One Post Office Square, Boston, MA 02109
Fund Type: GI - Growth and Income
Major Rating Factors: Middle of the road best describes Putnam Fund for Gr & Inc A whose TheStreet.com Investment Rating is currently a C+ (Fair). The fund currently has a performance rating of C+ (Fair) based on an average return of 16.00% over the last three years and 0.02% over the last three months. Factored into the performance evaluation is an expense ratio of 0.97% (low) and a 5.8% front-end load that is levied at the time of purchase.

The fund's risk rating is currently C+ (Fair). It carries a beta of 1.08, meaning that its performance tracks fairly well with that of the overall stock market. Volatility, as measured by both the semi-deviation and a drawdown factor, is considered low.

Robert D. Ewing has been running the fund for 7 years and currently receives a manager quality ranking of 48 (0=worst, 99=best). If you desire an average level of risk, then this fund may be an option.

Services Offered: Automated phone transactions, payroll deductions, an IRA investment plan, a 401K investment plan, a Keogh investment plan and a systematic withdrawal plan.

Data Date	Investment Rating	Net Assets ($Mil)	NAV	Performance Rating/Pts	Total Return Y-T-D	Risk Rating/Pts
3-15	C+	5,350	21.60	C+ / 6.4	0.02%	C+ / 6.9
2014	B+	5,346	21.65	B / 7.9	10.60%	C+ / 6.9
2013	B-	5,231	19.86	B- / 7.1	35.37%	C / 4.9
2012	C	4,256	14.85	C+ / 6.0	18.88%	C / 4.5
2011	D+	4,071	12.69	D+ / 2.8	-4.85%	C / 4.5
2010	C-	4,862	13.54	D+ / 2.5	14.08%	C / 4.7

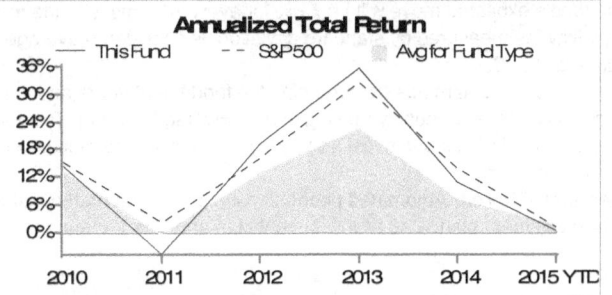

Schwab 1000 Index Fund (SNXFX)   B+   Good

Fund Family: Schwab Funds   **Phone:** (800) 407-0256
Address: P.O. Box 8283, Boston, MA 02266
Fund Type: GI - Growth and Income
Major Rating Factors: Strong performance is the major factor driving the B+
(Good) TheStreet.com Investment Rating for Schwab 1000 Index Fund. The
fund currently has a performance rating of B (Good) based on an average return
of 15.98% over the last three years and 1.54% over the last three months.
Factored into the performance evaluation is an expense ratio of 0.34% (very low)
and a 2.0% back-end load levied at the time of sale.

The fund's risk rating is currently B- (Good). It carries a beta of 1.01,
meaning that its performance tracks fairly well with that of the overall stock
market. Volatility, as measured by both the semi-deviation and a drawdown
factor, is considered low.

Ron Toll has been running the fund for 7 years and currently receives a
manager quality ranking of 65 (0=worst, 99=best). If you desire only a moderate
level of risk and strong performance, then this fund is an excellent option.
Services Offered: Automated phone transactions, payroll deductions, an IRA
investment plan, a 401K investment plan, a Keogh investment plan and wire
transfers.

Data Date	Investment Rating	Net Assets ($Mil)	NAV	Perfor-mance Rating/Pts	Total Return Y-T-D	Risk Rating/Pts
3-15	B+	6,824	53.29	B / 7.8	1.54%	B- / 7.0
2014	A-	6,750	52.48	B+ / 8.4	12.75%	B- / 7.0
2013	B+	6,046	48.68	B / 7.7	32.67%	C+ / 5.7
2012	C+	4,835	38.46	C+ / 6.9	15.77%	C / 5.4
2011	C+	4,491	35.37	C+ / 6.9	1.27%	C / 4.8
2010	C	4,556	37.18	C / 4.5	15.96%	C- / 4.2

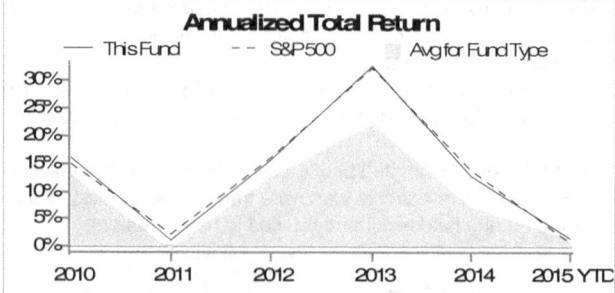

Schwab S&P 500 Index Fund (SWPPX)   A-   Excellent

Fund Family: Schwab Funds   **Phone:** (800) 407-0256
Address: P.O. Box 8283, Boston, MA 02266
Fund Type: IX - Index
Major Rating Factors: Strong performance is the major factor driving the A-
(Excellent) TheStreet.com Investment Rating for Schwab S&P 500 Index Fund.
The fund currently has a performance rating of B (Good) based on an average
return of 16.01% over the last three years and 0.90% over the last three months.
Factored into the performance evaluation is an expense ratio of 0.09% (very low)
and a 2.0% back-end load levied at the time of sale.

The fund's risk rating is currently B- (Good). It carries a beta of 1.00,
meaning that its performance tracks fairly well with that of the overall stock
market. Volatility, as measured by both the semi-deviation and a drawdown
factor, is considered low.

Ron Toll has been running the fund for 7 years and currently receives a
manager quality ranking of 66 (0=worst, 99=best). If you desire only a moderate
level of risk and strong performance, then this fund is an excellent option.
Services Offered: Automated phone transactions, payroll deductions, an IRA
investment plan, a Keogh investment plan and wire transfers.

Data Date	Investment Rating	Net Assets ($Mil)	NAV	Perfor-mance Rating/Pts	Total Return Y-T-D	Risk Rating/Pts
3-15	A-	21,704	32.45	B / 7.8	0.90%	B- / 7.3
2014	A	21,050	32.16	B+ / 8.6	13.57%	B- / 7.4
2013	A-	17,678	28.85	B / 7.8	32.27%	C+ / 6.2
2012	C+	12,827	22.19	C+ / 6.8	15.91%	C+ / 5.9
2011	C+	10,994	19.57	C+ / 6.7	2.07%	C / 4.9
2010	C-	9,999	19.57	C- / 3.9	14.97%	C / 4.5

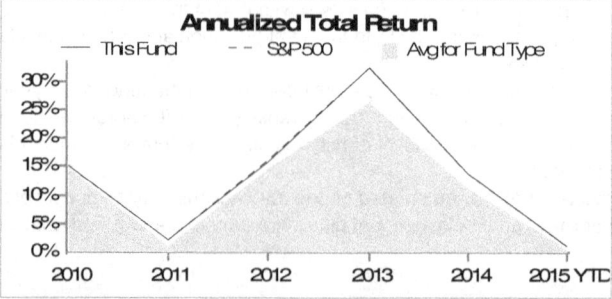

SEI Inst World Equity Ex US A (WEUSX)   D-   Weak

Fund Family: SEI Financial Management Corp   **Phone:** (800) 342-5734
Address: One Freedom Valley Drive, Oaks, PA 19456
Fund Type: EM - Emerging Market
Major Rating Factors: Disappointing performance is the major factor driving the
D- (Weak) TheStreet.com Investment Rating for SEI Inst World Equity Ex US A.
The fund currently has a performance rating of D+ (Weak) based on an average
return of 7.96% over the last three years and 3.73% over the last three months.
Factored into the performance evaluation is an expense ratio of 0.62% (very
low).

The fund's risk rating is currently C (Fair). It carries a beta of 0.79, meaning
the fund's expected move will be 7.9% for every 10% move in the market.
Volatility, as measured by standard deviation, is considered average for equity
funds at 12.36.

Robert A. Gillam has been running the fund for 10 years and currently
receives a manager quality ranking of 96 (0=worst, 99=best). This fund offers an
average level of risk but investors looking for strong performance will be
frustrated.
Services Offered: Automated phone transactions, bank draft capabilities, an
IRA investment plan, a 401K investment plan and wire transfers.

Data Date	Investment Rating	Net Assets ($Mil)	NAV	Perfor-mance Rating/Pts	Total Return Y-T-D	Risk Rating/Pts
3-15	D-	7,174	12.23	D+ / 2.7	3.73%	C / 5.3
2014	D-	6,611	11.79	D+ / 2.6	-2.65%	C / 5.3

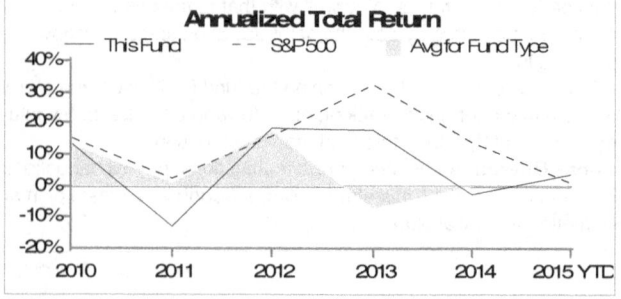

Sequoia Fund (SEQUX)   A+   Excellent

Fund Family: Sequoia Funds   **Phone:** (800) 686-6884
Address: 767 Fifth Avenue, New York, NY 10153
Fund Type: GR - Growth
Major Rating Factors: Exceptional performance is the major factor driving the A+ (Excellent) TheStreet.com Investment Rating for Sequoia Fund. The fund currently has a performance rating of A (Excellent) based on an average return of 17.63% over the last three years and 7.67% over the last three months. Factored into the performance evaluation is an expense ratio of 1.02% (low).

The fund's risk rating is currently B- (Good). It carries a beta of 0.77, meaning the fund's expected move will be 7.7% for every 10% move in the market. Volatility, as measured by both the semi-deviation and a drawdown factor, is considered low.

Robert D. Goldfarb has been running the fund for 35 years and currently receives a manager quality ranking of 93 (0=worst, 99=best). If you desire only a moderate level of risk and strong performance, then this fund is an excellent option.

Services Offered: Automated phone transactions, payroll deductions, an IRA investment plan, a Keogh investment plan and a systematic withdrawal plan. However, the fund is currently closed to new investors.

Data Date	Investment Rating	Net Assets ($Mil)	NAV	Performance Rating/Pts	Total Return Y-T-D	Risk Rating/Pts
3-15	A+	8,616	253.02	A / 9.5	7.67%	B- / 7.2
2014	B+	8,070	235.00	B / 7.7	7.55%	B- / 7.2
2013	A+	8,037	222.92	A+ / 9.6	34.58%	C+ / 6.8
2012	A+	5,828	168.31	A+ / 9.7	15.68%	C+ / 6.3
2011	A+	4,711	145.50	A- / 9.0	13.19%	C / 5.5
2010	B+	3,355	129.29	B / 8.1	19.50%	C / 5.4

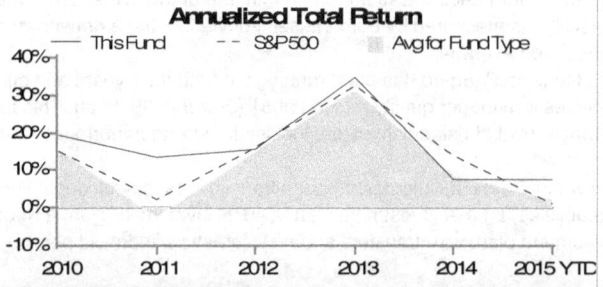

T Rowe Price Blue Chip Growth (TRBCX)   A   Excellent

Fund Family: T Rowe Price Funds   **Phone:** (800) 638-5660
Address: 100 East Pratt Street, Baltimore, MD 21202
Fund Type: GR - Growth
Major Rating Factors: Exceptional performance is the major factor driving the A (Excellent) TheStreet.com Investment Rating for T Rowe Price Blue Chip Growth. The fund currently has a performance rating of A (Excellent) based on an average return of 17.80% over the last three years and 5.96% over the last three months. Factored into the performance evaluation is an expense ratio of 0.74% (very low).

The fund's risk rating is currently C+ (Fair). It carries a beta of 1.01, meaning that its performance tracks fairly well with that of the overall stock market. Volatility, as measured by both the semi-deviation and a drawdown factor, is considered low.

Lawrence J. Puglia has been running the fund for 22 years and currently receives a manager quality ranking of 79 (0=worst, 99=best). If you desire only a moderate level of risk and strong performance, then this fund is an excellent option.

Services Offered: Automated phone transactions, payroll deductions, bank draft capabilities, an IRA investment plan, a 401K investment plan, a Keogh investment plan, wire transfers and a systematic withdrawal plan.

Data Date	Investment Rating	Net Assets ($Mil)	NAV	Performance Rating/Pts	Total Return Y-T-D	Risk Rating/Pts
3-15	A	25,005	71.28	A / 9.5	5.96%	C+ / 5.8
2014	B+	23,276	67.27	A / 9.4	9.28%	C+ / 5.6
2013	A+	19,448	64.60	A+ / 9.8	41.57%	C / 5.1
2012	B+	13,692	45.63	B+ / 8.3	18.41%	C / 4.8
2011	A+	10,661	38.65	A- / 9.1	1.50%	C / 5.5
2010	C+	10,483	38.13	C+ / 6.3	16.42%	C / 5.0

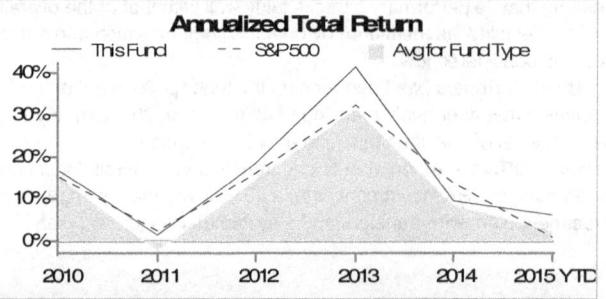

T Rowe Price Cap Appreciation (PRWCX)   B   Good

Fund Family: T Rowe Price Funds   **Phone:** (800) 638-5660
Address: 100 East Pratt Street, Baltimore, MD 21202
Fund Type: AA - Asset Allocation
Major Rating Factors: Strong performance is the major factor driving the B (Good) TheStreet.com Investment Rating for T Rowe Price Cap Appreciation. The fund currently has a performance rating of B- (Good) based on an average return of 14.11% over the last three years and 3.21% over the last three months. Factored into the performance evaluation is an expense ratio of 0.71% (very low).

The fund's risk rating is currently C+ (Fair). It carries a beta of 1.01, meaning that its performance tracks fairly well with that of the overall stock market. Volatility, as measured by both the semi-deviation and a drawdown factor, is considered low.

David R. Giroux has been running the fund for 9 years and currently receives a manager quality ranking of 88 (0=worst, 99=best). If you desire only a moderate level of risk and strong performance, then this fund is an excellent option.

Services Offered: Automated phone transactions, payroll deductions, bank draft capabilities, an IRA investment plan, a 401K investment plan, a Keogh investment plan, wire transfers and a systematic withdrawal plan.

Data Date	Investment Rating	Net Assets ($Mil)	NAV	Performance Rating/Pts	Total Return Y-T-D	Risk Rating/Pts
3-15	B	22,644	26.97	B- / 7.3	3.21%	C+ / 6.6
2014	C+	21,810	26.13	C+ / 6.6	12.25%	C+ / 6.7
2013	B-	18,006	25.66	C / 5.2	22.43%	B- / 7.2
2012	A+	13,380	22.25	B- / 7.5	14.70%	B- / 7.3
2011	A+	10,770	20.62	B+ / 8.3	3.19%	B- / 7.0
2010	A-	9,967	20.31	B / 8.2	14.07%	C+ / 6.2

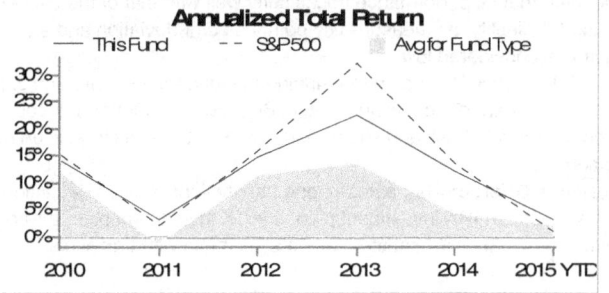

T Rowe Price Emerging Mkts Stk (PRMSX)
E+   Very Weak

Fund Family: T Rowe Price Funds   **Phone:** (800) 638-5660
Address: 100 East Pratt Street, Baltimore, MD 21202
Fund Type: EM - Emerging Market

Major Rating Factors: Very poor performance is the major factor driving the E+ (Very Weak) TheStreet.com Investment Rating for T Rowe Price Emerging Mkts Stk. The fund currently has a performance rating of E+ (Very Weak) based on an average return of 2.17% over the last three years and 3.61% over the last three months. Factored into the performance evaluation is an expense ratio of 1.24% (average) and a 2.0% back-end load levied at the time of sale.

The fund's risk rating is currently C (Fair). It carries a beta of 1.02, meaning that its performance tracks fairly well with that of the overall stock market. Volatility, as measured by both the semi-deviation and a drawdown factor, is considered average.

Gonzalo Pangaro has been running the fund for 7 years and currently receives a manager quality ranking of 81 (0=worst, 99=best). This fund offers an average level of risk but investors looking for strong performance will be frustrated.

Services Offered: Automated phone transactions, payroll deductions, bank draft capabilities, an IRA investment plan, a 401K investment plan, a Keogh investment plan, wire transfers and a systematic withdrawal plan.

Data Date	Investment Rating	Net Assets ($Mil)	NAV	Perfor-mance Rating/Pts	Total Return Y-T-D	Risk Rating/Pts
3-15	E+	8,168	33.55	E+ / 0.9	3.61%	C / 5.3
2014	E+	7,592	32.38	E+ / 0.8	1.41%	C / 5.2
2013	E	7,173	32.22	E / 0.3	-4.69%	C- / 3.3
2012	D+	7,090	34.06	C / 5.0	20.03%	C- / 3.2
2011	B-	5,806	28.51	B / 8.0	-18.84%	C- / 4.0
2010	D-	5,207	35.28	D+ / 2.7	18.75%	D / 2.1

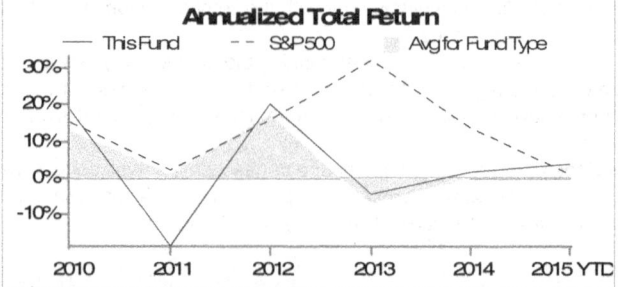

T Rowe Price Equity Income (PRFDX)
C+   Fair

Fund Family: T Rowe Price Funds   **Phone:** (800) 638-5660
Address: 100 East Pratt Street, Baltimore, MD 21202
Fund Type: IN - Income

Major Rating Factors: Middle of the road best describes T Rowe Price Equity Income whose TheStreet.com Investment Rating is currently a C+ (Fair). The fund currently has a performance rating of C+ (Fair) based on an average return of 13.31% over the last three years and -1.03% over the last three months. Factored into the performance evaluation is an expense ratio of 0.67% (very low).

The fund's risk rating is currently B- (Good). It carries a beta of 0.96, meaning that its performance tracks fairly well with that of the overall stock market. Volatility, as measured by both the semi-deviation and a drawdown factor, is considered low.

Brian C. Rogers has been running the fund for 30 years and currently receives a manager quality ranking of 40 (0=worst, 99=best). If you desire an average level of risk, then this fund may be an option.

Services Offered: Automated phone transactions, payroll deductions, bank draft capabilities, an IRA investment plan, a 401K investment plan, a Keogh investment plan, wire transfers and a systematic withdrawal plan.

Data Date	Investment Rating	Net Assets ($Mil)	NAV	Perfor-mance Rating/Pts	Total Return Y-T-D	Risk Rating/Pts
3-15	C+	27,934	32.35	C+ / 5.6	-1.03%	B- / 7.3
2014	B-	28,254	32.80	C+ / 6.7	7.49%	B- / 7.3
2013	C+	26,505	32.84	C+ / 6.8	29.75%	C+ / 5.9
2012	A-	22,111	26.45	B / 7.9	17.25%	C / 5.4
2011	C	19,081	23.06	C+ / 5.9	-0.72%	C- / 4.2
2010	C	17,321	23.69	C / 4.8	15.15%	C / 4.6

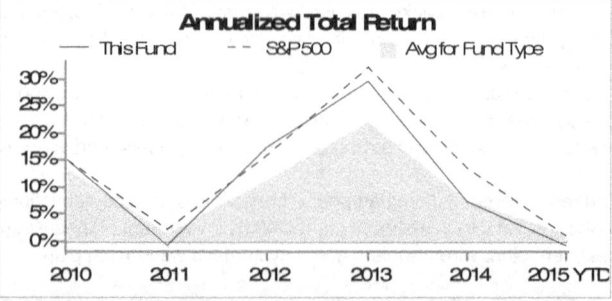

T Rowe Price Equity Index 500 (PREIX)
A-   Excellent

Fund Family: T Rowe Price Funds   **Phone:** (800) 638-5660
Address: 100 East Pratt Street, Baltimore, MD 21202
Fund Type: IX - Index

Major Rating Factors: Strong performance is the major factor driving the A- (Excellent) TheStreet.com Investment Rating for T Rowe Price Equity Index 500. The fund currently has a performance rating of B (Good) based on an average return of 15.82% over the last three years and 0.90% over the last three months. Factored into the performance evaluation is an expense ratio of 0.28% (very low) and a 0.5% back-end load levied at the time of sale.

The fund's risk rating is currently B- (Good). It carries a beta of 1.00, meaning that its performance tracks fairly well with that of the overall stock market. Volatility, as measured by both the semi-deviation and a drawdown factor, is considered low.

E. Frederick Bair has been running the fund for 13 years and currently receives a manager quality ranking of 64 (0=worst, 99=best). If you desire only a moderate level of risk and strong performance, then this fund is an excellent option.

Services Offered: Automated phone transactions, payroll deductions, bank draft capabilities, an IRA investment plan, a 401K investment plan, a Keogh investment plan, wire transfers and a systematic withdrawal plan.

Data Date	Investment Rating	Net Assets ($Mil)	NAV	Perfor-mance Rating/Pts	Total Return Y-T-D	Risk Rating/Pts
3-15	A-	25,248	55.70	B / 8.0	0.90%	B- / 7.3
2014	A	24,367	55.47	B+ / 8.7	13.40%	B- / 7.3
2013	A-	19,701	49.79	B / 7.9	32.02%	C+ / 6.0
2012	B	15,551	38.40	B- / 7.0	15.68%	C+ / 5.6
2011	C+	13,514	33.88	C+ / 6.9	1.87%	C / 5.0
2010	C	12,594	33.86	C- / 4.1	14.71%	C / 5.2

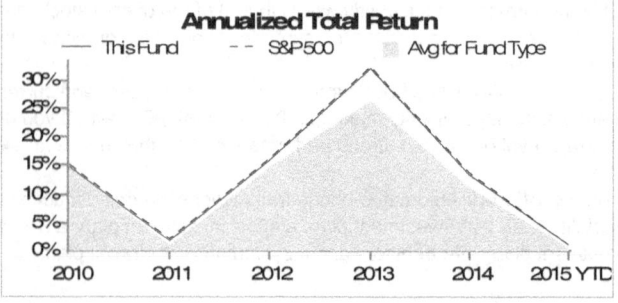

T Rowe Price Growth Stock (PRGFX)   B+   Good

Fund Family: T Rowe Price Funds   **Phone:** (800) 638-5660
Address: 100 East Pratt Street, Baltimore, MD 21202
Fund Type: GR - Growth
Major Rating Factors: Exceptional performance is the major factor driving the B+ (Good) TheStreet.com Investment Rating for T Rowe Price Growth Stock. The fund currently has a performance rating of A (Excellent) based on an average return of 17.05% over the last three years and 6.04% over the last three months. Factored into the performance evaluation is an expense ratio of 0.69% (very low).

The fund's risk rating is currently C (Fair). It carries a beta of 0.97, meaning that its performance tracks fairly well with that of the overall stock market. Volatility, as measured by both the semi-deviation and a drawdown factor, is considered average.

Joseph B. Fath has been running the fund for 1 year and currently receives a manager quality ranking of 79 (0=worst, 99=best). If you desire an average level of risk and strong performance, then this fund is a good option.
Services Offered: Automated phone transactions, payroll deductions, bank draft capabilities, an IRA investment plan, a 401K investment plan, a Keogh investment plan, wire transfers and a systematic withdrawal plan.

Data Date	Investment Rating	Net Assets ($Mil)	NAV	Performance Rating/Pts	Total Return Y-T-D	Risk Rating/Pts
3-15	B+	40,960	55.09	A / 9.3	6.04%	C / 5.0
2014	B	38,583	51.95	A- / 9.2	8.83%	C / 4.9
2013	A	36,132	52.57	A+ / 9.6	39.20%	C / 4.9
2012	B	27,354	37.78	B / 7.9	18.92%	C / 4.6
2011	A	22,672	31.83	B+ / 8.7	-0.97%	C / 5.3
2010	C+	21,237	32.15	C+ / 6.7	16.93%	C / 5.1

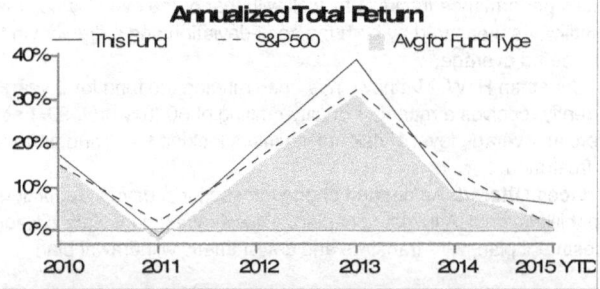

T Rowe Price Health Sciences (PRHSX)   A-   Excellent

Fund Family: T Rowe Price Funds   **Phone:** (800) 638-5660
Address: 100 East Pratt Street, Baltimore, MD 21202
Fund Type: HL - Health
Major Rating Factors: Exceptional performance is the major factor driving the A- (Excellent) TheStreet.com Investment Rating for T Rowe Price Health Sciences. The fund currently has a performance rating of A+ (Excellent) based on an average return of 36.57% over the last three years and 14.00% over the last three months. Factored into the performance evaluation is an expense ratio of 0.79% (very low).

The fund's risk rating is currently C (Fair). It carries a beta of 0.85, meaning the fund's expected move will be 8.5% for every 10% move in the market. Volatility, as measured by both the semi-deviation and a drawdown factor, is considered average.

Taymour R. Tamaddon has been running the fund for 2 years and currently receives a manager quality ranking of 99 (0=worst, 99=best). If you desire an average level of risk and strong performance, then this fund is a good option.
Services Offered: Automated phone transactions, payroll deductions, bank draft capabilities, an IRA investment plan, a 401K investment plan, a Keogh investment plan, wire transfers and a systematic withdrawal plan.

Data Date	Investment Rating	Net Assets ($Mil)	NAV	Performance Rating/Pts	Total Return Y-T-D	Risk Rating/Pts
3-15	A-	13,647	77.51	A+ / 9.9	14.00%	C / 5.0
2014	B+	11,770	67.99	A+ / 9.9	31.94%	C / 5.1
2013	A	8,431	57.80	A+ / 9.9	51.40%	C / 4.3
2012	A	5,016	41.22	A+ / 9.9	31.93%	C- / 4.0
2011	A	3,016	32.60	A / 9.4	11.01%	C / 4.6
2010	A-	2,309	30.28	B+ / 8.4	16.33%	C+ / 5.8

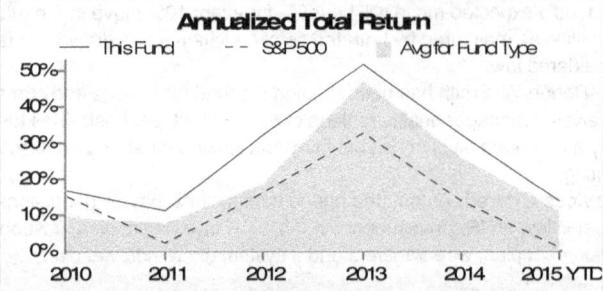

T Rowe Price Instl Lg Cap Gr (TRLGX)   B+   Good

Fund Family: T Rowe Price Funds   **Phone:** (800) 638-5660
Address: 100 East Pratt Street, Baltimore, MD 21202
Fund Type: GR - Growth
Major Rating Factors: Exceptional performance is the major factor driving the B+ (Good) TheStreet.com Investment Rating for T Rowe Price Instl Lg Cap Gr. The fund currently has a performance rating of A (Excellent) based on an average return of 17.69% over the last three years and 5.49% over the last three months. Factored into the performance evaluation is an expense ratio of 0.56% (very low).

The fund's risk rating is currently C (Fair). It carries a beta of 1.07, meaning that its performance tracks fairly well with that of the overall stock market. Volatility, as measured by both the semi-deviation and a drawdown factor, is considered average.

Robert W. Sharps has been running the fund for 13 years and currently receives a manager quality ranking of 70 (0=worst, 99=best). If you desire an average level of risk and strong performance, then this fund is a good option.
Services Offered: Automated phone transactions, bank draft capabilities, an IRA investment plan, a 401K investment plan, a Keogh investment plan, wire transfers and a systematic withdrawal plan.

Data Date	Investment Rating	Net Assets ($Mil)	NAV	Performance Rating/Pts	Total Return Y-T-D	Risk Rating/Pts
3-15	B+	12,332	28.99	A / 9.4	5.49%	C / 5.3
2014	B+	11,653	27.48	A / 9.5	8.72%	C / 5.2
2013	A	9,271	27.26	A+ / 9.8	44.44%	C / 4.8
2012	C+	5,698	18.88	B- / 7.3	17.55%	C / 4.4
2011	A+	3,251	16.12	A / 9.3	-1.40%	C / 5.3
2010	B+	2,283	16.38	B+ / 8.3	16.29%	C / 4.7

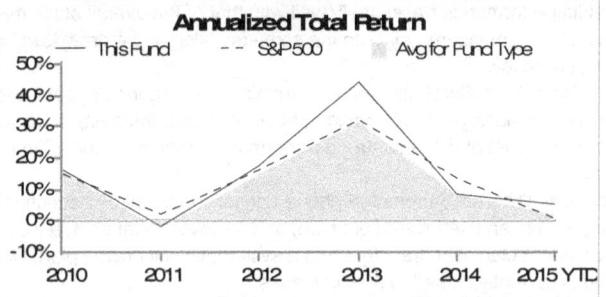

T Rowe Price Intl Gr and Inc (TRIGX)   D-   Weak

Fund Family: T Rowe Price Funds   **Phone:** (800) 638-5660
Address: 100 East Pratt Street, Baltimore, MD 21202
Fund Type: FO - Foreign
Major Rating Factors: Disappointing performance is the major factor driving the D- (Weak) TheStreet.com Investment Rating for T Rowe Price Intl Gr and Inc. The fund currently has a performance rating of D (Weak) based on an average return of 7.65% over the last three years and 3.92% over the last three months. Factored into the performance evaluation is an expense ratio of 0.85% (very low) and a 2.0% back-end load levied at the time of sale.

The fund's risk rating is currently C (Fair). It carries a beta of 0.94, meaning that its performance tracks fairly well with that of the overall stock market. Volatility, as measured by both the semi-deviation and a drawdown factor, is considered average.

Jonathan H. W. Matthews has been running the fund for 5 years and currently receives a manager quality ranking of 50 (0=worst, 99=best). This fund offers an average level of risk but investors looking for strong performance will be frustrated.

Services Offered: Automated phone transactions, payroll deductions, bank draft capabilities, an IRA investment plan, a 401K investment plan, a Keogh investment plan, wire transfers and a systematic withdrawal plan.

Data Date	Investment Rating	Net Assets ($Mil)	NAV	Performance Rating/Pts	Total Return Y-T-D	Risk Rating/Pts
3-15	D-	11,173	14.31	D / 1.9	3.92%	C / 5.1
2014	D-	10,020	13.77	D / 1.9	-5.32%	C / 5.3
2013	D	8,187	15.57	C- / 3.8	22.97%	C- / 3.9
2012	D-	5,936	12.96	D+ / 2.8	15.38%	C- / 3.8
2011	D-	4,154	11.52	D- / 1.3	-10.80%	C / 4.4
2010	D	3,040	13.31	D- / 1.2	10.49%	C- / 3.9

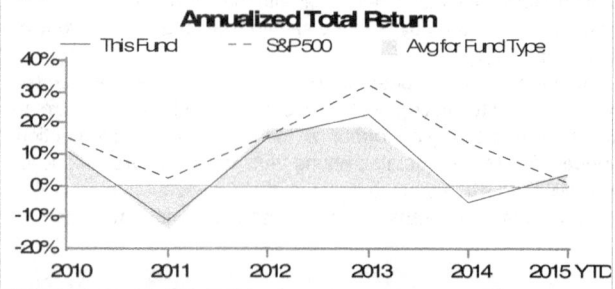

T Rowe Price Intl Stock (PRITX)   D   Weak

Fund Family: T Rowe Price Funds   **Phone:** (800) 638-5660
Address: 100 East Pratt Street, Baltimore, MD 21202
Fund Type: FO - Foreign
Major Rating Factors: Disappointing performance is the major factor driving the D (Weak) TheStreet.com Investment Rating for T Rowe Price Intl Stock. The fund currently has a performance rating of D+ (Weak) based on an average return of 7.92% over the last three years and 6.34% over the last three months. Factored into the performance evaluation is an expense ratio of 0.83% (very low) and a 2.0% back-end load levied at the time of sale.

The fund's risk rating is currently C+ (Fair). It carries a beta of 0.88, meaning the fund's expected move will be 8.8% for every 10% move in the market. Volatility, as measured by both the semi-deviation and a drawdown factor, is considered low.

Robert W. Smith has been running the fund for 8 years and currently receives a manager quality ranking of 62 (0=worst, 99=best). This fund offers only a moderate level of risk but investors looking for strong performance are still waiting.

Services Offered: Automated phone transactions, payroll deductions, bank draft capabilities, an IRA investment plan, a 401K investment plan, a Keogh investment plan, wire transfers and a systematic withdrawal plan.

Data Date	Investment Rating	Net Assets ($Mil)	NAV	Performance Rating/Pts	Total Return Y-T-D	Risk Rating/Pts
3-15	D	13,671	16.60	D+ / 2.9	6.34%	C+ / 5.6
2014	D	12,328	15.61	D+ / 2.4	-0.82%	C+ / 5.6
2013	D-	11,706	16.30	D / 1.8	14.27%	C- / 4.0
2012	C-	9,617	14.40	C / 5.2	18.72%	C- / 3.8
2011	C-	6,865	12.29	C / 4.5	-12.33%	C / 4.7
2010	D+	5,988	14.23	C- / 3.4	14.48%	C- / 3.6

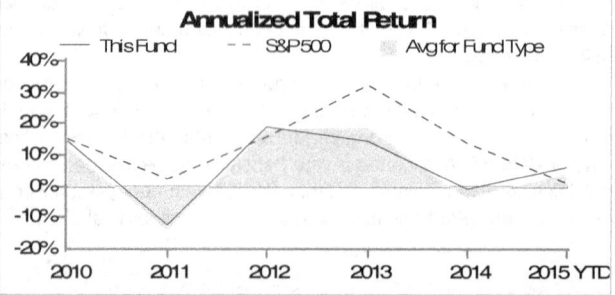

T Rowe Price Mid-Cap Growth (RPMGX)   A   Excellent

Fund Family: T Rowe Price Funds   **Phone:** (800) 638-5660
Address: 100 East Pratt Street, Baltimore, MD 21202
Fund Type: MC - Mid Cap
Major Rating Factors: Exceptional performance is the major factor driving the A (Excellent) TheStreet.com Investment Rating for T Rowe Price Mid-Cap Growth. The fund currently has a performance rating of A+ (Excellent) based on an average return of 18.41% over the last three years and 6.52% over the last three months. Factored into the performance evaluation is an expense ratio of 0.78% (very low).

The fund's risk rating is currently C+ (Fair). It carries a beta of 0.93, meaning that its performance tracks fairly well with that of the overall stock market. Volatility, as measured by both the semi-deviation and a drawdown factor, is considered low.

Brian W. H. Berghuis has been running the fund for 23 years and currently receives a manager quality ranking of 86 (0=worst, 99=best). If you desire only a moderate level of risk and strong performance, then this fund is an excellent option.

Services Offered: Automated phone transactions, payroll deductions, bank draft capabilities, an IRA investment plan, a 401K investment plan, a Keogh investment plan, wire transfers and a systematic withdrawal plan. However, the fund is currently closed to new investors.

Data Date	Investment Rating	Net Assets ($Mil)	NAV	Performance Rating/Pts	Total Return Y-T-D	Risk Rating/Pts
3-15	A	23,932	80.36	A+ / 9.7	6.52%	C+ / 5.8
2014	A-	22,677	75.44	A / 9.3	13.16%	C+ / 5.8
2013	B	21,410	72.78	B+ / 8.4	36.89%	C- / 4.1
2012	B	16,860	56.47	B+ / 8.6	13.91%	C- / 4.0
2011	A	16,699	52.73	A+ / 9.6	-1.21%	C / 4.6
2010	A-	17,806	58.53	A / 9.3	28.06%	C / 4.6

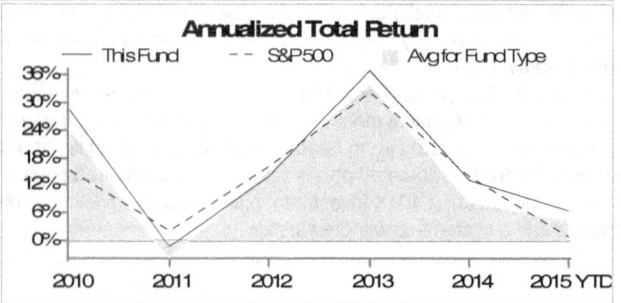

T Rowe Price Mid-Cap Value Fd (TRMCX)   B+   Good

Fund Family: T Rowe Price Funds   **Phone:** (800) 638-5660
Address: 100 East Pratt Street, Baltimore, MD 21202
Fund Type: MC - Mid Cap
Major Rating Factors: Strong performance is the major factor driving the B+ (Good) TheStreet.com Investment Rating for T Rowe Price Mid-Cap Value Fd. The fund currently has a performance rating of B+ (Good) based on an average return of 17.12% over the last three years and 2.88% over the last three months. Factored into the performance evaluation is an expense ratio of 0.80% (very low).

The fund's risk rating is currently C (Fair). It carries a beta of 0.88, meaning the fund's expected move will be 8.8% for every 10% move in the market. Volatility, as measured by both the semi-deviation and a drawdown factor, is considered average.

David J. Wallack has been running the fund for 15 years and currently receives a manager quality ranking of 84 (0=worst, 99=best). If you desire an average level of risk and strong performance, then this fund is a good option.
Services Offered: Automated phone transactions, payroll deductions, bank draft capabilities, an IRA investment plan, a 401K investment plan, a Keogh investment plan, wire transfers and a systematic withdrawal plan. However, the fund is currently closed to new investors.

Data Date	Investment Rating	Net Assets ($Mil)	NAV	Performance Rating/Pts	Total Return Y-T-D	Risk Rating/Pts
3-15	B+	11,520	29.65	B+ / 8.7	2.88%	C / 5.4
2014	B	11,112	28.82	B+ / 8.3	10.60%	C / 5.1
2013	C+	10,360	30.05	B- / 7.1	31.54%	C / 4.7
2012	B+	8,437	24.04	B+ / 8.3	19.63%	C / 4.8
2011	B+	7,627	21.39	B / 8.1	-4.82%	C / 4.8
2010	B+	7,723	23.71	B+ / 8.7	16.45%	C / 5.1

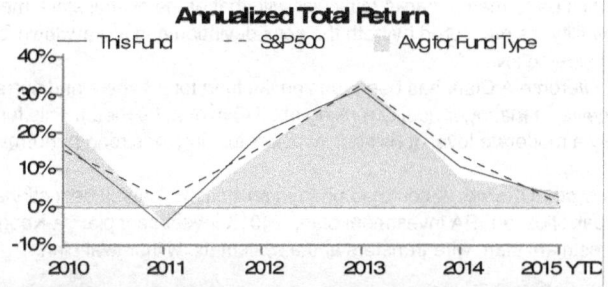

T Rowe Price New Horizons (PRNHX)   B   Good

Fund Family: T Rowe Price Funds   **Phone:** (800) 638-5660
Address: 100 East Pratt Street, Baltimore, MD 21202
Fund Type: SC - Small Cap
Major Rating Factors: Exceptional performance is the major factor driving the B (Good) TheStreet.com Investment Rating for T Rowe Price New Horizons. The fund currently has a performance rating of A+ (Excellent) based on an average return of 19.03% over the last three years and 6.40% over the last three months. Factored into the performance evaluation is an expense ratio of 0.80% (very low).

The fund's risk rating is currently C- (Fair). It carries a beta of 0.87, meaning the fund's expected move will be 8.7% for every 10% move in the market. Volatility, as measured by both the semi-deviation and a drawdown factor, is considered average.

Henry M. Ellenbogen has been running the fund for 5 years and currently receives a manager quality ranking of 92 (0=worst, 99=best). If you desire an average level of risk and strong performance, then this fund is a good option.
Services Offered: Automated phone transactions, payroll deductions, bank draft capabilities, an IRA investment plan, a 401K investment plan, a Keogh investment plan, wire transfers and a systematic withdrawal plan. However, the fund is currently closed to new investors.

Data Date	Investment Rating	Net Assets ($Mil)	NAV	Performance Rating/Pts	Total Return Y-T-D	Risk Rating/Pts
3-15	B	15,974	46.58	A+ / 9.6	6.40%	C- / 4.2
2014	B-	15,356	43.78	A / 9.3	6.10%	C- / 4.1
2013	B+	15,523	46.27	A+ / 9.9	49.11%	C- / 3.2
2012	B+	9,727	33.17	A+ / 9.8	16.20%	C- / 3.0
2011	B+	7,901	31.03	A+ / 9.9	6.63%	C- / 3.4
2010	A-	7,176	33.49	A+ / 9.7	34.67%	C / 4.5

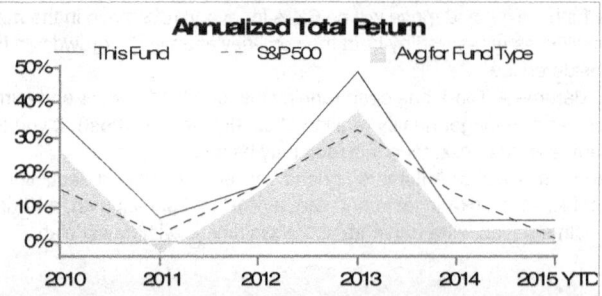

T Rowe Price Overseas Stock Fund (TROSX)   D+   Weak

Fund Family: T Rowe Price Funds   **Phone:** (800) 638-5660
Address: 100 East Pratt Street, Baltimore, MD 21202
Fund Type: FO - Foreign
Major Rating Factors: T Rowe Price Overseas Stock Fund receives a TheStreet.com Investment Rating of D+ (Weak). The fund currently has a performance rating of C- (Fair) based on an average return of 9.24% over the last three years and 5.63% over the last three months. Factored into the performance evaluation is an expense ratio of 0.84% (very low) and a 2.0% back-end load levied at the time of sale.

The fund's risk rating is currently C+ (Fair). It carries a beta of 0.91, meaning that its performance tracks fairly well with that of the overall stock market. Volatility, as measured by both the semi-deviation and a drawdown factor, is considered low.

Raymond A. Mills has been running the fund for 9 years and currently receives a manager quality ranking of 73 (0=worst, 99=best). If you desire an average level of risk, then this fund may be an option.
Services Offered: Automated phone transactions, payroll deductions, bank draft capabilities, an IRA investment plan, a 401K investment plan, wire transfers and a systematic withdrawal plan.

Data Date	Investment Rating	Net Assets ($Mil)	NAV	Performance Rating/Pts	Total Return Y-T-D	Risk Rating/Pts
3-15	D+	10,272	9.95	C- / 3.2	5.63%	C+ / 6.1
2014	D	9,367	9.42	D+ / 2.4	-4.49%	C+ / 6.2
2013	D	7,047	10.15	C- / 4.0	21.75%	C / 4.3
2012	C-	5,444	8.50	C / 5.0	18.59%	C- / 4.1
2011	D	3,785	7.32	D / 1.6	-10.12%	C / 4.7
2010	D	2,337	8.34	D- / 1.3	10.57%	C- / 4.0

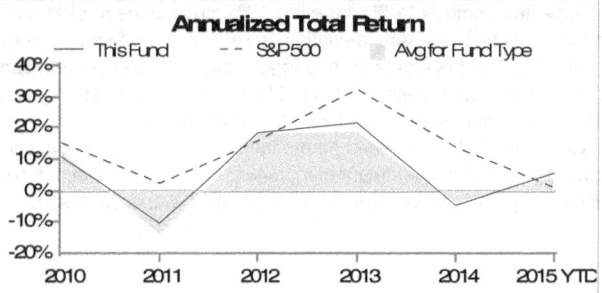

T Rowe Price Retirement 2010 (TRRAX)   C   Fair

Fund Family: T Rowe Price Funds   **Phone:** (800) 638-5660
Address: 100 East Pratt Street, Baltimore, MD 21202
Fund Type: AA - Asset Allocation
Major Rating Factors: Disappointing performance is the major factor driving the C (Fair) TheStreet.com Investment Rating for T Rowe Price Retirement 2010. The fund currently has a performance rating of D+ (Weak) based on an average return of 7.60% over the last three years and 1.75% over the last three months. Factored into the performance evaluation is an expense ratio of 0.59% (very low).

The fund's risk rating is currently B (Good). It carries a beta of 0.96, meaning that its performance tracks fairly well with that of the overall stock market. Volatility, as measured by both the semi-deviation and a drawdown factor, is considered low.

Jerome A Clark has been running the fund for 13 years and currently receives a manager quality ranking of 30 (0=worst, 99=best). This fund offers only a moderate level of risk but investors looking for strong performance are still waiting.

Services Offered: Automated phone transactions, payroll deductions, bank draft capabilities, an IRA investment plan, a 401K investment plan, a Keogh investment plan, wire transfers and a systematic withdrawal plan.

Data Date	Investment Rating	Net Assets ($Mil)	NAV	Perfor-mance Rating/Pts	Total Return Y-T-D	Risk Rating/Pts
3-15	C	5,233	18.04	D+ / 2.8	1.75%	B / 8.3
2014	C	5,178	17.73	C- / 3.0	4.99%	B / 8.4
2013	C	4,858	17.82	D+ / 2.5	11.93%	B- / 7.9
2012	B-	4,629	16.47	C / 4.7	12.44%	B- / 7.9
2011	B-	4,285	15.02	C+ / 6.0	0.54%	B- / 7.7
2010	A-	4,195	15.34	B- / 7.2	12.70%	C+ / 6.9

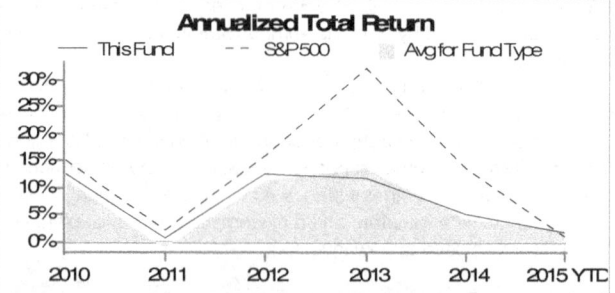

T Rowe Price Retirement 2015 (TRRGX)   C   Fair

Fund Family: T Rowe Price Funds   **Phone:** (800) 638-5660
Address: 100 East Pratt Street, Baltimore, MD 21202
Fund Type: GI - Growth and Income
Major Rating Factors: Middle of the road best describes T Rowe Price Retirement 2015 whose TheStreet.com Investment Rating is currently a C (Fair). The fund currently has a performance rating of C- (Fair) based on an average return of 8.88% over the last three years and 2.07% over the last three months. Factored into the performance evaluation is an expense ratio of 0.63% (very low).

The fund's risk rating is currently B (Good). It carries a beta of 0.64, meaning the fund's expected move will be 6.4% for every 10% move in the market. Volatility, as measured by both the semi-deviation and a drawdown factor, is considered low.

Jerome A. Clark has been running the fund for 11 years and currently receives a manager quality ranking of 52 (0=worst, 99=best). If you desire an average level of risk, then this fund may be an option.

Services Offered: Automated phone transactions, payroll deductions, bank draft capabilities, an IRA investment plan, a 401K investment plan, a Keogh investment plan, wire transfers and a systematic withdrawal plan.

Data Date	Investment Rating	Net Assets ($Mil)	NAV	Perfor-mance Rating/Pts	Total Return Y-T-D	Risk Rating/Pts
3-15	C	9,003	14.77	C- / 3.5	2.07%	B / 8.3
2014	C+	8,770	14.47	C- / 3.7	5.37%	B / 8.3
2013	C	7,732	14.32	C- / 3.2	15.18%	B- / 7.4
2012	B-	6,635	12.88	C+ / 5.8	13.81%	B- / 7.3
2011	B-	5,703	11.58	C+ / 6.7	-0.32%	B- / 7.2
2010	B+	5,009	11.89	B- / 7.2	13.79%	C+ / 6.2

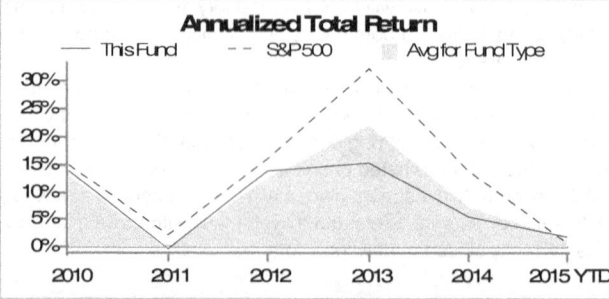

T Rowe Price Retirement 2020 (TRRBX)   C+   Fair

Fund Family: T Rowe Price Funds   **Phone:** (800) 638-5660
Address: 100 East Pratt Street, Baltimore, MD 21202
Fund Type: AA - Asset Allocation
Major Rating Factors: Middle of the road best describes T Rowe Price Retirement 2020 whose TheStreet.com Investment Rating is currently a C+ (Fair). The fund currently has a performance rating of C- (Fair) based on an average return of 10.03% over the last three years and 2.51% over the last three months. Factored into the performance evaluation is an expense ratio of 0.67% (very low).

The fund's risk rating is currently B (Good). It carries a beta of 1.23, meaning it is expected to move 12.3% for every 10% move in the market. Volatility, as measured by both the semi-deviation and a drawdown factor, is considered low.

Jerome A. Clark has been running the fund for 13 years and currently receives a manager quality ranking of 24 (0=worst, 99=best). If you desire an average level of risk, then this fund may be an option.

Services Offered: Automated phone transactions, payroll deductions, bank draft capabilities, an IRA investment plan, a 401K investment plan, a Keogh investment plan, wire transfers and a systematic withdrawal plan.

Data Date	Investment Rating	Net Assets ($Mil)	NAV	Perfor-mance Rating/Pts	Total Return Y-T-D	Risk Rating/Pts
3-15	C+	19,731	21.23	C- / 4.2	2.51%	B / 8.1
2014	C+	18,820	20.71	C / 4.3	5.63%	B / 8.0
2013	C+	15,342	20.39	C- / 4.0	18.05%	C+ / 6.9
2012	C+	12,612	17.88	C+ / 6.5	15.01%	C+ / 6.8
2011	A	10,271	15.91	B- / 7.1	-1.20%	C+ / 6.8
2010	B	8,912	16.44	B- / 7.1	14.74%	C / 5.5

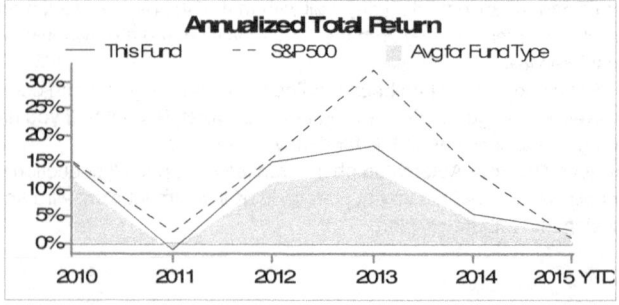

T Rowe Price Retirement 2025 (TRRHX)   C+   Fair

Fund Family: T Rowe Price Funds   **Phone:** (800) 638-5660
Address: 100 East Pratt Street, Baltimore, MD 21202
Fund Type: GI - Growth and Income
Major Rating Factors: Middle of the road best describes T Rowe Price Retirement 2025 whose TheStreet.com Investment Rating is currently a C+ (Fair). The fund currently has a performance rating of C (Fair) based on an average return of 11.05% over the last three years and 2.86% over the last three months. Factored into the performance evaluation is an expense ratio of 0.70% (very low).

The fund's risk rating is currently B- (Good). It carries a beta of 0.79, meaning the fund's expected move will be 7.9% for every 10% move in the market. Volatility, as measured by both the semi-deviation and a drawdown factor, is considered low.

Jerome A. Clark has been running the fund for 11 years and currently receives a manager quality ranking of 48 (0=worst, 99=best). If you desire an average level of risk, then this fund may be an option.

Services Offered: Automated phone transactions, payroll deductions, bank draft capabilities, an IRA investment plan, a 401K investment plan, a Keogh investment plan, wire transfers and a systematic withdrawal plan.

Data Date	Investment Rating	Net Assets ($Mil)	NAV	Perfor- mance Rating/Pts	Total Return Y-T-D	Risk Rating/Pts
3-15	C+	14,858	16.16	C / 4.9	2.86%	B- / 7.8
2014	C+	13,931	15.71	C / 4.8	5.84%	B- / 7.8
2013	C+	10,781	15.38	C / 4.6	20.78%	C+ / 6.5
2012	A-	8,266	13.12	B- / 7.1	16.00%	C+ / 6.2
2011	A-	6,403	11.58	B- / 7.3	-2.06%	C+ / 6.4
2010	C+	5,240	12.04	C+ / 6.9	15.37%	C / 5.2

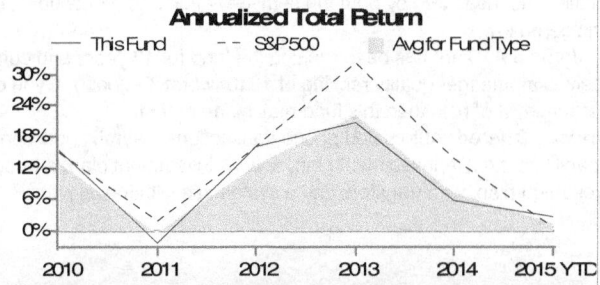

Annualized Total Return

T Rowe Price Retirement 2030 (TRRCX)   B-   Good

Fund Family: T Rowe Price Funds   **Phone:** (800) 638-5660
Address: 100 East Pratt Street, Baltimore, MD 21202
Fund Type: AA - Asset Allocation
Major Rating Factors: T Rowe Price Retirement 2030 receives a TheStreet.com Investment Rating of B- (Good). The fund currently has a performance rating of C (Fair) based on an average return of 11.88% over the last three years and 3.08% over the last three months. Factored into the performance evaluation is an expense ratio of 0.73% (very low).

The fund's risk rating is currently B- (Good). It carries a beta of 1.44, meaning it is expected to move 14.4% for every 10% move in the market. Volatility, as measured by both the semi-deviation and a drawdown factor, is considered low.

Jerome A Clark has been running the fund for 13 years and currently receives a manager quality ranking of 19 (0=worst, 99=best). If you desire an average level of risk, then this fund may be an option.

Services Offered: Automated phone transactions, payroll deductions, bank draft capabilities, an IRA investment plan, a 401K investment plan, a Keogh investment plan, wire transfers and a systematic withdrawal plan.

Data Date	Investment Rating	Net Assets ($Mil)	NAV	Perfor- mance Rating/Pts	Total Return Y-T-D	Risk Rating/Pts
3-15	B-	18,380	23.73	C / 5.4	3.08%	B- / 7.5
2014	C+	17,284	23.02	C / 5.3	6.05%	B- / 7.4
2013	C+	13,819	22.60	C / 5.1	23.09%	C+ / 6.0
2012	B+	10,773	18.92	B- / 7.5	16.82%	C+ / 5.8
2011	A-	8,170	16.54	B- / 7.5	-2.70%	C+ / 6.0
2010	C+	6,917	17.28	C+ / 6.9	16.01%	C / 4.9

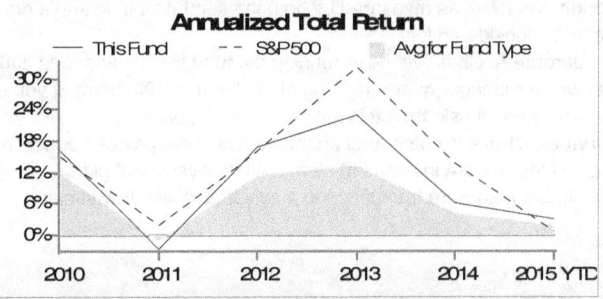

Annualized Total Return

T Rowe Price Retirement 2035 (TRRJX)   B-   Good

Fund Family: T Rowe Price Funds   **Phone:** (800) 638-5660
Address: 100 East Pratt Street, Baltimore, MD 21202
Fund Type: GI - Growth and Income
Major Rating Factors: T Rowe Price Retirement 2035 receives a TheStreet.com Investment Rating of B- (Good). The fund currently has a performance rating of C+ (Fair) based on an average return of 12.49% over the last three years and 3.36% over the last three months. Factored into the performance evaluation is an expense ratio of 0.75% (very low).

The fund's risk rating is currently B- (Good). It carries a beta of 0.89, meaning the fund's expected move will be 8.9% for every 10% move in the market. Volatility, as measured by both the semi-deviation and a drawdown factor, is considered low.

Jerome A. Clark has been running the fund for 11 years and currently receives a manager quality ranking of 44 (0=worst, 99=best). If you desire an average level of risk, then this fund may be an option.

Services Offered: Automated phone transactions, payroll deductions, bank draft capabilities, an IRA investment plan, a 401K investment plan, a Keogh investment plan, wire transfers and a systematic withdrawal plan.

Data Date	Investment Rating	Net Assets ($Mil)	NAV	Perfor- mance Rating/Pts	Total Return Y-T-D	Risk Rating/Pts
3-15	B-	10,716	17.22	C+ / 5.8	3.36%	B- / 7.2
2014	C+	9,950	16.66	C+ / 5.6	6.07%	B- / 7.2
2013	C+	7,620	16.28	C / 5.5	24.86%	C+ / 5.7
2012	B+	5,653	13.38	B / 7.7	17.35%	C / 5.4
2011	B+	4,178	11.66	B- / 7.5	-3.26%	C+ / 5.7
2010	C+	3,359	12.23	C+ / 6.9	16.34%	C / 4.8

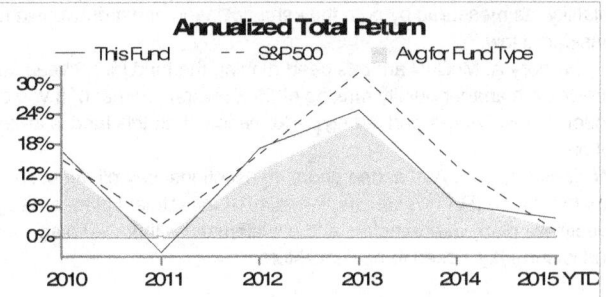

Annualized Total Return

T Rowe Price Retirement 2040 (TRRDX)   B-   Good

Fund Family: T Rowe Price Funds   **Phone:** (800) 638-5660
Address: 100 East Pratt Street, Baltimore, MD 21202
Fund Type: AA - Asset Allocation
Major Rating Factors: T Rowe Price Retirement 2040 receives a
TheStreet.com Investment Rating of B- (Good). The fund currently has a
performance rating of C+ (Fair) based on an average return of 12.87% over the
last three years and 3.47% over the last three months. Factored into the
performance evaluation is an expense ratio of 0.76% (very low).

The fund's risk rating is currently B- (Good). It carries a beta of 1.56,
meaning it is expected to move 15.6% for every 10% move in the market.
Volatility, as measured by both the semi-deviation and a drawdown factor, is
considered low.

Jerome A. Clark has been running the fund for 13 years and currently
receives a manager quality ranking of 16 (0=worst, 99=best). If you desire an
average level of risk, then this fund may be an option.

Services Offered: Automated phone transactions, payroll deductions, bank draft
capabilities, an IRA investment plan, a 401K investment plan, a Keogh
investment plan, wire transfers and a systematic withdrawal plan.

Data Date	Investment Rating	Net Assets ($Mil)	NAV	Performance Rating/Pts	Total Return Y-T-D	Risk Rating/Pts
3-15	B-	12,343	24.75	C+ / 6.0	3.47%	B- / 7.0
2014	C+	11,532	23.92	C+ / 5.8	6.18%	B- / 7.0
2013	C+	9,818	23.41	C+ / 5.7	25.93%	C+ / 5.6
2012	B+	7,139	19.09	B / 7.7	17.55%	C / 5.3
2011	B+	5,259	16.57	B- / 7.5	-3.49%	C+ / 5.7
2010	C+	4,354	17.42	B- / 7.0	16.51%	C / 4.4

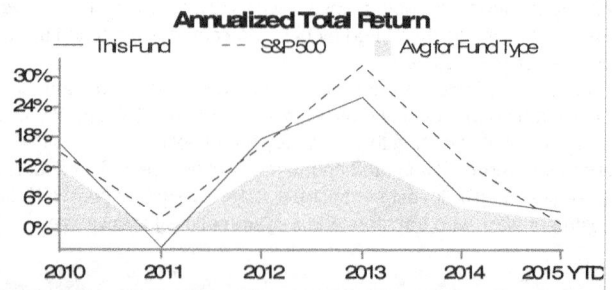
Annualized Total Return

T Rowe Price Retirement 2045 (TRRKX)   B-   Good

Fund Family: T Rowe Price Funds   **Phone:** (800) 638-5660
Address: 100 East Pratt Street, Baltimore, MD 21202
Fund Type: GI - Growth and Income
Major Rating Factors: T Rowe Price Retirement 2045 receives a
TheStreet.com Investment Rating of B- (Good). The fund currently has a
performance rating of C+ (Fair) based on an average return of 12.87% over the
last three years and 3.50% over the last three months. Factored into the
performance evaluation is an expense ratio of 0.76% (very low).

The fund's risk rating is currently B- (Good). It carries a beta of 0.92,
meaning that its performance tracks fairly well with that of the overall stock
market. Volatility, as measured by both the semi-deviation and a drawdown
factor, is considered low.

Jerome A. Clark has been running the fund for 10 years and currently
receives a manager quality ranking of 43 (0=worst, 99=best). If you desire an
average level of risk, then this fund may be an option.

Services Offered: Automated phone transactions, payroll deductions, bank draft
capabilities, an IRA investment plan, a 401K investment plan, a Keogh
investment plan, wire transfers and a systematic withdrawal plan.

Data Date	Investment Rating	Net Assets ($Mil)	NAV	Performance Rating/Pts	Total Return Y-T-D	Risk Rating/Pts
3-15	B-	6,023	16.56	C+ / 6.1	3.50%	B- / 7.1
2014	C+	5,544	16.00	C+ / 5.8	6.14%	B- / 7.0
2013	C+	4,153	15.61	C+ / 5.8	25.93%	C+ / 5.6
2012	B+	3,124	12.71	B / 7.8	17.62%	C / 5.3
2011	B+	2,191	11.03	B- / 7.5	-3.47%	C+ / 5.7
2010	C+	1,676	11.61	C+ / 6.9	16.44%	C / 4.8

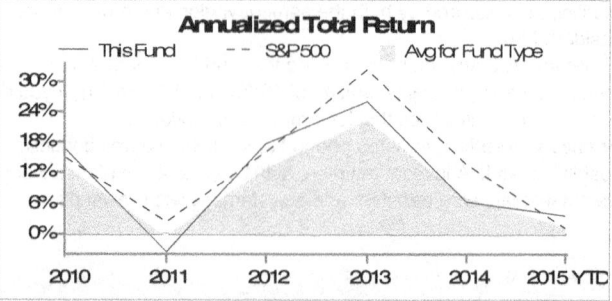
Annualized Total Return

T Rowe Price Small Cap Stock (OTCFX)   A-   Excellent

Fund Family: T Rowe Price Funds   **Phone:** (800) 638-5660
Address: 100 East Pratt Street, Baltimore, MD 21202
Fund Type: SC - Small Cap
Major Rating Factors: Strong performance is the major factor driving the A-
(Excellent) TheStreet.com Investment Rating for T Rowe Price Small Cap Stock.
The fund currently has a performance rating of B+ (Good) based on an average
return of 16.72% over the last three years and 3.90% over the last three months.
Factored into the performance evaluation is an expense ratio of 0.91% (low).

The fund's risk rating is currently C+ (Fair). It carries a beta of 0.87, meaning
the fund's expected move will be 8.7% for every 10% move in the market.
Volatility, as measured by both the semi-deviation and a drawdown factor, is
considered low.

Gregory A. McCrickard has been running the fund for 23 years and currently
receives a manager quality ranking of 86 (0=worst, 99=best). If you desire only a
moderate level of risk and strong performance, then this fund is an excellent
option.

Services Offered: Automated phone transactions, payroll deductions, bank draft
capabilities, an IRA investment plan, a 401K investment plan, a Keogh
investment plan, wire transfers and a systematic withdrawal plan. However, the
fund is currently closed to new investors.

Data Date	Investment Rating	Net Assets ($Mil)	NAV	Performance Rating/Pts	Total Return Y-T-D	Risk Rating/Pts
3-15	A-	9,111	46.05	B+ / 8.8	3.90%	C+ / 6.1
2014	B+	9,351	44.32	B+ / 8.4	6.90%	C+ / 6.0
2013	B	9,709	44.56	A- / 9.1	37.65%	C- / 3.5
2012	B	7,071	34.03	A+ / 9.6	18.01%	C- / 3.1
2011	B+	6,513	31.25	A+ / 9.6	-0.09%	C- / 3.6
2010	A	6,017	34.43	A+ / 9.7	32.53%	C / 4.8

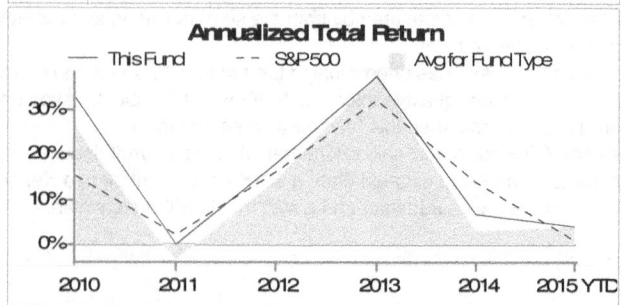
Annualized Total Return

T Rowe Price Small Cap Value (PRSVX)   C   Fair

Fund Family: T Rowe Price Funds   **Phone:** (800) 638-5660
Address: 100 East Pratt Street, Baltimore, MD 21202
Fund Type: SC - Small Cap
Major Rating Factors: Middle of the road best describes T Rowe Price Small Cap Value whose TheStreet.com Investment Rating is currently a C (Fair). The fund currently has a performance rating of C (Fair) based on an average return of 12.66% over the last three years and 1.13% over the last three months. Factored into the performance evaluation is an expense ratio of 0.96% (low) and a 1.0% back-end load levied at the time of sale.

The fund's risk rating is currently C+ (Fair). It carries a beta of 0.87, meaning the fund's expected move will be 8.7% for every 10% move in the market. Volatility, as measured by both the semi-deviation and a drawdown factor, is considered low.

Preston G. Athey has been running the fund for 24 years and currently receives a manager quality ranking of 49 (0=worst, 99=best). If you desire an average level of risk, then this fund may be an option.

Services Offered: Automated phone transactions, payroll deductions, bank draft capabilities, an IRA investment plan, a 401K investment plan, a Keogh investment plan, wire transfers and a systematic withdrawal plan.

Data Date	Investment Rating	Net Assets ($Mil)	NAV	Performance Rating/Pts	Total Return Y-T-D	Risk Rating/Pts
3-15	C	7,888	47.33	C / 5.1	1.13%	C+ / 5.9
2014	C	8,040	46.80	C / 5.3	0.14%	C+ / 6.0
2013	B	8,603	50.37	B / 8.0	32.74%	C / 4.6
2012	A-	6,744	39.17	A / 9.3	17.76%	C- / 4.1
2011	C+	5,859	34.48	B / 8.2	-0.60%	C- / 3.3
2010	B+	5,583	36.13	A / 9.3	25.25%	C / 4.3

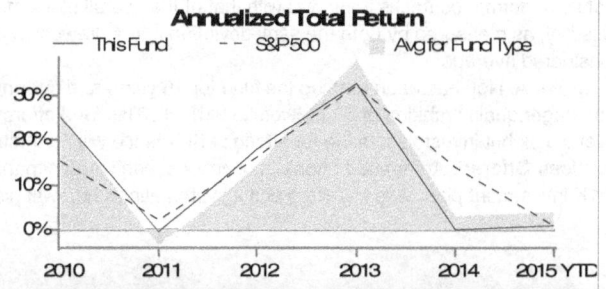

T Rowe Price Value (TRVLX)   A   Excellent

Fund Family: T Rowe Price Funds   **Phone:** (800) 638-5660
Address: 100 East Pratt Street, Baltimore, MD 21202
Fund Type: GI - Growth and Income
Major Rating Factors: Exceptional performance is the major factor driving the A (Excellent) TheStreet.com Investment Rating for T Rowe Price Value. The fund currently has a performance rating of A (Excellent) based on an average return of 18.65% over the last three years and 0.89% over the last three months. Factored into the performance evaluation is an expense ratio of 0.84% (very low).

The fund's risk rating is currently C+ (Fair). It carries a beta of 1.05, meaning that its performance tracks fairly well with that of the overall stock market. Volatility, as measured by both the semi-deviation and a drawdown factor, is considered low.

Mark S. Finn has been running the fund for 6 years and currently receives a manager quality ranking of 80 (0=worst, 99=best). If you desire only a moderate level of risk and strong performance, then this fund is an excellent option.

Services Offered: Automated phone transactions, payroll deductions, bank draft capabilities, an IRA investment plan, a 401K investment plan, a Keogh investment plan, wire transfers and a systematic withdrawal plan.

Data Date	Investment Rating	Net Assets ($Mil)	NAV	Performance Rating/Pts	Total Return Y-T-D	Risk Rating/Pts
3-15	A	22,100	34.96	A / 9.3	0.89%	C+ / 6.3
2014	A	21,583	34.65	A+ / 9.6	13.37%	C+ / 6.3
2013	A	17,266	33.77	A- / 9.0	37.31%	C / 5.2
2012	A-	13,319	26.38	B+ / 8.7	19.46%	C / 4.8
2011	B	11,391	22.54	B / 7.8	-2.00%	C / 4.4
2010	C+	10,546	23.34	C+ / 6.1	15.96%	C / 4.5

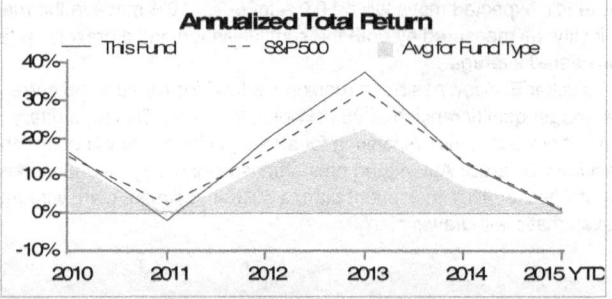

Templeton Growth A (TEPLX)   D+   Weak

Fund Family: Franklin Templeton Investments   **Phone:** (800) 342-5236
Address: One Franklin Parkway, San Mateo, CA 94403
Fund Type: GL - Global
Major Rating Factors: Templeton Growth A receives a TheStreet.com Investment Rating of D+ (Weak). The fund currently has a performance rating of C- (Fair) based on an average return of 11.97% over the last three years and 1.47% over the last three months. Factored into the performance evaluation is an expense ratio of 1.07% (low) and a 5.8% front-end load that is levied at the time of purchase.

The fund's risk rating is currently C+ (Fair). It carries a beta of 0.94, meaning that its performance tracks fairly well with that of the overall stock market. Volatility, as measured by both the semi-deviation and a drawdown factor, is considered low.

Tucker E. Scott has been running the fund for 8 years and currently receives a manager quality ranking of 88 (0=worst, 99=best). If you desire an average level of risk, then this fund may be an option.

Services Offered: Automated phone transactions, payroll deductions, bank draft capabilities, an IRA investment plan, a 401K investment plan and a systematic withdrawal plan.

Data Date	Investment Rating	Net Assets ($Mil)	NAV	Performance Rating/Pts	Total Return Y-T-D	Risk Rating/Pts
3-15	D+	13,002	24.16	C- / 3.3	1.47%	C+ / 6.2
2014	C-	12,827	23.81	C- / 3.9	-1.91%	C+ / 6.0
2013	C	14,475	24.97	C+ / 6.1	30.15%	C / 4.4
2012	C	12,186	19.43	C+ / 6.4	21.54%	C- / 4.2
2011	D-	11,449	16.29	D- / 1.2	-6.38%	C / 4.4
2010	D-	13,469	17.79	E / 0.4	7.54%	C- / 4.0

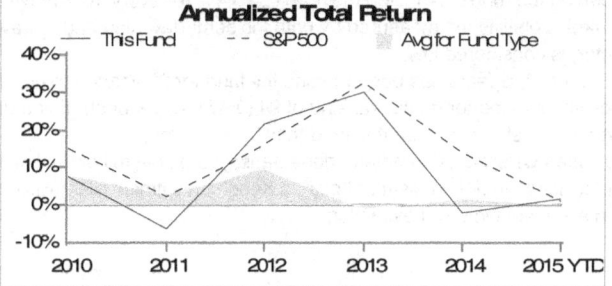

Templeton Inst-Foreign Eq Prm (TFEQX)

D-   **Weak**

Fund Family: Franklin Templeton Institutional Gr   **Phone:** (800) 321-8563
Address: 777 Mariners Island Blvd, San Mateo, CA 94404
Fund Type: FO - Foreign
Major Rating Factors: Disappointing performance is the major factor driving the D- (Weak) TheStreet.com Investment Rating for Templeton Inst-Foreign Eq Prm. The fund currently has a performance rating of D+ (Weak) based on an average return of 8.21% over the last three years and 5.29% over the last three months. Factored into the performance evaluation is an expense ratio of 0.79% (very low).

The fund's risk rating is currently C (Fair). It carries a beta of 0.96, meaning that its performance tracks fairly well with that of the overall stock market. Volatility, as measured by both the semi-deviation and a drawdown factor, is considered average.

Peter A. Nori has been running the fund for 16 years and currently receives a manager quality ranking of 55 (0=worst, 99=best). This fund offers an average level of risk but investors looking for strong performance will be frustrated.
Services Offered: Automated phone transactions, bank draft capabilities, a 401K investment plan, wire transfers and a systematic withdrawal plan.

Data Date	Investment Rating	Net Assets ($Mil)	NAV	Performance Rating/Pts	Total Return Y-T-D	Risk Rating/Pts
3-15	D-	6,305	21.11	D+ / 2.5	5.29%	C / 5.3
2014	D-	6,226	20.05	D / 1.8	-6.78%	C+ / 5.6
2013	D-	6,815	22.72	C- / 3.7	19.51%	C- / 3.0
2012	D+	5,828	19.60	C / 5.4	18.55%	D+ / 2.6
2011	E+	5,496	17.04	D- / 1.1	-10.90%	C- / 3.8
2010	D-	6,399	20.05	D- / 1.0	6.70%	C- / 3.9

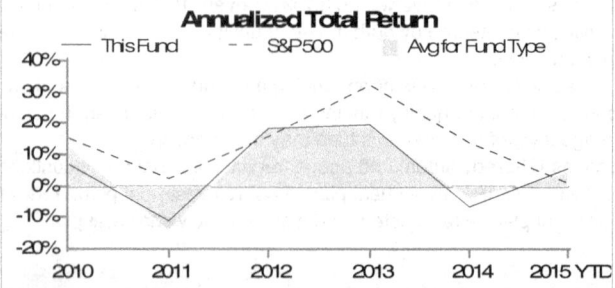

Annualized Total Return

Templeton World A (TEMWX)

D-   **Weak**

Fund Family: Franklin Templeton Investments   **Phone:** (800) 342-5236
Address: One Franklin Parkway, San Mateo, CA 94403
Fund Type: GL - Global
Major Rating Factors: Disappointing performance is the major factor driving the D- (Weak) TheStreet.com Investment Rating for Templeton World A. The fund currently has a performance rating of D+ (Weak) based on an average return of 10.84% over the last three years and 1.69% over the last three months. Factored into the performance evaluation is an expense ratio of 1.05% (low) and a 5.8% front-end load that is levied at the time of purchase.

The fund's risk rating is currently C (Fair). It carries a beta of 0.90, meaning the fund's expected move will be 9.0% for every 10% move in the market. Volatility, as measured by both the semi-deviation and a drawdown factor, is considered average.

Tucker E. Scott has been running the fund for 8 years and currently receives a manager quality ranking of 85 (0=worst, 99=best). This fund offers an average level of risk but investors looking for strong performance will be frustrated.
Services Offered: Automated phone transactions, payroll deductions, bank draft capabilities, an IRA investment plan, a 401K investment plan, wire transfers and a systematic withdrawal plan.

Data Date	Investment Rating	Net Assets ($Mil)	NAV	Performance Rating/Pts	Total Return Y-T-D	Risk Rating/Pts
3-15	D-	5,372	17.49	D+ / 2.7	1.69%	C / 5.0
2014	D	5,314	17.20	C- / 3.3	-3.16%	C+ / 5.6
2013	C	5,868	19.41	C+ / 5.9	29.89%	C / 5.0
2012	C	4,902	15.74	C / 5.2	19.40%	C / 4.7
2011	D	4,909	13.74	D / 1.6	-5.49%	C / 5.1
2010	D	5,704	14.84	D- / 1.2	7.99%	C / 4.7

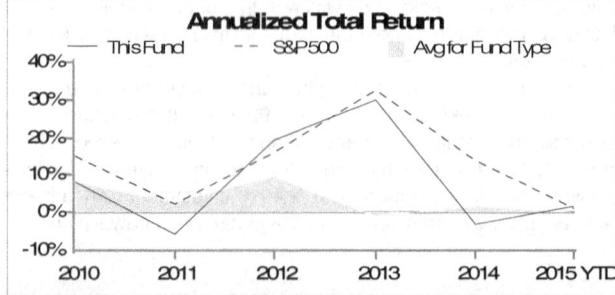

Annualized Total Return

Tweedy Browne Global Value (TBGVX)

C   **Fair**

Fund Family: Tweedy Browne Funds   **Phone:** (800) 432-4789
Address: 4400 Computer Drive, Westborough, MA 01581
Fund Type: FO - Foreign
Major Rating Factors: Middle of the road best describes Tweedy Browne Global Value whose TheStreet.com Investment Rating is currently a C (Fair). The fund currently has a performance rating of C- (Fair) based on an average return of 10.99% over the last three years and 3.57% over the last three months. Factored into the performance evaluation is an expense ratio of 1.38% (average) and a 2.0% back-end load levied at the time of sale.

The fund's risk rating is currently B- (Good). It carries a beta of 0.54, meaning the fund's expected move will be 5.4% for every 10% move in the market. Volatility, as measured by both the semi-deviation and a drawdown factor, is considered low.

John D. Spears has been running the fund for 22 years and currently receives a manager quality ranking of 94 (0=worst, 99=best). If you desire an average level of risk, then this fund may be an option.
Services Offered: Automated phone transactions, payroll deductions, bank draft capabilities, an IRA investment plan, a Keogh investment plan, wire transfers and a systematic withdrawal plan.

Data Date	Investment Rating	Net Assets ($Mil)	NAV	Performance Rating/Pts	Total Return Y-T-D	Risk Rating/Pts
3-15	C	9,596	26.97	C- / 4.1	3.57%	B- / 7.3
2014	C-	8,720	26.04	C- / 3.6	1.51%	B- / 7.2
2013	C	7,388	26.62	C- / 3.9	19.62%	C+ / 6.4
2012	A	5,221	23.24	B- / 7.4	18.38%	C+ / 6.3
2011	B-	4,368	21.85	C+ / 5.8	-4.13%	B- / 7.0
2010	C	4,663	23.82	C / 4.4	13.82%	C / 4.7

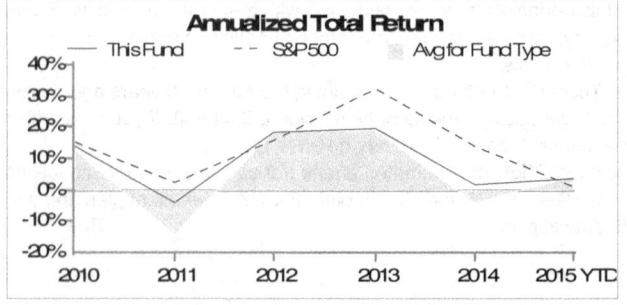

Annualized Total Return

Vanguard 500 Index Inv (VFINX) — A — Excellent

Fund Family: Vanguard Funds   **Phone:** (800) 662-7447
Address: Vanguard Financial Center, Valley Forge, PA 19482
Fund Type: IX - Index
Major Rating Factors: Strong performance is the major factor driving the A (Excellent) TheStreet.com Investment Rating for Vanguard 500 Index Inv. The fund currently has a performance rating of B (Good) based on an average return of 15.93% over the last three years and 0.91% over the last three months. Factored into the performance evaluation is an expense ratio of 0.17% (very low).

The fund's risk rating is currently B- (Good). It carries a beta of 1.00, meaning that its performance tracks fairly well with that of the overall stock market. Volatility, as measured by both the semi-deviation and a drawdown factor, is considered low.

Michael H. Buek has been running the fund for 24 years and currently receives a manager quality ranking of 65 (0=worst, 99=best). If you desire only a moderate level of risk and strong performance, then this fund is an excellent option.

Services Offered: Automated phone transactions, payroll deductions, an IRA investment plan, wire transfers and a systematic withdrawal plan.

Data Date	Investment Rating	Net Assets ($Mil)	NAV	Performance Rating/Pts	Total Return Y-T-D	Risk Rating/Pts
3-15	A	28,828	190.71	B / 8.2	0.91%	B- / 7.3
2014	A+	28,040	189.89	B+ / 8.9	13.51%	B- / 7.3
2013	A	27,758	170.36	B / 8.1	32.18%	C+ / 6.0
2012	B+	24,821	131.37	B- / 7.3	15.82%	C+ / 5.6
2011	B	25,967	115.80	B- / 7.2	1.97%	C / 5.0
2010	C	38,030	115.82	C / 4.4	14.91%	C / 4.9

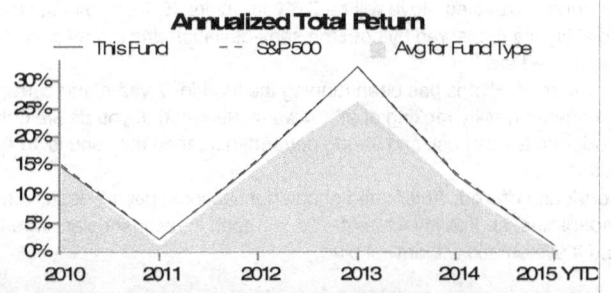

Vanguard Dividend Growth Inv (VDIGX) — A- — Excellent

Fund Family: Vanguard Funds   **Phone:** (800) 662-7447
Address: Vanguard Financial Center, Valley Forge, PA 19482
Fund Type: GI - Growth and Income
Major Rating Factors: Strong performance is the major factor driving the A- (Excellent) TheStreet.com Investment Rating for Vanguard Dividend Growth Inv. The fund currently has a performance rating of B- (Good) based on an average return of 15.01% over the last three years and 0.86% over the last three months. Factored into the performance evaluation is an expense ratio of 0.31% (very low).

The fund's risk rating is currently B- (Good). It carries a beta of 0.90, meaning the fund's expected move will be 9.0% for every 10% move in the market. Volatility, as measured by both the semi-deviation and a drawdown factor, is considered low.

Donald J. Kilbride has been running the fund for 9 years and currently receives a manager quality ranking of 73 (0=worst, 99=best). If you desire only a moderate level of risk and strong performance, then this fund is an excellent option.

Services Offered: Automated phone transactions, payroll deductions, bank draft capabilities, an IRA investment plan, a Keogh investment plan, wire transfers and a systematic withdrawal plan.

Data Date	Investment Rating	Net Assets ($Mil)	NAV	Performance Rating/Pts	Total Return Y-T-D	Risk Rating/Pts
3-15	A-	24,440	22.92	B- / 7.4	0.86%	B- / 7.7
2014	A-	23,436	23.09	B- / 7.3	11.85%	B- / 7.9
2013	A+	19,709	21.36	B / 8.0	31.53%	B- / 7.1
2012	C+	11,753	16.64	C+ / 6.0	10.39%	C+ / 6.8
2011	A+	7,710	15.42	B / 8.0	9.43%	C+ / 6.3
2010	C+	4,675	14.38	C+ / 6.4	11.42%	C+ / 6.6

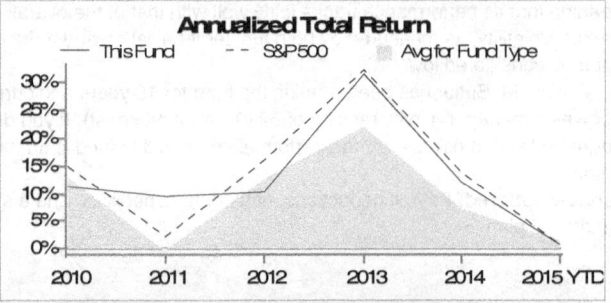

Vanguard Equity Income Inv (VEIPX) — B- — Good

Fund Family: Vanguard Funds   **Phone:** (800) 662-7447
Address: Vanguard Financial Center, Valley Forge, PA 19482
Fund Type: IN - Income
Major Rating Factors: Vanguard Equity Income Inv receives a TheStreet.com Investment Rating of B- (Good). The fund currently has a performance rating of C+ (Fair) based on an average return of 14.85% over the last three years and -0.07% over the last three months. Factored into the performance evaluation is an expense ratio of 0.29% (very low).

The fund's risk rating is currently B- (Good). It carries a beta of 0.94, meaning that its performance tracks fairly well with that of the overall stock market. Volatility, as measured by both the semi-deviation and a drawdown factor, is considered low.

James P. Stetler has been running the fund for 12 years and currently receives a manager quality ranking of 65 (0=worst, 99=best). If you desire an average level of risk, then this fund may be an option.

Services Offered: Automated phone transactions, payroll deductions, an IRA investment plan, a Keogh investment plan, wire transfers and a systematic withdrawal plan.

Data Date	Investment Rating	Net Assets ($Mil)	NAV	Performance Rating/Pts	Total Return Y-T-D	Risk Rating/Pts
3-15	B-	5,742	30.99	C+ / 6.9	-0.07%	B- / 7.6
2014	B+	5,676	31.21	B- / 7.3	11.29%	B- / 7.7
2013	A+	5,126	29.76	B+ / 8.3	30.07%	B- / 7.0
2012	A+	3,966	24.15	B+ / 8.4	13.49%	C+ / 6.7
2011	B+	3,328	21.90	B+ / 8.3	10.60%	C / 4.7
2010	C	2,626	20.38	C / 4.5	14.88%	C / 5.3

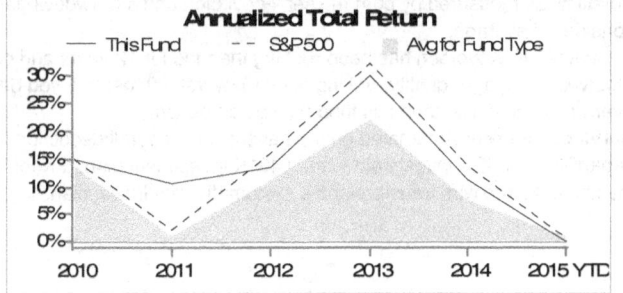

Vanguard Health Care Inv (VGHCX)　　　　A　Excellent

Fund Family: Vanguard Funds　　　　**Phone:** (800) 662-7447
Address: Vanguard Financial Center, Valley Forge, PA 19482
Fund Type: HL - Health
Major Rating Factors: Exceptional performance is the major factor driving the A (Excellent) TheStreet.com Investment Rating for Vanguard Health Care Inv. The fund currently has a performance rating of A+ (Excellent) based on an average return of 29.10% over the last three years and 9.64% over the last three months. Factored into the performance evaluation is an expense ratio of 0.35% (very low).

The fund's risk rating is currently C+ (Fair). It carries a beta of 0.76, meaning the fund's expected move will be 7.6% for every 10% move in the market. Volatility, as measured by both the semi-deviation and a drawdown factor, is considered low.

Jean M. Hynes has been running the fund for 7 years and currently receives a manager quality ranking of 99 (0=worst, 99=best). If you desire only a moderate level of risk and strong performance, then this fund is an excellent option.

Services Offered: Automated phone transactions, payroll deductions, bank draft capabilities, an IRA investment plan, a Keogh investment plan, wire transfers and a systematic withdrawal plan.

Data Date	Investment Rating	Net Assets ($Mil)	NAV	Performance Rating/Pts	Total Return Y-T-D	Risk Rating/Pts
3-15	A	12,287	225.70	A+ / 9.9	9.64%	C+ / 5.6
2014	A	11,252	211.71	A+ / 9.9	28.52%	C+ / 5.6
2013	A+	9,636	187.16	A+ / 9.8	43.19%	C+ / 6.6
2012	A+	8,143	143.27	B- / 7.2	15.11%	B- / 7.1
2011	C+	8,223	128.73	C+ / 6.7	11.45%	C+ / 6.3
2010	C+	8,426	122.40	C+ / 5.6	6.16%	C+ / 6.3

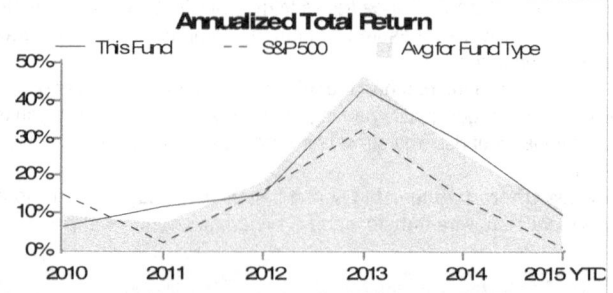

Vanguard Instl Index Inst (VINIX)　　　　A　Excellent

Fund Family: Vanguard Funds　　　　**Phone:** (800) 662-7447
Address: Vanguard Financial Center, Valley Forge, PA 19482
Fund Type: IX - Index
Major Rating Factors: Strong performance is the major factor driving the A (Excellent) TheStreet.com Investment Rating for Vanguard Instl Index Inst. The fund currently has a performance rating of B+ (Good) based on an average return of 16.08% over the last three years and 0.94% over the last three months. Factored into the performance evaluation is an expense ratio of 0.04% (very low).

The fund's risk rating is currently B- (Good). It carries a beta of 1.00, meaning that its performance tracks fairly well with that of the overall stock market. Volatility, as measured by both the semi-deviation and a drawdown factor, is considered low.

Donald M. Butler has been running the fund for 15 years and currently receives a manager quality ranking of 67 (0=worst, 99=best). If you desire only a moderate level of risk and strong performance, then this fund is an excellent option.

Services Offered: Payroll deductions, bank draft capabilities and a systematic withdrawal plan.

Data Date	Investment Rating	Net Assets ($Mil)	NAV	Performance Rating/Pts	Total Return Y-T-D	Risk Rating/Pts
3-15	A	106,126	188.84	B+ / 8.3	0.94%	B- / 7.3
2014	A+	102,114	188.67	A- / 9.0	13.65%	B- / 7.3
2013	A	87,843	169.28	B / 8.2	32.35%	C+ / 6.0
2012	B+	68,055	130.52	B- / 7.5	15.98%	C+ / 5.6
2011	B	58,399	115.04	B- / 7.3	2.09%	C / 5.0
2010	C	54,686	115.01	C / 4.5	15.05%	C / 4.9

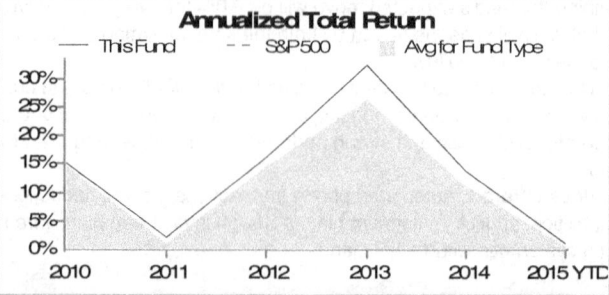

Vanguard International Growth Inv (VWIGX)　　　　D　Weak

Fund Family: Vanguard Funds　　　　**Phone:** (800) 662-7447
Address: Vanguard Financial Center, Valley Forge, PA 19482
Fund Type: FO - Foreign
Major Rating Factors: Vanguard International Growth Inv receives a TheStreet.com Investment Rating of D (Weak). The fund currently has a performance rating of C- (Fair) based on an average return of 8.83% over the last three years and 5.48% over the last three months. Factored into the performance evaluation is an expense ratio of 0.47% (very low).

The fund's risk rating is currently C (Fair). It carries a beta of 0.98, meaning that its performance tracks fairly well with that of the overall stock market. Volatility, as measured by both the semi-deviation and a drawdown factor, is considered average.

James K. Anderson has been running the fund for 12 years and currently receives a manager quality ranking of 60 (0=worst, 99=best). If you desire an average level of risk, then this fund may be an option.

Services Offered: Automated phone transactions, payroll deductions, bank draft capabilities, an IRA investment plan, a 401K investment plan, a Keogh investment plan, wire transfers and a systematic withdrawal plan.

Data Date	Investment Rating	Net Assets ($Mil)	NAV	Performance Rating/Pts	Total Return Y-T-D	Risk Rating/Pts
3-15	D	8,143	22.72	C- / 3.2	5.48%	C / 5.4
2014	D	7,819	21.54	D+ / 2.7	-5.63%	C / 5.5
2013	D	9,716	23.34	C / 4.4	22.95%	C- / 3.5
2012	C	9,411	19.27	B- / 7.0	20.01%	C- / 3.4
2011	D	9,320	16.35	D / 2.0	-13.68%	C- / 4.2
2010	C-	12,326	19.34	C- / 3.6	15.66%	C- / 3.8

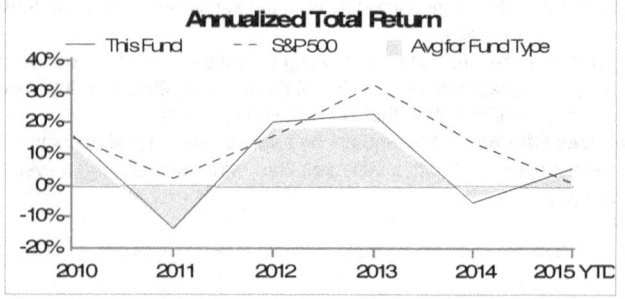

Vanguard International Value Inv (VTRIX)   D   Weak

Fund Family: Vanguard Funds   **Phone:** (800) 662-7447
Address: Vanguard Financial Center, Valley Forge, PA 19482
Fund Type: FO - Foreign
Major Rating Factors: Disappointing performance is the major factor driving the D (Weak) TheStreet.com Investment Rating for Vanguard International Value Inv. The fund currently has a performance rating of D+ (Weak) based on an average return of 8.33% over the last three years and 4.18% over the last three months. Factored into the performance evaluation is an expense ratio of 0.43% (very low).

The fund's risk rating is currently C+ (Fair). It carries a beta of 1.00, meaning that its performance tracks fairly well with that of the overall stock market. Volatility, as measured by both the semi-deviation and a drawdown factor, is considered low.

Alisdair G. M. Nairn has been running the fund for 7 years and currently receives a manager quality ranking of 50 (0=worst, 99=best). This fund offers only a moderate level of risk but investors looking for strong performance are still waiting.

Services Offered: Automated phone transactions, payroll deductions, bank draft capabilities and a systematic withdrawal plan.

Data Date	Investment Rating	Net Assets ($Mil)	NAV	Performance Rating/Pts	Total Return Y-T-D	Risk Rating/Pts
3-15	D	8,319	35.37	D+ / 2.5	4.18%	C+ / 5.6
2014	D-	7,879	33.95	D / 2.2	-6.69%	C+ / 5.7
2013	D	8,263	37.38	C- / 4.0	22.15%	C- / 4.1
2012	D+	6,808	31.18	C / 4.7	20.18%	C- / 3.8
2011	D-	6,081	26.63	E+ / 0.6	-14.58%	C / 4.4
2010	D	7,623	32.16	D- / 1.2	7.31%	C / 4.3

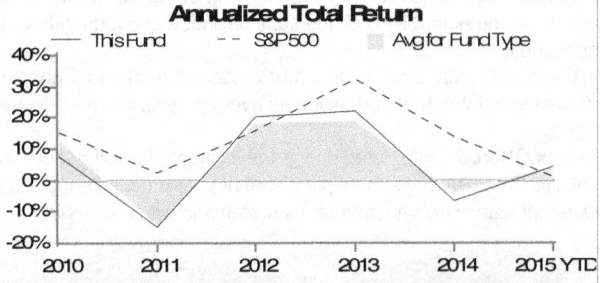

Vanguard LifeStrategy Consv Gr Inv (VSCGX)   C+   Fair

Fund Family: Vanguard Funds   **Phone:** (800) 662-7447
Address: Vanguard Financial Center, Valley Forge, PA 19482
Fund Type: AA - Asset Allocation
Major Rating Factors: Disappointing performance is the major factor driving the C+ (Fair) TheStreet.com Investment Rating for Vanguard LifeStrategy Consv Gr Inv. The fund currently has a performance rating of D+ (Weak) based on an average return of 7.36% over the last three years and 2.07% over the last three months. Factored into the performance evaluation is an expense ratio of 0.15% (very low).

The fund's risk rating is currently B+ (Good). It carries a beta of 0.69, meaning the fund's expected move will be 6.9% for every 10% move in the market. Volatility, as measured by both the semi-deviation and a drawdown factor, is considered very low.

This is team managed and currently receives a manager quality ranking of 67 (0=worst, 99=best). This fund offers only a moderate level of risk but investors looking for strong performance are still waiting.

Services Offered: Automated phone transactions, payroll deductions, bank draft capabilities, an IRA investment plan, a 401K investment plan, a Keogh investment plan, wire transfers and a systematic withdrawal plan.

Data Date	Investment Rating	Net Assets ($Mil)	NAV	Performance Rating/Pts	Total Return Y-T-D	Risk Rating/Pts
3-15	C+	7,693	18.74	D+ / 2.9	2.07%	B+ / 9.3
2014	C+	7,420	18.44	D+ / 2.7	6.93%	B+ / 9.3
2013	C	8,873	18.05	D / 1.9	9.08%	B+ / 9.0
2012	C+	7,504	16.97	D+ / 2.4	9.19%	B+ / 9.1
2011	B-	6,558	16.22	C- / 3.1	1.76%	B / 8.6
2010	A+	6,435	16.36	B- / 7.4	11.14%	B / 8.3

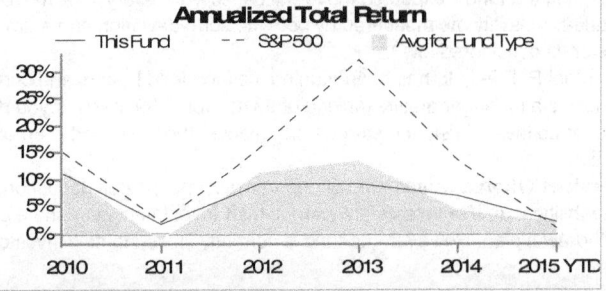

Vanguard LifeStrategy Growth Inv (VASGX)   B-   Good

Fund Family: Vanguard Funds   **Phone:** (800) 662-7447
Address: Vanguard Financial Center, Valley Forge, PA 19482
Fund Type: AA - Asset Allocation
Major Rating Factors: Vanguard LifeStrategy Growth Inv receives a TheStreet.com Investment Rating of B- (Good). The fund currently has a performance rating of C (Fair) based on an average return of 11.35% over the last three years and 2.33% over the last three months. Factored into the performance evaluation is an expense ratio of 0.17% (very low).

The fund's risk rating is currently B (Good). It carries a beta of 1.37, meaning it is expected to move 13.7% for every 10% move in the market. Volatility, as measured by both the semi-deviation and a drawdown factor, is considered low.

This is team managed and currently receives a manager quality ranking of 21 (0=worst, 99=best). If you desire an average level of risk, then this fund may be an option.

Services Offered: Automated phone transactions, payroll deductions, bank draft capabilities, an IRA investment plan, a 401K investment plan, a Keogh investment plan, wire transfers and a systematic withdrawal plan.

Data Date	Investment Rating	Net Assets ($Mil)	NAV	Performance Rating/Pts	Total Return Y-T-D	Risk Rating/Pts
3-15	B-	11,267	29.48	C / 5.1	2.33%	B / 8.0
2014	B-	10,774	28.81	C / 5.0	7.17%	B- / 7.9
2013	C	10,218	27.62	C / 4.4	21.20%	C+ / 6.2
2012	C+	7,960	23.30	C+ / 5.9	14.38%	C+ / 6.0
2011	C	7,187	21.10	C / 4.4	-2.28%	C+ / 5.6
2010	C	7,832	22.06	C / 4.9	15.06%	C / 5.1

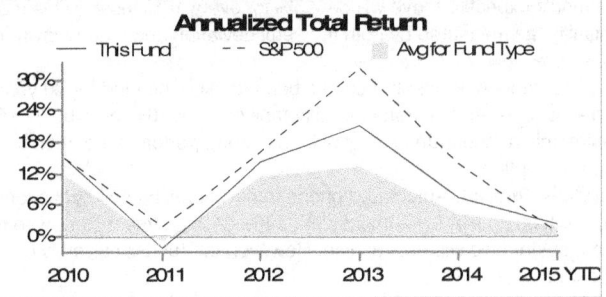

Vanguard LifeStrategy Mod Gro Inv (VSMGX)   C+   Fair

Fund Family: Vanguard Funds   **Phone:** (800) 662-7447
Address: Vanguard Financial Center, Valley Forge, PA 19482
Fund Type: AA - Asset Allocation
Major Rating Factors: Middle of the road best describes Vanguard LifeStrategy Mod Gro Inv whose TheStreet.com Investment Rating is currently a C+ (Fair). The fund currently has a performance rating of C- (Fair) based on an average return of 9.38% over the last three years and 2.20% over the last three months. Factored into the performance evaluation is an expense ratio of 0.16% (very low).

The fund's risk rating is currently B (Good). It carries a beta of 1.03, meaning that its performance tracks fairly well with that of the overall stock market. Volatility, as measured by both the semi-deviation and a drawdown factor, is considered low.

This is team managed and currently receives a manager quality ranking of 42 (0=worst, 99=best). If you desire an average level of risk, then this fund may be an option.

Services Offered: Automated phone transactions, payroll deductions, bank draft capabilities, an IRA investment plan, a 401K investment plan, a Keogh investment plan, wire transfers and a systematic withdrawal plan.

Data Date	Investment Rating	Net Assets ($Mil)	NAV	Perfor-mance Rating/Pts	Total Return Y-T-D	Risk Rating/Pts
3-15	C+	12,479	24.61	C- / 4.0	2.20%	B / 8.9
2014	C+	11,963	24.08	C- / 3.8	7.08%	B / 8.9
2013	C+	11,143	23.11	C- / 3.0	15.04%	B- / 7.9
2012	B-	8,908	20.55	C / 4.3	11.76%	B- / 7.9
2011	C+	7,952	19.16	C- / 3.9	0.26%	B- / 7.3
2010	C+	8,297	19.57	C+ / 5.9	13.31%	C+ / 6.7

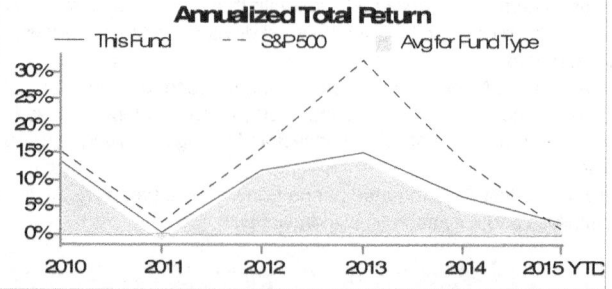

Vanguard PRIMECAP Core Inv (VPCCX)   A+   Excellent

Fund Family: Vanguard Funds   **Phone:** (800) 662-7447
Address: Vanguard Financial Center, Valley Forge, PA 19482
Fund Type: GR - Growth
Major Rating Factors: Exceptional performance is the major factor driving the A+ (Excellent) TheStreet.com Investment Rating for Vanguard PRIMECAP Core Inv. The fund currently has a performance rating of A+ (Excellent) based on an average return of 20.14% over the last three years and 1.85% over the last three months. Factored into the performance evaluation is an expense ratio of 0.50% (very low).

The fund's risk rating is currently B- (Good). It carries a beta of 0.90, meaning the fund's expected move will be 9.0% for every 10% move in the market. Volatility, as measured by both the semi-deviation and a drawdown factor, is considered low.

Joel P. Fried, Jr. has been running the fund for 11 years and currently receives a manager quality ranking of 93 (0=worst, 99=best). If you desire only a moderate level of risk and strong performance, then this fund is an excellent option.

Services Offered: Automated phone transactions, payroll deductions, bank draft capabilities, an IRA investment plan, a 401K investment plan and a systematic withdrawal plan. However, the fund is currently closed to new investors.

Data Date	Investment Rating	Net Assets ($Mil)	NAV	Perfor-mance Rating/Pts	Total Return Y-T-D	Risk Rating/Pts
3-15	A+	7,687	22.04	A+ / 9.7	1.85%	B- / 7.0
2014	A+	7,328	21.64	A+ / 9.8	19.29%	B- / 7.1
2013	A-	6,168	19.44	B / 8.2	36.14%	C+ / 5.8
2012	B	4,652	14.93	B- / 7.1	14.57%	C+ / 5.6
2011	A-	4,628	13.49	B / 7.7	-0.86%	C+ / 5.7
2010	B+	5,035	13.77	B / 8.2	14.88%	C / 5.5

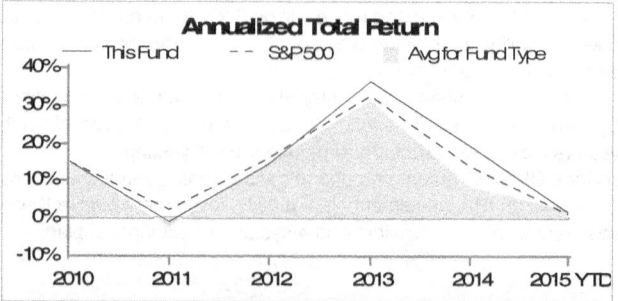

Vanguard PRIMECAP Inv (VPMCX)   A+   Excellent

Fund Family: Vanguard Funds   **Phone:** (800) 662-7447
Address: Vanguard Financial Center, Valley Forge, PA 19482
Fund Type: MC - Mid Cap
Major Rating Factors: Exceptional performance is the major factor driving the A+ (Excellent) TheStreet.com Investment Rating for Vanguard PRIMECAP Inv. The fund currently has a performance rating of A+ (Excellent) based on an average return of 21.00% over the last three years and 2.25% over the last three months. Factored into the performance evaluation is an expense ratio of 0.44% (very low).

The fund's risk rating is currently C+ (Fair). It carries a beta of 0.75, meaning the fund's expected move will be 7.5% for every 10% move in the market. Volatility, as measured by both the semi-deviation and a drawdown factor, is considered low.

Theofanis A. Kolokotrones has been running the fund for 30 years and currently receives a manager quality ranking of 96 (0=worst, 99=best). If you desire only a moderate level of risk and strong performance, then this fund is an excellent option.

Services Offered: Automated phone transactions, payroll deductions, bank draft capabilities, an IRA investment plan, a Keogh investment plan, wire transfers and a systematic withdrawal plan. However, the fund is currently closed to new investors.

Data Date	Investment Rating	Net Assets ($Mil)	NAV	Perfor-mance Rating/Pts	Total Return Y-T-D	Risk Rating/Pts
3-15	A+	9,938	105.16	A+ / 9.8	2.25%	C+ / 7.0
2014	A+	13,680	102.85	A+ / 9.8	18.72%	B- / 7.0
2013	A+	13,537	92.33	A- / 9.1	39.73%	C / 5.5
2012	C+	13,239	69.49	C+ / 6.2	15.27%	C / 5.4
2011	C+	14,935	61.74	C+ / 6.4	-1.84%	C / 5.3
2010	B-	17,883	65.80	B- / 7.4	12.89%	C / 4.8

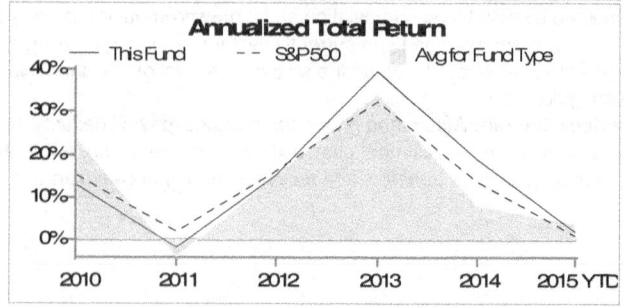

Vanguard Selected Value Inv (VASVX)   A   Excellent

Fund Family: Vanguard Funds   **Phone:** (800) 662-7447
Address: Vanguard Financial Center, Valley Forge, PA 19482
Fund Type: MC - Mid Cap

Major Rating Factors: Strong performance is the major factor driving the A (Excellent) TheStreet.com Investment Rating for Vanguard Selected Value Inv. The fund currently has a performance rating of B (Good) based on an average return of 16.95% over the last three years and 1.30% over the last three months. Factored into the performance evaluation is an expense ratio of 0.44% (very low).

The fund's risk rating is currently B- (Good). It carries a beta of 0.86, meaning the fund's expected move will be 8.6% for every 10% move in the market. Volatility, as measured by both the semi-deviation and a drawdown factor, is considered low.

James P. Barrow has been running the fund for 16 years and currently receives a manager quality ranking of 85 (0=worst, 99=best). If you desire only a moderate level of risk and strong performance, then this fund is an excellent option.

Services Offered: Automated phone transactions, payroll deductions, an IRA investment plan, a 401K investment plan, a Keogh investment plan and a systematic withdrawal plan.

Data Date	Investment Rating	Net Assets ($Mil)	NAV	Perfor-mance Rating/Pts	Total Return Y-T-D	Risk Rating/Pts
3-15	A	10,454	28.75	B / 8.1	1.30%	B- / 7.2
2014	B+	10,192	28.38	B / 7.8	6.36%	B- / 7.2
2013	A+	7,923	28.20	A / 9.5	42.04%	C+ / 5.6
2012	A	4,398	20.98	B+ / 8.5	15.25%	C / 5.3
2011	A	3,887	18.59	B+ / 8.7	0.82%	C / 5.1
2010	B+	3,954	18.76	B / 8.0	19.44%	C / 5.2

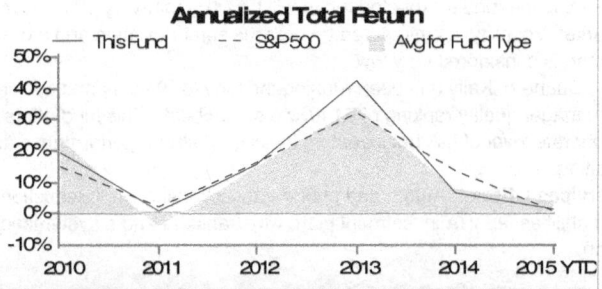

Vanguard STAR Fund (VGSTX)   B-   Good

Fund Family: Vanguard Funds   **Phone:** (800) 662-7447
Address: Vanguard Financial Center, Valley Forge, PA 19482
Fund Type: GI - Growth and Income

Major Rating Factors: Vanguard STAR Fund receives a TheStreet.com Investment Rating of B- (Good). The fund currently has a performance rating of C (Fair) based on an average return of 10.69% over the last three years and 2.60% over the last three months. Factored into the performance evaluation is an expense ratio of 0.34% (very low).

The fund's risk rating is currently B (Good). It carries a beta of 0.64, meaning the fund's expected move will be 6.4% for every 10% move in the market. Volatility, as measured by both the semi-deviation and a drawdown factor, is considered low.

This is team managed and currently receives a manager quality ranking of 73 (0=worst, 99=best). If you desire an average level of risk, then this fund may be an option.

Services Offered: Automated phone transactions, payroll deductions, an IRA investment plan, a 401K investment plan, a Keogh investment plan, wire transfers and a systematic withdrawal plan.

Data Date	Investment Rating	Net Assets ($Mil)	NAV	Perfor-mance Rating/Pts	Total Return Y-T-D	Risk Rating/Pts
3-15	B-	19,282	25.26	C / 4.7	2.60%	B / 8.6
2014	B-	18,749	24.62	C / 4.5	7.34%	B / 8.6
2013	C+	17,625	23.89	C- / 4.0	17.80%	B- / 7.8
2012	B-	15,029	20.80	C+ / 5.7	13.79%	B- / 7.8
2011	B-	13,597	18.73	C / 5.1	0.77%	B- / 7.7
2010	C+	13,927	19.08	C+ / 6.8	11.70%	C+ / 6.7

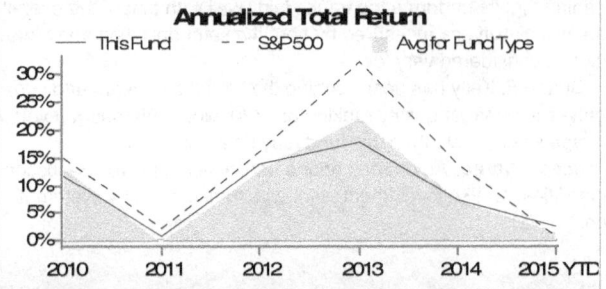

Vanguard Strategic Equity Inv (VSEQX)   A+   Excellent

Fund Family: Vanguard Funds   **Phone:** (800) 662-7447
Address: Vanguard Financial Center, Valley Forge, PA 19482
Fund Type: SC - Small Cap

Major Rating Factors: Exceptional performance is the major factor driving the A+ (Excellent) TheStreet.com Investment Rating for Vanguard Strategic Equity Inv. The fund currently has a performance rating of A+ (Excellent) based on an average return of 20.78% over the last three years and 5.16% over the last three months. Factored into the performance evaluation is an expense ratio of 0.27% (very low).

The fund's risk rating is currently C+ (Fair). It carries a beta of 0.76, meaning the fund's expected move will be 7.6% for every 10% move in the market. Volatility, as measured by both the semi-deviation and a drawdown factor, is considered low.

James D. Troyer has been running the fund for 9 years and currently receives a manager quality ranking of 96 (0=worst, 99=best). If you desire only a moderate level of risk and strong performance, then this fund is an excellent option.

Services Offered: Automated phone transactions, payroll deductions, bank draft capabilities, an IRA investment plan, a Keogh investment plan, wire transfers and a systematic withdrawal plan.

Data Date	Investment Rating	Net Assets ($Mil)	NAV	Perfor-mance Rating/Pts	Total Return Y-T-D	Risk Rating/Pts
3-15	A+	6,151	33.84	A+ / 9.8	5.16%	C+ / 6.7
2014	A+	5,781	32.18	A+ / 9.8	13.68%	C+ / 6.5
2013	A	4,771	30.00	A+ / 9.7	41.54%	C / 4.5
2012	A-	3,288	21.45	A / 9.4	18.90%	C- / 4.1
2011	B	3,053	18.34	B+ / 8.5	1.17%	C- / 3.8
2010	C+	3,315	18.32	C+ / 6.6	21.38%	C- / 4.0

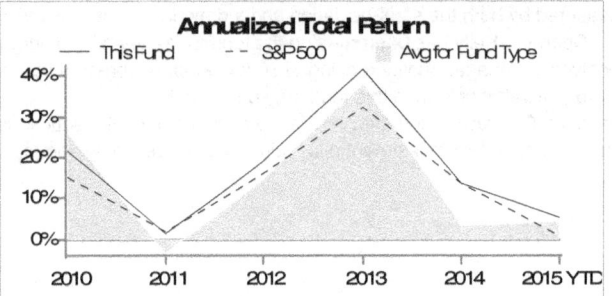

Vanguard Target Retirement 2010 Inv (VTENX)

C+   Fair

Fund Family: Vanguard Funds   **Phone:** (800) 662-7447
Address: Vanguard Financial Center, Valley Forge, PA 19482
Fund Type: AA - Asset Allocation
Major Rating Factors: Disappointing performance is the major factor driving the C+ (Fair) TheStreet.com Investment Rating for Vanguard Target Retirement 2010 Inv. The fund currently has a performance rating of D+ (Weak) based on an average return of 7.02% over the last three years and 1.86% over the last three months. Factored into the performance evaluation is an expense ratio of 0.16% (very low).

The fund's risk rating is currently B+ (Good). It carries a beta of 0.70, meaning the fund's expected move will be 7.0% for every 10% move in the market. Volatility, as measured by both the semi-deviation and a drawdown factor, is considered very low.

Duane F. Kelly has been running the fund for 9 years and currently receives a manager quality ranking of 61 (0=worst, 99=best). This fund offers only a moderate level of risk but investors looking for strong performance are still waiting.

Services Offered: Automated phone transactions, payroll deductions, bank draft capabilities, an IRA investment plan, wire transfers and a systematic withdrawal plan.

Data Date	Investment Rating	Net Assets ($Mil)	NAV	Performance Rating/Pts	Total Return Y-T-D	Risk Rating/Pts
3-15	C+	7,140	26.81	D+ / 2.6	1.86%	B+ / 9.3
2014	C+	7,011	26.32	D+ / 2.6	5.93%	B+ / 9.3
2013	C+	6,851	25.60	D / 2.1	9.10%	B+ / 9.2
2012	B+	6,435	24.13	C- / 3.6	10.12%	B+ / 9.2
2011	B	5,132	22.43	C / 4.8	3.37%	B / 8.3
2010	B-	4,510	22.31	C+ / 6.7	11.43%	B- / 7.9

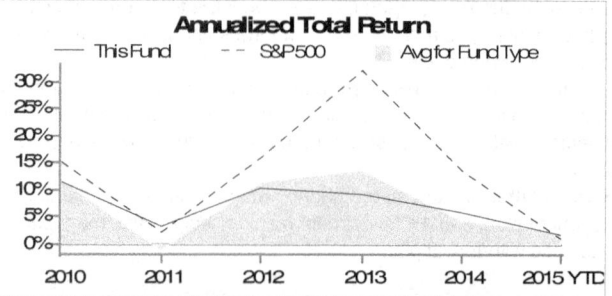

Annualized Total Return

Vanguard Target Retirement 2015 Inv (VTXVX)

C+   Fair

Fund Family: Vanguard Funds   **Phone:** (800) 662-7447
Address: Vanguard Financial Center, Valley Forge, PA 19482
Fund Type: AA - Asset Allocation
Major Rating Factors: Middle of the road best describes Vanguard Target Retirement 2015 Inv whose TheStreet.com Investment Rating is currently a C+ (Fair). The fund currently has a performance rating of C- (Fair) based on an average return of 8.49% over the last three years and 2.03% over the last three months. Factored into the performance evaluation is an expense ratio of 0.16% (very low).

The fund's risk rating is currently B+ (Good). It carries a beta of 0.92, meaning that its performance tracks fairly well with that of the overall stock market. Volatility, as measured by both the semi-deviation and a drawdown factor, is considered very low.

Duane F. Kelly has been running the fund for 12 years and currently receives a manager quality ranking of 47 (0=worst, 99=best). If you desire an average level of risk, then this fund may be an option.

Services Offered: Automated phone transactions, payroll deductions, bank draft capabilities, an IRA investment plan, wire transfers and a systematic withdrawal plan.

Data Date	Investment Rating	Net Assets ($Mil)	NAV	Performance Rating/Pts	Total Return Y-T-D	Risk Rating/Pts
3-15	C+	22,508	15.60	C- / 3.4	2.03%	B+ / 9.1
2014	C+	21,957	15.29	C- / 3.4	6.55%	B+ / 9.1
2013	C+	20,300	14.77	D+ / 2.7	13.00%	B / 8.5
2012	B	17,623	13.38	C- / 4.2	11.37%	B / 8.4
2011	B-	14,394	12.30	C / 4.8	1.71%	B- / 7.7
2010	B-	13,354	12.42	C+ / 6.6	12.47%	B- / 7.2

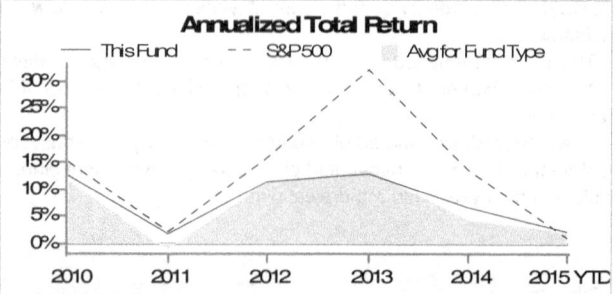

Annualized Total Return

Vanguard Target Retirement 2025 Inv (VTTVX)

B-   Good

Fund Family: Vanguard Funds   **Phone:** (800) 662-7447
Address: Vanguard Financial Center, Valley Forge, PA 19482
Fund Type: AA - Asset Allocation
Major Rating Factors: Vanguard Target Retirement 2025 Inv receives a TheStreet.com Investment Rating of B- (Good). The fund currently has a performance rating of C (Fair) based on an average return of 10.35% over the last three years and 2.24% over the last three months. Factored into the performance evaluation is an expense ratio of 0.17% (very low).

The fund's risk rating is currently B (Good). It carries a beta of 1.21, meaning it is expected to move 12.1% for every 10% move in the market. Volatility, as measured by both the semi-deviation and a drawdown factor, is considered low.

Duane F. Kelly has been running the fund for 12 years and currently receives a manager quality ranking of 30 (0=worst, 99=best). If you desire an average level of risk, then this fund may be an option.

Services Offered: Automated phone transactions, payroll deductions, bank draft capabilities, an IRA investment plan, wire transfers and a systematic withdrawal plan.

Data Date	Investment Rating	Net Assets ($Mil)	NAV	Performance Rating/Pts	Total Return Y-T-D	Risk Rating/Pts
3-15	B-	34,238	16.90	C / 4.5	2.24%	B / 8.5
2014	C+	32,318	16.53	C / 4.4	7.16%	B / 8.4
2013	C+	28,021	15.75	C- / 3.8	18.14%	B- / 7.4
2012	B-	21,269	13.59	C / 5.4	13.29%	B- / 7.2
2011	C+	16,357	12.27	C / 5.1	-0.37%	C+ / 6.7
2010	C+	14,987	12.62	C+ / 6.1	13.84%	C+ / 5.9

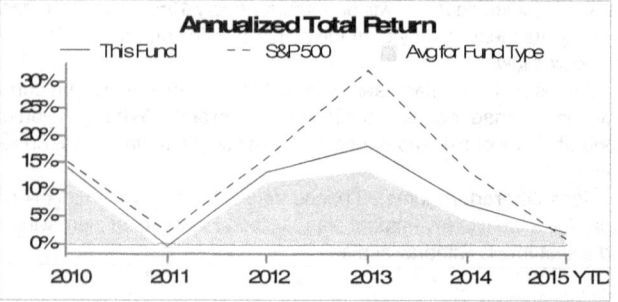

Annualized Total Return

Vanguard Target Retirement 2030 (VTHRX)   B-   Good

Fund Family: Vanguard Funds   **Phone:** (800) 662-7447
Address: Vanguard Financial Center, Valley Forge, PA 19482
Fund Type: AA - Asset Allocation
Major Rating Factors: Vanguard Target Retirement 2030 receives a
TheStreet.com Investment Rating of B- (Good). The fund currently has a
performance rating of C (Fair) based on an average return of 11.10% over the
last three years and 2.31% over the last three months. Factored into the
performance evaluation is an expense ratio of 0.17% (very low).

   The fund's risk rating is currently B (Good). It carries a beta of 1.33, meaning
it is expected to move 13.3% for every 10% move in the market. Volatility, as
measured by both the semi-deviation and a drawdown factor, is considered low.

   Duane F. Kelly has been running the fund for 9 years and currently receives
a manager quality ranking of 23 (0=worst, 99=best). If you desire an average
level of risk, then this fund may be an option.
Services Offered: Automated phone transactions, payroll deductions, bank draft
capabilities, an IRA investment plan, wire transfers and a systematic withdrawal
plan.

Data Date	Investment Rating	Net Assets ($Mil)	NAV	Perfor-mance Rating/Pts	Total Return Y-T-D	Risk Rating/Pts
3-15	B-	25,532	29.71	C / 4.9	2.31%	B / 8.1
2014	B-	23,824	29.04	C / 4.9	7.19%	B / 8.1
2013	C+	19,778	27.64	C / 4.4	20.49%	C+ / 6.9
2012	C+	13,816	23.38	C+ / 5.9	14.24%	C+ / 6.6
2011	C+	9,392	20.92	C / 5.4	-1.27%	C+ / 6.1
2010	C+	7,505	21.68	C+ / 5.8	14.43%	C / 5.4

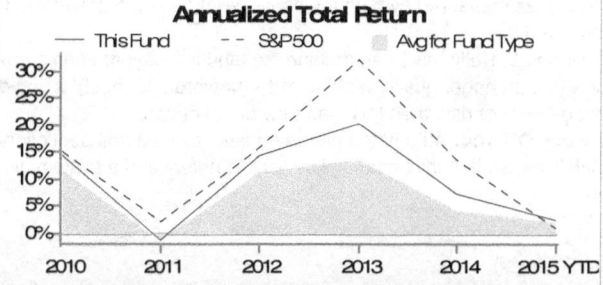

Vanguard Target Retirement 2035 Inv (VTTHX)   B-   Good

Fund Family: Vanguard Funds   **Phone:** (800) 662-7447
Address: Vanguard Financial Center, Valley Forge, PA 19482
Fund Type: AA - Asset Allocation
Major Rating Factors: Vanguard Target Retirement 2035 Inv receives a
TheStreet.com Investment Rating of B- (Good). The fund currently has a
performance rating of C (Fair) based on an average return of 11.85% over the
last three years and 2.35% over the last three months. Factored into the
performance evaluation is an expense ratio of 0.18% (very low).

   The fund's risk rating is currently B- (Good). It carries a beta of 1.46,
meaning it is expected to move 14.6% for every 10% move in the market.
Volatility, as measured by both the semi-deviation and a drawdown factor, is
considered low.

   Duane F. Kelly has been running the fund for 12 years and currently
receives a manager quality ranking of 17 (0=worst, 99=best). If you desire an
average level of risk, then this fund may be an option.
Services Offered: Automated phone transactions, payroll deductions, bank draft
capabilities, an IRA investment plan, wire transfers and a systematic withdrawal
plan.

Data Date	Investment Rating	Net Assets ($Mil)	NAV	Perfor-mance Rating/Pts	Total Return Y-T-D	Risk Rating/Pts
3-15	B-	26,044	18.26	C / 5.4	2.35%	B- / 7.7
2014	B-	24,514	17.84	C / 5.4	7.28%	B- / 7.7
2013	C+	21,131	16.98	C / 4.9	22.82%	C+ / 6.3
2012	C+	15,218	14.09	C+ / 6.4	15.16%	C+ / 6.0
2011	C+	11,361	12.51	C / 5.5	-2.24%	C+ / 5.6
2010	C+	10,353	13.09	C+ / 5.9	15.14%	C / 4.9

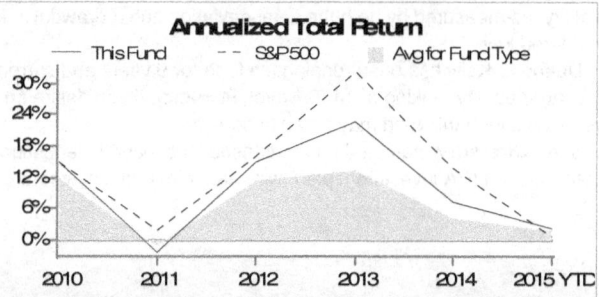

Vanguard Target Retirement 2040 Inv (VFORX)   B-   Good

Fund Family: Vanguard Funds   **Phone:** (800) 662-7447
Address: Vanguard Financial Center, Valley Forge, PA 19482
Fund Type: AA - Asset Allocation
Major Rating Factors: Vanguard Target Retirement 2040 Inv receives a
TheStreet.com Investment Rating of B- (Good). The fund currently has a
performance rating of C+ (Fair) based on an average return of 12.30% over the
last three years and 2.39% over the last three months. Factored into the
performance evaluation is an expense ratio of 0.18% (very low).

   The fund's risk rating is currently B- (Good). It carries a beta of 1.55,
meaning it is expected to move 15.5% for every 10% move in the market.
Volatility, as measured by both the semi-deviation and a drawdown factor, is
considered low.

   Duane F. Kelly has been running the fund for 9 years and currently receives
a manager quality ranking of 14 (0=worst, 99=best). If you desire an average
level of risk, then this fund may be an option.
Services Offered: Automated phone transactions, payroll deductions, bank draft
capabilities, an IRA investment plan, wire transfers and a systematic withdrawal
plan.

Data Date	Investment Rating	Net Assets ($Mil)	NAV	Perfor-mance Rating/Pts	Total Return Y-T-D	Risk Rating/Pts
3-15	B-	17,706	30.47	C+ / 5.6	2.39%	B- / 7.5
2014	B-	16,482	29.76	C+ / 5.6	7.15%	B- / 7.4
2013	C+	13,470	28.32	C / 5.3	24.37%	C+ / 6.1
2012	C+	8,797	23.18	C+ / 6.6	15.56%	C+ / 5.8
2011	C+	5,758	20.50	C / 5.3	-2.55%	C+ / 5.6
2010	C+	4,500	21.50	C+ / 6.0	15.17%	C / 5.0

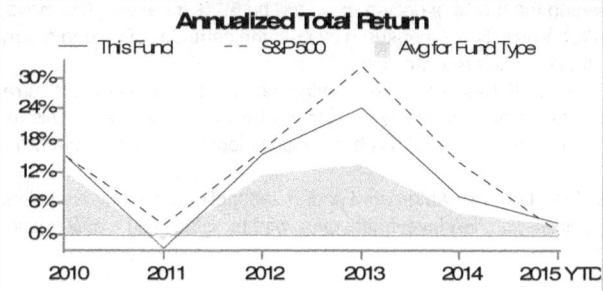

Vanguard Target Retirement 2045 Inv (VTIVX)   B-   Good

Fund Family: Vanguard Funds   **Phone:** (800) 662-7447
Address: Vanguard Financial Center, Valley Forge, PA 19482
Fund Type: AA - Asset Allocation

Major Rating Factors: Vanguard Target Retirement 2045 Inv receives a TheStreet.com Investment Rating of B- (Good). The fund currently has a performance rating of C+ (Fair) based on an average return of 12.31% over the last three years and 2.41% over the last three months. Factored into the performance evaluation is an expense ratio of 0.18% (very low).

The fund's risk rating is currently B- (Good). It carries a beta of 1.55, meaning it is expected to move 15.5% for every 10% move in the market. Volatility, as measured by both the semi-deviation and a drawdown factor, is considered low.

Duane F. Kelly has been running the fund for 12 years and currently receives a manager quality ranking of 14 (0=worst, 99=best). If you desire an average level of risk, then this fund may be an option.

Services Offered: Automated phone transactions, payroll deductions, bank draft capabilities, an IRA investment plan, wire transfers and a systematic withdrawal plan.

Data Date	Investment Rating	Net Assets ($Mil)	NAV	Perfor-mance Rating/Pts	Total Return Y-T-D	Risk Rating/Pts
3-15	B-	16,047	19.10	C+ / 5.6	2.41%	B- / 7.5
2014	B-	15,036	18.65	C+ / 5.6	7.14%	B- / 7.4
2013	C+	12,766	17.76	C / 5.3	24.37%	C+ / 6.1
2012	C+	8,758	14.55	C+ / 6.6	15.58%	C+ / 5.8
2011	C+	6,372	12.87	C / 5.3	-2.51%	C+ / 5.6
2010	C+	5,610	13.50	C+ / 6.0	15.19%	C / 4.9

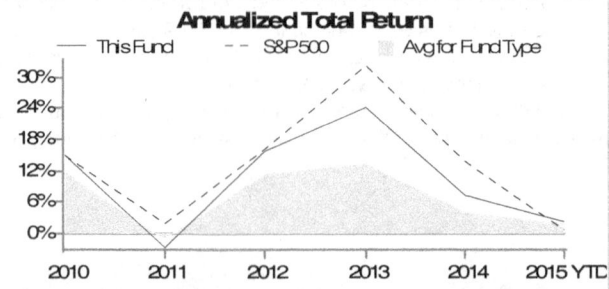

Vanguard Target Retirement 2050 Inv (VFIFX)   B-   Good

Fund Family: Vanguard Funds   **Phone:** (800) 662-7447
Address: Vanguard Financial Center, Valley Forge, PA 19482
Fund Type: AA - Asset Allocation

Major Rating Factors: Vanguard Target Retirement 2050 Inv receives a TheStreet.com Investment Rating of B- (Good). The fund currently has a performance rating of C+ (Fair) based on an average return of 12.30% over the last three years and 2.36% over the last three months. Factored into the performance evaluation is an expense ratio of 0.18% (very low).

The fund's risk rating is currently B- (Good). It carries a beta of 1.55, meaning it is expected to move 15.5% for every 10% move in the market. Volatility, as measured by both the semi-deviation and a drawdown factor, is considered low.

Duane F. Kelly has been running the fund for 9 years and currently receives a manager quality ranking of 14 (0=worst, 99=best). If you desire an average level of risk, then this fund may be an option.

Services Offered: Automated phone transactions, payroll deductions, bank draft capabilities, an IRA investment plan, wire transfers and a systematic withdrawal plan.

Data Date	Investment Rating	Net Assets ($Mil)	NAV	Perfor-mance Rating/Pts	Total Return Y-T-D	Risk Rating/Pts
3-15	B-	8,341	30.32	C+ / 5.6	2.36%	B- / 7.4
2014	B-	7,683	29.62	C+ / 5.6	7.19%	B- / 7.4
2013	C+	6,052	28.19	C / 5.2	24.34%	C+ / 6.1
2012	C+	3,820	23.09	C+ / 6.6	15.58%	C+ / 5.8
2011	C+	2,415	20.41	C / 5.3	-2.54%	C+ / 5.6
2010	C+	1,810	21.40	C+ / 6.0	15.20%	C / 5.0

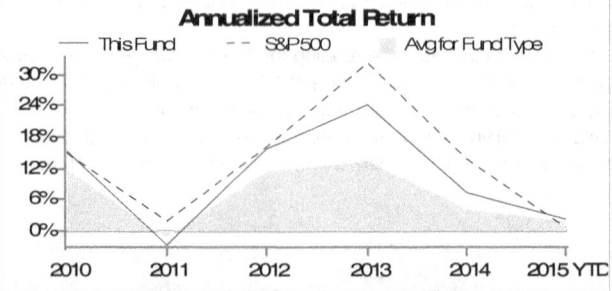

Vanguard Target Retirement Income (VTINX)   C   Fair

Fund Family: Vanguard Funds   **Phone:** (800) 662-7447
Address: Vanguard Financial Center, Valley Forge, PA 19482
Fund Type: AA - Asset Allocation

Major Rating Factors: Disappointing performance is the major factor driving the C (Fair) TheStreet.com Investment Rating for Vanguard Target Retirement Income. The fund currently has a performance rating of D (Weak) based on an average return of 5.79% over the last three years and 1.75% over the last three months. Factored into the performance evaluation is an expense ratio of 0.16% (very low).

The fund's risk rating is currently B+ (Good). It carries a beta of 0.51, meaning the fund's expected move will be 5.1% for every 10% move in the market. Volatility, as measured by both the semi-deviation and a drawdown factor, is considered very low.

Duane F. Kelly has been running the fund for 12 years and currently receives a manager quality ranking of 71 (0=worst, 99=best). This fund offers only a moderate level of risk but investors looking for strong performance are still waiting.

Services Offered: Automated phone transactions, payroll deductions, bank draft capabilities, an IRA investment plan, wire transfers and a systematic withdrawal plan.

Data Date	Investment Rating	Net Assets ($Mil)	NAV	Perfor-mance Rating/Pts	Total Return Y-T-D	Risk Rating/Pts
3-15	C	11,678	13.09	D / 2.0	1.75%	B+ / 9.6
2014	C	11,379	12.91	D / 1.9	5.58%	B+ / 9.6
2013	C+	10,338	12.50	D- / 1.5	5.87%	B+ / 9.6
2012	B-	9,711	12.19	D+ / 2.4	8.23%	B+ / 9.7
2011	B+	5,402	11.53	C- / 3.5	5.25%	B+ / 9.6
2010	A+	3,960	11.28	B / 7.8	9.39%	B+ / 9.7

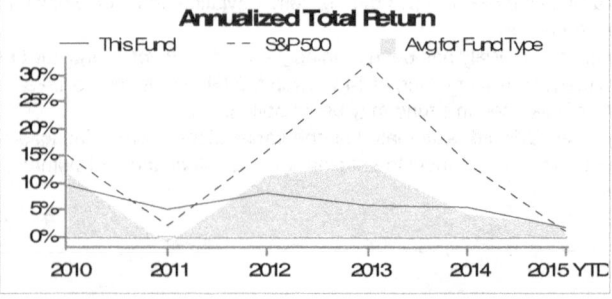

Vanguard Tax-Managed Cap Appr Adm (VTCLX)   A+   Excellent

Fund Family: Vanguard Funds   **Phone:** (800) 662-7447
Address: Vanguard Financial Center, Valley Forge, PA 19482
Fund Type: GR - Growth
Major Rating Factors: Strong performance is the major factor driving the A+ (Excellent) TheStreet.com Investment Rating for Vanguard Tax-Managed Cap Appr Adm. The fund currently has a performance rating of B+ (Good) based on an average return of 16.45% over the last three years and 1.92% over the last three months. Factored into the performance evaluation is an expense ratio of 0.12% (very low).

The fund's risk rating is currently B- (Good). It carries a beta of 1.02, meaning that its performance tracks fairly well with that of the overall stock market. Volatility, as measured by both the semi-deviation and a drawdown factor, is considered low.

Michael H. Buek has been running the fund for 21 years and currently receives a manager quality ranking of 68 (0=worst, 99=best). If you desire only a moderate level of risk and strong performance, then this fund is an excellent option.

Services Offered: Automated phone transactions, payroll deductions, bank draft capabilities, wire transfers and a systematic withdrawal plan.

Data Date	Investment Rating	Net Assets ($Mil)	NAV	Performance Rating/Pts	Total Return Y-T-D	Risk Rating/Pts
3-15	A+	5,972	105.80	B+ / 8.5	1.92%	B- / 7.2
2014	A+	5,760	103.82	B+ / 8.9	12.52%	B- / 7.2
2013	A+	5,040	93.70	B+ / 8.5	33.67%	B- / 7.6
2012	A	3,702	71.17	B / 7.8	16.35%	C+ / 6.2
2011	B	3,305	62.36	B- / 7.4	1.34%	C / 5.2
2010	C	589	31.09	C / 5.0	15.94%	C / 4.9

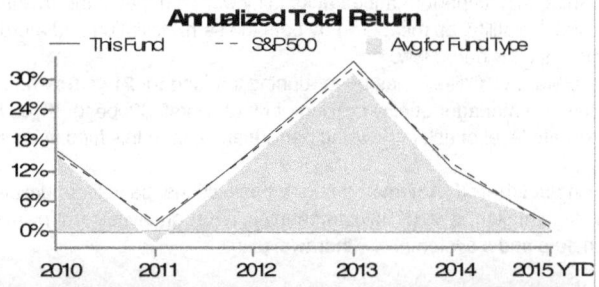

Vanguard Tgt Retirement 2020 Inv (VTWNX)   B-   Good

Fund Family: Vanguard Funds   **Phone:** (800) 662-7447
Address: Vanguard Financial Center, Valley Forge, PA 19482
Fund Type: AA - Asset Allocation
Major Rating Factors: Vanguard Tgt Retirement 2020 Inv receives a TheStreet.com Investment Rating of B- (Good). The fund currently has a performance rating of C- (Fair) based on an average return of 9.62% over the last three years and 2.18% over the last three months. Factored into the performance evaluation is an expense ratio of 0.16% (very low).

The fund's risk rating is currently B (Good). It carries a beta of 1.07, meaning that its performance tracks fairly well with that of the overall stock market. Volatility, as measured by both the semi-deviation and a drawdown factor, is considered low.

Duane F. Kelly has been running the fund for 9 years and currently receives a manager quality ranking of 38 (0=worst, 99=best). If you desire an average level of risk, then this fund may be an option.

Services Offered: Automated phone transactions, payroll deductions, bank draft capabilities, an IRA investment plan, wire transfers and a systematic withdrawal plan.

Data Date	Investment Rating	Net Assets ($Mil)	NAV	Performance Rating/Pts	Total Return Y-T-D	Risk Rating/Pts
3-15	B-	30,226	29.08	C- / 4.1	2.18%	B / 8.8
2014	C+	28,525	28.46	C- / 4.0	7.12%	B / 8.8
2013	C+	23,878	27.11	C- / 3.3	15.85%	B- / 7.9
2012	B-	17,324	23.83	C / 4.8	12.35%	B- / 7.8
2011	B-	12,288	21.69	C / 4.9	0.60%	B- / 7.2
2010	C+	10,071	22.10	C+ / 6.4	13.12%	C+ / 6.6

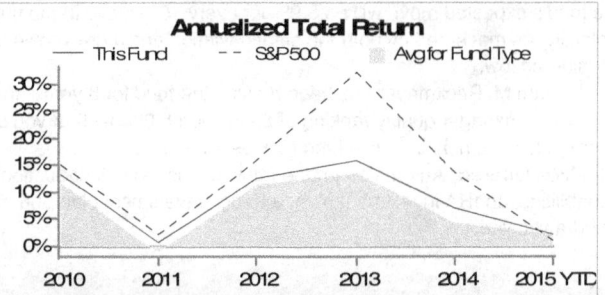

Vanguard Total Intl Stock Index Inv (VGTSX)   D-   Weak

Fund Family: Vanguard Funds   **Phone:** (800) 662-7447
Address: Vanguard Financial Center, Valley Forge, PA 19482
Fund Type: FO - Foreign
Major Rating Factors: Disappointing performance is the major factor driving the D- (Weak) TheStreet.com Investment Rating for Vanguard Total Intl Stock Index Inv. The fund currently has a performance rating of D (Weak) based on an average return of 6.55% over the last three years and 4.03% over the last three months. Factored into the performance evaluation is an expense ratio of 0.22% (very low).

The fund's risk rating is currently C+ (Fair). It carries a beta of 0.96, meaning that its performance tracks fairly well with that of the overall stock market. Volatility, as measured by both the semi-deviation and a drawdown factor, is considered low.

Michael Perre has been running the fund for 7 years and currently receives a manager quality ranking of 32 (0=worst, 99=best). This fund offers only a moderate level of risk but investors looking for strong performance are still waiting.

Services Offered: Automated phone transactions, payroll deductions, bank draft capabilities, an IRA investment plan, a Keogh investment plan and a systematic withdrawal plan.

Data Date	Investment Rating	Net Assets ($Mil)	NAV	Performance Rating/Pts	Total Return Y-T-D	Risk Rating/Pts
3-15	D-	54,433	16.13	D / 1.8	4.03%	C+ / 5.9
2014	D-	50,966	15.55	D / 1.8	-4.24%	C+ / 5.8
2013	D-	46,892	16.75	D / 1.8	15.04%	C- / 3.9
2012	D	37,659	14.98	C- / 4.0	18.14%	C- / 3.7
2011	D-	29,949	13.06	E+ / 0.9	-14.56%	C / 4.3
2010	D-	45,191	15.76	D / 1.6	11.12%	D+ / 2.9

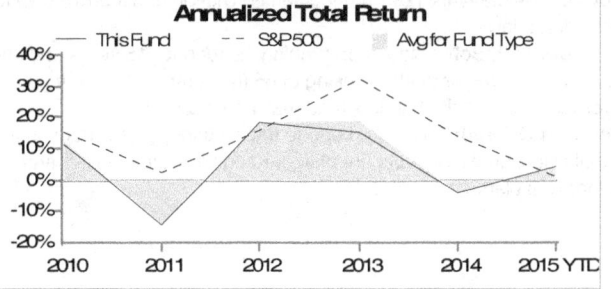

Vanguard Total Stock Mkt Index Inv (VTSMX)   A   Excellent

Fund Family: Vanguard Funds   **Phone:** (800) 662-7447
Address: Vanguard Financial Center, Valley Forge, PA 19482
Fund Type: GR - Growth
Major Rating Factors: Strong performance is the major factor driving the A (Excellent) TheStreet.com Investment Rating for Vanguard Total Stock Mkt Index Inv. The fund currently has a performance rating of B+ (Good) based on an average return of 16.24% over the last three years and 1.76% over the last three months. Factored into the performance evaluation is an expense ratio of 0.17% (very low).

The fund's risk rating is currently B- (Good). It carries a beta of 1.01, meaning that its performance tracks fairly well with that of the overall stock market. Volatility, as measured by both the semi-deviation and a drawdown factor, is considered low.

Gerard C. O'Reilly has been running the fund for 21 years and currently receives a manager quality ranking of 66 (0=worst, 99=best). If you desire only a moderate level of risk and strong performance, then this fund is an excellent option.

Services Offered: Automated phone transactions, payroll deductions, an IRA investment plan, a 401K investment plan, a Keogh investment plan, wire transfers and a systematic withdrawal plan.

Data Date	Investment Rating	Net Assets ($Mil)	NAV	Perfor-mance Rating/Pts	Total Return Y-T-D	Risk Rating/Pts
3-15	A	124,041	52.26	B+ / 8.4	1.76%	B- / 7.1
2014	A+	117,966	51.58	B+ / 8.8	12.43%	B / 8.0
2013	A-	105,008	46.67	B+ / 8.3	33.35%	C+ / 5.7
2012	B+	78,936	35.64	B / 7.9	16.25%	C / 5.3
2011	B	62,668	31.29	B / 7.6	0.96%	C / 4.9
2010	C+	61,363	31.56	C+ / 6.1	17.09%	C / 4.8

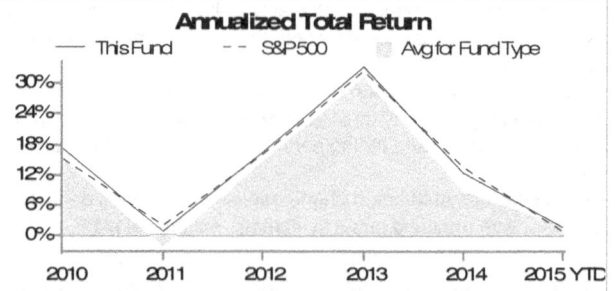

Vanguard Wellesley Income Inv (VWINX)   C+   Fair

Fund Family: Vanguard Funds   **Phone:** (800) 662-7447
Address: Vanguard Financial Center, Valley Forge, PA 19482
Fund Type: AA - Asset Allocation
Major Rating Factors: Middle of the road best describes Vanguard Wellesley Income Inv whose TheStreet.com Investment Rating is currently a C+ (Fair). The fund currently has a performance rating of C- (Fair) based on an average return of 8.25% over the last three years and 1.27% over the last three months. Factored into the performance evaluation is an expense ratio of 0.25% (very low).

The fund's risk rating is currently B (Good). It carries a beta of 0.59, meaning the fund's expected move will be 5.9% for every 10% move in the market. Volatility, as measured by both the semi-deviation and a drawdown factor, is considered low.

William M. Reckmeyer has been running the fund for 8 years and currently receives a manager quality ranking of 83 (0=worst, 99=best). If you desire an average level of risk, then this fund may be an option.

Services Offered: Automated phone transactions, payroll deductions, bank draft capabilities, an IRA investment plan, a Keogh investment plan and a systematic withdrawal plan.

Data Date	Investment Rating	Net Assets ($Mil)	NAV	Perfor-mance Rating/Pts	Total Return Y-T-D	Risk Rating/Pts
3-15	C+	12,774	25.72	C- / 3.2	1.27%	B / 9.0
2014	C+	12,324	25.57	C- / 3.1	8.07%	B+ / 9.0
2013	C+	11,363	24.85	D+ / 2.5	9.19%	B+ / 9.0
2012	B+	11,648	24.11	C+ / 5.8	10.06%	B+ / 9.3
2011	B	10,280	22.93	C+ / 6.8	9.63%	B / 8.7
2010	A+	8,323	21.70	B+ / 8.4	10.65%	B+ / 9.3

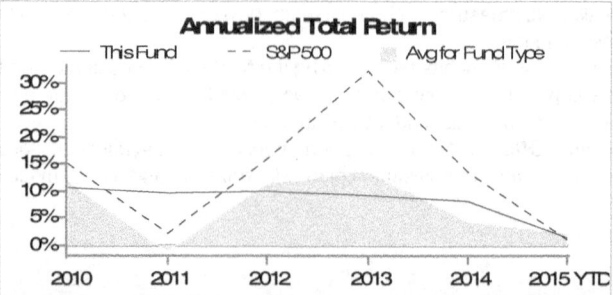

Vanguard Wellington Inv (VWELX)   B   Good

Fund Family: Vanguard Funds   **Phone:** (800) 662-7447
Address: Vanguard Financial Center, Valley Forge, PA 19482
Fund Type: BA - Balanced
Major Rating Factors: Vanguard Wellington Inv receives a TheStreet.com Investment Rating of B (Good). The fund currently has a performance rating of C (Fair) based on an average return of 11.53% over the last three years and 0.85% over the last three months. Factored into the performance evaluation is an expense ratio of 0.26% (very low).

The fund's risk rating is currently B (Good). It carries a beta of 1.07, meaning that its performance tracks fairly well with that of the overall stock market. Volatility, as measured by both the semi-deviation and a drawdown factor, is considered low.

Edward P. Bousa has been running the fund for 15 years and currently receives a manager quality ranking of 65 (0=worst, 99=best). If you desire an average level of risk, then this fund may be an option.

Services Offered: Automated phone transactions, payroll deductions, bank draft capabilities, an IRA investment plan, a Keogh investment plan and a systematic withdrawal plan.

Data Date	Investment Rating	Net Assets ($Mil)	NAV	Perfor-mance Rating/Pts	Total Return Y-T-D	Risk Rating/Pts
3-15	B	23,519	39.25	C / 5.1	0.85%	B / 8.3
2014	B	23,377	39.15	C / 5.2	9.82%	B / 8.3
2013	B-	26,920	37.94	C / 4.5	19.66%	B- / 7.6
2012	B-	26,746	33.84	C / 5.2	12.57%	B- / 7.7
2011	B-	25,506	31.34	C+ / 5.9	3.85%	B- / 7.6
2010	B-	26,692	31.10	C+ / 6.9	10.94%	B- / 7.3

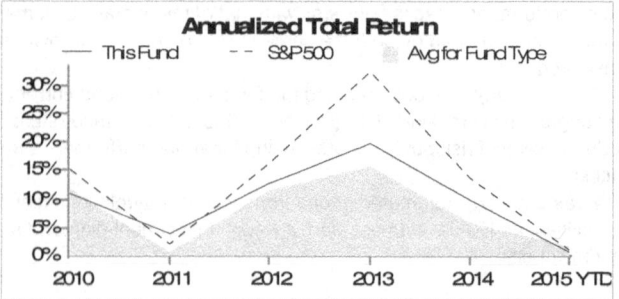

Vanguard Windsor-I Inv (VWNDX)   A+   Excellent

Fund Family: Vanguard Funds   **Phone:** (800) 662-7447
Address: Vanguard Financial Center, Valley Forge, PA 19482
Fund Type: MC - Mid Cap

Major Rating Factors: Strong performance is the major factor driving the A+ (Excellent) TheStreet.com Investment Rating for Vanguard Windsor-I Inv. The fund currently has a performance rating of B+ (Good) based on an average return of 17.69% over the last three years and 1.54% over the last three months. Factored into the performance evaluation is an expense ratio of 0.37% (very low).

The fund's risk rating is currently C+ (Fair). It carries a beta of 0.90, meaning the fund's expected move will be 9.0% for every 10% move in the market. Volatility, as measured by both the semi-deviation and a drawdown factor, is considered low.

James N. Mordy has been running the fund for 7 years and currently receives a manager quality ranking of 85 (0=worst, 99=best). If you desire only a moderate level of risk and strong performance, then this fund is an excellent option.

Services Offered: Automated phone transactions, payroll deductions, an IRA investment plan, a Keogh investment plan and a systematic withdrawal plan.

Data Date	Investment Rating	Net Assets ($Mil)	NAV	Perfor-mance Rating/Pts	Total Return Y-T-D	Risk Rating/Pts
3-15	A+	5,917	21.79	B+ / 8.9	1.54%	C+ / 6.8
2014	A+	5,956	21.46	A / 9.5	11.82%	C+ / 6.9
2013	B+	7,226	20.34	B+ / 8.6	36.08%	C / 5.1
2012	A-	6,638	15.10	B+ / 8.6	20.78%	C / 4.8
2011	C+	6,522	12.77	C+ / 6.4	-4.00%	C / 4.7
2010	C	7,771	13.51	C / 4.6	14.82%	C / 4.4

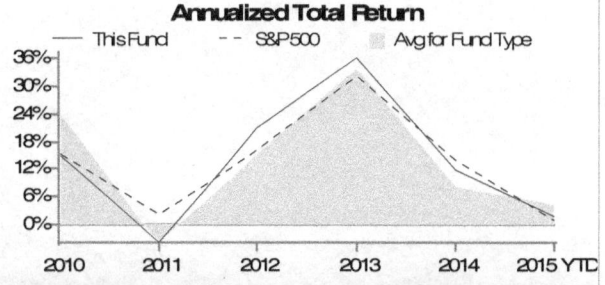

Annualized Total Return

Vanguard Windsor-II Inv (VWNFX)   C+   Fair

Fund Family: Vanguard Funds   **Phone:** (800) 662-7447
Address: Vanguard Financial Center, Valley Forge, PA 19482
Fund Type: GR - Growth

Major Rating Factors: Middle of the road best describes Vanguard Windsor-II Inv whose TheStreet.com Investment Rating is currently a C+ (Fair). The fund currently has a performance rating of C+ (Fair) based on an average return of 14.67% over the last three years and -0.08% over the last three months. Factored into the performance evaluation is an expense ratio of 0.36% (very low).

The fund's risk rating is currently C+ (Fair). It carries a beta of 1.00, meaning that its performance tracks fairly well with that of the overall stock market. Volatility, as measured by both the semi-deviation and a drawdown factor, is considered low.

James P. Barrow has been running the fund for 30 years and currently receives a manager quality ranking of 49 (0=worst, 99=best). If you desire an average level of risk, then this fund may be an option.

Services Offered: Automated phone transactions, payroll deductions, bank draft capabilities, an IRA investment plan, a 401K investment plan, a Keogh investment plan and a systematic withdrawal plan.

Data Date	Investment Rating	Net Assets ($Mil)	NAV	Perfor-mance Rating/Pts	Total Return Y-T-D	Risk Rating/Pts
3-15	C+	17,346	37.28	C+ / 6.7	-0.08%	C+ / 6.8
2014	A-	17,277	37.31	B / 7.9	11.16%	B- / 7.2
2013	A-	18,061	36.77	B / 7.7	30.69%	C+ / 6.1
2012	B+	17,893	29.38	B- / 7.2	16.72%	C+ / 5.6
2011	C+	18,387	25.78	C+ / 6.6	2.70%	C / 4.8
2010	C-	20,504	25.67	D+ / 2.7	10.62%	C / 4.8

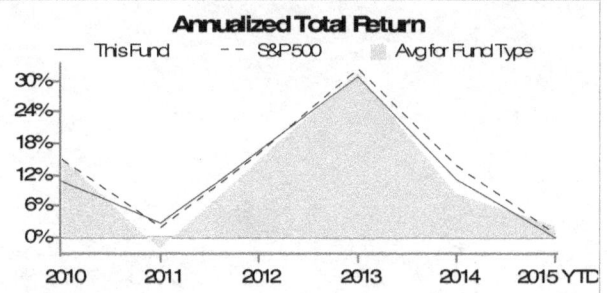

Annualized Total Return

Section III

Top 200
Stock Mutual Funds

A compilation of those

Equity Mutual Funds

receiving the highest TheStreet Investment Ratings.

Funds are listed in order by Overall Investment Rating.

Section III Contents

This section contains a summary analysis of each of the top 200 equity mutual funds as determined by their overall TheStreet Investment Rating. You can use this section to identify those mutual funds that have achieved the best possible combination of total return on investment and reduced volatility over the past three years. Consult each fund's individual Performance Rating and Risk Rating to find the fund that best matches your investing style.

In order to optimize the utility of our top and bottom fund lists, rather than listing all funds in a multi-class series, a single fund from each series is selected for display as the primary share class. Whenever possible, the selected fund is one that a retail investor would be most likely to choose. This share class may not be appropriate for every investor, so please consult with your financial advisor, the fund company, and the fund's prospectus before placing your trade.

1. Fund Type	The mutual fund's peer category based on an analysis of its investment portfolio.	

AG	Aggressive Growth		HL	Health
AA	Asset Allocation		IN	Income
BA	Balanced		IX	Index
CV	Convertible		MC	Mid Cap
EM	Emerging Market		OT	Other
EN	Energy/Natural Resources		PM	Precious Metals
FS	Financial Services		RE	Real Estate
FO	Foreign		SC	Small Cap
GL	Global		TC	Technology
GR	Growth		UT	Utilities
GI	Growth and Income			

A blank fund type means that the mutual fund has not yet been categorized.

2. Fund Name   The name of the mutual fund as stated in its prospectus, which can sometimes differ slightly from the name that the company uses for advertising. If you cannot find the particular mutual fund you are interested in, or if you have any doubts regarding the precise name, verify the information with your broker or on your account statement. Also, use the fund's ticker symbol for confirmation. (See column 3.)

3. Ticker Symbol   The unique alphabetic symbol used for identifying and trading a specific mutual fund. No two funds can have the same ticker symbol, and the ticker symbol for mutual funds always ends with an "X".

A handful of funds currently show no associated ticker symbol. This means that the fund is either small or new since the NASD only assigns a ticker symbol to funds with at least $25 million in assets or 1,000 shareholders.

4.	**Overall Investment Rating**	Our overall rating is measured on a scale from A to E based on each fund's risk-adjusted performance. Please see page 10 for specific descriptions of each letter grade. Also, refer to page 7 for information on how our ratings are derived. Most important, when using this rating, please be sure to consider the warnings beginning on page 11 regarding the ratings' limitations and the underlying assumptions.
5.	**Phone**	The telephone number of the company managing the fund. Call this number to receive a prospectus or other information about the fund.
6.	**Net Asset Value (NAV)**	The fund's share price as of the date indicated. A fund's NAV is computed by dividing the value of the fund's asset holdings, less accrued fees and expenses, by the number of its shares outstanding.
7.	**Performance Rating/Points**	A letter grade rating based solely on the mutual fund's financial performance over the trailing three years, without any consideration for the amount of risk the fund poses. Like the overall Investment Rating, the Performance Rating is measured on a scale from A to E for ease of interpretation. The points score indicates where the Performance Rating falls on a scale of 0 to 10.
8.	**1-Year Total Return**	The total return the fund has provided investors over the preceeding twelve months. This total return figure is computed based on the fund's dividend distributions and share price appreciation/depreciation during the period, net of the expenses and fees it imposes on its shareholders. Although the total return figure does not reflect an adjustment for any loads the fund may carry, such adjustments have been made in deriving TheStreet Investment Ratings.
9.	**1-Year Total Return Percentile**	The fund's percentile rank based on its one-year performance compared to that of all other equity funds in existence for at least one year. A score of 99 is the best possible, indicating that the fund outperformed 99% of the other mutual funds. Zero is the worst possible percentile score.
10.	**3-Year Total Return**	The total annual return the fund has provided investors over the preceeding three years.
11.	**3-Year Total Return Percentile**	The fund's percentile rank based on its three-year performance compared to that of all other equity funds in existence for at least three years. A score of 99 is the best possible, indicating that the fund outperformed 99% of the other mutual funds. Zero is the worst possible percentile score.
12.	**5-Year Total Return**	The total annual return the fund has provided investors over the preceeding five years.
13.	**5-Year Total Return Percentile**	The fund's percentile rank based on its five-year performance compared to that of all other equity funds in existence for at least five years. A score of 99 is the best possible, indicating that the fund outperformed 99% of the other mutual funds. Zero is the worst possible percentile score.

14. Risk Rating/Points

A letter grade rating based solely on the mutual fund's risk as determined by its monthly performance volatility over the trailing three years. The risk rating does not take into consideration the overall financial performance the fund has achieved or the total return it has provided to its shareholders. Like the overall Investment Rating, the Risk Rating is measured on a scale from A to E for ease of interpretation. The points score indicates where the Risk Rating falls on a scale of 0 to 10.

15. Manager Quality Percentile

The manager quality percentile is based on a ranking of the fund's alpha, a statistical measure representing the difference between a fund's actual returns and its expected performance given its level of risk. Fund managers who have been able to exceed the fund's statistically expected performance receive a high percentile rank with 99 representing the highest possible score. At the other end of the spectrum, fund managers who have actually detracted from the fund's expected performance receive a low percentile rank with 0 representing the lowest possible score.

16. Manager Tenure

The number of years the current manager has been managing the fund. Since fund managers who deliver substandard returns are usually replaced, a long tenure is usually a good sign that shareholders are satisfied that the fund is achieving its stated objectives.

Fund Type	Fund Name	Ticker Symbol	Overall Investment Rating	Phone	Net Asset Value As of 3/31/15	Performance Rating/Pts	1Yr / Pct	3Yr / Pct	5Yr / Pct	Risk Rating/Pts	Mgr. Quality Pct	Mgr. Tenure (Years)
GR	ProFunds-HlthCare UltraSector	HCPSX	A+	(888) 776-3637	44.30	A+ /9.9	38.24 /99	38.76 /99	27.38 /99	B- / 7.2	99	2
GR	ProFunds-Consumer Srvs Ultra	CYPSX	A+	(888) 776-3637	76.52	A+ /9.9	28.75 /99	31.46 /99	27.02 /99	C+ / 6.7	92	2
GR	ProFunds-Pharm UltraSector Svc	PHPSX	A+	(888) 776-3637	22.56	A+ /9.9	24.39 /98	32.15 /99	24.32 /99	C+ / 6.4	98	2
HL	Hartford Healthcare A	HGHAX	A+	(888) 843-7824	39.13	A+ /9.9	29.12 /99	29.34 /99	21.36 /99	C+ / 6.2	99	15
HL	Vanguard HealthCare Index Adm	VHCIX	A+	(800) 662-7447	67.68	A+ /9.9	27.85 /99	27.67 /99	20.76 /99	B / 8.2	99	11
HL	Rydex Health Care A	RYHEX	A+	(800) 820-0888	33.60	A+ /9.9	30.21 /99	26.61 /99	19.23 /98	C+ / 6.6	99	17
GR	LM CM Opportunity Trust A	LGOAX	A+	(877) 534-4627	20.06	A+ /9.9	12.95 /86	30.29 /99	13.37 /72	C+ / 5.9	95	16
GR	Fidelity Select Air Transport	FSAIX	A+	(800) 544-8888	73.26	A+ /9.9	21.54 /97	26.07 /99	18.41 /98	C+ / 6.8	98	3
HL	Fidelity Select Medical Delivery	FSHCX	A+	(800) 544-8888	90.32	A+ /9.9	29.21 /99	20.44 /98	18.89 /98	C+ / 6.0	97	3
HL	Oak Assoc-Live Oak Health	LOGSX	A+	(888) 462-5386	22.05	A+ /9.9	21.12 /97	23.05 /99	18.64 /98	C+ / 6.1	98	14
RE	Baron Real Estate Retail	BREFX	A+	(800) 992-2766	27.09	A+ /9.9	16.19 /94	24.10 /99	21.34 /99	C+ / 6.2	99	6
GR	● Vanguard Capital Opportunity Inv	VHCOX	A+	(800) 662-7447	54.97	A+ /9.9	17.69 /95	23.41 /99	15.71 /91	C+ / 6.8	96	17
GR	Eventide Gilead A	ETAGX	A+	(877) 453-7877	27.72	A+ /9.9	16.24 /94	24.76 /99	20.37 /99	C+ / 6.1	97	7
GR	Fidelity Select Transportation	FSRFX	A+	(800) 544-8888	91.17	A+ /9.8	19.69 /96	24.36 /99	18.33 /98	C+ / 6.9	98	3
GR	Fidelity Select Retailing	FSRPX	A+	(800) 544-8888	95.25	A+ /9.8	21.98 /97	20.99 /98	20.01 /99	C+ / 5.9	83	1
IN	Aquila Three Peaks Oppty Gro A	ATGAX	A+	(800) 437-1020	47.19	A+ /9.8	20.73 /97	23.71 /99	18.49 /98	C+ / 6.3	96	12
SC	Ariel Fund Investor	ARGFX	A+	(800) 292-7435	76.61	A+ /9.8	19.54 /96	21.60 /98	16.12 /94	C+ / 5.9	94	29
GR	Bridgeway Large-Cap Growth	BRLGX	A+	(800) 661-3550	23.91	A+ /9.8	22.54 /97	20.83 /98	16.24 /94	B- / 7.0	90	12
GR	Nicholas	NICSX	A+	(800) 544-6547	71.57	A+ /9.8	19.51 /96	21.92 /98	18.41 /98	C+ / 6.7	94	46
MC	Rydex Mid Cap 1.5x Strgy A	RYAHX	A+	(800) 820-0888	67.32	A+ /9.8	15.50 /92	23.07 /99	20.23 /99	C+ / 5.9	26	14
GR	Rydex Transportation A	RYTSX	A+	(800) 820-0888	48.41	A+ /9.8	16.34 /94	24.25 /99	16.70 /95	C+ / 6.9	96	17
OT	Lazard Global Listed Infr Open	GLFOX	A+	(800) 821-6474	14.82	A+ /9.8	18.18 /96	21.60 /98	14.45 /82	B- / 7.0	98	10
GR	Fidelity Select Multimedia	FBMPX	A+	(800) 544-8888	82.20	A+ /9.8	13.61 /88	23.14 /99	20.52 /99	C+ / 6.5	90	2
GI	Vanguard Cons Discn Idx Adm	VCDAX	A+	(800) 662-7447	63.35	A+ /9.8	17.09 /95	20.67 /98	19.95 /99	C+ / 6.8	86	5
GR	Glenmede Large Cap Growth Port	GTLLX	A+	(800) 442-8299	24.53	A+ /9.8	20.97 /97	19.99 /98	18.37 /98	C+ / 6.8	84	11
HL	Saratoga Adv Tr-Health & Biotech	SHPAX	A+	(800) 807-3863	31.71	A+ /9.8	19.51 /96	21.87 /98	17.78 /97	C+ / 6.4	97	10
SC	Vanguard Strategic Equity Inv	VSEQX	A+	(800) 662-7447	33.84	A+ /9.8	14.29 /90	20.78 /98	18.19 /98	C+ / 6.7	96	9
GR	● Smead Value Fund Investor	SMVLX	A+	(877) 807-4122	40.25	A+ /9.8	12.72 /86	21.57 /98	17.61 /97	B- / 7.5	91	7
SC	PNC Multi-Factor Small Cap Core	PLOAX	A+	(800) 551-2145	21.34	A+ /9.8	13.56 /88	22.34 /98	19.63 /99	C+ / 6.4	94	10
AG	Rydex Nova A	RYANX	A+	(800) 820-0888	46.40	A+ /9.8	17.09 /95	22.38 /98	19.28 /98	C+ / 6.6	33	19
MC	● Vanguard PRIMECAP Inv	VPMCX	A+	(800) 662-7447	105.16	A+ /9.8	15.58 /93	21.00 /98	15.91 /93	C+ / 7.0	96	30
GR	Fidelity Sel Defense and	FSDAX	A+	(800) 544-8888	129.39	A+ /9.8	13.61 /88	19.85 /98	17.08 /96	C+ / 6.5	92	3
MC	Harbor Mid Cap Value Inv	HIMVX	A+	(800) 422-1050	21.34	A+ /9.8	12.33 /84	20.98 /98	16.10 /93	B- / 7.3	91	11
SC	Hennessy Cornerstone Growth Inv	HFCGX	A+	(800) 966-4354	20.28	A+ /9.8	17.23 /95	19.68 /97	14.56 /83	C+ / 6.8	96	15
GR	Leuthold Select Industries	LSLTX	A+	(888) 200-0409	22.90	A+ /9.8	15.08 /92	20.01 /98	12.51 /64	B- / 7.1	78	2
MC	● T Rowe Price Instl Mid-Cap Eq Gr	PMEGX	A+	(800) 638-5660	46.00	A+ /9.8	18.05 /96	19.09 /97	17.60 /97	C+ / 6.2	86	19
SC	Hennessy Focus Investor	HFCSX	A+	(800) 966-4354	70.89	A+ /9.8	18.24 /96	19.04 /97	17.35 /97	C+ / 6.6	97	6
MC	Hennessy Cornerstone Mid Cap 30	HFMDX	A+	(800) 966-4354	19.69	A+ /9.7	15.42 /92	19.55 /97	17.26 /96	C+ / 6.1	86	12
MC	Janus Aspen Enterprise Inst	JAAGX	A+	(800) 295-2687	66.19	A+ /9.7	17.93 /95	17.84 /94	16.92 /96	C+ / 6.2	91	8
AG	Bridgeway Aggressive Investor 1	BRAGX	A+	(800) 661-3550	60.13	A+ /9.7	11.61 /81	20.83 /98	15.35 /89	C+ / 6.2	72	21
GR	● Vanguard PRIMECAP Core Inv	VPCCX	A+	(800) 662-7447	22.04	A+ /9.7	15.49 /92	20.14 /98	15.55 /90	B- / 7.0	93	11
GR	Parnassus Endeavor	PARWX	A+	(800) 999-3505	30.83	A+ /9.7	18.69 /96	19.20 /97	15.87 /92	C+ / 6.8	89	10
GR	Glenmede Large Cap core	GTLOX	A+	(800) 442-8299	22.52	A+ /9.7	15.24 /92	19.61 /97	17.30 /97	B- / 7.0	81	11
MC	Fidelity Mid Cap Enhanced Index	FMEIX	A+	(800) 544-8544	14.17	A+ /9.7	14.79 /91	19.63 /97	16.75 /95	C+ / 6.8	90	8
AG	Fidelity Growth Strategies Fd	FDEGX	A+	(800) 544-8544	34.41	A+ /9.7	19.73 /97	17.82 /94	14.50 /82	C+ / 6.3	71	2
SC	Vanguard Strategic Sm-Cp Equity	VSTCX	A+	(800) 662-7447	32.07	A+ /9.7	11.51 /80	19.59 /97	17.65 /97	C+ / 6.2	92	9
IN	Natixis ASG Managed Futures	AMFAX	A+	(800) 225-5478	12.27	A+ /9.7	39.33 /99	12.29 /55	--	B- / 7.7	96	5
MC	PRIMECAP Odyssey Growth Fd	POGRX	A+	(800) 729-2307	26.98	A+ /9.7	13.10 /87	19.63 /97	15.20 /88	C+ / 6.7	91	11
SC	Golden Small Cap Core Inst	GLDSX	A+	(800) 754-8757	18.45	A+ /9.7	14.27 /90	18.60 /96	16.66 /95	C+ / 6.4	92	10
MC	● VY JPMorgan Mid Cap Val Adv	IJMAX	A+	(800) 992-0180	23.28	A+ /9.7	15.28 /92	18.94 /97	16.57 /95	C+ / 6.6	94	11
GR	ProFunds-Consumer Goods Ultra	CNPSX	A+	(888) 776-3637	78.41	A+ /9.6	15.99 /93	19.22 /97	18.59 /98	C+ / 6.8	30	2
GR	Janus Portfolio Institutional	JAGRX	A+	(800) 295-2687	38.01	A+ /9.6	20.49 /97	16.78 /89	14.30 /80	C+ / 6.1	78	4

● Denotes fund is closed to new investors

Fund Type	Fund Name	Ticker Symbol	Overall Investment Rating	Phone	Net Asset Value As of 3/31/15	Performance Rating/Pts	Annualized Total Return Through 3/31/15 1Yr / Pct	3Yr / Pct	5Yr / Pct	Risk Rating/Pts	Mgr. Quality Pct	Mgr. Tenure (Years)
GR	Amer Beacon Bridgeway LC Val	BRLVX	A+	(800) 658-5811	24.32	A+ /9.6	12.45 /85	19.75 /98	15.85 /92	B- / 7.9	89	12
SC	Westwood SmallCap Value Inst	WHGSX	A+	(877) 386-3944	14.34	A+ /9.6	8.63 /67	19.62 /97	16.82 /96	C+ / 6.4	90	2
MC	Dreyfus Active MidCap A	DNLDX	A+	(800) 782-6620	59.40	A+ /9.6	18.36 /96	19.57 /97	14.96 /86	C+ / 6.9	83	3
MC ●	Principal MidCap A	PEMGX	A+	(800) 222-5852	23.00	A+ /9.6	18.04 /96	19.27 /97	18.56 /98	C+ / 6.8	91	15
IN	SEI Inst Inv Managed Vol Fund A	SVYAX	A+	(800) 342-5734	14.64	A /9.5	15.66 /93	18.42 /95	16.60 /95	C+ / 6.3	95	11
GR	NASDAQ-100 Index Direct	NASDX	A+	(800) 955-9988	11.14	A /9.5	21.69 /97	17.85 /94	18.46 /98	C+ / 6.6	74	12
GI	Lazard US Eqty Concentrated	LEVOX	A+	(800) 821-6474	13.91	A /9.5	19.71 /95	17.76 /93	13.77 /76	C+ / 6.7	81	10
GR	USAA Growth Fund	USAAX	A+	(800) 382-8722	25.02	A /9.5	16.22 /94	18.29 /95	15.48 /90	C+ / 6.6	77	8
GR ●	Sequoia Fund	SEQUX	A+	(800) 686-6884	253.02	A /9.5	13.77 /89	17.63 /93	17.69 /97	B- / 7.2	93	35
SC	Wasatch Small Cap Value Investor	WMCVX	A+	(800) 551-1700	6.44	A /9.5	10.84 /78	18.81 /96	15.97 /93	C+ / 6.6	93	16
GL	Brown Advisory SmCP Fund Val	BIAUX	A+	(800) 540-6807	24.11	A /9.5	10.00 /74	19.04 /97	17.44 /97	C+ / 6.7	99	7
MC	Fidelity Adv Mid Cap Value A	FMPAX	A+	(800) 522-7297	24.81	A /9.5	15.38 /92	20.25 /98	16.35 /94	B- / 7.1	92	2
GR	Vanguard FTSE Social Index Inv	VFTSX	A+	(800) 662-7447	13.49	A /9.5	14.60 /91	18.67 /96	14.96 /87	B- / 7.0	80	4
GR	Rydex Retailing A	RYRTX	A+	(800) 820-0888	26.85	A /9.5	19.44 /96	16.99 /90	16.95 /96	C+ / 6.5	52	17
MC	Virtus Mid-Cap Core Fund A	VMACX	A+	(800) 243-1574	23.00	A /9.5	22.75 /98	16.97 /90	15.46 /90	B- / 7.0	83	6
MC ●	J Hancock III Dsp Val Mid Cap A	JVMAX	A+	(800) 257-3336	20.19	A /9.5	13.78 /89	19.64 /97	17.18 /96	C+ / 6.9	90	15
GI	Transamerica Prt Large Core	DVGIX	A+	(888) 233-4339	33.88	A /9.5	16.36 /94	18.26 /95	15.70 /91	B- / 7.6	80	6
GI	Fidelity Value Fd	FDVLX	A+	(800) 544-8544	116.72	A /9.5	10.90 /78	18.97 /97	15.02 /87	C+ / 6.9	82	5
SC	Homestead Small Company Stock	HSCSX	A+	(800) 258-3030	40.95	A /9.5	11.30 /80	18.17 /95	17.71 /97	C+ / 6.5	91	16
GR	Natixis Vaughan Nelson Val Opp A	VNVAX	A+	(800) 225-5478	22.78	A /9.5	12.73 /86	19.64 /97	16.48 /95	C+ / 6.3	84	7
MC	Vanguard Mid-Cap Value Index Inv	VMVIX	A+	(800) 662-7447	36.08	A /9.5	12.44 /85	18.69 /96	15.48 /90	B- / 7.0	89	9
GR	TCW Concentrated Value N	TGFVX	A+	(800) 386-3829	20.00	A /9.5	15.51 /92	18.66 /96	13.02 /68	C+ / 6.7	76	11
AG	CB Aggressive Growth A	SHRAX	A+	(877) 534-4627	209.82	A /9.4	11.38 /80	20.93 /98	18.65 /98	C+ / 6.6	89	32
GR	LSV Value Equity Inst	LSVEX	A+	(866) 777-7818	24.02	A /9.4	9.20 /70	19.66 /97	15.06 /87	B- / 7.1	72	16
GR	Fidelity NASDAQ Composite Index	FNCMX	A+	(800) 544-8544	64.65	A /9.4	18.00 /95	17.88 /94	16.53 /95	C+ / 6.6	71	11
FS	Fidelity Select Insurance	FSPCX	A+	(800) 544-8888	67.08	A /9.4	11.31 /80	19.52 /97	13.49 /73	C+ / 6.7	85	2
GL	Janus Contrarian A	JCNAX	A+	(800) 295-2687	22.26	A /9.4	12.63 /85	20.63 /98	11.78 /59	C+ / 6.3	99	4
FO	Hennessy Japan Fund Investor	HJPNX	A+	(800) 966-4354	23.34	A /9.4	18.84 /96	15.52 /79	13.59 /74	B- / 7.3	98	9
MC	Vanguard Mid-Cap Index Inv	VIMSX	A+	(800) 662-7447	35.14	A /9.4	14.72 /91	17.76 /93	15.91 /92	C+ / 6.9	83	17
MC	Lazard US Mid Cap Eq Open	LZMOX	A+	(800) 821-6474	19.82	A /9.4	21.07 /97	15.22 /77	12.87 /67	C+ / 6.6	51	14
GR	PRIMECAP Odyssey Stock Fd	POSKX	A+	(800) 729-2307	24.25	A /9.4	13.56 /88	18.33 /95	14.44 /82	B- / 7.7	91	11
GR	American Century Veedot Inv	AMVIX	A+	(800) 345-6488	10.93	A /9.4	14.72 /91	18.16 /95	15.60 /91	B- / 7.1	80	16
GR	SunAmerica VAL Co I Nsdq 100	VCNIX	A+	(800) 858-8850	9.95	A /9.4	21.35 /97	17.26 /91	17.99 /97	C+ / 6.4	69	3
MC	Transamerica Prt Mid Value	DVMVX	A+	(888) 233-4339	21.95	A /9.4	13.99 /89	17.73 /93	15.09 /87	B- / 7.6	90	14
MC	Wells Fargo Adv Spec Mid Cp VI A	WFPAX	A+	(800) 222-8222	32.68	A /9.4	11.83 /82	19.88 /98	15.96 /93	C+ / 6.4	90	6
GR	American Century Leg Multi Cp	ACMFX	A+	(800) 345-6488	18.08	A /9.3	13.26 /87	17.70 /93	15.70 /91	B- / 7.3	85	8
SC	Vanguard Small-Cap Value Index	VISVX	A+	(800) 662-7447	26.20	A /9.3	10.45 /76	18.12 /95	14.94 /86	C+ / 6.8	90	17
GR	Tax Mgd US MktWide Val II Inst	DFMVX	A+	(800) 984-9472	24.91	A /9.3	9.89 /74	19.07 /97	15.54 /90	B- / 7.0	74	N/A
MC ●	JPMorgan Mid Cap Value A	JAMCX	A+	(800) 480-4111	37.77	A /9.3	15.15 /92	18.96 /97	16.68 /95	B- / 7.0	94	18
GR	USAA Nasdaq 100 Index	USNQX	A+	(800) 382-8722	12.53	A /9.3	21.08 /97	17.13 /91	17.76 /97	C+ / 6.6	67	9
TC	Guinness Atkinson Glob Innov	IWIRX	A+	(800) 915-6565	34.38	A /9.3	10.77 /77	18.90 /96	14.86 /86	C+ / 6.9	71	5
SC	PNC Small Cap A	PPCAX	A+	(800) 551-2145	21.81	A /9.3	9.74 /73	18.89 /96	17.68 /97	C+ / 6.8	92	11
GR	PNC Large Cap Growth A	PEWAX	A+	(800) 551-2145	28.93	A /9.3	22.83 /98	16.61 /88	15.90 /92	B- / 7.0	57	6
GR	J Hancock VIT Fund AC Core I	JEQAX	A+	(800) 257-3336	23.12	A /9.3	12.07 /83	18.21 /95	15.71 /91	C+ / 6.4	49	4
FO	Glenmede Total Market Port	GTTMX	A+	(800) 442-8299	15.22	A /9.3	11.23 /79	17.78 /93	15.32 /89	C+ / 6.5	98	9
GR	Vulcan Value Partners	VVPLX	A+	(877) 421-5078	19.44	A /9.3	14.59 /91	18.68 /96	15.96 /93	B- / 7.1	81	6
IN	SEI Instl Mgd Tr-US Mgd Volty A	SVOAX	A+	(800) 342-5734	17.11	A- /9.2	14.61 /91	17.60 /93	15.86 /92	C+ / 6.5	93	N/A
GI	Delaware Large Cap Value Eqty	DPDEX	A+	(800) 523-1918	27.65	A- /9.2	13.11 /87	18.13 /95	17.07 /96	B- / 7.8	92	9
GR	AMG FQ Tax-Managed US Equity	MFQAX	A+	(800) 835-3879	24.91	A- /9.2	12.35 /84	17.70 /93	16.48 /95	B- / 7.4	70	7
GL	Motley Fool Great America Investor	TMFGX	A+	(888) 863-8803	20.05	A- /9.2	13.32 /88	17.46 /92	--	C+ / 6.9	98	5
FS	Emerald Banking and Finance A	HSSAX	A+	(855) 828-9909	28.91	A- /9.2	4.37 /34	20.00 /98	14.27 /80	B- / 7.0	93	18
GR	J Hancock VIT All Cap Core I	JEACX	A+	(800) 257-3336	28.74	A- /9.2	13.09 /87	17.04 /90	14.27 /80	C+ / 6.9	65	5

● Denotes fund is closed to new investors

99 Pct = Best
0 Pct = Worst

Fund Type	Fund Name	Ticker Symbol	Overall Investment Rating	Phone	Net Asset Value As of 3/31/15	Performance Rating/Pts	Annualized Total Return Through 3/31/15 1Yr / Pct	3Yr / Pct	5Yr / Pct	Risk Rating/Pts	Mgr. Quality Pct	Mgr. Tenure (Years)
GI	Fidelity Value Discovery Fd	FVDFX	A+	(800) 544-8544	24.95	A- /9.1	12.11 /83	17.78 /93	14.25 /80	B- /7.8	80	3
GR	Hartford Core Equity A	HAIAX	A+	(888) 843-7824	23.30	A- /9.1	16.98 /95	18.20 /95	15.65 /91	B- /7.3	81	17
GR	Akre Focus Retail	AKREX	A+	(877) 862-9556	23.10	A- /9.1	12.02 /83	17.77 /93	18.21 /98	B- /7.1	82	6
MC	Prudential Mid-Cap Value A	SPRAX	A+	(800) 225-1852	21.35	A- /9.1	12.41 /84	19.13 /97	15.41 /90	C+ /6.8	89	8
MC	American Century VP Mid Cap Val	AVMTX	A+	(800) 345-6488	19.14	A- /9.1	13.62 /88	17.42 /92	14.56 /83	B- /7.2	92	11
GR	Olstein All Cap Value C	OFALX	A+	(800) 799-2113	21.90	A- /9.1	15.59 /93	16.79 /89	13.86 /76	B- /7.1	62	20
GI	JPMorgan Tax Aware Equity I	JPDEX	A+	(800) 480-4111	29.61	A- /9.1	14.28 /90	17.28 /91	14.54 /83	C+ /6.7	66	7
MC	Vanguard S&P Mid-Cap 400 Value	VMFVX	A+	(800) 662-7447	198.20	A- /9.1	10.75 /77	17.48 /92	--	C+ /6.6	67	2
GR	Fidelity Blue Chip Value	FBCVX	A+	(800) 544-8544	16.71	A- /9.0	14.24 /90	16.86 /89	11.29 /55	B- /7.2	58	1
GR	Wells Fargo Adv Large Cap Core A	EGOAX	A+	(800) 222-8222	15.82	A- /9.0	15.51 /92	18.55 /96	15.38 /89	B- /7.4	83	8
GR	Vanguard Structured Lg-Cp Eq Inst	VSLIX	A+	(800) 662-7447	40.44	A- /9.0	14.13 /90	17.32 /91	15.86 /92	B- /7.3	75	9
IN	Nicholas Equity Income	NSEIX	A+	(800) 544-6547	20.99	A- /9.0	13.13 /87	16.94 /90	14.83 /85	B- /7.0	84	22
GR	Vanguard US Value Inv	VUVLX	A+	(800) 662-7447	17.66	A- /9.0	10.12 /75	18.03 /94	15.13 /88	B- /7.4	80	7
GR	DFA US Large Cap Value II Inst	DFCVX	A+	(800) 984-9472	16.15	A- /9.0	8.25 /65	18.62 /96	14.93 /86	B- /7.1	70	14
IN	Parnassus Core Equity Inv	PRBLX	A+	(800) 999-3505	40.29	A- /9.0	12.70 /86	17.75 /93	13.69 /75	B- /7.1	87	14
GR	Rydex Leisure A	RYLSX	A+	(800) 820-0888	56.88	A- /9.0	10.86 /78	18.79 /96	17.50 /97	B- /7.1	82	17
GR	Fidelity LgCp Gr Enh Idx Fd	FLGEX	A+	(800) 544-8544	15.22	A- /9.0	16.35 /94	16.55 /87	15.52 /90	B- /7.1	72	8
GR	Robeco Boston Ptrs All Cap Val Inv	BPAVX	A+	(888) 261-4073	22.83	A- /9.0	10.58 /77	17.56 /93	13.92 /77	B- /7.2	68	8
GI	Vanguard Cons Stap Idx Adm	VCSAX	A+	(800) 662-7447	62.59	B+ /8.9	16.90 /94	16.43 /86	15.42 /90	B- /7.1	88	5
GI	Homestead Value	HOVLX	A+	(800) 258-3030	51.53	B+ /8.9	12.96 /86	17.19 /91	14.09 /79	B- /7.5	69	25
GR	Brown Advisory Flexible Equity Inv	BIAFX	A+	(800) 540-6807	16.07	B+ /8.9	13.19 /87	17.26 /91	14.56 /83	B- /7.3	77	7
GR	Columbia Large Cap Enh Core A	NMIAX	A+	(800) 345-6611	21.65	B+ /8.9	14.68 /91	16.99 /90	15.38 /89	B- /7.4	66	6
MC	Vanguard Windsor-I Inv	VWNDX	A+	(800) 662-7447	21.79	B+ /8.9	9.71 /73	17.69 /93	14.04 /78	C+ /6.8	85	7
FS	Burnham Financial Services A	BURKX	A+	(800) 462-2392	28.35	B+ /8.9	7.44 /59	19.65 /97	9.95 /44	B- /7.0	96	16
SC	FAM Value Inv	FAMVX	A+	(800) 932-3271	68.58	B+ /8.9	13.55 /88	16.28 /85	13.52 /73	B- /7.2	94	28
GR	Goldman Sachs LC Gro Insights A	GLCGX	A+	(800) 526-7384	22.74	B+ /8.8	17.89 /95	17.82 /94	16.06 /93	B- /7.3	75	4
GR	Vanguard Mega Cap Gr Index I	VMGAX	A+	(800) 662-7447	165.40	B+ /8.8	16.62 /94	16.38 /86	15.51 /90	B- /7.0	69	5
GR	SEI Inst Inv Tr-Tax Mgd Volty A	TMMAX	A+	(800) 342-5734	14.43	B+ /8.8	14.10 /90	16.63 /88	15.33 /89	B- /7.4	92	8
GR	Manor Growth Fund	MNRGX	A+	(800) 787-3334	20.82	B+ /8.8	15.14 /92	16.09 /84	14.77 /85	B- /7.1	65	16
GR	SunAmerica VAL Co II Soc Resp	VCSRX	A+	(800) 858-8850	19.49	B+ /8.8	13.51 /88	17.01 /90	14.88 /86	B- /7.1	73	3
GR	DFA TA US Core Equity 2 Inst	DFTCX	A+	(800) 984-9472	14.53	B+ /8.8	9.80 /74	17.24 /91	14.94 /86	C+ /6.9	59	3
GR	QS Batterymarch US Large Cap Eq	LMUSX	A+	(877) 534-4627	17.19	B+ /8.8	13.48 /88	16.73 /88	14.50 /82	B- /7.6	63	7
IN	DFA US Core Equity 2 Ptf Inst	DFQTX	A+	(800) 984-9472	17.82	B+ /8.7	9.51 /72	17.22 /91	14.89 /86	B- /7.0	59	3
OT	Vanguard Industrials Index Adm	VINAX	A+	(800) 662-7447	55.12	B+ /8.7	8.41 /66	17.40 /92	15.11 /88	B- /7.0	64	5
IN	DFA US Core Equity 1 Ptf Inst	DFEOX	A+	(800) 984-9472	18.26	B+ /8.7	10.75 /77	16.93 /89	14.97 /87	B- /7.0	64	3
GI	Vanguard Growth & Income Inv	VQNPX	A+	(800) 662-7447	42.34	B+ /8.7	13.83 /89	16.61 /88	14.77 /85	B- /7.1	72	4
MC	Touchstone Mid Cap A	TMAPX	A+	(800) 543-0407	25.95	B+ /8.7	12.73 /86	17.98 /94	15.68 /91	B- /7.1	88	4
IN	State Farm Equity A	SNEAX	A+	(800) 447-4930	10.02	B+ /8.6	15.83 /93	17.22 /91	13.97 /77	B- /7.2	75	N/A
GR	Fidelity LgCp Val Enh Idx Fd	FLVEX	A+	(800) 544-8544	11.22	B+ /8.6	10.50 /76	17.37 /92	14.40 /81	B- /7.4	75	8
IN	AQR Managed Futures Strategy N	AQMNX	A+	(866) 290-2688	11.44	B+ /8.6	26.37 /99	10.28 /41	5.70 /15	B /8.2	99	5
GR	Vanguard Instl TtlStk Mkt Inst	VITNX	A+	(800) 662-7447	47.27	B+ /8.6	12.37 /84	16.45 /87	14.80 /85	B- /7.1	68	14
IN	Transamerica Prt Large Value	DVEIX	A+	(888) 233-4339	27.95	B+ /8.5	9.51 /72	16.87 /89	14.75 /85	B- /7.4	64	6
GR	Vanguard Tax-Managed Cap Appr	VTCLX	A+	(800) 662-7447	105.80	B+ /8.5	12.29 /84	16.45 /87	14.69 /84	B- /7.2	68	21
GR	Northern Large Cap Core	NOLCX	A+	(800) 595-9111	15.42	B+ /8.4	10.81 /78	16.81 /89	14.82 /85	B- /7.5	64	4
GR	Federated MDT All Cap Core Fd A	QAACX	A+	(800) 341-7400	21.97	B+ /8.4	10.21 /75	18.35 /95	14.30 /80	B- /7.4	78	7
IN	T Rowe Price Dividend Growth	PRDGX	A+	(800) 638-5660	36.54	B+ /8.3	12.65 /85	15.82 /82	13.90 /77	B- /7.4	74	15
FS	Alpine Financial Services Inst	ADFSX	A+	(888) 785-5578	13.59	B+ /8.3	1.09 /19	18.28 /95	10.71 /50	B- /7.4	91	10
IN	Target Large Capitalization Val T	TALVX	A+	(800) 225-1852	16.41	B+ /8.3	10.04 /74	16.65 /88	12.82 /67	B- /7.5	61	10
MC	Boyar Value Fund	BOYAX	A+	(800) 266-5566	23.34	B /8.1	16.23 /94	16.95 /90	14.07 /78	B /8.1	94	17
GR	Delaware Value A	DDVAX	A+	(800) 523-1918	18.50	B /8.0	12.43 /84	17.53 /92	16.36 /94	B- /7.8	90	11
GR	Fidelity Adv Equity Value A	FAVAX	A+	(800) 522-7297	16.14	B /7.9	11.54 /81	17.29 /91	13.72 /75	B- /7.8	77	3
FO	FMI International	FMIJX	A+	(800) 811-5311	30.03	B /7.9	10.92 /78	14.85 /74	--	B- /7.8	98	N/A

● Denotes fund is closed to new investors

Fund Type	Fund Name	Ticker Symbol	Overall Investment Rating	Phone	Net Asset Value As of 3/31/15	Perform-ance Rating/Pts	Annualized Total Return Through 3/31/15			Risk Rating/Pts	Mgr. Quality Pct	Mgr. Tenure (Years)
	99 Pct = Best *0 Pct = Worst*						1Yr / Pct	3Yr / Pct	5Yr / Pct			
GR	Vanguard Russell 1000 Val Index	VRVIX	A+	(800) 662-7447	175.98	B /7.9	9.26 /71	16.34 /86	--	B- / 7.8	68	5
IX	American Beacon S&P 500 Idx Inv	AAFPX	A+	(800) 658-5811	27.96	B /7.7	12.03 /83	15.43 /78	13.78 /76	B / 8.0	58	11
GR	Weitz Funds Part III Oppty	WPOPX	A+	(800) 232-4161	17.31	B- /7.4	7.76 /61	14.90 /74	14.64 /84	B / 8.6	83	32
HL	BlackRock Health Sci Opps Inv A	SHSAX	A	(800) 441-7762	54.46	A+ /9.9	34.56 /99	30.02 /99	21.02 /99	C / 5.4	99	12
HL	Vanguard Health Care Inv	VGHCX	A	(800) 662-7447	225.70	A+ /9.9	29.47 /99	29.10 /99	21.70 /99	C+ / 5.6	99	7
AG	● PRIMECAP Odyssey Agg Growth	POAGX	A	(800) 729-2307	34.88	A+ /9.9	17.96 /95	26.39 /99	20.62 /99	C+ / 5.6	95	11
GR	Fidelity Select Constn and Housing	FSHOX	A	(800) 544-8888	60.87	A+ /9.9	21.85 /97	21.09 /98	19.13 /98	C+ / 5.7	88	3
SC	Roxbury/Hood River Sm-Cap Gr	RSCIX	A	(800) 336-9970	33.42	A+ /9.8	16.85 /94	21.31 /98	17.68 /97	C+ / 5.7	95	8
HL	Delaware Healthcare Fund A	DLHAX	A	(800) 523-1918	20.36	A+ /9.8	16.37 /94	23.61 /99	19.82 /99	C+ / 5.6	96	8
AG	Rydex Dow 2x Strategy A	RYLDX	A	(800) 820-0888	50.69	A+ /9.8	17.18 /95	22.98 /99	21.60 /99	C+ / 5.6	2	11
GR	Fidelity Select IT Serv Portfolio	FBSOX	A	(800) 544-8888	38.89	A+ /9.8	15.74 /93	20.31 /98	19.63 /99	C+ / 5.7	64	6
GL	Thornburg Globl Opportunities A	THOAX	A	(800) 847-0200	26.90	A+ /9.8	21.60 /97	20.32 /98	13.93 /77	C+ / 5.8	99	9
GR	ProFunds-Industrial UltraSector	IDPSX	A	(888) 776-3637	65.11	A+ /9.8	9.50 /72	21.61 /98	18.28 /98	C+ / 5.7	10	2
SC	JPMorgan Small Cap Core Sel	VSSCX	A	(800) 480-4111	56.48	A+ /9.7	12.79 /86	19.68 /97	16.68 /95	C+ / 5.9	87	11
SC	T Rowe Price Diversified Sm-Cap	PRDSX	A	(800) 638-5660	27.68	A+ /9.7	15.57 /93	18.97 /97	19.03 /98	C+ / 5.9	92	9
GR	Fidelity Blue Chip Growth Fd	FBGRX	A	(800) 544-8544	72.16	A+ /9.7	18.66 /96	18.79 /96	16.98 /96	C+ / 5.9	78	6
MC	● T Rowe Price Mid-Cap Growth	RPMGX	A	(800) 638-5660	80.36	A+ /9.7	17.20 /95	18.41 /95	17.02 /96	C+ / 5.8	86	23
GI	Olstein Strategic Opps Fd A	OFSAX	A	(800) 799-2113	18.49	A+ /9.7	16.55 /94	20.23 /98	16.72 /95	C+ / 5.8	77	9
GR	Federated Kaufmann Large Cap A	KLCAX	A	(800) 341-7400	19.34	A+ /9.7	19.73 /97	19.75 /98	17.40 /97	C+ / 5.8	90	8
GR	Fidelity Independence Fd	FDFFX	A	(800) 544-8544	41.03	A+ /9.6	13.50 /88	19.18 /97	15.29 /89	C+ / 5.7	85	9
SC	PNC Multi-Factor Small Cap	PLWAX	A	(800) 551-2145	20.58	A+ /9.6	13.75 /89	19.74 /98	19.21 /98	C+ / 6.0	90	10
GR	Golden Large Cap Core Inst	GLDLX	A	(800) 754-8757	14.67	A+ /9.6	15.90 /93	18.76 /96	15.42 /90	C+ / 5.9	84	20
GR	T Rowe Price Instl Lg Cap Core Gr	TPLGX	A	(800) 638-5660	26.36	A /9.5	17.17 /95	17.86 /94	17.06 /96	C+ / 6.0	80	12
SC	● Hotchkis and Wiley Small Cap Val	HWSAX	A	(866) 493-8637	61.24	A /9.5	10.76 /77	20.75 /98	17.24 /96	C+ / 6.0	93	20
GR	T Rowe Price Blue Chip Growth	TRBCX	A	(800) 638-5660	71.28	A /9.5	17.08 /95	17.80 /94	17.07 /96	C+ / 5.8	79	22
GL	Hodges Retail	HDPMX	A	(877) 232-1222	38.98	A /9.5	3.53 /29	21.71 /98	14.33 /81	C+ / 6.1	99	16
GR	GE Institutional Premier Gro Eq Inv	GEIPX	A	(800) 242-0134	14.77	A /9.5	17.52 /95	18.26 /95	15.40 /90	C+ / 5.8	79	16
GR	SunAmerica VAL Co I Bluechip Gro	VCBCX	A	(800) 858-8850	17.73	A /9.4	16.86 /94	17.57 /93	16.84 /96	C+ / 5.9	78	15
MC	Vanguard Mid-Cap Growth Index	VMGIX	A	(800) 662-7447	42.34	A /9.4	17.09 /95	16.68 /88	16.19 /94	C+ / 6.1	70	2
SC	Fidelity Sm Cap Enhanced Index	FCPEX	A	(800) 544-8544	13.38	A /9.4	11.86 /82	17.90 /94	16.70 /95	C+ / 6.0	85	8
MC	T Rowe Price Diversified MidCap	PRDMX	A	(800) 638-5660	24.91	A /9.4	16.13 /93	17.12 /90	16.23 /94	C+ / 6.0	72	12
SC	● AMG Mgrs Skyline Special Eqty	SKSEX	A	(800) 835-3879	41.10	A /9.4	6.99 /55	19.42 /97	17.10 /96	C+ / 6.2	84	14
SC	DFA Tax Mgd US Target Val Inst	DTMVX	A	(800) 984-9472	33.76	A /9.4	7.40 /58	18.83 /96	15.82 /92	C+ / 6.2	88	3
SC	Hodges Small Cap Retail	HDPSX	A	(877) 232-1222	20.43	A /9.4	8.78 /68	19.16 /97	20.30 /99	C+ / 6.0	91	8
MC	SEI Instl Managed Tr-MidCap Portf	SEMCX	A	(800) 342-5734	27.70	A /9.3	13.11 /87	17.88 /94	15.31 /89	C+ / 6.0	78	22
MC	Alger Mid Cap Growth Inst R	AGIRX	A	(800) 254-3796	22.70	A /9.3	14.76 /91	17.24 /91	13.44 /72	C+ / 6.0	75	5
GL	GF Multi-Factor Growth Equity Fd I	GFMGX	A	(800) 473-1155	17.89	B /9.3	17.14 /95	17.44 /92	15.85 /92	C+ / 6.4	98	6
MC	American Century NT Md Cp Val	ACLMX	A	(800) 345-6488	12.82	B /9.3	14.05 /89	17.82 /94	15.14 /88	C+ / 6.4	92	9
GI	Federated MDT Stock Tr IS	FMSTX	A	(800) 341-7400	28.61	A /9.3	8.75 /68	19.04 /97	15.54 /90	C+ / 6.2	68	6
GR	Wasatch Core Growth Investor	WGROX	A	(800) 551-1700	61.47	A /9.3	15.11 /92	16.75 /88	17.15 /96	C+ / 6.4	73	15
GI	T Rowe Price Value	TRVLX	A	(800) 638-5660	34.96	A /9.3	10.36 /76	18.65 /96	14.96 /87	C+ / 6.3	80	6
SC	● T Rowe Price Instl Small Cap Stk	TRSSX	A	(800) 638-5660	21.32	A /9.3	9.50 /72	17.63 /93	17.58 /97	C+ / 6.2	88	15
MC	T Rowe Price Extended Eq Mkt	PEXMX	A	(800) 638-5660	26.32	A- /9.2	10.38 /76	17.68 /93	16.08 /93	C+ / 6.2	61	13
SC	Nationwide HighMark Sm Cp Core	NWGPX	A	(800) 848-0920	32.55	A- /9.2	14.17 /90	18.34 /95	17.07 /96	C+ / 6.2	89	2

Section IV

Bottom 200
Stock Mutual Funds

A compilation of those

Equity Mutual Funds

receiving the lowest TheStreet Investment Ratings.

Funds are listed in order by Overall Investment Rating.

Section IV Contents

This section contains a summary analysis of each of the bottom 200 equity mutual funds as determined by their overall TheStreet Investment Rating. Typically, these funds have invested in stocks that are currently out of favor, presenting a risky investment proposition. As such, these are the funds that you should generally avoid since they have historically underperformed most other mutual funds given the level of risk in their underlying investments.

In order to optimize the utility of our top and bottom fund lists, rather than listing all funds in a multi-class series, a single fund from each series is selected for display as the primary share class. Whenever possible, the selected fund is one that a retail investor would be most likely to choose. This share class may not be appropriate for every investor, so please consult with your financial advisor, the fund company, and the fund's prospectus before placing your trade.

1. **Fund Type**   The mutual fund's peer category based on an analysis of its investment portfolio.

AG	Aggressive Growth	HL	Health
AA	Asset Allocation	IN	Income
BA	Balanced	IX	Index
CV	Convertible	MC	Mid Cap
EM	Emerging Market	OT	Other
EN	Energy/Natural Resources	PM	Precious Metals
FS	Financial Services	RE	Real Estate
FO	Foreign	SC	Small Cap
GL	Global	TC	Technology
GR	Growth	UT	Utilities
GI	Growth and Income		

A blank fund type means that the mutual fund has not yet been categorized.

2. **Fund Name**   The name of the mutual fund as stated in its prospectus, which can sometimes differ slightly from the name that the company uses for advertising. If you cannot find the particular mutual fund you are interested in, or if you have any doubts regarding the precise name, verify the information with your broker or on your account statement. Also, use the fund's ticker symbol for confirmation. (See column 3.)

3. **Ticker Symbol**   The unique alphabetic symbol used for identifying and trading a specific mutual fund. No two funds can have the same ticker symbol, and the ticker symbol for mutual funds always ends with an "X".

A handful of funds currently show no associated ticker symbol. This means that the fund is either small or new since the NASD only assigns a ticker symbol to funds with at least $25 million in assets or 1,000 shareholders.

4.	**Overall Investment Rating**	Our overall rating is measured on a scale from A to E based on each fund's risk-adjusted performance. Please see page 10 for specific descriptions of each letter grade. Also, refer to page 7 for information on how our ratings are derived. Most important, when using this rating, please be sure to consider the warnings beginning on page 11 regarding the ratings' limitations and the underlying assumptions.
5.	**Phone**	The telephone number of the company managing the fund. Call this number to receive a prospectus or other information about the fund.
6.	**Net Asset Value (NAV)**	The fund's share price as of the date indicated. A fund's NAV is computed by dividing the value of the fund's asset holdings, less accrued fees and expenses, by the number of its shares outstanding.
7.	**Performance Rating/Points**	A letter grade rating based solely on the mutual fund's financial performance over the trailing three years, without any consideration for the amount of risk the fund poses. Like the overall Investment Rating, the Performance Rating is measured on a scale from A to E for ease of interpretation. The points score indicates where the Performance Rating falls on a scale of 0 to 10.
8.	**1-Year Total Return**	The total return the fund has provided investors over the preceeding twelve months. This total return figure is computed based on the fund's dividend distributions and share price appreciation/depreciation during the period, net of the expenses and fees it imposes on its shareholders. Although the total return figure does not reflect an adjustment for any loads the fund may carry, such adjustments have been made in deriving TheStreet Investment Ratings.
9.	**1-Year Total Return Percentile**	The fund's percentile rank based on its one-year performance compared to that of all other equity funds in existence for at least one year. A score of 99 is the best possible, indicating that the fund outperformed 99% of the other mutual funds. Zero is the worst possible percentile score.
10.	**3-Year Total Return**	The total annual return the fund has provided investors over the preceeding three years.
11.	**3-Year Total Return Percentile**	The fund's percentile rank based on its three-year performance compared to that of all other equity funds in existence for at least three years. A score of 99 is the best possible, indicating that the fund outperformed 99% of the other mutual funds. Zero is the worst possible percentile score.
12.	**5-Year Total Return**	The total annual return the fund has provided investors over the preceeding five years.
13.	**5-Year Total Return Percentile**	The fund's percentile rank based on its five-year performance compared to that of all other equity funds in existence for at least five years. A score of 99 is the best possible, indicating that the fund outperformed 99% of the other mutual funds. Zero is the worst possible percentile score.

14.	**Risk Rating/Points**	A letter grade rating based solely on the mutual fund's risk as determined by its monthly performance volatility over the trailing three years. The risk rating does not take into consideration the overall financial performance the fund has achieved or the total return it has provided to its shareholders. Like the overall Investment Rating, the Risk Rating is measured on a scale from A to E for ease of interpretation. The points score indicates where the Risk Rating falls on a scale of 0 to 10.
15.	**Manager Quality Percentile**	The manager quality percentile is based on a ranking of the fund's alpha, a statistical measure representing the difference between a fund's actual returns and its expected performance given its level of risk. Fund managers who have been able to exceed the fund's statistically expected performance receive a high percentile rank with 99 representing the highest possible score. At the other end of the spectrum, fund managers who have actually detracted from the fund's expected performance receive a low percentile rank with 0 representing the lowest possible score.
16.	**Manager Tenure**	The number of years the current manager has been managing the fund. Since fund managers who deliver substandard returns are usually replaced, a long tenure is usually a good sign that shareholders are satisfied that the fund is achieving its stated objectives.

Fund Type	Fund Name	Ticker Symbol	Overall Investment Rating	Phone	Net Asset Value As of 3/31/15	Performance Rating/Pts	1Yr / Pct	3Yr / Pct	5Yr / Pct	Risk Rating/Pts	Mgr. Quality Pct	Mgr. Tenure (Years)
FO	Profunds-Ultra Short Japan Svc	UKPSX	E-	(888) 776-3637	14.07	E- /0.0	-48.02 / 0	-44.85 / 0	-33.50 / 0	E- / 0.0	0	6
PM	ProFunds-Precious Metals Ultra	PMPSX	E-	(888) 776-3637	6.68	E- /0.0	-42.21 / 0	-38.81 / 0	-25.71 / 0	D / 1.6	0	2
FO	ProFunds-Ultra Latin America Svc	UBPSX	E-	(888) 776-3637	3.25	E- /0.0	-47.92 / 0	-34.32 / 0	-23.49 / 0	D- / 1.1	0	6
GL	Encompass	ENCPX	E-	(888) 263-6443	3.66	E- /0.0	-39.40 / 0	-32.76 / 0	-17.80 / 0	D- / 1.1	0	9
SC	Rydex Inv Rusl 2000 2x Strtgy A	RYIUX	E-	(800) 820-0888	25.05	E- /0.0	-23.39 / 1	-33.63 / 0	-36.31 / 0	E- / 0.0	1	9
AG	Rydex Inv NASDAQ 100 2x Stgy A	RYVTX	E-	(800) 820-0888	19.36	E- /0.0	-37.04 / 0	-32.89 / 0	-36.00 / 0	E- / 0.0	2	15
GR	ProFunds Ultra Short	USPSX	E-	(888) 776-3637	12.53	E- /0.0	-38.26 / 0	-33.95 / 0	-36.81 / 0	E- / 0.0	2	2
PM	Midas Fund	MIDSX	E-	(800) 400-6432	0.96	E- /0.0	-34.25 / 0	-34.14 / 0	-24.17 / 0	D- / 1.3	0	13
SC	ProFunds-Ultra Short Small-Cap	UCPSX	E-	(888) 776-3637	18.95	E- /0.0	-24.05 / 1	-34.34 / 0	-37.51 / 0	E- / 0.0	1	2
FO	Direxion Mo Latin America Bl 2X	DXZLX	E-	(800) 851-0511	16.84	E- /0.0	-39.14 / 0	-29.99 / 0	-21.45 / 0	E- / 0.0	0	9
MC	ProFunds-Ultra Short Mid-Cap Svc	UIPSX	E-	(888) 776-3637	4.45	E- /0.0	-26.81 / 0	-33.27 / 0	-35.19 / 0	E- / 0.0	2	2
SC	Direxion Mo Small Cap Bear 2X Inv	DXRSX	E-	(800) 851-0511	30.75	E- /0.0	-23.07 / 1	-32.50 / 0	-33.42 / 0	E- / 0.0	2	11
PM	US Global Inv World Prec Min	UNWPX	E-	(800) 873-8637	4.43	E- /0.0	-31.95 / 0	-30.61 / 0	-20.17 / 0	D- / 1.3	0	26
AG	Rydex Inv S&P 500 2x Strategy A	RYTMX	E-	(800) 820-0888	23.87	E- /0.0	-25.38 / 0	-29.97 / 0	-30.46 / 0	E / 0.3	7	15
GR	ProFunds-Ultra Bear Svc	URPSX	E-	(888) 776-3637	5.31	E- /0.0	-26.14 / 0	-31.22 / 0	-31.57 / 0	E- / 0.0	3	6
FO	Profunds-Ultra Short China Svc	UHPSX	E-	(888) 776-3637	15.59	E- /0.0	-29.33 / 0	-29.92 / 0	-27.95 / 0	E- / 0.0	0	6
PM	Deutsche Gold & Prec Metals Fund	SGDAX	E-	(800) 728-3337	5.65	E- /0.0	-25.36 / 0	-27.39 / 0	-16.45 / 0	E / 0.4	1	4
PM	Oppenheimer Gold/Spec Min A	OPGSX	E-	(888) 470-0862	12.82	E- /0.0	-25.08 / 0	-27.27 / 0	-15.68 / 0	E+ / 0.7	1	18
GR	Direxion Mo S&P 500 Bear 2X Inv	DXSSX	E-	(800) 851-0511	29.20	E- /0.0	-24.53 / 0	-29.46 / 0	-29.11 / 0	E- / 0.0	12	9
PM	Franklin Gold & Precious Metals A	FKRCX	E-	(800) 342-5236	13.60	E- /0.0	-24.82 / 0	-26.63 / 0	-16.05 / 0	D- / 1.2	1	16
PM	Rydex Precious Metal A	RYMNX	E-	(800) 820-0888	24.28	E- /0.0	-28.13 / 0	-25.99 / 0	-15.48 / 0	E- / 0.2	1	22
PM	American Century Global Gold A	ACGGX	E-	(800) 345-6488	7.21	E- /0.0	-22.95 / 1	-26.63 / 0	-14.43 / 0	E- / 0.2	1	23
PM	Fidelity Adv Gold A	FGDAX	E-	(800) 522-7297	15.92	E- /0.0	-21.15 / 1	-26.59 / 0	-15.06 / 0	E / 0.4	2	8
AG	Rydex Inv Dow 2x Strategy A	RYIDX	E-	(800) 820-0888	30.36	E- /0.0	-22.85 / 1	-26.18 / 0	-28.42 / 0	E / 0.5	59	7
PM	USAA Precious Mtls&Minerals	USAGX	E-	(800) 382-8722	11.32	E- /0.0	-22.99 / 1	-27.15 / 0	-15.55 / 0	E+ / 0.6	1	7
GR	ProFunds-Ultra Short Dow 30 Svc	UWPSX	E-	(888) 776-3637	5.82	E- /0.0	-23.62 / 1	-27.30 / 0	-29.26 / 0	E- / 0.2	38	2
PM	Van Eck Intl Investors Gold A	INIVX	E-	(800) 826-1115	7.57	E- /0.0	-22.28 / 1	-25.00 / 0	-13.24 / 0	E- / 0.0	3	19
PM	Wells Fargo Adv Precious Mtls A	EKWAX	E-	(800) 222-8222	28.99	E- /0.0	-20.90 / 1	-24.56 / 0	-13.26 / 0	E+ / 0.7	2	8
PM	Invesco Gold and Precious Mtls A	IGDAX	E-	(800) 959-4246	3.60	E- /0.0	-21.40 / 1	-23.54 / 0	-12.23 / 0	E+ / 0.7	2	2
PM	Tocqueville Gold	TGLDX	E-	(800) 697-3863	30.05	E- /0.0	-21.15 / 1	-24.24 / 0	-11.44 / 0	E / 0.3	2	18
OT	Rydex Commodities Strgy A	RYMEX	E-	(800) 820-0888	9.01	E- /0.0	-41.00 / 0	-18.52 / 0	-9.92 / 0	E+ / 0.6	0	10
PM	OCM Gold Fund Investor	OCMGX	E-	(800) 628-9403	9.29	E- /0.0	-19.86 / 1	-23.46 / 0	-12.23 / 0	E+ / 0.6	5	19
PM	US Global Inv Gold & PMetals Fd	USERX	E-	(800) 873-8637	5.28	E- /0.0	-21.31 / 1	-24.65 / 0	-14.87 / 0	E+ / 0.7	2	26
PM	Gabelli Gold A	GLDAX	E-	(800) 422-3554	10.37	E- /0.0	-17.70 / 1	-22.74 / 0	-12.33 / 0	E / 0.4	11	21
PM	Vanguard Prec Metals & Mining Inv	VGPMX	E-	(800) 662-7447	8.68	E- /0.0	-20.37 / 1	-22.27 / 0	-13.00 / 0	E+ / 0.8	1	2
EM	ProFunds-Ultra Sh Intl Svc	UXPSX	E-	(888) 776-3637	22.16	E- /0.0	-6.18 / 4	-23.68 / 0	-24.93 / 0	E- / 0.0	0	6
GI	Goldman Sachs Commodity Strat A	GSCAX	E-	(800) 526-7384	3.63	E- /0.0	-36.76 / 0	-16.12 / 0	-7.47 / 1	D- / 1.1	0	8
EN	JPMorgan Glbl Natural Resources	JGNAX	E-	(800) 480-4111	7.03	E- /0.0	-26.74 / 0	-17.79 / 0	--	D- / 1.0	0	5
PM	First Eagle Gold A	SGGDX	E-	(800) 334-2143	13.94	E- /0.0	-15.36 / 2	-20.76 / 0	-9.95 / 0	E- / 0.0	6	2
EM	Fidelity Advisor Latin America Fd A	FLFAX	E-	(800) 544-8544	21.62	E- /0.0	-22.78 / 1	-16.96 / 0	-8.78 / 1	D- / 1.2	0	6
EN	US Global Inv Global Resources	PSPFX	E-	(800) 873-8637	5.83	E- /0.0	-38.31 / 0	-14.89 / 0	-6.86 / 1	D / 2.1	0	26
GR	ProFunds-Short OTC Svc	SOPSX	E-	(888) 776-3637	16.84	E- /0.0	-22.68 / 1	-20.13 / 0	-21.19 / 0	D / 2.2	5	6
IN	Comstock Capital Value A	DRCVX	E-	(800) 422-3554	7.89	E- /0.0	-17.81 / 1	-18.92 / 0	-17.70 / 0	D+ / 2.3	12	28
EN	Oppenheimer Comm Str Tot Retn	QRAAX	E-	(888) 470-0862	2.15	E- /0.0	-31.75 / 0	-15.07 / 0	-7.30 / 1	D / 1.7	0	2
AG	Rydex Inv NASDAQ 100 Strgy A	RYAPX	E-	(800) 820-0888	25.44	E- /0.0	-20.50 / 1	-17.77 / 0	-19.21 / 0	D+ / 2.4	17	17
SC	ProFunds-Short Small Cap Svc	SHPSX	E-	(888) 776-3637	20.12	E- /0.0	-13.05 / 2	-19.10 / 0	-20.00 / 0	D / 1.9	6	6
SC	Rydex Inv Russell 2000 Stgy A	RYAFX	E-	(800) 820-0888	29.22	E- /0.0	-11.48 / 2	-17.68 / 0	-18.45 / 0	D / 2.1	13	11
MC	Rydex Inv Mid-Cap Stgy A	RYAGX	E-	(800) 820-0888	30.76	E- /0.0	-13.47 / 2	-17.42 / 0	-17.83 / 0	D+ / 2.5	20	11
GR	Federated Prudent Bear Fund A	BEARX	E-	(800) 341-7400	2.18	E- /0.0	-15.18 / 2	-17.41 / 0	-15.63 / 0	D+ / 2.8	8	16
OT	PIMCO CommoditiesPLUS	PCLAX	E-	(800) 426-0107	7.16	E- /0.0	-32.54 / 0	-12.11 / 1	--	D+ / 2.8	0	5
OT	ProFunds-Rising Rates Opport Svc	RRPSX	E-	(888) 776-3637	5.06	E- /0.0	-28.83 / 0	-14.69 / 0	-18.76 / 0	D- / 1.4	0	6
IN	Arrow Commodity Strategy A	CSFFX	E-	(877) 277-6933	6.15	E- /0.0	-25.54 / 0	-12.98 / 1	--	C- / 3.6	0	5

• Denotes fund is closed to new investors

Fund Type	Fund Name	Ticker Symbol	Overall Investment Rating	Phone	Net Asset Value As of 3/31/15	Perform-ance Rating/Pts	1Yr / Pct	3Yr / Pct	5Yr / Pct	Risk Rating/Pts	Mgr. Quality Pct	Mgr. Tenure (Years)
RE	ProFunds Short Real Estate Svc	SRPSX	E-	(888) 776-3637	17.70	E- /0.0	-21.44 / 1	-15.85 / 0	-18.82 / 0	D+ / 2.9	14	2
IN	Van Eck CM Commodity Index A	CMCAX	E-	(800) 826-1115	5.69	E- /0.0	-27.33 / 0	-12.62 / 1	--	C- / 3.6	0	5
IN	PIMCO Commodity Real Ret Str A	PCRAX	E-	(800) 426-0107	4.17	E- /0.0	-28.12 / 0	-12.65 / 1	-4.19 / 1	D / 1.8	0	8
AG	Rydex Inv S&P 500 Stgry A	RYARX	E-	(800) 820-0888	13.59	E- /0.0	-13.49 / 2	-16.21 / 0	-15.97 / 0	D+ / 2.8	27	21
GR	ProFunds-Bear Fund Svc	BRPSX	E-	(888) 776-3637	9.13	E- /0.1	-14.67 / 2	-17.28 / 0	-17.06 / 0	D+ / 2.7	15	2
EN	BlackRock Energy & Resources Inv	SSGRX	E-	(800) 441-7762	23.34	E- /0.1	-31.99 / 0	-10.37 / 1	-5.48 / 1	D- / 1.4	0	2
OT	Eaton Vance Commodity Strategy	EACSX	E-	(800) 262-1122	6.26	E- /0.1	-26.62 / 0	-12.19 / 1	--	C- / 3.6	0	5
OT	ALPS CoreComm Mgt CompComm	JCRAX	E-	(866) 759-5679	7.94	E- /0.1	-25.38 / 0	-11.24 / 1	--	C- / 3.4	0	5
EN	Rydex Energy Srsvices A	RYESX	E-	(800) 820-0888	37.32	E- /0.1	-37.11 / 0	-8.42 / 1	-1.92 / 2	D / 1.9	1	17
FO	BlackRock Latin America Inv A	MDLTX	E-	(800) 441-7762	41.82	E- /0.1	-17.84 / 1	-12.16 / 1	-7.02 / 1	D- / 1.5	0	13
FO	JPMorgan Latin America A	JLTAX	E-	(800) 480-4111	13.80	E- /0.1	-20.06 / 1	-11.48 / 1	-5.32 / 1	D / 2.2	0	8
OT	● MFS Commodity Strategy Fund A	MCSAX	E-	(800) 225-2606	6.67	E- /0.1	-26.46 / 0	-11.17 / 1	--	C- / 3.6	0	5
BA	Invesco Balanced-Risk Com Str A	BRCAX	E-	(800) 959-4246	7.17	E- /0.1	-19.17 / 1	-13.11 / 1	--	D / 2.1	0	5
IN	Harbor Commodity Real Rtn Str	HACMX	E-	(800) 422-1050	4.39	E- /0.1	-28.03 / 0	-12.39 / 1	-3.93 / 1	D+ / 2.6	0	7
SC	Leuthold Grizzly Short	GRZZX	E-	(888) 200-0409	6.86	E- /0.1	-10.56 / 3	-16.25 / 0	-16.00 / 0	D / 2.1	8	9
OT	Fidelity Srs Commodity Strat Fund	FCSSX	E-	(800) 544-8544	6.12	E- /0.1	-27.57 / 0	-12.13 / 1	-6.36 / 1	D+ / 2.3	0	6
FO	T Rowe Price Latin America	PRLAX	E-	(800) 638-5660	20.46	E- /0.1	-18.26 / 1	-12.68 / 1	-8.13 / 1	D- / 1.2	0	1
EM	T Rowe Price Emer Europe	TREMX	E-	(800) 638-5660	12.44	E- /0.1	-25.78 / 0	-11.73 / 1	-7.90 / 1	D / 1.6	1	2
EN	● J Hancock II Natural Resources A	JNRAX	E-	(800) 257-3336	12.78	E- /0.1	-28.16 / 0	-9.97 / 1	-6.67 / 1	D+ / 2.3	1	10
GR	NYSA Fund	NYSAX	E-	(800) 535-9169	4.92	E- /0.1	-36.52 / 0	-10.66 / 1	-9.01 / 1	D / 1.6	0	2
EM	Profunds-Ultra Emerging Mkt Svc	UUPSX	E-	(888) 776-3637	8.86	E- /0.1	-9.68 / 3	-12.84 / 1	-11.13 / 0	D- / 1.3	1	6
EM	Rydex Emerging Mkts 2x Strat A	RYWTX	E-	(800) 820-0888	60.49	E- /0.1	-8.72 / 3	-11.54 / 1	--	D- / 1.3	1	5
EN	RS Global Natural Resources Fund	RSNRX	E-	(800) 766-3863	24.03	E- /0.1	-27.54 / 0	-8.70 / 1	-2.13 / 2	D / 2.0	1	10
FO	Deutsche Latin America Equity A	SLANX	E-	(800) 728-3337	21.04	E- /0.1	-19.29 / 1	-9.39 / 1	-6.33 / 1	D- / 1.0	0	2
GR	Direxion Mo Natural Res Bull 2X	DXCLX	E-	(800) 851-0511	44.17	E- /0.1	-31.90 / 0	-7.80 / 1	-3.71 / 1	E- / 0.0	0	10
EM	US Global Investors Em Europe	EUROX	E-	(800) 873-8637	6.18	E- /0.1	-21.23 / 1	-10.60 / 1	-7.43 / 1	E+ / 0.9	1	18
IN	DFA Commodity Strategy Port	DCMSX	E-	(800) 984-9472	6.64	E- /0.1	-25.52 / 0	-9.87 / 1	--	C- / 3.5	0	5
EN	Prudential Jennison Natural Res A	PGNAX	E-	(800) 225-1852	38.69	E- /0.1	-25.81 / 0	-7.47 / 1	-3.04 / 1	D / 2.2	1	10
EN	Franklin Natural Resources A	FRNRX	E-	(800) 342-5236	28.27	E- /0.1	-24.43 / 1	-7.72 / 1	-1.81 / 2	D+ / 2.3	1	16
EN	Aberdeen Global Natural Res A	GGNAX	E-	(866) 667-9231	13.14	E- /0.1	-19.15 / 1	-6.93 / 1	-3.39 / 1	C- / 3.3	2	5
EM	Voya Russia A	LETRX	E-	(800) 992-0180	23.43	E- /0.1	-14.41 / 2	-10.51 / 1	-7.24 / 1	D- / 1.5	1	3
RE	Thrivent Natural Resources A	TREFX	E-	(800) 847-4836	7.93	E- /0.1	-22.02 / 1	-6.38 / 1	-0.31 / 2	D+ / 2.6	1	4
EN	Putnam Global Energy Fund A	PGEAX	E-	(800) 225-1581	9.92	E- /0.1	-25.56 / 0	-4.77 / 2	-0.28 / 2	D / 2.0	2	3
EN	Fidelity Select Energy Svcs	FSESX	E-	(800) 544-8888	52.94	E- /0.1	-31.53 / 0	-3.81 / 2	0.71 / 3	D / 1.9	2	2
GL	Fidelity Adv Glb Commodity Stk A	FFGAX	E-	(800) 522-7297	12.00	E- /0.1	-14.45 / 2	-6.13 / 1	-3.30 / 1	C- / 3.7	0	6
EM	Pioneer Emerging Markets A	PEMFX	E-	(800) 225-6292	18.44	E- /0.1	-13.34 / 2	-6.31 / 1	-4.48 / 1	D+ / 2.9	4	2
EN	Van Eck Global Hard Assets A	GHAAX	E-	(800) 826-1115	39.21	E- /0.1	-20.11 / 1	-4.69 / 2	-1.01 / 2	D / 2.0	2	20
EN	Invesco Energy A	IENAX	E-	(800) 959-4246	31.22	E- /0.1	-24.16 / 1	-2.94 / 2	0.46 / 3	D / 2.0	4	2
GL	Stone Harbor Local Markets Inst	SHLMX	E-	(866) 699-8125	8.29	E- /0.2	-13.26 / 2	-6.50 / 1	--	D+ / 2.7	1	5
GI	Huntington Real Strategies Invst A	HRSAX	E-	(800) 253-0412	6.65	E- /0.2	-19.53 / 1	-3.53 / 2	0.46 / 3	C- / 3.1	0	8
EN	Voya Global Natural Resources A	LEXMX	E-	(800) 992-0180	8.46	E- /0.2	-18.01 / 1	-2.95 / 2	0.17 / 3	D+ / 2.9	4	5
EN	BlackRock AllCap Energy & Res	BACAX	E-	(800) 441-7762	12.61	E- /0.2	-17.52 / 1	-2.75 / 2	-0.83 / 2	D+ / 2.7	5	2
GL	Listed Pvt Eq Plus A	LPEAX	E-	(866) 900-4223	2.29	E- /0.2	-22.64 / 1	-1.72 / 3	-3.85 / 1	D / 2.1	2	8
FO	Janus Overseas A	JDIAX	E-	(800) 295-2687	31.24	E- /0.2	-14.12 / 2	-3.88 / 2	-4.72 / 1	C- / 3.3	1	14
EN	Saratoga Adv Tr Energy&Basic Mat	SBMBX	E-	(800) 807-3863	13.28	E- /0.2	-19.52 / 1	-2.28 / 3	0.29 / 3	D+ / 2.5	6	4
EN	Guinness Atkinson Glob Energy	GAGEX	E-	(800) 915-6565	25.04	E- /0.2	-25.81 / 0	-2.10 / 3	0.30 / 3	D+ / 2.3	5	11
EN	Ivy Global Nat Resource A	IGNAX	E-	(800) 777-6472	16.13	E- /0.2	-15.42 / 2	-3.10 / 2	-2.77 / 1	D+ / 2.8	5	2
EN	BlackRock Natural Resource Inv A	MDGRX	E-	(800) 441-7762	51.28	E- /0.2	-18.48 / 1	-1.75 / 3	1.37 / 4	D+ / 2.3	7	18
EN	ICON Energy A	ICEAX	E-	(800) 764-0442	13.91	E- /0.2	-22.68 / 1	-0.98 / 3	--	D- / 1.5	10	8
EN	Putnam Global Natural Resources	EBERX	E-	(800) 225-1581	18.81	E- /0.2	-16.58 / 2	-2.40 / 3	0.35 / 3	C- / 3.2	7	3
EN	Rydex Energy A	RYENX	E-	(800) 820-0888	21.94	E- /0.2	-21.49 / 1	-1.24 / 3	2.42 / 5	D+ / 2.5	8	17
FO	Direxion Mo Emerg Mkts Bull 2X	DXELX	E-	(800) 851-0511	44.35	E- /0.2	-5.58 / 5	-6.66 / 1	-6.60 / 1	E- / 0.0	0	10

● Denotes fund is closed to new investors

Data as of March 31, 2015

Fund Type	Fund Name	Ticker Symbol	Overall Investment Rating	Phone	Net Asset Value As of 3/31/15	Performance Rating/Pts	1Yr / Pct	3Yr / Pct	5Yr / Pct	Risk Rating/Pts	Mgr. Quality Pct	Mgr. Tenure (Years)
EN	ProFunds Oil Eqpt Svcs & Dist Svc	OEPSX	E-	(888) 776-3637	18.42	E- /0.2	-26.79 / 0	-0.66 / 4	2.56 / 5	D- / 1.5	5	2
EN	Columbia Gl Energy and Nat Res A	EENAX	E-	(800) 345-6611	18.03	E- /0.2	-15.64 / 2	-1.40 / 3	0.33 / 3	D+ / 2.8	10	4
EN	ProFunds Short Oil & Gas Svc	SNPSX	E-	(888) 776-3637	6.22	E- /0.2	6.51 /51	-9.06 / 1	-14.06 / 0	D+ / 2.3	7	2
EM	● Templeton Frontier Markets A	TFMAX	E-	(800) 342-5236	13.47	E- /0.2	-19.91 / 1	0.62 / 5	0.51 / 3	C- / 3.4	70	7
EM	Rydex Inverse Emg Mkts 2x Str A	RYWWX	E-	(800) 820-0888	16.88	E- /0.2	-7.96 / 3	-4.33 / 2	--	E- / 0.0	25	5
EM	Profunds-Ultra Sh Emer Mkt Svc	UVPSX	E-	(888) 776-3637	8.82	E- /0.2	-8.60 / 3	-5.44 / 2	-12.91 / 0	E- / 0.0	15	6
EM	American Beacon Emerg Mkts A	AEMAX	E-	(800) 658-5811	10.14	E- /0.2	-5.25 / 5	-0.98 / 3	--	C- / 3.5	42	15
EN	Fidelity Select Natural Gas	FSNGX	E-	(800) 544-8888	31.14	E- /0.2	-21.74 / 1	0.96 / 5	1.00 / 3	D+ / 2.9	28	3
EN	Vanguard Energy Inv	VGENX	E-	(800) 662-7447	52.80	E- /0.2	-17.67 / 1	-0.66 / 4	2.78 / 6	D+ / 2.7	14	23
EM	RS Emerging Markets Fund A	GBEMX	E-	(800) 766-3863	17.55	E /0.3	0.81 /18	-3.32 / 2	-0.42 / 2	D / 2.0	16	2
EM	Templeton Developing Markets A	TEDMX	E-	(800) 342-5236	17.36	E /0.3	-3.36 / 8	-2.10 / 3	0.08 / 3	D / 1.7	27	24
FO	Janus Aspen Overseas Inst	JAIGX	E-	(800) 295-2687	32.29	E /0.3	-12.54 / 2	-1.64 / 3	-2.35 / 2	D / 1.8	1	14
EN	ProFunds-Oil & Gas UltraSector	ENPSX	E-	(888) 776-3637	38.30	E /0.3	-21.79 / 1	1.43 / 6	6.50 /20	D / 2.0	14	2
SC	Aegis Value I	AVALX	E-	(800) 528-3780	12.43	E /0.3	-28.69 / 0	2.52 / 7	5.61 /15	D- / 1.4	2	17
EM	Sit Developing Mkts Growth Fund	SDMGX	E-	(800) 332-5580	14.66	E /0.3	-4.79 / 6	-1.99 / 3	-0.77 / 2	D+ / 2.7	28	18
EM	CGCM Emerging Mkts Eqty Invest	TEMUX	E-	(800) 444-4273	12.42	E /0.3	-3.20 / 8	-2.37 / 3	-0.13 / 2	C- / 3.1	24	6
EN	Fidelity Adv Energy A	FANAX	E-	(800) 522-7297	34.85	E /0.3	-13.85 / 2	2.31 / 7	5.12 /12	D+ / 2.5	40	9
GR	Valley Forge Fund	VAFGX	E-	(800) 548-1942	7.86	E /0.3	-20.07 / 1	1.63 / 6	3.98 / 8	D / 1.8	1	2
EN	Fidelity Select Natural Resources	FNARX	E-	(800) 544-8888	31.07	E /0.3	-13.93 / 2	0.72 / 5	3.93 / 8	D+ / 2.4	23	9
SC	Pacific Advisors Small Cap Value A	PASMX	E-	(800) 282-6693	42.26	E /0.3	-21.88 / 1	4.68 /12	10.37 /48	D / 1.8	1	22
SC	Wells Fargo Adv Sm/Mid Cp Val A	WFVAX	E-	(800) 222-8222	11.36	E /0.3	-16.66 / 2	2.53 / 7	3.86 / 8	D- / 1.1	2	18
EM	● SSgA Emerging Markets N	SSEMX	E-	(800) 843-2639	10.70	E /0.4	-1.54 /11	-1.63 / 4	0.26 / 3	D- / 1.5	33	8
EM	Delaware Emerging Markets II	DPEGX	E-	(800) 523-1918	8.18	E /0.4	-7.74 / 3	0.82 / 5	--	C- / 3.4	68	5
EN	Ivy Energy A	IEYAX	E-	(800) 777-6472	14.03	E /0.4	-14.35 / 2	3.43 / 9	4.78 /11	D+ / 2.6	60	9
EN	T Rowe Price New Era	PRNEX	E-	(800) 638-5660	34.23	E /0.4	-11.14 / 2	1.31 / 6	2.20 / 5	D / 1.9	35	5
EN	Waddell & Reed Adv Energy Fund	WEGAX	E-	(888) 923-3355	14.30	E /0.4	-13.75 / 2	3.79 /10	4.95 /12	D+ / 2.6	65	9
EM	Templeton Inst-Emerg Markets	TEEMX	E-	(800) 321-8563	4.68	E /0.4	-2.61 / 9	-0.82 / 4	2.03 / 4	D- / 1.3	45	22
EN	Fidelity Select Energy	FSENX	E-	(800) 544-8888	45.33	E /0.4	-13.80 / 2	2.48 / 7	5.31 /13	D+ / 2.4	43	9
FO	Fidelity Adv Canada A	FACNX	E-	(800) 522-7297	49.39	E /0.4	-3.40 / 8	3.04 / 8	2.86 / 6	C- / 3.4	22	7
EM	PIMCO EM Fdmtl Index+AR Str	PEFIX	E-	(800) 426-0107	9.44	E /0.5	-0.94 /13	0.20 / 4	3.24 / 6	C- / 3.1	59	1
AG	Stonebridge Small Cap Growth	SBSGX	E-	(800) 639-3935	8.31	E /0.5	-10.13 / 3	1.41 / 6	4.20 / 9	C- / 3.3	0	36
SC	Royce Low Priced Stock Svc	RYLPX	E-	(800) 221-4268	9.51	E /0.5	-4.81 / 6	0.91 / 5	4.26 / 9	D- / 1.0	1	2
GR	Newmark Risk-Managed	NEWRX	E-	(877) 772-7231	2.46	E /0.5	13.36 /88	-2.58 / 3	-9.65 / 0	C- / 3.3	0	2
SC	Williston Basin/Mid-Nrth Amer Stk	ICPAX	E-	(800) 601-5593	5.99	E /0.5	-13.23 / 2	5.14 /14	12.67 /65	D+ / 2.5	5	5
GR	Catalyst Hedged Insider Buying A	STVAX	E-	(866) 447-4228	10.36	E /0.5	-12.34 / 2	5.33 /14	--	C- / 3.1	3	5
GL	Forward Income & Growth Alloc A	AOLAX	E-	(800) 999-6809	11.10	E+ /0.6	0.78 /18	3.04 / 8	3.88 / 8	D+ / 2.8	40	N/A
RE	Alpine Emg Mkts Real Estate Inst	AEMEX	E-	(888) 785-5578	16.05	E+ /0.6	3.81 /31	1.66 / 6	2.74 / 5	D+ / 2.9	5	7
EN	Guinness Atkinson Alt Energy Fd	GAAEX	E-	(800) 915-6565	3.55	E+ /0.7	-15.88 / 2	5.05 /13	-9.42 / 0	D / 2.1	78	9
FO	Columbia Acorn International Sel A	LAFAX	E-	(800) 345-6611	22.35	E+ /0.7	-8.44 / 3	5.75 /16	7.13 /24	D+ / 2.6	67	14
SC	● Artisan Small Cap Value Inv	ARTVX	E-	(800) 344-1770	13.91	E+ /0.7	-9.00 / 3	3.74 /10	5.75 /15	D / 2.2	2	18
FO	Longleaf Partners International	LLINX	E-	(800) 445-9469	13.74	E+ /0.7	-17.61 / 1	5.74 /16	3.20 / 6	D+ / 2.9	12	17
SC	Schneider Small Cap Value	SCMVX	E-	(888) 520-3277	12.77	E+ /0.9	-16.23 / 2	7.75 /26	5.34 /13	D- / 1.0	3	17
EM	Forward Frontier Strategy Inv	FRONX	E-	(800) 999-6809	9.79	E+ /0.9	-6.89 / 4	6.76 /20	2.32 / 5	D- / 1.2	95	7
SC	Wells Fargo Adv Sm Cp Val A	SMVAX	E-	(800) 222-8222	27.51	D- /1.0	-7.29 / 4	7.22 /23	6.60 /21	D+ / 2.3	11	18
FO	RS International Fund A	GUBGX	E-	(800) 766-3863	10.31	D- /1.1	-2.49 / 9	5.86 /16	5.35 /14	D- / 1.3	24	6
FO	Frost International Equity Inv	FANTX	E-	(866) 777-7818	7.27	D- /1.2	1.57 /20	5.28 /14	4.54 /10	D- / 1.0	27	13
FO	ASTON/Barings International Fund	ABARX	E-	(800) 992-8151	6.14	D- /1.3	-0.14 /15	5.01 /13	4.56 /10	D+ / 2.5	24	7
GL	Federated Emerging Markets Eq	FGLEX	E-	(800) 341-7400	9.62	D- /1.3	-4.15 / 7	5.97 /17	--	D / 1.7	41	5
GL	Calamos Global Growth and	CVLOX	E-	(800) 582-6959	8.71	D- /1.4	3.78 /30	5.89 /16	6.68 /21	D / 2.0	75	19
SC	Paradigm Value	PVFAX	E-	(877) 593-8637	49.26	D /2.0	-1.29 /12	7.24 /23	9.47 /40	D- / 1.5	6	2
GR	MassMutual Select Lg Cap Val A	MMLAX	E-	(800) 542-6767	8.04	D /2.1	-0.14 /15	9.65 /37	8.59 /34	D- / 1.1	8	3
AA	● Lifetime Achievement	LFTAX	E-	(888) 339-4230	18.08	C- /3.3	2.56 /24	9.78 /38	9.06 /37	E- / 0.1	4	15

● Denotes fund is closed to new investors

Fund Type	Fund Name	Ticker Symbol	Overall Investment Rating	Phone	Net Asset Value As of 3/31/15	Perform-ance Rating/Pts	Annualized Total Return Through 3/31/15			Risk Rating/Pts	Mgr. Quality Pct	Mgr. Tenure (Years)
							1Yr / Pct	3Yr / Pct	5Yr / Pct			
EM	ProFunds-Ultra Intl Svc	UNPSX	E-	(888) 776-3637	14.91	C- /3.4	-8.47 / 3	10.50 /42	2.59 / 5	E / 0.4	98	6
GL	Schroder Global Multi-Cp Eq R6	SQQIX	E-	(800) 464-3108	12.03	C- /3.7	2.48 /24	10.55 /43	--	E- / 0.0	89	5
OT	Russell Commodity Strategies A	RCSAX	E	(800) 832-6688	6.34	E- /0.0	-27.38 / 0	-12.94 / 1	--	C- / 3.9	0	N/A
OT	Direxion Indexed Commodity Stg A	DXCTX	E	(800) 851-0511	16.44	E- /0.1	-12.74 / 2	-7.95 / 1	-8.93 / 1	C / 5.0	1	7
GR	GAMCO Mathers Fund	MATRX	E	(800) 422-3554	6.80	E- /0.1	-9.93 / 3	-10.04 / 1	-8.11 / 1	C / 4.5	19	41
OT	Hartford Global Real Asset A	HRLAX	E	(888) 843-7824	8.91	E- /0.1	-14.28 / 2	-5.87 / 2	--	C / 5.3	0	5
EM	Nuveen TW Emerging Markets A	NTEAX	E	(800) 257-8787	24.42	E- /0.1	-5.97 / 4	-7.22 / 1	-6.32 / 1	C- / 3.7	3	7
FO	Lazard Developing Markets Eq	LDMOX	E	(800) 821-6474	10.04	E- /0.2	-10.58 / 3	-6.68 / 1	-2.68 / 1	C- / 3.9	0	28
GR	Hussman Strategic Growth	HSGFX	E	(800) 487-7626	8.97	E- /0.2	-9.61 / 3	-7.20 / 1	-6.03 / 1	C / 5.2	37	15
EM	Templeton BRIC A	TABRX	E	(800) 342-5236	9.78	E- /0.2	-3.89 / 7	-5.59 / 2	-5.39 / 1	C- / 3.8	5	9
FO	SunAmerica Intl Dividend Strat A	SIEAX	E	(800) 858-8850	9.73	E- /0.2	-15.16 / 2	-3.08 / 2	-2.51 / 1	C- / 3.8	1	3
FO	AMG FQ Global Alternatives Inv	MGAAX	E	(800) 835-3879	6.83	E- /0.2	-10.66 / 3	-5.36 / 2	-4.86 / 1	C / 4.7	19	9
OT	Midas Perpetual Portfolio	MPERX	E	(800) 400-6432	0.98	E- /0.2	-9.42 / 3	-5.33 / 2	0.30 / 3	C / 4.5	1	7
EM	Schwab Fundmntl EM Large Co	SFENX	E	(800) 407-0256	7.64	E- /0.2	-8.36 / 3	-4.27 / 2	-1.77 / 2	C- / 4.1	10	3
EM	Dreyfus Emerging Markets A	DRFMX	E	(800) 782-6620	9.19	E- /0.2	-3.78 / 7	-2.70 / 2	-2.02 / 2	C / 4.9	20	19
EM	MassMutual Premier Str Em Mkts	MPASX	E	(800) 542-6767	10.98	E- /0.2	-4.80 / 6	-3.24 / 2	-1.97 / 2	C / 4.3	16	2
EM	Lazard Emerging Mkts Eq Blend	EMBOX	E	(800) 821-6474	9.80	E- /0.2	-7.79 / 3	-4.05 / 2	--	C / 4.5	11	5
AA	Federated Unconstrained Bond	FUBDX	E	(800) 341-7400	8.48	E- /0.2	-7.94 / 3	-3.64 / 2	--	C / 5.3	2	2
EM	MFS Emerging Mkt Equity Fund A	MEMAX	E	(800) 225-2606	27.34	E- /0.2	-4.58 / 6	-2.96 / 2	0.21 / 3	C / 4.6	19	7
EM	SA Emerging Markets Value	SAEMX	E	(800) 366-7266	8.95	E- /0.2	-7.51 / 4	-3.65 / 2	-2.04 / 2	C / 4.6	13	8
EM	Fidelity Adv Emerging EMEA A	FMEAX	E	(800) 522-7297	8.11	E- /0.2	-9.42 / 3	-1.19 / 3	1.70 / 4	C- / 4.0	39	7
EM	● Invesco Developing Markets A	GTDDX	E	(800) 959-4246	29.39	E- /0.2	-7.25 / 4	-1.45 / 3	2.13 / 5	C / 4.6	36	12
GL	STAAR Inv Trust International	SITIX	E	(800) 332-7738	10.76	E- /0.2	-13.57 / 2	-1.78 / 3	-0.74 / 2	C- / 3.6	0	18
EM	QS Batterymarch Emerging	LMRAX	E	(877) 534-4627	18.02	E- /0.2	-1.18 /12	-3.12 / 2	-2.04 / 2	C / 4.7	17	N/A
GI	Investment Partners Opportunities	IPOFX	E	(866) 390-0440	9.42	E- /0.2	-10.17 / 3	-0.84 / 4	0.33 / 3	C / 5.1	1	5
EM	USAA Emerging Markets Fund	USEMX	E	(800) 382-8722	15.74	E- /0.2	-7.22 / 4	-3.00 / 2	-2.26 / 2	C / 4.6	18	3
SC	Ave Maria Opportunity Fund	AVESX	E	(866) 283-6274	10.98	E- /0.2	-19.49 / 1	-0.12 / 4	4.46 /10	C- / 4.1	1	9
EM	Touchstone Emerging Mkts Eq A	TEMAX	E	(800) 543-0407	11.19	E- /0.2	0.71 /18	-3.10 / 2	0.03 / 2	C / 4.4	18	6
EM	Laudus Mondrian Emg Mkts Inv	LEMIX	E	(800) 407-0256	8.18	E /0.3	-3.46 / 8	-3.09 / 2	0.33 / 3	C / 4.4	17	8
EM	● Wells Fargo Adv Emerg Mkts Eq A	EMGAX	E	(800) 222-8222	19.82	E /0.3	-3.79 / 7	-1.76 / 3	1.25 / 4	C / 5.0	32	9
EM	GMO Emerging Markets II	GMEMX	E		9.86	E /0.3	-3.04 / 9	-3.19 / 2	-0.12 / 2	C / 4.8	16	22
EM	● GMO Emerging Countries III	GMCEX	E		8.86	E /0.3	-2.46 / 9	-3.34 / 2	-0.21 / 2	C / 4.5	15	18
FO	WHV International Equity A	WHVAX	E	(888) 739-1390	19.70	E /0.3	-13.34 / 2	1.25 / 5	1.83 / 4	C- / 4.2	5	7
EM	Delaware Emerging Markets A	DEMAX	E	(800) 523-1918	13.83	E /0.3	-10.78 / 3	1.27 / 6	1.26 / 4	C- / 3.5	73	9
GI	Catalyst/SMH Total Return Income	TRIFX	E	(866) 447-4228	5.02	E /0.3	-13.54 / 2	0.62 / 5	2.32 / 5	C / 4.7	2	7
FO	Voya Emerging Markets Equity Div	IFCAX	E	(800) 992-0180	12.09	E /0.3	-5.63 / 5	-0.30 / 4	0.39 / 3	C- / 3.6	4	3
EM	Artisan Emerging Markets Inv	ARTZX	E	(800) 344-1770	12.03	E /0.3	-2.47 / 9	-2.47 / 3	-2.58 / 1	C / 4.8	23	9
EM	J Hancock VIT Emerg Mkts Val		E	(800) 257-3336	8.87	E /0.3	-4.91 / 6	-2.25 / 3	-1.47 / 2	C- / 3.9	25	8
GR	CM Advisors	CMAFX	E	(800) 664-4888	11.26	E /0.3	-19.00 / 1	1.22 / 5	3.79 / 8	C / 4.8	1	12
EM	● Lazard Emerging Markets Open	LZOEX	E	(800) 821-6474	17.30	E /0.3	-5.90 / 5	-1.20 / 3	1.38 / 4	C / 4.3	38	21
EM	DFA Emerging Markets Val R2	DFEPX	E	(800) 984-9472	25.68	E /0.3	-4.14 / 7	-2.02 / 3	-1.01 / 2	C / 4.7	28	17
AA	PIMCO All Asset All Authority A	PAUAX	E	(800) 426-0107	9.08	E /0.3	-5.26 / 5	-0.03 / 4	3.39 / 7	C- / 3.7	3	12
EM	BNY Mellon Emerging Markets M	MEMKX	E	(800) 645-6561	9.30	E /0.3	-3.34 / 8	-1.68 / 3	-0.24 / 2	C / 5.1	32	15
EM	SEI Inst Intl Emerging Mkts Eqty A	SIEMX	E	(800) 342-5734	10.04	E /0.3	-3.86 / 7	-1.15 / 3	-0.47 / 2	C / 5.2	40	5

Section V

Performance:
100 Best and Worst
Stock Mutual Funds

A compilation of those

Equity Mutual Funds

receiving the highest and lowest Performance Ratings.

Funds are listed in order by Performance Rating.

Section V Contents

This section contains a summary analysis of each of the top 100 and bottom 100 equity mutual funds as determined by their TheStreet Performance Rating. Since the Performance Rating does not take into consideration the amount of risk a fund poses, the selection of funds presented here is based solely on each fund's financial performance over the past three years.

In order to optimize the utility of our top and bottom fund lists, rather than listing all funds in a multi-class series, a single fund from each series is selected for display as the primary share class. Whenever possible, the selected fund is one that a retail investor would be most likely to choose. This share class may not be appropriate for every investor, so please consult with your financial advisor, the fund company, and the fund's prospectus before placing your trade.

You can use this section to identify those funds that have historically given shareholders the highest returns on their investments. A word of caution though: past performance is not necessarily indicative of future results. While these funds have provided the highest returns, some of them may be currently overvalued and due for a correction.

1.	**Fund Type**	\multicolumn{2}{l}{The mutual fund's peer category based on an analysis of its investment portfolio.}

AG	Aggressive Growth	HL	Health
AA	Asset Allocation	IN	Income
BA	Balanced	IX	Index
CV	Convertible	MC	Mid Cap
EM	Emerging Market	OT	Other
EN	Energy/Natural Resources	PM	Precious Metals
FS	Financial Services	RE	Real Estate
FO	Foreign	SC	Small Cap
GL	Global	TC	Technology
GR	Growth	UT	Utilities
GI	Growth and Income		

A blank fund type means that the mutual fund has not yet been categorized.

2.   **Fund Name**   The name of the mutual fund as stated in its prospectus, which can sometimes differ slightly from the name that the company uses for advertising. If you cannot find the particular mutual fund you are interested in, or if you have any doubts regarding the precise name, verify the information with your broker or on your account statement. Also, use the fund's ticker symbol for confirmation. (See column 3.)

<table>
<tr><td>3.</td><td>**Ticker Symbol**</td><td>The unique alphabetic symbol used for identifying and trading a specific mutual fund. No two funds can have the same ticker symbol, and the ticker symbol for mutual funds always ends with an "X".

A handful of funds currently show no associated ticker symbol. This means that the fund is either small or new since the NASD only assigns a ticker symbol to funds with at least $25 million in assets or 1,000 shareholders.</td></tr>

<tr><td>4.</td><td>**Overall Investment Rating**</td><td>Our overall rating is measured on a scale from A to E based on each fund's risk-adjusted performance. Please see page 10 for specific descriptions of each letter grade. Also, refer to page 7 for information on how our ratings are derived. Most important, when using this rating, please be sure to consider the warnings beginning on page 11 regarding the ratings' limitations and the underlying assumptions.</td></tr>

<tr><td>5.</td><td>**Phone**</td><td>The telephone number of the company managing the fund. Call this number to receive a prospectus or other information about the fund.</td></tr>

<tr><td>6.</td><td>**Net Asset Value (NAV)**</td><td>The fund's share price as of the date indicated. A fund's NAV is computed by dividing the value of the fund's asset holdings, less accrued fees and expenses, by the number of its shares outstanding.</td></tr>

<tr><td>7.</td><td>**Performance Rating/Points**</td><td>A letter grade rating based solely on the mutual fund's financial performance over the trailing three years, without any consideration for the amount of risk the fund poses. Like the overall Investment Rating, the Performance Rating is measured on a scale from A to E for ease of interpretation. The points score indicates where the Performance Rating falls on a scale of 0 to 10.</td></tr>

<tr><td>8.</td><td>**1-Year Total Return**</td><td>The total return the fund has provided investors over the preceeding twelve months. This total return figure is computed based on the fund's dividend distributions and share price appreciation/depreciation during the period, net of the expenses and fees it imposes on its shareholders. Although the total return figure does not reflect an adjustment for any loads the fund may carry, such adjustments have been made in deriving TheStreet Investment Ratings.</td></tr>

<tr><td>9.</td><td>**1-Year Total Return Percentile**</td><td>The fund's percentile rank based on its one-year performance compared to that of all other equity funds in existence for at least one year. A score of 99 is the best possible, indicating that the fund outperformed 99% of the other mutual funds. Zero is the worst possible percentile score.</td></tr>

<tr><td>10.</td><td>**3-Year Total Return**</td><td>The total annual return the fund has provided investors over the preceeding three years.</td></tr>
</table>

11. 3-Year Total Return Percentile

The fund's percentile rank based on its three-year performance compared to that of all other equity funds in existence for at least three years. A score of 99 is the best possible, indicating that the fund outperformed 99% of the other mutual funds. Zero is the worst possible percentile score.

12. 5-Year Total Return

The total annual return the fund has provided investors over the preceeding five years.

13. 5-Year Total Return Percentile

The fund's percentile rank based on its five-year performance compared to that of all other equity funds in existence for at least five years. A score of 99 is the best possible, indicating that the fund outperformed 99% of the other mutual funds. Zero is the worst possible percentile score.

14. Risk Rating/Points

A letter grade rating based solely on the mutual fund's risk as determined by its monthly performance volatility over the trailing three years. The risk rating does not take into consideration the overall financial performance the fund has achieved or the total return it has provided to its shareholders. Like the overall Investment Rating, the Risk Rating is measured on a scale from A to E for ease of interpretation. The points score indicates where the Risk Rating falls on a scale of 0 to 10.

15. Manager Quality Percentile

The manager quality percentile is based on a ranking of the fund's alpha, a statistical measure representing the difference between a fund's actual returns and its expected performance given its level of risk. Fund managers who have been able to exceed the fund's statistically expected performance receive a high percentile rank with 99 representing the highest possible score. At the other end of the spectrum, fund managers who have actually detracted from the fund's expected performance receive a low percentile rank with 0 representing the lowest possible score.

16. Manager Tenure

The number of years the current manager has been managing the fund. Since fund managers who deliver substandard returns are usually replaced, a long tenure is usually a good sign that shareholders are satisfied that the fund is achieving its stated objectives.

Fund Type	Fund Name	Ticker Symbol	Overall Investment Rating	Phone	Net Asset Value As of 3/31/15	Performance Rating/Pts	Annualized Total Return Through 3/31/15			Risk Rating/Pts	Mgr. Quality Pct	Mgr. Tenure (Years)
							1Yr / Pct	3Yr / Pct	5Yr / Pct			
HL	Vanguard HealthCare Index Adm	VHCIX	A+	(800) 662-7447	67.68	A+ /9.9	27.85 /99	27.67 /99	20.76 /99	B / 8.2	99	11
GR	ProFunds-HlthCare UltraSector	HCPSX	A+	(888) 776-3637	44.30	A+ /9.9	38.24 /99	38.76 /99	27.38 /99	B- / 7.2	99	2
GR	● Vanguard Capital Opportunity Inv	VHCOX	A+	(800) 662-7447	54.97	A+ /9.9	17.69 /95	23.41 /99	15.71 /91	C+ / 6.8	96	17
GR	Fidelity Select Air Transport	FSAIX	A+	(800) 544-8888	73.26	A+ /9.9	21.54 /97	26.07 /99	18.41 /98	C+ / 6.8	98	3
GR	ProFunds-Consumer Srvs Ultra	CYPSX	A+	(888) 776-3637	76.52	A+ /9.9	28.75 /99	31.46 /99	27.02 /99	C+ / 6.7	92	2
HL	Rydex Health Care A	RYHEX	A+	(800) 820-0888	33.60	A+ /9.9	30.21 /99	26.61 /99	19.23 /98	C+ / 6.6	99	17
GR	ProFunds-Pharm UltraSector Svc	PHPSX	A+	(888) 776-3637	22.56	A+ /9.9	24.39 /98	32.15 /99	24.32 /99	C+ / 6.4	98	2
RE	Baron Real Estate Retail	BREFX	A+	(800) 992-2766	27.09	A+ /9.9	16.19 /94	24.10 /99	21.34 /99	C+ / 6.2	99	6
HL	Hartford Healthcare A	HGHAX	A+	(888) 843-7824	39.13	A+ /9.9	29.12 /99	29.34 /99	21.36 /99	C+ / 6.2	99	15
GR	Eventide Gilead A	ETAGX	A+	(877) 453-7877	27.72	A+ /9.9	16.24 /94	24.76 /99	20.37 /99	C+ / 6.1	97	7
HL	Oak Assoc-Live Oak Health	LOGSX	A+	(888) 462-5386	22.05	A+ /9.9	21.12 /97	23.05 /99	18.64 /98	C+ / 6.1	98	14
HL	Fidelity Select Medical Delivery	FSHCX	A+	(800) 544-8888	90.32	A+ /9.9	29.21 /99	20.44 /98	18.89 /98	C+ / 6.0	97	3
GR	LM CM Opportunity Trust A	LGOAX	A+	(877) 534-4627	20.06	A+ /9.9	12.95 /86	30.29 /99	13.37 /72	C+ / 5.9	95	16
GR	Fidelity Select Constn and Housing	FSHOX	A	(800) 544-8888	60.87	A+ /9.9	21.85 /97	21.09 /98	19.13 /98	C+ / 5.7	88	3
AG	● PRIMECAP Odyssey Agg Growth	POAGX	A	(800) 729-2307	34.88	A+ /9.9	17.96 /95	26.39 /99	20.62 /99	C+ / 5.6	95	11
HL	Vanguard Health Care Inv	VGHCX	A	(800) 662-7447	225.70	A+ /9.9	29.47 /99	29.10 /99	21.70 /99	C+ / 5.6	99	7
HL	BlackRock Health Sci Opps Inv A	SHSAX	A	(800) 441-7762	54.46	A+ /9.9	34.56 /99	30.02 /99	21.02 /99	C / 5.4	99	12
HL	Putnam Global Health Care Fund A	PHSTX	A-	(800) 225-1581	71.94	A+ /9.9	31.06 /99	29.35 /99	18.07 /97	C / 5.3	99	10
HL	Invesco Global Health Care A	GGHCX	A-	(800) 959-4246	46.56	A+ /9.9	25.57 /98	25.87 /99	18.51 /98	C / 5.3	98	N/A
HL	Deutsche Health and Wellness A	SUHAX	A-	(800) 728-3337	43.69	A+ /9.9	30.43 /99	28.59 /99	21.23 /99	C / 5.2	99	14
HL	SunAmerica VAL Co I Health Sci	VCHSX	A-	(800) 858-8850	25.70	A+ /9.9	41.62 /99	36.21 /99	28.54 /99	C / 5.2	99	2
AG	ProFunds-Ultra Bull Svc	ULPSX	A-	(888) 776-3637	89.74	A+ /9.9	20.88 /97	27.92 /99	22.68 /99	C / 5.2	9	2
HL	Fidelity Adv Health Care A	FACDX	A-	(800) 522-7297	43.08	A+ /9.9	34.53 /99	35.23 /99	26.32 /99	C / 5.2	99	7
AG	Rydex S&P 500 2x Strategy A	RYTTX	A-	(800) 820-0888	70.18	A+ /9.9	22.51 /97	29.80 /99	24.33 /99	C / 5.1	17	15
HL	Fidelity Select Pharmaceuticals	FPHAX	A-	(800) 544-8888	23.67	A+ /9.9	26.48 /99	27.58 /99	22.55 /99	C / 5.1	99	2
GR	Fidelity Select Medical Eqpmnt Sys	FSMEX	A-	(800) 544-8888	43.00	A+ /9.9	30.83 /99	25.97 /99	18.18 /98	C / 5.0	98	8
HL	T Rowe Price Health Sciences	PRHSX	A-	(800) 638-5660	77.51	A+ /9.9	41.92 /99	36.57 /99	28.92 /99	C / 5.0	99	2
GL	Janus Global Life Sciences A	JFNAX	B+	(800) 295-2687	58.93	A+ /9.9	42.25 /99	36.88 /99	26.86 /99	C / 4.9	99	8
HL	J Hancock VIT Hlth Sciences I	JEHSX	B+	(800) 257-3336	38.22	A+ /9.9	41.68 /99	36.38 /99	28.66 /99	C / 4.8	99	2
HL	Kinetics Medical Advisor A	KRXAX	B+	(800) 930-3828	32.48	A+ /9.9	21.21 /97	24.59 /99	16.56 /95	C / 4.8	97	14
HL	Schwab Health Care	SWHFX	B+	(800) 407-0256	27.37	A+ /9.9	26.92 /99	26.82 /99	21.25 /99	C / 4.7	98	3
HL	Fidelity Select Health Care	FSPHX	B	(800) 544-8888	243.32	A+ /9.9	35.12 /99	36.11 /99	26.96 /99	C- / 4.1	99	7
AG	ProFunds-Ultra Mid Cap Svc	UMPSX	B	(888) 776-3637	81.90	A+ /9.9	19.75 /97	29.78 /99	24.82 /99	C- / 4.1	14	2
GR	Direxion Mo S&P 500 Bull 2X Inv	DXSLX	B	(800) 851-0511	90.97	A+ /9.9	23.59 /98	30.47 /99	25.55 /99	C- / 4.0	23	9
GR	ProFunds-Ultra Nasdaq-100 Svc	UOPSX	B	(888) 776-3637	77.73	A+ /9.9	40.79 /99	31.48 /99	31.95 /99	C- / 4.0	13	2
AG	Rydex Dyn-NASDAQ 100 2x Strgy	RYVLX	B	(800) 820-0888	369.52	A+ /9.9	42.33 /99	33.02 /99	33.41 /99	C- / 3.8	23	15
HL	AllianzGI Health Sciences A	RAGHX	B-	(800) 988-8380	36.48	A+ /9.9	31.22 /99	24.94 /99	19.34 /98	C- / 3.4	98	10
HL	Fidelity Adv Biotechnology A	FBTAX	B-	(800) 522-7297	28.31	A+ /9.9	45.91 /99	42.13 /99	32.61 /99	C- / 3.2	99	10
HL	Rydex Biotechnology A	RYBOX	B-	(800) 820-0888	87.63	A+ /9.9	41.83 /99	37.84 /99	28.59 /99	C- / 3.2	99	17
HL	● Prudential Jennison Health Sci A	PHLAX	B-	(800) 225-1852	53.98	A+ /9.9	43.17 /99	36.97 /99	29.20 /99	C- / 3.2	99	16
HL	● Franklin Biotechnology Discvry A	FBDIX	B-	(800) 342-5236	192.85	A+ /9.9	43.56 /99	41.68 /99	31.02 /99	C- / 3.1	99	18
HL	Eaton Vance WW Health Sciences	ETHSX	C+	(800) 262-1122	13.35	A+ /9.9	29.82 /99	28.19 /99	19.67 /99	D+ / 2.9	99	26
SC	Rydex Russell 2000 2x Strgy A	RYRUX	C+	(800) 820-0888	349.40	A+ /9.9	11.52 /81	28.83 /99	22.08 /99	D+ / 2.8	10	9
SC	ProFunds-Ultra Small Cap Svc	UAPSX	C+	(888) 776-3637	36.94	A+ /9.9	10.53 /76	28.11 /99	21.54 /99	D+ / 2.7	8	2
HL	Fidelity Select Biotech Port	FBIOX	C+	(800) 544-8888	256.71	A+ /9.9	46.13 /99	43.52 /99	33.30 /99	D+ / 2.6	99	10
HL	Alger Health Sciences Fund A	AHSAX	C+	(800) 254-3796	24.40	A+ /9.9	30.51 /99	23.63 /99	17.14 /96	D+ / 2.5	99	10
FO	Matthews India Fund Inv	MINDX	C+	(800) 789-2742	29.20	A+ /9.9	57.70 /99	21.77 /98	11.48 /57	D / 2.0	98	10
HL	ICON Healthcare S	ICHCX	C	(800) 764-0442	20.11	A+ /9.9	29.72 /99	28.32 /99	20.75 /99	D- / 1.5	99	2
GR	ProFunds-Biotech Ultra Sector Svc	BIPSX	C	(888) 776-3637	57.28	A+ /9.9	55.44 /99	62.85 /99	40.79 /99	D- / 1.0	99	2
SC	ProFunds-Internet UltraSector Svc	INPSX	C-	(888) 776-3637	33.00	A+ /9.9	10.72 /77	27.61 /99	25.30 /99	E / 0.5	93	2
GI	PIMCO StockPlus Long Duration	PSLDX	C-	(800) 426-0107	7.56	A+ /9.9	29.07 /99	24.14 /99	24.94 /99	E- / 0.1	98	8
GR	Direxion Mo NASDAQ-100 Bull 2X	DXQLX	C-	(800) 851-0511	56.64	A+ /9.9	43.73 /99	33.97 /99	34.51 /99	E- / 0.0	33	9

● Denotes fund is closed to new investors

Fund Type	Fund Name	Ticker Symbol	Overall Investment Rating	Phone	Net Asset Value As of 3/31/15	Performance Rating/Pts	1Yr / Pct	3Yr / Pct	5Yr / Pct	Risk Rating/Pts	Mgr. Quality Pct	Mgr. Tenure (Years)
FO	ProFunds-Ultra Sh Latin America	UFPSX	D+	(888) 776-3637	19.84	A+ /9.9	41.00 /99	18.71 /96	-3.41 / 1	E- / 0.0	99	6
FO	Direxion Mo China Bull 2X Inv	DXHLX	D+	(800) 851-0511	49.79	A+ /9.9	57.81 /99	15.03 /75	0.37 / 3	E- / 0.0	55	8
SC	Direxion Mo Small Cap Bull 2X Inv	DXRLX	C-	(800) 851-0511	53.18	A+ /9.9	13.04 /87	30.96 /99	25.33 /99	E- / 0.0	24	11
FO	ProFunds-Ultra Japan Svc	UJPSX	C-	(888) 776-3637	19.22	A+ /9.9	55.50 /99	37.64 /99	12.68 /66	E- / 0.0	99	6
GR	● Smead Value Fund Investor	SMVLX	A+	(877) 807-4122	40.25	A+ /9.8	12.72 /86	21.57 /98	17.61 /97	B- / 7.5	91	7
MC	Harbor Mid Cap Value Inv	HIMVX	A+	(800) 422-1050	21.34	A+ /9.8	12.33 /84	20.98 /98	16.10 /93	B- / 7.3	91	11
GR	Leuthold Select Industries	LSLTX	A+	(888) 200-0409	22.90	A+ /9.8	15.08 /92	20.01 /98	12.51 /64	B- / 7.1	78	2
GR	Bridgeway Large-Cap Growth	BRLGX	A+	(800) 661-3550	23.91	A+ /9.8	22.54 /97	20.83 /98	16.24 /94	B- / 7.0	90	12
MC	● Vanguard PRIMECAP Inv	VPMCX	A+	(800) 662-7447	105.16	A+ /9.8	15.58 /93	21.00 /98	15.91 /93	C+ / 7.0	96	30
OT	Lazard Global Listed Infr Open	GLFOX	A+	(800) 821-6474	14.82	A+ /9.8	18.18 /96	21.60 /98	14.45 /82	B- / 7.0	98	10
GR	Rydex Transportation A	RYTSX	A+	(800) 820-0888	48.41	A+ /9.8	16.34 /94	24.25 /99	16.70 /95	C+ / 6.9	96	17
GR	Fidelity Select Transportation	FSRFX	A+	(800) 544-8888	91.17	A+ /9.8	19.69 /97	24.36 /99	18.33 /98	C+ / 6.9	98	3
GR	Glenmede Large Cap Growth Port	GTLLX	A+	(800) 442-8299	24.53	A+ /9.8	20.97 /97	19.99 /98	18.37 /98	C+ / 6.8	84	11
GI	Vanguard Cons Discn Idx Adm	VCDAX	A+	(800) 662-7447	63.35	A+ /9.8	17.09 /95	20.67 /98	19.95 /99	C+ / 6.8	86	5
SC	Hennessy Cornerstone Growth Inv	HFCGX	A+	(800) 966-4354	20.28	A+ /9.8	17.23 /95	19.68 /97	14.56 /83	C+ / 6.8	96	15
SC	Vanguard Strategic Equity Inv	VSEQX	A+	(800) 662-7447	33.84	A+ /9.8	14.29 /90	20.78 /98	18.19 /98	C+ / 6.7	96	9
GR	Nicholas	NICSX	A+	(800) 544-6547	71.57	A+ /9.8	19.51 /96	21.92 /98	18.41 /98	C+ / 6.7	94	46
AG	Rydex Nova A	RYANX	A+	(800) 820-0888	46.40	A+ /9.8	17.09 /95	22.38 /98	19.28 /98	C+ / 6.6	33	19
SC	Hennessy Focus Investor	HFCSX	A+	(800) 966-4354	70.89	A+ /9.8	18.24 /96	19.04 /97	17.35 /97	C+ / 6.6	97	6
GR	Fidelity Sel Defense and	FSDAX	A+	(800) 544-8888	129.39	A+ /9.8	13.61 /88	19.85 /98	17.08 /96	C+ / 6.5	92	3
GR	Fidelity Select Multimedia	FBMPX	A+	(800) 544-8888	82.20	A+ /9.8	13.61 /88	23.14 /99	20.52 /99	C+ / 6.5	90	2
SC	PNC Multi-Factor Small Cap Core	PLOAX	A+	(800) 551-2145	21.34	A+ /9.8	13.56 /88	22.34 /98	19.63 /99	C+ / 6.4	94	10
HL	Saratoga Adv Tr-Health & Biotech	SHPAX	A+	(800) 807-3863	31.71	A+ /9.8	19.51 /96	21.87 /98	17.78 /97	C+ / 6.4	97	10
IN	Aquila Three Peaks Oppty Gro A	ATGAX	A+	(800) 437-1020	47.19	A+ /9.8	20.73 /97	23.71 /99	18.49 /98	C+ / 6.3	96	12
MC	● T Rowe Price Instl Mid-Cap Eq Gr	PMEGX	A+	(800) 638-5660	46.00	A+ /9.8	18.05 /96	19.09 /97	17.60 /97	C+ / 6.2	86	19
MC	Rydex Mid Cap 1.5x Strgy A	RYAHX	A+	(800) 820-0888	67.32	A+ /9.8	15.50 /92	23.07 /99	20.23 /99	C+ / 5.9	26	14
GR	Fidelity Select Retailing	FSRPX	A+	(800) 544-8888	95.25	A+ /9.8	21.98 /97	20.99 /98	20.01 /99	C+ / 5.9	83	1
SC	Ariel Fund Investor	ARGFX	A+	(800) 292-7435	76.61	A+ /9.8	19.54 /96	21.60 /98	16.12 /94	C+ / 5.9	94	29
GL	Thornburg Globl Opportunities A	THOAX	A	(800) 847-0200	26.90	A+ /9.8	21.60 /97	20.32 /98	13.93 /77	C+ / 5.8	99	9
SC	Roxbury/Hood River Sm-Cap Gr	RSCIX	A	(800) 336-9970	33.42	A+ /9.8	16.85 /94	21.31 /98	17.68 /97	C+ / 5.7	95	8
GR	ProFunds-Industrial UltraSector	IDPSX	A	(888) 776-3637	65.11	A+ /9.8	9.50 /72	21.61 /98	18.28 /98	C+ / 5.7	10	2
GR	Fidelity Select IT Serv Portfolio	FBSOX	A	(800) 544-8888	38.89	A+ /9.8	15.74 /93	20.31 /98	19.63 /99	C+ / 5.7	64	6
AG	Rydex Dow 2x Strategy A	RYLDX	A	(800) 820-0888	50.69	A+ /9.8	17.18 /95	22.98 /99	21.60 /99	C+ / 5.6	2	11
HL	Delaware Healthcare Fund A	DLHAX	A	(800) 523-1918	20.36	A+ /9.8	16.37 /94	23.61 /99	19.82 /99	C+ / 5.6	96	8
GR	ProFunds-Ultra Dow 30 Svc	UDPSX	A-	(888) 776-3637	59.35	A+ /9.8	16.05 /93	21.72 /98	20.64 /99	C / 5.4	2	2
TC	USAA Science & Technology Fund	USSCX	A-	(800) 382-8722	21.64	A+ /9.8	20.82 /97	21.55 /98	18.24 /98	C / 5.3	93	13
AG	Rydex Russell 2000 1.5x Strgy A	RYAKX	B+	(800) 820-0888	58.05	A+ /9.8	9.48 /72	21.86 /98	18.22 /98	C / 4.9	6	15
SC	RS Small Cap Growth Fund K	RSEKX	B+	(800) 766-3863	67.54	A+ /9.8	16.48 /94	20.63 /98	18.23 /98	C / 4.9	92	8
FS	ProFunds-Financial UltraSector	FNPSX	B+	(888) 776-3637	13.08	A+ /9.8	12.86 /86	22.36 /98	12.04 /61	C / 4.9	16	2
GL	J Hancock II Technical Opport NAV		B	(800) 257-3336	13.89	A+ /9.8	11.90 /82	20.40 /98	10.39 /48	C / 4.3	99	6
IN	ASTON/LMCG Small Cap Growth	ACWDX	B+	(800) 992-8151	15.64	A+ /9.8	16.50 /94	21.27 /98	--	C / 4.3	92	5
RE	Phocas Real Estate	PHREX	B	(866) 746-2271	34.37	A+ /9.8	27.96 /99	16.45 /87	16.02 /93	C- / 4.2	81	9
TC	Fidelity Select Electronics Port	FSELX	B	(800) 544-8888	87.63	A+ /9.8	27.76 /99	18.59 /96	16.37 /94	C- / 4.2	61	6
GL	● Janus Venture D	JANVX	B	(800) 295-2687	68.52	A+ /9.8	18.51 /96	19.02 /97	18.19 /98	C- / 3.9	99	2
SC	● Longleaf Partners Small-Cap	LLSCX	B	(800) 445-9469	32.24	A+ /9.8	13.35 /88	20.28 /98	16.50 /95	C- / 3.9	98	26
GR	Hartford Growth Opps HLS Fd IA	HAGOX	B	(888) 843-7824	41.44	A+ /9.8	20.06 /97	19.93 /98	16.41 /94	C- / 3.7	88	14
SC	● Harbor Small Cap Growth Inv	HISGX	B-	(800) 422-1050	13.83	A+ /9.8	14.47 /90	19.90 /98	16.19 /94	C- / 3.4	92	15
AG	SunAmerica VAL Co I SmCp Agg	VSAGX	B-	(800) 858-8850	14.31	A+ /9.8	17.67 /95	21.28 /98	16.23 /94	C- / 3.2	93	4

Fund Type	Fund Name	Ticker Symbol	Overall Investment Rating (99 Pct = Best / 0 Pct = Worst)	Phone	Net Asset Value As of 3/31/15	Perform-ance Rating/Pts	Annualized Total Return Through 3/31/15 1Yr / Pct	3Yr / Pct	5Yr / Pct	Risk Rating/Pts	Mgr. Quality Pct	Mgr. Tenure (Years)
SC	ProFunds-Ultra Short Small-Cap	UCPSX	E-	(888) 776-3637	18.95	E- /0.0	-24.05 / 1	-34.34 / 0	-37.51 / 0	E- / 0.0	1	2
MC	ProFunds-Ultra Short Mid-Cap Svc	UIPSX	E-	(888) 776-3637	4.45	E- /0.0	-26.81 / 0	-33.27 / 0	-35.19 / 0	E- / 0.0	2	2
PM	First Eagle Gold A	SGGDX	E-	(800) 334-2143	13.94	E- /0.0	-15.36 / 2	-20.76 / 0	-9.95 / 0	E- / 0.0	6	2
AG	Rydex Inv NASDAQ 100 2x Stgy A	RYVTX	E-	(800) 820-0888	19.36	E- /0.0	-37.04 / 0	-32.89 / 0	-36.00 / 0	E- / 0.0	2	15
FO	Profunds-Ultra Short Japan Svc	UKPSX	E-	(888) 776-3637	14.07	E- /0.0	-48.02 / 0	-44.85 / 0	-33.50 / 0	E- / 0.0	0	6
EM	ProFunds-Ultra Sh Intl Svc	UXPSX	E-	(888) 776-3637	22.16	E- /0.0	-6.18 / 4	-23.68 / 0	-24.93 / 0	E- / 0.0	0	6
FO	Direxion Mo Latin America Bl 2X	DXZLX	E-	(800) 851-0511	16.84	E- /0.0	-39.14 / 0	-29.99 / 0	-21.45 / 0	E- / 0.0	0	9
GR	Direxion Mo S&P 500 Bear 2X Inv	DXSSX	E-	(800) 851-0511	29.20	E- /0.0	-24.53 / 0	-29.46 / 0	-29.11 / 0	E- / 0.0	12	9
SC	Rydex Inv Rusl 2000 2x Strtgy A	RYIUX	E-	(800) 820-0888	25.05	E- /0.0	-23.39 / 1	-33.63 / 0	-36.31 / 0	E- / 0.0	1	9
FO	Profunds-Ultra Short China Svc	UHPSX	E-	(888) 776-3637	15.59	E- /0.0	-29.33 / 0	-29.92 / 0	-27.95 / 0	E- / 0.0	0	6
GR	ProFunds Ultra Short	USPSX	E-	(888) 776-3637	12.53	E- /0.0	-38.26 / 0	-33.95 / 0	-36.81 / 0	E- / 0.0	2	2
GR	ProFunds-Ultra Bear Svc	URPSX	E-	(888) 776-3637	5.31	E- /0.0	-26.14 / 0	-31.22 / 0	-31.57 / 0	E- / 0.0	3	6
PM	Van Eck Intl Investors Gold A	INIVX	E-	(800) 826-1115	7.57	E- /0.0	-22.28 / 1	-25.00 / 0	-13.24 / 0	E- / 0.0	3	19
SC	Direxion Mo Small Cap Bear 2X Inv	DXRSX	E-	(800) 851-0511	30.75	E- /0.0	-23.07 / 1	-32.50 / 0	-33.42 / 0	E- / 0.0	2	11
GR	ProFunds-Ultra Short Dow 30 Svc	UWPSX	E-	(888) 776-3637	5.82	E- /0.0	-23.62 / 1	-27.30 / 0	-29.26 / 0	E- / 0.2	38	2
PM	Rydex Precious Metal A	RYMNX	E-	(800) 820-0888	24.28	E- /0.0	-28.13 / 0	-25.99 / 0	-15.48 / 0	E- / 0.2	1	22
PM	American Century Global Gold A	ACGGX	E-	(800) 345-6488	7.21	E- /0.0	-22.95 / 1	-26.63 / 0	-14.43 / 0	E- / 0.2	1	23
AG	Rydex Inv S&P 500 2x Strategy A	RYTMX	E-	(800) 820-0888	23.87	E- /0.0	-25.38 / 0	-29.97 / 0	-30.46 / 0	E / 0.3	7	15
PM	Tocqueville Gold	TGLDX	E-	(800) 697-3863	30.05	E- /0.0	-21.15 / 1	-24.24 / 0	-11.44 / 0	E / 0.3	2	18
PM	Gabelli Gold A	GLDAX	E-	(800) 422-3554	10.37	E- /0.0	-17.70 / 1	-22.74 / 0	-12.33 / 0	E / 0.4	11	21
PM	Fidelity Adv Gold A	FGDAX	E-	(800) 522-7297	15.92	E- /0.0	-21.15 / 1	-26.59 / 0	-15.06 / 0	E / 0.4	2	8
PM	Deutsche Gold & Prec Metals Fund	SGDAX	E-	(800) 728-3337	5.65	E- /0.0	-25.36 / 0	-27.39 / 0	-16.45 / 0	E / 0.4	1	4
AG	Rydex Inv Dow 2x Strategy A	RYIDX	E-	(800) 820-0888	30.36	E- /0.0	-22.85 / 1	-26.18 / 0	-28.42 / 0	E / 0.5	59	7
OT	Rydex Commodities Strgy A	RYMEX	E-	(800) 820-0888	9.01	E- /0.0	-41.00 / 0	-18.52 / 0	-9.92 / 0	E+ / 0.6	0	10
PM	USAA Precious Mtls&Minerals	USAGX	E-	(800) 382-8722	11.32	E- /0.0	-22.99 / 1	-27.15 / 0	-15.55 / 0	E+ / 0.6	1	7
PM	OCM Gold Fund Investor	OCMGX	E-	(800) 628-9403	9.29	E- /0.0	-19.86 / 1	-23.46 / 0	-12.23 / 0	E+ / 0.6	5	19
PM	Oppenheimer Gold/Spec Min A	OPGSX	E-	(888) 470-0862	12.82	E- /0.0	-25.08 / 0	-27.27 / 0	-15.68 / 0	E+ / 0.7	1	18
PM	Wells Fargo Adv Precious Mtls A	EKWAX	E-	(800) 222-8222	28.99	E- /0.0	-20.90 / 1	-24.56 / 0	-13.26 / 0	E+ / 0.7	2	8
PM	US Global Inv Gold & PMetals Fd	USERX	E-	(800) 873-8637	5.28	E- /0.0	-21.31 / 1	-24.65 / 0	-14.87 / 0	E+ / 0.7	2	26
PM	Invesco Gold and Precious Mtls A	IGDAX	E-	(800) 959-4246	3.60	E- /0.0	-21.40 / 1	-23.54 / 0	-12.23 / 0	E+ / 0.7	2	2
PM	Vanguard Prec Metals & Mining Inv	VGPMX	E-	(800) 662-7447	8.68	E- /0.0	-20.37 / 1	-22.27 / 0	-13.00 / 0	E+ / 0.8	1	2
EN	JPMorgan Glbl Natural Resources	JGNAX	E-	(800) 480-4111	7.03	E- /0.0	-26.74 / 0	-17.79 / 0	--	D- / 1.0	0	5
GI	Goldman Sachs Commodity Strat A	GSCAX	E-	(800) 526-7384	3.63	E- /0.0	-36.76 / 0	-16.12 / 0	-7.47 / 1	D- / 1.1	0	8
FO	ProFunds-Ultra Latin America Svc	UBPSX	E-	(888) 776-3637	3.25	E- /0.0	-47.92 / 0	-34.32 / 0	-23.49 / 0	D- / 1.1	0	6
GL	Encompass	ENCPX	E-	(888) 263-6443	3.66	E- /0.0	-39.40 / 0	-32.76 / 0	-17.80 / 0	D- / 1.1	0	9
PM	Franklin Gold & Precious Metals A	FKRCX	E-	(800) 342-5236	13.60	E- /0.0	-24.82 / 0	-26.63 / 0	-16.05 / 0	D- / 1.2	1	16
EM	Fidelity Advisor Latin America Fd A	FLFAX	E-	(800) 544-8544	21.62	E- /0.0	-22.78 / 1	-16.96 / 0	-8.78 / 1	D- / 1.2	0	6
PM	Midas Fund	MIDSX	E-	(800) 400-6432	0.96	E- /0.0	-34.25 / 0	-34.14 / 0	-24.17 / 0	D- / 1.3	0	13
PM	US Global Inv World Prec Min	UNWPX	E-	(800) 873-8637	4.43	E- /0.0	-31.95 / 0	-30.61 / 0	-20.17 / 0	D- / 1.3	0	26
OT	ProFunds-Rising Rates Opport Svc	RRPSX	E-	(888) 776-3637	5.06	E- /0.0	-28.83 / 0	-14.69 / 0	-18.76 / 0	D- / 1.4	0	6
PM	ProFunds-Precious Metals Ultra	PMPSX	E-	(888) 776-3637	6.68	E- /0.0	-42.21 / 0	-38.81 / 0	-25.71 / 0	D / 1.6	0	2
EN	Oppenheimer Comm Str Tot Retn	QRAAX	E-	(888) 470-0862	2.15	E- /0.0	-31.75 / 0	-15.07 / 0	-7.30 / 1	D / 1.7	0	2
IN	PIMCO Commodity Real Ret Str A	PCRAX	E-	(800) 426-0107	4.17	E- /0.0	-28.12 / 0	-12.65 / 1	-4.19 / 1	D / 1.8	0	8
SC	ProFunds-Short Small Cap Svc	SHPSX	E-	(888) 776-3637	20.12	E- /0.0	-13.05 / 2	-19.10 / 0	-20.00 / 0	D / 1.9	6	6
SC	Rydex Inv Russell 2000 Stgy A	RYAFX	E-	(800) 820-0888	29.22	E- /0.0	-11.48 / 2	-17.68 / 0	-18.45 / 0	D / 2.1	13	11
EN	US Global Inv Global Resources	PSPFX	E-	(800) 873-8637	5.83	E- /0.0	-38.31 / 0	-14.89 / 0	-6.86 / 1	D / 2.1	0	26
GR	ProFunds-Short OTC Svc	SOPSX	E-	(888) 776-3637	16.84	E- /0.0	-22.68 / 1	-20.13 / 0	-21.19 / 0	D / 2.2	5	6
IN	Comstock Capital Value A	DRCVX	E-	(800) 422-3554	7.89	E- /0.0	-17.81 / 1	-18.92 / 0	-17.70 / 0	D+ / 2.3	12	28
AG	Rydex Inv NASDAQ 100 Strgy A	RYAPX	E-	(800) 820-0888	25.44	E- /0.0	-20.50 / 1	-17.77 / 0	-19.21 / 0	D+ / 2.4	17	17
MC	Rydex Inv Mid-Cap Stgy A	RYAGX	E-	(800) 820-0888	30.76	E- /0.0	-13.47 / 2	-17.42 / 0	-17.83 / 0	D+ / 2.5	20	11
AG	Rydex Inv S&P 500 Stgry A	RYARX	E-	(800) 820-0888	13.59	E- /0.0	-13.49 / 2	-16.21 / 0	-15.97 / 0	D+ / 2.8	27	21
GR	Federated Prudent Bear Fund A	BEARX	E-	(800) 341-7400	2.18	E- /0.0	-15.18 / 2	-17.41 / 0	-15.63 / 0	D+ / 2.8	8	16

● Denotes fund is closed to new investors

Fund Type	Fund Name	Ticker Symbol	Overall Investment Rating	Phone	Net Asset Value As of 3/31/15	Performance Rating/Pts	1Yr / Pct	3Yr / Pct	5Yr / Pct	Risk Rating/Pts	Mgr. Quality Pct	Mgr. Tenure (Years)
OT	PIMCO CommoditiesPLUS	PCLAX	E-	(800) 426-0107	7.16	E- /0.0	-32.54 / 0	-12.11 / 1	--	D+ / 2.8	0	5
RE	ProFunds Short Real Estate Svc	SRPSX	E-	(888) 776-3637	17.70	E- /0.0	-21.44 / 1	-15.85 / 0	-18.82 / 0	D+ / 2.9	14	2
IN	Van Eck CM Commodity Index A	CMCAX	E-	(800) 826-1115	5.69	E- /0.0	-27.33 / 0	-12.62 / 1	--	C- / 3.6	0	5
IN	Arrow Commodity Strategy A	CSFFX	E-	(877) 277-6933	6.15	E- /0.0	-25.54 / 0	-12.98 / 1	--	C- / 3.6	0	5
OT	Russell Commodity Strategies A	RCSAX	E	(800) 832-6688	6.34	E- /0.0	-27.38 / 0	-12.94 / 1	--	C- / 3.9	0	N/A
GR	Direxion Mo Natural Res Bull 2X	DXCLX	E-	(800) 851-0511	44.17	E- /0.1	-31.90 / 0	-7.80 / 1	-3.71 / 1	E- / 0.0	0	10
EM	US Global Investors Em Europe	EUROX	E-	(800) 873-8637	6.18	E- /0.1	-21.23 / 1	-10.60 / 1	-7.43 / 1	E+ / 0.9	1	18
FO	Deutsche Latin America Equity A	SLANX	E-	(800) 728-3337	21.04	E- /0.1	-19.29 / 1	-9.39 / 1	-6.33 / 1	D- / 1.0	0	2
FO	T Rowe Price Latin America	PRLAX	E-	(800) 638-5660	20.46	E- /0.1	-18.26 / 1	-12.68 / 1	-8.13 / 1	D- / 1.2	0	1
EM	Profunds-Ultra Emerging Mkt Svc	UUPSX	E-	(888) 776-3637	8.86	E- /0.1	-9.68 / 3	-12.84 / 1	-11.13 / 0	D- / 1.3	1	6
EM	Rydex Emerging Mkts 2x Strat A	RYWTX	E-	(800) 820-0888	60.49	E- /0.1	-8.72 / 3	-11.54 / 1	--	D- / 1.3	1	5
EN	BlackRock Energy & Resources Inv	SSGRX	E-	(800) 441-7762	23.34	E- /0.1	-31.99 / 0	-10.37 / 1	-5.48 / 1	D- / 1.4	0	2
EM	Voya Russia A	LETRX	E-	(800) 992-0180	23.43	E- /0.1	-14.41 / 2	-10.51 / 1	-7.24 / 1	D- / 1.5	1	3
FO	BlackRock Latin America Inv A	MDLTX	E-	(800) 441-7762	41.82	E- /0.1	-17.84 / 1	-12.16 / 1	-7.02 / 1	D- / 1.5	0	13
GR	NYSA Fund	NYSAX	E-	(800) 535-9169	4.92	E- /0.1	-36.52 / 0	-10.66 / 1	-9.01 / 1	D / 1.6	0	2
EM	T Rowe Price Emer Europe	TREMX	E-	(800) 638-5660	12.44	E- /0.1	-25.78 / 0	-11.73 / 1	-7.90 / 1	D / 1.6	1	2
EN	Rydex Energy Srsvices A	RYESX	E-	(800) 820-0888	37.32	E- /0.1	-37.11 / 0	-8.42 / 1	-1.92 / 2	D / 1.9	1	17
EN	Fidelity Select Energy Svcs	FSESX	E-	(800) 544-8888	52.94	E- /0.1	-31.53 / 0	-3.81 / 2	0.71 / 3	D / 1.9	2	2
EN	Van Eck Global Hard Assets A	GHAAX	E-	(800) 826-1115	39.21	E- /0.1	-20.11 / 1	-4.69 / 2	-1.01 / 2	D / 2.0	2	20
EN	RS Global Natural Resources Fund	RSNRX	E-	(800) 766-3863	24.03	E- /0.1	-27.54 / 0	-8.70 / 1	-2.13 / 2	D / 2.0	1	10
EN	Putnam Global Energy Fund A	PGEAX	E-	(800) 225-1581	9.92	E- /0.1	-25.56 / 0	-4.77 / 2	-0.28 / 2	D / 2.0	2	3
EN	Invesco Energy A	IENAX	E-	(800) 959-4246	31.22	E- /0.1	-24.16 / 1	-2.94 / 2	0.46 / 3	D / 2.0	4	2
SC	Leuthold Grizzly Short	GRZZX	E-	(888) 200-0409	6.86	E- /0.1	-10.56 / 3	-16.25 / 0	-16.00 / 0	D / 2.1	8	9
BA	Invesco Balanced-Risk Com Str A	BRCAX	E-	(800) 959-4246	7.17	E- /0.1	-19.17 / 1	-13.11 / 1	--	D / 2.1	0	5
FO	JPMorgan Latin America A	JLTAX	E-	(800) 480-4111	13.80	E- /0.1	-20.06 / 1	-11.48 / 1	-5.32 / 1	D / 2.2	0	8
EN	Prudential Jennison Natural Res A	PGNAX	E-	(800) 225-1852	38.69	E- /0.1	-25.81 / 0	-7.47 / 1	-3.04 / 1	D / 2.2	1	10
EN	Franklin Natural Resources A	FRNRX	E-	(800) 342-5236	28.27	E- /0.1	-24.43 / 1	-7.72 / 1	-1.81 / 2	D+ / 2.3	1	16
OT	Fidelity Srs Commodity Strat Fund	FCSSX	E-	(800) 544-8544	6.12	E- /0.1	-27.57 / 0	-12.13 / 1	-6.36 / 1	D+ / 2.3	0	6
EN	● J Hancock II Natural Resources A	JNRAX	E-	(800) 257-3336	12.78	E- /0.1	-28.16 / 0	-9.97 / 1	-6.67 / 1	D+ / 2.3	1	10
RE	Thrivent Natural Resources A	TREFX	E-	(800) 847-4836	7.93	E- /0.1	-22.02 / 1	-6.38 / 1	-0.31 / 2	D+ / 2.6	1	4
IN	Harbor Commodity Real Rtn Str	HACMX	E-	(800) 422-1050	4.39	E- /0.1	-28.03 / 0	-12.39 / 1	-3.93 / 1	D+ / 2.6	0	7
GR	ProFunds-Bear Fund Svc	BRPSX	E-	(888) 776-3637	9.13	E- /0.1	-14.67 / 2	-17.28 / 0	-17.06 / 0	D+ / 2.7	15	2
EM	Pioneer Emerging Markets A	PEMFX	E-	(800) 225-6292	18.44	E- /0.1	-13.34 / 2	-6.31 / 1	-4.48 / 1	D+ / 2.9	4	2
EN	Aberdeen Global Natural Res A	GGNAX	E-	(866) 667-9231	13.14	E- /0.1	-19.15 / 1	-6.93 / 1	-3.39 / 1	C- / 3.3	2	5
OT	ALPS CoreComm Mgt CompComm	JCRAX	E-	(866) 759-5679	7.94	E- /0.1	-25.38 / 0	-11.24 / 1	--	C- / 3.4	0	5
IN	DFA Commodity Strategy Port	DCMSX	E-	(800) 984-9472	6.64	E- /0.1	-25.52 / 0	-9.87 / 1	--	C- / 3.5	0	5
OT	Eaton Vance Commodity Strategy	EACSX	E-	(800) 262-1122	6.26	E- /0.1	-26.62 / 0	-12.19 / 1	--	C- / 3.6	0	5
OT	● MFS Commodity Strategy Fund A	MCSAX	E-	(800) 225-2606	6.67	E- /0.1	-26.46 / 0	-11.17 / 1	--	C- / 3.6	0	5
GL	Fidelity Adv Glb Commodity Stk A	FFGAX	E-	(800) 522-7297	12.00	E- /0.1	-14.45 / 2	-6.13 / 1	-3.30 / 1	C- / 3.7	0	6
EM	Nuveen TW Emerging Markets A	NTEAX	E	(800) 257-8787	24.42	E- /0.1	-5.97 / 4	-7.22 / 1	-6.32 / 1	C- / 3.7	3	7
GR	GAMCO Mathers Fund	MATRX	E	(800) 422-3554	6.80	E- /0.1	-9.93 / 3	-10.04 / 1	-8.11 / 1	C / 4.5	19	41
OT	Direxion Indexed Commodity Stg A	DXCTX	E	(800) 851-0511	16.44	E- /0.1	-12.74 / 2	-7.95 / 1	-8.93 / 1	C / 5.0	1	7
OT	Hartford Global Real Asset A	HRLAX	E	(888) 843-7824	8.91	E- /0.1	-14.28 / 2	-5.87 / 2	--	C / 5.3	0	5
FS	● Merk Hard Currency Investor	MERKX	E+	(866) 637-5386	9.49	E- /0.1	-17.47 / 1	-6.22 / 1	-2.37 / 2	C+ / 5.8	1	10
EN	Deutsche Enhanced Comdty Strat	SKNRX	E+	(800) 728-3337	13.13	E- /0.1	-14.07 / 2	-6.80 / 1	-2.25 / 2	C+ / 5.9	3	5
FO	Direxion Mo Emerg Mkts Bull 2X	DXELX	E-	(800) 851-0511	44.35	E- /0.2	-5.58 / 5	-6.66 / 1	-6.60 / 1	E- / 0.0	0	10
EM	Profunds-Ultra Sh Emer Mkt Svc	UVPSX	E-	(888) 776-3637	8.82	E- /0.2	-8.60 / 3	-5.44 / 2	-12.91 / 0	E- / 0.0	15	6
EM	Rydex Inverse Emg Mkts 2x Str A	RYWWX	E-	(800) 820-0888	16.88	E- /0.2	-7.96 / 3	-4.33 / 2	--	E- / 0.0	25	5

● Denotes fund is closed to new investors

Section VI

Risk:
100 Best and Worst
Stock Mutual Funds

A compilation of those

Equity Mutual Funds

receiving the highest and lowest Risk Ratings.

Funds are listed in order by Risk Rating.

Section VI Contents

This section contains a summary analysis of each of the top 100 and bottom 100 mutual funds as determined by their TheStreet Risk Rating. Since the Risk Rating does not take into consideration a fund's overall financial performance, the selection of funds presented here is based solely on each fund's performance volatility over the past three years.

In order to optimize the utility of our top and bottom fund lists, rather than listing all funds in a multi-class series, a single fund from each series is selected for display as the primary share class. Whenever possible, the selected fund is one that a retail investor would be most likely to choose. This share class may not be appropriate for every investor, so please consult with your financial advisor, the fund company, and the fund's prospectus before placing your trade.

You can use this section to identify those funds that have historically given shareholders the most consistent returns on their investments. A word of caution though: consistency in the past is not necessarily indicative of future results. While these funds have provided the most stable returns, it is possible for a fund manager – especially a newly appointed fund manager – to suddenly shift the fund's investment focus which could lead to greater volatility.

1. **Fund Type**   The mutual fund's peer category based on an analysis of its investment portfolio.

AG	Aggressive Growth	HL	Health
AA	Asset Allocation	IN	Income
BA	Balanced	IX	Index
CV	Convertible	MC	Mid Cap
EM	Emerging Market	OT	Other
EN	Energy/Natural Resources	PM	Precious Metals
FS	Financial Services	RE	Real Estate
FO	Foreign	SC	Small Cap
GL	Global	TC	Technology
GR	Growth	UT	Utilities
GI	Growth and Income		

A blank fund type means that the mutual fund has not yet been categorized.

2. **Fund Name**   The name of the mutual fund as stated in its prospectus, which can sometimes differ slightly from the name that the company uses for advertising. If you cannot find the particular mutual fund you are interested in, or if you have any doubts regarding the precise name, verify the information with your broker or on your account statement. Also, use the fund's ticker symbol for confirmation. (See column 3.)

3. Ticker Symbol

The unique alphabetic symbol used for identifying and trading a specific mutual fund. No two funds can have the same ticker symbol, and the ticker symbol for mutual funds always ends with an "X".

A handful of funds currently show no associated ticker symbol. This means that the fund is either small or new since the NASD only assigns a ticker symbol to funds with at least $25 million in assets or 1,000 shareholders.

4. Overall Investment Rating

Our overall rating is measured on a scale from A to E based on each fund's risk-adjusted performance. Please see page 10 for specific descriptions of each letter grade. Also, refer to page 7 for information on how our ratings are derived. Most important, when using this rating, please be sure to consider the warnings beginning on page 11 regarding the ratings' limitations and the underlying assumptions.

5. Phone

The telephone number of the company managing the fund. Call this number to receive a prospectus or other information about the fund.

6. Net Asset Value (NAV)

The fund's share price as of the date indicated. A fund's NAV is computed by dividing the value of the fund's asset holdings, less accrued fees and expenses, by the number of its shares outstanding.

7. Performance Rating/Points

A letter grade rating based solely on the mutual fund's financial performance over the trailing three years, without any consideration for the amount of risk the fund poses. Like the overall Investment Rating, the Performance Rating is measured on a scale from A to E for ease of interpretation. The points score indicates where the Performance Rating falls on a scale of 0 to 10.

8. 1-Year Total Return

The total return the fund has provided investors over the preceeding twelve months. This total return figure is computed based on the fund's dividend distributions and share price appreciation/depreciation during the period, net of the expenses and fees it imposes on its shareholders. Although the total return figure does not reflect an adjustment for any loads the fund may carry, such adjustments have been made in deriving TheStreet Investment Ratings.

9. 1-Year Total Return Percentile

The fund's percentile rank based on its one-year performance compared to that of all other equity funds in existence for at least one year. A score of 99 is the best possible, indicating that the fund outperformed 99% of the other mutual funds. Zero is the worst possible percentile score.

10. 3-Year Total Return

The total annual return the fund has provided investors over the preceeding three years.

11. 3-Year Total Return Percentile

The fund's percentile rank based on its three-year performance compared to that of all other equity funds in existence for at least three years. A score of 99 is the best possible, indicating that the fund outperformed 99% of the other mutual funds. Zero is the worst possible percentile score.

12. 5-Year Total Return

The total annual return the fund has provided investors over the preceeding five years.

13. 5-Year Total Return Percentile

The fund's percentile rank based on its five-year performance compared to that of all other equity funds in existence for at least five years. A score of 99 is the best possible, indicating that the fund outperformed 99% of the other mutual funds. Zero is the worst possible percentile score.

14. Risk Rating/Points

A letter grade rating based solely on the mutual fund's risk as determined by its monthly performance volatility over the trailing three years. The risk rating does not take into consideration the overall financial performance the fund has achieved or the total return it has provided to its shareholders. Like the overall Investment Rating, the Risk Rating is measured on a scale from A to E for ease of interpretation. The points score indicates where the Risk Rating falls on a scale of 0 to 10.

15. Manager Quality Percentile

The manager quality percentile is based on a ranking of the fund's alpha, a statistical measure representing the difference between a fund's actual returns and its expected performance given its level of risk. Fund managers who have been able to exceed the fund's statistically expected performance receive a high percentile rank with 99 representing the highest possible score. At the other end of the spectrum, fund managers who have actually detracted from the fund's expected performance receive a low percentile rank with 0 representing the lowest possible score.

16. Manager Tenure

The number of years the current manager has been managing the fund. Since fund managers who deliver substandard returns are usually replaced, a long tenure is usually a good sign that shareholders are satisfied that the fund is achieving its stated objectives.

Fund Type	Fund Name	Ticker Symbol	Overall Investment Rating	Phone	Net Asset Value As of 3/31/15	Performance Rating/Pts	Annualized Total Return Through 3/31/15			Risk Rating/Pts	Mgr. Quality Pct	Mgr. Tenure (Years)
							1Yr / Pct	3Yr / Pct	5Yr / Pct			
GL	Fidelity Freedom Index Income	FIKFX	C	(800) 544-8544	11.52	D- /1.1	3.83 /31	3.52 / 9	3.99 / 8	B+ / 9.9	71	6
AA	● Fidelity Adv Inc Replacement 2016	FRJAX	C-	(800) 522-7297	51.26	E+ /0.6	1.29 /19	2.56 / 7	3.72 / 7	B+ / 9.9	66	8
AA	Epiphany FFV Strat Income A	EPIAX	C-		10.58	E+ /0.6	3.42 /29	2.82 / 8	--	B+ / 9.9	71	5
GR	American Century Eqty Mkt Ntrl A	ALIAX	C-	(800) 345-6488	11.04	E /0.5	-0.72 /14	1.62 / 6	2.27 / 5	B+ / 9.9	74	10
IN	JPMorgan Research Market Neut A	JMNAX	C-	(800) 480-4111	14.65	E /0.5	1.32 /19	1.33 / 6	-0.41 / 2	B+ / 9.9	60	1
AA	JPMorgan Multi-Cap Mrkt Netral A	OGNAX	C-	(800) 480-4111	9.89	E /0.4	0.61 /17	0.51 / 5	-0.22 / 2	B+ / 9.9	46	2
AA	MFS Lifetime Income A	MLLAX	C	(800) 225-2606	12.27	D- /1.1	3.81 /31	5.06 /13	5.91 /16	B+ / 9.8	58	N/A
AA	● Fidelity Adv Inc Replacement 2018	FRKAX	C-	(800) 522-7297	55.15	E+ /0.9	2.99 /26	4.51 /12	5.13 /12	B+ / 9.8	65	8
OT	Merk Asian Currency Investor	MEAFX	C-	(866) 637-5386	9.50	E /0.5	0.74 /18	-0.07 / 4	0.24 / 3	B+ / 9.8	33	7
GI	Fidelity Freedom Index 2005	FJIFX	C	(800) 544-8544	12.71	D /1.6	4.87 /38	5.10 /13	5.60 /15	B+ / 9.7	61	N/A
AA	Transamerica Asst All Short Hrzn	DVCSX	C	(888) 233-4339	11.66	D- /1.2	3.43 /29	3.87 /10	4.97 /12	B+ / 9.7	74	19
GL	DFA Global Allocation 25/75 R2	DFGPX	C-	(800) 984-9472	12.84	D- /1.1	2.37 /23	3.91 /10	4.37 /10	B+ / 9.7	84	N/A
AA	Hatteras Alpha Hedged Strat NL	ALPHX	C	(877) 569-2382	11.64	E+ /0.8	0.17 /16	2.53 / 7	2.72 / 5	B+ / 9.7	32	N/A
AA	Pacific Financial Stg Csv Inv	PFLSX	C	(800) 637-1380	9.55	E+ /0.7	1.53 /20	2.00 / 6	2.89 / 6	B+ / 9.7	78	8
AA	RBB Free Market Fixed Income	FMFIX	C-	(888) 261-4073	10.29	E+ /0.6	1.45 /20	0.66 / 5	1.46 / 4	B+ / 9.7	72	8
IN	JPMorgan Market Neutral A	HSKAX	C-	(800) 480-4111	14.58	E /0.3	1.32 /19	-0.77 / 4	-1.53 / 2	B+ / 9.7	34	1
AA	Schwab MarketTrack Consv Port	SWCGX	C	(800) 407-0256	16.22	D /2.2	5.69 /44	6.73 /20	6.95 /23	B+ / 9.6	53	7
AA	Vanguard Target Retirement	VTINX	C	(800) 662-7447	13.09	D /2.0	5.71 /44	5.79 /16	6.70 /21	B+ / 9.6	71	12
GL	Schwab Monthly Income Fund	SWKRX	C	(800) 407-0256	11.33	D /1.9	5.67 /44	5.43 /15	6.06 /17	B+ / 9.6	77	N/A
GL	UBS Equity Lg-Sht Multi-Strategy A	BMNAX	C	(888) 793-8637	11.01	D /1.7	10.53 /76	5.56 /15	--	B+ / 9.6	94	N/A
GL	Schwab Monthly Income Fund	SWLRX	C	(800) 407-0256	10.50	D- /1.3	5.29 /41	3.85 /10	4.50 /10	B+ / 9.6	80	N/A
GL	PACE Alternatives Strat Invst A	PASIX	C-	(888) 793-8637	11.03	D- /1.2	5.35 /41	5.65 /15	4.14 / 9	B+ / 9.6	89	9
AA	Fidelity Adv Inc Replacement 2020	FILAX	C	(800) 522-7297	56.35	D- /1.2	4.07 /32	5.83 /16	6.11 /17	B+ / 9.6	60	8
AA	SEI Asset Alloc-Defensive Strat A	SNSAX	C-	(800) 342-5734	9.82	E+ /0.8	2.18 /23	2.05 / 6	2.45 / 5	B+ / 9.6	69	N/A
GI	TIAA-CREF Lifecycle Idx Ret Inc	TRCIX	C+	(800) 842-2252	13.26	D+ /2.4	6.25 /49	6.67 /20	7.28 /25	B+ / 9.5	77	6
GR	Schwab Target 2010	SWBRX	C	(800) 407-0256	12.48	D /2.2	5.76 /44	6.85 /21	7.21 /24	B+ / 9.5	73	10
AA	Fidelity Adv Inc Replacement 2022	FRAMX	C	(800) 522-7297	58.70	D /1.6	4.76 /37	6.82 /20	6.83 /22	B+ / 9.5	56	8
GI	Fidelity Freedom K Income	FFKAX	C-	(800) 544-8544	12.01	D- /1.3	4.28 /34	4.37 /11	4.79 /11	B+ / 9.5	75	N/A
AA	Transamerica Inst Asst All Sht Hrz	DISHX	C-	(888) 233-4339	11.19	D- /1.3	3.92 /31	4.24 /11	5.34 /13	B+ / 9.5	78	19
GL	Guggenheim Multi-Hedge Strat A	RYMQX	C-	(800) 820-0888	24.59	D- /1.2	8.79 /68	3.40 / 9	4.03 / 8	B+ / 9.5	88	10
AA	Transamerica Multi-Mgr Alter Strg	IMUAX	C-	(888) 233-4339	10.61	E+ /0.9	4.86 /38	4.17 /11	3.65 / 7	B+ / 9.5	56	N/A
GI	AdvisorOne CLS Enh Long/Short N	CLEIX	C-	(866) 811-0225	10.45	E+ /0.9	0.74 /18	3.29 / 8	3.85 / 8	B+ / 9.5	39	6
IN	Glenmede Long/Short Portfolio	GTAPX	C	(800) 442-8299	11.31	D+ /2.4	4.72 /37	6.70 /20	6.10 /17	B+ / 9.4	76	9
GI	Fidelity Freedom Index 2010	FKIFX	C	(800) 544-8544	13.36	D /2.2	5.36 /41	6.40 /18	6.76 /22	B+ / 9.4	55	N/A
BA	New Covenant Balanced Income	NCBIX	C	(877) 835-4531	21.36	D /2.1	6.38 /50	5.93 /16	6.39 /19	B+ / 9.4	53	N/A
GI	Sterling Capital Strat Alloc Csv A	BCGAX	C	(800) 228-1872	10.81	D /1.6	6.30 /49	6.64 /20	6.71 /21	B+ / 9.4	77	N/A
AA	American Century One Chc	AONIX	C-	(800) 345-6488	11.90	D- /1.4	4.42 /34	4.62 /12	5.47 /14	B+ / 9.4	59	11
BA	Fidelity Freedom Income	FFFAX	C-	(800) 544-8544	11.75	D- /1.3	4.31 /34	4.35 /11	4.76 /11	B+ / 9.4	64	10
AA	Oppenheimer Conservative Inv A	OACIX	C-	(888) 470-0862	9.17	D- /1.1	4.32 /34	5.28 /14	5.90 /16	B+ / 9.4	39	10
GI	Praxis Genesis Conservative A	MCONX	C-	(800) 977-2947	11.47	D- /1.1	5.63 /43	5.52 /15	5.89 /16	B+ / 9.4	79	N/A
AA	Fidelity Adv Freedom Income A	FAFAX	C-	(800) 522-7297	11.07	E+ /0.8	3.63 /30	3.94 /10	4.44 /10	B+ / 9.4	59	12
AA	Vanguard LifeStrategy Consv Gr	VSCGX	C+	(800) 662-7447	18.74	D+ /2.9	7.11 /56	7.36 /23	7.31 /25	B+ / 9.3	67	N/A
AA	TIAA-CREF Lifecycle Index 2010	TLTRX	C+	(800) 842-2252	13.88	D+ /2.9	6.53 /51	7.50 /24	7.82 /29	B+ / 9.3	50	6
AA	American Century One Chc Conv	AOCIX	C+	(800) 345-6488	13.68	D+ /2.8	6.00 /46	7.39 /23	7.88 /29	B+ / 9.3	49	N/A
AA	Vanguard Target Retirement 2010	VTENX	C+	(800) 662-7447	26.81	D+ /2.6	6.12 /48	7.02 /21	7.63 /27	B+ / 9.3	61	9
AA	Fidelity Freedom 2005	FFFVX	C	(800) 544-8544	12.24	D /2.0	5.26 /41	5.89 /16	6.18 /18	B+ / 9.3	47	10
AA	Fidelity Adv Inc Replacement 2024	FRNAX	C	(800) 522-7297	59.25	D /1.9	5.23 /40	7.56 /24	7.36 /25	B+ / 9.3	52	8
AA	JPMorgan Investor Conserv Gr A	OICAX	C-	(800) 480-4111	12.88	D- /1.5	4.85 /37	6.06 /17	6.05 /17	B+ / 9.3	54	19
AA	MFS Conservative Alloc A	MACFX	C-	(800) 225-2606	14.95	D- /1.4	4.37 /34	6.41 /19	7.05 /23	B+ / 9.3	47	13
AA	SEI Asset Alloc-Cons Strat A	SVSAX	C-	(800) 342-5734	10.46	D- /1.2	3.39 /28	4.07 /10	4.44 /10	B+ / 9.3	73	12
GR	Oppenheimer Flexible Strategies A	QVOPX	C-	(888) 470-0862	26.85	D- /1.2	4.57 /36	5.72 /16	3.48 / 7	B+ / 9.3	88	4
AA	Wilmington Strat Alloc Conserv A	WCAAX	C-	(800) 336-9970	10.96	E+ /0.8	3.19 /27	3.67 / 9	4.58 /10	B+ / 9.3	51	N/A

● Denotes fund is closed to new investors

Fund Type	Fund Name	Ticker Symbol	Overall Investment Rating	Phone	Net Asset Value As of 3/31/15	Performance Rating/Pts	1Yr / Pct	3Yr / Pct	5Yr / Pct	Risk Rating/Pts	Mgr. Quality Pct	Mgr. Tenure (Years)
GR	Absolute Strategies R	ASFAX	D+	(800) 754-8757	10.88	E /0.4	-0.18 /15	-0.52 / 4	0.50 / 3	B+ / 9.3	82	N/A
AA	TIAA-CREF Lifecycle Index 2015	TLGRX	C+	(800) 842-2252	14.36	C- /3.3	6.67 /52	8.18 /28	8.29 /32	B+ / 9.2	44	6
GL	Schwab Monthly Income Fund	SWJRX	C	(800) 407-0256	11.39	D+ /2.6	6.14 /48	6.96 /21	7.25 /25	B+ / 9.2	75	N/A
GL	Fidelity Freedom Index 2015	FLIFX	C	(800) 544-8544	13.62	D+ /2.5	5.87 /45	6.87 /21	7.09 /24	B+ / 9.2	61	6
BA	Madison Diversified Income A	MBLAX	C	(800) 877-6089	14.91	D+ /2.4	5.61 /43	8.62 /31	9.15 /38	B+ / 9.2	60	17
AA	Fidelity Adv Inc Replacement 2026	FIOAX	C	(800) 522-7297	60.45	D /2.2	5.56 /43	8.08 /27	7.71 /28	B+ / 9.2	50	8
BA	Bridgeway Managed Volatility Fund	BRBPX	C	(800) 661-3550	14.23	D /2.1	4.77 /37	6.31 /18	5.83 /16	B+ / 9.2	75	14
AA	Vanguard LifeStrategy Income Inv	VASIX	C	(800) 662-7447	15.13	D /2.0	6.66 /52	5.32 /14	5.77 /16	B+ / 9.2	82	N/A
AA	Wells Fargo Adv DJ Tgt 2010 C	WFOCX	C-	(800) 222-8222	13.33	E+ /0.8	1.42 /20	2.24 / 7	3.58 / 7	B+ / 9.2	38	9
AA	Wells Fargo Adv DJ Tgt Today C	WFODX	C-	(800) 222-8222	11.06	E+ /0.7	1.16 /19	1.57 / 6	3.05 / 6	B+ / 9.2	40	9
GI	Kinetics Alternative Inc Advisor A	KWIAX	D+	(800) 930-3828	89.92	E+ /0.6	1.67 /21	3.31 / 8	1.39 / 4	B+ / 9.2	63	5
IX	State Farm Equity & Bond Legacy	SLBAX	B+	(800) 447-4930	11.43	C /5.1	11.67 /81	11.39 /48	10.04 /45	B+ / 9.1	84	N/A
AA	Vanguard Target Retirement 2015	VTXVX	C+	(800) 662-7447	15.60	C- /3.4	6.84 /54	8.49 /30	8.56 /34	B+ / 9.1	47	12
GL	Frost Moderate Allocation Inv	FASTX	C+	(866) 777-7818	12.84	D+ /2.8	6.53 /51	8.41 /29	7.43 /26	B+ / 9.1	92	9
GI	Sterling Capital Strat Alloc Bal A	BAMGX	C	(800) 228-1872	10.91	D+ /2.5	7.11 /56	8.39 /29	7.68 /28	B+ / 9.1	65	N/A
AA	Fidelity Adv Inc Replacement 2028	FARPX	C	(800) 522-7297	61.52	D+ /2.4	5.77 /44	8.45 /30	7.97 /30	B+ / 9.1	47	8
AA	Putnam Retirement Ready 2020 A	PRRMX	C	(800) 225-1581	19.11	D /1.9	6.21 /48	7.21 /22	6.68 /21	B+ / 9.1	71	N/A
AA	MFS Lifetime 2020 A	MFLAX	C	(800) 225-2606	13.45	D /1.8	4.45 /35	7.34 /23	8.02 /30	B+ / 9.1	38	10
BA	JPMorgan Smart Ret Inc A	JSRAX	C-	(800) 480-4111	17.85	D /1.6	5.53 /43	6.20 /18	6.68 /21	B+ / 9.1	46	9
AA	Fidelity Adv Freedom 2005 A	FFAVX	C-	(800) 522-7297	12.10	D- /1.2	4.60 /36	5.45 /15	5.89 /16	B+ / 9.1	40	12
AA	Putnam Retirement Ready 2015 A	PRRHX	C-	(800) 225-1581	18.43	D- /1.2	4.67 /36	5.45 /15	5.17 /13	B+ / 9.1	75	N/A
GR	JPMorgan Research Equity L/S A	JLSAX	C-	(800) 480-4111	16.73	D- /1.0	3.14 /27	5.34 /14	--	B+ / 9.1	51	1
AA	Touchstone Conservative Alloc A	TSAAX	C-	(800) 543-0407	11.14	E+ /0.9	2.50 /24	4.53 /12	5.13 /13	B+ / 9.1	50	N/A
GL	Nationwide Inv Dest Cons A	NDCAX	C-	(800) 848-0920	10.27	E+ /0.8	3.52 /29	3.78 /10	4.23 / 9	B+ / 9.1	75	N/A
AA	Nuveen Tactical Market Opps I	FGTYX	D+	(800) 257-8787	10.59	E /0.5	0.83 /18	-0.15 / 4	2.38 / 5	B+ / 9.1	43	6
BA	James Adv Bal Goldn Rainbow	GLRBX	C+	(888) 426-7640	25.24	C- /3.7	7.39 /58	8.74 /31	9.45 /40	B+ / 9.0	51	24
AA	Vanguard Wellesley Income Inv	VWINX	C+	(800) 662-7447	25.72	C- /3.2	6.63 /52	8.25 /28	9.19 /38	B / 9.0	83	8
BA	J Hancock VIT Lifestyle Bal I	JELBX	C	(800) 257-3336	14.17	D+ /2.9	4.93 /38	7.78 /26	7.81 /29	B+ / 9.0	35	N/A
GL	Fidelity Freedom Index 2020	FPIFX	C	(800) 544-8544	14.10	D+ /2.8	6.18 /48	7.36 /23	7.58 /27	B+ / 9.0	57	6
AA	Fidelity Freedom 2010	FFFCX	C	(800) 544-8544	15.74	D+ /2.7	5.84 /45	7.19 /22	7.28 /25	B+ / 9.0	36	10
AA	Voya Retirement Moderate Adv	IRMPX	C	(800) 992-0180	12.93	D+ /2.6	5.78 /45	7.09 /22	7.25 /25	B+ / 9.0	33	9
AA	Fidelity Adv Inc Replacement 2030	FRQAX	C	(800) 522-7297	61.08	D+ /2.6	5.90 /46	8.73 /31	8.17 /31	B+ / 9.0	46	8
GI	Westwood Income Opportunity A	WWIAX	C	(877) 386-3944	14.70	D+ /2.6	6.53 /51	8.86 /32	9.56 /41	B+ / 9.0	78	10
GI	American Century OneChoice	ARBMX	C	(800) 345-6488	12.28	D /2.1	5.78 /45	7.83 /26	8.26 /32	B+ / 9.0	63	7
AA	Principal LifeTime 2010 A	PENAX	C	(800) 222-5852	13.80	D /2.0	5.01 /39	7.19 /22	7.60 /27	B+ / 9.0	42	10
AA	J Hancock II Ret Choices at 2020 1	JRWOX	C	(800) 257-3336	12.24	D /2.0	5.03 /39	5.95 /17	--	B+ / 9.0	52	5
AA	T Rowe Price Retire Balanced	TRRIX	C	(800) 638-5660	15.01	D /1.9	3.96 /32	6.06 /17	6.51 /20	B+ / 9.0	34	13
GI	Oppenheimer Capital Income A	OPPEX	C-	(888) 470-0862	9.90	D /1.8	4.50 /35	7.32 /23	7.77 /28	B+ / 9.0	90	6
GL	Russell Mod Strategy A	RMLAX	C-	(800) 832-6688	11.87	D- /1.2	4.41 /34	5.55 /15	6.04 /17	B+ / 9.0	56	N/A
AA	Deutsche LifeCompass Retirement	SUCAX	C-	(800) 728-3337	12.68	D- /1.2	4.06 /32	5.77 /16	5.80 /16	B+ / 9.0	31	2
AA	AB Consv Wealth Strat A	ABPAX	C-	(800) 221-5672	12.52	D- /1.1	4.43 /35	4.70 /12	4.92 /12	B+ / 9.0	38	N/A
AA	Putnam Ret Income Fd Lifestyle 1	PRMAX	C-	(800) 225-1581	17.70	D- /1.1	4.28 /34	4.68 /12	4.26 / 9	B+ / 9.0	78	N/A
AA	Wells Fargo Adv DJ Tgt 2015 Inv	WFQEX	C-	(800) 222-8222	10.49	D- /1.1	2.63 /25	4.01 /10	5.15 /13	B+ / 9.0	40	N/A
GR	ASTON/Lake Partners LASSO	ALSNX	C-	(800) 992-8151	13.18	D- /1.1	0.92 /18	4.35 /11	4.21 / 9	B+ / 9.0	45	N/A
AA	J Hancock II Ret Choices at 2010 1	JRTOX	C-	(800) 257-3336	11.20	D- /1.0	3.28 /28	3.13 / 8	--	B+ / 9.0	78	3
GL	Russell Cons Strat A	RCLAX	C-	(800) 832-6688	10.89	E+ /0.8	3.53 /29	4.04 /10	4.86 /11	B+ / 9.0	69	N/A
AA	Nationwide Retirement Inc A	NWRAX	D+	(800) 848-0920	9.69	E+ /0.8	3.84 /31	3.57 / 9	3.67 / 7	B+ / 9.0	30	N/A
GR	EAS Crow Point Alternatives A	EASAX	D+		9.01	E+ /0.7	2.32 /23	3.38 / 9	2.22 / 5	B+ / 9.0	32	6

Fund Type	Fund Name	Ticker Symbol	Overall Investment Rating	Phone	Net Asset Value As of 3/31/15	Performance Rating/Pts	Annualized Total Return Through 3/31/15			Risk Rating/Pts	Mgr. Quality Pct	Mgr. Tenure (Years)
							1Yr / Pct	3Yr / Pct	5Yr / Pct			
SC	ProFunds-Ultra Short Small-Cap	UCPSX	E-	(888) 776-3637	18.95	E- /0.0	-24.05 / 1	-34.34 / 0	-37.51 / 0	E- / 0.0	1	2
MC	ProFunds-Ultra Short Mid-Cap Svc	UIPSX	E-	(888) 776-3637	4.45	E- /0.0	-26.81 / 0	-33.27 / 0	-35.19 / 0	E- / 0.0	2	2
PM	First Eagle Gold A	SGGDX	E-	(800) 334-2143	13.94	E- /0.0	-15.36 / 2	-20.76 / 0	-9.95 / 0	E- / 0.0	6	2
AG	Rydex Inv NASDAQ 100 2x Stgy A	RYVTX	E-	(800) 820-0888	19.36	E- /0.0	-37.04 / 0	-32.89 / 0	-36.00 / 0	E- / 0.0	2	15
FO	Profunds-Ultra Short Japan Svc	UKPSX	E-	(888) 776-3637	14.07	E- /0.0	-48.02 / 0	-44.85 / 0	-33.50 / 0	E- / 0.0	0	6
EM	ProFunds-Ultra Sh Intl Svc	UXPSX	E-	(888) 776-3637	22.16	E- /0.0	-6.18 / 4	-23.68 / 0	-24.93 / 0	E- / 0.0	0	6
FO	Direxion Mo Latin America Bl 2X	DXZLX	E-	(800) 851-0511	16.84	E- /0.0	-39.14 / 0	-29.99 / 0	-21.45 / 0	E- / 0.0	0	9
GR	Direxion Mo S&P 500 Bear 2X Inv	DXSSX	E-	(800) 851-0511	29.20	E- /0.0	-24.53 / 0	-29.46 / 0	-29.11 / 0	E- / 0.0	12	9
SC	Rydex Inv Rusl 2000 2x Strtgy A	RYIUX	E-	(800) 820-0888	25.05	E- /0.0	-23.39 / 1	-33.63 / 0	-36.31 / 0	E- / 0.0	1	9
FO	Profunds-Ultra Short China Svc	UHPSX	E-	(888) 776-3637	15.59	E- /0.0	-29.33 / 0	-29.92 / 0	-27.95 / 0	E- / 0.0	0	6
GR	ProFunds Ultra Short	USPSX	E-	(888) 776-3637	12.53	E- /0.0	-38.26 / 0	-33.95 / 0	-36.81 / 0	E- / 0.0	2	2
GR	ProFunds-Ultra Bear Svc	URPSX	E-	(888) 776-3637	5.31	E- /0.0	-26.14 / 0	-31.22 / 0	-31.57 / 0	E- / 0.0	3	6
PM	Van Eck Intl Investors Gold A	INIVX	E-	(800) 826-1115	7.57	E- /0.0	-22.28 / 1	-25.00 / 0	-13.24 / 0	E- / 0.0	3	19
SC	Direxion Mo Small Cap Bear 2X Inv	DXRSX	E-	(800) 851-0511	30.75	E- /0.0	-23.07 / 1	-32.50 / 0	-33.42 / 0	E- / 0.0	2	11
GR	Direxion Mo Natural Res Bull 2X	DXCLX	E-	(800) 851-0511	44.17	E- /0.1	-31.90 / 0	-7.80 / 1	-3.71 / 1	E- / 0.0	0	10
FO	Direxion Mo Emerg Mkts Bull 2X	DXELX	E-	(800) 851-0511	44.35	E- /0.2	-5.58 / 5	-6.66 / 1	-6.60 / 1	E- / 0.0	0	10
EM	Profunds-Ultra Sh Emer Mkt Svc	UVPSX	E-	(888) 776-3637	8.82	E- /0.2	-8.60 / 3	-5.44 / 2	-12.91 / 0	E- / 0.0	15	6
EM	Rydex Inverse Emg Mkts 2x Str A	RYWWX	E-	(800) 820-0888	16.88	E- /0.2	-7.96 / 3	-4.33 / 2	--	E- / 0.0	25	5
GL	Schroder Global Multi-Cp Eq R6	SQQIX	E-	(800) 464-3108	12.03	C- /3.7	2.48 /24	10.55 /43	--	E- / 0.0	89	5
FO	Profunds-Ultra China Svc	UGPSX	E+	(888) 776-3637	11.71	C+ /5.8	13.47 /88	12.38 /55	2.13 / 5	E- / 0.0	12	6
SC	Turner Small Cap Growth Fund	TSCEX	D-	(800) 224-6312	18.77	B- /7.3	7.48 /59	14.20 /69	13.54 /73	E- / 0.0	37	2
RE	PIMCO RealEstate RlRetrn Str A	PETAX	D+	(800) 426-0107	3.82	A /9.3	29.19 /99	13.54 /64	20.71 /99	E- / 0.0	5	8
GR	Direxion Mo NASDAQ-100 Bull 2X	DXQLX	C-	(800) 851-0511	56.64	A+ /9.9	43.73 /99	33.97 /99	34.51 /99	E- / 0.0	33	9
FO	ProFunds-Ultra Sh Latin America	UFPSX	D+	(888) 776-3637	19.84	A+ /9.9	41.00 /99	18.71 /96	-3.41 / 1	E- / 0.0	99	6
FO	Direxion Mo China Bull 2X Inv	DXHLX	D+	(800) 851-0511	49.79	A+ /9.9	57.81 /99	15.03 /75	0.37 / 3	E- / 0.0	55	8
SC	Direxion Mo Small Cap Bull 2X Inv	DXRLX	C-	(800) 851-0511	53.18	A+ /9.9	13.04 /87	30.96 /99	25.33 /99	E- / 0.0	24	11
FO	ProFunds-Ultra Japan Svc	UJPSX	C-	(888) 776-3637	19.22	A+ /9.9	55.50 /99	37.64 /99	12.68 /66	E- / 0.0	99	6
AA	● Lifetime Achievement	LFTAX	E-	(888) 339-4230	18.08	C- /3.3	2.56 /24	9.78 /38	9.06 /37	E- / 0.1	4	15
SC	Turner Emerging Growth Inv	TMCGX	E+	(800) 224-6312	31.34	C+ /6.5	2.57 /24	13.75 /65	14.22 /80	E- / 0.1	41	N/A
SC	● Universal Inst Small Co Growth II	USIIX	D-	(800) 869-6397	17.11	B- /7.2	-5.22 / 5	16.36 /86	14.94 /86	E- / 0.1	34	12
GI	PIMCO StockPlus Long Duration	PSLDX	C-	(800) 426-0107	7.56	A+ /9.9	29.07 /99	24.14 /99	24.94 /99	E- / 0.1	98	8
GR	ProFunds-Ultra Short Dow 30 Svc	UWPSX	E-	(888) 776-3637	5.82	E- /0.0	-23.62 / 1	-27.30 / 0	-29.26 / 0	E- / 0.2	38	2
PM	Rydex Precious Metal A	RYMNX	E-	(800) 820-0888	24.28	E- /0.0	-28.13 / 0	-25.99 / 0	-15.48 / 0	E- / 0.2	1	22
PM	American Century Global Gold A	ACGGX	E-	(800) 345-6488	7.21	E- /0.0	-22.95 / 1	-26.63 / 0	-14.43 / 0	E- / 0.2	1	23
AG	Rydex Inv S&P 500 2x Strategy A	RYTMX	E-	(800) 820-0888	23.87	E- /0.0	-25.38 / 0	-29.97 / 0	-30.46 / 0	E / 0.3	7	15
PM	Tocqueville Gold	TGLDX	E-	(800) 697-3863	30.05	E- /0.0	-21.15 / 1	-24.24 / 0	-11.44 / 0	E / 0.3	2	18
GR	Janus Adviser Forty A	JDCAX	D+	(800) 295-2687	32.41	A /9.3	19.89 /97	16.68 /88	12.55 /64	E / 0.3	72	2
PM	Gabelli Gold A	GLDAX	E-	(800) 422-3554	10.37	E- /0.0	-17.70 / 1	-22.74 / 0	-12.33 / 0	E / 0.4	11	21
PM	Fidelity Adv Gold A	FGDAX	E-	(800) 522-7297	15.92	E- /0.0	-21.15 / 1	-26.59 / 0	-15.06 / 0	E / 0.4	2	8
PM	Deutsche Gold & Prec Metals Fund	SGDAX	E-	(800) 728-3337	5.65	E- /0.0	-25.36 / 0	-27.39 / 0	-16.45 / 0	E / 0.4	2	4
EM	ProFunds-Ultra Intl Svc	UNPSX	E-	(888) 776-3637	14.91	C- /3.4	-8.47 / 3	10.50 /42	2.59 / 5	E / 0.4	98	6
MC	Turner Midcap Growth Inv	TMGFX	E+	(800) 224-6312	23.75	C+ /6.3	8.59 /67	12.77 /58	12.29 /62	E / 0.4	12	7
MC	TCM Small Mid Cap Growth	TCMMX	D+	(800) 536-3230	16.90	A /9.3	14.24 /90	17.06 /90	14.73 /85	E / 0.4	42	8
SC	Dreyfus/Boston Co Sm Cap Growth	SSETX	D+	(800) 221-4795	39.21	A /9.4	9.15 /70	17.40 /92	15.41 /90	E / 0.4	79	N/A
AG	Rydex Inv Dow 2x Strategy A	RYIDX	E-	(800) 820-0888	30.36	E- /0.0	-22.85 / 1	-26.18 / 0	-28.42 / 0	E / 0.5	59	7
MC	TCW Growth Equities N	TGDNX	E+	(800) 386-3829	12.48	C+ /5.9	6.53 /51	12.11 /53	11.43 /56	E / 0.5	4	3
SC	● AMG Frontier Small Cap Growth	MSSVX	D+	(800) 835-3879	15.66	A- /9.2	10.34 /76	16.61 /87	14.90 /86	E / 0.5	71	6
MC	Alger SMidCap Growth I2	AAMOX	C-	(800) 254-3796	8.00	A+ /9.7	9.44 /72	20.36 /98	16.79 /95	E / 0.5	75	7
GR	Janus Aspen Forty Inst	JACAX	C-	(800) 295-2687	43.43	A+ /9.7	20.22 /97	16.98 /90	12.83 /67	E / 0.5	79	2
SC	ProFunds-Internet UltraSector Svc	INPSX	C-	(888) 776-3637	33.00	A+ /9.9	10.72 /77	27.61 /99	25.30 /99	E / 0.5	93	2
OT	Rydex Commodities Strgy A	RYMEX	E-	(800) 820-0888	9.01	E- /0.0	-41.00 / 0	-18.52 / 0	-9.92 / 0	E+ / 0.6	0	10
PM	USAA Precious Mtls&Minerals	USAGX	E-	(800) 382-8722	11.32	E- /0.0	-22.99 / 1	-27.15 / 0	-15.55 / 0	E+ / 0.6	1	7

● Denotes fund is closed to new investors

Fund Type	Fund Name	Ticker Symbol	Overall Investment Rating	Phone	Net Asset Value As of 3/31/15	Performance Rating/Pts	1Yr / Pct	3Yr / Pct	5Yr / Pct	Risk Rating/Pts	Mgr. Quality Pct	Mgr. Tenure (Years)
	99 Pct = Best *0 Pct = Worst*							Annualized Total Return Through 3/31/15		RISK	FUND MGR	
PM	OCM Gold Fund Investor	OCMGX	E-	(800) 628-9403	9.29	E- /0.0	-19.86 / 1	-23.46 / 0	-12.23 / 0	E+ / 0.6	5	19
SC	Jacob Micro Cap Growth Inv	JMCGX	E	(888) 522-6239	17.25	C- /3.6	4.49 /35	8.03 /27	12.83 /67	E+ / 0.6	6	3
SC	Eagle Smaller Company A	EGEAX	E+	(800) 421-4184	13.24	C /5.1	3.10 /27	13.10 /60	12.90 /67	E+ / 0.6	47	N/A
RE	Ell Global Property Inst	EIIGX	E+	(888) 323-8912	9.74	C /5.3	11.72 /81	9.63 /37	10.15 /46	E+ / 0.6	47	9
MC	Wasatch Ultra Growth Investor	WAMCX	D-	(800) 551-1700	20.43	B- /7.2	7.05 /55	14.06 /68	15.17 /88	E+ / 0.6	13	3
SC	Sentinel Small Company Fd A	SAGWX	D-	(800) 282-3863	5.80	B- /7.3	11.40 /80	15.29 /77	15.31 /89	E+ / 0.6	88	3
PM	Oppenheimer Gold/Spec Min A	OPGSX	E-	(888) 470-0862	12.82	E- /0.0	-25.08 / 0	-27.27 / 0	-15.68 / 0	E+ / 0.7	1	18
PM	Wells Fargo Adv Precious Mtls A	EKWAX	E-	(800) 222-8222	28.99	E- /0.0	-20.90 / 1	-24.56 / 0	-13.26 / 0	E+ / 0.7	2	8
PM	US Global Inv Gold & PMetals Fd	USERX	E-	(800) 873-8637	5.28	E- /0.0	-21.31 / 1	-24.65 / 0	-14.87 / 0	E+ / 0.7	2	26
PM	Invesco Gold and Precious Mtls A	IGDAX	E-	(800) 959-4246	3.60	E- /0.0	-21.40 / 1	-23.54 / 0	-12.23 / 0	E+ / 0.7	2	2
SC	Alger Small Cap Growth Inst R	ASIRX	E+	(800) 254-3796	22.84	C+ /6.1	6.23 /48	12.12 /53	11.89 /60	E+ / 0.7	22	14
SC	BlackRock Small Cap Gr Equity Inv	CSGEX	D-	(800) 441-7762	15.74	C+ /6.2	7.67 /60	14.14 /68	13.69 /75	E+ / 0.7	21	2
SC	Frontier Netols Small Cap Value Y	FNSYX	D-	(888) 825-2100	10.99	C+ /6.9	5.16 /40	14.43 /70	12.42 /63	E+ / 0.7	41	10
MC	Westcore MIDCO Growth Rtl	WTMGX	D-	(800) 392-2673	5.73	C+ /6.9	7.68 /60	13.98 /67	13.51 /73	E+ / 0.7	14	10
GR	RidgeWorth Lrg-Cap Growth Stock	STCIX	D-	(888) 784-3863	8.75	B- /7.3	14.83 /91	14.68 /72	15.15 /88	E+ / 0.7	36	8
PM	ProFunds Short Precious Metals	SPPSX	D	(888) 776-3637	10.19	B /8.1	17.80 /95	14.49 /71	2.15 / 5	E+ / 0.7	57	2
PM	Vanguard Prec Metals & Mining Inv	VGPMX	E-	(800) 662-7447	8.68	E- /0.0	-20.37 / 1	-22.27 / 0	-13.00 / 0	E+ / 0.8	1	2
GR	Neuberger Berman Lg Cap Disp Gr	NLDAX	E	(800) 877-9700	4.00	C- /3.3	8.29 /65	9.75 /38	9.67 /42	E+ / 0.8	7	16
SC	AlphaMark Small Cap Growth Fund	AMSCX	E+	(866) 420-3350	12.32	C /5.1	7.52 /59	11.26 /47	14.60 /83	E+ / 0.8	45	7
SC	RidgeWorth Sm Cap Gr Stock A	SCGIX	D-	(888) 784-3863	13.23	C+ /6.2	4.21 /33	14.39 /70	13.98 /78	E+ / 0.8	37	8
SC	● Dreyfus/Boston Co Sm Cap Value I	STSVX	D-	(800) 221-4795	24.43	C+ /6.3	1.84 /21	14.22 /69	12.44 /64	E+ / 0.8	44	15
GR	● Wasatch Heritage Growth Investor	WAHGX	D-	(800) 551-1700	6.40	C+ /6.4	9.33 /71	13.00 /60	13.53 /73	E+ / 0.8	17	11
GR	Meridian Growth Legacy	MERDX	D-	(800) 446-6662	37.27	C+ /6.7	13.86 /89	12.77 /58	15.13 /88	E+ / 0.8	34	2
SC	Wells Fargo Adv Sm Cp Opp Adm	NVSOX	D+	(800) 222-8222	25.19	A- /9.0	11.75 /82	16.49 /87	13.70 /75	E+ / 0.8	89	12
SC	● Lord Abbett Developing Growth A	LAGWX	C-	(888) 522-2388	23.78	A /9.4	8.78 /68	19.61 /97	18.95 /98	E+ / 0.8	86	14
EM	US Global Investors Em Europe	EUROX	E-	(800) 873-8637	6.18	E- /0.1	-21.23 / 1	-10.60 / 1	-7.43 / 1	E+ / 0.9	1	18
GR	Nationwide HighMark Large Cp Gr	NWGLX	E+	(800) 848-0920	8.79	C /4.8	12.47 /85	11.40 /48	11.73 /59	E+ / 0.9	33	2
SC	Deutsche Small Cap Value A	KDSAX	E+	(800) 728-3337	26.48	C /5.1	4.95 /38	12.64 /57	10.16 /46	E+ / 0.9	28	2
GR	Columbia Global Infrastructure A	RRIAX	E+	(800) 345-6611	16.36	C+ /5.6	3.59 /29	15.00 /75	12.04 /61	E+ / 0.9	23	8
MC	Calamos Growth A	CVGRX	E+	(800) 582-6959	42.67	C+ /5.9	13.20 /87	12.28 /54	11.79 /59	E+ / 0.9	18	25
SC	TCW Small Cap Growth N	TGSNX	D-	(800) 386-3829	28.70	C+ /6.5	9.10 /70	12.09 /53	10.08 /45	E+ / 0.9	5	3
SC	Rice Hall James Small Cap Port	RHJMX	D	(866) 777-7818	13.98	B /8.1	10.56 /77	14.61 /72	17.10 /96	E+ / 0.9	49	19
MC	Principal MidCp Grw R3	PFPPX	C-	(800) 222-5852	7.17	A+ /9.6	16.80 /94	17.46 /92	15.99 /93	E+ / 0.9	73	N/A
EN	JPMorgan Glbl Natural Resources	JGNAX	E-	(800) 480-4111	7.03	E- /0.0	-26.74 / 0	-17.79 / 0	--	D- / 1.0	0	5
FO	Deutsche Latin America Equity A	SLANX	E-	(800) 728-3337	21.04	E- /0.1	-19.29 / 1	-9.39 / 1	-6.33 / 1	D- / 1.0	0	2
SC	Royce Low Priced Stock Svc	RYLPX	E-	(800) 221-4268	9.51	E /0.5	-4.81 / 6	0.91 / 5	4.26 / 9	D- / 1.0	1	2
SC	Schneider Small Cap Value	SCMVX	E-	(888) 520-3277	12.77	E+ /0.9	-16.23 / 2	7.75 /26	5.34 /13	D- / 1.0	3	17
FO	Frost International Equity Inv	FANTX	E-	(866) 777-7818	7.27	D- /1.2	1.57 /20	5.28 /14	4.54 /10	D- / 1.0	27	13
GR	AdvisorOne CLS Domestic Equity	CLDEX	E+	(866) 811-0225	9.26	C /4.8	9.54 /72	10.39 /42	10.02 /45	D- / 1.0	16	2
SC	● Columbia Small Cap Growth I A	CGOAX	E+	(800) 345-6611	27.25	C /5.1	3.19 /27	11.98 /52	12.40 /63	D- / 1.0	9	9
SC	Westport Select Cap R	WPSRX	E+	(888) 593-7878	18.24	C /5.4	5.03 /39	12.49 /56	10.34 /47	D- / 1.0	28	18
GR	Transparent Value LgCp Aggr A	TVAAX	E+	(888) 727-6885	7.54	C+ /5.6	8.24 /65	13.57 /64	--	D- / 1.0	5	5
SC	Lord Abbett Small Cap Value F	LRSFX	E+	(888) 522-2388	27.50	C+ /5.9	5.87 /45	12.19 /54	11.75 /59	D- / 1.0	34	2
GR	Transparent Value LgCp Market A	TVMAX	D-	(888) 727-6885	10.37	C+ /6.2	8.84 /68	14.61 /72	--	D- / 1.0	24	5
GR	Wells Fargo Adv Cap Gr A	WFCGX	D-	(800) 222-8222	17.14	C+ /6.3	12.80 /86	14.30 /69	13.65 /75	D- / 1.0	41	11
SC	Nuveen Small Cap Select A	EMGRX	D-	(800) 257-8787	11.57	C+ /6.3	10.83 /78	13.37 /62	13.56 /74	D- / 1.0	32	7
FO	Columbia Greater China A	NGCAX	D-	(800) 345-6611	39.44	C+ /6.5	17.38 /95	11.89 /52	6.20 /18	D- / 1.0	93	10
GR	Westcore Growth Rtl	WTEIX	D-	(800) 392-2673	13.30	C+ /6.9	12.79 /86	13.22 /61	13.41 /72	D- / 1.0	31	11

Section VII

Top-Rated
Stock Mutual Funds
by Risk Category

A compilation of those

Equity Mutual Funds

receiving the highest TheStreet Investment Ratings

within each risk grade.

Funds are listed in order by Overall Investment Rating.

Section VII Contents

This section contains a summary analysis of the top 100 rated stock mutual funds within each risk grade. Based on your personal risk tolerance, each page shows those funds that have achieved the best financial performance over the past three years.

In order to optimize the utility of our top and bottom fund lists, rather than listing all funds in a multi-class series, a single fund from each series is selected for display as the primary share class. Whenever possible, the selected fund is one that a retail investor would be most likely to choose. This share class may not be appropriate for every investor, so please consult with your financial advisor, the fund company, and the fund's prospectus before placing your trade.

Take the Investor Profile Quiz in the Appendix for assistance in determining your own risk tolerance level. Then you can use this section to identify those funds that are most appropriate for your investing style.

Note that increased risk does not always mean increased performance. Most of the riskiest mutual funds in the E (Very Weak) Risk Rating category have also provided very poor returns to their shareholders. Funds in the D and E Risk Rating categories generally represent speculative ventures that should not be entered into lightly.

1.	**Fund Type**	The mutual fund's peer category based on an analysis of its investment portfolio.	

AG	Aggressive Growth	HL	Health
AA	Asset Allocation	IN	Income
BA	Balanced	IX	Index
CV	Convertible	MC	Mid Cap
EM	Emerging Market	OT	Other
EN	Energy/Natural Resources	PM	Precious Metals
FS	Financial Services	RE	Real Estate
FO	Foreign	SC	Small Cap
GL	Global	TC	Technology
GR	Growth	UT	Utilities
GI	Growth and Income		

A blank fund type means that the mutual fund has not yet been categorized.

2.	**Fund Name**	The name of the mutual fund as stated in its prospectus, which can sometimes differ slightly from the name that the company uses for advertising. If you cannot find the particular mutual fund you are interested in, or if you have any doubts regarding the precise name, verify the information with your broker or on your account statement. Also, use the fund's ticker symbol for confirmation. (See column 3.)

3.	**Ticker Symbol**	The unique alphabetic symbol used for identifying and trading a specific mutual fund. No two funds can have the same ticker symbol, and the ticker symbol for mutual funds always ends with an "X".
		A handful of funds currently show no associated ticker symbol. This means that the fund is either small or new since the NASD only assigns a ticker symbol to funds with at least $25 million in assets or 1,000 shareholders.
4.	**Overall Investment Rating**	Our overall rating is measured on a scale from A to E based on each fund's risk-adjusted performance. Please see page 10 for specific descriptions of each letter grade. Also, refer to page 7 for information on how our ratings are derived. Most important, when using this rating, please be sure to consider the warnings beginning on page 11 regarding the ratings' limitations and the underlying assumptions.
5.	**Phone**	The telephone number of the company managing the fund. Call this number to receive a prospectus or other information about the fund.
6.	**Net Asset Value (NAV)**	The fund's share price as of the date indicated. A fund's NAV is computed by dividing the value of the fund's asset holdings, less accrued fees and expenses, by the number of its shares outstanding.
7.	**Performance Rating/Points**	A letter grade rating based solely on the mutual fund's financial performance over the trailing three years, without any consideration for the amount of risk the fund poses. Like the overall Investment Rating, the Performance Rating is measured on a scale from A to E for ease of interpretation. The points score indicates where the Performance Rating falls on a scale of 0 to 10.
8.	**1-Year Total Return**	The total return the fund has provided investors over the preceeding twelve months. This total return figure is computed based on the fund's dividend distributions and share price appreciation/depreciation during the period, net of the expenses and fees it imposes on its shareholders. Although the total return figure does not reflect an adjustment for any loads the fund may carry, such adjustments have been made in deriving TheStreet Investment Ratings.
9.	**1-Year Total Return Percentile**	The fund's percentile rank based on its one-year performance compared to that of all other equity funds in existence for at least one year. A score of 99 is the best possible, indicating that the fund outperformed 99% of the other mutual funds. Zero is the worst possible percentile score.
10.	**3-Year Total Return**	The total annual return the fund has provided investors over the preceeding three years.

11. 3-Year Total Return Percentile

The fund's percentile rank based on its three-year performance compared to that of all other equity funds in existence for at least three years. A score of 99 is the best possible, indicating that the fund outperformed 99% of the other mutual funds. Zero is the worst possible percentile score.

12. 5-Year Total Return

The total annual return the fund has provided investors over the preceeding five years.

13. 5-Year Total Return Percentile

The fund's percentile rank based on its five-year performance compared to that of all other equity funds in existence for at least five years. A score of 99 is the best possible, indicating that the fund outperformed 99% of the other mutual funds. Zero is the worst possible percentile score.

14. Risk Rating/Points

A letter grade rating based solely on the mutual fund's risk as determined by its monthly performance volatility over the trailing three years. The risk rating does not take into consideration the overall financial performance the fund has achieved or the total return it has provided to its shareholders. Like the overall Investment Rating, the Risk Rating is measured on a scale from A to E for ease of interpretation. The points score indicates where the Risk Rating falls on a scale of 0 to 10.

15. Manager Quality Percentile

The manager quality percentile is based on a ranking of the fund's alpha, a statistical measure representing the difference between a fund's actual returns and its expected performance given its level of risk. Fund managers who have been able to exceed the fund's statistically expected performance receive a high percentile rank with 99 representing the highest possible score. At the other end of the spectrum, fund managers who have actually detracted from the fund's expected performance receive a low percentile rank with 0 representing the lowest possible score.

16. Manager Tenure

The number of years the current manager has been managing the fund. Since fund managers who deliver substandard returns are usually replaced, a long tenure is usually a good sign that shareholders are satisfied that the fund is achieving its stated objectives.

Fund Type	Fund Name	Ticker Symbol	Overall Investment Rating	Phone	Net Asset Value As of 3/31/15	Perform-ance Rating/Pts	Annualized Total Return Through 3/31/15			Risk Rating/Pts	Mgr. Quality Pct	Mgr. Tenure (Years)
							1Yr / Pct	3Yr / Pct	5Yr / Pct			
HL	Vanguard HealthCare Index Adm	VHCIX	A+	(800) 662-7447	67.68	A+ /9.9	27.85 /99	27.67 /99	20.76 /99	B / 8.2	99	11
GR	ProFunds-HlthCare UltraSector	HCPSX	A+	(888) 776-3637	44.30	A+ /9.9	38.24 /99	38.76 /99	27.38 /99	B- / 7.2	99	2
GR ●	Smead Value Fund Investor	SMVLX	A+	(877) 807-4122	40.25	A+ /9.8	12.72 /86	21.57 /98	17.61 /97	B- / 7.5	91	7
MC	Harbor Mid Cap Value Inv	HIMVX	A+	(800) 422-1050	21.34	A+ /9.8	12.33 /84	20.98 /98	16.10 /93	B- / 7.3	91	11
GR	Leuthold Select Industries	LSLTX	A+	(888) 200-0409	22.90	A+ /9.8	15.08 /92	20.01 /98	12.51 /64	B- / 7.1	78	2
GR	Bridgeway Large-Cap Growth	BRLGX	A+	(800) 661-3550	23.91	A+ /9.8	22.54 /97	20.83 /98	16.24 /94	B- / 7.0	90	12
OT	Lazard Global Listed Infr Open	GLFOX	A+	(800) 821-6474	14.82	A+ /9.8	18.18 /96	21.60 /98	14.45 /82	B- / 7.0	98	10
IN	Natixis ASG Managed Futures	AMFAX	A+	(800) 225-5478	12.27	A+ /9.7	39.33 /99	12.29 /55	--	B- / 7.7	96	5
GR ●	Vanguard PRIMECAP Core Inv	VPCCX	A+	(800) 662-7447	22.04	A+ /9.7	15.49 /92	20.14 /98	15.55 /90	B- / 7.0	93	11
GR	Glenmede Large Cap core	GTLOX	A+	(800) 442-8299	22.52	A+ /9.7	15.24 /92	19.61 /97	17.30 /97	B- / 7.0	81	11
GR	Amer Beacon Bridgeway LC Val	BRLVX	A+	(800) 658-5811	24.32	A+ /9.6	12.45 /85	19.75 /98	15.85 /92	B- / 7.9	89	12
GI	Transamerica Prt Large Core	DVGIX	A+	(888) 233-4339	33.88	A /9.5	16.36 /94	18.26 /95	15.70 /91	B- / 7.6	80	6
GR ●	Sequoia Fund	SEQUX	A+	(800) 686-6884	253.02	A /9.5	13.77 /89	17.63 /93	17.69 /97	B- / 7.2	93	35
MC	Fidelity Adv Mid Cap Value A	FMPAX	A+	(800) 522-7297	24.81	A /9.5	15.38 /92	20.25 /98	16.35 /94	B- / 7.1	92	2
MC	Vanguard Mid-Cap Value Index Inv	VMVIX	A+	(800) 662-7447	36.08	A /9.5	12.44 /85	18.69 /96	15.48 /90	B- / 7.0	89	9
MC	Virtus Mid-Cap Core Fund A	VMACX	A+	(800) 243-1574	23.00	A /9.5	22.75 /98	16.97 /90	15.46 /90	B- / 7.0	83	6
GR	Vanguard FTSE Social Index Inv	VFTSX	A+	(800) 662-7447	13.49	A /9.5	14.60 /91	18.67 /96	14.96 /87	B- / 7.0	80	4
GR	PRIMECAP Odyssey Stock Fd	POSKX	A+	(800) 729-2307	24.25	A /9.4	13.56 /88	18.33 /95	14.44 /82	B- / 7.7	91	11
MC	Transamerica Prt Mid Value	DVMVX	A+	(888) 233-4339	21.95	A /9.4	13.99 /89	17.73 /93	15.09 /87	B- / 7.6	90	14
FO	Hennessy Japan Fund Investor	HJPNX	A+	(800) 966-4354	23.34	A /9.4	18.84 /96	15.52 /79	13.59 /74	B- / 7.3	98	9
GR	American Century Veedot Inv	AMVIX	A+	(800) 345-6488	10.93	A /9.4	14.72 /91	18.16 /95	15.60 /91	B- / 7.1	80	16
GR	LSV Value Equity Inst	LSVEX	A+	(866) 777-7818	24.02	A /9.4	9.20 /70	19.66 /97	15.06 /87	B- / 7.1	72	16
GR	American Century Leg Multi Cp	ACMFX	A+	(800) 345-6488	18.08	A /9.3	13.26 /87	17.70 /93	15.70 /91	B- / 7.3	85	8
GR	Vulcan Value Partners	VVPLX	A+	(877) 421-5078	19.44	A /9.3	14.59 /91	18.68 /96	15.96 /93	B- / 7.1	81	6
GR	Tax Mgd US MktWide Val II Inst	DFMVX	A+	(800) 984-9472	24.91	A /9.3	9.89 /74	19.07 /97	15.54 /90	B- / 7.0	74	N/A
GR	PNC Large Cap Growth A	PEWAX	A+	(800) 551-2145	28.93	A /9.3	22.83 /98	16.61 /88	15.90 /92	B- / 7.0	57	6
MC ●	JPMorgan Mid Cap Value A	JAMCX	A+	(800) 480-4111	37.77	A /9.3	15.15 /92	18.96 /97	16.68 /95	B- / 7.0	94	18
GI	Delaware Large Cap Value Eqty	DPDEX	A+	(800) 523-1918	27.65	A- /9.2	13.11 /87	18.13 /95	17.07 /96	B- / 7.8	92	9
GR	AMG FQ Tax-Managed US Equity	MFQAX	A+	(800) 835-3879	24.91	A- /9.2	12.35 /84	17.70 /93	16.48 /95	B- / 7.4	70	7
FS	Emerald Banking and Finance A	HSSAX	A+	(855) 828-9909	28.91	A- /9.2	4.37 /34	20.00 /98	14.27 /80	B- / 7.0	93	18
GI	Fidelity Value Discovery Fd	FVDFX	A+	(800) 544-8544	24.95	A- /9.1	12.11 /83	17.78 /93	14.25 /80	B- / 7.8	80	3
GR	Hartford Core Equity A	HAIAX	A+	(888) 843-7824	23.30	A- /9.1	16.98 /95	18.20 /95	15.65 /91	B- / 7.3	81	17
MC	American Century VP Mid Cap Val	AVMTX	A+	(800) 345-6488	19.14	A- /9.1	13.62 /88	17.42 /92	14.56 /83	B- / 7.2	92	11
GR	Olstein All Cap Value C	OFALX	A+	(800) 799-2113	21.90	A- /9.1	15.59 /93	16.79 /89	13.86 /76	B- / 7.1	62	20
GR	Akre Focus Retail	AKREX	A+	(877) 862-9556	23.10	A- /9.1	12.02 /83	17.77 /93	18.21 /98	B- / 7.1	82	6
GR	Wells Fargo Adv Large Cap Core A	EGOAX	A+	(800) 222-8222	15.82	A- /9.0	15.51 /92	18.55 /96	15.38 /89	B- / 7.4	83	8
GR	Vanguard US Value Inv	VUVLX	A+	(800) 662-7447	17.66	A- /9.0	10.12 /75	18.03 /94	15.13 /88	B- / 7.4	80	7
GR	Vanguard Structured Lg-Cp Eq Inst	VSLIX	A+	(800) 662-7447	40.44	A- /9.0	14.13 /90	17.32 /91	15.86 /92	B- / 7.3	75	9
GR	Fidelity Blue Chip Value	FBCVX	A+	(800) 544-8544	16.71	A- /9.0	14.24 /90	16.86 /89	11.29 /55	B- / 7.2	58	1
GR	Robeco Boston Ptrs All Cap Val Inv	BPAVX	A+	(888) 261-4073	22.83	A- /9.0	10.58 /77	17.56 /93	13.92 /77	B- / 7.2	68	8
GR	DFA US Large Cap Value II Inst	DFCVX	A+	(800) 984-9472	16.15	A- /9.0	8.25 /65	18.62 /96	14.93 /86	B- / 7.1	70	14
GR	Rydex Leisure A	RYLSX	A+	(800) 820-0888	56.88	A- /9.0	10.86 /78	18.79 /96	17.50 /97	B- / 7.1	82	17
GR	Fidelity LgCp Gr Enh Idx Fd	FLGEX	A+	(800) 544-8544	15.22	A- /9.0	16.35 /94	16.55 /87	15.52 /90	B- / 7.1	72	8
IN	Parnassus Core Equity Inv	PRBLX	A+	(800) 999-3505	40.29	A- /9.0	12.70 /86	17.75 /93	13.69 /75	B- / 7.1	87	14
IN	Nicholas Equity Income	NSEIX	A+	(800) 544-6547	20.99	A- /9.0	13.13 /87	16.94 /90	14.83 /85	B- / 7.0	84	22
GI	Homestead Value	HOVLX	A+	(800) 258-3030	51.53	B+ /8.9	12.96 /86	17.19 /91	14.09 /79	B- / 7.5	69	25
GR	Columbia Large Cap Enh Core A	NMIAX	A+	(800) 345-6611	21.65	B+ /8.9	14.68 /91	16.99 /90	15.38 /89	B- / 7.4	66	6
GR	Brown Advisory Flexible Equity Inv	BIAFX	A+	(800) 540-6807	16.07	B+ /8.9	13.19 /87	17.26 /91	14.56 /83	B- / 7.3	77	7
SC	FAM Value Inv	FAMVX	A+	(800) 932-3271	68.58	B+ /8.9	13.55 /88	16.28 /85	13.52 /73	B- / 7.2	94	28
GI	Vanguard Cons Stap Idx Adm	VCSAX	A+	(800) 662-7447	62.59	B+ /8.9	16.90 /94	16.43 /86	15.42 /90	B- / 7.1	88	5
FS	Burnham Financial Services A	BURKX	A+	(800) 462-2392	28.35	B+ /8.9	7.44 /59	19.65 /97	9.95 /44	B- / 7.0	96	16
GR	QS Batterymarch US Large Cap Eq	LMUSX	A+	(877) 534-4627	17.19	B+ /8.8	13.48 /88	16.73 /88	14.50 /82	B- / 7.6	63	7

● Denotes fund is closed to new investors

Fund Type	Fund Name	Ticker Symbol	Overall Investment Rating	Phone	Net Asset Value As of 3/31/15	Performance Rating/Pts	Annualized Total Return Through 3/31/15			Risk Rating/Pts	Mgr. Quality Pct	Mgr. Tenure (Years)
							1Yr / Pct	3Yr / Pct	5Yr / Pct			
GR	SEI Inst Inv Tr-Tax Mgd Volty A	TMMAX	A+	(800) 342-5734	14.43	B+ /8.8	14.10 /90	16.63 /88	15.33 /89	B- / 7.4	92	8
GR	Goldman Sachs LC Gro Insights A	GLCGX	A+	(800) 526-7384	22.74	B+ /8.8	17.89 /95	17.82 /94	16.06 /93	B- / 7.3	75	4
GR	Manor Growth Fund	MNRGX	A+	(800) 787-3334	20.82	B+ /8.8	15.14 /92	16.09 /84	14.77 /85	B- / 7.1	65	16
GR	SunAmerica VAL Co II Soc Resp	VCSRX	A+	(800) 858-8850	19.49	B+ /8.8	13.51 /88	17.01 /90	14.88 /86	B- / 7.1	73	3
GR	Vanguard Mega Cap Gr Index I	VMGAX	A+	(800) 662-7447	165.40	B+ /8.8	16.62 /94	16.38 /86	15.51 /90	B- / 7.0	69	5
MC	Touchstone Mid Cap A	TMAPX	A+	(800) 543-0407	25.95	B+ /8.7	12.73 /86	17.98 /94	15.68 /91	B- / 7.1	88	4
GI	Vanguard Growth & Income Inv	VQNPX	A+	(800) 662-7447	42.34	B+ /8.7	13.83 /89	16.61 /88	14.77 /85	B- / 7.1	72	4
OT	Vanguard Industrials Index Adm	VINAX	A+	(800) 662-7447	55.12	B+ /8.7	8.41 /66	17.40 /92	15.11 /88	B- / 7.0	64	5
IN	DFA US Core Equity 1 Ptf Inst	DFEOX	A+	(800) 984-9472	18.26	B+ /8.7	10.75 /77	16.93 /89	14.97 /87	B- / 7.0	64	3
IN	DFA US Core Equity 2 Ptf Inst	DFQTX	A+	(800) 984-9472	17.82	B+ /8.7	9.51 /72	17.22 /91	14.89 /86	B- / 7.0	59	3
IN	AQR Managed Futures Strategy N	AQMNX	A+	(866) 290-2688	11.44	B+ /8.6	26.37 /99	10.28 /41	5.70 /15	B / 8.2	99	5
GR	Fidelity LgCp Val Enh Idx Fd	FLVEX	A+	(800) 544-8544	11.22	B+ /8.6	10.50 /76	17.37 /92	14.40 /81	B- / 7.4	75	8
IN	State Farm Equity A	SNEAX	A+	(800) 447-4930	10.02	B+ /8.6	15.83 /93	17.22 /91	13.97 /77	B- / 7.2	75	N/A
GR	Vanguard Instl TtlStk Mkt Inst	VITNX	A+	(800) 662-7447	47.27	B+ /8.6	12.37 /84	16.45 /87	14.80 /85	B- / 7.1	68	14
IN	Transamerica Prt Large Value	DVEIX	A+	(888) 233-4339	27.95	B+ /8.5	9.51 /72	16.87 /89	14.75 /85	B- / 7.4	64	6
GR	Vanguard Tax-Managed Cap Appr	VTCLX	A+	(800) 662-7447	105.80	B+ /8.5	12.29 /84	16.45 /87	14.69 /84	B- / 7.2	68	21
GR	Northern Large Cap Core	NOLCX	A+	(800) 595-9111	15.42	B+ /8.4	10.81 /78	16.81 /89	14.82 /85	B- / 7.5	64	4
GR	Federated MDT All Cap Core Fd A	QAACX	A+	(800) 341-7400	21.97	B+ /8.4	10.21 /75	18.35 /95	14.30 /80	B- / 7.4	78	7
IN	Target Large Capitalization Val T	TALVX	A+	(800) 225-1852	16.41	B+ /8.3	10.04 /74	16.65 /88	12.82 /67	B- / 7.5	61	10
FS	Alpine Financial Services Inst	ADFSX	A+	(888) 785-5578	13.59	B+ /8.3	1.09 /19	18.28 /95	10.71 /50	B- / 7.4	91	10
IN	T Rowe Price Dividend Growth	PRDGX	A+	(800) 638-5660	36.54	B+ /8.3	12.65 /85	15.82 /82	13.90 /77	B- / 7.4	74	15
MC	Boyar Value Fund	BOYAX	A+	(800) 266-5566	23.34	B /8.1	16.23 /94	16.95 /90	14.07 /78	B / 8.1	94	17
GR	Delaware Value A	DDVAX	A+	(800) 523-1918	18.50	B /8.0	12.43 /84	17.53 /92	16.36 /94	B- / 7.8	90	11
GR	Vanguard Russell 1000 Val Index	VRVIX	A+	(800) 662-7447	175.98	B /7.9	9.26 /71	16.34 /86	--	B- / 7.8	68	5
FO	FMI International	FMIJX	A+	(800) 811-5311	30.03	B /7.9	10.92 /78	14.85 /74	--	B- / 7.8	98	N/A
GR	Fidelity Adv Equity Value A	FAVAX	A+	(800) 522-7297	16.14	B /7.9	11.54 /81	17.29 /91	13.72 /75	B- / 7.8	77	3
IX	American Beacon S&P 500 Idx Inv	AAFPX	A+	(800) 658-5811	27.96	B /7.7	12.03 /83	15.43 /78	13.78 /76	B / 8.0	58	11
GR	Weitz Funds Part III Oppty	WPOPX	A+	(800) 232-4161	17.31	B- /7.4	7.76 /61	14.90 /74	14.64 /84	B / 8.6	83	32
IN	AT Disciplined Equity Institutional	AWEIX	A	(800) 338-2550	15.92	B+ /8.7	14.94 /91	16.15 /84	14.72 /84	B- / 7.0	72	5
GR	DFA US Sustainability Core 1 Inst	DFSIX	A	(800) 984-9472	16.94	B+ /8.6	10.60 /77	16.85 /89	14.68 /84	B- / 7.0	60	3
IN	Vanguard Russell 3000 Index Inst	VRTTX	A	(800) 662-7447	185.88	B+ /8.5	12.32 /84	16.35 /86	--	B- / 7.2	67	5
GI	T Rowe Price Instl Lg Cap Val	TILCX	A	(800) 638-5660	20.54	B+ /8.5	9.99 /74	17.27 /91	13.61 /74	B- / 7.1	74	11
GI	Dodge & Cox Stk Fund	DODGX	A	(800) 621-3979	176.55	B+ /8.5	6.50 /51	18.20 /95	13.81 /76	B- / 7.0	73	N/A
GR	T Rowe Price Total Eq Mkt Index	POMIX	A	(800) 638-5660	23.85	B+ /8.4	12.09 /83	16.37 /86	14.54 /83	B- / 7.2	66	13
GI	Fidelity Spartan Total Mkt Idx F	FFSMX	A	(800) 544-8544	60.96	B+ /8.4	12.27 /84	16.34 /86	14.72 /84	B- / 7.2	67	11
IN	DFA Tax-Managed US Eq Inst	DTMEX	A	(800) 984-9472	22.56	B+ /8.4	11.85 /82	16.26 /85	14.61 /83	B- / 7.2	62	3
GI	MainStay Common Stock B	MOPBX	A	(800) 624-6782	18.43	B+ /8.4	11.97 /82	16.52 /87	13.07 /69	B- / 7.1	58	8
GR	Vantagepoint Broad Market Index II	VPBMX	A	(800) 669-7400	16.46	B+ /8.4	12.27 /84	16.18 /85	14.55 /83	B- / 7.1	65	11
GR	Vanguard Total Stock Mkt Index	VTSMX	A	(800) 662-7447	52.26	B+ /8.4	12.17 /83	16.24 /85	14.62 /83	B- / 7.1	66	21
IX	Vanguard Instl Index Inst	VINIX	A	(800) 662-7447	188.84	B+ /8.3	12.71 /86	16.08 /84	14.44 /82	B- / 7.3	67	15
GR	TIAA-CREF Equity Index Retire	TIQRX	A	(800) 842-2252	16.01	B+ /8.3	12.02 /83	16.09 /84	14.37 /81	B- / 7.1	65	10
GI	T Rowe Price Growth and Inc	PRGIX	A	(800) 638-5660	32.58	B+ /8.3	12.72 /86	15.88 /82	13.60 /74	B- / 7.1	68	8
GR	American Century Leg Foc Lg Cp	ACFDX	A	(800) 345-6488	16.84	B /8.2	11.00 /78	16.01 /83	13.20 /70	B- / 7.4	75	8
GR	Vanguard Large Cap Index Inv	VLACX	A	(800) 662-7447	38.44	B /8.2	12.56 /85	15.98 /83	14.37 /81	B- / 7.3	66	11
GR	JPMorgan Intrepid America A	JIAAX	A	(800) 480-4111	38.07	B /8.2	13.61 /88	17.31 /91	14.51 /82	B- / 7.3	72	10
IX	Northern Stock Index	NOSIX	A	(800) 595-9111	25.41	B /8.2	12.59 /85	15.98 /83	14.29 /80	B- / 7.3	65	9
IX	Vanguard 500 Index Inv	VFINX	A	(800) 662-7447	190.71	B /8.2	12.56 /85	15.93 /83	14.29 /80	B- / 7.3	65	24
IX	Fidelity Spartan 500 Index Inv	FUSEX	A	(800) 544-8544	73.52	B /8.2	12.62 /85	16.01 /83	14.37 /81	B- / 7.3	66	9

99 Pct = Best
0 Pct = Worst

Denotes fund is closed to new investors

Data as of March 31, 2015

Fund Type	Fund Name	Ticker Symbol	Overall Investment Rating	Phone	Net Asset Value As of 3/31/15	Performance Rating/Pts	Annualized Total Return Through 3/31/15			Risk Rating/Pts	Mgr. Quality Pct	Mgr. Tenure (Years)
							1Yr / Pct	3Yr / Pct	5Yr / Pct			
GR	● Vanguard Capital Opportunity Inv	VHCOX	A+	(800) 662-7447	54.97	A+ /9.9	17.69 /95	23.41 /99	15.71 /91	C+ / 6.8	96	17
GR	Fidelity Select Air Transport	FSAIX	A+	(800) 544-8888	73.26	A+ /9.9	21.54 /97	26.07 /99	18.41 /98	C+ / 6.8	98	3
GR	ProFunds-Consumer Srvs Ultra	CYPSX	A+	(888) 776-3637	76.52	A+ /9.9	28.75 /99	31.46 /99	27.02 /99	C+ / 6.7	92	2
HL	Rydex Health Care A	RYHEX	A+	(800) 820-0888	33.60	A+ /9.9	30.21 /99	26.61 /99	19.23 /98	C+ / 6.6	99	17
GR	ProFunds-Pharm UltraSector Svc	PHPSX	A+	(888) 776-3637	22.56	A+ /9.9	24.39 /98	32.15 /99	24.32 /99	C+ / 6.4	98	2
RE	Baron Real Estate Retail	BREFX	A+	(800) 992-2766	27.09	A+ /9.9	16.19 /94	24.10 /99	21.34 /99	C+ / 6.2	99	6
HL	Hartford Healthcare A	HGHAX	A+	(888) 843-7824	39.13	A+ /9.9	29.12 /99	29.34 /99	21.36 /99	C+ / 6.2	99	15
GR	Eventide Gilead A	ETAGX	A+	(877) 453-7877	27.72	A+ /9.9	16.24 /94	24.76 /99	20.37 /99	C+ / 6.1	97	7
HL	Oak Assoc-Live Oak Health	LOGSX	A+	(888) 462-5386	22.05	A+ /9.9	21.12 /97	23.05 /99	18.64 /98	C+ / 6.1	98	14
HL	Fidelity Select Medical Delivery	FSHCX	A+	(800) 544-8888	90.32	A+ /9.9	29.21 /99	20.44 /98	18.89 /98	C+ / 6.0	97	3
GR	LM CM Opportunity Trust A	LGOAX	A+	(877) 534-4627	20.06	A+ /9.9	12.95 /86	30.29 /99	13.37 /72	C+ / 5.9	95	16
MC	● Vanguard PRIMECAP Inv	VPMCX	A+	(800) 662-7447	105.16	A+ /9.8	15.58 /93	21.00 /98	15.91 /93	C+ / 7.0	96	30
GR	Rydex Transportation A	RYTSX	A+	(800) 820-0888	48.41	A+ /9.8	16.34 /94	24.25 /99	16.70 /95	C+ / 6.9	96	17
GR	Fidelity Select Transportation	FSRFX	A+	(800) 544-8888	91.17	A+ /9.8	19.69 /97	24.36 /99	18.33 /98	C+ / 6.9	98	3
GR	Glenmede Large Cap Growth Port	GTLLX	A+	(800) 442-8299	24.53	A+ /9.8	20.97 /97	19.99 /98	18.37 /98	C+ / 6.8	84	11
GI	Vanguard Cons Discn Idx Adm	VCDAX	A+	(800) 662-7447	63.35	A+ /9.8	17.09 /95	20.67 /98	19.95 /99	C+ / 6.8	86	5
SC	Hennessy Cornerstone Growth Inv	HFCGX	A+	(800) 966-4354	20.28	A+ /9.8	17.23 /95	19.68 /97	14.56 /83	C+ / 6.8	96	15
SC	Vanguard Strategic Equity Inv	VSEQX	A+	(800) 662-7447	33.84	A+ /9.8	14.29 /90	20.78 /98	18.19 /98	C+ / 6.7	96	9
GR	Nicholas	NICSX	A+	(800) 544-6547	71.57	A+ /9.8	19.51 /96	21.92 /98	18.41 /98	C+ / 6.7	94	46
AG	Rydex Nova A	RYANX	A+	(800) 820-0888	46.40	A+ /9.8	17.09 /95	22.38 /98	19.28 /98	C+ / 6.6	33	19
SC	Hennessy Focus Investor	HFCSX	A+	(800) 966-4354	70.89	A+ /9.8	18.24 /96	19.04 /97	17.35 /97	C+ / 6.6	97	6
GR	Fidelity Sel Defense and	FSDAX	A+	(800) 544-8888	129.39	A+ /9.8	13.61 /88	19.85 /94	17.08 /96	C+ / 6.5	92	3
GR	Fidelity Select Multimedia	FBMPX	A+	(800) 544-8888	82.20	A+ /9.8	13.61 /88	23.14 /99	20.52 /99	C+ / 6.5	90	2
SC	PNC Multi-Factor Small Cap Core	PLOAX	A+	(800) 551-2145	21.34	A+ /9.8	13.56 /88	22.34 /98	19.63 /99	C+ / 6.4	94	10
HL	Saratoga Adv Tr-Health & Biotech	SHPAX	A+	(800) 807-3863	31.71	A+ /9.8	19.51 /96	21.87 /98	17.78 /97	C+ / 6.4	97	10
IN	Aquila Three Peaks Oppty Gro A	ATGAX	A+	(800) 437-1020	47.19	A+ /9.8	20.73 /97	23.71 /99	18.49 /98	C+ / 6.3	96	12
MC	● T Rowe Price Instl Mid-Cap Eq Gr	PMEGX	A+	(800) 638-5660	46.00	A+ /9.8	18.05 /96	19.09 /97	17.60 /97	C+ / 6.2	86	19
MC	Rydex Mid Cap 1.5x Strgy A	RYAHX	A+	(800) 820-0888	67.32	A+ /9.8	15.50 /92	23.07 /99	20.23 /99	C+ / 5.9	26	14
GR	Fidelity Select Retailing	FSRPX	A+	(800) 544-8888	95.25	A+ /9.8	21.98 /97	20.99 /98	20.01 /99	C+ / 5.9	83	1
SC	Ariel Fund Investor	ARGFX	A+	(800) 292-7435	76.61	A+ /9.8	19.54 /96	21.60 /98	16.12 /94	C+ / 5.9	94	29
GR	Parnassus Endeavor	PARWX	A+	(800) 999-3505	30.83	A+ /9.7	18.69 /96	19.20 /97	15.87 /92	C+ / 6.8	89	10
MC	Fidelity Mid Cap Enhanced Index	FMEIX	A+	(800) 544-8544	14.17	A+ /9.7	14.79 /91	19.63 /97	16.75 /95	C+ / 6.8	90	8
MC	PRIMECAP Odyssey Growth Fd	POGRX	A+	(800) 729-2307	26.98	A+ /9.7	13.10 /87	19.63 /97	15.20 /88	C+ / 6.7	91	11
MC	● VY JPMorgan Mid Cap Val Adv	IJMAX	A+	(800) 992-0180	23.28	A+ /9.7	15.28 /92	18.94 /97	16.57 /95	C+ / 6.6	94	11
SC	Golden Small Cap Core Inst	GLDSX	A+	(800) 754-8757	18.45	A+ /9.7	14.27 /90	18.60 /96	16.66 /95	C+ / 6.4	92	10
AG	Fidelity Growth Strategies Fd	FDEGX	A+	(800) 544-8544	34.41	A+ /9.7	19.73 /97	17.82 /94	14.50 /82	C+ / 6.3	71	2
AG	Bridgeway Aggressive Investor 1	BRAGX	A+	(800) 661-3550	60.13	A+ /9.7	11.61 /81	20.83 /98	15.35 /89	C+ / 6.2	72	21
SC	Vanguard Strategic Sm-Cp Equity	VSTCX	A+	(800) 662-7447	32.07	A+ /9.7	11.51 /80	19.59 /97	17.65 /97	C+ / 6.2	92	9
MC	Janus Aspen Enterprise Inst	JAAGX	A+	(800) 295-2687	66.19	A+ /9.7	17.93 /95	17.84 /94	16.92 /96	C+ / 6.2	91	8
MC	Hennessy Cornerstone Mid Cap 30	HFMDX	A+	(800) 966-4354	19.69	A+ /9.7	15.42 /92	19.55 /97	17.26 /96	C+ / 6.1	86	12
MC	Dreyfus Active MidCap A	DNLDX	A+	(800) 782-6620	59.40	A+ /9.6	18.36 /96	19.57 /97	14.96 /86	C+ / 6.9	83	3
GR	ProFunds-Consumer Goods Ultra	CNPSX	A+	(888) 776-3637	78.41	A+ /9.6	15.99 /93	19.22 /97	18.59 /98	C+ / 6.8	30	2
MC	● Principal MidCap A	PEMGX	A+	(800) 222-5852	23.00	A+ /9.6	18.04 /96	19.27 /97	18.56 /98	C+ / 6.8	91	15
SC	Westwood SmallCap Value Inst	WHGSX	A+	(877) 386-3944	14.34	A+ /9.6	8.63 /67	19.62 /97	16.82 /96	C+ / 6.4	90	2
GR	Janus Portfolio Institutional	JAGRX	A+	(800) 295-2687	38.01	A+ /9.6	20.49 /97	16.78 /89	14.30 /80	C+ / 6.1	78	4
GI	Fidelity Value Fd	FDVLX	A+	(800) 544-8544	116.72	A /9.5	10.90 /78	18.97 /97	15.02 /87	C+ / 6.9	82	5
MC	● J Hancock III Dsp Val Mid Cap A	JVMAX	A+	(800) 257-3336	20.19	A /9.5	13.78 /89	19.64 /97	17.18 /96	C+ / 6.9	90	15
GI	Lazard US Eqty Concentrated	LEVOX	A+	(800) 821-6474	13.91	A /9.5	19.71 /97	17.76 /93	13.77 /76	C+ / 6.7	81	10
GL	Brown Advisory SmCP Fund Val	BIAUX	A+	(800) 540-6807	24.11	A /9.5	10.00 /74	19.04 /97	17.44 /97	C+ / 6.7	99	7
GR	TCW Concentrated Value N	TGFVX	A+	(800) 386-3829	20.00	A /9.5	15.51 /92	18.66 /96	13.02 /68	C+ / 6.7	76	11
SC	Wasatch Small Cap Value Investor	WMCVX	A+	(800) 551-1700	6.44	A /9.5	10.84 /78	18.81 /96	15.97 /93	C+ / 6.6	93	16
GR	USAA Growth Fund	USAAX	A+	(800) 382-8722	25.02	A /9.5	16.22 /94	18.29 /95	15.48 /90	C+ / 6.6	77	8

● Denotes fund is closed to new investors

99 Pct = Best
0 Pct = Worst

Fund Type	Fund Name	Ticker Symbol	Overall Investment Rating	Phone	Net Asset Value As of 3/31/15	Performance Rating/Pts	Annualized Total Return Through 3/31/15			Risk Rating/Pts	Mgr. Quality Pct	Mgr. Tenure (Years)
							1Yr / Pct	3Yr / Pct	5Yr / Pct			
GR	NASDAQ-100 Index Direct	NASDX	A+	(800) 955-9988	11.14	A /9.5	21.69 /97	17.85 /94	18.46 /98	C+ / 6.6	74	12
GR	Rydex Retailing A	RYRTX	A+	(800) 820-0888	26.85	A /9.5	19.44 /96	16.99 /90	16.95 /96	C+ / 6.5	52	17
SC	Homestead Small Company Stock	HSCSX	A+	(800) 258-3030	40.95	A /9.5	11.30 /80	18.17 /95	17.71 /97	C+ / 6.5	91	16
GR	Natixis Vaughan Nelson Val Opp A	VNVAX	A+	(800) 225-5478	22.78	A /9.5	12.73 /86	19.64 /97	16.48 /95	C+ / 6.3	84	7
IN	SEI Inst Inv Managed Vol Fund A	SVYAX	A+	(800) 342-5734	14.64	A /9.5	15.66 /93	18.42 /95	16.60 /95	C+ / 6.3	95	11
MC	Vanguard Mid-Cap Index Inv	VIMSX	A+	(800) 662-7447	35.14	A /9.4	14.72 /91	17.76 /93	15.91 /92	C+ / 6.9	83	17
FS	Fidelity Select Insurance	FSPCX	A+	(800) 544-8888	67.08	A /9.4	11.31 /80	19.52 /97	13.49 /73	C+ / 6.7	85	2
GR	Fidelity NASDAQ Composite Index	FNCMX	A+	(800) 544-8544	64.65	A /9.4	18.00 /95	17.88 /94	16.53 /95	C+ / 6.6	71	11
AG	CB Aggressive Growth A	SHRAX	A+	(877) 534-4627	209.82	A /9.4	11.38 /80	20.93 /98	18.65 /98	C+ / 6.6	89	32
MC	Lazard US Mid Cap Eq Open	LZMOX	A+	(800) 821-6474	19.82	A /9.4	21.07 /97	15.22 /77	12.87 /67	C+ / 6.6	51	14
GR	SunAmerica VAL Co I Nsdq 100	VCNIX	A+	(800) 858-8850	9.95	A /9.4	21.35 /97	17.26 /91	17.99 /97	C+ / 6.4	69	3
MC	Wells Fargo Adv Spec Mid Cp VI A	WFPAX	A+	(800) 222-8222	32.68	A /9.4	11.83 /82	19.88 /98	15.96 /93	C+ / 6.4	90	6
GL	Janus Contrarian A	JCNAX	A+	(800) 295-2687	22.26	A /9.4	12.63 /85	20.63 /98	11.78 /59	C+ / 6.3	99	4
TC	Guinness Atkinson Glob Innov	IWIRX	A+	(800) 915-6565	34.38	A /9.3	10.77 /77	18.90 /96	14.86 /86	C+ / 6.9	71	5
SC	Vanguard Small-Cap Value Index	VISVX	A+	(800) 662-7447	26.20	A /9.3	10.45 /76	18.12 /96	14.94 /86	C+ / 6.8	90	17
SC	PNC Small Cap A	PPCAX	A+	(800) 551-2145	21.81	A /9.3	9.74 /73	18.89 /96	17.68 /97	C+ / 6.8	92	11
GR	USAA Nasdaq 100 Index	USNQX	A+	(800) 382-8722	12.53	A /9.3	21.08 /97	17.13 /91	17.76 /97	C+ / 6.6	67	9
FO	Glenmede Total Market Port	GTTMX	A+	(800) 442-8299	15.22	A /9.3	11.23 /79	17.78 /93	15.32 /89	C+ / 6.5	98	9
GR	J Hancock VIT Fund AC Core I	JEQAX	A+	(800) 257-3336	23.12	A /9.3	12.07 /83	18.21 /95	15.71 /91	C+ / 6.4	49	4
GR	J Hancock VIT All Cap Core I	JEACX	A+	(800) 257-3336	28.74	A- /9.2	13.09 /87	17.04 /90	14.27 /80	C+ / 6.9	65	5
GL	Motley Fool Great America Investor	TMFGX	A+	(888) 863-8803	20.05	A- /9.2	13.32 /88	17.46 /92	--	C+ / 6.9	98	5
IN	SEI Instl Mgd Tr-US Mgd Volty A	SVOAX	A+	(800) 342-5734	17.11	A- /9.2	14.61 /91	17.60 /93	15.86 /92	C+ / 6.5	93	N/A
MC	Prudential Mid-Cap Value A	SPRAX	A+	(800) 225-1852	21.35	A- /9.1	12.41 /84	19.13 /97	15.41 /90	C+ / 6.8	89	8
GI	JPMorgan Tax Aware Equity I	JPDEX	A+	(800) 480-4111	29.61	A- /9.1	14.28 /90	17.28 /91	14.54 /83	C+ / 6.7	66	7
MC	Vanguard S&P Mid-Cap 400 Value	VMFVX	A+	(800) 662-7447	198.20	A- /9.1	10.75 /77	17.48 /92	--	C+ / 6.6	67	2
MC	Vanguard Windsor-I Inv	VWNDX	A+	(800) 662-7447	21.79	B+ /8.9	9.71 /73	17.69 /93	14.04 /78	C+ / 6.8	85	7
GR	DFA TA US Core Equity 2 Inst	DFTCX	A+	(800) 984-9472	14.53	B+ /8.8	9.80 /74	17.24 /91	14.94 /86	C+ / 6.9	59	3
GR	Fidelity Select Constn and Housing	FSHOX	A	(800) 544-8888	60.87	A+ /9.9	21.85 /97	21.09 /98	19.13 /98	C+ / 5.7	88	3
AG	● PRIMECAP Odyssey Agg Growth	POAGX	A	(800) 729-2307	34.88	A+ /9.9	17.96 /95	26.39 /99	20.62 /99	C+ / 5.6	95	11
HL	Vanguard Health Care Inv	VGHCX	A	(800) 662-7447	225.70	A+ /9.9	29.47 /99	29.10 /99	21.70 /99	C+ / 5.6	99	7
HL	BlackRock Health Sci Opps Inv A	SHSAX	A	(800) 441-7762	54.46	A+ /9.9	34.56 /99	30.02 /99	21.02 /99	C / 5.4	99	12
GL	Thornburg Globl Opportunities A	THOAX	A	(800) 847-0200	26.90	A+ /9.8	21.60 /97	20.32 /98	13.93 /77	C+ / 5.8	99	9
SC	Roxbury/Hood River Sm-Cap Gr	RSCIX	A	(800) 336-9970	33.42	A+ /9.8	16.85 /94	21.31 /98	17.68 /97	C+ / 5.7	95	8
GR	ProFunds-Industrial UltraSector	IDPSX	A	(888) 776-3637	65.11	A+ /9.8	9.50 /72	21.61 /98	18.28 /98	C+ / 5.7	10	2
GR	Fidelity Select IT Serv Portfolio	FBSOX	A	(800) 544-8888	38.89	A+ /9.8	15.74 /93	20.31 /98	19.63 /99	C+ / 5.7	64	6
AG	Rydex Dow 2x Strategy A	RYLDX	A	(800) 820-0888	50.69	A+ /9.8	17.18 /95	22.98 /99	21.60 /99	C+ / 5.6	2	11
HL	Delaware Healthcare Fund A	DLHAX	A	(800) 523-1918	20.36	A+ /9.8	16.37 /94	23.61 /99	19.82 /99	C+ / 5.6	96	8
SC	T Rowe Price Diversified Sm-Cap	PRDSX	A	(800) 638-5660	27.68	A+ /9.7	15.57 /93	18.97 /97	19.03 /98	C+ / 5.9	92	9
SC	JPMorgan Small Cap Core Sel	VSSCX	A	(800) 480-4111	56.48	A+ /9.7	12.79 /86	19.68 /97	16.68 /95	C+ / 5.9	87	11
GR	Fidelity Blue Chip Growth Fd	FBGRX	A	(800) 544-8544	72.16	A+ /9.7	18.66 /96	18.79 /96	16.98 /96	C+ / 5.9	78	6
GI	Olstein Strategic Opps Fd A	OFSAX	A	(800) 799-2113	18.49	A+ /9.7	16.55 /94	20.23 /98	16.72 /95	C+ / 5.8	77	9
GR	Federated Kaufmann Large Cap A	KLCAX	A	(800) 341-7400	19.34	A+ /9.7	19.73 /97	19.75 /98	17.40 /97	C+ / 5.8	90	8
MC	● T Rowe Price Mid-Cap Growth	RPMGX	A	(800) 638-5660	80.36	A+ /9.7	17.20 /95	18.41 /95	17.02 /96	C+ / 5.8	86	23
SC	PNC Multi-Factor Small Cap	PLWAX	A	(800) 551-2145	20.58	A+ /9.6	13.75 /89	19.74 /98	19.21 /98	C+ / 6.0	90	10
GR	Golden Large Cap Core Inst	GLDLX	A	(800) 754-8757	14.67	A+ /9.6	15.90 /93	18.76 /96	15.42 /90	C+ / 5.9	84	20
GR	Fidelity Independence Fd	FDFFX	A	(800) 544-8544	41.03	A+ /9.6	13.50 /88	19.18 /97	15.29 /89	C+ / 5.7	85	9
GL	Hodges Retail	HDPMX	A	(877) 232-1222	38.98	A /9.5	3.53 /29	21.71 /98	14.33 /81	C+ / 6.1	99	16
GR	T Rowe Price Instl Lg Cap Core Gr	TPLGX	A	(800) 638-5660	26.36	A /9.5	17.17 /95	17.86 /94	17.06 /96	C+ / 6.0	80	12

● Denotes fund is closed to new investors

Data as of March 31, 2015

99 Pct = Best
0 Pct = Worst

Fund Type	Fund Name	Ticker Symbol	Overall Investment Rating	Phone	Net Asset Value As of 3/31/15	Performance Rating/Pts	1Yr / Pct	3Yr / Pct	5Yr / Pct	Risk Rating/Pts	Mgr. Quality Pct	Mgr. Tenure (Years)
HL	Eaton Vance WW Health Sciences	ETHSX	C+	(800) 262-1122	13.35	A+ /9.9	29.82 /99	28.19 /99	19.67 /99	D+ / 2.9	99	26
SC	Rydex Russell 2000 2x Strtgy A	RYRUX	C+	(800) 820-0888	349.40	A+ /9.9	11.52 /81	28.83 /99	22.08 /99	D+ / 2.8	10	9
SC	ProFunds-Ultra Small Cap Svc	UAPSX	C+	(888) 776-3637	36.94	A+ /9.9	10.53 /76	28.11 /99	21.54 /99	D+ / 2.7	8	2
HL	Fidelity Select Biotech Port	FBIOX	C+	(800) 544-8888	256.71	A+ /9.9	46.13 /99	43.52 /99	33.30 /99	D+ / 2.6	99	10
HL	Alger Health Sciences Fund A	AHSAX	C+	(800) 254-3796	24.40	A+ /9.9	30.51 /99	23.63 /99	17.14 /96	D+ / 2.5	99	10
FO	Matthews India Fund Inv	MINDX	C+	(800) 789-2742	29.20	A+ /9.9	57.70 /99	21.77 /98	11.48 /57	D / 2.0	98	10
GR	ProFunds-Mble Telcm UltraSector	WCPSX	C+	(888) 776-3637	43.23	A+ /9.8	-8.98 / 3	26.05 /99	17.50 /97	D / 2.1	96	2
GR	ProFunds-Semicond UltraSector	SMPSX	C+	(888) 776-3637	25.23	A+ /9.7	33.49 /99	18.32 /95	15.68 /91	D+ / 2.6	2	2
SC	TFS Small Cap	TFSSX	C+	(800) 534-2001	14.28	A+ /9.7	9.97 /74	19.74 /98	16.70 /95	D+ / 2.5	90	9
RE	Manning & Napier Real Estate S	MNREX	C+	(800) 466-3863	16.20	A /9.5	24.46 /98	14.33 /70	15.11 /88	D+ / 2.9	70	6
SC	MFS Blended Research SC Eq		C+	(800) 225-2606	16.80	A /9.5	9.67 /73	18.70 /96	15.40 /90	D+ / 2.7	87	3
MC	BlackRock Mid Cap Growth Eq Inv	BMGAX	C+	(800) 441-7762	15.81	A /9.5	16.17 /93	18.57 /96	14.90 /86	D+ / 2.4	69	2
GR	Mount Lucas US Focused Eq I	BMLEX	C+	(844) 261-6483	10.04	A /9.4	9.78 /73	18.91 /96	14.89 /86	D+ / 2.9	63	N/A
HL	ICON Healthcare S	ICHCX	C	(800) 764-0442	20.11	A+ /9.9	29.72 /99	28.32 /99	20.75 /99	D- / 1.5	99	2
GR	ProFunds-Biotech Ultra Sector Svc	BIPSX	C	(888) 776-3637	57.28	A+ /9.9	55.44 /99	62.85 /99	40.79 /99	D- / 1.0	99	2
TC	T Rowe Price Global Technology	PRGTX	C	(800) 638-5660	12.83	A+ /9.8	21.40 /97	19.92 /98	20.12 /99	D- / 1.2	76	3
GR	TCM Small Cap Growth	TCMSX	C	(800) 536-3230	34.00	A+ /9.6	9.35 /71	18.89 /96	15.43 /90	D / 1.6	70	11
RE	Ell Realty Sec Inst	EIIRX	C	(888) 323-8912	5.19	A /9.5	24.16 /98	14.37 /70	16.69 /95	D / 2.2	72	11
GI	MainStay US Eqty Opportunities C	MYCCX	C	(800) 624-6782	7.74	A /9.5	15.47 /92	18.66 /96	15.19 /88	D / 1.9	77	8
GR	AMG Renaissance Large Cap Gro	MRLTX	C	(800) 835-3879	11.74	A /9.5	18.18 /96	18.14 /95	15.19 /88	D / 1.8	77	N/A
RE	Principal Real Est Securities A	PRRAX	C	(800) 222-5852	24.00	A /9.4	26.07 /98	14.90 /74	15.67 /91	D+ / 2.3	68	15
SC	CGCM Small Cap Growth Invest	TSGUX	C	(800) 444-4273	25.68	A /9.3	10.10 /75	17.28 /91	15.39 /89	D+ / 2.5	77	18
RE	J Hancock II Real Estate Sec 1	JIREX	C	(800) 257-3336	15.16	A /9.3	24.49 /98	13.49 /63	15.76 /92	D / 2.2	46	10
SC	William Blair Small Cap Gr N	WBSNX	C	(800) 742-7272	26.57	A /9.3	5.00 /39	18.76 /96	12.17 /62	D / 1.6	87	16
MC	Mutual of America Inst MCE Idx	MAMQX	C	(800) 914-8716	12.32	A- /9.1	12.08 /83	16.91 /89	16.67 /95	D / 2.2	66	1
MC	BlackRock US Opportunities Inv A	BMEAX	C	(800) 441-7762	38.19	B+ /8.9	15.10 /92	17.67 /93	13.88 /77	D+ / 2.8	72	17
GR	Transamerica Growth I2	TJNIX	C	(888) 233-4339	14.21	B+ /8.8	16.00 /93	15.73 /81	15.00 /87	D+ / 2.5	55	11
IN	Johnson Enhanced Return	JENHX	C	(800) 541-0170	16.01	B+ /8.7	13.26 /87	16.78 /89	15.50 /90	D+ / 2.7	73	10
GR	Vantagepoint Discovery Inv	VPDSX	C	(800) 669-7400	10.44	B+ /8.6	6.86 /54	16.43 /87	14.63 /84	D+ / 2.7	37	8
SC	Wasatch Micro Cap Value Investor	WAMVX	C	(800) 551-1700	2.93	B+ /8.5	4.34 /34	17.18 /91	13.40 /72	D+ / 2.8	85	12
MC	Schroder US Smll & Mid Cap Opp	SMDVX	C	(800) 464-3108	12.51	B+ /8.5	13.40 /88	16.08 /84	13.93 /77	D+ / 2.7	70	9
SC	● Buffalo Emerging Opportunities	BUFOX	C	(800) 492-8332	17.85	B+ /8.5	-0.71 /14	17.96 /94	18.63 /98	D+ / 2.7	58	4
SC	Mutual of America Inst SC Gro	MASSX	C	(800) 914-8716	12.89	B+ /8.4	11.87 /82	14.75 /73	14.47 /82	D+ / 2.5	50	8
SC	SunAmerica VAL Co II SmCp	VASMX	C	(800) 858-8850	18.07	B+ /8.3	5.68 /42	15.68 /84	15.70 /91	D+ / 2.6	43	8
MC	Madison Mid Cap Y	GTSGX	C-	(800) 336-3063	8.98	A- /9.2	13.72 /89	17.13 /90	16.73 /95	D- / 1.2	86	5
FO	Rydex Japan 2x Strategy Fd A	RYJSX	C-	(800) 820-0888	23.29	A- /9.0	20.61 /97	14.66 /72	7.15 /24	D- / 1.2	73	7
EM	Eaton Vance Greater India A	ETGIX	C-	(800) 262-1122	29.26	B+ /8.9	35.09 /99	12.73 /58	4.34 / 9	D / 1.6	98	8
SC	MassMutual Select Small Cap GE	MMGEX	C-	(800) 542-6767	14.95	B+ /8.7	11.00 /78	17.54 /92	14.71 /84	D- / 1.3	83	14
GL	Hartford Small/Mid Cap Eq HLS Fd	HMCVX	C-	(888) 843-7824	9.89	B+ /8.6	8.43 /66	16.23 /85	15.00 /87	D / 1.6	98	3
GR	INTECH US Managed Volatility A	JRSAX	C-	(800) 295-2687	10.62	B+ /8.5	11.36 /80	17.84 /94	14.44 /82	D / 1.9	87	10
SC	CRM Small Cap Value Inv	CRMSX	C-	(800) 276-2883	19.88	B+ /8.3	8.21 /64	15.90 /83	12.18 /62	D / 2.2	76	7
SC	Federated Kaufmann Sm Cap A	FKASX	C-	(800) 341-7400	26.86	B+ /8.3	12.27 /84	16.03 /84	15.54 /90	D / 1.8	55	N/A
GR	Commerce Growth	CFGRX	C-	(800) 995-6365	28.67	B /8.2	15.96 /93	14.89 /74	13.16 /70	D+ / 2.6	48	21
SC	Invesco Small Cap Discovery A	VASCX	C-	(800) 959-4246	11.28	B /8.2	10.77 /77	16.20 /85	14.78 /85	D+ / 2.4	82	15
MC	Harbor Mid Cap Growth Inv	HIMGX	C-	(800) 422-1050	9.69	B /8.1	9.74 /73	15.51 /79	13.78 /76	D / 2.2	45	10
FO	Oberweis China Opportunities	OBCHX	C-	(800) 245-7311	14.45	B /8.1	-2.19 /10	18.81 /96	7.51 /27	D / 1.9	99	10
FS	ProFunds-Banks UltraSector Svc	BKPSX	C-	(888) 776-3637	29.11	B /8.0	0.31 /16	18.58 /96	5.20 /13	D+ / 2.6	1	2
GR	Goldman Sachs Capital Growth A	GSCGX	C-	(800) 526-7384	25.87	B /7.9	16.36 /94	16.06 /84	14.07 /78	D+ / 2.8	59	15
MC	Transamerica Prt Mid Growth	DVMGX	C-	(888) 233-4339	10.79	B /7.9	13.55 /88	14.03 /67	13.87 /77	D+ / 2.7	16	2
SC	Hartford Small Company A	IHSAX	C-	(888) 843-7824	22.05	B /7.9	11.10 /79	16.42 /86	15.04 /87	D+ / 2.5	76	16
SC	Principal SmCp Gr I R3	PPNMX	C-	(800) 222-5852	11.23	B /7.9	7.28 /57	15.00 /75	16.53 /95	D / 1.9	53	N/A
SC	Thrivent Partner Small Cap Gr A	TPSAX	C-	(800) 847-4836	14.96	B /7.7	11.13 /79	15.42 /78	14.20 /80	D+ / 2.9	65	N/A

● Denotes fund is closed to new investors

99 Pct = Best
0 Pct = Worst

Fund Type	Fund Name	Ticker Symbol	Overall Investment Rating	Phone	Net Asset Value As of 3/31/15	Performance Rating/Pts	1Yr / Pct	3Yr / Pct	5Yr / Pct	Risk Rating/Pts	Mgr. Quality Pct	Mgr. Tenure (Years)
SC	● Dreyfus Opportunistic Small Cap	DSCVX	C-	(800) 645-6561	31.42	B /7.7	2.51 /24	16.07 /84	13.60 /74	D+ /2.9	34	10
GR	BlackRock Focus Growth Fd Inv A	MDFOX	C-	(800) 441-7762	3.02	B /7.7	16.89 /94	14.91 /74	13.44 /72	D+ /2.8	36	2
GR	Mutual of America Inst All Amer	MALLX	C-	(800) 914-8716	10.60	B /7.7	11.72 /81	15.08 /75	13.35 /72	D+ /2.6	55	12
RE	Invesco Real Estate A	IARAX	C-	(800) 959-4246	27.33	B /7.6	22.35 /97	12.68 /57	14.09 /79	D+ /2.5	50	N/A
MC	Franklin Small-Mid Cap Growth A	FRSGX	C-	(800) 342-5236	38.78	B /7.6	13.58 /88	15.43 /78	15.05 /87	D+ /2.5	38	23
RE	Columbia Real Estate Equity A	CREAX	C-	(800) 345-6611	16.51	B- /7.5	22.07 /97	12.22 /54	13.77 /76	D+ /2.7	29	9
GR	Neuberger Berman Focus A	NFAAX	C-	(800) 877-9700	16.61	B- /7.4	8.33 /65	17.09 /90	13.18 /70	D+ /2.5	80	7
EM	● Wells Fargo Adv Emerging Gr A	WEMAX	C-	(800) 222-8222	16.71	B- /7.3	10.74 /77	14.35 /70	17.64 /97	D+ /2.8	99	8
SC	Delaware Smid-Cap Growth Equity	DCGTX	C-	(800) 523-1918	18.68	B- /7.2	13.77 /89	12.88 /59	18.29 /98	D+ /2.9	75	10
GR	Chase Growth Fund	CHASX	D+	(888) 861-7556	13.67	B+ /8.8	15.91 /93	16.33 /86	14.53 /83	D- /1.0	73	18
RE	Natixis AEW Real Estate A	NRFAX	D+	(800) 225-5478	18.19	B+ /8.5	24.13 /98	13.20 /61	15.37 /89	D- /1.0	47	15
IX	Mutual of America Inst Eqty Idx	MAEQX	D+	(800) 914-8716	9.79	B /8.2	12.55 /85	16.01 /83	14.09 /79	D- /1.1	67	1
SC	● Bridgeway Ultra-SmCo	BRUSX	D+	(800) 661-3550	32.35	B /8.0	-1.64 /11	17.58 /93	14.40 /81	D /1.6	58	21
GR	Hartford Capital Apprec A	ITHAX	D+	(888) 843-7824	38.33	B /8.0	10.42 /76	17.46 /92	11.68 /58	D /1.6	63	19
GI	Natixis US Equity Opportunties A	NEFSX	D+	(800) 225-5478	28.04	B /7.9	12.05 /83	17.24 /91	15.54 /90	D /1.8	73	4
GR	Scotia Dynamic US Growth I	DWUGX	D+	(888) 261-4073	27.62	B /7.8	17.57 /95	12.77 /58	20.42 /99	D /1.9	29	6
SC	● BMO Small-Cap Growth Y	MRSCX	D+	(800) 236-3863	19.91	B /7.8	3.41 /29	15.13 /76	14.93 /86	D /1.6	32	11
SC	Northern Multi Mgr Small Cap	NMMSX	D+	(800) 595-9111	10.06	B /7.7	7.11 /56	15.19 /76	13.62 /74	D /1.8	70	5
GR	ICON Consumer Staples S	ICLEX	D+	(800) 764-0442	9.37	B- /7.5	15.79 /93	13.91 /66	12.83 /67	D /2.1	86	1
GR	US Lg-Cap Core Eqty Inv	GEIVX	D+	(800) 242-0134	9.67	B- /7.2	8.83 /68	15.30 /77	12.90 /67	D+ /2.4	44	13
SC	Dunham Small Cap Growth A	DADGX	D+	(888) 338-6426	17.72	B- /7.2	5.49 /42	15.62 /80	13.53 /73	D /2.2	61	11
MC	Nuveen Mid Cap Growth Opps A	FRSLX	D+	(800) 257-8787	42.98	B- /7.2	12.56 /85	15.26 /77	16.05 /93	D /2.0	39	10
GR	Principal LgCp Gr II R3	PPTMX	D+	(800) 222-5852	8.18	B- /7.0	13.40 /88	13.59 /64	12.79 /66	D+ /2.5	36	15
SC	CRM Small/Mid Cap Value Inv	CRMAX	D+	(800) 276-2883	15.34	C+ /6.9	6.99 /55	14.37 /70	13.10 /69	D+ /2.7	87	11
GR	BlackRock Capital Appr Inv A	MDFGX	D+	(800) 441-7762	24.87	C+ /6.9	15.40 /92	14.11 /68	12.38 /63	D+ /2.4	27	2
SC	Nuveen Small Cap Growth Opps A	FRMPX	D+	(800) 257-8787	23.35	C+ /6.8	9.30 /71	14.80 /73	14.53 /83	D+ /2.7	49	11
GR	Alger Growth Opportunities A	AOFAX	D+	(800) 254-3796	11.47	C+ /6.7	8.24 /64	14.40 /70	13.65 /74	D+ /2.9	38	N/A
GR	Morgan Stanley Multi Cap Gr Trust	CPOAX	D+	(800) 869-6397	33.41	C+ /6.6	9.44 /72	15.10 /76	16.02 /93	D+ /2.9	26	13
GI	Manning & Napier Tax Managed	EXTAX	D+	(800) 466-3863	27.40	C+ /6.6	6.80 /53	14.66 /72	11.17 /54	D+ /2.8	35	20
MC	Goldman Sachs Growth Opps A	GGOAX	D+	(800) 526-7384	25.34	C+ /6.6	11.36 /80	15.01 /75	14.08 /78	D+ /2.8	60	16
SC	Adv Inn Cir ICM Sm Co I	ICSCX	D+	(866) 777-7818	29.32	C+ /6.5	3.79 /30	13.85 /66	12.43 /64	D+ /2.7	37	16
GR	BNY Mellon Large Cap Stock M	MPLCX	D	(800) 645-6561	6.24	B /7.6	14.39 /90	14.76 /73	12.56 /65	D- /1.2	48	2
MC	CRM Large Cap Opportunity Inv	CRMGX	D	(800) 276-2883	9.33	B- /7.3	11.16 /79	14.48 /71	12.12 /61	D- /1.1	71	10
AG	Delaware Select 20 Port	DPCEX	D	(800) 523-1918	8.58	B- /7.2	15.54 /93	13.27 /62	16.26 /94	D /1.6	36	10
IN	Rainier Large Cap Equity Original	RIMEX	D	(800) 248-6314	25.43	B- /7.2	14.12 /90	13.90 /66	12.37 /63	D- /1.3	23	19
MC	CRM Mid Cap Value Inv	CRMMX	D	(800) 276-2883	28.44	B- /7.0	7.37 /58	14.52 /71	12.28 /62	D /2.0	66	17
GR	● Janus Twenty T	JAVLX	D	(800) 295-2687	58.66	C+ /6.8	10.92 /78	14.01 /67	10.97 /52	D /1.8	37	2
GR	Columbia Select Large Cap Equity	NSGAX	D	(800) 345-6611	12.72	C+ /6.7	13.10 /87	15.07 /75	13.11 /69	D+ /2.3	66	11
GR	Columbia Marsico Focused Eq A	NFEAX	D	(800) 345-6611	20.16	C+ /6.6	16.11 /93	14.94 /74	13.85 /76	D /2.2	63	18
GR	Principal LgCp Blend II R3	PPZMX	D	(800) 222-5852	9.97	C+ /6.6	9.52 /72	13.95 /67	12.11 /61	D /1.8	36	8
EM	T Rowe Price Inst Global Foc Gr	TRGSX	D	(800) 638-5660	11.35	C+ /6.5	10.17 /75	13.72 /65	10.62 /50	D+ /2.3	99	3
GI	Profit	PVALX	D	(888) 744-2337	21.61	C+ /6.5	10.51 /76	14.27 /69	12.84 /67	D /2.2	23	18
SC	Oberweis Emerging Growth	OBEGX	D	(800) 245-7311	27.84	C+ /6.4	-1.39 /12	14.13 /68	11.88 /60	D /2.2	17	14
GR	CRM All Cap Value Inv	CRMEX	D	(800) 276-2883	10.58	C+ /6.2	7.58 /60	13.12 /61	11.11 /54	D+ /2.8	20	5
SC	Paradigm Select	PFSLX	D	(877) 593-8637	34.09	C+ /6.2	11.16 /79	12.46 /56	13.78 /76	D+ /2.7	55	2
GR	Nuveen Large Cap Growth Opps A	FRGWX	D	(800) 257-8787	36.08	C+ /6.2	14.36 /90	13.00 /60	14.37 /81	D+ /2.5	18	13
SC	MassMutual Select Small Comp Gr	MRWAX	D	(800) 542-6767	11.79	C+ /6.1	9.11 /70	13.55 /64	14.97 /87	D+ /2.9	41	2
SC	Royce Value Plus Fd Svc	RYVPX	D	(800) 221-4268	14.91	C+ /6.1	5.25 /40	13.05 /60	11.24 /55	D+ /2.9	22	13

● Denotes fund is closed to new investors

99 Pct = Best
0 Pct = Worst

Fund Type	Fund Name	Ticker Symbol	Overall Investment Rating	Phone	Net Asset Value As of 3/31/15	Perform-ance Rating/Pts	Annualized Total Return Through 3/31/15			Risk Rating/Pts	Mgr. Quality Pct	Mgr. Tenure (Years)
							1Yr / Pct	3Yr / Pct	5Yr / Pct			
SC	ProFunds-Internet UltraSector Svc	INPSX	C-	(888) 776-3637	33.00	A+ /9.9	10.72 /77	27.61 /99	25.30 /99	E / 0.5	93	2
GI	PIMCO StockPlus Long Duration	PSLDX	C-	(800) 426-0107	7.56	A+ /9.9	29.07 /99	24.14 /99	24.94 /99	E- / 0.1	98	8
FO	ProFunds-Ultra Japan Svc	UJPSX	C-	(888) 776-3637	19.22	A+ /9.9	55.50 /99	37.64 /99	12.68 /66	E- / 0.0	99	6
GR	Direxion Mo NASDAQ-100 Bull 2X	DXQLX	C-	(800) 851-0511	56.64	A+ /9.9	43.73 /99	33.97 /99	34.51 /99	E- / 0.0	33	9
SC	Direxion Mo Small Cap Bull 2X Inv	DXRLX	C-	(800) 851-0511	53.18	A+ /9.9	13.04 /87	30.96 /99	25.33 /99	E- / 0.0	24	11
GR	Janus Aspen Forty Inst	JACAX	C-	(800) 295-2687	43.43	A+ /9.7	20.22 /97	16.98 /90	12.83 /67	E / 0.5	79	2
MC	Alger SMidCap Growth I2	AAMOX	C-	(800) 254-3796	8.00	A+ /9.7	9.44 /72	20.36 /98	16.79 /95	E / 0.5	75	7
MC	Principal MidCp Grw R3	PFPPX	C-	(800) 222-5852	7.17	A+ /9.6	16.80 /94	17.46 /92	15.99 /93	E+ / 0.9	73	N/A
SC	● Lord Abbett Developing Growth A	LAGWX	C-	(888) 522-2388	23.78	A /9.4	8.78 /68	19.61 /97	18.95 /98	E+ / 0.8	86	14
FO	Direxion Mo China Bull 2X Inv	DXHLX	D+	(800) 851-0511	49.79	A+ /9.9	57.81 /99	15.03 /75	0.37 / 3	E- / 0.0	55	8
FO	ProFunds-Ultra Sh Latin America	UFPSX	D+	(888) 776-3637	19.84	A+ /9.9	41.00 /99	18.71 /96	-3.41 / 1	E- / 0.0	99	6
SC	Dreyfus/Boston Co Sm Cap Growth	SSETX	D+	(800) 221-4795	39.21	A /9.4	9.15 /70	17.40 /92	15.41 /90	E / 0.4	79	N/A
MC	TCM Small Mid Cap Growth	TCMMX	D+	(800) 536-3230	16.90	A /9.3	14.24 /90	17.06 /90	14.73 /85	E / 0.4	42	8
GR	Janus Adviser Forty A	JDCAX	D+	(800) 295-2687	32.41	A /9.3	19.89 /97	16.68 /88	12.55 /64	E / 0.3	72	2
RE	PIMCO RealEstate RlRetrn Str A	PETAX	D+	(800) 426-0107	3.82	A /9.3	29.19 /99	13.54 /64	20.71 /99	E- / 0.0	5	8
SC	● AMG Frontier Small Cap Growth	MSSVX	D+	(800) 835-3879	15.66	A- /9.2	10.34 /76	16.61 /87	14.90 /86	E / 0.5	71	6
SC	Wells Fargo Adv Sm Cp Opp Adm	NVSOX	D+	(800) 222-8222	25.19	A- /9.0	11.75 /82	16.49 /87	13.70 /75	E+ / 0.8	89	12
SC	Rice Hall James Small Cap Port	RHJMX	D	(866) 777-7818	13.98	B /8.1	10.56 /77	14.61 /72	17.10 /96	E+ / 0.9	49	19
PM	ProFunds Short Precious Metals	SPPSX	D	(888) 776-3637	10.19	B /8.1	17.80 /95	14.49 /71	2.15 / 5	E+ / 0.7	57	2
GR	RidgeWorth Lrg-Cap Growth Stock	STCIX	D-	(888) 784-3863	8.75	B- /7.3	14.83 /91	14.68 /72	15.15 /88	E+ / 0.7	36	8
SC	Sentinel Small Company Fd A	SAGWX	D-	(800) 282-3863	5.80	B- /7.3	11.40 /80	15.29 /77	15.31 /89	E+ / 0.6	88	3
SC	Turner Small Cap Growth Fund	TSCEX	D-	(800) 224-6312	18.77	B- /7.3	7.48 /59	14.20 /69	13.54 /73	E- / 0.0	37	2
MC	Wasatch Ultra Growth Investor	WAMCX	D-	(800) 551-1700	20.43	B- /7.2	7.05 /55	14.06 /68	15.17 /88	E+ / 0.6	13	3
SC	● Universal Inst Small Co Growth II	USIIX	D-	(800) 869-6397	17.11	B- /7.2	-5.22 / 5	16.36 /86	14.94 /86	E- / 0.1	34	12
SC	Frontier Netols Small Cap Value Y	FNSYX	D-	(888) 825-2100	10.99	C+ /6.9	5.16 /40	14.43 /70	12.42 /63	E+ / 0.7	41	10
MC	Westcore MIDCO Growth Rtl	WTMGX	D-	(800) 392-2673	5.73	C+ /6.9	7.68 /60	13.98 /67	13.51 /73	E+ / 0.7	14	10
GR	Meridian Growth Legacy	MERDX	D-	(800) 446-6662	37.27	C+ /6.7	13.86 /89	12.77 /58	15.13 /88	E+ / 0.8	34	2
SC	TCW Small Cap Growth N	TGSNX	D-	(800) 386-3829	28.70	C+ /6.5	9.10 /70	12.09 /53	10.08 /45	E+ / 0.9	5	3
GR	● Wasatch Heritage Growth Investor	WAHGX	D-	(800) 551-1700	6.40	C+ /6.4	9.33 /71	13.00 /60	13.53 /73	E+ / 0.8	17	11
SC	● Dreyfus/Boston Co Sm Cap Value I	STSVX	D-	(800) 221-4795	24.43	C+ /6.3	1.84 /21	14.22 /69	12.44 /64	E+ / 0.8	44	15
SC	RidgeWorth Sm Cap Gr Stock A	SCGIX	D-	(888) 784-3863	13.23	C+ /6.2	4.21 /33	14.39 /70	13.98 /78	E+ / 0.8	37	8
SC	BlackRock Small Cap Gr Equity Inv	CSGEX	D-	(800) 441-7762	15.74	C+ /6.2	7.67 /60	14.14 /68	13.69 /75	E+ / 0.7	21	2
SC	Turner Emerging Growth Inv	TMCGX	E+	(800) 224-6312	31.34	C+ /6.5	2.57 /24	13.75 /65	14.22 /80	E- / 0.1	41	N/A
MC	Turner Midcap Growth Inv	TMGFX	E+	(800) 224-6312	23.75	C+ /6.3	8.59 /67	12.77 /58	12.29 /62	E / 0.4	12	7
SC	Alger Small Cap Growth Inst R	ASIRX	E+	(800) 254-3796	22.84	C+ /6.1	6.23 /48	12.12 /53	11.89 /60	E+ / 0.7	22	14
MC	Calamos Growth A	CVGRX	E+	(800) 582-6959	42.67	C+ /5.9	13.20 /87	12.28 /54	11.79 /59	E+ / 0.9	18	25
MC	TCW Growth Equities N	TGDNX	E+	(800) 386-3829	12.48	C+ /5.9	6.53 /51	12.11 /53	11.43 /56	E / 0.5	4	3
FO	Profunds-Ultra China Svc	UGPSX	E+	(888) 776-3637	11.71	C+ /5.8	13.47 /88	12.38 /55	2.13 / 5	E- / 0.0	12	6
GR	Columbia Global Infrastructure A	RRIAX	E+	(800) 345-6611	16.36	C+ /5.6	3.59 /29	15.00 /75	12.04 /61	E+ / 0.9	23	8
RE	Ell Global Property Inst	EIIGX	E+	(888) 323-8912	9.74	C /5.3	11.72 /81	9.63 /37	10.15 /46	E+ / 0.6	47	9
SC	Deutsche Small Cap Value A	KDSAX	E+	(800) 728-3337	26.48	C /5.1	4.95 /38	12.64 /57	10.16 /46	E+ / 0.9	28	2
SC	AlphaMark Small Cap Growth Fund	AMSCX	E+	(866) 420-3350	12.32	C /5.1	7.52 /59	11.26 /47	14.60 /83	E+ / 0.8	45	7
SC	Eagle Smaller Company A	EGEAX	E+	(800) 421-4184	13.24	C /5.1	3.10 /27	13.10 /60	12.90 /67	E+ / 0.6	47	N/A
GR	Nationwide HighMark Large Cp Gr	NWGLX	E+	(800) 848-0920	8.79	C /4.8	12.47 /85	11.40 /48	11.73 /59	E+ / 0.9	33	2
SC	Jacob Micro Cap Growth Inv	JMCGX	E	(888) 522-6239	17.25	C- /3.6	4.49 /35	8.03 /27	12.83 /67	E+ / 0.6	6	3
GR	Neuberger Berman Lg Cap Disp Gr	NLDAX	E	(800) 877-9700	4.00	C- /3.3	8.29 /65	9.75 /38	9.67 /42	E+ / 0.8	7	16
GL	Schroder Global Multi-Cp Eq R6	SQQIX	E-	(800) 464-3108	12.03	C- /3.7	2.48 /24	10.55 /43	--	E- / 0.0	89	5
EM	ProFunds-Ultra Intl Svc	UNPSX	E-	(888) 776-3637	14.91	C- /3.4	-8.47 / 3	10.50 /42	2.59 / 5	E / 0.4	98	6
AA	● Lifetime Achievement	LFTAX	E-	(888) 339-4230	18.08	C- /3.3	2.56 /24	9.78 /38	9.06 /37	E- / 0.1	4	15
EM	Profunds-Ultra Sh Emer Mkt Svc	UVPSX	E-	(888) 776-3637	8.82	E- /0.2	-8.60 / 3	-5.44 / 2	-12.91 / 0	E- / 0.0	15	6
FO	Direxion Mo Emerg Mkts Bull 2X	DXELX	E-	(800) 851-0511	44.35	E- /0.2	-5.58 / 5	-6.66 / 1	-6.60 / 1	E- / 0.0	0	10
EM	Rydex Inverse Emg Mkts 2x Str A	RYWWX	E-	(800) 820-0888	16.88	E- /0.2	-7.96 / 3	-4.33 / 2	--	E- / 0.0	25	5

● Denotes fund is closed to new investors

Fund Type	Fund Name	Ticker Symbol	Overall Investment Rating	Phone	Net Asset Value As of 3/31/15	Performance Rating/Pts	Annualized Total Return Through 3/31/15 1Yr / Pct	3Yr / Pct	5Yr / Pct	Risk Rating/Pts	Mgr. Quality Pct	Mgr. Tenure (Years)
	99 Pct = Best *0 Pct = Worst*											
EM	US Global Investors Em Europe	EUROX	E-	(800) 873-8637	6.18	E- /0.1	-21.23 / 1	-10.60 / 1	-7.43 / 1	E+ / 0.9	1	18
GR	Direxion Mo Natural Res Bull 2X	DXCLX	E-	(800) 851-0511	44.17	E- /0.1	-31.90 / 0	-7.80 / 1	-3.71 / 1	E- / 0.0	0	10
PM	Vanguard Prec Metals & Mining Inv	VGPMX	E-	(800) 662-7447	8.68	E- /0.0	-20.37 / 1	-22.27 / 0	-13.00 / 0	E+ / 0.8	1	2
PM	Invesco Gold and Precious Mtls A	IGDAX	E-	(800) 959-4246	3.60	E- /0.0	-21.40 / 1	-23.54 / 0	-12.23 / 0	E+ / 0.7	2	2
PM	Wells Fargo Adv Precious Mtls A	EKWAX	E-	(800) 222-8222	28.99	E- /0.0	-20.90 / 1	-24.56 / 0	-13.26 / 0	E+ / 0.7	2	8
PM	Oppenheimer Gold/Spec Min A	OPGSX	E-	(888) 470-0862	12.82	E- /0.0	-25.08 / 0	-27.27 / 0	-15.68 / 0	E+ / 0.7	1	18
PM	US Global Inv Gold & PMetals Fd	USERX	E-	(800) 873-8637	5.28	E- /0.0	-21.31 / 1	-24.65 / 0	-14.87 / 0	E+ / 0.7	2	26
PM	USAA Precious Mtls&Minerals	USAGX	E-	(800) 382-8722	11.32	E- /0.0	-22.99 / 1	-27.15 / 0	-15.55 / 0	E+ / 0.6	1	7
PM	OCM Gold Fund Investor	OCMGX	E-	(800) 628-9403	9.29	E- /0.0	-19.86 / 1	-23.46 / 0	-12.23 / 0	E+ / 0.6	5	19
OT	Rydex Commodities Strgy A	RYMEX	E-	(800) 820-0888	9.01	E- /0.0	-41.00 / 0	-18.52 / 0	-9.92 / 0	E+ / 0.6	0	10
AG	Rydex Inv Dow 2x Strategy A	RYIDX	E-	(800) 820-0888	30.36	E- /0.0	-22.85 / 1	-26.18 / 0	-28.42 / 0	E / 0.5	59	7
PM	Deutsche Gold & Prec Metals Fund	SGDAX	E-	(800) 728-3337	5.65	E- /0.0	-25.36 / 0	-27.39 / 0	-16.45 / 0	E / 0.4	1	4
PM	Gabelli Gold A	GLDAX	E-	(800) 422-3554	10.37	E- /0.0	-17.70 / 1	-22.74 / 0	-12.33 / 0	E / 0.4	11	21
PM	Fidelity Adv Gold A	FGDAX	E-	(800) 522-7297	15.92	E- /0.0	-21.15 / 1	-26.59 / 0	-15.06 / 0	E / 0.4	2	8
PM	Tocqueville Gold	TGLDX	E-	(800) 697-3863	30.05	E- /0.0	-21.15 / 1	-24.24 / 0	-11.44 / 0	E / 0.3	2	18
AG	Rydex Inv S&P 500 2x Strategy A	RYTMX	E-	(800) 820-0888	23.87	E- /0.0	-25.38 / 0	-29.97 / 0	-30.46 / 0	E / 0.3	7	15
GR	ProFunds-Ultra Short Dow 30 Svc	UWPSX	E-	(888) 776-3637	5.82	E- /0.0	-23.62 / 1	-27.30 / 0	-29.26 / 0	E- / 0.2	38	2
PM	Rydex Precious Metal A	RYMNX	E-	(800) 820-0888	24.28	E- /0.0	-28.13 / 0	-25.99 / 0	-15.48 / 0	E- / 0.2	1	22
PM	American Century Global Gold A	ACGGX	E-	(800) 345-6488	7.21	E- /0.0	-22.95 / 1	-26.63 / 0	-14.43 / 0	E- / 0.2	1	23
SC	Direxion Mo Small Cap Bear 2X Inv	DXRSX	E-	(800) 851-0511	30.75	E- /0.0	-23.07 / 1	-32.50 / 0	-33.42 / 0	E- / 0.0	2	11
PM	Van Eck Intl Investors Gold A	INIVX	E-	(800) 826-1115	7.57	E- /0.0	-22.28 / 1	-25.00 / 0	-13.24 / 0	E- / 0.0	3	19
GR	ProFunds-Ultra Bear Svc	URPSX	E-	(888) 776-3637	5.31	E- /0.0	-26.14 / 0	-31.22 / 0	-31.57 / 0	E- / 0.0	3	6
GR	ProFunds Ultra Short	USPSX	E-	(888) 776-3637	12.53	E- /0.0	-38.26 / 0	-33.95 / 0	-36.81 / 0	E- / 0.0	2	2
FO	Profunds-Ultra Short China Svc	UHPSX	E-	(888) 776-3637	15.59	E- /0.0	-29.33 / 0	-29.92 / 0	-27.95 / 0	E- / 0.0	0	6
SC	Rydex Inv Rusl 2000 2x Strtgy A	RYIUX	E-	(800) 820-0888	25.05	E- /0.0	-23.39 / 1	-33.63 / 0	-36.31 / 0	E- / 0.0	1	9
GR	Direxion Mo S&P 500 Bear 2X Inv	DXSSX	E-	(800) 851-0511	29.20	E- /0.0	-24.53 / 0	-29.46 / 0	-29.11 / 0	E- / 0.0	12	9
FO	Direxion Mo Latin America Bl 2X	DXZLX	E-	(800) 851-0511	16.84	E- /0.0	-39.14 / 0	-29.99 / 0	-21.45 / 0	E- / 0.0	0	9
EM	ProFunds-Ultra Sh Intl Svc	UXPSX	E-	(888) 776-3637	22.16	E- /0.0	-6.18 / 4	-23.68 / 0	-24.93 / 0	E- / 0.0	0	6
FO	Profunds-Ultra Short Japan Svc	UKPSX	E-	(888) 776-3637	14.07	E- /0.0	-48.02 / 0	-44.85 / 0	-33.50 / 0	E- / 0.0	0	6
AG	Rydex Inv NASDAQ 100 2x Stgy A	RYVTX	E-	(800) 820-0888	19.36	E- /0.0	-37.04 / 0	-32.89 / 0	-36.00 / 0	E- / 0.0	2	15
PM	First Eagle Gold A	SGGDX	E-	(800) 334-2143	13.94	E- /0.0	-15.36 / 2	-20.76 / 0	-9.95 / 0	E- / 0.0	6	2
MC	ProFunds-Ultra Short Mid-Cap Svc	UIPSX	E-	(888) 776-3637	4.45	E- /0.0	-26.81 / 0	-33.27 / 0	-35.19 / 0	E- / 0.0	2	2
SC	ProFunds-Ultra Short Small-Cap	UCPSX	E-	(888) 776-3637	18.95	E- /0.0	-24.05 / 1	-34.34 / 0	-37.51 / 0	E- / 0.0	1	2

Denotes fund is closed to new investors

Section VIII

Top-Rated
Stock Mutual Funds
by Fund Type

A compilation of those

Equity Mutual Funds

receiving the highest TheStreet Investment Rating

within each type of fund.

Funds are listed in order by Overall Investment Rating.

Section VIII Contents

This section contains a summary analysis of the top 100 rated mutual funds within each fund type. If you are looking for a particular type of mutual fund, these pages show those funds that have achieved the best combination of risk and financial performance over the past three years.

In order to optimize the utility of our top and bottom fund lists, rather than listing all funds in a multi-class series, a single fund from each series is selected for display as the primary share class. Whenever possible, the selected fund is one that a retail investor would be most likely to choose. This share class may not be appropriate for every investor, so please consult with your financial advisor, the fund company, and the fund's prospectus before placing your trade.

1.	**Fund Type**	The mutual fund's peer category based on an analysis of its investment portfolio.	

AG	Aggressive Growth	HL	Health
AA	Asset Allocation	IN	Income
BA	Balanced	IX	Index
CV	Convertible	MC	Mid Cap
EM	Emerging Market	OT	Other
EN	Energy/Natural Resources	PM	Precious Metals
FS	Financial Services	RE	Real Estate
FO	Foreign	SC	Small Cap
GL	Global	TC	Technology
GR	Growth	UT	Utilities
GI	Growth and Income		

A blank fund type means that the mutual fund has not yet been categorized.

2.	**Fund Name**	The name of the mutual fund as stated in its prospectus, which can sometimes differ slightly from the name that the company uses for advertising. If you cannot find the particular mutual fund you are interested in, or if you have any doubts regarding the precise name, verify the information with your broker or on your account statement. Also, use the fund's ticker symbol for confirmation. (See column 3.)

3.	**Ticker Symbol**	The unique alphabetic symbol used for identifying and trading a specific mutual fund. No two funds can have the same ticker symbol, and the ticker symbol for mutual funds always ends with an "X".

A handful of funds currently show no associated ticker symbol. This means that the fund is either small or new since the NASD only assigns a ticker symbol to funds with at least $25 million in assets or 1,000 shareholders.

4.	**Overall Investment Rating**	Our overall rating is measured on a scale from A to E based on each fund's risk-adjusted performance. Please see page 10 for specific descriptions of each letter grade. Also, refer to page 7 for information on how our ratings are derived. Most important, when using this rating, please be sure to consider the warnings beginning on page 11 regarding the ratings' limitations and the

underlying assumptions.

5.   Phone
The telephone number of the company managing the fund. Call this number to receive a prospectus or other information about the fund.

6.   Net Asset Value (NAV)
The fund's share price as of the date indicated. A fund's NAV is computed by dividing the value of the fund's asset holdings, less accrued fees and expenses, by the number of its shares outstanding.

7.   Performance Rating/Points
A letter grade rating based solely on the mutual fund's financial performance over the trailing three years, without any consideration for the amount of risk the fund poses. Like the overall Investment Rating, the Performance Rating is measured on a scale from A to E for ease of interpretation. The points score indicates where the Performance Rating falls on a scale of 0 to 10.

8.   1-Year Total Return
The total return the fund has provided investors over the preceeding twelve months. This total return figure is computed based on the fund's dividend distributions and share price appreciation/depreciation during the period, net of the expenses and fees it imposes on its shareholders. Although the total return figure does not reflect an adjustment for any loads the fund may carry, such adjustments have been made in deriving TheStreet Investment Ratings.

9.   1-Year Total Return Percentile
The fund's percentile rank based on its one-year performance compared to that of all other equity funds in existence for at least one year. A score of 99 is the best possible, indicating that the fund outperformed 99% of the other mutual funds. Zero is the worst possible percentile score.

10.   3-Year Total Return
The total annual return the fund has provided investors over the preceeding three years.

11.   3-Year Total Return Percentile
The fund's percentile rank based on its three-year performance compared to that of all other equity funds in existence for at least three years. A score of 99 is the best possible, indicating that the fund outperformed 99% of the other mutual funds. Zero is the worst possible percentile score.

12.   5-Year Total Return
The total annual return the fund has provided investors over the preceeding five years.

13.   5-Year Total Return Percentile
The fund's percentile rank based on its five-year performance compared to that of all other equity funds in existence for at least five years. A score of 99 is the best possible, indicating that the fund outperformed 99% of the other mutual funds. Zero is the worst possible percentile score.

14. Risk Rating/Points

A letter grade rating based solely on the mutual fund's risk as determined by its monthly performance volatility over the trailing three years. The risk rating does not take into consideration the overall financial performance the fund has achieved or the total return it has provided to its shareholders. Like the overall Investment Rating, the Risk Rating is measured on a scale from A to E for ease of interpretation. The points score indicates where the Risk Rating falls on a scale of 0 to 10.

15. Manager Quality Percentile

The manager quality percentile is based on a ranking of the fund's alpha, a statistical measure representing the difference between a fund's actual returns and its expected performance given its level of risk. Fund managers who have been able to exceed the fund's statistically expected performance receive a high percentile rank with 99 representing the highest possible score. At the other end of the spectrum, fund managers who have actually detracted from the fund's expected performance receive a low percentile rank with 0 representing the lowest possible score.

16. Manager Tenure

The number of years the current manager has been managing the fund. Since fund managers who deliver substandard returns are usually replaced, a long tenure is usually a good sign that shareholders are satisfied that the fund is achieving its stated objectives.

Fund Type	Fund Name	Ticker Symbol	Overall Investment Rating	Phone	Net Asset Value As of 3/31/15	PERFORMANCE Perform-ance Rating/Pts	Annualized Total Return Through 3/31/15 1Yr / Pct	3Yr / Pct	5Yr / Pct	RISK Risk Rating/Pts	FUND MGR Mgr. Quality Pct	Mgr. Tenure (Years)
	99 Pct = Best *0 Pct = Worst*											
AG	Rydex Nova A	RYANX	A+	(800) 820-0888	46.40	A+ /9.8	17.09 /95	22.38 /98	19.28 /98	C+ / 6.6	33	19
AG	Fidelity Growth Strategies Fd	FDEGX	A+	(800) 544-8544	34.41	A+ /9.7	19.73 /97	17.82 /94	14.50 /82	C+ / 6.3	71	2
AG	Bridgeway Aggressive Investor 1	BRAGX	A+	(800) 661-3550	60.13	A+ /9.7	11.61 /81	20.83 /98	15.35 /89	C+ / 6.2	72	21
AG	CB Aggressive Growth A	SHRAX	A+	(877) 534-4627	209.82	A /9.4	11.38 /80	20.93 /98	18.65 /98	C+ / 6.6	89	32
AG ●	PRIMECAP Odyssey Agg Growth	POAGX	A	(800) 729-2307	34.88	A+ /9.9	17.96 /95	26.39 /99	20.62 /99	C+ / 5.6	95	11
AG	Rydex Dow 2x Strategy A	RYLDX	A	(800) 820-0888	50.69	A+ /9.8	17.18 /95	22.98 /99	21.60 /99	C+ / 5.6	2	11
AG	ProFunds-Ultra Bull Svc	ULPSX	A-	(888) 776-3637	89.74	A+ /9.9	20.88 /97	27.92 /99	22.68 /99	C / 5.2	9	2
AG	Rydex S&P 500 2x Strategy A	RYTTX	A-	(800) 820-0888	70.18	A+ /9.9	22.51 /97	29.80 /99	24.33 /99	C / 5.1	17	15
AG	Rydex NASDAQ 100 A	RYATX	A-	(800) 820-0888	23.78	B /8.2	20.24 /97	16.16 /85	16.82 /96	C+ / 6.9	55	21
AG	First Inv Select Growth A	FICGX	A-	(800) 423-4026	12.34	B /8.0	15.99 /93	15.56 /80	16.35 /94	C+ / 6.9	45	8
AG	Rydex Russell 2000 1.5x Strgy A	RYAKX	B+	(800) 820-0888	58.05	A+ /9.8	9.48 /72	21.86 /98	18.22 /98	C / 4.9	6	15
AG	Permanent Portfolio Aggress Gr	PAGRX	B+	(800) 531-5142	70.22	B+ /8.3	7.58 /60	17.39 /92	13.50 /73	C+ / 6.0	34	12
AG	ProFunds-Nasdaq-100 Svc	OTPSX	B+	(888) 776-3637	113.70	B- /7.5	18.16 /96	14.13 /68	14.90 /86	B- / 7.2	29	2
AG	ProFunds-Ultra Mid Cap Svc	UMPSX	B	(888) 776-3637	81.90	A+ /9.9	19.75 /97	29.78 /99	24.82 /99	C- / 4.1	14	2
AG	Rydex Dyn-NASDAQ 100 2x Strgy	RYVLX	B	(800) 820-0888	369.52	A+ /9.9	42.33 /99	33.02 /99	33.41 /99	C- / 3.8	23	15
AG ●	Fidelity Fifty Fund	FFTYX	B	(800) 544-8544	30.41	B /7.7	7.21 /57	15.66 /80	14.10 /79	C+ / 6.2	61	4
AG	SunAmerica VAL Co I SmCp Agg	VSAGX	B-	(800) 858-8850	14.31	A+ /9.8	17.67 /95	21.28 /98	16.23 /94	C- / 3.2	93	4
AG	Meeder Aggressive Growth	FLAGX	B-	(800) 325-3539	10.71	B /8.1	13.59 /88	15.28 /77	12.03 /61	C / 4.9	41	10
AG	Franklin Growth Opportunities A	FGRAX	B-	(800) 342-5236	33.24	B /8.0	15.81 /93	15.36 /78	14.95 /86	C / 4.9	38	16
AG	Needham Aggressive Growth	NEAGX	B-	(800) 625-7071	24.45	B /7.6	14.25 /90	13.87 /66	13.56 /74	C / 5.4	22	5
AG	ProFunds-Bull Svc	BLPSX	B-	(888) 776-3637	81.35	C+ /5.8	9.44 /72	12.70 /57	11.06 /53	B- / 7.9	25	2
AG	Fund *X Aggressive Upgrader	HOTFX	C+	(866) 455-3863	58.64	C+ /6.7	9.05 /70	13.49 /63	10.50 /49	C+ / 6.2	29	13
AG	MassMutual Select Growth Opps A	MMAAX	C+	(800) 542-6767	11.04	C+ /6.6	11.73 /81	15.22 /77	17.38 /97	C / 5.3	39	11
AG	USAA Aggressive Growth Fund	USAUX	C	(800) 382-8722	40.47	B- /7.0	13.97 /89	13.61 /64	13.32 /71	C / 4.7	19	5
AG	Timothy Plan Aggressive Growth A	TAAGX	C	(800) 662-0201	9.14	C+ /6.5	10.29 /76	14.27 /69	16.07 /93	C / 5.1	19	7
AG	CAN SLIM Select Growth	CANGX	C	(800) 558-9105	14.19	C+ /6.2	7.99 /63	13.94 /67	11.57 /57	C / 5.2	46	7
AG	Midas Magic Fund	MISEX	C	(800) 400-6432	23.00	C /5.4	3.30 /28	13.42 /63	11.52 /57	C+ / 6.2	8	N/A
AG	MFS Aggressive Gr Alloc A	MAAGX	C	(800) 225-2606	20.41	C /4.4	5.87 /45	12.05 /53	11.19 /54	C+ / 6.9	25	13
AG	J Hancock II Lifestyle Agg A	JALAX	C	(800) 257-3336	16.80	C /4.3	6.06 /47	11.58 /50	9.98 /44	C+ / 6.8	22	N/A
AG ●	Delaware Select Growth A	DVEAX	C-	(800) 523-1918	50.28	C /5.5	11.88 /82	12.51 /56	16.44 /95	C / 5.2	19	10
AG	BlackRock Aggr Pre Inv A	BAAPX	C-	(800) 441-7762	12.40	C /5.3	8.78 /68	13.04 /60	11.25 /55	C / 5.3	20	8
AG	CGM Focus	CGMFX	C-	(800) 345-4048	41.79	C /5.3	6.09 /47	11.86 /51	6.35 /19	C / 4.7	1	18
AG	Gabelli Value 25 A	GABVX	C-	(800) 422-3554	18.40	C /4.9	3.71 /30	13.49 /63	13.49 /73	C+ / 5.8	21	26
AG	Oppenheimer Equity Inv A	OAAIX	C-	(888) 470-0862	15.53	C- /4.2	4.67 /36	11.90 /52	9.96 /44	C+ / 6.6	15	10
AG	J Hancock VIT Lifestyle Aggr I		C-	(800) 257-3336	10.87	C- /3.6	1.41 /20	10.08 /40	9.52 /41	C+ / 6.5	9	N/A
AG	Guggenheim Long Short Equity A	RYAMX	C-	(800) 820-0888	16.16	D+ /2.3	7.23 /57	6.89 /21	5.20 /13	B / 8.0	54	13
AG	Delaware Select 20 Port	DPCEX	D	(800) 523-1918	8.58	B- /7.2	15.54 /93	13.27 /62	16.26 /94	D / 1.6	36	10
AG	RidgeWorth Aggressive Gr Stock A	SAGAX	D	(888) 784-3863	20.76	C+ /5.6	4.47 /35	15.07 /75	13.41 /72	C- / 3.2	16	11
AG	ESG Managers Growth A	PAGAX	D	(800) 767-1729	13.20	C /4.9	8.58 /67	12.71 /58	10.05 /45	C- / 4.1	23	6
AG	Forward Multi-Strategy A	AGRRX	D	(800) 999-6809	14.66	E+ /0.9	1.76 /21	4.77 /12	4.41 /10	B- / 7.4	12	N/A
AG	RidgeWorth Aggr Gr Alloc Str A	SLAAX	E+	(888) 784-3863	7.87	C- /3.7	7.56 /60	10.53 /42	9.57 /41	C- / 3.1	18	23
AG	HSBC World Selection Aggr Strat A	HAAGX	E	(800) 728-8183	11.77	D+ /2.6	3.37 /28	9.22 /34	8.26 /32	D / 1.9	8	N/A
AG	Stonebridge Small Cap Growth	SBSGX	E-	(800) 639-3935	8.31	E /0.5	-10.13 / 3	1.41 / 6	4.20 / 9	C- / 3.3	0	36
AG	Rydex Inv S&P 500 Stgry A	RYARX	E-	(800) 820-0888	13.59	E- /0.0	-13.49 / 2	-16.21 / 0	-15.97 / 0	D+ / 2.8	27	21
AG	Rydex Inv NASDAQ 100 Strgy A	RYAPX	E-	(800) 820-0888	25.44	E- /0.0	-20.50 / 1	-17.77 / 0	-19.21 / 0	D+ / 2.4	17	17
AG	Rydex Inv Dow 2x Strategy A	RYIDX	E-	(800) 820-0888	30.36	E- /0.0	-22.85 / 1	-26.18 / 0	-28.42 / 0	E / 0.5	59	7
AG	Rydex Inv S&P 500 2x Strategy A	RYTMX	E-	(800) 820-0888	23.87	E- /0.0	-25.38 / 0	-29.97 / 0	-30.46 / 0	E / 0.3	7	15
AG	Rydex Inv NASDAQ 100 2x Stgy A	RYVTX	E-	(800) 820-0888	19.36	E- /0.0	-37.04 / 0	-32.89 / 0	-36.00 / 0	E- / 0.0	2	15

● Denotes fund is closed to new investors

Fund Type	Fund Name	Ticker Symbol	Overall Investment Rating	Phone	Net Asset Value As of 3/31/15	PERFORMANCE Perform-ance Rating/Pts	Annualized Total Return Through 3/31/15 1Yr / Pct	3Yr / Pct	5Yr / Pct	RISK Risk Rating/Pts	FUND MGR Mgr. Quality Pct	Mgr. Tenure (Years)
AA	Vanguard Diversified Equity Inv	VDEQX	A	(800) 662-7447	33.38	B+/8.7	12.31 /84	16.51 /87	14.62 /83	C+/6.7	29	N/A
AA	Rx Dynamic Growth Fund Inst	FMGRX	B	(877) 773-3863	12.75	B /7.9	13.61 /88	13.09 /60	10.08 /45	C+/5.6	18	1
AA	T Rowe Price Cap Appreciation	PRWCX	B	(800) 638-5660	26.97	B-/7.3	12.66 /85	14.11 /68	12.59 /65	C+/6.6	88	9
AA	Wells Fargo Adv Index Asst All A	SFAAX	B	(800) 222-8222	29.92	C+/6.1	14.58 /91	13.89 /66	13.25 /71	B /8.6	79	9
AA	T Rowe Price Retirement 2040	TRRDX	B-	(800) 638-5660	24.75	C+/6.0	8.34 /65	12.87 /59	11.75 /59	B- /7.0	16	13
AA ●	SEI Asset Alloc-Mkt Gr Str Alloc A	SGOAX	B-	(800) 342-5734	19.79	C+/5.8	6.83 /54	12.71 /58	11.45 /56	B- /7.3	12	12
AA ●	SEI Asset Alloc Core Mkt Str Al A	SKTAX	B-	(800) 342-5734	16.43	C+/5.8	6.84 /54	12.68 /57	11.39 /56	B- /7.3	13	12
AA ●	SEI Asset Alloc-Tax Mgd Agg Strgy	SISAX	B-	(800) 342-5734	18.12	C+/5.8	6.83 /54	12.73 /58	11.43 /56	B- /7.3	13	N/A
AA	Fidelity Four In One Index	FFNOX	B-	(800) 544-8544	38.10	C+/5.7	7.74 /61	12.40 /55	11.04 /53	B- /7.4	20	16
AA	Vanguard Target Retirement 2045	VTIVX	B-	(800) 662-7447	19.10	C+/5.6	7.92 /62	12.31 /55	11.06 /53	B- /7.5	14	12
AA	Putnam Retirement Ready 2045 A	PRVLX	B-	(800) 225-1581	19.40	C+/5.6	10.13 /75	13.32 /62	11.22 /55	B- /7.5	32	N/A
AA	Vanguard Target Retirement 2040	VFORX	B-	(800) 662-7447	30.47	C+/5.6	7.91 /62	12.30 /55	11.06 /53	B- /7.5	14	9
AA	TIAA-CREF Lifecycle Index 2050	TLLRX	B-	(800) 842-2252	16.52	C+/5.6	7.70 /60	12.25 /54	11.02 /53	B- /7.5	15	6
AA	TIAA-CREF Lifecycle Index 2045	TLMRX	B-	(800) 842-2252	16.54	C+/5.6	7.74 /61	12.25 /54	11.01 /53	B- /7.5	14	6
AA	TIAA-CREF Lifecycle Index 2040	TLZRX	B-	(800) 842-2252	16.62	C+/5.6	7.73 /61	12.27 /54	11.01 /53	B- /7.5	14	6
AA	Vanguard Target Retirement 2055	VFFVX	B-	(800) 662-7447	32.74	C+/5.6	7.90 /62	12.32 /55	--	B- /7.5	14	5
AA	Vanguard Target Retirement 2050	VFIFX	B-	(800) 662-7447	30.32	C+/5.6	7.91 /62	12.30 /55	11.06 /53	B- /7.4	14	9
AA	Vanguard Target Retirement 2035	VTTHX	B-	(800) 662-7447	18.26	C /5.4	7.92 /62	11.85 /51	10.76 /51	B- /7.7	17	12
AA	T Rowe Price Retirement 2030	TRRCX	B-	(800) 638-5660	23.73	C /5.4	7.70 /60	11.88 /52	11.10 /53	B- /7.5	19	13
AA	TIAA-CREF Lifecycle Index 2035	TLYRX	B-	(800) 842-2252	16.36	C /5.3	7.57 /60	11.70 /50	10.65 /50	B- /7.8	18	6
AA	American Century One Chc Agg	AOGIX	B-	(800) 345-6488	16.80	C /5.3	8.81 /68	11.41 /48	10.97 /52	B- /7.6	18	N/A
AA	Value Line Asset Allocation	VLAAX	B-	(800) 243-2729	28.88	C /5.2	8.39 /66	11.20 /47	12.47 /64	B /8.1	53	22
AA	Putnam Retirement Ready 2040 A	PRRZX	B-	(800) 225-1581	21.08	C /5.2	9.71 /73	12.81 /58	10.85 /51	B- /7.7	33	11
AA	Vanguard LifeStrategy Growth Inv	VASGX	B-	(800) 662-7447	29.48	C /5.1	7.79 /61	11.35 /48	10.34 /47	B /8.0	21	N/A
AA	Vanguard Target Retirement 2030	VTHRX	B-	(800) 662-7447	29.71	C /4.9	7.77 /61	11.10 /46	10.28 /47	B /8.1	23	9
AA	TIAA-CREF Lifecycle Index 2030	TLHRX	B-	(800) 842-2252	15.88	C /4.8	7.36 /58	10.86 /45	10.09 /45	B /8.2	23	6
AA	Putnam Dynamic Asset Alloc Bal A	PABAX	B-	(800) 225-1581	14.84	C /4.8	10.14 /75	11.93 /52	10.63 /50	B /8.2	62	13
AA	Vanguard Target Retirement 2025	VTTVX	B-	(800) 662-7447	16.90	C /4.5	7.65 /60	10.35 /42	9.78 /43	B /8.5	30	12
AA	Vanguard Tgt Retirement 2020 Inv	VTWNX	B-	(800) 662-7447	29.08	C- /4.1	7.51 /59	9.62 /37	9.27 /39	B /8.8	38	9
AA	USAA Growth & Tax Strategy Fund	USBLX	B-	(800) 382-8722	17.44	C- /4.1	8.56 /67	9.60 /37	9.50 /41	B /8.8	78	10
AA	VY T Rowe Price Cap App Adv	ITRAX	C+	(800) 992-0180	28.89	C+/6.9	12.17 /83	13.53 /64	12.02 /61	C+/6.6	86	9
AA	American Century One Chc	AOVIX	C+	(800) 345-6488	18.29	C+/6.4	9.78 /73	13.12 /60	12.03 /61	C+/6.8	11	N/A
AA	Vantagepoint Milestone 2045 Inv M	VPRJX	C+	(800) 669-7400	14.43	C+/5.7	6.87 /54	12.47 /56	11.06 /53	C+/6.2	11	5
AA	Transamerica Inst Asst All Lg Hrz	DILSX	C+	(888) 233-4339	11.35	C+/5.6	7.73 /61	11.85 /51	11.18 /54	B- /7.3	9	17
AA	TIAA-CREF Lifecycle 2040 Ret	TCLOX	C+	(800) 842-2252	13.77	C+/5.6	7.12 /56	12.22 /54	11.04 /53	C+/6.7	9	8
AA	MainStay Growth Allocation B	MGXBX	C+	(800) 624-6782	15.45	C /5.5	6.37 /50	12.34 /55	10.62 /50	C+/6.5	6	11
AA	Voya Strategic Alloc Gr Cl S	ISGRX	C+	(800) 992-0180	14.13	C /5.3	8.24 /65	11.56 /49	10.11 /46	B- /7.4	13	8
AA	JPMorgan Smart Ret 2040 A	SMTAX	C+	(800) 480-4111	20.16	C /5.3	9.55 /72	12.54 /56	11.21 /55	B- /7.3	15	9
AA	JPMorgan Smart Ret 2045 A	JSAAX	C+	(800) 480-4111	19.09	C /5.3	9.55 /72	12.58 /57	11.19 /55	B- /7.3	15	N/A
AA	Transamerica Asst All Lg Horizon	DVLSX	C+	(888) 233-4339	12.81	C /5.3	7.38 /58	11.48 /49	10.82 /51	B- /7.3	8	17
AA	IMS Dividend Growth Inst	IMSAX	C+		13.24	C /5.3	10.76 /77	11.46 /49	10.55 /49	B- /7.1	5	13
AA	TIAA-CREF Lifecycle 2035 Ret	TCLRX	C+	(800) 842-2252	13.44	C /5.3	6.98 /55	11.73 /51	10.73 /51	B- /7.0	11	8
AA	Eaton Vance Tax-Mgd Eqty A-Alloc	EAEAX	C+	(800) 262-1122	17.65	C /5.3	7.63 /60	13.50 /63	11.06 /53	C+/6.7	13	2
AA	JPMorgan Smart Ret 2050 A	JTSAX	C+	(800) 480-4111	19.04	C /5.2	9.49 /72	12.51 /56	11.24 /55	B- /7.3	15	N/A
AA	Principal LifeTime 2045 R5	LTRDX	C+	(800) 222-5852	11.82	C /5.2	7.30 /57	11.62 /50	10.60 /50	B- /7.2	12	7
AA	Voya Index Solution 2045 Adv	ISJAX	C+	(800) 992-0180	12.48	C /5.2	7.10 /56	11.68 /50	10.16 /46	C+/6.7	7	7
AA	JPMorgan Smart Ret 2035 A	SRJAX	C+	(800) 480-4111	18.80	C /5.1	9.36 /71	12.24 /54	11.01 /53	B- /7.4	17	8
AA	Principal LifeTime 2055 R3	LTFDX	C+	(800) 222-5852	12.00	C /5.1	6.98 /55	11.46 /49	10.27 /47	B- /7.1	8	7
AA	Principal SAM Strat Growth A	SACAX	C+	(800) 222-5852	21.07	C /5.1	8.51 /66	12.99 /60	11.58 /58	C+/6.8	12	15
AA	American Funds Tgt Dte Ret 2050	AALTX	C+	(800) 421-0180	12.95	C /5.0	7.43 /59	13.12 /61	11.20 /54	B- /7.5	28	8
AA	American Funds Tgt Dte Ret 2045	AAHTX	C+	(800) 421-0180	13.24	C /5.0	7.49 /59	13.15 /61	11.21 /54	B- /7.5	28	8
AA	American Funds Tgt Dte Ret 2040	AAGTX	C+	(800) 421-0180	13.17	C /5.0	7.36 /58	13.09 /60	11.18 /54	B- /7.5	29	8

● Denotes fund is closed to new investors

Data as of March 31, 2015

99 Pct = Best
0 Pct = Worst

99 Pct = Best
0 Pct = Worst

Fund Type	Fund Name	Ticker Symbol	Overall Investment Rating	Phone	Net Asset Value As of 3/31/15	Perform-ance Rating/Pts	Annualized Total Return Through 3/31/15 1Yr / Pct	3Yr / Pct	5Yr / Pct	Risk Rating/Pts	Mgr. Quality Pct	Mgr. Tenure (Years)
BA	Archer Balanced Fund	ARCHX	B	(800) 494-2755	11.88	C+ /5.8	14.51 /91	11.25 /47	8.45 /33	B /8.0	45	10
BA	Vanguard Wellington Inv	VWELX	B	(800) 662-7447	39.25	C /5.1	8.20 /64	11.53 /49	10.64 /50	B /8.3	65	15
BA	Transamerica Prt Balanced	DVIBX	B	(888) 233-4339	19.92	C /4.9	9.21 /70	10.91 /45	10.52 /49	B /8.6	62	5
BA	Wells Fargo Adv Dvsfd Cap Bldr A	EKBAX	B-	(800) 222-8222	10.01	C+ /6.8	12.02 /83	15.27 /77	12.59 /65	B- /7.2	44	8
BA	Alger Growth and Income A	ALBAX	B-	(800) 254-3796	33.28	C+ /6.1	12.09 /83	14.31 /69	12.68 /65	B- /7.6	27	4
BA	Madison Dividend Income Y	BHBFX	B-	(800) 336-3063	22.39	C+ /6.1	6.79 /53	13.73 /65	10.77 /51	B- /7.2	30	25
BA	Fidelity Balanced Fd	FBALX	B-	(800) 544-8544	23.28	C+ /5.7	10.60 /77	12.05 /53	11.26 /55	B- /7.5	60	7
BA	Green Century Balanced	GCBLX	B-	(800) 221-5519	24.70	C /5.3	9.34 /71	11.82 /51	10.29 /47	B- /7.8	32	10
BA	Mairs & Power Balanced Fund	MAPOX	B-	(800) 304-7404	86.97	C /4.9	6.73 /53	11.32 /48	11.21 /55	B /8.5	51	23
BA	Schwab Balanced Fund	SWOBX	B-	(800) 407-0256	15.46	C /4.5	10.16 /75	10.43 /42	10.04 /45	B /8.7	51	N/A
BA	Columbia Balanced A	CBLAX	B-	(800) 345-6611	36.75	C /4.5	9.97 /74	11.84 /51	10.80 /51	B /8.4	61	18
BA	Vanguard Tax-Managed Bal	VTMFX	B-	(800) 662-7447	27.05	C- /4.2	8.76 /68	9.76 /38	9.56 /41	B /8.9	75	16
BA	Tributary Balanced Fund Inst	FOBAX	C+	(800) 662-4203	17.66	C /5.2	9.40 /71	10.82 /44	11.55 /57	C+ /6.8	28	N/A
BA	AMG CEP Balanced Inv	MBEAX	C+	(800) 835-3879	15.57	C /5.2	10.90 /78	10.81 /44	10.55 /49	C+ /6.8	66	15
BA	MainStay Balanced C	MBACX	C+	(800) 624-6782	32.92	C /5.1	7.72 /61	11.48 /49	9.90 /44	B- /7.8	65	7
BA	T Rowe Price Balanced	RPBAX	C+	(800) 638-5660	23.43	C /4.7	7.63 /60	10.65 /43	10.15 /46	B- /7.4	40	4
BA	Sit Balanced Fund	SIBAX	C+	(800) 332-5580	21.62	C /4.6	10.60 /77	9.96 /39	9.45 /40	B /8.2	32	20
BA	Eaton Vance Balanced A	EVIFX	C+	(800) 262-1122	8.68	C /4.6	10.22 /75	11.88 /52	10.10 /45	B- /7.4	62	6
BA	Wells Fargo Adv Gro Bal A	WFGBX	C+	(800) 222-8222	40.46	C /4.5	8.78 /68	11.73 /51	10.75 /51	B- /7.8	27	10
BA	Jamestown Balanced	JAMBX	C+	(866) 738-1126	14.65	C /4.5	7.31 /58	10.57 /43	9.69 /42	B- /7.6	34	16
BA	Federated MDT Balanced Fund A	QABGX	C+	(800) 341-7400	16.82	C /4.4	8.04 /63	11.68 /50	9.59 /41	B /8.2	50	N/A
BA	Ivy Balanced A	IBNAX	C+	(800) 777-6472	25.65	C /4.4	9.06 /70	11.46 /49	11.18 /54	B- /7.9	29	1
BA	LKCM Balanced Institutional	LKBAX	C+	(800) 688-5526	20.34	C /4.4	6.46 /50	10.74 /44	10.22 /46	B- /7.9	29	18
BA	Fidelity Adv Balanced A	FABLX	C+	(800) 522-7297	19.55	C /4.4	10.07 /75	11.57 /49	10.82 /51	B- /7.8	53	7
BA	Hennessy Equity and Income	HEIFX	C+	(800) 966-4354	16.51	C /4.3	9.41 /71	9.89 /39	10.74 /51	B /8.5	67	8
BA	Boston Trust Asset Management	BTBFX	C+	(800) 282-8782	41.80	C /4.3	8.21 /64	10.02 /39	10.01 /45	B /8.2	23	20
BA	American Funds Amer Balncd Fd A	ABALX	C+	(800) 421-0180	24.75	C /4.3	8.08 /63	11.94 /52	11.42 /56	B /8.0	50	12
BA	Alpine Equity Income Institutional	ADBYX	C+	(888) 785-5578	14.17	C- /4.2	10.79 /77	9.47 /36	9.06 /37	B /8.2	16	14
BA	TIAA-CREF Mgd Alloc Ret	TIMRX	C+	(800) 842-2252	12.26	C- /4.1	6.69 /53	9.68 /37	9.43 /40	B /8.2	33	N/A
BA	Delaware Dividend Income A	DDIAX	C+	(800) 523-1918	13.75	C- /4.0	6.69 /53	11.47 /49	10.65 /50	B /8.3	68	9
BA	Transamerica Multi-Managed Bal A	IBALX	C+	(888) 233-4339	25.04	C- /3.9	9.27 /71	10.65 /43	12.32 /63	B /8.1	55	4
BA	FPA Crescent	FPACX	C+	(800) 982-4372	33.79	C- /3.8	4.67 /36	10.45 /42	9.73 /42	B /8.5	56	22
BA	American Beacon Balanced A	ABFAX	C+	(800) 658-5811	14.90	C- /3.8	7.11 /56	11.13 /46	--	B /8.2	55	28
BA	James Adv Bal Goldn Rainbow	GLRBX	C+	(888) 426-7640	25.24	C- /3.7	7.39 /58	8.74 /31	9.45 /40	B+ /9.0	51	24
BA	State Farm Balanced Fund	STFBX	C+	(800) 447-4930	67.53	C- /3.7	8.53 /67	8.98 /33	8.15 /31	B /8.8	53	24
BA	Janus Balanced A	JDBAX	C+	(800) 295-2687	30.87	C- /3.7	8.47 /66	10.56 /43	9.27 /39	B /8.1	59	10
BA	Schwab MarketTrack Bal Port Inv	SWBGX	C+	(800) 407-0256	19.39	C- /3.4	6.12 /48	9.04 /33	8.64 /34	B /8.8	32	7
BA	CGM Mutual	LOMMX	C	(800) 345-4048	31.39	C /5.4	12.39 /84	10.14 /40	7.61 /27	C+ /5.8	4	34
BA	Janus Aspen Balanced Inst	JABLX	C	(800) 295-2687	31.86	C /4.9	8.66 /67	11.09 /46	9.80 /43	C+ /6.8	64	10
BA	Waddell & Reed Adv Continentl Inc	UNCIX	C	(888) 923-3355	10.53	C /4.4	9.01 /69	11.46 /49	11.47 /57	B- /7.4	28	1
BA	T Rowe Price Personal Strategy	TRPBX	C	(800) 638-5660	22.86	C /4.4	6.98 /55	10.28 /41	10.06 /45	C+ /6.9	33	4
BA	BlackRock Bal Capital Inv A	MDCPX	C	(800) 441-7762	24.19	C /4.4	9.05 /70	11.55 /49	10.32 /47	C+ /6.6	53	9
BA	American Century Balanced Inv	TWBIX	C	(800) 345-6488	18.32	C /4.3	8.08 /63	10.10 /40	10.31 /47	B- /7.5	50	18
BA	Oakmark Equity and Income II	OARBX	C	(800) 625-6275	32.00	C /4.3	5.67 /44	10.30 /41	8.65 /34	B- /7.1	23	20
BA	Cavanal Hill Balanced NL Inv	APBAX	C	(800) 762-7085	13.88	C- /4.1	8.56 /67	9.32 /35	9.27 /39	B- /7.5	62	10
BA	Voya Balanced Inc S	IBPSX	C	(800) 992-0180	14.90	C- /4.1	6.93 /54	9.59 /37	8.87 /36	B- /7.2	20	8
BA	Prudential Asset Allocation A	PIBAX	C	(800) 225-1852	15.48	C- /4.1	9.07 /70	11.07 /46	10.49 /49	B- /7.0	54	10
BA	MainStay Income Builder B	MKTRX	C	(800) 624-6782	19.66	C- /4.1	5.16 /40	10.35 /41	9.94 /44	B- /7.0	35	6
BA	Plumb Balanced Fund	PLBBX	C	(866) 987-7888	22.75	C- /4.0	9.65 /73	9.15 /34	8.60 /34	B- /7.5	12	8
BA	Dreyfus Balanced Opport A	DBOAX	C	(800) 645-6561	21.41	C- /4.0	7.83 /62	11.14 /46	9.79 /43	B- /7.4	40	8
BA	JPMorgan Diversified A	JDVAX	C	(800) 480-4111	16.79	C- /3.9	7.79 /61	10.46 /42	9.73 /42	B- /7.3	31	21
BA	Lord Abbett Multi Asset Bal Opp A	LABFX	C	(888) 522-2388	12.12	C- /3.8	5.17 /40	10.18 /40	8.75 /35	B- /7.2	19	10

● Denotes fund is closed to new investors

Fund Type	Fund Name	Ticker Symbol	Overall Investment Rating	Phone	Net Asset Value As of 3/31/15	PERFORMANCE					RISK	FUND MGR	
	99 Pct = Best 0 Pct = Worst					Perform-ance Rating/Pts	Annualized Total Return Through 3/31/15			Risk Rating/Pts	Mgr. Quality Pct	Mgr. Tenure (Years)	
							1Yr / Pct	3Yr / Pct	5Yr / Pct				
CV	Columbia Convertible Securities A	PACIX	C+	(800) 345-6611	19.36	C /4.7	7.50 /59	12.46 /56	11.25 /55	B- / 7.4	48	9
CV	Fidelity Advisor Convertible Sec A	FACVX	C+	(800) 522-7297	32.43	C /4.6	7.80 /61	12.37 /55	10.72 /50	B- / 7.3	42	10
CV	Victory Invt Grade Conv A	SBFCX	C+	(800) 539-3863	14.08	C /4.5	8.69 /68	10.95 /45	8.71 /35	B / 8.1	68	19
CV	MainStay Convertible B	MCSVX	C	(800) 624-6782	17.01	C /4.6	7.08 /56	10.67 /43	9.05 /37	C+ / 6.4	26	14
CV ●	AllianzGI Convertible A	ANZAX	C	(800) 988-8380	34.61	C /4.5	5.94 /46	12.06 /53	11.68 /58	C+ / 6.5	20	21
CV	Putnam Convertible Securities A	PCONX	C	(800) 225-1581	24.99	C /4.3	6.65 /52	11.90 /52	10.23 /46	B- / 7.5	55	9
CV	Miller Convertible Bond A	MCFAX	C	(877) 441-4434	12.54	D+ /2.5	3.39 /28	8.97 /33	8.37 /32	B / 8.4	46	8
CV	Lord Abbett Convertible A	LACFX	C-	(888) 522-2388	12.22	C /4.8	6.32 /49	11.92 /52	9.16 /38	C / 5.5	29	12
CV	Vanguard Convertible Sec Inv	VCVSX	C-	(800) 662-7447	13.26	C /4.3	3.52 /29	10.25 /41	9.11 /38	C+ / 6.0	49	19
CV	Franklin Convertible Securities A	FISCX	C-	(800) 342-5236	18.42	C- /3.7	3.85 /31	11.13 /46	10.20 /46	B- / 7.0	27	13
CV	Invesco Convertible Securities A	CNSAX	C-	(800) 959-4246	24.19	C- /3.1	2.25 /23	10.27 /41	9.55 /41	B- / 7.2	34	17
CV	Gabelli Global Rising Inc & Div A	GAGAX	D+	(800) 422-3554	22.41	D- /1.3	2.20 /23	6.16 /17	4.97 /12	B / 8.4	31	21
CV	Northern Income Equity	NOIEX	D	(800) 595-9111	12.74	C+ /6.0	9.40 /71	12.69 /57	11.78 /59	D+ / 2.8	57	8
CV ●	PIMCO Convertible Bond Admin	PFCAX	D	(800) 426-0107	12.48	C /4.6	9.01 /69	10.56 /43	9.55 /41	C- / 4.2	29	5
CV	Calamos Convertible A	CCVIX	D	(800) 582-6959	17.63	D /2.2	4.60 /36	8.12 /28	6.98 /23	C+ / 6.4	9	30
CV	Matthews Asian Growth & Income	MACSX	D	(800) 789-2742	18.37	D /1.6	0.86 /18	6.69 /20	6.64 /21	C+ / 6.5	24	6

● Denotes fund is closed to new investors
www.thestreetratings.com
807
Data as of March 31, 2015

Fund Type	Fund Name	Ticker Symbol	Overall Investment Rating	Phone	Net Asset Value As of 3/31/15	Performance Rating/Pts	Annualized Total Return Through 3/31/15			Risk Rating/Pts	Mgr. Quality Pct	Mgr. Tenure (Years)
							1Yr / Pct	3Yr / Pct	5Yr / Pct			
EM	SEI Instl Mgd Tr-Glb Mngd Volty A	SVTAX	B+	(800) 342-5734	11.15	B /7.7	14.41 /90	14.57 /72	11.21 /55	C+ / 6.4	99	9
EM	Franklin India Growth Fund A	FINGX	B-	(800) 342-5236	13.24	A+ /9.6	39.39 /99	14.10 /68	7.47 /26	C- / 3.5	99	N/A
EM	Northern Glbl Sustainability Index	NSRIX	C	(800) 595-9111	12.29	C /5.0	5.82 /45	12.32 /55	9.76 /43	C+ / 6.6	99	7
EM	Vanguard Total Wld Stk Index Inv	VTWSX	C	(800) 662-7447	25.04	C /4.6	5.35 /41	11.04 /46	9.13 /38	C+ / 6.5	98	2
EM	Eaton Vance Greater India A	ETGIX	C-	(800) 262-1122	29.26	B+ /8.9	35.09 /99	12.73 /58	4.34 / 9	D / 1.6	98	8
EM ●	Wells Fargo Adv Emerging Gr A	WEMAX	C-	(800) 222-8222	16.71	B- /7.3	10.74 /77	14.35 /70	17.64 /97	D+ / 2.8	99	8
EM	Fidelity Adv Emerging Asia A	FEAAX	D+	(800) 522-7297	31.64	C- /3.3	13.16 /87	8.11 /28	7.39 /26	C+ / 6.0	96	5
EM	T Rowe Price Inst Global Foc Gr	TRGSX	D	(800) 638-5660	11.35	C+ /6.5	10.17 /75	13.72 /65	10.62 /50	D+ / 2.3	99	3
EM	Templeton Global Equity Series	TGESX	D	(800) 342-5236	9.90	C /5.0	-2.25 /10	13.11 /60	10.35 /47	C- / 3.5	99	7
EM	Pacific Financial Intl Inst	PFGIX	D	(800) 637-1380	5.86	D /2.1	0.17 /16	6.58 /19	1.29 / 4	C+ / 6.2	95	8
EM ●	Tweedy Browne Glbl Val II Cr	TBCUX	D	(800) 432-4789	14.02	D /1.6	-4.71 / 6	7.71 /25	7.72 /28	C+ / 6.9	96	6
EM	DFA International Value II Inst	DIVTX	D-	(800) 984-9472	5.28	D /2.1	-3.97 / 7	7.85 /26	4.78 /11	C / 5.0	96	17
EM	SEI Inst Screened World Eq Ex-US	SSEAX	D-	(800) 342-5734	9.21	D /1.9	-1.16 /13	6.87 /21	5.04 /12	C+ / 6.1	95	7
EM	RBB Free Market Intl Eq Inst	FMNEX	D-	(888) 261-4073	9.75	D /1.9	-5.02 / 5	7.56 /24	5.50 /14	C / 5.3	96	8
EM	Harding Loevner Frontier EM Inst	HLFMX	D-	(877) 435-8105	8.45	D- /1.4	-5.16 / 5	8.61 /30	4.47 /10	C+ / 6.6	97	7
EM	Templeton Emerg Mkts Small Cap	TEMMX	D-	(800) 342-5236	12.25	D- /1.1	5.40 /42	6.02 /17	3.05 / 6	C+ / 6.6	94	9
EM	Van Eck Emerging Mkts A	GBFAX	D-	(800) 826-1115	14.40	D- /1.1	0.56 /17	6.25 /18	5.89 /16	C+ / 5.9	94	17
EM	SA International Value Fund	SAHMX	E+	(800) 366-7266	11.12	D /1.6	-4.89 / 6	6.73 /20	3.88 / 8	C / 5.2	95	16
EM	American Century NT Emg Market	ACLKX	E+	(800) 345-6488	10.80	D- /1.3	5.17 /40	3.31 / 8	3.05 / 6	C / 5.3	87	9
EM ●	William Blair Emrg Mkts Gr N	WBENX	E+	(800) 742-7272	13.26	D- /1.2	5.41 /42	3.44 / 9	5.38 /14	C / 5.4	88	10
EM	Fidelity Emerging Markets Fd	FEMKX	E+	(800) 544-8544	24.99	D- /1.0	4.26 /33	3.41 / 9	2.60 / 5	C / 5.1	88	3
EM	Causeway Emerging Mkt Inv	CEMVX	E+	(866) 947-7000	12.04	E+ /0.9	4.35 /34	3.38 / 9	5.23 /13	C+ / 5.6	87	8
EM	AllianzGI Emerging Markets Opp A	AOTAX	E+	(800) 988-8380	26.35	E+ /0.9	6.25 /49	3.34 / 9	3.94 / 8	C / 5.5	87	8
EM	William Blair EM Leaders N	WELNX	E+	(800) 742-7272	9.25	E+ /0.9	4.54 /35	2.38 / 7	--	C / 5.4	82	7
EM	T Rowe Price Emerging Mkts Stk	PRMSX	E+	(800) 638-5660	33.55	E+ /0.9	5.73 /44	2.17 / 7	2.36 / 5	C / 5.3	81	7
EM	T Rowe Price Instl Emer Mkt Eqty	IEMFX	E+	(800) 638-5660	30.64	E+ /0.9	5.96 /46	2.31 / 7	2.60 / 5	C / 5.2	82	7
EM	American Century Emerging Mkt A	AEMMX	E+	(800) 345-6488	8.69	E+ /0.8	4.70 /36	3.20 / 8	2.91 / 6	C / 5.3	87	9
EM	Driehaus Emerging Markets	DREGX	E+	(800) 560-6111	30.59	E+ /0.8	-2.49 / 9	3.88 /10	5.11 /12	C / 5.2	89	7
EM	BMO LGM Emg Mkts Eqty Y	MEMYX	E+	(800) 236-3863	13.70	E+ /0.8	6.70 /53	2.16 / 6	1.52 / 4	C / 4.8	81	4
EM	Institutional Emerging Markets I	HLMEX	E+	(877) 435-8105	17.63	E+ /0.7	-1.23 /12	3.14 / 8	4.22 / 9	C / 5.5	87	10
EM	Thornburg Developing World A	THDAX	E+	(800) 847-0200	17.78	E+ /0.7	-4.77 / 6	4.64 /12	7.10 /24	C / 5.5	91	N/A
EM	Fidelity Srs Emerging Markets Fd	FEMSX	E+	(800) 544-8544	17.00	E+ /0.7	-0.07 /15	2.10 / 6	2.59 / 5	C / 5.3	80	6
EM	Columbia Emerging Markets A	EEMAX	E+	(800) 345-6611	10.31	E+ /0.7	1.48 /20	2.83 / 8	3.14 / 6	C / 5.2	85	7
EM	Fidelity Adv Emerging Markets A	FAMKX	E+	(800) 522-7297	23.05	E+ /0.7	3.83 /31	2.97 / 8	2.10 / 5	C / 5.1	86	3
EM	Sanford C Bernstein Emerg Mkts	SNEMX	E+	(212) 486-5800	27.48	E+ /0.7	4.68 /36	1.08 / 5	0.80 / 3	C / 5.1	71	4
EM	Harding Loevner Emerg Mrkt	HLEMX	E+	(877) 435-8105	46.27	E+ /0.7	-0.97 /13	3.24 / 8	4.19 / 9	C / 4.9	87	10
EM	Universal Inst Emer Markets Eqty II	UEMBX	E+	(800) 869-6397	14.35	E+ /0.6	-1.27 /12	1.07 / 5	2.24 / 5	C+ / 5.5	72	19
EM	Acadian Emerging Markets Inst	AEMGX	E+	(866) 777-7818	18.41	A+ /0.6	2.56 /24	1.04 / 5	2.96 / 6	C / 5.5	71	22
EM	Alger Emerging Markets A	AAEMX	E+	(800) 254-3796	9.23	E+ /0.6	-0.43 /14	2.67 / 7	--	C / 5.5	84	5
EM	DFA Emerging Markts Core Eqty	DFCEX	E+	(800) 984-9472	19.29	E+ /0.6	0.40 /17	0.98 / 5	2.29 / 5	C / 5.4	71	N/A
EM	Goldman Sachs EM Eqty Insights	GERAX	E+	(800) 526-7384	8.62	E+ /0.6	4.03 /32	1.62 / 6	2.76 / 6	C / 5.2	76	7
EM	Forward Emerg Markets Inv	PGERX	E+	(800) 999-6809	10.24	E+ /0.6	-3.70 / 7	1.82 / 6	1.18 / 4	C / 5.1	79	3
EM	DFA Emerging Markets II Inst	DFETX	E+	(800) 984-9472	24.63	E+ /0.6	0.19 /16	0.67 / 5	2.47 / 5	C / 5.1	N/A	17
EM	Cheswold Lane Intl High Div Inst	CLIDX	E+	(800) 771-4701	13.29	E+ /0.6	-9.80 / 3	3.87 /10	2.38 / 5	C / 5.0	90	10
EM	Schroder Emerging Market Equity	SEMVX	E	(800) 464-3108	12.97	E /0.5	0.62 /17	0.64 / 5	1.58 / 4	C / 5.4	67	9
EM	DFA Emerging Mkts Socl Core Eq	DFESX	E	(800) 984-9472	12.27	E /0.5	-0.02 /15	0.42 / 5	1.76 / 4	C / 5.4	64	N/A
EM	Pear Tree PanAgora Emg Markets	QFFOX	E	(800) 326-2151	21.94	E /0.5	0.49 /17	0.31 / 5	2.21 / 5	C / 5.3	62	9
EM	Neuberger Berman Emg Mkt Eq A	NEMAX	E	(800) 877-9700	16.10	E /0.4	-1.18 /12	1.29 / 6	0.90 / 3	C+ / 5.9	74	7
EM	PACE Intertl Emg Mkts Eq Inve A	PWEAX	E	(888) 793-8637	12.71	E /0.4	0.87 /18	0.01 / 4	1.67 / 4	C+ / 5.7	58	11
EM	Henderson Emerging Markets	HEMAX	E	(866) 443-6337	9.01	E /0.4	0.67 /17	-0.28 / 4	--	C+ / 5.6	53	5
EM	Dunham Emerging Markets Stock	DAEMX	E	(888) 338-6426	13.58	E /0.4	1.87 /21	-0.26 / 4	-0.17 / 2	C / 5.5	54	N/A
EM	BlackRock Emerg Mkt Inv A	MDDCX	E	(800) 441-7762	18.79	E /0.4	0.10 /16	-0.31 / 4	1.61 / 4	C / 5.4	52	6

● Denotes fund is closed to new investors

Fund Type	Fund Name	Ticker Symbol	Overall Investment Rating	Phone	Net Asset Value As of 3/31/15	Perform-ance Rating/Pts	1Yr / Pct	3Yr / Pct	5Yr / Pct	Risk Rating/Pts	Mgr. Quality Pct	Mgr. Tenure (Years)
EN	Hennessy Gas Utility Investor	GASFX	A-	(800) 966-4354	29.77	B /8.2	10.89 /78	16.85 /89	17.40 /97	C+ / 6.9	99	14
EN	Fidelity Select Envir and Alt Ener	FSLEX	C	(800) 544-8888	20.80	C+ /5.7	1.03 /19	13.67 /65	9.70 /42	C / 5.2	98	5
EN	Advisory Research MLP & Engy	INFIX	C		13.26	C /5.0	9.06 /70	12.84 /58	--	C+ / 6.4	98	5
EN	Center Coast MLP Focus A	CCCAX	D	(877) 766-0066	10.76	E+ /0.9	3.77 /30	6.00 /17		B- / 7.6	92	5
EN	Firsthand Alternative Energy Fd	ALTEX	D-	(888) 884-2675	6.78	C /5.2	-8.87 / 3	14.39 /70	-2.71 / 1	D / 1.9	98	8
EN	Deutsche Enhanced Comdty Strat	SKNRX	E+	(800) 728-3337	13.13	E- /0.1	-14.07 / 2	-6.80 / 1	-2.25 / 2	C+ / 5.9	3	5
EN	Calvert Global Energy Solutions A	CGAEX	E	(800) 368-2745	7.08	D- /1.1	-7.45 / 4	6.93 /21	-4.17 / 1	C / 4.4	91	8
EN	Dreyfus Natural Resources C	DLDCX	E	(800) 782-6620	26.99	E+ /0.6	-8.21 / 3	3.49 / 9	4.50 /10	C / 4.9	72	6
EN	Vanguard Energy Index Adm	VENAX	E	(800) 662-7447	54.55	E /0.5	-13.18 / 2	3.20 / 8	7.21 /24	C- / 3.5	57	5
EN	AllianzGI Global Natural Res A	ARMAX	E	(800) 988-8380	17.19	E /0.4	-10.38 / 3	2.12 / 6	2.03 / 4	C- / 4.0	50	11
EN	Guinness Atkinson Alt Energy Fd	GAAEX	E-	(800) 915-6565	3.55	E+ /0.7	-15.88 / 2	5.05 /13	-9.42 / 0	D / 2.1	78	9
EN	Waddell & Reed Adv Energy Fund	WEGAX	E-	(888) 923-3355	14.30	E /0.4	-13.75 / 2	3.79 /10	4.95 /12	D+ / 2.6	65	9
EN	Ivy Energy A	IEYAX	E-	(800) 777-6472	14.03	E /0.4	-14.35 / 2	3.43 / 9	4.78 /11	D+ / 2.6	60	9
EN	Fidelity Select Energy	FSENX	E-	(800) 544-8888	45.33	E /0.4	-13.80 / 2	2.48 / 7	5.31 /13	D+ / 2.4	43	9
EN	T Rowe Price New Era	PRNEX	E-	(800) 638-5660	34.23	E /0.4	-11.14 / 2	1.31 / 6	2.20 / 5	D / 1.9	35	5
EN	Fidelity Adv Energy A	FANAX	E-	(800) 522-7297	34.85	E /0.3	-13.85 / 2	2.31 / 7	5.12 /12	D+ / 2.5	40	9
EN	Fidelity Select Natural Resources	FNARX	E-	(800) 544-8888	31.07	E /0.3	-13.93 / 2	0.72 / 5	3.93 / 8	D+ / 2.4	23	9
EN	ProFunds-Oil & Gas UltraSector	ENPSX	E-	(888) 776-3637	38.30	E /0.3	-21.79 / 1	1.43 / 6	6.50 /20	D / 2.0	14	2
EN	Putnam Global Natural Resources	EBERX	E-	(800) 225-1581	18.81	E- /0.2	-16.58 / 2	-2.40 / 3	0.35 / 3	C- / 3.2	7	3
EN	Voya Global Natural Resources A	LEXMX	E-	(800) 992-0180	8.46	E- /0.2	-18.01 / 1	-2.95 / 3	0.17 / 3	D+ / 2.9	4	5
EN	Fidelity Select Natural Gas	FSNGX	E-	(800) 544-8888	31.14	E- /0.2	-21.74 / 1	0.96 / 5	1.00 / 3	D+ / 2.9	28	3
EN	Columbia Gl Energy and Nat Res A	EENAX	E-	(800) 345-6611	18.03	E- /0.2	-15.64 / 2	-1.40 / 3	0.33 / 3	D+ / 2.8	10	4
EN	Ivy Global Nat Resource A	IGNAX	E-	(800) 777-6472	16.13	E- /0.2	-15.42 / 2	-3.10 / 2	-2.77 / 1	D+ / 2.8	5	2
EN	Vanguard Energy Inv	VGENX	E-	(800) 662-7447	52.80	E- /0.2	-17.67 / 1	-0.66 / 4	2.78 / 6	D+ / 2.7	14	23
EN	BlackRock AllCap Energy & Res	BACAX	E-	(800) 441-7762	12.61	E- /0.2	-17.52 / 1	-2.75 / 2	-0.83 / 2	D+ / 2.7	5	2
EN	Saratoga Adv Tr Energy&Basic Mat	SBMBX	E-	(800) 807-3863	13.28	E- /0.2	-19.52 / 1	-2.28 / 3	0.29 / 3	D+ / 2.5	6	4
EN	Rydex Energy A	RYENX	E-	(800) 820-0888	21.94	E- /0.2	-21.49 / 1	-1.24 / 3	2.42 / 5	D+ / 2.5	8	17
EN	ProFunds Short Oil & Gas Svc	SNPSX	E-	(888) 776-3637	6.22	E- /0.2	6.51 /51	-9.06 / 1	-14.06 / 0	D+ / 2.3	7	2
EN	BlackRock Natural Resource Inv A	MDGRX	E-	(800) 441-7762	51.28	E- /0.2	-18.48 / 1	-1.75 / 3	1.37 / 4	D+ / 2.3	7	18
EN	Guinness Atkinson Glob Energy	GAGEX	E-	(800) 915-6565	25.04	E- /0.2	-25.81 / 0	-2.10 / 3	0.30 / 3	D+ / 2.3	5	11
EN	ProFunds Oil Eqpt Svcs & Dist Svc	OEPSX	E-	(888) 776-3637	18.42	E- /0.2	-26.79 / 0	-0.66 / 4	2.56 / 5	D- / 1.5	5	2
EN	ICON Energy A	ICEAX	E-	(800) 764-0442	13.91	E- /0.2	-22.68 / 1	-0.98 / 3	--	D- / 1.5	10	8
EN	Aberdeen Global Natural Res A	GGNAX	E-	(866) 667-9231	13.14	E /0.1	-19.15 / 1	-6.93 / 1	-3.39 / 1	C- / 3.3	2	5
EN	Franklin Natural Resources A	FRNRX	E-	(800) 342-5236	28.27	E /0.1	-24.43 / 1	-7.72 / 1	-1.81 / 2	D+ / 2.3	1	16
EN	● J Hancock II Natural Resources A	JNRAX	E-	(800) 257-3336	12.78	E /0.1	-28.16 / 0	-9.97 / 1	-6.67 / 1	D+ / 2.3	1	10
EN	Prudential Jennison Natural Res A	PGNAX	E-	(800) 225-1852	38.69	E /0.1	-25.81 / 0	-7.47 / 1	-3.04 / 1	D / 2.2	1	10
EN	Invesco Energy A	IENAX	E-	(800) 959-4246	31.22	E /0.1	-24.16 / 1	-2.94 / 2	0.46 / 3	D / 2.0	4	2
EN	RS Global Natural Resources Fund	RSNRX	E-	(800) 766-3863	24.03	E /0.1	-27.54 / 0	-8.70 / 1	-2.13 / 2	D / 2.0	1	10
EN	Putnam Global Energy Fund A	PGEAX	E-	(800) 225-1581	9.92	E /0.1	-25.56 / 0	-4.77 / 2	-0.28 / 2	D / 2.0	2	3
EN	Van Eck Global Hard Assets A	GHAAX	E-	(800) 826-1115	39.21	E /0.1	-20.11 / 1	-4.69 / 2	-1.01 / 2	D / 2.0	2	20
EN	Rydex Energy Srsvices A	RYESX	E-	(800) 820-0888	37.32	E /0.1	-37.11 / 0	-8.42 / 1	-1.92 / 2	D / 1.9	1	17
EN	Fidelity Select Energy Svcs	FSESX	E+	(800) 544-8888	52.94	E /0.1	-31.53 / 0	-3.81 / 2	0.71 / 3	D / 1.9	2	2
EN	BlackRock Energy & Resources Inv	SSGRX	E-	(800) 441-7762	23.34	E /0.1	-31.99 / 0	-10.37 / 1	-5.48 / 1	D- / 1.4	0	2
EN	US Global Inv Global Resources	PSPFX	E-	(800) 873-8637	5.83	E /0.0	-38.31 / 0	-14.89 / 0	-6.86 / 1	D / 2.1	0	26
EN	Oppenheimer Comm Str Tot Retn	QRAAX	E-	(888) 470-0862	2.15	E /0.0	-31.75 / 0	-15.07 / 0	-7.30 / 1	D / 1.7	0	2
EN	JPMorgan Glbl Natural Resources	JGNAX	E-	(800) 480-4111	7.03	E /0.0	-26.74 / 0	-17.79 / 0	--	D- / 1.0	0	5

Fund Type	Fund Name	Ticker Symbol	Overall Investment Rating	Phone	Net Asset Value As of 3/31/15	PERFORMANCE					RISK	FUND MGR	
	99 Pct = Best *0 Pct = Worst*					Perform-ance Rating/Pts	Annualized Total Return Through 3/31/15			Risk Rating/Pts	Mgr. Quality Pct	Mgr. Tenure (Years)	
							1Yr / Pct	3Yr / Pct	5Yr / Pct				
FS	Fidelity Select Insurance	FSPCX	A+	(800) 544-8888	67.08	A /9.4	11.31 /80	19.52 /97	13.49 /73	C+ / 6.7	85	2
FS	Emerald Banking and Finance A	HSSAX	A+	(855) 828-9909	28.91	A- /9.2	4.37 /34	20.00 /98	14.27 /80	B- / 7.0	93	18
FS	Burnham Financial Services A	BURKX	A+	(800) 462-2392	28.35	B+ /8.9	7.44 /59	19.65 /97	9.95 /44	B- / 7.0	96	16
FS	Alpine Financial Services Inst	ADFSX	A+	(888) 785-5578	13.59	B+ /8.3	1.09 /19	18.28 /95	10.71 /50	B- / 7.4	91	10
FS	T Rowe Price Financial Services	PRISX	A	(800) 638-5660	22.50	A- /9.0	9.50 /72	17.76 /93	10.89 /52	C+ / 6.3	55	5
FS	Franklin Mutual Financial Svcs A	TFSIX	A	(800) 342-5236	19.00	B- /7.2	13.08 /87	15.86 /82	10.55 /49	B / 8.3	92	6
FS	Burnham Financial Long/Short A	BURFX	A-	(800) 462-2392	15.49	B /8.2	10.40 /76	17.43 /92	8.04 /30	C+ / 6.9	90	11
FS	ProFunds-Financial UltraSector	FNPSX	B+	(888) 776-3637	13.08	A+ /9.8	12.86 /86	22.36 /98	12.04 /61	C / 4.9	16	2
FS	Vanguard Financial Index Fd Adm	VFAIX	B+	(800) 662-7447	24.69	B+ /8.4	10.21 /75	16.67 /88	10.83 /51	C+ / 6.2	57	5
FS	Fidelity Select Brkg and Inv Mgmt	FSLBX	B+	(800) 544-8888	74.56	B /8.2	6.33 /49	17.61 /93	9.16 /38	C+ / 5.9	21	2
FS	Schwab Financial Services Focus	SWFFX	B	(800) 407-0256	16.27	B /7.7	10.20 /75	16.09 /84	10.50 /49	C+ / 6.3	35	3
FS	Fidelity Select Financial Services	FIDSX	B	(800) 544-8888	88.84	B- /7.3	9.51 /72	15.37 /78	7.43 /26	C+ / 6.6	47	2
FS	1919 Financial Services A	SBFAX	B-	(844) 828-1919	19.27	C+ /6.9	6.10 /47	16.75 /88	12.66 /65	B- / 7.5	82	1
FS	J Hancock VIT Financial Indus I	JEFSX	B-	(800) 257-3336	17.00	C+ /5.9	7.74 /61	13.27 /62	10.19 /46	B- / 7.3	43	1
FS	J Hancock Financial Indust A	FIDAX	C+	(800) 257-3336	17.50	C+ /6.7	2.01 /22	16.91 /89	11.20 /54	C+ / 6.9	63	17
FS	Davis Financial A	RPFGX	C+	(800) 279-0279	39.49	C+ /6.7	12.18 /83	15.28 /77	11.21 /54	C+ / 5.9	69	24
FS	J Hancock Regional Bank A	FRBAX	C+	(800) 257-3336	18.60	C+ /6.6	3.74 /30	16.26 /85	11.03 /53	C+ / 6.4	59	17
FS	Diamond Hill Financial Lng-Sht A	BANCX	C+	(614) 255-3333	19.42	C+ /6.5	7.17 /56	15.77 /81	10.69 /50	C+ / 6.9	43	14
FS	ALPS/Red Rocks Listed Priv Eq A	LPEFX	C+	(866) 759-5679	6.82	C+ /6.5	0.26 /16	17.18 /91	12.44 /64	C+ / 6.7	86	8
FS	Fidelity Adv Financial Serv A	FAFDX	C+	(800) 522-7297	16.13	C+ /6.2	9.40 /71	15.23 /77	7.33 /25	C+ / 6.7	43	2
FS	Fidelity Select Banking Port	FSRBX	C+	(800) 544-8888	26.32	C+ /6.0	1.31 /19	14.70 /72	9.65 /42	C+ / 6.8	45	3
FS	Rydex Financial Srsvice A	RYFNX	C+	(800) 820-0888	109.65	C+ /5.9	8.89 /69	14.06 /68	9.31 /39	C+ / 6.1	38	17
FS	Fidelity Select Consumer Finance	FSVLX	C	(800) 544-8888	14.26	B+ /8.3	8.34 /65	16.72 /88	12.18 /62	C- / 3.4	74	3
FS	Hennessy Large Cap Financial Inv	HLFNX	C	(800) 966-4354	18.88	C+ /6.0	2.30 /23	14.81 /73	8.31 /32	C+ / 5.8	13	18
FS	ICON Financial S	ICFSX	C	(800) 764-0442	8.38	C /5.1	7.57 /60	11.48 /49	7.15 /24	C+ / 6.0	6	12
FS	ProFunds-Banks UltraSector Svc	BKPSX	C-	(888) 776-3637	29.11	B /8.0	0.31 /16	18.58 /96	5.20 /13	D+ / 2.6	1	2
FS	Hennessy Small Cap Financial Inv	HSFNX	D+	(800) 966-4354	21.73	C+ /6.0	-0.92 /13	13.67 /65	6.92 /23	C- / 3.8	13	18
FS	Saratoga Adv Tr Financial Service	SFPAX	D	(800) 807-3863	8.49	D+ /2.9	3.66 /30	11.05 /46	5.39 /14	C+ / 6.1	4	9
FS	Rydex Banking A	RYBKX	D	(800) 820-0888	57.76	D+ /2.9	-0.98 /13	10.75 /44	4.57 /10	C+ / 6.0	3	17
FS	Putnam Global Financials Fund A	PGFFX	E+	(800) 225-1581	11.91	C- /4.0	-0.54 /14	12.58 /57	5.97 /17	D / 2.0	4	7
FS	ProFunds-Rising Rates Opp 10	RTPSX	E+	(888) 776-3637	15.27	E- /0.2	-12.04 / 2	-6.73 / 1	-9.31 / 1	C+ / 5.9	1	6
FS	● Merk Hard Currency Investor	MERKX	E+	(866) 637-5386	9.49	E- /0.1	-17.47 / 1	-6.22 / 1	-2.37 / 2	C+ / 5.8	1	10
FS	Prudential Financial Services A	PFSAX	E	(800) 225-1852	13.24	D- /1.4	-7.79 / 3	9.26 /35	7.66 /28	D+ / 2.6	2	6

● Denotes fund is closed to new investors

Fund Type	Fund Name	Ticker Symbol	Overall Investment Rating	Phone	Net Asset Value As of 3/31/15	Perform-ance Rating/Pts	Annualized Total Return Through 3/31/15 1Yr / Pct	3Yr / Pct	5Yr / Pct	Risk Rating/Pts	Mgr. Quality Pct	Mgr. Tenure (Years)
FO	Hennessy Japan Fund Investor	HJPNX	A+	(800) 966-4354	23.34	A /9.4	18.84 /96	15.52 /79	13.59 /74	B- / 7.3	98	9
FO	Glenmede Total Market Port	GTTMX	A+	(800) 442-8299	15.22	A /9.3	11.23 /79	17.78 /93	15.32 /89	C+ / 6.5	98	9
FO	FMI International	FMIJX	A+	(800) 811-5311	30.03	B /7.9	10.92 /78	14.85 /74	--	B- / 7.8	98	N/A
FO	Matthews Japan Fund Inv	MJFOX	A	(800) 789-2742	18.43	A- /9.1	16.94 /94	15.52 /79	12.04 /61	C+ / 6.5	97	9
FO	Oberweis Internatl Opportunities	OBIOX	A-	(800) 245-7311	19.87	A /9.5	0.20 /16	21.16 /98	17.80 /97	C+ / 5.6	98	8
FO	JOHCM International Select I	JOHIX	B+	(866) 260-9549	20.55	A /9.5	16.27 /94	17.45 /92	14.55 /83	C / 5.3	97	6
FO	Fidelity Japan Small Companies	FJSCX	B+	(800) 544-8544	13.37	B+ /8.4	8.71 /68	16.85 /89	11.03 /53	C+ / 6.0	97	7
FO	Oppenheimer Intl Small Comp A	OSMAX	B+	(888) 470-0862	34.54	B+ /8.3	3.23 /28	18.61 /96	14.64 /84	C+ / 5.9	98	3
FO	Pear Tree Polaris Foreign VSC Ord	QUSOX	B+	(800) 326-2151	13.35	B- /7.1	2.54 /24	15.45 /79	9.83 /43	B- / 7.1	97	7
FO	Matthews India Fund Inv	MINDX	C+	(800) 789-2742	29.20	A+ /9.9	57.70 /99	21.77 /98	11.48 /57	D / 2.0	98	10
FO	Fidelity Adv Intl Real Estate A	FIRAX	C+	(800) 522-7297	10.60	C+ /6.0	8.24 /64	14.74 /73	9.64 /42	C+ / 6.3	95	5
FO	Papp Small and Mid Cap Growth	PAPPX	C+	(877) 370-7277	18.29	C+ /5.8	10.77 /77	11.45 /49	13.15 /70	C+ / 6.5	95	N/A
FO ●	Artisan International Value Inv	ARTKX	C+	(800) 344-1770	35.46	C+ /5.8	2.84 /26	14.06 /68	11.85 /60	C+ / 6.0	95	13
FO	Old Westbury Large Cap Strategies	OWLSX	C+	(800) 607-2200	13.31	C+ /5.7	8.64 /67	12.10 /53	8.62 /34	C+ / 6.3	93	4
FO	MFS Intl Value Fund A	MGIAX	C+	(800) 225-2606	35.24	C+ /5.6	6.94 /55	13.49 /63	10.92 /52	C+ / 6.9	95	N/A
FO	Matthews China Dividend Fund Inv	MCDFX	C+	(800) 789-2742	14.31	C+ /5.6	13.14 /87	11.04 /46	9.83 /43	C+ / 6.8	94	3
FO	Hennessy Japan Small Cap Inv	HJPSX	C	(800) 966-4354	9.94	B /8.1	10.33 /76	16.22 /85	13.07 /69	C- / 3.1	98	8
FO	Fidelity Adv China Region Fd A	FHKAX	C	(800) 522-7297	32.34	B- /7.1	14.70 /91	14.45 /70	9.12 /38	C / 4.4	97	4
FO	Fidelity Pacific Basin	FPBFX	C	(800) 544-8544	28.17	C+ /6.6	9.60 /72	13.48 /63	10.90 /52	C / 4.5	94	2
FO	Fidelity Nordic Fund	FNORX	C	(800) 544-8544	44.62	C+ /6.2	-3.21 / 8	15.58 /80	11.45 /56	C / 5.1	93	11
FO ●	Matthews Pacific Tiger Fund Inv	MAPTX	C	(800) 789-2742	28.57	C+ /6.0	17.47 /95	10.76 /44	9.75 /43	C / 5.4	91	9
FO	Wasatch International Opps Inv	WAIOX	C	(800) 551-1700	2.82	C+ /5.7	5.53 /43	13.41 /63	11.24 /55	C / 5.4	96	10
FO	Victory Trivalent Intl Sm Cap A	MISAX	C	(800) 539-3863	11.23	C+ /5.6	1.09 /19	14.52 /71	12.77 /66	C+ / 6.2	94	8
FO	JPMorgan China Region A	JCHAX	C	(800) 480-4111	23.00	C /5.5	14.82 /91	10.84 /45	6.24 /18	C+ / 6.3	91	8
FO	Janus Global Research A	JDWAX	C	(800) 295-2687	68.06	C /5.5	12.39 /84	12.05 /53	11.65 /58	C+ / 6.1	93	1
FO	Fidelity Series International SC F	FFSTX	C	(800) 544-8544	15.90	C /5.4	0.43 /17	12.58 /57	11.47 /57	C+ / 6.4	94	6
FO	Clough China A	CHNAX	C	(866) 759-5679	24.06	C /5.4	15.88 /93	11.31 /48	6.77 /22	C+ / 6.3	94	10
FO	Fidelity Overseas Fd	FOSFX	C	(800) 544-8544	40.87	C /5.4	2.52 /24	12.32 /55	8.15 /31	C+ / 6.1	90	3
FO	Fidelity International Cap App Fd	FIVFX	C	(800) 544-8544	17.03	C /5.3	6.87 /54	11.86 /51	9.72 /42	C+ / 5.7	90	7
FO	Brown Capital Mgmt Intl Eq	BCIIX	C	(877) 892-4226	12.63	C /5.0	0.40 /17	12.51 /56	6.87 /22	C+ / 6.7	92	10
FO	Matthews Asia Growth Fund Inv	MPACX	C	(800) 789-2742	22.51	C /5.0	10.83 /78	10.71 /44	9.38 /40	C+ / 6.5	90	8
FO	T Rowe Price Japan	PRJPX	C	(800) 638-5660	10.40	C /5.0	8.97 /69	10.55 /43	7.89 /29	C+ / 6.4	90	2
FO	Lazard Intl Strategic EquityOpen	LISOX	C	(800) 821-6474	14.49	C /5.0	1.72 /21	12.34 /55	9.71 /42	C+ / 6.0	89	10
FO	MainStay Intl Opportunities C	MYICX	C	(800) 624-6782	8.46	C /5.0	-0.15 /15	12.25 /54	8.51 /33	C+ / 5.9	88	8
FO	Artisan International Fund Inv	ARTIX	C	(800) 344-1770	31.23	C /4.9	5.16 /40	11.95 /52	10.30 /47	C+ / 6.9	91	20
FO	T Rowe Price Africa and Middle	TRAMX	C	(800) 638-5660	9.82	C /4.9	3.25 /28	13.41 /63	7.47 /26	C+ / 6.0	97	4
FO	Lazard Intl Small Cap Eq Open	LZSMX	C	(800) 821-6474	10.57	C /4.8	-1.28 /12	12.18 /54	10.18 /46	C+ / 6.3	92	24
FO ●	Matthews Asia Dividend Fund Inv	MAPIX	C	(800) 789-2742	16.56	C /4.7	10.50 /76	9.53 /36	8.15 /31	C+ / 6.9	89	4
FO	Pear Tree Polaris Foreign Val Ord	QFVOX	C	(800) 326-2151	18.67	C /4.7	-2.53 / 9	11.94 /52	9.33 /39	C+ / 6.3	88	17
FO	Wells Fargo Adv Asia Pac A	WFAAX	C	(800) 222-8222	12.63	C /4.6	12.03 /83	10.89 /45	8.17 /31	C+ / 6.7	92	22
FO	Tweedy Browne Global Value	TBGVX	C	(800) 432-4789	26.97	C- /4.1	3.69 /30	10.99 /45	9.25 /39	B- / 7.3	94	22
FO	Toews Hedged Growth Allocation	THGWX	C	(877) 558-6397	10.50	D /2.2	0.57 /17	7.44 /24	--	B / 8.6	89	5
FO	ProFunds-Ultra Japan Svc	UJPSX	C-	(888) 776-3637	19.22	A+ /9.9	55.50 /99	37.64 /99	12.68 /66	E- / 0.0	99	6
FO	Rydex Japan 2x Strategy Fd A	RYJSX	C-	(800) 820-0888	23.29	A- /9.0	20.61 /97	14.66 /72	7.15 /24	D- / 1.2	73	7
FO	Oberweis China Opportunities	OBCHX	C-	(800) 245-7311	14.45	B /8.1	-2.19 /10	18.81 /96	7.51 /27	D / 1.9	99	10
FO	DFA United Kingdom Small Co Inst	DFUKX	C-	(800) 984-9472	33.53	C+ /5.8	-7.48 / 4	15.27 /77	15.45 /90	C / 4.4	95	17
FO ●	Oakmark International II	OARIX	C-	(800) 625-6275	24.98	C /5.4	-0.41 /14	12.58 /57	9.34 /39	C / 5.4	86	23
FO	J Hancock Greater China Opp A	JCOAX	C-	(800) 257-3336	21.52	C /5.1	8.65 /67	11.85 /51	5.95 /17	C / 5.4	94	9
FO	Fidelity Advisor Worldwide A	FWAFX	C-	(800) 522-7297	23.24	C /5.0	5.07 /39	13.25 /61	11.47 /57	C / 5.0	94	9
FO ●	Dodge & Cox International Stock	DODFX	C-	(800) 621-3979	43.88	C /4.9	1.48 /20	12.25 /54	7.99 /30	C / 5.4	86	11
FO	AllianzGI China Equity A	ALQAX	C-	(800) 988-8380	17.66	C /4.7	17.89 /95	8.99 /33	--	C / 5.3	87	5
FO	Vanguard International Explorer Inv	VINEX	C-	(800) 662-7447	17.67	C /4.7	-0.14 /15	11.53 /49	8.61 /34	C / 5.2	88	15

99 Pct = Best
0 Pct = Worst

● Denotes fund is closed to new investors

Fund Type	Fund Name	Ticker Symbol	Overall Investment Rating	Phone	Net Asset Value As of 3/31/15	Performance Rating/Pts	Annualized Total Return Through 3/31/15 1Yr / Pct	3Yr / Pct	5Yr / Pct	Risk Rating/Pts	Mgr. Quality Pct	Mgr. Tenure (Years)
GL	Brown Advisory SmCP Fund Val	BIAUX	A+	(800) 540-6807	24.11	A /9.5	10.00 /74	19.04 /97	17.44 /97	C+ / 6.7	99	7
GL	Janus Contrarian A	JCNAX	A+	(800) 295-2687	22.26	A /9.4	12.63 /85	20.63 /98	11.78 /59	C+ / 6.3	99	4
GL	Motley Fool Great America Investor	TMFGX	A+	(888) 863-8803	20.05	A- /9.2	13.32 /88	17.46 /92	--	C+ / 6.9	98	5
GL	Thornburg Globl Opportunities A	THOAX	A	(800) 847-0200	26.90	A+ /9.8	21.60 /97	20.32 /98	13.93 /77	C+ / 5.8	99	9
GL	Hodges Retail	HDPMX	A	(877) 232-1222	38.98	A /9.5	3.53 /29	21.71 /98	14.33 /81	C+ / 6.1	99	16
GL	GF Multi-Factor Growth Equity Fd I	GFMGX	A	(800) 473-1155	17.89	A /9.3	17.14 /95	17.44 /92	15.85 /92	C+ / 6.4	98	6
GL	Janus Enterprise A	JDMAX	A	(800) 295-2687	91.22	A- /9.2	17.00 /95	16.95 /90	16.22 /94	C+ / 6.3	98	8
GL	Artisan Global Equity Inv	ARTHX	A-	(800) 344-1770	17.05	B+ /8.5	8.67 /67	17.03 /90	14.76 /85	C+ / 6.6	98	5
GL	Janus Global Life Sciences A	JFNAX	B+	(800) 295-2687	58.93	A+ /9.9	42.25 /99	36.88 /99	26.86 /99	C / 4.9	99	8
GL	Hartford MidCap HLS Fd IA	HIMCX	B+	(888) 843-7824	39.49	A+ /9.7	13.48 /88	19.15 /97	15.61 /91	C / 4.8	99	11
GL	Janus Research A	JRAAX	B+	(800) 295-2687	45.36	A- /9.2	18.38 /96	17.76 /93	15.55 /90	C / 5.2	98	1
GL	Hartford MidCap A	HFMCX	B+	(888) 843-7824	26.51	A- /9.1	12.88 /86	18.43 /95	15.10 /88	C / 5.4	98	11
GL	Polaris Global Value	PGVFX	B+	(888) 263-5594	22.19	B /7.8	4.43 /35	16.27 /85	13.53 /73	B- / 7.0	97	26
GL	Fidelity Adv Global Cap App-Cl A	FGEAX	B+	(800) 522-7297	16.24	B /7.7	8.63 /67	17.40 /92	10.81 /51	C+ / 6.5	97	5
GL	Convergence Core Plus Fund Inst	MARNX	B+	(877) 677-9414	18.25	B /7.6	10.72 /77	15.35 /78	15.60 /91	B- / 7.1	98	6
GL	Leuthold Global Industries Retail	LGINX	B+	(888) 200-0409	17.29	B- /7.3	5.69 /44	15.22 /77	--	B- / 7.0	96	5
GL	Schroder North American Equity	SNAVX	B+	(800) 464-3108	14.95	B- /7.0	10.62 /77	14.62 /72	13.13 /69	B- / 7.2	97	12
GL	J Hancock II Technical Opport NAV		B	(800) 257-3336	13.89	A+ /9.8	11.90 /82	20.40 /98	10.39 /48	C / 4.3	99	6
GL	● Janus Venture D	JANVX	B	(800) 295-2687	68.52	A+ /9.8	18.51 /96	19.02 /97	18.19 /98	C- / 3.9	99	2
GL	Janus Aspen Global Research Inst	JAWGX	B	(800) 295-2687	43.73	B /8.0	12.66 /85	14.96 /75	10.64 /50	C+ / 5.6	95	1
GL	RS Investors Fund A	RSINX	B	(800) 766-3863	12.96	B /7.8	0.75 /18	18.88 /96	15.17 /88	C+ / 6.0	98	10
GL	Private Capital Management Value	VFPAX	B	(888) 739-1390	16.91	B- /7.4	16.53 /94	15.26 /77	--	C+ / 6.1	97	5
GL	Dreyfus Dynamic Total Return A	AVGAX	B	(800) 782-6620	16.41	C /4.8	14.67 /91	10.30 /41	9.15 /38	B / 8.8	79	5
GL	Empiric 2500 A	EMCAX	B-	(800) 880-0324	34.70	B- /7.4	10.71 /77	16.17 /85	8.52 /33	C+ / 5.8	98	20
GL	QS Batterymarch Global Equity A	CFIPX	B-	(877) 534-4627	13.68	C+ /6.7	12.65 /85	14.77 /73	11.03 /53	B- / 7.1	96	4
GL	Janus Growth and Income A	JDNAX	B-	(800) 295-2687	48.50	C+ /6.1	10.51 /76	14.67 /72	12.22 /62	B- / 7.2	97	8
GL	AllianzGI NFJ Mid-Cap Value A	PQNAX	B-	(800) 988-8380	25.85	C+ /6.0	7.67 /60	14.93 /74	13.55 /73	B- / 7.3	97	6
GL	● Artisan Global Value Inv	ARTGX	B-	(800) 344-1770	15.59	C+ /5.9	3.69 /30	14.50 /71	12.97 /68	B- / 7.8	97	8
GL	Putnam Global Industrials Fund A	PGIAX	C+	(800) 225-1581	17.61	B /7.6	3.81 /31	17.60 /93	14.06 /78	C / 4.4	98	6
GL	GuideStone Growth Equity Inv	GGEZX	C+	(888) 984-8433	23.47	B- /7.4	12.96 /86	14.51 /71	14.75 /85	C / 4.6	97	12
GL	Buffalo Growth Fund	BUFGX	C+	(800) 492-8332	34.60	B- /7.3	11.32 /80	14.80 /73	14.56 /83	C / 5.2	96	4
GL	Cohen & Steers Inst Glbl Realty	GRSIX	C+	(800) 330-7348	26.24	B- /7.0	15.08 /92	12.01 /53	9.94 /44	C / 5.3	94	9
GL	VY Oppenheimer Global Adv	IGMAX	C+	(800) 992-0180	19.55	C+ /6.9	8.64 /67	13.73 /65	10.84 /51	C+ / 5.9	93	11
GL	Kinetics Small Cap Opps Advisor A	KSOAX	C+	(800) 930-3828	38.28	C+ /6.9	-3.16 / 8	19.01 /97	12.98 /68	C+ / 5.6	98	13
GL	Dodge & Cox Global Stock	DODWX	C+	(800) 621-3979	12.00	C+ /6.8	4.57 /36	15.42 /78	10.81 /51	C+ / 6.1	96	N/A
GL	Lord Abbett Sec Tr-Alpha Stratg A	ALFAX	C+	(888) 522-2388	31.28	C+ /6.8	5.93 /46	15.49 /79	13.96 /77	C+ / 5.8	97	17
GL	Quaker Global Tactical Alloc A	QTRAX	C+	(800) 220-8888	11.28	C+ /6.6	13.82 /89	14.42 /70	10.88 /52	C+ / 6.5	97	7
GL	AllianzGI Global Small Cap A	RGSAX	C+	(800) 988-8380	44.53	C+ /6.6	4.53 /35	15.28 /77	15.75 /92	C+ / 6.2	97	5
GL	T Rowe Price Global Stock	PRGSX	C+	(800) 638-5660	26.89	C+ /6.6	10.11 /75	13.81 /66	10.66 /50	C / 5.5	94	4
GL	Quaker Strategic Growth A	QUAGX	C+	(800) 220-8888	25.91	C+ /6.5	12.51 /85	14.86 /74	11.27 /55	C+ / 6.5	97	19
GL	Bright Rock Mid Cap Growth Inst	BQMGX	C+	(800) 273-7223	14.10	C+ /6.5	15.20 /92	11.22 /47	--	C / 5.5	93	3
GL	USAA World Growth Fund	USAWX	C+	(800) 382-8722	28.16	C+ /6.4	6.27 /49	13.79 /66	11.91 /60	C+ / 6.7	95	13
GL	Bright Rock Qual Lrg Cap Inst	BQLCX	C+	(800) 273-7223	14.35	C+ /6.4	8.22 /64	14.14 /68	--	C+ / 6.3	97	5
GL	Golub Group Equity Fund	GGEFX	C+	(866) 954-6682	18.89	C+ /6.2	8.55 /67	13.82 /66	12.21 /62	C+ / 6.4	97	6
GL	T Rowe Price Inst Glbl Gr Eq	RPIGX	C+	(800) 638-5660	22.80	C+ /6.2	12.06 /83	12.82 /58	10.43 /48	C+ / 5.7	94	7
GL	Vanguard Global Equity Inv	VHGEX	C+	(800) 662-7447	25.01	C+ /6.1	6.03 /47	13.27 /62	10.79 /51	C+ / 6.8	94	11
GL	Deutsche Glb Infrastructure A	TOLLX	C+	(800) 728-3337	14.73	C+ /6.1	9.71 /73	15.48 /79	15.55 /90	C+ / 6.5	98	N/A
GL	PMC Diversified Equity	PMDEX	C+	(866) 762-7338	24.94	C+ /5.9	7.10 /56	12.85 /59	11.57 /58	C+ / 6.5	95	6
GL	DFA Global Equity R2	DGERX	C+	(800) 984-9472	19.02	C+ /5.8	5.03 /39	12.99 /60	11.03 /53	C+ / 6.6	94	N/A
GL	Horizon Spin-off and Corp Res A	LSHAX	C+	(800) 207-7108	10.38	C+ /5.8	-0.76 /14	15.53 /79	11.94 /60	C+ / 6.1	95	8
GL	Pioneer Global Equity A	GLOSX	C+	(800) 225-6292	13.88	C+ /5.6	8.92 /69	13.93 /67	9.75 /43	B- / 7.0	96	5
GL	Alpine Global Infrastructure Inst	AIFRX	C+	(888) 785-5578	19.62	C /5.5	5.05 /39	13.12 /60	12.52 /64	C+ / 6.6	95	7

● Denotes fund is closed to new investors

Fund Type	Fund Name	Ticker Symbol	Overall Investment Rating	Phone	Net Asset Value As of 3/31/15	PERFORMANCE Perform-ance Rating/Pts	Annualized Total Return Through 3/31/15 1Yr / Pct	3Yr / Pct	5Yr / Pct	RISK Risk Rating/Pts	FUND MGR Mgr. Quality Pct	Mgr. Tenure (Years)
GR	ProFunds-HlthCare UltraSector	HCPSX	A+	(888) 776-3637	44.30	A+ /9.9	38.24 /99	38.76 /99	27.38 /99	B- / 7.2	99	2
GR	● Vanguard Capital Opportunity Inv	VHCOX	A+	(800) 662-7447	54.97	A+ /9.9	17.69 /95	23.41 /99	15.71 /91	C+ / 6.8	96	17
GR	Fidelity Select Air Transport	FSAIX	A+	(800) 544-8888	73.26	A+ /9.9	21.54 /97	26.07 /99	18.41 /98	C+ / 6.8	98	3
GR	ProFunds-Consumer Srvs Ultra	CYPSX	A+	(888) 776-3637	76.52	A+ /9.9	28.75 /99	31.46 /99	27.02 /99	C+ / 6.7	92	2
GR	ProFunds-Pharm UltraSector Svc	PHPSX	A+	(888) 776-3637	22.56	A+ /9.9	24.39 /98	32.15 /99	24.32 /99	C+ / 6.4	98	2
GR	Eventide Gilead A	ETAGX	A+	(877) 453-7877	27.72	A+ /9.9	16.24 /94	24.76 /99	20.37 /99	C+ / 6.1	97	7
GR	LM CM Opportunity Trust A	LGOAX	A+	(877) 534-4627	20.06	A+ /9.9	12.95 /86	30.29 /99	13.37 /72	C+ / 5.9	95	16
GR	● Smead Value Fund Investor	SMVLX	A+	(877) 807-4122	40.25	A+ /9.8	12.72 /86	21.57 /98	17.61 /97	B- / 7.5	91	7
GR	Leuthold Select Industries	LSLTX	A+	(888) 200-0409	22.90	A+ /9.8	15.08 /92	20.01 /98	12.51 /64	B- / 7.1	78	2
GR	Bridgeway Large-Cap Growth	BRLGX	A+	(800) 661-3550	23.91	A+ /9.8	22.54 /97	20.83 /98	16.24 /94	B- / 7.0	90	12
GR	Rydex Transportation A	RYTSX	A+	(800) 820-0888	48.41	A+ /9.8	16.34 /94	24.25 /99	16.70 /95	C+ / 6.9	96	17
GR	Fidelity Select Transportation	FSRFX	A+	(800) 544-8888	91.17	A+ /9.8	19.69 /96	24.36 /99	18.33 /98	C+ / 6.9	98	3
GR	Glenmede Large Cap Growth Port	GTLLX	A+	(800) 442-8299	24.53	A+ /9.8	20.97 /97	19.99 /98	18.37 /98	C+ / 6.8	84	11
GR	Nicholas	NICSX	A+	(800) 544-6547	71.57	A+ /9.8	19.51 /96	21.92 /98	18.41 /98	C+ / 6.7	94	46
GR	Fidelity Sel Defense and	FSDAX	A+	(800) 544-8888	129.39	A+ /9.8	13.61 /88	19.85 /98	17.08 /96	C+ / 6.5	92	3
GR	Fidelity Select Multimedia	FBMPX	A+	(800) 544-8888	82.20	A+ /9.8	13.61 /88	23.14 /99	20.52 /99	C+ / 6.5	90	2
GR	Fidelity Select Retailing	FSRPX	A+	(800) 544-8888	95.25	A+ /9.8	21.98 /97	20.99 /98	20.01 /99	C+ / 5.9	83	1
GR	● Vanguard PRIMECAP Core Inv	VPCCX	A+	(800) 662-7447	22.04	A+ /9.7	15.49 /92	20.14 /98	15.55 /90	B- / 7.0	93	11
GR	Glenmede Large Cap core	GTLOX	A+	(800) 442-8299	22.52	A+ /9.7	15.24 /92	19.61 /97	17.30 /97	B- / 7.0	81	11
GR	Parnassus Endeavor	PARWX	A+	(800) 999-3505	30.83	A+ /9.7	18.69 /96	19.20 /97	15.87 /92	C+ / 6.8	89	10
GR	Amer Beacon Bridgeway LC Val	BRLVX	A+	(800) 658-5811	24.32	A+ /9.6	12.45 /85	19.75 /98	15.85 /92	B- / 7.9	89	12
GR	ProFunds-Consumer Goods Ultra	CNPSX	A+	(888) 776-3637	78.41	A+ /9.6	15.99 /93	19.22 /97	18.59 /98	C+ / 6.8	30	2
GR	Janus Portfolio Institutional	JAGRX	A+	(800) 295-2687	38.01	A+ /9.6	20.49 /97	16.78 /89	14.30 /80	C+ / 6.1	78	4
GR	● Sequoia Fund	SEQUX	A+	(800) 686-6884	253.02	A /9.5	13.77 /89	17.63 /93	17.69 /97	B- / 7.2	93	35
GR	Vanguard FTSE Social Index Inv	VFTSX	A+	(800) 662-7447	13.49	A /9.5	14.60 /91	18.67 /96	14.96 /87	B- / 7.0	80	4
GR	TCW Concentrated Value N	TGFVX	A+	(800) 386-3829	20.00	A /9.5	15.51 /92	18.66 /96	13.02 /68	C+ / 6.7	76	11
GR	USAA Growth Fund	USAAX	A+	(800) 382-8722	25.02	A /9.5	16.22 /94	18.29 /95	15.48 /90	C+ / 6.6	77	8
GR	NASDAQ-100 Index Direct	NASDX	A+	(800) 955-9988	11.14	A /9.5	21.69 /97	17.85 /94	18.46 /98	C+ / 6.6	74	12
GR	Rydex Retailing A	RYRTX	A+	(800) 820-0888	26.85	A /9.5	19.44 /96	16.99 /90	16.95 /96	C+ / 6.5	52	17
GR	Natixis Vaughan Nelson Val Opp A	VNVAX	A+	(800) 225-5478	22.78	A /9.5	12.73 /86	19.64 /97	16.48 /95	C+ / 6.3	84	7
GR	PRIMECAP Odyssey Stock Fd	POSKX	A+	(800) 729-2307	24.25	A /9.5	13.56 /92	18.33 /94	14.44 /82	B- / 7.7	91	11
GR	American Century Veedot Inv	AMVIX	A+	(800) 345-6488	10.93	A /9.4	14.72 /91	18.16 /95	15.60 /91	B- / 7.1	80	16
GR	LSV Value Equity Inst	LSVEX	A+	(866) 777-7818	24.02	A /9.4	9.20 /70	19.66 /97	15.06 /87	B- / 7.1	72	16
GR	Fidelity NASDAQ Composite Index	FNCMX	A+	(800) 544-8544	64.65	A /9.4	18.00 /95	17.88 /94	16.53 /95	C+ / 6.6	71	11
GR	SunAmerica VAL Co I Nsdq 100	VCNIX	A+	(800) 858-8850	9.95	A /9.4	21.35 /97	17.26 /91	17.99 /97	C+ / 6.4	69	3
GR	American Century Leg Multi Cp	ACMFX	A+	(800) 345-6488	18.08	A /9.3	13.26 /87	17.70 /93	15.70 /91	B- / 7.3	85	8
GR	Vulcan Value Partners	VVPLX	A+	(877) 421-5078	19.44	A /9.3	14.59 /91	18.68 /96	15.96 /93	B- / 7.1	81	6
GR	Tax Mgd US MktWide Val II Inst	DFMVX	A+	(800) 984-9472	24.91	A /9.3	9.89 /74	19.07 /97	15.54 /90	B- / 7.0	74	N/A
GR	PNC Large Cap Growth A	PEWAX	A+	(800) 551-2145	28.93	A /9.3	22.83 /98	16.61 /88	15.90 /92	B- / 7.0	57	6
GR	USAA Nasdaq 100 Index	USNQX	A+	(800) 382-8722	12.53	A /9.3	21.08 /97	17.13 /91	17.76 /97	C+ / 6.6	67	9
GR	J Hancock VIT Fund AC Core I	JEQAX	A+	(800) 257-3336	23.12	A /9.3	12.07 /83	18.21 /95	15.71 /91	C+ / 6.4	49	4
GR	AMG FQ Tax-Managed US Equity	MFQAX	A+	(800) 835-3879	24.91	A- /9.2	12.35 /84	17.70 /93	16.48 /95	B- / 7.4	70	7
GR	J Hancock VIT All Cap Core I	JEACX	A+	(800) 257-3336	28.74	A- /9.2	13.09 /87	17.04 /90	14.27 /80	C+ / 6.9	65	5
GR	Hartford Core Equity A	HAIAX	A+	(888) 843-7824	23.30	A- /9.1	16.98 /95	18.20 /95	15.65 /91	B- / 7.3	81	17
GR	Olstein All Cap Value C	OFALX	A+	(800) 799-2113	21.90	A- /9.1	15.59 /93	16.79 /89	13.86 /76	B- / 7.1	62	20
GR	Akre Focus Retail	AKREX	A+	(877) 862-9556	23.10	A- /9.1	12.02 /83	17.77 /93	18.21 /98	B- / 7.1	82	6
GR	Wells Fargo Adv Large Cap Core A	EGOAX	A+	(800) 222-8222	15.82	A- /9.0	15.51 /92	18.55 /96	15.38 /89	B- / 7.4	83	8
GR	Vanguard US Value Inv	VUVLX	A+	(800) 662-7447	17.66	A- /9.0	10.12 /75	18.03 /94	15.13 /88	B- / 7.4	80	7
GR	Vanguard Structured Lg-Cp Eq Inst	VSLIX	A+	(800) 662-7447	40.44	A- /9.0	14.13 /90	17.32 /91	15.86 /92	B- / 7.3	75	9
GR	Fidelity Blue Chip Value	FBCVX	A+	(800) 544-8544	16.71	A- /9.0	14.24 /90	16.86 /89	11.29 /55	B- / 7.2	58	1
GR	Robeco Boston Ptrs All Cap Val Inv	BPAVX	A+	(888) 261-4073	22.83	A- /9.0	10.58 /77	17.56 /93	13.92 /77	B- / 7.2	68	8
GR	DFA US Large Cap Value II Inst	DFCVX	A+	(800) 984-9472	16.15	A- /9.0	8.25 /65	18.62 /96	14.93 /86	B- / 7.1	70	14

● Denotes fund is closed to new investors

Data as of March 31, 2015

99 Pct = Best
0 Pct = Worst

99 Pct = Best
0 Pct = Worst

Fund Type	Fund Name	Ticker Symbol	Overall Investment Rating	Phone	Net Asset Value As of 3/31/15	Performance Rating/Pts	Annualized Total Return Through 3/31/15			Risk Rating/Pts	Mgr. Quality Pct	Mgr. Tenure (Years)
							1Yr / Pct	3Yr / Pct	5Yr / Pct			
GI	Vanguard Cons Discn Idx Adm	VCDAX	A+	(800) 662-7447	63.35	A+ /9.8	17.09 /95	20.67 /98	19.95 /99	C+ / 6.8	86	5
GI	Transamerica Prt Large Core	DVGIX	A+	(888) 233-4339	33.88	A /9.5	16.36 /94	18.26 /95	15.70 /91	B- / 7.6	80	6
GI	Fidelity Value Fd	FDVLX	A+	(800) 544-8544	116.72	A /9.5	10.90 /78	18.97 /97	15.02 /87	C+ / 6.9	82	5
GI	Lazard US Eqty Concentrated	LEVOX	A+	(800) 821-6474	13.91	A /9.5	19.71 /97	17.76 /93	13.77 /76	C+ / 6.7	81	10
GI	Delaware Large Cap Value Eqty	DPDEX	A+	(800) 523-1918	27.65	A- /9.2	13.11 /87	18.13 /95	17.07 /96	B- / 7.8	92	9
GI	Fidelity Value Discovery Fd	FVDFX	A+	(800) 544-8544	24.95	A- /9.1	12.11 /83	17.78 /93	14.25 /80	B- / 7.8	80	3
GI	JPMorgan Tax Aware Equity I	JPDEX	A+	(800) 480-4111	29.61	A- /9.1	14.28 /90	17.28 /91	14.54 /83	C+ / 6.7	66	7
GI	Homestead Value	HOVLX	A+	(800) 258-3030	51.53	B+ /8.9	12.96 /86	17.19 /91	14.09 /79	B- / 7.5	69	25
GI	Vanguard Cons Stap Idx Adm	VCSAX	A+	(800) 662-7447	62.59	B+ /8.9	16.90 /94	16.43 /86	15.42 /90	B- / 7.1	88	5
GI	Vanguard Growth & Income Inv	VQNPX	A+	(800) 662-7447	42.34	B+ /8.7	13.83 /89	16.61 /88	14.77 /85	B- / 7.1	72	4
GI	Olstein Strategic Opps Fd A	OFSAX	A	(800) 799-2113	18.49	A+ /9.7	16.55 /94	20.23 /98	16.72 /95	C+ / 5.8	77	9
GI	T Rowe Price Value	TRVLX	A	(800) 638-5660	34.96	A /9.3	10.36 /76	18.65 /96	14.96 /87	C+ / 6.3	80	6
GI	Federated MDT Stock Tr IS	FMSTX	A	(800) 341-7400	28.61	A /9.3	8.75 /68	19.04 /97	15.54 /90	C+ / 6.2	68	6
GI	T Rowe Price Instl Lg Cap Val	TILCX	A	(800) 638-5660	20.54	B+ /8.5	9.99 /74	17.27 /91	13.61 /74	B- / 7.1	74	11
GI	Dodge & Cox Stk Fund	DODGX	A	(800) 621-3979	176.55	B+ /8.5	6.50 /51	18.20 /95	13.81 /76	B- / 7.0	73	N/A
GI	Fidelity Spartan Total Mkt Idx F	FFSMX	A	(800) 544-8544	60.96	B+ /8.4	12.27 /84	16.34 /86	14.72 /84	B- / 7.2	67	11
GI	MainStay Common Stock B	MOPBX	A	(800) 624-6782	18.43	B+ /8.4	11.97 /82	16.52 /87	13.07 /69	B- / 7.1	58	8
GI	T Rowe Price Growth and Inc	PRGIX	A	(800) 638-5660	32.58	B+ /8.3	12.72 /86	15.88 /82	13.60 /74	B- / 7.1	68	8
GI	SunAmerica Foc Dividend Strategy	FDSAX	A	(800) 858-8850	17.40	B /8.2	12.37 /84	17.64 /93	16.10 /93	B- / 7.2	87	2
GI	J Hancock VIT Amer Growth-Inc I		A	(800) 257-3336	24.38	B /8.1	10.59 /77	16.29 /85	12.75 /66	B- / 7.2	78	16
GI	JPMorgan Value Advtg A	JVAAX	A	(800) 480-4111	30.10	B /7.9	10.93 /78	17.18 /91	14.99 /87	B- / 7.6	82	10
GI	Goldman Sachs US Eqty Insights A	GSSQX	A	(800) 526-7384	41.71	B /7.9	13.64 /89	17.00 /90	15.00 /87	B- / 7.4	67	4
GI	Wright Selected Blue Chip Equities	WSBEX	A-	(800) 232-0013	13.07	A+ /9.6	13.79 /89	18.25 /95	16.07 /93	C / 5.4	67	7
GI	Voya Russell Mid Cap Index Adv	IRMAX	A-	(800) 992-0180	17.55	A- /9.1	12.67 /85	17.08 /90	15.20 /88	C+ / 5.8	75	3
GI	BMO Large Cap Value Y	MREIX	A-	(800) 236-3863	16.02	B+ /8.6	10.90 /78	16.91 /89	13.14 /69	C+ / 6.6	71	3
GI	Harbor Large Cap Value Inv	HILVX	A-	(800) 422-1050	12.09	B+ /8.4	9.44 /72	16.53 /87	13.14 /69	C+ / 6.6	45	3
GI	Invesco Equally-Weighted S&P	VADAX	A-	(800) 959-4246	49.73	B+ /8.3	12.55 /85	17.63 /93	15.36 /89	C+ / 6.9	73	5
GI	JPMorgan Disciplined Equity A	JDEAX	A-	(800) 480-4111	23.84	B+ /8.3	14.04 /89	17.32 /91	14.94 /86	C+ / 6.8	74	13
GI	Columbia Large Core Quant A	AQEAX	A-	(800) 345-6611	9.83	B /7.8	15.62 /93	16.48 /87	15.78 /92	B- / 7.2	54	5
GI	Matthew 25 Fund	MXXVX	A-	(888) 625-3863	31.82	B /7.8	9.09 /70	16.69 /88	20.89 /99	B- / 7.2	64	20
GI	SEI Instl Managed Tr-Lg Cap Val A	TRMVX	A-	(800) 342-5734	25.20	B /7.8	9.22 /70	16.18 /85	13.58 /74	B- / 7.1	48	21
GI	Wasatch Strategic Income Investor	WASIX	A-	(800) 551-1700	12.43	B /7.7	11.03 /78	16.05 /84	15.81 /92	B- / 7.5	75	9
GI	JPMorgan Growth and Income A	VGRIX	A-	(800) 480-4111	46.00	B /7.7	11.43 /80	17.12 /90	14.60 /83	B- / 7.3	73	13
GI	Vanguard Dividend Growth Inv	VDIGX	A-	(800) 662-7447	22.92	B- /7.4	10.72 /77	15.01 /75	14.11 /79	B- / 7.7	73	9
GI	Commerce Value	CFVLX	A-	(800) 995-6365	31.82	B- /7.2	8.08 /63	15.35 /78	14.33 /81	B- / 7.8	75	18
GI	Invesco Diversified Dividend A	LCEAX	A-	(800) 959-4246	18.61	B- /7.2	10.18 /75	16.19 /85	13.10 /69	B- / 7.8	88	13
GI	● SEI Asset Alloc Tr Tax Mgd Strgy A	SXMAX	A-	(800) 342-5734	19.71	B- /7.0	10.87 /78	14.05 /67	13.30 /71	B / 8.3	87	12
GI	Elfun Trusts	ELFNX	B+	(800) 242-0134	58.95	A- /9.2	15.19 /92	17.54 /92	15.34 /89	C / 5.5	73	27
GI	SunAmerica VAL Co I Lgcap Core	VLCCX	B+	(800) 858-8850	13.30	A- /9.0	13.47 /88	17.32 /91	15.16 /88	C / 5.2	67	4
GI	BNY Mellon Income Stock M	MPISX	B+	(800) 645-6561	9.14	B+ /8.8	10.75 /77	17.33 /91	14.36 /81	C+ / 6.0	75	4
GI	Dreyfus Growth and Income	DGRIX	B+	(800) 645-6561	21.14	B+ /8.4	10.08 /75	16.53 /87	14.54 /83	C+ / 6.2	53	7
GI	Deutsche Core Equity A	SUWAX	B+	(800) 728-3337	24.84	B+ /8.4	15.67 /93	17.20 /91	14.35 /81	C+ / 6.0	55	2
GI	JPMorgan US Equity A	JUEAX	B+	(800) 480-4111	14.74	B /8.0	13.59 /88	16.94 /89	14.31 /80	C+ / 6.3	65	9
GI	Schwab 1000 Index Fund	SNXFX	B+	(800) 407-0256	53.29	B /7.8	12.39 /84	15.98 /83	14.33 /81	B- / 7.0	65	7
GI	SEI Large Cap Fund A	SLGAX	B+	(800) 342-5734	14.91	B /7.7	11.09 /79	15.50 /79	13.62 /74	C+ / 6.4	51	6
GI	UBS US Large Cap Eq A	BNEQX	B+	(888) 793-8637	26.88	B /7.7	14.80 /91	16.38 /85	13.43 /72	C+ / 6.4	41	21
GI	Fidelity Growth and Income	FGRIX	B+	(800) 544-8544	30.32	B /7.6	9.49 /72	15.77 /81	14.09 /79	B- / 7.2	51	4
GI	Hotchkis and Wiley Large Cap Val	HWLAX	B+	(866) 493-8637	26.76	B /7.6	7.67 /60	17.74 /93	14.01 /78	B- / 7.1	68	27
GI	Hennessy Large Value Investor	HLVFX	B+	(800) 966-4354	34.44	B- /7.5	10.92 /78	15.11 /76	12.21 /62	B- / 7.2	49	8
GI	Hartford Value HLS Fd IB	HBVLX	B+	(888) 843-7824	17.06	B- /7.5	10.42 /76	15.17 /76	12.68 /66	B- / 7.1	44	14
GI	SunAmerica VAL Co I Growth & Inc	VCGAX	B+	(800) 858-8850	19.30	B- /7.4	12.75 /86	14.62 /72	12.19 /62	C+ / 6.9	46	N/A
GI	Putnam Capital Spectrum Fund A	PVSAX	B+	(800) 225-1581	38.19	B- /7.3	6.68 /52	17.51 /92	18.16 /98	B- / 7.0	95	6

● Denotes fund is closed to new investors

Fund Type	Fund Name	Ticker Symbol	Overall Investment Rating	Phone	Net Asset Value As of 3/31/15	Perform-ance Rating/Pts	Annualized Total Return Through 3/31/15			Risk Rating/Pts	Mgr. Quality Pct	Mgr. Tenure (Years)
							1Yr / Pct	3Yr / Pct	5Yr / Pct			
HL	Vanguard HealthCare Index Adm	VHCIX	A+	(800) 662-7447	67.68	A+ /9.9	27.85 /99	27.67 /99	20.76 /99	B /8.2	99	11
HL	Rydex Health Care A	RYHEX	A+	(800) 820-0888	33.60	A+ /9.9	30.21 /99	26.61 /99	19.23 /98	C+ /6.6	99	17
HL	Hartford Healthcare A	HGHAX	A+	(888) 843-7824	39.13	A+ /9.9	29.12 /99	29.34 /99	21.36 /99	C+ /6.2	99	15
HL	Oak Assoc-Live Oak Health	LOGSX	A+	(888) 462-5386	22.05	A+ /9.9	21.12 /97	23.05 /99	18.64 /98	C+ /6.1	98	14
HL	Fidelity Select Medical Delivery	FSHCX	A+	(800) 544-8888	90.32	A+ /9.9	29.21 /99	20.44 /98	18.89 /98	C+ /6.0	97	3
HL	Saratoga Adv Tr-Health & Biotech	SHPAX	A+	(800) 807-3863	31.71	A+ /9.8	19.51 /96	21.87 /98	17.78 /97	C+ /6.4	97	10
HL	Vanguard Health Care Inv	VGHCX	A	(800) 662-7447	225.70	A+ /9.9	29.47 /99	29.10 /99	21.70 /99	C+ /5.6	99	7
HL	BlackRock Health Sci Opps Inv A	SHSAX	A	(800) 441-7762	54.46	A+ /9.9	34.56 /99	30.02 /99	21.02 /99	C /5.4	99	12
HL	Delaware Healthcare Fund A	DLHAX	A	(800) 523-1918	20.36	A+ /9.8	16.37 /94	23.61 /99	19.82 /99	C+ /5.6	96	8
HL	Invesco Global Health Care A	GGHCX	A-	(800) 959-4246	46.56	A+ /9.9	25.57 /98	25.87 /99	18.51 /98	C /5.3	98	N/A
HL	Putnam Global Health Care Fund A	PHSTX	A-	(800) 225-1581	71.94	A+ /9.9	31.06 /99	29.35 /99	18.07 /97	C /5.3	99	10
HL	SunAmerica VAL Co I Health Sci	VCHSX	A-	(800) 858-8850	25.70	A+ /9.9	41.62 /99	36.21 /99	28.54 /99	C /5.2	99	2
HL	Fidelity Adv Health Care A	FACDX	A-	(800) 522-7297	43.08	A+ /9.9	34.53 /99	35.23 /99	26.32 /99	C /5.2	99	7
HL	Deutsche Health and Wellness A	SUHAX	A-	(800) 728-3337	43.69	A+ /9.9	30.43 /99	28.59 /99	21.23 /99	C /5.2	99	14
HL	Fidelity Select Pharmaceuticals	FPHAX	A-	(800) 544-8888	23.67	A+ /9.9	26.48 /99	27.58 /99	22.55 /99	C /5.1	99	2
HL	T Rowe Price Health Sciences	PRHSX	A-	(800) 638-5660	77.51	A+ /9.9	41.92 /99	36.57 /99	28.92 /99	C /5.0	99	2
HL	Kinetics Medical Advisor A	KRXAX	B+	(800) 930-3828	32.48	A+ /9.9	21.21 /97	24.59 /99	16.56 /95	C /4.8	97	14
HL	J Hancock VIT Hlth Sciences I	JEHSX	B+	(800) 257-3336	38.22	A+ /9.9	41.68 /99	36.38 /99	28.66 /99	C /4.8	99	2
HL	Schwab Health Care	SWHFX	B+	(800) 407-0256	27.37	A+ /9.9	26.92 /99	26.82 /99	21.25 /99	C /4.7	98	3
HL	Fidelity Select Health Care	FSPHX	B	(800) 544-8888	243.32	A+ /9.9	35.12 /99	36.11 /99	26.96 /99	C- /4.1	99	7
HL	AllianzGI Health Sciences A	RAGHX	B-	(800) 988-8380	36.48	A+ /9.9	31.22 /99	24.94 /99	19.34 /98	C- /3.4	98	10
HL	Rydex Biotechnology A	RYBOX	B-	(800) 820-0888	87.63	A+ /9.9	41.83 /99	37.84 /99	28.59 /99	C- /3.2	99	17
HL	● Prudential Jennison Health Sci A	PHLAX	B-	(800) 225-1852	53.98	A+ /9.9	43.17 /99	36.97 /99	29.20 /99	C- /3.2	99	16
HL	Fidelity Adv Biotechnology A	FBTAX	B-	(800) 522-7297	28.31	A+ /9.9	45.91 /99	42.13 /99	32.61 /99	C- /3.2	99	10
HL	● Franklin Biotechnology Discvry A	FBDIX	B-	(800) 342-5236	192.85	A+ /9.9	43.56 /99	41.68 /99	31.02 /99	C- /3.1	99	18
HL	Eaton Vance WW Health Sciences	ETHSX	C+	(800) 262-1122	13.35	A+ /9.9	29.82 /99	28.19 /99	19.67 /99	D+ /2.9	99	26
HL	Fidelity Select Biotech Port	FBIOX	C+	(800) 544-8888	256.71	A+ /9.9	46.13 /99	43.52 /99	33.30 /99	D+ /2.6	99	10
HL	Alger Health Sciences Fund A	AHSAX	C+	(800) 254-3796	24.40	A+ /9.9	30.51 /99	23.63 /99	17.14 /96	D+ /2.5	99	10
HL	Highland Long/Short Healthcare A	HHCAX	C+	(877) 665-1287	16.32	C+ /6.4	9.62 /73	13.66 /65	11.50 /57	C+ /6.5	95	N/A
HL	ICON Healthcare S	ICHCX	C	(800) 764-0442	20.11	A+ /9.9	29.72 /99	28.32 /99	20.75 /99	D- /1.5	99	2

	99 Pct = Best 0 Pct = Worst					PERFORMANCE				RISK	FUND MGR	
Fund Type	Fund Name	Ticker Symbol	Overall Investment Rating	Phone	Net Asset Value As of 3/31/15	Perform- ance Rating/Pts	Annualized Total Return Through 3/31/15			Risk Rating/Pts	Mgr. Quality Pct	Mgr. Tenure (Years)
							1Yr / Pct	3Yr / Pct	5Yr / Pct			
IN	Aquila Three Peaks Oppty Gro A	ATGAX	A+	(800) 437-1020	47.19	A+ /9.8	20.73 /97	23.71 /99	18.49 /98	C+ / 6.3	96	12
IN	Natixis ASG Managed Futures	AMFAX	A+	(800) 225-5478	12.27	A+ /9.7	39.33 /99	12.29 /55	--	B- / 7.7	96	5
IN	SEI Inst Inv Managed Vol Fund A	SVYAX	A+	(800) 342-5734	14.64	A /9.5	15.66 /93	18.42 /95	16.60 /95	C+ / 6.3	95	11
IN	SEI Instl Mgd Tr-US Mgd Volty A	SVOAX	A+	(800) 342-5734	17.11	A- /9.2	14.61 /91	17.60 /93	15.86 /92	C+ / 6.5	93	N/A
IN	Parnassus Core Equity Inv	PRBLX	A+	(800) 999-3505	40.29	A- /9.0	12.70 /86	17.75 /93	13.69 /75	B- / 7.1	87	14
IN	Nicholas Equity Income	NSEIX	A+	(800) 544-6547	20.99	A- /9.0	13.13 /87	16.94 /90	14.83 /85	B- / 7.0	84	22
IN	DFA US Core Equity 2 Ptf Inst	DFQTX	A+	(800) 984-9472	17.82	B+ /8.7	9.51 /72	17.22 /91	14.89 /86	B- / 7.0	59	3
IN	DFA US Core Equity 1 Ptf Inst	DFEOX	A+	(800) 984-9472	18.26	B+ /8.7	10.75 /77	16.93 /89	14.97 /87	B- / 7.0	64	3
IN	AQR Managed Futures Strategy N	AQMNX	A+	(866) 290-2688	11.44	B+ /8.6	26.37 /99	10.28 /41	5.70 /15	B / 8.2	99	5
IN	State Farm Equity A	SNEAX	A+	(800) 447-4930	10.02	B+ /8.6	15.83 /93	17.22 /91	13.97 /77	B- / 7.2	75	N/A
IN	Transamerica Prt Large Value	DVEIX	A+	(888) 233-4339	27.95	B+ /8.5	9.51 /72	16.87 /89	14.75 /85	B- / 7.4	64	6
IN	Target Large Capitalization Val T	TALVX	A+	(800) 225-1852	16.41	B+ /8.3	10.04 /74	16.65 /88	12.82 /67	B- / 7.5	61	10
IN	T Rowe Price Dividend Growth	PRDGX	A+	(800) 638-5660	36.54	B+ /8.3	12.65 /85	15.82 /82	13.90 /77	B- / 7.4	74	15
IN	Vanguard Extended Market Index	VEXMX	A	(800) 662-7447	70.11	A- /9.2	10.10 /75	17.35 /92	15.80 /92	C+ / 6.3	66	18
IN	AT Disciplined Equity Institutional	AWEIX	A	(800) 338-2550	15.92	B+ /8.7	14.94 /91	16.15 /84	14.72 /84	B- / 7.0	72	5
IN	Vanguard Russell 3000 Index Inst	VRTTX	A	(800) 662-7447	185.88	B+ /8.5	12.32 /84	16.35 /86	--	B- / 7.2	67	5
IN	DFA Tax-Managed US Eq Inst	DTMEX	A	(800) 984-9472	22.56	B+ /8.4	11.85 /82	16.26 /85	14.61 /83	B- / 7.2	62	3
IN	Vanguard High Div Yield Index Inv	VHDYX	A	(800) 662-7447	26.97	B- /7.4	10.93 /78	15.36 /78	14.78 /85	B / 8.0	72	9
IN	DFA U.S. Vector Equity Port Inst	DFVEX	A-	(800) 984-9472	17.01	B+ /8.5	7.15 /56	17.10 /90	14.65 /84	C+ / 6.6	41	3
IN	RBB Free Market US Equity Inst	FMUEX	A-	(888) 261-4073	17.09	B+ /8.3	6.69 /53	16.82 /89	14.43 /82	C+ / 6.6	39	8
IN	ASTON/LMCG Small Cap Growth	ACWDX	B+	(800) 992-8151	15.64	A+ /9.8	16.50 /94	21.27 /98	--	C / 4.3	92	5
IN	GuideStone Value Equity Inv	GVEZX	B+	(888) 984-8433	21.32	B /7.6	8.13 /64	15.90 /83	13.59 /74	C+ / 6.9	40	14
IN	TCW Relative Value Dividend App	TGIGX	B+	(800) 386-3829	17.26	B- /7.4	7.84 /62	15.78 /82	14.10 /79	B- / 7.0	29	14
IN	Fidelity Equity Dividend Income	FEQTX	B+	(800) 544-8544	26.72	B- /7.1	10.28 /75	14.73 /73	11.54 /57	B- / 7.7	66	4
IN	PIMCO SmallCap StkPlus AR Strat	PCKAX	B	(800) 426-0107	9.45	A /9.3	9.50 /72	19.01 /97	18.09 /97	C / 4.7	63	1
IN	RS Large Cap Alpha Fd A	GPAFX	B	(800) 766-3863	59.25	B+ /8.3	10.17 /75	18.11 /95	12.55 /65	C+ / 5.7	67	3
IN	Fidelity Strategic Advisers Core	FCSAX	B	(800) 544-8544	15.79	B /8.0	11.74 /81	15.71 /81	13.63 /74	C+ / 6.0	60	6
IN	Putnam Equity Income A	PEYAX	B	(800) 225-1581	21.23	B- /7.4	10.80 /78	16.76 /89	14.31 /81	C+ / 6.5	65	3
IN	Delaware US Growth A	DUGAX	B	(800) 523-1918	26.40	B- /7.4	15.60 /93	15.59 /80	16.48 /95	C+ / 6.0	56	10
IN	Principal Equity Inc Fd A	PQIAX	B	(800) 222-5852	26.69	C+ /5.8	9.27 /71	14.17 /68	13.15 /70	B- / 7.7	55	7
IN	PIMCO Fundamental IndexPLUS	PIXAX	B-	(800) 426-0107	6.32	B+ /8.4	8.24 /64	18.54 /96	18.11 /98	C / 4.8	75	1
IN	Vanguard Equity Income Inv	VEIPX	B-	(800) 662-7447	30.99	C+ /6.9	8.67 /67	14.85 /74	14.81 /85	B- / 7.6	65	12
IN	Adv Inn Cir FMC Select Fd	FMSLX	B-	(866) 777-7818	31.36	C+ /6.8	10.72 /77	13.72 /65	11.83 /59	B- / 7.7	59	5
IN	JPMorgan Equity Income A	OIEIX	B-	(800) 480-4111	14.00	C+ /6.7	10.70 /77	15.47 /79	15.29 /89	B- / 7.6	70	11
IN	American Century Fdmtl Equity A	AFDAX	B-	(800) 345-6488	21.78	C+ /6.7	12.95 /86	15.29 /77	14.26 /80	B- / 7.4	60	7
IN	Pioneer Equity Income A	PEQIX	B-	(800) 225-6292	34.59	C+ /6.4	10.94 /78	14.75 /73	14.26 /80	B- / 7.0	62	25
IN	Nationwide HighMark LC Core Eq	NWGHX	B-	(800) 848-0920	13.56	C+ /6.4	11.99 /82	14.93 /74	13.47 /73	B- / 7.0	49	2
IN	Voya Large Cap Value Adv	IPEAX	B-	(800) 992-0180	12.37	C+ /6.3	7.74 /61	13.99 /67	13.53 /73	B- / 7.7	39	4
IN	AB Value A	ABVAX	B-	(800) 221-5672	14.25	C+ /6.3	7.99 /63	15.29 /77	11.47 /57	B- / 7.2	34	6
IN	Fidelity Equity Income K	FEIKX	B-	(800) 544-8544	57.69	C+ /6.2	6.62 /52	14.05 /67	11.15 /54	B- / 7.2	56	4
IN	Zacks All-Cap Core A	CZOAX	B-	(800) 245-2934	24.26	C+ /6.1	12.48 /85	14.47 /71	13.17 /70	B- / 7.0	45	10
IN	Amana Income Investor	AMANX	B-	(800) 732-6262	46.55	C+ /6.0	7.54 /59	13.40 /63	11.55 /57	B- / 7.4	42	25
IN	Neiman Large Cap Value NL	NEIMX	B-		27.16	C+ /5.9	10.84 /78	12.22 /54	11.14 /54	B- / 7.1	56	12
IN	Nationwide Ziegler Equity Income	NWGYX	B-	(800) 848-0920	13.82	C+ /5.8	8.71 /68	14.35 /70	13.76 /75	B- / 7.7	63	6
IN	USAA Income Stock Fund	USISX	B-	(800) 382-8722	17.73	C+ /5.8	7.13 /56	13.46 /63	12.48 /64	B- / 7.5	40	5
IN	Schwab Dividend Equity Fund	SWDSX	C+	(800) 407-0256	17.08	B- /7.1	10.09 /75	15.28 /77	13.44 /72	C / 5.5	55	3
IN ●	ASTON/River Road Div All Cap Val	ARDEX	C+	(800) 992-8151	13.23	C+ /6.8	9.39 /71	14.28 /69	13.31 /71	C+ / 6.5	61	10
IN	FAM Equity-Income Inv	FAMEX	C+	(800) 932-3271	26.01	C+ /6.6	8.47 /66	13.75 /65	12.87 /67	C+ / 6.7	45	19
IN	Invesco American Franchise A	VAFAX	C+	(800) 959-4246	17.26	C+ /6.5	13.02 /87	14.64 /72	13.53 /73	C / 5.4	26	5
IN	TETON Westwood Equity A	WEECX	C+	(800) 422-3554	13.13	C+ /6.3	10.03 /74	14.36 /70	11.60 /58	C+ / 6.7	39	3
IN	Prudential Jennison Equity Income	SPQAX	C+	(800) 225-1852	17.64	C+ /6.2	10.19 /75	14.66 /72	13.31 /71	C+ / 6.7	57	15
IN	MassMutual Select Fundamental V	MFUAX	C+	(800) 542-6767	14.03	C+ /6.1	10.10 /75	14.71 /73	12.03 /61	C+ / 6.6	37	7

● Denotes fund is closed to new investors

Fund Type	Fund Name	Ticker Symbol	Overall Investment Rating	Phone	Net Asset Value As of 3/31/15	Performance Rating/Pts	1Yr / Pct	3Yr / Pct	5Yr / Pct	Risk Rating/Pts	Mgr. Quality Pct	Mgr. Tenure (Years)
						PERFORMANCE — Annualized Total Return Through 3/31/15				RISK	FUND MGR	
IX	American Beacon S&P 500 Idx Inv	AAFPX	A+	(800) 658-5811	27.96	B /7.7	12.03 /83	15.43 /78	13.78 /76	B /8.0	58	11
IX	Vanguard Instl Index Inst	VINIX	A	(800) 662-7447	188.84	B+ /8.3	12.71 /86	16.08 /84	14.44 /82	B- /7.3	67	15
IX	Northern Stock Index	NOSIX	A	(800) 595-9111	25.41	B /8.2	12.59 /85	15.98 /83	14.29 /80	B- /7.3	65	9
IX	Fidelity Spartan 500 Index Inv	FUSEX	A	(800) 544-8544	73.52	B /8.2	12.62 /85	16.01 /83	14.37 /81	B- /7.3	66	9
IX	Vanguard 500 Index Inv	VFINX	A	(800) 662-7447	190.71	B /8.2	12.56 /85	15.93 /83	14.29 /80	B- /7.3	65	24
IX	USAA S&P 500 Index Members	USSPX	A	(800) 382-8722	29.54	B /8.1	12.47 /85	15.83 /82	14.18 /79	B- /7.3	64	9
IX	GE Institutional S&P 500 Index Inv	GIDIX	A	(800) 242-0134	19.52	B /8.1	12.39 /84	15.88 /82	14.29 /80	B- /7.3	64	N/A
IX	Dreyfus Basic S&P 500 Stock Idx	DSPIX	A	(800) 645-6561	42.57	B /8.1	12.51 /85	15.90 /83	14.27 /80	B- /7.2	65	13
IX	Vantagepoint 500 Stock Index II	VPSKX	A	(800) 669-7400	15.23	B /8.1	12.52 /85	15.89 /82	14.26 /80	B- /7.2	65	11
IX	S&P 500 Index Direct	SPFIX	A	(800) 955-9988	41.66	B /8.0	12.46 /85	15.76 /81	14.21 /80	B- /7.3	62	12
IX	T Rowe Price Equity Index 500	PREIX	A-	(800) 638-5660	55.70	B /8.0	12.46 /85	15.82 /82	14.17 /79	B- /7.3	64	13
IX	TIAA-CREF S&P 500 Idx Retire	TRSPX	A-	(800) 842-2252	23.14	B /8.0	12.34 /84	15.74 /81	14.09 /79	B- /7.3	64	10
IX	GuideStone Equity Index Inv	GEQZX	A-	(888) 984-8433	23.06	B /7.9	12.20 /83	15.69 /81	14.25 /80	B- /7.3	61	14
IX	Columbia Large Cap Index A	NEIAX	A-	(800) 345-6611	39.94	B /7.9	12.20 /83	15.59 /80	13.97 /77	B- /7.3	61	6
IX	Schwab S&P 500 Index Fund	SWPPX	A-	(800) 407-0256	32.45	B /7.8	12.60 /85	16.01 /83	14.36 /81	B- /7.3	66	7
IX	Meeder Quantex	FLCGX	B+	(800) 325-3539	35.22	B+ /8.3	6.86 /54	17.30 /91	13.95 /77	C+ /6.1	39	10
IX	SEI Instl Managed Tr-S&P 500 Idx	SSPIX	B+	(800) 342-5734	50.85	B /7.9	12.29 /84	15.64 /80	14.06 /78	C+ /6.5	61	4
IX	Dreyfus S&P 500 Index Fund	PEOPX	B+	(800) 645-6561	52.11	B /7.8	12.16 /83	15.55 /80	13.92 /77	C+ /6.9	61	15
IX	Nuveen Equity Index A	FAEIX	B+	(800) 257-8787	28.18	B /7.7	12.09 /83	15.41 /78	13.77 /76	C+ /6.8	59	16
IX	Principal LgCap S&P 500 A	PLSAX	B+	(800) 222-5852	14.58	B- /7.5	12.18 /83	15.45 /79	13.79 /76	B- /7.3	59	4
IX	PNC S&P 500 Index A	PIIAX	B+	(800) 551-2145	16.32	B- /7.4	12.31 /84	15.56 /80	13.90 /77	B- /7.3	60	N/A
IX	Prudential Stock Index A	PSIAX	B+	(800) 225-1852	43.69	B- /7.2	12.14 /83	15.50 /79	13.90 /77	B- /7.1	60	23
IX	State Farm Equity & Bond Legacy	SLBAX	B+	(800) 447-4930	11.43	C /5.1	11.67 /81	11.39 /48	10.04 /45	B+ /9.1	84	N/A
IX	Deutsche S&P 500 Index A	SXPAX	B-	(800) 728-3337	26.00	C+ /6.8	11.95 /82	15.32 /77	13.74 /75	B- /7.1	58	8
IX	Invesco S&P 500 Index A	SPIAX	B-	(800) 959-4246	22.31	C+ /6.7	12.06 /83	15.47 /79	13.81 /76	B- /7.3	59	5
IX	● Wells Fargo Adv Index A	WFILX	B-	(800) 222-8222	65.90	C+ /6.7	12.15 /83	15.50 /79	13.86 /76	B- /7.2	60	2
IX	Rydex S&P 500 A	RYSOX	B-	(800) 820-0888	41.40	C+ /6.0	10.90 /78	14.23 /69	12.64 /65	B- /7.5	43	17
IX	PIMCO StocksPLUS Absolute	PTOAX	C+	(800) 426-0107	9.62	B+ /8.5	12.88 /86	17.68 /93	17.28 /96	C- /3.4	73	1
IX	PIMCO StocksPLUS A	PSPAX	C+	(800) 426-0107	8.98	B+ /8.4	12.89 /86	17.38 /92	15.58 /91	C- /3.9	75	1
IX	Victory Munder Index 500 A	MUXAX	C+	(800) 539-3863	22.29	B- /7.2	12.02 /83	15.32 /77	13.68 /75	C /5.5	57	7
IX	JPMorgan Equity Index A	OGEAX	C+	(800) 480-4111	41.21	C+ /6.8	12.21 /84	15.56 /80	13.94 /77	C+ /6.7	61	20
IX	Nationwide S&P 500 Index A	GRMAX	C+	(800) 848-0920	15.15	C+ /6.7	12.08 /83	15.46 /79	13.80 /76	C+ /6.8	58	4
IX	Russell US Core Equity A	RSQAX	C	(800) 832-6688	38.74	C+ /6.1	10.55 /77	14.58 /72	12.56 /65	C /5.5	32	N/A
IX	Franklin Global Real Estate A	FGRRX	C	(800) 342-5236	9.19	C+ /6.0	16.16 /93	11.71 /51	10.91 /52	C /5.2	91	5
IX	Mutual of America Inst Eqty Idx	MAEQX	D+	(800) 914-8716	9.79	B /8.2	12.55 /85	16.01 /83	14.09 /79	D- /1.1	67	1
IX	Forester Value N	FVALX	D+	(800) 388-0365	12.54	E+ /0.7	0.96 /18	1.87 / 6	1.84 / 4	B /8.5	30	16
IX	Parametric Absolute Return Inv	EOAAX	D-	(800) 262-1122	9.66	E+ /0.6	0.52 /17	0.98 / 5	--	C+ /6.9	94	5
IX	Absolute Credit Opportunities Inst	AOFOX	D-	(800) 754-8757	9.92	E /0.5	4.37 /34	-0.25 / 4	0.45 / 3	C+ /6.5	64	7
IX	Forward Tactical Enhanced A	FTEAX	E+	(800) 999-6809	22.48	E- /0.2	-7.41 / 4	-1.03 / 3	--	C+ /6.5	6	3

99 Pct = Best
0 Pct = Worst

● Denotes fund is closed to new investors

Fund Type	Fund Name	Ticker Symbol	Overall Investment Rating	Phone	Net Asset Value As of 3/31/15	Performance Rating/Pts	Annualized Total Return Through 3/31/15			Risk Rating/Pts	Mgr. Quality Pct	Mgr. Tenure (Years)
							1Yr / Pct	3Yr / Pct	5Yr / Pct			
MC	Harbor Mid Cap Value Inv	HIMVX	A+	(800) 422-1050	21.34	A+ /9.8	12.33 /84	20.98 /98	16.10 /93	B- / 7.3	91	11
MC	● Vanguard PRIMECAP Inv	VPMCX	A+	(800) 662-7447	105.16	A+ /9.8	15.58 /93	21.00 /98	15.91 /93	C+ / 7.0	96	30
MC	● T Rowe Price Instl Mid-Cap Eq Gr	PMEGX	A+	(800) 638-5660	46.00	A+ /9.8	18.05 /96	19.09 /97	17.60 /97	C+ / 6.2	86	19
MC	Rydex Mid Cap 1.5x Strgy A	RYAHX	A+	(800) 820-0888	67.32	A+ /9.8	15.50 /92	23.07 /99	20.23 /99	C+ / 5.9	26	14
MC	Fidelity Mid Cap Enhanced Index	FMEIX	A+	(800) 544-8544	14.17	A+ /9.7	14.79 /91	19.63 /97	16.75 /95	C+ / 6.8	90	8
MC	PRIMECAP Odyssey Growth Fd	POGRX	A+	(800) 729-2307	26.98	A+ /9.7	13.10 /87	19.63 /97	15.20 /88	C+ / 6.7	91	11
MC	● VY JPMorgan Mid Cap Val Adv	IJMAX	A+	(800) 992-0180	23.28	A+ /9.7	15.28 /92	18.94 /97	16.57 /95	C+ / 6.6	94	11
MC	Janus Aspen Enterprise Inst	JAAGX	A+	(800) 295-2687	66.19	A+ /9.7	17.93 /95	17.84 /94	16.92 /96	C+ / 6.2	91	8
MC	Hennessy Cornerstone Mid Cap 30	HFMDX	A+	(800) 966-4354	19.69	A+ /9.7	15.42 /92	19.55 /97	17.26 /96	C+ / 6.1	86	12
MC	Dreyfus Active MidCap A	DNLDX	A+	(800) 782-6620	59.40	A+ /9.6	18.36 /96	19.57 /97	14.96 /86	C+ / 6.9	83	3
MC	● Principal MidCap A	PEMGX	A+	(800) 222-5852	23.00	A+ /9.6	18.04 /96	19.27 /97	18.56 /98	C+ / 6.8	91	15
MC	Fidelity Adv Mid Cap Value A	FMPAX	A+	(800) 522-7297	24.81	A /9.5	15.38 /92	20.25 /98	16.35 /94	B- / 7.1	92	2
MC	Vanguard Mid-Cap Value Index Inv	VMVIX	A+	(800) 662-7447	36.08	A /9.5	12.44 /85	18.69 /96	15.48 /90	B- / 7.0	89	9
MC	Virtus Mid-Cap Core Fund A	VMACX	A+	(800) 243-1574	23.00	A /9.5	22.75 /98	16.97 /91	15.46 /90	B- / 7.0	83	6
MC	● J Hancock III Dsp Val Mid Cap A	JVMAX	A+	(800) 257-3336	20.19	A /9.5	13.78 /89	19.64 /97	17.18 /96	C+ / 6.9	90	15
MC	Transamerica Prt Mid Value	DVMVX	A+	(888) 233-4339	21.95	A /9.4	13.99 /89	17.73 /93	15.09 /87	B- / 7.6	90	14
MC	Vanguard Mid-Cap Index Inv	VIMSX	A+	(800) 662-7447	35.14	A /9.4	14.72 /91	17.76 /93	15.91 /92	C+ / 6.9	83	17
MC	Lazard US Mid Cap Eq Open	LZMOX	A+	(800) 821-6474	19.82	A /9.4	21.07 /97	15.22 /77	12.87 /67	C+ / 6.6	51	14
MC	Wells Fargo Adv Spec Mid Cp VI A	WFPAX	A+	(800) 222-8222	32.68	A /9.4	11.83 /82	19.88 /98	15.96 /93	C+ / 6.4	90	6
MC	● JPMorgan Mid Cap Value A	JAMCX	A+	(800) 480-4111	37.77	A /9.3	15.15 /92	18.96 /97	16.68 /95	B- / 7.0	94	18
MC	American Century VP Mid Cap Val	AVMTX	A+	(800) 345-6488	19.14	A- /9.1	13.62 /88	17.42 /92	14.56 /83	B- / 7.2	92	11
MC	Prudential Mid-Cap Value A	SPRAX	A+	(800) 225-1852	21.35	A- /9.1	12.41 /84	19.13 /97	15.41 /90	C+ / 6.8	89	8
MC	Vanguard S&P Mid-Cap 400 Value	VMFVX	A+	(800) 662-7447	198.20	A- /9.1	10.75 /77	17.48 /92	--	C+ / 6.6	67	2
MC	Vanguard Windsor-I Inv	VWNDX	A+	(800) 662-7447	21.79	B+ /8.9	9.71 /73	17.69 /93	14.04 /78	C+ / 6.8	85	7
MC	Touchstone Mid Cap A	TMAPX	A+	(800) 543-0407	25.95	B+ /8.7	12.73 /86	17.98 /94	15.68 /91	B- / 7.1	88	4
MC	Boyar Value Fund	BOYAX	A+	(800) 266-5566	23.34	B /8.1	16.23 /94	16.95 /90	14.07 /78	B / 8.1	94	17
MC	● T Rowe Price Mid-Cap Growth	RPMGX	A	(800) 638-5660	80.36	A+ /9.7	17.20 /95	18.41 /95	17.02 /96	C+ / 5.8	86	23
MC	Vanguard Mid-Cap Growth Index	VMGIX	A	(800) 662-7447	42.34	A /9.4	17.09 /95	16.68 /88	16.19 /94	C+ / 6.1	70	2
MC	T Rowe Price Diversified MidCap	PRDMX	A	(800) 638-5660	24.91	A /9.4	16.13 /93	17.12 /90	16.23 /94	C+ / 6.0	72	12
MC	American Century NT Md Cp Val	ACLMX	A	(800) 345-6488	12.82	A /9.3	14.05 /89	17.82 /94	15.14 /88	C+ / 6.4	92	9
MC	Alger Mid Cap Growth Inst R	AGIRX	A	(800) 254-3796	22.70	A /9.3	14.76 /91	17.24 /91	13.44 /72	C+ / 6.0	75	5
MC	SEI Instl Managed Tr-MidCap Portf	SEMCX	A	(800) 342-5734	27.70	A /9.3	13.11 /87	17.88 /94	15.31 /89	C+ / 6.0	78	22
MC	T Rowe Price Extended Eq Mkt	PEXMX	A	(800) 638-5660	26.32	A- /9.2	10.38 /76	17.68 /93	16.08 /93	C+ / 6.2	61	13
MC	Northern Midcap Index	NOMIX	A	(800) 595-9111	18.43	A- /9.1	11.98 /82	16.82 /89	15.45 /90	C+ / 6.5	65	9
MC	● JPMorgan Mid Cap Equity A	JCMAX	A	(800) 480-4111	46.73	A- /9.1	13.95 /89	18.20 /95	16.42 /94	C+ / 6.5	86	13
MC	Vanguard S&P Mid-Cap 400 Index	VSPMX	A	(800) 662-7447	204.78	A- /9.1	12.15 /83	16.97 /90	--	C+ / 6.5	67	2
MC	Vanguard S&P Mid-Cap 400 Gro	VMFGX	A	(800) 662-7447	209.97	A- /9.1	13.21 /87	16.39 /86	--	C+ / 6.5	64	2
MC	SunAmerica VAL Co I Midcap Idx	VMIDX	A	(800) 858-8850	28.46	A- /9.0	11.80 /82	16.68 /88	15.36 /89	C+ / 6.5	63	3
MC	Voya VP Index Plus MidCap S	IPMSX	A	(800) 992-0180	25.51	B+ /8.9	12.06 /83	16.65 /88	14.62 /83	C+ / 6.5	62	9
MC	Columbia Mid Cap Index A	NTIAX	A	(800) 345-6611	16.35	B+ /8.9	11.66 /81	16.49 /87	15.20 /88	C+ / 6.4	60	6
MC	Dreyfus MidCap Index Fund	PESPX	A	(800) 645-6561	39.52	B+ /8.9	11.75 /81	16.49 /87	15.18 /88	C+ / 6.4	61	15
MC	Principal MidCp Value III R3	PJPPX	A	(800) 222-5852	18.94	B+ /8.8	9.39 /71	17.26 /91	15.03 /87	C+ / 6.8	84	10
MC	Westcore Mid-Cap Value Div Rtl	WTMCX	A	(800) 392-2673	27.58	B+ /8.8	14.09 /90	16.22 /85	13.63 /74	C+ / 6.8	87	13
MC	TIAA-CREF Mid Cap Value Retail	TCMVX	A	(800) 842-2252	24.38	B+ /8.7	11.15 /79	16.58 /87	14.35 /81	C+ / 6.7	82	13
MC	Vanguard Selected Value Inv	VASVX	A	(800) 662-7447	28.75	B /8.1	5.50 /42	16.95 /90	14.55 /83	B- / 7.2	85	16
MC	Parnassus Mid Cap	PARMX	A	(800) 999-3505	27.90	B /8.0	13.22 /87	15.30 /77	14.79 /85	B- / 7.3	86	7
MC	Vanguard Mega Cap Index Inst	VMCTX	A	(800) 662-7447	138.66	B /8.0	12.27 /84	15.79 /82	14.22 /80	B- / 7.3	88	8
MC	William Blair Small-Mid Cap Gr N	WSMNX	A-	(800) 742-7272	20.12	A+ /9.7	15.21 /92	18.09 /95	16.33 /94	C / 5.5	71	12
MC	Ariel Appreciation Fund Investor	CAAPX	A-	(800) 292-7435	55.97	A+ /9.7	13.93 /89	19.21 /97	15.28 /89	C / 5.4	66	13
MC	Baron Partners Retail	BPTRX	A-	(800) 992-2766	37.68	A /9.4	7.32 /58	19.50 /97	16.98 /96	C / 5.5	58	23
MC	T Rowe Price Tax-Efficient Equity	PREFX	A-	(800) 638-5660	22.61	A- /9.2	16.50 /94	16.21 /85	15.73 /91	C+ / 6.0	75	15
MC	GuideMark Small/Mid Cap Core	GMSMX	A-	(800) 664-5345	17.31	A- /9.2	11.19 /79	17.23 /91	14.39 /81	C+ / 6.0	61	1

● Denotes fund is closed to new investors

Fund Type	Fund Name	Ticker Symbol	Overall Investment Rating	Phone	Net Asset Value As of 3/31/15	Perform-ance Rating/Pts	Annualized Total Return Through 3/31/15			Risk Rating/Pts	Mgr. Quality Pct	Mgr. Tenure (Years)
							1Yr / Pct	3Yr / Pct	5Yr / Pct			
OT	Lazard Global Listed Infr Open	GLFOX	A+	(800) 821-6474	14.82	A+ /9.8	18.18 /96	21.60 /98	14.45 /82	B- / 7.0	98	10
OT	Vanguard Industrials Index Adm	VINAX	A+	(800) 662-7447	55.12	B+ /8.7	8.41 /66	17.40 /92	15.11 /88	B- / 7.0	64	5
OT	Pacific Financial Explorer Inst	PFGPX	B	(800) 637-1380	10.35	B- /7.1	10.86 /78	14.07 /68	9.23 /38	C+ / 6.8	52	8
OT	ICON Consumer Discretionary S	ICCCX	B-	(800) 764-0442	14.99	B /7.9	9.24 /71	15.36 /78	17.53 /97	C / 5.1	60	4
OT	Davis Research Fund Class A	DRFAX	B-	(800) 279-0279	18.89	C+ /6.2	9.47 /72	14.47 /71	12.50 /64	B- / 7.1	32	N/A
OT	Guggenheim Managed Futures	RYMTX	C+	(800) 820-0888	26.07	C /4.5	26.29 /99	4.79 /12	0.44 / 3	B- / 7.8	91	8
OT	Putnam Global Consumer Fund A	PGCOX	C-	(800) 225-1581	18.07	C+ /6.0	7.05 /55	14.15 /68	13.45 /72	C / 4.7	30	7
OT	Wells Fargo Adv Endeavor Sel A	STAEX	C-	(800) 222-8222	13.28	C+ /5.8	11.30 /80	13.56 /64	13.29 /71	C / 4.5	37	15
OT	ICON Materials S	ICBMX	C-	(800) 764-0442	15.17	C- /4.1	2.61 /25	10.64 /43	10.41 /48	C+ / 6.6	6	8
OT	Merk Asian Currency Investor	MEAFX	C-	(866) 637-5386	9.50	E /0.5	0.74 /18	-0.07 / 4	0.24 / 3	B+ / 9.8	33	7
OT	Merk Abs Rtn Currency Investor	MABFX	D	(866) 637-5386	8.72	E /0.3	-6.59 / 4	-1.11 / 3	-0.98 / 2	B / 8.2	11	6
OT	Midas Perpetual Portfolio	MPERX	E	(800) 400-6432	0.98	E- /0.2	-9.42 / 3	-5.33 / 2	0.30 / 3	C / 4.5	1	7
OT	Hartford Global Real Asset A	HRLAX	E	(888) 843-7824	8.91	E- /0.1	-14.28 / 2	-5.87 / 2	--	C / 5.3	0	5
OT	Direxion Indexed Commodity Stg A	DXCTX	E	(800) 851-0511	16.44	E- /0.1	-12.74 / 2	-7.95 / 1	-8.93 / 1	C / 5.0	1	7
OT	Russell Commodity Strategies A	RCSAX	E	(800) 832-6688	6.34	E- /0.0	-27.38 / 0	-12.94 / 1	--	C- / 3.9	0	N/A
OT	Eaton Vance Commodity Strategy	EACSX	E-	(800) 262-1122	6.26	E- /0.1	-26.62 / 0	-12.19 / 1	--	C- / 3.6	0	5
OT	● MFS Commodity Strategy Fund A	MCSAX	E-	(800) 225-2606	6.67	E- /0.1	-26.46 / 0	-11.17 / 1	--	C- / 3.6	0	5
OT	ALPS CoreComm Mgt CompComm	JCRAX	E-	(866) 759-5679	7.94	E- /0.1	-25.38 / 0	-11.24 / 1	--	C- / 3.4	0	5
OT	Fidelity Srs Commodity Strat Fund	FCSSX	E-	(800) 544-8544	6.12	E- /0.1	-27.57 / 0	-12.13 / 1	-6.36 / 1	D+ / 2.3	0	6
OT	PIMCO CommoditiesPLUS	PCLAX	E-	(800) 426-0107	7.16	E- /0.0	-32.54 / 0	-12.11 / 1	--	D+ / 2.8	0	5
OT	ProFunds-Rising Rates Opport Svc	RRPSX	E-	(888) 776-3637	5.06	E- /0.0	-28.83 / 0	-14.69 / 0	-18.76 / 0	D- / 1.4	0	6
OT	Rydex Commodities Strgy A	RYMEX	E-	(800) 820-0888	9.01	E- /0.0	-41.00 / 0	-18.52 / 0	-9.92 / 0	E+ / 0.6	0	10

99 Pct = Best
0 Pct = Worst

● Denotes fund is closed to new investors

Fund Type	Fund Name	Ticker Symbol	Overall Investment Rating	Phone	Net Asset Value As of 3/31/15	Performance Rating/Pts	Annualized Total Return Through 3/31/15			Risk Rating/Pts	Mgr. Quality Pct	Mgr. Tenure (Years)
	99 Pct = Best 0 Pct = Worst						1Yr / Pct	3Yr / Pct	5Yr / Pct			
PM	Vanguard Materials Index Fd Adm	VMIAX	C	(800) 662-7447	55.29	C /4.7	3.99 /32	11.76 /51	11.10 /53	C+ / 6.3	99	5
PM	ProFunds Short Precious Metals	SPPSX	D	(888) 776-3637	10.19	B /8.1	17.80 /95	14.49 /71	2.15 / 5	E+ / 0.7	57	2
PM	Fidelity Adv Materials A	FMFAX	D-	(800) 522-7297	77.21	D /1.7	-2.51 / 9	9.05 /33	10.25 /46	C+ / 5.8	99	7
PM	ProFunds-Precious Metals Ultra	PMPSX	E-	(888) 776-3637	6.68	E- /0.0	-42.21 / 0	-38.81 / 0	-25.71 / 0	D / 1.6	0	2
PM	US Global Inv World Prec Min	UNWPX	E-	(800) 873-8637	4.43	E- /0.0	-31.95 / 0	-30.61 / 0	-20.17 / 0	D- / 1.3	0	26
PM	Midas Fund	MIDSX	E-	(800) 400-6432	0.96	E- /0.0	-34.25 / 0	-34.14 / 0	-24.17 / 0	D- / 1.3	0	13
PM	Franklin Gold & Precious Metals A	FKRCX	E-	(800) 342-5236	13.60	E- /0.0	-24.82 / 0	-26.63 / 0	-16.05 / 0	D- / 1.2	1	16
PM	Vanguard Prec Metals & Mining Inv	VGPMX	E-	(800) 662-7447	8.68	E- /0.0	-20.37 / 1	-22.27 / 0	-13.00 / 0	E+ / 0.8	1	2
PM	Invesco Gold and Precious Mtls A	IGDAX	E-	(800) 959-4246	3.60	E- /0.0	-21.40 / 1	-23.54 / 0	-12.23 / 0	E+ / 0.7	2	2
PM	Wells Fargo Adv Precious Mtls A	EKWAX	E-	(800) 222-8222	28.99	E- /0.0	-20.90 / 1	-24.56 / 0	-13.26 / 0	E+ / 0.7	2	8
PM	US Global Inv Gold & PMetals Fd	USERX	E-	(800) 873-8637	5.28	E- /0.0	-21.31 / 1	-24.65 / 0	-14.87 / 0	E+ / 0.7	2	26
PM	Oppenheimer Gold/Spec Min A	OPGSX	E-	(888) 470-0862	12.82	E- /0.0	-25.08 / 0	-27.27 / 0	-15.68 / 0	E+ / 0.7	1	18
PM	USAA Precious Mtls&Minerals	USAGX	E-	(800) 382-8722	11.32	E- /0.0	-22.99 / 1	-27.15 / 0	-15.55 / 0	E+ / 0.6	1	7
PM	OCM Gold Fund Investor	OCMGX	E-	(800) 628-9403	9.29	E- /0.0	-19.86 / 1	-23.46 / 0	-12.23 / 0	E+ / 0.6	5	19
PM	Deutsche Gold & Prec Metals Fund	SGDAX	E-	(800) 728-3337	5.65	E- /0.0	-25.36 / 0	-27.39 / 0	-16.45 / 0	E / 0.4	1	4
PM	Gabelli Gold A	GLDAX	E-	(800) 422-3554	10.37	E- /0.0	-17.70 / 1	-22.74 / 0	-12.33 / 0	E / 0.4	11	21
PM	Fidelity Adv Gold A	FGDAX	E-	(800) 522-7297	15.92	E- /0.0	-21.15 / 1	-26.59 / 0	-15.06 / 0	E / 0.4	2	8
PM	Tocqueville Gold	TGLDX	E-	(800) 697-3863	30.05	E- /0.0	-21.15 / 1	-24.24 / 0	-11.44 / 0	E / 0.3	2	18
PM	American Century Global Gold A	ACGGX	E-	(800) 345-6488	7.21	E- /0.0	-22.95 / 1	-26.63 / 0	-14.43 / 0	E- / 0.2	1	23
PM	Rydex Precious Metal A	RYMNX	E-	(800) 820-0888	24.28	E- /0.0	-28.13 / 0	-25.99 / 0	-15.48 / 0	E- / 0.2	1	22
PM	Van Eck Intl Investors Gold A	INIVX	E-	(800) 826-1115	7.57	E- /0.0	-22.28 / 1	-25.00 / 0	-13.24 / 0	E- / 0.0	3	19
PM	First Eagle Gold A	SGGDX	E-	(800) 334-2143	13.94	E- /0.0	-15.36 / 2	-20.76 / 0	-9.95 / 0	E- / 0.0	6	2

● Denotes fund is closed to new investors

Fund Type	Fund Name	Ticker Symbol	Overall Investment Rating	Phone	Net Asset Value As of 3/31/15	PERFORMANCE Performance Rating/Pts	Annualized Total Return Through 3/31/15 1Yr / Pct	3Yr / Pct	5Yr / Pct	RISK Risk Rating/Pts	FUND MGR Mgr. Quality Pct	Mgr. Tenure (Years)
RE	Baron Real Estate Retail	BREFX	A+	(800) 992-2766	27.09	A+ /9.9	16.19 /94	24.10 /99	21.34 /99	C+ / 6.2	99	6
RE	Third Avenue Real Estate Value	TVRVX	A-	(800) 443-1021	32.25	B /7.9	10.02 /74	15.83 /82	12.83 /67	B- / 7.3	97	17
RE	REMS Real Estate Value Opp Fd	HLPPX	B+	(800) 527-9525	18.22	A- /9.1	17.26 /95	15.77 /81	15.90 /92	C / 5.5	94	13
RE	Phocas Real Estate	PHREX	B	(866) 746-2271	34.37	A+ /9.8	27.96 /99	16.45 /87	16.02 /93	C- / 4.2	81	9
RE	Cohen and Steers Real Estate Sec	CSEIX	B	(800) 330-7348	17.00	A+ /9.7	27.35 /99	15.60 /80	15.76 /92	C- / 3.8	77	11
RE	J Hancock II Real Est Eq Nav		B	(800) 257-3336	12.69	A /9.4	24.64 /98	13.65 /65	15.71 /91	C / 4.6	64	9
RE	T Rowe Price Real Estate	TRREX	B	(800) 638-5660	28.23	A /9.4	24.49 /98	13.73 /65	15.86 /92	C / 4.5	66	18
RE	Stratton Real Estate Fund	STMDX	B	(800) 634-5726	38.00	A /9.4	25.52 /98	14.34 /70	14.74 /85	C- / 4.1	70	35
RE	TIAA-CREF Real Est Secs Retail	TCREX	B	(800) 842-2252	15.82	A /9.3	24.41 /98	13.19 /61	15.28 /89	C- / 4.2	61	10
RE	SEI Instl Managed Tr-Real Est A	SETAX	B	(800) 342-5734	19.89	A- /9.2	24.46 /98	13.16 /61	15.09 /87	C- / 4.2	48	12
RE	CGM Realty	CGMRX	B	(800) 345-4048	34.06	B /7.9	22.54 /97	11.25 /47	12.33 /63	C / 5.5	75	21
RE	Alpine Realty Inc and Growth Inst	AIGYX	B-	(888) 785-5578	23.06	A+ /9.6	26.09 /98	14.59 /72	16.26 /94	C- / 3.6	60	16
RE	Cohen & Steers Realty Shares	CSRSX	B-	(800) 330-7348	80.43	A /9.5	24.77 /98	13.93 /67	14.97 /87	C- / 3.7	56	10
RE	AMG Mgrs Real Estate Securities	MRESX	B-	(800) 835-3879	12.65	A /9.5	25.49 /98	13.93 /67	16.04 /93	C- / 3.6	52	11
RE	Cohen & Steers Inst Realty Shrs	CSRIX	B-	(800) 330-7348	52.37	A /9.5	24.85 /98	14.15 /68	15.20 /88	C- / 3.6	60	10
RE	Vanguard REIT Index Inv	VGSIX	B-	(800) 662-7447	28.02	A /9.4	23.95 /98	13.94 /67	15.68 /91	C- / 3.8	51	19
RE	DFA Real Estate Securities Ptf Inst	DFREX	B-	(800) 984-9472	34.34	A /9.4	24.59 /98	13.94 /67	15.80 /92	C- / 3.7	49	3
RE	● SSgA Clarion Real Estate N	SSREX	B-	(800) 843-2639	17.41	A /9.3	24.97 /98	13.33 /62	15.39 /89	C- / 3.9	45	2
RE	Dunham Real Estate Stock A	DAREX	B-	(888) 338-6426	20.11	A- /9.2	25.21 /98	14.39 /70	14.93 /86	C- / 3.9	62	3
RE	Fidelity Real Estate Investment	FRESX	B-	(800) 544-8544	42.67	A- /9.2	24.19 /98	13.37 /62	15.52 /90	C- / 3.9	45	18
RE	Oppenheimer Real Estate A	OREAX	B-	(888) 470-0862	30.02	A- /9.2	25.98 /98	14.21 /69	15.52 /90	C- / 3.8	57	13
RE	SA Real Estate Securities Fund	SAREX	B-	(800) 366-7266	11.20	A- /9.0	23.07 /98	12.94 /59	14.84 /86	C- / 3.9	38	3
RE	Universal Inst US Real Estate II	USRBX	B-	(800) 869-6397	20.87	B+ /8.9	23.34 /98	12.70 /57	14.56 /83	C / 4.5	58	18
RE	Eaton Vance Real Estate Fund A	EAREX	B-	(800) 262-1122	14.79	B+ /8.9	25.88 /98	13.29 /62	15.65 /91	C- / 4.2	59	9
RE	Ivy Real Estate Securities A	IRSAX	B-	(800) 777-6472	29.38	B+ /8.8	25.19 /98	13.38 /62	14.52 /82	C- / 4.1	56	9
RE	DFA Gl Real Estate Securities Port	DFGEX	B-	(800) 984-9472	10.87	B /8.2	18.68 /96	12.97 /59	13.86 /76	C / 4.9	54	N/A
RE	AB Inst Global RealEst II	ARIIX	B-	(800) 221-5672	11.10	B /7.8	16.54 /94	13.27 /61	12.12 /61	C / 5.4	77	3
RE	ProFunds-Real Est UltraSector Svc	REPSX	C+	(888) 776-3637	39.68	A+ /9.8	29.63 /99	15.77 /81	17.02 /96	C- / 3.1	9	2
RE	GE Investments Real Est Sec 1	GEIRX	C+	(800) 242-0134	15.46	A+ /9.6	25.47 /98	14.34 /70	16.51 /95	C- / 3.2	56	9
RE	Manning & Napier Real Estate S	MNREX	C+	(800) 466-3863	16.20	A /9.5	24.46 /98	14.33 /70	15.11 /88	D+ / 2.9	70	6
RE	VY Clarion Real Estate Adv	ICRPX	C+	(800) 992-0180	35.13	B+ /8.9	22.84 /98	12.75 /58	15.06 /87	C- / 3.8	39	13
RE	Fidelity Adv Real Estate A	FHEAX	C+	(800) 522-7297	24.24	B+ /8.9	24.68 /98	13.81 /66	15.34 /89	C- / 3.5	52	11
RE	Franklin Real Estate Sec A	FREEX	C+	(800) 342-5236	22.86	B+ /8.7	24.15 /98	13.50 /63	15.29 /89	C- / 4.0	47	5
RE	American Century Real Estate A	AREEX	C+	(800) 345-6488	31.22	B+ /8.7	24.55 /98	13.51 /63	16.07 /93	C- / 3.9	53	7
RE	JPMorgan Realty Income A	URTAX	C+	(800) 480-4111	14.47	B+ /8.6	24.79 /98	13.05 /60	15.48 /90	C- / 3.7	41	8
RE	Forward Progressive Real Est A	KREAX	C+	(800) 999-6809	18.03	B+ /8.5	23.13 /98	13.65 /65	14.75 /85	C / 4.3	71	5
RE	Pioneer Real Estate Shares A	PWREX	C+	(800) 225-6292	30.97	B+ /8.5	23.88 /98	13.16 /61	15.29 /89	C- / 4.0	47	11
RE	MSIF US Real Estate A	MUSDX	C+	(800) 354-8185	20.86	B+ /8.4	23.99 /98	13.19 /61	14.77 /85	C / 4.4	64	20
RE	Voya Real Estate A	CLARX	C+	(800) 992-0180	20.74	B+ /8.4	23.92 /98	13.08 /60	15.31 /89	C- / 3.9	39	19
RE	Goldman Sachs Real Estate Sec A	GREAX	C+	(800) 526-7384	20.50	B /8.2	23.16 /98	13.16 /61	15.46 /90	C- / 4.1	54	5
RE	Delaware RE Inv A	DPREX	C+	(800) 523-1918	16.08	B /8.1	22.76 /98	12.95 /59	15.36 /89	C- / 4.0	44	18
RE	Spirit Of America Real Estate A	SOAAX	C+	(800) 452-4892	13.56	B /8.0	24.09 /98	13.11 /60	13.72 /75	C / 4.7	68	N/A
RE	Davis Real Estate A	RPFRX	C+	(800) 279-0279	37.60	B /7.6	23.56 /98	11.61 /50	13.34 /71	C / 4.7	51	13
RE	Delaware Global RE Opps Inst	DGROX	C+	(800) 523-1918	7.40	B- /7.5	15.07 /92	13.25 /61	12.57 /65	C / 5.3	72	8
RE	J Hancock II Glb Real Est Nav		C+	(800) 257-3336	9.69	B- /7.5	16.28 /94	12.69 /57	11.19 /54	C / 5.1	64	9
RE	Principal Glb Real Est Sec A	POSAX	C+	(800) 222-5852	8.97	B- /7.3	16.30 /94	13.91 /66	12.61 /65	C / 5.2	79	8
RE	Commonwealth-Real Estate	CNREX	C+	(888) 345-1898	15.19	B- /7.0	15.34 /92	12.15 /53	10.15 /46	C / 5.5	88	N/A
RE	T Rowe Price Glbl Real Estate	TRGRX	C+	(800) 638-5660	21.00	C+ /6.6	15.59 /93	11.65 /50	11.94 /60	C / 5.5	57	7
RE	AB Glbl Real Est Inv A	AREAX	C+	(800) 221-5672	14.73	C+ /6.4	15.53 /93	12.48 /56	11.21 /54	C / 5.5	72	3
RE	Forward Select Income A	KIFAX	C+	(800) 999-6809	26.00	C /4.9	11.95 /82	11.59 /50	11.86 /60	B- / 7.7	96	14
RE	EII Realty Sec Inst	EIIRX	C	(888) 323-8912	5.19	A /9.5	24.16 /98	14.37 /70	16.69 /95	D / 2.2	72	11
RE	Principal Real Est Securities A	PRRAX	C	(800) 222-5852	24.00	A /9.4	26.07 /98	14.90 /74	15.67 /91	D+ / 2.3	68	15

● Denotes fund is closed to new investors

Fund Type	Fund Name	Ticker Symbol	Overall Investment Rating	Phone	Net Asset Value As of 3/31/15	Perform-ance Rating/Pts	Annualized Total Return Through 3/31/15			Risk Rating/Pts	Mgr. Quality Pct	Mgr. Tenure (Years)
	99 Pct = Best 0 Pct = Worst						1Yr / Pct	3Yr / Pct	5Yr / Pct			
SC	Hennessy Cornerstone Growth Inv	HFCGX	A+	(800) 966-4354	20.28	A+ /9.8	17.23 /95	19.68 /97	14.56 /83	C+ / 6.8	96	15
SC	Vanguard Strategic Equity Inv	VSEQX	A+	(800) 662-7447	33.84	A+ /9.8	14.29 /90	20.78 /98	18.19 /98	C+ / 6.7	96	9
SC	Hennessy Focus Investor	HFCSX	A+	(800) 966-4354	70.89	A+ /9.8	18.24 /96	19.04 /97	17.35 /97	C+ / 6.6	97	6
SC	PNC Multi-Factor Small Cap Core	PLOAX	A+	(800) 551-2145	21.34	A+ /9.8	13.56 /88	22.34 /98	19.63 /99	C+ / 6.4	94	10
SC	Ariel Fund Investor	ARGFX	A+	(800) 292-7435	76.61	A+ /9.8	19.54 /96	21.60 /98	16.12 /94	C+ / 5.9	94	29
SC	Golden Small Cap Core Inst	GLDSX	A+	(800) 754-8757	18.45	A+ /9.7	14.27 /90	18.60 /96	16.66 /95	C+ / 6.4	92	10
SC	Vanguard Strategic Sm-Cp Equity	VSTCX	A+	(800) 662-7447	32.07	A+ /9.7	11.51 /80	19.59 /97	17.65 /97	C+ / 6.2	92	9
SC	Westwood SmallCap Value Inst	WHGSX	A+	(877) 386-3944	14.34	A+ /9.6	8.63 /67	19.62 /97	16.82 /96	C+ / 6.4	90	2
SC	Wasatch Small Cap Value Investor	WMCVX	A+	(800) 551-1700	6.44	A /9.5	10.84 /78	18.81 /96	15.97 /93	C+ / 6.6	93	16
SC	Homestead Small Company Stock	HSCSX	A+	(800) 258-3030	40.95	A /9.5	11.30 /80	18.17 /95	17.71 /97	C+ / 6.5	91	16
SC	Vanguard Small-Cap Value Index	VISVX	A+	(800) 662-7447	26.20	A /9.3	10.45 /76	18.12 /95	14.94 /86	C+ / 6.8	90	17
SC	PNC Small Cap A	PPCAX	A+	(800) 551-2145	21.81	A /9.3	9.74 /73	18.89 /96	17.68 /97	C+ / 6.8	92	11
SC	FAM Value Inv	FAMVX	A+	(800) 932-3271	68.58	B+ /8.9	13.55 /88	16.28 /85	13.52 /73	B- / 7.2	94	28
SC	Roxbury/Hood River Sm-Cap Gr	RSCIX	A	(800) 336-9970	33.42	A+ /9.8	16.85 /94	21.31 /98	17.68 /97	C+ / 5.7	95	8
SC	T Rowe Price Diversified Sm-Cap	PRDSX	A	(800) 638-5660	27.68	A+ /9.7	15.57 /93	18.97 /97	19.03 /98	C+ / 5.9	92	9
SC	JPMorgan Small Cap Core Sel	VSSCX	A	(800) 480-4111	56.48	A+ /9.7	12.79 /86	19.68 /97	16.68 /95	C+ / 5.9	87	11
SC	PNC Multi-Factor Small Cap	PLWAX	A	(800) 551-2145	20.58	A+ /9.6	13.75 /89	19.74 /98	19.21 /98	C+ / 6.0	90	10
SC	● Hotchkis and Wiley Small Cap Val	HWSAX	A	(866) 493-8637	61.24	A /9.5	10.76 /77	20.75 /98	17.24 /96	C+ / 6.0	93	20
SC	● AMG Mgrs Skyline Special Eqty	SKSEX	A	(800) 835-3879	41.10	A /9.4	6.99 /55	19.42 /97	17.10 /96	C+ / 6.2	84	14
SC	DFA Tax Mgd US Target Val Inst	DTMVX	A	(800) 984-9472	33.76	A /9.4	7.40 /58	18.83 /96	15.82 /92	C+ / 6.2	88	3
SC	Hodges Small Cap Retail	HDPSX	A	(877) 232-1222	20.43	A /9.4	8.78 /68	19.16 /97	20.30 /99	C+ / 6.0	91	8
SC	Fidelity Sm Cap Enhanced Index	FCPEX	A	(800) 544-8544	13.38	A /9.4	11.86 /82	17.90 /94	16.70 /95	C+ / 6.0	85	8
SC	● T Rowe Price Instl Small Cap Stk	TRSSX	A	(800) 638-5660	21.32	A /9.3	9.50 /72	17.63 /93	17.58 /97	C+ / 6.2	88	15
SC	Value Line Small Cap	VLEOX	A	(800) 243-2729	49.50	A- /9.2	10.96 /78	17.13 /91	16.96 /96	C+ / 6.3	93	17
SC	Nationwide HighMark Sm Cp Core	NWGPX	A	(800) 848-0920	32.55	A- /9.2	14.17 /90	18.34 /95	17.07 /96	C+ / 6.2	89	2
SC	Vanguard Tax-Managed Small-Cap	VTMSX	A	(800) 662-7447	47.62	A- /9.2	9.27 /71	17.33 /92	16.25 /94	C+ / 6.2	84	16
SC	JPMorgan US Small Company A	JTUAX	A	(800) 480-4111	16.92	A- /9.2	11.00 /78	18.56 /96	15.98 /93	C+ / 6.1	83	11
SC	Vanguard Small-Cap Index Inv	NAESX	A	(800) 662-7447	58.49	A- /9.1	9.66 /73	17.40 /92	15.65 /91	C+ / 6.3	88	24
SC	Vanguard S&P SC 600 Indx Inst	VSMSX	A	(800) 662-7447	214.28	A- /9.1	8.67 /67	17.22 /91	--	C+ / 6.2	82	2
SC	PNC Multi-Factor Small Cap Value	PMRRX	A	(800) 551-2145	19.87	A- /9.0	12.90 /86	18.04 /94	15.69 /91	C+ / 6.6	87	10
SC	RBC Micro Cap Value A	TMVAX	A	(800) 422-2766	29.53	B+ /8.8	9.15 /70	18.86 /96	15.86 /92	C+ / 6.7	89	6
SC	SunAmerica VAL Co I Smcp Spl	VSSVX	A	(800) 858-8850	13.92	B+ /8.5	7.64 /60	16.38 /86	13.73 /75	C+ / 6.8	82	10
SC	Janus Triton A	JGMAX	A-	(800) 295-2687	24.87	A+ /9.6	18.87 /96	17.84 /94	18.43 /98	C+ / 5.7	93	N/A
SC	Wilshire Small Co Growth Inv	DTSGX	A-	(888) 200-6796	25.30	A /9.5	12.01 /83	17.51 /92	15.78 /92	C / 5.5	79	13
SC	VY Baron Growth Adv	IBSAX	A-	(800) 992-0180	31.88	A /9.4	9.71 /73	18.13 /95	16.89 /96	C+ / 5.9	95	13
SC	● Hartford SmallCap Growth A	HSLAX	A-	(888) 843-7824	52.12	A /9.4	12.60 /85	18.53 /96	18.79 /98	C+ / 5.6	85	6
SC	Wilshire Small Co Val Inv	DTSVX	A-	(888) 200-6796	23.63	A /9.4	8.68 /67	18.31 /95	13.72 /75	C+ / 5.6	83	8
SC	Northern Small Cap Core	NSGRX	A-	(800) 595-9111	22.26	A /9.3	10.33 /76	17.46 /92	15.83 /92	C+ / 5.9	84	5
SC	Glenmede Small Cap Equity Adv	GTCSX	A-	(800) 442-8299	27.26	A /9.3	6.92 /54	18.07 /94	17.17 /96	C+ / 5.8	83	19
SC	Pax World Small Cap Ind Inv	PXSCX	A-	(800) 767-1729	14.51	A /9.3	9.34 /71	18.11 /95	15.40 /90	C+ / 5.7	95	7
SC	S&P SmallCap Index Direct	SMCIX	A-	(800) 955-9988	21.78	A- /9.2	9.87 /74	17.18 /91	15.78 /92	C+ / 5.8	84	12
SC	● SSgA Dynamic Small Cap N	SVSCX	A-	(800) 843-2639	39.54	A- /9.1	7.84 /62	17.41 /92	18.20 /98	C+ / 6.2	83	5
SC	DFA Tax Managed US Sm Cap	DFTSX	A-	(800) 984-9472	38.50	A- /9.1	7.18 /57	17.66 /93	15.94 /93	C+ / 6.1	80	3
SC	● Fidelity Small Cap Discovery Fund	FSCRX	A-	(800) 544-8544	30.67	A- /9.1	8.47 /66	18.23 /95	17.77 /97	C+ / 6.1	90	9
SC	Nuveen NWQ Small Cap Value A	NSCAX	A-	(800) 257-8787	44.75	A- /9.1	8.51 /66	19.20 /97	17.51 /97	C+ / 5.9	88	11
SC	DFA US Small Cap Port Inst	DFSTX	A-	(800) 984-9472	32.33	A- /9.1	7.71 /60	17.52 /92	16.04 /93	C+ / 5.9	80	3
SC	Dreyfus Small Cap Stock Index Fd	DISSX	A-	(800) 645-6561	30.09	B+ /8.9	8.53 /66	16.93 /89	15.95 /93	C+ / 6.0	81	15
SC	● T Rowe Price Small Cap Stock	OTCFX	A-	(800) 638-5660	46.05	B+ /8.8	8.82 /68	16.72 /88	16.86 /96	C+ / 6.1	86	23
SC	Diamond Hill Small-Mid Cap Fd A	DHMAX	A-	(614) 255-3333	19.10	B+ /8.6	9.45 /72	18.02 /94	15.01 /87	C+ / 6.6	93	10
SC	Delaware Small Cap Core A	DCCAX	A-	(800) 523-1918	20.60	B+ /8.6	10.36 /76	17.89 /94	16.84 /96	C+ / 6.4	88	11
SC	Transamerica Prt Small Value	DVSVX	A-	(888) 233-4339	17.71	B+ /8.6	9.53 /72	15.93 /83	14.53 /83	C+ / 6.4	75	5
SC	Forward Total MarketPlus Inv	ACSIX	A-	(800) 999-6809	37.72	B /7.6	11.18 /79	15.15 /76	13.01 /68	B- / 7.3	92	5

● Denotes fund is closed to new investors

99 Pct = Best
0 Pct = Worst

Fund Type	Fund Name	Ticker Symbol	Overall Investment Rating	Phone	Net Asset Value As of 3/31/15	Performance Rating/Pts	1Yr / Pct	3Yr / Pct	5Yr / Pct	Risk Rating/Pts	Mgr. Quality Pct	Mgr. Tenure (Years)
TC	Guinness Atkinson Glob Innov	IWIRX	A+	(800) 915-6565	34.38	A / 9.3	10.77 / 77	18.90 / 96	14.86 / 86	C+ / 6.9	71	5
TC	USAA Science & Technology Fund	USSCX	A-	(800) 382-8722	21.64	A+ / 9.8	20.82 / 97	21.55 / 98	18.24 / 98	C / 5.3	93	13
TC	Ivy Science and Technology A	WSTAX	A-	(800) 777-6472	55.95	A / 9.4	8.48 / 66	20.73 / 98	17.03 / 96	C+ / 5.8	91	14
TC	Buffalo Discovery Fund	BUFTX	A-	(800) 492-8332	21.50	A / 9.4	15.56 / 93	17.53 / 92	16.94 / 96	C / 5.5	68	N/A
TC	Waddell & Reed Adv Science &	UNSCX	B+	(888) 923-3355	15.78	A+ / 9.6	7.52 / 59	21.68 / 98	17.54 / 97	C / 5.0	92	14
TC	Columbia Global Technology Gro A	CTCAX	B+	(800) 345-6611	18.72	A / 9.4	17.18 / 95	19.40 / 97	16.60 / 95	C / 5.4	76	13
TC	ICON Information Technology S	ICTEX	B+	(800) 764-0442	15.42	B+ / 8.4	22.87 / 98	12.29 / 55	12.84 / 67	C+ / 6.1	10	6
TC	Janus Aspen Global Technology	JGLTX	B+	(800) 295-2687	8.73	B+ / 8.4	14.10 / 90	15.52 / 79	14.65 / 84	C+ / 5.8	30	4
TC	Victory Munder Growth Opps A	MNNAX	B+	(800) 539-3863	44.55	B- / 7.5	17.74 / 95	14.89 / 74	13.99 / 78	C+ / 6.7	36	16
TC	Fidelity Select Electronics Port	FSELX	B	(800) 544-8888	87.63	A+ / 9.8	27.76 / 99	18.59 / 96	16.37 / 94	C- / 4.2	61	6
TC	Fidelity Adv Electronics A	FELAX	B	(800) 522-7297	16.33	A+ / 9.6	27.30 / 99	17.83 / 94	15.57 / 91	C- / 4.2	49	6
TC	Fidelity Select Sware and Comp	FSCSX	B	(800) 544-8888	117.15	B+ / 8.6	8.22 / 64	17.45 / 92	18.59 / 98	C / 4.9	55	1
TC	Matthews Asia Science and Tech	MATFX	B	(800) 789-2742	14.27	B / 8.1	15.17 / 92	15.85 / 82	11.56 / 57	C+ / 5.9	79	9
TC	Oak Assoc-Red Oak Technology	ROGSX	B	(888) 462-5386	16.69	B / 7.6	8.26 / 65	15.91 / 83	15.95 / 93	C+ / 6.5	24	9
TC	Vanguard Info Tech Ind Adm	VITAX	B	(800) 662-7447	54.36	B- / 7.5	17.37 / 95	14.01 / 67	14.68 / 84	C+ / 6.3	21	5
TC	Nationwide Ziegler NYSE Arc T100	NWJCX	B	(800) 848-0920	57.37	B- / 7.5	12.50 / 85	16.29 / 85	17.06 / 96	C+ / 6.1	48	2
TC	Firsthand Technology	TEFQX	B-	(888) 884-2675	8.84	B+ / 8.6	13.63 / 89	15.84 / 82	14.76 / 85	C / 4.5	54	16
TC	J Hancock VIT Science & Tech I	JESTX	B-	(800) 257-3336	27.81	B / 7.8	13.46 / 88	15.09 / 76	15.20 / 88	C / 5.1	22	6
TC	Rydex Electronics A	RYELX	C+	(800) 820-0888	78.62	B / 8.2	19.36 / 96	14.63 / 72	9.54 / 41	C / 4.3	7	17
TC	T Rowe Price Media and	PRMTX	C+	(800) 638-5660	67.02	B / 8.2	9.32 / 71	16.42 / 86	17.28 / 96	C- / 3.8	75	2
TC	Columbia Seligman Global Tech A	SHGTX	C+	(800) 345-6611	30.08	B / 8.0	24.46 / 98	13.48 / 63	13.19 / 70	C / 4.8	25	21
TC	ProFunds-Tech UltraSector Svc	TEPSX	C+	(888) 776-3637	53.39	B / 7.6	21.78 / 97	13.97 / 67	16.06 / 93	C / 4.5	1	2
TC	Franklin DynaTech A	FKDNX	C+	(800) 342-5236	48.64	B- / 7.3	14.40 / 90	15.36 / 78	15.07 / 87	C / 4.8	50	11
TC	Kinetics Internet Advisor A	KINAX	C+	(800) 930-3828	55.43	C+ / 6.5	5.54 / 43	16.64 / 88	14.88 / 86	C / 5.5	39	16
TC	T Rowe Price Global Technology	PRGTX	C	(800) 638-5660	12.83	A+ / 9.8	21.40 / 97	19.92 / 98	20.12 / 99	D- / 1.2	76	3
TC	Fidelity Select Technology	FSPTX	C	(800) 544-8888	120.51	B- / 7.3	14.23 / 90	13.76 / 65	14.86 / 86	C- / 4.1	42	8
TC	Wells Fargo Adv Spec Tech A	WFSTX	C	(800) 222-8222	10.74	B- / 7.1	13.24 / 87	15.78 / 82	15.67 / 91	C / 4.7	46	N/A
TC	Columbia Seligman Comm & Info A	SLMCX	C	(800) 345-6611	58.08	B- / 7.1	24.12 / 98	12.46 / 56	13.25 / 71	C / 4.3	13	25
TC	BlackRock Sci & Tech Opp Inv A	BGSAX	C	(800) 441-7762	15.19	C+ / 6.8	12.52 / 85	14.38 / 70	12.61 / 65	C / 5.0	26	15
TC	Northern Technology	NTCHX	C	(800) 595-9111	23.72	C+ / 6.5	15.54 / 93	11.50 / 49	14.33 / 81	C / 4.9	4	11
TC	Fidelity Adv Technology A	FADTX	C	(800) 522-7297	36.40	C+ / 6.0	14.11 / 90	13.33 / 62	14.44 / 82	C / 5.2	36	10
TC	MFS Technology A	MTCAX	C	(800) 225-2606	24.73	C / 5.5	10.56 / 77	13.44 / 63	15.18 / 88	C+ / 5.6	15	4
TC	Fidelity Adv Telecom A	FTUAX	C	(800) 522-7297	61.65	C / 4.5	5.73 / 44	12.57 / 56	11.36 / 56	C+ / 6.8	81	2
TC	Deutsche Communication A	TISHX	C	(800) 728-3337	24.12	C- / 3.9	3.31 / 28	11.97 / 52	11.99 / 60	B- / 7.0	50	5
TC	AllianzGI Technology A	RAGTX	C-	(800) 988-8380	56.63	B- / 7.4	13.01 / 87	16.34 / 86	15.90 / 92	C- / 3.3	49	N/A
TC	Rydex Internet A	RYINX	C-	(800) 820-0888	73.71	C+ / 6.8	6.12 / 48	16.33 / 86	14.26 / 80	C- / 4.0	32	15
TC	Janus Global Technology A	JATAX	C-	(800) 295-2687	22.30	C+ / 6.7	13.21 / 87	14.84 / 74	14.12 / 79	C- / 4.0	24	4
TC	Oak Assoc-Black Oak Emerging	BOGSX	C-	(888) 462-5386	4.52	C+ / 6.0	13.00 / 87	11.39 / 48	11.95 / 60	C / 4.3	2	9
TC	Goldman Sachs Tech Tollkeeper A	GITAX	C-	(800) 526-7384	18.40	C / 5.5	12.71 / 86	12.67 / 57	13.13 / 69	C / 4.8	14	16
TC	Rydex Technology A	RYTHX	C-	(800) 820-0888	57.69	C / 4.9	9.28 / 71	12.27 / 54	10.85 / 51	C / 5.4	5	17
TC	T Rowe Price Science and Tech	PRSCX	D+	(800) 638-5660	38.61	C+ / 6.8	13.53 / 88	13.41 / 63	14.10 / 79	C- / 3.0	6	6
TC	Fidelity Select Wireless Fund	FWRLX	D+	(800) 544-8888	9.26	C+ / 5.6	4.69 / 36	13.02 / 60	11.87 / 60	C- / 4.2	53	6
TC	● Invesco Technology Sector A	IFOAX	D+	(800) 959-4246	17.10	C / 4.4	14.00 / 89	9.65 / 37	10.74 / 51	C / 5.1	4	1
TC	AB Global Thematic Gr R	ATERX	D+	(800) 221-5672	88.46	C- / 4.2	8.02 / 63	9.34 / 35	6.15 / 18	C / 4.9	2	2
TC	Jacob Internet Fund Investor	JAMFX	D	(888) 522-6239	4.10	C+ / 5.6	8.03 / 64	12.38 / 55	14.32 / 81	C- / 3.1	35	16
TC	Fidelity Select Commun Equip Port	FSDCX	D	(800) 544-8888	31.66	C / 4.4	8.34 / 65	10.48 / 42	8.88 / 36	C- / 3.8	2	1
TC	Invesco Technology A	ITYAX	D	(800) 959-4246	38.58	C- / 4.2	13.48 / 88	9.30 / 35	12.47 / 64	C- / 4.0	3	7
TC	Saratoga Adv Tr Technology &	STPAX	D	(800) 807-3863	16.35	C- / 3.8	8.10 / 64	11.36 / 48	16.58 / 95	C / 4.7	7	4
TC	Wasatch World Innovators Investor	WAGTX	D	(800) 551-1700	20.76	C- / 3.7	-1.49 / 11	10.75 / 44	13.84 / 76	C / 4.7	8	7
TC	Putnam Global Technology Fund A	PGTAX	D	(800) 225-1581	21.28	C- / 3.5	12.99 / 86	9.93 / 39	10.11 / 46	C / 5.5	6	3
TC	Fidelity Select Computers Port	FDCPX	D	(800) 544-8888	79.11	C- / 3.3	5.49 / 42	9.44 / 36	13.78 / 76	C / 5.1	2	2
TC	GAMCO Global Telecom A	GTCAX	D	(800) 422-3554	23.97	D+ / 2.4	2.14 / 22	9.06 / 33	7.39 / 26	C+ / 6.3	3	22

● Denotes fund is closed to new investors

Data as of March 31, 2015

Fund Type	Fund Name	Ticker Symbol	Overall Investment Rating	Phone	Net Asset Value As of 3/31/15	Perform-ance Rating/Pts	Annualized Total Return Through 3/31/15			Risk Rating/Pts	Mgr. Quality Pct	Mgr. Tenure (Years)
	99 Pct = Best *0 Pct = Worst*						1Yr / Pct	3Yr / Pct	5Yr / Pct			
UT	Prudential Jennison Utility A	PRUAX	B	(800) 225-1852	15.34	B /7.9	11.02 /78	18.01 /94	16.06 /93	C+ / 5.9	98	15
UT	Invesco Dividend Income A	IAUTX	B-	(800) 959-4246	21.16	C+ /6.4	12.88 /86	14.48 /71	13.31 /71	B- / 7.5	97	6
UT	Eaton Vance Dividend Builder Fd A	EVTMX	B-	(800) 262-1122	14.54	C+ /6.0	12.93 /86	13.77 /65	11.79 /59	B- / 7.1	99	8
UT	ProFunds-Utilities UltraSector Svc	UTPSX	C+	(888) 776-3637	31.66	B /7.7	12.74 /86	15.69 /81	15.97 /93	C / 4.6	28	2
UT	Fidelity Select Utilities	FSUTX	C+	(800) 544-8888	73.01	C+ /6.6	7.22 /57	15.19 /76	14.33 /81	C+ / 6.2	92	9
UT	Fidelity Telecom and Utilities	FIUIX	C+	(800) 544-8544	24.20	C+ /6.5	7.15 /56	14.45 /70	14.37 /81	C+ / 6.8	96	10
UT	J Hancock VIT Utilities I	JEUTX	C+	(800) 257-3336	16.41	C+ /6.2	6.78 /53	13.94 /67	13.69 /75	C+ / 6.2	96	14
UT	Vanguard Utilities Index Adm	VUIAX	C+	(800) 662-7447	48.56	C+ /6.0	10.57 /77	12.99 /60	13.14 /69	C+ / 6.4	75	5
UT	ICON Utilities S	ICTUX	C+	(800) 764-0442	8.43	C+ /5.7	10.55 /77	12.26 /54	11.97 /60	C+ / 6.9	75	1
UT	AB Equity Income A	AUIAX	C+	(800) 221-5672	26.73	C /5.3	8.83 /68	13.15 /61	14.91 /86	C+ / 6.6	98	5
UT	Franklin Utilities A	FKUTX	C+	(800) 342-5236	16.95	C /5.2	10.80 /78	12.96 /59	13.61 /74	C+ / 6.7	84	17
UT	Cohen & Steers Glbl Infr A	CSUAX	C+	(800) 330-7348	18.91	C /5.1	6.61 /52	13.30 /62	10.64 /50	C+ / 6.8	96	11
UT	Fidelity Adv Utilities A	FUGAX	C	(800) 522-7297	26.32	C /5.4	6.77 /53	14.79 /73	13.99 /78	C+ / 6.0	92	9
UT	MFS Utilities A	MMUFX	C	(800) 225-2606	21.60	C /5.1	6.82 /54	13.70 /65	13.43 /72	C+ / 6.0	96	23
UT	American Century Utilities Inv	BULIX	C	(800) 345-6488	17.03	C /5.0	6.40 /50	12.21 /54	12.15 /62	C+ / 6.4	87	5
UT	Wells Fargo Adv Util and Tel A	EVUAX	C	(800) 222-8222	18.23	C- /4.1	4.82 /37	12.15 /53	12.01 /61	B- / 7.1	90	13
UT	Meeder Utilities and Infrastructure	FLRUX	C-	(800) 325-3539	30.47	C /4.7	4.33 /34	11.93 /52	10.80 /51	C / 5.5	96	20
UT	Rydex Utilities A	RYUTX	C-	(800) 820-0888	34.70	C- /4.1	8.78 /68	11.23 /47	11.69 /58	C+ / 6.2	60	15
UT	Virtus Global Dividend A	PGUAX	D+	(800) 243-1574	15.01	C- /3.1	3.73 /30	10.81 /44	11.29 /55	C+ / 6.5	93	11
UT	Gabelli Utilities A	GAUAX	D	(800) 422-3554	9.98	D+ /2.4	2.41 /24	9.53 /36	9.71 /42	C+ / 6.2	88	16
UT	Putnam Global Utilities Fund A	PUGIX	D	(800) 225-1581	12.35	D /1.9	2.60 /25	8.41 /29	5.41 /14	B- / 7.1	70	3

● Denotes fund is closed to new investors

Appendix

What is a Mutual Fund?

Picking individual stocks is difficult and buying individual bonds can be expensive. Mutual funds were introduced to allow the small investor to participate in the stock and bond market for just a small initial investment. Mutual funds are pools of stocks or bonds that are managed by investment professionals. First, an investment company organizes the fund and collects the money from investors. The company then takes that money and pays a portfolio manager to invest it in stocks, bonds, money market instruments and other types of securities.

Most funds fit within one of two main categories, open-ended funds or closed-end funds. Open-ended funds issue new shares when investors put in money and redeem shares when investors withdraw money. The price of a share is determined by dividing the total net assets of the fund by the number of shares outstanding.

On the other hand, closed-end funds issue a fixed number of shares in an initial public offering, trading thereafter in the open market like a stock. Open-end funds are the most common type of mutual fund. Investing in either class of funds means you own a share of the portfolio, so you participate in the fund's gains and losses.

There are approximately 27,000 different mutual funds, each with a stated investment objective. Here are descriptions for five of the most popular types of funds:

Stock funds: A mutual fund which invests mainly in stocks. These funds are more actively traded than other more conservative funds. The stocks chosen may vary widely according to the fund's investment strategy.

Bond funds: A mutual fund which invests in bonds, in an effort to provide stable income while preserving principal as much as possible. These funds invest in medium- to long-term bonds issued by corporations and governments.

Index funds: A mutual fund that aims to match the performance of a specific index, such as the S&P 500. Index funds tend to have fewer expenses than other funds because portfolio decisions are automatic and transactions are infrequent.

Balanced funds: A mutual fund that buys a combination of stocks and bonds, in order to supply both income and capital growth while ensuring a minimal amount of risk for investors.

Money market funds: An open-end mutual fund which invests only in stable, short-term securities. The fund seeks to preserve its value at a constant $1 per share. Money market funds are not insured by the FDIC, however may be covered by SIPC insurance. Investors should contact the firm administering their investment account to determine the insurance coverage of the funds or contact the FDIC and/or the SIPC directly.

Investing in a mutual fund has several advantages over owning a single stock or bond. For example, funds offer instant portfolio diversification by giving you ownership of many stocks or bonds simultaneously. This diversification protects you in case a part of your investment takes a sudden downturn. You also get the benefit of having a professional handling your investment, though a management fee is charged for these services, typically 1% or 2% a year.

You should be aware that the fund may also levy other fees and that you will likely have to pay a sales commission (known as a load) if you purchase the fund from a financial adviser. The fund manager's strategy is laid out in the fund's prospectus, which is the official name for the legal document that contains financial information about the fund, including its history, its officers and its performance. Mutual fund investments are fully liquid so you can easily get in or out by just placing an order through a broker.

Investor Profile Quiz

We recognize that each person approaches his or her investment decisions from a unique perspective. A mutual fund that is perfect for someone else may be totally inappropriate for you due to factors such as:

- How much risk you are comfortable taking
- Your age and the number of years you have before retirement
- Your income level and tax rate
- Your other existing investments and personal net worth
- Preconceived expectations about investment performance

The following quiz will help you quantify your tolerance for risk based on your own personal life situation. As you read through each question, circle the letter next to the single answer that you feel most accurately describes your current position. Keep in mind that there are no "correct" answers to this quiz, only answers that are helpful in assessing your investment style. So don't worry about how your answer might be perceived by others; just try to be as honest and accurate as possible.

Then at the end of the quiz, use the point totals listed on the right side of the page to compute your test score. Once you've added up your total points, refer to the corresponding investor profile for an evaluation of your personal risk tolerance. Each profile also lists the page number where you will find the top performing mutual funds matching your risk profile.

		Points	Your Score
1.	I am currently investing to pay for:		
	a. Retirement	0 pts	
	b. College	0 pts	
	c. A house	0 pts	
2.	I expect I will need to liquidate some or all of this investment in:		
	a. 2 years or less	0 pts	
	b. 2 to 5 years	5 pts	
	c. 5 to 10 years	8 pts	
	d. 10 years or more	10 pts	
3.	My age group is		
	a. Under 30	10 pts	
	b. 30 to 44	9 pts	
	c. 45 to 60	7 pts	
	d. 60 to 74	5 pts	
	e. 75 and older	1 pts	
4.	I am currently looking to invest money through:		
	a. An IRA or other tax-deferred account	0 pts	
	b. A fully taxable account	0 pts	

5.	I have a cash reserve equal to 3 to 6 months expenses.		
	a. Yes	10 pts	
	b. No	1 pts	
6.	My primary source of income is:		
	a. Salary and other earnings from my primary occupation	7 pts	
	b. Earnings from my investment portfolio	5 pts	
	c. Retirement pension and/or Social Security	3 pts	
7.	I will need regular income from this investment now or in the near future.		
	a. Yes	6 pts	
	b. No	10 pts	
8.	Over the long run, I expect this investment to average returns of:		
	a. 8% annually or less	0 pts	
	b. 8% to 12% annually	6 pts	
	c. 12% to 15% annually	8 pts	
	d. 15% to 20% annually	10 pts	
	e. Over 20% annually	18 pts	
9.	The worst loss I would be comfortable accepting on my investment is:		
	a. Less than 5%. Stability of principal is very important to me.	1 pts	
	b. 5% to 10%. Modest periodic declines are acceptable.	3 pts	
	c. 10% to 15%. I understand that there may be losses in the short run but over the long term, higher risk investments will offer highest returns.	8 pts	
	d. Over 15%. You don't get high returns without taking risk. I'm looking for maximum capital gains and understand that my funds can substantially decline.	15 pts	
10.	If the stock market were to suddenly decline by 15%, which of the following would most likely be your reaction?		
	a. I should have left the market long ago, at the first sign of trouble.	3 pts	
	b. I should have substantially exited the stock market by now to limit my exposure.	5 pts	
	c. I'm still in the stock market but I've got my finger on the trigger.	7 pts	
	d. I'm staying fully invested so I'll be ready for the next bull market.	10 pts	
11.	The best defense against a bear market is:		
	a. A defensive market timing system that avoids large losses.	4 pts	
	b. A potent offense that will make big gains in the next bull market.	10 pts	
12.	The best strategy to employ during bear markets is:		
	a. Move to cash. It's the only safe hiding place.	5 pts	
	b. Short the market and try to make a profit as it declines.	10 pts	
	c. Wait it out because the market will eventually recover.	8 pts	

13.	I would classify myself as:			
	a. A buy-and-hold investor who rides out all the peaks and valleys.		10 pts	
	b. A market timer who wants to capture the major bull markets.		7 pts	
	c. A market timer who wants to avoid the major bear markets.		5 pts	
14.	My attitude regarding trading activity is:			
	a. Active trading is costly and unproductive.		0 pts	
	b. I don't mind frequent trades as long as I'm making money		2 pts	
	c. Occasional trading is okay but too much activity is not good.		1 pts	
15.	If the S&P 500 advanced strongly over the last 12 months, my investment should have:			
	a. Grown even more than the market.		10 pts	
	b. Approximated the performance of the broad market.		5 pts	
	c. Focused on reducing the risk of loss in a bear market, even if it meant giving up some upside potential in the bull market.		2 pts	

16.	I have experience (extensive, some, or none) with the following types of investments.	Extensive	Some	None	
	a. U.S. stocks or stock mutual funds	2 pts	1 pts	0 pts	
	b. International stock funds	2 pts	1 pts	0 pts	
	c. Bonds or bond funds	1 pts	0 pts	0 pts	
	d. Futures and/or options	5 pts	3 pts	0 pts	
	e. Managed futures or funds	3 pts	1 pts	0 pts	
	f. Real estate	2 pts	1 pts	0 pts	
	g. Private hedge funds	3 pts	1 pts	0 pts	
	h. Privately managed accounts	2 pts	1 pts	0 pts	

17.	Excluding my primary residence, this investment represents ___% of my investment holdings.		
	a. Less than 5%	10 pts	
	b. 5% to 10%	7 pts	
	c. 10% to 20%	5 pts	
	d. 20% to 30%	3 pts	
	e. 30% or more	1 pts	
		TOTAL	

Under 58 pts   **Very Conservative.** You appear to be very risk averse with capital preservation as your primary goal. As such, most equity mutual funds may be a little too risky for your taste, especially in a turbulent market environment. We recommend you stick to the safest bond funds and money market mutual funds where your income stream is predictable and more secure. Those funds are not covered in this publication, but you can easily find them in Section VII of *TheStreet Ratings Guide to Bond and Money Market Mutual Funds.*

58 to 77 pts   **Conservative.** Based on your responses, it appears that you are more concerned about minimizing the risk to your principal than you are about maximizing your returns. Don't worry, there are plenty of good mutual funds that offer strong returns with very little volatility. As a starting point, we recommend you turn to page 790 where you will find a list of the top-rated funds receiving the best risk rating we issue to equity mutual funds (B– or better, meaning Good).

78 to 108 pts   **Moderate.** You are prepared to take on a little added risk in order to enhance your investment returns. This is probably the most common approach to mutual fund investing. To select a mutual fund matching your style, we recommend you turn to page 792. There you can easily pick from the top-rated mutual funds receiving a risk rating in the C (Fair) range.

109 to 129 pts   **Aggressive.** You appear to be ready to ride out almost any financial storm on your way toward maximizing your investment returns. You understand that the only way to make large returns on your investments is by taking on added risk, and your personal situation seems to allow for that approach. We recommend you use pages 792 - 795 as a starting point for selecting a top-rated mutual fund with a risk rating in the C (Fair) or D (Weak) range.

Over 129 pts   **Very Aggressive.** Based on your responses, you appear to be leaning heavily toward speculation. Your primary concern is maximizing your investment growth, and you are prepared to take on as much risk as necessary in order to do so. To this end, turn to page 796 where you'll find the top-rated mutual funds with a risk rating in the E (Very Weak) range. These investments have historically been extremely volatile, oftentimes investing in stocks that are currently out of favor. As such, they are highly speculative investments that could provide superior results if you can stomach the volatility and uncertainty. For a list of the top performing mutual funds regardless of risk category, turn to page 770. Also see section VI of *TheStreet Ratings Guide to Common Stocks.*

Performance Benchmarks

The following benchmarks represent the average performance for all mutual funds within each stock fund type category. Comparing an individual mutual fund's returns to these benchmarks is yet another way to assess its performance. For the top performing funds within each of the following categories, turn to Section VIII, Top-Rated Stock Mutual Funds By Fund Type, beginning on page 804. You can also use this information to compare the average performance of one category of funds to another (updated through March 31, 2015).

		3 Month Total Return %	1 Year Total Return %	Refer to page:
AA	Asset Allocation - Domestic	2.00%	4.86%	805
AG	Aggressive Growth	2.08%	6.15%	804
BA	Balanced - Domestic	1.72%	6.13%	806
CV	Convertible	2.23%	5.12%	807
EM	Emerging Market Equity	1.05%	-1.08%	808
EN	Sector - Energy/Natural Res	-1.70%	-13.93%	809
FO	Non-US Equity	4.49%	0.06%	811
FS	Sector - Financial Services	0.34%	2.35%	810
GI	Growth & Income	1.51%	6.97%	814
GL	Global Equity	2.46%	4.32%	812
GR	Growth	2.29%	9.80%	813
HL	Sector - Health/Biotechnology	10.95%	30.97%	815
IN	Equity Income	1.25%	7.12%	816
IX	S&P 500 Index	0.80%	10.21%	817
MC	Mid Cap	4.21%	10.37%	818
OT	Sector - Other	-1.99%	-8.95%	819
PM	Sector - Precious Metals	-3.45%	-20.39%	820
RE	Sector - Real Estate	4.15%	18.20%	821
SC	Small Cap	4.14%	6.53%	822
TC	Sector - Tech/Communications	3.05%	12.32%	823
UT	Sector - Utilities	-1.30%	7.69%	824

Fund Type Descriptions

<u>AG - Aggressive Growth</u> - Seeks maximum capital appreciation, by investing primarily in common stocks of companies that are believed to offer rapid growth potential. These funds tend to employ greater-than-average risk strategies than a typical growth fund in an attempt to gain a higher rate of return. Aggressive Growth funds have the flexibility to invest in companies with any capitalization.

<u>AA - Asset Allocation</u> - Seeks both income and capital appreciation by determining the optimal percentage of assets to place in stocks, bonds, and cash.

<u>BA - Balanced</u> - Seeks both income and capital appreciation by determining the optimal proportion of assets to place in stocks, bonds, and cash. The allocation across asset classes will remain relatively stable.

<u>CV - Convertible</u> - Invests at least 65% in convertible securities. Convertible securities are bonds or preferred stocks that are exchangeable for a set number of shares of common stock.

<u>EM - Emerging Market</u> - Seeks long term capital appreciation by investing primarily in emerging market equity securities. Income is usually incidental.

<u>EN - Energy/Natural Resources</u> - Invests primarily in equity securities of companies involved in the exploration, distribution, or processing of natural resources.

<u>FS - Financial</u> - Seeks capital appreciation by investing in equity securities of companies engaged in providing financial services. Typically, securities are from commercial banks, S&Ls, finance companies, securities brokerages, investment managers, insurance companies, and leasing companies.

<u>FO - Foreign</u> - Invests primarily in non-U.S. equity securities of any market capitalization. Income is usually incidental.

<u>GL - Global</u> - Invests primarily in domestic and foreign equity securities of any market capitalization. Income is usually incidental.

<u>GR - Growth</u> - Seeks long term capital appreciation by investing primarily in equity securities of any market capitalization. Income is usually incidental.

<u>GI - Growth and Income</u> - Seeks both capital appreciation and income primarily by investing in equities with a level or rising dividend stream.

<u>HL - Health</u> - Seeks capital appreciation by investing primarily in equities of companies engaged in the design, manufacture, or sale of products or services connected with health care or medicine.

<u>IN - Income</u> - Seeks current income by investing a minimum of 65% of its assets in income-producing equity securities.

<u>IX - Index</u> - Seeks to provide investment results comparable to that of a particular index by investing substantially in the securities of, or characteristically similar to those of, the index.

<u>MC - Mid Cap</u> - Seeks long term capital appreciation by investing in stocks of medium size companies, as determined by market capitalization. Typically, capitalizations between $1 billion and $5 billion are ranked as medium capitalization companies.

<u>OT - Other</u> - Funds which have a specific focus that do not fit into any of the existing categories.

<u>PM - Precious Metals</u> - Seeks capital appreciation by investing primarily in equity securities of companies involved in mining, distribution, processing, or dealing in gold, silver, platinum, diamonds, or other precious metals and minerals.

<u>RE - Real Estate</u> - Seeks capital appreciation and income by investing in equity securities of real estate investment trusts and other real estate industry companies.

<u>SC - Small Cap</u> - Seeks maximum capital appreciation, by investing primarily in stocks of small companies, as determined by market capitalization. Typically, capitalizations under $1 billion are classified as small capitalization companies.

<u>TC - Technology</u> - Seeks capital appreciation by investing a minimum of 65% of its assets in the technology sector.

<u>UT - Utilities</u> - Seeks a high level of current income by investing primarily in the equity securities of utility companies.

Share Class Descriptions

Many mutual funds have several classes of shares, each with different fees and associated sales charges. While there is no official standardization of mutual fund classes we have compiled a list of those most frequently seen. Ultimately you must consult a fund's prospectus for particular share class designations and what they mean. Federal regulation requires that the load, or sales charge, not exceed 8.5% of the investment purchase.

Class	Description
A	**Front End Load.** Sales charge is paid at the time of purchase and is deducted from the investment amount.
B	**Back End Load.** Also know as contingent deferred sales charge (CDSC); the sales charge is imposed if the fund is sold. Class B shares usually convert to Class A shares after six to eight years from the date of purchase.
C	**Level Load.** A set sales charge paid annually for as long as the fund is held. This class is especially beneficial to the short–term investor.
D	**Flexible.** Class D shares can be anything a fund company wants. Check the fund prospectus for the details regarding a specific fund's fee structure.
I	**Institutional.** No sales charge is collected due to the size of the order. This class usually requires a minimum investment of $100,000.
M	**Mid Load.** Similar to Class A, but with a lower front end load and higher expense ratio (see page 17 for more information on expense ratios).
N	**No Load.** No sales fee is imposed.
R	**No Load.** No sales fee is imposed and fund must be held in a qualified retirement account.
T	**Mid Load.** Similar to Class A, but with a lower front end load and higher expense ratio (see page 17 for more information on expense ratios).
Y	**Institutional.** No sales charge is collected due to the size of the order. This class usually requires a minimum investment of $100,000.
Z	**No Load.** Fund is only available for purchase to employees of the mutual fund company, as an employee benefit. No sales fee is imposed.